PRESENTED TO

_____

BY:

_____

ON:

_____

Then he said to me,
"These words are faithful and true."

–Revelation 22:6a

THE TONY EVANS STUDY BIBLE

ADVANCING GOD'S KINGDOM AGENDA

CSB
CHRISTIAN STANDARD BIBLE®

HOLMAN® BIBLES

Binding	ISBN
Hardcover	978-1-4336-0686-1
British Tan LeatherTouch	978-1-4336-0687-8
British Tan LeatherTouch, Indexed	978-1-4336-0688-5
Purple LeatherTouch	978-1-4336-0689-2
Purple LeatherTouch, Indexed	978-1-4336-0690-8
Black Genuine Leather	978-1-4336-0691-5
Black Genuine Leather, Indexed	978-1-4336-0692-2
Black/Brown LeatherTouch	978-1-5359-7113-3
Black/Brown LeatherTouch, Indexed	978-1-5359-7114-0
Teal/Earth LeatherTouch	978-1-0877-2030-2
Teal/Earth LeatherTouch, Indexed	978-1-0877-2181-1
Burgundy LeatherTouch	978-1-0877-5222-8
Burgundy LeatherTouch, Indexed	978-1-0877-5223-5
Goldenrod Cloth over Board	978-1-0877-5224-2
Goldenrod Cloth over Board, Indexed	978-1-0877-5225-9

Printed in Korea
6 7 8 — 23 22 21
SWP

TONY EVANS STUDY BIBLE

OLD TESTAMENT

NEW TESTAMENT

ADDITIONAL MATERIAL

STUDY BIBLE FEATURES

DR. TONY EVANS

Dr. Tony Evans is the founder and senior pastor of Oak Cliff Bible Fellowship in Dallas, is founder and president of The Urban Alternative, served as chaplain of the NBA's Dallas Mavericks and the NFL's Dallas Cowboys, and is author of over one hundred books, booklets, and Bible studies. The first African American to earn a doctorate of theology from Dallas Theological Seminary, he has been named one of the 12 Most Effective Preachers in the English-Speaking World by Baylor University.

Dr. Evans holds the honor of writing and publishing the first full-Bible commentary and study Bible by an African American. His radio broadcast, *The Alternative with Dr. Tony Evans*, can be heard on more than 1,300 US outlets daily and in more than 130 countries.

Dr. Evans launched the Tony Evans Training Center in 2017, an online learning platform providing quality seminary-style courses for a fraction of the cost to any person in any place. The goal is to increase biblical literacy and to advance God's kingdom agenda not only among lay people but also among those Christian leaders who cannot afford or find the time for formal ongoing education.

For more information, visit TonyEvans.org.

ACKNOWLEDGMENTS

A work of this magnitude requires an enormously committed support system. *The Tony Evans Study Bible* (and its companion *The Tony Evans Bible Commentary*) has been years in the making. It is for this reason I wish to express my heartfelt gratitude to all who enabled this project to reach its completion.

First of all, I want to thank the B&H Publishing family for their hard work. This includes Trevin Wax who oversaw the publishing of this work. I am also grateful for the investment of time and energy given by the managing editor, Chris Cowan, with whom I spent countless hours critiquing, constructing, and reviewing the content of my exposition of every paragraph of God's Holy Word. Thanks also to B&H's editorial and production team, J. D. Green, Lloyd Mullens, Garry Fulton, Dustin Curtis, and Bethany McShurley for the wonderful and professional way they put this project together. And I want to thank Jeremy Howard for his vision as we started this project nearly a decade ago and his involvement in helping establish the Study Bible features.

I'm grateful to my good friend Greg Thornton and Moody Publishers for their willingness to allow me to draw on and tweak some previously published content. A special thanks goes to my good friends Phil Rawley, Terry Glaspey, John Fortner, Scott Cyre, and Gabe Smith for their support and contributions to this work. Thanks also go to Jeff Godby and 2K/DENMARK for their design and typesetting expertise, as well as to Dylan Gerik, Tayte Gerik, Troy Black, and Vijay Prabhaker, who handled video and audio production.

I am also very grateful to my longtime executive assistant, Mrs. Sylvia Stewart, for the endless time and effort she put into keeping up with all the administrative duties connected with this project amidst all her other responsibilities. My appreciation goes to Mrs. Heather Hair who curated my preaching and written library and used it along with her creativity, marketing, organizational, video, and writing skills to bring about the unique elements you find in this Study Bible.

Finally, I want to express my deepest, heartfelt gratitude to my wife and ministry partner Lois Evans for her unending love, patience, support, and encouragement that made this legacy work possible.

INTRODUCTION

This study Bible is based on a simple yet profound biblical worldview: the glory of God through the advancement of his kingdom. This is the unifying theme of Scripture, from Genesis through Revelation. The concept of God's kingdom is what ties all of the Bible together. When this central point of connectivity is lost to the reader, it is easy for Scripture to seem like a series of disconnected stories, events, personalities, and doctrines that do not strategically and thematically connect to one another.

The word *kingdom* means "rule" or "authority." When linked to God, it refers to the rule of God in both heaven and earth encompassing both eternity and time. It is therefore comprehensive in nature. This kingdom is composed of a ruler (God), subjects (angels and people), a realm (creation), and regulations (laws).

The Bible unfolds how God's kingdom operates in the affairs of the world and how God receives glory through his kingdom rule, even when that rule is being opposed by both angels and human beings. While God's kingdom rule takes various forms with varying laws through varying administrations (i.e., dispensations), it nonetheless maintains its central goal of bringing God glory whether through blessing or judgment.

The *kingdom agenda*, then, is the visible manifestation of the comprehensive rule of God over every area of life. God's kingdom agenda is carried out through four covenantal spheres: the individual, the family, the church, and the government (i.e., nations). A covenant is a divinely created relational bond through which God administrates his kingdom program. It establishes a legal relationship in the spiritual realm that is to be lived out in the physical realm. To operate and function underneath the umbrella of God's kingdom covenants and guidelines is to position the specific covenantal relationship (i.e., individual, family, church, government) to experience God's greatest involvement and benefits within that covenantal sphere. Conversely, to operate outside of and in opposition to God's kingdom covenant is to experience the negative consequences of not being aligned and covenantally covered.

This study Bible is designed to reflect this kingdom perspective. My goal is that it will serve as a valuable study resource for serious students of the Bible by combining exegesis, exposition, and exhortation that creates a relevant kingdom mindset.

As you use this study Bible, remember:

I. Study the Scriptures with a view to meeting with God, not just learning about him.

II. Study the Scriptures by routinely asking, "What should I do in light of what I have learned?"

III. Study the Scriptures in their context in order to be accurate in your understanding of what the biblical authors are saying.

IV. Study the Scriptures in prayer and in dependency on the Holy Spirit to open up your mind and heart to the meaning and contemporary relevancy and application of the text.

V. Study the Scripture with a kingdom mindset, seeking to identify God's rule over every area of life.

While nothing can be added to or subtracted from God's inerrant Word, it is my sincere hope that the notes and features in this study Bible will aid you in your understanding and application of the Bible to your life. For additional exposition and application of the Scriptures, see also *The Tony Evans Bible Commentary: Advancing God's Kingdom Agenda*. Most importantly, it is my prayer that your reading, studying, and obedience to the written Word will lead you into a deeper, more intimate relationship with the living Word, Jesus Christ, as kingdom disciples as you live all of life under his kingdom rule.

WITHIN OUR HEARTS IS
A *desire* TO DISCOVER GOD.

TO SEE *Him.*

TO EXPERIENCE *Him.*

TO KNOW *His* STORY.

HOW TO USE THIS STUDY BIBLE

Throughout *The Tony Evans Study Bible*, there are various features designed to enhance your reading experience. Whether you have questions about a passage, are seeking additional inspiration, or desire a deeper understanding through serious study, these resources will help you.

STUDY NOTES – These notes provide my exegesis, exposition, and exhortation to help you understand and apply a given passage. Words in bold are directly from the Scripture text.

1:1 Most ancient creation accounts chronicle a struggle between good and evil, with earth popping up as an accidental by-product of struggle. In these accounts, the gods who created the world did so out of prior material. They could not truly create. Scripture's story is different: **In the beginning God** (*Elohim*, the Supreme One) **created** out of nothing. With a mere word he made the entire universe of time, space, and mat-

1:3–5 God made the light, but he also *named* it: **God called the light "day"** (1:5). By naming the parts of his creation, God expresses sovereign rule over them. Even the concept of light, which is fundamental to our world, only exists because God sustains it.

1:6–8 God placed some **water above the expanse** (1:7); this is the basis of our earthly water cycle. God created the atmosphere so

what was emanating light for the first three days? God himself was (see Rev 22:5). On day four, God handed over that responsibility to celestial representatives, so that they would **provide light on the earth** (Gen 1:17) and **serve as signs** (1:14).

1:20–23 As he had populated the ground with plants (1:11–13), God made birds and fish (1:21). What is unique here is that he blesses them with a commission to be fruitful . . . and fill

KINGDOM LIVING LESSONS – Practical lessons regarding your ability to live your life according to God's kingdom agenda, the visible manifestation of the comprehensive rule of God over every area of your life. These are divided into five categories: Kingdom, Personal, Family, Church, and Community.

Kingdom: This category considers the theology of the kingdom. Throughout the Bible, God reveals how he advances his kingdom, his all-encompassing dominion over all that he created.

Personal: God's Word was written to equip you for every good work. It is sufficient for preparing you for life in his kingdom, both here on earth and in heaven. The personal sphere of God's kingdom agenda focuses on your self-management and how you use your time, talents, and treasures as his kingdom disciple.

Family: God created the family to be the foundation of civilization. As the family goes, so goes the culture. These lessons focus on strengthening family relationships based on biblical principles.

Church: The church exists as God's central governing mechanism through which he enacts his heavenly intervention on earth. I seek to provide you with a spiritual framework for the purpose and power of the church.

Community: Christians are to function as kingdom citizens by personally modeling while also influencing government to maintain a safe, just, righteous, and compassionately-responsible society where freedom flourishes.

HOPE WORDS – Brief insights inspired by Scripture to empower and encourage you.

⇁ KINGDOM LIVING ⇽
FAMILY

A Photograph of God

Looking at Genesis 1, we read that God created the heavens and the earth in such a way that they are functional, vibrant, and pulsating with life. On the fifth day, God started forming the creatures that would live on the earth. Then, on the sixth day, he reached the pinnacle of his creative purposes with the creation of humankind.

Important truths arise from this account in Genesis 1:26-28. First, we see the word "us" referring to the triune God: Father, Son, and Spirit. The Trinity consists of three individual and unique persons who make up the unified reality of the Godhead. Second, we see the commission of humankind—which is to hear

---

⇁ HOPE WORDS ⇽

Faith is our positive response to what God has already provided.

You hold in your hands the preservation of his unique narrative, opening with creation and expanding his kingdom rule throughout history and into eternity. In these pages, chroniclers inspired by the Holy Spirit have presented the history, rules, redemption, and purposes of our King in what we call the Bible.

Additional articles, insights, inspirational thoughts, questions, videos, and more have been added to help you on this journey through the Word of God.

It is all here, ready to be explored, uncovered, understood, and applied—by you.

INSPIRATIONAL ARTICLES – Heart-felt articles providing you with knowledge and inspiration as you strive to understand and apply the biblical text in a deeper way.

Faith Works

I WAS ONCE BATTLING A COLD and couldn't shake it. I called my doctor, told him my symptoms, and he told me I didn't need to come in. He would call in a prescription for me. He told me what medicine he was prescribing and how he wanted me to take it.

To benefit from this conversation, I had to believe that I was talking to the person I thought I was talking to, because I couldn't see him. Ours was just a brief talk over the phone, so I had to listen to and trust his voice. Then I had

Video Devotional
"SUPER GAME SUNDAY"

We have been called to rule on behalf of God's kingdom while on earth.

VIDEO DEVOTIONALS – Brief videos on various topics, which you can access on your mobile device using the provided QR code. Some are devotional, others are segments from sermons. Each video is designed to enhance your study experience by helping you dive deeper on a topic or providing you with encouragement in your study.

Q&A WITH TONY EVANS
My answers to a variety of questions, including questions about my own life and ministry, how to understand various biblical texts and theological issues, and how to apply God's kingdom agenda in your daily life.

❧ Questions & Answers ❧

Q You have called *The Kingdom Agenda* your "magnum opus." Why do you view this book and philosophy of life as so critical and central to your life's work?

A *The Kingdom Agenda* is my life's work because of its comprehensive nature. When I saw that the whole Bible is the

BIBLE BOOK INTRODUCTIONS – Each book of the Bible includes an introduction that discusses matters of authorship, historical background, and purpose. Each is accompanied by a video that you can access on your mobile device using the provided QR code. In these videos, I expound briefly on the biblical book's message and key themes.

GENESIS

INTRODUCTION

Author

THOUGH THE BOOK OF GENESIS is anonymous (no author is listed), ancient Jewish and Christian traditions held that Moses authored the first five books of the Bible—referred to as the *Pentateuch* ("five vessels") or the *Torah* (a Hebrew word for "law" or "instruction"). That Moses stood behind these five books is attested to in both the Old and the New

In the meantime Genesis records the angelic conflict now being waged on earth to such an extent that God destroyed the earth with a flood and began again with Noah to establish his kingdom rule—for Genesis introduces us to a kingdom concept. The world after the flood also rebelled against God at Babylon, and God judged the people for trying to establish unity without him. Then God called one man, Abraham, through whom

APPLICATION QUESTIONS – Questions to help you engage the biblical text and apply God's Word to every area of your life.

APPLICATION QUESTIONS

READ GENESIS 1:26-27

- What do these verses teach about family?
- How have you experienced God's provision in your efforts to manage your family and your other spheres of life?

a 1:26 Gn 3:22; 11:7
b Gn 5:1,3; 9:6; Rm 8:29;
1Co 11:7; 15:49; 2Co 3:18;
4:4; Eph 4:24; Col 1:15;
Jms 3:9
c Gn 9:2; Ps 8:6-8; Jms 3:7
d 1:27 Gn 5:2; Mt 19:4;
Mk 10:6
e 1:28 Gn 9:1,7
f 1:29 Gn 9:3; Ps 104:14-15;
136:25; 145:15-16
g 1:30 Ps 147:9

SIDE-MARGIN CROSS REFERENCES – Other Bible passages that are related to the text on which you are focusing.

Cradled within the depths that define our humanity lies an unyielding fascination with kingdom. No matter what color, creed, or culture we examine, we find with even the most cursory glance into the accounts passed down by either pen or by tongue something intertwined with kingdom. Whether it be the great kings and rulers of Scripture such as David or Solomon, or whether it be Caesar, Alexander the Great, Charlemagne, Tutankhamun, and the like, these lives somehow captivate us, intriguing our imaginations.

Even rulers who did not hold the official title of "king" have left their legacies, for good or for bad, to enthrall us. There is Napoleon, the dominator of continental Europe, who possessed a formidable intellect and superior military mind. There is Khan, the evil and brutal ruler, who conquered most of the world during his time. There are the Pharaohs, most of whom possessed strength and skill to such a degree that for many centuries they progressed their nation beyond the others in academics, engineering, medicine, and writing. Then there are also the Monarchs spanning over sixteen hundred years of history, in one form or fashion, beginning humbly as the Angles, moving to Aengla Land, and eventually becoming what we know today as England.

Stories of conquerors, conquests, rebellions, and conspiracy mesmerize us. We tell them to our children in fairy tales riddled with kings, queens, princes, princesses and kingdoms. We read about them in history books, mythology, fables, legends, and fiction. We flock to movies to watch the rise or fall of power connected to a kingdom in epic adventures. Inevitably, we portray the king, or the prince, as reputedly handsome—when he is a good king. We portray him as sinister and ugly when he is bad.

Queens and princesses play a role in our fascination as well. From Cinderella to Nefertiti to Elizabeth I, we hold in highest regard that special strength of a woman who both utilizes and maintains her nobility in the face of constant and devastating betrayal and opposition in order to produce a greater good for her kingdom and her subjects.

The life of a king or a queen is often envied. Yet, that envy is naïve. Any true historian knows the utter fragility that comes with absolute power. As the playwright Shakespeare once wrote, "Uneasy lies the head that wears the crown." Kings, queens, and rulers frequently function in a culture of conflict, and even violence. Those around them might swear an oath of total allegiance while they simultaneously plot their destruction, or even their death.

As a result, history reminds us again and again, through what may seem like the same story just set on a different stage, that kings and rulers often resort to brute force and extreme taxation to protect their own personal interests and power. While uprisers such as the Scottish William Wallace (best known for being portrayed in the film *Braveheart*) could wind up hung and quartered in a meat factory, it wasn't only the uprisers who needed to fear the virtual paranoid wrath that sometimes appeared in a king. No one was safe when it came to the possibility of usurping his role, as we see with poisoning of family members and even the gruesome, bloody beheading of wives with Henry VIII.

Nowhere in any story of a king or in any story of a kingdom do we read about the ruler himself sacrificing his own greatest treasure simply for the benefit of others. Sure sacrifices were made. Lives were lost. But this always happened toward the aim of preserving power, rather than yielding it—that is, except for one instance. The true King of the Bible gave up his own Son, Jesus Christ, in order that those who believe on him—his death, burial, and resurrection—would be restored to the place of both fellowship and dominion with their king, something they had lost in the battle in the garden.

THE UNUSUAL KINGDOM

It is not unusual that this unusual action occurred by this very unusual king because his is an even more unusual kingdom. Jesus spoke of it plainly when he told Pilate that the ways of his kingdom do not reflect the ways of the kingdoms on earth, "My kingdom is not of this world." He said, "If my kingdom were of this world, my servants would fight, so that I wouldn't be handed over to the Jews. But as it is, my kingdom is not from here" (John 18:36).

When his followers asked him to tell them who is the greatest in this very unusual kingdom, Jesus pulled a child close and replied, "Therefore, whoever humbles himself like this child—this one is the greatest in the kingdom of heaven" (Matt 18:4). Then rather than requiring the pomp and circumstance typical of a king, he instructed his subjects on how he would like to be approached as their Ruler and Lord: "And whoever welcomes one child like this in my name welcomes me" (18:5).

This is a kingdom without borders, and a kingdom without time. To try and apply the rules, precepts, and writs of this world to this very unearthly kingdom would be similar to giving a football linebacker a horse and a polo stick and instructing him to get on with it and play. Neither the rules of this earth nor its tools govern the rules of God's kingdom. As

King, he determines the way it is both to operate and function.

In his kingdom, neither race nor gender delineate inequality. In his kingdom, power goes to the weak who recognize their weakness and humbly look to him. Forgiveness reigns preeminently, and the amount of money matters less than the heart that offers it, as we see in the case of the widow and her gift (Luke 21:1-4). Significance, in this unusual kingdom, is connected to service. Hope comes through helping others who may need it as well.

That is not to say there are no battles to fight or wars to win in this kingdom, or that this is a kingdom of rainbows, waterfalls, and unending bliss. There is a vile enemy still lurking and still seeking to dethrone the King because his kingdom is the greatest of all. Its origin lies in eternity past, and it will last forever.

In fact, before there ever was an earth at all, there was a kingdom. It existed solely in the heavenlies, and it was a place of glory, majesty, and beauty. Yet treason was committed in an attempt to steal the seat of power, and those caught in an attempt to lay siege to the throne were repudiated—kicked down into darkness, which would later be sculpted and called Earth. Satan, the leader of this primeval rebellion, now uses charm, deception, distraction, temptation, lust, pride, apathy, and evil to try and establish a rival kingdom whose subjects aim to defeat the subjects of the one, true King.

In the chancery known as the Holy Spirit, the story of this unique kingdom has been preserved for us, its subjects—followers of the Lord Jesus Christ—in what we call the Bible. Throughout Scripture, chroniclers—inspired by the Spirit—recorded, encouraged, equipped, lamented, and presented the history, rules, redemption, and purpose of our King and his kingdom. Unfortunately, today, many of us are living as followers of a King whom we also seek to dethrone, though perhaps not outrightly, through subtle ways of complacency, autonomy, independence, or just simply through a lack of a connection to him, his Word, and his covenants. As a result, we experience what anyone in any kingdom living apart from the rules of the King would. In our personal lives, homes, churches, communities, and our nation, we feel the chaos that comes from rebellion.

This is because in a kingdom, life is to be lived under the rule and authority of the King. The blessings of the covenantal charter of our King in his Word, imbued with the authority he gives us through his covenants, along with his promises and loyal love, come when we live all of our life under God. It comes when we live our lives on target with his goals and purposes as a kingdom disciple.

The unifying central theme throughout the Bible is the glory of God and the advancement of his kingdom. The conjoining thread from Genesis to Revelation—from beginning to end—is focused on one thing: God's glory through advancing his kingdom.

When you do not have that theme, the Bible becomes disconnected stories that are great for inspiration but seem to be unrelated in purpose and direction. The Bible exists to share God's movement in history toward the establishment and expansion of his kingdom. Understanding this theme increases the relevancy of this ancient book to your day-to-day living, because the kingdom is not only then, it is now.

Throughout the Bible, the kingdom of God is his rule, his plan, his program. God's kingdom is all-embracing. It covers everything in the universe. In fact, we can define the kingdom as God's comprehensive rule over all creation. It is the rule of God (theocracy) and not the rule of man (homocracy) that is paramount.

Now if God's kingdom is comprehensive, so is his kingdom agenda. The kingdom agenda, then, may be defined as *the visible demonstration of the comprehensive rule of God over every area of life.* The Greek word the Bible uses for kingdom is *basileia*, which basically means "rule" or "authority." Included in this definition is the concept of power. So when we talk about a kingdom, we're talking first about a king or a ruler. We are talking about someone who is in charge. Since there is a ruler, there also have to be "rulees," or kingdom subjects. In addition, a kingdom includes a realm—that is, a domain over which the king rules. Finally, if you're going to have a ruler, rulees, and a realm, you also need kingdom regulations, guidelines that govern the relationship between the ruler and the subjects. These are necessary so that the rulees will know whether they are doing what the ruler wants.

God's kingdom operates through his covenant. *A covenant is a divinely created relational bond through which God reveals himself and administers his kingdom program.* The four biblical covenantal spheres through which the kingdom operates are the individual, family, church, and community (or government).

Individual: The individual realm refers to each of us singularly as his kingdom disciple. A kingdom disciple can be defined as *a believer in Christ who takes part in the spiritual developmental process of progressively learning to live all of life under the lordship of Jesus Christ.* The goal of a kingdom disciple is to have a transformed life that transfers the values of the kingdom of God so that they replicate themselves in the lives of others. The result of such replication is God's exercising his rule from heaven to history through his kingdom disciples. Discipleship is the missing key to a life of authority under God. But surrender to Christ's lordship and obedience to his rule of love are the grooves and edges which make up that key, which (when used rightly) will unlock the power to bring heaven to bear on earth.

Family: The family realm refers to familial units, both immediate and extended. This can also include

variations on family due to death or adoption. The foundation of a family involves a husband and wife. A kingdom marriage is defined as *a covenantal union between a man and a woman who commit themselves to function in unison under divine authority in order to replicate God's image and expand his rule in the world through both their individual and joint callings.* Kingdom parenting can be defined as *the responsibility to intentionally oversee the generational transfer of a comprehensive Christian worldview so that children learn to consistently live all of life under God's divine authority.*

Church: The local church is the context and environment God has created to transform Christians into what we were created and redeemed to be: fully devoted followers of Jesus Christ. It is the spiritually redeemed body of believers that are to legislate the values of the kingdom of God from heaven to earth. A kingdom church can be defined as *a group of believers who covenant together to disciple its members in order to model and transfer heaven's values in history.* Discipleship is that process of the local church that seeks to bring believers from spiritual infancy to spiritual maturity so that they are then able to repeat that process with someone else.

Community: The community includes the multiple layers of society through which God works to establish order and ensure the freedoms and rights of all are carried out. This is obtained through biblical justice, which can be defined as *the equitable and impartial application of the rule of God's moral law in society.* Whether exercising itself through economic, political, social, or criminal justice, the one constant is the understanding and application of God's moral law within the social realm. It is the division of the sacred and the secular that has led to the cultural disintegration we are now experiencing (2 Chr 15:3-6). It was never the Creator's desire to have such a separation exist in his world. From Genesis to Revelation, it is inextricably clear that the spiritual and the social are always to be integrated if life is to be lived the way God intended.

The more these four covenantal spheres are properly connected to God and each other, the more ordered society will be. The less they are connected, the more conflict and chaos will occur.

It is my desire and prayer that this study Bible be used by God to guide, equip, strengthen, inspire, and inform you of all you need to fully experience both his power and his peace as you live under his rule. May it also awaken an even greater desire to discover more about our Lord himself as you explore his kingdom, anytime and anywhere.

Scan this code with your mobile device or follow this link for videos of Tony Evans teaching on the Kingdom Agenda.

www.bhpublishinggroup.com/qr/te/67-01

Scan these codes with your mobile device or follow these links for additional audio messages of Tony Evans teaching on the Kingdom Agenda.

KINGDOM AGENDA SERMONS

www.bhpublishinggroup.com/qr/te/67-02

KINGDOM LIFE SERMONS

www.bhpublishinggroup.com/qr/te/67-03

KINGDOM FAMILY SERMONS

www.bhpublishinggroup.com/qr/te/67-04

KINGDOM SOCIETY SERMONS

www.bhpublishinggroup.com/qr/te/67-05

HOW TO STUDY THE BIBLE

The Bible is a book unlike any other book. It is, in fact, a whole library of books, all bound together in one volume. These individual books were written by many different authors over an extended period of time. What makes the Bible so unique, though, is that its many human authors were all inspired by its one divine author—God himself! The Greek word Paul uses for "inspired by God" means "God-breathed." These words that carry God's breath are words that can change and transform our lives. Paul reminds us that all of Scripture "is inspired by God and is profitable for teaching, for rebuking, for correcting, for training in righteousness" (2 Tim 3:16).

If we want to understand who God is, what his purposes are, and how he has made himself known to the human race, we cannot afford to ignore the Bible. Whenever you purchase a complicated gadget it is usually accompanied by a set of instructions—a manufacturer's handbook. Without this handbook you'll find yourself having to guess at how it works. In a sense, the Bible is the "manufacturer's handbook" for life. The one who created us has plans and purposes for us. If we don't know the content of his manufacturer's handbook, we won't know his plans and purposes, nor will we know how to live as he intends.

Still, many people put little effort into reading the Bible. Sometimes the problem is just laziness or a wrong set of priorities. But that isn't the only reason. The Bible *can* be a difficult book to understand. While its most important teachings are understandable by a child, there is much in the pages of Scripture that is not easy to grasp without some extra effort and help. That's where a study Bible comes in handy. It will provide you with some background material and theological explanation that will bring biblical truths into sharper focus. But don't count on the study Bible to do all the work for you. If you want to get the most out of the Scripture you need to learn to read it for yourself and learn to interpret it by giving careful focus to the passage you are reading and by comparing what you learn there with the rest of what the Bible teaches.

What follows are some things you can do to help you get the most out of your biblical study.

READ CAREFULLY

Though the Bible is an exciting book, you can't read it in the same way you'd read a thrilling novel. If you race through the pages you will miss much of what it has to offer. Good Bible reading begins with reading slowly and carefully, and it is a good idea to have a pen and paper handy to jot down the things you observe. Or maybe you'll want to write in the margins of your Bible. Mark down the things that inspire, challenge, or puzzle you. If there is a key verse or key idea you discover, you might want to underline it. You can make a study Bible your own by recording *in* it the things you are learning *from* it.

As you read, pay close attention to words like *if*, *then*, and *therefore*, which will help you understand the relationships between the concepts it teaches. These little words may reveal requirements and expectations that you need to keep in mind. Many of the Bible's promises, for example, are conditional. There are things you are expected to do if that promise is to become real in your life. And in the New Testament letters, the word *therefore* is often a signal that what went before is the doctrinal basis on which a truth can be embraced and applied.

Read and read again. You might even try reading aloud as a way of forcing yourself to slow down and take in every thought. Above all, don't be in a hurry. Read slowly and think about what each sentence and paragraph means. Don't just hunt for an inspiring nugget of truth. Let every sentence speak to you!

ASK QUESTIONS

One of the common characteristics of children is that they are almost insatiably curious. They ask lots of questions, which can sometimes become exhausting for their parents. But it is the way they learn new things. One of the problems with adults is that they often stop asking questions as they grow older. So be more like a curious child as you read the Bible. Don't assume you already know what it says. Keep your curiosity high and keep your heart and mind open. One great way to do this is by cross-examining the passage you are reading in order to make sure you are noticing all it has to say. See if you can answer these questions: *who, what, where, when, why,* and *how?* Exploring the answers to these questions will open new depths of understanding.

PAY ATTENTION TO THE CONTEXT

Paying attention to *context* is extremely important if you want to accurately understand what the Bible is saying. Some people just search its pages for an

individual verse that speaks to their need of the moment, without paying much attention to the verses that surround it. Reading this way is like treating the Bible as a fortune cookie or as a collection of inspirational memes. As you read the Bible, sometimes a verse will stand out and engage your heart in a very personal way. But when that happens, it's important to see how that verse relates to the verses around it. If you don't pay attention to the context, you are in danger of trying to make the Bible say something that it doesn't actually say.

Every verse of the Bible is part of a chapter, and every chapter is part of a book, and every book of the Bible is part of one larger God-inspired message that unfolds across its pages. Many people don't realize that the Bible wasn't originally written in chapters and verses. Each book was one continuous text contained in a scroll, and it was not until the late Middle Ages that someone came up with the idea of dividing it into chapters and verses to make it more convenient for readers and as a tool for helping people locate specific passages they wanted to remember. You should keep that in mind before pulling a verse out of its context and applying it to your life.

As you read, pay attention to the immediate context of the neighboring verses and try to understand the main point that the biblical writer is making. Ask yourself how it fits in the context of the entire book. You should notice if the passage you are reading is part of a larger story or a larger argument and who is speaking or being spoken to. There are, for example, places in the Bible that contain the words of Satan or of a godless leader, and we don't want to treat those in the same way we'd treat the words of Jesus!

As we study the Bible, it is important to keep our focus upon the main points and the most important teachings, and not allow ourselves to be sidetracked too much by secondary issues. Make sure you understand the big picture through your *telescope* before you pull out your *microscope* to examine the details! The Bible isn't a puzzle book or a coded message, so don't look for complicated symbols and secret meanings. Ask yourself what it meant to the original readers and how that applies to you today.

BE READY TO OBEY

Applying what we read in the Bible to our daily lives is the highest purpose of Bible study. We don't study it so that we can win theological arguments or impress people with our knowledge. We read it so that God can use it to transform our lives. Therefore, we should read the Bible with humility and an open heart, being ready to be challenged and changed by God's Word. We should read it with an open mind, not assuming we already know what it means. The more

you read the Bible, the more new and fresh truths you will discover in its pages. It is inexhaustible.

The Bible speaks with God's own authority, so the proper response to such authority is obedience. James 1:23 tells us that the Bible is a mirror in which we can catch an honest glimpse of ourselves. As you read, you can perceive where you are falling short, where you are making improper compromises, where you are following your own desires instead of God's best, and where you are placing your cultural prejudices over God's truth. So, as you read Scripture, hear—and then obey.

PRAY

Since the Bible is a spiritual book, it must be approached spiritually. You approach studying the Bible spiritually by bathing your study in prayer. In this way, the Holy Spirit can illuminate your mind regarding the meaning and application of its truth to your life (1 Cor 2:9-16; Eph 6:18).

THE BIG STORY AND ALL THE LITTLE ONES

The Bible is filled with history, biographies, miracles, prophecies, songs, poems, letters, and practical teaching. Each element deserves your time and attention, and each book contains wisdom and guidance for your life. But as you read and study, you should never lose sight of the big over-arching story of the Bible, which is the story of God's redemptive love and his desire to be present with his people. It is a story about a King who will go to any lengths to invite his people into relationship with him and to join him in advancing his kingdom agenda in history.

The Old Testament tells the story of how that relationship grew and changed over time. It focuses upon the story of Israel, a people specially chosen by God to establish and advance his kingdom for his glory. He worked with his people in different ways through each of the covenants he made with them. The New Testament contains the fulfillment of these promises and covenants in the person of Jesus Christ, who is God in the flesh.

The Bible tells a story with a big narrative arc, and that arc points toward God's increasingly intimate dealings with his people. That's why it is important to pay attention to where you are in the big story as you read through the Bible.

The Pentateuch (Genesis–Deuteronomy) tells of the creation of the universe, the fall of humanity, the calling of Abraham to be the father of a chosen people, God's deliverance of his people from slavery through Moses, and the giving of the law as a sign of the covenant God made with his people. These five

books are the foundation for everything that follows in the establishing and expansion of God's kingdom.

The Historical Books (Joshua–Esther) record the many victories and failures of Israel. It is often not a pretty story! The historical books record the conquest of the land God had promised, the era of the judges, the rise of the monarchy, and the constant struggles against the temptations toward idolatry and immorality. They also tell of how Israel underwent a civil war and was divided into a northern kingdom (Israel) and a southern kingdom (Judah). This led to destruction and exile. The last few books reveal what happened when the Israelites finally emerged from exile.

The Poetical Books (Job–Song) were written at various times during the history of Israel, though the lion's share were penned during the high points of the monarchy under David and Solomon, who are traditionally considered to be the authors of much that is in these books. Job struggles with the question of why there is suffering in the lives of good people. Psalms is a book of songs, praises, and prayers. Proverbs offers bite-sized nuggets of wisdom for living, Ecclesiastes centers on the meaning of a truly good and purposeful life. The Song of Songs reflects upon human and divine love. Since poetry is less straightforward than prose, these books take a different path to revealing important truths about God and our walk with him.

The Prophetic Books (Isaiah–Malachi) record the stories and messages of the men God raised up to challenge Israel for its unfaithfulness, injustice, and hypocrisy. The prophets challenged the status quo and pointed toward the future with hope. They gestured toward a time when God will powerfully intervene in history and make himself known. Included in these books are prophecies of the coming Messiah, as well as the coming realization of the kingdom of God upon the earth.

The Gospels (Matthew–John) give us four different, but complementary, perspectives on the life of Jesus. We see in them the story of the one who embodies the kingdom of God and who offers a path to salvation based upon his love, his sacrifice, and his grace. The Gospels also record Jesus's kingdom teaching and the preparing of his disciples for the establishment of the church.

Acts is the story of the early church, focusing especially on the ministries of Peter and Paul. It shows how the power of the Holy Spirit was unleashed upon God's people so that they could bear witness to the truth—by miracles, healings, and especially by the powerful proclamation of the good news of Jesus Christ and his kingdom program.

The Epistles (Romans–Jude) are a collection of letters that the apostle Paul and other early church leaders wrote to inspire, instruct, and encourage the church—as well as to challenge false teachings that were beginning to creep into the early congregations. These letters give us a picture of the early Christian communities and offer practical advice about living the life of faith.

Revelation is the last book of the New Testament, and the last book of the Bible. Unquestionably the most complex and difficult biblical book to interpret, it has spawned a variety of different interpretations. But the central message is clear: A day is coming when God will defeat all the powers of darkness and establish his eternal worldwide kingdom with his people. This is the great and grand hope of Revelation.

As you read and study each book of the Bible, remember that the big story is one of God's love and redemption, and his desire to dwell with and in his people. The King is establishing a kingdom where he can rule in every heart, and where his grace will be the basis for relationship. Every page of the Bible is, in some way, pointing toward this ultimate hope.

Scan this code with your mobile device or follow this link for videos of Tony Evans leading you on an overview of the Old Testament.

Scan this code with your mobile device or follow this link for videos of Tony Evans leading you on an overview of the New Testament.

www.bhpublishinggroup.com/qr/te/67-07

www.bhpublishinggroup.com/qr/te/67-06

The Bible is God's revelation to humanity. It is our only source for completely reliable information about God, what happens when we die, and where history is headed. The Bible reveals these things because it is God's inspired Word, inerrant in the original manuscripts. Bible translation brings God's Word from the ancient languages (Hebrew, Greek, and Aramaic) into today's world. In dependence on God's Spirit to accomplish this sacred task, the CSB Translation Oversight Committee and Holman Bible Publishers present the Christian Standard Bible.

TEXTUAL BASE OF THE CSB

The textual base for the New Testament (NT) is the Nestle-Aland *Novum Testamentum Graece*, 28th edition, and the United Bible Societies' *Greek New Testament*, 5th corrected edition. The text for the Old Testament (OT) is the *Biblia Hebraica Stuttgartensia*, 4th edition.

Where there are significant differences among Hebrew, Aramaic, or Greek manuscripts, the translators follow what they believe is the original reading and indicate the main alternative(s) in footnotes. The CSB uses the traditional verse divisions found in most Protestant Bibles.

GOALS OF THIS TRANSLATION

- Provide English-speaking people worldwide with an accurate translation in contemporary English.
- Provide an accurate translation for personal study, sermon preparation, private devotions, and memorization.
- Provide a text that is clear and understandable, suitable for public reading, and shareable so that all may access its life-giving message.
- Affirm the authority of Scripture and champion its absolute truth against skeptical viewpoints.

TRANSLATION PHILOSOPHY OF THE CHRISTIAN STANDARD BIBLE

Most discussions of Bible translations speak of two opposite approaches: formal equivalence and dynamic equivalence. This terminology is meaningful, but Bible translations cannot be neatly sorted into these two categories. There is room for another category of translation philosophy that capitalizes on the strengths of the other two.

1. FORMAL EQUIVALENCE:

Often called "word-for-word" (or "literal") translation, the principle of formal equivalence seeks as nearly as possible to preserve the structure of the original language. It seeks to represent each word of the original text with an exact equivalent word in the translation so that the reader can see word for word what the original human author wrote. The merits of this approach include its consistency with the conviction that the Holy Spirit did inspire the very words of Scripture in the original manuscripts. It also provides the English Bible student some access to the structure of the text in the original language. Formal equivalence can achieve accuracy to the degree that English has an exact equivalent for each word and that the grammatical patterns of the original language can be reproduced in understandable English. However, it can sometimes result in awkward, if not incomprehensible, English or in a misunderstanding of the author's intent. The literal rendering of ancient idioms is especially difficult.

2. DYNAMIC OR FUNCTIONAL EQUIVALENCE:

Often called "thought-for-thought" translation, the principle of dynamic equivalence rejects as misguided the attempt to preserve the structure of the original language. It proceeds by extracting the meaning of a text from its form and then translating that meaning so that it makes the same impact on modern readers that the ancient text made on its original readers. Strengths of this approach include a high degree of clarity and readability, especially in places where the original is difficult to render word for word. It also acknowledges that accurate and effective translation may require interpretation. However, the meaning of a text cannot always be neatly separated from its form, nor can it always be precisely determined. A biblical author may have intended multiple meanings, but these may be lost with the elimination of normal structures. In striving for readability, dynamic equivalence also sometimes overlooks and loses some of the less prominent elements of meaning. Furthermore, lack of formal correspondence to the original makes it difficult to verify accuracy and thus can affect the usefulness of the translation for in-depth Bible study.

3. OPTIMAL EQUIVALENCE:

In practice, translations are seldom if ever purely formal or dynamic but favor one theory of Bible translation or the other to varying degrees. Optimal equivalence as a translation philosophy recognizes that form cannot always be neatly separated from meaning and should not be changed unless comprehension demands it. The primary goal of translation is to convey the sense of the original with as much clarity as the original text and the translation language permit. Optimal equivalence appreciates the goals

of formal equivalence but also recognizes its limitations.

Optimal equivalence starts with an exhaustive analysis of the text at every level (word, phrase, clause, sentence, discourse) in the original language to determine its original meaning and intention (or purpose). Then, relying on the latest and best language tools and experts, the nearest corresponding semantic and linguistic equivalents are used to convey as much of the information and intention of the original text with as much clarity and readability as possible. This process assures the maximum transfer of both the words and the thoughts contained in the original.

The CSB uses optimal equivalence as its translation philosophy. In the many places throughout the Bible where a word-for-word rendering is understandable, a literal translation is used. When a word-for-word rendering might obscure the meaning for a modern audience, a more dynamic translation is used. The Christian Standard Bible places equal value on fidelity to the original and readability for a modern audience, resulting in a translation that achieves both goals.

THE GENDER LANGUAGE USAGE IN BIBLE TRANSLATION

The goal of the translators of the Christian Standard Bible has not been to promote a cultural ideology but to translate the Bible faithfully. Recognizing modern usage of English, the CSB regularly translates the plural of the Greek word $\alpha\nu\theta\rho\omega\pi\sigma\varsigma$ ("man") as "people" instead of "men," and occasionally the singular as "one," "someone," or "everyone," when the supporting pronouns in the original languages validate such a translation. While the CSB avoids using "he" or "him" unnecessarily, the translation does not restructure sentences to avoid them when they are in the text.

HISTORY OF THE CSB

After several years of preliminary development, Holman Bible Publishers, the oldest Bible publisher in North America, assembled an international, interdenominational team of one hundred scholars, editors, stylists, and proofreaders, all of whom were committed to biblical inerrancy. Outside consultants and reviewers contributed valuable suggestions from their areas of expertise. Working from the original languages, an executive team of translators edited, polished, and reviewed the final manuscript, which was first published as the Holman Christian Standard Bible (HCSB) in 2004.

A standing committee was also formed to maintain the HCSB translation and look for ways to improve readability without compromising accuracy. As with the original translation team,

the committee that prepared this revision of the HCSB, renamed the Christian Standard Bible, is international and interdenominational, comprising evangelical scholars who honor the inspiration and authority of God's written Word.

TRADITIONAL FEATURES FOUND IN THE CSB

In keeping with a long line of Bible publications, the CSB has retained a number of features found in traditional Bibles:

1. Traditional theological vocabulary (for example, *justification, sanctification, redemption*) has been retained since such terms have no other translation equivalent that adequately communicates their exact meaning.
2. Traditional spellings of names and places found in most Bibles have been used to make the CSB compatible with most Bible study tools.
3. Some editions of the CSB will print the words of Christ in red letters to help readers easily locate the spoken words of the Lord Jesus Christ.
4. Descriptive headings, printed above each section of Scripture, help readers quickly identify the contents of that section.
5. OT passages quoted in the NT are indicated. In the CSB, they are set in boldface type.

HOW THE NAMES OF GOD ARE TRANSLATED

The Christian Standard Bible consistently translates the Hebrew names for God as follows:

Hebrew original:	CSB English:
Elohim	God
YHWH (Yahweh)	LORD
Adonai	Lord
Adonai Yahweh	Lord GOD
Yahweh Sabaoth	LORD of Armies
El Shaddai	God Almighty

FOOTNOTES

Footnotes are used to show readers how the original biblical language has been understood in the CSB.

I. OLD TESTAMENT (OT) TEXTUAL FOOTNOTES

OT textual notes show important differences among Hebrew (Hb) manuscripts and ancient OT versions, such as the Septuagint and the Vulgate. See the list of abbreviations on page XXI for a list of other ancient versions used.

Some OT textual notes (like NT textual notes) give only an alternate textual reading. However, other OT textual notes also give the support for the reading chosen by the editors

as well as for the alternate textual reading. For example, the CSB text of Psalm 12:7 reads,

> You, LORD, will guard us;
> you will protect us[A]
> from this generation forever.

The textual footnote for this verse reads,

[A] **12:7** Some Hb mss, LXX; other Hb mss read *him*

The textual note in this example means that there are two different readings found in the Hebrew manuscripts: some manuscripts read *us* and others read *him*. The CSB translators chose the reading *us*, which is also found in the Septuagint (LXX), and placed the other Hebrew reading *him* in the footnote.

Two other kinds of OT textual notes are

Alt Hb tradition reads ____
   a variation given by scribes in the Hebrew manuscript tradition (known as *Kethiv/Qere* and *Tiqqune Sopherim* readings)

Hb uncertain
   when it is unclear what the original Hebrew text was

2. NEW TESTAMENT (NT) TEXTUAL FOOTNOTES

NT textual notes indicate significant differences among Greek manuscripts (mss) and are normally indicated in one of three ways:

Other mss read _____
Other mss add _____
Other mss omit _____

In the NT, some textual footnotes that use the word "add" or "omit" also have square brackets before and after the corresponding verses in the biblical text. Examples of this use of square brackets are Mark 16:9-20 and John 7:53–8:11.

3. OTHER KINDS OF FOOTNOTES

Lit ____	a more literal rendering in English of the Hebrew, Aramaic, or Greek text
Or ____	an alternate or less likely English translation of the same Hebrew, Aramaic, or Greek text
=	an abbreviation for "it means" or "it is equivalent to"
Hb, Aramaic, Gk	the actual Hebrew, Aramaic, or Greek word is given using equivalent English letters
Hb obscure	the existing Hebrew text is especially difficult to translate
emend(ed) to ____	the original Hebrew text is so difficult to translate that competent scholars have conjectured or inferred a restoration of the original text based on the context, probable root meanings of the words, and uses in comparative languages

In some editions of the CSB, additional footnotes clarify the meaning of certain biblical texts or explain biblical history, persons, customs, places, activities, and measurements. Cross references are given for parallel passages or passages with similar wording, and in the NT, for passages quoted from the OT.

AD	In the year of our Lord
BC	before Christ
c.	century
ca	circa
chap(s).	chapter(s)
cp.	compare
DSS	Dead Sea Scrolls
e.g.	for example
Eng	English
etc.	et cetera
Gk	Greek
Hb	Hebrew
i.e.	that is
Lat	Latin
lit	literal(ly)
LXX	Septuagint—an ancient translation of the Old Testament into Greek
MT	Masoretic Text
NT	New Testament
ms(s)	manuscript(s)
OT	Old Testament
pl.	plural
Ps(s)	Psalm(s)
Sam	Samaritan Pentateuch
sg.	singular
Sym	Symmachus
Syr	Syriac
Tg	Targum
Theod	Theodotian
v./vv.	verse, verses
Vg	Vulgate—an ancient translation of the Bible into Latin
vol(s).	volume(s)

THE
OLD TESTAMENT

GENESIS

INTRODUCTION

Author

THOUGH THE BOOK OF GENESIS is anonymous (no author is listed), ancient Jewish and Christian traditions held that Moses authored the first five books of the Bible—referred to as the *Pentateuch* ("five vessels") or the *Torah* (a Hebrew word for "law" or "instruction"). That Moses stood behind these five books is attested to in both the Old and the New Testaments (see Neh 8:1; Mark 12:26).

Assuming Mosaic authorship does not prevent us from accepting that others would have provided some editorial additions later—for example, the details of Moses's death in Deuteronomy 34:5-12 and the mention of the city "Dan" in Genesis 14:14, which would not have been named until the time of the judges (see Judg 18:29). Thus, though many critical scholars today reject Mosaic authorship, we have good reason to accept the biblical tradition that Moses wrote the Pentateuch. For Genesis in particular, Moses probably used written sources and put them together to form this book.

Historical Background

Genesis covers the lengthy period from the creation of the heavens and the earth (1:1) to the death of Joseph, the son of Jacob, in Egypt (50:26). It includes an account of the origin of humankind and another of the origin of the nation of Israel. The rest of the Bible is dependent on the history and theology of Genesis. It is foundational for all that follows. Here we have the creation of the universe, man and woman made in the image of God, the mandate for humans to rule the earth, the first marriage, Satan's opposition to humanity, the fall of humanity into sin, God's promise to defeat Satan through the seed of the woman, Noah and the flood, the tower of Babylon, God's covenant with Abraham, the faith of Abraham, the sacrifice of Isaac, the introduction to the twelve sons of Jacob (that is, Israel), the story of Joseph, and more.

Message and Purpose

Genesis is the book of beginnings. It is critical because it sets the stage for the rest of Scripture. The best way to understand Genesis is through its personalities, beginning with the first couple: Adam and Eve. God gave his dominion covenant to humankind, to rule on his behalf on earth as a reflection of his dominion over all. This set the stage for the fall, when Adam and Eve sinned against God, bringing earth under the temporary control of Satan. But the episode recording the entrance of sin is also embedded with the prophecy of a Redeemer (3:15)—Jesus Christ—who will defeat Satan and restore God's kingdom rule over all.

In the meantime Genesis records the angelic conflict now being waged on earth to such an extent that God destroyed the earth with a flood and began again with Noah to establish his kingdom rule—for Genesis introduces us to a kingdom concept. The world after the flood also rebelled against God at Babylon, and God judged the people for trying to establish unity without him.

Then God called one man, Abraham, through whom he would reestablish his kingdom regime. Beginning with chapter 12, Genesis traces the history of Abraham and his family as God lays the foundation of his kingdom through the nation of Israel.

VIDEO | INTRO

www.bhpublishinggroup.com/qr/te/01_00

Outline

I. From Adam to Abram (1:1–11:9)
  A. Creation, Marriage, and the Fall into Sin (1:1–5:32)
  B. The Flood (6:1–8:22)
  C. A New Beginning—And a Dead End (9:1–11:9)

II. Abraham (11:10–24:67)
  A. Father Abraham and His Rocky Faith Journey (11:10–14:24)
  B. From Abram to Abraham: A Covenant Renewed (15:1–17:27)
  C. Sodom and Lot (18:1–19:38)
  D. Isaac: Birth, Sacrifice, and Quest for a Wife (20:1–24:67)

III. Jacob (25:1–36:43)
  A. Jacob the Deceiver and Esau the Impulsive (25:1–28:9)
  B. A Holy God, a Beautiful Woman, and a Deceptive Uncle (28:10–29:29)
  C. Jacob Multiplies, Struggles with God, and Meets Esau Again (29:30–33:20)
  D. The Defilement of Dinah and the Return to Bethel (34:1–36:43)

IV. Joseph (37:1–50:26)
  A. Joseph the Dreamer and Judah the Hypocrite (37:1–38:30)
  B. From Rags to Riches in Egypt (39:1–41:57)
  C. Family Reunion (42:1–47:31)
  D. The Blessings of Jacob and the Promises of God (48:1–50:26)

[a] 1:1 Ps 90:2; 102:12; Is
40:21; Jn 1:1-3; Eph 3:21
[b] Neh 9:6; Is 40:12-14;
43:7; Jr 10:12-16; Am 4:13;
Rm 1:25; 1Co 11:9; Col 1:16;
Rv 4:11
[c] 1:2 Jr 4:23
[d] Jb 26:13; 33:4; Ps 33:6;
104:30
[e] 1:3 2Co 4:6
[f] 1:6 Is 44:24; Jr 10:12
[g] 1:7 Ps 148:4
[h] 1:9 Jb 38:8-11; Ps 33:7;
136:6; Jr 5:22; 2Pt 3:5
[i] 1:11 Ps 65:9-13; 104:14

[j] 1:14 Jr 10:2
[k] Ps 104:19
[l] 1:16 Dt 4:19; Ps 136:7-9;
Is 40:26
[m] 1:18 Jr 31:35
[n] 1:21 Ps 104:25-28
[o] 1:22 Gn 8:17; 9:1

THE CREATION

1 In the beginning[a] God created the heavens and the earth. [A,b]

² Now the earth was formless and empty,[c] darkness covered the surface of the watery depths, and the Spirit of God was hovering over the surface of the waters.[d] ³ Then God said, "Let there be light,"[e] and there was light. ⁴ God saw that the light was good, and God separated the light from the darkness. ⁵ God called the light "day," and the darkness he called "night." There was an evening, and there was a morning: one day.

⁶ Then God said, "Let there be an expanse between the waters, separating water from water."[f] ⁷ So God made the expanse and separated the water under the expanse from the water above the expanse.[g] And it was so. ⁸ God called the expanse "sky."[B] Evening came and then morning: the second day.

⁹ Then God said, "Let the water under the sky be gathered into one place,[h] and let the dry land appear." And it was so. ¹⁰ God called the dry land "earth," and the gathering of the water he called "seas." And God saw that it was good. ¹¹ Then God said, "Let the earth produce vegetation: seed-bearing plants and fruit trees on the earth bearing fruit with seed in it according to their kinds."[i] And it was so. ¹² The earth produced vegetation: seed-bearing plants according to their kinds and trees bearing fruit with seed in it according to their kinds. And God saw that it was good. ¹³ Evening came and then morning: the third day.

¹⁴ Then God said, "Let there be lights in the expanse of the sky to separate the day from the night. They will serve as signs[j] for seasons[C] and for days and years.[k] ¹⁵ They will be lights in the expanse of the sky to provide light on the earth." And it was so. ¹⁶ God made the two great lights — the greater light to rule over the day and the lesser light to rule over the night — as well as the stars.[l] ¹⁷ God placed them in the expanse of the sky to provide light on the earth, ¹⁸ to rule the day and the night, and to separate light from darkness.[m] And God saw that it was good. ¹⁹ Evening came and then morning: the fourth day.

²⁰ Then God said, "Let the water swarm with[D] living creatures, and let birds fly above the earth across the expanse of the sky." ²¹ So God created the large sea-creatures[E] and every living creature that moves and swarms in the water,[n] according to their kinds. He also created every winged creature according to its kind. And God saw that it was good. ²² God blessed them: "Be fruitful, multiply, and fill the waters of the seas, and let the birds multiply on the earth."[o] ²³ Evening came and then morning: the fifth day.

²⁴ Then God said, "Let the earth produce living creatures according to their kinds: livestock, creatures that crawl, and the wildlife of the earth according to their kinds." And it was so. ²⁵ So God made the wildlife of the earth according to their kinds, the livestock according to their kinds, and all the creatures that crawl on the ground according to their kinds. And God saw that it was good.

[A] 1:1 Or *created the universe*   [B] 1:8 Or *"heavens."*   [C] 1:14 Or *for the appointed times*   [D] 1:20 Lit *with swarms of*   [E] 1:21 Or *created sea monsters*

1:1 Most ancient creation accounts chronicle a struggle between good and evil, with earth popping up as an accidental by-product of struggle. In these accounts, the gods who created the world did so out of prior material. They could not truly create. Scripture's story is different: **In the beginning God** (*Elohim*, the Supreme One) **created** out of nothing. With a mere word he made the entire universe of time, space, and matter—negating any possibility of atheistic evolution.

1:2 **Formless and empty** connotes a desolate, uninhabitable place. This suggests something happened between verses 1 and 2. Satan arrived on the scene. We get few details of Satan's fall here (Ezek 28 and Isa 14 provide more), but it appears his rebellion plunged earth into darkness (see Luke 10:18). Nevertheless, **the Spirit of God was hovering**, ready to bring order out of chaos.

1:3-5 God made the light, but he also *named* it: **God called the light "day"** (1:5). By naming the parts of his creation, God expresses sovereign rule over them. Even the concept of light, which is fundamental to our world, only exists because God sustains it.

1:6-8 God placed some **water above the expanse** (1:7); this is the basis of our earthly water cycle. God created the atmosphere so that life here is possible.

1:9-13 God **gathered into one place** (1:9) all the water, essentially pulling the land up to create continents. He then created vegetation, **according to . . . kinds** (1:12). God gave names to these new creations too. He also recognized that these things were **good** (1:10, 12).

1:14-19 God creates the **lights in the expanse of the sky** (1:14)—but just a few verses earlier, God had created light and darkness. So

what was emanating light for the first three days? God himself was (see Rev 22:5). On day four, God handed over that responsibility to celestial representatives, so that they would **provide light on the earth** (Gen 1:17) and **serve as signs** (1:14).

1:20-23 As he had populated the ground with plants (1:11-13), God made birds and fish (1:21). What is unique here is that he blesses them with a commission to **be fruitful . . . and fill the . . . earth** (1:22). God created a built-in capacity for his creation to reproduce and spread.

1:24-25 The threefold taxonomy of animals reflects the Jewish way of categorizing: **creatures that crawl** (1:24), or the tiny things we would call insects, rodents, and lizards; **livestock** (1:24), domesticated animals like cows, sheep, and goats; and the rest are **wildlife of the earth** (1:24). This would include the dinosaurs.

❧ KINGDOM LIVING ❧
FAMILY
A Photograph of God

Looking at Genesis 1, we read that God created the heavens and the earth in such a way that they are functional, vibrant, and pulsating with life. On the fifth day, God started forming the creatures that would live on the earth. Then, on the sixth day, he reached the pinnacle of his creative purposes with the creation of humankind.

Important truths arise from this account in Genesis 1:26-28. First, we see the word "us" referring to the triune God: Father, Son, and Spirit. The Trinity consists of three individual and unique persons who make up the unified reality of the Godhead. Second, we see the commission of humankind—which is to bear this Trinitarian image of God. God created humanity (body, soul, and spirit) to mirror him, and then he established them in the divine institution called family to reproduce his image. Therefore, the goal of people in general—and the family in particular—is to mirror God in the visible realm predicated on his reality in the invisible realm. The family unit is to serve as a visible photograph of God himself.

Simply put, the family's mission is the replication of the image of God in history and to carry out his divinely mandated dominion (Gen 1:26, 28). Personal and familial happiness is to be a benefit of a strong family, but it's not the mission. The mission is the reflection of God through the advancement of his kingdom and rule on earth. Happiness becomes the natural benefit when this goal is being actualized.

FOR THE NEXT FAMILY
KINGDOM LIVING LESSON SEE PAGE 5.

APPLICATION QUESTIONS

READ GENESIS 1:26-27

– What do these verses teach about family?
– How have you experienced God's provision in your efforts to manage your family and your other spheres of life?

---

26 Then God said, "Let us[a] make man[A] in[B] our image, according to our likeness.[b] They will rule the fish of the sea, the birds of the sky, the livestock, the whole earth,[c] and the creatures that crawl[D] on the earth."[c]
27 So God created man
    in his own image;
he created him in[E] the image of God;
    he created them male and female.[d]
28 God blessed them, and God said to them, "Be fruitful, multiply, fill the earth,[e] and subdue it. Rule the fish of the sea, the birds of the sky, and every creature that crawls[F] on the earth." **29** God also said, "Look, I have given you every seed-bearing plant on the surface of the entire earth and every tree whose fruit contains seed. This will be food for you,[f] **30** for all the wildlife of the earth, for every bird of the sky, and for every creature that crawls on the earth — everything having the breath of life in it — I have given[G] every green plant for food."[g] And it was so. **31** God saw all that he had made, and it was very good indeed.[h] Evening came and then morning: the sixth day.

2 So the heavens and the earth and everything in them were completed.[i] **2** On the seventh[H] day God had completed his work that he had done, and he rested[i] on the seventh day from all his work that he had done.[j] **3** God blessed the seventh day and declared it holy, for on it he rested[k] from all his work of creation.[j,l]

[a] 1:26 Gn 3:22; 11:7
[b] Gn 5:1,3; 9:6; Rm 8:29; 1Co 11:7; 15:49; 2Co 3:18; 4:4; Eph 4:24; Col 1:15; Jms 3:9
[c] Gn 9:2; Ps 8:6-8; Jms 3:7
[d] 1:27 Gn 5:2; Mt 19:4; Mk 10:6
[e] 1:28 Gn 9:1,7
[f] 1:29 Gn 9:3; Ps 104:14-15; 136:25; 145:15-16
[g] 1:30 Ps 147:9
[h] 1:31 1Tm 4:4
[i] 2:1 Neh 9:6; Ps 33:6; Is 34:4; 45:12
[j] 2:2 Ex 20:8-11; 31:17; Dt 5:12-14; Heb 4:4
[k] 2:3 Ex 31:17
[l] Ex 20:11; 31:17; Ps 121:2

[A] 1:26 Or *human beings*; Hb *'adam*, also in v. 27   [B] 1:26 Or *as*   [C] 1:26 Syr reads *sky, and over every animal of the land*   [D] 1:26 Or *scurry*   [E] 1:27 Or *man as his own image; he created him as*   [F] 1:28 Or *and all scurrying animals*   [G] 1:30 *I have given* added for clarity   [H] 2:2 Sam, LXX, Syr read *sixth*   [I] 2:2 Or *ceased*, also in v. 3   [J] 2:3 Lit *work that God created to make*

1:26-30 God made his crowning achievement: **Let us make man in our image, visibly mirroring God's spiritual nature, according to our likeness visibly mirroring God's functional actions** (1:26). "Let us" is a hint at the Trinity: God the Father, Son, and the Spirit agreed to make the first human family, and that family was supposed to reflect truths about God. Every human reflects the unity of God. But he also **created them male and female** (1:27), so our differences reflect the diversity of the Trinity too.

We humans are to rule on God's behalf, and we are to reproduce for his glory (1:28). Just as God handed over responsibility to the sun, so that it would shine *for God,* God handed over responsibility to us, so that we would govern and steward his world *for him.* This is the dominion covenant that is at the heart of the expansion of God's kingdom program in history through the rule of man (Ps 8:4-6; Heb 2:4-8).

1:31 Here God declared his world **very good indeed**. Humanity reflected the beauty and complexity of God like no other part of creation.

2:1-3 God **rested on the seventh day** (2:2) because he wanted to provide us a model.

If even God, who "does not slumber or sleep" (Ps 121:4), took an entire day off to enjoy the fruit of his labors, we too should pause.

2:4-7 "Adam," in Hebrew, refers to that which comes from the ground, because **the LORD God formed the man out of . . . the ground** (2:7). With the introduction of the name "Lord" (Yahweh), God introduced himself relationally. God also breathed into Adam **the breath of life** (2:7). God made us out of the most mundane material, but God also infused us with his Spirit, which gives us tremendous value and enables us to communicate with God.

a 2:4 Gn 5:1; 6:9; 10:1; 11:10,27; 25:12,19; 36:1,9; 37:2
b 2:5 Gn 1:11-12
c 2:7 Gn 3:19,23; 18:27; Ps 103:14; Ec 12:7; 1Co 15:47
d Gn 7:22; Jb 33:4; Is 2:22
e 1Co 15:45
f 2:8 Gn 13:10; Is 51:3; Ezk 28:13; 31:8; Jl 2:3
g 2:9 Gn 3:22; Rv 2:7; 22:2,14
h Pr 3:18
i 2:11 Gn 10:7,29; 25:18; 1Sm 15:7
j 2:14 Dn 10:4
k Gn 15:18
l 2:16 Gn 3:1-2
m 2:17 Gn 3:5; Dt 30:15,19-20; Rm 6:23; 1Tm 5:6; Jms 1:15
n 2:18 Pr 31:11-12; 1Co 11:9; 1Tm 2:13
o 2:19 Ps 8:6
p 2:21 Gn 15:12
q 2:22 1Co 11:8,12

MAN AND WOMAN IN THE GARDEN

4 These are the records*a* of the heavens and the earth, concerning their creation. At the time*A* that the LORD God made the earth and the heavens, **5** no shrub of the field*b* had yet grown on the land,*B* and no plant of the field had yet sprouted, for the LORD God had not made it rain on the land, and there was no man to work the ground. **6** But mist would come up from the earth and water all the ground. **7** Then the LORD God formed the man out of the dust from the ground*c* and breathed the breath of life into his nostrils,*d* and the man became a living being.*e*

8 The LORD God planted a garden in Eden, in the east,*f* and there he placed the man he had formed. **9** The LORD God caused to grow out of the ground every tree pleasing in appearance and good for food, including the tree of life in the middle of the garden,*g* as well as the tree of the knowledge of good and evil.*h*

10 A river went*C* out from Eden to water the garden. From there it divided and became the source of four rivers.*D* **11** The name of the first is Pishon, which flows through the entire land of Havilah,*E,i* where there is gold. **12** Gold from that land is pure;*F* bdellium*G* and onyx*H* are also there. **13** The name of the second river is Gihon, which flows through the entire land of Cush. **14** The name of the third river is Tigris,*j* which runs east of Assyria. And the fourth river is the Euphrates.*k*

15 The LORD God took the man and placed him in the garden of Eden to work it and watch over it. **16** And the LORD God commanded the man, "You are free to eat from any tree of the garden,*l* **17** but you must not eat from the tree of the knowledge of good and evil, for on the day you eat from it, you will certainly die."*m* **18** Then the LORD God said, "It is not good for the man to be alone. I will make a helper corresponding*n* to him." **19** The LORD God formed out of the ground every wild animal and every bird of the sky, and brought each to the man to see what he would call it.*o* And whatever the man called a living creature, that was its name. **20** The man gave names to all the livestock, to the birds of the sky, and to every wild animal; but for the man*i* no helper was found corresponding to him. **21** So the LORD God caused a deep sleep to come over the man,*p* and he slept. God took one of his ribs and closed the flesh at that place. **22** Then the LORD God made the rib he had taken from the man into a woman and brought her to the man.*q* **23** And the man said:

> **Questions & Answers**
>
> **Q** You have called *The Kingdom Agenda* your "magnum opus." Why do you view this book and philosophy of life as so critical and central to your life's work?
>
> **A** *The Kingdom Agenda* is my life's work because of its comprehensive nature. When I saw that the whole Bible is the summary of God's kingdom program and plan—and saw how all the pieces fit together—it made the Bible come alive to me. I began to see that things people often view as irrelevant are actually terribly relevant to our decision-making, our relationships, and every aspect of our lives. When I saw how comprehensive this is and how it knits together all the questions that I had, it became a driving force for everything I did. It became clear to me that God had given me a worldview based on his Word that, if understood by God's people, could be as transforming for their lives as it was for mine.
>
> FOR THE NEXT Q&A, SEE PAGE 7.

A 2:4 Lit *creation on the day*   *B* 2:5 Or *earth*   *C* 2:10 Or *goes*   *D* 2:10 Lit *became four heads*   *E* 2:11 Or *of the Havilah*   *F* 2:12 Lit *good*   *G* 2:12 A yellowish, transparent gum resin   *H* 2:12 Identity of this precious stone uncertain   *I* 2:20 Or *for Adam*

2:8-15 Adam was **to work** the garden **and watch over it** (2:15). He was also to guard and protect that which was under his responsibility. Since the only threat in existence was Satan, this introduces the angelic conflict and the fact that man was created to demonstrate God's greater glory to the angelic realm (see *Ps 8:4-6; Eph 3:10; 6:10-12*).

2:16-17 The LORD God commanded the man and expected him to obey (2:16). The commandment was simple: **you must not eat from the tree of the knowledge of good and evil** (2:17). Biblical freedom is the responsibility and opportunity to choose to maximize one's calling under God. God gave Adam a tremendous amount of freedom, allowing him to enjoy whatever God provided. But biblical freedom has healthy limits. When we misuse that freedom, the consequences are severe. Just as the rules in a football game *help the players and fans enjoy the game*, boundaries in our spiritual walk help us live the way God intended. Ignoring God's boundaries always ends in death.

2:18 When God saw Adam by himself, he responded this way: **It is not good for the man to be alone.** So he promises to make **a helper corresponding to him**. A wife is there to be a man's counterpart, equal to him and adding what he lacks. It would be the man's responsibility to provide, protect, and proclaim God's truth in the home. The woman is an essential contributor to the marriage—not a secondary servant to her mate.

2:21-22 God lovingly addressed Adam's need, creating a woman out of one of Adam's ribs. God formed Adam; he *fashioned* Eve. God then **brought her to the man** (2:22). Just like Adam, then, Eve had a relationship with God before she had a relationship with her spouse.

2:23-25 Adam—*ish* in Hebrew—gives his wife his name. **This one will be called "woman"**

a 2:23 Eph 5:28-30
b 2:24 Mal 2:15; Mt 19:5;
Mk 10:7-8; 1Co 6:16;
Eph 5:31
c 3:1 Mt 10:16; 2Co 11:3; Rv
12:9; 20:2

d 3:3 Gn 2:17
e 3:4 Jn 8:44
f 3:6 1Tm 2:14; Jms 1:14-15;
1Jn 2:16

☙ KINGDOM LIVING ❧
FAMILY
The Role of Helper

An unfortunate, yet common, belief in Christian circles is that since God made Eve as a "helper" for Adam, women are somehow less valuable than men. People frequently compare women to the Holy Spirit in his role of "helper" because he's the member of the Trinity who does a substantial amount of work but gets very little recognition. Yet a deeper examination of the word used for "helper" in the original language is eye-opening.

The Hebrew words translated "helper . . . corresponding to him" (Gen 2:20) in the creation story are important to examine because they are uniquely powerful. The words are *ezer* and *keneg-do*. The word *ezer* occurs twenty-one times in the Old Testament, with only two of those occurrences relating to a woman. In all the other instances, the word is used to refer directly to God the Father.

The term *kenegdo* was added to *ezer* in order to distinguish it from every other time in the Old Testament that it was used to refer to a strong help from God. The addition of *kenegdo* draws from its literal definition which is, "before your face, within your view or purpose." It can also be translated as a "counterpart to."

Through a careful look at the original language, it is easy to determine that Eve's role was not one of subservience, maid service, or even that of simply playing a support role. In the original language of Scripture, hers is a strong, visible help comparable to that provided by God the Father.

FOR THE NEXT FAMILY
KINGDOM LIVING LESSON SEE PAGE 9.

This one, at last, is bone of my bone and flesh of my flesh;
this one will be called "woman,"
for she was taken from man.*a*

24 This is why a man leaves his father and mother and bonds with his wife, and they become one flesh.*b* **25** Both the man and his wife were naked, yet felt no shame.

THE TEMPTATION AND THE FALL

3 Now the serpent was the most cunning of all the wild animals that the LORD God had made. He said to the woman, "Did God really say, 'You can't eat from any tree in the garden'?"*c*

2 The woman said to the serpent, "We may eat the fruit from the trees in the garden. **3** But about the fruit of the tree in the middle of the garden, God said, 'You must not eat it or touch it, or you will die.'"*d*

4 "No! You will not die," the serpent said to the woman.*e* **5** "In fact, God knows that when[A] you eat it your eyes will be opened and you will be like God,[B] knowing good and evil." **6** The woman saw that the tree was good for food and delightful to look at, and that it was desirable for obtaining wisdom. So she took some of its fruit and ate it; she also gave some to her husband, who was with her, and he ate it.*f* **7** Then the eyes of both of them were opened, and they knew they were naked; so they sewed fig leaves together and made coverings for themselves.

SIN'S CONSEQUENCES

8 Then the man and his wife heard the sound of the LORD God walking in the garden at the time of the evening breeze,[C]

[A] 3:5 Lit *on the day*   [B] 3:5 Or *gods*, or *divine beings*   [C] 3:8 Lit *at the wind of the day*

(2:23), he says, the Hebrew word for "woman" being *isha*. Together, **they become one flesh** (2:24), which is to say they share a unity of purpose while retaining their uniqueness as individuals. This is a pattern for all married couples. This also establishes the fact that marriage is only between a man and a woman (Matt 19:4-6).

3:1 **The serpent** that showed up is the devil in disguise. He approached **the woman** on purpose. Adam was supposed to lead his family by making sure that both he and Eve knew God's commands and walked in them. The serpent sought to reverse the divinely ordained roles in the family by bypassing the man and appealing to the woman. Satan also ignored the name *Lord* while retaining the name *God*, thus retaining religion while removing relationship.

Notice Satan's tactics. He intentionally misrepresented God, implying that God had commanded, **You can't eat from any tree in the garden.** One of Satan's oldest lies, as alluring today as then, is this: *God is holding out on you.*

3:4-5 Satan reveals two more classic lies. The first is that sin carries no consequences: **You will not die** (3:4). The second is that humans can become equal to God (3:5). The irony is that God intended for us to be like him, sharing in his reign and ruling over his world. But Satan tempted Adam and Eve to try to *take God's place.*

3:6 Eve sized up the fruit and concluded **that the tree was good for food,** and so she took a bite. Notice that Adam **was with her** this whole time. He became the responder instead of the leader, and literally all hell broke loose as a result.

3:7-8 The manifestation of death was emotional, spiritual, relational, environmental, and ultimately physical. Adam and Eve **sewed fig leaves together** for clothing (3:7). Awareness

a 3:8 Jb 34:22-23
b 3:12 Jb 31:33; Pr 28:13
c 3:13 Rm 7:11; 2Co 11:3;
    1Tm 2:14

d 3:14 Is 65:25; Mc 7:17
e 3:15 Heb 2:14; 1Jn 3:8
f 3:16 Jn 16:21; 1Tm 2:15
g Gn 4:7

❧ KINGDOM LIVING ❧
KINGDOM
Keeping "Lord" with God

The first conversation between the devil and a human was also about God. Not only that, but it was also about God's word. Satan asked Eve, "Did God really say . . . ?" (Gen 3:1). And Satan did this because he knew that in order to get rid of God's rule, he had to get rid of the authority of his word.

A very important part of Satan's strategy is that he did not seek to get rid of religion. The whole conversation was about God. In fact, he even went so far as to tell Eve that she could "be like God" (3:5). Satan doesn't mind religion. You can go to church all day long if you want. What he does mind, though, is when you acknowledge God as ruler over your life. This is evidenced through a clever maneuver Satan pulled on Eve.

Prior to the conversation between the woman and the snake, the Creator is referenced in Scripture as "Lord God." This means "ruler, absolute authority." Yet when Satan talked with Eve, he removed the name "Lord." He purposefully left out the fundamental principle that God is the rightful King over his kingdom. The issue in the garden was really about whose word would be final.

Will God be "Lord God" to you? Or will you just say that he is "God" while making your own decisions? Whenever you allow the evil one to cause you to question the ultimate authority of God in your life, you jeopardize your influence in God's kingdom. That is why so many Christians never fully live out their destinies.

In the garden, Satan also challenged God's authority by trying to persuade Eve to think that God was being jealous about the matter of deity. But Satan knew no one could be like God. How did he know? Because he had tried it already himself and gotten thrown out of heaven for his efforts. Nevertheless, Satan attempted to sell Eve the same exact lie he had once sold himself.

God created you for his glory. So whenever you try to take glory for yourself and live independently of him, you are living outside of your intended purpose.

FOR THE NEXT KINGDOM
KINGDOM LIVING LESSON SEE PAGE 783.

and they hid from the Lord God among the trees of the garden.*a* **9** So the Lord God called out to the man and said to him, "Where are you?"

10 And he said, "I heard you*A* in the garden, and I was afraid because I was naked, so I hid."

11 Then he asked, "Who told you that you were naked? Did you eat from the tree that I commanded you not to eat from?"

12 The man replied,*b* "The woman you gave to be with me — she gave me some fruit from the tree, and I ate."

13 So the Lord God asked the woman, "What is this you have done?"

And the woman said, "The serpent deceived me, and I ate."*c*

14 So the Lord God said to the serpent:
Because you have done this,
you are cursed more than any livestock
and more than
any wild animal.
You will move on your belly
and eat dust all the days
of your life.*d*
15 I will put hostility between you
and the woman,
and between your offspring
and her offspring.
He will strike your head,
and you will strike his heel.*e*
16 He said to the woman:
I will intensify
your labor pains;
you will bear children
with painful effort.*f*
Your desire*g* will be
for your husband,
yet he will rule over you.

A 3:10 Lit *the sound of you*

of their nakedness was a mark of emotional death, rather than life. When they heard God approaching, they **hid from the Lord God** (3:8). The spiritual relationship that nourished them and should have brought them their greatest joy had become a terror to them.
3:9-13 When God called to Adam, **Where are you?** (3:9), he was calling Adam to task

because Adam was the leader and had failed. To those men abandoning their families or failing to lead spiritually, God also says, "Where are you? Step up to be the men I created you to be."
3:14-19 The seeds of death spread. Adam and Eve's rebellion led to relational death, as God promised that the relationship between men

and women would become a battle (3:16). It caused economic death as God promised that work would become **painful** because Adam valued the word of his wife more than the word of God (3:17). And while Adam and Eve would not drop dead on the spot, their coming biological deaths were now guaranteed (3:19). They were like flowers cut off from the plant.

Questions & Answers

Q Can Christians be possessed by and under the control of the devil? How should we understand the role of our will and decision-making in the face of the devil's temptations?

A One comedian was famous for saying, "The devil made me do it," as a funny way of accounting for bad decisions. We are often tempted to do the same thing, chalking up our weaknesses, defeats, and pet sins to the power of the devil's temptations. This impulse to blame the devil for our sins goes all the way back to the garden of Eden, when Eve (after being blamed by Adam) blamed the serpent for her sin: "The serpent deceived me, and I ate" (Gen 3:13). While Christians cannot be possessed by the devil, they can be under satanic influence so that he is the dominant one prompting their decision-making.

Scripture makes it clear that Jesus's atoning death on the cross defeated the devil (see Col 2:14-15; Heb 2:14-15). So now the devil has to defeat us through deception, not through raw power, because God's power is greater (1 John 4:4) and we are "more than conquerors" in Christ (Rom 8:37). Though Satan is not more powerful than God, he can leverage influence in our lives if we give him authority that does not belong to him and attention that he should not receive. So, then, we are to relate to the devil as one who has great power, but not ultimate power. We are to resist the devil in the same way Jesus did—with the Word of God (see Luke 4:1-13). Satan is allergic to Scripture. When you resist him by using Scripture rightly, he'll "flee from you" (Jas 4:7) because he can't handle prolonged exposure to it.

FOR THE NEXT Q&A, SEE PAGE 69.

17 And he said to the man, "Because you listened to your wife and ate from the tree about which I commanded you, 'Do not eat from it':

The ground is cursed
  because of you.[a]
You will eat from it by means of
  painful labor[A]
all the days of your life.
18 It will produce thorns
  and thistles for you,
and you will eat the plants
  of the field.[b]
19 You will eat bread[B] by the sweat
  of your brow
until you return to the ground,[c]
since you were taken from it.
For you are dust,
and you will return to dust."

20 The man named his wife Eve[c] because she was the mother of all the living. **21** The LORD God made clothing from skins for the man and his wife, and he clothed them. **22** The LORD God said, "Since the man has become like one of us, knowing good and evil, he must not reach out, take from the tree of life, eat, and live forever."[d] **23** So the LORD God sent him away from the garden of Eden to work the ground from which he was taken. **24** He drove the man out and stationed the cherubim and the flaming, whirling sword east of the garden of Eden to guard the way to the tree of life.[e]

CAIN MURDERS ABEL

4 The man was intimate with his wife Eve, and she conceived and gave birth to Cain. She said, "I have had a male child with the LORD's help."[D] **2** She also gave birth to his brother Abel. Now Abel became a shepherd of flocks, but Cain worked the ground. **3** In the course of time Cain presented some of the land's produce as an offering to the LORD.[f] **4** And Abel also presented an offering — some of the firstborn of his flock and their fat portions.[g] The LORD had regard for Abel and his offering,[h] **5** but he did not have regard for

[a] 3:17 Gn 5:29; Rm 8:20-22; Heb 6:8
[b] 3:18 Gn 2:5
[c] 3:19 Ps 90:3; 104:29; Ec 12:7
[d] 3:22 Gn 2:9; Rv 2:7
[e] 3:24 Ex 25:18-22; Ps 104:4; Ezk 10:1-20; Heb 1:7
[f] 4:3 Ex 23:19; 34:26; Neh 10:35
[g] 4:4 Ex 13:12; Nm 18:17; Pr 3:9
[h] Heb 11:4

[A] 3:17 Lit it through pain [B] 3:19 Or food [C] 3:20 Lit Living, or Life [D] 4:1 Lit the LORD

3:20-24 Driving **the man out** of the garden and placing a **cherubim** with a **flaming . . . sword** at the entrance (3:24) was the kindest thing God could have done. If Adam's and Eve had eaten of the tree of life in their sinful state, they would have been locked into that sinful state and its consequences forever.

4:1-5 Though **the LORD had regard for Abel and his offering** (4:4), **he did not have regard for Cain** (4:5). Cain offered **produce** from a ground that was under the curse. But Abel was exercising dominion over the animals, as God had commanded (1:28). He was also offering the required sacrifice of shed blood (see Heb 9:22). True worship must be what

God will receive, not merely what we want to give.

4:5-7 Cain grew **furious** and **despondent** (4:5). That makes for a dangerous combination. God reminded Cain that if he did **what [was] right,** he would **be accepted** (4:7). The cure for emotional problems is found in spiritual realignment.

a 4:6 Jnh 4:4
b 4:7 Gn 3:16
c 4:8 Mt 23:35; Lk 11:51; 1Jn 3:12-15; Jd 11
d 4:10 Nm 35:33; Dt 21:1-9; Heb 12:24; Rv 6:9-10
e 4:12 Dt 28:16-18; Is 26:21
f 4:14 Nm 35:26-27
g 4:15 Ex 9:4; Ezk 9:4,6; Rv 13:16-17
h 4:26 Lk 3:38
i Gn 12:8; 26:25; 1Kg 18:24; Ps 116:17; Jl 2:32; Zph 3:9; 1Co 1:2
j 5:1 Gn 2:4

Cain and his offering. Cain was furious, and he looked despondent.[A]

6 Then the LORD said to Cain, "Why are you furious?[a] And why do you look despondent?[B] **7** If you do what is right, won't you be accepted? But if you do not do what is right, sin is crouching at the door. Its desire is for you, but you must rule over it."[b]

8 Cain said to his brother Abel, "Let's go out to the field."[c] And while they were in the field, Cain attacked his brother Abel and killed him.[c]

9 Then the LORD said to Cain, "Where is your brother Abel?"

"I don't know," he replied. "Am I my brother's guardian?"

10 Then he said, "What have you done? Your brother's blood cries out to me from the ground![d] **11** So now you are cursed, alienated from the ground that opened its mouth to receive your brother's blood you have shed.[D] **12** If you work the ground, it will never again give you its yield. You will be a restless wanderer on the earth."[e]

13 But Cain answered the LORD, "My punishment[E] is too great to bear! **14** Since you are banishing me today from the face of the earth, and I must hide from your presence and become a restless wanderer on the earth, whoever finds me will kill me."[f]

15 Then the LORD replied to him, "In that case,[F] whoever kills Cain will suffer vengeance seven times over."[G] And he placed a mark[g] on Cain so that whoever found him would not kill him. **16** Then Cain went out from the LORD's presence and lived in the land of Nod, east of Eden.

THE LINE OF CAIN

17 Cain was intimate with his wife, and she conceived and gave birth to Enoch. Then Cain became the builder of a city, and he named the city Enoch after his son. **18** Irad was born to Enoch, Irad fathered Mehujael, Mehujael fathered Methushael, and Methushael fathered Lamech. **19** Lamech took two wives for himself, one named Adah and the other named Zillah. **20** Adah bore Jabal; he was the father of the nomadic herdsmen.[H] **21** His brother was named Jubal; he was the father of all who play the lyre and the flute. **22** Zillah bore Tubal-cain, who made all kinds of bronze and iron tools. Tubal-cain's sister was Naamah.

23 Lamech said to his wives:

Adah and Zillah, hear my voice;
wives of Lamech, pay attention
to my words.
For I killed a man for wounding me,
a young man for striking me.
24 If Cain is to be avenged
seven times over,
then for Lamech it will be
seventy-seven times!

25 Adam was intimate with his wife again, and she gave birth to a son and named him Seth, for she said, "God has given[I] me another child[J] in place of Abel, since Cain killed him." **26** A son was born to Seth[h] also, and he named him Enosh. At that time people began to call on the name of the LORD.[i]

THE LINE OF SETH

5 This is the document containing the family[K] records[j] of Adam.[L] On the day that God created man,[M] he made him in the likeness of God; **2** he created them male and female. When they were created, he blessed them and called them mankind.[N]

3 Adam was 130 years old when he fathered a son in his likeness, according to his image, and named him Seth. **4** Adam lived 800 years after he fathered Seth, and he fathered other sons and daughters. **5** So Adam's life lasted 930 years; then he died.

6 Seth was 105 years old when he fathered Enosh. **7** Seth lived 807 years after he fathered Enosh, and he fathered other sons and daughters. **8** So Seth's life lasted 912 years; then he died.

A 4:5 Lit *and his face fell*   B 4:6 Lit *why has your face fallen*   C 4:8 Sam, LXX, Syr, Vg; MT omits *"Let's go out to the field."*   D 4:11 Lit *blood from your hand*   E 4:13 Or *sin*   F 4:15 LXX, Syr, Vg read *"Not so!"*   G 4:15 Or *suffer severely*   H 4:20 Lit *the dweller of tent and livestock*   I 4:25 The Hb word for *given* sounds like the name "Seth."   J 4:25 Lit *seed*   K 5:1 Lit *written family*   L 5:1 Or *mankind*   M 5:1 Or *Adam, human beings*   N 5:2 Hb *'adam*

4:8-16 Rather than listening to God's counsel, Cain nursed his emotions until they manifested as murder (4:8). This time, instead of the ground merely becoming cursed as had happened following Adam's rebellion, it **[would] never again give [Cain] its yield** (4:12).

4:17-24 Cain's murderous ways infect his family line. By the time we get to his great-great-great-grandson, we find a man *bragging* about his own violence. **I killed a man for wounding me,** Lamech boasts (4:23). Notice too that Lamech is talking to **his wives** (4:23). God's perfect design is only four chapters old, and already we find people reveling in bloodshed and ignoring his design for marriage. **4:25-5:32 In place of Abel** God granted Eve a son named **Seth** (4:25). In connection with Seth, **people began to call on . . . the LORD** (4:26). Hundreds of years later, Noah would come from Seth's line (5:28-32).

FAMILY
Families Rule on God's Behalf

Family was established to provide the opportunity and framework for individuals to collectively carry out the plan of God in history. In particular, that plan includes the replication of God's image and the implementation of his rule, or *dominion*, on earth. Dominion simply means ruling on God's behalf in history so that history comes under God's authority.

In Genesis we read about God creating humankind, male and female. After doing so, he gives them a common commission: to rule (Gen 1:26, 28). What we see in the surrounding verses is God delegating to humanity the full responsibility for managing his earthly creation. God decides to control the affairs of earth indirectly by letting humankind exercise direct dominion. He has placed an agent on earth to serve as his representative to carry out his desires in history.

Not only does God proffer the delegation to rule, but he also grants the freedom, responsibility, and the right to rule on his behalf as owner. But what he does not do is *force* man to rule. What that means is that you can have a happy family or a miserable family depending on whether or not you are exercising your rule in reflection of God's image. God isn't going to make you rule. He isn't going to make you have a productive and fulfilling home life. He sets up the fundamentals of the family and gives you the option of utilizing them.

FOR THE NEXT FAMILY
KINGDOM LIVING LESSON SEE PAGE 32.

9 Enosh was 90 years old when he fathered Kenan. **10** Enosh lived 815 years after he fathered Kenan, and he fathered other sons and daughters. **11** So Enosh's life lasted 905 years; then he died. **12** Kenan was 70 years old when he fathered Mahalalel. **13** Kenan lived 840 years after he fathered Mahalalel, and he fathered other sons and daughters. **14** So Kenan's life lasted 910 years; then he died.

15 Mahalalel was 65 years old when he fathered Jared. **16** Mahalalel lived 830 years after he fathered Jared, and he fathered other sons and daughters. **17** So Mahalalel's life lasted 895 years; then he died.

18 Jared was 162 years old when he fathered Enoch. **19** Jared lived 800 years after he fathered Enoch, and he fathered other sons and daughters. **20** So Jared's life lasted 962 years; then he died.

21 Enoch was 65 years old when he fathered Methuselah. **22** And after he fathered Methuselah, Enoch walked with God[a] 300 years and fathered other sons and daughters. **23** So Enoch's life lasted 365 years. **24** Enoch walked with God; then he was not there because God took him.[b]

25 Methuselah was 187 years old when he fathered Lamech. **26** Methuselah lived 782 years after he fathered Lamech, and he fathered other sons and daughters. **27** So Methuselah's life lasted 969 years; then he died.

28 Lamech was 182 years old when he fathered a son. **29** And he named him Noah,[A] saying, "This one will bring us relief from the agonizing labor of our hands, caused by the ground the LORD has cursed."[c] **30** Lamech lived 595 years after he fathered Noah, and he fathered other sons and daughters. **31** So Lamech's life lasted 777 years; then he died.

32 Noah was 500 years old, and he fathered Shem, Ham, and Japheth.

SONS OF GOD AND DAUGHTERS OF MANKIND

6 When mankind began to multiply on the earth and daughters were born to them, **2** the sons of God[d] saw that the daughters of mankind were beautiful, and they took any they chose as wives[B] for themselves.[e] **3** And the LORD said, "My Spirit will not remain[c] with[D] mankind forever,[f] because they are corrupt.[E,g] Their days will be 120 years." **4** The Nephilim[F] were on the earth both in those days and afterward, when the sons of God came to the daughters of mankind, who bore children to them. They were the powerful men of old, the famous men.

a 5:22 Gn 6:9; 17:1; 24:40; 48:15; Mc 6:8; Mal 2:6; 1Th 2:12
b 5:24 2Kg 2:11; Heb 11:5
c 5:29 Gn 3:17-19; 4:11
d 6:2 Jb 1:6; 2:1; 38:7
e 1Pt 3:19-20; Jd 6
f 6:3 Gl 5:16-17; 1Pt 3:20
g Ps 78:39

A 5:29 In Hb, the name *Noah* sounds like "bring us relief." B 6:2 Or *women* C 6:3 Or *strive* D 6:3 Or *in* E 6:3 Lit *flesh* F 6:4 Possibly means "fallen ones"; traditionally, "giants"; Nm 13:31-33

6:1-4 **The Nephilim** (6:4) are demonized men, whose sexual intimacy with women led to a demonized society. They had given themselves over to powers of darkness, yet their dark powers were no match for God, who looked down and decreed that **their days will be 120 years** (6:3). God thus announced a 120-year window for repentance, after which judgment would come.

*6:5 Gn 8:21; Ps 14:1-3; Pr
6:18; Mt 15:19; Rm 1:28-32
*6:6 Nm 23:19; 1Sm
15:11,29; 2Sm 24:16; Jl 2:13
*6:8 Gn 19:19; Ex 33:17;
Lk 1:30
*6:9 Gn 2:4
*Ps 37:39; 2Pt 2:5
*Gn 17:1; Dt 18:13; Jb 1:1
*Gn 5:22
*6:12 Jb 22:15-17; Ps 14:2-
3; 53:2-3
*6:17 Gn 7:4; 2Pt 2:5
*6:18 Gn 9:9-16; 17:7

*6:22 Gn 7:5
*7:1 Mt 24:38-39; Lk 17:26-
27; Heb 11:7
*7:2 Gn 8:20; Lv 11:1-31;
Dt 14:3-20
*7:5 Gn 6:22
*7:11 Gn 8:2; Pr 8:28;
Am 9:6

JUDGMENT DECREED

5 When the Lord saw that human wickedness was widespread on the earth and that every inclination of the human mind was nothing but evil all the time,*ᵃ* **6** the Lord regretted that he had made man on the earth,*ᵇ* and he was deeply grieved.*ᴬ* **7** Then the Lord said, "I will wipe mankind, whom I created, off the face of the earth, together with the animals, creatures that crawl, and birds of the sky — for I regret that I made them." **8** Noah, however, found favor with the Lord.*ᶜ*

GOD WARNS NOAH

9 These are the family records*ᵈ* of Noah. Noah was a righteous man,*ᵉ* blameless among his contemporaries;*ᶠ* Noah walked with God.*ᵍ* **10** And Noah fathered three sons: Shem, Ham, and Japheth.

11 Now the earth was corrupt in God's sight, and the earth was filled with wickedness.*ᴮ* **12** God saw how corrupt the earth was, for every creature had corrupted its way on the earth.*ʰ* **13** Then God said to Noah, "I have decided to put an end to every creature, for the earth is filled with wickedness because of them; therefore I am going to destroy them along with the earth.

14 "Make yourself an ark of gopher*ᶜ* wood. Make rooms in the ark, and cover it with pitch inside and outside. **15** This is how you are to make it: The ark will be 450 feet long, 75 feet wide, and 45 feet high.*ᴰ* **16** You are to make a roof,*ᴱ* finishing the sides of the ark to within eighteen inches*ᶠ* of the roof. You are to put a door in the side of the ark. Make it with lower, middle, and upper decks.

17 "Understand that I am bringing a flood — floodwaters on the earth*ⁱ* to destroy every creature under heaven with the breath of life in it. Everything on earth will perish. **18** But I will establish my covenant with you,*ʲ* and you will enter the ark with your sons, your wife, and your sons' wives. **19** You are also to bring into the ark

two of all the living creatures, male and female, to keep them alive with you. **20** Two of everything — from the birds according to their kinds, from the livestock according to their kinds, and from the animals that crawl on the ground according to their kinds — will come to you so that you can keep them alive. **21** Take with you every kind of food that is eaten; gather it as food for you and for them." **22** And Noah did this. He did everything that God had commanded him.*ᵏ*

ENTERING THE ARK

7 Then the Lord said to Noah, "Enter the ark, you and all your household, for I have seen that you alone are righteous before me in this generation.*ˡ* **2** You are to take with you seven pairs, a male and its female, of all the clean animals,*ᵐ* and two of the animals that are not clean, a male and its female, **3** and seven pairs, male and female, of the birds of the sky — in order to keep offspring alive throughout the earth. **4** Seven days from now I will make it rain on the earth forty days and forty nights, and every living thing I have made I will wipe off the face of the earth." **5** And Noah did everything that the Lord commanded him.*ⁿ*

6 Noah was six hundred years old when the flood came and water covered the earth. **7** So Noah, his sons, his wife, and his sons' wives entered the ark because of the floodwaters. **8** From the clean animals, unclean animals, birds, and every creature that crawls on the ground, **9** two of each, male and female, came to Noah and entered the ark, just as God had commanded him. **10** Seven days later the floodwaters came on the earth.

THE FLOOD

11 In the six hundredth year of Noah's life, in the second month, on the seventeenth day of the month, on that day all the sources of the vast watery depths burst open,*ᵒ* the floodgates of the sky

---

^6:6 Lit *was grieved to his heart*　ᴮ6:11 Or *injustice*, also in v. 13　ᶜ6:14 Unknown species of tree; perhaps pine or cypress　ᴰ6:15 Or *300 cubits long, 50 cubits wide, and 30 cubits high*　ᴱ6:16 Or *window*, or *hatch*; Hb uncertain　ᶠ6:16 Lit *to a cubit*

6:5-7 By this early point in history sin was in full bloom. God saw **that every inclination of the human mind was nothing but evil all the time** (6:5). People had become comprehensively corrupt. God issued a decree for their destruction (6:7).
6:8-13 **Noah . . . found favor** (6:8). He was exceptional because he walked with God. All believers should be exceptions in the midst of their own sinful generations.

6:14–7:5 God revealed his plan to Noah: **I am bringing a flood . . . to destroy every [land] creature** (6:17). The only escape would be through the ark that God commanded Noah to build, a flat-bottomed vessel enormous enough to preserve humans and land animals. God intended to start over.
Of the clean animals, Noah was to take with him **seven pairs** (7:2-3). These were

for Noah and his family to eat after exiting the ark and—as we will see at the end of this story—for Noah to sacrifice to God. In all this, Noah did **everything that the Lord commanded** (7:5). Obedience should be the supreme goal of God's people.
7:11-12 The water came from above as well as below. The result was a flood that impacted the whole earth, lasting **forty days and . . . nights** (7:12).

were opened,[a] [12] and the rain fell on the earth forty days and forty nights. [13] On that same day Noah and his three sons, Shem, Ham, and Japheth, entered the ark, along with Noah's wife and his three sons' wives. [14] They entered it with all the wildlife according to their kinds, all livestock according to their kinds, all the creatures that crawl on the earth according to their kinds, every flying creature — all the birds and every winged creature — according to their kinds. [15] Two of every creature that has the breath of life in it came to Noah and entered the ark. [16] Those that entered, male and female of every creature, entered just as God had commanded him. Then the LORD shut him in.

[17] The flood continued for forty days on the earth; the water increased and lifted up the ark so that it rose above the earth. [18] The water surged and increased greatly on the earth, and the ark floated on the surface of the water. [19] Then the water surged even higher on the earth, and all the high mountains under the whole sky were covered. [20] The mountains were covered as the water surged above them more than twenty feet.[A] [21] Every creature perished — those that crawl on the earth, birds, livestock, wildlife, and those that swarm[B] on the earth, as well as all mankind. [22] Everything with the breath of the spirit of life in its nostrils[b] — everything on dry land died. [23] He wiped out every living thing that was on the face of the earth, from mankind to livestock, to creatures that crawl, to the birds of the sky, and they were wiped off the earth. Only Noah was left, and those that were with him in the ark.[c] [24] And the water surged on the earth 150 days.

THE FLOOD RECEDES

8 God remembered Noah,[d] as well as all the wildlife and all the livestock that were with him in the ark. God caused a wind[c] to pass over the earth,[e] and the water began to subside. [2] The sources of the watery depths and the floodgates of the sky were closed, and the rain from the sky stopped.[f] [3] The water steadily receded from the earth, and by the end of 150 days the water had decreased significantly.[g] [4] The ark came to rest in the seventh month, on the seventeenth day of the month, on the mountains of Ararat.[h]

[5] The water continued to recede until the tenth month; in the tenth month, on the first day of the month, the tops of the mountains were visible. [6] After forty days Noah opened the window of the ark that he had made, [7] and he sent out a raven. It went back and forth until the water had dried up from the earth. [8] Then he sent out a dove to see whether the water on the earth's surface had gone down, [9] but the dove found no resting place for its foot. It returned to him in the ark because water covered the surface of the whole earth. He reached out and brought it into the ark to himself. [10] So Noah waited seven more days and sent out the dove from the ark again. [11] When the dove came to him at evening, there was a plucked olive leaf in its beak. So Noah knew that the water on the earth's surface had gone down. [12] After he had waited another seven days, he sent out the dove, but it did not return to him again. [13] In the six hundred and first year,[D] in the first month, on the first day of the month, the water that had covered the earth was dried up. Then Noah removed the ark's cover and saw that the surface of the ground was drying. [14] By the twenty-seventh day of the second month, the earth was dry.

THE LORD'S PROMISE

[15] Then God spoke to Noah, [16] "Come out of the ark, you, your wife, your sons, and your sons' wives with you. [17] Bring out all the living creatures[E] that are with you — birds, livestock, those that crawl on the earth — and they will spread over the earth and be fruitful and multiply on the earth."[i] [18] So Noah, along with his sons, his wife, and his sons' wives, came out. [19] All the animals, all the creatures that crawl, and all the flying creatures — everything that moves on the earth — came out of the ark by their families.

[20] Then Noah built an altar to the LORD. He took some of every kind of clean animal and every kind of clean bird and offered

[a] 7:11 2Kg 7:19; Ps 78:23; Is 24:18; Mal 3:10
[b] 7:22 Gn 2:7
[c] 7:23 1Pt 3:20; 2Pt 2:5
[d] 8:1 Gn 19:29; Ex 2:24; 1Sm 1:19; Ps 105:42
[e] Ex 14:21; 15:10; Jb 12:15; Ps 29:10; Is 44:27; Nah 1:4
[f] 8:2 Gn 7:11
[g] 8:3 Gn 7:24
[h] 8:4 2Kg 19:37; Is 37:38; Jr 51:27
[i] 8:17 Gn 1:22,28; 9:1

[A] 7:20 Lit *surged 15 cubits*   [B] 7:21 Lit *all the swarming swarms*   [C] 8:1 Or *spirit*; Gn 1:2   [D] 8:13 = of Noah's life   [E] 8:17 Lit *creatures of all flesh*

7:23-24 Not a drop of this judgment was more extensive than it needed to be. Great was the sin, so also was God's just judgment. Sitting on that boat while **the water surged on the earth 150 days** (7:24), Noah's family acted as a living reminder that the

God who fiercely judges sin is the same one who mercifully delivers.

8:20-22 Noah, overflowing with thanks for the way that God had saved him, made an offering (8:20). When he saw Noah's worship, God promised to **never again curse**

the ground because of human beings (8:21). God would providentially preserve the earth for the sake of humanity. God's promise gives us hope that when we respond to him in faith, he can renew something that has been lost.

a 8:21 Ex 29:18; Lv 1:9; Ezk 16:19; 20:41; 2Co 2:15; Eph 5:2; Php 4:18
b Gn 3:17; 5:29; 6:7; Is 54:9
c Gn 6:5; Ps 51:5; Jr 17:9; Rm 1:21; 3:23; Eph 2:1-3
d Gn 9:11,15
e 8:22 Jr 33:20,25
f 9:1 Gn 1:28; 8:17; 9:7; 35:11
g 9:3 Dt 12:15; 1Tm 4:3-4
h 9:1-3 Gn 1:28-30
i 9:4 Lv 3:17; 7:20; 17:10-16; 19:26; Dt 12:16,23; 15:23; 1Sm 14:34; Ac 15:20,29
j 9:5 Ex 21:28
k Gn 4:2,8
l 9:6 Ex 21:12-14; Lv 24:17; Nm 35:33; Mt 26:52
m Gn 1:26-27
n 9:7 Gn 1:28
o 9:9 Gn 6:18; 8:22; 17:2; Ex 6:4; 19:5; Lv 26:9

p 9:11 Is 54:9-10
q 9:12 Gn 17:11
r 9:13 Ezk 1:28; Rv 4:3; 10:1
s 9:15 Lv 26:42,45; Dt 7:9; 1Kg 8:23; Ezk 16:60
t 9:16 Gn 17:13; 2Sm 23:5; 1Ch 16:17; Is 24:5
u 9:19 Gn 9:1,7; 10:32; 1Ch 1:4
v 9:22 Lm 4:21; Hab 2:15

burnt offerings on the altar. [21] When the LORD smelled the pleasing aroma,[a] he said to himself, "I will never again curse the ground[b] because of human beings, even though the inclination of the human heart is evil from youth onward.[c] And I will never again strike down every living thing as I have done.[d]

[22] As long as the earth endures,
seedtime and harvest, cold and heat,
summer and winter, and day and night
will not cease."[e]

GOD'S COVENANT WITH NOAH

9 God blessed Noah and his sons and said to them, "Be fruitful and multiply and fill the earth.[f] [2] The fear and terror of you will be in every living creature on the earth, every bird of the sky, every creature that crawls on the ground, and all the fish of the sea. They are placed under your authority.[A] [3] Every creature that lives and moves will be food for you;[g] as I gave the green plants, I have given you everything.[h] [4] However, you must not eat meat with its lifeblood in it.[i] [5] And I will require a penalty for your lifeblood;[B] I will require it from any animal[j] and from any human; if someone murders a fellow human, I will require that person's life.[C,K]

[6] Whoever sheds human blood,
by humans his blood will be shed,[l]
for God made humans in his image.[m]

[7] But you, be fruitful and multiply; spread out over the earth and multiply on it."[n]

[8] Then God said to Noah and his sons with him, [9] "Understand that I am establishing my covenant[o] with you and your descendants after you, [10] and with every living creature that is with you — birds,

livestock, and all wildlife of the earth that are with you — all the animals of the earth that came out of the ark. [11] I establish my covenant with you that never again will every creature be wiped out by floodwaters; there will never again be a flood to destroy the earth."[p]

[12] And God said, "This is the sign of the covenant[q] I am making between me and you and every living creature with you, a covenant for all future generations: [13] I have placed my bow in the clouds,[r] and it will be a sign of the covenant between me and the earth. [14] Whenever I form clouds over the earth and the bow appears in the clouds, [15] I will remember my covenant[s] between me and you and all the living creatures:[D] water will never again become a flood to destroy every creature. [16] The bow will be in the clouds, and I will look at it and remember the permanent covenant[t] between God and all the living creatures[E] on earth." [17] God said to Noah, "This is the sign of the covenant that I have established between me and every creature on earth."

PROPHECIES ABOUT NOAH'S FAMILY

[18] Noah's sons who came out of the ark were Shem, Ham, and Japheth. Ham was the father of Canaan. [19] These three were Noah's sons, and from them the whole earth was populated.[u]

[20] Noah, as a man of the soil, began by planting[F] a vineyard. [21] He drank some of the wine, became drunk, and uncovered himself inside his tent. [22] Ham, the father of Canaan, saw his father naked and told his two brothers outside.[v] [23] Then Shem and Japheth took a cloak and placed it

---

[A] 9:2 Lit *are given in your hand* [B] 9:5 Lit *And your blood belonging to your life I will seek* [C] 9:5 Lit *any human; from the hand of a man his brother I will seek the life of the human.* [D] 9:15 Lit *and creatures of all flesh* [E] 9:16 Lit *creatures of all flesh* [F] 9:20 Or *Noah began to be a farmer and planted*

9:1 God recommissioned Noah with the command to **be fruitful and . . . fill the earth**—the commission given originally to Adam and Eve. God was not abandoning his original purposes, but resetting the scene so his original purposes could go forth.

9:2-6 Humanity was now free to eat meat. The only restriction God placed on this was to avoid eating meat **with its lifeblood in it** (9:4). Raw meat was off limits because it represented life (see Lev 17:11).

God also added another command about lifeblood: **Whoever sheds human blood, by humans his blood will be shed** (Gen 9:6). This is the basis of capital punishment, and it is grounded in the fact that **God made humans in his image** (9:6). Taking innocent human life is an attack on God.

9:7-11 God made a new covenant with Noah, promising **that never again will every creature be wiped out by floodwaters** (9:11). Nevertheless, a second judgment is indeed coming—one not carried along by waves but by flames (see 2 Pet 3:7).

9:12-17 Generally covenants are two-party agreements: I do this; you do that. But in this case God simply said, **Whenever . . . the bow appears . . . , I will remember my covenant** (9:14-15). God keeps his promises unconditionally, even in the face of our sin.

9:18-19 All humanity has its origin in Adam and the three sons of Noah: **Shem, Ham, and Japheth** (9:18; also see Acts 17:26). Because all races stem from the same root, it is absurd for any group to claim superiority over another. Each son is associated with nations of peoples, as is recorded in the "Table of Nations" in

Genesis 10. All races can take pride in the fact that it was God's intention that each unique group exist, survive, and function as nations of peoples, without any one group or ethnicity being superior in nature to any other.

9:20-29 Noah's sinful drunkenness provided the setting for another sinful act. Ham **saw his father naked.** And rather than covering his nakedness, Ham ridiculed his father to his brothers (9:22). This led to the curse on Ham's son, **Canaan.** This happened because some in Canaan's line would continue in unrighteousness, following in the footsteps of Ham's example (9:25).

Since Ham was the father of black people (see 10:6), and since his descendants were cursed to be **slaves** because of his sin (9:25-27), some have argued that Africans and their descendants are destined to be slaves.

over both their shoulders, and walking backward, they covered their father's nakedness. Their faces were turned away, and they did not see their father naked. [24] When Noah awoke from his drinking and learned what his youngest son had done to him, [25] he said:

Canaan is cursed.[a]
He will be the lowest of slaves
    to his brothers.[b]

[26] He also said:

Blessed be the LORD, the God of Shem;
Let Canaan be[A] Shem's slave.

[27]   Let God extend Japheth;[B]
let Japheth dwell in the tents of Shem;
let Canaan be Shem's slave.

[28] Now Noah lived 350 years after the flood. [29] So Noah's life lasted 950 years; then he died.

THE TABLE OF NATIONS

10 These are the family records[c] of Noah's sons, Shem, Ham, and Japheth. They also had sons after the flood. [2] Japheth's sons:[d] Gomer, Magog, Madai, Javan, Tubal, Meshech, and Tiras. [3] Gomer's sons: Ashkenaz, Riphath, and Togarmah. [4] And Javan's sons: Elishah, Tarshish,[e] Kittim, and Dodanim.[c] [5] From these descendants, the peoples of the coasts and islands spread out into their lands according to their clans in their nations, each with its own language.

[6] Ham's sons:[f] Cush, Mizraim, Put, and Canaan. [7] Cush's sons: Seba, Havilah, Sabtah, Raamah, and Sabteca. And Raamah's sons: Sheba and Dedan.

[8] Cush fathered Nimrod, who began to be powerful in the land. [9] He was a powerful hunter in the sight of the LORD. That is why it is said, "Like Nimrod, a powerful hunter

in the sight of the LORD." [10] His kingdom started with Babylon,[g] Erech,[D] Accad,[E] and Calneh,[F] in the land of Shinar.[G,h] [11] From that land he went to Assyria[i] and built Nineveh, Rehoboth-ir, Calah, [12] and Resen, between Nineveh and the great city Calah.

[13] Mizraim[H,j] fathered the people of Lud, Anam, Lehab, Naphtuh, [14] Pathrus, Casluh (the Philistines came from them), and Caphtor.[k]

[15] Canaan fathered Sidon his firstborn and Heth, [16] as well as the Jebusites, the Amorites, the Girgashites,[l] [17] the Hivites, the Arkites, the Sinites, [18] the Arvadites, the Zemarites, and the Hamathites. Afterward the Canaanite clans scattered. [19] The Canaanite border went from Sidon going toward Gerar as far as Gaza, and going toward Sodom, Gomorrah, Admah, and Zeboiim as far as Lasha.

[20] These are Ham's sons by their clans, according to their languages, in their lands and their nations.

[21] And Shem, Japheth's older brother, also had sons. Shem was the father of all the sons of Eber.[m] [22] Shem's sons[n] were Elam, Asshur, Arpachshad, Lud, and Aram. [23] Aram's sons: Uz, Hul, Gether, and Mash. [24] Arpachshad fathered[i] Shelah,[o] and Shelah fathered Eber. [25] Eber had two sons. One was named Peleg,[j] for during his days the earth was divided;[p] his brother was named Joktan. [26] And Joktan fathered Almodad, Sheleph, Hazarmaveth, Jerah, [27] Hadoram, Uzal, Diklah, [28] Obal, Abimael, Sheba, [29] Ophir, Havilah, and Jobab. All these were Joktan's sons. [30] Their settlements extended from Mesha to Sephar, the eastern hill country.

[31] These are Shem's sons by their clans, according to their languages, in their lands and their nations.

[a] 9:25 Dt 27:16
[b] Jos 9:23; Jdg 1:28; 1Kg 9:20-21
[c] 10:1 Gn 2:4
[d] 10:2-5 1Ch 1:5-7; Ezk 38:1-6
[e] 10:4 1Kg 10:22; Is 2:16
[f] 10:6-7 1Ch 1:8-10

[g] 10:10 Gn 11:9
[h] Gn 11:2; 14:1
[i] 10:11 Mc 5:6
[j] 10:13-18 1Ch 1:11-16
[k] 10:14 Jr 47:4; Am 9:7
[l] 10:16 Gn 15:19-21
[m] 10:21 Gn 11:13-14
[n] 10:22-29 1Ch 1:17-23
[o] 10:24 Gn 11:12; Lk 3:35
[p] 10:25 Gn 11:8; Ps 55:9

[A] 9:26 As a wish or prayer; others interpret the verbs in vv. 26-27 as prophecy: Canaan will be . . .   [B] 9:27 In Hb, the name Japheth sounds like the word "extend."   [C] 10:4 Some Hb mss, Sam, LXX read Rodanim; 1Ch 1:7   [D] 10:10 Or Uruk   [E] 10:10 Or Akkad   [F] 10:10 Or and all of them   [G] 10:10 Or in Babylonia   [H] 10:13 = Egypt   [I] 10:24 LXX reads fathered Cainan, and Cainan fathered; Gn 11:12-13; Lk 3:35-36   [J] 10:25 = Division

Due to this "curse of Ham" theory, there existed a myth of inferiority with apparent biblical roots in Christian history and culture. This myth became an authoritative one because it was rooted in a purported theology, and slave owners used this twisted belief system to sustain a perverted sociology. Unfortunately, this contributed to the establishing and continuation of a distorted myth of black inferiority in the American Christian psyche.

This interpretation of the "curse of Ham" is incorrect due to multiple reasons. Canaan, Ham's son, was cursed, not Ham himself. How then could all black people everywhere be cursed? The Bible also places limitations

on curses—only three or four generations at most (Exod 20:5). Moreover, the curse that Canaan and his descendants would be slaves finds its most obvious fulfillment in the ongoing defeat and subjugation of Canaan by Israel (see Josh 9:23; 1 Kgs 9:20-21). The descendants of Ham's other sons (Gen 10:6) have continued to this day as national peoples in Ethiopia (Cush), Egypt (Mizraim), and Libya (Put).

10:1-32 The author fast-forwards by using a genealogy that skips from Noah to the next big scene at the tower of Babylon (11:1-9). As we skip through these centuries, however, we see God creating the multitude of nations.

Though God would focus his redemptive plan through one line (Shem's), he cares for all nations and has a plan to redeem people from every group.

Noah's son Ham had four **sons: Cush, Mizraim, Put, and Canaan** (10:6). Cush was the progenitor of the Ethiopian people (Cush and Ethiopia are used interchangeably in the Scriptures). Mizraim was the progenitor of the Egyptian people, who are understood in Scripture to have been a Hamitic people, and thus African (see also Pss 78:51; 105:23, 26-27; 106:21-22). Put was the progenitor of Libya. Canaan was the progenitor of the Canaanites.

a 10:32 Gn 9:19
b 11:2 Gn 10:10; 14:1; Dn 1:2
c 11:3 Gn 14:10; Ex 2:3
d 11:4 Dt 1:28; 9:1; Ps 107:26
e 11:5 Gn 18:21; Ex 3:8; 19:11,18,20

f 11:8 Gn 11:4; Ps 92:9; Lk 1:51
g 11:9 Gn 10:10
h 11:10 Gn 2:4; 11:27

❧ KINGDOM LIVING ❧
COMMUNITY
A One-World Government

Any king, governing body, family, or institution that claims absolute power has rebelled against God. Since God has centralized all power within himself, whenever people try to centralize power in themselves, God intervenes to break up their attempts at autonomy and their declarations of independence. Just ask those who gathered at the tower of Babylon (see Gen 11:1-9).

Their building project was doomed because their objective was wrong from the beginning: "Come, let us build ourselves a city and a tower with its top in the sky" (Gen 11:4). Instead of being given a name by God or wearing his name, those building the tower sought to make a name for themselves. They sought to build a city (a civilization), a tower (a religious system), and a name (that is, independence) apart from God.

God looked down and saw what they were doing, and he didn't like it. God's concern was that the people were trying to concentrate power in their own hands. That would prove disastrous, so God confused their language—effectively disrupting their unity, thinking, ideology, faith, and common confession—so that they couldn't understand one another.

When humankind said, "Let's make ourselves a name. Let's concentrate power and build a one-world government that will rule the universe," God said, "Not in my universe, you won't!" (see Pss 2:1-4; 9:17-20; 33:9-12). What happened at the tower of Babylon is a prototype of any effort that defies God and raises itself up in pride through the centralization of power. Any attempt to be autonomous from God will produce divine intervention and decentralization so that men will once again seek God (see Acts 17:24-28).

FOR THE NEXT COMMUNITY
KINGDOM LIVING LESSON SEE PAGE 483.

---

32 These are the clans of Noah's sons, according to their family records, in their nations. The nations on earth spread out from these after the flood.*a*

THE TOWER OF BABYLON

11 The whole earth had the same language and vocabulary.*A* **2** As people*B* migrated from the east,*c* they found a valley in the land of Shinar and settled there.*b* **3** They said to each other, "Come, let us make oven-fired bricks." (They used brick for stone and asphalt*c* for mortar.) **4** And they said, "Come, let us build ourselves a city and a tower with its top in the sky.*d* Let us make a name for ourselves; otherwise, we will be scattered throughout the earth." **5** Then the LORD came down*e* to look over the city and the tower that the humans*D* were building. **6** The LORD said, "If they have begun to do this as one people all having the same language, then nothing they plan to do will be impossible for them. **7** Come, let's go down there and confuse their language so that they will not understand one another's speech." **8** So from there the LORD scattered them throughout the earth,*f* and they stopped building the city. **9** Therefore it is called Babylon,*E,F,g* for there the LORD confused the language of the whole earth, and from there the LORD scattered them throughout the earth.

FROM SHEM TO ABRAM

10 These are the family records*h* of Shem. Shem lived 100 years and fathered Arpachshad two years after the flood. **11** After he fathered Arpachshad, Shem

---

A 11:1 Lit *one lip and the same words*   *B* 11:2 Lit *they*   *C* 11:2 Or *migrated eastward*   *D* 11:5 Or *the descendants of Adam*   *E* 11:9 Hb *Babel*
F 11:9 In Hb, the name for "Babylon," *babel* sounds like the word for "confuse," *balal.*

11:1-2 A key theme hinges on this word **east** (11:2). When God pushed Adam and Eve out of the garden, he sent them east (3:24). After Cain killed his brother, he too went east (4:16). "East" represents a journey away from God. **11:3-5** The people at Babel made a declaration of independence from God himself. **Let us build ourselves a city** (i.e., civilization) **and a tower** (i.e., religious center). . . . **Let us make a name for ourselves** (since they did not want to carry God's name; 11:4). Instead of pursuing God's agenda—multiplying and filling the earth—they wanted to do everything to *prevent* being **scattered** (11:4). Their efforts would be man-centered, not God-centered. **11:6-7** **If they have begun to do this . . . then nothing . . . will be impossible for them** (11:6). God was not threatened by what humanity was doing. Rather he recognized that unified sinful humanity had enormous potential to sour God's creation. So in order to put the brakes on evil's proliferation, God decided to disunify them and **confuse their language** (11:7).

11:8-9 The people **stopped building the city** (11:8), and all of them—now speaking precursors of Arabic and German and Swahili—were *forced* to scatter (11:9).
11:10-32 The author transitions to the next move in God's redemptive plan. The genealogy slows as it approaches **Abram** (11:27-32). We pick up the action as Abram's father, Terah, moved his family from **Ur** (a wealthy city in Mesopotamia) **to go to . . . Canaan**, the promised land (11:31). **Terah**, however, stopped short in the land of **Haran**—modern day northern Syria (11:31).

Faith Works

I WAS ONCE BATTLING A COLD and couldn't shake it. I called my doctor, told him my symptoms, and he told me I didn't need to come in. He would call in a prescription for me. He told me what medicine he was prescribing and how he wanted me to take it.

To benefit from this conversation, I had to believe that I was talking to the person I thought I was talking to, because I couldn't see him. Ours was just a brief talk over the phone, so I had to listen to and trust his voice. Then I had to respond when he told me how to fix my problem. Now, I could've lain in bed and meditated. I could have believed him without leaving my bed, thinking about how good it was that I had a doctor who understood my problem and provided me with a solution. But all that lying around and thinking about the good words that the good doctor shared with me wouldn't make me better. It may have given me warm fuzzies, but I'd still be sick as a dog.

I had things to do. I had to get up, get in my car, drive to Walgreens, and say to the pharmacist, "Do you have a prescription with my name on it?" Though there was a lot of medicine in that pharmacy, I needed the one thing waiting with my name on it. I needed something personally prescribed for me. The doctor had told me it was there, and because I believed his word, I acted on it.

Taking this illustration further, I could have just received the medicine, gazed at it, and made sure that it looked acceptable to me. But, I'd still feel miserable. The doctor's instructions were not for me just to drive to Walgreens and get emotionally fixated on the look of the medicine. He told me to take it. By following his instructions, I allowed my faith in the doctor to match up with my works of obedience and began to feel much better.

A lot of us are spiritually sick, and every week we go to hear what the Great Physician has to say to us. But some of us just stop there and think about how good it was to hear from him. Some of us leave church feeling good about how great the prescription sounds, yet we remain sick as a spiritual dog because we don't ingest the prescription by acting on it. Therefore, we're not transformed.

Think about Abraham. God didn't just tell him that he would give him a bountiful land. He gave him a prescription: "Go out from your land, your relatives, and your father's house to the land that I will show you. I will make you into a great nation" (GEN 12:1-2). In order for Abraham to experience the goodness of what God wanted to give him, he needed to put his faith into action.

Abraham's story serves as an example that each of us should learn from. Hebrews 11 provides a list of other biblical heroes whose journeys of faith also provide us with inspiration and instruction about how to receive the full promises of God. This "large cloud of witnesses" (HEB 12:1) should remind us of something vital to our Christian walk: faith works.

On the other hand, "faith without works is dead" (JAS 2:26). Faith in God can't just be a good feeling about something you heard on Sunday morning. The Great Physician has prescribed a course of action for you, and in order for you to benefit from the medicine, you'll have to follow his instructions.

a 11:24 Jos 24:2
b 11:29 Gn 17:15; 20:12
c Gn 22:20,23; 24:15
d 11:30 Gn 25:21; 29:31; Ex 23:26; Jdg 13:2-3; 1Sm 2:5; Jb 24:21; Is 54:1; Lk 1:36; 23:29; Gl 4:27; Heb 11:11
e 11:31 Gn 15:7; Neh 9:7; Ac 7:4

f 12:1 Gn 15:7; Ac 7:3; Heb 11:8
g 12:2 Gn 17:4-6; 18:18; 46:3; Dt 26:5
h Gn 22:17
i Zch 8:13
j 12:3 Gn 27:29; Nm 24:9
k Gn 18:18; 26:4; 28:14; Ac 3:25; Gl 3:8
l 12:4 Gn 11:27,31
m 12:6 Gn 35:4; Dt 11:30; Heb 11:9
n 12:7 Gn 13:15; Ex 33:1; Ps 105:9-12; Ac 7:5; Gl 3:16
o 12:8 Gn 4:26; 21:33
p 12:10 Gn 26:1; 43:1

lived 500 years and fathered other sons and daughters. **12** Arpachshad lived 35 years[A] and fathered Shelah. **13** After he fathered Shelah, Arpachshad lived 403 years and fathered other sons and daughters. **14** Shelah lived 30 years and fathered Eber. **15** After he fathered Eber, Shelah lived 403 years and fathered other sons and daughters. **16** Eber lived 34 years and fathered Peleg. **17** After he fathered Peleg, Eber lived 430 years and fathered other sons and daughters. **18** Peleg lived 30 years and fathered Reu. **19** After he fathered Reu, Peleg lived 209 years and fathered other sons and daughters. **20** Reu lived 32 years and fathered Serug. **21** After he fathered Serug, Reu lived 207 years and fathered other sons and daughters. **22** Serug lived 30 years and fathered Nahor. **23** After he fathered Nahor, Serug lived 200 years and fathered other sons and daughters. **24** Nahor lived 29 years and fathered Terah.[a] **25** After he fathered Terah, Nahor lived 119 years and fathered other sons and daughters. **26** Terah lived 70 years and fathered Abram, Nahor, and Haran.

27 These are the family records of Terah. Terah fathered Abram, Nahor, and Haran, and Haran fathered Lot. **28** Haran died in his native land, in Ur of the Chaldeans, during his father Terah's lifetime. **29** Abram and Nahor took wives: Abram's wife was named Sarai,[b] and Nahor's wife was named Milcah.[c] She was the daughter of Haran, the father of both Milcah and Iscah. **30** Sarai was unable to conceive;[d] she did not have a child.

31 Terah took his son Abram, his grandson Lot (Haran's son), and his daughter-in-law Sarai, his son Abram's wife, and they set out together from Ur of the Chaldeans[e] to go to the land of Canaan. But when they came to Haran, they settled there. **32** Terah lived 205 years and died in Haran.

THE CALL OF ABRAM

12 The LORD said to Abram:
Go out from your land,
your relatives,
and your father's house
to the land that I will show you.[f]
2 I will make you into a great nation,[g]
I will bless you,[h]
I will make your name great,
and you will be a blessing.[i]
3 I will bless those who bless you,
I will curse anyone who treats you
with contempt,[j]
and all the peoples[B] on earth
will be blessed[c] through you.[D,k]

4 So Abram went, as the LORD had told him, and Lot went with him. Abram was seventy-five years old when he left Haran.[l] **5** He took his wife Sarai, his nephew Lot, all the possessions they had accumulated, and the people they had acquired in Haran, and they set out for the land of Canaan. When they came to the land of Canaan, **6** Abram passed through the land to the site of Shechem,[m] at the oak of Moreh. (At that time the Canaanites were in the land.) **7** The LORD appeared to Abram and said, "To your offspring[n] I will give this land." So he built an altar there to the LORD who had appeared to him. **8** From there he moved on to the hill country east of Bethel and pitched his tent, with Bethel on the west and Ai on the east. He built an altar to the LORD there, and he called on the name of the LORD.[o] **9** Then Abram journeyed by stages to the Negev.

ABRAM IN EGYPT

10 There was a famine in the land,[p] so Abram went down to Egypt to stay there for a while because the famine in the land was severe. **11** When he was about to enter Egypt, he said to his wife Sarai, "Look, I know what a beautiful woman you are.

[A] 11:12-13 LXX reads *years and fathered Cainan.* **13** *After he fathered Cainan, Arpachshad lived 430 years and fathered other sons and daughters, and he died. Cainan lived 130 years and fathered Shelah. After he fathered Shelah, Cainan lived 330 years and fathered other sons and daughters, and he died*; 10:24; Lk 3:35-36 [B] 12:3 Lit *clans* [C] 12:3 Or *will find blessing* [D] 12:3 Or *will bless themselves by you*

12:1-3 When God saw the wickedness in Noah's day, he chose to work out his kingdom purpose through one faithful man. God's desire was still to fill the earth with his glory and bless **all the peoples** (12:3), but he would work through an individual to accomplish it. Thus, God commanded Abram to leave his **father's house** to go to a new land (12:1).

Abram did not know where God was leading him. He only knew that if he would obey, God would respond by making him **into a great nation**, making his **name great**, and even using him to bring **blessing** to others (12:2).

God would advance his kingdom agenda through Abram's faith.

12:4-7 Abram left Haran with **his wife Sarai, his nephew Lot,** and all of the other **people** who were stepping out in faith with Abram (12:5). When he arrived **at the oak of Moreh** (12:6), most likely a Canaanite worship center, God promised to **give this land** to Abram's **offspring** (12:7). Abram's faith in action had led to further illumination, to greater clarity of God's will, purpose, and direction for his life.

12:10 Abram began his journey of faith well, but his faith soon gave way to fear. A **famine**

caused Abram and his family to travel to **Egypt** for food. This was a bad move because God had made it clear that he wanted Abram in Canaan, not Egypt. The moment Abram assessed the situation from a human perspective, he made a poor decision.

12:11-15 In Egypt, Abram worried that someone might see Sarai's beauty and kill him to get her (12:11-12). So Sarai was to say that she was Abram's **sister** (12:13)—which, according to 20:12, was half true. Abram was ready to give up his wife and abandon the promise of God for mere self-preservation.

12 When the Egyptians see you, they will
say, 'This is his wife.' They will kill me but
let you live.[a] 13 Please say you're my sister
so it will go well for me because of you,
and my life will be spared on your account." 14 When Abram entered Egypt, the
Egyptians saw that the woman was very
beautiful. 15 Pharaoh's officials saw her
and praised her to Pharaoh, so the woman was taken to Pharaoh's household. 16 He
treated Abram well because of her, and
Abram acquired flocks and herds, male
and female donkeys, male and female
slaves, and camels.
17 But the LORD struck Pharaoh and his
household with severe plagues because of
Abram's wife Sarai.[b] 18 So Pharaoh sent for
Abram and said, "What have you done to
me? Why didn't you tell me she was your
wife? 19 Why did you say, 'She's my sister,'
so that I took her as my wife? Now, here is
your wife. Take her and go!" 20 Then Pharaoh gave his men orders about him, and
they sent him away with his wife and all
he had.

ABRAM AND LOT SEPARATE

13 Abram went up from Egypt to the
Negev[c] — he, his wife, and all he
had, and Lot with him. 2 Abram was very
rich in livestock, silver, and gold. 3 He went
by stages from the Negev to Bethel, to the
place between Bethel and Ai where his
tent had formerly been, 4 to the site where
he had built the altar. And Abram called on
the name of the LORD there.[d]
5 Now Lot, who was traveling with
Abram, also had flocks, herds, and tents.
6 But the land was unable to support them
as long as they stayed together, for they
had so many possessions that they could
not stay together,[e] 7 and there was quarreling between the herdsmen of Abram's
livestock and the herdsmen of Lot's
livestock.[f] (At that time the Canaanites
and the Perizzites were living in the land.)[g]
8 So Abram said to Lot, "Please, let's not
have quarreling between you and me, or
between your herdsmen and my herdsmen, since we are relatives.[A] 9 Isn't the
whole land before you? Separate from me:
if you go to the left, I will go to the right;
if you go to the right, I will go to the left."
10 Lot looked out and saw that the entire plain[B] of the Jordan[h] as far as[C] Zoar[i]
was well watered everywhere like the
LORD's garden[j] and the land of Egypt.
(This was before the LORD destroyed
Sodom and Gomorrah.)[k] 11 So Lot chose
the entire plain of the Jordan for himself. Then Lot journeyed eastward, and
they separated from each other. 12 Abram
lived in the land of Canaan, but Lot lived
in the cities on the plain and set up his
tent near Sodom. 13 (Now the men of
Sodom were evil, sinning immensely[D]
against the LORD.)[l]
14 After Lot had separated from him,
the LORD said to Abram, "Look from the
place where you are. Look north and
south, east and west,[m] 15 for I will give
you and your offspring forever all the
land that you see.[n] 16 I will make your
offspring like the dust of the earth,[o] so
that if anyone could count the dust of
the earth, then your offspring could be
counted. 17 Get up and walk around the
land, through its length and width, for I
will give it to you."
18 So Abram moved his tent and went to
live near the oaks of Mamre at Hebron,[p]
where he built an altar to the LORD.

ABRAM RESCUES LOT

14 In those days King Amraphel of Shinar,[q] King Arioch of Ellasar, King
Chedorlaomer of Elam,[r] and King Tidal
of Goiim[E] 2 waged war against King Bera

[a] 12:12 Gn 20:1-18; 26:6-11
[b] 12:17 Gn 20:18; 1Ch 16:21; Ps 105:14
[c] 13:1 Gn 12:9
[d] 13:4 Gn 12:7,8
[e] 13:6 Gn 36:7
[f] 13:7 Gn 26:20
[g] Gn 12:6; 15:20-21
[h] 13:10 Gn 19:17-29
[i] Gn 14:2,8; Dt 34:3
[j] Gn 2:8-10
[k] Gn 19:24-25
[l] 13:13 Gn 18:20; Ezk 16:49; 2Pt 2:7-8
[m] 13:14 Gn 28:14
[n] 13:15 Gn 12:7; 15:18; 17:8; 24:7; 26:4; 28:13; 35:12; Dt 34:4; 2Ch 20:7; Ac 7:5
[o] 13:16 Gn 16:10; 28:14; Nm 23:10
[p] 13:18 Gn 14:13; 18:1; 23:17-19
[q] 14:1 Gn 10:10; 11:2
[r] Gn 10:22; Is 11:11; Dn 8:2

[A] **13:8** Lit *brothers* [B] **13:10** Lit *circle*; i.e., probably the large round plain where the Jordan River empties into the Dead Sea, also in v. 11 [C] **13:10** Lit *Jordan as you go to* [D] **13:13** Lit *evil and sinful* [E] **14:1** Or *nations*

12:17-20 God remains committed to his kingdom program and promises, even when his people fail. He sent **severe plagues** to Pharaoh's household (12:17), which immediately signaled to the people involved that they had been deceived. Sadly, Pharaoh acted with more integrity than Abram in giving Sarai back to her husband without punishing the couple (12:18-20).

13:1-7 Abram and his family gradually made their way back toward the land of promise. By this point Abram had become **rich in livestock** (13:2), but so had his nephew Lot (13:5). Their herds were too vast for any one area (13:6). There simply wasn't enough water and pasture.

13:8-9 Abram recognized that he and Lot had to separate. Surprisingly, though, Abram chose to preserve relationship over keeping the economic upper hand. He allowed Lot to pick his plot of land first (13:9). Abram had faith in God's promise and provision, so he was able to defer to Lot.

13:10-13 Lot looked at the two options and **saw that the entire plain of the Jordan . . . was well watered** (13:10). Yet he failed to see that God was going to judge the region soon, because **the men of Sodom were evil, sinning immensely** (13:13). Lot chose to get close to sin for material gain, journeying **eastward** toward Sodom and Gomorrah (13:11).

13:14-17 What God offered to Abram was long-term: **I will give you and your offspring forever all the land that you see** (13:15). Abram wouldn't have to do anything to make this happen. **I will give it to you** (13:17), God plainly told him.

13:18 Abram moved his tent near **the oaks of Mamre**, building there another **altar**. Unlike he'd done during his time in Egypt, Abram was again moving by faith, not by sight, which would be the foundation not only of *his* obedience but also of the obedience that God wants of all who follow him (see 2 Cor 5:7).

a 14:2 Hs 11:8
b Gn 19:22-23
c 14:3 Nm 34:12; Dt 3:17;
   Jos 3:16
d 14:5 Gn 15:20; Dt 2:11,20-
   21; 3:11,13; Jos 12:4
e Dt 1:4; Jos 9:10
f 14:6 Gn 36:20; Dt 2:12,22
g Gn 21:21; Nm 10:12
h 14:7 Nm 13:26
i 2Ch 20:2
j 14:10 Gn 19:17
k 14:12 Gn 13:12
l 14:13 Gn 39:14; 40:15
m 14:14 Gn 12:5; 15:3; 17:27;
   Ec 2:7
n Dt 34:1; Jdg 18:29; 1Kg
   15:20

o 14:17 2Sm 18:18
p 14:18 Ps 110:4; Heb
   5:6; 7:1
q Ps 57:2
r 14:20 Heb 7:4
s 15:1 1Sm 15:10; 2Sm 7:4;
   1Kg 6:11; Is 38:4; Jr 1:2
t Gn 26:24; Is 41:10; Jr
   30:10; Lk 1:13,30
u Dt 33:29; 2Sm 22:3,31; Ps
   3:3; 7:10

of Sodom, King Birsha of Gomorrah, King Shinab of Admah, and King Shemeber of Zeboiim,*a* as well as the king of Bela (that is, Zoar*b*). **3** All of these came as allies to the Siddim Valley (that is, the Dead Sea*c*). **4** They were subject to Chedorlaomer for twelve years, but in the thirteenth year they rebelled. **5** In the fourteenth year Chedorlaomer and the kings who were with him came and defeated the Rephaim*d* in Ashteroth-karnaim, the Zuzim in Ham,*e* the Emim in Shaveh-kiriathaim, **6** and the Horites*f* in the mountains of Seir, as far as El-paran*g* by the wilderness. **7** Then they came back to invade En-mishpat (that is, Kadesh*h*), and they defeated the whole territory of the Amalekites, as well as the Amorites who lived in Hazazon-tamar.*i*

8 Then the king of Sodom, the king of Gomorrah, the king of Admah, the king of Zeboiim, and the king of Bela (that is, Zoar) went out and lined up for battle in the Siddim Valley **9** against King Chedorlaomer of Elam, King Tidal of Goiim, King Amraphel of Shinar, and King Arioch of Ellasar — four kings against five. **10** Now the Siddim Valley contained many asphalt pits, and as the kings of Sodom and Gomorrah fled, some fell into them,*A* but the rest fled to the mountains.*j* **11** The four kings took all the goods of Sodom and Gomorrah and all their food and went on. **12** They also took Abram's nephew Lot and his possessions, for he was living in Sodom,*k* and they went on.

13 One of the survivors came and told Abram the Hebrew,*l* who lived near the oaks belonging to Mamre the Amorite, the brother of Eshcol and the brother of Aner. They were bound by a treaty with*B* Abram. **14** When Abram heard that his relative had been taken prisoner, he assembled*c* his 318 trained men, born in his household,*m* and they went in pursuit as far as Dan.*n* **15** And he and his servants

deployed against them by night, defeated them, and pursued them as far as Hobah to the north of Damascus. **16** He brought back all the goods and also his relative Lot and his goods, as well as the women and the other people.

MELCHIZEDEK'S BLESSING

17 After Abram returned from defeating Chedorlaomer and the kings who were with him, the king of Sodom went out to meet him in the Shaveh Valley (that is, the King's Valley*o*). **18** Melchizedek, king of Salem,*D,p* brought out bread and wine; he was a priest to God Most High.*q* **19** He blessed him and said:

> Abram is blessed
>   by God Most High,
>   Creator*E* of heaven and earth,
> **20** and blessed be God Most High
>   who has handed over
>   your enemies to you.

And Abram gave him a tenth of everything.*r* **21** Then the king of Sodom said to Abram, "Give me the people, but take the possessions for yourself."

22 But Abram said to the king of Sodom, "I have raised my hand in an oath to the LORD, God Most High, Creator of heaven and earth, **23** that I will not take a thread or sandal strap or anything that belongs to you, so you can never say, 'I made Abram rich.' **24** I will take nothing*F* except what the servants have eaten. But as for the share of the men who came with me — Aner, Eshcol, and Mamre — they can take their share."

THE ABRAHAMIC COVENANT

15 After these events, the word of the LORD came*s* to Abram in a vision:
> Do not be afraid,*t* Abram.
> I am your shield;*u*
> your reward will be
>   very great.

A 14:10 Sam, LXX; MT reads *fell there*   *B* 14:13 Lit *were possessors of a covenant of*   *C* 14:14 Sam; MT reads *poured out*   *D* 14:18 = Jerusalem
E 14:19 Or *Possessor*   *F* 14:24 Lit *nothing to me*

14:13-16 Word reached Abram that Lot had been captured (14:13-14), so he **assembled his 318 trained men** to go get his nephew back (14:14). With them, Abram pursued the armies. The only explanation for his amazing victory, though, was God fulfilling his word to Abram—that those who hurt Abram were hurting God, and God himself would defend Abram. God also wants to be our protector when circumstances raid our lives.
14:17-18 Abram's daring military venture also released several kings. One of them came to thank Abram. His name was **Melchizedek,**

king of Salem, called a **priest to God Most High** (14:18). Peculiarly, he's both a King and a priest. Kings rule over the people, while priests mediate between the people and God. No Jew ever occupied both offices. This is why the author of Hebrews said that Jesus was a priest and a king in "the order of Melchizedek" (Heb 5:10). He is the great high priest and ruling king who bridged the gap between God and humanity and acts on our behalf (Heb 4:14-16).
14:20 We see the first tithe here, as **Abram gave** Melchizedek **a tenth**. Notice Abram

only gave his tithe *after* Melchizedek had blessed him (14:18-19). In other words, Abram did not give to get God's blessing; he gave as a response to what God had done. Since Jesus came in "the order of Melchizedek," the tithe is still valid today as a response to God's goodness in our lives (see Heb 7:1-17).
14:22-24 Abram told the king that he would be keeping his own spoils and wouldn't touch even **a . . . sandal strap** belonging to him, because Abram wanted to make sure the king could never say, **I made Abram rich** (14:23). The victory was God's alone.

[2] But Abram said, "Lord GOD, what can you give me, since I am childless and the heir of my house is Eliezer of Damascus?"[A] [3] Abram continued, "Look, you have given me no offspring, so a slave born in[B] my house will be my heir."

[4] Now the word of the LORD came to him: "This one will not be your heir; instead, one who comes from your own body[C] will be your heir." [5] He took him outside and said, "Look at the sky and count the stars, if you are able to count them." Then he said to him, "Your offspring will be that numerous."[a]

⚮ HOPE WORDS ⚮

Faith is our positive response to what God has already provided.

[6] Abram believed the LORD, and he credited it to him as righteousness.[b]

[7] He also said to him, "I am the LORD who brought you from Ur of the Chaldeans to give you this land to possess."[c]

[8] But he said, "Lord GOD, how can I know[d] that I will possess it?"

[9] He said to him, "Bring me a three-year-old cow, a three-year-old female goat, a three-year-old ram, a turtledove, and a young pigeon."

[10] So he brought all these to him, cut them in half, and laid the pieces opposite each other, but he did not cut the birds[e] in half. [11] Birds of prey came down on the carcasses, but Abram drove them away. [12] As the sun was setting, a deep sleep[f] came over Abram, and suddenly great terror and darkness descended on him.

[13] Then the LORD said to Abram,[g] "Know this for certain: Your offspring will be resident aliens[h] for four hundred years[i] in a land that does not belong to them and will be enslaved and oppressed.[D] [14] However, I will judge the nation they serve,[j] and afterward they will go out with many possessions.[k] [15] But you will go to your fathers in peace and be buried at a good old age.[l] [16] In the fourth generation they will return here, for the iniquity of the Amorites has not yet reached its full measure."[E,m]

[17] When the sun had set and it was dark, a smoking fire pot and a flaming torch appeared and passed between the divided animals. [18] On that day the LORD made a covenant with Abram, saying, "I give this land to your offspring,[n] from the Brook of Egypt[o] to the great river, the Euphrates River: [19] the land of the Kenites, Kenizzites, Kadmonites, [20] Hethites, Perizzites, Rephaim, [21] Amorites, Canaanites, Girgashites, and Jebusites."

HAGAR AND ISHMAEL

16 Abram's wife Sarai had not borne any children for him, but she owned an Egyptian slave named Hagar. [2] Sarai said to Abram, "Since the LORD has prevented me from bearing children, go to my slave; perhaps through her I can build a family." And Abram agreed to what Sarai said.[f] [3] So Abram's wife Sarai took Hagar, her Egyptian slave, and gave her to her husband Abram as a wife for him. This happened after Abram had lived in the land of Canaan ten years. [4] He slept with[G] Hagar, and she became pregnant. When she saw that she was pregnant, her mistress became contemptible to her. [5] Then Sarai said to Abram, "You are responsible for my suffering![H] I put my slave in your

---

Cross references:
[a] 15:5 Gn 22:17; 26:4; Ex 32:13; Dt 1:10; 10:22; 1Ch 27:23; Rm 4:18; Heb 11:12
[b] 15:6 Rm 4:3,9,22; Gl 3:6; Jms 2:23
[c] 15:7 Gn 11:31; 12:1; Neh 9:7-8; Ac 7:2-4
[d] 15:8 Jdg 6:17; 2Kg 20:8; Ps 86:17; Is 7:11-13; Lk 1:18
[e] 15:10 Lv 1:17
[f] 15:12 Gn 2:21
[g] 15:13-14 Ac 7:6-7
[h] 15:13 Ex 22:21; 23:9
[i] Ex 12:40; Gl 3:17
[j] 15:14 Ex 6:6; 7:4; 12:12
[k] Ex 3:22
[l] 15:15 Gn 25:8; 47:30
[m] 15:16 Lv 18:24-28; Dn 8:23; Mt 23:32; 1Th 2:16
[n] 15:18 Gn 12:7; 13:15; 17:8; 24:7; 26:4; Nm 34:2; Dt 34:4; Jos 21:43; Neh 9:8; Ac 7:5
[o] Ex 23:31; Nm 34:1-15; Dt 1:7-8; 2Kg 24:7

[A] 15:2 Hb obscure [B] 15:3 Lit *a son of* [C] 15:4 Lit *loins* [D] 15:13 Lit *will serve them and they will oppress them* [E] 15:16 Lit *Amorites is not yet complete* [F] 16:2 Lit *Abram listened to the voice of Sarai* [G] 16:4 Lit *He came to* [H] 16:5 Or *"May my suffering be on you!*

15:4-5 God insisted that **one who comes from [Abram's] own body** would inherit his wealth (15:4). **Count the stars, if you are able** (15:5), God said. *That's* how many descendants you'll have. If God was powerful enough to create billions of stars out of nothing, he would prove powerful enough to create new life from an old man.
15:6 In spite of all the obstacles before him, Abram believed God's promise. God saw this faith and **credited it to him as righteousness.** The apostle Paul would pick up on this verse in Romans 4:3, using Abram as an example of how faith works. God spoke to Abram, and Abram took him at his word. That's the essence of faith. Because of this faith, God chose to count

Abram's faith as righteousness. That's the result of faith.
15:7-21 Abram did as instructed and then fell asleep (15:12). The key detail in what happened next is that God alone—in the form of **a smoking fire pot and a flaming torch**—passed through the path of the torn animals as he renewed his covenant with Abram (15:17). Both parties to the covenant were supposed to walk between the slain animals, signaling that if either one broke their side of the agreement, he would suffer a fate like that of the animals. But God's covenant was radically unique: Abram wasn't even awake when it was made. God walked through for both of them, promising to bear the fatal burden if *either* of them broke the covenant. Thus, this

was an unconditional covenant dependent on God alone for its fulfillment.
16:1-4 Abram and Sarai were both pushing the century mark, and the promise was still unfulfilled. So Sarai did what many do when they don't like God's timing: she produced a scheme to help God out. It was the custom of the day for a servant to act as a surrogate when the wife of the household couldn't conceive. Sarai, therefore, took **Hagar** and offered **her to her husband** (16:3). Abram quietly acquiesced (16:4), passively allowing his wife to overrule the will of God.
16:4-6 Hagar's pregnancy was hardly the panacea that Sarai hoped for. It only incited Sarai's jealousy and rage. **Sarai mistreated her so much that she ran away** (16:6).

a 16:5 Gn 31:49; Jos 22:25; 1Sm 24:12
b 16:7 Gn 22:11; Ex 3:2; Nm 22:22; Jdg 2:1; 2Sm 24:16; 1Kg 19:7; 2Kg 19:35; Ps 34:7
c 16:10 Gn 15:5; 17:2; 26:24; Lv 26:9; Dt 7:13; 30:5; Ps 107:38
d 16:12 Gn 25:18
e 16:13 Gn 32:30; Ex 33:23; Ps 139:1-12
f 17:1 Gn 28:3; 35:11; Ex 6:3
g Gn 6:9; Ps 15:2; Lk 1:6

h 17:5 Gn 35:11; 48:19; Rm 4:11-12,16-18
i 17:7 Gn 9:16
j Ex 6:7; Lv 11:45; 26:12,45; Dt 29:13; Heb 11:16; Rv 21:7
k 17:8 Gl 3:16
l Gn 48:4; Ac 7:5
m 17:11 Ex 12:48; Dt 10:16; Ac 7:8; Rm 4:11
n 17:12 Lv 12:3; Lk 1:59; 2:21; Php 3:5

arms,^A^ and when she saw that she was pregnant, I became contemptible to her. May the LORD judge between me and you."^a^

6 Abram replied to Sarai, "Here, your slave is in your hands; do whatever you want with her." Then Sarai mistreated her so much that she ran away from her. **7** The angel of the LORD^b^ found her by a spring in the wilderness, the spring on the way to Shur. **8** He said, "Hagar, slave of Sarai, where have you come from and where are you going?"

She replied, "I'm running away from my mistress Sarai."

9 The angel of the LORD said to her, "Go back to your mistress and submit to her authority." **10** The angel of the LORD said to her, "I will greatly multiply your offspring,^c^ and they will be too many to count."

11 The angel of the LORD said to her, "You have conceived and will have a son. You will name him Ishmael,^B^ for the LORD has heard your cry of affliction. **12** This man will be like a wild donkey. His hand will be against everyone, and everyone's hand will be against him; he will settle near all his relatives."^d^

13 So she named the LORD who spoke to her: "You are El-roi,"^c^ for she said, "In this place, have I actually seen^e^ the one who sees me?"^D^ **14** That is why the well is called Beer-lahai-roi.^E^ It is between Kadesh and Bered.

15 So Hagar gave birth to Abram's son, and Abram named his son (whom Hagar bore) Ishmael. **16** Abram was eighty-six years old when Hagar bore Ishmael to him.

COVENANT CIRCUMCISION

17 When Abram was ninety-nine years old, the LORD appeared to him, saying, "I am God Almighty.^f^ Live^f^ in my presence and be blameless.^g^ **2** I will set up my covenant between me and you, and I will multiply you greatly."

3 Then Abram fell facedown and God spoke with him: **4** "As for me, here is my covenant with you: You will become the father of many nations. **5** Your name will no longer be Abram;^G^ your name will be Abraham,^H^ for I will make you the father of many nations.^h^ **6** I will make you extremely fruitful and will make nations and kings come from you. **7** I will confirm my covenant that is between me and you and your future offspring throughout their generations. It is a permanent covenant^i^ to be your God and the God of your offspring after you.^j^ **8** And to you and your future offspring^k^ I will give the land where you are residing — all the land of Canaan — as a permanent possession,^l^ and I will be their God."

9 God also said to Abraham, "As for you, you and your offspring after you throughout their generations are to keep my covenant. **10** This is my covenant between me and you and your offspring after you, which you are to keep: Every one of your males must be circumcised. **11** You must circumcise the flesh of your foreskin to serve as a sign of the covenant between me and you.^l,m^ **12** Throughout your generations, every male among you is to be circumcised^n^ at eight days old — every male born in your household or purchased from any foreigner and not your offspring. **13** Whether born in your household or purchased, he must be circumcised. My covenant will be marked in your flesh as a permanent covenant. **14** If any male is not circumcised in the flesh of his foreskin, that man will be cut off from his people; he has broken my covenant."

15 God said to Abraham, "As for your wife Sarai, do not call her Sarai, for Sarah^J^ will

---

^A^ 16:5 Lit *bosom*   ^B^ 16:11 = God Hears   ^C^ 16:13 = God Sees Me   ^D^ 16:13 Hb obscure   ^E^ 16:14 = Well of the Living One Who Sees Me   ^F^ 17:1 Or *Walk*   ^G^ 17:5 = The Father Is Exalted   ^H^ 17:5 = Father of a Multitude   ^I^ 17:11 *You* in v. 11 is pl.   ^J^ 17:15 = Princess

---

16:7-11 God met Hagar in her place of despair. He guided her back to Abram and Sarai (16:9). He also promised that the child in her womb would be a son (16:11). God called his name **Ishmael**, which means "God hears" (16:11). God is near to the brokenhearted, and he hears their cries (see Ps 34:18). Single parents, then, are not alone.

16:12 Hagar's promised son would be **like a wild donkey**. His descendants would be unruly, bringing conflict into the household of God for generations to come. Sarai's scheme only led to more conflict.

16:13-16 In spite of the negative promises about Ishmael's future, Hagar **named the LORD who spoke to her: "You are El-roi"** (16:13), meaning "The God who sees." What greater comfort can there be than to *know* that God hears, sees, and cares?

17:1 Twenty-four years had passed since God first promised Abram a son, a promise that looked increasingly impossible if Sarai was to be the mother. But God assured Abram, **I am God Almighty**. He is full of power. All Abram needed to do was to fulfill his obligation to God: **Live in my presence and be blameless.**

17:4-8 Name changes in the Bible are always important. God changed Abram's name, even before the promise was fulfilled, from **Abram** to **Abraham** (17:5). *Abram* means "exalted father," but *Abraham* means "father of a multitude" because he would become the **father of many nations** (17:5). The promise had grown. Notice, however, that God still hadn't done anything to change the circumstances Abram could see. Instead, he changed Abram's name to fit his own promise.

17:9-14 The sign of God's renewed covenant with Abraham was that every male **must circumcise the flesh of [his] foreskin** (17:11). This painful procedure underscores the deep commitment God expected from those in covenant with him. Circumcision was a signal that men would carry the covenant, as we see this promise pass from Abraham to his son Isaac and so on. It was also to be a perpetual reminder to the people that God intended to remove impurity from their midst.

17:15-16 By God's command, **Sarai** became **Sarah**, meaning "princess" (17:15). With this

be her name. ¹⁶ I will bless her; indeed, I will give you a son by her.^a I will bless her, and she will produce nations; kings of peoples will come from her."

¹⁷ Abraham fell facedown. Then he laughed^b and said to himself, "Can a child be born to a hundred-year-old man? Can Sarah, a ninety-year-old woman, give birth?" ¹⁸ So Abraham said to God, "If only Ishmael were acceptable^A to you!"

¹⁹ But God said, "No. Your wife Sarah will bear you a son, and you will name him Isaac.^B I will confirm my covenant with him as a permanent covenant for his future offspring. ²⁰ As for Ishmael, I have heard you. I will certainly bless him; I will make him fruitful and will multiply him greatly. He will father twelve tribal leaders,^c and I will make him into a great nation. ²¹ But I will confirm my covenant with Isaac, whom Sarah will bear to you at this time next year."^d ²² When he finished talking with him, God withdrew^c from Abraham.^e

²³ So Abraham took his son Ishmael and those born in his household or purchased — every male among the members of Abraham's household — and he circumcised the flesh of their foreskin on that very day, just as God had said to him. ²⁴ Abraham was ninety-nine years old when the flesh of his foreskin was circumcised, ²⁵ and his son Ishmael was thirteen years old when the flesh of his foreskin was circumcised. ²⁶ On that same day Abraham and his son Ishmael were circumcised. ²⁷ And all the men of his household — whether born in his household or purchased from a foreigner — were circumcised with him.

ABRAHAM'S THREE VISITORS

18 The LORD appeared to Abraham at the oaks of Mamre^f while he was sitting at the entrance of his tent during the heat of the day. ² He looked up, and he saw three men standing near him.^g When he saw them, he ran from the entrance of the tent to meet them, bowed to the ground, ³ and said, "My lord, if I have found favor with you, please do not go on past your servant. ⁴ Let a little water be brought, that you may wash your feet and rest yourselves under the tree. ⁵ I will bring a bit of bread so that you may strengthen yourselves.^D This is why you have passed your servant's way. Later, you can continue on."

"Yes," they replied, "do as you have said."

⁶ So Abraham hurried into the tent and said to Sarah, "Quick! Knead three measures^E of fine flour and make bread."^F ⁷ Abraham ran to the herd and got a tender, choice calf. He gave it to a young man, who hurried to prepare it. ⁸ Then Abraham took curds^G and milk, as well as the calf that he had prepared, and set them before the men. He served^H them as they ate under the tree.

SARAH LAUGHS

⁹ "Where is your wife Sarah?" they asked him.

"There, in the tent," he answered.

¹⁰ The LORD said, "I will certainly come back to you in about a year's time, and your wife Sarah will have a son!"^h Now Sarah was listening at the entrance of the tent behind him.

¹¹ Abraham and Sarah were old and getting on in years.ⁱ Sarah had passed the age of childbearing.^{J,i} ¹² So she laughed to herself: "After I am worn out and my lord is old, will I have delight?"^j

¹³ But the LORD asked Abraham, "Why did Sarah laugh, saying, 'Can I really have a baby when I'm old?' ¹⁴ Is anything impossible for the LORD?^k At the appointed time I will come back to you, and in about a year she will have a son."

^a17:16 Gn 18:10
^b17:17 Gn 21:6-7; Rm 4:19
^c17:20 Gn 25:13-16
^d17:21 Gn 18:10,14; 21:1
^e17:22 Gn 35:13
^f18:1 Gn 13:18; 14:13; 23:17-19

^g18:2 Gn 18:16,22; 19:1; 32:24; Jos 5:13; Jdg 13:6-11; Heb 13:2
^h18:10 Gn 17:10; 21:1; Rm 9:9
ⁱ18:11 Gn 17:17; Rm 4:19; Heb 11:11-12
^j18:12 Gn 17:17; Lk 1:18; 1Pt 3:6
^k18:14 Jb 34:10; Jr 32:17,27; Mt 19:26; Mk 10:27; Lk 1:37; 18:27; Heb 6:18

^A17:18 Lit *alive*   ^B17:19 = He Laughs   ^C17:22 Lit *went up*, or *ascended*   ^D18:5 Lit *may sustain your heart*   ^E18:6 Lit *three seahs*; about 21 quarts   ^F18:6 A round, thin, unleavened bread   ^G18:8 Or *butter*   ^H18:8 Lit *was standing by*   ^I18:11 Lit *days*   ^J18:11 Lit *The way of women had ceased for Sarah*

new name comes the promise that **kings of peoples will come from her** (17:16).
17:17-22 Abraham found this difficult to believe, since he was pushing one hundred and Sarah was ninety. **He laughed** (17:17) because he couldn't take God seriously. God repeated the promise of a son, but added, **you will name him Isaac** (17:19)—the name *Isaac* meaning "he laughs." Every time Abraham would say his son's name, he would be reminded that he had laughed at the miracle God had promised. God always gets the last laugh.

17:23-27 Abraham obeyed the command to circumcise himself and his men (17:23). Importantly, circumcision no longer operates as the sign of God's kingdom. It has been replaced by baptism, the sign of the new covenant. Baptism serves as a sign that we are operating in accordance with God's covenant and allowing his kingdom rule to govern our lives.
18:1-2 The text makes it clear that these visitors were actually **the LORD** and two angels (18:1; 19:1). This was a "Christophany," a pre-

incarnate but visible manifestation of the Second Person of the Trinity.
18:3-8 God had decided to visit with Abraham, personally confirming what he had already promised. The picture here is surprisingly intimate: God sat and ate with Abraham for half a day, surrounding his promise with his presence.
18:13-15 In response to Sarah's laughter, God asked the most important question of faith: **Is anything impossible for the LORD?** (18:14). God invites us to let the facts be swallowed up by trust in him.

a 18:17 Am 3:7
b 18:18 Gn 12:3; 26:4; Gl 3:8
c 18:21 Gn 11:5; Ex 3:8;
Ps 14:2
d 18:22 Gn 19:1
e 18:23 Ex 23:7; Nm 16:22;
2Sm 24:17; Ps 11:4-7
f 18:25 Dt 1:16-17; 32:4; Jb
8:3,20; Ps 58:11; 94:2; Is
3:10-11; Rm 3:5-6
g 18:26 Jr 5:1

h 18:32 Jdg 6:39
i 19:1 Gn 18:2,22

15 Sarah denied it. "I did not laugh," she said, because she was afraid.

But he replied, "No, you did laugh."

ABRAHAM'S PLEA FOR SODOM

16 The men got up from there and looked out over Sodom, and Abraham was walking with them to see them off. **17** Then the LORD said, "Should I hide what I am about to do from Abraham?*a* **18** Abraham is to become a great and powerful nation, and all the nations of the earth will be blessed through him.*b* **19** For I have chosen^A him so that he will command his children and his house after him to keep the way of the LORD by doing what is right and just. This is how the LORD will fulfill to Abraham what he promised him." **20** Then the LORD said, "The outcry against Sodom and Gomorrah is immense, and their sin is extremely serious. **21** I will go down*c* to see if what they have done justifies the cry that has come up to me. If not, I will find out."

22 The men turned from there and went toward Sodom*d* while Abraham remained standing before the LORD.^B **23** Abraham stepped forward and said, "Will you really sweep away the righteous with the wicked?*e* **24** What if there are fifty righteous people in the city? Will you really sweep it away instead of sparing the place for the sake of the fifty righteous people who are in it? **25** You could not possibly do such a thing: to kill the righteous with the wicked, treating the righteous and the wicked alike. You could not possibly do that! Won't the Judge of the whole earth do what is just?"*f*

26 The LORD said, "If I find fifty righteous people in the city of Sodom, I will spare the whole place for their sake."*g*

27 Then Abraham answered, "Since I have ventured to speak to my lord — even though I am dust and ashes — **28** suppose the fifty righteous lack five. Will you destroy the whole city for lack of five?"

He replied, "I will not destroy it if I find forty-five there."

29 Then he spoke to him again, "Suppose forty are found there?"

He answered, "I will not do it on account of forty."

30 Then he said, "Let my lord not be angry, and I will speak further. Suppose thirty are found there?"

He answered, "I will not do it if I find thirty there."

31 Then he said, "Since I have ventured to speak to my lord, suppose twenty are found there?"

He replied, "I will not destroy it on account of twenty."

32 Then he said, "Let my lord not be angry, and I will speak one more time.*h* Suppose ten are found there?"

He answered, "I will not destroy it on account of ten." **33** When the LORD had finished speaking with Abraham, he departed, and Abraham returned to his place.

THE DESTRUCTION OF SODOM AND GOMORRAH

19 The two angels entered Sodom*i* in the evening as Lot was sitting in Sodom's gateway. When Lot saw them, he got up to meet them. He bowed with his face to the ground **2** and said, "My lords, turn aside to your servant's house, wash your feet, and spend the night. Then you can get up early and go on your way."

"No," they said. "We would rather spend the night in the square." **3** But he urged them so strongly that they followed him and went into his house. He prepared a feast and baked unleavened bread for them, and they ate.

4 Before they went to bed, the men of the city of Sodom, both young and old,

18:16-21 The fully omniscient God, of course, already had all the information against Sodom he needed. He just wanted to make it plain that the coming destruction was just. **Their sin was extremely serious** (18:20). It consisted of gross immorality, violence, and oppression of the poor (see Ezek 16:49-50).

18:18-19 Here God makes a beautiful statement about his vision for kingdom fathers, men who represent God the ultimate Father. Each of us has a world-altering destiny that God intends us to fulfill (18:18). A kingdom father bears the responsibility to **command his children . . . to keep the**

way of the LORD (18:19). This is a thrilling opportunity. Family plays a crucial role in the national expansion of God's kingdom agenda.

18:22-26 With the destruction of Sodom and Gomorrah imminent, God paused, yet again, to allow them another chance. This time Abraham would be a part of the forbearing process. Abraham appealed to God's justice, by saying, **Will you really sweep away the righteous with the wicked?** (18:23). What follows is a peculiar scene. Abraham was attempting to "talk God down," and surprisingly enough, God played along.

18:27-33 Each time God responded to Abraham's compassionate intercession by granting him his request. This scene corresponds with what we read in Matthew 5:13-16, where Jesus talks of believers as the "salt of the earth." Our job, as members of God's kingdom, is to act as a preserving influence in a dying world. **19:1-5** It was not long before **the men . . . of Sodom** began pounding on Lot's door (19:4), demanding that he release the strangers so they could **have sex with them** (19:5). Sodom had descended into such a den of sin that visitors to the city could not be left in public alone for even a few hours without fear of being raped (19:3, 5).

the whole population, surrounded the house. **5** They called out to Lot and said, "Where are the men who came to you tonight? Send them out to us so we can have sex with them! "[a]

6 Lot went out to them at the entrance and shut the door behind him. **7** He said, "Don't do this evil, my brothers. **8** Look, I've got two daughters who haven't been intimate with a man.[b] I'll bring them out to you, and you can do whatever you want[A] to them. However, don't do anything to these men, because they have come under the protection of my roof."

9 "Get out of the way! " they said, adding, "This one came here as an alien, but he's acting like a judge![c] Now we'll do more harm to you than to them." They put pressure on Lot and came up to break down the door. **10** But the angels[B] reached out, brought Lot into the house with them, and shut the door. **11** They struck the men who were at the entrance of the house, both young and old, with blindness[c] so that they were unable to find the entrance.[d]

12 Then the angels said to Lot, "Do you have anyone else here: a son-in-law, your sons and daughters, or anyone else in the city who belongs to you? Get them out of this place, **13** for we are about to destroy this place because the outcry against its people is so great before the LORD, that the LORD has sent us to destroy it."[e]

14 So Lot went out and spoke to his sons-in-law, who were going to marry[D] his daughters. "Get up," he said. "Get out of this place, for the LORD is about to destroy the city! "[f] But his sons-in-law thought he was joking.

15 At daybreak the angels urged Lot on: "Get up! Take your wife and your two daughters who are here, or you will be swept away in the punishment[E] of the city." **16** But he hesitated. Because of the LORD's compassion for him, the men grabbed his hand, his wife's hand, and the hands of his two daughters. They brought him out and left him outside the city.

17 As soon as the angels got them outside, one of them[f] said, "Run for your lives! Don't look back and don't stop anywhere on the plain! Run to the mountains, or you will be swept away! "

18 But Lot said to them, "No, my lords[G] — please. **19** Your servant has indeed found favor with you, and you have shown me great kindness by saving my life. But I can't run to the mountains; the disaster will overtake me, and I will die. **20** Look, this town is close enough for me to flee to. It is a small place. Please let me run to it — it's only a small place, isn't it? — so that I can survive."

21 And he said to him, "All right,[H] I'll grant your request[I] about this matter too and will not demolish the town you mentioned. **22** Hurry up! Run to it, for I cannot do anything until you get there." Therefore the name of the city is Zoar.[J,g]

23 The sun had risen over the land when Lot reached Zoar. **24** Then out of the sky the LORD rained on Sodom and Gomorrah burning sulfur from the LORD.[h] **25** He demolished these cities, the entire plain, all the inhabitants of the cities, and whatever grew on the ground. **26** But Lot's wife looked back and became a pillar of salt.[i]

27 Early in the morning Abraham went to the place where he had stood before the LORD.[j] **28** He looked down toward Sodom and Gomorrah and all the land of the plain, and he saw that smoke was going up from the land like the smoke of a furnace. **29** So it was, when God destroyed the cities of the plain, he remembered Abraham and brought Lot out of the middle of the upheaval when he demolished the cities where Lot had lived.

---

[a] 19:5 Lv 18:22; Jdg 19:22
[b] 19:8 Jdg 19:24
[c] 19:9 Ex 2:14
[d] 19:11 Dt 28:28–29; 2Kg 6:18; Ac 13:11
[e] 19:13 Gn 18:20–21; Ex 3:7; 22:23; 1Sm 9:16; Jb 27:9
[f] 19:14 Nm 16:21,26,45; Jr 51:6; Rv 18:4

[g] 19:22 Gn 14:2
[h] 19:24 Dt 29:23; Ps 11:6; Is 13:19; Jr 20:16; Ezk 16:49–50; Lk 17:28–29; 2Pt 2:6–8; Jd 7
[i] 19:26 Lk 17:32
[j] 19:27 Gn 18:22

[A] 19:8 Lit *do what is good in your eyes*   [B] 19:10 Lit *men*, also in v. 12   [C] 19:11 Or *a blinding light*   [D] 19:14 Lit *take*   [E] 19:15 Or *iniquity*, or *guilt*   [F] 19:17 LXX, Syr, Vg read *outside, they*   [G] 19:18 Or *my Lord*, or *my lord*   [H] 19:21 Or *"Look!*   [I] 19:21 Lit *I will lift up your face*   [J] 19:22 In Hb, the name *Zoar* is related to "small" in v. 20; its previous name was "Bela"; Gn 14:2.

19:6-8 Lot offered to give the riotous crowd his **two daughters** (19:8). This repulsive offer reveals Lot's failure to believe that God would protect him.
19:9-14 If **you have anyone else here**—anyone you want to rescue—now is the time to get them out (19:12), the angels warned. Lot tried, but was met with laughter from his daughters' husbands-to-be when he extended the invitation for them to leave town with him (19:14). How dangerous to hear the warnings of God and shrug them off as a joke!

19:15-29 Lot's family had become comfortable in a society that rejected God and his laws. Even though the angels strictly warned them, **Don't look back** (19:17), Lot's wife paused to do so, and instantly **became a pillar of salt** (19:26). She thus became a permanent monument of the serious consequences of disobedience and worldliness. In Luke 17:32 Jesus charged us to remember not the evil men of Sodom, but "Lot's wife." We are to be in the world, working for the good of our neighbors, but not to be contaminated by its rebellion against God.
19:30-38 Lot's daughters, their fiancés now dead, were so concerned about their marriage prospects that they devised a sinful scheme (19:31-32). The plan worked, and **both of Lot's daughters became pregnant** (19:36) by him. Their two sons, **Moab** and **Ben-ammi**, would become the patriarchs of the Moabites and Ammonites, ongoing enemies of God's people. When we try to solve God's "problems" for him, we only create more problems for ourselves.

a 19:37 Dt 2:9
b 19:38 Dt 2:19
c 20:1 Gn 26:1,6
d 20:2 Gn 12:13; 26:7

e 20:7 1Sm 7:5; 2Kg 5:11;
Jb 42:8
f 20:9 Gn 12:19; 26:9
g 20:11 Neh 5:15; Pr 16:6
h 20:13 Gn 12:1
i Gn 12:13; 20:5
j 20:15 Gn 13:9; 34:10; 47:6
k 20:17 Nm 12:13; 21:7;
Jms 5:16
l 21:1 Gn 17:16; 18:10;
Gl 4:23

THE ORIGIN OF MOAB AND AMMON

30 Lot departed from Zoar and lived in the mountains along with his two daughters, because he was afraid to live in Zoar. Instead, he and his two daughters lived in a cave. **31** Then the firstborn said to the younger, "Our father is old, and there is no man in the land to sleep with us as is the custom of all the land. **32** Come, let's get our father to drink wine so that we can sleep with him and preserve our father's line." **33** So they got their father to drink wine that night, and the firstborn came and slept with her father; he did not know when she lay down or when she got up. **34** The next day the firstborn said to the younger, "Look, I slept with my father last night. Let's get him to drink wine again tonight so you can go sleep with him and we can preserve our father's line." **35** That night they again got their father to drink wine, and the younger went and slept with him; he did not know when she lay down or when she got up. **36** So both of Lot's daughters became pregnant by their father. **37** The firstborn gave birth to a son and named him Moab.ᴬ He is the father of the Moabites of today.ᵃ **38** The younger also gave birth to a son, and she named him Ben-ammi.ᴮ He is the father of the Ammonites of today.ᵇ

SARAH RESCUED FROM ABIMELECH

20 From there Abraham traveled to the region of the Negev and settled between Kadesh and Shur. While he was staying in Gerar,ᶜ **2** Abraham said about his wife Sarah, "She is my sister."ᵈ So King Abimelech of Gerar had Sarah brought to him.

3 But God came to Abimelech in a dream by night and said to him, "You are about to die because of the woman you have taken, for she is a married woman."ᶜ **4** Now Abimelech had not approached her, so he said, "Lord, would you destroy a nation even though it is innocent? **5** Didn't he himself say to me, 'She is my sister'? And she herself said, 'He is my brother.' I did this with a clear conscienceᴰ and cleanᴱ hands."

6 Then God said to him in the dream, "Yes, I know that you did this with a clear conscience.ᶠ I have also kept you from sinning against me. Therefore I have not let you touch her. **7** Now return the man's wife, for he is a prophet,ᵉ and he will pray for you and you will live. But if you do not return her, know that you will certainly die, you and all who are yours."

8 Early in the morning Abimelech got up, called all his servants together, and personallyᴳ told them all these things, and the men were terrified.

9 Then Abimelech called Abraham in and said to him, "What have you done to us? How did I sin against you that you have brought such enormous guilt on me and on my kingdom? You have done things to me that should never be done."ᶠ **10** Abimelech also asked Abraham, "What made you do this?"

11 Abraham replied, "I thought, 'There is absolutely no fear of God in this place.ᵍ They will kill me because of my wife.' **12** Besides, she really is my sister, the daughter of my father though not the daughter of my mother, and she became my wife. **13** So when God had me wander from my father's house,ʰ I said to her: Show your loyalty to me wherever we go and say about me: 'He's my brother.'"ᶦ

14 Then Abimelech took flocks and herds and male and female slaves, gave them to Abraham, and returned his wife Sarah to him. **15** Abimelech said, "Look, my land is before you.ʲ Settle wherever you want."ᴴ **16** And he said to Sarah, "Look, I am giving your brother one thousand pieces of silver. It is a verification of your honorᶦ to all who are with you. You are fully vindicated."

17 Then Abraham prayed to God,ᵏ and God healed Abimelech, his wife, and his female slaves so that they could bear children, **18** for the Lᴏʀᴅ had completely closed all the wombs in Abimelech's household on account of Sarah, Abraham's wife.

THE BIRTH OF ISAAC

21 The Lᴏʀᴅ came to Sarah as he had said, and the Lᴏʀᴅ did for Sarah what he had promised.ᶦ **2** Sarah became

---

ᴬ**19:37** = From My Father   ᴮ**19:38** = Son of My People   ᶜ**20:3** Lit *is possessed by a husband*   ᴰ**20:5** Lit *with integrity of my heart*
ᴱ**20:5** Lit *cleanness of my*   ᶠ**20:6** Lit *with integrity of your heart*   ᴳ**20:8** Lit *in their ears*   ᴴ**20:15** Lit *Settle in the good in your eyes*   ᶦ**20:16** Lit *a covering of the eyes*

20:1-18 Though Sarah was ninety years old, she was apparently still attractive. The king immediately had her taken to the palace as a bride (20:2). But God told Abimelech about the real relationship between Abraham and Sarah in a dream (20:6-8). This is the first time we see Abraham called **a prophet** (20:7). Sadly, though, it is an unbelieving king, not Abraham, who does the virtuous and right thing (see 12:10-20).

21:1-7 It had taken twenty-five years, but **the Lᴏʀᴅ did for Sarah what he had promised** (21:1). She **bore a son** (21:2). Abraham and his wife demonstrated their faith by naming the boy Isaac, just as God had instructed (21:3). Though the laughter of Abraham and Sarah had previously been doubtful, it transformed into the laughter of joy.

pregnant and bore a son to Abraham in his old age, at the appointed time God had told him.[a] [3] Abraham named his son who was born to him — the one Sarah bore to him — Isaac.[b] [4] When his son Isaac was eight days old, Abraham circumcised him, as God had commanded him.[c] [5] Abraham was a hundred years old when his son Isaac was born to him.[d]

[6] Sarah said, "God has made me laugh, and everyone who hears will laugh with me."[A,e] [7] She also said, "Who would have told Abraham that Sarah would nurse children? Yet I have borne a son for him[B] in his old age."

HAGAR AND ISHMAEL SENT AWAY

[8] The child grew and was weaned, and Abraham held a great feast on the day Isaac was weaned. [9] But Sarah saw the son mocking — the one Hagar the Egyptian had borne to Abraham.[f] [10] So she said to Abraham, "Drive out this slave with her son, for the son of this slave will not be a coheir with my son Isaac!"[g] [11] This was very distressing to[c] Abraham because of his son. [12] But God said to Abraham, "Do not be distressed[D] about the boy and about your slave. Whatever Sarah says to you, listen to her, because your offspring will be traced through Isaac,[h] [13] and I will also make a nation of the slave's son[i] because he is your offspring."

[14] Early in the morning Abraham got up, took bread and a waterskin, put them on Hagar's shoulders, and sent her and the boy away. She left and wandered in the Wilderness of Beer-sheba. [15] When the water in the skin was gone, she left the boy under one of the bushes [16] and went and sat at a distance, about a bowshot away, for she said, "I can't bear to watch the boy die!" While she sat at a distance, she[E] wept loudly.[j] [17] God heard the boy crying, and the[F] angel of God called to Hagar from heaven and said to her, "What's wrong, Hagar? Don't be afraid, for God has heard the boy crying from the place where he is. [18] Get

up, help the boy up, and grasp his hand, for I will make him a great nation." [19] Then God opened her eyes,[k] and she saw a well. So she went and filled the waterskin and gave the boy a drink. [20] God was with the boy, and he grew; he settled in the wilderness and became an archer. [21] He settled in the Wilderness of Paran, and his mother got a wife for him from the land of Egypt.

ABRAHAM'S COVENANT WITH ABIMELECH

[22] At that time Abimelech, accompanied by Phicol the commander of his army,[l] said to Abraham, "God is with you in everything you do.[m] [23] Swear to me by God here and now, that you will not break an agreement with me or with my children and descendants. As I have been loyal to you, so you will be loyal to me and to the country where you are a resident alien."

[24] And Abraham said, "I swear it." [25] But Abraham complained to Abimelech because of the well that Abimelech's servants had seized.[n] [26] Abimelech replied, "I don't know who did this thing. You didn't report anything to me, so I hadn't heard about it until today."

[27] Abraham took flocks and herds and gave them to Abimelech, and the two of them made a covenant.[o] [28] Abraham separated seven ewe lambs from the flock. [29] And Abimelech said to Abraham, "Why have you separated these seven ewe lambs?" [30] He replied, "You are to accept the seven ewe lambs from me so that this act[G] will serve as my witness that I dug this well." [31] Therefore that place was called Beer-sheba[H,p] because it was there that the two of them swore an oath. [32] After they had made a covenant at Beer-sheba, Abimelech and Phicol, the commander of his army, left and returned to the land of the Philistines.

[33] Abraham planted a tamarisk tree in Beer-sheba, and there he called on the name of the LORD, the Everlasting God.[q]

[a] 21:2 Gn 17:21; 18:10,14; Heb 11:11
[b] 21:3 Gn 17:19
[c] 21:4 Gn 17:10,12; Ac 7:8
[d] 21:5 Gn 17:1,17; Rm 4:19
[e] 21:6 Gn 18:12-15
[f] 21:9 Gn 16:1,15; Gl 4:29
[g] 21:10 Gl 4:30
[h] 21:12 Rm 9:7; Heb 11:18
[i] 21:13 Gn 16:10; 21:18; 25:12-18
[j] 21:16 Jr 6:26; Am 8:10

[k] 21:19 Nm 22:31; 2Kg 6:17-18,20; Lk 24:16,31
[l] 21:22 Gn 20:2; 26:1,26
[m] Gn 26:28
[n] 21:25 Gn 26:15,18,20-22
[o] 21:27 Gn 26:31
[p] 21:31 Gn 26:33
[q] 21:33 Ps 45:6; 48:14; 90:2; 93:2; Is 40:28; Jr 10:10; Rm 16:26; Heb 13:8

[A] 21:6 Isaac = He Laughs; Gn 17:19   [B] 21:7 Sam, Tg Jonathan; MT omits *him*   [C] 21:11 Lit *was very bad in the eyes of*   [D] 21:12 Lit *"Let it not be bad in your eyes*   [E] 21:16 LXX reads *the boy*   [F] 21:17 Or *an*   [G] 21:30 Lit *that it*   [H] 21:31 = Well of the Oath, or Seven Wells

21:8-13 Ishmael—**the one Hagar . . . had borne to Abraham** (21:9)—began to mock his half brother Isaac. As a result, Sarah saw Ishmael as a threat to her son's inheritance (21:10). While God shared Sarah's concern that Ishmael **not be a coheir with . . . Isaac** (21:10), he did not share her animosity toward Ishmael. **21:14-21** As before, Hagar assumed that she would die in the wilderness. **She left** [Ishmael] **under one of the bushes** (21:15) and went a distance away to await their deaths. But **God . . . heard the [outcast] crying** (21:17). He met their physical needs and renewed the promise to **make [Ishmael] a great nation** (21:18-19), giving them spiritual hope for the journey ahead. **21:33-34** Planting trees signified that Abraham intended to coexist in the land with other nations. This **tamarisk tree in Beer-sheba** (21:33) would be a sign of peace, security, and the appropriate kind of godly compromise. Abraham was doing what all believers should do: pursuing peace with his unbelieving neighbors without compromising his kingdom principles.

[a] 22:1 Dt 8:2,16; 1Co 10:13;
　Heb 11:17; Jms 1:12-14;
　1Pt 1:6-7
[b] 22:2 Gn 22:12,16; Jr 6:26;
Am 8:10; Mk 12:6; Lk 7:12;
Jn 3:16; 1Jn 4:9
[c] 2Ch 3:1
[d] 22:3 Jos 3:1
[e] 22:4 Ex 19:11,16; Jos 9:17;
Jdg 20:30; 2Sm 1:2; 1Kg
12:12; 2Kg 20:5; Est 5:1; Hs
6:2; Mt 17:23
[f] 22:6 Jn 19:17
[g] Jdg 19:29; Pr 30:14
[h] 22:8 Gn 22:14
[i] 22:9 Heb 11:17; Jms 2:21

[j] 22:12 Rm 8:32
[k] 22:16 Ps 105:9; Lk 1:73;
Heb 6:13
[l] 22:17 Heb 6:14
[m] Gn 15:5; 26:4; Jr 33:22;
Heb 11:12
[n] Gn 13:16; 32:12
[o] Gn 24:60
[p] 22:18 Gn 12:3; 26:4; Ac
3:25; Gl 3:8
[q] 22:20 Gn 11:29
[r] 22:23 Gn 24:15

34 And Abraham lived as an alien in the land of the Philistines for many days.

THE SACRIFICE OF ISAAC

22 After these things God tested Abraham[a] and said to him, "Abraham!" "Here I am," he answered.

2 "Take your son," he said, "your only son Isaac, whom you love,[b] go to the land of Moriah,[c] and offer him there as a burnt offering on one of the mountains I will tell you about."

3 So Abraham got up early in the morning,[d] saddled his donkey, and took with him two of his young men and his son Isaac. He split wood for a burnt offering and set out to go to the place God had told him about. **4** On the third day[e] Abraham looked up and saw the place in the distance. **5** Then Abraham said to his young men, "Stay here with the donkey. The boy and I will go over there to worship; then we'll come back to you." **6** Abraham took the wood for the burnt offering and laid it on his son Isaac.[f] In his hand he took the fire and the knife,[g] and the two of them walked on together.

7 Then Isaac spoke to his father Abraham and said, "My father."

And he replied, "Here I am, my son."

Isaac said, "The fire and the wood are here, but where is the lamb for the burnt offering?"

8 Abraham answered, "God himself will provide[A,h] the lamb for the burnt offering, my son." Then the two of them walked on together.

9 When they arrived at the place that God had told him about, Abraham built the altar there and arranged the wood. He bound his son Isaac[B] and placed him on the altar[i] on top of the wood. **10** Then Abraham reached out and took the knife to slaughter his son. **11** But the angel of the Lord called to him from heaven and said, "Abraham, Abraham!"

He replied, "Here I am."

12 Then he said, "Do not lay a hand on the boy or do anything to him. For now I know that you fear God, since you have not withheld your only son from me."[j] **13** Abraham looked up and saw a ram[c] caught in the thicket by its horns. So Abraham went and took the ram and offered it as a burnt offering in place of his son. **14** And Abraham named that place The Lord Will Provide,[D] so today it is said: "It will be provided[E] on the Lord's mountain."

15 Then the angel of the Lord called to Abraham a second time from heaven **16** and said, "By myself I have sworn,"[k] this is the Lord's declaration: "Because you have done this thing and have not withheld your only son, **17** I will indeed bless you[l] and make your offspring as numerous as the stars of the sky[m] and the sand on the seashore.[n] Your offspring will possess the city gates of their enemies.[o] **18** And all the nations of the earth will be blessed[F] by your offspring[p] because you have obeyed my command."

19 Abraham went back to his young men, and they got up and went together to Beer-sheba. And Abraham settled in Beer-sheba.

REBEKAH'S FAMILY

20 Now after these things Abraham was told, "Milcah also has borne sons to your brother Nahor:[q] **21** Uz his firstborn, his brother Buz, Kemuel the father of Aram, **22** Chesed, Hazo, Pildash, Jidlaph, and Bethuel." **23** And Bethuel fathered Rebekah.[r] Milcah bore these eight to Nahor, Abraham's brother. **24** His concubine, whose name was Reumah, also bore Tebah, Gaham, Tahash, and Maacah.

[A] 22:8 Lit *see*　[B] 22:9 Or *Isaac hand and foot*　[C] 22:13 Some Hb mss, Sam, LXX, Syr, Tg; other Hb mss read *saw behind him a ram*
[D] 22:14 = *Yahweh-yireh*　[E] 22:14 Or *"He will be seen"*　[F] 22:18 Or *will bless themselves,* or *will find blessing*

22:1-3 How would Abraham respond to this test? **Abraham got up early in the morning**. He obeyed immediately. He avoided partial obedience and delayed obedience, following God boldly into the unknown.
22:4-6 When Abraham and Isaac reached the mountain, Abraham told his servants, **The boy and I will go . . . then we'll come back to you** (22:5). Somehow Abraham believed that he would be coming back down the mountain

with Isaac. The writer of Hebrews notes that Abraham "considered God to be able even to raise someone from the dead" (Heb 11:19). Abraham trusted God's promise that Isaac would continue the line of blessing—even if its fulfillment took another miracle. The same resurrecting power that brought Isaac into the world could somehow keep him in it.
22:13 The **ram** must have been there the entire time, but Abraham didn't notice it until God

wanted to reveal it. While Abraham walked up one side of the mountain with his problem, God had arranged it so that up the other side of the mountain was coming his answer. However the answer was not revealed until obedience was completed.
22:15-19 Here God makes an oath: **By myself I have sworn** (22:16; see Heb 6:13-18) God's oath means that he's *ready* to do what he's promised.

SARAH'S BURIAL

23 Now Sarah lived 127 years; these were all the years of her life. ² Sarah died in Kiriath-arba (that is, Hebron[a]) in the land of Canaan, and Abraham went to mourn for Sarah and to weep for her.

³ Then Abraham got up from beside his dead wife and spoke to the Hethites: ⁴ "I am an alien residing among you.[b] Give me burial property among you so that I can bury my dead." [A,C]

⁵ The Hethites replied to Abraham,[B] ⁶ "Listen to us, my lord. You are a prince of God[c] among us. Bury your dead in our finest burial place.[D] None of us will withhold from you his burial place for burying your dead."

⁷ Then Abraham rose and bowed down to the Hethites, the people of the land. ⁸ He said to them, "If you are willing for me to bury my dead, listen to me and ask Ephron son of Zohar on my behalf ⁹ to give me the cave of Machpelah that belongs to him; it is at the end of his field. Let him give it to me in your presence, for the full price, as burial property."

¹⁰ Ephron was sitting among the Hethites. So in the hearing[E] of all the Hethites who came to the gate of his city,[d] Ephron the Hethite answered Abraham: ¹¹ "No, my lord. Listen to me. I give you the field, and I give you the cave that is in it. I give it to you in the sight[F] of my people. Bury your dead."

¹² Abraham bowed down to the people of the land ¹³ and said to Ephron in the hearing of the people of the land, "Listen to me, if you please. Let me pay the price of the field. Accept it from me, and let me bury my dead there."

¹⁴ Ephron answered Abraham and said to him, ¹⁵ "My lord, listen to me. Land worth four hundred shekels of silver[e] — what is that between you and me? Bury your dead." ¹⁶ Abraham agreed with Ephron, and Abraham weighed out to Ephron the silver that he had agreed to in the hearing of the Hethites: four hundred standard shekels[G] of silver.[f] ¹⁷ So Ephron's field[g] at Machpelah near Mamre — the field with its cave and all the trees anywhere within the boundaries of the field — became ¹⁸ Abraham's possession in the sight of all the Hethites who came to the gate of his city. ¹⁹ After this, Abraham buried his wife Sarah in the cave of the field at Machpelah near Mamre (that is, Hebron) in the land of Canaan. ²⁰ The field with its cave passed from the Hethites to Abraham[h] as burial property.

A WIFE FOR ISAAC

24 Abraham was now old, getting on in years,[H,i] and the LORD had blessed him in everything. ² Abraham said to his servant, the elder of his household who managed all he owned, "Place your hand under my thigh,[j] ³ and I will have you swear by the LORD, God of heaven and God of earth, that you will not take a wife for my son from the daughters of the Canaanites among whom I live,[k] ⁴ but will go to my land and my family to take a wife for my son Isaac."

⁵ The servant said to him, "Suppose the woman is unwilling to follow me to this land? Should I have your son go back to the land you came from?"

⁶ Abraham answered him, "Make sure that you don't take my son back there. ⁷ The LORD, the God of heaven,[l] who took me from my father's house and from my native land,[m] who spoke to me and swore to me, 'I will give this land to your offspring'[n] — he will send his angel before you,[o] and you can take a wife for my son from there. ⁸ If the woman is unwilling to follow you, then you are free from this oath to me,[p] but don't let my son go back there." ⁹ So the servant placed his hand under his master Abraham's thigh and swore an oath to him concerning this matter.

¹⁰ The servant took ten of his master's camels, and with all kinds of his master's goods in hand, he went to Aram-naharaim,

---

a 23:2 Gn 35:27; Jos 14:15; 15:13; 21:11; Jdg 1:10
b 23:4 Gn 17:8; Lv 25:23; 1Ch 29:15; Ps 39:12; 105:12; Heb 11:9,13
c Gn 49:30; Ac 7:16
d 23:10 Gn 34:20,24; Ru 4:1
e 23:15 Ex 30:13; Ezk 45:12

f 23:16 Jr 32:9; Zch 11:12
g 23:17 Gn 25:9; 49:29-32; 50:13
h 23:20 Jr 32:10-14
i 24:1 Gn 18:11; Jos 13:1; 23:1-2; 1Kg 1:1
j 24:2 Gn 47:29; Ex 1:5
k 24:3 Gn 26:34,35; 27:46; Dt 7:3; 2Co 6:14
l 24:7 2Ch 36:23; Ezr 1:2
m Gn 12:1
n Gn 12:7; 13:15; 15:18; Ex 32:13
o Gn 16:7; 21:17; 22:11; Ex 23:20,23
p 24:8 Jos 2:17-20

---

^A 23:4 Lit *dead from before me*   ^B 23:5 Lit *Abraham, saying to him*   ^C 23:6 Or *a mighty prince*   ^D 23:6 Or *finest graves*   ^E 23:10 Lit *ears*, also in vv. 13,16   ^F 23:11 Lit *in the eyes of the sons*   ^G 23:16 Lit *400 shekels passing to the merchant*   ^H 24:1 Lit *days*

23:1 Sarah died at the age of **127 years.** Note God's gracious provision. Sarah was ninety when Isaac was born—apparently too old to spend any significant time with him. Yet God gave Sarah almost four decades with her son. **23:2-20** Abraham was **in the land of Canaan** (23:2). Abraham saw in his wife's death the opportunity to seize the firstfruits of God's promise. This explains why he insisted upon paying **the full price** for his plot (23:9, 13) rather than receiving it as a gift (23:6, 11).

This gave him a toehold in possessing the promised land.
24:1-4 Abraham had begun to inherit the promises of God by this point. But God had promised him descendants as plentiful as sand, so Isaac needed a wife. Abraham commissioned **the elder of his household** (24:2), essentially his chief of staff, to go to his **family to take a wife for . . . Isaac** (24:4). The selection of the girl was so important that he made the servant pledge an oath in an inti-

mate action commonly used in those days to affirm sacred agreements (24:2).
24:10-14 The key piece of prayer here is the specific request for **the girl** to respond to his inquiry by saying, **Drink, and I'll water your camels also** (24:14). It was customary in those days to offer water to strangers. It was incredibly rare, however, to offer to water a stranger's animals. Camels can drink up to twenty-five gallons of water, and Eliezer traveled with **ten** of them (24:10).

a 24:12 Gn 27:20
b 24:13-14 Gn 24:43-44
c 24:15 Gn 11:29; 22:23
d 24:16 Gn 12:11; 26:7;
29:17
e 24:26 Ex 4:31

f 24:27 Ru 2:20; Ezr 9:9;
Neh 9:17
g 24:29 Gn 25:20; 28:2;
29:5
h 24:31 Gn 26:29; Jdg 17:2;
Ru 3:10
i 24:32 Gn 43:24; Jdg 19:21
j 24:36 Gn 21:2
k Gn 25:5
l 24:40 Gn 17:1; 1Sm 2:30;
1Kg 2:4; 8:23; 2Kg 20:3;
Ps 116:9

to Nahor's town. ¹¹ At evening, the time when women went out to draw water, he made the camels kneel beside a well outside the town.

¹² "LORD, God of my master Abraham," he prayed, "make this happen for me today,ᵃ and show kindness to my master Abraham. ¹³ I am standing hereᵇ at the spring where the daughters of the men of the town are coming out to draw water. ¹⁴ Let the girl to whom I say, 'Please lower your water jug so that I may drink,' and who responds, 'Drink, and I'll water your camels also' — let her be the one you have appointed for your servant Isaac. By this I will know that you have shown kindness to my master."

¹⁵ Before he had finished speaking, there was Rebekah — daughter of Bethuel son of Milcah,ᶜ the wife of Abraham's brother Nahor — coming with a jug on her shoulder. ¹⁶ Now the girl was very beautiful,ᵈ a virgin — no man had been intimate with her. She went down to the spring, filled her jug, and came up. ¹⁷ Then the servant ran to meet her and said, "Please let me have a little water from your jug."

¹⁸ She replied, "Drink, my lord." She quickly lowered her jug to her hand and gave him a drink. ¹⁹ When she had finished giving him a drink, she said, "I'll also draw water for your camels until they have had enough to drink."ᴬ ²⁰ She quickly emptied her jug into the trough and hurried to the well again to draw water. She drew water for all his camels ²¹ while the man silently watched her to see whether or not the LORD had made his journey a success.

²² As the camels finished drinking, the man took a gold ring weighing half a shekel, and for her wrists two bracelets weighing ten shekels of gold. ²³ "Whose daughter are you?" he asked. "Please tell me, is there room in your father's house for us to spend the night?"

²⁴ She answered him, "I am the daughter of Bethuel son of Milcah, whom she bore to Nahor." ²⁵ She also said to him, "We have plenty of straw and feed and a place to spend the night."

²⁶ Then the man knelt low, worshiped the LORD,ᵉ ²⁷ and said, "Blessed be the LORD,

the God of my master Abraham, who has not withheld his kindness and faithfulness from my master.ᶠ As for me, the LORD has led me on the journey to the house of my master's relatives."

²⁸ The girl ran and told her mother's household about these things. ²⁹ Now Rebekah had a brother named Laban,ᵍ and Laban ran out to the man at the spring. ³⁰ As soon as he had seen the ring and the bracelets on his sister's wrists, and when he had heard his sister Rebekah's words — "The man said this to me!" — he went to the man. He was standing there by the camels at the spring.

³¹ Laban said, "Come, you who are blessed by the LORD.ʰ Why are you standing out here? I have prepared the house and a place for the camels." ³² So the man came to the house, and the camels were unloaded.ⁱ Straw and feed were given to the camels, and water was brought to wash his feet and the feet of the men with him.

³³ A meal was set before him, but he said, "I will not eat until I have said what I have to say."

So Laban said, "Please speak."

³⁴ "I am Abraham's servant," he said. ³⁵ "The LORD has greatly blessed my master, and he has become rich. He has given him flocks and herds, silver and gold, male and female slaves, and camels and donkeys. ³⁶ Sarah, my master's wife, bore a son to my master in herᴮ old age,ʲ and he has given him everything he owns.ᵏ ³⁷ My master put me under this oath: 'You will not take a wife for my son from the daughters of the Canaanites in whose land I live ³⁸ but will go to my father's family and to my clan to take a wife for my son.' ³⁹ But I said to my master, 'Suppose the woman will not come back with me?' ⁴⁰ He said to me, 'The LORD before whom I have walkedˡ will send his angel with you and make your journey a success, and you will take a wife for my son from my clan and from my father's family. ⁴¹ Then you will be free from my oath if you go to my family and they do not give her to you — you will be free from my oath.'

⁴² "Today when I came to the spring, I prayed: LORD, God of my master Abraham, if only you will make my journey successful! ⁴³ I am standing here at a spring. Let

ᴬ 24:19 Lit *they are finished drinking*   ᴮ 24:36 Sam, LXX read *his*

24:22-33 Eliezer had been given specific orders to take a wife from Abraham's clan (24:4). So imagine his relief when Rebekah introduced herself as **the daughter of Bethuel son of Milcah, whom she bore to Nahor** (24:24). Rebekah was Isaac's cousin. **24:34-48** We should not overlook the faithfulness of the servant throughout this story;

he kept his mission in front of him at all times. The purpose of marriage is not simply personal happiness, but kingdom fulfillment, so his task was vital.

the young woman[A] who comes out to draw water, and I say to her, 'Please let me drink a little water from your jug,' [44] and who responds to me, 'Drink, and I'll draw water for your camels also' — let her be the woman the LORD has appointed for my master's son.

[45] "Before I had finished praying silently,[a] there was Rebekah coming with her jug on her shoulder, and she went down to the spring and drew water. So I said to her, 'Please let me have a drink.' [46] She quickly lowered her jug from her shoulder and said, 'Drink, and I'll water your camels also.' So I drank, and she also watered the camels. [47] Then I asked her, 'Whose daughter are you?' She responded, 'The daughter of Bethuel son of Nahor, whom Milcah bore to him.' So I put the ring on her nose[b] and the bracelets on her wrists. [48] Then I knelt low, worshiped the LORD, and blessed the LORD, the God of my master Abraham, who guided me on the right way to take the granddaughter of my master's brother for his son. [49] Now, if you are going to show kindness and faithfulness to my master,[c] tell me; if not, tell me, and I will go elsewhere."[B]

[50] Laban and Bethuel answered, "This is from the LORD; we have no choice in the matter.[c,d] [51] Rebekah is here in front of you. Take her and go, and let her be a wife for your master's son, just as the LORD has spoken."

[52] When Abraham's servant heard their words, he bowed to the ground before the LORD. [53] Then he brought out objects of silver and gold, and garments, and gave them to Rebekah. He also gave precious gifts to her brother and her mother. [54] Then he and the men with him ate and drank and spent the night.

When they got up in the morning, he said, "Send me to my master."

[55] But her brother and mother said, "Let the girl stay with us for about ten days.[D] Then she[E] can go."

[56] But he responded to them, "Do not delay me, since the LORD has made my journey a success. Send me away so that I may go to my master."

[57] So they said, "Let's call the girl and ask her opinion."[F]

[58] They called Rebekah and said to her, "Will you go with this man?"

She replied, "I will go." [59] So they sent away their sister Rebekah with the one who had nursed and raised her,[G,e] and Abraham's servant and his men.

[60] They blessed Rebekah, saying to her:

Our sister, may you become
thousands upon ten thousands.[f]
May your offspring possess
the city gates of their[H] enemies.[g]

[61] Then Rebekah and her female servants got up, mounted the camels, and followed the man. So the servant took Rebekah and left.

[62] Now Isaac was returning from Beer-lahai-roi,[I,h] for he was living in the Negev region. [63] In the early evening Isaac went out to walk[J] in the field, and looking up he saw camels coming. [64] Rebekah looked up, and when she saw Isaac, she got down from her camel [65] and asked the servant, "Who is that man in the field coming to meet us?"

The servant answered, "It is my master." So she took her veil and covered herself. [66] Then the servant told Isaac everything he had done.

[67] And Isaac brought her into the tent of his mother Sarah and took Rebekah to be his wife. Isaac loved her, and he was comforted after his mother's death.[i]

ABRAHAM'S OTHER WIFE AND SONS

25 Abraham had taken[k] another wife, whose name was Keturah.[j] [2] and she bore him Zimran, Jokshan, Medan, Midian, Ishbak, and Shuah. [3] Jokshan fathered Sheba and Dedan. Dedan's sons were the Asshurim, Letushim, and Leummim. [4] And Midian's sons were Ephah, Epher, Hanoch, Abida, and Eldaah. All these were sons of Keturah. [5] Abraham gave everything he owned to Isaac.[k] [6] But Abraham gave gifts to the sons of his

[a] 24:45 1Sm 1:13
[b] 24:47 Ezk 16:11-12
[c] 24:49 Gn 47:29; Jos 2:14
[d] 24:50 Gn 31:24,29; 2Sm 13:22
[e] 24:59 Gn 35:8
[f] 24:60 Gn 17:16
[g] Gn 22:17
[h] 24:62 Gn 16:14; 25:11
[i] 24:67 Gn 23:1-2
[j] 25:1-4 1Ch 1:32-33
[k] 25:5 Gn 24:35-36

[A] 24:43 Or *the virgin*   [B] 24:49 Lit *go to the right or to the left*   [C] 24:50 Lit *we cannot say to you anything bad or good*   [D] 24:55 Lit *us days or tenth*   [E] 24:55 Or *you*   [F] 24:57 Lit *mouth*   [G] 24:59 Lit *with her wet nurse*; Gn 35:8   [H] 24:60 Lit *his*   [I] 24:62 = A Well of the Living One Who Sees Me   [J] 24:63 Or *pray*, or *meditate*; Hb obscure   [K] 25:1 Or *Abraham took*

24:49-59 The servant plainly asked Rebekah's family whether they would bless the marriage (24:49). Laban and Bethuel acknowledged that **this is from the LORD,** who clearly had orchestrated the entire event (24:50). Interestingly, Rebekah too approved of the marriage (24:58), even though she had never seen Isaac. Rebekah submitted her future to a husband she didn't even know, because she was convinced God was at work.

25:1-6 The author mentions Abraham taking **another wife** (25:1) without commenting on whether Sarah was still living when he did or the ethics surrounding the decision. Although God's established order was for marriage to be between one man and one woman (2:21-24), polygamy crept in early. Abraham **gave everything he owned to Isaac** (25:5). The **sons of his concubines** were only given a few gifts and sent eastward (25:6).

ª 25:6 Gn 21:14
ᵇ 25:8 Gn 15:15; 47:8-9
ᶜ Gn 25:17; 35:29; 49:29,33
ᵈ 25:9 Gn 23:17-18; 49:29-30; 50:13
ᵉ 25:10 Gn 23:16; 50:13
ᶠ 25:11 Gn 16:14; 24:62
ᵍ 25:12 Gn 2:4; 25:19
ʰ 25:12-16 1Ch 1:29-31
ⁱ 25:16 Gn 17:20
ʲ 25:18 Gn 16:12
ᵏ 25:19 Mt 1:2
ˡ 25:20 Gn 24:15,29,67
ᵐ Gn 22:23
ⁿ Gn 24:29
ᵒ 25:21 Gn 11:30; 29:31; Ex 23:26; Jdg 13:2-3; 1Sm 2:5; Jb 24:21; Is 54:1; Lk 1:36; 23:29; Gl 4:27; Heb 11:11
ᵖ 1Sm 1:17; 1Ch 5:20; 2Ch 33:13; Ezr 8:23; Ps 127:3; Rm 9:10
ᵠ 25:22 1Sm 9:9; 10:22
ʳ 25:23 2Sm 8:14; Ob 18-21
ˢ Gn 27:29; Mal 1:2-3; Rm 9:12
ᵗ 25:25 Gn 27:11,16,23
ᵘ 25:26 Hs 12:3
ᵛ Gn 27:36
ʷ 25:28 Gn 27:4-9

concubines, and while he was still alive he sent them eastward, away from his son Isaac, to the land of the East.ª

ABRAHAM'S DEATH

7 This is the length of Abraham's life:ᴬ 175 years. **8** He took his last breath and died at a good old age,ᵇ old and contented,ᴮ and he was gathered to his people.ᶜ **9** His sons Isaac and Ishmael buried him in the cave of Machpelahᵈ near Mamre, in the field of Ephron son of Zohar the Hethite. **10** This was the field that Abraham bought from the Hethites.ᵉ Abraham was buried there with his wife Sarah. **11** After Abraham's death, God blessed his son Isaac, who lived near Beer-lahai-roi.ᶠ

ISHMAEL'S FAMILY RECORDS

12 These are the family recordsᵍ of Abraham's son Ishmael,ʰ whom Hagar the Egyptian, Sarah's slave, bore to Abraham. **13** These are the names of Ishmael's sons; their names according to the family records are Nebaioth, Ishmael's firstborn, then Kedar, Adbeel, Mibsam, **14** Mishma, Dumah, Massa, **15** Hadad, Tema, Jetur, Naphish, and Kedemah. **16** These are Ishmael's sons, and these are their names by their settlements and encampments: twelve leadersᶜ,ʲ of their clans.ᴰ **17** This is the lengthᴱ of Ishmael's life: 137 years. He took his last breath and died, and was gathered to his people. **18** And theyᶠ settled from Havilah to Shur, which is opposite Egypt as you go toward Asshur.ᴳ Heᴴ stayed nearⁱ all his relatives.ʲ

THE BIRTH OF JACOB AND ESAU

19 These are the family records of Isaac son of Abraham. Abraham fathered Isaac.ᵏ **20** Isaac was forty years old when he took

as his wife Rebekahˡ daughter of Bethuel the Aramean from Paddan-aramᵐ and sister of Laban the Aramean.ⁿ **21** Isaac prayed to the LORD on behalf of his wife because she was childless.ᵒ The LORD was receptive to his prayer, and his wife Rebekah conceived.ᵖ **22** But the children inside her struggled with each other, and she said, "Why is this happening to me?"ʲ So she went to inquire of the LORD.ᵠ **23** And the LORD said to her:

Two nations are in your womb;
two peoples will come from you
   and be separated.
One people will be stronger
   than the other,ʳ
   and the older will serve
   the younger.ˢ

24 When her time came to give birth, there were indeed twins in her womb. **25** The first one came out red-looking,ᵏ covered with hairᴸ like a fur coat, and they named him Esau.ᵗ **26** After this, his brother came out grasping Esau's heel with his hand.ᵘ So he was named Jacob.ᴹ,ᵛ Isaac was sixty years old when they were born.

ESAU SELLS HIS BIRTHRIGHT

27 When the boys grew up, Esau became an expert hunter, an outdoorsman,ᴺ but Jacob was a quiet man who stayed at home.ᵒ **28** Isaac loved Esau because he had a taste for wild game, but Rebekah loved Jacob.ʷ

29 Once when Jacob was cooking a stew, Esau came in from the field exhausted. **30** He said to Jacob, "Let me eat some of that red stuff, because I'm exhausted." That is why he was also named Edom.ᵖ

31 Jacob replied, "First sell me your birthright."

ᴬ 25:7 Lit And these are the days of the years of the life of Abraham that he lived   ᴮ 25:8 Sam, LXX, Syr read full of days   ᶜ 25:16 Or chieftains
ᴰ 25:16 Or peoples   ᴱ 25:17 Lit And these are the years   ᶠ 25:18 LXX, Vg read he   ᴳ 25:18 Or Assyria   ᴴ 25:18 = Ishmael and his descendants
ⁱ 25:18 Or He settled down alongside   ʲ 25:22 Lit said, "If thus, why this I?"   ᵏ 25:25 In Hb, red-looking sounds like "Edom"; Gn 32:3.   ᴸ 25:25 In
Hb, hair sounds like "Seir"; Gn 32:3.   ᴹ 25:26 = He Grasps the Heel   ᴺ 25:27 Lit a man of the field   ᵒ 25:27 Lit man living in tents   ᵖ 25:30 = Red

25:7-10 When Abraham **died** (25:8), his estranged sons **buried him** (25:9). But the family strife had hardly been buried with the patriarch. **25:19-23** We aren't given as much insight into Rebekah's infertility struggle as we got with Sarah's, but note that she could not conceive for *twenty* years (25:20, 26). When God answered Isaac's prayer to let her conceive, though, he did so in duplicate! When Rebekah wondered why her pregnancy was so active (25:22), God answered, **Two nations are in your womb** (25:23). Even before their births, Jacob and Esau were battling one another, foreshadowing the coming conflict between their two nations, Israel and Edom.

25:24-26 The older twin was **covered with** red hair . . . and they named him Esau (25:25). He was also called "Edom" (see 25:30). The younger **came out grasping Esau's heel**, so they **named** him **Jacob**, which means, "he grasps the heel" (25:26). Jacob's name can also mean, "he deceives." Both meanings would prove prophetic. **25:27-28** These parents apparently chose favorites. **Isaac loved Esau** because he was a "man's man," and **Rebekah loved Jacob** because he loved spending time at home (25:28). Isaac and Rebekah were at fault in the feud between the boys. **25:29-34** We see here the character flaws of both sons. Jacob's "grasping" and deceiving

ways are on full display here, while Esau proved to be impulsive and shortsighted. When faced with the prospect of losing his double inheritance, he reasoned, **I'm about to die** (from hunger), **so what good is a birthright to me?** (25:32). He settled for temporary satisfaction over hanging on to something much more spiritually valuable. The author says **Esau despised his birthright**, because he considered it less significant than a single bowl of **stew** (25:34). The author of Hebrews cautions his readers to avoid being like Esau (Heb 12:16). Heed the warning: never let physical satisfaction take precedence over spiritual priorities.

32 "Look," said Esau, "I'm about to die, so what good is a birthright to me?"

33 Jacob said, "Swear to me first." So he swore to Jacob and sold his birthright to him. **34** Then Jacob gave bread and lentil stew to Esau; he ate, drank, got up, and went away. So Esau despised his birthright.[a]

THE PROMISE REAFFIRMED TO ISAAC

26 There was another famine in the land in addition to the one that had occurred in Abraham's time.[b] And Isaac went to Abimelech, king of the Philistines, at Gerar.[c] **2** The LORD appeared to him and said, "Do not go down to Egypt. Live in the land that I tell you about; **3** stay in this land as an alien, and I will be with you and bless you.[d] For I will give all these lands to you and your offspring,[e] and I will confirm the oath that I swore to your father Abraham.[f] **4** I will make your offspring as numerous as the stars of the sky, I will give your offspring all these lands, and all the nations of the earth will be blessed[A] by your offspring,[g] **5** because Abraham listened to me and kept my mandate, my commands, my statutes, and my instructions."[h] **6** So Isaac settled in Gerar.

ISAAC'S DECEPTION

7 When the men of the place asked about his wife, he said, "She is my sister,"[i] for he was afraid to say "my wife," thinking,[j] "The men of the place will kill me on account of Rebekah, for she is a beautiful woman."[k] **8** When Isaac had been there for some time, Abimelech king of the Philistines looked down from the window and was surprised to see[B] Isaac caressing his wife Rebekah.

9 Abimelech sent for Isaac and said, "So she is really your wife! How could you say, 'She is my sister'?"

Isaac answered him, "Because I thought I might die on account of her."

10 Then Abimelech said, "What is this you've done to us? One of the people could easily have slept with your wife, and you would have brought guilt on us."[i] **11** So Abimelech warned all the people, "Whoever harms this man or his wife will certainly be put to death."

CONFLICTS OVER WELLS

12 Isaac sowed seed in that land, and in that year he reaped[c] a hundred times what was sown. The LORD blessed him,[m] **13** and the man became rich and kept getting richer until he was very wealthy. **14** He had flocks of sheep, herds of cattle, and many slaves, and the Philistines were envious of him. **15** Philistines stopped up all the wells that his father's servants had dug in the days of his father Abraham,[n] filling them with dirt. **16** And Abimelech said to Isaac, "Leave us, for you are much too powerful for us."[D]

17 So Isaac left there, camped in the Gerar Valley, and lived there. **18** Isaac reopened the wells that had been dug in the days of his father Abraham and that the Philistines had stopped up after Abraham died. He gave them the same names his father had given them. **19** Then Isaac's servants dug in the valley and found a well of spring[E] water there. **20** But the herdsmen of Gerar quarreled with Isaac's herdsmen and said, "The water is ours!" So he named the well Esek[F] because they argued with him.[o] **21** Then they dug another well and quarreled over that one also, so he named it Sitnah.[G] **22** He moved from there and dug another, and they did not quarrel over it. He named it Rehoboth[H] and said, "For now the LORD has made space for us, and we will be fruitful in the land."

THE LORD APPEARS TO ISAAC

23 From there he went up to Beer-sheba, **24** and the LORD appeared to him that night and said, "I am the God of your father Abraham.[p] Do not be afraid, for I am with you.[q] I will bless you and multiply your offspring because of my servant Abraham."

[a] 25:34 Heb 12:16-17
[b] 26:1 Gn 12:10
[c] Gn 20:2
[d] 26:3 Gn 12:2; 26:24; 28:15; 31:3
[e] Gn 12:7; 13:15; 15:18
[f] Gn 22:16-18; Ps 105:9
[g] 26:4 Gn 12:3; 18:18; Ac 3:25; Gl 3:8
[h] 26:5 Lv 18:30; Dt 11:1
[i] 26:7 Gn 12:13; 20:5
[j] Pr 29:25
[k] Gn 24:16

[l] 26:10 Gn 20:8-10
[m] 26:12 Gn 24:1,35
[n] 26:15 Gn 21:30
[o] 26:20 Gn 21:25
[p] 26:24 Gn 17:7-8; 24:12; Ex 3:6; Ac 7:32
[q] Gn 21:17; Ex 20:20; 2Kg 6:16; Is 41:10; 43:1,5

[A] 26:4 Or *will bless themselves*   [B] 26:8 Or *and he looked and behold* —   [C] 26:12 Lit *found*   [D] 26:16 Or *are more numerous than we are*   [E] 26:19 Lit *living*   [F] 26:20 = Argument   [G] 26:21 = Hostility   [H] 26:22 = Open Spaces

26:1-11 In the midst of a scene about Isaac's fear and unfaithfulness, we find a repetition of God's covenant faithfulness to him. Isaac, like Abraham, was promised **lands, offspring,** and a blessing that would be for **all the nations** (26:3-4). This promise was unconditionally made to Abraham and passed on to Isaac despite his failings.
26:12-22 God's hand was on Isaac. **He reaped a hundred times what was sown,** and his flocks also multiplied (26:12-14). Unfortunately, the Philistines of the area grew envious, so they attempted to sabotage Isaac by stopping **up all the wells** (26:15). In an agrarian society, wells indicated dominion. Owning one meant that you essentially governed the surrounding area. Rather than quarrel over specific wells, however, Isaac constantly moved and dug new wells (26:19-21). Eventually God provided an uncontested well—and, by extension, a space for Isaac to **be fruitful in the land** (26:22).
26:23-25 God knew fear was a problem for Isaac, so while he confirmed his promise he also confirmed his presence. In response, Isaac did what we all should do, demonstrating faith by fresh worship (26:25).

a 26:25 Gn 8:20; 12:7;
13:18; 35:7; Ex 17:15;
Jos 8:30
b Gn 26:32
c 26:26 Gn 21:22
d 26:29 Gn 24:31; Ps 115:15

e 26:31 Gn 21:31
f 26:32 Gn 26:19
g 26:33 Gn 21:30-31
h 26:34 Gn 28:9; 36:2-3
i 26:35 Gn 27:46
j 27:1 Gn 48:10; 1Sm 3:2

⤳ KINGDOM LIVING ⤝
FAMILY

The Family Blessing

Parents blessing their children is a powerful biblical concept that is being rediscovered in our day. The blessing was a key part of family life in the Old Testament. The battle between Jacob and Esau in Genesis 27 was over who would get their father Isaac's blessing. The blessing involved a father transferring the family inheritance to his son and telling him of the future God had for him (see Gen 49). To be blessed meant that a child's significance was recognized by his father. The blessing told the child that he was the future, that his father was counting on him.

The best thing we fathers can do for our sons and daughters is to put our hands on them and bless them in the name of Jesus Christ. There's no way to measure the impact that your blessing can have on your children. Blessing is especially important because we parents are so quick to curse our kids. I don't mean that we use profanity on them. I'm talking about the kinds of discouraging comments that slip out of our mouths so quickly and easily: "You didn't do that right." "Why don't you change this?" "How come you're not better at that?" Our kids hear how they fall short. But do they also hear us blessing them?

The difference between encouragement and praise is important. We praise our children a lot, but we don't always encourage them. Praise focuses on what the child has accomplished. But encouragement is not related to what people achieve. It is tied to who they are. Encouragement says, "I want to affirm you as my child. You don't have to do anything spectacular. I love you because of who you are."

FOR THE NEXT FAMILY
KINGDOM LIVING LESSON SEE PAGE 206.

25 So he built an altar there,[a] called on the name of the LORD, and pitched his tent there. Isaac's servants also dug a well there.[b]

COVENANT WITH ABIMELECH

26 Now Abimelech came to him from Gerar with Ahuzzath his adviser and Phicol the commander of his army.[c] **27** Isaac said to them, "Why have you come to me? You hated me and sent me away from you."

28 They replied, "We have clearly seen how the LORD has been with you. We think there should be an oath between two parties — between us and you. Let us make a covenant with you: **29** You will not harm us, just as we have not harmed you but have done only what was good to you, sending you away in peace. You are now blessed by the LORD."[d]

30 So he prepared a banquet for them, and they ate and drank. **31** They got up early in the morning and swore an oath to each other.[A,e] Isaac sent them on their way, and they left him in peace. **32** On that same day Isaac's servants came to tell him about the well they had dug, saying to him, "We have found water!"[f] **33** He called it Sheba.[B] Therefore the name of the city is still Beer-sheba[C,g] today.

ESAU'S WIVES

34 When Esau was forty years old, he took as his wives Judith daughter of Beeri the Hethite, and Basemath daughter of Elon the Hethite.[h] **35** They made life bitter[D] for Isaac and Rebekah.[i]

THE STOLEN BLESSING

27 When Isaac was old and his eyes were so weak that he could not see,[j] he called his older son Esau and said to him, "My son."

And he answered, "Here I am."

A 26:31 Lit *swore, each man to his brother*   B 26:33 Or *Shibah*   C 26:33 = Well of the Oath   D 26:35 Lit *And they became bitterness of spirit*

26:26-33 Abimelech recognized that God was with Isaac, so he sought to make a treaty with him (26:28-29). This is a partial fulfillment of the promise to Abraham and Isaac that the Gentiles would share in the blessings of God's people. Abimelech even referred to God as **the LORD** (26:29), using God's covenant name. He had grown in his understanding of God through his association with Isaac — just as people today are meant to draw closer to God because of the witness of his people.

26:34-35 Esau was making **life bitter for Isaac and Rebekah** (26:35) because he'd married two **Hethite** women (26:34). Rebellion against his parents' wishes further illustrates why Esau was not fit to carry on the covenant. He'd aligned himself with the surrounding pagan culture.

27:1-4 As Isaac anticipated his death, he decided to impart his blessing to Esau. Jacob may have already stolen the birthright — the physical inheritance — but Esau still had the chance to inherit his father's blessing — a blessing representing the umbrella of God's operation in the family line. Isaac began the ritual by calling **Esau** to prepare **a delicious meal** (27:1, 4). Isaac preferred Esau's wild game and wanted him to hunt for an animal that they could share during the coming sacred time.

[2] He said, "Look, I am old and do not know the day of my death. [3] So now take your hunting gear, your quiver and bow, and go out in the field to hunt some game for me.[a] [4] Then make me a delicious meal that I love and bring it to me to eat, so that I can bless you before I die."[b]

[5] Now Rebekah was listening to what Isaac said to his son Esau. So while Esau went to the field to hunt some game to bring in, [6] Rebekah said to her son Jacob, "Listen! I heard your father talking with your brother Esau. He said, [7] 'Bring me game and make a delicious meal for me to eat so that I can bless you in the LORD's presence before I die.' [8] Now, my son, listen to me and do what I tell you. [9] Go to the flock and bring me two choice young goats, and I will make them into a delicious meal for your father — the kind he loves. [10] Then take it to your father to eat so that he may bless you before he dies."

[11] Jacob answered Rebekah his mother, "Look, my brother Esau is a hairy man, but I am a man with smooth skin.[c] [12] Suppose my father touches me. Then I will be revealed to him as a deceiver and bring a curse rather than a blessing on myself."

[13] His mother said to him, "Your curse be on me, my son. Just obey me and go get them for me."

[14] So he went and got the goats and brought them to his mother, and his mother made the delicious food his father loved. [15] Then Rebekah took the best clothes of her older son Esau, which were in the house, and had her younger son Jacob wear them. [16] She put the skins of the young goats on his hands and the smooth part of his neck. [17] Then she handed the delicious food and the bread she had made to her son Jacob.

[18] When he came to his father, he said, "My father."

And he answered, "Here I am. Who are you, my son?"

[19] Jacob replied to his father, "I am Esau, your firstborn. I have done as you told me.

Please sit up and eat some of my game so that you may bless me."

[20] But Isaac said to his son, "How did you ever find it so quickly, my son?"

He replied, "Because the LORD your God made it happen for me."

[21] Then Isaac said to Jacob, "Please come closer so I can touch you, my son. Are you really my son Esau or not?"

[22] So Jacob came closer to his father Isaac. When he touched him, he said, "The voice is the voice of Jacob, but the hands are the hands of Esau." [23] He did not recognize him, because his hands were hairy like those of his brother Esau; so he blessed him. [24] Again he asked, "Are you really my son Esau?"

And he replied, "I am."

[25] Then he said, "Bring it closer to me, and let me eat some of my son's game so that I can bless you." Jacob brought it closer to him, and he ate; he brought him wine, and he drank.

[26] Then his father Isaac said to him, "Please come closer and kiss me, my son." [27] So he came closer and kissed him. When Isaac smelled[A] his clothes, he blessed him and said:

> Ah, the smell of my son
> is like the smell of a field
> that the LORD has blessed.
> [28] May God give to you —
> from the dew of the sky[d]
> and from the richness of the land[e] —
> an abundance of grain
> and new wine.[f]
> [29] May peoples serve you[g]
> and nations bow in worship to you.
> Be master over your relatives;
> may your mother's sons bow
> in worship to you.
> Those who curse you will be cursed,
> and those who bless you
> will be blessed.[h]

[30] As soon as Isaac had finished blessing Jacob and Jacob had left the presence of his father Isaac, his brother Esau arrived

[a] 27:3 Gn 25:27-28
[b] 27:4 Gn 27:19,25,31; 48:9,15-16; Dt 33:1; Heb 11:20
[c] 27:11 Gn 25:25
[d] 27:28 Gn 27:39; Dt 32:2; 33:13,28; 2Sm 1:21; Pr 3:20; Is 18:4; Hs 14:5; Hg 1:10; Zch 8:12
[e] Nm 18:12
[f] Dt 7:13; Jl 2:19
[g] 27:29 Gn 25:23; Is 45:14; 49:7,23; 60:12-14
[h] Gn 12:3; Nm 24:9

[A] 27:27 Lit *smelled the smell of*

27:5-17 Esau went to . . . hunt (27:5) while his mother called in Jacob. She hatched this plot: Jacob would **go to the flock**, pick out **two . . . goats**, and mom would **make them into a delicious meal** for Isaac (27:9). Then Isaac, whose "eyes were . . . weak" (27:1), would be deceived and bless Jacob rather than Esau. When Jacob objected, **Esau is a hairy man, but I [have] smooth skin** (27:11), his mother said she would take **the skins of the young**

goats and put them on Jacob's **hands and the smooth part of his neck** (27:16). Evidently Esau was *so* hairy that the feel (and odor! cf. 27:27) of a dead goat was a sufficient disguise. 27:18-25 The ruse almost didn't work because of Jacob's unique **voice** (27:22). Three times Isaac asked Jacob if he was *really* Esau, and without a hesitation, Jacob the deceiver assured him (27:19, 21-22, 24). Worse, Jacob even used God's name in vain, explaining that

he was able to find the goat quickly because **God made it happen** (27:20). 27:28 Isaac passed on to Jacob his most valuable possession, the blessing he had received from his father Abraham. **May God give to you—from the dew of the sky and from the richness of the land—an abundance**. In other words, heaven would rain down everything he needed to get the promises of God fulfilled.

[a] 27:34 Heb 12:17
[b] 27:36 Gn 25:26,32-34
[c] 27:46 Gn 26:34-35; 28:8
[d] Gn 24:3
[e] 28:3 Gn 1:28
[f] Gn 48:4
[g] 28:4 Gn 12:1-3
[h] Gn 12:7; 15:18

from his hunting. [31] He had also made some delicious food and brought it to his father. He said to his father, "Let my father get up and eat some of his son's game, so that you may bless me."

[32] But his father Isaac said to him, "Who are you?"

He answered, "I am Esau your firstborn son."

[33] Isaac began to tremble uncontrollably. "Who was it then," he said, "who hunted game and brought it to me? I ate it all before you came in, and I blessed him. Indeed, he will be blessed!"

[34] When Esau heard his father's words, he cried out with a loud and bitter cry and said to his father, "Bless me too, my father!"[a]

[35] But he replied, "Your brother came deceitfully and took your blessing."

[36] So he said, "Isn't he rightly named Jacob?[A,b] For he has cheated me twice now. He took my birthright, and look, now he has taken my blessing." Then he asked, "Haven't you saved a blessing for me?"

[37] But Isaac answered Esau, "Look, I have made him a master over you, have given him all of his relatives as his servants, and have sustained him with grain and new wine. What then can I do for you, my son?"

[38] Esau said to his father, "Do you have only one blessing, my father? Bless me too, my father!" And Esau wept loudly.[B]

[39] His father Isaac answered him,
Look, your dwelling place will be
away from the richness of the land,
away from the dew of the sky above.
[40] You will live by your sword,
and you will serve your brother.
But when you rebel,[c]
you will break his yoke
from your neck.

ESAU'S ANGER

[41] Esau held a grudge against Jacob because of the blessing his father had given him. And Esau determined in his heart:

"The days of mourning for my father are approaching; then I will kill my brother Jacob."

[42] When the words of her older son Esau were reported to Rebekah, she summoned her younger son Jacob and said to him, "Listen, your brother Esau is consoling himself by planning to kill you. [43] So now, my son, listen to me. Flee at once to my brother Laban in Haran, [44] and stay with him for a few days until your brother's anger subsides — [45] until your brother's rage turns away from you and he forgets what you have done to him. Then I will send for you and bring you back from there. Why should I lose you both in one day?"

[46] So Rebekah said to Isaac, "I'm sick of my life because of these Hethite girls.[c] If Jacob marries someone from around here,[D] like these Hethite girls, what good is my life?"[d]

JACOB'S DEPARTURE

28 So Isaac summoned Jacob, blessed him, and commanded him, "Do not marry a Canaanite girl. [2] Go at once to Paddan-aram, to the house of Bethuel, your mother's father. Marry one of the daughters of Laban, your mother's brother. [3] May God Almighty bless you and make you fruitful and multiply you[e] so that you become an assembly of peoples.[f] [4] May God give you and your offspring the blessing of Abraham[g] so that you may possess the land where you live as a foreigner, the land God gave to Abraham."[h] [5] So Isaac sent Jacob to Paddan-aram, to Laban son of Bethuel the Aramean, the brother of Rebekah, the mother of Jacob and Esau.

[6] Esau noticed that Isaac blessed Jacob and sent him to Paddan-aram to get a wife there. When he blessed him, Isaac commanded Jacob, "Do not marry a Canaanite girl." [7] And Jacob listened to his father and mother and went to Paddan-aram. [8] Esau realized that his father Isaac disapproved

[A] 27:36 = He Grasps the Heel   [B] 27:38 Lit Esau lifted up his voice and wept   [C] 27:40 Hb obscure   [D] 27:46 Lit someone like these daughters of the land

27:30-34 Esau's response to the events that happened in his absence is simultaneously pitiful and tragic. **He cried out with a ... bitter cry** (27:34). This was a gut-wrenching wail from a man who realized that his entire future had been snatched away.
27:34-38 Esau's insistence on receiving some blessing from his father mirrors the heart cry of so many in our society: **Bless me too, my father** (27:34)! So many beg for their fathers to speak a simple word of blessing into their lives.

27:39-41 Esau received a prophetic word from his father, but it was far from a blessing (27:39). No wonder, then, that **Esau held a grudge against Jacob**, plotting to kill him (27:41).
27:42-46 Rebekah, ever the eavesdropper, found out about Esau's murderous intent. She decided Jacob should **flee at once** to her **brother Laban** (27:43), hiding out until Esau's rage cooled (27:44-45). She reasoned that Jacob would therefore be more inclined to marry someone from within their clan (27:46).

28:1-2 Isaac, in rare agreement with his wife, sent Jacob out with a commission against marrying **a Canaanite** (28:1). Even in the midst of Jacob's deception, God was at work to keep the line of succession distinct.
28:6-9 Attempting to please his father, Esau tried to emulate what Jacob was doing. He **went to Paddan-aram** (28:7) to get a wife, avoiding the **Canaanite women** that his **father Isaac disapproved of** (28:8). Yet **Esau went to Ishmael and married** (28:9). He never realized that this wasn't a righteous action God wanted.

of the Canaanite women,[a] [9] so Esau went to Ishmael and married, in addition to his other wives, Mahalath daughter of Ishmael, Abraham's son. She was the sister of Nebaioth.

JACOB AT BETHEL

[10] Jacob left Beer-sheba and went toward Haran. [11] He reached a certain place and spent the night there because the sun had set. He took one of the stones from the place, put it there at his head, and lay down in that place. [12] And he dreamed:[b] A stairway was set on the ground with its top reaching the sky, and God's angels were going up and down on it.[c] [13] The LORD was standing there beside him,[A] saying, "I am the LORD,[d] the God of your father Abraham and the God of Isaac. I will give you and your offspring the land on which you are lying. [14] Your offspring will be like the dust of the earth,[e] and you will spread out toward the west, the east, the north, and the south. All the peoples on earth will be blessed through you and your offspring.[f] [15] Look, I am with you and will watch over you wherever you go. I will bring you back to this land,[g] for I will not leave you until I have done what I have promised you."

[16] When Jacob awoke from his sleep, he said, "Surely the LORD is in this place, and I did not know it."[h] [17] He was afraid and said, "What an awesome place this is! This is none other than the house of God. This is the gate of heaven."

[18] Early in the morning Jacob took the stone that was near his head and set it up as a marker. He poured oil on top of it [19] and named the place Bethel,[B] though previously the city was named Luz.[i] [20] Then Jacob made a vow:[j] "If God will be with me and watch over me during this journey I'm making, if he provides me with food to eat and clothing to wear, [21] and if I return safely to my father's

family,[k] then the LORD will be my God.[l] [22] This stone that I have set up as a marker will be God's house, and I will give to you a tenth of all that you give me."[m]

JACOB MEETS RACHEL

29 Jacob resumed his journey[c] and went to the eastern country.[D,n] [2] He looked and saw a well in a field. Three flocks of sheep were lying there beside it because the sheep were watered from this well. But a large stone covered the opening of the well. [3] The shepherds would roll the stone from the opening of the well and water the sheep when all the flocks[E] were gathered there. Then they would return the stone to its place over the well's opening.

[4] Jacob asked the men at the well, "My brothers! Where are you from?"

"We're from Haran," they answered.

[5] "Do you know Laban grandson of Nahor?" Jacob asked them.

They answered, "We know him."

[6] "Is he well?" Jacob asked.

"Yes," they said, "and here is his daughter Rachel, coming with his sheep."

[7] Then Jacob said, "Look, it is still broad daylight. It's not time for the animals to be gathered. Water the flock, then go out and let them graze."

[8] But they replied, "We can't until all the flocks have been gathered and the stone is rolled from the well's opening. Then we will water the sheep."

[9] While he was still speaking with them, Rachel came with her father's sheep, for she was a shepherdess. [10] As soon as Jacob saw his uncle Laban's daughter Rachel with his sheep,[f] he went up and rolled the stone from the opening and watered his uncle Laban's sheep. [11] Then Jacob kissed Rachel and wept loudly.[G] [12] He told Rachel that he was her father's relative, Rebekah's son. She ran and told her father.

[a] 28:8 Gn 24:3; 26:34-35; 27:46
[b] 28:12 Gn 41:1; Nm 12:6; Jb 33:15-16
[c] Jn 1:51
[d] 28:13 Gn 15:7; Ex 6:8
[e] 28:14 Gn 13:16
[f] Gn 12:3
[g] 28:15 Gn 48:21; Dt 30:3; 1Kg 8:34; Zph 3:20
[h] 28:16 Ex 3:4-6; Jos 5:13-15; Ps 139:7-12
[i] 28:19 Gn 35:6; 48:3; Jdg 1:23,26
[j] 28:20 Gn 31:13

[k] 28:21 Gn 33:18; Jdg 11:31; 2Sm 15:7-9
[l] Dt 26:17
[m] 28:22 Gn 14:20; Lv 27:30; Dt 14:22
[n] 29:1 Nm 23:7; Jdg 6:3

[A] 28:13 Or *there above it* [B] 28:19 = House of God [C] 29:1 Lit *Jacob picked up his feet* [D] 29:1 Lit *the land of the children of the east* [E] 29:3 Sam, some LXX mss read *flocks and the shepherds* [F] 29:10 Lit *with the sheep of Laban his mother's brother* [G] 29:11 Lit *and he lifted his voice and wept*

28:10-12 Jacob, now a fugitive, found himself in circumstances so grim that the only pillow he had was a rock (28:11). Yet that night, **he dreamed** that **a stairway was set on the ground with its top reaching the sky** (28:12). While sleeping, Jacob was watching divine activity at work around him. Prior to this, all he could see was the mess he was in. But God opened his eyes to a spiritual reality that transformed his viewpoint.
28:13 God had always been watching over Jacob. Now Jacob got to *see* his presence.

28:14-15 This is the first time Jacob heard the promise from God himself. The information thus became real because he finally realized that it was God's promise—not just his father's. What a blessing it is when God illuminates his word so that we hear the Spirit speaking personally *to us*.
28:18-19 He woke up and gave the place a sacred name—**Bethel** (28:19), "house of God." What had been a dark place became a sacred space.
29:1-8 Jacob **resumed his journey** (29:1). Through providential circumstances, he met

Rachel, a woman of Laban's household, part of his extended family (29:5-6). The scene is similar to that preceding Isaac and Rebekah's meeting: Rachel, like Rebekah, proved her own industrious character by leading her sheep (29:9) even while the other shepherds were lazily lounging (29:8).
29:9-12 The stones covering wells in those days were intentionally large, meant to be moved by several men. But Jacob, smitten with love upon seeing the beautiful Rachel (29:17), shifted the thing all on his own (29:10).

[a]**29:14** Gn 2:23; 37:27;
Jdg 9:2; 2Sm 5:1; 19:12-13;
1Ch 11:1
[b]**29:18** Gn 30:26; 31:41;
Hs 12:12

[c]**29:30** Gn 31:41
[d]**29:31** Gn 25:28; Dt
21:15-16; 22:13; 24:3; Lk
14:26; 16:13
[e]Gn 30:22
[f]Gn 11:30; 25:21; Jdg 13:2-
3; 1Sm 2:5; Lk 1:36
[g]**29:32** Gn 31:42; Ex 3:7;
4:31; Dt 26:7
[h]**29:35** Gn 49:8; Mt 1:2
[i]**30:1** 1Sm 1:5-6

JACOB DECEIVED

[13] When Laban heard the news about his sister's son Jacob, he ran to meet him, hugged him, and kissed him. Then he took him to his house, and Jacob told him all that had happened.

[14] Laban said to him, "Yes, you are my own flesh and blood."[A,a]

After Jacob had stayed with him a month, [15] Laban said to him, "Just because you're my relative, should you work for me for nothing? Tell me what your wages should be."

[16] Now Laban had two daughters: the older was named Leah, and the younger was named Rachel. [17] Leah had tender eyes, but Rachel was shapely and beautiful. [18] Jacob loved Rachel, so he answered Laban, "I'll work for you seven years for your younger daughter Rachel."[b]

[19] Laban replied, "Better that I give her to you than to some other man. Stay with me." [20] So Jacob worked seven years for Rachel, and they seemed like only a few days to him because of his love for her.

[21] Then Jacob said to Laban, "Since my time is complete, give me my wife, so I can sleep with[B] her." [22] So Laban invited all the men of the place and sponsored a feast. [23] That evening, Laban took his daughter Leah and gave her to Jacob, and he slept with her. [24] And Laban gave his slave Zilpah to his daughter Leah as her slave.

[25] When morning came, there was Leah! So he said to Laban, "What is this you have done to me? Wasn't it for Rachel that I worked for you? Why have you deceived me?"

[26] Laban answered, "It is not the custom in this place to give the younger daughter in marriage before the firstborn. [27] Complete this week of wedding celebration, and we will also give you this younger one in return for working yet another seven years for me."

[28] And Jacob did just that. He finished the week of celebration, and Laban gave him his daughter Rachel as his wife. [29] And Laban gave his slave Bilhah to his daughter Rachel as her slave. [30] Jacob slept with Rachel also, and indeed, he loved Rachel more than Leah. And he worked for Laban another seven years.[c]

JACOB'S SONS

[31] When the LORD saw that Leah was unloved,[d] he opened her womb;[e] but Rachel was unable to conceive.[f] [32] Leah conceived, gave birth to a son, and named him Reuben,[c] for she said, "The LORD has seen my affliction;[g] surely my husband will love me now."

[33] She conceived again, gave birth to a son, and said, "The LORD heard that I am unloved and has given me this son also." So she named him Simeon.[D]

[34] She conceived again, gave birth to a son, and said, "At last, my husband will become attached to me because I have borne three sons for him." Therefore he was named Levi.[E]

[35] And she conceived again, gave birth to a son, and said, "This time I will praise the LORD." Therefore she named him Judah.[F,h] Then Leah stopped having children.

30 When Rachel saw that she was not bearing Jacob any children, she envied her sister. "Give me sons, or I will die!"[i] she said to Jacob.

[A]**29:14** Lit *my bone and my flesh*   [B]**29:21** Lit *can go to*   [C]**29:32** = See, a Son; in Hb, the name *Reuben* sounds like "has seen my affliction."
[D]**29:33** In Hb, the name *Simeon* sounds like "has heard."   [E]**29:34** In Hb, the name *Levi* sounds like "attached to."   [F]**29:35** In Hb, the name *Judah* sounds like "praise."

29:13-20 Laban rushed to Jacob, **hugged him, and took him to his house** (29:13). On the surface, Laban seemed to treat Jacob like close family. Yet when Jacob requested to marry his beloved daughter, Laban set him up. Jacob agreed to **work for . . . seven years** to afford a dowry for Laban's **younger daughter Rachel** (29:18). The years flew by for Jacob, **because of his love for her** (29:20).
29:21-25 On the honeymoon Jacob found that **Laban** had given him **his daughter Leah** instead (29:23). Jacob's surprise at seeing Leah's face in dawn's light is captured in what has to be the most profound understatement in the Bible: **When morning came, there was Leah!** (29:25).
29:26 Laban had out-tricked his nephew in much the same way that Jacob had manipulated his older brother Esau. The younger and

the older had been swapped, except this time Jacob was on the short end of the trick. He was experiencing what the apostle Paul calls the law of sowing and reaping (see Gal 6:7-8). Our actions, righteous or unrighteous, will always bear fruit in keeping with the roots.
29:27-30 Jacob, realizing he had no basis for "righteous" anger, accepted the marriage to Leah (29:27-28). But he was still in love with Rachel, so he agreed to marry her too for *another* seven years of labor (29:27-30).
29:30-35 Leah and Rachel, competing for Jacob's affection, began a race to produce children. Their sons would ultimately become the patriarchs of the twelve tribes of Israel.
   God, recognizing that **Leah was unloved, opened her womb** before Rachel's (29:31). The first child she named **Reuben**, which sounds like "has seen my affliction" (29:32)

in the Hebrew language. This suggests that in spite of the loveless relationship with her husband, Leah expressed faith in God, believing that he knew the reality of her circumstances. She named the second son **Simeon**, which sounds like "has heard" (29:33). Again, Leah knew that God had loved her even though Jacob had not. With the birth of a third son, **Levi**, whose name sounds like "attached to" in Hebrew, Leah hoped that Jacob would develop an attachment to her (29:34). But he wouldn't, so with son number four, **Judah**, which sounds like "praise," Leah turned her full attention to God. She chose to praise God *despite* her challenges (29:35).
30:1-8 Rachel **envied her sister** greatly (30:1). Jacob **became angry with Rachel** and didn't offer much reassurance, other than the true—but rather cold—reminder, God **has**

[2] Jacob became angry with Rachel and said, "Am I in God's place, who has withheld offspring[A] from you?"

[3] Then she said, "Here is my maid Bilhah. Go sleep with her, and she'll bear children for me[B,a] so that through her I too can build a family." [4] So Rachel gave her slave Bilhah to Jacob as a wife, and he slept with her. [5] Bilhah conceived and bore Jacob a son. [6] Rachel said, "God has vindicated me; yes, he has heard me and given me a son," so she named him Dan.[c]

[7] Rachel's slave Bilhah conceived again and bore Jacob a second son. [8] Rachel said, "In my wrestlings with God,[D] I have wrestled with my sister and won," and she named him Naphtali.[E]

[9] When Leah saw that she had stopped having children, she took her slave Zilpah and gave her to Jacob as a wife. [10] Leah's slave Zilpah bore Jacob a son. [11] Then Leah said, "What good fortune!"[F] and she named him Gad.[G]

[12] When Leah's slave Zilpah bore Jacob a second son, [13] Leah said, "I am happy that the women call me happy,"[b] so she named him Asher.[H]

[14] Reuben went out during the wheat harvest and found some mandrakes in the field.[c] When he brought them to his mother Leah, Rachel asked, "Please give me some of your son's mandrakes."

[15] But Leah replied to her, "Isn't it enough that you have taken my husband? Now you also want to take my son's mandrakes?"

"Well then," Rachel said, "he can sleep with you tonight in exchange for your son's mandrakes."

[16] When Jacob came in from the field that evening, Leah went out to meet him and said, "You must come with me, for I have hired you with my son's mandrakes." So Jacob slept with her that night.

[17] God listened to Leah, and she conceived and bore Jacob a fifth son. [18] Leah said, "God has rewarded me for giving my slave to my husband," and she named him Issachar.[I]

[19] Then Leah conceived again and bore Jacob a sixth son. [20] "God has given me a good gift," Leah said. "This time my husband will honor me because I have borne six sons for him," and she named him Zebulun.[J] [21] Later, Leah bore a daughter and named her Dinah.

[22] Then God remembered Rachel. He listened to her and opened her womb.[d] [23] She conceived and bore a son, and she said, "God has taken away my disgrace."[e] [24] She named him Joseph[K] and said, "May the LORD add another son to me."[f]

JACOB'S FLOCKS MULTIPLY

[25] After Rachel gave birth to Joseph, Jacob said to Laban, "Send me on my way so that I can return to my homeland. [26] Give me my wives and my children that I have worked for, and let me go.[g] You know how hard I have worked for you."

[27] But Laban said to him, "If I have found favor with you, stay. I have learned by divination that the LORD has blessed me because of you." [28] Then Laban said, "Name your wages, and I will pay them."[h]

[29] So Jacob said to him, "You know how I have served you and how your herds have fared with me.[i] [30] For you had very little before I came, but now your wealth has increased. The LORD has blessed you because of me. And now, when will I also do something for my own family?"

[31] Laban asked, "What should I give you?"

And Jacob said, "You don't need to give me anything. If you do this one thing for me, I will continue to shepherd and keep your flock. [32] Let me go through all your sheep today and remove every sheep that is speckled or spotted, every dark-colored sheep among the lambs, and the spotted and speckled among the female goats.

[a] 30:3 Gn 50:23
[b] 30:13 Lk 1:48
[c] 30:14 Sg 7:13
[d] 30:22 Gn 29:31
[e] 30:23 Is 4:1; Lk 1:25
[f] 30:24 Gn 35:17
[g] 30:26 Gn 29:18,20,27; Hs 12:12
[h] 30:28 Gn 29:15; 31:7,41
[i] 30:29 Gn 31:6,38-40

[A] 30:2 Lit the fruit of the womb   [B] 30:3 Lit bear on my knees   [C] 30:6 In Hb, the name Dan sounds like "has vindicated," or "has judged."   [D] 30:8 Or "With mighty wrestlings   [E] 30:8 In Hb, the name Naphtali sounds like "my wrestling."   [F] 30:11 Alt Hb tradition, LXX, Vg read "Good fortune has come!"   [G] 30:11 = Good Fortune   [H] 30:13 = Happy   [I] 30:18 In Hb, the name Issachar sounds like "reward."   [J] 30:20 In Hb, the name Zebulun sounds like "honored."   [K] 30:24 = He Adds

withheld offspring from you (30:2). So Rachel did what Sarah had done. She offered to Jacob her servant Bilhah as a surrogate, who would have kids on her behalf (30:3-4). This resulted in two sons—Dan and Naphtali (30:6-8). **30:9-13** Leah then offered *her* servant Zilpah to Jacob (30:9). Again, a human solution worked as well as Sarah's, and two more sons—**Gad** and **Asher**—entered the mix (30:11-13). **30:14-24** Finding **some mandrakes** (30:14), which were fruits believed to help women

conceive, Reuben contributed to the competition between his mother and aunt. He took them to his mother Leah, who agreed to share some with Rachel in exchange for another night with Jacob (30:15). Leah conceived again—and again—bearing **Issachar** and **Zebulun** (30:18, 20). Then Rachel finally had **Joseph** (30:22-24). The sisters' sinful tactics only continued to make matters more confusing and painful, yet God was gracious to mitigate against the damage.

30:25-36 Jacob desired to return to his **homeland** (30:25). Laban, however, knew how beneficial Jacob was to his business; he wanted to strike a deal for Jacob to stay (30:27-28). So Jacob offered to stay if only he could have the **speckled or spotted . . . dark-colored sheep** and goats (30:32). Laban immediately accepted the deal (30:34), but he separated the flock to protect his investment (30:36), thinking he had, once again, gotten the better of Jacob.

a 30:39 Gn 31:10-12
b 30:43 Gn 12:16; 13:2; 24:35; 26:13-14; 30:30

c 31:3 Gn 28:15; 32:10
d 31:6 Gn 30:29
e 31:8 Gn 30:32
f 31:12 Gn 30:37-40; Ex 3:7
g 31:13 Gn 28:18-19
h 31:15 Gn 29:19-30

Such will be my wages. ³³ In the future when you come to check on my wages, my honesty will testify for me. If I have any female goats that are not speckled or spotted, or any lambs that are not black, they will be considered stolen."

³⁴ "Good," said Laban. "Let it be as you have said."

³⁵ That day Laban removed the streaked and spotted male goats and all the speckled and spotted female goats — every one that had any white on it — and every dark-colored one among the lambs, and he placed his sons in charge of them. ³⁶ He put a three-day journey between himself and Jacob. Jacob, meanwhile, was shepherding the rest of Laban's flock.

³⁷ Jacob then took branches of fresh poplar, almond, and plane wood, and peeled the bark, exposing white stripes on the branches. ³⁸ He set the peeled branches in the troughs in front of the sheep — in the water channels where the sheep came to drink. And the sheep bred when they came to drink. ³⁹ The flocks bred in front of the branches and bore streaked, speckled, and spotted young.*a* ⁴⁰ Jacob separated the lambs and made the flocks face the streaked sheep and the completely dark sheep in Laban's flocks. Then he set his own stock apart and didn't put them with Laban's sheep.

⁴¹ Whenever the stronger of the flock were breeding, Jacob placed the branches in the troughs, in full view of the flocks, and they would breed in front of the branches. ⁴² As for the weaklings of the flocks, he did not put out the branches. So it turned out that the weak sheep belonged to Laban and the stronger ones to Jacob. ⁴³ And the man became very rich.*A* He had many flocks, female and male slaves, and camels and donkeys.*b*

JACOB SEPARATES FROM LABAN

31 Now Jacob heard what Laban's sons were saying: "Jacob has taken all that was our father's and has built this wealth from what belonged to our father." ² And Jacob saw from Laban's face that his attitude toward him was not the same as before.

³ The LORD said to him, "Go back to the land of your fathers and to your family, and I will be with you."*c*

⁴ Jacob had Rachel and Leah called to the field where his flocks were. ⁵ He said to them, "I can see from your father's face that his attitude toward me is not the same as before, but the God of my father has been with me. ⁶ You know that with all my strength I have served your father*d* ⁷ and that he has cheated me and changed my wages ten times. But God has not let him harm me. ⁸ If he said, 'The spotted sheep will be your wages,' then all the sheep were born spotted. If he said, 'The streaked sheep will be your wages,' then all the sheep were born streaked.*e* ⁹ God has taken away your father's herds and given them to me.

¹⁰ "When the flocks were breeding, I saw in a dream that the streaked, spotted, and speckled males were mating with the females. ¹¹ In that dream the angel of God said to me, 'Jacob!' and I said, 'Here I am.' ¹² And he said, 'Look up and see: all the males that are mating with the flocks are streaked, spotted, and speckled, for I have seen all that Laban has been doing to you.*f* ¹³ I am the God of Bethel, where you poured oil on the stone marker and made a solemn vow to me.*g* Get up, leave this land, and return to your native land.' "

¹⁴ Then Rachel and Leah answered him, "Do we have any portion or inheritance in our father's family? ¹⁵ Are we not regarded by him as outsiders? For he has sold us*h* and has certainly spent our purchase price. ¹⁶ In fact, all the wealth that God has taken away from our father belongs to us and to our children. So do whatever God has said to you."

¹⁷ So Jacob got up and put his children and wives on the camels. ¹⁸ He took all the livestock and possessions he had acquired in Paddan-aram, and he drove his herds to go to the land of Canaan, to his father

A 30:43 Lit *The man spread out very much, very much*

30:37-43 No husbandry manual teaches that animals that breed in the sight of peeled branches (30:38) produce speckled offspring. God was supernaturally guiding this breeding program. In the end, **the weak sheep belonged to Laban and the stronger ones to Jacob** (30:42). It doesn't matter how good a deal seems in human terms; the man on whose side God stands will get the better deal.

31:1-3 God was using the family conflict to drive Jacob **back to the land of [his] fathers** (31:3). God often allows conflicts to open new paths in our lives.

31:4-16 Jacob revealed his plans to his wives, letting them know that God himself had commanded him to **return to [his] native land** (31:13). Rachel and Leah responded by following Jacob's leadership (31:16), proving that the best way for a man to lead his

family is by communicating where God is leading him.

31:17-35 Laban rushed after Jacob (31:23). Their two parties met, and Laban scolded Jacob for sneaking away, taking his **daughters away like prisoners of war** (31:26). What had most irked Laban, however, was the disappearance of his household gods (31:30), which Rachel had stolen (see 31:19). Perhaps she took them because she, like her father,

Isaac. ¹⁹ When Laban had gone to shear his sheep, Rachel stole her father's household idols.ᵃ ²⁰ And Jacob deceivedᴬ Laban the Aramean, not telling him that he was fleeing. ²¹ He fled with all his possessions, crossed the Euphrates, and headed forᴮ the hill country of Gilead.

LABAN OVERTAKES JACOB

²² On the third day Laban was told that Jacob had fled. ²³ So he took his relatives with him, pursued Jacob for seven days, and overtook him in the hill country of Gilead. ²⁴ But God came to Laban the Aramean in a dream at night. "Watch yourself!" God warned him. "Don't say anything to Jacob, either good or bad."ᵇ
²⁵ When Laban overtook Jacob, Jacob had pitched his tent in the hill country, and Laban and his relatives also pitched their tents in the hill country of Gilead. ²⁶ Laban said to Jacob, "What have you done? You have deceived me and taken my daughters away like prisoners of war! ²⁷ Why did you secretly flee from me, deceive me, and not tell me? I would have sent you away with joy and singing, with tambourines and lyres, ²⁸ but you didn't even let me kiss my grandchildren and my daughters. You have acted foolishly. ²⁹ I could do you great harm, but last night the God of your father said to me: 'Watch yourself! Don't say anything to Jacob, either good or bad.' ³⁰ Now you have gone off because you long for your father's family — but why have you stolen my gods?"ᶜ
³¹ Jacob answered, "I was afraid, for I thought you would take your daughters from me by force. ³² If you find your gods with anyone here, he will not live!ᵈ Before our relatives, point out anything that is yours and take it." Jacob did not know that Rachel had stolen the idols.
³³ So Laban went into Jacob's tent, Leah's tent, and the tents of the two concubines,ᶜ but he found nothing. When he left Leah's tent, he went into Rachel's tent. ³⁴ Now Rachel had taken Laban's household idols, put them in the saddlebag of the camel, and sat on them. Laban searched the whole tent but found nothing. ³⁵ She said to her father, "Don't be angry, my lord, that I cannot stand up in your presence;ᵉ I am having my period."

So Laban searched, but could not find the household idols.

JACOB'S COVENANT WITH LABAN

³⁶ Then Jacob became incensed and brought charges against Laban. "What is my crime?" he said to Laban. "What is my sin, that you have pursued me? ³⁷ You've searched all my possessions! Have you found anything of yours?ᵈ Put it here before my relatives and yours, and let them decide between the two of us. ³⁸ I've been with you these twenty years. Your ewes and female goats have not miscarried, and I have not eaten the rams from your flock. ³⁹ I did not bring you any of the flock torn by wild beasts; I myself bore the loss. You demanded payment from me for what was stolen by day or by night. ⁴⁰ There I was — the heat consumed me by day and the frost by night, and sleep fled from my eyes. ⁴¹ For twenty years in your household I served you — fourteen years for your two daughters and six years for your flocksᶠ — and you have changed my wages ten times! ⁴² If the God of my father, the God of Abraham, the Fear of Isaac, had not been with me, certainly now you would have sent me off empty-handed. But God has seen my affliction and my hard work,ᴱ and he issued his verdict last night."
⁴³ Then Laban answered Jacob, "The daughters are my daughters; the sons, my sons; and the flocks, my flocks! Everything you see is mine! But what can I do today for these daughters of mine or for the children they have borne? ⁴⁴ Come now, let's make a covenant, you and I.ᵍ Let it be a witness between the two of us."
⁴⁵ So Jacob picked out a stone and set it up as a marker.ʰ ⁴⁶ Then Jacob said to his relatives, "Gather stones." And they took stones and made a mound, then ate there by the mound. ⁴⁷ Laban named the mound Jegar-sahadutha, but Jacob named it Galeed.ᶠ
⁴⁸ Then Laban said, "This mound is a witness between you and me today." Therefore the place was called Galeed ⁴⁹ and also Mizpah,ᴳ·ⁱ for he said, "May the LORD watch between you and me when we are out of each other's sight. ⁵⁰ If you mistreat my daughters or take other wives, though

ᵃ 31:19 Jdg 17:5; 1Sm 15:23; 19:13; Ezk 21:21; Hs 3:4; Zch 10:2
ᵇ 31:24 Gn 24:50; 31:29; 2Sm 13:22
ᶜ 31:30 Gn 31:19; Jos 24:2; Jdg 18:24
ᵈ 31:32 Gn 44:9
ᵉ 31:35 Lv 19:32

ᶠ 31:41 Gn 29:27,30
ᵍ 31:44 Gn 21:27,32; 26:28
ʰ 31:45 Jos 24:26-27
ⁱ 31:49 Jdg 11:29; 1Sm 7:5-6

ᴬ 31:20 Lit And he stole the heart of   ᴮ 31:21 Lit and set his face to   ᶜ 31:33 Lit servants   ᴰ 31:37 Lit What have you found from all of the possessions of your house?   ᴱ 31:42 Lit and the work of my hands   ᶠ 31:47 Jegar-sahadutha is Aramaic, and Galeed is Hb; both names = Mound of Witness   ᴳ 31:49 = Watchtower

---

believed they brought good luck. Perhaps she was just paying her father back for the terrible way he had treated her and Jacob.

31:36-55 Ultimately, Laban tried to limit his personal losses, proposing that a **covenant** be made between him and Jacob (31:44). The terms of the covenant were meant to keep Jacob and Laban apart (31:52).

a 31:50 Jdg 11:10; 1Sm 12:5;
  Jb 16:19; Jr 42:5; Mc 1:2
b 31:53 Jos 24:2
c 32:1 Ps 91:9-11
d 32:2 Jos 21:38; 2Sm 2:8;
  17:24,27; 1Kg 2:8
e 32:5 Gn 33:8,15
f 32:6 Gn 33:1
g 32:8 Gn 27:41
h 32:9 Gn 28:13; 31:42,53

i 32:9 Gn 31:3,13
j 32:12 Gn 28:13-15
k 32:13 Gn 43:11
l 32:22 Dt 2:37; 3:16;
  Jos 12:2
m 32:24 Hs 12:3-4

no one is with us, understand that God will be a witness between you and me."[a] [51] Laban also said to Jacob, "Look at this mound and the marker I have set up between you and me. [52] This mound is a witness and the marker is a witness that I will not pass beyond this mound to you, and you will not pass beyond this mound and this marker to do me harm. [53] The God of Abraham, and the gods[b] of Nahor — the gods of their father[A] — will judge between us." And Jacob swore by the Fear of his father Isaac. [54] Then Jacob offered a sacrifice on the mountain and invited his relatives to eat a meal. So they ate a meal and spent the night on the mountain. [55] Laban got up early in the morning, kissed his grandchildren and daughters, and blessed them. Then Laban left to return home.

PREPARING TO MEET ESAU

32 Jacob went on his way, and God's angels met him.[c] [2] When he saw them, Jacob said, "This is God's camp." So he called that place Mahanaim.[B,d]

[3] Jacob sent messengers ahead of him to his brother Esau in the land of Seir, the territory of Edom. [4] He commanded them, "You are to say to my lord Esau, 'This is what your servant Jacob says. I have been staying with Laban and have been delayed until now. [5] I have oxen, donkeys, flocks, and male and female slaves. I have sent this message to inform my lord, in order to seek your favor.' "[e]

[6] When the messengers returned to Jacob, they said, "We went to your brother Esau; he is coming to meet you — and he has four hundred men with him."[f] [7] Jacob was greatly afraid and distressed; he divided the people with him into two camps, along with the flocks, herds, and camels. [8] He thought, "If Esau comes to one camp and attacks it, the remaining one can escape."[g]

[9] Then Jacob said, "God of my father Abraham and God of my father Isaac,[h] the LORD who said to me, 'Go back to your land and to your family, and I will cause

you to prosper,'[i] [10] I am unworthy of all the kindness and faithfulness you have shown your servant. Indeed, I crossed over the Jordan with my staff, and now I have become two camps. [11] Please rescue me from my brother Esau, for I am afraid of him; otherwise, he may come and attack me, the mothers, and their children. [12] You have said, 'I will cause you to prosper, and I will make your offspring like the sand of the sea, too numerous to be counted.' "[j]

[13] He spent the night there and took part of what he had brought with him as a gift for his brother Esau:[k] [14] two hundred female goats, twenty male goats, two hundred ewes, twenty rams, [15] thirty milk camels with their young, forty cows, ten bulls, twenty female donkeys, and ten male donkeys. [16] He entrusted them to his slaves as separate herds and said to them, "Go on ahead of me, and leave some distance between the herds."

[17] And he told the first one: "When my brother Esau meets you and asks, 'Who do you belong to? Where are you going? And whose animals are these ahead of you?' [18] then tell him, 'They belong to your servant Jacob. They are a gift sent to my lord Esau. And look, he is behind us.' "

[19] He also told the second one, the third, and everyone who was walking behind the animals, "Say the same thing to Esau when you find him. [20] You are also to say, 'Look, your servant Jacob is right behind us.' " For he thought, "I want to appease Esau with the gift that is going ahead of me. After that, I can face him, and perhaps he will forgive me."

[21] So the gift was sent on ahead of him while he remained in the camp that night. [22] During the night Jacob got up and took his two wives, his two slave women, and his eleven sons, and crossed the ford of Jabbok.[l] [23] He took them and sent them across the stream, along with all his possessions.

JACOB WRESTLES WITH GOD

[24] Jacob was left alone, and a man wrestled with him until daybreak.[m] [25] When the

---

A 31:53 Two Hb mss, LXX omit *the gods of their father*   B 32:2 = Two Camps

---

32:1-2 Fresh out of a crisis with Laban and about to enter another potential crisis with his brother Esau, Jacob was in need of divine help. God sent **angels** to assure Jacob of God's presence and protection (32:1). The battle before him, like the battle behind him, would be primarily spiritual in nature.

32:3-8 Jacob sent messengers . . . to his brother Esau (32:3) in an attempt to **seek**

Esau's **favor** and reestablish their broken relationship (32:5). Imagine Jacob's surprise and dread, then, when a messenger returned with news that Esau was **coming** with **four hundred men** (32:6).

32:9-12 Fear drove Jacob to plead with God for deliverance (32:11). His short prayer is a model for the way we should pray, too: he approached God with humility (32:10), reminded God of

his promises (32:9), and asked God to act in accordance with them (32:12).

32:24-25 On the night before his big confrontation with his supposedly murderous brother, Jacob was suddenly jumped by **a man** who **wrestled with him until daybreak** (32:24). This mysterious stranger **dislocated his hip** (32:25). If Jacob had been unable to best Esau physically before this fight, now

man saw that he could not defeat him, he struck Jacob's hip socket as they wrestled and dislocated his hip. **26** Then he said to Jacob, "Let me go, for it is daybreak."

But Jacob said, "I will not let you go unless you bless me."

27 "What is your name?" the man asked. "Jacob," he replied.

28 "Your name will no longer be Jacob,"[a] he said. "It will be Israel[A] because you have struggled with God[b] and with men and have prevailed."

29 Then Jacob asked him, "Please tell me your name."

But he answered, "Why do you ask my name?"[c] And he blessed him there.

30 Jacob then named the place Peniel,[B] "For I have seen God face to face," he said, "yet my life has been spared."[d] **31** The sun shone on him as he passed by Penuel[c,e] — limping because of his hip. **32** That is why, still today, the Israelites don't eat the thigh muscle that is at the hip socket: because he struck Jacob's hip socket at the thigh muscle.[D]

JACOB MEETS ESAU

33 Now Jacob looked up and saw Esau coming toward him with four hundred men. So he divided the children among Leah, Rachel, and the two slave women. **2** He put the slaves and their children first, Leah and her children next, and Rachel and Joseph last. **3** He himself went on ahead and bowed to the ground[f] seven times until he approached his brother.

4 But Esau ran to meet him, hugged him, threw his arms around him, and kissed him. Then they wept.[g] **5** When Esau looked up and saw the women and children, he asked, "Who are these with you?"

He answered, "The children God has graciously given your servant."[h] **6** Then the slaves and their children approached

him and bowed down. **7** Leah and her children also approached and bowed down, and then Joseph and Rachel approached and bowed down.

8 So Esau said, "What do you mean by this whole procession[E] I met?"[i]

"To find favor with you, my lord,"[j] he answered.

9 "I have enough, my brother," Esau replied. "Keep what you have."

10 But Jacob said, "No, please! If I have found favor with you, take this gift from me. For indeed, I have seen your face, and it is like seeing God's face, since you have accepted me. **11** Please take my present that was brought to you, because God has been gracious to me and I have everything I need." So Jacob urged him until he accepted.

12 Then Esau said, "Let's move on, and I'll go ahead of you."

13 Jacob replied, "My lord knows that the children are weak, and I have nursing flocks and herds. If they are driven hard for one day, the whole herd will die. **14** Let my lord go ahead of his servant. I will continue on slowly, at a pace suited to the livestock and the children, until I come to my lord at Seir."

15 Esau said, "Let me leave some of my people with you."

But he replied, "Why do that? Please indulge me,[F] my lord."[k]

16 That day Esau started on his way back to Seir, **17** but Jacob went to Succoth. He built a house for himself and shelters for his livestock; that is why the place was called Succoth.[G,l]

18 After Jacob came from Paddan-aram, he arrived safely[m] at Shechem[n] in the land of Canaan and camped in front of the city. **19** He purchased a section of the field where he had pitched his tent from the sons of Hamor, Shechem's father, for

a 32:28 Gn 35:10; 2Kg 17:34
b Hs 12:3-4
c 32:29 Jdg 13:18
d 32:30 Gn 16:13; Ex 24:10-11; 33:20; Nm 12:8; Jdg 6:22; 13:22
e 32:31 Jdg 8:8
f 33:3 Gn 18:2; 42:6; 43:26
g 33:4 Gn 45:14
h 33:5 Gn 48:9; Ps 127:3; Is 8:18
i 33:8 Gn 32:13-16
j Gn 32:5
k 33:15 Gn 34:11; 47:25; Ru 2:13
l 33:17 Jos 13:27; Jdg 8:5; Ps 60:6
m 33:18 Gn 28:21
n Jos 24:1; Jdg 9:1; Ps 60:6; Ac 7:16

A 32:28 In Hb, the name *Israel* sounds like "he struggled (with) God."   **B** 32:30 = Face of God   **C** 32:31 Variant of *Peniel*   **D** 32:32 Or *tendon*   **E** 33:8 Lit *camp*   **F** 33:15 Lit *May I find favor in your eyes*   **G** 33:17 = Stalls or Huts

---

he couldn't even run from him. He was alone, afraid, and completely broken—just where God wanted him to be.

32:26-28 Bless me (32:26), Jacob demanded of the stranger, because he realized that this physical altercation was about something spiritual. The wrestler responded by asking, **What is your name** (32:27)? Jacob responded with the identity he had for himself: I'm a trickster, which is what the name **Jacob** means. But the man replied, **Your name will no longer be Jacob**, but **it will be Israel** (32:28). In other words, he said, you don't operate by schemes anymore. Now you'll be

identified by the fact that you've wrestled with God.

32:30-32 Jacob's life would never be the same, because he was now **limping** (32:31). This suggests that any man God blesses will possess a limp of sorts. God will create something in that person's life that makes him despair of his own strength and lean on the Lord's instead. Brokenness is the key to blessing.

33:8-11 Jacob insisted that Esau share in his blessing, **because God had been gracious** (33:11). This suggests that we become truly generous, not when we give out of

compulsion, but when we realize that God has given us all we possess.

33:12-17 Fearing a possible change of heart, Jacob avoided traveling any further with Esau. Using his **children** and his **flocks** as an excuse (33:13), he appealed to Esau to **go ahead** (33:14). Once Esau was out of sight and **on his way back to Seir** (33:16), Jacob **went to Succoth**, which was in the opposite direction (33:17).

33:18-20 Jacob **arrived safely . . . in the land of Canaan** (33:18) and, like Abraham, **set up an altar there** (34:20). He acknowledged that God had brought him back to the land of promise.

Where God Becomes Real to You Again

IN GENESIS 34, JACOB'S SONS had just put the family at great risk by attacking an entire city to avenge the rape of their sister. Jacob knew his entire household was in danger of a return attack. The family crisis had grown too big to handle, and the mess had no visible solution. The whole family was on the verge of being turned upside down.

Oftentimes, God does not show up until things are at their worst because it is then that he has our attention. As long as we think we can handle it, fix it, or work it out, he waits. But when we admit that we no longer know the solution, he shows up.

God told Jacob, "Get up! Go to Bethel and settle there. Build an altar there to the God who appeared to you when you fled from your brother Esau" (GEN 35:1). There, at Bethel, God met Jacob again. Twenty years earlier, Jacob had seen a stairway between heaven and earth there, with angels going up and down it (GEN 28). At Bethel, Jacob had seen heaven connect with earth.

Your personal Bethel is that place where God becomes real to you again. That place where the Bible becomes so alive that you *know* God is talking to you. Bethel is where God works out circumstances in your life in such a way that leaves you wondering what you were ever concerned about. Bethel is the place where God meets you intimately and transforms you into a different kind of person than you've ever been. And as a result, where you once were known for being mean, now you are known for being nice. Where you once were known for being strong-willed, now you are known for being submissive. Where you once were known for your lack of leadership, now you are known for godly leadership. Bethel is the place where God fixes you so that you can flourish in the life he has in store for you.

God turned things around for Jacob so that he brought him and his brother back together. He restored his family. He gave Jacob a heritage that blessed the world through his son Joseph, who provided food during a time of nationwide drought and famine.

God can do similar things for you if you will arise and go where he wants each of us to go—to Bethel. To get there, you need to seek to know him because in knowing him you'll find true and lasting revival.

a hundred pieces of silver.^{A,a} **20** And he set up an altar there and called it God, the God of Israel.^B

DINAH DEFILED

34 Leah's daughter^b Dinah, whom Leah bore to Jacob, went out to see some of the young women of the area. **2** When Shechem — son of Hamor the Hivite, who was the region's chieftain — saw her, he took her and raped her. **3** He became infatuated with Jacob's daughter Dinah. He loved the young girl and spoke tenderly to her.^c **4** "Get me this girl as a wife,"^c he told his father.

5 Jacob heard that Shechem had defiled his daughter Dinah, but since his sons were with his livestock in the field, he remained silent until they returned. **6** Meanwhile, Shechem's father Hamor came to speak with Jacob. **7** Jacob's sons returned from the field when they heard about the incident and were deeply grieved and very angry. For Shechem had committed an outrage against Israel by raping Jacob's daughter,^d and such a thing should not be done.

8 Hamor said to Jacob's sons, "My son Shechem has his heart set on your^D daughter. Please give her to him as a wife. **9** Intermarry with us; give your daughters to us, and take our daughters for yourselves. **10** Live with us. The land is before you. Settle here, move about, and acquire property in it."

11 Then Shechem said to Dinah's father and brothers, "Grant me this favor,^E and I'll give you whatever you say. **12** Demand of me a high compensation^F and gift; I'll give you whatever you ask me. Just give the girl to be my wife!"

13 But Jacob's sons answered Shechem and his father Hamor deceitfully because he had defiled their sister Dinah. **14** "We cannot do this thing," they said to them.

"Giving our sister to an uncircumcised man is a disgrace to us. **15** We will agree with you only on this condition: if all your males are circumcised as we are.^e **16** Then we will give you our daughters, take your daughters for ourselves, live with you, and become one people. **17** But if you will not listen to us and be circumcised, then we will take our daughter and go."

18 Their words seemed good to Hamor and his son Shechem. **19** The young man did not delay doing this, because he was delighted with Jacob's daughter. Now he was the most important in all his father's family. **20** So Hamor and his son Shechem went to the gate of their city^f and spoke to the men of their city.

21 "These men are peaceful toward us," they said. "Let them live in our land and move about in it, for indeed, the region is large enough for them. Let us take their daughters as our wives and give our daughters to them. **22** But the men will agree to live with us and be one people only on this condition: if all our men are circumcised as they are. **23** Won't their livestock, their possessions, and all their animals become ours? Only let us agree with them, and they will live with us."

24 All the men^g who had come to the city gates listened to Hamor and his son Shechem, and all those men were circumcised. **25** On the third day, when they were still in pain, two of Jacob's sons, Simeon and Levi,^h Dinah's brothers, took their swords, went into the unsuspecting city, and killed every male. **26** They killed Hamor and his son Shechem with their swords, took Dinah from Shechem's house, and went away. **27** Jacob's sons came to the slaughter and plundered the city because their sister had been defiled. **28** They took their flocks, herds, donkeys, and whatever was in the city and in the field. **29** They captured all their possessions, dependents,

^a **33:19** Jos 24:32; Jn 4:5
^b **34:1** Gn 30:21
^c **34:4** Jdg 14:2
^d **34:7** Dt 22:20–30; Jdg 20:6; 2Sm 13:12
^e **34:15** Gn 17:23–27
^f **34:20** Ru 4:1; 2Sm 15:2
^g **34:24** Gn 23:10
^h **34:25** Gn 49:5-7

---

^A **33:19** Lit *100 qesitahs*; the value of this currency is unknown   ^B **33:20** = *El-Elohe-Israel*   ^C **34:3** Lit *spoke to her heart*   ^D **34:8** The Hb word for *your* is pl, showing that Hamor is speaking to Jacob and his sons.   ^E **34:11** Lit *"May I find favor in your eyes*   ^F **34:12** Or *bride-price*, or *betrothal present*

34:1-4 Dinah, Jacob's daughter, **went out to see some of the young women of the area** (34:1). During her visiting, a man named **Shechem**, the son of **the region's chieftain . . . raped her** (34:2). He then decided that **he loved the young girl** (33:3) and wanted to marry her (34:4).

34:5-7 Jacob heard that Shechem had defiled . . . Dinah (34:5) and desired to marry her (34:8), but said little (34:5). Instead, it was **Jacob's sons** who became **deeply grieved**, rightly calling Shechem's actions an **outrage** (34:7).

34:8-24 Hamor seemed unaware of Jacob's sons' rage, presenting intermarriage between

their two families as a profitable situation for everybody involved (34:10). Jacob's sons, taking after their father's old ways, **answered . . . deceitfully** (34:13), plotting to take Shechem down by surprise. They required Shechem, Hamor, and all of their men to be **circumcised** (34:14-16). Hamor and company considered this a small price to pay for a bride (34:19) and all of Jacob's **possessions** (34:23), so they agreed (34:24).

34:25-31 The circumcision required was a ruse to weaken the men. **Simeon and Levi . . . killed** many and **plundered the city**

(34:25,27), leaving Hamor's people devastated (34:29). Jacob feared retribution from the other Canaanites in the area, who were much more numerous than his family (34:30). Most of the men in this story respond in ways that show little faith in God: Shechem did violence to an innocent woman; Jacob didn't trust that God would maintain his family in the land like he had promised; and Jacob's sons used a sacred covenant symbol as a trick to murder far more people than were guilty.

a 34:30 Jos 7:25
b Ex 5:21; 1Sm 13:4; 2Sm
10:6
c Gn 13:7; 34:2
d Gn 46:26-27; Dt 4:27;
1Ch 16:19; Ps 105:12
e 35:1 Gn 28:19
f Gn 27:43
g 35:2 Gn 31:19; Jos 24:23;
1Sm 7:3
h Ex 19:10
i 35:3 1Sm 7:9; 2Sm 24:25;
Jb 12:4; Ps 20:1; 34:4
j Gn 28:10-22
k 35:5 Ex 23:27
l 35:6 Gn 28:19; 48:3
m 35:8 Gn 24:59

n 35:10 Gn 17:5; 32:28
o 35:11 Gn 17:1; 28:3; Ex 6:3
p Gn 9:1,7
q Gn 48:4
r Gn 17:6,16; 36:31
s 35:12 Gn 12:7; 13:15; 26:3-
4; 28:13; Ex 32:13
t 35:13 Gn 17:22; 18:33
u 35:14 Gn 28:18-19; 31:45
v 35:17 Gn 30:24
w 35:19 Mc 5:2; Mt 2:18
x 35:22 Gn 49:3-4
y 35:22-26 1Ch 2:1-2

and wives and plundered everything in the houses.

30 Then Jacob said to Simeon and Levi, "You have brought trouble on me,[a] making me odious to the inhabitants of the land,[b] the Canaanites and the Perizzites.[c] We are few in number; if they unite against me and attack me, I and my household will be destroyed."[d]

31 But they answered, "Should he treat our sister like a prostitute?"

RETURN TO BETHEL

35 God said to Jacob, "Get up! Go to Bethel and settle there.[e] Build an altar there to the God who appeared to you when you fled from your brother Esau."[f]

2 So Jacob said to his family and all who were with him, "Get rid of the foreign gods that are among you.[g] Purify yourselves and change your clothes.[h] 3 We must get up and go to Bethel. I will build an altar there to the God who answered me in my day of distress.[i] He has been with me everywhere I have gone."[j]

4 Then they gave Jacob all their foreign gods and their earrings, and Jacob hid them under the oak near Shechem. 5 When they set out, a terror from God came over the cities around them, and they did not pursue Jacob's sons.[k] 6 So Jacob and all who were with him came to Luz (that is, Bethel[l]) in the land of Canaan. 7 Jacob built an altar there and called the place El-bethel[A] because it was there that God had revealed himself to him when he was fleeing from his brother.

8 Deborah, the one who had nursed and raised Rebekah,[B,m] died and was buried under the oak south of Bethel. So Jacob named it Allon-bacuth.[C]

9 God appeared to Jacob again after he returned from Paddan-aram, and he blessed him. 10 God said to him, "Your name is Jacob; you will no longer be named

Jacob, but your name will be Israel."[n] So he named him Israel. 11 God also said to him, "I am God Almighty.[o] Be fruitful and multiply.[p] A nation, indeed an assembly of nations, will come from you,[q] and kings will descend from you.[D,r] 12 I will give to you the land that I gave to Abraham and Isaac.[s] And I will give the land to your future descendants." 13 Then God withdrew[E,t] from him at the place where he had spoken to him.

14 Jacob set up a marker at the place where he had spoken to him — a stone marker. He poured a drink offering on it and anointed it with oil.[u] 15 Jacob named the place where God had spoken with him Bethel.

RACHEL'S DEATH

16 They set out from Bethel. When they were still some distance from Ephrath, Rachel began to give birth, and her labor was difficult. 17 During her difficult labor, the midwife said to her, "Don't be afraid, for you have another son."[v] 18 With her last breath — for she was dying — she named him Ben-oni,[F] but his father called him Benjamin.[G] 19 So Rachel died and was buried on the way to Ephrath (that is, Bethlehem[w]). 20 Jacob set up a marker on her grave; it is the marker at Rachel's grave still today.

ISRAEL'S SONS

21 Israel set out again and pitched his tent beyond the Tower of Eder.[H] 22 While Israel was living in that region, Reuben went in and slept with his father's concubine Bilhah, and Israel heard about it.[x]

Jacob had twelve sons:[y]
23 Leah's sons were Reuben (Jacob's firstborn),
Simeon, Levi, Judah,
Issachar, and Zebulun.
24 Rachel's sons were Joseph and Benjamin.

A 35:7 = God of Bethel   B 35:8 Lit Deborah, Rebekah's wet nurse; Gn 24:59   C 35:8 = Oak of Weeping   D 35:11 Lit will come from your loins
E 35:13 Lit went up   F 35:18 = Son of My Sorrow   G 35:18 = Son of the Right Hand   H 35:21 Or beyond Migdal-eder

---

35:1 Get up! Go to Bethel and settle there. God's timing is never accidental. He spoke to Jacob in the middle of a family crisis because he knew Jacob was desperate enough to listen.

35:2 It appears Jacob experienced a personal revival, which spilled over into a family revival. In Jacob's revival, we see the three steps that anyone should follow when returning to God. First, he said, **get rid of the foreign gods . . . among you.** For the last twenty years, apparently, Laban's idols had been stashed in Jacob's household. It was

time to make a clean break from them. Second, **purify yourselves.** This is an extension of the first point: remove the sin from your midst. Third, **change your clothes.** Changing garments symbolizes a reorienting of life. For instance, when a judge puts on his robe, he's not an ordinary man anymore; he has authority.

35:4-5 A few verses earlier, Jacob cowered in fear because of what his enemies might do to him. But when he set out for Bethel, suddenly **a terror from God came over the cities around [his family]** (35:5). What changed?

Jacob had stepped up to be the leader God called him to be. Thus, the same people he had been fearing turned to run.

35:16-18 Rachel gave birth and named her second son **Ben-oni,** which means "Son of My Sorrow," because she was dying (35:18). Jacob renamed the child **Benjamin,** which means "Son of the Right Hand," as an indication of the place the boy would have in Jacob's heart.

35:19-26 Since Benjamin was born **on the way to Ephrath** (35:19), he was the only son to be born inside the promised land. The others were born in **Paddan-aram** (35:26).

25 The sons of Rachel's slave Bilhah were Dan and Naphtali. **26** The sons of Leah's slave Zilpah were Gad and Asher. These are the sons of Jacob, who were born to him in Paddan-aram.

ISAAC'S DEATH

27 Jacob came to his father Isaac at Mamre[a] in Kiriath-arba (that is, Hebron[b]), where Abraham and Isaac had stayed. **28** Isaac lived 180 years. **29** He took his last breath and died, and was gathered to his people,[c] old and full of days. His sons Esau and Jacob buried him.

ESAU'S FAMILY

36 These are the family records[d] of Esau (that is, Edom[e]). **2** Esau took his wives from the Canaanite women: Adah daughter of Elon the Hethite,[f] Oholibamah daughter of Anah and granddaughter[A] of Zibeon the Hivite, **3** and Basemath daughter of Ishmael and sister of Nebaioth.[g] **4** Adah bore Eliphaz to Esau, Basemath bore Reuel, **5** and Oholibamah bore Jeush, Jalam, and Korah. These were Esau's sons, who were born to him in the land of Canaan.

6 Esau took his wives, sons, daughters, and all the people of his household, as well as his herds, all his livestock, and all the property he had acquired in Canaan; he went to a land away from his brother Jacob. **7** For their possessions were too many for them to live together,[h] and because of their herds, the land where they stayed could not support them.[i] **8** So Esau (that is, Edom) lived in the mountains of Seir.[j]

9 These are the family records of Esau, father of the Edomites in the mountains of Seir.

10 These are the names of Esau's sons:[k]
Eliphaz son of Esau's wife Adah,
and Reuel son of Esau's wife Basemath.
11 The sons of Eliphaz were
Teman, Omar, Zepho, Gatam,
and Kenaz.
12 Timna, a concubine of Esau's son Eliphaz,
bore Amalek to Eliphaz.
These are the sons of Esau's wife Adah.

13 These are Reuel's sons:
Nahath, Zerah, Shammah,
and Mizzah.
These are the sons of Esau's wife Basemath.

14 These are the sons of Esau's wife Oholibamah
daughter of Anah
and granddaughter[A] of Zibeon:
She bore Jeush, Jalam, and Korah to Edom.

15 These are the chiefs
among Esau's sons:
the sons of Eliphaz, Esau's firstborn:
chief Teman, chief Omar, chief Zepho, chief Kenaz,
16 chief Korah,[B] chief Gatam,
and chief Amalek.
These are the chiefs descended from Eliphaz
in the land of Edom.
These are the sons of Adah.

17 These are the sons of Reuel, Esau's son:
chief Nahath, chief Zerah, chief Shammah, and chief Mizzah.
These are the chiefs descended from Reuel
in the land of Edom.
These are the sons of Esau's wife Basemath.

18 These are the sons of Esau's wife Oholibamah:
chief Jeush, chief Jalam, and chief Korah.
These are the chiefs descended from Esau's wife Oholibamah
daughter of Anah.

19 These are the sons of Esau (that is, Edom),
and these are their chiefs.

SEIR'S FAMILY

20 These are the sons of Seir the Horite,[l]
the inhabitants of the land:
Lotan, Shobal, Zibeon, Anah,
21 Dishon, Ezer, and Dishan.
These are the chiefs among the Horites,
the sons of Seir, in the land of Edom.

[a] 35:27 Gn 13:18; 18:1; 23:19 [b] Jos 14:15 [c] 35:29 Gn 25:8,17; 49:33; Nm 20:24,26; Dt 32:50 [d] 36:1 Gn 2:4; 36:9 [e] Gn 25:30 [f] 36:2 Gn 26:34 [g] 36:3 Gn 28:9 [h] 36:7 Gn 13:6 [i] Gn 17:8; Heb 11:9 [j] 36:8 Dt 2:5 [k] 36:10-14 1Ch 1:35-37 [l] 36:20-28 Gn 14:6; Dt 2:12,22; 1Ch 1:38-42

[A] 36:2,14 Sam, LXX read Anah son [B] 36:16 Sam omits Korah

35:27-29 Isaac, thought to be on death's doorstep twenty years prior, finally passed away after living for **180 years** (35:28). Remarkably, **Esau and Jacob buried him** together in cooperation (35:29).

36:1-43 The author gives the genealogical record of **Esau** as a way of closing the book on Esau and his family, just as he had done for Cain in chapter 4, Noah's sons in chapter 10, Lot in chapter 19, and Ishmael in chapter 25. As God had promised, Esau's descendants would grow into a nation of his own—**the Edomites** (36:9).

a 36:31-43 Gn 17:6,16;
35:11; 1Ch 1:43-54

b 37:1 Gn 26:3
c 37:2 Gn 30:1-13
d 1Sm 2:22-24
e 37:3 Gn 44:20

22 The sons of Lotan were Hori
   and Heman.
   Timna was Lotan's sister.
23 These are Shobal's sons:
   Alvan, Manahath, Ebal, Shepho,
   and Onam.
24 These are Zibeon's sons:
   Aiah and Anah.
   This was the Anah who
   found the hot springs^A
   in the wilderness
   while he was pasturing the donkeys
   of his father Zibeon.
25 These are the children of Anah:
   Dishon and Oholibamah
   daughter of Anah.
26 These are Dishon's sons:
   Hemdan, Eshban, Ithran,
   and Cheran.
27 These are Ezer's sons:
   Bilhan, Zaavan, and Akan.
28 These are Dishan's sons:
   Uz and Aran.

29 These are the chiefs
   among the Horites:
   chief Lotan, chief Shobal, chief
   Zibeon, chief Anah,
30 chief Dishon, chief Ezer, and chief
   Dishan.
   These are the chiefs
   among the Horites,
   clan by clan,^B in the land of Seir.

RULERS OF EDOM

31 These are the kings who reigned
   in the land of Edom^a
   before any king reigned
   over the Israelites:
32 Bela son of Beor reigned in Edom;
   the name of his city was Dinhabah.
33 When Bela died, Jobab son of Zerah
   from Bozrah reigned in his place.
34 When Jobab died, Husham
   from the land of the Temanites
   reigned in his place.
35 When Husham died, Hadad
   son of Bedad reigned in his place.
   He defeated Midian in the field
   of Moab;
   the name of his city was Avith.

36 When Hadad died, Samlah
   from Masrekah reigned
   in his place.
37 When Samlah died, Shaul
   from Rehoboth on the
   Euphrates River reigned
   in his place.
38 When Shaul died, Baal-hanan
   son of Achbor reigned
   in his place.
39 When Baal-hanan son of Achbor
   died, Hadar^c reigned in his place.
   His city was Pau, and his wife's name
   was Mehetabel
   daughter of Matred daughter
   of Me-zahab.

40 These are the names of Esau's chiefs,
   according to their families
   and their localities,
   by their names:
   chief Timna, chief Alvah, chief
   Jetheth,
41 chief Oholibamah, chief Elah,
   chief Pinon,
42 chief Kenaz, chief Teman,
   chief Mibzar,
43 chief Magdiel, and chief Iram.
   These are Edom's chiefs,
   according to their settlements
   in the land they possessed.
   Esau^D was father of the Edomites.

JOSEPH'S DREAMS

37 Jacob lived in the land where his
father had stayed, the land of Canaan.^b 2 These are the family records of
Jacob.
   At seventeen years of age, Joseph tended sheep with his brothers. The young man
was working with the sons of Bilhah and
Zilpah, his father's wives,^c and he brought
a bad report about them to their father.^d
   3 Now Israel loved Joseph more than
his other sons because Joseph was a son
born to him in his old age,^e and he made a
robe of many colors^E for him. 4 When his
brothers saw that their father loved him
more than all his brothers, they hated him
and could not bring themselves to speak
peaceably to him.

---

^A 36:24 Syr, Vg; Tg reads *the mules*; Hb obscure   ^B 36:30 Lit *Horites, for their chiefs*   ^C 36:39 Many Hb mss, Sam, Syr read *Hadad*
^D 36:43 Lit *He Esau*   ^E 37:3 Or *robe with long sleeves*; see 2Sm 13:18,19

37:1-4 Jacob's family dysfunction contin-
ued into the next generation because of
favoritism. **Israel** (that is, Jacob) **loved
Joseph more than his other sons** because
Joseph was the son of his favorite wife,
Rachel (37:3). When Jacob **made a robe of**

many colors for Joseph (37:3), a garment
symbolizing the privilege of the firstborn,
the sibling rivalry erupted. Joseph's brothers **hated him** (37:4).
37:5-11 We aren't told at this point in the story
that Joseph's dreams were prophetic. Jacob

asked, **Am I . . . really going to come and bow
down . . . before you** (37:10)? Actually, *yes,*
Jacob, you will. God intended to lead Joseph
to a grand destiny. But Joseph would have a
lot of unexpected detours in his life before
he got there.

⁵ Then Joseph had a dream. When he told it to his brothers, they hated him even more. ⁶ He said to them, "Listen to this dream I had: ⁷ There we were, binding sheaves of grain in the field. Suddenly my sheaf stood up, and your sheaves gathered around it and bowed down to my sheaf."ᵃ

⁸ "Are you really going to reign over us?" his brothers asked him. "Are you really going to rule us?" So they hated him even more because of his dream and what he had said.

⁹ Then he had another dream and told it to his brothers. "Look," he said, "I had another dream, and this time the sun, moon, and eleven stars were bowing down to me."

¹⁰ He told his father and brothers, and his father rebuked him. "What kind of dream is this that you have had?" he said. "Am I and your mother and your brothers really going to come and bow down to the ground before you?"¹¹ His brothers were jealous of him,ᵇ but his father kept the matter in mind.ᶜ

JOSEPH SOLD INTO SLAVERY

¹² His brothers had gone to pasture their father's flocks at Shechem. ¹³ Israel said to Joseph, "Your brothers, you know, are pasturing the flocks at Shechem. Get ready. I'm sending you to them."

"I'm ready," Joseph replied.

¹⁴ Then Israel said to him, "Go and see how your brothers and the flocks are doing, and bring word back to me." So he sent him from the Hebronᵈ Valley, and he went to Shechem.

¹⁵ A man found him there, wandering in the field, and asked him, "What are you looking for?"

¹⁶ "I'm looking for my brothers," Joseph said. "Can you tell me where they are pasturing their flocks?"

¹⁷ "They've moved on from here," the man said. "I heard them say, 'Let's go to Dothan.'"ᵉ So Joseph set out after his brothers and found them at Dothan.

¹⁸ They saw him in the distance, and before he had reached them, they plotted to kill him.ᶠ ¹⁹ They said to one another, "Oh, look, here comes that dream expert!ᴬ ²⁰ So now, come on, let's kill him and throw him into one of the pits.ᴮ We can say that a vicious animal ate him. Then we'll see what becomes of his dreams!"

²¹ When Reuben heard this, he tried to save him from them.ᶜ He said, "Let's not take his life."ᵍ ²² Reuben also said to them, "Don't shed blood. Throw him into this pit in the wilderness, but don't lay a hand on him" — intending to rescue him from them and return him to his father.

²³ When Joseph came to his brothers, they stripped off Joseph's robe, the robe of many colors that he had on. ²⁴ Then they took him and threw him into the pit. The pit was empty, without water.

²⁵ They sat down to eat a meal,ʰ and when they looked up, there was a caravan of Ishmaelites coming from Gilead.ⁱ Their camels were carrying aromatic gum, balsam, and resin, going down to Egypt.ʲ ²⁶ Judah said to his brothers, "What do we gain if we kill our brother and cover up his blood? ²⁷ Come on, let's sell him to the Ishmaelites and not lay a hand on him, for he is our brother, our own flesh," and his brothers agreed. ²⁸ When Midianiteᵏ traders passed by, his brothers pulled Joseph out of the pit and sold him for twenty pieces of silver to the Ishmaelites, who took Joseph to Egypt.ˡ

²⁹ When Reuben returned to the pit and saw that Joseph was not there, he tore his clothes.ᵐ ³⁰ He went back to his brothers and said, "The boy is gone! What am I going to do?"ᴰ ³¹ So they took Joseph's robe, slaughtered a male goat, and dipped the robe in its blood. ³² They sent the robe of many colors to their father and said, "We found this. Examine it. Is it your son's robe or not?"

³³ His father recognized it. "It is my son's robe," he said. "A vicious animal has

ᵃ 37:7 Gn 42:6,9; 43:26; 44:14
ᵇ 37:11 Ac 7:9
ᶜ Dn 7:28; Lk 2:19,51
ᵈ 37:14 Gn 13:18; 35:27
ᵉ 37:17 2Kg 6:13

ᶠ 37:18 Ps 31:13; 37:12,32; Mk 14:1; Jn 11:53; Ac 23:12
ᵍ 37:21 Gn 42:22
ʰ 37:25 Gn 42:21
ⁱ Gn 39:1
ʲ Gn 43:11; Jr 8:22; 46:11
ᵏ 37:28 Dt 25:5,7; Jdg 8:22-24; Mt 22:24; Mk 12:19; Lk 20:28
ˡ Gn 45:4-5; Ps 105:17; Ac 7:9
ᵐ 37:29 Gn 44:13; Nm 14:6; 2Sm 1:11; 3:31; Jb 1:20

ᴬ 37:19 Lit comes the lord of the dreams   ᴮ 37:20 Or cisterns   ᶜ 37:21 Lit their hands   ᴰ 37:30 Lit And I, where am I going?

37:12-20 Joseph's brothers **saw him in the distance** and **plotted to kill him** (37:18). They couldn't stand his dreams, so they wanted to ensure that they would never come true. **37:19-24** Eldest brother **Reuben** reasoned with his siblings: **Throw him into this pit**, thinking that he could return later to **rescue [Joseph]** (37:22). And so, when Joseph arrived, **they stripped off [his] robe** and **threw him into the pit**, which was **empty** (37:23-24).

37:25-28 Joseph had been living large, like royalty, until his brothers **sold him for twenty pieces of silver** (37:27-28). Just like that, he became a slave. Little did he know that God was orchestrating something much bigger than he could imagine.
37:29 Reuben, it seems, wasn't with the brothers when they sold Joseph into slavery. So when he **returned to the pit and saw that Joseph was not there, he tore his clothes** in despair.

37:30-32 Together Joseph's older brothers **took Joseph's robe, slaughtered a male goat, and dipped the robe in its blood** (37:31). They then presented the robe to their father Jacob (37:32). There is irony here, since Jacob had used goat skins to deceive his brother years before; now Jacob is deceived by animal evidence. Jacob's deceptive character had been transferred to his sons.

a 37:33 Gn 44:28
b 38:1 Jos 15:35; 1Sm 22:1
c 38:3 Gn 46:12; Nm 26:19
d 38:7 1Ch 2:3
e 38:8 Dt 25:5-10
f Mt 22:24
g 38:11 Ru 1:12-13

h 38:12 Jos 15:10,57
i 38:14 Gn 24:65
j 38:16 Lv 18:15

devoured him. Joseph has been torn to pieces!"*a* **34** Then Jacob tore his clothes, put sackcloth around his waist, and mourned for his son many days. **35** All his sons and daughters tried to comfort him, but he refused to be comforted. "No," he said. "I will go down to Sheol to my son, mourning." And his father wept for him.

36 Meanwhile, the Midianites sold Joseph in Egypt to Potiphar, an officer of Pharaoh and the captain of the guards.

JUDAH AND TAMAR

38 At that time Judah left his brothers and settled near an Adullamite*b* named Hirah. **2** There Judah saw the daughter of a Canaanite named Shua; he took her as a wife and slept with her. **3** She conceived and gave birth to a son, and he named him Er.*c* **4** She conceived again, gave birth to a son, and named him Onan. **5** She gave birth to another son and named him Shelah. It was at Chezib that*A,B* she gave birth to him.

6 Judah got a wife for Er, his firstborn, and her name was Tamar. **7** Now Er, Judah's firstborn, was evil in the LORD's sight; he and the LORD put him to death.*d* **8** Then Judah said to Onan, "Sleep with your brother's wife. Perform your duty as her brother-in-law*e* and produce offspring for your brother."*f* **9** But Onan knew that the offspring would not be his, so whenever he slept with his brother's wife, he released his semen on the ground so that he would not produce offspring for his brother. **10** What he did was evil in the LORD's sight, so he put him to death also.

11 Then Judah said to his daughter-in-law Tamar, "Remain a widow in your father's house until my son Shelah grows up."*g* For he thought, "He might die too, like his brothers." So Tamar went to live in her father's house.

12 After a long time*c* Judah's wife, the daughter of Shua, died. When Judah had finished mourning, he and his friend Hirah the Adullamite went up to Timnah*h* to his sheepshearers. **13** Tamar was told, "Your father-in-law is going up to Timnah to shear his sheep." **14** So she took off her widow's clothes, veiled her face,*i* covered herself, and sat at the entrance to Enaim,*D* which is on the way to Timnah. For she saw that, though Shelah had grown up, she had not been given to him as a wife. **15** When Judah saw her, he thought she was a prostitute, for she had covered her face.

16 He went over to her and said, "Come, let me sleep with you," for he did not know that she was his daughter-in-law.*j*

She said, "What will you give me for sleeping with me?"

17 "I will send you a young goat from my flock," he replied.

But she said, "Only if you leave something with me until you send it."

18 "What should I give you?" he asked.

She answered, "Your signet ring, your cord, and the staff in your hand." So he gave them to her and slept with her, and she became pregnant by him. **19** She got up and left, then removed her veil and put her widow's clothes back on.

20 When Judah sent the young goat by his friend the Adullamite in order to get back the items he had left with the woman, he could not find her. **21** He asked the men of the place, "Where is the cult prostitute who was beside the road at Enaim?"

"There has been no cult prostitute here," they answered.

22 So the Adullamite returned to Judah, saying, "I couldn't find her, and besides, the men of the place said, 'There has been no cult prostitute here.'"

23 Judah replied, "Let her keep the items for herself; otherwise we will become a

A 38:5 LXX reads *She was at Chezib when* *B* 38:5 Or *He was at Chezib when* *C* 38:12 Lit *And there were many days, and* *D* 38:14 Or *sat by the mouth of the springs*

37:36 God was working through this family disaster to deliver Jacob and his sons to Egypt. Joseph's own departure would place him **in Egypt,** in the house of **Potiphar, an officer of Pharaoh** so that Joseph would be in a position to save his family from starvation. **38:1-2** To remind us of the line of succession to the covenant promise, the author briefly focuses on **Judah.** He would eventually inherit the promise and blessing of Abraham, but at this point in the story he was just another conniving member of a dysfunctional family. Judah married **the daughter of a Canaanite** (37:2), an inauspicious start.

38:3-10 Judah's eldest son, **Er,** married a woman named **Tamar** (37:6). Unfortunately, Er **was evil in the LORD's sight, and the LORD put him to death** (37:7), leaving Tamar with no husband and no children. The custom of the day in situations like this was for the next living brother of the deceased to marry the widow (see Deut 25:5-10). **Onan,** the brother in line for this task, was fine with taking Tamar as his wife, but because he **knew that the offspring would not be his,** but would be credited to his deceased brother, he intentionally avoided getting her pregnant (Gen 38:9). He was using Tamar.

38:11-15 Legally, Tamar could expect to marry **Shelah,** the third son. But Judah seemed to blame *Tamar* for the death of his other two boys, and he refused to arrange the marriage (38:11, 14). So Tamar **veiled her face,** and posed as a prostitute (38:14-15). Apparently Tamar suspected Judah's lustful ways, so she planned to lure him. **38:16-23** Judah agreed to pay the supposed prostitute with **a young goat** (38:17), and as a guarantee that he would, he left her his **signet ring** and his **staff** (38:18). Both would have had markings uniquely identifying Judah as their owner. The stage was set for blackmail.

laughingstock. After all, I did send this young goat, but you couldn't find her."

²⁴ About three months later Judah was told, "Your daughter-in-law, Tamar, has been acting like a prostitute, and now she is pregnant."

"Bring her out," Judah said, "and let her be burned to death!"ᵃ ²⁵ As she was being brought out, she sent her father-in-law this message: "I am pregnant by the man to whom these items belong." And she added, "Examine them. Whose signet ring, cord, and staff are these?"

²⁶ Judah recognized them and said, "She is more in the rightᴬ than I,ᵇ since I did not give her to my son Shelah." And he did not know her intimately again.

²⁷ When the time came for her to give birth, there were twins in her womb. ²⁸ As she was giving birth, one of them put out his hand, and the midwife took it and tied a scarlet thread around it, announcing, "This one came out first." ²⁹ But then he pulled his hand back, out came his brother, and she said, "What a breakout you have made for yourself!" So he was named Perez.ᴮ,ᶜ ³⁰ Then his brother, who had the scarlet thread tied to his hand, came out, and was named Zerah.ᶜ

JOSEPH IN POTIPHAR'S HOUSE

39 Now Joseph had been taken to Egypt. An Egyptian named Potiphar, an officer of Pharaoh and the captain of the guards, bought him from the Ishmaelitesᵈ who had brought him there. ² The LORD was with Joseph,ᵉ and he became a successful man, servingᴰ in the household of his Egyptian master. ³ When his master saw that the LORD was with him and that the LORD made everything he did successful,ᶠ ⁴ Joseph found favorᵍ with his master and became his personal attendant. Potiphar also put him in charge of his household and placed all that he owned under his authority.ᴱ ⁵ From the time that he put him in charge of his household and of all that he owned, the LORD blessed the Egyptian's house because of Joseph.ʰ The LORD's blessing was on all that he owned, in his house and in his fields. ⁶ He left all that he owned under Joseph's authority;ᶠ he did not concern himself with anything except the food he ate.

Now Joseph was well-built and handsome.ⁱ ⁷ After some timeᴳ his master's wife looked longingly at Joseph and said, "Sleep with me."

⁸ But he refused. "Look," he said to his master's wife, "with me here my master does not concern himself with anything in his house, and he has put all that he owns under my authority.ᴴ ⁹ No one in this house is greater than I am. He has withheld nothing from me except you, because you are his wife. So how could I do this immense evil, and how could I sin against God?"ʲ

¹⁰ Although she spoke to Joseph day after day, he refused to go to bed with her.ⁱ ¹¹ Now one day he went into the house to do his work, and none of the household servants were there.ʲ ¹² She grabbed him by his garment and said, "Sleep with me!" But leaving his garment in her hand, he escaped and ran outside. ¹³ When she saw that he had left his garment with her and had run outside, ¹⁴ she called her

ᵃ 38:24 Lv 20:14
ᵇ 38:26 1Sm 24:17
ᶜ 38:29 Gn 46:12; Nm 26:20; 1Ch 2:4; Mt 1:3
ᵈ 39:1 Gn 37:25,28,36; Ps 105:17
ᵉ 39:2 Gn 39:3,21,23; Ac 7:9

ᶠ 39:3 Ps 1:3
ᵍ 39:4 Gn 18:3; 19:19; 33:10
ʰ 39:5 Gn 30:27
ⁱ 39:6 Gn 29:17; 1Sm 16:12
ʲ 39:9 Gn 20:6; 42:18; 2Sm 12:13; Ps 51:4; Pr 6:29

ᴬ 38:26 Or more righteous   ᴮ 38:29 = Breaking Out   ᶜ 38:30 = Brightness of Sunrise; perhaps related to the scarlet thread   ᴰ 39:2 Lit and he was
ᴱ 39:4 Lit owned in his hand   ᶠ 39:6 Lit owned in Joseph's hand   ᴳ 39:7 Lit And after these things   ᴴ 39:8 Lit owns in my hand   ⁱ 39:10 Lit he did not
listen to her to lie beside her, to be with her   ʲ 39:11 Lit there in the house

38:24-26 Tamar responded to Judah's judgment that she be **burned** for harlotry (38:24) by sending his missing pledge to him, and asking, **Whose . . . are these** (38:25)? The question she posed bears a resemblance to the question Judah and his brothers posed to their father Jacob after faking Joseph's death (see 37:32). Judah immediately recognized his guilt, knowing that Tamar had acted desperately because he had withheld his son (38:26).
38:27-30 Tamar gave birth to **twins**, and just as with Jacob and Esau, the older of these two (**Zerah**, 38:30), would serve the younger (**Perez**, 38:29). Thus the line of Judah, which was the covenant line, was preserved and continued, even in the midst of sinful circumstances. God never causes, accepts, or condones sin, but he can use it to sovereignly accomplish his plan.

39:1-2 Joseph **had been taken to Egypt** as a slave. But because **the LORD was with Joseph . . . he became a successful man** in the house of **Potiphar** (39:1-2). Joseph's life proves the lesson taught by the sponge: when you fill a sponge with water and then add pressure, water comes out. Joseph was so full of God's presence that when life squeezed him, evidence of his dedication to God oozed out.
39:4-5 Joseph became the best employee in Potiphar's house. Potiphar **placed all that he owned under his authority** (39:4). Joseph thus shows us how we should conduct ourselves when working with and for non-Christians. We should be the most punctual, most productive, most trustworthy employees in our companies.
39:8-9 Joseph's reaction to Mrs. Potiphar's advances is a sort of template for how we

should resist temptation, sexual or otherwise. First, he saw that the consequences of sin would be damaging. Potiphar had placed all his possessions under Joseph's **authority** (39:8). To sleep with his master's wife would ruin that trust. More importantly, he recognized that what makes sin sinful is that it is an **immense evil** committed **against God** (39:9).
39:10-20 Potiphar's wife **spoke to Joseph day after day**, even though he kept rejecting her (39:10). Then, when no one was around, **she grabbed him by his garment** (39:12). Joseph bolted, which was the right move. But, in doing so, he **left his garment with her** (39:13). So Potiphar's wife spun a story about Joseph trying to rape her (39:14-18). Potiphar grew furious and **had [Joseph] thrown into prison** (39:20).

a 39:20 Gn 40:3; Ps 105:18
b 39:21 Gn 39:2; Ps 105:19; Ac 7:9
c Ex 3:21; 11:3; 12:36
d 39:23 Gn 39:2-3
e 40:1 Neh 1:11
f 40:3 Gn 39:20

g 40:7 Neh 2:2
h 40:8 Dn 2:11,20-24
i 40:12 Gn 41:12; Dn 2:36
j 40:13 Gn 40:19-22
k 40:15 Gn 37:28
l Gn 39:20

household servants. "Look," she said to them, "my husband brought a Hebrew man to make fools of us. He came to me so he could sleep with me, and I screamed as loud as I could. ¹⁵ When he heard me screaming for help,^A he left his garment beside me and ran outside."

¹⁶ She put Joseph's garment beside her until his master came home. ¹⁷ Then she told him the same story: "The Hebrew slave you brought to us came to make a fool of me, ¹⁸ but when I screamed for help,^B he left his garment beside me and ran outside."

¹⁹ When his master heard the story his wife told him — "These are the things your slave did to me" — he was furious ²⁰ and had him thrown into prison,^a where the king's prisoners were confined. So Joseph was there in prison.

JOSEPH IN PRISON

²¹ But the LORD was with Joseph and extended kindness to him.^b He granted him favor with the prison warden.^c ²² The warden put all the prisoners who were in the prison under Joseph's authority,^c and he was responsible for everything that was done there. ²³ The warden did not bother with anything under Joseph's authority,^D because the LORD was with him, and the LORD made everything that he did successful.^d

JOSEPH INTERPRETS TWO PRISONERS' DREAMS

40 After this, the king of Egypt's cupbearer^e and baker offended their master, the king of Egypt. ² Pharaoh was angry with his two officers, the chief cupbearer and the chief baker, ³ and put them in custody in the house of the captain of the guards^f in the prison where Joseph was confined. ⁴ The captain of the guards assigned Joseph to them as their personal attendant, and they were in custody for some time.^E

⁵ The king of Egypt's cupbearer and baker, who were confined in the prison, each had a dream. Both had a dream on the same night, and each dream had its own meaning. ⁶ When Joseph came to them in the morning, he saw that they looked distraught. ⁷ So he asked Pharaoh's officers who were in custody with him in his master's house, "Why do you look so sad today?"^g

⁸ "We had dreams," they said to him, "but there is no one to interpret them."

Then Joseph said to them, "Don't interpretations belong to God? Tell me your dreams."^h

⁹ So the chief cupbearer told his dream to Joseph: "In my dream there was a vine in front of me. ¹⁰ On the vine were three branches. As soon as it budded, its blossoms came out and its clusters ripened into grapes. ¹¹ Pharaoh's cup was in my hand, and I took the grapes, squeezed them into Pharaoh's cup, and placed the cup in Pharaoh's hand."

¹² "This is its interpretation,"^i Joseph said to him. "The three branches are three days. ¹³ In just three days Pharaoh will lift up your head^j and restore you to your position. You will put Pharaoh's cup in his hand the way you used to when you were his cupbearer. ¹⁴ But when all goes well for you, remember that I was with you. Please show kindness to me by mentioning me to Pharaoh, and get me out of this prison. ¹⁵ For I was kidnapped from the land of the Hebrews,^k and even here I have done nothing that they should put me in the dungeon."^F,l

¹⁶ When the chief baker saw that the interpretation was positive, he said to Joseph, "I also had a dream. Three baskets of white bread were on my head. ¹⁷ In the top basket were all sorts of baked goods for Pharaoh, but the birds were eating them out of the basket on my head."

---

^A 39:15 Lit *he heard that I raised my voice and I screamed*   ^B 39:18 Lit *I raised my voice and screamed*   ^C 39:22 Lit *prison in the hand of Joseph*   ^D 39:23 Lit *anything in his hand*   ^E 40:4 Lit *custody days*   ^F 40:15 Or *pit, or cistern*

39:21-23 We are reminded: **the LORD was with Joseph** (39:21). And before long, Joseph had gained such a good reputation that **the warden put all the prisoners . . . under Joseph's authority** (39:22). This is just the kind of thing God can do when we trust him in our detours. Living with God's presence in the middle of jail offers a truer freedom than living without God anywhere else ever could.

40:1-2 Joseph came into contact with two other prisoners—**the chief cupbearer and the chief baker** (40:2). Since both handled Pharaoh's food and drink, perhaps Pharaoh was con-

cerned about an assassination attempt, since capital punishment was possible (40:18-19, 22). **40:5-7** Joseph noticed that the cupbearer and baker **looked distraught** (40:6). He expressed concern for their emotional well-being (40:7). Even in his misery, Joseph was making time to minister to the hurting (see 2 Cor 1:3-7). By serving during his own suffering, Joseph was putting himself on the path toward future blessing.

40:8 The problem for these two prisoners was the same—troubling **dreams**. Joseph displayed confidence in God by reminding

them that only **God** could interpret dreams. Most striking, however, is his confidence that God *would use* him to reveal the dreams' meanings. In our suffering, a common temptation is to stop believing that God will use *us*.

40:14-15 Joseph tried to use the connections he had to get himself out of prison. **When all goes well for you**, he told the cupbearer, **show kindness to me by mentioning me to Pharaoh** (40:14). He must have been hopeful that this favor would soon lead to release.

---

18 "This is its interpretation," Joseph replied. "The three baskets are three days. **19** In just three days Pharaoh will lift up your head — from off you — and hang you on a tree.[A] Then the birds will eat the flesh from your body."[B]

20 On the third day, which was Pharaoh's birthday, he gave a feast for all his servants. He elevated[c] the chief cupbearer and the chief baker among his servants.[a] **21** Pharaoh restored the chief cupbearer to his position as cupbearer, and he placed the cup in Pharaoh's hand. **22** But Pharaoh hanged[D] the chief baker, just as Joseph had explained to them. **23** Yet the chief cupbearer did not remember Joseph; he forgot him.[b]

JOSEPH INTERPRETS PHARAOH'S DREAMS

41 At the end of two years Pharaoh had a dream: He was standing beside the Nile,[c] **2** when seven healthy-looking, well-fed cows came up from the Nile and began to graze among the reeds. **3** After them, seven other cows, sickly and thin, came up from the Nile and stood beside those cows along the bank of the Nile. **4** The sickly, thin cows ate the healthy, well-fed cows. Then Pharaoh woke up. **5** He fell asleep and dreamed a second time: Seven heads of grain, plump and good, came up on one stalk. **6** After them, seven heads of grain, thin and scorched by the east wind, sprouted up. **7** The thin heads of grain swallowed up the seven plump, full ones. Then Pharaoh woke up, and it was only a dream.

8 When morning came, he was troubled,[d] so he summoned all the magicians of Egypt and all its wise men.[e] Pharaoh told them his dreams, but no one could interpret them for him.

9 Then the chief cupbearer said to Pharaoh, "Today I remember my faults. **10** Pharaoh was angry with his servants, and he put me and the chief baker in the custody of the captain of the guards. **11** He and I had dreams on the same night; each dream had its own meaning. **12** Now a young Hebrew, a slave of the captain of the guards, was with us there. We told him our dreams, he interpreted our dreams for us, and each had its own interpretation. **13** It turned out just the way he interpreted them to us: I was restored to my position, and the other man was hanged."[f]

14 Then Pharaoh sent for Joseph, and they quickly brought him from the dungeon.[E,g] He shaved, changed his clothes, and went to Pharaoh.[h]

15 Pharaoh said to Joseph, "I have had a dream, and no one can interpret it. But I have heard it said about you that you can hear a dream and interpret it."[i]

16 "I am not able to,"[j] Joseph answered Pharaoh. "It is God who will give Pharaoh a favorable answer."[F,k]

17 So Pharaoh said to Joseph: "In my dream I was standing on the bank of the Nile, **18** when seven well-fed, healthy-looking cows came up from the Nile and grazed among the reeds. **19** After them, seven other cows — weak, very sickly, and thin — came up. I've never seen such sickly ones as these in all the land of Egypt. **20** Then the thin, sickly cows ate the first seven well-fed cows. **21** When they had devoured them, you could not tell that they had devoured them; their appearance was as bad as it had been before. Then I woke up. **22** In my dream I also saw seven heads of grain, full and good, coming up on one stalk. **23** After them, seven heads of grain — withered, thin, and scorched by the east wind — sprouted up. **24** The thin heads of grain swallowed the seven good ones. I told this to the magicians, but no one can tell me what it means."[l]

25 Then Joseph said to Pharaoh, "Pharaoh's dreams mean the same thing. God has revealed to Pharaoh what he is about to do.[m] **26** The seven good cows are seven

---

a 40:20 2Kg 25:27; Jr 52:31; Mt 14:6
b 40:23 Ec 9:15-16
c 41:1-7 Gn 41:17-23
d 41:8 Dn 2:1,3
e Ex 7:11,22; Dn 1:20; 2:2

f 41:13 Gn 40:1-22
g 41:14 Ps 105:20
h Dn 2:25
i 41:15 Dn 5:16
j 41:16 Dn 2:30
k Gn 40:8; Dn 2:22,28,47
l 41:24 Is 8:19; Dn 4:7
m 41:25 Dn 2:28-29,45; Rv 4:1

A 40:19 Or *and impale you on a pole*   B 40:19 Lit *eat your flesh from upon you*   C 40:20 Lit *He lifted up the head of*   D 40:22 Or *impaled*
E 41:14 Or *pit*, or *cistern*   F 41:16 Or *"God will answer Pharaoh with peace of mind."*

40:20-23 Three days later, everything happened **just as Joseph had explained** (40:22). Pharaoh **restored the chief cupbearer** to his original position (40:21) and **hanged the chief baker** (40:22). For a moment, it looked like Joseph was about to get his "get-out-of-jail-free card." **Yet the chief cupbearer did not remember Joseph** (40:23). This is how our circumstances go at times, too. Victory appears to be right on the horizon, then suddenly life takes a hard left and the joy we thought was coming disappears. Through his experiences,

however, Joseph continued to trust God. Though people may leave us and forget us, God never will.

41:1 Between Joseph interpreting the dreams of the prisoners and his next chance to get out of jail, **two years** passed. Joseph's life hadn't panned out as he had intended, yet God was at work on his behalf in someplace unexpected: the king's bedroom. **Pharaoh had a dream** that he couldn't figure out.

41:9-14 The wise men's discussion was overheard by the **cupbearer** (41:9). He realized he

had left the interpreter of dreams languishing. So he told Pharaoh all about Joseph and his gift, and **Pharaoh sent for Joseph** (41:10-14). The time of Joseph's testing had been completed (see Ps 105:17-19).

41:15-16 Joseph's reply shows that he had been letting God work on him during his imprisonment: **It is God who will give Pharaoh a favorable answer** (41:16). God's presence had been Joseph's constant companion, so God's preeminence was always on his mind.

a 41:27 2Kg 8:1
b 41:30 Gn 41:54,56; 47:13; Ps 105:16
c 41:38 Jb 32:8; Dn 4:8,9,18; 5:11,14
d 41:40 Ps 105:21; Ac 7:10

e 41:42 Est 3:10; 8:2; Dn 5:7,16,29
f 41:50 Gn 46:20; 48:5

years, and the seven good heads are seven years. The dreams mean the same thing. ²⁷ The seven thin, sickly cows that came up after them are seven years, and the seven worthless, scorched heads of grain are seven years of famine.ᵃ

²⁸ "It is just as I told Pharaoh: God has shown Pharaoh what he is about to do. ²⁹ Seven years of great abundance are coming throughout the land of Egypt. ³⁰ After them, seven years of famine will take place, and all the abundance in the land of Egypt will be forgotten. The famine will devastate the land.ᵇ ³¹ The abundance in the land will not be remembered because of the famine that follows it, for the famine will be very severe. ³² Since the dream was given twice to Pharaoh, it means that the matter has been determined by God, and he will carry it out soon.

³³ "So now, let Pharaoh look for a discerning and wise man and set him over the land of Egypt. ³⁴ Let Pharaoh do this: Let him appoint overseers over the land and take a fifth of the harvest of the land of Egypt during the seven years of abundance. ³⁵ Let them gather all the excess food during these good years that are coming. Under Pharaoh's authority, store the grain in the cities, so they may preserve it as food. ³⁶ The food will be a reserve for the land during the seven years of famine that will take place in the land of Egypt. Then the country will not be wiped out by the famine."

JOSEPH EXALTED

³⁷ The proposal pleased Pharaoh and all his servants, ³⁸ and he said to them, "Can we find anyone like this, a man who has God's spiritᴬ in him?"ᶜ ³⁹ So Pharaoh said to Joseph, "Since God has made all this known to you, there is no one as discerning and wise as you are. ⁴⁰ You will be over my house, and all my people will obey your commands.ᴮ,ᵈ Only I, as king,ᶜ will be greater than you." ⁴¹ Pharaoh also said to Joseph,

"See, I am placing you over all the land of Egypt." ⁴² Pharaoh removed his signet ring from his hand and put it on Joseph's hand, clothed him with fine linen garments, and placed a gold chain around his neck.ᵉ ⁴³ He had Joseph ride in his second chariot, and servants called out before him, "Make way!"ᴰ So he placed him over all the land of Egypt. ⁴⁴ Pharaoh said to Joseph, "I am Pharaoh and no one will be able to raise his hand or foot in all the land of Egypt without your permission." ⁴⁵ Pharaoh gave Joseph the name Zaphenath-paneah and gave him a wife, Asenath daughter of Potiphera, priest at On.ᴱ And Joseph went throughoutᶠ the land of Egypt.

JOSEPH'S ADMINISTRATION

⁴⁶ Joseph was thirty years old when he entered the service of Pharaoh king of Egypt. Joseph left Pharaoh's presence and traveled throughout the land of Egypt.

⁴⁷ During the seven years of abundance the land produced outstanding harvests. ⁴⁸ Joseph gathered all the excess food in the land of Egypt during the seven years and put it in the cities. He put the food in every city from the fields around it. ⁴⁹ So Joseph stored up grain in such abundance — like the sand of the sea — that he stopped measuring it because it was beyond measure.

⁵⁰ Two sons were born to Joseph before the years of famine arrived.ᶠ Asenath daughter of Potiphera, priest at On, bore them to him. ⁵¹ Joseph named the firstborn Manassehᴳ and said, "God has made me forget all my hardship and my whole family." ⁵² And the second son he named Ephraimᴴ and said, "God has made me fruitful in the land of my affliction."

⁵³ Then the seven years of abundance in the land of Egypt came to an end, ⁵⁴ and the seven years of famine began, just as Joseph had said. There was famine in every land, but in the whole land of Egypt there was food. ⁵⁵ When the whole land of Egypt

---

ᴬ 41:38 Or *the spirit of the gods*, or *a god's spirit*   ᴮ 41:40 Lit *will kiss your mouth*   ᶜ 41:40 Lit *Only the throne I*   ᴰ 41:43 Or *"Kneel!"*
ᴱ 41:45 Or *Heliopolis*, also in v. 50   ᶠ 41:45 Or *Joseph gained authority over*   ᴳ 41:51 In Hb, the name *Manasseh* sounds like the verb "forget."
ᴴ 41:52 In Hb, the name *Ephraim* sounds like the word for "fruitful."

41:32 Joseph pointed out a principle that is often presented throughout Scripture— when God intends to do something, he will confirm his Word with two or three witnesses. In this case, **since the dream was given twice to Pharaoh,** Joseph knew **the matter had been determined.**
41:33-36 Joseph went above the call of duty to advise Pharaoh on how to handle the impending crisis.

41:37-45 Pharaoh immediately recognized that Joseph was the man for the job of preparing for the agricultural crisis. Not only did he have wisdom to see things spiritually, but Joseph could also make right conclusions based on that wisdom (41:39). He gave Joseph power, gifts, and even **a wife** (41:45). In a single day, Joseph rose from the pit to the palace. **41:50-52** Joseph hadn't seen his family for thirteen years, but he did not forget his heritage.

Joseph gave his sons Hebrew names. The first, **Manasseh,** sounds like the Hebrew verb for "forget," because God made Joseph **forget** his **hardship** (41:51). The second, **Ephraim,** sounds like the word "fruitful," because God made him **fruitful in the land** of his **affliction** (41:52). Indeed Joseph could see that the loving arm of God had been guiding him.
41:53-57 Seven years of famine began, just as Joseph had said (41:54). In Egypt alone there

was stricken with famine, the people cried out to Pharaoh for food. Pharaoh told all Egypt, "Go to Joseph and do whatever he tells you." **56** Now the famine had spread across the whole region, so Joseph opened all the storehouses and sold grain to the Egyptians, for the famine was severe in the land of Egypt. **57** Every land came to Joseph in Egypt to buy grain, for the famine was severe in every land.[a]

JOSEPH'S BROTHERS IN EGYPT

42 When Jacob learned that there was grain in Egypt,[b] he said to his sons, "Why do you keep looking at each other? **2** Listen," he went on, "I have heard there is grain in Egypt. Go down there and buy some for us so that we will live and not die."[c] **3** So ten of Joseph's brothers went down to buy grain from Egypt. **4** But Jacob did not send Joseph's brother Benjamin with his brothers, for he thought, "Something might happen to him."

5 The sons of Israel were among those who came to buy grain, for the famine was in the land of Canaan. **6** Joseph was in charge of the country; he sold grain to all its people. His brothers came and bowed down before him with their faces to the ground.[d] **7** When Joseph saw his brothers, he recognized them, but he treated them like strangers and spoke harshly to them.

"Where do you come from?" he asked.

"From the land of Canaan to buy food," they replied.

8 Although Joseph recognized his brothers, they did not recognize him. **9** Joseph remembered his dreams about them[e] and said to them, "You are spies. You have come to see the weakness[A] of the land."

10 "No, my lord. Your servants have come to buy food," they said. **11** "We are all sons of one man. We are honest; your servants are not spies."

12 "No," he said to them. "You have come to see the weakness of the land."

13 But they replied, "We, your servants, were twelve brothers, the sons of one man in the land of Canaan. The youngest is now[B] with our father, and one is no longer living."

14 Then Joseph said to them, "I have spoken:[c] 'You are spies!' **15** This is how you will be tested: As surely as Pharaoh lives, you will not leave this place unless your youngest brother comes here. **16** Send one from among you to get your brother. The rest of you will be imprisoned so that your words can be tested to see if they are true. If they are not, then as surely as Pharaoh lives, you are spies!" **17** So Joseph imprisoned them together for three days.

18 On the third day Joseph said to them, "I fear God[f] — do this and you will live. **19** If you are honest, let one of you[D] be confined to the guardhouse, while the rest of you go and take grain to relieve the hunger of your households. **20** Bring your youngest brother to me so that your words can be confirmed; then you won't die." And they consented to this.

21 Then they said to each other, "Obviously, we are being punished for what we did to our brother. We saw his deep distress when he pleaded with us, but we would not listen. That is why this trouble has come to us."[g]

22 But Reuben replied: "Didn't I tell you not to harm the boy?[h] But you wouldn't listen. Now we must account for his blood!"[E]

23 They did not realize that Joseph understood them, since there was an interpreter between them. **24** He turned away from them and wept. When he turned back and spoke to them, he took Simeon from them and had him bound before their eyes. **25** Joseph then gave orders to fill their containers with grain, return each

[a] 41:57 Gn 12:10
[b] 42:1 Ac 7:12
[c] 42:2 Gn 43:8
[d] 42:6 Gn 37:7-10; 41:43; Is 60:14
[e] 42:9 Gn 37:5-11
[f] 42:18 Gn 39:9; Lv 25:43; Neh 5:15
[g] 42:21 Gn 37:26-28
[h] 42:22 Gn 37:22

[A] **42:9** Lit *nakedness*, also in v. 12   [B] **42:13** Or *today*, also in v. 32   [C] **42:14** Lit *"That which I spoke to you saying:*   [D] **42:19** Lit *your brothers*   [E] **42:22** Lit *Even his blood is being sought!"*

---

was food, so Egypt became the breadbasket of the world.

42:1-5 Jacob sent his sons to Egypt so that they would **not die** of famine (42:2). Jacob, however, **did not send Joseph's brother Benjamin** (42:4) because he didn't trust the brothers to protect him. He had already lost Joseph under suspicious circumstances, and he refused to lose the other son of Rachel.

42:6-17 When Joseph's brothers arrived in Egypt **and bowed down before him** (42:6), he immediately recognized them, but **they did not recognize him** (42:8). Joseph also saw in their

actions the fulfillment of his **dreams** (42:9). After twenty years, Joseph had finally been exalted over all of his brothers. To test them and draw out more information, Joseph accused them (42:9). God was working through Joseph to bring the brothers to a place of repentance, which would ultimately lead to restoration.

42:18-24 After letting his brothers languish in prison for three days, Joseph kept Simeon in custody and sent the others home, charging them to return with Benjamin (42:19-20, 24). At this point, the brothers began to realize their guilt. **Trouble has come to us,** they

said to one another. **We saw [Joseph's] deep distress . . . , but we would not listen** (42:21). They had ignored Joseph's cry for help, and they saw that they were reaping a similar response during *their* cry for help against unjust accusations.

42:25-28 Joseph sent his brothers back to Canaan **with grain,** but he also secretly put **each man's silver** back in **his sack** (42:25). When the brothers noticed their money had been returned, **their hearts sank,** because now it *really* looked like they were spies up to no good (42:28).

a 42:38 Gn 37:33-34; 42:13; 44:27-28

b Gn 44:29
c 43:1 Gn 12:10; 41:56-57; 47:20
d 43:5 Gn 42:18-20; 44:23
e 43:9 Gn 42:37; 44:32
f 43:11 Gn 37:25; Jr 8:22; Ezk 27:17

man's silver to his sack, and give them provisions for their journey. This order was carried out. **26** They loaded the grain on their donkeys and left there.

THE BROTHERS RETURN HOME

27 At the place where they lodged for the night, one of them opened his sack to get feed for his donkey, and he saw his silver there at the top of his bag. **28** He said to his brothers, "My silver has been returned! It's here in my bag." Their hearts sank. Trembling, they turned to one another and said, "What is this that God has done to us?"

29 When they reached their father Jacob in the land of Canaan, they told him all that had happened to them: **30** "The man who is the lord of the country spoke harshly to us and accused us of spying on the country. **31** But we told him: We are honest and not spies. **32** We were twelve brothers, sons of the same^ father. One is no longer living, and the youngest is now with our father in the land of Canaan. **33** The man who is the lord of the country said to us, 'This is how I will know if you are honest: Leave one brother with me, take food to relieve the hunger of your households, and go. **34** Bring back your youngest brother to me, and I will know that you are not spies but honest men. I will then give your brother back to you, and you can trade in the country.' "

35 As they began emptying their sacks, there in each man's sack was his bag of silver! When they and their father saw their bags of silver, they were afraid. **36** Their father Jacob said to them, "It's me that you make childless. Joseph is gone, and Simeon is gone. Now you want to take Benjamin. Everything happens to me!" **37** Then Reuben said to his father, "You can kill my two sons if I don't bring him back to you. Put him in my care,^B and I will return him to you." **38** But Jacob answered, "My son will not go down with you, for his brother is dead and he alone is left.^a If anything happens

to him on your journey, you will bring my gray hairs down to Sheol in sorrow."^b

DECISION TO RETURN TO EGYPT

43 Now the famine in the land was severe.^c **2** When they had used up the grain they had brought back from Egypt, their father said to them, "Go back and buy us a little food."

3 But Judah said to him, "The man specifically warned us: 'You will not see me again unless your brother is with you.' **4** If you will send our brother with us, we will go down and buy food for you. **5** But if you will not send him, we will not go, for the man said to us, 'You will not see me again unless your brother is with you.'"^d

6 "Why have you caused me so much trouble?" Israel asked. "Why did you tell the man that you had another brother?"

7 They answered, "The man kept asking about us and our family: 'Is your father still alive? Do you have another brother?' And we answered him accordingly. How could we know that he would say, 'Bring your brother here'?"

8 Then Judah said to his father Israel, "Send the boy with me. We will be on our way so that we may live and not die — neither we, nor you, nor our dependents. **9** I will be responsible for him. You can hold me personally accountable!^c If I do not bring him back to you and set him before you, I will be guilty before you forever.^e **10** If we had not delayed, we could have come back twice by now."

11 Then their father Israel said to them, "If it must be so, then do this: Put some of the best products of the land in your packs and take them down to the man as a gift — a little balsam and a little honey, aromatic gum and resin, pistachios and almonds.^f **12** Take twice as much silver with you. Return the silver that was returned to you in the top of your bags. Perhaps it was a mistake. **13** Take your brother also, and go back at once to the man. **14** May God Almighty cause the man to be merciful to you so that he will release your other brother

^A 42:32 Lit *of our*   ^B 42:37 Lit *hand*   ^C 43:9 Lit *can seek him from my hand*

42:29-38 Jacob's sons relayed **all that had happened** (42:29). When they mentioned the demand of **the lord of the country** that they must **bring back** their **youngest brother**, however, Jacob grew stubborn (42:33-36). He said, **Joseph is gone, and Simeon is gone** (42:36). With two sons lost, Jacob wouldn't risk something happening to Benjamin.

43:8-9 **Judah** stepped up to take responsibility for Benjamin: **If I do not bring him back … I will be guilty before you forever** (43:9). Interestingly, Judah was the man who spearheaded the conspiracy to sell Joseph into slavery in the first place. But God had been softening his heart over the last twenty years, shaping him into the sort of vessel that he could use.

43:10-14 Jacob reluctantly agreed to send his sons, Benjamin in tow, back to Egypt. He suggested that they take valuable local gifts to curry favor with Egypt's demanding leader. He also sent **twice as much silver** as before (43:12), thus replacing the returned silver that Joseph could have claimed was stolen and providing money for more grain.

and Benjamin to you. As for me, if I am deprived of my sons, then I am deprived."[a]

THE RETURN TO EGYPT

15 The men took this gift, double the amount of silver, and Benjamin. They immediately went down to Egypt and stood before Joseph.

16 When Joseph saw Benjamin with them, he said to his steward, "Take the men to my house. Slaughter an animal and prepare it, for they will eat with me at noon." **17** The man did as Joseph had said and brought them to Joseph's house.

18 But the men were afraid because they were taken to Joseph's house. They said, "We have been brought here because of the silver that was returned in our bags the first time. They intend to overpower us, seize us, make us slaves, and take our donkeys." **19** So they approached Joseph's steward[A] and spoke to him at the doorway of the house.

20 They said, "My lord, we really did come down here the first time only to buy food. **21** When we came to the place where we lodged for the night and opened our bags of grain, each one's silver was at the top of his bag![b] It was the full amount of our silver, and we have brought it back with us. **22** We have brought additional silver with us to buy food. We don't know who put our silver in the bags."

23 Then the steward said, "May you be well. Don't be afraid. Your God and the God of your father must have put treasure in your bags. I received your silver." Then he brought Simeon out to them. **24** The steward brought the men into Joseph's house, gave them water to wash their feet,[c] and got feed for their donkeys. **25** Since the men had heard that they were going to eat a meal there, they prepared their gift for Joseph's arrival at noon. **26** When Joseph came home, they brought him the gift they had carried into the house, and they bowed to the ground before him.

27 He asked if they were well, and he said, "How is your elderly father that you told me about? Is he still alive?"

28 They answered, "Your servant our father is well. He is still alive." And they knelt low and paid homage to him.

29 When he looked up and saw his brother Benjamin, his mother's son, he asked, "Is this your youngest brother that you told me about?" Then he said, "May God be gracious to you, my son." **30** Joseph hurried out because he was overcome with emotion for his brother, and he was about to weep. He went into an inner room and wept there. **31** Then he washed his face and came out. Regaining his composure,[d] he said, "Serve the meal."

32 They served him by himself, his brothers by themselves, and the Egyptians who were eating with him by themselves, because Egyptians could not eat with Hebrews, since that is detestable to them.[e] **33** They were seated before him in order by age, from the firstborn to the youngest. The men looked at each other in astonishment. **34** Portions were served to them from Joseph's table, and Benjamin's portion was five times larger than any of theirs.[f] They drank and became drunk with Joseph.

JOSEPH'S FINAL TEST

44 Joseph commanded his steward, "Fill the men's bags with as much food as they can carry, and put each one's silver at the top of his bag.[g] **2** Put my cup, the silver one, at the top of the youngest one's bag, along with the silver for his grain." So he did as Joseph told him.

3 At morning light, the men were sent off with their donkeys. **4** They had not gone very far from the city when Joseph said to his steward, "Get up. Pursue the men, and when you overtake them, say to them, 'Why have you repaid evil for good? **5** Isn't this the cup that my master drinks from and uses for divination?[h] What you have done is wrong!'"

6 When he overtook them, he said these words to them. **7** They said to him, "Why does my lord say these things? Your servants could not possibly do such a thing. **8** We even brought back to you

Right column marginal references:

[a] 43:14 Gn 42:36
[b] 43:21 Gn 42:27,35
[c] 43:24 Gn 18:4; 19:2; 24:32

[d] 43:31 Gn 45:1
[e] 43:32 Gn 46:34; Ex 8:26
[f] 43:34 Gn 35:24; 45:22
[g] 44:1 Gn 42:25
[h] 44:5 Gn 30:27; 44:15; Lv 19:26; Dt 18:10-14

[A] **43:19** Lit *approached the one who was over the house*

43:15-23 The brothers attempted to clear up the misunderstanding about the money (43:19-22). But the steward replied, **Your God . . . must have put treasure in your bags** (43:23). This suggests that Joseph's faith must have spread to his staff, because here was an Egyptian servant invoking the name of the God of the Hebrews!

43:32-34 It must have been a shock to Joseph's brothers to see that in the seating arrangements, **they were seated . . . in order by age** (43:33). How could this Egyptian ruler have known their birth order? **44:1-12** Joseph arranged for one final test. He had his steward put his **cup . . . at the top of the youngest one's bag** (44:2). He was

framing Benjamin for theft to see whether his brothers would defend him. The steward, following Joseph's orders, overtook his brothers and charged them with stealing (44:5). The brothers denied it, but **the cup was found** (44:12). The penalty for such an act would have been Benjamin becoming Joseph's **slave** (44:10).

a 44:9 Gn 31:32
b 44:13 Gn 37:29
c 44:14 Gn 37:7-10; 42:6;
43:26-28
d 44:18 Gn 37:7-8;
41:40-44
e 44:20 Gn 37:3; 43:8;
44:30
f 44:21 Gn 42:15,20
g 44:23 Gn 43:3,5
h 44:25 Gn 43:2
i 44:28 Gn 37:31-35
j 44:29 Gn 42:38
k 44:32 Gn 43:9
l 45:1 Ac 7:13

from the land of Canaan the silver we found at the top of our bags. How could we steal silver or gold from your master's house? **9** If it is found with one of us, your servants, he must die, and the rest of us will become my lord's slaves."*a*

10 The steward replied, "What you have said is right, but only the one who is found to have it will be my slave, and the rest of you will be blameless."

11 So each one quickly lowered his sack to the ground and opened it. **12** The steward searched, beginning with the oldest and ending with the youngest, and the cup was found in Benjamin's sack. **13** Then they tore their clothes,*b* and each one loaded his donkey and returned to the city.

14 When Judah and his brothers reached Joseph's house, he was still there. They fell to the ground before him.*c* **15** "What is this you have done?" Joseph said to them. "Didn't you know that a man like me could uncover the truth by divination?"

16 "What can we say to my lord?" Judah replied. "How can we plead? How can we justify ourselves? God has exposed your servants' iniquity. We are now my lord's slaves — both we and the one in whose possession the cup was found."

17 Then Joseph said, "I swear that I will not do this. The man in whose possession the cup was found will be my slave. The rest of you can go in peace to your father."

JUDAH'S PLEA FOR BENJAMIN

18 But Judah approached him and said, "My lord, please let your servant speak personally to my lord.*A* Do not be angry with your servant, for you are like Pharaoh.*d* **19** My lord asked his servants, 'Do you have a father or a brother?' **20** and we answered my lord, 'We have an elderly father and a younger brother, the child of his old age.*e* The boy's brother is dead. He is the only one of his mother's sons left, and his father loves him.' **21** Then you said to your servants, 'Bring him to me so that I can see

him.'*f* **22** But we said to my lord, 'The boy cannot leave his father. If he were to leave, his father would die.' **23** Then you said to your servants, 'If your younger brother does not come down with you, you will not see me again.'*g*

24 "This is what happened when we went back to your servant my father: We reported to him the words of my lord. **25** But our father said, 'Go again, and buy us a little food.'*h* **26** We told him, 'We cannot go down unless our younger brother goes with us. If our younger brother isn't with us, we cannot see the man.' **27** Your servant my father said to us, 'You know that my wife bore me two sons. **28** One is gone from me — I said he must have been torn to pieces — and I have never seen him again.'*i* **29** If you also take this one from me and anything happens to him, you will bring my gray hairs down to Sheol in sorrow.'*j*

30 "So if I come to your servant my father and the boy is not with us — his life is wrapped up with the boy's life — **31** when he sees that the boy is not with us, he will die. Then your servants will have brought the gray hairs of your servant our father down to Sheol in sorrow. **32** Your servant became accountable to my father for the boy, saying, 'If I do not return him to you, I will always bear the guilt for sinning against you, my father.'*k* **33** Now please let your servant remain here as my lord's slave, in place of the boy. Let him go back with his brothers. **34** For how can I go back to my father without the boy? I could not bear to see the grief that would overwhelm my father."

JOSEPH REVEALS HIS IDENTITY

45 Joseph could no longer keep his composure in front of all his attendants,*B* so he called out, "Send everyone away from me!" No one was with him when he revealed his identity to his brothers.*l* **2** But he wept so loudly that the Egyptians heard it, and also Pharaoh's household heard it. **3** Joseph said to his

---

A **44:18** Lit *speak a word in my lord's ears*   *B* **45:1** Lit *all those standing about him*

44:13-16 When Benjamin was exposed as the thief, the brothers **tore their clothes** (44:13). Not only did they grieve, but they refused to abandon Benjamin to his plight. **Each one loaded his donkey and returned to the city** (44:13), signaling to their youngest sibling that they were in the mess together. They offered themselves as willing **slaves** in solidarity (44:16).

44:17-34 **Judah** once again moved to the forefront. He gave an impassioned plea for Joseph to show mercy, both for Benjamin's sake and for the sake of his **father** Jacob (44:34). The pinnacle of Judah's appeal—the proof that he had truly experienced a change of heart—was the staggering offer he made to **remain . . . as [his] lord's slave, in place of the boy** (44:33). The character transformation was

complete, and God was ready to carry out the next step in his plan.

45:1-3 Alone with his brothers, Joseph revealed his identity, which could have been confirmed by his circumcision. The brothers sat in stunned silence, **terrified in his presence** (45:3). Joseph, the brother they had intended to kill, was now standing before them with all the power in the world. And

brothers, "I am Joseph! Is my father still living?" But they could not answer him because they were terrified in his presence.

4 Then Joseph said to his brothers, "Please, come near me," and they came near. "I am Joseph, your brother," he said, "the one you sold into Egypt.[a] **5** And now don't be grieved or angry with yourselves for selling me here, because God sent me ahead of you to preserve life.[b] **6** For the famine has been in the land these two years, and there will be five more years without plowing or harvesting. **7** God sent me ahead of you to establish you as a remnant within the land and to keep you alive by a great deliverance.[A] **8** Therefore it was not you who sent me here, but God. He has made me a father to Pharaoh, lord of his entire household, and ruler over all the land of Egypt.

9 "Return quickly to my father and say to him, 'This is what your son Joseph says: "God has made me lord of all Egypt. Come down to me without delay. **10** You can settle in the land of Goshen[c] and be near me — you, your children, and your grandchildren, your flocks, your herds, and all you have. **11** There I will sustain you, for there will be five more years of famine. Otherwise, you, your household, and everything you have will become destitute." '[d] **12** Look! Your eyes and the eyes of my brother Benjamin can see that I'm[B] the one speaking to you. **13** Tell my father about all my glory in Egypt and about all you have seen. And bring my father here quickly." '[e]

14 Then Joseph threw his arms around his brother Benjamin and wept, and Benjamin wept on his shoulder. **15** Joseph kissed each of his brothers as he wept,[c] and afterward his brothers talked with him.

THE RETURN FOR JACOB

16 When the news reached Pharaoh's palace, "Joseph's brothers have come," Pharaoh and his servants were pleased. **17** Pharaoh said to Joseph, "Tell your brothers, 'Do this: Load your animals and go on back to the land of Canaan. **18** Get your father and your families, and come back to me. I will give you the best of the land of Egypt, and you can eat from the richness of the land.' **19** You are also commanded to tell them, 'Do this: Take wagons from the land of Egypt for your dependents and your wives and bring your father here.[f] **20** Do not be concerned about your belongings, for the best of all the land of Egypt is yours.' "[g]

21 The sons of Israel did this. Joseph gave them wagons as Pharaoh had commanded, and he gave them provisions for the journey. **22** He gave each of the brothers changes of clothes,[h] but he gave Benjamin three hundred pieces of silver and five changes of clothes.[i] **23** He sent his father the following: ten donkeys carrying the best products of Egypt and ten female donkeys carrying grain, food, and provisions for his father on the journey. **24** So Joseph sent his brothers on their way, and as they were leaving, he said to them, "Don't argue[D] on the way."

25 So they went up from Egypt and came to their father Jacob in the land of Canaan. **26** They said, "Joseph is still alive, and he is ruler over all the land of Egypt!" Jacob was stunned,[E] for he did not believe them. **27** But when they told Jacob all that Joseph had said to them, and when he saw the wagons that Joseph had sent to transport him, the spirit of their father Jacob revived.

[a] 45:4 Gn 37:18-36
[b] 45:5 Gn 45:7-8; 50:20; Ps 105:17
[c] 45:10 Gn 46:34; 47:1, 4,6,11,27; 50:8; Ex 8:22; Jos 10:41
[d] 45:11 Gn 47:12; 50:21
[e] 45:13 Ac 7:14
[f] 45:19 Gn 46:5
[g] 45:20 Dt 32:9-14
[h] 45:22 2Kg 5:5
[i] Gn 43:34

[A] 45:7 Or *keep alive for you many survivors*   [B] 45:12 Lit *that my mouth is*   [C] 45:15 Lit *brothers, and he wept over them*   [D] 45:24 Or *be anxious*   [E] 45:26 Lit *Jacob's heart was numb*

to their surprise, he was extending not vengeance but mercy.

45:4-8 Joseph was able to see the hand of God in that evil thing the brothers had done. **God sent me ahead of you to preserve life** (45:5). The terrible string of events had all led Joseph to his position of privilege just in time to save the lives of tens of thousands, and he had noticed the connection (45:7-8). Joseph's life demonstrated the truth that Paul declared, "All things work together for the good of those who love God, who are called according to his purpose" (Rom 8:28).

45:9-13 Joseph told his brothers to **return quickly** to their **father** and give him the news (45:9). He invited Jacob to **settle in the land**

of Goshen with all of his **children** and everything else he owned (45:10). Thus Jacob and also Joseph's brothers came under Joseph's authority and care, just as God had long ago promised Joseph that they would.

45:16-23 The reunion was so exciting that even **Pharaoh** wanted to get involved. Out of gratitude to Joseph, he offered his entire family **the best of the land of Egypt** and **the richness of the land** (45:18). He also arranged for their transportation, so that the large caravan could make the long journey with all of their belongings (45:19-21). Jacob's family, seemingly on the cusp of starvation, had become fabulously wealthy in a moment.

45:24 Don't argue on the way. Joseph encouraged his brothers to move forward in their newfound unity rather than peering backward into the sinful disputes that had fractured their lives. God speaks to us a bold word of encouragement through this story: you are all fellow travelers and fellow sinners; don't argue on the way through life.

45:25-28 Jacob **did not believe** the report at first (45:26). But eventually the testimony of his sons, combined with the phenomenal gifts sent from Egypt, convinced him. And his **spirit . . . revived** (45:27). God's plan, when hidden from our eyes, can often lead us to despair. But if we can hold out until God is prepared to reveal what he is doing, our spirits will be revived.

a 46:1 Gn 21:14; 28:10; Jos 15:28; Jdg 20:1; 2Sm 24:7; 1Kg 19:3
b 46:2 Gn 15:1; Jb 33:14-15
c 46:3 Gn 12:2; 15:13-14; 35:11; Ex 1:7,9; Dt 26:5
d 46:4 Gn 15:16; 28:15; 48:21; 50:24; Ex 3:8
e Gn 50:1
f 46:5 Gn 45:19,21
g 46:6 Dt 26:5; Jos 24:4; Ps 105:23; Is 52:4; Ac 7:15
h 46:8-27 Ex 1:1-5; Nm 26:4-5
i 46:9 Ex 6:14
j 46:10 Ex 6:15
k 46:11 Ex 6:16; 1Ch 6:16
l 46:12 Gn 38:29; 1Ch 2:5
m 46:13 1Ch 7:1
n 46:17 1Ch 7:30-31
o 46:21 Nm 26:38-40; 1Ch 7:6-12; 8:1
p 46:24 1Ch 7:13
q 46:25 Gn 29:29; 30:5-8
r 46:27 Ex 1:5; Dt 10:22; Ac 7:14
s 46:28 Gn 45:10

28 Then Israel said, "Enough! My son Joseph is still alive. I will go to see him before I die."

JACOB LEAVES FOR EGYPT

46 Israel set out with all that he had and came to Beer-sheba,*a* and he offered sacrifices to the God of his father Isaac. 2 That night God spoke to Israel in a vision:*b* "Jacob, Jacob!" he said.

And Jacob replied, "Here I am."

3 God said, "I am God, the God of your father. Do not be afraid to go down to Egypt, for I will make you into a great nation there.*c* 4 I will go down with you to Egypt, and I will also bring you back.*d* Joseph will close your eyes when you die."*A,e*

5 Jacob left Beer-sheba. The sons of Israel took their father Jacob in the wagons Pharaoh had sent to carry him,*f* along with their dependents and their wives. 6 They also took their cattle and possessions they had acquired in the land of Canaan. Then Jacob and all his offspring with him came to Egypt.*g* 7 His sons and grandsons, his daughters and granddaughters, indeed all his offspring, he brought with him to Egypt.

JACOB'S FAMILY

8 These are the names of the sons of Israel who came to Egypt*h* — Jacob and his sons:
Jacob's firstborn: Reuben.
9 Reuben's sons:*i* Hanoch, Pallu, Hezron, and Carmi.
10 Simeon's sons:*j* Jemuel, Jamin, Ohad, Jachin, Zohar, and Shaul, the son of a Canaanite woman.
11 Levi's sons:*k* Gershon, Kohath, and Merari.
12 Judah's sons: Er, Onan, Shelah, Perez, and Zerah; but Er and Onan died in the land of Canaan.
The sons*l* of Perez were Hezron and Hamul.
13 Issachar's sons:*m* Tola, Puvah,*B* Jashub,*c* and Shimron.
14 Zebulun's sons: Sered, Elon, and Jahleel.
15 These were Leah's sons born to Jacob in Paddan-aram,

as well as his daughter Dinah. The total number of persons:*D* thirty-three.
16 Gad's sons: Ziphion, Haggi, Shuni, Ezbon, Eri, Arodi, and Areli.
17 Asher's sons:*n* Imnah, Ishvah, Ishvi, Beriah, and their sister Serah. Beriah's sons were Heber and Malchiel.
18 These were the sons of Zilpah — whom Laban gave to his daughter Leah — that she bore to Jacob: sixteen persons.
19 The sons of Jacob's wife Rachel: Joseph and Benjamin.
20 Manasseh and Ephraim were born to Joseph in the land of Egypt. They were born to him by Asenath daughter of Potiphera, a priest at On.*E*
21 Benjamin's sons:*o* Bela, Becher, Ashbel, Gera, Naaman, Ehi, Rosh, Muppim, Huppim, and Ard.
22 These were Rachel's sons who were born to Jacob: fourteen persons.
23 Dan's son:*F* Hushim.
24 Naphtali's sons:*p* Jahzeel, Guni, Jezer, and Shillem.
25 These were the sons of Bilhah, whom Laban gave to his daughter Rachel.*q* She bore to Jacob: seven persons.
26 The total number of persons belonging to Jacob — his direct descendants,*G* not including the wives of Jacob's sons — who came to Egypt: sixty-six.
27 And Joseph's sons who were born to him in Egypt: two persons. All those of Jacob's household who came to Egypt: seventy*H* persons.*r*

JACOB ARRIVES IN EGYPT

28 Now Jacob had sent Judah ahead of him to Joseph to prepare for his arrival*I* at Goshen.*s* When they came to the land of Goshen, 29 Joseph hitched the horses to his chariot and went up to Goshen to meet his

---

A 46:4 Lit *will put his hand on your eyes*   *B* 46:13 Sam, Syr read *Puah* ; 1Ch 7:1   *C* 46:13 Sam, LXX; MT reads *Iob*   *D* 46:15 Lit *All persons his sons and his daughters:*   *E* 46:20 Or *Heliopolis*   *F* 46:23 Alt Hb tradition reads *sons:*   *G* 46:26 Lit *Jacob who came out from his loins*   *H* 46:27 LXX reads *75* ; Ac 7:14   *I* 46:28 Lit *to give directions before him*

46:1-7 Would God lead his people back to Canaan if they left, en masse, for Egypt? God quieted any anxiety Jacob might have had on that point through a vision. The journey to Egypt would fulfill part of his promise; he would make Jacob

into a great nation there (46:3). At the appointed time, God would bring them back (46:4). Jacob was able to make the trek with hope.

46:8-27 Jacob's entire family numbered seventy persons (46:27). God's promise to

make Abraham's descendants as numerous as the stars in the sky was already on its way to fruition.

father Israel. Joseph presented himself to him, threw his arms around him, and wept for a long time.[a]

30 Then Israel said to Joseph, "I'm ready to die now because I have seen your face and you are still alive!"

31 Joseph said to his brothers and to his father's family, "I will go up and inform Pharaoh, telling him, 'My brothers and my father's family, who were in the land of Canaan, have come to me.[b] **32** The men are shepherds; they also raise livestock. They have brought their flocks and herds and all that they have.' **33** When Pharaoh addresses you and asks, 'What is your occupation?' **34** you are to say, 'Your servants, both we and our fathers, have raised livestock[A] from our youth until now.' Then you will be allowed to settle in the land of Goshen, since all shepherds are detestable to Egyptians."[c]

PHARAOH WELCOMES JACOB

47 So Joseph went and informed Pharaoh: "My father and my brothers, with their flocks and herds and all that they own, have come from the land of Canaan and are now in the land of Goshen."[d]

2 He took five of his brothers and presented them to Pharaoh.[e] **3** And Pharaoh asked his brothers, "What is your occupation?"

They said to Pharaoh, "Your servants, both we and our fathers, are shepherds."[f] **4** And they said to Pharaoh, "We have come to stay in the land for a while because there is no grazing land for your servants' sheep, since the famine in the land of Canaan has been severe.[g] So now, please let your servants settle in the land of Goshen."

5 Then Pharaoh said to Joseph, "Now that your father and brothers have come to you, **6** the land of Egypt is open before you; settle your father and brothers in the best part of the land.[h] They can live in the land of Goshen. If you know of any capable men among them, put them in charge of my livestock."[i]

7 Joseph then brought his father Jacob and presented him to Pharaoh, and Jacob blessed Pharaoh. **8** Pharaoh said to Jacob, "How many years have you lived?"

9 Jacob said to Pharaoh, "My pilgrimage[j] has lasted 130 years. My years have been few and hard,[k] and they have not reached the years of my fathers during their pilgrimages."[l] **10** So Jacob blessed Pharaoh and departed from Pharaoh's presence.

11 Then Joseph settled his father and brothers in the land of Egypt and gave them property in the best part of the land, the land of Rameses,[m] as Pharaoh had commanded. **12** And Joseph provided his father, his brothers, and all his father's family with food for their dependents.[n]

THE LAND BECOMES PHARAOH'S

13 But there was no food in the entire region, for the famine was very severe. The land of Egypt and the land of Canaan were exhausted by the famine. **14** Joseph collected all the silver to be found in the land of Egypt and the land of Canaan in exchange for the grain they were purchasing, and he brought the silver to Pharaoh's palace.[o] **15** When the silver from the land of Egypt and the land of Canaan was gone, all the Egyptians came to Joseph and said, "Give us food. Why should we die here in front of you? The silver is gone!"

16 But Joseph said, "Give me your livestock. Since the silver is gone, I will give you food in exchange for your livestock." **17** So they brought their livestock to Joseph, and he gave them food in exchange for the horses, the flocks of sheep, the herds of cattle, and the donkeys. That year he provided them with food in exchange for all their livestock.

18 When that year was over, they came the next year and said to him, "We cannot hide from our lord that the silver is gone and that all our livestock belongs to our lord. There is nothing left for our lord except our bodies and our land. **19** Why should we die here in front of you — both us and our land? Buy us and our land in exchange for food. Then we with our land will become Pharaoh's slaves. Give us seed so that we can live and not die, and so that the land won't become desolate."

20 In this way, Joseph acquired all the land in Egypt for Pharaoh, because every

[a] 46:29 Gn 45:14
[b] 46:31 Gn 47:1
[c] 46:34 Gn 43:32; Ex 8:26
[d] 47:1 Gn 45:10; 46:28
[e] 47:2 Ac 7:13
[f] 47:3 Gn 46:32-34
[g] 47:4 Gn 15:13; Dt 26:5
[h] 47:6 Gn 45:10,18; 47:11
[i] Ex 18:21,25; 1Kg 11:28; Pr 22:29
[j] 47:9 1Ch 29:15; Ps 39:12; 119:19,54; Heb 11:9,13
[k] Jb 14:1; Ps 39:4-5; Jms 4:14
[l] Gn 11:32; 25:7; 35:28 Ex 1:11; 12:37
[m] 47:11 Gn 45:10; Ex 1:11; 12:37
[n] 47:12 Gn 45:11; 50:21
[o] 47:14 Gn 41:56

[A] **46:34** Lit *fathers, are men of livestock*

46:31-34 Joseph gave his family a brief lesson in cross-cultural communication, helping them know how to interact with Pharaoh. Specifically, he encouraged them to emphasize not only that they were shepherds—**since all shepherds are detestable to Egyptians**—but also

that they had **raised livestock from** their **youth** (46:34). Joseph hoped to acquire for his family the land near Goshen, which was suitable for raising sheep and cattle.

47:7-12 Jacob's brief audience with Pharaoh hints at the fulfillment of another aspect of

God's covenant with Abraham. Jacob's family had already settled in the land. They had multiplied phenomenally. Here **Jacob blessed Pharaoh** as a firstfruits fulfillment of God's intention to bless all the nations of the world (47:7) through this line.

[a] **47:24** Gn 41:34
[b] **47:27** Gn 17:6; 26:4; 35:11; Ex 1:7; Dt 26:5; Ac 7:17
[c] **47:29** Dt 31:14; 1Kg 2:1
[d] Gn 24:2
[e] Gn 24:49
[f] **47:30** Gn 23:17-20; 25:9-10; 35:29; 49:29-32; 50:5,13; Ac 7:15-16
[g] **47:31** Gn 48:2; 1Kg 1:47; Heb 11:21
[h] **48:3** Gn 17:1
[i] Gn 28:13,19; 35:6,9
[j] **48:4** Gn 17:8
[k] Gn 35:9-12
[l] **48:5** Gn 41:50-52; 46:20
[m] Jos 13:7; 14:4; 17:17
[n] **48:7** Gn 35:9-19
[o] **48:9** Gn 27:4; 49:25-26; Heb 11:21
[p] **48:10** Gn 27:1
[q] Gn 27:27
[r] **48:12** Gn 18:2; 24:52; 33:3; 42:6; 43:26; Ex 34:8

Egyptian sold his field since the famine was so severe for them. The land became Pharaoh's, 21 and Joseph moved the people to the cities[A] from one end of Egypt to the other. 22 The only land he did not acquire belonged to the priests, for they had an allowance from Pharaoh. They ate from their allowance that Pharaoh gave them; therefore they did not sell their land.

23 Joseph said to the people, "Understand today that I have acquired you and your land for Pharaoh. Here is seed for you. Sow it in the land. 24 At harvest, you are to give a fifth of it to Pharaoh,[a] and four-fifths will be yours as seed for the field and as food for yourselves, your households, and your dependents."

25 "You have saved our lives," they said. "We have found favor with our lord and will be Pharaoh's slaves." 26 So Joseph made it a law, still in effect today in the land of Egypt, that a fifth of the produce belongs to Pharaoh. Only the priests' land does not belong to Pharaoh.

ISRAEL SETTLES IN GOSHEN

27 Israel settled in the land of Egypt, in the region of Goshen. They acquired property in it and became fruitful and very numerous.[b] 28 Now Jacob lived in the land of Egypt 17 years, and his life span was 147 years. 29 When the time approached for him to die,[c] he called his son Joseph and said to him, "If I have found favor with you, put your hand under my thigh[d] and promise me that you will deal with me in kindness and faithfulness.[e] Do not bury me in Egypt. 30 When I rest with my fathers, carry me away from Egypt and bury me in their burial place."[f]

Joseph answered, "I will do what you have asked."

31 And Jacob said, "Swear to me." So Joseph swore to him. Then Israel bowed in thanks at the head of his bed.[B,g]

JACOB BLESSES EPHRAIM AND MANASSEH

48 Some time after this, Joseph was told, "Your father is weaker." So he set out with his two sons, Manasseh and Ephraim. 2 When Jacob was told, "Your son Joseph has come to you," Israel summoned his strength and sat up in bed.

3 Jacob said to Joseph, "God Almighty[h] appeared to me at Luz[i] in the land of Canaan and blessed me. 4 He said to me, 'I will make you fruitful and numerous; I will make many nations come from you, and I will give this land as a permanent possession[j] to your future descendants.'[k] 5 Your two sons[l] born to you in the land of Egypt before I came to you in Egypt are now mine.[m] Ephraim and Manasseh belong to me just as Reuben and Simeon do. 6 Children born to you after them will be yours and will be recorded under the names of their brothers with regard to their inheritance. 7 When I was returning from Paddan, to my sorrow Rachel died along the way,[n] some distance from Ephrath in the land of Canaan. I buried her there along the way to Ephrath" (that is, Bethlehem).

8 When Israel saw Joseph's sons, he said, "Who are these?"

9 And Joseph said to his father, "They are my sons God has given me here."

So Israel said, "Bring them to me and I will bless them."[o] 10 Now his eyesight was poor because of old age; he could hardly[C] see.[p] Joseph brought them to him, and he kissed and embraced them.[q] 11 Israel said to Joseph, "I never expected to see your face again, but now God has even let me see your offspring." 12 Then Joseph took them from his father's knees and bowed with his face to the ground.[r]

EPHRAIM'S GREATER BLESSING

13 Then Joseph took them both — with his right hand Ephraim toward Israel's left, and with his left hand Manasseh toward

[A] **47:21** Sam, LXX, Vg read *and he made the people servants* [B] **47:31** Or *Israel worshiped while leaning on the top of his staff* [C] **48:10** Lit *he was not able to*

47:27-31 As Jacob neared death, he charged Joseph, **Do not bury me in Egypt** (47:29). He remembered the promises of God and wanted his bones to rest where his ancestors' did—in the promised land (47:30).

48:1-12 In saying that Joseph's sons **Ephraim and Manasseh belong to [him] just as Reuben and Simeon do** (48:5), Jacob expressed his desire for each son to receive a portion of the inheritance equal to that of the other true brothers. Thus the twelve portions became thirteen, and Joseph—once again the son of honor—would receive the double portion usually reserved for the firstborn.

48:13-20 Much to Joseph's shock and disagreement (48:17-18), Jacob switched his hands so that **Ephraim**, the younger, would receive the **firstborn** blessing (48:14). Jacob was continuing the pattern of reversal that God had used throughout the history of the Jewish patriarchs. God's ways are not ours. He was also demonstrating the wonderful opportunity grandparents have to speak blessing in their grandchildren's lives. The lesser blessing, that **they grow to be numerous** (48:16), is the sort of blessing that we all inherently want. It's a prayer for prosperity. But the greater blessing that Jacob gave was that **they be called by [his] name and the names of [his] fathers** (48:16). To be included in the family of God is a blessing that bears fruit for eternity.

It is important to remember that Manasseh and Ephraim were born to Joseph while he was in Egypt. Yet both were to be treated as Jacob's sons and to receive an inheritance in the land. The claim to inheritance was not a matter of skin color, but instead a matter of lineage.

Israel's right — and brought them to Israel. **14** But Israel stretched out his right hand and put it on the head of Ephraim, the younger, and crossing his hands, put his left on Manasseh's head, although Manasseh was the firstborn.[a] **15** Then he blessed Joseph and said:

The God before whom my fathers
    Abraham and Isaac walked,[b]
the God who has been my shepherd[c]
    all my life to this day,
16 the angel who has redeemed me
    from all harm[d] —
may he bless these boys.
And may they be called
    by my name
and the names of my fathers
    Abraham and Isaac,[e]
and may they grow to be numerous
    within the land.

17 When Joseph saw that his father had placed his right hand on Ephraim's head, he thought it was a mistake[A] and took his father's hand to move it from Ephraim's head to Manasseh's. **18** Joseph said to his father, "Not that way, my father! This one is the firstborn. Put your right hand on his head."

19 But his father refused and said, "I know, my son, I know! He too will become a tribe,[B] and he too will be great; nevertheless, his younger brother will be greater than he, and his offspring will become a populous nation."[C] **20** So he blessed them that day, putting Ephraim before Manasseh when he said, "The nation Israel will invoke blessings by you, saying, 'May God make you like Ephraim and Manasseh.'"

21 Israel said to Joseph, "Look, I am about to die, but God will be with you and will bring you back to the land of your fathers.[f] **22** Over and above what I am giving your brothers, I am giving you the one mountain slope[D] that I took from the Amorites with my sword and bow."[g]

JACOB'S LAST WORDS

49 Then Jacob called his sons and said, "Gather around, and I will tell you what will happen to you in the days to come.[E,h]

2   Come together and listen,
    sons of Jacob;
listen to your father Israel:

3   Reuben, you are my firstborn,[i]
my strength and the firstfruits
    of my virility,[j]
excelling in prominence,
    excelling in power.
4   Turbulent as water, you will
    not excel,
because you got
    into your father's bed[k]
and you defiled it — he[F] got
    into my bed.

5   Simeon and Levi are brothers;
their knives are vicious weapons.[l]
6   May I never enter their council;
may I never join their assembly.
For in their anger they kill men,
and on a whim they hamstring oxen.
7   Their anger is cursed, for it is strong,
and their fury, for it is cruel!
I will disperse them
    throughout Jacob
and scatter them throughout Israel.[m]

8   Judah, your brothers will
    praise you.[n]
Your hand will be on the necks
    of your enemies;
your father's sons will bow down
    to you.[o]
9   Judah is a young lion[p] —
my son, you return from the kill.
He crouches; he lies down like a lion
or a lioness — who dares
    to rouse him?
10   The scepter will not depart
    from Judah
or the staff from between his feet

[a] **48:14** Gn 25:23; 27:18-30
[b] **48:15** Gn 17:1; 24:40
[c] **48:16** Gn 28:13-15; 31:11;
Is 63:9; Ac 7:35
[d] **48:16** Dt 28:10; 2Ch 7:14; Is 4:1;
43:1; 48:1
[e] **48:21** Gn 46:4; 50:24
[g] **48:22** Gn 34:25-29; Jos
24:32; Jn 4:5

[h] **49:1** Nm 24:14; Dt 4:30;
31:29; Is 2:2; Jr 23:20; Dn
2:28; 10:14; Hs 3:5
[i] **49:3** Gn 29:32
[j] **49:4** Dt 21:17
[k] **49:4** Gn 35:22
[l] **49:5** Gn 34:25,30
[m] **49:7** Ex 32:28; Nm 3:5-
13; Dt 33:10; Jos 19:1-9;
1Ch 4:24-39; 2Ch 34:6;
Neh 11:25-28
[n] **49:8** Gn 29:35
[o] Gn 27:29; 1Ch 5:2
[p] **49:9** Nm 24:9; Ezk 19:5-
7; Mc 5:8; Rv 5:5

[A] **48:17** Or *he was displeased*; lit *head, it was bad in his eyes*   [B] **48:19** Lit *people*   [C] **48:19** Or *a multitude of nations*; lit *a fullness of nations*
[D] **48:22** Or *Shechem*, Joseph's burial place; lit *one shoulder*   [E] **49:1** Or *in the last days*   [F] **49:4** LXX, Syr, Tg read *you*

49:1-2 Jacob called his other sons to his bedside to tell them about **the days to come** (49:1). He issued prophetic words about the future of each son, reflecting the destinies that their tribes would live out.
49:3-4 The first three sons were rejected from being able to lead the messianic line. **Reuben**, Jacob's **firstborn** (49:3), would have been the most natural candidate for the job, but he had disqualified himself by defiling his **father's bed** (49:4; see 35:22).

49:5-7 Jacob said of the next two brothers, **Simeon and Levi** (49:5), that they were men of anarchy and violence. **In their anger they kill men** (49:6), Jacob said, remembering their deceitful attack against Shechem (34:24-29).
49:8-10 God had chosen Judah—in spite of his failings—to father the line of kings leading to Christ, as **the scepter will not depart from Judah or the staff from between his feet until he whose right it is comes** (49:10).

He would be the new leader of his brothers, full of power and majesty **like a lion** (49:8-9). From Judah would come the kingly line of David. More importantly, Jesus would be called the "Lion from the tribe of Judah" (Rev 5:5). He is the one **whose right it is** to carry the scepter throughout eternity, **and the obedience of the peoples belongs to him** (Gen 49:10).

[a] 49:10 Nm 2:9; 10:14; 24:17; Jdg 1:1-2; Ps 60:7; 108:8; Ezk 21:27
[b] Ps 2:6-9; 72:8-11; Is 42:1,4; 49:6
[c] 49:13 Dt 33:19; Jos 19:10-16
[d] 49:15 Jdg 5:15-16
[e] 49:16 Dt 33:22; Jdg 13:2,25; 18:25-27
[f] 49:19 Dt 33:20; 1Ch 5:18-22; Jr 49:1
[g] 49:20 Dt 33:24-25; Jos 19:24-31; Jdg 5:17; 1Kg 4:7
[h] 49:21 Jos 19:32-39

[i] 49:24 Gn 31:42; Ps 132:2,5; Is 1:24; 49:26
[j] Gn 48:15; Ps 23:1; Jr 31:10
[k] Ps 118:22; Is 28:16; 1Pt 2:6-8
[l] 49:26 Dt 33:15-16
[m] 49:27 Jdg 5:14; 20:21; 1Sm 14:47-48

until he whose right it is comes[A,a]
and the obedience of the peoples
   belongs to him.[b]
11 He ties his donkey to a vine,
and the colt of his donkey
   to the choice vine.
He washes his clothes in wine
and his robes in the blood of grapes.
12 His eyes are darker than wine,
and his teeth are whiter than milk.

13 Zebulun will live by the seashore
and will be a harbor for ships,
and his territory will be next to Sidon.[c]

14 Issachar is a strong donkey
lying down between the saddlebags.[B]
15 He saw that his resting place
   was good
and that the land was pleasant,
so he leaned his shoulder to bear
   a load
and became a forced laborer.[d]

16 Dan will judge his people[e]
as one of the tribes of Israel.
17 Dan will be a snake by the road,
a viper beside the path,
that bites the horse's heels
so that its rider falls backward.

18 I wait for your salvation, LORD.

19 Gad will be attacked by raiders,
but he will attack their heels.[f]

20 Asher's[c] food will be rich,
and he will produce royal delicacies.[g]

21 Naphtali is a doe set free
that bears beautiful fawns.[h]

22 Joseph is a fruitful vine,
a fruitful vine beside a spring;
its branches[D] climb over the wall.[E]
23 The archers attacked him,
shot at him, and were hostile
   toward him.
24 Yet his bow remained steady,
and his strong arms
   were made agile
by the hands of the Mighty One
   of Jacob,[i]
by the name of[F] the Shepherd,[j]
   the Rock of Israel,[k]
25 by the God of your father
   who helps you,
and by the Almighty
   who blesses you
with blessings
   of the heavens above,
blessings of the deep
   that lies below,
and blessings of the breasts
   and the womb.
26 The blessings of your father excel
the blessings of my ancestors[G]
and[H] the bounty of the ancient hills.[E,l]
May they rest on the head
   of Joseph,
on the brow of the prince
   of his brothers.

27 Benjamin is a wolf; he tears
   his prey.
In the morning he devours the prey,
and in the evening he divides
   the plunder."[m]

28 These are the tribes of Israel, twelve in all, and this is what their father said to them. He blessed them, and he blessed each one with a suitable blessing.

[A] 49:10 Or until tribute comes to him, or until Shiloh comes, or until he comes to Shiloh   [B] 49:14 Or sheep pens   [C] 49:19-20 LXX, Syr, Vg; MT reads their heel.   [20] From Asher   [D] 49:22 Lit daughters   [E] 49:22,26 Hb obscure   [F] 49:24 Syr, Tg; MT reads Jacob, from there   [G] 49:26 Or of the mountains   [H] 49:26 Lit to

49:13 **Zebulun will live by the seashore and will be a harbor for ships**, indicating the future trade of this son's descendants. When the people of Israel would return to the promised land and apportion the land, the tribe of Zebulun would be given land near the ocean. 49:14-15 **Issachar** would not fare well during the return to Canaan. Issachar **leaned his shoulder to bear a load and became a forced laborer** (49:15), a prophecy about the tribe's approach to the native inhabitants of the promised land. Even though Issachar had strength enough to drive the people out as God promised (49:14), they grew comfortable living alongside them. And what began as a seemingly harmless partnership between the groups eventually led to Issachar's slavery.

49:16-17 **Dan**, which sounds like the Hebrew word for "has judged," **will judge his people** (49:16). In their best moments, the people of Dan were to provide justice for the rest of the nation. But they proved to be treacherous, like **a snake by the road** (49:17). During Israel's conquest of the promised land, Dan quickly gave up on the land to which God had called them (see Judg 2:3-4), leaving the land to the Philistines. Worse, Dan appears to be the first tribe to plummet into full-scale idolatry (see Judg 18). 49:19-21 **Gad**, **Asher**, and **Naphtali** were given rapid-fire prophecies. Gad would **be attacked by raiders** (49:19), indicating the constant conflict that the tribe would experience. Asher, whose name means "blessed," would live a life worthy of the name, with rich food and **royal delicacies** (49:20). Naphtali would

be a free people, dwelling in the mountains to the north (49:21).
49:22-26 As in his life, so in his tribe's future, Joseph would be **a fruitful vine** (49:22), not only succeeding for his own sake, but blessing the lives of others. Joseph's tribe would continue to be one of the most prosperous of the twelve (49:25-26).
49:27-28 Though Jacob favored Benjamin personally, it appears that the future of this tribe would be mixed. Jacob characterized the Benjaminites like **a wolf** that **tears his prey** and **divides the plunder** (49:27). They would be a tribe with a violent spirit, which was seen perhaps most vividly in their two most famous descendants. King Saul, Israel's first king, was a Benjaminite; so too was the persecutor-turned-apostle Paul.

[a] 49:29 Gn 25:8
[b] Gn 47:30
[c] Gn 23:16-20; 50:13
[d] 49:30 Gn 23:3-20
[e] 49:31 Gn 23:19; 25:9
[f] Gn 35:29
[g] Gn 48:7

[h] 50:3 Gn 50:10; Nm 20:29; Dt 34:8
[i] 50:5 Gn 47:29-31
[j] 2Ch 16:14; Is 22:16; Mt 27:60

◈ KINGDOM LIVING ◈
PERSONAL
When You Feel Stuck

The life of Joseph provides a perfect example of how life's disappointments can actually be detours in disguise. When Joseph was seventeen, God gave him a series of dreams telling him that one day he would rule over his brothers. Joseph told his siblings about these dreams and, in their jealousy and anger, they threw him in a deep pit and left him for dead. Shortly thereafter, he was sold into slavery. And while serving, he was falsely accused of raping his master's wife and was thrown into prison. In total, Joseph spent thirteen years enduring one disappointment after another before God led him out of the pit and into the palace of Pharaoh.

But why would he put him through all that? Those disappointments in Joseph's life were the very events through which God prepared the man for his destiny, and the destiny for the man. As a seventeen-year-old, he wasn't ready for all that God had in store for him. God also needed to set the stage for Joseph's arrival; after all, it wasn't until Pharaoh had his own dreams and could find no one in his kingdom to interpret them that God delivered Joseph from prison and into his destiny. His disappointments were in fact blessings, and Joseph acknowledges this when he tells his brothers, "You planned evil against me; God planned it for good to bring about the present result—the survival of many people" (Gen 50:20).

You also have a destiny. Maybe you've been waiting for God to lead you into it, but lately it seems as though you're going nowhere or you're stuck in a rut. It looks like you're moving further away from your destiny, and in those moments disappointment can set in. Do not lose heart; God hasn't forgotten about you. He's just not taking you there in a straight line. Trust the detours God brings your way. He uses them to take you from where you are to where he wants you to be.

FOR THE NEXT PERSONAL
KINGDOM LIVING LESSON SEE PAGE 692.

JACOB'S BURIAL INSTRUCTIONS

29 Then he commanded them: "I am about to be gathered to my people.[a] Bury me with my fathers[b] in the cave in the field of Ephron the Hethite.[c] **30** The cave is in the field of Machpelah near Mamre, in the land of Canaan. This is the field Abraham purchased from Ephron the Hethite as burial property.[d] **31** Abraham and his wife Sarah are buried there,[e] Isaac and his wife Rebekah are buried there,[f] and I buried Leah there.[g] **32** The field and the cave in it were purchased from the Hethites." **33** When Jacob had finished giving charges to his sons, he drew his feet into the bed, took his last breath, and was gathered to his people.

JACOB'S BURIAL

50 Then Joseph, leaning over his father's face, wept and kissed him. **2** He commanded his servants who were physicians to embalm his father. So they embalmed Israel. **3** They took forty days to complete this, for embalming takes that long, and the Egyptians mourned for him seventy days.[h]

4 When the days of mourning were over, Joseph said to Pharaoh's household, "If I have found favor with you, please tell[A] Pharaoh that **5** my father made me take an oath,[i] saying, 'I am about to die. You must bury me there in the tomb that I made for myself in the land of Canaan.'[j] Now let me go and bury my father. Then I will return."

6 So Pharaoh said, "Go and bury your father in keeping with your oath." **7** Then Joseph went to bury his father, and all Pharaoh's servants, the elders of his household, and all the elders of the land of Egypt went with him, **8** along with all Joseph's family, his brothers, and his father's family. Only their dependents, their flocks, and their herds were left in the land of Goshen. **9** Horses and chariots went up

---

[A] **50:4** Lit *please speak in the ears of*

49:29-33 Jacob finally gave honor to his first wife, **Leah**, asking to be buried with her (49:31) rather than with his beloved Rachel.

50:1-13 Joseph ensured that Jacob was embalmed after the style of Egyptian royalty (50:3). The entire nation mourned for Jacob **seventy days** (50:3), a phenomenal show of respect by the Egyptians. Joseph obeyed his father's dying wishes, taking his body back to the land of Canaan for burial (50:5).

a 50:13 Gn 23:16-20
b 50:15 Gn 37:28; 42:21-22
c 50:17 Gn 43:30; 46:29;
50:1

d 50:19 Gn 3:5
e 50:20 Gn 45:7; Rm 8:28
f 50:21 Gn 45:11; 47:12
g 50:23 Jb 42:16; Ps 128:6
h Gn 30:3
i 50:24 Gn 48:21; Ex 3:16-
17; Heb 11:22
j Gn 13:15-17; 15:7-8
k Gn 26:3
l Gn 28:13; 35:12
m 50:25 Ex 13:19

with him; it was a very impressive procession. **10** When they reached the threshing floor of Atad, which is across the Jordan, they lamented and wept loudly, and Joseph mourned seven days for his father. **11** When the Canaanite inhabitants of the land saw the mourning at the threshing floor of Atad, they said, "This is a solemn mourning on the part of the Egyptians." Therefore the place is named Abel-mizraim.^A It is across the Jordan.

12 So Jacob's sons did for him what he had commanded them. **13** They carried him to the land of Canaan and buried him in the cave at Machpelah in the field near Mamre, which Abraham had purchased as burial property from Ephron the Hethite.^a **14** After Joseph buried his father, he returned to Egypt with his brothers and all who had gone with him to bury his father.

JOSEPH'S KINDNESS

15 When Joseph's brothers saw that their father was dead, they said to one another, "If Joseph is holding a grudge against us, he will certainly repay us for all the suffering we caused him."^b **16** So they sent this message to Joseph, "Before he died your father gave a command: **17** 'Say this to Joseph: Please forgive your brothers' transgression and their sin — the suffering they caused you.' Therefore, please forgive the transgression of the servants of the God of your father." Joseph wept^c when their message came to him. **18** His brothers also came to him,

HOPE WORDS

God can use the mess you are in to bring you to the place of your destiny.

bowed down before him, and said, "We are your slaves!"

19 But Joseph said to them, "Don't be afraid. Am I in the place of God?^d **20** You planned evil against me; God planned it for good to bring about the present result — the survival of many people.^e **21** Therefore don't be afraid. I will take care of you and your children."^f And he comforted them and spoke kindly to them.^B

JOSEPH'S DEATH

22 Joseph and his father's family remained in Egypt. Joseph lived 110 years. **23** He saw Ephraim's sons to the third generation;^g the sons of Manasseh's son Machir were recognized by^c,D Joseph.^h

24 Joseph said to his brothers, "I am about to die,^i but God will certainly come to your aid and bring you up from this land to the land he swore to give to Abraham,^j Isaac,^k and Jacob."^l **25** So Joseph made the sons of Israel take an oath: "When God comes to your aid, you are to carry my bones up from here."^m **26** Joseph died at the age of 110. They embalmed him and placed him in a coffin in Egypt.

^A 50:11 = Mourning of Egypt   ^B 50:21 Lit *spoke to their hearts*   ^C 50:23 Lit *were born on the knees of*   ^D 50:23 Referring to a ritual of adoption or of legitimation; Gn 30:3

50:16-18 The brothers were scared, so they lied. They sent a message to Joseph, claiming that their father had said, **Please forgive your brothers' transgression** (50:17). They even reverted to the same posture they assumed when they first came to Egypt, bowing down before Joseph (50:18).
50:19-21 Joseph had discovered the secret of forgiving your enemies: you need the right view of God. Vengeance belongs to him, and the longer we cherish an unforgiving attitude in our hearts, the more we harm ourselves. Unforgiveness acts like a leash that keeps snapping us back, painfully, to the past. Only when we choose to let God be the God of vengeance (and take ourselves off that lofty throne) does the leash disappear, allowing us to march forward toward the destiny God has in store for us, which will always include bringing kingdom benefits to the lives of others.
50:22-26 When the time came for Joseph to die, he remembered the promises made to his forefathers (50:24). Thus he made his brothers promise **to carry [his] bones** to the promised land (50:25). Years later, the Israelites did so (see Exod 13:19; Josh 24:32).

EXODUS

INTRODUCTION

Author

THE BOOK OF EXODUS, like the other books of the Pentateuch (the first five books of the Bible), names no particular author. Early Jewish and Christian tradition, however, affirmed that Moses was the writer. In several places, the book indicates that Moses wrote down God's instructions (see Exod 17:14; 24:4; 34:27-28). Thus, though the book is formally anonymous, there is every reason to accept the tradition that it was written by the main character in its storyline: Moses.

Historical Background

Exodus opens where the book of Genesis ends—with the death of Joseph in Egypt in about 1805 BC (see Gen 50:22-26). But by Exodus 1:8, the narrative has skipped forward three hundred years to the period of the Israelites' enslavement in Egypt. The first half of the book describes how Moses led the Israelites out of Egypt through the initiative and miraculous deliverance of God. The second half explains how God entered into a covenant relationship with Israel (in spite of their sins), gave them his law, and established the tabernacle.

Scholars debate the year of the exodus. But many conservative scholars arrive at a date of 1446 BC. In 1 Kings 6:1, the author indicates that Solomon began constructing the temple in the fourth year of his reign, which was "in the four hundred eightieth year after the Israelites came out of the land of Egypt." Since this date is determined to be 966 BC, the math brings us to the year 1446 BC for Israel's sojourn out of Egypt. If this is correct, then the Pharaoh who enslaved the Israelites would have been Thutmose III. The Pharaoh during the exodus would have been his son, Amenhotep II.

Message and Purpose

Exodus is the continuation of Genesis in that we see within it the fulfillment of God's promise to Abraham to make of him a great nation (Gen 12:2), the nation of Israel. To accomplish this, God brought the people of Israel—Abraham's biological descendants—out from bondage in Egypt through the deliverance of Moses and the plagues that he called down on the Egyptians. Exodus shows how God kept Pharaoh from continuing to oppress the Israelites and from destroying them.

The book also shows how God moved the people of Israel into the wilderness to begin the process of developing them into the nation he wanted them to become. This is a reminder that after deliverance comes development. It was in the wilderness, in fact, that Israel would learn to walk with God, trust him, and receive their national constitution, the Ten Commandments. These familiar rules were guidelines God gave the Israelites regarding how they were to relate to him and to each other.

God also gave strict guidelines for constructing the tabernacle and placing it at the very center of the Israelite camp in the wilderness. This was to teach the people that he was to be at the very heart of their worship and their lives. Thus, Exodus is a book about what it means to worship God and keep him at the center of life. These principles are at the heart of kingdom living.

www.bhpublishinggroup.com/qr/te/02_00

Outline

[a] 1:1 Gn 46:8
[b] 1:5 Gn 46:26-27; Dt 10:22
[c] 1:6 Gn 50:26
[d] 1:7 Gn 12:2; 46:3; Dt 26:5; Ac 7:17
[e] 1:9 Ps 105:24
[f] 1:10 Ps 83:3-4; Ac 7:19
[g] 1:11 Gn 15:13; Ex 2:11; 3:7; 5:4-5; 6:6; Dt 26:6
[h] Gn 47:11; 1Kg 9:19; 2Ch 8:4
[i] 1:13 Dt 4:20
[j] 1:14 Ex 2:23; Nm 20:15; Ac 7:19
[k] 1:17 Ex 1:21; Pr 16:6
[l] Dn 3:16-18; Ac 4:18-20; 5:29
[m] 1:19 Jos 2:4; 2Sm 17:20
[n] 1:20 Pr 11:18; Is 3:10
[o] 1:21 1Sm 2:35; 2Sm 7:11,27; 1Kg 11:38; Ps 127:1
[p] 1:22 Gn 41:1; Ac 7:19
[q] 2:1 Ex 6:20; Nm 26:59; 1Ch 23:14
[r] 2:2 Ac 7:20; Heb 11:23
[s] 2:4 Ex 15:20; Nm 26:59

ISRAEL OPPRESSED IN EGYPT

1 These are the names of the sons of Israel who came to Egypt with Jacob; each came with his family:[a] **2** Reuben, Simeon, Levi, and Judah; **3** Issachar, Zebulun, and Benjamin; **4** Dan and Naphtali; Gad and Asher. **5** The total number of Jacob's descendants[A] was seventy;[B,b] Joseph was already in Egypt.

6 Joseph and all his brothers and all that generation eventually died.[c] **7** But the Israelites were fruitful, increased rapidly, multiplied, and became extremely numerous[d] so that the land was filled with them.

8 A new king, who did not know about Joseph, came to power in Egypt. **9** He said to his people, "Look, the Israelite people are more numerous and powerful than we are.[e] **10** Come, let's deal shrewdly with them; otherwise they will multiply further, and when war breaks out, they will join our enemies, fight against us, and leave the country."[f] **11** So the Egyptians assigned taskmasters over the Israelites to oppress them with forced labor.[g] They built Pithom and Rameses as supply cities[h] for Pharaoh. **12** But the more they oppressed them, the more they multiplied and spread so that the Egyptians came to dread[c] the Israelites. **13** They worked the Israelites ruthlessly[i] **14** and made their lives bitter with difficult labor in brick and mortar and in all kinds of fieldwork. They ruthlessly imposed all this work on them.[j]

15 The king of Egypt said to the Hebrew midwives — the first whose name was Shiphrah and the second whose name was Puah — **16** "When you help the Hebrew women give birth, observe them as they deliver. If the child is a son, kill him, but if it's a daughter, she may live." **17** The midwives, however, feared God[k] and did not do as the king of Egypt had told them;[l] they let the boys live. **18** So the king of Egypt summoned the midwives and asked them, "Why have you done this and let the boys live?"

19 The midwives said to Pharaoh, "The Hebrew women are not like the Egyptian women, for they are vigorous and give birth before the midwife can get to them."[m]

20 So God was good to the midwives,[n] and the people multiplied and became very numerous. **21** Since the midwives feared God, he gave them families.[o] **22** Pharaoh then commanded all his people: "You must throw every son born to the Hebrews into the Nile, but let every daughter live."[p]

MOSES'S BIRTH AND ADOPTION

2 Now a man from the family of Levi married a Levite woman.[q] **2** The woman became pregnant and gave birth to a son; when she saw that he was beautiful,[D] she hid him for three months.[r] **3** But when she could no longer hide him, she got a papyrus basket for him and coated it with asphalt and pitch. She placed the child in it and set it among the reeds by the bank of the Nile. **4** Then his sister[s] stood at a distance in order to see what would happen to him.

5 Pharaoh's daughter went down to bathe at the Nile while her servant girls walked along the riverbank. She saw the basket among the reeds, sent her slave girl, took it, **6** opened it, and saw him, the child — and there he was, a little boy, crying. She felt sorry for him and said, "This is one of the Hebrew boys."

7 Then his sister said to Pharaoh's daughter, "Should I go and call a Hebrew woman who is nursing to nurse the boy for you?"

8 "Go," Pharaoh's daughter told her. So the girl went and called the boy's mother. **9** Then Pharaoh's daughter said to her, "Take this child and nurse him for me, and

---

[A] 1:5 Lit *of people issuing from Jacob's loins*   [B] 1:5 LXX, DSS read *75*; Gn 46:27; Ac 7:14   [C] 1:12 Or *Egyptians loathed*   [D] 2:2 Or *healthy*

1:1-7 Jacob's family had come to dwell in Egypt to escape the extensive famine. **Seventy** Israelites had **multiplied . . . so that the land was filled with them** (1:5-7). By this point in history, Israel consisted of "six hundred thousand able-bodied men . . . besides their families" (12:37). God was fulfilling his kingdom promise to give Abraham numerous descendants (see Gen 13:16).

1:8-10 After Joseph died, **a new king** ascended in Egypt. This pharaoh had no appreciation for Joseph's achievements (1:8). As he saw the **Israelite people** multiplying, he feared they might align with Egypt's enemies (1:9-10).

1:11 Years prior, God told Abraham that one day his offspring would be enslaved by

another nation (see Gen 15:13-14). That had finally come to pass.

1:12-14 In spite of Pharaoh's ill-treatment, the Israelites' numbers rose. In the midst of their suffering, God blessed them.

1:15-17 Pharaoh told the **Hebrew midwives** to **kill** any **son** the **Hebrew women** delivered (1:15-16). But the midwives **feared God** (1:17). Though Pharaoh had the power to execute them, these women knew God held ultimate power. God blessed them in spite of their deception. This teaches us the principle that, when faced with two sins, you must choose that which brings God the greatest glory.

1:18-21 The women lied to this wicked king — who didn't deserve the truth — in order to

prevent the murder of innocent children made in God's image. The principle here is that when God's people are faced with only sinful options, we are to choose that which brings God greater glory.

2:1-4 This **Levite woman . . . hid [her son] for three months**, trusting God over the power of Pharaoh's edict (2:1-2; see Heb 11:23). Then she placed her son in a **basket** and hoped that in the providence of God, the body of water in which babies were being drowned would serve as a means of deliverance for her child (Exod 2:3).

2:5-9 One moment the baby was under the threat of death, the next moment his mother was being paid by **Pharaoh's daughter** to raise him (2:9). This is the sovereignty of God

I will pay your wages." So the woman took the boy and nursed him. ¹⁰ When the child grew older, she brought him to Pharaoh's daughter, and he became her son. She named him Moses,^A "Because," she said, "I drew him out of the water."

MOSES IN MIDIAN

¹¹ Years later,^B after Moses had grown up, he went out to his own people^c and observed their forced labor.^d He saw an Egyptian striking a Hebrew, one of his people. ¹² Looking all around and seeing no one, he struck the Egyptian dead and hid him in the sand. ¹³ The next day he went out and saw two Hebrews fighting. He asked the one in the wrong, "Why are you attacking your neighbor?"^D

¹⁴ "Who made you a commander and judge over us?" the man replied. "Are you planning to kill me as you killed the Egyptian?"

Then Moses became afraid and thought, "What I did is certainly known."

¹⁵ When Pharaoh heard about this, he tried to kill Moses. But Moses fled from Pharaoh and went to live in the land of Midian,^b and sat down by a well.^c

¹⁶ Now the priest of Midian^d had seven daughters. They came to draw water and filled the troughs to water their father's flock. ¹⁷ Then some shepherds arrived and drove them away, but Moses came to their rescue and watered their flock. ¹⁸ When they returned to their father Reuel,^{E,e} he asked, "Why have you come back so quickly today?"

¹⁹ They answered, "An Egyptian rescued us from the shepherds. He even drew water for us and watered the flock."

²⁰ "So where is he?" he asked his daughters. "Why then did you leave the man behind? Invite him to eat dinner."

²¹ Moses agreed to stay with the man, and he gave his daughter Zipporah^f to Moses in marriage. ²² She gave birth to a son whom he named Gershom,^F for he said, "I have been a resident alien^g in a foreign land."

²³ After a long time, the king of Egypt died. The Israelites groaned because of their difficult labor; and they cried out;^h and their cry for help because of the difficult labor ascended to God. ²⁴ And God heard their groaning; and God rememberedⁱ his covenant with Abraham, with Isaac, and with Jacob;^j ²⁵ and God saw the Israelites; and God knew.^k

APPLICATION QUESTIONS

READ EXODUS 3:1-10

– How has your life been changed by meaningful encounters with God?
– When have you recently felt God directing you to make specific decisions or follow a certain path?
– What obstacles commonly prevent you from intentionally placing yourself in God's presence?
– How can you overcome these obstacles?

MOSES AND THE BURNING BUSH

3 Meanwhile, Moses was shepherding the flock of his father-in-law Jethro,^G the priest of Midian. He led the flock to the far side of the wilderness and came to Horeb,^H the mountain of God.^l ² Then the angel of the LORD appeared to him in a flame of fire within a bush.^m As Moses looked, he saw that the bush was on fire but was

^a2:11 Ex 1:11; Ac 7:23; Heb 11:24-26
^b2:15 Ac 7:29; Heb 11:27
^cGn 24:11; 29:2
^d2:16 Ex 3:1; 1Sm 9:11
^e2:18 Ex 3:1; 4:18; Nm 10:29
^f2:21 Ex 4:25; 18:2
^g2:22 Ex 18:3-4; Ac 7:29; Heb 11:13
^h2:23 Ex 3:7,9; Dt 26:7; Jms 5:4
ⁱ2:24 Gn 9:15; Ex 6:5; 1Ch 16:15; Ps 105:8; 106:45; 111:4
^jPs 22:23; Lk 1:33,55
^k2:25 Ex 3:7; 4:31; Lk 1:25
^l3:1 Ex 2:18; 18:5; 1Kg 19:8
^m3:2 Dt 33:16; Ac 7:30

at work. In the remarkable provision of the Lord, the midwives, the mother, the sister, and even Pharaoh's daughter, were used by God to care for a child whom God would use to bring about his kingdom purposes.

2:10 An Israelite child who was supposed to have been executed under royal orders was now being raised in the royal household—"educated in all the wisdom of the Egyptians" (Acts 7:22). In divine irony, the future prophet of God who would bring plagues upon Egypt and lead slaves to freedom was being nurtured under the enemy's nose.

2:11-15 Notwithstanding his advantages, Moses decided to identify with the Hebrews and help them. When he noticed an Egyptian beating a Hebrew, Moses killed the Egyptian and **hid** his body (2:11-12). But **the next day, two Hebrews** rejected Moses's attempts at

peacemaking. One asked Moses if he planned to kill him like he **killed the Egyptian** (2:14). And Moses realized that his actions had become **known.** When Pharaoh finally caught wind of things, he **tried to kill** Moses (2:14-15). **Moses** had to run for his life, fleeing to **Midian** (2:15), in modern-day Saudi Arabia.

Moses was well-intentioned in trying to help his native people, but impulsive. This is a reminder that we shouldn't attempt to do the right things in the wrong way. God's people need God's perspective on their situations.

2:16-22 In Midian, Moses came to the defense of the **daughters** of **the priest** there (2:16-17). As a result of Moses's kindness, this father gave him **his daughter Zipporah** as a wife (2:18-21). She bore Moses a **son** and Moses became a shepherd (2:22; 3:1). Moses

went from living as Pharaoh's protégé to working as a desert herdsman. But God was supernaturally working behind the scenes to prepare the deliverer of his people. Sometimes, to accomplish his purposes through you, God has to take you low before he will take you high.

2:23 Hardship forces us to turn our focus upward, to cry out for help.

3:1 By now, Moses was eighty (see Acts 7:23, 30), working for **his father-in-law**. He likely had come to accept this as his lot. But things changed dramatically at **Horeb**, another name for Mount Sinai (see Exod 3:12; Deut 1:19). Here God would soon enter into a covenant with the nation of Israel.

3:2-3 Moses saw that a **bush was on fire but was not consumed** (3:2). Such a contradictory marvel brings to my mind the Lord's words:

a **3:5** Jos 5:15; Ac 7:33
b **3:6** Gn 28:13; Mt 22:32;
Mk 12:26; Lk 20:37;
Ac 7:32
c **3:7** Ex 2:23-25; Neh 9:9;
Ps 106:44
d **3:8** Gn 50:24; Ex 6:6
e Gn 15:18-21; Ex 3:17; 13:5;
Dt 1:25; Jr 11:5; Ezk 20:6
f **3:9** Ex 1:14; 2:23
g **3:11** Ex 6:12; 1Sm 18:18

h **3:12** Gn 31:3; Jos 1:5;
Rm 8:31
i **3:14** Ex 6:3; Ps 68:4; Jn
8:58; Heb 13:8; Rv 1:4; 4:8
j **3:15** Ps 102:12; 135:13;
Hs 12:5
k **3:16** Ex 4:29; Lk 1:68
l **3:17** Gn 15:16; Jos 24:11
m **3:18** Ex 4:31; 5:1; Nm
23:3-4,15-16
n **3:19** Ex 5:2; 6:1

not consumed. **3** So Moses thought, "I must go over and look at this remarkable sight. Why isn't the bush burning up?" **4** When the LORD saw that he had gone over to look, God called out to him from the bush, "Moses, Moses!"

"Here I am," he answered.

5 "Do not come closer," he said. "Remove the sandals from your feet, for the place where you are standing is holy ground."*a* **6** Then he continued, "I am the God of your father,*A* the God of Abraham, the God of Isaac, and the God of Jacob."*b* Moses hid his face because he was afraid to look at God.

⟶ HOPE WORDS ⟵

God's calling on your life is bigger than what you can see.

7 Then the LORD said, "I have observed the misery of my people in Egypt, and have heard them crying out*c* because of their oppressors. I know about their sufferings, **8** and I have come down to rescue them from the power of the Egyptians and to bring them from that land to a good and spacious land, a land flowing with milk and honey*d* — the territory of the Canaanites, Hethites, Amorites, Perizzites, Hivites, and Jebusites.*e* **9** So because the Israelites' cry for help has come to me, and I have also seen the way the Egyptians are oppressing*f* them, **10** therefore, go. I am sending you to Pharaoh so that you may lead my people, the Israelites, out of Egypt."

11 But Moses asked God, "Who am I*g* that I should go to Pharaoh and that I should bring the Israelites out of Egypt?"

12 He answered, "I will certainly be with you,*h* and this will be the sign to you that I am the one who sent you: when you bring the people out of Egypt, you will all worship*B* God at this mountain."

13 Then Moses asked God, "If I go to the Israelites and say to them, 'The God of your fathers has sent me to you,' and they ask me, 'What is his name?' what should I tell them?"

14 God replied to Moses, "I AM WHO I AM.*c/* This is what you are to say to the Israelites: I AM has sent me to you." **15** God also said to Moses, "Say this to the Israelites: The LORD, the God of your fathers, the God of Abraham, the God of Isaac, and the God of Jacob, has sent me to you. This is my name forever;*j* this is how I am to be remembered in every generation.

16 "Go and assemble the elders of Israel and say to them: The LORD, the God of your fathers, the God of Abraham, Isaac, and Jacob, has appeared to me and said: I have paid close attention to you and to what has been done to you in Egypt.*k* **17** And I have promised you that I will bring you up from the misery of Egypt*l* to the land of the Canaanites, Hethites, Amorites, Perizzites, Hivites, and Jebusites — a land flowing with milk and honey. **18** They will listen to what you say. Then you, along with the elders of Israel, must go to the king of Egypt and say to him: The LORD, the God of the Hebrews, has met with us. Now please let us go on a three-day trip into the wilderness so that we may sacrifice to the LORD our God.*m*

19 "However, I know that the king of Egypt will not allow you to go, even under force from a strong hand.*n* **20** But when I stretch out my hand and strike Egypt with all my miracles that I will perform

A **3:6** Sam, some LXX mss read *fathers*; Ac 7:32   *B* **3:12** Or *serve*   *C* **3:14** Or *I AM BECAUSE I AM*, or *I WILL BE WHO I WILL BE*

"My thoughts are not your thoughts, and your ways are not my ways" (Isa 55:8). Moses's ordinary day was about to be invaded by God's extraordinary plan.
3:4-5 Moses was standing on a quarter inch of sandal sole. But in the presence of a holy God, he needed to humble himself. He also needed to be reminded of where he came from. Man was made "out of the dust from the ground" (Gen 2:7).
3:9-10 Moses may have thought that his life was nearly over as he passed time with the sheep as an octogenarian. But just as the Lord had given Moses forty years of uptown training in Egypt, he provided forty years of downtown training in the wilderness. That's what was necessary to get this shepherd ready to lead the sheep of Israel.

3:11-12 Gone was the brash man who had expected his fellow Hebrews to look up to him. He asked, **Who am I that I should go to Pharaoh?** (3:11). Notice how the Lord responded to his humility: **I will certainly be with you** (3:12). Moses's greatest need (and ours too) was not self-confidence; he needed God-confidence.

Here God revealed his purpose (3:12). God wasn't freeing the Israelites so they could sit around and be lazy. He was freeing them so that they could do what they had been created for: he wanted them to **worship** him. Whenever God delivers you *from* something, he also delivers you *to* something—himself.
3:13 Moses wanted to know on whose authority he was to say he was operating.
3:14-15 I AM is the English translation of the first-person singular Hebrew verb meaning

"to be." By describing himself this way, God was affirming that he is the personal, eternal, self-existing, and self-sufficient Creator and sustainer of all.

Many claim to believe in a generic "God." But Moses was to tell the Israelites that he had been sent by the one true God—"the Lord." He alone is "the God of Abraham, Isaac, and Jacob" (3:16), and he is the Father of our Lord Jesus. He is responsible for all that exists, and he sovereignly directs all things to accomplish his purposes. Though the world is ever-changing, HE IS.
3:19-22 Since the king would not consent, God would respond with miraculous displays of divine power to compel the king to release Israel (3:20). The Lord would also see to it that the Israelites didn't leave Egypt **empty-handed** (3:21). In fact, after all the

⇝ Questions & Answers ⇜

Q You have noted that when God called Moses to serve him, one of his basic questions was, "What is that in your hand?" (Exod 4:2). How does this practical question apply to discerning God's calling on our lives?

A To God's question, Moses responded, "A staff." This was a shepherd's staff because his job was leading sheep. Little did he know, however, that God would use that experience to prepare him to lead a different kind of sheep—the children of Israel—for forty years.

God places in our hands what he wants us to use for ministry. It's that thing that we have become good at, that gift, that ability that we have been able to hone over time. We may be exercising it in one realm, but God can take that same tool and use it for the advancement of his program. What has God placed in your capacity that can be used in his calling for your life? When you discover it and use it (like Moses's staff), it turns out to be more powerful than you thought.

FOR THE NEXT Q&A, SEE PAGE 87.

in it, after that, he will let you go.[a] **21** And I will give these people such favor with the Egyptians that when you go, you will not go empty-handed.[b] **22** Each woman will ask her neighbor and any woman staying in her house for silver and gold jewelry, and clothing, and you will put them on your sons and daughters. So you will plunder the Egyptians."[c]

MIRACULOUS SIGNS FOR MOSES

4 Moses answered, "What if they won't believe me and will not obey me but say, 'The LORD did not appear[d] to you'?"

2 The LORD asked him, "What is that in your hand?"

"A staff," he replied.

3 "Throw it on the ground," he said. So Moses threw it on the ground, it became a snake, and he ran from it. **4** The LORD told Moses, "Stretch out your hand and grab it by the tail." So he stretched out his hand and caught it, and it became a staff in his hand. **5** "This will take place," he continued, "so that they will believe that the LORD, the God of their fathers, the God of Abraham, the God of Isaac, and the God of Jacob, has appeared to you."[e]

6 In addition the LORD said to him, "Put your hand inside your cloak." So he put his hand inside his cloak, and when he took it out, his hand was diseased, resembling snow.[A,f] **7** "Put your hand back inside your cloak," he said. So he put his hand back inside his cloak, and when he took it out, it had again become like the rest of his skin.[g] **8** "If they will not believe you and will not respond to the evidence of the first sign, they may believe the evidence of the second sign. **9** And if they don't believe even these two signs or listen to what you say, take some water from the Nile and pour it on the dry ground. The water you take from the Nile will become blood on the ground."[h]

10 But Moses replied to the LORD, "Please, Lord, I have never been eloquent — either in the past or recently or since you have been speaking to your servant — because my mouth and my tongue are sluggish."[B,i]

11 The LORD said to him, "Who placed a mouth on humans? Who makes a person mute or deaf, seeing or blind? Is it not I, the LORD?[j] **12** Now go! I will help you speak[c] and I will teach you what to say."[k]

13 Moses said, "Please, Lord, send someone else."[D]

14 Then the LORD's anger burned against Moses, and he said, "Isn't Aaron the Levite your brother? I know that he can speak well. And also, he is on his way now to

---

[A] **4:6** A reference to whiteness or flakiness of the skin [B] **4:10** Lit *heavy of mouth and heavy of tongue* [C] **4:12** Lit *will be with your mouth* [D] **4:13** Lit *send by the hand of whom you will send*

---

suffering linked to the coming plagues, the Egyptians would gladly give Israel riches just to get rid of them. In a sense, the Israelites would receive the back-wages they deserved. **4:1-9** Moses was still nervous. Therefore, the Lord literally filled his hands with reason for confidence. The Lord assured his servant that with the aid of such miracles as the staff becoming a snake, the people of Israel would believe that **the God of Abraham** had **appeared to** him (4:5). **4:10-12** Whether Moses had a speech impediment, was a poor public speaker, or simply

didn't want to go, he argued, "Lord, you need someone else to be your mouthpiece" (4:10). God's response is for all who come up with excuses for why they are unable to obey his will (4:11). God was not unaware of Moses's weaknesses. Similarly, when he calls you to kingdom service, he knows about your fears and your shortcomings.

God didn't choose you to serve him because he desperately needed your qualities on his team. He chose you so you could reflect his glory to the world. Paul told the

Corinthians, "Not many were wise from a human perspective, not many powerful. . . . God has chosen what is foolish in the world to shame the wise" (1 Cor 1:26-27). **4:12** Ultimately, the exodus of God's people from Egypt wouldn't depend on Moses but on God. If God promises to inject his heavenly presence into your earthly reality, that's all you need. **4:13-17** The truth was out: Moses simply didn't want to go (4:13). But God wasn't taking "No" for an answer. God would speak to Moses, Moses would speak to **Aaron**, and Aaron would

a 4:15 Ex 7:1-2; Nm 23:5,12,16
b 4:17 Ex 4:2; 7:15
c 4:19 Ex 2:15,23; Mt 2:20
d 4:20 Ex 17:9; Nm 20:8-9
e 4:21 Ex 7:13; 9:12,35; 14:8; Dt 2:30; Jos 11:20; Is 63:17; Jn 12:40; Rm 9:18
f 4:22 Is 63:16; 64:8; Jr 31:9; Hs 11:1; Rm 9:4
g 4:23 Ex 11:5; 12:29
h 4:25 Gn 17:14; Jos 5:2-3

i 4:27 Ex 3:1; 4:14
j 4:31 Ex 2:25; 3:7,18; 4:8-9
k Gn 24:26; 1Ch 29:20
l 5:1 Ex 3:18; 10:9
m 5:2 1Sm 25:10; Pr 30:9; Jr 9:6
n Ex 3:19; 2Kg 18:35; Jb 21:15
o 5:3-5 Ex 1:7,9,11; 3:18

meet you. He will rejoice when he sees you. **15** You will speak with him and tell him what to say.[a] I will help both you and him to speak[A] and will teach you both what to do. **16** He will speak to the people for you. He will serve as a mouth for you, and you will serve as God to him. **17** And take this staff in your hand that you will perform the signs with."[b]

MOSES'S RETURN TO EGYPT

18 Then Moses went back to his father-in-law Jethro and said to him, "Please let me return to my relatives in Egypt and see if they are still living."

Jethro said to Moses, "Go in peace." **19** Now in Midian the LORD told Moses, "Return to Egypt, for all the men who wanted to kill you are dead."[c] **20** So Moses took his wife and sons, put them on a donkey, and returned to the land of Egypt. And Moses took God's staff[d] in his hand.

21 The LORD instructed Moses, "When you go back to Egypt, make sure you do before Pharaoh all the wonders that I have put within your power. But I will harden his heart[B,e] so that he won't let the people go. **22** And you will say to Pharaoh: This is what the LORD says: Israel is my firstborn son.[f] **23** I told you: Let my son go so that he may worship me, but you refused to let him go. Look, I am about to kill your firstborn son!"[g]

24 On the trip, at an overnight campsite, it happened that the LORD confronted him and intended to put him to death. **25** So Zipporah took a flint, cut off her son's foreskin, threw it at Moses's feet, and said, "You are a bridegroom of blood to me!"[h] **26** So he let him alone. At that time she said,

"You are a bridegroom of blood," referring to the circumcision.

REUNION OF MOSES AND AARON

27 Now the LORD had said to Aaron, "Go and meet Moses in the wilderness." So he went and met him at the mountain of God and kissed him.[i] **28** Moses told Aaron everything the LORD had sent him to say, and about all the signs he had commanded him to do. **29** Then Moses and Aaron went and assembled all the elders of the Israelites. **30** Aaron repeated everything the LORD had said to Moses and performed the signs before the people. **31** The people believed, and when they heard that the LORD had paid attention[j] to them and that he had seen their misery,[k] they knelt low and worshiped.

MOSES CONFRONTS PHARAOH

5 Later, Moses and Aaron went in and said to Pharaoh, "This is what the LORD, the God of Israel, says: Let my people go, so that they may hold a festival for me in the wilderness."[l]

2 But Pharaoh responded, "Who is the LORD that I should obey him by letting Israel go?[m] I don't know[c] the LORD, and besides, I will not let Israel go."[n]

3 They answered, "The God of the Hebrews has met with us. Please let us go on a three-day trip into the wilderness so that we may sacrifice to the LORD our God, or else he may strike us with plague or sword."

4 The king of Egypt said to them, "Moses and Aaron, why are you causing the people to neglect their work? Get to your labor!" **5** Pharaoh also said, "Look, the people of the land are so numerous, and you would stop them from their labor."[o]

A 4:15 Lit *will be with your mouth and with his mouth*   **B** 4:21 Or *will make him stubborn*   **C** 5:2 Or *recognize*

---

convey the message to Pharaoh (4:14-16). It was time for Moses to take courage, trust God, and start walking. Though he initially fought it, he was destined to be God's kingdom man.
4:21 God said he would **harden** Pharaoh's **heart** so that he wouldn't **let the people go**. Throughout this book, however, we'll see that God didn't harden Pharaoh's heart until Pharaoh first hardened himself. When Pharaoh repeatedly refused to listen (7:22; 8:15, 32), God told him, in a sense, "Have it your way." He used Pharaoh's rebellion to achieve his kingdom purpose.
4:22-23 Moses was to tell Pharaoh that the Lord said, **Israel is my firstborn son** (4:22). In other words, the ethnic group that the king was abusing wasn't just some random group; Creator God saw them as his son, making himself their *Father*. The firstborn held a position

of honor in the ancient Near East. Pharaoh had enslaved those to whom God demanded that he show respect. He would pay a high price: the life of his own **firstborn son** (4:23).
4:24-26 Why was God ready to execute the one whom he had chosen to deliver his people? Moses's wife's actions (4:25), which at first glance seem bizarre, provide the answer. As a descendent of Abraham (see Gen 17:1-27), Moses was to circumcise his son. He, however, had failed to lead his family and demonstrate his commitment to God's covenant. Moses was to serve as God's representative to lead God's firstborn son—that is, the Israelites—to worship him, but he hadn't even fulfilled his basic obligation. Fathers, the Lord calls us to lead our families in following Christ (see Eph 6:4). Wives are to help, but God has laid the responsibility at our feet.

Since Moses had been negligent, **Zipporah** circumcised their son and deflected God's judgment (Exod 4:25-26)—thus saving her husband's life. This suggests that many a life is saved as godly mothers obey the Lord when their husbands fail to do so.
4:31 Once the descendants of Israel knew of God's mercy on their **misery**, they **worshiped**. News of God's deliverance should always lead his people to praise.
5:1-2 Pharaoh could have avoided tremendous grief if he had heeded this simple request. Instead he refused to **obey** the Lord because he didn't **know** him (5:2). He didn't recognize him as a deity among Egypt's pantheon.
5:3-9 Instead of relenting, Pharaoh accused Moses and Aaron of enabling the people to be idle (5:4-5). He decided to prevent any further unruliness. His order, he reasoned, would

FURTHER OPPRESSION OF ISRAEL

6 That day Pharaoh commanded the overseers[a] of the people as well as their foremen: **7** "Don't continue to supply the people with straw for making bricks, as before. They must go and gather straw for themselves. **8** But require the same quota of bricks from them as they were making before; do not reduce it. For they are slackers — that is why they are crying out,[b] 'Let us go and sacrifice to our God.' **9** Impose heavier work on the men. Then they will be occupied with it and not pay attention to deceptive words."

10 So the overseers and foremen of the people went out and said to them, "This is what Pharaoh says:[c] 'I am not giving you straw. **11** Go get straw yourselves wherever you can find it, but there will be no reduction at all in your workload.'" **12** So the people scattered throughout the land of Egypt to gather stubble for straw. **13** The overseers insisted, "Finish your assigned work each day, just as you did when straw was provided." **14** Then the Israelite foremen, whom Pharaoh's slave drivers had set over the people, were beaten[d] and asked, "Why haven't you finished making your prescribed number of bricks yesterday or today, as you did before?"

15 So the Israelite foremen went in and cried for help to Pharaoh: "Why are you treating your servants this way? **16** No straw has been given to your servants, yet they say to us, 'Make bricks!' Look, your servants are being beaten, but it is your own people who are at fault."

17 But he said, "You are slackers. Slackers! That is why you are saying, 'Let us go sacrifice to the LORD.' **18** Now get to work. No straw will be given to you, but you must produce the same quantity of bricks."

19 The Israelite foremen saw that they were in trouble when they were told, "You cannot reduce your daily quota of bricks." **20** When they left Pharaoh, they confronted Moses and Aaron, who stood waiting to meet them.

21 "May the LORD take note of you and judge," they said to them, "because you have made us reek to Pharaoh and his officials — putting a sword in their hand to kill us!"[e]

22 So Moses went back to the LORD and asked, "Lord, why have you caused trouble for this people? And why did you ever send me?[f] **23** Ever since I went in to Pharaoh to speak in your name he has caused trouble for this people, and you haven't rescued your people at all."

6 But the LORD replied to Moses, "Now you will see what I will do to Pharaoh: because of a strong hand he will let them go, and because of a strong hand he will drive them from his land."[g]

GOD PROMISES FREEDOM

2 Then God spoke to Moses, telling him, "I am the LORD. **3** I appeared to Abraham, Isaac, and Jacob as God Almighty, but I was not known to them by my name 'the LORD.'[A,h] **4** I also established my covenant with them to give them the land of Canaan, the land they lived in as aliens.[i] **5** Furthermore, I have heard the groaning of the Israelites, whom the Egyptians are forcing to work as slaves, and I have remembered[j] my covenant.

6 "Therefore tell the Israelites: I am the LORD, and I will bring you out from the forced labor of the Egyptians and rescue you from slavery to them. I will redeem you with an outstretched arm[k] and great acts of judgment. **7** I will take you as my people,[l] and I will be your God. You will know[m] that I am the LORD your God, who brought you out from the forced labor of the Egyptians. **8** I will bring you to the land that I swore[B,n] to give to Abraham, Isaac, and Jacob, and I will give it to you as a possession. I am the LORD." **9** Moses told this to the Israelites, but they did not listen[o] to him because of their broken spirit and hard labor.

[a] 5:6 Ex 1:1; 3:7
[b] 5:8 Ex 2:23; 3:7; 5:15
[c] 5:10 Ex 4:22; 5:1
[d] 5:14 Is 10:24

[e] 5:21 Gn 34:30; Ex 6:9; 14:11
[f] 5:22 Nm 11:11; Jr 4:10
[g] 6:1 Ex 3:19; 12:31,33,39
[h] 6:3 Gn 17:1; Ex 3:14; Ps 68:4; 83:18; Jn 8:58
[i] 6:4 Gn 15:18; 28:4
[j] 6:5 Gn 9:15; Ex 2:24; 1Ch 16:15; Ps 105:8; 106:45; 111:4
[k] 6:6 Ex 3:17; Dt 7:8; 26:8; 1Ch 17:21
[l] 6:7 Dt 4:20; 2Sm 7:24
[m] Ex 16:12; 29:45; Is 41:20; Rv 21:7
[n] 6:8 Gn 14:22; 15:18; 26:3
[o] 6:9 Ex 5:21; Ac 7:25

A 6:3 LORD (in small capitals) stands for the personal name of God, which in Hb is *Yahweh*. There is a long tradition of substituting "LORD" for "Yahweh" out of reverence.   B 6:8 Lit *raised my hand*

keep the lazy **slackers** busy and avoid further whining about worshiping the Lord (5:8-9).
5:19-21 Upon leaving Pharaoh's presence, **the Israelite foremen . . . confronted Moses and Aaron** (5:19-20). They angrily blamed the brothers for making matters worse (5:21). If the Hebrews hadn't wanted Moses for a deliverer in the past (2:13-14), they certainly didn't want him now.
5:22-23 The people blamed Moses, so he shifted the blame to God. He had quickly

forgotten that God told him that Pharaoh's heart would be hard, that freedom would be won only by God's mighty power, and that it would be a fight to the death.
6:1-5 Things were about to get exciting. **Now**, God said, **you will see what I will do** (6:1). He reminded Moses that he had revealed himself to the patriarchs, though they had not known him **by [the] name 'the LORD'** (6:3). In recent days he had **heard the groaning** of their blood descendants and **remembered** his **covenant** (6:5).

When the Bible says that God "remembers," it doesn't mean that he called to mind something that he had forgotten. It means that, based on a covenant promise he made, he's ready to act to fulfill his obligation.
6:6 The Lord's **outstretched arm** refers to his supernatural power that would invade history to such an extent that people would still be talking about it thousands of years later.

a 6:12 Ex 4:10; 6:30; Jr 1:6
b 6:14 Gn 46:9; 1Ch 5:3
c 6:15 Gn 46:10; 1Ch 4:24
d 6:16 Gn 46:11; Nm 3:17
e 6:17-19 Nm 3:18-20; 1Ch
6:17-19; 23:21
f 6:20 Ex 2:1-2; Nm 26:59
g 6:21 Nm 16:1; 1Ch
6:37-38

h 6:22 Lv 10:4; Nm 3:30
i 6:23 Ru 4:19-20; 1Ch
2:10; Mt 1:4
j Lv 10:1; Nm 3:2; 26:60
k 6:24 Nm 26:11; 1Ch
6:22-23,37
l 6:25 Nm 25:7,11; Jos
24:33; Ps 106:30
m 6:26 Ex 7:4; 12:17,51;
Nm 33:1
n 6:29 Ex 6:11; 7:2
o 6:30 Ex 4:10; 6:12
p 7:3 Ex 4:21

[10] Then the LORD spoke to Moses, [11] "Go and tell Pharaoh king of Egypt to let the Israelites go from his land."

[12] But Moses said in the LORD's presence: "If the Israelites will not listen to me, then how will Pharaoh listen to me, since I am such a poor speaker?"[A,a] [13] Then the LORD spoke to Moses and Aaron and gave them commands concerning both the Israelites and Pharaoh king of Egypt to bring the Israelites out of the land of Egypt.

GENEALOGY OF MOSES AND AARON

[14] These are the heads of their fathers' families:

The sons of Reuben,[b] the firstborn
   of Israel:
Hanoch and Pallu, Hezron and Carmi.
These are the clans of Reuben.

[15]   The sons of Simeon:[c]
Jemuel, Jamin, Ohad, Jachin,
Zohar, and Shaul, the son
   of a Canaanite woman.
These are the clans of Simeon.

[16]   These are the names of the sons
   of Levi
according to their family records;
Gershon, Kohath, and Merari.[d]
Levi lived 137 years.
[17]   The sons of Gershon:
Libni and Shimei, by their clans.
[18]   The sons of Kohath:
Amram, Izhar, Hebron, and Uzziel.
Kohath lived 133 years.
[19]   The sons of Merari:
Mahli and Mushi.
These are the clans of the Levites[e]
according to their family records.

[20]   Amram married his father's sister
   Jochebed,
and she bore him Aaron and Moses.[f]
Amram lived 137 years.
[21]   The sons of Izhar:[g]
Korah, Nepheg, and Zichri.

[22]   The sons of Uzziel:
Mishael, Elzaphan,[h] and Sithri.
[23]   Aaron married Elisheba,
daughter of Amminadab[i] and sister
   of Nahshon.
She bore him Nadab and Abihu,
Eleazar and Ithamar.[j]
[24]   The sons of Korah:[k]
Assir, Elkanah, and Abiasaph.
These are the clans
   of the Korahites.
[25]   Aaron's son Eleazar married
one of the daughters
   of Putiel,
and she bore him Phinehas.[l]
These are the heads of the Levite
   families by their clans.

[26] It was this Aaron and Moses whom the LORD told, "Bring the Israelites out of the land of Egypt according to their military divisions."[m] [27] Moses and Aaron were the ones who spoke to Pharaoh king of Egypt in order to bring the Israelites out of Egypt.

MOSES AND AARON
BEFORE PHARAOH

[28] On the day the LORD spoke to Moses in the land of Egypt, [29] he said to him, "I am the LORD;[n] tell Pharaoh king of Egypt everything I am telling you."

[30] But Moses replied in the LORD's presence, "Since I am such a poor speaker,[o] how will Pharaoh listen to me?"

7 The LORD answered Moses, "See, I have made you like God to Pharaoh, and Aaron your brother will be your prophet. [2] You must say whatever I command you; then Aaron your brother must declare it to Pharaoh so that he will let the Israelites go from his land. [3] But I will harden Pharaoh's heart[p] and multiply my signs and wonders in the land of Egypt. [4] Pharaoh will not listen to you, but I will put my hand into Egypt and bring the military divisions of my people the Israelites out

---

[A] 6:12 Lit *I have uncircumcised lips*, also in v. 30

6:12 Moses pointed to his lack of eloquence as if that would somehow lead to the downfall of God's plan. But God intended to deliver the people through his "outstretched arm" (6:6), not through Moses's ability to captivate an audience.
6:25 The name **Phinehas** means "the Negro" or "Nubian," a dark-skinned people (also see 1 Chr 9:20). Phinehas was the son of **Eleazar** and his wife, a daughter of **Putiel**. Therefore, at least some of the citizens within Israel were giving birth to children whose names charac-

terized them as Nubian or Negroes. Thus, the children of Israel must have been heterogeneous. Putiel's name provides us with a possible understanding of who his people were. The first three letters of Putiel's name appear to have a lexical/etymological link to Put, one of the sons of Ham. Where the name Put is used in the Old Testament, it usually names African peoples (see also Jer 46:9; Ezek 27:10; 30:5; 38:5). This would certainly explain how Phinehas was born a Nubian in the midst of a Semitic congregation.

6:26 The statement that **it was this Aaron and Moses whom the LORD told** to lead the Israelites out of Egypt means that these two had the right family credentials for the work God had assigned them. They were Levites (6:14-25).
7:3-5 Since Pharaoh would refuse to **listen**, God would **stretch out [his] hand against Egypt** in judgment to deliver his people (7:4-5). This is a reminder that all people will experience the hand of God one way or another—either its hardness or its mercy.

The Majesty of You

G OD HAS PLACED A CROWN on your head. You are majestic. For real. The enemy does not want you to know this, however. Satan does not want you to know that you have glory, honor, and dominion from God. Why? As long as Satan can keep you from thinking like royalty, he can keep you from acting like royalty. As long as he can keep you thinking that you are nobody, or that you do not matter and you have no say, he can keep you acting like you are nobody, and that you do not matter, and that you have no say. As a result, Satan can keep the greatness of your future locked up and tucked away. But I want to let you in on a very powerful secret: you have something that Satan does not.

As a believer in Jesus Christ, you have spiritual authority. You have been crowned with majesty in God's kingdom. It is up to you to use the rights that come with the majesty you have been given. While God is the sovereign and absolute King, he has given you the authority to accomplish all that you need to do to fulfill your destiny.

Not only has God given you spiritual authority, but he also has empowered you with all you need to exercise it. If you only memorize one verse in your entire life, memorize this one. It is one of my favorites. "God is able to make every grace overflow to you, so that in every way, always having everything you need, you may excel in every good work" (2 COR 9:8). It is a promise.

It doesn't matter what opposition you face. It doesn't matter how big the Pharaohs are in your life (SEE EXOD 7:1-2). If you are doing what God has created you to do, he has empowered you with authority. You are majestic.

Keep in mind, though, that God won't force you to exercise your authority any more than he forced Moses to confront Pharaoh. That is up to you. Moses could have walked away and said, "You know what, God, that sounds good, and that is a great locker-room speech, but have you *seen* Pharaoh? Do you have any idea how many men he has at his disposal? I appreciate the vote of confidence you gave me, God, but you are just not being realistic." Moses could have said that and left. But as a result, we might be reading about someone else in Scripture whom God used to set his people free.

Many of us, unfortunately, have given away our spiritual authority. Satan didn't even have to battle us for it. Some simply examine their situations, see the size of the challenges, or look at their own inadequacies, and give up. In so doing, authority over that situation at work, that situation in the home, that problem, that addiction, that ambition, or that vision gets handed over to Satan.

[a] 7:5 Ex 7:17; 8:19,22; 14:4,18
[b] Ex 3:20; 6:6
[c] 7:7 Dt 29:5; 31:2; 34:7; Ac 7:23,30
[d] 7:9 Ex 4:2; Is 7:11; Jn 2:18; 6:30
[e] 7:11 Gn 41:8; 2Tm 3:8
[f] Ex 7:22; 8:7,18
[g] 7:13 Ex 4:21; 7:22; 8:15,19,32; 9:7,12,34; 10:1,20,27; 11:10; 14:8
[h] 7:14-15 Ex 4:2-3; 8:15; 10:1,20,27

[i] 7:19 Ex 8:5-6,16-17; 9:22; 10:12,21; 14:21,26
[j] 7:20 Ex 17:5; Ps 78:44; 105:29
[k] 8:1 Ex 3:12,18; 4:23
[l] 8:2 Ex 7:14; 9:2; Rv 16:13
[m] 8:3-5 Ex 7:19; 10:6
[n] 8:6 Ps 78:45; 105:30

of the land of Egypt by great acts of judgment. [5] The Egyptians will know that I am the LORD[a] when I stretch out my hand[b] against Egypt and bring out the Israelites from among them."

[6] So Moses and Aaron did this; they did just as the LORD commanded them. [7] Moses was eighty years old[c] and Aaron eighty-three when they spoke to Pharaoh.

[8] The LORD said to Moses and Aaron, [9] "When Pharaoh tells you, 'Perform a miracle,' tell Aaron, 'Take your staff and throw it down before Pharaoh. It will become a serpent.'"[d] [10] So Moses and Aaron went in to Pharaoh and did just as the LORD had commanded. Aaron threw down his staff before Pharaoh and his officials, and it became a serpent. [11] But then Pharaoh called the wise men and sorcerers — the magicians[e] of Egypt, and they also did the same thing by their occult practices.[f] [12] Each one threw down his staff, and it became a serpent. But Aaron's staff swallowed their staffs. [13] However, Pharaoh's heart was hard,[g] and he did not listen to them, as the LORD had said.

THE FIRST PLAGUE: WATER TURNED TO BLOOD

[14] Then the LORD said to Moses, "Pharaoh's heart is hard: He refuses to let the people go. [15] Go to Pharaoh in the morning. When you see him walking out to the water, stand ready to meet him by the bank of the Nile. Take in your hand the staff that turned into a snake.[h] [16] Tell him: The LORD, the God of the Hebrews, has sent me to tell you: Let my people go, so that they may worship[A] me in the wilderness, but so far you have not listened. [17] This is what the LORD says: Here is how you will know that I am the LORD. Watch. I am about to strike the water in the Nile with the staff in my hand, and it will turn to blood. [18] The fish in the Nile will die, the river will stink, and the Egyptians will be unable to drink water from it." [19] So the LORD said to Moses, "Tell Aaron: Take your staff and stretch out your

hand[i] over the waters of Egypt — over their rivers, canals, ponds, and all their water reservoirs — and they will become blood. There will be blood throughout the land of Egypt, even in wooden and stone containers."

[20] Moses and Aaron did just as the LORD had commanded; in the sight of Pharaoh and his officials, he raised the staff and struck the water in the Nile, and all the water in the Nile was turned to blood.[j] [21] The fish in the Nile died, and the river smelled so bad the Egyptians could not drink water from it. There was blood throughout the land of Egypt.

[22] But the magicians of Egypt did the same thing by their occult practices. So Pharaoh's heart was hard, and he would not listen to them, as the LORD had said. [23] Pharaoh turned around, went into his palace, and didn't take even this to heart. [24] All the Egyptians dug around the Nile for water to drink because they could not drink the water from the river. [25] Seven days passed after the LORD struck the Nile.

THE SECOND PLAGUE: FROGS

8 Then the LORD said to Moses, "Go in to Pharaoh and tell him: This is what the LORD says: Let my people go, so that they may worship me.[k] [2] But if you refuse to let them go, then I will plague all your territory with frogs.[l] [3] The Nile will swarm with frogs; they will come up and go into your palace, into your bedroom and on your bed, into the houses of your officials and your people, and into your ovens and kneading bowls. [4] The frogs will come up on you, your people, and all your officials."

[5] The LORD then said to Moses, "Tell Aaron: Stretch out your hand with your staff over the rivers, canals, and ponds, and cause the frogs to come up onto the land of Egypt."[m] [6] When Aaron stretched out his hand over the waters of Egypt, the frogs[n] came up and covered the land of Egypt.

[A] 7:16 Or *serve*; Ex 4:23

7:6-7 Moses and Aaron . . . did just as the LORD commanded them (7:6). There's no better commendation a person can receive than this. Those who do likewise will hear the Lord Jesus say, "Well done, good and faithful servant!" (Matt 25:23).

Notice that these two brothers began their ministry at age **eighty** and **eighty-three** (Exod 7:7). For the godly saint devoted to the King's agenda, the senior years can be the most fruitful.

7:8-13 Lest Pharaoh think his magic and the Lord's supernatural power were on equal footing, **Aaron's staff swallowed their staffs** (7:12).

7:17-18 The Nile, that which was a source of life for Egypt, would become a source of death.

7:19-24 All the water **turned to blood**, and the Egyptians **could not drink** it (7:20-21). Once again, Egypt's **magicians . . . did the same thing by their occult practices**, probably by some sort of sleight of hand—but

clearly on a much smaller scale (7:22). But even if they were able to mimic God's miracle, they were unable to reverse it. Pharaoh simply walked away from the first clear evidence of God's hand at work against him (7:23). Out of pride, he refused to submit to divine authority.

8:1-7 Once again, Pharaoh's **magicians** imitated this sign (8:7). Ridding the land of frogs would've demonstrated genuine spiritual power, but this they couldn't do.

⁷ But the magicians did the same thing by their occult practices and brought frogs up onto the land of Egypt.

⁸ Pharaoh summoned Moses and Aaron and said, "Appeal[a] to the LORD to remove the frogs from me and my people. Then I will let the people go and they can sacrifice to the LORD."

⁹ Moses said to Pharaoh, "You may have the honor of choosing. When should I appeal on behalf of you, your officials, and your people, that the frogs be taken away from you and your houses, and remain only in the Nile?"

¹⁰ "Tomorrow," he answered.

Moses replied, "As you have said, so that you may know there is no one like the LORD our God,[b] ¹¹ the frogs will go away from you, your houses, your officials, and your people. The frogs will remain only in the Nile." ¹² After Moses and Aaron went out from Pharaoh, Moses cried out to the LORD for help concerning the frogs that he had brought against Pharaoh. ¹³ The LORD did as Moses had said: the frogs in the houses, courtyards, and fields died. ¹⁴ They piled them in countless heaps, and there was a terrible odor in the land. ¹⁵ But when Pharaoh saw there was relief, he hardened his heart[c] and would not listen to them, as the LORD had said.

THE THIRD PLAGUE: GNATS

¹⁶ Then the LORD said to Moses, "Tell Aaron: Stretch out your staff and strike the dust of the land, and it will become gnats[A] throughout the land of Egypt." ¹⁷ And they did this. Aaron stretched out his hand with his staff, and when he struck the dust of the land, gnats were on people and animals. All the dust of the land became gnats throughout the land of Egypt. ¹⁸ The magicians tried to produce gnats using their occult practices,

but they could not. The gnats remained on people and animals.[d]

¹⁹ "This is the finger of God,"[e] the magicians said to Pharaoh. But Pharaoh's heart was hard, and he would not listen to them, as the LORD had said.

THE FOURTH PLAGUE: SWARMS OF FLIES

²⁰ The LORD said to Moses, "Get up early in the morning and present yourself to Pharaoh when you see him going out to the water. Tell him: This is what the LORD says: Let my people go, so that they may worship[B] me.[f] ²¹ But if you will not let my people go, then I will send swarms of flies[c] against you, your officials, your people, and your houses. The Egyptians' houses will swarm with flies, and so will the land where they live.[D] ²² But on that day I will give special treatment to the land of Goshen, where my people are living;[g] no flies will be there. This way you will know that I, the LORD, am in the land. ²³ I will make a distinction[E] between my people and your people. This sign will take place tomorrow."

²⁴ And the LORD did this. Thick swarms of flies went into Pharaoh's palace and his officials' houses. Throughout Egypt the land was ruined because of the swarms of flies.[h] ²⁵ Then Pharaoh summoned Moses and Aaron and said, "Go sacrifice to your God within the country."

²⁶ But Moses said, "It would not be right[F] to do that, because what we will sacrifice to the LORD our God is detestable to the Egyptians.[i] If we sacrifice what the Egyptians detest in front of them, won't they stone us? ²⁷ We must go a distance of three days into the wilderness and sacrifice to the LORD our God as he instructs us."

²⁸ Pharaoh responded, "I will let you go and sacrifice to the LORD your God in the wilderness, but don't go very far. Make an appeal[j] for me."

ᵃ 8:8 Ex 8:28; 9:28; 10:17
ᵇ 8:10 Ex 9:14; Dt 33:26; 2Sm 7:22; 1Ch 17:20; Is 46:9; Jr 10:6-7
ᶜ 8:15 Ex 7:4; Ec 8:11
ᵈ 8:18 Ex 7:11; 9:11; Dn 5:8
ᵉ 8:19 Ps 8:3; Lk 11:20
ᶠ 8:20 Ex 2:5; 7:15; 8:1; 9:13
ᵍ 8:22 Ex 9:4,6; 10:23; 11:7
ʰ 8:24 Ps 78:45; 105:31
ⁱ 8:26 Gn 43:32; 46:34
ʲ 8:28 Ex 8:8; 9:28; 1Kg 13:6

ᴬ 8:16 Perhaps sand fleas or mosquitoes   ᴮ 8:20 Or serve   ᶜ 8:21 Or insects   ᴰ 8:21 Lit are   ᴱ 8:23 LXX, Syr, Vg; MT reads will place redemption
ᶠ 8:26 Or allowable

8:8-14 Notice Moses's cunning reply: **You may have the honor of choosing. When should . . . the frogs be taken away?** (8:9). This would prevent Pharaoh from claiming that their coming and going was a freak act of nature (8:10-11).

8:15 **When Pharaoh saw there was relief, he hardened his heart** again. This is a warning to us all. When struggles are intense, we tend to cry to God for relief. Yet, as soon as it comes, we can easily fall back into business as usual.

Importantly, while the Lord could have wiped this arrogant Pharaoh off the map,

he gave him many chances to repent. God's kindness was intended to lead the king to repentance (see Rom 2:4).

8:16-19 Egypt's sorcerers were unable to replicate the plague of gnats by their magic arts (8:18). They realized they were in over their heads and confessed to Pharaoh, **This is the finger of God**. But Pharaoh **would not listen to** his own spiritual advisers (8:19).

8:20-23 This time God would **make a distinction** between the Israelites and the Egyptians by permitting **no flies** in Goshen, the

land of his people (8:22-23). God was giving further proof that his power was behind the ecological disasters.

8:24-27 Pharaoh decided he would try to strike a compromise and offered to let the people go to **sacrifice** to God **within the country** of Egypt (8:25). But Moses wouldn't haggle. If the Israelites remained in Egypt, the Egyptians would **stone** them because they would **detest** their sacrifices (8:26). The worship that the true God found acceptable clashed with the religious practices of pagan Egypt.

[a] 9:1-5 Ex 7:4,16; 8:1-2,22; 11:7
[b] 9:6 Ex 9:19; Ps 78:50
[c] 9:7 Ex 7:14; 8:32

[d] 9:9 Dt 28:27; Rv 16:2
[e] 9:11 Ex 8:18; 2Tm 3:9
[f] 9:12 Ex 4:21; 7:22
[g] 9:15 Ex 3:20; 8:10,20
[h] 9:16 Ex 14:17; Pr 16:4; Rm 9:17
[i] 9:18 Jos 10:11; Jb 38:22; Ps 18:12; Is 28:2; 30:30; Ezk 13:11; 38:22

[29] "As soon as I leave you," Moses said, "I will appeal to the Lord, and tomorrow the swarms of flies will depart from Pharaoh, his officials, and his people. But Pharaoh must not act deceptively again by refusing to let the people go and sacrifice to the Lord." [30] Then Moses left Pharaoh's presence and appealed to the Lord. [31] The Lord did as Moses had said: He removed the swarms of flies from Pharaoh, his officials, and his people; not one was left. [32] But Pharaoh hardened his heart this time also and did not let the people go.

THE FIFTH PLAGUE: DEATH OF LIVESTOCK

9 Then the Lord said to Moses, "Go in to Pharaoh and say to him: This is what the Lord, the God of the Hebrews, says: Let my people go, so that they may worship me. [2] But if you refuse to let them go and keep holding them, [3] then the Lord's hand will bring a severe plague against your livestock in the field — the horses, donkeys, camels, herds, and flocks. [4] But the Lord will make a distinction between the livestock of Israel and the livestock of Egypt, so that nothing of all that the Israelites own will die." [5] And the Lord set a time, saying, "Tomorrow the Lord will do this thing in the land."[a] [6] The Lord did this the next day. All the Egyptian livestock died,[b] but none among the Israelite livestock died. [7] Pharaoh sent messengers who saw that not a single one of the Israelite livestock was dead. But Pharaoh's heart was hard,[c] and he did not let the people go.

THE SIXTH PLAGUE: BOILS

[8] Then the Lord said to Moses and Aaron, "Take handfuls of furnace soot, and Moses is to throw it toward heaven in the sight of Pharaoh. [9] It will become fine dust over the entire land of Egypt. It will become festering boils[d] on people and animals throughout the land of Egypt." [10] So they took furnace soot and stood before Pharaoh. Moses threw it toward heaven, and it became festering boils on people and animals. [11] The magicians could not stand before Moses because of the boils, for the boils were on the magicians as well as on all the Egyptians.[e] [12] But the Lord hardened Pharaoh's heart[f] and he did not listen to them, as the Lord had told Moses.

THE SEVENTH PLAGUE: HAIL

[13] Then the Lord said to Moses, "Get up early in the morning and present yourself to Pharaoh. Tell him: This is what the Lord, the God of the Hebrews says: Let my people go, so that they may worship me. [14] For this time I am about to send all my plagues against you,[A] your officials, and your people. Then you will know there is no one like me on the whole earth. [15] By now I could have stretched out my hand and struck you and your people with a plague, and you would have been obliterated from the earth.[g] [16] However, I have let you live for this purpose: to show you my power[h] and to make my name known on the whole earth. [17] You are still acting arrogantly against[B] my people by not letting them go. [18] Tomorrow at this time I will rain down the worst hail[i] that has ever occurred in Egypt from the day it was founded until now. [19] Therefore give orders to bring your livestock and all that you have in the field into shelters. Every person and animal that is in the field and

[A] 9:14 Lit plagues to your heart   [B] 9:17 Or still obstructing

---

9:1-7 Again the Lord would **make a distinction** between Israel and Egypt; the livestock of the former would live while that of the latter would die (9:4). To this point, there had been no destruction of property or bodily suffering as a result of Pharaoh's obstinacy—unless you equate having frogs hopping on your pillow as a painful experience. But that leniency was about to change. The death of the livestock would have been a severe blow to the Egyptian economy.

9:8-12 With this sixth plague, painful physical suffering visited the Egyptians. Even Pharaoh's **magicians could not stand before Moses** because they were covered with boils (9:11). Yet Pharaoh was defiant, unmoved by the misery of his own subjects. Therefore, the Lord removed all restraint and finally supersized the hardness of Pharaoh's heart (see the note on 4:21).

9:15 Through his intermediaries God said to Pharaoh, **By now I could have ... struck you ... and you would have been obliterated** (9:15). It's as if Egypt's king is a petulant child who has talked back to his father one too many times, earning this response: "Do you understand whom you're talking to, young man?" Except, in the biblical case, the situation is incredibly magnified. Parents have limited authority over their children. God has complete, righteous authority over all his creatures. The king's life hung by a thread. He existed only by God's mercy.

9:16-17 Christians often quote the gracious promise of Romans 8:28: "All things work together for the good of those who love God, who are called according to his purpose." But there's a flip side to that reality: All things can work together for the bad of those who hate

God and resist his purposes. Would Pharaoh submit to God, or would he be run over by God's sovereignty tires? God will be glorified—through us or in spite of us.

If you cooperate with the sovereignty of God, it does not mean you won't experience hardship and suffering. Rather, it means you can be assured that the good, bad, and ugly of your life will be put into God's blender, ultimately bringing you to the place where he wants you to be.

9:17-21 Once more God tempered judgment with mercy and urged the man to bring all the surviving **livestock** into the **shelters** because **every person and animal** outside when the **hail** fell would be killed (9:19). Some of **Pharaoh's officials who feared the word of the Lord** brought their livestock in (9:20).

not brought inside will die when the hail falls on them." **20** Those among Pharaoh's officials who feared the word of the LORD made their servants and livestock flee to shelters, **21** but those who didn't take to heart the LORD's word left their servants and livestock in the field.

22 Then the LORD said to Moses, "Stretch out your hand toward heaven and let there be hail throughout the land of Egypt — on people and animals and every plant of the field in the land of Egypt." **23** So Moses stretched out his staff toward heaven, and the LORD sent thunder and hail.[a] Lightning struck the land, and the LORD rained hail on the land of Egypt. **24** The hail, with lightning flashing through it, was so severe that nothing like it had occurred in the land of Egypt since it had become a nation. **25** Throughout the land of Egypt, the hail struck down everything in the field, both people and animals. The hail beat down every plant of the field and shattered every tree in the field. **26** The only place it didn't hail was in the land of Goshen, where the Israelites were.[b]

27 Pharaoh sent for Moses and Aaron. "I have sinned this time," he said to them. "The LORD is the righteous[c] one, and I and my people are the guilty ones. **28** Make an appeal to the LORD. There has been enough of God's thunder and hail. I will let you go;[d] you don't need to stay any longer."

29 Moses said to him, "When I have left the city, I will spread out my hands[e] to the LORD. The thunder will cease, and there will be no more hail, so that you may know the earth[A,f] belongs to the LORD. **30** But as for you and your officials, I know that you still do not fear the LORD God."

31 The flax and the barley were destroyed because the barley was ripe[B] and the flax was budding,[g] **32** but the wheat and the spelt were not destroyed since they are later crops.[c]

33 Moses left Pharaoh and the city, and spread out his hands to the LORD. Then the thunder and hail ceased, and rain no longer poured down on the land. **34** When Pharaoh saw that the rain, hail, and thunder had ceased, he sinned again and hardened his heart, he and his officials. **35** So Pharaoh's heart was hard, and he did not let the Israelites go, as the LORD had said through Moses.

THE EIGHTH PLAGUE: LOCUSTS

10 Then the LORD said to Moses, "Go to Pharaoh, for I have hardened his heart and the hearts of his officials so that I may do these miraculous signs of mine among them,[D,H] **2** and so that you may tell[E] your son and grandson[i] how severely I dealt with the Egyptians and performed miraculous signs among them, and you will know that I am the LORD."

3 So Moses and Aaron went in to Pharaoh and told him, "This is what the LORD, the God of the Hebrews, says: How long will you refuse to humble yourself before me? Let my people go, that they may worship me.[j] **4** But if you refuse to let my people go, then tomorrow I will bring locusts[k] into your territory. **5** They will cover the surface of the land so that no one will be able to see the land. They will eat the remainder left[l] to you that escaped the hail; they will eat every tree you have growing in the fields. **6** They will fill your houses, all your officials' houses, and the houses of all the Egyptians — something your fathers and grandfathers never saw since the time they occupied the land until today." Then he turned and left Pharaoh's presence.

7 Pharaoh's officials asked him, "How long must this man be a snare[m] to us? Let

a 9:23 Ps 78:47-48; 105:32; 148:8; Rv 8:7; 11:19; 16:21
b 9:26 Ex 8:22; 9:4,6; 11:7; 12:13; Is 32:18
c 9:27 Ex 10:16; 2Ch 12:6; Ps 129:4; 145:17; Lm 1:18
d 9:28 Ex 8:8; 10:17
e 9:29 1Kg 8:22,38; Ps 143:6; Is 1:15
f Ps 24:1; 1Co 10:26
g 9:31 Ru 1:22; 2:23

h 10:1 Ex 4:21; 7:4,13
i 10:2 Ex 13:8,14; Dt 4:9; 6:20-22; Ps 44:1; 78:5-7; Jl 1:3
j 10:3 1Kg 21:29; Jms 4:10; 1Pt 5:6
k 10:4 Pr 30:27; Rv 9:3
l 10:5 Ex 9:32; Jl 1:4
m 10:7 Ex 23:33; Jos 23:13; 1Sm 18:21; Ec 7:26

A 9:29 Or land   B 9:31 Lit was ears of grain   C 9:32 Lit are late   D 10:1 Lit mine in his midst   E 10:2 Lit tell in the ears of

9:26 God again spared **the land of Goshen, where the Israelites were**. This distinction makes it clear that this was not the work of Mother Nature, a fictitious figure often wrongly credited with the marvels of the natural world; it was the work of Father God, the true Creator of all.
9:27-30 On the surface, it appeared that Pharaoh was changing. Moses therefore promised to appeal to the Lord, and the hail would stop (9:29). But God gave Moses spiritual insight into Pharaoh's heart. The king of Egypt was willing to say what was necessary to cause a change in his wretched circumstances, but there had been no spiritual change in his life.

9:31-35 Even in the midst of all this devastation, God had been merciful to Egypt. **The flax and the barley were destroyed**, but **the wheat and the spelt** were preserved because they were not yet in season (9:31-32). Shockingly, Pharaoh saw this as an opportunity to persist in rebellion.
10:1-2 The Lord wanted Israel to realize that the miracles weren't merely for the Egyptians— they were also for their sake. Israelites in the generations to come were to tell their offspring how the Lord had powerfully judged their enemies, so that they might **know** and revere **the LORD** (10:2). Similarly, Christian parents are to pass on their faith to their children (see Eph 6:4).

10:3 Pharaoh would eventually humble himself. But how much destruction and sorrow would he bring on himself and those under his care before he finally gave in? The true King will get his way. The only question is whether a person will submit to his agenda and experience his blessing or resist it and experience misery.
10:7 Pharaoh's advisers urged the king to release the Israelites. Even as Pharaoh continued to puff himself up, his nation was crumbling all around him. Sometimes a leader's arrogance—whether he rules a country or a home—prevents him from seeing what everyone around him can.

*a*10:8-9 Ex 5:1; 8:8
*b*10:14 Ps 78:46; 105:34; Jl 2:2
*c*10:15 Ex 10:5; Ps 105:35
*d*10:16-18 Ex 8:8,30; 9:27

*e*10:19 Ex 13:18; 15:4,22; 23:31; Nm 14:25; 21:4; 33:10-11
*f*10:20 Ex 4:21; 11:10
*g*10:22-23 Ex 8:22; Ps 105:28
*h*10:27 Ex 4:21; 10:20
*i*10:29 Heb 11:27

the men go, so that they may worship the LORD their God. Don't you realize yet that Egypt is devastated?"

⁸ So Moses and Aaron were brought back to Pharaoh. "Go, worship the LORD your God," Pharaoh said. "But exactly who will be going?"

⁹ Moses replied, "We will go with our young and with our old; we will go with our sons and with our daughters, with our flocks and with our herds because we must hold the LORD's festival."ᵃ

¹⁰ He said to them, "The Lord would have to be with you if I would ever let you and your families go! Look out — you're heading for trouble. ¹¹ No, go — just able-bodied men — worship the LORD, since that's what you want." And they were driven from Pharaoh's presence.

¹² The LORD then said to Moses, "Stretch out your hand over the land of Egypt, and the locusts will come up over it and eat every plant in the land, everything that the hail left." ¹³ So Moses stretched out his staff over the land of Egypt, and the LORD sent an east wind over the land all that day and through the night. By morning the east wind had brought in the locusts. ¹⁴ The locusts went up over the entire land of Egypt and settled on the whole territory of Egypt. Never before had there been such a large number of locusts, and there never will be again.ᵇ ¹⁵ They covered the surface of the whole land so that the land was black, and they consumed all the plants on the ground and all the fruit on the trees that the hail had left. Nothing green was left on the trees or the plants in the field throughout the land of Egypt.ᶜ

¹⁶ Pharaoh urgently sent for Moses and Aaron and said, "I have sinned against the LORD your God and against you. ¹⁷ Please forgive my sin once more and make an appeal to the LORD your God, so that he will just take this death away from me." ¹⁸ Moses left Pharaoh's presence and appealed to the LORD.ᵈ ¹⁹ Then the LORD changed the wind to a strong westᴬ wind, and it carried off the locusts and blew them into the Red Sea.ᵉ Not a single locust was left in all the territory of Egypt. ²⁰ But the LORD hardened Pharaoh's heart,ᶠ and he did not let the Israelites go.

THE NINTH PLAGUE: DARKNESS

²¹ Then the LORD said to Moses, "Stretch out your hand toward heaven, and there will be darkness over the land of Egypt, a darkness that can be felt." ²² So Moses stretched out his hand toward heaven, and there was thick darkness throughout the land of Egypt for three days. ²³ One person could not see another, and for three days they did not move from where they were. Yet all the Israelites had light where they lived.ᵍ

²⁴ Pharaoh summoned Moses and said, "Go, worship the LORD. Even your families may go with you; only your flocks and herds must stay behind."

²⁵ Moses responded, "You must also let us haveᴮ sacrifices and burnt offerings to prepare for the LORD our God. ²⁶ Even our livestock must go with us; not a hoof will be left behind because we will take some of them to worship the LORD our God. We will not know what we will use to worship the LORD until we get there."

²⁷ But the LORD hardened Pharaoh's heart,ʰ and he was unwilling to let them go. ²⁸ Pharaoh said to him, "Leave me! Make sure you never see my face again, for on the day you see my face, you will die."

²⁹ "As you have said," Moses replied, "I will never see your face again."ⁱ

THE TENTH PLAGUE: DEATH OF THE FIRSTBORN

11 The LORD saidᶜ to Moses, "I will bring one more plague on Pharaoh and on Egypt. After that, he will let you go from here. When he lets you go,ᴰ he will drive you out of here. ² Now announce to the people that both men and women should ask their neighbors for silver and gold items." ³ The LORD gaveᴱ the people favor with the Egyptians. In addition, Moses himself was very highly regardedᶠ in the

ᴬ10:19 Lit *sea*   ᴮ10:25 Lit *also give in our hand*   ᶜ11:1 Or *had said*   ᴰ11:1 Or *go, it will be finished —*   ᴱ11:3 Or *had given*   ᶠ11:3 Lit *was very great*

10:8-11 The king's offer to let only the **able-bodied men** go was a shrewd move because he knew that these husbands and fathers would certainly not run off and leave their wives and children behind (10:11). **10:21-23** Pharaoh was given no warning about the ninth plague. The Lord simply brought darkness on **the land . . . for three days** (10:22).

It was so oppressive and complete that the Egyptians didn't move during that time. But, miraculously, **the Israelites had light** (10:23). **10:24-29** Pharaoh again made a halfhearted attempt to submit by letting the Israelite **families** go but demanding that the **flocks and herds . . . stay** (10:24). But Moses knew partial obedience to God is disobedience.

11:1 God could have freed the Israelites with only one plague—or none. But he had planned to use ten from the beginning, to demonstrate conclusively his sovereign authority and power to the whole earth. **11:2-3** After years of slavery, Israel was receiving its just wages.

land of Egypt by[A] Pharaoh's officials and the people.[a]

[4] So Moses said, "This is what the LORD says: About midnight I will go throughout Egypt, [5] and every firstborn male in the land of Egypt will die, from the firstborn of Pharaoh who sits on his throne to the firstborn of the servant girl who is at the grindstones, as well as every firstborn of the livestock. [6] Then there will be a great cry of anguish through all the land of Egypt such as never was before or ever will be again. [7] But against all the Israelites, whether people or animals, not even a dog will snarl,[B] so that you may know that the LORD makes a distinction between Egypt and Israel. [8] All these officials of yours will come down to me and bow before me, saying: Get out, you and all the people who follow you.[c] After that, I will get out." And he went out from Pharaoh's presence fiercely angry.[b]

[9] The LORD said to Moses, "Pharaoh will not listen[c] to you, so that my wonders may be multiplied in the land of Egypt." [10] Moses and Aaron did all these wonders before Pharaoh, but the LORD hardened Pharaoh's heart,[d] and he would not let the Israelites go out of his land.

INSTRUCTIONS FOR THE PASSOVER

12 The LORD said to Moses and Aaron in the land of Egypt: [2] "This month is to be the beginning of months for you; it is the first month of your year.[e] [3] Tell the whole community of Israel that on the tenth day of this month they must each select an animal of the flock according to their fathers' families, one animal per family. [4] If the household is too small for a whole animal, that person and the neighbor nearest his house are to select one based on the combined number of people; you should apportion the animal according to what each will eat. [5] You must have an unblemished[f] animal, a year-old male; you may take it from either the sheep or the goats. [6] You are to keep it until the fourteenth day of this month; then the whole assembly of the community of Israel will slaughter the animals at twilight.[g] [7] They must take some of the blood and put it on the two doorposts and the lintel of the houses where they eat them. [8] They are to eat the meat that night; they should eat it, roasted over the fire along with unleavened bread and bitter herbs.[h] [9] Do not eat any of it raw or cooked in boiling[D] water, but only roasted[i] over fire — its head as well as its legs and inner organs. [10] You must not leave any of it until morning;[j] any part of it left until morning you must burn. [11] Here is how you must eat it: You must be dressed for travel,[E] your sandals on your feet, and your staff in your hand. You are to eat it in a hurry; it is the LORD's Passover.[k]

[12] "I will pass through[l] the land of Egypt on that night and strike every firstborn male in the land of Egypt, both people and animals. I am the LORD; I will execute judgments against all the gods of Egypt.[m] [13] The blood on the houses where you are staying will be a distinguishing mark for you; when I see the blood, I will pass over you. No plague will be among you to destroy you when I strike the land of Egypt.

[14] "This day is to be a memorial for you, and you must celebrate it as a festival to the LORD. You are to celebrate it throughout your generations as a permanent statute.[n] [15] You must eat unleavened bread for seven days. On the first day you must remove yeast[o] from your houses. Whoever eats what is leavened from the first day through the seventh day must be cut off[p] from Israel. [16] You are to hold a sacred assembly[q] on the first day and another sacred assembly on the seventh day. No work may be done on those days except for preparing what people need to eat — you may do only that.

[17] "You are to observe the Festival of Unleavened Bread because on this very day I brought your military divisions out of the land of Egypt.[r] You must observe this day throughout your generations as

[a]11:1-3 Ex 3:21-22; 12:35-36
[b]11:8 Ex 12:3; Am 5:17
[c]11:9 Ex 3:19; 7:4; 10:1
[d]11:10 Ex 4:21; 10:20,27
[e]12:2 Ex 13:4; 23:15; 34:18; Dt 16:1
[f]12:5 Lv 22:19-21; Mal 1:8,14
[g]12:6 Lv 23:5; Nm 9:3; Dt 16:6
[h]12:8 Ex 34:25; Nm 9:11; Dt 16:3; 1Co 5:8
[i]12:9 Dt 16:7; 2Ch 35:13
[j]12:10 Ex 23:18; 34:25
[k]12:11 Ex 12:27; Dt 16:5
[l]12:12 Ex 11:4-5; Am 5:17
[m]Ex 6:2; Nm 33:4
[n]12:14 Ex 12:17,43; 13:9-10; 2Kg 23:21
[o]12:15 Ex 13:6-7; 23:15; 34:18; Lv 23:6; Dt 16:3,8
[p]Gn 17:14; Nm 9:13
[q]12:16 Lv 23:7-8; Nm 28:18,25
[r]12:17 Ex 12:41,51; 13:3

[A]11:3 Or *in the eyes of*   [B]11:7 Lit *point its tongue*   [C]11:8 Lit *people at your feet*   [D]12:9 Or *or boiled at all in*   [E]12:11 Lit *must have your waist girded*

11:4-10 The final curse against Pharaoh and Egypt would be a plague on the firstborn. The Lord would **go throughout Egypt, and every firstborn male** would die—whether human or livestock (11:4-5). But again God would make **a distinction** so that no harm would befall his people Israel (11:7). As a result, the Egyptians would beg the Israelites to leave. 12:3-13 The name *Passover* arises from the fact that the Lord would **pass through the land** ...

and strike every firstborn male (12:12), but he would **pass over** homes bearing the **blood** (12:13). Passover foreshadowed the coming of the Lord Jesus and his atoning death. To make sure his followers didn't miss the connection, Paul told the church, "Christ our Passover lamb has been sacrificed" (1 Cor 5:7). It was through the events of the first Passover that Israel was set free from slavery. Through placing faith in Christ's substitutionary death, we

likewise are set free from slavery to sin (see Rom 6:17-18). God had our salvation, too, in mind on that fateful night in Egypt. 12:14-20 **Yeast**, sometimes called "leaven," is often symbolic of sin in the Bible (12:15; see Luke 12:1; 1 Cor 5:6-8). Eating unleavened bread would remind the Israelites of their hasty exodus. Their deliverance happened so quickly that there was no time to use yeast to allow the bread to rise before they hit the road.

a 12:18 Lv 23:5-8; Nm 28:16-25
b 12:21 Ex 12:3; Mk 14:12-16
c 12:22 Ex 12:7; Heb 11:28
d 12:23 Ezk 9:6; 1Co 10:10; Rv 7:3
e 12:26 Ex 10:2; 13:8,14; Dt 6:20; 32:7; Jos 4:6,21; Ps 78:3-6
f 12:27 Ex 4:31; 12:11
g 12:29 Ex 4:23; 11:4; Nm 8:17; 33:4; Ps 78:51; 135:8

h 12:30 Ex 11:6; Am 5:17
i 12:33 Ex 11:8; Ps 105:38
j 12:35 Gn 15:14; Ex 3:21; Ps 105:37
k 12:37 Gn 47:11; Nm 33:3,5
l Ex 38:26; Nm 1:46; 11:21
m 12:39 Ex 6:1; 12:33
n 12:40 Gn 15:13-16; Ac 7:6; Gl 3:17
o 12:42 Ex 13:10; Dt 16:1,6

a permanent statute. **18** You are to eat unleavened bread in the first month,[a] from the evening of the fourteenth day of the month until the evening of the twenty-first day. **19** Yeast must not be found in your houses for seven days. If anyone eats something leavened, that person, whether a resident alien or native of the land, must be cut off from the community of Israel. **20** Do not eat anything leavened; eat unleavened bread in all your homes."[A]

21 Then Moses summoned all the elders of Israel and said to them, "Go, select an animal from the flock according to your families, and slaughter the Passover animal.[b] **22** Take a cluster of hyssop, dip it in the blood[c] that is in the basin, and brush the lintel and the two doorposts with some of the blood in the basin. None of you may go out the door of his house until morning. **23** When the LORD passes through to strike Egypt and sees the blood on the lintel and the two doorposts, he will pass over the door and not let the destroyer enter your houses to strike you.[d]

24 "Keep this command permanently as a statute for you and your descendants. **25** When you enter the land that the LORD will give you as he promised, you are to observe this ceremony. **26** When your children[e] ask you, 'What does this ceremony mean to you?' **27** you are to reply, 'It is the Passover sacrifice[f] to the LORD, for he passed over the houses of the Israelites in Egypt when he struck the Egyptians and spared our homes.'" So the people knelt low and worshiped. **28** Then the Israelites went and did this; they did just as the LORD had commanded Moses and Aaron.

THE EXODUS

29 Now at midnight the LORD struck every firstborn male in the land of Egypt, from the firstborn of Pharaoh who sat on his throne to the firstborn of the prisoner who was in the dungeon, and every firstborn of the livestock.[g] **30** During the night Pharaoh got up, he along with all his officials and all the Egyptians, and there was

a loud wailing[h] throughout Egypt because there wasn't a house without someone dead. **31** He summoned Moses and Aaron during the night and said, "Get out immediately from among my people, both you and the Israelites, and go, worship the LORD as you have said. **32** Take even your flocks and your herds as you asked and leave, and also bless me."

33 Now the Egyptians pressured the people in order to send them quickly out of the country, for they said, "We're all going to die!"[i] **34** So the people took their dough before it was leavened, with their kneading bowls wrapped up in their clothes on their shoulders.

35 The Israelites acted on Moses's word and asked the Egyptians for silver and gold items and for clothing.[j] **36** And the LORD gave the people such favor with the Egyptians that they gave them what they requested. In this way they plundered the Egyptians.

37 The Israelites traveled from Rameses to Succoth,[k] about six hundred thousand[l] able-bodied men on foot, besides their families. **38** A mixed crowd also went up with them, along with a huge number of livestock, both flocks and herds. **39** The people baked the dough they had brought out of Egypt into unleavened loaves, since it had no yeast; for when they were driven[m] out of Egypt, they could not delay and had not prepared provisions for themselves.

40 The time that the Israelites lived in Egypt[B] was 430 years.[n] **41** At the end of 430 years, on that same day, all the LORD's military divisions went out from the land of Egypt. **42** It was a night of vigil in honor of the LORD, because he would bring them out of the land of Egypt. This same night is in honor of the LORD, a night vigil for all the Israelites throughout their generations.[o]

PASSOVER INSTRUCTION

43 The LORD said to Moses and Aaron, "This is the statute of the Passover: no foreigner may eat it. **44** But any slave a man has purchased may eat it, after you have

---

[A] **12:20** Or *settlements*   [B] **12:40** LXX, Sam add *and in Canaan*

12:21-28 The festival would provide a teaching tool for future generations. When Jewish **children** asked their parents the meaning of **Passover**, the parents were to explain how God had judged Egypt and delivered his people (12:26-27).

12:29-30 Pharaoh had led his nation to cruelly enslave Israel and rebelliously despise Israel's God. As a result, Egypt was drinking the cup of God's wrath.

12:37-42 With women and children, the people of Israel would have numbered over two million. The **mixed crowd** indicates that non-Israelites accompanied them (12:38). Marriages to Egyptians, much like those of Joseph and Eleazar, would have produced dark-skinned offspring such as Phinehas (see 6:25), as well as a merging of bloodlines between Nubians and Semites. The Israelites' **430 years** in Egypt had finally

come to an end (12:40-41), just as the Lord had promised Abraham that they would (Gen 15:13-14).

12:43-51 The Israelites were not permitted to **break any of [the Passover sacrifice's] bones** (12:46). According to the New Testament, this was also fulfilled in Jesus Christ, the true Passover Lamb (see the note on 12:3-13). When Jesus was crucified, the soldiers did not break his legs (see John 19:31-36).

circumcised him. **45** A temporary resident or hired worker may not eat the Passover.[a] **46** It is to be eaten in one house. You may not take any of the meat outside the house, and you may not break any of its bones.[b] **47** The whole community of Israel must celebrate^ it. **48** If an alien resides among you and wants to observe the LORD's Passover, every male in his household must be circumcised, and then he may participate;[B] he will become like a native of the land. But no uncircumcised person may eat it. **49** The same law will apply to both the native and the alien[c] who resides among you."

50 Then all the Israelites did this; they did just as the LORD had commanded Moses and Aaron. **51** On that same day the LORD brought the Israelites out of the land of Egypt according to their military divisions.[d]

13 The LORD spoke to Moses: **2** "Consecrate every firstborn male[e] to me, the firstborn from every womb among the Israelites, both man and domestic animal; it is mine."

3 Then Moses said to the people, "Remember this day when you came out of Egypt, out of the place of slavery, for the LORD brought you out of here by the strength of his hand. Nothing leavened may be eaten.[f] **4** Today, in the month of Abib,[c,g] you are going out. **5** When the LORD brings you into the land of the Canaanites, Hethites, Amorites, Hivites, and Jebusites,[D] which he swore to your fathers that he would give you, a land flowing with milk and honey,[h] you must carry out this ceremony in this month.[i] **6** For seven days you must eat unleavened bread, and on the seventh day there is to be a festival to the LORD. **7** Unleavened bread is to be eaten for those seven days. Nothing leavened may be found among you, and no yeast may be found among you in all your territory. **8** On that day explain to your son, 'This is because of what the LORD did for me when I came out of Egypt.'[j] **9** Let it serve as a sign for you on your hand and as a reminder on your forehead,[E,k] so that the

LORD's instruction may be in your mouth; for the LORD brought you out of Egypt with a strong hand. **10** Keep this statute at its appointed time from year to year.

11 "When the LORD brings you into the land of the Canaanites, as he swore to you and your fathers, and gives it to you, **12** you are to present to the LORD every firstborn male of the womb. All firstborn offspring of the livestock you own that are males will be the LORD's. **13** You must redeem every firstborn of a donkey with a flock animal, but if you do not redeem it, break its neck. However, you must redeem every firstborn among your sons.[l]

14 "In the future, when your son[m] asks you, 'What does this mean?' say to him, 'By the strength of his hand the LORD brought us out of Egypt, out of the place of slavery. **15** When Pharaoh stubbornly refused to let us go, the LORD killed every firstborn male in the land of Egypt, both the firstborn of humans and the firstborn of livestock. That is why I sacrifice to the LORD all the firstborn of the womb that are males, but I redeem all the firstborn of my sons.' **16** So let it be a sign on your hand and a symbol[F] on your forehead, for the LORD brought us out of Egypt by the strength of his hand."[n]

THE ROUTE OF THE EXODUS

17 When Pharaoh let the people go, God did not lead them along the road to the land of the Philistines, even though it was nearby; for God said, "The people will change their minds and return to Egypt if they face war."[o] **18** So he led the people around toward the Red Sea along the road of the wilderness. And the Israelites left the land of Egypt in battle formation.[p]

19 Moses took the bones of Joseph[q] with him, because Joseph had made the Israelites swear a solemn oath, saying, "God will certainly come to your aid; then you must take my bones with you from this place."

20 They set out from Succoth and camped at Etham on the edge of the wilderness. **21** The LORD went ahead of them in a pillar of cloud[r] to lead them on their

[a] 12:43-45 Gn 17:11-13; Lv 22:10; Nm 9:14
[b] 12:46 Nm 9:12; Ps 34:20; Jn 19:33,36
[c] 12:49 Nm 9:14; 15:15-16,19; Gl 3:28
[d] 12:51 Ex 6:26; 12:41
[e] 13:2 Ex 13:12-13,15; 22:29-30; Nm 3:13; Dt 15:9; Lk 2:23
[f] 13:3 Ex 6:1; 12:8,42; Dt 16:3
[g] 13:4 Ex 12:2; 23:15; 34:18; Dt 16:1
[h] 13:5 Ex 3:8; 33:3; Nm 16:14; Jos 5:6; Jr 32:22
[i] Ex 6:8; 12:25
[j] 13:8 Ex 3:14; 12:26-27
[k] 13:9 Ex 13:16; Dt 6:8; 11:18

[l] 13:13 Ex 34:20; Nm 3:46-47; 18:15
[m] 13:14 Ex 12:26-27; Dt 6:20
[n] 13:15-16 Ex 12:29; 13:9
[o] 13:17 Ex 14:11; Nm 14:1-4; Dt 17:16
[p] 13:18 Ex 14:2; Nm 33:6; Jos 1:14
[q] 13:19 Gn 50:25; Jos 24:32; Ac 7:16; Heb 11:22
[r] 13:21 Ex 14:19; Nm 9:15-16; Dt 1:33; Neh 9:12; Ps 78:14; 99:7; Is 4:5; 1Co 10:1

---

^ **12:47** Lit *do*   [B] **12:48** Lit *may come near to do it*   [C] **13:4** March–April; called Nisan in the post-exilic period; Neh 2:1; Est 3:7   [D] **13:5** DSS, Sam, LXX, Syr add *Girgashites* and *Perizzites* ; Jos 3:10   [E] **13:9** Lit *reminder between your eyes*   [F] **13:16** Or *phylactery*

13:11-13 When the Israelites arrived in **the land of the Canaanites**, every firstborn male—man and animal—was to be presented to the Lord since God had spared the firstborn of Israel (13:11–12). The people were to **redeem every firstborn** son by offering a sacrifice from their flocks.
13:14-16 Similarly, the acts of baptism and the Lord's Supper provide Christian parents visual

pictures to help them instruct their children about the redemptive work of God through Jesus Christ. Taking advantage of such opportunities is part of how we "Bring [children] up in the training and instruction of the Lord" (Eph 6:4).
13:17-22 When the Israelites departed Egypt, God did not lead them down the nearest road

because it led to **the Philistines.** God knew they were not ready to face opposition, so he led them **toward the Red Sea** and into the Sinai Peninsula (13:18).

In keeping with Joseph's wishes (see Gen 50:24-25), **Moses took [his] bones** with him so that they could bury him in the land God had promised their family (Exod 13:19).

[a] 14:2 Ex 13:18; Nm 33:7;
Jr 44:1
[b] 14:4 Ex 4:21; 7:5; Rm
9:17,22-23
[c] 14:8 Ex 6:1; 13:9; Nm
33:3; Ac 13:17
[d] 14:9 Ex 15:9; Jos 24:6
[e] 14:10 Jos 24:7; Neh 9:9;
Ps 34:17

[f] 14:12 Ex 5:21; Ps 106:7-8
[g] 14:13 Gn 15:1; 46:3;
Ex 20:20; 2Ch 20:15,17;
Is 41:10
[h] 14:14 Ex 14:25; Dt 1:30;
3:22; Jos 10:14; 2Ch 20:29;
Is 30:15
[i] 14:16 Ex 4:17; Nm 20:8-9;
Is 10:26
[j] 14:19 Ex 23:20,23; 32:34;
33:2
[k] Ex 13:21; Is 63:9

way during the day and in a pillar of fire to give them light at night, so that they could travel day or night. [22] The pillar of cloud by day and the pillar of fire by night never left its place in front of the people.

14 Then the LORD spoke to Moses: [2] "Tell the Israelites to turn back and camp in front of Pi-hahiroth, between Migdol and the sea; you must camp in front of Baal-zephon, facing it by the sea.[a] [3] Pharaoh will say of the Israelites: They are wandering around the land in confusion; the wilderness has boxed them in. [4] I will harden Pharaoh's heart so that he will pursue them. Then I will receive glory by means of Pharaoh and all his army, and the Egyptians will know that I am the LORD." So the Israelites did this.[b]

THE EGYPTIAN PURSUIT

[5] When the king of Egypt was told that the people had fled, Pharaoh and his officials changed their minds about the people and said: "What have we done? We have released Israel from serving us." [6] So he got his chariot ready and took his troops[A] with him; [7] he took six hundred of the best chariots and all the rest of the chariots of Egypt, with officers in each one. [8] The LORD hardened the heart of Pharaoh king of Egypt, and he pursued the Israelites, who were going out defiantly.[B,C] [9] The Egyptians — all Pharaoh's horses and chariots, his horsemen,[c] and his army — chased[d] after them and caught up with them as they camped by the sea beside Pi-hahiroth, in front of Baal-zephon.

[10] As Pharaoh approached, the Israelites looked up and there were the Egyptians coming after them! The Israelites were terrified and cried out[e] to the LORD for help. [11] They said to Moses: "Is it because there are no graves in Egypt that you have taken us away to die in the wilderness? What have you done to us by bringing us out

~ HOPE WORDS ~

Just because you can't see the way doesn't mean that God doesn't have the way.

of Egypt? [12] Isn't this what we told you in Egypt: Leave us alone so that we may serve the Egyptians? It would have been better for us to serve the Egyptians than to die in the wilderness."[f]

[13] But Moses said to the people, "Don't be afraid. Stand firm and see[g] the LORD's salvation that he will accomplish for you today; for the Egyptians you see today, you will never see again. [14] The LORD will fight for you, and you must be quiet."[h]

ESCAPE THROUGH THE RED SEA

[15] The LORD said to Moses, "Why are you crying out to me? Tell the Israelites to break camp. [16] As for you, lift up your staff, stretch out your hand over the sea, and divide it so that the Israelites can go through the sea on dry ground.[i] [17] As for me, I am going to harden the hearts of the Egyptians so that they will go in after them, and I will receive glory by means of Pharaoh, all his army, and his chariots and horsemen. [18] The Egyptians will know that I am the LORD when I receive glory through Pharaoh, his chariots, and his horsemen."

[19] Then the angel of God,[j] who was going in front of the Israelite forces, moved and went behind them. The pillar of cloud moved from in front of them and stood behind them.[k] [20] It came between the Egyptian and Israelite forces. There was cloud and darkness, it lit up the night, and neither group came near the other all night long.

[21] Then Moses stretched out his hand over the sea. The LORD drove the sea back

[A] 14:6 Lit *people*   [B] 14:8 Lit *with a raised hand*   [C] 14:9 Or *chariot drivers*

14:2-9 Pharaoh acted just as the Lord predicted (14:2-4). When he learned of the seemingly erratic actions of the Israelites, he asked, **What have we done?** (14:5). Then he took **six hundred . . . chariots** and sped after the people (14:6-9).
14:10 When the Israelites caught sight of their pursuers, they **were terrified and cried out.** They seemed to be caught between a rock and a hard place—between the sea and the Egyptian army. But God, in fact, had orchestrated the apparent disaster. And he often does similar things in our lives today. Sometimes he will place his people in a dilemma so that he

can be glorified as he teaches us more about himself and accomplishes his purposes.
14:11-12 Out of the Israelites' fear rose some fussing. The hero who had delivered them from slavery quickly became an object of their scorn.
14:13-14 Though their fear made them want to run, the Lord told them to **stand firm.** You too *can* choose not to fear by fulfilling your obligation as one under the protection of God—by acting in spite of your fear. When you're boxed in by a dilemma, you must trust in the Lord. God did not inaugurate the miracle until there was an act of faith by Moses holding out the rod and one by the people moving forward.

14:15-20 While the Israelites prepared to march toward the sea, **the angel of God**—who had been leading them with **the pillar of cloud**—now **stood behind them** as a guardian, preventing the Egyptians from overtaking them (14:19-20).
14:21-22 Not only did God split the sea in half, but he also dried the ground so they could walk through without getting all muddy. It suggests that we too should look for the lavish, unexpected miracles that often accompany the bigger, more obvious ways that God works to help us.

with a powerful east wind all that night and turned the sea into dry land. So the waters were divided,[a] **22** and the Israelites went through the sea on dry ground, with the waters like a wall to them on their right and their left.[b]

23 The Egyptians set out in pursuit — all Pharaoh's horses, his chariots, and his horsemen — and went into the sea after them. **24** During the morning watch, the LORD looked down at the Egyptian forces from the pillar of fire[c] and cloud, and threw the Egyptian forces into confusion. **25** He caused their chariot wheels to swerve[A,B] and made them drive[c] with difficulty. "Let's get away from Israel," the Egyptians said, "because the LORD is fighting for them against Egypt!"

26 Then the LORD said to Moses, "Stretch out your hand over the sea so that the water may come back on the Egyptians, on their chariots and horsemen." **27** So Moses stretched out his hand over the sea, and at daybreak the sea returned to its normal depth. While the Egyptians were trying to escape from it, the LORD threw them into the sea.[d] **28** The water came back and covered the chariots[e] and horsemen, plus the entire army of Pharaoh that had gone after them into the sea. Not even one of them survived. **29** But the Israelites had walked through the sea on dry ground, with the waters like a wall to them on their right and their left. **30** That day the LORD saved Israel from the power of the Egyptians, and Israel saw the Egyptians dead on the seashore. **31** When Israel saw the great power that the LORD used against the Egyptians, the people feared the LORD and believed[f] in him and in his servant Moses.

ISRAEL'S SONG

15 Then Moses and the Israelites sang this song to the LORD. They said:

I will sing to the LORD,
    for he is highly exalted;
he has thrown the horse
    and its rider into the sea.

2 The LORD is my strength
    and my song;[D]
he has become my salvation.[g]
This is my God,
    and I will praise him,
my father's God, and I will exalt
    him.[h]

3 The LORD is a warrior;[i]
    the LORD is his name.[j]

4 He threw Pharaoh's chariots
    and his army into the sea;
the elite of his officers
    were drowned in the Red Sea.[k]

5 The floods covered them;
    they sank to the depths
    like a stone.[l]

6 LORD, your right hand is glorious
    in power.
LORD, your right hand shattered
    the enemy.[m]

7 You overthrew your adversaries
    by your great majesty.
You unleashed your burning wrath;
    it consumed them like stubble.[n]

8 The water heaped up[o] at the blast
    from your nostrils;
the currents stood firm like a dam.
The watery depths congealed
    in the heart of the sea.

9 The enemy said:
"I will pursue, I will overtake,
I will divide the spoil.[p]
My desire will be gratified
    at their expense.
I will draw my sword;
    my hand will destroy[E] them."

10 But you blew with your breath,
    and the sea covered them.
They sank like lead
    in the mighty waters.

11 LORD, who is like you
    among the gods?
Who is like you, glorious
    in holiness,[q]
revered with praises,
    performing wonders?[r]

---

[a] 14:21 Ex 15:8; Jos 3:16; Neh 9:11; Ps 74:13; 114:3,5; Is 63:12-13
[b] 14:22 Ex 15:19; Ps 66:6; Is 63:13; Hab 3:10; 1Co 10:1; Heb 11:29
[c] 14:24 Ex 13:21; Nm 14:14; Neh 9:12
[d] 14:27 Ex 5:1,7; Jos 4:18; Ps 78:53; Heb 11:29
[e] 14:28 Ps 106:11; Heb 3:8,13
[f] 14:31 Ps 106:12; Jn 2:11

[g] 15:2 Ps 18:2; 59:17; Is 12:2; Hab 3:18
[h] Gn 28:21; Ex 3:6,15,18; Is 25:1
[i] 15:3 Ps 24:8; Rv 19:11
[j] Ex 6:3; Ps 83:18
[k] 15:4 Ex 13:18; 15:22; 23:31
[l] 15:5 Ex 14:28; 15:10; Neh 9:11
[m] 15:6 Ps 118:15-16
[n] 15:7 Dt 33:26; Is 5:24
[o] 15:8 Ex 14:21; Ps 78:13
[p] 15:9 Ex 14:9; Jdg 5:30; Is 53:12
[q] 15:11 Dt 3:24; 1Kg 8:23
[r] Ps 77:14; Is 6:3; Rv 4:8

14:23-25 Pharaoh's forces, having just survived the plagues, immediately realized what was happening: **The LORD is fighting for** the Israelites. And they knew what they should do in response: **Let's get away from Israel,** they said (14:25).
14:26-28 Finally, the Lord was ready to deliver the knockout punch. As the Egyptians tried to escape, the Lord caused the sea to flow back into its **normal** position (14:27). **The water . . .**

covered . . . the entire army. . . . Not even one of them survived (14:28). The Egyptian king who had defied the God of creation had his army wiped out by God's creation.
15:1-5 In a response of praise for this miraculous exodus, **Moses and the Israelites sang this song to the LORD** (15:1). They had seen for themselves that the God of their fathers—of Abraham, Isaac, and Jacob—had come to save his people (15:2). The **elite** troops of Egypt

were no match for their God: **the LORD is a warrior** (15:3-4).
15:6-10 Scripture often speaks of God accomplishing actions with his **right hand** as a way of referring to his mighty **power**. Like a boxer with a devastating right hook, the Lord **shattered the enemy** (15:6).
15:11 The Egyptian "gods" had proven powerless to stop the Lord because they were imaginary.

a 15:13 Ps 77:15,20; 78:54
b 15:15 Gn 36:15,40; Nm 22:3; Dt 2:4; Jos 5:1
c 15:16 Ex 23:27; Jos 2:9
d 1Sm 25:37; Ps 74:2; 1Pt 2:9
e 15:17 Ps 44:2; 78:54
f 15:18 Ps 10:16; 29:10; Is 57:15

g 15:20 Nm 26:59; Jdg 4:4
h Jdg 11:34; 1Sm 18:6; Ps 150:4
i 15:23-24 Ex 16:2; Nm 33:8
j 15:25 Ex 14:10; Dt 8:2,16; Jdg 2:22; 3:1,4; 2Kg 2:21; Ps 66:10
k 15:26 Ex 23:25; Dt 7:12,15; 28:27,60; Ps 103:3

12 You stretched out your right hand,
and the earth swallowed them.
13 With your faithful love,
you will lead the people
you have redeemed;
you will guide them
to your holy dwelling
with your strength.*a*

14 When the peoples hear,
they will shudder;
anguish will seize the inhabitants
of Philistia.
15 Then the chiefs of Edom will be
terrified;*b*
trembling will seize the leaders
of Moab;
all the inhabitants of Canaan
will panic;
16 terror*c* and dread will fall on them.
They will be as still*A* as a stone
because of your powerful arm
until your people pass by, Lord,
until the people
whom you purchased*B* pass by.*d*

17 You will bring them in and plant
them
on the mountain of your possession;*e*
Lord, you have prepared the place
for your dwelling;
Lord,*c* your hands have established
the sanctuary.
18 The Lord will reign*f* forever
and ever!

19 When Pharaoh's horses with his chariots and horsemen went into the sea, the
Lord brought the water of the sea back
over them. But the Israelites walked
through the sea on dry ground. **20** Then
the prophetess Miriam,*g* Aaron's sister,
took a tambourine in her hand, and all
the women came out following her with
tambourines and dancing.*h* **21** Miriam sang
to them:

Sing to the Lord,
for he is highly exalted;
he has thrown the horse
and its rider into the sea.

WATER PROVIDED

22 Then Moses led Israel on from the Red
Sea, and they went out to the Wilderness
of Shur. They journeyed for three days
in the wilderness without finding water.
23 They came to Marah, but they could not
drink the water at Marah because it was
bitter — that is why it was named Marah.*D*
24 The people grumbled to Moses, "What
are we going to drink?"*i* **25** So he cried out
to the Lord, and the Lord showed him a
tree. When he threw it into the water, the
water became drinkable.

The Lord made a statute and ordinance for them at Marah, and he tested
them there.*j* **26** He said, "If you will carefully obey the Lord your God, do what is
right in his sight, pay attention to his commands, and keep all his statutes, I will not
inflict any illnesses on you that I inflicted
on the Egyptians. For I am the Lord who
heals you."*k*

27 Then they came to Elim, where there
were twelve springs and seventy date
palms, and they camped there by the water.

A 15:16 Or *silent*   *B* 15:16 Or *created*   *C* 15:17 Some Hb mss, DSS, Sam, Tg read Lord   *D* 15:23 = Bitter or Bitterness

15:20-21 Moses's sister **Miriam** is the first woman to be identified in Scripture as a **prophetess**. Interestingly, Micah 6:4 speaks of her along with her brothers Moses and Aaron as playing a role in the deliverance of the people. Even in the early biblical witness, women were not marginalized but were critically involved in the kingdom program of God. Thus, the church must celebrate and encourage them.

15:22-24 Don't miss that the only way they could reach their destination was by going through **the wilderness**. This is a strong indicator that although you may sometimes experience "wilderness" moments in your life, you are not necessarily outside of God's will.

The Israelites' main problem three days into the exodus was that they could find no **water** (15:22). When the people finally encountered some, they discovered that **it was bitter** (15:23). Their reaction, given all

that God had done for them to this point, should raise our eyebrows. What makes their negativity ironic is that their previous crisis had involved a water problem for which there had been no visible solution in sight either, yet they immediately forecasted doom for themselves. We doubt what God can do only because we forget what God has done.

15:25 Don't miss God's purpose in allowing this water problem: **he tested them** through it. The Lord had expected Israel to learn from the Red Sea event. Demonstrating his miraculous deliverance before their eyes, in fact, was his way of telling them, "This is going to be on the test! Be ready to draw on this knowledge and apply it." The Israelites earned an F when the pop quiz of bitter water was placed before them.

15:26 God promised Israel that, if they trusted him and followed his instructions, they wouldn't suffer as Egypt had. Instead, he would be their healer as they encountered

sickness. But some try to stretch the promise of this verse too far, advocating a "health and wealth" gospel that assures all believers they will be disease free and rich too if only they trust in Christ. They say that you shouldn't become sick if you are truly saved. But this adds to what God was saying. The illnesses that God would prevent in ancient Israel and the healing he would provide did not keep them from deteriorating with age or even from contracting a virus or getting involved in an accident. We live in a fallen world, and these things inevitably happen.

Sometimes, though, people suffer maladies—physical, mental, or emotional ones—because, like the Egyptians, they live in rebellion against God and operate from an unbiblical worldview. To those suffering because they are living outside the will of God, the Great Physician says in effect, "Take your medicine—obey my Word. For I am the Lord who heals."

MANNA AND QUAIL PROVIDED

16 The entire Israelite community departed from Elim and came to the Wilderness of Sin, which is between Elim and Sinai, on the fifteenth day of the second month after they had left the land of Egypt.[a] ² The entire Israelite community grumbled[b] against Moses and Aaron in the wilderness. ³ The Israelites said to them, "If only we had died by the LORD's hand in the land of Egypt, when we sat by pots of meat and ate all the bread we wanted. Instead, you brought us into this wilderness to make this whole assembly die of hunger!"[c]

⁴ Then the LORD said to Moses, "I am going to rain bread from heaven for you. The people are to go out each day and gather enough for that day. This way I will test them to see whether or not they will follow my instructions.[d] ⁵ On the sixth day, when they prepare what they bring in, it will be twice as much as they gather on other days."[A]

⁶ So Moses and Aaron said to all the Israelites: "This evening you will know that it was the LORD who brought you out of the land of Egypt,[e] ⁷ and in the morning you will see the LORD's glory because he has heard your complaints about him. For who are we that you complain about us?"[f]

─ ∽ HOPE WORDS ∽ ─

When your level of complaining is at an all-time high, it could mean that your level of praise is at an all-time low.

⁸ Moses continued, "The LORD will give you meat to eat this evening and all the bread you want in the morning, for he has heard the complaints that you are raising against him. Who are we? Your complaints are not against us but against the LORD."[g]

⁹ Then Moses told Aaron, "Say to the entire Israelite community, 'Come before the LORD, for he has heard your complaints.'" ¹⁰ As Aaron was speaking to the entire Israelite community, they turned toward the wilderness, and there in a cloud the LORD's glory appeared.[h]

¹¹ The LORD spoke to Moses, ¹² "I have heard the complaints of the Israelites. Tell them: At twilight you will eat meat, and in the morning you will eat bread until you are full. Then you will know that I am the LORD your God."

¹³ So at evening quail[i] came and covered the camp. In the morning there was a layer of dew all around the camp. ¹⁴ When the layer of dew evaporated, there were fine flakes on the desert surface, as fine as frost on the ground. ¹⁵ When the Israelites saw it, they asked one another, "What is it?" because they didn't know what it was.

Moses told them, "It is the bread the LORD has given you to eat.[j] ¹⁶ This is what the LORD has commanded: 'Gather as much of it as each person needs to eat. You may take two quarts[B] per individual, according to the number of people each of you has in his tent.'"

¹⁷ So the Israelites did this. Some gathered a lot, some a little. ¹⁸ When they measured it by quarts,[c] the person who gathered a lot had no surplus, and the person who gathered a little had no shortage. Each gathered as much as he needed to eat.[k] ¹⁹ Moses said to them, "No one is to let any of it remain until morning." ²⁰ But they didn't listen to Moses; some people left part of it until morning, and it bred worms and stank. Therefore Moses was angry with them.

²¹ They gathered it every morning. Each gathered as much as he needed to eat, but when the sun grew hot, it melted. ²² On the sixth day they gathered twice as much food, four quarts[D] apiece, and all the leaders of the community came and reported this to Moses. ²³ He told them, "This is what the LORD has said: 'Tomorrow is a day of complete rest, a holy Sabbath[l] to the LORD. Bake what you want to bake, and boil what you want to boil, and set aside everything left over to be kept until morning.'"

²⁴ So they set it aside until morning as Moses commanded, and it didn't stink or

ᵃ16:1 Nm 33:10-11
ᵇ16:2 Ex 15:24; 1Co 10:10
ᶜ16:3 Nm 11:4-5; Lm 4:9
ᵈ16:4 Dt 8:2; Jn 6:31
ᵉ16:6 Ex 6:7; Nm 16:28-30
ᶠ16:7 Nm 14:27; 16:11; Is 35:2; 40:5
ᵍ16:8 1Sm 8:7; Lk 10:16; Rm 13:2
ʰ16:10 Ex 13:21-22; Nm 16:19; 1Kg 8:10
ⁱ16:13 Nm 11:9,31; Ps 78:27-28; 105:40
ʲ16:15 Ex 16:4; Jn 6:31
ᵏ16:18 2Co 8:15
ˡ16:23 Gn 2:3; Ex 20:8; 31:15; 35:3; Lv 23:3

ᴬ16:5 Lit *as gathering day to day*   ᴮ16:16 Lit *an omer*   ᶜ16:18 Lit *by an omer*   ᴰ16:22 Lit *two omers*

16:1-3 In the **second month** after leaving Egypt, the people began what would be a habitual pattern: grumbling **against Moses and Aaron** (16:1-2). But since they were the Lord's chosen servants, ultimately Israel's grumbling was directed against the Lord. When food ran low, they complained about how good they had it in Egypt (16:3). How sad

that Egyptian slavery with a full belly looked better to them than God-supplied freedom with a little hunger along the way. **16:4-5** These were fairly simple instructions God gave for the people to follow, yet a rebellious heart will ignore even simple instructions. **16:21-30** Moses explained why it was necessary to gather two days' worth on the sixth day. The

seventh day was **a holy Sabbath** (16:23, 29-30), which was a hint of a commandment to come (20:8-11). The people were not to gather on that day. Through his instructions God was teaching the Israelites the principle that he provides for his people one day at a time. Jesus articulates this kingdom provision in the Lord's Prayer: "Give us today our daily bread" (Matt 6:11).

*a*16:28 2Kg 17:14; Ps 78:10
*b*16:31 Ex 16:14; Nm 11:7;
Dt 8:3
*c*16:34 Ex 25:16,21; 27:21;
40:20; Nm 17:10
*d*16:35 Jos 5:12; Neh 9:20-
21; Jn 6:31,49

*e*17:1 Ex 16:1; Nm 33:12,14
*f*17:2 Nm 20:3; Dt 6:16; Ps
78:18,41; 1Co 10:9
*g*17:3 Ex 15:24; 16:2,7-8;
Nm 14:2,27,29,36; 16:11
*h*17:4 Nm 14:10; 1Sm 30:6;
Jn 8:59; 10:31
*i*17:6 Ex 20:10-11; Ps 114:8;
1Co 10:9
*j*17:7 Nm 20:13,24; Ps
81:7; 95:8
*k*17:8 Gn 36:12; Nm 13:29;
24:20; Dt 25:17; Jdg 3:13;
6:3; 10:12; 1Sm 14:48
*l*17:9 Ex 24:13; 32:17; 33:11;
Ac 7:45
*m*17:11 Ex 24:14; Jms 5:16

have maggots in it. **25** "Eat it today," Moses said, "because today is a Sabbath to the LORD. Today you won't find any in the field. **26** For six days you will gather it, but on the seventh day, the Sabbath, there will be none."

27 Yet on the seventh day some of the people went out to gather, but they did not find any. **28** Then the LORD said to Moses, "How long will you[A] refuse to keep my commands[a] and instructions? **29** Understand that the LORD has given you the Sabbath; therefore on the sixth day he will give you two days' worth of bread. Each of you stay where you are; no one is to leave his place on the seventh day." **30** So the people rested on the seventh day.

31 The house of Israel named the substance manna.[B,b] It resembled coriander seed, was white, and tasted like wafers made with honey. **32** Moses said, "This is what the LORD has commanded: 'Two quarts[c] of it are to be preserved throughout your generations, so that they may see the bread I fed you in the wilderness when I brought you out of the land of Egypt.'"

33 Moses told Aaron, "Take a container and put two quarts[D] of manna in it. Then place it before the LORD to be preserved throughout your generations." **34** As the LORD commanded Moses, Aaron placed it before the testimony[c] to be preserved. **35** The Israelites ate manna for forty years, until they came to an inhabited land. They ate manna until they reached the border of the land of Canaan.[d] **36** (They used a measure called an omer, which held two quarts.[E])

WATER FROM THE ROCK

17 The entire Israelite community left the Wilderness of Sin, moving from one place to the next according to the LORD's command. They camped at Rephidim, but there was no water for the people

to drink.[e] **2** So the people complained to Moses, "Give us water to drink."

"Why are you complaining to me?" Moses replied to them. "Why are you testing[f] the LORD?"

3 But the people thirsted there for water and grumbled against Moses. They said, "Why did you ever bring us up from Egypt to kill us and our children and our livestock with thirst?"[g]

4 Then Moses cried out to the LORD, "What should I do with these people? In a little while they will stone me!"[h]

5 The LORD answered Moses, "Go on ahead of the people and take some of the elders of Israel with you. Take the staff you struck the Nile with in your hand and go. **6** I am going to stand there in front of you on the rock at Horeb; when you hit the rock, water[i] will come out of it and the people will drink." Moses did this in the sight of the elders of Israel. **7** He named the place Massah[F] and Meribah[G,j] because the Israelites complained, and because they tested the LORD, saying, "Is the LORD among us or not?"

THE AMALEKITES ATTACK

8 At Rephidim, Amalek[H,k] came and fought against Israel. **9** Moses said to Joshua,[l] "Select some men for us and go fight against Amalek. Tomorrow I will stand on the hilltop with God's staff in my hand."

10 Joshua did as Moses had told him, and fought against Amalek, while Moses, Aaron, and Hur went up to the top of the hill. **11** While Moses held up his hand,[i] Israel prevailed, but whenever he put his hand[i] down, Amalek prevailed.[m] **12** When Moses's hands grew heavy, they took a stone and put it under him, and he sat down on it. Then Aaron and Hur supported his hands, one on one side and one on the other so that his hands remained

[A] **16:28** The Hb word for *you* is pl, referring to the whole nation. [B] **16:31** = what?; Ex 16:15 [C] **16:32** Lit *'A full omer* [D] **16:33** Lit *a full omer* [E] **16:36** Lit *(The omer is a tenth of an ephah.)* [F] **17:7** = Testing [G] **17:7** = Quarreling [H] **17:8** A seminomadic people descended from *Amalek,* a grandson of Esau; Gn 36:12 [i] **17:11** Sam, LXX, Syr, Tg, Vg read *hands*

16:31-36 Israel would eat manna every day for **forty years** until they entered **Canaan** (16:35; cf. Josh 5:12).
17:2-7 Though God provided for them in spite of their sin, the Israelites were setting themselves on a path of habitual disobedience that would lead to sorrow and disappointment. Later, the author of Psalm 95 would warn God's people not to test the Lord like the Israelites of Moses's day (see Ps 95:7-11). It's important to remember that all these things "were written for our instruction" (1 Cor 10:11).

17:8 Amalek was a grandson of Esau, brother of Jacob, who was a patriarch of the Israelites (see Gen 36:12). Both the Israelites and the Amalekites, then, could trace their ancestries back to Isaac and to Abraham.
17:10-11 What was happening below was inextricably tied to what Moses was doing on the mountain. Through his actions, Moses was engaging in spiritual intercession while the people were fighting. This tells us that both military force and spiritual commitment were needed. This is a reminder that we must avoid the extremes

of thinking that either we'll simply pray and let God take care of the life battles we face or that we must assume all responsibility and solve each problem alone. To prevail against enemy attack, you must *both* make contact with heaven *and* take responsibility for your actions on earth.
17:12-13 Eventually, Moses grew tired. So **Aaron and Hur** stood on either side of their leader and **supported his hands** (17:12). Moses was a godly leader and servant of the Lord. But he couldn't do the work he'd been assigned alone. You, too, need others in your

a 17:14 Ex 34:27; Dt 25:17-19; 1Sm 15:3
b 17:15 Ex 20:24-26; 24:4; Jdg 6:24
c 18:1 Ex 2:16,18; 3:1
d 18:2 Ex 2:21; 4:25
e 18:3 Ex 2:22; 4:20; Ac 7:29
f 18:4-5 Ex 3:1; 1Ch 23:15
g 18:7 Gn 29:13; Ex 18:2
h 18:8 Ex 15:6,16; Ps 81:7
i 18:10 Gn 14:20; 2Sm 18:28
j 18:11 2Ch 2:5; Lk 1:51

Questions & Answers

Q You have celebrated over forty years of fruitful, faithful ministry at your church. Looking back on that, what are some key things you would advise a young person to focus on in order to shape a life and ministry that wisely stewards resources for the kingdom of God?

A Looking back, I would say keep the balance between ministry and family clear because that can get out of balance really quickly. Ministry is never-ending and always demanding. The more people there are, the more demands increase. So you must be careful not to marginalize your family. If you find that you are doing so, make the necessary adjustments.

Also, make sure that you maintain the balance between ministering to others and ministering to yourself. Often we can become so burdened by the legitimate concerns of others that we run out of gas ourselves. And when we run out of fuel, we're not able to properly care for others because we're not growing deeper ourselves. So be sure to look to your own growth as you seek to help others grow.

Another wise aspect of ministry is raising up leaders. You need to invest in others with spiritual potential who can share the load with you. Moses had to learn this very thing (see Exod 18:13-26). You need other ministry leaders to grow well and assist because you are only human and can only accomplish so much on your own.

FOR THE NEXT Q&A, SEE PAGE 88.

recite it to Joshua: I will completely blot out the memory of Amalek under heaven."*a* ¹⁵ And Moses built an altar*b* and named it, "The LORD Is My Banner."*B* ¹⁶ He said, "Indeed, my hand is lifted up toward*c* the LORD's throne. The LORD will be at war with Amalek from generation to generation."

JETHRO'S VISIT

18 Moses's father-in-law Jethro, the priest of Midian,*c* heard about everything that God had done for Moses and for God's people Israel when the LORD brought Israel out of Egypt. ² Now Jethro, Moses's father-in-law, had taken in Zipporah,*d* Moses's wife, after he had sent her back, ³ along with her two sons, one of whom was named Gershom*D* (because Moses had said, "I have been a resident alien in a foreign land")*e* ⁴ and the other Eliezer (because he had said, "The God of my father was my helper and rescued me from Pharaoh's sword").*E* ⁵ Moses's father-in-law Jethro, along with Moses's wife and sons, came to him in the wilderness where he was camped at the mountain of God.*f* ⁶ He sent word to Moses, "I, your father-in-law Jethro, am coming to you with your wife and her two sons." ⁷ So Moses went out to meet his father-in-law, bowed down,*g* and then kissed him. They asked each other how they had been*F* and went into the tent. ⁸ Moses recounted to his father-in-law all that the LORD had done to Pharaoh and the Egyptians for Israel's sake, all the hardships that confronted them on the way, and how the LORD rescued them.*h* ⁹ Jethro rejoiced over all the good things the LORD had done for Israel when he rescued them from the power of the Egyptians. ¹⁰ "Blessed be the LORD,"*i* Jethro exclaimed, "who rescued you from the power of Egypt and from the power of Pharaoh. He has rescued the people from under the power of Egypt! ¹¹ Now I know that the LORD is greater than all gods, because he did wonders when the Egyptians acted arrogantly against Israel."*G,j*

steady until the sun went down. ¹³ So Joshua defeated Amalek and his army*A* with the sword. ¹⁴ The LORD then said to Moses, "Write this down on a scroll as a reminder and

A 17:13 Or *people*   *B* 17:15 = *Yahweh-nissi*   *C* 17:16 Or *hand was on*, or *hand was against*; Hb obscure   *D* 18:3 In Hb the name *Gershom* sounds like the phrase "a stranger there."   *E* 18:4 = My God Is Help   *F* 18:7 Lit *other about well-being*   *G* 18:11 Hb obscure

life—brothers and sisters in the Lord—who will be there to help you spiritually when times get heavy.
17:14 Because of the Amalekites' wicked hostility toward their kin Israel, the Lord planned to eradicate them. He would later command King Saul to accomplish their demise. But because of Saul's disobedience, the prophet

Samuel would have to finish the job (see 1 Sam 15:1-3, 32-33). The Amalekites' story reminds us that while God is patient in bringing his wrathful judgment, he never forgets to mete it out.
18:1-12 Moses's wife and **sons** had been staying with her father—probably as a means of protection during Moses's confrontation

with Pharaoh (18:2-3). Jethro was **the priest of Midian** (18:1). We know he had become a follower of the true God because he **brought . . . sacrifices to God** (18:12). Jethro was a Kenite (see Judg 1:16), part of the Canaanite tribes (see Gen 15:19) who descended from Ham of African descent. At that time, the Kenites had settled in the land of Midian.

a 18:15-16 Ex 24:14; Lv
24:12; Nm 15:34; Dt 17:8
b 18:18 Ex 3:12; 4:16;
Nm 27:5
c 18:20 Dt 1:18; 5:1; Ps
143:8
d 18:21 Ex 18:8; Dt 16:19;
Ac 6:3
e Dt 1:15; 2Ch 19:5-10
f 18:22 Lv 24:11; Nm 11:17;
Dt 1:17
g 18:25-27 Ex 18:22; Nm
10:29-30; Dt 1:15

❧ Questions & Answers ❧

Q What role should a proper understanding of covenant play in our interpretation of Jesus's life and ministry?

A Covenant is a critical part of Jesus's relationship to God. The first thing that Jesus said he came to do was to fulfill the law. The law was God's covenant with Israel. So in his earthly life, he had to keep the covenant that Israel broke in order to satisfy the demands of God and to demonstrate that he qualified to be our sinless Savior. God didn't want us to forget it, so he instituted Communion or the Lord's Supper (see Luke 22:19-20; 1 Cor 11:23-26). He said essentially, "This is the new covenant in my blood about the relationship I now have with this new entity I have established called the church. I am covenantally in sync with the Father. So when you are in sync with me, we are all on the same page. Through this divinely created bond, you can experience covenantal benefits from the Father through me." So stick with Jesus because he is in covenant with God and you're in covenant with him.

FOR THE NEXT Q&A, SEE PAGE 108.

12 Then Jethro, Moses's father-in-law, brought a burnt offering and sacrifices to God, and Aaron came with all the elders of Israel to eat a meal with Moses's father-in-law in God's presence.

13 The next day Moses sat down to judge the people, and they stood around Moses from morning until evening. **14** When Moses's father-in-law saw everything he was doing for them he asked, "What is this thing you're doing for the people? Why are you alone sitting as judge, while all the people stand around you from morning until evening?"

15 Moses replied to his father-in-law, "Because the people come to me to inquire of God. **16** Whenever they have a dispute, it comes to me, and I make a decision between one man and another. I teach them God's statutes and laws."*a*

17 "What you're doing is not good," Moses's father-in-law said to him. **18** "You will certainly wear out both yourself and these people who are with you, because the task is too heavy for you. You can't do it alone.*b* **19** Now listen to me; I will give you some advice, and God be with you. You be the one to represent the people before God and bring their cases to him. **20** Instruct them about the statutes and laws, and teach them the way to live and what they must do.*c* **21** But you should select from all the people able men, God-fearing, trustworthy, and hating dishonest profit.*d* Place them over the people as commanders of thousands, hundreds, fifties, and tens.*e* **22** They should judge the people at all times. Then they can bring you every major case but judge every minor case themselves. In this way you will lighten your load,^A and they will bear it with you.*f* **23** If you do this, and God so directs you, you will be able to endure, and also all these people will be able to go home satisfied."^B

24 Moses listened to his father-in-law and did everything he said. **25** So Moses chose able men from all Israel and made them leaders over the people as commanders of thousands, hundreds, fifties, and tens. **26** They judged the people at all times; they would bring the hard cases to Moses, but they would judge every minor case themselves.

27 Moses let his father-in-law go, and he journeyed to his own land.*g*

ISRAEL AT SINAI

19 In the third month from the very day the Israelites left the land of Egypt, they came to the Sinai Wilderness.

^A 18:22 Lit *lighten from on you*   ^B 18:23 Lit *go to their place in peace*

18:13-16 When Israel left Egypt, there were six hundred thousand men (12:37)—and that didn't include the women and children! Even at a large church, with multiple staff members, it can be difficult to schedule an appointment with one of the pastoral staff. So imagine what Moses was dealing with, and be patient with your leaders who work hard to shepherd the hearts of the people.
18:17-18 In other words, this man said to his son-in-law, "Have you lost your cotton-pickin' mind? This job's too big for one guy!" Moses's heart was right, but his plan in this case was bad. Moses was a good and capable man, but

he wasn't God. Both he and the people were going to **wear out** (18:18) physiologically and psychologically if he didn't get some help.
18:21 This strongly suggests that the priority in enlisting spiritual leadership should be identifying those who are living in a godly manner and are biblically focused in their dealings. When Paul listed qualifications for church leaders, in fact, the lists consisted primarily of character qualities (see 1 Tim 3:1-12; Titus 1:6-9).
18:22-23 Here I see a reminder that pastors cannot bear the burdens of the church alone. Wise, Word-centered church laypeople must share the load. By dividing the work in this

way, more Christians can be trained to think biblically about life, and they in turn can help their brothers and sisters in Christ to think and live biblically. This is how the body of Christ is built up. It was never intended to be a one-man job.
18:24-27 Moses listened to his father-in-law's advice and chose leaders to serve in the young nation's new judicial system (18:25-26). In this story God used a Gentile man of African descent to provide wise counsel for the effective administration of the entire Jewish nation.
19:1-4 Three months after the exodus from Egypt, Israel arrived at **the mountain** in

2 They traveled from Rephidim, came to the Sinai Wilderness, and camped in the wilderness. Israel camped there in front of the mountain.[a]

3 Moses went up the mountain to God, and the LORD called[b] to him from the mountain: "This is what you must say to the house of Jacob and explain to the Israelites: **4** 'You have seen what I did to the Egyptians and how I carried you on eagles' wings and brought you to myself.[c] **5** Now if you will carefully listen to me and keep my covenant,[d] you will be my own possession[e] out of all the peoples, although the whole earth is mine, **6** and you will be my kingdom of priests and my holy nation.'[f] These are the words that you are to say to the Israelites."

7 After Moses came back, he summoned the elders of the people and set before them all these words that the LORD had commanded him. **8** Then all the people responded together, "We will do all that the LORD has spoken."[g] So Moses brought the people's words back to the LORD.

9 The LORD said to Moses, "I am going to come to you in a dense cloud,[h] so that the people will hear when I speak[i] with you and will always believe you." Moses reported the people's words to the LORD, **10** and the LORD told Moses, "Go to the people and consecrate them today and tomorrow. They must wash their clothes[j] **11** and be prepared by the third day, for on the third day the LORD will come down on Mount Sinai in the sight of all the people.[k] **12** Put boundaries for the people all around the mountain and say: Be careful that you don't go up on the mountain or touch its base. Anyone who touches the mountain must be put to death.[l] **13** No hand may touch him;[A] instead he will be stoned or shot with arrows and not live, whether animal or human. When the ram's horn sounds a long blast, they may go up the mountain."

14 Then Moses came down from the mountain to the people and consecrated them, and they washed their clothes. **15** He said to the people, "Be prepared by the third day. Do not have sexual relations with women."

16 On the third day, when morning came, there was thunder and lightning, a thick cloud on the mountain, and a very loud trumpet sound, so that all the people in the camp shuddered. **17** Then Moses brought the people out of the camp to meet God, and they stood at the foot of the mountain. **18** Mount Sinai was completely enveloped in smoke because the LORD came down on it in fire.[m] Its smoke went up like the smoke of a furnace,[n] and the whole mountain shook violently.[o] **19** As the sound of the trumpet grew louder and louder, Moses spoke and God answered him in the thunder.[p]

20 The LORD came down on Mount Sinai at the top of the mountain. Then the LORD summoned Moses to the top of the mountain, and he went up. **21** The LORD directed Moses, "Go down and warn the people not to break through to see the LORD; otherwise many of them will die.[q] **22** Even the priests who come near the LORD must consecrate themselves, or the LORD will break out in anger against them."[r]

23 Moses responded to the LORD, "The people cannot come up Mount Sinai, since you warned us: Put a boundary around the mountain and consecrate it." **24** And the LORD replied to him, "Go down and come back with Aaron. But the priests and the people must not break through to come up to the LORD, or he will break out in anger against them." **25** So Moses went down to the people and told them.

THE TEN COMMANDMENTS

20 Then God spoke all these words: **2** I am the LORD your God, who brought you out of the land of Egypt, out of the place of slavery.[s]

[A]**19:13** Or *it*

[a]19:2 Ex 3:1; 17:1,8
[b]19:3 Ex 3:4; Ac 7:38
[c]19:4 Dt 29:2; Is 63:9
[d]19:5 Ex 15:26; Dt 5:2
[e]Dt 7:6; 14:2; 26:18; Ps 135:4; Ti 2:14
[f]19:6 Dt 26:19; Is 62:12; 1Pt 2:5,9
[g]19:8 Ex 24:3,7; Dt 5:27
[h]19:9 Ex 24:15-16; Mt 17:5
[i]Dt 4:12,36; Jn 12:29
[j]19:10 Gn 35:2; Lv 11:44-45; Heb 10:22
[k]19:11 Ex 19:16; 34:5
[l]19:12 Heb 12:20

[m]19:18 Ex 3:2; 24:17; Dt 4:11; 2Ch 7:1
[n]Ps 144:5; Rv 15:8
[o]Jdg 5:5; Ps 68:7; Jr 4:24; Heb 12:26
[p]19:19 Neh 9:13; Ps 81:7
[q]19:21 Ex 3:5; 1Sm 6:19
[r]19:22 Lv 10:3; 2Sm 6:7-8
[s]20:2 Ex 13:3; Hs 13:4

the **Sinai Wilderness** where God had first appeared to Moses (19:1-2). The Lord had promised Moses that Israel would worship him at this very spot (3:12).

19:5-6 God intended to enter a binding relationship with Israel—making them his **own possession**. If they kept the **covenant** stipulations, the end result would be their blessing (see Deut 29:9). Covenants are the instruments through which God's kingdom operates. If Israel would operate under the covering of God's covenant, they would be his **kingdom of priests** and his **holy nation** (Exod 19:6), experiencing the benefits and privileges

that his kingdom offers. As recorded in Old Testament history, however, the sinful people of Israel would repeatedly break God's covenant and forfeit his blessings.

Only God's Son Jesus Christ, descended from the Israelite people, perfectly kept the laws of the covenant and offered himself as an atoning sacrifice for sinners. By the shedding of his own blood, he established a new covenant. All those who trust in Christ's sacrifice receive full atonement for sins, are indwelt by the Holy Spirit, and have fellowship with God. As members of the new covenant, Christians now have the capacity to obey God, so that

they may experience his deliverance in their daily circumstances.

19:9-15 These regulations were meant to help reveal to Israel how special and holy this event was to be. That the people were to stay away from even the mountain's base is a vivid reminder of the glory of God and of the great chasm that exists between a holy God and sinful people.

20:1-2 The Ten Commandments present the minimum standards of righteousness that God set for his people—I say *minimum* because Jesus showed that the sin problem people face is not limited to external sins but

a 20:3 Dt 6:14; Jr 35:15
b 20:4 Lv 26:1; Dt 27:15
c 20:5 Ex 34:14; Dt 4:24; Is 44:15,19
d Nm 14:18; Ps 79:8; Jr 32:18

e 20:6 Dt 7:9
f 20:7 Lv 19:12; Mt 5:33
g 20:8 Ex 31:13-16; Lv 26:2
h 20:9 Ex 34:21; Lk 13:14
i 20:10 Gn 2:2-3; Neh 13:16-19
j 20:12 Lv 19:3; Mt 15:4; Mk 7:10; Lk 18:20; Eph 6:2
k 20:13 Mt 5:21; Rm 13:9

APPLICATION QUESTIONS

READ EXODUS 20:8-11

– How would you describe your attitudes and emotions about attending church services?

– What steps do you take to prepare yourself spiritually before attending church services?

– What steps do you take to spiritually prepare your family members before attending church services?

3   Do not have other gods besides me.*a*

4   Do not make an idol*b* for yourself, whether in the shape of anything in the heavens above or on the earth below or in the waters under the earth. ⁵ Do not bow in worship to them, and do not serve them; for I, the Lord your God, am a jealous God,*c* punishing the children for the fathers' iniquity, to the third and fourth generations*d* of those who hate me, ⁶ but showing faithful love to a thousand generations of those who love me and keep my commands.*e*

7   Do not misuse the name of the Lord your God, because the Lord will not leave anyone unpunished who misuses his name.*f*

8   Remember the Sabbath day, to keep it holy:*g* ⁹ You are to labor six days and do all your work,*h* ¹⁰ but the seventh day is a Sabbath to the Lord your God. You must not do any work — you, your son or daughter, your male or female servant, your livestock, or the resident alien who is within your city gates.*i* ¹¹ For the Lord made the heavens and the earth, the sea, and everything in them in six days; then he rested on the seventh day. Therefore the Lord blessed the Sabbath day and declared it holy.

12   Honor your father and your mother*j* so that you may have a long life in the land that the Lord your God is giving you.

13   Do not murder.*k*

---

even warps internal attitudes (see Matt 5:21-30). If God's people were to please him, they had to keep his commands.

Following the commandments gives people protection from themselves and from one another. Laws promote order in society and prevent chaos. They also show us that we are sinners (see Rom 7:7-13) in the same way that a mirror can show you what's wrong with your hair. They *reveal* our need for a Savior (see Gal 3:19-24).

In the preamble to the Ten Commandments, God established his identity and his relationship to Israel: **I am the Lord your God, who brought you out . . . of the place of slavery** (Exod 20:2). Israel, then, was about to enter a covenant relationship with the God of heaven and earth because of what he had done for them. This is a principle that is still at work in the New Testament era. Under the *new* covenant, Christ died so that those who trust him might "no longer live for themselves, but for the one who died for them and was raised" (2 Cor 5:15). The believer's motivation for obeying God's laws, then, is not to earn salvation (we can't). Rather, we obey because we want to please the One who delivered us from hell and judgment.

20:3 Do not have other gods besides me means you are to treat no other person, place, or thing in your life like God by looking to them as your source. Sometimes business contracts have exclusivity clauses. Such a clause requires that the persons entering the agreement engage in an *exclusive* relationship with each other—having no competing loyalties and no competing contractual obligations that could in any way hinder their own partnership. The first commandment is an exclusivity clause.

Importantly, you can't get this command wrong and expect to proceed to the other nine with success. A baseball player might hit an inside-the-park home run, getting around every base before the other team can throw him out. But if he actually missed tagging first base, it doesn't matter if he touched second, third, and home. He's still out.

God alone is able to save from hell, deliver from crises, and bless with his kingdom promises. Why would you rather serve anyone or anything else?

20:4-6 Making an idol is attempting to create a visible representation of the invisible God. Any such attempt will always misrepresent him. All idols do, in fact, is arouse God's jealousy: **I, the Lord your God, am a jealous God**, he says (20:5). However, jealousy in God is not sinful. Think of it as the righteous and loving jealousy of a husband who is zealous for the faithfulness of his wife and wants to keep her and their marriage from harm.

Not all idols are physical. Paul mentions several sinful desires—sexual immorality, impurity, lust, evil desire, and greed—and calls these "idolatry" (Col 3:5). Gratifying such things frequently becomes the ruling influence in a person's life. A person who seeks to satisfy one of those desires, in fact, often will do and sacrifice anything to serve his idol.

There is only one legitimate representation of God and therefore only one legitimate means of accessing him. I'm talking about the Word who became flesh, the God-Man (see John 1:1-2, 14). "[Christ] is the image of the invisible God" (Col 1:15)—the only true representation of God. Jesus told his disciples, "I am the way, the truth, and the life. No one comes to the Father except through

me. . . . The one who has seen me has seen the Father" (John 14:6, 9).

20:7 God does not want his name defamed or abused, but valued and honored. We are not to use his name casually or carelessly, but seriously and reverently. Too often, however, we use frivolous phrases like, "Thank God," or, "I swear to God." At its core, this kind of flippancy is treating God's name insignificantly; it is saying that *he* is insignificant.

20:8-11 Remember the Sabbath day, to keep it holy (20:8; see 31:12-17) revolves around a concept predicated on what God did at creation. He made the world **in six days; then he rested on the seventh** (20:11). God didn't "rest" because he was tired. Rather, he rested so that he could enjoy what he had done (see Gen 1:31). Likewise, after six days of work, we are also called to rest and enjoy the fruit of our labor. This is a valuable means of helping ourselves to avoid becoming so busy and preoccupied that we forget what God has done, too.

The early Christians did not gather for worship on the Jewish Sabbath—Saturday, the official seventh day of the week. They gathered for worship on Sunday, the first day of the week, because it was on that day that Jesus was raised from the dead. They kept the Sabbath principle while adjusting the day.

20:12 The parent-child relationship represents a chain of command: God the Father is in charge; we, his children, are not. No matter your age, to "honor" your parents means to respect and value them.

20:13 This commandment doesn't forbid all killing, only **murder**. This includes the taking of one's own life in suicide. Abortion is also prohibited, because the Bible makes clear that an unborn baby is a person, not mere tissue (see

14 Do not commit adultery.[a]

15 Do not steal.[b]

16 Do not give false testimony against your neighbor.[c]

17 Do not covet your neighbor's house. Do not covet your neighbor's wife, his male or female servant, his ox or donkey, or anything that belongs to your neighbor.[d]

THE PEOPLE'S REACTION

18 All the people witnessed[A] the thunder and lightning, the sound of the trumpet, and the mountain surrounded by smoke. When the people saw it[B] they trembled and stood at a distance.[e] **19** "You speak to us, and we will listen," they said to Moses, "but don't let God speak to us, or we will die."[f] **20** Moses responded to the people, "Don't be afraid, for God has come to test you, so that you will fear him and will not[c] sin."[g] **21** And the people remained standing at a distance as Moses approached the total darkness where God was.[h]

MOSES RECEIVES ADDITIONAL LAWS

22 Then the LORD told Moses, "This is what you are to say to the Israelites: You have seen that I have spoken to you from heaven.[i] **23** Do not make gods of silver to rival me; do not make gods of gold for yourselves.[j]

24 "Make an earthen altar for me, and sacrifice on it your burnt offerings and fellowship offerings, your flocks and herds. I will come to you and bless you in every place where I cause my name to be remembered.[k] **25** If you make a stone altar for me, do not build it out of cut stones. If you use your chisel on it, you will defile it.[l] **26** Do not go up to my altar on steps, so that your nakedness is not exposed on it.

21 "These are the ordinances that you are to set before them:

LAWS ABOUT SLAVES

2 "When you buy a Hebrew slave, he is to serve for six years; then in the seventh he is to leave as a free man[D] without paying anything.[m] **3** If he arrives alone, he is to leave alone; if he arrives with[E] a wife, his wife is to leave with him. **4** If his master gives him a wife and she bears him sons or daughters, the wife and her children belong to her master, and the man must leave alone.

5 "But if the slave declares, 'I love my master, my wife, and my children; I do not want to leave as a free man,'[F] **6** his master is to bring him to the judges[F] and then bring him to the door or doorpost. His master will pierce his ear with an awl, and he will serve his master for life.

[a] 20:14 Dt 5:18; Mt 5:27
[b] 20:15 Lv 19:11; Mt 19:18
[c] 20:16 Ex 23:1
[d] 20:17 Dt 5:21; Mt 5:28; Lk 12:15; Rm 7:7; 13:9; Eph 5:3,5; Heb 13:5
[e] 20:18 Ex 19:18; Heb 12:18
[f] 20:19 Dt 5:25,27; Gl 3:19; Is 8:13
[h] 20:21 Ex 19:16; Dt 5:22
[i] 20:22 Dt 4:36; Neh 9:13
[j] 20:23 Ex 20:3; 32:4

[k] 20:24 Gn 12:2; Dt 12:5; 16:6,11; 1Kg 9:3; 2Ch 6:6
[l] 20:25 Dt 27:5-6; Jos 8:31
[m] 21:2 Dt 4:14; Jr 34:14
[n] 21:5 Dt 15:16-17

[A] 20:18 Lit *saw*   [B] 20:18 Sam, LXX, Syr, Tg, Vg read *smoke. The people* (or *they*) *were afraid,*   [C] 20:20 Lit *that the fear of him may be in you, and you do not*   [D] 21:2 Lit *to go forth*   [E] 21:3 Lit *he is the husband of*   [F] 21:6 Or *to God*; that is, to his sanctuary or court

---

21:22-24; Ps 139:13-16; Jer 1:5). The reason murder is forbidden is that all humans are uniquely made in the image of God (see Gen 1:26-27; 9:6). A murderous attack against a human is an attack against the Creator.
20:14 Sex was intended to inaugurate and renew the marriage covenant between man and wife (see Gen 2:24). **Adultery**—sexual intercourse involving at least one married person—is a defiling of that bond. Think of sex like a fire, with marriage serving as a living room fireplace. If you allow sex to blaze outside of its intended boundary, you just might burn down your own home. In any case, you will unleash destruction.

Those who have sex according to their own parameters—whether that includes committing adultery or engaging in fornication or homosexuality—will experience God's judgment (see Rom 1:24-32; Heb 13:4). That's because sexual sin is primarily a sin against God (see Gen 39:9). But understand that sexual immorality defiles humans like no other sin can (see 1 Cor 6:18).

Jesus upped the ante in saying, "Everyone who looks at a woman lustfully has already committed adultery with her in his heart" (Matt 5:28). Thus, lustful thoughts and engaging in voyeurism by viewing pornography are all

condemned. Nonetheless, to those who have fallen into these traps, Jesus offers forgiveness: "Neither do I condemn you . . . Go, and from now on do not sin anymore" (John 8:11).
20:15 Theft can take a variety of forms, including kidnapping, plagiarism, accepting praise or credit that should have gone to another, not paying taxes, accepting a paycheck without earning it, and even withholding wages count. Theft also happens when we rob God by not contributing tithes (see Mal 3:8-10). Importantly, though, even career thieves can be forgiven (see Luke 23:39-43).
20:16 Bearing **false testimony** against another person—whether damaging a reputation through gossip, causing them material loss, or saying something untrue that results in a death is an intentional attempt to hurt someone through falsehood. Such actions imitate the devil who is "the father of lies" (John 8:44).
20:17 Coveting is a passionate longing to possess something that is not yours. A covetous person is never satisfied. He fails to trust God to provide for him and assumes God is holding out on him. The antidote for covetousness is contentment.
20:18-20 How could Moses tell the people, **don't be afraid** and **fear**, at the same time (20:20)? The answer lies in what it means to

fear God: it means to respect him and take him seriously. Consider electricity. We're not to be so scared of electricity that we're unwilling to plug anything in. But neither should we go around sticking screwdrivers into outlets. Awesome power must be treated with respect.
20:21 The people had already complained about wanting to return to Egypt (14:12; 16:3), so they kept their **distance** because they didn't want the Lord confronting their evil desires. If you are keeping God at an arm's length, it's time to ask why.
20:23 No gods of their own creation, of course, could **rival** what they had just witnessed (though they would soon forget this; see 32:1-35).
20:24-25 The altars were to be made of earth or uncut stones—natural materials that reflected God's holy handiwork alone.
21:1 The next three chapters provide various laws and **ordinances** that were specific applications of the more general Ten Commandments.
21:2-11 An Israelite might sell himself into slavery—that is, indentured servitude—for various reasons, such as paying off debt or surviving financial calamity. Since slaves were in a vulnerable position, provisions were made to ensure their proper treatment (21:7-11).

a 21:7 Neh 5:5
b 21:10 1Co 7:5
c 21:12 Gn 9:6; Mt 26:52
d 21:13 Nm 35:11,22-25; Dt 19:2-5; Jos 20:2-9; 1Sm 24:4,10,18
e 21:14 Dt 19:11-12; 1Kg 2:28-34
f 21:16 Gn 37:28; Ex 22:4; Dt 24:7
g 21:17 Lv 20:9; Mt 15:4; Mk 7:10
h 21:21 Lv 25:44-46

i 21:22 Ex 21:30; Dt 22:18-19
j 21:24 Lv 24:20; Dt 19:21; Mt 5:38
k 21:28 Gn 9:5
l 21:30 Nm 35:31
m 21:32 Zch 11:12; Mt 26:15; 27:3,9

7 "When a man sells his daughter as a concubine,^ she is not to leave as the male slaves do.*a* 8 If she is displeasing to her master, who chose her for himself, then he must let her be redeemed. He has no right to sell her to foreigners because he has acted treacherously toward her. 9 Or if he chooses her for his son, he must deal with her according to the customary treatment of daughters. 10 If he takes an additional wife, he must not reduce the food, clothing, or marital rights of the first wife.*b* 11 And if he does not do these three things for her, she may leave free of charge, without any payment.*B*

LAWS ABOUT PERSONAL INJURY

12 "Whoever strikes a person so that he dies must be put to death.*c* 13 But if he did not intend any harm,*c* and yet God allowed it to happen, I will appoint a place for you where he may flee.*d* 14 If a person schemes and willfully*D* acts against his neighbor to murder him, you must take him from my altar to be put to death.*e*

15 "Whoever strikes his father or his mother must be put to death.

16 "Whoever kidnaps a person must be put to death, whether he sells him or the person is found in his possession.*f*

17 "Whoever curses his father or his mother must be put to death.*g*

18 "When men quarrel and one strikes the other with a stone or his fist, and the injured man does not die but is confined to bed, 19 if he can later get up and walk around outside leaning on his staff, then the one who struck him will be exempt from punishment. Nevertheless, he must pay for his lost work time*E* and provide for his complete recovery.

20 "When a man strikes his male or female slave with a rod, and the slave dies under his abuse,*F* the owner must be punished.*G* 21 However, if the slave can stand up after a day or two, the owner should not be punished*H* because he is his owner's property.*i,h*

22 "When men get in a fight and hit a pregnant woman so that her children are born prematurely but there is no injury, the one who hit her must be fined as the woman's husband demands*i* from him, and he must pay according to judicial assessment. 23 If there is an injury, then you must give life for life, 24 eye for eye, tooth for tooth,*j* hand for hand, foot for foot, 25 burn for burn, bruise for bruise, wound for wound.

26 "When a man strikes the eye of his male or female slave and destroys it, he must let the slave go free in compensation for his eye. 27 If he knocks out the tooth of his male or female slave, he must let the slave go free in compensation for his tooth.

28 "When an ox*i* gores a man or a woman to death, the ox must be stoned,*k* and its meat may not be eaten, but the ox's owner is innocent. 29 However, if the ox was in the habit of goring, and its owner has been warned yet does not restrain it, and it kills a man or a woman, the ox must be stoned, and its owner must also be put to death. 30 If instead a ransom*l* is demanded of him, he can pay a redemption price for his life in the full amount demanded from him. 31 If it gores a son or a daughter, he is to be dealt with according to this same law. 32 If the ox gores a male or female slave, he must give thirty shekels*m* of silver*k* to the slave's master, and the ox must be stoned.

33 "When a man uncovers a pit or digs a pit, and does not cover it, and an ox or a donkey falls into it, 34 the owner of the pit must give compensation; he must pay to its owner, but the dead animal will become his.

35 "When a man's ox injures his neighbor's ox and it dies, they must sell the live ox and divide its proceeds; they must also divide the dead animal. 36 If, however, it is known that the ox was in the habit of goring, yet its owner has not restrained it, he must compensate fully, ox for ox; the dead animal will become his.

---

^21:7 Or *servant*   B 21:11 She doesn't have to pay any redemption price.   C 21:13 Lit *he was not lying in wait*   D 21:14 Or *maliciously*   E 21:19 Lit *his inactivity*   F 21:20 Lit *hand*   G 21:20 Or *must suffer vengeance*   H 21:21 Or *not suffer vengeance*   I 21:21 Lit *silver*   J 21:28 Or *a bull*, or *a steer*   K 21:32 About one pound of silver

---

21:12-14 The **death** penalty was prescribed for intentional homicide only (21:12,14). In the event of unintentional homicide, the person could **flee** to an appointed place (21:13)— what would become known as a "city of refuge" (see Num 35:9-34).
21:15-17 When parents exercised their authority legitimately, they were to be respected and honored. Physical or verbal abuse against one's parents was a capital crime.

21:18-19 Personal injuries not resulting in death still required compensation to the **injured** party.
21:20-27 Such laws limiting a slave owner's power and respecting the rights of slaves were unprecedented and unique to Israel in the ancient Near East.
The stipulation in 21:23-24 is commonly referred to by the Latin expression *lex talionis*, the "law of retaliation." The idea

behind **life for life, eye for eye, tooth for tooth** was to limit punishment given. Penalties were to match and not exceed the damage done.
21:28-36 Owners were accountable for any injuries or deaths caused by their animals (21:28-32, 35-36). If an animal had a history of causing harm and **the owner** refused to restrain it, he would pay with his life (21:29).

LAWS ABOUT THEFT

22 "When a man steals an ox or a sheep and butchers it or sells it, he must repay[a] five cattle for the ox or four sheep for the sheep. [2] If a thief is caught in the act of breaking in, and he is beaten to death, no one is guilty of bloodshed.[b] [3] But if this happens after sunrise, the householder is guilty of bloodshed. A thief must make full restitution. If he is unable, he is to be sold because of his theft.[c] [4] If what was stolen — whether ox, donkey, or sheep — is actually found alive in his possession, he must repay double.

LAWS ABOUT CROP PROTECTION

[5] "When a man lets a field or vineyard be grazed in, and then allows his animals to go and graze in someone else's field, he must repay[A] with the best of his own field or vineyard.

[6] "When a fire gets out of control, spreads to thornbushes, and consumes stacks of cut grain, standing grain, or a field, the one who started the fire must make full restitution for what was burned.

LAWS ABOUT PERSONAL PROPERTY

[7] "When a man gives his neighbor valuables[B] or goods to keep, but they are stolen from that person's house, the thief, if caught, must repay double. [8] If the thief is not caught, the owner of the house must present himself to the judges[c] to determine[D] whether or not he has taken his neighbor's property.[d] [9] In any case of wrongdoing involving an ox, a donkey, a sheep, a garment, or anything else lost, and someone claims, 'That's mine,'[E] the case between the two parties is to come before the judges.[F] The one the judges condemn[G] must repay double to his neighbor.

[10] "When a man gives his neighbor a donkey, an ox, a sheep, or any other animal to care for, but it dies, is injured, or is stolen, while no one is watching, [11] there must be an oath before the LORD between the two of them to determine whether or not he has taken his neighbor's property. Its owner must accept the oath, and the other man does not have to make restitution. [12] But if, in fact, the animal was stolen from his custody, he must make restitution to its owner.[e] [13] If it was actually torn apart by a wild animal, he is to bring it as evidence; he does not have to make restitution for the torn carcass.

[14] "When a man borrows an animal from his neighbor, and it is injured or dies while its owner is not there with it, the man must make full restitution. [15] If its owner is there with it, the man does not have to make restitution. If it was rented, the loss is covered by[H] its rental price.

LAWS ABOUT SEDUCTION

[16] "If a man seduces a virgin who is not engaged, and he sleeps with her, he must certainly pay the bridal price for her to be his wife. [17] If her father absolutely refuses to give her to him, he must pay an amount in silver equal to the bridal price for virgins.[f]

CAPITAL OFFENSES

[18] "Do not allow a sorceress[g] to live.
[19] "Whoever has sexual intercourse with an animal[h] must be put to death.
[20] "Whoever sacrifices to any gods, except the LORD alone, is to be set apart for destruction.[i]

LAWS PROTECTING THE VULNERABLE

[21] "You must not exploit a resident alien[j] or oppress him, since you were resident aliens in the land of Egypt.
[22] "You must not mistreat any widow or fatherless child.[k] [23] If you do mistreat them, they will no doubt cry to me, and I will certainly hear their cry.[l] [24] My anger will burn, and I will kill you with the sword; then your wives will be widows and your children fatherless.[m]

[a] 22:1 2Sm 12:6; Pr 6:31; Lk 19:8
[b] 22:2 Nm 35:27; Mt 24:43
[c] 22:3 Ex 21:2,16
[d] 22:8 Dt 17:8-9
[e] 22:11-12 Gn 31:39; Heb 6:16
[f] 22:16-17 Gn 34:12; Dt 22:28-29
[g] 22:18 Lv 20:27; Dt 18:11; 1Sm 28:3
[h] 22:19 Lv 18:23; 20:15; Dt 27:21
[i] 22:20 Dt 17:2-5
[j] 22:21 Lv 19:33; Dt 10:19
[k] 22:22 Dt 24:17; Jms 1:27
[l] 22:23 Ps 18:6; Lk 18:7
[m] 22:24 Ps 69:4; 109:9

[A] 22:5 LXX adds *from his field according to its produce. But if someone lets his animals graze an entire field, he must repay*; DSS, Sam also support this reading. [B] 22:7 Lit *silver* [C] 22:8 Or *to God* [D] 22:8 LXX, Tg, Vg read *swear* [E] 22:9 Lit *That is it* [F] 22:9 Or *before God* [G] 22:9 Or *one whom God condemns* [H] 22:15 Lit *rented, it comes with*

22:1-4 The high cost of repayment (22:1, 4) was meant to deter future thieves.

22:5-6 In an agrarian society, devastation to a man's crops could render him destitute. Therefore, if a man's field was damaged through the negligence of another, **restitution** was to be made.

22:16-17 Promiscuity was recognized as harmful to families and not tolerated. If a man seduced and slept with a **virgin**, he had to pay **the bridal price for her**.

22:18-20 Sorcery and idolatry were rejections of the first two commandments (20:3-4). Bestiality is a form of immorality that not only rejects marriage between a husband and wife as the proper framework for sexual intercourse (20:14), but also rejects God's created order. Man is no mere mammal.

22:21-27 Israel was expected to care for the vulnerable, remembering that they too were once **resident aliens** in **Egypt** (22:21). Loans to fellow Israelites were to help the **poor**, not to harm them by making their situations worse (22:25-27).

a 22:25 Lv 25:36-37; Dt
  23:20; Ps 15:5
b 22:26-27 Ex 34:6; Dt 24:6
c 22:28 Ec 10:20; Ac 23:5
d 22:29 Ex 13:2; 23:16
e 22:30 Lv 22:27; Dt 15:19
f 22:31 Ex 19:2; Ezk 4:14
g 23:1 Ps 35:11; 101:5;
  Ac 6:11
h 23:2 Dt 16:19; 24:17; 27:19
i 23:5 Dt 22:1,4; Rm 12:20
j 23:6-7 Ec 5:8; Eph 4:25
k 23:8 Dt 10:17; 16:19;
  Pr 15:27
l 23:9 Ex 22:21

m 23:10 Lv 25:3-4
n 23:12 Ex 20:9
o 23:13 Dt 4:9; Jos 23:7; Hs
  2:17; 1Tm 4:16
p 23:14 Ex 34:23; Dt 16:16
q 23:15 Ex 12:15; 34:20
r 23:16 Ex 34:22; Lv 23:39;
  Dt 16:13
s 23:18 Ex 34:25; Dt 16:4
t 23:19 Ex 22:29; 26:2,10;
  Dt 14:21
u 23:20 Ex 14:19; 15:16-17;
  23:23; 32:34; 33:2

25 "If you lend silver to my people, to the poor person among you, you must not be like a creditor to him; you must not charge him interest.[a]

26 "If you ever take your neighbor's cloak as collateral, return it to him before sunset. **27** For it is his only covering; it is the clothing for his body.[A] What will he sleep in? And if he cries out to me, I will listen because I am gracious.[b]

RESPECT FOR GOD

28 "You must not blaspheme God[B] or curse a leader among your people.[c]

29 "You must not hold back offerings[d] from your harvest or your vats. Give me the firstborn of your sons. **30** Do the same with your cattle and your flock. Let them stay with their mothers for seven days, but on the eighth day you are to give them to me.[e]

31 "Be my holy people. You must not eat the meat of a mauled animal[f] found in the field; throw it to the dogs.

LAWS ABOUT HONESTY AND JUSTICE

23 "You must not spread a false report. Do not join[c] the wicked to be a malicious witness.[g]

2 "You must not follow a crowd in wrongdoing. Do not testify in a lawsuit and go along with a crowd to pervert justice.[h] **3** Do not show favoritism to a poor person in his lawsuit.

4 "If you come across your enemy's stray ox or donkey, you must return it to him.

5 "If you see the donkey of someone who hates you lying helpless under its load, and you want to refrain from helping it, you must help with it.[D,i]

6 "You must not deny justice to a poor person among you in his lawsuit. **7** Stay far away from a false accusation. Do not kill the innocent and the just, because I will not justify the guilty.[j] **8** You must not take a bribe,[k] for a bribe blinds the clear-sighted and corrupts the words[E] of the righteous. **9** You must not oppress a resident alien;[l] you yourselves know how it feels to be a resident alien because you were resident aliens in the land of Egypt.

SABBATHS AND FESTIVALS

10 "Sow your land for six years and gather its produce.[m] **11** But during the seventh year you are to let it rest and leave it uncultivated, so that the poor among your people may eat from it and the wild animals may consume what they leave. Do the same with your vineyard and your olive grove.

12 "Do your work[n] for six days but rest on the seventh day so that your ox and your donkey may rest, and the son of your female slave as well as the resident alien may be refreshed.

13 "Pay strict attention to everything I have said to you. You must not invoke the names of other gods; they must not be heard on your lips.[F,o]

14 "Celebrate a festival in my honor three times a year.[p] **15** Observe the Festival of Unleavened Bread. As I commanded you, you are to eat unleavened bread for seven days at the appointed time in the month of Abib,[G] because you came out of Egypt in that month. No one is to appear before me empty-handed.[q] **16** Also observe the Festival of Harvest[H] with the firstfruits of your produce from what you sow in the field, and observe the Festival of Ingathering[I,r] at the end of the year, when you gather your produce[J] from the field. **17** Three times a year all your males are to appear before the Lord GOD.

18 "You must not offer the blood of my sacrifices with anything leavened. The fat of my festival offering must not remain until morning.[s]

19 "Bring the best of the firstfruits of your land to the house of the LORD your God.

"You must not boil a young goat in its mother's milk.[t]

PROMISES AND WARNINGS

20 "I am going to send an angel[u] before you to protect you on the way and bring you

---

A 22:27 Lit skin   B 22:28 Or judges   C 23:1 Lit join hands with   D 23:5 Or load, you must refrain from leaving it to him; you must set it free with him
E 23:8 Or and subverts the cause   F 23:13 Lit mouth   G 23:15 March–April; called Nisan in the post-exilic period; Neh 2:1; Est 3:7   H 23:16 The
Festival of Harvest is called Festival of Weeks elsewhere; Ex 34:22. In the NT it is called Pentecost; Ac 2:1.   I 23:16 The Festival of Ingathering is
called Festival of Shelters elsewhere; Lv 23:34-36.   J 23:16 Lit labors

---

22:29-30 The people were not to defraud God by withholding their **offerings** and **firstborn**, which belonged to him.

23:1-9 The Israelites were to deal honestly and fairly with all people. No one was to be treated with **favoritism**—not even the poor (23:3). And no one was to be treated with injustice—not even an enemy's animal (23:4-5).

23:10-13 The law regarding a weekly Sabbath of rest for people and animals (23:12; see 20:8-11) was expanded to Sabbatical years to provide **rest** for the land and food for the poor (23:10-11). It was a reminder that God owned the land; they were stewards on his behalf.
23:14-19 Each **festival** was a reminder of God's provision for his people.

The practice of boiling **a young goat in its mother's milk** may have been a pagan custom (23:19) that the Lord didn't want his people to adopt.

to the place I have prepared. [21] Be attentive to him and listen to him. Do not defy him, because he will not forgive your acts of rebellion, for my name is in him.[a] [22] But if you will carefully obey him and do everything I say, then I will be an enemy[b] to your enemies and a foe to your foes. [23] For my angel will go before you and bring you to the land of the Amorites, Hethites, Perizzites, Canaanites, Hivites, and Jebusites, and I will wipe them out.[c] [24] Do not bow in worship to their gods, and do not serve them. Do not imitate their practices. Instead, demolish them[A] and smash their sacred pillars to pieces.[d] [25] Serve the LORD your God, and he[B] will bless your bread and your water. I will remove illnesses from you.[e] [26] No woman will miscarry or be childless in your land. I will give you the full number of your days.[f]

[27] "I will cause the people ahead of you to feel terror[c] and will throw into confusion[g] all the nations you come to. I will make all your enemies turn their backs to you in retreat.[D] [28] I will send hornets[E,h] in front of you, and they will drive the Hivites, Canaanites, and Hethites away from you. [29] I will not drive them out ahead of you in a single year; otherwise, the land would become desolate, and wild animals would multiply against you. [30] I will drive them out little by little ahead of you until you have become numerous[f] and take possession of the land. [31] I will set your borders from the Red Sea to the Mediterranean Sea,[G] and from the wilderness to the Euphrates River.[H] For I will place the inhabitants of the land under your control, and you will drive them out ahead of you.[i] [32] You must not make a covenant[j] with them or their gods. [33] They must not remain in your land, or else they will make you sin against me. If you serve their gods, it will be a snare for you."[k]

THE COVENANT CEREMONY

24 Then he said to Moses, "Go up to the LORD, you and Aaron, Nadab, and Abihu, and seventy of Israel's elders,[l] and bow in worship at a distance. [2] Moses alone is to approach the LORD, but the others are not to approach, and the people are not to go up with him."

[3] Moses came and told the people all the commands of the LORD and all the ordinances. Then all the people responded with a single voice, "We will do everything that the LORD has commanded."[m] [4] And Moses wrote[n] down all the words of the LORD. He rose early the next morning and set up an altar and twelve pillars for the twelve tribes of Israel at the base of the mountain. [5] Then he sent out young Israelite men, and they offered burnt offerings and sacrificed bulls as fellowship offerings to the LORD. [6] Moses took half the blood and set it in basins; the other half of the blood he splattered on the altar. [7] He then took the covenant scroll and read it aloud to the people. They responded, "We will do and obey all that the LORD has commanded."

[8] Moses took the blood, splattered it on the people, and said, "This is the blood of the covenant that the LORD has made with you concerning all these words."[o]

[9] Then Moses went up with Aaron, Nadab, and Abihu, and seventy of Israel's elders, [10] and they saw[p] the God of Israel. Beneath his feet was something like a pavement made of lapis lazuli, as clear as the sky itself.[q] [11] God did not harm[i] the Israelite nobles; they saw[r] him, and they ate and drank.

[12] The LORD said to Moses, "Come up to me on the mountain and stay there so that I may give you the stone tablets[s] with the law and commandments I have written for their instruction."

[13] So Moses arose with his assistant Joshua and went up the mountain of God.[t]

[a]23:21 Nm 14:11; Dt 18:19; Ps 78:40,56
[b]23:22 Gn 12:3; Dt 30:7; Jr 30:20
[c]23:23 Ex 23:20; Jos 24:8
[d]23:24 Ex 20:5; 34:13; Nm 33:52; Dt 12:30
[e]23:25 Ex 15:26; Dt 6:13; 7:15; 28:5,8; Mt 4:10
[f]23:26 Dt 7:14; Jb 5:26; Mal 3:11
[g]23:27 Dt 2:25; 7:23
[h]23:28 Dt 7:20; Jos 24:12 Jos 21:44; 1Kg 4:21
[i]23:32 Ex 34:12,15; Dt 7:2
[k]23:33 Dt 7:16; Ps 106:36

[l]24:1 Ex 6:23; Lv 10:1-2; Nm 11:16
[m]24:3 Ex 19:8; Dt 5:27
[n]24:4 Gn 28:18; Dt 31:9
[o]24:6-8 Heb 9:18-20; 1Pt 1:2
[p]24:10 Jn 1:18; 1Jn 4:12
[q]Ezk 1:26; Mt 17:2; Rv 4:3
[r]24:11 Gn 32:30; Ex 19:21
[s]24:12 Ex 32:15; Dt 5:22
[t]24:13 Ex 3:1; 17:9

A23:24 Probably the idols   B23:25 LXX, Vg read *I*   C23:27 Lit *will send terror of me ahead of you*   D23:27 Or *I will give your enemies to you by the neck*   E23:28 Or *send panic*   F23:30 Lit *fruitful*   G23:31 Lit *the Sea of the Philistines*   H23:31 Lit *the River*   I24:11 Lit *not stretch out his hand against*

23:27-30 God thoughtfully promised to **drive** the Israelites' enemies out of the land gradually—or else **the land would become desolate** (23:29).
23:33 The people's failure to partner with God in driving the Canaanites out of the land would result in them being a **snare** to the Israelites. Their idolatrous beliefs and practices would lure Israel, leading God's people to **sin**.
24:3 The only reason we can truly know God is that he chooses to make himself known. We learn about him because he decides to tell us. But the proclamation of the Word of

God is not a mere opportunity for note taking. It's a call to respond to God. Scripture says, "Be doers of the word and not hearers only, deceiving yourselves" (Jas 1:22).
24:4-8 The reason we no longer need to offer bloody sacrifices to have fellowship with God is that the ultimate sacrifice has been made. Jesus Christ obtained our eternal redemption "not by the blood of goats and calves, but by his own blood" (Heb 9:12). Through his atoning sacrifice, the Son of God inaugurated a new covenant—one that provides complete forgiveness of your sins and grants you a new

heart, so that you have the capacity to obey him if you'll only place your faith in him (see the notes on Heb 8:7-12).
24:9-11 The Lord let these men see something of his glory in a manner similar to what Moses would later experience in a more dramatic fashion (see 33:18-23; 34:5-8). Israel, we must note, only saw God when they worshiped at his invitation, responded to his revelation, and received the blood of his consecration.

[a] 24:15 Ex 19:9; Mt 17:5
[b] 24:16 Ex 16:10
[c] 24:17 Ex 3:2; Dt 4:36; Heb 12:18,29
[d] 24:18 Ex 34:28; Dt 9:9
[e] 25:2 Ex 35:5,21; 1Ch 29:5; Ezr 2:68; Neh 11:2; 2Co 8:12; 9:7
[f] 25:5 Ex 26:14; 35:7,23; 36:19; 39:34
[g] 25:6 Ex 27:20; 30:23-24
[h] 25:7 Ex 28:4,6-15
[i] 25:8 Ex 36:1-5; Heb 9:12
[j] Ex 29:45; 1Kg 6:13; 2Co 6:16; Rv 21:3
[k] 25:9 Ex 25:40; 26:30; Ac 7:44; Heb 8:2,5
[l] 25:10 Ex 37:1,3-4; Dt 10:3; Heb 9:4

[m] 25:16 Ex 16:34; Dt 31:26; 1Kg 8:9
[n] 25:17 Ex 37:6; Rm 3:25; Heb 9:5
[o] 25:20 1Kg 8:7; 1Ch 28:18; Heb 9:5
[p] 25:21 Ex 25:16; 26:34
[q] 25:22 Nm 7:89; 1Sm 4:4; 2Sm 6:2; 2Kg 19:15; Ps 80:1; Is 37:16
[r] 25:23 Ex 25:17; 1Kg 7:48; 2Ch 4:8; Heb 9:2

[14] He told the elders, "Wait here for us until we return to you. Aaron and Hur are here with you. Whoever has a dispute should go to them." [15] When Moses went up the mountain, the cloud[a] covered it. [16] The glory of the LORD settled on Mount Sinai, and the cloud covered it for six days. On the seventh day he called to Moses from the cloud.[b] [17] The appearance of the LORD's glory to the Israelites was like a consuming fire[c] on the mountaintop. [18] Moses entered the cloud as he went up the mountain, and he remained on the mountain forty days and forty nights.[d]

OFFERINGS TO BUILD THE TABERNACLE

25 The LORD spoke to Moses: [2] "Tell the Israelites to take an offering for me. You are to take my offering from everyone who is willing to give.[e] [3] This is the offering you are to receive from them: gold, silver, and bronze; [4] blue, purple, and scarlet yarn; fine linen and goat hair; [5] ram skins dyed red[f] and fine leather;[A] acacia wood; [6] oil[g] for the light; spices for the anointing oil and for the fragrant incense; [7] and onyx[B] along with other gemstones for mounting on the ephod and breastpiece.[C,h]

[8] "They are to make a sanctuary[i] for me so that I may dwell[j] among them. [9] You must make it according to all that I show you — the pattern[k] of the tabernacle as well as the pattern of all its furnishings.

THE ARK

[10] "They are to make an ark[l] of acacia wood, forty-five inches long, twenty-seven inches wide, and twenty-seven inches high.[D] [11] Overlay it with pure gold; overlay it both inside and out. Also make a gold molding all around it. [12] Cast four gold rings for it and place them on its four feet, two rings on one side and two rings on the other side. [13] Make poles of acacia wood and overlay them with gold. [14] Insert the poles into the rings on the sides of the ark in order to carry the ark with them. [15] The poles are to remain in the rings of the ark; they must not be removed from it. [16] Put the tablets of[E] the testimony that I will give you into the ark.[m] [17] Make a mercy seat[n] of pure gold, forty-five inches long and twenty-seven inches wide.[F] [18] Make two cherubim of gold; make them of hammered work at the two ends of the mercy seat. [19] Make one cherub at one end and one cherub at the other end. At its two ends, make the cherubim of one piece with the mercy seat. [20] The cherubim are to have wings spread out above, covering[o] the mercy seat with their wings, and are to face one another. The faces of the cherubim should be toward the mercy seat. [21] Set the mercy seat on top of the ark and put the tablets of the testimony that I will give you into the ark.[p] [22] I will meet with you there above the mercy seat, between the two cherubim[q] that are over the ark of the testimony; I will speak with you from there about all that I command you regarding the Israelites.

THE TABLE

[23] "You are to construct a table[r] of acacia wood, thirty-six inches long, eighteen inches wide, and twenty-seven inches high.[G] [24] Overlay it with pure gold and make a gold molding all around it. [25] Make a three-inch[H] frame all around it and make a gold molding for it all around its frame. [26] Make four gold rings for it, and attach the rings to the four corners at its four legs. [27] The rings should be next to the frame as holders for the poles to carry the table. [28] Make the poles of acacia wood and overlay them with gold, and the table

---

[A] 25:5 Hb obscure [B] 25:7 Or carnelian [C] 25:7 Traditionally, breastplate [D] 25:10 Lit two and a half cubits its length, one and a half cubits its width, and one and a half cubits its height [E] 25:16 the tablets of supplied for clarity, also in v. 21 [F] 25:17 Lit two and a half cubits its length, one and a half cubits its width [G] 25:23 Lit two cubits its length, one cubit its width, and one and a half cubits its height [H] 25:25 Lit Make it a handbreadth

---

25:1-7 Through these details, God was showing his people how they were to worship him rightly. First, the Israelites were given an opportunity to make an **offering** of precious materials so that everything for the tabernacle could be constructed and prepared (25:2-7). Back when Israel departed Egypt, God gave the people favor with the Egyptians. As a result, they gave the Israelites whatever they wanted (12:36). This story gives us a wonderful insight into God's ways: he knows how to take the wealth of his enemies and use it for his kingdom purposes.

25:8-9 The tabernacle or **sanctuary** would be a tent where God could make his presence known and would **dwell among** his people (25:8). The **tabernacle** (25:9) could be taken down and reassembled as the people traveled from place to place. Eventually the tabernacle would be replaced by a temple (see 1 Kgs 6:1). **25:10-22** The first piece of furniture for the tabernacle was the **ark** (25:10). The lid or cover was referred to as the **mercy seat** (25:17). On top of it were **two** golden **cherubim**—glorious angelic beings facing each other (25:18-20). Inside the ark, Moses was

to place the two stone tablets on which God wrote the Ten Commandments (see 24:12). Thus, the ark was also called **the ark of the testimony**. **Above the mercy seat** was where God manifested his presence (25:22). Israel viewed the ark as God's throne on earth; he was enthroned above the mercy seat between the cherubim (see 1 Sam 4:4; 2 Sam 6:2; Pss 80:1; 99:1; Isa 37:16). **25:23-30** On the **table** the priests were to **put the Bread of the Presence** (25:30). This consisted of twelve flat loaves of bread, one representing each of the twelve tribes. The

can be carried by them. **29** You are also to make its plates[a] and cups, as well as its pitchers and bowls for pouring drink offerings. Make them out of pure gold. **30** Put the Bread of the Presence[b] on the table before me at all times.

THE LAMPSTAND

31 "You[c] are to make a lampstand[d] out of pure, hammered gold. It is to be made of one piece: its base and shaft, its ornamental cups, and its buds[A] and petals. **32** Six branches are to extend from its sides, three branches of the lampstand from one side and three branches of the lampstand from the other side. **33** There are to be three cups shaped like almond blossoms, each with a bud and petals, on one branch, and three cups shaped like almond blossoms, each with a bud and petals, on the next branch. It is to be this way for the six branches that extend from the lampstand. **34** There are to be four cups shaped like almond blossoms on the lampstand shaft along with its buds and petals. **35** For the six branches that extend from the lampstand, a bud must be under the first pair of branches from it, a bud under the second pair of branches from it, and a bud under the third pair of branches from it. **36** Their buds and branches are to be of one piece.[B] All of it is to be a single hammered piece of pure gold.

37 "Make its seven lamps,[e] and set them up so that they illuminate the area in front of it. **38** Its snuffers and firepans must be of pure gold. **39** The lampstand[c] with all these utensils is to be made from seventy-five pounds[D] of pure gold. **40** Be careful to make them according to the pattern[f] you have been shown on the mountain.

THE TABERNACLE

26 "You[g] are to construct the tabernacle itself with ten curtains. You must make them of finely spun linen, and blue, purple, and scarlet yarn, with a design of cherubim worked into them. **2** Each curtain should be forty-two feet[E] long and six feet[F] wide; all the curtains are to have

the same measurements. **3** Five of the curtains should be joined together, and the other five curtains joined together. **4** Make loops of blue yarn on the edge of the last curtain in the first set, and do the same on the edge of the outermost curtain in the second set. **5** Make fifty loops on the one curtain and make fifty loops on the edge of the curtain in the second set, so that the loops line up together. **6** Also make fifty gold clasps and join the curtains together with the clasps, so that the tabernacle may be a single unit.

7 "You are to make curtains of goat hair for a tent over the tabernacle; make eleven of these curtains. **8** Each curtain should be forty-five feet[G] long and six feet wide. All eleven curtains are to have the same measurements. **9** Join five of the curtains by themselves, and the other six curtains by themselves. Then fold the sixth curtain double at the front of the tent. **10** Make fifty loops on the edge of one curtain, the outermost in the first set, and make fifty loops on the edge of the corresponding curtain of the second set. **11** Make fifty bronze clasps; put the clasps through the loops and join the tent together so that it is a single unit. **12** As for the flap that remains from the tent curtains, the leftover half curtain is to hang over the back of the tabernacle. **13** What remains along the length of the tent curtains — a half yard[H] on one side and a half yard on the other side — should hang over the sides of the tabernacle on either side to cover it. **14** Make a covering for the tent from ram skins dyed red[h] and a covering of fine leather[i] on top of that.

15 "You are to make upright supports[J] of acacia wood[i] for the tabernacle. **16** Each support is to be fifteen feet[K] long and twenty-seven[L] inches wide. **17** Each support will have two tenons for joining. Do the same for all the supports of the tabernacle. **18** Make the supports for the tabernacle as follows: twenty supports for the south side, **19** and make forty silver bases under the twenty supports, two bases under the first support for its two tenons, and two bases under the next support for

[a] 25:29 Ex 37:16; Nm 4:7
[b] 25:30 Ex 35:13; 39:36; 40:23; Lv 24:5-9; Nm 4:7
[c] 25:31-39 Ex 37:17-24
[d] 25:31 1Kg 7:49; Zch 4:2; Heb 9:2; Rv 1:12
[e] 25:37 Ex 27:21; 37:23; Lv 24:3-4; Nm 8:2; 2Ch 13:11
[f] 25:40 Ex 26:30; Nm 8:4; 1Ch 28:11,19; Ac 7:44; Heb 8:5
[g] 26:1-37 Ex 36:8-38

[h] 26:14 Ex 25:5; 35:7; 36:19; 39:34; Nm 4:25
[i] 26:15 Ex 25:28; 26:37; 27:1,6; 30:1,5; 35:33; 36:20; 37:15; 38:6

[A] 25:31 = the outer covering of a flower [B] 25:36 Lit *piece with it* [C] 25:39 Lit *lt* [D] 25:39 Lit *a talent* [E] 26:2 Lit *28 cubits* [F] 26:2 Lit *four cubits*, also in v. 8 [G] 26:8 Lit *30 cubits* [H] 26:13 Lit *the cubit* [I] 26:14 Hb obscure [J] 26:15 Or *frames*, or *beams* [K] 26:16 Lit *10 cubits* [L] 26:16 Lit *a cubit and a half*

---

bread foreshadowed someone who would arrive on the scene later in history: the true "bread of God" is his Son Jesus, "the bread of life" (see John 6:33, 35).
25:31-40 The **lampstand** was to be kept burning every night by the priests with olive oil supplied by the Israelites (see 27:20-21;

Lev 24:2-4). This too foreshadowed Christ. Jesus declared, "I am the light of the world. Anyone who follows me will never walk in the darkness" (John 8:12).
26:1 As with the ark, visual representations of the angelic beings were included to give the tabernacle the appearance of heavenly glory.

26:15-30 The Israelites were to build the tabernacle based on **the plan** that God had **shown them** (26:30). This was not a structure that came out of man's imagination. God's instructions were precise and purposeful.

ª 26:30 Ex 25:9,40; Ac
7:44; Heb 8:5
ᵇ 26:31 Ex 36:35; 2Ch 3:14;
Mt 27:51; Heb 9:3
ᶜ 26:33 Ex 25:16; 40:21; Lv
16:2; Heb 9:2
ᵈ 26:34 Ex 25:21; 40:20;
Heb 9:5
ᵉ 26:35 Ex 40:22,24;
Heb 9:2

ᶠ 27:1-8 Ex 38:1-7; Ezk
43:13
ᵍ 27:2 Nm 16:38; Ps 118:27
ʰ 27:8 Ex 25:40; 26:30
ⁱ 27:9-19 Ex 38:9-20

its two tenons; **²⁰** twenty supports for the second side of the tabernacle, the north side, **²¹** along with their forty silver bases, two bases under the first support and two bases under each support; **²²** and make six supports for the west side of the tabernacle. **²³** Make two additional supports for the two back corners of the tabernacle. **²⁴** They are to be paired at the bottom, and joined together^ at the top in a single ring. So it should be for both of them; they will serve as the two corners. **²⁵** There are to be eight supports with their silver bases: sixteen bases; two bases under the first support and two bases under each support.

²⁶ "You are to make five crossbars of acacia wood for the supports on one side of the tabernacle, **²⁷** five crossbars for the supports on the other side of the tabernacle, and five crossbars for the supports of the back side of the tabernacle on the west. **²⁸** The central crossbar is to run through the middle of the supports from one end to the other. **²⁹** Then overlay the supports with gold, and make their rings of gold as the holders for the crossbars. Also overlay the crossbars with gold. **³⁰** You are to set up the tabernacle according to the plan for it that you have been shown on the mountain.ª

³¹ "You are to make a curtain of blue, purple, and scarlet yarn, and finely spun linen with a design of cherubim worked into it.ᵇ **³²** Hang it on four gold-plated pillars of acacia wood that have gold hooks and that stand on four silver bases. **³³** Hang the curtain under the claspsᵇ and bring the ark of the testimony there behind the curtain, so the curtain will make a separation for you between the holy placeᶜ and the most holy place. **³⁴** Put the mercy seat on the ark of the testimony in the most holy place.ᵈ **³⁵** Place the table outside the curtain and the lampstand on the south side of the tabernacle, opposite the table; put the table on the north side.ᵉ

³⁶ "For the entrance to the tent you are to make a screen embroideredᶜ with blue, purple, and scarlet yarn, and finely spun linen. **³⁷** Make five pillars of acacia wood for the screen and overlay them with gold; their hooks are to be gold, and you are to cast five bronze bases for them.

THE ALTAR OF BURNT OFFERING

27 "Youᶠ are to construct the altar of acacia wood. The altar must be square, 7 ½ feet long, and 7 ½ feet wide;ᴰ it must be 4 ½ feet high.ᴱ **²** Make horns for it on its four corners; the horns are to be of one piece.ᶠ Overlay it with bronze.ᵍ **³** Make its pots for removing ashes, and its shovels, basins, meat forks, and firepans; make all its utensils of bronze. **⁴** Construct a grate for it of bronze mesh, and make four bronze rings on the mesh at its four corners. **⁵** Set it below, under the altar's ledge,ᵍ so that the mesh comes halfway upᴴ the altar. **⁶** Then make poles for the altar, poles of acacia wood, and overlay them with bronze. **⁷** The poles are to be inserted into the rings so that the poles are on two sides of the altar when it is carried. **⁸** Construct the altar with boards so that it is hollow. They are to make it just as it was shown to you on the mountain.ʰ

THE COURTYARD

⁹ "Youⁱ are to make the courtyard for the tabernacle. Make hangings for the south side of the courtyard out of finely spun linen, 150 feetⁱ long on that side **¹⁰** including twenty posts and twenty bronze bases, with silver hooks and silver bandsʲ for the posts. **¹¹** And so make hangings 150 feet long for the north side, including twenty posts and their twenty bronze bases, with silver hooks and silver bands for the posts. **¹²** For the width of the courtyard, make hangings 75 feetᴷ long for the west side, including their ten posts and their ten bases. **¹³** And for the width of the courtyard on the east side toward the sunrise, 75 feet, **¹⁴** make hangings 22 ½ feetᴸ long for one side of the gate, including their

---

^ **26:24** Lit *and together they are to be complete*   ᴮ **26:33** The *clasps* that join the ten curtains of the tabernacle; Ex 26:6   ᶜ **26:36** Or *woven*   ᴰ **27:1** Lit *five cubits in length and five cubits in width*   ᴱ **27:1** Lit *wide; and its height three cubits*   ᶠ **27:2** Lit *piece with it*   ᴳ **27:5** Perhaps a *ledge* around the altar on which the priests could stand; Lv 9:22   ᴴ **27:5** Or *altar's rim, so that the grid comes halfway down*   ⁱ **27:9** Lit *100 cubits*, also in v. 11   ʲ **27:10** Or *connecting rods*, also in v. 11   ᴷ **27:12** Lit *50 cubits*, also in v. 13   ᴸ **27:14** Lit *15 cubits*, also in v. 15

26:31-37 A curtain was to be made to separate **the holy place**, which contained **the table** and **the lampstand**, from **the most holy place**, which contained **the mercy seat** (26:31-35). Only the high priest could pass through the curtain into the most holy place—and only once per year on the Day of Atonement (see

Lev 16:1-34; Heb 9:7). When Christ died on the cross, the curtain separating the most holy place in the temple was torn in two by an unseen hand (see Matt 27:51). This symbolized that Jesus had gained for his people full and eternal access to God's holy presence. No other sacrifice would ever be needed.

27:9-19 These verses describe the rectangular courtyard for the tabernacle. The height of the hangings constructing its walls prevented anyone from seeing inside them. One couldn't simply waltz into God's presence. There was only one **gate** for entrance (27:16).

three posts and their three bases. **15** And make hangings 22 ½ feet long for the other side, including their three posts and their three bases. **16** The gate of the courtyard is to have a 30-foot[A] screen[a] embroidered[B] with blue, purple, and scarlet yarn, and finely spun linen. It is to have four posts and their four bases.

17 "All the posts around the courtyard are to be banded with silver and have silver hooks and bronze bases. **18** The courtyard is to be 150 feet long, 75 feet wide at each end, and 7 ½ feet high,[c] all of it made of finely spun linen. The bases of the posts are to be bronze. **19** All the utensils of the tabernacle for every use and all its tent pegs as well as all the tent pegs of the courtyard are to be made of bronze.

THE LAMPSTAND OIL

20 "You are to command the Israelites to bring you pure oil from crushed olives for the light, in order to keep the lamp burning regularly. **21** In the tent of meeting outside the curtain that is in front of the testimony,[b] Aaron and his sons are to tend the lamp[c] from evening until morning before the LORD. This is to be a permanent statute[d] for the Israelites throughout their generations.

THE PRIESTLY GARMENTS

28 "Have your brother Aaron, with his sons, come to you from the Israelites to serve me as priest — Aaron, his sons Nadab and Abihu, Eleazar and Ithamar.[e] **2** Make holy garments[f] for your brother Aaron, for glory and beauty. **3** You are to instruct all the skilled artisans,[D,g] whom I have filled with a spirit of wisdom, to make Aaron's garments for consecrating him to serve me as priest. **4** These are the garments that they must make: a breastpiece, an ephod, a robe, a specially woven tunic,[E] a turban, and a sash. They are to make holy garments for your brother Aaron and his sons so that they may serve me as priests. **5** They should use[f] gold; blue, purple, and scarlet yarn; and fine linen.

THE EPHOD

6 "They[h] are to make the ephod of finely spun linen embroidered[B] with gold, and with blue, purple, and scarlet yarn. **7** It must have two shoulder pieces attached to its two edges so that it can be joined together. **8** The artistically woven waistband that is on the ephod[G] must be of one piece,[H] according to the same workmanship of gold, of blue, purple, and scarlet yarn, and of finely spun linen.

9 "Take two onyx stones and engrave on them the names of Israel's sons: **10** six of their names on the first stone and the remaining six names on the second stone, in the order of their birth. **11** Engrave the two stones with the names of Israel's sons as a gem cutter engraves a seal. Mount them, surrounded with gold filigree settings. **12** Fasten both stones on the shoulder pieces of the ephod as memorial stones for the Israelites. Aaron will carry their names on his two shoulders before the LORD as a reminder.[i] **13** Fashion gold filigree settings **14** and two chains of pure gold; you will make them of braided cord work, and attach the cord chains to the settings.

THE BREASTPIECE

15 "You[j] are to make an embroidered breastpiece for making decisions.[i] Make it with the same workmanship as the ephod; make it of gold, of blue, purple, and scarlet yarn, and of finely spun linen. **16** It must be square and folded double, nine inches long and nine inches wide.[j] **17** Place a setting of gemstones[K] on it, four rows of stones:

> The first row should be
> a row of carnelian, topaz,
> and emerald;[L]
> **18** the second row,
> a turquoise,[M] a lapis lazuli,
> and a diamond;[N]
> **19** the third row,
> a jacinth,[E] an agate, and an amethyst;
> **20** and the fourth row,
> a beryl, an onyx, and a jasper.

They should be adorned with gold filigree in their settings. **21** The twelve stones are to

*a*27:16 Ex 35:17; 38:18; 39:40; 40:8,33; Nm 3:26; 4:26
*b*27:21 Ex 30:8; 1Sm 3:3; 2Ch 13:11
*c*Ex 26:31,33; 28:43
*d*Ex 29:9; Lv 3:17; 16:34; Nm 18:23; 19:21
*e*28:1 Nm 18:7; Ps 99:6; Heb 5:1
*f*28:2 Ex 29:5,9; 31:10; 39:1-2; Lv 8:7,30; Nm 20:26,28
*g*28:3 Ex 31:6; 35:25; 36:1

*h*28:6-12 Ex 39:2-7; Lv 8:7
*i*28:12 Ex 28:29; Jos 4:7; Zch 6:14
*j*28:15-28 Ex 39:8-21

A27:16 Lit *20-cubit* B27:16; 28:6 Or *woven* C27:18 Lit *be 100 by the cubit, and the width 50 by 50, and the height five cubits* D28:3 Lit *all wise of heart* E28:4,19 Hb obscure F28:5 Lit *receive* G28:8 Lit *waistband of its ephod, which is on it* H28:8 Lit *piece with the ephod* I28:15 Used for determining God's will; Nm 27:21 J28:16 Lit *a span its length and a span its width* K28:17 Many of these stones cannot be identified with certainty. L28:17 Or *beryl* M28:18 Or *malachite*, or *garnet* N28:18 Hb obscure; LXX, Vg read *jasper*

28:1-5 God chose the descendants of Levi to care for and transport the tabernacle and all its furnishings (see Num 1:50). From the Levites, God chose **Aaron** and his descendants to serve as Israel's priests (Exod 28:1). They were to have **holy garments** appropriate to their holy role (28:2).
28:6-14 The **ephod** was an artistically embroidered vest-like garment that the priest was to wear (28:6-8). It would include **two onyx stones** engraved with **six** of the **names of Israel's sons**, since the priest would be representing the twelve tribes in his ministerial duties (28:9-11). This would serve as **a reminder** of God's covenant with his people (28:12).

a 28:30 Lv 8:8; Nm 27:21;
Dt 33:8; Ezr 2:63; Neh 7:65
b 28:31-40 Ex 39:22-31

c 28:36 Lv 8:9; Zch 14:20
d 28:38 Lv 10:17; 22:16; Nm
18:1; Is 53:11; Ezk 4:4-6; Jn
1:29; Heb 9:28; 1Pt 2:24
e 28:40 Ex 39:41; Ezk
44:17-18
f 28:41 Ex 29:7; 30:30;
40:15; Lv 10:7
g Ex 29:9; Heb 7:28
h 28:42 Lv 6:10; 16:4;
Ezk 44:18
i 28:43 Ex 20:26; Lv 5:1,17;
20:19
j Ex 27:21; Lv 17:7

correspond to the names of Israel's sons. Each stone must be engraved like a seal, with one of the names of the twelve tribes. [22] "You are to make braided chains[A] of pure gold cord work for the breastpiece. [23] Fashion two gold rings for the breastpiece and attach them to its two corners. [24] Then attach the two gold cords to the two gold rings at the corners of the breastpiece. [25] Attach the other ends of the two cords to the two filigree settings, and in this way attach them to the ephod's shoulder pieces in the front. [26] Make two other gold rings and put them at the two other corners of the breastpiece on the edge that is next to the inner border of the ephod. [27] Make two more gold rings and attach them to the bottom of the ephod's two shoulder pieces on its front, close to its seam,[B] and above the ephod's woven waistband. [28] The artisans are to tie the breastpiece from its rings to the rings of the ephod with a cord of blue yarn, so that the breastpiece is above the ephod's waistband and does not come loose from the ephod. [29] "Whenever he enters the sanctuary, Aaron is to carry the names of Israel's sons over his heart on the breastpiece for decisions, as a continual reminder before the LORD. [30] Place the Urim and Thummim[a] in the breastpiece for decisions, so that they will also be over Aaron's heart whenever he comes before the LORD. Aaron will continually carry the means of decisions for the Israelites over his heart before the LORD.

THE ROBE

[31] "You[b] are to make the robe of the ephod entirely of blue yarn. [32] There should be an opening at its top in the center of it. Around the opening, there should be a woven collar with an opening like that of body armor[c] so that it does not tear. [33] Make pomegranates of blue, purple, and scarlet yarn on its lower hem and all around it. Put gold bells between them all

the way around, [34] so that gold bells and pomegranates alternate around the lower hem of the robe. [35] The robe will be worn by Aaron whenever he ministers, and its sound will be heard when he enters the sanctuary before the LORD and when he exits, so that he does not die.

THE TURBAN

[36] "You are to make a pure gold medallion and engrave it, like the engraving of a seal:[c] HOLY TO THE LORD. [37] Fasten it to a cord of blue yarn so it can be placed on the turban; the medallion is to be on the front of the turban. [38] It will be on Aaron's forehead so that Aaron may bear the guilt[d] connected with the holy offerings that the Israelites consecrate as all their holy gifts. It is always to be on his forehead, so that they may find acceptance with the LORD.

OTHER PRIESTLY GARMENTS

[39] "You are to weave the tunic from fine linen, make a turban of fine linen, and make an embroidered sash. [40] Make tunics, sashes, and headbands for Aaron's sons to give them glory and beauty.[e] [41] Put these on your brother Aaron and his sons; then anoint,[f] ordain,[D] and consecrate[g] them, so that they may serve me as priests. [42] Make them linen undergarments[h] to cover their naked bodies; they must extend from the waist to the thighs. [43] These must be worn by Aaron and his sons whenever they enter the tent of meeting or approach the altar to minister in the sanctuary area, so that they do not incur guilt[i] and die. This is to be a permanent statute[j] for Aaron and for his future descendants.

INSTRUCTIONS
ABOUT CONSECRATION

29 "This is what you are to do for them to consecrate them to serve me as priests. Take a young bull and two unblemished rams, [2] with unleavened bread, unleavened cakes mixed with oil, and unleavened wafers coated with oil.

[A] 28:22 The same *chains* mentioned in v. 14   [B] 28:27 The place where the *shoulder pieces* join the front of the ephod   [C] 28:32 Hb obscure
[D] 28:41 Lit *anoint them, fill their hand*

28:29-30 The gemstones for each tribe reflected the fact that the priest was representing and interceding for the nation. He bore **the names of Israel's sons over his heart** (28:29). The reason it was called **the breastpiece for decisions** was because it included **the Urim and Thummim** (28:29-30). It is not clear exactly what these items were or exactly how they were used. But they were used for decision-making when Israel needed

an answer from the Lord (see Num 27:18-21; 1 Sam 14:41-42; 28:5-6; Ezra 2:63).
28:31-35 The priest's blue **robe** included **gold bells** attached to its **lower hem** (28:33-34). That way, others could hear the bells and know that the priest was ministering **before the LORD** (28:35).
28:36-38 The priest was set apart for God's service. He was to **bear the guilt** with regard to Israel's **holy offerings** (28:38). The only

high priest who would be perfectly holy and able to perfectly intercede for his people, however, would be Jesus Christ (see Heb 7:26-28).
28:39-43 Such artistically woven items of beautiful material set apart **Aaron's sons** and gave **them glory and beauty** (28:40). Those who were to minister in the name of a glorious God were to be dressed gloriously.

Make them out of fine wheat flour,[a] [3] put them in a basket, and bring them in the basket, along with the bull and two rams. [4] Bring Aaron and his sons to the entrance to the tent of meeting and wash them with water.[b] [5] Then take the garments and clothe Aaron with the tunic, the robe for the ephod, the ephod itself, and the breastpiece; fasten the ephod on him with its woven waistband.[c] [6] Put the turban on his head and place the holy diadem[d] on the turban. [7] Take the anointing oil, pour it on his head, and anoint[e] him. [8] You must also bring his sons and clothe them with tunics. [9] Tie the sashes on Aaron and his sons and fasten headbands on them. The priesthood is to be theirs by a permanent statute. This is the way you will ordain Aaron and[A] his sons.[f]

[10] "You are to bring the bull to the front of the tent of meeting, and Aaron and his sons must lay their hands on the bull's head.[g] [11] Slaughter the bull before the LORD at the entrance to the tent of meeting. [12] Take some of the bull's blood and apply it to the horns[h] of the altar with your finger; then pour out all the rest of the blood at the base of the altar. [13] Take all the fat[i] that covers the entrails, the fatty lobe of the liver, and the two kidneys with the fat on them, and burn them on the altar. [14] But burn the bull's flesh, its hide, and its waste outside the camp;[j] it is a sin offering.

[15] "Take one ram, and Aaron and his sons are to lay their hands on the ram's head.[k] [16] You are to slaughter the ram, take its blood, and splatter it on all sides of the altar. [17] Cut the ram into pieces. Wash its entrails and legs, and place them with its head and its pieces on the altar. [18] Then burn the whole ram on the altar; it is a burnt offering to the LORD. It is a pleasing aroma,[l] a fire offering to the LORD.

[19] "You are to take the second ram, and Aaron and his sons must lay their hands on the ram's head.[m] [20] Slaughter the ram, take some of its blood, and put it on Aaron's right earlobe, on his sons' right earlobes, on the thumbs of their right hands, and on the big toes of their right feet. Splatter the remaining blood on all sides of the altar. [21] Take some of the blood that is on the altar and some of the anointing oil,[n]

and sprinkle them on Aaron and his garments, as well as on his sons and their garments. So he and his garments will be holy, as well as his sons and their garments.

[22] "Take the fat from the ram, the fat tail, the fat covering the entrails, the fatty lobe of the liver, the two kidneys and the fat on them, and the right thigh (since this is a ram for ordination[B]); [23] take one loaf of bread, one cake of bread made with oil, and one wafer from the basket of unleavened bread that is before the LORD; [24] and put all of them in the hands of Aaron and his[c] sons and present them as a presentation offering before the LORD.[o] [25] Take them from their hands and burn them on the altar on top of the burnt offering, as a pleasing aroma before the LORD; it is a fire offering to the LORD.

[26] "Take the breast from the ram of Aaron's ordination and present it as a presentation offering before the LORD; it is to be your portion.[p] [27] Consecrate for Aaron and his sons[q] the breast of the presentation offering that is presented and the thigh of the contribution that is lifted up from the ram of ordination. [28] This will belong to Aaron and his sons as a regular portion from the Israelites, for it is a contribution. It will be the Israelites' contribution from their fellowship sacrifices, their contribution to the LORD.

[29] "The holy garments that belong to Aaron are to belong to his sons after him, so that they can be anointed and ordained[D] in them.[r] [30] Any priest who is one of his sons and who succeeds him and enters the tent of meeting to minister in the sanctuary must wear them for seven days.[s]

[31] "You are to take the ram of ordination and boil its flesh in a holy place. [32] Aaron and his sons are to eat the meat of the ram and the bread that is in the basket at the entrance to the tent of meeting.[t] [33] They must eat those things by which atonement was made at the time of their ordination[E] and consecration. An unauthorized person must not eat[u] them, for these things are holy. [34] If any of the meat of ordination or any of the bread is left until morning, burn what is left over. It must not be eaten because it is holy.

a 29:2 Lv 2:4; 6:19-23
b 29:4 Ex 40:12; Lv 8:6; Heb 10:22
c 29:5 Ex 28:2,8; Lv 8:7
d 29:6 Ex 28:36-37; Lv 8:9
e 29:7 Ex 30:25; Lv 8:12; 10:7; 21:10; Nm 35:25
f 29:9 Ex 28:41; Nm 18:7
g 29:10 Lv 1:4; 8:14
h 29:12 Ex 27:2; Lv 8:15
i 29:13 Lv 3:3-4
j 29:14 Lv 4:11-12,21; Heb 13:11
k 29:15 Lv 1:4; 8:18
l 29:18 Gn 8:21; Ex 29:25
m 29:19 Lv 29:3; Lv 8:22
n 29:21 Ex 30:25,31; Heb 9:22

o 29:23-24 Lv 7:30; 8:22
p 29:26 Lv 7:3; 8:29
q 29:27 Lv 7:31,34; Nm 18:11,18; Dt 18:3
r 29:29 Nm 18:8; 20:26,28
s 29:30 Lv 8:35; Nm 20:28
t 29:31-32 Lv 8:31; Mt 12:4
u 29:33 Lv 10:14-15,17; 22:10

A 29:9 Lit you will fill the hand of Aaron and the hand of; Ex 29:23-24   B 29:22 The priest would normally receive the right thigh to be eaten, but here it is burned; Lv 7:32-34.   C 29:24 Lit in the hands of his   D 29:29 Lit him for anointing in them and for filling their hand   E 29:33 Lit made to fill their hand

29:19-20 The blood from one of the slaughtered rams was to be placed on Aaron and his sons so that the whole body would be con-

secrated to the Lord's service—their ears to hear God's Word, their hands to do his work, and their feet to walk in his ways.

30:10 The atonement ceremony (30:10) is a reference to the Day of Atonement (see Lev 16:1-34).

[a] 29:36 Ex 40:10; Heb 10:11
[b] 29:37 Ex 30:29; Mt 23:19
[c] 29:38 Nm 28:3; 1Ch 16:40; Ezr 3:3; Dn 12:11
[d] 29:39 1Kg 18:29,36; 2Kg 16:15; Ezr 9:4–5; Ps 141:2; Ezk 46:13–15
[e] 29:42 Ex 25:22; 30:8
[f] 29:43 1Kg 8:11; 2Ch 5:14; Ezk 43:5; Hg 2:7,9
[g] 29:45 Zch 2:10; Jn 14:17
[h] Ex 25:8; Lv 26:12
[i] 29:46 Ex 20:2
[j] 30:1 Ex 37:25; Rv 8:3

[k] 30:7 Ex 27:21; 1Sm 2:28; 1Ch 23:13; Lk 1:9
[l] 30:9 Lv 10:1
[m] 30:10 Lv 16:18
[n] 30:12 Nm 1:2; 2Sm 24:2
[o] Nm 31:50; Mt 20:28
[p] Ex 12:13; 2Sm 24:13,21,25
[q] 30:13 Ex 38:26; Nm 3:47; Mt 17:24
[r] 30:15 Pr 22:2; Eph 6:9
[s] 30:16 Ex 38:25–28; Nm 16:40
[t] 30:18 Ex 38:8; 40:7,30; 1Kg 7:38

35 "This is what you are to do for Aaron and his sons based on all I have commanded you. Take seven days to ordain them. **36** Sacrifice a bull as a sin offering each day for atonement. Purify[A] the altar when you make atonement for it, and anoint it in order to consecrate it.[a] **37** For seven days you must make atonement for the altar and consecrate it. The altar will be especially holy. Whatever touches the altar will be consecrated.[b]

38 "This is what you are to offer regularly on the altar every day: two year-old lambs.[c] **39** In the morning offer one lamb, and at twilight offer the other lamb.[d] **40** With the first lamb offer two quarts[B] of fine flour mixed with one quart[C] of oil from crushed olives, and a drink offering of one quart of wine. **41** You are to offer the second lamb at twilight. Offer a grain offering and a drink offering with it, like the one in the morning, as a pleasing aroma, a fire offering to the LORD. **42** This will be a regular burnt offering throughout your generations at the entrance to the tent of meeting before the LORD, where I will meet you[D] to speak with you.[e] **43** I will also meet with the Israelites there, and that place will be consecrated by my glory.[f] **44** I will consecrate the tent of meeting and the altar; I will also consecrate Aaron and his sons to serve me as priests. **45** I will dwell[g] among the Israelites and be their God.[h] **46** And they will know that I am the LORD their God, who brought them out of the land of Egypt, so that I might dwell among them. I am the LORD their God.[i]

THE INCENSE ALTAR

30 "You are to make an altar for the burning of incense; make it of acacia wood.[j] **2** It must be square, eighteen inches long and eighteen inches wide;[E] it must be thirty-six inches high.[F] Its horns must be of one piece with it. **3** Overlay its top, all around its sides, and its horns with pure gold; make a gold molding all around it. **4** Make two gold rings for it under the molding on two of its sides; put these on opposite sides of it to be holders for the poles to carry it with. **5** Make the poles of acacia wood and overlay them with gold.

6 "You are to place the altar in front of the curtain by the ark of the testimony — in front of the mercy seat that is over the testimony — where I will meet with you. **7** Aaron must burn fragrant incense on it; he must burn it every morning when he tends the lamps.[k] **8** When Aaron sets up the lamps at twilight, he must burn incense. There is to be an incense offering before the LORD throughout your generations. **9** You must not offer unauthorized incense on it,[l] or a burnt or grain offering; you are not to pour a drink offering on it.

10 "Once a year Aaron is to perform the atonement ceremony for the altar. Throughout your generations he is to perform the atonement ceremony for[G] it once a year, with the blood of the sin offering for atonement on the horns.[m] The altar is especially holy to the LORD."

THE ATONEMENT MONEY

11 The LORD spoke to Moses: **12** "When you take a census[n] of the Israelites to register them, each of the men must pay a ransom[o] for his life to the LORD as they are registered. Then no plague[p] will come on them as they are registered. **13** Everyone who is registered must pay half a shekel[H] according to the sanctuary shekel (twenty gerahs to the shekel). This half shekel is a contribution to the LORD.[q] **14** Each man who is registered, twenty years old or more, must give this contribution to the LORD. **15** The wealthy may not give more and the poor may not give less[r] than half a shekel when giving the contribution to the LORD to atone for[I] your lives. **16** Take the atonement price[J] from the Israelites and use it for the service of the tent of meeting. It will serve as a reminder for the Israelites before the LORD to atone for your lives."[s]

THE BRONZE BASIN

17 The LORD spoke to Moses: **18** "Make a bronze basin[t] for washing and a bronze stand for it. Set it between the tent of meeting and the altar, and put water in it. **19** Aaron and his sons must wash their hands and feet from the basin. **20** Whenever they enter the tent of meeting or approach the altar to minister by burning an

[A] 29:36 Or *Make a sin offering on*   [B] 29:40 Lit *offer a tenth*   [C] 29:40 Lit *a fourth of a hin*   [D] 29:42 = Moses   [E] 30:2 Lit *one cubit its length and one cubit its width*   [F] 30:2 Lit *wide; and two cubits its height*   [G] 30:10 Or *on*   [H] 30:13 A shekel is about two-fifths of an ounce of silver   [I] 30:15 Or *to ransom*, also in v. 16   [J] 30:16 Lit *the silver of the atonement*

30:11-16 This **ransom** served two purposes. First, it served as an **atonement** for the men's lives and prevented **plague** from coming on them (30:12, 15-16). Second, the money was used to maintain **the tent of meeting** (30:16).
30:17-21 The **bronze basin** was used as a reservoir for water so that the priests could perform their ritual washing before approaching to minister in the tabernacle.

offering to the LORD, they must wash with water so that they will not die. **21** They must wash their hands and feet so that they will not die; this is to be a permanent statute[a] for them, for Aaron and his descendants throughout their generations."

THE ANOINTING OIL

22 The LORD spoke to Moses: **23** "Take for yourself the finest spices:[b] 12 ½ pounds[A] of liquid myrrh, half as much (6 ¼ pounds[B]) of fragrant cinnamon, 6 ¼ pounds of fragrant cane, **24** 12 ½ pounds of cassia (by the sanctuary shekel), and a gallon[c] of olive oil.[c] **25** Prepare from these a holy anointing oil, a scented blend, the work of a perfumer; it will be holy anointing oil.[d]

26 "With it you are to anoint[e] the tent of meeting, the ark of the testimony, **27** the table with all its utensils, the lampstand with its utensils, the altar of incense, **28** the altar of burnt offering with all its utensils, and the basin with its stand. **29** Consecrate them and they will be especially holy. Whatever touches them will be consecrated. **30** Anoint Aaron and his sons and consecrate[f] them to serve me as priests.

31 "Tell the Israelites: This will be my holy anointing oil throughout your generations. **32** It must not be used for ordinary anointing on a person's body, and you must not make anything like it using its formula. It is holy, and it must be holy to you. **33** Anyone who blends something like it or puts some of it on an unauthorized person must be cut off[g] from his people."

THE SACRED INCENSE

34 The LORD said to Moses: "Take fragrant spices: stacte, onycha, and galbanum; the spices and pure frankincense are to be in equal measures. **35** Prepare expertly blended incense from these; it is to be seasoned with salt, pure and holy. **36** Grind some of it into a fine powder and put some in front of the testimony in the tent of meeting, where I will meet with you. It must be especially holy[h] to you. **37** As for the incense you are making, you must not make any

for yourselves using its formula. It is to be regarded by you as holy — belonging to the LORD. **38** Anyone who makes something like it to smell its fragrance must be cut off from his people."

GOD'S PROVISION OF THE SKILLED WORKERS

31 The LORD also spoke to Moses: **2** "Look, I have appointed by name Bezalel[i] son of Uri, son of Hur, of the tribe of Judah. **3** I have filled him with God's Spirit, with wisdom, understanding, and ability in every craft[j] **4** to design artistic works in gold, silver, and bronze, **5** to cut gemstones for mounting, and to carve wood for work in every craft. **6** I have also selected Oholiab[D] son of Ahisamach, of the tribe of Dan, to be with him. I have put wisdom in the heart of every skilled artisan[E] in order to make all that I have commanded you: **7** the tent of meeting, the ark of the testimony, the mercy seat that is on top of it, and all the other furnishings of the tent[k] — **8** the table with its utensils, the pure gold lampstand with all its utensils, the altar of incense, **9** the altar of burnt offering with all its utensils, the basin with its stand — **10** the specially woven[F] garments, both the holy garments for the priest Aaron and the garments for his sons to serve as priests, **11** the anointing oil, and the fragrant incense for the sanctuary. They must make them according to all that I have commanded you."[l]

OBSERVING THE SABBATH

12 The LORD said to Moses: **13** "Tell the Israelites: You must observe my Sabbaths, for it is a sign between me and you throughout your generations, so that you will know that I am the LORD who consecrates you.[m] **14** Observe the Sabbath, for it is holy to you. Whoever profanes it must be put to death. If anyone does work on it, that person must be cut off from his people.[n] **15** Work may be done for six days, but on the seventh day there must be a Sabbath of complete rest,[o] holy to the LORD. Anyone who

[a] 30:21 Ex 27:21; 28:43
[b] 30:23 Sg 4:14; Ezk 27:22
[c] 30:24 Ex 29:40; Ps 45:8
[d] 30:25 Ex 37:29; Nm 35:25
[e] 30:26 Ex 40:9; Lv 8:10; Nm 7:1
[f] 30:30 Ex 29:7; Lv 8:12,30
[g] 30:33 Gn 17:14; Ex 30:38
[h] 30:36 Ex 29:37; Lv 2:3

[i] 31:2 Ex 35:30; 36:1; 1Ch 2:20
[j] 31:3 Ex 35:31; 1Kg 7:14
[k] 31:7 Ex 36:8–38; 37:1–6
[l] 31:8–11 Ex 30:25,31,34; 37:10–29; 38:1,8; 39:1,41
[m] 31:13 Lv 19:3,30; Ezk 20:12,20
[n] 31:14 Nm 15:35
[o] 31:15 Gn 2:2; Ex 16:23; 20:9

[A] **30:23** Lit *500* (shekels), also in v. 24   [B] **30:23** Lit *250* (shekels)   [C] **30:24** Lit *a hin*   [D] **31:6** LXX, Syr read *Eliab*   [E] **31:6** Lit *everyone wise of heart*
[F] **31:10** Hb obscure

30:22-33 God carefully described the ingredients for the **holy anointing oil** (30:22-25). Anything that didn't meet these specific requirements would be considered "unauthorized" (30:9). This oil was holy and not to be used for any other purpose (30:31-32). The things of God were to be held with the highest regard.

30:34-38 Like the anointing oil, the **incense** too would be used only in the tabernacle (30:35-36). Anyone who mixed a batch for his own use would be **cut off from his people** (30:38).

31:1-11 The Lord **appointed** two men to lead the construction work: **Bezalel** and **Oholiab** (31:2-6). This tells us that God not only pro-

vided precise instructions for everything needed, but he also endowed men with wisdom and skill to do the work. God also provides the means to accomplish what he calls you to do.

31:12-17 To reject **the Sabbath** was to reject the holy God. Thus, anyone who ignored the command was to be **put to death** (31:15).

*31:18 Ex 24:12; 32:15-16;
Dt 4:13; 5:22; 2Co 3:3
*32:1 Ex 13:21; 24:18; Dt
9:9; Ac 7:40
*32:2 Ex 35:22; Jdg 8:24-27
*32:4 Dt 9:16; Jdg 17:3-4;
1Kg 12:28; Neh 9:18; Ps
106:19; Ac 7:41
*32:5 Lv 23:2,37; 2Kg
10:20

*32:6 Nm 25:2; 1Co 10:7
*32:7 Gn 6:11-12; Dt 9:12
*32:8 Ex 20:3-4,23; 34:15;
Dt 32:17; 1Kg 12:28
*32:9 Ex 33:3,5; 34:9; 2Ch
30:8; Is 48:4; Ac 7:51
*32:10 Ex 22:24; Nm 14:12;
Dt 9:14
*32:11-12 Nm 14:13-16; Dt
9:18,26-29
*32:13 Gn 22:16-18;
Heb 6:13
*Gn 12:7; 13:15; 15:7,18;
26:4; 35:11-12
*32:14 2Sm 24:16;
Ps 106:45

does work on the Sabbath day must be put to death. **16** The Israelites must observe the Sabbath, celebrating it throughout their generations as a permanent covenant. **17** It is a sign forever between me and the Israelites, for in six days the LORD made the heavens and the earth, but on the seventh day he rested and was refreshed."

THE TWO STONE TABLETS

18 When he finished speaking with Moses on Mount Sinai, he gave him the two tablets of the testimony, stone tablets inscribed by the finger of God.ᵃ

THE GOLD CALF

32 When the people saw that Moses delayed in coming down from the mountain, they gathered around Aaron and said to him, "Come, make godsᴬ for us who will go before us because this Moses, the man who brought us up from the land of Egypt — we don't know what has happened to him!"ᵇ **2** Aaron replied to them, "Take off the gold ringsᶜ that are on the ears of your wives, your sons, and your daughters and bring them to me." **3** So all the people took off the gold rings that were on their ears and brought them to Aaron. **4** He took the gold from them, fashioned it with an engraving tool, and made it into an image of a calf.

Then they said, "Israel, these are your gods,ᴮ who brought you up from the land of Egypt!"ᵈ **5** When Aaron saw this, he built an altar in front of it and made an announcement: "There will be a festivalᵉ to the LORD tomorrow." **6** Early the next morning they arose, offered burnt offerings, and presented fellowship offerings. The

people sat down to eat and drink, and got up to party.ᶠ

7 The LORD spoke to Moses: "Go down at once! For your people you brought up from the land of Egypt have acted corruptly.ᵍ **8** They have quickly turned from the way I commanded them; they have made for themselves an image of a calf. They have bowed down to it, sacrificed to it, and said, 'Israel, these are your gods, who brought you up from the land of Egypt.'"ʰ **9** The LORD also said to Moses: "I have seen this people, and they are indeed a stiff-neckedⁱ people. **10** Now leave me alone, so that my anger can burn against them and I can destroy them. Then I will make you into a great nation."ʲ

11 But Moses sought the favor of the LORD his God: "LORD, why does your anger burn against your people you brought out of the land of Egypt with great power and a strong hand? **12** Why should the Egyptians say, 'He brought them out with an evil intent to kill them in the mountains and eliminate them from the face of the earth'? Turn from your fierce anger and relent concerning this disaster planned for your people.ᵏ **13** Remember your servants Abraham, Isaac, and Israel — you swore to them by yourselfˡ and declared, 'I will make your offspring as numerous as the stars of the sky and will give your offspring all this land that I have promised, and they will inherit it forever.'"ᵐ **14** So the LORD relentedⁿ concerning the disaster he had said he would bring on his people.

15 Then Moses turned and went down the mountain with the two tablets of the testimony in his hands. They were inscribed on both sides — inscribed front and back. **16** The tablets were the work of

---

ᴬ**32:1** Or *make a god*, also in v. 23   ᴮ**32:4** Or *"Israel, this is your god* or *"Israel, this is your God,* also in v. 8

32:1 Moses was on the mountain receiving instructions from the Lord for "forty days and forty nights" (see 24:18). Apparently, that was too long for the Israelites. They showed contempt for the one whom God used to deliver them: **this Moses, . . . we don't know what has happened to him!** They also demanded that Aaron make them an idol to lead them in Moses's place as well as the Lord's—which was a rejection of the first two commandments (20:3-4) and a repudiation of their vow to obey the Lord (24:7).
32:2-4 Aaron's choice to create **an image of a calf** is a significant choice because the Egyptians and the Canaanites, the native inhabitants of the land promised to Israel, were known for their deities shaped as calves. Thus, Israel had scorned the great "I AM" (3:14)

who had rescued them, and they worshiped instead a false god of the nations (32:4).
32:5-6 Don't miss that they called this idol **the LORD** as they made sacrifices that the real Lord had prescribed. Religious syncretism always results in false religion. If you mix idolatry with Christianity, you no longer have Christianity. Rejection of the true God was this party's foundation, and it likely incorporated corrupt cultic practices from other nations, including things like drunkenness and immorality. Paul quotes this verse when he warns the Corinthians, "Don't become idolaters" (1 Cor 10:7).
32:10-14 Rather than embrace the idea of being the patriarch of a nation without the existing Israelites, Moses pleaded with God not to destroy Israel (32:11). He appealed

not to any merit on their part, but to God's reputation and his character. As a result of Moses's intercession, **the LORD relented** (32:14).

God himself says that he does not change (see Mal 3:6). Yet he also declares that he may choose to relent and not bring threatened judgment upon a people should they change their ways (see Jer 18:8; 26:3). In other words, he might relent if the people repent or, as here, in response to intercessory prayer.

God's relenting from destroying Israel didn't imply that he'd changed his attitude toward their sin. In fact, though he didn't obliterate them, he did hold them accountable for their wickedness (Exod 32:27-28, 33-35). God thus upheld his reputation, remained faithful to his word, and displayed his grace.

God, and the writing was God's writing, engraved on the tablets.[a]

17 When Joshua heard the sound of the people as they shouted, he said to Moses, "There is a sound of war in the camp."

18 But Moses replied:

It's not the sound of a victory cry
and not the sound of a cry of defeat;
I hear the sound of singing!

19 As he approached the camp and saw the calf and the dancing, Moses became enraged and threw the tablets out of his hands, smashing them at the base of the mountain. **20** He took the calf they had made, burned it up, and ground it to powder. He scattered the powder over the surface of the water and forced the Israelites to drink the water.

21 Then Moses asked Aaron, "What did these people do to you that you have led them into such a grave sin?"

22 "Don't be enraged, my lord," Aaron replied. "You yourself know that the people are intent on evil.[b] **23** They said to me, 'Make gods for us who will go before us because this Moses, the man who brought us up from the land of Egypt — we don't know what has happened to him!' **24** So I said to them, 'Whoever has gold, take it off,' and they gave it to me. When I threw it into the fire, out came this calf!"

25 Moses saw that the people were out of control, for Aaron had let them get out of control, making them a laughingstock to their enemies.[A] **26** And Moses stood at the camp's entrance and said, "Whoever is for the LORD, come to me." And all the Levites gathered around him. **27** He told them, "This is what the LORD, the God of Israel, says, 'Every man fasten his sword to his side; go back and forth through the camp from entrance to entrance, and each

of you kill his brother, his friend, and his neighbor.'"[c] **28** The Levites did as Moses commanded, and about three thousand men fell dead that day among the people. **29** Afterward Moses said, "Today you have been dedicated[B] to the LORD, since each man went against his son and his brother. Therefore you have brought a blessing on yourselves today."[d]

30 The following day Moses said to the people, "You have committed a grave sin. Now I will go up to the LORD; perhaps I will be able to atone for your sin."[e] **31** So Moses returned to the LORD and said, "Oh, these people have committed a grave sin; they have made a god of gold for themselves.[f] **32** Now if you would only forgive their sin. But if not, please erase me from the book you have written."[g]

33 The LORD replied to Moses: "Whoever has sinned against me I will erase from my book.[h] **34** Now go, lead the people to the place I told you about; see, my angel will go before you. But on the day I settle accounts, I will hold them accountable for their sin."[i] **35** And the LORD inflicted a plague on the people for what they did with the calf Aaron had made.

THE TENT OUTSIDE THE CAMP

33 The LORD spoke to Moses: "Go up from here, you and the people you brought up from the land of Egypt, to the land I promised to Abraham, Isaac, and Jacob, saying: I will give it to your offspring.[j] **2** I will send an angel ahead of you and will drive out the Canaanites, Amorites, Hethites, Perizzites,[c] Hivites, and Jebusites.[k] **3** Go up to a land flowing with milk and honey. But I will not go up with you because you are a stiff-necked people; otherwise, I might destroy you on the way."[l] **4** When the

[a] 32:15-16 Ex 31:18; Dt 9:15
[b] 32:19-22 Gn 20:9; 26:10; Ex 14:11; Dt 9:16-17,21

[c] 32:27 Nm 25:5; Dt 33:9
[d] 32:29 Nm 25:11-13; Zch 13:3
[e] 32:30 1Sm 12:20; 2Sm 16:12
[f] 32:31 Ex 20:23; Dt 9:18
[g] 32:32 Ps 69:28; Dn 12:1; Rm 9:3; Php 4:3; Rv 3:5; 21:27
[h] 32:33 Dt 29:20; Ps 9:5
[i] 32:34 Dt 32:35; Rm 2:5-6
[j] 33:1 Gn 12:7; Ex 32:7
[k] 33:2 Ex 32:34; Jos 24:11
[l] 33:3 Ex 3:8; 32:9; Nm 16:21,45

[A]32:25 Hb obscure [B]32:29 Text emended; MT reads *Today dedicate yourselves*; LXX, Vg read *Today you have dedicated yourselves*
[C]33:2 Sam, LXX add *Girgashites*

32:21-24 Rather than fessing up about his wrong, Aaron merely shifted the blame to the people, as if they forced him to do it (32:22-23). Then he made this ridiculous claim: **When I threw** the gold **into the fire, out came this calf** (32:24). He thus falsely implied that the idol was supernaturally formed.
32:25-29 When the Levites gathered around him in response to his call, Moses sent them to act out God's judgment on those who persisted in their idolatry and immorality (32:27). As a result, **three thousand men** soon **fell dead** (32:28). Sin is no joke. It brings death (see Gen 3:17; Rom 6:23; Jas 1:15). Sometimes it may result in untimely physical death. But if one does not receive God's grace through

Jesus Christ, it will result in the second death, which is much worse: eternal judgment in the lake of fire (see Rev 20:14-15).
32:30-35 Moses was willing to lay down his life for this ungrateful, sinful people (32:32), but God would not allow him to take their sin upon himself and be punished in their place. Moses was himself a sinner, so he could not bear the sin of others. But one day a holy and righteous man would come—the God-Man, Jesus Christ. Jesus would be able to bear and take away the sin of the world (see John 1:29).
33:1-3 Because of the people's sin, God said he would **not go up** into the promised land with them, otherwise he **might destroy** them

(33:3). Thus, God would not dwell among his people any longer; the tabernacle would not be the place of his presence (25:8). This sobering passage tells us that it's possible to receive blessings (like **a land flowing with milk and honey,** 33:3) yet lack God's presence. Since knowing God—and not merely receiving his blessings—is the goal of a believer's life, we should be grieved at the thought of doing life without him.
33:4-6 The people **mourned** and took off **their jewelry** they had obtained from the Egyptians (12:35-36), knowing that some of that very wealth had been misused to make the golden calf (32:2-4). Removing it was a sign of remorse.

[a] 33:4 Nm 14:39; Ezk 24:17,23
[b] 33:7 Ex 29:42-43; Dt 4:29
[c] 33:9 Ex 13:21; 31:18; Ps 99:7
[d] 33:11 Ex 24:13; Nm 12:8; Dt 34:10
[e] 33:12 Ex 32:34; Jn 10:14-15; 2Tm 2:19
[f] 33:13 Ps 25:4; 86:11; 119:33
[g] Ex 34:9; Dt 9:26,29
[h] 33:14 Jos 21:44; 22:4; Is 63:9
[i] 33:16 Ex 34:10; Nm 14:14
[j] 33:18 Ex 33:20; 1Tm 6:16
[k] 33:19 Rm 9:15
[l] 33:20 Gn 32:30; Is 6:5
[m] 33:22 Ps 91:1,4; Is 2:21

people heard this bad news, they mourned and didn't put on their jewelry.[a]

[5] For the LORD said to Moses: "Tell the Israelites: You are a stiff-necked people. If I went up with you for a single moment, I would destroy you. Now take off your jewelry, and I will decide what to do with you." [6] So the Israelites remained stripped of their jewelry from Mount Horeb onward.

[7] Now Moses took a tent and pitched it outside the camp, at a distance from the camp; he called it the tent of meeting. Anyone who wanted to consult the LORD would go to the tent of meeting that was outside the camp.[b] [8] Whenever Moses went out to the tent, all the people would stand up, each one at the door of his tent, and they would watch Moses until he entered the tent. [9] When Moses entered the tent, the pillar of cloud would come down and remain at the entrance to the tent, and the LORD would speak with Moses.[c] [10] As all the people saw the pillar of cloud remaining at the entrance to the tent, they would stand up, then bow in worship, each one at the door of his tent. [11] The LORD would speak with Moses face to face, just as a man speaks with his friend, then Moses would return to the camp. His assistant, the young man Joshua son of Nun, would not leave the inside of the tent.[d]

THE LORD'S GLORY

[12] Moses said to the LORD, "Look, you have told me, 'Lead this people up,' but you have not let me know whom you will send

with me. You said, 'I know you by name,[e] and you have also found favor with me.' [13] Now if I have indeed found favor with you, please teach me your ways,[f] and I will know you, so that I may find favor with you. Now consider that this nation is your people."[g]

[14] And he replied, "My presence will go with you, and I will give you rest."[h]

[15] "If your presence does not go," Moses responded to him, "don't make us go up from here. [16] How will it be known that I and your people have found favor with you unless you go with us? I and your people will be distinguished by this from all the other people on the face of the earth."[i]

[17] The LORD answered Moses, "I will do this very thing you have asked, for you have found favor with me, and I know you by name."

[18] Then Moses said, "Please, let me see your glory."[j]

[19] He said, "I will cause all my goodness to pass in front of you, and I will proclaim the name 'the LORD' before you. I will be gracious to whom I will be gracious, and I will have compassion on whom I will have compassion."[k] [20] But he added, "You cannot see my face, for humans cannot see[l] me and live." [21] The LORD said, "Here is a place near me. You are to stand on the rock, [22] and when my glory passes by, I will put you in the crevice of the rock and cover you with my hand until I have passed by.[m] [23] Then I will take my hand

---

33:7-11 That Moses pitched his tent outside the camp indicated that God was serious about his threat not to go with them (33:3). Nevertheless, God had not completely abandoned them yet. **When Moses entered the tent**, the **cloud**—representing God's presence—descended, and **the LORD** spoke (33:9, 11). At that point, **anyone who wanted to consult the LORD would go . . . outside the camp** (33:7). So God's presence was still available. To take advantage of it, though, the people had to leave the camp and make their way to a special place. This trek they made is a reminder that God makes his blessed presence available to anyone who makes the effort to seek him (Jer 29:11-14).

Face to face (Exod 33:11) is a figure of speech that means "openly and honestly." To be friends with God requires openness and honesty. If you are a friend to the world's sinful ways, however, you will not come to God in this manner.

33:12-17 Though he had experienced the burning bush incident, the opening of the Red Sea, the water gushing from the rock, and he had eaten bread from heaven, all of that

was yesterday's news. Moses wanted a fresh, deeper knowledge of God. So Moses said to the Lord, **Please teach me your ways** (33:13). He wasn't satisfied to nibble on an appetizer and to sample the soup. He wanted to *feast* on all the Lord offers.

God doesn't want mere churchgoers. He wants people who are hungry and thirsty to know him (Matt 5:6). That, in fact, is the meaning of eternal life—to know God: "This is eternal life: that they may know you, the only true God, and the one you have sent—Jesus Christ" (John 17:3).

Moses made his position clear: **If your presence does not go . . . don't make us go up from here** (Exod 33:15). He had no faith in his people's ability to thrive without the Lord. In fact, he would rather be in the desert with God than in the promised land without him. He chose the Blesser over the blessing—a choice God wants all of his people to make.

33:18 In saying to the Lord, **Please, let me see your glory** (33:18), Moses wanted to see a visible manifestation of the invisible God. He wanted God to "go public" for him and provide an observable display of his glorious

deity. Are you satisfied with listening to a sermon and singing a few songs to God? Or do you constantly long to see more of God in your life, to grasp a greater sense of God's glory?

33:19-20 While God would let Moses see a portion of his glory, he would not show him his face—not the essence of his being. To be exposed to the unfiltered glory of God on this side of eternity would be like entering a nuclear reactor or traveling to the sun; the divine holiness would consume us.

33:21-23 The Lord was limiting Moses's exposure to his glory for Moses's own welfare. Of course, God who is spirit (see John 4:24) has no body, so he has no back—just as he has no arm (see the note on Exod 6:6). This is anthropomorphic language, or the use of human concepts to explain a spiritual reality. God's "arm" refers to his power. God's **back** refers to the amount of glory that Moses was able to handle (33:23). (Think of it like the exhaust that's left behind when a high-flying jet passes overhead.)

No one has ever seen God in all his glory, but the Son of God has revealed him (John

away, and you will see my back, but my face will not be seen."

NEW STONE TABLETS

34 The LORD said to Moses, "Cut two stone tablets like the first ones, and I will write on them the words that were on the first tablets, which you broke.[a] **2** Be prepared by morning. Come up Mount Sinai in the morning and stand before me on the mountaintop. **3** No one may go up with you; in fact, no one should be seen anywhere on the mountain. Even the flocks and herds are not to graze in front of that mountain."[b]

4 Moses cut two stone tablets like the first ones. He got up early in the morning, and taking the two stone tablets in his hand, he climbed Mount Sinai, just as the LORD had commanded him.

5 The LORD came down in a cloud, stood with him there, and proclaimed his name, "the LORD." **6** The LORD passed in front of him and proclaimed:

The LORD — the LORD is a compassionate and gracious God, slow to anger and abounding in faithful love and truth,[c] **7** maintaining faithful love to a thousand generations, forgiving iniquity, rebellion, and sin.[d] But he will not leave the guilty[e] unpunished, bringing the fathers' iniquity on the children and grandchildren to the third and fourth generation.

8 Moses immediately knelt low on the ground and worshiped. **9** Then he said, "My Lord, if I have indeed found favor with you, my Lord, please go with us (even though this is a stiff-necked people), forgive our iniquity and our sin, and accept us as your own possession."[f]

COVENANT OBLIGATIONS

10 And the LORD responded: "Look, I am making a covenant. I will perform wonders in the presence of all your people

that have never been done[A] in the whole earth or in any nation. All the people you live among will see the LORD's work, for what I am doing with you is awe-inspiring.[g] **11** Observe what I command you today. I am going to drive out before you the Amorites, Canaanites, Hethites, Perizzites, Hivites,[B] and Jebusites. **12** Be careful not to make a treaty with the inhabitants of the land that you are going to enter; otherwise, they will become a snare among you.[h] **13** Instead, you must tear down their altars, smash their sacred pillars, and chop down their Asherah poles.[i] **14** Because the LORD is jealous[j] for his reputation, you are never to bow down to another god.[c] He is a jealous God.

15 "Do not make a treaty with the inhabitants of the land, or else when they prostitute themselves with their gods and sacrifice to their gods, they will invite you, and you will eat their sacrifices.[k] **16** Then you will take some of their daughters as brides for your sons. Their daughters will prostitute themselves with their gods and cause your sons to prostitute themselves with their gods.[l]

17 "Do not make cast images[m] of gods for yourselves.

18 "Observe the Festival of Unleavened Bread. You are to eat unleavened bread for seven days at the appointed time in the month of Abib,[D] as I commanded you, for you came out of Egypt in the month of Abib.[n]

19 "The firstborn[o] male from every womb belongs to me, including all your male[E,F] livestock, the firstborn of cattle or sheep. **20** You may redeem the firstborn of a donkey with a sheep, but if you do not redeem it, break its neck.[p] You must redeem all the firstborn of your sons. No one is to appear before me empty-handed.

21 "You are to labor six days but you must rest[q] on the seventh day; you must even rest during plowing and harvesting times.

[a] 34:1 Ex 32:19; 34:28; Dt 10:2,4
[b] 34:2-3 Ex 19:12-13,20-21
[c] 34:6 Nm 14:18; Neh 9:17; Ps 86:15; 103:8; 108:4; Jl 2:13; Rm 2:4
[d] 34:7 Ex 20:6; Ps 103:3; 130:4; Dn 9:9; 1Jn 1:9
[e] Jos 24:19; Jb 10:14; Nah 1:3
[f] 34:9 Ex 33:15-16; Ps 33:12; 94:14
[g] 34:10 Dt 4:32; 5:2; Ps 77:14; 145:6
[h] 34:11-12 Ex 23:32-33; 33:2
[i] 34:13 Ex 23:24; Dt 12:3; 2Kg 18:4; 2Ch 34:3-4
[j] 34:14 Ex 20:3,5; Dt 4:24
[k] 34:15 Nm 25:2; Jdg 2:17; 1Co 8:4,7,10
[l] 34:16 Dt 7:3; 1Kg 11:2,4; Ezr 9:2; Neh 13:25
[m] 34:17 Ex 32:8; Lv 19:14
[n] 34:18 Ex 12:15; 13:4
[o] 34:19 Ex 13:2; 22:29
[p] 34:20 Ex 13:13,15; 23:15; Dt 16:16
[q] 34:21 Ex 20:9; Lk 13:14

[A]34:10 Lit *created* [B]34:11 DSS, Sam, LXX add *Girgashites* [C]34:14 Or *the LORD — his name is Jealous* or *the LORD, being jealous by nature* [D]34:18 March–April; called Nisan in the post-exilic period; Neh 2:1; Est 3:7 [E]34:19 LXX, Theod, Vg, Tg read *males* [F]34:19 Hb obscure

1:18). Jesus, in fact, told his disciples, "The one who has seen me has seen the Father" (John 14:9). One day, believers will see Jesus Christ in all his glory, as the apostle John did late in the biblical story (see Rev 1:12-16). This sight of God enabled Moses to see God's history and thus be able to pen the Pentateuch.

34:6-7 The Lord's words here tell us that God's love is not permissive. He is righteous and cannot overlook sin. That, in fact, is what

makes the gospel such good news. In the cross of Christ, God's justice and God's love met. He satisfied his own righteous demands, so that he could show grace to those who come to his Son in repentance and faith.

34:10-17 In spite of Israel's sin, God vowed to stay true to the **covenant** (34:10). He promised to **perform** further **wonders** and **drive out** the wicked inhabitants of the land he was giving them (34:10-11). Israel's job was to

observe what God commanded (34:11). They were to remember that **the LORD is jealous for his reputation** and they were thus never to **bow down to another god** (34:14).

34:18-26 Of special note here is that all of the **males** were to meet with the Lord three times per year. Don't miss that if the men would take their rightful place under God's kingdom rule, he would protect the whole nation (34:23-24).

^a34:23 Ex 23:14
^b34:24 Ex 33:2; Ps 78:55
^cDt 12:20; 19:8
^d34:25 Ex 12:10; 23:18
^e34:26 Ex 23:19; Dt 26:2

^f34:27 Ex 17:14; 24:4
^g34:28 Ex 24:18; 31:18; Dt 4:13; 10:2,4
^h34:29 Ex 32:15
ⁱ34:30 Ps 34:5; Mt 17:2; 2Co 3:7,13
^j34:34 Ex 24:3; 2Co 3:13-16
^k35:1 Ex 34:32
^l35:2 Ex 20:9; Lv 23:3
^m35:3 Ex 16:23

Questions & Answers

Q If you had to pick one, which name of God is most meaningful to you at this stage of your Christian journey?

A The name of God that really draws my attention in this stage of life is *Adonai* because *Adonai* means "boss." He's the one who tells us what to do. So much of our ministry is centered around the kingdom agenda worldview ("the visual manifestation of the comprehensive rule of God over every area of life"); therefore, it is essential that we recognize God as our *Adonai* and submit to his will. No matter what you think, how you feel, how you were raised, or what your experiences were, he expects you to come under his authority. Since the reality of God as *Adonai* dovetails so well with the kingdom agenda worldview, it gets my extra attention because he wants to be our boss, our Lord.

FOR THE NEXT Q&A, SEE PAGE 207.

22 "Observe the Festival of Weeks with the firstfruits of the wheat harvest, and the Festival of Ingathering^A at the turn of the agricultural year. **23** Three times a year^a all your males are to appear before the Lord God, the God of Israel. **24** For I will drive out nations^b before you and enlarge your territory.^c No one will covet your land when you go up three times a year to appear before the LORD your God.

25 "Do not present^B the blood for my sacrifice with anything leavened. The sacrifice of the Passover Festival must not remain until morning.^d

26 "Bring the best firstfruits^e of your land to the house of the LORD your God.

"You must not boil a young goat in its mother's milk."

27 The LORD also said to Moses, "Write^f down these words, for I have made a covenant with you and with Israel based on these words."

28 Moses was there with the LORD forty days and forty nights; he did not eat food or drink water. He wrote the Ten Commandments,^g the words of the covenant, on the tablets.

MOSES'S RADIANT FACE

29 As Moses descended from Mount Sinai — with the two tablets of the testimony in his hands as he descended the mountain — he did not realize that the skin of his face shone as a result of his speaking with the LORD.^{C,h} **30** When Aaron and all the Israelites saw Moses, the skin of his face shone!ⁱ They were afraid to come near him. **31** But Moses called out to them, so Aaron and all the leaders of the community returned to him, and Moses spoke to them. **32** Afterward all the Israelites came near, and he commanded them to do everything the LORD had told him on Mount Sinai. **33** When Moses had finished speaking with them, he put a veil over his face. **34** But whenever Moses went before the LORD to speak with him, he would remove the veil until he came out. After he came out, he would tell the Israelites what he had been commanded,^j **35** and the Israelites would see that Moses's face^D was radiant. Then Moses would put the veil over his face again until he went to speak with the LORD.

THE SABBATH COMMAND

35 Moses assembled the entire Israelite community and said to them, "These are the things that the LORD has commanded you to do:^k **2** For six days work is to be done, but on the seventh day you are to have a holy day, a Sabbath^l of complete rest to the LORD. Anyone who does work on it must be executed. **3** Do not light a fire in any of your homes on the Sabbath day."^m

^A34:22 The *Festival of Ingathering* is called Festival of Shelters elsewhere; Lv 23:34-36. ^B34:25 Lit *slaughter* ^C34:29 Lit *with him* ^D34:35 Lit *see Moses's face, that the skin of his face*

34:27 This lends strong support to the view that Moses is the author of the book of Exodus (as well as the entire Pentateuch).

34:28-35 When Moses finally descended the mountain, **he did not realize that the skin of his face shone as a result of his speaking with the LORD** (34:29). When Moses spent extended, uninterrupted time in God's presence, he began to glow.

God wants to transform you, too, and he wants others to see the transformation.

Paul reminds the Corinthians that the old covenant, which was written on stone and brought death (because the law can't save), made Moses's face glorious. So how much more glory does the new covenant, written on believers' hearts in this era marked by Christ's saving death and resurrection, bring

through the ministry of the Spirit? (see 2 Cor 3:7-10). As believers, we are transformed into the image of Christ by the Spirit of God as we peer into his Word (2 Cor 3:17-18). God is supposed to rub off on us more than he rubbed off on Moses, whose glory faded (2 Cor 3:13). We are to "shine like stars in the world" as a result of Christ's transforming influence in our lives (Phil 2:15).

BUILDING THE TABERNACLE

4 Then Moses said to the entire Israelite community, "This is what the Lord has commanded: **5** Take[a] up an offering among you for the Lord. Let everyone whose heart is willing bring this as the Lord's offering: gold, silver, and bronze; **6** blue, purple, and scarlet yarn; fine linen and goat hair; **7** ram skins dyed red and fine leather;[A] acacia wood; **8** oil for the light; spices for the anointing oil and for the fragrant incense; **9** and onyx with gemstones to mount on the ephod and breastpiece.

10 "Let all the skilled artisans[B] among you come and make everything that the Lord has commanded:[b] **11** the tabernacle — its tent and covering, its clasps and supports, its crossbars, its pillars and bases; **12** the ark with its poles, the mercy seat, and the curtain for the screen; **13** the table with its poles, all its utensils, and the Bread of the Presence; **14** the lampstand for light with its utensils and lamps as well as the oil for the light; **15** the altar of incense with its poles; the anointing oil and the fragrant incense; the entryway screen for the entrance to the tabernacle; **16** the altar of burnt offering with its bronze grate, its poles, and all its utensils; the basin with its stand; **17** the hangings of the courtyard, its posts and bases, and the screen for the gate of the courtyard; **18** the tent pegs for the tabernacle and the tent pegs for the courtyard, along with their ropes; **19** and the specially woven[A] garments for ministering in the sanctuary — the holy garments for the priest Aaron and the garments for his sons to serve as priests."[c]

20 Then the entire Israelite community left Moses's presence. **21** Everyone whose heart was moved and whose spirit prompted him came and brought an offering to the Lord for the work on the tent of meeting, for all its services, and for the holy garments.[d] **22** Both men and women came; all who had willing hearts brought brooches, earrings, rings, necklaces, and all kinds of gold jewelry — everyone who presented a presentation offering of gold to the Lord. **23** Everyone who possessed blue, purple, or scarlet yarn,[e] fine linen or goat hair, ram skins dyed red or fine leather,[A] brought them. **24** Everyone making an offering of silver or bronze brought it as a contribution to the Lord. Everyone who possessed acacia wood useful for any task in the work brought it. **25** Every skilled[c] woman[f] spun yarn with her hands and brought it: blue, purple, and scarlet yarn, and fine linen. **26** And all the women whose hearts were moved spun the goat hair by virtue of their skill. **27** The leaders[g] brought onyx and gemstones to mount on the ephod and breastpiece, **28** as well as the spice[h] and oil for the light, for the anointing oil, and for the fragrant incense. **29** So the Israelites brought a freewill offering to the Lord, all the men and women whose hearts prompted them to bring something for all the work that the Lord, through Moses, had commanded to be done.[i]

BEZALEL AND OHOLIAB

30 Moses[j] then said to the Israelites: "Look, the Lord has appointed by name Bezalel son of Uri, son of Hur, of the tribe of Judah. **31** He has filled him with God's Spirit, with wisdom, understanding, and ability in every kind of craft **32** to design artistic works in gold, silver, and bronze, **33** to cut gemstones for mounting, and to carve wood for work in every kind of artistic craft. **34** He has also given[D] both him and Oholiab son of Ahisamach, of the tribe of Dan, the ability to teach others. **35** He has filled them with skill[E] to do all the work[k] of a gem cutter; a designer; an embroiderer[F] in blue, purple, and scarlet yarn and fine linen; and a weaver. They can do every kind of craft and design artistic designs.

36 **1** Bezalel, Oholiab, and all the skilled[G] people are to work based on everything the Lord has commanded. The Lord has given them wisdom and understanding to know how to do all the work of constructing the sanctuary."[l]

2 So Moses summoned Bezalel, Oholiab, and every skilled person in whose heart the Lord had placed wisdom, all whose hearts moved them,[m] to come to the work

---

[a] 35:5-9 Ex 25:2-7
[b] 35:10 Ex 31:6
[c] 35:11-19 Ex 24:5-6; 25:10,23,30-31; 26:1-2; 27:1,9; 30:1,25,34; 31:10; 39:1,41; Lv 24:5-6; Nm 4:5
[d] 35:21 Ex 36:2

[e] 35:23 1Ch 29:8
[f] 35:25 Ex 28:3
[g] 35:27 1Ch 29:6; Ezr 2:68
[h] 35:28 Ex 30:23
[i] 35:29 Ex 35:21; 36:3; 1Ch 29:9
[j] 35:30-34 Ex 31:1-6; 2Ch 2:14
[k] 35:35 Ex 31:3,6; 1Kg 7:14
[l] 36:1 Ex 25:8; 28:3; 31:6; 35:10,35
[m] 36:2 Ex 25:2; 35:21,26; 1Ch 29:5

[A] 35:7,19,23 Hb obscure   [B] 35:10 Lit the wise of heart   [C] 35:25 Lit wise of heart   [D] 35:34 Lit also put in his heart   [E] 35:35 Lit with wisdom of heart
[F] 35:35 Or weaver   [G] 36:1 Lit wise of heart, also in v. 2

35:4-29 Moses called the Israelites to give sacrificially (35:5-9). In response to Moses's exhortation, everyone ... whose spirit prompted him ... brought an offering (35:21). This means the people gave willingly, not out of compulsion—which is the kind of giving that God loves (see 2 Cor 9:7).

36:1-7 Moses commissioned the artisans in their work. **The Lord had placed wisdom** in their hearts (36:2). Now, as good stewards under God, it was time to use their divine gifts for his service.

Don't miss that Moses had to order the people to stop giving because there was **more than enough** (36:6-7). (How often do churches today have to give an order like that?)

a 36:5 2Ch 31:10; 2Co 8:2-3
b 36:8-19 Ex 26:1-14
c 36:20-34 Ex 25:5; 26:15-29
d 36:35-38 Ex 26:31-37

and do it. ³ They took from Moses's presence all the contributions that the Israelites had brought for the task of making the sanctuary. Meanwhile, the people continued to bring freewill offerings morning after morning.

⁴ Then all the artisans who were doing all the work for the sanctuary came one by one from the work they were doing ⁵ and said to Moses, "The people are bringing more than is needed*a* for the construction of the work the LORD commanded to be done."

⁶ After Moses gave an order, they sent a proclamation throughout the camp: "Let no man or woman make anything else as an offering for the sanctuary." So the people stopped. ⁷ The materials were sufficient for them to do all the work. There was more than enough.

BUILDING THE TABERNACLE

⁸ All*b* the skilled artisans*A* among those doing the work made the tabernacle with ten curtains. Bezalel made them of finely spun linen, as well as blue, purple, and scarlet yarn, with a design of cherubim worked into them. ⁹ Each curtain was forty-two feet*B* long and six feet*c* wide; all the curtains had the same measurements. ¹⁰ He joined five of the curtains to each other, and the other five curtains he joined to each other. ¹¹ He made loops of blue yarn on the edge of the last curtain in the first set and did the same on the edge of the outermost curtain in the second set. ¹² He made fifty loops on the one curtain and fifty loops on the edge of the curtain in the second set, so that the loops lined up with each other. ¹³ He also made fifty gold clasps and joined the curtains to each other, so that the tabernacle became a single unit.

¹⁴ He made curtains of goat hair for a tent over the tabernacle; he made eleven of them. ¹⁵ Each curtain was forty-five feet*D* long and six feet wide. All eleven curtains had the same measurements. ¹⁶ He joined five of the curtains together, and the other six together. ¹⁷ He made fifty loops on the edge of the outermost curtain in the first set and fifty loops on the edge of the corresponding curtain in the second set. ¹⁸ He made fifty bronze clasps to join the tent together as a single unit. ¹⁹ He also made a covering for the tent from ram skins dyed red and a covering of fine leather*E* on top of it.

²⁰ He*c* made upright supports*F* of acacia wood for the tabernacle. ²¹ Each support was fifteen feet*G* long and twenty-seven inches*H* wide. ²² Each support had two tenons for joining one to another. He did the same for all the supports of the tabernacle. ²³ He made supports for the tabernacle as follows: twenty for the south side, ²⁴ and he made forty silver bases to put under the twenty supports, two bases under the first support for its two tenons, and two bases under each of the following supports for their two tenons; ²⁵ for the second side of the tabernacle, the north side, he made twenty supports, ²⁶ with their forty silver bases, two bases under the first support and two bases under each of the following ones; ²⁷ and for the back of the tabernacle, on the west side, he made six supports. ²⁸ He also made two additional supports for the two back corners of the tabernacle. ²⁹ They were paired at the bottom and joined together*I* at the*J* top in a single ring. This is what he did with both of them for the two corners. ³⁰ So there were eight supports with their sixteen silver bases, two bases under each one.

³¹ He made five crossbars of acacia wood for the supports on one side of the tabernacle, ³² five crossbars for the supports on the other side of the tabernacle, and five crossbars for those at the back of the tabernacle on the west. ³³ He made the central crossbar run through the middle of the supports from one end to the other. ³⁴ He overlaid them with gold and made their rings out of gold as holders for the crossbars. He also overlaid the crossbars with gold.

³⁵ Then*d* he made the curtain with blue, purple, and scarlet yarn, and finely spun linen. He made it with a design of cherubim worked into it. ³⁶ He made four pillars of acacia wood for it and overlaid them with gold; their hooks were of gold. And he cast four silver bases for the pillars.

³⁷ He made a screen embroidered*K* with blue, purple, and scarlet yarn, and finely spun linen for the entrance to the tent, ³⁸ together with its five pillars and their hooks. He overlaid the tops of the pillars and their bands with gold, but their five bases were bronze.

A 36:8 Lit the wise of heart   B 36:9 Lit 28 cubits   c 36:9 Lit four cubits, also in v. 15   D 36:15 Lit 30 cubits   E 36:19 Hb obscure   F 36:20 Or made frames
G 36:21 Lit 10 cubits   H 36:21 Lit a cubit and a half   I 36:29 Lit and together they are to be complete   J 36:29 Lit its   K 36:37 Or woven

MAKING THE ARK

37 Bezalel[a] made the ark of acacia wood, forty-five inches long, twenty-seven inches wide, and twenty-seven inches high.[A] **2** He overlaid it with pure gold inside and out and made a gold molding all around it. **3** He cast four gold rings for it, for its four feet, two rings on one side and two rings on the other side. **4** He made poles of acacia wood and overlaid them with gold. **5** He inserted the poles into the rings on the sides of the ark for carrying the ark.

6 He made a mercy seat of pure gold, forty-five inches long and twenty-seven inches wide.[B] **7** He made two cherubim of gold; he made them of hammered work at the two ends of the mercy seat, **8** one cherub at one end and one cherub at the other end. At each end, he made a cherub of one piece with the mercy seat. **9** They had wings spread out. They faced each other and covered the mercy seat with their wings. The faces of the cherubim were looking toward the mercy seat.

MAKING THE TABLE

10 He[b] constructed the table of acacia wood, thirty-six inches long, eighteen inches wide, and twenty-seven inches high.[C] **11** He overlaid it with pure gold and made a gold molding all around it. **12** He made a three-inch[D] frame all around it and made a gold molding all around its frame. **13** He cast four gold rings for it and attached the rings to the four corners at its four legs. **14** The rings were next to the frame as holders for the poles to carry the table. **15** He made the poles for carrying the table from acacia wood and overlaid them with gold. **16** He also made the utensils that would be on the table out of pure gold: its plates and cups, as well as its bowls and pitchers for pouring drink offerings.

MAKING THE LAMPSTAND

17 Then[c] he made the lampstand out of pure hammered gold. He made it all of one piece: its base and shaft, its ornamental cups, and its buds and petals. **18** Six branches extended from its sides, three branches of the lampstand from one side and three branches of the lampstand from the other side. **19** There were three cups shaped like almond blossoms, each with a bud and petals, on one branch, and three cups shaped like almond blossoms, each with a bud and petals, on the next branch. It was this way for the six branches that extended from the lampstand. **20** There were four cups shaped like almond blossoms on the lampstand shaft along with its buds and petals. **21** For the six branches that extended from it, a bud was under the first pair of branches from it, a bud under the second pair of branches from it, and a bud under the third pair of branches from it. **22** Their buds and branches were of one piece with it. All of it was a single hammered piece of pure gold. **23** He also made its seven lamps, snuffers, and firepans of pure gold. **24** He made it and all its utensils of seventy-five pounds[E] of pure gold.

MAKING THE ALTAR OF INCENSE

25 He[d] made the altar of incense out of acacia wood. It was square, eighteen inches long and eighteen inches wide; it was thirty-six inches high.[F] Its horns were of one piece with it. **26** He overlaid it, its top, all around its sides, and its horns with pure gold. Then he made a gold molding all around it. **27** He made two gold rings for it under the molding on two of its sides; he put these on opposite sides of it to be holders for the poles to carry it with. **28** He made the poles of acacia wood and overlaid them with gold.

29 He also made the holy anointing oil and the pure, fragrant, and expertly blended incense.[e]

MAKING THE ALTAR OF BURNT OFFERING

38 Bezalel[f] constructed the altar of burnt offering from acacia wood. It was square, 7½ feet long and 7½ feet wide,[G] and was 4½ feet[H] high. **2** He made horns for it on its four corners; the horns were of one piece with it. Then he overlaid it with bronze.

3 He made all the altar's utensils: the pots, shovels, basins, meat forks, and firepans; he made all its utensils of bronze. **4** He constructed for the altar a grate of bronze mesh under its ledge,[i] halfway up from the bottom. **5** He cast four rings at the four corners of the bronze grate as holders for the poles.

[a] 37:1-9 Ex 25:10-20
[b] 37:10-16 Ex 25:23-29
[c] 37:17-24 Ex 25:31-39

[d] 37:25-28 Ex 30:1-5
[e] 37:29 Ex 30:23-24,34-35
[f] 38:1-7 Ex 27:1-8

[A] 37:1 Lit two and a half cubits its length, one and a half cubits its width, and one and a half cubits its height   [B] 37:6 Lit two and a half cubits its length and one and a half cubits its width   [C] 37:10 Lit two cubits its length, one cubit its width, and one and a half cubits its height   [D] 37:12 Lit a handbreadth   [E] 37:24 Lit a talent   [F] 37:25 Lit a cubit its length, a cubit its width, and two cubits its height   [G] 38:1 Lit five cubits its length and five cubits its width   [H] 38:1 Lit three cubits   [i] 38:4 Or rim

ᵃ 38:8 Ex 30:18; 1Sm 2:22
ᵇ 38:9-20 Ex 27:9-19

ᶜ 38:21 Nm 1:50,53; 9:15;
10:11; 17:7-8; 2Ch 24:6;
Ac 7:44
ᵈ Nm 4:28,33
ᵉ 38:24 Ex 30:13; Lv 27:25;
Nm 3:47; 18:16
ᶠ 38:26-27 Ex
26:19,21,25,32; 30:13;
Nm 1:46

6 He made the poles of acacia wood and overlaid them with bronze. **7** Then he inserted the poles into the rings on the sides of the altar in order to carry it with them. He constructed the altar with boards so that it was hollow.

MAKING THE BRONZE BASIN

8 He made the bronze basin and its stand from the bronze mirrors of the women who served at the entrance to the tent of meeting.ᵃ

MAKING THE COURTYARD

9 Thenᵇ he made the courtyard. The hangings on the south side of the courtyard were of finely spun linen, 150 feetᴬ long, **10** including their twenty posts and their twenty bronze bases, with silver hooks and silver bandsᴮ for the posts. **11** The hangings on the north side were also 150 feet long, including their twenty posts and twenty bronze bases. The hooks and bands of the posts were silver. **12** The hangings on the west side were 75 feetᶜ long, including their ten posts and their ten bases, with silver hooks and silver bands for the posts. **13** And for the east side toward the sunrise, 75 feet long, **14** the hangings on one side of the gate were 22 ½ feet,ᴰ including their three posts and their three bases. **15** It was the same for the other side of the courtyard gate. The hangings were 22 ½ feet, including their three posts and their three bases. **16** All the hangings around the courtyard were of finely spun linen. **17** The bases for the posts were bronze; the hooks and bands of the posts were silver; and the plating for the tops of the posts was silver. All the posts of the courtyard were banded with silver.

18 The screen for the gate of the courtyard was made of finely spun linen, expertly embroideredᴱ with blue, purple, and scarlet yarn. It was 30 feetᶠ long, and like the hangings of the courtyard, 7 ½ feetᴳ high.ᴴ **19** It had four posts with their four bronze bases. Their hooks were silver, and their top plating and their bands were silver. **20** All the tent pegs for the tabernacle and for the surrounding courtyard were bronze.

INVENTORY OF MATERIALS

21 This is the inventory for the tabernacle, the tabernacle of the testimony,ᶜ that was recorded at Moses's command. It was the work of the Levites under the direction ofⁱ Ithamar son of Aaron the priest.ᵈ **22** Bezalel son of Uri, son of Hur, of the tribe of Judah, made everything that the LORD commanded Moses. **23** With him was Oholiab son of Ahisamach, of the tribe of Dan, a gem cutter, a designer, and an embroiderer with blue, purple, and scarlet yarn, and fine linen.

24 All the gold of the presentation offering that was used for the project in all the work on the sanctuary, was 2,193 pounds,ʲ according to the sanctuary shekel.ᵉ **25** The silver from those of the community who were registered was 7,544 pounds,ᴷ according to the sanctuary shekel — **26** one-fifth of an ounceᴸ per man, that is, half a shekel according to the sanctuary shekel, from everyone twenty years old or more who had crossed over to the registered group, 603,550 men. **27** There were 7,500 poundsᴹ of silver used to cast the bases of the sanctuary and the bases of the curtain — one hundred bases from 7,500 pounds, 75 poundsᴺ for each base.ᶠ **28** With the remaining 44 poundsᴼ he made the hooks for the posts, overlaid their tops, and supplied bands for them.

29 The bronze of the presentation offering totaled 5,310 pounds.ᴾ **30** He made with it the bases for the entrance to the tent of meeting, the bronze altar and its bronze grate, all the utensils for the altar, **31** the bases for the surrounding courtyard, the bases for the gate of the courtyard, all the tent pegs for the tabernacle, and all the tent pegs for the surrounding courtyard.

ᴬ 38:9 Lit *100 cubits*, also in v. 11   ᴮ 38:10 Or *connecting rods*, also in vv. 11,17,19,28   ᶜ 38:12 Lit *50 cubits*, also in v. 13   ᴰ 38:14 Lit *15 cubits*, also in v. 15   ᴱ 38:18 Or *woven*   ᶠ 38:18 Lit *20 cubits*   ᴳ 38:18 Lit *five cubits*   ᴴ 38:18 Lit *high in width*   ⁱ 38:21 Lit *Levites by the hand of*   ʲ 38:24 Lit *29 talents and 730 shekels*   ᴷ 38:25 Lit *100 talents and 1,775 shekels*   ᴸ 38:26 Lit *a beka*   ᴹ 38:27 Lit *100 talents*   ᴺ 38:27 Lit *one talent*   ᴼ 38:28 Lit *1,775 (shekels)*   ᴾ 38:29 Lit *70 talents and 2,400 shekels*

38:21-31 This was clearly a vast and expensive project. Tons of **gold, silver,** and **bronze** were incorporated (38:24-31). But God is worth every penny spent in his service.
39:32-43 Whether a student has written a paper or an employee has finished a project, there comes a time when an assessment of the effort must be made. When the Israelites had finished all of the work, Moses began his inspection (39:33). God is holy; therefore, the tabernacle, its furnishings, and the priestly garments had to meet the divine specifications precisely.

You too should serve the Lord with excellence in whatever work he has assigned you. He did not spare his own Son to save you (see Rom 8:32), and he sealed you with his promised Holy Spirit (see Eph 1:13). So why would you offer to him anything but your best?

MAKING THE PRIESTLY GARMENTS

39 They made specially woven[A] garments for ministry in the sanctuary, and the holy garments for Aaron from the blue, purple, and scarlet yarn, just as the LORD had commanded Moses.[a]

MAKING THE EPHOD

[2] Bezalel[b] made the ephod of gold, of blue, purple, and scarlet yarn, and of finely spun linen. [3] They hammered out thin sheets of gold, and he[B] cut threads from them to interweave with the blue, purple, and scarlet yarn, and the fine linen in a skillful design. [4] They made shoulder pieces for attaching it; it was joined together at its two edges. [5] The artistically woven waistband that was on the ephod was of one piece with the ephod, according to the same workmanship of gold, of blue, purple, and scarlet yarn, and of finely spun linen, just as the LORD had commanded Moses.

[6] Then they mounted the onyx stones surrounded with gold filigree settings, engraved with the names of Israel's sons as a gem cutter engraves a seal. [7] He fastened them on the shoulder pieces of the ephod as memorial stones for the Israelites, just as the LORD had commanded Moses.

MAKING THE BREASTPIECE

[8] He[c] also made the embroidered[c] breastpiece with the same workmanship as the ephod of gold, of blue, purple, and scarlet yarn, and of finely spun linen. [9] They made the breastpiece square and folded double, nine inches long and nine inches wide.[D] [10] They mounted four rows of gemstones[E] on it.

The first row was
a row of carnelian, topaz, and
emerald;[F]
[11] the second row,
a turquoise,[G] a lapis lazuli, and a
diamond;[H]
[12] the third row,
a jacinth,[A] an agate, and an
amethyst;
[13] and the fourth row,
a beryl, an onyx, and a jasper.
They were surrounded with gold filigree in their settings.

[14] The twelve stones corresponded to the names of Israel's sons. Each stone was engraved like a seal with one of the names of the twelve tribes.

[15] They made braided chains of pure gold cord for the breastpiece. [16] They also fashioned two gold filigree settings and two gold rings and attached the two rings to its two corners. [17] Then they attached the two gold cords to the two gold rings on the corners of the breastpiece. [18] They attached the other ends of the two cords to the two filigree settings, and in this way they attached them to the ephod's shoulder pieces in front. [19] They made two other gold rings and put them at the two other corners of the breastpiece on the edge that is next to the inner border of the ephod. [20] They made two more gold rings and attached them to the bottom of the ephod's two shoulder pieces on its front, close to its seam,[I] above the ephod's woven waistband. [21] Then they tied the breastpiece from its rings to the rings of the ephod with a cord of blue yarn, so that the breastpiece was above the ephod's waistband and did not come loose from the ephod. They did just as the LORD had commanded Moses.

MAKING THE ROBE

[22] They[d] made the woven robe of the ephod entirely of blue yarn. [23] There was an opening in the center of the robe like that of body armor[A] with a collar around the opening so that it would not tear. [24] They made pomegranates of finely spun blue, purple, and scarlet yarn[J] on the lower hem of the robe. [25] They made bells of pure gold and attached the bells between the pomegranates, all around the hem of the robe between the pomegranates, [26] a bell and a pomegranate alternating all around the lower hem of the robe[K] to be worn for ministry. They made it just as the LORD had commanded Moses.

THE OTHER PRIESTLY GARMENTS

[27] They made the tunics of fine woven linen for Aaron and his sons. [28] They made the turban and the ornate headbands[L] of fine linen, the linen undergarments of finely spun linen,[e] [29] and the sash of finely spun linen expertly embroidered with blue, purple, and scarlet yarn. They did just as the LORD had commanded Moses.

[a] 39:1 Ex 28:2,4; 31:10; 35:19,23; 39:41
[b] 39:2-7 Ex 28:6-12
[c] 39:8-21 Ex 28:15-28

[d] 39:22-26 Ex 28:31-34
[e] 39:28 Ex 28:39,42; Ezk 44:18

[A] 39:1,12,23 Hb obscure   [B] 39:3 Sam, Syr, Tg read *they*   [C] 39:8 Or *woven*   [D] 39:9 Lit *a span its length and a span its width*   [E] 39:10 Many of these stones cannot be identified with certainty.   [F] 39:10 Or *beryl*   [G] 39:11 Or *malachite*, or *garnet*   [H] 39:11 Hb uncertain; LXX, Vg read *jasper*   [I] 39:20 The place where the *shoulder pieces* join the front of the ephod   [J] 39:24 Sam, LXX, Vg add *and linen*   [K] 39:26 Lit *bell and pomegranate, bell and pomegranate, on the hem of the robe around*   [L] 39:28 Lit *and the headdresses of headbands*

a 39:30 Ex 28:36-37; 29:6
b 39:32 Ex 25:40; 39:42-43
c 39:33-42 Ex 25:31; 27:9-15; 30:3; 35:10
d 39:43 Lv 9:22-23; Nm 6:23-27; Jos 22:6; 2Sm 6:18; 1Kg 8:14; 2Ch 30:27
e 40:2 Ex 12:12; 13:4; 26:30
f 40:3 Ex 26:33; 40:21; Nm 4:5

g 40:7 Ex 30:18; 40:30
h 40:9 Ex 30:26; Lv 8:10
i 40:12 Lv 8:1-3
j 40:13 Ex 28:41
k 40:15 Ex 29:9; Nm 25:13
l 40:17 Ex 40:2; Nm 7:1
m 40:20 Ex 16:34; 25:16

MAKING THE HOLY DIADEM

30 They made a medallion, the holy diadem, out of pure gold and wrote on it an inscription like the engraving on a seal:[a] HOLY TO THE LORD. **31** They attached a cord of blue yarn to it in order to mount it on the turban, just as the LORD had commanded Moses.

MOSES'S INSPECTION OF THE TABERNACLE

32 So all the work for the tabernacle, the tent of meeting, was finished. The Israelites did everything just as the LORD had commanded Moses.[b] **33** They brought the tabernacle to Moses: the tent with all its furnishings, its clasps, its supports, its crossbars, and its pillars and bases; **34** the covering of ram skins dyed red and the covering of fine leather;[A] the curtain for the screen; **35** the ark of the testimony with its poles and the mercy seat; **36** the table, all its utensils, and the Bread of the Presence; **37** the pure gold lampstand, with its lamps arranged and all its utensils, as well as the oil for the light; **38** the gold altar; the anointing oil; the fragrant incense; the screen for the entrance to the tent; **39** the bronze altar with its bronze grate, its poles, and all its utensils; the basin with its stand; **40** the hangings of the courtyard, its posts and bases, the screen for the gate of the courtyard, its ropes and tent pegs, and all the furnishings for the service of the tabernacle, the tent of meeting; **41** and the specially woven[A] garments for ministering in the sanctuary, the holy garments for the priest Aaron and the garments for his sons to serve as priests. **42** The Israelites had done all the work according to everything the LORD had commanded Moses.[c] **43** Moses inspected all the work they had accomplished. They had done just as the LORD commanded. Then Moses blessed them.[d]

SETTING UP THE TABERNACLE

40 The LORD spoke to Moses: **2** "You are to set up the tabernacle, the tent of meeting, on the first day of the first month.[B,e] **3** Put the ark[f] of the testimony there and screen off the ark with the curtain. **4** Then bring in the table and lay out its arrangement; also bring in the lampstand and set up its lamps. **5** Place the gold altar for incense in front of the ark of the testimony. Put up the screen for the entrance to the tabernacle. **6** Position the altar of burnt offering in front of the entrance to the tabernacle, the tent of meeting. **7** Place the basin[g] between the tent of meeting and the altar, and put water in it. **8** Assemble the surrounding courtyard and hang the screen for the gate of the courtyard.

9 "Take the anointing oil and anoint[h] the tabernacle and everything in it; consecrate it along with all its furnishings so that it will be holy. **10** Anoint the altar of burnt offering and all its utensils; consecrate the altar so that it will be especially holy. **11** Anoint the basin and its stand and consecrate it.

12 "Then bring Aaron and his sons to the entrance to the tent of meeting and wash them with water.[i] **13** Clothe Aaron with the holy garments,[j] anoint him, and consecrate him, so that he can serve me as a priest. **14** Have his sons come forward and clothe them in tunics. **15** Anoint them just as you anointed their father, so that they may also serve me as priests. Their anointing will serve to inaugurate a permanent priesthood for them throughout their generations."[k]

16 Moses did everything just as the LORD had commanded him. **17** The tabernacle was set up in the first month of the second year, on the first day of the month.[C,l] **18** Moses set up the tabernacle: He laid its bases, positioned its supports, inserted its crossbars, and set up its pillars. **19** Then he spread the tent over the tabernacle and put the covering of the tent on top of it, just as the LORD had commanded Moses.

20 Moses took the testimony[m] and placed it in the ark, and attached the poles to the ark. He set the mercy seat on top of the ark. **21** He brought the ark into the tabernacle, put up the curtain for the screen, and screened off the ark of the testimony, just as the LORD had commanded him.

22 Moses placed the table in the tent of meeting on the north side of the tabernacle, outside the curtain. **23** He arranged the bread on it before the LORD, just as the LORD had commanded him. **24** He put the lampstand in the tent of meeting opposite the table on the south side of the tabernacle **25** and set up the lamps before the LORD, just as the LORD had commanded him.

[A] 39:34,41 Hb obscure   [B] 40:2 Lit *on the day of the first month, on the first of the month*   [C] 40:17 DSS, Sam, LXX add *of their coming out of Egypt*

40:1-33 Here we see that Moses followed the divine plan without deviation. That's a good habit to adopt.

26 Moses installed the gold altar in the tent of meeting, in front of the curtain, **27** and burned fragrant incense on it, just as the Lord had commanded him. **28** He put up the screen at the entrance to the tabernacle. **29** He placed the altar of burnt offering at the entrance to the tabernacle, the tent of meeting, and offered the burnt offering and the grain offering on it, just as the Lord had commanded him.

30 He set the basin between the tent of meeting and the altar and put water in it for washing. **31** Moses, Aaron, and his sons washed their hands and feet from it. **32** They washed whenever they came to the tent of meeting and approached the altar, just as the Lord had commanded Moses.

33 Next Moses set up the surrounding courtyard for the tabernacle and the altar and hung a screen for the gate of the courtyard. So Moses finished the work.[a]

THE LORD'S GLORY

34 The cloud covered the tent of meeting, and the glory of the Lord filled the tabernacle.[b] **35** Moses was unable to enter the tent of meeting because the cloud rested on it, and the glory of the Lord filled the tabernacle.

36 The Israelites set out whenever the cloud was taken up from the tabernacle throughout all the stages of their journey.[c] **37** If the cloud was not taken up, they did not set out until the day it was taken up.[d] **38** For the cloud of the Lord was over the tabernacle by day, and there was a fire inside the cloud by night, visible to the entire house of Israel throughout all the stages of their journey.

[a] 40:21-33 Ex 25:37; 26:33,35-36; 27:9,16; 29:38; 30:5-7,19-20; 40:1-7
[b] 40:34 Lv 16:2; Nm 9:15; 1Kg 8:10-11; 2Ch 5:13-14; 7:2; Is 6:4; Hg 2:7,9; Rv 15:8
[c] 40:36 Nm 9:17; Neh 9:19
[d] 40:37 Nm 9:19-22

40:34-35 When everything was in place, the **cloud** of God's **glory** descended and **filled the tabernacle** (40:34). When they obediently followed his agenda, he came and took up residence among his people. In fact, Moses couldn't even **enter the tent** because it was bursting with **the glory of the Lord** (40:35).

Importantly, when the Son of God took on flesh and came into the world, he "dwelt [lit., in Greek, "tabernacled"] among us" and displayed "his glory" (John 1:14). All those who trust in him receive the Holy Spirit to dwell within them. As a believer, "you are God's temple," and "the Spirit of God lives in you" (1 Cor 3:16). There's no room for anyone else but him.

40:36-38 When the glory **cloud** was in the **tabernacle**, Israel stayed put. When the cloud lifted, Israel went wherever the cloud led them (40:36-37; see Num 9:15-23). Thus, the book of Exodus ends with God's people following his direction, as he led a nation of former slaves to the promised land.

LEVITICUS

INTRODUCTION

Author

THE BOOK IS ANONYMOUS; no author's name is included. However, evidence from the Bible (see Rom 10:5), and ancient Jewish and Christian traditions points to Moses as the author of Leviticus—and of the Pentateuch (the first five books of the Old Testament) in general. As the book demonstrates, Moses was the Lord's intermediary, making his revelation known to the people of Israel (see Lev 1:1; 4:1; 5:14; 6:1, 8). Clearly, the author was familiar with the events recorded in Leviticus, so there is no reason to doubt that this writer was Moses.

Historical Background

From the time the Israelites arrived at Mount Sinai (see Exod 19:1-2) until they departed (see Num 10:11-13) was about one year. In that time, Moses received the Lord's covenant, constructed the tabernacle, and received all of the instructions recorded in Leviticus and in the early chapters of Numbers. The repeated expression found throughout the book, "The LORD spoke to Moses" (see Lev 4:1; 5:14), leaves no doubt that Leviticus contains divine revelation—not the ideas of Moses. The title of the book derives from the attention it gives to the duties of the Levites who were charged with the ministry of the tabernacle.

Message and Purpose

Leviticus is one of the most neglected and yet powerful books in the Bible. It establishes the guidelines by which God is to be known and worshiped. It is far more relevant to us than many realize.

The book distinguishes between the profane, the common, and the holy. Here's an illustration that may help to explain the differences between those concepts. When you have dirty dishes in your sink, they are profane. That is, they are unacceptable to use until they have been cleaned. Profane things in our lives are completely unacceptable to God because they bring dirt before him. The common dishes, by contrast, are those you use every day. There's nothing wrong with them; they just aren't special. And should we treat God as common, we don't hold him in the high regard his holiness deserves and demands.

Think about what's holy in relation to the china dishes secured behind the glass doors in the hutch in the dining room. These are the ones we only bring out on special occasions for honored guests. That picture gives insight into how Leviticus teaches us to treat God—the Holy One who is like no other. We are to relate to God and worship him as our unique, one-of-a-kind Lord, and King of his kingdom. He deserves only the best.

THE BURNT OFFERING

1 Then the LORD summoned Moses[a] and spoke to him from the tent of meeting:[b] **2** "Speak to the Israelites and tell them: When any of you brings an offering to the LORD from the livestock, you may bring your offering from the herd or the flock.

3 "If his offering is a burnt offering[c] from the herd, he is to bring an unblemished male.[d] He will bring it to the entrance to the tent of meeting so that he[A] may be accepted by the LORD.[e] **4** He is to lay his hand on[f] the head of the burnt offering so it can be accepted[g] on his behalf to make atonement for him.[h] **5** He is to slaughter the bull before the LORD; Aaron's sons the priests[i] are to present the blood[j] and splatter it[k] on all sides of the altar that is at the entrance to the tent of meeting. **6** Then he is to skin the burnt offering[l] and cut it into pieces.[B] **7** The sons of Aaron the priest will prepare a fire on the altar and arrange wood on the fire. **8** Aaron's sons the priests are to arrange the pieces, the head, and the fat[m] on top of the burning wood on the altar. **9** The offerer is to wash its entrails[n] and legs[o] with water. Then the priest will burn all of it on the altar as a burnt offering, a fire offering[p] of a pleasing aroma[q] to the LORD.

10 "But if his offering for a burnt offering is from the flock, from sheep or goats,[r] he is to present an unblemished male. **11** He will slaughter it on the north side of the altar before the LORD. Aaron's sons the priests will splatter its blood against the altar on all sides. **12** He will cut the animal into pieces with its head and its fat, and the priest will arrange them on top of the burning wood on the altar. **13** But he is to wash the entrails and legs with water. The priest will then present all of it and burn it on the altar; it is a burnt offering, a fire offering of a pleasing aroma to the LORD.

14 "If his offering to the LORD is a burnt offering of birds,[s] he is to present his offering from the turtledoves[t] or young pigeons.[C,u] **15** Then the priest is to bring it to the altar, and will twist off its head and burn it on the altar; its blood should be drained at the side of the altar. **16** He will remove its digestive tract,[D] cutting off the tail feathers, and throw it on the east side of the altar at the place for ashes.[v] **17** He will tear it open by its wings without dividing the bird.[w] Then the priest is to burn it on the altar on top of the burning wood. It is a burnt offering, a fire offering of a pleasing aroma to the LORD.

THE GRAIN OFFERING

2 "When anyone presents a grain offering[x] as an offering to the LORD, it is to consist of fine flour.[y] He is to pour olive oil[z] on it, put frankincense on it,[aa] **2** and bring it to Aaron's sons the priests. The priest will take a handful of fine flour and oil from it, along with all its frankincense, and will burn this memorial portion[ab] of it on the altar, a fire offering of a pleasing aroma to the LORD. **3** But the rest of the grain offering will belong to Aaron and his sons; it is the holiest part[ac] of the fire offerings to the LORD.

4 "When you present a grain offering baked in an oven, it is to be made of fine flour, either unleavened cakes[ad] mixed with oil or unleavened wafers[ae] coated with oil. **5** If your offering is a grain offering prepared on a griddle,[af] it is to be unleavened bread[ag] made of fine flour mixed with oil. **6** Break it into pieces and pour oil on it; it is a grain offering. **7** If your offering is a grain offering prepared in a pan,[ah] it

[a] 1:1 Ps 77:20; Mt 8:4; Heb 3:2
[b] Ex 27:21
[c] 1:3 Gn 22:2; Lv 3:5
[d] Ex 29:1
[e] Lv 19:5; Heb 9:14; 1Pt 1:19
[f] 1:4 Ex 29:10; Lv 3:2; 8:14,18,22; 16:21; Nm 8:10,12
[g] Gn 33:10; Lv 7:18; 19:7; 22:23,25,27
[h] Ex 30:15
[i] 1:5 Lv 4:16
[j] Heb 9:12
[k] Ex 24:6; 29:16,20
[l] 1:6 Lv 7:8; 9:11; 2Ch 29:34
[m] 1:8 Lv 1:12; 8:20
[n] 1:9 Ex 12:9; 29:13,22; Lv 1:13; 3:3
[o] Ex 12:9; 29:17; Lv 1:13; 4:11; 8:21; 9:14; Am 3:12
[p] Dt 18:1
[q] Lv 2:2; 23:13
[r] 1:10 Lv 4:23

[s] 1:14 Gn 40:17; Lv 17:13
[t] Gn 15:9; Lv 1:14; 5:7,11; 12:6,8; 14:22,30; 15:14,29; Nm 6:10; Ps 74:19; Sg 2:12; Jr 8:7
[u] Gn 8:8-12; Lv 5:7,11
[v] 1:16 Lv 4:12; 6:10-11; 1Kg 13:3,5; Jr 31:40
[w] 1:17 Gn 15:9-10
[x] 2:1 Ex 40:29
[y] Gn 18:6; Ex 29:2,40; Lv 2:1-7
[z] Gn 28:18; 35:14
[aa] Ex 30:34
[ab] 2:2 Lv 2:9,16; 5:12; 6:8; 24:7; Nm 5:26; Ac 10:4
[ac] 2:3 Lv 14:13
[ad] 2:4 Ex 29:2
[ae] Ex 29:2,23; Lv 7:12; 8:26; Nm 6:15,19; 1Ch 23:29
[af] 2:5 Lv 6:14; 7:9; 1Ch 23:29; Ezk 4:3
[ag] Ex 12:8; Mt 16:6,11-12; 1Co 5:6-8
[ah] 2:7 Lv 7:9

[A] 1:3 Or it [B] 1:6 Lit its pieces, also in v. 12 [C] 1:14 Or or pigeons [D] 1:16 Or its crop, or its crissum

1:1 The opening words of Leviticus give us the context we need to understand the importance of Israel getting their worship of God right. The regulations contained in Israel's book of worship came from **the LORD**.

1:2-9 In keeping with God's perfect holiness, the **burnt offering** was to be perfect (1:3). This was the most frequent of Israel's offerings, to be offered by God's priests every morning and evening (see 6:8-13). The offerer skinned and cut up the animal for burning by the **priests**, who also sprinkled its **blood** on the **altar** (1:5-9). This was a messy affair, a reminder that atoning for sin is serious business.

The Hebrew word for the burnt offering means "to ascend." The smoke from the fire ascended to God. God's pleasure with and acceptance of the sacrifice gave the wor-

shiper the assurance that he, despite being a sinner, was accepted and forgiven in God's holy presence.

1:10-17 No Israelite was left out of giving a burnt offering, no matter how poor he was. Those who could not afford the other animals mentioned could offer **turtledoves or young pigeons** (1:14). Poor people could bring birds for other offerings as well, as when Joseph and Mary presented birds at the temple for Jesus's dedication (see Luke 2:21-24).

2:1-16 These offerings provided a way for the people to acknowledge their dependence on God for their sustenance. The grain offerings were the only bloodless sacrifices, but they were still holy to the Lord. They were to be free of **yeast** (2:11). We know from other passages of Scripture

that yeast was often used as a symbol of sin (see 1 Cor 5:8).

The part of the offerings that was not burned up—**the holiest part**—belonged to **Aaron and his sons** (Lev 2:3, 10). In payment for their ministry, the consecrated priests were allowed to eat these offerings.

All of the grain offerings were to include **the salt of the covenant with your God** (2:13). Salt was a symbol of permanence; it was something that the ancients believed could not be destroyed even by fire. The concept of a "covenant of salt" appears in Numbers 18:19 and in 2 Chronicles 13:5, the latter referring to the permanence of God's covenant with David to establish his throne forever. (This covenant will be fulfilled when Jesus takes the throne of David at his second coming.)

a 2:10 Lv 7:9-10
b 2:11 Ex 12:14
c Jdg 14:8
d 2:12 Gn 49:3; Ex 23:16,19
e 2:13 Ex 19:5; Nm 18:19;
2Ch 13:5
f 3:1 Lv 7:11
g Ex 29:1
h 3:2 Lv 1:5
i 3:3 Ex 23:18; 29:13,22
j Ex 12:9
k 3:4 Lv 7:4

l 3:4 Lv 9:10
m 3:5 Lv 1:3-4
n 3:9 Ex 29:22; Lv 7:3;
8:25; 9:19
o Lv 1:9
p 3:11 Lv 3:16; 21:6,8,17,21-
22; 22:25; 26:5; Nm 28:24
q 3:12 Lv 4:23
r 3:17 Ex 28:43; Lv 11:46
s Lv 7:26; 17:10,14; 19:26;
Dt 12:16,23; 15:23
t 4:2 Nm 15:22,24

is to be made of fine flour with oil. **8** When you bring to the LORD the grain offering made in any of these ways, it is to be presented to the priest, and he will take it to the altar. **9** The priest will remove the memorial portion[A] from the grain offering and burn it on the altar, a fire offering of a pleasing aroma to the LORD. **10** But the rest of the grain offering will belong to Aaron and his sons;[a] it is the holiest part of the fire offerings to the LORD.

11 "No grain offering that you present to the LORD is to be made with yeast, for you are not to burn[b] any yeast[b] or honey[c] as a fire offering to the LORD. **12** You may present them to the LORD as an offering of firstfruits,[d] but they are not to be offered on the altar as a pleasing aroma. **13** You are to season each of your grain offerings with salt; you must not omit from your grain offering the salt of the covenant[e] with your God. You are to present salt with each of your offerings.

14 "If you present a grain offering of firstfruits to the LORD, you are to present fresh heads of grain, crushed kernels, roasted on the fire, for your grain offering of firstfruits. **15** You are to put oil and frankincense on it; it is a grain offering. **16** The priest will then burn some of its crushed kernels and oil with all its frankincense as a fire offering to the LORD.

THE FELLOWSHIP OFFERING

3 "If his offering is a fellowship sacrifice,[f] and he is presenting an animal from the herd, whether male or female, he is to present one without blemish[g] before the LORD. **2** He is to lay his hand on the head of his offering and slaughter it at the entrance to the tent of meeting. Then Aaron's sons the priests will splatter the blood on all sides of the altar.[h] **3** He will present part of the fellowship sacrifice as a fire offering to the LORD: the fat[i] surrounding the entrails,[j] all the fat that is on the entrails, **4** and the two kidneys[k] with the

fat on them at the loins; he will also remove the fatty lobe of the liver[l] with the kidneys. **5** Aaron's sons will burn it on the altar along with the burnt offering[m] that is on the burning wood, a fire offering of a pleasing aroma to the LORD.

6 "If his offering as a fellowship sacrifice to the LORD is from the flock, he is to present a male or female without blemish. **7** If he is presenting a lamb for his offering, he is to present it before the LORD. **8** He must lay his hand on the head of his offering, then slaughter it before the tent of meeting. Aaron's sons will splatter its blood on all sides of the altar. **9** He will then present part of the fellowship sacrifice as a fire offering to the LORD consisting of its fat and the entire fat tail,[n] which he is to remove close to the backbone. He will also remove the fat surrounding the entrails,[o] all the fat on the entrails, **10** the two kidneys with the fat on them at the loins, and the fatty lobe of the liver above the kidneys. **11** Then the priest will burn the food on the altar,[p] as a fire offering to the LORD.

12 "If his offering is a goat,[q] he is to present it before the LORD. **13** He must lay his hand on its head and slaughter it before the tent of meeting. Aaron's sons will splatter[C] its blood on all sides of the altar. **14** He will present part of his offering as a fire offering to the LORD: the fat surrounding the entrails, all the fat that is on the entrails, **15** and the two kidneys with the fat on them at the loins; he will also remove the fatty lobe of the liver with the kidneys. **16** Then the priest will burn the food on the altar, as a fire offering for a pleasing aroma.[D]

"All fat belongs to the LORD. **17** This is a permanent statute[r] throughout your generations, wherever you live: you must not eat any fat or any blood."[s]

THE SIN OFFERING

4 Then the LORD spoke to Moses: **2** "Tell the Israelites: When someone sins unintentionally[t] against any of the LORD's

---

A 2:9 Lit *portion of it*   B 2:11 Some Hb mss, Sam, LXX, Tg read *present*   C 3:13 Or *dash*   D 3:16 Sam, LXX add *to the LORD*

3:1-17 The distinctive element of the **fellowship sacrifice** is that the worshiper shared in it by eating the meat (3:1; 7:11-35; cf. Deut 12:7). In this case, birds were excluded from the offering since they were so small that nothing would be left to consume. The worshiper, his family, and friends were invited to eat the fellowship meal consisting of the meat returned to them by the priests. This was to be a festive meal expressing the offerer's joy in experiencing communion with God. That the fellowship offering is

often mentioned in conjunction with the burnt offering (as in Exod 20:24; 24:5) reinforces the picture of a worshiper first offering a sacrifice to atone for his sins before enjoying fellowship.

Various explanations for not eating the **fat** portions have been offered, including the suggestion that since the fat is the choicest part of the animal, God alone is worthy of it (Lev 3:14-16). The prohibition against eating **blood** (3:17) was established in God's covenant with Noah (see Gen 9:4).

4:1 That God himself had to initiate the rules for dealing with sin is obvious from the opening phrase: **The LORD spoke to Moses.** Making a way for sinners to be made right with him has always been important to God. Interestingly, the natural human reaction for dealing with sin is to hide, as Adam and Eve did in the garden (see Gen 3:8).

4:2 Israel's sin offering provided forgiveness and atonement for sins committed **unintentionally.** This is a broad statement that covers all kinds of situations, although in 5:1-6 the

commands and does anything prohibited
by them —
3 "If the anointed priest[a] sins, bringing
guilt[b] on the people, he is to present to the
LORD a young, unblemished[c] bull as a sin[A]
offering[d] for the sin he has committed.
4 He is to bring the bull to the entrance to
the tent of meeting before the LORD, lay
his hand on the bull's head, and slaughter
it before the LORD. 5 The anointed priest
will then take some of the bull's blood
and bring it into the tent of meeting. 6 The
priest is to dip his finger in the blood and
sprinkle some of it seven times[e] before
the LORD in front of the curtain[f] of the
sanctuary.[g] 7 The priest is to apply some
of the blood to the horns of the altar of
fragrant incense[h] that is before the LORD
in the tent of meeting. He must pour out
the rest of the bull's blood at the base of
the altar of burnt offering[i] that is at the
entrance to the tent of meeting. 8 He is to
remove all the fat from the bull of the sin
offering: the fat surrounding the entrails,
all the fat that is on the entrails, 9 and the
two kidneys with the fat on them at the
loins. He will also remove the fatty lobe
of the liver with the kidneys, 10 just as the
fat is removed from the ox of the fellowship sacrifice.[j] The priest is to burn them
on the altar of burnt offering. 11 But the
hide[k] of the bull and all its flesh, with its
head and legs, and its entrails and waste
— 12 all the rest of the bull — he must
bring to a ceremonially clean place[l] outside the camp[m] to the ash heap, and must
burn it on a wood fire. It is to be burned
at the ash heap.
13 "Now if the whole community of Israel[n] errs,[o] and the matter escapes the
notice of the assembly,[p] so that they violate any of the LORD's commands and
incur guilt[q] by doing what is prohibited,
14 then the assembly must present a young
bull as a sin offering. They are to bring it
before the tent of meeting when the sin
they have committed in regard to the command becomes known. 15 The elders[r] of the
community are to lay their hands on the
bull's head before the LORD and it is to be
slaughtered before the LORD. 16 The anointed priest will bring some of the bull's blood
into the tent of meeting. 17 The priest is to
dip his finger in the blood and sprinkle it
seven times before the LORD in front of the
curtain. 18 He is to apply some of the blood
to the horns of the altar that is before the
LORD in the tent of meeting. He will pour
out the rest of the blood at the base of the
altar of burnt offering that is at the entrance to the tent of meeting. 19 He is to
remove all the fat from it and burn it on
the altar. 20 He is to offer this bull just as
he did with the bull in the sin offering; he
will offer it the same way. So the priest will
make atonement[s] on their behalf, and they
will be forgiven.[t] 21 Then he will bring the
bull outside the camp[u] and burn it just as
he burned the first bull. It is the sin offering for the assembly.
22 "When a leader[B,v] sins and unintentionally violates any of the commands of
the LORD his God by doing what is prohibited, and incurs guilt, 23 or someone
informs him about the sin he has committed, he is to bring an unblemished male
goat[w] as his offering. 24 He is to lay his hand
on the head of the goat and slaughter it
at the place where the burnt offering[x] is
slaughtered before the LORD. It is a sin offering.[y] 25 Then the priest is to take some
of the blood from the sin offering with his
finger and apply it to the horns of the altar of burnt offering.[z] The rest of its blood
he is to pour out at the base of the altar of
burnt offering. 26 He must burn all its fat

[a] 4:3 Lv 4:16; 6:15
[b] Lv 6:5,7; 22:16
[c] Ex 29:1
[d] Ex 29:14
[e] 4:6 Lv 16:14
[f] Mk 15:38; Lk 23:45
[g] Ex 15:17; Lv 10:4
[h] 4:7 Ex 30:27
[i] Ex 3:5; 35:16
[j] 4:8-10 Lv 7:11
[k] 4:11 Lv 7:8
[l] 4:12 Lv 6:4; 10:14; Nm 19:9
[m] Lv 8:17; Heb 13:11-13
[n] 4:13 Ex 12:47
[o] Nm 15:22
[p] Ex 16:3; Lv 4:21; Nm 10:7; 15:15; 20:6,10
[q] Nm 5:6; Ps 68:21
[r] 4:15 Ex 18:12
[s] 4:20 Ex 30:15
[t] Lv 5:16; 6:7
[u] 4:21 Lv 8:17
[v] 4:22 Ex 34:31
[w] 4:23 Lv 9:3; 16:5; 23:19; Nm 7:16-82
[x] 4:24 Gn 22:2; Ex 20:24; Lv 3:5
[y] Ex 29:14
[z] 4:25 Lv 5:9

[A] 4:3 Or *purification* [B] 4:22 Or *ruler*

Lord gave four specific examples of unintentional sins needing atonement. The only atonement for deliberate, intentional sin was the death of the offender.

4:3-35 Chapter 4 outlines the **sin offering** requirements for four groups in Israel. These groups were **the anointed priest** (4:3), **the whole community** of Israel (4:13), leaders (4:22), and **the common people** (4:27). The word "common," of course, had nothing to do with their intrinsic value to God. Rather, it was a recognition of their diverse positions within the community and the potential impact their sins would have on the nation.

The entire sacrificial system would grind to a halt if **the anointed priest**—the high priest—was carrying unforgiven sin that would disqualify him from ministering before the Lord. His sin would bring guilt on the entire nation, so his sacrifice had to be the costliest animal mentioned (4:3).

No one who sinned was left without a remedy—but addressing the offense always required the shedding of blood.

4:4 The priest would **lay his hand on the bull's head**, signifying that this animal was bearing his sin. The phrase **before the LORD** occurs ten times in chapter 4 alone, and many times afterward. Through these rituals people were constantly being reminded that their sin was first an offense against the holy God they worshiped; thus, it was him they needed to satisfy. David showed he understood this truth when he said, "Against you [Lord]—you alone—I have sinned and done this evil" (Ps 51:4).

4:13 The second set of sin offering procedures was for **the whole community of Israel**. This signals a logical progression because if the congregation as a whole was under God's displeasure for sin, nothing good was going to happen at the individual level. Similarly, in the church, God's people need to keep short their sin accounts with the Lord, so that we can move ahead as one to advance his kingdom on earth.

4:22-26 **A leader** could refer to either a tribal leader or an official in one of the clans of a particular tribe.

^a 4:32 Lv 9:3
^b 5:1 Gn 4:13; Ex 20:5;
Lv 16:21-22; Nm 5:15,31;
Dt 19:15
^c 5:2 Lv 11:4; Nm 19:13
^d Lv 26:6
^e Lv 11:24-40; Dt 14:8

^f 5:2 Nm 5:6; Ps 68:21
^g 5:3 Lv 14:19
^h Lv 11:24
ⁱ 5:4 Ps 106:33; Pr 12:18
^j 5:5 Lv 16:21
^k 5:6 Lv 14:12
^l Ex 30:15
^m 5:7 Lv 1:14
ⁿ 5:8 Gn 15:10; Lv 1:15,17
^o 5:9 Lv 4:25,30
^p 5:10 Lv 1:14-17
^q 5:11 Lk 2:24
^r Lv 2:1
^s 5:12 Lv 2:2
^t 5:13 Lv 2:3,10

on the altar, like the fat of the fellowship sacrifice. In this way the priest will make atonement on his behalf for that person's sin, and he will be forgiven.

²⁷ "Now if any of the common people[A] sins unintentionally by violating one of the LORD's commands, does what is prohibited, and incurs guilt, ²⁸ or if someone informs him about the sin he has committed, then he is to bring an unblemished female goat as his offering for the sin that he has committed. ²⁹ He is to lay his hand on the head of the sin offering and slaughter it at the place of the burnt offering. ³⁰ Then the priest is to take some of its blood with his finger and apply it to the horns of the altar of burnt offering. He is to pour out the rest of its blood at the base of the altar. ³¹ He is to remove all its fat just as the fat is removed from the fellowship sacrifice. The priest is to burn it on the altar as a pleasing aroma to the LORD. In this way the priest will make atonement on his behalf, and he will be forgiven.

³² "Or if the offering that he brings as a sin offering is a lamb,[a] he is to bring an unblemished female. ³³ He is to lay his hand on the head of the sin offering and slaughter it as a sin offering at the place where the burnt offering is slaughtered. ³⁴ Then the priest is to take some of the blood of the sin offering with his finger and apply it to the horns of the altar of burnt offering. He is to pour out the rest of its blood at the base of the altar. ³⁵ He is to remove all its fat just as the fat of the lamb is removed from the fellowship sacrifice. The priest will burn it on the altar along with the fire offerings to the LORD. In this way the priest will make atonement on his behalf for the sin he has committed, and he will be forgiven.

CASES REQUIRING SIN OFFERINGS

5 "When someone sins in any of these ways:
If he has seen, heard, or known about something he has witnessed, and did not respond to a public call to testify, he will bear his iniquity.[b]
² Or if someone touches anything unclean[c] — a carcass of an unclean wild animal,[d] or unclean livestock, or an unclean swarming creature[e]

— without being aware of it, he is unclean and incurs guilt.[f]

³ Or if he touches human uncleanness[g] — any uncleanness by which one can become defiled[h] — without being aware of it, but later recognizes it, he incurs guilt.

⁴ Or if someone swears rashly[i] to do what is good or evil — concerning anything a person may speak rashly in an oath — without being aware of it, but later recognizes it, he incurs guilt in such an instance.

⁵ If someone incurs guilt in one of these cases, he is to confess[j] he has committed that sin. ⁶ He must bring his penalty for guilt[k] for the sin he has committed to the LORD: a female lamb or goat from the flock as a sin offering. In this way the priest will make atonement[l] on his behalf for his sin.

⁷ "But if he cannot afford an animal from the flock, then he may bring to the LORD two turtledoves or two young pigeons[m] as penalty for guilt for his sin — one as a sin offering and the other as a burnt offering. ⁸ He is to bring them to the priest, who will first present the one for the sin offering. He is to twist its head at the back of the neck without severing it.[n] ⁹ Then he will sprinkle some of the blood of the sin offering on the side of the altar, while the rest of the blood is to be drained out at the base of the altar;[o] it is a sin offering. ¹⁰ He will prepare the second bird as a burnt offering according to the regulation.[p] In this way the priest will make atonement on his behalf for the sin he has committed, and he will be forgiven.

¹¹ "But if he cannot afford two turtledoves or two young pigeons,[q] he may bring two quarts[B] of fine flour[C,r] as an offering for his sin. He must not put olive oil or frankincense on it, for it is a sin offering. ¹² He is to bring it to the priest, who will take a handful from it as its memorial portion[s] and burn it on the altar along with the fire offerings to the LORD; it is a sin offering. ¹³ In this way the priest will make atonement on his behalf concerning the sin he has committed in any of these cases, and he will be forgiven. The rest will belong to the priest, like the grain offering."[t]

[A] 4:27 Lit the people of the land   [B] 5:11 Lit one-tenth of an ephah   [C] 5:11 Lit flour as a sin offering

5:1-4 The four conditions mentioned here could be categorized as sins of omission or neglect. The things outlined may sound like minor offenses, but God was using them to teach his people the important difference between being clean and unclean—between being holy and profane.

THE GUILT OFFERING

14 Then the LORD spoke to Moses: **15** "If someone offends[a] by sinning unintentionally[b] in regard to any of the LORD's holy things,[A] he must bring his penalty for guilt to the LORD: an unblemished ram from the flock (based on your assessment of its value in silver shekels, according to the sanctuary shekel[c]) as a guilt offering. **16** He is to make restitution[d] for his sin regarding any holy[e] thing, adding a fifth of its value to it,[f] and give it to the priest. Then the priest will make atonement on his behalf with the ram of the guilt offering, and he will be forgiven.[g]

17 "If someone sins and without knowing it violates any of the LORD's commands concerning anything prohibited, he is guilty, and he will bear his iniquity. **18** He must bring an unblemished ram from the flock according to your assessment of its value as a guilt offering to the priest. Then the priest will make atonement on his behalf for the error he has committed unintentionally, and he will be forgiven. **19** It is a guilt offering; he is indeed guilty before the LORD."

6 The LORD spoke to Moses: **2** "When someone sins and offends the LORD by deceiving[h] his neighbor in regard to a deposit,[i] a security,[B] or a robbery;[j] or defrauds[k] his neighbor; **3** or finds something lost and lies about it;[l] or swears falsely[m] about any of the sinful things a person may do — **4** once he has sinned[n] and acknowledged his guilt[o] — he must return what he stole or defrauded, or the deposit entrusted to him, or the lost item he found, **5** or anything else about which he swore falsely. He will make full restitution for it and add a fifth of its value to it.[p] He is to pay it to its owner on the day he acknowledges his guilt.[q] **6** Then he is to bring his guilt offering[r] to the LORD: an unblemished[s] ram from the flock according to your assessment of its value as a guilt offering to the priest. **7** In this way the priest

will make atonement on his behalf before the LORD, and he will be forgiven for anything he may have done to incur guilt."[t]

THE BURNT OFFERING

8 The LORD spoke to Moses: **9** "Command Aaron and his sons: This is the law of the burnt offering; the burnt offering itself must remain on the altar's hearth all night until morning, while the fire of the altar is kept burning on it. **10** The priest is to put on his linen robe and linen undergarments.[C,u] He is to remove the ashes of the burnt offering the fire has consumed on the altar, and place them beside the altar. **11** Then he will take off his garments, put on other clothes,[v] and bring the ashes outside the camp to a ceremonially clean place. **12** The fire on the altar is to be kept burning; it must not go out. Every morning the priest will burn wood on the fire. He is to arrange the burnt offering on the fire and burn the fat portions from the fellowship offerings[w] on it. **13** Fire must be kept burning on the altar continually; it must not go out.

THE GRAIN OFFERING

14 "Now this is the law of the grain offering:[x] Aaron's sons will present it before the LORD in front of the altar. **15** The priest is to remove a handful of fine flour and olive oil from the grain offering, with all the frankincense that is on the offering, and burn its memorial portion on the altar as a pleasing aroma to the LORD. **16** Aaron and his sons may eat the rest of it.[y] It is to be eaten in the form of unleavened bread[z] in a holy place;[aa] they are to eat it in the courtyard[ab] of the tent of meeting. **17** It must not be baked with yeast; I have assigned it as their portion[ac] from my fire offerings.[ad] It is especially holy, like the sin offering[ae] and the guilt offering. **18** Any male among Aaron's descendants[af] may eat it. It is a permanent portion[D,ag] throughout your generations from the fire offerings to the

a 5:15 Dt 32:51
b Nm 15:24
c Lv 27:3; Nm 3:47
d 5:16 Lv 14:12; 24:18
e Lv 25:12
f Lv 27:13
g Lv 4:20,26,31,35; 6:7
h 6:2 Lv 19:11
i Ex 22:7-13
j Is 61:8; Ezk 22:29
k Dt 24:14
l 6:3 Ex 23:4; Dt 22:1-3
m Ex 22:11; Lv 19:12
n 6:4 Gn 44:32; Jdg 10:10; Neh 1:6; Ps 39:1; Is 1:4
o Lv 4:3
p 6:5 Lv 27:13
q 6:4-5 Ex 22:9-12; 23:4-5; Dt 22:13; Mt 5:23-24; Lk 19:8-9
r 6:6 Lv 14:12
s Ex 29:1

t 6:7 Lv 5:10,13,18
u 6:10 Ex 28:42-43; Lv 16:4; Ezk 44:17-19
v 6:11 Lv 16:23; Ezk 42:14; 44:19
w 6:12 Lv 1:2; 7:11
x 6:14-18 Lv 2:1-16
y 6:16 1Co 9:13
z Ex 12:8; 1Co 5:8
aa Lv 16:24
ab Ex 27:9
ac 6:17 Lv 6:10; Nm 18:20; 31:36; Dt 10:9; 12:12
ad Dt 18:1
ae Ex 29:14
af 6:18 Lv 21:18-23
ag Lv 7:34; Heb 13:10

5:14-19 The **guilt offering** introduced the concept of **restitution** when one sinned against any holy thing or defrauded "his neighbor" (5:16; 6:2-3). A fine was added to this offering in recognition that a wrong had been done against God or the injured party (5:16).

The offense against any **holy** thing (5:14-16) could involve anything from mishandling the portion of a sacrifice meant for the priest, to failure to give God the tithe, to not keeping a vow. Since the offense was against God, the

extra penalty was paid to his representative, **the priest** (5:16). Note that even when sin is done in ignorance, it is still considered sin (5:17). **6:1-7** Having to pay back the full value plus twenty percent was a strong deterrent to crime (6:5).

Once full restitution was made, the sin was forgiven by God and the clear implication is that the two human parties involved would put the matter behind them and move on. Instead of this justice and closure in our

current cultural system, however, we have offenders warehoused in prisons where they learn to be better criminals while their victims must seek restitution by other means— which all too often ends with nothing being restored. We lock offenders away so that they cannot repay their victims with kindness and cash even if they want to. If the principles of biblical justice were implemented in our society today, we wouldn't have prisons full to overflowing.

a 6:18 Ex 29:37; Lk 11:2
b 6:23 Dt 13:17; 33:10; 1Sm 7:9; Ps 51:19
c 6:25 Ex 29:14
d 6:26 Lv 16:24; 1Co 9:13
e 7:1 Lv 14:12-13
f 7:2 Gn 22:2; Lv 3:5; Nm 6:11; Jos 8:31; 1Ch 16:1; Ps 20:3; Mc 6:6
g 7:3 Lv 3:9

h 7:4 Lv 9:10
7:5 Dt 18:1
j 7:6 1Co 9:13
k Lv 16:24
l Lv 14:13
m 7:7 Ex 29:14
n Lv 14:13
o Ex 30:15
p 7:9 Ex 40:29
q 7:11 Lv 3:1,3,6,9
7:12 Lv 22:29
s Ex 12:8
t Lv 2:4
u 7:14 Ex 36:3
v 7:15 Lv 22:30
w Ex 12:10; 34:25; Lv 19:5-8; Dt 16:4
x 7:16 Lv 27:8
y Ex 35:29
z 7:17 Lv 19:6
aa 7:18 Lv 1:4

LORD. Anything that touches the offerings will become holy."[a]

19 The LORD spoke to Moses: **20** "This is the offering that Aaron and his sons are to present to the LORD on the day that he is anointed: two quarts[A] of fine flour as a regular grain offering, half of it in the morning and half in the evening. **21** It is to be prepared with oil on a griddle; you are to bring it well-kneaded. You are to present it as a grain offering of baked pieces,[B] a pleasing aroma to the LORD. **22** The priest, who is one of Aaron's sons and will be anointed to take his place, is to prepare it. It must be completely burned as a permanent portion for the LORD. **23** Every grain offering for a priest will be a whole burnt offering;[b] it is not to be eaten."

THE SIN OFFERING

24 The LORD spoke to Moses: **25** "Tell Aaron and his sons: This is the law of the sin offering.[c] The sin offering is most holy and must be slaughtered before the LORD at the place where the burnt offering is slaughtered. **26** The priest who offers it as a sin offering will eat it. It is to be eaten in a holy place,[d] in the courtyard of the tent of meeting. **27** Anything that touches its flesh will become holy, and if any of its blood spatters on a garment, then you must wash that garment[c] in a holy place. **28** A clay pot in which the sin offering is boiled is to be broken; if it is boiled in a bronze vessel, it is to be scoured and rinsed with water. **29** Any male among the priests may eat it; it is especially holy. **30** But no sin offering may be eaten if its blood has been brought into the tent of meeting to make atonement in the holy place; it must be burned.

THE GUILT OFFERING

7 "Now this is the law of the guilt[D] offering;[e] it is especially holy. **2** The guilt offering is to be slaughtered at the place where the burnt offering[f] is slaughtered, and the priest is to splatter its blood on all sides of the altar. **3** The offerer is to present all the fat from it: the fat tail,[g] the fat

surrounding the entrails,[E] **4** and the two kidneys with the fat on them at the loins; he will also remove the fatty lobe of the liver[h] with the kidneys. **5** The priest will burn them on the altar as a fire offering[i] to the LORD; it is a guilt offering. **6** Any male among the priests may eat it.[j] It is to be eaten in a holy place;[k] it is especially holy.[l]

7 "The guilt offering is like the sin offering;[m] the law is the same for both. It belongs to the priest[n] who makes atonement[o] with it. **8** As for the priest who presents someone's burnt offering, the hide of the burnt offering he has presented belongs to him; it is the priest's. **9** Any grain offering[p] that is baked in an oven or prepared in a pan or on a griddle belongs to the priest who presents it; it is his. **10** But any grain offering, whether dry or mixed with oil, belongs equally to all of Aaron's sons.

THE FELLOWSHIP SACRIFICE

11 "Now this is the law of the fellowship sacrifice[q] that someone may present to the LORD: **12** If he presents it for thanksgiving, in addition to the thanksgiving sacrifice,[r] he is to present unleavened cakes[s] mixed with olive oil, unleavened wafers[t] coated with oil, and well-kneaded cakes of fine flour mixed with oil. **13** He is to present as his offering cakes of leavened bread with his thanksgiving sacrifice of fellowship. **14** From the cakes he is to present one portion of each offering as a contribution[u] to the LORD. It will belong to the priest who splatters the blood of the fellowship offering; it is his. **15** The meat of his thanksgiving sacrifice of fellowship must be eaten on the day he offers it;[v] he may not leave any of it until morning.[w]

16 "If the sacrifice he offers is a vow[x] or a freewill offering,[y] it is to be eaten on the day he presents his sacrifice, and what is left over may be eaten on the next day. **17** But what remains of the sacrificial meat by the third day must be burned.[z] **18** If any of the meat of his fellowship sacrifice is eaten on the third day, it will not be accepted.[aa]

A 6:20 Lit *a tenth of an ephah* B 6:21 Hb obscure C 6:27 Lit *wash what it spattered on* D 7:1 Or *restitution* E 7:3 LXX, Sam add *and all the fat that is on the entrails*; Lv 3:3,9,14; 4:8

6:20 The reference to the day that the priest is **anointed** suggests that this was a praise offering for God's mercy in providing a mediator between him and his people and ensuring the continuation of the priestly line through Aaron's descendants. For New Testament believers, by virtue of his sinless life, atoning death, and resurrection, Jesus

Christ is our ever-living, merciful high priest (see Heb 4:14-16).

7:7-10 These verses summarize the parts of the offerings that went to the priests as their food, since they would not have lands and crops of their own given the way the promised land was to be distributed among the tribes. God's provision for his servants is a biblical principle

that can be traced from the law of Moses to the church today (see 1 Cor 9:1-12; 1 Tim 5:17-18).

7:11-21 The name of **the fellowship sacrifice** explains its purpose. The worshiper sought to draw near to God by making an offering either in **thanksgiving** as a testimony to God's goodness (7:12-15), or as an offering in fulfillment of a **vow**, or simply as a **freewill offering** (7:16-18).

It will not be credited to the one who presents it; it is repulsive.[a] The person who eats any of it will bear his iniquity.[A]

19 "Meat that touches anything unclean must not be eaten; it is to be burned. Everyone who is clean may eat any other meat. **20** But the one who eats meat from the LORD's fellowship sacrifice while he is unclean, that person must be cut off from his people.[b] **21** If someone touches anything unclean, whether human uncleanness, an unclean animal, or any unclean, abhorrent[B,c] creature, and eats meat from the LORD's fellowship sacrifice, that person is to be cut off from his people."

FAT AND BLOOD PROHIBITED

22 The LORD spoke to Moses: **23** "Tell the Israelites: You are not to eat any fat[d] of an ox, a sheep, or a goat. **24** The fat of an animal that dies naturally or is mauled by wild beasts[c,e] may be used for any other purpose, but you must not eat it.[f] **25** If anyone eats animal fat from a fire offering presented to the LORD, the person who eats it is to be cut off from his people. **26** Wherever you live, you must not eat the blood[g] of any bird or animal. **27** Whoever eats any blood is to be cut off from his people."

THE PORTION FOR THE PRIESTS

28 The LORD spoke to Moses: **29** "Tell the Israelites: The one who presents a fellowship sacrifice to the LORD is to bring an offering to the LORD from his sacrifice. **30** His own hands will bring the fire offerings to the LORD. He will bring the fat together with the breast. The breast is to be presented as a presentation offering[h] before the LORD. **31** The priest is to burn the fat on the altar, but the breast belongs to Aaron and his sons. **32** You are to give the right thigh[i] to the priest as a contribution

from your fellowship sacrifices. **33** The son of Aaron who presents the blood of the fellowship offering and the fat will have the right thigh as a portion. **34** I have taken from the Israelites the breast of the presentation offering and the thigh of the contribution from their fellowship sacrifices, and have assigned them to the priest Aaron and to his sons as a permanent portion[D,j] from the Israelites."

35 This is the portion from the fire offerings to the LORD for Aaron and his sons[k] since the day they were presented to serve the LORD as priests. **36** The LORD commanded this to be given to them by the Israelites on the day he anointed them.[l] It is a permanent portion throughout their generations.

37 This is the law for the burnt offering, the grain offering, the sin offering, the guilt offering, the ordination offering,[m] and the fellowship sacrifice, **38** which the LORD commanded Moses on Mount Sinai[n] on the day he commanded the Israelites to present their offerings to the LORD in the Wilderness of Sinai.[o]

ORDINATION OF AARON AND HIS SONS

8 The LORD spoke to Moses: **2** "Take Aaron, his sons with him, the garments, the anointing oil,[p] the bull of the sin[E] offering, the two rams, and the basket[q] of unleavened bread, **3** and assemble the whole community[r] at the entrance to the tent of meeting." **4** So Moses did as the LORD commanded him, and the community assembled at the entrance to the tent of meeting. **5** Moses said to them, "This is what the LORD has commanded to be done."

6 Then Moses presented Aaron and his sons and washed them with water. **7** He put the tunic on Aaron, wrapped the sash

[a] 7:18 Lv 19:7; Is 65:4; Ezk 4:14;
[b] 7:20 Gn 17:14; Lv 7:27; 19:8; Nm 9:13
[c] 7:21 Lv 11:10-13,20,23,41-42; Is 66:17; Ezk 8:10
[d] 7:23 Lv 3:16-17
[e] 7:24 Lv 17:15; 22:8
[f] Ex 22:31; Lv 3:17; 17:15; 22:8; Dt 14:21; Ezk 4:14; 44:31
[g] 7:26 Gn 9:3-4; Lv 17:10-12; Dt 12:16,23
[h] 7:30 Ex 29:24
[i] 7:32 Ex 29:22; Lv 8:25-26; 9:21; Nm 18:18
[j] 7:34 Ex 29:28; 30:21; Lv 6:11,15; 10:15; 24:9; Nm 18:8,11,19; Jr 5:22
[k] 7:35 Mt 10:10; 1Co 9:13-14; 1Tm 5:17-18
[l] 7:36 Ex 40:13-15; Lv 8:12,30
[m] 7:37 Lv 8:22
[n] 7:38 Ex 34:2
[o] Ex 31:18; 34:32; Lv 26:46; Neh 9:13
[p] 8:2 Ex 29:7
[q] Gn 40:16
[r] 8:3 Ex 12:47

[A] 7:18 Or *will bear his guilt*   [B] 7:21 Some Hb mss, Sam, Syr, Tg read *swarming*   [C] 7:24 Lit *fat of a carcass or the fat of a mauled beast*
[D] 7:34 Or *statute*, also in v. 36   [E] 8:2 Or *purification*

7:22-27 God had set aside the **fat** portion of the offerings (7:23-25), the choicest part of the animals, as his alone (see the note on 3:1-17), reminding the Israelites that their great God deserved their best. Since life itself is a creation of God, and since **blood** (the stuff of life) was used as the means of atonement for sin, it was not an appropriate source of nutrition for the Israelites (7:26-27). The complete absence of blood in any meat is still a requirement for observant Jews today.
7:28-36 The **breast** of the sacrifice was **presented as a presentation offering** (7:30), a ritual in which the offerer held the breast in his hands while the priest placed his own hands

under those of the worshiper. Together they lifted the piece to symbolize that it belonged to the Lord, who then graciously gave it back **to Aaron and his sons** to eat (7:31). **The right thigh** was given to the officiating priest (7:33).
7:37-38 Connecting these instructions to the giving of the law on **Mount Sinai** firmly established their authority as coming from the **LORD** (7:38).
8:1-5 Everything concerning the priests' consecration was to be done according to divine revelation. The ordination was to be a public ceremony.
8:6-9 The service began with a ceremonial washing of Aaron and his sons, symbolizing

the fact that they as sinful humans were intrinsically unclean and needed to be purified before they could minister before a holy God (8:6). Then Moses dressed Aaron in the high priest's garments, including a beautiful **breastpiece** with its twelve precious stones representing the twelve tribes of Israel (8:8; see Exod 28:15-30). This symbolized the fact that the high priest carried the people close to his heart and represented them before the Lord.

We assume the **Urim and Thummim** were two named stones that were used to determine God's will in circumstances when the people needed special guidance.

[a] 8:7 Ex 28:4
[b] 8:8 Ex 28:30; Nm 27:21; Dt 33:8; 1Sm 28:6; Ezr 2:63; Neh 7:65
[c] 8:9 Lv 16:4
[d] 8:1-9 Ex 28:1-43; 29:1-8; 39:1-31
[e] 8:10 Ex 19:10,14,23; 20:11
[f] 8:10-11 Ex 30:18-28; 38:8; 40:7-11
[g] 8:12 Ex 29:7; 30:30; Lv 21:10-12
[h] 8:15 Ex 29:36; Lv 14:49,52; Nm 19:19; Ps 51:7; Ezk 43:22-23; 45:18
[i] 8:14-15 Ex 29:10-12,36-37; Lv 4:7
[j] 8:16 Lv 7:4
[k] 8:17 Ex 29:13; Lv 4:7-10 4:12,21; 6:4; 9:11; 10:4-5; 13:46; 14:3; 16:27; 17:3; 24:14,23
[m] 8:20 Lv 1:8

[n] 8:22 Ex 29:22,26-34; Lv 7:37; 8:28-33
[o] 8:23 Ex 29:20; Lv 14:14,17,25,28
[p] 8:25 Lv 3:9
[q] 8:26 Ex 29:3,23; Lv 7:32; Nm 6:15-19
[r] 8:30 Ex 29:21; Is 6:6-7; Heb 10:22
[s] 8:31 Lv 6:16,18; 10:12; 1Co 9:13-14
[t] 8:32 Ex 29:34

around him, clothed him with the robe, and put the ephod[a] on him. He put the woven band of the ephod around him and fastened it to him. **8** Then he put the breastpiece on him and placed the Urim and Thummim[b] into the breastpiece. **9** He also put the turban[c] on his head and placed the gold medallion, the holy diadem, on the front of the turban, as the LORD had commanded Moses.[d]

10 Then Moses took the anointing oil and anointed the tabernacle and everything in it to consecrate[e] them. **11** He sprinkled some of the oil on the altar seven times, anointing the altar with all its utensils, and the basin with its stand, to consecrate them.[f] **12** He poured some of the anointing oil on Aaron's head and anointed and consecrated him.[g] **13** Then Moses presented Aaron's sons, clothed them with tunics, wrapped sashes around them, and fastened headbands on them, as the LORD had commanded Moses.

14 Then he brought the bull near for the sin offering, and Aaron and his sons laid their hands on the head of the bull for the sin offering. **15** Then Moses slaughtered it,[A] took the blood, and applied it with his finger to the horns of the altar on all sides, purifying[h] the altar. He poured out the blood at the base of the altar and consecrated it so that atonement can be made on it.[B,i] **16** Moses took all the fat that was on the entrails, the fatty lobe of the liver, and the two kidneys[j] with their fat, and he burned them on the altar.[k] **17** He burned the bull with its hide, flesh, and waste outside the camp,[l] as the LORD had commanded Moses.

18 Then he presented the ram for the burnt offering, and Aaron and his sons laid their hands on the head of the ram. **19** Moses slaughtered it and[C] splattered the blood on all sides of the altar. **20** Moses cut the ram into pieces and burned the head, the pieces, and the fat,[m] **21** but he washed the entrails and legs with water. He then burned the entire ram on the altar. It was a burnt offering for a pleasing aroma, a fire offering to the LORD as he had commanded Moses.

22 Next he presented the second ram, the ram of ordination,[n] and Aaron and his sons laid their hands on the head of the ram. **23** Moses slaughtered it,[D] took some of its blood, and put it on Aaron's right earlobe, on the thumb of his right hand, and on the big toe of his right foot.[o] **24** Moses also presented Aaron's sons and put some of the blood on their right earlobes, on the thumbs of their right hands, and on the big toes of their right feet. Then Moses splattered the blood on all sides of the altar. **25** He took the fat — the fat tail,[p] all the fat that was on the entrails, the fatty lobe of the liver, and the two kidneys with their fat — as well as the right thigh. **26** From the basket of unleavened bread that was before the LORD he took one cake of unleavened bread, one cake of bread made with oil, and one wafer, and placed them on the fat portions and the right thigh.[q] **27** He put all these in the hands of Aaron and his sons and presented them before the LORD as a presentation offering. **28** Then Moses took them from their hands and burned them on the altar with the burnt offering. This was an ordination offering for a pleasing aroma, a fire offering to the LORD. **29** He also took the breast and presented it before the LORD as a presentation offering; it was Moses's portion of the ordination ram as the LORD had commanded him.

30 Then Moses took some of the anointing oil and some of the blood that was on the altar and sprinkled them on Aaron and his garments, as well as on his sons and their garments. In this way he consecrated Aaron and his garments, as well as his sons and their garments.[r]

31 Moses said to Aaron and his sons, "Boil the meat at the entrance to the tent of meeting and eat it there with the bread that is in the basket for the ordination offering as I commanded:[E] Aaron and his sons are to eat it.[s] **32** Burn up what remains of the meat and bread.[t] **33** Do not go outside the entrance to the tent of meeting

---

[A] 8:14-15 Or *offering, and he slaughtered it.* [A] *Then Moses*   [B] 8:15 Or *it by making atonement for it*   [C] 8:18-19 Or *ram,* [19] *and he slaughtered it. Moses*
[D] 8:22-23 Or *ram,* [23] *and he slaughtered it. Moses*   [E] 8:31 LXX, Syr, Tg read *was commanded*; Ex 29:31-32

8:12 The anointing of Aaron wasn't done by dabbing a mere drop of oil on his forehead. In the Psalms, David referred to the "fine oil on the head, running down on the beard, running down Aaron's beard onto his robes" (Ps 133:2). **8:22-24** The **ordination** offering involved a unique element: the application of the blood to the **right earlobe**, the right **thumb**, and

the right **big toe** of both Aaron and his sons (8:23-24). These parts could have been chosen because they stood for the activities of hearing, doing, and walking (or obeying)— all of which needed to be consecrated to the Lord's use. **8:31-36** Food for the **ordination** meal came from the parts of the ordination ram and the

consecrated bread that were not burned. The priests also had to observe a seven-day confinement period, during which they could not leave the area around the tabernacle under penalty of death (8:33-35). Then they were fully ordained to serve the Lord.

for seven days, until the time your days of ordination are completed, because it will take seven days to ordain you.[A] [34] The Lord commanded what has been done today in order to make atonement for you.[a] [35] You must remain at the entrance to the tent of meeting day and night for seven days and keep the Lord's charge[b] so that you will not die,[c] for this is what I was commanded." [36] So Aaron and his sons did everything the Lord had commanded through Moses.

THE PRIESTLY MINISTRY INAUGURATED

9 On the eighth day Moses summoned Aaron, his sons, and the elders of Israel.[d] [2] He said to Aaron, "Take a young bull for a sin[B] offering and a ram for a burnt offering, both without blemish,[e] and present them before the Lord. [3] And tell the Israelites:[C] Take a male goat for a sin offering; a calf and a lamb, male yearlings without blemish, for a burnt offering; [4] an ox and a ram for a fellowship offering to sacrifice before the Lord; and a grain offering mixed with oil. For today the Lord is going to appear[f] to you."

[5] They brought what Moses had commanded to the front of the tent of meeting, and the whole community came forward and stood before the Lord. [6] Moses said, "This is what the Lord commanded you to do, that the glory of the Lord[g] may appear to you." [7] Then Moses said to Aaron, "Approach the altar and sacrifice your sin offering and your burnt offering; make atonement for yourself and the people.[D,h] Sacrifice the people's offering and make atonement for them, as the Lord commanded."

[8] So Aaron approached the altar and slaughtered the calf as a sin offering for himself. [9] Aaron's sons brought the blood to him, and he dipped his finger in the blood and applied it to the horns of the altar. He poured out the blood at the base of the altar. [10] He burned the fat, the kidneys, and the fatty lobe of the liver from the sin offering on the altar, as the Lord had commanded Moses. [11] He burned the flesh and the hide[i] outside the camp.[j]

[12] Then he slaughtered the burnt offering. Aaron's sons brought him the blood, and he splattered it on all sides of the altar. [13] They brought him the burnt offering piece by piece, along with the head, and he burned them on the altar. [14] He washed the entrails and the legs and burned them with the burnt offering on the altar.

[15] Aaron presented the people's offering. He took the male goat for the people's sin offering, slaughtered it, and made a sin offering with it as he did before. [16] He presented the burnt offering and sacrificed it according to the regulation.[k] [17] Next he presented the grain offering, took a handful of it, and burned it on the altar in addition to the morning burnt offering.[l]

[18] Finally, he slaughtered the ox and the ram as the people's fellowship sacrifice. Aaron's sons brought him the blood, and he splattered it on all sides of the altar. [19] They also brought the fat portions from the ox and the ram — the fat tail, the fat surrounding the entrails, the kidneys, and the fatty lobe of the liver — [20] and placed these on the breasts. Aaron burned the fat portions on the altar, [21] but he presented the breasts[m] and the right thigh as a presentation offering[n] before the Lord, as Moses had commanded.[E]

[22] Aaron lifted up his hands toward the people and blessed[o] them. He came down after sacrificing the sin offering, the burnt offering, and the fellowship offering. [23] Moses and Aaron then entered the tent of meeting. When they came out, they blessed the people, and the glory of the Lord appeared to all the people. [24] Fire came from the Lord and

[a] 8:33-34 Ex 29:35-37; Heb 7:28
[b] 8:35 Gn 26:5
[c] Lv 10:1-2
[d] 9:1 Ex 18:12
[e] 9:2 Ex 29:1
[f] 9:4 Gn 35:9
[g] 9:6 Ex 40:34; Lk 9:32
[h] 9:7 Heb 5:1-3; 7:26-27

[i] 9:11 Lv 7:8
[j] Ex 29:14; Lv 4:8-10,12,21; 8:17; 16:27
[k] 9:16 Lv 18:26
[l] 9:17 Ex 29:38-42; Lv 2:2
[m] 9:21 Ex 29:26-27; Lv 7:30-34; 8:26; 10:14-15; Nm 6:20; 18:18
[n] Ex 29:24
[o] 9:22 Gn 14:19; Nm 6:24-26

[A] 8:33 Lit because he will fill your hands for seven days   [B] 9:2 Or purification   [C] 9:3 Sam, LXX read elders of Israel   [D] 9:7 LXX reads and your household   [E] 9:21 Some Hb mss, LXX, Sam read as the Lord commanded Moses

9:1-7 On **the eighth day** following the seven days the priests spent in separation, the people brought the required sacrifices to the tabernacle as Moses had commanded (9:1-4). Everyone stood in front of the altar (9:5) as Moses turned to Aaron and gave him the go-ahead to officially begin Israel's sacrificial system.

9:8-14 Many Bible teachers have pointed out the irony that Aaron was instructed to offer a **calf** as his sin offering, a glaring reminder that he had made the golden calf idol in the wilderness in disobedience to God (see Exod 32). Nevertheless, Aaron's sin was forgiven and he was authorized to serve as high priest.

9:15 The **people's offering** made it possible for God to dwell among them without contaminating his holiness or having to judge the people for their sins. Such forgiveness and fellowship is what the Israelites needed then; it's also what we need today.

9:24 The people's response was one of worship but also of godly fear. They knew God's fire could just as easily have consumed them as it did a sacrifice.

As believers whose sins have been forgiven by Christ's death on the cross, we are truly in a privileged position today. The writer to the Hebrews says that God's awesome, holy presence was so terrifying in the days of Moses that even he trembled in fear (see Heb 12:18-24). Incredibly, we can come into God's presence with assurance and joy, and even share in his holiness, through the work of Christ.

[a] 9:24 1Kg 18:38-39;
2Ch 7:1
[b] Ps 35:27; Is 12:6; 24:14
[c] Nm 16:4
[d] 10:1 Ex 6:23; 28:1; Nm
3:2,4; 26:60-61; 1Ch 6:3
[e] Ex 24:1
[f] Ex 27:3; 38:3; 1Kg 7:50;
2Kg 25:15; Jr 52:19
[g] Ex 30:7-9; Lv 16:12; Nm
16:17,46
[h] Ex 30:9; Nm 3:4; 26:61; Jr
2:25; 3:13; Hs 5:7
[i] 10:2 Gn 4:14
[j] Nm 26:61; Dt 4:24;
2Sm 6:7
[k] 10:3 Nm 20:13; Ezk
20:41; 28:22,25; 36:23;
38:16; 39:27
[l] Dt 30:14; Heb 7:19
[m] Ex 14:4,17-18; Is 26:15;
Ezk 28:22; 39:13; Hg 1:8
[n] 10:4 Ex 6:22
[o] Nm 3:19
[p] Lv 8:17; Heb 13:11-13
[q] 10:6 Ex 6:23
[r] Lv 13:45; 21:10; Nm 5:18;
Jdg 5:2
[s] Lv 21:10; Mk 14:63
[t] Ex 16:20
[u] Gn 37:34
[v] 10:7 Ex 29:7; Lv 21:12
[w] 10:9 Gn 9:21
[x] Nm 6:3-4; Dt 7:13; 11:14;
Jdg 13:4; Pr 20:1; Ezk
44:21; Dn 1:3-16; 10:3;
Am 2:12; Mk 4:23-25; Lk
1:15; Jn 2:1-11; Rm 14:21;
1Tm 3:3,8
[y] Ex 28:43; Lv 11:46
[z] 10:10 Lv 20:25
[aa] Ezk 22:26; 42:20; 44:23;
48:15; Ac 10:28
[ab] Lv 11:4; Nm 19:13
[ac] 10:11 Gn 47:26

[ad] 10:12 Dt 18:1
[ae] 10:15 Ex 29:28; 30:21;
Lv 6:11,15; 24:9; Nm
18:8,11,19; Jr 5:22
[af] 10:17 Lv 6:26,29
[ag] Nm 5:31
[ah] Ex 28:38; Hs 14:2; Jn 1:29
[ai] 10:18 Lv 6:26,29-30
[aj] 11:2 Lv 11:1-23; Dt 14:3-
21; Dn 1:3-16; Ac 10:9-16;
11:3; Rm 14:2; Gl 2:11-14
[ak] Dt 14:4-21; Ac 10:9-16;
Rm 14:14

consumed[a] the burnt offering and the fat portions on the altar. And when all the people saw it, they shouted[b] and fell facedown.[c]

NADAB AND ABIHU

10 Aaron's sons Nadab[d] and Abihu[e] each took his own firepan,[f] put fire in it, placed incense on it,[g] and presented unauthorized[h] fire before the LORD, which he had not commanded them to do. [2] Then fire came from the LORD[i] and consumed them, and they died before the LORD.[j] [3] Moses said to Aaron, "This is what the LORD has spoken:

I will demonstrate my holiness[A,k]
to those who are near me,[l]
and I will reveal my glory[B,m]
before all the people."

And Aaron remained silent.

[4] Moses summoned Mishael and Elzaphan,[n] sons of Aaron's uncle Uzziel,[o] and said to them, "Come here and carry your relatives away from the front of the sanctuary to a place outside the camp."[p] [5] So they came forward and carried them in their tunics outside the camp, as Moses had said.

[6] Then Moses said to Aaron and his sons Eleazar and Ithamar,[q] "Do not let your hair hang loose[r] and do not tear your clothes,[s] or else you will die, and the LORD will become angry[t] with the whole community. However, your brothers, the whole house of Israel, may weep[u] over the conflagration the LORD ignited. [7] You must not go outside the entrance to the tent of meeting or you will die, for the LORD's anointing oil[v] is on you." So they did as Moses said.

REGULATIONS FOR PRIESTS

[8] The LORD spoke to Aaron: [9] "You and your sons are not to drink wine[w] or beer[x] when you enter the tent of meeting, or else you will die; this is a permanent statute[y] throughout your generations. [10] You must distinguish[z] between the holy and the common,[aa] and the clean and the unclean,[ab] [11] and teach the Israelites all the statutes[ac] that the LORD has given to them through Moses."

[12] Moses spoke to Aaron and his remaining sons, Eleazar and Ithamar: "Take the grain offering that is left over from the fire offerings[ad] to the LORD, and eat it prepared without yeast beside the altar, because it is especially holy. [13] You must eat it in a holy place because it is your portion[c] and your sons' from the fire offerings to the LORD, for this is what I was commanded. [14] But you and your sons and your daughters may eat the breast of the presentation offering and the thigh of the contribution in any ceremonially clean place, because these portions have been assigned to you and your children from the Israelites' fellowship sacrifices. [15] They are to bring the thigh of the contribution and the breast of the presentation offering, together with the offerings of fat portions made by fire, to present as a presentation offering before the LORD. It will belong permanently[ae] to you and your children, as the LORD commanded."

[16] Then Moses inquired carefully about the male goat of the sin offering, but it had already been burned up. He was angry with Eleazar and Ithamar, Aaron's surviving sons, and asked, [17] "Why didn't you eat the sin offering in the sanctuary area?[af] For it is especially holy, and he has assigned it to you to take away the guilt[ag] of the community[ah] and make atonement for them before the LORD. [18] Since its blood was not brought inside the sanctuary, you should have eaten it in the sanctuary area, as I commanded."[ai]

[19] But Aaron replied to Moses, "See, today they presented their sin offering and their burnt offering before the LORD. Since these things have happened to me, if I had eaten the sin offering today, would it have been acceptable in the LORD's sight?" [20] When Moses heard this, it was acceptable to him.[D]

CLEAN AND UNCLEAN LAND ANIMALS

11 The LORD spoke to Moses and Aaron: [2] "Tell the Israelites: You may eat[aj] all these kinds of land animals.[ak] [3] You may eat any animal with divided hooves and that

---

[A] 10:3 Or *will be treated as holy*   [B] 10:3 Or *will be glorified*   [C] 10:13 Or *statute*   [D] 10:20 Lit *acceptable in his sight*

10:1-3 After the rebellion, Moses reminded Aaron that it was critical for all the people to understand the Lord's **holiness** (10:3). God's people must understand that the Lord isn't our pal. He's our God. He is "holy, holy, holy" (Isa 6:3; Rev 4:8)—the pure, perfect, and powerful Creator of the universe. When he issues a command, he means for it to be obeyed.

10:4-5 The sin of Nadab and Abihu led them from the place of God's presence to a place that came to symbolize being rejected and discarded. **10:16-20** It wouldn't be surprising if Aaron and his sons showed reluctance to carry on with the sacrifices for fear of displeasing the Lord and sharing the fate of Nadab and Abihu. Sure enough, **Eleazar and Ithamar** burned a part of

the sin offering they were supposed to have eaten (10:16-18). Moses was **angry** about this, but **Aaron** explained that their mistake was due either to fear of offending the Lord or maybe grief (10:19). God obviously forgave Aaron's sons since they were not struck down (10:20). **11:1-7** Much speculation surrounds the reasons behind Israel's dietary restrictions, but

chews the cud. **4** But among the ones that chew the cud or have divided hooves you are not to eat these:

camels,[a] though they chew the cud, do not have divided hooves — they are unclean for you;

5 hyraxes,[b] though they chew the cud, do not have hooves — they are unclean for you;

6 hares, though they chew the cud, do not have hooves — they are unclean for you;

7 pigs, though they have divided hooves, do not chew the cud — they are unclean for you.

8 Do not eat any of their meat or touch their carcasses — they are unclean for you.[c]

CLEAN AND UNCLEAN AQUATIC ANIMALS

9 "This is what you may eat from all that is in the water: You may eat everything in the water that has fins and scales, whether in the seas or streams. **10** But these are to be abhorrent to you: everything in the seas or streams that does not have fins and scales among all the swarming things and other living creatures[d] in the water. **11** They are to remain abhorrent to you; you must not eat any of their meat, and you must abhor their carcasses. **12** Everything in the water that does not have fins and scales will be abhorrent to you.

UNCLEAN BIRDS

13 "You are to abhor these birds. They must not be eaten because they are abhorrent:

eagles,[A,e] bearded vultures, Egyptian vultures,[B] **14** kites,[c] any kind of falcon,[D,f]

15 every kind of raven, **16** ostriches,[E] short-eared owls, gulls,[F] any kind of hawk,[g]

17 little[G] owls, cormorants,[H] long-eared owls,[I,h]

18 barn[J] owls, eagle owls,[K,j] ospreys, **19** storks,[L]

any kind of heron,[M] hoopoes, and bats.

CLEAN AND UNCLEAN FLYING INSECTS

20 "All winged insects that walk on all fours are to be abhorrent to you. **21** But you may eat these kinds of all the winged insects that walk on all fours: those that have jointed legs above their feet for hopping on the ground. **22** You may eat these:

any kind of locust,[j] katydid, cricket, and grasshopper.

23 All other winged insects that have four feet are to be abhorrent to you.

PURIFICATION AFTER TOUCHING DEAD ANIMALS

24 "These will make you unclean. Whoever touches their carcasses will be unclean[k] until evening, **25** and whoever carries any of their carcasses is to wash his clothes and will be unclean until evening.[l] **26** All animals that have hooves but do not have a divided hoof and do not chew the cud are unclean for you. Whoever touches them becomes unclean. **27** All the four-footed animals[m] that walk on their paws are unclean for you. Whoever touches their carcasses will be unclean until evening, **28** and anyone who carries their carcasses is to wash his clothes and will be unclean until evening. They are unclean for you.

29 "These creatures that swarm[n] on the ground are unclean for you:

weasels,[N] mice,[o] any kind of large lizard,[o]

30 geckos, monitor lizards,[P] common lizards,[Q] skinks,[R] and chameleons.[S]

31 These are unclean for you among all the swarming creatures. Whoever touches them when they are dead will be unclean until evening. **32** When any one of them dies and falls on anything it becomes unclean — any item of wood, clothing, leather, sackcloth,[p] or any implement used for work. It is to be rinsed with water and

[a]11:4 Gn 24:64; 31:34; Dt 14:7; Jr 2:23; Mt 19:24; 23:24; Mk 10:25; Lk 18:25
[b]11:5 Dt 14:7; Ps 104:18; Pr 30:26
[c]11:8 Lv 7:21; 11:24-27; Is 52:11; 2Co 6:17
[d]11:10 Gn 1:20; 2:19; Lv 11:46
[e]11:13 Dt 14:12; 28:49; 32:11; Pr 23:5; Is 40:31
[f]11:14 Dt 14:13; Jb 28:7
[g]11:16 Dt 14:15; Jb 39:26
[h]11:17 Dt 14:16
[i]11:18 Dt 14:17; Ps 102:6; Is 34:11; Zph 2:14

[j]11:22 Dt 28:38
[k]11:24 Ezk 22:3-4; 23:17; 44:25; Mc 2:10; Hg 2:13
[l]11:25 Lv 16:28; 17:15-16; 22:6; Nm 19:7-10
[m]11:27 Rv 18:2
[n]11:29 Ex 8:3
[o]1Sm 6:4-5,11,18; Is 66:17
[p]11:32 Gn 37:34

A 11:13 Or griffon-vultures   B 11:13 Or ospreys, or bearded vultures   C 11:14 Or hawks   D 11:14 Or buzzards, or hawks   E 11:16 Or eagle owls
F 11:16 Or long-eared owls   G 11:17 Or tawny   H 11:17 Or pelicans   I 11:17 Or ibis   J 11:18 Or pelicans, or horned owls   K 11:19 Or herons   M 11:19 Or cormorants, or hawks   N 11:29 Or mole rats, or rats   O 11:29 Or of thorn-tailed, or dabb lizard, or of crocodile   P 11:30 Or spotted lizards, or chameleons   Q 11:30 Or geckos, or newts, or salamanders   R 11:30 Or sand lizards, or newts, or snails   S 11:30 Or salamanders, or moles

God used them to set Israel apart from the pagan nations around them. There may also have been health reasons for the distinctions. And some of the animals listed, including pigs, were used in pagan religious ceremonies. But the main source of the distinction between the two categories of animals is sim-

ply the revealed will of God. Even though the prohibition against pork is probably the most well known of the Jewish dietary restrictions, the text does not single out swine as any more **unclean** than other unclean animals.
11:9-23 God used the word **abhorrent** in relation to unclean fish, birds, and insects (11:10-

13, 20, 23), meaning they were to be especially detestable to the Jews. The **birds** listed are birds of prey (11:13-19), which would be prohibited because they ate flesh that still had the blood in it—something forbidden to the Israelites. The clean **insects** that could be eaten included the **locust** and **grasshopper** (11:20-22).

a 11:34 Lv 26:5
b 11:44 Nm 15:41
c Ex 19:22; Lv 20:7; Nm 11:18; Ezk 38:23
d Lv 19:2; 20:7,26; 1Pt 1:16
e 11:45 Ex 6:7; 20:2; Lv 25:38,42; 26:13,45
f Lv 21:8

g 11:47 Lv 26:6
h 12:2 Lv 10:14
i Lv 15:19
j 12:3 Ex 4:25
k Gn 34:14
l Gn 17:12-13; 21:4; Lk 2:21; Gl 3:5; 5:6; 6:15
m 12:4 Lv 14:2
n Lk 8:43
o 12:8 Lv 14:21
p Lk 2:24
q 13:2 Lv 14:3,7,32,44,54-57; Dt 24:8; 2Kg 5:3,6-7,27; 2Ch 26:19

will remain unclean until evening; then it will be clean. 33 If any of them falls into any clay pot, everything in it will become unclean; you are to break it. 34 Any edible food[a] coming into contact with that unclean water will become unclean, and any drinkable liquid in any container will become unclean. 35 Anything one of their carcasses falls on will become unclean. If it is an oven or stove, it is to be smashed; it is unclean and will remain unclean for you. 36 A spring or cistern containing water will remain clean, but someone who touches a carcass in it will become unclean. 37 If one of their carcasses falls on any seed that is to be sown, it is clean; 38 but if water has been put on the seed and one of their carcasses falls on it, it is unclean for you.

39 "If one of the animals that you use for food dies, anyone who touches its carcass will be unclean until evening. 40 Anyone who eats some of its carcass is to wash his clothes and will be unclean until evening. Anyone who carries its carcass must wash his clothes and be unclean until evening.

UNCLEAN SWARMING CREATURES

41 "All the creatures that swarm on the earth are abhorrent; they must not be eaten. 42 Do not eat any of the creatures that swarm on the earth, anything that moves on its belly or walks on all fours or on many feet,[A] for they are abhorrent. 43 Do not become contaminated by any creature that swarms; do not become unclean or defiled by them. 44 For I am the LORD your God,[b] so you must consecrate yourselves[c] and be holy because I am holy.[d] Do not defile yourselves by any swarming creature that crawls on the ground. 45 For I am the LORD, who brought you up from the land of Egypt to be your God,[e] so you must be holy because I am holy.[f]

46 "This is the law concerning animals, birds, all living creatures that move in the water, and all creatures that swarm on the ground, 47 in order to distinguish between the unclean and the clean, between the animals[g] that may be eaten and those that may not be eaten."

PURIFICATION AFTER CHILDBIRTH

12 The LORD spoke to Moses: 2 "Tell the Israelites: When a woman becomes pregnant and gives birth to a male child,[h] she will be unclean seven days, as she is during the days of her menstrual impurity.[i] 3 The flesh of his foreskin[j] must be circumcised[k] on the eighth day.[l] 4 She will continue in purification[m] from her bleeding[n] for thirty-three days. She must not touch any holy thing or go into the sanctuary until completing her days of purification. 5 But if she gives birth to a female child, she will be unclean for two weeks as she is during her menstrual impurity. She will continue in purification from her bleeding for sixty-six days.

6 "When her days of purification are complete, whether for a son or daughter, she is to bring to the priest at the entrance to the tent of meeting a year-old male lamb for a burnt offering, and a young pigeon or a turtledove for a sin[B] offering. 7 He will present them before the LORD and make atonement on her behalf; she will be clean from her discharge of blood. This is the law for a woman giving birth, whether to a male or female. 8 But if she doesn't have sufficient means[C,o] for a sheep, she may take two turtledoves or two young pigeons,[p] one for a burnt offering and the other for a sin offering. Then the priest will make atonement on her behalf, and she will be clean."

SKIN DISEASES

13 The LORD spoke to Moses and Aaron: 2 "When a person has a swelling,[D] scab,[E] or spot on the skin of his body, and it may be a serious disease on the skin[q] of his

---

A 11:42 Lit fours, to anything multiplying pairs of feet   B 12:6 Or purification, also in v. 8   C 12:8 Lit if her hand cannot obtain what is sufficient   D 13:2 Or discoloration   E 13:2 Or rash, or eruption

---

11:33-40 Not just people, but clothing or household items were rendered unclean by contact with an unclean animal. A **clay pot** so contaminated had to be broken (11:33), and an unclean **oven or stove** had to be **smashed** (11:35). Even contact with the carcasses of clean animals defiled a person, if the animals died in any way other than in the rituals of worship.

11:44 Holiness is still a requirement for God's people today. Sinners are made acceptable to God only through the atoning sacrifice of Jesus Christ when they place their faith in him. But

after coming to saving faith, we are called to live lives that please God. The New Testament, in fact, is filled with commands about honoring the Lord with lives dedicated to his service (see Rom 12:1; 1 Thess 4:7; 1 Pet 1:15-16; 2 Pet 3:11).

12:1-8 It wasn't a child's birth that made the mother unclean, but the flow of blood that followed. The mother needed only ritual **purification** after delivery (12:4) so she could enter the tabernacle and worship God again.

A male child was to be circumcised **on the eighth day** after birth (12:3), after his mother had observed seven days of ceremonial

uncleanness. Then she was to take a **burnt offering** and a **sin offering** to the tabernacle (12:8). In Luke 2:21-24 we find that even giving birth to the sinless Son of God did not exempt Mary from obeying the law of Moses concerning purification.

13:1-8 **A serious disease on the skin** (13:1) that might be infectious is a threat anytime people live in close proximity. This was definitely the case among the Israelites who lived in the wilderness before germs were understood and hospitals could help contain them. Yet the real thrust of chapters 13—15 is not the

body, he is to be brought to the priest Aaron or to one of his sons, the priests. **3** The priest will examine the sore[a] on the skin of his body. If the hair in the sore has turned white and the sore appears to be deeper than the skin of his body, it is in fact a serious skin disease. After the priest examines him, he must pronounce him unclean. **4** But if the spot on the skin of his body is white and does not appear to be deeper than the skin, and the hair in it has not turned white, the priest will quarantine the stricken person for seven days.[b] **5** The priest will then reexamine him on the seventh day. If he sees that the sore remains unchanged and has not spread on the skin, the priest will quarantine him for another seven days. **6** The priest will examine him again on the seventh day. If the sore has faded and has not spread on the skin, the priest is to pronounce him clean;[c] it is a scab. The person is to wash his clothes and will become clean. **7** But if the scab spreads further on his skin after he has presented himself to the priest for his cleansing,[d] he is to present himself again to the priest. **8** The priest will examine him, and if the scab has spread on the skin, then the priest must pronounce him unclean; he has a serious skin disease.

9 "When a case of serious skin disease may have developed on a person, he is to be brought to the priest. **10** The priest will examine him. If there is a white swelling on the skin that has turned the hair white, and there is a patch of raw flesh in the swelling, **11** it is a chronic serious disease on the skin of his body, and the priest must pronounce him unclean.[e] He need not quarantine him, for he is unclean. **12** But if the skin disease breaks out all over the skin so that it covers all the skin of the stricken person from his head to his feet so far as the priest can see, **13** the priest will look, and if the skin disease has covered his entire body, he is to pronounce the stricken person clean.[f] Since he has turned totally white, he is clean. **14** But whenever raw flesh appears on him, he will be unclean. **15** When the priest examines the raw flesh, he must pronounce him unclean. Raw flesh is unclean; this is a serious skin disease. **16** But if the raw flesh changes[A] and[B] turns white, he is to go to the priest. **17** The priest will examine him, and if the sore has turned white, the priest must pronounce the stricken person clean; he is clean.

18 "When a boil appears on the skin[g] of someone's body[h] and it heals, **19** and a white swelling or a reddish-white spot develops where the boil was, the person is to present himself to the priest. **20** The priest will make an examination, and if the spot seems to be beneath the skin and the hair in it has turned white, the priest must pronounce him unclean; it is a case of serious skin disease that has broken out in the boil. **21** But when the priest examines it, if there is no white hair in it, and it is not beneath the skin but is faded, the priest will quarantine him seven days. **22** If it spreads further on the skin, the priest must pronounce him unclean; it is in fact a disease. **23** But if the spot remains where it is and does not spread, it is only the scar from the boil. The priest is to pronounce him clean.

24 "When there is a burn on the skin of one's body produced by fire, and the patch made raw by the burn becomes reddish-white or white, **25** the priest is to examine it. If the hair in the spot has turned white and the spot appears to be deeper than the skin, it is a serious skin disease that has broken out in the burn. The priest must pronounce him unclean; it is a serious skin disease. **26** But when the priest examines it, if there is no white hair in the spot and it is not beneath the skin but is faded, the priest will quarantine him seven days. **27** The priest will reexamine him on the seventh day. If it has spread further on the skin, the priest must pronounce him unclean; it is in fact a case of serious skin disease. **28** But if the spot has remained where it was and has not spread on the skin but is faded, it is the swelling from the burn. The priest is to pronounce him clean, for it is only the scar from the burn.

29 "When a man or woman has a condition on the head or chin, **30** the priest is to examine the condition. If it appears to be deeper than the skin,[i] and the hair

a 13:3 Ex 11:1; Dt 17:8; 21:5; Is 53:8
b 13:4 Nm 12:14-15; 2Kg 15:5
c 13:6 Nm 8:6-7; Ps 51:2; Ezk 24:13
d 13:7 Lv 14:2
e 13:11 Lv 11:4
f 13:13 Lv 10:10

g 13:18 Lv 13:2
h Ex 9:9-11; Dt 28:27,35; Jb 2:7
i 13:30 Lv 13:2

A 13:16 Or *recedes*   B 13:16 Or *flesh again*

---

medical implications of these conditions, but the fact that many of them made the sufferer ceremonially unclean and thus excluded from the presence of God. This doesn't mean, however, that God assigned moral blame to people with skin diseases.

13:9-17 Note that if a person's skin turns **totally white** over his **entire body**, he is pronounced **clean** (13:12-13). This symptom actually refers to a condition known as leukoderma, which cannot be passed from one person to another. **Raw flesh**, by contrast,

indicated a much more serious problem (13:10, 14-16).
13:18-28 The best outcome for either a **boil** or a **burn** (13:18, 24) was when the spot turned out to be just the related **scar** (13:23, 28).

[a]13:33 Gn 41:14; Lv 14:8-9; 21:5; Nm 6:9,18-19; Dt 21:12; Jdg 16:17,19,22
[b]13:40 2Kg 2:23
[c]13:42 2Ch 26:19-20

[d]13:44 Ex 4:6; Lv 14:2-3; 22:4; Nm 5:2; 12:10
[e]13:45 Lv 10:6; 21:10
[f]Ezk 24:17,22; Mc 3:7
[g]13:46 Nm 5:1-4; 8:17; 12:14-15
[h]13:51 Lv 11:24; 15:10-12,21-27; Hg 2:12-13

in it is yellow and sparse, the priest must pronounce the person unclean. It is a scaly outbreak, a serious skin disease of the head or chin. [31] When the priest examines the scaly condition, if it does not appear to be deeper than the skin, and there is no black hair in it, the priest will quarantine the person with the scaly condition for seven days. [32] The priest will reexamine the condition on the seventh day. If the scaly outbreak has not spread and there is no yellow hair in it and it does not appear to be deeper than the skin, [33] the person is to shave himself[a] but not shave the scaly area. Then the priest will quarantine the person who has the scaly outbreak for another seven days. [34] The priest will examine the scaly outbreak on the seventh day, and if it has not spread on the skin and does not appear to be deeper than the skin, the priest is to pronounce the person clean. He is to wash his clothes, and he will be clean. [35] But if the scaly outbreak spreads further on the skin after his cleansing, [36] the priest is to examine the person. If the scaly outbreak has spread on the skin, the priest does not need to look for yellow hair; the person is unclean. [37] But if as far as he can see, the scaly outbreak remains unchanged and black hair has grown in it, then it has healed; he is clean. The priest is to pronounce the person clean.

[38] "When a man or a woman has white spots on the skin of the body, [39] the priest is to make an examination. If the spots on the skin of the body are dull white, it is only a rash[h] that has broken out on the skin; the person is clean.

[40] "If a man loses the hair of his head, he is bald,[b] but he is clean. [41] Or if he loses the hair at his hairline, he is bald on his forehead, but he is clean. [42] But if there is a reddish-white condition on the bald head or forehead, it is a serious skin disease breaking out on his head or forehead.[c] [43] The priest is to examine him, and if the swelling of the condition on his bald head or forehead is reddish-white, like the appearance of a serious skin disease on his body, [44] the man is afflicted with a serious skin disease;[d] he is unclean. The priest must pronounce him unclean; the infection is on his head.

[45] "The person who has a case of serious skin disease is to have his clothes torn[e] and his hair hanging loose, and he must cover his mouth[f] and cry out, 'Unclean, unclean!' [46] He will remain unclean as long as he has the disease; he is unclean. He must live alone in a place outside the camp.[g]

CONTAMINATED FABRICS

[47] "If a fabric is contaminated with mildew — in wool or linen fabric, [48] in the warp or weft of linen or wool, or in leather or anything made of leather — [49] and if the contamination is green or red in the fabric, the leather, the warp, the weft, or any leather article, it is a mildew contamination and is to be shown to the priest. [50] The priest is to examine the contamination and quarantine the contaminated fabric for seven days. [51] The priest is to reexamine the contamination on the seventh day. If it has spread in the fabric, the warp, the weft, or the leather, regardless of how it is used, the contamination is harmful mildew; it is unclean.[h] [52] He is to burn the fabric, the warp or weft in wool or linen, or any leather article, which is contaminated. Since it is harmful mildew it must be burned.

[53] "When the priest examines it, if the contamination has not spread in the fabric, the warp or weft, or any leather article, [54] the priest is to order whatever is contaminated to be washed and quarantined for another seven days. [55] After it has been washed, the priest is to reexamine the contamination. If the appearance of the contaminated article has not changed, it is unclean. Even though the contamination has not spread, you must burn the

[h]13:39 Hb obscure

13:40-44 You might smile to discover that being **bald** was also included in a chapter on skin diseases. However, baldness itself did not make a man unclean (13:40-41); the presence of a **skin disease** on the scalp did (13:42-44).

13:45-46 A person with an infectious skin disease had **his clothes torn and his hair hanging loose** (13:45). This alone would make the person repulsive to the eyes of others. But he also had to **cry out, "Unclean, unclean!"** (13:45), signaling that

he could potentially spread any infection he carried. Worse, he had to **live alone . . . outside the camp** (13:46). The holy standards of God, the well-being of the community, and a person's life and family were at stake when disease was found within the camp. To banish a person was significant, so it was vital that the correct diagnosis was made. With this background in mind, imagine the joy and gratitude overflowing from those Jesus healed from skin diseases (see Luke 17:11-19). He made a way for even those

who'd once thought themselves hopelessly unclean to find total physical restoration. And that's a picture of what he can do for people spiritually, too.

13:47-59 Clothing and other garments could be rendered unclean by the appearance of something abnormal on them. This was not just a spot on the surface of a fabric, but a contamination that went deep to the core of the piece (13:48), signaling that the problem had intertwined itself with the fabric and could not be cleansed away.

fabric. It is a fungus^A^ on the front or back of the fabric.

56 "If the priest examines it, and the contamination has faded after it has been washed, he is to cut the contaminated section out of the fabric, the leather, or the warp or weft. **57** But if it reappears in the fabric, the warp or weft, or any leather article, it has broken out again. You must burn whatever is contaminated. **58** But if the contamination disappears from the fabric, the warp or weft, or any leather article, which have been washed, it is to be washed again, and it will be clean.

59 "This is the law concerning a mildew contamination in wool or linen fabric, warp or weft, or any leather article, in order to pronounce it clean or unclean."^a^

CLEANSING OF SKIN DISEASES

14 The LORD spoke to Moses: **2** "This is the law^b^ concerning the person afflicted with a skin disease on the day of his cleansing.^c^ He is to be brought to the priest,^d^ **3** who will go outside the camp^e^ and examine him.^f^ If the skin disease has disappeared from the afflicted person,^B^ **4** the priest will order that two live clean birds,^g^ cedar wood,^h^ scarlet^i^ yarn, and hyssop^j^ be brought for the one who is to be cleansed. **5** Then the priest will order that one of the birds be slaughtered over fresh water in a clay pot. **6** He is to take the live bird together with the cedar wood, scarlet yarn, and hyssop, and dip them all into the blood of the bird that was slaughtered over the fresh water. **7** He will then sprinkle the blood seven times on the one who is to be cleansed from the skin disease. He is to pronounce him clean and release the live bird over the open countryside.^k^ **8** The one who is to be cleansed must wash his clothes, shave off all his hair, and bathe with water; he is clean. Afterward he may enter the camp, but he must remain outside his tent for seven days. **9** He is to shave off all his hair again on the seventh day: his head, his beard, his eyebrows, and the rest of his hair. He is to wash his clothes and bathe himself with water; he is clean.

10 "On the eighth day he must take two unblemished^i^ male lambs, an unblemished year-old ewe lamb, a grain offering of six quarts^c^ of fine flour mixed with olive oil, and one-third of a quart^D^ of olive oil. **11** The priest who performs the cleansing will place the person who is to be cleansed, together with these offerings, before the LORD at the entrance to the tent of meeting. **12** The priest is to take one male lamb and present it as a guilt offering,^m^ along with the one-third quart of olive oil, and he will present them as a presentation offering^n^ before the LORD. **13** He is to slaughter the male lamb at the place in the sanctuary area where the sin offering^o^ and burnt offering^p^ are slaughtered,^q^ for like the sin offering, the guilt offering belongs to the priest;^r^ it is especially holy.^s^ **14** The priest is to take some of the blood from the guilt offering and put it on the lobe of the right ear of the one to be cleansed, on the thumb of his right hand, and on the big toe of his right foot.^t^ **15** Then the priest will take some of the one-third quart of olive oil and pour it into his left palm. **16** The priest will dip his right finger into the oil in his left palm and sprinkle some of the oil with his finger seven times before the LORD. **17** From the oil remaining in his palm the priest will put some on the lobe of the right ear of the one to be cleansed, on the thumb of his right hand, and on the big toe of his right foot, on top of the blood of the guilt offering.^u^ **18** What is left of the oil in the priest's palm he is to put on the head of the one to be cleansed. In this way the priest will make atonement for him before the LORD. **19** The priest is to sacrifice the sin offering and make atonement for the one to be cleansed from his uncleanness.^v^ Afterward he will slaughter the burnt offering. **20** The priest is to offer the burnt offering and the grain

^a^13:59 Lv 10:10-11
^b^14:2 Lv 11:46
^c^Lv 12:4-5; Nm 6:9; Ezk 44:26
^d^Lv 4:16
^e^14:3 Lv 8:17
^f^Lv 13:2-3
^g^14:4 Gn 40:17
^h^Jdg 9:15; 2Sm 5:11; 7:2,7; 1Kg 5:13; 6:9-10; Ps 29:5; Sg 1:17; 8:9; Am 2:9; Zch 11:1-2
^i^Ex 25:4; Nm 4:8; 19:6
^j^Ex 12:22
^k^14:7 Lv 14:53; 16:21-22

^l^14:10 Ex 29:1
^m^14:12 Lv 5:6-19
^n^Ex 29:24
^o^14:13 Ex 29:14
^p^Gn 22:2; Lv 3:5; Nm 6:11; Jos 8:31; 1Ch 16:1; Ps 20:3; Mc 6:6
^q^Lv 1:11; 6:25; 7:2
^r^Lv 7:7
^s^Lv 2:3; 6:10; 7:1,6; 10:12; 24:9; 27:28
^t^14:14 Ex 29:20; Lv 8:23-24; 14:25,28
^u^14:17 Lv 14:14
^v^14:19 Lv 5:3

14:2-9 A person who believed he had been cured of his disease would send for the **priest** (14:2) If the priest verified that the cleansing had taken place, he took two birds, **slaughtered** one, and caught its blood in a **pot** (14:4-5). Then the priest performed a unique ceremony. **The live bird together with . . . cedar wood, scarlet yarn, and hyssop** were dipped into the blood, which was then sprinkled **seven times** on the patient. The **live bird** was then released, prob-

ably as a symbol of the person's cleansing and release from his isolation (14:6-7). (Seeing that bird fly away had to be a happy moment for one who had been in isolation for days or even weeks.) Now pronounced **clean**, the person was allowed to **enter the camp**, but only after washing thoroughly and shaving off his hair (14:7-8). Of course, a person who looked like this was a dramatic illustration to passersby that his life was beginning over (14:8-9).

14:10-20 The similarity between what we see here and the consecration ceremony for the priests outlined in chapter 8 cannot be a coincidence. It must have symbolized that just as the priests had been fully consecrated and were ready to bring sacrifices to God, so was this cleansed person. Even the remaining **oil** from this ceremony was poured **on the head** of the worshiper (14:18), also in imitation of the priests' ordination ceremony.

[a] 14:20 Mt 8:1-4; Mk 1:21-44; Lk 5:12-14
[b] 14:21 Am 5:11
[c] Lv 5:7-13; 12:8
[d] 14:29 Lv 14:18
[e] 14:34 Gn 37:1
[f] Gn 17:8; 23:4; 36:43; 47:11; 48:4; 49:30; 50:13; Dt 32:49; Jos 21:12,41

offering on the altar. The priest will make atonement for him, and he will be clean.[a]

[21] "But if he is poor[b] and cannot afford these,[c] he is to take one male lamb for a guilt offering to be presented in order to make atonement for him, along with two quarts[A] of fine flour mixed with olive oil for a grain offering, one-third of a quart of olive oil, [22] and two turtledoves or two young pigeons, whatever he can afford, one to be a sin offering and the other a burnt offering. [23] On the eighth day he is to bring these things for his cleansing to the priest at the entrance to the tent of meeting before the LORD. [24] The priest will take the male lamb for the guilt offering and the one-third quart of olive oil, and present them as a presentation offering before the LORD. [25] After he slaughters the male lamb for the guilt offering, the priest is to take some of the blood of the guilt offering and put it on the right earlobe of the one to be cleansed, on the thumb of his right hand, and on the big toe of his right foot. [26] Then the priest will pour some of the oil into his left palm. [27] With his right finger the priest will sprinkle some of the oil in his left palm seven times before the LORD. [28] The priest will also put some of the oil in his palm on the right earlobe of the one to be cleansed, on the thumb of his right hand, and on the big toe of his right foot, on the same place as the blood of the guilt offering. [29] What is left of the oil in the priest's palm he is to put on the head of the one to be cleansed to make atonement for him before the LORD.[d] [30] He is to then sacrifice one type of what he can afford, either the turtledoves or young pigeons, [31] one as a sin offering and the other as a burnt offering, sacrificing what he can afford together with the grain offering. In this way the priest will make atonement before the LORD for the one to be cleansed. [32] This is the law for someone who has[s] a skin disease and cannot afford the cost of his cleansing."

CLEANSING OF CONTAMINATED OBJECTS

[33] The LORD spoke to Moses and Aaron: [34] "When you enter the land of Canaan[e] that I am giving you as a possession,[f] and I place a mildew contamination in a house in the land you possess,[c] [35] the owner of the house is to come and tell the priest: Something like mildew contamination has appeared[D] in my house. [36] The priest must order them to clear the house before he enters to examine the contamination, so that nothing in the house becomes unclean. Afterward the priest will come to examine the house. [37] He will examine it, and if the contamination in the walls of the house consists of green or red indentations[E] that appear to be beneath the surface of the wall, [38] the priest is to go outside the house to its doorway and quarantine the house for seven days. [39] The priest is to return on the seventh day and examine it. If the contamination has spread on the walls of the house, [40] the priest must order that the stones with the contamination be pulled out and thrown into an unclean place outside the city. [41] He is to have the inside of the house completely scraped, and have the plaster[f] that is scraped off dumped in an unclean place outside the city. [42] Then they are to take different stones to replace the former ones and take additional plaster to replaster the house.

[43] "If the contamination reappears in the house after the stones have been pulled out, and after the house has been scraped and replastered, [44] the priest is to come and examine it. If the contamination has spread in the house, it is harmful mildew; the house is unclean. [45] It must be torn down with its stones, its beams, and all its plaster, and taken outside the city to an unclean place. [46] Whoever enters the house during any of the days the priest quarantines it will be unclean until evening. [47] Whoever lies down in the house is to wash his clothes, and whoever eats in it is to wash his clothes.

[48] "But when the priest comes and examines it, if the contamination has not spread in the house after it was replastered, he is to pronounce the house clean because the contamination has disappeared.[G] [49] He is to take two birds, cedar wood, scarlet yarn, and hyssop to purify the house, [50] and he is to slaughter one of the birds over a clay pot containing fresh water. [51] He will take the

---

[A] 14:21 Lit *him, and one-tenth*; probably one-tenth of an ephah   [B] 14:32 Lit *someone on whom there is*   [C] 14:34 Lit *land of your possession*   [D] 14:35 Lit *appeared to me*   [E] 14:37 Or *eruptions*; Hb obscure   [F] 14:41 Lit *dust*, also in v. 42   [G] 14:48 Lit *healed*

14:30-32 Here again we see the significance of the mediating role of the **priest**—making **atonement** in order to reconcile God and humanity (14:31). This is what our great high priest Jesus came to do (see Heb 10:10-21).

14:33-57 Since the Israelites were living in tents when these instructions were given, the regulations for examining a house (and either cleansing it or tearing it down) were for future use, when they took possession of **Canaan** (14:34).

cedar wood, the hyssop, the scarlet yarn, and the live bird, dip them in the blood of the slaughtered bird and the fresh water, and sprinkle the house seven times. ⁵² He will purify the house with the blood of the bird, the fresh water, the live bird, the cedar wood, the hyssop, and the scarlet yarn. ⁵³ Then he is to release the live bird into the open countryside^a outside the city. In this way he will make atonement for the house, and it will be clean.

⁵⁴ "This is the law for any skin disease or mildew, for a scaly outbreak, ⁵⁵ for mildew in clothing or on a house, ⁵⁶ and for a swelling, scab, or spot, ⁵⁷ to determine when something is unclean or clean. This is the law regarding skin disease and mildew."

BODILY DISCHARGES

15 The LORD spoke to Moses and Aaron: ² "Speak to the Israelites and tell them: When any man has a discharge^b from his member, he is unclean. ³ This is uncleanness of his discharge: Whether his member secretes the discharge or retains it, he is unclean. All the days that his member secretes or retains anything because of his discharge,^A he is unclean. ⁴ Any bed the man with the discharge lies on will be unclean, and any furniture he sits on will be unclean. ⁵ Anyone who touches his bed is to wash his clothes and bathe with water, and he will remain unclean until evening. ⁶ Whoever sits on furniture that the man with the discharge was sitting on is to wash his clothes and bathe with water, and he will remain unclean until evening. ⁷ Whoever touches the body^B of the man with a discharge is to wash his clothes and bathe with water, and he will remain unclean until evening. ⁸ If the man with the discharge spits on anyone who is clean, he is to wash his clothes and bathe with water, and he will remain unclean until evening. ⁹ Any saddle the man with the discharge rides on will be unclean.^c ¹⁰ Whoever touches anything that was under him will be unclean until evening, and whoever carries such things is to wash his clothes and bathe with water, and he will remain unclean until evening. ¹¹ If the man with the discharge touches anyone

without first rinsing his hands in water,^d the person who was touched is to wash his clothes and bathe with water, and he will remain unclean until evening. ¹² Any clay pot that the man with the discharge touches must be broken, while any wooden utensil is to be rinsed with water.^e

¹³ "When the man with the discharge has been cured of it, he is to count seven days for his cleansing, wash his clothes, and bathe his body in fresh water; he will be clean. ¹⁴ He must take two turtledoves or two young pigeons on the eighth day, come before the LORD at the entrance to the tent of meeting, and give them to the priest. ¹⁵ The priest is to sacrifice them, one as a sin offering and the other as a burnt offering.^f In this way the priest will make atonement for him before the LORD because of his discharge.

¹⁶ "When a man has an emission of semen,^g he is to bathe himself completely with water, and he will remain unclean until evening. ¹⁷ Any clothing or leather on which there is an emission of semen is to be washed with water, and it will remain unclean until evening. ¹⁸ If a man sleeps with a woman and has an emission of semen, both of them are to bathe with water, and they will remain unclean until evening.^h

¹⁹ "When a woman has a discharge, and it consists of blood from her body, she will be unclean because of her menstruationⁱ for seven days. Everyone who touches her will be unclean until evening. ²⁰ Anything she lies on during her menstruation will become unclean, and anything she sits on will become unclean. ²¹ Everyone who touches her bed is to wash his clothes and bathe with water, and he will remain unclean until evening. ²² Everyone who touches any furniture she was sitting on is to wash his clothes and bathe with water, and he will remain unclean until evening. ²³ If discharge is on the bed or the furniture she was sitting on, when he touches it he will be unclean until evening. ²⁴ If a man sleeps with her, and blood from her menstruation gets on him, he will be unclean for seven days, and every bed he lies on will become unclean.^j

^a 14:53 Lv 14:7
^b 15:2 Lv 15:33; 22:4; Nm 5:2; 2Sm 3:29
^c 15:9 Gn 31:34-35
^d 15:11 Ex 30:19; Mt 15:2; Mk 7:3
^e 15:12 Lv 6:28; 11:33
^f 15:15 Gn 22:2; Lv 3:5; Nm 6:11; Jos 8:31; 1Ch 16:1; Ps 20:3; Mc 6:6
^g 15:16 Lv 15:32; 19:20; 22:4; Nm 5:13
^h 15:18 2Sm 11:2-4
ⁱ 15:19 Lv 12:2,5; 18:19; Ezk 22:10; 36:17
^j 15:24 Lv 18:19; 20:18; Ezk 18:6

15:1-18 Interestingly, the man with a **discharge** was not sent outside the camp as were those with skin diseases. Some argue that this was because the discharge was not infectious. Once the discharge had stopped and the man

had waited **seven days**, he could **wash** and be clean, and then offer the sacrifices of **cleansing** (15:13-15). Semen **emission**, possibly during intercourse (15:16-18), brought uncleanness to the man and the **woman** involved.

15:19-24 A woman's monthly menstruation resulted in her uncleanness. The man who came in contact with her flow—like the woman herself (15:19)—was unclean for **seven days** (15:24).

a 15:28 Lv 15:13; Mt
          9:20-22
b 15:31 Ex 25:9; Nm 5:2-3
          c 16:1 Gn 4:14
          d Lv 10:1-2

e 16:2 Heb 6:19
          f Mk 15:38
          g Ex 31:7
          h Ex 16:10
i Nm 7:89; 16:42; 1Kg 8:10-
          12; Heb 9:5
j 16:3 Lv 4:1-12; Heb
          9:7,24-25
k Gn 22:2; Lv 3:5; Nm 6:11;
Jos 8:31; 1Ch 16:1; Ps 20:3;
          Mc 6:6
l 16:4 Ex 28:42-43; Lv 6:10;
          8:7-8; Ezk 44:17-19
m 16:5 Lv 4:23-24; 8:18-
          21; 9:15
n 16:8 Nm 26:55
          o Lv 16:26
p 16:9 Nm 29:11
          q 16:10 Gn 14:6
          r 16:12 Nm 7:14
          s Mk 15:38
          t 16:13 Ex 16:10
          u Ex 31:18
v Lv 10:1; Nm 16:46-48; Ps
          141:2; Rv 8:3-5
w 16:14 Heb 9:22

25 "When a woman has a discharge of her blood for many days, though it is not the time of her menstruation, or if she has a discharge beyond her period, she will be unclean all the days of her unclean discharge, as she is during the days of her menstruation. **26** Any bed she lies on during the days of her discharge will be like her bed during menstrual impurity; any furniture she sits on will be unclean as in her menstrual period. **27** Everyone who touches them will be unclean; he must wash his clothes and bathe with water, and he will remain unclean until evening. **28** When she is cured of her discharge, she is to count seven days, and after that she will be clean.*a* **29** On the eighth day she must take two turtledoves or two young pigeons and bring them to the priest at the entrance to the tent of meeting. **30** The priest is to sacrifice one as a sin offering and the other as a burnt offering. In this way the priest will make atonement for her before the Lord because of her unclean discharge.

31 "You must keep the Israelites from their uncleanness, so that they do not die by defiling my tabernacle*b* that is among them. **32** This is the law for someone with a discharge: a man who has an emission of semen, becoming unclean by it; **33** a woman who is in her menstrual period; anyone who has a discharge, whether male or female; and a man who sleeps with a woman who is unclean."

THE DAY OF ATONEMENT

16 The Lord spoke to Moses after the death of two of Aaron's sons when they approached the presence*c* of*A* the Lord and died.*d* **2** The Lord said to Moses: "Tell your brother Aaron that he may not come whenever he wants into the holy place*e* behind the curtain*f* in front of the mercy seat*g* on the ark or else he will die, because I appear in the cloud*h* above the mercy seat.*i*

3 "Aaron is to enter the most holy place*j* in this way: with a young bull for a sin offering and a ram for a burnt offering.*k* **4** He is to wear a holy linen tunic, and linen undergarments are to be on his body. He is to tie a linen sash around him and wrap his head with a linen turban.*l* These are holy garments; he must bathe his body with water before he wears them. **5** He is to take from the Israelite community two male goats for a sin offering and one ram for a burnt offering.*m*

6 "Aaron will present the bull for his sin offering and make atonement for himself and his household. **7** Next he will take the two goats and place them before the Lord at the entrance to the tent of meeting. **8** After Aaron casts lots*n* for the two goats, one lot for the Lord and the other for an uninhabitable place,*B,C,o* **9** he is to present the goat chosen by lot for the Lord and sacrifice it as a sin offering.*p* **10** But the goat chosen by lot for an uninhabitable place is to be presented alive before the Lord to make atonement with it by sending it into the wilderness*q* for an uninhabitable place.

11 "When Aaron presents the bull for his sin offering and makes atonement for himself and his household, he will slaughter the bull for his sin offering. **12** Then he is to take a firepan full of blazing coals from the altar before the Lord and two handfuls of finely ground fragrant incense,*r* and bring them inside the curtain.*s* **13** He is to put the incense on the fire before the Lord, so that the cloud*t* of incense covers the mercy seat that is over the testimony,*u* or else he will die.*v* **14** He is to take some of the bull's blood*w* and sprinkle it with his

---

A 16:1 LXX, Tg, Syr, Vg read *they brought strange fire before*; Nm 3:4   *B* 16:8 Lit *for Azazel*, also in vv. 10 (2x),26   *C* 16:8 Perhaps a term that means "for the goat that departs," or "for removal," or "for a rough, difficult place," or "for a goat-demon"; Hb obscure; also in vv. 10,26

15:25-30 A woman with a chronic discharge of blood was considered **unclean** during her entire illness (15:25). This brings to mind the New Testament era woman who had suffered bleeding for twelve years before she touched Jesus and was healed (see Matt 9:20-22). According to the law, she should not have touched Jesus. And this may explain why she came "with fear and trembling" when Jesus called her forward (Mark 5:33). But no contamination, of course, could make Jesus unclean!

15:31 God's holiness, and his demand for holiness from his people, gave these laws life-and-death importance.

16:1-10 The Day of Atonement was the most solemn day on Israel's calendar. The emphasis in this chapter is on the necessity of sin being atoned for so that God's people may be forgiven and reconciled to him.

Aaron, the high priest, was the central figure in this drama. He could not enter whenever he wanted into **the holy place** where the **ark** of the covenant was. If he did, he would **die**. Why? Because, the Lord said, **I appear** there **in the cloud above the mercy seat**—the gold cover over the ark (16:2). In other words, this small cubicle in the tabernacle, and later the temple, literally housed the glorious, holy presence of God. Thus,

God alone would decide who could enter his throne room and under what circumstances it could happen.

16:11-15 Aaron entered and left the most holy place three times during the day's sacrifices and rituals (16:12-15). The first time was to burn **fragrant incense** before the Lord (16:12-13). The second time was to get some of **the bull's blood** from his sin offering and sprinkle it **against the east side of the mercy seat** and **before the mercy seat** (16:14). His third entrance into the most holy place was to bring the blood of the **male goat for the people's sin offering** and sprinkle it on and in front of the **mercy seat** (16:15).

finger against the east side of the mercy seat; then he will sprinkle some of the blood with his finger before the mercy seat seven times.[a]

15 "When he slaughters the male goat for the people's sin offering and brings its blood inside the curtain, he will do the same with its blood as he did with the bull's blood: He is to sprinkle it against the mercy seat and in front of it. **16** He will make atonement for the most holy place in this way for all their sins because of the Israelites' impurities and rebellious acts.[b] He will do the same for the tent of meeting that remains among them, because it is surrounded by their impurities. **17** No one may be in the tent of meeting from the time he enters to make atonement in the most holy place until he leaves after he has made atonement for himself, his household, and the whole assembly of Israel.[c] **18** Then he will go out to the altar that is before the LORD and make atonement for it. He is to take some of the bull's blood and some of the goat's blood and put it on the horns on all sides of the altar. **19** He is to sprinkle some of the blood on it with his finger seven times to cleanse and set it apart[d] from the Israelites' impurities.[e] **20** "When he has finished making atonement for the most holy place, the tent of meeting, and the altar, he is to present the live male goat. **21** Aaron will lay both his hands on the head of the live goat and confess[f] over it all the Israelites' iniquities[g] and rebellious acts — all their sins.[h] He is to put them on the goat's head and send it away into the wilderness[i] by the man appointed for the task.[A] **22** The goat will carry all their iniquities into a desolate land,[j] and the man will release it there.

23 "Then Aaron is to enter the tent of meeting, take off the linen garments[k] he wore when he entered the most holy place, and leave them there. **24** He will bathe his body with water in a holy place[l] and put

on his clothes.[m] Then he must go out and sacrifice his burnt offering and the people's burnt offering; he will make atonement for himself and for the people. **25** He is to burn the fat of the sin offering on the altar. **26** The man who released the goat for an uninhabitable place is to wash his clothes and bathe his body with water; afterward he may reenter the camp. **27** The bull for the sin offering and the goat for the sin offering, whose blood was brought into the most holy place to make atonement, must be brought outside the camp[n] and their hide,[o] flesh, and waste burned.[p] **28** The one who burns them is to wash his clothes and bathe himself with water; afterward he may reenter the camp.

29 "This is to be a permanent statute[q] for you: In the seventh month, on the tenth day of the month you are to practice self-denial[r] and do no work,[s] both the native and the alien[t] who resides among you. **30** Atonement will be made for you on this day to cleanse you,[u] and you will be clean from all your sins before the LORD. **31** It is a Sabbath[v] of complete rest for you,[w] and you must practice self-denial; it is a permanent statute. **32** The priest who is anointed and ordained[B,x] to serve as high priest[y] in place of his father will make atonement. He will put on the linen garments, the holy garments, **33** and make atonement for the most holy place. He will make atonement for the tent of meeting and the altar and will make atonement for the priests and all the people of the assembly. **34** This is to be a permanent statute for you, to make atonement for the Israelites once a year[z] because of all their sins." And all this was done as the LORD commanded Moses.

FORBIDDEN SACRIFICES

17 The LORD spoke to Moses: **2** "Speak to Aaron, his sons, and all the Israelites and tell them: This is what the LORD

[a] 16:14 Lv 4:6; Heb 9:4-5
[b] 16:16 Ex 22:9
[c] 16:17 1Tm 2:5; Heb 9:7
[d] 16:19 Lv 8:10
[e] 16:17-19 Heb 9:11-14
[f] 16:21 Lv 5:5; 26:40; Nm 5:7; 2Ch 30:22; Neh 1:6; 9:2; Dn 9:4,20
[g] Lv 5:1
[h] Ezr 10:1; Neh 9:2-3; Dn 9:20; 2Co 5:21; Jms 5:16; 1Jn 1:9
[i] Lv 14:7
[j] 16:22 Ps 103:12; Is 53:4,6,11-12; Jn 1:29; Heb 9:28; 1Pt 2:24; 1Jn 3:5
[k] 16:23 Lv 6:11
[l] 16:24 Ex 29:31; Lv 6:16,26-27; 7:6; 10:13; 24:9; Ec 8:10; Ezk 42:13
[m] 16:24 Lv 8:6-9
[n] 16:27 Lv 8:17
[o] Lv 7:8
[p] Lv 4:11-12; Heb 13:11-12
[q] 16:29 Ex 28:43; Lv 11:46
[r] Lv 23:27-32; Nm 29:7; Ps 35:13; Is 58:3,5; Dn 10:12
[s] Ex 12:16; Lv 23:3,28,31; Nm 29:7; Jr 17:22
[t] Ex 12:49; Lv 17:15; 18:26
[u] 16:30 Lv 13:6
[v] 16:31 Gn 2:2
[w] Ex 16:23; 31:15; 35:2; Lv 23:3,24,32,39; 25:4-5
[x] 16:32 Ex 29:33
[y] Lv 8:12,33
[z] 16:34 Heb 9:7

[A] 16:21 Lit *wilderness in the hand of a ready man*   [B] 16:32 Lit *and will fill his hand*

16:20-22 Aaron was to **lay both his hands on the head of the live goat and confess over it** all the **sins** of the people (16:21). In this way he ceremonially transferred the nation's sins to the goat, which was sent into the wilderness—symbolizing the removal of their sins from the camp. The word "scapegoat" may come to mind when you read this since the goat was to bear the nation's sins.

For believers in Jesus Christ, this ceremony offers strong encouragement. Since our sins too have been sent away, so to speak, we cannot lose our salvation. The scapegoat isn't coming back tomorrow to return to us all the sins we thought

were gone. If you have trusted Jesus Christ as your Savior, your sins have been removed "as far as the east is from the west" (Ps 103:12).

Watching the goat being led away served as a vivid illustration to the Israelites that their sins had been removed and fully atoned for. Yet, it's important to remember that this ritual had to be repeated annually (see Lev 16:34). Only through Christ do sinful people have a sacrifice that was offered "once for all time" (Heb 10:10-14).

16:27 The unused parts of the offering were **brought outside the camp** and **burned**. The author of Hebrews alludes to the practice and

says this was also true of Jesus Christ who "suffered outside the gate" of the city (Heb 13:11-12). Therefore, Christians should identify with their Lord and "go to him outside the camp." In other words, we must be willing to bear "his disgrace" (Heb 13:13).

16:32-34 The Day of Atonement was to be established as an annual event. When Jesus offered himself as our great high priest, he made atonement for our sins once and for all (see Heb 10:10). The Day of Atonement was fulfilled in him.

17:1-6 Beginning with chapter 17, the focus of Leviticus turns to the subject of how God's people were to be holy in their everyday

[a] 17:3 Dt 12:5-21
[b] 17:4 Ex 22:1; Lv 20:9; Nm 35:27; Dt 19:10; Ps 55:23; Is 33:15
[c] Gn 9:6
[d] Nm 9:13
[e] 17:5 Gn 46:1; Ex 34:25
[f] Lv 7:11
[g] 17:7 2Ch 11:15; Is 13:21; 34:14
[h] Dt 22:21
[i] Gn 26:5; Ex 12:14; Lv 3:17; Nm 9:3; Dt 6:2; 8:11
[j] 17:8 Gn 19:9; Ex 2:22
[k] 17:10 Gn 9:4; Lv 3:17
[l] 17:11 Mt 26:28; Mk 14:24; Rm 3:25; 5:9; Eph 1:7; Col 1:14,20; Heb 13:12; 1Jn 1:7; Rv 1:5

[m] 17:13 Gn 25:27
[n] Ex 29:12; Lv 17:4; Dt 12:16,24; 15:23; Ezk 24:7
[o] 17:14 Lv 3:17
[p] 17:15 Lv 16:29
[q] Ex 22:31; Lv 7:24; 22:8; Dt 14:21
[r] 18:2 Nm 15:41
[s] 18:3 Lv 11:45; 19:34,36
[t] Dt 18:9-12
[u] Ex 23:24; Lv 18:24-30; 2Kg 17:7-8
[v] 18:4 Lv 18:26; Nm 29:18; Jos 6:15; Ezr 3:4; Jb 9:19; Ps 119:13; Is 1:17; Ezk 18:5
[w] Lv 7:7
[x] 18:5 Dt 4:1; Neh 9:29; Ezk 20:13,21,25; 33:12; Rm 7:10; Php 1:21
[y] Dt 6:24; Pr 6:23; Lk 10:26-28; Rm 7:10; 10:5; Gl 3:12
[z] 18:6 Gn 20:4
[aa] 1Tm 4:3
[ab] 18:7 Ezk 22:10
[ac] 18:8 Gn 35:22; 49:4; Lv 20:11; 2Sm 16:21-22; Am 2:7; 1Co 5:1
[ad] Lv 20:11
[ae] 18:9 Lv 20:17; Dt 27:22; 2Sm 13:11-14; Ezk 22:11

has commanded: **3** Anyone from the house of Israel who slaughters[a] an ox, sheep, or goat in the camp, or slaughters it outside the camp, **4** instead of bringing it to the entrance to the tent of meeting to present it as an offering to the LORD before his tabernacle — that person will be considered guilty.[A,b] He has shed blood[c] and is to be cut off from his people.[d] **5** This is so the Israelites will bring to the LORD the sacrifices[e] they have been offering in the open country. They are to bring them to the priest at the entrance to the tent of meeting and offer them as fellowship sacrifices[f] to the LORD. **6** The priest will then splatter the blood on the LORD's altar at the entrance to the tent of meeting and burn the fat as a pleasing aroma to the LORD. **7** They must no longer offer their sacrifices to the goat-demons[g] that they have prostituted[h] themselves with. This will be a permanent statute[i] for them throughout their generations.

8 "Say to them: Anyone from the house of Israel or from the aliens[j] who reside among them who offers a burnt offering or a sacrifice **9** but does not bring it to the entrance to the tent of meeting to sacrifice it to the LORD, that person is to be cut off from his people.

EATING BLOOD AND CARCASSES PROHIBITED

10 "Anyone from the house of Israel or from the aliens who reside among them who eats any blood,[k] I will turn[B] against that person who eats blood and cut him off from his people. **11** For the life of a creature is in the blood, and I have appointed it to you to make atonement on the altar for[C] your lives, since it is the lifeblood that makes atonement.[l] **12** Therefore I say to the Israelites: None of you and no alien who resides among you may eat blood.

13 "Any Israelite or alien residing among them, who hunts[m] down a wild animal or bird that may be eaten must drain its blood[n] and cover it with dirt. **14** Since the life of every creature is its blood, I have told the Israelites: You are not to eat the blood of any creature,[o] because the life of every creature is its blood; whoever eats it must be cut off.

15 "Every person, whether the native or the resident alien,[p] who eats an animal that died a natural death or was mauled by wild beasts[q] is to wash his clothes and bathe with water, and he will remain unclean until evening; then he will be clean. **16** But if he does not wash his clothes and bathe himself, he will bear his iniquity."

PROHIBITED PAGAN PRACTICES

18 The LORD spoke to Moses: **2** "Speak to the Israelites and tell them: I am the LORD your God.[r] **3** Do not follow the practices of the land of Egypt,[s] where you used to live, or follow the practices of the land of Canaan,[t] where I am bringing you. You must not follow their customs.[u] **4** You are to practice my ordinances[v] and you are to keep my statutes[w] by following them; I am the LORD your God. **5** Keep my statutes and ordinances; a person will live[x] if he does them.[y] I am the LORD.

6 "You are not to come near[z] any close relative[D] for sexual intercourse;[aa] I am the LORD. **7** You are not to violate the intimacy that belongs to your father[ab] and mother.[E] She is your mother; you must not have sexual intercourse with her. **8** You are not to have sex with your father's wife;[ac] she is your father's family.[ad] **9** You are not to have sexual intercourse with your sister, either your father's daughter or your mother's,[ae] whether born at home or born elsewhere. You are not to have sex with her. **10** You are not to have sexual intercourse with your son's daughter or your daughter's

[A] 17:4 Lit tabernacle — blood will be charged against that person   [B] 17:10 Lit will set my face   [C] 17:11 Or to ransom   [D] 18:6 Lit any flesh of his flesh
[E] 18:7 Lit Do not uncover your father's nakedness and your mother's nakedness

lives. For this reason, these chapters are often called Israel's "Holiness Code."

The first command was a prohibition against sacrificing animals anywhere except at the **tabernacle**. Sacrifices were to be performed by the Lord's authorized priest in the proper way (17:3-4). This not only ensured the proper worship of Israel's holy God, but also prevented the Israelites from joining in the detestable practice of offering sacrifices to the false gods of the nations around them. **17:7-9** Apparently some Israelites had been offering sacrifices to **goat-demons**, which

the Lord considered an act of spiritual prostitution (17:7).

17:10-12 Blood is not merely *a* means of atonement but *the* means of atonement. That's why the author of Hebrews insisted that "without the shedding of blood there is no forgiveness" (Heb 9:22). The animal was to die as a substitute for the sinner. Ultimately all of these sacrificial animals pointed to the Savior who fulfilled Israel's sacrificial system (see Heb 9:25-26). Jesus is the Lamb of God who takes away the sin of the world (see John 1:29).

18:1-5 What's the connection between his identity as their God and the Israelites' sex lives (18:1-5, 6-20)? Since they were God's people, Israel's sexual practices were to be completely different from those of the land where they came from (**Egypt**) and where they were going (**Canaan**). God's people were to follow his holy **statutes** rather than pagan **customs** (18:3-5). The Lord designed sex, so he gets to decide the parameters in which it is to happen. We can trust that engaging in it his way will always bring us the most joy and will save us from devastating consequences.

daughter, for they are your family.[A] [11] You are not to have sexual intercourse with your father's wife's daughter, who is adopted by[B] your father; she is your sister. [12] You are not to have sexual intercourse with your father's sister;[a] she is your father's close relative. [13] You are not to have sexual intercourse with your mother's sister,[b] for she is your mother's close relative. [14] You are not to violate the intimacy that belongs to[c] your father's brother by approaching his wife to have sexual intercourse; she is your aunt.[c] [15] You are not to have sexual intercourse with your daughter-in-law.[d] She is your son's wife; you are not to have sex with her. [16] You are not to have sexual intercourse with your brother's wife; she is your brother's family.[e] [17] You are not to have sexual intercourse with a woman and her daughter.[f] You are not to marry her son's daughter or her daughter's daughter and have sex with her. They are close relatives; it is depraved.[g] [18] You are not to marry a woman as a rival to her sister and have sexual intercourse with her during her sister's lifetime.[h]

[19] "You are not to approach[i] a woman during her menstrual impurity to have sexual intercourse with her.[j] [20] You are not to have sexual intercourse with[D] your neighbor's wife, defiling yourself with her.[k]

[21] "You are not to sacrifice any of your children in the fire[E] to Molech.[l] Do not profane the name[m] of your God; I am the LORD. [22] You are not to sleep with a man as with a woman;[n] it is detestable.[o] [23] You are not to have sexual intercourse with[F] any animal, defiling yourself with it; a woman is not to present herself to an animal to mate with it;[p] it is a perversion.

[24] "Do not defile yourselves by any of these practices, for the nations I am driving out before you have defiled themselves by all these things. [25] The land has become

defiled, so I am punishing it for its iniquity, and the land will vomit out its inhabitants.[q] [26] But you are to keep my statutes and ordinances. You must not commit any of these detestable acts — not the native or the alien who resides among you. [27] For the people who were in the land prior to you have committed all these detestable acts, and the land has become defiled. [28] If you defile the land, it will vomit[r] you out as it has vomited out the nations that were before you. [29] Any person who does any of these detestable practices is to be cut off from his people. [30] You must keep my instruction to not do any of the detestable customs[s] that were practiced before you, so that you do not defile yourselves by them; I am the LORD your God."

LAWS OF HOLINESS

19 The LORD spoke to Moses: [2] "Speak to the entire Israelite community and tell them: Be holy[t] because I, the LORD your God, am holy.[u]

[3] "Each of you is to respect his mother and father.[v] You are to keep my Sabbaths; I am the LORD your God. [4] Do not turn to idols[w] or make cast images[x] of gods for yourselves;[y] I am the LORD your God.

[5] "When you offer a fellowship sacrifice to the LORD, sacrifice it so that you may be accepted. [6] It is to be eaten on the day you sacrifice it or on the next day, but what remains on the third day must be burned.[z] [7] If any is eaten on the third day, it is a repulsive thing; it will not be accepted.[aa] [8] Anyone who eats it will bear his iniquity, for he has profaned what is holy to the LORD. That person is to be cut off from his people.[ab]

[9] "When you reap the harvest of your land, you are not to reap to the very edge of your field or gather the gleanings[ac] of your harvest. [10] Do not strip your vineyard bare or gather its fallen grapes. Leave

[a] 18:12 Ex 6:20
[b] 18:13 Lv 20:19
[c] 18:14 Lv 20:20
[d] 18:15 Gn 38:16; Lv 20:12; Ezk 22:11
[e] 18:16 Lv 20:21; Dt 25:5-10; Mt 14:3-4; Mk 6:18
[f] 18:17 Lv 20:14; Dt 27:23; Am 2:7
[g] Lv 19:29
[h] 18:18 Gn 29:21-28
[i] 18:19 Gn 20:4
[j] Lv 15:19-24; 20:18; Ezk 18:6
[k] 18:20 Ex 20:14; Lv 20:10; Nm 5:11-31; Dt 22:22; 1Co 6:9; Heb 13:4
[l] 18:21 Lv 20:2-5; Dt 18:10; 1Kg 11:7; 2Kg 23:10; Jr 32:35; Ac 7:43
[m] Ex 20:7; Lv 20:3; Jn 10:25
[n] 18:22 Gn 19:5; Lv 20:13; Dt 23:18; Rm 1:26-27; 1Co 6:9-11; Gl 5:21; 1Tm 1:10; Rv 21:8
[o] Gn 46:34
[p] 18:23 Ex 22:19

[q] 18:25 Nm 35:33-34; Dt 9:4; Ezr 9:11; Is 24:5-6; Jr 2:7; Ezk 36:1
[r] 18:28 Lv 20:22; Dt 8:20
[s] 18:30 Lv 7:7
[t] 19:2 Ex 19:5-6
[u] Lv 11:44; 21:8
[v] 19:3 Ex 20:12; 21:15
[w] 19:4 Lv 26:1
[x] Nm 33:52
[y] Ex 20:3,23; 32:31; Dt 4:15-16
[z] 19:6 Lv 7:17
[aa] 19:7 Lv 1:4
[ab] 19:7-8 Lv 7:18,20
[ac] 19:9 Lv 23:22; Dt 24:19-22; Ru 2:2-7,15-19,23; Is 17:5

18:6-24 All these things had been practiced by the Canaanite inhabitants of the land (18:24).

18:21 The command **not to sacrifice any ... children in the fire to Molech,** the pagan god of the Ammonites, is a reminder of the great depravity of which humans are capable. Religious fervor sometimes drove ancient peoples to sacrifice their own children to appease the "gods"—who were really demons in disguise (see Ps 106:37; 1 Cor 10:20). Today child sacrifice is more likely to take place at the altar of sexual freedom. The abortion industry has slaughtered millions.

18:24-26 That God was about to make the land **vomit out its inhabitants** sounds harsh in our day of political correctness because so many people hold to such a low view of God (18:25). To them, he is just a tame god of their own creation whose role is to affirm their lifestyle choices—whether they are based on Scripture or not. Our true Creator, however, is a holy and righteous God who considers sin **detestable** (18:26). This is the God with whom we are confronted.

19:1-2 Many have the mistaken notion that keeping religious laws or performing rituals is all it takes to please God. But Leviticus 19

makes it clear that holy living in every aspect of life is what our holy God requires. It's what provides access to his blessings.

19:9-10 In Scripture, extending charity included providing an opportunity to work. God's people were told to leave a portion in their fields, so that the poor could gather it for themselves. People thus could turn poverty into productivity in response to the charitable opportunities provided. This is much more helpful to someone who has fallen on hard times than simply lining up for a check from the government. If a person *can* work, then biblically he is expected *to* work (see

www.bhpublishinggroup.com/qr/te/03-19

them for the poor[a] and the resident alien;[b] I am the LORD your God.

11 "Do not steal.[c] Do not act deceptively[d] or lie[e] to one another. **12** Do not swear falsely by my name, profaning the name of your God;[f] I am the LORD.

13 "Do not oppress[g] your neighbor or rob[h] him. The wages due a hired worker[i] must not remain with you until morning. **14** Do not curse the deaf or put a stumbling block in front of the blind,[j] but you are to fear your God;[k] I am the LORD.[l]

15 "Do not act unjustly[m] when deciding a case. Do not be partial[n] to the poor or give preference to the rich;[o] judge your neighbor fairly. **16** Do not go about spreading slander[p] among your people; do not jeopardize[A] your neighbor's life; I am the LORD.

17 "Do not harbor hatred against your brother.[B,q] Rebuke your neighbor directly, and you will not incur guilt because of him.[r] **18** Do not take revenge[s] or bear a grudge against members of your community, but love your neighbor as yourself;[t] I am the LORD.

19 "You are to keep my statutes. Do not crossbreed two different kinds of your livestock, sow your fields with two kinds of seed, or put on a garment made of two kinds of material.[u]

20 "If a man has sexual intercourse with a woman who is a slave designated for another man, but she has not been redeemed[v] or given her freedom, there must be punishment.[c] They are not to be put to death, because she had not been freed. **21** However, he must bring a ram as his guilt[D] offering to the LORD at the entrance to the tent of meeting.[W] **22** The priest will make atonement on his behalf before the LORD with the ram of the guilt offering for the sin he has committed, and he will be forgiven for the sin he committed.

23 "When you come into the land and plant any kind of tree for food, you are to consider the fruit forbidden.[E] It will be forbidden to you for three years; it is not to be eaten. **24** In the fourth year all its fruit is to be consecrated as a praise offering[x] to the LORD. **25** But in the fifth year you may eat its fruit. In this way its yield will increase for you;[y] I am the LORD your God.

26 "You are not to eat anything with blood in it.[F,z] You are not to practice divination[aa] or witchcraft.[ab] **27** You are not to cut off the hair at the sides of your head or mar the edge of your beard.[ac] **28** You are not to make gashes on your bodies for the dead[ad] or put tattoo marks on yourselves; I am the LORD.

29 "Do not debase[G,ae] your daughter by making her a prostitute,[af] or the land will be prostituted and filled with depravity. **30** Keep my Sabbaths and revere my sanctuary;[ag] I am the LORD.

31 "Do not turn to mediums[H,ah] or consult spiritists,[I,ai] or you will be defiled by them; I am the LORD your God.

32 "You are to rise in the presence of the elderly and honor the old.[aj] Fear your God; I am the LORD.

33 "When an alien resides with you in your land, you must not oppress[ak] him. **34** You will regard the alien who resides with you as the native-born among you. You are to love him as yourself,[al] for you were aliens in the land of Egypt;[am] I am the LORD your God.

35 "Do not be unfair[an] in measurements of length, weight, or volume. **36** You are to have honest balances,[ao] honest weights, an honest dry measure,[J] and an honest liquid measure;[K,ap] I am the LORD your God, who brought you out of the land of

---

[a] 19:10 Dt 15:11
[b] Ex 2:22; Dt 24:20-21; Is 17:5-6; 24:13
[c] 19:11 Ex 20:15; 22:1; Rm 13:9; Eph 4:28
[d] Pr 30:9; Is 30:9; 59:13; Jr 5:12; Hs 4:2; 7:3; 9:2; 10:13; Nah 3:1; Hab 3:17; Zch 13:4
[e] Gn 21:23; Ex 20:16; 1Sm 15:29; Ps 44:18; 89:34; Is 63:8; Eph 4:25
[f] 19:12 Ex 20:7; Lv 18:21; 20:3; Mal 3:5; Jms 5:12
[g] 19:13 Dt 24:14
[h] Dt 28:29
[i] Ex 12:45; 22:14; Lv 22:10; 25:6,40,50,53; Is 7:20; Jr 46:21; Ezk 18:7; Mal 3:5; Jms 5:4
[j] 19:14 Ex 4:11; Dt 27:18
[k] Ps 147:11; Pr 1:7; Ac 10:2; Rv 14:7
[l] Ex 31:13
[m] 19:15 Dt 25:16
[n] Ex 23:2-3; Dt 1:17; Jms 2:9
[o] Gn 24:35; Jb 34:19
[p] 19:16 Ps 15:3; Jr 6:28; 9:4; Lk 6:22; 2Co 6:8; 12:20; Eph 4:31; Col 3:8; Ti 3:2; 1Pt 2:1; 4:4; Rv 2:9
[q] 19:17 2Th 3:15; 1Jn 2:9,11; 3:15; 4:20
[r] Pr 9:8; 27:5; Ezk 3:18; Mt 18:15; Gl 6:1
[s] 19:18 Dt 32:35; Pr 20:22; Rm 12:17,19; Heb 10:30; Rv 19:2
[t] Pr 17:17; Mt 5:43; 22:39; Mk 12:31; Lk 10:27; Rm 13:9; Gl 5:14; Jms 2:8

[u] 19:19 Dt 22:9-11   [v] 19:20 Ex 6:6; 21:7-11; Lv 27:29; Dt 22:23-27

[W] 19:21 Ex 27:21   [X] 19:24 Jdg 9:27   [Y] 19:25 Lv 25:18-22   [Z] 19:26 Gn 9:4; Lv 3:17; 17:10-12; 1Sm 14:32-35; Ezk 33:25   [aa] 1Kg 20:33   [ab] Dt 18:10,14; Jdg 9:37; 2Kg 21:6; 2Ch 33:6; Is 2:6; 57:3; Jr 27:9   [ac] 19:27 Lv 21:5; Dt 14:1; 2Sm 10:4-5; Jr 41:5; 48:37; Ezk 5:1-5; 44:20   [ad] 19:28 1Kg 18:28; Jr 16:6; 41:5; 47:5; 48:37   [ae] 19:29 Lv 21:12   [af] Ex 34:31; Lv 21:9; Dt 23:17-18   [ag] 19:30 Ex 15:17; Lv 20:3; 26:2; Nm 19:20   [ah] 19:31 Lv 20:6   [ai] Dt 18:11; Ac 16:16   [aj] 19:32 Jb 12:12; 32:4; Pr 23:22; Lm 5:12; 1Tm 5:1   [ak] 19:33 Dt 23:16   [al] 19:34 Lv 19:18   [am] Ex 23:9; Lv 18:3; Dt 10:19; 23:7   [an] 19:35 Dt 25:16   [ao] 19:36 Hs 12:8; Am 8:5; Mc 6:11   [ap] Dt 25:13-16; Pr 16:11; Ezk 45:10

[A] 19:16 Lit *not stand against*   [B] 19:17 Or *your fellow Israelite*   [C] 19:20 Or *compensation*   [D] 19:21 Or *restitution*   [E] 19:23 Lit *uncircumcised*   [F] 19:26 Or *anything over its blood*   [G] 19:29 Lit *profane*   [H] 19:31 Or *spirits of the dead*   [I] 19:31 Or *familiar spirits*   [J] 19:36 Lit *honest ephah*   [K] 19:36 Lit *honest hin*

---

2 Thess 3:10). Gleaning provided the opportunity for **the poor** to help themselves. This gave opportunity to maximize personal God-given potential and live with dignity. In the book of Ruth, Naomi and her daughter-in-law benefited from this system (see Ruth 2).

19:11-18 In all things, Israel was to follow this principle: **love your neighbor as yourself** (19:18). As both Jesus and Paul pointed out, Scripture is summed up in the commands to love God and neighbor (see Mark 12:29-31; Gal 5:14).

19:26,29-31 Prohibitions against occult practices and consulting **mediums** were intended to establish and set apart the Israelites as God's holy people (19:31). Saul, Israel's first king, would stray so far from following God that he would turn to the world of the occult for guidance (see 1 Sam 28:3-25)!

19:32 The exhortation to **honor the old** is still needed today. In a culture that worships youthfulness, we need to be reminded that "gray hair is a glorious crown" (Prov 16:31).

Godly older men and women have experience, maturity, and wisdom that young people can ignore—but only to their own peril. Make time for the aged.

19:34 Many foreigners attached themselves to Israel as the nation moved through the wilderness and settled in Canaan, and they were to be treated well. The Israelites were to consider them as their own brothers and sisters—and treat them accordingly.

Egypt. ³⁷Keep all my statutes and all my ordinances and do them; I am the LORD."

MOLECH WORSHIP AND SPIRITISM

20 The LORD spoke to Moses: ² "Say to the Israelites: Any Israelite or alien residing in Israel who gives any of his children to Molech^a must be put to death; the people of the country are to stone him.^b ³ I will turn^A against that man and cut him off from his people, because he gave his offspring to Molech, defiling my sanctuary^c and profaning my holy name.^d ⁴ But if the people of the country look the other way when that man^B gives any of his children to Molech, and do not put him to death, ⁵ then I will turn against that man and his family, and cut off from their people both him and all who follow^c him in prostituting^e themselves with Molech.

⁶ "Whoever turns to mediums^{D,f} or spiritists^E and prostitutes himself with them, I will turn against that person and cut him off from his people. ⁷ Consecrate yourselves and be holy, for I am the LORD your God. ⁸ Keep my statutes and do them; I am the LORD who sets you apart.

FAMILY AND SEXUAL OFFENSES

⁹ "If anyone curses his father or mother, he must be put to death.^g He has cursed his father or mother; his death is his own fault.^F

¹⁰ "If a man commits adultery^h with a married woman — if he commits adultery with his neighbor's wife — both the adulterer and the adulteress must be put to death. ¹¹ If a man sleeps with his father's wife, he has violated the intimacy that belongs to his father.^{G,i} Both of them must be put to death; their death is their own fault.^H ¹² If a man sleeps with his daughter-in-law,^j both of them must be put to death. They have acted perversely; their death is their own fault. ¹³ If a man sleeps with a man as with a woman,^k they have both committed a detestable act.^I They must be put to

death; their death is their own fault. ¹⁴ If a man marriesⁱ a woman and her mother,^m it is depraved. Both he and they must be burned,ⁿ so that there will be no depravity among you. ¹⁵ If a man has sexual intercourse with^j an animal, he must be put to death; you are also to kill the animal. ¹⁶ If a woman approaches any animal and mates with it, you are to kill the woman and the animal.^o They must be put to death; their death is their own fault. ¹⁷ If a man marries his sister,^p whether his father's daughter or his mother's daughter, and they have sexual relations,^{K,q} it is a disgrace.^r They are to be cut off publicly from their people. He has had sexual intercourse with his sister; he will bear his iniquity. ¹⁸ If a man sleeps with a menstruating woman and has sexual intercourse with her, he has exposed the source of her flow, and she has uncovered the source of her blood.^s Both of them are to be cut off from their people. ¹⁹ You must not have sexual intercourse with your mother's sister or your father's sister,^t for it is exposing one's own blood relative; both people will bear their iniquity. ²⁰ If a man sleeps with his aunt, he has violated the intimacy that belongs to his uncle;^{L,u} they will bear their guilt and die childless. ²¹ If a man marries his brother's wife, it is impurity.^v He has violated the intimacy that belongs to his brother;^{M,w} they will be childless.

HOLINESS IN THE LAND

²² "You are to keep all my statutes and all my ordinances, and do them, so that the land where I am bringing you to live will not vomit you out.^x ²³ You must not follow the statutes of the nations I am driving out before you, for they did all these things, and I abhorred them.^y ²⁴ And I promised you: You will inherit their land, since I will give it to you to possess, a land flowing with milk and honey.^z I am the LORD your God who set you apart from the peoples.

^a 20:2 Lv 18:21; Dt 18:10; 2Kg 23:10; Ac 7:43
^b Lv 24:14; Nm 15:35–36; Dt 17:2–7; 21:21; Jos 7:25
^c 20:3 Ex 15:17
^d Lv 18:21; 19:12; 22:2,32; Jr 34:16; Ezk 36:20; 39:7; Am 2:7
^e 20:5 Dt 22:21
^f 20:6 Lv 19:31; 20:27; Dt 18:11; 1Sm 28:3,7–9; 2Kg 21:6; 23:24; 1Ch 10:13; 2Ch 33:6; Is 8:19; 19:3; 29:4
^g 20:9 Ex 21:17; Dt 21:18–21; 27:16; Pr 20:20; 30:11; Mt 15:4; Mk 7:10
^h 20:10 Ex 20:14; Dt 5:18; 22:22; 31:16; Pr 6:32; Mal 3:5; Mt 5:27–28,32; 19:9,18
ⁱ 20:11 Lv 18:8; Dt 22:30; 27:20; 1Co 5:1
^j 20:12 Gn 38:16; Lv 18:15; Ezk 22:11
^k 20:13 Gn 19:5
^l Gn 46:34

^m 20:14 Lv 18:17
ⁿ Gn 38:24; Lv 18:22; 21:9; Jdg 14:15; Rv 17:16
^o 20:15–16 Ex 22:19
^p 20:17 Lv 18:13
^q Lv 18:9
^r Lv 19:29
^s 20:18 Lv 18:19
^t 20:19 Ex 6:20; Lv 18:12–13
^u 20:20 Lv 18:14
^v 20:21 Mk 6:18
^w Lv 18:16
^x 20:22 Lv 18:25
^y 20:23 Ex 23:24; Lv 18:3
^z 20:24 Ex 3:8; 13:5; Nm 14:8; 16:13–14

^A 20:3 Lit *will set my face*, also in vv. 5,6   ^B 20:4 Lit *country ever close their eyes from that man when he*   ^C 20:5 Lit *prostitute themselves with*   ^D 20:6 Or *spirits of the dead*   ^E 20:6 Or *familiar spirits*   ^F 20:9 Lit *his blood on him*   ^G 20:11 Lit *has uncovered his father's nakedness*   ^H 20:11 Lit *their blood on them*, also in vv. 12,13,16,27   ^I 20:14 Lit *takes*, also in vv. 17,21   ^J 20:15 Lit *man gives his emission to*   ^K 20:17 Lit *and he sees her nakedness and she sees his nakedness*   ^L 20:20 Lit *has uncovered his uncle's nakedness*   ^M 20:21 Lit *has uncovered his brother's nakedness*

20:1-5 To give one's **children to Molech** (19:2-5) no doubt meant to burn them as a child sacrifice (see the note on 18:21).
20:7-8 To be sanctified or set apart is to be separated from the common and ordinary and made special. Many of us have "sanctified" places in our homes. When I was growing up, our living room was off limits most of the time. It was set apart for guests.

Leviticus teaches that God has set apart his people for his use and glory. Yet, God's people are also to **consecrate** themselves and **be holy** (20:7). This paradox points to what we could call the dynamic tension of the Christian life. We are set apart by God, in the sense of being his chosen people, at the moment each one of us is saved. But we are also to set ourselves apart in the decisions and choices we make.

Sanctification (becoming more like Jesus) is not some passive process whereby we simply go through our days expecting God to rubber stamp our choices and bless us. He sanctifies, but he also calls us to sanctify ourselves by choosing to live according to his standards.
20:22-23 If God's people followed in the tracks of the Canaanites, they would be expelled from the land too.

25 Therefore you are to distinguish the clean animal from the unclean one, and the unclean bird from the clean one. Do not become contaminated[a] by any land animal, bird, or whatever crawls on the ground; I have set these apart as unclean for you.[b] **26** You are to be holy to me because I, the LORD, am holy, and I have set you apart from the nations to be mine.[c]

27 "A man or a woman who is[A] a medium or a spiritist must be put to death. They are to be stoned; their death is their own fault."

THE HOLINESS OF THE PRIESTS

21 The LORD said to Moses: "Speak to Aaron's sons, the priests, and tell them: A priest is not to make himself ceremonially unclean for a dead person among his relatives,[d] **2** except for his immediate family: his mother, father, son, daughter, or brother. **3** He may make himself unclean for his unmarried virgin sister in his immediate family. **4** He is not to make himself unclean for those related to him by marriage[B] and so defile himself.

5 "Priests may not make bald spots on their heads, shave the edge of their beards, or make gashes on their bodies.[e] **6** They are to be holy to their God and not profane the name of their God.[f] For they present the fire offerings to the LORD, the food of their God, and they must be holy. **7** They are not to marry a woman defiled by prostitution.[C,g] They are not to marry one divorced[h] by her husband, for the priest is holy to his God. **8** You are to consider him holy since he presents the food of your God. He will be holy to you because I, the LORD who sets you apart, am holy. **9** If a priest's daughter defiles herself by promiscuity,[D,i] she defiles her father; she must be burned to death.[j]

10 "The priest who is highest among his brothers, who has had the anointing oil poured on his head and has been ordained[E] to wear the clothes, must not dishevel his hair[F] or tear his clothes.[k] **11** He must not go near any dead person or make himself unclean even for his father or mother.[l] **12** He must not leave the sanctuary or he will desecrate the sanctuary of his God, for the consecration of

the anointing oil of his God is on him;[m] I am the LORD.

13 "He is to marry a woman who is a virgin. **14** He is not to marry a widow,[n] a divorced woman,[o] or one defiled by prostitution. He is to marry a virgin from his own people, **15** so that he does not corrupt his bloodline[G] among his people, for I am the LORD who sets him apart."

PHYSICAL DEFECTS AND PRIESTS

16 The LORD spoke to Moses: **17** "Tell Aaron: None of your descendants throughout your generations who has a physical defect[p] is to come near to present the food[q] of his God. **18** No man who has any defect is to come near: no man who is blind, lame, facially disfigured, or deformed; **19** no man who has a broken foot or hand, **20** or who is a hunchback or a dwarf,[H,r] or who has an eye defect, a festering rash, scabs,[s] or a crushed testicle.[t] **21** No descendant of the priest Aaron who has a defect is to come near to present the fire offerings to the LORD. He has a defect and is not to come near to present the food of his God. **22** He may eat the food of his God from what is especially holy as well as from what is holy. **23** But because he has a defect, he must not go near the curtain[u] or approach the altar. He is not to desecrate my holy places, for I am the LORD who sets them apart."[v] **24** Moses said this to Aaron and his sons and to all the Israelites.

PRIESTS AND THEIR FOOD

22 The LORD spoke to Moses: **2** "Tell Aaron and his sons to deal respectfully with the holy offerings of the Israelites that they have consecrated to me, so they do not profane my holy name;[w] I am the LORD. **3** Say to them: If any man from any of your descendants throughout your generations is in a state of uncleanness yet approaches the holy offerings that the Israelites consecrate to the LORD, that person will be cut off from my presence; I am the LORD. **4** No man of Aaron's descendants who has a skin disease[I] or a discharge is to eat from the holy offerings until he is clean. Whoever touches anything made unclean by

---

A 20:27 Lit *is in them*　B 21:4 Lit *unclean a husband among his people*　C 21:7 Or *a prostitute, or a defiled woman*　D 21:9 Or *prostitution*　E 21:10 Lit *and one has filled his hand*　F 21:10 Or *not uncover his head*　G 21:15 Lit *not profane his seed*　H 21:20 Or *or emaciated*　I 22:4 Or *has leprosy* or *scale disease*

21:5 These prohibitions had to do with pagan rituals.
21:7, 9, 13-15 The reputations of a priest's wife and daughters were also relevant to his fitness to serve in the sanctuary.

21:16-24 Priests were restricted from service based on various physical defects and deformities. Such people were no less humans who bear God's image. Rather, Moses was emphasizing the necessity for

priests to represent wholeness in serving a holy God. Priests with physical limitations, then, could not perform the ceremonies. However, they were not shunned, but were provided for (21:22).

a dead person or by a man who has an emission of semen, [5] or whoever touches any swarming creature that makes him unclean or any person who makes him unclean — whatever his uncleanness — [6] the man who touches any of these will remain unclean until evening[a] and is not to eat from the holy offerings unless he has bathed his body with water. [7] When the sun has set, he will become clean, and then he may eat from the holy offerings, for that is his food.[b] [8] He must not eat an animal that died naturally or was mauled by wild beasts, [A,c] making himself unclean by it; I am the LORD. [9] They must keep my instruction,[d] or they will be guilty and die because they profane it; I am the LORD who sets them apart.

[10] "No one outside a priest's family[B,e] is to eat the holy offering. A foreigner staying with a priest or a hired worker is not to eat the holy offering. [11] But if a priest purchases someone with his own silver, that person may eat it, and those born in his house may eat his food. [12] If the priest's daughter is married to a man outside a priest's family,[c] she is not to eat from the holy contributions.[D] [13] But if the priest's daughter becomes widowed or divorced, has no children, and returns to her father's house as in her youth, she may share her father's food. But no outsider may share it. [14] If anyone eats a holy offering in error,[f] he is to add a fifth to its value and give the holy offering to the priest.[g] [15] The priests must not profane the holy offerings the Israelites give to the LORD [16] by letting the people eat their holy offerings and having them bear the penalty of restitution.[h] For I am the LORD who sets them apart."

ACCEPTABLE SACRIFICES

[17] The LORD spoke to Moses: [18] "Speak to Aaron, his sons, and all the Israelites and tell them: Any man of the house of Israel or of the resident aliens[i] in Israel who presents his offering[j] — whether they present payment of vows or freewill gifts to the LORD as burnt offerings — [19] must offer an unblemished male[k] from the cattle, sheep, or goats in order for you to be accepted. [20] You are not to present anything that has a defect,

because it will not be accepted on your behalf.

[21] "When a man presents a fellowship sacrifice to the LORD to fulfill a vow or as a freewill offering from the herd or flock, it has to be unblemished to be acceptable; there must be no defect in it. [22] You are not to present any animal to the LORD that is blind, injured, maimed, or has a running sore, festering rash,[l] or scabs; you may not put any of them on the altar as a fire offering to the LORD.[m] [23] You may sacrifice as a freewill offering any animal from the herd or flock that has an elongated or stunted limb, but it is not acceptable as a vow offering. [24] You are not to present to the LORD anything that has bruised, crushed, torn, or severed testicles;[n] you must not sacrifice them in your land. [25] Neither you nor[E] a foreigner are to present food to your God from any of these animals. They will not be accepted for you because they are deformed and have a defect."[o]

[26] The LORD spoke to Moses: [27] "When an ox, sheep, or goat is born, it is to remain with[F] its mother for seven days; from the eighth day[p] on, it will be acceptable as an offering, a fire offering to the LORD. [28] But you are not to slaughter an animal from the herd or flock on the same day as its young.[q] [29] When you sacrifice a thank offering[r] to the LORD, sacrifice it so that you may be accepted. [30] It is to be eaten on the same day.[s] Do not let any of it remain until morning; I am the LORD.

[31] "You are to keep my commands and do them; I am the LORD. [32] You must not profane my holy name; I must be treated as holy[t] among the Israelites. I am the LORD who sets you apart, [33] the one who brought you out of the land of Egypt to be your God; I am the LORD."

HOLY DAYS

23

The LORD spoke to Moses: [2] "Speak to the Israelites and tell them: These are my appointed times,[u] the times of the LORD that you will proclaim as sacred assemblies.[v]

[3] "Work may be done for six days, but on the seventh day there is to be a Sabbath of complete rest,[w] a sacred assembly. You are not to do any work; it is a Sabbath[x] to the LORD wherever you live.

[a] 22:6 Lv 11:24-28,31-32,39-40
[b] 22:7 Lv 6:16-18,29; 7:7-10,32-36; 26:5
[c] 22:8 Ex 22:31; Lv 7:24; 17:15; Ezk 44:31
[d] 22:9 Gn 26:5; Lv 18:30
[e] 22:10 Ex 29:33; Nm 3:10; 18:4,7
[f] 22:14 Nm 15:22,24
[g] Lv 5:14-16
[h] 22:16 Lv 14:12
[i] 22:18 Ex 2:22
[j] Lv 1:2
[k] 22:19 Ex 29:1

[l] 22:22 Dt 28:27; 2Sm 23:38; 1Ch 11:40; Jr 31:39
[m] Lv 21:18-20; Is 28:20
[n] 22:24 Lv 21:20
[o] 22:25 Mal 1:14
[p] 22:27 Ex 22:30
[q] 22:28 Ex 23:19; Dt 22:6-7
[r] 22:29 Lv 7:12-15; 2Ch 29:31; 33:16; Ps 56:13; Jr 17:26; 33:11; Am 4:5
[s] 22:30 Ex 34:25; Lv 7:15; 19:6-7
[t] 22:32 Lv 19:12; 21:6-8,23; 22:2; Lk 11:2
[u] 23:2 Lv 23:37,44; Nm 10:10; 2Ch 2:3; Ezr 3:5
[v] Ex 12:16; Lv 23:21,24,27,35-37; Nm 28:18,25-26; 29:1,7,12
[w] 23:3 Ex 31:15; 35:2; Lv 16:31; 23:32; 25:4
[x] Gn 2:2-3

A 22:8 Lit *eat a carcass or a mauled beast*   B 22:10 Lit *"No stranger*   c 22:12 Lit *to a stranger*   D 22:12 Lit *the contribution of holy offerings*   E 22:25 Lit *nor from the hand of*   F 22:27 Lit *under*

22:31-33 The Israelites needed no higher reason to honor and obey God by living holy lives—and neither do we. God sacrificed his own Son to save you from his righteous judgment. Why would you choose any other path but to live for him?

a 23:5 Ex 12:11
b 23:6 Ex 12:17
c 23:12 Ex 29:1
d 23:15 Ex 34:22; Nm 28:26; Dt 16:10; Ac 2:1
e Ex 29:24

f 23:17 Lv 2:12; 1Co 15:20; Rv 14:4
g 23:22 Ex 2:22; Lv 19:9-10; Ac 6:1; 11:29
h 23:24 Lv 25:9; Nm 5:15
i Nm 29:1; Ps 81:3
j 23:27 Ex 30:10; Lv 16:29-30; 25:9; Nm 29:7-11
k Ac 27:9

4 "These are the LORD's appointed times, the sacred assemblies you are to proclaim at their appointed times. 5 The Passover*a* to the LORD comes in the first month, at twilight on the fourteenth day of the month. 6 The Festival of Unleavened Bread*b* to the LORD is on the fifteenth day of the same month. For seven days you must eat unleavened bread. 7 On the first day you are to hold a sacred assembly; you are not to do any daily work. 8 You are to present a fire offering to the LORD for seven days. On the seventh day there will be a sacred assembly; do not do any daily work."

9 The LORD spoke to Moses: 10 "Speak to the Israelites and tell them: When you enter the land I am giving you and reap its harvest,*A* you are to bring the first sheaf of your harvest to the priest. 11 He will present the sheaf before the LORD so that you may be accepted; the priest is to present it on the day after the Sabbath. 12 On the day you present the sheaf, you are to offer a year-old male lamb*B* without blemish*c* as a burnt offering to the LORD. 13 Its grain offering is to be four quarts*c* of fine flour mixed with oil as a fire offering to the LORD, a pleasing aroma, and its drink offering will be one quart*D* of wine. 14 You must not eat bread, roasted grain, or any new grain*E* until this very day, and until you have brought the offering to your God. This is to be a permanent statute throughout your generations wherever you live.

15 "You are to count seven*F* complete weeks*G,d* starting from the day after the Sabbath, the day you brought the sheaf of the presentation offering.*e* 16 You are to count fifty days until the day after the seventh Sabbath and then present an offering of new grain to the LORD. 17 Bring two loaves of bread from your settlements as a presentation offering, each of them made from four quarts of fine flour, baked with yeast, as firstfruits*f* to the LORD. 18 You are to present with the bread seven unblemished male lambs a year old, one young bull, and two rams. They will be a burnt offering to the LORD, with their grain offerings and drink offerings, a fire offering of a pleasing aroma to the LORD. 19 You are also to prepare one male goat as a sin offering, and two male lambs a year old as a fellowship sacrifice. 20 The priest will present the lambs with the bread of firstfruits as a presentation offering before the LORD; the bread and the two lambs will be holy to the LORD for the priest. 21 On that same day you are to make a proclamation and hold a sacred assembly. You are not to do any daily work. This is to be a permanent statute wherever you live throughout your generations. 22 When you reap the harvest of your land, you are not to reap all the way to the edge of your field or gather the gleanings of your harvest. Leave them for the poor and the resident alien;*g* I am the LORD your God."

23 The LORD spoke to Moses: 24 "Tell the Israelites: In the seventh month, on the first day of the month, you are to have a day of complete rest, commemoration, and trumpet blasts*h* — a sacred assembly.*i* 25 You must not do any daily work, but you must present a fire offering to the LORD."

26 The LORD again spoke to Moses: 27 "The tenth day of this seventh month is the Day of Atonement.*j* You are to hold a sacred assembly and practice self-denial;*k* you are to present a fire offering to the LORD. 28 On this particular day you are not to do any work, for it is a Day of Atonement to make atonement for yourselves before the LORD your God. 29 If any person does not

---

A 23:10 = the barley harvest   *B* 23:12 Or *a male lamb in its first year*   *c* 23:13 Lit *two-tenths of an ephah*, also in v. 17   *D* 23:13 Lit *one-fourth of a hin*
E 23:14 Grain or bread from the new harvest   *f* 23:15 Lit *count; they will be seven*   *G* 23:15 Or *Sabbaths*

23:4-5 The festivals or **sacred assemblies** (23:4) God commanded Israel to observe celebrated his provision. Perhaps the most well known is the **Passover** (23:5), commemorating the night God delivered Israel from Egypt. Jesus celebrated it with his disciples before his crucifixion (see Luke 22:7-15), and he fulfills it because he is "our Passover lamb" (1 Cor 5:7). **23:9-14** This custom became known as the Feast of Firstfruits, honoring God for the firstfruits of the spring barley harvest. It acknowledged his provision and signaled their ongoing trust in his future provision. In the New Testament, Paul describes the risen Lord Jesus as the "firstfruits" of those who have died (1 Cor 15:20). His resurrection is the promise that all

those who trust in him will also be raised to life when he comes (see 1 Cor 15:22-23). **23:15-22 Fifty days** after the Feast of First-fruits, the Israelites were to celebrate the Festival of Weeks (23:15-16). Seven weeks from that day brought the people to late spring and the wheat harvest. Thus, the offerings included **bread . . . as firstfruits to the LORD** (23:17). The festival also became known as "Pentecost" from the Greek word for "fiftieth." This, along with Passover and the Festival of Shelters, was one of the three "pilgrim feasts," for which God required the attendance of every Jewish man in Jerusalem. It was at Pentecost, when thousands of Jewish pilgrims were in Jerusalem, in fact, that

the first disciples of Christ would receive the Holy Spirit, thus marking the church's birthday (see Acts 2:1-4). **23:23-25** This became known as the Festival of Trumpets—modern day Rosh Hashanah, the Jewish New Year. In the Old Testament, **trumpet blasts** called God's people to worship or to war. In the New Testament, trumpet blasts are said to precede the rapture (see 1 Thess 4:16-17) and God's end-time acts of judgment (see Rev 8). **23:26-32** On **the Day of Atonement** (23:27), the high priest was to enter the most holy place to make atonement for the sins of the people (see Lev 16). Christ is the once-for-all "atoning sacrifice" for sins (Rom 3:25; 1 John 4:10).

practice self-denial on this particular day, he is to be cut off from his people. **30** I will destroy among his people anyone who does any work on this same day. **31** You are not to do any work. This is a permanent statute throughout your generations wherever you live. **32** It will be a Sabbath of complete rest for you, and you must practice self-denial. You are to observe your Sabbath from the evening of the ninth day of the month until the following evening."

33 The LORD spoke to Moses: **34** "Tell the Israelites: The Festival of Shelters^A,a to the LORD begins on the fifteenth day of this seventh month and continues for seven days. **35** There is to be a sacred assembly on the first day; you are not to do any daily work. **36** You are to present a fire offering to the LORD for seven days. On the eighth day you are to hold a sacred assembly and present a fire offering to the LORD. It is a solemn gathering;^b you are not to do any daily work.

37 "These are the LORD's appointed times that you are to proclaim as sacred assemblies for presenting fire offerings to the LORD, burnt offerings and grain offerings, sacrifices and drink offerings, each on its designated day. **38** These are in addition to the offerings for the LORD's Sabbaths, your gifts, all your vow offerings, and all your freewill offerings that you give to the LORD.

39 "You are to celebrate the LORD's festival on the fifteenth day of the seventh month for seven days after you have gathered the produce of the land. There will be complete rest on the first day and complete rest on the eighth day. **40** On the first day you are to take the product^c of majestic trees — palm fronds,^d boughs of leafy trees,^e and willows of the brook^f — and rejoice before the LORD your God for seven days. **41** You are to celebrate it as a festival to the LORD seven days each year. This is a permanent statute for you throughout your generations; celebrate it in the seventh month. **42** You are to live in shelters^g for seven days. All the native-born of Israel must live in shelters, **43** so that your generations may know that I made the Israelites live in shelters when I brought them out of the land of Egypt; I am the LORD your God." **44** So Moses declared the LORD's appointed times to the Israelites.

TABERNACLE OIL AND BREAD

24 The LORD spoke to Moses: **2** "Command the Israelites to bring you pure oil from crushed olives for the light, in order to keep the lamp burning regularly.^h **3** Aaron is to tend it continually from evening until morning before the LORD outside the curtain^i of the testimony^j in the tent of meeting. This is a permanent statute throughout your generations. **4** He must continually tend the lamps on the pure gold lampstand in the LORD's presence.^k

5 "Take fine flour and bake it into twelve loaves;^l each loaf is to be made with four quarts.^B **6** Arrange them in two rows, six to a row, on the pure gold table^m before the LORD. **7** Place pure frankincense^n near each row, so that it may serve as a memorial portion^o for the bread and a fire offering^p to the LORD. **8** The bread is to be set out before the LORD every Sabbath day as a permanent covenant^q obligation on the part of the Israelites. **9** It belongs to Aaron and his sons, who are to eat it in a holy place, for it is the holiest portion for him from the fire offerings to the LORD; this is a permanent rule."

A CASE OF BLASPHEMY

10 Now the son of an Israelite mother and an Egyptian father was^c among the Israelites. A fight broke out in the camp between the Israelite woman's son and an Israelite man. **11** Her son cursed and blasphemed the Name,^r and they brought him to Moses. (His mother's name was Shelomith, a daughter of Dibri of the tribe of Dan.^s)

^a 23:34 Ex 23:16; Jn 7:37
^b 23:36 Nm 29:35
^c 23:40 Gn 1:11
^d Ex 15:27; Nm 33:9; Jdg 4:5; Neh 8:15; Ps 92:12; Sg 7:8-9; Jl 1:12; Rv 7:9
^e Neh 8:15; Ezk 6:13; 20:28
^f Jb 40:22; Is 44:4

^g 23:42 Gn 33:17; Dt 16:13,16; 31:10; Neh 8:14-17; Am 9:11; Jnh 4:5
^h 24:2 Ex 25:37
^i 24:3 Mk 15:38; Heb 6:19
^j Ex 31:18
^k 24:4 Gn 4:14; Ex 25:31; 37:17; Zch 4:2
^l 24:5 Ex 25:30
^m 24:6 Ex 25:23; Heb 9:2
^n 24:7 Ex 30:34
^o Lv 2:2
^p Dt 18:1
^q 24:8 Ex 19:5
^r 24:11 Ex 20:7; Lv 24:16; Nm 15:30; 1Sm 3:13; Neh 9:18
^s Gn 49:16

---

^A **23:34** Or *Tabernacles*, or *Booths*   ^B **24:5** Lit *two-tenths of an ephah*   ^C **24:10** Lit *went out*

23:33-43 The Festival of Shelters (or "Tabernacles" or "Booths") was named for the temporary structures the Israelites were to build and live in during the festival to commemorate God's provision for them during the years when they lived in the wilderness (23:42-43). John records an occasion when Jesus was in Jerusalem for the Festival of Shelters (see John 7:2, 10).
24:1-4 Chapter 24 turns to the responsibilities of the priests in the tabernacle. The first of these duties was **to keep the lamp burning** (24:2). This is a reference to the . . . lamp-

stand in the LORD's presence (24:4). Later Jesus, who was foreshadowed by this lamp, would later say of himself, "I am the light of the world" (John 8:12). You'll never have to worry about his light going out.
24:5-9 These **twelve loaves** represented the twelve tribes, and the bread was known as "the Bread of the Presence" (Exod 25:30). Bread was a common staple in the Israelite diet. To live, you ate bread. Thus later in history, when Jesus said, "I am the bread of life" (John 6:35), his meaning was clear: come to me if you want to live.

24:10-23 The LORD spoke (24:13) with regard to the man who had **blasphemed the Name** (24:11). The witnesses put their hands on the man's head as a sign that their testimony was true, and the people **stoned him** to death (24:23). This was a lasting reminder to the community that blasphemy was not to be tolerated. The penalty for cursing covenant God was as severe as it could be, reminding us that his name should never be used as a swear word.

a 24:12 Gn 40:3-7; 41:10; 42:17

b Nm 3:39; 15:32-36

c 24:14 Lv 20:2,27; 24:16,23; Nm 14:10; 15:35-36; Dt 21:21; Jos 7:25; 1Kg 12:18; Ezk 16:40; 23:47; Jn 10:33

d 24:16 Ex 20:7; 22:28; 1Kg 21:10,13; Jn 8:59; 19:7; 2Tm 2:19

e 24:17 Gn 9:5-6; Ex 20:13; 21:12-14; Nm 35:30-31

f 24:19-20 Ex 21:24; Dt 19:21; Mt 5:38-39; 7:12

g 24:21 Nm 35:30-33

h 25:4 Lv 16:31

i 25:9 Lv 23:27

j 25:10 Lv 27:17-24; Nm 36:4; Dt 15:1

k 25:14 Dt 23:16

12 They put him in custody*a* until the LORD's decision*b* could be made clear to them.

13 Then the LORD spoke to Moses: **14** "Bring the one who has cursed to the outside of the camp and have all who heard him lay their hands on his head; then have the whole community stone him.*c* **15** And tell the Israelites: If anyone curses his God, he will bear the consequences of his sin. **16** Whoever blasphemes the name of the LORD must be put to death;*d* the whole community is to stone him. If he blasphemes the Name, he is to be put to death, whether the resident alien or the native.

17 "If a man kills anyone, he must be put to death.*e* **18** Whoever kills an animal is to make restitution for it, life for life. **19** If any man inflicts a permanent injury on his neighbor, whatever he has done is to be done to him: **20** fracture for fracture, eye for eye, tooth for tooth. Whatever injury he inflicted on the person, the same is to be inflicted on him.*f* **21** Whoever kills an animal is to make restitution for it, but whoever kills a person is to be put to death.*g* **22** You are to have the same law for the resident alien and the native, because I am the LORD your God."

23 After Moses spoke to the Israelites, they brought the one who had cursed to the outside of the camp and stoned him. So the Israelites did as the LORD had commanded Moses.

SABBATH YEARS AND JUBILEE

25 The LORD spoke to Moses on Mount Sinai: **2** "Speak to the Israelites and tell them: When you enter the land I am giving you, the land will observe a Sabbath to the LORD. **3** You may sow your field for six years, and you may prune your vineyard and gather its produce for six years. **4** But there will be a Sabbath of complete rest*h* for the land in the seventh year, a Sabbath to the LORD: you are not to sow your field or prune your vineyard. **5** You are not to reap what grows by itself from your crop, or harvest the grapes of your untended vines. It is to be a year of complete rest for the land. **6** Whatever the land produces during the Sabbath year can be food for you — for yourself, your male or female slave, and the hired worker or alien who resides with you. **7** All of its growth may serve as food for your livestock and the wild animals in your land.

8 "You are to count seven sabbatical years, seven times seven years, so that the time period of the seven sabbatical years amounts to forty-nine. **9** Then you are to sound a trumpet loudly in the seventh month, on the tenth day of the month; you will sound it throughout your land on the Day of Atonement.*i* **10** You are to consecrate the fiftieth year and proclaim freedom in the land for all its inhabitants. It will be your Jubilee,*j* when each of you is to return to his property and each of you to his clan. **11** The fiftieth year will be your Jubilee; you are not to sow, reap what grows by itself, or harvest its untended vines. **12** It is to be holy to you because it is the Jubilee; you may only eat its produce directly from the field.

13 "In this Year of Jubilee, each of you will return to his property. **14** If you make a sale to your neighbor or a purchase from him, do not cheat*k* one another. **15** You are to make the purchase from your neighbor based on the number of years since the

---

25:1-7 The **Sabbath year** was to be observed once the people of Israel were living in Canaan and planting crops (25:6). They could plant and harvest for six years in succession, but there was to be **complete rest for the land in the seventh year** (25:4). Thus, the land itself enjoyed a Sabbath rest in the seventh year, even as God provided a Sabbath rest for his people every seventh day.

Skipping the harvest for a year sounds like a risky idea for an agriculturally dependent people, but remember that the Israelites were not ordinary farmers. They were the people of God who needed constant reminders of their utter dependence on him for provision. Tragically, as time passed, Israel disregarded God's command to observe the Sabbath year—not for a mere decade or two but for 490 years! That's seventy Sabbath years they would neglect to observe, and God would keep count. When he sent them into exile

in Babylon, they remained there for seventy years—one year for each Sabbath year they violated (see 26:33-35; 2 Chron 36:20-21).

25:8-10 In the year of **Jubilee** the Israelites were to **proclaim freedom in the land** (25:10). All those in servitude were set free and property reverted to its original owners. This was to begin with **the Day of Atonement** (25:9; see 16:1-34; 23:26-32), the day set aside to atone for the individual and corporate sins of the nation of Israel. The Day of Atonement marked the time when Israel got right with God through the shedding of blood—that is, through the slaying of a sacrifice. In other words, they didn't get to enjoy the Jubilee (i.e., God's involvement in their economy, society, and politics) without first getting their sins addressed by God.

Many people want God to do things for them without coming to him for atonement (or even recognizing that they need it). They cry out for justice, or ask God to pay this, fix

that, or vindicate them, while skipping the very thing that inaugurates God's Jubilee—that is, addressing personal and corporate sin. You can't have deliverance from your problems without King Jesus, who delivers.

25:13-34 A primary feature of the Jubilee was the **return** of all **property** in Israel to its original owners (25:13-17)—the only exception to this rule involved property in walled cities (25:29-30). This was based on the following principle: **The land is not to be permanently sold because it is [God's], and [the people] are only . . . temporary residents on [his] land** (25:23). There were occasions when Israelites had to sell their land or sell themselves into servitude because of poverty. But since they and their land really belonged to God, any such sale was temporary. God made it clear that no one could refuse to allow the redemption of land during Jubilee. Notice that God did not use the word *own*, but **occupy** (25:24).

last Jubilee. He is to sell to you based on the number of remaining harvest years. **16** You are to increase its price in proportion to a greater amount of years, and decrease its price in proportion to a lesser amount of years, because what he is selling to you is a number of harvests. **17** You are not to cheat one another, but fear your God, for I am the LORD your God.

18 "You are to keep my statutes and ordinances and carefully observe them, so that you may live securely in the land.ᵃ **19** Then the land will yield its fruit, so that you can eat, be satisfied, and live securely in the land. **20** If you wonder: 'What will we eat in the seventh year if we don't sow or gather our produce?' **21** I will appoint my blessing for you in the sixth year, so that it will produce a crop sufficient for three years. **22** When you sow in the eighth year, you will be eating from the previous harvest. You will be eating this until the ninth year when its harvest comes in.

23 "The land is not to be permanently sold because it is mine, and you are only aliens and temporary residents on my land.^(A,b) **24** You are to allow the redemption of any land you occupy. **25** If your brother becomes destitute and sells part of his property, his nearest relative may come and redeem what his brother has sold. **26** If a man has no family redeemer, but he prospersᴮ and obtains enough to redeem his land, **27** he may calculate the years since its sale, repay the balance to the man he sold it to, and return to his property. **28** But if he cannot obtain enough to repay him, what he sold will remain in the possession of its purchaser until the Year of Jubilee. It is to be released at the Jubilee, so that he may return to his property.

29 "If a man sells a residence in a walled city, his right of redemption will last until a year has passed after its sale; his right of redemption will last a year. **30** If it is not redeemed by the end of a full year, then the house in the walled city is permanently

transferred to its purchaser throughout his generations. It is not to be released on the Jubilee. **31** But houses in settlements that have no walls around them are to be classified as open fields. The right to redeem such houses stays in effect, and they are to be released at the Jubilee.

32 "Concerning the Levitical cities,ᶜ the Levites always have the right to redeem houses in the cities they possess. **33** Whatever property one of the Levites can redeemᶜ — a house sold in a city they possess — is to be released at the Jubilee, because the houses in the Levitical cities are their possession among the Israelites. **34** The open pastureland around their cities may not be sold, for it is their permanent possession.

35 "If your brother becomes destitute and cannot sustain himself amongᴰ you, you are to support him as an alien or temporary resident, so that he can continue to live among you. **36** Do not profit or take interest from him,ᵈ but fear your God and let your brother live among you. **37** You are not to lend him your silver with interest or sell him your food for profit. **38** I am the LORD your God, who brought you out of the land of Egypt to give you the land of Canaan and to be your God.

39 "If your brother among you becomes destitute and sells himself to you,ᵉ you must not force him to do slave labor. **40** Let him stay with you as a hired worker or temporary resident; he may work for you until the Year of Jubilee. **41** Then he and his children are to be released from you, and he may return to his clan and his ancestral property.ᶠ **42** They are not to be sold as slaves,ᴱ because they are my servantsᶠ that I brought out of the land of Egypt. **43** You are not to rule over them harshlyᵍ but fear your God. **44** Your male and female slaves are to be from the nations around you; you may purchase male and female slaves. **45** You may also purchase them from the aliens residing with you, or from their

ᵃ 25:18 Lv 18:4-5,26; 19:37; 20:8,22; 26:3-5
ᵇ 25:23 1Ch 29:15; Heb 11:13
ᶜ 25:32 Nm 35:1-8; Dt 18:1-2; 19:2-9; Jos 21; 1Ch 6:54-81
ᵈ 25:36 Ex 22:25; Dt 23:19-20; Ezk 22:12
ᵉ 25:39 2Kg 4:1; Neh 5:5; Is 50:1; Mt 18:25
ᶠ 25:41 Ex 21:3-6
ᵍ 25:43 Ex 1:13-14

25:35-55 The rules of Jubilee also concerned the people of Israel who were poor, who had been sold, or who had sold themselves into a form of indentured servitude to pay a debt (25:35-43). If an Israelite sold himself for service, he was to be treated as **a hired worker** instead of as a slave (25:39-40). His station was only a temporary condition that was to be reversed during the **Year of Jubilee** (25:40-41). Israelites were not to be **sold as**

slaves because they were God's **servants** whom he **brought out of . . . Egypt** (25:42). Foreigners whom the Israelites had purchased were not eligible for release during the Year of Jubilee (25:44-46). Often in ancient Israel foreign peoples became slaves as a result of war. Such refugees might have no other means of subsistence. So in contrast to other nations in the ancient Near East, Israel was required to grant protection

and justice to slaves (see Exod 21:20-21, 26-27; Deut 23:15-16; and the note on Eph 6:5-9).

The principles of Jubilee relating to servitude, redemption, and freedom have great meaning to us as believers today. We are God's possession since he bought us back from slavery to sin by the blood of Jesus Christ. We are free from sin and death, but we are servants of God.

a 25:55 Ex 4:10
b 26:1 Ex 20:3-4; Ps 81:9
c 26:2 Ex 15:17; Lv 19:30;
Ezk 20:13,16,21; 23:38

d 26:3-5 Lv 25:18-19; Dt
28:1-2,12; Is 30:21-23;
Am 9:13
e 26:6 Dt 4:4; Ezk
34:25,28; Mc 4:4
f 26:7-8 Dt 3:22; 32:30; Jos
10:19; 23:3,10
g 26:11 Ex 25:8; 29:45-46;
Lv 26:44; 1Kg 6:13
h 26:12 Jr 7:23; Lk 1:68; 2Co
6:16; Rv 21:3
i 26:13 Ex 6:6-7; Is 9:4; Jr
5:5; 28:10-11
j 26:16 Ps 78:33; Is 65:23;
Jr 15:8
k 26:17 Ex 12:23; Dt 28:25
l 26:18 Gn 4:15,24; Heb
12:4-11

families living among you — those born in your land. These may become your property. **46** You may leave them to your sons after you to inherit as property; you can make them slaves for life. But concerning your brothers, the Israelites, you must not rule over one another harshly.

47 "If an alien or temporary resident living among you prospers, but your brother living near him becomes destitute and sells himself to the alien living among you, or to a member of the resident alien's clan, **48** he has the right of redemption after he has been sold. One of his brothers may redeem him. **49** His uncle or cousin may redeem him, or any of his close relatives from his clan may redeem him. If he prospers, he may redeem himself. **50** The one who purchased him is to calculate the time from the year he sold himself to him until the Year of Jubilee. The price of his sale will be determined by the number of years. It will be set for him like the daily wages of a hired worker. **51** If many years are still left, he must pay his redemption price in proportion to them based on his purchase price. **52** If only a few years remain until the Year of Jubilee, he will calculate and pay the price of his redemption in proportion to his remaining years. **53** He will stay with him like a man hired year by year. A resident alien is not to rule over him harshly in your sight. **54** If he is not redeemed in any of these ways, he and his children are to be released at the Year of Jubilee. **55** For the Israelites are my servants.*a* They are my servants that I brought out of the land of Egypt; I am the LORD your God.

COVENANT BLESSINGS AND DISCIPLINE

26 "Do not make idols for yourselves,*b* set up a carved image or sacred pillar for yourselves, or place a sculpted stone in your land to bow down to it, for I am the LORD your God. **2** Keep my Sabbaths and revere my sanctuary;*c* I am the LORD.

3 "If you follow my statutes and faithfully observe my commands, **4** I will give you rain at the right time, and the land will yield its produce, and the trees of the field will bear their fruit. **5** Your threshing will continue until grape harvest, and the grape harvest will continue until sowing time; you will have plenty of food to eat and live securely in your land.*d* **6** I will give peace to the land, and you will lie down with nothing to frighten you. I will remove dangerous animals from the land, and no sword will pass through your land.*e* **7** You will pursue your enemies, and they will fall before you by the sword. **8** Five of you will pursue a hundred, and a hundred of you will pursue ten thousand; your enemies will fall before you by the sword.*f*

9 "I will turn to you, make you fruitful and multiply you, and confirm my covenant with you. **10** You will eat the old grain of the previous year and will clear out the old to make room for the new. **11** I will place my residence[A] among you, and I will not reject you.*g* **12** I will walk among you and be your God, and you will be my people.*h* **13** I am the LORD your God, who brought you out of the land of Egypt, so that you would no longer be their slaves. I broke the bars of your yoke*i* and enabled you to live in freedom.[B]

14 "But if you do not obey me and observe all these commands — **15** if you reject my statutes and despise my ordinances, and do not observe all my commands — and break my covenant, **16** then I will do this to you: I will bring terror*j* on you — wasting disease and fever that will cause your eyes to fail and your life to ebb away. You will sow your seed in vain because your enemies will eat it. **17** I will turn[C] against you, so that you will be defeated by your enemies. Those who hate you will rule over you, and you will flee even though no one is pursuing you.*k*

18 "But if after these things you will not obey me, I will proceed to discipline you seven times for your sins.*l* **19** I will break down your strong pride. I will make your sky like iron and your land like bronze,

---

[A] 26:11 Or *tabernacle*　[B] 26:13 Lit *to walk uprightly*　[C] 26:17 Lit *will set my face*

26:3-13 Here we find the blessings God would provide in return for faithfulness. None of this was because the Israelites had sought him out—but because he had sought them out (26:13). This is in line with a well-known New Testament teaching: "We love because [God] first loved us" (1 John 4:19).
26:14-17 If Israel rejected the Lord and his covenant, God would rain down curses on Israel—literally reversing the blessings God had just laid out for obedience. In fact, things would get so bad that they would **flee** in paranoid terror even when the enemy wasn't after them (26:17).
26:18-22 The warning that God would make **the sky like iron and [the] land like bronze** (26:19) is a graphic picture of drought that would produce a famine so severe that the people's efforts to raise crops would be useless (26:18-20). The Lord also would send **wild animals** into the land that would kill people as well as their **livestock** (26:22), a sharp contrast to the promise that God would "remove dangerous animals from the land" (26:6).

²⁰ and your strength will be used up for nothing.ᵃ Your land will not yield its produce, and the trees of the land will not bear their fruit.

²¹ "If you act with hostility toward me and are unwilling to obey me, I will multiply your plagues seven times for your sins.ᵇ ²² I will send wild animals against you that will deprive you of your children, ravage your livestock, and reduce your numbers until your roads are deserted.ᶜ

²³ "If in spite of these things you do not accept my discipline, but act with hostility toward me, ²⁴ then I will act with hostility toward you; I also will strike you seven times for your sins. ²⁵ I will bring a sword against youᵈ to execute the vengeance of the covenant. Though you withdraw into your cities, I will send a pestilence among you, and you will be delivered into enemy hands. ²⁶ When I cut off your supply of bread, ten women will bake your bread in a single oven and ration out your bread by weight, so that you will eat but not be satisfied.ᵉ

²⁷ "And if in spite of this you do not obey me but act with hostility toward me, ²⁸ I will act with furious hostility toward you; I will also discipline you seven times for your sins. ²⁹ You will eat the flesh of your sons; you will eat the flesh of your daughters.ᶠ ³⁰ I will destroy your high places, cut down your shrines,^ and heap your lifeless bodies on the lifeless bodies of your idols;ᵍ I will reject you. ³¹ I will reduce your cities to ruins and devastate your sanctuaries. I will not smell the pleasing aroma of your sacrifices.ʰ ³² I also will devastate the land, so that your enemies who come to live there will be appalled by it. ³³ But I will scatter you among the nations, and I will draw a sword to chase after you. So your land will become desolate, and your cities will become ruins.

³⁴ "Then the land will make up for its Sabbath years during the time it lies desolate, while you are in the land of your enemies. At that time the land will rest and make up for its Sabbaths. ³⁵ As long as it lies desolate, it will have the rest it did not have during your Sabbaths when you lived there.

³⁶ "I will put anxiety in the hearts of those of you who survive in the lands of their enemies. The sound of a wind-driven leaf will put them to flight, and they will flee as one flees from a sword, and fall though no one is pursuing them. ³⁷ They will stumble over one another as if fleeing from a sword though no one is pursuing them. You will not be able to stand against your enemies. ³⁸ You will perish among the nations; the land of your enemies will devour you. ³⁹ Thoseᴮ who survive in the lands of your enemies will waste away because of their iniquity; they will also waste away because of their fathers' iniquities along with theirs.

⁴⁰ "But when they confess their iniquity and the iniquity of their fathers — their unfaithfulness that they practiced against me, and how they acted with hostility toward me, ⁴¹ and I acted with hostility toward them and brought them into the land of their enemies — and when their uncircumcised hearts are humbledⁱ and

ᵃ 26:20 Dt 28:23; Am 4:7-8
ᵇ 26:21 Gn 4:15,24
ᶜ 26:22 Dt 32:24; Jdg 5:6; Is 33:8; Lm 1:1-4; Ezk 14:15; Zch 7:14
ᵈ 26:25 Ezk 14:21
ᵉ 26:26 Is 3:1; Ezk 4:16; 14:13; Am 4:6; Mc 6:14
ᶠ 26:29 Dt 28:53-57; 2Kg 6:28-29; Jr 19:9; Lm 4:10; Mc 3:2-3
ᵍ 26:30 Gn 31:19; Ezk 6:3-6
ʰ 26:31 Gn 8:21; 1Sm 26:19; Am 5:21-22

ⁱ 26:41 Dt 30:6; Jr 4:4; 9:25; Ezk 44:7,9

---

^ 26:30 Or *incense altars*   ᴮ 26:39 Lit *Those of you*

26:27-29 Should God's patience with Israel's stubborn unfaithfulness finally run out, he would send their enemies against them and conditions would become so desperate in the accompanying siege that the people would resort to cannibalism (29:29).

26:33, 36-39 Eventually, the people would be exiled from the land (26:33). Yet even in captivity the Israelites who survived all the other disasters would be subjected to fear and would ultimately die in exile **because of their [sin]** and **because of their fathers' [sins]** (26:39).

Anyone who feels the Lord was being too harsh in the punishments he threatened should reread the various phrases describing Israel's deliberate and prideful disobedience. Note the "if" clauses (26:14, 15, 18, 21, 23, 27) and the statement about the people rejecting God's **ordinances and [abhorring his] statutes** (26:43). The Israelites would not be innocent bystanders who ignorantly displeased God. They would quickly grow into a nation that established a lengthy pattern of idolatry and hatred toward the God who had rescued them, ignoring his warnings and expecting his blessings anyway.

26:39-40 The phrase **because of their fathers' iniquities along with theirs** (26:39) hints at the reality of the generational curse, which may be defined as a pattern of behavior passed down from one generation to another due to rebellion against God. Some sins, attitudes, and tendencies get handed down from generation to generation in some families. Grandpa's alcoholism or Great-Grandma's explosive temper can and often does show up in their descendants.

The point of trying to identify and frankly discuss any generational curses that might be alive in our families, though, is to break them—not to bemoan what our fathers and mothers did. We often want to blame our sin on our pasts: "Well, you know, my daddy did this, therefore I . . ." or "My momma used to tell me, so I . . . ." Instead, we need to own up to our iniquity and confess our part in any generational problems that have a hold on us.

God teaches that the first step in breaking such a curse is to confess and repent of our participation in it. God called on the Israelites to confess both their sins and the sins of their fathers (26:40), which were not dealt with in their fathers' generation and so continued to poison the stream of Israel's relationship with God. Confession and repentance are a potent remedy. Taking this radical step can break the chains of iniquity that have shackled generations.

26:40-45 There would remain a ray of hope amid all the suffering promised. This is an indicator that there is always hope for people who will turn to God in humble sincerity, brokenness, and repentance. If the people experiencing God's judgment were to do this (26:41-42), God would **remember the covenant** and restore them (26:45).

[a] 26:44 Gn 17:8; Ezk 36:22;
Hs 11:8-9; Zch 10:9
[b] 27:2 Lv 27:8
[c] 27:3 2Kg 15:20
[d] Ex 30:13; Lv 5:15; 27:25;
Nm 3:47
[e] 27:4 Ex 21:32
[f] 27:5 Gn 37:28
[g] 27:6 Nm 3:46-47;
18:15-16

[h] 27:10 Mal 1:8
[i] 27:13 Gn 47:24; Lv
5:16; 6:5
[j] 27:14-15 Lv 25:29-31
[k] 27:17 Lv 25:10

they make amends for their iniquity, [42] then I will remember my covenant with Jacob. I will also remember my covenant with Isaac and my covenant with Abraham, and I will remember the land. [43] For the land abandoned by them will make up for its Sabbaths by lying desolate without the people, while they make amends for their iniquity, because they rejected my ordinances and abhorred my statutes. [44] Yet in spite of this, while they are in the land of their enemies, I will not reject or abhor them so as to destroy them and break my covenant with them, since I am the LORD their God.[a] [45] For their sake I will remember the covenant with their fathers, whom I brought out of the land of Egypt in the sight of the nations to be their God; I am the LORD."

[46] These are the statutes, ordinances, and laws the LORD established between himself and the Israelites through Moses on Mount Sinai.

FUNDING THE SANCTUARY

27 The LORD spoke to Moses: [2] "Speak to the Israelites and tell them: When someone makes a special vow[b] to the LORD that involves the assessment of people, [3] if the assessment concerns a male from twenty to sixty years old, your assessment is fifty silver shekels[c] measured by the standard sanctuary shekel.[d] [4] If the person is a female, your assessment is thirty shekels.[e] [5] If the person is from five to twenty years old, your assessment for a male is twenty shekels[f] and for a female ten shekels. [6] If the person is from one month to five years old, your assessment for a male is five silver shekels,[g] and for a female your assessment is three shekels of silver. [7] If the person is sixty years or more, your assessment is fifteen shekels for a male and ten shekels for a female. [8] But if one is too poor to pay the assessment, he is to present the person before the priest and the priest will set a value for him. The priest will set a value for him according to what the one making the vow can afford.

[9] "If the vow involves one of the animals that may be brought as an offering to the LORD, any of these he gives to the LORD will be holy. [10] He may not replace it or make a substitution for it, either good for bad, or bad for good.[h] But if he does substitute one animal for another, both that animal and its substitute will be holy.

[11] "If the vow involves any of the unclean animals that may not be brought as an offering to the LORD, the animal must be presented before the priest. [12] The priest will set its value, whether high or low; the price will be set as the priest makes the assessment for you. [13] If the one who brought it decides to redeem it, he must add a fifth to the[A] assessed value.[i]

[14] "When a man consecrates his house as holy to the LORD, the priest will assess its value, whether high or low. The price will stand just as the priest assesses it. [15] But if the one who consecrated his house redeems it, he must add a fifth to the assessed value, and it will be his.[j]

[16] "If a man consecrates to the LORD any part of a field that he possesses, your assessment of value will be proportional to the seed needed to sow it, at the rate of fifty silver shekels for every five bushels[B] of barley seed.[C] [17] If he consecrates his field during the Year of Jubilee,[k] the price will stand according to your assessment. [18] But if he consecrates his field after the Jubilee, the priest will calculate the price for him in proportion to the years left until the next Year of Jubilee, so that your assessment will be reduced. [19] If the one who consecrated the field decides to redeem it, he must add a fifth to the assessed value, and the field will transfer back to him. [20] But if he does not redeem the field or if he has sold it to another man, it is no longer redeemable. [21] When the field is released in the Jubilee, it will be holy to the LORD like a field permanently set apart; it becomes the priest's property.

[22] "If a person consecrates to the LORD a field he has purchased that is not part of his inherited landholding, [23] then the priest will calculate for him the amount

[A] 27:13 Lit *your*, also in vv. 15,19,23   [B] 27:16 Lit *for a homer*   [C] 27:16 Or *grain*

27:1-8 It makes sense that a book which began with the sacrifices the Israelites were obliged to make would conclude with offerings and vows that they were under no obligation to make, but which God took just as seriously (see Eccl 5:4-5). The first category of vows included dedicating a person to the Lord in some special way (Lev 27:2-8). These ways are not spelled out, but we have an example later in Scripture of what one might involve. We find it in the story of Hannah, who dedicated her yet-to-be-conceived son Samuel to the Lord: "I will give him to the Lord all the days of his life," she promised (1 Sam 1:11). Had she wished to keep the child upon his birth, she would have been required to pay a price to the tabernacle that was equivalent to the boy's value. The price to release a man in the prime of his productive years from a vow was **fifty silver shekels** (27:3), a high price that represented that many months' wages.

of the assessment up to the Year of Jubilee, and the person will pay the assessed value on that day as a holy offering to the LORD. [24] In the Year of Jubilee the field will return to the one he bought it from,[a] the original owner. [25] All your assessed values will be measured by the standard sanctuary shekel,[A] twenty gerahs to the shekel.[b]

[26] "But no one can consecrate a firstborn of the livestock, whether an animal from the herd or flock, to the LORD, because a firstborn already belongs to the LORD.[c] [27] If it is one of the unclean livestock, it can be ransomed according to your assessment by adding a fifth of its value to it. If it is not redeemed, it can be sold according to your assessment.[d]

[28] "Nothing that a man permanently sets apart to the LORD from all he owns, whether a person, an animal, or his inherited landholding, can be sold or redeemed; everything set apart is especially holy to the LORD. [29] No person who has been set apart for destruction is to be ransomed; he must be put to death.[e]

[30] "Every tenth of the land's produce, grain from the soil or fruit from the trees, belongs to the LORD;[f] it is holy to the LORD. [31] If a man decides to redeem any part of this tenth, he must add a fifth to its value. [32] Every tenth animal from the herd or flock, which passes under the shepherd's rod,[g] will be holy to the LORD. [33] He is not to inspect whether it is good or bad, and he is not to make a substitution for it. But if he does make a substitution, both the animal and its substitute will be holy;[h] they cannot be redeemed."[i]

[34] These are the commands the LORD gave Moses for the Israelites on Mount Sinai.[j]

[a] 27:24 Lv 25:28
[b] 27:25 Ex 30:13; Nm 18:16; Ezk 45:12
[c] 27:26 Ex 13:2,15; 34:19; Nm 18:15
[d] 27:27 Ex 13:13; 34:20

[e] 27:29 Nm 21:1-3; 31:7,13-17; Jos 6:17; 1Sm 15:17-33
[f] 27:30 Nm 18:21-32; Dt 14:22-29; Neh 10:37-39
[g] 27:32 Gn 28:22; 2Ch 31:6; Jr 33:13
[h] 27:33 Lv 12:4; 25:12
[i] Lv 27:10
[j] 27:34 Nm 36:13

[A] 27:25 A *shekel* is about two-fifths of an ounce of silver

---

27:30-34 Vows were voluntary, but tithes were required. **Every tenth of the land's produce . . . belongs to the LORD; it is holy** (27:30). God expected his people to return to him a portion of what he already owned and had graciously lent to them. (When we approach giving with the mindset that everything belongs to God, we realize what a blessing it is that he allows us to give these resources back to him to be used for his glorious purposes.) Not only did the tithe feed the priests, but it was also a reminder to the Israelites, and to us today, that even though we might earn our salaries by the sweat of our brows, we are not the originators of our blessings. "You may say to yourself, 'My power and my own ability have gained this wealth for me,' but remember that the Lord your God gives you the power to gain wealth" (Deut 8:17-18).

NUMBERS

INTRODUCTION

Author

THE BOOK OF NUMBERS IS formally anonymous—that is, it does not indicate the name of its writer. But ancient Jewish and Christian tradition affirms that Moses was the author—not only of Numbers but also of the entire Pentateuch (the first five books of the Old Testament). We read repeatedly that "The LORD spoke to Moses" (1:1), and we are informed that "Moses wrote down" what God told him (33:2). So, even though it's likely that a later editor added some things (such as 12:3) to the text, we have every reason to trust the claim that Moses authored the book.

Historical Background

Numbers picks up where Exodus left off—recounting events that happened one month later than what is recorded there (see Exod 40:2; Num 1:1). As the narrative opens, the Israelites have been free from Egyptian bondage for one year, have entered into a covenant with the Lord, and have received God's law through the hand of his servant Moses. As a result of Israel's national sin, the people descended from Israel (Jacob) would wander in the wilderness for forty years. Numbers covers the period from their departure from Sinai (1:1) to their arrival "by the Jordan across from Jericho" (36:13)—that is, it ends with God's people being on the verge of entering the promised land.

Message and Purpose

Numbers begins with a focus on the first generation out of Egypt, acknowledging their wanderings in the wilderness. It closes with the second generation preparing to enter the promised land.

As God's people left slavery, they had to move through the ins and outs of learning to trust their Deliverer daily. Through all their experiences, God was teaching them what it means to walk by faith, to move from the point of initial deliverance to their destiny as heirs of the promise. But a major factor on that journey was the wilderness itself. Living as nomads called to trust in a God they could not see for even the daily basics of food and water was difficult for the people. Though they obediently followed God through the

wilderness, they consistently displayed a lack of faith in him at the same time.

Nothing brings out the people's failure to trust God more than Numbers 14 does. There the people chose to believe the majority report that said the promised land couldn't be taken. In doing so, they rejected the report of Joshua and Caleb, who wisely said they could take it indeed if only they would believe God. As a result, that faithless generation was sentenced to die in the wilderness.

The rest of the book centers on the second generation of Israelites, who learned to walk in faith so that they could realize the destiny their parents had failed to gain: God's blessings in the promised land that was prepared for them. Numbers is a great reminder that kingdom benefits can only be secured by faith.

www.bhpublishinggroup.com/qr/te/04_00

Outline

I. Preparing to Travel to the Promised Land (1:1–10:10)
   A. The Numbering and Organization of the Twelve Tribes (1:1–4:49)
   B. Instructions for the Journey (5:1–10:10)

II. Israel on the Journey to the Promised Land (10:11–21:35)
   A. Traveling from Sinai to Kadesh (10:11–15:41)
   B. God's Discipline of the People (16:1–20:13)
   C. Traveling from Kadesh to Moab (20:14–21:35)

III. Israel on the Edge of the Promised Land (22:1–36:13)
   A. God's Faithfulness and Israel's Unfaithfulness (22:1–25:18)
   B. Preparations for Entering the Promised Land (26:1–30:16)
   C. Midianites Defeated and Transjordan Settled (31:1–32:42)
   D. Exhorting a New Generation and Dividing the Land (33:1–36:13)

THE CENSUS OF ISRAEL

1 The LORD spoke to Moses in the tent of meeting[a] in the Wilderness of Sinai,[b] on the first day of the second month of the second year[c] after Israel's departure from the land of Egypt: [2] "Take a census[d] of the entire Israelite community by their clans and their fathers' families,[A] counting the names of every male one by one. [3] You and Aaron are to register those who are twenty years old or more by their military divisions — everyone who can serve in Israel's army.[B,e] [4] A man from each tribe is to be with you, each one the head of his ancestral family.[C,f] [5] These are the names of the men who are to assist you:[g]

Elizur son of Shedeur from Reuben;
6   Shelumiel son of Zurishaddai
        from Simeon;
7   Nahshon son of Amminadab
        from Judah;
8   Nethanel son of Zuar from Issachar;
9   Eliab son of Helon from Zebulun;
10   from the sons of Joseph:
        Elishama son of Ammihud
        from Ephraim,
        Gamaliel son of Pedahzur
        from Manasseh;
11   Abidan son of Gideoni
        from Benjamin;
12   Ahiezer son of Ammishaddai
        from Dan;
13   Pagiel son of Ochran from Asher;
14   Eliasaph son of Deuel[D] from Gad;
15   Ahira son of Enan from Naphtali.

[16] These are the men called from the community; they are leaders of their ancestral tribes,[h] the heads of Israel's clans."[i]

[17] So Moses and Aaron took these men who had been designated by name,[j] [18] and they assembled the whole community on the first day of the second month. They recorded their ancestry by their clans and their ancestral families, counting one by one the names of those twenty years old or more, [19] just as the LORD commanded Moses. He registered them in the Wilderness of Sinai:

[20] The descendants of Reuben,[k] the firstborn of Israel: according to their family records by their clans and their ancestral families, counting one by one the names of every male twenty years old or more, everyone who could serve in the army, [21] those registered for the tribe of Reuben numbered 46,500.

[22] The descendants of Simeon:[l] according to their family records by their clans and their ancestral families, those registered counting one by one the names of every male twenty years old or more, everyone who could serve in the army, [23] those registered for the tribe of Simeon numbered 59,300.

[24] The descendants of Gad:[m] according to their family records by their clans and their ancestral families, counting the names of those twenty years old or more, everyone who could serve in the army, [25] those registered for the tribe of Gad numbered 45,650.

[26] The descendants of Judah:[n] according to their family records by their clans and their ancestral families, counting the names of those twenty years old or more, everyone who could serve in the army, [27] those registered for the tribe of Judah numbered 74,600.

[28] The descendants of Issachar:[o] according to their family records by their clans and their ancestral families, counting the names of those twenty years old or more, everyone who could serve in the army, [29] those registered for the tribe of Issachar numbered 54,400.

[30] The descendants of Zebulun:[p] according to their family records by their clans and their ancestral families, counting the names of those twenty years old or more, everyone who could serve in the army, [31] those registered for the tribe of Zebulun numbered 57,400.

[32] The descendants of Joseph:[q]

The descendants of Ephraim:[r] according to their family records by their

a 1:1 Ex 27:21; 40:2,6-7,34-35
b Ex 19:1; Nm 33:16
c Ex 12:40-41; 19:1; 40:17
d 1:2 Ex 30:11-16; Nm 26:2
e 1:3 Ex 30:14; Nm 14:29; 32:11; 1Ch 23:24,27; Ezr 3:8
f 1:4 Nm 1:16; Jos 22:14
g 1:5-15 Nm 2:3-30; 7:12-83; 10:14-27
h 1:16 Nm 1:47; 13:2; 26:55; 33:54; 36:4-8
i Nm 10:4; Jos 22:21,30
j 1:17 1Ch 12:31; 16:41; 2Ch 28:15; 31:19; Ezr 8:20
k 1:20 Gn 29:32; 49:3-4; 1Ch 5:1

l 1:22 Gn 29:33; 42:14-24; 49:5-7
m 1:24 Gn 30:11; 49:19
n 1:26 Gn 29:35; 49:8-12; Mt 1:2-3; Rv 5:5
o 1:28 Gn 30:18; 49:14-15
p 1:30 Gn 30:20; 49:13
q 1:32 Gn 30:22-24; 49:22-26
r Gn 46:20; 48:13-20

A **1:2** Lit *the house of their fathers,* also in vv. 18,20,22,24,26,28,30,32,34,36,38,40,42,45   B **1:3** Lit *everyone going out to war in Israel*   C **1:4** Lit *the house of his fathers,* also in v. 44   D **1:14** LXX, Syr read *Reuel*

1:1-46 Over two million souls had to be organized into an orderly traveling community. **The LORD** got this massive process started with a command to Moses: **Take a census of the entire Israelite community . . . register** . . . **everyone who can serve in Israel's army** (1:1-3). This count also assessed Israel's preparedness for war. **1:17-46** The twelve tribes listed descended from the sons of Jacob (1:20-43), except for **Ephraim** and **Manasseh** (1:32-35). They replaced the priestly tribe of Levi who would not receive a land inheritance. These two tribes descended from Jacob's son, **Joseph.**

ᵃ1:34 Gn 46:20; 48:13-20
ᵇ1:36 Gn 35:18; 49:27
ᶜ1:38 Gn 30:6; 49:16-17
ᵈ1:40 Gn 30:13; 49:20
ᵉ1:42 Gn 30:8; 49:21

ᶠ1:46 Ex 12:37; Nm 26:51
ᵍ1:47 Gn 34:25,30; 49:5-7;
Ex 32:26-29; Nm 3:6,12-
13,40-43; 8:16-19; 18:1; Dt
10:8-9; 18:1-2; 21:5; Jos
13:14,33
ʰ1:51 Ex 29:33; 30:33; Nm
3:10,38; 16:40; 18:4,7
ⁱEx 19:12; Nm 3:10,38;
8:19; 18:7
ʲ1:53 Nm 3:7; 18:4-5; 1Ch
23:32; Ezk 44:15-16
ᵏ1:54 Ex 39:32,42; Nm 9:5;
36:10; Jos 14:5
ˡ2:3 Nm 1:3,52; 2:9-10;
10:14; 33:1; Jdg 8:6
ᵐEx 6:23; Nm 1:7; 7:12,17;
10:14; 1Ch 2:10-11; Mt 1:4;
Lk 3:32

clans and their ancestral families, counting the names of those twenty years old or more, everyone who could serve in the army, ³³ those registered for the tribe of Ephraim numbered 40,500.

³⁴ The descendants of Manasseh:ᵃ according to their family records by their clans and their ancestral families, counting the names of those twenty years old or more, everyone who could serve in the army, ³⁵ those registered for the tribe of Manasseh numbered 32,200.

³⁶ The descendants of Benjamin:ᵇ according to their family records by their clans and their ancestral families, counting the names of those twenty years old or more, everyone who could serve in the army, ³⁷ those registered for the tribe of Benjamin numbered 35,400.

³⁸ The descendants of Dan:ᶜ according to their family records by their clans and their ancestral families, counting the names of those twenty years old or more, everyone who could serve in the army, ³⁹ those registered for the tribe of Dan numbered 62,700.

⁴⁰ The descendants of Asher:ᵈ according to their family records by their clans and their ancestral families, counting the names of those twenty years old or more, everyone who could serve in the army, ⁴¹ those registered for the tribe of Asher numbered 41,500.

⁴² The descendants of Naphtali:ᵉ according to their family records by their clans and their ancestral families, counting the names of those twenty years old or more, everyone who could serve in the army, ⁴³ those registered for the tribe of Naphtali numbered 53,400.

⁴⁴ These are the men Moses and Aaron registered, with the assistance of the twelve leaders of Israel; each represented his ancestral family. ⁴⁵ So all the Israelites twenty years old or more, everyone who could serve in Israel's army, were registered by their ancestral families. ⁴⁶ All those registered numbered 603,550.ᶠ

DUTIES OF THE LEVITES

⁴⁷ But the Levitesᵍ were not registered with them by their ancestral tribe. ⁴⁸ For the LORD had told Moses: ⁴⁹ "Do not register or take a census of the tribe of Levi with the other Israelites. ⁵⁰ Appoint the Levites over the tabernacle of the testimony, all its furnishings, and everything in it. They are to transport the tabernacle and all its articles, take care of it, and camp around it. ⁵¹ Whenever the tabernacle is to move, the Levites are to take it down, and whenever it is to stop at a campsite, the Levites are to set it up. Any unauthorizedʰ person who comes near it is to be put to death.ⁱ

⁵² "The Israelites are to camp by their military divisions, each man with his encampment and under his banner. ⁵³ The Levites are to camp around the tabernacle of the testimony and watch over it, so that no wrath will fall on the Israelite community."ʲ ⁵⁴ The Israelites did everything just as the LORD had commanded Moses.ᵏ

ORGANIZATION OF THE CAMPS

2 The LORD spoke to Moses and Aaron: ² "The Israelites are to camp under their respective banners beside the flags of their ancestral families.ᴬ They are to camp around the tent of meeting at a distance from it:

³ Judah's military divisionsˡ will camp on the east side toward the sunrise under their banner. The leader of the descendants of Judah is Nahshonᵐ son of Amminadab. ⁴ His military division numbers 74,600. ⁵ The tribe of Issachar will camp next to it. The leader of the Issacharites is Nethanel son of Zuar. ⁶ His military division numbers 54,400.

ᴬ2:2 Lit the house of their fathers, also in v. 32

1:47-50 That **the Levites were not registered** (1:47) indicates that even in the event of war, worship was to remain paramount. The Levites were set aside to care for **the tabernacle** (1:50).
1:52-53 The Israelite **camp** was laid out in a cross shape (based on the placements and tribal sizes given in Num 2), with three tribes grouped on each side of the tabernacle, which was situated in the middle. The Levites camped **around the tabernacle** and thus stood between the people and God's dwelling (1:53). Even in the physical layout of the Israelite nation on the move, the people needed a human mediator to stand between them and God. The ultimate mediator would come in God's Son, Jesus Christ, who would die on a cross (see 1 Tim 2:5).
2:3-4 **The east** was the direction in which the tabernacle faced. This meant that the tribe of **Judah** led the way when the nation traveled (2:3). It was the appropriate position for the tribe from which kings, including David and Jesus Christ, would come.

7 The tribe of Zebulun will be next. The leader of the Zebulunites is Eliab son of Helon. **8** His military division numbers 57,400. **9** The total number in their military divisions who belong to Judah's encampment is 186,400; they will move out first.

10 Reuben's military divisions will camp on the south side under their banner. The leader of the Reubenites is Elizur son of Shedeur. **11** His military division numbers 46,500. **12** The tribe of Simeon will camp next to it. The leader of the Simeonites is Shelumiel son of Zurishaddai. **13** His military division numbers 59,300. **14** The tribe of Gad will be next. The leader of the Gadites is Eliasaph son of Deuel.^A **15** His military division numbers 45,650. **16** The total number in their military divisions who belong to Reuben's encampment is 151,450; they will move out second.

17 The tent of meeting is to move out with the Levites' camp, which is in the middle of the camps. They are to move out just as they camp, each in his place,^B with their banners.

18 Ephraim's military divisions will camp on the west side under their banner. The leader of the Ephraimites is Elishama son of Ammihud. **19** His military division numbers 40,500. **20** The tribe of Manasseh will be next to it. The leader of the Manassites is Gamaliel son of Pedahzur. **21** His military division numbers 32,200. **22** The tribe of Benjamin will be next. The leader of the Benjaminites is Abidan son of Gideoni. **23** His military division numbers 35,400. **24** The total in their military divisions who belong to Ephraim's encampment number 108,100; they will move out third.

25 Dan's military divisions will camp on the north side under their banner. The leader of the Danites is Ahiezer son of Ammishaddai. **26** His military division numbers 62,700. **27** The tribe of Asher will camp next to it. The leader of the Asherites is Pagiel son of Ochran. **28** His military division numbers 41,500. **29** The tribe of Naphtali will be next. The leader of the Naphtalites is Ahira son of Enan. **30** His military division numbers 53,400. **31** The total number who belong to Dan's encampment is 157,600; they are to move out last, with their banners."

32 These are the Israelites registered by their ancestral families. The total number in the camps by their military divisions is 603,550. **33** But the Levites were not registered among the Israelites, just as the LORD had commanded Moses.^a **34** The Israelites did everything the LORD commanded Moses; they camped by their banners in this way and moved out the same way, each man by his clan and by his ancestral family.^c,b

AARON'S SONS AND THE LEVITES

3 These are the family records of Aaron and Moses at the time the LORD spoke with Moses on Mount Sinai.^c **2** These are the names of Aaron's sons: Nadab, the firstborn, and Abihu, Eleazar, and Ithamar. **3** These are the names of Aaron's sons, the anointed priests, who were ordained to serve as priests. **4** But Nadab and Abihu died in the LORD's presence when they presented unauthorized fire^d before the LORD in the Wilderness of Sinai, and they had no sons. So Eleazar and Ithamar served as priests under the direction of Aaron their father.^e

5 The LORD spoke to Moses: **6** "Bring the tribe of Levi near and present them to the priest Aaron to assist him. **7** They are to perform duties for^D him and the entire community before the tent of meeting by attending to the service of the tabernacle. **8** They are to take care of all the furnishings of the tent of meeting^f and perform duties for the Israelites by attending to the service of the tabernacle. **9** Assign the Levites to Aaron and his sons; they have been assigned exclusively to him^E from the Israelites.^g **10** You are to appoint Aaron and his sons to carry out their priestly responsibilities, but any unauthorized

^a 2:33 Nm 1:47-49
^b 2:34 Nm 10:10-28
^c 3:1 Ex 19:3
^d 3:4 Lv 10:1-2
^e Lv 10:6; Nm 4:16,28,33
^f 3:8 Nm 1:50,53
^g 3:9 Nm 8:16,19,22; 18:6

---

^A 2:14 Some Hb mss, Sam, Vg; other Hb mss read *Reuel* ^B 2:17 Lit *each on his hand* ^C 2:34 Lit *the house of his fathers* ^D 3:7 Or *to guard*, also in v. 8 ^E 3:9 Some Hb mss, LXX, Sam read *me*; Nm 8:16

2:17 The tribes were **to move out just as they** camped, **each in his place, with their banners.** Their migration must've been an awesome sight!
3:1-3 While both Moses and Aaron were descendants of Levi, only Aaron and his descendants were chosen by God to serve as priests (3:3). The rest of the Levites were commanded to assist and to care for the tabernacle.
3:4 Nadab and Abihu, Aaron's eldest sons who were also priests, had **died in the LORD's** presence when they presented unauthorized fire (see Lev 10:1-2). That left **Eleazar and Ithamar** to do the job.
3:6-10 The Levites' duties explained here in general terms are given in more detail in chapter 4.

person who comes near the sanctuary is to be put to death."[a]

11 The LORD spoke to Moses: 12 "See, I have taken the Levites from the Israelites in place of every firstborn Israelite from the womb.[b] The Levites belong to me, 13 because every firstborn belongs to me. At the time I struck down every firstborn in the land of Egypt,[c] I consecrated every firstborn in Israel to myself, both man and animal. They are mine; I am the LORD."[d]

THE LEVITICAL CENSUS

14 The LORD spoke to Moses in the Wilderness of Sinai: 15 "Register the Levites by their ancestral families[A] and their clans. You are to register every male one month old or more." 16 So Moses registered them in obedience to the LORD as he had been commanded:

17 These were Levi's sons by name: Gershon, Kohath, and Merari. 18 These were the names of Gershon's sons by their clans: Libni and Shimei. 19 Kohath's sons by their clans were Amram, Izhar, Hebron, and Uzziel. 20 Merari's sons by their clans were Mahli and Mushi. These were the Levite clans by their ancestral families.[e]

21 The Libnite clan and the Shimeite clan came from Gershon; these were the Gershonite clans. 22 Those registered, counting every male one month old or more, numbered 7,500. 23 The Gershonite clans camped behind the tabernacle on the west side,[f] 24 and the leader of the Gershonite families[B] was Eliasaph son of Lael. 25 The Gershonites' duties[g] at the tent of meeting involved the tabernacle, the tent, its covering, the screen for the entrance to the tent of meeting,[h] 26 the hangings of the courtyard, the screen for the entrance[i] to the courtyard that surrounds the tabernacle and the altar, and the tent ropes — all the work relating to these.

27 The Amramite clan, the Izharite clan, the Hebronite clan, and the Uzzielite clan came from Kohath; these were the Kohathites. 28 Counting every male one month old or more, there were 8,600[C] responsible for the duties of[D] the sanctuary. 29 The clans of the Kohathites camped on the south side of the tabernacle,[j] 30 and the leader of the families of the Kohathite clans was Elizaphan son of Uzziel. 31 Their duties involved the ark, the table, the lampstand, the altars, the sanctuary utensils that were used with these, and the screen[E,k] — and all the work relating to them.[l] 32 The chief of the Levite leaders was Eleazar[m] son of Aaron the priest; he had oversight of those responsible for the duties of the sanctuary.

33 The Mahlite clan and the Mushite clan came from Merari; these were the Merarite clans. 34 Those registered, counting every male one month old or more, numbered 6,200. 35 The leader of the families of the Merarite clans was Zuriel son of Abihail; they camped on the north side of the tabernacle.[n] 36 The assigned duties of Merari's descendants involved the tabernacle's supports, crossbars, pillars, bases, all its equipment, and all the work related to these,[o] 37 in addition to the posts of the surrounding courtyard with their bases, tent pegs, and ropes.

38 Moses, Aaron, and his sons, who performed the duties of[F] the sanctuary as a service on behalf of the Israelites, camped in front of the tabernacle on the east,[p] in front of the tent of meeting toward the sunrise. Any unauthorized person who came near it was to be put to death.[q]

39 The total number of all the Levite males one month old or more that Moses and Aaron[G] registered by their clans at the LORD's command was 22,000.

REDEMPTION OF THE FIRSTBORN

40 The LORD told Moses: "Register every firstborn male of the Israelites[r] one month

[a] 3:10 Nm 1:51; 3:38; 8:19; 18:7
[b] 3:12 Ex 13:1-2; 32:26-29; Nm 3:6,12-13,40-43; 8:16-18; 18:1
[c] 3:13 Ex 13:15-16
[d] Ex 3:14-16; 6:6-7; Nm 3:41,45
[e] 3:17-20 Ex 6:17-19; 1Ch 6:1,16,20-29
[f] 3:23 Nm 2:18-24
[g] 3:25-26 Nm 4:24-26
[h] 3:25 Ex 26:7,14,36-37; 35:11,15
[i] 3:26 Ex 27:9-19; 35:17-18; 38:9-31
[j] 3:29 Nm 2:10-16
[k] 3:31 Ex 35:12
[l] Ex 25:10–27:21
[m] 3:32 Ex 6:23-25; 28:1; Lv 10:6,12,16; Nm 3:2,4
[n] 3:35 Nm 2:25-31
[o] 3:36-37 Ex 35:1-13; Nm 4:31-32
[p] 3:38 Nm 2:3-9
[q] Nm 1:51; 3:10; 8:19; 18:7
[r] 3:40 Ex 13:1-2; Nm 8:16-18

A 3:15 Lit *the house of their fathers*, also in v. 20 B 3:24 Lit *a father's house*, also in vv. 30,35 C 3:28 LXX reads *8,300* D 3:28 Or *for guarding*, also in v. 32 E 3:31 The screen between the most holy place and the holy place; Ex 35:12 F 3:38 Or *who guarded* G 3:39 Some Hb mss, Sam, Syr omit *and Aaron*

3:11-13 God could have claimed every firstborn male in Israel to be set aside for his service at the tabernacle; instead, he chose the Levites to serve **in place of every firstborn Israelite** (3:12).
3:17 Duties and positions related to worship were divvied up to **Levi's sons**, who are listed **by name**.
3:23-26 **The Gershonite clans** were responsible for **the tabernacle** itself (3:23; see 4:21-26).
3:29-31 The Kohathites' **duties involved** caring for the furnishings of the tabernacle, including **the ark** and **lampstand** (3:31).
3:33-37 **The Merarite clans** were to dismantle, carry, and set up **the tabernacle's** wooden framework and all connecting items that supported it. They were the heavy haulers (see 4:29-33).
3:40-51 A precise count was made to ensure there were enough Levites to redeem **every firstborn male** in the camp (3:40-42). The Levite count was 22,000 (3:39), but the firstborn count

old or more, and list their names. 41 You are to take the Levites for me — I am the LORD — in place of every firstborn among the Israelites, and the Levites' cattle in place of every firstborn among the Israelites' cattle." 42 So Moses registered every firstborn among the Israelites, as the LORD commanded him. 43 The total number of the firstborn males one month old or more listed by name was 22,273.

44 The LORD spoke to Moses again: 45 "Take the Levites in place of every firstborn among the Israelites, and the Levites' cattle in place of their cattle. The Levites belong to me; I am the LORD.[a] 46 As the redemption price for the 273 firstborn Israelites who outnumber the Levites, 47 collect five shekels for each person, according to the standard sanctuary shekel — twenty gerahs to the shekel.[A,b] 48 Give the silver to Aaron and his sons as the redemption price for those who are in excess among the Israelites."

49 So Moses collected the redemption amount from those in excess of the ones redeemed by the Levites. 50 He collected the silver from the firstborn Israelites: 1,365 shekels[B] measured by the standard sanctuary shekel. 51 He gave the redemption silver to Aaron and his sons in obedience to the LORD, just as the LORD commanded Moses.

DUTIES OF THE KOHATHITES

4 The LORD spoke to Moses and Aaron: 2 "Among the Levites, take a census of the Kohathites[c] by their clans and their ancestral families,[C] 3 men from thirty years old to fifty years old — everyone who is qualified[D] to do work at the tent of meeting.

4 "The service of the Kohathites at the tent of meeting concerns the most holy objects.[d] 5 Whenever the camp is about to move on, Aaron and his sons are to go in, take down the screening curtain, and cover the ark of the testimony with it.[e] 6 They are to place over this a covering made of fine leather,[E,f] spread a solid blue cloth on top, and insert its poles.[g]

7 "They are to spread a blue cloth over the table of the Presence and place the plates and cups on it, as well as the bowls and pitchers for the drink offering. The regular bread offering is to be on it.[h] 8 They are to spread a scarlet cloth over them, cover them with a covering made of fine leather, and insert the poles in the table.[i]

9 "They are to take a blue cloth and cover the lampstand[j] used for light, with its lamps, snuffers, and firepans,[k] as well as its jars of oil by which they service it. 10 Then they are to place it with all its utensils inside a covering made of fine leather and put them on the carrying frame.

11 "They are to spread a blue cloth over the gold altar,[l] cover it with a covering made of fine leather, and insert its poles.[m] 12 They are to take all the serving utensils they use in the sanctuary, place them in a blue cloth, cover them with a covering made of fine leather, and put them on a carrying frame.

13 "They are to remove the ashes from the bronze altar, spread a purple cloth over it, 14 and place all the equipment on it that they use in serving: the firepans, meat forks, shovels, and basins — all the equipment of the altar.[n] They are to spread a covering made of fine leather over it and insert its poles.[F,o]

15 "Aaron and his sons are to finish covering the holy objects and all their equipment whenever the camp is to move on. The Kohathites will come and carry them, but they are not to touch the holy objects or they will die.[p] These are the transportation duties of the Kohathites regarding the tent of meeting.

16 "Eleazar, son of Aaron the priest, has oversight of the lamp oil,[q] the fragrant incense,[r] the daily grain offering,[s] and the anointing oil.[t] He has oversight of the entire tabernacle and everything in it, the holy objects and their utensils."[G]

17 Then the LORD spoke to Moses and Aaron: 18 "Do not allow the Kohathite tribal clans to be wiped out from the Levites. 19 Do this for them so that they may live and not die when they come near the most holy objects:[u] Aaron and his sons are to go in and assign each man his task and transportation duty. 20 The Kohathites are not to

[a] 3:45 Nm 3:13,41; 10:10; 15:40-41
[b] 3:47 Nm 18:16
[c] 4:2 Ex 6:16,18; Nm 3:27-31; 1Ch 6:22-28
[d] 4:4 Nm 3:30-31; 4:15-19
[e] 4:5 Ex 25:10-22; 26:31-33
[f] 4:6 Ex 25:5; 26:14; 35:7,23; 36:19,34
[g] Ex 25:13-15
[h] 4:7 Ex 25:30; Lv 24:5-9
[i] 4:8 Ex 25:26-28
[j] 4:9 Ex 25:31-35; 26:35; 37:17-20
[k] Ex 25:38; 37:23; Nm 4:14
[l] 4:11 Ex 30:1-3; 31:8; 39:38; 40:5,26
[m] Ex 30:4; 35:15
[n] 4:14 Ex 27:3; 38:3; Nm 7:13–8:4
[o] Ex 27:7
[p] 4:15 Nm 1:51; 4:20; 8:19; 18:7
[q] 4:16 Ex 25:6; 27:20; Lv 4:2
[r] Ex 25:6; 30:7; Lv 4:7
[s] Lv 6:20-22
[t] Ex 25:6; 29:7,21; Lv 8:2,10,12,30
[u] 4:19 Nm 3:31; 4:4

[A] 3:47 A shekel is about two-fifths of an ounce of silver [B] 3:50 Over 34 pounds of silver [C] 4:2 Lit *the house of their fathers*, also in vv. 22,29,34, 38,40,42,46 [D] 4:3 Lit *everyone entering the service* [E] 4:6 Hb obscure, also in vv. 8,10,11,12,14,25 [F] 4:14 Sam, LXX add *They are to take a purple cloth and cover the wash basin and its base. They are to place them in a covering made of fine leather and put them on the carrying frame.* [G] 4:16 Or *the sanctuary and its furnishings*

among the Israelites was **22,273** (3:43). A collection of **five shekels** of silver was taken up for each of the **273** males as their redemption price. It was given to **Aaron and his sons** (3:46-51).

4:2-3 Those performing service among the Levites had to be **from thirty years old to fifty** (4:3).

4:9-15 Once everything was properly covered and organized, **the Kohathites** could **carry** the tabernacle furnishings. But if they touched any of **the holy objects**, they would **die** (4:15). Their duty was not to be taken lightly.

ᵃ4:22 Nm 3:17,21-26
ᵇ4:25 Ex 26:1-13; 36:8-17
ᶜ4:28 Ex 6:23; 28:1; 38:21
ᵈ4:29 Ex 6:16,19; Nm 3:17,33-37

ᵉ5:2 Ex 4:6; Lv 13:42-44; Nm 12:10
ᶠLv 15:2-33; 22:4; 2Sm 3:29

go in and look at the holy objects as they are covered^ or they will die."

DUTIES OF THE GERSHONITES

²¹ The LORD spoke to Moses: ²² "Take a census of the Gershonites^a also, by their ancestral families and their clans. ²³ Register men from thirty years old to fifty years old, everyone who is qualified to perform service, to do work at the tent of meeting. ²⁴ This is the service of the Gershonite clans regarding work and transportation duties: ²⁵ They are to transport the tabernacle curtains,^b the tent of meeting with its covering and the covering made of fine leather on top of it, the screen for the entrance to the tent of meeting, ²⁶ the hangings of the courtyard, the screen for the entrance at the gate of the courtyard that surrounds the tabernacle and the altar, along with their ropes and all the equipment for their service. They will carry out everything that needs to be done with these items.

²⁷ "All the service of the Gershonites, all their transportation duties and all their other work, is to be done at the command of Aaron and his sons; you are to assign to them all that they are responsible to carry. ²⁸ This is the service of the Gershonite clans at the tent of meeting, and their duties will be under the direction of Ithamar son of Aaron the priest.^c

DUTIES OF THE MERARITES

²⁹ "As for the Merarites, you are to register them by their clans^d and their ancestral families. ³⁰ Register men from thirty years old to fifty years old, everyone who is qualified to do the work of the tent of meeting. ³¹ This is what they are responsible to carry as the whole of their service at the tent of meeting: the supports of the tabernacle, with its crossbars, pillars, and bases, ³² the posts of the surrounding courtyard with their bases, tent pegs, and ropes, including all their equipment and all the work related to them. You are to assign by name the items that they are responsible to carry. ³³ This is the service of the Merarite clans regarding all their work at the tent of meeting, under the direction of Ithamar son of Aaron the priest."

CENSUS OF THE LEVITES

³⁴ So Moses, Aaron, and the leaders of the community registered the Kohathites by their clans and their ancestral families, ³⁵ men from thirty years old to fifty years old, everyone who was qualified for work at the tent of meeting. ³⁶ The men registered by their clans numbered 2,750. ³⁷ These were the registered men of the Kohathite clans, everyone who could serve at the tent of meeting. Moses and Aaron registered them at the LORD's command through Moses.

³⁸ The Gershonites were registered by their clans and their ancestral families, ³⁹ men from thirty years old to fifty years old, everyone who was qualified for work at the tent of meeting. ⁴⁰ The men registered by their clans and their ancestral families numbered 2,630. ⁴¹ These were the registered men of the Gershonite clans. At the LORD's command Moses and Aaron registered everyone who could serve at the tent of meeting.

⁴² The men of the Merarite clans were registered by their clans and their ancestral families, ⁴³ those from thirty years old to fifty years old, everyone who was qualified for work at the tent of meeting. ⁴⁴ The men registered by their clans numbered 3,200. ⁴⁵ These were the registered men of the Merarite clans; Moses and Aaron registered them at the LORD's command through Moses.

⁴⁶ Moses, Aaron, and the leaders of Israel registered all the Levites by their clans and their ancestral families, ⁴⁷ from thirty years old to fifty years old, everyone who was qualified to do the work of serving at the tent of meeting and transporting it. ⁴⁸ Their registered men numbered 8,580. ⁴⁹ At the LORD's command they were registered under the direction of Moses, each one according to his work and transportation duty, and his assignment was as the LORD commanded Moses.

ISOLATION OF THE UNCLEAN

5 The LORD instructed Moses: ² "Command the Israelites to send away anyone from the camp who is afflicted with a skin disease,^e anyone who has a discharge,^f or anyone who is defiled

^4:20 Or objects, even long enough to swallow,

4:46-49 A total of **8,580** Levites were set apart for the Lord's service (4:48). Thus, the work of transporting the tabernacle could be shared among them. No one would be over-burdened. This cooperative approach should carry over into the church.
5:1-4 God's holiness was manifested visibly in the tabernacle, which was in the center of the Israelites' camp and served as the symbol of his presence in their midst. The regulations of chapter 5 spell out several stipulations regarding how the people were called to be

because of a corpse.[a] [3] Send away both male or female; send them outside the camp, so that they will not defile their camps where I dwell among them." [4] The Israelites did this, sending them outside the camp. The Israelites did as the LORD instructed Moses.

COMPENSATION FOR WRONGDOING

[5] The LORD spoke to Moses: [6] "Tell the Israelites: When a man or woman commits any sin against another, that person acts unfaithfully toward the LORD[b] and is guilty.[c] [7] The person is to confess[d] the sin he has committed. He is to pay full compensation, add a fifth of its value to it, and give it to the individual he has wronged.[e] [8] But if that individual has no relative[f] to receive compensation, the compensation goes to the LORD for the priest, along with the atonement ram by which the priest will make atonement for the guilty person.[g] [9] Every holy contribution the Israelites present to the priest will be his.[h] [10] Each one's holy contribution is his to give; what each one gives to the priest will be his."

THE JEALOUSY RITUAL

[11] The LORD spoke to Moses: [12] "Speak to the Israelites and tell them: If any man's wife goes astray, is unfaithful to him, [13] and sleeps with another,[A] but it is concealed from her husband, and she is undetected, even though she has defiled herself, since there is no witness against her, and she wasn't caught in the act; [14] and if a feeling of jealousy[i] comes over the husband and he becomes jealous because of his wife who has defiled herself — or if a feeling of jealousy comes over him and he becomes jealous of her though she has not defiled herself — [15] then the man is to bring his wife to the priest. He is also to bring an offering for her of two quarts[B] of barley flour. He is not to pour oil over it or put frankincense on it because it is a grain offering of jealousy, a grain offering for remembrance to draw attention to guilt.

[16] "The priest is to bring her forward and have her stand before the LORD. [17] Then the priest is to take holy water in a clay bowl, take some of the dust from the tabernacle floor, and put it in the water. [18] After the priest has the woman stand before the LORD, he is to let down her hair[c] and place in her hands the grain offering for remembrance, which is the grain offering of jealousy. The priest is to hold the bitter water that brings a curse. [19] The priest will require the woman to take an oath and will say to her, 'If no man has slept with you, if you have not gone astray and become defiled while under your husband's authority, be unaffected by this bitter water that brings a curse. [20] But if you have gone astray while under your husband's authority, if you have defiled yourself and a man other than your husband has slept with you' — [21] at this point the priest will make the woman take the oath with the sworn curse, and he is to say to her — 'May the LORD make you into an object of your people's cursing and swearing when he makes your womb[D] shrivel and your belly swell. [22] May this water that brings a curse enter your stomach, causing your belly to swell and your womb to shrivel.'

"And the woman will reply, 'Amen, Amen.'

[23] "Then the priest is to write these curses on a scroll and wash them off into the bitter water. [24] He will require the woman to drink the bitter water that brings a curse, and it will enter her to cause bitter suffering. [25] The priest is to take the grain offering of jealousy from the woman, present the offering before the LORD, and bring it to the altar. [26] The priest is to take a handful of the grain offering as a memorial portion[j] and burn it on the altar. Afterward, he will require the woman to drink the water. [27] "When he makes her drink the water, if she has defiled herself and been unfaithful to her husband, the water that brings a curse will enter her to cause bitter suffering; her belly will swell, and her

[a] 5:2 Lv 14:2-3; 15:2; 22:4; Nm 9:6-7
[b] 5:6 Lv 6:2; Nm 31:16; Jos 22:22; 2Ch 28:19
[c] Lv 4:13,22,27; 5:2-5,17-19; 6:4; Ezk 22:4; 25:12
[d] 5:7 Lv 5:5; 26:40; Neh 1:6
[e] Lv 5:16; 6:1-5; 22:14; 27:13,15,19,27,31
[f] 5:8 Lv 25:25,48-49; Jr 32:7
[g] Lv 6:6-7
[h] 5:9 Ex 25:2-3; 29:27-28; Lv 7:14,32,34
[i] 5:14 Jb 5:2; Pr 6:34; 14:30; 27:4; 2Co 12:20; Gl 5:20

[j] 5:26 Lv 2:2,9,16; 5:12; 6:15; 24:7

[A] 5:13 Lit and man lies with her and has an emission of semen   [B] 5:15 Lit a tenth of an ephah   [C] 5:18 Or to uncover her head   [D] 5:21 Lit thigh, also in vv. 22,27

---

holy because their Lord is holy (see Lev 19:2). The "unclean" among them had to go **outside the camp** so that they didn't **defile** the encampment (Num 5:3). The issue here was ceremonial uncleanness—not any inherent spiritual inferiority within those who were suffering.
5:6 Everyone needed to be reminded that *any* sin in Israel's kingdom community was

ultimately a sin against **the LORD**. King David would understand this. Though he committed adultery (wronging both Bathsheba and her husband Uriah) and murder (by having Uriah killed), David knew that he had offended God most of all. For it was God who said, "Do not murder," and "Do not commit adultery" (Exod 20:13-14). This is why David prayed, "Against you—you alone—I have sinned" (Ps 51:4).

5:11-31 The point here is that if the woman were innocent, no harm would come to her (5:28). But if she were guilty, the curse would supernaturally render her sterile (5:27). Some modern critics of the Bible cite this as an example of how the Bible affirms the oppression of women, but it is actually an example of how God supernaturally protected women before there was any other way to prove their innocence.

[a] 6:2 Jdg 13:5,7; 16:17; Am 2:11-12
[b] 6:3 Jdg 13:4,7,14
[c] 6:6 Nm 19:11-16
[d] 6:8 Nm 6:5; Dt 7:6; 14:2,21; 26:19; 2Ch 35:3
[e] 6:9 Nm 19:11
[f] 6:10 Ex 29:42-43; Lv 5:7; Nm 6:18
[g] 6:11 Lv 1:14-17; 5:7-10

[h] 6:11 Lv 15:13-15
[i] 6:12 Lv 5:14-19; 7:1-6
[j] 6:13 Lv 14:11; Nm 8:9
[k] 6:14 Ac 21:24
[l] Lv 1:10-13; 3:1-5; 4:32-35
[m] 6:15 Ex 29:40-41; Lv 23:12-13,18; Nm 15:1-12
[n] Ex 29:2; Lv 2:4-11; 7:12
[o] 6:19 Ex 29:24; Lv 2:4-11
[p] 6:20 Ex 29:25-27
[q] Ex 25:2-3; 29:27-28; Lv 7:14,32,34
[r] 6:21 Ac 21:24

womb will shrivel. She will become a curse among her people. [28] But if the woman has not defiled herself and is pure, she will be unaffected and will be able to conceive children.

[29] "This is the law regarding jealousy when a wife goes astray and defiles herself while under her husband's authority, [30] or when a feeling of jealousy comes over a husband and he becomes jealous of his wife. He is to have the woman stand before the Lord, and the priest will carry out all these instructions for her. [31] The husband will be free of guilt, but that woman will bear her iniquity."

THE NAZIRITE VOW

6 The Lord instructed Moses: [2] "Speak to the Israelites and tell them: When a man or woman makes a special vow, a Nazirite vow,[a] to consecrate himself to the Lord, [3] he is to abstain from wine and beer.[b] He must not drink vinegar made from wine or from beer. He must not drink any grape juice or eat fresh grapes or raisins. [4] He is not to eat anything produced by the grapevine, from seeds to skin, during the period of his consecration.

[5] "You must not cut his hair[A] throughout the time of his vow of consecration. He may be holy until the time is completed during which he consecrates himself to the Lord; he is to let the hair of his head grow long. [6] He must not go near a dead body during the time he consecrates himself to the Lord.[c] [7] He is not to defile himself for his father or mother, or his brother or sister, when they die, while the mark of consecration to his God is on his head. [8] He is holy to the Lord[d] during the time of consecration.

[9] "If someone suddenly dies near him, defiling his consecrated head, he must shave his head on the day of his purification; he is to shave it on the seventh day.[e] [10] On the eighth day he is to bring two turtledoves or two young pigeons to the priest at the entrance to the tent of meeting.[f] [11] The priest is to offer one as a sin offering and the other as a burnt offering[g] to make atonement on behalf

of the Nazirite, since he incurred guilt because of the corpse. On that day he is to consecrate his head again.[h] [12] He is to rededicate his time of consecration to the Lord and to bring a year-old male lamb as a guilt offering.[i] But do not count the initial period of consecration because it became defiled.

[13] "This is the law of the Nazirite: On the day his time of consecration is completed, he is to be brought to the entrance to the tent of meeting.[j] [14] He is to present an offering to the Lord[k] of one unblemished year-old male lamb as a burnt offering, one unblemished year-old female lamb as a sin offering, one unblemished ram as a fellowship offering,[l] [15] along with their grain offerings and drink offerings,[m] and a basket of unleavened cakes made from fine flour mixed with oil, and unleavened wafers coated with oil.[n]

[16] "The priest is to present these before the Lord and sacrifice the Nazirite's sin offering and burnt offering. [17] He will also offer the ram as a fellowship sacrifice to the Lord, together with the basket of unleavened bread. Then the priest will offer the accompanying grain offering and drink offering.

[18] "The Nazirite is to shave his consecrated head at the entrance to the tent of meeting, take the hair from his head, and put it on the fire under the fellowship sacrifice. [19] The priest is to take the boiled shoulder from the ram, one unleavened cake from the basket, and one unleavened wafer, and put them into the hands[o] of the Nazirite after he has shaved his consecrated head. [20] The priest is to present them as a presentation offering before the Lord.[p] It is a holy portion for the priest, in addition to the breast of the presentation offering and the thigh of the contribution.[q] After that, the Nazirite may drink wine.

[21] "These are the instructions about the Nazirite who vows his offering to the Lord for his consecration,[r] in addition to whatever else he can afford; he must fulfill whatever vow he makes in keeping with the instructions for his consecration."

[A] 6:5 Lit "A razor is not to pass over his head

6:1-8 Any Israelite could consecrate himself to the Lord for a time of special devotion by taking **a Nazirite vow** (6:2). Usually this was done for a limited period of time (see 6:8). But in the case of two famous Old Testament Nazirites, Samuel (see 1 Sam 1:11) and Samson (see Judg 13:5), their vows were lifelong. Three stipulations highlighted the separateness of consecration: abstinence from **anything produced by the grapevine**; no cutting of the **hair throughout** the **vow**, and no going **near a dead body** (Num 6:3-6). These indicated the Nazirite was set apart for the Lord's service.

6:13-17 The **burnt offering** symbolized complete consecration to God, the **sin offering** atoned for any sins the Nazirite may have unintentionally committed during his vow period, and the **fellowship offering** denoted that he and the Lord were in harmony (6:14).

THE PRIESTLY BLESSING

[22] The LORD spoke to Moses: [23] "Tell Aaron and his sons, 'This is how you are to bless the Israelites. You should say to them,

[24] "May the LORD bless you
        and protect you;[a]
[25] may the LORD make his face shine
        on you
        and be gracious to you;[b]
[26] may the LORD look with favor
        on you[A]
        and give you peace.' "[C]

[27] In this way they will pronounce my name over[B] the Israelites, and I will bless them."

OFFERINGS FROM THE LEADERS

7 On the day Moses finished setting up the tabernacle,[d] he anointed and consecrated it and all its furnishings, along with the altar and all its utensils. After he anointed and consecrated these things, [2] the leaders of Israel, the heads of their ancestral families,[c] presented an offering. They were the tribal leaders who supervised the registration.[e] [3] They brought as their offering before the LORD six covered carts and twelve oxen, a cart from every two leaders and an ox from each one, and presented them in front of the tabernacle. [4] The LORD said to Moses, [5] "Accept these from them to be used in the work of the tent of meeting, and give this offering to the Levites, to each division according to their service."

[6] So Moses took the carts and oxen and gave them to the Levites. [7] He gave the Gershonites two carts and four oxen corresponding to their service,[f] [8] and gave the Merarites four carts and eight oxen corresponding to their service,[g] under the direction of Ithamar son of Aaron the priest. [9] But he did not give any to the Kohathites, since their responsibility was service related to the holy objects[h] carried on their shoulders.[i]

[10] The leaders also presented the dedication gift for the altar when it was anointed.[j] The leaders presented their offerings in front of the altar. [11] The LORD told Moses, "Each day have one leader present his offering for the dedication of the altar."[k]

[12] The one who presented his offering on the first day was Nahshon son of Amminadab[l] from the tribe of Judah. [13] His offering was one silver dish weighing 3 ¼ pounds[D] and one silver basin weighing 1 ¾ pounds,[E] measured by the standard sanctuary shekel, both of them full of fine flour mixed with oil for a grain offering;[m] [14] one gold bowl weighing four ounces,[F] full of incense; [15] one young bull, one ram, and one male lamb a year old, for a burnt offering;[n] [16] one male goat for a sin offering;[o] [17] and two bulls, five rams, five male goats, and five male lambs a year old, for the fellowship sacrifice.[p] This was the offering of Nahshon son of Amminadab.

[18] On the second day Nethanel son of Zuar,[q] leader of Issachar, presented an offering. [19] As his offering, he presented one silver dish weighing 3 ¼ pounds and one silver basin weighing 1 ¾ pounds, measured by the standard sanctuary shekel, both of them full of fine flour mixed with oil for a grain offering; [20] one gold bowl weighing four ounces, full of incense; [21] one young bull, one ram, and one male lamb a year old, for a burnt offering; [22] one male goat for a sin offering; [23] and two bulls, five rams, five male goats, and five male lambs a year old, for the fellowship sacrifice. This was the offering of Nethanel son of Zuar.

[24] On the third day Eliab son of Helon,[r] leader of the Zebulunites, presented an offering. [25] His offering was one

[a] 6:24 Ps 121:4,7; 128:5; 134:3
[b] 6:25 Ps 67:1; 80:3; 89:15; 119:135
[c] 6:26 Ps 4:6; 147:14
[d] 7:1 Ex 39:32; 40:17; Nm 9:15
[e] 7:2 Nm 1:4-16
[f] 7:7 Nm 4:23-28,32
[g] 7:8 Nm 3:36-37; 4:30-33
[h] 7:9 Nm 4:4-16
[i] Nm 3:28-31; 4:4-20

[j] 7:10 Nm 7:11,84,88; 1Kg 8:62-64; 2Ch 7:4-9; Neh 12:27
[k] 7:11 Ex 40:10
[l] 7:12 Nm 1:7; 2:3; 10:14
[m] 7:13 Lv 2:1-2; 6:14-18
[n] 7:15 Lv 1:1-13; 6:8-13
[o] 7:16 Lv 4:1–5:13; 6:24-30; Nm 28:11-15
[p] 7:17 Lv 3:1-17; 7:11-21
[q] 7:18 Nm 1:8; 2:5; 10:15
[r] 7:24 Nm 1:9; 2:7; 10:16

[A] 6:26 Lit LORD lift his face to you [B] 6:27 Or put my name on [C] 7:2 Lit the house of their fathers [D] 7:13 Lit dish, 130 its shekel-weight, also in vv. 19,25,31,37,43,49,55,61,67,73,79 [E] 7:13 Lit 70 shekels, also in vv. 19,25,31,37,43,49,55,61,67,73,79 [F] 7:14 Lit 10 (shekels), also in vv. 20,26,32, 38,44,50,56,62,68,74,80,86

6:22-27 God's instruction to Moses, **This is how you are to bless the Israelites** (6:23), is similar to Jesus's introduction to the Lord's Prayer for his disciples: "You should pray like this" (Matt 6:9). This blessing, then, is a formula that acts as a guide for God's people to bless others.

7:6-9 **Carts and oxen** were distributed based on the duties of the various Levitical families (7:6). Moses did not give them **to the**

Kohathites, since their responsibility was service related to the holy objects carried on their shoulders (7:9). These men carried the ark and the altars on poles rather than on carts so that no one would touch these sacred objects (see 4:1-20). Later, King David's failure to transport the ark in the right way would cost Uzzah his life when he reached out to steady the ark as it was transported by ox and cart (see 2 Sam 6:1-8).

7:12-83 The presentation of gifts began with **Nahshon ... from the tribe of Judah** (7:12), the tribe that led the way when Israel moved out. His offering is generous (7:13-17). The leaders of the other eleven tribes followed suit, coming on each of the next eleven days in the same order as the arrangement of the tribes encamped around the tabernacle (7:18-83; see 2:3-31). They brought offerings identical to Nahshon's.

[a] 7:30 Nm 1:5; 2:10; 10:18
[b] 7:36 Nm 1:6; 2:12; 10:19
[c] 7:42 Nm 1:14; 2:14; 10:20

[d] 7:48 Nm 1:10; 2:18; 10:22
[e] 7:54 Nm 1:10; 2:20; 10:23
[f] 7:60 Nm 1:11; 2:22; 10:24

silver dish weighing 3 ¼ pounds and one silver basin weighing 1 ¾ pounds, measured by the standard sanctuary shekel, both of them full of fine flour mixed with oil for a grain offering; [26] one gold bowl weighing four ounces, full of incense; [27] one young bull, one ram, and one male lamb a year old, for a burnt offering; [28] one male goat for a sin offering; [29] and two bulls, five rams, five male goats, and five male lambs a year old, for the fellowship sacrifice. This was the offering of Eliab son of Helon.

[30] On the fourth day Elizur son of Shedeur,[a] leader of the Reubenites, presented an offering. [31] His offering was one silver dish weighing 3 ¼ pounds and one silver basin weighing 1 ¾ pounds, measured by the standard sanctuary shekel, both of them full of fine flour mixed with oil for a grain offering; [32] one gold bowl weighing four ounces, full of incense; [33] one young bull, one ram, and one male lamb a year old, for a burnt offering; [34] one male goat for a sin offering; [35] and two bulls, five rams, five male goats, and five male lambs a year old, for the fellowship sacrifice. This was the offering of Elizur son of Shedeur.

[36] On the fifth day Shelumiel son of Zurishaddai,[b] leader of the Simeonites, presented an offering. [37] His offering was one silver dish weighing 3 ¼ pounds and one silver basin weighing 1 ¾ pounds, measured by the standard sanctuary shekel, both of them full of fine flour mixed with oil for a grain offering; [38] one gold bowl weighing four ounces, full of incense; [39] one young bull, one ram, and one male lamb a year old, for a burnt offering; [40] one male goat for a sin offering; [41] and two bulls, five rams, five male goats, and five male lambs a year old, for the fellowship sacrifice. This was the offering of Shelumiel son of Zurishaddai.

[42] On the sixth day Eliasaph son of Deuel,[A,c] leader of the Gadites, presented an offering. [43] His offering was one silver dish weighing 3 ¼ pounds and one silver basin weighing 1 ¾ pounds, measured by the standard sanctuary

shekel, both of them full of fine flour mixed with oil for a grain offering; [44] one gold bowl weighing four ounces full of incense; [45] one young bull, one ram, and one male lamb a year old, for a burnt offering; [46] one male goat for a sin offering; [47] and two bulls, five rams, five male goats, and five male lambs a year old, for the fellowship sacrifice. This was the offering of Eliasaph son of Deuel.[A]

[48] On the seventh day Elishama son of Ammihud,[d] leader of the Ephraimites, presented an offering. [49] His offering was one silver dish weighing 3 ¼ pounds and one silver basin weighing 1 ¾ pounds, measured by the standard sanctuary shekel, both of them full of fine flour mixed with oil for a grain offering; [50] one gold bowl weighing four ounces, full of incense; [51] one young bull, one ram, and one male lamb a year old, for a burnt offering; [52] one male goat for a sin offering; [53] and two bulls, five rams, five male goats, and five male lambs a year old, for the fellowship sacrifice. This was the offering of Elishama son of Ammihud.

[54] On the eighth day Gamaliel son of Pedahzur,[e] leader of the Manassites, presented an offering. [55] His offering was one silver dish weighing 3 ¼ pounds and one silver basin weighing 1 ¾ pounds, measured by the standard sanctuary shekel, both of them full of fine flour mixed with oil for a grain offering; [56] one gold bowl weighing four ounces, full of incense; [57] one young bull, one ram, and one male lamb a year old, for a burnt offering; [58] one male goat for a sin offering; [59] and two bulls, five rams, five male goats, and five male lambs a year old, for the fellowship sacrifice. This was the offering of Gamaliel son of Pedahzur.

[60] On the ninth day Abidan son of Gideoni,[f] leader of the Benjaminites, presented an offering. [61] His offering was one silver dish weighing 3 ¼ pounds and one silver basin weighing 1 ¾ pounds, measured by the standard sanctuary shekel, both of them full of fine flour mixed with oil for a grain

[A] 7:42,47 LXX, Syr read Reuel

offering; **62** one gold bowl weighing four ounces, full of incense; **63** one young bull, one ram, and one male lamb a year old, for a burnt offering; **64** one male goat for a sin offering; **65** and two bulls, five rams, five male goats, and five male lambs a year old, for the fellowship sacrifice. This was the offering of Abidan son of Gideoni.

66 On the tenth day Ahiezer son of Ammishaddai,[a] leader of the Danites, presented an offering. **67** His offering was one silver dish weighing 3 1/4 pounds and one silver basin weighing 1 3/4 pounds, measured by the standard sanctuary shekel, both of them full of fine flour mixed with oil for a grain offering; **68** one gold bowl weighing four ounces, full of incense; **69** one young bull, one ram, and one male lamb a year old, for a burnt offering; **70** one male goat for a sin offering; **71** and two bulls, five rams, five male goats, and five male lambs a year old, for the fellowship sacrifice. This was the offering of Ahiezer son of Ammishaddai.

72 On the eleventh day Pagiel son of Ochran,[b] leader of the Asherites, presented an offering. **73** His offering was one silver dish weighing 3 1/4 pounds and one silver basin weighing 1 3/4 pounds, measured by the standard sanctuary shekel, both of them full of fine flour mixed with oil for a grain offering; **74** one gold bowl weighing four ounces, full of incense; **75** one young bull, one ram, and one male lamb a year old, for a burnt offering; **76** one male goat for a sin offering; **77** and two bulls, five rams, five male goats, and five male lambs a year old, for the fellowship sacrifice. This was the offering of Pagiel son of Ochran.

78 On the twelfth day Ahira son of Enan,[c] leader of the Naphtalites, presented an offering. **79** His offering was one silver dish weighing 3 1/4 pounds and one silver basin weighing 1 3/4 pounds, measured by the standard sanctuary shekel, both of them full of fine flour mixed with oil for a grain offering; **80** one gold bowl weighing four

ounces, full of incense; **81** one young bull, one ram, and one male lamb a year old, for a burnt offering; **82** one male goat for a sin offering; **83** and two bulls, five rams, five male goats, and five male lambs a year old, for the fellowship sacrifice. This was the offering of Ahira son of Enan.

84 This was the dedication gift from the leaders of Israel for the altar when it was anointed:[d] twelve silver dishes, twelve silver basins, and twelve gold bowls. **85** Each silver dish weighed 3 1/4 pounds,[A] and each basin 1 3/4 pounds.[B] The total weight of the silver articles was 60 pounds[c] measured by the standard sanctuary shekel. **86** The twelve gold bowls full of incense each weighed four ounces measured by the standard sanctuary shekel. The total weight of the gold bowls was 3 pounds.[D] **87** All the livestock for the burnt offering[e] totaled twelve bulls, twelve rams, and twelve male lambs a year old, with their grain offerings, and twelve male goats for the sin offering.[f] **88** All the livestock for the fellowship sacrifice[g] totaled twenty-four bulls, sixty rams, sixty male goats, and sixty male lambs a year old. This was the dedication gift for the altar after it was anointed.

89 When Moses entered the tent of meeting to speak with the LORD, he heard the voice speaking to him[h] from above the mercy seat that was on the ark of the testimony, from between the two cherubim.[i] He spoke to him that way.

THE LIGHTING IN THE TABERNACLE

8 The LORD spoke to Moses: **2** "Speak to Aaron and tell him: When you set up the lamps, the seven lamps are to give light in front of the lampstand." **3** So Aaron did this; he set up its lamps to give light in front of the lampstand just as the LORD had commanded Moses. **4** This is the way the lampstand was made: it was a hammered work of gold, hammered from its base to its flower petals. The lampstand was made according to the pattern the LORD had shown Moses.[j]

CONSECRATION OF THE LEVITES

5 The LORD spoke to Moses: **6** "Take the Levites from among the Israelites and ceremonially cleanse them. **7** Do this to them

a 7:66 Nm 1:12; 2:25; 10:25
b 7:72 Nm 1:13; 2:27; 10:26
c 7:78 Nm 1:15; 2:29; 10:27

d 7:84 Nm 7:1,10
e 7:87 Lv 1:1-13; 6:8-13
f Lv 4:22-26; 6:24-30; Nm 28:11-15
g 7:88 Lv 3:1-17; 7:11-21
h 7:89 Nm 12:8
i Ex 25:10-22; 37:1-9; 1Kg 6:25
j 8:2-4 Ex 25:31-40

A 7:85 Lit 130 (shekels)   B 7:85 Lit 70 (shekels)   C 7:85 Lit 2,400 (shekels)   D 7:86 Lit 120 (shekels)

7:89 This was a pivotal moment establishing a new level of communication between God and his people. Moses spoke directly to God in his sanctuary, and God spoke directly to Moses.

ᵃ 8:7 Lv 14:51; Nm 19:7,13,17,20; Heb 9:13,23
ᵇ Lv 8:1-6; 14:8-9; Nm 6:19
ᶜ 8:9 Ex 29:4; Lv 8:1-6
ᵈ 8:11 Nm 1:50,53; 3:6-7
ᵉ 8:12 Lv 1:3-5; 4:3-4
ᶠ 8:14 Nm 3:12,45; 16:8-9
ᵍ 8:15 Ex 29:26-27; Lv 8:26-29; Nm 6:20
ʰ 8:16 Nm 3:9; 18:6
ⁱ Ex 13:2,12,15; 32:26-29; Nm 3:6,12-13,41-45; 8:16-19; 18:1; Dt 10:8-9; 18:1-2; 21:5
ʲ 8:17 Ex 13:1-2,11-12,15-16
ᵏ 8:19 Nm 1:51,53; 16:1-3,32-50; 18:1-7

ˡ 8:24 Nm 4:3,23,30
ᵐ 8:26 Nm 3:7-8
ⁿ 9:1 Ex 19:1-2; Nm 1:1; 3:4,14
ᵒ 9:2 Ex 13:10; 23:15
ᵖ 9:3 Ex 12:2-27; Lv 23:4-8; Nm 28:16-25; Dt 16:1-8
ᑫ 9:6 2Ch 30:3

for their purification: Sprinkle them with the purification water.ᵃ Have them shave their entire bodies and wash their clothes, and so purify themselves.ᵇ

⁸ "They are to take a young bull and its grain offering of fine flour mixed with oil, and you are to take a second young bull for a sin offering. ⁹ Bring the Levites before the tent of meeting and assemble the entire Israelite community.ᶜ ¹⁰ Then present the Levites before the LORD, and have the Israelites lay their hands on them. ¹¹ Aaron is to present the Levites before the LORD as a presentation offering from the Israelites, so that they may perform the LORD's work.ᵈ ¹² Next the Levites are to lay their hands on the heads of the bulls. Sacrifice one as a sin offering and the other as a burnt offering to the LORD, to make atonement for the Levites.ᵉ

¹³ "You are to have the Levites stand before Aaron and his sons, and you are to present them before the LORD as a presentation offering. ¹⁴ In this way you are to separate the Levites from the rest of the Israelites so that the Levites will belong to me.ᶠ ¹⁵ After that the Levites may come to serve at the tent of meeting, once you have ceremonially cleansed them and presented them as a presentation offering.ᵍ ¹⁶ For they have been exclusively assigned to me from the Israelites.ʰ I have taken them for myself in place of all who come first from the womb, every Israelite firstborn.ⁱ ¹⁷ For every firstborn among the Israelites is mine, both man and animal. I consecrated them to myselfʲ on the day I struck down every firstborn in the land of Egypt. ¹⁸ But I have taken the Levites in place of every firstborn among the Israelites. ¹⁹ From the Israelites, I have given the Levites exclusively to Aaron and his sons to perform the work for the Israelites at the tent of meeting and to make atonement on their behalf, so that no plague will come against the Israelites when they approach the sanctuary."ᵏ

²⁰ Moses, Aaron, and the entire Israelite community did this to the Levites. The Israelites did everything to them the LORD commanded Moses regarding the Levites. ²¹ The Levites purified themselves and washed their clothes; then Aaron presentedᴬ them before the LORD as a presentation offering. Aaron also made atonement for them to cleanse them ceremonially. ²² After that, the Levites came to do their work at the tent of meeting in the presence of Aaron and his sons. So they did to them as the LORD had commanded Moses concerning the Levites.

²³ The LORD spoke to Moses: ²⁴ "In regard to the Levites: From twenty-five years old or more, a man enters the service in the work at the tent of meeting.ˡ ²⁵ But at fifty years old he is to retire from his service in the work and no longer serve. ²⁶ He may assist his brothers to fulfill responsibilitiesᴮ at the tent of meeting,ᵐ but he must not do the work. This is how you are to deal with the Levites regarding their duties."

THE SECOND PASSOVER

9 In the first month of the second year after their departure from the land of Egypt, the LORD told Moses in the Wilderness of Sinai:ⁿ ² "The Israelites are to observe the Passover at its appointed time.ᵒ ³ You must observe it at its appointed time on the fourteenth day of this month at twilight; you are to observe it according to all its statutes and ordinances."ᵖ ⁴ So Moses told the Israelites to observe the Passover, ⁵ and they observed it in the first month on the fourteenth day at twilight in the Wilderness of Sinai. The Israelites did everything as the LORD had commanded Moses.

⁶ But there were some men who were unclean because of a human corpse, so they could not observe the Passover on that day.ᑫ These men came before Moses and Aaron the same day ⁷ and said to him, "We are unclean because of a human corpse. Why should we be excluded from presenting the LORD's offering at its appointed time with the other Israelites?"

⁸ Moses replied to them, "Wait here until I hear what the LORD commands for you."

ᴬ 8:21 Lit waved   ᴮ 8:26 Or to keep guard

8:9-12 Aaron was to **have the Israelites lay their hands on** the Levites in a service we would recognize today as a form of ordination (8:10). It was called **a presentation offering** to the Lord from the Israelites, so that the Levites could **perform the LORD's work** (8:11). Thus, the Levites were a gift to the Lord, and the people were investing them with the authority to execute their

ministry. The sin offering atoned for sin, and the burnt offering symbolized total commitment to God (8:12).
8:20 The people's posture of obedience here will contrast sharply with the rebellion of the Israelites once they hit the road toward Canaan. The Israelites often failed to trust God when the going got tough—a tendency that we too can easily adopt.

8:25-26 This was a merciful provision that would prevent men who might not be physically able from failing in their duties and simultaneously bringing defilement on the nation.
9:1-5 It was through the events of the first **Passover** that the Lord delivered his people from slavery. So it was appropriate to celebrate it again **in the first month** of the nation's **second year** out from Egypt (9:1-2).

9 Then the LORD spoke to Moses: **10** "Tell the Israelites: When any one of you or your descendants is unclean because of a corpse*ᵃ* or is on a distant journey, he may still observe the Passover to the LORD. **11** Such people are to observe it in the second month, on the fourteenth day at twilight. They are to eat the animal with unleavened bread and bitter herbs;*ᵇ* **12** they may not leave any of it until morning or break any of its bones.*ᶜ* They must observe the Passover according to all its statutes.

13 "But the man who is ceremonially clean, is not on a journey, and yet fails to observe the Passover is to be cut off from his people, because he did not present the LORD's offering at its appointed time. That man will bear the consequences of his sin.

14 "If an alien resides with you and wants to observe the Passover to the LORD,*ᵈ* he is to do it according to the Passover statute and its ordinances. You are to apply the same statute to both the resident alien and the native of the land."*ᵉ*

GUIDANCE BY THE CLOUD

15 On the day the tabernacle was set up, the cloud covered the tabernacle, the tent of the testimony,*ᶠ* and it appeared like fire above the tabernacle from evening until morning. **16** It remained that way continuously: the cloud would cover it,*ᴬ* appearing like fire at night.*ᵍ* **17** Whenever the cloud was lifted up above the tent, the Israelites would set out; at the place where the cloud stopped, there the Israelites camped.*ʰ* **18** At the LORD's command the Israelites set out, and at the LORD's command they camped. As long as the cloud stayed over the tabernacle, they camped.

19 Even when the cloud stayed over the tabernacle many days, the Israelites carried out the LORD's requirement and did not set out. **20** Sometimes the cloud remained over the tabernacle for only a few days. They would camp at the LORD's command and set out at the LORD's command. **21** Sometimes the cloud remained only from evening until morning; when the cloud lifted in the morning, they set out. Or if it remained a day and a night, they moved out when the cloud lifted. **22** Whether it was two days, a month, or longer,*ᴮ* the Israelites camped and did not set out as long as the cloud stayed over the tabernacle. But when it was lifted, they set out. **23** They camped at the LORD's command, and they set out at the LORD's command. They carried out the LORD's requirement according to his command through Moses.

TWO SILVER TRUMPETS

10 The LORD spoke to Moses: **2** "Make two trumpets of hammered silver to summon the community*ʲ* and have the camps set out. **3** When both are sounded in long blasts, the entire community is to gather before you at the entrance to the tent of meeting. **4** However, if one is sounded, only the leaders, the heads of Israel's clans,*ʲ* are to gather before you.

5 "When you sound short blasts, the camps pitched on the east*ᵏ* are to set out. **6** When you sound short blasts a second time, the camps pitched on the south*ˡ* are to set out. Short blasts are to be sounded for them to set out. **7** When calling the assembly together, you are to sound long blasts, not short ones. **8** The sons of Aaron, the priests, are to sound the trumpets. Your use of these is a permanent statute throughout your generations.

9 "When you enter into battle in your land against an adversary who is attacking you, sound short blasts on the trumpets, and you will be remembered before the LORD your God and be saved from your enemies.*ᵐ* **10** You are to sound the trumpets over your burnt offerings and your fellowship sacrifices and on your joyous occasions, your appointed festivals, and the beginning of each of your months. They

*ᵃ*9:10 Lv 21:1-3; Nm 5:2; 6:6-12
*ᵇ*9:11 Ex 12:8,15; Dt 16:3-4,8
*ᶜ*9:12 Ex 12:10,46; Ps 34:20; Jn 19:36
*ᵈ*9:14 Ex 12:48
*ᵉ*Ex 12:49; Lv 24:22; Nm 15:14-16
*ᶠ*9:15 Ex 40:17,34; Nm 7:1
*ᵍ*9:16 Ex 13:21-22; 40:38
*ʰ*9:17 Ex 40:36-38; Nm 10:11,33-34

*ʲ*10:2 Jl 2:15-16
*ʲ*10:4 Nm 1:5-16
*ᵏ*10:5 Nm 2:3-9; 10:14-16
*ˡ*10:6 Nm 2:10-16; 10:18-20
*ᵐ*10:9 Dt 20:4; 2Ch 13:12; Ps 18:3

ᴬ9:16 LXX, Vg, Syr, Tg read *it by day*   **ᴮ**9:22 Or *a year*

9:9-11 God's answer to the men prevented from celebrating Passover at the proper time (see 9:6-8) was gracious and provided an ordinance for future generations. Those in a similar situation could wait a month to observe the Passover (9:11), still keeping all of the required regulations. They wouldn't have to miss out. **9:13** An Israelite who simply skipped the Passover was to be **cut off**, which would have meant banishment or death. Interestingly, in the New Testament era, similar

mistreatment of the Lord's Supper by the Corinthians resulted in sickness or death (see 1 Cor 11:28-30). **9:15-18** The Israelites had a divine GPS guiding them during their time in the wilderness. They were directed by the Lord's **cloud** that **covered the tabernacle** (9:15). When the cloud hovered low over it, the Israelites remained in camp; when the cloud **lifted**, the Israelites broke camp and followed until the cloud stopped over a new location (9:17-18).

10:2-10 Trumpets could call either the entire congregation or their leaders to rally at the tabernacle or **set out** as needed (10:2-5). The trumpet sound during battle was especially important as a reminder to the Israelites that **the LORD** was going before them and would save them from their enemies (10:9). Trumpets also became a key part of Israel's sacrifices and festivals, serving as auditory reminders that the Lord alone was their God (10:10).

[a]10:10 Ex 6:7; Lv 18:2,4,30; 19:2-4
[b]10:12 Ex 17:1; 19:1; Nm 1:1
[c]Gn 21:21; Nm 12:16; 13:3,26; 1Sm 25:1
[d]10:13 Nm 9:18-23
[e]10:14 Nm 1:7; 2:3; 7:12; 1Ch 2:10
[f]10:15 Nm 1:8; 2:5; 7:18
[g]10:19 Nm 1:6; 2:12; 7:36
[h]10:21 Nm 3:27-31; 4:2-4,15,18-20
[i]10:22 Nm 1:10; 2:18; 7:48

[j]10:25 Nm 1:12; 2:25; 7:66
[k]10:29 Ex 2:16-18; 3:1; 4:18; Jdg 4:11
[l]Gn 12:7; 13:14-17; 15:7; Ac 7:5
[m]Ex 18:9
[n]10:32 Jdg 1:16; 4:11
[o]10:33 Dt 1:33
[p]10:35 Ps 68:1
[q]10:36 Gn 15:5; Dt 1:8,10
[r]11:1 Ex 22:24; 32:10-11; Nm 11:1,33; 32:13; Dt 6:15
[s]1Kg 18:38; 19:12; Is 66:16

Video Devotional

"GOD IS UP TO SOMETHING GREAT"

Adjust your expectations to God's promises, and he will do something great both in you and through you.

will serve as a reminder for you before your God: I am the LORD your God."[a]

FROM SINAI TO PARAN

[11] During the second year, in the second month on the twentieth day of the month, the cloud was lifted up above the tabernacle of the testimony. [12] The Israelites traveled on from the Wilderness of Sinai, moving from one place to the next[b] until the cloud stopped in the Wilderness of Paran.[c] [13] They set out for the first time according to the LORD's command through Moses.[d]

[14] The military divisions of the camp of Judah's descendants with their banner set out first, and Nahshon son of Amminadab[e] was over their divisions. [15] Nethanel son of Zuar[f] was over the division of the tribe of Issachar's descendants, [16] and Eliab son of Helon was over the division of the tribe of Zebulun's descendants. [17] The tabernacle was then taken down, and the Gershonites and the Merarites set out, transporting the tabernacle.

[18] The military divisions of the camp of Reuben with their banner set out, and Elizur son of Shedeur was over their divisions. [19] Shelumiel son of Zurishaddai[g] was over the division of the tribe of Simeon's descendants, [20] and Eliasaph son of Deuel[A] was over the division of the tribe of Gad's descendants. [21] The Kohathites then set out, transporting the holy objects;[h] the tabernacle was to be set up before their arrival.

[22] Next the military divisions of the camp of Ephraim's descendants with their banner set out, and Elishama son of Ammihud[i] was over their divisions. [23] Gamaliel son of Pedahzur was over the division of the tribe of Manasseh's descendants, [24] and Abidan son of Gideoni was over the division of the tribe of Benjamin's descendants.

[25] The military divisions of the camp of Dan's descendants with their banner set out, serving as rear guard for all the camps,

and Ahiezer son of Ammishaddai[j] was over their divisions. [26] Pagiel son of Ochran was over the division of the tribe of Asher's descendants, [27] and Ahira son of Enan was over the division of the tribe of Naphtali's descendants. [28] This was the order of march for the Israelites by their military divisions as they set out.

[29] Moses said to Hobab, descendant of Reuel[k] the Midianite and Moses's relative by marriage: "We're setting out for the place the LORD promised: 'I will give it to you.'[l] Come with us, and we will treat you well, for the LORD has promised good things to Israel."[m] [30] But he replied to him, "I don't want to go. Instead, I will go to my own land and my relatives." [31] "Please don't leave us," Moses said, "since you know where we should camp in the wilderness, and you can serve as our eyes. [32] If you come with us, whatever good the LORD does for us we will do for you."[n]

[33] They set out from the mountain of the LORD on a three-day journey with the ark of the LORD's covenant traveling ahead of them for those three days to seek a resting place for them.[o] [34] Meanwhile, the cloud of the LORD was over them by day when they set out from the camp.

[35] Whenever the ark set out, Moses would say:

Arise, LORD!
Let your enemies be scattered,
   and those who hate you flee
   from your presence.[p]

[36] When it came to rest, he would say:
Return, LORD,
   to the countless thousands of Israel.[q]

COMPLAINTS ABOUT HARDSHIP

[11] Now the people began complaining openly before[B] the LORD about hardship. When the LORD heard, his anger burned,[r] and fire[s] from the LORD blazed

---

[A]10:20 LXX, Syr read *Reuel*   [B]11:1 Lit *in the ears of*

10:11-13 The people had been parked at Sinai for almost a year, awaiting this momentous next step toward Canaan. The cloud's first stop en route was **in the Wilderness of Paran** (10:12), a long stretch of barren land.
10:14-28 Moses summarized what must have been an awe-inspiring sight: **This was the order of march for the Israelites by their military divisions** (10:28).
10:21 This tells us that by the time the ark of the covenant, the altars, and the holy utensils used in worship arrived at a stopping point, the tabernacle would already be ready to house them.

10:29-32 To Moses's disappointment, Hobab preferred to return home (10:30). Since Hobab knew the region, Moses had hoped to draw on his knowledge for the best routes through a harsh and dangerous land (10:31-32).
10:33-34 The presence of **the ark** (10:33) must have been a tremendous comfort to Moses and all Israel, for it was to serve as the Lord's throne among his people; he dwelled above it, between its decorative cherubim (see 2 Sam 6:2; Ps 99:1; Is 37:16).
10:35 These words were a reminder to Israel that war laid ahead. They would eventually

encounter hostile forces that despised the Lord and, therefore, despised his people. I see here another reminder for Christians: we should not expect acceptance from a world that rejects God. Jesus articulated this to his disciples: "If the world hates you, understand that it hated me before it hated you" (John 15:18).
10:36 This is essentially a request for God's comforting presence and protection over the Israelites.
11:1-2 In spite of his remarkable provision, Israel didn't try to hide their gripes from God. As a result, God's **anger burned**. He became,

among them and consumed the outskirts of the camp. ² Then the people cried out to Moses, and he prayed to the LORD, and the fire died down. ³ So that place was named Taberah,^,ᵃ because the LORD's fire had blazed among them.

COMPLAINTS ABOUT FOOD

⁴ The riffraffᴮ among themᵇ had a strong cravingᶜ for other food. The Israelites wept again and said, "Who will feed us meat? ⁵ We remember the free fish we ate in Egypt,ᵈ along with the cucumbers, melons, leeks, onions, and garlic. ⁶ But now our appetite is gone;ᶜ there's nothing to look at but this manna!"

⁷ The mannaᵉ resembled coriander seed, and its appearance was like that of bdellium.ᴰ ⁸ The people walked around and gathered it. They ground it on a pair of grinding stones or crushed it in a mortar, then boiled it in a cooking pot and shaped it into cakes. It tasted like a pastry cooked with the finest oil. ⁹ When the dew fell on the camp at night, the manna would fall with it.ᶠ

¹⁰ Moses heard the people, family after family, weeping at the entrance of their tents. The LORD was very angry;ᵍ Moses was also provoked.ᴱ ¹¹ So Moses asked the LORD, "Why have you brought such trouble on your servant? Why are you angry with me,ᶠ and why do you burden me with all these people?ʰ ¹² Did I conceive all these people? Did I give them birth so you should tell me, 'Carry them at your breast, as a nanny carries a baby,'ⁱ to the land that you swore to give their fathers?'ʲ ¹³ Where can I get meat to give all these people? For they are weeping to me, 'Give us meat to eat!' ¹⁴ I can't carry all these people by myself. They are too much for me. ¹⁵ If you are going to

treat me like this, please kill me right nowᵏ if I have found favor with you, and' don't let me see my miseryᴳ anymore."

SEVENTY ELDERS ANOINTED

¹⁶ The LORD answered Moses, "Bring me seventy men from Israel known to you as elders and officers of the people. Take them to the tent of meeting and have them stand there with you. ¹⁷ Then I will come down and speak with you there. I will take some of the Spirit who is on you and put the Spirit on them.ᵐ They will help you bear the burden of the people, so that you do not have to bear it by yourself.ⁿ

¹⁸ "Tell the people: Consecrate yourselves in readiness for tomorrow, and you will eat meat because you wept in the LORD's hearing, 'Who will feed us meat? We were better off in Egypt.' The LORD will give you meat and you will eat. ¹⁹ You will eat, not for one day, or two days, or five days, or ten days, or twenty days, ²⁰ but for a whole month — until it comes out of your nostrils and becomes nauseating to you — because you have rejected the LORD who is among you, and wept before him: 'Why did we ever leave Egypt?'"ᵒ

²¹ But Moses replied, "I'm in the middle of a people with six hundred thousand foot soldiers,ᵖ yet you say, 'I will give them meat, and they will eat for a month.' ²² If flocks and herds were slaughtered for them, would they have enough? Or if all the fish in the sea were caught for them, would they have enough?"ᑫ

²³ The LORD answered Moses, "Is the LORD's arm weak?ᴴ,ʳ Now you will see whether or not what I have promised will happen to you."

²⁴ Moses went out and told the people the words of the LORD. He brought seventy

ᵃ11:3 Dt 9:22
ᵇ11:4 Ex 12:38
ᶜNm 11:34; Ps 78:29–31; 106:14–15; 1Co 10:5–6
ᵈ11:5 Ex 16:3
ᵉ11:7 Ex 16:4–35; Dt 8:3,16; Jos 5:12; Neh 9:20; Ps 78:24; Jn 6:48–51; Rv 2:17
ᶠ11:9 Ex 16:13–14
ᵍ11:10 Ex 22:24; 32:10–11; Nm 11:1,33; 32:13; Dt 6:15
ʰ11:11 Ex 5:22; Dt 1:9–13
ⁱ11:12 Is 40:11; 66:11–12
ʲGn 12:7; 26:3–4; Nm 14:16,23; Dt 6:10,23

ᵏ11:15 Ex 32:32; Jb 6:9; 7:15–16
ˡGn 6:8; Ex 33:12–17; Ru 2:2,10,13
ᵐ11:17 2Kg 2:9,15
ⁿEx 18:18; Dt 1:9–13; Ac 6:1–6
ᵒ11:20 Ex 17:3
ᵖ11:21 Ex 12:37; Nm 1:45–46; 2:32; 26:51
ᑫ11:22 Mt 15:33; Mk 6:37; 8:4
ʳ11:23 Jb 38:1–42:6; Is 50:2; 59:1

---

^11:3 = Blaze   ᴮ11:4 Or *The mixed multitude*; Hb obscure   ᶜ11:6 Or *our lives are wasting away*, or *our throat is dry*   ᴰ11:7 A yellowish, transparent gum resin   ᴱ11:10 Lit *and it was evil in the eyes of Moses*   ᶠ11:11 Lit *Why have I not found favor in your eyes*   ᴳ11:15 Alt Hb tradition reads *your misery*   ᴴ11:23 Lit *the LORD's arm too short*

---

literally, as mad as a fire is hot. In fact, he sent **fire** that **consumed the outskirts of the camp** (11:1). Once again, Moses interceded for his wayward Israelite brothers, praying for grace (11:2). **11:4-9** God graciously and supernaturally provided **manna**—bread from heaven (11:7-9). But these complainers couldn't stand **to look at** it (11:6). They were tired of the Lord's menu. Shockingly, they preferred **the free** food they had back **in Egypt** (11:5). **11:10-15** The people were **weeping** like children whining about what they had to eat for dinner (11:10). So in Moses's prayer, he basically said, "Lord, what did I do to make you so mad at me that you loaded me down with this nation

of crybabies?" His exasperation brings us to an important aside. Moses wouldn't be the last ministry leader to be overwhelmed by the spiritual immaturity of those under his care. But shepherding Israel was *God's project*, not his. Those who lead and feed God's people are under-shepherds; the chief Shepherd is the One who's really in charge (see 1 Pet 5:1-4). And not only is he able to supply his under-shepherds with the resources they need to do the work he has called them to do, but he will also reward them for their faithfulness. **11:16-17** God provided Moses **seventy … elders and officers** to share the leadership load (11:16). They needed to be competent and trustworthy

men, but they also needed something even more important: the Holy **Spirit** (11:17). **11:19-20** God declared he would take action to deal with those who clamored for meat, but the people would soon wish they'd never asked for it. God heard their complaints as a rejection of himself (11:20). Complaining about God's provision is rejecting him. **11:21-23** Moses was at the end of his rope (11:21-22). His attitude was essentially this: "Lord, these people are such a mess I don't think even *you* can do anything for them!" But God rebuked his prophet in no uncertain terms. The all-powerful Creator is not **weak**; if he promised it, he will do it (11:23).

*a*11:25 Ex 19:9; 33:9-10;
  Nm 12:5-8
*b*1Sm 10:6-10; 19:20-24; Is
  63:11; Jl 2:28
*c*11:29 Nm 12:2; 16:3
*d*11:31 Ex 14:21
*e*Ex 16:12-13; Ps 78:26-28
*f*11:32 2Sm 17:19; Ezk
  26:5,14
*g*11:33 Ex 22:24; 32:10-11;
  Nm 11:1,10; 32:13; Dt 6:15

*h*11:33 Ps 78:29-31;
  106:14-15
*i*11:35 Nm 12:16; 33:16-17
*j*12:1 Ex 15:20-21; Nm 20:1;
  26:59; Dt 24:9
*k*12:5 Dt 31:15
*l*12:6 1Sm 3:15; Ezk 1:1; Dn
  10:7-8,16; Rv 1:10-12
*m*12:7 Heb 3:2,5
*n*12:8 Ex 33:11; Nm 7:89;
  Jdg 6:22
*o*1Co 13:12
*p*12:9 Ex 22:24; 32:10-11;
  Nm 11:1,10,33; 32:13;
  Dt 6:15

men from the elders of the people and had them stand around the tent. ²⁵ Then the LORD descended in the cloud and spoke to him.*ᵃ* He took some of the Spirit that was on Moses and placed the Spirit on the seventy elders. As the Spirit rested on them, they prophesied,*ᵇ* but they never did it again. ²⁶ Two men had remained in the camp, one named Eldad and the other Medad; the Spirit rested on them — they were among those listed, but had not gone out to the tent — and they prophesied in the camp. ²⁷ A young man ran and reported to Moses, "Eldad and Medad are prophesying in the camp."

²⁸ Joshua son of Nun, assistant to Moses since his youth,*ᴬ* responded, "Moses, my lord, stop them!"

²⁹ But Moses asked him, "Are you jealous on my account?*ᶜ* If only all the LORD's people were prophets and the LORD would place his Spirit on them!" ³⁰ Then Moses returned to the camp along with the elders of Israel.

QUAIL IN THE CAMP

³¹ A wind sent by the LORD*ᵈ* came up and blew quail in from the sea; it dropped them all around the camp. They were flying three feet*ᴮ* off*ᶜ* the ground for about a day's journey in every direction.*ᵉ* ³² The people were up all that day and night and all the next day gathering the quail — the one who took the least gathered fifty bushels*ᴰ* — and they spread them out all around the camp.*ᴱ,ᶠ* ³³ While the meat was still between their teeth, before it was chewed, the LORD's anger burned*ᵍ* against the people, and the LORD struck them with a very

severe plague.*ʰ* ³⁴ So they named that place Kibroth-hattaavah,*ᶠ* because there they buried the people who had craved the meat.

³⁵ From Kibroth-hattaavah the people moved on to Hazeroth*ᴳ,ⁱ* and remained there.

MIRIAM AND AARON REBEL

12 Miriam*ʲ* and Aaron criticized Moses because of the Cushite woman he married (for he had married a Cushite woman). ² They said, "Does the LORD speak only through Moses? Does he not also speak through us?" And the LORD heard it. ³ Moses was a very humble man, more so than anyone on the face of the earth.

⁴ Suddenly the LORD said to Moses, Aaron, and Miriam, "You three come out to the tent of meeting." So the three of them went out. ⁵ Then the LORD descended in a pillar of cloud,*ᵏ* stood at the entrance to the tent, and summoned Aaron and Miriam. When the two of them came forward, ⁶ he said:

"Listen to what I say:
If there is a prophet among you
    from the LORD,
I make myself known to him
    in a vision;*ˡ*
I speak with him in a dream.
⁷ Not so with my servant Moses;
    he is faithful in*ᴴ* all my household.*ᵐ*
⁸ I speak with him*ⁿ* directly,*ⁱ*
    openly, and not in riddles;
    he sees the form of the LORD.*ᵒ*

So why were you not afraid to speak against my servant Moses?" ⁹ The LORD's anger burned against them,*ᵖ* and he left.

¹⁰ As the cloud moved away from the tent, Miriam's skin suddenly became diseased,

---

ᴬ11:28 Or *Moses, from his elite young men*   ᴮ11:31 Lit *two cubits*   ᶜ11:31 Or *They were three feet deep on*   ᴰ11:32 Lit *10 homers*   ᴱ11:32 To dry or cure the meat; 2Sm 17:19; Ezk 26:5,14   ᶠ11:34 = Graves of Craving   ᴳ11:35 = Settlements; Nm 12:16; 33:16-17   ᴴ12:7 Or *is entrusted with*
ⁱ12:8 Lit *mouth to mouth*

11:26-29 Joshua sought to protect Moses from what he saw as a challenge to his leadership (11:28). But Moses demonstrated why God's Word calls him, "a very humble man" (12:3). Rather than seeing the men as competition, Moses saw them as God's blessing intended to bring more glory to God. Similarly, the more people who know, obey, and teach God's Word, the more the church is edified and God is glorified.

11:31-35 God's meat delivery service rolled up to the camp in the form of **quail** that fell in droves (11:31). (It was grilling time!) Yet **before [this meat] was chewed, the LORD's anger burned against the people, and the LORD struck them with a very severe plague** (11:33). Thus, the ingrates had craved their way to the grave, so the survivors called

the place **Kibroth-hattaavah**, "Graves of Craving" (11:34).

12:1-2 Regardless of what really motivated their attack, the siblings used Moses's marriage to a woman of a different ethnicity to challenge his authority. Moses had married a woman from a region called Cush, which today is Ethiopia. This means this Jewish forefather chose a woman of African descent; she was a descendant of Noah's son Ham, through Cush (see Gen 10:6).

This story reveals that there is no place for racial hatred and division among God's people (Num 12:9-15). Undoubtedly Moses's wife, like her husband, had embraced faith in the one true God. The couple serves as a reminder to us that Christians are to marry "in the Lord"—that is, we are to marry those who

share the same faith in God through Jesus Christ that we do (see 1 Cor 7:39). Marriage is to be faith-based—not race-based.

12:6-8 What distinguished Moses's leadership was his ability and willingness to submit himself to the will of God. In a word, Moses was **faithful** (12:7). Therefore, the Lord had great confidence in his **servant** and granted him intimate relationship (12:7-8). Jesus promised that all believers who are faithful with the responsibilities God has given them will one day hear their Master say, "Well done, good and faithful servant! You were faithful over a few things; I will put you in charge of many" (Matt 25:21).

12:10 Don't miss the appropriateness of the punishment. Miriam had condemned Moses because of the color of his wife's **skin**. The penalty fit her crime.

resembling snow.[A] When Aaron turned toward her, he saw that she was diseased [11] and said to Moses, "My lord, please don't hold against us this sin we have so foolishly committed. [12] Please don't let her be like a dead baby[B] whose flesh is half eaten away when he comes out of his mother's womb."

[13] Then Moses cried out to the LORD, "God, please heal her! "[a]

[14] The LORD answered Moses, "If her father had merely spit in her face, wouldn't she remain in disgrace for seven days? Let her be confined outside the camp[b] for seven days;[c] after that she may be brought back in." [15] So Miriam was confined outside the camp for seven days, and the people did not move on until Miriam was brought back in.[d] [16] After that, the people set out from Hazeroth and camped in the Wilderness of Paran.

SCOUTING OUT CANAAN

13 The LORD spoke to Moses: [2] "Send men to scout out the land of Canaan[e] I am giving to the Israelites. Send one man who is a leader among them from each of their ancestral tribes." [3] Moses sent them from the Wilderness of Paran at the LORD's command. All the men were leaders in Israel.[f] [4] These were their names:

Shammua son of Zaccur from the tribe of Reuben;

[5] Shaphat son of Hori from the tribe of Simeon;

[6] Caleb[g] son of Jephunneh from the tribe of Judah;

[7] Igal son of Joseph from the tribe of Issachar;

[8] Hoshea son of Nun[h] from the tribe of Ephraim;

[9] Palti son of Raphu from the tribe of Benjamin;

[10] Gaddiel son of Sodi from the tribe of Zebulun;

[11] Gaddi son of Susi from the tribe of Manasseh (from the tribe of Joseph);

[12] Ammiel son of Gemalli from the tribe of Dan;

[13] Sethur son of Michael from the tribe of Asher;

[14] Nahbi son of Vophsi from the tribe of Naphtali;

[15] Geuel son of Machi from the tribe of Gad.

[16] These were the names of the men Moses sent to scout out the land, and Moses renamed Hoshea son of Nun, Joshua.

[17] When Moses sent them to scout out the land of Canaan, he told them, "Go up this way to the Negev, then go up into the hill country. [18] See what the land is like, and whether the people who live there are strong or weak, few or many. [19] Is the land they live in good[i] or bad? Are the cities they live in encampments or fortifications?[j] [20] Is the land fertile or unproductive?[k] Are there trees in it or not? Be courageous. Bring back some fruit from the land." It was the season for the first ripe grapes.[l]

[21] So they went up and scouted out the land from the Wilderness of Zin[c] as far as Rehob near the entrance to Hamath.[D] [22] They went up through the Negev and came to Hebron, where Ahiman, Sheshai, and Talmai, the descendants of Anak,[m] were living. Hebron was built seven years before Zoan[n] in Egypt. [23] When they came to the Valley of Eshcol,[o] they cut down a

[a]12:13 Gn 20:17; Ex 15:26; Lv 14:3; Dt 32:39
[b]12:14 Lv 13:46; Nm 5:1-4; 2Kg 15:5
[c]Lv 13:4
[d]12:15 Lv 14:2,8
[e]13:2 Dt 1:22-26
[f]13:3 Ex 18:25-26; Dt 1:13-18
[g]13:6 Nm 14:6,24,30,38; 26:65
[h]13:8 Ex 33:11; Nm 14:30,38; 27:18-23

[i]13:19 Nm 14:7; Dt 1:25
[j]Dt 1:28; 3:5; 9:1; Jos 14:12
[k]13:20 Neh 9:25,35; Is 30:23; Ezk 34:14,20
[l]Nm 13:23
[m]13:22 Nm 13:28,33; Dt 1:28; 2:10-11,21
[n]13:22 Ps 78:12; Is 19:11; 30:4; Ezk 30:14
[o]13:23 Nm 32:9; Dt 1:24

[A]12:10 A reference to whiteness or flakiness of the skin [B]12:12 Alt Hb tradition reads *baby who comes out of our mother's womb and our flesh is half eaten away.* [C]13:21 Southern border of the promised land [D]13:21 Or *near Lebo-hamath*

12:11-16 The lesson here is that racism in any form is a sin, whether it is based on ethnic origin or the color of one's skin (see 12:1). To judge people on the basis of so-called race is to reject the truth that all humans are created in God's image. We are all descendants of Adam and Eve.

The cross of Christ is the answer to hate rooted in perceived differences. The atoning death of Jesus tears down the divisions that separate humanity. This doesn't mean that the gospel obliterates distinctions like ethnicity. Rather, it means that the gospel and the power of the Holy Spirit enable us as believers—no matter where we come from or what we look like—to embrace differences because we share a common commitment to God. Because we have peace with God through

Christ, we can have peace with one another and become a part of a whole new race made up of members from every tribe, language, and nation. I'm talking about heaven's new community, the church (see Eph 2:11-17).

13:1-16 These scouts included **Caleb** and **Hoshea**, who would become heroes in Israel's history (13:6, 8). We know Hoshea better as **Joshua** (13:16); he would fight the battle of Jericho and succeed Moses to lead Israel. Interestingly, Joshua hailed from the tribe that descended from **Ephraim**, one of two sons of Joseph and his Egyptian wife (13:8; see Gen 41:50-52). The people of Egypt were descended from Noah's son Ham and his grandson Mizraim. This means the Egyptians were a Hamitic, and thus an African people (see the notes on Gen 9:18-29). Caleb was the son of

Jephunneh the Kenizzite (Num 13:6; see Josh 14:6); the Kenizzites were a part of the Canaanite tribes and also descendants of Ham. Moreover, Caleb also came from the tribe of Judah. Judah, the progenitor of the tribe, fathered twin sons by Tamar, who was a Hamitic descendant (see Gen 38). Thus, Hamitic (that is, dark-skinned) peoples were crucial to the program of God throughout Old Testament history.

13:17-27 Moses's instructions contained a number of questions (13:17-20). The spies did their recon work and brought back the answers, both verbally and visually, supplying **a single cluster of grapes** harvested during the **forty days** they were gone (13:23-25). They reported that the land was awesome, figuratively **flowing with milk and honey** (13:27)—just as God had promised (see Exod 3:8, 17).

a 13:23 Nm 20:5; Dt 8:8
b 13:25 Nm 14:33-34; 32:13;
Ps 95:10
c 13:26 Nm 32:9; Dt
1:24-25
d 13:27 Ex 3:8; Lv 20:24;
Nm 14:8; 16:13-14
e 13:28 Dt 1:28; 3:5; 9:1;
Jos 14:12
f Nm 13:22,33; Dt 1:28;
2:10-11,21
g 13:29 Ex 17:8-16; Nm
14:25,43,45; Dt 25:17-19
h 13:30 Nm 14:6,24,30,38;
26:65
i 13:33 Gn 6:4
j Dt 2:10-11,20-21

k 14:2 Ex 16:2,7-8; 17:3; Nm
14:27; 16:11,41; Ps 59:15
l 14:3 Gn 34:29; Nm 14:31
m Nm 11:5; Dt 17:16; Neh
9:17; Ac 7:39
n 14:7 Ex 3:8; Nm 13:27; Dt
1:25; 3:25
o 14:8 Ex 3:8; Lv 20:24; Nm
13:17; 16:13-14
p 14:9 Nm 14:3
q Ps 17:8; 36:7; 57:1; 63:7;
91:1; Is 49:2; 51:16
r 14:10 Ex 17:4; Mt 23:37
s 14:11 Ex 4:1-12:31;
14:11,21-22; Nm 14:22
t 14:12 Gn 12:2; Ex 32:10

branch with a single cluster of grapes, which was carried on a pole by two men. They also took some pomegranates and figs.*a* 24 That place was called the Valley of Eshcol[A] because of the cluster of grapes the Israelites cut there. 25 At the end of forty days*b* they returned from scouting out the land.

REPORT ABOUT CANAAN

26 The men went back to Moses, Aaron, and the entire Israelite community in the Wilderness of Paran at Kadesh. They brought back a report for them and the whole community, and they showed them the fruit of the land.*c* 27 They reported to Moses: "We went into the land where you sent us. Indeed it is flowing with milk and honey,*d* and here is some of its fruit. 28 However, the people living in the land are strong, and the cities are large and fortified.*e* We also saw the descendants of Anak*f* there. 29 The Amalekites*g* are living in the land of the Negev; the Hethites, Jebusites, and Amorites live in the hill country; and the Canaanites live by the sea and along the Jordan."

30 Then Caleb*h* quieted the people in the presence of Moses and said, "Let's go up now and take possession of the land because we can certainly conquer it!"

31 But the men who had gone up with him responded, "We can't attack the people because they are stronger than we are!" 32 So they gave a negative report to the Israelites about the land they had scouted: "The land we passed through to explore is one that devours its inhabitants, and all the people we saw in it are men of great size. 33 We even saw the Nephilim*i* there — the descendants of Anak come from the Nephilim!*j* To ourselves we seemed like grasshoppers, and we must have seemed the same to them."

ISRAEL'S REFUSAL TO ENTER CANAAN

14 Then the whole community broke into loud cries, and the people wept that night. 2 All the Israelites complained about Moses and Aaron,*k* and the whole community told them, "If only we had died in the land of Egypt, or if only we had died in this wilderness! 3 Why is the LORD bringing us into this land to die by the sword? Our wives and children will become plunder.*l* Wouldn't it be better for us to go back to Egypt?"*m* 4 So they said to one another, "Let's appoint a leader and go back to Egypt."

5 Then Moses and Aaron fell facedown in front of the whole assembly of the Israelite community. 6 Joshua son of Nun and Caleb son of Jephunneh, who were among those who scouted out the land, tore their clothes 7 and said to the entire Israelite community: "The land we passed through and explored is an extremely good land.*n* 8 If the LORD is pleased with us, he will bring us into this land, a land flowing with milk and honey,*o* and give it to us. 9 Only don't rebel against the LORD, and don't be afraid of the people of the land, for we will devour them.*p* Their protection*q* has been removed from them, and the LORD is with us. Don't be afraid of them!"

10 While the whole community threatened to stone them,*r* the glory of the LORD appeared to all the Israelites at the tent of meeting.

GOD'S JUDGMENT OF ISRAEL'S REBELLION

11 The LORD said to Moses, "How long will these people despise me? How long will they not trust in me despite all the signs I have performed among them?*s* 12 I will strike them with a plague and destroy them. Then I will make you into a greater and mightier nation than they are."*t*

13:28-33 After seeing Canaan's tall inhabitants and towering, walled **cities** (13:28-29), ten of the spies **gave a negative report** and declared, **We can't attack . . . because they are stronger than we are!** (13:31-32). They planted a defeatist mentality in the people's minds (13:33). As a result of their "brave" leaders wimping out on them, the people decided to cower in the desert.
14:1-2 Though Caleb had tried to counter the fearful spies' report in 13:30, negative thinking multiplied rapidly. **The whole community . . . wept** (14:1). The Israelites were crying because of their refusal to move forward in the will of God. They literally preferred death

in the land of slavery or death in the wilderness to trusting in God's promises (14:2).
14:3-4 The people sealed their doom by accusing God of dragging them out of their comfortable slavery to let them die in the desert (14:3). They cried, **Let's appoint a leader and go back to Egypt** (14:4). In other words, they had rejected God's deliverance, God's leader, and God's provision.
14:6-10 **Joshua** and **Caleb** made an impassioned plea for the Israelites to forget their rebellion and take the promised land God had given (14:7-8). Though Canaan's inhabitants looked impressive, the Lord had **removed** their **protection** (14:9). The God

who had destroyed Pharaoh's army in the Red Sea was the same God who would lead the Israelites to victory over the Canaanites. But even as they spoke, **the whole community threatened to stone them** (14:10). They were actually ready to put God's leaders to death!
14:11-16 As he had done before (see Exod 32:7-10), God vowed to **destroy** Israel and make Moses into an even **mightier nation** (Num 14:11-12). But, as then, Moses interceded for his kinsmen. Moses prayed for God to spare them so that he might preserve the glory of his great **fame** among the **nations** (14:13-16).

13 But Moses replied to the LORD, "The Egyptians will hear about it, for by your strength you brought up this people from them. **14** They will tell it to the inhabitants of this land.[a] They have heard that you, LORD, are among these people, how you, LORD, are seen face to face, how your cloud stands over them, and how you go before them in a pillar of cloud by day and in a pillar of fire by night.[b] **15** If you kill this people with a single blow,[A,c] the nations that have heard of your fame[d] will declare, **16** 'Since the LORD wasn't able to bring this people into the land he swore to give them,[e] he has slaughtered them in the wilderness.'[f]

17 "So now, may my Lord's power be magnified just as you have spoken: **18** The LORD is slow to anger and abounding in faithful love,[g] forgiving iniquity and rebellion.[h] But he will not leave the guilty unpunished,[i] bringing the consequences of the fathers' iniquity on the children to the third and fourth generation.[j] **19** Please pardon the iniquity of this people, in keeping with the greatness of your faithful love,[k] just as you have forgiven them from Egypt until now."

20 The LORD responded, "I have pardoned them as you requested. **21** Yet as surely as I live and as the whole earth is filled with the LORD's glory,[l] **22** none of the men who have seen my glory and the signs I performed in Egypt and in the wilderness, and have tested me these ten times and did not obey me, **23** will ever see the land I swore to give their fathers.[m] None of those who have despised me[n] will see it. **24** But since my servant Caleb has a different spirit and has remained loyal to me, I will bring him into the land where he has gone, and his descendants will inherit it.[o] **25** Since the Amalekites and Canaanites are living in the lowlands,[B] turn back tomorrow and head for the wilderness in the direction of the Red Sea."[p]

26 Then the LORD spoke to Moses and Aaron: **27** "How long must I endure this evil community that keeps complaining about me? I have heard the Israelites' complaints that they make against me.[q] **28** Tell them: As surely as I live — this is the LORD's declaration — I will do to you exactly as I heard you say. **29** Your corpses will fall in this wilderness — all of you who were registered in the census, the entire number of you twenty years old or more[r] — because you have complained about me. **30** I swear that none of you will enter the land I promised[c] to settle you in, except Caleb son of Jephunneh and Joshua son of Nun. **31** I will bring your children whom you said would become plunder[s] into the land you rejected, and they will enjoy it.[t] **32** But as for you, your corpses will fall in this wilderness. **33** Your children will be shepherds in the wilderness for forty years and bear the penalty for your acts of unfaithfulness until all your corpses lie scattered in the wilderness. **34** You will bear the consequences of your iniquities forty years based on the number of the forty days that you scouted the land, a year for each day.[D,u] You will know my displeasure.[E] **35** I, the LORD, have spoken. I swear that I will do this to the entire evil community that has conspired against me.[v] They will come to an end in the wilderness, and there they will die."[w]

36 So the men Moses sent to scout out the land, and who returned and incited the entire community to complain about him by spreading a negative report about the land — **37** those men who spread the negative report about the land were struck down by the LORD. **38** Only Joshua son of Nun and Caleb son of Jephunneh remained alive of those men who went to scout out the land.

ISRAEL ROUTED

39 When Moses reported these words to all the Israelites, the people were overcome

[a]14:14 Ex 15:13-15; Dt 2:25
[b]Ex 13:21-22; Nm 9:16-17; Dt 1:33
[c]14:15 Ex 32:9-12
[d]Dt 2:25; Jos 2:10; 9:9; Is 66:19; Hab 3:2
[e]14:16 Gn 12:7; 13:14-17; 15:7; Ac 7:5
[f]Dt 9:28
[g]14:18 Neh 9:17; Ps 86:5,15; 103:8; 145:8; Jl 2:13; Jnh 4:2
[h]Ezr 9:13; Ps 78:38; 85:2; Is 43:25; 44:22
[i]Pr 11:21; Jr 25:29; Nah 1:3
[j]Ex 20:5; 34:6-7; Dt 5:9; Jr 32:18
[k]14:19 Ex 34:9; Ps 25:11; 86:5; Jl 2:13
[l]14:21 Ps 72:19; Hab 2:14
[m]14:23 Gn 12:7; 13:14-17; 15:7; Ac 7:5
[n]Nm 14:11; Dt 31:20; Ps 74:18
[o]14:24 Jos 14:6-15; Jdg 1:10-12,20
[p]14:25 Nm 21:4; Dt 1:40; 2:1

[q]14:27 Ex 16:2,7-8; 17:3; Nm 14:29,36; 16:11,41; Dt 1:27
[r]14:29 Nm 1:3
[s]14:31 Nm 14:3
[t]Dt 1:39
[u]14:34 Nm 13:25; 32:13; Dt 2:14; Ps 95:10; Ezk 4:6
[v]14:35 Nm 16:11; 27:3; Ps 2:1-3
[w]Nm 14:30; 26:64-65; 1Co 10:5

14:18-19 In verse 18 Moses quoted the Lord's own words back to him (see Exod 34:6-7). In pointing to the truth of God's character, Moses pleaded with him to **pardon** Israel **in keeping with the greatness of [his] faithful love** (Num 14:19). Moses prayed for things consistent with God's character; he was deeply concerned that God be glorified. We are wise to follow his example.

14:20-25 God's Word affirms that "the prayer of a righteous person is very powerful" (Jas 5:16). We see that in action here as once more God responded positively to the great intercessory prayer of Moses and **pardoned** Israel

(14:20). He would not forsake the nation. Nevertheless, he swore that he would "not leave the guilty unpunished," which is a move consistent with his character (Num 14:18): **none of the men who have seen my glory and the signs I performed in Egypt and in the wilderness, and have tested me these ten times and did not obey me, will ever see the land,** God said (14:22-23). Because of their loyalty to God, **Caleb** and Joshua were exceptions to this (14:24; see 13:30; 14:6-9, 30, 38).

14:26-34 Frankly, the Israelites had sentenced themselves. They had lamented, "If only we had died in this wilderness!" (14:2). So God said, "You

want to perish in this desert you're wandering in? You got it." (14:28-29). And to make sure they wouldn't fail to remember their part in their own demise, the length of time they and their children would still have to wander before that first generation had died off was determined by the length of time the rebels had spent scouting the land, **a year for each day** (14:34).

14:39-40 The people's response was typical of those who get caught doing wrong and are suddenly "repentant," wanting everything to go back to the way it was before judgment fell. They were like children who realized they were in trouble and were now ready to obey to

ᵃ14:40 Dt 1:41-44
ᵇ14:45 Nm 21:3; Jdg 1:17
ᶜ15:2 Lv 14:34
ᵈ15:3 Ex 29:18; Lv 1:9;
21:6; Nm 15:10,13-14,25;
18:17; 28:2; Dt 18:1
ᵉLv 22:21; 27:2; Nm 15:8
ᶠLv 1:9,13,17
ᵍ15:5 Ex 29:40; Lv 23:13
ʰ15:6 Lv 23:13; Nm 28:9,12
ⁱ15:9 Nm 28:12

ʲ15:15 Ex 27:21; Lv 3:17;
7:36; 10:9; 23:14,31,41;
24:3; Nm 10:8; 18:23
ᵏ15:16 Ex 12:19,49; Lv
16:29-31; 17:8-16; Nm 9:14;
15:26,29; 19:10; 35:15
ˡ15:20 Neh 10:37; Ezk
44:30
ᵐLv 2:14
ⁿ15:22 Lv 4:2
ᵒ15:25 Lv 4:20,26,31,35;
19:20; Jr 5:1

with grief. **40** They got up early the next morning and went up the ridge of the hill country, saying, "Let's go to the place the LORD promised, for we were wrong."ᵃ **41** But Moses responded, "Why are you going against the LORD's command? It won't succeed. **42** Don't go, because the LORD is not among you and you will be defeated by your enemies. **43** The Amalekites and Canaanites are right in front of you, and you will fall by the sword. The LORD won't be with you, since you have turned from following him."

44 But they dared to go up the ridge of the hill country, even though the ark of the LORD's covenant and Moses did not leave the camp. **45** Then the Amalekites and Canaanites who lived in that part of the hill country came down, attacked them, and routed them as far as Hormah.ᵇ

LAWS ABOUT OFFERINGS

15 The LORD instructed Moses: **2** "Speak to the Israelites and tell them: When you enter the land I am giving you to settle in,ᶜ **3** and you make a fire offeringᵈ to the LORD from the herd or flock — either a burnt offering or a sacrifice, to fulfill a vow,ᵉ or as a freewill offering, or at your appointed festivals — to produce a pleasing aroma for the LORD,ᶠ **4** the one presenting his offering to the LORD is also to present a grain offering of two quartsᴬ of fine flour mixed with a quartᴮ of oil. **5** Prepare a quart of wine as a drink offeringᵍ with the burnt offering or sacrifice of each lamb.

6 "If you prepare a grain offering with a ram, it is to be four quartsᶜ of fine flour mixed with a third of a gallonᴰ of oil.ʰ **7** Also present a third of a gallon of wine for a drink offering as a pleasing aroma to the LORD.

8 "If you prepare a young bull as a burnt offering or as a sacrifice, to fulfill a vow, or as a fellowship offering to the LORD, **9** a grain offering of six quartsᴱ of fine flour mixed with two quartsᶠ of oil is to be presented with the bull.ⁱ **10** Also present two quarts of wine as a drink offering. It is a fire offering of pleasing aroma to the LORD. **11** This is to be done for each ox, ram, lamb, or goat. **12** This is how you are to prepare each of them, no matter how many.

13 "Every Israelite is to prepare these things in this way when he presents a fire offering as a pleasing aroma to the LORD. **14** When an alien resides with you or someone else is among you and wants to prepare a fire offering as a pleasing aroma to the LORD, he is to do exactly as you do throughout your generations. **15** The assembly is to have the same statute for both you and the resident alien as a permanent statute throughout your generations.ʲ You and the alien will be alike before the LORD. **16** The same law and the same ordinance will apply to both you and the alien who resides with you."ᵏ

17 The LORD instructed Moses: **18** "Speak to the Israelites and tell them: After you enter the land where I am bringing you, **19** you are to offer a contribution to the LORD when you eat from the food of the land. **20** You are to offer a loaf from your first batch of doughˡ as a contribution; offer it just like a contribution from the threshing floor.ᵐ **21** Throughout your generations, you are to give the LORD a contribution from the first batch of your dough.

22 "When you sin unintentionally and do not obey all these commands that the LORD spoke to Mosesⁿ — **23** all that the LORD has commanded you through Moses, from the day the LORD issued the commands and onward throughout your generations — **24** and if it was done unintentionally without the community's awareness, the entire community is to prepare one young bull for a burnt offering as a pleasing aroma to the LORD, with its grain offering and drink offering according to the regulation, and one male goat as a sin offering. **25** The priest will then make atonement for the entire Israelite community so that they may be forgiven,ᵒ for the sin was unintentional. They are to bring their offering, one made by fire to the LORD, and their

---

ᴬ15:4 Lit *a tenth* (of an ephah) ᴮ15:4 Lit *a fourth hin*, also in v. 5 ᶜ15:6 Lit *two-tenths* (of an ephah) ᴰ15:6 Lit *a third*, also in v. 7 ᴱ15:9 Lit *three-tenths* (of an ephah) ᶠ15:9 Lit *a half hin*, also in v. 10

---

avoid punishment: "Okay, okay. We'll do what you asked us to do. Just don't ground us!"
14:42 Moses's warning brings up an important principle: just as you can't be defeated with the Lord at your side, you can't be victorious without him.
14:44-45 The people had become too spiritually dull to understand the foolishness of going ahead without God's blessing. As a result, **the Amalekites and Canaanites** thrashed them (14:45).
15:1-30 Though the Israelite generation that had left Egypt would not enter the promised land, their children would. The offerings described in 15:3-16 were not for sin or guilt, but were to be presented as voluntary sacrifices of praise, thanksgiving, and fellowship. They were designed to show the Lord how much the people valued his covenant faithfulness.
15:22-26 **The entire community** could be guilty of a sin of omission without even being aware of it, which nevertheless required **atonement** so that the people might **be forgiven** (15:24-25).

sin offering before the LORD for their unintentional sin. **26** The entire Israelite community and the alien who resides among them will be forgiven, since it happened to all the people unintentionally.

27 "If one person sins unintentionally,[a] he is to present a year-old female goat as a sin offering. **28** The priest will then make atonement before the LORD on behalf of the person who acts in error sinning unintentionally, and when he makes atonement for him, he will be forgiven. **29** You are to have the same law for the person who acts in error, whether he is an Israelite or an alien who resides among you.

30 "But the person who acts defiantly,[A] whether native or resident alien, blasphemes the LORD.[b] That person is to be cut off from his people. **31** He will certainly be cut off, because he has despised the LORD's word and broken his command; his guilt remains on him."

SABBATH VIOLATION

32 While the Israelites were in the wilderness, they found a man gathering wood on the Sabbath day.[c] **33** Those who found him gathering wood brought him to Moses, Aaron, and the entire community. **34** They placed him in custody because it had not been decided what should be done to him. **35** Then the LORD told Moses, "The man is to be put to death. The entire community is to stone him outside the camp."[d] **36** So the entire community brought him outside the camp and stoned him to death, as the LORD had commanded Moses.

TASSELS FOR REMEMBRANCE

37 The LORD said to Moses, **38** "Speak to the Israelites and tell them that throughout their generations they are to make tassels[e]

for the corners of their garments, and put a blue cord on the tassel at each corner. **39** These will serve as tassels for you to look at, so that you may remember all the LORD's commands and obey them and not prostitute yourselves by following your own heart[f] and your own eyes.[g] **40** This way you will remember and obey all my commands and be holy to your God. **41** I am the LORD your God who brought you out of the land of Egypt to be your God; I am the LORD your God."[h]

KORAH INCITES REBELLION

16 Now Korah son of Izhar, son of Kohath, son of Levi,[i] with Dathan and Abiram,[j] sons of Eliab, and On son of Peleth, sons of Reuben, took **2** two hundred and fifty prominent Israelite men who were leaders of the community and representatives in the assembly, and they rebelled against Moses. **3** They came together against Moses and Aaron and told them, "You have gone too far! Everyone in the entire community is holy, and the LORD is among them.[k] Why then do you exalt yourselves above the LORD's assembly?"

4 When Moses heard this, he fell facedown. **5** Then he said to Korah and all his followers, "Tomorrow morning the LORD will reveal who belongs to him, who is set apart, and the one he will let come near[l] him. He will let the one he chooses[m] come near him. **6** Korah, you and all your followers are to do this: take firepans,[n] and tomorrow **7** place fire in them and put incense on them before the LORD.[o] Then the man the LORD chooses will be the one who is set apart.[p] It is you Levites who have gone too far!"

8 Moses also told Korah, "Now listen, Levites! **9** Isn't it enough for you that the

a 15:27 Lv 4:27
b 15:30 2Kg 19:6,22; Is 37:6,23; Ezk 20:27
c 15:32 Ex 35:2-3
d 15:35 Lv 20:27; 24:14,23; Nm 14:10; Jos 7:25; Ezk 16:40; Mt 21:35; Ac 14:19; 2Co 11:25; Heb 11:37; 12:20
e 15:38 Dt 22:12; Mt 9:20; 14:36; 23:5

f 15:39 Jr 3:17; 9:14; 16:12; 18:12; Ezk 14:7; 20:16; 33:31
g Jb 31:7
h 15:41 Ex 29:46; Lv 19:36; 25:38; 26:13
i 16:1 Ex 6:16-21
j Nm 26:9; Dt 11:6; Ps 106:16-18
k 16:3 Nm 14:14; Ezk 37:26-28
l 16:5 Ex 40:12-15
m Nm 17:5; Jdg 10:14; 1Sm 10:24; 2Sm 6:21; 1Kg 8:44; 11:32; Ps 105:26
n 16:6 Ex 27:3; 38:3; Nm 4:9,14; 16:17,37-39
o 16:7 Lv 10:1-2; 16:12
p Nm 17:5

A 15:30 Lit *with a high hand*

15:32-36 Mention is made of **a man gathering wood on the Sabbath** (15:32)—in a blatant and defiant violation of a clear command. The Lord himself pronounced sentence: **The entire community is to stone him** (15:35). It isn't hard to imagine the fear of God this execution instilled in the participants.

Defiant sin is no small matter. Sometimes the judgment it brings is immediate physical death (see Acts 5:1-11). And without the perpetrator placing faith in the atoning death of Jesus Christ before he or she passes, it will bring God's eternal judgment.

15:37-41 These embellishments were to serve as visible reminders of the people's covenant God, so that they would obey him.

16:1-2 Notably, these men already held positions of great honor when they decided to

make a play for further power. This story is a reminder that sin doesn't play favorites; it infects all.

16:3 Korah and his followers claimed to be as **holy** as Moses and Aaron. One has to wonder if they had been paying any attention at all. It is mind-blowing that they thought they could pull off a successful rebellion against Moses given what had befallen Miriam and all God had done through Moses to this point. Not one of these previous incidents or God's responses, however, penetrated their hard hearts. Their accusation even included Aaron, the high priest, suggesting that they were challenging both the religious and governmental leadership of God's kingdom structure.

16:4-7 **Moses** knew that, ultimately, Korah and crew were not sinning against him but

against the Lord. So **he fell facedown** in worship and prayer before God (16:4). He must have been there long enough to get instructions from God for the event that would take place the next day at the entrance to the tabernacle.

16:8-11 Korah wasn't content to take care of the **tabernacle** as a Levite. He wanted to usurp the role of a priest, even though God had given that ministry to Aaron and his family alone among the descendants of Levi (16:9-10). God had **brought [Korah] near** (16:10) by sanctifying him for ministry, but that wasn't good enough for him. Thus, Korah and his friends decided to conspire **against the LORD** (16:11).

[a] 16:9 Gn 8:9; Ex 19:4
[b] Dt 10:8; 21:5; 2Ch 29:11; Ezk 40:46; 44:11,15-16
[c] 16:10 Ex 29:9; Nm 18:7; 25:13; Neh 7:64; 13:29
[d] 16:11 Nm 14:35; 27:3; Ps 2:1-3
[e] 16:13 Ex 3:8,17
[f] 16:14 1Sm 11:2
[g] 16:19 Ex 16:7,10
[h] 16:21 Nm 16:45; Jos 24:20; Jr 14:12; Ezk 43:8
[i] 16:22 Gn 17:3; Lv 9:24; Nm 16:4,45
[j] Nm 27:16
[k] Gn 18:24-26

[l] 16:26 Is 52:11
[m] Gn 19:15,17
[n] 16:28 Ex 3:10-12; Zch 2:9,11; 4:9; 6:15
[o] 16:30 Is 5:14
[p] 16:32 Ex 15:12; Nm 26:10
[q] 16:35 Gn 19:24; Lv 10:1-2; Nm 11:1; 2Kg 1:10

God of Israel has separated you from the Israelite community to bring you near to himself,[a] to perform the work at the LORD's tabernacle, and to stand before the community to minister to them?[b] [10] He has brought you near, and all your fellow Levites who are with you, but you are pursuing the priesthood[c] as well. [11] Therefore, it is you and all your followers who have conspired against the LORD![d] As for Aaron, who is he[A] that you should complain about him?"

[12] Moses sent for Dathan and Abiram, the sons of Eliab, but they said, "We will not come! [13] Is it not enough that you brought us up from a land flowing with milk and honey to kill us in the wilderness?[e] Do you also have to appoint yourself as ruler over us? [14] Furthermore, you didn't bring us to a land flowing with milk and honey or give us an inheritance of fields and vineyards. Will you gouge out the eyes of these men?[f] We will not come!"

[15] Then Moses became angry and said to the LORD, "Don't respect their offering. I have not taken one donkey from them or mistreated a single one of them." [16] So Moses told Korah, "You and all your followers are to appear before the LORD tomorrow — you, they, and Aaron. [17] Each of you is to take his firepan, place incense on it, and present his firepan before the LORD — 250 firepans. You and Aaron are each to present your firepan also."

[18] Each man took his firepan, placed fire in it, put incense on it, and stood at the entrance to the tent of meeting along with Moses and Aaron. [19] After Korah assembled the whole community against them at the entrance to the tent of meeting, the glory of the LORD[g] appeared to the whole community. [20] The LORD spoke to Moses and Aaron, [21] "Separate yourselves from this community so I may consume them instantly."[h]

[22] But Moses and Aaron fell facedown[i] and said, "God, God who gives breath to all,[B,j] when one man sins, will you vent your wrath on the whole community?"[k]

[23] The LORD replied to Moses, [24] "Tell the community: Get away from the dwellings of Korah, Dathan, and Abiram."

[25] Moses got up and went to Dathan and Abiram, and the elders of Israel followed him. [26] He warned the community, "Get away now from the tents of these wicked men. Don't touch anything that belongs to them,[l] or you will be swept away because of all their sins."[m] [27] So they got away from the dwellings of Korah, Dathan, and Abiram. Meanwhile, Dathan and Abiram came out and stood at the entrance of their tents with their wives, children, and infants.

[28] Then Moses said, "This is how you will know that the LORD sent me[n] to do all these things and that it was not of my own will: [29] If these men die naturally as all people would, and suffer the fate of all, then the LORD has not sent me. [30] But if the LORD brings about something unprecedented, and the ground opens its mouth and swallows them along with all that belongs to them so that they go down alive into Sheol,[o] then you will know that these men have despised the LORD."

[31] Just as he finished speaking all these words, the ground beneath them split open. [32] The earth opened its mouth and swallowed them and their households, all Korah's people,[p] and all their possessions. [33] They went down alive into Sheol with all that belonged to them. The earth closed over them, and they vanished from the assembly. [34] At their cries, all the people of Israel who were around them fled because they thought, "The earth may swallow us too!" [35] Fire also came out from the LORD and consumed the 250 men who were presenting the incense.[q]

[36] Then the LORD spoke to Moses: [37] "Tell Eleazar son of Aaron the priest to remove the firepans from the burning debris, because they are holy, and scatter the fire far away. [38] As for the firepans of those who sinned at the cost of their own lives, make them into hammered sheets as plating for the altar, for they presented them before

[A] 16:11 Or Aaron, what has he done [B] 16:22 Or God of the spirits of all flesh

16:12-14 The claim made by Dathan and Abiram was outrageous. In their minds, Egypt—the land in which they had been enslaved—was **a land flowing with milk and honey** (16:13). So not only had Moses yanked them out of their "paradise" in Egypt, but he had also failed to give them the land that had been promised. They felt Moses had so deceived the people that the only way he could hide his true intention to **kill** everyone **in the wilderness** was to **gouge out the eyes** of the rebels who knew the real truth (16:13-14). They were delusional. 16:15 Everything Dathan and Abiram said was a lie; the opposite, in fact, was true: Moses had cared for and interceded for Israel. (See the note on 16:12-14.) 16:19 Korah's prominence within the camp is on display here because he was able to assemble **the whole community against** Moses and Aaron. Yet his popularity did not mean his heart was right or that he was worth following. 16:31-40 What followed was a terrifying scene of judgment. As Moses predicted and through the supernatural work of God, **the earth** consumed **all Korah's people** (16:32).

the LORD, and the firepans are holy. They will be a sign to the Israelites."

39 So the priest Eleazar took the bronze firepans that those who were burned had presented, and they were hammered into plating for the altar, **40** just as the LORD commanded him through Moses. It was to be a reminder for the Israelites that no unauthorized person outside the lineage of Aaron should approach to offer incense before the LORD[a] and become like Korah and his followers.

41 The next day the entire Israelite community complained about Moses and Aaron,[b] saying, "You have killed the LORD's people!" **42** When the community assembled against them, Moses and Aaron turned toward the tent of meeting, and suddenly the cloud covered it, and the LORD's glory appeared.

43 Moses and Aaron went to the front of the tent of meeting, **44** and the LORD said to Moses, **45** "Get away from this community so that I may consume them instantly."[c] But they fell facedown.

46 Then Moses told Aaron, "Take your firepan, place fire from the altar in it, and add incense. Go quickly to the community and make atonement for them, because wrath has come from the LORD; the plague has begun." **47** So Aaron took his firepan as Moses had ordered, ran into the middle of the assembly, and saw that the plague had begun among the people. After he added incense, he made atonement for the people. **48** He stood between the dead and the living, and the plague was halted. **49** But those who died from the plague numbered 14,700, in addition to those who died because of the Korah incident. **50** Aaron then returned to Moses at the entrance to the tent of meeting, since the plague had been halted.[d]

AARON'S STAFF CHOSEN

17 The LORD instructed Moses: **2** "Speak to the Israelites and take one staff from them for each ancestral tribe,[A]

twelve staffs from all the leaders of their tribes.[B] Write each man's name on his staff. **3** Write Aaron's name on Levi's staff, because there is to be one staff for the head of each tribe. **4** Then place them in the tent of meeting in front of the testimony where I meet with you. **5** The staff of the man I choose will sprout, and I will rid myself of the Israelites' complaints that they have been making about you."

6 So Moses spoke to the Israelites, and each of their leaders gave him a staff, one for each of the leaders of their tribes, twelve staffs in all. Aaron's staff was among them.[e] **7** Moses placed the staffs before the LORD in the tent of the testimony.

8 The next day Moses entered the tent of the testimony and saw that Aaron's staff, representing the house of Levi, had sprouted, formed buds, blossomed, and produced almonds! **9** Moses then brought out all the staffs from the LORD's presence to all the Israelites. They saw them, and each man took his own staff. **10** The LORD told Moses, "Put Aaron's staff back in front of the testimony to be kept as a sign[f] for the rebels, so that you may put an end to their complaints before me, or else they will die."[g] **11** So Moses did as the LORD commanded him.

12 Then the Israelites declared to Moses, "Look, we're perishing! We're lost; we're all lost! **13** Anyone who comes near the LORD's tabernacle will die.[h] Will we all perish?"

PROVISION FOR THE PRIESTHOOD

18 The LORD said to Aaron, "You, your sons, and your ancestral family[c,i] will be responsible for iniquity against the sanctuary. You and your sons will be responsible for iniquity involving your priesthood. **2** But also bring your relatives with you from the tribe of Levi, your ancestral tribe, so they may join you and assist you and your sons in front of the tent of the testimony.[j] **3** They are to perform duties for you and for the whole tent. They must not come near the sanctuary

*a*16:40 Ex 28:1; Nm 3:10,38; 18:4,7
*b*16:41 Ex 16:2,7-8; 17:3; Nm 14:2,27; 16:3; 17:6; 20:2; 26:9; 1Co 10:10
*c*16:45 Nm 16:21
*d*16:47-50 Nm 25:1-9; 2Sm 24:15-25

*e*17:6 Ex 7:12
*f*17:10 Heb 9:4
*g*Ex 28:35; 30:20-21; Lv 8:35; 10:6,9; 15:31; 16:2,13; Nm 4:19; 18:3,32; 35:12
*h*17:13 Nm 3:10,38; 8:19; 18:7
*i*18:1 Nm 10:21
*j*18:2 Nm 8:5-26

16:41 The **community** had witnessed the truth for themselves. Their outrageous claim testifies that humans can be tenacious in their willingness to deny the truth and believe a lie—no matter how obviously the facts are presented. **16:45-50** The **plague** mentioned in verse 46 led to a fresh revelation of God's fierce holiness that no doubt put reverential fear in the hearts of the remaining Israelites, so that they might not sin against the Lord. The Lord is a

holy God. The worst thing you can do is fail to take him seriously.

17:1-5 God took a decisive step to clarify that he had invested only Aaron's family with the priesthood. Each tribal leader's name was written on his staff, with **Aaron's name on Levi's** (17:3). Then all the staffs were placed in the tabernacle (17:4). The wooden staff of God's chosen priest would supernaturally **sprout** (17:5).

17:8-10 Aaron's staff didn't just blossom; it **produced almonds** (17:8). God told Moses to put the rod **back in** the tabernacle (see Heb 9:4) as a warning to the **rebels** to think twice before they challenged God's leaders again—lest they **die** (Num 17:10).

17:12-13 It's interesting that we get no mention of Moses trying to soothe the people's fears here. He was probably glad to see the fear of God finally grip their hearts.

[a]18:5 Nm 1:53; 16; 17:12-13; 1Ch 9:19; Ezk 44:11
[b]18:7 Nm 3:10
[c]Nm 1:51; 3:10,38
[d]18:8 Ex 36:3; Lv 22:12; Nm 18:19; Dt 12:6,11,17; Neh 10:39; 12:44; 13:5; Ezk 20:40; Mal 3:8
[e]Lv 22:2-7,15-16; Nm 18:32; Ezk 42:13
[f]Lv 10:12-15; Nm 5:9
[g]18:11 Ex 29:24-27; 35:22; 38:24,29; Lv 7:30,34; 8:27,29; 9:21; 10:14-15; 14:12,24; 23:15,17,20; Nm 6:20; 8:11-21
[h]Lv 7:34-36
[i]18:12 Dt 7:13; 11:14; 12:17; 14:23; 18:4; 28:51; Neh 10:37-39
[j]Gn 49:3; Ex 23:16,19; 34:22,26; Lv 2:12,14; 23:17,20; Nm 28:26; Jr 2:3; Rm 8:23; 11:16; 1Co 15:20,23; 16:15; Jms 1:18; Rv 14:4
[k]18:14 Lv 27:28

[l]18:15 Ex 13:11-16
[m]18:16 Lv 27:6; Nm 3:46-47
[n]18:19 Lv 2:13; 2Ch 13:5
[o]18:20 Dt 10:9; Jos 18:7; Ezk 44:28-30
[p]18:21 Dt 26:12; 2Ch 31:12; Neh 10:37-38; Heb 7:5
[q]18:23 Dt 10:8-9; 18:1-2; Jos 13:14,33

equipment or the altar; otherwise, both they and you will die. [4] They are to join you and guard the tent of meeting, doing all the work at the tent, but no unauthorized person may come near you.

[5] "You are to guard the sanctuary and the altar so that wrath may not fall on the Israelites again.[a] [6] Look, I have selected your fellow Levites from the Israelites as a gift for you, assigned by the LORD to work at the tent of meeting. [7] But you and your sons will carry out your priestly responsibilities[b] for everything concerning the altar and for what is inside the curtain, and you will do that work. I am giving you the work of the priesthood as a gift,[A] but an unauthorized person who comes near the sanctuary will be put to death."[c]

SUPPORT FOR THE PRIESTS AND LEVITES

[8] Then the LORD spoke to Aaron, "Look, I have put you in charge of the contributions[d] brought to me. As for all the holy offerings[e] of the Israelites, I have given them to you and your sons as a portion and a permanent statute.[f] [9] A portion of the holiest offerings kept from the fire will be yours; every one of their offerings that they give me, whether the grain offering, sin offering, or guilt offering will be most holy for you and your sons. [10] You are to eat it as a most holy offering.[B] Every male may eat it; it is to be holy to you.

[11] "The contribution of their gifts also belongs to you. I have given all the Israelites' presentation offerings[g] to you and to your sons and daughters as a permanent statute.[h] Every ceremonially clean person in your house may eat it. [12] I am giving you all the best of the fresh oil, new wine, and grain,[i] which the Israelites give to the LORD as their firstfruits.[j] [13] The firstfruits of all that is in their land, which they bring to the LORD, belong to you. Every clean person in your house may eat them.

[14] "Everything in Israel that is permanently dedicated to the LORD[k] belongs to you. [15] The firstborn of every living thing, human or animal, presented to the LORD belongs to you. But you must certainly redeem a human firstborn,[l] and redeem the firstborn of an unclean animal. [16] You will pay the redemption price for a month-old male according to your assessment: five shekels[c] of silver by the standard sanctuary shekel, which is twenty gerahs.[m]

[17] "However, you must not redeem the firstborn of an ox, a sheep, or a goat; they are holy. You are to splatter their blood on the altar and burn their fat as a fire offering for a pleasing aroma to the LORD. [18] But their meat belongs to you. It belongs to you like the breast of the presentation offering and the right thigh.

[19] "I give to you and to your sons and daughters all the holy contributions that the Israelites present to the LORD as a permanent statute. It is a permanent covenant of salt[n] before the LORD for you as well as your offspring."

[20] The LORD told Aaron, "You will not have an inheritance in their land; there will be no portion among them for you. I am your portion and your inheritance among the Israelites.[o]

[21] "Look, I have given the Levites every tenth[p] in Israel as an inheritance in return for the work they do, the work of the tent of meeting. [22] The Israelites must never again come near the tent of meeting, or they will incur guilt and die. [23] The Levites will do the work of the tent of meeting, and they will bear the consequences of their iniquity. The Levites will not receive an inheritance among the Israelites;[q] this is a permanent statute throughout your generations. [24] For I have given them the tenth that the Israelites present to the LORD as a contribution for their inheritance. That is why I told them that they would not receive an inheritance among the Israelites."

[25] The LORD instructed Moses, [26] "Speak to the Levites and tell them: When you receive from the Israelites the tenth that I have given you as your inheritance, you

---

[A]18:7 Or curtain. So you are to perform the service; a gift of your priesthood I grant   [B]18:10 Or it in a most holy place   [C]18:16 A shekel is about two-fifths of an ounce

---

18:8-19 God provided for Aaron and his sons to be supported from **the contributions from all the holy offerings of the Israelites** (18:8). Since their daily labor revolved around the tabernacle, the priests and their families were to receive provision for daily life through the offerings made by their fellow Israelites.

In the New Testament era, Paul recognized a ministry principle here that applies today.

Ministers of the gospel have a legitimate right to make a living from their work on behalf of the gospel—even though Paul, a tentmaker by trade, had declined to use that right himself. He said to the Corinthians, "Don't you know that those who perform the temple services eat the food from the temple? . . . In the same way, the Lord has commanded that those who preach the gospel should earn their living by the gospel" (1 Cor 9:13-14).

18:21-31 God set aside a **tenth** of the Israelites' offerings for the Levites to live on, since they also would **not receive an inheritance among the Israelites** (18:21, 23). But unlike the priests, the Levites had to tithe back to God on their tithe from the people (18:26). The Levites could then eat of their own offerings as their **wage in return for [their] work at the tent of meeting** (18:30-31).

are to present part of it as an offering to the LORD — a tenth of the tenth. **27** Your offering will be credited to you as if it were your grain from the threshing floor or the full harvest from the winepress. **28** You are to present an offering to the LORD from every tenth you receive from the Israelites. Give some of it to the priest Aaron as an offering to the LORD. **29** You must present the entire offering due the LORD from all your gifts. The best part of the tenth[a] is to be consecrated.

30 "Tell them further: Once you have presented the best part of the tenth, and it is credited to you Levites as the produce of the threshing floor or the winepress, **31** then you and your household may eat it anywhere. It is your wage in return for your work at the tent of meeting. **32** You will not incur guilt because of it once you have presented the best part of it, but you must not defile the Israelites' holy offerings, so that you will not die."

PURIFICATION RITUAL

19 The LORD spoke to Moses and Aaron, **2** "This is the legal statute that the LORD has commanded: Instruct the Israelites to bring you an unblemished red cow that has no defect and has never been yoked.[b] **3** Give it to the priest Eleazar,[c] and he will have it brought outside the camp and slaughtered in his presence. **4** The priest Eleazar is to take some of its blood with his finger and sprinkle it seven times toward the front of the tent of meeting. **5** The cow is to be burned in his sight. Its hide, flesh, and blood, are to be burned along with its waste. **6** The priest is to take cedar wood, hyssop, and crimson yarn,[d] and throw them onto the fire where the cow is burning. **7** Then the priest must wash his clothes and bathe his body in water; after that he may enter the camp, but he will remain ceremonially unclean until evening. **8** The one who burned the cow must also wash his clothes and bathe his body in water, and he will remain unclean until evening.

9 "A man who is clean is to gather up the cow's ashes and deposit them outside the camp in a ceremonially clean place. The ashes will be kept by the Israelite community for preparing the water to remove impurity; it is a sin offering.[e] **10** Then the one who gathers up the cow's ashes must wash his clothes, and he will remain unclean until evening. This is a permanent statute for the Israelites and for the alien who resides among them.

11 "The person who touches any human corpse will be unclean for seven days. **12** He is to purify himself with the water[A] on the third day and the seventh day; then he will be clean.[f] But if he does not purify himself on the third and seventh days, he will not be clean. **13** Anyone who touches a body of a person who has died, and does not purify himself, defiles the tabernacle of the LORD. That person will be cut off from Israel. He remains unclean because the water for impurity has not been sprinkled on him, and his uncleanness is still on him.

14 "This is the law when a person dies in a tent: everyone who enters the tent and everyone who is already in the tent will be unclean for seven days, **15** and any open container without a lid tied on it is unclean. **16** Anyone in the open field who touches a person who has been killed by the sword or has died, or who even touches a human bone, or a grave, will be unclean for seven days. **17** For the purification of the unclean person, they are to take some of the ashes of the burnt sin offering, put them in a jar, and add fresh water to them. **18** A person who is clean is to take hyssop, dip it in the water, and sprinkle the tent, all the furnishings, and the people who were there. He is also to sprinkle the one who touched a bone, a grave, a corpse, or a person who had been killed.

19 "The one who is clean is to sprinkle the unclean person on the third day and the seventh day. After he purifies the unclean person on the seventh day, the one being purified must wash his clothes and bathe in water, and he will be clean by evening. **20** But a person who is unclean and does not purify himself, that person will be cut off from the assembly because he has defiled the sanctuary of the LORD.[g] The water

[a]18:29 Nm 18:12
[b]19:2 Dt 21:3; 1Sm 6:7; Heb 9:13
[c]19:3 Ex 6:23-25; 28:1; Lv 10:6,12,16; Nm 3:2,4,32; 4:16; 16:37,39
[d]19:6 Lv 14:4-7,49-52; Heb 9:19

[e]19:9 Lv 4
[f]19:12 Nm 31:19
[g]19:20 1Co 6:19-20

[A]19:12 Or *ashes*; lit *with it*

19:1-8 Every step of this cleansing ritual underscored that death is the ultimate symbol of sin; it cannot remain in God's presence. It must, by God's prescription, be washed away.
19:11-13 To remind the congregation that these were not just ceremonial regulations with little spiritual ramification, God commanded that anyone who touched a corpse and failed to **purify himself** would defile the tabernacle. That person was to be **cut off** (19:13).
19:14-18 The practicality of these rules can be seen with regard to someone who died in a **tent** or someone who came upon a dead body **in the open field** (19:14, 16), two places where a nomadic group would spend their time.
19:22 At work here is a timeless spiritual principle. Sin that isn't dealt with contaminates that which is holy.

for impurity has not been sprinkled on
him; he is unclean. 21 This is a permanent
statute for them. The person who sprin-
kles the water for impurity is to wash his
clothes, and whoever touches the water
for impurity will be unclean until evening.
22 Anything the unclean person touches
will become unclean, and anyone who
touches it will be unclean until evening."

WATER FROM THE ROCK

20 The entire Israelite community entered the Wilderness of Zin[a] in the
first month, and they[A] settled in Kadesh.[b]
Miriam[c] died and was buried there.
2 There was no water for the community, so they assembled against Moses and
Aaron. 3 The people quarreled with Moses
and said,[d] "If only we had perished when
our brothers perished before the LORD.[e]
4 Why have you brought the LORD's assembly into this wilderness[f] for us and
our livestock to die here?[g] 5 Why have you
led us up from Egypt to bring us to this
evil place? It's not a place of grain, figs,
vines, and pomegranates,[h] and there is no
water to drink! "
6 Then Moses and Aaron went from
the presence of the assembly to the
doorway of the tent of meeting. They
fell facedown, and the glory of the LORD
appeared to them. 7 The LORD spoke to
Moses, 8 "Take the staff[i] and assemble the
community. You and your brother Aaron are to speak to the rock[j] while they
watch, and it will yield its water. You will
bring out water for them from the rock
and provide drink for the community
and their livestock."
9 So Moses took the staff from the LORD's
presence[k] just as he had commanded him.
10 Moses and Aaron summoned the assembly in front of the rock, and Moses said to
them, "Listen, you rebels! Must we bring
water out of this rock for you? " 11 Then
Moses raised his hand and struck the rock
twice with his staff, so that abundant water gushed out, and the community and
their livestock drank.[l]
12 But the LORD said to Moses and Aaron,
"Because you did not trust me to demonstrate my holiness in the sight of the Israelites, you will not bring this assembly
into the land I have given them."[m] 13 These
are the Waters of Meribah,[B,n] where the Israelites quarreled with the LORD, and he
demonstrated his holiness to them.[o]

EDOM DENIES PASSAGE

14 Moses sent messengers from Kadesh to
the king of Edom, "This is what your brother Israel[p] says, 'You know all the hardships
that have overtaken us. 15 Our fathers went
down to Egypt, and we lived in Egypt many
years, but the Egyptians treated us and
our fathers badly. 16 When we cried out
to the LORD, he heard our plea,[C] and sent
an angel,[D,q] and brought us out of Egypt.
Now look, we are in Kadesh, a city on the
border of your territory. 17 Please let us
travel through your land. We won't travel through any field or vineyard, or drink
any well water. We will travel the King's
Highway; we won't turn to the right or the
left until we have traveled through your
territory.'"[r]
18 But Edom answered him, "You will not
travel through our land, or we will come
out and confront you with the sword."
19 "We will go on the main road," the Israelites replied to them, "and if we or our
herds drink your water, we will pay its
price.[s] There will be no problem; only let
us travel through on foot."
20 Yet Edom insisted, "You may not travel
through." And they came out to confront
them with a large force of heavily-armed
people.[E] 21 Edom refused to allow Israel to
travel through their territory, and Israel
turned away from them.

[a] **20:1** Nm 13:21; 27:14; 33:36; 34:3; Dt 32:51; Jos 15:1
[b] Nm 13:26; 27:14; 33:36-37; Dt 1:46; Jdg 11:16-17; Ps 29:8
[c] Ex 15:20-21; Nm 12:1; 26:59; Dt 24:9
[d] **20:3** Ex 17:2
[e] Nm 16:31-35,41-50
[f] **20:4** Nm 11:11
[g] Gn 47:15,19; Ex 14:11-12; Nm 21:5
[h] **20:5** Ex 13:5; Nm 13:23-27; Dt 8:8
[i] **20:8** Ex 4:2-5; 7:15,17,20; 17:4-9; Nm 17:8; 2Kg 4:31
[j] Gn 49:24; Ex 17:6; Dt 32:13-18; Neh 9:15; Jb 29:6; Ps 78:20; 81:16; 114:8
[k] **20:9** Nm 17:10
[l] **20:11** Ex 17:6; Ps 78:15; 1Co 10:4
[m] **20:12** Nm 27:12-14; Dt 1:37; 3:26; 32:51
[n] **20:13** Ex 17:7; Nm 27:14; Dt 32:51; Ps 95:8; 106:32
[o] Nm 27:14; Ezk 28:22; 38:23
[p] **20:14** Gn 25:23-26,30; 36:8
[q] **20:16** Ex 3:7-10; 14:19; 23:20
[r] **20:17** Nm 21:22; Dt 2:27
[s] **20:19** Dt 2:1-7

[A] **20:1** Lit *the people* [B] **20:13** = Quarreling [C] **20:16** Lit *voice* [D] **20:16** Or *a messenger* [E] **20:20** Lit *with numerous people and a strong hand*

20:1 **The first month** referred to here was actually in the fortieth year of Israel's wandering in the wilderness. We can date this confidently because 33:38 says Aaron died in that fortieth year, and his death is recorded in 20:22-29. The nation was back **in Kadesh** where they had rebelled against the Lord and refused to take the promised land. What happened between the second and fortieth year of Israel's wandering isn't discussed in Scripture.

20:2-13 God commanded Moses to take his **staff**, gather the people, and **speak to the rock** (20:8). But Moses was frustrated with the people and said to them, **Must we bring water out of this rock for you?** (20:10). Then he **struck the rock twice** (20:11).

Don't miss what might at first seem to be only a minor breach of obedience here. Moses totally failed to obey, striking the rock instead of speaking to it. Equally jarring are his words. He publicly attributed to his own efforts the authority that belonged to God alone. The result would be disastrous for God's servant. Moses and Aaron lost their opportunity to enter the promised land. This judgment once again directed attention to the Lord's **holiness**, which the pair had failed to honor (20:12-13).

20:14-17 Moses hoped for passage to Canaan through the land of **Edom**. He sent an appeal to their king, essentially signing the spoken query with the name **your brother Israel** (20:14), since the Edomites were the descendants of Israelite patriarch Jacob's brother Esau. The two people groups shared common ancestors in Abraham and Isaac.

20:18-21 The Edomite king turned Moses down cold (20:18) and came out with such a large army to underscore his refusal that the Israelites had no choice but to turn away (20:19-21). (So much for that plea to brotherhood Moses had been counting on.)

AARON'S DEATH

22 After they set out from Kadesh, the entire Israelite community came to Mount Hor.[a] **23** The LORD said to Moses and Aaron at Mount Hor on the border of the land of Edom, **24** "Aaron will be gathered to his people; he will not enter the land I have given the Israelites, because you both rebelled against my command at the Waters of Meribah. **25** Take Aaron and his son Eleazar and bring them up Mount Hor. **26** Remove Aaron's garments and put them on his son Eleazar. Aaron will be gathered to his people and die there."

27 So Moses did as the LORD commanded, and they climbed Mount Hor in the sight of the whole community. **28** After Moses removed Aaron's garments and put them on his son Eleazar, Aaron died there on top of the mountain. Then Moses and Eleazar came down from the mountain. **29** When the whole community saw that Aaron had passed away, the entire house of Israel mourned for him thirty days.

CANAANITE KING DEFEATED

21 When the Canaanite king of Arad,[b] who lived in the Negev, heard that Israel was coming on the Atharim road, he fought against Israel and captured some prisoners. **2** Then Israel made a vow to the LORD, "If you will hand this people over to us, we will completely destroy their cities."[c] **3** The LORD listened to Israel's request and handed the Canaanites over to them, and Israel completely destroyed them and their cities. So they named the place Hormah.[A,d]

THE BRONZE SNAKE

4 Then they set out from Mount Hor by way of the Red Sea to bypass the land of Edom, but the people became impatient because of the journey. **5** The people spoke against God and Moses: "Why have you led us up from Egypt to die in the wilderness? There is no bread or water, and we detest this wretched food!" **6** Then the LORD sent poisonous[B] snakes among the people, and they bit them so that many Israelites died.[e]

7 The people then came to Moses and said, "We have sinned by speaking against the LORD and against you. Intercede with the LORD so that he will take the snakes away from us." And Moses interceded for the people.

8 Then the LORD said to Moses, "Make a snake image and mount it on a pole. When anyone who is bitten looks at it, he will recover."[f] **9** So Moses made a bronze snake and mounted it on a pole. Whenever someone was bitten, and he looked at the bronze snake, he recovered.

JOURNEY AROUND MOAB

10 The Israelites set out and camped at Oboth.[g] **11** They set out from Oboth and camped at Iye-abarim in the wilderness that borders Moab on the east. **12** From there they went and camped at Zered Valley. **13** They set out from there and camped on the other side of the Arnon River, in the wilderness that extends from the Amorite border, because the Arnon was the Moabite border between Moab and the Amorites. **14** Therefore it is stated in the Book of the LORD's Wars:

> Waheb in Suphah
> and the ravines of the Arnon,
> **15** even the slopes of the ravines
> that extend to the site of Ar[h]
> and lie along the border of Moab.

16 From there they went to Beer,[c] the well the LORD told Moses about, "Gather the people so I may give them water." **17** Then Israel sang this song:

> Spring up, well — sing to it!
> **18** The princes dug the well;
> the nobles of the people
> hollowed it out
> with a scepter and with their staffs.

---

[a]20:22 Nm 21:4; 33:37-41; Dt 32:50
[b]21:1 Nm 33:40; Jos 12:14; Jdg 1:16
[c]21:2 Dt 2:34; 13:16-17; Jos 6:18,21
[d]21:3 Nm 14:45; Dt 1:44; Jdg 1:17

[e]21:6 1Co 10:9
[f]21:8 2Kg 18:4; Jn 3:14-15
[g]21:10-11 Nm 33:43-44
[h]21:15 Nm 21:28; Dt 2:9,18,29; Is 15:1

[A]21:3 = Destruction   [B]21:6 Lit *Burning*   [C]21:16 = Well

---

20:23-27 It must have been hard for Aaron's son **Eleazar** to take part in Aaron's burial preparations even before he had died, but that was God's command (20:25-26). The entire nation watched as **Aaron's** priestly **garments** were removed and put on Eleazar (20:27-28). The first generation out of Egypt was rapidly coming to an end. Only Moses remained.
21:1-3 Instead of letting the Israelites pass, **the Canaanite king of Arad** attacked them and **captured some prisoners** (21:1). Israel, understandably piqued, pledged to **completely destroy** their attacker's **cities** if God gave them victory over this people (21:2). So God made Israel victorious, and they renamed the place **Hormah**, meaning "Destruction" (21:3).
21:4-6 The arduous journey intended to skirt hostile Edom frustrated the Israelites who resorted to their favorite complaint against God and Moses: **Why have you led us up from Egypt to die in the wilderness?** (21:5). For forty years God had preserved them. To assume the worst of him at this point was scandalous. So, since they were determined to complain about dying, God gave them something to actually complain about. He **sent poisonous snakes** (21:6).
21:7-9 Anyone who looked at **the bronze snake** in faith that God would heal him as promised **recovered** (21:9). Later in history, Jesus compared the lifting up of the bronze snake to his being lifted up on the cross as an antidote for the world's sin problem. It's a wonderful illustration of the necessity of looking to the Lord in faith to be saved (see John 3:14-15).

a 21:20 Nm 23:14; Dt 3:17,27; 4:49; 34:1; Jos 12:3; 13:20
b Nm 23:28
c 21:21 Nm 32:33; Dt 1:4; 2:24–4:46
d 21:22 Nm 20:17; Dt 2:26-33
e 21:23 Dt 2:32; Jdg 11:20; 1Ch 6:78
f 21:21-24 Jdg 11:19-22
g 21:27-29 Jdg 11:24; 1Kg 11:7,33; Jr 48:45-47
h 21:30 Nm 32:34; Neh 11:25; Jr 48:18,22

i 21:30 Jos 13:9,16; 1Ch 19:7; Is 15:2
j 21:33 Nm 32:33; Dt 3:1-13; 4:47
k Dt 3:1,10; Jos 12:4; 13:12,31
l 21:34 Dt 3:2
m 21:35 Ps 135:10-11
n 22:2 Jos 24:9-10; Jdg 11:25; Mc 6:5; Rv 2:14
o Dt 4:46; Jos 10:12
p 22:3 Gn 47:27; Ex 1:7,9; 32:13; 2Sm 17:11; 1Kg 4:20; 1Ch 27:23
q 22:5 Dt 23:3-5; Jos 24:9-10; Mc 6:5; 2Pt 2:15-16; Jd 11; Rv 2:14
r Ex 10:5
s 22:6 Gn 27:29; Nm 24:9

They went from the wilderness to Mattanah, 19 from Mattanah to Nahaliel, from Nahaliel to Bamoth, 20 from Bamoth to the valley in the territory of Moab near the Pisgah highlands*a* that overlook the wasteland.*A,b*

AMORITE KINGS DEFEATED

21 Israel sent messengers to say to King Sihon*c* of the Amorites: 22 "Let us travel through your land. We won't go into the fields or vineyards. We won't drink any well water. We will travel the King's Highway until we have traveled through your territory."*d* 23 But Sihon would not let Israel travel through his territory. Instead, he gathered his whole army and went out to confront Israel in the wilderness. When he came to Jahaz,*e* he fought against Israel. 24 Israel struck him with the sword and took possession of his land from the Arnon to the Jabbok,*f* but only up to the Ammonite border, because it was fortified.*B*

25 Israel took all the cities and lived in all these Amorite cities, including Heshbon and all its surrounding villages. 26 Heshbon was the city of King Sihon of the Amorites, who had fought against the former king of Moab and had taken control of all his land as far as the Arnon. 27 Therefore the poets*c* say:

Come to Heshbon, let it be rebuilt;
let the city of Sihon be restored.*D*

28 For fire came out of Heshbon,
a flame from the city of Sihon.
It consumed Ar of Moab,
the citizens of Arnon's heights.

29 Woe to you, Moab!
You have been destroyed,
   people of Chemosh!*g*
He gave up his sons as refugees,
and his daughters into captivity
to Sihon the Amorite king.

30 We threw them down;
Heshbon has been destroyed
   as far as Dibon.*h*

We caused desolation
   as far as Nophah,
   which reaches as far as Medeba.*i*
31 So Israel lived in the Amorites' land. 32 After Moses sent spies to Jazer, Israel captured its surrounding villages and drove out the Amorites who were there.

33 Then they turned and went up the road to Bashan, and King Og of Bashan*j* came out against them with his whole army to do battle at Edrei.*k* 34 But the LORD said to Moses, "Do not fear him, for I have handed him over to you along with his whole army and his land. Do to him as you did to King Sihon of the Amorites, who lived in Heshbon."*l* 35 So they struck him, his sons, and his whole army until no one was left,*E* and they took possession of his land.*m*

BALAK HIRES BALAAM

22 The Israelites traveled on and camped in the plains of Moab near the Jordan across from Jericho. 2 Now Balak*n* son of Zippor saw all that Israel had done to the Amorites.*o* 3 Moab was terrified of the people because they were numerous,*p* and Moab dreaded the Israelites. 4 So the Moabites said to the elders of Midian, "This horde will devour everything around us like an ox eats up the green plants in the field."

Since Balak son of Zippor was Moab's king at that time, 5 he sent messengers to Balaam*q* son of Beor at Pethor, which is by the Euphrates in the land of his people.*F,G* Balak said to him: "Look, a people has come out of Egypt; they cover the surface of the land*r* and are living right across from me. 6 Please come and put a curse on these people for me because they are more powerful than I am. I may be able to defeat them and drive them out of the land, for I know that those you bless are blessed and those you curse are cursed."*s*

A 21:20 Or overlook Jeshimon   *B* 21:24 LXX reads because the Ammonite border was Jazer   *C* 21:27 Lit ones who speak proverbs   *D* 21:27 Or firmly founded   *E* 21:35 Lit left to him   *F* 22:5 Sam, Vg, Syr read of the Ammonites   *G* 22:5 Or of the Amawites

21:21-23 Just like Edom's king, **Sihon of the Amorites** refused to allow the Israelites to pass through his land and **fought against Israel** (21:23). This was a foolish move.
21:27-30 This is an ancient Amorite poem of Sihon's conquest of the Moabites. It's included because what Sihon had taken from Moab, Israel wrenched away from Sihon. (Talk about poetic justice.)
21:33-35 **Og of Bashan** (21:33) was another Amorite king who presented no threat to Israel because the Lord had already given him

into Israel's hands. Og's defeat was a foregone conclusion before he even put on his armor. After the battle, Israel also **took possession of his land** (21:35).
22:1 **Near the Jordan** River **across from** the city of **Jericho** is where the book of Deuteronomy opens, as well as the book of Joshua.
22:4-6 **Balaam** was essentially a prophet-for-hire in an area where the false god Baal was worshiped (22:5-6). Apparently, he had a reputation for getting results through the

words he spoke. But the Lord's reputation is flawless: if he says something will happen, it will. This is important to understanding what happened next because God had promised Abraham many years before that he would, "make [him] into a great nation. . . . [He would] bless those who bless [Abraham], . . . curse anyone who treats [Abraham] with contempt" (Gen 12:2-3). These promises would extend to the Israelites, Abraham's blood descendants. King Balak's plan, then, was failed from the start.

7 The elders of Moab and Midian departed with fees for divination[a] in hand.[b] They came to Balaam and reported Balak's words to him. **8** He said to them, "Spend the night here, and I will give you the answer the LORD tells me." So the officials of Moab stayed with Balaam.

9 Then God came to Balaam and asked, "Who are these men with you?"

10 Balaam replied to God, "Balak son of Zippor, king of Moab, sent this message to me: **11** 'Look, a people has come out of Egypt, and they cover the surface of the land. Now come and put a curse on them for me. I may be able to fight against them and drive them away.'"

12 Then God said to Balaam, "You are not to go with them. You are not to curse this people, for they are blessed."

13 So Balaam got up the next morning and said to Balak's officials, "Go back to your land, because the LORD has refused to let me go with you."

14 The officials of Moab arose, returned to Balak, and reported, "Balaam refused to come with us."

15 Balak sent officials again who were more numerous and higher in rank than the others. **16** They came to Balaam and said to him, "This is what Balak son of Zippor says: 'Let nothing keep you from coming to me, **17** for I will greatly honor you and do whatever you ask me. So please come and put a curse on these people for me!'"

18 But Balaam responded to the servants of Balak, "If Balak were to give me his house full of silver and gold, I could not go against the command of the LORD my God to do anything small or great. **19** Please stay here overnight as the others did, so that I may find out what else the LORD has to tell me."

20 God came to Balaam at night and said to him, "Since these men have come to summon you, get up and go with them, but you must only do what I tell you." **21** When he got up in the morning, Balaam saddled his donkey and went with the officials of Moab.

BALAAM'S DONKEY AND THE ANGEL

22 But God was incensed that Balaam was going, and the angel of the LORD[c] took his stand on the path to oppose him. Balaam was riding his donkey, and his two servants were with him. **23** When the donkey saw the angel of the LORD standing on the path with a drawn sword in his hand, she turned off the path and went into the field. So Balaam hit her to return her to the path. **24** Then the angel of the LORD stood in a narrow passage between the vineyards, with a stone wall on either side. **25** The donkey saw the angel of the LORD and pressed herself against the wall, squeezing Balaam's foot against it. So he hit her once again. **26** The angel of the LORD went ahead and stood in a narrow place where there was no room to turn to the right or the left. **27** When the donkey saw the angel of the LORD, she crouched down under Balaam. So he became furious and beat the donkey with his stick.

28 Then the LORD opened the donkey's mouth, and she asked Balaam, "What have I done to you that you have beaten me these three times?"[d]

29 Balaam answered the donkey, "You made me look like a fool. If I had a sword in my hand, I'd kill you now!"

30 But the donkey said, "Am I not the donkey you've ridden all your life until today? Have I ever treated you this way before?"

"No," he replied.

31 Then the LORD opened Balaam's eyes, and he saw the angel of the LORD standing in the path with a drawn sword in his hand. Balaam knelt low and bowed in worship on his face. **32** The angel of the LORD asked him, "Why have you beaten your donkey these three times? Look, I came out to oppose you, because I consider what you are doing to be evil.^ **33** The donkey saw me and turned away from me these three times. If

[a] 22:7 Gn 30:27; 44:5,15; Lv 19:26; Nm 23:23; Dt 18:10; 1Sm 15:23; 2Kg 17:17; 21:6; Is 2:6; Jr 14:14; Ezk 12:24; 13:7,23; 21:21; Mc 3:11
[b] 2Pt 2:15; Jd 11

[c] 22:22 Gn 16:7; 22:11; Ex 3:2; Jdg 2:1; 5:23; 6:1; 13:3; 2Sm 24:16; 1Kg 19:7; 2Kg 1:3; 19:35; Zch 1:11; 3:1; 12:8
[d] 22:28 2Pt 2:15-16

---

^22:32 Lit *because your way is perverse before me*

22:8-12 Although Balaam practiced God-forbidden sorcery, he refused to go with the men Balak sent until he had received an answer from **the LORD** about it (22:8). The implication seems to be that he intended to do whatever God told him to do, no matter how good the money was—which is exactly what he did at most points in the story. So that night God graciously condescended to appear (22:9) to this sorcerer, who generally was not committed to living in a manner pleasing to him (see Rev 2:14). God warned him not to curse his people (Num 22:10-12). **22:22** God was so **incensed that Balaam was going** to Moab that he appeared in the road as **the angel of the LORD . . . to oppose him.** Now 2 Peter 2:15 says, "Balaam . . . loved the wages of wickedness." So it seems that Balaam really was a mercenary prophet at heart. He cared nothing for Israel and out of greedy motivation was prepared to curse Israel for the reward—despite God's instructions.

22:23-27 Duplicity within the prophet led to the humorous scene between an animal with keen spiritual sense and a human being who was as dumb as a rock spiritually. **22:28-30** Don't miss that this is a conversation between a faithful donkey and an unfaithful prophet (22:29-30).

a 23:1 1Ch 15:26; 2Ch
29:21; Jb 42:8; Ezk 45:23

b 23:7 Dt 23:4
c Nm 22:6,17
d 23:9 Dt 33:28
e 23:10 Gn 13:16
f 23:12 Nm 22:38
g 23:13 Nm 23:27
h 23:14 Nm 21:20; Dt
3:17,27; 4:49; 34:1; Jos
12:3; 13:20

she had not turned away from me, I would have killed you by now and let her live."

³⁴ Balaam said to the angel of the LORD, "I have sinned, for I did not know that you were standing in the path to confront me. And now, if it is evil in your sight, I will go back."

³⁵ Then the angel of the LORD said to Balaam, "Go with the men, but you are to say only what I tell you." So Balaam went with Balak's officials.

³⁶ When Balak heard that Balaam was coming, he went out to meet him at the Moabite city^A on the Arnon border at the edge of his territory. ³⁷ Balak asked Balaam, "Did I not send you an urgent summons? Why didn't you come to me? Am I really not able to reward you?"

³⁸ Balaam said to him, "Look, I have come to you, but can I say anything I want? I must speak only the message God puts in my mouth." ³⁹ So Balaam went with Balak, and they came to Kiriath-huzoth.^B ⁴⁰ Balak sacrificed cattle, sheep, and goats and sent for Balaam and the officials who were with him.

⁴¹ In the morning, Balak took Balaam and brought him to Bamoth-baal.^C From there he saw the outskirts of the people's camp.

BALAAM'S ORACLES

23 Then Balaam said to Balak, "Build me seven altars here and prepare seven bulls and seven rams for me."^a ² So Balak did as Balaam directed, and they offered a bull and a ram on each altar. ³ Balaam said to Balak, "Stay here by your burnt offering while I am gone. Maybe the LORD will meet with me. I will tell you whatever he reveals to me." So he went to a barren hill.

⁴ God met with him and Balaam said to him, "I have arranged seven altars and offered a bull and a ram on each altar." ⁵ Then

the LORD put a message in Balaam's mouth and said, "Return to Balak and say what I tell you."

⁶ So he returned to Balak, who was standing there by his burnt offering with all the officials of Moab.

BALAAM'S FIRST ORACLE

⁷ Balaam proclaimed his poem:

Balak brought me from Aram;^b
    the king of Moab,
    from the eastern mountains:
"Come, put a curse on Jacob for me;
    come, denounce Israel!"^c
⁸   How can I curse someone
        God has not cursed?
How can I denounce someone
    the LORD has not denounced?
⁹   I see them from the top of rocky cliffs,
    and I watch them from the hills.
There is a people living alone;^d
    it does not consider itself
        among the nations.
¹⁰   Who has counted the dust of Jacob^e
    or numbered even one-fourth
        of Israel?
Let me die the death of the upright;
    let the end of my life be like theirs.

¹¹ "What have you done to me?" Balak asked Balaam. "I brought you to curse my enemies, but look, you have only blessed them!"

¹² He answered, "Shouldn't I say exactly what the LORD puts in my mouth?"^f

BALAAM'S SECOND ORACLE

¹³ Then Balak said to him, "Please come with me to another place^g where you can see them. You will only see the outskirts of their camp; you won't see all of them. From there, put a curse on them for me." ¹⁴ So Balak took him to Lookout Field^D on top of Pisgah,^h built seven altars, and offered a bull and a ram on each altar.

---

^A 22:36 Or *at Ir-moab*, or *at Ar of Moab*   ^B 22:39 = The City of Streets   ^C 22:41 = The High Places of Baal   ^D 23:14 Or *to the field of Zophim*

22:36-41 King Balak was shaking in his sandals at the sight of the Israelite horde camped in the desert at the edge of his land, ready to devour his culture like a swarm of locusts descending on a barley crop. So he was a little edgy when Balaam finally arrived (22:36-37). Though Balaam warned him that he was only going to say what God put in his **mouth** (22:38), Balak ignored it. He offered a sacrifice to his false god Baal and hustled Balaam to a place called **Bamoth-baal** (22:40-41). Thus, Balak was calling on an idol to curse Israel and expected Balaam to serve as his spiritual megaphone.

23:3 Repeatedly in this story Balaam pointed out that he could do nothing without the approval of God—Creator God whom the Israelites worshiped—and yet Balak never objected or complained, "What are you doing consulting with the God of the Israelites? They're the enemies I'm paying you to curse!" Clearly he put little stock in the Lord's say in the matter.

23:7-10 Balaam delivered the first of four poetic messages, or oracles, of blessing on Israel. First, he rehearsed why he was there: he'd been summoned to **denounce Israel** (23:7). Yet he asked how anyone could **curse**

someone God has not (23:8). Then he considered Israel's vast numbers, a fact that was likely common knowledge, and said that even to be identified with Israel in **death** was a blessing (23:10).

23:13-17 Balak thought a change of scenery would help Balaam get back on task (23:13). So the Moabite king took the sorcerer to **Lookout Field on top of [Mount] Pisgah** (23:14). When Balaam returned from inquiring of the Lord this time, Balak even asked, **What did the LORD say?** (23:17). (He apparently held out hope that the God of the Israelites had finally decided to curse his own people.)

15 Balaam said to Balak, "Stay here by your burnt offering while I seek the LORD over there."

16 The LORD met with Balaam and put a message in his mouth. Then he said, "Return to Balak and say what I tell you."

17 So he returned to Balak, who was standing there by his burnt offering with the officials of Moab. Balak asked him, "What did the LORD say?"

18 Balaam proclaimed his poem:
Balak, get up and listen;
    son of Zippor, pay attention to what
        I say!
19   God is not a man, that he might lie,
    or a son of man, that he might
        change his mind.[a]
    Does he speak and not act,
    or promise and not fulfill?[b]
20   I have indeed received a command
        to bless;
    since he has blessed,[A] I cannot change it.
21   He considers no disaster for Jacob;
    he sees no trouble for Israel.[B]
    The LORD their God is with them,[c]
    and there is rejoicing over the King
        among them.
22   God brought them out of Egypt;
    he is like the horns of a wild ox
        for them.[C,d]
23   There is no magic curse against Jacob
    and no divination against Israel.
    It will now be said about Jacob
        and Israel,
    "What great things God has done!"
24   A people rise up like a lioness;
    they rouse themselves like a lion.[e]
    They will not lie down
        until they devour the prey
    and drink the blood of the slain.

25 Then Balak told Balaam, "Don't curse them and don't bless them!"

26 But Balaam answered him, "Didn't I tell you: Whatever the LORD says, I must do?"[f]

BALAAM'S THIRD ORACLE

27 Again Balak said to Balaam, "Please come. I will take you to another place. Maybe it will be agreeable to God that you can put a curse on them for me there."
28 So Balak took Balaam to the top of Peor, which overlooks the wasteland.[D,g]
29 Balaam told Balak, "Build me seven altars here and prepare seven bulls and seven rams for me."[h] **30** So Balak did as Balaam said and offered a bull and a ram on each altar.

24 Since Balaam saw that it pleased the LORD to bless Israel, he did not go to seek omens as on previous occasions, but turned[E] toward the wilderness. **2** When Balaam looked up and saw Israel encamped tribe by tribe, the Spirit of God[i] came on him, **3** and he proclaimed his poem:
The oracle of Balaam son of Beor,
    the oracle of the man whose eyes
        are opened,
4   the oracle of one who hears
        the sayings of God,
    who sees a vision
        from the Almighty,[j]
    who falls into a trance with his eyes
        uncovered:
5   How beautiful are
        your tents, Jacob,
    your dwellings, Israel.
6   They stretch out like river valleys,[F]
    like gardens beside a stream,
    like aloes the LORD has planted,
    like cedars beside the water.
7   Water will flow from his buckets,
    and his seed will be
        by abundant water.

[a] 23:19 1Sm 15:29; Mal 3:6; Ti 1:2; Heb 6:17-18
[b] Ps 33:10-11; Pr 19:21; Is 14:24; 31:2; 45:23; 46:9-11; 48:3; 55:11; Rm 11:29; Eph 1:11; 2Tm 2:13
[c] 23:21 Gn 28:15; Nm 14:9; Dt 2:7; 20:1; Jos 1:17; Jdg 6:13; 2Ch 20:17; Ps 46:11; Is 8:10; 41:10; Jr 1:19; 15:20; Zph 3:17; Hg 2:4; Rv 21:3
[d] 23:22 Nm 24:8
[e] 23:24 Nm 24:9

[f] 23:26 Nm 22:38
[g] 23:28 Nm 21:20
[h] 23:29 Nm 23:1-2
[i] 24:2 Ex 35:31; Nm 11:17,25-26,29; 1Sm 10:10
[j] 24:4 Is 13:6,9; Ezk 30:2-3; Jl 2:1-2,11,31

[A] **23:20** Sam, LXX read *since I will bless*   [B] **23:21** Or *He does not observe sin in Jacob; he does not see wrongdoing in Israel*   [C] **23:22** Or *Egypt; they have the horns of a wild ox*   [D] **23:28** Or *overlooks Jeshimon*   [E] **24:1** Lit *set his face*   [F] **24:6** Or *like date palms*

23:18-20 Balaam began with a personalized call that should have made the king catch his breath: **Balak, get up and listen; son of Zippor, pay attention to what I say!** (23:18). Then, under the inspiration of the Holy Spirit, the idolatrous prophet uttered a glorious statement of God's immutable nature (23:19). Because of who God is and the promises he had made, Balaam had been given a command to bless Israel. **I cannot change it**, he said (23:20).
23:23 Balaam said Israel was a force against which **no magic curse** or **divination**, like the kind of tricks Balak was trying to employ, could work.

23:27-30 In the ancient Near East where these men lived, people often believed that certain gods had power over certain geographical areas. This makes it less surprising that Balak thought a new location might somehow change the results he was getting.
24:1-4 Balaam looked out over Israel, which was encamped below according to the careful pattern God had laid out (see the note on 1:52-53). When he saw the vast nation **encamped tribe by tribe, the Spirit of God came on him** (24:2). Then the prophet essentially described the Lord's influence on him. His **eyes** were **opened**, he heard **the sayings of God**, he saw a **vision from the Almighty**

(24:3-4). In this state Balaam uttered another poetic tribute to God's hand of blessing on Israel.
24:7 Balaam referred to Israel as a **kingdom**, even though their first king (Saul) would not rule until hundreds of years had passed.

The mention of **Agag** is curious. A future king of the Amalekites named Agag would be executed by the prophet Samuel during King Saul's day (see 1 Sam 15). However, in the ancient Near East, kings often carried the same throne name down through the decades—as we see in the case of Egypt's Pharaoh or Philistia's Abimelech. So Amalek's current king probably bore the name

a 24:7 Ex 17:14-16; 1Sm 15:8-33
b 24:8 Nm 23:22
c 24:9 Gn 49:9; Nm 23:24
d Gn 12:3; 27:29
e 24:11 Nm 22:17
f 24:13 Nm 22:18,38
g 24:15-16 Nm 24:3-4

h 24:17 Gn 49:10; Mt 2:2; Rv 22:16
i 24:18 Gn 32:3
j 24:20 Ex 17:8-16; 1Sm 15
k 24:24 Gn 10:4; Is 23:1,12; Jr 2:10; Dn 11:30
l Gn 10:21,24-25; 11:14-27
m 25:1 Nm 33:49; Jos 2:1; 3:1; Mc 6:5
n 25:2 Ex 34:15-16; 1Co 10:8; Rv 2:14

His king will be greater than Agag,[a]
and his kingdom will be exalted.
8 God brought him out of Egypt;
he is like[A] the horns of a wild ox
for them.[b]
He will feed on enemy nations
and gnaw their bones;
he will strike them with his arrows.
9 He crouches, he lies down like a lion
or a lioness — who dares
to rouse him?[c]
Those who bless you will be blessed,
and those who curse you
will be cursed.[d]

¹⁰ Then Balak became furious with Balaam, struck his hands together, and said to him, "I summoned you to put a curse on my enemies, but instead, you have blessed them these three times. ¹¹ Now go to your home! I said I would reward you richly,[e] but look, the Lord has denied you a reward." ¹² Balaam answered Balak, "Didn't I previously tell the messengers you sent me: ¹³ If Balak were to give me his house full of silver and gold, I could not go against the Lord's command, to do anything good or bad of my own will? I will say whatever the Lord says.[f] ¹⁴ Now I am going back to my people, but first, let me warn you what these people will do to your people in the future."

BALAAM'S FOURTH ORACLE

¹⁵ Then he proclaimed his poem:
The oracle of Balaam son of Beor,
the oracle of the man whose eyes
are opened;
16   the oracle of one who hears
the sayings of God
and has knowledge
from the Most High,
who sees a vision
from the Almighty,
who falls into a trance with his
eyes uncovered:[g]

17   I see him, but not now;
I perceive him, but not near.
A star will come from Jacob,
and a scepter will arise from Israel.[h]
He will smash the forehead[B]
of Moab
and strike down[c] all the Shethites.[D]
18   Edom will become a possession;
Seir[i] will become a possession
of its enemies,
but Israel will be triumphant.
19   One who comes from Jacob
will rule;
he will destroy the city's survivors.

²⁰ Then Balaam saw Amalek and proclaimed his poem:
Amalek was first
among the nations,[j]
but his future is destruction.

²¹ Next he saw the Kenites and proclaimed his poem:
Your dwelling place is enduring;
your nest is set in the cliffs.
22   Kain will be destroyed
when Asshur takes you captive.

²³ Once more he proclaimed his poem:
Ah, who can live
when God does this?
24   Ships will come from the coast
of Kittim;[k]
they will carry out raids against
Asshur and Eber,[l]
but they too will come
to destruction.
²⁵ Balaam then arose and went back to his homeland, and Balak also went his way.

ISRAEL WORSHIPS BAAL

25 While Israel was staying in the Acacia Grove,[E,m] the people began to prostitute themselves with the women of Moab. ² The women invited them to the sacrifices for their gods, and the people ate and bowed in worship to their gods.[n]

A 24:8 Or he has   B 24:17 Or frontiers   C 24:17 Sam reads and the skulls of; Jr 48:45   D 24:17 Or Sethites   E 25:1 Or in Shittim

---

Agag, too. Assuming that this is so, we should consider that this wasn't the first prophecy regarding the Amalekites. This nation had attacked Israel after the exodus (see Exod 17:8-16). So the Lord had promised at that time, "I will completely blot out the memory of Amalek under heaven" (Exod 17:14). Balaam, then, prophesied Israel's future dominance over the Amalekite kingdom.

24:8-9 Balaam emphasized God's strength in bringing Israel out of **Egypt** and defeating **enemy nations** before them (24:8). The latter

was exactly what Balak was afraid of. Balaam concluded with a chilling announcement: **Those who curse [Israel] will be cursed** (24:9). By seeking to curse Israel, King Balak had sealed his own fate.

24:17-20 Balaam gave a prophecy of the coming of Israel's Messiah. Incredibly, he made predictions about the future rising of the **star ... from Jacob** and a **scepter ... from Israel**; these are references to the Christ, a descendant of Israel and the "morning star" of Revelation 22:16 (Num 24:17). He also foresaw

Israel's victories over **Moab** (Balak's people), the Edomites, and the Amalekites (24:17-20). The cursing of Israel had failed.

25:1-3 Though he was unable to curse Israel, Balaam still offered advice to their enemies. We read this in 31:16: "at Balaam's advice, [the Midianite women] incited the Israelites to unfaithfulness against the Lord in the Peor incident." Later, the risen Lord Jesus would say this about the matter, "Balaam ... taught Balak to place a stumbling block in front of the Israelites: to eat meat sacrificed to idols

³ So Israel aligned itself with Baal of Peor,ᵃ and the LORD's anger burned against Israel.ᵇ ⁴ The LORD said to Moses, "Take all the leaders of the people and executeᴬ them in broad daylight before the LORD so that his burning anger may turn away from Israel."

⁵ So Moses told Israel's judges, "Kill each of the men who aligned themselves with Baal of Peor."

PHINEHAS INTERVENES

⁶ An Israelite man came bringing a Midianite woman to his relatives in the sight of Moses and the whole Israelite community while they were weeping at the entrance to the tent of meeting. ⁷ When Phinehas son of Eleazar, son of Aaron the priest, saw this, he got up from the assembly, took a spear in his hand, ⁸ followed the Israelite man into the tent,ᴮ and drove it through both the Israelite man and the woman — through her belly. Then the plague on the Israelites was stopped, ⁹ but those who died in the plague numbered twenty-four thousand.ᶜ

¹⁰ The LORD spoke to Moses, ¹¹ "Phinehas son of Eleazar, son of Aaron the priest, has turned back my wrath from the Israelites because he was zealous among them with my zeal,ᶜ·ᵈ so that I did not destroy the Israelites in my zeal. ¹² Therefore declare: I grant him my covenant of peace.ᵉ ¹³ It will be a covenant of perpetual priesthood for him and his future descendants,ᶠ because he was zealous for his God and made atonement for the Israelites."

¹⁴ The name of the slain Israelite man, who was struck dead with the Midianite woman, was Zimri son of Salu, the leader of a Simeonite family.ᴰ ¹⁵ The name of the slain Midianite woman was Cozbi, the daughter of Zur, a tribal head of a family in Midian.

VENGEANCE AGAINST THE MIDIANITES

¹⁶ The LORD told Moses: ¹⁷ "Attack the Midianites and strike them dead. ¹⁸ For they attacked you with the treachery that they used against you in the Peor incident. They did the same in the case involving their sister Cozbi, daughter of the Midianite leader who was killed the day the plague came at Peor."

THE SECOND CENSUS

26 After the plague, the LORD said to Moses and Eleazar son of Aaron the priest, ² "Take a census of the entire Israelite community by their ancestral familiesᴱ of those twenty years old or more who can serve in Israel's army."ᵍ

³ So Moses and the priest Eleazar said to them in the plains of Moabʰ by the Jordan across from Jericho, ⁴ "Take a census of those twenty years old or more, as the LORD had commanded Moses and the Israelites who came out of the land of Egypt."ⁱ

⁵   Reubenʲ was the firstborn
        of Israel.
    Reuben's descendants:

ᵃ 25:3 Nm 23:28
ᵇ Dt 4:3; Ps 106:28-29; Hs 9:10
ᶜ 25:9 1Co 10:8
ᵈ 25:11 Ex 34:14; Zch 8:2
ᵉ 25:12 Is 54:10; Ezk 34:25; 37:26; Mal 2:5
ᶠ 25:13 Ex 40:15; Ps 106:30-31

ᵍ 26:2 Nm 1:2-3; 4:2,22; 2Sm 24:10; 2Kg 12:4; 1Ch 27:24; 2Ch 2:17
ʰ 26:3 Nm 22:1; 26:63; 31:12; 33:48-50; 35:1; 36:13; Dt 34:1,8; Jos 13:32
ⁱ 26:4 Nm 1
ʲ 26:5 Gn 46:8-27; Ex 6:14-25

ᴬ 25:4 Or impale, or hang, or expose; Hb obscure   ᴮ 25:8 Perhaps a tent shrine or bridal tent   ᶜ 25:11 Or jealousy   ᴰ 25:14 Lit a father's house, also in v. 15   ᴱ 26:2 Lit the house of their fathers

---

and to commit sexual immorality" (Rev 2:14). So, in spite of what Balaam said in Numbers 22–24, at heart he was a wicked enemy of the true God and his people.

Don't miss that since Israel's enemies couldn't get the Lord to be unfaithful to his people, they chose to lead his people to be unfaithful to him. And as a direct result of this maneuver, God's people **began to prostitute themselves** (25:1). The Lord had protected his people by refusing to let Balaam curse Israel, but now Israel was essentially cursing the Lord through actions. Therefore, God's **anger burned** (25:3).
25:4-6 In light of this obviously public execution and the national **weeping** it brought, it is almost beyond comprehension that an Israelite man would dare to march his Midianite girlfriend into camp and into his tent **in the sight of . . . the whole Israelite community** (25:6). Yet that's exactly what happened. Spurred by lust, this man dared to flout God and his law in front of everyone.

25:7-13 Phinehas was **zealous** for God's holiness (25:11), so he left the service of repentance at the tabernacle, **took a spear**, ran into the man's **tent, and drove it through both the Israelite man and the woman** (25:7-8). (This is a clear indication that they were having sexual relations when he found them.)

Meanwhile, God had apparently sent a **plague** among the people for their sin. Phinehas's righteous action **stopped** it, but only after **twenty-four thousand** Israelites died (25:8-9). God praised Phinehas for his zeal and promised a **perpetual priesthood** to **him** (25:12-13). This meant that the Aaronic priesthood would remain with Phinehas and his family.
25:14-15 If the men involved in these sins were mostly Simeonites, this could explain the drastic decrease in their number of males from the first census of "59,300" (1:23) to "22,200" (26:14). **Zimri** was from a prominent family and brought great destruction on his people with his blatant sin. Thus, once

again Scripture warns that our sin always affects others.
25:16-18 The Moabites and Midianites appeared together in the Balaam narratives because they lived in the same area and were both involved in hiring Balaam to curse Israel (see 22:4, 7). The Israelites didn't attack the Moabites, who were descendants of Abraham through Lot. But the Lord commanded Israel to **attack the Midianites** because they had been involved in inciting the Israelites to worship Baal (25:17; see also 31:15-16).
26:1-4 By this time most of Moses's generation had died according to God's decree. It was time to **take a census** of the new generation (26:1-2). Israelite soldiers would be needed to battle the inhabitants of the promised land. The census was taken **across from Jericho** (26:3). This was the first fortified city Israel would encounter in Canaan. What happened there would mark Israel's first victory in the long-anticipated conquest (see Josh 6:1-27).

a 26:9 Nm 16:1-3
b 26:10 Nm 16:31-35
c 26:12 Gn 46:10; Ex 6:15; 1Ch 4:24
d 26:19 Gn 38:3-4,6-11
e 26:20 Gn 38:29; 46:12; Ru 4:12,18; 1Ch 2:4; 4:1; 9:4; 27:3; Mt 1:3; Lk 3:33

f 26:23 1Ch 7:1
g 26:29 Nm 1:34; 32:39; Jos 14:4; 17:2; 1Ch 9:3
h 26:33 Nm 27:1-11; 36:10-11; Jos 17:3; 1Ch 7:15

the Hanochite clan from Hanoch;
the Palluite clan from Pallu;
6 the Hezronite clan from Hezron;
the Carmite clan from Carmi.
7 These were the Reubenite clans,
and their registered men
numbered 43,730.
8 The son of Pallu was Eliab.
9 The sons of Eliab were Nemuel,
Dathan, and Abiram.
(It was Dathan and Abiram, chosen
by the community, who fought
against Moses and Aaron; they and
Korah's followers fought against the
LORD.*a* 10 The earth opened its mouth
and swallowed them with Korah,
when his followers died and the fire
consumed 250 men.*b* They serve as
a warning sign. 11 The sons of Korah,
however, did not die.)

12 Simeon's descendants by their clans:
the Nemuelite clan
from Nemuel;*c*
the Jaminite clan from Jamin;
the Jachinite clan from Jachin;
13 the Zerahite clan from Zerah;
the Shaulite clan from Shaul.
14 These were the Simeonite clans,
numbering 22,200 men.

15 Gad's descendants by their clans:
the Zephonite clan from Zephon;
the Haggite clan from Haggi;
the Shunite clan from Shuni;
16 the Oznite clan from Ozni;
the Erite clan from Eri;
17 the Arodite clan from Arod;
the Arelite clan from Areli.
18 These were the Gadite
clans numbered by their
registered men: 40,500.

19 Judah's sons included Er and Onan,
but they died in the land of Canaan.*d*
20 Judah's descendants by their
clans:
the Shelanite clan from Shelah;
the Perezite clan from Perez;*e*
the Zerahite clan from Zerah.
21 The descendants of Perez:
the Hezronite clan from Hezron;
the Hamulite clan from Hamul.
22 These were Judah's clans numbered
by their registered men: 76,500.

23 Issachar's descendants
by their clans:
the Tolaite clan from Tola;
the Punite clan from Puvah;*A,f*
24 the Jashubite clan from Jashub;
the Shimronite clan from Shimron.
25 These were Issachar's
clans numbered by their
registered men: 64,300.

26 Zebulun's descendants
by their clans:
the Seredite clan from Sered;
the Elonite clan from Elon;
the Jahleelite clan from Jahleel.
27 These were the Zebulunite
clans numbered by their
registered men: 60,500.

28 Joseph's descendants by their clans
from Manasseh and Ephraim:
29 Manasseh's descendants:*g*
the Machirite clan from Machir.
Machir fathered Gilead;
the Gileadite clan from Gilead.
30 These were Gilead's descendants:
the Iezerite clan from Iezer;
the Helekite clan from Helek;
31 the Asrielite clan from Asriel;
the Shechemite clan
from Shechem;
32 the Shemidaite clan from Shemida;
the Hepherite clan from Hepher;
33 Zelophehad son of Hepher had no
sons — only daughters. The names
of Zelophehad's daughters were
Mahlah, Noah, Hoglah, Milcah, and
Tirzah.*h*
34 These were Manasseh's
clans, numbered by their
registered men: 52,700.
35 These were Ephraim's descendants
by their clans:
the Shuthelahite clan
from Shuthelah;
the Becherite clan from Becher;
the Tahanite clan from Tahan.
36 These were
Shuthelah's descendants:
the Eranite clan from Eran.
37 These were the Ephraimite
clans numbered by their
registered men: 32,500.
These were Joseph's descendants
by their clans.

A 26:23 Sam, LXX, Vg, Syr read *Puite clan from Puah*; 1Ch 7:1

26:11 The note that **the sons of Korah . . . did not die** acknowledges that grace had been extended, allowing Korah's family line to continue in spite of his rebellion (see ch. 16). Sons that did not follow his example would have an inheritance in the promised land.

38 Benjamin's descendants
   by their clans:
   the Belaite clan from Bela;
   the Ashbelite clan from Ashbel;
   the Ahiramite clan from Ahiram;
39 the Shuphamite clan
   from Shupham;[A]
   the Huphamite clan from Hupham.
40 Bela's descendants from Ard
   and Naaman:
   the Ardite clan from Ard;
   the Naamite clan from Naaman.
41 These were the Benjaminite
   clans numbered by their
   registered men: 45,600.

42 These were Dan's descendants
   by their clans:
   the Shuhamite clan from Shuham.
   These were the clans of Dan
   by their clans.
43 All the Shuhamite clans numbered
   by their registered men: 64,400.

44 Asher's descendants by their clans:
   the Imnite clan from Imnah;
   the Ishvite clan from Ishvi;
   the Beriite clan from Beriah.
45 From Beriah's descendants:
   the Heberite clan from Heber;
   the Malchielite clan
   from Malchiel.
46 And the name of Asher's daughter
   was Serah.
47 These were the Asherite
   clans numbered by their
   registered men: 53,400.

48 Naphtali's descendants
   by their clans:
   the Jahzeelite clan from Jahzeel;
   the Gunite clan from Guni;
49 the Jezerite clan from Jezer;
   the Shillemite clan from Shillem.
50 These were the Naphtali
   clans numbered by their
   registered men: 45,400.

51 These registered Israelite men
   numbered 601,730.

52 The LORD spoke to Moses, **53** "The land is to be divided among them as an inheritance based on the number of names. **54** Increase the inheritance for a large tribe and decrease it for a small one. Each is to be given its inheritance according to those who were registered in it. **55** The land is to be divided by lot; they will receive an inheritance according to the names of their ancestral tribes. **56** Each inheritance will be divided by lot among the larger and smaller tribes."[a]

57 These were the Levites registered
   by their clans:
   the Gershonite clan from Gershon;
   the Kohathite clan from Kohath;
   the Merarite clan from Merari.
58 These were the Levite family
   groups:
   the Libnite clan,
   the Hebronite clan,
   the Mahlite clan,
   the Mushite clan,
   and the Korahite clan.[b]

Kohath was the ancestor of Amram.[c] **59** The name of Amram's wife was Jochebed, a descendant of Levi, born to Levi in Egypt. She bore to Amram: Aaron, Moses, and their sister Miriam. **60** Nadab, Abihu, Eleazar, and Ithamar were born to Aaron,[d] **61** but Nadab and Abihu died when they presented unauthorized fire before the LORD.[e] **62** Those registered were 23,000, every male one month old or more; they were not registered among the other Israelites, because no inheritance was given to them among the Israelites.

63 These were the ones registered by Moses and the priest Eleazar when they registered the Israelites on the plains of Moab by the Jordan across from Jericho. **64** But among them there was not one of those who had been registered by Moses and the priest Aaron when they registered the Israelites in the Wilderness of Sinai.[f] **65** For the LORD had said to them that they would all die in the wilderness. None of them was left except Caleb son of Jephunneh and Joshua son of Nun.

[a]26:56 Nm 33:53-54; 34:13; 36:2; Jos 14:2; 18:6-11; 19:51; 21:4-8; 1Ch 6:61,63,65; Ps 78:55; Ezk 45:1
[b]26:58 Ex 6:21,24; Nm 3:17-20
[c]Ex 6:18-20
[d]26:60 Ex 6:23; 24:1,9; 28:1; Nm 3:2,4; 1Ch 6:3
[e]26:61 Lv 10:1-2; 1Ch 24:1-2
[f]26:64 Nm 1:17-46; 3:39

[A]26:39 Some Hb mss, Sam, LXX, Syr, Tg, Vg; other Hb mss read *Shephupham*

26:51 The total number of fighting men was calculated: **601,730.** This figure was quite close to the original count of "603,550," taken almost four decades earlier (1:46). Though the exodus generation died off and Israel suffered a number of severe judgments on their way to Canaan, God prospered his people so that they were ready to cross the Jordan at full strength.

26:55-56 The census was followed by the casting of a **lot** to determine where each tribe's inheritance in the promised land would be located. The actual dividing of the land would come later.

26:58-59 In discussing **the Levite family groups,** Moses included a note about his own family.

26:63-65 Only two men of Moses's generation had stood firm in faith and were still alive at the new census: **Caleb** and **Joshua** (26:65). These two, who had witnessed the plagues of Egypt and God's every provision in the wilderness, would enter the land.

a 27:3 Nm 16:1-3,11
b 27:7 Jos 17:4
c 27:12-14 Dt 32:48-51

d 27:13 Nm 20:22-29
e 27:14 Nm 20:2-13
f 27:16 Nm 16:22
g 27:17 Jos 14:11; 1Sm 18:13-16; 2Sm 5:2; 11:1; 1Kg 3:7; 2Kg 11:9
h 1Kg 22:17; 2Ch 18:16; Ezk 34:5; Mt 9:36; Mk 6:34
i 27:18 Dt 34:9
j 27:19 Dt 31:14,23; Ps 91:11; Is 10:6
k 27:21 Ex 28:30
l 28:2 Lv 3:11,16; 22:25; Nm 28:24

A CASE OF DAUGHTERS' INHERITANCE

27 The daughters of Zelophehad approached; Zelophehad was the son of Hepher, son of Gilead, son of Machir, son of Manasseh from the clans of Manasseh, the son of Joseph. These were the names of his daughters: Mahlah, Noah, Hoglah, Milcah, and Tirzah. ² They stood before Moses, the priest Eleazar, the leaders, and the entire community at the entrance to the tent of meeting and said, ³ "Our father died in the wilderness, but he was not among Korah's followers, who gathered together against the LORD.*a* Instead, he died because of his own sin, and he had no sons. ⁴ Why should the name of our father be taken away from his clan? Since he had no son, give us property among our father's brothers."

⁵ Moses brought their case before the LORD, ⁶ and the LORD answered him, ⁷ "What Zelophehad's daughters say is correct. You are to give them hereditary property among their father's brothers and transfer their father's inheritance to them.*b* ⁸ Tell the Israelites: When a man dies without having a son, transfer his inheritance to his daughter. ⁹ If he has no daughter, give his inheritance to his brothers. ¹⁰ If he has no brothers, give his inheritance to his father's brothers. ¹¹ If his father has no brothers, give his inheritance to the nearest relative of his clan, and he will take possession of it. This is to be a statutory ordinance for the Israelites as the LORD commanded Moses."

JOSHUA COMMISSIONED TO SUCCEED MOSES

¹² Then the LORD said to Moses,*c* "Go up this mountain of the Abarim range*A* and see the land that I have given the Israelites. ¹³ After you have seen it, you will also be gathered to your people, as Aaron your brother was.*d* ¹⁴ When the community quarreled in the Wilderness of Zin, both of you rebelled against my command to demonstrate my holiness in their sight at the waters." Those were the Waters of Meribah-kadesh*B* in the Wilderness of Zin.*e*

¹⁵ So Moses appealed to the LORD, ¹⁶ "May the LORD, the God who gives breath to all,*C,f* appoint a man over the community ¹⁷ who will go out before them and come back in before them,*g* and who will bring them out and bring them in, so that the LORD's community won't be like sheep without a shepherd."*h*

¹⁸ The LORD replied to Moses, "Take Joshua son of Nun, a man who has the Spirit in him, and lay your hands on him.*i* ¹⁹ Have him stand before the priest Eleazar and the whole community, and commission*j* him in their sight. ²⁰ Confer some of your authority on him so that the entire Israelite community will obey him. ²¹ He will stand before the priest Eleazar who will consult the LORD for him with the decision of the Urim.*k* He and all the Israelites with him, even the entire community, will go out and come back in at his command."

²² Moses did as the LORD commanded him. He took Joshua, had him stand before the priest Eleazar and the entire community, ²³ laid his hands on him, and commissioned him, as the LORD had spoken through Moses.

PRESCRIBED OFFERINGS

28 The LORD spoke to Moses, ² "Command the Israelites and say to them: Be sure to present to me at its appointed time my offering and my food*l* as my fire

---

A 27:12 = Mount Nebo; Nm 33:47-48; Dt 32:49; Jr 22:20   *B* 27:14 = Quarreling   *C* 27:16 Or *God of the spirits of all flesh*

27:1-11 A man named **Zelophehad** from the tribe of **Manasseh** died without a son but left behind five **daughters** (27:1). Under Israel's laws of inheritance, in which property was reckoned through the male head of the family, these women were facing a bleak future when the nation divided up the promised land. They said, **Since [our father] had no son, give us property among our father's brothers** (27:4). God agreed with their position, and he established a new rule of inheritance that covered this family's dilemma and underscored his care not just for men, but women too (27:5-11).
27:12-14 God took Moses to Mount Nebo in the **Abarim range** just across from Jericho where he could look out over **the land that**

God had **given the Israelites** (27:12). Seeing the land from afar was the best Moses could hope for, since he and Aaron had **rebelled against** God at **Meribah** (27:14; see 20:1-13).
27:15-17 As death neared, Moses made a plea that God would give his people a godly, qualified leader who would lead them with courage. He asked for someone to **go out before them** as their military commander, while also directing them like a tender and caring **shepherd** (26:17).
27:18-20 Certainly Joshua, **a man who [had] the Spirit in him** (27:18), was already well known and well respected among the Israelites for his close association with Moses, his record of bravery regarding Canaan years before, and his advanced age. All he lacked

was the public stamp of approval from the Lord through a ceremony in which Moses would symbolically transfer leadership (27:19-20).
27:21-23 With Joshua committed to consulting the Lord through **the priest Eleazar**, Israel's future leadership was secured.
28:1-3 One important element of the offerings described in chapters 28 and 29 was that whether they were daily, weekly (on the Sabbath), monthly, or presented for annual festivals such as Passover or Pentecost, each was to be made **at its appointed time** (28:2). The offering of the sacrificial animals also emphasized the tremendous offense that sin is to God. Only blood can atone for it and bring the sinner into fellowship with him.

offering, a pleasing aroma to me.[a] [3] And say to them: This is the fire offering you are to present to the LORD:[b]

DAILY OFFERINGS

"Each day present two unblemished year-old male lambs as a regular burnt offering. [4] Offer one lamb in the morning and the other lamb at twilight, [5] along with two quarts[A] of fine flour for a grain offering mixed with a quart[B] of olive oil from crushed olives.[c] [6] It is a regular burnt offering established at Mount Sinai for a pleasing aroma, a fire offering to the LORD. [7] The drink offering is to be a quart with each lamb. Pour out the offering of beer to the LORD in the sanctuary area. [8] Offer the second lamb at twilight, along with the same kind of grain offering and drink offering as in the morning. It is a fire offering, a pleasing aroma to the LORD.

SABBATH OFFERINGS

[9] "On the Sabbath day present two unblemished year-old male lambs, four quarts[c] of fine flour mixed with oil as a grain offering, and its drink offering. [10] It is the burnt offering for every Sabbath, in addition to the regular burnt offering and its drink offering.[d]

MONTHLY OFFERINGS

[11] "At the beginning of each of your months[e] present a burnt offering to the LORD: two young bulls, one ram, seven male lambs a year old — all unblemished — [12] with six quarts[D] of fine flour mixed with oil as a grain offering for each bull, four quarts of fine flour mixed with oil as a grain offering for the ram, [13] and two quarts[E] of fine flour mixed with oil as a grain offering for each lamb. It is a burnt offering, a pleasing aroma, a fire offering to the LORD. [14] Their drink offerings are to be two quarts[F] of wine with each bull, one and a third quarts[G] with the ram, and one quart[H]

with each male lamb. This is the monthly burnt offering for all the months of the year. [15] And one male goat is to be offered as a sin offering to the LORD, in addition to the regular burnt offering with its drink offering.

OFFERINGS FOR PASSOVER

[16] "The Passover[f] to the LORD comes in the first month, on the fourteenth day of the month. [17] On the fifteenth day of this month there will be a festival; unleavened bread is to be eaten for seven days. [18] On the first day there is to be a sacred assembly; you are not to do any daily work.[g] [19] Present a fire offering, a burnt offering to the LORD: two young bulls, one ram, and seven male lambs a year old. Your animals are to be unblemished.[h] [20] The grain offering with them is to be of fine flour mixed with oil; offer six quarts with each bull and four quarts with the ram. [21] Offer two quarts with each of the seven lambs [22] and one male goat for a sin offering to make atonement for yourselves. [23] Offer these with the morning burnt offering that is part of the regular burnt offering. [24] You are to offer the same food each day for seven days as a fire offering,[i] a pleasing aroma to the LORD. It is to be offered with its drink offering and the regular burnt offering. [25] On the seventh day you are to hold a sacred assembly; you are not to do any daily work.

OFFERINGS FOR THE FESTIVAL OF WEEKS

[26] "On the day of firstfruits, you are to hold a sacred assembly when you present an offering of new grain to the LORD at your Festival of Weeks;[j] you are not to do any daily work. [27] Present a burnt offering for a pleasing aroma to the LORD: two young bulls, one ram, and seven male lambs a year old, [28] with their grain offering of fine flour mixed with oil, six quarts with each bull, four quarts with the ram, [29] and

[a] 28:2 Ex 29:18; Lv 1:9; 2:2; 3:5; 8:21; 23:13; Nm 15:3; 18:17; 29:6; Am 5:25
[b] 28:3-8 Ex 29:38-41
[c] 28:5 Ex 27:20; Lv 2:1; 24:2; Nm 15:4
[d] 28:10 Ezk 46:4-5
[e] 28:11 1Sm 20:5; 1Ch 23:31; 2Ch 2:4; Ezr 3:5; Is 1:13-14; Ezk 45:17; 46:6; Hs 2:11; Col 2:16
[f] 28:16-17 Ex 12:18; Lv 23:5-6; Ezk 45:21
[g] 28:18 Ex 12:16; Lv 23:3,7,28; Nm 29:7
[h] 28:19 Lv 22:20; Nm 29:8,13; Dt 15:21; 17:1
[i] 28:24-25 Ex 12:16; 13:6; Lv 23:8
[j] 28:26 Ex 23:16; 34:22; Lv 23:10,15; Dt 16:9-10; Ac 2:1

[A] 28:5 Lit *one-tenth of an ephah* [B] 28:5 Lit *a fourth of a hin*, also in v. 7 [C] 28:9 Lit *two-tenths* (of an ephah), also in vv. 12,20,28 [D] 28:12 Lit *three-tenths* (of an ephah), also in vv. 20,28 [E] 28:13 Lit *one-tenth* (of an ephah), also in vv. 21,29 [F] 28:14 Lit *a half hin* [G] 28:14 Lit *bull, a third hin* [H] 28:14 Lit *a fourth hin*

28:3-6 The **burnt offering** (28:3) had been given to Israel at Sinai as the means by which God would come down to his people, fellowship with them, and be their God as he smelled the aroma of their pleasing sacrifices (see Exod 29:42-46).
28:9-10 Weekly **Sabbath** offerings involved an entirely new set of offerings in addition to the day's regular burnt offerings. If any Israelite thought worship was cheap or easy, or that the Lord would accept any leftover

his followers tossed his way, these regulations were intended to shake him into reality. (Tragically, many Christians offer their leftover time, talents, and treasures to the same God who has always demanded the first and best of his people.)
28:16-25 **The Passover** was the holy festival that commemorated Israel's freedom from Egyptian bondage (28:16). The people were to eat **unleavened bread . . . for seven days** (28:17) as their parents and grandparents

had on the night of the first Passover so they could leave Egypt in haste.
28:26-31 The **Festival of Weeks** occurred fifty days after Passover: this is also called "Pentecost" (28:26). Although the fact isn't emphasized here, the people were also to bring the firstfruits of their fields to celebrate it—clearly pointing forward to the day when they would take the promised land and establish themselves there.

a 29:1 Ex 12:16
b Lv 23:23-25
c 29:7 Lv 23:27-28

d 29:12 Lv 23:34-35
e 29:18 Nm 15:1-12

two quarts with each of the seven lambs, ³⁰ and one male goat to make atonement for yourselves. ³¹ Offer them with their drink offerings in addition to the regular burnt offering and its grain offering. Your animals are to be unblemished.

FESTIVAL OF TRUMPETS OFFERINGS

29 "You are to hold a sacred assembly in the seventh month, on the first day of the month, and you are not to do any daily work. *a* This will be a day of trumpet blasts for you. *b* ² Offer a burnt offering as a pleasing aroma to the LORD: one young bull, one ram, seven male lambs a year old — all unblemished — ³ with their grain offering of fine flour mixed with oil, six quarts*A* with the bull, four quarts*B* with the ram, ⁴ and two quarts*C* with each of the seven male lambs. ⁵ Also offer one male goat as a sin offering to make atonement for yourselves. ⁶ These are in addition to the monthly and regular burnt offerings with their prescribed grain offerings and drink offerings. They are a pleasing aroma, a fire offering to the LORD.

OFFERINGS FOR THE DAY OF ATONEMENT

⁷ "You are to hold a sacred assembly on the tenth day of this seventh month and practice self-denial;*c* do not do any work. ⁸ Present a burnt offering to the LORD, a pleasing aroma: one young bull, one ram, and seven male lambs a year old. All your animals are to be unblemished. ⁹ Their grain offering is to be of fine flour mixed with oil, six quarts with the bull, four quarts with the ram, ¹⁰ and two quarts with each of the seven lambs. ¹¹ Offer one male goat for a sin offering. The regular burnt offering with its grain offering and drink offerings are in addition to the sin offering of atonement.

OFFERINGS FOR THE FESTIVAL OF SHELTERS

¹² "You are to hold a sacred assembly on the fifteenth day of the seventh month;*d* you do not do any daily work. You are to celebrate a seven-day festival for the LORD. ¹³ Present a burnt offering, a fire offering as a pleasing aroma to the LORD: thirteen young bulls, two rams, and fourteen male lambs a year old. They are to be unblemished. ¹⁴ Their grain offering is to be of fine flour mixed with oil, six quarts with each of the thirteen bulls, four quarts with each of the two rams, ¹⁵ and two quarts with each of the fourteen lambs. ¹⁶ Also offer one male goat as a sin offering. These are in addition to the regular burnt offering with its grain and drink offerings.

¹⁷ "On the second day present twelve young bulls, two rams, and fourteen male lambs a year old — all unblemished — ¹⁸ with their grain and drink offerings*e* for the bulls, rams, and lambs, in proportion to their number. ¹⁹ Also offer one male goat as a sin offering. These are in addition to the regular burnt offering with its grain and drink and their drink offerings.

²⁰ "On the third day present eleven bulls, two rams, fourteen male lambs a year old — all unblemished — ²¹ with their grain and drink offerings for the bulls, rams, and lambs, in proportion to their number. ²² Also offer one male goat as a sin offering. These are in addition to the regular burnt offering with its grain and drink offerings.

²³ "On the fourth day present ten bulls, two rams, fourteen male lambs a year old — all unblemished — ²⁴ with their grain and drink offerings for the bulls, rams, and lambs, in proportion to their number. ²⁵ Also offer one male goat as a sin offering. These are in addition to the regular burnt offering with its grain and drink offerings.

A 29:3 Lit *three-tenths* (of an ephah), also in vv. 9,14   *B* 29:3 Lit *two-tenths* (of an ephah), also in vv. 9,14   *C* 29:4 Lit *one-tenth* (of an ephah), also in vv. 10,15

29:1-40 The Lord gave Moses instructions for offerings associated with three more holy observances: the Festival of Trumpets, the Day of Atonement, and the Festival of Shelters.
29:1-6 The first day of **the seventh month** was a special day that later came to be known as Rosh Hashanah ("the head of the year"; 29:1). This marked the Jewish New Year. An offering equal to the regular New Moon offerings was to be made, along with **the . . . regular burnt offerings** (29:6). Notice that the requirement for acceptable

worship never decreases with the addition of special days and even weeks; it always increases.
29:7-11 The Day of Atonement ("Yom Kippur" in Hebrew) was and still is the most sacred day on the Jewish calendar. It was to be a day of confession and mourning for sin. It was also the one day of the year when the high priest entered the most holy place to sprinkle blood on the mercy seat of the ark of the covenant to make atonement for the people (see Lev 16:1-34). On that day, a **male goat** was to be sacrificed

for a sin offering (Num 29:11). For believers in Jesus Christ, full atonement for sin was made in his substitutionary death on the cross, which is why such sacrifices as those we read about here no longer need to be offered (see Heb 9:28).
29:12-38 During the Festival of Shelters, the Israelites were to leave their homes and live in shelters of sticks and greenery as a reminder of their forebears' years of wilderness wanderings and as a commemoration of God's promised deliverance out of that season.

26 "On the fifth day present nine bulls, two rams, fourteen male lambs a year old — all unblemished — **27** with their grain and drink offerings for the bulls, rams, and lambs, in proportion to their number. **28** Also offer one male goat as a sin offering. These are in addition to the regular burnt offering with its grain and drink offerings.

29 "On the sixth day present eight bulls, two rams, fourteen male lambs a year old — all unblemished — **30** with their grain and drink offerings for the bulls, rams, and lambs, in proportion to their number. **31** Also offer one male goat as a sin offering. These are in addition to the regular burnt offering with its grain and drink offerings.

32 "On the seventh day present seven bulls, two rams, and fourteen male lambs a year old — all unblemished — **33** with their grain and drink offerings for the bulls, rams, and lambs, in proportion to their number. **34** Also offer one male goat as a sin offering. These are in addition to the regular burnt offering with its grain and drink offerings.

35 "On the eighth day you are to hold a solemn assembly; you are not to do any daily work.[a] **36** Present a burnt offering, a fire offering as a pleasing aroma to the LORD: one bull, one ram, seven male lambs a year old — all unblemished — **37** with their grain and drink offerings for the bulls, rams, and lambs, in proportion to their number. **38** Also offer one male goat as a sin offering. These are in addition to the regular burnt offering with its grain and drink offerings.

39 "Offer these to the LORD at your appointed times in addition to your vow and freewill offerings, whether burnt, grain, drink, or fellowship offerings." **40** So Moses told the Israelites everything the LORD had commanded him.

REGULATIONS ABOUT VOWS

30 Moses told the leaders of the Israelite tribes,[b] "This is what the LORD has commanded: **2** When a man makes a vow to the LORD or swears an oath to put himself under an obligation, he must not break his word; he must do whatever he has promised.[c]

3 "When a woman in her father's house during her youth makes a vow to the LORD or puts herself under an obligation, **4** and her father hears about her vow or the obligation she put herself under, and he says nothing to her, all her vows and every obligation she put herself under are binding. **5** But if her father prohibits her on the day he hears about it, none of her vows and none of the obligations she put herself under are binding. The LORD will release her because her father has prohibited her.

6 "If a woman marries while her vows or the rash commitment she herself made are binding, **7** and her husband hears about it and says nothing to her when he finds out, her vows are binding, and the obligations she put herself under are binding. **8** But if her husband prohibits her when he hears about it, he will cancel her vow that is binding or the rash commitment she herself made, and the LORD will release her.

9 "Every vow a widow or divorced woman puts herself under is binding on her.

10 "If a woman in her husband's house has made a vow or put herself under an obligation with an oath, **11** and her husband hears about it, says nothing to her, and does not prohibit her, all her vows are binding, and every obligation she put herself under is binding. **12** But if her husband cancels them on the day he hears about it, nothing that came from her lips, whether her vows or her obligation, is binding. Her husband has canceled them, and the LORD will release her. **13** Her husband may confirm or cancel any vow or any sworn obligation to deny herself. **14** If her husband says nothing at all to her from day to day, he confirms all her vows and obligations, which are binding. He has confirmed them because he said nothing to her when he heard about them. **15** But if he cancels them

30:1-2 Vows were entirely voluntary. So God was well within his rights to demand complete faithfulness from an Israelite who made one. Such a person **must not break his word** (30:2). Many years later, Solomon gave this advice about vows to reinforce their solemnity: "God . . . does not delight in fools. Fulfill what you vow. Better that you do not vow than that you vow and not fulfill it" (Eccl 5:4-5). **30:3-5** This is a divine protection for an underage woman who spoke rashly. The **woman** in view was not yet an adult and was under parental authority (30:3). If such a girl made a vow to the Lord that put her under obligation, her father had the authority either to let the vow stand—in which case his daughter was bound to it—or to declare it void and **release** her (30:4-5). That Daddy got the last word was a loving provision and a reminder that Israelite women needed the covering of the covenant through their fathers before their release to the protection and covering of their husbands.

30:6-9 Like the previous one in 30:3-5, this situation illustrates the divinely appointed authority in the home. If an unmarried woman was bound by a vow that her father approved, she would carry that vow into her marriage, where her husband had the same choice as her father regarding whether or not she'd have to keep it from that point. (30:6-8). By contrast, **every vow a widow or divorced woman [put] herself under [was] binding**: she would make her own calls (30:9).

a 31:2 Nm 20:24-26; 27:13;
Dt 32:50
b 31:3 Ps 18:47; 79:10; 94:1;
Jr 11:20
c 31:7 Gn 34:25; 1Kg 11:16
d 31:8 Jos 13:21-22; Jdg
8:5,12,26
e Nm 22:5-24:25
f 31:9 Gn 34:28-29; Dt
20:13-14

g 31:16 Nm 25; Dt 20:18;
2Pt 2:15; Rv 2:14
h 31:17 Jdg 21:11-12
i 31:18 Dt 21:10-14
j 31:19 Lv 11:31; 22:4; Nm
5:2; 19:11,18; Hg 2:13
k 31:19-20 Lv 11:32; Nm
19:11-20
l 31:23 Nm 19:1-9,17-20
m 31:24 Ex 19:10; Lv
11:25,28,40; 13:6,34; 14:8;
15:5; 16:26; 17:15; Nm
8:7; 19:7
n 31:27 Jos 22:8; 1Sm 30:24

after he hears about them, he will be responsible for her commitment."[A]

16 These are the statutes that the LORD commanded Moses concerning the relationship between a man and his wife, or between a father and his daughter in his house during her youth.

WAR WITH MIDIAN

31 The LORD spoke to Moses, **2** "Execute vengeance for the Israelites against the Midianites. After that, you will be gathered to your people."[a]

3 So Moses spoke to the people, "Equip some of your men for war. They will go against Midian to inflict the LORD's vengeance[b] on them. **4** Send one thousand men to war from each Israelite tribe." **5** So one thousand were recruited from each Israelite tribe out of the thousands[B] in Israel — twelve thousand equipped for war. **6** Moses sent one thousand from each tribe to war. They went with Phinehas son of Eleazar the priest, in whose care were the holy objects and signal trumpets.

7 They waged war against Midian, as the LORD had commanded Moses, and killed every male.[c] **8** Along with the others slain by them, they killed the Midianite kings — Evi, Rekem, Zur, Hur, and Reba, the five kings of Midian.[d] They also killed Balaam son of Beor[e] with the sword. **9** The Israelites took the Midianite women and their dependents captive, and they plundered all their cattle, flocks, and property.[f] **10** Then they burned all the cities where the Midianites lived, as well as all their encampments, **11** and took away all the spoils of war and the captives, both people and animals. **12** They brought the prisoners, animals, and spoils of war to Moses, the priest Eleazar, and the Israelite community at the camp on the plains of Moab by the Jordan across from Jericho.

13 Moses, the priest Eleazar, and all the leaders of the community went to meet them outside the camp. **14** But Moses became furious with the officers, the commanders of thousands and commanders of hundreds, who were returning from the military campaign. **15** "Have you let every female live?" he asked them. **16** "Yet they are the ones who, at Balaam's advice, incited the Israelites to unfaithfulness against the LORD in the Peor incident, so that the plague came against the LORD's community.[g] **17** So now, kill every male among the dependents and kill every woman who has gone to bed with a man,[h] **18** but keep alive for yourselves all the young females who have not gone to bed with a man.[i]

19 "You are to remain outside the camp for seven days. All of you and your prisoners who have killed a person or touched the dead are to purify yourselves on the third day and the seventh day.[j] **20** Also purify everything: garments, leather goods, things made of goat hair, and every article of wood."[k]

21 Then the priest Eleazar said to the soldiers who had gone to battle, "This is the legal statute the LORD commanded Moses: **22** The gold, silver, bronze, iron, tin, and lead — **23** everything that can withstand fire — you are to pass through fire, and it will be clean. It must still be purified with the purification water.[l] Anything that cannot withstand fire, pass through the water. **24** On the seventh day wash your clothes, and you will be clean.[m] After that you may enter the camp."

25 The LORD told Moses, **26** "You, the priest Eleazar, and the family heads of the community are to take a count of what was captured, people and animals. **27** Then divide the captives between the troops who went out to war and the entire community.[n] **28** Set aside a tribute for the LORD from what belongs to the fighting men who went out to war: one out of every five hundred people, cattle, donkeys, sheep, and goats. **29** Take the tribute from their half and give it to the priest Eleazar as a contribution to the LORD. **30** From the

---

[A] **30:15** Or *will bear her guilt*   [B] **31:5** Or *clans*

31:1-2 God's vengeance **against the Midianites** would be fierce because of their part in seducing Israel into the degrading worship of Baal (see 25:1-18).
31:3-6 Each tribe had been affected by the sin of Baal worship, so each tribe would be involved in cleansing the source of this sin. **Phinehas son of Eleazar**, who had been zealous for God's holiness in the event to be avenged (see 25:6-13), accompanied the troops (31:6).
31:8 One of those killed along with the soldiers and **the Midianite kings** was Balaam son

of Beor, who suffered the consequences of his sin (see 31:16; Rom 6:23).
31:9-18 The Israelite troops failed to follow the Lord's command. They **took the Midianite women and their dependents captive** (31:9) as they destroyed the Midianites' dwellings and took **all the spoils** (31:11).

Moses couldn't believe it. Some of the women whom they had captured were the very ones who had **incited the Israelites to unfaithfulness** in the first place (31:15-16). They had lured Israelite men to commit

sexual immorality in worshiping Baal, resulting in the very plague that killed twenty-four thousand Israelites (see 25:1-18). So Moses gave the following command: **kill every woman who has gone to bed with a man** (31:17). In other words, those who had not participated in the immorality of the Peor incident were permitted to live (31:18). The execution of the others was a necessary purge of evil lest the Midianites' ways be allowed to further influence—and endanger—God's covenant people.

Israelites' half, take one out of every fifty from the people, cattle, donkeys, sheep, and goats, all the livestock, and give them to the Levites who perform the duties of[A] the LORD's tabernacle."

³¹ So Moses and the priest Eleazar did as the LORD commanded Moses. ³² The captives remaining from the plunder the army had taken totaled:
675,000 sheep and goats,
³³   72,000 cattle,
³⁴   61,000 donkeys,
³⁵   and 32,000 people, all the females
       who had not gone to bed
       with a man.

³⁶ The half portion for those who went out to war numbered:
337,500 sheep and goats,
³⁷   and the tribute to the LORD was 675
       from the sheep and goats;
³⁸   from the 36,000 cattle,
       the tribute to the LORD was 72;
³⁹   from the 30,500 donkeys,
       the tribute to the LORD was 61;
⁴⁰   and from the 16,000 people,
       the tribute to the LORD
       was 32 people.
⁴¹ Moses gave the tribute to the priest Eleazar as a contribution for the LORD, as the LORD had commanded Moses.

⁴² From the Israelites' half, which Moses separated from the men who fought, ⁴³ the community's half was:
337,500 sheep and goats,
⁴⁴   36,000 cattle,
⁴⁵   30,500 donkeys,
⁴⁶   and 16,000 people.
⁴⁷ Moses took one out of every fifty, selected from the people and the livestock of the Israelites' half. He gave them to the Levites who perform the duties of the LORD's tabernacle, as the LORD had commanded him.
⁴⁸ The officers who were over the thousands of the army, the commanders of

thousands and of hundreds, approached Moses ⁴⁹ and told him, "Your servants have taken a census of the fighting men under our command, and not one of us is missing. ⁵⁰ So we have presented to the LORD an offering of the gold articles each man found — armlets, bracelets, rings, earrings, and necklaces — to make atonement for ourselves before the LORD."[a]

⁵¹ Moses and the priest Eleazar received from them all the articles made out of gold. ⁵² All the gold of the contribution they offered to the LORD, from the commanders of thousands and of hundreds, was 420 pounds.[B] ⁵³ Each of the soldiers had taken plunder for himself.[b] ⁵⁴ Moses and the priest Eleazar received the gold from the commanders of thousands and of hundreds and brought it into the tent of meeting as a memorial for the Israelites before the LORD.

TRANSJORDAN SETTLEMENTS

32 The Reubenites and Gadites had a very large number of livestock. When they surveyed the lands of Jazer[c] and Gilead, they saw that the region was a good one for livestock. ² So the Gadites and Reubenites came to Moses, the priest Eleazar, and the leaders of the community and said: ³ "The territory of Ataroth, Dibon, Jazer, Nimrah, Heshbon, Elealeh, Sebam,[c] Nebo, and Beon,[d] ⁴ which the LORD struck down[e] before the community of Israel,[f] is good land for livestock, and your servants own livestock." ⁵ They said, "If we have found favor with you, let this land be given to your servants as a possession. Don't make us cross the Jordan."

⁶ But Moses asked the Gadites and Reubenites, "Should your brothers go to war while you stay here? ⁷ Why are you discouraging the Israelites from crossing into the land the LORD has given them? ⁸ That's what your fathers did when I sent

[a] 31:50 Ex 30:12-16
[b] 31:53 Dt 20:14
[c] 32:1 Nm 21:32; Jos 13:25; 21:39; 2Sm 24:5
[d] 32:3 Nm 21:30; 33:47; Dt 32:49; 1Ch 5:8; Is 15:2; 46:1; Jr 48:1,22
[e] 32:4 Nm 21:24
[f] Nm 21:24,34

[A] 31:30 Or *who protect*   [B] 31:52 Lit *16,750 shekels*   [C] 32:3 Sam, LXX read *Sibmah* (v. 38); Syr reads *Sebah*

31:48-50 The Midianite campaign had been a tremendous success. But the leaders of the troops who had fought had one more blessing to report—and a gift of thanks to offer. They informed Moses that not one of their soldiers was **missing** after the battle. None had been lost (31:49). They recognized how incredible this was and wanted to make a sacrificial offering of thanks to God for his divine protection.

To suffer no casualties in a battle of this size is unheard of, and these soldiers knew it. Their offering was given entirely of their own freewill, and it was over-the-top generous

because they knew what God had done for them and their fellow troops. The **atonement** they spoke of (31:50) was probably not a reference to some sin, but rather a recognition that God's faithfulness to them was far more than they deserved.

31:51-52 , 54 This offering recognized that everything the Israelites possessed came from the hand of the Lord and served as a reminder that he is able to supply every need. God loves it when giving is done willingly, cheerfully, and generously (see 2 Cor 9:6-8). **32:1-5** While the Israelites were still camped on the east side of the Jordan River opposite

Canaan, the tribes of Reuben and Gad looked around and **saw that the region was a good one for livestock**—of which they had huge numbers (32:1). These tribes came to Moses and the other leaders with a special request: **let this land be given to your servants as a possession. Don't make us cross the Jordan** (32:5). They were happy to stay right where they were while the rest of the tribes entered the promised land proper.

32:6-7 Moses questioned their courage. Did they really prefer the land on the east side of the Jordan? Or were they actually trying to avoid plunging into battle in support of

a 32:8 Nm 13:1–3,32–33;
Dt 1:22–28
b 32:10 Dt 1:34–36
c 32:11–12 Nm 14:22–
24,29–30
d 32:11 Nm 14:29
e 32:12 Nm 14:6,24,30,38;
26:65; Dt 1:36; Jos 14:6,8–
9; 15:7
f Ex 33:11; Nm 27:18–23
g 32:13 Nm 14:33–35;
26:64–65
h 32:15 Jos 22:16–18; 2Ch
7:19–20
i 32:17 Dt 3:18; Jos 1:13–15;
4:12–13
j 32:18 Jos 22:4,9
k 32:19 Jos 13:8

l 32:24 Nm 30:2; Jos 1:12–
18; 4:12
m 32:29 Jos 22:9

them from Kadesh-barnea to see the land.*a* **9** After they went up as far as Eshcol Valley and saw the land, they discouraged the Israelites from entering the land the Lord had given them. **10** So the Lord's anger burned that day, and he swore an oath:*b* **11** 'Because they did not remain loyal to me,*c* none of the men twenty years old or more who came up from Egypt will see the land I swore to give Abraham, Isaac, and Jacob*d* — **12** none except Caleb*e* son of Jephunneh the Kenizzite and Joshua*f* son of Nun, because they did remain loyal to the Lord.' **13** The Lord's anger burned against Israel, and he made them wander in the wilderness forty years until the whole generation that had done what was evil in the Lord's sight was gone.*g* **14** And here you, a brood of sinners, stand in your fathers' place adding even more to the Lord's burning anger against Israel. **15** If you turn back from following him,*h* he will once again leave this people in the wilderness, and you will destroy all of them."

16 Then they approached him and said, "We want to build sheep pens here for our livestock and cities for our dependents. **17** But we will arm ourselves and be ready to go ahead of the Israelites until we have brought them into their place.*i* Meanwhile, our dependents will remain in the fortified cities because of the inhabitants of the land. **18** We will not return to our homes until each of the Israelites has taken possession of his inheritance.*j* **19** Yet we will not have an inheritance with them across the Jordan and beyond, because our inheritance will be across the Jordan to the east."*k*

20 Moses replied to them, "If you do this — if you arm yourselves for battle before the Lord, **21** and every one of your armed men crosses the Jordan before the Lord

until he has driven his enemies from his presence, **22** and the land is subdued before the Lord — afterward you may return and be free from obligation to the Lord and to Israel. And this land will belong to you as a possession before the Lord. **23** But if you don't do this, you will certainly sin against the Lord; be sure your sin will catch up with you. **24** Build cities for your dependents and pens for your flocks, but do what you have promised."*l*

25 The Gadites and Reubenites answered Moses, "Your servants will do just as my lord commands. **26** Our dependents, wives, livestock, and all our animals will remain here in the cities of Gilead, **27** but your servants are equipped for war before the Lord and will go across to the battle as my lord orders."

28 So Moses gave orders about them to the priest Eleazar, Joshua son of Nun, and the family heads of the Israelite tribes. **29** Moses told them, "If the Gadites and Reubenites cross the Jordan with you, every man in battle formation before the Lord, and the land is subdued before you, you are to give them the land of Gilead as a possession.*m* **30** But if they don't go across with you in battle formation, they must accept land in Canaan with you."

31 The Gadites and Reubenites replied, "What the Lord has spoken to your servants is what we will do. **32** We will cross over in battle formation before the Lord into the land of Canaan, but we will keep our hereditary possession across the Jordan."

33 So Moses gave them — the Gadites, Reubenites, and half the tribe of Manasseh son of Joseph — the kingdom of King Sihon of the Amorites and the kingdom of King Og of Bashan, the land including its cities with the territories surrounding

---

their fellow Israelites? Moses's words got more pointed: **Why are you discouraging the Israelites from crossing into the land the Lord has given?** (32:7). He wanted them to recognize that their decision would affect the rest of the nation deeply.

There is a principle here that is applicable to the church. Some who claim to follow Christ insist that their similar actions—whether they are choosing to worship at home each Sunday when they could just as easily join a local fellowship or deciding not to serve in their churches but only to sit and soak—are not hurting anyone. But sinful choices do affect those around us. We must take care not to cause our fellow Christians discouragement. A discouraged Christian is an unfruitful Christian.

32:8-15 Since it was looking like the children of the previous generation wanted to follow in their parents' wicked footsteps, Moses didn't hold back. He said, **If you turn back from following [God], he will once again leave this people in the wilderness, and you will destroy all of them** (32:15).

32:16-19 The leaders of Reuben and Gad asked permission **to build sheep pens** for their **livestock** and **cities for [their] dependents** before they, the fighting men, joined their brothers in battle across the Jordan (32:16). They would stay on the job until the promised land was secure in Israel's hand (32:17-18) and would not expect **an inheritance . . . across the Jordan** (32:19).

32:20-24 Moses strictly warned them of the consequences of failing to stand by their promise. His words are chilling: **If you don't do**

this, you will certainly sin against the Lord; be sure your sin will catch up with you (32:23).

Sin's consequences can't be escaped. Though through trusting in the atoning sacrifice of Jesus Christ, you will escape God's eternal judgment, that doesn't mean you will escape all the consequences for sin in this life. As Paul reminded the Galatians, "God is not mocked. For whatever a person sows he will also reap" (Gal 6:7).

32:33-42 In anticipation of the fulfillment of their promises, Moses gave Gad and Reuben their inheritance. But Moses also included **half the tribe of Manasseh** in this allotment (32:33). Apparently, they shared a desire to dwell east of the Jordan, since they had defeated a number of enemies there and captured their land (32:39-41).

them.[a] 34 The Gadites rebuilt Dibon, Ataroth, Aroer, 35 Atroth-shophan, Jazer, Jogbehah, 36 Beth-nimrah, and Beth-haran[b] as fortified cities, and built sheep pens. 37 The Reubenites rebuilt Heshbon, Elealeh, Kiriathaim, 38 as well as Nebo and Baal-meon (whose names were changed), and Sibmah. They gave names to the cities they rebuilt.

39 The descendants of Machir[c] son of Manasseh went to Gilead, captured it, and drove out the Amorites who were there. 40 So Moses gave Gilead to the clan of Machir son of Manasseh, and they settled in it.[d] 41 Jair, a descendant of Manasseh, went and captured their villages, which he renamed Jair's Villages.[A,e] 42 Nobah went and captured Kenath with its surrounding villages and called it Nobah after his own name.

WILDERNESS TRAVELS REVIEWED

33 These were the stages of the Israelites' journey when they went out of the land of Egypt by their military divisions under the leadership of Moses and Aaron. 2 At the LORD's command, Moses wrote down the starting points for the stages of their journey; these are the stages listed by their starting points:

3 They traveled from Rameses[f] in the first month, on the fifteenth day of the month. On the day after the Passover[g] the Israelites went out defiantly[B,h] in the sight of all the Egyptians. 4 Meanwhile, the Egyptians were burying every firstborn male the LORD had struck down among them, for the LORD had executed judgment against their gods.[i] 5 The Israelites traveled from Rameses and camped at Succoth.[j] 6 They traveled from Succoth and camped at Etham,[k] which is on the edge of the wilderness. 7 They traveled from Etham and turned back to Pi-hahiroth, which faces Baal-zephon, and they camped before Migdol.[l] 8 They traveled from Pi-hahiroth[c] and crossed through the middle of the sea[m] into the wilderness. They took a three-day journey into the Wilderness of Etham and camped at Marah.[n] 9 They traveled from Marah and came to Elim.[o] There were twelve springs

and seventy date palms at Elim, so they camped there. 10 They traveled from Elim and camped by the Red Sea. 11 They traveled from the Red Sea and camped in the Wilderness of Sin.[p] 12 They traveled from the Wilderness of Sin and camped in Dophkah. 13 They traveled from Dophkah and camped at Alush. 14 They traveled from Alush and camped at Rephidim,[q] where there was no water for the people to drink.[r] 15 They traveled from Rephidim and camped in the Wilderness of Sinai.[s] 16 They traveled from the Wilderness of Sinai and camped at Kibroth-hattaavah.[t] 17 They traveled from Kibroth-hattaavah and camped at Hazeroth.[u] 18 They traveled from Hazeroth and camped at Rithmah. 19 They traveled from Rithmah and camped at Rimmon-perez. 20 They traveled from Rimmon-perez and camped at Libnah. 21 They traveled from Libnah and camped at Rissah. 22 They traveled from Rissah and camped at Kehelathah. 23 They traveled from Kehelathah and camped at Mount Shepher. 24 They traveled from Mount Shepher and camped at Haradah. 25 They traveled from Haradah and camped at Makheloth. 26 They traveled from Makheloth and camped at Tahath. 27 They traveled from Tahath and camped at Terah. 28 They traveled from Terah and camped at Mithkah. 29 They traveled from Mithkah and camped at Hashmonah. 30 They traveled from Hashmonah and camped at Moseroth. 31 They traveled from Moseroth and camped at Bene-jaakan.[v] 32 They traveled from Bene-jaakan and camped at Hor-haggidgad. 33 They traveled from Hor-haggidgad and camped at Jotbathah. 34 They traveled from Jotbathah and camped at Abronah.

[a] 32:33 Dt 3:12-17; 29:8; Jos 12:6; 13:8; 22:4
[b] 32:36 Jos 13:27
[c] 32:39 Gn 50:23; Nm 26:29; Jos 17:1,3
[d] 32:40 Jos 13:31
[e] 32:41 Dt 3:14; Jos 13:30; 1Kg 4:13; 1Ch 2:23
[f] 33:3 Gn 47:11; Ex 1:11; 12:37
[g] Ex 12:11-48; Lv 23:5; Nm 9:2-14
[h] Ex 14:8
[i] 33:4 Ex 12:12
[j] 33:5 Ex 12:37
[k] 33:6 Ex 13:20
[l] 33:7 Ex 14:2,9; Jr 46:14; Ezk 30:6
[m] 33:8 Ex 14:22-26
[n] Ex 15:23
[o] 33:9 Ex 15:27; 16:1

[p] 33:11 Ex 16:1; 17:1
[q] 33:14 Ex 17:1,8; 19:2
[r] Ex 17:1-7
[s] 33:15 Ex 19:1-2
[t] 33:16 Nm 11:34-35; Dt 9:22
[u] 33:17 Nm 11:35; 12:16; Dt 1:1
[v] 33:31-33 Dt 10:6-7

[A] 32:41 Or renamed Havvoth-jair   [B] 33:3 Lit with a raised hand; Ex 14:8   [C] 33:8 Some Hb mss, Sam, Syr, Vg; other Hb mss read from before Hahiroth

---

33:1-49 Moses kept a highly detailed travelogue of the Israelites' journey from the time they left **the land of Egypt** (33:1).

a 33:35 Dt 2:8; 1Kg 9:26
b 33:36 Nm 10:12
c 33:37 Nm 21:4; 33:37-41; Dt 32:50
d 33:38 Nm 20:23-29
e 33:40 Nm 21:1-3
f 33:43 Nm 21:10-11
g 33:44 Nm 21:11
h 33:45 Nm 32:34; Neh 11:25; Jr 48:18,22
i 33:46 Jr 48:22
j 33:47 Nm 27:12; Dt 32:49; Jr 22:20
k Dt 32:49; 34:1
l 33:48 Nm 22:1
m 33:49 Jos 12:7; 15:18; Ezk 25:9
n Nm 25:1; Jos 2:1; 3:1; Jl 3:18; Mc 6:5

o 33:52 Lv 26:1; Ezk 8:12
p Ex 32:4,8; 34:17; Lv 19:4; Dt 27:15
q 33:53 Gn 12:7; 15:18; 24:7; 35:12
r 33:56 Dt 28:15
s 34:4 Jos 15:3; Jdg 1:36
t 34:4-5 Jos 15:4
u 34:5 Jos 15:47; Is 27:12; Ezk 47:19
v 34:7 Nm 20:22-28; 33:37-56

35 They traveled from Abronah and camped at Ezion-geber.*a* **36** They traveled from Ezion-geber and camped in the Wilderness of Zin*b* (that is, Kadesh). **37** They traveled from Kadesh and camped at Mount Hor*c* on the edge of the land of Edom. **38** At the LORD's command, the priest Aaron climbed Mount Hor and died there on the first day of the fifth month in the fortieth year after the Israelites went out of the land of Egypt.*d* **39** Aaron was 123 years old when he died on Mount Hor. **40** At that time the Canaanite king of Arad, who lived in the Negev in the land of Canaan,*e* heard the Israelites were coming.

41 They traveled from Mount Hor and camped at Zalmonah. **42** They traveled from Zalmonah and camped at Punon. **43** They traveled from Punon and camped at Oboth.*f* **44** They traveled from Oboth and camped at Iye-abarim on the border of Moab.*g* **45** They traveled from Iyim*A* and camped at Dibon-gad.*h* **46** They traveled from Dibon-gad and camped at Almon-diblathaim.*i* **47** They traveled from Almon-diblathaim and camped in the Abarim*j* range facing Nebo.*k* **48** They traveled from the Abarim range and camped on the plains of Moab by the Jordan across from Jericho.*l* **49** They camped by the Jordan from Beth-jeshimoth*m* to the Acacia Meadow*B,n* on the plains of Moab.

INSTRUCTIONS FOR OCCUPYING CANAAN

50 The LORD spoke to Moses in the plains of Moab by the Jordan across from Jericho. **51** "Tell the Israelites: When you cross the Jordan into the land of Canaan, **52** you must drive out all the inhabitants of the land before you, destroy all their stone images*o* and cast images,*p* and demolish all their high places. **53** You are to take possession of the land and settle in it because I have given you the land*q* to possess. **54** You are to receive the land as an inheritance by lot according to your clans. Increase the inheritance for a large clan and decrease it for a small one. Whatever place the lot indicates for someone will be his. You will receive an inheritance according to your ancestral tribes. **55** But if you don't drive out the inhabitants of the land before you, those you allow to remain will become barbs for your eyes and thorns for your sides; they will harass you in the land where you will live. **56** And what I had planned to do to them, I will do to you."*r*

BOUNDARIES OF THE PROMISED LAND

34 The LORD spoke to Moses, **2** "Command the Israelites and say to them: When you enter the land of Canaan, it will be allotted to you as an inheritance*c* with these borders:

3 Your southern side will be from the Wilderness of Zin along the boundary of Edom. Your southern border on the east will begin at the east end of the Dead Sea. **4** Your border will turn south of the Scorpions' Ascent,*D* proceed to Zin, and end south of Kadesh-barnea. It will go to Hazar-addar and proceed to Azmon.*s* **5** The border will turn from Azmon*t* to the Brook of Egypt,*u* where it will end at the Mediterranean Sea.

6 Your western border will be the coastline of the Mediterranean Sea; this will be your western border.

7 This will be your northern border: From the Mediterranean Sea draw a line to Mount Hor;*v* **8** from Mount Hor draw a line to the entrance of

---

A 33:45 A shortened form of Iye-abarim   *B* 33:49 Or to Abel-shittim   *C* 34:2 Lit inheritance — the land of Canaan   *D* 34:4 Lit of Scorpions; Jos 15:3; Jdg 1:36

33:36 The Wilderness of Zin (that is, Kadesh) lives in infamy. It was because of Israel's rebellion there that the nation would wander in the wilderness for forty years.
33:50-53 Moses emphasized the total spiritual depravity of the Canaanites they would encounter, as well as the Lord's command concerning them. The Israelites were to **drive out all the inhabitants of the land . . . destroy all their . . . images, and demolish all their**

high places (33:52). There could be no compromises. The nation had entered a covenant relationship with the Lord alone, and through their obedience he would judge the Canaanites for many years of extreme wickedness.
33:55-56 If Israel were to disobey their covenant God and fail in their assignment, the native inhabitants would prove to be a snare to them. Israel would ultimately adopt their idolatrous ways and be driven out.

Tragically, this warning would prove prophetic. Eventually, after years of covenant unfaithfulness—and years of the Lord's abundant patience—they would be cast from the land in stages.
34:1-29 Before the transition of leadership from Moses to Joshua, the Lord gave Moses boundaries for the land (34:1-15) and identified the leaders from the tribes who would oversee the distribution in his stead (34:16-29).

Hamath,[A,a] and the border will reach Zedad.[b] 9 Then the border will go to Ziphron and end at Hazar-enan.[c] This will be your northern border.

10 For your eastern border, draw a line from Hazar-enan to Shepham. 11 The border will go down from Shepham to Riblah east of Ain.[d] It will continue down and reach the eastern slope of the Sea of Chinnereth.[B,e] 12 Then the border will go down to the Jordan and end at the Dead Sea. This will be your land defined by its borders on all sides."

13 So Moses commanded the Israelites, "This is the land you are to receive by lot as an inheritance, which the LORD commanded to be given to the nine and a half tribes. 14 For the tribe of Reuben's descendants and the tribe of Gad's descendants have received their inheritance according to their ancestral families,[c] and half the tribe of Manasseh has received its inheritance. 15 The two and a half tribes have received their inheritance[f] across the Jordan east of Jericho, toward the sunrise."

LEADERS FOR DISTRIBUTING THE LAND

16 The LORD spoke to Moses, 17 "These are the names of the men who are to distribute the land as an inheritance for you: the priest Eleazar and Joshua son of Nun. 18 Take one leader from each tribe to distribute the land. 19 These are the names of the men:

Caleb[g] son of Jephunneh from the tribe of Judah;
20 Shemuel son of Ammihud from the tribe of Simeon's descendants;
21 Elidad son of Chislon from the tribe of Benjamin;
22 Bukki son of Jogli, a leader from the tribe of Dan's descendants;
23 from the sons of Joseph:
Hanniel son of Ephod, a leader from the tribe of Manasseh's descendants,

24 Kemuel son of Shiphtan, a leader from the tribe of Ephraim's descendants;
25 Eli-zaphan son of Parnach, a leader from the tribe of Zebulun's descendants;
26 Paltiel son of Azzan, a leader from the tribe of Issachar's descendants;
27 Ahihud son of Shelomi, a leader from the tribe of Asher's descendants;
28 Pedahel son of Ammihud, a leader from the tribe of Naphtali's descendants."

29 These are the ones the LORD commanded to distribute the inheritance to the Israelites in the land of Canaan.

CITIES FOR THE LEVITES

35 The LORD again spoke to Moses in the plains of Moab by the Jordan across from Jericho:[h] 2 "Command the Israelites to give cities out of their hereditary property for the Levites to live in and pastureland around the cities.[i] 3 The cities will be for them to live in, and their pasturelands will be for their herds, flocks, and all their other animals. 4 The pasturelands of the cities you are to give the Levites will extend from the city wall five hundred yards[D] on every side. 5 Measure a thousand yards[E] outside the city for the east side, a thousand yards for the south side, a thousand yards for the west side, and a thousand yards for the north side, with the city in the center. This will belong to them as pasturelands for the cities.

6 "The cities you give the Levites will include six cities of refuge,[j] which you will provide so that the one who kills someone may flee there; in addition to these, give forty-two other cities.[k] 7 The total number of cities you give the Levites will be forty-eight, along with their pasturelands.[l] 8 Of the cities that you give from the Israelites' territory, you should take more from a larger tribe and less from a smaller one.[m] Each tribe is to give some of its cities to the Levites in proportion to the inheritance it receives."

a 34:8 Nm 13:21; 2Kg 14:25; 2Ch 7:8; Ezk 48:1
b Ezk 47:15
c 34:9 Ezk 47:17; 48:1
d 34:11 Jos 15:32
e Jos 12:3; 13:27; Lk 5:1
f 34:15 Nm 32:33
g 34:19 Nm 14:6,24,30,38; 26:65

h 35:1 Nm 22:1; 26:3,63; 31:12; 33:48-50; 36:13; Dt 34:1,8; Jos 13:32
i 35:2 Jos 14:3-4; 21:2-3; Ezk 45:1-5; 48:8-14
j 35:6 Ex 21:12-14; Dt 4:41-43; 19:1-13; Jos 20:2,7-9; 21:3,13,21,27,32,36,38; 1Ch 6:57,67
k Jos 21:13
l 35:7 Jos 21:41
m 35:8 Nm 26:54; 33:54

A 34:8 Or to Lebo-hamath   B 34:11 = the Sea of Galilee; Jos 12:3; 13:27; Lk 5:1   C 34:14 Lit the house of their fathers   D 35:4 Lit 1,000 cubits
E 35:5 Lit 2,000 cubits

34:18 God gave Moses the name of **one leader from each tribe to distribute the land** to ensure that each tribe was fairly represented. 35:2-5 By God's **command,** the **Levites** were to have dwellings scattered throughout Israel (35:2). Not only did this provide practically for the Levites who would receive no

specific territory, but it was also spiritually strategic. If they lived in cities that were dispersed throughout the nation, the Levites were thus accessible to all the people. They were well positioned to "teach the Israelites all the statutes that the Lord [had] given" (Lev 10:11).

35:6-15 **Cities of refuge** (35:6-7) were places where **a person who [killed] someone unintentionally [might] flee . . . until he [stood] trial** (35:11-12). These cities were to be equally divided so that those living throughout the area could access them (35:14).

a 35:11 Dt 4:42; 19:3-4,6;
Jos 20:3-6
b 35:12 Gn 9:5-6; Dt
19:6,12; Jos 20:5,9; 2Sm
14:11; 1Th 4:6
c 35:14 Dt 4:41; Jos 20:8
d 35:16 Ex 21:12-14; Lv
24:17; Dt 19:11-12
e 35:19 Dt 19:6,12; Jos
20:3,5

f 35:22-25 Ex 21:13
g 35:30 Dt 17:6; 19:15;
Mt 18:16
h 35:33 Ps 106:38; Is 24:5;
Jr 3:9
i 36:1 Nm 26:29

CITIES OF REFUGE

9 The LORD said to Moses, **10** "Speak to the Israelites and tell them: When you cross the Jordan into the land of Canaan, **11** designate cities to serve as cities of refuge for you, so that a person who kills someone unintentionally may flee there.*a* **12** You will have the cities as a refuge from the avenger,*b* so that the one who kills someone will not die until he stands trial before the assembly. **13** The cities you select will be your six cities of refuge. **14** Select three cities across the Jordan and three cities in the land of Canaan to be cities of refuge.*c* **15** These six cities will serve as a refuge for the Israelites and for the alien or temporary resident among them, so that anyone who kills a person unintentionally may flee there.

16 "If anyone strikes a person with an iron object and death results, he is a murderer; the murderer must be put to death.*d* **17** If anyone has in his hand a stone capable of causing death and strikes another person and he dies, the murderer must be put to death. **18** If anyone has in his hand a wooden object capable of causing death and strikes another person and he dies, the murderer must be put to death. **19** The avenger of blood himself is to kill the murderer; when he finds him, he is to kill him.*e* **20** Likewise, if anyone in hatred pushes a person or throws an object at him with malicious intent and he dies, **21** or if in hostility he strikes him with his hand and he dies, the one who struck him must be put to death; he is a murderer. The avenger of blood is to kill the murderer when he finds him.

22 "But if anyone suddenly pushes a person without hostility or throws any object at him without malicious intent **23** or without looking drops a stone that could kill a person and he dies, but he was not his enemy and didn't intend to harm him, **24** the assembly is to judge between the person who kills someone and the avenger of blood according to these ordinances. **25** The assembly is to protect the one who kills someone from the avenger of blood. Then the assembly will return him to the city of refuge he fled to, and he must live there until the death of the high priest who was anointed with the holy oil.*f* **26** "If the one who kills someone ever goes outside the border of the city of refuge he fled to, **27** and the avenger of blood finds him outside the border of his city of refuge and kills him, the avenger will not be guilty of bloodshed, **28** for the one who killed a person was supposed to live in his city of refuge until the death of the high priest. Only after the death of the high priest may the one who has killed a person return to the land he possesses. **29** These instructions will be a statutory ordinance for you throughout your generations wherever you live.

30 "If anyone kills a person, the murderer is to be put to death based on the word of witnesses. But no one is to be put to death based on the testimony of one witness.*g* **31** You are not to accept a ransom for the life of someone who is guilty of murder; he must be put to death. **32** Neither should you accept a ransom for the person who flees to his city of refuge, allowing him to return and live in the land before the death of the high priest.

33 "Do not defile the land where you live, for bloodshed defiles the land,*h* and there can be no atonement for the land because of the blood that is shed on it, except by the blood of the person who shed it. **34** Do not make the land unclean where you live and where I dwell; for I, the LORD, reside among the Israelites."

THE INHERITANCE OF ZELOPHEHAD'S DAUGHTERS

36 The family heads from the clan of the descendants of Gilead — the son of Machir, son of Manasseh*i* — who

---

35:16-29 There was no refuge for the person who committed premeditated murder. Fittingly, this required the **death** penalty (35:16). The idea behind the descriptions given here is the presence of **hatred** and **malicious intent** (35:17-21). In such cases, **the avenger of blood himself [was] to kill the murderer** (35:19). This individual was a family member of the victim. It was his responsibility to carry out justice.

In the case of an accidental death or an incident of manslaughter—when death was caused **without hostility** (35:22)—the cities of refuge provided a safe haven for the guilty party until the case could be heard and emotions could cool. If the court ruled for the defendant,

he would live safely in his city of refuge, where he was required to stay **until the death of the high priest** (35:25), after which he was free to return home. In this mention we see that there was an atoning effect in even the high priest's death in that it signaled a cleansing and forgiveness of past sins in the nation and a fresh start for people who had accidentally taken a life.

Importantly, if the person violated the terms of his house arrest by leaving his **city of refuge** before the high priest's death, **the avenger** could kill him without guilt (35:26-28). Wise King Solomon would one day employ a similar precedent in his dealings with Shimei (see 1 Kgs 2:36-46).

35:30 The requirement for multiple **witnesses** was a provision to prevent miscarriages of justice.

35:31 Once a murderer had been convicted, no amount of money could buy him his life back. The *only* acceptable payment a murderer could make was to forfeit his own life for the death of his victim.

35:33-34 Bloodshed defiles the land (35:33). It could not be tolerated because **the LORD** himself resided **among the Israelites** (35:34). God is holy and requires holiness from his people.

36:1-4 The problem these men faced was significant for a nation in which a family's land

were from the clans of the sons of Joseph, approached and addressed Moses and the leaders who were heads of the Israelite families. ² They said, "The LORD commanded my lord to give the land as an inheritance by lot to the Israelites. My lord was further commanded by the LORD to give our brother Zelophehad's inheritance to his daughters.ᵃ ³ If they marry any of the men from the other Israelite tribes, their inheritance will be taken away from our fathers' inheritance and added to that of the tribe into which they marry. Therefore, part of our allotted inheritance would be taken away. ⁴ When the Jubileeᵇ comes for the Israelites, their inheritance will be added to that of the tribe into which they marry, and their inheritance will be taken away from the inheritance of our ancestral tribe."

⁵ So Moses commanded the Israelites at the word of the LORD, "What the tribe of Joseph's descendants says is right. ⁶ This is what the LORD has commanded concerning Zelophehad's daughters: They may marry anyone they like provided they marry within a clan of their ancestral tribe. ⁷ No inheritance belonging to the Israelites is to transfer from tribe to tribe, because each of the Israelites is to retain the inheritance of his ancestral tribe.ᶜ ⁸ Any daughter who possesses an inheritance from an Israelite tribe must marry someone from the clan of her ancestral tribe, so that each of the Israelites will possess the inheritance of his fathers. ⁹ No inheritance is to transfer from one tribe to another, because each of the Israelite tribes is to retain its inheritance."

¹⁰ The daughters of Zelophehad did as the LORD commanded Moses. ¹¹ Mahlah, Tirzah, Hoglah, Milcah, and Noah, the daughters of Zelophehad, married cousins on their father's side. ¹² They married men from the clans of the descendants of Manasseh son of Joseph, and their inheritance remained within the tribe of their father's clan.

¹³ These are the commands and ordinances the LORD commanded the Israelites through Moses in the plains of Moab by the Jordan across from Jericho.

ᵃ 36:2 Nm 26:33; 27:1-11; Jos 17:3; 1Ch 7:15
ᵇ 36:4 Lv 25:8-55; 27:7-24

ᶜ 36:7 Lv 25:23-24; 1Kg 21:3

---

was a sacred grant from the Lord that was never to be permanently sold. (One generation used it and then passed it along to the next, as if it were on lease to a family from God.) They realized that if these **daughters** married outside of their tribe—while owning their father's land—that land would pass to others (36:2-4).

36:5-9 To address the problem raised in 36:1-4, Israelite daughters who owned an inheritance were to marry within their own **clan** (36:8).

DEUTERONOMY

INTRODUCTION

Author

DEUTERONOMY 1:1 TESTIFIES that the book's recorded words were spoken by Moses. Moreover, later biblical books quote from Deuteronomy and attribute the words to Moses (see Matt 19:7; Acts 3:22; Rom 10:19). Surely a final editor added some things, like the account of Moses's death in Deuteronomy 34:5-12, but since Moses was Israel's God-appointed leader who wrote things down at God's command (see Num 33:2), we have no reason to doubt the traditional Jewish and Christian position that Moses is the author of this book.

Historical Background

After the Lord delivered the nation of Israel from Egyptian slavery, he led them to the Sinai Wilderness, entered into a covenant with them, and gave them his law. One year later, they departed Sinai, and God led them to the edge of the promised land. However, because the people feared the inhabitants of Canaan, they refused to take possession of it. Therefore, God caused the Israelites to wander in the wilderness for forty years as punishment for their unbelief in his ability to provide—until every Israelite from that generation had died. At the end of the book of Numbers and the beginning of the book of Deuteronomy, Israel was once again on the edge of the promised land. They were encamped across the Jordan River, not far from the Canaanite city of Jericho. Here Moses reviewed the Lord's covenant and laws with the new generation. The title of the book comes from the Greek translation of the Old Testament (the Septuagint). *Deuteronomy* means "second law" (*deutero nomos*) or "repetition of the law."

Message and Purpose

This fifth and final book of the Pentateuch is Moses's farewell address to the second generation of Israelites, those whose once enslaved parents came out of Egypt on their way to the promised land of Canaan. Deuteronomy is structured like the treaties of that day, in which a king would spell out the laws, standards, and stipulations by which he would rule the vassals, or servants, who made up his nation. God was (in a very real sense)

Israel's King, the people of Israel were his servants, and the standards of his kingdom had been spelled out in the covenant he made with them at Sinai.

Moses's message to this new generation of Israelites was that their choice to obey or disobey God's law—to submit to their King or not—would determine the kind of life they would have once they entered Canaan. In fact, the people's obedience to God would be the very thing to bring them the blessings of the covenant that stretched all the way back to Abraham—land, national identity, and a promise of bringing blessing to the nations. But tied to the choice they faced were curses for disobedience, too. Deuteronomy is thus a covenantal book. Through it, God tells his people that he will bond with them based on their adherence to the covenant of his kingdom.

www.bhpublishinggroup.com/qr/te/05_00

Outline

INTRODUCTION

1 These are the words Moses spoke to all Israel across the Jordan in the wilderness,[a] in the Arabah[b] opposite Suph,[A] between Paran[c] and Tophel, Laban, Hazeroth,[d] and Di-zahab. [2] It is an eleven-day journey from Horeb[e] to Kadesh-barnea[f] by way of Mount Seir.[g] [3] In the fortieth year,[h] in the eleventh month, on the first of the month, Moses told the Israelites everything the LORD had commanded him to say to them. [4] This was after he had defeated King Sihon of the Amorites, who lived in Heshbon, and King Og of Bashan, who lived in Ashtaroth, at Edrei.[i] [5] Across the Jordan in the land of Moab, Moses began to explain this law, saying:

DEPARTURE FROM HOREB

[6] "The LORD our God spoke to us at Horeb: 'You have stayed at this mountain long enough. [7] Resume your journey and go to the hill country of the Amorites[j] and their neighbors in the Arabah, the hill country, the Judean foothills,[B] the Negev[k] and the sea coast — to the land of the Canaanites and to Lebanon as far as the great river, the Euphrates River.[l] [8] See, I have set the land before you. Enter and take possession of the land[m] the LORD swore to give to your fathers[n] Abraham, Isaac, and Jacob and their future descendants.'[o]

LEADERS FOR THE TRIBES

[9] "I said to you at that time: I can't bear the responsibility for you on my own. [10] The LORD your God has so multiplied you that today you are as numerous as the stars of the sky.[p] [11] May the LORD, the God of your fathers, increase you a thousand times more, and bless you as he promised you. [12] But how can I bear your troubles, burdens, and disputes by myself? [13] Appoint for yourselves wise, understanding, and respected men from each of your tribes, and I will make them your leaders.

[14] "You replied to me, 'What you propose to do is good.'

[15] "So I took the leaders of your tribes, wise and respected men, and set them over you as leaders: commanders for thousands, hundreds, fifties, and tens, and officers for your tribes. [16] I commanded your judges at that time: Hear the cases between your brothers, and judge rightly between a man and his brother or his resident alien. [17] Do not show partiality when deciding a case;[q] listen to small and great alike. Do not be intimidated by anyone, for judgment belongs to God.[r] Bring me any case too difficult for you, and I will hear it. [18] At that time I commanded you about all the things you were to do.[s]

ISRAEL'S DISOBEDIENCE AT KADESH-BARNEA

[19] "We then set out from Horeb and went across all the great and terrible wilderness you saw on the way to the hill country of the Amorites, just as the LORD our God had commanded us. When we reached Kadesh-barnea, [20] I said to you: You have reached the hill country of the Amorites, which the LORD our God is giving us. [21] See, the LORD your God has set the land before you. Go up and take possession of it as the LORD, the God of your fathers, has told you. Do not be afraid or discouraged.

[22] "Then[t] all of you approached me and said, 'Let's send men ahead of us, so that they may explore the land for us and bring us back a report about the route we should go up and the cities we will come to.' [23] The plan seemed good to me, so I selected twelve men from among you, one man for each tribe. [24] They left and went up into the hill country and came to the Valley of Eshcol, scouting the land. [25] They took some of the fruit from the land in their hands, carried it down to us, and brought

[a] 1:1 Gn 50:10-11; Dt 4:41,46-47; 11:30; Jos 1:14-15
[b] Dt 3:17; 4:49; Jos 12:3,8; Jr 50:12; Ezk 47:8
[c] Nm 12:16; Dt 33:2
[d] Nm 11:35
[e] 1:2 Dt 3:1; Dt 4:10,15; 5:2; 18:16; 1Kg 8:9; 19:8; Ps 106:19; Mal 4:4
[f] Nm 13:26; 20:1,14,16,22; 27:14; 32:8; Dt 2:14; 9:23; Jos 14:6-7
[g] Gn 32:3; 36:8-9,20-21; Dt 2:12; 33:2; Jdg 5:4; Ezk 35:2-3,7,15
[h] 1:3 Ex 16:35; Nm 14:33-34; 32:13; Dt 2:7; 8:2,4; 29:5; Jos 5:6; Neh 9:21; Ps 95:10; Am 2:10; 5:25; Ac 7:36,42; 13:18; Heb 3:17
[i] 1:4 Nm 21:21-35; 32:33; Dt 2:24-3:11; 29:7; 31:4; Jos 2:10; 9:10; 12:1-5; Jdg 11:19-21; Ps 135:10-12; 136:17-21
[j] 1:7 Gn 15:16; 48:22; Ex 3:8,17; 13:5; 23:23; Nm 13:29; 21:13; 22:2; 32:39; Jos 10:12; 11:3; 12:8; 24:8
[k] Gn 12:9; 13:3; Nm 13:29; Dt 34:3; Jos 15:21; Ps 126:4; Is 30:6; Ob 19-20
[l] Dt 11:24
[m] 1:8 Dt 4:1; 6:10,18; 8:1; 10:11; 11:8
[n] Dt 1:35; 9:5; 11:9,21; 26:3; 28:11; 29:13; 30:20; 31:7; Jos 5:6
[o] Gn 15:18-21; 26:3; 35:12; Ex 3:16; 6:8; 33:1; Nm 32:11; Dt 34:4; Ac 3:13
[p] 1:10 Gn 22:17; 26:4; Ex 32:13

[q] 1:17 Lv 19:15; Dt 16:19; Pr 24:23
[r] 2Ch 19:6
[s] 1:9-18 Ex 18:13-26
[t] 1:22-46 Nm 13–14

[A] 1:1 LXX, Tg, Vg read the Red Sea   [B] 1:7 Or the Shephelah

1:5 Deuteronomy opens with a new generation standing at the edge of the promised land. Why was a review of the **law** necessary? Forty years before, their parents had received God's law. They were to enter the land shortly thereafter, but they rebelled and refused. This led to the Lord's decree that all the adults of that generation would die in the wilderness for failing to trust him. The children of the exodus generation needed to hear afresh what God expected of them as they prepared to lay hold of their inheritance as his people.

1:6-8 When the Lord **spoke** to the Israelites **at Horeb** (which is another name for Mount Sinai, where the Ten Commandments were given), he commanded them to go to **the land** he promised to **Abraham, Isaac, and Jacob and their future descendants** (1:6, 8). But notice that even though he had **set the land before** them, Israel still had to **take possession of** it (1:8).

This is an important principle for modern believers. Whatever God promises, he delivers. But laying hold of those promises still requires our obedience. We do not inherit the promises of God by sitting in our easy chairs. We love, work, serve, pray, and fight the good fight of the faith because this is our kingdom role in fulfilling the King's agenda.

1:19 The Israelites' journey from **Horeb** to **Kadesh-barnea**, the location from which twelve spies would be sent out to scout the promised land, had been anything but easy.

a 1:25 Dt 8:7
b 1:27 Ps 106:25
c 1:28 Jos 14:8
d Dt 9:1-2
e Dt 2:10; 9:2; Jos 11:21; 14:12
f 1:29 Dt 31:6
g 1:30 Ex 23:23; 32:34; Dt 31:8; Jdg 4:14; Is 52:12
h Ex 14:14; Dt 20:4; Jdg 9:17
i 1:35 Dt 1:8; 6:18; 10:11; 11:21; 30:20; 31:7,20; Ezk 20:42
j 1:37 Nm 20:12
k 1:38 Nm 27:12-21

l 1:40 Nm 14:25
m 1:42 Nm 14:42
n 1:44 Nm 14:45
o 2:1 Ex 10:19; 13:18; 15:4,22; 23:31; Nm 21:4; Dt 1:40
p 2:3 Dt 1:6

us back a report: 'The land the LORD our God is giving us is good.'[a]

26 "But you were not willing to go up. You rebelled against the command of the LORD your God. 27 You grumbled in your tents[b] and said, 'The LORD brought us out of the land of Egypt to hand us over to the Amorites in order to destroy us, because he hates us. 28 Where can we go? Our brothers have made us lose heart,[A,c] saying: The people are larger and taller than we are; the cities are large, fortified to the heavens.[d] We also saw the descendants of the Anakim[e] there.'

29 "So I said to you: Don't be terrified or afraid of them![f] 30 The LORD your God who goes before you[g] will fight for you,[h] just as you saw him do for you in Egypt. 31 And you saw in the wilderness how the LORD your God carried you as a man carries his son all along the way you traveled until you reached this place. 32 But in spite of this you did not trust the LORD your God, 33 who went before you on the journey to seek out a place for you to camp. He went in the fire by night and in the cloud by day to guide you on the road you were to travel.

34 "When the LORD heard your[B] words, he grew angry and swore an oath: 35 'None of these men in this evil generation will see the good land I swore to give your fathers,[i] 36 except Caleb the son of Jephunneh. He will see it, and I will give him and his descendants the land on which he has set foot, because he remained loyal to the LORD.'

37 "The LORD was angry with me also because of you and said: 'You will not enter there either.'[j] 38 Joshua son of Nun, who attends you, will enter it. Encourage him, for he will enable Israel to inherit it.[k] 39 Your children, whom you said would be plunder, your sons who[c] don't yet know good from evil, will enter there. I will give them the land, and they will take possession of it. 40 But you are to turn back and head for the wilderness by way of the Red Sea.'[l]

41 "You answered me, 'We have sinned against the LORD. We will go up and fight just as the LORD our God commanded us.' Then each of you put on his weapons of war and thought it would be easy to go up into the hill country.

42 "But the LORD said to me, 'Tell them: Don't go up and fight, for I am not with you to keep you from being defeated by your enemies.'[m] 43 So I spoke to you, but you didn't listen. You rebelled against the LORD's command and defiantly went up into the hill country. 44 Then the Amorites who lived there came out against you and chased you like a swarm of bees. They routed you from Seir as far as Hormah.[n] 45 When you returned, you wept before the LORD, but he didn't listen to your requests or pay attention to you. 46 For this reason you stayed in Kadesh as long as you did.[D]

JOURNEY PAST SEIR

2 "Then we turned back and headed for the wilderness by way of the Red Sea,[o] as the LORD had told me, and we traveled around the hill country of Seir for many days. 2 The LORD then said to me, 3 'You've been traveling around this hill country long enough; turn north.[p] 4 Command the people: You are about to travel through the territory of your brothers, the descendants of Esau, who live in Seir. They will be afraid of you, so be very careful. 5 Don't provoke them, for I will not give you any of their land, not even a foot of it,[E] because I have given Esau the hill country of Seir

---

1:26-28 Fearful of the scouts' claim that the native inhabitants of the promised land were giants living in cities **fortified to the heavens** (1:28), the exodus generation had the audacity to claim that God had brought them out of Egypt to let the Amorites slaughter them—because he hated them (1:27). Years later, the Lord would testify, "When Israel was a child, I loved him, and out of Egypt I called my son" (Hos 11:1). But the people of Israel, the very ones for whom he so tenderly and graciously provided, described the *love* of God as *hatred*. **1:29-36** Moses tried to rally the people with the reminder that the Lord would go before them and fight for them, as he had done in Egypt and in the wilderness (1:29-31). But the Israelites' fear had made them deaf and blind

to God's goodness. Sadly, they **did not trust** him (1:32). Thus, only **Caleb** (1:36) and **Joshua** (1:38), the two scouts who responded faithfully when confronted with seeming obstacles, would receive their inheritance in the promised land. **1:37-38** In mentioning the prior incident, Moses wasn't blaming the people for his sin, but he was reminding them that their grumbling had been so contagious that it caused him to sin too (1:37). Nonetheless, **Joshua**, Moses's faithful servant, would lead the people in his place (1:38). **1:39-40** Fearful Israel had refused to enter the land, claiming that their children would be **plunder** for the nations living there (1:39). Ironically, God turned their excuse against

them. In reality they would be excluded from the promised land and die in the wilderness, while their children inherited the land. **1:45** The people **wept** without any genuine repentance. Because of their rebellious hearts, God ignored their **requests**. He wants to be approached with sincere repentance and humility. **2:4-23** Moses recalls how they had encountered three groups of relatives, whom the Lord told them not to pick a fight with: the Edomites, the Moabites, and the Ammonites. The former group descended from their forefather Jacob's twin brother Esau. The latter two were related to the patriarch Abraham since they were descended from his nephew Lot.

as his possession.[a] **6** You may purchase food from them, so that you may eat, and buy water from them to drink.[b] **7** For the LORD your God has blessed you in all the work of your hands.[c] He has watched over your journey through this immense wilderness. The LORD your God has been with you this past forty years, and you have lacked nothing.'[d]

JOURNEY PAST MOAB

8 "So we bypassed our brothers, the descendants of Esau, who live in Seir. We turned away from the Arabah road and from Elath and Ezion-geber.[e] We traveled along the road to the Wilderness of Moab. **9** The LORD said to me, 'Show no hostility toward Moab, and do not provoke them to battle, for I will not give you any of their land as a possession, since I have given Ar as a possession to the descendants of Lot.'"[f]

10 The Emim, a great and numerous people as tall as the Anakim,[g] had previously lived there. **11** They were also regarded as Rephaim,[h] like the Anakim, though the Moabites called them Emim.[i] **12** The Horites[j] had previously lived in Seir, but the descendants of Esau drove them out, destroying them completely[A] and settling in their place, just as Israel did in the land of its possession the LORD gave them.

13 "The LORD said, 'Now get up and cross the Zered Valley.' So we crossed the Zered Valley.[k] **14** The time we spent traveling from Kadesh-barnea until we crossed the Zered Valley was thirty-eight years until the entire generation of fighting men had perished from the camp, as the LORD had sworn to them. **15** Indeed, the LORD's hand was against them, to eliminate[j] them from the camp until they had all perished.[m]

JOURNEY PAST AMMON

16 "When all the fighting men had died among the people, **17** the LORD spoke to me,

18 'Today you are going to cross the border of Moab at Ar. **19** When you get close to the Ammonites, don't show any hostility to them or provoke them, for I will not give you any of the Ammonites' land as a possession; I have given it as a possession to the descendants of Lot.'"[n]

20 This too used to be regarded as the land of the Rephaim. The Rephaim lived there previously, though the Ammonites called them Zamzummim,[o] **21** a great and numerous people, tall as the Anakim. The LORD destroyed the Rephaim at the advance of the Ammonites, so that they drove them out and settled in their place. **22** This was just as he had done for the descendants of Esau who lived in Seir, when he destroyed the Horites before them; they drove them out and have lived in their place until now. **23** The Caphtorim, who came from Caphtor,[B,p] destroyed the Avvites, who lived in villages as far as Gaza, and settled in their place.

DEFEAT OF SIHON THE AMORITE

24 "The LORD also said, 'Get up, move out, and cross the Arnon Valley. See, I have handed the Amorites' King Sihon of Heshbon and his land over to you. Begin to take possession of it; engage[c] him in battle.[q] **25** Today I will begin to put the fear and dread of you on the peoples everywhere under heaven. They will hear the report about you, tremble, and be in anguish because of you.'[r]

26 "So I sent messengers with an offer of peace[s] to King Sihon of Heshbon from the Wilderness of Kedemoth, saying, **27** 'Let us travel through your land; we will keep strictly to the highway. We will not turn to the right or the left.[t] **28** You can sell us food in exchange for silver so we may eat, and give us water for silver so we may drink. Only let us travel through on foot, **29** just as the descendants of Esau who live in Seir

---

[a] 2:5 Ezk 25:12-14
[b] 2:1-6 Nm 20:14-21
[c] 2:7 Dt 30:9
[d] Dt 8:2-4; 29:5; Neh 9:21
[e] 2:8 Nm 33:35-36; 1Kg 9:26
[f] 2:9 Gn 19:36-37; Ezk 25:8-11; Am 2:1-2; Mc 6:5; Zph 2:8-9
[g] 2:10 Dt 1:28; Jos 11:21-22
[h] 2:11 Gn 14:5; 15:20; Jos 13:12; 2Sm 21:15-22
[i] Gn 14:5
[j] 2:12 Gn 14:6; 36:21,29-30
[k] 2:8-13 Nm 21:10-20
[l] 2:15 Ex 14:24; 23:27; Dt 7:23
[m] 1Co 10:1-5; Jd 5

[n] 2:19 Gn 19:36,38; Nm 21:24; Jdg 10:9-18; 1Sm 11:11; 12:12; Neh 4:7
[o] 2:20 Gn 14:5
[p] 2:23 Gn 10:14; 1Ch 1:12; Jr 47:4; Am 9:7
[q] 2:24 Dt 1:27
[r] 2:25 Ex 15:14-16; 23:27; Dt 11:25; Jos 2:9-11; 5:1; 9:3-6
[s] 2:26 Dt 20:10; Jdg 21:13
[t] 2:27 Nm 20:17

[A] **2:12** Lit *them before them*   [B] **2:23** Probably Crete   [C] **2:24** Or *provoke*

2:7 Moses wanted to instill in the new generation the confidence that, just as God had been faithful to their parents, he would be faithful to them.

2:10-12 The mention that **previously**, a very **tall** and impressive-looking people group lived in Moab, but had been driven out (2:10) was no doubt intended to encourage Israel that the tall inhabitants of Canaan were certainly not undefeatable either.

2:14-15 These **fighting men** didn't perish simply as a result of growing old (2:14). This is a solemn reminder that no matter how healthy, wealthy, or powerful you are, you will not suc-

ceed if you reject the Lord's will. His hand will be against you. Conversely, if you submit to his kingdom agenda, he will help you in your circumstances.

2:20-23 The land of the Ammonites had been previously inhabited by a **numerous** and **tall** people who had been driven out (2:21). This served as a message of encouragement to Israel that they could similarly displace the seeming giants that dwelled in the land of Canaan.

2:24-30 Moses had made **an offer of peace to King Sihon** (2:26-29). But the Lord knew in advance that the Amorite king would reject peace

with Israel. **God had made his . . . heart obstinate in order to hand him over to** them (2:30).

God similarly hardened Pharaoh's heart back in Egypt so that he could display his own great power and glory. The hardness of Pharaoh's heart, though, began with Pharaoh. He repeatedly defied God, stubbornly setting himself against him (see Exod 7:22; 8:15, 32). Finally, God gave Pharaoh what he wanted and hardened his heart even further (see Exod 9:12). Like Pharaoh, Sihon had been obstinate to begin with. A day arrived when God used his obstinacy to bring righteous judgment upon him.

*a*2:30 Ex 4:21; 7:3; Nm 21:23; 2Ch 36:13
*b*2:33 Dt 7:2,23; 20:13; 21:10; 31:5; Jos 8:7; 11:8
*c*2:34 Dt 20:16-18; 1Sm 15:9
*d*2:36 Nm 13:28; Ps 139:6; Pr 18:10-11; Is 2:11,17; 26:5
e Jos 13:9,16
*f*2:37 Nm 21:24; Jos 12:2
*g*2:24-37 Nm 21:21-31
*h*3:1 Nm 21:33; 32:33; Dt 1:4; 4:43,47; 29:7; 32:14; 33:22; Jos 9:10; 12:4-5; 13:11-12,30-31; 17:1; 20:8; 1Kg 4:19; Neh 9:22; Ps 22:12; 68:15; 135:11; 136:20; Is 2:13; Ezk 27:6
i Nm 21:33,35; Dt 1:4; 3:10; 29:6-7; Jos 12:4; 13:12,31
*j*3:2 Nm 21:23-26,34; Dt 2:33; Jdg 11:21
*k*3:3 Dt 2:34

*l*3:1-7 Nm 21:32-35
*m*3:8 Gn 50:10-11; Dt 1:1,5; Jos 1:14-15
*n*3:10 Jos 13:11
*o*3:11 Gn 14:5; 15:20; Dt 2:11,20-21
p Jos 13:25; 15:60; 2Sm 11:1; 12:29; Jr 49:2
q 1Sm 17:4
*r*3:12 Gn 28:4; Lv 20:24; Dt 4:5; 6:1; 7:1; 8:1; 12:29; 30:5

did for us, and the Moabites who live in Ar, until we cross the Jordan into the land the LORD our God is giving us.' ³⁰ But King Sihon of Heshbon would not let us travel through his land, for the LORD your God had made his spirit stubborn and his heart obstinate in order to hand him over to you, as has now taken place.*a*

³¹ "Then the LORD said to me, 'See, I have begun to give Sihon and his land to you. Begin to take possession of it.' ³² So Sihon and his whole army came out against us for battle at Jahaz. ³³ The LORD our God handed him over to us,*b* and we defeated him, his sons, and his whole army. ³⁴ At that time we captured all his cities and completely destroyed the people of every city, including the women and children. We left no survivors.*c* ³⁵ We took only the livestock and the spoil from the cities we captured as plunder for ourselves. ³⁶ There was no city that was inaccessible to*A,d* us, from Aroer on the rim of the Arnon Valley, along with the city in the valley, even as far as Gilead.*e* The LORD our God gave everything to us. ³⁷ But you did not go near the Ammonites' land, all along the bank of the Jabbok River,*f* the cities of the hill country, or any place that the LORD our God had forbidden.*g*

DEFEAT OF OG OF BASHAN

3 "Then we turned and went up the road to Bashan, and King Og of Bashan*h* came out against us with his whole army to do battle at Edrei.*i* ² But the LORD said to me, 'Do not fear him, for I have handed him over to you along with his whole army and his land. Do to him as you did to King Sihon of the Amorites,*j* who lived in Heshbon.' ³ So the LORD our God also handed over King Og of Bashan and his whole army to us. We struck him until there was no survivor left.*k* ⁴ We captured all his cities at that time. There wasn't a city that we didn't take from them: sixty cities, the entire region of Argob, the kingdom of Og in Bashan. ⁵ All these were fortified with high walls, gates, and bars, besides a large number of rural villages. ⁶ We completely destroyed them, as we had done to King Sihon of Heshbon, destroying the men, women, and children of every city. ⁷ But we took all the livestock and the spoil from the cities as plunder for ourselves.*l*

THE LAND OF THE TRANSJORDAN TRIBES

⁸ "At that time we took the land from the two Amorite kings across the Jordan,*m* from the Arnon Valley as far as Mount Hermon, ⁹ which the Sidonians call Sirion, but the Amorites call Senir, ¹⁰ all the cities of the plateau, Gilead, and Bashan as far as Salecah and Edrei, cities of Og's kingdom in Bashan.*n* ¹¹ (Only King Og of Bashan was left of the remnant of the Rephaim.*o* His bed*B* was made of iron. Isn't it in Rabbah of the Ammonites?*p* It is 13 ½ feet long and 6 feet wide by a standard measure.*C*)*q*

¹² "At that time we took possession of this land.*r* I gave to the Reubenites and Gadites the area extending from Aroer by the Arnon Valley, and half the hill country of Gilead along with its cities. ¹³ I gave to half the tribe of Manasseh the rest of Gilead and all Bashan, the kingdom of Og. The entire region of Argob, the whole territory of Bashan, used to be called the land of the Rephaim. ¹⁴ Jair, a descendant of Manasseh, took over the entire region of Argob as far as the border of the Geshurites and Maacathites. He called Bashan by his own name, Jair's Villages,*D* as it is today. ¹⁵ I gave Gilead to Machir, ¹⁶ and I gave to the Reubenites and Gadites the area extending from Gilead to the Arnon Valley (the middle of the valley was the border) and up to the Jabbok River, the border of the Ammonites. ¹⁷ The Arabah and Jordan are also borders from Chinnereth*E* as far as the Sea of the Arabah,

---

*A*2:36 Or *was too high for*   *B*3:11 Or *sarcophagus*   *C*3:11 Lit *nine cubits its length and four cubits its width, by a man's cubit*   *D*3:14 Or *Havvoth-jair*
*E*3:17 = the Sea of Galilee; Jos 12:3; 13:27; Lk 5:1

2:31 Though God makes promises to his children, we must obey him to secure them. God feeds the birds of the sky (see Matt 6:26). But they don't sit in their nests waiting for a special delivery of worms. They go out and obtain the food that God has provided.
2:32-36 The Amorites were **destroyed**, and Israel took all of their possessions (2:34-35). **There was no city that was inaccessible** (2:36). Compare this victory to what is recorded in 1:28, where the faithless scouts complained that the Canaanite cities were "fortified to the heavens." Moses wanted the new generation, which was about to face Canaan's fortified cities, to know that nothing could stand in their way if they gave themselves fully to obeying the Lord.
3:1-7 In Og's kingdom Israel captured **sixty cities**, which had **high walls** (3:4-6). High-walled cities were no barrier when God decided to hand an enemy over. The most spectacular example of that truth would come later at Jericho (see Josh 6:1-21).

3:11 King Og was the last **remnant of** a people group of gigantic physical size. **His bed was 13 ½ feet long and 6 feet wide.** Clearly, he was no puny king. His takedown testifies to the truth that the Lord is no puny god.
3:12-20 The **Reubenites**, the **Gadites**, and **half the tribe of Manasseh** had asked to dwell on the already-conquered east side of the Jordan rather than accompany the other tribes into Canaan (3:12-13; see Num 32:1-42). Yet they promised to help their brothers conquer the promised land before returning home (Deut 3:18-20).

the Dead Sea, under the slopes of Pisgah on the east.[a]

18 "I commanded you at that time: The LORD your God has given you this land to possess. All your valiant men will cross over in battle formation ahead of your brothers the Israelites. **19** But your wives, dependents, and livestock — I know that you have a lot of livestock — will remain in the cities I have given you[b] **20** until the LORD gives rest[c] to your brothers as he has to you, and they also take possession of the land the LORD your God is giving them across the Jordan. Then each of you may return to his possession that I have given you.[d]

THE TRANSFER OF ISRAEL'S LEADERSHIP

21 "I commanded Joshua at that time: Your own eyes have seen everything the LORD your God has done to these two kings. The LORD will do the same to all the kingdoms you are about to enter. **22** Don't be afraid of them, for the LORD your God fights for you. **23** "At that time I begged the LORD: **24** Lord GOD, you have begun to show your greatness and your strong hand to your servant, for what god is there in heaven or on earth who can perform deeds and mighty acts like yours? **25** Please let me cross over and see the beautiful land[e] on the other side of the Jordan, that good hill country and Lebanon.

26 "But the LORD was angry with me because of you[A] and would not listen to me. The LORD said to me, 'That's enough! Do not speak to me again about this matter. **27** Go to the top of Pisgah and look to the west, north, south, and east, and see it with your own eyes, for you will not cross the Jordan.[f] **28** But commission Joshua and

encourage and strengthen him, for he will cross over ahead of the people and enable them to inherit this land that you will see.'[g] **29** So we stayed in the valley facing Beth-peor.

CALL TO OBEDIENCE

4 "Now, Israel, listen to the statutes and ordinances[h] I am teaching you to follow, so that you may live,[i] enter, and take possession of the land the LORD, the God of your fathers,[j] is giving you. **2** You must not add anything to what I command you or take anything away from it,[k] so that you may keep the commands of the LORD your God I am giving you. **3** Your eyes have seen what the LORD did at Baal-peor, for the LORD your God destroyed every one of you who followed Baal of Peor.[l] **4** But you who have remained faithful[B] to the LORD your God are all alive today. **5** Look, I have taught you statutes and ordinances as the LORD my God has commanded me, so that you may follow them in the land you are entering to possess. **6** Carefully follow them, for this will show your wisdom and understanding in the eyes of the peoples. When they hear about all these statutes, they will say, 'This great nation is indeed a wise and understanding people.' **7** For what great nation is there that has a god near to it as the LORD our God is to us whenever we call to him?[m] **8** And what great nation has righteous statutes and ordinances like this entire law I set before you today?[n]

9 "Only be on your guard and diligently watch yourselves,[o] so that you don't forget[p] the things your eyes have seen and so that they don't slip from your mind[c] as long as you live. Teach them to your children and your grandchildren.[q] **10** The day

[a] 3:8-17 Nm 32:1-19,33-42; Jos 12:2-3
[b] 3:19 Dt 1:39; 2:35; 3:7
[c] 3:20 Gn 2:15; Ex 20:11; 23:12; 33:14; Nm 10:33,36; Dt 12:9-10; 25:19; 28:65; Jos 1:13,15; 21:44; 22:4; 23:1; Ru 1:9; 3:1; 2Sm 7:1,11; 1Kg 5:4; 8:56; 1Ch 6:31; 22:9; 28:2; 2Ch 6:41; Ps 23:2; 95:11; 116:7; 132:8,14; Is 11:10; 14:3,7; 28:12; 32:18; 63:14; 66:1; Heb 3:11–4:11
[d] 3:18-20 Nm 32:20-32; Jos 1:14-15
[e] 3:25 Dt 8:7
[f] 3:26-27 Nm 20:1-13

[g] 3:27-28 Nm 27:12-23
[h] 4:1 Ex 15:25; Lv 26:46; Dt 5:1; 11:32; 12:1; 26:16-17; Jos 24:25; 1Sm 30:25; 1Kg 9:4; Ezr 7:10; Ps 81:4; 147:19; Ezk 11:12; 20:18,25; 36:27; Mal 4:4
[i] Lv 25:18; Dt 4:40; 5:16,33; 8:1; 11:9; 26:15; 30:16; 2Kg 18:32; Ezk 18:9; Am 5:14
[j] Ex 3:13,15-16; Dt 1:11,21; 6:3; 12:1; 27:3; Jos 18:3; 2Ch 13:12; 28:9; 29:5; Ezr 8:28; 10:11
[k] 4:2 Dt 12:32; Pr 30:6; Mk 7:9-13; Rv 22:18-19
[l] 4:3 Ps 106:28; Hs 9:10; 1Co 10:8
[m] 4:7 1Kg 8:52; Ps 4:3; Is 55:6; Jr 11:14; Hs 11:7; Rm 10:12,14
[n] 4:8 Dt 11:26,32
[o] 4:9 Jos 22:5; Pr 13:3; 16:17; 19:16; 22:5
[p] Dt 6:12; 8:11; Pr 3:1; 4:5
[q] 4:9-10 Ex 12:26; Dt 6:7,20-25; 11:2-7,18-21; 31:12-13,19-22; 32:46; Jos 4:6,21-22; 8:35; Ps 34:11; 78:5

[A] 3:26 Or *me for your sake*   [B] 4:4 Lit *have held on*   [C] 4:9 Or *don't depart from your heart*

3:21-22 In other words, Moses said to his successor, "Don't worry about the enemies in the promised land, Joshua, because you've just seen what God can do to those who oppose him" **Don't be afraid of them, for the LORD your God fights for you** (3:22). (You too can be courageous to follow God's will for your life because he has your back.)

3:23-25 It seems the victories he had led in the Transjordan gave Moses hope that God was open to changing his mind about allowing him into Canaan (see Num 20:1-13). So Moses, whose intercessory prayers had been effective previously, **begged** God to let him **cross over** to **the beautiful land** (Deut 3:23, 25).

3:26-27 God, like a parent putting his foot down with regard to whether he would go

back on a decision, said to Moses, **That's enough!** (3:26). All he allowed Moses to do was to ascend Mount **Pisgah** and view the land from afar (3:27).

4:1-4 The people were to obey God and worship him alone, but in their short time as God's covenant people, Israel had repeatedly failed. Moses reminded them of one example with the mention of **Baal-peor** (4:3). There Israelite men were enticed into physical and spiritual adultery with Moabite women, worshiping the false god Baal (see Num 25:1-18; 31:13-16). God **destroyed** every Israelite **who followed Baal** (Deut 4:3). Yet Moses made a clear contrast between that group and his hearers: **But you who have remained faithful to the LORD your God are all alive today** (4:4). Obedience to the

Lord brings life and blessings; disobedience brings death and cursing. That's the message of Deuteronomy.

4:5-8 This is a wonderful indicator that when you faithfully follow the agenda of your divine King, those who don't know him will take notice that there is something different about your approach to life and will seek to learn about it.

4:9 Humans have an amazing tendency to forget God's goodness and fall into sin again and again. One way to help the people avoid this pitfall involved them regularly teaching God's ways to their **children** and **grandchildren**—that is, they needed to establish a godly legacy within their homes. Living faithfully as God's people requires that we transmit our faith to our offspring.

[a] 4:10 Gn 18:22; 19:27; Lv 9:5; Dt 10:8; 1Sm 6:20; 1Kg 22:21; 2Ch 20:13
[b] Dt 5:29; Is 57:11; Jr 5:22; 32:39; Zph 3:7; Mal 3:5
[c] 4:11 Ex 24:4; 32:19
[d] Ex 3:2; 19:18; Dt 5:23; 9:15; Heb 12:18
[e] Gn 15:12; Ex 20:21; Dt 5:22; 2Sm 22:10; 1Kg 8:12; 2Ch 6:1; Ps 18:9; 97:2; Is 60:2; Jr 13:16; Ezk 34:12; Jl 2:2; Zph 1:15
[f] 4:12 Ex 3:2-4; Dt 4:33,36; 5:4,22-26; 9:10; 10:4; 33:16; Ezk 1:4; Ac 7:30,35
[g] 4:9-12 Ex 19:10-19; Dt 5:8; Heb 12:18-19
[h] 4:13 Ex 2:24; 19:5; Lv 26:9,15,42,44; Dt 7:12; 8:18; 17:2; 31:16,20; Jos 7:11; Jdg 2:1,20; 2Kg 17:15; 18:12; Ps 25:10,14; 78:37; 103:18; 105:8; 106:45; 111:5,9
[i] Ex 34:28; Dt 10:4
[j] Ex 34:1,4; Dt 5:22; 10:1,3
[k] 4:19 Dt 17:3; Ezk 8:16; Zph 1:5; Ac 7:42
[l] Ps 19:1
[m] 4:20 1Kg 8:51; Jr 11:4
[n] 4:21 Dt 1:37
[o] Dt 8:7
[p] Dt 15:4

[q] 4:22 Dt 34:1-8
[r] 4:24 Ex 24:17; Dt 9:3; 2Sm 22:9; Is 29:6; 30:27,30; 34:14
[s] 4:23-24 Ex 20:5; 34:14; Dt 5:9; 6:15; Jos 24:19; Heb 12:29
[t] 4:26 Dt 8:19
[u] 4:27 Lv 26:33; Dt 28:64; 1Kg 14:15; Neh 1:8; Est 3:8; Ps 44:11; 106:27; Jr 9:16; 31:10; Ezk 6:8; 11:16-17; 12:15; Zch 1:19,21; 2:6
[v] 4:29 Jr 29:13
[w] 4:31 Lv 26:45; Dt 5:3; 7:12; 8:18; 31:20
[x] Ex 34:6

you stood before the Lord your God[a] at Horeb, the Lord said to me, 'Assemble the people before me, and I will let them hear my words, so that they may learn to fear me[b] all the days they live on the earth and may instruct their children.' [11] You came near and stood at the base of the mountain,[c] a mountain blazing with fire[d] into the heavens and enveloped in a totally black cloud.[e] [12] Then the Lord spoke to you from the fire.[f] You kept hearing the sound of the words, but didn't see a form; there was only a voice.[g] [13] He declared his covenant[h] to you. He commanded you to follow the Ten Commandments,[i] which he wrote on two stone tablets.[j] [14] At that time the Lord commanded me to teach you statutes and ordinances for you to follow in the land you are about to cross into and possess.

WORSHIPING THE TRUE GOD

[15] "Diligently watch yourselves — because you did not see any form on the day the Lord spoke to you out of the fire at Horeb — [16] so you don't act corruptly and make an idol for yourselves in the shape of any figure: a male or female form, [17] or the form of any animal on the earth, any winged creature that flies in the sky, [18] any creature that crawls on the ground, or any fish in the waters under the earth. [19] When you look to the heavens and see the sun, moon, and stars — all the stars in the sky — do not be led astray to bow in worship to them and serve them.[k] The Lord your God has provided them for all people everywhere under heaven.[l] [20] But the Lord selected you and brought you out of Egypt's iron furnace[m] to be a people for his inheritance, as you are today.

[21] "The Lord was angry with me on your account.[n] He swore that I would not cross the Jordan and enter the good land[o] the Lord your God is giving you as an inheritance.[p] [22] I won't be crossing the Jordan because I am going to die in this land.[q] But you are about to cross over and take possession of this good land. [23] Be careful not to forget the covenant of the Lord your God that he made with you, and make an idol for yourselves in the shape of anything he has forbidden you. [24] For the Lord your God is a consuming fire,[r] a jealous God.[s]

[25] "When you have children and grandchildren and have been in the land a long time, and if you act corruptly, make an idol in the form of anything, and do what is evil in the sight of the Lord your God, angering him, [26] I call heaven and earth as witnesses against you today that you will quickly perish[t] from the land you are about to cross the Jordan to possess. You will not live long there, but you will certainly be destroyed. [27] The Lord will scatter you among the peoples,[u] and you will be reduced to a few survivors[A] among the nations where the Lord your God will drive you. [28] There you will worship man-made gods of wood and stone, which cannot see, hear, eat, or smell. [29] But from there, you will search for the Lord your God, and you will find him when you seek him with all your heart and all your soul.[v] [30] When you are in distress and all these things have happened to you, in the future you will return to the Lord your God and obey him. [31] He will not leave you, destroy you, or forget the covenant[w] with your fathers that he swore to them by oath, because the Lord your God is a compassionate God.[x]

[32] "Indeed, ask about the earlier days that preceded you, from the day God created mankind[B] on the earth and from one end of the heavens to the other: Has anything like this great event ever happened, or has anything like it been heard of? [33] Has a people heard God's voice speaking from the fire as you have, and lived? [34] Or has a god attempted to go and take a nation as his own out of another nation,

[A] 4:27 Lit be left few in number   [B] 4:32 Or Adam

4:12 The people had been given no image to associate with their deity. God did not reveal himself in a physical **form**; therefore, Israel was not to worship physical images.
4:13-14 Instead of revealing an image of himself, the Lord revealed his own character and his will for his people in the form of **the Ten Commandments** (4:13). If they truly had reverential awe of him, they would fear disobeying his Word (4:14).
4:15-20 Moses pointed out that on the day Israel entered a covenant with the Lord, they saw no **form** of the Lord—no shape of

a person or animal (4:15). To worship an **idol** in the shape of anything would only corrupt them; the Lord was not to be represented in such a manner (4:16-19).
4:23-24 Idolatry is spiritual adultery, a theme that will be highlighted throughout the Old Testament. Like a faithful husband whose wife has broken the marriage covenant, the Lord expresses righteous jealousy for his people when they turn from his love and their own promises to cozy up to strangers.
4:29-31 Moses said, **You will search for the Lord your God, and you will find him when**

you seek him with all your heart (4:29). This, in fact, is a promise that is still available today. Though you may have strayed far from God, if you turn to him in true repentance, he will not hide from you but will allow himself to be found. He is **a compassionate God** (4:30-31).
4:32-40 What should knowledge of the unique and incomparable God drive people of all times to do? To **keep his statutes and commands . . . so that [we and our] children after [us] may prosper** (4:40).

by trials, signs, wonders, and war, by a strong hand and an outstretched arm, by great terrors, as the LORD your God did for you in Egypt before your eyes? **35** You were shown these things so that you would know that the LORD is God; there is no other besides him.*ᵃ* **36** He let you hear his voice from heaven to instruct you.*ᵇ* He showed you his great fire on earth, and you heard his words from the fire.*ᶜ* **37** Because he loved*ᵈ* your fathers, he chose their descendants after them and brought you out of Egypt by his presence and great power, **38** to drive out before you nations greater and stronger than you and to bring you in and give you their land as an inheritance,*ᵉ* as is now taking place. **39** Today, recognize and keep in mind that the LORD is God in heaven above and on earth below; there is no other. **40** Keep his statutes and commands, which I am giving you today, so that you and your children after you may prosper and so that you may live long in the land the LORD your God is giving you for all time."

CITIES OF REFUGE

41 Then Moses set apart three cities across the Jordan to the east. **42** Someone could flee there who committed manslaughter, killing his neighbor accidentally without previously hating him. He could flee to one of these cities and stay alive: **43** Bezer in the wilderness on the plateau land, belonging to the Reubenites; Ramoth in Gilead, belonging to the Gadites; or Golan in Bashan, belonging to the Manassites.*ᶠ*

INTRODUCTION TO THE LAW

44 This is the law Moses gave the Israelites. **45** These are the decrees, statutes, and ordinances Moses proclaimed to them after they came out of Egypt, **46** across the Jordan in the valley facing Beth-peor in the land of King Sihon of the Amorites. He lived in Heshbon, and Moses and the Israelites defeated him after they came out of

Egypt. **47** They took possession of his land and the land of Og king of Bashan, the two Amorite kings who were across the Jordan to the east, **48** from Aroer on the rim of the Arnon Valley as far as Mount Sion (that is, Hermon) **49** and all the Arabah on the east side of the Jordan as far as the Dead Sea below the slopes of Pisgah.

THE TEN COMMANDMENTS

5 Moses summoned all Israel and said to them, "Israel, listen to the statutes and ordinances I am proclaiming as you hear them today. Learn and follow them carefully. **2** The LORD our God made a covenant*ᵍ* with us at Horeb. **3** He did not make this covenant with our fathers,*ʰ* but with all of us who are alive here today. **4** The LORD spoke to you face to face from the fire on the mountain. **5** At that time I was standing between the LORD and you to report the word*^* of the LORD to you, because you were afraid of the fire and did not go up the mountain. And he said:

6   I am the LORD your God,*ⁱ* who brought you out of the land of Egypt, out of the place of slavery.*ʲ*

7   Do not have other gods besides me.

8   Do not make an idol for yourself in the shape of anything in the heavens above or on the earth below or in the waters under the earth. **9** Do not bow in worship to them, and do not serve them, because I, the LORD your God, am a jealous God, punishing the children for the fathers' iniquity to the third and fourth generations of those who hate me,*ᵏ* **10** but showing faithful love to a thousand generations of those who love me and keep my commands.

11   Do not misuse the name*ˡ* of the LORD your God, because the LORD will not leave anyone unpunished who misuses his name.

12   Be careful to remember the Sabbath day, to keep it holy as the LORD your

ᵃ 4:35 1Kg 8:60; Is 43:11; 44:8; 45:5-6,18-22; 46:9; Dn 3:29; Jl 2:27; Mk 12:32
ᵇ 4:36 Ex 20:22
ᶜ Ex 19:18
ᵈ 4:37 Dt 7:6-8; 10:15; 23:5; 33:3; Jr 31:3; Hs 11:1; Mal 1:2
ᵉ 4:38 Lv 20:24
ᶠ 4:41-43 Nm 35:6-15; Dt 19:2-13; Jos 20:7-9

ᵍ 5:2 Dt 31:16
ʰ 5:3 Dt 4:31
ⁱ 5:6-21 Ex 20:2-17; Dt 8:14
ʲ 5:6 Lv 26:13; Dt 6:12; 8:14; 13:5,10; Jos 24:17; Jr 34:13
ᵏ 5:9 Ex 34:7; Nm 14:18; Dt 7:10; Ezk 18
ˡ 5:11 Ex 3:13; 6:3; 33:19

*^*5:5 One Hb ms, DSS, Sam, LXX, Syr, Vg read *words*

5:1-21 Israel was to **learn and follow** the **statutes and ordinances** they had received (5:1-2). Notice the imperatives: "Learn *and* follow." If you get no further than acquiring an intellectual knowledge of the Bible, you haven't gone far enough. A football team might have an expert understanding of the rules of the game. But, if the coach and players fail to put those rules into practice, the only thing they will obtain will be a losing record.

5:3-4 In effect Moses was telling those standing before him in verse 3, "This isn't merely your father's covenant I'm talking about; this is *your* covenant. Your fathers are gone; now *you* are God's covenant partners. He expects obedience from *you*." When God **spoke** with the previous generation of Israelites **from the fire** years before (5:4), he was speaking to all future generations.

5:6 This preamble to the commands sets the context for them: **I am the LORD your**

God, who brought you . . . out of the place of slavery. This is a reminder that the law was not given for Israel's redemption; they had already been redeemed from Egypt when he gave it to them. No one is saved by keeping the law, then. Rather, the law provided the means for a redeemed people to express their reciprocal love for the holy God who had saved them.

5:7-21 See Exod 20:1-17 and the notes there on the Ten Commandments.

*a*5:16–20 Mt 19:18–19; Mk 10:19; Lk 18:20; Rm 13:9
*b*5:16 Mt 15:4; Mk 7:10; Eph 6:2–3
*c*5:17 Mt 5:21; Jms 2:11
*d*5:18 Mt 5:27
*e*5:20 Pr 25:18

*f*5:16–21 Mt 19:18–19; Mk 10:19; Lk 18:20; Rm 13:9
*g*5:22–27 Ex 20:18–21

❧ KINGDOM LIVING ❧
FAMILY
A Parent's Task to Teach

If you have children, you are responsible to make sure that the truth you are learning is transmitted to them. After all, if you don't teach God's Word to your family, there is someone else out there who has another word he would be glad to share.

Satan has his own message, kingdom, and effective instructors who would be glad to teach your children for you. Some of these teachers are on the streets, some are in the school system, and some may even attend your church. In fact, your child could be sitting next to another kid in Sunday school whose lack of regard for God will rub off on him or her.

Therefore, we have to teach our children diligently—not occasionally. That may mean turning off the television and using the time for teaching. In any case, you have to carve out time with your family to teach the Word. Neither the government nor the church has been charged to do what parents are supposed to do. But if you as a kingdom parent will go about raising kingdom kids, I have good news for you. If you give your kids God's Word early in life, the Holy Spirit has something to hook on to and bring them back should they take a bad turn.

If you are single and don't have your own children, then look for children in your circle of influence who may not have Christian parents involved in their lives. They could be nieces, nephews, or kids at a local school or church whom you could mentor in God's Word. In the body of Christ, everyone is part of a family.

FOR THE NEXT FAMILY
KINGDOM LIVING LESSON SEE PAGE 733.

God has commanded you. **13** You are to labor six days and do all your work, **14** but the seventh day is a Sabbath to the Lord your God. Do not do any work — you, your son or daughter, your male or female slave, your ox or donkey, any of your livestock, or the resident alien who lives within your city gates, so that your male and female slaves may rest as you do.

15 Remember that you were a slave in the land of Egypt, and the Lord your God brought you out of there with a strong hand and an outstretched arm. That is why the Lord your God has commanded you to keep the Sabbath day.

16 Honor your father and your mother,*a* as the Lord your God has commanded you, so that you may live long and so that you may prosper in the land the Lord your God is giving you.*b*

17 Do not murder.*c*

18 Do not commit adultery.*d*

19 Do not steal.

20 Do not give dishonest testimony against your neighbor.*e*

21 Do not covet your neighbor's wife or desire your neighbor's house, his field, his male or female slave, his ox or donkey, or anything that belongs to your neighbor.*f*

THE PEOPLE'S RESPONSE

22 "The Lord spoke these commands in a loud voice to your entire assembly from the fire, cloud, and total darkness on the mountain; he added nothing more. He wrote them on two stone tablets and gave them to me. **23** All of you approached me with your tribal leaders and elders when you heard the voice from the darkness and while the mountain was blazing with fire. **24** You said, 'Look, the Lord our God has shown us his glory and greatness, and we have heard his voice from the fire. Today we have seen that God speaks with a person, yet he still lives. **25** But now, why should we die? This great fire will consume us and we will die if we hear the voice of the Lord our God any longer. **26** For who out of all mankind has heard the voice of the living God speaking from the fire, as we have, and lived? **27** Go near and listen to everything the Lord our God says. Then you can tell us everything the Lord our God tells you; we will listen and obey.'*g*

28 "The Lord heard your^A words when you spoke to me. He said to me, 'I have

^5:28 Lit *the sound of your*

5:27 It would take the new covenant sacrifice of Jesus Christ to make it possible for those who trust him to receive new hearts with the capacity to obey him steadfastly as the people had promised to do (see Heb 8:7-13).

➵ Questions & Answers ➴

Q You have described a time in your journey when your conceptual or intellectual knowledge of God was not matched with an experiential, loving knowledge of God. What are some ways we can avoid this split between our heads and our hearts when it comes to knowing God better?

A There exists a tendency to accumulate data in the brain that doesn't change the life. In seminary, because I was being overwhelmed with information to learn and study, I found myself drying up. I found myself acquiring knowledge upon knowledge, while lacking spiritual growth.

The secret to experiencing the God about whom you are learning is to identify something you wish to apply based on the information you are receiving. The moment application is connected to information, there is the transfer of the information into experience. When you keep application and information separate from each other, you accumulate data without it having any effect on you. As a result, you may be able to quote the Bible and expound theology, but it's not doing anything for you, to you, through you, or in you. Thus, the key is to marry application with information, while depending on the Holy Spirit to make it experiential in your life.

FOR THE NEXT Q&A, SEE PAGE 234.

heard the words that these people have spoken to you. Everything they have said is right. ²⁹ If only they had such a heart to fear me and keep all my commands always, so that they and their children would prosper forever. ³⁰ Go and tell them: Return to your tents. ³¹ But you stand here with me, and I will tell you every command — the statutes and ordinances — you are to teach them, so that they may follow them in the land I am giving them to possess.'

³² "Be careful to do as the LORD your God has commanded you; you are not to turn aside to the right or the left. ³³ Follow the whole instruction the LORD your God has commanded you, so that you may live, prosper, and have a long life in the land you will possess.

THE GREATEST COMMAND

6 "This is the command — the statutes and ordinances — the LORD your God has commanded me to teach you, so that you may follow them in the land you are about to enter and possess.^a ² Do this so that you may fear^b the LORD your God^c all the days of your life^d by keeping all his statutes and commands I am giving you, your son, and your grandson, and so that you may have a long life.^e ³ Listen, Israel, and be careful to follow them, so that you may prosper and multiply greatly, because the LORD, the God of your fathers, has promised you a land flowing with milk and honey.^f

---

APPLICATION QUESTIONS

READ DEUTERONOMY 6:4-9

– What emotions do you experience when you read these verses?
– How do these verses emphasize the importance of first seeking God and his kingdom?

---

⁴ "Listen, Israel: The LORD our God, the LORD is one.^{A,g} ⁵ Love the LORD your God with all your heart, with all your soul, and with all your strength.^h ⁶ These words that I am giving you today are to be in your heart.ⁱ ⁷ Repeat them to your children.^j Talk about them when you sit in your house and when you walk along the road, when you lie down and when you get up. ⁸ Bind them as a sign on your hand and let them

---

^A 6:4 Or *the LORD is our God; the LORD is one*, or *The LORD is our God, the LORD alone*, or *The LORD our God is one LORD*

6:3-9 These verses are known in Judaism as the *Shema*, which is the Hebrew word that begins 6:4; it means "listen, hear." Moses was calling the people to sit up and take notes on what he was about to say because of its importance.
6:5 Jesus would later call this "the greatest and most important command" (Matt 22:37-39).
6:7 If the Israelites were going to thrive in the promised land, the family unit would have to become the primary place where faith in and love for the Lord was modeled and transferred. Parents are to teach God's ways

regularly to their children in the everyday events of life.
    While it's good for families to have formal teaching times, the powerful witness of a godly lifestyle that incorporates God's Word in each day's routine cannot be overstated. Notice how regularly Israel was to speak of the things of God: **when you sit in your house and when you walk along the road, when you lie down and when you get up.** That effort to welcome the Lord to be part of all aspects of life is how parents can transfer to their children a biblical worldview so that God is their

point of reference as they navigate choices. The family carries the primary responsibility for passing along the torch of faith as the church supports parents in that work.
6:8 Many Jews took the command to **bind** God's words on their **forehead** literally. They wrote Deuteronomy 6:4-9 on tiny scrolls, placed them in small boxes called phylacteries, and tied them to their foreheads. This was the practice that Jesus would have in view when he condemned scribes and Pharisees who enlarged their phylacteries to draw attention to themselves (see Matt 23:5).

a 6:8 Ex 13:16; Dt 11:18
b 6:10-11 Jos 24:13
c 6:11 Dt 8:10; Neh 9:25
d 6:12 Lv 26:13; Dt 5:6;
8:14; 13:5,10; Jos 24:17;
Jr 34:13
e 6:13 Dt 10:12,20; 13:4; Jos
24:14; 1Sm 12:24; Mt 4:10;
Lk 4:8; Rv 14:7
f 6:15 Dt 5:9
g 6:16 Ex 15:25; 16:4; Nm
14:22; Ps 78:18,41,56;
106:14; Mal 3:15; Mt 4:7;
Lk 4:12
h Ex 17:1-7; Dt 9:22; 33:8;
Ps 95:8-9
i 6:18 Dt 8:7
j Dt 1:35
k 6:19 Ex 34:11
l 6:20 Jos 4:21
m 6:21 Ex 3:19; 6:1; 13:9;
32:11; Nm 20:20; Dt 4:34;
5:15; 7:8; 9:26; 26:8; Ps
136:12; Jr 32:21; Ezk 20:33-
34; Dn 9:15
n 6:22 Neh 9:10; Ps 135:9;
Is 20:3; Jr 32:20

o 7:1-5 Ex 23:23-26
p 7:1 Dt 3:12
q Ac 13:19
r Ex 1:9
s 7:2 Dt 20:17
t Pr 6:34; Is 9:17; 13:18;
27:11; 47:6; Jr 13:14; Hs
1:6,8; 2:4,23
u 7:3 Jos 23:12-13; 1Kg 11:1-
2; Ezr 9:12,14
v 7:4 Dt 13:6,13; 17:3;
28:36,64; 29:26; Jos 23:16;
24:16; 1Sm 26:19; Jr 16:13
w Ex 22:24; Dt 11:17; 31:17;
Jos 23:16
x 7:5 Ex 34:13; Dt 12:2-3;
Jdg 2:2
y 7:6 Ex 22:31; Dt 14:2,21;
26:19; 28:9; Ps 16:3; Is
62:12; 63:18; Dn 8:24; 12:7
z Ex 19:5; Dt 14:2; 26:18-19;
Ps 135:4; Ec 2:8; Mal 3:17
aa 7:8 Dt 4:37

be a symbol[A] on your forehead.[B,a] **9** Write them on the doorposts of your house and on your city gates.

REMEMBERING GOD THROUGH OBEDIENCE

10 "When the LORD your God brings you into the land he swore to your fathers Abraham, Isaac, and Jacob that he would give you — a land with large and beautiful cities that you did not build, **11** houses full of every good thing that you did not fill them with, cisterns that you did not dig, and vineyards and olive groves that you did not plant[b] — and when you eat and are satisfied,[c] **12** be careful not to forget the LORD who brought you out of the land of Egypt, out of the place of slavery.[d] **13** Fear the LORD your God, worship him, and take your oaths in his name.[e] **14** Do not follow other gods, the gods of the peoples around you, **15** for the LORD your God, who is among you, is a jealous God.[f] Otherwise, the LORD your God will become angry with you and obliterate you from the face of the earth. **16** Do not test[g] the LORD your God as you tested him at Massah.[h] **17** Carefully observe the commands of the LORD your God, the decrees and statutes he has commanded you. **18** Do what is right and good in the LORD's sight, so that you may prosper and so that you may enter and possess the good land[i] the LORD your God swore to give your fathers,[j] **19** by driving out all your enemies before you, as the LORD has said.[k]

20 "When your son asks you in the future, 'What is the meaning[l] of the decrees, statutes, and ordinances that the LORD our God has commanded you?' **21** tell him, 'We were slaves of Pharaoh in Egypt, but the LORD brought us out of Egypt with a strong hand.[m] **22** Before our eyes the LORD inflicted great and devastating signs and wonders on Egypt,[n] on Pharaoh, and on all his household, **23** but he brought us from there in order to lead us in and give us the land that he swore to our fathers. **24** The LORD commanded us to follow all these statutes and to fear the LORD our God for our prosperity always and for our preservation, as it is today. **25** Righteousness will be ours if we are careful to follow every one of these commands before the LORD our God, as he has commanded us.'

ISRAEL TO DESTROY IDOLATROUS NATIONS

7 "When the LORD your God brings you into the land[o] you are entering to possess,[p] and he drives out many nations before you — the Hethites, Girgashites, Amorites, Canaanites, Perizzites, Hivites and Jebusites, seven nations[q] more numerous and powerful than you[r] — **2** and when the LORD your God delivers them over to you and you defeat them, you must completely destroy[s] them. Make no treaty with them and show them no mercy.[t] **3** You must not intermarry with them, and you must not give your daughters to their sons or take their daughters for your sons,[u] **4** because they will turn your sons away from me to worship other gods.[v] Then the LORD's anger will burn against you,[w] and he will swiftly destroy you. **5** Instead, this is what you are to do to them: tear down their altars, smash their sacred pillars, cut down their Asherah poles,[x] and burn their carved images. **6** For you are a holy people[y] belonging to the LORD your God. The LORD your God has chosen you to be his own possession[z] out of all the peoples on the face of the earth.

7 "The LORD had his heart set on you and chose you, not because you were more numerous than all peoples, for you were the fewest of all peoples. **8** But because the LORD loved[aa] you and kept the oath he

---

[A]6:8 Or *phylactery*; Mt 23:5   [B]6:8 Lit *symbol between your eyes*

6:10-12 The Israelites were about to enter a **land** of instant prosperity. There were abundant **cities . . . houses . . . cisterns . . . vineyards and olive groves** in Canaan—none of which Israel had lifted a finger to develop (6:10-11). All they had to do was take the land and enjoy its riches. Moses had spent forty years in the wilderness with these people's parents, and he knew the sinful human tendency to **forget** God's past deliverance and provision when times are good (6:12). Thus, he gave this warning.
6:14-15 If Israel ceased to **fear the LORD** and turned instead to **follow other gods** (6:13-14), the Lord would **obliterate** them (6:15). This taking over of Canaan was no game. Israel

was to represent the one true and living God to the surrounding nations. His glory was at stake.
6:16 *Massah* means "testing." There Israel had complained against Moses and the Lord because they had no water (see Exod 17:1-7).
6:20-25 When Israelite children would ask their parents what these **decrees, statutes, and ordinances** meant (6:20), the parents were to give a God-glorifying answer. Notice that they were expected to be informed and quick to reply with truth. This is the kind of informed teaching that children need today. We must remind them of God's miraculous acts of grace, exhorting them to trust and obey him for the blessings promised.

7:1-2 Moses could speak of the conquest as if it were an accomplished fact because the Lord would deliver their enemies into their hands. Israel was to **completely destroy them** (7:2) because of the wicked practices of the Canaanites (see Lev 18:1-30; Deut 18:9-14).
7:5-6 The only safeguard against idolatry's spread was the destruction of the Canaanite idols. The Lord is a holy God; therefore, his people are to live as **holy people** (7:6).
7:7-8 This passage reminds us as Christians that we were not saved because we were something special or because we sought God's help. It all began with God's love: "He loved us and sent his Son to be the atoning sacrifice for our sins" (1 John 4:10).

swore to your fathers, he brought you out with a strong hand and redeemed[a] you from the place of slavery, from the power of Pharaoh king of Egypt. **9** Know that the LORD your God is God, the faithful God who keeps his gracious covenant loyalty for a thousand generations with those who love him and keep his commands.[b] **10** But he directly pays back[A] and destroys those who hate him.[c] He will not hesitate to pay back directly[B] the one who hates him. **11** So keep the command — the statutes and ordinances — that I am giving you to follow today.

12 "If you listen to and are careful to keep these ordinances, the LORD your God will keep his covenant loyalty with you, as he swore to your fathers.[d] **13** He will love you, bless you, and multiply you. He will bless your offspring,[c,e] and the produce of your land — your grain, new wine, and fresh oil — the young of your herds, and the newborn of your flocks, in the land he swore to your fathers that he would give you. **14** You will be blessed above all peoples; there will be no infertile male or female among you or your livestock. **15** The LORD will remove all sickness from you; he will not put on you[f] all the terrible diseases of Egypt that you know about, but he will inflict them on all who hate you. **16** You must destroy all the peoples the LORD your God is delivering over to you and not look on them with pity. Do not worship their gods, for that will be a snare to you.

17 "If you say to yourself, 'These nations are greater than I; how can I drive them out?' **18** do not be afraid of them. Be sure to remember what the LORD your God did to Pharaoh and all Egypt: **19** the great trials that you saw, the signs and wonders, the strong hand and outstretched arm, by which the LORD your God brought you out. The LORD your God will do the same to all the peoples you fear. **20** The LORD your

God will also send hornets against them until all the survivors and those hiding from you perish.[g] **21** Don't be terrified of them, for the LORD your God, a great and awesome God, is among you. **22** The LORD your God will drive out these nations before you little by little. You will not be able to destroy them all at once; otherwise, the wild animals will become too numerous for you.[h] **23** The LORD your God will give them over to you and throw them into great confusion until they are destroyed. **24** He will hand their kings over to you, and you will wipe out their names under heaven. No one will be able to stand against you; you will annihilate them. **25** Burn up the carved images of their gods. Don't covet the silver and gold on the images and take it for yourself, or else you will be ensnared by it, for it is detestable to the LORD your God. **26** Do not bring any detestable thing into your house, or you will be set apart for destruction like it. You are to abhor and detest it utterly because it is set apart for destruction.

REMEMBER THE LORD

8 "Carefully follow every command I am giving you today, so that you may live and increase, and may enter and take possession of the land[i] the LORD swore to your fathers. **2** Remember that the LORD your God led you on the entire journey these forty years in the wilderness, so that he might humble you and test you to know what was in your heart, whether or not you would keep his commands. **3** He humbled you by letting you go hungry; then he gave you manna to eat, which you and your fathers had not known, so that you might learn that man does not live on bread alone but on every word that comes from the mouth of the LORD.[j] **4** Your clothing did not wear out, and your feet did not swell these forty years.[k] **5** Keep in mind that the

[a] 7:8 Dt 9:26; 15:15; 24:18
[b] 7:9 Neh 1:5; Dn 9:4
[c] 7:10 Ex 34:6-7
[d] 7:12 Dt 4:31
[e] 7:13 Dt 28:4
[f] 7:15 Ex 15:26; 23:25; Dt 28:27,60

[g] 7:20 Ex 23:28; Jos 24:12
[h] 7:22 Ex 23:29-30
[i] 8:1 Dt 3:12
[j] 8:3 Mt 4:4; Lk 4:4
[k] 8:4 Dt 29:5; Neh 9:21

[A] 7:10 Lit *He pays back to their faces*   [B] 7:10 Lit *to pay back to their faces*   [C] 7:13 Lit *bless the fruit of your womb*

7:9-11 Given this insight into God's character (7:9-10), the only wise thing Israel could do was to keep the commands and ordinances of God that Moses was laying out for them (7:11). This principle is still applicable to us.

7:17-24 Even as seemingly weak Israel prepared to walk into the future God had prepared for them, Pharaoh's mighty chariot army lay at the bottom of the Red Sea. So Moses said, **The LORD your God will do the same to all the peoples you fear.... Don't be terrified** (7:19, 21). The ultimate cure for fear is awareness of the presence and power of God.

7:25-26 As the gold in the tabernacle was holy because it was devoted to the Lord's service, so the **gold** of the Canaanites was **detestable** because it was devoted to **the images** of their gods (7:25). Thus, the possessions of the Canaanites were to be devoted to **destruction** (7:26).

8:2 God's classroom for teaching the Israelites humble dependence on and obedience to him was **the wilderness**, where he tested them to find out if they **would keep his commands**. In a sense, all believers must go through a wilderness of testing before God will let us reach our destinies. Israel needed to find out if

their faith in God would hold strong in a place where they had to depend on him for everything: food, water, clothing, protection. The testing of our faith gives us similar insight.

8:3 The **manna** that sustained their lives arrived by God's word, as did everything good they received. Keeping God's Word and past provision at the forefront of our thoughts in times of testing will bring us spiritual victory.

8:5 God is the ultimate parent who **disciplines** his children for their own good. Hebrews reminds us, "No discipline seems enjoyable at the time, but painful. Later on, however, it yields the peaceful fruit of righteousness" (Heb 12:11).

[a]8:7 Ex 3:8; Nm 14:7; Dt 1:25,35; 3:25; 4:21-22; 6:18; 8:10; 9:6; 11:17; Jos 23:16
[b]8:10 Dt 11:15
[c]Dt 8:7
[d]8:14 Lv 26:13; Dt 5:6; 6:12; 13:5,10; Jos 24:17; Jr 34:13
[e]8:16 Ex 16:4
[f]8:18 Dt 4:31
[g]8:19 Dt 4:26
[h]9:1 Dt 4:38; 11:23; Jos 17:18; Jdg 1:19
[i]Dt 1:28
[j]9:2 Dt 2:10; Jos 11:21-22; 14:12,15
[k]Nm 13:22; Jos 15:13-14; 21:11; Jdg 1:20
[l]9:3 Dt 31:3; Jos 3:11
[m]Ex 24:17; Dt 4:24; Is 29:6; 30:27,30; 33:14; Ezk 15:7; 19:12
[n]Dt 12:2; Jos 23:13
[o]9:4 Ps 31:1; 89:16; 119:40; Ezk 14:14,20; 18:22
[p]Pr 11:5
[q]9:6 Dt 8:7
[r]Ex 32:9; 33:3,5; 34:9; Dt 9:13
[s]9:7–10:11 Ex 32–34

LORD your God has been disciplining you
just as a man disciplines his son. 6 So keep
the commands of the LORD your God by
walking in his ways and fearing him. 7 For
the LORD your God is bringing you into a
good land,[a] a land with streams, springs,
and deep water sources, flowing in both
valleys and hills; 8 a land of wheat, barley,
vines, figs, and pomegranates; a land of olive oil and honey; 9 a land where you will
eat food without shortage, where you will
lack nothing; a land whose rocks are iron
and from whose hills you will mine copper. 10 When you eat and are full,[b] you will
bless the LORD your God for the good land[c]
he has given you.
11 "Be careful that you don't forget the
LORD your God by failing to keep his commands, ordinances, and statutes that I am
giving you today. 12 When you eat and are
full, and build beautiful houses to live in,
13 and your herds and flocks grow large,
and your silver and gold multiply, and
everything else you have increases, 14 be
careful that your heart doesn't become
proud and you forget the LORD your God
who brought you out of the land of Egypt,
out of the place of slavery.[d] 15 He led you
through the great and terrible wilderness
with its poisonous[A] snakes and scorpions,
a thirsty land where there was no water.
He brought water out of the flint rock
for you. 16 He fed you in the wilderness
with manna,[e] which your fathers had not
known, in order to humble and test you,
so that in the end he might cause you to
prosper. 17 You may say to yourself, 'My
power and my own ability have gained
this wealth for me,' 18 but remember that
the LORD your God gives you the power to
gain wealth, in order to confirm his covenant he swore to your fathers,[f] as it is today. 19 If you ever forget the LORD your God
and follow other gods to serve them and
bow in worship to them, I testify against
you today that you will perish.[g] 20 Like the
nations the LORD is about to destroy before
you, you will perish if you do not obey the
LORD your God.

WARNING AGAINST SELF-RIGHTEOUSNESS

9 "Listen, Israel: Today you are about
to cross the Jordan to enter and drive
out nations greater and stronger than
you,[h] with large cities fortified to the heavens.[i] 2 The people are strong and tall, the
descendants of the Anakim.[j] You know
about them and you have heard it said
about them, 'Who can stand up to the sons
of Anak?'[k] 3 But understand that today the
LORD your God will cross over ahead of
you[l] as a consuming fire;[m] he will devastate and subdue them before you. You will
drive them out and destroy them swiftly,[n]
as the LORD has told you. 4 When the LORD
your God drives them out before you, do
not say to yourself, 'The LORD brought me
in to take possession of this land because of
my righteousness.'[o] Instead, the LORD will
drive out these nations before you because
of their wickedness.[p] 5 You are not going
to take possession of their land because
of your righteousness or your integrity.
Instead, the LORD your God will drive out
these nations before you because of their
wickedness, in order to fulfill the promise
he swore to your fathers, Abraham, Isaac,
and Jacob. 6 Understand that the LORD
your God is not giving you this good land[q]
to possess because of your righteousness,
for you are a stiff-necked people.[r]

ISRAEL'S REBELLION AND MOSES'S INTERCESSION

7 "Remember[s] and do not forget how you
provoked the LORD your God in the wilderness. You have been rebelling against
the LORD from the day you left the land
of Egypt until you reached this place.
8 You provoked the LORD at Horeb, and he
was angry enough with you to destroy
you. 9 When I went up the mountain to
receive the stone tablets, the tablets of

[A]8:15 Lit *burning*

8:6-11 With prosperity comes the temptation to **forget the LORD . . . by failing to keep his commands** (8:11).

8:12-17 There's little worse than a person who has come from humble circumstances through the help and mercy of others acting like his change of fortune came about by his own merit, essentially claiming, **My power and my own ability have gained this wealth for me** (8:17). Later, Paul told the Romans, "I tell everyone among you not to think of himself more highly than he should" (Rom 12:3). And Peter said, "God resists the proud but gives grace to the humble" (1 Pet 5:5).

8:18 God doesn't give us **wealth** just so that we can lavish it on ourselves. Prosperity is inextricably tied to his kingdom agenda for his people.

8:19-20 The Israelites were warned that if they acted like the Canaanites, God would treat them like Canaanites. God doesn't play favorites. He doesn't let his people live as they please.

9:4-6 Moses cautioned against spiritual pride. Israel was receiving the promised land because God hates wickedness and keeps his promises. If Israel was tempted to think of themselves as inherently righteous, they needed to nip that idea in the bud. Moses pulled no punches when he said, **You are a stiff-necked people** (9:6).

9:7-12 Moses wanted to drive home how easy it is for God's people to go off the rails even in the face of his constant mercy and faithfulness, so he reminded them of the quintessential example of Israel's sin: the golden calf incident (see Exod 32:1-35).

the covenant[a] the LORD made with you, I stayed on the mountain forty days and forty nights. I did not eat food or drink water. [10] On the day of the assembly the LORD gave me the two stone tablets, inscribed by God's finger.[b] The exact words were on them, which the LORD spoke to you from the fire on the mountain.[c] [11] The LORD gave me the two stone tablets, the tablets of the covenant, at the end of the forty days and forty nights.

[12] "The LORD said to me, 'Get up and go down immediately from here. For your people whom you brought out of Egypt have acted corruptly. They have quickly turned from the way that I commanded them; they have made a cast image for themselves.'[d] [13] The LORD also said to me, 'I have seen this people, and indeed, they are a stiff-necked people. [14] Leave me alone, and I will destroy them and blot out their name under heaven.[e] Then I will make you into a nation stronger and more numerous than they.'

[15] "So I went back down the mountain, while it was blazing with fire, and the two tablets of the covenant were in my hands. [16] I saw how you had sinned against the LORD your God; you had made a calf image for yourselves. You had quickly turned from the way the LORD had commanded for you. [17] So I took hold of the two tablets and threw them from my hands, shattering them before your eyes.[f] [18] I fell down like the first time in the presence of the LORD for forty days and forty nights; I did not eat food or drink water because of all the sin you committed, doing what was evil in the LORD's sight and angering him. [19] I was afraid of the fierce anger the LORD had directed against you,[g] because he was about to destroy you. But again the LORD listened to me on that occasion.[h] [20] The LORD was angry enough with Aaron to destroy him. But I prayed for Aaron at that time also. [21] I took the sinful calf you had made and burned it. I crushed it, thoroughly grinding it to powder as fine as dust, and threw its dust into the stream that came down from the mountain.[i]

[22] "You continued to provoke the LORD at Taberah, Massah, and Kibroth-hattaavah.[j] [23] When the LORD sent you from Kadesh-barnea, he said, 'Go up and possess

HOPE WORDS

Faith is about believing that the One you believe in is believable.

the land I have given you'; you rebelled against the command of the LORD your God. You did not believe or obey him.[k] [24] You have been rebelling against the LORD ever since I have[A] known you.[l]

[25] "I fell down in the presence of the LORD forty days and forty nights because the LORD had threatened to destroy you. [26] I prayed to the LORD:

Lord GOD, do not annihilate your people, your inheritance, whom you redeemed[m] through your greatness and brought out of Egypt with a strong hand. [27] Remember your servants Abraham, Isaac, and Jacob. Disregard this people's stubbornness, and their wickedness and sin. [28] Otherwise, those in the land you brought us from will say, 'Because the LORD wasn't able to bring them into the land he had promised them, and because he hated them, he brought them out to kill them in the wilderness.'[n] [29] But they are your people, your inheritance, whom you brought out by your great power and outstretched arm.[o]

THE COVENANT RENEWED

10 "The LORD said to me at that time, 'Cut two stone tablets like the first ones and come to me on the mountain and make a wooden ark. [2] I will write on the tablets the words that were on the first tablets you broke, and you are to place them in the ark.' [3] So I made an ark of acacia wood,[p] cut two stone tablets like the first ones, and climbed the mountain with the two tablets in my hand. [4] Then on the day of the assembly, the LORD wrote on the tablets what had been written previously, the Ten Commandments that he had spoken to you on the mountain from the fire. The LORD gave them to me, [5] and I went back down the mountain and placed the tablets in the ark I had made. And they have remained there, as the LORD commanded me."[q]

[a] 9:9 Ex 24:12; 31:18; Dt 9:11,15; Heb 9:4
[b] 9:10 Ex 8:19; 31:18; Lk 11:20; Jn 8:6
[c] Dt 5:4,22; 10:4
[d] 9:12 Ex 32:4,8; 34:17; Lv 19:4; Nm 33:52; Dt 27:15
[e] 9:14 Ex 17:14; Dt 25:19; 29:20; 32:26; 2Kg 14:27; Ps 51:1,9; Jr 18:23
[f] 9:17 Ex 32:19
[g] 9:19 Heb 12:21
[h] Dt 10:10
[i] 9:21 Ex 32:20
[j] 9:22 Ex 17:1-7; Nm 11:1-35
[k] 9:23 Nm 13-14
[l] 9:24 Ps 95; 106
[m] 9:26 Dt 7:8; 15:15; 24:18
[n] 9:28 Nm 14:16
[o] 9:29 2Kg 17:36; Neh 1:10; Jr 27:5; 32:17
[p] 10:3 Ex 25:10; 37:1
[q] 10:5 Ex 25:16; 1Kg 8:9; Heb 9:4

[A] 9:24 Sam, LXX read *since he has*

9:13-21 Israel's story consisted of rebellion, divine anger, intercession by Moses, divine grace, repeat. They'd not been chosen for their inherent goodness: we haven't been either.

*a*10:6 Nm 20:22-29
*b*10:6-7 Nm 33:31-33
*c*10:8 Ex 27:21–28:1;
32:26-29; Nm 3:45; 18:19;
25:12-13; Dt 33:8-11
*d*10:9 Lv 25:32-34; Nm
18:20; 26:62; Dt 18:1-2; Jos
13:14,33; Ezk 44:28-30
*e*10:10 Dt 9:19
*f*10:11 Dt 1:35
*g*10:12 Dt 14:23
*h*Dt 6:5; 11:13; 13:3; 30:6;
Jos 22:5; Mt 22:37
*i*10:13 Ex 15:26; Dt 4:40;
11:1; 26:17; 28:45; 30:16;
1Kg 2:3; 3:14; 6:12; 8:58,61;
9:6-7; 11:38; 2Kg 17:13; 23:3
*j*10:14 Ps 24:1
*k*10:15 Dt 4:37
*l*Dt 7:7; Ezk 20:5
*m*10:16 Dt 30:6; Jr 4:4;
Rm 2:29
*n*10:17 Jos 22:22; Ps 50:1;
136:2; Dn 2:47; 11:36
*o*Ps 136:3; 1Tm 6:15; Rv
17:14; 19:6
*p*2Ch 19:7; Jb 34:19; Mt
22:16
*q*10:18 Dt 27:19; Jr 22:3;
Mal 3:5
*r*10:19 Lv 19:34

*s*10:20 Dt 6:13; 13:4
*t*10:22 Gn 46:27; Ex 1:5
*u*Gn 15:5; 22:17; 26:4
*v*11:2 1Kg 8:42; 2Ch 6:32
*w*11:3 Ex 7–12
*x*11:4 Ex 14
*y*11:6 Nm 16
*z*11:7 Dt 3:21; 4:3; 29:2-3;
Jos 24:7
*aa*11:9 Dt 4:40; 5:16; 25:15
*ab*Ex 3:17; Lv 20:24; Nm
13:27; Dt 6:3; 26:9,15;
27:3; 31:20; Jos 5:6; Jr 11:5;
Ezk 20:6

6 The Israelites traveled from Beeroth Bene-jaakan[A] to Moserah. Aaron died and was buried there, and Eleazar his son became priest in his place.*a* **7** They traveled from there to Gudgodah, and from Gudgodah to Jotbathah, a land with flowing streams.*b* **8** "At that time the LORD set apart the tribe of Levi*c* to carry the ark of the LORD's covenant, to stand before the LORD to serve him, and to pronounce blessings in his name, as it is today. **9** For this reason, Levi does not have a portion or inheritance like his brothers; the LORD is his inheritance, as the LORD your God told him.*d*

10 "I stayed on the mountain forty days and forty nights like the first time. The LORD also listened to me on this occasion;*e* he agreed not to annihilate you. **11** Then the LORD said to me, 'Get up. Continue your journey ahead of the people, so that they may enter and possess the land I swore to give their fathers.'*f*

WHAT GOD REQUIRES

12 "And now, Israel, what does the LORD your God ask of you except to fear*g* the LORD your God by walking in all his ways, to love him, and to worship the LORD your God with all your heart and all your soul?*h* **13** Keep the LORD's commands and statutes I am giving you today, for your own good.*i* **14** The heavens, indeed the highest heavens, belong to the LORD your God, as does the earth and everything in it.*j* **15** Yet the LORD had his heart set on your fathers and loved them.*k* He chose their descendants after them — he chose you out of all the peoples, as it is today.*l* **16** Therefore, circumcise your hearts*m* and don't be stiff-necked any longer. **17** For the LORD your God is the God of gods*n* and Lord of lords,*o* the great, mighty, and awe-inspiring God, showing no partiality and taking no bribe.*p* **18** He executes justice for the fatherless and the widow, and loves the resident alien, giving him food and clothing.*q* **19** You are also to love the resident alien, since you were resident aliens in the land of Egypt.*r* **20** You are to fear the LORD your God and

worship him. Remain faithful[B] to him and take oaths in his name.*s* **21** He is your praise and he is your God, who has done for you these great and awe-inspiring works your eyes have seen. **22** Your fathers went down to Egypt, seventy people in all,*t* and now the LORD your God has made you numerous, like the stars of the sky.*u*

REMEMBER AND OBEY

11 "Therefore, love the LORD your God and always keep his mandate and his statutes, ordinances, and commands. **2** Understand today that it is not your children who experienced or saw the discipline of the LORD your God:

His greatness, strong hand, and outstretched arm;*v* **3** his signs and the works he did in Egypt to Pharaoh king of Egypt and all his land;*w* **4** what he did to Egypt's army, its horses and chariots, when he made the water of the Red Sea flow over them as they pursued you, and he destroyed them*x* completely;[C] **5** what he did to you in the wilderness until you reached this place; **6** and what he did to Dathan and Abiram, the sons of Eliab the Reubenite, when in the middle of the whole Israelite camp the earth opened its mouth and swallowed them, their households, their tents, and every living thing with them.*y*

7 Your own eyes have seen*z* every great work the LORD has done.

8 "Keep every command I am giving you today, so that you may have the strength to cross into and possess the land you are to inherit, **9** and so that you may live long*aa* in the land the LORD swore to your fathers to give them and their descendants, a land flowing with milk and honey.*ab* **10** For the land you are entering to possess is not like the land of Egypt, from which you have come, where you sowed your seed and irrigated by hand[D] as in a vegetable garden. **11** But the land you are entering to possess is a land of mountains and valleys, watered by rain from the sky. **12** It is a land

---

A 10:6 Or *from the wells of Bene-jaakan,* or *from the wells of the Jaakanites*　　**B** 10:20 Lit *Hold on*　　**C** 11:4 Lit *to this day*　　**D** 11:10 Lit *foot*

10:12 What does a person do who **fears** the Lord? He or she walks in his ways, loves him, and worships him. Such a person takes God seriously—so seriously that he or she does what God says.

10:14-22 The only appropriate response the people of Israel could make to God's grace toward them was to **circumcise** their

hearts—that is, to bow in submission to God and be **stiff-necked** no longer (10:16; see 9:6).

11:1 Sincere **love** for God is always accompanied by obedience.

11:10-17 Egypt had to be **irrigated by hand** in order for anything to grow (11:10). By contrast, Canaan was **watered by rain** (11:11). This didn't come from the hand of a fictional

Mother Nature, but from the hand of Father God (11:12). So if Israel was careful to **obey . . . love . . . and worship** the Lord, they could count on him to bless their produce (11:13-15). For an agrarian society, that's everything. But if they turned to **worship** false **gods**, they would find that their **produce** wouldn't grow (11:16-17)—a devastating situation.

the LORD your God cares for. He is always watching over it[a] from the beginning to the end of the year.

[13] "If you carefully obey my commands I am giving you today, to love the LORD your God and worship him with all your heart and all your soul, [14] I[A] will provide rain for your land in the proper time, the autumn and spring rains,[b] and you will harvest your grain, new wine, and fresh oil.[c] [15] I[B] will provide grass in your fields for your livestock. You will eat and be satisfied.[d] [16] Be careful[e] that you are not enticed to turn aside, serve, and bow in worship to other gods.[f] [17] Then the LORD's anger will burn against you.[g] He will shut the sky, and there will be no rain;[h] the land will not yield its produce, and you will perish quickly from the good land[i] the LORD is giving you.

[18] "Imprint these words of mine on your hearts and minds, bind them as a sign on your hands, and let them be a symbol[c] on your foreheads.[D] [19] Teach them to your children,[j] talking about them when you sit in your house and when you walk along the road, when you lie down and when you get up. [20] Write them on the doorposts of your house and on your city gates,[k] [21] so that as long as the heavens are above the earth, your days and those of your children may be many in the land the LORD swore to give your fathers.[l] [22] For if you carefully observe every one of these commands I am giving you to follow — to love the LORD your God, walk in all his ways, and remain faithful[E] to him — [23] the LORD will drive out all these nations before you, and you will drive out nations greater and stronger than you are.[m] [24] Every place the sole of your foot treads will be yours.[n] Your territory will extend from the wilderness to Lebanon and from the Euphrates River[F] to the Mediterranean Sea.[o] [25] No one will be able to stand against you; the LORD your God will put fear and dread of you in all the land where you set foot, as he has promised you.[p]

A BLESSING AND A CURSE

[26] "Look, today I set before you a blessing and a curse:[q] [27] there will be a blessing, if you obey the commands of the LORD your God I am giving you today, [28] and a curse, if you do not obey the commands of the LORD your God and you turn aside from the path I command you today by following other gods you have not known. [29] When the LORD your God brings you into the land you are entering to possess, you are to proclaim the blessing at Mount Gerizim and the curse at Mount Ebal. [30] Aren't these mountains across the Jordan, beyond the western road in the land of the Canaanites, who live in the Arabah, opposite Gilgal, near the oaks[G] of Moreh? [31] For you are about to cross the Jordan to enter and take possession of the land the LORD your God is giving you. When you possess it and settle in it, [32] be careful to follow all the statutes and ordinances I set before you today.

THE CHOSEN PLACE OF WORSHIP

12 "Be careful to follow these statutes and ordinances in the land that the LORD, the God of your fathers,[r] has given you to possess all the days you live on the earth. [2] Destroy completely all the places where the nations that you are driving out worship their gods[s] — on the high mountains, on the hills, and under every green tree.[t] [3] Tear down their altars, smash their sacred pillars, burn their Asherah poles, cut down the carved images of their gods, and wipe out their names from every[H] place.[u] [4] Don't worship the LORD your God this way. [5] Instead, turn to the place the LORD your God chooses[v] from all your tribes to put his name for his dwelling and go there. [6] You are to bring there your burnt offerings and sacrifices, your tenths and personal contributions,[I] your vow offerings and freewill offerings, and the firstborn of your herds and flocks. [7] You will eat there in the presence of the LORD your

[a] 11:12 Is 27:3
[b] 11:14 Jr 5:24; Jms 5:7
[c] Dt 7:13; 14:23; 18:4; 2Ch 32:28; Neh 10:39; 13:5,12; Hs 2:22; Jl 2:19,24
[d] 11:15 Lv 25:19; Dt 6:11; 8:10; 31:20
[e] 11:16 Ex 34:12; Dt 4:23; 6:12; 8:11; 12:13,19,30; 15:9
[f] Dt 17:3; 29:26; 30:17; Jos 23:16; Jdg 2:17; 2Ch 7:19,22
[g] 11:17 Ex 22:24; Dt 7:4; 31:17; Jos 23:16
[h] 1Kg 8:35; 2Ch 2:6; 6:26; 7:13
[i] Dt 8:7
[j] 11:19 Dt 4:9-10
[k] 11:18-20 Dt 6:6-9
[l] 11:21 Dt 1:35
[m] 11:23 Dt 4:38; 9:1
[n] 11:24-25 Jos 1:3-5
[o] 11:24 Gn 15:18-20; Ex 23:31
[p] 11:25 Dt 2:25

[q] 11:26 Dt 30:15; Jr 21:8
[r] 12:1 Ex 3:13,15-16; Dt 1:11,21; 4:1; 6:3; 27:3; Jos 18:3; Ezr 10:11; Ac 7:32
[s] 12:2 Ex 23:23-26; 34:13; Dt 7:1-5
[t] 1Kg 14:23; 2Kg 16:4; 17:10; 2Ch 28:4; Is 57:5; Jr 2:20; 3:6,13; Ezk 6:13
[u] 12:3 Ex 34:13; Dt 7:5; 2Kg 23:14; 2Ch 14:3; 31:1; 34:4,7; Is 27:9
[v] 12:5 Dt 14:23-25; 15:20; 16:2,7,11,15-16; 17:8,10; 18:6; 26:2; 31:11; Jos 9:27

11:18-25 The antidote to forgetfulness and idolatry was stated in 6:4-9 and is repeated here in 11:18-21. God was providing Israel with the perfect means to achieve guaranteed results. We should apply it.

12:1-4 In Canaan the Israelites would see various Canaanite worship centers, which were typically erected **on the high moun-**tains, on the hills, and under every green tree (12:2). These sites honored the Canaanite god and goddess of fertility, Baal and Asherah (12:3). Moses knew that the people might be intrigued by forms of worship that included sexual symbols and immoral sexual acts. The Israelites had fallen for such debauchery before (see Num 25:1-9). But Israel was not to **worship** the Lord **this way** (Deut 12:4).

12:5-7 Rather than permitting worship on any high place or under any green tree, God intended to centralize Israel's worship. The ultimate fulfillment of this would be at the temple in Jerusalem. Until that was built, the divinely ordained place for worship was the tabernacle.

[a]12:8 Ex 15:26; Jdg 17:6; 21:25
[b]12:9 Dt 3:20; 5:14; 25:19; 28:65
[c]Dt 15:4
[d]12:10 Dt 15:4
[e]12:11 Dt 14:23; 16:2,6,11; 26:2
[f]12:12 Lv 23:40; Dt 14:26; 16:11-15; 26:11; 27:7
[g]Ex 20:10; Nm 18:20; Dt 5:14; 12:18; 14:21,27,29; 16:11,14; 23:16
[h]12:15-16 Dt 15:22-23
[i]12:16 Lv 17:10-14

[j]12:20 Ex 34:24
[k]12:23 Lv 17:11,14
[l]12:24 Lv 3:17; 7:26; 17:14; 19:26; Dt 15:23; 1Sm 14:34; Ezk 33:25
[m]12:29 Dt 19:1
[n]Dt 3:12
[o]12:30 Ex 23:33; 34:12; Dt 7:16,25; Jos 23:13; Jdg 8:27; Ps 106:36; Heb 12:1

God and rejoice with your household in everything you do,[A] because the LORD your God has blessed you.

8 "You are not to do as we are doing here today; everyone is doing whatever seems right in his own sight.[a] 9 Indeed, you have not yet come into the resting place[b] and the inheritance[c] the LORD your God is giving you. 10 When you cross the Jordan and live in the land the LORD your God is giving you to inherit,[d] and he gives you rest from all the enemies around you and you live in security, 11 then the LORD your God will choose the place to have his name dwell.[e] Bring there everything I command you: your burnt offerings, sacrifices, offerings of the tenth, personal contributions,[B] and all your choice offerings you vow to the LORD. 12 You will rejoice[f] before the LORD your God — you, your sons and daughters, your male and female slaves, and the Levite who is within your city gates, since he has no portion or inheritance among you.[g] 13 Be careful not to offer your burnt offerings in all the sacred places you see. 14 You must offer your burnt offerings only in the place the LORD chooses in one of your tribes, and there you must do everything I command you.

SLAUGHTERING ANIMALS TO EAT

15 "But whenever you want, you may slaughter and eat meat within any of your city gates,[h] according to the blessing the LORD your God has given you. Those who are clean or unclean may eat it, as they would a gazelle or deer, 16 but you must not eat the blood; pour it on the ground like water.[i] 17 Within your city gates you may not eat the tenth of your grain, new wine, or fresh oil; the firstborn of your herd or flock; any of your vow offerings that you pledge; your freewill offerings; or your personal contributions.[C] 18 You are to eat them in the presence of the LORD your God at the place the LORD your God chooses — you, your son and daughter, your male and female slave, and the Levite who is within

your city gates. Rejoice before the LORD your God in everything you do, 19 and be careful not to neglect the Levite, as long as you live in your land.

20 "When the LORD your God enlarges your territory as he has promised you,[j] and you say, 'I want to eat meat' because you have a strong desire to eat meat, you may eat it whenever you want. 21 If the place where the LORD your God chooses to put his name is too far from you, you may slaughter any of your herd or flock he has given you, as I have commanded you, and you may eat it within your city gates whenever you want. 22 Indeed, you may eat it as the gazelle and deer are eaten; both the clean and the unclean may eat it. 23 But don't eat the blood, since the blood is the life, and you must not eat the life with the meat.[k] 24 Do not eat blood; pour it on the ground like water.[l] 25 Do not eat it, so that you and your children after you will prosper, because you will be doing what is right in the LORD's sight. 26 "But you are to take the holy offerings you have and your vow offerings and go to the place the LORD chooses. 27 Present the meat and blood of your burnt offerings on the altar of the LORD your God. The blood of your other sacrifices is to be poured out beside the altar of the LORD your God, but you may eat the meat. 28 Be careful to obey all these things I command you, so that you and your children after you may prosper forever, because you will be doing what is good and right in the sight of the LORD your God.

29 "When the LORD your God annihilates the nations before you,[m] which you are entering to take possession of,[n] and you drive them out and live in their land, 30 be careful not to be ensnared by their ways[o] after they have been destroyed before you. Do not inquire about their gods, asking, 'How did these nations worship their gods? I'll also do the same.' 31 You must not do the same to the LORD your God, because they practice every detestable act, which

---

[A]12:7 Lit you put your hand to, also in v. 18   [B]12:11 Lit tenth, the contributions from your hands   [C]12:17 Lit or the contributions from your hands

---

12:8 Previously God had commanded the people to "do what [was] right in [God's] sight" (Exod 15:26). This highlights a great divide. Will we follow the destructive path that looks good to our faulty eyes? Or will we follow God's way?
12:15-16 Though animals could only be sacrificed in one place, this did not prevent Israelite fathers from hunting animals for family meals (12:15). Nevertheless, consuming blood

was strictly prohibited because "the life of every creature is its blood" (Lev 17:14) and "without the shedding of blood there is no forgiveness" (Heb 9:22). This prohibition pointed to the ultimate blood sacrifice. By Jesus's own blood, he has "obtained eternal redemption" (Heb 9:12).
12:20-28 The instructions here (12:21-28) may strike us as unnecessary repetition (see 12:15-19). But given the sinful human tendency

to forget, any good teacher of God's Word knows the value of repetition, as illustrated by the apostle Peter: "I will always remind you about these things, even though you know them. . . . I think it is right . . . to wake you up with a reminder" (2 Pet 1:12-13).
12:29-32 What we worship drives how we live: as part of their idolatry, the Canaanites burned **their sons and daughters** (12:31). Worldview matters. Ideas have consequences.

the LORD hates, for their gods. They even burn their sons and daughters in the fire to their gods. ³² Be careful to do everything I command you; do not add anything to it or take anything away from it.^a

THE FALSE PROPHET

13 "If a prophet or someone who has dreams^b arises among you and proclaims a sign or wonder to you, ² and that sign or wonder he has promised you comes about, but he says, 'Let us follow other gods,' which you have not known, 'and let us worship them,' ³ do not listen to that prophet's words or to that dreamer. For the LORD your God is testing you to know whether you love the LORD your God with all your heart and all your soul.^c ⁴ You must follow the LORD your God and fear him. You must keep his commands and listen to him; you must worship him and remain faithful^A to him.^d ⁵ That prophet or dreamer must be put to death,^e because he has urged rebellion against the LORD your God who brought you out of the land of Egypt and redeemed you from the place of slavery,^f to turn you from the way the LORD your God has commanded you to walk. You must purge the evil from you.^g

DON'T TOLERATE IDOLATRY

⁶ "If your brother, the son of your mother,^B or your son or daughter, or the wife you embrace, or your closest friend secretly entices you, saying, 'Let us go and worship other gods' — which neither you nor your fathers have known, ⁷ any of the gods of the peoples around you, near you or far from you, from one end of the earth to the other — ⁸ do not yield to him or listen to him. Show him no pity,^c and do not spare him or shield him.^h ⁹ Instead, you must kill him. Your hand is to be the first against him to put him to death, and then the hands of all the people.ⁱ ¹⁰ Stone him to death for trying to turn you away from the LORD your God who brought you out of

the land of Egypt, out of the place of slavery.^j ¹¹ All Israel will hear and be afraid, and they will no longer do anything evil like this among you.^k

¹² "If you hear it said about one of your cities the LORD your God is giving you to live in, ¹³ that wicked men have sprung up among you, led the inhabitants of their city astray, and said, 'Let us go and worship other gods,' which you have not known,^l ¹⁴ you are to inquire, investigate, and interrogate thoroughly. If the report turns out to be true that this detestable act has been done among you, ¹⁵ you must strike down the inhabitants of that city with the sword. Completely destroy everyone in it as well as its livestock with the sword. ¹⁶ You are to gather all its spoil in the middle of the city square and completely burn the city and all its spoil for the LORD your God. The city is to remain a mound of ruins forever;^m it is not to be rebuilt. ¹⁷ Nothing set apart for destruction is to remain in your hand, so that the LORD will turn from his burning anger and grant you mercy, show you compassion, and multiply you as he swore to your fathers. ¹⁸ This will occur if you obey the LORD your God, keeping all his commands I am giving you today, doing what is right in the sight of the LORD your God.

FORBIDDEN PRACTICES

14 "You are sons of the LORD your God;ⁿ do not cut yourselves or make a bald spot on your head^D on behalf of the dead,^o ² for you are a holy people belonging to the LORD your God. The LORD has chosen you to be his own possession^p out of all the peoples on the face of the earth.

CLEAN AND UNCLEAN FOODS

³ "You must not eat any detestable thing. ⁴ These are the animals you may eat:
   oxen, sheep, goats,
⁵ deer, gazelles, roe deer,
   wild goats, ibexes, antelopes,
   and mountain sheep.

^a 12:32 Dt 4:2; Rv 22:18-19
^b 13:1 1Sm 28:6,15; Jr 23:27,32; 29:8; Zch 10:2
^c 13:3 Dt 6:5; 11:13; Jos 22:5; Mt 22:37
^d 13:4 Dt 10:20; Jr 13:10; 25:6
^e 13:5 Jos 1:18
^f Lv 26:13; Dt 5:6; 6:12; 8:14; 13:10; Jos 24:17; Jr 34:13
^g Dt 17:7,12; 19:13,19; 21:9,21; 22:21-24; 24:7; Ezk 20:38; 22:15
^h 13:8 Dt 7:16; 19:13,21; 25:12
ⁱ 13:9 Dt 17:7

^j 13:10 Lv 24:16; Dt 17:5; 21:21; 1Kg 21:13
^k 13:11 Dt 19:20
^l 13:12-15 Dt 17:2-5
^m 13:16 Jr 25:9; 49:13; Mal 1:4
ⁿ 14:1 Ex 4:22-23; Dt 32:6
^o Lv 19:28
^p 14:2 Ex 19:5; Dt 7:6

^A 13:4 Lit and hold on   ^B 13:6 DSS, Sam, LXX read *If the son of your father or the son of your mother*   ^C 13:8 Lit *Your eye must not pity him*
^D 14:1 Or *forehead*

13:1-3 Moses said the test of a true prophet is not his *magic* but his *message*. No matter what a prophet, magician, or soothsayer did to dazzle the Israelites, Moses said in effect, "It's his theology that matters."
13:3 Though God never tempts us, he does permit us to encounter temptation in order to test our faithfulness and reveal what is in our hearts.
13:5 False doctrine is not to be tolerated in the church either. The church has the authority (and responsibility) to carry out

church discipline and exclude people from membership who propagate false teachings about the essentials of the faith and seek to lead Christians astray.
13:6-11 Israel's love for God was so paramount that it superseded even love of family (see Matt 10:37). The death sentence was meant as a powerful deterrent.
14:1-2 The Israelites were not to **cut themselves** or **make a bald spot on [their heads] on behalf of the dead** (14:1). These mourning

rituals were banned because they were part of the Canaanite religions and were thus unfit for God's **holy people** (14:2).
14:3-21 A major day-to-day aspect of Israel's covenant with God involved keeping the nation's food laws. We have only one clear reason why God declared some food clean and some unclean for Israel: **You are a holy people belonging to the LORD** (14:21). Food laws, then, were another way of setting Israel apart to be the unique people of God.

[a]14:4-8 Lv 11:1-8
[b]14:9-10 Lv 11:9-12
[c]14:11-18 Lv 11:13-19
[d]14:19-20 Lv 11:20-23

[e]14:23 Dt 12:11
[f]Dt 4:10; 6:2; 10:12; 17:19;
31:12-13; Jos 4:24; 24:14;
1Sm 12:14; 2Kg 17:25;
Ps 15:4
[g]14:26-27 Dt 12:12,18-19
[h]14:28-29 Dt 26:12
[i]14:29 Dt 30:9
[j]15:1 Ex 22:25-27; Lv 25
[k]15:4 Ex 32:13; Lv 20:24;
Dt 4:21; 12:10; 16:20;
19:10; 21:23; 24:4; 25:19;
26:1; 29:8; Jos 1:6

6 You may eat any animal that has hooves divided in two and chews the cud.[A] **7** But among the ones that chew the cud or have divided hooves, you are not to eat these: camels, hares, and hyraxes, though they chew the cud, they do not have hooves — they are unclean for you; **8** and pigs, though they have hooves, they do not chew the cud — they are unclean for you. Do not eat their meat or touch their carcasses.[a]

9 "You may eat everything from the water that has fins and scales, **10** but you may not eat anything that does not have fins and scales — it is unclean for you.[b]

11 "You may eat every clean bird, **12** but these are the ones you may not eat: eagles, bearded vultures, black vultures, **13** the kites, any kind of falcon,[B] **14** every kind of raven, **15** ostriches, short-eared owls, gulls, any kind of hawk, **16** little owls, long-eared owls, barn owls, **17** eagle owls, ospreys, cormorants, **18** storks, any kind of heron, hoopoes, and bats.[C,c]

19 All winged insects are unclean for you; they may not be eaten. **20** But you may eat every clean flying creature.[d]

21 "You are not to eat any carcass; you may give it to a resident alien within your city gates, and he may eat it, or you may sell it to a foreigner. For you are a holy people belonging to the LORD your God. Do not boil a young goat in its mother's milk.

A TENTH FOR THE LORD

22 "Each year you are to set aside a tenth of all the produce grown in your fields. **23** You are to eat a tenth of your grain, new wine, and fresh oil, and the firstborn of your herd and flock, in the presence of the LORD your God at the place where he chooses

to have his name dwell,[e] so that you will always learn to fear[f] the LORD your God. **24** But if the distance is too great for you to carry it, since the place where the LORD your God chooses to put his name is too far away from you and since the LORD your God has blessed you, **25** then exchange it for silver, take the silver in your hand, and go to the place the LORD your God chooses. **26** You may spend the silver on anything you want: cattle, sheep, goats, wine, beer, or anything you desire. You are to feast there in the presence of the LORD your God and rejoice with your family. **27** Do not neglect the Levite within your city gates, since he has no portion or inheritance among you.[g]

28 "At the end of every three years, bring a tenth of all your produce for that year and store it within your city gates. **29** Then the Levite, who has no portion or inheritance among you, the resident alien, the fatherless, and the widow within your city gates may come, eat, and be satisfied.[h] And the LORD your God will bless you in all the work of your hands that you do.[i]

DEBTS CANCELED

15 "At the end of every seven years you must cancel debts.[j] **2** This is how to cancel debt: Every creditor[D] is to cancel what he has lent his neighbor. He is not to collect anything from his neighbor or brother, because the LORD's release of debts has been proclaimed. **3** You may collect something from a foreigner, but you must forgive whatever your brother owes you.

4 "There will be no poor among you, however, because the LORD is certain to bless you in the land the LORD your God is giving you to possess as an inheritance[k] — **5** if only you obey the LORD your God and are careful to follow every one of these commands I am giving you today. **6** When the LORD your God blesses you as he has promised you, you will lend to

[A]14:6 The Hb does not specify chewing the cud, but bringing up partially digested food and swallowing it again.   [B]14:13 Some Hb mss, Sam, LXX; other Hb mss, Vg read *the falcon, the various kinds of kite*   [C]14:5-18 The identification of some of these animals is uncertain.
[D]15:2 Lit *owner of a loan of his hand*

14:22-29 Giving to God is a test of faith. Israel lived in an agrarian society, so the people were dependent on their harvest to survive. When they gave God the first portion of their crops (14:22), they were trusting him to bless them and provide for their needs so that they could feed their families and be charitable to others. Giving to God first is crucial because it shows how much you value him, and it expresses

your faith in his ability and willingness to provide for you. When Israel gave the Lord their tithe, they were not saying that ten percent belonged to God while the other ninety percent belonged to them. Instead, giving a tenth to God was their way of acknowledging that *everything* they had was from him.
15:1-3 To us, this sounds like an impossible way to run a country, but it was part of God's

original plan and will for Israel. It's a reminder that God's kingdom does not operate according to the principles by which the banker downtown conducts business.
15:4-6 The people had the opportunity to ensure that there would be **no poor among** them (15:4-5). Sadly, history would show that Israel was unfaithful to God's economic commands. Too often the church similarly fails to take action that empowers the poor.

many nations but not borrow; you will rule many nations, but they will not rule you.

LENDING TO THE POOR

7 "If there is a poor person among you, one of your brothers within any of your city gates in the land the LORD your God is giving you, do not be hardhearted or tightfisted toward your poor brother. **8** Instead, you are to open your hand to him and freely loan him enough for whatever need he has. **9** Be careful that there isn't this wicked thought in your heart, 'The seventh year, the year of canceling debts, is near,' and you are stingy toward your poor brother and give him nothing. He will cry out to the LORD against you, and you will be guilty. **10** Give to him, and don't have a stingy heart^A when you give, and because of this the LORD your God will bless you in all your work and in everything you do.^B **11** For there will never cease to be poor people in the land;^a that is why I am commanding you, 'Open your hand willingly to your poor and needy brother in your land.'

RELEASE OF SLAVES

12 "If your fellow Hebrew, a man or woman, is sold to you and serves you six years, you must set him free in the seventh year.^b **13** When you set him free, do not send him away empty-handed. **14** Give generously to him from your flock, your threshing floor, and your winepress. You are to give him whatever the LORD your God has blessed you with. **15** Remember that you were a slave in the land of Egypt and the LORD your God redeemed^c you; that is why I am giving you this command today.^d **16** But if your slave says to you, 'I don't want to leave you,' because he loves you and your family, and is well off with you, **17** take an awl and pierce through his ear into the door, and he will become your slave for life. Also treat your female slave the same way. **18** Do not regard it as a hardship^c when you set him free, because he worked for you six

years — worth twice the wages of a hired worker. Then the LORD your God will bless you in everything you do.^e

CONSECRATION OF FIRSTBORN ANIMALS

19 "Consecrate to the LORD your God every firstborn male produced by your herd and flock.^f You are not to put the firstborn of your oxen to work or shear the firstborn of your flock. **20** Each year you and your family are to eat it before the LORD your God in the place the LORD chooses. **21** But if there is a defect in the animal, if it is lame or blind or has any serious defect, you may not sacrifice it to the LORD your God. **22** Eat it within your city gates; both the unclean person and the clean may eat it, as though it were a gazelle or deer. **23** But you must not eat its blood; pour it on the ground like water.^g

THE FESTIVAL OF PASSOVER

16 "Set aside the month of Abib^D,^h and observe the Passover to the LORD your God, because the LORD your God brought you out of Egypt by night in the month of Abib.^i **2** Sacrifice to the LORD your God a Passover animal from the herd or flock in the place where the LORD chooses to have his name dwell.^j **3** Do not eat leavened bread with it.^k For seven days you are to eat unleavened bread with it, the bread of hardship — because you left the land of Egypt in a hurry^l — so that you may remember for the rest of your life the day you left the land of Egypt. **4** No yeast is to be found anywhere in your territory for seven days,^m and none of the meat you sacrifice in the evening of the first day is to remain until morning.^n **5** You are not to sacrifice the Passover animal in any of the towns the LORD your God is giving you. **6** Sacrifice the Passover animal only at the place where the LORD your God chooses to have his name dwell. Do this in the evening as the sun sets at the same time of

^a 15:11 Mt 26:11
^b 15:12 Jr 34:14
^c 15:15 Ex 15:13; Dt 7:8; 9:26; 24:18
^d Dt 24:18,22

^e 15:12-18 Ex 21:2-11
^f 15:19 Lv 23:9-14
^g 15:22-23 Dt 12:15-16,22-24
^h 16:1-8 Ex 12
^i 16:1 Ex 13:4; 23:15; 34:18
^j 16:2 Dt 12:11
^k 16:3 Ex 12:15; 13:6-7; 23:15; 34:18; Lv 23:6; Nm 28:17; 2Ch 30:21; 35:17; Ezr 6:22; Ezk 45:21; Ac 20:6
^l Ex 12:11
^m 16:4 Ex 12:39; 13:7
^n Ex 12:10; Lv 7:17; 8:32

---

^A 15:10 Lit and let not your heart be grudging   ^B 15:10 Lit you put your hand to   ^C 15:18 Lit Let it not be hard in your sight   ^D 16:1 March–April; called Nisan in the post-exilic period; Neh 2:1; Est 3:7

15:9-11 The Sabbath year, with its debt forgiveness and care for the poor, was not really about financial transactions; it was a test of whether God's people would trust him even when doing so didn't make sense on the ledger. Furthermore, to provide for someone in need is the fulfillment of the second-most important commandment: "love your neighbor as yourself" (Lev 19:18; Mark 12:28-31).

15:12 A **fellow Hebrew** who was too poor to repay his debts could sell himself to his debtor as an indentured servant. **In the seventh year**, he was to be set free (see Lev 25:39-42).
15:13-15 A Hebrew, that is an Israelite, was to **give generously** to his former servant based on how the Lord had **blessed** him (15:14). He was also to **remember** that he was once worse off than an indentured servant—he was **a slave in . . . Egypt** (15:15).

15:21-22 Animals which had a **defect** of some kind could not be offered as sacrifices, but they could still be eaten at home.
16:4 There was to be **no yeast . . . anywhere** in Israel's **territory** during Passover, the first of three national holiday gatherings. The word yeast is frequently representative of sin in Scripture.

a 16:9–12 Lv 23:15–21
b 16:10 Ex 34:22; Nm 28:26; 2Ch 8:13
c Ex 35:29; Lv 7:16; 22:21,23; Nm 15:3; Ezr 1:4,6; 8:28; Ps 54:6
d 16:11 Lv 23:40; Dt 12:12; 14:26; 26:11; 27:7
e 16:13 Lv 23:34; Dt 31:10; 2Ch 8:13; Ezr 3:4; Zch 14:16–19
f 16:13–15 Lv 23:33–43
g 16:15 Ex 23:14,17; 34:23–24; 1Kg 9:25
h 16:16 Ex 23:14,17; 34:23–24; 1Kg 9:25; Lk 2:42
i Ex 3:21; 23:15; 34:20

j 16:19 Ex 23:8; Dt 10:17; 27:25; 1Sm 12:3; 2Ch 19:7; Ps 15:5; Pr 17:23; Is 33:15; Ezk 22:12; Am 5:12
k 16:19–20 Ex 23:2–9
l 16:21–22 Dt 7:1–5; 12:2–3; 2Kg 23:2–6
m 17:1 Lv 3:1,6; 9:2–3; 21:17–23; 22:17–25; 23:12; Nm 19:2; Dt 15:21; Mal 1:8; Heb 9:14; 1Pt 1:19; 2Pt 3:14
n 17:2 Dt 31:16
o 17:3 Dt 13:6,13; Jos 23:16
p Dt 4:19; 2Kg 23:5; Jb 31:26–28; Ps 148:3; Is 24:23; 60:19–20; Jr 8:2
q 17:2–5 Dt 13:12–15; 29:18
r 17:5 Dt 22:24
s 17:6 Dt 19:15; Mt 18:16; 2Co 13:1; 1Tm 5:19; Heb 10:28

day you departed from Egypt. **7** You are to cook and eat it in the place the Lord your God chooses, and you are to return to your tents in the morning. **8** Eat unleavened bread for six days. On the seventh day there is to be a solemn assembly to the Lord your God; do not do any work.

THE FESTIVAL OF WEEKS

9 "You are to count seven weeks, counting the weeks from the time the sickle is first put to the standing grain.[a] **10** You are to celebrate the Festival of Weeks[b] to the Lord your God with a freewill offering[c] that you give in proportion to how the Lord your God has blessed you. **11** Rejoice[d] before the Lord your God in the place where he chooses to have his name dwell — you, your son and daughter, your male and female slave, the Levite within your city gates, as well as the resident alien, the fatherless, and the widow among you. **12** Remember that you were slaves in Egypt; carefully follow these statutes.

THE FESTIVAL OF SHELTERS

13 "You are to celebrate the Festival of Shelters[e] for seven days when you have gathered in everything from your threshing floor and winepress.[f] **14** Rejoice during your festival — you, your son and daughter, your male and female slave, as well as the Levite, the resident alien, the fatherless, and the widow within your city gates. **15** You are to hold a seven-day festival for the Lord your God in the place he chooses, because the Lord your God will bless you in all your produce and in all the work of your hands,[g] and you will have abundant joy.

16 "All your males are to appear three times a year[h] before the Lord your God in the place he chooses: at the Festival of Unleavened Bread, the Festival of Weeks, and the Festival of Shelters. No one is to appear before the Lord empty-handed.[i] **17** Everyone must appear with a gift suited

to his means, according to the blessing the Lord your God has given you.

APPOINTING JUDGES AND OFFICIALS

18 "Appoint judges and officials for your tribes in all your towns the Lord your God is giving you. They are to judge the people with righteous judgment. **19** Do not deny justice or show partiality to anyone. Do not accept a bribe, for it blinds the eyes of the wise and twists the words of the righteous.[j] **20** Pursue justice and justice alone, so that you will live and possess the land the Lord your God is giving you.[k]

FORBIDDEN WORSHIP

21 "Do not set up an Asherah of any kind of wood next to the altar you will build for the Lord your God, **22** and do not set up a sacred pillar; the Lord your God hates them.[l]

17 "Do not sacrifice to the Lord your God an ox or sheep with a defect or any serious flaw, for that is detestable to the Lord your God.[m]

THE JUDICIAL PROCEDURE FOR IDOLATRY

2 "If a man or woman among you in one of your towns that the Lord your God will give you is discovered doing evil in the sight of the Lord your God and violating his covenant[n] **3** and has gone to serve other gods[o] by bowing in worship to the sun, moon, or all the stars in the sky[p] — which I have forbidden[q] — **4** and if you are told or hear about it, then investigate it thoroughly. If the report turns out to be true that this detestable act has been done in Israel, **5** you are to bring out to your city gates that man or woman who has done this evil thing and stone them to death.[r] **6** The one condemned to die is to be executed on the testimony of two or three witnesses.[s] No one is to be executed on the testimony of a single witness. **7** The witnesses' hands are to be the first in putting him to death, and

---

16:9–12 The gathering called the **Festival of Weeks** (16:10), also known as Pentecost (from the Greek term meaning "fiftieth"), occurred fifty days after the Feast of Firstfruits. This was a joyful celebration of God's abundant provision in the harvest.

16:13–15 The **Festival of Shelters**, also known as Tabernacles or Booths (16:13), was a seven-day observance in which the Israelites were commanded to build and live in temporary shelters as a reminder of God's care for them during their wanderings (see Lev 23:42–43).

16:16 As the heads of their families, the men were to lead the way in worshiping the Lord. This principle carries over into our time.

16:18 Biblical Israel was a theocracy, meaning that the country had a form of government in which God served as the nation's King. This meant that the nation's civil leaders, its **judges and officials**, were charged with judging the people **with righteous judgment** — just as the Lord would.

16:20 God's leaders — those of yesterday and today — are not to pursue selfish gain but to **pursue justice**.

16:21–17:1 The sudden subject change from the duties of judges to forbidden forms of worship points to how the two topics were intricately related. In Israel, even the civil rulers were responsible for guarding the nation's purity of worship and punishing offenders.

17:6–7 Here we see both a provision to protect someone from being falsely accused (17:6), and a strong deterrent against sin; the latter principle was always at work behind the death penalty (17:7).

after that, the hands of all the people.[a] You must purge the evil from you.[b]

DIFFICULT CASES

8 "If a case is too difficult for you — concerning bloodshed,[c] lawsuits,[d] or assaults[e] — cases disputed at your city gates,[f] then go up to the place the LORD your God chooses. **9** You are to go to the Levitical priests and to the judge who presides at that time. Ask, and they will give you a verdict in the case. **10** You must abide by the verdict they give you at the place the LORD chooses. Be careful to do exactly as they instruct you. **11** You must abide by the instruction they give you and the verdict they announce to you. Do not turn to the right or the left from the decision they declare to you. **12** The person who acts arrogantly, refusing to listen either to the priest who stands there serving the LORD your God or to the judge, must die. You must purge the evil from Israel. **13** Then all the people will hear about it, be afraid, and no longer behave arrogantly.

APPOINTING A KING

14 "When you enter the land the LORD your God is giving you,[g] take possession of it, live in it, and say, 'I will set a king over me like all the nations around me,' **15** you are to appoint over you the king the LORD your God chooses.[h] Appoint a king from your brothers. You are not to set a foreigner over you, or one who is not of your people.[i] **16** However, he must not acquire many horses for himself or send the people back to Egypt to acquire many horses, for the LORD has told you, 'You are never to go back that way again.'[j] **17** He must not acquire many wives for himself so that his heart won't go astray.[k] He must not acquire very large amounts of silver and gold for himself.[l] **18** When he is seated on his royal throne, he is to write a copy of this instruction for himself on a scroll in the presence of the Levitical priests. **19** It is to remain with him, and he is to read from it all the days of his life, so that he may learn to fear[m] the LORD his God, to observe all the words of this instruction, and to do these statutes. **20** Then his heart will not be exalted above his countrymen, he will not turn from this command to the right or the left, and he and his sons will continue reigning many years[A] in Israel.

PROVISIONS FOR THE LEVITES

18 "The Levitical priests, the whole tribe of Levi, will have no portion or inheritance with Israel. They will eat the LORD's fire offerings; that is their[B,C] inheritance. **2** Although Levi has no inheritance among his brothers, the LORD is his inheritance, as he promised him.[n] **3** This is the priests' share from the people who offer a sacrifice, whether it is an ox, a sheep, or a goat; the priests are to be given the shoulder, jaws, and stomach. **4** You are to give him the firstfruits of your grain, new wine, and fresh oil,[o] and the first sheared wool of your flock. **5** For the LORD your God has chosen him and his sons from all your tribes to stand and minister in his name from now on.[D] **6** When a Levite leaves one of your towns in Israel where he was staying and wants to go to the place the LORD chooses, **7** he may serve in the name of the LORD his God like all his fellow Levites who minister there in the presence of the LORD. **8** They will eat equal portions besides what he has received from the sale of the family estate.[E,p]

OCCULT PRACTICES VERSUS PROPHETIC REVELATION

9 "When you enter the land the LORD your God is giving you, do not imitate the detestable customs of those nations.[q] **10** No

[a] 17:7 Dt 13:9
[b] Dt 13:5; 19:19; 21:21; 22:21-24; 24:7; 1Co 5:13
[c] 17:8 Ex 21:12-14,18-25; Nm 35:9-34; Dt 19:1-13; 25:7
[d] Ex 22:6-14
[e] Ex 21:22-26; Lv 24:19-20
[f] Dt 21:19; 22:15
[g] 17:14 Dt 26:1
[h] 17:14-15 1Sm 8:4-22
[i] 17:15 Gn 17:6,16; 35:11; Nm 24:17-19
[j] 17:16 1Kg 10:28-29
[k] 17:17 1Kg 11:3-4
[l] 1Kg 10:21-25

[m] 17:19 Dt 14:23
[n] 18:2 Nm 18:20; Dt 12:12; 14:27-29; Jos 14:4
[o] 18:4 Dt 14:23; Neh 10:39; 13:5,12
[p] 18:8 Nm 18:8-32
[q] 18:9 Ex 23:24; Dt 20:18; 1Kg 14:24; 2Kg 17:15; Ezk 16:47

[A] 17:20 Lit *will lengthen days on his kingdom*   [B] 18:1 LXX; MT reads *his*   [C] 18:1 Or *his*   [D] 18:5 Lit *name all the days*   [E] 18:8 Hb obscure

---

17:11 The leaders were ruling on God's behalf, so judgment had to be followed. No appeals would be heard.

17:14-20 In their early years in the promised land, Israel would be ruled by judges and priests. But eventually, Israel would clamor for a king **like all the nations around** them (17:14; see 1 Sam 8:4-5). In advance of that, Moses specified that Israel's king had to be an Israelite (Deut 17:15). Moreover, **he must not acquire many horses**—which would require going **back to Egypt** in violation of God's command (17:16). He was also not to **acquire many wives** or **very large amounts of silver and gold** (17:17). And, most importantly, he was to **write a copy of this instruction for himself** and **read from it all the days of his life** (17:18-20).

Sadly, though King Solomon would be called the wisest man who ever lived, in his sinfulness he broke all of these commandments for kings. Just because a person has access to wisdom doesn't guarantee he'll use it.

18:1 Levitical priests were those men set apart by the Lord to offer sacrifices and administer other duties in the tabernacle (and later in the temple). Not all Levites were priests—only those who were the descendants of Aaron. The others were also consecrated to serve God by assisting the priests with the tabernacle and its furnishings.

18:9-11 The various demonically inspired **customs** mentioned here were intended to influence or manipulate the gods to act in favor of the person seeking help (18:9). The most horrific practice of the nations was to **sacrifice** one's child **in the fire** to the gods (18:10).

Other forbidden occult practices can be summarized in three basic categories, beginning with **divination** (18:10). Divination is an attempt to get secret knowledge by interpreting omens or looking to astrology. Lest you think of this as an ancient practice, many people today read their horoscopes before they make any

a 18:10 Lv 18:21; 2Kg 16:3; 17:17; 21:6; 23:10; Jr 32:35; Ezk 20:26,31; 23:37
b 18:11 Lv 19:26,31; 20:6,27; Nm 22:7; 23:23; 1Sm 28:3; 2Kg 23:24; 2Ch 33:6; Is 2:6; 8:19; Jr 14:14; Ezk 13:7; 21:21; Mc 3:11
c 18:15 Mt 21:11; Lk 2:25-34; 7:16; 24:19; Jn 1:21,25; 4:19; Ac 3:22; 7:37
d 18:16 Ex 20:19; Dt 5:23-27
e 18:19 Ac 3:23
f 19:1 Dt 12:29
g 19:2-13 Nm 35:6-34; Jos 20
h 19:10 Dt 15:4

one among you is to sacrifice his son or daughter in the fire,[A,a] practice divination, tell fortunes, interpret omens, practice sorcery, [11] cast spells, consult a medium or a spiritist, or inquire of the dead.[b] [12] Everyone who does these acts is detestable to the LORD, and the LORD your God is driving out the nations before you because of these detestable acts. [13] You must be blameless before the LORD your God. [14] Though these nations you are about to drive out listen to fortune-tellers and diviners, the LORD your God has not permitted you to do this.

[15] "The LORD your God will raise up for you a prophet like me from among your own brothers.[c] You must listen to him. [16] This is what you requested from the LORD your God at Horeb on the day of the assembly when you said, 'Let us not continue to hear the voice of the LORD our God or see this great fire any longer, so that we will not die!'[d] [17] Then the LORD said to me, 'They have spoken well. [18] I will raise up for them a prophet like you from among their brothers. I will put my words in his mouth, and he will tell them everything I command him. [19] I will hold accountable whoever does not listen to my words that he speaks in my name.[e] [20] But the prophet who presumes to speak a message in my name that I have not commanded him to speak, or who speaks in the name of other gods — that prophet must die.' [21] You may say to yourself, 'How can we recognize a message the LORD has not spoken?' [22] When a prophet speaks in the LORD's name, and the message does not come true or is not fulfilled, that is a message the LORD has not spoken. The prophet has spoken it presumptuously. Do not be afraid of him.

CITIES OF REFUGE

19 "When the LORD your God annihilates the nations whose land he is giving you,[f] so that you drive them out and live in their cities and houses, [2] you are to set apart three cities for yourselves within the land the LORD your God is giving you to possess.[g] [3] You are to determine the distances[B] and divide the land the LORD your God is granting you as an inheritance into three regions, so that anyone who commits manslaughter can flee to these cities.[c]

[4] "Here is the law concerning a case of someone who kills a person and flees there to save his life, having killed his neighbor accidentally without previously hating him: [5] If, for example, he goes into the forest with his neighbor to cut timber, and his hand swings the ax to chop down a tree, but the blade flies off the handle and strikes his neighbor so that he dies, that person may flee to one of these cities and live. [6] Otherwise, the avenger of blood in the heat of his anger[D] might pursue the one who committed manslaughter, overtake him because the distance is great, and strike him dead. Yet he did not deserve to die,[E] since he did not previously hate his neighbor. [7] This is why I am commanding you to set apart three cities for yourselves. [8] If the LORD your God enlarges your territory as he swore to your fathers, and gives you all the land he promised to give them — [9] provided you keep every one of these commands I am giving you today and follow them, loving the LORD your God and walking in his ways at all times — you are to add three more cities to these three. [10] In this way, innocent blood will not be shed, and you will not become guilty of bloodshed in the land the LORD your God is giving you as an inheritance.[h] [11] But if someone hates his

---

A 18:10 Lit *to make his son or daughter pass through the fire*   B 19:3 Or *to prepare the roads*   C 19:3 Lit *flee there*   D 19:6 Lit *heart*   E 19:6 Lit *did not have a judgment of death*

---

decisions—yet they refuse to seek the guidance of the God who made them, which is found in the Scriptures.

The second category is magic, which includes **sorcery** and **spells** (18:10-11). This is not to be confused with the art of illusion. Moses was talking about witchcraft, through which humans attempt to accomplish in the spiritual realm what human power alone can't pull off.

The third category is spiritism, which involves the attempt to get in touch with spiritual intermediaries by contacting the **dead** (18:11). Holding séances and playing with Ouija boards are modern expressions of spiritism.

18:15 Here we find a wonderful prophecy. Moses told the people that the Lord would provide another mediator after he was gone—an in-between person who would speak on God's behalf and help the people to access God. Centuries later, Jesus Christ would rise up from among his brothers, fully human (see John 1:14; Heb 2:14-18). But God the Father also declared him to be fully divine, his own "beloved Son," and commanded the disciples to "Listen to him!" (Matt 17:5). The apostle Peter declared that Moses's words were fulfilled in Jesus (see Acts 3:22-23). He is our perfect Mediator (see 1 Tim 2:5).

18:19 God warned that he would **hold accountable whoever** did not **listen** to this

prophet, the Messiah (see the note on 18:15). Indeed, there are serious consequences to ignoring Christ: it's a matter of life and death. **18:20-22** God gave Israel a measuring stick to hold up against any prophet who claimed to speak in his name.

19:4-13 By having the three cities spaced throughout the land, Israel allowed the person who committed manslaughter a city of refuge within a close enough distance that he could get to it before being overtaken. By contrast, someone who had clearly hated his neighbor and killed him in cold blood was to be given no refuge (19:11-13).

neighbor, lies in ambush for him, attacks him, and strikes him fatally, and flees to one of these cities, ¹² the elders of his city are to send for him, take him from there, and hand him over to the avenger of blood and he will die. ¹³ Do not look on him with pity but purge from Israel the guilt of shedding innocent blood, and you will prosper.

BOUNDARY MARKERS

¹⁴ "Do not move your neighbor's boundary marker,^a established at the start in the inheritance you will receive in the land the LORD your God is giving you to possess.

WITNESSES IN COURT

¹⁵ "One witness cannot establish any iniquity or sin against a person, whatever that person has done.^b A fact must be established by the testimony of two or three witnesses.^c

¹⁶ "If a malicious witness^d testifies against someone accusing him of a crime, ¹⁷ the two people in the dispute are to stand in the presence of the LORD before the priests and judges in authority at that time. ¹⁸ The judges are to make a careful investigation, and if the witness turns out to be a liar who has falsely accused his brother, ¹⁹ you must do to him as he intended to do to his brother. You must purge the evil from you. ²⁰ Then everyone else will hear and be afraid, and they will never again do anything evil like this among you.^e ²¹ Do not show pity: life for life, eye for eye, tooth for tooth, hand for hand, and foot for foot.^f

RULES FOR WAR

20 "When you go out to war against your enemies and see horses, chariots, and an army larger than yours,^g do not be afraid of them, for the LORD your God, who brought you out of the land of Egypt,^h is with you. ² When you are about to engage in battle, the priest is to come forward and address the army.ⁱ ³ He is to say to them: 'Listen, Israel: Today you are about to engage in battle with your enemies. Do not be cowardly. Do not be afraid, alarmed, or terrified because of them. ⁴ For the LORD your God is the one who goes with you to fight for you^j against your enemies to give you victory.'

⁵ "The officers are to address the army, 'Has any man built a new house and not dedicated it? Let him leave and return home. Otherwise, he may die in battle and another man dedicate it. ⁶ Has any man planted a vineyard and not begun to enjoy its fruit?^A Let him leave and return home. Otherwise he may die in battle and another man enjoy its fruit.^B ⁷ Has any man become engaged to a woman and not married her? Let him leave and return home. Otherwise he may die in battle and another man marry her.' ⁸ The officers will continue to address the army and say, 'Is there any man who is afraid or cowardly? Let him leave and return home, so that his brothers won't lose heart as he did.'^{c,k} ⁹ When the officers have finished addressing the army, they will appoint military commanders to lead it.

¹⁰ "When you approach a city to fight against it, make an offer of peace. ¹¹ If it accepts your offer of peace and opens its gates to you, all the people found in it will become forced laborers for you and serve you.^l ¹² However, if it does not make peace with you but wages war against you, lay siege to it. ¹³ When the LORD your God hands it over to you, strike down all its males with the sword.^m ¹⁴ But you may take the women, dependents, animals, and whatever else is in the city — all its spoil — as plunder. You may enjoy the spoil of

^a 19:14 Dt 27:17; Pr 22:28; Hs 5:10
^b 19:15 Nm 35:30
^c Mt 18:16; Jn 8:17; 2Co 13:1
^d 19:16 Ex 23:1
^e 19:20 Dt 13:11
^f 19:21 Ex 21:23-25; Lv 24:19-20; Mt 5:38
^g 20:1 Jos 17:18; 2Ch 32:8; Ps 20:7; Is 31:1
^h 20:1 Dt 1:26-40
ⁱ 20:2 2Ch 13:12; 32:8
^j 20:4 Ex 14:14; Dt 1:30; 3:22; 31:6,8; Jos 23:10; Jdg 9:17; Jr 42:11
^k 20:8 Jdg 7:3
^l 20:11 Ex 1:11; Jos 16:10; 17:13; Jdg 1:28-35; 2Sm 20:24; 1Kg 5:13-14; 9:21
^m 20:13 Nm 31:7

---

^A20:6 Lit *not put it to use*   ^B20:6 Lit *man put it to use*   ^C20:8 Lit *brothers' hearts won't melt like his own*

19:14 To move a **neighbor's boundary marker** was to encroach upon someone else's rightful property, essentially stealing land that God himself had allotted to the tribes of Israel (see Exod 20:15).

19:18-21 The **eye for eye** principle outlined here (19:21) has often been referred to by the Latin expression *lex talionis*—that is, the "law of retaliation." This means that the punishment was to fit the crime. In fact, it *limited* the punishment to fit the crime so that if someone knocked out your tooth, you couldn't bust out four of his in response. Through this law, God wisely prevented both leniency and excess punishment in his legal system.

20:2-4 The priest's exhortation was extremely important. The previous generation of Israelites died in the wilderness because they had succumbed to fear of Canaan's inhabitants and failed to trust that God would provide for them (see Num 13:1–14:45). Therefore, the current generation needed to learn from the mistake of their ancestors.

We too often fail to follow the Lord and do as his Word commands because we fear the world—what they will think of us or do to us. Instead, we must trust that our King will provide the means to accomplish the kingdom agenda that he commands.

20:5-8 Each of the first three exemptions involves a lack of fulfillment in pursuing one of life's basic pleasures (20:5-7). They may have been chosen by God to illustrate the ways in which he intended his people to enjoy the good land he was giving them. The fourth exemption involved a soldier with a **cowardly** heart. He was sent home, not for his own sake, but so that he wouldn't demoralize **his brothers** (20:8).

20:10-14 Enemy cities outside the promised land were to be offered terms of **peace**, which they could accept on the condition of becoming **forced laborers** of Israel (20:10-11). Refusing the offer, however, led to **siege**, the death of all a city's men, and the taking of their goods (20:12-14).

a 20:17-18 Dt 7:1-5

your enemies that the LORD your God has given you. **15** This is how you are to treat all the cities that are far away from you and are not among the cities of these nations. **16** However, you must not let any living thing survive among the cities of these people the LORD your God is giving you as an inheritance. **17** You must completely destroy them — the Hethite, Amorite, Canaanite, Perizzite, Hivite, and Jebusite — as the LORD your God has commanded you, **18** so that they won't teach you to do all the detestable acts they do for their gods, and you sin against the LORD your God.[a]

19 "When you lay siege to a city for a long time, fighting against it in order to capture it, do not destroy its trees by putting an ax to them, because you can get food from them. Do not cut them down. Are trees of the field human, to come under siege by you? **20** But you may destroy the trees that you know do not produce food. You may cut them down to build siege works against the city that is waging war against you, until it falls.

UNSOLVED MURDERS

21 "If a murder victim is found lying in a field in the land the LORD your God is giving you to possess, and it is not known who killed him, **2** your elders and judges are to come out and measure the distance from the victim to the nearby cities. **3** The elders of the city nearest to the victim are to get a young cow that has not been yoked or used for work. **4** The elders of that city will bring the cow down to a continually flowing stream, to a place not tilled or sown, and they will break its neck there by the stream. **5** Then the priests, the sons of Levi, will come forward, for the LORD your God has chosen them to serve him and pronounce blessings in his name, and they are to give a ruling in[A] every dispute

and case of assault. **6** All the elders of the city nearest to the victim will wash their hands by the stream over the young cow whose neck has been broken. **7** They will declare, 'Our hands did not shed this blood; our eyes did not see it. **8** LORD, wipe away the guilt of your people Israel whom you redeemed, and do not hold the shedding of innocent blood against them.' Then the responsibility for bloodshed will be wiped away from them. **9** You must purge from yourselves the guilt of shedding innocent blood, for you will be doing what is right in the LORD's sight.

FAIR TREATMENT OF CAPTURED WOMEN

10 "When you go to war against your enemies and the LORD your God hands them over to you and you take some of them prisoner, and **11** if you see a beautiful woman among the captives, desire her, and want to take her as your wife, **12** you are to bring her into your house. She is to shave her head, trim her nails, **13** remove the clothes she was wearing when she was taken prisoner, live in your house, and mourn for her father and mother a full month. After that, you may have sexual relations with her and be her husband, and she will be your wife. **14** Then if you are not satisfied with her, you are to let her go where she wants, but you must not sell her or treat her as merchandise,[B] because you have humiliated her.

THE RIGHT OF THE FIRSTBORN

15 "If a man has two wives, one loved and the other unloved, and both the loved and the unloved bear him sons, and if the unloved wife has the firstborn son, **16** when that man gives what he has to his sons as an inheritance, he is not to show favoritism to the son of the loved wife as

---

[A] 21:5 Lit and according to their mouth will be   [B] 21:14 Hb obscure

---

20:15-18 No offer of peace was to be made to the Canaanites. Israel was to **completely destroy** them (20:16-17). Otherwise, survivors would teach the Israelites **to do all the detestable acts they** did and cause the people to **sin against the LORD** (20:18).
20:19-20 Israel was to refrain from the common practice in ancient warfare of punishing a defeated enemy by decimating its land. After all, Canaan was to be Israel's possession.
21:10-14 Should an Israelite soldier want to marry a woman **among the captives** from one of the cities outside of Canaan (21:11), the woman was allowed to undergo a certain physical and spiritual ritual to separate

her from her old life, including a month-long period of mourning **for her father and mother** (21:12-13)—either because they had been killed or in recognition of the fact that she would not be going back to them. A provision was also made for divorce if the husband was not pleased with his wife, but he could **not sell her** or mistreat her in any way (21:14). Though other nations often brutally mistreated women during times of war, this law provided a woman of a subjugated country protection.
21:15-17 Polygamy was tolerated in Old Testament times, but it was never God's standard for marriage—which was to be between one

man and one woman (see Gen 2:22-24). The culturally accepted practice of taking more than one wife always led to problems among God's people. (See, for example, the experiences of grief that polygamy brought into the lives of Jacob, David, and Solomon.) Jealousy was just one of those problems; it could cause one wife to push her son forward as the favorite, even if he were not the first born. Nevertheless, fathers was strictly forbidden to play that game and were commanded to give their **firstborn** sons **two shares of** their estates, because those sons—whether or not their mothers held their fathers' hearts—had **the rights of the firstborn** (Deut 21:17).

his firstborn over the firstborn of the unloved wife. **17** He must acknowledge the firstborn, the son of the unloved wife, by giving him two shares[A,B] of his estate, for he is the firstfruits of his virility; he has the rights of the firstborn.[a]

A REBELLIOUS SON

18 "If a man has a stubborn and rebellious son who does not obey his father or mother and doesn't listen to them even after they discipline him, **19** his father and mother are to take hold of him and bring him to the elders of his city, to the gate[b] of his hometown. **20** They will say to the elders of his city, 'This son of ours is stubborn and rebellious; he doesn't obey us. He's a glutton and a drunkard.' **21** Then all the men of his city will stone him to death.[c] You must purge the evil from you, and all Israel will hear and be afraid.

DISPLAY OF EXECUTED PEOPLE

22 "If anyone is found guilty of an offense deserving the death penalty and is executed, and you hang his body on a tree, **23** you are not to leave his corpse on the tree overnight but are to bury him that day, for anyone hung on a tree is under God's curse.[d] You must not defile the land the LORD your God is giving you as an inheritance.[e]

CARING FOR YOUR BROTHER'S PROPERTY

22 "If you see your brother Israelite's ox or sheep straying, do not ignore it; make sure you return it to your brother. **2** If your brother does not live near you or you don't know him, you are to bring the animal to your home to remain with you until your brother comes looking for it; then you can return it to him. **3** Do the same for his donkey, his garment, or anything your brother has lost and you have found. You must not ignore it.[f] **4** If you see your brother's donkey or ox fallen down on the road, do not ignore it; help him lift it up.

PRESERVING NATURAL DISTINCTIONS

5 "A woman is not to wear male clothing, and a man is not to put on a woman's garment, for everyone who does these things is detestable to the LORD your God.

6 "If you come across a bird's nest with chicks or eggs, either in a tree or on the ground along the road, and the mother is sitting on the chicks or eggs, do not take the mother along with the young. **7** You may take the young for yourself, but be sure to let the mother go free, so that you may prosper and live long. **8** If you build a new house, make a railing around your roof, so that you don't bring bloodguilt on your house if someone falls from it. **9** Do not plant your vineyard with two types of seed; otherwise, the entire harvest, both the crop you plant and the produce of the vineyard, will be defiled. **10** Do not plow with an ox and a donkey together. **11** Do not wear clothes made of both wool and linen.[g] **12** Make tassels on the four corners of the outer garment you wear.[h]

[a] 21:15-17 Gn 29:30-33; 49:3
[b] 21:19 Dt 17:8; 22:15; 25:7
[c] 21:21 Ex 21:17; Lv 20:9
[d] 21:23 Gl 3:13
[e] Dt 15:4

[f] 22:1-3 Ex 23:4
[g] 22:11 Lv 19:19
[h] 22:12 Nm 15:38-39

[A] 21:17 Lit *him mouth of two*, or *two mouthfuls*   [B] 21:17 Or *two-thirds*

21:18-21 The son in view here was not a teenager who fell into sassy speech on occasion. This was a son who, though his parents would **discipline him**, refused to repent (21:18). Instead, his **stubborn and rebellious** nature mirrored that of Egypt's hard-hearted Pharaoh, and it even included his being known as a **drunkard** (21:20). Such rebellion was a capital offense in God's eyes, because left unpunished it would destroy Israel's home life and eventually the entire community. The bottom line here is that this young man refused to submit to the Lord as his King and to his parents as his God-ordained authority.

21:22-23 Anyone hung on a tree is under God's curse (21:23). Sinless Jesus Christ redeemed us by his death on the cross—being hung on a tree—thus enduring God's curse against our sin in our place (see Gal 3:13).

22:1-4 The command to care for an **ox or sheep** or any other possession that was **lost** (22:1-3) was a practical way to live out the command to "love your neighbor as yourself" (Lev 19:18).

22:5 The prohibition against **a woman** wearing **male clothing** and vice versa is a reminder of the gender distinctions God designed. Men and women equally share in bearing the image of God, but he has designed us to be distinct from and complementary toward one another (see Gen 1:27). The gender confusion that exists in our culture is a clear rejection of God's good design.

In many places, homosexuality and transgenderism are aggressively promoted. But the people of God should promote his kingdom agenda through biblically based kingdom political involvement and sincere love for others. This is to be done not by violent revolution from the top down, but by social transformation based on spiritual principles that work from the bottom up. What God wants from his people is not revolution, but transformation.

22:6-8 The command to leave a **mother** bird behind while taking her **chicks or eggs** (22:6-7) helped guarantee a continual food supply. The command to build a **railing** around the flat roofs of Israelite houses prevented falls. Both promote the application of wisdom in daily life.

22:9-11 The common theme in these verses is the mixing of unlike things. Teaching the Israelites to recognize distinctions would help them see the importance of being holy and distinct in a sinful world. Paul uses a similar idea to **not plow with an ox and a donkey together** (22:10) when he warns believers not to enter into partnership with unbelievers (2 Cor 6:14). Though believers must live in this fallen world, God wants us to live lives distinct from the wickedness around us.

22:12 The **tassels** mentioned here served as visual reminders to obey God's laws (see Num 15:37-41).

^a 22:15 Dt 17:8; 21:19; 25:7
^b 22:18 Dt 25:1-3

^c 22:28-29 Ex 22:16-17
^d 22:30 Lv 18:8; 20:10-11
^e 23:3-4 Neh 13:1-2
^f 23:4 Nm 22:5-6

VIOLATIONS OF PROPER SEXUAL CONDUCT

13 "If a man marries a woman, has sexual relations with her, and comes to hate her, **14** and accuses her of shameful conduct, and gives her a bad name, saying, 'I married this woman and was intimate with her, but I didn't find any evidence of her virginity,' **15** the young woman's father and mother will take the evidence of her virginity and bring it to the city elders at the city gate.^a **16** The young woman's father will say to the elders, 'I gave my daughter to this man as a wife, but he hates her. **17** He has accused her of shameful conduct, saying: "I didn't find any evidence of your daughter's virginity," but here is the evidence of my daughter's virginity.' They will spread out the cloth before the city elders. **18** Then the elders of that city will take the man and punish him.^b **19** They will also fine him a hundred silver shekels and give them to the young woman's father, because that man gave an Israelite virgin a bad name. She will remain his wife; he cannot divorce her as long as he lives. **20** But if this accusation is true and no evidence of the young woman's virginity is found, **21** they will bring the woman to the door of her father's house, and the men of her city will stone her to death. For she has committed an outrage in Israel by being promiscuous while living in her father's house. You must purge the evil from you.

22 "If a man is discovered having sexual relations with another man's wife, both the man who had sex with the woman and the woman must die. You must purge the evil from Israel. **23** If there is a young woman who is a virgin engaged to a man, and another man encounters her in the city and sleeps with her, **24** take the two of them out to the gate of that city and stone them to death — the young woman because she did not cry out in the city and the man because he has violated his neighbor's fiancée. You must purge the evil from you. **25** But if the man encounters an engaged woman in the open country, and he seizes and rapes her, only the man who raped her must die. **26** Do nothing to the young woman, because she is not guilty of an offense deserving death. This case is just like one in which a man attacks his neighbor and murders him. **27** When he found her in the field, the engaged woman cried out, but there was no one to rescue her. **28** If a man encounters a young woman, a virgin who is not engaged, takes hold of her and rapes her, and they are discovered, **29** the man who raped her is to give the young woman's father fifty silver shekels, and she will become his wife because he violated her.^c He cannot divorce her as long as he lives.

30 "A man is not to marry his father's wife; he must not violate his father's marriage bed.^{A,d}

EXCLUSION AND INCLUSION

23 "No man whose testicles have been crushed^B or whose penis has been cut off may enter the LORD's assembly. **2** No one of illegitimate birth may enter the LORD's assembly; none of his descendants, even to the tenth generation, may enter the LORD's assembly. **3** No Ammonite or Moabite may enter the LORD's assembly; none of their descendants, even to the tenth generation, may ever enter the LORD's assembly. **4** This is because they did not meet you with food and water on the journey after you came out of Egypt, and because Balaam son of Beor from Pethor in Aram-naharaim was hired to curse you.^f **5** Yet the LORD your God would not listen to Balaam, but he turned the curse

^A 22:30 Lit *not uncover the edge of his father's garment* ; Ru 3:9; Ezk 16:8 · ^B 23:1 Lit *man bruised by crushing*

22:13-21 Given human sinfulness, God knew there would be marital problems. So he gave Moses regulations to be applied in the case of a husband who came to **hate** his wife and claimed she wasn't a virgin when he married her (22:13-14). If her parents could prove her pre-marital purity by providing **evidence of her virginity**, her husband was given a stiff fine and prohibited from ever divorcing his wife (22:15-19). Being prepared to show evidence of virginity was a customary practice that perhaps involved a blood-stained cloth from the wedding night.
22:22-24 Adultery was a capital offense under the Mosaic law, and an engaged woman was treated the same way as a married woman in a case in which sex was consensual. Importantly, Israel's violations of the covenant with God were described as spiritual "adultery" (see Hos 2:2), another indicator that God holds marital fidelity in high regard.
22:25-29 Rape was a capital offense if the victim was **engaged**. If she wasn't, the perpetrator had to pay the victim's father a fine, marry the woman, and live with her for the rest of his life to provide for her because he stole her virginity.
22:30 Moses prohibited a man from marrying his stepmother. Note Paul's application of this principle in his letter to the Corinthians (see 1 Cor 5:1).

23:1 The prohibition against a eunuch participating in worship at the tabernacle was not a matter of the person's sin; it was a ceremonial rule meant to teach Israel the need for perfection before the Lord.
23:2 The ban on people of **illegitimate birth** would have meant primarily those born of a union between an Israelite and a non-Israelite (for instance, a Canaanite). Their ban was permanent, which is the practical meaning behind the idea of **the tenth generation**.
23:3-6 The Ammonites and Moabites were barred because of their cruel treatment of the Israelites during their travels in the wilderness and because the Moabites hired **Balaam** to **curse** Israel (23:4).

into a blessing for you because the LORD your God loves[a] you.[b] 6 Never pursue their welfare or prosperity as long as you live. 7 Do not despise an Edomite, because he is your brother. Do not despise an Egyptian, because you were a resident alien in his land. 8 The children born to them in the third generation may enter the LORD's assembly.

CLEANLINESS OF THE CAMP

9 "When you are encamped against your enemies, be careful to avoid anything offensive. 10 If there is a man among you who is unclean because of a bodily emission during the night, he must go outside the camp; he may not come anywhere inside the camp. 11 When evening approaches, he is to wash with water, and when the sun sets he may come inside the camp.[c] 12 You are to have a place outside the camp and go there to relieve yourself. 13 You are to have a digging tool in your equipment; when you relieve yourself, dig a hole with it and cover up your excrement. 14 For the LORD your God walks throughout your camp to protect you and deliver your enemies to you; so your encampments must be holy. He must not see anything indecent among you or he will turn away from you.

FUGITIVE SLAVES

15 "Do not return a slave to his master when he has escaped from his master to you. 16 Let him live among you wherever he wants within your city gates. Do not mistreat him.

CULT PROSTITUTION FORBIDDEN

17 "No Israelite woman is to be a cult prostitute, and no Israelite man is to be a cult prostitute. 18 Do not bring a female prostitute's wages or a male prostitute's[A] earnings into the house of the LORD your God to fulfill any vow, because both are detestable to the LORD your God.

INTEREST ON LOANS

19 "Do not charge your brother interest on silver, food, or anything that can earn interest. 20 You may charge a foreigner interest, but you must not charge your brother Israelite interest, so that the LORD your God may bless you in everything you do[B] in the land you are entering to possess.[d]

KEEPING VOWS

21 "If you make a vow to the LORD your God, do not be slow to keep it, because he will require it of you, and it will be counted against you as sin. 22 But if you refrain from making a vow, it will not be counted against you as sin. 23 Be careful to do whatever comes from your lips, because you have freely vowed what you promised[c] to the LORD your God.[e]

NEIGHBOR'S CROPS

24 "When you enter your neighbor's vineyard, you may eat as many grapes as you want until you are full, but do not put any in your container. 25 When you enter your neighbor's standing grain, you may pluck heads of grain with your hand, but do not put a sickle to your neighbor's grain.

MARRIAGE AND DIVORCE LAWS

24 "If a man marries a woman, but she becomes displeasing to him[D] because he finds something indecent about her, he may write her a divorce certificate, hand it to her, and send her away from his house.[f] 2 If after leaving his house she goes and becomes another man's wife, 3 and the second man hates her, writes her a divorce certificate, hands it to her, and sends her away from his house or if he dies, 4 the first husband who sent her away may not marry her again after she has been defiled, because that would be detestable to the LORD. You must not bring guilt on the land the LORD your God is giving you as an inheritance.[g]

---

a 23:5 Dt 4:37
b Nm 23:11; 24:10
c 23:11 Lv 15:16-17

d 23:19-20 Ex 22:25
e 23:21-23 Nm 30:2-15; Jb 22:27; Ps 50:14; 56:12; 61:8; Pr 20:25; Ec 5:4-7; Mal 1:14
f 24:1 Mt 5:31; 19:7; Mk 10:4
g 24:4 Dt 15:4

A 23:18 Lit *a dog's*   B 23:20 Lit *you put your hand to*   C 23:23 Lit *promised with your mouth*   D 24:1 Lit *she does not find favor in his eyes*

23:7 The Edomites descended from Israelite patriarch Jacob's twin brother Esau.
23:9-14 The camp was to be ceremonially clean so that the holy God could dwell among his people.
23:15-16 The Lord wanted fugitive slaves to feel welcome in the Israelite camp. The righteous thing to do was to give such people sanctuary.
23:17-18 Wicked forms of pagan worship—whether one was visiting a **cult prostitute** or

acting as one—were contrary to the sexual ethic the Lord established.
23:19 This honored the law's command to "love your neighbor as yourself" (Lev 19:18).
23:21-23 Vows to God were completely voluntary, but once made they were to be kept.
23:24-25 It was acceptable to pluck **grapes** or **heads of grain** to eat while on a neighbor's property, but this did not give anyone license to show up with a **sickle** and start harvesting.

24:1-4 **Divorce** was not part of God's ideal for marriage, even though he permitted it here. Jesus told his disciples that this concession was made because of the hardness of the Israelites' hearts—that is, their refusal to submit to divine standards (see Matt 19:8).
24:5 This would allow the couple time to adjust to life together and prevent a new bride from losing her husband in war before having a chance to enjoy married life and possibly conceive.

a 24:7 Gn 40:15; Ex 21:16;
22:1; 1Sm 30:2-3,5;
1Tm 1:10
b 24:9 Nm 12:1-15; Dt 25:17
c 24:12-13 Ex 22:26-27
d 24:14-15 Lv 19:13

e 24:16 2Kg 14:6; 2Ch 25:4;
Ezk 18:20; 33:10-20
f 24:18 Dt 7:8; 9:26; 15:15
g Dt 15:15; 24:22
h 24:18-19 Ex 23:2-3,6-9;
Dt 30:9
i 24:19-22 Ex 22:26-27; Lv
19:9-10,13,15
j 25:4 1Co 9:9; 1Tm 5:18

5 "When a man takes a bride, he must not go out with the army or be liable for any duty. He is free to stay at home for one year, so that he can bring joy to the wife he has married.

SAFEGUARDING LIFE

6 "Do not take a pair of grindstones or even the upper millstone as security for a debt, because that is like taking a life as security. 7 "If a man is discovered kidnapping[a] one of his Israelite brothers, whether he treats him as a slave or sells him, the kidnapper must die. You must purge the evil from you.

8 "Be careful with a person who has a case of serious skin disease, following carefully everything the Levitical priests instruct you to do. Be careful to do as I have commanded them. 9 Remember what the LORD your God did to Miriam on the journey after you left Egypt.[b]

CONSIDERATION FOR PEOPLE IN NEED

10 "When you make a loan of any kind to your neighbor, do not enter his house to collect what he offers as security. 11 Stand outside while the man you are making the loan to brings the security out to you. 12 If he is a poor man, do not sleep with the garment he has given as security. 13 Be sure to return it[A] to him at sunset. Then he will sleep in it and bless you, and this will be counted as righteousness to you before the LORD your God.[c]

14 "Do not oppress a hired worker who is poor and needy, whether one of your Israelite brothers or one of the resident aliens in a town[B] in your land. 15 You are to pay him his wages each day before the sun sets, because he is poor and depends on them.[d] Otherwise he will cry out to the LORD against you, and you will be held guilty.

16 "Fathers are not to be put to death for their children, and children are not to be put to death for their fathers; each person

will be put to death for his own sin.[e] 17 Do not deny justice to a resident alien or fatherless child, and do not take a widow's garment as security. 18 Remember that you were a slave in Egypt, and the LORD your God redeemed[f] you from there. Therefore I am commanding you to do this.[g]

19 "When you reap the harvest in your field, and you forget a sheaf in the field, do not go back to get it. It is to be left for the resident alien, the fatherless, and the widow, so that the LORD your God may bless you in all the work of your hands.[h] 20 When you knock down the fruit from your olive tree, do not go over the branches again. What remains will be for the resident alien, the fatherless, and the widow. 21 When you gather the grapes of your vineyard, do not glean what is left. What remains will be for the resident alien, the fatherless, and the widow. 22 Remember that you were a slave in the land of Egypt. Therefore I am commanding you to do this.[i]

FAIRNESS AND MERCY

25 "If there is a dispute between men, they are to go to court, and the judges will hear their case. They will clear the innocent and condemn the guilty. 2 If the guilty party deserves to be flogged, the judge will make him lie down and be flogged in his presence with the number of lashes appropriate for his crime. 3 He may be flogged with forty lashes, but no more. Otherwise, if he is flogged with more lashes than these, your brother will be degraded in your sight.

4 "Do not muzzle an ox while it treads out grain.[j]

PRESERVING THE FAMILY LINE

5 "When brothers live on the same property[c] and one of them dies without a son, the wife of the dead man may not marry a stranger outside the family. Her brother-in-law is to take her as his wife, have

---

A 24:13 Lit *return what he has given as security*   B 24:14 Lit *within the city gates*   C 25:5 Lit *live together*

24:6 In ancient Israel, there were no refrigerators in which to store food, no closets full of clothes, no heaters to turn on when the weather got cold, and no banks. A man worked each day, got paid each evening, and bought or harvested his food for that night's dinner. Taking his **grindstones . . . as security** was cruel because it meant that he couldn't prepare his daily bread.
24:7 **Kidnapping** a fellow Israelite to enslave or sell him was an offense rightly punishable

by death. This is a stiff warning against human trafficking.
24:8 A **serious skin disease** was a matter of great concern, since it required the affected person to be quarantined and to endure extensive procedures with **the Levitical priests** in order to be pronounced clean again (see Lev 13:1-46; 14:1-32).
24:10-15 If anything was to mark the people of God, it was compassion for those in need—a trait in short supply both then and now.

24:19-22 Of all the peoples who should understand the pain of injustice, it was the Israelites. Therefore, they were commanded to care for the three most vulnerable groups within their society: **the resident alien, the fatherless, and the widow.** If you have been comforted by God, he expects you to share that comfort with others who have experienced similar suffering (see 2 Cor 1:4).
25:4 So important was the concept of justice to God that he even cared about it being offered to the animals that served the Israelites.

sexual relations with her, and perform the duty of a brother-in-law for her. **6** The first son she bears will carry on the name of the dead brother, so his name will not be blotted out from Israel.[a] **7** But if the man doesn't want to marry his sister-in-law, she is to go to the elders at the city gate[b] and say, 'My brother-in-law refuses to preserve his brother's name in Israel. He isn't willing to perform the duty of a brother-in-law for me.' **8** The elders of his city will summon him and speak with him. If he persists and says, 'I don't want to marry her,' **9** then his sister-in-law will go up to him in the sight of the elders, remove his sandal from his foot, and spit in his face. Then she will declare, 'This is what is done to a man who will not build up his brother's house.' **10** And his family name in Israel will be 'The house of the man whose sandal was removed.'[c]

11 "If two men are fighting with each other, and the wife of one steps in to rescue her husband from the one striking him, and she puts out her hand and grabs his genitals, **12** you are to cut off her hand. Do not show pity.

HONEST WEIGHTS AND MEASURES

13 "Do not have differing weights[A] in your bag, one heavy and one light.[d] **14** Do not have differing dry measures in your house, a larger and a smaller. **15** You must have a full and honest weight, a full and honest dry measure, so that you may live long in the land the LORD your God is giving you. **16** For everyone who does such things and acts unfairly is detestable to the LORD your God.[e]

REVENGE ON THE AMALEKITES

17 "Remember what the Amalekites did to you on the journey after you left Egypt.[f] **18** They met you along the way and attacked all your stragglers from behind when you were tired and weary. They did not fear God. **19** When the LORD your God gives you rest[g] from all the enemies around you in the land the LORD your God is giving you

to possess as an inheritance,[h] blot out the memory of Amalek under heaven. Do not forget.[i]

GIVING THE FIRSTFRUITS

26 "When you enter the land the LORD your God is giving you as an inheritance,[j] and you take possession of it and live in it, **2** take some of the first of all the land's produce that you harvest from the land the LORD your God is giving you and put it in a basket. Then go to the place where the LORD your God chooses to have his name dwell.[k] **3** When you come before the priest who is serving at that time, say to him, 'Today I declare to the LORD your[B] God that I have entered the land the LORD swore to our fathers to give us.'

4 "Then the priest will take the basket from you and place it before the altar of the LORD your God. **5** You are to respond by saying in the presence of the LORD your God:

My father was a wandering Aramean.[l] He went down to Egypt with a few people and resided there as an alien.[m] There he became a great, powerful, and populous nation. **6** But the Egyptians mistreated and oppressed us, and forced us to do hard labor. **7** So we called out to the LORD, the God of our fathers, and the LORD heard our cry and saw our misery, hardship, and oppression.[n] **8** Then the LORD brought us out of Egypt with a strong hand and an outstretched arm, with terrifying power, and with signs and wonders. **9** He led us to this place and gave us this land, a land flowing with milk and honey.[o] **10** I have now brought the first of the land's produce that you, LORD, have given me.

You will then place the container before the LORD your God and bow down to him. **11** You, the Levites, and the resident aliens among you will rejoice[p] in all the good things the LORD your God has given you and your household.

[a] 25:5-6 Gn 38:8; Mt 22:24; Mk 12:19; Lk 20:28
[b] 25:7 Dt 17:8; 21:19; 22:15
[c] 25:10 Gn 38; Ru 4:1-12
[d] 25:13 Pr 20:10
[e] 25:16 Lv 19:35-36
[f] 25:17 Dt 24:9
[g] 25:19 Dt 3:20; 5:14; 12:9-11; 28:65

[h] 25:19 Dt 15:4
[i] Ex 17:8-16; 1Sm 15; 30
[j] 26:1 Dt 15:4; 17:14
[k] 26:2 Dt 12:11
[l] 26:5 Gn 28:5
[m] Ex 1:1-3
[n] 26:7 Ex 3:7
[o] 26:9 Dt 11:9; Jr 32:22
[p] 26:11 Lv 23:40; Dt 12:12; 14:26; 16:11; 27:7

[A] **25:13** Lit *have a stone and a stone*　　[B] **26:3** LXX reads *my*

25:11-12 Having and raising children was highly valued in ancient Israel. "Sons are indeed a heritage from the Lord, offspring, a reward. Like arrows in the hand of a warrior are the sons born in one's youth. Happy is the man who has filled his quiver with them" (Ps 127:3-5). Thus, harming a man's reproductive ability incurred a severe penalty.

25:13-16 The Israelites should not be tempted to put a thumb on the scales, so to speak, when God had promised to prosper them in everything they did if only they would honor and obey him.

26:1-3 Offering the firstfruits of their harvest was an opportunity for the people to remind themselves and declare publicly that God had indeed given them the land

as promised and that the produce was the proof.

26:5 The **wandering Aramean** is a reference both to Jacob (also called Israel) and to the Israelites' father Abraham. He spent years in Aram on his way to Canaan. His grandson Jacob married Rachel, who was from the Aramean side of his family, too.

[a] 26:12 Dt 14:28-29
[b] 26:14 Jr 16:7; Ezk 24:17;
        Hs 9:4
[c] 26:19 Dt 7:6
[d] 27:2-8 Jos 8:30-32

[e] 27:3 Dt 11:9
[f] 27:5-7 Ex 20:25
[g] 27:12-13 Dt 11:29-30; Jos
        8:33-35

THE TENTH IN THE THIRD YEAR

12 "When you have finished paying all the tenth of your produce in the third year,[a] the year of the tenth, you are to give it to the Levites, resident aliens, fatherless children and widows, so that they may eat in your towns and be satisfied. **13** Then you will say in the presence of the LORD your God:

I have taken the consecrated portion out of my house; I have also given it to the Levites, resident aliens, fatherless children, and widows, according to all the commands you gave me. I have not violated or forgotten your commands. **14** I have not eaten any of it while in mourning, or removed any of it while unclean, or offered any of it for the dead.[b] I have obeyed the LORD my God; I have done all you commanded me. **15** Look down from your holy dwelling, from heaven, and bless your people Israel and the land you have given us as you swore to our fathers, a land flowing with milk and honey.

COVENANT SUMMARY

16 "The LORD your God is commanding you this day to follow these statutes and ordinances. Follow them carefully with all your heart and all your soul. **17** Today you have affirmed that the LORD is your God and that you will walk in his ways, keep his statutes, commands, and ordinances, and obey him. **18** And today the LORD has affirmed that you are his own possession as he promised you, that you are to keep all his commands, **19** that he will elevate you to praise, fame, and glory above all the nations he has made, and that you will be a holy people[c] to the LORD your God as he promised."

THE LAW WRITTEN ON STONES

27 Moses and the elders of Israel commanded the people, "Keep every command I am giving you today. **2** When you cross the Jordan into the land the LORD your God is giving you, set up large stones and cover them with plaster.[d] **3** Write all the words of this law on the stones after you cross to enter the land the LORD your

God is giving you, a land flowing with milk and honey,[e] as the LORD, the God of your fathers, has promised you. **4** When you have crossed the Jordan, you are to set up these stones on Mount Ebal, as I am commanding you today, and you are to cover them with plaster. **5** Build an altar of stones there to the LORD your God — do not use any iron tool on them.[f] **6** Use uncut stones to build the altar of the LORD your God and offer burnt offerings to the LORD your God on it. **7** There you are to sacrifice fellowship offerings, eat, and rejoice in the presence of the LORD your God. **8** Write clearly all the words of this law on the plastered stones."

THE COVENANT CURSES

9 Moses and the Levitical priests spoke to all Israel, "Be silent, Israel, and listen! This day you have become the people of the LORD your God. **10** Obey the LORD your God and follow his commands and statutes I am giving you today."

11 On that day Moses commanded the people, **12** "When you have crossed the Jordan, these tribes will stand on Mount Gerizim to bless the people: Simeon, Levi, Judah, Issachar, Joseph, and Benjamin. **13** And these tribes will stand on Mount Ebal to deliver the curse: Reuben, Gad, Asher, Zebulun, Dan, and Naphtali.[g] **14** The Levites will proclaim in a loud voice to every Israelite:

15 'The person who makes a carved idol or cast image, which is detestable to the LORD, the work of a craftsman, and sets it up in secret is cursed.'

And all the people will reply, 'Amen!'

16 'The one who dishonors his father or mother is cursed.'

And all the people will say, 'Amen!'

17 'The one who moves his neighbor's boundary marker is cursed.'

And all the people will say, 'Amen!'

18 'The one who leads a blind person astray on the road is cursed.'

And all the people will say, 'Amen!'

19 'The one who denies justice to a resident alien, a fatherless child, or a widow is cursed.'

And all the people will say, 'Amen!'

26:12 There is debate as to whether the tithe prescribed here to be brought **in the third year** was the regular third-year tithe Moses had already taught about (see 14:28-29), a one-time offering like the firstfruits offering above, or a second tithe to be made every third year.

26:16 Obedience was not to be grudging or mechanical. As people who were called to love the Lord their God with all of their being, they were to obey him willingly and fully, **heart** and **soul**.

27:4 **Mount Ebal** was located about thirty-five miles north of Jerusalem, which would one day be Israel's capital.

27:12-13 The people were to divide themselves into two groups of six tribes between **Mount Gerizim** and **Mount Ebal** to participate in reading the blessings and curses antiphonally.

27:14-26 The people would affirm that they understood each point through following it with an **Amen!** (27:15-26). They were pledging their obedience before God on each point and also giving him permission to bring down on them the curse attached to committing the sin described.

20 'The one who sleeps with his father's wife is cursed, for he has violated his father's marriage bed.'^A

And all the people will say, 'Amen!'

21 'The one who has sexual intercourse with any animal is cursed.'

And all the people will say, 'Amen!'

22 'The one who sleeps with his sister, whether his father's daughter or his mother's daughter is cursed.'

And all the people will say, 'Amen!'

23 'The one who sleeps with his mother-in-law is cursed.'

And all the people will say, 'Amen!'

24 'The one who secretly kills his neighbor is cursed.'

And all the people will say, 'Amen!'

25 'The one who accepts a bribe to kill an innocent person is cursed.'

And all the people will say, 'Amen!'

26 'Anyone who does not put the words of this law into practice is cursed.'

And all the people will say, 'Amen!'

BLESSINGS FOR OBEDIENCE

28 "Now^a if you faithfully obey the LORD your God^b and are careful to follow all his commands I am giving you today,^c the LORD your God will put you far above all the nations of the earth.^d **2** All these blessings will come and overtake^e you, because you obey the LORD your God:

3 You will be blessed in the city
   and blessed in the country.^f
4 Your offspring^B will be blessed,
   and your land's produce,
   and the offspring of your livestock,
   including the young of your herds
   and the newborn of your flocks.^g
5 Your basket and kneading bowl
   will be blessed.
6 You will be blessed
   when you come in
   and blessed when you go out.^h

7 "The LORD will cause the enemies who rise up against you to be defeated before you. They will march out against you from one direction but flee from you in seven directions. **8** The LORD will grant you a blessing on your barns and on everything you do;^c,j he will bless you in the land the LORD your God is giving you.^j **9** The LORD will establish you as his holy people,^k as he swore to you, if you obey the commands of the LORD your God and walk in his ways. **10** Then all the peoples of the earth will see that you bear the LORD's name,^l and they will stand in awe of you.^m **11** The LORD will make you prosper abundantly with offspring,^D the offspring of your livestock, and your land's produce in the land the LORD swore to your fathers to give you. **12** The LORD will open for you his abundant storehouse,^n the sky, to give your land rain in its season and to bless all the work of your hands.^o You will lend to many nations, but you will not borrow. **13** The LORD will make you the head and not the tail;^p you will only move upward and never downward if you listen to the LORD your God's commands I am giving you today and are careful to follow them. **14** Do not turn aside to the right or the left from all the things I am commanding you today,^q and do not follow other gods to worship them.

CURSES FOR DISOBEDIENCE

15 "But if you do not obey the LORD your God by carefully following all his commands and statutes I am giving you today, all these curses will come and overtake^r you:^s

16 You will be cursed in the city
    and cursed in the country.
17 Your basket and kneading bowl
    will be cursed.

^a 28:1-14 Lv 26:3-13
^b 28:1 Ex 15:26; 19:5; 23:22; Dt 11:13; 15:5; Jr 17:24; Zch 6:15
^c Dt 13:18; 30:8
^d Gn 18:18; 22:18; Jr 33:9; Zch 12:3
^e 28:2 Dt 28:15,45; Is 35:10; 51:11; Zch 1:6
^f 28:3 Dt 28:16
^g 28:4 Dt 7:13
^h 28:6 Dt 28:19; 2Kg 19:27; Is 37:28

^i 28:8 Pr 3:10
^j Dt 15:4; 30:16
^k 28:9 Ex 22:31; Dt 7:6; 14:2,21; 26:19; Is 62:12; 63:18
^l 28:10 1Kg 8:60; 2Ch 6:33; Zph 3:20
^m Dt 2:4; Mc 7:17
^n 28:12 Ps 135:7; Jr 10:13; 51:16
^o Dt 2:7; 14:29; 16:15; 24:19; 30:9
^p 28:13 Dt 28:44
^q 28:14 1Sm 6:12; 12:21; 1Kg 15:5; 2Kg 22:2; 2Ch 34:2
^r 28:15 Jb 27:20; Ps 7:5; 40:12; 69:24; Hs 10:9; Zch 1:6
^s 28:15-68 Lv 26:14-46

---

^A 27:20 Lit *has uncovered the edge of his father's garment*; Ru 3:9; Ezk 16:8   ^B 28:4 Lit *The fruit of your womb*, also in v. 18   ^C 28:8 Lit *you put your hand to*, also in v. 20   ^D 28:11 Lit *abundantly in the fruit of your womb*

27:26 This verse pronounced a sentence no Israelite—or anyone else for that matter—could escape. But as Israel would learn in the years ahead, they would prove incapable of perfectly keeping God's law. That's because the law doesn't give one the power to obey. It simply points out your shortcomings without granting you the ability to overcome them. In this way, the law is like a mirror—it shows what you look like but doesn't clean you up. The law is intended to show people our need for a Savior (see Gal 3:10-14).
28:1-68 Chapter 28 is hugely imbalanced: fourteen verses are devoted to blessings and

fifty-four to curses. (Clearly God knew the tendency of his people to disobey.)
28:13 This summary blessing provides a wonderful picture: Israel would be **the head and not the tail** among the nations, moving always **upward** if the people would be **careful to follow** God's commands. By living under God's authority and according to his agenda, you too get to live as the "head" rather than the "tail," experiencing God's blessings instead of being wagged this way and that as a result of sinful choices and their fallout.
28:15 Transitional words are like flags signaling that an important change in thought, a

conclusion, or a needed action step is coming. Here we see one of those transitional words: **But**. It's a sad word here because it was followed by a barrage of curses that are gruesome in their detail. Unfortunately, future generations of Israelites would live to see these curses imposed.
28:16-19 It would have been bad enough if the curses had stopped with these verses, which reversed the blessings of 28:3-6. But that described only the beginning of the terrible national fallout of living in opposition to the Lord.

[a] 28:20 Ezk 7:7
[b] Dt 7:23,24; 28:45,48,51,61; Jos 23:15
[c] Jr 4:4; 21:12; 26:3; 44:22
[d] 28:21 1Sm 15:18; Jr 9:16; 49:37
[e] 28:22 Am 4:9
[f] 28:25 Dt 28:7
[g] 2Ch 29:8; Jr 15:4; 24:9; 29:18; 34:17
[h] 28:26 Ps 79:2; Is 5:25; 34:3; Jr 7:33; 16:4; 19:7; 34:20; Ezk 6:5; Nah 3:3
[i] 28:27 Ex 9:9-11
[j] 28:28 2Kg 9:20; Zch 12:4
[k] 28:28-29 Jb 5:14; Ps 91:6; Is 59:9-10; Am 8:9; Mt 27:45
[l] 28:29 Dt 22:27; 1Sm 11:3; 2Sm 22:42; Ps 18:41; Is 47:15
[m] 28:30 Ac 1:20
[n] 28:32 Neh 5:5
[o] 28:33 Jdg 10:8; Jb 20:19; Hs 5:11; Am 4:1
[p] 28:35 Jb 2:7; Is 1:6
[q] 28:36 Dt 4:28; 28:64; Dn 5:23
[r] 28:37 Dt 4:27; 1Kg 9:7; 2Ch 7:20; Jr 24:9

18 Your offspring will be cursed,
and your land's produce,
the young of your herds,
and the newborn of your flocks.
19 You will be cursed
when you come in
and cursed when you go out.
20 The LORD will send against you curses, confusion,[a] and rebuke in everything
you do until you are destroyed and quickly perish,[b] because of the wickedness of
your actions in abandoning me.[c] 21 The
LORD will make pestilence cling to you until he has exterminated you from the land
you are entering to possess.[d] 22 The LORD
will afflict you with wasting disease, fever, inflammation, burning heat, drought,[A]
blight, and mildew;[e] these will pursue you
until you perish. 23 The sky above you will
be bronze, and the earth beneath you iron.
24 The LORD will turn the rain of your land
into falling[B] dust; it will descend on you
from the sky until you are destroyed. 25 The
LORD will cause you to be defeated before
your enemies. You will march out against
them from one direction but flee from
them in seven directions.[f] You will be an
object of horror[g] to all the kingdoms of the
earth. 26 Your corpses will be food for all
the birds of the sky and the wild animals of
the earth, with no one to scare them away.[h]
27 "The LORD will afflict you with the
boils of Egypt,[i] tumors, a festering rash,
and scabies, from which you cannot be
cured. 28 The LORD will afflict you with
madness, blindness, and mental confusion,[j] 29 so that at noon you will grope as a
blind person gropes in the dark.[k] You will
not be successful in anything you do. You
will only be oppressed and robbed continually, and no one will help you.[l] 30 You
will become engaged to a woman, but another man will rape her. You will build a
house but not live in it.[m] You will plant a
vineyard but not enjoy its fruit. 31 Your ox
will be slaughtered before your eyes, but
you will not eat any of it. Your donkey will
be taken away from you and not returned
to you. Your flock will be given to your
enemies, and no one will help you. 32 Your
sons and daughters will be given to another people, while your eyes grow weary looking for them every day. But you will
be powerless to do anything.[C,n] 33 A people
you don't know will eat your land's produce and everything you have labored for.
You will only be oppressed and crushed
continually.[o] 34 You will be driven mad by
what you see. 35 The LORD will afflict you
with painful and incurable boils on your
knees and thighs — from the sole of your
foot to the top of your head.[p]
36 "The LORD will bring you and your
king that you have appointed to a nation
neither you nor your fathers have known,
and there you will worship other gods,
of wood and stone.[q] 37 You will become
an object of horror, scorn, and ridicule
among all the peoples where the LORD
will drive you.[r]
38 "You will sow much seed in the field
but harvest little, because locusts will
devour it. 39 You will plant and cultivate
vineyards but not drink the wine or gather
the grapes, because worms will eat them.
40 You will have olive trees throughout
your territory but not moisten your skin
with oil, because your olives will drop off.
41 You will father sons and daughters, but
they will not remain yours, because they
will be taken prisoner. 42 Buzzing insects
will take possession of all your trees and
your land's produce. 43 The resident alien
among you will rise higher and higher
above you, while you sink lower and lower. 44 He will lend to you, but you won't lend
to him. He will be the head, and you will
be the tail.
45 "All these curses will come, pursue,
and overtake you until you are destroyed,

[A] 28:22 Or *sword* [B] 28:24 Lit *powder and* [C] 28:32 Lit *day, and not for power your hand*

28:20-29 If God's people chose to live as his enemies, he would treat them as such. In the centuries to come, the curses were to have a teaching purpose, because when the people found themselves in an awful mess, they could see in God's promises a clear reminder that it was because they had failed to obey their good God in times of prosperity. Moses's desire was that future generations would read these words and commit themselves to avoiding the sins of their ancestors.

28:30-68 The worst horrors among the coming curses were the siege and the exile of Israel, two terrible judgments that would eventually come true (28:52, 63-64). The idea of exile is first mentioned in 28:36-37. The real horrors associated with it are found in 28:49-57.

In the distant future, the **nation from far away** that would **swoop down on** Jerusalem (28:49) would be Babylon. Its army would besiege Jerusalem until its people resorted to the unimaginable degradation of cannibalism on their own children as all human compassion and dignity melted under the madness of hunger (28:53; see Lam 2:20; 4:10). The same thing would happen even sooner when the Arameans laid siege to the city of Samaria (see 2 Kgs 6:24-29).

Such destruction would come because Israel forgot the Lord and worshiped false gods. Therefore, the Lord would give them what they wanted: indeed they would **worship other gods**, make-believe deities with no power to hear them, let alone help (Deut 28:64). And as a result, the Israelites would find themselves where they were before God had rescued them—as **slaves** (28:68).

Neither the generation to whom Moses spoke nor all those to follow could say they hadn't been warned.

since you did not obey the LORD your God and keep the commands and statutes he gave you. **46** These curses will be a sign and a wonder[a] against you and your descendants forever. **47** Because you didn't serve the LORD your God with joy and a cheerful heart,[b] even though you had an abundance of everything, **48** you will serve your enemies the LORD will send against you, in famine, thirst, nakedness, and a lack of everything. He will place an iron yoke[c] on your neck until he has destroyed you. **49** The LORD will bring a nation from far away, from the ends of the earth,[d] to swoop down on you like an eagle,[e] a nation whose language you won't understand,[f] **50** a ruthless nation,[A] showing no respect for the old and not sparing the young. **51** They will eat the offspring of your livestock and your land's produce until you are destroyed. They will leave you no grain, new wine, fresh oil, young of your herds, or newborn of your flocks until they cause you to perish. **52** They will besiege you within all your city gates until your high and fortified walls, that you trust in, come down throughout your land. They will besiege you within all your city gates throughout the land the LORD your God has given you.

53 "You will eat your offspring,[B] the flesh of your sons and daughters the LORD your God has given you[g] during the siege and hardship your enemy imposes on you. **54** The most sensitive and refined man among you will look grudgingly[c] at his brother, the wife he embraces,[D] and the rest of his children, **55** refusing to share with any of them his children's flesh that he will eat because he has nothing left during the siege and hardship your enemy imposes on you in all your towns. **56** The most sensitive and refined woman among you, who would not venture to set the sole of her foot on the ground because of her refinement and sensitivity, will begrudge the husband she embraces, her son, and her daughter, **57** the afterbirth that comes out from between her legs and the children she bears, because she will secretly eat them for lack of anything else during the

siege and hardship your enemy imposes on you within your city gates.

58 "If you are not careful to obey all the words of this law, which are written in this scroll, by fearing this glorious and awe-inspiring name — the LORD, your God — **59** he will bring wondrous plagues on you and your descendants, severe and lasting plagues, and terrible and chronic sicknesses. **60** He will afflict you again with all the diseases of Egypt,[h] which you dreaded, and they will cling to you. **61** The LORD will also afflict you with every sickness and plague not recorded in the book of this law, until you are destroyed. **62** Though you were as numerous as the stars of the sky, you will be left with only a few people, because you did not obey the LORD your God. **63** Just as the LORD was glad to cause you to prosper and to multiply you, so he will also be glad to cause you to perish and to destroy you. You will be ripped out of the land you are entering to possess. **64** Then the LORD will scatter you among all peoples from one end of the earth to the other,[i] and there you will worship other gods, of wood and stone,[j] which neither you nor your fathers have known.[k] **65** You will find no peace among those nations, and there will be no resting place[l] for the sole of your foot. There the LORD will give you a trembling heart, failing eyes, and a despondent spirit. **66** Your life will hang in doubt before you. You will be in dread night and day, never certain of survival. **67** In the morning you will say, 'If only it were evening!' and in the evening you will say, 'If only it were morning!' — because of the dread you will have in your heart and because of what you will see. **68** The LORD will take you back in ships to Egypt by a route that I said you would never see again.[m] There you will sell yourselves to your enemies as male and female slaves, but no one will buy you."

RENEWING THE COVENANT

29 These are the words of the covenant[n] the LORD commanded Moses to make with the Israelites in the land of Moab, in addition to the covenant he had made with them at Horeb.[o] **2** Moses

---

[a] 28:46 Ex 7:3; Dt 4:34; 6:22; 7:19; 26:8; Is 8:18; Jr 32:20
[b] 28:47 Pr 15:15; Ec 9:7
[c] 28:48 Jr 28:13-14
[d] 28:49 Is 5:26
[e] Jr 48:40; 49:22
[f] Jr 5:15
[g] 28:53 Lv 26:29; 2Kg 6:25-29; Jr 19:9; Lm 2:20; 4:10; Ezk 5:10

[h] 28:60 Dt 7:15
[i] 28:64 Lv 26:33; Dt 4:27; Neh 1:8; Ezk 22:15
[j] Dt 4:28; 28:36; 2Kg 19:18; Ezk 20:32; Dn 5:4,23
[k] Dt 8:16; 13:6; 28:36
[l] 28:65 Gn 8:9; Dt 12:9
[m] 28:68 Dt 17:16
[n] 29:1 Dt 31:16
[o] Ex 3:1; 17:6; 33:6; Dt 1:2,6,19; 4:10,15; 5:2; 18:16; 1Kg 8:9; 2Ch 5:10

[A] 28:50 Lit *a nation strong of face*   [B] 28:53 Lit *eat the fruit of your womb*   [C] 28:54 Lit *you his eye will be evil*   [D] 28:54 Lit *wife of his bosom*

29:1 The covenant was initiated by God, and God set the covenant parameters, but it was mediated through Moses, who was the Lord's chosen representative. That's why to reject Moses was to reject God, because Moses

spoke God's words to the people (see Num 12:1-10; 14:1-12).

As members of God's kingdom and participants in the new covenant, Christians are called to live under God's covenant in obedi-

ence to the covenant Mediator, Jesus Christ. To reject Christ is to reject God.
29:2-4 This was a sad recognition that even as the people stood there on the plains of Moab with all of God's miraculous deliverance

a 29:2 Dt 4:34; 6:22;
Jos 24:7,17
b 29:3 Ex 7:3; Dt 6:22; 7:19;
26:8; 34:11; Neh 9:10; Ps
135:9; Jr 32:20-21
c 29:4 Is 6:9-10; Ezk 12:2;
Mt 13:14; Ac 28:26-27;
Rm 11:8
d 29:5 Dt 8:4; Neh 9:21
e 29:6 Ex 6:7; 7:5,17;
8:10,22; 9:14; 10:2; 14:4;
Ezk 6:7,10,13-14
f 29:7 Dt 2:26-3:17
g 29:7-8 Nm 21:21-35;
32:1-42; Jos 1:12
h 29:9 Dt 31:16
i Jos 1:8; Ps 1:2-3
j 29:13 Dt 7:8,12-13;
8:18; 9:5

k 29:17 2Ch 15:8; Jr 4:1;
Ezk 16:36
l 29:18 Heb 12:15
m 29:20 Dt 9:14
n 29:23 Gn 14:2,8; 19:23-29

summoned all Israel and said to them, "You have seen with your own eyes[a] everything the LORD did in Egypt to Pharaoh, to all his officials, and to his entire land. [3] You saw with your own eyes the great trials and those great signs and wonders.[b] [4] Yet to this day the LORD has not given you a mind to understand, eyes to see, or ears to hear.[c] [5] I led you forty years in the wilderness; your clothes and the sandals on your feet did not wear out;[d] [6] you did not eat food or drink wine or beer — so that you might know that I am the LORD your God.[e] [7] When you reached this place, King Sihon of Heshbon and King Og of Bashan came out against us in battle, but we defeated them.[f] [8] We took their land and gave it as an inheritance to the Reubenites, the Gadites, and half the tribe of Manasseh.[g] [9] Therefore, observe the words of this covenant[h] and follow them, so that you will succeed in everything you do.[i]

[10] "All of you are standing today before the LORD your God — your leaders, tribes, elders, officials, all the men of Israel, [11] your dependents, your wives, and the resident aliens in your camps who cut your wood and draw your water — [12] so that you may enter into the covenant of the LORD your God, which he is making with you today, so that you may enter into his oath [13] and so that he may establish you today as his people and he may be your God as he promised you and as he swore to your fathers Abraham, Isaac, and Jacob.[j] [14] I am making this covenant and this oath not only with you, [15] but also with those who are standing here with us today in the presence of the LORD our God and with those who are not here today.

ABANDONING THE COVENANT

[16] "Indeed, you know how we lived in the land of Egypt and passed through the nations where you traveled. [17] You saw their abhorrent images and idols made of wood, stone, silver, and gold, which were among them.[k] [18] Be sure there is no man, woman, clan, or tribe among you today whose heart turns away from the LORD our God to go and worship the gods of those nations. Be sure there is no root among you bearing poisonous and bitter fruit.[l] [19] When someone hears the words of this oath, he may consider himself exempt,[A] thinking, 'I will have peace even though I follow my own stubborn heart.' This will lead to the destruction of the well-watered land as well as the dry land. [20] The LORD will not be willing to forgive him. Instead, his anger and jealousy will burn against that person, and every curse written in this scroll will descend on him. The LORD will blot out his name under heaven,[m] [21] and single him out for harm from all the tribes of Israel, according to all the curses of the covenant written in this book of the law.

[22] "Future generations of your children who follow you and the foreigner who comes from a distant country will see the plagues of that land and the sicknesses the LORD has inflicted on it. [23] All its soil will be a burning waste of sulfur and salt, unsown, producing nothing, with no plant growing on it, just like the fall of Sodom and Gomorrah, Admah and Zeboiim, which the LORD demolished in his fierce anger.[n] [24] All the nations will ask, 'Why has the LORD done this to this land? Why this intense outburst of anger?' [25] Then people will answer, 'It is because they abandoned

[A] 29:19 Lit *may bless himself in his heart*

and sustaining power in their memories, they had not yet fully grasped the spiritual significance of what he'd done. They would not operate according to the instructions of God's covenant and receive its blessings without it.

29:5-8 Moses's approach here reminds us that history is not self-interpreting. An unbeliever could look at Israel's history and conclude that they were simply a resourceful and lucky people. But Moses provided the divine perspective on their experiences—that is, the only reliable perspective. Every blessing, provision, and victory Israel received was from the Lord.

If you recognize that a similar truth governs your own life story, you will understand your utter dependence on God. If you don't,

it won't be long before you believe in your own self-sufficiency, operate outside of his covenant, and find yourself living as the "tail" rather than the "head" (see 28:13).

29:9 God's covenants are designed to benefit his people. As members of the new covenant, Christians trust in Jesus Christ for forgiveness of sins. But, as his people, we are also called to live by the principles of and under the cover of his covenant. If you operate within God's covenant, you will experience the flow of his power. If you operate outside of it, you will not receive the covenant benefits but will be subject to being oppressed by sin, the world, and Satan. God's covenant is like an umbrella. It doesn't stop the rain from falling, but it keeps you from getting wet—*if* you keep it over your head.

29:14-15 The Lord looked ahead to generations yet unborn, calling on his listeners to obey God not only for their blessings but also for the sake of their children and grandchildren.

29:18 The author of Hebrews made reference to this verse when he warned his readers to make sure that "no root of bitterness springs up" among God's people (Heb 12:15). When one of God's people experiences trying circumstances, he needs the encouragement of the rest of the body of Christ. Otherwise difficulties can make people bitter and cause them to turn to sin, eventually poisoning the church.

29:19-21 Nothing can be hidden from God, and he would have no trouble picking out and punishing an individual guilty of such thoughts (29:21).

the covenant of the Lord, the God of their fathers, which he had made with them when he brought them out of the land of Egypt. **26** They began to serve other gods, bowing in worship to gods they had not known[a] — gods that the Lord had not permitted them to worship.[b] **27** Therefore the Lord's anger burned against this land, and he brought every curse written in this book on it. **28** The Lord uprooted them from their land in his anger, rage, and intense wrath, and threw them into another land where they are today.' **29** The hidden things belong to the Lord our God, but the revealed things belong to us and our children forever, so that we may follow all the words of this law.

RETURNING TO THE LORD

30 "When all these things happen to you — the blessings and curses I have set before you — and you come to your senses while you are in all the nations where the Lord your God has driven you,[c] **2** and you and your children return to the Lord your God and obey him with all your heart and all your soul[d] by doing[A] everything I am commanding you today, **3** then he will restore your fortunes,[B,e] have compassion on you, and gather you again from all the peoples where the Lord your God has scattered you.[f] **4** Even if your exiles are at the farthest horizon,[c] he will gather you and bring you back from there.[g] **5** The Lord your God will bring you into the land your fathers possessed, and you will take possession of it.[h] He will cause you to prosper and multiply you more than he did your fathers.[i] **6** The Lord your God will circumcise your heart[j] and the hearts of your descendants, and you will love him with all your heart and all your

soul so that you will live.[k] **7** The Lord your God will put all these curses on your enemies who hate and persecute you. **8** Then you will again obey him and follow all his commands I am commanding you today. **9** The Lord your God will make you prosper abundantly in all the work of your hands,[i] your offspring,[D] the offspring of your livestock, and the produce of your land. Indeed, the Lord will again delight in your prosperity, as he delighted in that of your fathers, **10** when you obey the Lord your God by keeping his commands and statutes that are written in this book of the law and return to him with all your heart and all your soul.

CHOOSE LIFE

11 "This command that I give you today is certainly not too difficult or beyond your reach. **12** It is not in heaven so that you have to ask, 'Who will go up to heaven, get it for us, and proclaim it to us so that we may follow it?' **13** And it is not across the sea so that you have to ask, 'Who will cross the sea, get it for us, and proclaim it to us so that we may follow it?' **14** But the message is very near you, in your mouth and in your heart, so that you may follow it.[m] **15** See, today I have set before you life and prosperity, death and adversity.[n] **16** For[E] I am commanding you today to love the Lord your God, to walk in his ways, and to keep his commands, statutes, and ordinances, so that you may live[F] and multiply, and the Lord your God may bless you in the land you are entering to possess. **17** But if your heart turns away and you do not listen and you are led astray to bow in worship to other gods and serve them, **18** I tell you today that you will certainly perish and will not prolong your days in the land

[a]29:26 Dt 32:17
[b]Dt 4:19; 1Kg 9:8-9; Jr 22:8-9
[c]30:1 Jr 23:12; Am 4:3; 9:4; Zph 3:18
[d]30:2 Dt 4:29; 6:5; 10:12; 11:13; 13:4; 26:16; Jos 22:5; 23:14; 1Kg 2:4; 8:48; 2Kg 23:25; 2Ch 15:12; 34:31
[e]30:3 Jr 29:14; Zph 2:7
[f]Lv 26:40-45; 1Kg 8:46-50; Jr 29:14; Ezk 16:53; Zph 3:20
[g]30:4 Neh 1:9
[h]30:5 Dt 3:12
[i]Dt 6:3; 28:63
[j]30:6 Dt 10:16; Jr 4:4

[k]30:6 Dt 16:20; Is 55:3
[l]30:9 Dt 2:7; 14:29; 16:15; 24:19; 28:12; Ec 5:6; Hg 2:17
[m]30:12-14 Rm 10:6-8
[n]30:15 Dt 11:26; Jr 21:8

A 30:2 Lit soul according to   B 30:3 Or will end your captivity   C 30:4 Lit skies   D 30:9 Lit hands in the fruit of your womb   E 30:16 LXX reads If you obey the commands of the Lord your God that   F 30:16 LXX reads ordinances, then you will live

29:29 The Lord is infinite and transcendent. Whatever knowledge he chooses to keep from us is beyond our ability to obtain. Nevertheless, he has **revealed** to us everything that we need to know. God's Holy Word contains all that we (**and our children**) need in order to understand, trust, and obey him.

30:1-10 Moses foresaw Israel's future apostasy and even exile from the land (30:1). So he gave them a promise of future regathering and blessing that his immediate audience and later generations of Israelites must have wondered about in terms of its fulfillment. This first half of the chapter

is a prophecy, the interpretation of which requires that the full lens of Scripture be used. Moses was speaking about Israel's full spiritual restoration and material blessing in the kingdom age, which will not come about until the return of Jesus Christ in his millennial kingdom. In other words, we're still waiting for it.

But at that time God will give the people of Israel new hearts to **obey him** (30:2, 6), and they will believe in Jesus as their Messiah. They will enjoy a time of blessing in Christ's millennial kingdom greater than the nation had ever known before (30:5). All the blessings that Moses had recited to

the nation will be realized when the people of Israel become circumcised in heart to **love** God as he has commanded (30:6). It will be God's great delight to bless his people with abundant **prosperity** when they return to him wholeheartedly and obey him (30:9-10).

30:11-14 The law was not some hard-to-understand code the Israelites couldn't figure out or a strange teaching they were hearing for the first time. It was not a buried treasure they had to search for before reaping its benefits (30:12-13). Instead, Moses argued, God's law was **very near** to them; God had graciously made it known (30:14).

[a]30:19 Dt 4:1; 5:33; 6:24;
8:1,3; 16:20; 32:46-47
[b]30:20 Dt 1:35
[c]31:2 Jos 14:10
[d]Dt 3:27
[e]31:3 Ex 23:31; Dt 9:3
[f]Dt 3:28
[g]31:4 Nm 21:21-35; Dt
29:6; Jos 2:10
[h]31:6 Dt 31:23; Jos 1:6-
7,9,18; 10:25
[i]Dt 1:29; 7:21; 20:3
[j]Heb 13:5
[k]31:7 Dt 1:8,35; 8:1;
11:9,21; 31:20; Ezk 20:42
[l]31:8 Ex 23:23; 32:34; Dt
1:30; Jdg 4:14; Is 52:12
[m]Jos 1:5; 1Ch 28:20;
Heb 13:5

✒ Questions & Answers ✒

Q Why is it important to understand that humankind was made by God to rule over his creation? Practically speaking, what does it look like to exercise God's command to rule over a portion of his creation?

A It is absolutely critical to understand what God gave us when he told Adam and Eve to rule over creation. What it means is that God is going to respect our decision-making. He did not stop Adam from eating the fruit. He let him make that decision. Why? Because human decisions matter. Moses told Israel that they were to "choose" between life and death, between blessing and curse (Deut 30:19). So choose life! You know why our choices matter? Because we matter. God created us as moral agents. He says to us in effect, "You matter so much that, within sovereign boundaries, I'm going to let you choose. Now, there will be consequences for your choices—positive or negative—but you choose."

We have all landed on both sides of that equation. We have made choices with both positive and negative outcomes, and we have seen the repercussions of both. So why does it matter? It matters because we will make choices in life for or against God based on his Word. Which way do you want the results to fall? Do you want to see God working on your behalf—or working against you because he cannot go along with your choice? The same is true in our human relationships: our loved ones make choices. Sometimes they are good for us; sometimes they are bad for us. Our children make choices, our employers make choices, and our politicians make choices. And those choices matter. God wants us to know that we matter so much that he respects our choices. But he urges us, "Choose me."

FOR THE NEXT Q&A, SEE PAGE 316.

you are entering to possess across the Jordan. [19] I call heaven and earth as witnesses against you today that I have set before you life and death, blessing and curse. Choose life[a] so that you and your descendants may live, [20] love the LORD your God, obey him, and remain faithful[A] to him. For he is your life, and he will prolong your days as you live in the land the LORD swore to give to your fathers[b] Abraham, Isaac, and Jacob."

JOSHUA TAKES MOSES'S PLACE

31 Then Moses continued to speak these[B] words to all Israel, [2] saying, "I am now 120 years old;[c] I can no longer act as your leader.[c] The LORD has told me, 'You will not cross the Jordan.'[d] [3] The LORD your God is the one who will cross ahead of you.[e] He will destroy these nations before you, and you will drive them out. Joshua is the one who will cross ahead of you, as the LORD has said.[f] [4] The LORD will deal with them as he did Sihon and Og, the kings of the Amorites, and their land when he destroyed them.[g] [5] The LORD will deliver them over to you, and you must do to them exactly as I have commanded you. [6] Be strong and courageous;[h] don't be terrified or afraid of them. For the LORD your God is the one who will go with you;[i] he will not leave you or abandon you."[j]

[7] Moses then summoned Joshua and said to him in the sight of all Israel, "Be strong and courageous, for you will go with[D] this people into the land the LORD swore to give to their fathers.[k] You will enable them to take possession of it.

⌁ HOPE WORDS ⌁

Illegitimate fear will always interrupt faith.

[8] The LORD is the one who will go before you.[l] He will be with you; he will not leave you or abandon you.[m] Do not be afraid or discouraged."

[A]30:20 Lit *and hold on* [B]31:1 Some Hb mss, DSS, LXX, Syr, Vg read *all these* [C]31:2 Lit *no longer go out or come in* [D]31:7 Some Hb mss, Sam, Syr, Vg read *you will bring*

30:19-20 In other words, Moses argued, no other decision made sense: God himself is the **life** of his people. He is the only one who could **prolong** their **days** in the promised land (30:20). Therefore, to experience the favor of God, his people must choose obedience to divine revelation over their own autonomous human reasoning.
31:2 Even though Moses was **120 years old**, his age was not what would prevent him from entering the promised land (see Num 20:1-13).
31:6-8 Moses gave the Israelites an exhortation that later became God's rallying call to Joshua: **Be strong and courageous** (Deut 31:6; see Josh 1:6-7, 9, 18). He knew the human tendency to be **afraid** and **discouraged** (Deut 31:8).

⁹ Moses wrote down this law and gave it to the priests, the sons of Levi, who carried the ark of the LORD's covenant, and to all the elders of Israel. ¹⁰ Moses commanded them, "At the end of every seven years, at the appointed time in the year of debt cancellation,ᵃ during the Festival of Shelters,ᵇ ¹¹ when all Israel assemblesᴬ in the presence of the LORD your God at the place he chooses,ᶜ you are to read this law aloud before all Israel.ᵈ ¹² Gather the people — men, women, dependents, and the resident aliens within your city gates — so that they may listen and learn to fearᵉ the LORD your God and be careful to follow all the words of this law. ¹³ Then their childrenᶠ who do not know the law will listen and learn to fear the LORD your God as long as you live in the land you are crossing the Jordan to possess."

¹⁴ The LORD said to Moses, "The time of your death is now approaching. Call Joshua and present yourselves at the tent of meeting so that I may commission him." When Moses and Joshua went and presented themselves at the tent of meeting, ¹⁵ the LORD appeared at the tent in a pillar of cloud,ᵍ and the cloud stood at the entrance to the tent.ʰ

¹⁶ The LORD said to Moses, "You are about to rest with your fathers,ⁱ and these people will soon prostitute themselves with the foreign godsʲ of the land they are entering. They will abandon meᵏ and break the covenantˡ I have made with them. ¹⁷ My anger will burn against them on that day;ᵐ I will abandon them and hide my face from them so that they will become easy prey.ᴮ,ⁿ Many troubles and afflictions will come to them. On that day they will say, 'Haven't these troubles come to us because our God is no longer with us?' ¹⁸ I will certainly hide my face on that day because of all the evil they have done by turning to other gods. ¹⁹ Therefore write down this songᵒ for yourselves and teach it to the Israelites; have them sing it,ᶜ so that this song may be a witness for me against the Israelites. ²⁰ When I bring them into the land I swore to give their fathers, a land flowing with milk and honey,ᵖ they will eat their fillᵍ and prosper.ᵇ They will turn to other gods and worship them, despising meʳ and breaking my covenant.ˢ ²¹ And when many troubles and afflictions come to them, this song will testify against them, becauseᴱ their descendants will not have forgotten it. For I know what they are prone to do,ᶠ even before I bring them into the land I swore to give them." ²² So Moses wrote down this song on that day and taught it to the Israelites.

²³ The LORD commissioned Joshua son of Nun, "Be strong and courageous, for you will bring the Israelites into the land I swore to them, and I will be with you."ᵗ

MOSES WARNS THE PEOPLE

²⁴ When Moses had finished writing down on a scroll every single wordᴳ of this law, ²⁵ he commanded the Levites who carried the ark of the LORD's covenant, ²⁶ "Take this book of the law and place it beside the ark of the covenant of the LORD your God so that it may remain there as a witness against you. ²⁷ For I know how rebellious and stiff-necked you are. If you are rebelling against the LORD now, while I am still alive, how much more will you rebel after I am dead! ²⁸ Assemble all your tribal elders and officers before me so that I may speak these words directly to them and call heaven and earth as witnesses against them.ᵘ ²⁹ For I know that after my death you will become completely corrupt and turn from the path I have commanded you. Disaster will come to you in the future, because you will do what is evil in the LORD's sight, angering him with what your hands have made."ᵛ ³⁰ Then Moses recited aloud every single wordᴴ of this song to the entire assembly of Israel:

SONG OF MOSES

32 Pay attention, heavens, and I
    will speak;
  listen, earth, to the words
    from my mouth.ʷ
² Let my teaching fall like rain
    and my word settle like dew,

ᵃ 31:10 Dt 15:1-2
ᵇ 31:10 Lv 23:34; Dt 16:3
ᶜ 31:11 Dt 12:14; 14:23; 15:20; 16:2; 23:16
ᵈ 31:10-11 Jos 8:34; 2Kg 22:8; Neh 8:3,8,18; 9:3; Jr 2:8; Mal 2:1-9
ᵉ 31:12 Dt 14:23; 17:19
ᶠ 31:13 Dt 4:9-10
ᵍ 31:15 Ex 13:21-22; 33:9-10; Ps 99:7
ʰ Nm 12:5
ⁱ 31:16 Gn 47:30; 2Sm 7:12; 1Kg 2:10; 11:43; 14:20,31
ʲ Jr 5:7; 7:9; Hs 3:1
ᵏ Dt 28:20; Jdg 10:13; 1Sm 8:8; 1Kg 11:33; 2Kg 22:17; Jr 1:16; 2:13; 5:7,19; 16:11; 19:4
ˡ Dt 4:13,23; 5:2-3; 17:2; 29:1,9-14,21,25
ᵐ 31:17 Nm 32:10; Is 13:9,13; Lm 1:12
ⁿ Ps 63:10; Jr 2:14; Ezk 34:8
ᵒ 31:19 Dt 32:1-43

ᵖ 31:20 Dt 11:9
ᵍ Dt 11:15
ʳ Nm 14:11,23; 1Sm 2:29-30; 2Sm 12:10; Jr 23:17; Mal 1:6
ˢ Lv 26:15,44; Dt 4:31; Jos 23:16
ᵗ 31:23 Jos 1:1-9
ᵘ 31:28 Dt 4:26; 30:19
ᵛ 31:27-29 Dt 4:25; Jdg 2:6-13
ʷ 32:1 Jdg 5:3; Pr 4:20; Is 1:2; 28:23; 34:1; 49:1; Mc 1:2

ᴬ 31:11 Lit comes to appear ᴮ 31:17 Lit will be for devouring ᶜ 31:19 Lit Israelites; put it in their mouths ᴰ 31:20 Lit be fat ᴱ 31:21 Lit because the mouths of ᶠ 31:21 Or know the plans they are devising ᴳ 31:24 Lit scroll the words to their completion ᴴ 31:30 Lit recited the words to their completion

31:9-13 A public reading of the law would have the benefits of review and education: the people would **listen and learn to fear the LORD** through hearing it (31:12). In addition, the **children who [did] not [yet] know the law** would be taught **to fear the LORD** (31:13).

31:14-15 The appearance of the glory of God in **a pillar of cloud** (31:15) would have provided all the confirmation that Israel needed: Joshua was God's man who would lead in Moses's absence.

31:19-22 God gave Moses a **song** whose purpose was to remind his people of the reason for the **troubles and afflictions** they would encounter, showing them the path to forgiveness by means of his grace (31:19-21).

32:1-12 The Song of Moses is an incredible teaching instrument that traces God's dealings with the nation. As if in a courtroom, Moses called the **heavens** and the **earth** as

[a] 32:3 Ex 33:19; Ps 22:22;
71:16,18; 89:1
[b] 32:4 Gn 49:24; Dt
32:15,18,30–31; 1Sm 23:28;
2Sm 23:3; Is 30:29; 44:8;
Hab 1:12
[c] 2Sm 22:31; Ps 10:5; 18:30;
25:10; 145:17; Lm 1:18;
Dn 4:37
[d] Dt 7:9; Ps 59:10,17
[e] 32:5 Ex 32:7; Dt 4:16,25;
9:12; Jdg 2:19; Neh 1:7;
Zph 3:7
[f] Dt 32:20; Ps 78:8; Jr 2:31;
Mt 11:16; 12:39; 16:4; 17:7;
Ac 2:40; Php 2:15
[g] 32:6 Jr 4:22; 5:21; 10:8
[h] Mal 2:10
[i] 32:8 Gn 11:1–9
[j] Ac 17:26
[k] 32:9 Nm 18:20; Dt 10:9;
Zch 2:12
[l] 32:10 Ezk 16:6–14
[m] Pr 7:2
[n] 32:11 Ex 19:4; Ps 91:4
[o] 32:13 Is 58:14

[p] 32:14 Ps 22:12; Ezk 39:18;
Am 4:1; Mc 7:14
[q] 32:15 Is 44:2
[r] 32:16 Ex 20:5; 34:14; Dt
4:24; 5:9; 6:15; 29:20; Jos
24:19; 1Kg 14:22; Ps 78:58;
Nah 1:2; Zph 1:18; 3:8
[s] 32:17 Ps 106:37; 1Co
10:19–20
[t] 32:20 Dt 31:17–18; Jb
13:24; 34:29; Ps 10:11; 13:1;
22:24; 27:9; 30:7; 69:17;
88:14; 102:2; 104:29; 143:7;
Is 8:17; 54:8; 59:2; 64:7; Jr
33:5; Ezk 39:23–24; 39:29;
Mc 3:4
[u] 32:21 1Kg 16:13,26; 2Kg
17:15; Jr 10:8
[v] Dt 32:6; Ps 74:18; Rm
10:19; 11:14

like gentle rain on new grass
and showers on tender plants.
3 For I will proclaim the LORD's name.[a]
Declare the greatness of our God!
4 The Rock[b] — his work is perfect;
all his ways are just.[c]
A faithful God,[d] without bias,
he is righteous and true.

5 His people have acted corruptly
toward him;[e]
this is their defect[A] — they are not
his children
but a devious and crooked generation.[f]
6 Is this how you repay the LORD,
you foolish and senseless people?[g]
Isn't he your Father and Creator?[B,h]
Didn't he make you and sustain you?
7 Remember the days of old;
consider the years of past
generations.
Ask your father, and he will tell you,
your elders, and they will teach you.
8 When the Most High gave
the nations their inheritance[C]
and divided the human race,[i]
he set the boundaries of the peoples[j]
according to the number
of the people of Israel.[D]
9 But the LORD's portion is his people,
Jacob, his own inheritance.[k]

10 He found him in a desolate land,
in a barren, howling wilderness;
he surrounded him, cared for him,[l]
and protected him as the pupil
of his eye.[m]
11 He watches over[E] his nest
like an eagle
and hovers over his young;
he spreads his wings, catches him,
and carries him on his feathers.[n]
12 The LORD alone led him,
with no help from a foreign god.[F]
13 He made him ride on the heights
of the land[o]
and eat the produce of the field.

He nourished him with honey
from the rock
and oil from flinty rock,
14 curds from the herd and milk
from the flock,
with the fat of lambs,
rams from Bashan,[p] and goats,
with the choicest grains of wheat;
you drank wine
from the finest grapes.[G]

15 Then[H] Jeshurun[I,q] became fat
and rebelled —
you became fat, bloated, and gorged.
He abandoned the God
who made him
and scorned the Rock of his salvation.
16 They provoked his jealousy
with different gods;
they enraged him
with detestable practices.[r]
17 They sacrificed to demons, not God,
to gods they had not known,
new gods that had just arrived,
which your fathers did not fear.[s]
18 You ignored the Rock
who gave you birth;
you forgot the God who gave birth
to you.

19 When the LORD saw this,
he despised them,
angered by his sons and daughters.
20 He said: "I will hide my face
from them;[t]
I will see what will become of them,
for they are
a perverse generation —
unfaithful children.
21 They have provoked my jealousy
with what is not a god;[J]
they have enraged me
with their worthless idols.[u]
So I will provoke their jealousy
with what is not a people;[K]
I will enrage them
with a foolish nation.[v]

[A] 32:5 Or *him; through their fault* ; Hb obscure   [B] 32:6 Or *Possessor*   [C] 32:8 Or *Most High divided the nations*   [D] 32:8 One DSS reads *number of the sons of God* ; LXX reads *number of the angels of God*   [E] 32:11 Or *He stirs up*   [F] 32:12 Lit *him, and no foreign god with him*   [G] 32:14 Lit *drank the blood of grapes, fermenting wine*   [H] 32:15 DSS, Sam, LXX add *Jacob ate his fill;*   [I] 32:15 = Upright One, referring to Israel   [J] 32:21 Lit *with no gods*   [K] 32:21 Lit *with no people*

---

witnesses to the truth of what he was about to say, beginning with his testimony to **the greatness of our God** (32:1-4). In contrast to God's greatness and faithfulness to Israel, his people **acted corruptly toward him** by becoming **a devious and crooked generation**—it was a wretched way to repay the love and kindness shown them (32:5-12).

32:15 Jeshurun is a term of affection for Israel meaning "Upright One" (see CSB note). The idea here is that the nation **became fat, bloated, and gorged** like a rebellious, stupid animal that kicks at the master who feeds it even as it chews what he's provided.
32:17 Notice that **demons** masquerade behind the mask of an idolatrous image.

32:20 When the God who made and sustains you turns his back on you, there is absolutely no hope. We see a similar phrase used in the book of Esther when Queen Esther revealed that Haman had plotted to kill her and the Jews. Once King Ahasuerus passed sentence on Haman, "they covered Haman's face" (Esth 7:8) to hide the king's face from him. This symbolized that he was out of appeals.

22 For fire has been kindled because of
       my anger
   and burns to the depths of Sheol;[a]
   it devours the land and its produce,
   and scorches the foundations
       of the mountains.

23 "I will pile disasters on them;
   I will use up my arrows
       against them.

24 They will be weak from hunger,
       ravaged by pestilence
       and bitter plague;
   I will unleash on them wild beasts
       with fangs,
   as well as venomous snakes
       that slither in the dust.

25 Outside, the sword will take
       their children,
   and inside, there will be terror;
   the young man and the young
       woman will be killed,
   the infant and the gray-haired man.[b]

26 "I would have said: I will cut them
       to pieces[A]
   and blot out the memory of them
       from mankind,[c]

27 if I had not feared provocation
       from the enemy,
   or feared that these foes
       might misunderstand
   and say: 'Our own hand
       has prevailed;
   it wasn't the LORD who did all this.' "

28 Israel is a nation lacking sense
   with no understanding at all.[B,d]

29 If only they were wise,
       they would comprehend this;
   they would understand their fate.

30 How could one pursue a thousand,
   or two put ten thousand to flight,[e]
   unless their Rock had sold them,
   unless the LORD had given
       them up?[f]

31 But their "rock" is not like our Rock,
   as even our enemies concede.

32 For their vine is from the vine
       of Sodom
   and from the fields of Gomorrah.
   Their grapes are poisonous;
   their clusters are bitter.

33 Their wine is serpents' venom,
   the deadly poison of cobras.[g]

34 "Is it not stored up with me,
   sealed up in my vaults?

35 Vengeance[c] belongs to me;
       I will repay.[D,h]
   In time their foot will slip,
   for their day of disaster is near,
   and their doom is coming quickly."

36 The LORD will indeed vindicate
       his people
   and have compassion
       on his servants[i]
   when he sees that their strength
       is gone
   and no one is left — slave or free.[E]

37 He will say: "Where are their gods,
   the 'rock' they found refuge in?

38 Who ate the fat of their sacrifices
   and drank the wine
       of their drink offerings?
   Let them rise up and help you;
   let it[f] be a shelter for you.

39 See now that I alone am he;
   there is no God but me.[j]
   I bring death and I give life;
   I wound and I heal.
   No one can rescue anyone
       from my power.[k]

40 I raise my hand to heaven
       and declare:
   As surely as I live forever,

41 when I sharpen my flashing sword,
   and my hand takes hold
       of judgment,
   I will take vengeance
       on my adversaries
   and repay those who hate me.

[a] 32:22 Ps 86:13; Pr 9:18; Is 7:11
[b] 32:22-25 Is 5:8-30; Jr 9:17-21
[c] 32:26 Ex 17:14; Dt 9:14; 25:19; 29:20; 2Kg 14:27
[d] 32:28 Is 44:19; Jr 29:7
[e] 32:30 Lv 26:36
[f] Ps 127:1; Lm 3:37; Mk 13:20

[g] 32:33 Jb 20:14
[h] 32:35 1Sm 24:12; 2Sm 22:48; Jr 11:20; 51:36; Nah 1:2; Rm 12:19; Heb 10:30
[i] 32:36 Ps 135:14
[j] 32:39 Is 40:25; 43:11-13; 46:9; Ezk 36:23
[k] Dt 30:15,19; 1Sm 2:6-8; 4:8; Jr 21:8; Hs 2:10

[A] 32:26 LXX reads *will scatter them*   [B] 32:28 Lit *understanding in them*   [c] 32:35 Sam, LXX read *On a day of vengeance*   [D] 32:35 LXX, Tg, Vg read *me; and recompense I will recompense*   [E] 32:36 Or *left — even the weak and impaired*; Hb obscure   [f] 32:38 Sam, LXX, Tg, Vg read *them*

32:28-29 You have to wonder what Moses's hearers were thinking when they heard him say, **Israel is a nation lacking sense with no understanding at all** (32:28). They could consider the example of their parents' generation—those who had been buried in the wilderness because they failed to trust God and blew their chance to enjoy the promised land. But perhaps this new generation thought to themselves that they wouldn't be like that. If so, they would have benefited

from Paul's warning to the Corinthians: "Whoever thinks he stands must be careful not to fall" (1 Cor 10:12).
32:30 We all would like to think that we'll do better than those who have gone before us. But we would be wiser to recognize that we are prone to failure and to pray to the Lord, "Do not bring us into temptation, but deliver us from the evil one" (Matt 6:13).
32:34-39 Moses concluded his song with a word of deliverance for Israel after God's

fierce judgment had run its course. God would take **vengeance** on Israel's enemies once he saw that the nation had come to the end of its **strength** and turned back to him (32:34-36). But Israel had to learn a hard lesson first—the futility of depending on false **gods** for **help** in their time of disaster (32:37-38). Only then would they be ready to come back in repentance to the Lord, who **alone** could **heal** them (32:39).

42 I will make my arrows drunk
with blood
while my sword devours flesh —
the blood of the slain
and the captives,
the heads of the enemy leaders."[A]

43 Rejoice, you nations,
concerning his people,[B,a]
for he will avenge the blood
of his servants.[C]
He will take vengeance
on his adversaries;[D,b]
he will purify his land
and his people.[E]

44 Moses came with Joshua[F] son of Nun
and recited all the words of this song in
the presence of the people. 45 After Moses finished reciting all these words to all
Israel, 46 he said to them, "Take to heart
all these words I am giving as a warning
to you today,[c] so that you may command
your children to follow all the words of
this law carefully.[d] 47 For they are not
meaningless words to you but they are
your life,[e] and by them you will live long
in the land you are crossing the Jordan
to possess."

MOSES'S IMPENDING DEATH

48 On that same day the LORD spoke
to Moses,[f] 49 "Go up Mount Nebo[g] in
the Abarim range in the land of Moab,
across from Jericho, and view the land
of Canaan I am giving the Israelites as
a possession. 50 Then you will die on the
mountain that you go up, and you will
be gathered to your people,[h] just as your
brother Aaron died on Mount Hor and
was gathered to his people.[i] 51 For both of
you broke faith with me among the Israelites at the Waters of Meribath-kadesh
in the Wilderness of Zin by failing to treat
me as holy in their presence. 52 Although
from a distance you will view the land
that I am giving the Israelites, you will
not go there."[j]

MOSES'S BLESSINGS

33 This is the blessing that Moses, the
man of God, gave the Israelites before his death.[k] 2 He said:

The LORD came from Sinai
and appeared to them from Seir;[l]
he shone on them
from Mount Paran[m]
and came with ten thousand
holy ones,[G]
with lightning[H] from his right hand[I]
for them.[n]
3 Indeed he loves the people.[J,o]
All your[K] holy ones are in your hand,
and they assemble[L] at your feet.
Each receives your words.
4 Moses gave us instruction,
a possession for the assembly
of Jacob.
5 So he became King in Jeshurun[M,p]
when the leaders of the people
gathered
with the tribes of Israel.

6 Let Reuben live and not die
though his people become few.[q]

7 He said this about Judah:
LORD, hear Judah's cry
and bring him to his people.
He fights for his cause[N]
with his own hands,
but may you be a help
against his foes.

8 He said about Levi:
Your Thummim and Urim[r] belong to
your faithful one;[O]
you tested him at Massah
and contended with him
at the Waters of Meribah.[s]
9 He said about his father and mother,
"I do not regard them."
He disregarded his brothers
and didn't acknowledge his sons,
for they kept your word
and maintained your covenant.[t]
10 They will teach your ordinances
to Jacob
and your instruction to Israel;[u]

[a] 32:43 Rm 15:10
[b] Ps 79:10; Jr 46:10; Mc 5:15; Nah 1:2
[c] 32:46 Dt 11:18; Ezk 3:10; Mal 2:2
[d] Dt 29:29; 31:12
[e] 32:47 Dt 30:20; Pr 4:13
[f] 32:48-51 Nm 27:12-14
[g] 32:49 Dt 34:1
[h] 32:50 Gn 25:8,17; 35:29; 49:33; Nm 27:13; 31:2
[i] Nm 20:22-29
[j] 32:51-52 Nm 20:2-13

[k] 33:1-29 Gn 49:1-33
[l] 33:2 Gn 14:6; 32:3; 36:8; Dt 1:2; Jdg 5:4
[m] Gn 21:21; Nm 10:12; 12:16; Dt 1:1; Hab 3:3
[n] Jdg 5:4-5; Ps 68:7-8; Hab 3:3
[o] 33:3 Dt 4:37; Mal 1:2
[p] 33:5 Dt 32:15; 33:26; Is 44:2
[q] 33:6 Gn 49:3-4; Jdg 5:15-16
[r] 33:8 Ex 28:30; Lv 8:8; Ezr 2:63; Neh 7:65
[s] Ex 17:1-7; Nm 20:2-13; Dt 6:16; 9:22; Ps 95:8
[t] 33:9 Ex 32:25-29
[u] 33:10 Dt 31:9-13

[A] 32:42 Or *the long-haired heads of the enemy* [B] 32:43 LXX reads *Rejoice, you heavens, along with him, and let all the sons of God worship him; rejoice, you nations, with his people, and let all the angels of God strengthen themselves in him*; DSS read *Rejoice, you heavens, along with him, and let all the angels worship him*; Heb 1:6 [C] 32:43 DSS, LXX read *sons* [D] 32:43 DSS, LXX add *and he will recompense those who hate him*; v. 41 [E] 32:43 Syr, Tg; DSS, Sam, LXX, Vg read *his people's land* [F] 32:44 LXX, Syr, Vg; MT reads *Hoshea*; Nm 13:8,16 [G] 33:2 LXX reads *Mount Paran with ten thousands from Kadesh* [H] 33:2 Or *fiery law*; Hb obscure [I] 33:2 Or *ones, from his southland to the mountain slopes* [J] 33:3 Or *peoples* [K] 33:3 Lit *his*, or *its* [L] 33:3 Hb obscure [M] 33:5 = Upright One, referring to Israel, also in v. 26 [N] 33:7 Or *He contends for them* [O] 33:8 DSS, LXX read *Give to Levi your Thummim, your Urim to your favored one*

33:1-29 The blessing Moses gave in this chapter served as something of a last will and testament. It was modeled on the blessing Jacob (also called Israel) imparted to each of his sons, the patriarchs of Israel's tribes, who shared their names (see Gen 49:1-28). One difference is that the tribe of Simeon is omitted and Joseph is counted as one, although his two sons Manasseh and Ephraim are mentioned. Judging from the statement in Deuteronomy 34:1, it seems Moses pronounced his blessing to the people before making the final climb up Mount Nebo. It was appropriate for Moses to bless the children of Israel as their "father" who was present at the nation's birth in the exodus from Egypt.

they will set incense before you
and whole burnt offerings
  on your altar.
11 LORD, bless his possessions,[A]
and accept the work of his hands.
Break the back[B] of his adversaries
  and enemies,
so that they cannot rise again.
12 He said about Benjamin:
The LORD's beloved rests[C] securely
  on him.
He[D] shields him all day long,
and he rests on his shoulders.[E]
13 He said about Joseph:
May his land be blessed
  by the LORD
with the dew of heaven's bounty
and the watery depths
  that lie beneath;[a]
14 with the bountiful harvest
  from the sun
and the abundant yield
  of the seasons;
15 with the best products
  of the ancient mountains
and the bounty of the eternal hills;[b]
16 with the choice gifts of the land
and everything in it;
and with the favor of him
who appeared[f] in the burning bush.[c]
May these rest on the head
  of Joseph,
on the brow of the prince
  of his brothers.[d]
17 His firstborn bull has[G] splendor,
and horns like[H] those of a wild ox;
he gores all the peoples with them
to the ends of the earth.
Such are the ten thousand
  of Ephraim,
and such are the thousands
  of Manasseh.
18 He said about Zebulun:
Rejoice, Zebulun, in your journeys,
and Issachar, in your tents.
19 They summon the peoples
  to a mountain;
there they offer
  acceptable sacrifices.
For they draw from the wealth
  of the seas

and the hidden treasures
  of the sand.[e]
20 He said about Gad:
The one who enlarges
  Gad's territory
will be blessed.
He lies down like a lion
and tears off an arm
  or even a head.[f]
21 He chose the best part
  for himself,
because a ruler's portion
  was assigned there for him.
He came with the leaders
  of the people;
he carried out the LORD's justice
and his ordinances for Israel.[g]
22 He said about Dan:
Dan is a young lion,
leaping out of Bashan.[h]
23 He said about Naphtali:
Naphtali, enjoying approval,
full of the LORD's blessing,
take[i] possession to the west
  and the south.
24 He said about Asher:
May Asher[j] be the most blessed
  of the sons;
may he be the most favored
  among his brothers
and dip his foot in olive oil.[i]
25 May the bolts of your gate be iron
  and bronze,
and your strength last as long as
  you live.

26 There is none like the God
  of Jeshurun,
who rides the heavens
  to your aid,
the clouds in his majesty.[j]
27 The God of old is
  your dwelling place,[k]
and underneath are
  the everlasting arms.
He drives out the enemy before you
and commands, "Destroy!"
28 So Israel dwells securely;[l]
Jacob lives untroubled[K,m]
in a land of grain and new wine;
even his skies drip with dew.[n]

[a] 33:13 Pr 3:20
[b] 33:15 Gn 49:26; Hab 3:6
[c] 33:16 Ex 3:2-4
[d] Gn 49:26

[e] 33:18-19 Gn 49:13; Jdg 5:15,18
[f] 33:20 1Ch 12:8
[g] 33:20-21 Nm 32:1-38
[h] 33:22 Jdg 5:17
[i] 33:24 Gn 49:20
[j] 33:26 2Sm 22:8-20; Ps 18:7-19; 68:4,33; Is 19:1
[k] 33:27 Ps 91:9
[l] 33:28 Lv 25:18-19; 26:5; Dt 12:10; 33:12; Jr 23:6; 33:16; Ezk 28:26; 34:28; 39:6
[m] Nm 23:9
[n] Dt 8:7-9

[A] 33:11 Or *abilities*   [B] 33:11 Or *waist*   [C] 33:12 Or *Let the LORD's beloved rest*   [D] 33:12 LXX reads *The Most High*   [E] 33:12 Or *and he dwells among his mountain slopes*   [F] 33:16 Lit *dwelt*   [G] 33:17 Some DSS, Sam, LXX, Syr, Vg read *A firstborn bull — he has*   [H] 33:17 Lit *and his horns are*   [I] 33:23 Sam, LXX, Syr, Vg, Tg read *he will take*   [J] 33:24 = Happy or Blessed; Gn 30:13   [K] 33:28 Text emended; MT reads *Jacob's fountain is alone*

33:13-17 Joseph was Jacob's favorite son, born through his beloved Rachel. He was a type of Christ (that is, a foreshadowing of Christ) in that he was the redeemer of his family in a situation that would've ended in their deaths. The blessing on Joseph's **land** (33:13) was realized by his sons, **Manasseh** and **Ephraim** (33:17), since his portion among his brothers was given to his offspring (see Gen 48:1-20).

33:26 See the note on 32:15 for insight on **Jeshurun**.

[a] 33:29 2Sm 22:44-46; Ps 18:43-45

[b] Dt 32:13; Hab 3:19

[c] 34:1-4 Dt 3:27; 32:48; Jos 13:20

[d] 34:4 Gn 12:7; 15:18-20; 26:3; 35:12; Ex 33:1; 1Kg 4:24

[e] 34:5 Jos 24:29; Jdg 2:8; 2Sm 3:18; 7:5,8; 1Kg 11:13; 14:8; 2Kg 18:12; 19:34; 21:8; Jb 1:8; 42:8; Is 20:3; 41:8-9; 42:1; 44:1; 52:13; 53:11

[f] 34:6 Nm 21:20

[g] Jd 9

[h] 34:8 Nm 20:29

[i] Mt 17:3

[j] 34:9 Ex 28:3; 31:3-6; 1Kg 4:29; 5:12; 7:14; 2Ch 1:10-12; Is 11:2; Ac 6:3; Eph 1:17

[k] Nm 11:16-30; 27:18; 1Sm 10:1,10; 16:13

[l] Nm 26:65; 27:15-23; 34:17; Dt 1:38; 3:28; 31:3-8,14-23

[m] 34:10 Ex 33:11

[n] 34:12 Ex 7:3; Dt 4:34; 6:22; 7:19; 26:8; 29:3; Neh 9:10; Ps 78:43; 105:27

29 How happy you are, Israel!
Who is like you,
a people saved by the LORD?
He is the shield that protects you,
the sword you boast in.
Your enemies will cringe
   before you,[a]
and you will tread on their backs.[A,b]

MOSES'S DEATH

34 Then Moses went up from the plains of Moab to Mount Nebo, to the top of Pisgah,[c] which faces Jericho, and the LORD showed him all the land: Gilead as far as Dan, **2** all of Naphtali, the land of Ephraim and Manasseh, all the land of Judah as far as the Mediterranean[B] Sea, **3** the Negev, and the plain in the Valley of Jericho, the City of Palms, as far as Zoar. **4** The LORD then said to him, "This is the land I promised Abraham, Isaac, and Jacob, 'I will give it to your descendants.'[d] I have let you see it with your own eyes, but you will not cross into it."

5 So Moses the servant of the LORD[e] died there in the land of Moab, according to the LORD's word. **6** He buried him[c] in the valley[f] in the land of Moab facing Beth-peor, and no one to this day knows where his grave is.[g] **7** Moses was one hundred twenty years old when he died; his eyes were not weak, and his vitality had not left him. **8** The Israelites wept for Moses in the plains of Moab thirty days.[h] Then the days of weeping and mourning for Moses came to an end.[i]

9 Joshua son of Nun was filled with the spirit of wisdom[j] because Moses had laid his hands on him.[k] So the Israelites obeyed him and did as the LORD had commanded Moses.[l] **10** No prophet has arisen again in Israel like Moses, whom the LORD knew face to face.[m] **11** He was unparalleled for all the signs and wonders the LORD sent him to do against the land of Egypt — to Pharaoh, to all his officials, and to all his land, **12** and for all the mighty acts of power[D] and terrifying deeds that Moses performed in the sight of all Israel.[n]

[A] 33:29 Or *high places*   [B] 34:2 Lit *Western*   [C] 34:6 Or *he was buried*   [D] 34:12 Lit *the strong hand*

34:5-12 The closing tribute to Moses demonstrates the truth that **no prophet** like him ever arose again in Israel—a prophet **whom the LORD knew face to face** and who performed **mighty acts of power and terrifying deeds . . . in the sight of all Israel** (34:10-12). Nevertheless, one day a new kind of prophet—an even better one—would arise (see 18:15; Acts 3:22-23). He would be a man—but far more than a man (see John 1:1-14). He would be the Son of God (see Matt 3:17). Though God knew Moses face to face, God's glory would truly shine in the face of Jesus Christ (see 2 Cor 4:6). Moses was faithful in God's household, but the Son would be worthy of more honor, in the same way that a "builder has more honor than the house" (see Heb 3:2-3). For the law came through Moses, but grace and truth would come through Jesus Christ (see John 1:17).

JOSHUA

INTRODUCTION

Author

THE BOOK OF JOSHUA IS anonymous; no author is identified in the text. It's certainly possible that Joshua himself wrote much of it. If he did not, then the book was penned by someone who both knew him and had access to his testimony and deeds. Regardless of whether or not Joshua was personally involved in its authorship, the book was clearly completed after his death, given the final words in 24:29-33.

Historical Background

The events in Joshua take place after the death of Moses (1:1), who appointed Joshua as his successor in obedience to the Lord (see Num 27:15-23; Deut 34:9). The people of Israel had come out of Egypt, entered into a covenant with God, spent forty years in the wilderness for their disobedience, and were now on the verge of crossing the Jordan River and entering the promised land (Josh 1:2-4). According to 1 Kings 6:1, "the fourth year" of King Solomon's reign over Israel (966 BC) happened 480 years after the Israelites had departed Egypt. Allowing for the forty years Israel spent in the wilderness, that would mean the book of Joshua opens in approximately 1400 BC—that is, fourteen hundred years before the birth of Christ.

Message and Purpose

The book of Joshua shows how God was faithful to fulfill his covenant with Israel to give them the land of Canaan. It also shows the participation of the people in the fulfillment of that plan as they conquered what God had already said he would give them. Israel had experienced a forty-year delay in claiming the promised land because of the disobedience of Moses's generation. But now the new generation would see that indeed God was faithful to his promises every step of the way—from the parting of the Jordan River, to making the sun stand still, to collapsing the walls of Jericho.

The lesson of Joshua for us is twofold: God is faithful to keep his Word, and we are to participate in his kingdom work through our obedience to him. Joshua refused to succumb to the pressures around him, and he challenged God's people to do the same. May we declare with Joshua, "As for me and my family, we will worship the LORD" (Josh 24:15).

VIDEO INTRO

www.bhpublishinggroup.com/qr/te/06_00

Outline

I. Entering the Promised Land (1:1–5:12)
  A. Joshua Assumes Command (1:1-18)
  B. The Faith of Rahab (2:1-24)
  C. Crossing the Jordan (3:1–5:12)
II. Claiming the Promised Land (5:13–12:24)
  A. Victory at Jericho (5:13–6:27)
  B. Defeat and Victory at Ai (7:1–8:35)
  C. Deceived by Gibeon (9:1-27)
  D. Victory throughout the Land (10:1–12:24)
III. Dividing the Promised Land (13:1–21:45)
IV. Serving God in the Promised Land (22:1–24:33)

a 1:1 Dt 34:5
b Ex 17:8-13; 33:11; Nm 13:8,16; 14:6-9; 27:18-23; Dt 31:2-8; 1Ch 7:20,27
c 1:2 Dt 34:5-8
d Jos 1:11
e 1:3-5 Dt 11:24-25
f 1:4 Gn 15:18; Nm 34:3
g Gn 10:15; 15:19-21
h Dt 11:24; 1Kg 4:21,24-25; 8:65
i 1:5 Dt 7:24
j Dt 31:6-8; Heb 13:5
k 1:6 Jos 1:18; 10:25; 1Kg 2:2-3; 1Ch 22:13; 28:20; Ps 27:14; 31:24
l Gn 15:18; Ex 32:13; Dt 15:4
m 1:7 Dt 5:32; 20:1-2; 21:1-3
n 1:8 Dt 31:24; Jos 8:34
o Dt 29:9; Ps 1:1-3
p 1:9 Dt 31:7-8; Jos 10:25

q 1:11 Jos 3:2
r 1:12 Nm 32:20-22
s 1:13-15 Dt 3:18-20
t 1:15 Jos 22:4
u Jos 1:1
v 1:17 Jos 1:5,9
w 1:18 Dt 31:7; Jos 1:6-7,9; 10:25
x 2:1 Gn 42:9; Nm 13:2,16-17; Jos 7:2; Jdg 18:2
y Heb 11:31; Jms 2:25

ENCOURAGEMENT OF JOSHUA

1 After the death of Moses[a] the LORD's servant, the LORD spoke to Joshua son of Nun,[b] Moses's assistant: **2** "Moses my servant is dead.[c] Now you and all the people prepare to cross over the Jordan[d] to the land I am giving the Israelites. **3** I have given you every place where the sole of your foot treads,[e] just as I promised Moses. **4** Your territory will be from the wilderness and Lebanon[f] to the great river, the Euphrates River — all the land of the Hittites[g] — and west to the Mediterranean Sea.[A,h] **5** No one will be able to stand against you as long as you live.[i] I will be with you, just as I was with Moses. I will not leave you or abandon you.[j]

6 "Be strong and courageous,[k] for you will distribute the land I swore to their fathers to give them as an inheritance.[l] **7** Above all, be strong and very courageous to observe carefully the whole instruction my servant Moses commanded you.[m] Do not turn from it to the right or the left, so that you will have success wherever you go. **8** This book of instruction must not depart from your mouth;[n] you are to meditate on[B] it day and night so that you may carefully observe everything written in it. For then you will prosper and succeed in whatever you do.[o] **9** Haven't I commanded you: be strong and courageous?[p] Do not be afraid or discouraged, for the LORD your God is with you wherever you go."

HOPE WORDS

When you allow God to lead you through a trial, you get to see him for yourself.

JOSHUA PREPARES THE PEOPLE

10 Then Joshua commanded the officers of the people: **11** "Go through the camp and tell the people, 'Get provisions ready for yourselves, for within three days you will be crossing the Jordan to go in and take possession of the land the LORD your God is giving you to inherit.'"[q]

12 Joshua said to the Reubenites, the Gadites, and half the tribe of Manasseh:[r] **13** "Remember what Moses the LORD's servant commanded you when he said, 'The LORD your God will give you rest, and he will give you this land.'[s] **14** Your wives, dependents, and livestock may remain in the land Moses gave you on this side of the Jordan. But your best soldiers must cross over in battle formation[C] ahead of your brothers and help them **15** until the LORD gives your brothers rest, as he has given you, and they too possess the land the LORD your God is giving them. You may then return to the land of your inheritance[t] and take possession of what Moses the LORD's servant[u] gave you on the east side of the Jordan."

16 They answered Joshua, "Everything you have commanded us we will do, and everywhere you send us we will go. **17** We will obey you, just as we obeyed Moses in everything. Certainly the LORD your God will be with you, as he was with Moses.[v] **18** Anyone who rebels against your order and does not obey your words in all that you command him, will be put to death. Above all, be strong and courageous!"[w]

SPIES SENT TO JERICHO

2 Joshua son of Nun secretly sent two men as spies[x] from the Acacia Grove,[D] saying, "Go and scout the land, especially Jericho." So they left, and they came to the house of a prostitute named Rahab,[y] and stayed there.

[A] 1:4 Lit *and to the Great Sea, the going down of the sun*   [B] 1:8 Or *to recite*   [C] 1:14 Or *over armed*   [D] 2:1 Or *from Shittim*

1:1-2 Israel had to stop looking back to the good old days when **Moses** had led, look ahead to the milk and honey of the promised land (Exod 3:7-8), and embrace new leadership.

It's important to remember the past: we should appreciate the good and learn from the bad. But in the walk of faith, you can't live with your eyes on the rearview mirror. You've got to face forward.

1:3-6 God reminded Joshua that the promised land—Israel's inheritance—was already given to them. That didn't mean, however, that they were to sit and wait for the local inhabitants to simply abandon Canaan to them. Actions of faith were required to make

literal what God had already made legal. This is an example of the intersection of God's sovereignty and human responsibility. God makes promises, but we are called to obey in order to secure them. Consider a parent who pays for a child's education. If the child doesn't go to class or study, it is not the promise of a free education that will inevitably fail. The problem is that the promise wasn't embraced.

1:8 Ultimately, success for a Christian is fulfilling your God-given purpose in life. To do that, you (like Israel) must **meditate on** Scripture and **carefully observe everything written in it**. To meditate on something is to roll it over and over in your mind in much the same way

that a cow chews its cud. When you do, the Word of God is driven deeply into your soul so that your actions can be driven by God's perspective rather than your feelings or opinion.

1:16-18 The Israelites were fully on board with the plan. All they wanted was for their leader to obey the Lord. Believers must expect the same of their church leaders. They are to be followed inasmuch as they follow God.

2:1 The two **spies** chose to hide in Jericho's red light district. It could be that **Rahab** was running an inn for travelers. If so, staying there would have helped the spies to look inconspicuous. Importantly, these men were in town for righteous purposes—not for wickedness.

2 The king of Jericho was told, "Look, some of the Israelite men have come here tonight to investigate the land." **3** Then the king of Jericho sent word to Rahab and said, "Bring out the men who came to you and entered your house,[a] for they came to investigate the entire land."

4 But the woman had taken the two men and hidden them.[b] So she said, "Yes, the men did come to me, but I didn't know where they were from. **5** At nightfall, when the city gate was about to close, the men went out, and I don't know where they were going. Chase after them quickly, and you can catch up with them!" **6** But she had taken them up to the roof and hidden them[c] among the stalks of flax that she had arranged on the roof. **7** The men pursued them along the road to the fords of the Jordan, and as soon as they left to pursue them, the city gate was shut.

THE PROMISE TO RAHAB

8 Before the men fell asleep, she went up on the roof **9** and said to them, "I know that the LORD has given you this land[d] and that the terror of you has fallen on us,[e] and everyone who lives in the land is panicking because of you.[A,f] **10** For we have heard how the LORD dried up the water of the Red Sea before you when you came out of Egypt,[g] and what you did to Sihon and Og, the two Amorite kings you completely destroyed[h] across the Jordan. **11** When we heard this, we lost heart,[i] and everyone's courage failed[B] because of you,[j] for the LORD your God is God in heaven above and on earth below.[k] **12** Now please swear to me by the LORD that you will also show kindness to my father's family,[c] because I showed kindness to you.[l] Give me a sure sign[D] **13** that you will spare the lives of my father, mother, brothers, sisters, and all

who belong to them, and save us from death."

14 The men answered her, "We will give our lives for yours. If you don't report our mission, we will show kindness and faithfulness to you when the LORD gives us the land."

15 Then she let them down by a rope through the window, since she lived in a house that was built into the wall of the city. **16** "Go to the hill country so that the men pursuing you won't find you," she said to them. "Hide there for three days until they return; afterward, go on your way."

17 The men said to her, "We will be free from this oath you made us swear, **18** unless, when we enter the land, you tie this scarlet cord to the window through which you let us down. Bring your father, mother, brothers, and all your father's family into your house. **19** If anyone goes out the doors of your house, his death will be his own fault,[E,m] and we will be innocent. But if anyone with you in the house should be harmed,[F] his death will be our fault.[G] **20** And if you report our mission, we are free from the oath you made us swear."

21 "Let it be as you say," she replied, and she sent them away. After they had gone, she tied the scarlet cord to the window.

22 So the two men went into the hill country and stayed there three days until the pursuers had returned. They searched all along the way, but did not find them. **23** Then the men returned, came down from the hill country, and crossed the Jordan. They went to Joshua son of Nun and reported everything that had happened to them. **24** They told Joshua, "The LORD has handed over the entire land to us. Everyone who lives in the land is also panicking because of us."[H]

[a] 2:3 Gn 19:5
[b] 2:4 2Sm 17:19
[c] 2:6 Jms 2:25
[d] 2:9 Nm 20:24; Jos 9:24
[e] Ex 15:16; 23:27; Ezr 3:3; Jb 9:34; 13:21; Is 33:18; Jr 50:38
[f] Ex 15:15; Jos 2:24; 1Sm 14:16
[g] 2:10 Ex 14:21-30
[h] Nm 21:23-30,33-35; Dt 2:32-34; 3:1-3; Jos 6:21
[i] 2:11 Dt 1:28; 20:8; Jos 5:1; 7:5; 2Sm 17:10; Is 13:7; 19:1; Ezk 21:7; Nah 2:10
[j] Jos 5:1; 7:5; Ps 22:14; Is 13:7; 19:1
[k] Dt 4:39; 1Kg 8:23
[l] 2:12 Gn 21:23; Jdg 1:24; 2Sm 2:5; 10:2

[m] 2:19 Mt 27:25

2:3-7 Rahab got around the king's demand by engaging in some righteous risky business: she hid the men and lied to the authorities (2:4-6). So, when is it acceptable to lie? Rahab was confronted with two sinful options, lying or abetting the execution of God's representatives, and she chose the option that would bring the most glory to God—protecting his people. **2:11-12** When Rahab confessed that **the LORD . . . is God** (2:11) and showed **kindness** to his people (2:12), she expressed personal faith in the true God's ability to work on behalf of those aligned with him and acted on it.

2:14-21 Remarkably, though Jericho's walls would soon fall down (6:20), this woman's house that was constructed within them was left standing (6:22-23). Rahab submitted in faith to God's program. As a result, she came under the covering of Israel, and her family did too (2:18). **2:24** Why were the spies so certain of victory? Much of it came down to the words and actions of an unlikely ally, Rahab. This woman's significance in God's kingdom plan cannot be overstated. Her story is a beautiful reminder that God's grace can meet us

where we are and use us to accomplish his purposes. Throughout Scripture, Rahab is repeatedly identified by her occupation as a *prostitute* (2:1; 6:17, 22, 25)—even in the New Testament (Heb 11:31; Jas 2:25). In the Bible, repetition is emphasis. God wants us to understand that no matter how wretched our pasts, he can do great things through anyone who righteously connects to him through faith. In God's providence, Rahab would become a link in the family chain leading to Jesus Christ (see Matt 1:5).

[a]3:2 Jos 1:11
[b]3:3 Dt 17:9,18; 18:1; 31:9; Jos 8:33; 2Ch 23:18; Jr 33:18,21
[c]3:5 Ex 19:10; Nm 11:18; Jos 7:13; 1Sm 16:5; 1Ch 15:12; 2Ch 29:5; 30:3,17; 35:6
[d]Ps 72:18; 86:10; 98:1; 106:22; 119:18; Mc 7:15
[e]3:7 Jos 4:14
[f]Dt 31:23; Jos 1:5; Jdg 6:16; 1Kg 11:38; Is 43:2; Jr 1:8; 30:11; 46:28
[g]3:10 Dt 5:26; Jr 10:10; Hs 1:10; 2Co 3:3
[h]Ex 33:2; Dt 7:1
[i]3:11 Ps 97:5; Mc 4:13; Zch 6:5
[j]3:12 Jos 4:2

[k]3:13 Ex 15:8
[l]3:14 Ac 7:44-45
[m]3:15 1Ch 12:15; Jr 12:5; 49:19
[n]3:16 Dt 1:1
[o]3:17 Ex 14:29
[p]4:1 Jos 3:17
[q]4:2 Jos 3:12
[r]4:3 Ex 28:21; 39:14; Jos 4:9,20; 1Kg 18:31

CROSSING THE JORDAN

3 Joshua started early the next morning and left the Acacia Grove[A] with all the Israelites. They went as far as the Jordan and stayed there before crossing. [2] After three days the officers went through the camp[a] [3] and commanded the people: "When you see the ark of the covenant of the LORD your God carried by the Levitical priests,[b] you are to break camp and follow it. [4] But keep a distance of about a thousand yards[B] between yourselves and the ark. Don't go near it, so that you can see the way to go, for you haven't traveled this way before."[c]

[5] Joshua told the people, "Consecrate yourselves,[c] because the LORD will do wonders[d] among you tomorrow." [6] Then he said to the priests, "Carry the ark of the covenant and go on ahead of the people." So they carried the ark of the covenant and went ahead of them.

[7] The LORD spoke to Joshua: "Today I will begin to exalt you in the sight of all Israel,[e] so they will know that I will be with you just as I was with Moses.[f] [8] Command the priests carrying the ark of the covenant: When you reach the edge of the water,[D] stand in the Jordan."

[9] Then Joshua told the Israelites, "Come closer and listen to the words of the LORD your God." [10] He said: "You will know that the living God is among you[g] and that he will certainly dispossess before you the Canaanites, Hethites, Hivites, Perizzites, Girgashites, Amorites, and Jebusites[h] [11] when the ark of the covenant of the Lord of the whole earth[i] goes ahead of you into the Jordan. [12] Now choose twelve men from the tribes of Israel, one man for each tribe.[j] [13] When the feet[E] of the priests who carry the ark of the LORD, the Lord of

the whole earth, come to rest in the Jordan's water, its water will be cut off. The water flowing downstream will stand up in a mass."[k]

[14] When the people broke camp to cross the Jordan, the priests carried the ark of the covenant[l] ahead of the people. [15] Now the Jordan overflows its banks throughout the harvest season.[m] But as soon as the priests carrying the ark reached the Jordan, their feet touched the water at its edge [16] and the water flowing downstream stood still, rising up in a mass that extended as far as[F] Adam, a city next to Zarethan. The water flowing downstream into the Sea of the Arabah[n] — the Dead Sea — was completely cut off, and the people crossed opposite Jericho. [17] The priests carrying the ark of the LORD's covenant stood firmly on dry ground in the middle of the Jordan,[o] while all Israel crossed on dry ground until the entire nation had finished crossing the Jordan.

THE MEMORIAL STONES

4 After the entire nation had finished crossing the Jordan,[p] the LORD spoke to Joshua: [2] "Choose twelve men from the people, one man for each tribe,[q] [3] and command them: Take twelve stones[r] from this place in the middle of the Jordan where the priests[G] are standing, carry them with you, and set them down at the place where you spend the night."

[4] So Joshua summoned the twelve men he had selected from the Israelites, one man for each tribe, [5] and said to them, "Go across to the ark of the LORD your God in the middle of the Jordan. Each of you lift a stone onto his shoulder, one for each[H] of the Israelite tribes, [6] so that this will be a sign among you. In the future, when your

[A]3:1 Or left Shittim   [B]3:4 Lit 2,000 cubits   [C]3:4 Lit yesterday and the day before   [D]3:8 Lit waters of the Jordan   [E]3:13 Lit soles of the feet   [F]3:16 Alt Hb tradition reads mass at   [G]4:3 Lit feet of the priests, also in v. 9   [H]4:5 Lit shoulder according to the number

---

3:1-4 When Israel crossed **the Jordan,** God's presence would be manifested by the golden **ark of the covenant** (3:1, 3), a box containing the Ten Commandments that was covered by the "mercy seat," which had two cherubim on it. It was between the cherubim that God promised to meet with Moses (see Exod 25:22). Since the Israelites understood the Lord to be "enthroned" there (1 Sam 4:4; 2 Kgs 19:15), this was a visual reminder that Israel's King would personally lead them into the promised land. **3:5** Most people wouldn't meet the president of the United States without first taking a shower and dressing appropriately—though a human leader is a sinner just like the rest of us. How much more, then, should we pre-

pare (or **consecrate**) ourselves spiritually if we want to encounter God? **3:13** The Lord would stop the **water** of the Jordan River from **flowing** so that the soldiers and people could cross—but only after the priests stepped into the river. Why not stop the waters first? Because God wanted to see faith in action before he provided the miracle. **3:17** The Lord quick dried the earth where the river had been. No feet stuck in the mud; no cart wheels bogged down. This was no freak act of nature. It was an act of God. **4:1-3** These **twelve stones** from the riverbed would be used as a memorial (4:2). A memorial helps people remember important things. The national park service, for instance,

manages sites with memorials of significant people, places, or battles from America's past. The football and baseball halls of fame have memorials to special athletes and their achievements. Even the church has memorials. The greatest of these is Communion, a special ceremony through which we remember the accomplishment of the sacrificial death of Christ (see 1 Cor 11:23-26). **4:6-7** That the people were to use the rocks to tell their descendants the history of God's work on their behalf suggests that we must not only remember the times in our lives when God has stepped into a difficult situation or done something extraordinary, but we must also give testimony about them.

children ask you, 'What do these stones mean to you?'[a7] you should tell them, 'The water of the Jordan was cut off in front of the ark of the LORD's covenant. When it crossed the Jordan, the Jordan's water was cut off.' Therefore these stones will always be a memorial for the Israelites."[b]

8 The Israelites did just as Joshua had commanded them. The twelve men took stones from the middle of the Jordan, one for each[A] of the Israelite tribes, just as the LORD had told Joshua. They carried them to the camp and set them down there. **9** Joshua also set up twelve stones in the middle[B] of the Jordan where the priests who carried the ark of the covenant were standing. The stones are still there today.[c]

10 The priests carrying the ark continued standing in the middle of the Jordan until everything was completed that the LORD had commanded Joshua to tell the people, in keeping with all that Moses had commanded Joshua. The people hurried across, **11** and after everyone had finished crossing, the priests with the ark of the LORD crossed in the sight of the people. **12** The Reubenites, Gadites, and half the tribe of Manasseh went in battle formation in front of the Israelites,[d] as Moses had instructed them. **13** About forty thousand equipped for war crossed to the plains of Jericho in the LORD's presence.

14 On that day the LORD exalted Joshua in the sight of all Israel, and they revered him throughout his life, as they had revered Moses.[e] **15** The LORD told Joshua, **16** "Command the priests who carry the ark of the testimony[f] to come up from the Jordan."

17 So Joshua commanded the priests, "Come up from the Jordan." **18** When the priests carrying the ark of the LORD's covenant came up from the middle of the Jordan, and their feet[c] stepped out on solid ground, the water of the Jordan resumed its course, flowing over all the banks as before.

19 The people came up from the Jordan on the tenth day of the first month,[g] and camped at Gilgal on the eastern limits of Jericho.[h] **20** Then Joshua set up in Gilgal the twelve stones they had taken from the Jordan, **21** and he said to the Israelites, "In the future, when your children ask their fathers, 'What is the meaning of these stones?' **22** you should tell your children, 'Israel crossed the Jordan on dry ground.' **23** For the LORD your God dried up the water of the Jordan before you until you had crossed over,[j] just as the LORD your God did to the Red Sea, which he dried up before us until we had crossed over. **24** This is so that all the peoples of the earth may know[k] that the LORD's hand is mighty,[l] and so that you may always fear the LORD your God."[m]

CIRCUMCISION OF THE ISRAELITES

5 When all the Amorite kings across the Jordan to the west and all the Canaanite kings near the sea[n] heard how the LORD had dried up the water of the Jordan before the Israelites until they had crossed over,[o] they lost heart and their courage failed[D] because of the Israelites.

2 At that time the LORD said to Joshua, "Make flint knives and circumcise the Israelite men again."[p] **3** So Joshua made flint knives and circumcised the Israelite men at Gibeath-haaraloth.[E] **4** This is the reason Joshua circumcised them: All the people who came out of Egypt who were males — all the men of war — had died in the wilderness along the way after they had come out of Egypt. **5** Though all the people who came out were circumcised, none of the people born in the wilderness along the way were circumcised after they had come out of Egypt. **6** For the Israelites wandered in the wilderness forty years

---

[a] 4:6 Ex 12:26-27; 13:8-9,14; Dt 6:20-24; Jos 4:21-22
[b] 4:7 Ex 12:14; 28:12; 39:7; Lv 2:2; Nm 16:40; 31:54; Is 57:8; Zch 6:14
[c] 4:9 Jos 6:25
[d] 4:12 Nm 32:17
[e] 4:14 Jos 3:7
[f] 4:16 Ex 25:16

[g] 4:19 Ex 12:3; Ezk 40:1
[h] Dt 11:30
[i] 4:22 Jos 3:17
[j] 4:23 Ex 14:21
[k] 4:24 Ex 9:14-16; 14:31; 1Kg 8:42
[l] Nm 11:23; Ps 89:13; Is 41:20; 59:1; 66:14
[m] Ex 14:31; Dt 6:2; 10:12; 14:23; 31:12-13
[n] 5:1 Nm 13:29; Dt 1:7; Jos 11:3
[o] Jos 2:11
[p] 5:2 Gn 17:10-14; Ex 4:24-26; 12:44,48; Lv 12:3

[A] 4:8 Lit *Jordan according to the number* [B] 4:9 Or *Now Joshua set up the twelve stones that had been in the middle* [c] 4:18 Lit *and the soles of the feet of the priests* [D] 5:1 Lit *and they did not have spirit in them any more* [E] 5:3 Or *The Hill of Foreskins*

4:9 Knowing that the rocks stood there, long after the river covered them over, would encourage Joshua in later years that nothing could stand in Israel's path with the Lord leading the way.

4:14 On that day the LORD exalted Joshua so that Israel **revered** Joshua **as they had revered Moses**, through whom God had worked to part the Red Sea four decades prior. God wanted all Israel to know: Joshua is my man. Follow him.

4:20-24 Focus on verse 24. The Israelites were to report God's deeds **so that all the peoples of the earth** (including you and me) **[might] know that the LORD's hand is mighty, and so that [they would] always fear the LORD**.

God's people, past and present, are to work to spread his fame.

5:2-9 Circumcision was the sign of the covenant between God and the descendants of Abraham (see Gen 17:9-14). Even though the men who **had come out of Egypt** had been circumcised, their children had not (Josh 5:4-6).

What did God mean when he said, **Today I have rolled away the disgrace of Egypt from you** (5:9)? In Egypt, the Israelites had been slaves. And even in the wilderness, many Israelites were longing to return there. But in the men's submission to the act of circumcision, this disgrace had been rolled back. It signaled that they were finally, truly free.

One of the great spiritual truths of the New Testament is that believers in Jesus Christ are free from slavery to sin (John 8:34-36). Though it lures us, we don't have to submit to it. Yet throughout our lifetimes, the devil works to deceive us, to cause us to think and act like we're still slaves to his will. He works to keep us from believing the truth of our freedom because the one who believes that he's truly free might actually start acting like it. If you find yourself falling for his tricks, it's time to ask the Lord to "roll away" the disgrace of your past so that you can move forward in victory.

[a]5:6 Dt 2:7,14
[b]Nm 14:23-24; Dt 11:9
[c]5:8 Dt 30:6; Hs 6:1-2
[d]5:9 Jos 6:25
[e]5:10 Ex 12:11,18,21; Lv 23:5; Nm 28:16; Ezk 45:21
[f]5:11 Lv 23:14
[g]5:12 Ex 16:35; Ps 78:25; Jn 6:48-51
[h]5:13 Gn 18:2; 32:24; Nm 22:31
[i]5:14 Ex 7:4; 12:41; 1Sm 17:45
[j]Gn 17:3
[k]5:15 Ex 3:5

[l]6:2 Dt 7:24; Jos 2:9,24; 8:1; Neh 9:24
[m]6:4 Ex 19:13; Ps 24:7; Is 18:3; 1Co 15:52; 1Th 4:16; Rv 11:15
[n]6:9 Is 52:12

until all the nation's men of war who came out of Egypt had died off because they did not obey the LORD.[a] So the LORD vowed never to let them see the land he had sworn to their fathers to give us, a land flowing with milk and honey.[b] 7 He raised up their sons in their place; it was these Joshua circumcised. They were still uncircumcised, since they had not been circumcised along the way. 8 After the entire nation had been circumcised, they stayed where they were in the camp until they recovered.[c] 9 The LORD then said to Joshua, "Today I have rolled away the disgrace of Egypt from you." Therefore, that place is still called Gilgal today.[d]

FOOD FROM THE LAND

10 While the Israelites camped at Gilgal on the plains of Jericho, they observed the Passover on the evening of the fourteenth day of the month.[e] 11 The day after Passover they ate unleavened bread and roasted grain from the produce of the land.[f] 12 And the day after they ate from the produce of the land, the manna ceased.[g] Since there was no more manna for the Israelites, they ate from the crops of the land of Canaan that year.

COMMANDER OF THE LORD'S ARMY

13 When Joshua was near Jericho, he looked up and saw a man standing in front of him with a drawn sword in his hand.[h] Joshua approached him and asked, "Are you for us or for our enemies?"

14 "Neither," he replied. "I have now come as commander of the LORD's army."[i]

Then Joshua bowed with his face to the ground in worship[j] and asked him, "What does my lord want to say to his servant?"

15 The commander of the LORD's army said to Joshua, "Remove the sandals from your feet, for the place where you are standing is holy."[k] And Joshua did that.

THE CONQUEST OF JERICHO

6 Now Jericho was strongly fortified because of the Israelites — no one leaving or entering. 2 The LORD said to Joshua, "Look, I have handed Jericho, its king, and its best soldiers over to you.[l] 3 March around the city with all the men of war, circling the city one time. Do this for six days. 4 Have seven priests carry seven ram's-horn trumpets in front of the ark. But on the seventh day, march around the city seven times, while the priests blow the trumpets.[m] 5 When there is a prolonged blast of the horn and you hear its sound, have all the troops give a mighty shout. Then the city wall will collapse, and the troops will advance, each man straight ahead."

6 So Joshua son of Nun summoned the priests and said to them, "Take up the ark of the covenant and have seven priests carry seven trumpets in front of the ark of the LORD." 7 He said to the troops, "Move forward, march around the city, and have the armed men go ahead of the ark of the LORD."

8 After Joshua had spoken to the troops, seven priests carrying seven trumpets before the LORD moved forward and blew the trumpets; the ark of the LORD's covenant followed them. 9 While the trumpets were blowing, the armed men went in front of the priests who blew the trumpets, and the rear guard went behind the ark.[n] 10 But Joshua had commanded the troops: "Do not shout or let your voice be heard. Don't let one word come out of your mouth until the time I say, 'Shout!' Then you are to shout." 11 So the ark of the LORD was carried around the city, circling it once. They returned to the camp and spent the night there.[A]

12 Joshua got up early the next morning. The priests took the ark of the LORD, 13 and the seven priests carrying seven trumpets marched in front of the ark of the LORD.

[A]6:11 Lit at the camp

5:12 For the last forty years, God had provided **manna**—bread from heaven—for them to eat (see Exod 16). But from this point forward, if they were going to eat, they would have to act on his promises.

Here I see an application to a person's spiritual development. Babies have to be fed. But if you're spoon-feeding your twelve-year-old, there's a serious problem! Similarly, as you grow in Christian maturity, God expects you to exercise increasing responsibility for your spiritual growth.

5:13-15 Many Bible teachers recognize this visitor as an earthly manifestation of the Son

of God. Why? First, when he recognized that he was outranked by him, **Joshua bowed . . . in worship** (5:14). We are to worship God alone, and angels rightly reject worship (see Rev 19:10; 22:9). This stranger accepted it as his due. Though Joshua didn't understand the Trinitarian nature of God (that is, the fact that God is one in three persons), he clearly recognized that this was a visible manifestation of the divine presence. Second, **the commander** told Joshua to **remove [his] sandals** because he was standing on **holy** ground (Josh 5:14). If these words sound familiar, it's because we have heard them before. As the man who had

taken Moses's place, Joshua was having his own burning bush moment, complete with the command to remove his shoes (see Exod 3:1-6). Holy ground is God-occupied space. Only God can turn an ordinary place into sacred territory. **6:4** Notice the repetition of the number **seven** in this verse. In Scripture, "seven" is the number of completion. God created the world in six days and rested on the seventh. The seven churches of Revelation represent all churches. In these instructions, then, God was emphasizing to Joshua that he must follow the instructions completely if he wanted God to bring down his problem.

While the trumpets were blowing, the armed men went in front of them, and the rear guard went behind the ark of the LORD. **14** On the second day they marched around the city once and returned to the camp. They did this for six days.

15 Early on the seventh day, they started at dawn and marched around the city seven times in the same way. That was the only day they marched around the city seven times. **16** After the seventh time, the priests blew the trumpets, and Joshua said to the troops, "Shout! For the LORD has given you the city. **17** But the city and everything in it are set apart to the LORD for destruction.ᵃ Only Rahab the prostitute and everyone with her in the house will live,ᵇ because she hid the messengers we sent. **18** But keep yourselves from the things set apart, or you will be set apart for destruction. If youᴬ take any of those things, you will set apart the camp of Israel for destruction and make trouble for it. **19** For all the silver and gold, and the articles of bronze and iron, are dedicated to the LORD and must go into the LORD's treasury."ᶜ

20 So the troops shouted, and the trumpets sounded. When they heard the blast of the trumpet, the troops gave a great shout, and the wall collapsed.ᵈ The troops advanced into the city, each man straight ahead, and they captured the city. **21** They completely destroyedᵉ everything in the city with the sword — every man and woman, both young and old, and every ox, sheep, and donkey.

RAHAB AND HER FAMILY SPARED

22 Joshua said to the two men who had scouted the land, "Go to the prostitute's house and bring the woman out of there, and all who are with her, just as you swore to her."ᶠ **23** So the young men who had scouted went in and brought out Rahab and her father, mother, brothers, and all who belonged to her. They brought out her whole family and settled them outside the camp of Israel.

24 They burned the city and everything in it, but they put the silver and gold and the articles of bronze and iron into the treasury of the LORD's house. **25** However, Joshua spared Rahab the prostitute, her father's family, and all who belonged to her, because she hid the messengers Joshua had sent to spy on Jericho, and she still lives in Israelᵍ today.ʰ

26 At that time Joshua imposed this curse:

The man who undertakes
the rebuilding of this city, Jericho,
is cursed before the LORD.ⁱ
He will lay its foundation
at the cost of his firstborn;
he will finish its gates
at the cost of his youngest.ʲ

27 And the LORD was with Joshua,ᵏ and his fame spread throughout the land.

DEFEAT AT AI

7 The Israelites, however, were unfaithfulˡ regarding the things set apart for destruction. Achan son of Carmi, son of Zabdi, son of Zerah, of the tribe of Judah, took some of what was set apart, and the LORD's anger burned against the Israelites.

2 Joshua sent men from Jericho to Ai, which is near Beth-aven,ᵐ east of Bethel, and told them, "Go up and scout the land." So the men went up and scouted Ai.

3 After returning to Joshua they reported to him, "Don't send all the people, but send about two thousand or three thousandᴮ men to attack Ai. Since the people of Ai are so few, don't wear out all our people there." **4** So about three thousand menᶜ went up there, but they fled from the men of Ai.ⁿ **5** The men of Ai struck down about thirty-six of them and chased them from outside the city gate to the quarries,ᴰ striking them down on the descent. As a result, the people lost heart.ᴱ,ᵒ

6 Then Joshua tore his clothes and fell facedown to the ground before the ark of the LORD until evening,ᵖ as did the elders of Israel; they all put dust on their heads.ᵠ

ᵃ **6:17** Lv 27:29; Dt 7:26; 13:17; Jos 7:1
ᵇ **6:18** Dt 7:2
ᶜ **6:19** 1Kg 7:51; 14:26; 15:18
ᵈ **6:20** Heb 11:30
ᵉ **6:21** Jos 2:10; 8:26
ᶠ **6:22** Jos 2:14

ᵍ **6:25** Ex 6:23; Ru 4:21-22; 1Ch 2:10-12; Mt 1:4-5
ʰ **Jos** 4:9; 5:9; 7:26; 14:14; 15:63
ⁱ **6:26** Dt 27:15; 1Sm 14:24; Jr 11:3; 20:15
ʲ **1Kg** 16:34
ᵏ **6:27** Gn 39:2,21; Jdg 1:19,22; 2:18; 1Sm 3:19; 18:12; 1Kg 1:37; 2Kg 18:7; 1Ch 9:20; 2Ch 17:3
ˡ **7:1** Lv 6:2; Nm 5:27; 31:16; Dt 32:51; Jos 22:16; Ezr 9:2-4
ᵐ **7:2** Jos 18:12; 1Sm 13:5; 14:23
ⁿ **7:4** Lv 26:17; Dt 28:25
ᵒ **7:5** Dt 20:8; Jos 2:11; 5:1; 2Sm 17:10; Ps 22:14; Is 13:7; 19:1; Ezk 21:7
ᵖ **7:6** Jb 1:20
ᵠ **Neh** 9:1; Lm 2:10; Ezk 27:30; Rv 18:19

ᴬ **6:18** LXX reads *you covet and*; Jos 7:21   ᴮ **7:3** Or *send two or three military units of*   ᶜ **7:4** Lit *men from the people*   ᴰ **7:5** Or *to Shebarim*
ᴱ **7:5** Lit *people's hearts melted and became like water*

6:18-19 The Israelites were not to pocket any of the things they found in Jericho. Everything of value in the city was either to be destroyed or preserved for **the LORD's treasury** (6:19)—a prohibition that will be very important to the events of chapter 7.
6:20 God's hand orchestrated even the direction in which Jericho's wall fell. When **the troops advanced into the city, each man straight ahead**, they could see that God had

turned the barrier that stood in their way into steppingstones leading to their goal.
6:26-27 Whoever sought to rebuild the city would do so at the cost of his own children (6:26). This would be fulfilled centuries later (see 1 Kgs 16:34).
7:1 Why was God angry with the whole nation when only **Achan** had sinned? This is a reminder of the corporate nature of the people of God. The Israelites were like

a football team in one sense. Thus, if one player committed an infraction of the rules, the entire team was penalized. This, in fact, is why the author of Hebrews urges believers to "encourage each other daily . . . so that none of [us are] hardened by sin's deception" (Heb 3:13). What seems an isolated problem can have systemic reach.
7:6-12 Earlier, at Mount Sinai, the Lord had made a **covenant** with Israel—a divinely

7 "Oh, Lord GOD," Joshua said, "why did you ever bring these people across the Jordan to hand us over to the Amorites for our destruction? If only we had been content to remain on the other side of the Jordan! **8** What can I say, Lord, now that Israel has turned its back and run from its enemies? **9** When the Canaanites and all who live in the land hear about this, they will surround us and wipe out our name from the earth.*ª* Then what will you do about your great name?"*ᵇ*

10 The LORD then said to Joshua, "Stand up! Why have you fallen facedown? **11** Israel has sinned. They have violated my covenant that I appointed for them. They have taken some of what was set apart. They have stolen, deceived, and put those things with their own belongings.*ᶜ* **12** This is why the Israelites cannot stand against their enemies. They will turn their backs and run from their enemies, because they have been set apart for destruction.*ᵈ* I will no longer be with you unless you remove from among you what is set apart.

13 "Go and consecrate the people. Tell them to consecrate themselves for tomorrow,*ᵉ* for this is what the LORD, the God of Israel, says: There are things that are set apart among you, Israel. You will not be able to stand against your enemies until you remove what is set apart. **14** In the morning, present yourselves tribe by tribe. The tribe the LORD selects is to come forward clan by clan. The clan the LORD selects is to come forward family by family. The family the LORD selects is to come forward man by man. **15** The one who is caught with the things set apart must be burned, along with everything he has, because he has violated the LORD's covenant and committed an outrage in Israel."*ᶠ*

ACHAN JUDGED

16 Joshua got up early the next morning. He had Israel come forward tribe by tribe, and the tribe of Judah was selected. **17** He had the clans of Judah come forward, and the Zerahite clan was selected. He had the Zerahite clan come forward by heads of families,*ᴬ* and Zabdi was selected. **18** He then had Zabdi's family come forward man by man, and Achan son of Carmi, son of Zabdi, son of Zerah, of the tribe of Judah, was selected.

19 So Joshua said to Achan, "My son, give glory to the LORD, the God of Israel,*ᵍ* and make a confession to him.*ᴮ* I urge you, tell me what you have done. Don't hide anything from me."

20 Achan replied to Joshua, "It is true. I have sinned against the LORD, the God of Israel.*ʰ* This is what I did: **21** When I saw among the spoils a beautiful cloak from Babylon,*ᶜ* five pounds*ᴰ* of silver, and a bar of gold weighing a pound and a quarter,*ᴱ* I coveted them and took them.*ⁱ* You can see for yourself. They are concealed in the ground inside my tent, with the silver under the cloak." **22** So Joshua sent messengers who ran to the tent, and there was the cloak, concealed in his tent, with the silver underneath. **23** They took the things from inside the tent, brought them to Joshua and all the Israelites, and spread them out in the LORD's presence.

24 Then Joshua and all Israel with him took Achan son of Zerah, the silver, the cloak, and the bar of gold, his sons and daughters, his ox, donkey, and sheep, his tent, and all that he had, and brought them up to the Valley of Achor.*ʲ* **25** Joshua said, "Why have you brought us trouble?*ᴷ* Today the LORD will bring you trouble!" So all Israel stoned them*ᶠ* to death. They burned their bodies, threw stones on them, **26** and raised over him a large pile of rocks that remains still today.*ˡ* Then the LORD turned from his burning anger. Therefore that place is called the Valley of Achor*ᴳ* still today.

CONQUEST OF AI

8 The LORD said to Joshua, "Do not be afraid or discouraged.*ᵐ* Take all the troops with you and go attack Ai. Look, I have handed over to you the king of Ai,

---

orchestrated agreement (7:11). Under it, he would be their God and deliver them, provided that they obeyed his instructions. By taking **some of what was set apart**, they had **stolen** from God (7:11). Joshua would have to deal with the sin in order for God to fight for them again (7:12).
7:14 Revealing the guilty party through such a lengthy process demonstrated to everyone the seriousness of this sin, which had affected the entire nation. It also allowed the people to see that God really did know each of them and their deeds intimately. And it gave Achan opportunity to come clean.
7:16-26 Joshua pronounced sentence on Achan and his children—who were apparently co-conspirators in his sin—and had them put **to death** (7:24-26) in accordance with the Lord's command (7:15).

Some may consider this judgment too severe. But we must be careful not to softpedal Achan's sin. He willfully disobeyed a clear prohibition and was responsible for the deaths of thirty-six innocent men! And he invited those consequences simply so that he could enrich himself with a few trinkets.

his people, city, and land.[a] **2** Treat Ai and its king as you did Jericho and its king,[b] except that you may plunder its spoil and livestock for yourselves.[c] Set an ambush behind the city."[d]

3 So Joshua and all the troops set out to attack Ai. Joshua selected thirty thousand of his best soldiers and sent them out at night. **4** He commanded them: "Pay attention. Lie in ambush behind the city, not too far from it, and all of you be ready.[e] **5** Then I and all the people who are with me will approach the city. When they come out against us as they did the first time, we will flee from them. **6** They will come after us until we have drawn them away from the city, for they will say, 'They are fleeing from us as before.' While we are fleeing from them, **7** you are to come out of your ambush and seize the city. The LORD your God will hand it over to you. **8** After taking the city, set it on fire. Follow the LORD's command — see that you do as I have ordered you." **9** So Joshua sent them out, and they went to the ambush site and waited between Bethel and Ai, to the west of Ai. But he spent that night with the troops.

10 Joshua started early the next morning and mobilized them. Then he and the elders of Israel led the troops up to Ai. **11** All those[A] who were with him went up and approached the city, arriving opposite Ai, and camped to the north of it, with a valley between them and the city. **12** Now Joshua had taken about five thousand men and set them in ambush between Bethel and Ai, to the west of the city. **13** The troops were stationed in this way: the main[B] camp to the north of the city and its rear guard to the west of the city. And that night Joshua went into the valley.

14 When the king of Ai saw the Israelites, the men of the city hurried and went out early in the morning so that he and all his people could engage Israel in battle at a suitable place facing the Arabah. But he did not know there was an ambush waiting for him behind the city. **15** Joshua and all Israel pretended to be beaten back by them and fled toward the wilderness.[f]

16 Then all the troops of Ai were summoned to pursue them, and they pursued Joshua and were drawn away from the city. **17** Not a man was left in Ai or Bethel who did not go out after Israel, leaving the city exposed while they pursued Israel.

18 Then the LORD said to Joshua, "Hold out the javelin in your hand toward Ai, for I will hand the city over to you." So Joshua held out his javelin toward it. **19** When he held out his hand, the men in ambush rose quickly from their position. They ran, entered the city, captured it, and immediately set it on fire.

20 The men of Ai turned and looked back, and smoke from the city was rising to the sky! They could not escape in any direction, and the troops who had fled to the wilderness now became the pursuers. **21** When Joshua and all Israel saw that the men in ambush had captured the city and that smoke was rising from it, they turned back and struck down the men of Ai. **22** Then men in ambush came out of the city against them, and the men of Ai were trapped between the Israelite forces, some on one side and some on the other. They struck them down until no survivor or fugitive remained,[g] **23** but they captured the king of Ai alive and brought him to Joshua.

24 When Israel had finished killing everyone living in Ai who had pursued them into the open country, and when every last one of them had fallen by the sword, all Israel returned to Ai and struck it down with the sword. **25** The total of those who fell that day, both men and women, was twelve thousand — all the people of Ai. **26** Joshua did not draw back his hand that was holding the javelin until all the inhabitants of Ai were completely destroyed.[h] **27** Israel plundered only the cattle and spoil of that city for themselves, according to the LORD's command that he had given Joshua.

28 Joshua burned Ai and left it a permanent ruin, still desolate today.[i] **29** He hung[C] the body of the king of Ai on a tree[D] until evening, and at sunset Joshua commanded that they take his body down from the

a 8:1 Jos 6:2
b 8:2 Jos 6:17
c Dt 20:14; Jos 8:27
d Jdg 9:32-35,43; 20:29; 1Sm 15:5
e 8:4 Jdg 20:29
f 8:15 Jdg 20:36

g 8:22 Dt 7:2
h 8:26 Nm 21:2-3; Dt 2:34; Jos 2:10; 6:21; 10:1,28,35-40; 11:11-12,20-21; 24:20
i 8:28 Dt 13:16; Jos 6:25

A 8:11 Lit *the people of war*   B 8:13 Lit *way: all the*   C 8:29 Or *impaled*   D 8:29 Or *wooden stake*

8:2 In the second battle against Ai, they were to employ a strategy that differed from those used previously. We must not presume to know God's plan for a given situation. His strategies are diverse, so God's people need to stay close to him in order to make sure we do as he wants. God's ways are not our ways (see Isa 55:8).

8:28-29 Ai was destroyed and the king's body was **hung** on a **tree**. At **evening**, Joshua ordered the Israelites to take down the king's **body** (8:29). It's easy to miss the significance of this. Earlier God had commanded Israel that if they executed a guilty person by hanging him on a tree, "[they were] not to leave his corpse on the

tree overnight but [were] to bury him." To disobey the Lord in this would be to "defile the land [their] God [was] giving" (Deut 21:22-23). So here we see that Joshua was not only a talented military tactician, but he was also a godly leader. He understood the dangers of disobeying God's Word (see Josh 7).

a 8:29 Dt 21:21-23
b 8:30 Dt 27:4-6
c 8:31 Ex 20:24-25; Dt 27:5-7
d 8:32 Dt 27:2-3
e 8:33 Dt 11:29
f Dt 27:12-13
g 8:35 Dt 31:12; Neh 8:2-3; 13:1
h 9:1 Jos 3:10
i Nm 34:6

j 9:3 Jos 10:2
k 9:6 Jos 5:10
l 9:7 Ex 23:32; Dt 7:2-5; 20:10-18
m 9:8 2Sm 15:15; 2Kg 10:5
n 9:14 Ex 17:1; Lv 24:12; Nm 3:16; 9:18; 22:18; 27:21; Dt 1:26; 8:3; Jr 23:16

tree.[a] They threw it down at the entrance of the city gate and put a large pile of rocks over it, which still remains today.

RENEWED COMMITMENT TO THE LAW

30 At that time Joshua built an altar on Mount Ebal[b] to the LORD, the God of Israel, 31 just as Moses the LORD's servant had commanded the Israelites. He built it according to what is written in the book of the law of Moses: an altar of uncut stones on which no iron tool has been used.[c] Then they offered burnt offerings to the LORD and sacrificed fellowship offerings on it. 32 There on the stones, Joshua copied the law of Moses, which he had written in the presence of the Israelites.[d] 33 All Israel — resident alien and citizen alike — with their elders, officers, and judges, stood on either side of the ark of the LORD's covenant facing the Levitical priests who carried it. Half of them were in front of Mount Gerizim and half in front of Mount Ebal,[e] as Moses the LORD's servant had commanded earlier concerning blessing the people of Israel.[f] 34 Afterward, Joshua read aloud all the words of the law — the blessings as well as the curses — according to all that is written in the book of the law. 35 There was not a word of all that Moses had commanded that Joshua did not read before the entire assembly of Israel, including the women, the dependents, and the resident aliens who lived[A] among them.[g]

DECEPTION BY GIBEON

9 When all the kings heard about Jericho and Ai, those who were west of the Jordan in the hill country,[h] in the Judean foothills,[B] and all along the coast of the Mediterranean Sea[i] toward Lebanon — the Hethites, Amorites, Canaanites, Perizzites, Hivites, and Jebusites — 2 they formed a unified alliance to fight against Joshua and Israel.

3 When the inhabitants of Gibeon heard what Joshua had done to Jericho and Ai,[j] 4 they acted deceptively. They gathered provisions[c] and took worn-out sacks on their donkeys and old wineskins, cracked and mended. 5 They wore old, patched sandals on their feet and threadbare clothing on their bodies. Their entire provision of bread was dry and crumbly. 6 They went to Joshua in the camp at Gilgal and said to him and the men of Israel, "We have come from a distant land. Please make a treaty with us."[k]

7 The men of Israel replied to the Hivites, "Perhaps you live among us. How can we make a treaty with you?"[l]

8 They said to Joshua, "We are your servants."[m]

Then Joshua asked them, "Who are you and where do you come from?"

9 They replied to him, "Your servants have come from a faraway land because of the reputation of the LORD your God. For we have heard of his fame, and all that he did in Egypt, 10 and all that he did to the two Amorite kings beyond the Jordan — King Sihon of Heshbon and King Og of Bashan, who was in Ashtaroth. 11 So our elders and all the inhabitants of our land told us, 'Take provisions with you for the journey; go and meet them and say, "We are your servants. Please make a treaty with us." ' 12 This bread of ours was warm when we took it from our houses as food on the day we left to come to you; but see, it is now dry and crumbly. 13 These wineskins were new when we filled them; but see, they are cracked. And these clothes and sandals of ours are worn out from the extremely long journey." 14 Then the men of Israel took some of their provisions, but did not seek the LORD's decision.[n] 15 So Joshua established peace with them and made a treaty to let them live,

---

8:34-35 Israel's future experience in the promised land would depend on the people's response to God. Whether they lived or died, whether they prospered or went hungry, whether they experienced blessing or cursing depended on their choices. Would they serve God or themselves? Moses had admonished them to "choose life so that [they] and [their] descendants [might] live" (Deut 30:19). But only by heeding God's covenant commands could Israel maximize what the promised land had to offer. Similarly, by choosing God's way, you will maximize the blessings God has for your life.

9:1-2 Joshua and the people had made a name for themselves. But mostly, it was God's reputation and fame that had become well known (see 9:9).

9:3-13 When the Gibeonites heard the news about the two fallen cities, they pretended they had traveled **from a distant land**—that is, from outside the promised land—to **make a treaty with** Israel (9:6). So complete was their ruse that before leaving home, they had put on raggedy **clothing** and **sandals** to make it look like they had journeyed a great distance. (9:5). One thing they said was true:

They had come to make a treaty **because of the reputation of the LORD [Israel's] God. For [they had] heard of his fame** (9:9). (When God does amazing things through you, people will take notice. And they might even try to get in on the blessings.)

9:14-15 The Israelites allowed themselves to be deceived into doing exactly what God had commanded them not to do (see Deut 7:1-2). They'd been flimflammed. This is a reminder that Satan can deceive you into sinning, too, so you must remain alert.

and the leaders of the community swore an oath to them.[a]

GIBEON'S DECEPTION DISCOVERED

[16] Three days after making the treaty with them, they heard that the Gibeonites were their neighbors, living among them. [17] So the Israelites set out and reached the Gibeonite cities on the third day. Now their cities were Gibeon, Chephirah, Beeroth, and Kiriath-jearim.[b] [18] But the Israelites did not attack them, because the leaders of the community had sworn an oath[c] to them by the LORD, the God of Israel. Then the whole community grumbled against the leaders.

[19] All the leaders answered them, "We have sworn an oath to them by the LORD, the God of Israel, and now we cannot touch them. [20] This is how we will treat them: we will let them live, so that no wrath will fall on us because of the oath we swore to them." [21] They also said, "Let them live." So the Gibeonites became woodcutters and water carriers[d] for the whole community, as the leaders had promised them.

[22] Joshua summoned the Gibeonites and said to them, "Why did you deceive us by telling us you live far away from us, when in fact you live among us? [23] Therefore you are cursed and will always be slaves — woodcutters and water carriers for the house of my God."

[24] The Gibeonites answered him, "It was clearly communicated to your servants that the LORD your God had commanded his servant Moses to give you all the land and to destroy all the inhabitants of the land before you. We greatly feared for our lives because of you, and that is why we did this.[e] [25] Now we are in your hands. Do to us whatever you think is right."[A,f] [26] This is what Joshua did to them: he rescued them from the Israelites, and they did not kill them. [27] On that day he made them woodcutters and water carriers — as they are

today — for the community and for the LORD's altar at the place he would choose.[g]

THE DAY THE SUN STOOD STILL

10 Now King Adoni-zedek of Jerusalem heard that Joshua had captured Ai and completely destroyed[h] it, treating Ai and its king as he had Jericho and its king, and that the inhabitants of Gibeon[i] had made peace with Israel and were living among them.[j] [2] So Adoni-zedek and his people were[B] greatly alarmed because Gibeon was a large city like one of the royal cities;[k] it was larger than Ai, and all its men were warriors. [3] Therefore King Adoni-zedek of Jerusalem sent word to King Hoham of Hebron, King Piram of Jarmuth, King Japhia of Lachish, and King Debir of Eglon, saying, [4] "Come up and help me. We will attack Gibeon, because they have made peace with Joshua and the Israelites." [5] So the five Amorite kings — the kings of Jerusalem, Hebron, Jarmuth, Lachish, and Eglon — joined forces, advanced with all their armies, besieged Gibeon, and fought against it.

[6] Then the men of Gibeon sent word to Joshua in the camp at Gilgal: "Don't give up on[c] your servants. Come quickly and save us! Help us, for all the Amorite kings living in the hill country have joined forces against us." [7] So Joshua and all his troops, including all his best soldiers, came from Gilgal.[l]

[8] The LORD said to Joshua, "Do not be afraid of them,[m] for I have handed them over to you.[n] Not one of them will be able to stand against you."[o]

[9] So Joshua caught them by surprise, after marching all night from Gilgal. [10] The LORD threw them into confusion[p] before Israel. He defeated them in a great slaughter at Gibeon, chased them through the ascent of Beth-horon, and struck them down as far as Azekah and Makkedah. [11] As they fled before Israel, the LORD threw large

[a] 9:15 2Sm 21:1-2
[b] 9:17 Jos 18:25
[c] 9:18 Ps 15:1-4; Ezk 17:16-20
[d] 9:21 Dt 29:11
[e] 9:24 Jos 10:2
[f] 9:25 Gn 16:6; Jr 26:14; 38:5

[g] 9:27 Dt 12:5
[h] 10:1 Jos 8:26; 10:28,35-40; 11:11-12,20-21; 24:20; Jdg 1:17; 21:11
[i] Jos 8:22
[j] Jos 9:15
[k] 10:2 Jos 13:31; 1Sm 27:5
[l] 10:7 Jos 8:1
[m] 10:8 Jos 1:5
[n] Gn 14:20; Nm 21:34; Dt 2:30; 7:24
[o] Dt 7:24; 11:25; Jos 1:5; 21:44; 23:9
[p] 10:10 Ex 14:24; 23:27; 1Sm 7:10

A 9:25 Lit *us as is good and as is right in your eyes do*   B 10:2 One Hb ms, Syr, Vg read *So he was*   C 10:6 Lit *Don't withdraw your hands from*

9:16-20 Although **the whole community grumbled against** Israel's **leaders** over what happened, there was nothing they could do. They had **sworn an oath** and could not retaliate against the Gibeonites (9:18-19). If they were to break their promise of peace, judgment would fall on them.
9:21-27 Since the Gibeonites had practiced deception, they would become **woodcutters and water carriers for the whole community** (9:21) and **for the LORD's altar** (9:27). They had heard of the Lord's reputation (9:9); from this

point forward, they would be made to work for him.
10:1-5 Gibeon wasn't a tiny village but a major **city** whose **men were warriors** (10:2). If a significant place like that teamed up with the Israelite invaders, it was only a matter of time before Jerusalem would be attacked. So its king **joined forces** with four other **Amorite kings** (10:3-5). They determined to put a stop to Israel's growing strength before all the peoples of the land fell like dominoes before their God.

10:9-11 This time, when Joshua and his men confronted their enemies, **the LORD … threw large hailstones on them** (10:10-11). Now, if God throws anything, he's not going to miss. So this was a dark day indeed for the men allied against him.
Notice, though, that this miraculous intervention on behalf of his people didn't happen until Israel's army marched. And when those on the earth were obedient, heaven intervened in history. Sometimes Christians declare that they're waiting on God to act in their situations.

ᵃ10:11 Ps 18:12-14
ᵇ10:12 Hab 3:11
ᶜ10:14 Ex 14:14,25; Dt
1:30; 3:22; 20:4; Jos 10:42;
23:3,10; 2Ch 20:29; 32:8;
Ps 35:1; Zch 14:3

ᵈ10:25 Dt 31:7; Jos
1:6-7,9,18
ᵉ10:26 Jos 8:29
ᶠ10:27 Dt 21:22-23
ᵍJos 6:25
ʰ10:28 Jos 6:21
ⁱ10:29 Jos 7:24; 10:15,31,36
ⁱJos 21:13

hailstones on them[a] from the sky along the descent of Beth-horon all the way to Azekah, and they died. More of them died from the hail than the Israelites killed with the sword.

¹² On the day the LORD gave the Amorites over to the Israelites, Joshua spoke to the LORD in the presence of Israel:

"Sun,[b] stand still over Gibeon,
and moon, over the Valley
of Aijalon."

¹³ And the sun stood still
and the moon stopped
until the nation took vengeance
on its enemies.

Isn't this written in the Book of Jashar?[A] So the sun stopped
in the middle of the sky
and delayed its setting
almost a full day.

¹⁴ There has been no day like it before or since, when the LORD listened to a man, because the LORD fought for Israel.[c] ¹⁵ Then Joshua and all Israel with him returned to the camp at Gilgal.

EXECUTION OF THE FIVE KINGS

¹⁶ Now the five defeated kings had fled and hidden in the cave at Makkedah. ¹⁷ It was reported to Joshua: "The five kings have been found; they are hiding in the cave at Makkedah."

¹⁸ Joshua said, "Roll large stones against the mouth of the cave, and station men by it to guard the kings. ¹⁹ But as for the rest of you, don't stay there. Pursue your enemies and attack them from behind. Don't let them enter their cities, for the LORD your God has handed them over to you." ²⁰ So Joshua and the Israelites finished inflicting a terrible slaughter on them until they were destroyed, although a few survivors ran away to the fortified cities.

²¹ The people returned safely to Joshua in the camp at Makkedah. And no one dared to threaten[B] the Israelites.

²² Then Joshua said, "Open the mouth of the cave, and bring those five kings to me out of there." ²³ That is what they did. They brought the five kings of Jerusalem, Hebron, Jarmuth, Lachish, and Eglon to Joshua out of the cave. ²⁴ When they had brought the kings to him, Joshua summoned all the men of Israel and said to the military commanders who had accompanied him, "Come here and put your feet on the necks of these kings." So the commanders came forward and put their feet on their necks. ²⁵ Joshua said to them, "Do not be afraid or discouraged. Be strong and courageous,[d] for the LORD will do this to all the enemies you fight."

²⁶ After this, Joshua struck them down and executed them. He hung[c] their bodies on five trees[D] and they were there until evening.[e] ²⁷ At sunset Joshua commanded that they be taken down from the trees[f] and thrown into the cave where they had hidden. Then large stones were placed against the mouth of the cave, and the stones are still there today.[g]

CONQUEST OF SOUTHERN CITIES

²⁸ On that day Joshua captured Makkedah and struck it down with the sword, including its king. He completely destroyed it[E] and everyone in it, leaving no survivors. So he treated the king of Makkedah as he had the king of Jericho.[h]

²⁹ Joshua and all Israel with him[i] crossed from Makkedah to Libnah and fought against Libnah.[j] ³⁰ The LORD also handed it and its king over to Israel. He struck it down, putting everyone in it to the sword, and left no survivors in it. He treated Libnah's king as he had the king of Jericho.

A10:13 Or of the Upright   B10:21 Lit No one sharpened his tongue against   C10:26 Or impaled   D10:26 Or wooden stakes, also in v. 27   E10:28 Some Hb mss read them

---

But they don't realize that God is often waiting on them to obey him first.

10:12-13 Critics claim that passages like this prove that the Bible is fictional. After all, they argue, science shows us that the sun is already "standing still." It's the earth that's moving—spinning on its axis and orbiting around the sun. But when people today talk about the sun rising and setting, they don't mean that they think the sun is literally moving up and down in the sky or that the sun is orbiting the earth. They're simply using the language of observation. This passage is merely describing the way things appeared.

Nevertheless, if the earth slowed its rotation, it would be catastrophic—unless the

author of creation was multi-tasking behind the scenes to keep everything in order. And that's what happened. Mother Nature is answerable to Father God.

10:14 I love that **the LORD listened to a man** regarding such an outlandish request (see 10:12-13). For those committed to making God's agenda their own, even the wildest prayer requests just might be granted.

10:24-26 Joshua had **the military commanders** place their **feet on the necks of [the enemy] kings** (10:24)—a pose illustrating the triumph of Israel and the subjugation of their foes. We see this imagery of the victor's feet on the enemy's head expressed repeatedly in the Bible, beginning with the

promise that the "offspring" of the woman would "strike" the serpent's "head" (Gen 3:15). In Psalms, the Lord instructs his Messiah, "Sit at my right hand until I make your enemies your footstool" (Ps 110:1). In the New Testament, both Jesus and Paul emphasize that indeed Christ will be victorious in this way (see Matt 22:43-44; 1 Cor 15:24-25). But what is true of the King will also be true of the faithful members of his kingdom: "The God of peace will soon crush Satan under your feet" (Rom 16:20). So keep walking with Jesus. The devil may be spiritually attacking you now (see Eph 6:10-18), but he's destined to have your foot on his head.

31 From Libnah, Joshua and all Israel with him crossed to Lachish. They laid siege to it and attacked it. **32** The Lord handed Lachish over to Israel, and Joshua captured it on the second day. He struck it down, putting everyone in it to the sword, just as he had done to Libnah. **33** At that time King Horam of Gezer went to help Lachish,[a] but Joshua struck him down along with his people, leaving no survivors.

34 Then Joshua crossed from Lachish to Eglon and all Israel with him. They laid siege to it and attacked it. **35** On that day they captured it and struck it down, putting everyone in it to the sword. He completely destroyed it that day, just as he had done to Lachish.

36 Next, Joshua and all Israel with him went up from Eglon to Hebron[b] and attacked it. **37** They captured it and struck down its king, all its villages, and everyone in it with the sword. He left no survivors, just as he had done at Eglon. He completely destroyed Hebron and everyone in it.

38 Finally, Joshua turned toward Debir[c] and attacked it. And all Israel was with him. **39** He captured it — its king and all its villages. They struck them down with the sword and completely destroyed everyone in it, leaving no survivors. He treated Debir and its king as he had treated Hebron and as he had treated Libnah and its king.

40 So Joshua conquered the whole region[d] — the hill country, the Negev, the Judean foothills,[A] and the slopes — with all their kings, leaving no survivors. He completely destroyed every living being, as the Lord, the God of Israel, had commanded.[e] **41** Joshua conquered everyone from Kadesh-barnea to Gaza, and all the land of Goshen[f] as far as Gibeon. **42** Joshua captured all these kings and their land in one campaign,[B] because the Lord, the God of Israel, fought for Israel.[g] **43** Then Joshua returned with all Israel to the camp at Gilgal.

CONQUEST OF NORTHERN CITIES

11 When King Jabin of Hazor heard this news, he sent a message to: King Jobab of Madon, the kings of Shimron and Achshaph, **2** and the kings of the north in the hill country, the Arabah south of Chinnereth,[h] the Judean foothills,[c] and the Slopes of Dor[D] to the west, **3** the Canaanites in the east and west, the Amorites, Hethites, Perizzites, and Jebusites in the hill country, and the Hivites at the foot of Hermon in the land of Mizpah.[i] **4** They went out with all their armies — a multitude as numerous as the sand on the seashore[j] — along with a vast number of horses and chariots. **5** All these kings joined forces; they came and camped together at the Waters of Merom to attack Israel.[k]

6 The Lord said to Joshua, "Do not be afraid of them, for at this time tomorrow I will cause all of them to be killed before Israel.[l] You are to hamstring their horses and burn their chariots."[m] **7** So Joshua and all his troops surprised them at the Waters of Merom and attacked them. **8** The Lord handed them over to Israel, and they struck them down, pursuing them as far as greater Sidon and Misrephoth-maim, and to the east as far as the Valley of Mizpeh.[n] They struck them down, leaving no survivors.[o] **9** Joshua treated them as the Lord had told him; he hamstrung their horses and burned their chariots.

10 At that time Joshua turned back, captured Hazor, and struck down its king with the sword, because Hazor had formerly been the leader of all these kingdoms. **11** They struck down everyone in it with the sword, completely destroying[p] them; he left no one alive. Then he burned Hazor.

12 Joshua captured all these kings and their cities and struck them down with the sword. He completely destroyed them, as Moses the Lord's servant[q] had commanded. **13** However, Israel did not burn any of the cities that stood on their mounds except Hazor, which Joshua burned. **14** The Israelites plundered all the spoils and cattle of these cities for themselves. But they struck down every person with the sword until they had annihilated them, leaving no one alive. **15** Just as the Lord had commanded his servant Moses, Moses commanded Joshua. That is what Joshua did, leaving nothing undone of all that the Lord had commanded Moses.

SUMMARY OF CONQUESTS

16 So Joshua took all this land — the hill country, all the Negev, all the land of Goshen,[r] the foothills, the Arabah, and the

[a] 10:33 Jos 16:10; Jdg 1:29; 1Kg 9:16-17
[b] 10:36 Jdg 1:10
[c] 10:38 Jos 15:15; Jdg 1:11
[d] 10:40 Dt 19:8; 34:1; Jos 2:24; 9:24; 11:16,23; 21:43
[e] Dt 20:16
[f] 10:41 Jos 15:50
[g] 10:42 Jos 10:14
[h] 11:2 Dt 3:17; Jos 12:3; 13:27; 19:35; 1Kg 15:20; Mt 14:34; Lk 5:1

[i] 11:3 Jdg 3:3
[j] 11:4 Gn 22:17; Jdg 7:12; 1Sm 13:5; 1Kg 4:29
[k] 11:5 Jdg 7:12
[l] 11:6 Jos 10:8
[m] 2Sm 8:4; Ps 20:7
[n] 11:8 Jos 13:6
[o] Dt 2:34; Jos 10:28,30,33, 37,39-40
[p] 11:11 Jos 10:1; 24:20; Jdg 1:17; 21:11; 1Sm 15:3; 2Ch 8:8; Jr 25:9
[q] 11:12 Dt 20:16-17
[r] 11:16 Jos 15:51

[A] **10:40** Or *the Shephelah*   [B] **10:42** Lit *land at one time*   [C] **11:2** Or *Shephelah*, also in v. 16   [D] **11:2** Or *and in Naphoth-dor*

11:6 God's people were about to face vast combined forces, the likes of which they had never seen. But God told Joshua, **Do not be afraid**. This command appears often in Scripture. God can counteract and overcome whatever strikes fear into our hearts. **11:16-23** **Joshua waged war . . . a long time** (11:18). And **no city made peace with the** **Israelites except . . . Gibeon** (11:19; see 9:1-27). Why? Because **it was the Lord's intention to harden their hearts, so that they would engage Israel in battle** (11:20). As a

a 11:17 Jos 12:7
b Dt 7:24
c 11:19 Jos 9:3,7
d 11:20 Ex 4:21; 7:3; 14:4,17;
Is 63:17; Rm 9:18
e 11:21 Nm 13:22,28,33
f 11:22 1Sm 17:4
g 11:23 Jos 14:15; 21:44;
2Ch 14:6; Hs 2:18; Heb 4:8
h 12:1 Dt 3:8-9
i 12:2 Dt 2:36
j Dt 3:16
k 12:3 Jos 13:20
l Jos 11:2
m 12:4 Dt 1:4
n 12:5 Dt 3:10,14

o 12:6 Nm 32:33; Dt 3:12;
Jos 1:1,13,15; 8:31,33; 11:12;
13:8; 14:7; 18:7; 22:2,4-5
p Nm 21:21-35; Dt
2:26–3:11; 29:7; 31:4; Ps
135:11; 136:19-20; Neh
9:22-25
q Dt 3:12-17; 29:8
r 12:7 Jos 11:16-17
s 12:9 Jos 6:2
t Jos 8:29
u 12:10 Jos 10:23

hill country of Israel with its foothills — **17** from Mount Halak,[a] which ascends to Seir, as far as Baal-gad in the Valley of Lebanon at the foot of Mount Hermon. He captured all their kings and struck them down, putting them to death.[b] **18** Joshua waged war with all these kings for a long time. **19** No city made peace with the Israelites except the Hivites who inhabited Gibeon;[c] all of them were taken in battle. **20** For it was the LORD's intention to harden their hearts,[d] so that they would engage Israel in battle, be completely destroyed without mercy, and be annihilated, just as the LORD had commanded Moses.

21 At that time Joshua proceeded to exterminate the Anakim[e] from the hill country — Hebron, Debir, Anab — all the hill country of Judah and of Israel. Joshua completely destroyed them with their cities. **22** No Anakim were left in the land of the Israelites, except for some remaining in Gaza, Gath,[f] and Ashdod.

23 So Joshua took the entire land, in keeping with all that the LORD had told Moses. Joshua then gave it as an inheritance to Israel according to their tribal allotments. After this, the land had rest from war.[g]

TERRITORY EAST OF THE JORDAN

12 The Israelites struck down the following kings of the land and took possession of their land beyond the Jordan to the east and from the Arnon River to Mount Hermon, including all the Arabah eastward:[h] **2** King Sihon of the Amorites lived in Heshbon. He ruled from Aroer[i] on the rim of the Arnon River, along the middle of the valley, and half of Gilead up to the Jabbok River (the border of the Ammonites[j]), **3** the Arabah east of the Sea of Chinnereth to the Sea of Arabah (that is, the Dead Sea), eastward through Beth-jeshimoth[k] and southward[A] below the slopes of Pisgah.[l] **4** King Og[B] of Bashan, of the remnant of the Rephaim, lived in Ashtaroth and Edrei.[m] **5** He ruled over Mount Hermon, Salecah, all Bashan up to the Geshurite and Maacathite border, and half of Gilead to the border of King Sihon of Heshbon.[n]

6 Moses the LORD's servant[o] and the Israelites struck them[p] down. And Moses the LORD's servant gave their land as an inheritance to the Reubenites, Gadites, and half the tribe of Manasseh.[q]

TERRITORY WEST OF THE JORDAN

7 Joshua and the Israelites struck down the following kings of the land beyond the Jordan to the west, from Baal-gad in the Valley of Lebanon to Mount Halak,[r] which ascends toward Seir (Joshua gave their land as an inheritance to the tribes of Israel according to their allotments: **8** the hill country, the Judean foothills,[c] the Arabah, the slopes, the wilderness, and the Negev — the lands of the Hethites, Amorites, Canaanites, Perizzites, Hivites, and Jebusites):

9	the king of Jericho[s]	one
	the king of Ai,[t] which is next to Bethel	one
10	the king of Jerusalem[u]	one
	the king of Hebron	one
11	the king of Jarmuth	one
	the king of Lachish	one
12	the king of Eglon	one
	the king of Gezer	one
13	the king of Debir	one
	the king of Geder	one
14	the king of Hormah	one
	the king of Arad	one
15	the king of Libnah	one
	the king of Adullam	one
16	the king of Makkedah	one
	the king of Bethel	one
17	the king of Tappuah	one
	the king of Hepher	one
18	the king of Aphek	one
	the king of Lasharon	one
19	the king of Madon	one
	the king of Hazor	one
20	the king of Shimron-meron	one
	the king of Achshaph	one
21	the king of Taanach	one
	the king of Megiddo	one
22	the king of Kedesh	one
	the king of Jokneam in Carmel	one
23	the king of Dor in Naphath-dor[D]	one
	the king of Goiim in Gilgal[E]	one
24	the king of Tirzah	one
	the total number of all kings:	thirty-one.

[A]12:3 Or *and from Teman*   [B]12:4 LXX; MT reads *The territory of Og*   [C]12:8 Or *the Shephelah*   [D]12:23 Or *in the Slopes of Dor*   [E]12:23 LXX reads *Galilee*

result, Israel defeated the peoples and **took the entire land** (11:23).

The Bible has a lot to say about God hardening the hearts of sinners. The first occurrence of this expression is in the book of Exodus where God hardened Pharaoh's heart (see Exod 9:12; 10:27; 11:10). But it's important to recognize that God only hardened Pharaoh's heart after Pharaoh first hardened it himself (see Exod 7:22; 8:15, 32). God does not harden those who are seeking him, but those who are defiantly rejecting him. Doing so helps accomplish his purposes.

12:9-24 Future generations would read this list and know that these stories were not fairy tales, but history.

UNCONQUERED LANDS

13 Joshua was now old, advanced in age,[a] and the LORD said to him, "You have become old, advanced in age, but a great deal of the land remains to be possessed.[b] 2 This is the land that remains: All the districts of the Philistines and the Geshurites: 3 from the Shihor east of Egypt to the border of Ekron on the north (considered to be Canaanite territory) — the five Philistine rulers of Gaza, Ashdod, Ashkelon, Gath, and Ekron, as well as the Avvites 4 in the south; all the land of the Canaanites, from Arah of the Sidonians to Aphek and as far as the border of the Amorites; 5 the land of the Gebalites;[c] and all Lebanon east from Baal-gad below Mount Hermon to the entrance of Hamath[A,d] — 6 all the inhabitants of the hill country from Lebanon to Misrephoth-maim,[e] all the Sidonians. I will drive them out before the Israelites, only distribute the land as an inheritance for Israel, as I have commanded you. 7 Therefore, divide this land as an inheritance to the nine tribes and half the tribe of Manasseh."

THE INHERITANCE EAST OF THE JORDAN

8 With the other half of the tribe of Manasseh, the Reubenites and Gadites had received the inheritance Moses gave them beyond the Jordan to the east, just as Moses the LORD's servant had given them:[f] 9 From Aroer on the rim of the Arnon Valley, along with the city in the middle of the valley,[g] all the Medeba plateau as far as Dibon, 10 and all the cities of King Sihon of the Amorites, who reigned in Heshbon, to the border of the Ammonites; 11 also Gilead[h] and the territory of the Geshurites and Maacathites, all Mount Hermon, and all Bashan to Salecah — 12 the whole kingdom of Og in Bashan, who reigned in Ashtaroth and Edrei; he was one of the remaining Rephaim. Moses struck them down and drove them out,[i] 13 but the Israelites did not drive out the Geshurites and Maacathites. So Geshur and Maacath still live in Israel today.[k] 14 He did not, however, give any inheritance to the tribe of Levi. This was their inheritance, just as he had promised: the

offerings made by fire to the LORD, the God of Israel.[l]

REUBEN'S INHERITANCE

15 To the tribe of Reuben's descendants by their clans, Moses gave 16 this as their territory: From Aroer on the rim of the Arnon Valley, along with the city in the middle of the valley, the whole plateau as far as[B] Medeba, 17 with Heshbon and all its cities on the plateau — Dibon, Bamoth-baal, Beth-baal-meon, 18 Jahaz, Kedemoth, Mephaath,[m] 19 Kiriathaim, Sibmah, Zereth-shahar on the hill in the valley,[n] 20 Beth-peor, the slopes of Pisgah, and Beth-jeshimoth — 21 all the cities of the plateau, and all the kingdom of King Sihon of the Amorites, who reigned in Heshbon. Moses had killed him and the chiefs of Midian — Evi, Rekem, Zur, Hur, and Reba — the princes of Sihon who lived in the land.[o] 22 Along with those the Israelites put to death, they also killed the diviner, Balaam son of Beor, with the sword. 23 The border of the Reubenites was the Jordan and its plain. This was the inheritance of the Reubenites by their clans, with the cities and their settlements.

GAD'S INHERITANCE

24 To the tribe of the Gadites by their clans, Moses gave 25 this as their territory: Jazer and all the cities of Gilead, and half the land of the Ammonites to Aroer, near Rabbah; 26 from Heshbon to Ramath-mizpeh and Betonim, and from Mahanaim to the border of Debir;[c] 27 in the valley: Beth-haram, Beth-nimrah, Succoth, and Zaphon — the rest of the kingdom of King Sihon of Heshbon. Their land also included the Jordan and its territory as far as the edge of the Sea of Chinnereth on the east side of the Jordan.[D] 28 This was the inheritance of the Gadites by their clans, with the cities and their settlements.

EAST MANASSEH'S INHERITANCE

29 And to half the tribe of Manasseh (that is, to half the tribe of Manasseh's descendants by their clans) Moses gave 30 this as their territory:

a 13:1 Gn 18:11; 24:1; Jos 14:10; 23:1-2; 1Kg 1:1
b Ex 23:27-33
c 13:5 1Kg 5:18
d Jos 12:7
e 13:6 Jos 11:8
f 13:8 Jos 12:6
g 13:9 Dt 2:36; Jos 13:16
h 13:11 Dt 3:10
i 13:12 Nm 21:24
j 13:13 Jos 16:10; 17:12-13; Jdg 1:1-2:5
k Jos 4:9; 5:9; 6:25; 7:26; 8:28-29; 10:27; 14:14; 15:63; 16:10; 22:17; 23:8-9

l 13:14 Nm 18:20; Dt 10:9; 18:1-2; Jos 13:33; 14:3-4; 18:7; 21:1-42
m 13:18 Nm 21:23
n 13:19 Nm 32:37
o 13:21 Nm 31:8

A 13:5 Or to Lebo-hamath   B 13:16 Some Hb mss read plateau near   C 13:26 Or Lidbir, or Lo-debar   D 13:27 Lit Chinnereth beyond the Jordan to the east

13:1-7 There was still much land that remained for the Israelites to acquire (13:1-6). But in light of God's promise, Israel was to **divide** the promised land **as an inheritance** among the **tribes** (13:7).

a 13:30 Nm 32:41
b 13:33 Dt 18:1-2; Jos 13:14
c 14:1 Nm 34:17-18
d Jos 19:51
e 14:2 Nm 33:54; 34:13
f 14:5 Nm 35:1-2; Jos 21:2

g 14:6 Nm 14:24,30
h 14:7 Nm 13:1-29
i 14:8 Nm 13:30–14:3
j 14:9 Dt 1:36
k 14:10 Nm 14:30; 26:65; 32:12
l 14:11 Dt 34:7
m 14:12 Dt 1:28; 2:10-11,21; 9:2; Jos 11:21-22
n Nm 13:28
o 14:13-15 Jos 15:13; Jdg 1:10,20
p 14:14 Jos 6:25
q 14:15 Nm 13:33
r Ex 33:14; Dt 3:20; 12:10; 25:19; Jos 1:13,15; 11:23; 21:44; 22:4; 23:1; 2Sm 7:1,11,12; 1Kg 5:4; 8:56; Ps 95:11; Mt 11:28-29; Heb 4:1
s 15:1 Nm 34:3

From Mahanaim through all Bashan — all the kingdom of King Og of Bashan, including all of Jair's Villages^A,a that are in Bashan — sixty cities. **31** But half of Gilead, and Og's royal cities in Bashan — Ashtaroth and Edrei — are for the descendants of Machir son of Manasseh (that is, half the descendants of Machir by their clans).

32 These were the portions Moses gave them on the plains of Moab beyond the Jordan east of Jericho. **33** But Moses did not give a portion to the tribe of Levi. The LORD, the God of Israel, was their inheritance, just as he had promised them.^b

ISRAEL'S INHERITANCE IN CANAAN

14 The Israelites received these portions that the priest Eleazar,^c Joshua son of Nun, and the family heads of the Israelite tribes gave them in the land of Canaan.^d **2** Their inheritance was by lot^e as the LORD commanded through Moses for the nine and a half tribes, **3** because Moses had given the inheritance to the two and a half tribes beyond the Jordan. But he gave no inheritance among them to the Levites. **4** The descendants of Joseph became two tribes, Manasseh and Ephraim. No portion of the land was given to the Levites except cities to live in, along with pasturelands for their cattle and livestock. **5** So the Israelites did as the LORD commanded Moses,^f and they divided the land.

CALEB'S INHERITANCE

6 The descendants of Judah approached Joshua at Gilgal, and Caleb son of Jephunneh the Kenizzite said to him, "You know what the LORD promised Moses the man of God at Kadesh-barnea about you and me.^g **7** I was forty years old when Moses the LORD's servant sent me from Kadesh-barnea to scout the land, and I brought back an honest report.^h **8** My brothers who went with me caused the people to lose heart,^B but I followed the LORD my God completely.^i **9** On that day Moses swore to me: 'The land where you have set foot will be an inheritance for you and your descendants forever, because you have followed the LORD my God completely.'^j

10 "As you see, the LORD has kept me alive these forty-five years as he promised,^k since the LORD spoke this word to Moses while Israel was journeying in the wilderness. Here I am today, eighty-five years old. **11** I am still as strong today as I was the day Moses sent me out. My strength for battle and for daily tasks^C is now as it was then.^l **12** Now give me this hill country the LORD promised me on that day, because you heard then that the Anakim are there,^m as well as large fortified cities.^n Perhaps the LORD will be with me and I will drive them out as the LORD promised."

13 Then Joshua blessed Caleb son of Jephunneh and gave him Hebron as an inheritance.^o **14** Therefore, Hebron still belongs to Caleb son of Jephunneh the Kenizzite as an inheritance today^p because he followed the LORD, the God of Israel, completely. **15** Hebron's name used to be Kiriath-arba; Arba was the greatest man among the Anakim.^q After this, the land had rest from war.^r

JUDAH'S INHERITANCE

15 Now the allotment for the tribe of the descendants of Judah by their clans^s was in the southernmost region, south to the Wilderness of Zin and over to the border of Edom.

---

^A 13:30 Or *all of Havvoth-jair*   ^B 14:8 Lit *people's hearts to melt with fear*   ^C 14:11 Lit *for going out and coming in*

13:33 The only tribe that did not receive an inheritance of land was **Levi**. This is because the Levites had been chosen by God to perform the work of maintaining the tabernacle (and later the temple) and providing priests to do the work of ministry. When the Israelites brought offerings to the Lord, a portion would be given to the Levites, to provide for them (see Num 18:8-32).
14:6-13 Many years previously, **Caleb** and Joshua had been two of the twelve spies whom Moses had sent to scout out the land (see Num 13:1-25). Though all twelve men had brought back a good report of Canaan, all but Joshua and Caleb said it was full of fortified cities that would be impossible to conquer (see Num 13:26-33). While Caleb and Joshua

brought back an honest report, the other ten **caused the people to lose heart** (Josh 14:7-8).
As a result, Israel rebelled against God and Moses and ended up wandering in the wilderness for forty years until nearly all of that first generation out of Egypt dropped dead (see Num 14:1-38). Only two adults survived the punishment, the faithful spies. Caleb was promised an **inheritance** in the land because he **followed the LORD [his] God completely** (14:9). In other words, Caleb didn't follow the crowd. He stood by his convictions without compromise. As a result, God remembered him. He can do the same for you as you choose to be influenced not by those who say God can't make a way but by the knowledge that there is nothing too big for him.

15:1-12 The borders of **Judah**, which is the name by which the area would be called, are described here. As the biblical storyline unfolds, Judah will become increasingly prominent. This is because in Genesis, Israelite forefather Jacob (Israel) prophesied that a kingly dynasty would arise from his son Judah, eventually resulting in the Messiah (see Gen 49:9-10). This prophecy would first become a realty when God had the prophet Samuel anoint a young shepherd named David to be king of Israel (see 1 Sam 16:1-13). Though in Joshua's day, the tribe of **Judah could not drive out the Jebusites who lived in Jerusalem** (Josh 15:63), King David would not only defeat the Jebusites, but he would also claim Jerusalem as his capital (see 2 Sam 5:6-9).

2 Their southern border began at the tip of the Dead Sea on the south bay[A] **3** and went south of the Scorpions' Ascent,[B] proceeded to Zin, ascended to the south of Kadesh-barnea, passed Hezron, ascended to Addar, and turned to Karka. **4** It proceeded to Azmon and to the Brook of Egypt[a] and so the border ended at the Mediterranean Sea. This is your[c] southern border.

5 Now the eastern border was along the Dead Sea to the mouth of the Jordan.

The border on the north side was from the bay of the sea at the mouth of the Jordan. **6** It ascended to Beth-hoglah, proceeded north of Beth-arabah, and ascended to the Stone of Bohan son of Reuben. **7** Then the border ascended to Debir from the Valley of Achor, turning north to the Gilgal that is opposite the Ascent of Adummim, which is south of the ravine. The border proceeded to the Waters of En-shemesh and ended at En-rogel. **8** From there the border ascended Ben Hinnom Valley to the southern Jebusite slope (that is, Jerusalem) and ascended to the top of the hill that faces Hinnom Valley on the west, at the northern end of Rephaim Valley. **9** From the top of the hill the border curved to the spring of the Waters of Nephtoah, went to the cities of Mount Ephron, and then curved to Baalah (that is, Kiriath-jearim[b]). **10** The border turned westward from Baalah to Mount Seir, went to the northern slope of Mount Jearim (that is, Chesalon), descended to Beth-shemesh, and proceeded to Timnah.[c] **11** Then the border reached to the slope north of Ekron, curved to Shikkeron, proceeded to Mount Baalah, went to Jabneel, and ended at the Mediterranean Sea.

12 Now the western border was the coastline of the Mediterranean Sea.

This was the boundary of the descendants of Judah around their clans.

CALEB AND OTHNIEL

13 He gave Caleb son of Jephunneh the following portion among the descendants of Judah based on the LORD's instruction to Joshua: Kiriath-arba (that is, Hebron; Arba was the father of Anak). **14** Caleb drove out from there the three sons of Anak: Sheshai, Ahiman, and Talmai, descendants of Anak.[d] **15** From there he marched against the inhabitants of Debir, which used to be called Kiriath-sepher,[e] **16** and Caleb said, "Whoever attacks and captures Kiriath-sepher, I will give my daughter Achsah to him as a wife." **17** So Othniel[f] son of Caleb's brother, Kenaz, captured it, and Caleb gave his daughter Achsah to him as a wife.[g] **18** When she arrived, she persuaded Othniel to ask her father for a field. As she got off her donkey, Caleb asked her, "What can I do for you?" **19** She replied, "Give me a blessing. Since you have given me land in the Negev, give me the springs also." So he gave her the upper and lower springs.

JUDAH'S CITIES

20 This was the inheritance of the tribe of the descendants of Judah by their clans. **21** These were the outermost cities of the tribe of the descendants of Judah toward the border of Edom in the Negev: Kabzeel, Eder, Jagur,[h] **22** Kinah, Dimonah, Adadah, **23** Kedesh, Hazor, Ithnan, **24** Ziph, Telem, Bealoth, **25** Hazor-hadattah, Kerioth-hezron (that is, Hazor), **26** Amam, Shema, Moladah, **27** Hazar-gaddah, Heshmon, Beth-pelet, **28** Hazar-shual, Beer-sheba, Biziothiah,[i] **29** Baalah, Iim, Ezem, **30** Eltolad, Chesil, Hormah, **31** Ziklag, Madmannah, Sansannah,[j] **32** Lebaoth, Shilhim, Ain, and Rimmon — twenty-nine cities in all, with their settlements.

33 In the Judean foothills:[D] Eshtaol, Zorah, Ashnah, **34** Zanoah, En-gannim, Tappuah,[E] Enam, **35** Jarmuth, Adullam,[k] Socoh,[F] Azekah, **36** Shaaraim, Adithaim, Gederah, and Gederothaim — fourteen cities, with their settlements; **37** Zenan, Hadashah, Migdal-gad,

a 15:4 Jos 15:47; 1Kg 8:65; 2Kg 24:7; Is 27:12; 2Ch 7:8
b 15:9 1Ch 13:6
c 15:10 Gn 38:13; Jdg 14:1

d 15:14 Nm 13:22,28,33; Dt 9:2; Jos 21:11
e 15:15-19 Jdg 1:11-15
f 15:17 Jdg 3:8-11
g 1Sm 17:25
h 15:21 Gn 35:21
i 15:28 Gn 21:31
j 15:31 1Sm 27:6; 30:1
k 15:35 1Sm 22:1

A 15:2 Lit *Sea at the tongue that turns southward*   B 15:3 Lit *of scorpions*   C 15:4 LXX reads *their*   D 15:33 Or *the Shephelah*
E 15:34 Or *En-gannim-tappuah*   F 15:35 Or *Adullam-socoh*

15:17-19 Caleb looked after **his daughter Achsah** and gave her an inheritance (15:18-19). In God's economy, the family is the foundation of society. Thus, in Israel the family was the basis for passing down not only the physical blessings but also the spiritual heritage (see Deut 6:4-9). The family unit is under attack today. Satan is undermining and redefining this unit because he wants to stop the blessings and favor of God from being passed on generationally. Christian parents—and especially fathers—must determine to pass on to the next generation not a legacy of brokenness and spiritual compromise but one of blessing and training in God's Word.

a 15:63 Jdg 1:21; 2Sm 5:5-9
b Jos 6:25; 16:10; 22:17;
    23:8-9
c 16:1 Jos 8:15; 18:12

d 16:2 Jos 18:13
e 16:3 Jos 10:33
f 16:4 Jos 17:14
g Gn 48:5-20
h 16:5 Jos 18:13
i 16:6 Jos 17:7
j 16:7 1Ch 7:28
k 16:8 Jos 17:8
l 16:10 Jdg 1:29; 1Kg 9:16
m Jos 6:25
n 17:1 Gn 41:51; 46:20;
    48:18
o 1Ch 28:3

38 Dilan, Mizpeh, Jokthe-el, **39** Lachish, Bozkath, Eglon, **40** Cabbon, Lahmam, Chitlish, **41** Gederoth, Beth-dagon, Naamah, and Makkedah — sixteen cities, with their settlements; **42** Libnah, Ether, Ashan, **43** Iphtah, Ashnah, Nezib, **44** Keilah, Achzib, and Mareshah — nine cities, with their settlements; **45** Ekron, with its surrounding villages and settlements; **46** from Ekron to the sea, all the cities near Ashdod, with their settlements; **47** Ashdod, with its surrounding villages and settlements; Gaza, with its surrounding villages and settlements, to the Brook of Egypt and the coastline of the Mediterranean Sea.

48 In the hill country: Shamir, Jattir, Socoh, **49** Dannah, Kiriath-sannah (that is, Debir), **50** Anab, Eshtemoh, Anim, **51** Goshen, Holon, and Giloh — eleven cities, with their settlements; **52** Arab, Dumah,[A] Eshan, **53** Janim, Beth-tappuah, Aphekah, **54** Humtah, Kiriath-arba (that is, Hebron), and Zior — nine cities, with their settlements; **55** Maon, Carmel, Ziph, Juttah, **56** Jezreel, Jokdeam, Zanoah, **57** Kain, Gibeah, and Timnah — ten cities, with their settlements; **58** Halhul, Beth-zur, Gedor, **59** Maarath, Beth-anoth, and Eltekon — six cities, with their settlements;[B] **60** Kiriath-baal (that is, Kiriath-jearim), and Rabbah — two cities, with their settlements.

61 In the wilderness: Beth-arabah, Middin, Secacah, **62** Nibshan, the City of Salt,[C] and En-gedi — six cities, with their settlements. **63** But the descendants of Judah could not drive out the Jebusites who lived in Jerusalem.[a] So the Jebusites still live in Jerusalem among the descendants of Judah today.[b]

JOSEPH'S INHERITANCE

16 The allotment for the descendants of Joseph went from the Jordan at Jericho to the Waters of Jericho on the east, through the wilderness[c]

ascending from Jericho into the hill country of Bethel. **2** From Bethel it went to Luz and proceeded to the border of the Archites by Ataroth.[d] **3** It then descended westward to the border of the Japhletites as far as the border of lower Beth-horon, then to Gezer,[e] and ended at the Mediterranean Sea. **4** So Ephraim and Manasseh, the sons of Joseph,[f] received their inheritance.[g]

EPHRAIM'S INHERITANCE

5 This was the territory of the descendants of Ephraim by their clans:
The border of their inheritance went from Ataroth-addar[h] on the east to Upper Beth-horon. **6** In the north the border went westward from Michmethath;[i] it turned eastward from Taanath-shiloh and passed it east of Janoah. **7** From Janoah it descended to Ataroth and Naarah,[j] and then reached Jericho and went to the Jordan. **8** From Tappuah the border went westward along the Brook of Kanah and ended at the Mediterranean Sea.[k]

This was the inheritance of the tribe of the descendants of Ephraim by their clans, together with **9** the cities set apart for the descendants of Ephraim within the inheritance of the descendants of Manasseh — all these cities with their settlements. **10** However, they did not drive out the Canaanites who lived in Gezer.[l] So the Canaanites still live in Ephraim today,[m] but they are forced laborers.

WEST MANASSEH'S INHERITANCE

17 This was the allotment for the tribe of Manasseh[n] as Joseph's firstborn. Gilead and Bashan were given to Machir, the firstborn of Manasseh and the father of Gilead, because he was a man of war.[o] **2** So the allotment was for the rest of Manasseh's descendants by their clans, for the sons of Abiezer, Helek, Asriel, Shechem, Hepher, and Shemida. These are the male descendants of Manasseh son of Joseph, by their clans.

A 15:52 Some Hb mss read *Rumah*   B 15:59 LXX adds *Tekoa, Ephrathah (that is, Bethlehem), Peor, Etam, Culom, Tatam, Sores, Carem, Gallim, Baither, and Manach — eleven cities, with their settlements*   C 15:62 Or *Ir-hamelach*

16:10 The Canaanites and their idolatrous religious practices would slowly work against Israel like a cancer, as we will learn in the book of Judges. In growing negligent to drive out the enemy as instructed, Israel was setting itself up for a fall.

17:3-13 Since a land inheritance was to be passed down from fathers to sons, these **daughters** would have received no inheritance (17:3). Others would have owned their father's land, and their father's name would have been forgotten. But years earlier, these daughters

had wisely implored Moses to allow them an inheritance within the territory of Manasseh (see Num 27:1-4). When Moses asked the Lord about the matter, God commanded, "When a man dies without having a son, transfer his inheritance to his daughter" (Num 27:8).

³ Now Zelophehad son of Hepher, son of Gilead, son of Machir, son of Manasseh, had no sons, only daughters. These are the names of his daughters: Mahlah, Noah, Hoglah, Milcah, and Tirzah.ᵃ ⁴ They came before the priest Eleazar, Joshua son of Nun, and the leaders, saying, "The LORD commanded Moses to give us an inheritance among our male relatives." So they gave them an inheritance among their father's brothers, in keeping with the LORD's instruction.ᵇ ⁵ As a result, ten tracts fell to Manasseh, besides the land of Gilead and Bashan, which are beyond the Jordan,^ ⁶ because Manasseh's daughters received an inheritance among his sons. The land of Gilead belonged to the rest of Manasseh's sons.

⁷ The border of Manasseh went from Asher to Michmethath near Shechem. It then went southward toward the inhabitants of En-tappuah. ⁸ The region of Tappuah belonged to Manasseh, but Tappuah itself on Manasseh's borderᶜ belonged to the descendants of Ephraim. ⁹ From there the border descended to the Brook of Kanah; south of the brook, cities belonged to Ephraim among Manasseh's cities. Manasseh's border was on the north side of the brook and ended at the Mediterranean Sea. ¹⁰ Ephraim's territory was to the south and Manasseh's to the north, with the Sea as its border. They reached Asher on the north and Issachar on the east. ¹¹ Within Issachar and Asher, Manasseh had Beth-shean, Ibleam, and the inhabitants of Dor with their surrounding villages;ᵈ the inhabitants of En-dor, Taanach, and Megiddo — the three cities of ᴮ Naphath — with their surrounding villages.ᵉ ¹² The descendants of Manasseh could not possess these cities, because the Canaanites were determined to stay in this land. ¹³ However, when the Israelites grew stronger, they imposed forced labor on the Canaanites but did not drive them out completely.ᶠ

JOSEPH'S ADDITIONAL INHERITANCE

¹⁴ Joseph's descendants said to Joshua, "Why did you give us only one tribal allotmentᶜ as an inheritance? We have many people, because the LORD has been blessing us greatly."

¹⁵ "If you have so many people," Joshua replied to them, "go to the forest and clear an area for yourselves there in the land of the Perizzites and the Rephaim, because Ephraim's hill country is too small for you."

¹⁶ But the descendants of Joseph said, "The hill country is not enough for us, and all the Canaanites who inhabit the valley area have iron chariots, both at Beth-shean with its surrounding villages and in the Jezreel Valley."

¹⁷ So Joshua replied to Joseph's family (that is, Ephraim and Manasseh), "You have many people and great strength. You will not have just one allotment, ¹⁸ because the hill country will be yours also. It is a forest; clear it and its outlying areas will be yours. You can also drive out the Canaanites, even though they have iron chariots and are strong."

LAND DISTRIBUTION AT SHILOH

18 The entire Israelite community assembled at Shilohᵍ and set up the tent of meeting there. The land had been subdued before them, ² but seven tribes among the Israelites were left who had not divided up their inheritance. ³ So Joshua asked the Israelites, "How long will you delay going out to take possession of the land that the LORD, the God of your fathers, gave you?ʰ ⁴ Appoint for yourselves three men from each tribe, and I will send them out. They are to go and survey the land, write a description of it for the purpose of their inheritance, and return to me. ⁵ Then they are to divide it into seven portions. Judah is to remain in its territory in the south and Joseph's family in their territory in the north.ⁱ ⁶ When you have written a description of the seven portions of land and brought it to me, I will cast lotsʲ for you here in the presence of the LORD our God.ᵏ

ᵃ 17:3 Nm 26:33
ᵇ 17:4 Nm 27:1-11
ᶜ 17:8 Jos 16:8-9
ᵈ 17:11 1Ch 7:29
ᵉ Jos 11:2; 12:23
ᶠ 17:13 Jdg 1:27-28

ᵍ 18:1 Jos 19:51; Jdg 18:31; 1Sm 1:9; 3:3
ʰ 18:3 Jdg 18:9
ⁱ 18:5 Jos 15:1
ʲ 18:6 1Ch 24:31; 25:8; 26:13-14; Neh 10:34; 11:1; Ps 22:18; Jnh 1:7
ᵏ Jos 14:2

---

^ 17:5 = east of the Jordan River   ᴮ 17:11 LXX, Vg read *the third is*   ᶜ 17:14 Lit *one lot and one territory*, also in v. 17

17:14-18 Since Joseph's descendants (Ephraim and Manasseh) were so numerous, they asked Joshua for more land (17:14). When Joshua directed them to an additional portion, however, the people were fearful of the Canaanites there (17:15-16). Joshua encouraged them that they *could* **drive out the Canaanites** (17:18). Whereas these people saw their own vast numbers as a problem, Joshua saw a strength: working together they could clear additional land and rid it of their enemies.

18:1-10 Joshua reprimanded them and basically said, "Look, this land isn't going to divide up itself." Again we're reminded that though God's promises may be within our reach, they may not be in our hands. God had promised Israel the land, but the people still had to do the work of taking it. Similarly, God feeds the birds of the sky (see Matt 6:26), but they still have to hunt for their worms. God has a purpose for your life, but you must walk with him by faith to see that purpose become a reality.

a 18:7 Jos 13:33
b 18:12 Jos 16:1
c 18:13 Jos 16:3

d 18:17 Jos 15:6
e 19:2 1Ch 4:28

7 But the Levites among you do not get a portion, because their inheritance is the priesthood of the LORD.*a* Gad, Reuben, and half the tribe of Manasseh have taken their inheritance beyond the Jordan to the east, which Moses the LORD's servant gave them."

8 As the men prepared to go, Joshua commanded them^A to write down a description of the land, saying, "Go and survey the land, write a description of it, and return to me. I will then cast lots for you here in Shiloh in the presence of the LORD." **9** So the men left, went through the land, and described it by towns in a document of seven sections. They returned to Joshua at the camp in Shiloh. **10** Joshua cast lots for them at Shiloh in the presence of the LORD where he distributed the land to the Israelites according to their divisions.

BENJAMIN'S INHERITANCE

11 The lot came up for the tribe of Benjamin's descendants by their clans, and their allotted territory lay between Judah's descendants and Joseph's descendants. **12** Their border on the north side began at the Jordan, ascended to the slope of Jericho on the north, through the hill country westward, and ended at the wilderness around Beth-aven.*b* **13** From there the border went toward Luz, to the southern slope of Luz (that is, Bethel); it then went down by Ataroth-addar, over the hill south of Lower Beth-horon.*c*

14 On the west side, from the hill facing Beth-horon on the south, the border curved, turning southward, and ended at Kiriath-baal (that is, Kiriath-jearim), a city of the descendants of Judah. This was the west side of their border.

15 The south side began at the edge of Kiriath-jearim, and the border extended westward; it went to the spring at the Waters of Nephtoah. **16** The border descended to the foot of the hill that faces Ben Hinnom Valley at the northern end of Rephaim Valley. It ran down Hinnom Valley toward the south Jebusite slope and downward to En-rogel. **17** It curved northward and went to

En-shemesh and on to Geliloth, which is opposite the Ascent of Adummim, and continued down to the Stone of Bohan*d* son of Reuben. **18** Then it went north to the slope opposite the Arabah*B* and proceeded into the plains.*c* **19** The border continued to the north slope of Beth-hoglah and ended at the northern bay of the Dead Sea, at the southern end of the Jordan. This was the southern border.

20 The Jordan formed the border on the east side.

This was the inheritance of Benjamin's descendants, by their clans, according to its surrounding borders.

BENJAMIN'S CITIES

21 These were the cities of the tribe of Benjamin's descendants by their clans:
Jericho, Beth-hoglah, Emek-keziz, **22** Beth-arabah, Zemaraim, Bethel, **23** Avvim, Parah, Ophrah, **24** Chephar-ammoni, Ophni, and Geba — twelve cities, with their settlements; **25** Gibeon, Ramah, Beeroth, **26** Mizpeh, Chephirah, Mozah, **27** Rekem, Irpeel, Taralah, **28** Zela, Haeleph, Jebus*D* (that is, Jerusalem), Gibeah, and Kiriath*E* — fourteen cities, with their settlements.

This was the inheritance for Benjamin's descendants by their clans.

SIMEON'S INHERITANCE

19 The second lot came out for Simeon, for the tribe of his descendants by their clans, but their inheritance was within the inheritance given to Judah's descendants. **2** Their inheritance included Beer-sheba (or Sheba*e*), Moladah, **3** Hazar-shual, Balah, Ezem, **4** Eltolad, Bethul, Hormah, **5** Ziklag, Beth-marcaboth, Hazar-susah, **6** Beth-lebaoth, and Sharuhen — thirteen cities, with their settlements; **7** Ain, Rimmon, Ether, and Ashan — four cities, with their settlements; **8** and all the settlements surrounding these cities as far as Baalath-beer (Ramah in the south*f*).

This was the inheritance of the tribe of Simeon's descendants by their clans. **9** The inheritance of Simeon's descendants was within the territory of Judah's

^A 18:8 Lit *the ones going around*   ^B 18:18 LXX reads *went northward to Beth-arabah*   ^C 18:18 Or *the Arabah*   ^D 18:28 Lit *Jebusite*   ^E 18:28 LXX, Syr read *Kiriath-jearim*   ^F 19:8 Or *the Negev*

18:11 Casting lots was something like rolling dice, but Israel understood that nothing happens by chance (see Prov 16:33). By casting lots, Joshua was acknowledging that it was God's decision to decide which tribe received which section.

descendants, because the share for Judah's descendants was too large. So Simeon's descendants received an inheritance within Judah's portion.

ZEBULUN'S INHERITANCE

¹⁰ The third lot came up for Zebulun's descendants by their clans.

The territory of their inheritance stretched as far as Sarid; ¹¹ their border went up westward to Maralah, reached Dabbesheth, and met the brook east of Jokneam. ¹² From Sarid, it turned due east along the border of Chisloth-tabor, went to Daberath, and went up to Japhia. ¹³ From there, it went due east to Gath-hepher and to Eth-kazin; it extended to Rimmon, curving around to Neah. ¹⁴ The border then circled around Neah on the north to Hannathon and ended at Iphtah-el Valley, ¹⁵ along with Kattath, Nahalal, Shimron, Idalah, and Bethlehem — twelve cities, with their settlements. ¹⁶ This was the inheritance of Zebulun's descendants by their clans, these cities, with their settlements.

ISSACHAR'S INHERITANCE

¹⁷ The fourth lot came out for the tribe of Issachar's descendants by their clans.

¹⁸ Their territory went to Jezreel, and included Chesulloth, Shunem,ᵃ ¹⁹ Hapharaim, Shion, Anaharath, ²⁰ Rabbith, Kishion, Ebez, ²¹ Remeth, En-gannim, En-haddah, and Beth-pazzez. ²² The border reached Tabor, Shahazumah, and Beth-shemesh, and ended at the Jordan — sixteen cities, with their settlements. ²³ This was the inheritance of the tribe of Issachar's descendants by their clans, the cities, with their settlements.

ASHER'S INHERITANCE

²⁴ The fifth lot came out for the tribe of Asher's descendants by their clans.

²⁵ Their boundary included Helkath, Hali, Beten, Achshaph, ²⁶ Allammelech, Amad, and Mishal and reached westward to Carmel and Shihor-libnath. ²⁷ It turned eastward to Beth-dagon, reached Zebulun and Iphtah-el Valley, north toward Beth-emek and Neiel, and went north to Cabul,ᵇ ²⁸ Ebron, Rehob, Hammon, and Kanah, as far as

greater Sidon. ²⁹ The boundary then turned to Ramah as far as the fortified city of Tyre; it turned back to Hosah and ended at the Mediterranean Sea, including Mahalab, Achzib,ᴬ ³⁰ Ummah, Aphek, and Rehob — twenty-two cities, with their settlements. ³¹ This was the inheritance of the tribe of Asher's descendants by their clans, these cities with their settlements.

NAPHTALI'S INHERITANCE

³² The sixth lot came out for Naphtali's descendants by their clans.

³³ Their boundary went from Heleph and from the oak in Zaanannim, including Adami-nekeb and Jabneel, as far as Lakkum, and ended at the Jordan. ³⁴ To the west, the boundary turned to Aznoth-tabor and went from there to Hukkok, reaching Zebulun on the south, Asher on the west, and Judahᴮ at the Jordan on the east. ³⁵ The fortified cities were Ziddim, Zer, Hammath, Rakkath, Chinnereth, ³⁶ Adamah, Ramah, Hazor, ³⁷ Kedesh, Edrei, En-hazor, ³⁸ Iron, Migdal-el, Horem, Beth-anath, and Beth-shemesh — nineteen cities, with their settlements. ³⁹ This was the inheritance of the tribe of Naphtali's descendants by their clans, the cities with their settlements.

DAN'S INHERITANCE

⁴⁰ The seventh lot came out for the tribe of Dan's descendants by their clans.

⁴¹ The territory of their inheritance included Zorah, Eshtaol, Ir-shemesh, ⁴² Shaalabbin, Aijalon,ᶜ Ithlah, ⁴³ Elon, Timnah, Ekron, ⁴⁴ Eltekeh, Gibbethon, Baalath, ⁴⁵ Jehud, Bene-berak, Gath-rimmon, ⁴⁶ Me-jarkon, and Rakkon, with the territory facing Joppa.ᵈ ⁴⁷ When the territory of the descendants of Dan slipped out of their control, they went up and fought against Leshem, captured it, and struck it down with the sword. So they took possession of it, lived there, and renamed Leshem after their ancestor Dan.ᵉ ⁴⁸ This was the inheritance of the tribe of Dan's descendants by their clans, these cities with their settlements.

JOSHUA'S INHERITANCE

⁴⁹ When they had finished distributing the land into its territories, the Israelites

ᵃ 19:18 1Sm 28:4
ᵇ 19:27 1Kg 9:13

ᶜ 19:42 Jdg 1:35
ᵈ 19:46 2Ch 2:16; Ezr 3:7
ᵉ 19:47 Jdg 1:34,35; 18:1

ᴬ19:29 Or *Sea, in the region of Achzib*   ᴮ19:34 LXX omits *Judah*

19:49-50 Like a good leader, Joshua made sure that all the people had received their territories before settling down in his own.

a 19:50 Jos 24:30
b 19:51 Jos 14:1
c 20:2 Nm 35:6-34; Dt
4:41-43; 19:1-13
d 20:3 Nm 5:5-8; Dt 19:6
e 20:4 Ru 4:1
f 20:6 Nm 35:12; Dt 21:1-9
g 20:7 1Ch 6:76
h Jos 21:11; Lk 1:39
i 20:9 Nm 35:15

j 21:2 Nm 35:4-5
k 21:11 1Ch 6:55

gave Joshua son of Nun an inheritance among them. **50** By the LORD's command, they gave him the city Timnath-serah in the hill country of Ephraim,*a* which he requested. He rebuilt the city and lived in it. **51** These were the portions that the priest Eleazar, Joshua son of Nun, and the family heads distributed to the Israelite tribes by lot at Shiloh in the LORD's presence at the entrance to the tent of meeting.*b* So they finished dividing up the land.

CITIES OF REFUGE

20 Then the LORD spoke to Joshua, **2** "Tell the Israelites: Select your cities of refuge, as I instructed you through Moses,*c* **3** so that a person who kills someone unintentionally or accidentally may flee there. These will be your refuge from the avenger of blood.*d* **4** When someone flees to one of these cities, stands at the entrance of the city gate, and states his case before^ the elders of that city, they are to bring him into the city and give him a place to live among them.*e* **5** And if the avenger of blood pursues him, they must not hand the one who committed manslaughter over to him, for he killed his neighbor accidentally and did not hate him beforehand. **6** He is to stay in that city until he stands trial before the assembly and until the death of the high priest serving at that time.*f* Then the one who committed manslaughter may return home to his own city from which he fled."

7 So they designated Kedesh in the hill country of Naphtali in Galilee,*g* Shechem in the hill country of Ephraim, and Kiriath-arba (that is, Hebron) in the hill country of Judah.*h* **8** Across the Jordan east of Jericho, they selected Bezer on the wilderness plateau from Reuben's tribe, Ramoth in Gilead from Gad's tribe, and Golan in Bashan from Manasseh's tribe. **9** These are the cities appointed for all the Israelites and the aliens residing among them,*i* so that anyone who kills a person unintentionally may flee there and not die at the hand of the avenger of blood until he stands before the assembly.

CITIES OF THE LEVITES

21 The Levite family heads approached the priest Eleazar, Joshua son of Nun, and the family heads of the Israelite tribes. **2** At Shiloh, in the land of Canaan, they told them, "The LORD commanded through Moses that we be given cities to live in, with their pasturelands for our livestock."*j* **3** So the Israelites, by the LORD's command, gave the Levites these cities with their pasturelands from their inheritance.

4 The lot came out for the Kohathite clans: The Levites who were the descendants of the priest Aaron received thirteen cities by lot from the tribes of Judah, Simeon, and Benjamin. **5** The remaining descendants of Kohath received ten cities by lot from the clans of the tribes of Ephraim, Dan, and half the tribe of Manasseh.

6 Gershon's descendants received thirteen cities by lot from the clans of the tribes of Issachar, Asher, Naphtali, and half the tribe of Manasseh in Bashan.

7 Merari's descendants received twelve cities for their clans from the tribes of Reuben, Gad, and Zebulun.

8 The Israelites gave these cities with their pasturelands around them to the Levites by lot, as the LORD had commanded through Moses.

CITIES OF AARON'S DESCENDANTS

9 The Israelites gave these cities by name from the tribes of the descendants of Judah and Simeon **10** to the descendants of Aaron from the Kohathite clans of the Levites, because they received the first lot. **11** They gave them Kiriath-arba*k* (that is, Hebron; Arba was the father of Anak) with its surrounding pasturelands in the hill country of Judah. **12** But they gave the fields and settlements of the city to Caleb son of Jephunneh as his possession.

13 They gave to the descendants of the priest Aaron:

Hebron, the city of refuge for the one who commits manslaughter, with its

^20:4 Lit *in the ears of*

pasturelands, Libnah with its pasturelands, ¹⁴ Jattir with its pasturelands, Eshtemoa with its pasturelands, ¹⁵ Holon with its pasturelands, Debir with its pasturelands, ¹⁶ Ain with its pasturelands, Juttah with its pasturelands, and Beth-shemesh with its pasturelands — nine cities from these two tribes.

¹⁷ From the tribe of Benjamin they gave: Gibeon with its pasturelands, Geba with its pasturelands, ¹⁸ Anathoth with its pasturelands, and Almon with its pasturelands — four cities. ¹⁹ All thirteen cities with their pasturelands were for the priests, the descendants of Aaron.

CITIES OF KOHATH'S OTHER DESCENDANTS

²⁰ The allotted cities to the remaining clans of Kohath's descendants, who were Levites, came from the tribe of Ephraim. ²¹ The Israelites gave them:
Shechem,[a] the city of refuge for the one who commits manslaughter, with its pasturelands in the hill country of Ephraim, Gezer with its pasturelands, ²² Kibzaim with its pasturelands, and Beth-horon with its pasturelands — four cities.

²³ From the tribe of Dan they gave: Elteke with its pasturelands, Gibbethon with its pasturelands, ²⁴ Aijalon with its pasturelands, and Gath-rimmon with its pasturelands — four cities.

²⁵ From half the tribe of Manasseh they gave:
Taanach with its pasturelands and Gath-rimmon[A] with its pasturelands — two cities.
²⁶ All ten cities with their pasturelands were for the clans of Kohath's other descendants.

CITIES OF GERSHON'S DESCENDANTS

²⁷ From half the tribe of Manasseh, they gave to the descendants of Gershon,[b] who were one of the Levite clans:
Golan, the city of refuge for the one who commits manslaughter, with its pasturelands in Bashan, and Beeshterah with its pasturelands — two cities.

²⁸ From the tribe of Issachar they gave: Kishion with its pasturelands, Daberath with its pasturelands, ²⁹ Jarmuth with its pasturelands, and En-gannim with its pasturelands — four cities.

³⁰ From the tribe of Asher they gave: Mishal with its pasturelands, Abdon with its pasturelands, ³¹ Helkath with its pasturelands, and Rehob with its pasturelands — four cities.

³² From the tribe of Naphtali they gave: Kedesh in Galilee, the city of refuge for the one who commits manslaughter, with its pasturelands, Hammoth-dor with its pasturelands, and Kartan with its pasturelands — three cities.
³³ All thirteen cities with their pasturelands were for the Gershonites by their clans.

CITIES OF MERARI'S DESCENDANTS

³⁴ From the tribe of Zebulun, they gave to the clans of the descendants of Merari,[c] who were the remaining Levites:
Jokneam with its pasturelands, Kartah with its pasturelands, ³⁵ Dimnah with its pasturelands, and Nahalal with its pasturelands — four cities.

³⁶ From the tribe of Reuben they gave: Bezer[d] with its pasturelands, Jahzah[B] with its pasturelands, ³⁷ Kedemoth with its pasturelands, and Mephaath with its pasturelands — four cities.[c]

³⁸ From the tribe of Gad they gave: Ramoth in Gilead, the city of refuge for the one who commits manslaughter, with its pasturelands, Mahanaim with its pasturelands, ³⁹ Heshbon with its pasturelands, and Jazer with its pasturelands — four cities in all. ⁴⁰ All twelve cities were allotted to the clans of Merari's descendants, the remaining Levite clans.

⁴¹ Within the Israelite possession there were forty-eight cities in all with their pasturelands for the Levites.[e] ⁴² Each of these cities had its own surrounding pasturelands; this was true for all the cities.

THE LORD'S PROMISES FULFILLED

⁴³ So the LORD gave Israel all the land he had sworn to give their fathers, and they took possession of it and settled there. ⁴⁴ The

[a] 21:21 Jos 20:7
[b] 21:27 1Ch 6:71
[c] 21:34 1Ch 6:77
[d] 21:36-38 Jos 20:8
[e] 21:41 Nm 35:7

[A] 21:25 Or *Ibleam*　[B] 21:36 Or *Jahaz*　[c] 21:36-37 Some Hb mss omit these vv.

[a] 21:45 Jos 23:14
[b] 22:2 Dt 3:18-20
[c] 22:5 Dt 6:5; 10:12-13; 11:13-17
[d] 22:6 Jos 14:13
[e] 22:7 Nm 32:33; Jos 17:5
[f] 22:8 Nm 31:27; 1Sm 30:24
[g] 22:9 Nm 32:1,26,29

[h] 22:12 Lv 17:8-9; Dt 13:12-15
[i] 22:13 Ex 6:25; Nm 25:7
[j] 22:14 Nm 1:4,16
[k] 22:17 Dt 10:17; Ps 50:1; 136:2; Dn 2:47; 11:36
[l] Jos 6:25
[m] 22:18 Nm 16:22
[n] 22:20 Jos 7:1-26

LORD gave them rest on every side according to all he had sworn to their fathers. None of their enemies were able to stand against them, for the LORD handed over all their enemies to them. **45** None of the good promises the LORD had made to the house of Israel failed. Everything was fulfilled.[a]

EASTERN TRIBES RETURN HOME

22 Joshua summoned the Reubenites, Gadites, and half the tribe of Manasseh **2** and told them, "You have done everything Moses the LORD's servant commanded you[b] and have obeyed me in everything I commanded you. **3** You have not deserted your brothers even once this whole time but have carried out the requirement of the command of the LORD your God. **4** Now that he has given your brothers rest, just as he promised them, return to your homes in your own land that Moses the LORD's servant gave you across the Jordan. **5** Only carefully obey the command and instruction that Moses the LORD's servant gave you: to love the LORD your God, walk in all his ways, keep his commands, be loyal to him, and serve him with all your heart and all your soul."[c]

6 Joshua blessed them and sent them on their way,[d] and they went to their homes. **7** Moses had given territory to half the tribe of Manasseh in Bashan, but Joshua had given territory to the other half,[A] with their brothers, on the west side of the Jordan.[e] When Joshua sent them to their homes and blessed them, **8** he said, "Return to your homes with great wealth: a huge number of cattle, and silver, gold, bronze, iron, and a large quantity of clothing. Share the spoil of your enemies with your brothers."[f]

EASTERN TRIBES BUILD AN ALTAR

9 The Reubenites, Gadites, and half the tribe of Manasseh left the Israelites at Shiloh in the land of Canaan to return to their own land of Gilead,[g] which they took possession of according to the LORD's command through Moses. **10** When they came to the region of[B] the Jordan in the land of Canaan, the Reubenites, Gadites, and half the tribe of Manasseh built a large, impressive altar there by the Jordan.

11 Then the Israelites heard it said, "Look, the Reubenites, Gadites, and half the tribe of Manasseh have built an altar on the frontier of the land of Canaan at the region of[c] the Jordan, on the Israelite side." **12** When the Israelites heard this, the entire Israelite community assembled at Shiloh to go to war against them.[h]

EXPLANATION OF THE ALTAR

13 The Israelites sent Phinehas son of Eleazar the priest to the Reubenites, Gadites, and half the tribe of Manasseh, in the land of Gilead.[i] **14** They sent ten leaders with him — one family leader for each tribe of Israel. All of them were heads of their ancestral families[D] among the clans of Israel.[j] **15** They went to the Reubenites, Gadites, and half the tribe of Manasseh, in the land of Gilead, and told them, **16** "This is what the LORD's entire community says: 'What is this treachery you have committed today against the God of Israel by turning away from the LORD and building an altar for yourselves, so that you are in rebellion against the LORD today? **17** Wasn't the iniquity of Peor,[k] which brought a plague on the LORD's community, enough for us? We have not cleansed ourselves from it even to this day,[l] **18** and now would you turn away from the LORD? If you rebel against the LORD today, tomorrow he will be angry with the entire community of Israel.[m] **19** But if the land you possess is defiled, cross over to the land the LORD possesses where the LORD's tabernacle stands, and take possession of it among us. But don't rebel against the LORD or against us by building for yourselves an altar other than the altar of the LORD our God. **20** Wasn't Achan son of Zerah unfaithful regarding what was set apart for destruction, bringing wrath on the entire community of Israel? He was not the only one who perished because of his iniquity.' "[n]

21 The Reubenites, Gadites, and half the tribe of Manasseh answered the heads of

[A] 22:7 Lit *to his half*   [B] 22:10 Or *to Geliloth by*   [c] 22:11 Or *at Geliloth by*   [D] 22:14 Lit *the house of their fathers*

21:45 This is the central affirmation of the book of Joshua. Hundreds of years prior, God had promised a pilgrim named Abram that he would give the land of Canaan to his offspring (see Gen 12:1-7). Though it had taken many years and there were delays for various reasons, God was faithful in keeping that word.

We live in a world full of broken promises. But the author of Hebrews says, "Let us hold on to . . . our hope without wavering, since he

who promised is faithful" (Heb 10:23). Every one of God's promises is "Yes" in Jesus Christ (2 Cor 1:20).

22:1-6 With the land acquired and at rest, Joshua sent the tribes of Reuben, Gad, and the half tribe of Manasseh back to their homes on the east side of **the Jordan** (22:4).

22:9-12 But the only acceptable place for Israel to worship was in Shiloh at the tabernacle. So as far as the rest of Israel was

concerned, idolatry was brewing in the east among their brothers. They didn't want to pay the price when God's resulting wrath visited the entire nation (22:10-12).

22:21-29 The tribes on the east side of the Jordan responded to the accusation that they were doing something rebellious in building an altar. This repetition of three different Hebrew names for God (22:21-22) was a way of making an extreme oath. **May the LORD**

the Israelite clans, ²² "The Mighty One, God, the LORD! The Mighty One, God, the LORD!^{A,a} He knows,^b and may Israel also know. Do not spare us today, if it was in rebellion or treachery against the LORD ²³ that we have built for ourselves an altar to turn away from him. May the LORD himself hold us accountable if we intended to offer burnt offerings and grain offerings on it, or to sacrifice fellowship offerings on it. ²⁴ We actually did this from a specific concern that in the future your descendants might say to our descendants, 'What relationship do you have with the LORD, the God of Israel? ²⁵ For the LORD has made the Jordan a border between us and you descendants of Reuben and Gad. You have no share in the LORD!' So your descendants may cause our descendants to stop fearing the LORD.

²⁶ "Therefore we said: Let us take action and build an altar for ourselves, but not for burnt offering or sacrifice. ²⁷ Instead, it is to be a witness between us and you,^c and between the generations after us, so that we may carry out the worship of the LORD in his presence with our burnt offerings, sacrifices, and fellowship offerings.^d Then in the future, your descendants will not be able to say to our descendants, 'You have no share in the LORD!' ²⁸ We thought that if they said this to us or to our generations in the future, we would reply: Look at the replica of the LORD's altar that our fathers made, not for burnt offering or sacrifice, but as a witness between us and you. ²⁹ We would never ever rebel against the LORD or turn away from him today by building an altar for burnt offering, grain offering, or sacrifice, other than the altar of the LORD our God, which is in front of his tabernacle."

CONFLICT RESOLVED

³⁰ When the priest Phinehas and the community leaders, the heads of Israel's clans who were with him, heard what the descendants of Reuben, Gad, and Manasseh had to say, they were pleased. ³¹ Phinehas son of Eleazar the priest said to the descendants of Reuben, Gad, and Manasseh, "Today we know that the LORD is among us, because you have not committed this treachery against him.^e As a result, you have rescued the Israelites from the LORD's power."

³² Then the priest Phinehas son of Eleazar and the leaders returned from the Reubenites and Gadites in the land of Gilead to the Israelites in the land of Canaan and brought back a report to them. ³³ The Israelites were pleased with the report, and they blessed God.^f They spoke no more about going to war against them to ravage the land where the Reubenites and Gadites lived. ³⁴ So the Reubenites and Gadites named the altar: It^B is a witness between us that the LORD is God.

JOSHUA'S FAREWELL ADDRESS

23 A long time after the LORD had given Israel rest from all the enemies around them,^g Joshua was old, advanced in age.^h ² So Joshua summoned all Israel, including its elders, leaders, judges, and officers,ⁱ and said to them, "I am old, advanced in age, ³ and you have seen for yourselves everything the LORD your God did to all these nations on your account, because it was the LORD your God who was fighting for you.^j ⁴ See, I have allotted these remaining nations to you as an inheritance for your tribes,^k including all the nations I have destroyed, from the Jordan westward to the Mediterranean Sea. ⁵ The LORD your God will force them back on your account and drive them out before you so that you can take possession of their land,^l as the LORD your God promised you.

⁶ "Be very strong^m and continue obeying all that is written in the book of the law of Moses, so that you do not turn from it to the right or left ⁷ and so that you do not associate with these nations remaining

^a22:22 Dt 10:17; Ps 50:1; 136:2; Dn 2:47; 11:36
^b1Kg 8:39
^c22:27 Gn 31:48,52; Dt 31:19,26; Jos 24:27; Is 19:20
^dDt 12:6

^e22:31 Lv 26:11-12
^f22:33 1Ch 29:20; Dn 2:19; Lk 2:28
^g23:1 Jos 21:44
^hJos 13:1
ⁱ23:2 Jos 24:1
^j23:3 Dt 1:30; Jos 10:14
^k23:4 Ex 23:30
^l23:5 Nm 33:53
^m23:6 Dt 5:32; Jos 1:7

---

^A22:22 Or *The LORD is the God of gods! The LORD is the God of gods!*   ^B22:34 Some Hb mss, Syr, Tg read *altar Witness because it*

---

himself hold us accountable if **we intended** to do wrong, they swore (22:23). They had only intended their altar to be a replica of the true altar at Shiloh, to bear witness to future generations that all the tribes on the east side of the Jordan were true Israelites who worshiped the Lord like their brothers did.

22:30-34 There are two important lessons to be learned from the wise actions of these leaders. The first is this: don't act hastily. It is "foolishness and disgrace" to give an answer before listening (Prov 18:13). Instead of imme-

diately going on the offensive, the western tribes wisely asked the others to explain themselves. Too often people attack when they feel offended instead of first seeking clarity over the issue of concern. The second lesson is this: take a stand. Though we don't want to be hasty, nevertheless, we must not compromise. These leaders didn't want anything to stand in the way of their family's relationship with the Lord. The only way we can experience God's blessing together is when we deal with sin biblically and honestly.

23:3-5 While it was true that the Israelites had done the fighting, they were only victorious because God had worked through them.

23:6-8 What does being **very strong** like this look like (23:6)? First, they were to **continue obeying all that is written in the book of the law of Moses, so that [they would] not turn from it to the right or left** (23:6). This is a reminder to us not to add to God's Word or take away from it (see Rev 22:18-19). God doesn't need your help revising Scripture; he knew exactly what he wanted to say when he

a 23:7 Ex 23:13; Ps 16:4
b 23:8 Jos 6:25
c 23:9 Ex 23:30
d Jos 1:5
e 23:10 Jdg 15:15-16
f Lv 26:8
g 23:12 Ex 34:16
h Dt 7:3
i 23:13 Ex 23:33; Dt 7:16;
    Jdg 2:3
j 23:14 1Kg 2:2
k Jos 21:45
l 23:15 Lv 26:14-33; Dt
    28:15

m 24:1 Gn 12:1-7
n Jos 23:2
o 24:2 Gn 11:27-32
p 24:3 Gn 12:1
q Gn 21:3
r 24:4 Gn 25:25-26
s Gn 36:8; Dt 2:5
t Gn 46:6
u 24:5 Ex 4:14
v 24:6 Ex 14:2
w 24:8 Nm 21:21-32

among you. Do not call on the names of their gods or make an oath to them;[a] do not serve them or bow in worship to them. [8] Instead, be loyal to the LORD your God, as you have been to this day.[b]

[9] "The LORD has driven out great and powerful nations before you,[c] and no one is able to stand against you to this day.[d] [10] One of you routed a thousand[e] because the LORD your God was fighting for you, as he promised.[A,f] [11] So diligently watch yourselves! Love the LORD your God! [12] If you ever turn away and become loyal to the rest of these nations remaining among you,[g] and if you intermarry or associate with them[h] and they with you, [13] know for certain that the LORD your God will not continue to drive these nations out before you. They will become a snare and a trap for you,[i] a sharp stick[B] for your sides and thorns in your eyes, until you disappear from this good land the LORD your God has given you.

[14] "I am now going the way of the whole earth,[j] and you know with all your heart and all your soul that none of the good promises the LORD your God made to you has failed. Everything was fulfilled for you; not one promise has failed.[k] [15] Since every good thing the LORD your God promised you has come about, so he will bring on you every bad thing until he has annihilated you from this good land the LORD your God has given you.[l] [16] If you break the covenant of the LORD your God, which he commanded you, and go and serve other gods, and bow in worship to them, the LORD's anger will burn against you, and

you will quickly disappear from this good land he has given you."

REVIEW OF ISRAEL'S HISTORY

24 Joshua assembled all the tribes of Israel at Shechem[m] and summoned Israel's elders, leaders, judges, and officers, and they presented themselves before God.[n] [2] Joshua said to all the people, "This is what the LORD, the God of Israel, says: 'Long ago your ancestors, including Terah,[o] the father of Abraham and Nahor, lived beyond the Euphrates River and worshiped other gods. [3] But I took your father Abraham from the region beyond the Euphrates River, led him throughout the land of Canaan, and multiplied his descendants.[p] I gave him Isaac,[q] [4] and to Isaac I gave Jacob and Esau.[r] I gave the hill country of Seir to Esau as a possession.[s]

"'Jacob and his sons, however, went down to Egypt.[t] [5] I sent Moses and Aaron,[u] and I defeated Egypt by what I did within it, and afterward I brought you out. [6] When I brought your fathers out of Egypt and you reached the Red Sea,[v] the Egyptians pursued your fathers with chariots and horsemen as far as the sea. [7] Your fathers cried out to the LORD, so he put darkness between you and the Egyptians, and brought the sea over them, engulfing them. Your own eyes saw what I did to Egypt. After that, you lived in the wilderness a long time.

[8] "'Later, I brought you to the land of the Amorites who lived beyond the Jordan.[w] They fought against you, but I handed them over to you. You possessed their

---

A **23:10** Lit *promised you*   B **23:13** Or *a whip*; Hb obscure

---

put together his Word. Your job is to believe what you find in it and, with the help of the Holy Spirit, to obey it. The second way to "be very strong" is to **be loyal to the LORD** (Josh 23:8) by not compromising with the world. We have to live *in* the world, but we're not to be *of* the world (see John 17:11, 16). God's people are to be distinct and reflect his character. **23:10** This tells us that when God fights for us, we don't need to worry about the number of folks working against us. If you're on God's team, the odds are always in your favor.
23:12-13 Joshua exhorted the Israelites not to **intermarry** with the surrounding peoples (23:12). There is no scriptural prohibition against marrying someone of another *race*. Joseph and Moses both had interracial marriages in that sense (see Gen 41:45; Exod 2:16, 21; Judg 1:16), and all people groups descend from Adam and Eve and are of equal worth (see Gen 3:20; Acts 17:26). But there is a prohibition against marrying someone of another *religion*—that is, marrying someone who

believes in and worships other gods rather than the one true God.
    If you're a believer seeking a spouse, you need to marry someone who is going in the same direction spiritually. And this is the reasoning behind God's intermarriage prohibition to Israel. Ignoring it could turn their hearts away from God.
23:15-16 To enjoy the promises in the land, the people would be required to give God their loyalty and commitment. Unfortunately, the next book of the Bible, Judges, shows Israel failing to do just that. In time, they would lose the land and the blessings that God had for them as a result.
24:2-13 The speaker here is Joshua, but the message is from God. Notice that throughout the rehearsal of Israel's history, God insisted that *he* was the star of the show and the performer of the action: **I took** (24:3), **I gave** (24:3-4, 13), **I sent** (24:5, 12), **I defeated** (24:5), **I brought** (24:5-6, 8), **I did** (24:7), **I handed** (24:8), **I annihilated** (24:8), **I would not listen**

(24:10), **I rescued** (24:10). In summary, God was telling them, "You got from slavery to here because of me. When you sinned and were unfaithful, I came through. I never bailed. I enabled you to succeed."
    In saying, **I gave you a land you did not labor for** (24:13), God reminded the Israelites that they were living in homes they hadn't built, eating food they hadn't grown, and sitting under shade trees they hadn't planted. Importantly, he used the unrighteous to get all this ready for them. The Canaanites did all the work, enjoying the fruit of their labors up until the day God evicted them for their wickedness. This reminds us that even the ungodly are God's ungodly—not by relationship but by sovereignty. Similarly, even the devil is God's devil, because he can only do what God permits. Israel needed to remember that they were like turtles on fence posts, which hadn't gotten to their safe place by their own power. Whatever blessings we

land, and I annihilated them before you. [9] Balak son of Zippor, king of Moab,[a] set out to fight against Israel. He sent for Balaam son of Beor to curse you, [10] but I would not listen to Balaam. Instead, he repeatedly blessed you, and I rescued you from him.

[11] " 'You then crossed the Jordan and came to Jericho.[b] Jericho's citizens — as well as the Amorites, Perizzites, Canaanites, Hethites, Girgashites, Hivites, and Jebusites — fought against you, but I handed them over to you. [12] I sent hornets[A,c] ahead of you, and they drove out the two Amorite kings[d] before you. It was not by your sword or bow. [13] I gave you a land you did not labor for, and cities you did not build,[e] though you live in them; you are eating from vineyards and olive groves you did not plant.'

THE COVENANT RENEWAL

[14] "Therefore, fear the Lord and worship him in sincerity and truth.[f] Get rid of the gods your fathers worshiped[g] beyond the Euphrates River and in Egypt, and worship the Lord. [15] But if it doesn't please you to worship the Lord, choose for yourselves today: Which will you worship — the gods your fathers worshiped beyond the Euphrates River or the gods of the Amorites in whose land you are living?[h] As for me and my family, we will worship the Lord."

[16] The people replied, "We will certainly not abandon the Lord to worship other gods! [17] For the Lord our God brought us and our fathers out of the land of Egypt, out of the place of slavery,[i] and performed these great signs before our eyes. He also protected us all along the way we went

and among all the peoples whose lands we traveled through. [18] The Lord drove out before us all the peoples, including the Amorites who lived in the land. We too will worship the Lord, because he is our God."

[19] But Joshua told the people, "You will not be able to worship the Lord, because he is a holy God. He is a jealous God;[j] he will not forgive your transgressions and sins.[k] [20] If you abandon the Lord and worship foreign gods, he will turn against you, harm you, and completely destroy[l] you, after he has been good to you."

[21] "No!" the people answered Joshua. "We will worship the Lord."

[22] Joshua then told the people, "You are witnesses against yourselves that you yourselves have chosen to worship the Lord."

"We are witnesses," they said.

[23] "Then get rid of the foreign gods that are among you and turn your hearts to the Lord, the God of Israel."

[24] So the people said to Joshua, "We will worship the Lord our God and obey him."

[25] On that day Joshua made a covenant for the people at Shechem and established a statute and ordinance for them. [26] Joshua recorded these things in the book of the law of God;[m] he also took a large stone and set it up there under the oak at the sanctuary of the Lord. [27] And Joshua said to all the people, "You see this stone — it will be a witness against us,[n] for it has heard all the words the Lord said to us, and it will be a witness against you, so that you will not deny your God." [28] Then Joshua sent the people away, each to his own inheritance.

[a] 24:9 Nm 22:5
[b] 24:11 Jos 3:14,17
[c] 24:12 Ex 23:27-28; Dt 7:20
[d] Nm 21:21-35; Dt 2:26-3:11; 29:7
[e] 24:13 Dt 6:10-11
[f] 24:14 Dt 10:12; 1Sm 12:24
[g] Gn 35:4
[h] 24:15 Jdg 6:10
[i] 24:17 Lv 26:13; Dt 5:6; 6:12; 8:14; 13:5,10; Jr 34:13

[j] 24:19 Lv 19:2
[k] Ex 23:21
[l] 24:20 Jos 10:1; 11:11; Jdg 1:17
[m] 24:26 Dt 31:24
[n] 24:27 Jos 22:27,34

[A] 24:12 Or sent terror

---

have received, we should give him all the thanks and praise.

24:14 To **fear** God means to take him seriously, rather than having a mere casual relationship with him and trying to keep him on the periphery of life.

That the people were to **Get rid of the gods [their] fathers worshiped** is likely a reference to the false gods mentioned in the Old Testament story, but an idol isn't merely a statue before which someone bows. An idol is any unauthorized person, place, or thing that a person looks to as a source of purpose, promise, or provision. Therefore, an idol can be money, power, popularity, sex, influence, or a person, and the list goes on. You have only one ultimate source to meet your needs—God.

24:15 Joshua spoke like a kingdom man. He couldn't control the hearts of the people of

Israel, but he knew whose agenda he himself would follow and who would lead his home. He was determined to serve the Lord. He called the Israelites to make the same crucial decision.

24:16-20 Joshua's response to the people's promise that they would **certainly not abandon** God may seem a little odd (24:16-18). But Joshua said this because he recognized the danger of not putting your money where your mouth is. Talk is cheap, but actions prove our words.

The warning that God **is a jealous God** gives insight into the Lord's character (24:19-20). Indeed, God is jealous—righteously jealous—for his people, just as an honorable husband would be righteously jealous if he saw his wife acting inappropriately with another man.

24:21-22 If the people were to fail in this pledge of fidelity, their own words would

call down a curse on them and justify the judgment of God. They had testified against themselves in advance.

24:23 Many people ask God why he's not working in their circumstances, while they're hugging their idol of choice at the same time (see the note on 24:14). They don't stop to consider that God's inactivity may be a result of the fact that, like many in Israel, they aren't willing to discard their idols.

24:27 Previously, Joshua had set up memorial stones to remind Israel of what God had done for them (see 4:1-9) and to remind them of the seriousness of sinning against God (see 7:26). This time, however, the memorial stone was to point them to their agreement to worship God. Every time they passed by it, the stone would silently whisper, "Do **not deny your God**; practice what you preach" (24:27).

BURIAL OF THREE LEADERS

a 24:30 Jos 19:49-50
b 24:31 Jdg 2:7

c 24:32 Gn 50:25; Ex 13:19
d Gn 33:19; Jb 42:11
e 24:33 Jos 22:13

29 After these things, the LORD's servant, Joshua son of Nun, died at the age of 110. **30** They buried him in his allotted territory at Timnath-serah, in the hill country of Ephraim[a] north of Mount Gaash. **31** Israel worshiped the LORD throughout Joshua's lifetime and during the lifetimes of the elders who outlived Joshua[b] and who had experienced all the works the LORD had done for Israel.

32 Joseph's bones, which the Israelites had brought up from Egypt,[c] were buried at Shechem in the parcel of land Jacob had purchased from the sons of Hamor, Shechem's father, for a hundred pieces of silver.[A,d] It was an inheritance for Joseph's descendants.

33 And Eleazar son of Aaron died, and they buried him at Gibeah,[B] which had been given to his son Phinehas[e] in the hill country of Ephraim.

[A] **24:32** Lit *a hundred qesitahs*   [B] **24:33** = the Hill

---

24:29-31 How would Joshua be remembered? As **the LORD's servant** (24:29). And as a testimony to his faithfulness, we are given this insight: **Israel worshiped the LORD throughout Joshua's lifetime** (24:31). Unfortunately, as the book of Judges will reveal, that pattern would soon change.

24:32 Many years before, when Joseph was about to die, he made the sons of Israel—his brothers—vow to carry his remains to the land God swore to give to Abraham (see Gen 50:24-26). So, when Moses led the Israelites out of Egypt, he "took the bones of Joseph" (Exod 13:19). Once Israel was in the land God had promised, they buried **Joseph's bones** (Josh 24:32).

Though he would not live to see the outcome of the promise, Joseph believed that God would keep his word to his family. And if you think about it, Christians are essentially called to do the same thing. We wait for entry into the divine promised land where God will dwell among his people forever. So with that truth ever in view, walk with God and trust him for what he has planned for your life. Because none of his promises fail.

JUDGES

INTRODUCTION

Author

THE AUTHOR OF THE BOOK of Judges is unknown. The date of composition is also uncertain. The most we can say is that it was probably composed after the rise of Israel's monarchy, given the book's repeated refrain, "In those days there was no king in Israel" (17:6; 18:1; 19:1; 21:25).

Historical Background

Judges covers a period of about three hundred years, explaining what happened in the promised land between its conquest under Joshua and the rise of the monarchy under Saul and David. The title of the book comes from the title given to the leaders who arose during this period to give Israel deliverance from their enemies (2:16). These were dark years of religious compromise and moral decay for the descendants of Jacob. There was no divine standard operating in the nation because the people had quickly forgotten the rules of the covenant they had made with God in Moses's day and reaffirmed in his successor's. Thus, "Everyone did whatever seemed right to him" (17:6; 21:25). And that caused countless problems. (It always does.)

Message and Purpose

The book of Judges is about cycles—cycles of disobedience, discipline, repentance, and deliverance. The Israelites' disobedience brought God's discipline. But in each instance that the people repented, God raised up a judge to bring about deliverance.

The generation after Joshua did not remain faithful to God, which led to cultural decline and horrific sin.

Judges shows what happens to a society when it drifts away from following God and living in respect of his moral standards. Yet Judges also offers hope: it shows how even in the darkest days God can use men and women to accomplish his plan—even though they are flawed themselves. The book serves as a warning that disaster will ultimately befall a people who reject God's kingdom rule over them, and it emphasizes the necessity of repentance before God will intervene to deliver and restore them to a place of blessing.

VIDEO | INTRO

www.bhpublishinggroup.com/qr/te/07_00

Outline

EXPOSITION OF JUDGES

www.bhpublishinggroup.com/qr/te/21-22

[a] 1:1 Jos 1:1; 24:29-31
[b] Jdg 20:23,27; 1Sm 10:22; 23:2,4; 28:6
[c] 1:2 Gn 29:35; 49:8-12
[d] 1:1-2 Jdg 20:18
[e] 1:2 Gn 35:12; Ex 6:8
[f] 1:4 Gn 13:7; Dt 7:1; Jos 3:10; Ezr 9:1
[g] 1Sm 11:8
[h] 1:6 2Sm 4:12
[i] 1:10 Gn 13:18; 23:2
[j] Gn 23:2; 35:27; Jos 14:15
[k] Nm 13:22; Jos 15:13-14
[l] 1:11 Jos 10:38-39; 11:21; 15:7; 21:15; 1Ch 6:58
[m] 1:12 Nm 13:6,13; 14:6,24,30,38; 26:65; 32:12
[n] 1Ch 2:49
[o] 1:13 Jdg 3:9,11; 1Ch 4:13

[p] 1:15 Gn 12:9; 13:1,3; Nm 13:17,22,29; 2Sm 24:7; Ps 126:4
[q] 1:11-15 Jos 15:15-19
[r] 1:16 Ex 2:18; 3:1; 4:18; 18:1-12; Nm 10:29
[s] Dt 34:3; Jdg 3:13; 2Ch 28:15
[t] Nm 21:1; 33:40; Jos 12:14
[u] 1:17 Nm 21:3; Dt 1:44
[v] 1:19 Gn 39:2,21; Jos 6:27; Jdg 2:18; 1Sm 18:12
[w] Jos 15:63
[x] Jos 17:16,18; Jdg 4:3,13
[y] 1:20 Dt 1:36; Jos 14:9
[z] Nm 13:22
[aa] 1:21 Jos 15:63
[ab] 1:22 Gn 39:2,21; Jos 6:27; Jdg 2:18; 1Sm 18:12

JUDAH'S LEADERSHIP AGAINST THE CANAANITES

1 After the death of Joshua,[a] the Israelites inquired of the LORD,[b] "Who will be the first to fight for us against the Canaanites?"

2 The LORD answered, "Judah[c] is to go.[d] I have handed the land over to him."[e]

3 Judah said to his brother Simeon, "Come with me to my allotted territory, and let us fight against the Canaanites. I will also go with you to your allotted territory." So Simeon went with him.

4 When Judah attacked, the LORD handed the Canaanites and Perizzites[f] over to them. They struck down ten thousand men in Bezek.[g] 5 They found Adoni-bezek in Bezek, fought against him, and struck down the Canaanites and Perizzites.

6 When Adoni-bezek fled, they pursued him, caught him, and cut off his thumbs and big toes.[h] 7 Adoni-bezek said, "Seventy kings with their thumbs and big toes cut off used to pick up scraps[A] under my table. God has repaid me for what I have done." They brought him to Jerusalem, and he died there.

8 The men of Judah fought against Jerusalem, captured it, put it to the sword, and set the city on fire. 9 Afterward, the men of Judah marched down to fight against the Canaanites who were living in the hill country, the Negev, and the Judean foothills.[B] 10 Judah also marched against the Canaanites who were living in Hebron[i] (Hebron was formerly named Kiriath-arba[j]). They struck down Sheshai, Ahiman, and Talmai.[k] 11 From there they marched against the residents of Debir[l] (Debir was formerly named Kiriath-sepher).

12 Caleb[m] said, "Whoever attacks and captures Kiriath-sepher, I will give my daughter Achsah[n] to him as a wife." 13 So Othniel[o] son of Kenaz, Caleb's youngest brother, captured it, and Caleb gave his daughter Achsah to him as his wife.

14 When she arrived, she persuaded Othniel to ask her father for a field. As she got off her donkey, Caleb asked her, "What do you want?" 15 She answered him, "Give me a blessing. Since you have given me land in the Negev,[p] give me springs also." So Caleb gave her both the upper and lower springs.[q]

16 The descendants of the Kenite, Moses's father-in-law,[r] had gone up with the men of Judah from the City of Palms[c,s] to the Wilderness of Judah, which was in the Negev of Arad.[t] They went to live among the people.

17 Judah went with his brother Simeon, struck the Canaanites who were living in Zephath, and completely destroyed the town. So they named the town Hormah.[u] 18 Judah captured Gaza and its territory, Ashkelon and its territory, and Ekron and its territory. 19 The LORD was with[v] Judah and enabled them to take possession of the hill country, but they could not drive out[w] the people who were living in the valley because those people had iron chariots.[x]

20 Judah gave Hebron to Caleb, just as Moses had promised.[y] Then Caleb drove out the three sons of Anak[z] who lived there.

BENJAMIN'S FAILURE

21 At the same time the Benjaminites did not drive out the Jebusites who were living in Jerusalem. The Jebusites have lived among the Benjaminites in Jerusalem to this day.[aa]

SUCCESS OF THE HOUSE OF JOSEPH

22 The house of Joseph also attacked Bethel, and the LORD was with[ab] them. 23 They sent spies to Bethel (the town was formerly

---

[A] 1:7 Lit *toes cut off are gathering*   [B] 1:9 Or *the Shephelah*   [C] 1:16 = Jericho; Dt 34:3; Jdg 3:13; 2Ch 28:15

1:1-2 It was up to the people to carry out the mopping-up operations against **the Canaanites**. They wisely asked the Lord for direction, which was the right way to begin their season of transition (1:1). When we have uncertainty, we must inquire of him.

1:8 In Scripture, **fire** is used as a means of judgment to remove all evil. In time, **Jerusalem** would become Israel's capital.

1:11 **Debir** comes from the Hebrew term that means "word," and **Kiriath-sepher** means "The City of the Scribe." This was the town where the records of the Canaanites were held; it was the repository for details about their history, culture, and background.

1:12 **Caleb** was one of two faithful spies who had survived from Moses's time (see Num 14:36-38). His challenge is a tall order for a father to make: "If you want this girl, I've got to see you fight and succeed." The high value he placed on his daughter is a reminder that every father ought to have high standards regarding the man who wants to marry his own. Fathers need to look for kingdom men for their girls: leaders and providers committed to loving their wives and future children.

1:13 **Othniel** became Caleb's son-in-law. In time he would also become Israel's first judge (see 3:9).

1:19 Why wasn't Judah fully victorious? The problem was that the Israelites' faith on **the hill** outmatched their faith **in the valley**. God was with them in both places, but they allowed what seemed an insurmountable problem in the valley to limit their faith.

When you're following the will of God, don't despair when circumstances are daunting. Remember what Caleb said earlier when the Israelites feared entering Canaan altogether. He kept his eyes on God's promise and declared, "We can certainly conquer it!" (Num 13:30). Don't let the size of your problem become bigger than the size of your God.

named Luz[a]). [24] The spies saw a man coming out of the town and said to him, "Please show us how to get into town, and we will show you kindness."[b] [25] When he showed them the way into the town, they put the town to the sword but released the man and his entire family. [26] Then the man went to the land of the Hittites, built a town, and named it Luz. That is its name still today.

FAILURE OF THE OTHER TRIBES

[27] At that time Manasseh failed to take possession of Beth-shean[c] and Taanach[d] and their surrounding villages, or the residents of Dor,[e] Ibleam,[f] and Megiddo[g] and their surrounding villages; the Canaanites were determined to stay in this land.[h] [28] When Israel became stronger, they made the Canaanites serve as forced labor but never drove them out completely.[i]

[29] At that time Ephraim failed to drive out the Canaanites who were living in Gezer, so the Canaanites have lived among them in Gezer.[j]

[30] Zebulun failed to drive out the residents of Kitron or the residents of Nahalol,[k] so the Canaanites lived among them and served as forced labor.

[31] Asher failed to drive out the residents of Acco or of Sidon, or Ahlab, Achzib, Helbah, Aphik, or Rehob. [32] The Asherites lived among the Canaanites who were living in the land, because they failed to drive them out.

[33] Naphtali did not drive out the residents of Beth-shemesh or the residents of Beth-anath. They lived among the Canaanites who were living in the land, but the residents of Beth-shemesh and Beth-anath served as their forced labor.

[34] The Amorites[l] forced the Danites into the hill country and did not allow them to go down into the valley. [35] The Amorites were determined to stay in[A] Har-heres,

Aijalon,[m] and Shaalbim. When the house of Joseph got the upper hand,[B] the Amorites[C] were made to serve as forced labor. [36] The territory of the Amorites extended from the Scorpions' Ascent,[n] that is from Sela[o] upward.

PATTERN OF SIN AND JUDGMENT

2 The angel of the LORD[p] went up from Gilgal to Bochim and said, "I brought you out of Egypt and led you into the land[q] I had promised to your fathers.[r] I also said: I will never break my covenant with you. [2] You are not to make a covenant[s] with the inhabitants of this land. You are to tear down their altars.[t] But you have not obeyed me. What is this you have done? [3] Therefore, I now say: I will not drive out these people before you.[u] They will be thorns[D,E] in your sides,[v] and their gods will be a trap for you."[w] [4] When the angel of the LORD had spoken these words to all the Israelites, the people wept loudly. [5] So they named that place Bochim[F] and offered sacrifices there to the LORD.

JOSHUA'S DEATH

[6] Previously, when Joshua had sent the people away, the Israelites had gone to take possession of the land, each to his own inheritance.[x] [7] The people worshiped the LORD throughout Joshua's lifetime and during the lifetimes of the elders who outlived[G] Joshua. They had seen all the LORD's great works[y] he had done for Israel.

[8] Joshua son of Nun, the servant of the LORD, died at the age of 110. [9] They buried him in the territory of his inheritance, in Timnath-heres, in the hill country of Ephraim,[z] north of Mount Gaash. [10] That whole generation was also gathered to their ancestors. After them another generation rose up who did not know the LORD[aa] or the works he had done for Israel.

[a]1:23 Gn 28:19; 35:6; 48:3
[b]1:24 Jos 2:12,14; 2Sm 9:1,3,7
[c]1:27 Jos 17:11,16; 1Sm 31:10,12; 2Sm 21:12
[d]Jos 21:25; Jdg 5:19
[e]Jos 11:2; 12:23; 17:11; 1Kg 4:11
[f]Jos 17:11; 2Kg 9:27
[g]Jdg 5:19; 1Kg 9:15; 2Kg 23:29-30
[h]Jdg 1:35; Hs 5:11
[i]1:27-28 Jos 17:12-13
[j]1:29 Jos 16:10
[k]1:30 Jos 19:15; 21:35
[l]1:34 Jos 18:3; Nm 13:29; 21:31; Jos 2:10

[m]1:35 Jos 10:12; 1Sm 14:31; 1Ch 8:13; 2Ch 28:18
[n]1:36 Nm 34:4; Jos 15:3
[o]2Kg 14:7; Is 16:1
[p]2:1 Gn 22:11; Ex 3:2; Ps 34:7; 35:5-6
[q]Ex 6:8; Nm 14:3,8; Ezk 20:15
[r]Nm 14:23; Dt 6:10,23; 10:11; Jos 1:6
[s]2:2 Ex 23:32; Dt 7:2
[t]Ex 34:13; Dt 7:5; 12:3; Jdg 6:30-32; 2Ch 34:7
[u]2:3 Ex 23:29
[v]Nm 33:55
[w]Ex 23:33; 34:12; Dt 7:16; Jos 23:13
[x]2:6 Dt 9:4; 11:31; Jos 1:11; 18:3; Jdg 18:9; Neh 9:15
[y]2:7 Dt 11:7
[z]2:9 Jos 19:50; 1Sm 1:1; 14:22; 1Ch 6:67
[aa]2:10 Ex 5:2; 1Sm 2:12

[A]1:35 Or Amorites determined to live in   [B]1:35 Lit When the hand of the house of Joseph was heavy   [C]1:35 LXX reads Joseph became strong on the Amorites, they   [D]2:3 LXX reads affliction   [E]2:3 Lit traps   [F]2:5 Or Weeping   [G]2:7 Lit extended their days after

1:27-35 All of this marks the beginning of a cycle of compromise and partial obedience. Perhaps the Israelites excused their failure to drive out their enemies with thoughts like, "Hey, the Canaanites could be beneficial to us. There's no need to get rid of all of them." But in Deuteronomy 7:1-6 God had commanded them to fully remove the Canaanites and destroy their idols because he knows that "a little leaven leavens the whole batch of dough" (1 Cor 5:6). Just as sure as a small cancer will metastasize, leaving pockets of Canaanites within the promised land would grow into a major problem.

2:1 The **angel of the LORD** is a Christophany—that is, a preincarnate manifestation of the Son of God showing up in the Old Testament's narrative. We can conclude this because he claimed to have **brought** them **out of Egypt and led** them into the promised **land.** These were the actions of God himself. **2:2** A covenant is a bond—entering one is like being glued together with that other party. God had made a covenant with Israel (2:1), and one of its stipulations was that they were **not to make a covenant with the inhabitants of** Canaan. To make a treaty with Canaan, in fact, was to make a covenant with its gods.

The native inhabitants of Canaan were people wholeheartedly connected to a worldview that contradicted the God who had delivered Israel. This is the principle behind Paul's words: "Don't become partners with those who do not believe" (2 Cor 6:14). There can be no true equality between one who worships the true Creator and one in league with his competition.

2:3 In other words, Israel's disobedience to God's clear order would boomerang back to slap them. Similarly, if the thing or person with whom you choose to bond is contrary to God, it will lead you astray and cause harm.

[a] 2:11 Nm 32:12; Dt 4:25; 31:29; 1Kg 11:6
[b] Jdg 3:7; 8:33; 1Sm 12:10; 2Kg 17:16; Jr 2:23; 9:14
[c] 2:12 Dt 6:14; 13:7
[d] 1Kg 14:15; 15:30; 2Kg 17:11; 2Ch 28:25
[e] 2:13 Jdg 10:6; 1Sm 7:3-4; 12:10; 1Kg 11:5,33; 2Kg 23:13
[f] 2:14 Jdg 3:8; 4:2,9; 10:7; Ps 44:12; Is 50:1; Ezk 30:12; Jl 3:8
[g] 2:15 Dt 2:15
[h] Lv 26:14-46; Dt 28:15-68
[i] 2:16 Jdg 3:9,15; 1Kg 11:14; 14:14
[j] 2:17 Dt 4:30; 1Sm 13:6; 30:6; 2Sm 22:7; Jb 20:22; Ps 59:16; Hs 5:15
[k] Ex 32:8; Dt 9:12,16
[l] 2:18 Gn 39:2,21; Jos 6:27; 1Sm 18:12
[m] 2:19 Gn 6:12; Dt 31:29; Is 1:4
[n] 2:19 Ex 32:9; Dt 9:6,13; Ezk 2:4
[o] 2:20 Jos 7:11,15; 23:16; Jr 34:18; Hs 6:7
[p] Jdg 3:4; 1Kg 8:58; 2Kg 17:13; Ps 78:5; Jr 11:4
[q] 2:21 Jos 13:1-7; 23:1-16
[r] Jos 24:29-30
[s] 2:22 Gn 18:19; 2Sm 22:22; Ps 138:5
[t] Jos 24:31
[u] 3:1 Jos 1-12
[v] 3:3 Jos 13:3; 1Sm 5:8,11
[w] Gn 10:14; Ex 13:17
[x] Jos 13:4; 1Kg 5:6; Ezk 32:30
[y] Ex 38:17; Dt 20:17; Jos 9:1,7
[z] 3:4 1Kg 8:58; 2Kg 17:13; Ps 78:5; Jr 11:4
[aa] 3:6 Ex 23:33; Dt 7:16

[11] The Israelites did what was evil in the LORD's sight.[a] They worshiped the Baals[b] [12] and abandoned the LORD, the God of their fathers, who had brought them out of Egypt. They followed other gods from the surrounding peoples[c] and bowed down to them. They angered the LORD,[d] [13] for they abandoned him and worshiped Baal and the Ashtoreths.[e]

[14] The LORD's anger burned against Israel, and he handed them over to marauders who raided them. He sold[f] them to[A] the enemies around them, and they could no longer resist their enemies. [15] Whenever the Israelites went out, the LORD[B] was against them[g] and brought disaster on them, just as he had promised and sworn to them.[h] So they suffered greatly.

[16] The LORD raised up[i] judges, who saved them from the power of their marauders, [17] but they did not listen to their judges. Instead, they prostituted[j] themselves with other gods, bowing down to them. They quickly turned from the way[k] of their fathers, who had walked in obedience to the LORD's commands. They did not do as their fathers did. [18] Whenever the LORD raised up a judge for the Israelites, the LORD was with[l] him and saved the people from the power of their enemies while the judge was still alive.[C] The LORD was moved to pity whenever they groaned because of those who were oppressing and afflicting them. [19] Whenever the judge died, the Israelites would act even more corruptly[m] than their fathers, following other gods to serve them and bow in worship to them.

They did not turn from their evil practices or their obstinate[n] ways.

[20] The LORD's anger burned against Israel, and he declared, "Because this nation has violated my covenant[o] that I made with their fathers[p] and disobeyed me, [21] I will no longer drive out before them any of the nations Joshua left[q] when he died.[r] [22] I did this to test Israel and to see whether or not they would keep the LORD's way[s] by walking in it, as their fathers had."[t] [23] The LORD left these nations and did not drive them out immediately. He did not hand them over to Joshua.

THE LORD TESTS ISRAEL

3 These are the nations the LORD left in order to test all those in Israel who had experienced[D] none of the wars in Canaan.[u] [2] This was to teach the future generations of the Israelites how to fight in battle, especially those who had not fought before.[E] [3] These nations included the five rulers[v] of the Philistines[w] and all of the Canaanites, the Sidonians,[x] and the Hivites[y] who lived in the Lebanese mountains from Mount Baal-hermon as far as the entrance to Hamath.[F] [4] The LORD left them to test Israel, to determine if they would keep the LORD's commands he had given their fathers through[G] Moses.[z] [5] But they settled among the Canaanites, Hethites, Amorites, Perizzites, Hivites, and Jebusites. [6] The Israelites took their daughters as wives for themselves, gave their own daughters to their sons, and worshiped their gods.[aa]

[A] 2:14 Lit *into the hand of*   [B] 2:15 Lit *the hand of the LORD*   [C] 2:18 Lit *enemies all the days of the judge*   [D] 3:1 Lit *had known*   [E] 3:2 Lit *not known it*
[F] 3:3 Or *as Lebo-hamath*   [G] 3:4 Lit *by the hand of*

2:10 That **another generation rose up who did not know the LORD or the works he had done** tells us that Israelite parents had failed to transfer their faith to their children. The resulting spiritual breakdown would bring about decline in the culture. This is a sharp warning for us: we need to take seriously the spiritual development of our children, because not only do they depend on it, but society is also banking on it. While children may not see the benefit of spiritual training as it's offered—or even want it—one day they're going to need it.

2:11-13 Baal was a dominant idol among the Canaanites. To them, he was the god of fertility—though he was really a god of *futility*. The Israelites had lost faith in God as their source and began to look to the natural realm.

Not only did the Israelites fail to rub off on the culture, but they had also allowed their enemies' culture to rub off on them. This

should make us ask: What ungodly aspects of today's culture are rubbing off on us?

2:14 Since the Israelites submitted themselves to the local, evil system of thinking, God allowed that system to rule them. When we wander from serving the true God, false humanistic worldviews fill the vacuum, taking his place in our hearts and ultimately wielding control over us.

2:15 From the people's perspective, the bad things that happened might have just seemed like bad luck, but in reality God himself was working against them. If God is against you, it doesn't matter what you have going for you. And if God is for you, it doesn't matter who is against you (see Rom 8:31). It's your obedience to his Word that will make the difference.

2:16-19 These verses provide a summary of the book of Judges. Israel sinfully departed from the Lord, their enemies oppressed them, the Lord felt sorry for them when they cried for help, he raised up a deliverer, the deliverer

defeated their enemies, the deliverer died, and Israel returned to their idols.

2:20-23 Here we get insight into God's mysterious ways. He said that he would leave Israel a problem—some Canaanites within their borders—specifically **to test Israel** (2:22). A *test* is a negative reality that God allows in your life so that *you* can see how serious (or lacking) your spiritual devotion to him is. God already knows how you'll respond to such tests, but they enable *you* to know the strength of your commitment.

3:1-6 In settling **among the Canaanites**, merging their families together, and even worshiping the natives' **gods** (3:5-6), the Israelites received an "F" on their spiritual report card.

When you are tempted to bend God's rules, know that "our struggle is not against flesh and blood, but against the rulers, against the authorities, against the cosmic powers of this darkness, against evil, spiritual forces in the heavens" (Eph 6:12), and choose to obey him.

OTHNIEL, THE FIRST JUDGE

7 The Israelites did what was evil in the LORD's sight; they forgot the LORD their God[a] and worshiped the Baals and the Asherahs. **8** The LORD's anger burned against Israel, and he sold them to[A] King Cushan-rishathaim[B] of Aram-naharaim,[C,b] and the Israelites served him eight years.

9 The Israelites cried out to the LORD.[c] So the LORD raised up Othniel son of Kenaz, Caleb's youngest brother,[d] as a deliverer[e] to save the Israelites. **10** The Spirit of the LORD came on him, and he judged Israel. Othniel went out to battle, and the LORD handed over King Cushan-rishathaim of Aram to him, so that Othniel overpowered him. **11** Then the land had peace for[f] forty years, and Othniel son of Kenaz died.

EHUD

12 The Israelites again did what was evil in the LORD's sight. He gave King Eglon of Moab[g] power over Israel, because they had done what was evil in the LORD's sight. **13** After Eglon convinced the Ammonites and the Amalekites to join forces with him, he attacked and defeated Israel and took possession of the City of Palms.[D,h] **14** The Israelites served King Eglon of Moab eighteen years.

15 Then the Israelites cried out to the LORD, and he raised up Ehud son of Gera, a left-handed[i] Benjaminite,[E] as a deliverer for them. The Israelites sent him with the tribute[j] for King Eglon of Moab. **16** Ehud made himself a double-edged sword eighteen inches long.[F] He strapped it to his right thigh under his clothes **17** and brought the tribute to King Eglon of Moab, who was an extremely fat man. **18** When Ehud had finished presenting the tribute, he dismissed the people who had carried it. **19** At the carved images near Gilgal he returned and said, "King Eglon, I have a secret message for you." The king said, "Silence!" and all his attendants left him. **20** Then Ehud approached him while he was sitting alone in his upstairs room where it was cool. Ehud said, "I have a message from God for you," and the king stood up from his throne. **21** Ehud reached with his left hand, took the sword from his right thigh, and plunged it into Eglon's belly. **22** Even the handle went in after the blade, and Eglon's fat closed in over it, so that Ehud did not withdraw the sword from his belly. And the waste came out.[G] **23** Ehud escaped by way of the porch, closing and locking the doors of the upstairs room behind him.

24 Ehud was gone when Eglon's servants came in. They looked and found the doors of the upstairs room locked and thought he was relieving himself[H] in the cool room. **25** The servants waited until they became embarrassed and saw that he had still not opened the doors of the upstairs room. So they took the key and opened the doors — and there was their lord lying dead on the floor!

26 Ehud escaped while the servants waited. He passed the Jordan near the carved images and reached Seirah. **27** After he arrived, he sounded the ram's horn throughout the hill country of Ephraim. The Israelites came down with him from the hill country, and he became their leader. **28** He told them, "Follow me, because the LORD has handed over your enemies, the Moabites, to you." So they followed him, captured the fords of the Jordan leading to Moab, and did not allow anyone

a **3:7** Dt 8:11,14,19; 1Sm 12:9; Jr 3:21
b **3:8** Gn 24:10; Dt 23:3-4; 1Ch 19:6; Ps 60 title
c **3:9** Jdg 3:15; 6:6-7; 10:10
d Jdg 1:13
e Dt 28:29,31; Jdg 6:36; 1Sm 14:39; Is 19:20; 43:11; Hs 13:4
f **3:11** Jdg 3:30; 5:31; 8:28; 2Ch 14:1,5-6
g **3:12** Nm 22:3; Dt 2:8-9; 32:49
h **3:13** Dt 34:3; Jdg 1:16; 2Ch 28:15
i **3:15** Jdg 20:16
j 2Sm 8:2,6; 2Ch 9:24; 17:11

[A] **3:8** Lit *into the hand of*   [B] **3:8** Lit *Doubly-Evil*   [C] **3:8** = Mesopotamia   [D] **3:13** = Jericho; Dt 34:3; Jdg 1:16; 2Ch 28:15   [E] **3:15** = son of the right hand
[F] **3:16** Lit *sword a gomed in length*   [G] **3:22** Or *And Eglon's bowels discharged*   [H] **3:24** Lit *was covering his feet*

3:8-9 "Crying out" speaks of a prayer of desperation (3:9). That's why God let things get so bad in the first place—so that they would come to the end of themselves. Unfortunately, it took them **eight years** to come to their senses (3:8). How long does it take you to cry out to the Lord when experiencing difficulties? **3:9-11** That God raised up **a deliverer to save** them means that he appointed a judge (3:9). A *judge* was basically a civil ruler whom God selected to take vengeance against his enemies.

The Spirit of the LORD came on Othniel to supernaturally enable him to fulfill the task (3:10). He was so successful that **the land had peace for forty years** (3:11). Don't miss that it was the Israelites' desperate cry to God that turned eight years of slavery into forty years of

victory. If you find yourself experiencing year after year of defeat, it's time to cry out to God. **3:12-14** God handed the Israelites to **King Eglon of Moab** (3:12), and he possessed the **City of Palms**, which was Jericho (3:13). They **served** Eglon for **eighteen years** (3:14). So not only were the Israelites being plagued from the Canaanites within their borders, but they were also being picked on by the surrounding nations.

Why wait eighteen years to cry for God's help? Sometimes we can stray so far from God that we're not conscious of how far we've gone or how long we've been gone. We can get so used to being a slave that we don't even look to the divine Deliverer. **3:16** The author of Hebrews describes the living Word of God as being "effective and

sharper than any **double-edged sword"** (Heb 4:12). It will pierce the conscience and the heart, exposing motives and sin, laying its hearers bare to the penetrating gaze of omniscient God.

3:18-30 In this story we see not only that God providentially directed the course of history, but was also involved in the small details. For instance, it was significant that Ehud was left-handed (3:15). It kept the sword on **his right thigh** safe from detection because no one would've expected a sword to be hidden there (3:21). We tend to look for evidence of God at work in the major events and fail to notice how the little things fit together to make major events possible. Keep your eyes open for how God orders minor details before he provides deliverance.

a 3:28 Jdg 12:5-6
b 4:2 Jos 11:1; Ps 83:9
c 1Sm 12:9
d Jdg 5:20-30; 1Sm 12:9;
Ps 83:9
e 4:3 Ex 14:10; Nm 12:13;
Dt 26:7; Ps 34:17
f 4:4 Ex 15:20; 2Kg 22:14;
Neh 6:14; Is 8:3
g 4:5 Nm 35:12; 2Ch 19:8;
Ps 9:4; 76:8-9; Is 3:13-14;
Ezk 44:24
h 4:6 Ex 5:1; Dt 6:4; Ps
41:13
i Jos 19:12,22,34; Ps 89:12
j Gn 30:8; 49:21
k Gn 30:20; 49:13
l 4:7 Jdg 5:21; 1Kg 18:40;
Ps 83:9
m Dt 2:30; Jdg 7:9; 2Sm
5:19; 1Ch 14:10; Is 47:6

n 4:11 Nm 10:29
o Ex 3:1; 4:18; 18:1-27
p Jos 19:33
q 4:15 Ex 14:24; 23:27; Jos
10:10; Ps 18:14; 144:6

to cross over.[a] [29] At that time they struck down about ten thousand Moabites, all stout and able-bodied men. Not one of them escaped. [30] Moab became subject to Israel that day, and the land had peace for eighty years.

SHAMGAR

[31] After Ehud, Shamgar son of Anath became judge. He also delivered Israel, striking down six hundred Philistines with a cattle prod.

DEBORAH AND BARAK

4 The Israelites again did what was evil in the sight of the LORD after Ehud had died. [2] So the LORD sold them to King Jabin[b] of Canaan, who reigned in Hazor.[c] The commander of his army was Sisera[d] who lived in Harosheth of the Nations.[A] [3] Then the Israelites cried out[e] to the LORD, because Jabin had nine hundred iron chariots, and he harshly oppressed them twenty years.

[4] Deborah, a prophetess[f] and the wife of Lappidoth, was judging Israel at that time. [5] She would sit under the palm tree of Deborah between Ramah and Bethel in the hill country of Ephraim, and the Israelites went up to her to settle disputes.[g] [6] She summoned Barak son of Abinoam from Kedesh in Naphtali and said to him, "Hasn't the LORD, the God of Israel,[h] commanded you: 'Go, deploy the troops on Mount Tabor,[i] and take with you ten thousand men from the Naphtalites[j] and Zebulunites?[k] [7] Then I will lure Sisera commander of Jabin's army, his chariots, and his infantry at the Wadi Kishon[l] to fight against you, and I will hand him over to you.' "[m]

[8] Barak said to her, "If you will go with me, I will go. But if you will not go with me, I will not go."

[9] "I will gladly go with you," she said, "but you will receive no honor on the road you are about to take, because the LORD will sell Sisera to a woman." So Deborah got up and went with Barak to Kedesh. [10] Barak summoned Zebulun and Naphtali to Kedesh; ten thousand men followed him, and Deborah also went with him.

[11] Now Heber the Kenite had moved away from the Kenites, the sons of Hobab,[n] Moses's father-in-law,[o] and pitched his tent beside the oak tree of Zaanannim,[p] which was near Kedesh.

[12] It was reported to Sisera that Barak son of Abinoam had gone up Mount Tabor. [13] Sisera summoned all his nine hundred iron chariots and all the troops who were with him from Harosheth of the Nations to the Wadi Kishon. [14] Then Deborah said to Barak, "Go! This is the day the LORD has handed Sisera over to you. Hasn't the LORD gone before you?" So Barak came down from Mount Tabor with ten thousand men following him.

[15] The LORD threw Sisera, all his charioteers, and all his army into a panic[q] before Barak's assault. Sisera left his chariot and fled on foot. [16] Barak pursued the chariots and the army as far as Harosheth of the Nations, and the whole army of Sisera fell by the sword; not a single man was left.

[17] Meanwhile, Sisera had fled on foot to the tent of Jael, the wife of Heber the Kenite, because there was peace between King Jabin of Hazor and the family of Heber the Kenite. [18] Jael went out to greet Sisera and said to him, "Come in, my lord. Come in with me. Don't be afraid." So he went

---

A 4:2 Or *Harosheth-ha-goiim*, also in vv. 13,16

3:31 Likely **Shamgar** was a farmer because his only weapon was **a cattle prod**, a pole with a sharp point on the end used to goad livestock. How do you kill six hundred Philistines with that? Probably gradually and consistently over time. If so, Shamgar was an ordinary man who was dissatisfied with the Philistine oppression and used what he had to do something about it. With God's help, he turned his ordinary cattle prod into something extraordinary.

You don't need extraordinary resources or gifts to be used of the Lord, to make a difference in the culture. You just need to be faithful with what the Lord has given you.

4:4-5 A prophet or **prophetess** communicates God's will about a specific scenario (4:4). He or she tells others how they ought to respond in accordance with God's Word.

4:6-7 Kedesh was a Levitical city (4:6; see Josh 21:1-3, 32), which suggests that Barak was a Levite. Deborah understood that Israel needed spiritual deliverance from their social reality, and it would come in the form of a literal battle.

Through Deborah, God told Barak what he was going to do and what he wanted Barak to do. This brings to mind Paul's insight, which says that we are "working together with [God]" (2 Cor 6:1). God sovereignly works to accomplish his purposes, but he expects our participation. Too often believers are waiting for God to act, when he is actually waiting for us to step up.

4:8-9 In other words, Barak was going to miss out on blessing because he balked at obeying God's command to assume leadership (4:8). Make no mistake: if God can't find the

right man to take care of a task, he will find a good **woman**. Many women have had to act because the men who should have been leading the way chose passivity (4:9).

4:17-21 Soundly defeated, Sisera ran to the tent **of Heber the Kenite**, because Sisera's king, Jabin, was at **peace** with Heber (4:17). Unknown to Sisera, however, Heber's wife Jael had decided to align herself with the Lord and his people. Once he was cozy, Jael **took a tent peg** and **hammered [it] into his temple** (4:21). Jael knew that Sisera and Jabin were wicked enemies of God's people, and she recognized that a wife is not to follow her husband into rebellion against the Lord. When given opportunity to fight back against the enemies of Israel, Jael took action.

into her tent, and she covered him with a blanket. ¹⁹ He said to her, "Please give me a little water to drink for I am thirsty." She opened a container of milk, gave him a drink, and covered him again. ²⁰ Then he said to her, "Stand at the entrance to the tent. If a man comes and asks you, 'Is there a man here?' say, 'No.'" ²¹ While he was sleeping from exhaustion, Heber's wife Jael took a tent peg, grabbed a hammer, and went silently to Sisera. She hammered the peg into his temple and drove it into the ground, and he died.

²² When Barak arrived in pursuit of Sisera, Jael went out to greet him and said to him, "Come and I will show you the man you are looking for." So he went in with her, and there was Sisera lying dead with a tent peg through his temple!

²³ That day God subdued King Jabin of Canaan before the Israelites. ²⁴ The power of the Israelites continued to increase against King Jabin of Canaan until they destroyed him.

DEBORAH'S SONG

5 On that day Deborah and Barak son of Abinoam sang:

² When the leaders lead[A] in Israel,
 when the people volunteer,
 blessed be the LORD.

³ Listen, kings! Pay attention, princes!
 I will sing to the LORD;
 I will sing praise to the LORD God
 of Israel.

⁴ LORD, when you came from Seir,[a]
 when you marched from the fields
 of Edom,
 the earth trembled,[b]
 the skies poured[c] rain,
 and the clouds poured water.

⁵ The mountains melted
 before the LORD,
 even Sinai,[B] before the LORD, the God
 of Israel.[d]

⁶ In the days of Shamgar[e]
 son of Anath,
 in the days of Jael,[f]
 the main roads were deserted

because travelers kept
 to the side roads.

⁷ Villages were deserted,[c]
 they were deserted in Israel,
 until I,[D] Deborah, arose,
 a mother in Israel.

⁸ Israel chose new gods,
 then there was war in the city gates.
 Not a shield or spear was seen
 among forty thousand in Israel.

⁹ My heart is with the leaders
 of Israel,
 with the volunteers of the people.
 Blessed be the LORD!

¹⁰ You who ride on white[c] donkeys,
 who sit on saddle blankets,
 and who travel on the road,
 give praise!

¹¹ Let them tell the righteous acts[g]
 of the LORD,
 the righteous deeds of his warriors
 in Israel,
 with the voices of the singers
 at the watering places.[c]

Then the LORD's people went down
 to the city gates.

¹² "Awake! Awake, Deborah!
 Awake! Awake, sing a song!
 Arise, Barak,
 and take your prisoners,
 son of Abinoam!"

¹³ Then the survivors[h] came down
 to the nobles;[i]
 the LORD's people came down to me[E]
 with the warriors.

¹⁴ Those with their roots in Amalek[F]
 came from Ephraim;
 Benjamin came with your people
 after you.
 The leaders came down
 from Machir,[j]
 and those who carry
 a marshal's staff came
 from Zebulun.

¹⁵ The princes of Issachar were
 with Deborah;
 Issachar was with Barak;
 they were under his leadership[G,k]
 in the valley.

[a] 5:4 Gn 14:6; 36:8-9; Dt 2:1
[b] 2Sm 22:8; Ps 18:7; Is 13:13; Ezk 38:20
[c] Jb 29:22; Ps 68:8; Pr 5:3; Jl 3:18
[d] 5:5 Ex 5:1; Dt 6:4; Ps 41:13
[e] 5:6 Jdg 3:31
[f] Jdg 4:17-22

[g] 5:11 1Sm 12:7; Ps 103:6; Is 45:24; Mc 6:5
[h] 5:13 Nm 21:35; Dt 2:34; Is 1:9
[i] Jdg 5:25; 2Ch 23:20; Neh 3:5; 10:29; Ps 16:3; Jr 14:3; Nah 2:5; 3:18
[j] 5:14 Gn 50:23; Nm 26:29; 32:39-40; Jos 17:1; 2Sm 9:4-5
[k] 5:15 Jdg 4:10

A 5:2 Or *the locks of hair are loose*　B 5:5 Or LORD, *this one of Sinai*　C 5:7,10,11 Hb obscure　D 5:7 Or *you*　E 5:13 LXX reads *down for him*　F 5:14 LXX reads *in the valley*　G 5:15 Lit *they set out as his feet*

4:22 As Deborah had prophesied in 4:9, a woman, Jael, was given credit for Sisera's demise.

4:23-24 As God and Israel worked together, **the power of the Israelites continued to increase** until **they destroyed** Jabin altogether (4:24). God and man working in partnership

against their common enemy is the principle behind spiritual warfare.

5:7 Don't miss that Deborah was **a mother in Israel**. Mothers experience spiritual victory in their unique role of raising children to submit to God's kingdom and battle the forces of darkness in his name. Motherhood is a noble

role through which God works to undermine Satan's work.

5:12-31 After recounting the battle (5:12-23), the song praises **Jael** as the **most blessed of women** (5:24). Though her husband was at peace with Jabin and Sisera (4:17), Jael knew Sisera was the enemy of God's people (5:25-27).

a 5:17 Gn 31:25; Nm 32:40;
Jdg 10:17–11:11
b 5:20–21 Jdg 4:15
c 5:25 Gn 18:8; Dt 32:14;
2Sm 17:29; Jb 20:17; 29:6;
Pr 30:3; Is 7:15,22

d 6:1 Jdg 2:11; 3:7,12; 4:1;
10:6; 13:1
e Jos 11:8; Jdg 11:32; 12:3;
13:1; 1Sm 14:10,12
f 6:2 Jdg 3:10
g 1Sm 23:14,19; 1Ch 11:7; Is
33:16; Jr 48:41
h 6:3 Gn 29:1; 1Kg 4:30;
Is 11:14
i 6:5 Jdg 7:12; Jr 46:23
j 6:6 Jdg 3:9,15; 4:3; 10:10

There was great searching[A] of heart
    among the clans of Reuben.
16 Why did you sit among the sheep
    pens[B]
listening to the playing of pipes
    for the flocks?
There was great searching of heart
    among the clans of Reuben.
17 Gilead[a] remained
    beyond the Jordan.
Dan, why did you linger at the ships?
Asher remained at the seashore
    and stayed in his harbors.
18 The people of Zebulun defied death,
Naphtali also, on the heights
    of the battlefield.

19 Kings came and fought.
Then the kings of Canaan fought
at Taanach by the Waters
    of Megiddo,
but they did not plunder the silver.
20 The stars fought from the heavens;
the stars fought with Sisera
    from their paths.
21 The river Kishon swept them away,[b]
the ancient river, the river Kishon.
March on, my soul, in strength!
22 The horses' hooves then
    hammered —
the galloping, galloping
    of his[c] stallions.
23 "Curse Meroz," says the angel
    of the LORD,
"Bitterly curse her inhabitants,
for they did not come to help
    the LORD,
to help the LORD with the warriors."

24 Jael is most blessed of women,
the wife of Heber the Kenite;
she is most blessed among
    tent-dwelling women.
25 He asked for water; she gave him
    milk.
She brought him cream[c]
    in a majestic bowl.
26 She reached for a tent peg,
her right hand,
    for a workman's hammer.
Then she hammered Sisera —
she crushed his head;
she shattered and pierced
    his temple.

27 He collapsed, he fell, he lay down
    between her feet;
he collapsed, he fell
    between her feet;
where he collapsed, there he fell —
    dead.

28 Sisera's mother looked
    through the window;
she peered through the lattice,
    crying out:
"Why is his chariot so long
    in coming?
Why don't I hear the hoofbeats
    of his horses?"[D]
29 Her wisest princesses answer her;
she even answers herself:[E]
30 "Are they not finding and dividing
    the spoil —
a girl or two[F] for each warrior,
the spoil of colored garments
    for Sisera,
the spoil of an embroidered garment
    or two for my neck?"[G]

31 LORD, may all your enemies perish
    as Sisera did.[H]
But may those who love him
be like the rising of the sun
    in its strength.

And the land had peace for forty years.

MIDIAN OPPRESSES ISRAEL

6 The Israelites did what was evil in the sight of the LORD.[d] So the LORD handed[e] them over to Midian seven years, ² and they oppressed Israel.[f] Because of Midian, the Israelites made hiding places[g] for themselves in the mountains, caves, and strongholds. ³ Whenever the Israelites planted crops, the Midianites, Amalekites, and the Qedemites[h] came and attacked them. ⁴ They encamped against them and destroyed the produce of the land, even as far as Gaza. They left nothing for Israel to eat, as well as no sheep, ox, or donkey. ⁵ For the Midianites came with their cattle and their tents like a great swarm of locusts.[i] They and their camels were without number, and they entered the land to lay waste to it. ⁶ So Israel became poverty-stricken because of Midian, and the Israelites cried out to the LORD.[j]

A 5:15 Some Hb mss, Syr read *There were great resolves* B 5:16 Or *the campfires* C 5:22 = *Sisera's* D 5:28 Lit *Why have the hoofbeats of his chariots delayed* E 5:29 Lit *answers her words* F 5:30 Lit *a womb or two wombs* G 5:30 Hb obscure H 5:31 Lit *perish in this way*

6:1-2 When the Lord **handed [disobedient Israel] over to Midian** (6:1), the oppression grew so bad that they had to hide in **caves** (6:2). This is a reminder that when we stray from the Lord, he will sometimes allow a crisis in our lives to compel our return.

7 When the Israelites cried out to him because of Midian, **8** the LORD sent a prophet[a] to them. He said to them, "This is what the LORD[b] God of Israel says: 'I brought you out of Egypt and out of the place of slavery.[c] **9** I rescued you from the power of Egypt and the power of all who oppressed[d] you. I drove them out before you and gave you their land. **10** I said to you: I am the LORD your God. Do not fear the gods of the Amorites whose land you live in.[e] But you did not obey me.'"

THE LORD CALLS GIDEON

11 The angel of the LORD[f] came, and he sat under the oak that was in Ophrah,[g] which belonged to Joash, the Abiezrite. His son Gideon was threshing wheat in the winepress in order to hide it from the Midianites. **12** Then the angel of the LORD appeared to him and said: "The LORD is with you, valiant warrior."[h]

13 Gideon said to him, "Please, my lord, if the LORD is with us, why has all this happened? And where are all his wonders that our fathers told us about? They said, 'Hasn't the LORD brought us out of Egypt?' But now the LORD has abandoned us and handed us over to Midian."

14 The LORD turned to him and said, "Go in the strength you have and deliver Israel from the grasp of Midian. I am sending you!"[i]

15 He said to him, "Please, Lord, how can I deliver Israel? Look, my family is the weakest in Manasseh, and I am the youngest in my father's family."

16 "But I will be with you,"[j] the LORD said to him. "You will strike Midian down as if it were one man."

17 Then he said to him, "If I have found favor with you,[k] give me a sign[l] that you are speaking with me. **18** Please do not leave this place until I return to you. Let me bring my gift and set it before you."

And he said, "I will stay until you return."

19 So Gideon went and prepared a young goat and unleavened bread from a half bushel[A] of flour. He placed the meat in a basket and the broth in a pot. He brought them out and offered them to him under the oak.

20 The angel of God[m] said to him, "Take the meat with the unleavened bread, put it on this stone, and pour the broth on it." So he did that.

21 The angel of the LORD extended the tip of the staff that was in his hand and touched the meat and the unleavened bread. Fire came up from the rock and consumed the meat and the unleavened bread. Then the angel of the LORD vanished from his sight.

22 When Gideon realized that he was the angel of the LORD, he said, "Oh no, Lord GOD![n] I have seen the angel of the LORD face to face!"[o]

23 But the LORD said to him, "Peace to you. Don't be afraid, for you will not die."

24 So Gideon built an altar to the LORD there and called it The LORD Is Peace.[B] It is still in Ophrah of the Abiezrites today.

GIDEON TEARS DOWN A BAAL ALTAR

25 On that very night the LORD said to him, "Take your father's young bull and a second bull seven years old. Then tear down the altar of Baal[p] that belongs to your father and cut down the Asherah pole beside it. **26** Build a well-constructed altar to the LORD your God on the top of this mound.[q] Take the second bull and offer it as a burnt offering with the wood of the Asherah pole you cut down." **27** So Gideon took ten of his male servants and did as the LORD had told him. But because he was too afraid of his father's family and the men of the city to do it in the daytime, he did it at night.

28 When the men of the city got up in the morning, they found Baal's altar torn down, the Asherah pole beside it cut down,

[a] **6:8** Gn 20:7; Ex 7:1; Nm 11:29; 12:6; Dt 18:15,18,20,22; 34:10
[b] **6:8** Ex 4:22; 5:1; Dt 6:4; Jos 7:13
[c] **6:8** Ex 13:3,14; 20:2; Dt 5:6; 7:8; Jr 34:13; Mc 6:4
[d] **6:9** Ex 3:9; 1Sm 10:18; Ps 106:42
[e] **6:10** Ex 23:24; Dt 7:16; 8:19; 11:16; Jos 24:14
[f] **6:11** Ex 3:2
[g] **6:12** Jos 11:4; 8:3; 2Kg 24:14; 1Ch 12:8
[h] **6:14** Ex 3:10; 1Sm 9:16; 16:1; Jr 1:7; 25:15; Ezk 2:3-4; Mal 4:5; Jn 20:21
[i] **6:16** Gn 26:3; Ex 3:12
[j] **6:17** Gn 6:8; 18:3; Ex 33:12-13; Ru 2:2,10,13; Est 5:8; 7:3
[l] **6:17** Ex 3:12; 1Sm 10:7,9; Is 7:11,14

[m] **6:20** Gn 31:11; Ex 14:19; Jdg 13:6,9; 2Sm 14:17,20; 2Ch 36:16
[n] **6:22** Jos 7:7; Jr 1:6; Ezk 4:14
[o] **6:22** Gn 32:20; Ex 24:10-11; 33:19-23; Jdg 13:21-23; Is 6:5
[p] **6:25** Jdg 2:11,13; 10:6; 1Kg 18:21; 2Ch 33:3; Jr 2:23; Zph 1:4
[q] **6:26** Neh 8:10; Ps 27:1; 37:39; Pr 10:29; Is 17:9-10

[A] **6:19** Lit *an ephah* [B] **6:24** = *Yahweh-shalom*

6:11-12 Normally **wheat** is threshed in a place that catches a breeze so that the chaff is blown away. But Gideon was **threshing wheat in the winepress . . . to hide it from the Midianites** (6:11). That Gideon was going to such lengths to stay out of sight makes it surprising that the heavenly visitor said to him, **The LORD is with you, valiant warrior** (6:12). Indeed, Gideon's success would be dependent on whether or not the Lord was with him. **6:13** Gideon could only see his own circumstances and not the big picture. Yes, God had saved Israel from **Egypt**, but he had saved them *for* a covenant relationship with him. They "did not obey" him (6:10) and were thus suffering the covenant consequences. **6:15-16** God responded to Gideon's feelings of inadequacy just as he had responded to Moses's concerns years prior: **I will be with you** (6:16; see Exod 3:11-12). The key to accomplishing an impossible task is always walking in the presence of God. **6:22-23** Likely in verse 22 Gideon had in mind the Lord's words to Moses, "You cannot see my face, for humans cannot see me and live" (Exod 33:20). But in response to Gideon's fear, the Lord assured him that he would live (Judg 6:23). It's clear, then, that Gideon did not see the full, unshielded expression of God's glory. **6:25-27** It took two bulls and **ten . . . male servants** to tear down the altar (6:25, 27), so it was obviously a major presence on Gideon's father's property. There's a principle at work here: don't expect God to do something *outside* of your home base if you're not willing to get things right *inside* it.

a 6:33 Jos 17:16; 1Sm
29:1,11; 1Kg 21:1
b 6:34 Jdg 3:10; 11:29;
13:25; 14:6,19; 15:14; 1Sm
10:6; 16:13-14

c 7:3 Gn 31:21,23,25;
Dt 3:12
d 7:7 Dt 20:4; Jr 42:11; Ezk
36:29; 37:23; Zch 8:13
e 7:9 Dt 2:30; Jdg 4:7;
20:28; 2Sm 5:19; 1Kg 20:13

and the second bull offered up on the altar that had been built. 29 They said to each other, "Who did this?" After they made a thorough investigation, they said, "Gideon son of Joash did it."

30 Then the men of the city said to Joash, "Bring out your son. He must die, because he tore down Baal's altar and cut down the Asherah pole beside it."

31 But Joash said to all who stood against him, "Would you plead Baal's case for him? Would you save him? Whoever pleads his case will be put to death by morning! If he is a god, let him plead his own case because someone tore down his altar." 32 That day he was called Jerubbaal, since Joash said, "Let Baal contend with him," because he tore down his altar.

THE SIGN OF THE FLEECE

33 All the Midianites, Amalekites, and Qedemites gathered together, crossed over the Jordan, and camped in the Jezreel Valley.a 34 The Spirit of the LORD enveloped^ Gideon,b and he blew the ram's horn and the Abiezrites rallied behind him. 35 He sent messengers throughout all of Manasseh, who rallied behind him. He also sent messengers throughout Asher, Zebulun, and Naphtali, who also came to meet him.

36 Then Gideon said to God, "If you will deliver Israel by my hand, as you said, 37 I will put a wool fleece here on the threshing floor. If dew is only on the fleece, and all the ground is dry, I will know that you will deliver Israel by my strength, as you said." 38 And that is what happened. When he got up early in the morning, he squeezed the fleece and wrung dew out of it, filling a bowl with water. 39 Gideon then said to God, "Don't be angry with me; let me speak one more time. Please allow me to make one more test with the fleece. Let it remain dry, and the dew be all over the ground." 40 That night God did as Gideon requested: only the fleece was dry, and dew was all over the ground.

GOD SELECTS GIDEON'S ARMY

7 Jerubbaal (that is, Gideon) and all the troops who were with him, got up early and camped beside the spring of Harod. The camp of Midian was north of them, below the hill of Moreh, in the valley. 2 The LORD said to Gideon, "You have too many troops for me to hand the Midianites over to them, or else Israel might elevate themselves over me and say,B 'My own strength saved me.' 3 Now announce to the troops: 'Whoever is fearful and trembling may turn back and leave Mount Gilead.' "c So twenty-two thousand of the troops turned back, but ten thousand remained.

4 Then the LORD said to Gideon, "There are still too many troops. Take them down to the water, and I will test them for you there. If I say to you, 'This one can go with you,' he can go. But if I say about anyone, 'This one cannot go with you,' he cannot go." 5 So he brought the troops down to the water, and the LORD said to Gideon, "Separate everyone who laps water with his tongue like a dog. Do the same with everyone who kneels to drink." 6 The number of those who lapped with their hands to their mouths was three hundred men, and all the rest of the troops knelt to drink water. 7 The LORD said to Gideon, "I will deliver youd with the three hundred men who lapped and hand the Midianites over to you. But everyone else is to go home." 8 So Gideon sent all the Israelites to their tents but kept the three hundred troops, who took the provisions and their trumpets. The camp of Midian was below him in the valley.

GIDEON SPIES ON THE MIDIANITE CAMP

9 That night the LORD said to him, "Get up and attack the camp, for I have handed it over to you.e 10 But if you are afraid to attack the camp, go down with Purah your servant. 11 Listen to what they say, and then you will be encouragedc to attack the camp." So he went down with Purah

---

^ 6:34 Lit clothed; 1Ch 12:18; 2Ch 24:20   B 7:2 Lit brag against me   c 7:11 Lit then your hands will be strengthened

---

6:30-32 This scene shows just how rampant idolatry had become in Israel. These people wanted to kill a man who had torn down an idol and erected in its place an altar for the God who had rescued them from Egypt! Perhaps Gideon's father saw the irony in that when he argued that **Baal**, if he was real, didn't need them to fight his battles (6:31). Surely, he said in effect, a god can defend himself. Thus, by God's grace Gideon earned a reputation as **Jerubbaal**, "Baal Fighter" (6:32).

6:37 Gideon was asking God to interrupt the natural order of things with a deviation from the usual. This is the definition of a miracle. 6:38-39 Gideon was like the man who told Jesus, "I do believe; help my unbelief!" (Mark 9:24). Though he'd had a divine visit and God did as Gideon requested (Judg 6:38), that wasn't enough. This time, he asked for the reverse as a sign: dry **fleece** and wet **ground**. (6:39). 7:2-3 In 6:5 the Midianites were said to be "without number" and "like a great swarm of

locusts." So if anything, Gideon probably was hoping for more warriors to join his army. But God was thinking of his own glory and the good of his people. God knew that if Israel fought with superior numbers, they **might elevate themselves over** him and say, **My own strength saved me** (7:2). So, to keep them from proudly trusting in themselves, God reduced their number by more than half (7:3). 7:6-7 Those who **lapped** from their hands were alert to what was happening around them.

his servant to the outpost of the troops[A] who were in the camp.

12 Now the Midianites, Amalekites, and all the Qedemites had settled down in the valley like a swarm of locusts, and their camels were as innumerable as the sand on the seashore. **13** When Gideon arrived, there was a man telling his friend about a dream. He said, "Listen, I had a dream:[a] a loaf of barley bread came tumbling into the Midianite camp, struck a tent, and it fell. The loaf turned the tent upside down so that it collapsed."

14 His friend answered: "This is nothing less than the sword of Gideon son of Joash, the Israelite. God has handed the entire Midianite camp over to him."

GIDEON ATTACKS THE MIDIANITES

15 When Gideon heard the account of the dream and its interpretation, he bowed in worship. He returned to Israel's camp and said, "Get up, for the Lord has handed the Midianite camp over to you." **16** Then he divided the three hundred men into three companies and gave each of the men a trumpet in one hand and an empty pitcher with a torch inside it in the other hand.

17 "Watch me," he said to them, "and do what I do. When I come to the outpost of the camp, do as I do. **18** When I and everyone with me blow our trumpets, you are also to blow your trumpets all around the camp. Then you will say, 'For the Lord and for Gideon!'"

19 Gideon and the hundred men who were with him went to the outpost of the camp at the beginning of the middle watch after the sentries had been stationed. They blew their trumpets and broke the pitchers that were in their hands. **20** The three companies blew their trumpets and shattered their pitchers. They held their torches in their left hands, their trumpets[B] in their right hands, and shouted, "A sword for the Lord and for Gideon!" **21** Each Israelite took his position around the camp, and the entire Midianite army began to run, and they cried out as they fled. **22** When Gideon's men blew their

three hundred trumpets, the Lord caused the men in the whole army to turn on each other with their swords.[b] They fled to Acacia House[c] in the direction of Zererah as far as the border of Abel-meholah[c] near Tabbath. **23** Then the men of Israel were called from Naphtali, Asher, and Manasseh, and they pursued the Midianites.

THE MEN OF EPHRAIM JOIN THE BATTLE

24 Gideon sent messengers throughout the hill country of Ephraim with this message: "Come down to intercept the Midianites and take control of the watercourses ahead of them as far as Beth-barah and the Jordan." So all the men of Ephraim[d] were called out, and they took control of the watercourses as far as Beth-barah and the Jordan. **25** They captured Oreb and Zeeb, the two princes of Midian; they killed Oreb at the rock of Oreb and Zeeb at the winepress of Zeeb, while they were pursuing the Midianites. They brought the heads of Oreb and Zeeb to Gideon across the Jordan.

8 The men of Ephraim said to him, "Why have you done this to us, not calling us when you went to fight against the Midianites?" And they argued with him violently.

2 So he said to them, "What have I done now compared to you? Is not the gleaning[e] of Ephraim better than the grape harvest[f] of Abiezer? **3** God handed over to you Oreb and Zeeb, the two princes of Midian. What was I able to do compared to you?" When he said this, their anger against him subsided.

GIDEON PURSUES THE KINGS OF MIDIAN

4 Gideon and the three hundred men came to the Jordan and crossed it. They were exhausted but still in pursuit. **5** He said to the men of Succoth,[g] "Please give some loaves of bread to the troops under my command,[D] because they are exhausted, for I am pursuing Zebah and Zalmunna, the kings of Midian."

[a]**7:13** Gn 37:5-6,8-10; 40:5,8-9,16; 41; 42:9; Nm 12:6; Dn 1:17

[b]**7:22** 1Sm 14:20
[c]1Kg 4:12; 19:16
[d]**7:24** Jdg 8:3; Ps 83:11; Is 10:26
[e]**8:2** Lv 19:9-10; 23:22; Dt 24:19-20; Ru 2
[f]Lv 26:5; Is 24:13; 32:10; Mc 7:1
[g]**8:5** Gn 33:17; Jos 13:27; 1Kg 7:46; 2Ch 4:17; Ps 60:6

[A]**7:11** Lit *of those who were arranged in companies of 50*   [B]**7:20** Lit *trumpets to blow*   [C]**7:22** Or *Beth-shittah*   [D]**8:5** Lit *troops at my feet*

7:16-25 Gideon **divided the three hundred men into three** groups, and they circled the enemy camp in the middle of the night (7:16; see 7:12). Then each man shattered a clay pitcher, uncovered a torch, blew a trumpet, and shouted, **A sword for the Lord and for Gideon!** (7:20). The noise

startled the Midianites from sleep. They assumed they were being overrun by a superior force. God created such confusion among them that they began fighting one another (7:22).

Midianites were shattered by the power of God working through the people of

God in the midst of dark circumstances. Let the church take notice. Even when we don't understand things and think the odds are against us, God calls us to do what he says—individually and collectively—and then watch him work.

*8:8 Gn 32:31-32; 1Kg
12:25
ᵇ8:11 Nm 32:42

ᶜ8:22 Gn 3:16; 4:7; 37:8
ᵈ8:27 Ex 25:7; 28:12; 39:12;
Jdg 18:14,17-20; 2Sm 6:14;
Hs 3:4
ᵉ8:28 Jdg 3:11; 5:31
ᶠ8:31 Gn 12:6; 37:12-14; Jos
21:22; Ps 60:6; 108:7

6 But the princes of Succoth asked, "Are^A Zebah and Zalmunna now in your hands that we should give bread to your army?" **7** Gideon replied, "Very well, when the LORD has handed Zebah and Zalmunna over to me, I will tear^B your flesh with thorns and briers from the wilderness!" **8** He went from there to Penuel and asked the same thing from them. The men of Penuel*a* answered just as the men of Succoth had answered. **9** He also told the men of Penuel, "When I return safely, I will tear down this tower!"

10 Now Zebah and Zalmunna were in Karkor, and with them was their army of about fifteen thousand men, who were all those left of the entire army of the Qedemites. Those who had been killed were one hundred twenty thousand armed men.^C **11** Gideon traveled on the caravan route^D east of Nobah*b* and Jogbehah and attacked their army while the army felt secure. **12** Zebah and Zalmunna fled, and he pursued them. He captured these two kings of Midian and routed the entire army.

13 Gideon son of Joash returned from the battle by the Ascent of Heres. **14** He captured a youth from the men of Succoth and interrogated him. The youth wrote down for him the names of the seventy-seven leaders and elders of Succoth. **15** Then he went to the men of Succoth and said, "Here are Zebah and Zalmunna. You taunted me about them, saying, 'Are Zebah and Zalmunna now in your power that we should give bread to your exhausted men?'" **16** So he took the elders of the city, and he took some thorns and briers from the wilderness, and he disciplined the men of Succoth with them. **17** He also tore down the tower of Penuel and killed the men of the city.

18 He asked Zebah and Zalmunna, "What kind of men did you kill at Tabor?"

"They were like you," they said. "Each resembled the son of a king."

19 So he said, "They were my brothers, the sons of my mother! As the LORD lives, if you had let them live, I would not kill you." **20** Then he said to Jether, his firstborn, "Get up and kill them." The youth did not draw his sword, for he was afraid because he was still a youth.

21 Zebah and Zalmunna said, "Get up and strike us down yourself, for a man is judged by his strength." So Gideon got up, killed Zebah and Zalmunna, and took the crescent ornaments that were on the necks of their camels.

GIDEON'S LEGACY

22 Then the Israelites said to Gideon, "Rule over us,^C you as well as your sons and your grandsons, for you delivered us from the power of Midian."

23 But Gideon said to them, "I will not rule over you, and my son will not rule over you; the LORD will rule over you." **24** Then he said to them, "Let me make a request of you: Everyone give me an earring from his plunder." Now the enemy had gold earrings because they were Ishmaelites.

25 They said, "We agree to give them." So they spread out a cloak, and everyone threw an earring from his plunder on it. **26** The weight of the gold earrings he requested was forty-three pounds^E of gold, in addition to the crescent ornaments and ear pendants, the purple garments on the kings of Midian, and the chains on the necks of their camels. **27** Gideon made an ephod*d* from all this and put it in Ophrah, his hometown. Then all Israel prostituted themselves by worshiping it there, and it became a snare to Gideon and his household.

28 So Midian was subdued before the Israelites, and they were no longer a threat.^F The land had peace for forty years*e* during the days of Gideon. **29** Jerubbaal (that is, Gideon) son of Joash went back to live at his house.

30 Gideon had seventy sons, his own offspring, since he had many wives. **31** His concubine who was in Shechem*f* also bore

^A 8:6 Lit *Are the hands of*, also in v. 15   ^B 8:7 Lit *thresh*   ^C 8:10 Lit *men who drew the sword*   ^D 8:11 Lit *on the route of those who live in tents*
^E 8:26 Lit *1,700 shekels*   ^F 8:28 Lit *they no longer raised their head*

8:16-17 Neither the leaders of **Succoth** nor the men **of Penuel** had been willing to join *their kinsmen Gideon* in siding against God's enemies through supplying his men with provisions (see 8:4-9).
8:22 Gideon was already the deliverer God provided, but the Israelites wanted more: they wanted a king. But God didn't want them to have a monarchy until they had learned to live under him. When men do not know how to be ruled properly under God, they are willing to be ruled improperly by man—who sometimes will seek to become a god.
8:24-27 An ephod was a priestly article that fit like a vest. There was only one official ephod; it was to be used only by a Levitical priest in the tabernacle (see Exod 28:6-14). Thus, Gideon chose to make something that he shouldn't have to use in a place where such a thing didn't belong. In doing so, he assumed an illegitimate position of religious authority that had not been assigned to him. And as the Israelites looked to him in his ephod to be a spiritual guide, they were unfaithful to God's program.
8:30-31 Whenever you see polygamy in the Bible, you've got a messy situation that contrasts with God's stated design for marriage (see Gen 2:23-24). As if Gideon's **many wives** aren't alarming enough (8:30), he also had a

him a son, and he named him Abimelech. ³² Then Gideon son of Joash died at a good old age and was buried in the tomb of his father Joash in Ophrah of the Abiezrites.

³³ When Gideon died, the Israelites turned and prostituted[a] themselves by worshiping the Baals and made Baal-berith[A] their god. ³⁴ The Israelites did not remember the LORD their God[b] who had rescued them from the hand of the enemies around them. ³⁵ They did not show kindness[c] to the house of Jerubbaal (that is, Gideon) for all the good he had done for Israel.

ABIMELECH BECOMES KING

9 Abimelech son of Jerubbaal went to Shechem and spoke to his uncles and to his mother's whole clan, saying, ² "Please speak in the hearing of all the citizens of Shechem, 'Is it better for you that seventy men, all the sons of Jerubbaal,[d] rule over you or that one man rule over you?' Remember that I am your own flesh and blood."[B]

³ His mother's relatives spoke all these words about him in the hearing of all the citizens of Shechem, and they were favorable to Abimelech, for they said, "He is our brother." ⁴ So they gave him seventy pieces of silver from the temple of Baal-berith.[A] Abimelech used it to hire worthless and reckless men, and they followed him. ⁵ He went to his father's house in Ophrah and killed his seventy brothers, the sons of Jerubbaal, on top of a large stone. But Jotham, the youngest son of Jerubbaal, survived, because he hid. ⁶ Then all the citizens of Shechem and of Beth-millo gathered together and proceeded to make Abimelech king at the oak of the pillar in Shechem.

JOTHAM'S PARABLE

⁷ When they told Jotham, he climbed to the top of Mount Gerizim,[e] raised his voice, and called to them:

Listen to me, citizens of Shechem,
and may God listen to you:

⁸ The trees decided
to anoint a king over themselves.
They said to the olive tree,
"Reign over us."
⁹ But the olive tree said to them,
"Should I stop giving my oil
that people use to honor both God
and men,
and rule[c] over the trees?"

¹⁰ Then the trees said to the fig tree,
"Come and reign over us."
¹¹ But the fig tree said to them,
"Should I stop giving
my sweetness and my good fruit,
and rule over trees?"

¹² Later, the trees said to the grapevine,
"Come and reign over us."
¹³ But the grapevine said to them,
"Should I stop giving my wine
that cheers both God and man,
and rule over trees?"

¹⁴ Finally, all the trees said
to the bramble,
"Come and reign over us."
¹⁵ The bramble said to the trees,
"If you really are anointing me
as king over you,
come and find refuge in my shade.
But if not,
may fire come out from the bramble
and consume the cedars
of Lebanon."

a8:33 Ex 34:15-16; Dt 31:16; 2Ch 21:13; Is 23:17; Jr 3:6,8; Ezk 16:15-17,26-28; Hs 4:12
b8:34 Gn 40:23; Ex 23:13; Jos 23:7; Is 17:10; 57:11; Zch 13:2
c8:35 Gn 24:12,49; Ex 20:6; 2Sm 22:51; Ps 18:50
d9:2 Jdg 6:32

e9:7 Dt 11:29; 27:12; Jos 8:33

A8:33; 9:4 Lit *Baal of the Covenant*, or *Lord of the Covenant*   B9:2 Lit *your bone and your flesh*   C9:9 Lit *and go to sway*, also in vv. 11,13

---

concubine (that's a mistress); and he named their son **Abimelech**, which means—get ready for this—"My Father Is King" (8:31). It seems that the power Gideon got from acting like a priest had gone to his head, and he was setting the stage for a dynasty. That's just the kind of overreach that can happen when someone is given unlimited power without accountability.
8:33-35 Sadly, the Israelites started worshiping **Baal-berith**, "Baal of the covenant" (8:33). In other words, they were practicing religious syncretism, trying to merge the worship of Baal with the idea of God's covenant with them. This is much like what happened when a previous generation made a golden-calf idol and called it the one who brought Israel up from Egypt (see Exod 32:4-5).

9:1-6 Gideon's son **Abimelech**, having aspirations to rule, decided to get rid of Gideon's other **seventy** sons—the competition (9:1-2). He hired **worthless . . . men** to kill all of them—though one escaped (9:4-5). Don't miss that this deed was carried out **on top of a large stone** (9:5). Since such stones were used as altars, we are to understand that this was human sacrifice. The man literally sacrificed his family for political power. And the local citizens **proceeded to make** him their **king** (9:6)!
9:7-21 Gideon's youngest son, **Jotham**, who had escaped the slaughter, stood on **Mount Gerizim**, the place of blessing (see Deut 11:29), when he received the news that Abimelech had been named king (Judg 9:7). He

told the people a parable about how the trees were looking for a leader to rule over them. Finally, in their desperation to be ruled, the trees asked the **bramble**—a thorn bush—to lead them (9:14). Importantly, the bramble is unproductive and is a symbol of the curse (see Gen 3:18). To be called a bramble was no compliment; to have put one in leadership was stupid.

The bramble effectively said, "If you don't let me rule over you like I want, I will destroy you" (Judg 9:15). That was Jotham's warning that Abimelech planned to rule the people with totalitarian authority, which is an illegitimate use of rule, biblically speaking. He wouldn't share power with God; he'd simply destroy anyone who opposed him.

ᵃ 9:16 1Sm 12:24; 1Kg 2:4;
Ps 111:8; Pr 29:14; Jr 32:41
ᵇ Jos 24:14; Ps 84:11
ᶜ 9:23 1Sm 16:14-23; 18:10-
12; 19:9; 2Kg 19:7
ᵈ 9:25 Jos 8:2; 1Sm 15:5;
2Ch 20:22; Ezr 8:31; Ps
10:9; Pr 1:11; Jr 9:8
ᵉ 9:27 Lv 19:24; Jdg
21:20-21
ᶠ 9:28 Gn 33:19; 34:2-26;
Jos 24:32

ᵍ 9:37 Ezk 38:12
ʰ 9:40 1Sm 17:52; 2Ch
13:17; Ezk 6:4,7; Dn 11:26

16 "Now if you have acted faithfully[a] and honestly[b] in making Abimelech king, if you have done well by Jerubbaal and his family, and if you have rewarded him appropriately for what he did — 17 for my father fought for you, risked his life, and rescued you from Midian, 18 and now you have attacked my father's family today, killed his seventy sons on top of a large stone, and made Abimelech, the son of his slave woman, king over the citizens of Shechem 'because he is your brother' — 19 so if you have acted faithfully and honestly with Jerubbaal and his house this day, rejoice in Abimelech and may he also rejoice in you. 20 But if not, may fire come from Abimelech and consume the citizens of Shechem and Beth-millo, and may fire come from the citizens of Shechem and Beth-millo and consume Abimelech." 21 Then Jotham fled, escaping to Beer, and lived there because of his brother Abimelech.

ABIMELECH'S PUNISHMENT

22 When Abimelech had ruled over Israel three years, 23 God sent an evil spirit[c] between Abimelech and the citizens of Shechem. They treated Abimelech deceitfully, 24 so that the crime against the seventy sons of Jerubbaal might come to justice and their blood would be avenged on their brother Abimelech, who killed them, and on the citizens of Shechem, who had helped him[A] kill his brothers. 25 The citizens of Shechem rebelled against him by putting men in ambush[d] on the tops of the mountains, and they robbed everyone who passed by them on the road. So this was reported to Abimelech.

26 Gaal son of Ebed came with his brothers and crossed into Shechem, and the citizens of Shechem trusted him. 27 So they went out to the countryside and harvested grapes from their vineyards. They trampled the grapes and held a celebration.[e] Then they went to the house of their god, and as they ate and drank, they cursed Abimelech. 28 Gaal son of Ebed said, "Who is Abimelech and who is Shechem that we should serve him? Isn't he the son of Jerubbaal, and isn't Zebul his officer? You are to serve the men of Hamor, the father of Shechem.[f] Why should we serve Abimelech? 29 If only these people were in my power, I would remove Abimelech." So he

said[B] to Abimelech, "Gather your army and come out."

30 When Zebul, the ruler of the city, heard the words of Gaal son of Ebed, he was angry. 31 So he secretly sent messengers to Abimelech, saying, "Beware! Gaal son of Ebed, with his brothers, have come to Shechem and are turning the city against you.[c] 32 Now tonight, you and the troops with you, come and wait in ambush in the countryside. 33 Then get up early, and at sunrise attack the city. When he and the troops who are with him come out against you, do to him whatever you can." 34 So Abimelech and all the troops with him got up at night and waited in ambush for Shechem in four units.

35 Gaal son of Ebed went out and stood at the entrance of the city gate. Then Abimelech and the troops who were with him got up from their ambush. 36 When Gaal saw the troops, he said to Zebul, "Look, troops are coming down from the mountaintops!" But Zebul said to him, "The shadows of the mountains look like men to you."

37 Then Gaal spoke again, "Look, troops are coming down from the central part of the land,[g] and one unit is coming from the direction of the Diviners' Oak." 38 Zebul replied, "What do you have to say now? You said, 'Who is Abimelech that we should serve him?' Aren't these the troops you despised? Now go and fight them!"

39 So Gaal went out leading the citizens of Shechem and fought against Abimelech, 40 but Abimelech pursued him, and Gaal fled before him. Numerous bodies were strewn[h] as far as the entrance of the city gate. 41 Abimelech stayed in Arumah, and Zebul drove Gaal and his brothers from Shechem.

42 The next day when the people of Shechem[D] went into the countryside, this was reported to Abimelech. 43 He took the troops, divided them into three companies, and waited in ambush in the countryside. He looked, and the people were coming out of the city, so he arose against them and struck them down. 44 Then Abimelech and the units that were with him rushed forward and took their stand at the entrance of the city gate. The other two units rushed against all who were in the countryside and struck them down. 45 So Abimelech

---

ᴬ 9:24 Lit had strengthened his hands   ᴮ 9:29 DSS read They said; LXX reads I would say   ᶜ 9:31 Hb obscure   ᴰ 9:42 of Shechem supplied for clarity

---

9:23 Notice who did the action. God and the devil do not battle as equals. God is sovereign; Satan is not. God can use the devil to mess up a situation that is offensive to his will.

fought against the city that entire day, captured it, and killed the people who were in it. Then he tore down the city and sowed it with salt.[a]

46 When all the citizens of the Tower of Shechem heard, they entered the inner chamber[A] of the temple of El-berith.[B] **47** Then it was reported to Abimelech that all the citizens of the Tower of Shechem had gathered. **48** So Abimelech and all the troops who were with him went up to Mount Zalmon. Abimelech took his ax in his hand and cut a branch from the trees. He picked up the branch, put it on his shoulder, and said to the troops who were with him, "Hurry and do what you have seen me do." **49** Each of the troops also cut his own branch and followed Abimelech. They put the branches against the inner chamber and set it on fire; about a thousand men and women died, including all the men of the Tower of Shechem.

50 Abimelech went to Thebez,[b] camped against it, and captured it. **51** There was a strong tower inside the city,[c] and all the men, women, and citizens of the city fled there. They locked themselves in and went up to the roof of the tower. **52** When Abimelech came to attack the tower, he approached its entrance to set it on fire. **53** But a woman threw the upper portion of a millstone on Abimelech's head and fractured his skull. **54** He quickly called his armor-bearer and said to him, "Draw your sword and kill me, or they'll say about me, 'A woman killed him.'" So his armor-bearer ran him through, and he died. **55** When the Israelites saw that Abimelech was dead, they all went home.

56 In this way, God brought back Abimelech's evil—the evil that Abimelech had done to his father when he killed his seventy brothers. **57** God also brought back to the men of Shechem all their evil.[d] So the curse of Jotham son of Jerubbaal came upon them.[e]

TOLA AND JAIR

10 After Abimelech, Tola son of Puah, son of Dodo became judge and began to deliver Israel. He was from Issachar and lived in Shamir in the hill country of Ephraim. **2** Tola judged Israel twenty-three years and when he died, was buried in Shamir.

3 After him came Jair the Gileadite,[f] who judged Israel twenty-two years. **4** He had thirty sons who rode on thirty donkeys. They had thirty towns[c] in Gilead, which are still called Jair's Villages[D] today. **5** When Jair died, he was buried in Kamon.

ISRAEL'S REBELLION AND REPENTANCE

6 Then the Israelites again did what was evil in the sight of the LORD.[g] They worshiped the Baals and the Ashtoreths, the gods of Aram, Sidon, and Moab, and the gods of the Ammonites and the Philistines.[h] They abandoned the LORD and did not worship him.[i] **7** So the LORD's anger burned against Israel, and he sold them to[E] the Philistines and the Ammonites.[j] **8** They shattered and crushed the Israelites that year, and for eighteen years they did the same to all the Israelites who were on the other side of the Jordan[k] in the land of the Amorites[l] in Gilead. **9** The Ammonites also crossed the Jordan to fight against Judah, Benjamin, and the house of Ephraim. Israel was greatly oppressed, **10** so they cried out to the LORD, saying, "We have sinned against you.[m] We have abandoned our God and worshiped the Baals."

11 The LORD said to the Israelites, "When the Egyptians,[n] Amorites, Ammonites, Philistines, **12** Sidonians, Amalekites, and Maonites[f,o] oppressed you, and you cried out to me, did I not deliver you from them? **13** But you have abandoned me and worshiped other gods. Therefore, I will not deliver you again. **14** Go and cry out to the gods you have chosen.[p] Let them deliver you whenever you are oppressed."

[a] 9:45 Dt 29:23; Ezk 47:11; Zph 2:9
[b] 9:50 2Sm 11:21
[c] 9:51 Ps 61:3; Pr 18:10
[d] 9:57 Jos 2:19; 1Sm 25:39; 1Kg 2:37,44; 8:32; 2Ch 6:23; Ps 7:16; Ezk 9:10; 11:21; 17:19; 22:31; 33:4; Jl 3:4; Ob 15
[e] Jdg 9:20

[f] 10:3 Nm 26:29-30; Jos 17:1,3; Jdg 11:1-2; 1Ch 2:12-24; 7:14-17
[g] 10:6 Jdg 3:12; 4:1
[h] 1Kg 11:33
[i] Ex 20:5; 23:24; Dt 5:9; Jos 23:7; 2Kg 17:35; Neh 9:35; Is 60:12; Mal 3:18
[j] 10:7 Jdg 2:14; 3:8
[k] 10:8 Gn 50:10-11; Dt 1:1,5; 3:8,20,25; Jos 12:17; Jdg 5:17
[l] Nm 21:31; Jos 24:8; Jdg 11:21; Am 2:10
[m] 10:10 Neh 1:6; Jr 14:20; Dn 9:8
[n] 10:11 Ex 1-15
[o] 10:12 Jos 15:5; 1Sm 23:24-25
[p] 10:14 Dt 32:37-38; Jr 2:28; 11:12

[A] **9:46** Or *the crypt,* or *the vault*   [B] **9:46** = God of the Covenant   [C] **10:4** LXX; MT reads *donkeys*   [D] **10:4** Or *called Havvoth-jair*   [E] **10:7** Lit *into the hand of*   [F] **10:12** LXX reads *Midianites*

9:46-49 The leaders of Shechem holed up in the **temple of El-berith**, meaning "God of the Covenant," because they thought the god of their syncretic religion would protect them. When Abimelech set **fire** to the temple and everyone died, there could be no doubt that this so-called deity was powerless (9:46, 49). Thus, Jotham's curse: "May fire come from Abimelech and consume the citizens of Shechem" (9:20) was fulfilled.

9:50-55 As the people of **Thebez** huddled on the roof of their tower for protection against invasion, Abimelech attacked (9:50-52). A **woman** above him **threw the upper portion of a millstone on Abimelech's head** (9:53). As Abimelech realized the severity of his injuries, he called on his right hand man to kill him so that people could not say that he had been killed by a girl. Though his armor-bearer obeyed, Scripture reports the truth of his embarrassing end.

9:56-57 Righteous **Jotham** had gone to the place of blessing and called on God to show justice, and—in his perfect timing—God dealt with the situation (see 9:7, 16-20).

10:6-7 At work here is a sobering spiritual principle. If you demand to worship false gods, God will eventually let you be ruled by your preferences.

10:11-14 If God is finished with you, then where will you appeal in an oppressive situation? If the people were honest with

a 10:15 1Sm 12:10; 1Ch 16:35; Ps 79:9

b 10:16 Gn 35:2; Jos 24:33; 1Sm 7:3; 2Ch 33:15

c Ex 10:7-8; 12:31; Dt 10:12; Jos 24:14-15; 2Ch 30:8

d Nm 21:4; Jdg 16:16; Mc 2:7; Zch 11:8

e 10:17 Gn 31:49; Jdg 11:11,34; Hs 5:1

f 11:1 1Sm 12:11; Heb 11:32

g Jdg 6:12; Ru 2:1; 1Sm 9:1; 16:18; 1Kg 11:28; 2Kg 5:1

h 11:3 2Sm 10:6,8

i 11:13 Nm 21:24; Dt 2:37; 3:16

j 11:17 Nm 20:14-21

k 11:19 Nm 21:25,28,30,34; Dt 3:2,6; Neh 9:22; Is 15:4

l 11:21 Nm 21:24; Dt 4:47; Jos 12:1; Jdg 1:19

15 But the Israelites said, "We have sinned. Deal with us as you see fit;[A] only rescue us[a] today!" **16** So they got rid of the foreign gods[b] among them and worshiped the LORD,[c] and he became weary[d] of Israel's misery.

17 The Ammonites were called together, and they camped in Gilead. So the Israelites assembled and camped at Mizpah.[e] **18** The rulers[B] of Gilead said to one another, "Which man will begin the fight against the Ammonites? He will be the leader of all the inhabitants of Gilead."

JEPHTHAH BECOMES ISRAEL'S LEADER

11 Jephthah[f] the Gileadite was a valiant warrior,[g] but he was the son of a prostitute, and Gilead was his father. **2** Gilead's wife bore him sons, and when they grew up, they drove Jephthah out and said to him, "You will have no inheritance in our father's family, because you are the son of another woman." **3** So Jephthah fled from his brothers and lived in the land of Tob.[h] Then some worthless men joined Jephthah and went on raids with him.

4 Some time later, the Ammonites fought against Israel. **5** When the Ammonites made war with Israel, the elders of Gilead went to get Jephthah from the land of Tob. **6** They said to him, "Come, be our commander, and let's fight the Ammonites."

7 Jephthah replied to the elders of Gilead, "Didn't you hate me and drive me out of my father's family? Why then have you come to me now when you're in trouble?"

8 They answered Jephthah, "That's true. But now we turn to you. Come with us, fight the Ammonites, and you will become leader of all the inhabitants of Gilead."

9 So Jephthah said to them, "If you are bringing me back to fight the Ammonites and the LORD gives them to me, I will be your leader."

10 The elders of Gilead said to Jephthah, "The LORD is our witness if we don't do as you say." **11** So Jephthah went with the elders of Gilead. The people made him their leader and commander, and Jephthah repeated all his terms in the presence of the LORD at Mizpah.

JEPHTHAH REJECTS AMMONITE CLAIMS

12 Jephthah sent messengers to the king of the Ammonites, asking, "What do you have against me that you have come to fight me in my land?"

13 The king of the Ammonites said to Jephthah's messengers, "When Israel came from Egypt, they seized my land from the Arnon to the Jabbok[i] and the Jordan. Now restore it peaceably."

14 Jephthah again sent messengers to the king of the Ammonites **15** to tell him, "This is what Jephthah says: Israel did not take away the land of Moab or the land of the Ammonites. **16** But when they came from Egypt, Israel traveled through the wilderness to the Red Sea and came to Kadesh. **17** Israel sent messengers to the king of Edom, saying, 'Please let us travel through your land,' but the king of Edom would not listen. They also sent messengers to the king of Moab, but he refused. So Israel stayed in Kadesh.[j]

18 "Then they traveled through the wilderness and around the lands of Edom and Moab. They came to the east side of the land of Moab and camped on the other side of the Arnon but did not enter into the territory of Moab, for the Arnon was the boundary of Moab.

19 "Then Israel sent messengers to Sihon king of the Amorites, king of Heshbon.[k] Israel said to him, 'Please let us travel through your land to our country,' **20** but Sihon would not trust Israel to pass through his territory. Instead, Sihon gathered all his troops, camped at Jahaz, and fought with Israel. **21** Then the LORD God of Israel handed over Sihon and all his troops to Israel, and they defeated them. So Israel took possession[l] of the entire land of the Amorites who lived in that country. **22** They took possession of all the territory of the Amorites from the Arnon to the Jabbok and from the wilderness to the Jordan.

A **10:15** Lit *Do to us what is good in your eyes*   B **10:18** Lit *The people, rulers*

---

themselves, there was no one else to whom they could go.

10:15-16 When Israel said in effect, "We've sinned, please deliver us," *and* they got rid of their gods (10:16), God was willing to act on their behalf (10:16). When our actions realign us with God's will, doors of blessing can open to us that were previously closed.

11:1 Why did the author tell us this detail about Jephthah's mother? Because as the man's story unfolds, we'll see that your background doesn't determine your usefulness to God. Rahab the harlot, for instance, cast herself on the mercy of the Lord and ended up being in the lineage of Jesus Christ (see Josh 2:1; 6:22-23; Matt 1:5).

11:14-23 Jephthah set the record straight (see 11:13-14). When Israel asked to pass through the same general area when they came out of Egypt (11:19), **Sihon** wouldn't let them and attacked Israel instead (11:20). So the Lord helped Israel defeat Sihon's people and gave them their land (11:21-23).

²³ "The LORD God of Israel has now driven out the Amorites before his people Israel, and will you now force us out? ²⁴ Isn't it true that you can have whatever your god Chemosh conquers for you, and we can have whatever the LORD our God conquers for us? ²⁵ Now are you any better than Balak son of Zippor, king of Moab? Did he ever contend with Israel or fight against them? ²⁶ While Israel lived three hundred years in Heshbon and Aroer and their surrounding villages, and in all the cities that are on the banks of the Arnon, why didn't you take them back at that time? ²⁷ I have not sinned against you, but you are doing me wrong by fighting against me. Let the LORD who is the judge[a] decide today between the Israelites and the Ammonites." ²⁸ But the king of the Ammonites would not listen to Jephthah's message that he sent him.

JEPHTHAH'S VOW AND SACRIFICE

²⁹ The Spirit of the LORD came on Jephthah, who traveled through Gilead and Manasseh, and then through Mizpah of Gilead. He crossed over to the Ammonites from Mizpah of Gilead. ³⁰ Jephthah made this vow[b] to the LORD: "If you in fact hand over the Ammonites to me, ³¹ whoever comes out the doors of my house to greet me when I return safely from the Ammonites will belong to the LORD, and I will offer that person as a burnt offering."[c]

³² Jephthah crossed over to the Ammonites to fight against them, and the LORD handed them over[d] to him. ³³ He defeated twenty of their cities with a great slaughter from Aroer all the way to the entrance of Minnith and to Abel-keramim. So the Ammonites were subdued[e] before the Israelites.

³⁴ When Jephthah went to his home in Mizpah, there was his daughter, coming out to meet him with tambourines and dancing![f] She was his only child; he had no other son or daughter besides her. ³⁵ When he saw her, he tore his clothes and said, "No! Not my daughter! You have devastated me! You have brought great misery on

me.[A] I have given my word to the LORD and cannot take it back."

³⁶ Then she said to him, "My father, you have given your word to the LORD. Do to me as you have said, for the LORD brought vengeance on your enemies, the Ammonites." ³⁷ She also said to her father, "Let me do this one thing: Let me wander two months through the mountains with my friends and mourn my virginity."

³⁸ "Go," he said. And he sent her away two months. So she left with her friends and mourned her virginity as she wandered through the mountains. ³⁹ At the end of two months, she returned to her father, and he kept the vow he had made about her. And she had never been intimate with a man. Now it became a custom in Israel ⁴⁰ that four days each year the young women of Israel would commemorate the daughter of Jephthah the Gileadite.

CONFLICT WITH EPHRAIM

12 The men of Ephraim were called together and crossed the Jordan to Zaphon.[g] They said to Jephthah, "Why have you crossed over to fight against the Ammonites but didn't call us to go with you? We will burn your house with you in it!"

² Then Jephthah said to them, "My people and I had a bitter conflict with the Ammonites. So I called for you, but you didn't deliver me from their power. ³ When I saw that you weren't going to deliver me, I took my life in my own hands and crossed over to the Ammonites, and the LORD handed them over to me. Why then have you come today to fight against me?"

⁴ Then Jephthah gathered all of the men of Gilead. They fought and defeated Ephraim, because Ephraim had said, "You Gileadites are Ephraimite fugitives in the territories of Ephraim and Manasseh." ⁵ The Gileadites captured the fords of the Jordan leading to Ephraim. Whenever a fugitive from Ephraim said, "Let me cross over," the Gileadites asked him, "Are you an Ephraimite?" If he answered, "No," ⁶ they told him, "Please say Shibboleth." If he said, "Sibboleth," because he could not

11:27 Gn 18:25; Jb 9:15; 23:7; Ps 7:11; 50:6; 75:7; Is 33:22
[b] **11:30** Gn 28:20; Nm 30:2; 1Sm 1:11
[c] **11:31** Ps 66:13
[d] **11:32** Jdg 12:3; 1Sm 14:10
[e] **11:33** Lv 26:41; Jdg 3:30; 8:28; 1Sm 7:13; 1Ch 20:4; 2Ch 13:18; Ps 106:42
[f] **11:34** Ex 15:20; 32:19; Jdg 21:21; Sg 6:13

[g] **12:1** Jos 13:27

[A] **11:35** Lit *have been among those who trouble me*

11:34-37 As a result of her father's vow (11:30-31), the girl would not be able to marry and have a family. Thus, when Jephthah's daughter, his only offspring, came out of his house to meet him, any dynasty plans he had were thwarted.
12:1-6 The men of Ephraim were upset because they hadn't been called into the

battle right away (12:1; see 8:1). The dispute resulted in Israel's tribes fighting each other. And ultimately, **forty-two thousand** were killed because of wounded pride (12:6).
Pride means thinking more of yourself than you ought, and it's the very thing that led to Satan's fall. He wanted to be like

God—that is, he wanted to be more than he was created to be (see Ezek 28:14-17). To battle against pride successfully, you must remember that (1) God hates pride and (2) you're not him.

a **12:8** Gn 35:19; Ru 1:1-2; Mc 5:2
b **12:13** 2Sm 23:30; 1Ch 11:31; 27:14
c **12:15** Gn 14:7; Nm 14:45; 2Sm 1:8,13
d **13:1** Jdg 3:12; 4:1; 10:6
e **13:2** Jos 19:42; Jdg 13:25; 16:31; 18:2,8,11
f **13:4** Nm 6:3
g Lv 7:19,21; 22:8; Dt 12:22; 14:10; 15:22; Hs 9:3-4
h **13:5** Nm 6:2
i **13:8** Gn 25:21; Ex 10:18; Jb 33:26
j **13:9** Gn 16:11; Ex 16:8; Dt 1:45; 33:7; Jos 10:14; Ps 27:7
k **13:15** Gn 18:5

pronounce it correctly, they seized him and executed him at the fords of the Jordan. At that time forty-two thousand from Ephraim died.

7 Jephthah judged Israel six years, and when he died, he was buried in one of the cities of Gilead.^A

IBZAN, ELON, AND ABDON

8 Ibzan, who was from Bethlehem,^a judged Israel after Jephthah **9** and had thirty sons. He gave his thirty daughters in marriage to men outside the tribe and brought back thirty wives for his sons from outside the tribe. Ibzan judged Israel seven years, **10** and when he died, he was buried in Bethlehem.

11 Elon, who was from Zebulun, judged Israel after Ibzan. He judged Israel ten years, **12** and when he died, he was buried in Aijalon in the land of Zebulun.

13 After Elon, Abdon son of Hillel, who was from Pirathon,^b judged Israel. **14** He had forty sons and thirty grandsons, who rode on seventy donkeys. Abdon judged Israel eight years, **15** and when he died, he was buried in Pirathon in the land of Ephraim, in the hill country of the Amalekites.^c

BIRTH OF SAMSON

13 The Israelites again did what was evil in the LORD's sight,^d so the LORD handed them over to the Philistines forty years. **2** There was a certain man from Zorah,^e from the family of Dan, whose name was Manoah; his wife was unable to conceive and had no children. **3** The angel of the LORD appeared to the woman and said to her, "It is true that you are unable to conceive and have no children, but you will conceive and give birth to a son. **4** Now please be careful not to drink wine or beer,^f or to eat anything unclean;^g **5** for indeed, you will conceive and give birth

to a son. You must never cut his hair,^B because the boy will be a Nazirite^h to God from birth, and he will begin to save Israel from the power of the Philistines."

6 Then the woman went and told her husband, "A man of God came to me. He looked like the awe-inspiring angel of God. I didn't ask him where he came from, and he didn't tell me his name. **7** He said to me, 'You will conceive and give birth to a son. Therefore, do not drink wine or beer, and do not eat anything unclean, because the boy will be a Nazirite to God from birth until the day of his death.'"

8 Manoah prayed^i to the LORD and said, "Please, Lord, let the man of God you sent come again to us and teach us what we should do for the boy who will be born."

9 God listened^j to^c Manoah, and the angel of God came again to the woman. She was sitting in the field, and her husband Manoah was not with her. **10** The woman ran quickly to her husband and told him, "The man who came to me the other day has just come back!"

11 So Manoah got up and followed his wife. When he came to the man, he asked, "Are you the man who spoke to my wife?"

"I am," he said.

12 Then Manoah asked, "When your words come true, what will be the boy's responsibilities and work?"

13 The angel of the LORD answered Manoah, "Your wife needs to do everything I told her. **14** She must not eat anything that comes from the grapevine or drink wine or beer. And she must not eat anything unclean. Your wife must do everything I have commanded her."

15 "Please stay here," Manoah told him, "and we will prepare a young goat^k for you."

16 The angel of the LORD said to him, "If I stay, I won't eat your food. But if you want to prepare a burnt offering, offer it to the

---

^A **12:7** LXX reads *in his city in Gilead*   ^B **13:5** Lit *And a razor is not to go up on his head*   ^C **13:9** Lit *to the voice of*

12:8-15 The repeated use of the word *died* in this section brings us to a sobering reality: unless Christ comes first, we're all going to die. And how we will be remembered will come down to the choices we make: will we, like these judges, serve God or something else?

If you want to be a doctor, but you don't want to go to medical school, then you don't really want to be a doctor, because you're not doing what is necessary to achieve what you want. Similarly, if you want to reign with Christ, you have to trust and follow Christ in the here and now.

13:2-3 Here the author introduces us to a couple that **was unable to conceive** (13:2). The

woman's barrenness was outside of their control, but it was fully under the control of the sovereign God of heaven. He was getting ready to do something remarkable, to send them Israel's next deliverer.

When you're discouraged and can't see your way past a difficult time, seek God and ask him what he's up to behind the scenes. Your trying circumstances may be just the opportunity through which God will work remarkably.

13:4-5 The promised boy was to be consecrated to God as **a Nazirite** even in the womb (13:5; see Num 6:1-21). This is wonderful evidence that personhood begins at conception.

Every moral issue has a spiritual component to it. Abortion, for instance, is a spiritual matter because it's the destruction of a person created in the image of God. Throughout his Word, God condemns those who shed innocent blood (see Prov 6:16-17). No blood is more innocent than that of an unborn child. **13:17-18** When Manoah asked for the visitor's name, he replied, **it is beyond understanding** (13:18). This cryptic statement is a reminder that while we often think we understand what God is going to do in our lives, the Lord likes to shock us with his marvelous ways. So don't put God in a box. He can bust right past all your preconceived ideas.

LORD." (Manoah did not know he was the angel of the LORD.)

¹⁷ Then Manoah said to him, "What is your name, so that we may honor you when your words come true?"

¹⁸ "Why do you ask my name," the angel of the LORD asked him, "since it is beyond understanding."[a]

¹⁹ Manoah took a young goat and a grain offering and offered them on a rock to the LORD, who did something miraculous[A] while Manoah and his wife were watching. ²⁰ When the flame went up from the altar to the sky, the angel of the LORD went up in its flame. When Manoah and his wife saw this, they fell facedown on the ground. ²¹ The angel of the LORD did not appear again to Manoah and his wife. Then Manoah realized that it was the angel of the LORD.

²² "We're certainly going to die," he said to his wife, "because we have seen God!"[b]

²³ But his wife said to him, "If the LORD had intended to kill us, he wouldn't have accepted the burnt offering and the grain offering from us, and he would not have shown us all these things or spoken to us like this."

²⁴ So the woman gave birth to a son and named him Samson.[c] The boy grew,[d] and the LORD blessed him. ²⁵ Then the Spirit of the LORD began to stir him in the Camp of Dan,[B] between Zorah and Eshtaol.[e]

SAMSON'S RIDDLE

14 Samson went down to Timnah[f] and saw a young Philistine woman there. ² He went back and told his father and his mother: "I have seen a young Philistine woman in Timnah. Now get her for me as a wife."

³ But his father and mother said to him, "Can't you find a young woman among your relatives or among any of our people? Must you go to the uncircumcised Philistines for a wife?"

But Samson told his father, "Get her for me. She's the right one for me." ⁴ Now his father and mother did not know this was from the LORD,[g] who wanted the Philistines to provide an opportunity for a confrontation.[c] At that time, the Philistines were ruling Israel.

⁵ Samson went down to Timnah with his father and mother and came to the vineyards of Timnah. Suddenly a young lion came roaring at him, ⁶ the Spirit of the LORD came powerfully on[h] him, and he tore the lion apart with his bare hands as he might have torn a young goat. But he did not tell his father or mother what he had done. ⁷ Then he went and spoke to the woman, because she seemed right to Samson.

⁸ After some time, when he returned to marry her, he left the road to see the lion's carcass, and there was a swarm of bees with honey in the carcass. ⁹ He scooped some honey into his hands and ate it as he went along. When he came to his father and mother, he gave some to them and they ate it. But he did not tell them that he had scooped the honey from the lion's carcass.[i]

¹⁰ His father went to visit the woman, and Samson prepared a feast there, as young men were accustomed to do. ¹¹ When the Philistines saw him, they brought thirty men to accompany him.

¹² "Let me tell you a riddle,"[j] Samson said to them. "If you can explain it to me during the seven days of the feast and figure it out, I will give you thirty linen garments and thirty changes of clothes. ¹³ But if you can't explain it to me, you must give me thirty linen garments and thirty changes of clothes."

"Tell us your riddle," they replied.[D] "Let's hear it."

ᵃ 13:18 Gn 32:29
ᵇ 13:22 Gn 33:10; Ex 24:10; 33:20; Jdg 6:22; Is 6:5
ᶜ 13:24 Heb 11:32
ᵈ 1Sm 3:19; Lk 1:80
ᵉ 13:25 Jos 15:33; Jdg 16:31; 18:2,8,11; 1Ch 2:53
ᶠ 14:1 Jos 15:10; 19:43; 2Ch 28:18

ᵍ 14:4 Jos 11:20; 1Kg 12:15; 2Kg 6:33
ʰ 14:6 Jdg 14:19; 15:14; 1Sm 10:6,10; 11:6; 16:13; 18:10
ⁱ 14:9 Lv 11:27
ʲ 14:12 Nm 12:8; Ps 49:4; Pr 1:6; Ezk 17:2; Dn 8:23

---

^A 13:19 LXX reads *to the LORD, to the one who works wonders*   ^B 13:25 Or *in Mahaneh-dan*   ^C 14:4 *for a confrontation* supplied for clarity   ^D 14:13 Lit *replied to him*

13:19-23 Manoah rightly equated **the angel of the LORD** with God (13:20-22). This is another Old Testament Christophany—a preincarnate but visible manifestation of Christ (see 2:1-2). Jesus Christ, the Second Person of the Trinity, is the manifestation of God in history. The eternal Father, who existed before time and who initiated it, routes his activity in time through Jesus. Just as the sun is the center of our solar system, the Son is the center of God's working in history.

14:1-4 Samson's parents tried to tell him he should not marry someone who was not a part of God's people (14:3). They didn't know God would use Samson's fascination with this woman to create an **opportunity** to deliver them (14:4). Importantly, the Lord *had* warned his people not to intermarry with the surrounding nations because they didn't worship the one true God (see Deut 7:1-3). A couple that is unequally yoked spiritually is likely to run into trouble.

14:5-9 On the way to Timnah, **the Spirit of the LORD came powerfully on [Samson], and he tore [an attacking] lion apart with his bare hands** (14:6). This was a clear sign that indeed he had been elected and empowered by God for a supernatural purpose. But later, when he discovered that **bees** had made a hive in the **carcass**, Samson blatantly ignored the law of Moses regarding unclean foods and took some of their **honey** (14:8-9).

14:12-14 Samson posed **a riddle** to the **Philistines**. The prize for answering it within a week would be **thirty changes of clothes** (14:12). (In biblical days, an additional set of clothing was a sign of honor and dignity.) Samson, his recent kill and the accompanying honey on his mind, said, **Out of the eater came something to eat, and out of the strong came something sweet** (14:14).

ᵃ 14:16 Jdg 16:15
ᵇ 15:1 Gn 30:14; Ex 34:22;
1Sm 6:13; 12:17

ᶜ 15:3 Nm 5:19,28,31; 1Sm
26:9; Jr 2:35
ᵈ 15:4 Neh 4:3; Ps 63:10;
Sg 2:15; Lm 5:18; Ezk 13:4
ᵉ 15:5 Ex 22:6
ᶠ 15:11 Lv 26:25; Dt
28:43; Jdg 13:1; 14:4; Ps
106:40-42

¹⁴ So he said to them:

Out of the eater came something
to eat,
and out of the strong came
something sweet.

After three days, they were unable to explain the riddle. ¹⁵ On the fourthᴬ day they said to Samson's wife, "Persuade your husband to explain the riddle to us, or we will burn you and your father's family to death. Did you invite us here to rob us?"

¹⁶ So Samson's wife came to him, weeping, and said, "You hate me and don't love me!ᵃ You told my people the riddle, but haven't explained it to me."

"Look," he said,ᴮ "I haven't even explained it to my father or mother, so why should I explain it to you?"

¹⁷ She wept the whole seven days of the feast, and at last, on the seventh day, he explained it to her, because she had nagged him so much. Then she explained it to her people. ¹⁸ On the seventh day, before sunset, the men of the city said to him:

What is sweeter than honey?
What is stronger than a lion?

So he said to them:

If you hadn't plowed with
my young cow,
you wouldn't know
my riddle now!

¹⁹ The Spirit of the LORD came powerfully on him, and he went down to Ashkelon and killed thirty of their men. He stripped them and gave their clothes to those who had explained the riddle. In a rage, Samson returned to his father's house, ²⁰ and his wife was given to one of the men who had accompanied him.

SAMSON'S REVENGE

15 Later on, during the wheat harvest,ᵇ Samson took a young goat as a gift and visited his wife. "I want to go to my wife in her room," he said. But her father would not let him enter.

² "I was sure you hated her," her father said, "so I gave her to one of the men who accompanied you. Isn't her younger sister more beautiful than she is? Why not take her instead?"

³ Samson said to them, "This time I will be blamelessᶜ when I harm the Philistines." ⁴ So he went out and caught three hundred foxes.ᵈ He took torches, turned the foxes tail-to-tail, and put a torch between each pair of tails. ⁵ Then he ignited the torches and released the foxes into the standing grain of the Philistines. He burned the piles of grain and the standing grain as well as the vineyards and olive groves.ᵉ

⁶ Then the Philistines asked, "Who did this?"

They were told, "It was Samson, the Timnite's son-in-law, because he took Samson's wife and gave her to his companion." So the Philistines went to her and her father and burned them to death.

⁷ Then Samson told them, "Because you did this, I swear that I won't rest until I have taken vengeance on you." ⁸ He tore them limb from limbᶜ and then went down and stayed in the cave at the rock of Etam.

⁹ The Philistines went up, camped in Judah, and raided Lehi. ¹⁰ So the men of Judah said, "Why have you attacked us?"

They replied, "We have come to tie Samson up and pay him back for what he did to us."

¹¹ Then three thousand men of Judah went to the cave at the rock of Etam, and they asked Samson, "Don't you realize that the Philistines rule us?ᶠ What have you done to us?"

"I have done to them what they did to me," he answered.ᴰ

¹² They said to him, "We've come to tie you up and hand you over to the Philistines."

Then Samson told them, "Swear to me that you yourselves won't kill me."

¹³ "No," they said,ᴱ "we won't kill you, but we will tie you up securely and hand you over to them." So they tied him up with

---

ᴬ 14:15 LXX, Syr; MT reads *seventh*   ᴮ 14:16 Lit *said to her*   ᶜ 15:8 Lit *He struck them hip and thigh with a great slaughter*   ᴰ 15:11 Lit *answered them*
ᴱ 15:13 Lit *said to him*

14:16-18 Because she had nagged him so much (14:17), Samson finally told his bride the answer to his riddle. Later, when the Philistine men parroted the answer (14:18), Samson knew how they had obtained it.
15:1-8 Samson wanted to visit his wife, but **her father would not let him enter** her room (15:1). He had given her to another man because he

assumed Samson was not happy with her after the riddle business (see 14:15-20). Samson was enraged. Since the Philistines had interfered with his family "harvest"—his plan to start a family with this woman—he decided to interfere with their harvest. He destroyed their crops with fire (15:3-5). In response, the Philistines killed **Samson's wife** and her father

(15:6). And Samson, in turn, avenged the murders with his bare hands (15:8).
15:9-13 Three thousand men of Judah went to arrest Samson, saying that he had brought trouble on them by riling up the Philistine oppressors (15:11). (Don't miss the irony here. They chose to hand over the man God had sent to save them *from* the Philistines *to* the Philistines.)

two new ropes[a] and led him away from the rock.

14 When he came to Lehi, the Philistines came to meet him shouting. The Spirit of the LORD came powerfully on him, and the ropes that were on his arms and wrists became like burnt flax and fell off. **15** He found a fresh jawbone of a donkey, reached out his hand, took it, and killed a thousand men with it. **16** Then Samson said:

With the jawbone of a donkey
I have piled them in heaps.
With the jawbone of a donkey
I have killed a thousand men.

17 When he finished speaking, he threw away the jawbone and named that place Ramath-lehi.[A] **18** He became very thirsty and called out to the LORD: "You have accomplished this great victory through your servant. Must I now die of thirst and fall into the hands of the uncircumcised?" **19** So God split a hollow place in the ground at Lehi, and water came out of it. After Samson drank, his strength returned, and he revived.[b] That is why he named it En-hakkore,[B] which is still in Lehi today. **20** And he judged Israel twenty years in the days of the Philistines.

SAMSON AND DELILAH

16 Samson went to Gaza,[c] where he saw a prostitute and went to bed with her. **2** When the Gazites heard that Samson was there, they surrounded the place and waited in ambush for him all that night at the city gate. They kept quiet all night, saying, "Let's wait until dawn; then we will kill him." **3** But Samson stayed in bed only until midnight. Then he got up, took hold of the doors of the city gate along with the two gateposts, and pulled them out, bar and all. He put them on his shoulders and took them to the top of the mountain overlooking Hebron.

4 Some time later, he fell in love with a woman named Delilah, who lived in the Sorek Valley. **5** The Philistine leaders[d] went to her and said, "Persuade him to tell you[C] where his great strength comes from, so we can overpower him, tie him up, and make him helpless. Each of us will then give you 1,100 pieces of silver."

6 So Delilah said to Samson, "Please tell me, where does your great strength come from? How could someone tie you up and make you helpless?"

7 Samson told her, "If they tie me up with seven fresh bowstrings that have not been dried, I will become weak and be like any other man."

8 The Philistine leaders brought her seven fresh bowstrings that had not been dried, and she tied him up with them. **9** While the men in ambush were waiting in her room, she called out to him, "Samson, the Philistines are here!"[D] But he snapped the bowstrings as a strand of yarn snaps when it touches fire. The secret of his strength remained unknown.

10 Then Delilah said to Samson, "You have mocked me and told me lies! Won't you please tell me how you can be tied up?"

11 He told her, "If they tie me up with new ropes that have never been used,[e] I will become weak and be like any other man."

12 Delilah took new ropes, tied him up with them, and shouted, "Samson, the Philistines are here!" But while the men in ambush were waiting in her room, he snapped the ropes off his arms like a thread.

13 Then Delilah said to Samson, "You have mocked me all along and told me lies! Tell me how you can be tied up."

He told her, "If you weave the seven braids on my head into the fabric on a loom—"[E]

14 She fastened the braids with a pin and called to him, "Samson, the Philistines are

a 15:13 Jdg 16:11-12
b 15:19 Gn 45:27; 1Kg 17:22; 2Kg 13:21; Is 38:16,21; Ezk 37:3,14
c 16:1 Jos 15:47

d 16:5 Jos 13:3
e 16:11 Jdg 15:13

A **15:17** = High Place of the Jawbone   B **15:19** = Spring of the One Who Cried Out   C **16:5** Lit *him and see*   D **16:9** Lit *are on you*, also in vv. 12,14,20
E **16:13-14** LXX reads *loom and fasten them with a pin into the wall and I will become weak and be like any other man."* **14**And while he was sleeping, Delilah wove the seven braids on his head into the loom.

15:14-15 Whenever **the Spirit of the LORD came** on Samson (15:14), supernatural activity followed. In the Old Testament, the Spirit of the Lord came on people specifically related to certain events. Since New Testament times, however, the Spirit comes to indwell every believer (see Eph 1:13-14; Rom 8:9). On this side of the cross the supernatural presence of God is not related to the Spirit coming on believers, but to the fullness of the Spirit at work within us.
16:1 For years the people of Israel had "prostituted themselves with other gods" (2:17; 8:27,

33). They had blatantly compromised with the surrounding culture and betrayed the Lord. By this season of his life, Samson the leader was openly living in a way that reflected what Israel had been doing. This trend would be his downfall.
16:3 You and I couldn't carry these massive **doors** a block's distance on level ground! This scene serves as proof that though Samson was outside of the will of God in what he was doing, God had not left him—*yet.*

16:4-5 It is not clear whether **Delilah** was a Philistine woman, but her loyalties lay with them and their **silver** (16:5).
16:6-17 Delilah steadily wore Samson down. In the end, she used the very trick Samson's bride had once employed when she betrayed him to the Philistines. She pleaded, **How can you say, "I love you" . . . when your heart is not with me?** (16:15; see 14:15-19). Of course, if she really loved *him*, she wouldn't set him up.

a 16:15 Jdg 14:6
b 16:17 Nm 6:5; Jdg 13:5
c 16:20 Nm 14:9,42-43;
Jos 7:12; 1Sm 16:14; 18:12;
28:15-16; 2Ch 15:2
d 16:23 Jos 15:41; 19:27;
1Sm 5:2-5,7; 1Ch 10:10

e 16:24 Dn 5:4
f 16:28 Jr 15:15

here!" He awoke from his sleep and pulled out the pin, with the loom and the web.

15 "How can you say, 'I love you,'*a* she told him, "when your heart is not with me? This is the third time you have mocked me and not told me what makes your strength so great!"

16 Because she nagged him day after day and pleaded with him until she wore him out,*A* 17 he told her the whole truth and said to her, "My hair has never been cut,*B* because I am a Nazirite*b* to God from birth. If I am shaved, my strength will leave me, and I will become weak and be like any other man."

18 When Delilah realized that he had told her the whole truth, she sent this message to the Philistine leaders: "Come one more time, for he has told me the whole truth." The Philistine leaders came to her and brought the silver with them.

19 Then she let him fall asleep on her lap and called a man to shave off the seven braids on his head. In this way, she made him helpless, and his strength left him. 20 Then she cried, "Samson, the Philistines are here!" When he awoke from his sleep, he said, "I will escape as I did before and shake myself free." But he did not know that the LORD had left him.*c*

SAMSON'S DEFEAT AND DEATH

21 The Philistines seized him and gouged out his eyes. They brought him down to Gaza and bound him with bronze shackles, and he was forced to grind grain in the prison. 22 But his hair began to grow back after it had been shaved.

23 Now the Philistine leaders gathered together to offer a great sacrifice to their god Dagon.*d* They rejoiced and said:

Our god has handed over
our enemy Samson to us.

24 When the people saw him, they praised their god*e* and said:

Our god has handed over to us
our enemy who destroyed our land
and who multiplied our dead.

25 When they were in good spirits,*c* they said, "Bring Samson here to entertain us." So they brought Samson from prison, and he entertained them. They had him stand between the pillars.

26 Samson said to the young man who was leading him by the hand, "Lead me where I can feel the pillars supporting the temple, so I can lean against them." 27 The temple was full of men and women; all the leaders of the Philistines were there, and about three thousand men and women were on the roof watching Samson entertain them. 28 He called out to the LORD: "Lord GOD, please remember me.*f* Strengthen me, God, just once more. With one act of vengeance, let me pay back the Philistines for my two eyes." 29 Samson took hold of the two middle pillars supporting the temple and leaned against them, one on his right hand and the other on his left. 30 Samson said, "Let me die with the Philistines." He pushed with all his might, and the temple fell on the leaders and all the people in it. And those he killed at his death were more than those he had killed in his life.

31 Then his brothers and all his father's family came down, carried him back, and buried him between Zorah and Eshtaol in the tomb of his father Manoah. So he judged Israel twenty years.

MICAH'S PRIEST

17 There was a man from the hill country of Ephraim named Micah. 2 He said to his mother, "The 1,100 pieces of silver taken from you, and that I heard

---

A 16:16 Lit *him and he became short to death*   B 16:17 Lit *A razor has not gone up on my head*   C 16:25 Or *When they were feeling good*

16:20 Samson let his relationship with Delilah take priority over his commitments to God, and it cost him dearly. This is evidence that no human relationship, no matter how close, is to trump your relationship with the Lord.
16:21 The enemies of God were suddenly in control of Samson's every move. When God is no longer in a life's equation, Satan controls the situation.
16:22 This is a hint that God wasn't done with Samson yet. The secret to his strength had begun to **grow back**. Its return was an outward symbol that he was inwardly repentant and turning back to God.
16:23-24 There was a problem with the Philistines' reasoning: **Dagon** hadn't handed

Samson over to them at all; God had. Thus, the battle between Samson and his tormentors was not merely personal or political but theological.

When we are in conflict, we should retreat as quickly as we can to the spiritual nature of the battle, as young David would do years later when facing off against this same people group and their champion, Goliath (see 1 Sam 17:45-47). David heard the challenge the man made in defiance of God and quickly realized that the battle to be fought was spiritual in nature, even though it would be played out in the physical arena. He saw it as a conflict between the god of the Philistines and the true God. We must follow the example of

these men, recognizing that our conflicts are spiritual and theological—not merely physical or emotional.
16:28-30 In Hebrews 11:32-34 Samson is included in the "Hall of Faith," alongside upright Old Testament people like Daniel. That inclusion ought to birth hope in every heart. While Samson was not even close to being a perfect man, he got this right: he *believed* God could use him to accomplish his will. Therefore, let us trust God, submit to his agenda for our lives, and give him everything we have.
17:1-3 **Micah** stole from his own **mother**. Only when he heard her **curse** the silver so that it would fail to be an advantage to whoever

you place a curse on — here's the silver. I took it."

Then his mother said, "My son, may you be blessed by the LORD!"[a]

[3] He returned the 1,100 pieces of silver to his mother, and his mother said, "I personally consecrate[b] the silver to the LORD for my son's benefit to make a carved image and a silver idol.[A] I will give it back to you." [4] So he returned the silver to his mother, and she took five pounds of silver and gave it to a silversmith. He made it into a carved image and a silver idol, and it was in Micah's house.

[5] This man Micah had a shrine, and he made an ephod and household idols,[c] and installed one of his sons to be his priest. [6] In those days there was no king in Israel;[d] everyone did whatever seemed right to him.

[7] There was a young man, a Levite from Bethlehem in Judah, who was staying within the clan of Judah.[e] [8] The man left the town of Bethlehem in Judah to stay wherever he could find a place. On his way he came to Micah's home in the hill country of Ephraim.

[9] "Where do you come from?" Micah asked him.

He answered him, "I am a Levite from Bethlehem in Judah, and I'm going to stay wherever I can find a place."

[10] Micah replied,[B] "Stay with me and be my father[f] and priest, and I will give you four ounces of silver a year, along with your clothing and provisions." So the Levite went in [11] and agreed to stay with the man, and the young man became like one of his sons. [12] Micah consecrated the Levite, and the young man became his priest[g] and lived in Micah's house. [13] Then Micah said, "Now I know that the LORD

will be good to me, because a Levite has become my priest."

DAN'S INVASION AND IDOLATRY

18 In those days, there was no king in Israel,[h] and the Danite tribe was looking for territory to occupy.[i] Up to that time no territory had been captured by them among the tribes of Israel. [2] So the Danites sent out five brave men[j] from all their clans, from Zorah and Eshtaol,[k] to scout[l] out the land and explore it. They told them, "Go and explore the land."

They came to the hill country of Ephraim as far as the home of Micah and spent the night there. [3] While they were near Micah's home, they recognized the accent of the young Levite. So they went over to him and asked, "Who brought you here? What are you doing in this place? What is keeping you here?" [4] He told them, "This is what Micah has done for me: He has hired me, and I became his priest."

[5] Then they said to him, "Please inquire of God[m] for us to determine if we will have a successful journey."

[6] The priest told them, "Go in peace. The LORD is watching over the journey you are going on."

[7] The five men left and came to Laish. They saw that the people who were there were living securely, in the same way as the Sidonians, quiet and unsuspecting. There was nothing lacking[c] in the land and no oppressive ruler. They were far from the Sidonians, having no alliance with anyone.[D]

[8] When the men went back to their relatives at Zorah and Eshtaol,[n] their relatives asked them, "What did you find out?"

[9] They answered, "Come on, let's attack them, for we have seen the land, and it is

[a] 17:2 Ru 2:20; 1Sm 15:13
[b] 17:3 Lv 22:2-3; 27:14-19; 1Ch 18:11; 26:26-28; 2Ch 30:17
[c] 17:5 Gn 31:19,34-35; Jdg 18:14; 1Sm 19:13; 2Kg 23:24; Hs 3:4
[d] 17:6 Jdg 18:1; 19:1; 21:25
[e] 17:7 Dt 18:6-7
[f] 17:10 Gn 45:8; Jdg 18:19; Jr 3:19
[g] 17:12 Jdg 18:30

[h] 18:1 Jdg 17:6; 19:1; 21:25; Jos 19:47-48; Jdg 1:34
[i] 18:2 Dt 3:18; 1Sm 14:52; 18:17; 2Sm 2:7; 13:28; 17:10; 1Kg 1:52; 2Kg 2:16
[j] 18:2 Jos 19:40-41; Jdg 13:2,25; Nm 13:17; Jos 2:1
[k] 18:2 Jos 19:40-41; Jdg 13:2,25
[m] 18:5 Gn 25:22; Ex 18:15; Jdg 1:1; 20:18; 1Sm 9:9; 10:22; 14:37; 22:10; 23:2; 28:6
[n] 18:8 Jos 15:33; 19:41; Jdg 13:2,25; 16:31

[A] 17:3 Or *image and a cast image*, also in v. 4   [B] 17:10 Lit *replied to him*   [C] 18:7 Hb obscure   [D] 18:7 MT; some LXX mss, Sym, Old Lat, Syr read *Aram*

---

stole it, did he return her money (17:1-2). At his admission, his mother said, **I personally consecrate the silver to the LORD for my son's benefit to make . . . a silver idol** (17:3).

Clearly, we have problems here. The Lord had commanded Israel, "Do not make an idol for yourself" (Exod 20:4). The woman's blatant double-mindedness is just what we would expect to develop in a culture that tries to blend the worship of the true God with the world's pagan ways.

17:5 Micah used both an **ephod** to determine God's will and **household idols** to determine the pagan gods' preferences. Then he made one of his own sons his personal **priest**. Micah was from the tribe of Ephraim, and only Levites could be priests. Thus, this was a further flagrant disregard for God's commands.

17:6 The people had completely forgotten that the Lord was to be their King. Instead, everyone followed his own standard, his own god.

17:7-12 Priests and Levites were supposed to steer the people away from idolatry toward the worship of God, teaching them right from wrong (see Lev 10:8-11; Ezek 44:23). But during the time period covered in these final five chapters, everyone simply ignored the rules God had given to Moses. Even the Levites were complicit in the decline and debauchery.

A **young man, a Levite**, was looking for a **place** to stay (17:7-8). Micah invited him to be his personal **priest** (17:10). The Levite **agreed** (17:11). And while only another priest could consecrate a priest, **Micah consecrated**

him (17:12). So while Micah was an idolater, the Levite was just as far away from God's standards of holiness in his thinking and practices.

17:13 Micah was convinced that having a Levite of his own was a sign of the Lord's blessing, but it most certainly was *not*. He was living outside God's stated will.

18:1 The tribe of Dan had failed to conquer what they were supposed to have conquered in the power of the Lord (1:34), so they searched for a people weak enough that they would be able to take their land away.

18:6 This is the kind of thing the Levite was expected to say—what he was paid to say. The Danites weren't paying him to give them bad news. But in truth, if you only get good news from a preacher, he's not doing his full job.

a 18:10 Dt 8:9
b 18:12 Jos 9:17; 1Ch 13:5-6; 2Ch 1:4; Jr 26:20
c 18:19 Jb 21:5; 29:9; 40:4; Mc 7:16

d 18:27 Dt 13:16; Jos 6:24; Jdg 1:8,25; 4:15-16; 1Sm 30:3; Jr 32:29; 34:2
e 18:28 Jb 5:4; Ps 7:2; 50:22; 71:11; Is 5:29; 42:22; Dn 8:4; Hs 5:14; Mc 5:8
f 18:30 2Kg 15:29
g 18:31 Jos 18:1; Jdg 21:12; 1Sm 1:3; 3:21; Ps 78:60; Jr 7:12,14; 26:6,9
h 19:1 Jdg 17:6; 18:1; 21:25

very good. Why wait? Don't hesitate to go and invade and take possession of the land! **10** When you get there, you will come to an unsuspecting people and a spacious land, for God has handed it over to you. It is a place where nothing on earth is lacking."*a* **11** Six hundred Danites departed from Zorah and Eshtaol armed with weapons of war. **12** They went up and camped at Kiriath-jearim*b* in Judah. This is why the place is still called the Camp of Dan*A* today; it is west of Kiriath-jearim. **13** From there they traveled to the hill country of Ephraim and arrived at Micah's house.

14 The five men who had gone to scout out the land of Laish told their brothers, "Did you know that there are an ephod, household gods, and a carved image and a silver idol*B* in these houses? Now think about what you should do." **15** So they detoured there and went to the house of the young Levite at the home of Micah and greeted him. **16** The six hundred Danite men were standing by the entrance of the city gate, armed with their weapons of war. **17** Then the five men who had gone to scout out the land went in and took the carved image, the ephod, the household idols, and the silver idol,*c* while the priest was standing by the entrance of the city gate with the six hundred men armed with weapons of war.

18 When they entered Micah's house and took the carved image, the ephod, the household idols, and the silver idol, the priest said to them, "What are you doing?" **19** They told him, "Be quiet. Keep your mouth shut.*D,c* Come with us and be a father and a priest to us. Is it better for you to be a priest for the house of one person or for you to be a priest for a tribe and family in Israel?" **20** So the priest was pleased and took his ephod, household idols, and carved image, and went with the people. **21** They prepared to leave, putting their dependents, livestock, and possessions in front of them.

22 After they were some distance from Micah's house, the men who were in the houses near it were mustered and caught up with the Danites. **23** They called to the Danites, who turned to face them, and said to Micah, "What's the matter with you that you mustered the men?" **24** He said, "You took the gods I had made and the priest, and went away. What do I have left? How can you say to me, 'What's the matter with you?'" **25** The Danites said to him, "Don't raise your voice against us, or angry men will attack you, and you and your family will lose your lives." **26** The Danites went on their way, and Micah turned to go back home, because he saw that they were stronger than he was.

27 After they had taken the gods Micah had made and the priest that belonged to him, they went to Laish, to a quiet and unsuspecting people. They killed them with their swords and burned the city.*d* **28** There was no one to rescue them*e* because it was far from Sidon and they had no alliance with anyone. It was in a valley that belonged to Beth-rehob. They rebuilt the city and lived in it. **29** They named the city Dan, after the name of their ancestor Dan, who was born to Israel. The city was formerly named Laish.

30 The Danites set up the carved image for themselves. Jonathan son of Gershom, son of Moses,*E* and his sons were priests for the Danite tribe until the time of the exile from the land.*f* **31** So they set up for themselves Micah's carved image that he had made, and it was there as long as the house of God was in Shiloh.*g*

OUTRAGE IN BENJAMIN

19 In those days, when there was no king in Israel,*h* a Levite staying in a remote part of the hill country of Ephraim acquired a woman from Bethlehem in Judah as his concubine. **2** But she was unfaithful to*F* him and left him for her

A 18:12 Or *called Mahaneh-dan*   *B* 18:14 Or *image, the cast image*   *c* 18:17 Or *the cast image*, also in v. 18   *D* 18:19 Lit *Put your hand on your mouth*
E 18:30 Some Hb mss, LXX, Vg; other Hb mss read *Manasseh*   *F* 19:2 LXX reads *was angry with*

18:14 What they should have done was "destroy" the idols and "drive out" the idol worshiper (see Num 33:52). But given how spiritually dark Israel had become, it doesn't take a genius to figure out what the Danites planned to do to Micah's trove of religious items.
18:19-20 In other words, the Danites appealed to the priest's pride and materialism. They said in effect, "We're giving you an opportunity for promotion: leave this house church and come lead our mega-church." Thus, a compromised

priest who'd been serving in a compromised house was now moving on to serve in a compromised community. Idolatry was spreading.
18:24 Any god that can be stolen is no god at all, but no one involved in this saga seemed to grasp that.
18:27-29 The Danite army burned and rebuilt Laish and named it **Dan** after their patriarch, who was one of the sons of Israel (that is, Jacob; 18:29). It would become the northernmost city in Israel, a fact often acknowl-

edged in the phrase "from Dan to Beer-sheba (Israel's southernmost city)" which appears throughout the Old Testament.
18:30-31 In other words, the Danites had created an idolatrous stronghold. And though they still kept the Lord in the equation, used his name, and even inquired of him, they were not truly worshiping the Lord. They were worshiping a god of their own making.
19:1 Concubines, or mistresses, were typically slaves.

father's house in Bethlehem in Judah. She was there for four months. ³ Then her husband got up and followed her to speak kindly to her^A,a and bring her back. He had his servant with him and a pair of donkeys. So she brought him to her father's house, and when the girl's father saw him, he gladly welcomed him. ⁴ His father-in-law, the girl's father, detained him, and he stayed with him for three days. They ate, drank, and spent the nights there.

⁵ On the fourth day, they got up early in the morning and prepared to go, but the girl's father said to his son-in-law, "Have something to eat to keep up your strength^b and then you can go." ⁶ So they sat down and the two of them ate and drank together. Then the girl's father said to the man, "Please agree to stay overnight and enjoy yourself."^c ⁷ The man got up to go, but his father-in-law persuaded him, so he stayed and spent the night there again. ⁸ He got up early in the morning of the fifth day to leave, but the girl's father said to him, "Please keep up your strength." So they waited until late afternoon and the two of them ate. ⁹ The man got up to go with his concubine and his servant, when his father-in-law, the girl's father, said to him, "Look, night is coming. Please spend the night. See, the day is almost over. Spend the night here, enjoy yourself, then you can get up early tomorrow for your journey and go home."

¹⁰ But the man was unwilling to spend the night. He got up, departed, and arrived opposite Jebus (that is, Jerusalem^d). The man had his two saddled donkeys and his concubine with him. ¹¹ When they were near Jebus and the day was almost gone, the servant^e said to his master, "Please, why not let us stop at this Jebusite city and spend the night here?"

¹² But his master replied to him, "We will not stop at a foreign city where there are no Israelites. Let's move on to Gibeah."^f ¹³ "Come on," he said,^B "let's try to reach one of these places and spend the night in Gibeah or Ramah." ¹⁴ So they continued on their journey, and the sun set as they neared Gibeah in Benjamin. ¹⁵ They stopped^c to go in and spend the night in Gibeah. The Levite went in and sat down in the city square, but no one took them into their home to spend the night.

¹⁶ In the evening, an old man came in from his work in the field. He was from the hill country of Ephraim,^g but he was residing in Gibeah where the people were Benjaminites. ¹⁷ When he looked up and saw the traveler in the city square, the old man asked, "Where are you going, and where do you come from?"

¹⁸ He answered him, "We're traveling from Bethlehem in Judah to the remote hill country of Ephraim, where I am from. I went to Bethlehem in Judah, and now I'm going to the house of the LORD.^D No one has taken me into his home, ¹⁹ although there's straw and feed for the donkeys, and I have bread and wine for me, my concubine, and the servant^E with us. There is nothing we lack."

²⁰ "Welcome!" said the old man. "I'll take care of everything you need. Only don't spend the night in the square." ²¹ So he brought him to his house and fed the donkeys. Then they washed their feet and ate and drank.^h ²² While they were enjoying themselves, all of a sudden, wicked men of the city^i surrounded the house and beat on the door. They said to the old man who was the owner of the house, "Bring out the man who came to your house so we can have sex with him!"

²³ The owner of the house went out and said to them, "Please don't do this evil, my brothers. After all, this man has come into my house. Don't commit this horrible outrage.^j ²⁴ Here, let me bring out my virgin daughter^k and the man's concubine now.

^a 19:3 Gn 34:3; 50:21
^b 19:5 Gn 18:5
^c 19:6 Jdg 16:25; 19:22; Ru 3:7; 1Kg 21:7; Est 1:10
^d 19:10 Jos 18:28; 1Ch 11:4-5
^e 19:11 Jdg 19:19

^f 19:12 Jos 18:28; 1Sm 10:26; 22:6; Hs 5:8; 9:9; 10:9
^g 19:16 Jdg 19:1
^h 19:21 Gn 24:32-33
^i 19:22 Gn 19:4-5; Dt 13:13; 1Sm 2:12; 1Kg 21:10; Ezk 16:46-48
^j 19:23 Gn 34:7; Dt 22:21; Jdg 20:6; 2Sm 13:12; Jb 42:8
^k 19:24 Gn 19:8

---

^A 19:3 Lit speak to her heart   ^B 19:13 Lit said to his servant   ^C 19:15 Lit stopped there   ^D 19:18 LXX reads to my house   ^E 19:19 Some Hb mss, Syr, Tg, Vg; other Hb mss read servants

---

19:10-12 The Levite traveled as far as **Jebus** (which would one day be called **Jerusalem** (19:10). His servant suggested they stay within its borders for the night, but the Levite insisted, **We will not stop at a foreign city where there are no Israelites. Let's move on to Gibeah,** which was a town in the territory of Benjamin (19:12). Unfortunately, finding a city of Israelites would bring perversion instead of provision.
19:15 Hospitality was a valued practice in the ancient Near East. It was customary to

offer a stranger a place to stay. That nobody would do even that basic service for his fellow Israelites shows that at this point in history there really was no spiritual standard among the people—and that's a recipe for disaster.
19:20 Clearly, the elderly man didn't think it would be safe to camp out in that neighborhood.
19:22 In Genesis 19, Abraham's nephew Lot lived in the city of Sodom and welcomed into his home two angels. But the wicked men of the city demanded, "Where are the

men who came to you tonight? Send them out to us so we can have sex with them!" (Gen 19:5). The author of Judges wants us to see a sad reality: God's people—who were called to be holy—had become just like the Canaanites whom they had driven out.
19:24 This is horrific! Even he, apparently among the city's finest given his hospitality, was completely without conscience with regard to how women should be treated.

ᵃ19:24 Jdg 20:5; 2Sm 13:12,14; Lm 5:11
ᵇ19:28 Jdg 20:5
ᶜ20:1 Gn 21:14; 22:19; 1Sm 3:20; 1Kg 4:25
ᵈJdg 11:11; 21:1,5,8; 1Sm 7:5-16; 10:17
ᵉ20:2 1Sm 14:38; Is 19:13

ᶠ20:6 Lv 18:17; 19:29; Jr 13:27; Ezk 16:27,43
ᵍ20:11 Dt 29:10; Jos 10:24; Jdg 20:33; 1Sm 11:15; 17:19; 2Sm 16:18; 17:14,24; 19:41; 20:2; 1Kg 8:2; 1Ch 10:7; 2Ch 5:3
ʰ20:13 Dt 13:13; Jdg 19:22; 1Sm 2:12; 10:27; 25:17; 1Kg 21:10,13; 2Ch 13:7
ⁱDt 13:5; 17:7,12; 19:19; 21:21; 22:21-24; 24:7
ʲ20:15 Nm 1:36-37; 2:23; 26:41
ᵏ20:18 Nm 27:21; Jdg 18:5; 1Sm 14:37; 1Ch 14:10

Abuse themᵃ and do whatever you wantᴬ to them. But don't commit this outrageous thing against this man."

²⁵ But the men would not listen to him, so the man seized his concubine and took her outside to them. They rapedᴮ her and abused her all night until morning. At daybreak they let her go. ²⁶ Early that morning, the woman made her way back, and as it was getting light, she collapsed at the doorway of the man's house where her master was.

²⁷ When her master got up in the morning, opened the doors of the house, and went out to leave on his journey, there was the woman, his concubine, collapsed near the doorway of the house with her hands on the threshold. ²⁸ "Get up," he told her. "Let's go." But there was no response.ᵇ So the man put her on his donkey and set out for home.

²⁹ When he entered his house, he picked up a knife, took hold of his concubine, cut her into twelve pieces, limb by limb, and then sent her throughout the territory of Israel. ³⁰ Everyone who saw it said, "Nothing like this has ever happened or has been seen since the day the Israelites came out of the land of Egypt until now.ᶜ Think it over, discuss it, and speak up!"

WAR AGAINST BENJAMIN

20 All the Israelites from Dan to Beer-sheabaᶜ and from the land of Gilead came out, and the community assembled as one body before the Lᴏʀᴅ at Mizpah.ᵈ ² The leadersᵉ of all the people and of all the tribes of Israel presented themselves in the assembly of God's people: four hundred thousand armedᴰ foot soldiers. ³ The Benjaminites heard that the Israelites had gone up to Mizpah.

The Israelites asked, "Tell us, how did this evil act happen?"

⁴ The Levite, the husband of the murdered woman, answered: "I went to Gibeah in Benjamin with my concubine to spend the night. ⁵ Citizens of Gibeah came to attack me and surrounded the house at night. They intended to kill me, but they raped my concubine, and she died. ⁶ Then I took my concubine and cut her in pieces, and sent her throughout Israel's territory, because they have committed a wicked outrage inᶠ Israel. ⁷ Look, all of you are Israelites. Give your judgment and verdict here and now."

⁸ Then all the people stood united and said, "None of us will go to his tent or return to his house. ⁹ Now this is what we will do to Gibeah: we will attack it. By lot ¹⁰ we will take ten men out of every hundred from all the tribes of Israel, and one hundred out of every thousand, and one thousand out of every ten thousand to get provisions for the troops when they go to Gibeah in Benjamin to punish them for all the outrage they committed in Israel."

¹¹ So all the men of Israelᵍ gathered united against the city. ¹² Then the tribes of Israel sent men throughout the tribe of Benjamin, saying, "What is this evil act that has happened among you? ¹³ Hand over the wicked menʰ in Gibeah so we can put them to death and eradicate evilⁱ from Israel." But the Benjaminites would not listen to their fellow Israelites. ¹⁴ Instead, the Benjaminites gathered together from their cities to Gibeah to go out and fight against the Israelites. ¹⁵ On that day the Benjaminites mobilized twenty-six thousand armed menᴱʲ from their cities, besides seven hundred fit young men rallied by the inhabitants of Gibeah. ¹⁶ There were seven hundred fit young men who were left-handed among all these troops; all could sling a stone at a hair and not miss.

¹⁷ The Israelites, apart from Benjamin, mobilized four hundred thousand armed men, every one an experienced warrior. ¹⁸ They set out, went to Bethel, and inquired of God.ᵏ The Israelites asked, "Who

19:25-27 The Levite grew so concerned for his own safety that he cruelly delivered his concubine over to be **raped** by these men all night! He slept while she was **abused** (19:25). **19:29-30** After the terrible events in Gibeah, the man cut his murdered concubine **into twelve pieces . . . and then sent her throughout the territory of Israel** (19:29). Those who saw the grim deliveries said, **Nothing like this has ever happened . . . since the day the Israelites came out of the land of Egypt** (19:30).

When people within a nation move away from honoring God, debauchery, decline, and chaos inevitably set in. It doesn't matter who is in power. Until the spiritual aspect gets rectified and idols are dismissed—specifically among God's people—there will be no divine standard operating within that country that can stop the downhill race into tragedy. **20:9-14** The Israelites decided to **attack** Gibeah **to punish them for all the outrage they committed** (20:9-10). Then they sent

messengers throughout Benjamin (since Gibeah was in the territory of Benjamin) saying, **Hand over the wicked men in Gibeah so we can . . . eradicate evil from Israel** (20:13). The result would be a civil war.

The Benjaminites preferred to defend their own evil tribesmen rather than let the instigators face judgment (20:14). Their misplaced loyalty should make us ask whether we are willing to endorse what is wrong for the sake of a relationship.

is to go first to fight for us against the Benjaminites?"

And the LORD answered, "Judah will be first."

19 In the morning, the Israelites set out and camped near Gibeah. **20** The men of Israel went out to fight against Benjamin and took their battle positions against Gibeah. **21** The Benjaminites came out of Gibeah and slaughtered twenty-two thousand men of Israel on the field that day. **22** But the Israelite troops rallied and again took their battle positions in the same place where they positioned themselves on the first day. **23** They went up, wept[a] before the LORD until evening,[b] and inquired of him: "Should we again attack our brothers the Benjaminites?"

And the LORD answered: "Fight against them."

24 On the second day the Israelites advanced against the Benjaminites. **25** That same day the Benjaminites came out from Gibeah to meet them and slaughtered an additional eighteen thousand Israelites on the field; all were armed.[A]

26 The whole Israelite army went to Bethel where they wept and sat before the LORD.[c] They fasted that day until evening and offered burnt offerings and fellowship offerings to the LORD. **27** Then the Israelites inquired of the LORD. In those days, the ark of the covenant[d] of God was there, **28** and Phinehas son of Eleazar, son of Aaron,[e] was serving before it. The Israelites asked: "Should we again fight against our brothers the Benjaminites or should we stop?"

The LORD answered: "Fight, because I will hand them over to you tomorrow."[f] **29** So Israel set up an ambush[g] around Gibeah. **30** On the third day the Israelites fought against the Benjaminites and took their battle positions against Gibeah as before. **31** Then the Benjaminites came out against the troops and were drawn away from the city.[h] They began to attack the troops as before, killing about thirty men of Israel on the highways, one of which goes up to Bethel and the other to Gibeah through the open country. **32** The Benjaminites said, "We are defeating them as before."

But the Israelites said, "Let's flee and draw them away from the city to the highways." **33** So all the men of Israel got up from their places and took their battle positions at Baal-tamar, while the Israelites in ambush charged out of their places west of[B] Geba.[i] **34** Then ten thousand fit young men from all Israel made a frontal assault against Gibeah, and the battle was fierce, but the Benjaminites did not know that disaster was about to strike them. **35** The LORD defeated Benjamin in the presence of Israel, and on that day the Israelites slaughtered 25,100 men of Benjamin; all were armed. **36** Then the Benjaminites realized they had been defeated.

The men of Israel had retreated before Benjamin, because they were confident in the ambush they had set against Gibeah. **37** The men in ambush had rushed quickly against Gibeah; they advanced and put the whole city to the sword.[j] **38** The men of Israel had a prearranged signal with the men in ambush: when they sent up a great cloud of smoke from the city, **39** the men of Israel would return to the battle. When Benjamin had begun to strike them down, killing about thirty men of Israel, they said, "They're defeated before us, just as they were in the first battle."[k] **40** But when the column of smoke began to go up from the city, Benjamin looked behind them, and the whole city was going up in smoke.[c] **41** Then the men of Israel returned, and the men of Benjamin were terrified when they realized that disaster had struck them. **42** They retreated before the men of Israel toward the wilderness,[l] but the battle overtook them, and those who came out of the cities[D] slaughtered those between them. **43** They surrounded the Benjaminites, pursued them, and easily overtook them near Gibeah toward the east. **44** There were eighteen thousand men who died from Benjamin; all were warriors. **45** Then Benjamin turned and fled toward the wilderness to Rimmon Rock,[m] and Israel killed five thousand men on the highways. They overtook them at Gidom and struck two thousand more dead.

46 All the Benjaminites who died that day were twenty-five thousand armed men; all were warriors. **47** But six

[a] 20:23 Jos 7:6-7
[b] 2Sm 1:12
[c] 20:26 Jdg 21:2
[d] 20:27 1Sm 4:4; 2Sm 15:24; 1Ch 16:6
[e] 20:28 Nm 25:7,11
[f] Jdg 7:9
[g] 20:29 Jos 8:4
[h] 20:31 Jos 8:31

[i] 20:33 Jos 8:19
[j] 20:37 Dt 13:15; Jos 10:37,39; 11:12,14; Jdg 1:8,25; 18:27; 20:48; 1Sm 22:19; 2Sm 15:14; 2Kg 10:25; Jr 21:7; Ezk 5:2
[k] 20:39 Jdg 20:32
[l] 20:42 Jos 8:15,24
[m] 20:45 Jdg 21:13

[A] **20:25** Lit *were drawing the sword*, also in v. 35　[B] **20:33** LXX, Syr, Vg; MT reads *places in the plain of*, or *places in the cave of*　[C] **20:40** Lit *up to the sky*　[D] **20:42** LXX, Vg read *city*

20:35 In the first two battles (20:19-25) the Israelites prayed and inquired of God while allowing unaddressed sin to linger in their midst. But before battle number three, they offered a sacrifice for their sins and a fellowship offering to make sure there was harmony between them and the Lord (20:26). If you have a request to make of God, make sure you deal with any known sin in your life before expecting him to overrule your circumstances (see Jas 1:19-21).

*21:1 Jdg 21:7,18
*21:2 Jdg 20:26
*21:4 2Sm 24:25
*21:10 Nm 31:17

*21:13 Dt 20:10
*21:19 Jos 18:1; Jdg 18:31;
          1Sm 1:3
*21:21 Ex 15:20; Jdg 11:34
*21:23 Jdg 20:48
*21:25 Jdg 17:6; 18:1; 19:1

hundred men escaped into the wilderness to Rimmon Rock and stayed there four months. ⁴⁸ The men of Israel turned back against the other Benjaminites and killed them with their swords — the entire city, the animals, and everything that remained. They also burned all the cities that remained.

BRIDES FOR BENJAMIN

21 The men of Israel had sworn an oath at Mizpah: "None of us will give his daughter to a Benjaminite in marriage."ᵃ ² So the people went to Bethel and sat there before Godᵇ until evening. They wept loudly and bitterly, ³ and cried out, "Why, LORD God of Israel, has it occurredᴬ that one tribe is missing in Israel today?" ⁴ The next day the people got up early, built an altar there,ᶜ and offered burnt offerings and fellowship offerings. ⁵ The Israelites asked, "Who of all the tribes of Israel didn't come to the LORD with the assembly?" For a great oath had been taken that anyone who had not come to the LORD at Mizpah would certainly be put to death.

⁶ But the Israelites had compassion on their brothers, the Benjaminites, and said, "Today a tribe has been cut off from Israel. ⁷ What should we do about wives for the survivors? We've sworn to the LORD not to give them any of our daughters as wives." ⁸ They asked, "Which city among the tribes of Israel didn't come to the LORD at Mizpah?" It turned out that no one from Jabesh-gilead had come to the camp and the assembly. ⁹ For when the roll was called, no men were there from the inhabitants of Jabesh-gilead.

¹⁰ The congregation sent twelve thousand brave warriorsᴮ there and commanded them: "Go and kill the inhabitants of Jabesh-gilead with the sword,ᵈ including women and dependents. ¹¹ This is what you should do: Completely destroy every male, as well as every woman who has gone to bed with a man." ¹² They found among the inhabitants of Jabesh-gilead four hundred young virgins, who had not gone to bed with a man,

and they brought them to the camp at Shiloh in the land of Canaan.

¹³ The whole congregation sent a message of peaceᵉ to the Benjaminites who were at Rimmon Rock. ¹⁴ Benjamin returned at that time, and Israel gave them the women they had kept alive from Jabesh-gilead. But there were not enough for them.

¹⁵ The people had compassion on Benjamin, because the LORD had made this gap in the tribes of Israel. ¹⁶ The elders of the congregation said, "What should we do about wives for those who are left, since the women of Benjamin have been destroyed?" ¹⁷ They said, "There must be heirs for the survivors of Benjamin, so that a tribe of Israel will not be wiped out. ¹⁸ But we can't give them our daughters as wives." For the Israelites had sworn, "Anyone who gives a wife to a Benjaminite is cursed." ¹⁹ They also said, "Look, there's an annual festival to the LORD in Shiloh,ᶠ which is north of Bethel, east of the highway that goes up from Bethel to Shechem, and south of Lebonah."

²⁰ Then they commanded the Benjaminites: "Go and hide in the vineyards. ²¹ Watch, and when you see the young women of Shiloh come out to perform the dances,ᵍ each of you leave the vineyards and catch a wife for yourself from the young women of Shiloh, and go to the land of Benjamin. ²² When their fathers or brothers come to us and protest, we will tell them, 'Show favor to them, since we did not get enough wives for each of them in the battle. You didn't actually give the women to them, soᶜ you are not guilty of breaking your oath.'"

²³ The Benjaminites did this and took the number of women they needed from the dancers they caught. They went back to their own inheritance, rebuilt their cities,ʰ and lived in them. ²⁴ At that time, each of the Israelites returned from there to his own tribe and family. Each returned from there to his own inheritance.

²⁵ In those days there was no king in Israel;ⁱ everyone did whatever seemed right to him.

ᴬ21:3 Lit *has this occurred in Israel*   ᴮ21:10 Lit *twelve thousand of their sons of valor*   ᶜ21:22 Lit *at this time*

21:8-14 Since the city of **Jabesh-gilead** had not come out to fight against Benjamin (21:8), the Israelites decided to put the city to death and take its **virgins** as wives for the Benjaminites (21:12). Thus, in spite of a season of repentance, Israel continued to slide into moral darkness. **21:22** Fallen human beings are good at justifying their actions and explaining away their guilt.

21:25 Judges ends with an indictment against the people of God—who looked nothing like "people of God." They had turned from God to idols, and there wasn't even a king to steer the people back to God through his example.

Thankfully, this is no longer the case. Though the judges and even the later kings of Israel were always imperfect and often wicked, we now have a Judge and King like no other: Jesus Christ. He alone can turn sinners to the living and true God, making them holy and upright. Will you submit to his kingdom rule over your life?

RUTH

INTRODUCTION

Author

THOUGH ANCIENT JEWISH SOURCES ATTRIBUTED the authorship of Ruth to the prophet Samuel, there is no mention in the book of the writer's identity. Given the genealogy at the end (4:18-22), the book was written during or after the reign of King David, who ruled from 1011 to 971 BC.

Historical Background

The book is set "during the time of the judges" (1:1), which the author of Judges describes as a sad period in Israel's history when "there was no king in Israel" and "everyone did whatever seemed right to him" (Judg 21:25). The period lasted about three hundred years, from Joshua's death until the rise of Israel's monarchy. Though we don't know when the events of the book of Ruth took place within this frame, "there was a famine in the land" at the time (Ruth 1:1).

Ruth, the book's namesake, was a Moabitess. The land of Moab was to the west of Judah, on the far side of the Dead Sea. The people of Moab were descended from Lot (Abraham's nephew) and his firstborn daughter (see Gen 19:30-38). Though Ruth was a Gentile descended from these humble circumstances, she worshiped the God of Israel, married into God's chosen people, and became the ancestress of King David and Jesus Christ.

Message and Purpose

This book is personal, prophetic, and full of theology. Written during the dark days of the period of Israel's judges, Ruth centers on a Gentile woman by that name. Through her experiences, we see the demonstration of God's providence, grace, love, and redemption.

Ruth was from Moab. Her mother-in-law, an Israelite named Naomi, was living in Moab when her husband and two sons (one of them being Ruth's husband) died. Ruth made a faith decision to go back to Israel with Naomi because she had adopted the true God of Israel as her own. In Bethlehem, Ruth experienced God's providential provision—his invisible hand at work through the glove of history. She made a connection with a man named Boaz, who "was one of [their] family redeemers" (Ruth 2:20). That role was designed to ensure that a man's lineage continued even if he had no heirs. The couple's story provides an illustration of God's love for Gentiles within the framework of his covenant with Israel.

Through Ruth's marriage to Boaz, she became the grandmother of King David, the ancestor of Jesus Christ. In her story we see the lengths to which God went to ensure that Jesus legally qualified to be Israel's Messiah and Savior of the world. This is why Ruth's name appears in Jesus's genealogy (see Matt 1:5). The book of Ruth shows how God can take messes and make miracles in order to advance his kingdom program, plan, and agenda.

VIDEO | INTRO

www.bhpublishinggroup.com/qr/te/08_00

Outline

I. Disappointment (1:1-22)
II. Service (2:1-23)
III. Hope (3:1-18)
IV. Redemption (4:1-22)

NAOMI'S FAMILY IN MOAB

1 During the time[A] of the judges,[a] there was a famine in the land.[b] A man left Bethlehem[B,c] in Judah with his wife and two sons to stay in the territory of Moab for a while. **2** The man's name was Elimelech,[c] and his wife's name was Naomi.[D] The names of his two sons were Mahlon[E] and Chilion.[F] They were Ephrathites[d] from Bethlehem in Judah. They entered the fields of Moab and settled there. **3** Naomi's husband Elimelech died, and she was left with her two sons. **4** Her sons took Moabite women as their wives: one was named Orpah and the second was named Ruth. After they lived in Moab about ten years, **5** both Mahlon and Chilion also died, and Naomi was left without her two children and without her husband.

RUTH'S LOYALTY TO NAOMI

6 She and her daughters-in-law set out to return from the territory of Moab, because she had heard in Moab that the LORD had paid attention to his people's need by providing them food.[e] **7** She left the place where she had been living, accompanied by her two daughters-in-law, and traveled along the road leading back to the land of Judah.

8 Naomi said to them, "Each of you go back to your mother's home.[f] May the LORD show kindness to you as you have shown to the dead and to me. **9** May the LORD grant each of you rest[g] in the house of a new husband." She kissed them, and they wept loudly.

10 They said to her, "We insist on returning with you to your people."

11 But Naomi replied, "Return home, my daughters. Why do you want to go with me? Am I able to have any more sons who could become your husbands?[h] **12** Return home, my daughters. Go on, for I am too old to have

another husband. Even if I thought there was still hope for me to have a husband tonight and to bear sons, **13** would you be willing to wait for them to grow up? Would you restrain yourselves from remarrying?[G] No, my daughters, my life is much too bitter for you to share,[H] because the LORD's hand has turned against me."[I] **14** Again they wept loudly, and Orpah kissed her mother-in-law, but Ruth clung to her. **15** Naomi said, "Look, your sister-in-law has gone back to her people and to her gods.[J] Follow your sister-in-law."

16 But Ruth replied:

Don't plead with me
  to abandon you
or to return and not follow you.
For wherever you go, I will go,
  and wherever you live, I will live;
your people will be my people,
  and your God will be my God.
17 Where you die, I will die,
  and there I will be buried.
May the LORD punish me,[I,k]
  and do so severely,
if anything but death separates you
  and me.

18 When Naomi saw that Ruth was determined to go with her, she stopped talking to her.

19 The two of them traveled until they came to Bethlehem. When they entered Bethlehem, the whole town was excited about their arrival[J,l] and the local women exclaimed, "Can this be Naomi?"

20 "Don't call me Naomi,"[K] she answered, "for the Almighty[m] has made me very bitter.[n] **21** I went away full, but the LORD has brought me back empty. Why do you call me Naomi, since the LORD has opposed[L] me, and the Almighty has afflicted me?"

22 So Naomi came back from the territory of Moab with her daughter-in-law Ruth

[a]1:1 Jdg 2:16-18
[b]Gn 12:10; 26:1; 43:1; 2Kg 8:1
[c]Jdg 17:7; 19:1
[d]1:2 Gn 35:19; 1Sm 17:12; 1Ch 4:4; Mc 5:2
[e]1:6 Ex 4:31; 1Sm 2:21
[f]1:8 Gn 24:28
[g]1:9 Ru 3:1
[h]1:11 Gn 38:11; Dt 25:5
[i]1:13 Jdg 2:15; Jb 19:21; Ps 32:4; 38:2; 39:10
[j]1:15 Jdg 11:24; 1Kg 11:7; Jr 48:7,13,46
[k]1:17 1Sm 3:17; 2Sm 3:9,35; 1Kg 2:23; 2Kg 6:31
[l]1:19 Mt 21:10
[m]1:20 Gn 49:25; Ex 6:3; Nm 24:4; Jb 6:4
[n]Ex 15:23
[o]1:21 Ru 3:17

[A]1:1 Lit In the days of the judging   [B]1:1 = House of Bread   [C]1:2 = My God Is King   [D]1:2 = Pleasant   [E]1:2 = Sickly   [F]1:2 = Weak or Failing   [G]1:13 Lit marrying a man   [H]1:13 Lit daughters, for more bitter to me than you   [I]1:17 A solemn oath formula; 1Sm 3:17; 2Sm 3:9,35; 1Kg 2:23; 2Kg 6:31   [J]1:19 Lit excited because of them   [K]1:20 = Bitter   [L]1:21 LXX, Syr, Vg read has humiliated

1:1 The time of the judges was a miserable period in Israel's history when a vicious cycle kept repeating itself: the people fell into idolatry, God let their enemies oppress them, they cried out for deliverance, God raised up a judge to rescue them, and they fell into idolatry again. Thus, the **famine** mentioned here was likely a result of God judging Israel's idolatry. **1:5** In other words, Naomi's circumstances had spiraled down to a point at which she had no way to provide for herself in Moab. **1:6-7** When Naomi heard that the famine back in her native Israel had ended, she determined to return home to **Judah** (1:7).

1:13 Naomi felt **the LORD's hand [had] turned against** her, yet it was through her difficult situation that God would work in a big way. **1:16-17** Ruth preferred widowhood and its challenges to abandoning Naomi and her God—a fact suggesting that she'd probably come to place faith in him, at least in part through the woman's witness. In renouncing the idolatry of the Moabites and embracing Israel's God as her own, Ruth made a complete break with her past. **1:20-22** While Naomi was truly in despair, it was time for **the barley harvest** (1:22). She

could see that God had ended the famine, the very thing that had driven her family off and to their graves. There was hope in the midst of her hopelessness.

Through this story God was preparing sleepy **Bethlehem** (1:22), hometown to Naomi and the male lead to whom we are introduced in the next chapter, as the site of his miraculous interruption at a later point in history (see Mic 5:2; Matt 2:1).

the Moabitess. They arrived in Bethlehem at the beginning of the barley harvest.[a]

RUTH AND BOAZ MEET

2 Now Naomi had a relative on her husband's side. He was a prominent man of noble character[b] from Elimelech's family. His name was Boaz.

[2] Ruth the Moabitess asked Naomi, "Will you let me go into the fields and gather fallen grain[c] behind someone with whom I find favor?"

Naomi answered her, "Go ahead, my daughter." [3] So Ruth left and entered the field to gather grain behind the harvesters. She happened[d] to be in the portion of the field belonging to Boaz, who was from Elimelech's family.

[4] Later, when Boaz arrived from Bethlehem, he said to the harvesters, "The LORD be with you."[e]

"The LORD bless you,"[f] they replied.

[5] Boaz asked his servant who was in charge of the harvesters, "Whose young woman is this?"

[6] The servant answered, "She is the young Moabite woman who returned with Naomi from the territory of Moab. [7] She asked, 'Will you let me gather fallen grain among the bundles behind the harvesters?' She came and has been on her feet since early morning, except that she rested a little in the shelter."[A]

[8] Then Boaz said to Ruth, "Listen, my daughter.[B] Don't go and gather grain in another field, and don't leave this one, but stay here close to my female servants. [9] See which field they are harvesting, and follow them. Haven't I ordered the young men not to touch you?[c] When you are thirsty, go and drink from the jars the young men have filled."

[10] She fell facedown, bowed to the ground,[g] and said to him, "Why have I found favor with you, so that you notice me, although I am a foreigner?"

[11] Boaz answered her, "Everything you have done for your mother-in-law since your husband's death has been fully reported to me: how you left your father and mother and your native land, and how you came to a people you didn't previously know. [12] May the LORD reward you for what you have done,[h] and may you receive a full reward from the LORD God of Israel, under whose wings you have come for refuge."[i]

[13] "My lord," she said, "I have found favor with you, for you have comforted and encouraged[D] your servant, although I am not like one of your female servants."

[14] At mealtime Boaz told her, "Come over here and have some bread and dip it in the vinegar sauce." So she sat beside the harvesters, and he offered her roasted grain. She ate and was satisfied and had some left over.

[15] When she got up to gather grain, Boaz ordered his young men, "Let her even gather grain among the bundles, and don't humiliate her. [16] Pull out some stalks from the bundles for her and leave them for her to gather. Don't rebuke her." [17] So Ruth gathered grain in the field until evening. She beat out what she had gathered, and it was about twenty-six quarts[E] of barley. [18] She picked up the grain and went into the town, where her mother-in-law saw what she had gleaned. She brought out what she had left over from her meal and gave it to her.

[19] Her mother-in-law said to her, "Where did you gather barley today, and where did you work? May the LORD bless the man who noticed you."[j]

Ruth told her mother-in-law whom she had worked with and said, "The name of the man I worked with today is Boaz."

[20] Then Naomi said to her daughter-in-law, "May the LORD[k] bless him because he has not abandoned his kindness to the living or the dead."[l] Naomi continued, "The man is a close relative. He is one of our family redeemers."[m]

[a] 1:22 Ex 9:31; Lv 23:10-11
[b] 2:1 Ru 1:2
[c] 2:2 Lv 19:9-10; 23:22
[d] 2:3 Pr 16:33; 20:24
[e] 2:4 1Sm 20:13
[f] Nm 6:24
[g] 2:10 1Sm 25:23,41

[h] 2:12 1Sm 24:19
[i] Ru 1:16; Ps 17:8; 36:7; 57:1; 63:7
[j] 2:19 Ps 41:1
[k] 2:20 2Sm 2:5
[l] Ru 1:8
[m] Lv 25:25-26; Ru 3:9,12; 4:1-8,14; Ps 19:14; Is 41:14

[A] 2:7 LXX reads *morning, and until evening she has not rested in the field a little*; Vg reads *morning until now and she did not return to the house*; Hb uncertain
[B] 2:8 Lit *"Haven't you heard, my daughter?"*   [C] 2:9 Either sexual or physical harassment   [D] 2:13 Lit *and spoken to the heart of*   [E] 2:17 Lit *about an ephah*

2:1 **Boaz** was a wealthy **relative** of Elimelech and, as Matthew 1:5 reveals, the son of Rahab, the same former prostitute who hid Israel's spies and survived the collapse of Jericho because of her faith in God (see Josh 2:1-24; 6:22-25).
2:2 The law of Moses (as if it had been given with Ruth and Naomi in mind) provided for the poor by commanding the Israelites to leave behind some grain at harvest time so that the poor could gather it and have food (see Lev 19:9-10; 23:22; Deut 24:19-21).

2:3 Seemingly by chance, Ruth **happened to [find herself working] in the portion of the field belonging to Boaz**. Of course nothing happens by chance, and no one just happens to be anywhere. The use of "happened to be" is the author's way of acknowledging the providential working of God in Ruth's life.
2:11-12 Boaz essentially told Ruth that she was simply reaping the blessings of the kind of life she had sown. Her kindness, service to her **mother-in-law** (2:11), and decision to take **refuge** under the Lord's provision (2:12) had

brought blessing on her own head. Because of Ruth's faithful commitment, Boaz pronounced a blessing on her, asking that the Lord—**under whose wings [she had] come for** protection—would provide a spiritual covering for her (2:12).
2:20 As a "family redeemer" (or kinsmen redeemer), Boaz could fulfill the law of levirate marriage (see Deut 25:5-10). This was an ancient provision that meant that if an Israelite man were to die without having a son as an heir to carry on his family

a 2:23 Dt 16:9
b 3:2 Dt 25:5-10
c 3:9 Ezk 16:8
d Ru 2:12

e 3:10 Ru 2:20
f 3:11 Ru 2:1; Pr 12:4; 31:10
g 3:13 Dt 25:5; Ru 4:5
h Jdg 8:19; 1Sm 14:39,45;
19:6; 2Sm 4:9; 12:5; 2Kg
2:2,6
i 4:1 Ru 3:11-12; 2Sm 15:2;
18:4,24,33; 19:8; Ps 127:5
j 4:2 Dt 19:12; 21:3-6; 1Kg
21:8; Pr 31:23

21 Ruth the Moabitess said, "He also told me, 'Stay with my young men until they have finished all of my harvest.'"

22 So Naomi said to her daughter-in-law Ruth, "My daughter, it is good for you to work[A] with his female servants, so that nothing will happen to you in another field." **23** Ruth stayed close to Boaz's female servants and gathered grain until the barley and the wheat harvests were finished.[a] And she lived with[B] her mother-in-law.

RUTH'S APPEAL TO BOAZ

3 Ruth's mother-in-law Naomi said to her, "My daughter, shouldn't I find rest for you, so that you will be taken care of? **2** Now isn't Boaz our relative?[b] Haven't you been working with his female servants? This evening he will be winnowing barley on the threshing floor. **3** Wash, put on perfumed oil, and wear your best clothes. Go down to the threshing floor, but don't let the man know you are there until he has finished eating and drinking. **4** When he lies down, notice the place where he's lying, go in and uncover his feet, and lie down. Then he will explain to you what you should do."

5 So Ruth said to her, "I will do everything you say."[C] **6** She went down to the threshing floor and did everything her mother-in-law had charged her to do. **7** After Boaz ate, drank, and was in good spirits,[D] he went to lie down at the end of the pile of barley, and she came secretly, uncovered his feet, and lay down.

8 At midnight, Boaz was startled, turned over, and there lying at his feet was a woman! **9** So he asked, "Who are you?"

"I am Ruth, your servant," she replied. "Take me under your wing,[E,c] for you are a family redeemer."[d]

10 Then he said, "May the LORD bless you,[e] my daughter. You have shown more kindness now than before,[F] because you have not pursued younger men, whether rich or poor. **11** Now don't be afraid, my daughter. I will do for you whatever you say,[G] since all the people in my town[H] know that you are a woman of noble character.[f] **12** Yes, it is true that I am a family redeemer, but there is a redeemer closer than I am. **13** Stay here tonight, and in the morning, if he wants to redeem you, that's good.[g] Let him redeem you. But if he doesn't want to redeem you, as the LORD lives,[h] I will. Now lie down until morning."

14 So she lay down at his feet until morning but got up while it was still dark.[I] Then Boaz said, "Don't let it be known that a[J] woman came to the threshing floor." **15** And he told Ruth, "Bring the shawl you're wearing and hold it out." When she held it out, he shoveled six measures of barley into her shawl, and she[K] went into the town.

16 She went to her mother-in-law, Naomi, who asked her, "What happened,[L] my daughter?"

Then Ruth told her everything the man had done for her. **17** She said, "He gave me these six measures of barley, because he said,[M] 'Don't go back to your mother-in-law empty-handed.'"

18 Naomi said, "My daughter, wait until you find out how things go, for he won't rest unless he resolves this today."

RUTH AND BOAZ MARRY

4 Boaz went to the gate of the town[i] and sat down there. Soon the family redeemer Boaz had spoken about came by. Boaz said, "Come over here[N] and sit down." So he went over and sat down. **2** Then Boaz took ten men of the town's elders[j] and said,

A 2:22 Lit *go out*   B 2:23 Some Hb mss, Vg read *she returned to*   C 3:5 Alt Hb tradition reads *say to me*   D 3:7 Lit *and his heart was glad*   E 3:9 Or *"Spread the edge of your garment;* lit *"Spread the wing of your garment;* Ru 2:12   F 3:10 Lit *kindness at the last than at the first*   G 3:11 Some Hb mss, Orig, Syr, Tg, Vg read *say to me*   H 3:11 Lit *all the gate of my people*   I 3:14 Lit *up before a man could recognize his companion*   J 3:14 LXX; MT reads *the*   K 3:15 Some Hb mss, Aramaic, Syr, Vg; other Hb mss read *he*   L 3:16 Lit *"Who are you*   M 3:17 Alt Hb tradition, LXX, Syr, Tg read *said to me*   N 4:1 Or *said, "Come here Mr. So-and-so*

name, the man's brother could provide for the deceased by marrying his widow. Then "the first son she [bore would] carry on the name of the dead brother, so his name [would] not be blotted out from Israel" (Deut 25:6).

3:1-4 Naomi decided to become a matchmaker (3:1). She told Ruth to go to Boaz's **threshing floor** that night. The threshing floor was where the **winnowing** would take place, separating the **barley** from the inedible chaff (3:2). During the harvest, Boaz would have spent the night there to prevent theft of his grain. Naomi advised Ruth to **uncover his feet, and lie down** after he finished **eating**

and drinking and went to sleep for the night. Once Boaz realized she was there, he would **explain** what she **should do** next (3:3-4).

3:6-9 Through her words and actions here Ruth was making a marriage proposal. She was requesting that Boaz perform his legal responsibility as a family redeemer (see 2:19-20). By asking him to take her **under [his] wing,** Ruth was reminding him of the blessing he had pronounced on her previously (3:9; see 2:12). Ruth was challenging him to become the human expression of God's divine covering.

3:12-13 The word **redeem** appears multiple times here. Through its use, Boaz is presented as an Old Testament picture of Jesus Christ,

who redeemed or "bought back" sinners from slavery to sin. Through Christ our Redeemer, we are forgiven, set free from sin, made new creations, and have a new relationship with God (see Rom 3:23-24; Gal 3:13-14; 4:4-5; Eph 1:13-14; Col 1:13-14; Heb 9:11-12). If Boaz were to redeem Ruth, she'd be bought out of slavery to her impoverished circumstances and formally adopted into God's chosen family.

3:14 Ruth arose and **left while it was still dark** so that no one would see her and misconstrue the night's events, bringing harm to their reputations.

4:1 Boaz went to the gate of the town, where business and civic activities were conducted.

"Sit here." And they sat down. ³ He said to the redeemer, "Naomi, who has returned from the territory of Moab, is selling the portion of the field that belonged to our brother Elimelech.ᵃ ⁴ I thought I should inform you:ᴬ Buy it back in the presence of those seated here and in the presence of the elders of my people. If you want to redeem it, do it. But if you doᴮ not want to redeem it, tell me so that I will know, because there isn't anyone other than you to redeem it, and I am next after you."

"I want to redeem it," he answered.

⁵ Then Boaz said, "On the day you buy the field from Naomi, you will acquireᶜ Ruth the Moabitess, the wife of the deceased man, to perpetuate the man's name on his property."ᴰ,ᵇ

⁶ The redeemer replied, "I can't redeem it myself, or I will ruin my own inheritance. Take my right of redemption, because I can't redeem it."

⁷ At an earlier period in Israel, a man removed his sandalᶜ and gave it to the other party in order to make any matter legally binding concerning the right of redemption or the exchange of property. This was the method of legally binding a transaction in Israel.

⁸ So the redeemer removed his sandal and said to Boaz, "Buy back the property yourself."

⁹ Boaz said to the elders and all the people, "You are witnesses today that I am buying from Naomi everything that belonged to Elimelech, Chilion, and Mahlon. ¹⁰ I have also acquired Ruth the Moabitess, Mahlon's widow, as my wife, to perpetuate the deceased man's name on his property, so that his name will not disappear among his relatives or from the gate of his hometown. You are witnesses today."

¹¹ All the people who were at the city gate, including the elders, said, "We are witnesses. May the LORD make the woman who is entering your house like Rachel and Leah,ᵈ who together built the house of Israel. May you be powerful in Ephrathah and your name well known in Bethlehem. ¹² May your house become like the house of Perez, the son Tamar bore to Judah,ᵉ because of the offspring the LORD will give you by this young woman."

¹³ Boaz took Ruth and she became his wife. He slept with her, and the LORD granted conception to her, and she gave birth to a son. ¹⁴ The women said to Naomi, "Blessed be the LORD, who has not left you without a family redeemer today. May his name become well known in Israel. ¹⁵ He will renew your life and sustain you in your old age. Indeed, your daughter-in-law, who loves you and is better to you than seven sons,ᶠ has given birth to him." ¹⁶ Naomi took the child, placed him on her lap, and became his nanny. ¹⁷ The neighbor women said, "A son has been born to Naomi," and they named him Obed.ᴱ He was the father of Jesse, the father of David.

DAVID'S GENEALOGY FROM JUDAH'S SON

¹⁸ Now these are the family records of Perez:
   Perez fathered Hezron,
¹⁹ Hezron fathered Ram,ᶠ
   Ram fathered Amminadab,
²⁰ Amminadab fathered Nahshon,
   Nahshon fathered Salmon,
²¹ Salmon fathered Boaz,
   Boaz fathered Obed,
²² Obed fathered Jesse,
   and Jesse fathered David.ᵍ

ᵃ 4:3 Lv 25:25
ᵇ 4:5 Gn 38:6-11; Lv 25:23-34; Dt 25:5-10
ᶜ 4:7 Dt 25:8-10
ᵈ 4:11 Gn 29:25-30; 35:16-18
ᵉ 4:12 Gn 38; 46:12; Ru 4:18
ᶠ 4:15 Ru 1:16-17; 2:11-12
ᵍ 4:18-22 Mt 1:3-6

ᴬ **4:4** Lit *should uncover your ear, saying*   ᴮ **4:4** Some Hb mss, LXX, Syr, Vg; other Hb mss read *if he does*   ᶜ **4:5** Lit *Naomi and from*   ᴰ **4:5** Alt Hb tradition reads *Naomi, I will have already acquired from Ruth the Moabitess, the wife of the dead man, the privilege of raising up the name of the dead man on his property*   ᴱ **4:17** = *Servant*   ᶠ **4:19** LXX reads *Aram*; Mt 1:3-4

Boaz invited the man to **sit down** with him and asked **ten** of **the town's elders** to join them. These men would serve as witnesses of the legal proceedings that were about to transpire. **4:3-5** Since he was the closest relation, the unnamed man had first rights to buy Naomi's land. When he jumped at the chance (4:4), Boaz noted that if the guy redeemed the land, he would also be redeeming the widow Ruth for a wife **to perpetuate the [deceased] man's name on his property** (4:5). That meant that with the economic acquisition came a social acquisition. **4:7-9** At that time in Israel you couldn't sign some legal documents and have them notarized. So a **legally binding** transaction of this nature was ratified by the custom of a man

giving **his sandal** to another party with whom he was doing business (4:7). **4:10** Boaz acquired Ruth and the property out of concern for others—**to perpetuate the deceased man's name on his property, so that his name [would] not disappear among his relatives.** This sacrifice brings to mind this New Testament principle: "Whoever wants to save his life will lose it, but whoever loses his life because of me will find it" (Matt 16:25). Often blessings follow when we lay down our priorities for the sake of God's kingdom. **4:11 Rachel and Leah** gave birth to many of the fathers of the tribes of Israel. **4:12** Little did they know how famous Boaz would become or how great his offspring would be (see Matt 1:5-17)!

4:17-22 Ruth and Boaz's son **Obed** (4:17) would be grandfather to David, the great king of Israel. The ancient Israelites to whom the author was writing knew of this amazing heritage.

What they didn't know was that there was an even greater descendant to come from this bloodline. The kingly line of David would ultimately lead to the Messiah, Jesus Christ (see Matt 1:1-16), who would be born in his ancestral home: Bethlehem. Though Boaz and Ruth were unaware of it, their lives and decisions were part of God's kingdom program. By submitting yourself to the Lord's agenda, you open yourself to his sovereign purposes—not only for your own benefit but also potentially for the benefit of generations after you.

1 SAMUEL

INTRODUCTION

Author

THE BOOKS OF 1 AND 2 SAMUEL are named for the prophet who first appears in 1 Samuel and who anointed both Saul and David as king. Ancient Jewish tradition, in fact, attributes at least some of the material to Samuel. Since his death is reported in 1 Samuel 25, it's possible he was responsible for chapters 1–24. Additional Jewish tradition claims that the prophets Gad (who appears in 1 Sam 22) and Nathan (who appears in 2 Samuel 7;12) compiled the rest of the books (see 1 Chr 29:29). But, ultimately, the text of 1–2 Samuel does not name any author.

Historical Background

First Samuel follows on the heels of the book of Judges, which chronicles the time period after Joshua's death and before Israel's monarchy. During the time of the judges, the Israelites fell into repeated cycles of disobedience to the Lord, oppression by enemies, and deliverance by God-appointed judges. First Samuel opens in the eleventh century at the end of this period. The initial chapters describe the calling of Samuel to his ministry and the transition to a monarchy beginning with Saul. The final event in 2 Samuel (the building of David's altar at the threshing floor of Araunah) occurred in about 975 BC.

Message and Purpose

The books of 1 and 2 Samuel highlight the life and influences of the prophet Samuel—especially in the early chapters of 1 Samuel, which record his miraculous birth and his prophetic calling. Through Samuel's prophetic office, God allowed and established a king in Israel. Though God wanted to be his people's King, they wanted to have a human king like those over other nations. So he gave them Saul and then later David, the two monarchs who are the main focus of 1–2 Samuel.

These books not only show Samuel's influence over Israel in bringing God's Word to his people, they also teach some powerful spiritual lessons. We see the consequences of disobedience as Saul's failure to obey God cost him his kingdom rule. But we also see

the emergence of David as the "man after [God's] own heart" (1 Sam 13:14).

In 2 Samuel, David is anointed as king, and God makes a covenant with him to establish his royal line forever—a line through which the Messiah would come. Thus, David is a key figure in God's kingdom agenda—not only for Israel but for the whole world. Second Samuel is about spiritual priorities and obedience, but it is also about grace. When David sinned greatly, God did not take his life. He showed him mercy.

Both books teach us to walk under God's kingdom rule so that we can experience the full benefit of his kingdom blessing as kingdom people.

https://www.bhpublishinggroup.com/qrpage/introduction-to-1-2-samuel/

Outline

I. Samuel and the Transition to the Monarchy (1:1–8:22)
   A. Samuel's Birth and Early Life (1:1–3:21)
   B. The Capture and Restoration of the Ark (4:1–7:17)
   C. Israel's Demand for a King (8:1-22)

II. The Rise and Fall of King Saul (9:1–15:35)
   A. Saul's Anointing and Early Successes (9:1–12:25)
   B. Saul's Decline and Rejection (13:1–15:35)

III. David's Anointing and History under Saul (16:1–28:2)
   A. David's Anointing and Service to Saul (16:1-23)
   B. David's Defeat of Goliath (17:1-58)
   C. David's Service in Saul's Court (18:1–20:42)
   D. David's Fugitive Years (21:1–28:2)

IV. Saul's Sad Final Days and Death (28:3–31:13)
   A. Saul Consults a Medium (28:3-25)
   B. David's Movements (29:1–30:31)
   C. Saul's Death at Gilboa (31:1-13)

HANNAH'S VOW

1 There was a man from Ramathaim-zo-phim[a] in[A] the hill country of Ephraim.[b] His name was Elkanah[c] son of Jeroham, son of Elihu, son of Tohu, son of Zuph, an Ephraimite. **2** He had two wives,[d] the first named Hannah[e] and the second Peninnah. Peninnah had children, but Hannah was childless. **3** This man would go up from his town every year[f] to worship and to sacrifice[g] to the LORD of Armies at Shiloh,[h] where Eli's two sons, Hophni and Phinehas, were the LORD's priests.

4 Whenever Elkanah offered a sacrifice, he always gave portions of the meat[i] to his wife Peninnah and to each of her sons and daughters. **5** But he gave a double[B] portion[j] to Hannah, for he loved her even though the LORD had kept her from conceiving. **6** Her rival would taunt her severely just to provoke her, because the LORD had kept Hannah from conceiving. **7** Year after year, when she went up to the LORD's house,[k] her rival taunted her in this way. Hannah would weep and would not eat. **8** "Hannah, why are you crying?" her husband Elkanah would ask. "Why won't you eat? Why are you troubled? Am I not better to you than ten sons?"[l]

9 On one occasion, Hannah got up after they ate and drank at Shiloh.[c] The priest Eli was sitting on a chair by the doorpost of the LORD's temple.[m] **10** Deeply hurt, Hannah prayed to the LORD and wept with many tears.[n] **11** Making a vow,[o] she pleaded, "LORD of Armies, if you will take notice of your servant's affliction,[p] remember and not forget me, and give your servant a son,[D] I will give him to the LORD all the days of his life, and his hair will never be cut."[E,q]

12 While she continued praying in the LORD's presence, Eli watched her mouth. **13** Hannah was praying silently,[F,r] and though her lips were moving, her voice could not be heard. Eli thought she was drunk **14** and said to her, "How long are you going to be drunk?[s] Get rid of your wine!"

15 "No, my lord," Hannah replied. "I am a woman with a broken heart. I haven't had any wine or beer; I've been pouring out my heart before the LORD.[t] **16** Don't think of me as a wicked woman;[u] I've been praying from the depth of my anguish and resentment."[v]

17 Eli responded, "Go in peace,[w] and may the God of Israel grant the request you've made of him."[x]

18 "May your servant find favor with you,"[y] she replied. Then Hannah went on her way; she ate and no longer looked despondent.[G,z]

SAMUEL'S BIRTH AND DEDICATION

19 The next morning Elkanah and Hannah got up early to worship before the LORD. Afterward, they returned home to Ramah.[aa] Then Elkanah was intimate with his wife Hannah, and the LORD remembered her.[ab] **20** After some time,[H] Hannah conceived and gave birth to a son. She named him Samuel,[I] because she said, "I requested him from the LORD."

21 When Elkanah and all his household went up to make the annual sacrifice[ac] and his vow offering to the LORD, **22** Hannah did not go and explained to her husband, "After the child is weaned, I'll take him to appear in the LORD's presence[ad] and to stay there permanently."[ae]

23 Her husband Elkanah replied, "Do what you think is best,[J,af] and stay here until you've weaned him. May the LORD

Cross references

[a] 1:1 1Sm 1:19
[b] Jos 17:14-18; Jdg 17:1
[c] 1Ch 6:22-28,33-38
[d] 1:2 Dt 21:15-17
[e] Lk 2:36
[f] 1:3 Ex 34:23; Dt 16:16; Lk 2:41
[g] Ex 23:14-17
[h] Jos 18:1
[i] 1:4 Dt 12:17-18
[j] 1:5 Gn 43:34; 48:22
[k] 1:7 Jos 18:1
[l] 1:8 Ru 4:15
[m] 1:9 1Sm 3:3
[n] 1:10 1Sm 30:6; 2Kg 4:27
[o] 1:11 Nm 30:6-11
[p] Gn 29:32
[q] Nm 6:5; Jdg 13:5; 16:7
[r] 1:13 Gn 24:42-45
[s] 1:14 Ac 2:4,13
[t] 1:15 Ps 62:8
[u] 1:16 1Sm 2:12
[v] Lk 6:45
[w] 1:17 1Sm 25:35; 2Kg 5:19; Mk 5:34
[x] Ru 2:13
[y] 1:18 Ru 2:13
[z] Rm 15:13
[aa] 1:19 1Sm 1:1; 2:11
[ab] Gn 8:1; 30:22; 1Sm 1:11
[ac] 1:21 Dt 12:11; 1Sm 1:3
[ad] 1:22 Lk 2:22
[ae] 1Sm 1:11,28
[af] 1:23 Nm 30:10-11

Footnotes

[A] 1:1 Or *from Ramathaim, a Zuphite from*　[B] 1:5 Or *gave only one*; Hb obscure　[C] 1:9 LXX adds *and presented herself before the LORD*　[D] 1:11 Lit *a seed of men*　[E] 1:11 Lit *and no razor will go up on his head*　[F] 1:13 Lit *praying to her heart*　[G] 1:18 Lit *and her face was not to her again*　[H] 1:20 Lit *in the turning of the days*　[I] 1:20 In Hb, the name *Samuel* sounds like the phrase "requested from God."　[J] 1:23 Lit *what is good in your eyes*

Study notes

1:1 Elkanah, who was Samuel's father, was a descendant of the priestly tribe of Levi (see 1 Chr 6:33-34) even though he is identified here as an **Ephraimite**—which referred to the territory in which he lived.

1:2 Having **two wives** was a violation of God's design for marriage (see Gen 2:18, 21-24). **Peninnah** was likely the younger woman given cultural practices of the day and her behavior throughout the story. While a second wife was sometimes taken in the case of a childless first marriage, bigamy or polygamy was never God's perfect plan.

1:3 Elkanah was a godly man, as attested by his faithfulness to go **every year to worship and to sacrifice to the LORD** at the tabernacle.

1:6 Since the commonly held view of childlessness in ancient Israel was that it was a curse from God, Hannah had to bear the bitter taunting of **her rival**.

1:9-11 Hannah vowed that if God would **give [her] a son**, she would dedicate him back to God all **of his life**. By promising that **his hair [would] never be cut** (1:11), Hannah was offering to raise him in accordance with the Nazirite vow, which included abstinence from alcohol and untrimmed hair as signs of a person's dedication to God (see Num 6:1-21).

1:19 The phrase, **the LORD remembered** Hannah, is important. Why? Because the Lord "had kept" her from conceiving (1:6). The

inclusion of these parallel truths signals to us that if God causes a problem, only God can fix it.

1:20 The **birth** of **Samuel** gave Hannah reason to put away her grief, and his arrival also heralded a gift of incalculable value to Israel. Samuel would be the last of the judges as well as a prophet and priest. He would serve as the great transitional figure from the lawless days of the judges to the relative structure and orderliness associated with Israel's monarchy.

[a] 1:23 Nm 30:13
[b] 1:24 Nm 15:9-10
[c] Jos 18:1; 1Sm 4:3-4
[d] 1:26 2Kg 2:2,4,6
[e] 1:27 1Sm 1:11-13
[f] 1Sm 1:17,20
[g] 1:28 1Sm 1:11
[h] 2:1 Ps 72:20; Hab 3:1; Lk 1:46-55
[i] Ps 75:4-5,10; 92:10
[j] Is 12:2-3
[k] 2:2 Ex 15:11
[l] 2Sm 22:32
[m] 2Sm 7:22; Ps 18:31
[n] 2:3 Pr 16:2; 24:12
[o] 2:4 Ps 37:15; 46:9
[p] Ps 18:39; Heb 11:32-34
[q] 2:5 Ru 4:15; Ps 113:9
[r] Jr 15:9
[s] 2:6 Dt 32:39

[t] 2:6 Is 26:19
[u] 2:7 Dt 8:17-18
[v] Jb 15:11; Jms 4:10
[w] 2:8 Jb 42:10-12; Ps 75:7
[x] 2Sm 7:8; Dn 2:48; Jms 2:5
[y] Jb 36:7
[z] Jb 38:4-6; Ps 75:3
[aa] Ps 113:7-8
[ab] 2:9 Ps 91:11-12; 1Pt 1:5
[ac] Mt 8:12
[ad] Ps 33:16-17
[ae] 2:10 Ps 2:9
[af] 1Sm 7:10; Ps 18:13-14
[ag] Ps 96:13; 98:9
[ah] 1Sm 2:35; 12:3; 16:6; Ps 89:24
[ai] 2:11 1Sm 1:1,19
[aj] 1Sm 1:28; 2:18; 3:1
[ak] 2:12 1Sm 1:15
[al] Jr 2:8; 9:3,6

confirm your[A] word."[a] So Hannah stayed there and nursed her son until she weaned him. [24] When she had weaned him, she took him with her to Shiloh, as well as a three-year-old bull,[B] half a bushel[C] of flour, and a clay jar of wine.[b] Though the boy was still young,[D] she took him to the Lord's house at Shiloh.[c] [25] Then they slaughtered the bull and brought the boy to Eli.

[26] "Please, my lord," she said, "as surely as you live,[d] my lord, I am the woman who stood here beside you praying to the Lord. [27] I prayed for this boy,[e] and since the Lord gave me what I asked him for,[f] [28] I now give the boy to the Lord. For as long as he lives, he is given to the Lord."[g] Then he[E] worshiped the Lord there.[f]

HANNAH'S TRIUMPHANT PRAYER

2 Hannah prayed:[h]
My heart rejoices in the Lord;[i]
      my horn is lifted up by the Lord.
My mouth boasts over my enemies,
      because I rejoice in your salvation.[j]
[2] There is no one holy like the Lord.[k]
      There is no one besides you![l]
      And there is no rock like our God.[m]
[3] Do not boast so proudly,
      or let arrogant words come out of
         your mouth,
      for the Lord is a God of knowledge,
      and actions are weighed by him.[n]
[4] The bows of the warriors
         are broken,[o]
      but the feeble are clothed
         with strength.[p]
[5] Those who are full hire themselves
         out for food,
      but those who are starving hunger
         no more.
      The woman who is childless
         gives birth to seven,[q]
      but the woman with many sons
         pines away.[r]
[6] The Lord brings death
      and gives life;[s]

he sends some down to Sheol,
      and he raises others up.[t]
[7] The Lord brings poverty and gives
         wealth;[u]
      he humbles and he exalts.[v]

⌇ HOPE WORDS ⌇

*In God's kingdom, the way
up the ladder is down it.*

---

[8] He raises the poor from the dust[w]
      and lifts the needy from the trash
         heap.[x]
      He seats them with noblemen[y]
      and gives them a throne of honor.[G]
      For the foundations of the earth
         are the Lord's;[z]
      he has set the world on them.[aa]
[9] He guards the steps[H]
         of his faithful ones,[ab]
      but the wicked perish in darkness,[ac]
      for a person does not prevail by
         his own strength.[ad]
[10] Those who oppose the Lord
         will be shattered;[I,ae]
      he will thunder in the heavens
         against them.[af]
      The Lord will judge the ends
         of the earth.[ag]
      He will give power to his king;
      he will lift up the horn
         of his anointed.[J,ah]

[11] Elkanah went home to Ramah,[ai] but the boy served the Lord in the presence of the priest Eli.[aj]

ELI'S FAMILY JUDGED

[12] Eli's sons were wicked men;[ak] they did not respect the Lord[al] [13] or the priests' share of the sacrifices from the people. When anyone offered a sacrifice, the priest's servant would come with a three-pronged meat

---

[A] 1:23 DSS, LXX, Syr; MT reads *his* [B] 1:24 DSS, LXX, Syr; MT reads *Shiloh with three bulls* [C] 1:24 Lit *bull and an ephah* [D] 1:24 Lit *And the youth was a youth* [E] 1:28 DSS read *she*; some Hb mss, Syr, Vg read *they* [F] 1:28 LXX reads *Then she left him there before the Lord* [G] 2:8 DSS, LXX add *He gives the vow of the one who makes a vow and he blesses the years of the just.* [H] 2:9 Lit *feet* [I] 2:10 DSS, LXX read *The Lord shatters those who dispute with him* [J] 2:10 Or *Messiah*

2:1-10 The themes of Hannah's prayer were the holiness, sovereignty, and power of God displayed among his people and in her own life. It exalts the Lord for all his actions on behalf of his people: He is **holy**, a **rock**, and full **of knowledge** (2:2-3). He **brings death and gives life** (2:6). He **brings poverty and gives wealth** (2:7). **He guards the steps of his faithful ones** (2:9). Those

who align themselves with him, then, are on the winning side.
2:11 Elkanah and Hannah went back home, but Samuel stayed at Shiloh and **served the Lord** in fulfillment of his mother's promise.
2:12-17 Samuel entered the Lord's service at a difficult time. The situation at Shiloh was terrible and would soon become disastrous. This summary statement sets the scene: **Eli's sons**

were wicked men; they did not respect the **Lord or the priests' share of the sacrifices from the people** (2:12-13). The sacrifices made were holy to the Lord, yet these men named Hophni and Phinehas—descendants of Aaron—stole the choicest parts of the meat for themselves and threatened violence on any worshiper who objected (2:13-16). They showed **contempt** for God's offerings (2:17).

fork while the meat was boiling [14] and plunge it into the container, kettle, cauldron, or cooking pot.[a] The priest would claim for himself whatever the meat fork brought up. This is the way they treated all the Israelites who came there to Shiloh. [15] Even before the fat was burned,[b] the priest's servant would come and say to the one who was sacrificing, "Give the priest some meat to roast, because he won't accept boiled meat from you — only raw." [16] If that person said to him, "The fat must be burned first; then you can take whatever you want for yourself,"[c] the servant would reply, "No, I insist that you hand it over right now. If you don't, I'll take it by force!" [17] So the servants' sin was very severe in the presence of the LORD, because the men treated the LORD's offering with contempt.[d]

[18] Samuel served in the LORD's presence[e]—this mere boy was dressed in the linen ephod.[f] [19] Each year his mother made him a little robe[g] and took it to him when she went with her husband to offer the annual sacrifice.[h] [20] Eli would bless Elkanah and his wife:[i] "May the LORD give you children by this woman in place of the one she[A] has given to the LORD."[j] Then they would go home.

[21] The LORD paid attention to Hannah's need,[k] and she conceived and gave birth to three sons and two daughters. Meanwhile, the boy Samuel grew up in the presence of the LORD.[l]

[22] Now Eli was very old. He heard about everything his sons were doing to all Israel[m] and how they were sleeping with the women who served at the entrance to the tent of meeting.[n] [23] He said to them, "Why are you doing these things? I have heard about your evil actions from all these people. [24] No, my sons, the news I hear the LORD's people spreading is not good. [25] If one person sins against another, God can intercede for him, but if a person sins against the LORD, who can intercede for him?"[o] But they would not listen to their father, since the LORD intended to kill

them.[p] [26] By contrast, the boy Samuel grew in stature and in favor with the LORD and with people.[q]

[27] A man of God came to Eli and said to him,[r] "This is what the LORD says: 'Didn't I reveal myself to your forefather's family[B] when they were in Egypt and belonged to Pharaoh's palace?[s] [28] Out of all the tribes of Israel, I chose your house[c] to be my priests, to offer sacrifices on my altar, to burn incense, and to wear an ephod in my presence.[t] I also gave your forefather's family all the Israelite fire offerings. [29] Why, then, do all of you despise my sacrifices and offerings that I require at the place of worship?[u] You have honored your sons more than me,[v] by making yourselves fat with the best part of all of the offerings of my people Israel.'

[30] "Therefore, this is the declaration of the LORD, the God of Israel: 'I did say that your family and your forefather's family would walk before me forever.'[w] But now,' this is the LORD's declaration, 'no longer! For those who honor me I will honor,[x] but those who despise me will be disgraced.[y] [31] Look, the days are coming when I will cut off your strength and the strength of your forefather's house, so that none in your family will reach old age.[z] [32] You will see distress in the place of worship,[aa] in spite of all that is good in Israel, and no one in your family will ever again reach old age.[ab] [33] Any man from your family I do not cut off from my altar will bring grief[D] and sadness to you. All your descendants will die violently.[E,F] [34] This will be the sign that will come to you concerning your two sons Hophni and Phinehas:[ac] both of them will die on the same day.[ad]

[35] "Then I will raise up a faithful priest[ae] for myself. He will do whatever is in my heart and mind. I will establish a lasting dynasty for him,[af] and he will walk before my anointed one for all time.[ag] [36] Anyone who is left in your family will come and bow down to him for a piece of silver or a loaf of bread. He will say: Please appoint me to some priestly office so I can have a piece of bread to eat.' "

[a] 2:14 Lv 7:29-34
[b] 2:15 Lv 3:3-5,16
[c] 2:16 Lv 7:25
[d] 2:17 Mal 2:7-9
[e] 2:18 1Sm 2:11; 3:1
[f] 1Sm 2:28
[g] 2:19 Ex 28:31
[h] 1Sm 1:3,21
[i] 2:20 Lk 2:34
[j] 1Sm 1:11,22,28
[k] 2:21 Gn 21:1
[l] 1Sm 2:26; 3:19-21; Lk 2:40
[m] 2:22 1Sm 2:13-17
[n] Ex 38:8
[o] 2:25 Nm 15:30-31; Heb 10:26-27

[p] 2:25 Ex 5:2; 14:17-18; Jos 11:18-20
[q] 2:26 Lk 2:52
[r] 2:27 Dt 33:1; Jdg 13:6
[s] 2:27 Ex 28:1-4
[t] 2:28 Ex 28:1-4
[u] 2:29 Dt 12:5-7
[v] Mt 10:37
[w] 2:30 Ex 29:9; 40:12-15; Nm 25:10-13
[x] 1Kg 2:26-27
[y] 2:31 1Sm 4:11-18; 22:17-20
[aa] 2:32 1Kg 2:26-27
[ab] Zch 8:4
[ac] 2:34 1Sm 10:7-9; 1Kg 13:3
[ad] 1Sm 4:11
[ae] 2:35 1Sm 3:20
[af] 1Sm 8:3-5; 1Kg 11:38
[ag] 1Sm 10:9-10; 12:3; 16:13

[A] 2:20 DSS; MT reads *he*　[B] 2:27 Lit *the palace of your father*　[C] 2:28 Lit *selected him*　[D] 2:33 Lit *grief to your eyes*　[E] 2:33 DSS, LXX read *die by the sword of men*　[F] 2:33 Lit *die men*

2:18 The contrast between a **mere boy** serving the Lord well and two grown men functioning as wicked priests couldn't be greater.

2:22-24 Though Eli knew what his sons were up to, he did nothing to stop his boys except to scold them. In essence Eli said, "Now, you boys, stop that," as if one halfhearted rebuke would set them on the right

track. But he never appears to have made an attempt to restrain them or remove them from service.

2:27-35 The judgment outlined would be severe because Eli's failure to discipline his sons revealed that at heart he despised God's **sacrifices and offerings** too. By [his] actions, Eli had **honored [his] sons more**

than God (2:29). Thus, Eli's family would lose its priestly privileges, which were transferred to the family of Zadok later in Israel's history (see 1 Kgs 2:26-27, 35). The **faithful priest** whom God promised to **raise up**, in fact, could have been Zadok himself. He would serve God's kings—first David and then Solomon (1 Sam 2:35).

a 3:1 1Sm 2:11,18
b Ps 74:9; Ezk 7:26; Am 8:11-12
c 3:2 1Sm 4:15
d 3:3 Ex 27:20-21
e 3:11 2Kg 21:12; Jr 19:3
f 3:12 1Sm 2:27-36
g 3:13 Dt 17:12; 21:18
h 3:14 Lv 15:31; Is 22:14
i 3:17 2Sm 3:35
j 3:18 Ex 34:5-7; Lv 10:3; Jb 2:10; Is 39:8
k 3:19 1Sm 2:21
l Gn 21:22; 28:15
m 1Sm 9:6
n 3:20 1Sm 2:35
o 3:21 1Sm 3:10
p 4:1 1Sm 7:12
q Jos 12:18; 1Sm 29:1
r 4:3 Jos 7:7-8
s Nm 10:35; Jos 6:6

SAMUEL'S CALL

3 The boy Samuel served the Lord in Eli's presence.*a* In those days the word of the Lord was rare and prophetic visions were not widespread.*b*

2 One day Eli, whose eyesight was failing,*c* was lying in his usual place. **3** Before the lamp of God had gone out,*d* Samuel was lying down in the temple of the Lord, where the ark of God was located.

4 Then the Lord called Samuel,*A* and he answered, "Here I am." **5** He ran to Eli and said, "Here I am; you called me."

"I didn't call," Eli replied. "Go back and lie down." So he went and lay down.

6 Once again the Lord called, "Samuel!" Samuel got up, went to Eli, and said, "Here I am; you called me."

"I didn't call, my son," he replied. "Go back and lie down."

7 Now Samuel did not yet know the Lord, because the word of the Lord had not yet been revealed to him. **8** Once again, for the third time, the Lord called Samuel. He got up, went to Eli, and said, "Here I am; you called me."

Then Eli understood that the Lord was calling the boy. **9** He told Samuel, "Go and lie down. If he calls you, say, 'Speak, Lord, for your servant is listening.'" So Samuel went and lay down in his place.

10 The Lord came, stood there, and called as before, "Samuel, Samuel!"

Samuel responded, "Speak, for your servant is listening."

11 The Lord said to Samuel, "I am about to do something in Israel that everyone who hears about it will shudder.*B,e* **12** On that day I will carry out against Eli everything I said about his family, from beginning to end.*f* **13** I told him that I am going to judge his family forever because of the iniquity he knows about: his sons are cursing God,*C* and he has not stopped them.*g* **14** Therefore, I have sworn to Eli's family:

The iniquity of Eli's family will never be wiped out by either sacrifice or offering."*h*

15 Samuel lay down until the morning; then he opened the doors of the Lord's house. He was afraid to tell Eli the vision, **16** but Eli called him and said, "Samuel, my son."

"Here I am," answered Samuel.

17 "What was the message he gave you?" Eli asked. "Don't hide it from me. May God punish you and do so severely if you hide anything from me that he told you."*i* **18** So Samuel told him everything and did not hide anything from him. Eli responded, "He is the Lord. Let him do what he thinks is good."*D,j*

19 Samuel grew,*k* and the Lord was with him,*l* and he fulfilled everything Samuel prophesied.*E,m* **20** All Israel from Dan to Beer-sheba knew that Samuel was a confirmed prophet of the Lord.*n* **21** The Lord continued to appear in Shiloh, because there he revealed himself to Samuel by

4 his word.*o* **1** And Samuel's words came to all Israel.

THE ARK CAPTURED BY THE PHILISTINES

Israel went out to meet the Philistines in battle and*F* camped at Ebenezer*p* while the Philistines camped at Aphek.*q* **2** The Philistines lined up in battle formation against Israel, and as the battle intensified, Israel was defeated by the Philistines, who struck down about four thousand men on the battlefield.

3 When the troops returned to the camp, the elders of Israel asked, "Why did the Lord defeat us today before the Philistines?*r* Let's bring the ark of the Lord's covenant from Shiloh. Then it*G* will go with us and save us from our enemies."*s* **4** So the people sent men to Shiloh to bring back the ark of the covenant of the Lord of Armies, who is enthroned between the

---

A 3:4 DSS, LXX read *called, "Samuel! Samuel!"*   *B* 3:11 Lit *about it, his two ears will tingle*; Hb obscure   *C* 3:13 LXX, Old Lat; MT reads *them*   *D* 3:18 Lit *what is good in his eyes*   *E* 3:19 Lit *he let none of his words fall to the ground*   *F* 4:1 LXX reads *In those days the Philistines gathered together to fight against Israel, and Israel went out to engage them in battle. They*   *G* 4:3 Or *he*

3:1 Samuel may have been in his teens by the time his call from the Lord took place. The word translated **boy** means a young man. It's the same word translated "youth" to describe David when he killed Goliath (see 17:33).

It's important not to skim over the acknowledgement that God didn't reveal himself much in those days **and prophetic visions were not widespread**. With Eli and his worthless sons in charge of Israel's house of worship and ministry, that's not surprising.

3:10-14 The first message Samuel would deliver as God's prophet was one of judgment on Eli and his family for his sons' sins and for Eli's failure to stop them.

4:1-3 Verse 1 suggests that since Eli was a leader in Israel, the nation would have to suffer along with him—a spiritual principle that we see repeatedly in the Old Testament. Sure enough, a day came when **Israel went out to meet the Philistines in battle** (4:1). The Israelites were beaten badly (4:2), and from the reaction of **the elders of Israel**, it seems that the lame spiritual

leadership of Eli and his sons had definitely penetrated the attitudes of the people. Instead of seeking God for the reason Israel had been routed, they simply decided to **bring the ark of the Lord's covenant from Shiloh** (4:3). In other words, they were treating it like a good luck charm that would guarantee victory.

4:4-5 As **Hophni and Phinehas** set out with the ark in tow, these wicked priests probably thought they were going as heroes to bring Israel a victory; instead, they were actually going to their own funerals.

cherubim.[a] Eli's two sons, Hophni and Phinehas, were there with the ark of the covenant of God. **5** When the ark of the covenant of the LORD entered the camp, all the Israelites raised such a loud shout that the ground shook.[b]

6 The Philistines heard the sound of the war cry and asked, "What's this loud shout in the Hebrews' camp?" When the Philistines discovered that the ark of the LORD had entered the camp, **7** they panicked. "A god has entered their camp!" they said. "Woe to us, nothing like this has happened before.[A] **8** Woe to us, who will rescue us from these magnificent gods? These are the gods that slaughtered the Egyptians with all kinds of plagues in the wilderness. **9** Show some courage and be men, Philistines![c] Otherwise, you'll serve the Hebrews just as they served you.[d] Now be men and fight!"

10 So the Philistines fought, and Israel was defeated,[e] and each man fled to his tent.[f] The slaughter was severe — thirty thousand of the Israelite foot soldiers fell. **11** The ark of God was captured, and Eli's two sons, Hophni and Phinehas, died.[g]

ELI'S DEATH AND ICHABOD'S BIRTH

12 That same day, a Benjaminite man ran[h] from the battle and came to Shiloh. His clothes were torn,[i] and there was dirt on his head. **13** When he arrived, there was Eli sitting on his chair beside the road watching,[j] because he was anxious about the ark of God. When the man entered the city to give a report, the entire city cried out. **14** Eli heard the outcry and asked, "Why this commotion?" The man quickly came and reported to Eli. **15** At that time Eli was ninety-eight years old, and his eyes didn't move[B] because he couldn't see.[k]

16 The man said to Eli, "I'm the one who came from the battle.[c] I fled from there today."

"What happened, my son?"[l] Eli asked.

17 The messenger answered, "Israel has fled from the Philistines, and also there was a great slaughter among the people. Your two sons, Hophni and Phinehas, are both dead, and the ark of God has been captured." **18** When he mentioned the ark of God, Eli fell backward off the chair by the city gate,[m] and since he was old and heavy, his neck broke and he died. Eli had judged Israel forty years.

19 Eli's daughter-in-law, the wife of Phinehas, was pregnant and about to give birth. When she heard the news about the capture of God's ark and the deaths of her father-in-law and her husband, she collapsed and gave birth because her labor pains came on her. **20** As she was dying,[D] the women taking care of her said, "Don't be afraid. You've given birth to a son!"[n] But she did not respond or pay attention. **21** She named the boy Ichabod,[E] saying, "The glory has departed from Israel,"[o] referring to the capture of the ark of God[p] and to the deaths of her father-in-law and her husband. **22** "The glory has departed from Israel," she said, "because the ark of God has been captured."

THE ARK IN PHILISTINE HANDS

5 After the Philistines had captured the ark of God, they took it from Ebenezer[q] to Ashdod.[r] **2** brought it into the temple of Dagon[F,s] and placed it next to his statue.[G] **3** When the people of Ashdod got up early the next morning, there was Dagon, fallen

a 4:4 Ex 25:22; Nm 7:89
b 4:5 Jos 6:5,20
c 4:9 1Co 16:13
d Jdg 13:1; 1Sm 14:21
e 4:10 Dt 28:15,25; 1Sm 4:2
f 2Sm 18:17; 2Kg 14:12
g 4:11 1Sm 2:34; Ps 78:56-64
h 4:12 Jos 7:22; 1Sm 8:11
i Jos 7:6; 2Sm 1:2; 15:32; Neh 9:1
j 4:13 1Sm 1:9; 4:18
k 4:15 1Kg 14:4
l 4:16 2Sm 1:4
m 4:18 1Sm 4:13
n 4:20 Gn 35:16-19
o 4:21 Ps 26:8; Jr 2:11
p 1Sm 4:11
q 5:1 1Sm 4:1; 7:12
r Jos 13:3
s 5:2 Jdg 16:23-24; 1Ch 10:8-10

4:6-11 The Philistines knew something of the history of their enemy. When they discovered that **the ark**, God's throne, had entered the camp, they assumed they were in serious trouble: Israel's God had come to fight for them (4:6-8). Yet the Philistine army rallied and inflicted a **slaughter** on the Israelites that included Eli's **sons** (4:10-11). Worse yet, the Philistines **captured** the **ark** (4:11). This was the judgment of God at work.

4:17-22 Not only did Eli die at the news that **the ark of God [had]** been captured (4:17-18), but the widow of Eli's son **Phinehas** also died giving birth to a son. With her last breaths, **she named the boy Ichabod** because **the glory [had] departed from Israel** (4:19-22). This means that the glory of God left the tabernacle with the ark because the Israelites had defamed God's glory.

5:1 To crush an enemy, strip him of his god, and bring it back home to display as a trophy was the ultimate symbol of victory for an ancient army. It also was a statement that the winner's god was stronger than the loser's. But since they knew the stories of how the ark had brought Israel such great and miraculous victories when they battled in the promised land, it could be that the Philistines believed that by possessing the ark they would inherit its related power.

The irony at work here is that Israel often operated by faulty theological thinking, too. Many Israelites, for instance, believed their spiritual condition didn't matter simply because they were God's people. This is what led John the Baptist to tell the Pharisees not to presume that their Jewish heritage would

save them because "God is able to raise up children for Abraham from . . . stones" (Matt 3:9). God cannot be obligated, and he expects obedience from his children. To put this in modern terms, merely showing up to church on Sunday mornings won't save you or give you God's blessings. You need to repent and place your faith in Jesus.

5:2-5 Nobody mocks God and gets away with it. The Lord humiliated Dagon in his own house. The Philistines' idol fell **before the ark** as if in humiliation and worship (5:3). The second time this happened, **Dagon's head and both of his hands were broken off** (5:4). Now, in that time period, severing the head and hands of an enemy was often done in battle, so these were trophies of victory. Dagon was nothing before the Lord.

a 5:3 Is 46:1-9
b 5:6 Ex 9:3; 1Sm 5:7,11
c 1Sm 6:5
d Dt 28:27; Ps 78:66
e 5:8 1Sm 5:11; 29:6-11
f 5:9 1Sm 5:11; 7:13
g 1Sm 5:6
h 5:11 1Sm 5:8
i 1Sm 5:6,9
j 5:12 Ex 12:30

k 6:2 Gn 41:8; Ex 7:11; Is 2:6
l 6:3 Dt 16:16
m Lv 5:15-16
n 6:4 1Sm 5:6,9,12; 6:17
o Jos 13:3; Jdg 3:3; 1Sm 6:17-18
p 6:5 Jos 7:19; Is 42:2
q 1Sm 5:6,11
r 1Sm 5:3-4,7
s 6:6 Ex 8:15,32; 9:34
t Ex 4:21; 12:31
u 6:7 Nm 19:2
v 6:8 1Sm 6:4-5
w 1Sm 6:3
x 6:9 Jos 15:10
y 1Sm 6:3

with his face to the ground before the ark of the LORD.[a] So they took Dagon and returned him to his place. [4] But when they got up early the next morning, there was Dagon, fallen with his face to the ground before the ark of the LORD. This time, Dagon's head and both of his hands were broken off and lying on the threshold. Only Dagon's torso remained.[A] [5] That is why, still today, the priests of Dagon and everyone who enters the temple of Dagon in Ashdod do not step on Dagon's threshold.

[6] The LORD's hand was heavy on the people of Ashdod.[b] He terrified[c] the people of Ashdod and its territory and afflicted them with tumors.[B,C,d] [7] When the people of Ashdod saw what was happening, they said, "The ark of Israel's God must not stay here with us, because his hand is strongly against us and our god Dagon." [8] So they called all the Philistine rulers together[e] and asked, "What should we do with the ark of Israel's God?"

"The ark of Israel's God should be moved to Gath," they replied. So they moved the ark of Israel's God. [9] After they had moved it, the LORD's hand was against the city of Gath,[f] causing a great panic. He afflicted the people of the city, from the youngest to the oldest, with an outbreak of tumors.[g]

[10] The people of Gath then sent the ark of God to Ekron, but when it got there, the Ekronites cried out, "They've moved the ark of Israel's God to us to kill us and our people!"[D]

[11] The Ekronites called all the Philistine rulers together.[h] They said, "Send the ark of Israel's God away. Let it return to its place so it won't kill us and our people!"[E] For the fear of death pervaded the city; God's hand was oppressing them.[i] [12] Those who did not die were afflicted with tumors, and the outcry of the city went up to heaven.[j]

THE RETURN OF THE ARK

6 When the ark of the LORD had been in Philistine territory for seven months, [2] the Philistines summoned the priests and the diviners[k] and pleaded, "What should we do with the ark of the LORD? Tell us how we can send it back to its place."

[3] They replied, "If you send the ark of Israel's God away, do not send it without an offering.[l] Send back a guilt offering to him,[m] and you will be healed. Then the reason his hand hasn't been removed from you will be revealed."[F]

[4] They asked, "What guilt offering should we send back to him?"

And they answered, "Five gold tumors and five gold mice[n] corresponding to the number of Philistine rulers,[o] since there was one plague for both you[G] and your rulers. [5] Make images of your tumors and of your mice that are destroying the land. Give glory to Israel's God,[p] and perhaps he will stop oppressing you,[H,q] your gods, and your land.[r] [6] Why harden your hearts as the Egyptians and Pharaoh hardened theirs?[s] When he afflicted them, didn't they send Israel away, and Israel left?[t]

[7] "Now then, prepare one new cart and two milk cows that have never been yoked.[u] Hitch the cows to the cart, but take their calves away and pen them up. [8] Take the ark of the LORD, place it on the cart, and put the gold objects that you're sending him as a guilt offering in a box[v] beside the ark.[w] Send it off and let it go its way. [9] Then watch: If it goes up the road to its homeland toward Beth-shemesh,[x] it is the LORD who has made this terrible trouble for us. However, if it doesn't, we will know that it was not his hand that punished[y] us — it was just something that happened to us by chance."

[10] The men did this: They took two milk cows, hitched them to the cart, and

---

[A] 5:4 LXX; Hb reads *Only Dagon remained on it* [B] 5:6 LXX adds *He brought up mice against them, and they swarmed in their ships. Then mice went up into the land and there was a mortal panic in the city.* [C] 5:6 Perhaps bubonic plague [D] 5:10 DSS, LXX read "*Why have you moved . . . people?*" [E] 5:11 DSS, LXX read "*Why don't you return it to . . . people?*" [F] 6:3 DSS, LXX read *healed, and an atonement shall be made for you. Shouldn't his hand be removed from you?*" [G] 6:4 Some Hb mss, LXX; other Hb mss read *them* [H] 6:5 Lit *will lighten the heaviness of his hand from you*

5:6 Tumors could be anything from boils to something like the bubonic plague.

5:9-12 The ark of God had become a deadly hot potato that none of the Philistines wanted to handle. Finally, the people demanded that it be sent back **to its place** (5:11).

6:1-3 Over the course of **seven months** (6:1), the pagan leaders had seen ample evidence that the God of Israel was a powerful deity who needed to be appeased. So they proposed returning the ark with a **guilt**

offering to remove **his hand** of affliction from Philistia (6:3).

6:4 The mention of rodents here suggests God had sent **mice** to cause the tumors that had afflicted the Philistines.

6:5 The Philistines were to **give glory to Israel's God** so that he might stop **oppressing** them. This is a reminder that God *will* ultimately receive glory even from his enemies.

6:6 The Philistine religious leaders had enough sense not to repeat the mistake of **the**

Egyptians and Pharaoh who had decided to **harden [their] hearts** against **Israel**, resulting in their defeat.

6:7-9 To make sure they hadn't just hit a run of bad luck unrelated to their prize, the Philistines devised a test for returning it that they believed would prove whether these events were from the hand of **the LORD** or had simply happened **by chance** (6:9).

6:10-12 The idea behind the Philistines' plan was that the cows' maternal instincts, and

confined their calves in the pen. **11** Then they put the ark of the LORD on the cart, along with the box containing the gold mice and the images of their tumors. **12** The cows went straight up the road to Beth-shemesh.[a] They stayed on that one highway,[b] lowing as they went; they never strayed to the right or to the left. The Philistine rulers were walking behind them to the territory of Beth-shemesh.

13 The people of Beth-shemesh were harvesting wheat in the valley, and when they looked up and saw the ark, they were overjoyed to see it. **14** The cart came to the field of Joshua of Beth-shemesh and stopped there near a large rock. The people of the city chopped up the cart and offered the cows as a burnt offering to the LORD.[c] **15** The Levites[d] removed the ark of the LORD, along with the box containing the gold objects, and placed them on the large rock. That day the people of Beth-shemesh offered burnt offerings and made sacrifices to the LORD. **16** When the five Philistine rulers[e] observed this, they returned to Ekron that same day.

17 As a guilt offering to the LORD, the Philistines had sent back one gold tumor for each city:[f] Ashdod, Gaza, Ashkelon, Gath, and Ekron. **18** The number of gold mice also corresponded to the number of Philistine cities of the five rulers, the fortified cities and the outlying villages.[g] The large rock[A,h] on which the ark of the LORD was placed is still in the field of Joshua of Beth-shemesh today.

19 God struck down the people of Beth-shemesh because they looked inside the ark of the LORD.[B,i] He struck down seventy persons.[c] The people mourned because the LORD struck them with a great slaughter. **20** The people of Beth-shemesh asked, "Who is able to stand in the presence of the

LORD this holy God?[j] To whom should the ark go from here?"

21 They sent messengers to the residents of Kiriath-jearim,[k] saying, "The Philistines have returned the ark of the LORD. Come down and get it."[D]

7 So the people of Kiriath-jearim came for the ark of the LORD and took it to Abinadab's house on the hill.[l] They consecrated his son Eleazar to take care of it.

VICTORY AT MIZPAH

2 Time went by until twenty years had passed since the ark had been taken to Kiriath-jearim. Then the whole house of Israel longed for the LORD. **3** Samuel told them, "If you[m] are returning to the LORD[n] with all your heart,[o] get rid of the foreign gods[p] and the Ashtoreths that are among you, dedicate yourselves to[E] the LORD, and worship only him.[q] Then he will rescue you from the Philistines." **4** So the Israelites removed the Baals and the Ashtoreths[r] and only worshiped the LORD.

5 Samuel said, "Gather all Israel at Mizpah,[s] and I will pray to the LORD on your behalf."[t] **6** When they gathered at Mizpah, they drew water and poured it out in the LORD's presence.[u] They fasted that day,[v] and there they confessed, "We have sinned against the LORD."[w] And Samuel judged the Israelites at Mizpah.

7 When the Philistines heard that the Israelites had gathered at Mizpah, their rulers marched up toward Israel. When the Israelites heard about it, they were afraid because of the Philistines. **8** The Israelites said to Samuel, "Don't stop crying out to the LORD our God for us, so that he will save us from the Philistines."

9 Then Samuel took a young lamb[x] and offered it as a whole burnt offering to the LORD. He cried out to the LORD on behalf

[a] 6:12 1Sm 6:9
[b] Nm 20:19
[c] 6:14 1Kg 19:21
[d] 6:15 Nm 4:1-33
[e] 6:16 Jos 13:3
[f] 6:17 1Sm 6:4
[g] 6:18 Dt 3:5
[h] 1Sm 6:14-15
[i] 6:19 Nm 4:15-20; 2Sm 6:7

[j] 6:20 Nm 17:13; Ps 76:7; Ezk 44:9-16
[k] 6:21 Jos 9:17; 15:9,60
[l] 7:1 2Sm 6:3-4
[m] 7:3 Ex 20:3
[n] Dt 13:4; 1Ch 19:3
[o] Dt 6:5; 30:10; Jl 2:12-14
[p] Jos 24:14,23; Jdg 10:16
[q] Dt 6:13; Mt 4:10
[r] 7:4 Jdg 2:13
[s] 7:5 Jdg 20:1
[t] 1Sm 8:6; 12:17,19,23
[u] 7:6 1Sm 1:15; Ps 62:8; Lm 2:19
[v] Lv 16:29; Neh 9:1
[w] Jdg 10:10
[x] 7:9 Lv 22:27

[A] 6:18 Some Hb mss, DSS, LXX, Tg; other Hb mss read *meadow*   [B] 6:19 LXX reads *But the sons of Jeconiah did not rejoice with the men of Beth-shemesh when they saw the ark of the LORD.*   [C] 6:19 Some Hb mss, Josephus; other Hb mss read *70 men, 50,000 men*   [D] 6:21 Lit *and bring it up to you*   [E] 7:3 Lit *you and set your hearts on*

---

their unfamiliarity with a yoke, would naturally cause them to want to throw off their restraints and turn back toward their bawling babies. So if they didn't fight the yoke and turn back, but **went straight**, the Philistines would know that the God of Israel had caused their troubles (6:12). Once again, the Lord proved himself to be the true God.

6:13-18 The Israelites did the right thing in using **the cart** and **the cows as a burnt offering to the Lord** (6:14). They also did well in calling for **the Levites** to handle the ark's removal from the cart. That was a crucial step, in fact, because only the priestly lead-

ers were consecrated to deal with the Lord's holy things (6:15).

6:19-20 Keep in mind that under normal circumstances the ark was to be kept in the tabernacle, "screened off" from view (see Exod 40:21). This incident tells us that God's people were, in one sense, as spiritually insensitive as the Philistines.

7:3-4 Baal was the chief deity of the Canaanites, the god of the sky who controlled everything. Ashtoreth was the female fertility deity whose worship involved debauchery. Israel, in worshiping the two, had fallen far from God. Samuel urged them to **get rid of** his competition (7:3).

7:5-7 Samuel led the nation in a service of repentance at **Mizpah**, located about seven miles north of Jerusalem (7:5). God was going to use the occasion to give Israel a resounding victory over their enemies, a fact implying that he accepted their repentance as genuine.

The Philistines apparently considered this Israelite gathering a threat to their security (7:7). The Israelites were immediately struck with fear over their approach. They had not been successful against the Philistines in the past (4:2, 10), so they didn't have high hopes of escaping another whipping.

[a] 7:9 Ps 99:6; Jr 15:1
[b] 7:10 1Sm 2:10; 2Sm 22:14
[c] Ex 23:27; Jos 10:10;
   Jdg 4:15
[d] 7:12 Jos 4:9
[e] 7:13 Jdg 13:1-15
[f] 1Sm 13:5
[g] 7:15 1Sm 7:6; 12:11
[h] 7:17 1Sm 1:1,19; 2:11
[i] 8:1 Dt 16:18-19
[j] 8:2 Gn 22:19; 1Kg 19:3;
   Am 5:5
[k] 8:3 Ex 23:1-9
[l] 8:4 1Sm 7:17
[m] 8:5 Dt 17:14-15

[n] 8:7 Ex 16:8; 1Sm 10:19
[o] 8:9 Ezk 3:18
[p] 8:12 Nm 31:14; 1Sm 22:7
[q] 8:14 1Kg 21:7; Ezk 46:18
[ ] 8:18 Is 8:21
[s] Pr 1:25-28; Mc 3:4
[t] 8:20 Nm 27:17; 1Sm 18:13;
   2Ch 1:10
[u] 8:22 1Sm 8:7

of Israel, and the LORD answered him.[a] [10] Samuel was offering the burnt offering as the Philistines approached to fight against Israel. The LORD thundered loudly[b] against the Philistines that day and threw them into such confusion that they were defeated by Israel.[c] [11] Then the men of Israel charged out of Mizpah and pursued the Philistines striking them down all the way to a place below Beth-car.

[12] Afterward, Samuel took a stone and set it upright[d] between Mizpah and Shen. He named it Ebenezer,[A] explaining, "The LORD has helped us to this point." [13] So the Philistines were subdued[e] and[g] did not invade Israel's territory again.[f] The LORD's hand was against the Philistines all of Samuel's life. [14] The cities from Ekron to Gath, which they had taken from Israel, were restored; Israel even rescued their surrounding territories from Philistine control. There was also peace between Israel and the Amorites.

[15] Samuel judged Israel throughout his life.[g] [16] Every year he would go on a circuit to Bethel, Gilgal, and Mizpah and would judge Israel at all these locations. [17] Then he would return to Ramah[h] because his home was there, he judged Israel there, and he built an altar to the LORD there.

ISRAEL'S DEMAND FOR A KING

8 When Samuel grew old, he appointed his sons as judges over Israel.[i] [2] His firstborn son's name was Joel and his second was Abijah. They were judges in Beersheba.[j] [3] However, his sons did not walk in his ways — they turned toward dishonest profit, took bribes, and perverted justice.[k]

[4] So all the elders of Israel gathered together and went to Samuel at Ramah.[l] [5] They said to him, "Look, you are old, and your sons do not walk in your ways. Therefore, appoint a king to judge us the same as all the other nations have."[m]

[6] When they said, "Give us a king to judge us," Samuel considered their demand wrong, so he prayed to the LORD.

[7] But the LORD told him, "Listen to the people and everything they say to you. They have not rejected you; they have rejected me as their king.[n] [8] They are doing the same thing to you that they have done to me,[c] since the day I brought them out of Egypt until this day, abandoning me and worshiping other gods. [9] Listen to them, but solemnly warn them[o] and tell them about the customary rights of the king who will reign over them."

[10] Samuel told all the LORD's words to the people who were asking him for a king. [11] He said, "These are the rights of the king who will reign over you: He will take your sons and put them to his use in his chariots, on his horses, or running in front of his chariots. [12] He can appoint them for his use as commanders of thousands or commanders of fifties,[p] to plow his ground and reap his harvest, or to make his weapons of war and the equipment for his chariots. [13] He can take your daughters to become perfumers, cooks, and bakers. [14] He can take your best fields, vineyards, and olive orchards and give them to his servants.[q] [15] He can take a tenth of your grain and your vineyards and give them to his officials and servants. [16] He can take your male servants, your female servants, your best young men,[D] and your donkeys and use them for his work. [17] He can take a tenth of your flocks, and you yourselves can become his servants. [18] When that day comes, you will cry out because of the king you've chosen for yourselves,[r] but the LORD won't answer you on that day."[s]

[19] The people refused to listen to Samuel. "No!" they said. "We must have a king over us. [20] Then we'll be like all the other nations: our king will judge us, go out before us,[t] and fight our battles."

[21] Samuel listened to all the people's words and then repeated them to the LORD.[E] [22] "Listen to them," the LORD told Samuel. "Appoint a king for them."[u]

Then Samuel told the men of Israel, "Each of you, go back to your city."

[A] 7:12 = Stone of Help   [B] 7:13 LXX reads *The LORD humbled the Philistines and they*   [C] 8:8 LXX; MT omits *to me*   [D] 8:16 LXX reads *best cattle*
[E] 8:21 Lit *them in the LORD's ears*

7:10-13 God's thunder sent the invaders into such confusion that Israel was able to defeat them (7:10). That day, God proved himself to be Israel's **Ebenezer**, their "Stone of Help" (7:12). The Philistines were pushed completely out of **Israel's territory** (7:13).

8:1-5 The obvious way to correct the problem outlined in verses 1-3 would have been to remove Samuel's sons from their positions

and reform the system. But instead, **all the elders of Israel** took matters into their own hands and asked Samuel to **appoint a king to judge** the nation (8:4-5).

8:6-7 Israel already had a king—the King of kings in fact—who was also the Lord of all the earth. They preferred to be led by a fallible human.

8:9-18 Importantly, it wasn't the people's request for a king per se that was wrong. A

king was in God's sovereign plan for his people (see Deut 17:14-15). The issue, then, was more that they wanted a human ruler alone. Nevertheless, this was not the time of God's perfect choosing—nor were these the right circumstances for the next season of Israel's development.

8:19 In other words, they refused to listen to the Lord who spoke through Samuel.

SAUL ANOINTED KING

9 There was a prominent man of Benjamin named Kish[a] son of Abiel, son of Zeror, son of Becorath, son of Aphiah, son of a Benjaminite. **2** He had a son named Saul, an impressive young man.[b] There was no one more impressive among the Israelites than he. He stood a head taller than anyone else.[A,c]

3 One day the donkeys of Saul's father Kish wandered off. Kish said to his son Saul, "Take one of the servants with you and go look for the donkeys." **4** Saul and his servant went through the hill country of Ephraim[d] and then through the region of Shalishah,[e] but they didn't find them. They went through the region of Shaalim[f] — nothing. Then they went through the Benjaminite region but still didn't find them.

5 When they came to the land of Zuph,[g] Saul said to the servant who was with him, "Come on, let's go back, or my father will stop worrying about the donkeys and start worrying about us."[h]

6 "Look," the servant said, "there's a man of God[i] in this city who is highly respected; everything he says is sure to come true.[j] Let's go there now. Maybe he'll tell us which way we should go."[k]

7 "Suppose we do go," Saul said to his servant, "what do we take the man? The food from our packs is gone, and there's no gift to take to the man of God.[l] What do we have?"

8 The servant answered Saul: "Here, I have a little[B] silver. I'll give it to the man of God, and he will tell us which way we should go."

9 Formerly in Israel, a man who was going to inquire of God would say, "Come, let's go to the seer," for the prophet of today was formerly called the seer.[m]

10 "Good," Saul replied to his servant. "Come on, let's go." So they went to the city where the man of God was. **11** As they were climbing the hill to the city, they found some young women coming out to draw water[n] and asked, "Is the seer here?"

12 The women answered, "Yes, he is ahead of you. Hurry, he just now entered the city, because there's a sacrifice[o] for the people at the high place[p] today. **13** As soon as you enter the city, you will find him before he goes to the high place to eat. The people won't eat until he comes because he must bless the sacrifice; after that, the guests can eat. Go up immediately — you can find him now." **14** So they went up toward the city.

Saul and his servant were entering the city when they saw Samuel coming toward them on his way to the high place. **15** Now the day before Saul's arrival, the LORD had informed Samuel,[C,q] **16** "At this time tomorrow I will send you a man from the land of Benjamin. Anoint him ruler over my people Israel.[r] He will save them from the Philistines because I have seen the affliction of my people,[s] for their cry has come to me." **17** When Samuel saw Saul, the LORD told him, "Here is the man I told you about;[t] he will govern my people."

18 Saul approached Samuel in the city gate and asked, "Would you please tell me where the seer's house is?"

19 "I am the seer," Samuel answered.[D] "Go up ahead of me to the high place and eat with me today. When I send you off in the morning, I'll tell you everything that's in your heart. **20** As for the donkeys that wandered away from you three days ago,[u] don't worry about them because they've been found. And who does all Israel desire[v] but you and all your father's family?"

21 Saul responded, "Am I not a Benjaminite[w] from the smallest of Israel's tribes and isn't my clan the least important of all the clans of the Benjaminite tribe?[x] So why have you said something like this to me?"

22 Samuel took Saul and his servant, brought them to the banquet hall, and gave them a place at the head of the thirty[E] or so men who had been invited. **23** Then Samuel said to the cook, "Get the portion of meat that I gave you and told you to set aside."

[a] 9:1 1Sm 14:51; 1Ch 9:36-39	
[b] 9:2 1Sm 10:24	
[c] 1Sm 10:23	
[d] 9:4 Jos 24:33	
[e] 2Kg 4:42	
[f] Jos 19:42	
[g] 9:5 1Sm 1:1	
[h] 1Sm 10:2	
[i] 9:6 Dt 33:1; 2Kg 5:8	
[j] 1Sm 3:19	
[k] Gn 24:42	
[l] 9:7 1Kg 14:3; 2Kg 5:15; 8:8-9; Ezk 13:19	
[m] 9:9 2Sm 24:11; 1Ch 9:22; 26:28; Is 30:10	
[n] 9:11 Gn 24:15; 29:9; Ex 2:16	
[o] 9:12 Nm 28:11-15	
[p] 1Sm 7:17; 10:5	
[q] 9:15 1Sm 15:1; Ac 13:21	
[r] 9:16 1Sm 10:1	
[s] Ex 3:7,9	
[t] 9:17 1Sm 16:12	
[u] 9:20 1Sm 9:3	
[v] 1Sm 8:5; 12:13	
[w] 9:21 1Sm 15:17	
[x] Jdg 20:46-48	

[A] 9:2 Lit *From his shoulder and up higher than any of the people*   [B] 9:8 Lit *a quarter of a shekel* (about a tenth of an ounce)   [C] 9:15 Lit *had uncovered Samuel's ear, saying*   [D] 9:19 Lit *answered Saul*   [E] 9:22 LXX reads *70*

9:1-2 The point here is that **Saul** came from good stock. He was **impressive** and **a head taller than anyone else** (9:2). These are qualities that would inspire confidence in the people. But, as things would turn out, they were all that Saul had going for them. God was no doubt giving Israel the kind of king they wanted—someone who looked the part. But later, after the people saw the disaster that was King Saul, God would choose a king for them whose heart was right for the job (see 16:7).

9:7-8 Apparently, it was customary to bring a **gift** when seeking a prophet's advice.

9:16 God's specific assignment for Saul was to **save** his people **from the Philistines** who were oppressing them. Indeed, Saul would have early success against the Philistines (14:47), but he would cower in fear with the rest of his army when Goliath defied Israel (17:11). And in the end, after God had rejected Saul and his life fell apart, he would die ingloriously at their hands (see 31:1-10).

9:22 Seating Saul **at the head of the thirty . . . men** in attendance probably was a way of getting Saul's name and face out there; it signaled he was a person to notice.

[a] **9:24** Ex 29:22,27; Lv 7:32-33; Nm 18:18
[b] **9:25** Dt 22:8; Ac 10:9
[c] **10:1** Ex 30:23-33; 1Sm 16:13; 2Kg 9:3,6
[d] 2Kg 9:1-3
[e] 1Sm 16:13; 26:9; 2Sm 1:14
[f] Dt 32:9; Ps 78:71
[g] **10:2** Gn 35:19-20
[h] 1Sm 9:3-5
[i] **10:3** Gn 35:8
[j] Gn 28:19; 35:1,3,7
[k] **10:5** 1Sm 13:2-3
[l] 1Sm 19:20; 2Kg 2:3,5,15
[m] 2Kg 3:15; 1Ch 25:1-6
[n] **10:6** Nm 11:25,29; Jdg 14:6
[o] Ec 9:10

[p] **10:6** 1Sm 19:23-24
[q] **10:7** Jos 1:5
[r] **10:11** 1Sm 19:24; Am 7:14-15; Mt 13:54-57
[s] **10:12** Gn 45:8; Jdg 17:10
[t] **10:14** 1Sm 14:50
[u] 1Sm 9:4-6
[v] **10:17** 1Sm 7:5
[w] **10:18** Jdg 6:8-9
[x] **10:19** 1Sm 8:6-7

24 The cook picked up the thigh[a] and
what was attached to it and set it before
Saul. Then Samuel said, "Notice that the
reserved piece is set before you. Eat it because it was saved for you for this solemn
event at the time I said, 'I've invited the
people.'" So Saul ate with Samuel that day.
25 Afterward, they went down from the
high place to the city, and Samuel spoke
with Saul on the roof.[A,b]
26 They got up early, and just before
dawn, Samuel called to Saul on the roof,
"Get up, and I'll send you on your way!"
Saul got up, and both he and Samuel went
outside. **27** As they were going down to the
edge of the city, Samuel said to Saul, "Tell
the servant to go on ahead of us, but you
stay for a while, and I'll reveal the word of
God to you." So the servant went on.

10 Samuel took the flask of oil,[c] poured
it out on Saul's head,[d] kissed him,
and said, "Hasn't the LORD anointed you[e]
ruler over his inheritance?[B,f] **2** Today when
you leave me, you'll find two men at Rachel's Grave[g] at Zelzah in the territory of
Benjamin. They will say to you, 'The donkeys you went looking for have been
found,[h] and now your father has stopped
being concerned about the donkeys and is
worried about you, asking: What should I
do about my son?'
3 "You will proceed from there until you
come to the oak of Tabor.[i] Three men going
up to God at Bethel[j] will meet you there,
one bringing three goats, one bringing
three loaves of bread, and one bringing a
clay jar of wine. **4** They will ask how you
are and give you two loaves[C] of bread,
which you will accept from them.
5 "After that you will come to Gibeah
of God[k] where there are Philistine garrisons.[D] When you arrive at the city, you
will meet a group of prophets[l] coming
down from the high place prophesying.[m]
They will be preceded by harps, tambourines, flutes, and lyres. **6** The Spirit of the
LORD will come powerfully on you,[n] you
will prophesy with them,[o] and you will
be transformed.[p] **7** When these signs have
happened to you, do whatever your circumstances require[E,q] because God is with
you. **8** Afterward, go ahead of me to Gilgal.
I will come to you to offer burnt offerings
and to sacrifice fellowship offerings. Wait
seven days until I come to you and show
you what to do."
9 When Saul turned around[F] to leave
Samuel, God changed his heart,[G] and all
the signs came about that day. **10** When
Saul and his servant arrived at Gibeah, a
group of prophets met him. Then the Spirit
of God came powerfully on him, and he
prophesied along with them.
11 Everyone who knew him previously
and saw him prophesy with the prophets
asked each other, "What has happened to
the son of Kish? Is Saul also among the
prophets?"[r]
12 Then a man who was from there
asked, "And who is their father?"[s]
As a result, "Is Saul also among the prophets?" became a popular saying. **13** Then Saul
finished prophesying and went to the high
place.
14 Saul's uncle[t] asked him and his servant, "Where did you go?"
"To look for the donkeys," Saul answered. "When we saw they weren't there,
we went to Samuel."[u]
15 "Tell me," Saul's uncle asked, "what did
Samuel say to you?"
16 Saul told him, "He assured us the donkeys had been found." However, Saul did
not tell him what Samuel had said about
the matter of kingship.

SAUL RECEIVED AS KING

17 Samuel summoned the people to the
LORD at Mizpah[v] **18** and said to the Israelites, "This is what the LORD, the God of Israel, says:[w] 'I brought Israel out of Egypt,
and I rescued you from the power of the
Egyptians and all the kingdoms that were
oppressing you.' **19** But today you have rejected your God,[x] who saves you from all
your troubles and afflictions. You said to

[A] **9:25** LXX reads *city. They prepared a bed for Saul on the roof, and he slept.* [B] **10:1** LXX adds *And you will reign over the LORD's people, and you will save them from the hand of their enemies all around. And this is the sign to you that the LORD has anointed you ruler over his inheritance.* [C] **10:4** DSS, LXX read *wave offerings* [D] **10:5** Or *governors* [E] **10:7** Lit *do for yourself whatever your hand finds* [F] **10:9** Lit *turned his shoulder* [G] **10:9** Lit *God turned to him another heart*

10:9 The expression **God changed his heart** could refer to the Holy Spirit coming upon Saul in power to accomplish his kingship, just as the Spirit came upon other leaders in the Old Testament for specific purposes.

10:11 Don't miss the expression of amazement that Saul of all people was suddenly exercising the prophetic gift.

10:17-19 Samuel summoned the people to present their new king to them (10:17). But as time would reveal, since the people were not wholly devoted to him, God was giving them a king who would not be wholly devoted to him either.

10:20-22 To make sure there could be no doubt about God's choice, Samuel brought all the **tribes** and **clans** forward. Samuel worked his way down to smaller and smaller groups—probably by casting lots (see Josh 7:16-18)—until **Saul son of Kish was selected** (1 Sam 10:20-21). But Saul, as it turned out, was hiding (10:22)—apparently overcome with either modesty or fear of the glare of the spotlight.

him, 'You[A] must set a king over us.'[a] Now therefore present yourselves before the LORD by your tribes and clans."[b]

20 Samuel had all the tribes of Israel come forward, and the tribe of Benjamin was selected. **21** Then he had the tribe of Benjamin come forward by its clans, and the Matrite clan was selected.[B] Finally, Saul son of Kish was selected.[c] But when they searched for him, they could not find him. **22** They again inquired of the LORD,[d] "Has the man come here yet?"

The LORD replied, "There he is, hidden among the supplies."

23 They ran and got him from there. When he stood among the people, he stood a head taller than anyone else.[c,e] **24** Samuel said to all the people, "Do you see the one the LORD has chosen?[f] There is no one like him among the entire population."

And all the people shouted,[D] "Long live the king!"[g]

25 Samuel proclaimed to the people the rights of kingship.[h] He wrote them on a scroll, which he placed in the presence of the LORD.[i] Then Samuel sent all the people home.

26 Saul also went to his home in Gibeah,[j] and brave men whose hearts God had touched went with him. **27** But some wicked men said, "How can this guy save us?" They despised him and did not bring him a gift,[k] but Saul said nothing.[E,F]

SAUL'S DELIVERANCE
OF JABESH-GILEAD

11 Nahash[G,l] the Ammonite came up and laid siege to Jabesh-gilead.[m] All the men of Jabesh said to him, "Make a treaty[n] with us, and we will serve you."

2 Nahash the Ammonite replied, "I'll make one with you on this condition: that I gouge out everyone's right eye[o] and humiliate all Israel."[p]

3 "Don't do anything to us for seven days," the elders of Jabesh said to him, "and let us send messengers throughout the territory of Israel. If no one saves us, we will surrender to you."

4 When the messengers came to Gibeah,[q] Saul's hometown, and told the terms to[H] the people, all wept aloud.[r] **5** Just then Saul was coming in from the field behind his oxen. "What's the matter with the people? Why are they weeping?" Saul inquired, and they repeated to him the words of the men from Jabesh.

6 When Saul heard these words, the Spirit of God suddenly came powerfully on him,[s] and his anger burned furiously. **7** He took a team of oxen, cut them in pieces,[t] and sent them throughout the territory of Israel by messengers who said, "This is what will be done to the ox of anyone who doesn't march behind Saul and Samuel."[u] As a result, the terror of the LORD fell on the people, and they went out united.[v]

8 Saul counted them at Bezek.[w] There were three hundred thousand[l,x] Israelites and thirty thousand[J] men from Judah. **9** He told the messengers who had come, "Tell this to the men of Jabesh-gilead: 'Deliverance will be yours tomorrow by the time the sun is hot.'" So the messengers told the men of Jabesh, and they rejoiced.

10 Then the men of Jabesh said to Nahash, "Tomorrow we will come out, and you can do whatever you want[K] to us."

11 The next day Saul organized the troops into three divisions.[y] During the morning watch, they invaded the Ammonite camp and slaughtered them until the heat of the day. There were survivors, but they were

[a]10:19 1Sm 8:19
[b]Jos 7:14–18; 24:1; Pr 16:33
[c]10:20–21 Jos 7:16–18
[d]10:22 Ex 28:30; Nm 27:21; 1Sm 23:2,4,9–11
[e]10:23 1Sm 9:2
[f]10:24 Dt 17:15; 2Sm 21:6
[g]1Kg 1:25,34,39
[h]10:25 1Sm 8:11–17
[i]Dt 17:18–20
[j]10:26 1Sm 11:4; 15:34
[k]10:27 1Kg 10:25; 2Ch 17:5
[l]11:1 1Sm 12:12
[m]1Sm 12:12; 31:11
[n]1Kg 20:34; Ezk 17:13

[o]11:2 Nm 16:14
[p]1Sm 17:26; Ps 44:13
[q]11:4 1Sm 10:26; 15:34
[r]Gn 27:38; Jdg 2:4
[s]11:6 Jdg 14:6; 1Sm 10:10
[t]11:7 Jdg 19:29
[u]Jdg 21:5,8,10
[v]Jdg 20:1
[w]11:8 Jdg 1:5
[x]Jdg 20:2
[y]11:11 Jdg 7:16

[A]10:19 Some Hb mss, LXX, Syr, Vg read *You said, 'No, you*   [B]10:21 LXX adds *And he had the Matrite clan come forward, man by man.*
[C]10:23 Lit *people, and he was higher than any of the people from his shoulder and up*   [D]10:24 LXX reads *acknowledged and said*   [E]10:27 DSS add *Nahash king of the Ammonites had been severely oppressing the Gadites and Reubenites. He gouged out the right eye of each of them and brought fear and trembling on Israel. Of the Israelites beyond the Jordan none remained whose right eye Nahash, king of the Ammonites, had not gouged out. But there were seven thousand men who had escaped from the Ammonites and entered Jabesh-gilead.*   [F]10:27 Lit *gift, and he was like a mute person*
[G]11:1 DSS, LXX read *About a month later, Nahash*   [H]11:4 Lit *in the ears of*   [I]11:8 LXX reads *600,000*   [J]11:8 DSS, LXX read *70,000*   [K]11:10 Lit *do what is good in your eyes*

11:1-3 Nahash the Ammonite and his army, the first test of Saul's reign, **laid siege to Jabesh-gilead**, located about twenty-five miles south of the Sea of Galilee (11:1). The townspeople were so ill-prepared to defend themselves that they agreed to Nahash's humiliating and crippling **treaty** terms (11:1-2). Nahash was so confident that no one would come to rescue them that he agreed to give them a week to send out an SOS and await response (11:3).

11:4-6 Israel's new king was out plowing (11:5), apparently having returned to his former life for the time being, when he heard about Nahash's threats against his people. He was suddenly empowered by **the Spirit of God** and his fierce **anger** (11:6).

11:7-11 A great victory over an enemy that had been menacing Israel solidified Saul's position as king in the eyes of the people (see 8:20). And according to Samuel's speech in chapter 12 (see 12:12), that he'd dealt with

Nahash in particular made Saul's victory even more impressive (11:10).

11:12-13 People were so taken with Saul that they wanted to execute his naysayers (11:12), maybe the same wicked men who had snubbed him at his coronation (see 10:27). But Saul extended grace, acknowledging that **the LORD [had] provided deliverance** (11:13). Unfortunately, this would be the spiritual high point of Saul's reign.

a 11:12 1Sm 10:27
b Lk 19:27
c 11:13 Ex 14:13; 1Sm 19:5
d 11:15 1Sm 10:17
e 1Sm 10:8
f 12:1 1Sm 8:5-22
g 12:3 Ex 20:17; Nm 16:15
h Dt 16:19
i 12:5 Ac 23:9; 24:20
j Ex 22:4

k 12:6 Ex 6:26
l 12:8 Ex 2:23-25
m Ex 3:1-10
n 12:9 Jdg 4:1-2
o Jdg 2:11-15
p 12:10 Jdg 2:18
q 12:11 Jdg 6:11-12,32
r Jdg 4:6; 11:1
s Jdg 11:1
t 1Sm 7:10-14
u 12:13 1Sm 10:24
v 1Sm 8:5; Hs 13:11
w 12:14 Jos 24:14
x 12:15 Jos 24:20; Is 1:20
y 1Sm 5:9
z Lv 26:14-33; Jos 24:14-27

so scattered that no two of them were left together.

SAUL'S CONFIRMATION AS KING

12 Afterward, the people said to Samuel, "Who said that Saul should not[A] reign over us?[a] Give us those men so we can kill them!"[b]

13 But Saul ordered, "No one will be executed this day, for today the LORD has provided deliverance in Israel."[c]

14 Then Samuel said to the people, "Come, let's go to Gilgal, so we can renew the kingship there." **15** So all the people went to Gilgal, and there in the LORD's presence[d] they made Saul king. There they sacrificed fellowship offerings[e] in the LORD's presence, and Saul and all the men of Israel rejoiced greatly.

SAMUEL'S FINAL PUBLIC SPEECH

12 Then Samuel said to all Israel, "I have carefully listened to everything you said to me and placed a king over you.[f] **2** Now you can see that the king is leading you. As for me, I'm old and gray, and my sons are here with you. I have led you from my youth until now. **3** Here I am. Bring charges against me before the LORD and his anointed: Whose ox or donkey have I taken?[g] Whom have I wronged or mistreated? From whom have I accepted a bribe to overlook something?[B,C,h] I will return it to you."

4 "You haven't wronged us, you haven't mistreated us, and you haven't taken anything from anyone," they responded.

5 He said to them, "The LORD is a witness against you, and his anointed is a witness today that you haven't found anything[i] in my hand."[j]

"He is a witness," they said.

6 Then Samuel said to the people, "The LORD, who appointed Moses and Aaron[k] and who brought your ancestors up from the land of Egypt, is a witness.[D] **7** Now present yourselves, so I may confront you before the LORD about all the righteous acts he has done for you and your ancestors.

8 "When Jacob went to Egypt,[E] your ancestors cried out to the LORD,[l] and he sent them Moses and Aaron, who led your ancestors out of Egypt and settled them in this place.[m] **9** But they forgot the LORD their God, so he handed them over to Sisera[n] commander of the army of Hazor, to the Philistines, and to the king of Moab.[o] These enemies fought against them. **10** Then they cried out to the LORD and said, 'We have sinned, for we abandoned the LORD and worshiped the Baals and the Ashtoreths. Now rescue us from the power of our enemies,[p] and we will serve you.' **11** So the LORD sent Jerubbaal,[q] Barak,[f,r] Jephthah,[s] and Samuel.[t] He rescued you from the power of the enemies around you, and you lived securely. **12** But when you saw that Nahash king of the Ammonites was coming against you, you said to me, 'No, we must have a king reign over us' — even though the LORD your God is your king.

13 "Now here is the king you've chosen,[u] the one you requested.[v] Look, this is the king the LORD has placed over you. **14** If you fear the LORD,[w] worship and obey him, and if you don't rebel against the LORD's command, then both you and the king who reigns over you will follow the LORD your God. **15** However, if you disobey the LORD[x] and rebel against his command, the LORD's hand will be against you[y] as it was against your ancestors.[G,z]

16 "Now, therefore, present yourselves and see this great thing that the LORD will

---

[A] 11:12 Some Hb mss, LXX; other Hb mss omit *not*   [B] 12:3 LXX reads *bribe or a pair of shoes? Testify against me.*   [C] 12:3 Lit *bribe and will hide my eyes with it?*   [D] 12:6 LXX; MT omits *is a witness*   [E] 12:8 LXX reads *"When Jacob and his sons went to Egypt and Egypt humbled them*   [F] 12:11 LXX, Syr; MT reads *Bedan*; Jdg 4:6; Heb 11:32   [G] 12:15 LXX *against you and against your king*

11:14 Gilgal was a historic site where the Israelites had first camped after entering the promised land during the conquest under Joshua (see Josh 5:10-12). The purpose of the meeting was two-fold: to confirm Saul as Israel's king and to confirm the people's commitment to him as such.

12:1-5 Following Saul's victory and the people's obvious enthusiasm for him, Samuel decided it was time for him to step aside and officially hand the reins of political leadership over to Saul. Samuel began his farewell speech by reestablishing the credibility of his long ministry as Israel's judge—an office in which honesty and integrity were essential. He put himself in the dock, confident that

no one could prove a charge of corruption against him. (All spiritual leaders ought to be able to similarly point to their lives as being "above reproach," 1 Tim 3:2.)

12:6-7 Here we learn why Samuel wanted to reassert his authority in 12:3. He switched out of judge mode to speak as a prophet with a message from the Lord. His call to the people to **present** themselves was a reminder that they were **before the LORD** (12:7)—that is, they were in his presence, which meant they had no excuse for not heeding what Samuel was about to tell them. He began his message in a pattern that would become a familiar one to the later writing prophets. He gave a recap of God's **righteous acts** (12:7) before starting

to outline the forgetfulness and ingratitude of the people that led them back into the sins from which he had delivered them.

12:11 The men listed were among Israel's judges. **Jerubbaal** was another name for Gideon.

12:13-15 In verses 13 and 14 it seems Samuel offered a word of grace from the Lord, saying essentially, "What's done is done, so let's move forward." If the Israelites would **fear the LORD, worship and obey him**, and not **rebel**, then they and the king would be blessed (12:14). But if they chose to disobey, God's judgment would fall on them like a ton of bricks—just as their **ancestors** had experienced (12:15).

12:16-17 Samuel proposed a sign that would prove the accuracy of his words, a thunderstorm

do before your eyes.[a] 17 Isn't the wheat harvest today?[b] I will call on the LORD, and he
will send thunder and rain so that you
will recognize[A] what an immense evil you
committed in the LORD's sight by requesting a king for yourselves."[c] 18 Samuel called
on the LORD, and on that day the LORD sent
thunder and rain. As a result, all the people
greatly feared the LORD and Samuel.[d]
19 They pleaded with Samuel, "Pray to
the LORD your God for your servants[e] so
we won't die! For we have added to all our
sins the evil of requesting a king for ourselves."[f]
20 Samuel replied, "Don't be afraid. Even
though you have committed all this evil,
don't turn away from following the LORD.[g]
Instead, worship the LORD with all your
heart. 21 Don't turn away to follow worthless[B] things that can't profit or rescue you;
they are worthless.[h] 22 The LORD will not
abandon his people,[i] because of his great
name and because he has determined to
make you his own people.[j]
23 "As for me, I vow that I will not sin
against the LORD by ceasing to pray for
you.[k] I will teach you the good and right
way. 24 Above all, fear the LORD and worship him faithfully with all your heart;
consider the great things he has done
for you.[l] 25 However, if you continue to do
what is evil, both you and your king will
be swept away."[m]

SAUL'S FAILURE

13 Saul was thirty years[C] old when he
became king, and he reigned for-
ty-two years[D] over Israel.[E] 2 He chose three
thousand men from Israel for himself: two
thousand were with Saul at Michmash[n]
and in Bethel's hill country, and one thousand were with Jonathan in Gibeah[o] of
Benjamin. He sent the rest of the troops
away, each to his own tent.
3 Jonathan attacked the Philistine garrison[F,p] that was in Geba,[q] and the Philistines heard about it. So Saul blew the ram's
horn throughout the land[r] saying, "Let the
Hebrews hear!"[G,s] 4 And all Israel heard
the news, "Saul has attacked the Philistine garrison, and Israel is now repulsive
to the Philistines." Then the troops were
summoned to join Saul at Gilgal.
5 The Philistines also gathered to fight
against Israel: three thousand[H] chariots,
six thousand horsemen, and troops as numerous as the sand on the seashore.[t] They
went up and camped at Michmash, east of
Beth-aven.[I,u]
6 The men of Israel saw that they were
in trouble because the troops were in a
difficult situation. They hid in caves, in
thickets, among rocks, and in holes and
cisterns.[v] 7 Some Hebrews even crossed the
Jordan to the land of Gad and Gilead.
Saul, however, was still at Gilgal, and
all his troops were gripped with fear. 8 He
waited seven days for the appointed time
that Samuel had set,[w] but Samuel didn't
come to Gilgal, and the troops were deserting him. 9 So Saul said, "Bring me the
burnt offering and the fellowship offerings." Then he offered the burnt offering.
10 Just as he finished offering the burnt
offering, Samuel arrived. So Saul went out
to greet him, 11 and Samuel asked, "What
have you done?"
Saul answered, "When I saw that the
troops were deserting me and you didn't
come within the appointed days and the
Philistines were gathering at Michmash,
12 I thought, 'The Philistines will now descend on me at Gilgal, and I haven't sought
the LORD's favor.' So I forced myself to offer
the burnt offering."
13 Samuel said to Saul, "You have been
foolish.[x] You have not kept the command
the LORD your God gave you.[y] It was at this

[a] 12:16 Ex 14:13
[b] 12:17 Pr 26:1
[c] 1Sm 8:7
[d] 12:18 Ex 9:23-25,31; 1Kg 18:37-39; Pr 26:1
[e] 12:19 Ex 9:28; Jr 15:1
[f] 1Sm 17:20
[g] 12:20 Dt 11:16
[h] 12:21 Is 44:9-20; Jr 2:8,11; Hab 2:18
[i] 12:22 Jos 7:9; Ezk 36:22-28
[j] Dt 7:6-9; 1Pt 2:9
[k] 12:23 Nm 21:7; 1Sm 7:5-9; Rm 1:9-10
[l] 12:24 Dt 10:21; Ps 103:2-14
[m] 12:25 2Kg 17:6-7
[n] 13:2 1Sm 14:31
[o] 1Sm 10:26

[p] 13:3 1Sm 10:5
[q] 1Sm 13:16; 14:5
[r] Jdg 3:27; 6:34
[s] Nm 10:9; Jdg 3:27; 6:34
[t] 13:5 Jos 11:4
[u] 1Sm 14:23
[v] 13:6 Jdg 6:2
[w] 13:8 1Sm 10:8
[x] 13:13 2Ch 16:9
[y] 1Sm 15:22,28

[A] 12:17 Lit *know and see* [B] 12:21 LXX reads *away after empty* [C] 13:1 Some LXX mss; MT reads *was one year* [D] 13:1 Text emended; MT reads *two years* [E] 13:1 Some LXX mss omit v. 1 [F] 13:3 Or *governor*, also in v. 4 [G] 13:3 LXX reads *"The slaves have revolted"* [H] 13:5 One LXX ms, Syr; MT reads *30,000* [I] 13:5 LXX reads *Michmash, opposite Beth-horon to the south*

during the **wheat harvest** when rain was rare. The point of the miracle was to emphasize the sin the people had committed and, thus, the urgency of their need to repent and follow the Lord with all their hearts.

13:1 In spite of his long reign, it didn't take long for Saul's personal and spiritual defects to manifest themselves. He was an impatient and impulsive person who made bad decisions under pressure and then tried to justify himself instead of admitting his wrongs, as chapters 13 through 15 illustrate.

13:2-5 Saul's son **Jonathan**, introduced in verse 2, was a brave soldier like his father. While Saul was mustering his troops, Jonathan pulled off a raid against a **Philistine garrison** that brought the huge Philistine army to set up camp against Saul (13:3-5).

13:6-12 The Israelites got one look at the enemy horde and **hid** behind or under any rock they could find (13:6). Previously, Saul and Samuel had apparently agreed that the king would wait for Samuel to come and offer the appropriate sacrifices seeking the Lord's help for victory (13:8). But Saul got tired of waiting and sinned by usurping the priest's role (13:9). Samuel arrived, took in the scene, and asked ominously, **What have you done?** (13:10-11).

Saul's excuse sounded plausible, at least to him (13:11-12). He was a military commander with a deserting army, a massive enemy who might pounce on him at any moment, and a priest who was nowhere to be found on the last day of their agreed-on waiting period. Saul was clearly hoping Samuel could see the tight spot he was in and understand. He would be disappointed.

^a13:13 1Sm 1:22
^b13:14 1Sm 15:28
^c1Sm 16:7; Ac 13:22
^d13:16 1Sm 13:2-3
^e13:17 1Sm 14:15
^fJos 18:23
^g13:18 Jos 18:13-14
^hNeh 11:34
ⁱ13:19 Jdg 5:8; 2Kg 24:14
^j13:22 Jdg 5:8
^k13:23 1Sm 14:1; 2Sm 23:14
^l14:2 Is 10:28
^m1Sm 13:15-16

⇌ Questions & Answers ⇌

Q Two key biblical leaders, Moses and David, each had a mentor or a wise older friend who helped them discern their calling: Jethro helped Moses and Samuel aided David. Did you have mentors who helped you in the process of discerning your calling? What advice would you give to others in seeking out wise mentors/counselors to help them discern their calling?

A Mentors, those who disciple and direct you, are critical in helping you discover what God has for you. I'm grateful for the mentors in my own life. My passion for evangelism came from B. Sam Hart, the evangelist who inspired me to go into ministry. Then, my desire to pursue pastoral ministry grew because of the influence of Reuben Conner and Gene Getz. So at different stages of life, God provides different people to teach us different emphases as we are ready to learn and grow. Haddon Robinson mentored me in expository preaching, and Zane Hodges and Charles Ryrie were awesome mentors in theology and biblical exegesis.

The best places to find a spiritual mentor are in your family and in your church. Local churches should have older spiritual men influencing younger men, and older spiritual women influencing younger women (see, e.g., Titus 2:1-5). Spiritual influence is to be passed down from one generation to the next. Godly parents routinely do this. They see potential in their children, and they offer them counsel and guidance. Spiritual mentors do the same, when they see spiritual potential in a believer's life. Seek out spiritual mentors in your circle of influence. Let them get to know you so that they can observe the spiritual potential God has placed in you.

FOR THE NEXT Q&A, SEE PAGE 670.

time that the LORD would have permanently established your reign over Israel,^a ¹⁴ but now your reign will not endure.^b The LORD has found a man after his own heart,^{A,c} and the LORD has appointed him as ruler over his people, because you have not done what the LORD commanded." ¹⁵ Then Samuel went^B from Gilgal to Gibeah in Benjamin. Saul registered the troops who were with him, about six hundred men.

¹⁶ Saul, his son Jonathan, and the troops who were with them were staying in Geba^d of Benjamin, and the Philistines were camped at Michmash. ¹⁷ Raiding parties^e went out from the Philistine camp in three divisions. One division headed toward the Ophrah^f road leading to the land of Shual. ¹⁸ The next division headed toward the Beth-horon^g road, and the last division headed down the border road that looks out over the Zeboim Valley^h toward the wilderness.

¹⁹ No blacksmith could be found in all the land of Israelⁱ because the Philistines had said, "Otherwise, the Hebrews will make swords or spears." ²⁰ So all the Israelites went to the Philistines to sharpen their plows, mattocks, axes, and sickles.^c ²¹ The price was two-thirds of a shekel^D for plows and mattocks, and one-third of a shekel for pitchforks and axes, and for putting a point on a cattle prod. ²² So on the day of battle not a sword or spear could be found in the hand of any of the troops who were with Saul^j and Jonathan; only Saul and his son Jonathan had weapons.

JONATHAN'S VICTORY OVER THE PHILISTINES

²³ Now a Philistine garrison^k took control

14 of the pass at Michmash. ¹ That same day Saul's son Jonathan said to the attendant who carried his weapons, "Come on, let's cross over to the Philistine garrison on the other side." However, he did not tell his father.

² Saul was staying under the pomegranate tree in Migron^l on the outskirts of Gibeah.^{E,m} The troops with him numbered

^A13:14 Lit *man according to his heart* ^B13:15 LXX reads *Samuel left Gilgal and went on his way, and the rest of the people followed Saul to join the people in his army. They went* ^C13:20 LXX; MT reads *plowshares* ^D13:21 Lit *of a pim*; about one-fourth ounce of silver ^E14:2 LXX reads *on top of the hill*

13:13 Here we see the interplay between God's sovereignty and human responsibility. God had already made it abundantly clear that Saul was not his choice, and earlier biblical prophecy foretold that God's king would come from the tribe of Judah (see Gen 49:8-10). Nevertheless, Saul was still responsible for his actions and could have enjoyed God's blessing on his reign.
13:14 The writer wants his readers to see how circumstances under Saul ushered God's chosen, covenantal ruler, **a man after his own heart,** to the throne.

13:19, 22 One reason for the Philistines' military superiority was their decision to rid Israel of blacksmiths. Saul's army had few real weapons.
14:1-2 Jonathan, who was armed, attempted another daring raid against a **Philistine garrison** (14:1). If successful, it could demoralize

about six hundred.[a] [3] Ahijah,[b] who was wearing an ephod,[c] was also there. He was the son of Ahitub, the brother of Ichabod[d] son of Phinehas, son of Eli the LORD's priest at Shiloh.[e] But the troops did not know that Jonathan had left.

[4] There were sharp columns[A] of rock on both sides of the pass[f] that Jonathan intended to cross to reach the Philistine garrison. One was named Bozez and the other Seneh; [5] one stood to the north in front of Michmash and the other to the south in front of Geba. [6] Jonathan said to the attendant who carried his weapons, "Come on, let's cross over to the garrison of these uncircumcised men.[g] Perhaps the LORD will help us. Nothing can keep the LORD from saving, whether by many or by few."[h]

[7] His armor-bearer responded, "Do what is in your heart. You choose. I'm right here with you whatever you decide."

[8] "All right," Jonathan replied, "we'll cross over to the men and then let them see us. [9] If they say, 'Wait until we reach you,' then we will stay where we are and not go up to them. [10] But if they say, 'Come on up,' then we'll go up, because the LORD has handed them over to us — that will be our sign."

[11] They let themselves be seen by the Philistine garrison, and the Philistines said, "Look, the Hebrews are coming out of the holes where they've been hiding!" [12] The men of the garrison called to Jonathan and his armor-bearer. "Come on up, and we'll teach you a lesson!" they said.

"Follow me," Jonathan told his armor-bearer, "for the LORD has handed them over to Israel."[i] [13] Jonathan climbed up using his hands and feet, with his armor-bearer behind him. Jonathan cut them down, and his armor-bearer followed and finished them off. [14] In that first assault Jonathan and his armor-bearer struck down about twenty men in a half-acre field.

A DEFEAT FOR THE PHILISTINES

[15] Terror spread through the Philistine camp and the open fields to all the troops. Even the garrison and the raiding parties[j] were terrified. The earth shook,[k] and terror spread from God.[B,l] [16] When Saul's watchmen in Gibeah of Benjamin looked, they saw the panicking troops scattering in every direction. [17] So Saul said to the troops with him, "Call the roll and determine who has left us." They called the roll and saw that Jonathan and his armor-bearer were gone.

[18] Saul told Ahijah, "Bring the ark of God," for it was with the Israelites[c] at that time. [19] While Saul spoke to the priest,[m] the panic in the Philistine camp increased in intensity. So Saul said to the priest, "Stop what you're doing."[D]

[20] Saul and all the troops with him assembled and marched to the battle, and there the Philistines were, fighting against each other in great confusion![n] [21] There were Hebrews from the area who had gone earlier into the camp to join the Philistines, but even they joined the Israelites[o] who were with Saul and Jonathan. [22] When all the Israelite men who had been hiding in the hill country of Ephraim[p] heard that the Philistines were fleeing, they also joined Saul and Jonathan in the battle. [23] So the LORD saved Israel that day.[q]

SAUL'S RASH OATH

The battle extended beyond Beth-aven, [24] and the men of Israel were worn out that day, for Saul had[E] placed the troops under an oath:[r] "The man who eats food before evening, before I have taken vengeance on my enemies is cursed." So none of the troops tasted any food.

[25] Everyone[F] went into the forest, and there was honey on the ground. [26] When the troops entered the forest, they saw the flow of honey, but none of them ate any of it[G] because they feared the oath. [27] However, Jonathan had not heard his father make the troops swear the oath. He reached out with the end of the staff he was carrying and dipped it into the honeycomb.[s] When he ate the honey,[H] he had renewed

[a] 14:2 1Sm 13:15
[b] 14:3 1Sm 22:9-12,20
[c] 1Sm 2:28
[d] 1Sm 4:21
[e] 1Sm 1:3
[f] 14:4 1Sm 13:23
[g] 14:6 1Sm 17:26,36; Jr 9:25-26
[h] Jdg 7:4-7
[i] 14:12 2Sm 5:24

[j] 14:15 1Sm 13:17-18
[k] 1Sm 7:10
[l] 2Kg 7:6
[m] 14:19 Nm 27:21
[n] 14:20 Jdg 7:22; 2Ch 20:23
[o] 14:21 1Sm 29:4
[p] 14:22 1Sm 13:6
[q] 14:23 Ex 14:30
[r] 14:24 Jos 6:26
[s] 14:27 1Sm 14:43

[A] 14:4 Lit There was a tooth   [B] 14:15 Or and a great terror spread   [C] 14:18 LXX reads "Bring the ephod." For he wore the ephod before Israel   [D] 14:19 Lit "Withdraw your hand"   [E] 14:24 LXX adds committed a great act of ignorance and   [F] 14:25 Lit All the land   [G] 14:26 Lit but there was none who raised his hand to his mouth   [H] 14:27 Lit he returned his hand to his mouth

---

the enemy and swing the momentum Israel's way despite the Philistines' military superiority. Meanwhile, Saul was resting with his **troops** (14:2).

14:3 Ahijah was **wearing an ephod**, a priestly garment housing the Urim and Thummim, which were objects used to determine God's

will in a specific situation (see Exod 28:6-30). Perhaps Saul was waiting for divine guidance. **14:6 Valiant** Jonathan thought of the Philistines as **uncircumcised men** who were defying the armies of Israel's savior, God. (David would say essentially the same about Goliath in the near future; see 17:26.) This

tells us Jonathan had deep confidence in God's ability to deliver his people. And as a result, "the Lord [would save] Israel that day" (14:23).

14:24-26 Saul's impetuous action weakened his troops, just when they had their enemies on the run and needed all their strength.

ª14:27 1Sm 30:12
ᵇ14:29 1Kg 18:17-18
ᶜ14:31 1Sm 14:5
ᵈJos 10:12
ᵉ14:32 1Sm 15:19
Gn 9:4; Lv 17:10-12
ᵍ14:35 1Sm 7:12,17
ʰ14:36 1Sm 14:3,18-19
ⁱJdg 18:5-6
ʲ14:37 1Sm 10:22
ᵏ1Sm 28:6

ˡ14:41 Ac 1:24
ᵐ14:43 Jos 7:19
ⁿ1Sm 14:27
ᵒ14:44 1Sm 25:22
ᵖ14:45 2Sm 14:11; 1Kg
1:52; Ac 27:34
ᵠJn 3:21
ʳ14:47 1Sm 11:1-13
ˢ2Sm 8:3-10
ᵗ14:48 1Sm 15:3,7
ᵘ14:49 1Sm 31:2; 1Ch 10:2
ᵛ1Sm 18:17-19
ʷ1Sm 18:20,27; 19:12; 2Sm
6:20-23

energy.ᴬ,ª **28** Then one of the troops said, "Your father made the troops solemnly swear, 'The man who eats food today is cursed,' and the troops are exhausted."

29 Jonathan replied, "My father has brought trouble to the land.ᵇ Just look at how I have renewed energyᴮ because I tasted a little of this honey. **30** How much better if the troops had eaten freely today from the plunder they took from their enemies! Then the slaughter of the Philistines would have been much greater."

31 The Israelites struck down the Philistines that day from Michmashᶜ all the way to Aijalon.ᵈ Since the Israelites were completely exhausted, **32** they rushed to the plunder,ᵉ took sheep, goats, cattle, and calves, slaughtered them on the ground, and ate meat with the blood still in it. **33** Some reported to Saul: "Look, the troops are sinning against the LORD by eating meat with the blood still in it."ᶠ

Saul said, "You have been unfaithful. Roll a large stone over here at once." **34** He then said, "Go among the troops and say to them, 'Let each man bring me his ox or his sheep. Do the slaughtering here and then you can eat. Don't sin against the LORD by eating meat with the blood in it.'" So everyone of the troops brought his ox that night and slaughtered it there. **35** Then Saul built an altar to the LORD; it was the first time he had built an altar to the LORD.ᵍ

36 Saul said, "Let's go down after the Philistines tonight and plunder them until morning. Don't let even one remain!"

"Do whatever you want,"ᶜ the troops replied.

But the priestʰ said, "Let's approach God here."ⁱ

37 So Saul inquired of God,ʲ "Should I go after the Philistines? Will you hand them over to Israel?" But God did not answer him that day.ᵏ

38 Saul said, "All you leaders of the troops, come here. Let us investigateᴰ how this sin has occurred today. **39** As surely as the LORD lives who saves Israel, even if it is

because of my son Jonathan, he must die!" Not one of the troops answered him.

40 So he said to all Israel, "You will be on one side, and I and my son Jonathan will be on the other side."

And the troops replied, "Do whatever you want."

41 So Saul said to the LORD, "God of Israel, why have you not answered your servant today? If the unrighteousness is in me or in my son Jonathan, LORD God of Israel, give Urim; but if the fault is in your people Israel, give Thummim."ᴱ,ʲ Jonathan and Saul were selected, and the troops were cleared of the charge.

42 Then Saul said, "Cast the lot between me and my son Jonathan," and Jonathan was selected. **43** Saul commanded him, "Tell me what you did."ᵐ

Jonathan told him, "I tasted a little honeyⁿ with the end of the staff I was carrying. I am ready to die!"

44 Saul declared to him, "May God punish me and do so severelyᵒ if you do not die, Jonathan!"

45 But the people said to Saul, "Must Jonathan die, who accomplished such a great deliverance for Israel? No, as the LORD lives, not a hair of his head will fall to the ground,ᵖ for he worked with God's help today."ᵠ So the people redeemed Jonathan, and he did not die. **46** Then Saul gave up the pursuit of the Philistines, and the Philistines returned to their own territory.

SUMMARY OF SAUL'S KINGSHIP

47 When Saul assumed the kingship over Israel, he fought against all his enemies in every direction: against Moab, the Ammonites,ʳ Edom, the kings of Zobah,ˢ and the Philistines. Wherever he turned, he caused havoc.ᶠ **48** He fought bravely, defeated the Amalekites,ᵗ and rescued Israel from those who plundered them.

49 Saul's sonsᵘ were Jonathan, Ishvi, and Malchishua. The names of his two daughters were Merab,ᵛ his firstborn, and Michal,ʷ the younger. **50** The name of Saul's

---

ᴬ14:27 Lit *his eyes became bright*   ᴮ14:29 Lit *how my eyes became bright*   ᶜ14:36 Lit *Do what is good in your eyes*, also in v. 40   ᴰ14:38 Lit *know and see*   ᴱ14:41 LXX; MT reads *said to the LORD, "God of Israel, give us the right decision."*   ᶠ14:47 LXX reads *he was victorious*

14:33 To eat animals without first draining **the blood** was a violation of the law of Moses.

14:42-44 Saul was ready to kill his son for disobeying his order (even though he hadn't heard it until it was too late; see 14:24-30).

15:1-3 If God's enemies were ranked on a scale of how deeply they had offended him, **the Amalekites** would be high on that list. God

had seen what they did to his people **as they were coming out of Egypt** (15:2; see Exod 17:8-16). He promised at that time to eventually "blot out the memory of Amalek under heaven" (Exod 17:14). So God appointed Saul to take care of business.

15:6 The **Kenites**, a nomadic people living near the Amalekites, were the people of Moses's father-in-law Jethro (see Judg 1:16).

15:7-9 As the battle raged and the Israelites got the upper hand, Saul apparently got a big head. Though he struck down the Amalekites, he spared **King Agag** and **the best of the . . . animals**. In spite of the Lord's explicit command, Saul and his troops **were not willing to destroy** what God said to destroy (15:8-9). They kept them as spoils of war.

wife was Ahinoam daughter of Ahimaaz. The name of the commander of his army was Abner son of Saul's uncle Ner.[a] [51] Saul's father was Kish.[b] Abner's father was Ner son of Abiel.

[52] The conflict with the Philistines was fierce all of Saul's days, so whenever Saul noticed any strong or valiant man, he enlisted him.[c]

SAUL REJECTED AS KING

15 Samuel told Saul, "The LORD sent me to anoint you as king over his people Israel.[d] Now, listen to the words of the LORD. [2] This is what the LORD of Armies says: 'I witnessed[A] what the Amalekites did to the Israelites when they opposed them along the way as they were coming out of Egypt.[e] [3] Now go and attack the Amalekites and completely destroy everything they have.[f] Do not spare them. Kill men and women, infants and nursing babies, oxen and sheep, camels and donkeys.'"[g]

[4] Then Saul summoned the troops and counted them at Telaim: two hundred thousand foot soldiers and ten thousand men from Judah. [5] Saul came to the city of Amalek and set up an ambush in the wadi. [6] He warned the Kenites,[h] "Since you showed kindness to all the Israelites when they came out of Egypt,[i] go on and leave! Get away from the Amalekites, or I'll sweep you away with them." So the Kenites withdrew from the Amalekites.

[7] Then Saul struck down the Amalekites[j] from Havilah[k] all the way to Shur,[l] which is next to Egypt. [8] He captured King Agag[m] of Amalek alive, but he completely destroyed all the rest of the people with the sword.[n] [9] Saul and the troops spared Agag, and the best of the sheep, goats, cattle, and choice animals,[B] as well as the young rams and the best of everything else. They were not willing to destroy them, but they did destroy all the worthless and unwanted things.

[10] Then the word of the LORD came to Samuel, [11] "I regret that I made Saul king,[o] for he has turned away from following me

and has not carried out my instructions."[p] So Samuel became angry and cried out to the LORD all night.[q]

[12] Early in the morning Samuel got up to confront Saul, but it was reported to Samuel, "Saul went to Carmel[r] where he set up a monument for himself. Then he turned around and went down to Gilgal."[s] [13] When Samuel came to him, Saul said, "May the LORD bless you.[t] I have carried out the LORD's instructions."

[14] Samuel replied, "Then what is this sound of sheep, goats,[c] and cattle I hear?"

[15] Saul answered, "The troops brought them from the Amalekites and spared the best sheep, goats, and cattle in order to offer a sacrifice to the LORD your God,[u] but the rest we destroyed."[v]

[16] "Stop!" exclaimed Samuel. "Let me tell you what the LORD said to me last night."

"Tell me," he replied.

[17] Samuel continued, "Although you once considered yourself unimportant,[w] have you not become the leader of the tribes of Israel? The LORD anointed you king over Israel [18] and then sent you on a mission and said: 'Go and completely destroy the sinful Amalekites. Fight against them until you have annihilated them.' [19] So why didn't you obey the LORD? Why did you rush on the plunder[x] and do what was evil in the LORD's sight?"

[20] "But I did obey the LORD!" Saul answered.[D] "I went on the mission the LORD gave me: I brought back King Agag of Amalek, and I completely destroyed the Amalekites. [21] The troops took sheep, goats, and cattle from the plunder — the best of what was set apart for destruction — to sacrifice to the LORD your God at Gilgal."[y]

[22] Then Samuel said:

Does the LORD[z] take pleasure
   in burnt offerings and sacrifices
as much as in obeying the LORD?

Look: to obey is better than sacrifice,
to pay attention is better than the fat
   of rams.[aa]
[23] For rebellion is like the sin
   of divination,[ab]

[a] 14:50 2Sm 2:8
[b] 14:51 1Sm 9:1,21
[c] 14:52 1Sm 8:11
[d] 15:1 1Sm 9:16
[e] 15:2 Ex 17:8-16; Nm 24:20; Dt 25:17-19
[f] 15:3 Nm 24:20; Dt 20:16-18
[g] Jos 6:17-21; 1Sm 22:19
[h] 15:6 Jdg 1:16; 4:11
[i] Ex 18:9-10; Nm 10:29-32
[j] 15:7 1Sm 14:48
[k] Gn 16:7; 25:17-18
[l] Ex 15:22; 1Sm 27:8
[m] 15:8 Nm 24:7; Est 3:1
[n] 1Sm 27:8; 30:1; 2Sm 8:12
[o] 15:11 Gn 6:6-7; Ex 32:14; 2Sm 24:16

[p] 15:11 1Kg 9:6-7
[q] Ex 32:11-13; Lk 6:12
[r] 15:12 Jos 15:55; 1Sm 25:2
[s] 1Sm 13:13-14
[t] 15:13 Gn 14:19; 2Sm 2:5
[u] 15:15 Gn 3:12-13
[v] 15:14-15 Ex 32:21-24
[w] 15:17 1Sm 9:21
[x] 15:19 1Sm 14:32
[y] 15:21 Ex 32:22-23
[z] 15:22 Ps 40:6-8; 51:16-17; Is 1:11-15; Mc 6:6-8
[aa] Heb 10:5-7
[ab] 15:23 Dt 18:10

[A] 15:2 LXX reads *I will avenge*   [B] 15:9 Lit *and the second ones*   [C] 15:14 Lit *sheep in my ears*   [D] 15:20 Lit *answered Samuel*

15:10-11 Clearly, God is omniscient and knew how Saul's reign would turn out. Nevertheless, he was genuinely grieved by Saul's rebellion against him. Samuel likewise was affected. He **became angry and cried out . . . all night** (15:11). No one sins in a vacuum. Our disobedience affects God, and it affects the people in our lives.

15:12 Self-glorification seems to have been Saul's intent in disobeying orders, because when Samuel came to **confront** him, he was told that the king had gone to **Carmel** to **set up a monument for himself**.

15:15 In other words, Saul said, "I slightly modified God's commands so that I might worship him." But you can't honor God by

defying him. You can't glorify the King by rejecting his kingdom agenda.

15:22 The lesson here is that the Lord calls people to submit to his agenda, not to attempt to honor him with their own agendas.

[a] 15:23 Gn 31:19,34
[b] 1Sm 8:7
[c] 15:24 Nm 22:34; 2Sm 12:13; Ps 51:3-4
[d] Pr 29:25; Is 51:12-13
[e] 15:25 Ex 10:17
[f] 15:26 1Sm 13:14; 16:1
[g] 15:28 1Sm 28:17-18
[h] 15:27-28 1Kg 11:30-36
[i] 15:29 1Ch 29:11; Ps 18:1-2
[j] Nm 23:19; Ezk 24:14
[k] 15:30 Jn 12:43
    Is 29:13
[m] 15:33 Gn 9:6; Jdg 1:7; Mt 7:2

[n] 15:34 1Sm 7:17
[o] 1Sm 11:4
[p] 15:35 1Sm 19:24
[q] 1Sm 16:1
[r] 16:1 1Sm 15:35
[s] 1Sm 13:13-14; 15:23
[t] 1Sm 9:16; 10:1; 2Kg 9:1
[u] Ru 4:17-22
[v] 16:2 1Sm 20:29
[w] 16:3 Ex 4:15; Ac 9:6
[x] Dt 17:14-15; 1Sm 9:16
[y] 16:4 Gn 48:7; Lk 2:4
[z] 1Kg 2:13; 2Kg 9:22; 1Ch 12:17-18
[aa] 16:5 Gn 35:2; Ex 19:10
[ab] 16:6 1Sm 17:13
[ac] 16:7 1Kg 8:39; Jr 17:10; Lk 16:15; Jn 2:24-25
[ad] 16:8 1Sm 17:13

and defiance is like wickedness[a] and idolatry.

Because you have rejected the word of the LORD,
he has rejected you as king.[b]

24 Saul answered Samuel, "I have sinned.[c] I have transgressed the LORD's command[d] and your words. Because I was afraid of the people, I obeyed them. 25 Now therefore, please forgive my sin[e] and return with me so I can worship the LORD."

26 Samuel replied to Saul, "I will not return with you. Because you rejected the word of the LORD,[f] the LORD has rejected you from being king over Israel." 27 When Samuel turned to go, Saul grabbed the corner of his robe, and it tore. 28 Samuel said to him, "The LORD has torn the kingship of Israel away from you today[g] and has given it to your neighbor who is better than you.[h] 29 Furthermore, the Eternal One of Israel[i] does not lie or change his mind, for he is not man who changes his mind."[j]

30 Saul said, "I have sinned. Please honor me[k] now before the elders of my people and before Israel. Come back with me so I can bow in worship to the LORD your God."[l] 31 Then Samuel went back, following Saul, and Saul bowed down to the LORD.

32 Samuel said, "Bring me King Agag of Amalek."

Agag came to him trembling,[A] for he thought, "Certainly the bitterness of death has come."[B,C]

33 Samuel declared:

As your sword has made women childless,
so your mother will be childless among women.[m]

Then he hacked Agag to pieces before the LORD at Gilgal.

34 Samuel went to Ramah,[n] and Saul went up to his home in Gibeah[o] of Saul. 35 Even to the day of his death, Samuel never saw Saul again.[p] Samuel mourned for Saul,[q] and the LORD regretted he had made Saul king over Israel.

SAMUEL ANOINTS DAVID

16 The LORD said to Samuel, "How long are you going to mourn for Saul,[r] since I have rejected him as king over Israel?[s] Fill your horn with oil[t] and go. I am sending you to Jesse of Bethlehem[u] because I have selected a king from his sons." 2 Samuel asked, "How can I go? Saul will hear about it and kill me!"

The LORD answered, "Take a young cow with you and say, 'I have come to sacrifice to the LORD.'[v] 3 Then invite Jesse to the sacrifice, and I will let you know what you are to do.[w] You are to anoint for me the one I indicate to you."[x]

4 Samuel did what the LORD directed and went to Bethlehem.[y] When the elders of the town met him, they trembled[D] and asked, "Do[E] you come in peace?"[z]

5 "In peace," he replied. "I've come to sacrifice to the LORD. Consecrate yourselves[aa] and come with me to the sacrifice."[F] Then he consecrated Jesse and his sons and invited them to the sacrifice. 6 When they arrived, Samuel saw Eliab[ab] and said, "Certainly the LORD's anointed one is here before him."

7 But the LORD said to Samuel, "Do not look at his appearance or his stature because I have rejected him. Humans do not see what the LORD sees,[G] for humans see what is visible,[H] but the LORD sees the heart."[ac]

8 Jesse called Abinadab[ad] and presented him to Samuel. "The LORD hasn't chosen

---

[A] 15:32 Hb obscure [B] 15:32 LXX reads *Is death bitter in this way?* [C] 15:32 Lit *turned* [D] 16:4 LXX reads *were astonished* [E] 16:4 DSS, LXX read *"Seer, do* [F] 16:5 LXX reads *and rejoice with me today* [G] 16:7 LXX reads *God does not see as a man sees* [H] 16:7 Lit *for the man sees according to the eyes*

15:24 Saul revealed that he feared humans more than he feared God. That's a trap to avoid.

15:27-28 That Saul **grabbed** and **tore** Samuel's **robe** (15:27) shows a desperate man grasping for a straw of hope, but even that became a prophetic sign against him (15:28).

15:30-33 When Saul pleaded with Samuel to **honor** him **before the elders**, Samuel eventually agreed (15:30-31). But it didn't change God's decree that he'd lose the throne, even though Saul would rule for many more years. Samuel's greater mission in returning with Saul was to finish the job this failed king was supposed to have accomplished (15:31-33).

15:35 The statement that **Samuel never saw Saul again** does not contradict Saul's appearance before Samuel in 19:24. The verb *see* can also mean "to have regard for, to take notice of." As far as Samuel was concerned, then, his relationship with Saul was over.

16:1 Samuel's grief over Saul's failure was understandable. But apparently God felt it had gone on for too **long**. He roused his elderly prophet to action, giving him the most important assignment of his ministry. Saul's replacement was at hand. And through that individual's line, God would fulfill his covenant promise to send an eternal Ruler, his Messiah.

16:4 Ironically, **the elders** of Bethlehem **trembled** with fear at the sight of Samuel, perhaps expecting him to deliver some message of judgment.

16:6-7 As soon as he looked at Jesse's sons, Samuel began sizing them up. He may have recalled that when Saul was identified as king of Israel he "stood a head taller than anyone else" (10:23). It certainly seems Samuel had physical characteristics in mind when he just looked at Jesse's firstborn **Eliab and said, "Certainly the LORD's anointed one is here"** (16:6). But as Samuel would find out, God's selection wasn't based on physical **appearance** or **stature**. People tend to **see what is visible, but the LORD sees the heart** (16:7).

this one either," Samuel said. **9** Then Jesse presented Shammah,[a] but Samuel said, "The LORD hasn't chosen this one either." **10** After Jesse presented seven of his sons to him, Samuel told Jesse, "The LORD hasn't chosen any of these." **11** Samuel asked him, "Are these all the sons you have?"

"There is still the youngest,"[b] he answered, "but right now he's tending the sheep." Samuel told Jesse, "Send for him. We won't sit down to eat until he gets here." **12** So Jesse sent for him. He had beautiful eyes and a healthy,[A] handsome appearance.[c]

Then the LORD said, "Anoint him, for he is the one."[d] **13** So Samuel took the horn of oil and anointed him[e] in the presence of his brothers, and the Spirit of the LORD came powerfully on David from that day forward.[f] Then Samuel set out and went to Ramah.

DAVID IN SAUL'S COURT

14 Now the Spirit of the LORD had left Saul,[g] and an evil spirit sent from the LORD began to torment him, **15** so Saul's servants said to him, "You see that an evil spirit from God is tormenting you. **16** Let our lord command your servants here in your presence to look for someone who knows how to play the lyre. Whenever the evil spirit from God comes on you, that person can play the lyre, and you will feel better."[h]

17 Then Saul commanded his servants, "Find me someone who plays well and bring him to me."

18 One of the young men answered, "I have seen a son of Jesse of Bethlehem who knows how to play the lyre. He is also a valiant man,[i] a warrior, eloquent, handsome, and the LORD is with him."[j]

19 Then Saul dispatched messengers to Jesse and said, "Send me your son David, who is with the sheep." **20** So Jesse took a donkey loaded with bread, a wineskin, and one young goat and sent them by his son David to Saul.[k] **21** When David came to Saul[l] and entered his service, Saul loved him very much, and David became his armor-bearer. **22** Then Saul sent word to Jesse: "Let David remain in my service, for he has found favor with me." **23** Whenever the spirit from God came on Saul,[m] David would pick up his lyre and play, and Saul would then be relieved, feel better, and the evil spirit would leave him.

DAVID VERSUS GOLIATH

17 The Philistines[n] gathered their forces for war at Socoh in Judah and camped between Socoh[o] and Azekah[p] in Ephes-dammim.[q] **2** Saul and the men of Israel gathered and camped in the Valley of Elah;[r] then they lined up in battle formation to face the Philistines.

3 The Philistines were standing on one hill, and the Israelites were standing on another hill with a ravine between them. **4** Then a champion named Goliath, from Gath,[s] came out from the Philistine camp. He was nine feet, nine inches[B,C] tall **5** and wore a bronze helmet[D] and bronze scale armor that weighed one hundred twenty-five pounds.[E] **6** There was bronze armor on his shins, and a bronze javelin[t] was slung between his shoulders. **7** His spear shaft[u] was like a weaver's beam, and the iron point of his spear weighed fifteen

---

[a] 16:9 1Sm 17:13
[b] 16:11 1Sm 17:12; 2Sm 13:3
[c] 16:12 1Sm 17:42
[d] 1Sm 9:17
[e] 16:13 1Sm 10:1
[f] Ps 51:10-12; Ezk 36:27; Ac 2:1-17
[g] 16:14 1Sm 11:6; 18:12; 28:15
[h] 16:16 1Sm 18:10; 19:9; 2Kg 3:15

[i] 16:18 1Sm 17:32-36
[j] 1Sm 3:19; 18:12-14
[k] 16:20 1Sm 10:4,27; Pr 18:16
[l] 16:21 Gn 41:46; Pr 22:29
[m] 16:23 1Sm 16:14-16
[n] 17:1 1Sm 13:5
[o] 2Ch 28:18
[p] Jos 10:10
[q] 1Ch 11:13
[r] 17:2 1Sm 21:9
[s] 17:4 2Sm 21:18-22; 1Ch 20:4-8
[t] 17:6 1Sm 17:45
[u] 17:7 2Sm 21:19; 1Ch 11:23

A **16:12** Or *ruddy*　B **17:4** DSS, LXX read *four cubits and a span*　C **17:4** Lit *was six cubits and a span*　D **17:5** Lit *helmet on his head*
E **17:5** Lit *5,000 shekels*

16:13 Importantly, Jesse and his sons knew that David was being **anointed** in some ritual way, but they may not have known why. They certainly couldn't view the inner reality taking place: **The Spirit of the LORD came powerfully on David from that day forward.** Suddenly, David was not just a man after God's own heart (see 13:14), but was filled with the Holy Spirit. Not only was that the right combination for the king of God's people, it's the right combination for any kingdom citizen.

In time, David would be remembered as one of the greatest kings in Israel's history. Notably, David's great-grandmother Rahab was a Canaanite (which indicates that she was of a dark-skinned lineage). David's grandmother was Ruth, a Moabite, from a people who were Canaanites as well, also of African descent. Thus, David, one of the heroes of the faith, hailed from mixed Jewish and Hamitic ances-

try (see Gen 10:6) and stands as a leader of whom blacks can be proud to call our own.
16:14-15 This **spirit** (16:14) was most likely a demon sovereignly appointed by God to trouble Saul mentally and emotionally, demonstrating God's power over Satan and his kingdom. That this problem came **from God** (16:15) signals to the reader that God was in control of Saul's demise and David's eventual rise to the throne.

In response to the way God used Satan's kingdom to terrorize Saul, Saul should have responded with repentance for his rebellious acts against the gracious God who had made him king. He needed to turn back to the Lord, and ask him to lift his hand of judgment.
16:22 This illustrates the warning Samuel had given to the Israelites when they first demanded a king, telling them that a ruler would press their sons into his service (see 8:11-12).

17:1-11 Once again Saul and the Israelite army faced off against their archenemies, **the Philistines** (17:1-2). **Goliath**, the enemy **champion** (17:4), **stood and shouted** his dare for a winner-take-all contest against any Israelite (17:8-9). He declared, **I defy the ranks of Israel** (17:10-11). But importantly, Goliath wasn't merely defying Israel and their king, he was defying Israel's God. Though this would be clear to David when he heard the giant's arrogant words (see 17:26), King Saul was so **terrified** that he apparently missed it (17:11). Saul stood head and shoulders above all the people—he was *Israel's champion*, the logical choice to represent Israel and go fight Goliath. But he wanted no part of the action.

Your level of fear can reveal your closeness to God. In general, the more you are afraid, the farther you are from God.

a 17:7 1Sm 17:41
b 17:8 1Sm 8:17
c 17:8-9 2Sm 2:12-16
d 17:10 1Sm 17:26,36,45
e 17:12 Gn 35:19
f 1Sm 16:10-11; 1Ch 2:13-15
g 17:13 1Sm 16:6,8-9
h 17:14 1Sm 16:11
i 17:15 1Sm 16:21-23
j 17:17 1Sm 25:18
k 17:18 Gn 37:13-14
l 17:20 1Sm 26:5,7

m 17:22 Jdg 18:21; Is 10:28
n 17:23 1Sm 17:8-10
o 17:25 Jos 15:16
p 1Sm 8:11
q 17:26 1Sm 11:2
r 1Sm 14:6; 17:36; Jr 9:25-26
s 1Sm 17:10
t Dt 5:26; 2Kg 19:4
u 17:27 1Sm 17:25
v 17:28 Gn 37:4,8-36
w 17:30 1Sm 17:26-27
x 17:32 Dt 20:1-4
y 1Sm 16:18

pounds.[A] In addition, a shield-bearer[a] was walking in front of him.

[8] He stood and shouted to the Israelite battle formations: "Why do you come out to line up in battle formation?" He asked them, "Am I not a Philistine and are you not servants of Saul?[b] Choose one of your men and have him come down against me. [9] If he wins in a fight against me and kills me, we will be your servants. But if I win against him and kill him, then you will be our servants and serve us."[c] [10] Then the Philistine said, "I defy the ranks of Israel today.[d] Send me a man so we can fight each other!" [11] When Saul and all Israel heard these words from the Philistine, they lost their courage and were terrified.

[12] Now David was the son of the Ephrathite[e] from Bethlehem of Judah named Jesse. Jesse had eight sons[f] and during Saul's reign was already an old man. [13] Jesse's three oldest sons had followed Saul to the war, and their names[g] were Eliab, the firstborn, Abinadab, the next, and Shammah, the third, [14] and David was the youngest.[h] The three oldest had followed Saul, [15] but David kept going back and forth from Saul[i] to tend his father's flock in Bethlehem.

[16] Every morning and evening for forty days the Philistine came forward and took his stand. [17] One day Jesse had told his son David: "Take this half-bushel[B] of roasted grain along with these ten loaves of bread[j] for your brothers and hurry to their camp. [18] Also take these ten portions of cheese to the field commander.[C] Check on the well-being of your brothers[k] and bring a confirmation from them. [19] They are with Saul and all the men of Israel in the Valley of Elah fighting with the Philistines."

[20] So David got up early in the morning, left the flock with someone to keep it, loaded up, and set out as Jesse had charged him. He arrived at the perimeter of the camp[l] as the army was marching out to its battle formation shouting their battle cry.

[21] Israel and the Philistines lined up in battle formation facing each other. [22] David left his supplies in the care of the quartermaster[m] and ran to the battle line. When he arrived, he asked his brothers how they were. [23] While he was speaking with them, suddenly the champion named Goliath, the Philistine from Gath, came forward from the Philistine battle line and shouted his usual words,[n] which David heard. [24] When all the Israelite men saw Goliath, they retreated from him terrified.

[25] Previously, an Israelite man had declared: "Do you see this man who keeps coming out? He comes to defy Israel. The king will make the man who kills him very rich and will give him his daughter.[o] The king will also make the family of that man's father exempt from paying taxes in Israel."[p]

[26] David spoke to the men who were standing with him: "What will be done for the man who kills that Philistine and removes this disgrace from Israel?[q] Just who is this uncircumcised Philistine[r] that he should defy the armies[s] of the living God?"[t]

[27] The troops told him about the offer, concluding, "That is what will be done for the man who kills him."[u]

[28] David's oldest brother Eliab listened as he spoke to the men, and he became angry with him.[v] "Why did you come down here?" he asked. "Who did you leave those few sheep with in the wilderness? I know your arrogance and your evil heart — you came down to see the battle!"

[29] "What have I done now?" protested David. "It was just a question." [30] Then he turned from those beside him to others in front of him and asked about the offer. The people gave him the same answer as before.[w]

[31] What David said was overheard and reported to Saul, so he had David brought to him. [32] David said to Saul, "Don't let anyone be discouraged by[D] him;[x] your servant will go[y] and fight this Philistine!"

[33] But Saul replied, "You can't go fight this Philistine. You're just a youth, and he's been a warrior since he was young."

17:15 Though David was officially in Saul's service (see 16:22), he went back and forth to help care for **his father's flock** since Jesse was aged (see 17:12).

17:23-27 David was concerned about removing Israel's **disgrace** at the hands of an **uncircumcised Philistine**, who was defying **the armies of the living God** (17:26). Don't miss that where the rest of the army saw a terrifying warrior (17:24), David saw an *uncircumcised* opponent—that is, someone who was not a part of God's covenant community and, therefore, not under God's covering. In spite of Goliath's size, he lacked the authority and power to which David had access as a covenant member.

17:28 It's possible that **Eliab** was jealous of David's anointing at the hands of Samuel the prophet (see the note on 16:13). Regardless, it's clear that Eliab despised his baby brother as a cocky kid who was showing off and neglecting his duties.

17:32 David was full of courage, zealous to protect those under his care, and bursting with trust in his covenant God.

34 David answered Saul: "Your servant has been tending his father's sheep. Whenever a lion or a bear came and carried off a lamb from the flock, **35** I went after it, struck it down, and rescued the lamb from its mouth.[a] If it reared up against me, I would grab it by its fur,[A] strike it down, and kill it. **36** Your servant has killed lions and bears; this uncircumcised Philistine will be like one of them, for he has defied the armies of the living God." **37** Then David said, "The Lord who rescued me from the paw of the lion and the paw of the bear will rescue me from the hand of this Philistine."[b]

Saul said to David, "Go, and may the Lord be with you."[c]

⟣ HOPE WORDS ⟣

God doesn't need a lot to do a lot.
All David had was five stones.
And all David used was one.

---

38 Then Saul had his own military clothes put on David. He put a bronze helmet on David's head and had him put on armor. **39** David strapped his sword on over the military clothes and tried to walk, but he was not used to them. "I can't walk in these," David said to Saul, "I'm not used to them." So David took them off. **40** Instead, he took his staff in his hand[d] and chose five smooth stones from the wadi and put them in the pouch, in his shepherd's bag. Then, with his sling in his hand, he approached the Philistine.

41 The Philistine came closer and closer to David, with the shield-bearer in front of him. **42** When the Philistine looked and saw David, he despised him[e] because he was just a youth, healthy[B,f] and handsome. **43** He said to David, "Am I a dog[g] that you come against me with sticks?"[c] Then he cursed David by his gods.[h] **44** "Come here," the Philistine called to David, "and I'll give your flesh to the birds of the sky and the wild beasts!"[i]

45 David said to the Philistine: "You come against me with a sword, spear, and javelin, but I come against you in the name of the Lord of Armies, the God of the ranks of Israel — you have defied him.[j] **46** Today, the Lord will hand you over to me. Today, I'll strike you down, remove your head, and give the corpses[D] of the Philistine camp to the birds of the sky and the wild creatures of the earth. Then all the world will know that Israel has a God,[k] **47** and this whole assembly will know that it is not by sword or by spear that the Lord saves,[l] for the battle is the Lord's.[m] He will hand you over to us." **48** When the Philistine started forward to attack him, David ran quickly to the battle line to meet the Philistine.[n] **49** David put his hand in the bag, took out a stone, slung it, and hit the Philistine on his forehead. The stone sank into his forehead, and he fell facedown to the ground. **50** David defeated the Philistine with a sling and a stone. David overpowered the Philistine and killed him without having a sword. **51** David ran and stood over him. He grabbed the Philistine's sword,[o] pulled it from its sheath, and used it to kill him. Then he cut off his head. When the Philistines saw that their hero was dead, they fled.[p] **52** The men of Israel and Judah rallied, shouting their battle cry, and chased the Philistines to the entrance of the valley and to the gates of Ekron.[E,q] Philistine bodies were strewn all along the Shaaraim road[r] to Gath and Ekron. **53** When the Israelites returned from the pursuit of the Philistines, they plundered their camps. **54** David took Goliath's[F] head and brought it to Jerusalem, but he put Goliath's weapons in his own tent.

55[G] When Saul had seen David going out to confront the Philistine, he asked Abner the commander of the army, "Whose son is this youth, Abner?"[s]

"Your Majesty, as surely as you live, I don't know," Abner replied.

56 The king said, "Find out whose son this young man is!"

57 When David returned from killing the Philistine, Abner took him and brought

[a] 17:35 Am 3:12
[b] 17:37 2Tm 4:17-18
[c] 1Sm 20:13
[d] 17:40 Jdg 20:16
[e] 17:42 Pr 16:18
[f] 1Sm 16:12
[g] 17:43 1Sm 24:14
[h] 1Kg 20:10
[i] 17:44 1Sm 17:46

[j] 17:45 2Ch 32:7-8; Ps 124:8; Heb 11:34
[k] 17:46 1Kg 18:36; 2Kg 19:19; Is 37:20
[l] 17:47 Hs 1:7
[m] Ex 14:13-14; Ps 33:16-22; 44:4-8
[n] 17:48 Ps 27:3
[o] 17:51 1Sm 21:9
[p] Heb 11:34
[q] 17:52 Jos 15:11
[r] Jos 15:36
[s] 17:55 1Sm 16:17-22; 17:25

[A] **17:35** LXX reads *throat*; lit *beard*   [B] **17:42** Or *ruddy*   [C] **17:43** Some LXX mss add *and stones?" And David said, "No! Worse than a dog!"*   [D] **17:46** LXX reads *give your limbs and the limbs*   [E] **17:52** LXX reads *Ashkelon*   [F] **17:54** Lit *the Philistine's*   [G] **17:55** LXX omits 1Sm 17:55–18:5

17:40 Rejecting Saul's armor, David went to war armed with **his sling** and a few **smooth stones** and the Creator of the universe on his side.

17:42-44 Little did Goliath know that his taunts had put him under a curse by the only true God (see Gen 12:3).

17:47 Don't miss the youth's bold declaration: **The battle is the Lord's. He will hand**

you over to us. No obstacle is too large and no circumstance is too menacing when you realize that God is sovereign over all.

17:48-49 Goliath, who stood for all that was evil, was a terrifying presence. But like our enemy Satan (see 1 Pet 5:8), Goliath was a toothless lion despite his roaring because David was fighting in the Lord's name and strength. In the end, it was no contest. As

thousands watched, David **slung** his **stone** and Goliath toppled (1 Sam 17:49).

17:57 In David's grisly trophy, we have a glimpse of what God promised that his Messiah would do to the serpent, the devil: "He will strike your head" (Gen 3:15). As David vanquished the giant, so Christ the Son of David will vanquish all his enemies.

a 17:57 1Sm 17:54
b 17:58 1Sm 17:12
c 18:1 1Sm 20:17; 2Sm 1:26
d 18:3 1Sm 20:8,16; 23:18
e 18:4 Gn 41:42
f 18:6 Ex 15:20-21; Jdg 11:34
g 18:7 1Sm 21:11; 29:5
h 18:8 1Sm 15:28; 24:20
i 18:10 1Sm 16:14; 19:9

j 18:10 1Sm 16:23
k 1Sm 19:9
l 18:11 1Sm 19:10; 20:33
m 18:12 1Sm 18:15,29
n 1Sm 16:13,18
o 1Sm 16:14; 17:36,47; 2Sm 5:2
p 18:13 2Sm 5:2
q 18:14 1Sm 3:19; 16:18
r 18:16 1Sm 18:5
s 18:17 1Sm 17:25
t Nm 21:14; 1Sm 17:36-37; 25:28
u 1Sm 18:21,25
v 18:18 1Sm 9:21; 18:23; 2Sm 7:18
w 18:19 Jdg 7:22; 2Sm 21:8; 1Kg 19:16
x 18:20 1Sm 18:28
y 18:21 1Sm 18:17
z 1Sm 18:20

him before Saul with the Philistine's head still in his hand.*a* **58** Saul said to him, "Whose son are you, young man?"

"The son of your servant Jesse of Bethlehem,"*b* David answered.

DAVID'S SUCCESS

18 When David had finished speaking with Saul, Jonathan was bound to David in close friendship,*A* and loved him as much as he loved himself.*c* **2** Saul kept David with him from that day on and did not let him return to his father's house. **3** Jonathan made a covenant with David*d* because he loved him as much as himself. **4** Then Jonathan removed the robe he was wearing and gave it to David,*e* along with his military tunic, his sword, his bow, and his belt.

5 David marched out with the army and was successful in everything Saul sent him to do. Saul put him in command of the fighting men, which pleased all the people and Saul's servants as well.

6 As the troops were coming back, when David was returning from killing the Philistine, the women came out from all the cities of Israel to meet King Saul,*f* singing and dancing with tambourines, with shouts of joy, and with three-stringed instruments. **7** As they danced, the women sang:

Saul has killed his thousands,
but David his tens of thousands.*g*

8 Saul was furious and resented this song.*B* "They credited tens of thousands to David," he complained, "but they only credited me with thousands. What more can he have but the kingdom?"*h* **9** So Saul watched David jealously from that day forward.

SAUL ATTEMPTS TO KILL DAVID

10 The next day an evil spirit sent from God came powerfully on Saul,*i* and he began to rave*c* inside the palace. David was playing the lyre as usual,*j* but Saul was holding a spear,*k* **11** and he threw it, thinking, "I'll pin David to the wall."*l* But David got away from him twice.

12 Saul was afraid of David,*m* because the LORD was with David*n* but had left Saul.*o* **13** Therefore, Saul sent David away from him and made him commander over a thousand men. David led the troops*p* **14** and continued to be successful in all his activities because the LORD was with him.*q* **15** When Saul observed that David was very successful, he dreaded him. **16** But all Israel and Judah loved David*r* because he was leading their troops. **17** Saul told David, "Here is my oldest daughter Merab. I'll give her to you as a wife,*s* if you will be a warrior for me and fight the LORD's battles."*t* But Saul was thinking, "I don't need to raise a hand against him; let the hand of the Philistines be against him."*u*

18 Then David responded, "Who am I,*v* and what is my family or my father's clan in Israel that I should become the king's son-in-law?" **19** When it was time to give Saul's daughter Merab to David, she was given to Adriel the Meholathite as a wife.*w*

DAVID'S MARRIAGE TO MICHAL

20 Now Saul's daughter Michal*x* loved David, and when it was reported to Saul, it pleased him.*D* **21** "I'll give her to him," Saul thought. "She'll be a trap for him, and the hand of the Philistines will be against him."*y* So Saul said to David a second time, "You can now be my son-in-law."*z*

22 Saul then ordered his servants, "Speak to David in private and tell him, 'Look, the king is pleased with you, and all his servants love you. Therefore, you should become the king's son-in-law.'"

23 Saul's servants reported these words directly to David,*E* but he replied, "Is it

---

A 18:1 Lit *the life of Jonathan was bound to the life of David*   *B* 18:8 Lit *furious; this saying was evil in his eyes*   *C* 18:10 Or *prophesy*   *D* 18:20 Lit *Saul, the thing was right in his eyes*   *E* 18:23 Lit *words in David's ears*

17:58 Saul was seeking to find out the name of David's father so he could properly reward the family of **Jesse of Bethlehem** (see 17:25). **18:1** The person who **loved** David the most was Saul's oldest son and heir **Jonathan**. We don't know when Jonathan realized that David, not he, would be Israel's next king (see 20:14-15). **18:2** That **Saul kept David with him** from the day he defeated Goliath means that David became a permanent leader in the army. **18:7-9** At the song's refrain, the fire of Saul's jealousy was ignited: David had been given more credit than he. In other words, the king let

his pride take over, ultimately fulfilling the truth of Proverbs 16:18: "Pride comes before destruction, and an arrogant spirit before a fall."

Saul wrongly assumed that David was seeking an opportunity to seize the throne (1 Sam 18:8). But nothing could be further from the truth. David was God's man and was living in God's timing. God had elevated him from the sheep pasture, and David was determined to leave his destiny in God's hands (see 24:1-22).

18:17-19 Since Saul had already reneged on his promise to give his daughter in marriage to

the warrior who would kill Goliath (see 17:25), it's not surprising to learn that he still had no real intention of making David his son-in-law. Instead, he expected **the Philistines** to kill him in battle first (18:17).

At work here is the truth that the more honorably David acted, the more treacherous Saul became. Sometimes living righteously and being determined to follow God leads the furnace of contempt and rejection to become even hotter.

trivial in your sight to become the king's son-in-law? I am a poor commoner."[a]

24 The servants reported back to Saul, "These are the words David spoke."

25 Then Saul replied, "Say this to David: 'The king desires no other bride-price[b] except a hundred Philistine foreskins, to take revenge on his enemies.'"[c] Actually, Saul intended to cause David's death at the hands of the Philistines.[d]

26 When the servants reported these terms to David, he was pleased[A] to become the king's son-in-law. Before the wedding day arrived,[B] **27** David and his men went out and killed two hundred[C] Philistines. He brought their foreskins and presented them as full payment to the king to become his son-in-law. Then Saul gave his daughter Michal to David as his wife.[e] **28** Saul realized[D] that the LORD was with David and that his daughter Michal loved him, **29** and he became even more afraid of David. As a result, Saul was David's enemy from then on.

30 Every time the Philistine commanders came out to fight,[f] David was more successful than all of Saul's officers.[g] So his name became well known.

DAVID DELIVERED FROM SAUL

19 Saul ordered his son Jonathan and all his servants to kill David.[h] But Saul's son Jonathan liked David very much,[i] **2** so he told him: "My father Saul intends to kill you. Be on your guard in the morning, and hide in a secret place and stay there. **3** I'll go out and stand beside my father in the field where you are and talk to him about you. When I see what he says, I'll tell you."[j]

4 Jonathan spoke well of David to his father Saul. He said to him: "The king should not sin against his servant David.[k] He hasn't sinned against you; in fact, his actions have been a great advantage to you. **5** He took his life in his hands when he struck down the Philistine,[l] and the LORD brought about a great victory for all Israel.[m] You saw it and rejoiced, so why would

you sin against innocent blood by killing David for no reason?"[n]

6 Saul listened to Jonathan's advice and swore an oath: "As surely as the LORD lives, David will not be killed." **7** So Jonathan summoned David and told him all these words. Then Jonathan brought David to Saul, and he served him as he did before.[o]

8 When war broke out again, David went out and fought against the Philistines. He defeated them with such great force that they fled from him.

9 Now an evil spirit sent from the LORD[p] came on Saul as he was sitting in his palace holding a spear.[q] David was playing the lyre,[r] **10** and Saul tried to pin David to the wall with the spear.[s] As the spear struck the wall, David eluded Saul, ran away, and escaped that night. **11** Saul sent agents to David's house to watch for him and kill him in the morning.[t] But his wife Michal[u] warned David, "If you don't escape tonight, you will be dead tomorrow!" **12** So she lowered David from the window, and he fled and escaped.[v] **13** Then Michal took the household idol and put it on the bed, placed some goat hair on its head, and covered it with a garment. **14** When Saul sent agents to seize David, Michal said, "He's sick."[w]

15 Saul sent the agents back to see David and said, "Bring him on his bed so I can kill him." **16** When the agents arrived, to their surprise, the household idol was on the bed with some goat hair on its head.

17 Saul asked Michal, "Why did you deceive me like this? You sent my enemy away, and he has escaped!"

She answered him, "He said to me, 'Let me go! Why should I kill you?'"

18 So David fled and escaped and went to Samuel at Ramah[x] and told him everything Saul had done to him. Then he and Samuel left and stayed at Naioth.[y]

19 When it was reported to Saul that David was at Naioth in Ramah, **20** he sent agents to seize David.[z] However, when they saw the group of prophets prophesying[aa] with Samuel leading them, the Spirit of

[a] 18:23 Gn 29:20; 34:12
[b] 18:25 Gn 34:12; Ex 22:17
[c] 1Sm 14:24
[d] 1Sm 18:17
[e] 18:27 2Sm 3:14
[f] 18:30 2Sm 11:1
[g] 1Sm 18:5
[h] 19:1 1Sm 18:8-9
[i] 1Sm 18:1-3
[j] 19:3 1Sm 20:32-33
[k] 19:4 Gn 44:22; Pr 17:13; Jr 18:20
[l] 19:5 1Sm 17:42-51
[m] 1Sm 11:13

[n] 19:5 Dt 19:10-13; 1Sm 20:32
[o] 19:7 1Sm 16:21; 18:2,10,13
[p] 19:9 1Sm 16:14; 18:10-11
[q] 1Sm 18:10
[r] 1Sm 16:14-16; 18:10
[s] 19:10 1Sm 18:11; 20:33
[t] 19:11 Ps 59 title
[u] 1Sm 18:20
[v] 19:12 Jos 2:15; Ac 9:23-25
[w] 19:14 Jos 2:5
[x] 19:18 1Sm 7:17
[y] 2Kg 6:1-2
[z] 19:20 1Sm 19:11; Jn 7:32
[aa] 1Sm 10:5-6,10

[A] **18:26** Lit *David, it was right in David's eyes*　　[B] **18:26** Lit *And the days were not full*　　[C] **18:27** LXX reads *100*　　[D] **18:28** Lit *saw and knew*

18:27 When David returned with twice the number of required Philistine trophies (see 18:25), Saul had no choice but to give Michal to him.
18:28-30 The wretched king continued to poison himself with his own bitterness of heart, watching David's star rise as his own faded.
19:4-7 Jonathan's defense of David was passionate and apparently hit home with Saul

during one of his saner moments (19:4-6). The king **swore an oath** that David would not be harmed (19:6). Jonathan believed his father's vow, and David believed Jonathan, so David came back to the royal court.
19:9-10 That the **evil spirit sent from the LORD came on Saul** again revealed Saul's lack of genuine repentance and his murderous heart.

19:19-24 Three teams of Saul's **agents** were overcome with a spirit of prophecy, which some commentators believe was a power that immobilized them so they could not harm David (19:19-21). When Saul finally went himself, he experienced the same phenomenon, causing him to collapse (19:22-24). Once again, as a result of divine intervention, it was clear that the Lord was with David. Yet Saul refused to repent.

[a]**19:21** Nm 11:25
[b]**19:23** 1Sm 10:10
[c]**19:24** Is 20:2; Mc 1:8
[d]**19:20-24** 1Sm 10:5-13
[e]**20:1** 1Sm 24:9
[f]**20:3** 1Sm 25:26; 2Kg 2:6
[g]**20:5** Nm 10:10; 28:11-15;
Am 8:5
[h]**1Sm 20:24,27
[i]**1Sm 19:2
[j]**20:6** 1Sm 17:58
[k]**Dt 12:5

[l]**20:8** 1Sm 18:3; 20:16;
23:18
[m]**2Sm 14:32
[n]**20:13** Ru 1:17; 1Sm 3:17
[o]**1Sm 18:12
[p]**20:15** 2Sm 9:1
[q]**20:16** 1Sm 18:3; 23:18
[r]**Dt 23:21
[s]**20:17** 1Sm 18:1
[t]**20:18** Nm 10:10
[u]**20:22** 1Sm 20:37

God came on Saul's agents, and they also started prophesying. [21] When they reported to Saul, he sent other agents, and they also began prophesying.[a] So Saul tried again and sent a third group of agents, and even they began prophesying. [22] Then Saul himself went to Ramah. He came to the large cistern at Secu and asked, "Where are Samuel and David?"

"At Naioth in Ramah," someone said.

[23] So he went to Naioth in Ramah. The Spirit of God also came on him,[b] and as he walked along, he prophesied until he entered Naioth in Ramah. [24] Saul then removed his clothes and also prophesied before Samuel; he collapsed and lay naked[c] all that day and all that night. That is why they say, "Is Saul also among the prophets?"[d]

JONATHAN PROTECTS DAVID

20 David fled from Naioth in Ramah and came to Jonathan and asked, "What have I done?[e] What did I do wrong? How have I sinned against your father so that he wants to take my life?"

[2] Jonathan said to him, "No, you won't die. Listen, my father doesn't do anything, great or small, without telling me.[A] So why would he hide this matter from me? This can't be true."

[3] But David said, "Your father certainly knows that I have found favor with you. He has said, 'Jonathan must not know of this, or else he will be grieved.'" David also swore, "As surely as the LORD lives and as you yourself live, there is but a step between me and death."[f]

[4] Jonathan said to David, "Whatever you say, I will do for you."

[5] So David told him, "Look, tomorrow is the New Moon,[g] and I'm supposed to sit down and eat with the king.[h] Instead, let me go, and I'll hide in the countryside for the next two nights.[B,i] [6] If your father misses me at all, say, 'David urgently requested my permission to go quickly to his hometown Bethlehem[j] for an annual sacrifice[k] there involving the whole clan.' [7] If he says, 'Good,' then your servant is safe, but if he

becomes angry, you will know he has evil intentions. [8] Deal kindly with[c] your servant, for you have brought me into a covenant with you before the LORD.[l] If I have done anything wrong,[m] then kill me yourself; why take me to your father?"

[9] "No!" Jonathan responded. "If I ever find out my father has evil intentions against you, wouldn't I tell you about it?"

[10] So David asked Jonathan, "Who will tell me if your father answers you harshly?"

[11] He answered David, "Come on, let's go out to the countryside." So both of them went out to the countryside. [12] "By the LORD, the God of Israel, I will sound out my father by this time tomorrow or the next day. If I find out that he is favorable toward you, will I not send for you and tell you?[D] [13] If my father intends to bring evil on you, may the LORD punish Jonathan and do so severely[n] if I do not tell you[E] and send you away so you may leave safely. May the LORD be with you,[o] just as he was with my father. [14] If I continue to live, show me kindness[f] from the LORD, but if I die, [15] don't ever withdraw your kindness from my household — not even when the LORD cuts off every one of David's enemies from the face of the earth."[p] [16] Then Jonathan made a covenant with the house of David,[q] saying, "May the LORD hold David's enemies accountable."[G,r] [17] Jonathan once again swore to David[H] in his love for him, because he loved him as he loved himself.[s]

[18] Then Jonathan said to him, "Tomorrow is the New Moon;[t] you'll be missed because your seat will be empty. [19] The following day hurry down and go to the place where you hid on the day this incident began and stay beside the rock Ezel. [20] I will shoot three arrows beside it as if I'm aiming at a target. [21] Then I will send a servant and say, 'Go and find the arrows!' Now, if I expressly say to the servant, 'Look, the arrows are on this side of you — get them,' then come, because as the LORD lives, it is safe for you and there is no problem. [22] But if I say this to the youth, 'Look, the arrows are beyond you!'[u] then go, for the LORD is

[A]**20:2** Lit *without uncovering my ear*   [B]**20:5** Lit *countryside until the third night*   [C]**20:8** Or *Show loyalty to*   [D]**20:12** Lit *and uncover your ear*
[E]**20:13** Lit *severely — I will uncover your ear*   [F]**20:14** Or *loyalty*, also in v. 15   [G]**20:16** Lit *LORD require it from the hand of David's enemies*
[H]**20:17** LXX; MT reads *Jonathan once again made David swear*

20:2 Jonathan was evidently unaware that his father had sent death squads to hunt down David. He still believed in Saul's oath not to harm David (see 19:6).

20:5 The **New Moon** was a festival that involved special meals, which David would

be expected to attend at Saul's table since he was a member of the king's court.

20:14-16 Jonathan expressed to David his awareness that David would not only live, but also inherit the kingdom from Saul someday. By this point, then, Jonathan

clearly understood that his father was under God's judgment. Though he was the king's son, Jonathan knew he would not be king himself. Nevertheless, he submitted himself to God's will.

sending you away. ²³ As for the matter you and I have spoken about,ᵃ the LORD will be a witnessᴬ between you and me forever."ᵇ ²⁴ So David hid in the countryside.

At the New Moon, the king sat down to eat the meal. ²⁵ He sat at his usual place on the seat by the wall. Jonathan sat facing himᴮ and Abner took his place beside Saul, but David's place was empty.ᶜ ²⁶ Saul did not say anything that day because he thought, "Something unexpected has happened; he must be ceremonially unclean — yes, that's it, he is unclean."ᵈ

²⁷ However, the day after the New Moon, the second day, David's place was still empty, and Saul asked his son Jonathan, "Why didn't Jesse's son come to the meal either yesterday or today?"

²⁸ Jonathan answered, "David asked for my permission to go to Bethlehem.ᵉ ²⁹ He said, 'Please let me go because our clan is holding a sacrifice in the town, and my brother has told me to be there. So now, if I have found favor with you, let me go so I can see my brothers.' That's why he didn't come to the king's table."

³⁰ Then Saul became angry with Jonathan and shouted, "You son of a perverse and rebellious woman! Don't I know that you are siding with Jesse's son to your own shame and to the disgrace of your mother?ᶜ ³¹ Every day Jesse's son lives on earth you and your kingship are not secure. Now send for him and bring him to me — he must die!"ᶠ

³² Jonathan answered his father back: "Why is he to be killed? What has he done?"ᵍ

³³ Then Saul threw his spear at Jonathan to kill him,ʰ so he knew that his father was determined to kill David.ⁱ ³⁴ He got up from the table fiercely angry and did not eat any food that second day of the New Moon, for he was grieved because of his father's shameful behavior toward David.

³⁵ In the morning Jonathan went out to the countryside for the appointed meeting with David. A young servant was with him. ³⁶ He said to the servant, "Run and find the arrows I'm shooting."ʲ As the servant ran, Jonathan shot an arrow beyond him. ³⁷ He came to the location of the arrow that Jonathan had shot, but Jonathan called to him and said, "The arrow is beyond you, isn't it?"ᵏ ³⁸ Then Jonathan called to him, "Hurry up and don't stop!" Jonathan's servant picked up the arrow and returned to his master. ³⁹ He did not know anything; only Jonathan and David knew the arrangement. ⁴⁰ Then Jonathan gave his equipment to the servant who was with him and said, "Go, take it back to the city."

⁴¹ When the servant had gone, David got up from the south side of the stone Ezel, fell facedown to the ground, and paid homage three times.ˡ Then he and Jonathan kissed each other and wept with each other, though David wept more.ᵐ

⁴² Jonathan then said to David, "Go in the assurance the two of us pledged in the name of the LORD when we said: The LORD will be a witness between you and me and between my offspring and your offspring forever."ⁿ Then David left, and Jonathan went into the city.

DAVID FLEES TO NOB

21 David went to the priest Ahimelechᵒ at Nob.ᵖ Ahimelech was afraid to meet David, so he said to him, "Why are you alone and no one is with you?"

² David answered the priest Ahimelech, "The king gave me a mission, but he told me, 'Don't let anyone know anything about the mission I'm sending you on or what I have ordered you to do.' I have stationed my young men at a certain place. ³ Now what do you have on hand? Give me five loaves of bread or whatever can be found."

⁴ The priest told him, "There is no ordinary bread on hand. However, there is consecrated bread,�q but the young men may eat itᴰ only if they have kept themselves from women."ʳ

ᵃ20:23 1Sm 20:14-15
ᵇGn 31:49,53
ᶜ20:25 1Sm 20:18
ᵈ20:26 Lv 7:20-21; Nm 10:10
ᵉ20:28 1Sm 20:6
ᶠ20:31 2Sm 12:5
ᵍ20:32 1Sm 19:5
ʰ20:33 1Sm 18:11; 19:10
ⁱ1Sm 20:7

ʲ20:36 1Sm 20:20-21
ᵏ20:37 1Sm 20:22
ˡ20:41 Gn 42:6
ᵐ1Sm 18:3
ⁿ20:42 1Sm 20:15-23
ᵒ21:1 1Sm 14:3; Mk 2:26
ᵖ1Sm 22:19
q21:4 Ex 25:30; Lv 24:5-9; Mt 12:3-4
ʳEx 19:15

ᴬ20:23 LXX; MT omits a witness   ᴮ20:25 Text emended; MT reads Jonathan got up   ᶜ20:30 Lit your mother's nakedness   ᴰ21:4 DSS; MT omits may eat it

20:30-31 Saul thought that Jonathan couldn't see what was obvious: David posed a huge threat to Jonathan's succession to the throne (20:31). What Saul didn't know was that Jonathan and David had already settled that issue. Although Saul was king, his son far surpassed him as a kingdom man.

21:1 David was a true fugitive. He fled south to Nob, a priestly sanctuary about one mile north of Jerusalem. The priest Ahimelech was apparently suspicious when he saw that David was alone. That's why he was afraid. Matthew 12:1-8 reveals that David actually traveled with a group of men, who were apparently in hiding here.

21:2 David lied to the priest by telling him that he and his men were on a secret mission for Saul.

21:3-6 Ahimelech had nothing on hand but the consecrated bread that was set apart and could only be eaten by the priests (21:4; see Lev 24:5-9). He gave David the day-old bread that had been replaced with fresh (1 Sam 21:6). This bread was holy, but this was an extraordinary circumstance. David was God's chosen future king, who was fleeing for his life. So as long as David and anyone traveling with him met ceremonial requirements, it was acceptable nourishment. Later, Jesus compared his disciples' actions to those of David eating the consecrated bread that was technically not lawful to eat (see Matt 12:1-8). In both cases an overly strict interpretation of the law of Moses would have caused the needy to go hungry.

[a]21:5 2Sm 11:11
[b]1Th 4:4
[c]21:6 Mt 12:3-4; Mk 2:25
[d]Lv 24:5-9
[e]21:7 1Sm 22:9; Ps 52 title
[f]21:9 1Sm 17:51
[g]21:10 Ps 56 title
[h]21:11 1Sm 18:7; 29:5
[i]21:13 Ps 34 title
[j]21:13-15 Ps 34 title
[k]22:1 Pss 57, 142 titles
[l]22:2 1Sm 23:13; 25:13
[m]22:5 1Ch 21:9; 29:29; 2Ch 29:25
[n]22:6 Jdg 4:5; 1Sm 14:2
[o]22:7 1Sm 8:12
[p]22:8 1Sm 18:3; 20:16
[q]1Sm 23:21
[r]22:9 Ps 52 title

5 David answered him, "I swear that women are being kept from us, as always when I go out to battle.[a] The young men's bodies[A] are consecrated[b] even on an ordinary mission, so of course their bodies are consecrated today." 6 So the priest gave him the consecrated bread,[c] for there was no bread there except the Bread of the Presence[d] that had been removed from the presence of the LORD. When the bread was removed, it had been replaced with warm bread.

7 One of Saul's servants, detained before the LORD, was there that day. His name was Doeg the Edomite,[e] chief of Saul's shepherds.

8 David said to Ahimelech, "Do you have a spear or sword on hand? I didn't even bring my sword or my weapons since the king's mission was urgent."

9 The priest replied, "The sword of Goliath the Philistine,[f] whom you killed in the Valley of Elah, is here, wrapped in a cloth behind the ephod. If you want to take it for yourself, then take it, for there isn't another one here."

"There's none like it!" David said. "Give it to me."

DAVID FLEES TO GATH

10 David fled that day from Saul's presence and went to King Achish of Gath.[g] 11 But Achish's servants said to him, "Isn't this David, the king of the land? Don't they sing about him during their dances:

Saul has killed his thousands,
but David his tens
of thousands?"[h]

12 David took this to heart[B] and became very afraid of King Achish of Gath, 13 so he pretended to be insane in their presence.[i] He acted like a madman around them,[C] scribbling[D] on the doors of the city gate and letting saliva run down his beard.

14 "Look! You can see the man is crazy," Achish said to his servants. "Why did you bring him to me? 15 Do I have such a shortage of crazy people that you brought this one to act crazy around me? Is this one going to come into my house?"[j]

SAUL'S INCREASING PARANOIA

22 So David left Gath and took refuge in the cave of Adullam.[k] When David's brothers and his father's whole family heard, they went down and joined him there. 2 In addition, every man who was desperate, in debt, or discontented rallied around him, and he became their leader. About four hundred men were with him.[l]

3 From there David went to Mizpeh of Moab where he said to the king of Moab, "Please let my father and mother stay with you until I know what God will do for me." 4 So he left them in the care of the king of Moab, and they stayed with him the whole time David was in the stronghold.

5 Then the prophet Gad[m] said to David, "Don't stay in the stronghold. Leave and return to the land of Judah." So David left and went to the forest of Hereth.

6 Saul heard that David and his men had been discovered. At that time Saul was in Gibeah, sitting under the tamarisk tree[n] at the high place. His spear was in his hand, and all his servants were standing around him. 7 Saul said to his servants, "Listen, men of Benjamin: Is Jesse's son going to give all of you fields and vineyards? Do you think he'll make all of you commanders of thousands and commanders of hundreds?[o] 8 That's why all of you have conspired against me! Nobody tells me[E] when my own son makes a covenant with Jesse's son.[p] None of you cares about me[q] or tells me[F] that my son has stirred up my own servant to wait in ambush for me, as is the case today."

9 Then Doeg the Edomite,[r] who was in charge of Saul's servants, answered: "I saw Jesse's son come to Ahimelech son

[A]21:5 Lit *vessels* [B]21:12 Lit *David placed these words in his heart* [C]21:13 Lit *madman in their hand* [D]21:13 LXX reads *drumming* [E]22:8 Lit *No one uncovers my ear* [F]22:8 Lit *or uncovers my ear*

21:7 The Edomites were longtime enemies of Israel.

21:10 That David chose to hide in Goliath's hometown reveals his desperation.

21:11-15 Perhaps Achish didn't kill David because of an ancient superstition against killing an insane person based on the belief that insanity was a divine judgment not to be interfered with. David's act worked as Achish sent him packing.

22:1-2 When they learned of his whereabouts, David's family joined him **in the cave**, since their lives would also have been in danger from Saul (22:1). And **every man who was desperate, in debt, or discontented**—that is, those whom we would call the disenfranchised or who had a gripe against the way Saul was running things—joined up with David (22:2).

22:3-4 David then took his family to **the king of Moab** for protection (22:3), perhaps because Moab was the home of David's great-grandmother, Ruth (see Ruth 4:21-22).

22:6-9 Saul's twisted charge that Jonathan was against him and that David was actually waiting **in ambush for** him shows how deranged and dangerous Saul had become (22:8). **Doeg** saw his chance to ingratiate himself with the king, so he reported what he had seen and heard at **Nob** (22:9-10; see 21:7). Doeg's malice combined with

of Ahitub at Nob.[a] [10] Ahimelech inquired of the LORD for him[b] and gave him provisions.[c] He also gave him the sword of Goliath the Philistine."[d]

SLAUGHTER OF THE PRIESTS

[11] The king sent messengers to summon the priest Ahimelech son of Ahitub, and his father's whole family, who were priests in Nob. All of them came to the king. [12] Then Saul said, "Listen, son of Ahitub!"

"I'm at your service,[e] my lord," he said.

[13] Saul asked him, "Why did you and Jesse's son conspire against me? You gave him bread and a sword and inquired of God for him, so he could rise up against me and wait in ambush, as is the case today."[f]

[14] Ahimelech replied to the king: "Who among all your servants is as faithful as David?[g] He is the king's son-in-law, captain of your bodyguard, and honored in your house. [15] Was today the first time I inquired of God for him?[h] Of course not! Please don't let the king make an accusation against your servant or any of my father's family, for your servant didn't have any idea[A] about all this."

[16] But the king said, "You will die, Ahimelech — you and your father's whole family!"

[17] Then the king ordered the guards standing by him, "Turn and kill the priests of the LORD[i] because they sided with David. For they knew he was fleeing, but they didn't tell me."[B] But the king's servants would not lift a hand to execute the priests of the LORD.

[18] So the king said to Doeg, "Go and execute the priests!" So Doeg the Edomite went and executed the priests himself. On that day, he killed eighty-five men[j] who wore linen ephods.[k] [19] He also struck down Nob, the city of the priests, with the sword — both men and women, infants and nursing babies, oxen, donkeys, and sheep.[l]

[20] However, one of the sons of Ahimelech son of Ahitub escaped. His name was Abiathar,[m] and he fled to David.[n] [21] Abiathar told David that Saul had killed the priests of the LORD. [22] Then David said to Abiathar, "I knew that Doeg the Edomite[o] was there that day and that he was sure to report to Saul. I myself am responsible for[c] the lives of everyone in your father's family. [23] Stay with me. Don't be afraid, for the one who wants to take my life wants to take your life.[p] You will be safe with me."

DELIVERANCE AT KEILAH

23 It was reported to David: "Look, the Philistines are fighting against Keilah[q] and raiding the threshing floors." [2] So David inquired of the LORD:[r] "Should I launch an attack against these Philistines?"

The LORD answered David, "Launch an attack against the Philistines and rescue Keilah."

[3] But David's men said to him, "Look, we're afraid here in Judah; how much more if we go to Keilah against the Philistine forces!"

[4] Once again, David inquired of the LORD, and the LORD answered him: "Go at once to Keilah, for I will hand the Philistines over to you."[s] [5] Then David and his men went to Keilah, fought against the Philistines, drove their livestock away, and inflicted heavy losses on them. So David rescued the inhabitants of Keilah. [6] Abiathar son of Ahimelech fled to David at Keilah, and he brought an ephod with him.

[7] When it was reported to Saul that David had gone to Keilah, he said, "God has handed him over to me, for he has trapped himself by entering a town with barred gates." [8] Then Saul summoned all the troops to go to war at Keilah and besiege David and his men.

[9] When David learned that Saul was plotting evil against him, he said to the priest Abiathar,[t] "Bring the ephod."[u]

[a] 22:9 1Sm 21:1; Ps 52 title
[b] 22:10 1Sm 10:22
[c] 1Sm 21:6,9
[d] 1Sm 21:2-9
[e] 22:12 1Sm 3:4-6; 2Sm 1:7
[f] 22:13 1Sm 22:8
[g] 22:14 1Sm 19:4-5
[h] 22:15 2Sm 5:19,23
[i] 22:17 2Kg 10:25; 2Ch 12:10
[j] 22:18 1Sm 2:31
[k] Ex 28:4; 1Sm 2:28
[l] 22:19 1Sm 2:18

[m] 22:20 1Sm 23:9; 30:7; 2Sm 2:1; 1Kg 2:26-27
[n] 1Sm 2:33
[o] 22:22 1Sm 21:7
[p] 22:23 1Kg 2:26
[q] 23:1 Jos 15:44; Neh 3:17-18
[r] 23:2 1Sm 23:4,6,9-12; 2Sm 5:19,23
[s] 23:4 Jos 8:7; Jdg 7:7
[t] 23:9 1Sm 22:20
[u] 1Sm 23:6; 30:7

[A] 22:15 Lit didn't know a thing, small or large [B] 22:17 Lit didn't uncover my ear [c] 22:22 LXX, Syr, Vg; MT reads I myself turn in

Saul's paranoia could produce nothing but calamity.

22:11-16 Ahimelech . . . and his father's whole family were called to stand trial for treason (22:11-13). But it was a kangaroo court. As far as Saul was concerned, Ahimelech was guilty by association.

22:17-19 Saul's **guards** apparently still had enough of the fear of the Lord in them that they **would not lift a hand to execute the priests** (22:17). **Doeg the Edomite**, however, not only killed all **eighty-five** priests at Nob,

but he also massacred every person and animal in town (22:18-19).

22:20-23 Only **Abiathar**, a son of Ahimelech, **escaped** and **fled to David** to tell him what happened (22:20-21). Abiathar stayed with David and would later serve in the priesthood when David became king (22:23).

The heading of Psalm 52 indicates that David wrote that psalm when he learned of Doeg's treachery. David knew that God would be faithful to bring down this wicked man, so David trusted and praised God for

his steadfast love (see Ps 52:5-9). His example is a reminder that regardless of how bad things look, we are to worship. God is still on his throne, and he will ultimately right every wrong.

23:1-2 David did more than merely hide from Saul during his days as a fugitive. He was still a loyal son of Israel and member of the tribe of Judah. When the Philistines attacked the Judean town of **Keilah**, David was concerned for his countrymen.

a 23:12 Jdg 15:10-13; 1Sm 23:20
b 23:13 1Sm 22:2; 25:13
  c 2Sm 15:20
d 23:14 Jos 15:55; 2Ch 11:8
  e Ps 32:7
  f 23:16 1Sm 30:6
g 23:17 1Sm 16:1-13; 24:20-22
  h 1Sm 20:31
i 23:18 1Sm 18:3; 20:12-17,42
j 23:19 1Sm 26:1; Ps 54 title

k 23:20 1Sm 23:12
  l 23:21 1Sm 22:8
m 23:24 Jos 15:55; 1Sm 25:2
  n 23:26 Ps 17:9
o 23:29 Jos 15:62; 2Ch 20:2
p 24:1 1Sm 23:28-29
  q 1Sm 23:19
r 24:2 1Sm 13:2; 26:2
  s 24:3 Jdg 3:24

10 Then David said, "LORD God of Israel, your servant has reliable information that Saul intends to come to Keilah and destroy the town because of me. **11** Will the citizens of Keilah hand me over to him? Will Saul come down as your servant has heard? LORD God of Israel, please tell your servant."

The LORD answered, "He will come down."

12 Then David asked, "Will the citizens of Keilah hand me and my men over to Saul?"

"They will,"*a* the LORD responded.

13 So David and his men, numbering about six hundred,*b* left Keilah at once and moved from place to place.*c* When it was reported to Saul that David had escaped from Keilah, he called off the expedition. **14** David then stayed in the wilderness strongholds and in the hill country of the Wilderness of Ziph.*d* Saul searched for him every day, but God did not hand David over to him.*e*

A RENEWED COVENANT

15 David was in the Wilderness of Ziph in Horesh when he saw that Saul had come out to take his life. **16** Then Saul's son Jonathan came to David in Horesh and encouraged him in his faith*A* in God,*f* **17** saying, "Don't be afraid, for my father Saul will never lay a hand on you. You yourself will be king over Israel,*g* and I'll be your second-in-command. Even my father Saul knows it is true."*h* **18** Then the two of them made a covenant in the LORD's presence.*i* Afterward, David remained in Horesh, while Jonathan went home.

DAVID'S NARROW ESCAPE

19 Some Ziphites*j* came up to Saul at Gibeah and said, "David is*B* hiding among us in the strongholds in Horesh on the hill of Hachilah south of Jeshimon. **20** Now, whenever the king wants to come down, let him come down. Our part will be to hand him over to the king."*k*

21 "May you be blessed by the LORD," replied Saul, "for you have shown concern for me.*l* **22** Go and check again. Investigate*C* where he goes*D* and who has seen him there; they tell me he is extremely cunning. **23** Investigate*E* all the places where he hides. Then come back to me with accurate information, and I'll go with you. If it turns out he really is in the region, I'll search for him among all the clans*F* of Judah." **24** So they went to Ziph ahead of Saul.

Now David and his men were in the wilderness near Maon*m* in the Arabah south of Jeshimon, **25** and Saul and his men went to look for him. When David was told about it, he went down to the rock and stayed in the Wilderness of Maon. Saul heard of this and pursued David there.

26 Saul went along one side of the mountain and David and his men went along the other side. Even though David was hurrying to get away from Saul, Saul and his men were closing in on David and his men to capture them.*n* **27** Then a messenger came to Saul saying, "Come quickly, because the Philistines have raided the land!" **28** So Saul broke off his pursuit of David and went to engage the Philistines. Therefore, that place was named the Rock of Separation. **29** From there David went up and stayed in the strongholds of En-gedi.*o*

DAVID SPARES SAUL

24 When Saul returned from pursuing the Philistines,*p* he was told, "David is in the wilderness near En-gedi."*q* **2** So Saul took three thousand of Israel's fit young men*r* and went to look for David and his men in front of the Rocks of the Wild Goats. **3** When Saul came to the sheep pens along the road, a cave was there, and he went in to relieve himself.*G,s* David and his men were staying in the recesses of

A 23:16 Lit *and strengthened his hand*   *B* 23:19 Lit "*Is David not . . . Jeshimon?*   *C* 23:22 Lit *Know and see*   *D* 23:22 Lit *watch his place where his foot will be*   *E* 23:23 Lit *See and know*   *F* 23:23 Or *thousands*   *G* 24:3 Lit *to cover his feet*

23:12 The people of Keilah probably knew what happened to the people of Nob, and they wanted no part of protecting David at such a cost.

23:16 God sent Jonathan to David and **encouraged him in his faith in God**. Similarly, when other believers are at spiritual low points, we as Christians are to be faithful Jonathans to them. This is what it is to love your neighbor as yourself.

23:17 Jonathan was looking forward to serving as David's **second-in-command** one day, but sadly that would never happen. This would

be the last time these two friends would see one another.

23:19 Perhaps the **Ziphites** wanted to ingratiate themselves with the king, or maybe they wanted to avoid being accused of knowing where David was and not telling.

23:26-28 Because of David's heart-stopping escape, the site was named **the Rock of Separation** to commemorate God's deliverance (23:28).

24:1-7 Even though David was God's anointed choice as king, he refused to take the throne by violence but determined to wait on God's

timing. God has a plan for every believer's life. The question is, Will you seek his will for you at any cost, or will you pursue it according to God's agenda and timetable?

Instead of burying his knife in Saul's back, David only **cut off the corner of Saul's robe** (24:4). David's **conscience** was so sensitive that even that act bothered him (24:5). In spite of his wickedness, Saul was still **the LORD's anointed** (24:6), and David intended to leave him in the hands of the Lord.

the cave,[a] [4] so they said to him, "Look, this is the day the LORD told you about: 'I will hand your enemy over to you so you can do to him whatever you desire.'" Then David got up and secretly cut off the corner of Saul's robe.

[5] Afterward, David's conscience bothered[A,b] him because he had cut off the corner of Saul's robe.[B] [6] He said to his men, "I swear before the LORD: I would never do such a thing to my lord, the LORD's anointed.[c] I will never lift my hand against him, since he is the LORD's anointed."[d] [7] With these words David persuaded[c] his men, and he did not let them rise up against Saul.

Then Saul left the cave and went on his way. [8] After that, David got up, went out of the cave, and called to Saul, "My lord the king!" When Saul looked behind him, David knelt low with his face to the ground and paid homage.[e] [9] David said to Saul, "Why do you listen to the words of people who say, 'Look, David intends to harm you'? [10] You can see with your own eyes that the LORD handed you over to me today in the cave.[f] Someone advised me to kill you,[g] but I[D,E] took pity on you and said: I won't lift my hand against my lord, since he is the LORD's anointed. [11] Look, my father!"[n] Look at the corner of your robe in my hand, for I cut it off, but I didn't kill you. Recognize[F] that I've committed no crime or rebellion. I haven't sinned against you even though you are hunting me down to take my life.[i]

[12] "May the LORD judge between me and you, and may the LORD take vengeance on you for me, but my hand will never be against you.[j] [13] As the old proverb says, 'Wickedness comes from wicked people.'[k] My hand will never be against you. [14] Who has the king of Israel come after? What are you chasing after? A dead dog? A single flea?[l] [15] May the LORD be judge and decide between you and me. May he take notice and plead my case and deliver[G] me from you."[m]

[16] When David finished saying these things to him, Saul replied, "Is that your voice, David my son?"[n] Then Saul wept aloud [17] and said to David, "You are more righteous than I, for you have done what is good to me though I have done what is evil to you.[o] [18] You yourself have told me today what good you did for me: when the LORD handed me over to you, you didn't kill me.[p] [19] When a man finds his enemy, does he let him go unharmed?[H,q] May the LORD repay you with good for what you've done for me today.

[20] "Now I know for certain you will be king, and the kingdom of Israel will be established[I] in your hand.[r] [21] Therefore swear to me by the LORD that you will not cut off my descendants or wipe out my name from my father's family."[s] [22] So David swore to Saul. Then Saul went back home, and David and his men went up to the stronghold.[t]

DAVID, NABAL, AND ABIGAIL

25 Samuel died,[u] and all Israel assembled to mourn for him,[v] and they buried him by his home in Ramah.[w] David then went down to the Wilderness of Paran.[J,x]

[2] A man in Maon[y] had a business in Carmel;[z] he was a very rich man with three thousand sheep and one thousand goats and was shearing his sheep in Carmel. [3] The man's name was Nabal, and his wife's name, Abigail. The woman was intelligent and beautiful, but the man, a Calebite,[aa] was harsh and evil in his dealings.

[4] While David was in the wilderness, he heard that Nabal was shearing sheep, [5] so David sent ten young men instructing them, "Go up to Carmel, and when you come to Nabal, greet him[K] in my name. [6] Then say this: 'Long life to you,[L] and peace to you, peace to your family, and peace to all that is yours.[ab] [7] I hear that you are shearing.[M] When your shepherds were with us, we did not harass them, and nothing of theirs was missing the whole time they were in Carmel.[ac] [8] Ask your young men, and they will tell you. So let my young men find favor with you, for we have come

[a] 24:3 Pss 57, 142 titles
[b] 24:5 2Sm 24:10
[c] 24:6 1Sm 26:9-11
[d] 1Sm 10:1
[e] 24:8 1Sm 25:23-24; 1Kg 1:31
[f] 24:10 Ps 7:3-4
[g] 1Sm 24:4
[h] 24:11 2Kg 5:13
[i] 1Sm 23:14,23; 26:20
[j] 24:12 1Sm 26:10-11,23
[k] 24:13 Mt 7:16-20; Lk 6:43-45
[l] 24:14 1Sm 26:20; 2Sm 9:8
[m] 24:15 Ps 35:1

[n] 24:16 1Sm 26:17
[o] 24:17 1Sm 26:21
[p] 24:18 1Sm 26:23
[q] 24:19 1Sm 23:17; Pr 16:29
[r] 24:20 1Sm 13:14; 16:1-13
[s] 24:21 Gn 21:23; 1Sm 20:14-17; 2Sm 21:6-8
[t] 24:22 1Sm 23:29
[u] 25:1 1Sm 28:3
[v] Dt 34:8
[w] 2Kg 21:18; 2Ch 33:20
[x] Gn 21:21; Nm 10:12; 13:3
[y] 25:2 1Sm 23:24
[z] Jos 15:55
[aa] 25:3 Jos 15:13; 1Sm 30:14
[ab] 25:6 1Ch 12:18
[ac] 25:7 1Sm 23:24-25; 25:15-16

[A] 24:5 Lit David's heart struck   [B] 24:5 Some Hb mss, LXX, Syr, Vg; other Hb mss omit robe   [C] 24:7 Or restrained   [D] 24:10 LXX, Syr, Tg; MT reads she or it   [E] 24:10 Or my eye   [F] 24:11 Lit Know and see   [G] 24:15 Lit render a verdict for   [H] 24:19 Lit go on a good way   [I] 24:20 Or will flourish   [J] 25:1 LXX reads to Maon   [K] 25:5 Or Nabal, ask him for peace   [L] 25:6 Lit 'To life   [M] 25:7 Lit you have shearers

---

24:16-19 In the hearing of his troops and David's men, Saul confessed his treachery and David's innocence.
24:22 Interestingly, David did not return with Saul and his army to Gibeah. Instead he stayed in **the stronghold**. Clearly, David was

not thoroughly convinced of the sincerity of Saul's repentance.
25:1 The last of the judges and the prophet who anointed Israel's first king (Saul) and its future king (David) was no more.

25:5-8 David asked for food in light of the safety he and his men had provided for Nabal's flocks.

*a*25:8 Neh 8:10-12
*b*25:10 Jdg 9:28
*c*25:13 1Sm 23:13; 30:9-10
*d*25:14 1Sm 13:10; 15:13
*e*25:15 1Sm 25:7,21
*f*25:16 Ex 14:22
*g*25:18 2Sm 16:1; 1Ch 12:40
*h*25:19 Gn 32:16,20

*i*25:22 1Sm 3:17; 20:13
*j*1Kg 14:10
*k*25:23 1Sm 20:41
*l*25:26 Heb 10:30
*m*2Sm 18:32
*n*25:27 Gn 33:11; 1Sm 30:26
*o*25:28 1Sm 25:24
*p*1Sm 2:35; 22:14; 2Sm 7:11,16
*q*1Sm 18:17
*r*1Sm 24:11; Ps 7:3
*s*25:29 Jr 10:18
*t*25:30 1Sm 13:14
*u*25:31 Gn 40:14; 1Sm 25:30
*v*25:32 Ex 18:10

on a feast[A] day.[a] Please give whatever you have on hand to your servants and to your son David.'"

9 David's young men went and said all these things to Nabal on David's behalf,[B] and they waited.[c] 10 Nabal asked them, "Who is David?[b] Who is Jesse's son? Many slaves these days are running away from their masters. 11 Am I supposed to take my bread, my water, and my meat that I butchered for my shearers and give them to these men? I don't know where they are from."

12 David's young men retraced their steps. When they returned to him, they reported all these words. 13 He said to his men, "All of you, put on your swords!" So each man put on his sword, and David also put on his sword. About four hundred men followed David while two hundred stayed with the supplies.[c]

14 One of Nabal's young men informed Abigail, Nabal's wife: "Look, David sent messengers from the wilderness to greet our master,[d] but he screamed at them. 15 The men treated us very well. When we were in the field, we weren't harassed[e] and nothing of ours was missing the whole time we were living among them. 16 They were a wall around us, both day and night,[f] the entire time we were with them herding the sheep. 17 Now consider carefully[D] what you should do, because there is certain to be trouble for our master and his entire family. He is such a worthless fool nobody can talk to him!"

18 Abigail hurried, taking two hundred loaves of bread, two clay jars of wine, five butchered sheep, a bushel[E] of roasted grain, one hundred clusters of raisins, and two hundred cakes of pressed figs, and loaded them on donkeys.[g] 19 Then she said to her male servants, "Go ahead of me. I will be right behind you."[h] But she did not tell her husband Nabal.

20 As she rode the donkey down a mountain pass hidden from view, she saw David and his men coming toward her and met them. 21 David had just said, "I guarded

everything that belonged to this man in the wilderness for nothing. He was not missing anything, yet he paid me back evil for good. 22 May God punish me[F] and do so severely[i] if I let any of his males[G] survive until morning."[j]

23 When Abigail saw David, she quickly got off the donkey and knelt down with her face to the ground and paid homage to David.[k] 24 She knelt at his feet and said, "The guilt is mine, my lord, but please let your servant speak to you directly. Listen to the words of your servant. 25 My lord should pay no attention to this worthless fool Nabal, for he lives up to his name:[H] His name means 'stupid,' and stupidity is all he knows.[i] I, your servant, didn't see my lord's young men whom you sent. 26 Now my lord, as surely as the LORD lives and as you yourself live— it is the LORD who kept you from participating in bloodshed and avenging yourself[l] by your own hand—may your enemies and those who intend to harm my lord be like Nabal.[m] 27 Let this gift[n] your servant has brought to my lord be given to the young men who follow my lord. 28 Please forgive your servant's offense,[o] for the LORD is certain to make a lasting dynasty for my lord[p] because he fights the LORD's battles.[q] Throughout your life, may evil[j] not be found in you.[r]

29 "Someone is pursuing you and intends to take your life. My lord's life is tucked safely in the place[k] where the LORD your God protects the living, but he is flinging away your enemies' lives like stones from a sling.[s] 30 When the LORD does for my lord all the good he promised you and appoints you ruler over Israel,[t] 31 there will not be remorse or a troubled conscience for my lord because of needless bloodshed or my lord's revenge. And when the LORD does good things for my lord, may you remember me your servant."[u]

32 Then David said to Abigail, "Blessed be the LORD God of Israel,[v] who sent you to meet me today! 33 May your discernment

---

^A^25:8 Lit *good*   ^B^25:9 Lit *name*   ^C^25:9 LXX reads *and he became arrogant*   ^D^25:17 Lit *Now know and see*   ^E^25:18 Lit *sheep, five seahs*
^F^25:22 LXX; MT reads *David's enemies*   ^G^25:22 Lit *of those of his who are urinating against the wall*   ^H^25:25 Lit *for as is his name, so he is*
^i^25:25 Lit *and foolishness is with him*   ^J^25:28 Or *trouble*   ^K^25:29 Lit *bundle*

25:14-17 Apparently Nabal's character was an open topic of discussion in the household because this servant didn't hesitate in pointing it out to the lady of the house: **He is such a worthless fool nobody can talk to him!** (25:17). 25:18-22 Abigail chose to intercede for her household and for Nabal. She was as wise

as Nabal was foolish, for David intended to kill every male in the household (25:22). If she didn't intercede, innocent lives would be lost and David would come to regret his actions.
25:23, 28 Abigail tactfully **paid homage to David** as to a king (25:23) and acknowledged

that he fought **the LORD's battles** (25:28). She is an example of the "wife of noble character" discussed in Proverbs 31:10-31. She didn't let her fool of a husband prevent her from fearing and obeying the Lord. She was a true kingdom woman.

be blessed, and may you be blessed. Today you kept me from participating in bloodshed and avenging myself by my own hand.[a] [34] Otherwise, as surely as the LORD God of Israel lives, who prevented me from harming you, if you had not come quickly to meet me, Nabal wouldn't have had any males[A] left by morning light." [35] Then David accepted what she had brought him and said, "Go home in peace.[b] See, I have heard what you said and have granted your request."[c]

[36] Then Abigail went to Nabal, and there he was in his house, holding a feast fit for a king.[d] Nabal's heart was cheerful,[B] and he was very drunk, so she didn't say anything[c] to him[e] until morning light. [37] In the morning when Nabal sobered up,[D] his wife told him about these events. His heart died[E] and he became a stone. [38] About ten days later, the LORD struck Nabal dead.[f]

[39] When David heard that Nabal was dead, he said, "Blessed be the LORD who championed my cause against Nabal's insults[g] and restrained his servant from doing evil.[h] The LORD brought Nabal's evil deeds back on his own head."[i]

Then David sent messengers to speak to Abigail about marrying him. [40] When David's servants came to Abigail at Carmel, they said to her, "David sent us to bring you to him as a wife."

[41] She stood up, paid homage with her face to the ground,[j] and said, "Here I am, your servant, a slave to wash the feet of my lord's servants."[k] [42] Then Abigail got up quickly, and with her five female servants accompanying her, rode on the donkey following David's messengers.[l] And so she became his wife.

[43] David also married Ahinoam of Jezreel,[m] and the two of them became his wives. [44] But Saul gave his daughter Michal, David's wife, to Palti[n] son of Laish, who was from Gallim.[o]

DAVID AGAIN SPARES SAUL

26 Then the Ziphites came to Saul at Gibeah saying, "David is hiding on the hill of Hachilah opposite Jeshimon."[p] [2] So Saul, accompanied by three thousand of the fit young men of Israel,[q] went immediately to the Wilderness of Ziph to search for David there. [3] Saul camped beside the road at the hill of Hachilah[r] opposite Jeshimon. David was living in the wilderness and discovered Saul had come there after him.[s] [4] So David sent out spies and knew for certain that Saul had come. [5] Immediately, David went to the place where Saul had camped. He saw the place where Saul and Abner son of Ner,[t] the commander of his army, were lying down. Saul was lying inside the inner circle of the camp with the troops camped around him. [6] Then David asked Ahimelech the Hethite[u] and Joab's brother Abishai[v] son of Zeruiah, "Who will go with me into the camp[w] to Saul?"

"I'll go with you," answered Abishai.

[7] That night, David and Abishai came to the troops, and Saul was lying there asleep in the inner circle of the camp with his spear stuck in the ground by his head. Abner and the troops were lying around him. [8] Then Abishai said to David, "Today God has delivered your enemy to you. Let me thrust the spear through him into the ground just once. I won't have to strike him twice!"

[9] But David said to Abishai, "Don't destroy him, for who can lift a hand against the LORD's anointed and be innocent?"[x] [10] David added, "As the LORD lives, the LORD will certainly strike him down:[y] either his day will come and he will die, or he will go into battle and perish. [11] However, because of the LORD, I will never lift my hand against the LORD's anointed.[z] Instead, take the spear and the water jug by his head, and let's go."

[12] So David took the spear and the water jug by Saul's head, and they went their

---

[a] 25:33 1Sm 25:26
[b] 25:35 1Sm 20:42; 2Kg 5:19
[c] Gn 19:21
[d] 25:36 2Sm 13:23
[e] 1Sm 25:19
[f] 25:38 1Sm 26:10
[g] 25:39 1Sm 24:15
[h] 1Sm 25:26,34
[i] 2Sm 3:28-29
[j] 25:41 1Sm 25:23
[k] Mk 1:7
[l] 25:42 Gn 24:61-67
[m] 25:43 Jos 15:56
[n] 25:44 1Sm 18:27; 2Sm 3:14-15
[o] Is 10:30

[p] 26:1 1Sm 23:19; Ps 54 title
[q] 26:2 1Sm 13:2; 24:2
[r] 26:3 1Sm 24:3
[s] 1Sm 23:15
[t] 26:5 1Sm 14:50-51; 17:55
[u] 26:6 Gn 26:34; Jos 3:10; 1Kg 10:29; 2Kg 7:6
[v] 1Ch 2:15-16
[w] Jdg 7:10-11
[x] 26:9 1Sm 10:1; 24:6-7; 2Sm 1:14,16
[y] 26:10 1Sm 25:26,38
[z] 26:11 Dt 32:35; 1Sm 24:6; 25:39; Rm 12:19

[A] 25:34 Lit *had anyone urinating against a wall*   [B] 25:36 Lit *Nabal's heart was good on him*   [C] 25:36 Lit *anything at all*   [D] 25:37 Lit *when the wine had gone out of Nabal*   [E] 25:37 Lit *Then his heart died within him*

25:36-38 Having saved the day, Abigail went home to find a drunken husband who had no idea how close to death he had come (25:36). When Nabal finally **sobered up** and Abigail told him everything, he had a stroke or heart attack (25:37). After **ten days**, God **struck [him] dead** in judgment (25:38).
25:40-44 Though his action was clearly intended to honor this godly woman, David was already **married** (25:43-44). Polygamy was never God's ideal for his people. And in

David's case, polygamous marriage would result in horrific family dysfunction (including rape and murder among his children).
26:2-3 In spite of his earlier repentance for unjustly pursuing David (see 24:16-20), Saul again brought his troops to catch David in his hiding place.
26:6 Brave **Abishai** would later become one of David's mighty men (see 1 Chr 11:20-21).
26:7-11 Militarily speaking, two against three thousand didn't make for a good plan. But

this was not a military operation. David made it clear to Abishai that he had no violent intent toward Saul. The author of 1 Samuel wanted us to know that the Lord was leading David on this midnight adventure to demonstrate again that though he was the legitimate king of Israel, he was not a usurper.
26:12 Possessing Saul's **spear and the water jug** would serve as evidence of David's good will and Saul's close brush with death.

[a] 26:12 Gn 2:21; 15:12
[b] 26:16 1Sm 20:31
[c] 26:17 1Sm 24:16; 26:21,25
[d] 26:18 1Sm 24:11
[e] 26:19 2Sm 16:11
[f] Gn 8:21
[g] 1Sm 24:9
[h] Jos 22:25-27
[i] 26:20 1Sm 24:14
[j] 26:21 1Sm 15:24,30; 24:17

[k] 26:23 1Sm 24:19
[l] 1Sm 24:10-12; 26:10-11
[m] 26:24 1Sm 18:30
[n] Ps 54:7
[o] 26:25 1Sm 24:19
[p] 1Sm 24:22
[q] 27:1 1Sm 26:19
[r] 27:2 1Sm 25:13
[s] 1Sm 2:10; 1Kg 2:39
[t] 27:3 1Sm 30:3; 2Sm 2:3
[u] 1Sm 25:42-44
[v] 27:6 Jos 15:31; 19:5; Neh 11:28
[w] 27:7 1Sm 29:1-11
[x] 27:8 Jos 13:2,13
[y] Ex 17:8; 1Sm 15:7-8
[z] Ex 15:22

way. No one saw them, no one knew, and no one woke up; they all remained asleep because a deep sleep from the LORD[a] came over them. [13] David crossed to the other side and stood on top of the mountain at a distance; there was a considerable space between them. [14] Then David shouted to the troops and to Abner son of Ner: "Aren't you going to answer, Abner?"

"Who are you who calls to the king?" Abner asked.

[15] David called to Abner, "You're a man, aren't you? Who in Israel is your equal? So why didn't you protect your lord the king when one of the people came to destroy him? [16] What you have done is not good. As the LORD lives, all of you deserve to die[A] since you didn't protect your lord, the LORD's anointed.[b] Now look around; where are the king's spear and water jug that were by his head?"

[17] Saul recognized David's voice and asked, "Is that your voice, my son David?"[c]

"It is my voice, my lord and king," David said. [18] Then he continued, "Why is my lord pursuing his servant? What have I done? What crime have I committed?[d] [19] Now, may my lord the king please hear the words of his servant: If it is the LORD who has incited you against me,[e] then may he accept an offering.[f] But if it is people,[g] may they be cursed in the presence of the LORD, for today they have banished me from sharing in the inheritance of the LORD saying,[h] 'Go and worship other gods.' [20] So don't let my blood fall to the ground far from the LORD's presence, for the king of Israel has come out to search for a single flea,[i] like one who pursues a partridge in the mountains."

[21] Saul responded, "I have sinned.[j] Come back, my son David, I will never harm you again because today you considered my life precious. I have been a fool! I've committed a grave error."

[22] David answered, "Here is the king's spear; have one of the young men come over and get it. [23] The LORD will repay every man for his righteousness[k] and his loyalty. I wasn't willing to lift my hand against the LORD's anointed, even though the LORD handed you over to me today.[l] [24] Just as I considered your life valuable today, so may the LORD consider my life valuable[m] and rescue me from all trouble."[n]

[25] Saul said to him, "You are blessed, my son David. You will certainly do great things and will also prevail."[o] Then David went on his way, and Saul returned home.[p]

DAVID FLEES TO ZIKLAG

27 David said to himself, "One of these days I'll be swept away by Saul. There is nothing better for me than to escape immediately to the land of the Philistines.[q] Then Saul will give up searching for me everywhere in Israel, and I'll escape from him." [2] So David set out with his six hundred men[r] and went over to Achish son of Maoch,[s] the king of Gath. [3] David and his men stayed with Achish in Gath. Each man had his family with him,[t] and David had his two wives: Ahinoam of Jezreel and Abigail of Carmel,[u] Nabal's widow. [4] When it was reported to Saul that David had fled to Gath, he no longer searched for him.

[5] Now David said to Achish, "If I have found favor with you, let me be given a place in one of the outlying towns, so I can live there. Why should your servant live in the royal city with you?" [6] That day Achish gave Ziklag[v] to him, and it still belongs to the kings of Judah today. [7] The length of time that David stayed in Philistine territory amounted to a year and four months.[w]

[8] David and his men went up and raided the Geshurites,[x] the Girzites,[B] and the Amalekites.[y] From ancient times they had been the inhabitants of the region through Shur[z] as far as the land of Egypt. [9] Whenever David attacked the land, he did not leave a single person alive, either man or woman, but he took flocks, herds, donkeys,

---

[A] 26:16 Lit *you are sons of death*   [B] 27:8 Alt Hb tradition reads *Gezerites*

26:13-16 Once David was again at a safe distance from the camp, he called out to Abner and Saul's troops, ridiculing them for failing to protect their king (26:14-15). Abner must have felt as if his pockets had been picked when he awoke to find someone had gotten to the king without his even knowing it.
26:21 Saul admitted, **I have been a fool!** (That's putting it mildly.) Unfortunately, Saul would not reform his ways. There is no point in acknowledging your foolishness if you insist on continuing to walk a foolish road.

27:1-4 It's hard to know what kind of reception David expected in enemy territory, but clearly he believed it couldn't be any worse than the fugitive life he had been living. This risky move makes more sense when we remember that David was responsible for six hundred **men** and their families as well as his own—quite an entourage to provide for in a barren wilderness (27:3).
27:5-6 Achish and the Philistines had become convinced that David really was a mortal enemy of Saul and could never go back to Israel. This made him a potentially valuable ally in their ongoing war with the Israelites.
27:7-11 David wanted to be away from Gath to be out from under the king's close scrutiny. David used Ziklag as his headquarters for the next sixteen months (27:7). From there David and his men carried out raids against various desert tribes that were enemies of Israel, including the nation's bitter and ancient foes, **the Amalekites** (27:8). David made sure that no one survived these raids to go to Gath and report to Achish what he was really doing (27:11).

camels, and clothing.[a] Then he came back
to Achish, 10 who inquired, "Where did you
raid today?"[A,b]
David replied, "The south country of
Judah," "The south country of the Jerahmeelites,"[c] or "The south country of the
Kenites."[d]
11 David did not let a man or woman live
to be brought to Gath, for he said, "Or they
will inform on us and say, 'This is what David did.'" This was David's custom during
the whole time he stayed in the Philistine
territory. 12 So Achish trusted David, thinking, "Since he has made himself repulsive
to his people Israel, he will be my servant
forever."

SAUL AND THE MEDIUM

28 At that time, the Philistines[e] gathered their military units into one
army to fight against Israel. So Achish
said to David, "You know, of course, that
you and your men must march out in the
army[B] with me."
2 David replied to Achish, "Good, you
will find out what your servant can do."
So Achish said to David, "Very well, I
will appoint you as my permanent bodyguard."[f]
3 By this time Samuel had died,[g] all Israel had mourned for him and buried him
in Ramah, his city,[h] and Saul had removed
the mediums and spiritists from the land.[i]
4 The Philistines gathered and camped at
Shunem. So Saul gathered all Israel, and
they camped at Gilboa. 5 When Saul saw
the Philistine camp, he was afraid and
his heart pounded. 6 He inquired of the
LORD, but the LORD did not answer him in
dreams or by the Urim or by the prophets.[j]
7 Saul then said to his servants, "Find me a
woman who is a medium, so I can go and
consult her."
His servants replied, "There is a woman
at En-dor[k] who is a medium."[l]
8 Saul disguised himself[m] by putting on
different clothes and set out with two of
his men. They came to the woman at night,
and Saul said, "Consult a spirit for me.[n]
Bring up for me the one I tell you."[o]
9 But the woman said to him, "You surely
know what Saul has done,[p] how he has cut
off the mediums and spiritists from the
land. Why are you setting a trap for me to
get me killed?"
10 Then Saul swore to her by the LORD:
"As surely as the LORD lives, no punishment
will come to you[C] from this."
11 "Who is it that you want me to bring
up for you?" the woman asked.
"Bring up Samuel for me," he answered.
12 When the woman saw Samuel, she
screamed, and then she asked Saul, "Why
did you deceive me? You are Saul!"
13 But the king said to her, "Don't be
afraid. What do you see?"
"I see a spirit form[D] coming up out of the
earth," the woman answered.
14 Then Saul asked her, "What does he
look like?"
"An old man is coming up," she replied.
"He's wearing a robe."[q] Then Saul knew
that it was Samuel, and he knelt low with
his face to the ground and paid homage.[r]
15 "Why have you disturbed me by bringing me up?" Samuel asked Saul.
"I'm in serious trouble," replied Saul.
"The Philistines are fighting against
me and God has turned away from me.[s]
He doesn't answer me anymore,[t] either
through the prophets or in dreams. So I've
called on you to tell me what I should do."
16 Samuel answered, "Since the LORD
has turned away from you and has become your enemy, why are you asking me?
17 The LORD has done[E] exactly what he said
through me: The LORD has torn the kingship out of your hand and given it to your
neighbor David.[u] 18 You did not obey the
LORD and did not carry out his burning anger against Amalek;[v] therefore the LORD
has done this to you today. 19 The LORD will
also hand Israel over to the Philistines
along with you. Tomorrow you and your

[a] 27:9 1Sm 15:3; Jb 1:3
[b] 27:10 1Sm 23:27
[c] 1Sm 30:29; 1Ch 2:9,25
[d] Jdg 1:16; 4:11
[e] 28:1 1Sm 29:1
[f] 28:2 1Sm 1:22,28
[g] 28:3 1Sm 25:1
[h] 1Sm 7:17
[i] Lv 19:31; 20:27; Dt 18:10-11
[j] 28:6 Ex 28:30; Nm 27:21; 1Kg 3:5
[k] 28:7 Jos 17:1; Ps 83:10
[l] Ac 16:16
[m] 28:8 2Ch 18:29; 35:21-22
[n] 28:8 Is 8:19
[o] Dt 18:10-11
[p] 28:9 1Sm 28:3
[q] 28:14 1Sm 15:27
[r] 1Sm 24:8
[s] 28:15 1Sm 16:13-14; 18:12
[t] 1Sm 28:6
[u] 28:17 1Sm 15:28
[v] 28:18 1Sm 15:1-9

A 27:10 Some Hb mss, Syr, Tg; LXX, Vg, DSS read *"Against whom did you raid today?"* B 28:1 DSS, LXX read *battle* C 28:10 Or *lives, you will not incur guilt* D 28:13 Or *a god*, or *a divine being* E 28:17 Some Hb, some LXX mss, Vg read *done to you*

28:1 As far as Achish was concerned, David and his men were now loyal comrades of the Philistines. So when the time came for the next battle between these two armies, Achish didn't give David an option. He had to **fight** with the Philistines **against Israel.**

Like any good drama, the book of 1 Samuel leaves the reader in suspense regarding what happened next, pausing to turn attention back to King Saul.

28:3-13 Previously, **Saul had removed the mediums and spiritists from the land** (28:3) in obedience to the law of Moses: "Do not turn to mediums or consult spiritists, or you will be defiled by them" (Lev 19:31; see also Deut 18:9-12). But here, facing war and desperate for supernatural guidance, Saul resorted to that which God had clearly prohibited.

28:14-19 The text presents the spirit of Samuel in a straightforward way, rather than as a demon impersonating Samuel or suggesting the medium merely used her wiles to trick Saul. It's doubtful that Saul would have been fooled by an impersonator, and Samuel's message of judgment on Saul—including his loss of the kingdom to David, his impending death, and Israel's defeat—were exactly what would come to pass. Thus, it would appear that God used an otherwise forbidden means to convey his verdict on a rebellious Saul.

a 28:19 1Sm 31:2; Jb 3:17-19
b 28:21 1Sm 19:5
c 28:23 2Kg 5:13
d Est 1:6; Ezk 23:41
e 28:24 Gn 18:6-7
f 29:1 1Sm 28:1-2
g Jos 12:18; 1Sm 4:1
h 1Kg 18:19; 21:1; 2Kg 9:30
i 29:2 1Sm 28:1-2
j 29:3 1Sm 27:4-12
k 29:4 1Sm 27:6
l 1Sm 14:21

m 29:5 1Sm 18:7; 21:11
n 29:6 1Sm 27:8-12; 29:3
o 29:8 1Sm 27:10-12
p 29:9 2Sm 14:17,20; 19:27
q 1Sm 29:4
r 29:10 1Ch 12:19,22
s 30:1-18 Gn 14:1-16
t 30:1 1Sm 27:6,8
u 1Sm 15:7; 27:8-10
v 30:2 1Sm 27:11

sons will be with me,[A,a] and the LORD will hand Israel's army over to the Philistines."

20 Immediately, Saul fell flat on the ground. He was terrified by Samuel's words and was also weak because he had not eaten anything all day and all night. **21** The woman came all over to Saul, and she saw that he was terrified and said to him, "Look, your servant has obeyed you. I took my life in my hands[b] and did what you told me to do. **22** Now please listen to your servant. Let me set some food in front of you. Eat and it will give you strength so you can go on your way."

23 He refused, saying, "I won't eat," but when his servants and the woman urged him, he listened to them.[c] He got up off the ground and sat on the bed.[d]

24 The woman had a fattened calf at her house, and she quickly slaughtered it.[e] She also took flour, kneaded it, and baked unleavened bread. **25** She served it to Saul and his servants, and they ate. Afterward, they got up and left that night.

PHILISTINES REJECT DAVID

29 The Philistines[f] brought all their military units together at Aphek[g] while Israel was camped by the spring in Jezreel.[h] **2** As the Philistine leaders were passing in review with their units of hundreds and thousands, David and his men[i] were passing in review behind them with Achish. **3** Then the Philistine commanders asked, "What are these Hebrews doing here?"

Achish answered the Philistine commanders, "That is David, servant of King Saul of Israel. He has been with me a considerable period of time. From the day he defected until today, I've found no fault with him."[j]

4 The Philistine commanders, however, were enraged with Achish and told him, "Send that man back and let him return to the place you assigned him.[k] He must not go down with us into battle only to become our adversary during the battle.[l]

What better way could he ingratiate himself with his master than with the heads of our men? **5** Isn't this the David they sing about during their dances:

Saul has killed his thousands,
　but David his tens of thousands?"[m]

6 So Achish summoned David and told him, "As the LORD lives, you are an honorable man. I think it is good[c] to have you fighting[D] in this unit with me, because I have found no fault in you from the day you came to me until today.[n] But the leaders don't think you are reliable. **7** Now go back quietly and you won't be doing anything the Philistine leaders think is wrong."

8 "But what have I done?"[o] David replied to Achish. "From the first day I entered your service until today, what have you found against your servant to keep me from going to fight against the enemies of my lord the king?"

9 Achish answered David, "I'm convinced that you are as reliable as an angel of God.[p] But the Philistine commanders have said, 'He must not go into battle with us.'[q] **10** So get up early in the morning, you and your masters' servants who came with you.[E,r] When you've all gotten up early, go as soon as it's light." **11** So David and his men got up early in the morning to return to the land of the Philistines. And the Philistines went up to Jezreel.

DAVID'S DEFEAT
OF THE AMALEKITES

30 David and his men[s] arrived in Ziklag[t] on the third day. The Amalekites[u] had raided the Negev and attacked and burned Ziklag. **2** They also had kidnapped the women and everyone[F] in it from youngest to oldest. They had killed no one but had carried them off[v] as they went on their way. **3** When David and his men arrived at the town, they found it burned. Their wives, sons, and daughters had been kidnapped.

A 28:19 LXX reads *sons will fall*　**B** 29:3 Hb obscure　**C** 29:6 Lit *It was good in my eyes*　**D** 29:6 Lit *you going out and coming in*　**E** 29:10 LXX adds *and go to the place I appointed you to. Don't take this evil matter to heart, for you are good before me.*　**F** 30:2 LXX; MT omits *and everyone*

29:1-5 When the text left David (27:12), he and his six hundred men were facing a dilemma as they were expected to serve the Philistines militarily against the Israelites. God providentially intervened. **The Philistine commanders** accused Achish of taking an incredibly dangerous risk in assuming that David would actually fight with them against his own people, instead of turning on them in order to **ingratiate himself with his master,**

Saul (29:4). Though Achish had come to trust David, the song sung about David in Israel was still well known in the land of Philistia (29:5). **29:6-8** David was no doubt delighted that he was no longer expected to go to war against Israel. But he played along with the charade, protesting this decision and emphasizing his past allegiance to the Philistines (29:8). **30:6** The men probably blamed David for the decision to leave Ziklag defenseless as they

fled to Gath to escape Saul. **But David found strength in the LORD.** He remembered that God had delivered him from lions and bears when he was a young shepherd (17:37), and he had delivered him from the hand of Saul numerous times. David knew where to turn for help. As he operated in the earthly realm, his true strength and protection lay in the heavenly realm.

To whom do you turn first when life's troubles visit you?

4 David and the troops with him wept loudly until they had no strength left to weep. **5** David's two wives,[a] Ahinoam the Jezreelite and Abigail the widow of Nabal the Carmelite, had also been kidnapped. **6** David was in an extremely difficult position because the troops talked about stoning him,[b] for they were all very bitter over the loss of their sons and daughters. But David found strength in the LORD his God.[c]

7 David said to the priest Abiathar son of Ahimelech, "Bring me the ephod."[d] So Abiathar brought it to him, **8** and David asked the LORD:[e] "Should I pursue these raiders? Will I overtake them?"[f]

The LORD replied to him, "Pursue them, for you will certainly overtake them and rescue the people."[g]

9 So David and the six hundred men with him[h] went. They came to the Wadi Besor, where some stayed behind.[i] **10** David and four hundred of the men continued the pursuit, while two hundred stopped because they were too exhausted to cross the Wadi Besor.

11 David's men found an Egyptian in the open country and brought him to David. They gave him some bread to eat and water to drink. **12** Then they gave him some pressed figs and two clusters of raisins. After he ate he revived,[j] for he hadn't eaten food or drunk water for three days and three nights.

13 Then David said to him, "Who do you belong to? Where are you from?"

"I'm an Egyptian, the slave of an Amalekite man," he said. "My master abandoned me when I got sick three days ago. **14** We raided the south country of the Cherethites,[k] the territory of Judah, and the south country of Caleb,[l] and we burned Ziklag."[m]

15 David then asked him, "Will you lead me to these raiders?"

He said, "Swear to me by God that you won't kill me or turn me over to my master, and I will lead you to them."

16 So he led him, and there were the Amalekites, spread out over the entire area, eating, drinking, and celebrating because of the great amount of plunder[n] they had taken from the land of the Philistines and the land of Judah. **17** David slaughtered them from twilight until the evening of the next day.[o] None of them escaped, except four hundred young men who got on camels and fled.[p]

18 David recovered everything the Amalekites had taken; he also rescued his two wives. **19** Nothing of theirs was missing from the youngest to the oldest, including the sons and daughters, and all the plunder the Amalekites had taken. David got everything back.[q] **20** He took all the flocks and herds, which were driven ahead of the other livestock, and the people shouted, "This is David's plunder!"[r]

21 When David came to the two hundred men who had been too exhausted to go with him and had been left at the Wadi Besor,[s] they came out to meet him and to meet the troops with him. When David approached the men, he greeted them, **22** but all the corrupt and worthless men among those who had gone with David argued, "Because they didn't go with us, we will not give any of the plunder we recovered to them except for each man's wife and children. They may take them and go."

23 But David said, "My brothers, you must not do this with what the LORD has given us. He protected us and handed over to us the raiders who came against us. **24** Who can agree to your proposal? The share of the one who goes into battle is to be the same as the share of the one who remains with the supplies. They will share equally."[t] **25** And it has been so from that day forward. David established this policy[A] as a law and an ordinance for Israel and it still continues today.

26 When David came to Ziklag, he sent some of the plunder to his friends, the elders of Judah, saying, "Here is a gift for

---

a 30:5 1Sm 25:42-43
b 30:6 Ex 17:4
c 1Sm 23:16; Ps 18:2; 27:14
d 30:7 1Sm 23:6-9
e 30:8 1Sm 23:2,4
f Ex 15:9
g 1Sm 30:18
h 30:9 1Sm 27:2
i 1Sm 30:21
j 30:12 Jdg 15:19
k 30:14 1Sm 30:16; 2Sm 8:18; Ezk 25:16
l Jos 14:13; 21:11-12
m 1Sm 30:1

n 30:16 1Sm 30:14
o 30:17 1Sm 11:11
p Jdg 7:12; 1Sm 15:3
q 30:19 1Sm 30:8
r 30:20 1Sm 30:26-31
s 30:21 1Sm 30:9-10
t 30:24 Nm 31:25-27; Jos 22:8

A 30:25 *this policy* supplied for clarity

30:11-15 David and the rest of his men met **an Egyptian** slave whose Amalekite master had left him behind when he couldn't keep up with the raiders who'd plundered David's camp (30:11, 14). God had providentially placed this man in David's path, for he agreed to **lead** David to the Amalekites (30:15).

30:16-20 David's army arrived at the Amalekite camp at the best possible time. The bad guys were in the worst possible military and physical condition to defend themselves:

they were **spread out over the entire area, eating, drinking, and celebrating** (30:16). So David decimated them and took the spoil (30:17-20).

30:21-25 As David prepared to divide the plunder among his men, he intended to include **the two hundred men** who had become too weary to continue the pursuit (30:21; see 30:9-10). His principle of equal sharing became **an ordinance for Israel** (30:25).

30:26 David made a wise and diplomatic move by sending gifts from the plunder **to his friends, the elders of Judah**, his own tribe. These gifts helped to reaffirm David's loyalty to his people after his time among the Philistines. The Egyptian slave had told David that "the territory of Judah" was among the places the Amalekite raiders had looted (30:14). So in returning the plunder to these Judean cities, David was restoring what they had lost.

a 30:26 1Sm 25:27
b 1Sm 18:17; 25:28
c 30:27 Jos 15:30; 19:4
    d Jos 19:8
e Jos 15:48; 21:14
f 30:28 1Ch 11:44
g 1Ch 27:27
h Jos 15:50
i 30:29 1Sm 27:10
    j 1Sm 15:6
k 30:30 Jos 12:14; 15:30;
    19:4
l Jos 15:42; 19:7
m 30:31 Nm 13:22; Jos
    14:13-15; 21:11-13
n 1Sm 23:22
o 31:1-13 2Sm 1:12; 1Ch
    10:1-12
p 31:1 1Sm 28:4
q 31:3 2Sm 1:6
r 31:4 Jdg 9:54
    s Jdg 14:3
t 2Sm 1:6,10

u 31:9 2Sm 1:20
v Jdg 16:23-24
w 31:10 Jdg 2:13; 1Sm 7:3
x 1Sm 31:12; 2Sm 21:14
    y Jos 17:11
z 31:11 1Sm 11:1-13
aa 31:12 2Sm 2:4-7
    ab 2Ch 16:14
ac 31:13 1Sm 22:6
ad 2Sm 2:4-7; 21:12-14

you[a] from the plunder of the LORD's enemies."[b] 27 He sent gifts[A] to those in Bethel,[c] in Ramoth of the Negev,[d] and in Jattir;[e] 28 to those in Aroer,[f] in Siphmoth,[g] and in Eshtemoa;[h] 29 to those in Racal, in the towns of the Jerahmeelites,[i] and in the towns of the Kenites;[j] 30 to those in Hormah,[k] in Bor-ashan,[l] and in Athach; 31 to those in Hebron,[m] and to those in all the places where David and his men had roamed.[n]

THE DEATH OF SAUL AND HIS SONS

31 The Philistines fought against Israel,[o] and Israel's men fled from them and were killed on Mount Gilboa.[p] 2 The Philistines pursued Saul and his sons and killed his sons, Jonathan, Abinadab, and Malchishua. 3 When the battle intensified against Saul,[q] the archers found him and severely wounded him.[B] 4 Then Saul said to his armor-bearer,[r] "Draw your sword and run me through with it, or these uncircumcised men[s] will come and run me through and torture me!" But his armor-bearer would not do it because he was terrified. Then Saul took his sword and fell on it.[t] 5 When his armor-bearer saw that Saul was dead, he also fell on his own sword and died with him. 6 So on that

day, Saul died together with his three sons, his armor-bearer, and all his men.

7 When the men of Israel on the other side of the valley and on the other side of the Jordan saw that Israel's men had fled and that Saul and his sons were dead, they abandoned the cities and fled. So the Philistines came and settled in them.

8 The next day when the Philistines came to strip the slain, they found Saul and his three sons dead on Mount Gilboa. 9 They cut off Saul's head, stripped off his armor, and sent messengers throughout the land of the Philistines to spread the good news[u] in the temples of their idols[v] and among the people. 10 Then they put his armor in the temple of the Ashtoreths[w] and hung his body[x] on the wall of Beth-shan.[y]

11 When the residents of Jabesh-gilead[z] heard what the Philistines had done to Saul, 12 all their brave men[aa] set out, journeyed all night, and retrieved the body of Saul and the bodies of his sons from the wall of Beth-shan. When they arrived at Jabesh, they burned the bodies there.[ab] 13 Afterward, they took their bones and buried them under the tamarisk tree[ac] in Jabesh[ad] and fasted seven days.

[A] 30:27 *He sent gifts* supplied for clarity   [B] 31:3 LXX reads *and he was wounded under the ribs*

30:27-31 Each of the cities mentioned here was in the territories of Judah and Simeon. David's actions helped cement Judah's loyalty to him. **Hebron** is worth noting (30:31) because David would be anointed king of Israel there and would rule from Hebron for over seven years before capturing Jerusalem and moving his capital there (see 2 Sam 5:1-5). **31:8-10** That the Philistines couldn't torture Saul and display him as a trophy while he was alive (see 31:4) didn't keep them from dishonoring his body. They beheaded him, pinned his corpse on the wall at **Beth-shan**, a few miles from Gilboa, and put his armor

in the **temple of** their gods as a sign of the power of their deities over the Lord (31:9-10). The author of 1 Chronicles summarized Saul's reign this way: "Saul died for his unfaithfulness to the Lord because he did not keep the Lord's word. He even consulted a medium for guidance. . . . So the Lord put him to death and turned the kingdom over to David son of Jesse" (1 Chr 10:13-14). **31:11-13** The people **of Jabesh-gilead** had been rescued from the Ammonites by Saul many years earlier (see 11:1-11), and here they showed their gratitude. **Their brave men** made a dangerous, all-night trip to recover

the bodies of Saul and his sons from Beth-shan and dispose of them properly (31:12). The people of Jabesh **buried** their bones and observed **seven days** of fasting for Saul and his sons (31:13).

The grief they expressed in this fast was genuine. All Israel could rightly share in it. King Saul's sin and rejection of the Lord's will had brought destruction and shame on the whole kingdom. The nation had reached a low point that only God could lift it out of. As it turned out, he was prepared to do just that through another king, one who was a "man after his own heart" (13:14).

2 SAMUEL

INTRODUCTION

Author

See discussion in 1 Samuel.

Historical Background

See discussion in 1 Samuel.

Message and Purpose

See discussion in 1 Samuel.

Outline

I. Coronation and Conflicts (1:1–5:5)

II. Jerusalem, the Davidic Covenant, and Military Victory (5:6–10:19)

III. David's Sin and Its Consequences (11:1–14:33)

IV. A Son's Rebellion and Its Consequences (15:1–20:26)

V. Final Years as King (21:1–24:25)

VIDEO | INTRO

https://www.bhpublishinggroup.com/qrpage/introduction-to-1-2-samuel/

a 1:1 1Sm 31:1–5
b 1Sm 30:1–20
c 1:2 Jos 7:6; 1Sm 4:12
d 1:4 1Sm 31:6
e 1:6–10 1Sm 31:1–5; 1Ch 10:1–6
f 1:8 Gn 36:12,16; Ex 17:8–16; Nm 24:20; Dt 25:19; 1Sm 15:1–34; 30:1–20; 1Ch 1:36
g 1:9 Jdg 9:54
h 1:11 Jos 7:6; 2Sm 3:31; 13:31
i 1:12 2Sm 3:35

j 1:14 1Sm 24:6; 26:6–12; 31:4
k 1:15 2Sm 4:10
l 1:16 Jos 2:19; Mt 27:24–25; Ac 18:5–6
m 1:17 2Sm 3:33; 2Ch 35:24–25
n 1:18 Jos 10:12–13
o 1:20 1Sm 31:8–9
p 1:21 1Sm 31:4
q 1Sm 10:1

RESPONSES TO SAUL'S DEATH

1 After the death of Saul,*a* David returned from defeating the Amalekites*b* and stayed at Ziklag two days. **2** On the third day a man with torn clothes and dust on his head*c* came from Saul's camp. When he came to David, he fell to the ground and paid homage. **3** David asked him, "Where have you come from?"

He replied to him, "I've escaped from the Israelite camp."

4 "What was the outcome? Tell me," David asked him.

"The troops fled from the battle," he answered. "Many of the troops have fallen and are dead. Also, Saul and his son Jonathan are dead."*d*

5 David asked the young man who had brought him the report, "How do you know Saul and his son Jonathan are dead?"

6 "I happened to be on Mount Gilboa,"*e* he replied, "and there was Saul, leaning on his spear. At that very moment the chariots and the cavalry were closing in on him. **7** When he turned around and saw me, he called out to me, so I answered: I'm at your service. **8** He asked me, 'Who are you?' I told him: I'm an Amalekite.*f* **9** Then he begged me, 'Stand over me and kill me, for I'm mortally wounded,*A* but my life still lingers.'*g* **10** So I stood over him and killed him because I knew that after he had fallen he couldn't survive. I took the crown that was on his head and the armband that was on his arm, and I've brought them here to my lord."

11 Then David took hold of his clothes and tore them,*h* and all the men with him did the same. **12** They mourned, wept, and fasted until the evening*i* for those who died by the sword — for Saul, his son Jonathan, the Lord's people, and the house of Israel.

13 David inquired of the young man who had brought him the report, "Where are you from?"

"I'm the son of a resident alien," he said. "I'm an Amalekite."

14 David questioned him, "How is it that you were not afraid to lift your hand to destroy the Lord's anointed?"*j* **15** Then David summoned one of his servants and said, "Come here and kill him!" The servant struck him, and he died.*k* **16** For David had said to the Amalekite, "Your blood is on your own head*l* because your own mouth testified against you by saying, 'I killed the Lord's anointed.'"

17 David sang the following lament*m* for Saul and his son Jonathan, **18** and he ordered that the Judahites be taught The Song of the Bow. It is written in the Book of Jashar:*B,n*

19   The splendor of Israel lies slain
          on your heights.
       How the mighty have fallen!
20   Do not tell it in Gath,
       don't announce it
          in the marketplaces
          of Ashkelon,
       or the daughters of the Philistines
          will rejoice,*o*
       and the daughters
          of the uncircumcised
          will celebrate.
21   Mountains of Gilboa,
       let no dew or rain be on you,
       or fields of offerings,*c*
       for there the shield of the mighty
          was defiled*p* —
       the shield of Saul, no longer
          anointed with oil.*q*
22   Jonathan's bow never retreated,
       Saul's sword never returned
          unstained,*D*
       from the blood of the slain,
       from the flesh*E* of the mighty.
23   Saul and Jonathan,
       loved and delightful,
       they were not parted in life
          or in death.

A **1:9** LXX reads *for terrible darkness has taken hold of me*   *B* **1:18** Or *of the Upright*   *C* **1:21** LXX reads *firstfruits*   *D* **1:22** Lit *empty*   *E* **1:22** Lit *fat*

1:1-2 The opening verses of 2 Samuel pick up right where 1 Samuel left off. David had just defeated **the Amalekites** (see 1 Sam 30), the people group to which his dusty visitor was related (see 2 Sam 1:8, 13).
1:6-10 Clearly, the man lied about his role in Saul's death. The author of 1–2 Samuel has already informed us that Saul committed suicide (see 1 Sam 31:4-6). That the man "happened to be on Mount Gilboa" (2 Sam 1:6) at the moment of a major battle is a pretty sketchy story. Most likely, he was robbing corpses after the battle (and before "the next day" when "the Philistines came to strip the slain"; see 1 Sam

31:8). When he found Saul dead, he probably saw it as an opportunity to curry favor with the soon-to-be king (2 Sam 1:10).
1:13-16 David judged the man by his own testimony. As a **resident alien**, he should have shown reverence for the king rather than a willingness to take his life. *Strike one.* He was also **an Amalekite** (1:13). The Amalekites had opposed Israel during the exodus, and the Lord had commanded Saul to destroy them all (see 1 Sam 15:1-3). *Strike two.* By his own admission (whether true or not), the man **killed the Lord's anointed** (2 Sam 1:10, 16). Even David, who'd been hunted by Saul, had

chosen to leave him in God's hands (see 1 Sam 24, 26). This Amalekite should have done the same. *Strike three* (2 Sam 1:15).
1:17 David became well-known as a poet and musician in Israel. Many of the Psalms bear his name.
1:21 Heartsick over what had happened, David called down a curse on the **mountains of Gilboa**, the place where Saul and Jonathan fell.
1:22-23 Saul had proved to be unfit spiritually to be Israel's king, but indeed he was a brave warrior who led his army in many battles. And Jonathan had proven his own courage, leading daring raids that helped turn the tide for Israel.

They were swifter than eagles,
    stronger than lions.
24 Daughters of Israel, weep for Saul,
    who clothed you in scarlet,
        with luxurious things,
    who decked your garments
        with gold ornaments.*a*
25 How the mighty have fallen
    in the thick of battle!
    Jonathan lies slain on your heights.
26 I grieve for you, Jonathan,
    my brother.
    You were such a friend to me.
    Your love for me was
        more wondrous
    than the love of women.*b*
27 How the mighty have fallen
    and the weapons of war
        have perished!

DAVID, KING OF JUDAH

2 Some time later, David inquired of the
    LORD:*c* "Should I go to one of the towns
of Judah?"
    The LORD answered him, "Go."
    Then David asked, "Where should I go?"
    "To Hebron,"*d* the LORD replied.
2 So David went there with his two
wives, Ahinoam the Jezreelite and Abigail,
the widow of Nabal the Carmelite.*e* 3 In addition, David brought the men who were
with him, each one with his family, and
they settled in the towns near Hebron.*f*
4 Then the men of Judah came, and there
they anointed David king over the house
of Judah.*g* They told David: "It was the men
of Jabesh-gilead who buried Saul."*h*
5 David sent messengers to the men
of Jabesh-gilead and said to them, "The
LORD bless you, because you have shown
this kindness to Saul your lord when you
buried him. 6 Now, may the LORD show
kindness and faithfulness to you, and I
will also show the same goodness to you
because you have done this deed. 7 Therefore, be strong*A* and valiant, for though
Saul your lord is dead, the house of Judah
has anointed me king over them."

8 Abner son of Ner, commander of
Saul's army,*i* took Saul's son Ish-bosheth*B,C* and moved him to Mahanaim.
9 He made him king over Gilead, Asher,
Jezreel, Ephraim, Benjamin — over all Israel. 10 Saul's son Ish-bosheth was forty
years old when he became king over Israel; he reigned for two years. The house
of Judah, however, followed David. 11 The
length of time that David was king in Hebron over the house of Judah was seven
years and six months.*j*
12 Abner son of Ner and soldiers of Ish-
bosheth son of Saul marched out from
Mahanaim to Gibeon. 13 So Joab son of
Zeruiah and David's soldiers marched out
and met them by the pool of Gibeon.*k* The
two groups took up positions on opposite
sides of the pool.
14 Then Abner said to Joab, "Let's have
the young men get up and compete in
front of us."
    "Let them get up," Joab replied.
15 So they got up and were counted off —
twelve for Benjamin and Ish-bosheth son
of Saul, and twelve from David's soldiers.
16 Then each man grabbed his opponent by
the head and thrust his sword into his opponent's side so that they all died together.
So this place, which is in Gibeon, is named
Field of Blades.*D*
17 The battle that day was extremely
fierce, and Abner and the men of Israel
were defeated by David's soldiers. 18 The
three sons of Zeruiah were there: Joab,
Abishai, and Asahel.*l* Asahel was a fast
runner, like one of the wild gazelles.*m*
19 He chased Abner and did not turn to
the right or the left in his pursuit of him.
20 Abner glanced back and said, "Is that
you, Asahel?"
    "Yes it is," Asahel replied.
21 Abner said to him, "Turn to your right
or left, seize one of the young soldiers,
and take whatever you can get from him."
But Asahel would not stop chasing him.
22 Once again, Abner warned Asahel, "Stop
chasing me. Why should I strike you to the

*a*1:24 Ezk 16:1-11
*b*1:26 1Sm 18:1-3
*c*2:1 1Sm 23:1-12
*d*1Sm 30:26-31; 2Sm
2:11; 5:5; 1Kg 2:11; 1Ch
3:4; 29:27
*e*2:2 1Sm 25:42-43
*f*2:3 1Sm 27:2-3; 30:9; 1Ch
12:1,23-37
*g*2:4 1Sm 16:13; 2Sm 5:3-5
*h*1Sm 31:11-13

*i*2:8 1Sm 14:50
*j*2:11 2Sm 5:5; 1Kg 2:11
*k*2:13 Jr 41:11-12
*l*2:18 1Ch 2:16
*m*1Ch 12:8; Sg 8:14

---

^A^2:7 Lit *Therefore, strengthen your hands*   ^B^2:8 Some LXX mss read *Ishbaal*; 1Ch 8:33; 9:39   ^C^2:8 = Man of Shame   ^D^2:16 Or *Helkath-hazzurim*

1:26 David and Jonathan had made a covenant
of friendship and loyalty to each other (see
1 Sam 20:14-17, 42).
2:1-7 At **Hebron**, located about twenty miles
south of Jerusalem (2:1-3), **the men of Judah . . .
anointed David king over the house of Judah**
(2:4). But he was not yet king over all of Israel,
a fact serving as an early indication of the coming division between the northern territories
that would one day become Israel and the
southern territories that would be called Judah.

2:8-9 The extent of the division between
north and south became evident when
Abner, the **commander of Saul's army**, set
up Saul's weak son **Ish-bosheth** (whose name
meant "Man of shame"; 2:8) as king **over all
Israel** instead of recognizing David's legitimate rule (2:9). Abner, though, was the real
power behind the throne (see 3:11).
2:10 Rebellion against David (and against the
Lord) led to civil war for the **two years** Ish-
bosheth reigned over Israel.

2:12-17 Just as David and Goliath had fought
as representatives of their armies to determine the outcome of the battle between
the Israelites and the Philistines (see 1 Sam
17), Abner suggested a similar contest to
Joab, his counterpart as the commander
of David's army (2 Sam 2:12-14). When the
contest ended in a tie, a **fierce** battle broke
out (2:17).

a 2:22 2Sm 3:27
b 2:27 2Sm 2:14
c 2:29 2Sm 2:8
d 3:1 1Sm 20:16; 1Kg 12:19;
2Ch 21:7; Ps 122:5; Is
22:22; Zch 12:8,10; 13:1;
Lk 1:27
e Jb 17:9
f 3:2 2Sm 13:1-29
g 1Sm 25:42-43
h 3:3 1Sm 25:3-42

i 3:3 2Sm 13:34;
14:23-25,33; 15:6,10-14;
18:9-12,33
j 1Sm 27:8; 2Sm 13:37-38;
14:32; 15:8
k 3:4 1Kg 1:5
l 3:5 1Ch 3:1-5
m 3:6 2Sm 2:8-9
n 3:7 2Sm 21:8-10
o 3:8 Ex 22:31; 1Sm 17:43;
24:14; 2Sm 9:8; 16:9
p 3:10 1Sm 15:28; 16:1-13;
28:17; 1Ch 12:23
q 3:13 1Sm 14:49
r 3:14 1Sm 18:20-27
s 3:15 1Sm 25:44

ground? How could I ever look your brother Joab in the face?"[a]

23 But Asahel refused to turn away, so Abner hit him in the stomach with the butt of his spear. The spear went through his body, and he fell and died right there. As they all came to the place where Asahel had fallen and died, they stopped, **24** but Joab and Abishai pursued Abner. By sunset, they had gone as far as the hill of Ammah, which is opposite Giah on the way to the wilderness of Gibeon.

25 The Benjaminites rallied to Abner; they formed a unit and took their stand on top of a hill. **26** Then Abner called out to Joab: "Must the sword devour forever? Don't you realize this will only end in bitterness? How long before you tell the troops to stop pursuing their brothers?"

27 "As God lives," Joab replied, "if you had not spoken up, the troops wouldn't have stopped pursuing their brothers until morning."[b] **28** Then Joab blew the ram's horn, and all the troops stopped; they no longer pursued Israel or continued to fight. **29** So Abner and his men marched through the Arabah all that night. They crossed the Jordan, marched all morning,[A] and arrived at Mahanaim.[c]

30 When Joab had turned back from pursuing Abner, he gathered all the troops. In addition to Asahel, nineteen of David's soldiers were missing, **31** but they had killed 360 of the Benjaminites and Abner's men. **32** Afterward, they carried Asahel to his father's tomb in Bethlehem and buried him. Then Joab and his men marched all night and reached Hebron at dawn.

CIVIL WAR

3 During the long war between the house of Saul and the house of David,[d] David was growing stronger[e] and the house of Saul was becoming weaker.

2 Sons were born to David in Hebron:
His firstborn was Amnon,[f]
by Ahinoam[g] the Jezreelite;
3 his second was Chileab,
by Abigail,[h] the widow of Nabal
the Carmelite;

the third was Absalom,[i]
son of Maacah the daughter
of King Talmai of Geshur;[j]
4 the fourth was Adonijah,[k]
son of Haggith;
the fifth was Shephatiah,
son of Abital;
5 the sixth was Ithream,
by David's wife Eglah.
These were born to David in Hebron.[l]

6 During the war between the house of Saul and the house of David, Abner kept acquiring more power in the house of Saul.[m] **7** Now Saul had a concubine whose name was Rizpah[n] daughter of Aiah, and Ish-bosheth questioned Abner, "Why did you sleep with my father's concubine?"

8 Abner was very angry about Ish-bosheth's accusation. "Am I a dog's head[B,o] who belongs to Judah?" he asked. "All this time I've been loyal to the family of your father Saul, to his brothers, and to his friends and haven't betrayed you to David, but now you accuse me of wrongdoing with this woman! **9** May God punish Abner and do so severely if I don't do for David what the LORD swore to him: **10** to transfer the kingdom from the house of Saul and establish the throne of David over Israel and Judah[p] from Dan to Beer-sheba." **11** Ish-bosheth did not dare respond to Abner because he was afraid of him.

12 Abner sent messengers as his representatives to say to David, "Whose land is it? Make your covenant with me, and you can be certain I am on your side to turn all Israel over to you."

13 David replied, "Good, I will make a covenant with you. However, there's one thing I require of you: You will not see my face unless you first bring Saul's daughter Michal[q] when you come to see me."

14 Then David sent messengers to say to Ish-bosheth son of Saul, "Give me back my wife, Michal. I was engaged to her for the price of a hundred Philistine foreskins."[r]

15 So Ish-bosheth sent someone to take her away from her husband, Paltiel son of Laish.[s] **16** Her husband followed her,

---

[A] 2:29 Or *marched through the Bithron*   [B] 3:8 = a despised person

2:23 Joab would not forget what Abner had done to his brother Asahel. He would wait for the right moment to take his revenge.
3:2-5 The author lists David's first six sons, each born to a different mother. Though acquiring many wives was a practice of ancient kings, it was not to be the practice of Israel's (see Deut 17:17). **Amnon**, **Absalom**,

and **Adonijah** (2 Sam 3:2-4) will appear later in David's story. These three sons would commit heinous sins.
3:7 The action of which Ish-bosheth accused Abner was considered an attempt to lay claim to a king's throne.
3:12 Irritated by Ish-bosheth's accusation (see 3:7-8), Abner turned the tide of the civil war

by pledging his loyalty to David and offering to make a **covenant** with him.
3:13-15 **Michal** was Saul's daughter whom he had given to David; later he gave her to another man while David was a fugitive (3:13-14; see 1 Sam 18:27; 25:44). There had never been a divorce, so Michal was taken from **Paltiel** and given back to David (2 Sam 3:15).

weeping all the way to Bahurim. Abner said to him, "Go back." So he went back.

THE ASSASSINATION OF ABNER

17 Abner conferred with the elders of Israel: "In the past you wanted David to be king over you. **18** Now take action, because the LORD has spoken concerning David: 'Through my servant David I will save my people Israel from the power of the Philistines and the power of all Israel's enemies.' "

19 Abner also informed the Benjaminites and went to Hebron to inform David about all that was agreed on by Israel and the whole house of Benjamin.[a] **20** When Abner and twenty men came to David at Hebron, David held a banquet for him and his men.

21 Abner said to David, "Let me now go and I will gather all Israel to my lord the king. They will make a covenant with you,[b] and you will reign over all you desire." So David dismissed Abner, and he went in peace.

22 Just then David's soldiers and Joab returned from a raid and brought a large amount of plundered goods with them. Abner was not with David in Hebron because David had dismissed him, and he had gone in peace. **23** When Joab and his whole army arrived, Joab was informed, "Abner son of Ner came to see the king, the king dismissed him, and he went in peace."

24 Joab went to the king and said, "What have you done? Look here, Abner came to you. Why did you dismiss him? Now he's getting away. **25** You know that Abner son of Ner came to deceive you and to find out about your military activities[A] and everything you're doing." **26** Then Joab left David and sent messengers after Abner. They brought him back from the well[B] of Sirah, but David was unaware of it. **27** When Abner returned to Hebron, Joab pulled him aside to the middle of the city gate, as if to speak to him privately, and there Joab stabbed him in the stomach. So Abner died in revenge for the death of Asahel,[c] Joab's brother.[c]

28 David heard about it later and said: "I and my kingdom are forever innocent before the LORD concerning the blood of Abner son of Ner. **29** May it hang over Joab's head and his father's whole family, and may the house of Joab never be without someone who has a discharge or a skin disease,[d] or a man who can only work a spindle,[D] or someone who falls by the sword or starves." **30** Joab and his brother Abishai killed Abner because he had put their brother Asahel to death in the battle at Gibeon.[e]

31 David then ordered Joab and all the people who were with him, "Tear your clothes, put on sackcloth,[f] and mourn over Abner." And King David walked behind the coffin.[E]

32 When they buried Abner in Hebron, the king wept aloud at Abner's tomb. All the people wept, **33** and the king sang a lament for Abner:[g]

Should Abner die as a fool dies?
34 Your hands were not bound,
your feet not placed in bronze shackles.
You fell like one who falls victim
to criminals.
And all the people wept over him even more.

35 Then they came to urge David to eat food while it was still day, but David took an oath: "May God punish me and do so severely if I taste bread or anything else before sunset!"[h] **36** All the people took note of this, and it pleased them. In fact, everything the king did pleased them. **37** On that day all the troops and all Israel were convinced that the king had no part in the killing of Abner son of Ner.

38 Then the king said to his soldiers, "You must know that a great leader has fallen in Israel today. **39** As for me, even though I

[a]3:19 1Ch 12:29
[b]3:21 2Sm 3:12
[c]3:27 2Sm 2:23; 1Kg 2:5,32
[d]3:29 Lv 14:2-8
[e]3:30 2Sm 2:23
[f]3:31 Gn 37:34; Jos 7:6
[g]3:33 2Sm 1:17; 2Ch 35:25
[h]3:35 2Sm 12:17

[A]3:25 Lit *your going out and your coming in*   [B]3:26 Or *cistern*   [c]3:27 Lit *And he died for the blood of Asahel*   [D]3:29 LXX reads *who uses a crutch*   [E]3:31 Or *the bier*; lit *the bed*

3:17-19 Abner set about building support for David among **the elders of Israel** (3:17). He rehearsed for them God's promise that David was God's chosen **servant** to **save** his people from **all [their] enemies** (3:18). Abner also approached **the Benjaminites**, Saul's own tribe, to get their agreement to back David (3:19).
3:21-23 Abner promised to go throughout **all Israel** and unite the people as one under David so that he could be king over the entire nation (3:21). David was obviously pleased, and the author is careful to note three times

that David sent Abner on his mission **in peace** (3:21-23). That would become important in light of what was about to happen.
3:24-25 Joab was furious that the killer of his brother Asahel had been treated kindly by David. He went to the king to accuse Abner of deceiving him as a spy. It's hard to know for certain what Joab's motives were. Revenge? Protection of David's throne? Jealousy that Abner might be a rival for command of David's army? Perhaps all of the above.
3:28-29 David had made a covenant with Abner to bring about peace in Israel and to

consolidate his kingdom (see 3:12-13). Thus, he wanted to avoid the appearance that he had anything to do with Joab's underhanded plot. David declared his own innocence and pronounced a severe curse on Joab and his descendants.
3:31-35 David showed his grief for Abner in every way possible. Consolidating all of Israel under his rule depended on it. He knew how important it was that the people of Israel understand that he was not gaining the throne through evil means.

a 3:39 2Sm 16:10; 19:22
b Ps 28:4; 2Tm 4:14
c 4:4 2Sm 9:3-7
d 4:7 Dt 1:1

e 4:9 1Kg 1:29
f 4:10 2Sm 1:2-15
g 4:11 Gn 9:5-6
h 4:12 2Sm 3:32
i 5:1-3 1Ch 11:1-3
j 5:1 Gn 29:14
k 5:2 1Sm 18:5,12-16
l 5:3 2Sm 3:12-13,21
m 5:4-5 1Kg 2:11; 1Ch 29:26-27
n 5:6 Jos 15:63; Jdg 1:21

am the anointed king, I have little power today. These men, the sons of Zeruiah, are too fierce for me.[a] May the LORD repay the evildoer according to his evil!"[b]

THE ASSASSINATION OF ISH-BOSHETH

4 When Saul's son Ish-bosheth heard that Abner had died in Hebron, he gave up,[A] and all Israel was dismayed. [2] Saul's son had two men who were leaders of raiding parties: one named Baanah and the other Rechab, sons of Rimmon the Beerothite of the Benjaminites. Beeroth is also considered part of Benjamin, [3] and the Beerothites fled to Gittaim and still reside there as aliens today.

[4] Saul's son Jonathan had a son whose feet were crippled. He was five years old when the report about Saul and Jonathan came from Jezreel. His nanny[B] picked him up and fled, but as she was hurrying to flee, he fell and became lame. His name was Mephibosheth.[c]

[5] Rechab and Baanah, the sons of Rimmon the Beerothite, set out and arrived at Ish-bosheth's house during the heat of the day while the king was taking his midday nap. [6] They entered the interior of the house as if to get wheat and stabbed him in the stomach. Then Rechab and his brother Baanah escaped. [7] They had entered the house while Ish-bosheth was lying on his bed in his bedroom and stabbed and killed him. They removed his head, took it, and traveled by way of the Arabah[d] all night. [8] They brought Ish-bosheth's head to David at Hebron and said to the king, "Here's the head of Ish-bosheth son of Saul, your enemy who intended to take your life. Today the LORD has granted vengeance to my lord the king against Saul and his offspring."

[9] But David answered Rechab and his brother Baanah, sons of Rimmon the Beerothite, "As the LORD lives, the one who has redeemed my life from every distress,[e] [10] when the person told me, 'Look, Saul is dead,' he thought he was a bearer of good news, but I seized him and put him to death at Ziklag.[f] That was my reward to him for his news! [11] How much more when wicked men kill a righteous man in his own house on his own bed! So now, should I not require his blood from you and purge you from the earth?"[g]

[12] So David gave orders to the young men, and they killed Rechab and Baanah. They cut off their hands and feet and hung their bodies by the pool in Hebron, but they took Ish-bosheth's head and buried it in Abner's tomb in Hebron.[h]

DAVID, KING OF ISRAEL

5 All the tribes of Israel came to David at Hebron[i] and said, "Here we are, your own flesh and blood.[C,j] [2] Even while Saul was king over us, you were the one who led us out to battle and brought us back.[k] The LORD also said to you, 'You will shepherd my people Israel, and you will be ruler over Israel.'"

[3] So all the elders of Israel came to the king at Hebron. King David made a covenant with them[l] at Hebron in the LORD's presence, and they anointed David king over Israel.

[4] David was thirty years old when he began his reign;[m] he reigned forty years. [5] In Hebron he reigned over Judah seven years and six months, and in Jerusalem he reigned thirty-three years over all Israel and Judah.

[6] The king and his men marched to Jerusalem against the Jebusites[n] who inhabited the land. The Jebusites had said

A 4:1 Lit his hands dropped   B 4:4 Lit His nurse   C 5:1 Lit your bone and your flesh

3:39 David lamented the violent nature of Joab and his brother, **the sons of Zeruiah**, but he did not discipline them. That Zeruiah was David's half-sister may explain his reluctance to take action (see 17:25; 1 Chr 2:13-16).
4:1 **Ish-bosheth** was a weak ruler, and with Abner gone his people may have feared that David would invade and conquer them.
4:4 **Mephibosheth** was the son of David's trusted friend. The author includes this note about him here to prepare the reader for the later story of David's kindness to Mephibosheth, offered out of his love for Jonathan (see ch. 9).
4:5-8 **Rechab and Baanah** cold-heartedly assassinated Ish-bosheth when he was defenseless in **his bed** (4:5-7). That they

were evil men with selfish motives becomes even more evident in that they immediately tried to curry favor with David as the new king of Israel (4:8). Little did they know that another man had similarly hoped for the king's approval by eradicating David's rival, but things didn't turn out so well for him (see 1:1-16).
4:12 Cutting off the killers' **hands and feet**—the parts of their bodies used in the murder—served as a gruesome way of denouncing their wicked actions and warning anyone else who might think of committing a similar act. David was making it clear to all of Israel that he'd had nothing to do with their deed.
5:1 That they were all **flesh and blood** means they were members of the twelve tribes of

Israel, descendants of Abraham, Isaac, and Jacob.
5:3 Previously, the men of Judah, David's own tribe, had anointed him king (see 2:4). But now **all the elders of Israel** came to **Hebron** and **anointed David king over Israel**. Through all the twists and turns of the years leading up to this event, David had trusted the Lord and waited on his perfect timing. His willingness to obtain God's purpose for him in God's way is a model to follow.
5:4-5 The Davidic dynasty had begun. And through it the Son of David, the Messiah, would one day come (see Matt 1:1).
5:6 David set out to conquer a new capital. In time his choice would become the place of God's temple. Since it would be a capital

to David: "You will never get in here. Even the blind and lame can repel you" thinking, "David can't get in here."

7 Yet David did capture the stronghold of Zion, that is, the city of David.[a] **8** He said that day, "Whoever attacks the Jebusites must go through the water shaft to reach the lame and the blind who are despised by David."[A] For this reason it is said, "The blind and the lame will never enter the house."[B]

9 David took up residence in the stronghold, which he named the city of David. He built it up all the way around from the supporting terraces inward. **10** David became more and more powerful,[b] and the LORD God of Armies was with him.[c] **11** King Hiram of Tyre sent envoys to David; he also sent cedar logs, carpenters, and stonemasons,[d] and they built a palace for David. **12** Then David knew that the LORD had established him as king over Israel and had exalted his kingdom for the sake of his people Israel.

13 After he arrived from Hebron, David took more concubines and wives from Jerusalem, and more sons and daughters were born to him. **14** These are the names of those born to him in Jerusalem: Shammua, Shobab, Nathan,[e] Solomon, **15** Ibhar, Elishua, Nepheg, Japhia, **16** Elishama, Eliada, and Eliphelet.[f]

17 When the Philistines heard that David had been anointed king over Israel,[g] they all went in search of David, but he heard about it and went down to the stronghold.[h] **18** So the Philistines came and spread out in the Valley of Rephaim.

19 Then David inquired of the LORD:[i] "Should I attack the Philistines? Will you hand them over to me?"

The LORD replied to David, "Attack, for I will certainly hand the Philistines over to you."

20 So David went to Baal-perazim and defeated them there and said, "Like a bursting flood, the LORD has burst out against my enemies before me."[j] Therefore, he named that place The Lord Bursts Out.[c] **21** The Philistines abandoned their idols there, and David and his men carried them off.

22 The Philistines came up again and spread out in the Valley of Rephaim. **23** So David inquired of the LORD, and he answered, "Do not attack directly, but circle around behind them and come at them opposite the balsam trees. **24** When you hear the sound of marching in the tops of the balsam trees, act decisively, for then the LORD will have gone out ahead of you to strike down the army of the Philistines."[k] **25** So David did exactly as the LORD commanded him, and he struck down the Philistines all the way from Geba to Gezer.

DAVID MOVES THE ARK

6 David again assembled all the fit young men in Israel:[l] thirty thousand. **2** He and all his troops set out[m] to bring the ark of God from Baale-judah.[D] The ark bears the Name, the name of the LORD of Armies who is enthroned between the cherubim.[n] **3** They set the ark of God on a new cart and transported it from Abinadab's house, which was on the hill. Uzzah and Ahio,[E] sons of Abinadab, were guiding the cart[o] **4** and brought it with the ark of God from Abinadab's house on the hill. Ahio walked in front of the ark. **5** David and the whole house of Israel were dancing before the LORD with all kinds of fir wood

[a] 5:7 Lk 2:4
[b] 5:10 2Sm 3:1
[c] 1Ch 11:9
[d] 5:11 1Kg 5:1,10,18
[e] 5:14 Lk 3:31
[f] 5:11-16 1Ch 3:5-8; 14:1-7
[g] 5:17-25 1Ch 14:8-17
[h] 5:17 1Sm 22:4-5; 2Sm 23:14
[i] 5:19 2Sm 2:1
[j] 5:20 Is 28:21
[k] 5:24 2Kg 7:6
[l] 6:1 2Sm 10:9; 1Ch 19:10
[m] 6:2-11 1Ch 13:6-14
[n] 6:2 Ex 25:22; 1Sm 4:4
[o] 6:3 1Ch 15:2,12-15

[A] 5:8 Alt Hb tradition, LXX, Tg, Syr read *who despise David*   [B] 5:8 Or *temple*, or *palace*   [C] 5:20 Or *Baal-perazim*; 2Sm 6:8; 1Ch 13:11
[D] 6:2 = Kiriath-jearim in 1Sm 7:1; 1Ch 13:6; 2Ch 1:4   [E] 6:3 Or *And his brothers*

---

city for a united Israel that was past the hostility of the civil war between Saul's house and David's, it would need to be in neutral territory. So David selected a city on the border of the lands of Benjamin and Judah—the tribes of Saul and David.

The Jebusites, one of the Canaanite peoples, didn't think much of Israel's new ruler. In fact, they felt so secure in their mountain stronghold of Jerusalem (formerly, Jebus; see Josh 18:28) that they claimed **the blind and lame** among their people could **repel** David's troops. The city was easily defensible on three sides, an important feature in the ancient world.

5:8 According to 1 Chronicles 11:6, Joab found the access and was given the command of David's army.

5:10 Tremendous earthly strength is useless unless heaven is on your side. David was powerful because the heavenly armies were fighting for him—as he would soon learn (see the note on 5:24).

5:17-19 Some foreign powers didn't take kindly to the new king. **The Philistines**, whom David had battled and deceived for years, were determined to bring him down (5:17-18). But the Lord vowed to **hand [them] over** to David (5:19).

5:24 In other words, God himself would lead the armies of heaven in the charge against David's enemies.

6:1-2 David turned his attention to God's throne—**the ark** of the covenant (6:2). This sacred chest had been neglected during Saul's reign. But David was zealous for the worship of the Lord. He understood the importance of the

ark to Israel's worship and spiritual well-being. Moreover, David knew that God was the heavenly King who stood behind his own earthly kingship. Therefore, it was essential that God's throne be brought into Israel's capital city.

6:3-5 For some inexplicable reason, David disobeyed God's explicit commands regarding how the ark was to be transported. The Levites alone were to carry the ark with poles inserted through its rings (see Exod 37:3-5; Deut 10:8). But David and his men **set the ark of God on a new cart** (2 Sam 6:3). The ark was once transported this way—by the Philistines (see 1 Sam 6:7). But God's people should have known better. They had God's revealed Word available to them. All their sincere worship (2 Sam 6:5) could not make up for neglecting God's will.

a 6:5 Ps 150:3-5
b 6:7 Ex 25:14; Nm 4:5,15,20
c 1Sm 6:19-20
d 6:10 Lk 2:4
e 6:11 1Ch 26:4-8
f 6:12 1Ch 15:25
g 6:13 1Kg 8:1-5
h 6:14 Ex 28:4-28; 1Sm 2:18
i 6:16 Lk 2:4
j 6:17 1Ch 15:1; 2Ch 1:4

k 6:12-19 1Ch 15:25–16:3
l 6:20 1Ch 16:43
m 6:21 1Sm 13:14; 15:28
n 7:1 2Sm 5:11
o 7:2 2Sm 12:1-7; 1Kg 1:8-11,34-45; 2Ch 9:29; 29:25
p Ex 26:1; 1Ch 17:1
q 7:5 1Kg 5:3; 8:19; 1Ch 22:8; 28:3

instruments,[A] lyres, harps, tambourines, sistrums,[B] and cymbals.[a] [6] When they came to Nacon's threshing floor, Uzzah reached out to the ark of God and took hold of it because the oxen had stumbled. [7] Then the LORD's anger burned against Uzzah,[b] and God struck him dead on the spot for his irreverence,[c] and he died there next to the ark of God. [8] David was angry because of the LORD's outburst against Uzzah, so he named that place Outburst Against Uzzah,[c] as it is today. [9] David feared the LORD that day and said, "How can the ark of the LORD ever come to me?" [10] So he was not willing to bring the ark of the LORD to the city of David;[d] instead, he diverted it to the house of Obed-edom of Gath. [11] The ark of the LORD remained in his house three months, and the LORD blessed Obed-edom[e] and his whole family.

[12] It was reported to King David: "The LORD has blessed Obed-edom's family and all that belongs to him because of the ark of God." So David went and had the ark of God brought up from Obed-edom's house to the city of David with rejoicing.[f] [13] When those carrying the ark of the LORD advanced six steps, he sacrificed an ox and a fattened calf.[g] [14] David was dancing[D] with all his might before the LORD wearing a linen ephod.[h] [15] He and the whole house of Israel were bringing up the ark of the LORD with shouts and the sound of the ram's horn. [16] As the ark of the LORD was entering the city of David,[i] Saul's daughter Michal looked down from the window and saw King David leaping and dancing before the LORD, and she despised him in her heart.

[17] They brought the ark of the LORD and set it in its place inside the tent David had pitched for it.[j] Then David offered burnt offerings and fellowship offerings in the LORD's presence. [18] When David had finished offering the burnt offering and the fellowship offerings, he blessed the people in the name of the LORD of Armies. [19] Then he distributed a loaf of bread, a date cake, and a raisin cake to each one in the entire Israelite community, both men and women.[k] Then all the people went home.

[20] When David returned home to bless his household,[l] Saul's daughter Michal came out to meet him. "How the king of Israel honored himself today!" she said. "He exposed himself today in the sight of the slave girls of his subjects like a vulgar person would expose himself."

[21] David replied to Michal, "It was before the LORD who chose me over your father and his whole family to appoint me ruler over the LORD's people Israel.[m] I will dance before the LORD, [22] and I will dishonor myself and humble myself even more.[E,F] However, by the slave girls you spoke about, I will be honored." [23] And Saul's daughter Michal had no child to the day of her death.

THE LORD'S COVENANT WITH DAVID

7 When the king had settled into his palace[n] and the LORD had given him rest on every side from all his enemies, [2] the king said to the prophet Nathan,[o] "Look, I am living in a cedar house while the ark of God sits inside tent curtains."[p]

[3] So Nathan told the king, "Go and do all that is on your mind, for the LORD is with you."

[4] But that night the word of the LORD came to Nathan: [5] "Go to my servant David and say, 'This is what the LORD says: Are you to build me a house to dwell in?[q] [6] From the time I brought the Israelites out of Egypt until today I have not dwelt

---

[A] 6:5 DSS, LXX read *with tuned instruments with strength, with songs*; 1Ch 13:8　　[B] 6:5 = an Egyptian percussion instrument　　[C] 6:8 Or *Perez-uzzah*; 2Sm 5:20　　[D] 6:14 Or *whirling*　　[E] 6:22 LXX reads *more and I will be humble in your eyes*　　[F] 6:22 Lit *more and I will be humble in my own eyes*

6:6-7 The Israelites had failed to treat God as holy or "set apart" from his creation. "Holy, holy, holy is the Lord of Armies," the seraphim would declare to Isaiah. "His glory fills the whole earth" (Isa 6:3). Forgetting that was a costly mistake.

6:8-10 Was David **angry** with God—a sin for which he later repented? Was he angry with Uzzah for touching the ark? Or was he angry with himself for being foolish? Regardless, **David feared the LORD that day** (6:9). Even though he sincerely loved God, he had not taken him seriously enough. As a result of what happened, he realized the awesome holiness of the Lord in a new way.

6:16-20 As David was **dancing before the LORD** in worship, his wife **Michal** saw him. As far as she was concerned, these were not the dignified actions of a king. So **she despised him** (6:16). Three times in this chapter Michal is referred to as **Saul's daughter** (6:16; also 6:20, 23). By emphasizing this relationship, the author wants us to know that Michal had the same uncaring attitude toward the ark and the true worship of God that her father had.

6:21-23 David was willing to **dishonor** and **humble** himself, if God were exalted in the process (6:22). Michal viewed the extravagant worship of God from an earthly perspective and considered it vulgar and embarrassing (6:20). As a result, God closed her womb (6:23). David viewed the worship of God from a heavenly perspective, and it brought him tremendous joy. For this, he was **honored** (6:22). Will you live life from God's perspective or from your own?

7:1 The author makes it clear that **the LORD had given [David] rest on every side**. All that David had was from God. (That's a truth that too many believers are quick to forget with relation to themselves.)

7:2 David felt uneasy living in his **cedar** palace, while **the ark of God** was housed in a mere **tent**.

7:4-10 With regard to David building him a temple, God's response was essentially, "Thanks, but no thanks." Far from needing provision, God had always been the Provider.

in a house; instead, I have been moving around with a tent as my dwelling.[a] **7** In all my journeys with all the Israelites, have I ever spoken a word to one of the tribes of Israel, whom I commanded to shepherd my people Israel, asking: Why haven't you built me a house of cedar?'

8 "So now this is what you are to say to my servant David: 'This is what the LORD of Armies says: I took you from the pasture, from tending the flock, to be ruler over my people Israel.[b] **9** I have been with you wherever you have gone, and I have destroyed all your enemies before you. I will make a great name[c] for you like that of the greatest on the earth.[d] **10** I will designate a place[e] for my people Israel and plant them,[f] so that they may live there and not be disturbed again. Evildoers will not continue to oppress them as they have done **11** ever since the day I ordered judges to be over my people Israel.[g] I will give you rest from all your enemies.

" 'The LORD declares to you: The LORD himself will make a house for you. **12** When your time comes and you rest with your fathers, I will raise up after you your descendant, who will come from your body, and I will establish his kingdom.[h] **13** He is the one who will build a house for my name,[i] and I will establish the throne of his kingdom forever.[j] **14** I will be his father, and he will be my son.[k] When he does wrong, I will discipline him with a rod of men and blows from mortals. **15** But my faithful love will never leave him[l] as it did when I removed it from Saul, whom I removed from before you.[m] **16** Your house and kingdom will endure before me[A] forever,[n] and your throne will be established forever.' "[o]

17 Nathan reported all these words and this entire vision to David.

DAVID'S PRAYER OF THANKSGIVING

18 Then King David went in,[p] sat in the LORD's presence, and said,

Who am I, Lord GOD, and what is my house that you have brought me this far? **19** What you have done so far[B] was a little thing to you, Lord GOD, for you have also spoken about your servant's house in the distant future. And this is a revelation[c] for mankind, Lord GOD. **20** What more can David say to you? You know your servant,[q] Lord GOD. **21** Because of your word and according to your will, you have revealed all these great things to your servant.

22 This is why you are great,[r] Lord GOD. There is no one like you, and there is no God besides you,[s] as all we have heard confirms. **23** And who is like your people Israel? God came to one nation on earth in order to redeem a people for himself, to make a name for himself, and to perform for them[D] great and awesome acts,[E] driving out nations and their gods before your people you redeemed for yourself from Egypt.[t] **24** You established your people Israel to be your own people forever, and you, LORD, have become their God.[u]

25 Now, LORD God, fulfill the promise forever that you have made to your servant and his house. Do as you have promised, **26** so that your name will be exalted forever, when it is said, "The LORD of Armies is God over Israel." The house of your servant David[v] will be established before you **27** since you, LORD of Armies, God of Israel, have revealed this to your servant when you said, "I will build a house for you." Therefore, your servant has found the courage to pray this prayer to you. **28** Lord GOD, you are God; your words are true, and you have promised this good thing to your servant. **29** Now, please bless your servant's house so

[a]**7:6** Ex 25:8-9; 26:1
[b]**7:8** 1Sm 16:11-13
[c]**7:9** Gn 11:4; 12:2; 2Sm 7:23; Neh 9:10; Is 55:13; 63:14; Jr 32:20
[d]**1**Sm 18:14; 2Sm 5:10; 8:6
[e]**7:10** 1Kg 8:21
[f]**Ex** 15:17; Ps 44:2; 80:8,16; Is 5:2; Jr 1:10; 2:21; 11:17; 12:2; 18:9; 24:6; 31:28; 32:41; 42:10; 45:4; Am 9:15
[g]**7:11** Jdg 2:14-16; 1Sm 12:9-11
[h]**7:12** Ac 13:23
[i]**7:13** 1Kg 5:2-5; 6:12; 8:18-19; Ac 7:47
[j]**Lk** 1:32-33
[k]**7:14** Ps 2:7; Heb 1:5; Rv 21:7
[l]**7:15** Ps 89:21,28,33
[m]**1**Sm 15:24-28
[n]**7:16** Lk 1:32-33
[o]**Ps** 89:3-4,26-37; Ezk 34:23-24; Rv 11:15
[p]**7:18-29** 1Ch 17:16-27

[q]**7:20** Ps 139:1-4
[r]**7:22** 1Ch 16:25; 2Ch 2:5
[s]**Mk** 12:32
[t]**7:23** Dt 4:32-38
[u]**7:24** Ex 6:7; Dt 26:18
[v]**7:26** Lk 1:69

[A]**7:16** Some Hb mss, LXX, Syr; other Hb mss read *you*   [B]**7:19** Lit *Yet this*   [C]**7:19** Or *custom,* or *instruction*   [D]**7:23** Some Hb mss, Tg, Vg, Syr; other Hb mss read *you*   [E]**7:23** LXX; MT reads *acts for your land*

7:11 Don't miss the shock value of this statement: **The LORD himself will make a house for you.** God was engaging in word play. Instead of David building God a house (that is, constructing a temple for him), God would build David a house (that is, he would raise up a kingly dynasty for him).

7:12-16 It was David's **descendant** who would **build a house** (a temple) for the **name** of the Lord (7:12-13). **Faithful love** would never depart from him (7:15). Thus, the **house and kingdom** and **throne** of David would be estab-

lished forever (7:16). The near-term fulfillment of these promises would be David's son Solomon. God would indeed establish his kingdom, paving the way for Israel's golden age.

Ultimately, however, it would take more than a mere man to fulfill the promises of this Davidic covenant. To have a kingdom and throne established forever, the God-man, Jesus Christ, was needed. Jesus in his humanity is a descendant of David and heir to the throne (see Matt 1:1-16; Luke 3:23-38). He is "the Son of the Most High, and the Lord God

will give him the throne of his father David" (Luke 1:32). "He will reign forever and ever" (Rev 11:15). Jesus will rule from David's throne in Jerusalem when he returns in glory to reign in his millennial kingdom.

7:25-29 Here we see a reminder that when you don't know what else to pray, you should ask God to fulfill his promises, because "if we ask anything according to his will, he hears us" (1 John 5:14). Like David, pray that the promises God has made in eternity become a reality in your history.

^a7:29 2Sm 22:51; Ps 89:28-29
^b8:1-18 1Ch 18:1-17
^c8:1 2Sm 3:18
^d8:2 Nm 24:17
^e8:3 2Sm 10:16-19
^f8:4 Jos 11:6
^g8:5 Gn 14:15; Ac 9:2-27
^h8:6 2Sm 8:14
ⁱ8:7 2Kg 11:10; 2Ch 23:9
^j8:9 Gn 10:15-18; Ezk 47:16-17

^k8:11 1Kg 7:51; 1Ch 26:26
^l8:13 2Sm 7:9
^m2Kg 14:7
ⁿ8:14 Gn 25:23; 27:29-40; Nm 24:18
^oDt 20:4; 2Sm 8:6
^p8:15 1Kg 10:9; Ps 99:4; Jr 9:23; 22:3,15; 23:5; 33:15; Ezk 18:5
^q8:18 2Sm 23:20-23
^r9:1 Gn 19:19; 24:12; 40:14; 47:29; Jos 2:12; Jdg 8:35; 2Sm 2:6
^s1Sm 18:3; 20:14-17,42
^t9:2 2Sm 16:1-4
^u9:3 2Sm 4:4

that it will continue before you forever. For you, Lord GOD, have spoken, and with your blessing your servant's house will be blessed forever.^a

DAVID'S VICTORIES

8 After this, David defeated the Philistines,^b subdued them, and took Metheg-ammah^A from Philistine control.^{B,C} ² He also defeated the Moabites, and after making them lie down on the ground, he measured them off with a cord. He measured every two cord lengths of those to be put to death and one full length of those to be kept alive. So the Moabites became David's subjects and brought tribute.^d

³ David also defeated Hadadezer^e son of Rehob, king of Zobah, when he went to restore his control at the Euphrates River. ⁴ David captured seventeen hundred horsemen^c and twenty thousand foot soldiers from him, and he hamstrung all the horses^f and kept a hundred chariots.^D ⁵ When the Arameans of Damascus^g came to assist King Hadadezer of Zobah, David struck down twenty-two thousand Aramean men. ⁶ Then he placed garrisons in Aram of Damascus, and the Arameans became David's subjects and brought tribute. The LORD made David victorious wherever he went.^h

⁷ David took the gold shields of Hadadezer's officers and brought them to Jerusalem.ⁱ ⁸ King David also took huge quantities of bronze from Betah^E and Berothai, Hadadezer's cities. ⁹ When King Toi of Hamath^j heard that David had defeated the entire army of Hadadezer, ¹⁰ he sent his son Joram to King David to greet him and to congratulate him because David had fought against Hadadezer and defeated him, for Toi and Hadadezer had fought many wars. Joram had items of silver, gold, and bronze with

him. ¹¹ King David also dedicated these to the LORD, along with the silver and gold he had dedicated from all the nations he had subdued^k — ¹² from Edom,^F Moab, the Ammonites, the Philistines, the Amalekites, and the spoil of Hadadezer son of Rehob, king of Zobah.

¹³ David made a reputation^l for himself when he returned from striking down eighteen thousand Edomites^G in Salt Valley.^{H,m} ¹⁴ He placed garrisons throughout Edom, and all the Edomites were subject to David.ⁿ The LORD made David victorious wherever he went.^o

¹⁵ So David reigned over all Israel, administering justice and righteousness for all his people.^p

¹⁶   Joab son of Zeruiah was
      over the army;
    Jehoshaphat son of Ahilud was
      court historian;
¹⁷   Zadok son of Ahitub and Ahimelech
      son of Abiathar were priests;
    Seraiah was court secretary;
¹⁸   Benaiah son of Jehoiada
      was over the Cherethites
      and the Pelethites;^q
    and David's sons were
      chief officials.^I

DAVID'S KINDNESS
TO MEPHIBOSHETH

9 David asked, "Is there anyone remaining from the family of Saul I can show kindness^r to for Jonathan's sake?"^s ² There was a servant of Saul's family named Ziba.^t They summoned him to David, and the king said to him, "Are you Ziba?"

"I am your servant," he replied.

³ So the king asked, "Is there anyone left of Saul's family that I can show the kindness of God to?"

Ziba said to the king, "There is still Jonathan's son who was injured in both feet."^u

^A8:1 Or *took control of the mother city*; Hb obscure   ^B8:1 LXX reads *them, and David took tribute out of the hand of the Philistines*   ^C8:4 LXX, DSS read *1,000 chariots and 7,000 horsemen*   ^D8:4 Or *chariot horses*   ^E8:8 Some LXX mss, Syr read *Tebah*   ^F8:12 Some Hb mss, LXX, Syr; other Hb mss read *Aram*; 1Ch 18:11   ^G8:13 Some Hb mss, LXX, Syr; other Hb mss read *Arameans*; 1Ch 18:12   ^H8:13 = the Dead Sea region   ^I8:18 LXX; MT reads *were priests*; 1Ch 18:17

8:1-6 David's expansion of his kingdom continued in every direction. The reason for David's unbroken success was unmistakable: **The LORD** made David victorious (8:6). **8:9-12 Toi** was so glad **that David had defeated the entire army of Hadadezer** that he sent his son to David with expensive gifts to congratulate him on his victory, because **Toi and Hadadezer had fought many wars** (8:9-10). As he did with all his spoil and gifts, David **dedicated these to the LORD** (8:11). In this I see a pattern: "The Lord made David

victorious" (8:6), and David dedicated his spoils to the Lord (8:11). The gracious provision of God should inspire our gratefulness and giving, too. **8:14** David subjugated the **Edomites,** descendants of Esau who proved to be bitter enemies of the Israelites, to make sure they didn't rise up against him again. **8:17** The priests **Zadok** and **Ahimelech** were from two different priestly lines descended from Aaron. Ahimelech was from the line of Eli, whose family was cursed because of the

sins of Hophni and Phinehas and Eli's failure to restrain them. Samuel had said this family line would come to an end (see 1 Sam 3:10-14). The line of Zadok, however, would continue on through the end of the Old Testament. **9:1** David never forgot his covenant promise of friendship with Saul's son Jonathan. **9:3-4** Ziba had been a servant in Saul's house and had kept up with the family (9:2). He knew Jonathan's crippled son was living on the opposite side of the Jordan River—possibly in hiding.

4 The king asked him, "Where is he?"

Ziba answered the king, "You'll find him in Lo-debar at the house of Machir son of Ammiel." **5** So King David had him brought from the house of Machir son of Ammiel in Lo-debar.

6 Mephibosheth son of Jonathan son of Saul came to David, fell facedown, and paid homage. David said, "Mephibosheth!"

"I am your servant," he replied.

7 "Don't be afraid," David said to him, "since I intend to show you kindness for the sake of your father Jonathan. I will restore to you all your grandfather Saul's fields, and you will always eat meals at my table."[a]

8 Mephibosheth paid homage and said, "What is your servant that you take an interest in a dead dog[b] like me?"

9 Then the king summoned Saul's attendant Ziba and said to him, "I have given to your master's grandson all that belonged to Saul and his family. **10** You, your sons, and your servants are to work the ground for him, and you are to bring in the crops so your master's grandson will have food to eat. But Mephibosheth, your master's grandson, is always to eat at my table." Now Ziba had fifteen sons and twenty servants.

11 Ziba said to the king, "Your servant will do all my lord the king commands."

So Mephibosheth ate at David's[A] table just like one of the king's sons. **12** Mephibosheth had a young son whose name was Mica.[c] All those living in Ziba's house were Mephibosheth's servants. **13** However, Mephibosheth lived in Jerusalem because he always ate at the king's table. His feet had been injured.

WAR WITH THE AMMONITES

10 Some time later, the king of the Ammonites died, and his son Hanun became king in his place.[d] **2** Then David said, "I'll show kindness to Hanun

son of Nahash, just as his father showed kindness to me."

So David sent his emissaries to console Hanun concerning his father. However, when they arrived in the land of the Ammonites, **3** the Ammonite leaders said to Hanun their lord, "Just because David has sent men with condolences for you, do you really believe he's showing respect for your father? Instead, hasn't David sent his emissaries in order to scout out the city, spy on it, and demolish it?"[e] **4** So Hanun took David's emissaries, shaved off half their beards,[f] cut their clothes in half at the hips, and sent them away.[g]

5 When this was reported to David, he sent someone to meet them, since they were deeply humiliated. The king said, "Stay in Jericho until your beards grow back; then return."

6 When the Ammonites realized they had become repulsive to David, they hired twenty thousand foot soldiers from the Arameans of Beth-rehob and Zobah, one thousand men from the king of Maacah, and twelve thousand men from Tob.

7 David heard about it and sent Joab and all the elite troops. **8** The Ammonites marched out and lined up in battle formation at the entrance to the city gate while the Arameans of Zobah and Rehob and the men of Tob and Maacah were in the field by themselves. **9** When Joab saw that there was a battle line in front of him and another behind him, he chose some of Israel's finest young men and lined up in formation to engage the Arameans. **10** He placed the rest of the forces under the command of his brother Abishai. They lined up in formation to engage the Ammonites.

11 "If the Arameans are too strong for me," Joab said, "then you will be my help. However, if the Ammonites are too strong for you, I'll come to help you. **12** Be strong! Let's prove ourselves strong for our people

[a] 9:7 1Kg 2:7
[b] 9:8 1Sm 24:14; 2Sm 16:9
[c] 9:12 1Ch 8:34
[d] 10:1-19 1Ch 19:1-19

[e] 10:3 1Sm 11:1-10
[f] 10:4 Is 50:6
[g] Is 7:20; 20:4

[A] 9:11 LXX; Syr reads *the king's*; Vg reads *your*; MT reads *my*

9:6-7 Mephibosheth bowed to David, perhaps not knowing the fate that awaited him as the heir of the disgraced former king (9:6). David quickly laid the young man's fears to rest by repeating his covenant promise to **Jonathan** and assuring Mephibosheth that he was to be the recipient of that blessing (9:7).

9:8-13 Mephibosheth's change in circumstances came as a result of sheer grace. There was no precedent in the ancient world for what David did on his behalf. But then there was no king like David, a type and forerunner

of Jesus Christ, who took mercy on us as crippled sinners and extended to us his kindness (see Titus 3:4-5).

10:1-2 The late king, **Nahash**, had been an enemy to Saul and Israel many years earlier (see 1 Sam 11:1-10). But in later years he had apparently shown some unnamed **kindness to** David. So David wanted to express his condolences to his son.

10:3-5 Without evidence, Hanun's foolish counselors accused David of sending his delegation as spies to scope out the capital so he could come and **demolish it** (10:3).

Unfortunately for Hanun and his people, he listened and humiliated David's representatives by shaving their **beards** and exposing their nakedness (10:4). David would not let the insult pass.

10:6-7 Taking on a formidable enemy like David would require extra troops, so Hanun hired tens of thousands of mercenaries **from the Arameans** and from smaller kingdoms (10:6). Meanwhile, David **sent Joab and all the elite troops** (10:7), which were soon divided to deal with the enemy's split forces. God gave Israel great victory (see 10:13-14).

a 10:12 Dt 31:6; Jos 1:6
b Ac 21:14
c 11:1 2Sm 12:26-29;
1Ch 20:1

d 11:3 2Sm 12:24; Ps 51
e Mt 1:6
f 11:4 Lv 15:18-30; 18:19
g 11:11 1Sm 21:5

and for the cities of our God.*a* May the LORD's will be done."*A,b*

13 Joab and his troops advanced to fight against the Arameans, and they fled before him. 14 When the Ammonites saw that the Arameans had fled, they too fled before Abishai and entered the city. So Joab withdrew from the attack against the Ammonites and went to Jerusalem.

15 When the Arameans saw that they had been defeated by Israel, they regrouped. 16 Hadadezer sent messengers to bring the Arameans who were beyond the Euphrates River, and they came to Helam with Shobach, commander of Hadadezer's army, leading them.

17 When this was reported to David, he gathered all Israel, crossed the Jordan, and went to Helam. Then the Arameans lined up to engage David in battle and fought against him. 18 But the Arameans fled before Israel, and David killed seven hundred of their charioteers and forty thousand foot soldiers.*B* He also struck down Shobach commander of their army, who died there. 19 When all the kings who were Hadadezer's subjects saw that they had been defeated by Israel, they made peace with Israel and became their subjects. After this, the Arameans were afraid to ever help the Ammonites again.

DAVID'S ADULTERY WITH BATHSHEBA

11 In the spring when kings march out to war, David sent Joab with his officers and all Israel. They destroyed the Ammonites and besieged Rabbah, but David remained in Jerusalem.*c*

2 One evening David got up from his bed and strolled around on the roof of the palace. From the roof he saw a woman bathing — a very beautiful woman. 3 So David sent someone to inquire about her, and he said, "Isn't this Bathsheba,*d* daughter of Eliam and wife of Uriah*e* the Hethite?"*c*

4 David sent messengers to get her, and when she came to him, he slept with her. Now she had just been purifying herself from her uncleanness.*f* Afterward, she returned home. 5 The woman conceived and sent word to inform David: "I am pregnant."

6 David sent orders to Joab: "Send me Uriah the Hethite." So Joab sent Uriah to David. 7 When Uriah came to him, David asked how Joab and the troops were doing and how the war was going. 8 Then he said to Uriah, "Go down to your house and wash your feet." So Uriah left the palace, and a gift from the king followed him. 9 But Uriah slept at the door of the palace with all his master's servants; he did not go down to his house.

10 When it was reported to David, "Uriah didn't go home," David questioned Uriah, "Haven't you just come from a journey? Why didn't you go home?"

11 Uriah answered David, "The ark, Israel, and Judah are dwelling in tents, and my master Joab and his soldiers*D* are camping in the open field. How can I enter my house to eat and drink and sleep with my wife? As surely as you live and by your life, I will not do this!"*g*

12 "Stay here today also," David said to Uriah, "and tomorrow I will send you back." So Uriah stayed in Jerusalem that day and the next. 13 Then David invited Uriah to eat and drink with him, and David got him drunk. He went out in the evening to lie down on his cot with his master's servants, but he did not go home.

URIAH'S DEATH ARRANGED

14 The next morning David wrote a letter to Joab and sent it with Uriah. 15 In the letter he wrote:

A 10:12 Lit the LORD do what is good in his eyes   *B* 10:18 Some LXX mss; MT reads horsemen; 1Ch 19:18   *C* 11:3 DSS add Joab's armor-bearer
D 11:11 Lit servants

10:18-19 That David killed **Shobach commander of their army** was a devastating psychological blow to the Aramean troops (10:18). At last the Arameans realized that fighting against David was a hopeless cause, so **they … became [Israel's] subjects** (10:19). **11:1** David had been a faithful follower of God as a young shepherd, an unjustly persecuted fugitive, and then as a powerful king. His fame and power were at their height. Unfortunately, it was at this point that he faltered.

The problem began **in the spring when kings march out to war.** Instead of joining his men in battle, David **sent Joab** and his army out while he **remained in Jerusalem**— for unnamed reasons. It's often when we're not doing what we ought to be doing that temptation pounces.

In the ancient world, kings could suppress records of their failures. But this is not the case with the biblical records of kings. Chapters like this one are included by inspiration of the Holy Spirit. They serve as a warning to us (see 1 Cor 10:6): none of us is above sin.

11:3-4 Ultimately, we don't know how **Bathsheba** (11:3) felt about what happened in verse 4. But we are given no reason to think that she was trying to seduce David. *He* stayed behind while his troops were fighting battles. *He* strolled on his rooftop when he should have been sleeping. *He* had another man's wife brought to him. David was the king, and his every order was to be obeyed.

11:5-8 Instead of seeking to stop the damage by repentance, David made things infinitely worse by scheming. David brought **Uriah** back home from the battlefield and encouraged him to go home for a few days and enjoy time with his wife. David assumed that he would take advantage of the opportunity to sleep with her, think the coming baby was his own, and David would be off the hook (11:6-8).

11:9-13 The contrast between David's underhanded plotting and Uriah's open integrity could not be greater.

Put Uriah[a] at the front of the fiercest fighting, then withdraw from him so that he is struck down and dies.

[16] When Joab was besieging the city, he put Uriah in the place where he knew the best enemy soldiers were. [17] Then the men of the city came out and attacked Joab, and some of the men from David's soldiers fell in battle; Uriah the Hethite also died.

[18] Joab sent someone to report to David all the details of the battle. [19] He commanded the messenger, "When you've finished telling the king all the details of the battle — [20] if the king's anger gets stirred up and he asks you, 'Why did you get so close to the city to fight? Didn't you realize they would shoot from the top of the wall? [21] At Thebez, who struck Abimelech son of Jerubbesheth?[A,B] Didn't a woman drop an upper millstone on him from the top of the wall so that he died?[b] Why did you get so close to the wall?' — then say, 'Your servant Uriah the Hethite is dead also.'"

[22] Then the messenger left.

When he arrived, he reported to David all that Joab had sent him to tell. [23] The messenger reported to David, "The men gained the advantage over us and came out against us in the field, but we counterattacked right up to the entrance of the city gate. [24] However, the archers shot down on your servants from the top of the wall, and some of the king's servants died. Your servant Uriah the Hethite is also dead."

[25] David told the messenger, "Say this to Joab: 'Don't let this matter upset you because the sword devours all alike. Intensify your fight against the city and demolish it.' Encourage him."

[26] When Uriah's[c] wife heard that her husband Uriah had died, she mourned for him.[c] [27] When the time of mourning ended, David had her brought to his house. She became his wife and bore him a son. However, the LORD considered what David had done to be evil.[d]

NATHAN'S PARABLE AND DAVID'S REPENTANCE

12 So the LORD sent Nathan to David.[e] When he arrived, he said to him: There were two men in a certain city, one rich and the other poor. [2] The rich man had very large flocks and herds, [3] but the poor man had nothing except one small ewe lamb that he had bought. He raised her, and she grew up with him and with his children. From his meager food she would eat, from his cup she would drink, and in his arms she would sleep. She was like a daughter to him. [4] Now a traveler came to the rich man, but the rich man could not bring himself to take one of his own sheep or cattle to prepare for the traveler who had come to him. Instead, he took the poor man's lamb and prepared it for his guest.[D]

[5] David was infuriated with the man and said to Nathan: "As the LORD lives, the man who did this deserves to die! [6] Because he has done this thing and shown no pity, he must pay four lambs for that lamb."[f]

[7] Nathan replied to David, "You are the man! This is what the LORD God of Israel says: 'I anointed you king over Israel,[g] and I rescued you from Saul. [8] I gave your master's house to you and your master's wives into your arms,[E] and I gave you the house of Israel and Judah, and if that was not enough, I would have given you even more. [9] Why then have you despised the LORD's command by doing what I consider[F] evil?[h] You struck down Uriah[i] the Hethite with the sword and took his wife as your own wife — you murdered him with

[a] 11:15 Mt 1:6
[b] 11:21 Jdg 9:50-54
[c] 11:26 Mt 1:6

[d] 11:27 2Sm 12:9; 15:19
[e] 12:1 Ps 51 title
[f] 12:6 Ex 22:1; Lk 19:8
[g] 12:7 1Sm 16:13
[h] 12:9 Nm 15:30-31; 1Sm 15:19
[i] Mt 1:6

[A]11:21 LXX reads *Jerubbaal*   [B]11:21 = Gideon   [C]11:26 Lit *her husband*   [D]12:4 Lit *for the man who had come to him*   [E]12:8 Lit *bosom*
[F]12:9 Alt Hb tradition reads *what he considers*

11:14-15 David was so desperate to bury his sin that he decided to bury Uriah. This is what sin will do to you, if you refuse to confess it and deal with it.

11:24-25 David's descent into sinful choices had led the man after God's own heart to grow increasingly coldhearted. If sin is not dealt with, eventually the sinner's heart grows calloused.

11:27 As far as David was concerned, the child would appear legitimate and the matter could be put to rest. But he had forgotten about his omniscient and omnipresent God, the one about whom David himself would write, "You understand my thoughts . . . Where can I flee

from your presence? . . . Even the darkness is not dark to you" (Ps 139:2, 7, 12). David had acted in secret. But nothing is hidden from the God who sees and knows all.

12:1-6 Nathan told a story of injustice (12:1-4), and the crime was so obvious and cruel that David jumped to the defense of the injured party. He said, **the man who did this deserves to die! Because he has done this thing and shown no pity, he must pay four lambs for that lamb** (12:5-6). Sadly, though, David had no idea that the tale was a parable of his own actions. The rich man represented David, the poor man represented Uriah, and

the ewe lamb represented Bathsheba. David's sin had blinded him. In condemning the rich man, he condemned himself.

12:7-12 In short, David had repaid the Lord with wickedness (12:7-9) after God had graciously placed under his authority and control everything that belonged to King Saul (including Saul's wives, who would become servants of the king and his kingdom since there is no indication that David married them). As a result, **the sword [would] never leave [his] house** (12:10). From that day forward, David's **family** would be plagued by rape, murder, and rebellion (12:11).

a 12:9 2Sm 11:14-17
b 12:10 2Sm 12:18; 13:28-
29; 18:14-18; 1Kg 2:22-25;
2Kg 11:1
c 12:11-12 2Sm 16:21-22
d 12:13 2Sm 24:10; Ps
32:5; 51:4
e Lv 20:10; 24:17; Ps 32:1-5;
Pr 28:13
f 12:14 2Sm 12:18
g 12:15 Mt 1:6
h 12:16 2Sm 13:31; Jb 1:20

i 12:23 Jb 7:8-10
j 12:24 Gn 37:35; Ps 23:4;
119:76,82
k 1Ch 22:9
l 12:26-31 1Ch 20:1-3
m 12:31 Ex 1:13-14
n 13:1 2Sm 3:3
o 2Sm 14:27; 1Ch 3:9
p 2Sm 3:2

the Ammonite's sword.[a] **10** Now therefore, the sword will never leave your house[b] because you despised me and took the wife of Uriah the Hethite to be your own wife.'

11 "This is what the LORD says,[c] 'I am going to bring disaster on you from your own family: I will take your wives and give them to another[A] before your very eyes, and he will sleep with them in broad daylight.[B] **12** You acted in secret, but I will do this before all Israel and in broad daylight.'"[c]

13 David responded to Nathan, "I have sinned against the LORD."[d]

Then Nathan replied to David, "And the LORD has taken away your sin; you will not die.[e] **14** However, because you treated[D] the LORD with such contempt in this matter, the son born to you will die."[f] **15** Then Nathan went home.

THE DEATH OF BATHSHEBA'S SON

The LORD struck the baby that Uriah's[g] wife had borne to David, and he became deathly ill. **16** David pleaded with God for the boy. He fasted, went home, and spent the night lying on the ground.[h] **17** The elders of his house stood beside him to get him up from the ground, but he was unwilling and would not eat anything with them.

18 On the seventh day the baby died. But David's servants were afraid to tell him the baby was dead. They said, "Look, while the baby was alive, we spoke to him, and he wouldn't listen to us. So how can we tell him the baby is dead? He may do something desperate."

19 When David saw that his servants were whispering to each other, he guessed that the baby was dead. So he asked his servants, "Is the baby dead?"

"He is dead," they replied.

20 Then David got up from the ground. He washed, anointed himself, changed his clothes, went to the LORD's house, and worshiped. Then he went home and requested something to eat. So they served him food, and he ate.

21 His servants asked him, "Why have you done this? While the baby was alive,

you fasted and wept, but when he died, you got up and ate food."

22 He answered, "While the baby was alive, I fasted and wept because I thought, 'Who knows? The LORD may be gracious to me and let him live.' **23** But now that he is dead, why should I fast? Can I bring him back again? I'll go to him, but he will never return to me."[i]

THE BIRTH OF SOLOMON

24 Then David comforted[j] his wife Bathsheba; he went to her and slept with her. She gave birth to a son and named[E] him Solomon.[F,k] The LORD loved him, **25** and he sent a message through the prophet Nathan, who named[G] him Jedidiah,[H] because of the LORD.

CAPTURE OF THE CITY OF RABBAH

26 Joab fought against Rabbah of the Ammonites[l] and captured the royal fortress. **27** Then Joab sent messengers to David to say, "I have fought against Rabbah and have also captured its water supply. **28** Now therefore, assemble the rest of the troops, lay siege to the city, and capture it. Otherwise I will be the one to capture the city, and it will be named after me." **29** So David assembled all the troops and went to Rabbah; he fought against it and captured it. **30** He took the crown from the head of their king,[i] and it was placed on David's head. The crown weighed seventy-five pounds[j] of gold, and it had a precious stone in it. In addition, David took away a large quantity of plunder from the city. **31** He removed the people who were in the city and put them to work with saws, iron picks, and iron axes, and to labor at brickmaking.[m] He did the same to all the Ammonite cities. Then he and all his troops returned to Jerusalem.

AMNON RAPES TAMAR

13 Some time passed. David's son Absalom[n] had a beautiful sister named Tamar,[o] and David's son Amnon[p] was infatuated with her. **2** Amnon was frustrated to the point of making himself sick over

A 12:11 Or *to your neighbor*   **B** 12:11 Lit *in the eyes of this sun*   **C** 12:12 Lit *and before the sun*   **D** 12:14 Alt Hb tradition, one LXX ms; MT reads *treated the enemies of*; DSS read *treated the word of*   **E** 12:24 Alt Hb tradition reads *he named*   **F** 12:24 In Hb, the name *Solomon* sounds like "peace."   **G** 12:25 Or *prophet to name*   **H** 12:25 = Beloved of the LORD   **I** 12:30 LXX reads *of Milcom*; some emend to *Molech*; 1Kg 11:5,33   **J** 12:30 Lit *a talent*

12:13-14 According to the law of Moses, David deserved to **die** for adultery and murder. Yet God graciously forgave him and spared his life (12:13). Nevertheless, there would still be serious consequences, beginning with the death of Bathsheba's baby (12:14).

12:24-25 The name **Solomon** sounds like the Hebrew word for "peace" (12:24). But the Lord named him **Jedidiah**, which means "Beloved of the LORD." This was a gracious sign that God had not removed his love from David (12:25).

12:26-28 **Joab** urged David to come to **Rabbah** and finish the battle—lest Joab win the fight and gain the honor instead of the king. **13:1-7** In this chapter polygamy came back to haunt David in one of many disastrous consequences for his family that unfolded as a

his sister Tamar because she was a virgin, but it seemed impossible to do anything to her. ³ Amnon had a friend named Jonadab, a son of David's brother Shimeah.^a Jonadab was a very shrewd man, ⁴ and he asked Amnon, "Why are you, the king's son, so miserable^b every morning? Won't you tell me?"

Amnon replied, "I'm in love with Tamar, my brother Absalom's sister."

⁵ Jonadab said to him, "Lie down on your bed and pretend you're sick. When your father comes to see you, say to him, 'Please let my sister Tamar come and give me something to eat. Let her prepare a meal in my presence^c so I can watch and eat from her hand.'"

⁶ So Amnon lay down and pretended to be sick. When the king came to see him, Amnon said to him, "Please let my sister Tamar come and make a couple of cakes in my presence so I can eat from her hand."

⁷ David sent word to Tamar at the palace: "Please go to your brother Amnon's house and prepare a meal for him."

⁸ Then Tamar went to his house while Amnon was lying down. She took dough, kneaded it, made cakes in his presence, and baked them. ⁹ She brought the pan and set it down in front of him, but he refused to eat. Amnon said, "Everyone leave me!" And everyone left him. ¹⁰ "Bring the meal to the bedroom," Amnon told Tamar, "so I can eat from your hand." Tamar took the cakes she had made and went to her brother Amnon's bedroom. ¹¹ When she brought them to him to eat, he grabbed her and said,^A "Come sleep with me, my sister!"

¹² "Don't, my brother!" she cried. "Don't disgrace^d me, for such a thing should never be done in Israel.^e Don't commit this outrage!^f ¹³ Where could I ever go with my humiliation? And you — you would be like one of the outrageous fools in Israel! Please, speak to the king, for he won't keep me from you." ¹⁴ But he refused to listen to her, and because he

was stronger than she was, he disgraced her by raping her.

¹⁵ So Amnon hated Tamar with such intensity that the hatred he hated her with was greater than the love he had loved her with. "Get out of here!" he said.

¹⁶ "No," she cried,^B "sending me away is much worse than the great wrong you've already done to me!"

But he refused to listen to her. ¹⁷ Instead, he called to the servant who waited on him: "Get this away from me, throw her out, and bolt the door behind her!" ¹⁸ Amnon's servant threw her out and bolted the door behind her. Now Tamar was wearing a long-sleeved^c garment, because this is what the king's virgin daughters wore. ¹⁹ Tamar put ashes on her head and tore the long-sleeved garment she was wearing. She put her hand on her head^g and went away crying out.

²⁰ Her brother Absalom said to her: "Has your brother Amnon been with you? Be quiet for now, my sister. He is your brother. Don't take this thing to heart." So Tamar lived as a desolate woman^h in the house of her brother Absalom.

ABSALOM MURDERS AMNON

²¹ When King David heard about all these things, he was furious.^D ²² Absalom didn't say anything to Amnon, either good or bad, because he hated Amnon since he disgraced his sister Tamar.

²³ Two years later, Absalom's sheepshearers were at Baal-hazor near Ephraim, and Absalom invited all the king's sons. ²⁴ Then he went to the king and said, "Your servant has just hired sheepshearers. Will the king and his servants please come with your servant?"

²⁵ The king replied to Absalom, "No, my son, we should not all go, or we would be a burden to you." Although Absalom urged him, he wasn't willing to go, though he did bless him.

²⁶ "If not," Absalom said, "please let my brother Amnon go with us."

^a13:3 1Sm 16:9; 17:13; 1Ch 2:13
^b13:4 Gn 41:19; 2Sm 3:1
^c13:5 Jr 7:18
^d13:12 Dt 21:14; Ru 2:15; 2Sm 19:3; Jb 19:3; Ps 35:4; 44:9; 136:23; Pr 28:7; Jr 14:3; 50:12; Ezk 36:32; 2Co 12:21
^eGn 20:9; 34:7; Lv 18:9; 20:17
^fDt 22:21; Jos 7:15; Jdg 19:23–24; 20:6; Jr 29:23

^g13:19 Jr 2:37
^h13:20 Is 54:1; 62:4

^A13:11 Lit *said to her*   ^B13:16 Lit *she said to him*   ^C13:18 Or *an ornamented*; Gn 37:3   ^D13:21 LXX, DSS add *but he did not grieve the spirit of Amnon his son, for he loved him because he was his firstborn*; 1Kg 1:6

result of his sin. **David's son Amnon became infatuated with** his half-sister **Tamar**, the full sister of **Absalom** (13:1). He would use David, who was clueless about his intentions, to help him satisfy his lust for the girl (13:6-7). **13:12-14** Like his father David before him (11:2-4), Amnon was blinded by lust and couldn't see the inevitable consequences of such actions.

13:15-18 True to his low character, **Amnon** quickly **hated Tamar with such intensity that the hatred he hated her with was greater than the love he had loved her with** (13:15). Clearly, his "love" was nothing more than self-centered lust. To cast her out following his actions would be **much worse than the great wrong [he'd] already done** (13:16). But Amnon didn't care (13:17-18). Rather than set-

ting things right, Amnon compounded his sin—just as his father had done. **13:21-22** Amazingly, it appears the king did nothing to punish Amnon. Perhaps his moral resolve had been weakened by the knowledge of his own past sexual sin. **Absalom**, though, would act. He **hated Amnon** for disgracing **his sister** (13:22). He'd patiently bide his time, looking for a chance at revenge.

a 13:28 Jos 1:9
b 13:31 2Sm 1:11
c 13:32 2Sm 13:3-5
d 13:37 2Sm 3:3; 1Ch 3:2

e 14:2 2Ch 20:20; Am 1:1
f 2Sm 13:3; 14:20; 20:16;
   Jb 5:13
g Dn 10:2-3
h 14:4 1Sm 20:41; 25:23;
   2Ch 20:18
i 14:5 2Sm 12:1
j 14:7 Nah 1:14
k 14:9 1Sm 25:24
l 14:11 Nm 35:19-21; Dt
   19:12
m 1Sm 14:45; Dn 3:27; Lk
   21:18; Ac 27:34

The king asked him, "Why should he go with you?" **27** But Absalom urged him, so he sent Amnon and all the king's sons. ^A

28 Now Absalom commanded his young men, "Watch Amnon until he is in a good mood from the wine. When I order you to strike Amnon, then kill him. Don't be afraid. Am I not the one who has commanded you? Be strong and valiant!" ^a **29** So Absalom's young men did to Amnon just as Absalom had commanded. Then all the rest of the king's sons got up, and each fled on his mule.

30 While they were on the way, a report reached David: "Absalom struck down all the king's sons; not even one of them survived!" **31** In response the king stood up, tore his clothes, and lay down on the ground, and all his servants stood by with their clothes torn. ^b

32 But Jonadab, son of David's brother Shimeah, ^c spoke up: "My lord must not think they have killed all the young men, the king's sons, because only Amnon is dead. In fact, Absalom has planned this ^B ever since the day Amnon disgraced his sister Tamar. **33** So now, my lord the king, don't take seriously the report that says all the king's sons are dead. Only Amnon is dead."

34 Meanwhile, Absalom had fled. When the young man who was standing watch looked up, there were many people coming from the road west of him from the side of the mountain. ^c **35** Jonadab said to the king, "Look, the king's sons have come! It's exactly like your servant said." **36** Just as he finished speaking, the king's sons entered and wept loudly. Then the king and all his servants also wept very bitterly. **37** But Absalom fled and went to Talmai son of Ammihud, king of Geshur. ^d And David mourned for his son ^D every day.

38 After Absalom had fled to Geshur and had been there three years, **39** King David ^E longed to go to Absalom, for David had finished grieving over Amnon's death.

ABSALOM RESTORED TO DAVID

14 Joab son of Zeruiah realized that the king's mind was on Absalom. **2** So Joab sent someone to Tekoa ^e to bring a wise ^f woman from there. He told her, "Pretend to be in mourning: dress in mourning clothes and don't put on any oil. ^g Act like a woman who has been mourning for the dead for a long time. **3** Go to the king and speak these words to him." Then Joab told her exactly what to say. ^F

4 When the woman from Tekoa came ^G to the king, she fell facedown to the ground, paid homage, ^h and said, "Help me, Your Majesty!"

5 "What's the matter?" the king asked her.

"Sadly, I am a widow; my husband died," she said. ^i **6** "Your servant had two sons. They were fighting in the field with no one to separate them, and one struck the other and killed him. **7** Now the whole clan has risen up against your servant and said, 'Hand over the one who killed his brother so we may put him to death for the life of the brother he murdered. We will eliminate the heir!' They would extinguish my one remaining ember by not preserving my husband's name or posterity on earth." ^j

8 The king told the woman, "Go home. I will issue a command on your behalf."

9 Then the woman of Tekoa said to the king, "My lord the king, may any blame be on me ^k and my father's family, and may the king and his throne be innocent."

10 "Whoever speaks to you," the king said, "bring him to me. He will not trouble you again!"

11 She replied, "Please, may the king invoke the LORD your God, so that the avenger of blood will not increase the loss, and they will not eliminate my son!" ^l

"As the LORD lives," he vowed, "not a hair of your son will fall to the ground." ^m

12 Then the woman said, "Please, may your servant speak a word to my lord the king?"

"Speak," he replied.

13 The woman asked, "Why have you devised something similar against the

---

^A 13:27 LXX adds *And Absalom prepared a feast like a royal feast.*   ^B 13:32 Lit *In fact, it was established on the mouth of Absalom*   ^C 13:34 LXX adds *And the watchman came and reported to the king saying, "I see men on the Horonaim road on the side of the mountain."*   ^D 13:37 Probably Amnon   ^E 13:39 DSS, LXX, Tg read *David's spirit*   ^F 14:3 Lit *Joab put the words into her mouth*   ^G 14:4 Some Hb mss, LXX, Syr, Tg, Vg; other Hb mss read *spoke*

13:28-29 Absalom's opportunity to avenge his sister's honor came "two years" after Amnon's attack (13:23). During a feast to which David's sons had been invited, **Absalom's young men** followed their master's orders and killed **Amnon**.

13:37-38 To escape punishment, Absalom went to the home of his maternal grandfather (see 3:3), where he stayed for **three years** (13:38).

14:1-17 David wanted Absalom back, but he couldn't just send for him and pretend everything was fine or the people might think the king didn't take Absalom's crime of murder seriously. Finally **Joab**, David's army commander, came up with a reunion plan and persuaded a **wise woman** from **Tekoa**, located about ten miles south of Jerusalem, to carry it out (14:1-3). Her words were a ruse to show David that while he was willing to grant clemency to some unnamed murderer, he'd not granted it to his own son (14:4-17).

people of God? When the king spoke as he did about this matter, he has pronounced his own guilt. The king has not brought back his own banished one. **14** We will certainly die[a] and be like water poured out on the ground, which can't be recovered. But God would not take away a life; he would devise plans so that the one banished from him does not remain banished.

15 "Now therefore, I've come to present this matter to my lord the king because the people have made me afraid. Your servant thought: I must speak to the king. Perhaps the king will grant his servant's request. **16** The king will surely listen in order to keep his servant from the grasp of this man who would eliminate both me and my son from God's inheritance. **17** Your servant thought: May the word of my lord the king bring relief, for my lord the king is able to discern the good and the bad like the angel of God.[b] May the LORD your God be with you."

18 Then the king answered the woman, "I'm going to ask you something; don't conceal it from me!"

"Let my lord the king speak," the woman replied.

19 The king asked, "Did Joab put you up to[A] all this?"

The woman answered. "As you live, my lord the king, no one can turn to the right or left from all my lord the king says. Yes, your servant Joab is the one who gave orders to me; he told your servant exactly what to say.[B] **20** Joab your servant has done this to address the issue indirectly,[C] but my lord has wisdom like the wisdom of the angel of God, knowing everything on earth."

21 Then the king said to Joab, "I hereby grant this request. Go, bring back the young man Absalom."

22 Joab fell with his face to the ground in homage and blessed the king. "Today," Joab said, "your servant knows I have found favor with you, my lord the king, because the king has granted the request of your servant."

23 So Joab got up, went to Geshur, and brought Absalom[c] to Jerusalem. **24** However, the king added, "He may return to his house, but he may not see my face." So Absalom returned to his house, but he did not see the king.[D]

25 No man in all Israel was as handsome[d] and highly praised as Absalom. From the sole of his foot to the top of his head, he did not have a single flaw. **26** When he shaved his head — he shaved it at the end of every year because his hair got so heavy for him that he had to shave it off — he would weigh the hair from his head and it would be five pounds[E] according to the royal standard.

27 Three sons were born to Absalom, and a daughter named Tamar, who was a beautiful woman. **28** Absalom resided in Jerusalem two years but never saw the king. **29** Then Absalom sent for Joab in order to send him to the king, but Joab was unwilling to come to him. So he sent again, a second time, but he still would not come. **30** Then Absalom said to his servants, "See, Joab has a field right next to mine, and he has barley there. Go and set fire to it!" So Absalom's servants set the field on fire.[F]

31 Then Joab came to Absalom's house and demanded, "Why did your servants set my field on fire?"

32 "Look," Absalom explained to Joab, "I sent for you and said, 'Come here. I want to send you to the king to ask: Why have I come back from Geshur? I'd be better off if I were still there.' So now, let me see the king. If I am guilty, let him kill me."

33 Joab went to the king and told him. So David summoned Absalom, who came to the king and paid homage with his face to the ground before him. Then the king kissed Absalom.

ABSALOM'S REVOLT

15 After this, Absalom got himself a chariot, horses, and fifty men to run before him.[e] **2** He would get up early and stand beside the road leading to

[a]14:14 Jn 8:51
[b]14:17 2Sm 19:27

[c]14:23 2Sm 13:38
[d]14:25 Gn 39:6; 1Sm 16:12,18; 17:42; 1Kg 1:6; Ps 45:2
[e]15:1 1Sm 8:11; 1Kg 1:5

[A]**14:19** Lit "Is the hand of Joab in   [B]**14:19** Lit he put all these words into the mouth of your servant   [C]**14:20** Lit to go around the face of the matter   [D]**14:24** Lit king's face   [E]**14:26** Lit 200 shekels   [F]**14:30** DSS, LXX add So Joab's servants came to him with their clothes torn and said, "Absalom's servants have set the field on fire!"

14:21, 24 David gave Joab permission to bring Absalom back to Jerusalem (14:21), yet under one condition: **he may not see [David's] face** (14:24). Such a half-hearted attempt at reconciliation was bound to fail.
14:25-26 The physical attributes described here would become important in helping explain how Absalom would be able to raise such a large following against his father. Yet

while the text says, **he did not have a single [physical] flaw** (14:25), he did develop one fatal character flaw: pride.
14:30-33 Like a sulky child, Absalom had Joab's barley **field** set **on fire** to get his attention (14:30). As a result, Joab interceded for Absalom and **went to the king**. Unfortunately, the reunion between David and his son would prove to be a case of too little too late (14:33).

15:1-6 Absalom, still disgruntled, knew exactly how to begin his plot to take his father's throne. He didn't need an army. He had charm and good looks—traits any good politician knows how to use to advantage. He also had a shrewd political strategy: identify the shortcomings of the current administration and make promises of better days under his own leadership. Over

[a] 15:2 Ru 4:1-11; 2Sm 19:8;
  Jb 29:7
[b] 15:5 Gn 29:13; Ex 18:7;
  1Sm 10:1; 2Sm 19:39
[c] 15:8 2Sm 13:37-38
[d] Gn 28:20-21; 1Sm 1:11
[e] 15:9 Ex 4:18; Jdg 18:6;
  1Sm 1:17; 2Kg 5:19; Lk
  7:50; 8:48
[f] 15:10 2Sm 6:15; 1Kg 1:41;
  Jr 4:19,21; 6:17; 42:14;
  Am 2:2
[g] 1Kg 1:11,18,33-34; 2Kg
  9:13
[h] 15:12 1Ch 27:33; Ps 41:9;
  55:12-14
[i] 15:14 Ps 3 title

[j] 15:18 1Sm 27:2-7
[k] 15:19 2Sm 18:2
[l] 15:21 Ru 1:16
[m] 15:24 2Sm 8:17; 20:25
[n] 15:25 1Sm 4:3

the city gate.[a] Whenever anyone had a grievance to bring before the king for settlement, Absalom called out to him and asked, "What city are you from?" If he replied, "Your servant is from one of the tribes of Israel," [3] Absalom said to him, "Look, your claims are good and right, but the king does not have anyone to listen to you." [4] He added, "If only someone would appoint me judge in the land. Then anyone who had a grievance or dispute could come to me, and I would make sure he received justice." [5] When a person approached to pay homage to him, Absalom reached out his hand, took hold of him, and kissed him.[b] [6] Absalom did this to all the Israelites who came to the king for a settlement. So Absalom stole the hearts of the men of Israel.

[7] When four[A] years had passed, Absalom said to the king, "Please let me go to Hebron to fulfill a vow I made to the Lord. [8] For your servant made a vow when I lived in Geshur of Aram,[c] saying: If the Lord really brings me back to Jerusalem, I will worship the Lord in Hebron."[B,d] [9] "Go in peace," the king said to him.[e] So he went to Hebron.

[10] Then Absalom sent agents throughout the tribes of Israel with this message: "When you hear the sound of the ram's horn,[f] you are to say, 'Absalom has become king in Hebron!'"[g] [11] Two hundred men from Jerusalem went with Absalom. They had been invited and were going innocently, for they did not know the whole situation. [12] While he was offering the sacrifices, Absalom sent for David's adviser Ahithophel the Gilonite,[h] from his city of Giloh. So the conspiracy grew strong, and the people supporting Absalom continued to increase.

[13] Then an informer came to David and reported, "The hearts of the men of Israel are with Absalom." [14] David said to all the servants with him in Jerusalem, "Get up. We have to flee, or we will not escape from Absalom![i] Leave quickly, or he will overtake us quickly, heap disaster on us, and strike the city with the edge of the sword."

[15] The king's servants said to the king, "Whatever my lord the king decides, we are your servants." [16] Then the king set out, and his entire household followed him. But he left behind ten concubines to take care of the palace. [17] So the king set out, and all the people followed him. They stopped at the last house [18] while all his servants marched past him. Then all the Cherethites, the Pelethites, and the people of Gath— six hundred men who came with him from there[j] — marched past the king.

[19] The king said to Ittai of Gath,[k] "Why are you also going with us? Go back and stay with the new king since you're both a foreigner and an exile from your homeland. [20] Besides, you only arrived yesterday; should I make you wander around with us today while I go wherever I can? Go back and take your brothers with you. May the Lord show you[c] kindness and faithfulness."

[21] But in response, Ittai vowed to the king, "As the Lord lives and as my lord the king lives, wherever my lord the king is, whether it means life or death, your servant will be there!"[l]

[22] "March on," David replied to Ittai. So Ittai of Gath marched past with all his men and the dependents who were with him. [23] Everyone in the countryside was weeping loudly while all the people were marching out of the city. As the king was crossing the Kidron Valley, all the people were marching past on the road that leads to the wilderness.

[24] Zadok was also there, and all the Levites with him were carrying the ark of the covenant of God. They set the ark of God down, and Abiathar offered sacrifices[D] until the people had finished marching past.[m] [25] Then the king instructed Zadok, "Return the ark of God to the city.[n] If I find favor with the Lord, he will

---

[A] 15:7 Some LXX mss, Syr, Vg; other LXX mss, MT read 40   [B] 15:8 Some LXX mss; MT omits in Hebron   [C] 15:20 LXX; MT omits Lit May the Lord show you   [D] 15:24 Or Abiathar went up

---

time, Absalom **stole the hearts of the men of Israel** (15:6).

15:7-12 After **four years** of conniving, Absalom had himself proclaimed king. The insurrection was in full swing.

15:13-14 Word of the rebellion reached David, and he instantly ordered an evacuation of his entire household from Jerusalem—to avoid bloodshed and to spare Jerusalem from certain destruction.

15:16 This detail regarding the **concubines** is sadly important because it would become part of God's judgment on David for his sins (see 12:11-12).

15:23 The sight of the king, his household, and troops on the run from Absalom caused **all the people** in the **countryside** to weep **loudly**. The king of Israel was going into exile.

15:24-26 David insisted that the Levites **return the ark of God to the city.** Though

the king was on the run, he was firmly convinced that God's throne should not. **If I find favor with the Lord**, David said, **he will bring me back and allow me to see both it and its dwelling place** (15:25). In other words, David was leaving his fate in the hands of his sovereign God.

bring me back and allow me to see both it and its^A dwelling place.^a 26 However, if he should say, 'I do not delight in you,' then here I am — he can do with me whatever pleases him."^B,b

27 The king also said to the priest Zadok,^c "Look,^c return to the city in peace and your two sons with you: your son Ahimaaz and Abiathar's son Jonathan. 28 Remember, I'll wait at the fords^D of the wilderness until word comes from you to inform me." 29 So Zadok and Abiathar returned the ark of God to Jerusalem and stayed there.

30 David was climbing the slope of the Mount of Olives,^d weeping as he ascended. His head was covered,^e and he was walking barefoot.^f All of the people with him covered their heads and went up, weeping as they ascended.

31 Then someone reported to David: "Ahithophel is among the conspirators with Absalom."

"Lord," David pleaded, "please turn the counsel of Ahithophel into foolishness!"^g

32 When David came to the summit where he used to worship God, Hushai the Archite^h was there to meet him with his robe torn and dust on his head. 33 David said to him, "If you go away with me, you'll be a burden to me, 34 but if you return to the city and tell Absalom, 'I will be your servant, Your Majesty! Previously, I was your father's servant, but now I will be your servant,' then you can counteract Ahithophel's counsel for me. 35 Won't the priests Zadok and Abiathar be there with you? Report everything you hear from the palace to the priests Zadok and Abiathar. 36 Take note: their two sons are there with them—Zadok's son Ahimaaz and Abiathar's son Jonathan. Send them to tell me everything you hear." 37 So Hushai,^i David's personal adviser, entered Jerusalem just as Absalom was entering the city.

ZIBA HELPS DAVID

16 When David had gone a little beyond the summit,^E Ziba, Mephibosheth's servant,^i was right there to meet him. He had a pair of saddled donkeys loaded with two hundred loaves of bread, one hundred clusters of raisins, one hundred bunches of summer fruit, and a clay jar of wine. 2 The king said to Ziba, "Why do you have these?"

Ziba answered, "The donkeys are for the king's household to ride, the bread and summer fruit are for the young men to eat, and the wine is for those to drink who become exhausted in the wilderness."

3 "Where is your master's grandson?" the king asked.

"Why, he's staying in Jerusalem," Ziba replied to the king, "for he said, 'Today, the house of Israel will restore my grandfather's kingdom to me.'"^k

4 The king said to Ziba, "All that belongs to Mephibosheth is now yours!"^l

"I bow before you," Ziba said. "May I find favor with you, my lord the king!"

SHIMEI CURSES DAVID

5 When King David got to Bahurim, a man belonging to the family of the house of Saul was just coming out.^m His name was Shimei son of Gera,^n and he was yelling curses as he approached. 6 He threw stones at David and at all the royal^F servants, the people and the warriors on David's right and left. 7 Shimei said as he cursed: "Get out, get out, you man of bloodshed, you wicked man!^o 8 The Lord has paid you back for all the blood of the house of Saul in whose place you became king, and the Lord has handed the kingdom over to your son Absalom. Look, you are in trouble because you're a man of bloodshed!"

9 Then Abishai son of Zeruiah said to the king, "Why should this dead dog^p curse my lord the king?^q Let me go over and remove his head!"

^a 15:25 Ps 43:3
^b 15:26 1Sm 3:18
^c 15:27 2Sm 8:17; 20:25-26; 1Kg 1:7-8
^d 15:30 Zch 14:4; Mt 21:1; 24:3; 26:30; Ac 1:12
^e Est 6:12; Jr 14:3-4
^f Jb 12:17,19; Is 20:2-4; Mc 1:8
^g 15:31 2Sm 16:21; 17:14,23
^h 15:32 Jos 16:2
^i 15:37 1Ch 27:33

^j 16:1 2Sm 9:12
^k 16:3 2Sm 19:26-27
^l 16:4 2Sm 9:3-11
^m 16:5 2Sm 3:16
^n 2Sm 19:16; 1Kg 2:8-9,36-46
^o 16:7 Ex 22:28
^p 16:9 1Sm 24:14; 2Sm 9:8
^q Ex 22:28

---

^A 15:25 Or *his*   ^B 15:26 Lit *me what is good in his eyes*   ^C 15:27 LXX; MT reads *"Are you a seer?*   ^D 15:28 Alt Hb tradition reads *plains*
^E 16:1 = Mount of Olives   ^F 16:6 Lit *all King David's*

15:32-37 The king realized that Hushai would be the perfect person to send back to Jerusalem under the guise of joining the conspiracy and offering his counsel to Absalom. He could **counteract Ahithophel's** savvy advice and also gather valuable intelligence to send to David through the priests (15:33-36). This gave David the eyes and ears he desperately needed in Jerusalem to find out what Absalom's plans were. God was answering David's prayer recorded in verse 31.

16:3 Ziba was accusing Mephibosheth of treason (see 9:8-9). Later, Mephibosheth would testify that Ziba had slandered him to the king (see 19:24-30).
16:5-8 Though David had done no violence to Saul or his family, Shimei falsely accused him of being responsible **for all the blood of the house of Saul** (16:8).
16:9 Abishai suggested killing Shimei for his bad behavior, and this wasn't the first time he'd leaped to violence as a solution. Years

before, Abishai had urged David to kill King Saul when he had the opportunity (see 1 Sam 26:7-11).

16:10-11 David took Shimei's cursing as a rebuke from God, which he needed to hear. After all, though he was not guilty of Saul's blood, David was indeed guilty of sinful bloodshed (see 11:14-27). Besides, he had much bigger issues to worry about than this man yelling at him.

^a16:10 2Sm 3:39; 19:22
^b1Sm 17:43; 2Sm 16:5; Ec 7:21-22
^c2Sm 12:11
^d16:11 2Sm 12:10-11
^e16:16 1Sm 10:24; 1Kg 1:25; 2Kg 11:12
^f16:19 2Sm 15:34
^g16:21 2Sm 15:16; 20:3

^h16:22 2Sm 12:11-12
ⁱ16:23 2Sm 15:12
^j17:2 1Kg 22:31
^k17:8 Pr 17:12; Hs 13:8
^l17:10 Am 3:8

10 The king replied, "Sons of Zeruiah, do we agree on anything?^a He curses^b me this way because the LORD^A told him, 'Curse David!'^c Therefore, who can say, 'Why did you do that?' " **11** Then David said to Abishai and all his servants, "Look, my own son, my own flesh and blood,^B intends to take my life^d—how much more now this Benjaminite! Leave him alone and let him curse me; the LORD has told him to. **12** Perhaps the LORD will see my affliction^c and restore goodness to me instead of Shimei's curses today." **13** So David and his men proceeded along the road as Shimei was going along the ridge of the hill opposite him. As Shimei went, he cursed David, threw stones at him, and kicked up dust. **14** Finally, the king and all the people with him arrived^D exhausted, so they rested there.

ABSALOM'S ADVISERS

15 Now Absalom and all the Israelites came to Jerusalem. Ahithophel was also with him. **16** When David's friend Hushai the Archite came to Absalom, Hushai said to Absalom, "Long live the king! Long live the king!"^e

17 "Is this your loyalty to your friend?" Absalom asked Hushai. "Why didn't you go with your friend?"

18 "Not at all," Hushai answered Absalom. "I am on the side of the one that the LORD, this people, and all the men of Israel have chosen. I will stay with him. **19** Furthermore, whom will I serve if not his son? As I served in your father's presence, I will also serve in yours."^f

20 Then Absalom said to Ahithophel, "Give me your advice. What should we do?"

21 Ahithophel replied to Absalom, "Sleep with your father's concubines whom he left to take care of the palace.^g When all Israel hears that you have become repulsive to your father, everyone with you will be encouraged."^E **22** So they pitched a tent for Absalom on the roof, and he slept with his father's concubines in the sight of all Israel.^h

23 Now the advice Ahithophel gave in those days was like someone asking about a word from Godⁱ—such was the regard that both David and Absalom had for Ahithophel's advice. **1** Ahithophel said to Absalom, "Let me choose twelve thousand men, and I will set out in pursuit of David tonight. **2** I will attack him while he is weary and discouraged,^F throw him into a panic, and all the people with him will scatter. I will strike down only the king^j **3** and bring all the people back to you. When everyone returns except the man you're looking for, all^G the people will be at peace." **4** This proposal seemed right to Absalom and all the elders of Israel.

5 Then Absalom said, "Summon Hushai the Archite also. Let's hear what he has to say as well."

6 So Hushai came to Absalom, and Absalom told him: "Ahithophel offered this proposal. Should we carry out his proposal? If not, what do you say?"

7 Hushai replied to Absalom, "The advice Ahithophel has given this time is not good." **8** Hushai continued, "You know your father and his men. They are warriors and are desperate like a wild bear robbed of her cubs.^k Your father is an experienced soldier who won't spend the night with the people. **9** He's probably already hiding in one of the caves^H or some other place. If some of our troops fallⁱ first, someone is sure to hear and say, 'There's been a slaughter among the people who follow Absalom.' **10** Then, even a brave man with the heart of a lionⁱ will lose heart^j because all Israel knows that your father and the valiant men with him are

^A16:10 Alt Hb tradition reads *If he curses, and if the LORD*   ^B16:11 Lit *son who came from my belly*   ^C16:12 Some Hb mss, LXX, Syr, Vg; one Hb tradition reads *iniquity* ; alt Hb tradition reads *eyes* ; another Hb tradition reads *will look with his eye*   ^D16:14 LXX adds *at the Jordan*   ^E16:21 Lit *father, the hands of everyone with you will be strong*   ^F17:2 Lit *and weak of hands*   ^G17:3 LXX reads *to you as a bride returns to her husband. You seek the life of only one man, and all*   ^H17:9 Or *pits, or ravines*   ⁱ17:9 Lit *And it will be when a falling on them at*   ^J17:10 Lit *melt*

16:15, 23 In Jerusalem, David's former trusted adviser **Ahithophel** was at Absalom's side. Getting Ahithophel to switch off of David was a big coup as far as Absalom was concerned because **the advice Ahithophel gave . . . was like someone asking about a word from God** (16:23). But God was going to thwart his counsel and use it against Absalom.

16:21 In publicly taking the king's harem as his own, Absalom would demonstrate to all that he was claiming the throne and would

humiliate David, ending any possibility of reconciliation.

17:5-7 In God's providence, Absalom asked to hear Hushai's counsel too regarding when and how David should be pursued (17:5-6). Hushai no doubt agreed that Ahithophel's advice (17:1-3) was sound. That's why, as David's friend, he immediately declared that it was **not good** (17:7).

17:8-14 Hushai's reasons for rejecting Ahithophel's plan for an immediate attack were a stroke of storytelling genius (17:8-13). Hushai

did a masterful job of instilling fear and raising doubt about Ahithophel's advice.

When Absalom took the bait suggesting that he personally lead his troops against his father (17:11), he didn't know that **the LORD had decreed that Ahithophel's good advice be undermined in order to bring about Absalom's ruin** (17:14). This brings to mind the truth that "A king's heart is like channeled water in the Lord's hand: He directs it wherever he chooses" (Prov 21:1).

warriors. **11** Instead, I advise that all Israel from Dan to Beer-sheba — as numerous as the sand by the sea[a] — be gathered to you and that you personally go into battle. **12** Then we will attack David wherever we find him, and we will descend on him like dew on the ground. Not even one will be left—neither he nor any of the men with him. **13** If he retreats to some city, all Israel will bring ropes to that city, and we will drag its stones[A] into the valley until not even a pebble can be found there." **14** Since the Lord had decreed[b] that Ahithophel's good advice be undermined[c] in order to bring about Absalom's ruin, Absalom and all the men of Israel said, "The advice of Hushai the Archite is better than Ahithophel's advice."

DAVID INFORMED OF ABSALOM'S PLANS

15 Hushai then told the priests Zadok and Abiathar, "This is what[B] Ahithophel advised Absalom and the elders of Israel, and this is what[c] I advised. **16** Now send someone quickly and tell David, 'Don't spend the night at the wilderness ford,[D] but be sure to cross over the Jordan,[E,d] or the king and all the people with him will be devoured.' "

17 Jonathan and Ahimaaz were staying at En-rogel, where a servant girl would come and pass along information to them. They in turn would go and inform King David, because they dared not be seen entering the city. **18** However, a young man did see them and informed Absalom. So the two left quickly and came to the house of a man in Bahurim. He had a well in his courtyard, and they climbed down into it. **19** Then his wife took the cover, placed it over the mouth of the well, and scattered grain on it so nobody would know anything. **20** Absalom's servants came to the woman at the house and asked, "Where are Ahimaaz and Jonathan?"

"They passed by toward the water,"[F] the woman replied to them. The men searched but did not find them, so they returned to Jerusalem.

21 After they had gone, Ahimaaz and Jonathan climbed out of the well and went and informed King David. They told him, "Get up and immediately ford the river, for Ahithophel has given this advice against you." **22** So David and all the people with him got up and crossed the Jordan. By daybreak, there was no one who had not crossed the Jordan. **23** When Ahithophel realized that his advice had not been followed, he saddled his donkey and set out for his house in his hometown. He set his house in order and hanged himself.[e] So he died and was buried in his father's tomb.

24 David had arrived at Mahanaim by the time Absalom crossed the Jordan with all the men of Israel. **25** Now Absalom had appointed Amasa[f] over the army in Joab's place. Amasa was the son of a man named Ithra[G] the Israelite;[H,g] Ithra had married Abigail daughter of Nahash.[i] Abigail was a sister to Zeruiah, Joab's mother. **26** And Israel and Absalom camped in the land of Gilead. **27** When David came to Mahanaim, Shobi son of Nahash[h] from Rabbah[j] of the Ammonites, Machir son of Ammiel from Lo-debar,[J] and Barzillai the Gileadite from Rogelim[K] **28** brought beds, basins,[J] and pottery items. They also brought wheat, barley, flour, roasted grain, beans, lentils,[K] **29** honey, curds, sheep, goats, and cheese[L] from the herd for David and the people with him to eat. They had reasoned, "The people must be hungry, exhausted, and thirsty in the wilderness."

ABSALOM'S DEFEAT

18 David reviewed his troops and appointed commanders of thousands and of hundreds over them. **2** He then sent out the troops, a third under Joab, a third under Joab's brother Abishai son of Zeruiah, and a third under Ittai of Gath. The king said to the troops, "I must also march out with you."

3 "You must not go!"[J] the people pleaded. "If we have to flee, they will not pay

[a] 17:11 Gn 22:17
[b] 17:14 Pr 21:30; 1Co 1:19
[c] 2Sm 15:31-34
[d] 17:16 2Sm 15:28

[e] 17:23 Mt 27:5
[f] 17:25 2Sm 19:13; 20:9-12; 1Kg 2:5,32
[g] 1Ch 2:13-17
[h] 17:27 2Sm 10:1-2
[i] 2Sm 12:26-29
[j] 2Sm 9:4
[k] 2Sm 19:31-32; 1Kg 2:7; Ezr 2:61
[l] 18:3 2Sm 21:17

[A] 17:13 Lit *drag it*   [B] 17:15 Lit *"Like this and like this*   [c] 17:15 Lit *and like this and like this*   [D] 17:16 Some Hb mss; MT reads *plains*   [E] 17:16 *the Jordan* supplied for clarity   [F] 17:20 Or *brook*; Hb obscure   [G] 17:25 Or *Jether*   [H] 17:25 Some LXX mss read *Ishmaelite*   [i] 17:25 Some LXX mss read *Jesse*   [J] 17:28 LXX reads *brought 10 embroidered beds with double coverings, 10 vessels*   [K] 17:28 LXX, Syr; MT adds *roasted grain*   [L] 17:29 Hb obscure

---

17:15-16 Even though Hushai had undercut Ahithophel's counsel, Absalom was still a threat. Placing distance between the king and his usurper was wise.

17:23 Ahithophel knew that Absalom was a fool for preferring Hushai's plan. It would only be a matter of time before David regained the throne. And when that happened, Ahithophel would be executed for rebellion.

17:25 Absalom's new commander **Amasa** was related to David and his commander Joab.

18:3-4 The people **pleaded** with David, reasoning that if David died their whole cause would be lost (18:3), until he relented in his plan to fight alongside them (18:4). Thus, David would not be on the battlefield when Absalom faced the inevitable consequences of his actions.

[a] 18:12 2Sm 18:5
[b] 18:17 Jos 7:24-26; 8:29
[c] 1Sm 4:10; 2Sm 19:8;
20:1,22; 2Kg 8:21
[d] 18:18 Gn 28:18; Dt 16:22;
1Sm 15:12; 2Kg 18:4
[e] Gn 14:17
[f] 2Sm 14:27
[g] 18:19 2Sm 15:36
[h] 18:24 2Sm 15:8
[i] 2Sm 13:34; 2Kg 9:17

any attention to us. Even if half of us die, they will not pay any attention to us because you are worth[A] ten thousand of us. Therefore, it is better if you support us from the city."

4 "I will do whatever you think is best," the king replied to them. So he stood beside the city gate while all the troops marched out by hundreds and thousands. 5 The king commanded Joab, Abishai, and Ittai, "Treat the young man Absalom gently for my sake." All the people heard the king's orders to all the commanders about Absalom.

6 Then David's forces marched into the field to engage Israel in battle, which took place in the forest of Ephraim. 7 Israel's army was defeated by David's soldiers, and the slaughter there was vast that day — twenty thousand dead. 8 The battle spread over the entire area, and that day the forest claimed more people than the sword.

ABSALOM'S DEATH

9 Absalom was riding on his mule when he happened to meet David's soldiers. When the mule went under the tangled branches of a large oak tree, Absalom's head was caught fast in the tree. The mule under him kept going, so he was suspended in midair.[B] 10 One of the men saw him and informed Joab. He said, "I just saw Absalom hanging in an oak tree!"

11 "You just saw him!" Joab exclaimed.[C] "Why didn't you strike him to the ground right there? I would have given you ten silver pieces[D] and a belt!"

12 The man replied to Joab, "Even if I had the weight of a thousand pieces of silver[E] in my hand, I would not raise my hand against the king's son. For we heard the king command you, Abishai, and Ittai, 'Protect the young man Absalom for me.'[F,a] 13 If I had jeopardized my own[G] life — and nothing is hidden from the king — you would have abandoned me."

14 Joab said, "I'm not going to waste time with you!" He then took three spears in his hand and thrust them into Absalom's chest. While Absalom was still alive in the oak tree, 15 ten young men who were Joab's armor-bearers surrounded Absalom, struck him, and killed him. 16 Joab blew the ram's horn, and the troops broke off their pursuit of Israel because Joab restrained them. 17 They took Absalom, threw him into a large pit in the forest, and raised up a huge mound of stones over him.[b] And all Israel fled, each to his tent.[c]

18 When he was alive, Absalom had taken a pillar and raised it up[d] for himself in the King's Valley,[e] since he thought, "I have no son[f] to preserve the memory of my name." So he named the pillar after himself. It is still called Absalom's Monument today.

19 Ahimaaz son of Zadok[g] said, "Please let me run and tell the king the good news that the LORD has vindicated him by freeing him from his enemies."

20 Joab replied to him, "You are not the man to take good news today. You may do it another day, but today you aren't taking good news, because the king's son is dead." 21 Joab then said to a Cushite, "Go tell the king what you have seen." The Cushite bowed to Joab and took off running.

22 However, Ahimaaz son of Zadok persisted and said to Joab, "No matter what, please let me also run behind the Cushite!"

Joab replied, "My son, why do you want to run since you won't get a reward?"[H]

23 "No matter what, I want to run!"

"Then run!" Joab said to him. So Ahimaaz ran by way of the plain and outran the Cushite.

24 David was sitting between the city gates[h] when the watchman went up to the roof of the city gate and over to the wall.[i] The watchman looked out and saw a man running alone. 25 He called out and told the king.

The king said, "If he's alone, he bears good news."

As the first runner came closer, 26 the watchman saw another man running. He called out to the gatekeeper, "Look! Another man is running alone!"

[A] 18:3 Some Hb mss, LXX, Vg; other Hb mss read *because there would now be about*   [B] 18:9 Lit *was between heaven and earth*   [C] 18:11 Lit *Joab said to the man who told him*   [D] 18:11 About four ounces of silver   [E] 18:12 About 25 pounds of silver   [F] 18:12 Some Hb mss, LXX, Tg, Vg; other Hb mss read *'Protect, whoever, the young man Absalom'*; Hb obscure   [G] 18:13 Alt Hb tradition reads *jeopardized his*   [H] 18:22 Or *you have no good news?*

18:5 Even on the verge of a battle that would determine the future of his kingdom, David told his three commanders, **Treat the young man Absalom gently**. David's rebel son was forefront in his mind.

18:8-9 The treacherous nature of the wooded area played a significant role in the battle when Absalom's head—perhaps because of his long hair—became caught in **the tangled branches of a large oak tree**, leaving him suspended in midair (18:9).

18:12, 14 The man didn't want to harm Absalom given David's clear instructions (18:12; see 18:5). Joab had no such qualms (18:14).

18:16 Once the leader of the rebellion was dead, **Joab blew the ram's horn** to call his soldiers back from the battle.

18:19-20 Ahimaaz was too young to know what happened to messengers who brought David that kind of **good** news (18:19; see 1:1-16; 4:5-12).

"This one is also bringing good news," said the king.

27 The watchman said, "The way the first man runs looks to me like the way Ahimaaz son of Zadok runs."[a]

"This is a good man; he comes with good news,"[b] the king commented.

28 Ahimaaz called out to the king, "All is well," and paid homage to the king with his face to the ground. He continued, "Blessed be the LORD your God! He delivered up the men who rebelled against my lord the king."

29 The king asked, "Is the young man Absalom all right?"

Ahimaaz replied, "When Joab sent the king's servant and your servant, I saw a big disturbance, but I don't know what it was."

30 The king said, "Move aside and stand here." So he stood to one side.

31 Just then the Cushite came and said, "May my lord the king hear the good news: The LORD has vindicated you today by freeing you from all who rise against you!"

32 The king asked the Cushite, "Is the young man Absalom all right?"

The Cushite replied, "I wish that the enemies of my lord the king, along with all who rise up against you with evil intent, would become like that young man."[c]

33 The king was deeply moved and went up to the chamber above the city gate and wept. As he walked, he cried, "My son Absalom! My son, my son Absalom! If only I had died instead of you, Absalom, my son, my son!"[d]

DAVID'S KINGDOM RESTORED

19 It was reported to Joab, "The king is weeping. He's mourning over Absalom." **2** That day's victory was turned into mourning for all the troops because on that day the troops heard, "The king is grieving over his son." **3** So they returned to the city quietly that day like troops come in when they are humiliated after fleeing in battle. **4** But the king covered his face[e] and cried loudly, "My son Absalom! Absalom, my son, my son!"

5 Then Joab went into the house to the king and said, "Today you have shamed all your soldiers — those who saved your life as well as your sons, your wives, and your concubines — **6** by loving your enemies and hating those who love you! Today you have made it clear that the commanders and soldiers mean nothing to you. In fact, today I know that if Absalom were alive and all of us were dead, it would be fine with you![A]

7 "Now get up! Go out and encourage[B] your soldiers, for I swear by the LORD that if you don't go out, not a man will remain with you tonight.[f] This will be worse for you than all the trouble that has come to you from your youth until now!"

8 So the king got up and sat in the city gate,[g] and all the people were told: "Look, the king is sitting in the city gate." Then they all came into the king's presence.

Meanwhile, each Israelite had fled to his tent.[h] **9** People throughout all the tribes of Israel were arguing among themselves, saying, "The king rescued us from the grasp of our enemies,[i] and he saved us from the grasp of the Philistines,[j] but now he has fled from the land because of Absalom.[k] **10** But Absalom, the man we anointed over us, has died in battle. So why do you say nothing about restoring the king?"

11 King David sent word to the priests Zadok and Abiathar:[l] "Say to the elders of Judah, 'Why should you be the last to restore the king to his palace? The talk of all Israel has reached the king at his house. **12** You are my brothers, my flesh and blood.[C,m] So why should you be the last to restore the king?' **13** And tell Amasa,[n] 'Aren't you my

---

[a] 18:27 2Kg 9:20
[b] 1Kg 1:42
[c] 18:32 1Sm 25:26
[d] 18:33 2Sm 19:4

[e] 19:4 2Sm 15:30
[f] 19:7 Pr 14:28
[g] 19:8 2Sm 18:4,24,33
[h] 2Sm 18:17
[i] 19:9 2Sm 8:1-14
[j] 2Sm 5:20; 8:1
[k] 2Sm 15:14
[l] 19:11 2Sm 15:29
[m] 19:12 Gn 29:14; 2Sm 5:1
[n] 19:13 2Sm 17:25

[A] 19:6 Lit be right in your eyes   [B] 19:7 Lit speak to the heart of   [C] 19:12 Lit my bone and my flesh

---

18:29 Ahimaaz knew the answer to David's question (see 18:19-20), but he pulled back and blew smoke instead: **I saw a big disturbance, but I don't know what it was.** Whether he'd planned all along to let the Cushite be the bearer of the bad news or just lost his nerve when King David looked him in the eye, the hanging question would soon be answered.

18:31-33 Given the manner in which he announced the news, the Cushite assumed that David would be overjoyed at what had happened to this **young man** who rose up against him **with evil intent** (18:32). But David went to his **chamber** and **wept**, overwhelmed with grief (18:33). David's kingdom had been spared, but his rebel son had not.

19:2-3 Thousands of brave men had just put their lives on the line to save David, his family, and his throne. Likely many had died. Although a parent's grief over the death of a child—even an estranged one—is understandable, David was on the verge of communicating the wrong message to his supporters.

19:5-7 In other words, David would have a serious morale and loyalty problem on his hands if he didn't pull himself together.

19:9-10 With Absalom dead, the northern tribes of Israel faced a dilemma. They had rallied behind Absalom, but with the throne now empty, they had to ask whether they should invite David to return. Opinions were divided. Some of the people argued that

David had been an effective leader in the past and should be restored. But others were hesitant, possibly because they had backed Absalom and worried about reprisals.

19:11-12 David sensed that the place to start in recovering his throne was with **Judah** (19:11). If any tribe was going to **restore the king**, it should be his own (19:12). If Judah delayed, it would send the wrong message to the nation.

19:13-14 Absalom had appointed **Amasa** over his army; thus, David was demonstrating that he bore no animosity toward those who had sided with Absalom. Furthermore, the demotion of Joab was no doubt a response to Joab's execution of Absalom—something he'd done against the king's order. This gesture **won over all the men of Judah** (19:14).

a 19:16 2Sm 16:5; 1Kg 2:8
b 19:17 2Sm 16:1-4
c 19:19 2Sm 16:5-13
d 19:21 Ex 22:28
e 19:22 2Sm 3:39; 16:10
f 19:23 1Kg 2:8-9,37,46
g 19:24 2Sm 9:6

h 19:26 2Sm 4:4; 9:3
i 19:27 2Sm 16:1-4
j 2Sm 14:17,20
k 19:28 2Sm 9:1-13
l 19:29 2Sm 9:9; 16:4
m 19:31 1Kg 2:7
n 19:32 2Sm 17:27-29
o 19:35 Ps 90:10
p 2Sm 15:33

flesh and blood?[A] May God punish me and do so severely if you don't become commander of my army from now on instead of Joab!'"

¹⁴ So he won over[B] all the men of Judah, and they unanimously sent word to the king: "Come back, you and all your servants." ¹⁵ Then the king returned. When he arrived at the Jordan, Judah came to Gilgal to meet the king and escort him across the Jordan.

¹⁶ Shimei son of Gera,[a] the Benjaminite from Bahurim, hurried down with the men of Judah to meet King David. ¹⁷ There were a thousand men from Benjamin with him. Ziba, an attendant from the house of Saul,[b] with his fifteen sons and twenty servants also rushed down to the Jordan ahead of the king. ¹⁸ They forded the Jordan to bring the king's household across and do whatever the king desired.[c]

When Shimei son of Gera crossed the Jordan, he fell facedown before the king ¹⁹ and said to him, "My lord, don't hold me guilty, and don't remember your servant's wrongdoing on the day my lord the king left Jerusalem.[c] May the king not take it to heart. ²⁰ For your servant knows that I have sinned. But look! Today I am the first one of the entire house of Joseph to come down to meet my lord the king."

²¹ Abishai son of Zeruiah asked, "Shouldn't Shimei be put to death for this, because he cursed the LORD's anointed?"[d]

²² David answered, "Sons of Zeruiah, do we agree on anything?[e] Have you become my adversary today? Should any man be killed in Israel today? Am I not aware that today I'm king over Israel?" ²³ So the king said to Shimei, "You will not die." Then the king gave him his oath.[f]

²⁴ Mephibosheth,[g] Saul's grandson, also went down to meet the king. He had not taken care of his feet, trimmed his mustache, or washed his clothes from the day the king left until the day he returned safely. ²⁵ When he came from Jerusalem to meet the king, the king asked him, "Mephibosheth, why didn't you come with me?"

²⁶ "My lord the king," he replied, "my servant Ziba betrayed me. Actually your servant said: 'I'll saddle the donkey for myself[D] so that I may ride it and go with the king'—for your servant is lame.[h] ²⁷ Ziba slandered your servant to my lord the king.[i] But my lord the king is like the angel of God,[j] so do whatever you think best.[E] ²⁸ For my grandfather's entire family deserves death from my lord the king, but you set your servant among those who eat at your table.[k] So what further right do I have to keep on making appeals to the king?"

²⁹ The king said to him, "Why keep on speaking about these matters of yours? I hereby declare: you and Ziba are to divide the land."[l]

³⁰ Mephibosheth said to the king, "Instead, since my lord the king has come to his palace safely, let Ziba take it all!"

³¹ Barzillai the Gileadite[m] had come down from Rogelim and accompanied the king to the Jordan River to see him off at the Jordan. ³² Barzillai was a very old man—eighty years old—and since he was a very wealthy man, he had provided for the needs of the king while he stayed in Mahanaim.[n]

³³ The king said to Barzillai, "Cross over with me, and I'll provide for you[E] at my side in Jerusalem."

³⁴ Barzillai replied to the king, "How many years of my life are left that I should go up to Jerusalem with the king? ³⁵ I'm now eighty years old.[o] Can I discern what is pleasant and what is not? Can your servant taste what he eats or drinks? Can I still hear the voice of male and female singers? Why should your servant be an added burden to my lord the king?[p] ³⁶ Since your servant is only going with the king a little way across the Jordan, why should the king repay me with such a reward? ³⁷ Please let your servant return so that I may die in my own city near the tomb of my father and mother. But here

[A] 19:13 Lit *my bone and my flesh?*   [B] 19:14 Lit *he turned the heart of*   [C] 19:18 Lit *do what is good in his eyes*   [D] 19:26 LXX, Syr, Vg read *said to him, 'Saddle the donkey for me*   [E] 19:27 Lit *do what is good in your eyes*   [F] 19:33 LXX reads *for your old age*; Ru 4:15

19:16-17 During King David's triumphant return trip to Jerusalem, Shimei showed up with **a thousand men from Benjamin**, showing that Saul's tribe was attempting to link itself with Judah now that David was fully in control of the throne again (19:17). **19:20** Shimei said he was **the first one of the entire house of Joseph** to welcome David back. This was a reference to the large tribe of Ephraim, Joseph's son, standing for the northern tribes of Israel as a whole. **19:23** David granted his former attacker a stay of execution (but see 1 Kgs 2:8-9). **19:24-30** Given the competing claims between Mephibosheth and Ziba, David divided the estate between them (19:29). **19:31-37 Barzillai** had **provided for the needs of the king** during his brief exile (19:31-32). David wanted him to go to **Jerusalem** with him so he could take care of him, but aged Barzillai wanted to live out his remaining years at home. He asked that David take **Chimham**, possibly Barzillai's son, to enjoy whatever reward David intended (19:33-37).

is your servant Chimham:[a] let him cross over with my lord the king. Do for him what seems good to you."[A]

38 The king replied, "Chimham will cross over with me, and I will do for him what seems good to you, and whatever you desire from me I will do for you." **39** So all the people crossed the Jordan, and then the king crossed. The king kissed Barzillai and blessed him, and Barzillai returned to his home.

40 The king went on to Gilgal, and Chimham went with him. All the troops of Judah and half of Israel's escorted the king. **41** Suddenly, all the men of Israel came to the king. They asked him, "Why did our brothers, the men of Judah, take you away secretly and transport the king and his household across the Jordan, along with all of David's men?"

42 All the men of Judah responded to the men of Israel, "Because the king is our relative. Why does this make you angry? Have we ever eaten anything of the king's or been honored at all?"[B]

43 The men of Israel answered the men of Judah: "We have ten shares in the king,[b] so we have a greater claim to David than you. Why then do you despise us? Weren't we the first to speak of restoring our king?"[c] But the words of the men of Judah were harsher than those of the men of Israel.

SHEBA'S REVOLT

20 Now a wicked man, a Benjaminite named Sheba son of Bichri, happened to be there. He blew the ram's horn and shouted:

We have no portion in David,
no inheritance in Jesse's son.
Each man to his tent,[c] Israel!

2 So all the men of Israel deserted David and followed Sheba son of Bichri, but the men of Judah from the Jordan all the way to Jerusalem remained loyal to their king.[d]

3 When David came to his palace in Jerusalem, he took the ten concubines he had left to take care of the palace and placed them under guard.[e] He provided for them,

but he was not intimate with them. They were confined until the day of their death, living as widows.

4 The king said to Amasa, "Summon the men of Judah to me within three days and be here yourself." **5** Amasa went to summon Judah, but he took longer than the time allotted him. **6** So David said to Abishai, "Sheba son of Bichri will do more harm to us than Absalom. Take your lord's soldiers and pursue him, or he will find fortified cities and elude us."[D]

7 So Joab's men, the Cherethites, the Pelethites, and all the warriors marched out under Abishai's command;[E] they left Jerusalem to pursue Sheba son of Bichri. **8** They were at the great stone in Gibeon when Amasa joined them. Joab was wearing his uniform and over it was a belt around his waist with a sword in its sheath. As he approached, the sword fell out. **9** Joab asked Amasa, "Are you well, my brother?" Then with his right hand Joab grabbed Amasa by the beard to kiss him.[f] **10** Amasa was not on guard against the sword in Joab's hand, and Joab stabbed him in the stomach with it and spilled his intestines out on the ground. Joab did not stab him again, and Amasa died.[g]

Joab and his brother Abishai pursued Sheba son of Bichri. **11** One of Joab's young men had stood over Amasa saying, "Whoever favors Joab and whoever is for David, follow Joab!" **12** Now Amasa had been writhing in his blood in the middle of the highway, and the man had seen that all the troops stopped. So he moved Amasa from the highway to the field and threw a garment over him because he realized that all those who encountered Amasa were stopping. **13** When he was removed from the highway, all the men passed by and followed Joab to pursue Sheba son of Bichri.

14 Sheba passed through all the tribes of Israel to Abel of Beth-maacah. All the Berites[F] came together and followed him. **15** Joab's troops came and besieged Sheba in Abel of Beth-maacah. They built a siege ramp[h] against the outer wall of the city.

[a] 19:37 1Kg 2:7; Jr 41:17
[b] 19:43 1Kg 11:31
[c] 2Sm 19:9-10
[d] 20:1-2 1Kg 12:16-17
[e] 20:3 2Sm 15:16; 16:21-22

[f] 20:9 Mt 26:49; Mk 14:45; Lk 22:47
[g] 20:10 1Kg 2:5
[h] 20:15 2Kg 19:32; Is 37:33; Jr 6:6; Ezk 4:2; 26:8

[A] 19:37 Lit *what is good in your eyes*, also in v. 38   [B] 19:42 LXX reads *king's or has he given us a gift or granted us a portion*   [C] 20:1 Alt Hb tradition reads *gods*   [D] 20:6 Lit *and snatch away our eyes*   [E] 20:7 Lit *out following him*   [F] 20:14 LXX, Vg read *Bichrites*

19:41-43 The men of Israel accused **Judah** of sneaking down to the Jordan to bring David back without telling them (19:41). The men of Judah shot back that David was one of their own biologically (19:42). But Israel responded that since they had ten tribes, they had **ten shares in the king**—and thus **a greater claim to David** than Judah did (19:43). Again, the author of Samuel shows his readers the roots of the nation's coming bitter division.

20:1-2 Sheba called **Israel** to officially war against Judah (20:1). Thus, the battle lines were drawn (20:2).

20:8-10 Joab had long been known as a violent man, but it was at this point that he showed his full treachery. He pretended to greet Amasa, whom David had elected as his replacement (see 19:13), with a **kiss** of brotherly kindness and then gutted him like an animal. Then Joab went on after **Sheba** as if nothing had happened (20:9-10).

a 20:22 Ec 9:14-15
b 20:23-26 2Sm 8:16-18;
1Kg 4:3-6
c 20:24 1Kg 12:18

d 21:2 Jos 9:3-17
e 21:4 Nm 35:31-32
f Lv 24:21-22
g 21:6 Nm 25:4
h 1Sm 15:34
i 1Sm 10:24
j 21:7 1Sm 18:3; 20:12-17;
23:18
k 21:8 2Sm 3:7
l 1Sm 18:19

While all the troops with Joab were battering the wall to make it collapse, [16] a wise woman called out from the city, "Listen! Listen! Please tell Joab to come here and let me speak with him."

[17] When he had come near her, the woman asked, "Are you Joab?"

"I am," he replied.

"Listen to the words of your servant," she said to him.

He answered, "I'm listening."

[18] She said, "In the past they used to say, 'Seek counsel in Abel,' and that's how they settled disputes. [19] I am one of the peaceful and faithful in Israel, but you're trying to destroy a city that is like a mother in Israel. Why would you devour the LORD's inheritance?"

[20] Joab protested: "Never! I would never devour or demolish! [21] That is not the case. There is a man named Sheba son of Bichri, from the hill country of Ephraim, who has rebelled against King David. Deliver this one man, and I will withdraw from the city."

The woman replied to Joab, "Watch! His head will be thrown over the wall to you."
[22] The woman went to all the people with her wise counsel,[a] and they cut off the head of Sheba son of Bichri and threw it to Joab. So he blew the ram's horn, and they dispersed from the city, each to his own tent. Joab returned to the king in Jerusalem.

[23] Joab commanded the whole army of
      Israel;[b]
      Benaiah son of Jehoiada was over
          the Cherethites and Pelethites;
[24] Adoram[A] was over forced labor;[c]
      Jehoshaphat son of Ahilud was
          court historian;
[25] Sheva was court secretary;
      Zadok and Abiathar were priests;
[26] and in addition, Ira the Jairite was
          David's priest.

JUSTICE FOR THE GIBEONITES

21 During David's reign there was a famine for three successive years, so David inquired[B] of the LORD. The LORD answered, "It is due to Saul and to his bloody family, because he killed the Gibeonites."

[2] The Gibeonites were not Israelites but rather a remnant of the Amorites. The Israelites had taken an oath concerning them,[d] but Saul had tried to kill them in his zeal for the Israelites and Judah. So David summoned the Gibeonites and spoke to them. [3] He asked the Gibeonites, "What should I do for you? How can I make atonement so that you will bring a blessing on[c] the LORD's inheritance?"

[4] The Gibeonites said to him, "We are not asking for silver and gold from Saul or his family,[e] and we cannot put anyone to death in Israel."[f]

"Whatever you say, I will do for you," he said.

[5] They replied to the king, "As for the man who annihilated us and plotted to destroy us so we would not exist within the whole territory of Israel, [6] let seven of his male descendants be handed over to us so we may hang[D] them in the presence of the LORD[g] at Gibeah of Saul,[h] the LORD's chosen."[i]

The king answered, "I will hand them over."

[7] David spared Mephibosheth, the son of Saul's son Jonathan, because of the oath of the LORD that was between David and Jonathan, Saul's son.[j] [8] But the king took Armoni and Mephibosheth, who were the two sons whom Rizpah[k] daughter of Aiah had borne to Saul, and the five sons whom Merab[E,l] daughter of Saul had borne to Adriel son of Barzillai the Meholathite [9] and handed them over to the Gibeonites. They hanged[f] them on the hill in the presence of the LORD; the seven of them died together. They were executed in the first days of the harvest at the beginning of the barley harvest.[G]

THE BURIAL OF SAUL'S FAMILY

[10] Rizpah, Aiah's daughter, took sackcloth and spread it out for herself on the rock from the beginning of the harvest[H] until the rain poured down from heaven on the

---

[A] 20:24 Some Hb mss, LXX, Syr read *Adoniram*; 1Kg 4:6; 5:14   [B] 21:1 Lit *sought the face of*   [C] 21:3 Lit *will bless*   [D] 21:6 Or *impale, or expose*   [E] 21:8 Some Hb mss, LXX, Syr, Tg; other Hb mss read *Michal*   [F] 21:9 Or *impaled, or exposed*, also in v. 13   [G] 21:9 = March–April   [H] 21:10 = April to October

---

20:21-22 That the people of the city so readily agreed to give up Sheba shows that not everyone in Israel had the stomach for another rebellion.

20:23 Given all of the rebellion, killing, and intrigue of the past days, perhaps David had decided that enough was enough and therefore kept **Joab** in his position as a key administrator over the nation. Eventually, however,

Joab's murderous spirit would cost him his life (see 1 Kgs 21:28-35).

21:1-2 The incident regarding Saul's actions is not recorded in Scripture, but it clearly violated a covenant Joshua had made with these non-Israelites years before (21:2; see Josh 9:15-21).

21:5-6 Saul had no doubt killed far more Gibeonites, but the number **seven** (21:6) was

likely chosen as the number of completeness. This would bring full satisfaction for the wrongs Saul and his family had committed against these people. As grim as this request seems to us, it is a reminder that sin is a great offense to God.

21:10 The **rain** signified the Lord's lifting of the curse and the end of the drought brought on by Saul's actions (see 21:1).

bodies. She kept the birds of the sky from them by day and the wild animals by night. **11** When it was reported to David what Saul's concubine Rizpah daughter of Aiah had done, **12** he went and got the bones of Saul and his son Jonathan from the citizens of Jabesh-gilead. They had stolen them from the public square of Beth-shan where the Philistines had hung the bodies the day the Philistines killed Saul at Gilboa.[a] **13** David had the bones brought from there. They gathered up the bones of Saul's family who had been hanged **14** and buried the bones of Saul and his son Jonathan at Zela in the land of Benjamin in the tomb of Saul's father Kish. They did everything the king commanded. After this, God was receptive to prayer for the land.[b]

THE PHILISTINE GIANTS

15 The Philistines again waged war against Israel. David went down with his soldiers, and they fought the Philistines, but David became exhausted. **16** Then Ishbi-benob, one of the descendants of the giant,[A] whose bronze spear weighed about eight pounds[B] and who wore new armor, intended to kill David. **17** But Abishai son of Zeruiah came to his aid, struck the Philistine, and killed him. Then David's men swore to him: "You must never again go out with us to battle. You must not extinguish the lamp of Israel."[C]

18 After this,[d] there was another battle with the Philistines at Gob. At that time Sibbecai the Hushathite killed Saph, who was one of the descendants of the giant. **19** Once again there was a battle with the Philistines at Gob, and Elhanan son of Jaare-oregim the Bethlehemite killed[c] Goliath of Gath. The shaft of his spear was like a weaver's beam.[e] **20** At Gath there was still another battle. A huge man was there with six fingers on each hand and six toes on each foot

—twenty-four in all. He, too, was descended from the giant. **21** When he taunted Israel, Jonathan, son of David's brother Shimei, killed him.

22 These four were descended from the giant in Gath and were killed by David and his soldiers.

DAVID'S SONG OF THANKSGIVING

22 David spoke the words of this song to the LORD on the day the LORD rescued him from the grasp of all his enemies and from the grasp of Saul. **2** He said:[f]

The LORD is my rock, my fortress,[g]
　　and my deliverer,
3　my God,[D] my rock where I seek
　　refuge.
My shield, the horn of my salvation,[h]
　　my stronghold,[i] my refuge,[j]
and my Savior, you save me
　　from violence.
4　I called to the LORD, who is worthy
　　of praise,[k]
and I was saved from my enemies.
5　For the waves of death engulfed me;[l]
　　the torrents of destruction
　　terrified me.
6　The ropes of Sheol entangled me;
　　the snares of death confronted me.[m]

7　I called to the LORD in my distress;
　　I called to my God.[n]
From his temple he heard my voice,
　　and my cry for help reached his ears.
8　Then the earth shook and quaked;
　　the foundations of the heavens[E]
　　trembled;[o]
they shook because he burned
　　with anger.[p]
9　Smoke rose from his nostrils,
　　and consuming fire came
　　from his mouth;
　　coals were set ablaze by it.[F]
10　He bent the heavens
　　and came down,[q]

[a] 21:12 1Sm 31:11-13
[b] 21:14 2Sm 24:25
[c] 21:17 2Sm 18:3; 1Kg 11:36; 15:4; 2Ch 21:7; Ps 132:17
[d] 21:18-22 1Ch 20:4-8
[e] 21:19 1Sm 17:7

[f] 22:2-51 Ps 18:2-50
[g] 22:2 Ps 31:3; 71:3
[h] 22:3 Lk 1:69
[i] Ps 9:9; 59:9,16-17; 62:2,6
[j] Ps 14:6; 71:7; Jr 16:19
[k] 22:4 1Ch 16:25; Ps 48:1; 96:4
[l] 22:5 Ps 42:7; Jnh 2:3
[m] 22:6 Ps 116:3
[n] 22:7 Ps 116:4; 120:1; Jnh 2:2
[o] 22:8 Jdg 5:4; Ps 77:18; 97:4
[p] Jb 26:11
[q] 22:10 Ps 144:5; Is 64:1

[A] **21:16** Or *Raphah*, also in vv. 18,20,22　[B] **21:16** Lit *300* (shekels)　[C] **21:19** 1Ch 20:5 adds *the brother of*　[D] **22:3** LXX, Ps 18:2 read *my God*; MT reads *God of*　[E] **22:8** Some Hb mss, Syr, Vg read *mountains*; Ps 18:7　[F] **22:9** Or *him*

21:15-17 By this point, David was no longer an energetic young warrior, and he soon **became exhausted** (21:15). The close call with **Ishbi-benob** led David's soldiers to make him promise not to go into battle again (21:16-17).

22:1-51 David's song of praise in this chapter is virtually identical to Psalm 18. The final stanza ties God's attributes to the ways God had worked through them on David's behalf. God was David's protector—**a shield to all who take refuge in him** (2 Sam 22:31), as well as a **rock** in whom David could find protection

(22:32). To underscore his point, David asked two questions in 22:32 to which he knew the answer: **Who is God besides the LORD? And who is a rock?** There is no solid and immovable rock like the Lord. God was the one who subdued David's **enemies** (22:38-41) and delivered David from harm (22:47-51). If the **king** of Israel looked to God as his **tower of salvation**, surely all of God's people should do the same (22:51).

23:2-3 Here David seems to claim divine inspiration for his writings, an idea which is fully expressed in the New Testament but which

the Old Testament prophets claimed in many places when they said things like, "The word of the Lord came to me" (see Jer 1:11; Ezek 6:1). **23:5** The heart of David's reign is the Davidic covenant (see 7:12-16) that will be fulfilled when Jesus Christ returns in glory to reign on David's throne in his coming millennial kingdom (see Luke 1:31-33). **23:6** In contrast to God's faithfulness, the wicked are like **thorns** that are completely useless and are only good for the fire of God's judgment.

a 22:12 Ps 97:2
b 22:14 Jb 37:4
c 22:15 Dt 32:23; Ps 7:13;
77:17; Hab 3:11
d Ps 144:6
e 22:16 Jb 4:9; Is 30:33
f Ex 15:8
g 22:17 Ps 144:7
h 22:20 Ps 31:8; 118:5
i 22:21 1Sm 26:23; 1Kg
8:32; Ps 7:8
j Ps 24:3-4
k 22:22 Pr 8:32
l 22:23 Ps 119:30,102

m 22:28 Ps 72:12-13
n Is 2:11-12,17; Lk 1:51
o 22:29 Jb 29:3; Ps 27:1
p 22:30 2Sm 5:6-9
q 22:31 Dt 32:4
r Ps 119:140
s 22:35 Ps 144:1
t 22:36 Eph 6:16-17
u 22:40 Ps 44:5

total darkness beneath his feet.
11 He rode on a cherub and flew,
    soaring[A] on the wings of the wind.
12 He made darkness a canopy
        around him,
    a gathering[B] of water
        and thick clouds.[a]
13 From the radiance of his presence,
    blazing coals were ignited.
14 The LORD thundered from heaven;
    the Most High made his voice
        heard.[b]
15 He shot arrows and scattered them;[c]
    he hurled lightning bolts
        and routed them.[d]
16 The depths of the sea became visible,
    the foundations of the world
        were exposed
    at the rebuke of the LORD,
    at the blast of the breath[e]
        of his nostrils.[f]

17 He reached down from on high
    and took hold of me;
    he pulled me out of deep water.[g]
18 He rescued me
        from my powerful enemy
    and from those who hated me,
    for they were too strong for me.
19 They confronted me in the day
        of my calamity,
    but the LORD was my support.
20 He brought me out
        to a spacious place;[h]
    he rescued me because he delighted
        in me.

21 The LORD rewarded me
    according to my righteousness;[i]
    he repaid me
    according to the cleanness
        of my hands.[j]
22 For I have kept the ways
        of the LORD[k]
    and have not turned from my God
        to wickedness.
23 Indeed, I let all his ordinances[l]
        guide me[c]
    and have not disregarded
        his statutes.
24 I was blameless before him
    and kept myself from my iniquity.
25 So the LORD repaid me
    according to my righteousness,

according to my cleanness[D]
    in his sight.
26 With the faithful
    you prove yourself faithful,
    with the blameless
    you prove yourself blameless,
27 with the pure
    you prove yourself pure;
    but with the crooked
    you prove yourself shrewd.
28 You rescue an oppressed people,[m]
    but your eyes are set
        against the proud —
    you humble them.[n]
29 LORD, you are my lamp;
    the LORD illuminates my darkness.[o]
30 With you I can attack a barricade,[E]
    and with my God I can leap
        over a wall.[p]
31 God — his way is perfect;[q]
    the word of the LORD is pure.[r]
    He is a shield to all who take refuge
        in him.[s]
32 For who is God besides the LORD?
    And who is a rock? Only our God.
33 God is my strong refuge;[F]
    he makes my way perfect.[G]
34 He makes my feet like
        the feet of a deer
    and sets me securely
        on the[H] heights.[i]
35 He trains my hands for war;[s]
    my arms can bend a bow of bronze.
36 You have given me the shield
        of your salvation;[t]
    your help[j] exalts me.
37 You make a spacious place
        beneath me for my steps,
    and my ankles do not give way.
38 I pursue my enemies
        and destroy them;
    I do not turn back until they are
        wiped out.
39 I wipe them out and crush them,
    and they do not rise;
    they fall beneath my feet.
40 You have clothed me with strength
        for battle;[u]
    you subdue my adversaries
        beneath me.
41 You have made my enemies retreat
        before me;[k]

[A] **22:11** Some Hb mss; other Hb mss, Syr, Tg read *he was seen*   [B] **22:12** Or *sieve,* or *mass;* Hb obscure   [C] **22:23** Lit *Indeed, all his ordinances have been in front of me*   [D] **22:25** LXX, Syr, Vg read *to the cleanness of my hands;* Ps 18:24   [E] **22:30** Or *a ridge,* or *raiders*   [F] **22:33** DSS, some LXX mss, Syr, Vg read *God clothes me with strength;* Ps 18:32   [G] **22:33** Some LXX mss, Syr; MT reads *he sets free the blameless his way;* Hb obscure   [H] **22:34** LXX; some Hb mss read *my;* other Hb mss read *his*   [i] **22:34** Or *on my high places*   [j] **22:36** LXX reads *humility;* Ps 18:35   [k] **22:41** Lit *you gave me the neck of my enemies*

I annihilate those who hate me.
42 They look, but there is no one
to save them —
they look to the LORD, but he does
not answer them.[a]
43 I pulverize them like dust
of the earth;
I crush them and trample them
like mud in the streets.[b]

44 You have freed me from the feuds
among my people;[c]
you have preserved me as head
of nations;
a people I had not known serve me.[d]
45 Foreigners submit to me cringing;
as soon as they hear, they obey me.
46 Foreigners lose heart
and come trembling
from their fortifications.[e]

47 The LORD lives —
blessed be my rock!
God, the rock of my salvation,[f]
is exalted.
48 God — he grants me vengeance
and casts down peoples under me.[g]
49 He frees me from my enemies.
You exalt me above my adversaries;
you rescue me from violent men.[h]

50 Therefore I will give thanks to you
among the nations, LORD;
I will sing praises about your name.[i]
51 He is a tower of salvation
for[A] his king;
he shows loyalty to his anointed,
to David and his descendants
forever.[j]

DAVID'S LAST WORDS

23 These are the last words of David:
The declaration of David
son of Jesse,[k]
the declaration of the man
raised on high,[B]
the one anointed by the God
of Jacob.[l]

This is the most delightful
of Israel's songs.
2 The Spirit of the LORD spoke
through me,
his word was on my tongue.[m]
3 The God of Israel spoke;
the Rock of Israel said to me,
"The one who rules the people
with justice,
who rules in the fear of God,[n]
4 is like the morning light
when the sun rises
on a cloudless morning,
the glisten of rain
on sprouting grass."

5 Is it not true my house is with God?
For he has established
a permanent covenant[o] with me,
ordered and secured in every detail.[p]
Will he not bring about
my whole salvation
and my every desire?
6 But all the wicked are like thorns
raked aside;
they can never be picked up
by hand.
7 The man who touches them
must be armed with iron
and the shaft of a spear.
They will be completely burned up
on the spot.

EXPLOITS OF DAVID'S WARRIORS

8 These are the names of David's warriors:[q]
Josheb-basshebeth the Tahchemonite
was chief of the officers.[C] He wielded his
spear[D] against eight hundred men that he
killed at one time.
9 After him, Eleazar son of Dodo son of
an Ahohite was among the three warriors
with David when they defied the Philistines. The men of Israel retreated in the
place they had gathered for battle, 10 but
Eleazar stood his ground and attacked
the Philistines until his hand was tired
and stuck to his sword. The LORD brought
about a great victory that day. Then the

[a] 22:42 1Sm 28:6; Pr 1:28
[b] 22:43 Is 10:6; Mc 7:10; Zch 10:5
[c] 22:44 2Sm 2:8-10; 15:1-6; 20:1-2
[d] 2Sm 8:1-14; Is 55:5
[e] 22:46 Mc 7:17
[f] 22:47 Ps 89:26; 95:1
[g] 22:48 Ps 144:2
[h] 22:49 Ps 140:1
[i] 22:50 Rm 15:9
[j] 22:51 2Sm 7:12-16; Lk 1:55
[k] 23:1 Lk 3:32
[l] 1Sm 16:12-13; Ps 89:20

[m] 23:2 Mt 22:43; 2Pt 1:21
[n] 23:3 Ps 72:1-3; Is 11:1-5
[o] 23:5 Gn 9:16; 17:7,19; 1Ch 16:17; Ps 105:10
[p] 2Sm 7:12-16; Ps 89:29; Is 55:3
[q] 23:8-39 1Ch 11:11-47

[A] 22:51 DSS read *he gives great victory to*   [B] 23:1 Or *raised up by the high God*   [C] 23:8 Some Hb mss, LXX read *Three*   [D] 23:8 Some Hb mss; other Hb mss, LXX read *He was Adino the Eznite*

23:8-39 The remainder of this chapter is devoted to the names and exploits of **David's warriors** (23:8). The stories herein are better than those credited to any comic-book superhero—and they're true (see especially 23:20-21)! Interestingly, among all the names, "Joab" is not included. His brothers **Abishai** and **Asahel** are, and each is designated as **Joab's brother** (23:18, 24).

Joab was certainly a great warrior who was the commander of David's entire army for most of his reign. But Joab was also an extremely violent and brutal man who did not hesitate to kill his own kinsmen when they got in his way.

Don't miss that this list includes **Uriah the Hethite** (22:39). His privileged role underscores the power that sin can have, even in

the life of a dedicated believer like David, when it takes over. Uriah wasn't just a good and loyal soldier. He was one of David's best, a man who had taken a vow to defend the king at the cost of his own life. Ironically, being David's soldier did cost Uriah his life, but his death was to David's great shame (see ch. 11).

a 23:13 1Sm 22:1
b 23:14 1Sm 22:4-5
c 23:18 1Sm 26:3-6
d 23:19 1Ch 11:21
e 23:20 2Sm 8:18; 20:23

f 23:24 2Sm 2:18-23;
    1Ch 27:7
g 23:34 2Sm 15:12
h 23:39 Mt 1:6
i 2Sm 11:3-26
j 24:1-25 1Ch 21:1-28

troops came back to him, but only to plunder the dead.

11 After him was Shammah son of Agee the Hararite. The Philistines had assembled in formation where there was a field full of lentils. The troops fled from the Philistines, **12** but Shammah took his stand in the middle of the field, defended it, and struck down the Philistines. So the Lord brought about a great victory.

13 Three of the thirty leading warriors went down at harvest time and came to David at the cave of Adullam,*a* while a company of Philistines was camping in the Valley of Rephaim. **14** At that time David was in the stronghold,*b* and a Philistine garrison was at Bethlehem. **15** David was extremely thirsty*A* and said, "If only someone would bring me water to drink from the well at the city gate of Bethlehem!" **16** So three of the warriors broke through the Philistine camp and drew water from the well at the gate of Bethlehem. They brought it back to David, but he refused to drink it. Instead, he poured it out to the Lord. **17** David said, "Lord, I would never do such a thing! Is this not the blood of men who risked their lives?" So he refused to drink it. Such were the exploits of the three warriors.

18 Abishai, Joab's brother and son of Zeruiah,*c* was leader of the Three.*B* He wielded his spear against three hundred men and killed them, gaining a reputation among the Three. **19** Was he not more honored than the Three? He became their commander even though he did not become one of the Three.*d*

20 Benaiah son of Jehoiada*e* was the son of a brave man from Kabzeel, a man of many exploits. Benaiah killed two sons*c* of Ariel*D* of Moab, and he went down into a pit on a snowy day and killed a lion. **21** He also killed an Egyptian, an impressive man. Even though the Egyptian had a spear in his hand, Benaiah went down to him with a club, snatched the spear out of the Egyptian's hand, and then killed him with his own spear. **22** These were the exploits of Benaiah son of Jehoiada, who had a reputation among the three

warriors. **23** He was the most honored of the Thirty, but he did not become one of the Three. David put him in charge of his bodyguard.

24 Among the Thirty were
Joab's brother Asahel,*f*
Elhanan son of Dodo of Bethlehem,
25 Shammah the Harodite,
Elika the Harodite,
26 Helez the Paltite,
Ira son of Ikkesh the Tekoite,
27 Abiezer the Anathothite,
Mebunnai the Hushathite,
28 Zalmon the Ahohite,
Maharai the Netophathite,
29 Heleb son of Baanah
the Netophathite,
Ittai son of Ribai from Gibeah
of the Benjaminites,
30 Benaiah the Pirathonite,
Hiddai from the wadis of Gaash,*E*
31 Abi-albon the Arbathite,
Azmaveth the Barhumite,
32 Eliahba the Shaalbonite,
the sons of Jashen,
Jonathan son of*F* **33** Shammah
the Hararite,
Ahiam son of Sharar the Hararite,
34 Eliphelet son of Ahasbai
son of the Maacathite,
Eliam son of Ahithophel
the Gilonite,*g*
35 Hezro the Carmelite,
Paarai the Arbite,
36 Igal son of Nathan from Zobah,
Bani the Gadite,
37 Zelek the Ammonite,
Naharai the Beerothite,
the armor-bearer for Joab
son of Zeruiah,
38 Ira the Ithrite,
Gareb the Ithrite,
39 and Uriah*h* the Hethite.*i*
There were thirty-seven in all.

DAVID'S MILITARY CENSUS

24 The Lord's anger burned against Israel again, and he stirred up David against them to say: "Go, count the people of Israel and Judah."*j*

A **23:15** Lit *And David craved*   *B* **23:18** Some Hb mss, Syr read *the Thirty*   *C* **23:20** LXX; MT omits *sons*   *D* **23:20** Or *two warriors*   *E* **23:30** Or *from Nahale-gaash*   *F* **23:32** Some LXX mss; MT omits *son of*; 1Ch 11:34

24:1-2 The story of David's census is an example of the mysterious interplay between God's sovereignty and human responsibility. Here the text says that the Lord **stirred up David** to take this census (24:1). But according to 1 Chronicles 21:1, "Satan rose up against Israel and incited David to count the people

of Israel." So, who did the action? The Lord or Satan? The answer is both.

God was angry with Israel apparently because the people had sinned in some way. So he allowed Satan to tempt David to arrogantly count the size of the troops under his command. This interplay between

God and Satan is similar to God allowing Satan to trouble Job (see Job 1:1–2:7). Ultimately, though, it was God who was sovereign over Job's circumstances. Job understood that he had suffered because of "all the adversity the Lord had brought on him" (Job 42:11). Though Satan had meant

² So the king said to Joab, the commander of his army, "Go through all the tribes of Israel from Dan to Beer-sheba and register the troops so I can know their number."[a]

³ Joab replied to the king, "May the LORD your God multiply the troops a hundred times more than they are[b] — while my lord the king looks on! But why does my lord the king want to do this?"

⁴ Yet the king's order prevailed over Joab and the commanders of the army. So Joab and the commanders of the army left the king's presence to register the troops of Israel.

⁵ They crossed the Jordan and camped in Aroer,[c] south of the town in the middle of the valley, and then proceeded toward Gad and Jazer. ⁶ They went to Gilead and to the land of the Hittites[A] and continued on to Dan-jaan and around to Sidon. ⁷ They went to the fortress of Tyre and all the cities of the Hivites and Canaanites. Afterward, they went to the Negev of Judah at Beer-sheba.

⁸ When they had gone through the whole land, they returned to Jerusalem at the end of nine months and twenty days. ⁹ Joab gave the king the total of the registration of the troops. There were eight hundred thousand valiant armed men[B] from Israel and five hundred thousand men from Judah.[d]

¹⁰ David's conscience troubled him[e] after he had taken a census of the troops. He said to the LORD, "I have sinned greatly in what I've done. Now, LORD, because I've been very foolish,[f] please take away your servant's guilt."

DAVID'S PUNISHMENT

¹¹ When David got up in the morning, the word of the LORD had come to the prophet Gad,[g] David's seer:[h] ¹² "Go and say to David, 'This is what the LORD says: I am offering you three choices. Choose one of them, and I will do it to you.'"

¹³ So Gad went to David, told him the choices, and asked him, "Do you want three[c] years of famine to come on your land, to flee from your foes three months while they pursue you, or to have a plague in your land three days? Now, consider carefully[D] what answer I should take back to the one who sent me."

¹⁴ David answered Gad, "I have great anxiety. Please, let us fall into the LORD's hands because his mercies are great,[i] but don't let me fall into human hands."

¹⁵ So the LORD sent a plague on Israel from that morning until the appointed time, and from Dan to Beer-sheba seventy thousand men died. ¹⁶ Then the angel extended his hand toward Jerusalem to destroy it,[j] but the LORD relented concerning the destruction[k] and said to the angel who was destroying[j] the people, "Enough, withdraw your hand now!" The angel of the LORD was then at the threshing floor of Araunah[E] the Jebusite.[m]

¹⁷ When David saw the angel striking the people, he said to the LORD, "Look, I am the one who has sinned; I am the one[F] who has done wrong. But these sheep, what have they done? Please, let your hand be against me and my father's family."

DAVID'S ALTAR

¹⁸ Gad came to David that day and said to him, "Go up and set up an altar to the LORD on the threshing floor of Araunah the Jebusite." ¹⁹ David went up in obedience to Gad's command, just as the LORD had commanded. ²⁰ Araunah looked down and saw the king and his servants coming toward him, so he went out and paid homage to the king with his face to the ground. ²¹ Araunah said, "Why has my lord the king come to his servant?"

[a] 24:2 Nm 1:2-3; 1Sm 13:15
[b] 24:3 Dt 1:11
[c] 24:5 Dt 2:36; Jos 13:19,16
[d] 24:9 Nm 1:45-46
[e] 24:10 1Sm 24:5
[f] Nm 12:9-12; 1Sm 13:13
[g] 24:11 1Sm 22:5
[h] 1Sm 9:9

[i] 24:14 Ps 103:8-18; 119:156
[j] 24:16 2Kg 19:35
[k] Ex 32:14; Am 7:3-6
[l] 1Co 10:10
[m] 2Ch 3:1

[A] 24:6 LXX; MT reads *of Tahtim-hodshi*; Hb obscure   [B] 24:9 Lit *men of valor drawing the sword*   [C] 24:13 LXX; MT reads *seven*; 1Ch 21:12   [D] 24:13 Lit *Now, know and see*   [E] 24:16 = Ornan in 1Ch 21:15-28; 2Ch 3:1   [F] 24:17 LXX reads *shepherd*

---

the adversity for evil, however, God had meant it for Job's good.

In principle, it isn't sinful for a commander to count his troops in order to know if he has sufficient numbers to go to battle. But the Lord had made it clear to David that he—not the army—was the source of Israel's strength. Satan had tempted David to meet a legitimate desire (to win Israel's battles) by an illegitimate means (the number of his forces) rather than a legitimate means (relying completely on the Lord).

24:3 On this occasion, **Joab** was more spiritually aware than David. He objected to David's order because he saw it for what it was—a needless attempt by David to take pride in and feel secure in his military might instead of trusting the Lord.

24:11-13 Sin, even forgiven sin, always has consequences. So the Lord gave the king a choice of **three** very painful judgments. They increase in severity from a **famine** to a **plague**, but decrease in length from **three years** to **three days** (24:13).

24:14-17 David had experienced years of fleeing from his enemies, so he knew he would find no mercy from them. Knowing the Lord's **mercies are great**, David placed himself in God's hands (24:14). Therefore, **the LORD sent a plague on Israel**, which resulted in

seventy thousand deaths (24:15). The plague stopped only when God spared **Jerusalem** in that mercy David had counted on (24:16). This happened **at the threshing floor of Araunah the Jebusite** (24:16). (In 1 Chronicles, Araunah is known by his alternate name, Ornan; see 1 Chr 21:18-28.)

David pleaded with God on behalf of his people. He recognized that the sin was his and begged God to let the judgment be against his family alone (2 Sam 24:17). This is a reminder that while you may think that your sinful choices affect no one but you, they leave spiritual harm in your wake—whether or not you see the results immediately.

a 24:21 Nm 16:44-50
b 24:22 1Sm 6:14; 1Kg 19:21

c 24:25 2Sm 21:14

David replied, "To buy the threshing floor from you in order to build an altar to the LORD, so the plague on the people may be halted."[a] **22** Araunah said to David, "My lord the king may take whatever he wants[A] and offer it. Here are the oxen for a burnt offering and the threshing sledges and ox yokes for the wood.[b] **23** Your Majesty, Araunah gives everything here to the king." Then he said to the king, "May the LORD your God accept you."

24 The king answered Araunah, "No, I insist on buying it from you for a price, for I will not offer to the LORD my God burnt offerings that cost me nothing." David bought the threshing floor and the oxen for twenty ounces[B] of silver. **25** He built an altar to the LORD there and offered burnt offerings and fellowship offerings. Then the LORD was receptive to prayer for the land,[c] and the plague on Israel ended.

[A] 24:22 Lit *take what is good in his eyes*   [B] 24:24 Lit *50 shekels*

24:24 Here David stated one of the great biblical principles of sacrificial giving: **I will not offer to the LORD my God burnt offerings that cost me nothing**. This should make us ask what we give to the Lord and his kingdom work (prayers, time, service, money, resources) that costs us little in terms of sacrifice.

Importantly, the piece of land that David **bought** was Mount Moriah, the spot where Abraham once offered his son Isaac to the Lord and where Solomon would one day build the Lord's temple (see Gen 22; 2 Chr 3:1). God allowed Satan's wickedness and David's sin to run their course until what would become Israel's holiest site was selected.

Through the events of the book of 2 Samuel, showing both the king's vulnerability to sin and his sensitivity to turn to the Lord in repentance, God calls all kingdom men and women to be on guard regarding their own vulnerability to sin and to maintain hearts sensitive to the Holy Spirit's convicting work.

1 KINGS

INTRODUCTION

Author

THE AUTHOR OF 1 AND 2 KINGS is unknown. Though ancient Jewish tradition attributed the books to the prophet Jeremiah, the books themselves are silent with regard to their writer. Clearly, the author was interested in showing how God's people had failed to live up to the requirements of the covenant, particularly as they are laid out in Deuteronomy. The books were completed sometime after the final event they mention: the pardoning of Jehoiachin (see 2 Kgs 25:27-30) in 561 BC. Given the time frame and the theological emphases, Jeremiah is certainly a good candidate.

Historical Background

First Kings begins with King David's final days, and 2 Kings ends with "the thirty-seventh year of the exile of Judah's King Jehoiachin, in the year Evil-merodach became king of Babylon" (2 Kgs 25:27). Thus, the books take readers from the golden age of Israel's monarchy to the exile of Judah's king, a period spanning four hundred years. Though 1–2 Chronicles cover much of the same ground, 1–2 Kings consider the kings and history of both the northern and southern kingdoms (Israel and Judah), while 1–2 Chronicles focus on Judah. In 1–2 Kings, readers see the construction of Solomon's temple (960 BC), the split of the nation into two kingdoms (930 BC), the exile of Israel to Assyria (722 BC), and the exile of Judah to Babylon (587 BC).

Message and Purpose

Written to the Jews living in captivity in Babylon, this two-volume work is a history of the united, and then divided, kingdom of Israel. The books describe the reigns of the kings of both Israel and Judah: there were nineteen kings in the northern kingdom (Israel) and twenty kings in the southern kingdom (Judah).

The message of 1–2 Kings was the same message God gave to Moses in Deuteronomy: God would provide blessing for obedience to him and judgment for disobedience. The writer wanted his readers to know that they were in captivity because of disobedience, but obedience to God would bring deliverance. The

prophetic ministries of Elijah, Elisha, and Isaiah are highlighted in these books, as these prophets called the people back to God so they could avoid the consequences of rebelling against their covenant with him.

The sweep of history within these works, from David's time through the broken kingdom era, shows us that no human ruler can fulfill God's ultimate demands. It reveals humanity's need for the ultimate King, the final Son of David, who alone could satisfy God's requirements and bring his people deliverance. Reading 1–2 Kings causes us to look forward to the righteous kingdom rule of David's final Son, the Messiah and our Savior.

Outline

https://www.bhpublishinggroup.com/qrpage/introduction-to-1-2-kings/

I. The United Kingdom (1:1–11:43)
   A. The Rise of King Solomon (1:1–2:46)
   B. Solomon's Wisdom, Administration, and Fame (3:1–4:34)
   C. The Construction and Dedication of the Temple (5:1–8:66)
   D. Solomon's Kingdom, Wealth, and Downfall (9:1–11:43)

II. The Divided Kingdom (12:1–22:53)
   A. Rehoboam, Jeroboam, and the Dividing of Israel (12:1–14:31)
   B. The Reigns of Abijam and Asa in Judah (15:1-24)
   C. The Reigns of Five Evil Kings in Israel (15:25–16:28)
   D. The Reign of Ahab and the Ministry of Elijah (16:29–22:40)
   E. The Reigns of Jehoshaphat in Judah and Ahaziah in Israel (22:41-53)

a 1:1 2Sm 5:4; 1Kg 2:10–11; 1Ch 23:1
b Ec 4:11
c 1:2 Est 2:2
d 1:3 1Kg 1:15; 2:17
e Jos 19:18; 1Sm 28:4
f 1:4 Est 2:7
g 1:5 2Sm 3:4
h 2Sm 15:1
i 1:6 1Sm 3:13
j 2Sm 13:21
k 2Sm 14:25
l 2Sm 3:3–4
m 1:7 1Ch 11:6
n 1Sm 22:20–23; 2Sm 20:25
o 1Kg 2:22
p 1:8 2Sm 20:25; 1Ch 16:39–40
q 2Sm 8:18
r 2Sm 7:2; 2:1–25
s 1Kg 4:18
t 2Sm 23:8–39
u 1:9 Jos 15:7; 18:16; 2Sm 17:17
v 2Sm 15:11–12
w 1:10 1Kg 1:8,26
x 1:11 2Sm 12:1,25; 1Kg 1:8,10
y 2Sm 12:24
z 2Sm 15:10; 1Kg 1:25; 2:15
aa 2Sm 3:26; 1Kg 1:18; 2:32
ab 1:12 Pr 15:22
ac 1Kg 15:29; 2Kg 10:11
ad 1:13 1Kg 1:17,30; 1Ch 22:9–13
ae 1:14 1Kg 1:22–27
af 1:15 1Kg 1:1–4
ag 1:21 Dt 31:16; 2Sm 7:12; 1Kg 2:10
ah 1Kg 1:12
ai 1:22 1Kg 1:14

DAVID'S LAST DAYS

1 Now King David was old and advanced in age.[a] Although they covered him with bedclothes, he could not get warm.[b] **2** So his servants said to him: "Let us[A] search for a young virgin for my lord the king. She is to attend the king and be his caregiver. She is to lie by your side so that my lord the king will get warm." **3** They searched for a beautiful girl throughout the territory of Israel; they found Abishag[d] the Shunammite[B,e] and brought her to the king. **4** The girl was of unsurpassed beauty,[f] and she became the king's caregiver. She attended to him, but he was not intimate with[c] her.

ADONIJAH'S BID FOR POWER

5 Adonijah son of Haggith[g] kept exalting himself, saying, "I will be king!" He prepared chariots, cavalry, and fifty men to run ahead of him.[D,h] **6** But his father had never once infuriated[i] him by asking, "Why did you do that?"[j] In addition, he was quite handsome[k] and was born after Absalom.[l] **7** He conspired[E] with Joab son of Zeruiah[m] and with the priest Abiathar.[n] They supported[o] Adonijah, **8** but the priest Zadok,[p] Benaiah son of Jehoiada,[q] the prophet Nathan,[r] Shimei,[s] Rei, and David's royal guard[F,t] did not side with Adonijah.

9 Adonijah sacrificed sheep, goats, cattle, and fattened cattle near the stone of Zoheleth, which is next to En-rogel.[u] He invited all his royal brothers and all the men of Judah, the servants of the king,[v] **10** but he did not invite the prophet Nathan, Benaiah, the royal guard, or his brother Solomon.[w]

NATHAN'S AND BATHSHEBA'S APPEALS

11 Then Nathan[x] said to Bathsheba, Solomon's mother,[y] "Have you not heard that Adonijah son of Haggith has become king[z] and our lord David does not know it?[aa] **12** Now please come and let me advise you.[ab] Save your life and the life of your son Solomon.[ac] **13** Go, approach King David and say to him, 'My lord the king, did you not swear to your servant: Your son Solomon is to become king after me, and he is the one who is to sit on my throne?[ad] So why has Adonijah become king?' **14** At that moment, while you are still there speaking with the king, I'll come in after you and confirm your words."[ae]

15 So Bathsheba went to the king in his bedroom. Since the king was very old, Abishag the Shunammite was attending to him.[af] **16** Bathsheba knelt low and paid homage to the king, and he asked, "What do you want?"

17 She replied, "My lord, you swore to your servant by the LORD your God, 'Your son Solomon is to become king after me, and he is the one who is to sit on my throne.' **18** Now look, Adonijah has become king. And,[G] my lord the king, you didn't know it. **19** He has lavishly sacrificed oxen, fattened cattle, and sheep. He invited all the king's sons, the priest Abiathar, and Joab the commander of the army, but he did not invite your servant Solomon. **20** Now, my lord the king, the eyes of all Israel are on you to tell them who will sit on the throne of my lord the king after him. **21** Otherwise, when my lord the king rests with his fathers,[ag] I and my son Solomon will be regarded as criminals."[ah]

22 At that moment, while she was still speaking with the king, the prophet Nathan arrived,[ai] **23** and it was announced to the king, "The prophet Nathan is here." He came into the king's presence and paid homage to him with his face to the ground. **24** "My lord the king," Nathan said, "did you say, 'Adonijah is to become king after me, and he is the one who is to sit on my throne'? **25** For today he went down and lavishly sacrificed oxen, fattened cattle, and sheep. He invited all the sons of the king, the commanders of the army, and the priest Abiathar. And look! They're eating and drinking in his presence, and they're saying, 'Long live King Adonijah!' **26** But he did not invite me — me, your servant

---

[A] **1:2** Lit *them*   [B] **1:3** Shunem was a town in the hill country of Issachar at the foot of Mt. Moreh; Jos 19:17–18.   [C] **1:4** Lit *he did not know*   [D] **1:5** Heralds announcing his procession   [E] **1:7** Lit *His words were*   [F] **1:8** Lit *David's warriors*   [G] **1:18** Some Hb mss, LXX, Vg, Syr; other Hb mss read *And now*

1:1–2 Elderly David was unable to keep **warm**, no matter how well he was covered (1:1). So the king's servants suggested that they find **a young virgin** who could provide him with warmth and also be his **caregiver** (1:2).
1:3 Abishag was from the village of Shunem in the tribal territory of Issachar.
1:5–10 It seems Adonijah had a lot in common with Absalom (see 2 Sam 15:1–10). He **kept exalting himself** and declared, **I will be king!** (1 Kgs 1:5). And like Absalom, he won over many followers by his good looks and charm.
1:11–14 Nathan and **Bathsheba** soon realized how serious the situation had become (1:11). They developed a plan to convince David that, unless he acted quickly and decisively, Adonijah would be king. And then, those loyal to David, including Bathsheba and Solomon, would be put to death (1:12–14).
1:24–27 Nathan the prophet essentially asked the king, "Did I miss something? Did you endorse Adonijah without letting us know about it?"

— or the priest Zadok or Benaiah son of Jehoiada or your servant Solomon. **27** I'm certain my lord the king would not have let this happen without letting your servant[A] know who will sit on my lord the king's throne after him."

SOLOMON CONFIRMED KING

28 King David responded by saying, "Call in Bathsheba for me." So she came into the king's presence and stood before him. **29** The king swore an oath and said, "As the LORD lives, who has redeemed my life from every difficulty,[a] **30** just as I swore to you by the LORD God of Israel: Your son Solomon is to become king after me, and he is the one who is to sit on my throne in my place,[b] that is exactly what I will do this very day."[c]

31 Bathsheba knelt low with her face to the ground, paying homage to the king,[d] and said, "May my lord King David live forever!"[e]

32 King David then said, "Call in the priest Zadok, the prophet Nathan, and Benaiah son of Jehoiada for me."[f] So they came into the king's presence. **33** The king said to them, "Take my servants[g] with you, have my son Solomon ride on my own mule,[h] and take him down to Gihon.[i] **34** There, the priest Zadok and the prophet Nathan are to anoint him as king over Israel.[j] You are to blow the ram's horn[k] and say, 'Long live King Solomon!'[l] **35** You are to come up after him, and he is to come in and sit on my throne. He is the one who is to become king in my place; he is the one I have commanded to be ruler[m] over Israel and Judah."[n]

36 "Amen," Benaiah son of Jehoiada replied to the king. "May the LORD, the God of my lord the king, so affirm it.[o] **37** Just as the LORD was with my lord the king,[p] so may he[B] be with Solomon and make his throne greater than the throne of my lord King David."[q]

38 Then the priest Zadok, the prophet Nathan, Benaiah son of Jehoiada, the Cherethites, and the Pelethites[r] went down, had Solomon ride on King David's mule, and took him to Gihon. **39** The priest Zadok took the horn of oil from the tabernacle and anointed Solomon.[s] Then they blew the ram's horn,[t] and all the people proclaimed, "Long live King Solomon!"[U] **40** All the people went up after him, playing flutes and rejoicing with such a great joy[v] that the earth split open from the sound.[c]

ADONIJAH HEARS OF SOLOMON'S CORONATION

41 Adonijah and all the invited guests who were with him[w] heard the noise as they finished eating. Joab heard the sound of the ram's horn and said, "Why is the town in such an uproar?"[x] **42** He was still speaking when Jonathan son of Abiathar the priest,[y] suddenly arrived. Adonijah said, "Come in, for you are an important man, and you must be bringing good news."[z]

43 "Unfortunately not," Jonathan answered him. "Our lord King David has made Solomon king. **44** And with Solomon, the king has sent the priest Zadok, the prophet Nathan, Benaiah son of Jehoiada, the Cherethites, and the Pelethites, and they have had him ride on the king's mule. **45** The priest Zadok and the prophet Nathan have anointed him king in Gihon.[aa] They have gone up from there rejoicing. The town has been in an uproar; that's the noise you heard. **46** Solomon has even taken his seat on the royal throne.[ab] **47** "The king's servants have also gone to congratulate our lord King David, saying, 'May your God make the name of Solomon more well known than your name, and may he make his throne greater than your throne.'[ac] Then the king bowed in worship on his bed.[ad] **48** And the king went on to say this: 'Blessed be the LORD God of Israel! Today he has provided one to sit on my throne,[ae] and I am a witness.'"[D]

49 Then all of Adonijah's guests got up trembling and went their separate ways. **50** Adonijah was afraid of Solomon, so he got up and went to take hold of the horns of the altar.[af] **51** It was reported to Solomon: "Look, Adonijah fears King Solomon, and he has taken hold of the horns of the altar, saying, 'Let King Solomon first[E] swear to me that he will not kill his servant with the sword.'"

[a]1:29 2Sm 4:9
[b]1:30 1Kg 1:13
[c]1:30 1Kg 1:33-35
[d]1:31 1Kg 1:16
[e]Neh 2:3; Dn 2:4; 3:9
[f]1:32 1Kg 1:8,10,26
[g]1:33 2Sm 20:6
[h]2Sm 18:9; Est 6:8; Zch 9:9; Jn 12:14-15
[i]2Ch 32:30; 33:14
[j]1:34 1Sm 10:1; 16:3,13
[k]2Sm 15:10
[l]1Sm 10:24; 1Kg 1:25
[m]1:35 1Sm 13:14
[n]2Sm 2:4; 5:3
[o]1:36 Jr 28:6
[p]1:37 1Sm 20:13
[q]1Kg 1:47
[r]1:38 2Sm 8:18

[s]1:39 1Ch 29:22
[t]2Kg 11:14
[u]1Sm 10:24
[v]1:40 Ezr 6:16
[w]1:41 1Kg 1:5,7-10
[x]2Kg 11:12-13
[y]1:42 2Sm 15:27,36
[z]2Sm 18:26-27
[aa]1:43-45 1Kg 1:33-35
[ab]1:46 1Ch 29:23
[ac]1:47 1Kg 1:37
[ad]Gn 47:31
[ae]1:48 2Sm 7:12; 1Kg 3:6
[af]1:50 Ex 21:12-14; 1Kg 2:28

[A]1:27 Some Hb mss, LXX; alt Hb tradition reads *servants*   [B]1:37 Alt Hb tradition reads *so he will*   [C]1:40 LXX reads *the land resounded with their noise*   [D]1:48 Lit *and my eyes are seeing*   [E]1:51 Some Hb mss, LXX, Syr, Vg read *today*

1:28-30 Though David was feeble, he wasn't feeble-minded. From his sickbed, he took steps to keep his previous promise to place Solomon on his **throne** (1:30).

1:41 Gihon, location of Solomon's coronation (see 1:33), was only about half a mile from where the usurper Adonijah and his crowd were celebrating. From where Adonijah sat, it wouldn't be hard to hear the noise the people were making. **1:50-51** Adonijah ran to the tabernacle in Jerusalem for sanctuary. He grabbed **the horns of the altar** as a way of pleading for his life.

a 1:52 1Sm 14:45; 2Sm 14:11; Ac 27:34
b 1Kg 2:23-25
c 2:1 Gn 47:29; Nm 27:13
d 2:2 Jos 23:14
e Jos 1:6-7,9
f 2:3 Dt 29:9; 1Ch 22:12-13
g 2:4 Dt 6:5; Mt 22:37
h 2Sm 7:12-13; 1Kg 8:25; 9:5
i 2:5 2Sm 18:5,12,14
j 2Sm 3:27
k 2Sm 20:10
l 2:7 2Sm 9:7; 19:28
m 2Sm 19:31-39
n 2:8 2Sm 16:5-13

o 2:8 2Sm 19:16-23
p 2:10 Ac 2:29; 13:36
q 2Sm 5:7
r 2:11 2Sm 5:4-5; 1Ch 29:27
s 2:12 1Kg 2:46; 1Ch 17:14
t 2:13 1Kg 1:5,51-53
u 1Sm 16:4-5
v 2:15 1Kg 1:11
w 1Kg 1:38-46
x 1Ch 23:9-10; 28:5,7; Dn 2:21; 4:17; Jn 19:11; Rm 13:1
y 2:17 1Kg 1:3-4,15
z 2:19 2Sm 15:16; 1Kg 15:13
aa Ps 110:1; Mt 20:21

52 Then Solomon said, "If he is a man of character, not a single hair of his will fall to the ground,*a* but if evil is found in him, he dies."*b* **53** So King Solomon sent for him, and they took him down from the altar. He came and paid homage to King Solomon, and Solomon said to him, "Go to your home."

DAVID'S DYING INSTRUCTIONS TO SOLOMON

2 As the time approached for David to die,*c* he ordered his son Solomon, **2** "As for me, I am going the way of all the earth.*d* Be strong and be a man,*e* **3** and keep your obligation to the LORD your God to walk in his ways and to keep his statutes, commands, ordinances, and decrees. This is written in the law of Moses, so that you will have success in everything you do*f* and wherever you turn, **4** and so that the LORD will fulfill his promise that he made to me: 'If your sons guard their way to walk faithfully before me with all their heart and all their soul,*g* you will never fail to have a man on the throne of Israel.'*h*

5 "You also know what Joab son of Zeruiah did to me*i* and what he did to the two commanders of Israel's army, Abner son of Ner*j* and Amasa son of Jether.*k* He murdered them in a time of peace to avenge blood shed in war. He spilled that blood on his own waistband and on the sandals of his feet.*A* **6** Act according to your wisdom, and do not let his gray head descend to Sheol in peace.

7 "Show kindness to the sons of Barzillai the Gileadite and let them be among those who eat at your table*l* because they supported me when I fled from your brother Absalom.*m*

8 "Keep an eye on Shimei son of Gera, the Benjaminite from Bahurim who is with you. He uttered malicious curses against me the day I went to Mahanaim.*n* But he

came down to meet me at the Jordan River, and I swore to him by the LORD: 'I will never kill you with the sword.'*o* **9** So don't let him go unpunished, for you are a wise man. You know how to deal with him to bring his gray head down to Sheol with blood."

10 Then David rested with his fathers*p* and was buried in the city of David.*q* **11** The length of time David reigned over Israel was forty years: he reigned seven years in Hebron and thirty-three years in Jerusalem.*r* **12** Solomon sat on the throne of his father David, and his kingship was firmly established.*s*

ADONIJAH'S FOOLISH REQUEST

13 Now Adonijah son of Haggith*t* came to Bathsheba, Solomon's mother. She asked, "Do you come peacefully?"

"Peacefully," he replied,*u* **14** and then asked, "May I talk with you?"*B*

"Go ahead," she answered.

15 "You know the kingship was mine,"*v* he said. "All Israel expected me to be king, but then the kingship was turned over to my brother,*w* for the LORD gave it to him.*x* **16** So now I have just one request of you; don't turn me down."*c*

She said to him, "Go on."

17 He replied, "Please speak to King Solomon since he won't turn you down. Let him give me Abishag the Shunammite*y* as a wife."

18 "Very well," Bathsheba replied. "I will speak to the king for you."

19 So Bathsheba went to King Solomon to speak to him about Adonijah. The king stood up to greet her, bowed to her, sat down on his throne, and had a throne placed for the king's mother.*z* So she sat down at his right hand.*aa*

20 Then she said, "I have just one small request of you. Don't turn me down."

"Go ahead and ask, mother," the king replied, "for I won't turn you down."

A 2:5 LXX, Old Lat read *on my waistband and . . . my feet*; v. 31   *B* 2:14 Lit *then said, "I have a word for you."*   *C* 2:16 Lit *don't make me turn my face*

2:3-4 If Solomon would be careful to put God's Word at the center of his reign, he would **have success in everything** (2:3). David's words were especially important given the covenant God had made with David, granting him an eternal dynasty and establishing his throne forever (see 2 Sam 7:8-16), because it required that Solomon and his sons after him **walk faithfully before** God (1 Kgs 2:4).

Though ultimately Solomon and his descendants would fail in this, God would fulfill his own covenant requirements. When the time was right, he would send his perfect

Son, born of the line of David. Jesus Christ would fulfill the demands of God's law, offer his life as an atoning sacrifice for sin, and then rise from the dead. He will sit on David's throne and reign forever (see Isa 9:6-7).

2:5-6 In the United States, election winners enter office and the losers go do something else. Most of us don't know what it's like to live in a monarchy in which the king must always be on guard against the plotting of his enemies who want to assassinate him and usurp his throne. **Joab** (2:5) had proved to be fierce and self-serving. His loyalty could not be trusted; he would be a liability to Solomon.

2:8-9 It was about time for **Shimei** to answer for cursing the Lord's anointed (2:8 ; also see 2:36-46).

2:15-17 The scheming Adonijah reminded Bathsheba—cue the sad music—that he and **all Israel expected [him] to be king** but that it was taken away from him (2:15). **Abishag** had been David's concubine. To acquire a woman from a king's harem was to have grounds for claiming the crown (see 2 Sam 3:6-7; 16:21-22). **2:18** Whether Bathsheba was oblivious to what Adonijah's request meant or understood it all too well, she relayed it (see the note on 2:15-17).

21 So she said, "Let Abishag the Shunammite be given to your brother Adonijah as
a wife."
22 King Solomon answered his mother, "Why are you requesting Abishag the
Shunammite for Adonijah? Since he is
my elder brother,[a] you might as well ask
the kingship for him,[b] for the priest Abiathar, and for Joab son of Zeruiah."[A,c] 23 Then
King Solomon took an oath by the LORD:
"May God punish me and do so severely[d]
if Adonijah has not made this request at
the cost of his life. 24 And now, as the LORD
lives — the one who established me, seated me on the throne of my father David,
and made me a dynasty as he promised[e]
— I swear Adonijah will be put to death today!" 25 Then King Solomon dispatched Benaiah son of Jehoiada,[f] who struck down
Adonijah, and he died.

ABIATHAR'S BANISHMENT

26 The king said to the priest Abiathar,[g]
"Go to your fields in Anathoth.[h] Even
though you deserve to die, I will not put
you to death today, since you carried the
ark of the Lord GOD in the presence of my
father David[i] and you suffered through all
that my father suffered."[j] 27 So Solomon
banished Abiathar from being the LORD's
priest, and it fulfilled the LORD's prophecy he had spoken at Shiloh against Eli's
family.[k]

JOAB'S EXECUTION

28 The news reached Joab. Since he had
supported Adonijah[l] but not Absalom,[m]
Joab fled to the LORD's tabernacle and took
hold of the horns of the altar.[n]
29 It was reported to King Solomon: "Joab
has fled to the LORD's tabernacle and is
now beside the altar." Then Solomon sent[B]
Benaiah son of Jehoiada[o] and told him, "Go
and strike him down!"[p]
30 So Benaiah went to the tabernacle and
said to Joab, "This is what the king says:
'Come out!'"[q]
But Joab said, "No, for I will die here."
So Benaiah took a message back to the
king, "This is what Joab said, and this is
how he answered me."
31 The king said to him, "Do just as he
says. Strike him down and bury him in
order to remove from me and from my
father's family the blood that Joab shed
without just cause.[r] 32 The LORD will bring
back his own blood on his head because
he struck down two men more righteous
and better than he, without my father
David's knowledge. With his sword, Joab
murdered Abner[s] son of Ner, commander of Israel's army, and Amasa[t] son of Jether, commander of Judah's army. 33 The
responsibility for their deaths will come
back to Joab and to his descendants[C] forever, but for David, his descendants, his dynasty, and his throne, there will be peace
from the LORD forever."[u]
34 Benaiah son of Jehoiada[v] went up,
struck down Joab, and put him to death.
He was buried at his house in the wilderness.[w] 35 Then the king appointed Benaiah
son of Jehoiada in Joab's place over the
army,[x] and he appointed the priest Zadok
in Abiathar's place.

SHIMEI'S BANISHMENT AND EXECUTION

36 Then the king summoned Shimei[y] and
said to him, "Build a house for yourself in
Jerusalem and live there, but don't leave
there and go anywhere else. 37 On the day
you do leave and cross the Kidron Valley,[z]
know for sure that you will certainly die.
Your blood will be on your own head."[aa]
38 Shimei said to the king, "The sentence
is fair; your servant will do as my lord the
king has spoken." And Shimei lived in Jerusalem for a long time.
39 But then, at the end of three years, two
of Shimei's slaves ran away to Achish[ab] son
of Maacah, king of Gath.[ac] Shimei was informed, "Look, your slaves are in Gath."
40 So Shimei saddled his donkey and set out
to Achish at Gath to search for his slaves.
He went and brought them back from Gath.

[a]2:22 1Kg 1:6; 1Ch 3:2,5
[b]2Sm 16:20-22
[c]1Kg 1:7
[d]2:23 Ru 1:17; 1Sm 3:17
[e]2:24 2Sm 7:11-13
[f]2:25 1Kg 1:8,26,38
[g]2:26 1Kg 1:7,19
[h]Jos 21:18; Jr 1:1
[i]2Sm 15:24-25,29
[j]1Sm 22:20-23; 2Sm 19:11
[k]2:27 1Sm 2:31-35
[l]2:28 1Kg 1:7
[m]2Sm 18:1-5
[n]Ex 21:12-14; 1Kg 1:50
[o]2:29 1Kg 1:8
[p]Ex 12:12,14; 2Sm 3:27; 18:14; 20:10
[q]2:30 Ex 21:14
[r]2:31 Nm 35:33; Dt 21:8-9
[s]2:32 2Sm 3:26-27
[t]2Sm 20:8-10
[u]2:33 2Sm 3:28-29
[v]2:34 2Kg 2:25
[w]2Sm 2:32
[x]2:35 1Kg 4:4
[y]2:36 2Sm 16:5-13; 1Kg 2:8-9
[z]2:37 Jn 18:1
[aa]Gn 2:17; 2Sm 1:16
[ab]2:39 1Sm 27:2
[ac]Jos 13:3; 1Sm 6:16-17; 21:10

[A]2:22 LXX, Vg, Syr read *kingship for him, and on his side are Abiathar the priest and Joab son of Zeruiah* [B]2:29 LXX adds *Joab a message: "What is the matter with you, that you have fled to the altar?" And Joab replied, "Because I feared you, I have fled to the Lord." And Solomon the king sent* [C]2:33 Lit *Their blood will return on the head of Joab and on the head of his seed*

2:22-24 Adonijah's request was really an act of treason. Since Adonijah had been next in line in the normal succession of kings, marrying Abishag would have given him *two* claims to the throne in the eyes of Israel's people (see the note on 2:15-17).

2:25 Years before, David pronounced judgment on himself when he thought he was passing judgment on the villain of Nathan's story about a rich man eating a poor man's pet sheep. He'd said, "The man who did this deserves to die! . . . He must pay four lambs for that lamb" (2 Sam 12:5).

Up to this point, David had paid for his sins with the lives of three "lambs": his sons Amnon (see 2 Sam 13:21-29), Absalom (see 2 Sam 18:9-15), and the unnamed baby boy resulting from his adultery (see 2 Sam 12:15-23). **Adonijah** was the fourth untimely loss. The lesson is clear: even forgiven sin has consequences.

2:26-27 In Abiathar's dismissal for having conspired with Adonijah we see that while God's wheels of judgment often grind slowly, he is as faithful to judge as he is to pardon and forgive.

[a]2:44 1Kg 2:8-9
[b]2:45 2Sm 7:13
[c]2:46 1Kg 2:12; 2Ch 1:1
[d]3:1 Dt 7:3; 1Kg 7:8; 9:24; Ezr 9:14
[e]2Sm 5:7; 7:8; 9:10
[f]2Sm 7:1-2
[g]2Sm 6:1,14; 1Kg 6:37; 7:51
[h]1Kg 9:15
[i]3:2 Dt 12:13-14
[j]Dt 14:23
[k]3:3 Dt 6:5
[l]1Kg 3:14
[m]3:4 Jos 9:3-27; 21:17
[n]2Ch 1:3,6
[o]3:5-15 2Ch 1:7-13
[p]3:5 Nm 12:6; 1Kg 9:2; 11:9
[q]Mt 7:7; Jn 15:7
[r]3:6 1Kg 1:48
[s]1Kg 2:4; 9:4; 2Ch 1:8

[t]3:7 2Ch 1:8
[u]1Ch 29:1; Jr 1:6-7
[v]3:8 Ex 19:5-6; Dt 7:6
[w]Gn 15:5; 22:17
[x]3:9 Dt 1:16-17
[y]2Ch 1:10
[z]3:11 Jms 4:3
[aa]1Ch 22:12
[ab]3:12 1Jn 5:14-15
[ac]1Kg 4:29-31; 10:23-24
[ad]3:13 Mt 6:33; Lk 12:31
[ae]1Kg 10:23
[af]3:14 1Kg 3:6; Pr 3:1-2
[ag]3:15 Gn 41:7
[ah]Dn 2:3; 4:5
[ai]2Sm 6:12
[aj]1Sm 11:15
[ak]1Kg 8:65
[al]3:16 Dt 16:18-19; 2Sm 15:2-4

41 It was reported to Solomon that Shimei had gone from Jerusalem to Gath and
had returned. 42 So the king summoned
Shimei and said to him, "Didn't I make you
swear by the LORD and warn you, saying,
'On the day you leave and go anywhere
else, know for sure that you will certainly die'? And you said to me, 'The sentence
is fair; I will obey.' 43 So why have you not
kept the LORD's oath and the command
that I gave you?" 44 The king also said, "You
yourself know all the evil that you did to
my father David.[a] Therefore, the LORD has
brought back your evil on your head, 45 but
King Solomon will be blessed, and David's
throne will remain established before the
LORD forever."[b]
46 Then the king commanded Benaiah
son of Jehoiada, and he went out and
struck Shimei down, and he died. So the
kingdom was established in Solomon's
hand.[c]

THE LORD APPEARS TO SOLOMON

3 Solomon made an alliance[A] with Pharaoh king of Egypt by marrying Pharaoh's daughter.[d] Solomon brought her to
the city of David[e] until he finished building his palace,[f] the LORD's temple,[g] and the
wall surrounding Jerusalem.[h] 2 However,
the people were sacrificing on the high
places,[i] because until that time a temple
for the LORD's name[j] had not been built.
3 Solomon loved the LORD[k] by walking in
the statutes of his father David,[l] but he
also sacrificed and burned incense on
the high places.
4 The king went to Gibeon[m] to sacrifice
there because it was the most famous high
place. He offered a thousand burnt offerings on that altar.[n] 5 At Gibeon the LORD appeared to Solomon[o] in a dream at night.[p]
God said, "Ask.[q] What should I give you?"
6 And Solomon replied, "You have shown
great and faithful love to your servant, my
father David, because he walked before
you in faithfulness, righteousness, and integrity.[B] You have continued this great and
faithful love for him by giving him a son to
sit on his throne,[r] as it is today.[s]
7 "LORD my God, you have now made
your servant king in my father David's
place.[t] Yet I am just a youth with no experience in leadership.[C,u] 8 Your servant is
among your people you have chosen,[v] a
people too many to be numbered or counted.[w] 9 So give your servant a receptive
heart to judge[x] your people and to discern
between good and evil. For who is able to
judge this great people of yours?"[y]
10 Now it pleased the Lord that Solomon had requested this. 11 So God said to
him, "Because you have requested this
and did not ask for long life[D] or riches for
yourself,[z] or the death[E] of your enemies,
but you asked discernment for yourself
to administer justice,[aa] 12 I will therefore
do what you have asked.[ab] I will give you
a wise and understanding heart, so that
there has never been anyone like you before and never will be again.[ac] 13 In addition, I will give you what you did not ask
for: both riches and honor,[ad] so that no
king will be your equal during your entire life.[ae] 14 If you walk in my ways and
keep my statutes and commands just as
your father David did, I will give you a
long life."[af]
15 Then Solomon woke up[ag] and realized
it had been a dream.[ah] He went to Jerusalem, stood before the ark of the Lord's
covenant,[ai] and offered burnt offerings
and fellowship offerings.[aj] Then he held a
feast[ak] for all his servants.

SOLOMON'S WISDOM

16 Then two women who were prostitutes
came to the king and stood before him.[al]
17 One woman said, "Please, my lord, this
woman and I live in the same house, and
I had a baby while she was in the house.
18 On the third day after I gave birth, she
also had a baby and we were alone. No
one else[F] was with us in the house; just
the two of us were there. 19 During the
night this woman's son died because she
lay on him. 20 She got up in the middle of
the night and took my son from my side
while your servant was asleep. She laid
him in her arms, and she put her dead son

[A]3:1 Lit *Solomon made himself a son-in-law* [B]3:6 Lit *and uprightness of heart with you* [C]3:7 Lit *am a little youth and do not know to go out or come in* [D]3:11 Lit *for many days* [E]3:11 Lit *life* [F]3:18 Lit *No stranger*

3:1 Solomon was not hesitant to use marriage as a political strategy, and he would eventually take foreign marriages to dizzying heights. In Old Testament times, God tolerated polygamy among his people, but it always cost them because it was outside his will.

3:2 The people of Israel were engaging in a pagan practice they learned from their Canaanite neighbors that was in violation of the Mosaic law (see Lev 17:3-4).

3:5-9 Solomon's response to God's question showed that in one sense, he was already wise beyond his twenty-or-so years. The young man recognized his inadequacies. The first step toward becoming a kingdom man is to realize your desperate need for God.

3:14 Notice the word ***if*** here. God's promises were sure, but they had to be accessed by obedience.

in my arms. **21** When I got up in the morning to nurse my son, I discovered he was dead. That morning, when I looked closely at him I realized that he was not the son I gave birth to."

22 "No," the other woman said. "My son is the living one; your son is the dead one."

The first woman said, "No, your son is the dead one; my son is the living one." So they argued before the king.

23 The king replied, "This woman says, 'This is my son who is alive, and your son is dead,' but that woman says, 'No, your son is dead, and my son is alive.' " **24** The king continued, "Bring me a sword." So they brought the sword to the king. **25** And the king said, "Cut the living boy in two and give half to one and half to the other."

26 The woman whose son was alive spoke to the king because she felt great compassion^A,a for her son. "My lord, give her the living baby," she said, "but please don't have him killed!"

But the other one said, "He will not be mine or yours. Cut him in two!"

27 The king responded, "Give the living baby to the first woman, and don't kill him. She is his mother." **28** All Israel heard about the judgment the king had given, and they stood in awe of the king because they saw that God's wisdom^b was in him to carry out justice.

SOLOMON'S OFFICIALS

4 King Solomon reigned over all Israel,^c **2** and these were his officials:^d

Azariah son of Zadok, priest;
3 Elihoreph and Ahijah the sons of Shisha, secretaries;
Jehoshaphat son of Ahilud, court historian;
4 Benaiah son of Jehoiada, in charge of the army;
Zadok and Abiathar, priests;
5 Azariah son of Nathan, in charge of the deputies;
Zabud son of Nathan, a priest and adviser to the king;
6 Ahishar, in charge of the palace;
and Adoniram son of Abda, in charge of forced labor.

7 Solomon had twelve deputies for all Israel. They provided food for the king and his household; each one made provision for one month out of the year.^e **8** These were their names:

Ben-hur, in the hill country of Ephraim;
9 Ben-deker, in Makaz, Shaalbim, Beth-shemesh, and Elon-beth-hanan;
10 Ben-hesed, in Arubboth (he had Socoh and the whole land of Hepher);
11 Ben-abinadab, in all Naphath-dor (Taphath daughter of Solomon was his wife);
12 Baana son of Ahilud, in Taanach, Megiddo, and all Beth-shean which is beside Zarethan below Jezreel, from Beth-shean to Abel-meholah, as far as the other side of Jokmeam;
13 Ben-geber, in Ramoth-gilead (he had the villages of Jair son of Manasseh, which are in Gilead, and he had the region of Argob, which is in Bashan, sixty great cities with walls and bronze bars);
14 Ahinadab son of Iddo, in Mahanaim;
15 Ahimaaz, in Naphtali (he also had married a daughter of Solomon — Basemath);
16 Baana son of Hushai, in Asher and Bealoth;
17 Jehoshaphat son of Paruah, in Issachar;
18 Shimei son of Ela, in Benjamin;
19 Geber son of Uri, in the land of Gilead, the country of King Sihon of the Amorites and of King Og of Bashan.
There was one deputy in the land of Judah.^B

SOLOMON'S PROVISIONS

20 Judah and Israel were as numerous as the sand by the sea;^f they were eating, drinking, and rejoicing. **21** Solomon ruled all the kingdoms from the Euphrates River to the land of the Philistines and as far as the border of Egypt.^g They offered tribute and served Solomon all the days of his life.^h

22 Solomon's provisions for one day were 150 bushels^c of fine flour and 300 bushels^D of meal, **23** ten fattened cattle,

^a3:26 Gn 43:30; Jr 31:20; Hs 11:8
^b3:28 2Sm 14:20; 1Kg 3:9,11-12
^c4:1 2Sm 5:5; 8:15
^d4:2 1Kg 12:6

^e4:7 1Kg 4:27
^f4:20 Gn 22:17; 1Kg 3:8
^g4:21 Gn 15:18; 2Ch 9:26
^h2Sm 8:2,6

---

^A3:26 Lit *because her compassion grew hot*   ^B4:19 LXX; MT omits *of Judah*   ^C4:22 Lit *30 cors*   ^D4:22 Lit *60 cors*

3:23-27 Left without the help of a DNA test, the average judge would be stumped by the women's conflicting claims. But with his God-given insight into human nature, Solomon knew just what to do. God had given him not just smarts, but the ability to see the world from a spiritual perspective and apply it. The book of Proverbs, written mostly by Solomon, is further demonstration that God had blessed the king with the ability to put spiritual truth into action.

4:20 This line shows the fulfillment of God's promise in Genesis 22:17.

4:21 That the king exacted **tribute** from the nations under his rule is a reminder that God is able to take the resources of unbelievers and use them for his kingdom purposes.

[a] 4:22-23 1Kg 10:5; Neh 5:18
[b] 4:25 Jdg 20:1; 1Sm 3:20
[c] Mc 4:3-4; Zch 3:10
[d] 4:26 Dt 17:16; 1Kg 10:26; 2Ch 1:14
[e] 4:28 Est 8:10,14
[f] 4:29 1Kg 3:12
[g] 4:30 Gn 29:1
[h] Is 19:11; Ac 7:22
[i] 1Ch 15:19; Pss 88, 89 titles
[k] 1Ch 2:6
[l] 1Kg 10:1,6
[m] 4:32 Pr 1:1; Ec 9:12
[n] Sg 1:1
[o] 4:34 1Kg 10:1,6
[p] 5:1 2Ch 2:3
[q] 1Kg 1:34,39
[r] 2Sm 5:11; 1Ch 14:1

[s] 5:3 1Ch 28:2-3
[t] 5:4 1Kg 4:24-25
[u] 5:5 2Ch 2:4
[v] 2Sm 7:12-13
[w] 5:6 2Ch 2:8
[x] 5:7 1Kg 10:9

[y] 5:9 2Ch 2:16; Ezr 3:7
[z] 5:11 2Ch 2:10
[aa] 5:12 1Kg 3:12
[ab] 1Kg 15:19
[ac] 5:13 1Kg 4:6; 9:15

twenty range cattle, and a hundred sheep and goats, besides deer, gazelles, roebucks, and pen-fed poultry,[A,a] 24 for he had dominion over everything west of the Euphrates from Tiphsah to Gaza and over all the kings west of the Euphrates. He had peace on all his surrounding borders. 25 Throughout Solomon's reign, Judah and Israel lived in safety from Dan to Beer-sheba,[b] each person under his own vine and his own fig tree.[c] 26 Solomon had forty thousand[B] stalls of horses for his chariots, and twelve thousand horsemen.[d] 27 Each of those deputies for a month in turn provided food for King Solomon and for everyone who came to King Solomon's table. They neglected nothing. 28 Each man brought the barley and the straw for the chariot teams and the other horses[e] to the required place according to his assignment.[c]

SOLOMON'S WISDOM AND LITERARY GIFTS

29 God gave Solomon wisdom, very great insight, and understanding[f] as vast as the sand on the seashore. 30 Solomon's wisdom was greater than the wisdom of all the people of the East,[g] greater than all the wisdom of Egypt.[h] 31 He was wiser than anyone[i] — wiser than Ethan the Ezrahite,[j] and Heman, Calcol, and Darda, sons of Mahol.[k] His reputation extended to all the surrounding nations.[l]

32 Solomon spoke 3,000 proverbs,[m] and his songs numbered 1,005.[n] 33 He spoke about trees, from the cedar in Lebanon to the hyssop growing out of the wall. He also spoke about animals, birds, reptiles, and fish. 34 Emissaries of all peoples, sent by every king on earth who had heard of his wisdom, came to listen to Solomon's wisdom.[o]

HIRAM'S BUILDING MATERIALS

5 King Hiram of Tyre[p] sent his emissaries to Solomon when he heard that he had been anointed king in his father's place,[q] for Hiram had always been friends with David.[r]

2 Solomon sent this message to Hiram: 3 "You know my father David was not able to build a temple for the name of the LORD his God. This was because of the warfare all around him until the LORD put his enemies under his feet.[s] 4 The LORD my God has now given me rest on every side; there is no enemy or crisis.[t] 5 So I plan to build a temple for the name of the LORD my God,[u] according to what the LORD promised my father David: 'I will put your son on your throne in your place, and he will build the temple for my name.'[v]

6 "Therefore, command that cedars from Lebanon be cut down for me. My servants will be with your servants, and I will pay your servants' wages according to whatever you say, for you know that not a man among us knows how to cut timber like the Sidonians."[w]

7 When Hiram heard Solomon's words, he rejoiced greatly and said, "Blessed be the LORD today![x] He has given David a wise son to be over this great people!" 8 Then Hiram sent a reply to Solomon, saying, "I have heard your message; I will do everything you want regarding the cedar and cypress timber. 9 My servants will bring the logs down from Lebanon to the sea, and I will make them into rafts to go by sea to the place you indicate. I will break them apart there, and you can take them away. You then can meet my needs by providing my household with food."[y]

10 So Hiram provided Solomon with all the cedar and cypress timber he wanted, 11 and Solomon provided Hiram with one hundred thousand bushels[D] of wheat as food for his household and one hundred ten thousand gallons[E] of oil from crushed olives.[z] Solomon did this for Hiram year after year.

12 The LORD gave Solomon wisdom, as he had promised him.[aa] There was peace between Hiram and Solomon, and the two of them made a treaty.[ab]

SOLOMON'S WORKFORCE

13 Then King Solomon drafted forced laborers from all Israel;[ac] the labor force numbered thirty thousand men. 14 He sent ten thousand to Lebanon each month in shifts; one month they were in Lebanon, two

---

[A] 4:23 Hb obscure   [B] 4:26 2Ch 9:25 reads 4,000 stalls   [C] 4:28 Lit judgment   [D] 5:11 Lit 20,000 cors   [E] 5:11 LXX reads 20,000 baths; MT reads 20 cors

---

4:30 That Solomon's wisdom far surpassed **the wisdom of all the people of the East** and **all the wisdom of Egypt** was significant; these regions were fabled for their wisdom. 4:31-33 A consideration of Solomon's ancestry is instructive. He was David's son by Bathsheba.

We know of her lineage because Bathsheba literally means "the daughter of Sheba." The Table of Nations (Gen 10) identifies Sheba in the line of Ham, making Sheba a man from an African nation (see Gen 10:6-7). So Solomon's mother (as well as his ancestors Rahab and

Ruth; see the note on 1 Sam 16:13) gave him roots within the black community. They thus place him as an example of black achievement as well as black history in biblical culture. 5:10-12 Solomon conducted negotiations in the wisdom God gave him.

months they were at home. Adoniram was in charge of the forced labor. [15] Solomon had seventy thousand porters and eighty thousand stonecutters in the mountains,[a] [16] not including his thirty-three hundred[A] deputies[b] in charge of the work. They supervised the people doing the work. [17] The king commanded them to quarry large, costly stones to lay the foundation of the temple with dressed stones.[c] [18] So Solomon's builders and Hiram's builders,[d] along with the Gebalites,[e] quarried the stone and prepared the timber and stone for the temple's construction.

BUILDING THE TEMPLE

6 Solomon began to build the temple for the Lord in the four hundred eightieth year[f] after the Israelites came out of the land of Egypt, in the fourth year of his reign over Israel, in the month of Ziv, which is the second month.[B,g] [2] The temple that King Solomon built for the Lord[h] was ninety feet[c] long, thirty feet[D] wide, and forty-five feet[E] high.[i] [3] The portico in front of the temple sanctuary was thirty feet long extending across the temple's width, and fifteen feet deep[F] in front of the temple.[j] [4] He also made windows with beveled frames[G] for the temple.[k]

[5] He then built a chambered structure[H] along the temple wall, encircling the walls of the temple, that is, the sanctuary and the inner sanctuary.[i] And he made side chambers[i] all around.[m] [6] The lowest chamber was 7 ½ feet[j] wide, the middle was 9 feet[K] wide, and the third was 10 ½ feet[L] wide. He also provided offset ledges for the temple all around the outside so that nothing would be inserted into the temple walls. [7] The temple's construction used finished stones cut at the quarry so that no hammer, chisel, or any iron tool was heard in the temple while it was being built.[n]

[8] The door for the lowest[M] side chamber was on the right side of the temple. They[N] went up a stairway[G] to the middle chamber, and from the middle to the third. [9] When he finished building the temple,[o] he paneled it with boards and planks of cedar. [10] He built the chambers along the entire temple, joined to the temple with cedar beams;[p] each story was 7 ½ feet high.

[11] The word of the Lord came to Solomon:[q] [12] "As for this temple you are building — if you walk in my statutes, observe my ordinances, and keep all my commands by walking in them,[r] I will fulfill my promise to you, which I made to your father David.[s] [13] I will dwell among the Israelites and not abandon my people Israel."[t]

[14] When Solomon finished building the temple,[o,u] [15] he paneled the interior temple walls with cedar boards; from the temple floor to the surface of the ceiling he overlaid the interior with wood. He also overlaid the floor with cypress boards.[v] [16] Then he lined thirty feet of the rear of the temple with cedar boards from the floor to the surface of the ceiling,[p] and he built the interior as an inner sanctuary, the most holy place.[w] [17] The temple, that is, the sanctuary in front of the most holy place,[q] was sixty feet[R] long. [18] The cedar paneling inside the temple was carved with ornamental gourds[x] and flower blossoms. Everything was cedar;[y] not a stone could be seen.

[19] He prepared the inner sanctuary[z] inside the temple to put the ark of the Lord's covenant[aa] there. [20] The interior of the sanctuary was thirty feet long, thirty feet wide, and thirty feet high; he overlaid it with pure gold.[ab] He also overlaid the cedar altar. [21] Next, Solomon overlaid the interior of the temple with pure gold, and he hung[s] gold chains[ac] across the front of the inner sanctuary[ad] and overlaid it with gold. [22] So he added the gold overlay to the

[a] 5:15 2Ch 2:17-18
[b] 5:16 1Kg 9:23
[c] 5:17 1Kg 6:7; 1Ch 22:2
[d] 5:18 1Kg 5:6,9
[e] 6:1 Ac 13:20
[f] 6:1 1Kg 6:37; 2Ch 3:1-2; Ezr 3:8
[g] 6:2 Ezr 5:11
[h] 2Ch 3:3; Ezk 41:1
[i] 6:3 2Ch 3:4; Ezk 40:49
[j] 6:4 Ezk 41:16
[k] 6:5 1Kg 6:16,19-21
[l] Jr 35:2; Ezk 41:5-6
[m] 6:7 1Kg 5:17

[n] 6:9 1Kg 6:1,14,38
[o] 6:9-10 1Kg 5:6,8,10
[p] 6:11 1Kg 3:5,11-15; 9:2
[q] 6:12 1Kg 11:10
[r] 2Sm 7:12-16; 1Kg 9:5
[s] 6:13 Lv 26:11; Jos 1:5-6; Heb 13:5
[t] 6:14 1Kg 6:1,38
[u] 6:15 1Kg 5:8,10; 7:7; Ezk 41:16
[v] 6:16 Ex 26:33-34; 1Kg 8:6; Heb 9:3
[w] 6:18 1Kg 7:24
[x] 1Kg 5:8,10
[y] 6:19 Ezk 41:3-4
[z] 6:20 2Ch 3:8-9
[aa] 6:21 2Ch 3:14; Mt 27:51
[ab] 2Ch 3:16

[A] 5:16 Some LXX mss read 3,600; 2Ch 2:2,18 [B] 6:1 April–May [C] 6:2 Lit 60 cubits [D] 6:2 Lit 20 cubits, also in vv. 3,16,20 [E] 6:2 Lit 30 cubits [F] 6:3 Lit 10 cubits wide [G] 6:4,8 Hb obscure [H] 6:5 Lit built the temple of chamber [I] 6:5 Lit made ribs or sides [J] 6:6 Lit five cubits, also in vv. 10,24 [K] 6:6 Lit six cubits [L] 6:6 Lit seven cubits [M] 6:8 LXX, Tg; MT reads middle [N] 6:8 = People [O] 6:11-14 LXX omits these vv. [P] 6:16 LXX; MT omits of the ceiling; 1Kg 6:15 [Q] 6:17 Lit front of me; Hb obscure [R] 6:17 Lit 40 cubits [S] 6:21 Lit he caused to pass across

6:1 This statement allows us to fix several key dates in Israel's history. It is generally agreed that Solomon reigned from 971 to 931 BC. So **the fourth year of his reign** would have been about 966 BC. Going back 480 years from this allows us to arrive at a date for the exodus: 1446 BC.

Solomon's charge to build the temple was the key feature of his reign. From this point onward, the attitude of Israel's and Judah's kings toward the temple, and by extension toward the Lord and his covenant, would be the basis for their evaluation in God's eyes.

6:2-4 Solomon's temple was not huge in terms of square footage, but its size was the only modest thing about it. Its outer appearance must have been stunning.

6:7 Making sure that each piece was precut so that it would sit perfectly in place would have required amazing skill. Just as the Lord had provided skilled workers to build the tabernacle (see Exod 31:1-11), he provided the same for the construction of his holy temple.

6:11-13 God was more concerned about the people's hearts and their obedience to him

than he was with the building they were working on.

6:19-20 The inner sanctuary, the most holy place, was a **thirty**-foot cube. Here the **ark of the Lord's covenant** would rest. The ark was considered the throne of God; he was enthroned between the cherubim above its cover, the mercy seat (see 1 Sam 4:4; Isa 37:16). According to 2 Chronicles 3:8, the weight of gold overlaying the most holy place was "forty-five thousand pounds"! The one true God deserved a temple of unequaled grandeur.

[a] 6:22 1Kg 7:48; Heb 9:3-4
[b] 6:23-27 Ex 25:18-22; 2Ch 3:10-13
[c] 6:27 2Ch 5:8
[d] 6:29 Ezk 41:18,25
[e] 6:31-32 Ezk 41:23
[f] 6:34-35 Ezk 41:23-25
[g] 6:36 2Ch 4:9; Jr 36:10
[h] 1Kg 7:12; Ezr 6:4

[i] 6:38 1Kg 6:1,14
[j] 1Kg 7:1
[k] 7:1 1Kg 9:10; 2Ch 8:1
[l] 7:2 1Kg 10:21; 2Ch 9:16
[m] 7:3-4 1Kg 10:16-17
[n] 7:7 1Kg 3:16-28
[o] 7:8 1Kg 3:1; 9:24; 2Ch 8:11
[p] 7:12 1Kg 6:36
[q] 7:13 1Kg 5:1-11; 2Ch 2:13-14
[r] 7:14 Ex 31:2-5

entire temple until everything was completely finished, including the entire altar[a] that belongs to the inner sanctuary.

[23] In the inner sanctuary he made two cherubim[b] 15 feet[A] high out of olive wood. [24] One wing of the first cherub was 7 ½ feet long, and the other wing was 7 ½ feet long. The wingspan was 15 feet from tip to tip. [25] The second cherub also was 15 feet; both cherubim had the same size and shape. [26] The first cherub's height was 15 feet and so was the second cherub's. [27] Then he put the cherubim inside the inner temple. Since their wings were spread out, the first one's wing touched one wall while the second cherub's wing touched the other[B] wall, and in the middle of the temple their wings were touching wing to wing.[c] [28] He also overlaid the cherubim with gold.

[29] He carved all the surrounding temple walls with carved engravings — cherubim,[d] palm trees, and flower blossoms — in the inner and outer sanctuaries. [30] He overlaid the temple floor with gold in both the inner and the outer sanctuaries.

[31] For the entrance of the inner sanctuary, he made olive wood doors.[e] The pillars of the doorposts were five-sided.[c] [32] The two doors were made of olive wood. He carved cherubim, palm trees, and flower blossoms on them and overlaid them with gold, hammering gold over the cherubim and palm trees. [33] In the same way, he made four-sided[c] olive wood doorposts for the sanctuary entrance. [34] The two doors[f] were made of cypress wood; the first door had two folding sides, and the second door had two folding panels. [35] He carved cherubim, palm trees, and flower blossoms on them and overlaid them with gold applied evenly over the carving. [36] He built the inner courtyard[g] with three rows of dressed stone[h] and a row of trimmed cedar beams.

[37] The foundation of the LORD's temple was laid in Solomon's fourth year in the month of Ziv. [38] In his eleventh year in the month of Bul, which is the eighth month,[D]

the temple was completed in every detail and according to every specification.[i] So he built it in seven years.[j]

SOLOMON'S PALACE COMPLEX

7 Solomon completed his entire palace complex after thirteen years of construction.[k] [2] He built the House of the Forest of Lebanon.[l] It was one hundred fifty feet[E] long, seventy-five feet[F] wide, and forty-five feet[G] high on four rows of cedar pillars, with cedar beams on top of the pillars. [3] It was paneled above with cedar at the top of the chambers that rested on forty-five pillars, fifteen per row. [4] There were three rows of window frames, facing each other[H] in three tiers.[l,m] [5] All the doors and doorposts had rectangular frames, the openings facing each other[J] in three tiers. [6] He made the hall of pillars seventy-five feet long and forty-five feet wide. A portico was in front of the pillars, and a canopy with pillars[c] was in front of them. [7] He made the Hall of the Throne where he would judge[n] — the Hall of Judgment. It was paneled with cedar from the floor to the rafters.[K] [8] Solomon's own palace where he would live, in the other courtyard behind the hall, was of similar construction. And he made a house like this hall for Pharaoh's daughter, his wife.[L,o]

[9] All of these buildings were of costly stones, cut to size and sawed with saws on the inner and outer surfaces, from foundation to coping and from the outside to the great courtyard. [10] The foundation was made of large, costly stones twelve and fifteen feet[M] long. [11] Above were also costly stones, cut to size, as well as cedar wood. [12] Around the great courtyard, as well as the inner courtyard of the LORD's temple and the portico of the temple, were three rows of dressed stone and a row of trimmed cedar beams.[p]

[13] King Solomon had Hiram[N,q] brought from Tyre. [14] He was a widow's son from the tribe of Naphtali, and his father was a man of Tyre, a bronze craftsman. Hiram had great skill,[r] understanding, and

[A] 6:23 Lit 10 cubits, also in vv. 24,25,26　[B] 6:27 Lit the second　[C] 6:31, 33; 7:6 Hb obscure　[D] 6:38 = October–November　[E] 7:2 Lit 100 cubits　[F] 7:2 Lit 50 cubits, also in v. 6　[G] 7:2 Lit 30 cubits, also in vv. 6,23　[H] 7:4 Lit frames, window to window　[I] 7:4 Lit three times; = at 3 different places, also in v. 5　[J] 7:5 Lit frames, opposing window to window　[K] 7:7 Syr, Vg; MT reads floor　[L] 7:8 Lit daughter he had taken　[M] 7:10 Lit ten cubits and eight cubits　[N] 7:13 = Huram in 2Ch 4:11

7:1 It took Solomon almost twice as long to build his **palace complex** as it took to build the temple.

7:2 The **House of the Forest of Lebanon** was probably so named because cedar from Lebanon was used extensively in its construction (see 5:6).

7:7 Within the larger complex was **the Hall of the Throne**, the place where Solomon **would judge**; thus, it is further described as **the Hall of Judgment**.

7:13-14 This man was not the king of **Tyre** (see 5:1-12). That he was brought in suggests his

skill was beyond anything Solomon could find locally (7:14).

knowledge to do every kind of bronze work. So he came to King Solomon and carried out all his work.[a]

THE BRONZE PILLARS

15 He cast two bronze pillars,[b] each 27 feet[A] high and 18 feet[B] in circumference.[C,c] **16** He also made two capitals[d] of cast bronze to set on top of the pillars; 7 ½ feet[D] was the height of the first capital, and 7 ½ feet was also the height of the second capital. **17** The capitals on top of the pillars had gratings of latticework, wreaths[E] made of chainwork — seven for the first capital and seven for the second.

18 He made the pillars with two encircling rows of pomegranates on the one grating to cover the capital on top; he did the same for the second capital. **19** And the capitals on top of the pillars in the portico were shaped like lilies, six feet[F] high. **20** The capitals on the two pillars were also immediately above the rounded surface next to the grating, and two hundred pomegranates[e] were in rows encircling each[G] capital. **21** He set up the pillars at the portico[f] of the sanctuary: he set up the right pillar and named it Jachin;[H] then he set up the left pillar and named it Boaz.[i,g] **22** The tops of the pillars were shaped like lilies. Then the work of the pillars was completed.[n]

THE BASIN

23 He made the cast metal basin,[i,j] 15 feet[K] from brim to brim, perfectly round. It was 7 ½ feet high and 45 feet in circumference. **24** Ornamental gourds[j] encircled it below the brim, ten every half yard,[L] completely encircling the basin.[k] The gourds were cast in two rows when the basin was cast. **25** It stood on twelve oxen,[l] three facing north, three facing west, three facing south, and three facing east. The basin was on top of them and all their hindquarters were toward the center. **26** The basin was three inches[M] thick, and its rim was fashioned like the brim of a cup or of a lily blossom. It held eleven thousand gallons.[N]

THE BRONZE WATER CARTS

27 Then he made ten bronze water carts.[o,m] Each water cart was 6 feet long, 6 feet wide, and 4 ½ feet[p] high. **28** This was the design of the carts: They had frames; the frames were between the cross-pieces, **29** and on the frames between the cross-pieces were lions, oxen, and cherubim.[n] On the cross-pieces there was a pedestal above, and below the lions and oxen were wreaths of hanging[o] work. **30** Each cart[o] had four bronze wheels with bronze axles. Underneath the four corners of the basin were cast supports, each next to a wreath. **31** And the water cart's opening inside the crown on top was eighteen inches[R] wide. The opening was round, made as a pedestal twenty-seven inches[S] wide. On it were carvings, but their frames were square, not round. **32** There were four wheels under the frames, and the wheel axles were part of the water cart; each wheel was twenty-seven inches[T] tall. **33** The wheels' design was similar to that of chariot wheels: their axles, rims, spokes, and hubs were all of cast metal. **34** Four supports were at the four corners of each water cart; each support was one piece with the water cart. **35** At the top of the cart was a band nine inches[u] high encircling it; also, at the top of the cart, its braces and its frames were one piece with it. **36** He engraved cherubim, lions, and palm trees[p] on the plates of its braces and on its frames, wherever each had space, with encircling wreaths. **37** In this way he made the ten water carts using the same casting, dimensions, and shape for all of them.

BRONZE BASINS AND OTHER UTENSILS

38 Then he made ten bronze basins[q] — each basin held 220 gallons[v] and each was six feet wide — one basin for each of the ten water carts. **39** He set five water carts on the right side of the temple and five on the left side. He put the basin near the right side of the temple toward the southeast.[r] **40** Then Hiram made[s] the basins, the shovels, and the sprinkling basins.

[a]7:14 2Ch 4:11
[b]7:15 2Kg 25:16–17; 2Ch 3:15
[c]1Kg 7:41
[d]7:16 1Kg 7:42; 2Kg 25:17
[e]7:20 2Ch 3:16; 4:13
[f]7:21 1Kg 6:3
[g]2Ch 3:17
[h]7:22 2Kg 25:17
[i]7:23 2Kg 25:13; 1Ch 18:8; 2Ch 4:6
[j]7:24 1Kg 6:18
[k]2Ch 4:3
[l]7:25 2Kg 16:17; 2Ch 4:4–5; Jr 52:20

[m]7:27 2Kg 25:13; 2Ch 4:14
[n]7:29 1Kg 6:29,32
[o]7:30 2Kg 16:17
[p]7:36 6:29
[q]7:38 Ex 30:18; 2Ch 4:6
[r]7:39 2Ch 4:10
[s]7:40–51 2Ch 4:11–5:1

[A]7:15 Lit *18 cubits*   [B]7:15 Lit *12 cubits*   [C]7:15 LXX adds *and the thickness of the pillar was four fingers hollowed and similarly the second pillar*   [D]7:16 Lit *five cubits*, also in v. 23   [E]7:17 Lit *tassels*   [F]7:19 Lit *four cubits*, also in vv. 27,38   [G]7:20 Lit *encircling the second*   [H]7:21 = He Will Establish   [i]7:21 = In Him Is Strength   [j]7:23 Lit *sea*   [K]7:23 Lit *10 cubits*   [L]7:24 Lit *10 per cubit*   [M]7:26 Lit *a handbreadth*   [N]7:26 Lit *2,000 baths*   [o]7:27 Lit *bronze stands*   [p]7:27 Lit *three cubits*   [q]7:29 Or *hammered-down*   [R]7:31 Lit *a cubit*   [S]7:31 Lit *one and a half cubits*   [T]7:32 Lit *was one and a half cubits*   [u]7:35 Lit *half a cubit*   [v]7:38 Lit *40 baths*

7:21 Jachin and **Boaz**, meaning "He Will Establish" and "In Him Is Strength," respectively, are a testimony to the security and strength the Lord offered to his people.

7:23-26 The **basin** would be used by the priests to wash themselves (see 2 Chr 4:6). **7:40-47** Hiram's extensive work was cataloged without attempt to summarize the

amount of **bronze** used (7:45, 47). It was too much to keep up with!

a 7:41 1Kg 7:15
b 1Kg 7:17
c 7:42 1Kg 7:20
d 7:43 1Kg 7:27
e 1Kg 7:38
f 7:44 1Kg 7:23
g 1Kg 7:25
h 7:45 Ex 27:3
i 7:46 Gn 33:17
j Jos 3:16; 1Kg 4:12
k 7:47 1Ch 22:3,14
l 7:48 Ex 25:30; 30:1-3;
      2Ch 29:18
m 7:49 Ex 25:31-36
n 7:50 2Kg 25:15
o 7:51 1Kg 6:37-38
p 2Sm 8:9-12; 2Ch 5:1
q 2Ch 36:18
r 8:1 Ex 3:16; Nm 11:16
s 8:1-11 2Ch 5:2-14
t 8:1 Nm 1:5-16; 7:2

u 8:1 2Sm 5:7
v 2Sm 6:12-15,17
w 8:2 Lv 23:34; Dt 16:13-15;
      1Kg 8:65
x 8:3 Nm 11:16
y Dt 31:9; Jos 3:3,6
z 2Sm 6:12,17
aa 8:4 2Ch 1:3
ab 2Ch 5:4-5
ac 8:5 2Ch 1:6; 30:24
ad 8:6 1Kg 6:19
ae 8:6-7 1Kg 6:23-28
af 8:8 Ex 25:13-15; 37:4-5
ag 8:9 Ex 25:21; Dt 10:5
ah Ex 24:7-8; Dt 4:13
ai 8:10 Ex 40:34-35;
      2Ch 7:1
aj 8:11 2Ch 7:2; Ezk 10:4,18-
      19; 43:4-5
ak 8:12 Ex 20:21; Lv 16:2;
      Dt 5:22
al 8:13 2Sm 7:13
am Ps 132:14
an 8:14 Ex 39:43; 2Sm 6:18;
      1Kg 8:55

COMPLETION OF THE BRONZE WORKS

So Hiram finished all the work that he was doing for King Solomon on the LORD's temple: **41** two pillars;[a] bowls for the capitals that were on top of the two pillars; the two gratings for covering both bowls of the capitals that were on top of the pillars;[b] **42** the four hundred pomegranates for the two gratings (two rows of pomegranates for each grating covering both capitals' bowls on top of the pillars[c]); **43** the ten water carts;[d] the ten basins on the water carts;[e] **44** the basin;[f] the twelve oxen underneath the basin;[g] **45** and the pots, shovels, and sprinkling basins.[h] All the utensils that Hiram made for King Solomon at the LORD's temple were made of burnished bronze. **46** The king had them cast in clay molds in the Jordan Valley between Succoth[i] and Zarethan.[j] **47** Solomon left all the utensils unweighed because there were so many; the weight of the bronze was not determined.[k]

COMPLETION OF THE GOLD FURNISHINGS

48 Solomon also made all the equipment in the LORD's temple: the gold altar; the gold table that the Bread of the Presence was placed on;[l] **49** the pure gold lampstands in front of the inner sanctuary, five on the right and five on the left;[m] the gold flowers, lamps, and tongs; **50** the pure gold ceremonial bowls, wick trimmers, sprinkling basins, ladles,[A] and firepans;[n] and the gold hinges for the doors of the inner temple (that is, the most holy place) and for the doors of the temple sanctuary.

51 So all the work King Solomon did in the LORD's temple was completed.[o] Then Solomon brought in the consecrated things of his father David[p] — the silver, the gold, and the utensils — and put them in the treasuries of the LORD's temple.[q]

SOLOMON'S DEDICATION OF THE TEMPLE

8 At that time Solomon assembled the elders[r] of Israel,[s] all the tribal heads[t] and the ancestral leaders of the Israelites before him at Jerusalem in order to bring the ark of the LORD's covenant from the city of David,[u] that is Zion.[v] **2** So all the men of Israel were assembled in the presence of King Solomon in the month of Ethanim, which is the seventh month,[B] at the festival.[w]

3 All the elders[x] of Israel came, and the priests[y] picked up the ark.[z] **4** The priests and the Levites brought the ark of the LORD, the tent of meeting,[aa] and the holy utensils that were in the tent.[ab] **5** King Solomon and the entire congregation of Israel, who had gathered around him and were with him in front of the ark, were sacrificing sheep, goats, and cattle that could not be counted or numbered, because there were so many.[ac] **6** The priests brought the ark of the LORD's covenant to its place, into the inner sanctuary of the temple, to the most holy place[ad] beneath the wings of the cherubim. **7** For the cherubim were spreading their wings over[c] the place of the ark, so that the cherubim covered the ark and its poles from above.[ae] **8** The poles were so long that their ends were seen from the holy place in front of the inner sanctuary, but they were not seen from outside the sanctuary; they are still there today.[af] **9** Nothing was in the ark except the two stone tablets that Moses had put there at Horeb,[D,ag] where the LORD made a covenant with the Israelites when they came out of the land of Egypt.[ah]

10 When the priests came out of the holy place, the cloud filled the LORD's temple,[ai] **11** and because of the cloud, the priests were not able to continue ministering, for the glory[aj] of the LORD filled the temple. **12** Then Solomon said:

> The LORD said that he would dwell
> in total darkness.[ak]
13   I have indeed built
> an exalted temple[al] for you,
> a place for your dwelling forever.[am]

14 The king turned around and blessed[an] the entire congregation of Israel while they were standing. **15** He said:

> Blessed be the LORD God of Israel!

[A] 7:50 Or *dishes*, or *spoons*; lit *palms*   [B] 8:2 = September–October   [C] 8:7 LXX; MT reads *toward*   [D] 8:9 = Sinai

---

8:1 The temple dedication began with the transport and installation of **the ark of the LORD's covenant** from its place on Mount **Zion** (see 2 Sam 6:12-17).

8:6-8 In contrast with David's first attempt to move the ark as recorded in 2 Samuel 6:1-10, **the ark** was carried the proper way this time, by **the priests** using **poles** attached through rings on the sides of the ark so that no one would touch it (see Exod 25:12-15; Deut 10:8).

8:9 The contents pointed to the fact that the primary concern for Israel was to obey the law of their divine King. (Previously, the **covenant** that God made with Israel at Sinai— here called **Horeb**—had often been neglected and disobeyed by the people.) The purpose of the whole dedication ceremony, in fact, was to reiterate that Solomon and Israel still saw themselves as bound to the Lord's covenant, as indeed they were.

8:10 This was a visible symbol of the Lord's presence, and what an awe-inspiring sight that must have been! Interestingly, the same thing had happened when the tabernacle was dedicated in Moses's day (see Exod 40:34).

8:11 When God manifests his **glory**, all activity must cease. Israel's great King had come to dwell with his people.

8:20 The construction of the temple had been planned and promised by God. Nevertheless,

He spoke directly to my father David,
and he has fulfilled the promise[a]
　　by his power.
He said,

16 "Since the day I brought
　　my people Israel out of Egypt,[b]
I have not chosen a city to build
　　a temple in
among any of the tribes of Israel,
so that my name[c] would be there.
But I have chosen David to rule
　　my people Israel."[d]

17 My father David had his heart set
on building a temple for the name
　　of the LORD, the God of Israel.[e]

18 But the LORD said to my father David,
"Since your heart was set
　　on building a temple for my name,
you have done well to have
　　this desire.[A,f]

19 Yet you are not the one to build it;
instead, your son,
　　your own offspring,
will build it for my name."[g]

20 The LORD has fulfilled
　　what he promised.
I have taken the place
　　of my father David,[h]
and I sit on the throne of Israel,
as the LORD promised.[i]
I have built the temple for the name
of the LORD, the God of Israel.

21 I have provided a place there
　　for the ark,
where the LORD's covenant is
that he made with our ancestors
when he brought them out
　　of the land of Egypt.[j]

SOLOMON'S PRAYER

22 Then Solomon stood[k] before the altar
of the LORD in front of the entire congregation of Israel and spread out his hands
toward heaven.[l] **23** He said:
　　LORD God of Israel,

there is no God like you
in heaven above or on earth below,[m]
who keeps the gracious covenant
with your servants who walk
　　before you
with all their heart.[n]

24 You have kept what you promised
to your servant, my father David.
You spoke directly to him
and you fulfilled your promise
　　by your power
as it is today.[o]

25 Therefore, LORD God of Israel,
keep what you promised
to your servant, my father David:
You will never fail to have a man
to sit before me on the throne
　　of Israel,[p]
if only your sons take care to walk
　　before me
as you have walked before me.[q]

26 Now LORD[B] God of Israel,
please confirm what you promised
to your servant, my father David.[r]

27 But will God indeed live on earth?
Even heaven, the highest heaven,
　　cannot contain you,
much less this temple I have built.[s]

28 Listen[c] to your servant's prayer
　　and his petition,[t]
LORD my God,
so that you may hear the cry
　　and the prayer
that your servant prays
　　before you today,

29 so that your eyes may watch over
　　this temple night and day,[u]
toward the place where you said,
"My name will be there,"[v]
and so that you may hear the prayer
that your servant prays
　　toward this place.

30 Hear the petition of your servant[w]
and your people Israel,

[a]8:15 2Sm 7:15-16,25
[b]8:16 2Sm 7:6; 1Ch 17:5
[c]Dt 12:5,11
[d]1Sm 16:1; 2Sm 7:8
[e]8:17 2Sm 7:2-3; 1Ch 22:7
[f]8:18 2Ch 6:8
[g]8:19 2Sm 7:12-13; 1Kg
5:5; Ac 7:47
[h]8:20 2Sm 7:12
[i]1Ch 28:5-6
[j]8:21 Dt 31:26; 1Kg 8:9
[k]8:22-53 2Ch 6:12-42
[l]8:22 1Kg 8:54; 2Ch 6:12

[m]8:23 1Sm 2:2; 2Sm 7:22
[n]Dt 7:16; Neh 1:5; Dn 9:4
[o]8:24 2Sm 7:15-16
[p]8:25 1Kg 2:4; 9:5
[q]1Kg 9:4-9; 2Ch 7:17-22
[r]8:26 2Sm 7:25
[s]8:27 2Ch 2:6; Ac 7:47;
17:24
[t]8:28 Php 4:6
[u]8:29 2Ch 7:15; Neh 1:6
[v]Dt 12:11
[w]8:30 Neh 1:6; Dn 9:4

[A]8:18 Lit *well because it was with your heart*　[B]8:26 Some Hb mss, LXX, Syr, Tg, Vg, 2Ch 6:16; other Hb mss omit LORD　[C]8:28 Lit *Turn*

God didn't miraculously cause the temple to appear out of thin air; its existence required careful obedience from Solomon. This is divine sovereignty and human responsibility in action. **8:21** The purpose of the temple was to serve as a home for **the ark**. The Lord had intended this end hundreds of years earlier when he **brought [Israel] out of the land of Egypt**. We often expect or even demand God to act immediately. But God brings about his promises and plans in his perfect timing. He knows what we need; he also knows when we need it.

8:23 This is one of the greatest affirmations of the person and work of God in Scripture. The nations beyond Israel's borders boasted of their powerful gods, but those pretenders were all talk and no action. The Lord, by contrast, demonstrated that he alone is God because he kept **the gracious covenant** that he had made with the children of Israel. **8:25** In order for the promise to continue, David's sons would have to **take care to walk before** the Lord in faithfulness. Unfortunately, as the books of 1–2 Kings and 1–2 Chronicles bear witness, the sons of David who reigned on his throne after him frequently failed.

Ultimately, God himself would fulfill the requirements in the person of his Son, Jesus Christ. As a descendant of David, he would qualify to sit on the throne (see Matt 1:1; Rom 1:3; Rev 22:16). And as the sinless and eternal Son of God, he alone can fulfill God's promise to "establish the throne of his kingdom forever" (2 Sam 7:13). **8:27** The king was not so naïve as to think that the Lord of heaven and earth actually needed a home and could be confined to it. **8:29** Solomon prayed that God would fulfill his promise to make his **name**—a synonym for his presence and character—dwell in the **temple**.

[a] 8:30 Dn 6:10
[b] 8:31 Ex 22:11; Jos 7:19; Jn 9:24
[c] 8:32 Dt 25:1
[d] 8:33 Lv 26:17,25,39
[e] 8:33-34 Lv 26:40-42
[f] 8:35 Dt 28:23-24
[g] Dt 30:1-3; Am 4:7-8
[h] 8:36 1Sm 12:23
[i] Dt 11:14; Jl 2:23

[j] 8:37 Lv 26:16,25-26
[k] 8:38 2Ch 6:29
[l] Ex 9:29; 2Ch 6:29
[m] 8:39 1Sm 16:7; 1Ch 28:9
[n] 8:40 Dt 6:13
[o] Dt 12:1
[p] 8:41 Lv 24:22; Dt 10:18-19
[q] 8:42 Dt 3:24
[r] 1Kg 10:1
[s] 8:43 Jos 4:24; 1Sm 17:46

which they pray toward this place.[a]
May you hear in your dwelling place
  in heaven.
May you hear and forgive.

31 When a man sins
    against his neighbor
  and is forced to take an oath,[A,b]
  and he comes to take an oath
  before your altar in this temple,
32 may you hear in heaven and act.
  May you judge your servants,
  condemning the wicked man
    by bringing
  what he has done on his own head
  and providing justice
    for the righteous
  by rewarding him according to
    his righteousness.[c]

33 When your people Israel
    are defeated before an enemy,
  because they have sinned
    against you,[d]
  and they return to you and praise
    your name,
  and they pray and plead with you
    for mercy in this temple,
34 may you hear in heaven
  and forgive the sin
    of your people Israel.
  May you restore them to the land
  you gave their ancestors.[e]

35 When the skies are shut and there is
    no rain,
  because they have sinned against you,[f]
  and they pray toward this place
  and praise your name,
  and they turn from their sins
  because you are afflicting them,[g]
36 may you hear in heaven
  and forgive the sin of your servants
  and your people Israel,
  so that you may teach them
    the good way
  they should walk in.[h]
  May you send rain on your land
  that you gave your people
    for an inheritance.[i]

37 When there is famine in the land,
  when there is pestilence,
  when there is blight or mildew,
    locust or grasshopper,[j]
  when their enemy besieges them
  in the land and its cities,[B]
  when there is any plague or illness,
38 every prayer or petition
  that any person or that all
    your people Israel may have —
  they each know
    their own affliction[c,k] —
  as they spread out their hands
    toward this temple,[l]
39 may you hear in heaven,
    your dwelling place,
  and may you forgive, act, and give to
    everyone
  according to all their ways,
    since you know each heart,
  for you alone know
    every human heart,[m]
40 so that they may fear[n] you
  all the days they live on the land[o]
  you gave our ancestors.

41 Even for the foreigner who is not
    of your people Israel
  but has come from a distant land[p]
  because of your name —
42 for they will hear
    of your great name,
  strong hand,[q] and outstretched arm,
  and will come[r] and pray
    toward this temple —
43 may you hear in heaven,
    your dwelling place,
  and do according to all
    the foreigner asks.
  Then all peoples of earth will know[s]
    your name,
  to fear you as your people Israel do
  and to know that this temple
    I have built
  bears your name.

44 When your people go out to fight
    against their enemies,[D]
  wherever you send them,
  and they pray to the LORD

[A] 8:31 Lit and he lifts a curse against him to curse him   [B] 8:37 Lit land of its gates   [C] 8:38 Lit know in his heart of a plague   [D] 8:44 Some Hb mss, some ancient versions, 2Ch 6:34; other Hb mss read enemy

---

8:30 This established the custom that subsequent Jews would follow of turning toward Jerusalem when they prayed (Dan 6:10).
8:33-34 The readers of 1-2 Kings would have felt a special pain in reading these verses, since they knew God had taken away all the land and sent his people into exile for their disobedience.
8:37-40 By disciplining people in the ways spelled out in verse 37 and by forgiving them when they repent, God leads his people to take him seriously—to **fear** (that is, to honor and respect) him (8:40).

8:41 This referred to the non-Israelite who attached himself to Israel because of his faith in the Lord.
8:44-45 Facing Jerusalem in prayer was not a magic formula. It represented Israel's acknowledgement that the God who alone could deliver them dwelled in his temple as promised.

in the direction of the city
  you have chosen[a]
and the temple I have built
  for your name,
45 may you hear their prayer
    and petition in heaven
    and uphold their cause.[b]

46 When they sin against you —
  for there is no one
    who does not sin[c] —
  and you are angry with them
  and hand them over to the enemy,
  and their captors deport them
    to the enemy's country[d] —
  whether distant or nearby —
47 and when they come to their senses[A]
  in the land where
    they were deported
  and repent and petition you
    in their captors' land:
  "We have sinned and done wrong;
  we have been wicked,"[e]
48 and when they return to you
    with all their heart and all their
      soul
  in the land of their enemies
    who took them captive,[f]
  and when they pray to you
    in the direction of their land
  that you gave their ancestors,
  the city you have chosen,[g]
  and the temple I have built
    for your name,
49 may you hear in heaven,
    your dwelling place,
  their prayer and petition and uphold
    their cause.
50 May you forgive your people
  who sinned against you
  and all their rebellions[B]
    against you,
  and may you grant
    them compassion
  before their captors,
  so that they may treat them
    compassionately.[h]
51 For they are your people
    and your inheritance;[i]
  you brought them out of Egypt,
  out of the middle
    of an iron furnace.[j]
52 May your eyes be open
    to your servant's petition

and to the petition
  of your people Israel,
listening to them whenever they call
  to you.
53 For you, Lord GOD, have set them
  apart as your inheritance
from all peoples of the earth,
  as you spoke
    through your servant Moses
  when you brought our ancestors
    out of Egypt.[k]

SOLOMON'S BLESSING

54 When Solomon finished praying this entire prayer and petition to the LORD, he got up from kneeling before the altar of the LORD, with his hands spread out toward heaven,[l] 55 and he stood and blessed the whole congregation of Israel[m] with a loud voice: 56 "Blessed be the LORD! He has given rest[n] to his people Israel according to all he has said. Not one of all the good promises he made through his servant Moses has failed.[o] 57 May the LORD our God be with us as he was with our ancestors. May he not abandon us or leave us[p] 58 so that he causes us to be devoted[c] to him,[q] to walk in all his ways, and to keep his commands, statutes, and ordinances, which he commanded our ancestors. 59 May my words with which I have made my petition before the LORD be near the LORD our God day and night. May he uphold his servant's cause and the cause of his people Israel, as each day requires.[r] 60 May all the peoples of the earth know that the LORD is God. There is no other![s] 61 Be wholeheartedly devoted to the LORD our God[t] to walk in his statutes and to keep his commands, as it is today."

62 The king and all Israel with him were offering sacrifices in the LORD's presence. 63 Solomon offered a sacrifice of fellowship offerings to the LORD: twenty-two thousand cattle and one hundred twenty thousand sheep and goats.[u] In this manner the king and all the Israelites dedicated[v] the LORD's temple.[w]

64 On the same day, the king consecrated the middle of the courtyard that was in front of the LORD's temple because that was where he offered the burnt offering, the grain offering, and the fat of the fellowship offerings[x] since the bronze altar before the LORD was too small to

[a] 8:44 Dt 12:11; 1Ch 5:20; 2Ch 14:11
[b] 8:45 Ps 9:4; 140:12
[c] 8:46 Rm 3:10,23
[d] Lv 26:33-34
[e] 8:47 Lv 26:40-42; Neh 1:6; Dn 9:5
[f] 8:48 Jr 29:10-14
[g] Dn 6:10
[h] 8:50 2Kg 25:28; 2Ch 30:9
[i] 8:51 Ex 32:11; Dt 9:26,29
[j] Dt 4:20

[k] 8:53 Ex 19:5-6; Dt 9:26-29
[l] 8:54 2Ch 6:12-13
[m] 8:55 Nm 6:23-26; 2Sm 6:18
[n] 8:56 Dt 12:10; 1Ch 22:18; Heb 3:18-19
[o] Jos 21:45; 23:15
[p] 8:57 Dt 31:6; Jos 1:5; Heb 13:5
[q] 8:58 Jos 24:23; Jr 31:33; Php 2:13
[r] 8:59 Pr 30:8; Mt 6:11
[s] 8:60 Dt 6:4; Jos 4:24; Mk 12:32
[t] 8:61 Dt 6:5; 1Kg 9:4; 11:4
[u] 8:62-63 1Ch 29:21; 2Ch 7:4-5; Ezr 6:16-17
[v] 8:63 Dt 20:5; Ezr 6:16; Neh 12:27
[w] 2Ch 7:5
[x] 8:64 Lv 6–7

[A] 8:47 Lit they return to their heart   [B] 8:50 Lit rebellions that they have rebelled   [C] 8:58 Lit causes our hearts to be inclined

---

8:46-50 To be driven from the land and deported to an **enemy's country** was the worst fate Israel could imagine (8:46). Sadly, Solomon's final petition was prophetic.

8:65 The worship and joy that Israel experienced in the Lord's **presence** is a picture of what the church should experience on a regular basis. It is also a foretaste of the tre-

mendous joy that we will know in the ages to come with Jesus Christ as our King.

a 8:64 2Ch 7:7
b 8:65 Nm 13:21; 34:8
c Gn 15:18
d Lv 23:36; 1Kg 8:2
e 2Ch 7:9
f 8:66 2Ch 7:10
g 9:1-9 2Ch 7:11-22
h 9:1 1Kg 7:1-2; 2Ch 7:11
i 9:2 1Kg 3:5; 11:9
j 9:3 1Kg 8:29
k 2Ch 6:40
l 9:4 1Kg 3:6,14; 11:4,6;
   1Ch 28:9
m 9:5 2Sm 7:12,15-16;
   1Kg 2:4

n 9:6 Dt 28:15; 1Kg 11:10;
   1Ch 28:9
o 9:7 Lv 26:33; Dt 28:63
p Dt 12:5; 1Kg 8:20
q Dt 28:37
r 9:8 Lv 26:32; Dt 29:24;
   Mt 23:38
s 9:9 Dt 29:25; 31:29
t 9:10 1Kg 6:38; 7:1; 2Ch 8:1
u 9:11 1Kg 5:1
v Dt 17:17
w 1Kg 5:10
x 9:11-13 2Ch 8:2
y 9:14 Dt 17:17
z 9:15 1Kg 5:13-16
aa 2Sm 5:9
ab 1Kg 3:1
ac Jos 11:1
ad Jos 17:11
ae Jdg 1:29

accommodate the burnt offerings, the grain offerings, and the fat of the fellowship offerings.[a]

65 Solomon and all Israel with him — a great assembly, from the entrance of Hamath[A,b] to the Brook of Egypt[c] — observed the festival at that time[d] in the presence of the Lord our God, seven days, and seven more days — fourteen days.[B,e] 66 On the fifteenth day[C] he sent the people away. So they blessed the king and went to their homes[D] rejoicing and with happy hearts for all the goodness that the Lord had done for his servant David and for his people Israel.[f]

THE LORD'S RESPONSE

9 When Solomon finished building the temple of the Lord,[g] the royal palace, and all that Solomon desired to do,[h] 2 the Lord appeared to Solomon a second time just as he had appeared to him at Gibeon.[i] 3 The Lord said to him:

I have heard your prayer and petition you have made before me. I have consecrated this temple you have built, to put[E] my name there forever;[j] my eyes and my heart will be there at all times.[k]

4 As for you, if you walk before me as your father David walked, with a heart of integrity and in what is right, doing everything I have commanded you, and if you keep my statutes and ordinances,[l] 5 I will establish your royal throne over Israel forever, as I promised your father David: You will never fail to have a man on the throne of Israel.[m]

6 If you or your sons turn away from following me and do not keep my commands — my statutes that I have set before you — and if you go and serve other gods and bow in worship

to them,[n] 7 I will cut off Israel from the land I gave them,[o] and I will reject[F] the temple I have sanctified for my name.[p] Israel will become an object of scorn and ridicule among all the peoples.[q] 8 Though this temple is now exalted,[G] everyone who passes by will be appalled and will scoff.[H] They will say: Why did the Lord do this to this land and this temple?[r] 9 Then they will say: Because they abandoned the Lord their God who brought their ancestors out of the land of Egypt. They held on to other gods and bowed in worship to them and served them. Because of this, the Lord brought all this ruin on them.[s]

KING HIRAM'S TWENTY TOWNS

10 At the end of twenty years during which Solomon had built the two houses, the Lord's temple and the royal palace[t] — 11 King Hiram of Tyre[u] having supplied him with cedar and cypress logs and gold[v] for his every wish[w] — King Solomon gave Hiram twenty towns in the land of Galilee. 12 So Hiram went out from Tyre to look over the towns that Solomon had given him, but he was not pleased with them. 13 So he said, "What are these towns you've given me, my brother?" So he called them the Land of Cabul,[I] as they are still called today.[x] 14 Now Hiram had sent the king nine thousand pounds[J] of gold.[y]

SOLOMON'S FORCED LABOR

15 This is the account of the forced labor[z] that King Solomon had imposed to build the Lord's temple, his own palace, the supporting terraces,[aa] the wall of Jerusalem,[ab] and Hazor,[ac] Megiddo,[ad] and Gezer.[ae] 16 Pharaoh king of Egypt had attacked and captured Gezer. He then burned it, killed the Canaanites who lived in the city, and gave it as a dowry to his daughter, Solomon's

---

A 8:65 Or from Lebo-hamath   B 8:65 Temple dedication lasted seven days, and the Festival of Shelters lasted seven days.   C 8:66 Lit the eighth day   D 8:66 Lit tents   E 9:3 Or by putting   F 9:7 Lit send from my presence   G 9:8 Some ancient versions read temple will become a ruin   H 9:8 Lit hiss   I 9:13 = Like Nothing   J 9:14 Lit 120 talents

---

9:2 Again God spoke to Solomon in a dream (see 3:1-15).

9:6-9 Was it really possible that Israel could fall into idolatry after God had manifested his glorious presence? Tragically, it had happened before. The generation that Moses led out of the wilderness, in fact, witnessed the Lord's spectacular signs and wonders over and over again. Yet they rejected him—over and over again. Sure enough, then, not only would Israel bow down to other gods in the future, but King Solomon himself would too.

9:10 Solomon ruled forty years. When he completed the temple and his palace at the end of twenty years, he had reached the midpoint of his reign.

9:11-14 Hiram wasn't happy with his gift, calling the towns Solomon gave him the Land of Cabul, a Hebrew word meaning "Like Nothing" (9:13). So although Hiram had given Solomon nine thousand pounds of gold (9:14), Solomon gave him "nothing" in response. It seems the author was indicating that Solomon's character was beginning to crack.

9:15-23 The record of Solomon's forced labor (9:15) shows how he acquired the workers needed to complete the temple and his palace complex. The slaves he used came from the peoples who remained of Israel's enemies, that is, their descendants (9:20-21). And while the Israelites weren't consigned to slavery, they served as his soldiers and his servants (9:22-23). This heavy workload would prove to be a problem for Solomon's successor (see 12:2-4).

wife.[a] **17** Then Solomon rebuilt Gezer, Lower Beth-horon,[b] **18** Baalath,[c] Tamar[A,B] in the Wilderness of Judah, **19** all the storage cities that belonged to Solomon, the chariot cities,[d] the cavalry cities,[e] and whatever Solomon desired to build[f] in Jerusalem, Lebanon, or anywhere else in the land of his dominion.

20 As for all the peoples who remained of the Amorites, Hethites, Perizzites, Hivites, and Jebusites, who were not Israelites — **21** their descendants who remained in the land after them, those whom the Israelites were unable to destroy completely[g] — Solomon imposed forced labor on them; it is still this way today.[h] **22** But Solomon did not consign the Israelites to slavery;[i] they were soldiers, his servants, his commanders, his captains, and commanders of his chariots and his cavalry. **23** These were the deputies[j] who were over Solomon's work: 550 who supervised the people doing the work.[k]

SOLOMON'S OTHER ACTIVITIES

24 Pharaoh's daughter moved from the city of David[l] to the house that Solomon had built for her;[m] he then built the terraces.[n]

25 Three times a year Solomon offered burnt offerings and fellowship offerings on the altar he had built for the LORD, and he burned incense with them in the LORD's presence.[o] So he completed the temple.[p]

26 King Solomon put together a fleet of ships at Ezion-geber,[q] which is near Eloth on the shore of the Red Sea in the land of Edom. **27** With the fleet, Hiram sent his servants, experienced seamen, along with Solomon's servants. **28** They went to Ophir[r] and acquired gold there — sixteen tons[c] — and delivered it to Solomon.[s]

THE QUEEN OF SHEBA

10 The queen of Sheba[t] heard about Solomon's fame[u] connected with the name of the LORD and came to test him with riddles.[v] **2** She came to Jerusalem with a very large entourage, with camels bearing[w] spices, gold in great abundance, and precious stones.[x] She came to Solomon and spoke to him about everything that was on her mind. **3** So Solomon answered all her questions; nothing was too difficult for the king to explain to her. **4** When the queen of Sheba observed all of Solomon's wisdom, the palace he had built,[y] **5** the food at his table,[z] his servants' residence, his attendants' service and their attire, his cupbearers, and the burnt offerings he offered at the LORD's temple, it took her breath away.

6 She said to the king, "The report I heard in my own country about your words and about your wisdom is true. **7** But I didn't believe the reports until I came and saw with my own eyes. Indeed, I was not even told half. Your wisdom and prosperity far exceed the report I heard.[aa] **8** How happy are your men.[b] How happy are these servants of yours, who always stand in your presence hearing your wisdom.[ab] **9** Blessed be the LORD your God! He delighted in you and put you on the throne of Israel,[ac] because of the LORD's eternal love for Israel.[ad] He has made you king to carry out justice and righteousness."[ae]

10 Then she gave the king four and a half tons[E] of gold,[af] a great quantity of spices, and precious stones. Never again did such a quantity of spices arrive as those the queen of Sheba gave to King Solomon.

11 In addition, Hiram's fleet that carried gold from Ophir brought from Ophir a large quantity of almug[F] wood and precious stones.[ag] **12** The king made the almug wood into steps for the LORD's temple and the king's palace and into lyres and harps for the singers. Never before did such almug wood arrive, and the like has not been seen again.

13 King Solomon gave the queen of Sheba her every desire — whatever she asked — besides what he had given her out of his royal bounty. Then she, along with her servants, returned to her own country.[ah]

SOLOMON'S WEALTH

14 The weight[ai] of gold that came to Solomon annually was twenty-five tons,[G] **15** besides what came from merchants,[aj]

[a] 9:16 1Kg 3:1; 7:8
[b] 9:17 Jos 16:3; 2Ch 8:5
[c] 9:18 Jos 19:44
[d] 9:19 1Kg 10:26
[e] 1Kg 4:26
[f] 1Kg 9:1
[g] 9:20-21 Jdg 1:21-36; 3:1; 2Ch 8:7-8
[h] 9:21 Jdg 1:28,35; Ezr 2:55,58
[i] 9:22 Lv 25:39
[j] 9:23 1Kg 5:16
[k] 9:22-23 2Ch 8:9-10
[l] 9:24 2Sm 5:7
[m] 1Kg 7:8; 2Ch 8:11
[n] 9:15; 11:27; 2Ch 32:5
[o] 9:25 Dt 16:16
[p] 2Ch 8:16
[q] 9:26 Nm 33:48; 1Kg 22:48
[r] 9:27-28 1Kg 10:11; 22:48-49
[s] 9:28 1Kg 9:11,14
[t] 10:1 2Ch 9:1; Mt 12:42
[u] 10:1-10 2Ch 9:1-12
[v] 10:1 Jdg 14:12-14
[w] 10:2 Gn 24:10
[x] 1Kg 10:10

[y] 10:4 1Kg 7:1
[z] 10:5 1Kg 4:22-23
[aa] 10:7 1Ch 29:25
[ab] 10:8 Pr 8:34
[ac] 10:9 2Sm 22:20; 1Kg 5:7
[ad] 1Ch 17:22; 2Ch 2:11
[ae] 2Sm 8:15
[af] 10:10 1Kg 9:28
[ag] 10:11 1Kg 9:27-28
[ah] 10:12-13 2Ch 9:11-12
[ai] 10:14-25 2Ch 9:13-24
[aj] 10:15 2Ch 1:16

[A] 9:18 Alt Hb traditions, LXX, Syr, Tg, Vg read *Tadmor*; 2Ch 8:4　　[B] 9:18 Tamar was a city in southern Judah; Ezk 47:19; 48:28.　　[C] 9:28 Lit *420 talents*
[D] 10:8 LXX, Syr read *your wives*　　[E] 10:10 Lit *120 talents*　　[F] 10:11 = algum in 2Ch 2:8; 9:10-11　　[G] 10:14 Lit *666 talents*

10:1-13 This story shows that God was blessing the peoples of the world through his chosen people, just as he had promised Abraham (see Gen 12:3). True spiritual blessings for all peoples of the earth would eventually come through the true seed (descendant) of Abraham, Jesus Christ (see Gal 3:14, 16, 29).

Sheba (1 Kgs 10:1) was an Arabian kingdom located in modern-day Yemen; the country lay about 1,200 miles from Jerusalem. Later, Jesus mentioned its queen (also called "the queen of the south") in his condemnation of the scribes and Pharisees (Matt 12:42). She was willing to travel hundreds of miles to hear Solomon's wisdom. But though the Son of God far exceeded Solomon in wisdom and glory, the Jewish religious leaders only scoffed at him. According to Jesus, at the final judgment, the queen of Sheba will point her finger at them in condemnation. They will have no excuse for having rejected the Messiah.

a10:14-15 1Kg 9:28; 10:2
b10:17 1Kg 7:2-5
c10:21 1Kg 7:2-5
d1Kg 9:28
e10:22 Jnh 1:3
f1Kg 9:26-28; 22:48
g10:23 1Kg 3:13
h10:24 1Kg 3:28; 10:1
i10:23-25 2Ch 9:22-24
j10:26 1Kg 4:26
k1Kg 9:19
l10:27 Dt 17:17
m1Kg 5:10; 2Ch 1:15

n10:28 Dt 17:16; 2Ch 9:28
o10:29 2Ch 1:17
p11:1 1Kg 3:1; 7:8
q Neh 13:23-27
r11:2 Dt 7:3-4
s11:3 2Sm 5:13; Est 2:14-
15; Sg 6:8
t Dt 17:17
u11:4 1Kg 8:61; 9:4;
15:3,14; 1Ch 29:19
v11:5 Jdg 2:13; 10:6;
1Kg 11:33
w Lv 18:21
x Jdg 2:13; 1Sm 7:3-4
y11:7 Nm 33:52; 1Kg 3:2-3
z Nm 21:29
aa 1Kg 11:33
ab 2Kg 23:13
ac11:9 1Kg 3:5; 9:2

traders' merchandise, and all the Arabian kings and governors of the land.[a]

16 King Solomon made two hundred large shields of hammered gold; fifteen pounds[A] of gold went into each shield. **17** He made three hundred small shields of hammered gold; nearly four pounds[B] of gold went into each shield. The king put them in the House of the Forest of Lebanon.[b]

18 The king also made a large ivory throne and overlaid it with fine gold. **19** The throne had six steps; there was a rounded top at the back of the throne, armrests on either side of the seat, and two lions standing beside the armrests. **20** Twelve lions were standing there on the six steps, one at each end. Nothing like it had ever been made in any other kingdom.

21 All of King Solomon's drinking cups were gold, and all the utensils of the House of the Forest of Lebanon[c] were pure gold.[d] There was no silver, since it was considered as nothing in Solomon's time, **22** for the king had ships of Tarshish[e] at sea with Hiram's fleet, and once every three years the ships of Tarshish would arrive bearing gold, silver, ivory, apes, and peacocks.[c,f]

23 King Solomon surpassed all the kings of the world in riches and in wisdom.[g] **24** The whole world wanted an audience with Solomon to hear the wisdom that God had put in his heart.[h] **25** Every man would bring his annual tribute: items[D] of silver and gold, clothing, weapons,[E] spices, and horses and mules.[f]

26 Solomon accumulated 1,400 chariots and 12,000 horsemen[j] and stationed them in the chariot cities and with the king in Jerusalem.[k] **27** The king made silver as common in Jerusalem as stones,[l] and he made cedar[m] as abundant as sycamore in the Judean foothills. **28** Solomon's horses were imported from Egypt and Kue.[F] The king's traders bought them from Kue at the going price.[n] **29** A chariot was imported from Egypt for fifteen pounds[G] of silver, and a horse for nearly four pounds.[H] In the same way, they exported them to all the kings of the Hittites and to the kings of Aram through their agents.[o]

SOLOMON'S UNFAITHFULNESS TO GOD

11 King Solomon loved many foreign women in addition to Pharaoh's daughter:[p] Moabite, Ammonite, Edomite, Sidonian, and Hittite women[q] **2** from the nations about which the LORD had told the Israelites, "You must not intermarry with them, and they must not intermarry with you, because they will turn your heart away to follow their gods."[r] To these women Solomon was deeply attached[s] in love. **3** He had seven hundred wives who were princesses and three hundred who were concubines,[s] and they turned his heart away.[t]

4 When Solomon was old, his wives turned his heart away to follow other gods. He was not wholeheartedly devoted to the LORD his God, as his father David had been.[u] **5** Solomon followed Ashtoreth,[v] the goddess of the Sidonians, and Milcom,[w] the abhorrent idol of the Ammonites.[x] **6** Solomon did what was evil in the LORD's sight, and unlike his father David, he did not remain loyal to the LORD.

7 At that time, Solomon built a high place[y] for Chemosh,[z] the abhorrent idol of Moab, and for Milcom,[J,aa] the abhorrent idol of the Ammonites,[ab] **8** He did the same for all his foreign wives, who were burning incense and offering sacrifices to their gods.

9 The LORD was angry with Solomon, because his heart had turned away from the LORD, the God of Israel, who had appeared to him twice.[ac] **10** He had commanded him about this, so that he would not follow

---

10:16-17 These **shields** were evidently used for ceremonial or ornamental purposes.

10:26-28 The Lord had told Moses that when God appointed a king for his people, the king was not to "acquire many horses for himself or send the people back to Egypt to acquire many" (Deut 17:16). Moreover, he was not to "acquire very large amounts of silver and gold for himself" (Deut 17:17). Descriptions like these make us wonder at what point Solomon began putting his trust in his wealth, his **chariots** (1 Kgs 10:26), and his **horses** (10:28) instead of in the Lord.

11:1-3 Solomon's polygamy was first a problem because it was contrary to God's original design of one man and one woman being united together (see Gen 2:22-24). Second, marrying these women from the surrounding nations was clearly forbidden, for God had warned that such women would **turn** the Israelites' **heart away to follow their gods** (1 Kgs 11:2; see Deut 7:3-4). And third, as God had told Moses, the king in particular was "not [to] acquire many wives for himself so that his heart [wouldn't] go astray" (Deut 17:17). Tragically, Solomon overlooked these truths *hundreds* of times.

11:4-6 The contrast with **David** was inevitable, because Solomon was the heir of God's promise to give David an everlasting throne. While David had sinned greatly too, he had repented. Solomon, however, only continued in his downward slide.

11:7-8 How ironic that the king who had built the magnificent temple for the one true God was now constructing sites of devotion and veneration for idols.

other gods, but Solomon did not do what the LORD had commanded.[a]

[11] Then the LORD said to Solomon, "Since you have done this[A] and did not keep my covenant and my statutes, which I commanded you, I will tear the kingdom away from you and give it to your servant.[b] [12] However, I will not do it during your lifetime for the sake of your father David;[c] I will tear it out of your son's hand. [13] Yet I will not tear the entire kingdom away from him. I will give one tribe to your son[d] for the sake of my servant David and for the sake of Jerusalem that I chose."

SOLOMON'S ENEMIES

[14] So the LORD raised up[e] Hadad the Edomite as an enemy against Solomon. He was of the royal family in Edom. [15] Earlier, when David was in Edom, Joab, the commander of the army, had gone to bury the dead and had struck down every male in Edom. [16] For Joab and all Israel had remained there six months, until he had killed every male in Edom.[f] [17] Hadad fled to Egypt, along with some Edomites from his father's servants. At the time Hadad was a small boy. [18] Hadad and his men set out from Midian and went to Paran.[g] They took men with them from Paran and went to Egypt, to Pharaoh king of Egypt,[h] who gave Hadad a house, ordered that he be given food, and gave him land. [19] Pharaoh liked Hadad so much[B] that he gave him a wife, the sister of his own wife, Queen Tahpenes. [20] Tahpenes's sister gave birth to Hadad's son Genubath. Tahpenes herself weaned him in Pharaoh's palace, and Genubath lived there along with Pharaoh's sons.

[21] When Hadad heard in Egypt that David rested with his fathers and that Joab, the commander of the army, was dead, Hadad said to Pharaoh, "Let me leave, so I may go to my own country."

[22] But Pharaoh asked him, "What do you lack here with me for you to want to go back to your own country?"

"Nothing," he replied, "but please let me leave."

[23] God raised up Rezon son of Eliada as an enemy[i] against Solomon. Rezon had fled from his master King Hadadezer of Zobah.[j] [24] and gathered men to himself. He became leader of a raiding party when David killed the Zobaites. He[c] went to Damascus,[k] lived there, and became king in Damascus. [25] Rezon was Israel's enemy throughout Solomon's reign, adding to the trouble Hadad had caused. He reigned over Aram[D,J] and loathed Israel.

[26] Now Solomon's servant,[m] Jeroboam son of Nebat, was an Ephraimite from Zeredah. His widowed mother's name was Zeruah. Jeroboam rebelled[n] against Solomon, [27] and this is the reason he rebelled against the king: Solomon had built the supporting terraces[o] and repaired the opening in the wall of the city of his father David. [28] Now the man Jeroboam was capable, and Solomon noticed the young man because he was getting things done. So he appointed him over the entire labor force of the house of Joseph.[p]

[29] During that time, the prophet Ahijah the Shilonite[q] met Jeroboam on the road as Jeroboam came out of Jerusalem. Now Ahijah had wrapped himself with a new cloak, and the two of them were alone in the open field. [30] Then Ahijah took hold of the new cloak he had on, tore it into twelve pieces,[r] [31] and said to Jeroboam, "Take ten pieces for yourself, for this is what the LORD God of Israel says: 'I am about to tear the kingdom out of Solomon's hand. I will give you ten tribes, [32] but one tribe will remain his for the sake of my servant David[s] and for the sake of Jerusalem, the city I chose out of all the tribes of Israel.[t] [33] For they have abandoned me; they have bowed down to Ashtoreth, the goddess of the Sidonians, to Chemosh, the god of Moab, and to Milcom, the god of the Ammonites.[u] They have not walked in my ways to do what is right in my sight and to carry out my

[a] 11:10 1Kg 6:12; 9:6-7
[b] 11:11 1Kg 11:29-31
[c] 11:12 2Sm 7:12-16; 2Kg 19:34; 20:6
[d] 11:12-13 1Kg 11:31-32
[e] 11:14 1Kg 5:4; 1Ch 5:26
[f] 11:15-16 2Sm 8:13-14; 1Ch 18:12-13
[g] 11:18 Nm 10:12; Dt 1:1
[h] 1Kg 3:1

[i] 11:23 1Kg 5:4
[j] 2Sm 8:3
[k] 11:24 2Sm 8:5
[l] 11:25 Gn 10:22; 2Sm 10:19
[m] 11:26 1Kg 11:11
[n] 1Kg 11:40; 2Ch 13:6
[o] 11:27 1Kg 9:15,24
[p] 11:28 1Kg 5:13-16; 12:4
[q] 11:29 1Kg 12:15; 14:2
[r] 11:30 1Sm 15:27-28; 1Kg 11:11-13
[s] 11:32 2Sm 7:15-16
[t] 11:30-32 1Kg 11:11-13
[u] 11:33 1Kg 11:5,7

[A] 11:11 Lit "Since this was with you   [B] 11:19 Lit Hadad found much favor in Pharaoh's eyes   [C] 11:24 LXX; Hb reads They   [D] 11:25 Some Hb mss, LXX, Syr read Edom

11:14-22 In response to Solomon's sin, God **raised up** foes against the kingdom. **Hadad the Edomite** was a survivor of the slaughter of his people that occurred in David's day (11:14-16). Hadad had been a boy at the time and a member of the royal house in Edom, Israel's ancient enemy to the southeast that was descended from Esau, Abraham's grandson. He was no doubt seething with hatred toward Israel and looking for revenge (11:21-22).

11:23-25 **Rezon** too was **raised up** by **God** to be a thorn in Solomon's side (11:23). He'd become the leader of a **raiding party** in David's day that harassed Israel **throughout Solomon's reign** (1:24-25). Rezon eventually became king of **Aram and loathed Israel** (11:25).

11:26-28 By far the most significant of Solomon's enemies was the man described as his "servant" (11:11). Capable **Jeroboam** was from the tribe of Ephraim, the leading tribe

in the north (11:26). Solomon had **appointed him over the entire labor force of . . . Joseph** (11:28). But eventually, Jeroboam **rebelled** (11:27). Jeroboam's rebellion in particular was part of God's plan to tear the kingdom apart because of Solomon's sin (see 11:11-13).

11:31-32 The missing tribe, that is the tribe that would bring the total to twelve, is Benjamin, who would side with Judah (see 12:21).

*a*11:33 1Kg 3:14; 11:9-11
*b*11:36 1Kg 12:16-17
*c*11:34-36 1Kg 3:14;
11:12-13
*d*11:36 2Sm 21:17; 1Kg 15:4;
2Kg 8:19
*e*1Kg 8:29; 11:13
*f*11:37 1Kg 11:11
*g*1Kg 14:7
*h*2Sm 3:21
*i*11:38 Jos 1:5; 1Kg 3:14;
11:11
*j*2Sm 7:11,27
*k*11:39 Ezk 37:15-28; Am
9:11-12
*l*11:40 1Kg 11:26-28
*m*1Kg 12:2
*n*1Kg 14:25-26; 2Ch 12:2-9
*o*11:41 1Kg 15:7,23; 2Ch
9:29
*p*11:42 2Sm 5:5
*q*11:43 1Kg 12:1
*r*11:42-43 2Ch 9:30-31
*s*12:1-19 2Ch 10:1-19
*t*12:1 Jos 12:1; 1Kg 12:25
*u*2Sm 20:1-2; 1Kg 12:16-17
*v*Jdg 9:6

*w*12:2 1Kg 11:40
*x*12:4 1Sm 8:11-18
*y*1Kg 4:20
*z*12:6 1Kg 4:2-19
*aa*12:7 2Ch 10:7; Pr 15:1
*ab*12:8 Lv 19:32
*ac*12:10-11 Ex 1:13-14; 5:6-
9; 2Ch 10:10-11

statutes and my judgments as his father David did. *a*

34 " 'However, I will not take the whole kingdom from him but will let him be ruler all the days of his life for the sake of my servant David, whom I chose and who kept my commands and my statutes. **35** I will take ten tribes of the kingdom from his son and give them to you. **36** I will give one tribe *b* to his son, *c* so that my servant David will always have a lamp before me *d* in Jerusalem, the city I chose for myself to put my name there. *e* **37** I will appoint you, *f* and you will reign as king *g* over all you want, *h* and you will be king over Israel.

38 " 'After that, if you obey all I command you, walk in my ways, and do what is right in my sight in order to keep my statutes and my commands as my servant David did, I will be with you. *i* I will build you a lasting dynasty just as I built for David, *j* and I will give you Israel. **39** I will humble David's descendants, because of their unfaithfulness, but not forever.' " *A,k*

40 Therefore, Solomon tried to kill Jeroboam, *l* but he fled to Egypt, *m* to King Shishak of Egypt, *n* where he remained until Solomon's death.

SOLOMON'S DEATH

41 The rest of the events of Solomon's reign, along with all his accomplishments and his wisdom, are written in the Book of Solomon's Events. *o* **42** The length of Solomon's reign in Jerusalem over all Israel totaled forty years. *p* **43** Solomon rested with his fathers and was buried in the city of his father David. His son Rehoboam *q* became king in his place. *r*

THE KINGDOM DIVIDED

12 Then Rehoboam *s* went to Shechem, *t* for all Israel *u* had gone to Shechem to make him king. *v* **2** When Jeroboam son of Nebat heard about it, he stayed in Egypt,

where he had fled from King Solomon's presence. *w* Jeroboam stayed in Egypt. *B* **3** But they summoned him, and Jeroboam and the whole assembly of Israel came and spoke to Rehoboam: **4** "Your father made our yoke harsh. *x* You, therefore, lighten your father's harsh service and the heavy yoke he put on us, *y* and we will serve you."

5 Rehoboam replied, "Go away for three days and then return to me." So the people left. **6** Then King Rehoboam consulted with the elders *z* who had served his father Solomon when he was alive, asking, "How do you advise me to respond to this people?"

7 They replied, "Today if you will be a servant to this people and serve them, and if you respond to them by speaking kind words to them, they will be your servants forever." *aa*

8 But he rejected the advice of the elders who had advised him *ab* and consulted with the young men who had grown up with him and attended him. **9** He asked them, "What message do you advise that we send back to this people who said to me, 'Lighten the yoke your father put on us'?"

10 Then the young men who had grown up with him told him, "This is what you should say to this people who said to you, 'Your father made our yoke heavy, but you, make it lighter on us!' This is what you should tell them: 'My little finger is thicker than my father's waist! **11** Although my father burdened you with a heavy yoke, I will add to your yoke; my father disciplined you with whips, but I will discipline you with barbed whips.' " *C,ac*

12 So Jeroboam and all the people came to Rehoboam on the third day, as the king had ordered: "Return to me on the third day." **13** Then the king answered the people harshly. He rejected the advice the elders had given him **14** and spoke to them according to the young men's advice: "My father made your yoke heavy, but I will

---

*A*11:38-39 LXX omits *and I will give . . . but not forever*   *B*12:2 LXX, Vg read *Jeroboam returned from Egypt*; 2Ch 10:2   *C*12:11 Lit *with scorpions*, also in v. 14

11:37-39 As Solomon had appointed Jeroboam over the "labor force of the house of Joseph" (11:28), God would appoint him as **king over Israel** (11:37). God even promised to build Jeroboam **a lasting dynasty**—if he would obey him (11:38). Unfortunately, in spite of this prospect and high hopes, Jeroboam would fail royally.

11:40 Solomon apparently learned about the prophecy Ahijah spoke to his rival because he **tried to kill Jeroboam**.

12:1 Shechem was an important historical site for the nation. Upon Abraham's arrival in Canaan, God appeared to him there and

promised the land to his offspring (see Gen 12:4-7). Later, Jacob settled in Shechem (see Gen 33:18-20). Then, after the exodus from Egypt and the conquest of the promised land, Joseph was buried there (see Josh 24:32). It was located in the valley between Mount Ebal and Mount Gerizim and was the place where the Israelites under Joshua pledged to keep the law (see Josh 24:16-22). It was a good choice for Rehoboam's coronation.

12:2-4 That the people called **Jeroboam** back from exile and made him their spokesman hints at the political power he already wielded.

12:6-7 The senior court officials knew that provoking the people would only inflame divisions that already existed in the nation. They encouraged Rehoboam to be **a servant to [the] people** so that they in turn would serve him (12:7). That's pretty sound advice because leaders should serve those under their authority by governing in their best interest. As Jesus said, "whoever leads" should be "like the one serving" (Luke 22:26).

12:8-11 The young men were attendants from Rehoboam's own generation (12:8). They encouraged him to come down on the people rather than pacify them.

add to your yoke; my father disciplined you with whips, but I will discipline you with barbed whips."

15 The king did not listen to the people, because this turn of events came from the LORD[a] to carry out his word, which the LORD had spoken through Ahijah the Shilonite to Jeroboam son of Nebat.[b] **16** When all Israel saw that the king had not listened to them, the people answered him:

What portion do we have in David?
We have no inheritance in the son
    of Jesse.[c]
Israel, return to your tents;
David, now look
    after your own house![d]

So Israel went to their tents, **17** but Rehoboam reigned over the Israelites living in the cities of Judah.[e]

18 Then King Rehoboam sent Adoram,[A,f] who was in charge of forced labor, but all Israel stoned him to death. King Rehoboam managed to get into the chariot and flee to Jerusalem. **19** Israel is still in rebellion against the house of David today.[g]

REHOBOAM IN JERUSALEM

20 When all Israel heard that Jeroboam had come back,[h] they summoned him to the assembly and made him king over all Israel.[i] No one followed the house of David except the tribe of Judah alone.[j] **21** When Rehoboam arrived in Jerusalem,[k] he mobilized one hundred eighty thousand fit young soldiers from the entire house of Judah and the tribe of Benjamin[l] to fight against the house of Israel to restore the kingdom to Rehoboam son of Solomon. **22** But the word of God came to Shemaiah,[m] the man of God: **23** "Say to Rehoboam son of Solomon, king of Judah, to the whole house of Judah and Benjamin, and to the rest of the people, **24** 'This is what the LORD says: You

are not to march up and fight against your brothers, the Israelites. Each of you return home, for this situation is from me.' "[n] So they listened to the word of the LORD and went back according to the word of the LORD.

JEROBOAM'S IDOLATRY

25 Jeroboam built Shechem[o] in the hill country of Ephraim and lived there. From there he went out and built Penuel.[p] **26** Jeroboam said to himself, "The kingdom might now return to the house of David.[q] **27** If these people regularly go to offer sacrifices in the LORD's temple in Jerusalem,[r] the heart of these people will return to their lord, King Rehoboam of Judah. They will kill me and go back to the king of Judah." **28** So the king sought advice.

Then he made two golden calves, and he said to the people, "Going to Jerusalem is too difficult for you. Israel, here are your gods[B] who brought you up from the land of Egypt."[s] **29** He set up one in Bethel,[t] and put the other in Dan.[u] **30** This led to sin;[v] the people walked in procession before one of the calves all the way to Dan.[C,w] **31** Jeroboam also made shrines[D] on the high places[x] and made priests from the ranks of the people who were not Levites.[y] **32** Jeroboam made a festival in the eighth month on the fifteenth day of the month, like the festival in Judah.[z] He offered sacrifices on the altar; he made this offering in Bethel to sacrifice to the calves he had made. He also stationed the priests in Bethel for the high places he had made.[aa] **33** He offered sacrifices on[E] the altar he had set up in Bethel on the fifteenth day of the eighth month. He chose this month on his own.[ab] He made a festival for the Israelites, offered sacrifices on the altar, and burned incense.[ac]

[A] 12:18 LXX reads *Adoniram*; 1Kg 4:6; 5:14   [B] 12:28 Or *here is your God*, or *here is your god*   [C] 12:30 Some LXX mss read *calves to Bethel and the other to Dan*   [D] 12:31 Lit *a house*   [E] 12:33 Or *He went up to*

12:15 This turn of events came from the LORD to carry out his word (12:15). This line underscores the truth of Proverbs 21:1: "A king's heart is like channeled water in the Lord's hand: He directs it wherever he chooses."

12:16 This cry of protest was similar to the battle cry Sheba gave when he rebelled against David (see 2 Sam 20:1).

12:17 Only **Judah** remained loyal to Rehoboam—along with Benjamin, the small tribe whose territory was next door to them and who remained loyal to the house of David (see 12:21).

12:18-19 The extent of Rehoboam's unpopularity in the north was proven when the people stoned to death **Adoram**, his head of

forced labor, and almost killed **Rehoboam** himself (12:18). Thus, what was supposed to have been Rehoboam's coronation (see 12:1) almost became his assassination.

12:20 The land was henceforth divided into the northern kingdom of Israel and the southern kingdom of Judah, each with its own king.

12:21-24 Rehoboam was determined not to allow the north to secede, so he amassed an army to defeat the new rival regime (12:21). But the Lord commanded **Judah and Benjamin** not to go to war against their **brothers**, and this time Rehoboam wisely **listened** (12:22-24).

12:26-27 Despite God's promises to make his kingdom thrive if he would be faithful, Israel's new king was paranoid.

12:28-30 The author summed up succinctly the effect these actions had on the people: **This led to sin** (12:30). How could it not? Jeroboam had effectively recapitulated the sin Israel had committed at the foot of Mount Sinai. Back then, while Moses was on the mountain receiving God's law for his people, Israel made a golden calf and worshiped it as the god that had delivered them from Egyptian slavery (see Exod 32:1-6). Jeroboam had apparently learned nothing from his people's history because he did the exact same thing that had gotten them into such trouble (see Exod 32:35)—only he gave the people two golden calves for the price of one!

ᵃ13:1 1Kg 12:22; 2Kg 23:17
ᵇ1Kg 12:32-33
ᶜ13:2 2Kg 23:15-16
ᵈ13:3 Is 7:14
ᵉJn 2:11,18
ᶠ13:6 Jms 5:16
ᵍ13:7 1Sm 9:7; 2Kg 5:15
ʰ13:8 Nm 22:18; Est 5:3;
   Mk 6:23

ⁱ13:9 1Kg 13:1
ʲ13:11 1Kg 12:32; 13:1
ᵏ1Kg 13:2-6
ˡ13:16-17 1Kg 13:8-9
ᵐ13:18 1Jn 4:1
ⁿDt 13:1-3

JUDGMENT ON JEROBOAM

13 A man of God[a] came, however, from Judah to Bethel by the word of the LORD while Jeroboam was standing beside the altar to burn incense.[b] **2** The man of God cried out against the altar by the word of the LORD: "Altar, altar, this is what the LORD says, 'A son will be born to the house of David, named Josiah, and he will sacrifice on you the priests of the high places who are burning incense on you. Human bones will be burned on you.'"[c] **3** He gave a sign[d] that day. He said, "This is the sign that the LORD has spoken: 'The altar will now be ripped apart, and the ashes that are on it will be poured out.'"[e]

4 When the king heard the message that the man of God had cried out against the altar at Bethel, Jeroboam stretched out his hand from the altar and said, "Arrest him!" But the hand he stretched out against him withered, and he could not pull it back to himself. **5** The altar was ripped apart, and the ashes poured from the altar, according to the sign that the man of God had given by the word of the LORD.

6 Then the king responded to the man of God, "Plead for the favor of the LORD your God and pray for me[f] so that my hand may be restored to me." So the man of God pleaded for the favor of the LORD, and the king's hand was restored to him and became as it had been at first.

7 Then the king declared to the man of God, "Come home with me, refresh yourself, and I'll give you a reward."[g] **8** But the man of God replied, "If you were to give me half your house,[h] I still wouldn't go with you, and I wouldn't eat food or drink water in this place, **9** for this is what I was commanded by the word of the LORD:[i] 'You must not eat food or drink water or go back the way you came.'" **10** So he went another way; he did not go back by the way he had come to Bethel.

THE OLD PROPHET AND THE MAN OF GOD

11 Now a certain old prophet was living in Bethel.[j] His son[A] came and told him all the deeds that the man of God had done that day in Bethel. His sons also told their father the words that he had spoken to the king.[k] **12** Then their father asked them, "Which way did he go?" His sons had seen[B] the way taken by the man of God who had come from Judah. **13** Then he said to his sons, "Saddle the donkey for me." So they saddled the donkey for him, and he got on it. **14** He followed the man of God and found him sitting under an oak tree. He asked him, "Are you the man of God who came from Judah?"

"I am," he said.

15 Then he said to him, "Come home with me and eat some food."

16 But he answered, "I cannot go back with you or accompany you; I will not eat food or drink water with you in this place. **17** For a message came to me by the word of the LORD: 'You must not eat food or drink water there[l] or go back by the way you came.'"

18 He said to him, "I am also a prophet[m] like you. An angel spoke to me by the word of the LORD: 'Bring him back with you to your house so that he may eat food and drink water.'" The old prophet deceived him,[n] **19** and the man of God went back with him, ate food in his house, and drank water.

ᴬ13:11 Some Hb mss, LXX, Syr, Vg read *sons* ᴮ13:12 LXX, Syr, Tg, Vg read *sons showed him*

13:1-2 The message of God's coming judgment on the nation came by way of a **man of God . . . from Judah** (13:1). That insight tells us the man was living under God's authority rather than under Jeroboam's rule. His prophecy is amazing because it named King **Josiah** from **the house of David** who would someday **sacrifice** on the altar **the priests of the high places** whom Jeroboam had appointed and defile it by burning **human bones** on it (13:2). While Josiah would not be born for almost three centuries, he would indeed do exactly what the man of God said he would (see 2 Kgs 23:15-20).
13:4 Jeroboam didn't want to hear more; he **stretched out his hand** in a kingly gesture of authority and ordered the man of God arrested. But God gave Jeroboam an unmistakable lesson in who was really in charge by withering the king's hand. Suddenly, arresting the prophet didn't seem like such a good idea.

13:7-10 Behind the offer of **reward** made in verse 7, Jeroboam may have been thinking, "Whew! That was close. I need this guy on my side." But the man had his orders. He was not to associate with Jeroboam and was to go home a different way (13:8-10). In other words, true prophets of God are not for sale. Doing the work of the true King is its own reward.
13:11-24 This story served as a graphic object lesson on the need for complete obedience to the word of the Lord; it was a lesson that God wanted Jeroboam and the people of Israel to take to heart. The Bethel prophet rode after the man of God and found him on his way back home (13:13-14). The old prophet may have been jealous over the other prophet's ministry. We simply don't know why he did what he did. But whatever his motives, the old prophet (like Jeroboam) invited the prophet from Judah to go back to Bethel

and eat with him. The man of God knew what God had commanded him, but **the old prophet deceived him**, saying that **the word of the LORD** had come to him and changed God's original command (13:18). The prophet from Judah should have known better than to believe a prophet from Bethel—a place where Jeroboam's idolatry ran rampant. But he foolishly ignored his charge from the Lord and went back to Bethel (13:19).

At dinner, God's word came upon the old prophet, and he uttered God's judgment on the disobedient prophet (13:20-22). This unusual story continued with the prophet from Judah being killed by **a lion** on his way home (13:23-24). And then, unnaturally, the **lion** and the man's **donkey** remained **standing** still beside **the corpse** (13:24). In other words, this was no accidental death, but the work of God.

20 While they were sitting at the table, the word of the LORD came to the prophet who had brought him back, **21** and the prophet cried out to the man of God who had come from Judah, "This is what the LORD says: 'Because you rebelled against the LORD's command and did not keep the command that the LORD your God commanded you — **22** but you went back and ate food and drank water in the place that he said to you, "Do not eat food and do not drink water"[a] — your corpse will never reach the grave of your fathers.'"[b]

23 So after he had eaten food and after he had drunk, the old prophet saddled the donkey for the prophet he had brought back. **24** When he left,[A] a lion attacked[B] him along the way and killed him.[C] His corpse was thrown on the road, and the donkey was standing beside it; the lion was standing beside the corpse too.

25 There were men passing by who saw the corpse thrown on the road and the lion standing beside it, and they went and spoke about it in the city where the old prophet lived. **26** When the prophet who had brought him back from his way heard about it, he said, "He is the man of God who disobeyed the LORD's command. The LORD has given him to the lion, and it has mauled and killed him, according to the word of the LORD that he spoke to him."

27 Then the old prophet instructed his sons, "Saddle the donkey for me." They saddled it,[d] **28** and he went and found the corpse thrown on the road and the donkey and the lion standing beside the corpse. The lion had not eaten the corpse or mauled the donkey. **29** So the prophet lifted the corpse of the man of God and laid it on the donkey and brought it back. The old prophet came into the city to mourn and to bury him. **30** Then he laid the corpse in his own grave,[e] and they mourned over him: "Oh, my brother!"[f]

31 After he had buried him, he said to his sons, "When I die, bury me in the grave where the man of God is buried; lay my bones beside his bones, **32** for the message

that he cried out by the word of the LORD against the altar in Bethel[g] and against all the shrines of the high places[h] in the cities of Samaria[i] is certain to happen."[j]

33 Even after this,[k] Jeroboam did not repent[l] of his evil way but again made priests for the high places from the ranks of the people.[m] He ordained whoever so desired it, and they became priests of the high places.[n] **34** This was the sin that caused the house of Jeroboam to be cut off and obliterated from the face of the earth.[o]

DISASTER ON THE HOUSE OF JEROBOAM

14 At that time Abijah son of Jeroboam became sick.[p] **2** Jeroboam said to his wife, "Go disguise yourself,[q] so they won't know that you're Jeroboam's wife, and go to Shiloh.[r] The prophet Ahijah is there; it was he who told about me becoming king over this people.[s] **3** Take with you ten loaves of bread, some cakes, and a jar of honey,[t] and go to him. He will tell you what will happen to the boy."

4 Jeroboam's wife did that: she went to Shiloh and arrived at Ahijah's house. Ahijah could not see; he was blind[c] due to his age.[u] **5** But the LORD had said to Ahijah, "Jeroboam's wife is coming soon to ask you about her son, for he is sick. You are to say such and such to her. When she arrives, she will be disguised."[v]

6 When Ahijah heard the sound of her feet entering the door, he said, "Come in, wife of Jeroboam! Why are you disguised?[w] I have bad news for you. **7** Go tell Jeroboam, 'This is what the LORD God of Israel says: I raised you up from among the people, appointed you ruler over my people Israel, **8** tore the kingdom away from the house of David, and gave it to you.[x] But you were not like my servant David, who kept my commands and followed me with all his heart, doing only what is right in my sight. **9** You behaved more wickedly than all who were before you.[y] In order to anger me, you have proceeded to make for yourself other gods and cast images,[z] but you have flung me behind your back.[aa]

[a] 13:21-22 1Kg 13:8-9
[b] 13:22 1Kg 13:30
[c] 13:24 1Kg 20:36
[d] 13:27 1Kg 13:13
[e] 13:30 1Kg 13:22,24
[f] Jr 22:18

[g] 13:32 1Kg 13:1-3
[h] 1Kg 12:31-32; 2Kg 17:29
[i] 1Kg 16:28-29,32
[j] 2Kg 23:16
[k] 13:33 1Kg 13:1-6,24
[l] 1Kg 12:28-33; 13:1; Ac 26:20
[m] 1Kg 12:31
[n] Jdg 17:5; 2Ch 13:9
[o] 13:34 1Kg 12:28-33; 2Kg 17:21-23
[p] 14:1 1Kg 14:12,17-18
[q] 14:2 1Sm 28:8; 2Sm 14:2-3
[r] Jos 18:1
[s] 1Kg 11:29-39
[t] 14:3 1Sm 9:7-8
[u] 14:4 1Sm 3:2; 4:15
[v] 14:5 2Sm 14:1-2
[w] 14:6 1Sm 28:12
[x] 14:7-8 1Kg 11:28-31; 16:2
[y] 14:9 1Kg 16:25,30
[z] 1Kg 11:33; 12:28-33
[aa] Neh 9:26; Ps 50:17

[A] 13:23-24 LXX reads *donkey, and he turned* **24** *and left, and* [B] 13:24 Lit *met* [C] 14:4 Lit *see, for his eyes stood*; 1Sm 4:15

13:33 Apparently the events of 13:11-32 were public knowledge.

14:1-3 The demise of Jeroboam's family and kingdom did not take long to begin. His young son **Abijah** became **sick**, which prompted the king to send his **wife** to see the prophet at **Shiloh**, in an attempt to secure the boy's healing (14:1-2). Ahijah had prophesied

Jeroboam's rise to power, so the king hoped for a favorable word on his son. It's not clear why Jeroboam wanted his wife to **disguise** herself (14:2). It could be that he didn't want the people of Israel knowing that his wife was visiting a prophet of the Lord.

14:4-5 The great irony here is that despite her disguise and the prophet's blindness he knew

who she was, because the Lord had revealed it to him (14:5). God had a message of doom for Jeroboam that he wanted the prophet to deliver. So in a sense it was Ahijah who was sent to the king's wife, not vice versa.

14:6 The blind and elderly prophet must have stunned his visitor with his greeting: **Come in, wife of Jeroboam!**

a 14:10 1Kg 15:29; 21:21-22
b 14:11 1Kg 16:4; 21:24
c 14:12 1Kg 14:17
d 14:13 2Ch 12:12; 19:3
e 14:14 1Kg 15:27-29
f 14:15 Dt 29:28
g 2Kg 15:29; 17:6
h Ex 34:14-15; Dt 12:3-4
i 14:16 1Kg 12:28-33; 13:34; 15:30
j 14:17 1Kg 15:33; Sg 6:4
k 14:18 1Kg 14:12-13
l 14:19 1Kg 14:30; 2Ch 13:2-20

m 14:20 1Kg 15:25-26
n 14:21 1Kg 12:1-24
o Dt 12:5; 1Kg 9:3; 11:32,36
p 2Ch 12:13
q 14:22 2Kg 17:19; 2Ch 12:1,14
r Dt 32:21
s 14:23 1Kg 3:2; 12:31
t Ex 23:24; Dt 16:21-22
u 14:24 Dt 23:17
v Ex 23:24; Dt 18:9; 2Kg 16:3; 17:15; 21:2; 3Jn 11
w 14:25 1Kg 11:40
x 14:25-28 2Ch 12:2-11
y 14:26 1Kg 10:16-17
z 14:27 1Sm 22:17; 2Sm 15:1
aa 14:28 1Kg 10:17
ab 14:29-31 2Ch 12:15-16

10 Because of all this, I am about to bring disaster on the house of Jeroboam:

I will wipe out all of
    Jeroboam's males,[A]
both slave and free,[B] in Israel;
I will sweep away the house
    of Jeroboam
as one sweeps away dung until it is
    all gone![a]

11 Anyone who belongs to Jeroboam
    and dies in the city,
the dogs will eat,
and anyone who dies in the field,
the birds[c] will eat,[b]
for the LORD has spoken!'

12 "As for you, get up and go to your house. When your feet enter the city, the boy will die.[c] 13 All Israel will mourn for him and bury him. He alone out of Jeroboam's house will be given a proper burial because out of the house of Jeroboam something favorable to the LORD God of Israel was found in him.[d] 14 The LORD will raise up for himself a king over Israel, who will wipe out the house of Jeroboam.[e] This is the day, yes,[D] even today! 15 For the LORD will strike Israel so that they will[E] shake as a reed shakes in water. He will uproot Israel from this good soil that he gave to their ancestors.[f] He will scatter them beyond the Euphrates[g] because they made their Asherah poles, angering the LORD.[h] 16 He will give up Israel because of Jeroboam's sins that he committed and caused Israel to commit."[i]

17 Then Jeroboam's wife got up and left and went to Tirzah.[j] As she was crossing the threshold of the house, the boy died. 18 He was buried, and all Israel mourned for him, according to the word of the LORD he had spoken through his servant the prophet Ahijah.[k]

19 As for the rest of the events of Jeroboam's reign, how he waged war[l] and how he reigned, note that they are written in the Historical Record of Israel's Kings. 20 The length of Jeroboam's reign was twenty-two years. He rested with his fathers, and his son Nadab became king in his place.[m]

JUDAH'S KING REHOBOAM

21 Now Rehoboam, Solomon's son, reigned in Judah.[n] Rehoboam was forty-one years old when he became king; he reigned seventeen years in Jerusalem, the city where the LORD had chosen from all the tribes of Israel to put his name.[o] Rehoboam's mother's name was Naamah the Ammonite.[p] 22 Judah did what was evil in the LORD's sight.[q] They provoked him to jealous anger[r] more than all that their ancestors had done with the sins they committed. 23 They also built for themselves high places,[s] sacred pillars,[t] and Asherah poles on every high hill and under every green tree; 24 there were even male cult prostitutes in the land.[u] They imitated all the detestable practices of the nations the LORD had dispossessed before the Israelites.[v]

25 In the fifth year of King Rehoboam, King Shishak of Egypt[w] went to war against Jerusalem.[x] 26 He seized the treasuries of the LORD's temple and the treasuries of the royal palace. He took everything. He took all the gold shields that Solomon had made.[y] 27 King Rehoboam made bronze shields to replace them and committed them into the care of the captains of the guards[F,z] who protected the entrance to the king's palace. 28 Whenever the king entered the LORD's temple, the guards would carry the shields, then they would take them back to the armory.[G,aa]

29 The rest of the events of Rehoboam's reign,[ab] along with all his accomplishments, are written about in the Historical Record of Judah's Kings. 30 There was

---

[A]14:10 Lit eliminate Jeroboam's one who urinates against the wall   [B]14:10 Or males, even the weak and impaired; Hb obscure   [C]14:11 Lit birds of the sky   [D]14:14 Hb obscure   [E]14:15 so that they will supplied for clarity   [F]14:27 Lit the runners   [G]14:28 Lit the chamber of the runners

---

14:10-11 Jeroboam had sinned so deeply that God was ready to **bring disaster** on his **house.** The prophetic picture is graphic.
14:12-13 The boy's more immediate death was a sure sign that the more distant parts of the prophecy would come to pass. Interestingly, he would be the only male member of Jeroboam's house to receive **a proper burial because . . . something favorable to the LORD . . . was found in him** (14:13).
14:14 This would be fulfilled in the next chapter (15:27-30). God's prophecy was so certain that Ahijah could say, **This is the day,** even though the pronouncement of Israel's scat-

tering (14:15-16) would not be fulfilled until 722 BC when the northern kingdom of Israel would be swept off the map by the Assyrians.
14:19 This was a historical document that's been lost to history.
14:20 Jeroboam's death would usher in a continuing parade of wicked kings that would march the nation all the way to the Assyrian invasion. As David had set a high spiritual standard for Judah's kings, Jeroboam had set a miserably low one for Israel's.
14:21-23 When last we saw Rehoboam, his reign in Judah began with foolishness (12:1-19). Things didn't improve. During his

seventeen years in Jerusalem (14:21), Judah (like the northern kingdom) fell into gross idolatry. The people did **what was evil in the LORD's sight**—this would become a familiar refrain throughout the books of 1-2 Kings. In the end, the sin in Rehoboam's day was even worse than that of Judah's **ancestors,** a strong indictment considering their history (14:22).
14:24 If Israel wanted to live like idolatrous **nations,** God would treat them like an idolatrous nation.
14:25-28 These things are sad indicators that the mighty kingdom of David and Solomon was no longer on top.

war between Rehoboam and Jeroboam throughout their reigns.[a] [31] Rehoboam rested with his fathers and was buried with his fathers in the city of David. His mother's name was Naamah the Ammonite.[b] His son Abijam[A,c] became king in his place.

JUDAH'S KING ABIJAM

15 In the eighteenth year of Israel's King Jeroboam son of Nebat, Abijam became king over Judah, [2] and he reigned three years in Jerusalem.[d] His mother's name was Maacah[e] daughter[B] of Abishalom.

[3] Abijam walked in all the sins his father before him had committed,[f] and he was not wholeheartedly devoted to the LORD his God as his ancestor David had been.[g] [4] But for the sake of David, the LORD his God gave him a lamp in Jerusalem by raising up his son after him and by preserving Jerusalem.[h] [5] For David did what was right in the LORD's sight, and he did not turn aside from anything he had commanded him all the days of his life,[i] except in the matter of Uriah[j] the Hethite.

[6] There had been war between Rehoboam and Jeroboam all the days of Rehoboam's life.[k] [7] The rest of the events of Abijam's reign, along with all his accomplishments, are written in the Historical Record of Judah's Kings.[l] There was also war between Abijam and Jeroboam.[m] [8] Abijam rested with his fathers and was buried in the city of David.[n] His son Asa became king in his place.[o]

JUDAH'S KING ASA

[9] In the twentieth year of Israel's King Jeroboam,[p] Asa became king of Judah, [10] and he reigned forty-one years in Jerusalem. His grandmother's[c] name was Maacah[q] daughter of Abishalom.

[11] Asa did what was right in the LORD's sight, as his ancestor David had done.[r] [12] He banished the male cult prostitutes[s] from the land and removed all of the idols that his fathers had made.[t] [13] He also[u] removed his grandmother[D] Maacah from being queen mother because she had made an obscene image of Asherah. Asa chopped down her obscene image and burned it[v] in the Kidron Valley.[w] [14] The high places were not taken away,[x] but Asa was wholeheartedly devoted to the LORD his entire life.[y] [15] He brought his father's consecrated gifts and his own consecrated gifts into the LORD's temple: silver, gold, and utensils.[z]

[16] There was war between Asa and King Baasha of Israel throughout their reigns.[aa] [17] Israel's King Baasha went to war against Judah.[ab] He built Ramah[ac] in order to keep anyone from leaving or coming to King Asa of Judah. [18] So Asa withdrew all the silver and gold that remained in the treasuries of the LORD's temple[ad] and the treasuries of the royal palace and gave it to his servants. Then King Asa sent them to Benhadad[ae] son of Tabrimmon son of Hezion king of Aram who lived in Damascus,[af] saying, [19] "There is a treaty between me and you, between my father and your father.[ag] Look, I have sent you a gift of silver and gold. Go and break your treaty with King Baasha of Israel[ah] so that he will withdraw from me."

[20] Ben-hadad listened to King Asa and sent the commanders of his armies against the cities of Israel. He attacked Ijon,[ai] Dan,[aj] Abel-beth-maacah,[ak] all Chinnereth,[al] and the whole land of Naphtali.[am] [21] When Baasha heard about it, he quit building Ramah and stayed in Tirzah.[an] [22] Then King Asa gave a command to everyone without exception in Judah, and they carried away the stones of Ramah and the timbers

[a] 14:30 1Kg 12:21-24; 15:6
[b] 14:31 1Kg 14:21
[c] 1Kg 15:1-8; 2Ch 11:20; 13:1-14:1
[d] 15:1-2 2Ch 13:1-2
[e] 15:2 1Kg 15:10,13; 2Ch 13:2
[f] 15:3 1Kg 14:21-22
[g] 1Kg 9:4; 11:4
[h] 15:4 2Sm 21:17; 1Kg 11:36; 2Ch 21:7
[i] 15:5 1Kg 9:4; 14:8
[j] 2Sm 11:3,15-17; 12:9-10
[k] 15:6 1Kg 14:30; 2Ch 12:15
[l] 15:7 1Kg 14:29
[m] 2Ch 13:4-20
[n] 15:8 1Kg 14:31; 2Ch 14:1
[o] 1Kg 14:31; 2Ch 14-16
[p] 15:9 1Kg 15:1
[q] 15:10 1Kg 15:2

[r] 15:11 1Kg 9:4-5; 2Ch 14:2
[s] 15:12 Dt 23:17; 1Kg 14:24
[t] 15:11-12 1Kg 11:7; 14:23; 2Ch 14:3,5
[u] 15:13-15 2Ch 15:16-18
[v] 15:13 Ex 32:20
[w] 2Kg 23:6
[x] 15:14 1Kg 22:43
[y] 1Kg 8:61; 15:3
[z] 15:15 1Kg 7:51
[aa] 15:16 1Kg 15:32
[ab] 15:17-22 2Ch 16:1-6
[ac] 15:17 Jos 18:25
[ad] 15:18 1Kg 14:26
[ae] 1Kg 20:1
[af] 1Kg 11:23-24
[ag] 15:19 1Kg 5:12; 2Ch 16:7
[ah] 1Kg 15:27-28
[ai] 15:20 2Kg 15:29
[aj] Jdg 18:29; 1Kg 12:29
[ak] 2Sm 20:15; 2Kg 15:29
[al] Jos 11:2; 12:3
[am] Jos 19:32-39; 1Kg 20:34
[an] 15:21 1Kg 14:17; 15:33; 16:8,15-18

[A] 14:31 = Abijah in 2Ch 13   [B] 15:2 Possibly granddaughter, also in v. 10; 2Ch 13:2   [C] 15:10 Lit *mother's*   [D] 15:13 Lit *mother*

15:1-4 Rehoboam's son was a chip off the old royal block. **Abijam walked in all the sins his father . . . had committed** (15:3). Instead of being a defender of true worship, as the king was expected to be, he perpetuated idolatrous practices. **He was not wholeheartedly devoted to the LORD his God as his ancestor David had been** (15:3). Yes, David had sinned greatly by committing adultery with the wife of **Uriah** (15:5), but he repented of his deeds. Moreover, he didn't succumb to idolatry as Solomon and his descendants had done. Thus, for Judah's kings, the standard of success was how they compared to David. After all, it was **for the sake of David** that the Lord preserved his royal line (15:4).

15:9-15 **Asa** was a good king—one of a few such blessings to Judah. He reigned one more year than either David or Solomon had, and he even passed the most important test for a king of Judah: **Asa did what was right in the LORD's sight, as his ancestor David had done** (15:11). Asa was a shining light of truth in Judah, pointing the way through the fog of apostasy.
15:16-17 **King Baasha** started the **war against Judah** by fortifying **Ramah** (15:17), which lay on the border of Israel and Judah and was only four miles north of Jerusalem. Likely this was an effort to isolate the southern kingdom and control the traffic between the two nations.
15:18-22 Instead of turning to the Lord for help, Asa emptied **the treasuries of the LORD's temple and . . . the royal palace** to persuade **Ben-hadad**, the **king of Aram** (modern-day Syria) to break his **treaty** with Baasha and attack Israel to relieve the pressure on Judah (15:18-19). Ben-hadad agreed to the deal and attacked Israel from the north, taking a good amount of territory and forcing Baasha to withdraw from Ramah (15:20-21). Asa then had Ramah torn down and built his own defensive towns of **Geba** and **Mizpah** with the building materials (15:22).

*a*15:22 Jos 18:24; 21:17
*b*Jos 11:3; 2Ch 16:6
*c*15:23-24 2Ch 16:11-14
*d*15:23 1Kg 14:29; 15:7
*e*2Ch 16:12
*f*15:24 1Kg 14:31; 15:8
*g*1Kg 22:41-50
*h*15:25 1Kg 14:20
*i*15:26 1Kg 14:16; 15:30,34
*j*15:27 1Kg 14:14; 15:16
*k*Jos 19:44; 1Kg 14:5
*l*15:28 1Kg 15:8-24; 2Ch 14-16
*m*1Kg 16:8-10
*n*15:29 1Kg 13:34
*o*1Kg 14:10
*p*15:30 1Kg 14:7-9
*q*15:31 1Kg 14:19; 16:5
*r*15:32 1Kg 15:16

*s*15:33 1Kg 15:21
*t*15:34 1Kg 14:16
*u*16:1 1Kg 16:7; 2Ch 19:2
*v*2Ch 16:7-10
*w*16:2 1Sm 2:8
*x*1Kg 14:7
*y*1Kg 15:26,34
*z*16:3 1Kg 14:10; 15:29
*aa*16:4 1Kg 14:11; 21:24
*ab*16:5 1Kg 14:19; 15:31
*ac*16:7 1Kg 16:1; 2Ch 19:2
*ad*1Kg 15:27,29
*ae*16:8 1Kg 15:21

Baasha had built it with. Then King Asa built Geba[a] of Benjamin and Mizpah[b] with them.

²³ The rest of all the events of Asa's reign,[c] along with all his might, all his accomplishments, and the cities he built, are written in the Historical Record of Judah's Kings.[d] But in his old age he developed a disease in his feet.[e] ²⁴ Then Asa rested with his fathers and was buried in the city of his ancestor David.[f] His son Jehoshaphat[g] became king in his place.

ISRAEL'S KING NADAB

²⁵ Nadab son of Jeroboam[h] became king over Israel in the second year of Judah's King Asa; he reigned over Israel two years. ²⁶ Nadab did what was evil in the LORD's sight and walked in the ways of his father and the sin he had caused Israel to commit.[i]

²⁷ Then Baasha[j] son of Ahijah of the house of Issachar conspired against Nadab, and Baasha struck him down at Gibbethon[k] of the Philistines while Nadab and all Israel were besieging Gibbethon. ²⁸ In the third year of Judah's King Asa,[l] Baasha killed Nadab[m] and reigned in his place.

²⁹ When Baasha became king, he struck down the entire house of Jeroboam.[n] He did not leave Jeroboam any survivors but[A] destroyed his family according to the word of the LORD he had spoken through his servant Ahijah the Shilonite.[o] ³⁰ This was because Jeroboam had angered[B] the LORD God of Israel by the sins he had committed and had caused Israel to commit.[p]

³¹ The rest of the events of Nadab's reign, along with all his accomplishments, are written in the Historical Record of Israel's Kings.[q] ³² There was war between Asa and King Baasha of Israel throughout their reigns.[r]

ISRAEL'S KING BAASHA

³³ In the third year of Judah's King Asa, Baasha son of Ahijah became king over all Israel, and he reigned in Tirzah[s] twenty-four years. ³⁴ He did what was evil in the LORD's sight and walked in the ways of Jeroboam and the sin he had caused Israel to commit.[t]

16 Now the word of the LORD came to Jehu[u] son of Hanani[v] against Baasha: ² "Because I raised you up from the dust[w] and made you ruler over my people Israel,[x] but you have walked in the ways of Jeroboam and have caused my people Israel to sin,[y] angering me with their sins, ³ take note: I will eradicate Baasha and his house, and I will make your house like the house of Jeroboam son of Nebat:[z]

⁴ Anyone who belongs to Baasha
    and dies in the city,
    the dogs will eat,
    and anyone who is his and dies
      in the field,
    the birds[c] will eat."[aa]

⁵ The rest of the events of Baasha's reign, along with all his accomplishments and might, are written in the Historical Record of Israel's Kings.[ab] ⁶ Baasha rested with his fathers and was buried in Tirzah. His son Elah became king in his place. ⁷ But through the prophet Jehu[ac] son of Hanani the word of the LORD also had come against Baasha and against his house because of all the evil he had done in the LORD's sight. His actions angered the LORD, and Baasha's house became like the house of Jeroboam, because he had struck it down.[ad]

ISRAEL'S KING ELAH

⁸ In the twenty-sixth year of Judah's King Asa, Elah son of Baasha became king over Israel, and he reigned in Tirzah[ae] two years.

---

^A15:29 Lit *Jeroboam anyone breathing until he*   ^B15:30 Lit *provoked in the provocation of*   ^C16:4 Lit *birds of the sky*

15:24 Jehoshaphat's reign is not covered until the end of 1 Kings. Between the accounts of kings Asa and Jehoshaphat of Judah come the stories of five kings of the northern kingdom of Israel. The reason five straight stories of Israel's kings are given without mention of Judah's kings is that Asa had a long reign of forty-one years (15:10), which spanned the reigns of several kings in Israel.

15:28-29 These things were done in fulfillment of **the word of the LORD** that he spoke against **Jeroboam** for his own sins and for leading Israel away from God (15:29; see 14:14). Thus, Nadab's death closed the book on Jeroboam.

15:33 Tirzah would serve as the capital for Israel's kings down to the time of Omri (see 16:23-24).

15:34 In the same way that Judah's kings were compared with David, Baasha and the kings of Israel were compared with **Jeroboam** (see 14:10-11).

16:1-4 Baasha was not only an evil king, but he followed the worst example: **Jeroboam** (16:2). Therefore, God declared the same judgment on Baasha that he had pronounced on Jeroboam. He said, **I will eradicate Baasha and his house**; his descendants would be eaten by **dogs** and **birds** (16:3-4; see 14:10-11). This

was a dose of divine irony. The king whom the Lord had raised up to wipe out Jeroboam's family would now have his own family wiped out because he imitated Jeroboam's idolatry and wickedness.

16:5 Wicked Baasha's reign included **accomplishments** that he achieved by his **might**. This kind of thing is repeated in some form in many cases with the kings of Israel. This tells us they weren't necessarily unsuccessful from the human standpoint. But whatever a person accomplishes is of no consequence in God's eyes if he or she isn't obeying him and living for his glory.

9 His servant Zimri,[a] commander of half his chariots, conspired against him while Elah was in Tirzah getting drunk[b] in the house of Arza, who was in charge of the household[c] at Tirzah. **10** In the twenty-seventh year of Judah's King Asa, Zimri went in, struck Elah down, killing him. Then Zimri became king in his place.[d]

11 When he became king, as soon as he was seated on his throne, Zimri struck down the entire house of Baasha. He did not leave a single male,[A,e] including his kinsmen and his friends. **12** So Zimri destroyed the entire house of Baasha, according to the word of the LORD he had spoken against Baasha through the prophet Jehu.[f] **13** This happened because of all the sins of Baasha and those of his son Elah, which they committed and caused Israel to commit, angering the LORD God of Israel[g] with their worthless idols.[h]

14 The rest of the events of Elah's reign, along with all his accomplishments, are written in the Historical Record of Israel's Kings.[i]

ISRAEL'S KING ZIMRI

15 In the twenty-seventh year of Judah's King Asa, Zimri became king for seven days in Tirzah.[j] Now the troops were encamped against Gibbethon of the Philistines.[k] **16** When these troops heard that Zimri had not only conspired but had also struck down the king, then all Israel made Omri, the army commander, king over Israel that very day in the camp. **17** Omri along with all Israel marched up from Gibbethon and besieged Tirzah.[l] **18** When Zimri saw that the city was captured, he entered the citadel of the royal palace and burned it down over himself. He died **19** because of the sin he committed by doing what was evil in the LORD's sight and by walking in the ways of Jeroboam and the sin he caused Israel to commit.[m]

20 The rest of the events of Zimri's reign, along with the conspiracy that he instigated, are written in the Historical Record of Israel's Kings. **21** At that time the people of Israel were divided: half the people followed Tibni son of Ginath, to make him king, and half followed Omri. **22** However, the people who followed Omri proved stronger than those who followed Tibni son of Ginath. So Tibni died and Omri became king.

ISRAEL'S KING OMRI

23 In the thirty-first year of Judah's King Asa, Omri became king over Israel, and he reigned twelve years. He reigned six years in Tirzah,[n] **24** then he bought the hill of Samaria[o] from Shemer for 150 pounds[B] of silver, and he built up the hill. He named the city he built Samaria[c] based on the name Shemer, the owner of the hill.

25 Omri did what was evil in the LORD's sight; he did more evil than all who were before him.[p] **26** He walked in all the ways of Jeroboam son of Nebat in every respect and continued in his sins that he caused Israel to commit, angering the LORD God of Israel with their worthless idols.[q] **27** The rest of the events of Omri's reign, along with his accomplishments and the might he exercised, are written in the Historical Record of Israel's Kings. **28** Omri rested with his fathers and was buried in Samaria. His son Ahab became king in his place.

ISRAEL'S KING AHAB

29 Ahab son of Omri became king over Israel in the thirty-eighth year of Judah's King Asa; Ahab son of Omri reigned over Israel in Samaria twenty-two years. **30** But Ahab son of Omri did what was evil in the LORD's sight more than all who were before him.[r] **31** Then, as if following the sin of Jeroboam son of Nebat were not enough, he married Jezebel,[s] the daughter of Ethbaal king of the Sidonians,[t] and then proceeded to serve Baal and bow in worship to him.[u] **32** He set up an altar for Baal in the temple of Baal[v] that he had built in Samaria. **33** Ahab also made an Asherah pole.[w] Ahab did more to anger the LORD

a 16:9 2Kg 9:30-33
b 1Sm 25:36; 1Kg 20:12,16; Pr 31:4-5; Eph 5:18
c 1Kg 18:3
d 16:10 1Kg 15:28
e 16:11 1Sm 25:22; 1Kg 15:29
f 16:12 1Kg 16:1-4
g 16:13 1Kg 15:26,30
h Dt 32:21; 1Kg 12:28-33
i 16:14 1Kg 15:31
j 16:15 1Kg 15:21
k 1Kg 15:27
l 16:17 1Kg 14:17
m 16:19 1Kg 12:28-33

n 16:23 1Kg 15:21
o 16:24 1Kg 13:32
p 16:25 1Kg 14:9; 16:30
q 16:25-26 1Kg 16:13,19
r 16:30 1Kg 14:9; 16:25
s 16:31 Dt 7:3-4; 1Kg 18:4,13; Rv 2:20
t 1Kg 11:5
u Jdg 2:11
v 16:32 2Kg 10:21,26-27
w 16:33 2Kg 13:6

A **16:11** Lit *leave him one who urinates against the wall*   B **16:24** Lit *for two talents*   C **16:24** = Belonging to Shemer's Clan

16:15-16 Zimri may have been a tool in the Lord's hand for judgment, but he was no hero. His reign lasted only **seven days**, making it the shortest in Israel's history (16:15). Zimri's actions were so unpopular that when word of his murder of his successor reached the army, its commanders pulled off a coup and **made Omri, the army commander, king over Israel** instead (16:16).
16:20-22 The story of Zimri illustrates how far the northern kingdom had descended

into chaos. Following his death **the people of Israel were divided** (16:21). A man named **Tibni** had the support of **half the people**, while the other half backed Omri. The conflict lasted for six years, but since Omri's followers were stronger (probably because he had the support of the army), they won out (16:22).
16:23-24 Omri moved the Israelite capital to **Samaria**, where it remained until the northern kingdom was destroyed by Assyria.

16:25 The second half of this sentence is a stunning statement given the heinous sins that the kings who came before him committed!
16:29-30 Omri's wickedness goes a long way toward explaining the total corruption and evil of his son. **Ahab** would earn the shameful title of Israel's worst king.
16:31-33 **Baal** was the fertility god of the Canaanites. **Asherah** was a fertility goddess and the mother of Baal (16:33).

[a] 16:33 1Kg 16:30
[b] 16:34 Jos 6:26
[c] 17:1 1Kg 17–19; 2Kg 1–2;
Mal 4:5; Mt 11:14
[d] Jdg 12:4
[e] 1Kg 18:10; 22:14
[f] Dt 11:16-17; Jms 5:17;
Rv 11:6
[g] 17:3 1Kg 18:4
[h] 17:4 1Kg 17:9; Jb 38:41;
Lk 12:24
[i] 17:6 Ex 16:8
[j] 17:9 Ob 20; Lk 4:26

[k] 17:10 Gn 24:17; Jn 4:7
[l] 17:12 1Kg 17:1
[m] 2Kg 4:2-7
[n] Gn 21:14,16
[o] 17:14 1Kg 17:1; Php 4:19
[p] 17:15 Mt 6:11
[q] 17:17 Ac 9:37
[r] 17:18 1Kg 22:22
[s] 2Sm 16:10; 2Kg 3:13
[t] Lk 5:8

God of Israel than all the kings of Israel who were before him.[a]

34 During his reign, Hiel the Bethelite built Jericho. At the cost of Abiram his firstborn, he laid its foundation, and at the cost of Segub his youngest, he finished its gates, according to the word of the LORD he had spoken through Joshua son of Nun.[b]

ELIJAH ANNOUNCES FAMINE

17 Now Elijah[c] the Tishbite, from the Gilead settlers,[A,d] said to Ahab, "As the LORD God of Israel lives,[e] in whose presence I stand, there will be no dew or rain during these years except by my command!"[f]

2 Then the word of the LORD came to him: **3** "Leave here, turn eastward, and hide[g] at the Wadi Cherith where it enters the Jordan. **4** You are to drink from the wadi. I have commanded the ravens[h] to provide for you there."

5 So he proceeded to do what the LORD commanded. Elijah left and lived at the Wadi Cherith where it enters the Jordan. **6** The ravens kept bringing him bread and meat in the morning and in the evening,[i] and he would drink from the wadi. **7** After a while, the wadi dried up because there had been no rain in the land.

ELIJAH AND THE WIDOW

8 Then the word of the LORD came to him: **9** "Get up, go to Zarephath[j] that belongs to Sidon and stay there. Look, I have commanded a woman who is a widow to provide for you there." **10** So Elijah got up and went to Zarephath. When he arrived at the city gate, there was a widow gathering wood. Elijah called to her and said, "Please bring me a little water in a cup and let me drink."[k] **11** As she went to get it, he called to her and said, "Please bring me a piece of bread in your hand."

12 But she said, "As the LORD your God lives,[l] I don't have anything baked — only a handful of flour in the jar and a bit of oil[m] in the jug. Just now, I am gathering a couple of sticks in order to go prepare it for myself and my son so we can eat it and die."[n]

13 Then Elijah said to her, "Don't be afraid; go and do as you have said. But first make me a small loaf from it and bring it out to me. Afterward, you may make some for yourself and your son, **14** for this is what the LORD God of Israel says, 'The flour jar will not become empty and the oil jug will not run dry until the day the LORD sends rain on the surface of the land.'"[o]

15 So she proceeded to do according to the word of Elijah. Then the woman, Elijah, and her household ate for many days.[p] **16** The flour jar did not become empty, and the oil jug did not run dry, according to the word of the LORD he had spoken through[B] Elijah.

THE WIDOW'S SON RAISED

17 After this, the son of the woman who owned the house became ill. His illness got worse until he stopped breathing.[q] **18** She said to Elijah, "Man of God,[r] why are you here?[s] Have you come to call attention to my iniquity[t] so that my son is put to death?"

[A] 17:1 LXX reads *from Tishbe of Gilead*   [B] 17:16 Lit *by the hand of*

16:34 Hiel decided to defy the curse God had pronounced through **Joshua** (see Josh 6:26). The curse was specific: the rebuilder of **Jericho** would succeed only at the cost of his **firstborn** and **youngest** sons, a price that Hiel paid. The point of this account may be to illustrate two things. First, neglect of God's Word was rampant during the days of Ahab. Second, just as God's Word was fulfilled in the case of Hiel, it would also be fulfilled in the case of Ahab. Israel's worst king wouldn't escape divine judgment. No matter how many years go by, God doesn't forget.

17:1 That there would be **no dew or rain**, except as **Elijah** commanded was a direct attack on Baal, a fertility god. His worshipers depended on *him* to provide rain to ensure *good crops*. Elijah would demonstrate that the Lord alone was in control of the natural world. He was their source.

Years before, God had warned the people through Moses to "be careful that you are not enticed to turn aside, serve, and bow in worship to other gods. Then the LORD's anger will burn against you. He will shut the sky, and there will be no rain; the land will not yield its produce, and you will perish quickly from the good land the LORD is giving you" (Deut 11:16-17). Once again, the author of 1 Kings, who knew Deuteronomy well, highlights how Israel's unfaithfulness to God's covenant was causing his judgment to fall on their heads. Or, in this case, how it was keeping his blessing of rain from falling on their heads.

17:4 Ravens were unclean birds. Importantly, this would make it easier for the prophet to receive help from a Gentile later.

17:9 God sent Elijah to Gentile country, where a Gentile **widow** would **provide for** him.

Through that encounter God would teach his prophet that he could produce whatever was needed both for him and for others. God would also use this opportunity to bring his blessing to a particular Sidonian household. If the king of Israel, its false prophets, and its people preferred to worship Baal (see ch. 19), the Lord would elicit praise from the mouth of a woman outside the promised land's borders instead (see 17:24). **Zarephath** was a hot, dry village located in modern-day Lebanon. This was the home turf of Jezebel (see 16:31), so in a sense God had sent Elijah to the idolatrous *Baal Belt*. Elijah was going into enemy territory to demonstrate that the Lord is the true God who alone has power over creation and can even provide in the den of Satan.

17:10-12 It seems **Zarephath** was suffering from the drought brought about by Israel's sin, too.

17:13-14 Elijah challenged the widow to act on faith and feed him first with the last of her flour for bread (17:13). She knew that the Lord was his God (17:12), and Elijah was declaring that **the LORD** would supply her needs if she trusted him (17:14).

17:15-16 Even in the face of certain death, this woman acted on faith, trusting in the God of the living God. And he provided. This reinforces a New Testament principle: we should give others the very thing we wish God would give to us (see Luke 6:38).

17:18 Having been exposed to the holiness of God through his miraculous works, the

¹⁹ But Elijah said to her, "Give me your son." So he took him from her arms, brought him up to the upstairs room[a] where he was staying, and laid him on his own bed. ²⁰ Then he cried out to the LORD[b] and said, "LORD my God, have you also brought tragedy on the widow I am staying with by killing her son?" ²¹ Then he stretched himself out over the boy three times.[c] He cried out to the LORD and said, "LORD my God, please let this boy's life come into him again!"

²² So the LORD listened to Elijah, and the boy's life came into him again, and he lived.[d] ²³ Then Elijah took the boy, brought him down from the upstairs room into the house, and gave him to his mother.[e] Elijah said, "Look, your son is alive."

²⁴ Then the woman said to Elijah, "Now I know you are a man of God[f] and the LORD's word from your mouth is true."[g]

ELIJAH'S MESSAGE TO AHAB

18 After a long time, the word of the LORD[h] came to Elijah in the third year:[i] "Go and present yourself to Ahab.[j] I will send rain on the surface of the land." ² So Elijah went to present himself to Ahab.

The famine was severe in Samaria.[k] ³ Ahab called for Obadiah, who was in charge of the palace.[l] Obadiah was a man who greatly feared the LORD[m] ⁴ and took a hundred prophets and hid them, fifty men to a cave, and provided them with food and water when Jezebel[n] slaughtered the LORD's prophets.[o] ⁵ Ahab said to Obadiah, "Go throughout the land to every spring and to every wadi. Perhaps we'll find grass so we can keep the horses and mules alive and not have to destroy any cattle."[p] ⁶ They divided the land between them in order to cover it. Ahab went one way by himself, and Obadiah went the other way by himself.

⁷ While Obadiah was walking along the road, Elijah suddenly met him.[q] When Obadiah recognized him, he fell facedown and said, "Is it you, my lord Elijah?"

⁸ "It is I," he replied. "Go tell your lord, 'Elijah is here!'"[A]

⁹ But Obadiah said, "What sin have I committed,[r] that you are handing your servant over to Ahab to put me to death? ¹⁰ As the LORD your God lives, there is no nation or kingdom where my lord has not sent someone to search for you. When they said, 'He is not here,' he made that kingdom or nation swear they had not found you. ¹¹ Now you say, 'Go tell your lord, "Elijah is here!"'¹² But when I leave you, the Spirit of the LORD may carry you off[s] to some place I don't know. Then when I go report to Ahab and he doesn't find you, he will kill me. But I, your servant, have feared the LORD from my youth. ¹³ Wasn't it reported to my lord what I did when Jezebel slaughtered the LORD's prophets? I hid a hundred of the prophets of the LORD, fifty men to a cave, and I provided them with food and water. ¹⁴ Now you say, 'Go tell your lord, "Elijah is here!"' He will kill me!"

¹⁵ Then Elijah said, "As the LORD of Armies lives,[t] in whose presence I stand, today I will present myself to Ahab."

¹⁶ Obadiah went to meet Ahab and told him. Then Ahab went to meet Elijah. ¹⁷ When Ahab saw Elijah, Ahab said to him, "Is that you, the one ruining Israel?"[u]

¹⁸ He replied, "I have not ruined Israel, but you and your father's family have, because you have abandoned the LORD's commands[v] and followed the Baals.[w] ¹⁹ Now summon all Israel to meet me at Mount Carmel,[x] along with the 450 prophets of Baal and the 400 prophets of Asherah[y] who eat at Jezebel's table."

ELIJAH AT MOUNT CARMEL

²⁰ So Ahab summoned all the Israelites and gathered the prophets at Mount Carmel. ²¹ Then Elijah approached all the people

a 17:19 Ac 9:37,39
b 17:20 2Kg 4:33
c 17:21 2Kg 4:34; Ac 20:10
d 17:22 Lk 7:14
e 17:23 Lk 7:15; Heb 11:35
f 17:24 Jn 3:2
g 1Kg 22:16; Jn 17:17
h 18:1 1Kg 17:8
i 1Kg 17:1; Jms 5:17
j 1Kg 16:29-33
k 18:2 1Kg 16:24,29
l 18:3 1Kg 16:9
m Neh 7:2; Pr 3:5-6
n 18:4 1Kg 16:31; Rv 2:20
o 1Kg 18:13
p 18:5 Gn 47:4
q 18:7 2Kg 1:6-8

r 18:9 1Kg 17:18
s 18:12 2Kg 2:16; Ac 8:39
t 18:15 1Kg 17:1
u 18:17 Jos 7:25; 1Kg 21:20
v 18:18 1Kg 9:9; 16:25-26
w 1Kg 16:31-32
x 18:19 Jos 19:26; 2Kg 2:25
y 1Kg 16:33; 22:6

A **18:8** The Hb words translated *'Elijah is here'* also mean *'Look, my God is the LORD'*

---

woman believed her sin had come to God's attention through Elijah's presence in her home. Thus, in her mind, God was punishing her for her sin by putting her **son...to death.**
17:23-24 Seeing her son returned to life confirmed the woman's faith in the Lord as the true God (17:24). The miracle also no doubt strengthened Elijah's faith for the tests he was about to face as he returned to Israel to confront Ahab and the prophets of Baal.
18:3-5 Obadiah was a faithful believer. Like Joseph, Daniel, and Nehemiah, he held a position of trust and responsibility in the palace of an unbelieving ruler.

18:9-10 Obadiah feared Elijah was pronouncing his death sentence. Ahab had put a price on Elijah's head. He reasoned that if he told the king that he had found Elijah, and then the prophet failed to appear, surely Ahab would put his servant to death.
18:17-18 Ahab immediately cast the blame for Israel's woes on Elijah. The wicked king wouldn't accept responsibility for his nation's suffering. King Ahab had integrated idolatry into a system that was supposed to be run on God's agenda because the Israelites were his people. Israel was suffering because of failed leadership.

18:19 These numbers indicate the extent to which Jezebel had plunged Israel into gross idolatry. It was time for a face-off.
18:20 That Ahab took up Elijah's challenge means he must have been confident of the outcome. Elijah was a powerful prophet, but 850 to 1 were pretty good odds.
18:21 This mass gathering set the stage for addressing one of the most important questions in all of Scripture: Who is the true God? The Lord had declared to Israel that he alone was God. Now the people were going to have to make up their minds. Would they believe in the God of their fathers? Or

a 18:21 2Kg 17:41
b Jos 24:15; Mt 6:24
c 18:22 1Kg 19:10,14
d 18:24 Gn 4:26; Rm 10:13
e 18:26 Jr 10:5; 1Co 8:4
f 18:27 Hab 2:19
g 18:28 Lv 19:28; Dt 14:1
h 18:29 Ex 29:39,41
i 1Sm 4:20; 2Kg 19:16; Ps 115:4-8; Is 16:12

j 18:30 1Kg 19:10
k 18:31 Gn 32:28; 35:10; 2Kg 17:34
l 18:32 Gn 12:7,8; 22:9
m 18:36 1Kg 18:29
n Ex 3:6; 4:5
o Nm 16:28
p 18:37 Jos 4:24; Jn 11:42
q 18:39 Lv 9:24; Mt 17:6
r 1Kg 18:21,24

and said, "How long will you waver between two opinions?[A],[a] If the LORD is God, follow him. But if Baal, follow him."[b] But the people didn't answer him a word.

22 Then Elijah said to the people, "I am the only remaining prophet of the LORD,[c] but Baal's prophets are 450 men. **23** Let two bulls be given to us. They are to choose one bull for themselves, cut it in pieces, and place it on the wood but not light the fire. I will prepare the other bull and place it on the wood but not light the fire. **24** Then you call on the name of your god, and I will call on the name of the LORD.[d] The God who answers with fire, he is God."

All the people answered, "That's fine."

25 Then Elijah said to the prophets of Baal, "Since you are so numerous, choose for yourselves one bull and prepare it first. Then call on the name of your god but don't light the fire."

26 So they took the bull that he gave them, prepared it, and called on the name of Baal from morning until noon, saying, "Baal, answer us!" But there was no sound;[e] no one answered. Then they danced[B] around the altar they had made.

27 At noon Elijah mocked them. He said, "Shout loudly, for he's a god! Maybe he's thinking it over; maybe he has wandered away;[c] or maybe he's on the road. Perhaps he's sleeping and will wake up!"[f] **28** They shouted loudly, and cut themselves[g] with knives and spears, according to their custom, until blood gushed over them. **29** All afternoon they kept on raving until the offering of the evening sacrifice,[h] but there was no sound; no one answered, no one paid attention.[i]

30 Then Elijah said to all the people, "Come near me." So all the people approached him. Then he repaired the LORD's altar that had been torn down:[j] **31** Elijah took twelve stones — according to the number of the tribes of the sons of Jacob, to whom the word of the LORD had come, saying, "Israel will be your name"[k] — **32** and he built an altar[l] with the stones in the name of the LORD. Then he made a trench around the altar large enough to hold about four gallons.[D],[E] **33** Next, he arranged the wood, cut up the bull, and placed it on the wood. He said, "Fill four water pots with water and pour it on the offering to be burned and on the wood." **34** Then he said, "A second time!" and they did it a second time. And then he said, "A third time!" and they did it a third time. **35** So the water ran all around the altar; he even filled the trench with water.

36 At the time for offering the evening sacrifice,[m] the prophet Elijah approached the altar and said, "LORD, the God of Abraham, Isaac, and Israel,[n] today let it be known[o] that you are God in Israel and I am your servant, and that at your word I have done all these things. **37** Answer me, LORD! Answer me so that this people will know that you, the LORD, are God[p] and that you have turned their hearts back."

38 Then the LORD's fire fell and consumed the burnt offering, the wood, the stones, and the dust, and it licked up the water that was in the trench. **39** When all the people saw it, they fell facedown[q] and said, "The LORD, he is God! The LORD, he is God!"[r]

A 18:21 Lit *you hobble on two crutches?* B 18:26 Or *hobbled* C 18:27 Or *has turned aside*; possibly to relieve himself D 18:32 LXX reads *trench containing two measures of seed* E 18:32 Lit *altar corresponding to a house of two seahs of seed*

---

would they continue to follow the gods of the nations?

There is no place for double-mindedness on spiritual matters; you can't have God and the world (see Jas 4:8). Israel was like an intoxicated man who couldn't walk a straight line but weaved from side to side, and Elijah's question implied that Israel's two-timing of God had been going on too long. It was time to choose sides: **If the LORD is God, follow him. But if Baal, follow him.** There is no such thing as neutrality when it comes to the true God and his demand for exclusive worship (see Matt 12:30).

Shockingly, **the people didn't answer** Elijah's impassioned challenge. The descendants of Abraham, Isaac, and Jacob couldn't even bring themselves to affirm that the Lord is the one true God.

18:22-24 Did the people really expect to see a supernatural response that day? Or did they have no expectations? Regardless, it's unlikely that they thought the out-gunned Elijah would come out on top.
18:27 Since Ahab and his prophets had led the people of Israel astray, Elijah wanted to make it clear that their false god and his religion were a lie and a disgrace that had caused the Lord to judge his people. Baal deserved to be **mocked.**
18:29 Here we see the outcome for those who trust in anyone or anything besides the true God: **No one answered, no one paid attention.**
18:30-31 Elijah called the people to **the LORD's altar** (18:30). Then Elijah took the **twelve stones** (18:31), representing the twelve tribes of Israel, and **repaired the LORD's altar.** This was a significant object lesson for the crowd. Even though the nation was divided at this time, they were

still the one people of God; they consisted of the descendants of the twelve sons of Jacob. Elijah was preparing the Israelites to see their God work by calling them to unity.
18:32-35 Elijah's elaborate preparations of the altar were designed to leave no doubt in anyone's mind that the Lord is the only true God. No human could light such a mess.
18:36-37 A prayer for God to be glorified and for his people to be edified is the kind of prayer that God answers.
18:38 God's dramatic response to Elijah's prayer was heightened by the fact that it was now evening (18:36). The perfect time for a divine fireworks display!

Given that the flames even **licked up the water,** it would have been obvious to everyone present that the supernatural had invaded the natural world; the spiritual had touched the physical; eternity had invaded history.

40 Then Elijah ordered them, "Seize the prophets of Baal![a] Do not let even one of them escape." So they seized them, and Elijah brought them down to the Wadi Kishon[b] and slaughtered them there.[c] **41** Elijah said to Ahab, "Go up, eat and drink, for there is the sound of a rainstorm."[d]

42 So Ahab went to eat and drink, but Elijah went up to the summit of Carmel.[e] He bent down on the ground and put his face between his knees.[f] **43** Then he said to his servant, "Go up and look toward the sea."

So he went up, looked, and said, "There's nothing."

Seven times Elijah said, "Go back."

44 On the seventh[g] time, he reported, "There's a cloud as small as a man's hand coming up from the sea."

Then Elijah said, "Go and tell Ahab, 'Get your chariot ready and go down so the rain doesn't stop you.'"

45 In a little while, the sky grew dark with clouds and wind, and there was a downpour. So Ahab got in his chariot and went to Jezreel.[h] **46** The power of the LORD[i] was on Elijah, and he tucked his mantle under his belt[j] and ran ahead of Ahab to the entrance of Jezreel.

ELIJAH'S JOURNEY TO HOREB

19 Ahab told Jezebel[k] everything that Elijah had done[l] and how he had killed all the prophets with the sword.[m] **2** So Jezebel sent a messenger to Elijah, saying, "May the gods punish me and do so severely[n] if I don't make your life like the life of one of them by this time tomorrow!"

3 Then Elijah became afraid[A,o] and immediately ran for his life.[p] When he came to Beer-sheba[q] that belonged to Judah, he left his servant there,[r] **4** but he went on a day's journey into the wilderness. He sat down under a broom tree[s] and prayed that he might die. He said, "I have had enough! LORD, take my life,[t] for I'm no better than my fathers." **5** Then he lay down and slept under the broom tree.

Suddenly, an angel touched him.[u] The angel told him, "Get up and eat." **6** Then he looked, and there at his head was a loaf of bread baked over hot stones, and a jug of water.[v] So he ate and drank and lay down again. **7** Then the angel of the LORD[w] returned for a second time and touched him. He said, "Get up and eat, or the journey will be too much for you." **8** So he got up, ate, and drank. Then on the strength from that food, he walked forty days and forty nights[x] to Horeb, the mountain of God.[y] **9** He entered a cave[z] there and spent the night.

ELIJAH'S ENCOUNTER WITH THE LORD

Suddenly, the word of the LORD came to him, and he said to him, "What are you doing here, Elijah?"[aa]

10 He replied, "I have been very zealous[ab] for the LORD God of Armies, but the Israelites have abandoned your covenant,[ac] torn down your altars,[ad] and killed your prophets[ae] with the sword. I alone am left,[af] and they are looking for me to take my life."[ag]

11 Then he said, "Go out and stand on the mountain in the LORD's presence."[ah]

A 19:3 Some Hb mss, LXX, Syr, Vg; other Hb mss read *He saw*

a 18:40 1Kg 18:19,22
b Jdg 4:7; 5:21
c Dt 13:5; 2Kg 10:24-25
d 18:41 1Kg 17:1; 18:1
e 18:42 1Kg 18:19
f 1Sm 12:17; Jms 5:18
g 18:44 Jos 6:15; Lk 12:54
h 18:45 Jos 17:16; Jdg 6:33
i 18:46 2Kg 3:15
j Ex 12:11; 2Kg 4:29; 9:1; Jr 1:17; 1Pt 1:13
k 19:1 1Kg 16:31; 18:4,14
l 1Kg 18:30-38
m 1Kg 18:40
n 19:2 1Sm 3:17; 1Kg 20:10; 2Kg 6:31
o 19:3 Pr 29:25
p Gn 31:21
q Gn 21:31; Jdg 20:1
r Gn 22:5; Mt 14:23; 26:36
s 19:4 Jb 30:4
t Nm 11:15; Jnh 4:3,8
u 19:5 Gn 28:11-16
v 19:6 1Kg 17:10-11
w 19:7 Gn 16:7,9,11
x 19:8 Ex 24:18; Mt 4:2
y Ex 3:1; 4:27
z 19:9 Ex 33:22
aa Gn 3:9
ab 19:10 Nm 25:13; Ac 22:3
ac Dt 31:16
ad 1Kg 18:30
ae 1Kg 18:4,13; Ac 7:52
af 1Kg 18:22
ag 1Kg 19:2,14; Rm 11:3
ah 19:11 Ex 19:20

18:40 With the event's outcome so one-sided, **the prophets of Baal** were shown to be the frauds that they were. Their fate was sealed.

18:41-46 With the greatness and uniqueness of the Lord vindicated and confessed, it was time to lift the drought and famine from the land (see 18:1). The prophet informed Ahab that **a rainstorm** was approaching and went **to the summit of Carmel** to pray (18:42). Elijah persisted in his intercession until the Lord answered with **a downpour** (18:45). In other words, he took the mental position of a woman in the travail of childbirth as he kept praying. After seven times (the number of completion), the answer came. He even received the bonus blessing of supernatural strength, which enabled him to outrun Ahab's **chariot** to **Jezreel** (18:43-45). Without a doubt, **the power of the LORD was on Elijah** (18:46). He was on a spiritual mountaintop. But he was about to enter the valley of the shadow of death.

19:1-2 Jezebel's god Baal had been mocked and her **prophets** had been **killed**—all

because of this upstart prophet of the Lord (19:1). Therefore, she threatened to make Elijah like her own prophets—that is, dead—by the following day (19:2).

19:3-4 The irony of Elijah's fear of a godless queen could not be greater, coming on the heels of his greatest victory. But there he was, exhausted, discouraged, and praying to **die** (19:4). Even the strongest saints have weaknesses. Spiritual depression strikes when we least expect it—especially following on the heels of spiritual victory. Remember that even Jesus was attacked after his glorious baptism (see Matt 3:16–4:1).

19:5-8 Sometimes what we need is simply a good meal and a good night's sleep. **Horeb** was the ancient name for Mount Sinai, where Moses had met God in the burning bush (see Exod 3:1-2) and where God had entered into a covenant with his people (see Deut 5:2). Just as sure as Elijah needed food and rest, he also needed time in God's presence to get his spiritual feet back under him.

19:9 God asked the prophet, **What are you doing here?** Of course, the obvious answer was, "I'm resting." But God wasn't asking Elijah what he was *doing* at Horeb but what he was doing *at Horeb*. Why had he fled so far from Israel, where the Lord had called him to minister?

19:10 Elijah had done everything God had asked of him. But nothing had changed. In effect Elijah wailed, "Israel is still in rebellion; your prophets have been killed; and now they're after me!" As far as he knew, he was the last man in Israel who still followed God. His answer could have been construed as saying, "God, your power was great, but it wasn't enough. We won the battle, but we've lost the war."

19:11-13 God didn't rebuke Elijah for his frankness in verse 10 but gave him supernatural illumination. Elijah was awed by it, and the message behind it was this: things were well under control. God's power had not diminished.

a 19:11 Ex 33:21-22
b Ezk 1:4; Ac 2:2
c Am 1:1; Rv 6:12; 16:18
d 19:12 Ex 3:2
e Zch 4:6,10
f 19:13 Ex 3:6
g 19:14 1Kg 19:10; Rm 11:3
h 19:15 2Kg 8:8-15
i 19:16 2Kg 9:1-10
j 1Kg 19:19
k 19:17 2Kg 9:14–10:25
l 2Kg 2:24; 8:1
m 19:18 Rm 11:4
n 1Kg 16:31
o Hs 13:2
p 19:19 1Kg 19:16-17
q 2Kg 2:8,13-14
r 19:20 Mt 8:21-22
s 19:21 1Sm 6:14; 2Sm 24:22

t 19:21 Lk 14:26,33
u 20:1 1Kg 15:18,20
v 1Kg 22:31
w 1Kg 16:24,29
x 20:3 2Kg 24:14-16; Dn 1:3-4
y 20:6 Lm 2:4; Ezk 24:16,21,25
z 20:7 2Kg 5:7
aa 20:10 1Kg 19:2; 2Kg 6:31
ab 2Sm 22:43
ac 20:11 Pr 27:1
ad 20:12 1Kg 16:9

At that moment, the LORD passed by.[a] A great and mighty wind[b] was tearing at the mountains and was shattering cliffs before the LORD, but the LORD was not in the wind. After the wind there was an earthquake,[c] but the LORD was not in the earthquake. [12] After the earthquake there was a fire,[d] but the LORD was not in the fire. And after the fire there was a voice, a soft whisper.[e] [13] When Elijah heard it, he wrapped his face in his mantle[f] and went out and stood at the entrance of the cave.

Suddenly, a voice came to him and said, "What are you doing here, Elijah?"

[14] "I have been very zealous for the LORD God of Armies," he replied, "but the Israelites have abandoned your covenant, torn down your altars, and killed your prophets with the sword. I alone am left, and they're looking for me to take my life."[g]

[15] Then the LORD said to him, "Go and return by the way you came to the Wilderness of Damascus. When you arrive, you are to anoint Hazael[h] as king over Aram. [16] You are to anoint Jehu[i] son of Nimshi as king over Israel and Elisha[j] son of Shaphat from Abel-meholah as prophet in your place. [17] Then Jehu will put to death whoever escapes the sword of Hazael,[k] and Elisha will put to death whoever escapes the sword of Jehu.[l] [18] But I will leave seven thousand in Israel[m] — every knee that has not bowed to Baal[n] and every mouth that has not kissed him."[o]

ELISHA'S APPOINTMENT AS ELIJAH'S SUCCESSOR

[19] Elijah left there and found Elisha[p] son of Shaphat as he was plowing. Twelve teams of oxen were in front of him, and he was with the twelfth team. Elijah walked by him and threw his mantle over him.[q] [20] Elisha left the oxen, ran to follow Elijah, and said, "Please let me kiss my father and mother, and then I will follow you."[r]

"Go on back," he replied, "for what have I done to you?"

[21] So he turned back from following him, took the team of oxen, and slaughtered[A] them. With the oxen's wooden yoke and plow,[s] he cooked the meat and gave it to the people, and they ate. Then he left, followed Elijah, and served him.[t]

VICTORY OVER BEN-HADAD

20 Now King Ben-hadad[u] of Aram assembled his entire army. Thirty-two kings,[v] along with horses and chariots, were with him. He marched up, besieged Samaria,[w] and fought against it. [2] He sent messengers into the city to King Ahab of Israel and said to him, "This is what Ben-hadad says: [3] 'Your silver and your gold are mine! And your best wives and children are mine as well!'"[x]

[4] Then the king of Israel answered, "Just as you say, my lord the king: I am yours, along with all that I have."

[5] The messengers then returned and said, "This is what Ben-hadad says: 'I have sent messengers to you, saying: You are to give me your silver, your gold, your wives, and your children. [6] But at this time tomorrow I will send my servants to you,[B,y] and they will search your palace and your servants' houses. They will lay their hands on and take away whatever is precious to you.'"

[7] Then the king of Israel called for all the elders of the land and said, "Recognize[c] that this one is only looking for trouble,[z] for he demanded my wives, my children, my silver, and my gold, and I didn't turn him down."

[8] All the elders and all the people said to him, "Don't listen or agree."

[9] So he said to Ben-hadad's messengers, "Say to my lord the king, 'Everything you demanded of your servant the first time, I will do, but this thing I cannot do.'" So the messengers left and took word back to him.

[10] Then Ben-hadad sent messengers to him and said, "May the gods punish me and do so severely[aa] if Samaria's dust[ab] amounts to a handful for each of the people who follow me."

[11] The king of Israel answered, "Say this: 'Don't let the one who puts on his armor boast[ac] like the one who takes it off.'"

[12] When Ben-hadad heard this response, while he and the kings were drinking[ad] in their quarters,[D] he said to his servants,

---

[A] 19:21 Or *sacrificed*   [B] 20:6 Lit *take all the delight of your eyes*   [C] 20:7 Lit *"Know and see"*   [D] 20:12 Lit *booths,* also in v. 16

19:15-18 Far from being thwarted, the Lord was about to wipe the throne of Israel clean and remove Baal worship from the nation. And now that Elijah had experienced a spiritual retreat of sorts, God informed him of his next assignment. He commanded the prophet to return to the north and anoint **Hazael as king over Aram** and anoint **Jehu . . . as king over Israel** (19:15-16). These men would exact God's vengeance on Israel's sin.

God also told Elijah to anoint his successor: **Elisha son of Shaphat** (19:16), indicating that Elijah wasn't as alone as he had feared (19:10). There were other servants of the Lord in the land: **seven thousand** (19:18).

20:1-6 Here events began to unfold that would bring about God's judgment on the house of Ahab and on Israel's worship of Baal.

"Take your positions." So they took their positions against the city.

13 A prophet approached King Ahab of Israel and said, "This is what the LORD says: 'Do you see this whole huge army? Watch, I am handing it over to you today so that you may know that I am the LORD.'"[a]

14 Ahab asked, "By whom?"

And the prophet said, "This is what the LORD says: 'By the young men of the provincial leaders.'"

Then he asked, "Who is to start the battle?"[b] He said, "You."

15 So Ahab mobilized the young men of the provincial leaders, and there were 232. After them he mobilized all the Israelite troops: 7,000.[c] **16** They marched out at noon while Ben-hadad and the thirty-two kings[d] who were helping him were getting drunk in their quarters. **17** The young men of the provincial leaders marched out first. Then Ben-hadad sent out scouts, and they reported to him, saying, "Men are marching out of Samaria."[e]

18 So he said, "If they have marched out in peace,[f] take them alive, and if they have marched out for battle, take them alive."

19 The young men of the provincial leaders and the army behind them marched out from the city, **20** and each one struck down his opponent.[g] So the Arameans fled and Israel pursued them,[h] but King Ben-hadad of Aram escaped on a horse with the cavalry. **21** Then the king of Israel marched out and attacked the cavalry and the chariots. He inflicted a severe slaughter on Aram.

22 The prophet approached the king of Israel and said to him, "Go and strengthen yourself, then consider carefully[A] what you should do, for in the spring[i] the king of Aram will attack you."

23 Now the king of Aram's servants said to him, "Their gods are gods of the hill country.[j] That's why they were stronger than we were. Instead, we should fight with them on the plain; then we will certainly be stronger than they are. **24** Also do this: remove each king from his position and appoint captains in their place. **25** Raise another army for yourself like the army you lost — horse for horse, chariot for chariot — and let's fight with them on

the plain; and we will certainly be stronger than they are." The king listened to them and did it.

26 In the spring, Ben-hadad mobilized the Arameans and went up to Aphek[k] to battle Israel. **27** The Israelites mobilized, gathered supplies, and went to fight them. The Israelites camped in front of them like two little flocks of goats, while the Arameans filled the landscape.[l]

28 Then the man of God[m] approached and said to the king of Israel, "This is what the LORD says: 'Because the Arameans have said: The LORD is a god of the mountains and not a god of the valleys,[n] I will hand over all this whole huge army to you. Then you will know that I am the LORD.'"[o]

29 They camped opposite each other for seven days. On the seventh day,[p] the battle took place, and the Israelites struck down the Arameans — one hundred thousand foot soldiers in one day. **30** The ones who remained fled into the city of Aphek, and the wall fell on those twenty-seven thousand remaining men.

Ben-hadad also fled and went into an inner room[q] in the city. **31** His servants said to him, "Consider this: we have heard that the kings of the house of Israel are merciful kings. So let's put sackcloth around our waists[r] and ropes around our heads, and let's go out to the king of Israel. Perhaps he will spare your life."

32 So they dressed with sackcloth around their waists and ropes around their heads, went to the king of Israel, and said, "Your servant Ben-hadad says, 'Please spare my life.'"

So he said, "Is he still alive? He is my brother."

33 Now the men were looking for a sign of hope, so they quickly picked up on this[B] and responded, "Yes, it is your brother Ben-hadad."

Then he said, "Go and bring him."

So Ben-hadad came out to him, and Ahab had him come up into the chariot. **34** Then Ben-hadad said to him, "I restore to you the cities that my father took from your father,[s] and you may set up marketplaces for yourself in Damascus, like my father set up in Samaria."[t]

a 20:13 1Kg 20:28
b 20:14 Jdg 1:1; 20:18
c 20:15 Jdg 7:2
d 20:16 1Kg 20:1
e 20:17 1Kg 16:24
f 20:18 2Kg 14:8
g 20:20 2Sm 2:15-16
h 20:22 2Sm 11:1
i 20:23 1Kg 14:23; Ps 139:7-12

k 20:26 2Kg 13:17
l 20:27 Jdg 6:5; 1Sm 13:5
m 20:28 1Kg 17:18
n 1Kg 20:23
o 1Kg 20:13
p 20:29 Jos 6:15
q 20:30 1Kg 22:25
r 20:31 Gn 37:34
s 20:34 1Kg 15:20
t 2Sm 8:6

A **20:22** Lit *then know and see*   B **20:33** Some Hb mss, alt Hb tradition, LXX; other Hb mss read *they hastened and caught hold;* "*Is this it?*"

20:13 This encouragement came not because Ahab deserved deliverance or even asked the Lord for help. Rather, the victory over Aram was intended to teach Ahab that the Lord was the true God. Would Ahab learn the lesson?

20:23 Ben-hadad's counselors gave him bad advice concerning the power of the Lord, so he planned the next battle for **the plain** where Aram would have an advantage—or so he thought.

20:32-34 Ahab accepted Ben-hadad's surren-

der and even **made a treaty with him** (20:34). God had handed over Ahab's enemy so that Ahab might defeat him and worship God. Instead, Ahab made friends with his enemy and forgot about God.

a 20:35 2Kg 2:3,5,7
b 20:36 1Kg 13:24
c 20:38 1Kg 14:2
d 20:39 Jos 2:14; 2Kg 10:24
e 20:40 2Sm 12:5
f 20:42 1Kg 19:16
g 20:43 1Kg 21:4
h 21:1 Jdg 6:33; 1Kg 18:45
i 1Kg 20:1
j 21:2 1Sm 8:14

k 21:3 Lv 25:23; Nm 36:7
l 21:4 1Kg 20:43
m 2Kg 20:2
n 1Sm 28:23
o 21:7 1Sm 8:14
p 21:8 2Sm 11:14
q Est 3:12; 8:8,10
r 1Kg 20:7
s 21:9 1Sm 7:5-6; 2Ch 20:2-4
t 21:10 Dt 13:13
u Ex 20:16; 23:1; Dt 5:20; Ac 6:11
v Lv 24:15-16
w 21:14 Lv 24:16

Ahab responded, "On the basis of this treaty, I release you." So he made a treaty with him and released him.

AHAB REBUKED BY THE LORD

35 One of the sons of the prophets*a* said to his fellow prophet by the word of the LORD, "Strike me!" But the man refused to strike him.

36 He told him, "Because you did not listen to the LORD, mark my words: When you leave me, a lion will kill you."*b* When he left him, a lion attacked and killed him.

37 The prophet found another man and said to him, "Strike me!" So the man struck him, inflicting a wound. **38** Then the prophet went and waited for the king on the road. He disguised*c* himself with a bandage over his eyes. **39** As the king was passing by, he cried out to the king and said, "Your servant marched out into the middle of the battle. Suddenly, a man turned aside and brought someone to me and said, 'Guard this man! If he is ever missing, it will be your life in place of his life,*d* or you will weigh out seventy-five pounds^A of silver.' **40** But while your servant was busy here and there, he disappeared."

The king of Israel said to him, "That will be your sentence; you yourself have decided it."*e*

41 He quickly removed the bandage from his eyes. The king of Israel recognized that he was one of the prophets. **42** The prophet said to him, "This is what the LORD says: 'Because you released from your hand the man I had set apart for destruction,*f* it will be your life in place of his life and your people in place of his people.'" **43** The king of Israel left for home resentful and angry,*g* and he entered Samaria.

AHAB AND NABOTH'S VINEYARD

21 Some time passed after these events. Naboth the Jezreelite had a vineyard; it was in Jezreel*h* next to the palace of King Ahab of Samaria.*i* **2** So Ahab spoke to Naboth, saying, "Give me your vineyard*j* so I can have it for a vegetable garden, since it is right next to my palace. I will give you a better vineyard in its place, or if you prefer, I will give you its value in silver."

3 But Naboth said to Ahab, "I will never give my fathers' inheritance*k* to you."

4 So Ahab went to his palace resentful and angry*l* because of what Naboth the Jezreelite had told him. He had said, "I will not give you my fathers' inheritance." He lay down on his bed, turned his face away,*m* and didn't eat any food.*n*

5 Then his wife Jezebel came to him and said to him, "Why are you so upset that you refuse to eat?"

6 "Because I spoke to Naboth the Jezreelite," he replied. "I told him: Give me your vineyard for silver, or if you wish, I will give you a vineyard in its place. But he said, 'I won't give you my vineyard!'"

7 Then his wife Jezebel said to him, "Now, exercise your royal power over Israel. Get up, eat some food, and be happy. For I will give you the vineyard of Naboth the Jezreelite."*o* **8** So she wrote letters*p* in Ahab's name and sealed them with his seal.*q* She sent the letters to the elders*r* and nobles who lived with Naboth in his city. **9** In the letters, she wrote:

Proclaim a fast*s* and seat Naboth at the head of the people. **10** Then seat two wicked men*t* opposite him and have them testify against him, saying, "You have cursed God and the king!"*u* Then take him out and stone him to death.*v*

11 The men of his city, the elders and nobles who lived in his city, did as Jezebel had sent word to them, just as it was written in the letters she had sent them. **12** They proclaimed a fast and seated Naboth at the head of the people. **13** The two wicked men came in and sat opposite him. Then the wicked men testified against Naboth in the presence of the people, saying, "Naboth has cursed God and the king!" So they took him outside the city and stoned him to death with stones. **14** Then they sent word to Jezebel: "Naboth has been stoned to death."*w*

^A 20:39 Lit *a talent*

20:35-36 These men knew each other; they shared the role of divine spokesmen; and the first prophet was speaking **by the word of the LORD** (20:35). So the second prophet should have known better than to ignore it. What God says is to be obeyed. The consequences for failing to obey can be catastrophic.
20:37-42 The **wound** the prophet received allowed him to disguise himself **with a** **bandage** (20:37-38). With it he approached King Ahab with a story (20:39-40) reminiscent of the tale Nathan told to King David after he had sinned—a tale that was designed to entrap him (see 2 Sam 12:1-10). Its point was that Ahab had committed a grave sin in releasing Ben-hadad when God had **set apart** that king **for destruction** (1 Kgs 20:42). Since Ahab had failed to carry out the Lord's will, he and Israel would suffer.
21:4 The king acted like a spoiled child when he didn't get what he wanted.
21:7-10 In other words, the evil queen set in motion a coldhearted plan to have **Naboth** executed under trumped-up charges so her weak-willed husband could have what he wanted.

15 When Jezebel heard that Naboth had been stoned to death, she said to Ahab, "Get up and take possession of the vineyard of Naboth the Jezreelite who refused to give it to you for silver,[a] since Naboth isn't alive, but dead." **16** When Ahab heard that Naboth was dead, he got up to go down to the vineyard of Naboth the Jezreelite to take possession of it.

THE LORD'S JUDGMENT ON AHAB

17 Then the word of the LORD came to Elijah the Tishbite:[b] **18** "Get up and go to meet King Ahab of Israel,[c] who is in Samaria.[d] He's in Naboth's vineyard, where he has gone to take possession of it. **19** Tell him, 'This is what the LORD says: Have you murdered[e] and also taken possession?'[f] Then tell him, 'This is what the LORD says: In the place where the dogs licked up Naboth's blood, the dogs will also lick up your blood!'"[g]

20 Ahab said to Elijah, "So, my enemy, you've found me, have you?"[h]

He replied, "I have found you because you devoted[i] yourself to do what is evil in the LORD's sight. **21** This is what the LORD says:[A] 'I am about to bring disaster on you and will eradicate your descendants:

I will wipe out all of Ahab's males,[B]
both slave and free,[C] in Israel;[j]

22 I will make your house like the house of Jeroboam[k] son of Nebat and like the house of Baasha[l] son of Ahijah, because you have angered me and caused Israel to sin.'[m] **23** The LORD also speaks of Jezebel: 'The dogs will eat Jezebel in the plot of land[D] at Jezreel:[n]

24 Anyone who belongs to Ahab
and dies in the city, the dogs
will eat,
and anyone who dies in the field,
the birds[E] will eat.'"[o]

25 Still, there was no one like Ahab, who devoted himself to do what was evil in the LORD's sight, because his wife Jezebel

incited him.[p] **26** He committed the most detestable acts by following idols[q] as the Amorites[r] had, whom the LORD had dispossessed before the Israelites.

27 When Ahab heard these words, he tore his clothes, put sackcloth over his body, and fasted. He lay down in sackcloth[s] and walked around subdued. **28** Then the word of the LORD came to Elijah the Tishbite: **29** "Have you seen how Ahab has humbled himself before me? I will not bring the disaster during his lifetime,[t] because he has humbled himself before me. I will bring the disaster on his house during his son's lifetime."[u]

JEHOSHAPHAT'S ALLIANCE WITH AHAB

22 There was[v] a lull of three years[w] without war between Aram and Israel. **2** However, in the third year, King Jehoshaphat[x] of Judah went to visit the king of Israel.[y] **3** The king of Israel had said to his servants, "Don't you know that Ramoth-gilead[z] is ours, but we're doing nothing to take it from the king of Aram?" **4** So[aa] he asked Jehoshaphat, "Will you go with me to fight Ramoth-gilead?"[ab]

Jehoshaphat replied to the king of Israel, "I am as you are, my people as your people, my horses as your horses."[ac] **5** But Jehoshaphat said to the king of Israel, "First, please ask what the LORD's will is."[ad]

6 So the king of Israel gathered the prophets, about four hundred men,[ae] and asked them, "Should I go against Ramoth-gilead for war or should I refrain?"

They replied, "March up, and the Lord will hand it over to the king."[af]

7 But Jehoshaphat asked, "Isn't there a prophet of the LORD here anymore?[ag] Let's ask him."

8 The king of Israel said to Jehoshaphat, "There is still one man who can inquire of the LORD, but I hate him[ah] because he never prophesies good about me,[ai] but only disaster. He is Micaiah son of Imlah."

a 21:15 1Kg 21:2-3
b 21:17 1Kg 17:2,8
c 21:18 1Kg 18:1
d 1Kg 16:29; 2Ch 22:9
e 21:19 Ex 20:13; Dt 5:17
f Lv 25:23
g 1Kg 22:38
h 21:20 1Kg 18:17
i 2Kg 17:17; Rm 7:14
j 21:21 2Kg 9:8
k 21:22 1Kg 14:10-11
l 1Kg 16:3-4
m 1Kg 12:30
n 21:23 2Kg 9:10,30-37
o 21:24 1Kg 14:11; 16:4

p 21:25 1Kg 16:30-33
q 21:26 2Kg 17:12
r Gn 15:16; 2Kg 21:11
s 21:27 Gn 37:34; 2Sm 3:31; 2Kg 6:30
t 21:29 2Kg 20:19; 2Ch 32:26
u 2Kg 9:25-37; 10:6-11
v 22:1-9 2Ch 18:1-8
w 22:1 1Kg 20:1,26
x 22:2 1Kg 15:24
y 2Ch 18:2
z 22:3 Dt 4:43; Jos 20:8; 1Kg 4:13
aa 22:4-6 2Kg 3:7-8
ab 22:4 2Kg 8:18,27
ac 2Kg 3:7
ad 22:5 1Sm 23:1-5; Jms 4:15
ae 22:6 1Kg 18:19
af 1Kg 13:18
ag 22:7 2Kg 1:3; 3:11; 5:8
ah 22:8 1Kg 18:17; 21:20
ai Am 5:10

A 21:21 LXX; MT omits *This is what the LORD says* 　B 21:21 Lit *eliminate Ahab's one who urinates against the wall* 　C 21:21 Or *males, even the weak and impaired*; Hb obscure 　D 21:23 Some Hb mss, Syr, Tg, Vg, 2Kg 9:36; other Hb mss, LXX read *the rampart* 　E 21:24 Lit *birds of the sky*

21:21-24 As a result of Jezebel's monstrous act, the king's posterity would be utterly destroyed—just as the Lord had done to the houses of **Jeroboam** and **Baasha** (21:22). The same judgment that had been pronounced on these kings, in fact, was now pronounced on Ahab (21:24; see 14:11; 16:4). For slaughtering the Lord's faithful servants over the years, **Jezebel**, too, would finally receive what she deserved (21:23).

21:27 These were physical actions intended to convey his repentance.
22:3-4 The **fight** discussed here would set in motion Ahab's demise (22:4).
22:5 This is the reader's first clue that Jehoshaphat was not like Ahab.
22:6 The fact that the king of Israel called **about four hundred** false, lying prophets to join them rather than bringing in a prophet of the Lord signals that Ahab's repentance

(in 21:27) hadn't brought about true reform in his life.
22:7 Apparently, Jehoshaphat sensed something wasn't right and thus wanted a second opinion—this time from **a prophet of the LORD**.
22:8 This answer laid bare the heart of the king. He didn't want to hear the truth; he only wanted to hear what was in his favor. Unfortunately, too many people feel the same way. Are you willing to accept the truth of the

a 22:10-12 2Ch 18:9-11
b 22:10 Jdg 6:37
c 22:11 1Kg 22:24
d Dt 33:17; Zch 1:18-21
e 22:12 1Kg 4:13
f 22:13-28 2Ch 18:12-27
g 22:14 1Kg 18:10,15
h Nm 22:28; 24:13
i 22:17 Nm 27:16-17; Mt 9:36; Mk 6:34
j 1Kg 22:35-36

k 22:19 Is 6:1; Dn 7:9
l Jb 1:6; Dn 7:10; Heb 1:7
m 22:20 1Kg 22:4
n 22:22 Jdg 9:23; 1Sm 16:14; Jr 20:7; Ezk 14:9
o 2Th 2:11
p 22:24 1Kg 22:11
q 2Ch 18:23
r 22:25 1Kg 20:30
s 22:26 1Kg 22:40
t 22:27 2Ch 16:10; Heb 11:36
u 22:28 Dt 18:22
v Mc 1:2
w 22:29-33 2Ch 18:28-32
x 22:29 1Kg 22:4
y 22:30 1Sm 28:8
z 2Ch 35:22

"The king shouldn't say that!" Jehoshaphat replied.

⁹ So the king of Israel called an officer and said, "Hurry and get Micaiah son of Imlah!"

¹⁰ Now the king of Israel and King Jehoshaphat of Judah,*a* clothed in royal attire, were each sitting on his own throne. They were on the threshing floor*b* at the entrance to the gate of Samaria, and all the prophets were prophesying in front of them. ¹¹ Then Zedekiah*c* son of Chenaanah made iron horns*d* and said, "This is what the LORD says: 'You will gore the Arameans with these until they are finished off.'" ¹² And all the prophets were prophesying the same: "March up to Ramoth-gilead*e* and succeed, for the LORD will hand it over to the king."

MICAIAH'S MESSAGE OF DEFEAT

¹³ The messenger*f* who went to call Micaiah instructed him, "Look, the words of the prophets are unanimously favorable for the king. So let your words be like theirs, and speak favorably."

¹⁴ But Micaiah said, "As the LORD lives,*g* I will say whatever the LORD says to me."*h*

¹⁵ So he went to the king, and the king asked him, "Micaiah, should we go to Ramoth-gilead for war, or should we refrain?"

Micaiah told him, "March up and succeed. The LORD will hand it over to the king."

¹⁶ But the king said to him, "How many times must I make you swear not to tell me anything but the truth in the name of the LORD?"

¹⁷ So Micaiah said:

I saw all Israel scattered on the hills
like sheep without a shepherd.*i*
And the LORD said,
"They have no master;
let everyone return home in peace."*j*

¹⁸ So the king of Israel said to Jehoshaphat, "Didn't I tell you he never prophesies good about me, but only disaster?"

¹⁹ Then Micaiah said, "Therefore, hear the word of the LORD: I saw the LORD sitting on his throne,*k* and the whole heavenly army*l* was standing by him at his right hand and at his left hand. ²⁰ And the LORD said, 'Who will entice Ahab to march up and fall at Ramoth-gilead?'*m* So one was saying this and another was saying that.

²¹ "Then a spirit came forward, stood in the LORD's presence, and said, 'I will entice him.'

²² "The LORD asked him, 'How?'

"He said, 'I will go and become a lying spirit*n* in the mouth of all his prophets.'

"Then he said, 'You will certainly entice him and prevail.*o* Go and do that.'

²³ "You see, the LORD has put a lying spirit into the mouth of all these prophets of yours, and the LORD has pronounced disaster against you."

²⁴ Then Zedekiah*p* son of Chenaanah came up, hit Micaiah on the cheek, and demanded, "Did*A* the Spirit of the LORD leave me to speak to you?"*q*

²⁵ Micaiah replied, "You will soon see when you go to hide in an inner chamber on that day."*r*

²⁶ Then the king of Israel ordered, "Take Micaiah and return him to Amon, the governor of the city, and to Joash, the king's son,*s* ²⁷ and say, 'This is what the king says: Put this guy in prison*t* and feed him only a little bread and water*B* until I come back safely.'"

²⁸ But Micaiah said, "If you ever return safely, the LORD has not spoken through me."*u* Then he said, "Listen, all you people!"*C,v*

AHAB'S DEATH

²⁹ Then*w* the king of Israel and Judah's King Jehoshaphat went up to Ramoth-gilead.*x* ³⁰ But the king of Israel said to Jehoshaphat, "I will disguise*y* myself and go into battle, but you wear your royal attire." So the king of Israel disguised himself and went into battle.*z*

A 22:24 Lit "Which way did   *B* 22:27 Lit *him on bread of oppression and water of oppression*   *C* 22:28 LXX omits *Then he said, "Listen, all you people!"*

---

word of God when it tells you what you don't want to hear?

22:9-12 As the kings of Israel and Judah waited for Micaiah, Ahab's prophets foretold his victory over Aram. One of them, **Zedekiah**, predicted a glorious triumph (22:11). And to this, all of his fellow lying prophets said, "Amen" (22:12).

22:13-15 Before Micaiah entered the king's presence, he was coached not to disagree with the other prophets. Micaiah disdained this charade; he was God's prophet (22:14).

But when he appeared before Ahab, he said what the king wanted to hear: **March up and succeed. The LORD will hand it over to** you (22:15).

22:16 Ahab recognized that Micaiah was being sarcastic, so he insisted on **the truth.**

22:22-23 A **lying spirit** volunteered to lead King Ahab astray by telling lies through **his prophets** (22:22). As you process that insight into what took place in the Lord's throne room, note that God did not lie. He permitted this lying spirit's actions to accomplish

his purposes. This is no different than God allowing Satan to act with evil intent so that God can achieve his good kingdom intentions in spite of Satan's plans (see Gen 50:20).

22:24 Like so many of God's faithful prophets, Micaiah was treated violently for speaking the truth.

22:28 Indeed, Ahab wouldn't be coming back—at least, not alive.

22:30-34 Ahab tried to **disguise** himself in order to steer the enemy's fire away from him, but you can't hide from divine judgment

31 Now the king of Aram had ordered his thirty-two chariot commanders,[a] "Do not fight with anyone at all[A] except the king of Israel."[b] **32** When the chariot commanders saw Jehoshaphat, they shouted, "He must be the king of Israel!" So they turned to fight against him, but Jehoshaphat cried out. **33** When the chariot commanders saw that he was not the king of Israel, they turned back from pursuing him.

34 But a man drew his bow[c] without taking special aim and struck the king of Israel through the joints of his armor. So he said to his charioteer, "Turn around and take me out of the battle,[B] for I am badly wounded!"[d] **35** The battle raged throughout that day, and the king was propped up in his chariot facing the Arameans. He died that evening,[e] and blood from his wound flowed into the bottom of the chariot. **36** Then the cry rang out in the army as the sun set, declaring:

Each man to his own city,
and each man to his own land![f]

37 So the king died and was brought to Samaria. They buried the king in Samaria.[g] **38** Then someone washed the chariot at the pool of Samaria. The dogs licked up his blood, and the prostitutes bathed in it, according to the word of the LORD that he had spoken.[h]

39 The rest of the events of Ahab's reign, along with all his accomplishments, including the ivory palace[i] he built, and all the cities he built, are written in the Historical Record of Israel's Kings.[j] **40** Ahab rested with his fathers,[k] and his son Ahaziah[l] became king in his place.

JUDAH'S KING JEHOSHAPHAT

41 Jehoshaphat[m] son of Asa became king over Judah in the fourth year of Israel's King Ahab. **42** Jehoshaphat was thirty-five years old when he became king; he reigned twenty-five years in Jerusalem. His mother's name was Azubah daughter of Shilhi. **43** He walked in all the ways of his father Asa;[n] he did not turn away from them but did what was right in the LORD's sight. However, the high places were not taken away;[c] the people still sacrificed and burned incense on the high places.[o] **44** Jehoshaphat also made peace with the king of Israel.[p]

45 The rest of the events of Jehoshaphat's reign, along with the might he exercised and how he waged war, are written in the Historical Record of Judah's Kings.[q] **46** He eradicated from the land the rest of the male cult prostitutes who were left from the days of his father Asa.[r] **47** There was no king in Edom;[s] a deputy served as king. **48** Jehoshaphat made ships of Tarshish[t] to go to Ophir[u] for gold, but they did not go because the ships were wrecked at Ezion-geber.[v] **49** At that time, Ahaziah[w] son of Ahab said to Jehoshaphat, "Let my servants go with your servants in the ships," but Jehoshaphat was not willing. **50** Jehoshaphat rested with his fathers and was buried with them in the city of his ancestor David.[x] His son Jehoram[y] became king in his place.

ISRAEL'S KING AHAZIAH

51 Ahaziah[z] son of Ahab became king over Israel in Samaria[aa] in the seventeenth year of Judah's King Jehoshaphat,[ab] and he reigned over Israel two years. **52** He did what was evil in the LORD's sight.[ac] He walked in the ways of his father,[ad] in the ways of his mother,[ae] and in the ways of Jeroboam son of Nebat, who had caused Israel to sin.[af] **53** He served Baal and bowed in worship to him.[ag] He angered the LORD God of Israel just as his father had done.[ah]

[a] 22:31 1Kg 20:1,16
[b] 2Ch 18:30
[c] 22:34 2Kg 9:24
[d] 2Ch 35:23
[e] 22:34-35 1Kg 22:17,28; 2Ch 18:33-34
[f] 22:36 2Sm 20:1; 1Kg 12:16; 22:17; 2Kg 14:12
[g] 22:37 1Kg 16:28
[h] 22:38 1Kg 21:19
[i] 22:39 Am 3:15
[j] 1Kg 16:27
[k] 22:40 1Kg 16:28
[l] 2Kg 1:2
[m] 22:41 2Ch 20:31

[n] 22:43 1Kg 15:11
[o] 1Kg 15:14
[p] 22:44 1Kg 22:2,4
[q] 22:45 1Kg 15:23; 2Ch 20:34
[r] 22:46 1Kg 15:12
[s] 22:47 2Sm 8:14; 2Kg 3:9
[t] 22:48 1Kg 10:22
[u] 1Kg 9:28
[v] 1Kg 9:26
[w] 22:49 1Kg 22:40,51
[x] 22:50 1Kg 15:24; 2Ch 21:1
[y] 2Kg 1:17
[z] 22:51 1Kg 22:40
[aa] 1Kg 16:24
[ab] 1Kg 22:41-50
[ac] 22:52 1Kg 15:26
[ad] 1Kg 21:25-26
[ae] 1Kg 16:31; 18:4; 21:25
[af] 1Kg 12:28-33
[ag] 22:53 Jdg 2:11; 1Kg 16:32
[ah] 1Kg 16:33; 21:25

[A] 22:31 Lit *with small or with great*   [B] 22:34 LXX; MT reads *camp*   [C] 22:43 LXX, Syr, Vg read *he did not remove the high places*

(22:30). A warrior from Aram shot a random arrow and **struck the king of Israel through the joints of his armor** (22:34). God takes random shots and makes them hit the bull's-eye. **22:37-38** These events happened just as the Lord had foretold through Elijah (21:19). **22:41-50 Jehoshaphat,** a king in **Judah,** was a reformer like his father Asa, walking in the Lord's ways (22:41-43, 46). Unfortunately,

Jehoshaphat's alliances with Ahab and his son Ahaziah proved to be disastrous (22:44, 48-49). And for these alliances, Jehoshaphat was rebuked by the Lord (see 2 Chr 19:1-2; 20:35-37). **22:51-53** Ahaziah learned well from three bad examples. He embraced their idolatry and wickedness, and he **angered the LORD God of Israel** as they had (22:53).

The story of the kings of Israel and Judah is often a depressing one. But there are moments when God's goodness and grace come shining through. In spite of the sins of his covenant people, the Lord was committed to fulfilling his kingdom purposes. The story continues in 2 Kings.

2 KINGS

INTRODUCTION

Author

See discussion in 1 Kings.

Historical Background

See discussion in 1 Kings.

Message and Purpose

See discussion in 1 Kings.

Outline

https://www.bhpublishinggroup.com/qrpage/introduction-to-1-2-kings/

AHAZIAH'S SICKNESS AND DEATH

1 After Ahab's death, Moab[a] rebelled against Israel.[b] **2** Ahaziah[c] had fallen through the latticed window of his upstairs room in Samaria[d] and was injured. So he sent messengers, instructing them, "Go inquire of Baal-zebub,[A,e] the god of Ekron,[f] whether I will recover from this injury."[g]

3 But the angel of the LORD said to Elijah the Tishbite,[h] "Go and meet the messengers of the king of Samaria[i] and say to them, 'Is it because there is no God in Israel that you are going to inquire of Baal-zebub, the god of Ekron? **4** Therefore, this is what the LORD says: You will not get up from your sickbed; you will certainly die.'" Then Elijah left.

5 The messengers returned to the king, who asked them, "Why have you come back?"

6 They replied, "A man came to meet us and said, 'Go back to the king who sent you and declare to him: This is what the LORD says: Is it because there is no God in Israel that you're sending these men to inquire of Baal-zebub, the god of Ekron? Therefore, you will not get up from your sickbed; you will certainly die.'"

7 The king asked them, "What sort of man came up to meet you and spoke those words to you?"

8 They replied, "A hairy man with a leather belt around his waist."[j]

He said, "It's Elijah the Tishbite."[k]

9 So King Ahaziah sent a captain with his fifty men[l] to Elijah. When the captain went up to him, he was sitting on top of the hill. He announced, "Man of God,[m] the king declares, 'Come down!'"

10 Elijah responded to the captain, "If I am a man of God, may fire come down from heaven and consume you and your fifty men." Then fire came down from heaven and consumed him and his fifty men.[n]

11 So the king sent another captain with his fifty men to Elijah. He took in the situation[B] and announced, "Man of God, this is what the king says: 'Come down immediately!'"

12 Elijah responded, "If I am a man of God, may fire come down from heaven and consume you and your fifty men." So a divine fire[c] came down from heaven and consumed him and his fifty men.

13 Then the king sent a third captain with his fifty men. The third captain went up and fell on his knees in front of Elijah and begged him, "Man of God,[o] please let my life and the lives of these fifty servants of yours be precious to you.[p] **14** Already fire has come down from heaven and consumed the first two captains with their companies, but this time let my life be precious to you."

15 The angel of the LORD[q] said to Elijah, "Go down with him. Don't be afraid of him."[r] So he got up and went down with him to the king.

16 Then Elijah said to King Ahaziah, "This is what the LORD says: 'Because you have sent messengers to inquire of Baal-zebub, the god of Ekron — is it because there is no God in Israel for you to inquire of his will? — you will not get up from your sickbed; you will certainly die.'"

17 Ahaziah died according to the word of the LORD that Elijah had spoken. Since he had no son, Joram[D,s] became king in his place. This happened in the second year of Judah's King Jehoram[t] son of Jehoshaphat.[E] **18** The rest of the events of Ahaziah's reign, along with his accomplishments, are written in the Historical Record of Israel's Kings.[F,u]

ELIJAH IN THE WHIRLWIND

2 The time had come for the LORD to take Elijah up to heaven[v] in a whirlwind.[w] Elijah and Elisha[x] were traveling from Gilgal,[y] **2** and Elijah said to Elisha,[z] "Stay here;[aa] the LORD is sending me on to Bethel."[ab]

Cross references (right margin):

[a] 1:1 Gn 19:37; 2Sm 8:2
[b] 2Kg 3:5
[c] 1:2 1Kg 22:40,51-53
[d] 1Kg 16:24; 22:51
[e] Jdg 10:6
[f] Jos 13:3; 2Kg 1:16
[g] 2Kg 8:8-9
[h] 1:3 1Kg 19:7
[i] 1Sm 28:7-8
[j] 1:8 Zch 13:4; Mt 3:4
[k] 1Kg 17:1
[l] 1:9 2Kg 6:13-14
[m] 1Kg 13:1
[n] 1:10 1Kg 18:36-38

[o] 1:13 1Kg 13:1
[p] 1Sm 26:21; Ps 72:14
[q] 1:15 1Kg 19:7; 2Kg 1:3
[r] Jr 1:17; Ezk 2:6
[s] 1:17 2Kg 3:1-3
[t] 1Kg 22:50
[u] 1:18 1Kg 22:39
[v] 2:1 Gn 5:24; Heb 11:5
[w] 2Kg 2:11
[x] 1Kg 19:16-21
[y] Jos 4:19; 2Kg 4:38
[z] 2:2 1Kg 19:16,19-21
[aa] Ru 1:15
[ab] 1Kg 12:28-29

[A] 1:2 = Lord of the Flies   [B] 1:11 Lit *He answered*   [C] 1:12 Lit *a fire of God*   [D] 1:17 Lit *Jehoram*; 2Kg 8:16   [E] 1:17 LXX omits *in the second year* . . . *Jehoshaphat*   [F] 1:18 LXX adds 4 more vv. here similar to 2Kg 3:1-3.

1:1 The international political landscape was changing, leading to an approaching war.
1:2 Ahab's son **Ahaziah** sought a word from **Baal-zebub, the god of Ekron**, rather than the Lord. Baal-zebub means "Lord of the Flies." Perhaps with this term the author was intentionally mocking this false god, changing the name Baal-zebul, which means "Lord of Glory," to something less impressive. Regardless, Ahaziah chose to look to a Philistine idol (Ekron was a Philistine city) for help.

1:4 As a result of the king's failure to seek God, Elijah sent him a divine prognosis: he would **certainly die.**
1:7-9 Interestingly, the king only needed a physical description to know exactly who the prophet of doom was: **Elijah the Tishbite** (1:8). Apparently Ahaziah had learned nothing from his father's famous encounters with Elijah, though. This was the same prophet who had stood on a mountain and called down fire from heaven (see 1Kgs 18:30-40). Nevertheless, the king sent **men** to take Elijah into custody (2Kgs 1:9).

1:11-12 The second captain made the same demand of Elijah as the first but insisted that he obey **immediately** (1:11). The only thing that happened immediately, however, was a doubling of the body count (1:12).
1:13-15 It seems the king was short on wisdom and long on expendable troops because— incredibly—he sent a third detachment.
2:1 Elisha, the man whom God appointed to be Elijah's helper and successor (see 1Kgs 19:16, 19-21), was aware of what was about to happen, as the following narrative makes plain.

a 2:2 1Sm 1:26; 2Kg 4:30
b 2:3 1Sm 10:5; 1Kg 20:35; 2Kg 4:1,38
c Gn 5:24
d 2:4 Jos 6:16; 1Kg 16:34
e 2:6 Jos 3:8; Mt 3:5–6,13
f 2:8 1Kg 19:13,19
g Ex 14:21-22; Jos 3:14-17
h 2:9 Nm 11:16-25; Dt 21:15-17
i 2:10 Ac 1:9-11
j 2:11 2Kg 6:17

k 2:11 2Kg 2:1
l 2:12 2Kg 13:14
m Gn 37:29,34
n 2:13 1Kg 19:19
o 2:16 1Kg 18:12; Ac 8:39
p 2:17 Jdg 3:25; 2Kg 8:11
q 2:18 2Kg 2:4
r 2:19 Dt 28:15-18; Jos 6:26; 1Kg 16:34

But Elisha replied, "As the LORD lives and as you yourself live, I will not leave you."[a] So they went down to Bethel.

³ Then the sons of the prophets[b] who were at Bethel came out to Elisha and said, "Do you know that the LORD will take your master away from you today?"[c]

He said, "Yes, I know. Be quiet."

⁴ Elijah said to him, "Elisha, stay here; the LORD is sending me to Jericho."[d]

But Elisha said, "As the LORD lives and as you yourself live, I will not leave you." So they went to Jericho.

⁵ Then the sons of the prophets who were in Jericho came up to Elisha and said, "Do you know that the LORD will take your master away from you today?"

He said, "Yes, I know. Be quiet."

⁶ Elijah said to him, "Stay here; the LORD is sending me to the Jordan."[e]

But Elisha said, "As the LORD lives and as you yourself live, I will not leave you." So the two of them went on.

⁷ Fifty men from the sons of the prophets came and stood observing them at a distance while the two of them stood by the Jordan. ⁸ Elijah took his mantle,[f] rolled it up, and struck the water, which parted to the right and left. Then the two of them crossed over on dry ground.[g] ⁹ When they had crossed over, Elijah said to Elisha, "Tell me what I can do for you before I am taken from you."

So Elisha answered, "Please, let me inherit two shares of your spirit."[h]

¹⁰ Elijah replied, "You have asked for something difficult. If you see me being taken from you,[i] you will have it. If not, you won't."

¹¹ As they continued walking and talking, a chariot of fire with horses of fire[j] suddenly appeared and separated the two of them. Then Elijah went up into heaven in the whirlwind.[k] ¹² As Elisha watched, he kept crying out, "My father, my father, the chariots and horsemen of Israel!"[l]

ELISHA SUCCEEDS ELIJAH

When he could see him no longer, he took hold of his own clothes, tore them in two,[m] ¹³ picked up the mantle[n] that had fallen off Elijah, and went back and stood on the bank of the Jordan. ¹⁴ He took the mantle Elijah had dropped, and he struck the water. "Where is the LORD God of Elijah?" he asked. He struck the water himself, and it parted to the right and the left, and Elisha crossed over.

¹⁵ When the sons of the prophets from Jericho who were observing saw him, they said, "The spirit of Elijah rests on Elisha." They came to meet him and bowed down to the ground in front of him.

¹⁶ Then the sons of the prophets said to Elisha, "Since there are fifty strong men here with your servants, please let them go and search for your master. Maybe the Spirit of the LORD has carried him away and put him on one of the mountains or into one of the valleys."[o]

He answered, "Don't send them."

¹⁷ However, they urged him to the point of embarrassment,[p] so he said, "Send them." They sent fifty men, who looked for three days but did not find him. ¹⁸ When they returned to him in Jericho[q] where he was staying, he said to them, "Didn't I tell you not to go?"

¹⁹ The men of the city said to Elisha, "My lord can see that even though the city's location is good, the water is bad and the land unfruitful."[r]

2:3 Sons of the prophets doesn't mean "children of the prophets"; instead, it was apparently some sort of school or seminary (a prophet training center). Thus, these men had divine insight.

2:4 If Elijah was testing his protégé to see if he was ready to accept his coming divine responsibility, Elisha showed no sign of turning back from his calling. He declared, **I will not leave you.** Elisha's insistence demonstrated his commitment to accepting the mantle of leadership.

2:5 See the note on 2:3.

2:6 This is a reference to the **Jordan** River. Interestingly, each of the locations along the men's route was a place where God's presence and power had been demonstrated. It seems, then, that Elijah wanted Elisha to review with him key locations memorializing God's acts to build up Elisha's confidence in God's presence and power being with him.

2:7 These men knew prophetically that it was time for Elijah to depart, so they had traveled to say farewell to Israel's faithful prophet. They would also serve as witnesses to the transfer of prophetic authority.

2:8 Elijah parted the Jordan with his **mantle,** a sleeveless outer garment.

2:9 Elisha was likely thinking of Deuteronomy 21:17, which states that a "firstborn" son was entitled to "two shares" of his father's estate. Based on God's own testimony (see 1 Kgs 19:16), Elisha was to be anointed prophet in Elijah's "place." Elijah was his spiritual "father" (see 2 Kgs 2:12), and Elisha was his heir, so to speak. Elisha knew he would need an extra dose of divine enablement for the tasks ahead.

2:11-12 Though Elijah didn't die, Elisha grieved over the loss of his mentor. It appears he called Elijah both **my father,** a title of respect, and **the chariots and horsemen**

of Israel, an acknowledgment that Israel's true strength was not in their army but in this one who faithfully delivered the word of God (2:12).

2:14 Elisha showed that he knew the power wasn't in him or in the garment. It was in **the LORD God.**

2:16-17 It's not clear why the men were so determined to **search for** Elijah (2:16). They may have thought he would make a landing somewhere after his supernatural flight. (After all, it's not every day that someone rides to heaven in a fiery chariot never to be seen again!) Or, it could be that they thought God would leave his body behind somewhere so that they could bury it.

Their efforts would prove fruitless: Elijah wouldn't be seen again—until several hundred years later when he appeared with Moses on a mountain, talking with the Son of God (see Matt 17:1-3).

20 He replied, "Bring me a new bowl and put salt in it."[a]

After they had brought him one, **21** Elisha went out to the spring, threw salt in it,[b] and said, "This is what the LORD says: 'I have healed this water. No longer will death or unfruitfulness result from it.'" **22** Therefore, the water still remains healthy today according to the word that Elisha spoke.

23 From there Elisha went up to Bethel.[c] As he was walking up the path, some small boys came out of the city and jeered at him,[d] chanting, "Go up, baldy! Go up, baldy!" **24** He turned around, looked at them, and cursed them in the name of the LORD.[e] Then two female bears came out of the woods and mauled forty-two of the children. **25** From there Elisha went to Mount Carmel,[f] and then he returned to Samaria.[g]

ISRAEL'S KING JORAM

3 Joram son of Ahab became king over Israel in Samaria during the eighteenth year of Judah's King Jehoshaphat, and he reigned twelve years.[h] **2** He did what was evil in the LORD's sight, but not like his father and mother,[i] for he removed the sacred pillar of Baal his father had made. **3** Nevertheless, Joram clung to the sins that Jeroboam son of Nebat had caused Israel to commit.[j] He did not turn away from them.

MOAB'S REBELLION AGAINST ISRAEL

4 King Mesha of Moab[k] was a sheep breeder. He used to pay[l] the king of Israel one hundred thousand lambs and the wool of one hundred thousand rams,[m] **5** but when Ahab died, the king of Moab rebelled against the king of Israel.[n] **6** So King Joram marched out from Samaria at that time and mobilized all Israel. **7** Then he sent a message to King Jehoshaphat[o] of Judah:

"The king of Moab has rebelled against me.[p] Will you go with me to fight against Moab?"

Jehoshaphat said, "I will go. I am as you are, my people as your people, my horses as your horses."[q]

8 He asked, "Which route should we take?"

He replied, "The route of the Wilderness of Edom."

9 So the king of Israel, the king of Judah, and the king of Edom[r] set out. After they had traveled their indirect route for seven days, they had no water for the army or the animals with them.

10 Then the king of Israel said, "Oh no, the LORD has summoned these three kings, only to hand them over to Moab."

11 But Jehoshaphat said, "Isn't there a prophet of the LORD here? Let's inquire of the LORD through him."[s]

One of the servants of the king of Israel answered, "Elisha son of Shaphat,[t] who used to pour water on Elijah's hands, is here."

12 Jehoshaphat affirmed, "The word of the LORD is with him." So the king of Israel and Jehoshaphat and the king of Edom went to him.[u]

13 However, Elisha said to King Joram of Israel, "What do we have in common? Go to the prophets of your father and your mother!"[v]

But the king of Israel replied, "No, because it is the LORD who has summoned these three kings to hand them over to Moab."

14 Elisha responded, "By the life of the LORD of Armies,[w] before whom I stand: If I did not have respect for King Jehoshaphat of Judah,[x] I wouldn't look at you; I would not take notice of you. **15** Now, bring me a musician."[y]

While the musician played,[z] the LORD's hand[aa] came on Elisha. **16** Then he said,

---

[a] 2:20 Lv 2:13; Nm 18:19
[b] 2:21-22 Ex 15:25-26; 2Kg 4:41; 6:6
[c] 2:23 2Kg 2:2-3
[d] 2Ch 36:16; Ps 31:17-18
[e] 2:24 Lv 26:21-22; Neh 13:25
[f] 2:25 1Kg 18:19-20
[g] 1Kg 16:24; 2Kg 1:2
[h] 3:1 2Kg 1:17
[i] 3:2 1Kg 21:25-26
[j] 3:3 1Kg 16:31-32
[k] 3:4 Gn 19:37; 2Kg 1:1
[l] 2Sm 8:2
[m] Is 16:1-2
[n] 3:5 2Kg 1:1
[o] 3:7 1Kg 22:41-50

[p] 3:7 2Kg 1:1
[q] 1Kg 22:4
[r] 3:9 1Kg 22:47; 2Kg 8:20
[s] 3:11 1Kg 22:7
[t] 1Kg 19:16,19-21; 2Kg 2:9
[u] 3:12 2Kg 2:25
[v] 3:13 1Kg 18:19,22; 22:6
[w] 3:14 1Kg 17:1; 2Kg 5:16
[x] 1Kg 22:41-50
[y] 3:15 1Sm 10:5
[z] 1Sm 16:23
[aa] Ezk 3:14

2:23-24 The phrase translated **small boys** here could refer to young men. No matter their ages, they mocked God's prophet by saying, **Go up, baldy!** (2:23). Apparently, they wanted Elisha to go away, to "go up" like Elijah had done—never to be seen again.

While what happened to the boys may seem harsh, we must remember that this is exactly what God warned Israel about when he made his covenant with them. In Leviticus, the Lord told his people what he would do if they were hostile toward him and refused to obey: "I will send wild animals against you that will deprive you of your children" (Lev 26:21-22). Ultimately, then, this scene is a judgment upon godless parenting. Parents

have a responsibility to lead their children to God.

3:4-9 Moab had been subject to Israel, paying tribute to them (3:4). But Mesha, **the king of Moab**, evidently sensed a weakness in Israel with the quick changes in leadership and **rebelled** (3:5). **Joram** thus gathered his army and asked good **King Jehoshaphat of Judah** to join him in attacking Moab (3:6-7). Jehoshaphat agreed, and **Edom** joined the alliance. But as the three kings and their armies marched down the eastern shore of the Dead Sea toward Moab, their **water** supply suddenly ran out (3:8-9).

3:10-12 The idol-worshiping **king of Israel** blamed the Lord for their predicament

(3:10). But Jehoshaphat wouldn't let Joram's blasphemous charge stand. So he called for **a prophet of** God to speak to the dilemma. When he heard that **Elisha . . . who used to pour water on Elijah's hands**—that is, serve Elijah—was available, Joram probably shuddered (3:11). For even if Joram didn't know of Elisha, he surely remembered Elijah—the one who had prophesied judgment and death on both his father Ahab and his brother Ahaziah.

3:13-14 In other words, he said in verse 13, "You're an idolater, Joram! What are you doing coming to see me? Go ask your idols for advice!" The only thing that kept Elisha from showing Joram to the door was his **respect for King Jehoshaphat** (3:14).

[a] 3:17 Ps 107:35; Is 32:2
[b] 3:18 Gn 18:14
[c] 2Kg 3:7
[d] 3:20 Ex 29:39-40
[e] 3:21 2Kg 3:9
[f] 3:22 Ex 7:17,20
[g] 3:23 2Kg 3:9
[h] 3:25 Jr 48:31,36
[i] 1Kg 16:3
[j] 3:27 Dt 12:31; 2Kg 16:3

[k] 4:1 2Kg 2:3,15
Pr 1:7; 9:10
[m] Lv 25:39-41
[n] 4:2 1Kg 17:12
[o] 4:3 2Kg 3:16
[p] 4:5 Mt 14:17-21
[q] 4:7 1Kg 12:22
[r] 1Kg 17:16
[s] 4:8 Jos 19:18
[t] Mt 10:40-42; 3Jn 5-8
[u] 4:10 1Kg 17:19
[v] 4:12 2Kg 4:29-31; 5:20-27

"This is what the LORD says: 'Dig ditch after ditch in this wadi.' [17] For the LORD says, 'You will not see wind or rain, but the wadi will be filled with water,[a] and you will drink — you and your cattle and your animals.' [18] This is easy in the LORD's sight.[b] He will also hand Moab over to you.[c] [19] Then you will attack every fortified city and every choice city. You will cut down every good tree and stop up every spring. You will ruin every good piece of land with stones."

[20] About the time for the grain offering[d] the next morning, water suddenly came from the direction of Edom and filled the land.

[21] All Moab had heard that the kings[e] had come up to fight against them. So all who could bear arms, from the youngest to the oldest, were summoned and took their stand at the border. [22] When they got up early in the morning, the sun was shining on the water, and the Moabites saw that the water across from them was red like blood.[f] [23] "This is blood!" they exclaimed. "The kings[g] have crossed swords[A] and their men have killed one another. So, to the spoil, Moab!"

[24] However, when the Moabites came to Israel's camp, the Israelites attacked them, and they fled from them. So Israel went into the land attacking the Moabites. [25] They would destroy the cities, and each of them would throw a stone to cover every good piece of land. They would stop up every spring and cut down every good tree. This went on until only the buildings of Kir-haresheth[h] were left. Then men with slings surrounded the city and attacked it.

[26] When the king of Moab saw that the battle was too fierce for him, he took seven hundred swordsmen with him to try to break through to the king of Edom,[i] but they could not do it. [27] So he took his firstborn son,[j] who was to become king in his place, and offered him as a burnt offering on the city wall. Great wrath was on the Israelites, and they withdrew from him and returned to their land.

THE WIDOW'S OIL MULTIPLIED

4 One of the wives of the sons of the prophets[k] cried out to Elisha, "Your servant, my husband, has died. You know that your servant feared the LORD.' Now the creditor is coming to take my two children as his slaves."[m]

[2] Elisha asked her, "What can I do for you? Tell me, what do you have in the house?"

She said, "Your servant has nothing in the house except a jar of oil."[n]

[3] Then he said, "Go out and borrow empty containers from all your neighbors. Do not get just a few.[o] [4] Then go in and shut the door behind you and your sons, and pour oil into all these containers. Set the full ones to one side." [5] So she left.

After she had shut the door behind her and her sons, they kept bringing her containers, and she kept pouring.[p] [6] When they were full, she said to her son, "Bring me another container."

But he replied, "There aren't any more." Then the oil stopped.

[7] She went and told the man of God,[q] and he said, "Go sell the oil and pay your debt; you and your sons can live on the rest."[r]

THE SHUNAMMITE WOMAN'S HOSPITALITY

[8] One day Elisha went to Shunem.[s] A prominent woman who lived there persuaded him to eat some food. So whenever he passed by, he stopped there to eat.[t] [9] Then she said to her husband, "I know that the one who often passes by here is a holy man of God, [10] so let's make a small, walled-in upper room and put a bed, a table, a chair, and a lamp there for him. Whenever he comes, he can stay there."[u]

THE SHUNAMMITE WOMAN'S SON

[11] One day he came there and stopped at the upstairs room to lie down. [12] He ordered his attendant Gehazi,[v] "Call this Shunammite woman." So he called her and she stood before him.

[13] Then he said to Gehazi, "Say to her, 'Look, you've gone to all this trouble for

[A] 3:23 Or have been laid waste

3:20-25 Everything happened just as Elisha predicted in verses 17-18. Not only was the **water** supply a miracle in itself, but God used it to fool the Moabite army into thinking that the ground was soaked in the **blood** of their enemies as if they'd been fighting each other (3:20-23). When they approached to steal the spoils, Moab's army had to flee because Israel attacked and pushed them all the way back to **Kir-haresheth**, Moab's major city (3:24-25).

3:26-27 King Mesha grew so desperate that he committed the heinous sin of human sacrifice, hoping that the gods would see and help him. **4:1** This woman was in an economic, emotional, familial, and spiritual crisis. Her destitution may have resulted from the fact that true **prophets** were not honored in the largely apostate northern kingdom of Israel. In going to Elisha, she was seeking a spiritual solution for her dilemma.

4:2-7 This story is a reminder that God is God, and we're not. Blessings—sometimes physical but always spiritual—come when we respond to his Word with faith and obedience. **4:8-10** This faithful woman was **prominent** and had a **husband** (4:8-9)—unlike the late prophet's poor widow (see 4:1-7). These cultural advantages made God no less mindful of her faith. **4:13** That Elisha was willing to speak **on [her] behalf to the king** is remarkable given that

us. What can we do for you?[a] Can we speak on your behalf to the king or to the commander of the army?'"

She answered, "I am living among my own people."

14 So he asked, "Then what should be done for her?"

Gehazi answered, "Well, she has no son, and her husband is old."

15 "Call her," Elisha said. So Gehazi called her, and she stood in the doorway. **16** Elisha said, "At this time next year you will have a son in your arms."[b]

Then she said, "No, my lord. Man of God, do not lie to your servant."[c]

17 The woman conceived and gave birth to a son at the same time the following year, as Elisha had promised her.

THE SHUNAMMITE'S SON RAISED

18 The child grew and one day went out to his father and the harvesters.[d] **19** Suddenly he complained to his father, "My head! My head!"

His father told his servant, "Carry him to his mother." **20** So he picked him up and took him to his mother. The child sat on her lap until noon and then died. **21** She went up and laid him on the bed of the man of God, shut him in, and left.

22 She summoned her husband and said, "Please send me one of the servants and one of the donkeys, so I can hurry to the man of God and come back again."

23 But he said, "Why go to him today? It's not a New Moon or a Sabbath."[e]

She replied, "Everything is all right."[f]

24 Then she saddled the donkey and said to her servant, "Go fast; don't slow the pace for me unless I tell you." **25** So she came to the man of God at Mount Carmel.[g]

When the man of God saw her at a distance, he said to his attendant Gehazi,[h] "Look, there's the Shunammite woman.[i] **26** Run out to meet her and ask, 'Are you all right? Is your husband all right? Is your son all right?'"

And she answered, "Everything's all right."

27 When she came up to the man of God at the mountain, she clung to his feet.[j]

Gehazi came to push her away, but the man of God said, "Leave her alone — she is in severe anguish,[k] and the LORD has hidden it from me. He hasn't told me."

28 Then she said, "Did I ask my lord for a son? Didn't I say, 'Do not lie to me?'"[l]

29 So Elisha said to Gehazi, "Tuck your mantle[m] under your belt, take my staff with you, and go. If you meet anyone, don't stop to greet him, and if a man greets you, don't answer him.[n] Then place my staff on the boy's face."

30 The boy's mother said to Elisha, "As the LORD lives and as you yourself live, I will not leave you."[o] So he got up and followed her.

31 Gehazi went ahead of them and placed the staff on the boy's face, but there was no sound or sign of life, so he went back to meet Elisha and told him, "The boy didn't wake up."[p]

32 When Elisha got to the house, he discovered the boy lying dead on his bed.[q] **33** So he went in, closed the door behind the two of them, and prayed to the LORD.[r] **34** Then he went up and lay on the boy:[s] he put mouth to mouth, eye to eye, hand to hand. While he bent down over him, the boy's flesh became warm.[t] **35** Elisha got up, went into the house, and paced back and forth. Then he went up and bent down over him again. The boy sneezed seven times and opened his eyes.[u]

36 Elisha called Gehazi and said, "Call the Shunammite woman." He called her and she came. Then Elisha said, "Pick up your son." **37** She came, fell at his feet, and bowed to the ground; she picked up her son and left.[v]

THE DEADLY STEW

38 When Elisha returned to Gilgal,[w] there was a famine[x] in the land. The sons of the prophets[y] were sitting before him.[z] He said to his attendant, "Put on the large pot and make stew for the sons of the prophets."

39 One went out to the field to gather herbs and found a wild vine from which he gathered as many wild gourds as his garment would hold. Then he came back

[a] 4:13 2Kg 4:2
[b] 4:16 Gn 18:9–14; Lk 1:7–13
[c] 2Kg 4:28
[d] 4:18 Ru 2:3
[e] 4:23 Nm 10:10; 28:11
[f] 2Sm 18:28; 2Kg 4:26
[g] 4:25 1Kg 18:19–20
[h] 2Kg 4:12
[i] 2Kg 4:8,12
[j] 4:27 Mt 28:9

[k] 4:27 Ru 1:19–21; 1Sm 1:15; Zch 12:10
[l] 4:28 2Kg 4:16
[m] 4:29 1Kg 18:46; 2Kg 9:1
[n] Lk 10:4
[o] 4:30 2Kg 2:2,4,6
[p] 4:31 Jn 11:11
[q] 4:32 2Kg 4:21
[r] 4:33 Mt 6:6
[s] 4:34 1Kg 17:21–23
[t] Ac 20:10
[u] 4:35 2Kg 8:5
[v] 4:37 Heb 11:35
[w] 4:38 2Kg 2:1
[x] Lv 26:26; 2Kg 8:1
[y] 2Kg 2:3,5,7
[z] Lk 10:39; Ac 22:3

Elisha was talking about the evil King Joram. Clearly, Elisha had influence even though he spoke for God amid an idolatrous administration. God can give his people influence in the civil government when they are faithfully serving him in their primary sphere of spiritual authority.
4:14-17 For the earliest readers of 1–2 Kings, both those who experienced Babylonian

exile and their descendants, this story served as a reminder that God honors faithfulness to him.
4:32-37 This miracle was a foretaste of the power Jesus Christ would wield as he raised people to life (see Luke 7:11-17; 8:52-56; John 11:1-44). And Christ's miraculous resurrections, of course, were just a foretaste of his own resurrection that would serve as

a promise of resurrection for all those who believe in him (see John 11:25-26; Acts 26:23; 1 Cor 15:20-23).
4:38-41 Only when the substance of **flour** was added was the food made edible (4:41). Similarly, only when the substance of God's truth is poured in and emphasized can the contaminating effects of false religion be overcome.

a 4:40 Ex 10:17
b 4:41 Is 15:25; 2Kg 2:21
c 4:42 1Sm 9:4
d Mt 14:17
e 4:43 Lk 9:13; Jn 6:9
f 4:43-44 Mt 14:20
g 5:1 Lk 4:27
h Ex 11:3
i 2Kg 7:3,8
j 5:2 2Kg 6:23; 13:20

k 5:5 Jdg 14:12; 2Kg 5:22
l 5:7 Gn 37:29; 2Kg 11:14
m Gn 30:2
n 1Kg 20:7
o 5:8 1Kg 22:7
p 5:10 Nm 5:1-4
q Jn 9:7
r Lv 14:7
s 5:11 Ex 7:19
t 5:12 Is 8:6
u Pr 14:17; 19:11
v 5:13 2Kg 2:12; 6:21; 13:14

and cut them up into the pot of stew, but they were unaware of what they were.[A]

40 They served some for the men to eat, but when they ate the stew they cried out, "There's death in the pot,[a] man of God!" And they were unable to eat it.

41 Then Elisha said, "Get some flour." He threw it into the pot and said, "Serve it for the people to eat." And there was nothing bad in the pot.[b]

THE MULTIPLIED BREAD

42 A man from Baal-shalishah[c] came to the man of God with his sack full of[B] twenty loaves of barley bread from the first bread of the harvest. Elisha said, "Give it to the people to eat."[d]

43 But Elisha's attendant asked, "What? Am I to set this before a hundred men?"[e]

"Give it to the people to eat," Elisha said, "for this is what the LORD says: 'They will eat, and they will have some left over.'"

44 So he set it before them, and as the LORD had promised, they ate and had some left over.[f]

NAAMAN'S DISEASE HEALED

5 Naaman,[g] commander of the army for the king of Aram, was a man important to his master and highly regarded[h] because through him, the LORD had given victory to Aram. The man was a valiant warrior, but he had a skin disease.[i]

2 Aram had gone on raids[j] and brought back from the land of Israel a young girl who served Naaman's wife. **3** She said to her mistress, "If only my master were with the prophet who is in Samaria, he would cure him of his skin disease."

4 So Naaman went and told his master what the girl from the land of Israel had said. **5** Therefore, the king of Aram said,

"Go, and I will send a letter with you to the king of Israel."

So he went and took with him 750 pounds[c] of silver, 150 pounds[D] of gold, and ten sets of clothing.[k] **6** He brought the letter to the king of Israel, and it read:

When this letter comes to you, note that I have sent you my servant Naaman for you to cure him of his skin disease.

7 When the king of Israel read the letter, he tore his clothes[l] and asked, "Am I God,[m] killing and giving life that this man expects me to cure a man of his skin disease? Recognize[E] that he is only picking a fight with me."[n]

8 When Elisha the man of God heard that the king of Israel had torn his clothes, he sent a message to the king, "Why have you torn your clothes? Have him come to me, and he will know there is a prophet in Israel."[o] **9** So Naaman came with his horses and chariots and stood at the door of Elisha's house.

10 Then Elisha sent him a messenger,[p] who said, "Go wash[q] seven times[r] in the Jordan and your skin will be restored and you will be clean."

11 But Naaman got angry and left, saying, "I was telling myself: He will surely come out, stand and call on the name of the LORD his God, and wave his hand[s] over the place and cure the skin disease. **12** Aren't Abana and Pharpar, the rivers of Damascus, better than all the waters of Israel?[t] Couldn't I wash in them and be clean?" So he turned and left in a rage.[u]

13 But his servants approached and said to him, "My father,[v] if the prophet had told you to do some great thing, would you not have done it? How much more should you

A 4:39 of what they were added for clarity   B 4:42 Or with some heads of fresh grain and   C 5:5 Lit 10 talents   D 5:5 Lit 6,000 shekels
E 5:7 Lit Know and see

4:42-44 Here we see a foretaste of the miracles of Jesus, who would feed thousands with only a few loaves and fish and have basketfuls left over (see Mark 6:30-44; 8:1-9). **5:1** The Lord had promised Abraham that he would bless all the peoples of the earth through him (see Gen 12:3), and God was determined to glorify his own name—even among the Gentiles. Naaman was a mighty and proud **commander of the army for... Aram**, a nation that often warred against Israel's evil kings. He was a Gentile who nevertheless experienced God's favor in battle. But he had a significant problem—the incurable **skin disease** of leprosy. **5:2-3** The kindness of this girl who'd been kidnapped from her homeland and her confidence in the God of Israel would turn

Naaman's life around. Rather than allowing her circumstances to make her bitter, she sought to be a blessing. **5:7** Israel's wicked King Joram had no faith in God, so he had no faith that even the prophet Elisha could fix Naaman's problem. In fact, Israel's king saw nothing spiritual in the request at all. Joram reasoned that if he told Aram's king that he couldn't heal his commander, Aram would invade. And instead of laying the letter before the Lord and asking for his guidance and protection, Joram essentially had a nervous breakdown. (For a dramatic contrast to this, see 2 Kgs 19:14-19.) **5:8** In other words he said, "You, Israel's king, don't believe in the God of Israel. But when I finish with this foreign general, he will."

5:9-10 This humbling lack of reception suggests that though Elisha intended to heal Naaman's physical problem, he also intended to deal with his spiritual problem—his pride. **5:11** Naaman just wanted a quick fix to his flesh without recognizing that his real problem was his heart. A lot of people today have the same attitude. **5:12** This conceited commander with his ideas about the superiority of his own homeland wasn't about to be humiliated by some two-bit prophet from a country that he had been routinely beating up. But Naaman did not yet realize that his victories hadn't been his own doing. They had been gifts from the God whose help he desperately needed (see 5:1).

do it when he only tells you, 'Wash and be clean'?" [14] So Naaman went down and dipped himself in the Jordan seven times, according to the command of the man of God. Then his skin was restored and became like the skin of a small boy, and he was clean.[a]

[15] Then Naaman and his whole company went back to the man of God, stood before him, and declared, "I know there's no God in the whole world except in Israel.[b] Therefore, please accept a gift[c] from your servant."

[16] But Elisha said, "As the LORD lives,[d] in whose presence I stand, I will not accept it."[e] Naaman urged him to accept it, but he refused.

[17] Naaman responded, "If not, please let your servant be given as much soil as a pair of mules can carry,[f] for your servant will no longer offer a burnt offering or a sacrifice to any other god but the LORD.[g] [18] However, in a particular matter may the LORD pardon your servant: When my master, the king of Aram, goes into the temple of Rimmon to bow in worship while he is leaning on my arm,[A,h] and I have to bow in the temple of Rimmon — when I bow[B] in the temple of Rimmon, may the LORD pardon your servant in this matter."

[19] So he said to him, "Go in peace."[i]

GEHAZI'S GREED PUNISHED

After Naaman had traveled a short distance from Elisha, [20] Gehazi,[j] the attendant of Elisha the man of God, thought, "My master has let this Aramean Naaman off lightly by not accepting from him what he brought. As the LORD lives,[k] I will run after him and get something from him."

[21] So Gehazi pursued Naaman. When Naaman saw someone running after him, he got down from the chariot to meet him and asked, "Is everything all right?"

[22] Gehazi said, "It's all right.[l] My master has sent me to say, 'I have just now

discovered that two young men from the sons of the prophets have come to me from the hill country of Ephraim. Please give them seventy-five pounds[c] of silver and two sets of clothing.'"[m]

[23] But Naaman insisted, "Please, accept one hundred fifty pounds."[D] He urged Gehazi and then packed one hundred fifty pounds of silver in two bags with two sets of clothing. Naaman gave them to two of his attendants who carried them ahead of Gehazi. [24] When Gehazi came to the hill,[E,n] he took the gifts from them and deposited them in the house. Then he dismissed the men, and they left.

[25] Gehazi came and stood by his master. "Where did you go, Gehazi?" Elisha asked him.

He replied, "Your servant didn't go anywhere."

[26] "And my heart didn't go[F,o] when the man got down from his chariot to meet you," Elisha said. "Is this a time to accept silver and clothing, olive orchards and vineyards, flocks and herds, and male and female slaves? [27] Therefore, Naaman's skin disease will cling to you and your descendants forever." So Gehazi went out from his presence diseased, resembling snow.[G,p]

THE FLOATING AX HEAD

6 The sons of the prophets[q] said to Elisha, "Please notice that the place where we live under your supervision[H] is too small for us. [2] Please let us go to the Jordan where we can each get a log and can build ourselves a place to live there."

"Go," he said.

[3] Then one said, "Please come with your servants."

"I'll come," he answered.

[4] So he went with them, and when they came to the Jordan, they cut down trees. [5] As one of them was cutting down a tree, the iron ax head fell into the water, and he cried out, "Oh, my master, it was borrowed!"[r]

[a] 5:14 Lk 4:27
[b] 5:15 Jos 2:11; 1Sm 17:46-47
[c] Gn 33:11
[d] 5:16 1Kg 17:1; 2Kg 3:14
[e] Gn 14:22-23
[f] 5:17 Ex 20:24
[g] Dt 6:4
[h] 5:18 2Kg 7:2
[i] 5:19 1Sm 1:17
[j] 5:20 2Kg 4:12,31
[k] Ex 20:7
[l] 5:21-22 2Kg 4:26

[m] 5:22 2Kg 5:5
[n] 5:24 2Kg 1:9
[o] 5:26 2Kg 2:9,15
[p] 5:27 Ex 4:6; Nm 12:10
[q] 6:1 1Sm 10:5; 2Kg 2:3,5,7; 4:38
[r] 6:5 Ex 22:14

5:15 Naaman had been cured, but he had also been humbled. Notice that when he spoke to Elisha, he referred to himself as **servant**. 5:16 Elisha was God's servant doing God's work. He wanted to make it clear to everyone that his services were not for sale. With Elisha's refusal of his "gift" (5:15), Naaman left in God's debt—not the other way around. 5:17 Previously, Naaman thought the rivers of his homeland were "better than all the waters of Israel" (5:12). But by this point he'd

realized that even Aramean dirt wasn't good enough for erecting an altar for Israel's God. If he were to make **a burnt offering** to the Lord, he would do it on an altar made from the land that the Lord had blessed. 5:25 Elisha's leading question is a reminder that you can't escape the gaze of the all-knowing God. 5:27 The faithlessness of this Israelite had earned him the **diseased** skin that the believing Aramean had left behind.

6:1 That one of the schools of the prophets in the northern kingdom was growing was no doubt a tribute to Elisha's ministry and **supervision**. 6:5-7 This student prophet was no doubt poor, making the item difficult to replace. Living as a spokesman for the true God during those dark days in Israel was not a profitable line of work (see 4:1-7). Yet Elisha's miraculous recovery of the lost tool showed God's concern for even the smallest needs of his people (6:6-7).

a 6:6 2Kg 4:8-9
b Ex 15:25; 2Kg 2:21; 4:41
c 6:8 2Kg 8:28-29
d 6:9 2Kg 4:8-9
e 6:13 Gn 37:17
f 6:16 Ex 14:13
g 2Ch 32:7

h 6:17 2Kg 2:11; Ps 34:7
i 6:18 Gn 19:11
j 6:19 1Kg 16:24; 2Kg 3:6
k 6:21 2Kg 2:12; 5:13
l 6:22 2Ch 28:8-15; Rm 12:20
m 6:23 2Kg 5:2; 24:2
n 6:24 1Kg 20:1
o 6:25 2Kg 4:38; 8:1
p Lv 26:26
q 6:27 Hs 9:2
r 6:26-28 2Sm 14:4-5

⁶ Then the man of God[a] asked, "Where did it fall?"

When he showed him the place, the man of God cut a piece of wood, threw it there, and made the iron float.[b] ⁷ Then he said, "Pick it up." So he reached out and took it.

THE ARAMEAN WAR

⁸ When the king of Aram[c] was waging war against Israel, he conferred with his servants, "My camp will be at such and such a place."

⁹ But the man of God[d] sent word to the king of Israel: "Be careful passing by this place, for the Arameans are going down there." ¹⁰ Consequently, the king of Israel sent word to the place the man of God had told him about. The man of God repeatedly[A] warned the king, so the king would be on his guard.

¹¹ The king of Aram was enraged because of this matter, and he called his servants and demanded of them, "Tell me, which one of us is for the king of Israel?"

¹² One of his servants said, "No one, my lord the king. Elisha, the prophet in Israel, tells the king of Israel even the words you speak in your bedroom."

¹³ So the king said, "Go and see where he is, so I can send men to capture him."

When he was told, "Elisha is in Dothan,"[e] ¹⁴ he sent horses, chariots, and a massive army there. They went by night and surrounded the city.

∽ HOPE WORDS ∽

You get sight in the spiritual realm when you exercise faith in the physical realm.

¹⁵ When the servant of the man of God got up early and went out, he discovered an army with horses and chariots surrounding the city. So he asked Elisha, "Oh, my master, what are we to do?"

¹⁶ Elisha said, "Don't be afraid,[f] for those who are with us outnumber those who are with them."[g]

¹⁷ Then Elisha prayed, "Lord, please open his eyes and let him see." So the Lord opened the servant's eyes, and he saw that the mountain was covered with horses and chariots of fire[h] all around Elisha.

¹⁸ When the Arameans came against him, Elisha prayed to the Lord, "Please strike this nation with blindness."[B] So he struck them with blindness,[i] according to Elisha's word. ¹⁹ Then Elisha said to them, "This is not the way, and this is not the city. Follow me, and I will take you to the man you're looking for." And he led them to Samaria.[j] ²⁰ When they entered Samaria, Elisha said, "Lord, open these men's eyes and let them see." So the Lord opened their eyes, and they saw that they were in the middle of Samaria.

²¹ When the king of Israel saw them, he said to Elisha, "Should I kill them,[k] should I kill them, my father?"

²² Elisha replied, "Don't kill them. Do you kill those you have captured with your sword or your bow? Set food and water in front of them so they can eat and drink and go to their master."[l]

²³ So he prepared a big feast for them. When they had eaten and drunk, he sent them away, and they went to their master. The Aramean raiders[m] did not come into Israel's land again.

THE SIEGE OF SAMARIA

²⁴ Some time later, King Ben-hadad[n] of Aram brought all his military units together and marched up and laid siege to Samaria. ²⁵ So there was a severe famine[o] in Samaria, and they continued the siege against it until a donkey's head sold for thirty-four ounces[c] of silver, and a cup[D] of dove's dung[E] sold for two ounces[F] of silver.[p]

²⁶ As the king of Israel was passing by on the wall, a woman cried out to him, "My lord the king, help!"

²⁷ He answered, "If the Lord doesn't help you, where can I get help for you? From the threshing floor or the winepress?"[q]

²⁸ Then the king asked her, "What's the matter?"[r]

She said, "This woman said to me, 'Give up your son, and we will eat him today.

A 6:10 Lit *not once and not twice*   B 6:18 Or *a blinding light*   C 6:25 Lit *for 80*; "shekels" is assumed   D 6:25 Lit *a fourth of a kab*   E 6:25 Or *seedpods, or wild onions*   F 6:25 Lit *for five*; "shekels" is assumed

6:8 This is most likely a reference to the same king who sent Naaman to Israel (see 5:1).
6:16 Elisha's certainty here bears similarities with the apostle John's exhortation to believers: "The one who is in you is greater than the one who is in the world" (1 John 4:4). When

we align ourselves with God, our enemy is always outnumbered.
6:24-31 Eventually, **Aram** invaded the northern kingdom again and **laid siege to Samaria** (6:24). Things got so bad that the city disintegrated into the horrors of cannibalism. The

Lord had warned Israel that such tragedies would befall them if they rejected him as their King (see Deut 28:53-57). Yet instead of crying out to the Lord in repentance and pleading for salvation, Israel's king just breathed murderous threats against Elisha (2 Kgs 6:31).

God Does Some of His Best Work
in the Dark

I LOVE THE HEAT. I WAS born in Baltimore, but I got to Dallas as quickly as I could. My wife, Lois, and I moved there so that I could attend seminary in the 1970s. When we did, I discovered a benefit to my new home—the city is known for its heat. Another great thing about Dallas is the immensity of the Texas sky. Sometimes it seems as if you can look straight into eternity when you look at the Texas sky.

An interesting thing happened one day as I looked at the sky around dusk. I saw one lone star in the enormous expanse while the rest of the sky appeared empty. A few minutes later, I looked again. This time the sky had gotten a little darker, so I could see a couple of stars. A few minutes later, I looked again. More stars. All those tiny lights reminded me of a spiritual truth: *all* of the stars were already in place when I looked up that very first time. I just couldn't see them.

What I want you to remember is that God has already given you everything you need to fight, and win, the spiritual battle you are facing. It is already inside of you. When you placed your faith in Christ for the forgiveness of your sins, you received the full impartation of the Holy Spirit within you. You received access to the authority you need to defeat the enemy on all accounts. But seeing, or realizing, that you have that access might be another story. Sometimes, in fact, we need help to see clearly. So sometimes things need to get darker for us to recognize God's hand better. God does some of his best work in the dark.

[a] 6:28-29 Lv 26:29; Dt 28:53,57
[b] 6:30 1Kg 21:27
[c] Gn 37:34
[d] 6:31 1Kg 19:2
[e] 6:32 Ezk 8:1; 14:1
[f] Lk 12:31-32
[g] 6:33 Jb 2:9; Is 8:21
[h] 7:1 2Kg 7:18
[i] 7:2 2Kg 5:18; 7:17
[j] 2Kg 4:8-9
[k] Mal 3:10
[l] 2Kg 7:17
[m] 7:3 Nm 5:2-4; 2Kg 5:1
[n] 7:4 2Kg 6:24

[o] 7:6 2Sm 5:24; 2Kg 5:16-17
[p] 1Kg 10:29
[q] 2Ch 12:2-3
[r] 7:7 Jdg 7:21
[s] 7:8 Jos 7:21
[t] 7:9 Pr 15:27; 21:17-18
[u] 7:12 2Kg 6:25
[v] Jos 8:4-12

Then we will eat my son tomorrow.' [29] So we boiled my son and ate him, and I said to her the next day, 'Give up your son, and we will eat him,'[a] but she has hidden her son."

[30] When the king heard the woman's words, he tore his clothes.[b] Then, as he was passing by on the wall, the people saw that there was sackcloth[c] under his clothes next to his skin. [31] He announced, "May God punish me and do so severely[d] if the head of Elisha son of Shaphat remains on his shoulders today."

[32] Elisha was sitting in his house, and the elders[e] were sitting with him. The king sent a man ahead of him, but before the messenger got to him, Elisha said to the elders, "Do you see how this murderer[f] has sent someone to remove my head? Look, when the messenger comes, shut the door to keep him out. Isn't the sound of his master's feet behind him?"

[33] While Elisha was still speaking with them, the messenger[A] came down to him. Then he said, "This disaster is from the LORD. Why should I wait for the LORD any longer?"[g]

7 Elisha replied, "Hear the word of the LORD! This is what the LORD says: 'About this time tomorrow at Samaria's gate, six quarts[B] of fine flour will sell for a half ounce of silver[c] and twelve quarts[D] of barley will sell for a half ounce of silver.'"[h]

[2] Then the captain, the king's right-hand man,[E,j] responded to the man of God,[j] "Look, even if the LORD were to make windows in heaven, could this really happen?"[k]

Elisha announced, "You will in fact see it with your own eyes, but you won't eat any of it."[l]

[3] Now four men with a skin disease[m] were at the entrance to the city gate. They said to each other, "Why just sit here until we die? [4] If we say, 'Let's go into the city,' we will die there because the famine is in the city, but if we sit here, we will also die. So now, come on. Let's surrender to the Arameans' camp.[n] If they let us live, we will live; if they kill us, we will die."

[5] So the diseased men got up at twilight to go to the Arameans' camp. When they came to the camp's edge, they discovered that no one was there, [6] for the Lord[F] had caused the Aramean camp to hear the sound of chariots, horses, and a large army.[o] The Arameans had said to each other, "The king of Israel must have hired the kings of the Hittites[p] and the kings of Egypt[q] to attack us." [7] So they had gotten up and fled[r] at twilight, abandoning their tents, horses, and donkeys. The camp was intact, and they had fled for their lives.

[8] When these diseased men came to the edge of the camp, they went into a tent to eat and drink. Then they picked up the silver, gold, and clothing and went off and hid them. They came back and entered another tent, picked things up, and hid them.[s] [9] Then they said to each other, "We're not doing what is right. Today is a day of good news.[t] If we are silent and wait until morning light, our punishment will catch up with us. So let's go tell the king's household."

[10] The diseased men came and called to the city's gatekeepers and told them, "We went to the Aramean camp and no one was there — no human sounds. There was nothing but tethered horses and donkeys, and the tents were intact." [11] The gatekeepers called out, and the news was reported to the king's household.

[12] So the king got up in the night and said to his servants, "Let me tell you what the Arameans have done to us. They know we are starving,[u] so they have left the camp to hide in the open country, thinking, 'When they come out of the city, we will take them alive and go into the city.'"[v]

[13] But one of his servants responded, "Please, let messengers take five of the horses that are left in the city. Their fate is like the entire Israelite community who will die,[G] so let's send them and see."

[14] The messengers took two chariots with horses, and the king sent them after the Aramean army, saying, "Go and see." [15] So they followed them as far as the Jordan. They saw that the whole way was littered with clothes and equipment the Arameans had thrown off in their haste. The messengers returned and told the king.

[A] 6:33 Some emend to king   [B] 7:1 Lit a seah, also in vv. 16,18   [C] 7:1 Lit for a shekel, also in vv. 16,18   [D] 7:1 Lit two seahs, also in vv. 16,18   [E] 7:2 Lit captain, upon whose hand the king leaned, also in v. 17   [F] 7:6 Some Hb mss read LORD   [G] 7:13 Some Hb mss, LXX, Syr, Vg; other Hb mss read left in it. Indeed, they are like the whole multitude of Israel that are left in it; indeed, they are like the whole multitude of Israel who will die.

7:1-2 **The king's right-hand man** was incredulous because such an abundance of food as what Elisha prophesied sounded impossible given their dire situation. Because of the man's unwillingness to believe, Elisha promised him that he would indeed see the provision, but he wouldn't **eat any of it** (7:2).

7:6-7 Assuming that Israel's king had hired foreign warriors to save them, the terrified Arameans fled—thus lifting their long siege of the city.

7:12-13 In this story, cool-headed wisdom had to come from the **servants** and outcasts because the king of Israel had none.

16 Then the people went out and plundered the Aramean camp.[a] It was then that six quarts of fine flour sold for a half ounce of silver and twelve quarts of barley sold for a half ounce of silver, according to the word of the LORD.[b] **17** The king had appointed the captain, his right-hand man,[c] to be in charge of the city gate, but the people trampled him in the gate. He died, just as the man of God had predicted when the king had come to him. **18** When the man of God had said to the king, "About this time tomorrow twelve quarts of barley will sell for a half ounce of silver and six quarts of fine flour will sell for a half ounce of silver at Samaria's gate," **19** this captain had answered the man of God, "Look, even if the LORD were to make windows in heaven, could this really happen?" Elisha had said, "You will in fact see it with your own eyes, but you won't eat any of it."[d] **20** This is what happened to him: the people trampled him in the city gate, and he died.

THE SHUNAMMITE'S LAND RESTORED

8 Elisha said to the woman whose son he had restored to life,[e] "Get ready, you and your household, and go live as a resident alien wherever you can. For the LORD has announced a seven-year famine,[f] and it has already come to the land." **2** So the woman got ready and did what the man of God said. She and her household lived as resident aliens in the land of the Philistines for seven years. **3** When the woman returned from the land of the Philistines at the end of seven years,[g] she went to appeal to the king for her house and field.[h] **4** The king had been speaking to Gehazi,[i] the attendant of the man of God, saying, "Tell me all the great things Elisha has done." **5** While he was telling the king how Elisha restored the dead son to life, the woman whose son he had restored to life

came to appeal to the king for her house and field. So Gehazi said, "My lord the king, this is the woman and this is the son Elisha restored to life."[j]

6 When the king asked the woman, she told him the story. So the king appointed a court official for her, saying, "Restore all that was hers, along with all the income from the field from the day she left the country until now."

ARAM'S KING HAZAEL

7 Elisha came to Damascus[k] while King Ben-hadad[l] of Aram was sick, and the king was told, "The man of God[m] has come here." **8** So the king said to Hazael,[n] "Take a gift[o] with you and go meet the man of God. Inquire of the LORD through him, 'Will I recover from this sickness?'"[p] **9** Hazael went to meet Elisha, taking with him a gift: forty camel-loads of all the finest products of Damascus. When he came and stood before him, he said, "Your son,[q] King Ben-hadad of Aram, has sent me to ask you, 'Will I recover from this sickness?'" **10** Elisha told him, "Go say to him, 'You are sure to[A] recover.' But the LORD has shown me that he is sure to die." **11** Then he stared steadily at him until he was ashamed.[r]

The man of God wept,[s] **12** and Hazael asked, "Why is my lord weeping?"

He replied, "Because I know the evil you will do to the people of Israel. You will set their fortresses on fire. You will kill their young men with the sword. You will dash their children to pieces. You will rip open their pregnant women."[t]

13 Hazael said, "How could your servant, a mere dog,[u] do such a mighty deed?"

Elisha answered, "The LORD has shown me that you will be king over Aram."[v]

14 Hazael left Elisha and went to his master, who asked him, "What did Elisha say to you?"

He responded, "He told me you are sure to recover." **15** The next day Hazael took a heavy cloth, dipped it in water, and spread

[a] 7:16 2Kg 7:8
[b] 2Kg 7:1-2
[c] 7:17 2Kg 7:2
[d] 7:18-19 2Kg 7:1-2
[e] 8:1 2Kg 4:8-37
[f] Gn 41:27,54
[g] 8:3 2Kg 7:1-2
[h] Dt 15:1-6
[i] 8:4 2Kg 4:12; 5:20-27
[j] 8:5 2Kg 4:35
[k] 8:7 1Kg 11:24
[l] 2Kg 6:24
[m] 2Kg 5:20
[n] 8:8 1Kg 19:15,17
[o] 1Kg 14:3
[p] 2Kg 1:2
[q] 8:9 2Kg 5:13
[r] 8:11 Jdg 3:25; 2Kg 2:17
[s] Lk 19:41
[t] 8:12 1Kg 19:17; 2Kg 10:32-33; 13:3
[u] 8:13 2Sm 9:8
[v] 8:13-15 1Kg 19:15

A 8:10 Alt Hb tradition reads *You will not*

7:16-20 In their mad stampede for food, the starving people of Samaria rushed toward the spoils and **trampled** the king's **right-hand man**. Therefore, **he died** just as Elisha had **predicted** (7:17; see 7:2).

8:4-6 The timing of this encounter happened not by chance, but by divine intervention. There are no chance encounters in your life either.

You may wonder what **Gehazi** (8:4) was doing in the presence of the king in light of the judgment God placed on him for his greed (see 5:20-27). One answer is that he

must have been restored due to passing a retest God gave him. Sometimes God gives us retests in order to offer opportunities to reverse the consequences of our sin.

I think it's likely that Gehazi was one of the diseased men in 7:3-11. If so, as one of these lepers who went into the Aramean camp, he said it would not be good to selfishly consume the bounty in secret (7:9)—which is an offense not unlike the deed that brought about his leprosy in the first place. From experience, then, he knew

that concealing the sin of greed would bring punishment.

8:10-15 At first glance, Elisha's contradictory answer is confusing. If Ben-hadad was **sure to recover**, why would the king **die** (8:10)? When Hazael asked why Elisha was crying, however, everything became clear. In time Hazael himself would assume the throne of Aram and then slaughter Israel's people (8:11-13). Thus, Ben-hadad *would have* recovered from his illness. But before he could, Hazael would assassinate him (8:14-15).

[a] 8:16-24 2Ch 21:5-20
[b] 8:16 2Kg 1:17; 3:1
[c] 2Ch 21:1
[d] 1Kg 22:50
[e] 8:17 2Ch 21:6
[f] 8:18 2Ch 21:6
[g] 8:19 1Kg 11:36; 15:4
[h] 2Ch 21:7
[i] 8:20 1Kg 22:47; 2Kg 3:9
[j] 8:21 2Sm 18:17; 19:8
[k] 8:22 Jos 21:13; 2Kg 19:8
[l] 8:23 1Kg 22:39; 2Kg 1:18
[m] 8:24 1Kg 22:40; 2Kg 1:17
[n] 8:25-29 2Ch 22:1-6
[o] 8:25 2Kg 9:29
[p] 8:26 1Kg 16:23; 2Ch 22:2

[q] 8:27 2Ch 22:3
[r] 8:28 1Kg 19:15
[s] 1Kg 22:3,29
[t] 8:29 1Kg 21:1
[u] 2Kg 9:15
[v] 9:1 2Kg 2:3,5,7
[w] 2Kg 4:29
[x] 1Sm 10:1; 16:1; 1Kg 1:39
[y] 1Kg 22:3,29; 2Kg 8:28-29
[z] 9:2 1Kg 19:16-17; 2Kg 9:14
[aa] 9:3 2Ch 22:7
[ab] 9:7 1Kg 18:4; 21:15
[ac] 9:8 1Kg 21:21; 2Kg 10:17

it over the king's face. Ben-hadad died, and Hazael reigned in his place.

JUDAH'S KING JEHORAM

16 In the fifth year[a] of Israel's King Joram[b] son of Ahab, Jehoram[A,c] son of Jehoshaphat became king of Judah, replacing his father.[B,d] **17** He was thirty-two years old when he became king, and he reigned eight years in Jerusalem.[e] **18** He walked in the ways of the kings of Israel, as the house of Ahab had done, for Ahab's daughter was his wife. He did what was evil in the LORD's sight.[f] **19** For the sake of his servant David, the LORD was unwilling to destroy Judah, since he had promised to give a lamp[g] to David and his sons forever.[h]

20 During Jehoram's reign, Edom rebelled against Judah's control and appointed their own king.[i] **21** So Jehoram crossed over to Zair with all his chariots. Then at night he set out to attack the Edomites who had surrounded him and the chariot commanders, but his troops fled to their tents.[j] **22** So Edom is still in rebellion against Judah's control today. Libnah[k] also rebelled at that time.

23 The rest of the events of Jehoram's reign, along with all his accomplishments, are written in the Historical Record of Judah's Kings.[l] **24** Jehoram rested with his fathers and was buried with his fathers in the city of David, and his son Ahaziah became king in his place.[m]

JUDAH'S KING AHAZIAH

25 In the twelfth year of Israel's King Joram son of Ahab,[n] Ahaziah son of Jehoram became king of Judah.[o] **26** Ahaziah was twenty-two years old when he became king, and he reigned one year in Jerusalem. His mother's name was Athaliah, granddaughter of Israel's King Omri.[p] **27** He walked in the ways of the house of Ahab and did what was evil in the LORD's sight

like the house of Ahab,[q] for his father had married into[c] the house of Ahab.

28 Ahaziah went with Joram son of Ahab to fight against King Hazael[r] of Aram in Ramoth-gilead,[s] and the Arameans wounded Joram. **29** So King Joram returned to Jezreel[t] to recover from the wounds that the Arameans had inflicted on him in Ramoth-gilead[D] when he fought against Aram's King Hazael.[u] Then Judah's King Ahaziah son of Jehoram went down to Jezreel to visit Joram son of Ahab since Joram was ill.

JEHU ANOINTED AS ISRAEL'S KING

9 The prophet Elisha called one of the sons of the prophets[v] and said, "Tuck your mantle[w] under your belt, take this flask of oil[x] with you, and go to Ramoth-gilead.[y] **2** When you get there, look for Jehu[z] son of Jehoshaphat, son of Nimshi. Go in, get him away from his colleagues, and take him to an inner room. **3** Then take the flask of oil, pour it on his head, and say, 'This is what the LORD says: "I anoint you king over Israel."'[aa] Open the door and escape. Don't wait." **4** So the young prophet[E] went to Ramoth-gilead.

5 When he arrived, the army commanders were sitting there, so he said, "I have a message for you, commander."

Jehu asked, "For which one of us?"

He answered, "For you, commander."

6 So Jehu got up and went into the house. The young prophet poured the oil on his head and said, "This is what the LORD God of Israel says: 'I anoint you king over the LORD's people, Israel. **7** You are to strike down the house of your master Ahab so that I may avenge the blood shed by the hand of Jezebel — the blood of my servants the prophets and of all the servants of the LORD.[ab] **8** The whole house of Ahab will perish, and I will wipe out all of Ahab's males,[f] both slave and free,[G] in Israel.[ac] **9** I will make the house of Ahab like the house

---

[A] 8:16 = The LORD is Exalted   [B] 8:16 Lit *Judah; Jehoshaphat had been king of Judah*   [C] 8:27 Lit *for he was related by marriage to*   [D] 8:29 Lit *Ramah*
[E] 9:4 Or *the young man, the attendant of the prophet*   [F] 9:8 Lit *wipe out Ahab's one who urinates against a wall*   [G] 9:8 Or *males, even the weak and impaired*; Hb obscure

---

8:16-18 For the first time in 2 Kings, the focus shifts to Judah in the south. Unfortunately, **Jehoram** was condemned as **evil in the LORD's sight** because he was greatly influenced by his wife, who was wicked **Ahab's daughter** (8:16,18). Thus, Ahab's legacy flowed, not only through the kings of Israel, but now also through the kings of Judah.
8:19 Ultimately, the **forever** of this promise will be fulfilled in Jesus Christ.

8:26-29 Like his father, **Ahaziah** also came under the influence of **Athaliah**, his mother, the daughter of Ahab (8:26). Ahaziah joined with **Joram** of the northern kingdom **to fight against . . . Aram**, but Joram was wounded and went to Jezreel to **recover**. Ahaziah went to **visit Joram** there (8:28-29); it would be a fatal choice.
9:1-3 The time had finally come for the Lord to eradicate the descendants of Ahab and Jezebel from Israel. Years before, God had

told Elijah to anoint Jehu for this stated purpose (see 1 Kgs 19:16-17). But the assignment of anointing Jehu actually fell to Elisha, who sent one of his student prophets to meet with **Jehu son of Jehoshaphat** (not Jehoshaphat the former king of Judah) in a private ceremony and **anoint** him as **king over Israel** in place of the wounded King Joram (see 2 Kgs 8:28-29).
9:7-10 These predictions were consistent with what Elijah had previously announced (see 1 Kgs 21:22-24).

of Jeroboam son of Nebat and like the house of Baasha son of Ahijah.[a] [10] The dogs will eat Jezebel in the plot of land at Jezreel — no one will bury her.'"[b] Then the young prophet opened the door and escaped.

[11] When Jehu came out to his master's servants, they asked, "Is everything all right? Why did this crazy person[c] come to you?"

Then he said to them, "You know the sort and their ranting."

[12] But they replied, "That's a lie! Tell us!"

So Jehu said, "He talked to me about this and that and said, 'This is what the LORD says: I anoint you king over Israel.'"

[13] Each man quickly took his garment and put it under Jehu on the bare steps.[A,d] They blew the ram's horn[e] and proclaimed, "Jehu is king!"[f]

[14] Then Jehu son of Jehoshaphat, son of Nimshi, conspired against Joram.[g] Joram and all Israel had been at Ramoth-gilead on guard against King Hazael of Aram. [15] But King Joram had returned to Jezreel to recover from the wounds that the Arameans had inflicted on him when he fought against Aram's King Hazael. Jehu said, "If you commanders wish to make me king,[B] then don't let anyone escape from the city to go tell about it in Jezreel."

JEHU KILLS JORAM AND AHAZIAH

[16] Jehu got into his chariot and went to Jezreel since Joram was laid up there and King Ahaziah of Judah had gone down to visit Joram. [17] Now the watchman[h] was standing on the tower in Jezreel. He saw Jehu's mob approaching and shouted, "I see a mob!"

Joram responded, "Choose a rider and send him to meet them and have him ask, 'Do you come in peace?'"[i]

[18] So a horseman went to meet Jehu and said, "This is what the king asks: 'Do you come in peace?'"

Jehu replied, "What do you have to do with peace?[c] Fall in behind me."

The watchman reported, "The messenger reached them but hasn't started back."

[19] So he sent out a second horseman, who went to them and said, "This is what the king asks: 'Do you come in peace?'"

Jehu answered, "What do you have to do with peace? Fall in behind me."

[20] Again the watchman reported, "He reached them but hasn't started back. Also, the driving is like that of Jehu son of Nimshi[j] — he drives like a madman."

[21] "Get the chariot ready!" Joram shouted, and they got it ready. Then King Joram of Israel and King Ahaziah of Judah set out, each in his own chariot, and met Jehu at the plot of land of Naboth the Jezreelite.[k] [22] When Joram saw Jehu he asked, "Do you come in peace, Jehu?"

He answered, "What peace can there be as long as there is so much prostitution and sorcery from your mother Jezebel?"[l]

[23] Joram turned around and fled, shouting to Ahaziah, "It's treachery,[m] Ahaziah!"

[24] Then Jehu drew his bow and shot Joram between the shoulders. The arrow went through his heart, and he slumped down in his chariot.[n] [25] Jehu said to Bidkar his aide, "Pick him up and throw him on the plot of ground belonging to Naboth the Jezreelite.[o] For remember when you and I were riding side by side behind his father Ahab, and the LORD uttered this pronouncement against him: [26] 'As surely as I saw the blood of Naboth and the blood of his sons yesterday' — this is the LORD's declaration — 'so will I repay you on this plot of land' — this is the LORD's declaration. So now, according to the word of the LORD, pick him up and throw him on the plot of land."[p]

[27] When King Ahaziah of Judah saw what was happening, he fled up the road toward Beth-haggan. Jehu pursued him, shouting, "Shoot him too!" So they shot him in his chariot[D] at Gur Pass near Ibleam,[q] but he fled to Megiddo[r] and died there.[s] [28] Then his servants carried him to Jerusalem in a chariot and buried him in his fathers' tomb in the city of David.[t] [29] It was in the eleventh year of Joram son of Ahab that Ahaziah had become king over Judah.[u]

JEHU KILLS JEZEBEL

[30] When Jehu came to Jezreel, Jezebel heard about it, so she painted her eyes,[v] fixed her

[a] 9:9 1Kg 16:3–5,11–12
[b] 9:10 1Kg 21:23; 2Kg 9:30–37
[c] 9:11 1Sm 10:11; Mk 3:21
[d] 9:13 Mt 21:8
[e] 2Sm 15:10
[f] 1Kg 1:39
[g] 9:14–16 2Kg 8:28–29; 2Ch 22:6
[h] 9:17 1Sm 14:16
[i] 1Sm 16:4
[j] 9:20 1Kg 19:17; 2Kg 9:2
[k] 9:21 1Kg 21:1–7
[l] 9:22 1Kg 16:30–33; 2Ch 21:13
[m] 9:23 2Kg 11:14
[n] 9:24 1Kg 22:34–35
[o] 9:25 1Kg 21:1
[p] 9:25–26 1Kg 21:13,19,24
[q] 9:27 Jos 17:11; Jdg 1:27
[r] 2Kg 23:29
[s] 2Ch 22:7,9
[t] 9:27–28 2Kg 23:30; 2Ch 22:9
[u] 9:29 2Kg 8:25
[v] 9:30 Jr 4:30; Ezk 23:40

[A] 9:13 Lit on the bones of the steps   [B] 9:15 Lit "If your desire exists   [C] 9:18 Lit What to you and to peace, also in v. 19   [D] 9:27 LXX, Syr, Vg; MT omits So they shot him

---

9:15 Jehu told his new subjects not to let anyone leave Ramoth-gilead and not to tell Joram in **Jezreel** so that he wouldn't have time to mount a defense before Jehu could get there. 9:16 Jehu, God's words to him from verses 7-8 in mind, made his way to **Jezreel** where King

Joram of Israel and **King Ahaziah of Judah** (both members of Ahab's house) were. 9:21 **The plot of land** mentioned was the very acreage that King Ahab had claimed as his own after Queen Jezebel had Naboth murdered (see 1 Kgs 21:1-16). It would, therefore,

be a fitting place for their wicked descendants to be put to death. 9:30-31 Queen **Jezebel heard about** what Jehu had done. So she **painted her eyes** and **fixed her hair** (9:30), probably in mock tribute to Israel's new king. She also derisively called

a 9:31 1Kg 16:9-20
b 9:32 Est 1:10; 2:14
c 9:33 Ps 7:5
d 9:34 1Kg 21:21-24
e 1Kg 16:31
f 9:36 1Kg 21:23; 2Kg 9:10
g 9:37 Jr 8:1-2; Zph 1:17
h 10:1 1Kg 16:24,29
i 1Kg 21:1; 2Kg 9:30
j 10:2 2Kg 5:6
k 10:4 2Kg 9:24,27

l 10:5 Jos 9:8,11; 1Kg
20:4,32; 2Kg 18:14
m 10:9 2Kg 9:14-24
n 10:10 2Kg 9:7-10
o 1Kg 21:19-29
p 10:13 2Kg 9:27-29
q 1Kg 2:19
r 10:14 2Ch 22:8
s 10:15 Jr 35:6-19

hair,[A] and looked down from the window. **31** As Jehu entered the city gate, she said, "Do you come in peace, Zimri,[a] killer of your master?"

32 He looked up toward the window and said, "Who is on my side? Who?" Two or three eunuchs[b] looked down at him, **33** and he said, "Throw her down!" So they threw her down, and some of her blood splattered on the wall and on the horses, and Jehu rode over her.[c]

34 Then he went in, ate and drank, and said, "Take care of this cursed[d] woman and bury her, since she's a king's daughter."[e] **35** But when they went out to bury her, they did not find anything but the skull, the feet, and the hands. **36** So they went back and told him, and he said, "This fulfills the LORD's word that he spoke through his servant Elijah the Tishbite: 'In the plot of land at Jezreel, the dogs will eat Jezebel's flesh.[f] **37** Jezebel's corpse will be like manure[g] on the surface of the ground in the plot of land at Jezreel so that no one will be able to say: This is Jezebel.'"

JEHU KILLS THE HOUSE OF AHAB

10 Since Ahab had seventy sons in Samaria,[h] Jehu wrote letters and sent them to Samaria to the rulers of Jezreel,[i] to the elders, and to the guardians of Ahab's sons,[B] saying: **2** Your master's sons are with you, and you have chariots, horses, a fortified city, and weaponry, so when this letter[j] arrives **3** select the most qualified[c] of your master's sons, set him on his father's throne, and fight for your master's house.

4 However, they were terrified and reasoned, "Look, two kings[k] couldn't stand against him; how can we?" **5** So the overseer of the palace, the overseer of the city, the elders, and the guardians sent a message to Jehu: "We are your servants, and we will do whatever you tell us. We will not make anyone king. Do whatever you think is right."[D,i]

6 Then Jehu wrote them a second letter, saying:

If you are on my side, and if you will obey me, bring me the heads of your master's sons[E] at this time tomorrow at Jezreel.

All seventy of the king's sons were being cared for by the city's prominent men. **7** When the letter came to them, they took the king's sons and slaughtered all seventy, put their heads in baskets, and sent them to Jehu at Jezreel. **8** When the messenger came and told him, "They have brought the heads of the king's sons," the king said, "Pile them in two heaps at the entrance of the city gate until morning."

9 The next morning when he went out and stood at the gate, he said to all the people, "You are innocent. It was I who conspired against my master and killed him.[m] But who struck down all these? **10** Know, then, that not a word the LORD spoke against the house of Ahab will fail,[n] for the LORD has done what he promised through his servant Elijah."[o] **11** So Jehu killed all who remained of the house of Ahab in Jezreel — all his great men, close friends, and priests — leaving him no survivors.

12 Then he set out and went to Samaria. On the way, while he was at Beth-eked of the Shepherds, **13** Jehu met the relatives of King Ahaziah of Judah and asked, "Who are you?"

They answered, "We're Ahaziah's[p] relatives. We've come down to greet the king's sons and the queen mother's[q] sons."

14 Then Jehu ordered, "Take them alive." So they took them alive and then slaughtered them at the pit of Beth-eked — forty-two men. He didn't spare any of them.[r]

15 When he left there, he found Jehonadab son of Rechab[s] coming to meet him. He greeted him and then asked, "Is your heart one with mine?"[F]

"It is," Jehonadab replied.

[A] **9:30** Lit *made her head pleasing*   [B] **10:1** LXX; MT reads *of Ahab*   [C] **10:3** Lit *the good and the upright*   [D] **10:5** Lit *Do what is good in your eyes*   [E] **10:6** Lit *heads of the men of the sons of your master*   [F] **10:15** Lit *heart upright like my heart is with your heart*

---

him **Zimri** (9:31), a reference to the man who had killed Israel's king, reigned seven days before killing himself, and was replaced by Ahab's father Omri (see 1 Kgs 16:9-20). Jezebel was implying that Jehu would meet the same fate.

9:32-33 Jehu rightly assumed the wicked queen's servants would be willing to **throw** her to her death.

10:1-3 Jehu knew his position wasn't secure as long as there were officials in the kingdom who were still loyal to Ahab's house. Especially concerning were the guardians of Ahab's **seventy** (seventy!) **sons in Samaria** (10:1). So Jehu penned correspondence to everyone who had connection to the royal house and challenged them to **select the most qualified** son of Ahab to **fight** him for the **throne** (10:2-3).

10:4-7 These leaders had heard what happened to Joram, Ahaziah, and Jezebel, and they wanted no part of Jehu's fury. So they promptly agreed to join his side and obeyed his grisly order.

10:8-9 Displaying his trophies so publicly was silent but effective evidence that he had succeeded in conquering the dynasty of Ahab. Any resistance against him was futile.

Jehu said, "If it is,^A give me your hand."^a

So he gave him his hand, and Jehu pulled him up into the chariot with him. **16** Then he said, "Come with me and see my zeal^b for the LORD!" So he let him ride with him in his chariot. **17** When Jehu came to Samaria, he struck down all who remained from the house of Ahab in Samaria until he had annihilated his house, according to the word of the LORD spoken to Elijah.^c

JEHU KILLS THE BAAL WORSHIPERS

18 Then Jehu brought all the people together and said to them, "Ahab served Baal^d a little, but Jehu will serve him a lot. **19** Now, therefore, summon to me all the prophets of Baal, all his servants, and all his priests.^e None must be missing, for I have a great sacrifice for Baal. Whoever is missing will not live." However, Jehu was acting deceptively in order to destroy the servants of Baal. **20** Jehu commanded, "Consecrate a solemn assembly^f for Baal." So they called one.

21 Then Jehu sent messengers throughout all Israel, and all the servants of Baal^B came; no one failed to come.^g They entered the temple of Baal,^h and it was filled from one end to the other. **22** Then he said to the custodian of the wardrobe, "Bring out the garments for all the servants of Baal." So he brought out their garments.

23 Then Jehu and Jehonadab son of Rechab entered the temple of Baal, and Jehu said to the servants of Baal, "Look carefully to see that there are no servants of the LORD here among you — only servants of Baal." **24** Then they went in to offer sacrifices and burnt offerings.

Now Jehu had stationed eighty men outside, and he warned them, "Whoever allows any of the men I am placing in your hands to escape will forfeit his life for theirs."^i **25** When he finished offering the burnt offering, Jehu said to the guards and officers, "Go in and kill them. Don't let anyone out."^j So they struck them down with the sword. Then the guards and officers threw the bodies out and went into the inner room of the temple of Baal. **26** They brought out the pillar of the temple of Baal and burned it, **27** and they tore down the pillar^k of Baal. Then they tore down the temple of Baal and made it a latrine^l — which it still is today.

EVALUATION OF JEHU'S REIGN

28 Jehu eliminated Baal worship from Israel, **29** but he did not turn away from the sins that Jeroboam son of Nebat had caused Israel to commit — worshiping the gold calves that were in Bethel and Dan.^m **30** Nevertheless, the LORD said to Jehu, "Because you have done well in carrying out what is right in my sight and have done to the house of Ahab all that was in my heart, four generations of your sons will sit on the throne of Israel."^n

31 Yet Jehu was not careful to follow the instruction of the LORD God of Israel with all his heart. He did not turn from the sins that Jeroboam had caused Israel to commit.

32 In those days the LORD began to reduce the size of Israel.^o Hazael^p defeated the Israelites throughout their territory **33** from the Jordan eastward: the whole land of Gilead — the Gadites, the Reubenites, and the Manassites — from Aroer^q which is by the Arnon Valley^r through Gilead to Bashan.^C

34 The rest of the events of Jehu's reign, along with all his accomplishments and all his might, are written in the Historical Record of Israel's Kings.^s **35** Jehu rested with his fathers and was buried in Samaria. His son Jehoahaz^t became king in his place. **36** The length of Jehu's reign over Israel in Samaria was twenty-eight years.^u

---

^a 10:15 Ezr 10:19
^b 10:16 1Kg 19:10
^c 10:17 1Kg 21:19-21; 2Kg 9:8
^d 10:18 1Kg 16:31-32
^e 10:19 1Kg 18:19; 22:6
^f 10:20 Jl 1:14
^g 10:21 1Kg 22:6
^h 1Kg 16:32
^i 10:24 1Kg 20:39

^j 10:25 1Kg 18:40
^k 10:27 1Kg 14:23; 2Kg 3:2
^l Ezr 6:11
^m 10:29 1Kg 12:28-29
^n 10:30 2Kg 15:12
^o 10:32 2Kg 13:25
^p 1Kg 19:17; 2Kg 8:12
^q 10:33 Dt 2:36; Jdg 11:26
^r Nm 21:13
^s 10:34 2Kg 1:18
^t 10:35 2Kg 13:1
^u 10:36 2Kg 1:17

---

^A 10:15 LXX, Syr, Vg; MT reads *mine?*" *Jehonadab said, "It is and it is*   ^B 10:21 LXX adds *— all his priests and all his prophets —*   ^C 10:33 Lit *Arnon Valley and Gilead and Bashan*

10:18-27 In preparation for the largest house-cleaning of Baal worship since Elijah's contest on Mount Carmel (see 1 Kgs 18), Jehu called **all the prophets of Baal** to come to a great **sacrifice**. But **Jehu was acting deceptively**, perhaps because he still wasn't confident of his level of support in Samaria (10:19). In the end, **all the servants of Baal came** (10:21). They were excited to find that the new king embraced the new "faith" of Israel that they had dedicated themselves to. When Jehu confirmed that there were no servants of the true God present (10:23), he sprang his trap (10:24-27).

10:28-30 While Jehu eradicated a great demonic evil in the land (Baal) and its human representatives (the house of Ahab and Baal's priests), Jehu nevertheless failed to follow the Lord wholeheartedly. This truth points to the sad reality that Israel would never be fully cleansed of its idolatry. That's why God would eventually bring his judgment on the northern kingdom, ejecting them from their land. In spite of Jehu's spiritual failings, God promised him a dynasty of **four generations of . . . sons** who would rule in Israel (10:30).
10:32-33 God demonstrated his displeasure with the idolatrous northern kingdom by

allowing their land to be reduced through conquests by the king of Aram.

11:1-3 Jehu had destroyed all of Ahab's family in the north, but this was not the end of Ahab's descendants in the southern kingdom of Judah. None was more dangerous than **Athaliah**, the **mother** of King Ahaziah (whom Jehu killed). Importantly, she was the daughter of Ahab and Jezebel. **She proceeded to annihilate all the royal heirs** when she saw her opportunity to seize the throne (11:1). But **Jehosheba, who was . . . Ahaziah's sister**, rescued Ahaziah's son (and Athaliah's grandson) **Joash** and, in God's providence, hid him (11:2-3).

a 11:1 2Ch 22:10
b 2Kg 8:26
c 2Kg 9:27
d 11:2 2Kg 11:21; 12:1
e 2Kg 8:25
f 11:4-16 2Ch 23:1-15
g 11:4 2Kg 11:15,17
h 2Kg 11:19
i 11:5 1Ch 9:25
j 11:4-6 2Ch 23:1-2
k 11:8 Nm 27:16-17
l 11:9 2Ch 23:8
m 11:10 2Sm 8:7; 1Ch 18:7

n 11:12 2Sm 1:10
o Ex 31:18; 2Kg 23:3
p 1Kg 1:39
q 1Sm 10:24
r 11:13 2Kg 11:1
s 2Ch 23:12
t 11:14 2Kg 23:3; 2Ch 34:31
u Nm 10:7-10; 1Kg 1:39-40
v 2Kg 9:23
w 11:15 2Kg 11:4
x 1Kg 11:4; 2Ch 23:1
y 1Kg 2:30
z 11:16 Neh 3:28
aa Gn 9:6; Lv 24:17; 2Kg 11:1
ab 11:17-20 2Ch 23:16-21
ac 11:17 Jos 24:25; 2Ch 34:31
ad 1Sm 10:25; 2Sm 5:3
ae 11:18 Dt 12:2-3; 2Kg 10:26-27
af 1Kg 18:40
ag 2Ch 23:18
ah 11:19 2Kg 11:4,6
ai 2Kg 11:2-3,12

ATHALIAH USURPS THE THRONE

11 When Athaliah,*a* Ahaziah's mother,*b* saw that her son was dead,*c* she proceeded to annihilate all the royal heirs. **2** Jehosheba,*d* who was King Jehoram's daughter and Ahaziah's*e* sister, secretly rescued Joash son of Ahaziah from among the king's sons who were being killed and put him and the one who nursed him in a bedroom. So he was hidden from Athaliah and was not killed. **3** Joash was in hiding with her in the LORD's temple six years while Athaliah reigned over the land.

ATHALIAH OVERTHROWN

4 In*f* the seventh year, Jehoiada*g* sent for the commanders of hundreds, the Carites, and the guards.*h* He had them come to him in the LORD's temple, where he made a covenant with them and put them under oath. He showed them the king's son **5** and commanded them, "This is what you are to do: A third of you who come on duty on the Sabbath*i* are to provide protection for the king's palace. **6** A third are to be at the Foundation*A* Gate and a third at the gate behind the guards. You are to take turns providing protection for the palace.*B,j* **7** "Your two divisions that go off duty on the Sabbath are to provide the king protection at the LORD's temple. **8** Completely surround the king with weapons in hand. Anyone who approaches the ranks is to be put to death. Be with the king in all his daily tasks."*C,k*

9 So the commanders of hundreds did everything the priest Jehoiada commanded. They each brought their men — those coming on duty on the Sabbath and those going off duty — and came to the priest Jehoiada.*l* **10** The priest gave to the commanders of hundreds King David's spears and shields*m* that were in the LORD's temple. **11** Then the guards stood with their weapons in hand surrounding the king — from the right side of the temple to the left side, by the altar and by the temple.

12 Jehoiada brought out the king's son, put the crown*n* on him, gave him the testimony,*b,o* and made him king. They anointed*p* him and clapped their hands and cried, "Long live the king!"*q*

13 When Athaliah*r* heard the noise from the guard and the crowd, she went out to the people at the LORD's temple.*s* **14** She looked, and there was the king standing by the pillar*t* according to the custom. The commanders and the trumpeters were by the king, and all the people of the land were rejoicing and blowing trumpets.*u* Athaliah tore her clothes and screamed "Treason! Treason!"*v*

15 Then the priest Jehoiada*w* ordered the commanders of hundreds*x* in charge of the army, "Take her out between the ranks, and put to death by the sword anyone who follows her," for the priest had said, "She is not to be put to death in the LORD's temple."*y* **16** So they arrested her, and she went through the horse entrance*z* to the king's palace, where she was put to death.*aa*

JEHOIADA'S REFORMS

17 Then*ab* Jehoiada made a covenant between the LORD, the king, and the people that they would be the LORD's people*ac* and another covenant between the king and the people.*E,ad* **18** So all the people of the land went to the temple of Baal and tore it down. They smashed its altars and images to pieces,*ae* and they killed Mattan, the priest of Baal, at the altars.*af*

Then Jehoiada the priest appointed guards for the LORD's temple.*ag* **19** He took the commanders of hundreds, the Carites, the guards,*ah* and all the people of the land, and they brought the king from the LORD's temple. They entered the king's palace by way of the guards' gate. Then Joash*ai* sat on the throne of the kings. **20** All the people of the land rejoiced, and the city was quiet, for they had put Athaliah to death by the sword in the king's palace.

A 11:6 See 2Ch 23:5; MT here reads *Sur*   *B* 11:6 Hb obscure   *C* 11:8 Lit *king when he goes out and when he comes in*   *D* 11:12 Or *him the copy of the covenant,* or *him a diadem,* or *him jewels*   *E* 11:17 Some Gk versions, 2Ch 23:16 omit *and another covenant between the king and the people*

11:4-8 After six years of concealing the crown prince, the high priest **Jehoiada** gathered a loyal band of men, **showed them** Joash, and planned a coup against Athaliah (11:4).
11:12-16 The commotion of the young king's coronation attracted Athaliah to the scene, as Jehoiada hoped. When she saw (no doubt with wide eyes) Joash—whom she'd assumed was as dead as his siblings—she cried out, **Treason!** (11:14). (Given her treachery in murdering the "royal heirs" [11:1], it's absurd that she would have the gall to accuse others of treason!) But it was too late for anyone to save her. The **commanders** were loyal to the rightful king (11:15-16).
11:18 The people of Judah were obviously tired of Athaliah's wickedness and devotion to Baal worship, and at this stage in the nation's history they were still sensitive to the Lord's honor.

JUDAH'S KING JOASH

21 Joash[A,a] was seven years old when he **12** became king.[b] **1** In the seventh year of Jehu, Joash became king, and he reigned forty years in Jerusalem. His mother's name was Zibiah; she was from Beer-sheba.[c] **2** Throughout the time the priest Jehoiada[d] instructed[e] him, Joash did what was right in the LORD's sight.[f] **3** Yet the high places were not taken away; the people continued sacrificing and burning incense on the high places.[g]

REPAIRING THE TEMPLE

4 Then[h] Joash said to the priests, "All the dedicated silver brought to the LORD's temple,[i] census silver,[j] silver from vows,[k] and all silver voluntarily given[l] for the LORD's temple — **5** each priest is to take it from his assessor[B] and repair whatever damage is found in the temple."[C,m]

6 But by the twenty-third year[n] of the reign of King Joash, the priests had not repaired the damage[D] to the temple.[o] **7** So King Joash called the priest Jehoiada[p] and the other priests and asked, "Why haven't you repaired the temple's damage? Since you haven't, don't take any silver from your assessors; instead, hand it over for the repair of the temple." **8** So the priests agreed that they would receive no silver from the people and would not be the ones to repair the temple's damage.

9 Then the priest Jehoiada took a chest,[q] bored a hole in its lid, and set it beside the altar on the right side as one enters the LORD's temple; the priests who guarded the threshold put into the chest all the silver that was brought to the LORD's temple.[r] **10** Whenever they saw there was a large amount of silver in the chest, the king's secretary[s] and the high priest would go bag up and tally the silver found in the LORD's temple.[t] **11** Then they would give the weighed silver to those doing the work — those who oversaw the LORD's temple. They in turn would pay it out to those working on the LORD's temple — the carpenters, the builders, **12** the masons, and the stonecutters — and would use it to buy timber and quarried stone to repair the damage to the LORD's temple[u] and for all expenses for temple repairs.

13 However, no silver bowls, wick trimmers, sprinkling basins, trumpets, or any articles of gold or silver[v] were made for the LORD's temple from the contributions[E] brought to the LORD's temple. **14** Instead, it was given to those doing the work, and they repaired the LORD's temple with it. **15** No accounting was required from the men who received the silver to pay those doing the work, since they worked with integrity.[w] **16** The silver from the guilt offering and the sin offering was not brought to the LORD's temple since it belonged to the priests.[x]

ARAMEAN INVASION OF JUDAH

17 At that time King Hazael[y] of Aram marched up and fought against Gath and captured it. Then he planned to attack Jerusalem.[z] **18** So King Joash of Judah took all the items consecrated by himself and by his ancestors — Judah's kings Jehoshaphat, Jehoram, and Ahaziah — as well as all the gold found in the treasuries of the LORD's temple and in the king's palace, and he sent them to King Hazael of Aram.[aa] Then Hazael withdrew from Jerusalem.

JOASH ASSASSINATED

19 The rest of the events of Joash's reign, along with all his accomplishments, are written in the Historical Record of Judah's Kings.[ab] **20** Joash's servants conspired against him and attacked him[ac] at Beth-millo[ad] on the road that goes down to Silla. **21** It was his servants Jozabad[F] son of Shimeath and Jehozabad son of Shomer who attacked him. He died[ae] and they buried him with his fathers in the city of David, and his son Amaziah became king in his place.[af]

[a] 11:21–12:3 2Ch 24:1-4
[b] 11:21 2Kg 11:2
[c] 12:1 2Kg 11:2,21; 2Ch 24:1
[d] 12:2 2Kg 11:4,17
[e] Mal 2:6-7
[f] Dt 12:25; 2Sm 8:15
[g] 12:3 1Kg 3:3; 2Kg 14:4; 15:35
[h] 12:4-12 2Ch 24:5-12
[i] 12:4 2Kg 22:4
[j] Ex 30:13-16
[k] Lv 27:2-28
[l] Ex 35:5
[m] 12:5 2Kg 22:5
[n] 12:6 2Kg 11:21
[o] 2Ch 24:5
[p] 12:7-8 2Kg 11:4-6
[q] 12:9 2Ch 23:1; 24:8
[r] Mk 12:41; Lk 21:1
[s] 12:10 2Sm 8:17; 2Kg 19:2
[t] 2Ch 24:11

[u] 12:11-12 2Kg 22:5-6; 2Ch 24:11-12
[v] 12:13 1Kg 7:48,50-51; 2Ch 24:14
[w] 12:15 2Kg 22:7; 2Ch 34:12
[x] 12:16 Lv 4:24,29; 5:15-18; 7:7
[y] 12:17 1Kg 19:17; 2Kg 8:12; 10:32
[z] 12:17-21 2Ch 24:23-27
[aa] 12:18 2Kg 16:8; 18:15-16
[ab] 12:19 1Kg 22:45
[ac] 12:20 2Kg 14:5
[ad] Jdg 9:6
[ae] 12:21 2Ch 24:26
[af] 2Kg 14:1; 2Ch 24:27

[A] 11:21 = The LORD Has Bestowed   [B] 12:5 Hb obscure   [C] 12:5 Lit repair the breach of the temple wherever there is found a breach   [D] 12:6 Lit breach in 2Kg 12:5-12   [E] 12:13 Lit silver   [F] 12:21 Some Hb mss, LXX read Jozacar; 2Ch 24:26 reads Zabad

12:1-3 Joash's rule was a mixed bag. He did what was right in God's sight, but only as long as his godly mentor, **the priest Jehoiada**, was alive to keep him on track (12:2; see 2 Chr 24:15-25). Thus, Joash was a weak ruler whose devotion to God was only outward. Is your faith superficial, or does it go deep down to the heart?
12:4-5 The **temple** would have been about one hundred years old by this time.

12:9-12 The king had a box installed by the **altar** with **a hole in its lid**. Instead of the priests receiving silver for repair work, it was to be placed in this box (12:9). This helped to ensure integrity with regard to the financial resources.
12:17 When Jehoiada, his spiritual mentor, died, Joash became an apostate. Thus, the attack by **King Hazael of Aram** in view here was God's judgment against Joash and Judah because they had abandoned the Lord (see 2 Chr 24:24).

12:18-21 Joash didn't repent or seek the Lord's help; instead, he bought off King Hazael by using the **treasuries** of the **temple** and **the king's palace** (12:18). So Hazael departed, but the seeds had been sown for Joash's destruction. His **servants conspired against him** and assassinated him (12:20-21). The king had thought he could escape God's judgment by scheming. But the only way to escape God's judgment is by turning to God in repentance and faith.

a 13:1 2Kg 12:1
b 2Kg 10:35
c 13:2 1Kg 12:26-33
d 13:3 Dt 31:17; Jdg 2:14
e 2Kg 8:12; 12:17
f 2Kg 13:24-25
g 13:4 Ex 3:7-9; Nm 21:7-9;
2Kg 14:26
h 13:5 Jdg 2:18; 2Kg 13:25;
14:25,27
i 13:6 2Kg 13:2
j 13:7 2Kg 10:32-33
k Am 1:3
l 13:8-9 2Kg 1:17-18;
10:34-36

m 13:11 1Kg 12:28-33
n 13:12-13 2Kg 14:15-16
o 13:13 2Kg 14:23
p 13:14 2Kg 2:12
q 13:15 1Sm 20:20
r 13:17 Jos 8:18
s 1Kg 20:26
t 13:19 2Kg 5:20
u 13:20 2Kg 2:1,11

ISRAEL'S KING JEHOAHAZ

13 In the twenty-third year of Judah's King Joash[a] son of Ahaziah, Jehoahaz[b] son of Jehu became king over Israel in Samaria, and he reigned seventeen years. **2** He did what was evil in the LORD's sight and followed the sins that Jeroboam son of Nebat had caused Israel to commit; he did not turn away from them.[c] **3** So the LORD's anger burned against Israel,[d] and he handed them over to King Hazael[e] of Aram and to his son Ben-hadad[f] during their reigns.

4 Then Jehoahaz sought the LORD's favor, and the LORD heard him, for he saw the oppression the king of Aram inflicted on Israel.[g] **5** Therefore, the LORD gave Israel a deliverer,[h] and they escaped from the power of the Arameans. Then the people of Israel returned to their former way of life,[A] **6** but they didn't turn away from the sins that the house of Jeroboam had caused Israel to commit. Jehoahaz continued them,[i] and the Asherah pole also remained standing in Samaria. **7** Jehoahaz did not have an army left, except for fifty horsemen, ten chariots, and ten thousand foot soldiers, because the king of Aram had destroyed them,[j] making them like dust at threshing.[k]

8 The rest of the events of Jehoahaz's reign, along with all his accomplishments and his might, are written in the Historical Record of Israel's Kings.[l] **9** Jehoahaz rested with his fathers, and he was buried in Samaria. His son Jehoash[s] became king in his place.

ISRAEL'S KING JEHOASH

10 In the thirty-seventh year of Judah's King Joash, Jehoash son of Jehoahaz became king over Israel in Samaria, and he reigned sixteen years. **11** He did what was evil in the LORD's sight. He did not turn away from all the sins that Jeroboam son of Nebat had caused Israel to commit, but he continued them.[m]

12 The rest of the events of Jehoash's reign, along with all his accomplishments and the power he had to wage war against Judah's King Amaziah,[n] are written in the Historical Record of Israel's Kings. **13** Jehoash rested with his fathers, and Jeroboam[o] sat on his throne. Jehoash was buried in Samaria with the kings of Israel.

ELISHA'S DEATH

14 When Elisha became sick with the illness from which he died, King Jehoash of Israel went down and wept over him and said, "My father, my father, the chariots and horsemen of Israel!"[p]

15 Elisha responded, "Get a bow and arrows." So he got a bow and arrows.[q] **16** Then Elisha said to the king of Israel, "Grasp the bow." So the king grasped it, and Elisha put his hands on the king's hands. **17** Elisha said, "Open the east window." So he opened it. Elisha said, "Shoot!" So he shot.[r] Then Elisha said, "The LORD's arrow of victory, yes, the arrow of victory over Aram. You are to strike down the Arameans in Aphek[s] until you have put an end to them."

18 Then Elisha said, "Take the arrows!" So he took them. Then Elisha said to the king of Israel, "Strike the ground!" So he struck the ground three times and stopped. **19** The man of God[t] was angry with him and said, "You should have struck the ground five or six times. Then you would have struck down Aram until you had put an end to them, but now you will strike down Aram only three times." **20** Then Elisha died and was buried.[u]

13:1-3 Jehoahaz was the first of the four generations of Jehu's descendants whom God promised would occupy Israel's throne (13:1; see 10:30). Sadly, though, none of the four was anything to write home about. Jehoahaz **did what was evil** in God's eyes by following steadfastly in **the sins** of **Jeroboam**, the idolatrous founder of the northern kingdom (13:2). So once again God used a foreign power (**Aram**) to serve as an instrument of judgment against his rebellious people (13:3). **13:4-5** When **Jehoahaz sought the LORD's favor** (13:4), God graciously provided **a deliverer** who gave Israel relief from the Arameans (13:5). This person's identity is unknown. **13:7** Because of their idolatrous ways, God kept Israel weak, allowing them only a piti-

ful army that could easily have been blown away **like dust**. **13:14** This was the same way that Elisha had addressed Elijah when the latter was taken away in a fiery chariot from heaven (see 2:11–12). Thus, in spite of his flaws, **King Jehoash** had great respect for the aged prophet before him. The king also recognized that Elisha was his divine lifeline if Israel was to receive any aid during its crisis with Aram. **13:15-17** This scene is a picture of the natural being sanctified by the supernatural when God places his hands on it. When Jehoash had enough faith to follow Elisha's instructions, the arrow that left his bow was no longer his but, as Elisha said, **the LORD's . . . arrow of victory over Aram** (13:17). The battle was now

a spiritual one—not just a physical one, since the weapons of war were now sanctified. **13:18-19** It's not clear whether the prophet wanted the king to shoot his arrows into the ground (as he did with the first arrow), or instead to hold them in his hand and hit the ground. Regardless, the king lacked the zeal that Elisha said he should have displayed. Therefore, Israel would experience only a partial victory rather than a total one, since he'd refused to use all the resources at his disposal, indicating a lack of faith and commitment. Complete obedience and engagement are needed for complete victory. **13:20-21** The power of Elisha didn't cease at his death. That's because the power he'd wielded in life was not his own.

Now Moabite raiders[a] used to come into the land in the spring of the year. **21** Once, as the Israelites were burying a man, suddenly they saw a raiding party, so they threw the man into Elisha's tomb. When he touched Elisha's bones, the man revived and stood up![b]

GOD'S MERCY ON ISRAEL

22 King Hazael[c] of Aram oppressed Israel throughout the reign of Jehoahaz, **23** but the LORD was gracious to them, had compassion on them,[d] and turned toward them because of his covenant with Abraham, Isaac, and Jacob.[e] He was not willing to destroy them. Even now he has not banished them from his presence.[f]

24 King Hazael of Aram died, and his son Ben-hadad[g] became king in his place. **25** Then Jehoash son of Jehoahaz took back from Ben-hadad son of Hazael the cities that Hazael had taken in war from Jehoash's father Jehoahaz. Jehoash defeated Ben-hadad three times and recovered the cities of Israel.[h]

JUDAH'S KING AMAZIAH

14 In[i] the second year of Israel's King Jehoash[A,j] son of Jehoahaz,[B] Amaziah[k] son of Joash became king of Judah. **2** He was twenty-five years old when he became king, and he reigned twenty-nine years in Jerusalem. His mother's name was Jehoaddan;[c] she was from Jerusalem. **3** He did what was right in the LORD's sight, but not like his ancestor David. He did everything his father Joash had done.[l] **4** Yet the high places were not taken away, and the people continued sacrificing and burning incense on the high places.[m]

5 As soon as the kingdom was firmly in his grasp, Amaziah killed his servants who had killed his father the king.[n] **6** However, he did not put the children of the killers to death, as it is written in the book of the

law of Moses where the LORD commanded, "Fathers are not to be put to death because of children, and children are not to be put to death because of fathers; instead, each one will be put to death for his own sin."[o]

7 Amaziah killed ten thousand Edomites in Salt Valley.[p] He took Sela[q] in battle and called it Joktheel,[r] which is still its name today. **8** Amaziah then sent messengers to Jehoash son of Jehoahaz, son of Jehu, king of Israel, and challenged him: "Come, let's meet face to face."[s]

9 King Jehoash of Israel sent word to King Amaziah of Judah, saying, "The thistle in Lebanon once sent a message to the cedar[t] in Lebanon,[u] saying, 'Give your daughter to my son as a wife.' Then a wild animal in Lebanon passed by and trampled the thistle. **10** You have indeed defeated Edom, and you have become overconfident.[D,v] Enjoy your glory and stay at home. Why should you stir up such trouble that you fall — you and Judah with you?"

11 But Amaziah would not listen, so King Jehoash of Israel advanced. He and King Amaziah of Judah met face to face at Beth-shemesh[w] that belonged to Judah. **12** Judah was routed before Israel, and each man fled to his own tent.[x] **13** King Jehoash of Israel captured Judah's King Amaziah son of Joash,[E] son of Ahaziah, at Beth-shemesh. Then Jehoash went to Jerusalem and broke down two hundred yards[F] of Jerusalem's wall from the Ephraim Gate[y] to the Corner Gate.[z] **14** He took all the gold and silver, all the articles found in the LORD's temple and in the treasuries of the king's palace, and some hostages.[aa] Then he returned to Samaria.

JEHOASH'S DEATH

15 The rest of the events of Jehoash's reign, along with his accomplishments, his might, and how he waged war against

[a] 13:20 2Kg 3:7; 24:2
[b] 13:21 Mt 27:52
[c] 13:22 1Kg 19:17; 2Kg 8:12-13
[d] 13:23 1Kg 8:28
[e] Ex 2:24
[f] 2Kg 14:27
[g] 13:24 2Kg 13:3
[h] 13:25 2Kg 10:32
[i] 14:1-14 2Ch 25:1-24
[j] 14:1 2Ch 25:1
[k] 2Kg 13:10
[l] 14:3 2Kg 12:2
[m] 14:4 1Kg 3:3; 2Kg 12:3; 16:4
[n] 14:5 2Kg 12:20

[o] 14:6 Dt 24:16; Jr 31:30; Ezk 18:4,20
[p] 14:7 2Sm 8:13
[q] Jdg 1:36
[r] Jos 15:38
[s] 14:8 2Sm 2:14-17
[t] 14:9 1Kg 4:33
[u] Jdg 9:8-15
[v] 14:10 Dt 8:14; 2Ch 26:16; 34:25
[w] 14:11 Jos 19:38; 21:16
[x] 14:12 2Sm 18:17; 1Kg 22:36
[y] 14:13 Neh 8:16; 12:39
[z] 2Ch 25:23; Zch 14:10
[aa] 14:14 1Kg 7:51; 14:26; 2Kg 12:18

[A] 14:1 Lit *Joash*, also in vv. 23,27   [B] 14:1 Lit *Joahaz*   [C] 14:2 Alt Hb tradition, some Hb mss, Syr, Tg, Vg, 2Ch 25:1; other Hb mss, LXX read *Jehoaddin*   [D] 14:10 Lit *and your heart has lifted you*   [E] 14:13 Lit *Jehoash*   [F] 14:13 Lit *400 cubits*

13:23 That God had not yet **banished** Israel **from his presence** after all their rebellion was a beautiful reminder that the Lord is "slow to anger and abounding in faithful love and truth" (Exod 34:6). But eventually, his patience would run out.

13:25 As Elisha had prophesied, King Jehoash **defeated** Aram **three times**, regaining **cities** that Israel had lost.

14:3 All the kings of Judah were measured against **David**, Judah's greatest king who kept God's law and received the promise of the Messiah coming from his line.

14:4 **High places** were sites where the people practiced forbidden worship.

14:6 This detail indicates Amaziah's respect for the law.

14:7 **Sela** is the famous rock fortress of Petra in Jordan.

14:8-10 Amaziah was apparently feeling strong and cocky after the Edomite campaign, so he looked north. Israel's army was weak after years of being battered by Aram, so perhaps Amaziah thought this was a good time for Judah to stick it to **Israel** (14:8). **Jehoash** answered with a parable

that ridiculed Judah's strength (14:9). Then he warned Amaziah in no uncertain terms: **Stay at home** (14:10).

14:12-14 Just as Jehoash had warned in verses 9-10, the battle was a complete disaster for the southern kingdom. Even worse, Jehoash **captured** Amaziah and plundered the **temple** (14:13-14). All this happened because of Amaziah's stubborn pride.

a 14:15-16 2Kg 13:12-13
b 14:17 2Ch 25:25-28
c 14:18 2Kg 12:19
d 14:19 2Ch 25:27
e Jos 10:31; 2Kg 18:14
f 14:20 2Kg 9:28
g 2Kg 12:21
h 14:21 2Kg 15:13; 2Ch 26:1-2
i 14:22 1Kg 9:26; 2Kg 16:6
j 14:23 2Kg 13:13
k 14:24 1Kg 12:30; 15:30
l 14:25 2Kg 13:25
m 1Kg 8:65
n Nm 34:3-9
o Jnh 1:1; Mt 12:39
p Jos 19:13
q 14:26 Ex 3:7-9; Dt 32:36; 2Kg 13:4
r 14:27 Dt 29:20; 2Kg 13:3
s Jdg 6:14
t 14:28 2Sm 8:5; 1Kg 11:24
u 2Sm 8:9; 2Ch 8:3
v 2Kg 13:8
w 14:29 2Kg 13:12-13; 15:8
x 15:1 2Kg 14:21
y 15:1-3 2Ch 26:3-5
z 15:3 1Kg 14:8
aa 15:4 2Kg 14:3-4
ab 15:5 2Ch 26:16-21
ac Lv 13:46
ad 2Kg 15:32; 2Ch 27:1; Mc 1:1
ae 2Ch 26:16-21
af 15:6 2Kg 14:18
ag 15:6-7 2Ch 26:22-23
ah 15:8 2Kg 14:29

King Amaziah of Judah, are written in the Historical Record of Israel's Kings.[a] 16 Jehoash rested with his fathers, and he was buried in Samaria with the kings of Israel. His son Jeroboam became king in his place.

AMAZIAH'S DEATH

17 Judah's King Amaziah son of Joash lived fifteen years after the death of Israel's King Jehoash son of Jehoahaz.[b] 18 The rest of the events of Amaziah's reign are written in the Historical Record of Judah's Kings.[c] 19 A conspiracy was formed against him in Jerusalem,[d] and he fled to Lachish.[e] However, men were sent after him to Lachish, and they put him to death there. 20 They carried him back[f] on horses, and he was buried in Jerusalem with his fathers in the city of David.[g]

21 Then all the people of Judah took Azariah,[A,h] who was sixteen years old, and made him king in place of his father Amaziah. 22 After Amaziah the king rested with his fathers, Azariah rebuilt Elath[B,i] and restored it to Judah.

ISRAEL'S KING JEROBOAM

23 In the fifteenth year of Judah's King Amaziah son of Joash, Jeroboam[j] son of Jehoash became king of Israel in Samaria, and he reigned forty-one years. 24 He did what was evil in the LORD's sight. He did not turn away from all the sins Jeroboam son of Nebat had caused Israel to commit.[k]

25 He restored Israel's border[l] from Lebo-hamath[m] as far as the Sea of the Arabah,[n] according to the word the LORD, the God of Israel, had spoken through his servant, the prophet Jonah[o] son of Amittai from Gath-hepher.[p] 26 For the LORD saw that the affliction of Israel was very bitter[q] for both slaves and free people.[c] There was no one to help Israel. 27 The LORD had not

said he would blot out the name of Israel under heaven,[r] so he delivered[s] them by the hand of Jeroboam son of Jehoash.

28 The rest of the events of Jeroboam's reign — along with all his accomplishments, the power he had to wage war, and how he recovered for Israel Damascus[t] and Hamath,[u] which had belonged to Judah[D] — are written in the Historical Record of Israel's Kings.[v] 29 Jeroboam rested with his fathers, the kings of Israel. His son Zechariah became king in his place.[w]

JUDAH'S KING AZARIAH

15 In the twenty-seventh year of Israel's King Jeroboam, Azariah[E,x] son of Amaziah became king of Judah.[y] 2 He was sixteen years old when he became king, and he reigned fifty-two years in Jerusalem. His mother's name was Jecoliah; she was from Jerusalem. 3 Azariah did what was right in the LORD's sight[z] just as his father Amaziah had done. 4 Yet the high places were not taken away; the people continued sacrificing and burning incense on the high places.[aa]

5 The LORD afflicted the king, and he had a serious skin disease until the day of his death.[ab] He lived in quarantine,[F,ac] while Jotham,[ad] the king's son, was over the household governing the people of the land.[ae]

6 The rest of the events of Azariah's reign, along with all his accomplishments, are written in the Historical Record of Judah's Kings.[af] 7 Azariah rested with his fathers and was buried with his fathers in the city of David. His son Jotham became king in his place.[ag]

ISRAEL'S KING ZECHARIAH

8 In the thirty-eighth year of Judah's King Azariah, Zechariah[ah] son of Jeroboam reigned over Israel in Samaria for six months. 9 He did what was evil in the LORD's sight as his

A 14:21 = Uzziah in 2Ch 26:1   B 14:22 = Eloth in 2Ch 26:2   C 14:26 Hb obscure   D 14:28 Lit recovered Damascus and for Judah in Israel; Hb obscure   E 15:1 = Uzziah in 2Ch 26:3   F 15:5 Lit in a house of exemption from duty

14:16 Jehoash's death was recorded for a second time here, probably because of his battle with Amaziah, an insight that fleshes out what was revealed previously (13:12). This Jeroboam was the third of the four kings in Jehu's dynasty, as promised to him by the Lord.
14:23-24 Jeroboam son of Jehoash is often referred to as Jeroboam II to distinguish him from the first king of Israel by the same name (mentioned in 14:24).
14:25-28 Jeroboam II was a successful military commander who regained much territory that Israel had lost to Aram. A prophecy con-

cerning this restoration of land was made by Jonah son of Amittai (14:25). This is the same Jonah tasked with prophesying to Nineveh (see Jonah 1:1).
15:1-7 Dismissing Azariah's fifty-two years with only a few verses may seem odd, especially since he was commended as a king who did what was right in the LORD's sight, except for leaving the high places intact (which almost all the kings of Judah did; 15:2-4). The only other thing included about Azariah was that God afflicted him with a serious skin disease (15:5), which required him to live separately in the later years of his

reign while his son Jotham administered. So what happened?
Azariah was also known as Uzziah (see 15:13, 30). In 2 Chronicles we find some helpful details about him. Uzziah was one of the most effective kings of Judah, expanding its territory and following the Lord—until he became proud, usurped the role of the priest, and was struck by God with a skin disease for his arrogance (see 2 Chr 26:1-23). Perhaps God left it to the author of 2 Chronicles to fill in the details of Azariah's reign since 1–2 Chronicles take a special interest in Judah's kings (see the introduction to 1–2 Chronicles).

fathers had done.[a] He did not turn away from the sins Jeroboam son of Nebat had caused Israel to commit.[b]

10 Shallum son of Jabesh conspired against Zechariah. He struck him down publicly,[A] killed him, and became king in his place.[c] **11** As for the rest of the events of Zechariah's reign, they are written in the Historical Record of Israel's Kings.[d] **12** The word of the LORD that he spoke to Jehu was, "Four generations of your sons will sit on the throne of Israel,"[e] and it was so.

ISRAEL'S KING SHALLUM

13 In the thirty-ninth year of Judah's King Uzziah,[B] Shallum son of Jabesh became king; he reigned in Samaria[a] a full month. **14** Then Menahem son of Gadi came up from Tirzah[g] to Samaria and struck down Shallum son of Jabesh there. He killed him and became king in his place. **15** As for the rest of the events of Shallum's reign, along with the conspiracy that he formed, they are written in the Historical Record of Israel's Kings.

ISRAEL'S KING MENAHEM

16 At that time, starting from Tirzah, Menahem attacked Tiphsah,[h] all who were in it, and its territory because they wouldn't surrender.[i] He ripped open all the pregnant women.[j]

17 In the thirty-ninth year of Judah's King Azariah, Menahem son of Gadi became king over Israel, and he reigned ten years in Samaria. **18** He did what was evil in the LORD's sight. Throughout his reign, he did not turn away from the sins Jeroboam son of Nebat had caused Israel to commit.[k]

19 King Pul[c,l] of Assyria invaded the land, so Menahem gave Pul seventy-five thousand pounds[D] of silver so that Pul would support him to strengthen his grasp on the kingdom.[m] **20** Then Menahem exacted twenty ounces[E] of silver from each of the prominent men of Israel to give to the king of Assyria. So the king of Assyria withdrew and did not stay there in the land.[n]

21 The rest of the events of Menahem's reign, along with all his accomplishments, are written in the Historical Record of Israel's Kings. **22** Menahem rested with his fathers, and his son Pekahiah became king in his place.[o]

ISRAEL'S KING PEKAHIAH

23 In the fiftieth year of Judah's King Azariah, Pekahiah son of Menahem became king over Israel in Samaria, and he reigned two years. **24** He did what was evil in the LORD's sight and did not turn away from the sins Jeroboam son of Nebat had caused Israel to commit.[p]

25 Then his officer, Pekah[q] son of Remaliah, conspired against him[r] and struck him down in Samaria at the citadel of the king's palace[s] — with Argob and Arieh.[F] There were fifty Gileadite men with Pekah. He killed Pekahiah and became king in his place.

26 As for the rest of the events of Pekahiah's reign, along with all his accomplishments, they are written in the Historical Record of Israel's Kings.

ISRAEL'S KING PEKAH

27 In the fifty-second year of Judah's King Azariah, Pekah son of Remaliah became king over Israel in Samaria, and he reigned twenty years. **28** He did what was evil in the LORD's sight. He did not turn away from the sins Jeroboam son of Nebat had caused Israel to commit.

29 In the days of King Pekah of Israel, King Tiglath-pileser[t] of Assyria came and captured Ijon,[u] Abel-beth-maacah, Janoah, Kedesh, Hazor, Gilead, and Galilee — all the land of Naphtali[v] — and deported the people to Assyria.[w]

30 Then Hoshea[x] son of Elah organized a conspiracy against Pekah son of Remaliah. He attacked him, killed him,[y] and became king in his place in the twentieth year of Jotham son of Uzziah.

31 As for the rest of the events of Pekah's reign, along with all his accomplishments, they are written in the Historical Record of Israel's Kings.

JUDAH'S KING JOTHAM

32 In the second year of Israel's King Pekah son of Remaliah, Jotham[z] son of Uzziah became king of Judah. **33** He was twenty-five years old when he became king,[aa] and he

---

[a] 15:9 2Kg 14:24
[b] 1Kg 12:28–33; 13:33–34
[c] 15:10 2Kg 12:20
[d] 15:11 2Kg 13:8
[e] 15:12 2Kg 10:30
[f] 15:13 1Kg 16:24
[g] 15:14 1Kg 14:17
[h] 15:16 1Kg 4:24
[i] Dt 20:11
[j] 2Kg 8:12; Hs 13:16; Am 1:13
[k] 15:18 1Kg 12:28–33; 15:26
[l] 15:19 1Ch 5:25–26
[m] 2Kg 14:5
[n] 15:20 2Kg 12:18

[o] 15:22 2Kg 14:29
[p] 15:24 1Kg 12:28–33
[q] 15:25 2Ch 28:6
[r] 2Kg 12:20
[s] 1Kg 16:8
[t] 15:29 1Ch 5:6,26
[u] 1Kg 15:29
[v] Jos 19:32–39
[w] 2Kg 17:6
[x] 15:30 2Kg 17:1
[y] 2Kg 12:20
[z] 15:32 2Kg 15:5,7
[aa] 15:33–35 2Ch 27:1–3

[A] 15:10 Some LXX mss read *down at Ibleam*; Hb uncertain   [B] 15:13 = Azariah, also in vv. 30,32,34   [C] 15:19 = Tiglath-pileser   [D] 15:19 Lit *1,000 talents*
[E] 15:20 Lit *50 shekels*   [F] 15:25 Hb obscure

15:16-18 Menahem demonstrated his brutality by attacking a town because its people wouldn't acknowledge him as king. His murder of **all the pregnant women** and their children was especially barbaric (15:16). It highlights the horror and cruelty of which fallen humans are capable.

15:19 Pul was the throne name of the powerful King Tiglath-pileser III. This is the first mention of **Assyria** we find in 2 Kings, but it won't be the last. (In time this foreign power would conquer Israel.)

[a] 15:34-35 2Kg 15:3-4
[b] 15:35 2Ch 27:3
[c] 15:36-38 2Ch 27:7-9
[d] 15:36 2Kg 14:18
[e] 15:37 2Kg 16:5; Is 7:1
[f] 15:38 2Kg 15:7
[g] 16:1-4 2Ch 28:1-4
[h] 16:1 Is 1:1; 7:1
[i] 16:2 1Kg 14:8
[j] 16:3 2Kg 17:9-10
[k] Dt 18:10; 2Kg 21:6;
2Ch 33:6
[l] 16:4 1Kg 22:17
[m] Dt 12:2
[n] 16:5-6 2Ch 28:5-6;
Is 7:1-9
[o] 16:5 2Kg 15:37; Is 7:1
[p] 16:6 1Kg 9:26

[q] 16:6 2Ch 26:2
[r] 16:7 2Ch 28:16
[s] 2Kg 15:29; 1Ch 5:26
[t] 16:8 1Kg 15:19; 2Kg 12:17-
18; 18:15
[u] 16:9 2Ch 28:21
[v] Am 1:3-5
[w] Is 22:6; Am 9:7
[x] 16:10 2Kg 15:29
[y] Is 8:2
[z] 16:12 2Ch 26:16
[aa] 16:13 Ex 29:40
[ab] Lv 7:11-21
[ac] 16:14 Ex 40:24

reigned sixteen years in Jerusalem. His mother's name was Jerusha daughter of Zadok. [34] He did what was right in the LORD's sight just as his father Uzziah had done.[a] [35] Yet the high places were not taken away; the people continued sacrificing and burning incense on the high places.

Jotham built the Upper Gate of the LORD's temple.[b] [36] The rest[c] of the events of Jotham's reign, along with all his accomplishments, are written in the Historical Record of Judah's Kings.[d] [37] In those days the LORD began sending Aram's King Rezin and Pekah son of Remaliah against Judah.[e] [38] Jotham rested with his fathers and was buried with his fathers in the city of his ancestor David.[f] His son Ahaz became king in his place.

JUDAH'S KING AHAZ

16 In the seventeenth year of Pekah son of Remaliah,[g] Ahaz[h] son of Jotham became king of Judah. [2] Ahaz was twenty years old when he became king, and he reigned sixteen years in Jerusalem. He did not do what was right in the sight of the LORD his God like his ancestor David[i] [3] but walked in the ways of the kings of Israel.[j] He even sacrificed his son in the fire,[A] imitating the detestable practices of the nations the LORD had dispossessed before the Israelites.[k] [4] He sacrificed and burned incense[l] on the high places, on the hills, and under every green tree.[m]

[5] Then[n] Aram's King Rezin and Israel's King Pekah son of Remaliah came to wage war against Jerusalem. They besieged Ahaz but were not able to conquer him.[o] [6] At that time Aram's King Rezin recovered Elath for Aram and expelled the Judahites from Elath.[p] Then the Arameans came to Elath, and they still live there today.[q]

[7] So Ahaz sent messengers[r] to King Tiglath-pileser[s] of Assyria, saying, "I am your servant and your son. March up and save me from the grasp of the king of Aram and of the king of Israel, who are rising up against me." [8] Ahaz also took the silver and gold found in the LORD's temple and in the treasuries of the king's palace and sent them to the king of Assyria as a bribe.[t] [9] So the king of Assyria listened to him[u] and marched up to Damascus and captured it.[v] He deported its people to Kir[w] but put Rezin to death.

AHAZ'S IDOLATRY

[10] King Ahaz went to Damascus to meet King Tiglath-pileser[x] of Assyria. When he saw the altar that was in Damascus, King Ahaz sent a model of the altar and complete plans for its construction to the priest Uriah.[y] [11] Uriah built the altar according to all the instructions King Ahaz sent from Damascus. Therefore, by the time King Ahaz came back from Damascus, the priest Uriah had completed it. [12] When the king came back from Damascus, he saw the altar. Then he approached the altar[z] and ascended it.[B] [13] He offered his burnt offering[aa] and his grain offering, poured out his drink offering, and splattered the blood of his fellowship offerings[ab] on the altar. [14] He took the bronze altar[ac] that was before the LORD in front of the temple between his altar and the LORD's temple, and put it on the north side of his altar.

[15] Then King Ahaz commanded the priest Uriah, "Offer on the great altar the morning burnt offering, the evening grain offering, and the king's burnt offering and

---

[A] 16:3 Lit even made his son pass through the fire   [B] 16:12 Or and offered on it:

15:34-35 Happily, just as the bad kings of Israel followed their predecessors in doing evil, Jotham of Judah followed Uzziah (also called Azariah) in doing **what was right** (15:34). However, like most of Judah's kings, he failed to destroy Judah's **high places**—the alternate places of worship that God had forbidden through Moses (15:35).

16:2-3 Hundreds of years earlier, the Lord had warned the people through Moses not to "imitate the detestable customs" of the nations that the Israelites were driving out of Canaan. The first item on the list of forbidden practices was to "sacrifice [one's] son or daughter in the fire" (Deut 18:9-10). Yet here was the king of Israel, destroying the most vulnerable members of society. He killed his own son, who was made in God's image (Gen 1:26)! Make no mistake: left unchecked, false theology leads to corruption and violence.

16:5-9 If the trouble described in verse 5 was a test of faith for Ahaz, he failed it miserably. He did not call out to God for deliverance. Instead, Judah's king pledged allegiance to Assyria if it would only save him from **Aram** and **Israel** (16:7). But for this Ahaz had to pay protection money: **silver and gold** from the **temple** and **the king's palace** (16:8). Judah was delivered—for now. But in ignoring God, Ahaz was cutting off his nation from the only one who could provide lasting deliverance.

16:10-15 The event of verse 10 was no meeting of equals because Ahaz was now the vassal of the Assyrian king and had to be careful not to do anything to offend him. Perhaps that's why Ahaz sent back to Jerusalem **complete plans** for the **altar** he saw in Damascus so his high **priest Uriah** could build it (16:10-11). Tiglath-pileser probably made it known to Ahaz that he wanted the worship of Assyrian gods to be observed in Judah, and Ahaz was ungodly enough to comply.

By the time Ahaz returned to Jerusalem, the altar was **completed** (16:11-13). Then Ahaz further offended God by moving the **bronze altar**, that Solomon had made, so he could put his new altar in its prominent place (16:14)! He also ordered the faithless **priest Uriah** to offer on this abomination of an altar three of Israel's most important offerings (16:15).

his grain offering. Also offer the burnt offering of all the people of the land, their grain offering, and their drink offerings. Splatter on the altar all the blood of the burnt offering and all the blood of sacrifice. The bronze altar will be for me to seek guidance."^A **16** The priest Uriah did everything King Ahaz commanded.

17 Then King Ahaz cut off the frames of the water carts^B,^a and removed the bronze basin from each of them. He took the basin^C,^b from the bronze oxen that were under it and put it on a stone pavement. **18** To satisfy the king of Assyria, he removed from the LORD's temple the Sabbath canopy they had built in the palace, and he closed the outer entrance for the king.

AHAZ'S DEATH

19 The rest^c of the events of Ahaz's reign, along with his accomplishments, are written in the Historical Record of Judah's Kings.^d **20** Ahaz rested with his fathers^e and was buried with his fathers in the city of David, and his son Hezekiah became king in his place.

ISRAEL'S KING HOSHEA

17 In the twelfth year of Judah's King Ahaz, Hoshea^f son of Elah became king over Israel in Samaria, and he reigned nine years. **2** He did what was evil in the LORD's sight, but not like the kings of Israel who preceded him.^g

3 King Shalmaneser^h of Assyria attacked him,^i and Hoshea became his vassal and paid him tribute. **4** But the king of Assyria caught Hoshea in a conspiracy: He had sent envoys to So king of Egypt^j and had not paid tribute to the king of Assyria as in previous years.^D Therefore the king of Assyria arrested him and put him in prison. **5** The king of Assyria invaded the whole land, marched up to Samaria, and besieged it for three years.^k

THE FALL OF SAMARIA

6 In the ninth year of Hoshea,^l the king of Assyria captured Samaria. He deported^m the Israelites to Assyria and settled them in Halah, along the Habor (Gozan's river), and in the cities of the Medes.^n

WHY ISRAEL FELL

7 This disaster happened because the people of Israel sinned against the LORD their God who had brought them out of the land of Egypt from the power of Pharaoh king of Egypt^o and because they worshiped^E other gods.^p **8** They lived according to the customs of the nations that the LORD had dispossessed before the Israelites^q and according to what the kings of Israel did.^r **9** The Israelites secretly did things^F against the LORD their God that were not right. They built high places in all their towns from watchtower^s to fortified city. **10** They set up for themselves sacred pillars^t and Asherah poles^u on every high hill and under every green tree.^v **11** They burned incense there on all the high places just like the nations that the LORD had driven out before them had done. They did evil things, angering the LORD. **12** They served idols, although the LORD had told them, "You must not do this."^w **13** Still, the LORD warned^x Israel and Judah through every prophet and every seer, saying, "Turn from your evil ways and keep my commands and statutes according to the whole law I commanded your ancestors and sent to you through my servants the prophets."^y

14 But they would not listen. Instead they became obstinate like^G their ancestors who did not believe the LORD their God.^z **15** They rejected his statutes and his covenant he had made with their ancestors^aa and the warnings he had given them. They followed worthless idols and became worthless themselves,^ab following the surrounding nations the LORD had commanded them not to imitate.^ac

^a 16:17 1Kg 7:27-28
^b 1Kg 7:23-25
^c 16:19-20 2Ch 28:26-27
^d 16:19 2Kg 15:36
^e 16:20 Is 14:28
^f 17:1 2Kg 15:30
^g 17:2 2Kg 15:24,28
^h 17:3 Hs 10:14
^i 2Kg 18:9-12
^j 17:4 Is 31:1
^k 17:5 2Kg 18:9-10; Hs 13:16

^l 17:6 Hs 1:4; 13:16
^m Dt 28:64; 29:27-28
^n 1Ch 5:26
^o 17:7 Jos 24:5-7
^p Jdg 6:10
^q 17:8 Lv 18:3; Dt 18:9
^r 2Kg 16:3; 17:19
^s 17:9 2Kg 18:8
^t 17:10 Ex 23:24
^u 1Kg 14:15,23; 15:13; 2Kg 18:4
^v Dt 12:2
^w 17:12 Ex 20:4-5
^x 17:13 Neh 9:29-30
^y 1Kg 9:6-9; 18:18-21
^z 17:14 Ex 32:9; 33:3; Nm 14:11
^aa 17:15 Ex 24:6-8
^ab Jr 2:5; Rm 1:21-23
^ac Dt 12:30-31

---

^A 16:15 Hb obscure   ^B 16:17 Lit *the stands*   ^C 16:17 Lit *sea*   ^D 17:4 Lit *as year by year*   ^E 17:7 Lit *feared*   ^F 17:9 Or *Israelites spoke words*   ^G 17:14 Lit *they stiffened their neck like the neck of*

16:20 The only good thing that came out of Ahaz's life was his son **Hezekiah**. He serves as a wonderful example of the fact that our futures are not predetermined by the character of our parents. Even if your parents didn't follow God, you can follow a different path—a God-honoring path—by God's grace and your willingness to make a change.
17:1 Hoshea was the northern kingdom's last leader.
17:6 When Samaria finally fell in 722 BC, Shalmaneser **deported the Israelites to Assyria**.

The northern kingdom had lasted just over two centuries. Twenty kings had sat on its throne—every one of them judged as evil in God's sight.
17:8-10 The offenses of God's people had really piled up. The Israelites imitated **the customs of the nations** that God had driven out of the promised land—customs that God had explicitly forbidden through Moses (see Deut 18:9). Israel's own **kings**—the men who were to lead the people in holiness and faithfulness—adopted these rebellious ways, and

the people followed their lead (2 Kgs 17:8). They thought they were doing these things **secretly** while still carrying on the pretense of worshiping God, as if he would be fooled (17:9). But God is omniscient (all knowing) and omnipresent (everywhere present). Nothing we do is in secret.
17:15 Psalm 115:4-7 drives this point about idolatry home. The psalmist wrote this about idol worshipers: "Those who make them are just like them" (Ps 115:8). Take note: you become like what you worship.

a 17:16 1Kg 12:28
b 1Kg 14:15,23
c 2Kg 21:3
d 1Kg 16:31-33; Am 5:26;
Zph 1:5
e 17:17 2Kg 16:3
f Lv 19:26; Dt 18:10-12;
2Kg 16:3
g 1Kg 21:20
h 17:18 2Kg 17:6
i 1Kg 11:13,32,36
j 17:19 1Kg 14:22-23
k 2Kg 16:3
l 17:20 2Kg 15:29; 17:6
m 17:21 1Kg 11:11,31
n 1Kg 12:20
o 17:21-22 1Kg 12:28-33
p 17:23 2Kg 17:6,13
q 17:24 Ezr 4:10

r 17:25 1Kg 13:24
s 17:27 2Kg 17:6
t 17:28 1Kg 12:29,32-33
u 17:29 1Kg 12:31; 13:32
v 17:31 2Kg 17:17
w 17:32 Jdg 17:5-13; 1Kg
12:31; 13:33
x 17:33 Zph 1:5
y 17:34 Gn 32:28; 35:10

16 They abandoned all the commands of the LORD their God. They made cast images*a* for themselves, two calves, and an Asherah pole.*b* They bowed in worship to all the stars in the sky*c* and served Baal.*d* **17** They sacrificed their sons and daughters in the fire*A,e* and practiced divination and interpreted omens.*f* They devoted themselves to do what was evil in the LORD's sight and angered him.*g*

18 Therefore, the LORD was very angry with Israel, and he removed them from his presence.*h* Only the tribe of Judah remained.*i* **19** Even Judah did not keep the commands of the LORD their God*j* but lived according to the customs Israel had practiced.*k* **20** So the LORD rejected all the descendants of Israel, punished them, and handed them over to plunderers until he had banished them from his presence.*l*

SUMMARY OF ISRAEL'S HISTORY

21 When the LORD tore*m* Israel from the house of David, Israel made Jeroboam son of Nebat king.*n* Then Jeroboam led Israel away from following the LORD and caused them to commit immense sin. **22** The Israelites persisted in all the sins that Jeroboam committed and did not turn away from them.*o* **23** Finally, the LORD removed Israel from his presence just as he had declared through all his servants the prophets. So Israel has been exiled to Assyria from their homeland to this very day.*p*

FOREIGN REFUGEES IN ISRAEL

24 Then the king of Assyria brought people from Babylon, Cuthah, Avva, Hamath, and Sepharvaim and settled them in place of the Israelites in the cities of Samaria. The settlers took possession of Samaria and lived in its cities.*q* **25** When they first lived there, they did not fear the LORD. So the LORD sent lions among them, which

killed some of them.*r* **26** The settlers said to the king of Assyria, "The nations that you have deported and placed in the cities of Samaria do not know the requirements of the god of the land. Therefore he has sent lions among them that are killing them because the people don't know the requirements of the god of the land."

27 Then the king of Assyria issued a command: "Send back one of the priests you deported.*s* Have him go and live there so he can teach them the requirements of the god of the land." **28** So one of the priests they had deported came and lived in Bethel,*t* and he began to teach them how they should fear the LORD.

29 But the people of each nation were still making their own gods in the cities where they lived and putting them in the shrines of the high places that the people of Samaria had made.*u* **30** The men of Babylon made Succoth-benoth, the men of Cuth made Nergal, the men of Hamath made Ashima, **31** the Avvites made Nibhaz and Tartak, and the Sepharvites burned their children in the fire*v* to Adrammelech and Anammelech, the gods of Sepharvaim. **32** They feared the LORD, but they also made from their ranks priests for the high places, who were working for them at the shrines of the high places.*w* **33** They feared the LORD, but they also worshiped their own gods*x* according to the practice of the nations from which they had been deported.

34 They are still observing the former practices to this day. None of them fear the LORD or observe the statutes and ordinances, the law and commandments that the LORD had commanded the descendants of Jacob, whom he had given the name Israel.*y* **35** The LORD made a covenant with Jacob's descendants and commanded them, "Do not fear other gods; do

A 17:17 Lit *They made their sons and daughters pass through the fire*

17:17 The most vulnerable members of society were put to death by their own parents! Tragically, this sounds like our own culture in which the appalling practice of abortion is so prevalent. God will not turn a blind eye to the destruction of his image bearers (see Gen 1:26). **17:19** In time, **Judah** would suffer a fate similar to Israel's.

17:23 The author helpfully notes that Israel's people were still in Assyria in his **day**, years after their homeland's collapse.

17:24 When rulers in the ancient Near East conquered a nation and took its people into exile, they would often settle peoples from other conquered nations into the newly-conquered land. This separation of the

people from their lands—and supposedly from their gods—was intended to prevent nationalistic sentiment from arising. Exiling the people and mixing the stragglers with other peoples would make them less likely to rebel.

17:28-29 The **priest** may have been one of the very people who'd led Israel to worship the golden calves erected by Jeroboam (17:28). So the fact that he taught these unbelievers what the Lord required was no guarantee that he lived by those standards or was above blending in with the people as they made and worshiped **their own gods** too (17:29).

17:34 Here we get a general indictment against the new inhabitants of what had been

Israel. This explains the origin of the syncretistic Samaritan people of Jesus's earthly ministry (see John 4:1-42). Many of the Israelites who were still in the land following Israel's overthrow intermarried with the foreign peoples over time until the distinctiveness of Israel's religion was systematically dismantled and replaced by a smorgasbord of religion in which the Lord was just one deity among many.

17:35-38 God had pledged his faithfulness and protection to **Jacob's descendants**, but in return they were to be faithful to him. They were to honor him exclusively as their King and live from the perspective of being citizens of his kingdom.

not bow in worship to them;[a] do not serve them; do not sacrifice to them.[b] **36** Instead fear the LORD, who brought you up from the land of Egypt with great power[c] and an outstretched arm.[d] You are to bow down to him, and you are to sacrifice to him. **37** You are to be careful always[e] to observe the statutes, the ordinances, the law, and the commandments he wrote for you; do not fear other gods. **38** Do not forget the covenant that I have made with you.[f] Do not fear other gods, **39** but fear the LORD your God, and he will rescue you from all your enemies."[g]

40 However, these nations would not listen but continued observing their former practices. **41** They feared the LORD but also served their idols. Still today, their children and grandchildren continue doing as their fathers did.[h]

JUDAH'S KING HEZEKIAH

18 In the third year of Israel's King Hoshea[i] son of Elah, Hezekiah[j] son of Ahaz became king of Judah. **2** He was twenty-five years old when he became king, and he reigned twenty-nine years in Jerusalem. His mother's name was Abi[A] daughter of Zechariah. **3** He did what was right in the LORD's sight just as his ancestor David had done.[k] **4** He removed the high places, shattered the sacred pillars, and cut down the Asherah poles.[l] He broke into pieces the bronze snake that Moses made,[m] for until then the Israelites were burning incense to it. It was called Nehushtan.[B]

5 Hezekiah relied on the LORD God of Israel;[n] not one of the kings of Judah was like him, either before him or after him.[o] **6** He remained faithful to the LORD[p] and did not turn from following him but kept the commands the LORD had commanded Moses.

7 The LORD was with him, and wherever he went he prospered.[q] He rebelled against the king of Assyria and did not serve him.[r] **8** He defeated the Philistines as far as Gaza and its borders,[s] from watchtower[t] to fortified city.

REVIEW OF ISRAEL'S FALL

9 In the fourth year of King Hezekiah, which was the seventh year of Israel's King Hoshea son of Elah, Assyria's King Shalmaneser marched against Samaria and besieged it.[u] **10** The Assyrians captured it at the end of three years. In the sixth year of Hezekiah, which was the ninth year of Israel's King Hoshea, Samaria was captured. **11** The king of Assyria deported the Israelites to Assyria and put them in Halah, along the Habor (Gozan's river), and in the cities of the Medes,[v] **12** because they did not listen to the LORD their God but violated his covenant — all he had commanded Moses the servant of the LORD. They did not listen, and they did not obey.[w]

SENNACHERIB'S INVASION

13 In the fourteenth year of King Hezekiah, Assyria's King Sennacherib attacked all the fortified cities of Judah and captured them.[x] **14** So King Hezekiah of Judah sent word to the king of Assyria at Lachish:[y] "I have done wrong;[z] withdraw from me. Whatever you demand from me, I will pay." The king of Assyria demanded eleven tons[c] of silver and one ton[D] of gold from King Hezekiah of Judah. **15** So Hezekiah gave him all the silver found in the LORD's temple and in the treasuries of the king's palace.

16 At that time Hezekiah stripped the gold from the doors of the LORD's sanctuary and from the doorposts he had overlaid and gave it to the king of Assyria.[aa]

17 Then the king of Assyria sent the field marshal,[ab] the chief of staff, and his royal spokesman, along with a massive army, from Lachish to King Hezekiah at Jerusalem.[ac] They advanced and came to Jerusalem, and[E] they took their position by the aqueduct of the upper pool, by the road to the Launderer's Field.[ad] **18** They called for the king, but Eliakim[ae] son of Hilkiah, who was in charge of the palace, Shebnah[af] the court secretary, and Joah son of Asaph, the court historian, came out to them.[ag]

[a] 17:35 Ex 20:5; Dt 5:9;
[b] Dt 5:9
[c] 17:36 Ex 14:15-30
[d] Ex 6:6; 9:15
[e] 17:37 Dt 5:32
[f] 17:38 Dt 4:23; 6:12
[g] 17:39 Ex 23:22; Dt 20:1-4; 23:14
[h] 17:41 1Kg 8:21; Ezr 4:2; Mt 6:24
[i] 18:1 2Kg 17:1
[j] 2Ch 28:27
[k] 18:2-3 2Ch 29:1-2
[l] 18:4 2Kg 17:10; 18:22; 2Ch 31:1
[m] Nm 21:5-9
[n] 18:5 2Kg 19:10
[o] 1Kg 3:12; 2Kg 23:25
[p] 18:6 Dt 10:20; Jos 23:8
[q] 18:7 Gn 39:2-3; 1Sm 18:14
[r] 2Kg 16:7
[s] 18:8 2Ch 28:18; Is 14:29
[t] 2Kg 17:9

[u] 18:9 2Kg 17:3-7
[v] 18:10-11 2Kg 17:6; 1Ch 5:26
[w] 18:12 1Kg 9:6; 2Kg 17:7-18; Dn 9:6,10
[x] 18:13 2Ch 32:1; Is 36:1
[y] 18:14 2Kg 19:8
[z] Is 24:5; 33:8
[aa] 18:15-16 2Kg 12:18; 16:8; 2Ch 16:2
[ab] 18:17 Is 20:1
[ac] 2Ch 32:9
[ad] 2Kg 20:20; Is 7:3
[ae] 18:18 2Kg 19:2; Is 22:20
[af] Is 22:15
[ag] 18:17-18 Is 36:2-3

[A] 18:2 = Abijah in 2Ch 29:1 [B] 18:4 = A Bronze Thing [C] 18:14 Lit *300 talents* [D] 18:14 Lit *30 talents* [E] 18:17 LXX, Syr, Vg; MT reads *and came and*

17:40-41 When people from other **nations** came to live in the land of Israel—even though they knew what happened to the former inhabitants—they **continued...their former practices** (17:40). They taught their offspring to mix worship of the Lord with worship of their **idols** (17:41). What a sad outcome.
18:4 Hezekiah destroyed **the bronze snake that Moses made** centuries before (see Num

21:8-9), which **was called Nehushtan**, meaning "A Bronze Thing." How sad that this object which God had used to deliver his people had become a thing of worship!
18:7-8 As Hezekiah looked to God as his source of deliverance, God helped him.
18:13 Sennacherib was the successor to Shalmaneser, who had conquered Israel. Soon God would circle the Assyrians around

Jerusalem itself to test Hezekiah's faith and to demonstrate his own mighty power to his people.
18:17 Either Hezekiah's ransom described in verses 15-16 wasn't enough for Sennacherib or he was looking for a pretext to attack Jerusalem and complete his conquest of Judah anyway.

a 18:19-37 Is 36:4-22
b 18:19 2Kg 18:5; 2Ch 32:10
c 18:20 2Kg 18:7
d 18:21 Is 30:2-3,7
e Ezk 29:6-7
f 18:22 2Kg 18:4; 2Ch 31:1; 32:11-12
g 18:24 Is 10:8
h 18:25 2Kg 19:6,22; 24:3; 2Ch 35:21
i 18:26 Ezr 4:7; Dn 2:4
j 18:26-27 Is 36:11-12

k 18:29 2Kg 19:10
l 2Ch 32:15
m 18:30 2Ch 32:18
n 18:31 1Kg 4:25
o 18:32 Dt 8:7-9; 11:12
p Dt 30:19
q 18:33 2Kg 9:12; Is 10:10-11
r 18:34 2Kg 17:24; 19:13
s 18:35 2Ch 32:14; Ps 2:1-4; Dn 3:15
t 18:37 2Kg 18:26; 19:2
u 2Kg 6:30; Is 33:7
v 19:1 1Kg 21:27; 2Kg 18:37; Ps 69:11
w 2Ch 32:20; Is 37:1

THE ROYAL SPOKESMAN'S SPEECH

19 Then[a] the royal spokesman said to them, "Tell Hezekiah this is what the great king, the king of Assyria, says: 'What are you relying on?[A,b] **20** You think mere words are strategy and strength for war. Who are you now relying on so that you have rebelled against me?[c] **21** Now look, you are relying on Egypt, that splintered reed of a staff[d] that will pierce the hand of anyone who grabs it and leans on it.[e] This is what Pharaoh king of Egypt is to all who rely on him. **22** Suppose you say to me, "We rely on the LORD our God." Isn't he the one whose high places and altars Hezekiah has removed,[f] saying to Judah and to Jerusalem, "You must worship at this altar in Jerusalem"?'

23 "So now, make a bargain with my master the king of Assyria. I'll give you two thousand horses if you're able to supply riders for them! **24** How then can you drive back a single officer[g] among the least of my master's servants? How can you rely on Egypt for chariots and for horsemen? **25** Now, have I attacked this place to destroy it without the LORD's approval?[h] The LORD said to me, 'Attack this land and destroy it.'"

26 Then Eliakim son of Hilkiah, Shebnah, and Joah said to the royal spokesman, "Please speak to your servants in Aramaic,[i] since we understand it. Don't speak with us in Hebrew[B] within earshot of the people on the wall."

27 But the royal spokesman said to them, "Has my master sent me to speak these words only to your master and to you? Hasn't he also sent me to the men who sit on the wall, destined with you to eat their own excrement and drink their own urine?"[j]

28 The royal spokesman stood and called out loudly in Hebrew: "Hear the word of the great king, the king of Assyria. **29** This is what the king says: 'Don't let Hezekiah deceive[k] you; he can't rescue you from my power.[l] **30** Don't let Hezekiah persuade you to rely on the LORD by saying, "Certainly the LORD will rescue us! This city will not be handed over to the king of Assyria."'[m]

31 "Don't listen to Hezekiah, for this is what the king of Assyria says: 'Make peace[c] with me and surrender to me. Then each of you may eat from his own vine and his own fig tree,[n] and each may drink water from his own cistern **32** until I come and take you away to a land like your own land — a land of grain and new wine, a land of bread and vineyards, a land of olive trees and honey[o] — so that you may live[p] and not die. But don't listen to Hezekiah when he misleads you, saying, "The LORD will rescue us." **33** Has any of the gods of the nations ever rescued[q] his land from the power of the king of Assyria? **34** Where are the gods of Hamath and Arpad? Where are the gods of Sepharvaim, Hena, and Ivvah?[D] Have they rescued Samaria from my power?[r] **35** Who among all the gods of the lands has rescued his land from my power? So will the LORD rescue Jerusalem from my power?'"[s]

36 But the people kept silent; they did not answer him at all, for the king's command was, "Don't answer him." **37** Then Eliakim son of Hilkiah, who was in charge of the palace, Shebna the court secretary, and Joah son of Asaph, the court historian,[t] came to Hezekiah with their clothes torn[u] and reported to him the words of the royal spokesman.

HEZEKIAH SEEKS ISAIAH'S COUNSEL

19 When King Hezekiah heard their report, he tore his clothes, covered himself with sackcloth,[v] and went into the LORD's temple.[w] **2** He sent Eliakim, who was

---

A 18:19 Lit *'What is this trust which you trust*   **B** 18:26 Lit *Judahite*, also in v. 28   **C** 18:31 Lit *a blessing*   **D** 18:34 Some LXX mss, Old Lat read *Sepharvaim? Where are the gods of the land of Samaria?*

18:19-25 In 18:26 we learn that there were citizens gathered "on the wall," listening in on this conversation between the enemy king's **royal spokesman** and Hezekiah's men (18:19). The former made what he thought was a slam-dunk case for Hezekiah and his people to open their gates and surrender, essentially claiming, "Hey, your God is on my side!" This point was a lie, but to the demoralized people of Jerusalem, it certainly may have looked as if he was right. After all, their northern neighbors had fallen to these same cruel conquerors.

18:26-27 The request made in verse 26 was designed to shield the listeners from the threats. But the Assyrian spokesman wanted everyone to fear his king's ultimatum. He even loudly threatened them in Hebrew in the most repulsive way imaginable (18:27). Given this diatribe, how long would the people of Judah continue to trust their king?

18:31-32 Similarly, Satan tempts believers with offers that sound inviting, but sin never delivers all it promises.

18:33-37 The speech concluded with six rhetorical questions. Their essence was this: **The gods of the nations** had not rescued their followers from **the power of the king of Assyria**. And neither would **the LORD rescue Jerusalem** (18:33-35). Intimidated by this encounter, Hezekiah's men took their report back to the king **with their clothes torn** in distress (18:37).

19:1-2 Surely the king wondered how such a terrible turn of events had happened. After all, he had been faithful to God. He had reformed Judah's worship. He had kept the Lord's commands.

This account, then, is a good reminder that faithfulness to God does not keep you from trials. However, it *does* prepare you to meet them. By living life with a divine perspective, you will be equipped to deal with trouble and suffering; to rely on God in the bad times as you've relied on him in the good. And you will have an opportunity to see God at work.

In spite of his distress, King Hezekiah **went into the LORD's temple** to worship (19:1). He also did what so many of his predecessors

in charge of the palace, Shebna the court secretary,[a] and the leading priests, who were wearing sackcloth,[b] to the prophet Isaiah[c] son of Amoz. **3** They said to him, "This is what Hezekiah says: 'Today is a day of distress, rebuke, and disgrace, for children have come to the point of birth,[d] but there is no strength to deliver them. **4** Perhaps the LORD your God[e] will hear[f] all the words of the royal spokesman, whom his master the king of Assyria sent to mock the living God, and will rebuke[g] him for the words that the LORD your God has heard. Therefore, offer a prayer for the surviving remnant.'"[h]

5 So the servants of King Hezekiah went to Isaiah, **6** who said to them, "Tell your master, 'The LORD says this: Don't be afraid[i] because of the words you have heard, with which the king of Assyria's attendants[j] have blasphemed[k] me. **7** I am about to put a spirit in him, and he will hear a rumor and return to his own land,[l] where I will cause him to fall by the sword.'"[m]

SENNACHERIB'S DEPARTING THREAT

8 When[n] the royal spokesman heard that the king of Assyria had pulled out of Lachish,[o] he left and found him fighting against Libnah.[p] **9** The king had heard concerning King Tirhakah of Cush, "Look, he has set out to fight against you." So he again sent messengers to Hezekiah, saying, **10** "Say this to King Hezekiah of Judah: 'Don't let your God, on whom you rely,[q] deceive you by promising that Jerusalem will not be handed over to the king of Assyria.' **11** Look, you have heard what the kings of Assyria have done to all the countries: They completely destroyed them. Will you be rescued? **12** Did the gods of the nations[s] that my predecessors destroyed rescue them — nations such as Gozan,[t] Haran,[u] Rezeph, and the Edenites[v] in Telassar? **13** Where is the king of Hamath, the king of Arpad, the king of the city of[A] Sepharvaim, Hena, or Ivvah?'"[w]

HEZEKIAH'S PRAYER

14 Hezekiah took[x] the letter[y] from the messengers' hands, read it, then went up to the LORD's temple, and spread it out before the LORD.[z] **15** Then Hezekiah prayed before the LORD:

LORD God of Israel, enthroned between the cherubim,[aa] you are God — you alone — of all the kingdoms of the earth. You made the heavens and the earth.[ab] **16** Listen closely, LORD, and hear; open your eyes, LORD, and see.[ac] Hear the words that Sennacherib has sent to mock the living God.[ad] **17** LORD, it is true that the kings of Assyria have devastated the nations and their lands.[ae] **18** They have thrown their gods into the fire, for they were not gods but made by human hands — wood and stone.[af] So they have destroyed them. **19** Now, LORD our God, please save us from his power so that all the kingdoms of the earth may know that you, LORD, are God — you alone.[ag]

GOD'S ANSWER THROUGH ISAIAH

20 Then[ah] Isaiah son of Amoz sent a message to Hezekiah: "The LORD, the God of Israel says, 'I have heard your prayer[ai] to me about King Sennacherib of Assyria.'[aj] **21** This is the word the LORD has spoken against him:

Virgin Daughter Zion[ak]
despises you and scorns you;
Daughter Jerusalem
shakes her head behind your back.[al]
22 Who is it you mocked
and blasphemed?[am]
Against whom have you raised
your voice
and lifted your eyes in pride?
Against the Holy One of Israel![an]
23 You have mocked the Lord[B] through[C]
your messengers.[ao]
You have said, 'With my many chariots[ap]
I have gone up to the heights
of the mountains,
to the far recesses of Lebanon.
I cut down its tallest cedars,

[a] 19:2 2Kg 18:26,37
[b] 2Sm 3:31
[c] Is 1:1; 2:1
[d] 19:3 Hs 13:13
[e] 19:4 1Sm 17:26; 2Kg 18:35
[f] Jos 14:12; 2Sm 16:12
[g] Ps 50:21
[h] 2Kg 19:30; Is 1:9
[i] 19:6 Is 37:6
[j] 2Kg 18:17
[k] 2Kg 18:22-25,30,35
[l] 19:7 2Kg 7:6
[m] 2Kg 19:35-37
[n] 19:8-13 Is 37:8-13
[o] 19:8 2Kg 18:14
[p] Jos 10:29
[q] 19:10 2Kg 18:5
[r] 2Kg 18:29-30
[s] 19:12 2Kg 18:33,35
[t] 2Kg 17:6
[u] Gn 11:31
[v] Is 37:12
[w] 19:13 2Kg 18:34

[x] 19:14-19 Is 37:14-20
[y] 19:14 2Kg 5:7
[z] Is 37:14
[aa] 19:15 Ex 25:22
[ab] 19:15 Gn 1:1; 2Kg 5:15; Is 44:6
[ac] 19:16 Dn 9:18
[ad] 2Kg 19:4; Ps 31:2; Is 37:17
[ae] 19:17 2Kg 18:34
[af] 19:18 Is 44:9-20; Jr 10:3-5; Ac 17:29
[ag] 19:19 1Kg 8:42-43; Is 43:10-11
[ah] 19:20-34 Is 37:21-35
[ai] 19:20 2Kg 20:5
[aj] Is 37:21
[ak] 19:21 Jr 14:17; Lm 2:13
[al] Ps 22:7-8; 109:25; Mt 27:39
[am] 19:22 2Kg 19:4,6
[an] Is 5:24; 30:11-15; Jr 51:5
[ao] 19:23 2Kg 18:17; 19:4
[ap] Ps 20:7; Jr 50:37

[A] 19:13 Or *king of Lair,*   [B] 19:23 Many mss read LORD   [C] 19:23 Lit *by the hand of*

---

had not. He sought a word from the Lord by sending a delegation to **Isaiah** the prophet (19:2).

19:6 Don't be afraid is repeated often in Scripture. It's God's way of calming his people, filling them with confidence, and assuring them, "I have everything under control. You can trust me." Not only had the Lord heard the blasphemous words of the Assyrian king's lackey, but he also planned to do something about them.

19:8 Sennacherib's **royal spokesman** was probably camped at the walls of Jerusalem waiting for an answer from Hezekiah when a report came that the king had **pulled** his army **out of Lachish** and was fighting at **Libnah,** twenty-five miles southwest of Jerusalem. **19:15-19** Hezekiah saw Sennacherib's letter as an attack on God's character (19:16), and he pleaded with God to vindicate himself and his people (19:19). Hezekiah was reminding him that answering his prayer would bring

God great glory. This prayer is a model for believers in distress.

19:21-28 This poetic response ridicules Sennacherib and exalts God's sovereign rule over the nations. Though the man credited himself for his victories, the bigheaded Assyrian king was just a pawn on God's kingdom chessboard. Sennacherib couldn't even make a move or have a private thought that God didn't know about. His personal judgment day was coming (19:27-28).

[a] 19:24 Is 19:6
[b] 19:25 Is 40:21; 45:7
[c] Is 10:5
[d] 19:26 Ps 129:6
[e] 19:27 Ps 139:1-2
[f] 19:28 Ezk 19:9; 29:4; 38:4
[g] 19:29 Ex 3:14; 2Kg 20:8-9; Is 7:14
[h] 19:30 2Kg 19:4; 2Ch 32:22-23
[i] 19:31 Is 10:20
[j] Is 9:7
[k] 19:32 Is 8:7-10
[l] 19:34 1Kg 11:12-13; 2Kg 20:6; Is 31:5
[m] 19:35 2Ch 32:21; Is 37:36
[n] 19:36 Jnh 1:2
[o] 19:37 2Kg 17:31
[p] Gn 8:4; Jr 51:27
[q] Gn 10:11; Ezr 4:2
[r] 20:1-11 Is 38:1-8
[s] 20:1 2Ch 32:24
[t] Is 1:1; 2:1
[u] 2Sm 17:23
[v] 20:2 1Kg 21:4
[w] 20:3 Neh 5:19; 13:14,22,31
[x] 2Kg 18:3-6
[y] 2Sm 12:21-22
[z] 20:5 1Sm 9:16; 10:1

its choice cypress trees.
I came to its farthest outpost,
its densest forest.
24 I dug wells
and drank water in foreign lands.
I dried up all the streams of Egypt[a]
with the soles of my feet.'

25 Have you not heard?[b]
I designed it long ago;
I planned it in days gone by.
I have now brought it to pass,[c]
and you have crushed fortified cities
into piles of rubble.
26 Their inhabitants have
become powerless,
dismayed, and ashamed.
They are plants of the field,
tender grass,
grass on the rooftops,[d]
blasted by the east wind.[A]

27 But I know your sitting down,[e]
your going out and your coming in,
and your raging against me.
28 Because your raging against me
and your arrogance have reached
my ears,
I will put my hook in your nose[f]
and my bit in your mouth;
I will make you go back
the way you came.

29 "This will be the sign[g] for you: This year
you will eat what grows on its own, and in
the second year what grows from that. But
in the third year sow and reap, plant vineyards and eat their fruit. 30 The surviving
remnant[h] of the house of Judah will again
take root downward and bear fruit upward.
31 For a remnant will go out from Jerusalem,
and survivors, from Mount Zion.[i] The zeal
of the LORD of Armies will accomplish this.[j]
32 Therefore, this is what the LORD says
about the king of Assyria:
He will not enter this city,
shoot an arrow here,
come before it with a shield,
or build up a siege ramp against it.[k]
33 He will go back
the way he came,
and he will not enter this city.
This is the LORD's declaration.
34 I will defend this city and rescue it
for my sake and for the sake of my
servant David."[l]

HOPE WORDS

You will know God is showing up when he shows up in a way that you can't explain.

DEFEAT AND DEATH OF SENNACHERIB

35 That night the angel of the LORD went out
and struck down one hundred eighty-five
thousand in the camp of the Assyrians.
When the people got up the next morning
— there were all the dead bodies![m] 36 So
King Sennacherib of Assyria broke camp
and left. He returned home and lived in
Nineveh.[n]
37 One day, while he was worshiping in
the temple of his god Nisroch, his sons
Adrammelech[o] and Sharezer struck him
down with the sword and escaped to the
land of Ararat.[p] Then his son Esar-haddon[q]
became king in his place.

HEZEKIAH'S ILLNESS AND RECOVERY

20 In those days[r] Hezekiah became
terminally ill.[s] The prophet Isaiah[t]
son of Amoz came and said to him, "This
is what the LORD says: 'Set your house in
order, for you are about to die; you will not
recover.'"[u]
2 Then Hezekiah turned his face to the
wall[v] and prayed to the LORD, 3 "Please,
LORD, remember[w] how I have walked before you faithfully and wholeheartedly
and have done what pleases you."[B,x] And
Hezekiah wept bitterly.[y]
4 Isaiah had not yet gone out of the inner courtyard when the word of the LORD
came to him: 5 "Go back and tell Hezekiah,
the leader[z] of my people, 'This is what the

[A] 19:26 DSS; MT reads *blasted before standing grain*; Is 37:27 [B] 20:3 Lit *what is good in your eyes*

19:29-31 God gave an apt word of comfort to a king and people facing a seemingly unavoidable siege and starvation.
19:37 The Assyrian king had ridiculed the Lord for being unable to protect Jerusalem. But, in the end, it was Sennacherib's god who was unable to protect his devoted follower—even in his own temple.
20:1-3 Sometimes biblical authors do not put events in chronological order. Rather, they order events in their narratives to fit their purposes. It's likely that the account of Hezekiah's illness (20:1-21) actually happened before the account of Sennacherib's invasion (18:13–19:37; see 20:6; Isa 38:6).
20:5 God does not lie (see Num 23:19), and he does not change (see Mal 3:6). Yet he *is* relational. His declaration of death for Hezekiah in verse 1 was real. But God is free to change—not in his character or in his ultimate purposes—but with regard to his actions within his purposes. When God threatens judgment on sin, he is free to show mercy and grace in response to repentance (see Jonah 3:4-10). When he proclaims his intent to do something—sometimes as a test of faith—he is free to alter his actions in response to prayer (see Exod 32:11-14) or obedience (see Gen 22:1-18) because people have adjusted their relationship to him.

LORD God of your ancestor David says: I have heard your prayer;[a] I have seen your tears. Look, I will heal you. On the third day from now you will go up to the LORD's temple. [6] I will add fifteen years to your life. I will rescue you and this city from the grasp of the king of Assyria. I will defend this city for my sake and for the sake of my servant David.'[b]

[7] Then Isaiah said, "Bring a lump of pressed figs." So they brought it and applied it to his infected skin, and he recovered.[c]

[8] Hezekiah had asked Isaiah, "What is the sign[d] that the LORD will heal me and that I will go up to the LORD's temple on the third day?"

[9] Isaiah said, "This is the sign[e] to you from the LORD that he will do what he has promised: Should the shadow go ahead ten steps or go back ten steps?"

[10] Then Hezekiah answered, "It's easy for the shadow to lengthen ten steps. No, let the shadow go back ten steps." [11] So the prophet Isaiah called out to the LORD, and he brought the shadow[A] back the ten steps it had descended on the stairway of Ahaz.[B,f]

HEZEKIAH'S FOLLY

[12] At that time[g] Merodach-baladan[c] son of Baladan, king of Babylon, sent letters and a gift to Hezekiah since he heard that he had been sick. [13] Hezekiah listened to the letters and showed the envoys his whole treasure house — the silver, the gold, the spices, and the precious oil — and his armory, and everything that was found in his treasuries. There was nothing in his palace and in all his realm that Hezekiah did not show them.[h]

[14] Then the prophet Isaiah came to King Hezekiah and asked him, "Where did these men come from and what did they say to you?"

Hezekiah replied, "They came from a distant country, from Babylon."

[15] Isaiah asked, "What have they seen in your palace?"

Hezekiah answered, "They have seen everything in my palace. There isn't anything in my treasuries that I didn't show them."

[16] Then Isaiah said to Hezekiah, "Hear the word of the LORD: [17] 'Look, the days are coming when everything in your palace and all that your fathers have stored up until today will be carried off to Babylon; nothing will be left,'[i] says the LORD. [18] 'Some of your descendants — who come from you, whom you father — will be taken away,[j] and they will become eunuchs[D] in the palace of the king of Babylon.'"[k]

[19] Then Hezekiah said to Isaiah, "The word of the LORD that you have spoken is good,"[l] for he thought: Why not, if there will be peace and security during my lifetime?

HEZEKIAH'S DEATH

[20] The rest of the events of Hezekiah's reign, along with all his might and how he made the pool[m] and the tunnel and brought water into the city,[n] are written in the Historical Record of Judah's Kings.[o] [21] Hezekiah rested with his fathers, and his son Manasseh became king in his place.[p]

JUDAH'S KING MANASSEH

21 Manasseh[q] was twelve years old when he became king, and he reigned fifty-five years in Jerusalem. His mother's name was Hephzibah.[r] [2] He did what was evil in the LORD's sight,[s] imitating the detestable practices of the nations that the LORD had dispossessed before the Israelites.[t] [3] He rebuilt the high places that his father Hezekiah had destroyed[u] and reestablished the altars for Baal. He made an Asherah,[v] as King Ahab of Israel had done;[w] he also bowed in worship to all the stars in the sky[x] and served them. [4] He built altars in the LORD's temple,[y] where the LORD had said, "Jerusalem is where I will put my name."[z] [5] He built altars to all the stars in the sky[aa] in both courtyards of the LORD's temple.[ab] [6] He sacrificed his son in the fire,[E,ac] practiced witchcraft and divination, and consulted mediums and spiritists.[ad] He did a huge amount of evil in the LORD's sight, angering him.[ae]

[7] Manasseh set up the carved image of Asherah, which he made, in the temple

[a] 20:5 Ps 39:12
[b] 20:6 2Kg 19:34
[c] 20:7 Is 38:21
[d] 20:8 Jdg 6:17,37,39
[e] 20:9 Is 38:7
[f] 20:11 Jos 10:12-14; Is 38:8
[g] 20:12-19 Is 39:1-8
[h] 20:13 2Ch 32:27

[i] 20:17 2Kg 24:13; 2Ch 36:10
[j] 20:18 2Kg 24:12; 2Ch 33:11
[k] Dn 1:3-7,11
[l] 20:19 1Sm 3:18; 2Kg 22:20
[m] 20:20 Neh 3:16; Is 7:3
[n] 2Ch 32:30
[o] 2Kg 16:19
[p] 20:20-21 2Ch 32:32-33
[q] 21:1-9 2Ch 33:1-9
[r] 21:1 Is 62:4
[s] 21:2 2Kg 20:16; Jr 15:4
[t] 2Kg 16:3
[u] 21:3 2Kg 18:4; 2Ch 31:1
[v] 2Kg 23:26
[w] 1Kg 16:32-33
[x] 2Kg 17:16; 23:5
[y] 21:4 2Kg 16:10-16
[z] Dt 12:11,14; 1Kg 11:13
[aa] 21:5 2Kg 23:4-5
[ab] 1Kg 7:12; 2Kg 23:12
[ac] 21:6 Lv 18:21; 2Kg 16:3; 2Ch 28:3
[ad] Lv 19:26,31; Dt 18:10-12; 2Kg 23:24
[ae] 2Kg 23:26

[A] 20:11 Lit shadow on the steps   [B] 20:11 Tg, Vg; DSS read on the steps of Ahaz's roof chamber; Is 38:8   [C] 20:12 Some Hb mss, LXX, Syr, Tg, some Vg mss, Is 39:1; other Hb mss read Berodach-baladan   [D] 20:18 Or court officials   [E] 21:6 Lit He made his son pass through the fire

20:7 Isaiah commanded that a medicinal **lump of pressed figs** be **applied** to the king's infection in order to draw out the poison. This tells us that prayer, medication, and the word of God worked together to bring about healing. 20:12-13 Assyria was the world power at this time, and (like Judah) Babylon was feeling the pressure. The **gift** sent to congratulate Hezekiah was probably an effort to secure his support in an alliance against Assyria (20:12). This visit was likely prior to the threatened Assyrian invasion since Hezekiah's **treasuries** that he showed to the Babylonians were full (20:13; see the note on 20:1-3). When Sennacherib threatened Jerusalem, Hezekiah emptied them to keep the city safe (see 18:15-16). 20:17-18 Judah's impending Babylonian captivity was over one hundred years in the future. 21:1-2 **Manasseh** was an Israelite physically, but he was a Canaanite spiritually.

a 21:7 Dt 12:5; 1Kg 11:32
b 21:8 2Sm 7:10; 1Kg 9:1-9
c 21:9 1Kg 14:9
d 21:11 2Kg 21:2; 24:3-4
e Gn 15:16; 1Kg 21:16
f 21:12 1Sm 3:11; Jr 19:3
g 21:13 Is 34:11; Am 7:7-8
h 2Kg 23:27
i 21:14 2Kg 19:4; Jr 6:9
j 21:15 Ex 32:22; Jr 25:7
k 21:16 2Kg 24:4
l 21:17-18 2Ch 33:18-20

m 21:17 2Kg 20:20
n 21:19-24 2Ch 33:21-25
o 21:20 2Kg 21:2-7,11,16
p 21:21 2Kg 16:2
q 21:22 1Kg 11:33
r 2Kg 22:17
s 21:23 2Kg 12:20; 14:19
t 21:24 2Kg 14:5
u 2Kg 22:1
v 22:1-2 2Ch 34:1-2
w 22:1 Jos 15:39
x 22:2 1Kg 14:8
y Dt 5:32; Jos 1:7

that the LORD had spoken about to David and his son Solomon: "I will establish my name forever in this temple and in Jerusalem, which I have chosen out of all the tribes of Israel.*a* *8* I will never again cause the feet of the Israelites to wander from the land I gave to their ancestors if only they will be careful to do all I have commanded them — the whole law that my servant Moses commanded them."*b* *9* But they did not listen; Manasseh caused them to stray so that they did worse evil than the nations the LORD had destroyed before the Israelites.*c*

10 The LORD said through his servants the prophets, *11* "Since King Manasseh of Judah has committed all these detestable acts*d* — worse evil than the Amorites*e* who preceded him had done — and by means of his idols has also caused Judah to sin, *12* this is what the LORD God of Israel says: 'I am about to bring such disaster on Jerusalem and Judah that everyone who hears about it will shudder.*A,f* *13* I will stretch over Jerusalem the measuring line used on Samaria and the mason's level used on the house of Ahab,*g* and I will wipe*h* Jerusalem clean as one wipes a bowl — wiping it and turning it upside down. *14* I will abandon the remnant*i* of my inheritance and hand them over to their enemies. They will become plunder and spoil to all their enemies, *15* because they have done what is evil in my sight and have angered me from the day their ancestors came out of Egypt until today.'"*j* *16* Manasseh also shed so much innocent blood that he filled Jerusalem with it from one end to another.*k* This was in addition to his sin that he caused Judah to commit, so that they did what was evil in the LORD's sight.

MANASSEH'S DEATH

17 The rest*l* of the events of Manasseh's reign, along with all his accomplishments

and the sin that he committed, are written in the Historical Record of Judah's Kings.*m* *18* Manasseh rested with his fathers and was buried in the garden of his own house, the garden of Uzza. His son Amon became king in his place.

JUDAH'S KING AMON

19 Amon was twenty-two years old when he became king,*n* and he reigned two years in Jerusalem. His mother's name was Meshullemeth daughter of Haruz; she was from Jotbah. *20* He did what was evil in the LORD's sight, just as his father Manasseh had done.*o* *21* He walked in all the ways his father had walked; he served the idols his father had served, and he bowed in worship to them.*p* *22* He abandoned the LORD God of his ancestors*q* and did not walk in the ways of the LORD.*r*

23 Amon's servants conspired against him and put the king to death in his own house.*s* *24* The common people*B* killed*t* all who had conspired against King Amon, and they made his son Josiah*u* king in his place.

25 The rest of the events of Amon's reign, along with his accomplishments, are written in the Historical Record of Judah's Kings. *26* He was buried in his tomb in the garden of Uzza, and his son Josiah became king in his place.

JUDAH'S KING JOSIAH

22 Josiah*v* was eight years old when he became king, and he reigned thirty-one years in Jerusalem. His mother's name was Jedidah the daughter of Adaiah; she was from Bozkath.*w* *2* He did what was right in the LORD's sight and walked in all the ways of his ancestor David;*x* he did not turn to the right or the left.*y*

JOSIAH REPAIRS THE TEMPLE

3 In the eighteenth year of King Josiah, the king sent the court secretary Shaphan son

A 21:12 Lit *about it, his two ears will tingle*; Hb obscure　　*B* 21:24 Lit *The people of the land*

21:10-11 One of **the prophets** who delivered this message of judgment may have been Isaiah, who, according to Jewish tradition, was sawn in two under Manasseh's orders (21:10; see Heb 11:37 for a possible reference to this incident). Comparing Manasseh's evil to that of **the Amorites** (2 Kgs 21:11) was one way of putting it in context, since they were one of the most morally deficient people groups of Joshua's day. 21:12 Importantly, the people of **Jerusalem** in particular thought themselves bulletproof. Why? Because they lived in God's holy city with his holy temple in their midst. They were

confident he would never allow an enemy to destroy it.
21:13 God's word of doom on Judah included two names—references that would have made even the smuggest resident of Jerusalem break out in a cold sweat. He was **measuring** Jerusalem for the same kind of disaster that befell **Samaria** (Israel's capital), and he was using **the mason's level** to draw a straight line of destruction on Manasseh the way he did on the house of **Ahab**.
21:16 The **innocent blood that** Manasseh spilled certainly included his child sacrifices,

but it also possibly included the innocent people he may have eliminated to hold on to power.
22:1 **Josiah** obviously needed the help of advisers in his early years.
22:2 The statement that Josiah, son of the wicked Amon, **did what was right in the LORD's sight** and was worthy of comparison with **David** is a testimony to God's grace. You are not condemned to follow in the footsteps of unfaithful parents either.
22:3-7 The temple in Jerusalem had been desecrated by the idolatrous altars and images that Manasseh had placed in it. The procedure

of Azaliah, son of Meshullam, to the LORD's temple,[a] saying, **4** "Go up to the high priest Hilkiah so that he may total up the silver brought into the LORD's temple — the silver the doorkeepers have collected from the people.[b] **5** It is to be given to those doing the work — those who oversee the LORD's temple. They in turn are to give it to the workmen in the LORD's temple to repair the damage.[c] **6** They are to give it to the carpenters, builders, and masons to buy timber and quarried stone to repair the temple.[d] **7** But no accounting is to be required from them for the silver given to them since they work with integrity."[e]

THE BOOK OF THE LAW FOUND

8 The high priest Hilkiah told the court secretary Shaphan, "I have found the book of the law[f] in the LORD's temple," and he gave the book to Shaphan, who read it.

9 Then the court secretary Shaphan went to the king and reported,[A] "Your servants have emptied out the silver that was found in the temple and have given it to those doing the work — those who oversee the LORD's temple." **10** Then the court secretary Shaphan told the king, "The priest Hilkiah has given me a book," and Shaphan read it in the presence of the king.[g]

11 When the king heard the words of the book of the law, he tore his clothes.[h] **12** Then he commanded the priest Hilkiah, Ahikam[i] son of Shaphan, Achbor[j] son of Micaiah, the court secretary Shaphan, and the king's servant Asaiah: **13** "Go and inquire of the LORD for me, the people, and all Judah about the words in this book that has been found. For great is the LORD's wrath that is kindled against us because our ancestors have not obeyed the words of this book in order to do everything written about us."[k]

HULDAH'S PROPHECY OF JUDGMENT

14 So[l] the priest Hilkiah, Ahikam, Achbor, Shaphan, and Asaiah went to the prophetess[m] Huldah, wife of Shallum son of

Tikvah,[n] son of Harhas, keeper of the wardrobe. She lived in Jerusalem in the Second District.[o] They spoke with her.

15 She said to them, "This is what the LORD God of Israel says: Say to the man who sent you to me, **16** 'This is what the LORD says: I am about to bring disaster on this place and on its inhabitants, fulfilling[B] all the words of the book that the king of Judah has read,[p] **17** because they have abandoned me and burned incense to other gods in order to anger me with all the work of their hands. My wrath will be kindled against this place, and it will not be quenched.'[q] **18** Say this to the king of Judah who sent you to inquire of the LORD: 'This is what the LORD God of Israel says: As for the words that you heard,[r] **19** because your heart was tender and you humbled yourself before the LORD[s] when you heard what I spoke against this place and against its inhabitants, that they would become a desolation and a curse,[t] and because you have torn your clothes and wept before me, I myself have heard' — this is the LORD's declaration. **20** 'Therefore, I will indeed gather you to your fathers, and you will be gathered to your grave in peace.[u] Your eyes will not see all the disaster that I am bringing on this place.'"

Then they reported[c] to the king.

COVENANT RENEWAL

23 So the king sent messengers,[v] and they gathered all the elders[w] of Judah and Jerusalem to him. **2** Then the king went to the LORD's temple with all the men of Judah and all the inhabitants of Jerusalem, as well as the priests and the prophets — all the people from the youngest to the oldest. He read in their hearing all the words of the book of the covenant[x] that had been found in the LORD's temple.[y] **3** Next, the king stood by the pillar[D,z] and made a covenant[aa] in the LORD's presence to follow the LORD and to keep his commands, his decrees, and his statutes with

[a] 22:3 2Ch 34:8
[b] 22:4 2Kg 12:4,9-10
[c] 22:5 2Kg 12:5
[d] 22:6 2Kg 12:11-12
[e] 22:7 2Kg 12:15; 1Co 4:2
[f] 22:8 Dt 31:24-26; 2Ch 34:14-15
[g] 22:10 Dt 17:18-20
[h] 22:11 Gn 37:34; Jos 7:6
[i] 22:12 2Kg 25:22; Jr 26:24
[j] 2Ch 34:20
[k] 22:13 Dt 29:24-28; 31:17-18
[l] 22:14-20 2Ch 34:22-28
[m] 22:14 Ex 15:20

[n] 22:14 2Ch 34:22
[o] Zph 1:10
[p] 22:16 Dt 29:27; Dn 9:11-14
[q] 22:17 Dt 29:25-26; 1Kg 9:9
[r] 22:18 2Ch 34:26
[s] 22:19 1Sm 24:5; 1Kg 21:29
[t] Dt 28:15; Jr 26:6
[u] 22:20 2Kg 20:19; 23:30
[v] 23:1 2Ch 34:29-32
[w] 2Kg 10:1
[x] 23:2 Dt 31:10-13
[y] 2Kg 22:8
[z] 23:3 1Kg 7:15; 2Kg 11:14
[aa] 2Kg 11:17

[A] **22:9** Lit *and returned a word to the king and said*   [B] **22:16** *fulfilling* supplied for clarity   [C] **22:20** Lit *returned a word*   [D] **23:3** 2Ch 34:31 reads *platform*

---

described here is very similar to that used by an earlier reformer (King Joash; see 12:1-16) in that the priests collected the money and gave it to **the workmen . . . to repair the damage** (22:5). Like their earlier counterparts, these workers did the work **with integrity** (22:7).
22:8 This could have been a copy of the entire Pentateuch (that is, the first five books of the Bible). Evidently Manasseh had made sure the Word of God would not be available to mess up his program of idolatry, and he may have destroyed any other copies.

22:11 The immediate, earnest response of grief by the king suggests that the law was not part of Judah's life and worship for a long time. This is what it looks like when God's Word delivers its convicting power.
22:18-20 The Lord's word to Josiah personally was one of mercy. For his **tender** heart and humility, and his tears of repentance on behalf of himself and his people, Josiah would be spared the coming **disaster** that God would bring on Judah in the form of the Babylonian captivity (22:19-20). (Josiah

would die in 609 BC, just four years before Nebuchadnezzar's first invasion of Judah.)
23:1-3 When Josiah learned God wouldn't bring his judgment on Judah during his reign, the young king could have simply said, "Whew," and returned to business as usual. Instead, Josiah was rightly zealous in his desire to please and glorify the Lord. Josiah was not managing his own kingdom; he was managing *God's* kingdom. So he wasn't about to be negligent with regard to an opportunity he saw. Chapter 23 essentially records how Josiah rolled up his

a 23:3 Dt 6:4-6; 13:4
b Ex 24:3-8; Jos 24:14-28
c 23:4 2Kg 22:8,14
d 2Kg 25:18; Jr 35:4; 52:24
e 2Kg 21:3,7; 2Ch 33:3
f 2Kg 23:15
g 23:5 2Kg 16:4
h 2Kg 21:3
i 23:6 1Kg 14:15,23; 2Kg 18:4; 21:7
j 1Kg 15:13
k 2Kg 23:15
l 2Ch 34:4; Jr 26:23
m 23:7 Dt 23:17; 1Kg 14:24; 15:12
n Ex 38:8; Ezk 16:16
o 23:8 2Kg 18:4
p Jos 21:17; 1Kg 15:22
q 1Sm 3:20
r 23:9 Ezk 44:10-14
s 23:10 Is 30:33; Jr 7:31-32
t Jos 15:8
u Lv 18:21; 20:2-5
v 1Kg 11:7; Jr 32:35

w 23:11 Dt 4:19; Ezk 8:16
x 23:12 Jr 19:13; Zph 1:4-5
y 2Kg 20:11
z 2Kg 21:5; 2Ch 33:5
aa 23:13 1Kg 11:5-8
ab 23:14 Ex 23:24
ac 2Kg 18:4
ad 23:15 1Kg 13:1-3
ae 1Kg 12:28-33
af 2Kg 23:6
ag 23:16 2Ch 34:5
ah 1Kg 13:2
ai 23:17 1Kg 13:1,31-32
aj 23:18 1Kg 13:29-31
ak 23:19 2Ch 34:6-7

all his heart and with all his soul*a* in order to carry out the words of this covenant that were written in this book; all the people agreed to*A* the covenant.*b*

JOSIAH'S REFORMS

4 Then the king commanded the high priest Hilkiah*c* and the priests of the second rank*d* and the doorkeepers to bring out of the LORD's sanctuary all the articles made for Baal, Asherah, and all the stars in the sky.*e* He burned them outside Jerusalem in the fields of the Kidron and carried their ashes to Bethel.*f* **5** Then he did away with the idolatrous priests the kings of Judah had appointed to burn incense at the high places*g* in the cities of Judah and in the areas surrounding Jerusalem. They had burned incense to Baal, and to the sun, moon, constellations, and all the stars in the sky.*h* **6** He brought out the Asherah pole*i* from the LORD's temple to the Kidron Valley outside Jerusalem. He burned it at the Kidron Valley,*j* beat it to dust,*k* and threw its dust on the graves of the common people.*B,l* **7** He also tore down the houses of the male cult prostitutes*m* that were in the LORD's temple, in which the women were weaving tapestries*C* for Asherah.*n*

8 Then Josiah brought all the priests from the cities of Judah, and he defiled the high places*o* from Geba*p* to Beer-sheba,*q* where the priests had burned incense. He tore down the high places of the city gates at the entrance of the gate of Joshua the governor of the city (on the left at the city gate). **9** The priests of the high places, however, did not come up to the altar of the LORD in Jerusalem; instead, they ate unleavened bread with their fellow priests.*r*

10 He defiled Topheth,*s* which is in Ben Hinnom Valley,*t* so that no one could sacrifice his son or daughter in the fire*D,u* to Molech.*v* **11** He did away with the horses that the kings of Judah had dedicated to

the sun. They had been at the entrance of the LORD's temple in the precincts by the chamber of Nathan-melech, the eunuch. He also burned the chariots of the sun.*w* **12** The king tore down the altars that the kings of Judah had made on the roof*x* of Ahaz's upper chamber.*y* He also tore down the altars that Manasseh had made*z* in the two courtyards of the LORD's temple. Then he smashed them*E* there and threw their dust into the Kidron Valley. **13** The king also defiled the high places that were across from Jerusalem, to the south of the Mount of Destruction, which King Solomon of Israel had built for Ashtoreth, the abhorrent idol of the Sidonians; for Chemosh, the abhorrent idol of Moab; and for Milcom, the detestable idol of the Ammonites.*aa* **14** He broke the sacred pillars into pieces,*ab* cut down the Asherah poles,*ac* then filled their places with human bones.

15 He even tore down the altar at Bethel*ad* and the high place*ae* that had been made by Jeroboam son of Nebat, who caused Israel to sin. He burned the high place, crushed it to dust, and burned the Asherah.*af* **16** As Josiah turned, he saw the tombs there on the mountain. He sent someone to take the bones out of the tombs, and he burned them on the altar.*ag* He defiled it according to the word of the LORD proclaimed by the man of God*F* who proclaimed these things.*ah* **17** Then he said, "What is this monument I see?"

The men of the city told him, "It is the tomb of the man of God who came from Judah and proclaimed these things that you have done to the altar at Bethel."*ai*

18 So he said, "Let him rest. Don't let anyone disturb his bones." So they left his bones undisturbed with the bones of the prophet who came from Samaria.*aj*

19 Josiah also removed all the shrines of the high places that were in the cities of Samaria, which the kings of Israel had made to anger the LORD.*ak* Josiah did the

---

A 23:3 Lit *people took a stand in*   *B* 23:6 Lit *the sons of the people*   *C* 23:7 Or *clothing*   *D* 23:10 Lit *could make his son or daughter pass through the fire*
E 23:12 Text emended; MT reads *he ran from*   *F* 23:16 LXX adds *when Jeroboam stood by the altar of the feast. And he turned and raised his eyes to the tomb of the man of God*

---

sleeves and set about destroying every vestige of false worship in the vicinity and establishing worship of the true and living God.
23:4 Josiah started his spiritual cleanup campaign in the temple, which his grandfather Manasseh had turned into a shrine to false gods. His efforts are a reminder that when you identify areas of temptation in your life, you are not merely to throw them in a closet or shove them under a rug. You must eradicate them.

23:8 Josiah **defiled the high places from Geba** in the far north of Judah to **Beer-sheba** in the far south. He was a man on a mission.
23:13 The false worship sites Josiah destroyed even included some built centuries before by **King Solomon** after his heart was led astray (see 1 Kgs 11:1-6).
23:15 Josiah went so far as to destroy the idolatry at neighboring **Bethel**, tearing down the **altar** and the **high place** that Israel's King **Jeroboam** had built.

23:16-20 While in Bethel, Josiah saw the **tomb** of the prophet who many years earlier had foretold of him and predicted his future actions (23:17; see 1 Kgs 13:2-3). That Josiah was able to freely move in this region that was part of the Assyrian Empire may suggest how weak Assyria was by this time; it was in the waning years of its power.

same things to them that he had done at Bethel. **20** He slaughtered on the altars all the priests of those high places,[a] and he burned human bones on the altars.[b] Then he returned to Jerusalem.

PASSOVER OBSERVED

21 The king commanded all the people, "Observe the Passover of the LORD your God as written in the book of the covenant."[c] **22** No such Passover had ever been observed from the time of the judges who judged Israel through the entire time of the kings of Israel and Judah. **23** But in the eighteenth year of King Josiah, the LORD's Passover was observed in Jerusalem.[d]

FURTHER ZEAL FOR THE LORD

24 In addition, Josiah eradicated the mediums, the spiritists,[e] household idols,[f] images, and all the abhorrent things[g] that were seen in the land of Judah and in Jerusalem. He did this in order to carry out the words of the law that were written in the book that the priest Hilkiah found in the LORD's temple.[h] **25** Before him there was no king like him who turned to the LORD with all his heart and with all his soul and with all his strength[i] according to all the law of Moses, and no one like him arose after him.[j]

26 In spite of all that, the LORD did not turn from the fury of his intense burning anger, which burned against Judah because of all the affronts with which Manasseh had angered him.[k] **27** For the LORD had said, "I will also remove Judah from my presence just as I have removed Israel.[l] I will reject this city Jerusalem, that I have chosen, and the temple about which I said, 'My name will be there.' "[m]

JOSIAH'S DEATH

28 The rest of the events of Josiah's reign,[n] along with all his accomplishments, are written in the Historical Record of Judah's Kings. **29** During his reign, Pharaoh Neco king of Egypt[o] marched up to help the king of Assyria at the Euphrates River. King Josiah went to confront him, and at Megiddo[p] when Neco saw him he killed him. **30** From Megiddo his servants carried his dead body in a chariot, brought him into Jerusalem, and buried him in his own tomb.[q] Then the common people[A] took Jehoahaz son of Josiah, anointed him, and made him king in place of his father.[r]

JUDAH'S KING JEHOAHAZ

31 Jehoahaz[s] was[t] twenty-three years old when he became king, and he reigned three months in Jerusalem. His mother's name was Hamutal[u] daughter of Jeremiah; she was from Libnah. **32** He did what was evil in the LORD's sight just as his ancestors had done.[v] **33** Pharaoh Neco imprisoned him at Riblah[w] in the land of Hamath[x] to keep him from reigning in Jerusalem, and he imposed on the land a fine of seventy-five hundred pounds[B] of silver and seventy-five pounds[c] of gold.

JUDAH'S KING JEHOIAKIM

34 Then[y] Pharaoh Neco made Eliakim[z] son of Josiah king in place of his father Josiah and changed Eliakim's name to Jehoiakim.[aa] But Neco took Jehoahaz and went to Egypt, and he died there.[ab] **35** So Jehoiakim gave the silver and the gold to Pharaoh, but at Pharaoh's command he taxed the land to give it. He exacted the silver and the gold from the common people, each according to his assessment,[ac] to give it to Pharaoh Neco.

36 Jehoiakim was twenty-five years old when he became king, and he reigned eleven years in Jerusalem. His mother's name was Zebidah daughter of Pedaiah; she was from Rumah. **37** He did what was evil[ad] in the LORD's sight just as his ancestors had done.

[a]23:20 1Kg 12:31; 13:2
[b]2Kg 10:25; 11:18; 2Ch 34:5
[c]23:21 Nm 9:1-14; Dt 16:1-8; 2Ch 35:1-6
[d]23:22-23 2Ch 35:18-19
[e]23:24 Lv 19:31; 2Kg 21:6
[f]Gn 31:19
[g]Dt 7:26; 2Kg 16:3
[h]2Kg 22:8; 23:2-3
[i]23:25 Dt 6:4-9; 2Kg 23:3
[j]1Kg 3:12; 2Kg 18:5
[k]23:26 2Kg 21:11-13; Jr 15:4
[l]23:27 2Kg 18:11-12
[m]Dt 12:11; 1Kg 9:3; 2Kg 21:4
[n]23:28-30 2Ch 35:20-27

[o]23:29 Jr 46:2
[p]Jdg 5:19
[q]23:30 2Kg 9:28
[r]2Ch 36:1
[s]23:31 1Ch 3:15; Jr 22:11
[t]23:31-33 2Ch 36:2-3
[u]23:31 2Kg 24:18
[v]23:32 2Kg 21:2-7
[w]23:33 2Kg 25:6
[x]1Kg 8:65
[y]23:34-37 2Ch 36:4-5
[z]23:34 1Ch 3:15
[aa]2Kg 24:17; 2Ch 36:4
[ab]Jr 22:11-12; Ezk 19:3-4
[ac]23:35 Ex 30:12-16; Lv 27:2-8
[ad]23:37 Jr 22:13-19; 36:1-26

[A]23:30 Lit *the people of the land*, also in v. 35   [B]23:33 Lit *100 talents*   [c]23:33 Lit *one talent*

23:22 The reference here is to a period of five centuries! How sad that God's people had neglected his law for so long, yet how good and right it was for Josiah to lead them in reforming their ways.

23:28-30 Josiah's death was tragic, but it was also part of God's plan in executing his judgment on Judah. He mercifully removed his faithful king from the scene before pouring out his wrath on his unfaithful people (see 22:19-20). Josiah's son **Jehoahaz** (23:30) and the kings who followed him (three of whom were Josiah's sons!)

were hollow shells compared to their godly ancestors.

23:31-32 God wouldn't put up with the first king in this section's hall of shame for very long. "The common people" had made Jehoahaz king (23:30), which could mean they hoped he would continue the good reign of his father. If that was the case, they were sorely disappointed. Jehoahaz immediately reverted to the **evil** of **his ancestors** (23:32), for which he and Judah were **dearly**.

23:33 To the informed reader, the name **Riblah** has an ominous sound; there Nebuchadnezzar

would set up his headquarters during the destruction of Judah, and he would also execute many of the nation's leaders.

23:34-37 Pharaoh Neco put Jehoahaz's older brother **Eliakim** on the throne in Jerusalem and changed his name to **Jehoiakim** (23:34) as a way of showing that he (that is, Pharaoh) was in charge. The **common people** suffered heavily under the taxation needed to pay the tribute Neco demanded, yet Jehoiakim spent **eleven years** doing **evil in the LORD's sight** (23:35-37).

a 24:1-6 2Ch 36:6-8
b 24:1 2Kg 23:26-27
c 2Kg 24:10-11; Dn 1:1
d 2Kg 20:14
e Jr 35:11
f 24:2 2Kg 6:23
g 2Kg 13:20
h 2Kg 23:27
i 24:3 2Kg 18:25
j 2Kg 23:26
k 24:4 2Kg 21:16
l 24:5 2Kg 23:28
m 24:5-6 Jr 22:18-19
n 24:7 Jr 37:5-7
o Jr 46:2
p Gn 15:18; 1Kg 4:21;
   Is 27:12
q 24:8-9 2Ch 36:9; Jr
   22:24-30
r 24:10-17 2Ch 36:10
s 24:10 2Kg 24:1; Dn 1:1
t 24:12 2Kg 25:27; Jr
   22:24-30
u 24:13 1Kg 7:48-50
v 2Kg 20:16-18; Is 39:5-7
w 24:14 Jr 24:1
x Jr 52:28
y Jr 24:1; 29:2
z 2Kg 25:12
aa 24:15 2Ch 36:10; Jr
   22:24-28
ab 24:17 1Ch 3:15; 2Ch
   36:11; Jr 1:3
ac 24:18 Jr 27:1; 28:1
ad 24:18-20 2Ch 36:11-12;
   Jr 52:1-3
ae 24:18 2Kg 23:31
af 24:19 2Kg 23:37
ag 24:20 Dt 4:26; 29:27;
   2Kg 23:26
ah 2Kg 13:23
ai 2Ch 36:13; Ezk 17:15
aj 25:1 Jr 32:1
ak 25:1-7 Jr 39:1-7; 52:4-11

JEHOIAKIM'S REBELLION AND DEATH

24 During[a] Jehoiakim's reign,[b] King Nebuchadnezzar[c] of Babylon[d] attacked.[e] Jehoiakim became his vassal for three years, and then he turned and rebelled against him. **2** The LORD sent Chaldean, Aramean,[f] Moabite,[g] and Ammonite raiders against Jehoiakim. He sent them against Judah to destroy it, according to the word of the LORD he had spoken through his servants the prophets.[h] **3** Indeed, this happened to Judah at the LORD's command to remove them from his presence.[i] It was because of the sins of Manasseh, according to all he had done,[j] **4** and also because of all the innocent blood he had shed. He had filled Jerusalem with innocent blood,[k] and the LORD was not willing to forgive.

5 The rest of the events of Jehoiakim's reign, along with all his accomplishments, are written in the Historical Record of Judah's Kings.[l] **6** Jehoiakim rested with his fathers, and his son Jehoiachin became king in his place.[m]

7 Now the king of Egypt did not march out of his land again,[n] for the king of Babylon took everything that had belonged to the king of Egypt,[o] from the Brook of Egypt to the Euphrates River.[p]

JUDAH'S KING JEHOIACHIN

8 Jehoiachin was eighteen years old when he became king, and he reigned three months in Jerusalem. His mother's name was Nehushta daughter of Elnathan; she was from Jerusalem.[q] **9** He did what was evil in the LORD's sight just as his father had done.

DEPORTATIONS TO BABYLON

10 At that time[r] the servants of King Nebuchadnezzar[s] of Babylon marched up to Jerusalem, and the city came under siege. **11** King Nebuchadnezzar of Babylon came to the city while his servants were besieging it. **12** King Jehoiachin of Judah, along with his mother, his servants, his commanders, and his officials,[A] surrendered to the king of Babylon.[t]

So the king of Babylon took him captive in the eighth year of his reign. **13** He also carried off from there all the treasures of the LORD's temple and the treasures of the king's palace, and he cut into pieces all the gold articles that King Solomon of Israel had made[u] for the LORD's sanctuary, just as the LORD had predicted.[v] **14** He deported all Jerusalem and all the commanders and all the best soldiers[w] — ten thousand captives[x] including all the craftsmen and metalsmiths.[y] Except for the poorest people of the land,[z] no one remained.

15 Nebuchadnezzar deported Jehoiachin to Babylon. He took the king's mother, the king's wives, his officials, and the leading men of the land into exile from Jerusalem to Babylon.[aa] **16** The king of Babylon brought captive into Babylon all seven thousand of the best soldiers and one thousand craftsmen and metalsmiths — all strong and fit for war. **17** And the king of Babylon made Mattaniah, Jehoiachin's[B] uncle, king in his place and changed his name to Zedekiah.[ab]

JUDAH'S KING ZEDEKIAH

18 Zedekiah[ac] was twenty-one years old when he became king,[ad] and he reigned eleven years in Jerusalem. His mother's name was Hamutal[ae] daughter of Jeremiah; she was from Libnah. **19** Zedekiah did what was evil in the LORD's sight just as Jehoiakim had done.[af] **20** Because of the LORD's anger,[ag] it came to the point in Jerusalem and Judah that he finally banished them from his presence.[ah] Then Zedekiah rebelled against the king of Babylon.[ai]

NEBUCHADNEZZAR'S SIEGE OF JERUSALEM

25 In the ninth year[aj] of Zedekiah's reign,[ak] on the tenth day of the tenth month, King Nebuchadnezzar of Babylon advanced against Jerusalem with

---

A 24:12 Or *eunuchs*   B 24:17 Lit *his*

24:1 Nebuchadnezzar appears for the first time in 2 Kings in connection with his initial attack against Judah in 605 BC, during which he took Daniel of lions' den fame and other captives back to Babylon in the first of three deportations. He had recently established **Babylon** as the next world superpower. He attacked Judah to firm up his control in that region, and **Jehoiakim** submitted to him for **three years** before rebelling. This rebellion, though, was contrary to God's will for Judah: Nebuchadnezzar was his instrument of judgment.

24:8-17 Nebuchadnezzar had sent troops to besiege **Jerusalem** because of Jehoiakim's rebellion, but apparently by the time the Babylonian king arrived in 597 BC Jehoiakim was gone and Jehoiachin was ruling (24:10-11). Undeterred, Nebuchadnezzar took captive Jehoiachin and many other **officials** and took them to **Babylon**, along with a haul of treasures—a total of **ten thousand** people in all (24:12-14), including the prophet Ezekiel. Nebuchadnezzar left another puppet king named **Mattaniah**, a son of Josiah, on the

throne in Jerusalem and **changed his name to Zedekiah** (24:17).

24:18-20 Zedekiah was last in the line of evil kings whom God appointed to occupy the throne in Judah's final years. The writer first summed up the result of Zedekiah's reign as the time in which the cup of God's **anger** finally ran over, and he **banished** his people **from his presence** (24:20).

25:1-7 Zedekiah's rebellion (24:20) was the historical event God used to destroy Judah. Nebuchadnezzar's siege of Jerusalem

his entire army.[a] They laid siege to the city and built a siege wall against it all around.[b] ² The city was under siege until King Zedekiah's eleventh year.

³ By the ninth day of the fourth month the famine was so severe in the city that the common people had no food.[c] ⁴ Then the city was broken into,[d] and all the warriors fled[e] at night by way of the city gate between the two walls near the king's garden,[f] even though the Chaldeans surrounded the city. As the king made his way along the route to the Arabah,[g] ⁵ the Chaldean army pursued him and overtook him in the plains of Jericho. Zedekiah's entire army left him and scattered.[h] ⁶ The Chaldeans seized the king[i] and brought him up to the king of Babylon[j] at Riblah,[k] and they passed sentence on him. ⁷ They slaughtered Zedekiah's sons before his eyes. Finally, the king of Babylon blinded Zedekiah, bound him in bronze chains, and took him to Babylon.[l]

JERUSALEM DESTROYED

⁸ On[m] the seventh day of the fifth month — which was the nineteenth year of King Nebuchadnezzar of Babylon — Nebuzaradan, the captain of the guards, a servant of the king of Babylon, entered Jerusalem.[n] ⁹ He burned the LORD's temple,[o] the king's palace,[p] and all the houses of Jerusalem; he burned down[q] all the great houses. ¹⁰ The whole Chaldean army with the captain of the guards tore down the walls[r] surrounding Jerusalem. ¹¹ Nebuzaradan, the captain of the guards, deported the rest of the people who remained in the city, the deserters who had defected to the king of Babylon, and the rest of the population.[s] ¹² But the captain of the guards left some of the poorest of the land to be vinedressers and farmers.[t]

¹³ Now[u] the Chaldeans broke into pieces the bronze pillars[v] of the LORD's temple, the water carts, and the bronze basin,[A,w] which were in the LORD's temple, and carried the bronze to Babylon.[x] ¹⁴ They also took the pots, shovels, wick trimmers, dishes, and all the bronze articles used in the priests' service.[y] ¹⁵ The captain of the guards took away the firepans and sprinkling basins — whatever was gold or silver.[z]

¹⁶ As for the two pillars, the one basin, and the water carts that Solomon had made for the LORD's temple, the weight of the bronze of all these articles was beyond measure.[aa] ¹⁷ One pillar was twenty-seven feet[B] tall and had a bronze capital on top of it. The capital, encircled by a grating and pomegranates of bronze, stood five feet[c] high. The second pillar was the same, with its own grating.[ab] ¹⁸ The captain of the guards[ac] also took away Seraiah[ad] the chief priest, Zephaniah[ae] the priest of the second rank, and the three doorkeepers. ¹⁹ From the city he took a court official[D] who had been appointed over the warriors; five trusted royal aides[E,af] found in the city; the secretary of the commander of the army, who enlisted the people of the land for military duty; and sixty men from the common people[F] who were found within the city. ²⁰ Nebuzaradan, the captain of the guards, took them and brought them to the king of Babylon at Riblah.[ag] ²¹ The king of Babylon put them to death at Riblah in the land of Hamath. So Judah went into exile from its land.[ah]

GEDALIAH MADE GOVERNOR

²² King Nebuchadnezzar of Babylon appointed Gedaliah[ai] son of Ahikam, son of Shaphan, over the rest of the people he left in the land of Judah.[aj] ²³ When all the commanders of the armies — they and their men — heard that the king of Babylon had appointed Gedaliah, they came to Gedaliah at Mizpah.[ak] The commanders included Ishmael son of Nethaniah, Johanan son of Kareah, Seraiah son of Tanhumeth the Netophathite, and Jaazaniah son of the Maacathite — they and their men.[al] ²⁴ Gedaliah swore an oath to them and their men, assuring them, "Don't be afraid of the servants of the Chaldeans. Live in the land and serve the king of Babylon, and it will go well for you."[am]

[a] 25:1 Jr 21:2; 34:1-2; Ezk 24:2
[b] Ezk 21:22
[c] 25:3 2Kg 6:24-25; Lm 4:9-10
[d] 25:4 Jr 39:2
[e] Ezk 33:21
[f] Neh 3:15
[g] Dt 2:8
[h] 25:5 Lv 26:36; Ezk 12:14; 17:21
[i] 25:6 Jr 34:21-22
[j] Jr 32:4
[k] Nm 34:11; 2Kg 23:33; Jr 52:9
[l] 25:7 Jr 39:6-7; Ezk 12:13
[m] 25:8-12 Jr 39:8-10; 52:12-16
[n] 25:8 2Kg 24:12; Jr 39:9; 52:12
[o] 25:9 1Kg 9:8; 2Ch 36:19
[p] Jr 39:8; Am 2:5
[q] Jr 17:27
[r] 25:10 2Kg 24:13; Neh 1:3; Jr 50:15
[s] 25:11 2Ch 36:20; Jr 5:19; 39:1-9
[t] 25:12 2Kg 24:14; Jr 39:10; 40:7
[u] 25:13-21 Jr 52:17-27
[v] 25:13 2Kg 20:17; 2Ch 36:18; Jr 52:17
[w] 1Kg 7:23; 2Ch 4:2-4
[x] Jr 27:19-22
[y] 25:14 Ex 27:3; 1Kg 7:47-50; 2Ch 4:16
[z] 25:15 2Kg 24:13; Jr 15:13; 20:5
[aa] 25:16 1Kg 7:47
[ab] 25:17 1Kg 7:15-22
[ac] 25:18 Jr 39:9-13; 52:12-16,24
[ad] 1Ch 6:14; Ezr 7:1
[ae] Jr 21:1; 29:25,29
[af] 25:19 Jr 52:25
[ag] 25:20 2Kg 23:33
[ah] 25:21 Dt 28:63-64; 2Kg 23:27
[ai] 25:22 Jr 39:14; 40:7-9
[aj] Is 1:9; Jr 40:5
[ak] 25:23 Jos 18:26
[al] Jr 40:7-8
[am] 25:24 Jr 40:9

[A] 25:13 Lit sea　[B] 25:17 Lit 18 cubits　[C] 25:17 Lit three cubits　[D] 25:19 Or eunuch　[E] 25:19 Lit five men who look on the king's face　[F] 25:19 Lit the people of the land

---

brought hunger to the people and caused the city's defenders, including Zedekiah, to try and escape **at night** when the Babylonians (here called the **Chaldeans**) broke through into the city in 586 BC (25:1-4). Nevertheless, the invaders easily captured Zedekiah. Soon his fearful sentence was carried out (25:6), and he was taken **to Babylon** in chains (25:7). **25:8-21** Nebuchadnezzar sent his troops to Jerusalem to destroy everything of impor-

tance, including **the walls** (25:10) and the **temple** (25:13-16).

There was no mercy for **Seraiah the chief priest**, an ancestor of that great priest Ezra (25:18; see Ezra 7:1), or for the seventy-one other priests and leaders in Jerusalem. They were arrested and executed (25:20-21). Jerusalem was a smoking ruin. **25:22-24 Gedaliah** was the grandson of **Shaphan**, who had been one of Josiah's offi-

cials (25:22). Gedaliah was apparently a good man, who befriended the prophet Jeremiah (see Jer 39:14). He obviously believed Jeremiah's counsel that the people left in the land should **serve the king of Babylon** so that it might go well for them (25:24; see Jer 39:11-14; 40:6, 9-10). But unfortunately for him, there were still those left in Judah who (unwisely) wanted to fight the Babylonians.

a 25:25 Jr 41:1-2
b 25:26 Is 30:2; Jr 43:4-7
c 25:27-30 Jr 52:31-34

d 25:27 2Kg 24:12
e Gn 40:13,20
f 25:28 1Kg 8:50
g Ezr 5:5; 7:6,28
h 25:29 2Sm 9:7
i 25:30 Gn 43:34; Neh 12:47

25 In the seventh month, however, Ishmael son of Nethaniah, son of Elishama, of the royal family, came with ten men and struck down Gedaliah, and he died. Also, they killed the Judeans and the Chaldeans who were with him at Mizpah.[a] **26** Then all the people, from the youngest to the oldest, and the commanders of the army, left and went to Egypt, for they were afraid of the Chaldeans.[b]

JEHOIACHIN PARDONED

27 On[c] the twenty-seventh day of the twelfth month of the thirty-seventh year of the exile of Judah's King Jehoiachin, in the year Evil-merodach became king of Babylon, he pardoned King Jehoiachin[d] of Judah and released him[A] from prison.[e] **28** He spoke kindly[f] to him and set his throne over the thrones of the kings who were with him in Babylon.[g] **29** So Jehoiachin changed his prison clothes, and he dined regularly in the presence of the king of Babylon for the rest of his life.[h] **30** As for his allowance, a regular allowance[i] was given to him by the king, a portion for each day, for the rest of his life.

[A] 25:27 *and released him* supplied for clarity

25:25-26 The people fled to **Egypt** in fear of Nebuchadnezzar's reprisals over the murder of his representative (25:26).
25:27 The date of the kindness shown to **King Jehoiachin** by Nebuchadnezzar's successor, **Evil-merodach**, moves the history forward to somewhere between 562 and 560 BC. The Babylonian king may have done this to curry favor with the Jews (those who had been imported from Judah), as some historians suggest. But God was also working his sovereign plan to preserve his people even in captivity.

1 CHRONICLES

INTRODUCTION

Author

ANCIENT TRADITION CLAIMS THAT EZRA wrote 1–2 Chronicles. The author must have lived after the Babylonian exile and the return of the Jews to the land of Israel. He also must have had access to historical records and had an interest in the reimplementation of the law and the temple. All of this makes Ezra a good candidate. Furthermore, the final verses of 2 Chronicles are the first verses of Ezra. In the end, however, 1–2 Chronicles do not claim Ezra as author. Thus, the writer will be referred to here as the Chronicler.

Historical Background

First Chronicles begins with extensive genealogies covering the time of Adam to the period of the Jewish nation's return from exile. The book focuses on the reign of David and concludes with David's death and the transition of power to Solomon. Second Chronicles begins with Solomon and follows the reigns of subsequent kings up to the Babylonian exile and the restoration. It covers the same time period as 1–2 Kings except that 2 Chronicles focuses exclusively on the kings of Judah. The books of 1 and 2 Chronicles were written after the return from exile, perhaps in the middle of the fifth century BC. Clearly the Chronicler makes use of material from the books of 1–2 Samuel and 1–2 Kings, but he uses it for his own purposes and adds much of his own material.

Message and Purpose

In these books, the Chronicler records the history of the southern kingdom of Judah, focusing on the reigns of the Davidic kings, as well as giving attention to the priesthood. Thus, we see in these books the wedding of the kingship and the priesthood, with a focus on the temple as the place of God's presence.

The message of 1–2 Chronicles was one of hope for the readers, who were struggling in Babylonian exile.

They were reminded that while God ruled over them as King, he also related to them through the priesthood. God's rule over and relationship with his people are the key aspects of his kingdom identity with them.

These books use the historical ups and downs of the kingdom of Judah to show the need for a leader who could perfectly fulfill the roles of king and priest. Ultimately, this would happen in the Messiah, the Lord Jesus Christ, who would be both King and high priest. He rules us and rescues us.

www.bhpublishinggroup.com/qr/te/13_00

Outline

FROM ADAM TO ABRAHAM

a1:1-4 Gn 4:25–5:32
b1:5-7 Gn 10:2-4
c1:11-16 Gn 10:13-18
d1:12 Dt 2:23; Am 9:7
e1:17-23 Gn 10:21-29
f1:24-27 Gn 11:10-26;
   Lk 3:34-36

g1:29-31 Gn 25:12-16
h1:32-33 Gn 25:1-4
i1:34 1Ch 1:28
j Gn 25:24-26; 32:28
k1:35-37 Gn 36:4-5,9-14
l1:38-42 Gn 36:20-30
m1:43-50 Gn 36:31-39

1 Adam,[a] Seth, Enosh, [2] Kenan, Mahalalel, Jared, [3] Enoch, Methuselah, Lamech, [4] Noah, Noah's sons:[A] Shem, Ham, and Japheth.

[5] Japheth's[b] sons: Gomer, Magog, Madai, Javan, Tubal, Meshech, and Tiras. [6] Gomer's sons: Ashkenaz, Riphath,[B] and Togarmah. [7] Javan's sons: Elishah, Tarshish, Kittim, and Rodanim.[c]

[8] Ham's sons: Cush, Mizraim,[D] Put, and Canaan. [9] Cush's sons: Seba, Havilah, Sabta, Raama, and Sabteca. Raama's sons: Sheba and Dedan. [10] Cush fathered Nimrod, who was the first to become a great warrior on earth. [11] Mizraim[c] fathered the people of Lud, Anam, Lehab, Naphtuh, [12] Pathrus, Casluh (the Philistines came from them), and Caphtor.[d] [13] Canaan fathered Sidon as his firstborn and Heth, [14] as well as the Jebusites, Amorites, Girgashites, [15] Hivites, Arkites, Sinites, [16] Arvadites, Zemarites, and Hamathites.

[17] Shem's[e] sons: Elam, Asshur, Arpachshad, Lud, Aram, Uz, Hul, Gether, and Meshech. [18] Arpachshad fathered Shelah, and Shelah fathered Eber. [19] Two sons were born to Eber. One of them was named Peleg[E] because the earth was divided during his lifetime, and the name of his brother was Joktan. [20] Joktan fathered Almodad, Sheleph, Hazarmaveth, Jerah, [21] Hadoram, Uzal, Diklah, [22] Ebal, Abimael, Sheba, [23] Ophir, Havilah, and Jobab. All of these were Joktan's sons.

[24] Shem,[f] Arpachshad, Shelah, [25] Eber, Peleg, Reu,

[26] Serug, Nahor, Terah, [27] and Abram (that is, Abraham).

ABRAHAM'S DESCENDANTS

[28] Abraham's sons: Isaac and Ishmael.

[29] These[g] are their family records: Nebaioth, Ishmael's firstborn, Kedar, Adbeel, Mibsam, [30] Mishma, Dumah, Massa, Hadad, Tema, [31] Jetur, Naphish, and Kedemah. These were Ishmael's sons.

[32] The sons[h] born to Keturah, Abraham's concubine: Zimran, Jokshan, Medan, Midian, Ishbak, and Shuah. Jokshan's sons: Sheba and Dedan. [33] Midian's sons: Ephah, Epher, Hanoch, Abida, and Eldaah. All of these were Keturah's descendants.

[34] Abraham[i] fathered Isaac. Isaac's sons: Esau and Israel.[j] [35] Esau's[k] sons: Eliphaz, Reuel, Jeush, Jalam, and Korah. [36] Eliphaz's sons: Teman, Omar, Zephi, Gatam, and Kenaz; and by Timna, Amalek.[F] [37] Reuel's sons: Nahath, Zerah, Shammah, and Mizzah.

THE EDOMITES

[38] Seir's[l] sons: Lotan, Shobal, Zibeon, Anah, Dishon, Ezer, and Dishan. [39] Lotan's sons: Hori and Homam. Timna was Lotan's sister. [40] Shobal's sons: Alian, Manahath, Ebal, Shephi, and Onam. Zibeon's sons: Aiah and Anah. [41] Anah's son: Dishon. Dishon's sons: Hamran, Eshban, Ithran, and Cheran. [42] Ezer's sons: Bilhan, Zaavan, and Jaakan. Dishan's sons: Uz and Aran.

[43] These[m] were the kings who reigned in the land of Edom

A1:4 LXX; MT omits *Noah's sons*   B1:6 Some Hb mss, LXX, Vg; other Hb mss read *Diphath*; Gn 10:3   C1:7 Some Hb mss, Syr read *Dodanim*; Gn 10:4   D1:8 = Egypt   E1:19 = Division   F1:36 LXX; MT reads *and Timna and Amalek*; Gn 36:12

1:1-4 Genealogical lists can bog down even the most faithful Bible readers. But 2 Timothy 3:16-17 says, "All Scripture [yes, even the genealogies] is inspired by God and is profitable for teaching, for rebuking, for correcting, for training in righteousness, so that the man of God may be complete, equipped for every good work."

God does not list names because he ran out of material. He always has purposes in

mind. The genealogies of 1 Chronicles show the development of Israel's theocracy, focusing on the messianic line of David in the tribe of Judah, from which God's promises and Savior would come, and the priestly line of Levi, which was crucial to the ministry of the temple. Thus, the genealogies of 1 Chronicles 1–9 are like a compressed history of Israel. That chapter 1 begins with the mention of **Adam** (1:1) served to connect

the history of Israel with the beginning of God's creative work.

1:17 **Shem's** was the godly line through which the Messiah (that is, Jesus) would come.

1:38-54 Though Esau's line, the Edomites, did not figure prominently in messianic or Levitical history, he was a grandson of Abraham and the brother of Jacob (also called Israel). Their descendants had a stormy history.

before any king reigned
over the Israelites:
Bela son of Beor.
Bela's town was named Dinhabah.
44 When Bela died, Jobab son of Zerah
from Bozrah[a] reigned in his place.
45 When Jobab died, Husham
from the land of the Temanites[b]
reigned in his place.
46 When Husham died, Hadad
son of Bedad, who defeated
Midian in the territory of Moab,
reigned in his place.
Hadad's town was named Avith.
47 When Hadad died, Samlah
from Masrekah reigned
in his place.
48 When Samlah died, Shaul
from Rehoboth on the Euphrates
River reigned in his place.
49 When Shaul died, Baal-hanan
son of Achbor reigned
in his place.
50 When Baal-hanan died, Hadad
reigned in his place.
Hadad's city was named Pai, and his
wife's name was Mehetabel
daughter of Matred, daughter
of Me-zahab.
51 Then Hadad died.

Edom's[c] chiefs: Timna, Alvah,[A] Jetheth,
52 Oholibamah, Elah, Pinon, 53 Kenaz,
Teman, Mibzar, 54 Magdiel, and Iram.
These were Edom's chiefs.

ISRAEL'S SONS

2 These[d] were Israel's sons:
Reuben, Simeon, Levi,
Judah, Issachar, Zebulun,
2 Dan, Joseph, Benjamin,
Naphtali, Gad, and Asher.

JUDAH'S DESCENDANTS

3 Judah's[e] sons: Er, Onan, and Shelah.[f] These three were born to him
by Bath-shua the Canaanite woman.
Er, Judah's firstborn, was evil in the
LORD's sight, so he put him to death.
4 Judah's daughter-in-law Tamar bore
Perez and Zerah to him. Judah had five
sons in all.

5 Perez's sons: Hezron and Hamul.
6 Zerah's sons: Zimri, Ethan, Heman,
Calcol, and Dara[B,g] — five in all.
7 Carmi's son: Achar,[c,h] who brought
trouble on Israel when he was
unfaithful by taking the things set
apart for destruction.
8 Ethan's son: Azariah.
9 Hezron's sons, who were born to him:
Jerahmeel, Ram, and Chelubai.[D]

10 Ram fathered Amminadab, and
Amminadab fathered Nahshon, a
leader of Judah's descendants.
11 Nahshon fathered Salma, and Salma
fathered Boaz.
12 Boaz fathered Obed, and Obed
fathered Jesse.
13 Jesse fathered Eliab, his firstborn;
Abinadab was born second, Shimea
third, 14 Nethanel fourth, Raddai fifth,
15 Ozem sixth, and David seventh.
16 Their sisters were Zeruiah and
Abigail. Zeruiah's three sons: Abishai,
Joab, and Asahel. 17 Amasa's mother
was Abigail, and his father was Jether
the Ishmaelite.

18 Caleb son of Hezron had children
by his wife Azubah and by Jerioth.
These were Azubah's sons: Jesher,
Shobab, and Ardon. 19 When Azubah
died, Caleb married Ephrath, and she
bore Hur to him. 20 Hur fathered Uri,
and Uri fathered Bezalel. 21 After this,
Hezron slept with the daughter of
Machir the father of Gilead.[i] Hezron
had married her when he was sixty
years old, and she bore Segub to him.
22 Segub fathered Jair, who possessed
twenty-three towns in the land of Gilead. 23 But Geshur and Aram captured[E]
Jair's Villages[F] along with Kenath
and its surrounding villages — sixty
towns. All these were the descendants
of Machir father of Gilead. 24 After
Hezron's death in Caleb-ephrathah, his
wife Abijah bore[G] Ashhur to him. He
was the father of Tekoa.

25 The sons of Jerahmeel, Hezron's
firstborn: Ram, his firstborn, Bunah,

[a] 1:44 Is 34:6
[b] 1:45 Jb 2:11
[c] 1:51-54 Gn 36:40-43
[d] 2:1-2 Gn 35:22-26; 46:8-25
[e] 2:3-4 Gn 38:6-30
[f] 2:3 Gn 38:2-5; 46:12; Nm 26:19-22

[g] 2:6 1Kg 4:31
[h] 2:7 Jos 7:1,16-26
[i] 2:21 Nm 26:29

A 1:51 Alt Hb tradition reads *Aliah* B 2:6 Some Hb mss, LXX, Syr, Tg, Vg read *Darda*; 1Kg 4:31 C 2:7 = Trouble; Achan in Jos 7:1,16-26 D 2:9 = Caleb E 2:23 Lit *took from them* F 2:23 Or *captured Havvoth-jair* G 2:24 LXX, Vg read *death, Caleb slept with Ephrath (Hezron's wife was Abijah) and she bore*

2:1-2 Israel is crucial to the Jewish nation's history; he was the father of **Israel's** twelve tribes (2:1). God had changed Jacob's name to Israel after his smackdown with the angel that's described in Genesis 32:24-28. It's sig-

nificant when God changes a person's name; it means he has a new purpose and direction for that person's life.
2:3-55 **Judah** (2:3-5) was not the first son of Jacob's sons in birth order, but he became

prominent because God promised that Israel's rulers would come from his line; this promise included the Messiah (see Gen 49:10).

a 3:1-4a 2Sm 3:2-5
b 3:4 2Sm 2:11; 5:4-5
c 3:5-8 2Sm 5:14-16; 1Ch 14:4-7
d 3:5 2Sm 12:24-25
e 2Sm 11:3

Oren, Ozem, and Ahijah. ²⁶ Jerahmeel had another wife named Atarah, who was the mother of Onam. ²⁷ The sons of Ram, Jerahmeel's firstborn: Maaz, Jamin, and Eker. ²⁸ Onam's sons: Shammai and Jada. Shammai's sons: Nadab and Abishur. ²⁹ Abishur's wife was named Abihail, who bore Ahban and Molid to him. ³⁰ Nadab's sons: Seled and Appaim. Seled died without children. ³¹ Appaim's son: Ishi. Ishi's son: Sheshan. Sheshan's descendant: Ahlai. ³² The sons of Jada, brother of Shammai: Jether and Jonathan. Jether died without children. ³³ Jonathan's sons: Peleth and Zaza. These were the descendants of Jerahmeel. ³⁴ Sheshan had no sons, only daughters, but he did have an Egyptian servant whose name was Jarha. ³⁵ Sheshan gave his daughter in marriage to his servant Jarha, and she bore Attai to him.

³⁶ Attai fathered Nathan, and Nathan fathered Zabad. ³⁷ Zabad fathered Ephlal, and Ephlal fathered Obed. ³⁸ Obed fathered Jehu, and Jehu fathered Azariah. ³⁹ Azariah fathered Helez, and Helez fathered Elasah. ⁴⁰ Elasah fathered Sismai, and Sismai fathered Shallum. ⁴¹ Shallum fathered Jekamiah, and Jekamiah fathered Elishama.

⁴² The sons of Caleb brother of Jerahmeel: Mesha, his firstborn, fathered Ziph, and Mareshah, his second son,ᴬ fathered Hebron. ⁴³ Hebron's sons: Korah, Tappuah, Rekem, and Shema. ⁴⁴ Shema fathered Raham, who fathered Jorkeam, and Rekem fathered Shammai. ⁴⁵ Shammai's son was Maon, and Maon fathered Beth-zur. ⁴⁶ Caleb's concubine Ephah was the mother of Haran, Moza, and Gazez. Haran fathered Gazez.

⁴⁷ Jahdai's sons: Regem, Jotham, Geshan, Pelet, Ephah, and Shaaph. ⁴⁸ Caleb's concubine Maacah was the mother of Sheber and Tirhanah. ⁴⁹ She was also the mother of Shaaph, Madmannah's father, and of Sheva, the father of Machbenah and Gibea. Caleb's daughter was Achsah. ⁵⁰ These were Caleb's descendants.

The sons of Hur, Ephrathah's firstborn: Shobal fathered Kiriath-jearim; ⁵¹ Salma fathered Bethlehem, and Hareph fathered Beth-gader.

⁵² These were the descendants of Shobal the father of Kiriath-jearim: Haroeh, half of the Manahathites,ᴮ ⁵³ and the families of Kiriath-jearim — the Ithrites, Puthites, Shumathites, and Mishraites. The Zorathites and Eshtaolites descended from these.

⁵⁴ Salma's descendants: Bethlehem, the Netophathites, Atroth-beth-joab, and half of the Manahathites, the Zorites, ⁵⁵ and the families of scribes who lived in Jabez — the Tirathites, Shimeathites, and Sucathites. These are the Kenites who came from Hammath, the father of Rechab's family.

DAVID'S DESCENDANTS

3 Theseᵃ were David's sons who were born to him in Hebron:
Amnon was the firstborn, by Ahinoam of Jezreel;
Daniel was born second, by Abigail of Carmel;
² Absalom son of Maacah, daughter of King Talmai of Geshur, was third;
Adonijah son of Haggith was fourth;
³ Shephatiah, by Abital, was fifth;
and Ithream, by David's wife Eglah, was sixth.
⁴ Six sons were born to David in Hebron, where he reigned seven years and six months, and he reigned in Jerusalem thirty-three years.ᵇ
⁵ Theseᶜ sons were born to him in Jerusalem:
Shimea, Shobab, Nathan, and Solomon.ᵈ These four were born to him by Bath-shuaᵉ daughter of Ammiel.

ᴬ **2:42** Lit *and the sons of Mareshah* ᴮ **2:52** Lit *Manuhoth*

3:1-24 David was the nation's most important king, which is why his progeny receive so much attention here (3:1-9). God made a covenant with David to give him a kingly dynasty—culminating in the Messiah (see ch. 17). Thus, David was not just the head of Judah's royal line but also the ancestor of Jesus. Chapter 3 especially lists the Davidic kings of Judah (3:10-16) before following the Davidic line after the Babylonian exile (3:17-24).

6 David's other sons: Ibhar, Elishua,[A,a] Eliphelet, **7** Nogah, Nepheg, Japhia, **8** Elishama, Eliada, and Eliphelet — nine sons. **9** These were all David's sons, with their sister Tamar,[b] in addition to the sons by his concubines.

JUDAH'S KINGS

10 Solomon's son was Rehoboam; his son was Abijah, his son Asa, his son Jehoshaphat, **11** his son Jehoram,[B,C] his son Ahaziah, his son Joash, **12** his son Amaziah, his son Azariah, his son Jotham, **13** his son Ahaz, his son Hezekiah, his son Manasseh, **14** his son Amon, and his son Josiah. **15** Josiah's sons: Johanan was the firstborn, Jehoiakim second, Zedekiah third, and Shallum fourth. **16** Jehoiakim's sons: his sons Jeconiah and Zedekiah.

DAVID'S LINE AFTER THE EXILE

17 The sons of Jeconiah the captive: his sons Shealtiel, **18** Malchiram, Pedaiah, Shenazzar, Jekamiah, Hoshama, and Nedabiah. **19** Pedaiah's sons: Zerubbabel and Shimei. Zerubbabel's sons: Meshullam and Hananiah, with their sister Shelomith; **20** and five others — Hashubah, Ohel, Berechiah, Hasadiah, and Jushab-hesed. **21** Hananiah's descendants: Pelatiah, Jeshaiah, and the sons of Rephaiah, Arnan, Obadiah, and Shecaniah.[D]

22 The son[E] of Shecaniah: Shemaiah. Shemaiah's sons: Hattush, Igal, Bariah, Neariah, and Shaphat — six. **23** Neariah's sons: Elioenai, Hizkiah, and Azrikam — three. **24** Elioenai's sons: Hodaviah, Eliashib, Pelaiah, Akkub, Johanan, Delaiah, and Anani — seven.

JUDAH'S DESCENDANTS

4 Judah's sons:[c] Perez, Hezron, Carmi, Hur, and Shobal. **2** Reaiah son of Shobal fathered Jahath, and Jahath fathered Ahumai and Lahad. These were the families of the Zorathites. **3** These were Etam's sons:[F] Jezreel, Ishma, and Idbash, and their sister was named Hazzelelponi. **4** Penuel fathered Gedor, and Ezer fathered Hushah. These were the sons of Hur, Ephrathah's firstborn and the father of Bethlehem: **5** Ashhur fathered Tekoa and had two wives, Helah and Naarah. **6** Naarah bore Ahuzzam, Hepher, Temeni, and Haahashtari to him. These were Naarah's sons. **7** Helah's sons: Zereth, Zohar,[G] and Ethnan. **8** Koz fathered Anub, Zobebah,[H] and the families of Aharhel son of Harum.

9 Jabez[I] was more honored than his brothers. His mother named him Jabez and said, "I gave birth to him in pain." **10** Jabez called out to the God of Israel: "If only you would bless me, extend my border, let your hand be with me, and keep me

[a]3:6 2Sm 5:15; 1Ch 14:5
[b]3:9 2Sm 13:1

[c]4:1 1Ch 2:5,18,50

[A]3:6 Lit *Elishama*; 2Sm 5:15; 1Ch 14:5   [B]3:11 Lit *Joram*   [C]3:11 = The LORD is Exalted   [D]3:21 LXX reads *Jeshaiah, his son Rephaiah, his son Arnan, his son Obadiah, and his son Shecaniah*   [E]3:22 LXX; MT reads *sons*   [F]4:3 LXX; MT reads *father*   [G]4:7 Alt Hb tradition reads *Izhar*   [H]4:8 Or *Hazzobebah*   [I]4:9 In Hb, the name *Jabez* sounds like "he causes pain."

4:9-10 Jabez was singled out only because of his simple, powerful prayer of faith that moved God to respond. Jabez said, **If only you would bless me, extend my border, let your hand be with me, and keep me from harm, so that I will not experience pain** (4:10).

Much about this man is left to speculation, but we know a few things. First, his name means **pain**, so something happened surrounding his birth that caused his mother to give Jabez this unusual name (4:9). Now, a name like that is quite a burden to overcome. I believe God wanted us to read about this man in part as a reminder that pain doesn't have to be the last word in our lives.

Second, Jabez realized that he didn't just need *someone* to bless him; he needed the impartation of spiritual favor that comes from God alone. It's interesting that Jabez's request is open-ended instead of specific. Jabez did not try to make a deal with God; after all, when you do that you are limited to the terms of your deal. The beautiful thing about just throwing yourself on the mercy of God is that he decides what's in your best interest. Jabez brought God an empty cup and asked him to fill it as he saw fit. That's a prayer of faith. Let God decide what to fill your cup with and how high.

Third, Jabez wanted God to expand his borders. In essence, he prayed, "God, broaden my frontier." The problem with too many of us is that we have become complacent with our little plots of land in the kingdom when God wants to use us to expand the influ-ence of his kingdom in history. People who are complacent aren't motivated to ask God for anything, so they don't receive anything from God. Jabez wanted his kingdom impact to grow, and he knew the Lord could deliver.

Fourth, Jabez knew that God was capable of keeping him from harm, from pain. Why did he pray that? I suspect Jabez did not want the blessings he anticipated to become a source of pain by allowing them to disconnect him from God. So he asked God to put a restraining order on the devil, as it were. The more God blesses you, the more Satan sets his sights on you. Success, then, is a great opportunity for failure if we are not alert. When received, blessings like those Jabez requested can dull our sense of dependency on God.

a 4:24 Gn 46:10

b 4:40 Jdg 18:7-10
c 4:41 1Ch 4:33-38
d Nm 21:3; Dt 2:34; 7:2;
13:15; Jos 6:17-21

from harm, so that I will not experience pain."[A] And God granted his request. [11] Chelub brother of Shuhah fathered Mehir, who was the father of Eshton. [12] Eshton fathered Beth-rapha, Paseah, and Tehinnah the father of Irnahash. These were the men of Recah. [13] Kenaz's sons: Othniel and Seraiah. Othniel's sons: Hathath and Meonothai.[B] [14] Meonothai fathered Ophrah, and Seraiah fathered Joab, the ancestor of those in the Craftsmen's Valley,[C] for they were craftsmen. [15] The sons of Caleb son of Jephunneh: Iru, Elah, and Naam. Elah's son: Kenaz. [16] Jehallelel's sons: Ziph, Ziphah, Tiria, and Asarel. [17] Ezrah's sons: Jether, Mered, Epher, and Jalon. Mered's wife Bithiah gave birth to Miriam, Shammai, and Ishbah the father of Eshtemoa. [18] These were the sons of Pharaoh's daughter Bithiah; Mered had married her. His Judean wife gave birth to Jered the father of Gedor, Heber the father of Soco, and Jekuthiel the father of Zanoah. [19] The sons of Hodiah's wife, the sister of Naham: the father of Keilah the Garmite and the father of Eshtemoa the Maacathite. [20] Shimon's sons: Amnon, Rinnah, Ben-hanan, and Tilon. Ishi's sons: Zoheth and Ben-zoheth.

[21] The sons of Shelah son of Judah: Er the father of Lecah, Laadah the father of Mareshah, the families of the guild[D] of linen workers at Beth-ashbea, [22] Jokim, the men of Cozeba; and Joash and Saraph, who married Moabites[E] and returned to Lehem.[F] These names are from ancient records. [23] They were the potters and residents of Netaim and Gederah. They lived there in the service of the king.

SIMEON'S DESCENDANTS

[24] Simeon's sons:[a] Nemuel, Jamin, Jarib, Zerah, and Shaul;

[25] Shaul's sons: his son Shallum, his son Mibsam, and his son Mishma. [26] Mishma's sons: his son Hammuel, his son Zaccur, and his son Shimei.

[27] Shimei had sixteen sons and six daughters, but his brothers did not have many children, so their whole family did not become as numerous as the Judeans. [28] They lived in Beer-she-ba, Moladah, Hazar-shual, [29] Bilhah, Ezem, Tolad, [30] Bethuel, Hormah, Ziklag, [31] Beth-marcaboth, Hazar-susim, Beth-biri, and Shaaraim. These were their cities until David became king. [32] Their villages were Etam, Ain, Rimmon, Tochen, and Ashan — five cities, [33] and all their surrounding villages as far as Baal. These were their settlements, and they kept a genealogical record for themselves.

[34] Meshobab, Jamlech, Joshah son of Amaziah, [35] Joel, Jehu son of Joshibiah, son of Seraiah, son of Asiel, [36] Elioenai, Jaakobah, Jeshohaiah, Asaiah, Adiel, Jesimiel, Benaiah, [37] and Ziza son of Shiphi, son of Allon, son of Jedaiah, son of Shimri, son of Shemaiah —

[38] these mentioned by name were leaders in their families. Their ancestral houses increased greatly. [39] They went to the entrance of Gedor, to the east side of the valley to seek pasture for their flocks. [40] They found rich, good pasture, and the land was broad, peaceful, and quiet,[b] for some Hamites had lived there previously.

[41] These[c] who were recorded by name came in the days of King Hezekiah of Judah, attacked the Hamites' tents and the Meunites who were found there, and set them apart for destruction,[d] as they are today. Then they settled in their place because there was pasture for their flocks. [42] Now five hundred men from these sons of Simeon went with Pelatiah, Neariah,

[A] 4:10 Or *not cause any pain*   [B] 4:13 LXX, Vg; MT omits *and Meonothai*   [C] 4:14 Or *the Ge-harashim*   [D] 4:21 Lit *house*   [E] 4:22 Or *who ruled over Moab*   [F] 4:22 Tg, Vg; MT reads *and Jashubi Lehem*

4:40 That **rich, good pasture** was found **for some Hamites had lived [in a particular area] previously** suggests that Hamitic (that is, dark-skinned) people living in Canaan had positively contributed to community life, productivity, and social well-being. This verse refutes the so-called "curse of Ham" (which is really a misunderstanding of Noah's curse of Ham's son Canaan) as applying to an entire race or subset of humanity (see the note on Gen 9:20-29). **4:42-43** **The Amalekites** had attacked Israel without provocation, leading to the famous incident in which Aaron and Hur held up Moses's hands so Israel could prevail against them (4:43; see Exod 17:8-13). After the battle, God said, "I will completely blot out the memory of Amalek under heaven" (Exod 17:14). But when given the chance to blot out

Rephaiah, and Uzziel, the descendants of Ishi, as their leaders to Mount Seir.[a] **43** They struck down[b] the remnant of the Amalekites who had escaped, and they still live there today.

REUBEN'S DESCENDANTS

5 These were the sons of Reuben the firstborn of Israel. He was the firstborn,[c] but his birthright was given to the sons of Joseph[d] son of Israel, because Reuben defiled his father's bed.[e] He is not listed in the genealogy according to birthright. **2** Although Judah became strong among his brothers[f] and a ruler came from him,[g] the birthright was given to Joseph.

3　The sons of Reuben, Israel's firstborn:[h] Hanoch, Pallu, Hezron, and Carmi.

4　Joel's sons: his son Shemaiah, his son Gog, his son Shimei,

5　his son Micah, his son Reaiah, his son Baal, **6** and his son Beerah.

Beerah was a leader of the Reubenites, and King Tiglath-pileser[A] of Assyria took him into exile. **7** His relatives by their families as they are recorded in their family records:[i]

Jeiel the chief, Zechariah,

8 and Bela son of Azaz,

son of Shema, son of Joel.

They settled in Aroer[j] as far as Nebo and Baal-meon. **9** They also settled in the east as far as the edge of the desert that extends to the Euphrates River, because their herds had increased in the land of Gilead.[k] **10** During Saul's reign they waged war against the Hagrites,[l] who were defeated by their power. And they lived in their tents throughout the region east of Gilead.

GAD'S DESCENDANTS

11 The sons[m] of Gad lived next to them in the land of Bashan as far as Salecah:[n] **12** Joel the chief, Shapham the second in command, Janai, and Shaphat in Bashan.

13 Their relatives according to their ancestral houses: Michael, Meshullam, Sheba, Jorai, Jacan, Zia, and Eber — seven.

14 These were the sons of Abihail son of Huri,

son of Jaroah, son of Gilead,

son of Michael, son of Jeshishai,

son of Jahdo, son of Buz.

15 Ahi son of Abdiel, son of Guni, was head of their ancestral family.[B] **16** They lived in Gilead, in Bashan and its surrounding villages, and throughout the pasturelands of Sharon.[o] **17** All of them were registered in the genealogies during the reigns of Judah's King Jotham[p] and Israel's King Jeroboam.[q]

18 The descendants of Reuben and Gad and half the tribe of Manasseh had 44,760 warriors who could serve[r] in the army — men who carried shield and sword, drew the bow, and were trained for war. **19** They waged war against the Hagrites,[s] Jetur,[t] Naphish, and Nodab. **20** They received help against these enemies because they cried out to God in battle, and the Hagrites and all their allies were handed over to them.[u] He was receptive to their prayer because they trusted in him.[v] **21** They captured the Hagrites' livestock — fifty thousand of their camels, two hundred fifty thousand sheep, and two thousand donkeys — as well as one hundred thousand people. **22** Many of the Hagrites were killed because it was God's battle.[w] And they lived there in the Hagrites' place[x] until the exile.[y]

HALF THE TRIBE OF MANASSEH

23 The descendants of half the tribe of Manasseh settled in the land from Bashan to Baal-hermon (that is, Senir[z] or Mount Hermon); they were numerous. **24** These were the heads of their ancestral families: Epher, Ishi, Eliel, Azriel, Jeremiah, Hodaviah, and

---

[a] 4:42 Gn 36:8-9
[b] 4:43 1Sm 15:7-8; 30:17
[c] 5:1 Gn 29:32; 1Ch 2:1
[d] Gn 48:15-22
[e] Gn 35:22; 49:4
[f] 5:2 Gn 49:8-10
[g] Mc 5:2; Mt 2:6
[h] 5:3 Gn 46:9; Nm 26:5-9
[i] 5:7 1Ch 5:17
[j] 5:8 Nm 32:34; Jos 12:2
[k] 5:9 Jos 22:8-9
[l] 5:10 1Ch 5:19-21; 11:38; 27:31
[m] 5:11-12 Gn 46:16; Nm 26:15-18
[n] 5:11 Dt 3:10

[o] 5:16 1Ch 27:29
[p] 5:17 2Kg 15:5,32
[q] 2Kg 14:16,28
[r] 5:18 Nm 1:3
[s] 5:19 1Ch 5:10
[t] 1Ch 1:31
[u] 5:20 2Ch 14:11-13
[v] Ps 9:10; 20:7-8
[w] 5:22 Jos 23:10; 2Ch 32:8
[x] 1Ch 4:41
[y] 2Kg 15:29; 17:6
[z] 5:23 Dt 3:9

[A] **5:6** LXX; MT reads *Tilgath-pilneser*　　[B] **5:15** Lit *the house of their fathers*, also in v. 24

---

the Amalekites, King Saul failed (see 1 Sam 15). Rather than eradicating the Amalekites and everything they owned, Saul kept back the best of the livestock for sacrifice and spared their king, Agag.

About five hundred years after Saul, Queen Esther, a Jewish exile living in Persia, had to take her life in her hands to beg King Xerxes not to allow "Haman . . . the Agagite" to annihilate her people (Esth 3:1). Haman was likely a descendant of King Agag of Saul's day and, thus, a descendant of the Amalekites whom Israel evidently did not destroy as God commanded. If so, that disobedience almost led to an Old Testament holocaust at the hands of Haman. It appears that Simeon's descendants had attempted to finish the job left incomplete in Saul's day (1 Chr 4:42).

5:1-2 That **Reuben defiled his father's bed** is a way of saying he committed adultery with his father's concubine Bilhah (see Gen 35:22; 30:4). Reuben's sin was detestable to God, so Reuben forfeited his birthright **to Joseph**

(1 Chr 5:2) for the same reason Esau did earlier: both men cared more about their physical appetites than their spiritual heritage (see Gen 25:32).

The accounts of Esau and Reuben teach an important principle at work in God's kingdom. Through his sovereign power, God can do more with the lesser creatures (in these cases, Esau's younger brother Jacob and Reuben's younger brother Joseph) than the devil can do with the greater creatures when the lesser are devoted to him.

ᵃ5:25 Ex 34:15
ᵇ2Kg 17:7-8
ᶜ5:26 2Kg 15:19,29
ᵈ6:1-3 Gn 46:11; Ex
6:16,18,20,23; Nm
26:57-60
ᵉ6:4 Ex 6:25
ᶠ6:15 2Kg 24:1-2,10,14;
25:1,8,11,21; 1Ch 9:1
ᵍ6:16-19 Ex 6:16-19

ʰ6:28 1Sm 8:2
ⁱ6:31 1Ch 15:16-22; 16:4-6
ʲ2Sm 6:17; 1Ch 15:25−16:1

Jahdiel. They were valiant warriors, famous men, and heads of their ancestral houses. ²⁵ But they were unfaithful to the God of their ancestors. They prostituted themselvesᵃ with the gods of the nationsᴬ God had destroyed before them.ᵇ ²⁶ So the God of Israel roused the spirit of King Pulᶜ (that is, Tiglath-pileserᴮ) of Assyria, and he took the Reubenites, Gadites, and half the tribe of Manasseh into exile. He took them to Halah, Habor, Hara, and Gozan's river, where they are until today.

THE LEVITES

6 Levi'sᵈ sons: Gershom,ᶜ Kohath, and Merari.

² Kohath's sons: Amram, Izhar, Hebron, and Uzziel.

³ Amram's children: Aaron, Moses, and Miriam.

Aaron's sons: Nadab, Abihu, Eleazar, and Ithamar.

⁴ Eleazar fathered Phinehas;ᵉ Phinehas fathered Abishua;

⁵ Abishua fathered Bukki; Bukki fathered Uzzi;

⁶ Uzzi fathered Zerahiah; Zerahiah fathered Meraioth;

⁷ Meraioth fathered Amariah; Amariah fathered Ahitub;

⁸ Ahitub fathered Zadok; Zadok fathered Ahimaaz;

⁹ Ahimaaz fathered Azariah; Azariah fathered Johanan;

¹⁰ Johanan fathered Azariah, who served as priest in the temple that Solomon built in Jerusalem;

¹¹ Azariah fathered Amariah; Amariah fathered Ahitub;

¹² Ahitub fathered Zadok; Zadok fathered Shallum;

¹³ Shallum fathered Hilkiah; Hilkiah fathered Azariah;

¹⁴ Azariah fathered Seraiah; and Seraiah fathered Jehozadak.

¹⁵ Jehozadak went into exile when the LORD sent Judah and Jerusalem into exile at the hands of Nebuchadnezzar.ᶠ

¹⁶ Levi'sᵍ sons: Gershom, Kohath, and Merari.

¹⁷ These are the names of Gershom's sons: Libni and Shimei.

¹⁸ Kohath's sons: Amram, Izhar, Hebron and Uzziel.

¹⁹ Merari's sons: Mahli and Mushi. These are the Levites' families according to their fathers:

²⁰ Of Gershom: his son Libni, his son Jahath, his son Zimmah,

²¹ his son Joah, his son Iddo, his son Zerah, and his son Jeatherai.

²² Kohath's sons: his son Amminadab, his son Korah, his son Assir,

²³ his son Elkanah, his son Ebiasaph, his son Assir, ²⁴ his son Tahath, his son Uriel, his son Uzziah, and his son Shaul.

²⁵ Elkanah's sons: Amasai and Ahimoth,

²⁶ his son Elkanah, his son Zophai, his son Nahath, ²⁷ his son Eliab, his son Jeroham, and his son Elkanah.

²⁸ Samuel's sons: his firstborn Joel,ᴰ,ʰ and his second son Abijah.

²⁹ Merari's sons: Mahli, his son Libni, his son Shimei, his son Uzzah,

³⁰ his son Shimea, his son Haggiah, and his son Asaiah.

THE MUSICIANS

³¹ These are the men David put in charge of the music in the LORD's templeⁱ after the ark came to rest there.ʲ ³² They ministered with song in front of the tabernacle, the tent of meeting, until Solomon built the LORD's temple in Jerusalem, and they performed their task according to the regulations given to them. ³³ These are the men who served with their sons.

From the Kohathites:

Heman the singer, son of Joel, son of Samuel,

³⁴ son of Elkanah, son of Jeroham, son of Eliel, son of Toah,

³⁵ son of Zuph, son of Elkanah, son of Mahath, son of Amasai,

³⁶ son of Elkanah, son of Joel, son of Azariah, son of Zephaniah,

³⁷ son of Tahath, son of Assir, son of Ebiasaph, son of Korah,

³⁸ son of Izhar, son of Kohath, son of Levi, son of Israel.

³⁹ Heman's relative was Asaph, who stood at his right hand: Asaph son of Berechiah, son of Shimea,

ᴬ5:25 Lit *the peoples of the land*   ᴮ5:26 LXX; MT reads *Tilgath-pilneser*   ᶜ6:1 In Hb Levi's son's name is spelled "Gershon" here and many other places   ᴰ6:28 Some LXX mss, Syr, Arabic; other Hb mss omit *Joel*; 1Sm 8:2

6:1-81 To the original readers, this was a vital record of the priestly descent so the Israelites who'd returned from the Babylonian exile could be assured that the priests serving them were legitimate.

40 son of Michael, son of Baaseiah,
son of Malchijah, **41** son of Ethni,
son of Zerah, son of Adaiah,
42 son of Ethan, son of Zimmah,
son of Shimei, **43** son of Jahath,
son of Gershom, son of Levi.

44 On the left, their relatives were
Merari's sons:
Ethan son of Kishi, son of Abdi,
son of Malluch, **45** son of Hashabiah,
son of Amaziah, son of Hilkiah,
46 son of Amzi, son of Bani,
son of Shemer, **47** son of Mahli,
son of Mushi, son of Merari,
son of Levi.

AARON'S DESCENDANTS

48 Their relatives, the Levites, were assigned to all the service of the tabernacle, God's temple. **49** But Aaron and his sons did all the work of the most holy place. They presented the offerings on the altar of burnt offerings[a] and on the altar of incense[b] to make atonement for Israel according to all that Moses the servant of God had commanded.[c] **50** These[d] are Aaron's sons: his son Eleazar,
his son Phinehas, his son Abishua,
51 his son Bukki, his son Uzzi,
his son Zerahiah, **52** his son Meraioth,
his son Amariah, his son Ahitub,
53 his son Zadok, and his son Ahimaaz.

THE SETTLEMENTS OF THE LEVITES

54 These were the places assigned to Aaron's descendants from the Kohathite family for their settlements in their territory, because the first lot was for them.[e] **55** They[f] were given Hebron in the land of Judah and its surrounding pasturelands, **56** but the fields and settlements around the city were given to Caleb son of Jephunneh. **57** Aaron's descendants were given:[g]
Hebron (a city of refuge), Libnah and its pasturelands, Jattir, Eshtemoa and its pasturelands, **58** Hilen[A] and its pasturelands, Debir and its pasturelands, **59** Ashan and its pasturelands, and Bethshemesh and its pasturelands. **60** From the tribe of Benjamin they were given Geba and its pasturelands, Alemeth and its pasturelands, and Anathoth and its pasturelands. They had thirteen towns in all among their families.

61 To the rest of the Kohathites, ten towns from half the tribe of Manasseh were assigned by lot.[h]
62 The Gershomites were assigned thirteen towns from the tribes of Issachar, Asher, Naphtali, and Manasseh in Bashan according to their families.
63 The Merarites were assigned by lot twelve towns from the tribes of Reuben, Gad, and Zebulun according to their families.[i] **64** So the Israelites gave these towns and their pasturelands to the Levites.[j] **65** They assigned by lot the towns named above[k] from the tribes of the descendants of Judah, Simeon, and Benjamin.
66 Some[l] of the families of the Kohathites were given towns from the tribe of Ephraim for their territory:
67 Shechem (a city of refuge) with its pasturelands in the hill country of Ephraim, Gezer and its pasturelands, **68** Jokmeam and its pasturelands, Bethhoron and its pasturelands, **69** Aijalon and its pasturelands, and Gath-rimmon and its pasturelands. **70** From half the tribe of Manasseh, Aner and its pasturelands, and Bileam and its pasturelands were given to the rest of the families of the Kohathites.

71 The Gershomites received:
Golan in Bashan and its pasturelands, and Ashtaroth and its pasturelands from the families of half the tribe of Manasseh. **72** From the tribe of Issachar they received Kedesh and its pasturelands, Daberath and its pasturelands, **73** Ramoth and its pasturelands, and Anem and its pasturelands. **74** From the tribe of Asher they received Mashal and its pasturelands, Abdon and its pasturelands, **75** Hukok and its pasturelands, and Rehob and its pasturelands. **76** From the tribe of Naphtali they received Kedesh in Galilee and its pasturelands, Hammon and its pasturelands, and Kiriathaim and its pasturelands.

77 The rest of the Merarites received:
From the tribe of Zebulun they received Rimmono and its pasturelands and Tabor and its pasturelands. **78** From the tribe of Reuben across the Jordan at Jericho, to the east of the Jordan, they received Bezer in the desert and its pasturelands, Jahzah and its pasturelands,

[a] 6:49 Ex 27:1-8
[b] Ex 30:1-7
[c] Ex 30:10-16
[d] 6:50-53 1Ch 6:4-8
[e] 6:54 Jos 21:4,10
[f] 6:55-56 Jos 14:13; 15:13
[g] 6:57 Jos 21:13,19

[h] 6:61 Jos 21:5; 1Ch 6:66-70
[i] 6:63 Jos 21:7; 1Ch 6:77-81
[j] 6:64 Jos 21:3,41-42
[k] 6:65 1Ch 6:57-60
[l] 6:66-81 Jos 21:20-40

a 7:1 Gn 46:13
b 7:2 2Sm 24:1-9
c 7:6-12 Gn 46:21; Nm
26:38-41; 1Ch 8
d 7:13 Gn 46:24-25

e 7:14-19 Nm 26:29-34
f 7:20-21a Nm 26:35-36
g 7:24 Jos 16:3,5
h 7:27 Ex 17:9-14; 24:13
i 7:28 Jos 16:2

79 Kedemoth and its pasturelands, and Mephaath and its pasturelands. **80** From the tribe of Gad they received Ramoth in Gilead and its pasturelands, Mahanaim and its pasturelands, **81** Heshbon and its pasturelands, and Jazer and its pasturelands.

ISSACHAR'S DESCENDANTS

7 Issachar's sons:*a* Tola, Puah, Jashub, and Shimron — four. **2** Tola's sons: Uzzi, Rephaiah, Jeriel, Jahmai, Ibsam, and Shemuel, the heads of their ancestral families.^A During David's reign, 22,600 descendants of Tola were recorded as valiant warriors in their family records.*b* **3** Uzzi's son: Izrahiah. Izrahiah's sons: Michael, Obadiah, Joel, Isshiah. All five of them were chiefs. **4** Along with them, they had 36,000 troops for battle according to the family records of their ancestral families, for they had many wives and children. **5** Their tribesmen who were valiant warriors belonging to all the families of Issachar totaled 87,000 in their genealogies.

BENJAMIN'S DESCENDANTS

6 Three*c* of Benjamin's sons: Bela, Becher, and Jediael. **7** Bela's sons: Ezbon, Uzzi, Uzziel, Jerimoth, and Iri — five. They were valiant warriors and heads of their ancestral families; 22,034 were listed in their genealogies. **8** Becher's sons: Zemirah, Joash, Eliezer, Elioenai, Omri, Jeremoth, Abijah, Anathoth, and Alemeth; all these were Becher's sons. **9** Their family records were recorded according to the heads of their ancestral families — 20,200 valiant warriors. **10** Jediael's son: Bilhan. Bilhan's sons: Jeush, Benjamin, Ehud, Chenaanah, Zethan, Tarshish, and Ahishahar. **11** All these sons of Jediael listed by family heads were valiant warriors; there were 17,200 who could serve in the army. **12** Shuppim and Huppim were sons of Ir, and the Hushim were the sons of Aher.

NAPHTALI'S DESCENDANTS

13 Naphtali's sons:*d* Jahziel, Guni, Jezer, and Shallum — Bilhah's sons.

MANASSEH'S DESCENDANTS

14 Manasseh's*e* sons through his Aramean concubine: Asriel and Machir the father of Gilead. **15** Machir took wives from Huppim and Shuppim. The name of his sister was Maacah. Another descendant was named Zelophehad, but he had only daughters. **16** Machir's wife Maacah gave birth to a son, and she named him Peresh. His brother was named Sheresh, and his sons were Ulam and Rekem. **17** Ulam's son: Bedan. These were the sons of Gilead son of Machir, son of Manasseh. **18** His sister Hammolecheth gave birth to Ishhod, Abiezer, and Mahlah. **19** Shemida's sons: Ahian, Shechem, Likhi, and Aniam.

EPHRAIM'S DESCENDANTS

20 Ephraim's*f* sons: Shuthelah, and his son Bered, his son Tahath, his son Eleadah, his son Tahath, **21** his son Zabad, his son Shuthelah, also Ezer, and Elead.

The men of Gath, born in the land, killed them because they went down to raid their cattle. **22** Their father Ephraim mourned a long time, and his relatives^B came to comfort him. **23** He slept with his wife, and she conceived and gave birth to a son. So he named him Beriah, because there had been misfortune in his home.^C **24** His daughter was Sheerah, who built Lower and Upper Beth-horon*g* and Uzzen-sheerah,

25 his son Rephah,*D* his son Resheph, his son Telah, his son Tahan, **26** his son Ladan, his son Ammihud, his son Elishama, **27** his son Nun, and his son Joshua.*h*

28 Their holdings and settlements were Bethel*i* and its surrounding villages; Naaran to the east, Gezer and its villages to the west, and Shechem and its villages as far as Ayyah and its villages, **29** and along the borders of the descendants of Manasseh, Beth-shean, Taanach, Megiddo, and Dor with their surrounding villages. The sons

---

^A 7:2 Lit *the house of their fathers*, also in vv. 4,7,9,40   ^B 7:22 Or *his brothers*   ^C 7:23 In Hb, the name *Beriah* sounds like "in misfortune."
^D 7:25 Probably Ephraim's son

of Joseph son of Israel lived in these towns.

ASHER'S DESCENDANTS

[30] Asher's[a] sons: Imnah, Ishvah, Ishvi, and Beriah, with their sister Serah. [31] Beriah's sons: Heber, and Malchiel, who fathered Birzaith. [32] Heber fathered Japhlet, Shomer, and Hotham, with their sister Shua. [33] Japhlet's sons: Pasach, Bimhal, and Ashvath. These were Japhlet's sons. [34] Shemer's sons: Ahi, Rohgah, Hubbah, and Aram. [35] His brother Helem's sons: Zophah, Imna, Shelesh, and Amal. [36] Zophah's sons: Suah, Harnepher, Shual, Beri, Imrah, [37] Bezer, Hod, Shamma, Shilshah, Ithran, and Beera. [38] Jether's sons: Jephunneh, Pispa, and Ara. [39] Ulla's sons: Arah, Hanniel, and Rizia. [40] All these were Asher's descendants. They were the heads of their ancestral families, chosen men, valiant warriors, and chiefs among the leaders.
The number of men listed in their genealogies for military service was 26,000.

BENJAMIN'S DESCENDANTS

8 Benjamin[b] fathered Bela, his firstborn; Ashbel was born second, Aharah third, [2] Nohah fourth, and Rapha fifth. [3] Bela's sons: Addar, Gera, Abihud,[A] [4] Abishua, Naaman, Ahoah, [5] Gera, Shephuphan, and Huram. [6] These were Ehud's sons, who were the heads of the families living in Geba and who were deported to Manahath: [7] Naaman, Ahijah, and Gera. Gera deported them and was the father of Uzza and Ahihud. [8] Shaharaim had sons in the territory of Moab after he had divorced his wives Hushim and Baara. [9] His sons by his wife

Hodesh: Jobab, Zibia, Mesha, Malcam, [10] Jeuz, Sachia, and Mirmah. These were his sons, family heads. [11] He also had sons by Hushim: Abitub and Elpaal. [12] Elpaal's sons: Eber, Misham, and Shemed who built Ono and Lod and its surrounding villages, [13] Beriah and Shema, who were the family heads of Aijalon's residents and who drove out the residents of Gath, [14] Ahio,[B] Shashak, and Jeremoth. [15] Zebadiah, Arad, Eder, [16] Michael, Ishpah, and Joha were Beriah's sons. [17] Zebadiah, Meshullam, Hizki, Heber, [18] Ishmerai, Izliah, and Jobab were Elpaal's sons. [19] Jakim, Zichri, Zabdi, [20] Elienai, Zillethai, Eliel, [21] Adaiah, Beraiah, and Shimrath were Shimei's sons. [22] Ishpan, Eber, Eliel, [23] Abdon, Zichri, Hanan, [24] Hananiah, Elam, Anthothijah, [25] Iphdeiah, and Penuel were Shashak's sons. [26] Shamsherai, Shehariah, Athaliah, [27] Jaareshiah, Elijah, and Zichri were Jeroham's sons. [28] These[c] were family heads, chiefs according to their family records; they lived in Jerusalem.

[29] Jeiel[c,d] fathered Gibeon and lived in Gibeon. His wife's name was Maacah. [30] Abdon was his firstborn son, then Zur, Kish, Baal, Nadab, [31] Gedor, Ahio, Zecher, [32] and Mikloth who fathered Shimeah. These also lived opposite their relatives in Jerusalem, with their other relatives. [33] Ner fathered Kish, Kish fathered Saul, and Saul fathered Jonathan, Malchishua, Abinadab, and Esh-baal.[D] [34] Jonathan's son was Merib-baal,[E] and Merib-baal fathered Micah. [35] Micah's sons: Pithon, Melech, Tarea, and Ahaz. [36] Ahaz fathered Jehoaddah, Jehoaddah fathered Alemeth,

[a] 7:30-31 Gn 46:17; Nm 26:44-46
[b] 8:1-5 Gn 46:21; Nm 26:38-41; 1Ch 7:6-12
[c] 8:28-38 1Ch 9:34-44
[d] 8:29 1Ch 9:35

[A] 8:3 Or *Gera father of Ehud*; Jdg 3:15   [B] 8:13-14 LXX reads *Gath* [14]*and their brother*   [C] 8:29 LXX; MT omits *Jeiel*; 1Ch 9:35   [D] 8:33 = Man of Baal
[E] 8:34 = Baal Contends

7:40 Asher's sons had four outstanding qualities: **They were the heads of their ancestral families, chosen men, valiant warriors, and chiefs among the leaders**. A summary of these qualities reveals traits that seem to be in short supply today.

First, Asher's sons were "heads" of their families. That suggests Asher raised his sons to be leaders. They weren't just hanging around the house, eating and taking up space.

Second, they were "chosen men." That phrase suggests Asher raised his boys to be the cream of the crop. They were the kind of men a father would choose for his daughter to marry, men of high character and strong ethical standards who accepted responsibility.

Third, they were "valiant warriors"—that is, they were men of valor, like those who fought alongside David in his many battles. These guys had a sense of conviction and were ready to take a stand when a stand needed to be taken.

Fourth, Asher's sons are described as "chiefs among the leaders." Another word for *leader* is "prince," and a prince is just a king waiting to happen. Asher's sons were outstanding even among the literal princes of Israel.

Our country and church need godly, committed men to take up the reins of leadership. **8:1-40** Benjamin's tribe was small, but important since it was the tribe of **Saul**, Israel's first king (8:33).

a 9:1 1Ch 6:15
b 9:2-9 Neh 11:3-9
c 9:2 Ezr 2:43,58; 8:20
d 9:9 Neh 11:8
e 9:10-16 Neh 11:10-18

f 9:11 Jr 20:1
g 9:17-22a 1Ch 26:1-19; Ezr 2:42; Neh 7:45; 11:19
h 9:18 Ezk 46:1-2
i 9:19 Nm 4:1-20; 26:11; 1Ch 6:22
j 9:20 Nm 25:7-13
k 9:21 1Ch 26:2,14

Azmaveth, and Zimri, and Zimri fathered Moza.
[37] Moza fathered Binea. His son was Raphah, his son Elasah, and his son Azel.
[38] Azel had six sons, and these were their names: Azrikam, Bocheru, Ishmael, Sheariah, Obadiah, and Hanan. All these were Azel's sons.
[39] His brother Eshek's sons: Ulam was his firstborn, Jeush second, and Eliphelet third.
[40] Ulam's sons were valiant warriors and archers.[A] They had many sons and grandsons — 150 of them.
All these were among Benjamin's sons.

AFTER THE EXILE

9 All Israel was registered in the genealogies that are written in the Book of the Kings of Israel. But Judah was exiled[a] to Babylon because of their unfaithfulness. [2] The first[b] to live in their towns on their own property again were Israelites, priests, Levites, and temple servants.[c]
[3] These people from the descendants of Judah, Benjamin, Ephraim, and Manasseh settled in Jerusalem:
[4] Uthai son of Ammihud, son of Omri, son of Imri, son of Bani, a descendant[B] of Perez son of Judah;
[5] from the Shilonites:
Asaiah the firstborn and his sons;
[6] and from the descendants of Zerah: Jeuel and their relatives — 690 in all.

[7] The Benjaminites: Sallu son of Meshullam, son of Hodaviah, son of Hassenuah;
[8] Ibneiah son of Jeroham;
Elah son of Uzzi, son of Michri;
Meshullam son of Shephatiah, son of Reuel, son of Ibnijah;
[9] and their relatives according to their family records — 956[d] in all. All these men were heads of their ancestral families.[c]

[10] The priests:[e] Jedaiah; Jehoiarib; Jachin;

[11] Azariah son of Hilkiah, son of Meshullam, son of Zadok, son of Meraioth, son of Ahitub, the chief official[f] of God's temple;
[12] Adaiah son of Jeroham, son of Pashhur, son of Malchijah;
Maasai son of Adiel, son of Jahzerah, son of Meshullam, son of Meshillemith, son of Immer;
[13] and their relatives, the heads of their ancestral families — 1,760 in all. They were capable men employed in the ministry of God's temple.

[14] The Levites: Shemaiah son of Hasshub, son of Azrikam, son of Hashabiah of the Merarites;
[15] Bakbakkar, Heresh, Galal, and Mattaniah, son of Mica, son of Zichri, son of Asaph;
[16] Obadiah son of Shemaiah, son of Galal, son of Jeduthun;
and Berechiah son of Asa, son of Elkanah who lived in the settlements of the Netophathites.

[17] The gatekeepers:[g] Shallum, Akkub, Talmon, Ahiman, and their relatives. Shallum was their chief; [18] he was previously stationed at the King's Gate on the east side.[h] These were the gatekeepers from the camp of the Levites.
[19] Shallum son of Kore, son of Ebiasaph, son of Korah and his relatives from his father's family,[D] the Korahites, were assigned to guard the thresholds of the tent.[E] Their ancestors had been assigned to the LORD's camp as guardians of the entrance.[i] [20] In earlier times Phinehas son of Eleazar had been their leader, and the LORD was with him.[j] [21] Zechariah son of Meshelemiah was the gatekeeper at the entrance to the tent of meeting.[k]

[22] The total number of those chosen to be gatekeepers at the thresholds was 212. They were registered by genealogy in their settlements. David and the seer Samuel

---

[A] 8:40 Lit *valiant ones who string the bow*   [B] 9:4 Lit *Bani, from the sons*   [C] 9:9 Lit *the house of their fathers*, also in v. 13   [D] 9:19 Lit *the house of his father*   [E] 9:19 = the temple

---

9:1 Mentioning the Babylonian captivity in passing as the Chronicler does here would serve to remind the book's earliest audiences of the gross sin, idolatry, and apostasy that had led to the exile and destruction of the Jerusalem temple and the land of Judah. It was far more than a history lesson, then. It was a powerful reminder that the current generation must live faithfully. 9:2-34 This passage emphasizes the **priests** (9:10-13), **Levites** (9:14-16), **gatekeepers** (9:17-26), and other **servants** of God who officiated in and cared for the **temple** (9:2). This, then, is one of the places in which we can see that the Chronicler had a definite theological or spiritual purpose for his work and wasn't merely compiling historical facts. He wanted the people to read their history from the divine perspective so they could bring all of life under the lordship of their great Creator God. Similarly, God wants the

had appointed them[a] to their trusted positions. 23 So they and their sons were assigned as guards to the gates of the LORD's temple, which had been the tent-temple. 24 The gatekeepers were on the four sides: east, west, north, and south. 25 Their relatives came from their settlements[b] at fixed times to be with them seven days,[c] 26 but the four chief gatekeepers, who were Levites, were entrusted with the rooms and the treasuries of God's temple.[d] 27 They spent the night in the vicinity of God's temple, because they had guard duty and were in charge of opening it every morning.[e]

28 Some of them were in charge of the utensils used in worship. They would count them when they brought them in and when they took them out. 29 Others were put in charge of the furnishings and all the utensils of the sanctuary,[f] as well as the fine flour,[g] wine, oil, incense, and spices. 30 Some of the priests' sons mixed the spices.[h] 31 A Levite called Mattithiah, the firstborn of Shallum the Korahite, was entrusted with baking the bread.[A] 32 Some of the Kohathites' relatives were responsible for preparing the rows of the Bread of the Presence[i] every Sabbath.

33 The singers,[j] the heads of the Levite families, stayed in the temple chambers and were exempt from other tasks because they were on duty day and night.[k] 34 These[l] were the heads of the Levite families, chiefs according to their family records; they lived in Jerusalem.

SAUL'S FAMILY

35 Jeiel fathered Gibeon and lived in Gibeon. His wife's name was Maacah. 36 Abdon was his firstborn son, then Zur, Kish, Baal, Ner, Nadab, 37 Gedor, Ahio, Zechariah, and Mikloth. 38 Mikloth fathered Shimeam. These also lived opposite their relatives in Jerusalem with their other relatives. 39 Ner fathered Kish, Kish fathered Saul, and Saul fathered Jonathan, Malchishua, Abinadab, and Esh-baal. 40 Jonathan's son was Merib-baal, and Merib-baal fathered Micah. 41 Micah's sons: Pithon, Melech, Tahrea, and Ahaz.[B] 42 Ahaz fathered Jarah;

Jarah fathered Alemeth, Azmaveth, and Zimri; Zimri fathered Moza. 43 Moza fathered Binea. His son was Rephaiah, his son Elasah, and his son Azel. 44 Azel had six sons, and these were their names: Azrikam, Bocheru, Ishmael, Sheariah, Obadiah, and Hanan. These were Azel's sons.

THE DEATH OF SAUL AND HIS SONS

10 The Philistines[m] fought against Israel, and Israel's men fled from them. Many were killed on Mount Gilboa. 2 The Philistines pursued Saul and his sons and killed his sons Jonathan, Abinadab, and Malchishua. 3 When the battle intensified against Saul, the archers spotted him and severely wounded him. 4 Then Saul said to his armor-bearer, "Draw your sword and run me through with it, or these uncircumcised men will come and torture me." But his armor-bearer would not do it because he was terrified. Then Saul took his sword and fell on it. 5 When his armor-bearer saw that Saul was dead, he also fell on his own sword and died. 6 So Saul and his three sons died — his whole house died together.

7 When all the men of Israel in the valley saw that the army had fled and that Saul and his sons were dead, they abandoned their cities and fled. So the Philistines came and settled in them.

8 The next day when the Philistines came to strip the slain, they found Saul and his sons dead on Mount Gilboa. 9 They stripped Saul, cut off his head, took his armor, and sent messengers throughout the land of the Philistines to spread the good news to their idols and the people. 10 Then they put his armor in the temple of their gods and hung his skull in the temple of Dagon.[n]

11 When all Jabesh-gilead heard of everything the Philistines had done to Saul, 12 all their brave men set out and retrieved the body of Saul and the bodies of his sons and brought them to Jabesh. They buried their bones under the oak[c] in Jabesh[o] and fasted seven days.

13 Saul died for his unfaithfulness to the LORD because he did not keep the LORD's

a 9:22 1Ch 26:1
b 9:25 1Ch 9:16
c 2Kg 11:5,7; 2Ch 23:8
d 9:26 Neh 12:25
e 9:27 1Sm 3:3,15; 1Ch 23:30-32
f 9:29 Nm 3:31
g 1Ch 23:29
h 9:30 Ex 30:23-25
i 9:32 Lv 24:5-9
j 9:33 1Ch 6:31-47; 25:1
k Ps 134:1
l 9:34-44 1Ch 8:28-38

m 10:1-12 1Sm 31:1-13
n 10:10 1Sm 5:1-4; 17:54
o 10:12 2Sm 21:12-14

A 9:31 Lit with things prepared in pans   B 9:41 LXX, Syr, Tg, Vg, Arabic; MT omits and Ahaz; 1Ch 8:35   C 10:12 Or terebinth, or large tree

church to comprehensively bring every area of life under the lordship of Jesus Christ so that his people live all of life the way God intended.

10:3-9 The sad, pitiful end of Israel's first king provides a strong lesson for us and illustrates the difference between living for a kingdom agenda and living for a selfish, personal agenda. Saul's life followed the path of convenience, regardless of God's Word or priorities.

a 10:13 1Sm 13:13-14; 15:23
  b 1Sm 28:7
c 10:14 1Sm 15:28; 1Ch
          12:23
d 11:1-3 2Sm 5:1-3
e 11:3 1Sm 16:1-13
f 11:4-9 2Sm 5:6-10
g 11:4 Jos 15:8,63; Jdg 1:21
h 11:6 2Sm 8:16; 1Ch 18:15
  i 11:9 2Sm 3:1

j 11:10 1Ch 11:3
k 11:11-25 2Sm 23:8-23
  11:11 1Ch 12:18
m 11:12 1Ch 27:4
n 11:13 2Sm 23:11-12
  11:15 1Sm 22:1
  p 1Ch 14:9
q 11:16 1Sm 22:4-5;
          2Sm 5:9
  r 1Sm 10:5
s 11:20 1Sm 26:6; 2Sm 18:2
  11:22 2Sm 8:18; 20:23;
  23:20-23; 1Kg 1:8; 1Ch
          18:17; 27:5-6,34

word.[a] He even consulted a medium for guidance,[b] 14 but he did not inquire of the LORD. So the LORD put him to death and turned the kingdom over to David son of Jesse.[c]

DAVID'S ANOINTING AS KING

11 All Israel[d] came together to David at Hebron and said, "Here we are, your own flesh and blood.[A] 2 Even previously when Saul was king, you were leading Israel out to battle and bringing us back. The LORD your God also said to you, 'You will shepherd my people Israel, and you will be ruler over my people Israel.'"

3 So all the elders of Israel came to the king at Hebron. David made a covenant with them at Hebron in the LORD's presence, and they anointed David king over Israel, in keeping with the LORD's word through Samuel.[e]

DAVID'S CAPTURE OF JERUSALEM

4 David[f] and all Israel marched to Jerusalem (that is, Jebus); the Jebusites who inhabited the land were there.[g] 5 The inhabitants of Jebus said to David, "You will never get in here." Yet David did capture the stronghold of Zion, that is, the city of David.

6 David said, "Whoever is the first to kill a Jebusite will become chief commander." Joab[h] son of Zeruiah went up first, so he became the chief.

7 Then David took up residence in the stronghold; therefore, it was called the city of David. 8 He built up the city all the way around, from the supporting terraces to the surrounding parts, and Joab restored the rest of the city. 9 David steadily grew more powerful,[i] and the LORD of Armies was with him.

EXPLOITS OF DAVID'S WARRIORS

10 The following were the chiefs of David's warriors who, together with all Israel, strongly supported him in his reign to make him king according to the LORD's

word about Israel.[j] 11 This[k] is the list of David's warriors:

Jashobeam son of Hachmoni was chief[l] of the Thirty;[B] he wielded his spear against three hundred and killed them at one time.

12 After him, Eleazar son of Dodo[m] the Ahohite was one of the three warriors. 13 He was with David at Pas-dammim when the Philistines had gathered there for battle. There was a portion of a field full of barley, where the troops had fled from the Philistines.[n] 14 But Eleazar and David[c] took their stand in the middle of the field and defended it. They killed the Philistines, and the LORD gave them a great victory.

15 Three of the thirty chief men went down to David, to the rock at the cave of Adullam,[o] while the Philistine army was encamped in the Valley of Rephaim.[p] 16 At that time David was in the stronghold,[q] and a Philistine garrison[r] was at Bethlehem. 17 David was extremely thirsty[D] and said, "If only someone would bring me water to drink from the well at the city gate of Bethlehem!" 18 So the Three broke through the Philistine camp and drew water from the well at the gate of Bethlehem. They brought it back to David, but he refused to drink it. Instead, he poured it out to the LORD. 19 David said, "I would never do such a thing in the presence of my God! How can I drink the blood of these men who risked their lives?" For they brought it at the risk of their lives. So he would not drink it. Such were the exploits of the three warriors.

20 Abishai,[s] Joab's brother, was the leader of the Three.[E] He raised his spear against three hundred men and killed them, gaining a reputation among the Three. 21 He was more honored than the Three and became their commander even though he did not become one of the Three.

22 Benaiah son of Jehoiada[t] was the son of a brave man[F] from Kabzeel, a man of many exploits. Benaiah killed two sons of Ariel of Moab,[G] and he went down into a pit on a snowy day and killed a lion. 23 He

11:1-3 That all Israel came to Hebron for the anointing (11:1) was a significant statement of national unity for the readers of 1 Chronicles who had returned from the Babylonian exile. Israel had been divided, tribe against tribe, from the time of Solomon's death until the exile—a period of several hundred years. Now that the people were back in the land, unity was crucial.

11:4-5 In time, the place David captured would house the temple. Thus, Jerusalem would be home to the throne of King David and, more importantly, to the throne of the King of kings (11:4).
11:10-47 The exploits of these men sound like something out of a superhero movie, telling us that David had an incredible office staff! Nevertheless, the Chronicler makes it clear

that David and his warriors were not victorious merely because of their brute strength and military cunning. Though they possessed these qualities, the LORD gave them ... great victory (11:14). So don't pat yourself on the back and forget the true source of your victory either.

also killed an Egyptian who was seven and a half feet tall.[A] Even though the Egyptian had a spear in his hand like a weaver's beam,[a] Benaiah went down to him with a club, snatched the spear out of the Egyptian's hand, and then killed him with his own spear. **24** These were the exploits of Benaiah son of Jehoiada, who had a reputation among the three warriors. **25** He was the most honored of the Thirty, but he did not become one of the Three. David put him in charge of his bodyguard.

26 The best soldiers[b] were
Joab's brother Asahel,[c]
Elhanan son of Dodo of Bethlehem,
27 Shammoth the Harorite,
Helez the Pelonite,
28 Ira son of Ikkesh the Tekoite,
Abiezer the Anathothite,
29 Sibbecai the Hushathite,
Ilai the Ahohite,
30 Maharai the Netophathite,
Heled son of Baanah
the Netophathite,
31 Ithai son of Ribai from Gibeah
of the Benjaminites,
Benaiah the Pirathonite,
32 Hurai from the wadis of Gaash,
Abiel the Arbathite,
33 Azmaveth the Baharumite,
Eliahba the Shaalbonite,
34 the sons of[B,d] Hashem the Gizonite,
Jonathan son of Shagee the Hararite,
35 Ahiam son of Sachar the Hararite,
Eliphal son of Ur,
36 Hepher the Mecherathite,
Ahijah the Pelonite,
37 Hezro the Carmelite,
Naarai son of Ezbai,
38 Joel the brother of Nathan,
Mibhar son of Hagri,
39 Zelek the Ammonite,
Naharai the Beerothite,
the armor-bearer for Joab
son of Zeruiah,
40 Ira the Ithrite,
Gareb the Ithrite,
41 Uriah the Hethite,
Zabad son of Ahlai,
42 Adina son of Shiza the Reubenite,
chief of the Reubenites, and thirty
with him,
43 Hanan son of Maacah,
Joshaphat the Mithnite,
44 Uzzia the Ashterathite,
Shama and Jeiel the sons of Hotham
the Aroerite,
45 Jediael son of Shimri and his brother
Joha the Tizite,
46 Eliel the Mahavite,
Jeribai and Joshaviah, the sons
of Elnaam,
Ithmah the Moabite,
47 Eliel, Obed, and Jaasiel
the Mezobaite.

DAVID'S FIRST SUPPORTERS

12 The following were the men who came to David at Ziklag while he was still banned from the presence of Saul son of Kish.[e] They were among the warriors who helped him in battle. **2** They were archers who could use either the right or left hand, both to sling stones and shoot arrows from a bow.[f] They were Saul's relatives[g] from Benjamin:

3 Their chief was Ahiezer son of
Shemaah the Gibeathite.
Then there was his brother Joash;
Jeziel and Pelet sons of Azmaveth;
Beracah, Jehu the Anathothite;
4 Ishmaiah the Gibeonite, a warrior
among the Thirty and a leader over the
Thirty;
Jeremiah, Jahaziel, Johanan, Jozabad
the Gederathite;
5 Eluzai, Jerimoth, Bealiah, Shemariah,
Shephatiah the Haruphite;
6 Elkanah, Isshiah, Azarel, Joezer, and
Jashobeam, the Korahites;
7 and Joelah and Zebadiah, the sons of
Jeroham from Gedor.

8 Some Gadites defected to David at his stronghold in the desert. They were valiant warriors, trained for battle, expert with shield and spear. Their faces were like the faces of lions, and they were as swift as gazelles on the mountains.[h] **9** Ezer was the chief, Obadiah second, Eliab third, **10** Mishmannah fourth, Jeremiah fifth, **11** Attai sixth, Eliel seventh, **12** Johanan eighth, Elzabad ninth, **13** Jeremiah tenth, and Machbannai eleventh. **14** These Gadites were army commanders; the least of them was a match for a hundred, and the greatest of them for a thousand.[i] **15** These are the men who crossed the Jordan in the first month[c] when it was overflowing all its banks,[j] and put to flight all those in the valleys to the east and to the west.

[a] 11:23 1Sm 17:7; 1Ch 20:5
[b] 11:26-47 2Sm 23:24-39
[c] 11:26 2Sm 2:18-23
[d] 11:34 2Sm 23:32

[e] 12:1 1Sm 27:1-7
[f] 12:2 Jdg 3:15; 20:16
[g] 1Ch 12:29
[h] 12:8 2Sm 2:18
[i] 12:14 Lv 26:8; Dt 32:30; Is 30:17
[j] 12:15 Jos 3:15; 4:18

[A] 11:23 Lit *who measured five cubits*   [B] 11:34 LXX omits *the sons of*; 2Sm 23:32   [C] 12:15 = Nisan (March–April)

a12:16 1Sm 22:1-2
b12:18 Jdg 6:34; 2Ch 24:20
c1Ch 2:17
d1Sm 25:5-6
e12:19 1Sm 29:1-11
f12:21 1Sm 30:1-20
g12:22 Gn 32:1-2; Jos 5:13-15
h12:23 1Sm 15:28; 1Ch 10:14
i1Ch 11:10
j12:28 2Sm 8:17; 1Ch 6:8,53; 9:11; 15:11; 16:39

k12:29 1Ch 12:2
l12:32 Est 1:13
m12:33 Ps 12:2
n12:38 2Sm 5:1-3

16 Other Benjaminites and men from Judah also went to David at the stronghold.[a] **17** David went out to meet them and said to them, "If you have come in peace to help me, my heart will be united with you, but if you have come to betray me to my enemies even though my hands have done no wrong, may the God of our ancestors look on it and judge."

18 Then the Spirit enveloped[A,b] Amasai,[c] chief of the Thirty, and he said:

We are yours, David,
we are with you, son of Jesse!
Peace, peace to you,
and peace to him who helps you,[d]
for your God helps you.

So David received them and made them leaders of his troops.

19 Some Manassites defected to David when he went with the Philistines to fight against Saul. However, they did not help the Philistines because the Philistine rulers sent David away after a discussion. They said, "It will be our heads if he defects to his master Saul."[e] **20** When David went to Ziklag, some men from Manasseh defected to him: Adnah, Jozabad, Jediael, Michael, Jozabad, Elihu, and Zillethai, chiefs of thousands in Manasseh. **21** They helped David against the raiders,[f] for they were all valiant warriors and commanders in the army. **22** At that time, men came day after day to help David until there was a great army, like an army of God.[B,g]

DAVID'S SOLDIERS IN HEBRON

23 The numbers of the armed troops who came to David at Hebron to turn Saul's kingdom over to him,[h] according to the LORD's word,[i] were as follows:

24 From the Judahites: 6,800 armed troops bearing shields and spears.

25 From the Simeonites: 7,100 valiant warriors ready for war.

26 From the Levites: 4,600 **27** in addition to Jehoiada, leader of the house of Aaron, with 3,700 men; **28** and Zadok,[j] a young valiant warrior, with 22 commanders from his father's family.[c]

29 From the Benjaminites, the relatives of Saul:[k] 3,000 (up to that time the majority of the Benjaminites maintained their allegiance to the house of Saul).

30 From the Ephraimites: 20,800 valiant warriors who were famous men in their ancestral families.[D]

31 From half the tribe of Manasseh: 18,000 designated by name to come and make David king.

32 From the Issacharites, who understood the times[l] and knew what Israel should do: 200 chiefs with all their relatives under their command.

33 From Zebulun: 50,000 who could serve in the army, trained for battle with all kinds of weapons of war, with one purpose[m] to help David.[E]

34 From Naphtali: 1,000 commanders accompanied by 37,000 men with shield and spear.

35 From the Danites: 28,600 trained for battle.

36 From Asher: 40,000 who could serve in the army, trained for battle.

37 From across the Jordan — from the Reubenites, Gadites, and half the tribe of Manasseh: 120,000 men equipped with all the military weapons of war.

38 All these warriors, lined up in battle formation, came to Hebron wholeheartedly determined to make David king over all Israel. All the rest of Israel was also of one mind to make David king.[n] **39** They spent three days there eating and drinking with David, for their relatives had provided for them. **40** In addition, their neighbors from as far away as Issachar, Zebulun, and Naphtali came and brought food on donkeys, camels, mules, and oxen

---

A12:18 Lit *clothed*; Jdg 6:34; 2Ch 24:20   B12:22 Or *like the ultimate army*   C12:28 Lit *the house of his father*   D12:30 Lit *the house of their fathers*   E12:33 LXX; MT omits *David*

12:18 So clear was it to **Amasai, chief of the Thirty**, that God was with David that he and his men pledged their loyalty to him. How did Amasai come by this insight? After all, at the time described in verses 1–22, David was hiding out (12:8, 16). The answer is that **the Spirit enveloped Amasai**—that is, he received a direct revelation from the Lord who said of David, "This is my man." Small wonder, then, that when all the soldiers gathered to David, it looked "like an army of God" (12:22).

12:32 This group **understood the times and knew what Israel should do.** That insight tells us that somebody raised those boys to understand what was happening around them, and they were ready to serve. They're a faithful example of kingdom living.

Parents, teach your children to be observant about the dangerous times we live in and to follow God's path of wisdom. Let's raise up followers of Christ of whom it is one day said, "They understood the times and knew what the church should do."

12:38 As a group of football players with diverse roles become a team when united in purpose, so God's people are truly united when his kingdom purposes become theirs. As the apostle Paul affirms, true unity is a spiritual issue (see Eph 4:3).

— abundant provisions of flour, fig cakes, raisins, wine and oil, herds, and flocks.[a] Indeed, there was joy in Israel.

DAVID AND THE ARK

13 David consulted with all his leaders, the commanders of hundreds and of thousands. [2] Then he said to the whole assembly of Israel, "If it seems good to you, and if this is from the LORD our God, let us spread out and send the message to the rest of our relatives in all the districts of Israel, including the priests and Levites in their cities with pasturelands,[b] that they should gather together with us. [3] Then let us bring back the ark of our God, for we did not inquire of him[A,C] in Saul's days." [4] Since the proposal seemed right to all the people, the whole assembly agreed to do it.

[5] So David assembled all Israel,[d] from the Shihor of Egypt to the entrance of Hamath,[B,e] to bring the ark of God from Kiriath-jearim.[f] [6] David[g] and all Israel went to Baalah[h] (that is, Kiriath-jearim that belongs to Judah) to take from there the ark of God, which bears the name of the LORD who is enthroned between the cherubim.[i] [7] At Abinadab's house[j] they set the ark of God on a new cart. Uzzah and Ahio[c] were guiding the cart.

[8] David and all Israel were dancing with all their might before God with songs and with lyres, harps, tambourines, cymbals, and trumpets.[k] [9] When they came to Chidon's threshing floor,[l] Uzzah reached out to hold the ark because the oxen had stumbled. [10] Then the LORD's anger burned against Uzzah, and he struck him dead because he had reached out to the ark.[m] So he died there in the presence of God.[n]

[11] David was angry because of the LORD's outburst against Uzzah, so he named that place Outburst Against Uzzah,[D] as it is still named today. [12] David feared God that day and said, "How can I ever bring the ark of God to me?" [13] So David did not bring the ark of God home[E] to the city of David; instead, he diverted it to the house of Obed-edom of Gath.[o] [14] The ark of God remained with Obed-edom's family in his house for three months, and the LORD blessed his family and all that he had.

GOD'S BLESSING ON DAVID

14 King Hiram of Tyre sent envoys to David,[p] along with cedar logs, stonemasons, and carpenters to build a palace for him. [2] Then David knew that the LORD had established him as king over Israel and that his kingdom had been exalted for the sake of his people Israel.

[3] David took more wives in Jerusalem, and he became the father of more sons and daughters. [4] These[q] are the names of the children born to him in Jerusalem: Shammua, Shobab, Nathan, Solomon, [5] Ibhar, Elishua, Elpelet, [6] Nogah, Nepheg, Japhia, [7] Elishama, Beeliada, and Eliphelet.

[8] When the Philistines heard that David had been anointed king over all Israel, they all went in search of David; when David heard of this, he went out to face them. [9] Now the Philistines had come and raided in the Valley of Rephaim,[r] [10] so David inquired of God, "Should I attack the Philistines? Will you hand them over to me?"

The LORD replied, "Attack, and I will hand them over to you."

[11] So the Israelites went up to Baal-perazim, and David defeated the Philistines there. Then David said, "Like a bursting flood, God has used me to burst out against my enemies." Therefore, they named that place The Lord Bursts Out.[F]

[a] 12:40 1Sm 25:18
[b] 13:2 Nm 35:1-8
[c] 13:3 1Sm 7:1-2; 1Ch 10:14; 15:13
[d] 13:5 2Sm 6:1; 1Ch 15:3
[e] 1Kg 8:65
[f] 1Sm 6:21; 7:1
[g] 13:6-14 2Sm 6:2-11
[h] 13:6 Jos 15:9
[i] 2Kg 19:15
[j] 13:7 1Sm 7:1
[k] 13:8 1Ch 15:16
[l] 13:9 2Sm 6:6
[m] 13:10 1Ch 15:13,15
[n] Lv 10:2

[o] 13:13 1Ch 26:4-5; 2Ch 25:23-24
[p] 14:1-17 2Sm 5:11-25
[q] 14:4-7 1Ch 3:5-8
[r] 14:9 1Ch 11:15; 14:13

[A] 13:3 Or did not seek it   [B] 13:5 Or to Lebo-hamath   [C] 13:7 Or And his brothers   [D] 13:11 Or Perez-uzzah   [E] 13:13 Lit to himself   [F] 14:11 Or Baal-perazim

---

13:7-13 The story recorded here reminds us that worship must be more than heartfelt. It must be carried out in the way God prescribes. God had given Israel strict instructions about how to transport the ark. Only the Levites were to carry it and only by using poles inserted through rings in its side (see Exod 25:12-15; 37:3-5; Deut 10:8). Yet when David transported the ark, it was placed **on a new cart** pulled by oxen (1 Chr 13:7). That detail is important because this was how the godless Philistines had moved the ark (see 1 Sam 6:7).

God's worshipers aren't free to just make things up as they go along, and the parade didn't end well. **Uzzah**, one of those guiding the cart, **reached out to hold the ark because the oxen had stumbled** (1 Chr 13:9). As a result, God **struck him dead** (13:10). Through this response God was reminding David and Israel that he is holy—that is, "separate" or "set apart." He is separate from his creation, unstained by sin, and is the standard of righteousness. We are to approach him as such.

If you were in charge of transporting the President of the United States, you wouldn't have the freedom to simply show up at the White House on horseback and tell the leader of the free world to climb aboard. So, how much more important was it for Israel to submit to the agenda of their holy and transcendent King "who is enthroned between the cherubim" on the ark when it was time to transport it (13:6)?

14:10, 14 To inquire of God—to pray—is to seek heavenly intervention in an earthly situation. It is the established means by which God relates to his people and we relate to him. God has wired the world of his people, in fact, to work through prayer.

Think of God's power like the electricity in your home. Your home has been wired for power; that's the way it was built. The electric company will provide your home with all the power you need, but you have to plug in the toaster to get the benefits of that power. You have to flip the switch. Similarly, if you are a Christian, you are wired for divine power. But unless it is activated through prayer, you'll never see heavenly power working on earth. You've got to flip the switch.

Prayer is calling forth in history what God has determined in eternity. Specific prayer for

a 14:17 Ex 15:14-16; Dt 2:25
15:1 1Ch 16:1; 17:1-5
c 15:2 Nm 4:15; Dt 10:8
d 15:3 1Ch 13:5
e 2Sm 6:12,17; 1Ch 15:12
15:11 1Ch 12:28; 18:16;
24:3,6,31; 27:17; 29:22
g 1Sm 22:20-23; 1Kg 1:7;
2:26-27,35; 1Ch 27:34
h 15:12 Ex 19:14; 2Ch 35:6
i 1Ch 15:1,3

j 15:13 2Sm 6:3; 1Ch 13:7
15:15 Ex 25:12-15; Nm
4:6,15
l 15:16 1Ch 13:8; 25:1
m 15:24 1Ch 16:6
n 15:25-29 2Sm 6:12-16
15:25 1Ch 13:13
p 15:26 Nm 23:1-4,29

12 The Philistines abandoned their idols there, and David ordered that they be burned in the fire.

13 Once again the Philistines raided in the valley. 14 So David again inquired of God, and God answered him, "Do not pursue them directly. Circle around them and attack them opposite the balsam trees. 15 When you hear the sound of marching in the tops of the balsam trees, then go out to battle, for God will have gone out ahead of you to strike down the army of the Philistines." 16 So David did as God commanded him, and they struck down the Philistine army from Gibeon to Gezer. 17 Then David's fame spread throughout the lands, and the Lord caused all the nations to be terrified of him.a

THE ARK COMES TO JERUSALEM

15 David built houses for himself in the city of David, and he prepared a place for the ark of God and pitched a tent for it.b 2 Then David said, "No one but the Levites may carry the ark of God, because the Lord has chosen them to carry the ark of the Lord and to minister before him forever."c

3 David assembled all Israel at Jerusalemd to bring the ark of the Lord to the place he had prepared for it.e 4 Then he gathered together the descendants of Aaron and the Levites:

5 From the Kohathites, Uriel the leader and 120 of his relatives; 6 from the Merarites, Asaiah the leader and 220 of his relatives; 7 from the Gershomites,A Joel the leader and 130 of his relatives; 8 from the Elizaphanites, Shemaiah the leader and 200 of his relatives; 9 from the Hebronites, Eliel the leader and 80 of his relatives; 10 from the Uzzielites, Amminadab the leader and 112 of his relatives.

11 David summoned the priests Zadokf and Abiatharg and the Levites Uriel, Asaiah, Joel, Shemaiah, Eliel, and Amminadab. 12 He said to them, "You are the heads of the Levite families. You and your relatives must consecrate yourselvesh so that you may bring the ark of the Lord God of Israel to the place I have prepared for it.i

13 For the Lord our God burst out in anger against us because you Levites were not with us the first time, for we didn't inquire of him about the proper procedures."j 14 So the priests and the Levites consecrated themselves to bring up the ark of the Lord God of Israel. 15 Then the Levites carried the ark of God the way Moses had commanded according to the word of the Lord: on their shoulders with the poles.k

16 Then David told the leaders of the Levites to appoint their relatives as singers and to have them raise their voices with joy accompanied by musical instruments — harps, lyres, and cymbals.l 17 So the Levites appointed Heman son of Joel; from his relatives, Asaph son of Berechiah; and from their relatives the Merarites, Ethan son of Kushaiah. 18 With them were their relatives second in rank: Zechariah, Jaaziel,B Shemiramoth, Jehiel, Unni, Eliab, Benaiah, Maaseiah, Mattithiah, Eliphelehu, Mikneiah, and the gatekeepers Obed-edom and Jeiel. 19 The singers Heman, Asaph, and Ethan were to sound the bronze cymbals; 20 Zechariah, Aziel, Shemiramoth, Jehiel, Unni, Eliab, Maaseiah, and Benaiah were to play harps according to *Alamoth*;c 21 and Mattithiah, Eliphelehu, Mikneiah, Obed-edom, Jeiel, and Azaziah were to lead the music with lyres according to the *Sheminith*. 22 Chenaniah, the leader of the Levites in music, was to direct the music because he was skillful. 23 Berechiah and Elkanah were to be gatekeepers for the ark. 24 The priests, Shebaniah, Joshaphat, Nethanel, Amasai, Zechariah, Benaiah, and Eliezer, were to blow trumpetsm before the ark of God. Obed-edom and Jehiah were also to be gatekeepers for the ark.

25 David,n the elders of Israel, and the commanders of thousands went with rejoicing to bring the ark of the covenant of the Lord from the house of Obed-edom.o 26 Because God helped the Levites who were carrying the ark of the covenant of the Lord, with God's help, they sacrificed seven bulls and seven rams.p 27 Now David was dressed in a robe of fine linen, as were all the Levites who were

A 15:7 = Gershonites　B 15:18 Some Hb mss, LXX; other Hb mss read *Zechariah son and Jaaziel*　C 15:20 This may refer to a high pitch, perhaps a tune sung by soprano voices; the Hb word means "young women"; Ps 46 title

each sitation allows the Holy Spirit to give decision-making guidance for life's challenges (John 14:16-18; 16:13).

15:1-26 This time, the transport mission was done right. **No one but the Levites** carried the ark (15:2), and they accomplished the task **according to the word of the Lord** (15:15).

The Bible—the written Word of God—is no mere book. It's the authoritative voice of God. Mixing a human viewpoint with the divine viewpoint can be deadly (13:9-10). David took what God said seriously, and we should too. **15:27-29** David had married Michal, a daughter of Saul who was apparently quite a diva.

(Saul even chuckled to himself when he gave Michal to David because he hoped she would be a trap to bring him down; see 1 Sam 18:20-21). **As the ark of the covenant of the Lord was entering the city,** Michal saw David **dancing.** But instead of worshiping with him, **she despised him in her heart** (1 Chr 15:29).

carrying the ark, as well as the singers and Chenaniah, the music leader of the singers. David also wore a linen ephod. **28** So all Israel brought up the ark of the covenant of the LORD with shouts, the sound of the ram's horn, trumpets, and cymbals, and the playing of harps and lyres. **29** As the ark of the covenant of the LORD was entering the city of David, Saul's daughter Michal looked down from the window and saw King David leaping[A] and dancing, and she despised him in her heart.

16 They[a] brought the ark of God and placed it inside the tent David had pitched for it.[b] Then they offered burnt offerings and fellowship offerings in God's presence. **2** When David had finished offering the burnt offerings and the fellowship offerings, he blessed the people in the name of the LORD. **3** Then he distributed to each and every Israelite, both men and women, a loaf of bread, a date cake, and a raisin cake.

4 David appointed some of the Levites to be ministers before the ark of the LORD, to celebrate the LORD God of Israel, and to give thanks and praise to him. **5** Asaph was the chief and Zechariah was second to him. Jeiel, Shemiramoth, Jehiel, Mattithiah, Eliab, Benaiah, Obed-edom, and Jeiel played the harps and lyres, while Asaph sounded the cymbals **6** and the priests Benaiah and Jahaziel blew the trumpets regularly before the ark of the covenant of God.

DAVID'S PSALM OF THANKSGIVING

7 On that day David decreed for the first time that thanks be given to the LORD by Asaph and his relatives:

8 Give thanks[c] to the LORD; call on
    his name;
proclaim his deeds among
    the peoples.[d]
9 Sing to him; sing praise to him;
    tell about all his wondrous works!
10 Honor his holy name;
    let the hearts of those who seek the
    LORD rejoice.

11 Seek the LORD and his strength;
    seek his face always.[e]

⟶ HOPE WORDS ⟵

Don't worry that you may pray poorly. Worry if you don't pray at all.

---

12 Remember the wondrous works
    he has done,[f]
his wonders, and the judgments
    he has pronounced,[B,g]
13 you offspring of Israel his servant,
    Jacob's descendants —
    his chosen ones.

14 He is the LORD our God;
    his judgments govern
    the whole earth.[h]
15 Remember his covenant forever —
    the promise he ordained
    for a thousand generations,
16 the covenant he made
    with Abraham,
swore[c] to Isaac,[i]
17 and confirmed to Jacob as a decree,
    and to Israel
    as a permanent covenant:[j]
18 "I will give the land of Canaan
    to you
    as your inherited portion."[k]

19 When they[D] were few in number,
    very few indeed,[l] and resident aliens
    in Canaan
20 wandering from nation to nation
    and from one kingdom to another,
21 he allowed no one to oppress them;
    he rebuked kings on their behalf:[m]
22 "Do not touch my anointed ones
    or harm my prophets."[n]

23 Let the whole earth sing[o] to
    the LORD.

[a] 16:1-3 2Sm 6:17-19
[b] 16:1 1Ch 15:1
[c] 16:8-22 Ps 105:1-15
[d] 16:8 1Kg 8:43; 2Kg 19:19
[e] 16:11 Ps 24:6
[f] 16:12 Ps 103:2
[g] Ps 78:43-68
[h] 16:14 Ps 48:10
[i] 16:16 Gn 17:2; 22:16-18; 26:3
[j] 16:17 Gn 35:11-12
[k] 16:18 Gn 13:15
[l] 16:19 Gn 34:30; Dt 7:7
[m] 16:21 Gn 12:17; 20:3; Ex 7:15-18
[n] 16:22 Gn 20:7
[o] 16:23-33 Ps 96

[A] 15:29 Or *whirling*   [B] 16:12 Lit *judgments of his mouth*   [C] 16:16 Lit *and his oath*   [D] 16:19 One Hb ms, LXX, Vg; other Hb mss read *you*

What happened in this passage is why Christians ought not be "partners with" or "unequally yoked" with (as the KJV put it) unbelievers (2 Cor 6:14). A believer's marriage to someone who refuses to place himself or herself under God's kingdom rule will result in having two radically different agendas trying to operate under the same roof. Be careful whom you marry *before* you marry.

16:8-36 This great hymn to the Lord combines portions of three Psalms: 95, 105, and 106.

17:8-10 These big promises are a reminder not to place God in a box. He "is able to do above and beyond all that we ask or think" (Eph 3:20).

There's great significance to the last part of 1 Chronicles 17:10. David had proposed building a house for God. But God said, **I will build a house for you**. The house God had in mind wasn't composed of bricks. He was talking about a royal dynasty.

17:11-14 The near term referent in these verses is Solomon; he would build God's temple (see 2 Chr 2:1–7:11). Ultimately, though, this covenant with David couldn't be fulfilled by a mere man. It required a God-man. Only Jesus Christ could fulfill the Davidic covenant and rule as an eternal King. "He . . . will be called the Son of the Most High, and the Lord God will give him the throne of his father David" (Luke 1:32), and "he will reign forever" (Rev 11:15).

17:23 If you sometimes wonder what to pray, ask God to fulfill the promises he has made to his children. If he promises it, you know it's his will. So pray that he makes that which is settled in heaven a reality in your earthly history.

a16:25 Ps 144:3-6
b Ps 89:7
c16:26 Lv 19:4
d Ps 102:25
e16:29 Ps 29:2
f16:30-31 Ps 93:1
g16:31 Is 44:23; 49:13
h16:32 Ps 98:7
i16:34 Ps 106:1; 136:1
j16:35-36a Ps 106:47-48
k16:36 1Kg 8:15,56; Ps 72:18
l16:37 1Ch 16:4-5

m16:37 2Ch 8:14; Ezr 3:4
n16:38 1Ch 13:13
o1Ch 26:10
p16:39 1Kg 3:4; 1Ch 21:29
q16:40 Ex 29:38-42; Nm 28:3-4
r16:41 1Ch 6:33
s1Ch 25:1-6
t2Ch 5:13
u16:42 1Ch 25:7; 2Ch 7:6; 29:27
v16:43 2Sm 6:19-20
w17:1-2 2Sm 7:1-3
x17:1 Hg 1:4
y17:3-15 2Sm 7:4-17
z17:4 1Ch 22:7-8; 28:2-3
aa17:5 Ex 40:2-3; 2Sm 7:6
ab17:6 2Sm 7:7
ac17:7 1Sm 16:11-13
ad17:9 Ex 15:17

Proclaim his salvation from day
to day.
24 Declare his glory among the nations,
his wondrous works
among all peoples.

25 For the LORD is great
and highly praised;[a]
he is feared above all gods.[b]
26 For all the gods of the peoples
are idols,[c]
but the LORD made the heavens.[d]
27 Splendor and majesty are
before him;
strength and joy are in his place.
28 Ascribe to the LORD, families
of the peoples,
ascribe to the LORD glory
and strength.
29 Ascribe to the LORD the glory
of his name;
bring an offering and come
before him.
Worship the LORD
in the splendor of his holiness;[e]
30 let the whole earth tremble[f]
before him.

The world is firmly established;
it cannot be shaken.
31 Let the heavens be glad
and the earth rejoice,[g]
and let them say among the nations,
"The LORD reigns!"
32 Let the sea and all that fills it resound;
let the fields and everything in them
exult.[h]
33 Then the trees of the forest
will shout for joy before the LORD,
for he is coming to judge the earth.

34 Give thanks to the LORD,
for he is good;
his faithful love endures forever.[i]
35 And say:[j] "Save us,
God of our salvation;
gather us and rescue us from
the nations
so that we may give thanks to
your holy name
and rejoice in your praise.
36 Blessed be the LORD God of Israel[k]
from everlasting to everlasting."
Then all the people said, "Amen" and
"Praise the LORD."

37 So David left Asaph and his relatives
there before the ark of the LORD's covenant to minister regularly[l] before the ark

according to the daily requirements.[m] 38 He
assigned Obed-edom[n] and his[A] sixty-eight
relatives. Obed-edom son of Jeduthun and
Hosah[o] were to be gatekeepers. 39 David
left the priest Zadok and his fellow priests
before the tabernacle of the LORD at the
high place in Gibeon[p] 40 to offer burnt offerings regularly, morning and evening, to
the LORD on the altar of burnt offerings
and to do everything that was written in
the law of the LORD, which he had commanded Israel to keep.[q] 41 With them were
Heman,[r] Jeduthun, and the rest who were
chosen and designated by name[s] to give
thanks to the LORD — for his faithful love
endures forever.[t] 42 Heman and Jeduthun
had with them trumpets and cymbals to
play and musical instruments of God.[u] Jeduthun's sons were at the city gate.

43 Then all the people went home, and
David returned home to bless his household.[v]

THE LORD'S COVENANT WITH DAVID

17 When David[w] had settled into his
palace, he said to the prophet Nathan, "Look! I am living in a cedar house
while the ark of the LORD's covenant is under tent curtains."[x]
2 So Nathan told David, "Do all that is on
your mind, for God is with you."
3 But that night[y] the word of God came to
Nathan: 4 "Go to David my servant and say,
'This is what the LORD says: You are not the
one to build me a house to dwell in.[z] 5 From
the time I brought Israel out of Egypt until
today I have not dwelt in a house; instead, I
have moved from one tent site to another,
and from one tabernacle location to another.[B,aa] 6 In all my journeys throughout
Israel, have I ever spoken a word to even
one of the judges of Israel, whom I commanded to shepherd my people, asking:
Why haven't you built me a house of cedar?'[ab]
7 "So now this is what you are to say to
my servant David: 'This is what the LORD of
Armies says: I took you from the pasture,
from tending the flock, to be ruler over
my people Israel.[ac] 8 I have been with you
wherever you have gone, and I have destroyed all your enemies before you. I will
make a name for you like that of the greatest on the earth. 9 I will designate a place
for my people Israel and plant them,[ad] so
that they may live there and not be disturbed again. Evildoers will not continue
to oppress them as they have done 10 ever

since the day I ordered judges to be over my people Israel. I will also subdue all your enemies.

" 'Furthermore, I declare to you that the LORD himself will build a house for you. **11** When your time comes to be with your fathers, I will raise up after you your descendant, who is one of your own sons, and I will establish his kingdom. **12** He is the one who will build a house for me,[a] and I will establish his throne forever. **13** I will be his father, and he will be my son.[b] I will not remove my faithful love from him as I removed it from the one who was before you.[c] **14** I will appoint him over my house and my kingdom forever, and his throne will be established forever.' "[d]

15 Nathan reported all these words and this entire vision to David.

DAVID'S PRAYER OF THANKSGIVING

16 Then[e] King David went in, sat in the LORD's presence, and said,

Who am I, LORD God, and what is my house that you have brought me this far? **17** This was a little thing to you,[A] God, for you have spoken about your servant's house in the distant future. You regard me as a man of distinction,[B] LORD God. **18** What more can David say to you for honoring your servant? You know your servant. **19** LORD, you have done this whole great thing, making known all these great promises for the sake of your servant and according to your will.[f] **20** LORD, there is no one like you, and there is no God besides you, as all we have heard confirms. **21** And who is like your people Israel? God, you came to one nation on earth to redeem a people for yourself, to make a name for yourself through great and awesome works by driving out nations before your people you redeemed from Egypt.[g] **22** You made your people Israel your own people forever, and you, LORD, have become their God.[h]

23 Now, LORD, let the word that you have spoken concerning your servant and his house be confirmed forever, and do as you have promised. **24** Let your name be confirmed and magnified forever in the saying, "The LORD of Armies, the God of Israel, is God over Israel." May the house of your servant David be established before you. **25** Since you, my God, have revealed to[c,i] your servant that you will build him a house, your servant has found courage to pray in your presence. **26** LORD, you indeed are God, and you have promised this good thing to your servant. **27** So now, you have been pleased to bless your servant's house that it may continue before you forever. For you, LORD, have blessed it, and it is blessed forever.

DAVID'S MILITARY CAMPAIGNS

18 After this,[i] David defeated the Philistines, subdued them, and took Gath and its surrounding villages from Philistine control. **2** He also defeated the Moabites, and they became David's subjects and brought tribute.

3 David also defeated King Hadadezer of Zobah at Hamath when he went to establish his control at the Euphrates River. **4** David captured one thousand chariots, seven thousand horsemen, and twenty thousand foot soldiers from him, hamstrung all the horses, and kept a hundred chariots.[D]

5 When the Arameans of Damascus came to assist King Hadadezer of Zobah,[k] David struck down twenty-two thousand Aramean men. **6** Then he placed garrisons[E,l] in Aram of Damascus, and the Arameans became David's subjects and brought tribute. The LORD made David victorious wherever he went.

7 David took the gold shields carried by Hadadezer's officers and brought them to Jerusalem. **8** From Tibhath and Cun, Hadadezer's cities, David also took huge quantities of bronze, from which Solomon made the bronze basin,[f] the pillars, and the bronze articles.[m]

9 When King Tou of Hamath heard that David had defeated the entire army of King Hadadezer of Zobah, **10** he sent his son Hadoram to King David to greet him and

[a] 17:12 1Kg 5:2-5; 6:14,38; 8:17-20; 2Ch 6:2
[b] 17:13 Heb 1:5
[c] 1Sm 15:23-28; 1Ch 10:14
[d] 17:14 Ps 89:29,36
[e] 17:16-27 2Sm 7:18-29
[f] 17:19 Is 37:35
[g] 17:21 Dt 4:32-38
[h] 17:22 Ex 6:7; 19:5-6

[i] 17:25 Ex 6:7; 19:5-6
[j] 18:1-13 2Sm 8:1-14
[k] 18:5 1Ch 18:9; 19:6
[l] 18:6 2Sm 8:6
[m] 18:8 1Kg 7:15-47; 2Ch 3:15-4:18

[A] 17:17 Lit *thing in your eyes*   [B] 17:17 Hb obscure   [C] 17:25 Lit *have uncovered the ear of*   [D] 18:4 Or *chariot horses*   [E] 18:6 Some Hb mss, LXX, Vg; other Hb mss omit *garrisons*; 2Sm 8:6   [F] 18:8 Lit *sea*

18:1-17 The battles listed here are not necessarily in chronological order but were probably chosen to demonstrate the greatness of David's rule as he consolidated and expanded his kingdom. No superpowers stood in his way because **the LORD made David victori**ous wherever he went (18:6, 13). With this repeated phrase, the Chronicler wants his readers to remember that God was the power behind David's sword.

Don't miss verse 11. David's **dedicated** tribute and plunder served as a good illustration of the principle found in Proverbs 13:22: "the sinner's wealth is stored up for the righteous." A kingdom-minded economic agenda recognizes that God often providentially transfers the resources of the wicked to be used for kingdom purposes.

[a]18:14-17 2Sm 8:15-18
[b]18:15 1Ch 11:6
[c]18:16 2Sm 8:17; 1Ch
24:6,31
[d]18:17 2Sm 23:20-23
[e]19:1-5 2Sm 10:1-5
19:4 Is 7:20; 20:4

[g]19:6-19 2Sm 10:6-19
[h]19:6 1Ch 18:5,9
[i]19:7 Nm 21:30; Jos
13:9,16; Is 15:2
[j]19:10 2Sm 6:1
[k]19:13 Jos 1:6

to congratulate him because David had fought against Hadadezer and defeated him, for Tou and Hadadezer had fought many wars. Hadoram brought all kinds of gold, silver, and bronze items. **11** King David also dedicated these to the LORD, along with the silver and gold he had carried off from all the nations — from Edom, Moab, the Ammonites, the Philistines, and the Amalekites.

12 Abishai son of Zeruiah struck down eighteen thousand Edomites in the Salt Valley. **13** He put garrisons in Edom, and all the Edomites were subject to David. The LORD made David victorious wherever he went.

14 So David reigned over all Israel,[a] administering justice and righteousness for all his people.

15   Joab[b] son of Zeruiah was
      over the army;
   Jehoshaphat son of Ahilud was
      court historian;
16   Zadok son of Ahitub and
      Ahimelech[A,C] son of Abiathar
      were priests;
   Shavsha was court secretary;
17   Benaiah son of Jehoiada[d] was over
      the Cherethites and the Pelethites;
   and David's sons were
      the chief officials
      at the king's side.

WAR WITH THE AMMONITES

19 Some time later,[e] King Nahash of the Ammonites died, and his son became king in his place. **2** Then David said, "I'll show kindness to Hanun son of Nahash, because his father showed kindness to me."

So David sent messengers to console him concerning his father. However, when David's emissaries arrived in the land of the Ammonites to console him, **3** the Ammonite leaders said to Hanun, "Just because David has sent men with condolences for you, do you really believe he's showing respect for your father? Instead, haven't his emissaries come in order to scout out, overthrow, and spy on the land?" **4** So Hanun took David's emissaries, shaved them, cut their clothes in half at the hips, and sent them away.[f]

5 It was reported to David about his men, so he sent messengers to meet them, since the men were deeply humiliated. The king said, "Stay in Jericho until your beards grow back; then return."

6 When the Ammonites realized[g] they had made themselves repulsive to David, Hanun and the Ammonites sent thirty-eight tons[B] of silver to hire chariots and horsemen from Aram-naharaim, Aram-maacah, and Zobah.[h] **7** They hired thirty-two thousand chariots and the king of Maacah with his army, who came and camped near Medeba.[i] The Ammonites also came together from their cities for the battle.

8 David heard about this and sent Joab and all the elite troops. **9** The Ammonites marched out and lined up in battle formation at the entrance of the city while the kings who had come were in the field by themselves. **10** When Joab saw that there was a battle line in front of him and another behind him, he chose some of Israel's finest young men[c,j] and lined up in formation to engage the Arameans. **11** He placed the rest of the forces under the command of his brother Abishai. They lined up in formation to engage the Ammonites.

12 "If the Arameans are too strong for me," Joab said, "then you'll be my help. However, if the Ammonites are too strong for you, I'll help you. **13** Be strong! Let's prove ourselves strong for our people and for the cities of our God.[k] May the LORD's will be done."[D]

14 Joab and the people with him approached the Arameans for battle, and they fled before him. **15** When the Ammonites saw that the Arameans had fled, they likewise fled before Joab's brother Abishai and entered the city. Then Joab went to Jerusalem.

16 When the Arameans realized that they had been defeated by Israel, they sent messengers to summon the Arameans who were beyond the Euphrates River. They were led by Shophach, the commander of Hadadezer's army.

17 When this was reported to David, he gathered all Israel and crossed the Jordan. He came up to the Arameans and lined up against them. When David lined up to engage them, they fought against him. **18** But the Arameans fled before Israel, and David killed seven thousand of their charioteers and forty thousand foot soldiers. He also killed Shophach, commander of the army.

[A]18:16 Some Hb mss, LXX, Syr, Vg; other Hb mss read *Abimelech*; 2Sm 8:17   [B]19:6 Lit *1,000 talents*   [C]19:10 Lit *Israel's choice ones*   [D]19:13 Lit *the LORD do what is good in his eyes*

19:1-19 This story demonstrates the need for leaders to have wise counselors.

19 When Hadadezer's subjects saw that they had been defeated by Israel, they made peace with David and became his subjects. After this, the Arameans were never willing to help the Ammonites again.

CAPTURE OF THE CITY OF RABBAH

20 In the spring[A] when kings march out to war,[a] Joab led the army and destroyed the Ammonites' land. He came to Rabbah and besieged it, but David remained in Jerusalem.[b] Joab attacked Rabbah and demolished it. **2** Then David took the crown from the head of their king,[B,C,c] and it was placed on David's head. He found that the crown weighed seventy-five pounds[D] of gold, and there was a precious stone in it. In addition, David took away a large quantity of plunder from the city. **3** He brought out the people who were in it and put them to work with saws,[E] iron picks, and axes.[F,d] David did the same to all the Ammonite cities. Then he and all his troops returned to Jerusalem.

THE PHILISTINE GIANTS

4 After this,[e] a war broke out with the Philistines at Gezer. At that time Sibbecai the Hushathite killed Sippai, a descendant of the Rephaim,[G,f] and the Philistines were subdued.

5 Once again there was a battle with the Philistines, and Elhanan son of Jair killed Lahmi the brother of Goliath of Gath. The shaft of his spear was like a weaver's beam.[g]

6 There was still another battle at Gath where there was a man of extraordinary stature with six fingers on each hand and six toes on each foot — twenty-four in all. He, too, was descended from the giant.[H] **7** When he taunted Israel, Jonathan son of David's brother Shimei killed him.

8 These were the descendants of the giant in Gath killed by David and his soldiers.

DAVID'S MILITARY CENSUS

21 Satan[I,h] rose up against Israel and incited David[I] to count the people of Israel. **2** So David said to Joab and the commanders of the troops, "Go and count Israel from Beer-sheba to Dan and bring a report to me so I can know their number."[J]

3 Joab replied, "May the LORD multiply the number of his people a hundred times over![k] My lord the king, aren't they all my lord's servants? Why does my lord want to do this? Why should he bring guilt on Israel?"

4 Yet the king's order prevailed over Joab. So Joab left and traveled throughout Israel and then returned to Jerusalem. **5** Joab gave the total troop registration to David. In all Israel there were one million one hundred thousand armed men[J] and in Judah itself four hundred seventy thousand armed men. **6** But he did not include Levi and Benjamin in the count because the king's command was detestable to him. **7** This command was also evil in God's sight, so he afflicted Israel.

8 David said to God, "I have sinned greatly because I have done this thing. Now, please take away your servant's guilt, for I've been very foolish."[l]

DAVID'S PUNISHMENT

9 Then[m] the LORD instructed Gad,[n] David's seer.[o] **10** "Go and say to David, 'This is what the LORD says: I am offering you three choices. Choose one of them for yourself, and I will do it to you.'"

11 So Gad went to David and said to him, "This is what the LORD says: 'Take your choice: **12** three years of famine, or three months of devastation by your foes with

a 20:1-3 2Sm 12:26-31
b 20:1 2Sm 11:1
c 20:2 1Kg 11:5,7
d 20:3 2Sm 12:31
e 20:4-8 2Sm 21:18-22
f 20:4 Gn 14:5; Dt 2:11
g 20:5 1Sm 17:7; 1Ch 11:23

h 21:1 Jb 1:6; Zch 3:1-2
i 21:1-8 2Sm 24:1-10
j 21:2 1Ch 27:23-24
k 21:3 Dt 1:11
l 21:8 2Sm 12:13
m 21:9-17 2Sm 24:11-17
n 21:9 1Ch 29:29
o 1Sm 9:9; 2Sm 24:11;
1Ch 25:5

A 20:1 Lit At the time of the return of the year   B 20:2 LXX, Vg read of Milcom   C 20:2 = Molech; 1Kg 11:5,7   D 20:2 Lit a talent   E 20:3 Text emended; MT reads and sawed them with the saw; 2Sm 12:31   F 20:3 Text emended; MT reads saws; 2Sm 12:31   G 20:4 Or the Rephaites   H 20:6 Or Raphah, also in v. 8   I 21:1 Or An adversary; Jb 1:6; Zch 3:1-2   J 21:5 Lit men drawing the sword

20:1 The beginning of this verse may sound familiar. It hints of the infamous occasion when David stayed in Jerusalem (while his army went to battle) and ended up committing adultery with Bathsheba (see 2 Sam 11:1-27). Recording that event in detail didn't fit with the Chronicler's purpose of showing God's favor to his people through his blessing of David; besides, it was likely well known. **21:1** Interestingly, in 2 Samuel 24:1 it says, "The Lord's anger burned against Israel again, and he stirred up David against them to say: 'Go, count the people of Israel and Judah.'" So what happened? Did God stir David to take a census of the people, or did Satan? The answer is both.

To execute his own judgment on some sin the people of Israel had committed, God allowed Satan to lay a snare for David by tempting him to take pride in the size of his kingdom and in the number of his troops rather than trusting in God. In other words, God put Satan on a short leash that allowed him permission to work on David. (This is similar to the scene in Job 1–2 in which God permits Satan to do a number on Job for his purposes.)

Satan likes to mess with our minds, our thoughts. So we must remember that while our legitimate desires are God-given, the enemy wants to influence how we decide to satisfy them. Satan wants our desires to

master us. And while he can't make us do anything, he can build castles of warped desire in our minds that lure us to do wrongful things. **21:8** Whereas before Satan had appealed to David's desires to lead him to sin, the Holy Spirit apparently worked on David's conscience to lead him to repent (see 2 Sam 24:10). He confessed to God: **I have sinned greatly . . . . I've been very foolish** (1 Chr 21:8). To repent means to change one's mind and reverse direction. It's like reversing course when you realize you've been traveling the wrong road. David's *confession* of his sin was what the Lord was waiting for, but it did not eliminate the *consequences* of his sin.

[a]21:13 Ps 51:1; 130:4,7
[b]21:15 Ex 32:14; 1Sm 15:11;
2Sm 24:16; Am 7:3,6; Jnh
3:9-10
[c]21:16 1Kg 21:27
[d]21:18-27 2Sm 24:18-25
[e]21:18 2Ch 3:1

[f]21:26 Lv 9:24; Jdg 6:21
[g]21:29 1Kg 3:4; 1Ch 16:39
[h]22:1 1Ch 21:18-28;
2Ch 3:1
[i]22:2 1Kg 9:20-21; 2Ch
2:17
[j]1Kg 5:17-18
[k]22:3 1Ch 29:2,7

the sword of your enemy overtaking you, or three days of the sword of the LORD — a plague on the land, the angel of the LORD bringing destruction to the whole territory of Israel.' Now decide what answer I should take back to the one who sent me."

[13] David answered Gad, "I'm in anguish. Please, let me fall into the LORD's hands because his mercies are very great,[a] but don't let me fall into human hands."

[14] So the LORD sent a plague on Israel, and seventy thousand Israelite men died. [15] Then God sent an angel to Jerusalem to destroy it, but when the angel was about to destroy the city,[A] the LORD looked, relented concerning the destruction,[b] and said to the angel who was destroying the people, "Enough, withdraw your hand now!" The angel of the LORD was then standing at the threshing floor of Ornan[B] the Jebusite. [16] When David looked up and saw the angel of the LORD standing between earth and heaven, with his drawn sword in his hand stretched out over Jerusalem, David and the elders, clothed in sackcloth,[c] fell facedown. [17] David said to God, "Wasn't I the one who gave the order to count the people? I am the one who has sinned and acted very wickedly. But these sheep, what have they done? LORD my God, please let your hand be against me and against my father's family, but don't let the plague be against your people."

DAVID'S ALTAR

[18] So the angel of the LORD ordered Gad[d] to tell David to go and set up an altar to the LORD on the threshing floor of Ornan the Jebusite.[e] [19] David went up at Gad's command spoken in the name of the LORD. [20] Ornan was threshing wheat when he turned and saw the angel. His four sons, who were with him, hid. [21] David came to Ornan, and when Ornan looked and saw David, he left the threshing floor and bowed to David with his face to the ground.

[22] Then David said to Ornan, "Give me this threshing-floor plot so that I may build an altar to the LORD on it. Give it to me for the full price, so the plague on the people may be stopped."

[23] Ornan said to David, "Take it! My lord the king may do whatever he wants.[c] See, I give the oxen for the burnt offerings, the threshing sledges for the wood, and the wheat for the grain offering — I give it all."

[24] King David answered Ornan, "No, I insist on paying the full price, for I will not take for the LORD what belongs to you or offer burnt offerings that cost me nothing."

[25] So David gave Ornan fifteen pounds of gold[D] for the plot. [26] He built an altar to the LORD there and offered burnt offerings and fellowship offerings. He called on the LORD, and he answered him with fire from heaven on the altar of burnt offering.[f] [27] Then the LORD spoke to the angel, and he put his sword back into its sheath. [28] At that time, David offered sacrifices there when he saw that the LORD answered him at the threshing floor of Ornan the Jebusite. [29] The tabernacle of the LORD, which Moses made in the wilderness, and the altar of burnt offering were at the high place in Gibeon,[g] [30] but David could not go before it to inquire of God, because he was terrified of the sword of the LORD's

22

angel. [1] Then David said, "This is the house of the LORD God, and this is the altar of burnt offering for Israel."[h]

DAVID'S PREPARATIONS FOR THE TEMPLE

[2] So David gave orders to gather the resident aliens that were in the land of Israel,[i] and he appointed stonecutters to cut finished stones for building God's house.[j] [3] David supplied a great deal of iron to make the nails for the doors of the gates and for the fittings, together with an immeasurable quantity of bronze,[k] [4] and

---

[A]21:15 Lit but as he was destroying　[B]21:15-28 = Araunah in 2Sm 24:16-24　[C]21:23 Lit do what is good in his eyes　[D]21:25 Lit 600 shekels of gold by weight

---

21:11-13 Each of the disciplinary measures offered was horrific, so David chose to appeal to God's grace. He said, **Let me fall into the LORD's hands because his mercies are very great** (21:13). David knew that the Lord acts toward his children not with vengeance as toward an enemy, but with love for his children. **21:16** Angelic figures in the Bible aren't pictured as sweet cherubs with rosy cheeks. When visible in all their glory, they're overwhelming and fearsome-looking (see Dan 10:5-9; Rev 22:8-9).

21:17 David called what he'd done what it was: sin. He accepted full responsibility for it, and he pleaded with God to punish him instead of the people. When the Holy Spirit convicts you of your sin, humbly agree with him. **21:24** If churches were infused with this kind of attitude toward God and Christian service, we would have fewer problems. David understood that sacrifice isn't sacrifice if it doesn't hurt. Likewise, service isn't service if it doesn't cost you something.

22:1 David rightly concluded that Ornan's old threshing floor was where God wanted Israel to build him a temple. This is confirmed in 2 Chronicles 3:1, which says, "Solomon began to build the Lord's temple in Jerusalem on Mount Moriah where the Lord had appeared to his father David, at the site David had prepared on the threshing floor of Ornan the Jebusite." In his sovereignty and providence, then, God directed the sinful actions of David into a positive outcome by leading him to the very place, Mount

innumerable cedar logs because the Sidonians and Tyrians had brought a large quantity of cedar logs to David.[a] [5] David said, "My son Solomon is young and inexperienced, and the house that is to be built for the LORD must be exceedingly great and famous and glorious in all the lands.[b] Therefore, I will make provision for it." So David made lavish preparations for it before his death.

[6] Then he summoned his son Solomon and charged him to build a house for the LORD God of Israel. [7] "My son," David said to Solomon, "It was in my heart to build a house for the name of the LORD my God,[c] [8] but the word of the LORD came to me: 'You have shed much blood and waged great wars. You are not to build a house for my name because you have shed so much blood on the ground before me.[d] [9] But a son will be born to you; he will be a man of rest. I will give him rest from all his surrounding enemies,[e] for his name will be Solomon,[A,f] and I will give peace and quiet to Israel during his reign.[g] [10] He is the one who will build a house for my name. He will be my son, and I will be his father. I will establish the throne of his kingdom over Israel forever.'[h]

[11] "Now, my son, may the LORD be with you,[i] and may you succeed in building the house of the LORD your God, as he said about you. [12] Above all, may the LORD give you insight and understanding when he puts you in charge of Israel so that you may keep the law of the LORD your God.[j] [13] Then you will succeed if you carefully follow the statutes and ordinances the LORD commanded Moses for Israel.[k] Be

strong and courageous. Don't be afraid or discouraged.[l]

[14] "Notice I have taken great pains to provide for the house of the LORD — 3,775 tons of gold, 37,750 tons of silver,[B,m] and bronze and iron that can't be weighed because there is so much of it. I have also provided timber and stone, but you will need to add more to them. [15] You also have many workers: stonecutters, masons, carpenters, and people skilled in every kind of work [16] in gold, silver, bronze, and iron — beyond number. Now begin the work, and may the LORD be with you."[n]

[17] Then David ordered all the leaders of Israel to help his son Solomon: [18] "The LORD your God is with you, isn't he? And hasn't he given you rest on every side?[o] For he has handed the land's inhabitants over to me, and the land has been subdued before the LORD and his people. [19] Now determine in your mind and heart to seek the LORD your God.[p] Get started building the LORD God's sanctuary so that you may bring the ark of the LORD's covenant and the holy articles of God to the temple that is to be built[q] for the name of the LORD."[r]

THE DIVISIONS OF THE LEVITES

23 When David was old and full of days,[s] he installed his son Solomon as king over Israel.[t] [2] Then he gathered all the leaders of Israel, the priests, and the Levites. [3] The Levites thirty years old or more were counted;[u] the total number of men was thirty-eight thousand by headcount.[v] [4] "Of these," David said, "twenty-four thousand are to be in charge of the work on the LORD's temple,[w] six thousand are to be

[a] 22:4 1Kg 5:6-10
[b] 22:5 1Ch 29:1
[c] 22:7 2Sm 7:2-3; 1Ch 17:1-2; 28:2
[d] 22:8 1Ch 28:3
[e] 22:9 1Kg 4:20,25
[f] 2Sm 12:24-25
[g] 1Ch 28:5
[h] 22:10 2Sm 7:13-14; 1Ch 17:12-13; 28:6-7
[i] 22:11 1Ch 22:16
[j] 22:12 1Kg 3:9-12; 2Ch 1:10-12
[k] 22:13 1Ch 28:7

[l] 22:13 Jos 1:6-9
[m] 22:14 1Ch 29:4
[n] 22:16 1Ch 22:11
[o] 22:18 1Ch 22:9; 23:25
[p] 22:19 1Ch 28:9
[q] 1Kg 8:6,21; 2Ch 5:7
[r] 1Ch 22:7
[s] 23:1 1Ch 29:28
[t] 1Ch 28:5; 29:22
[u] 23:3 Nm 4:3-49
[v] 1Ch 23:24
[w] 23:4 Ezr 3:8-9

[A] 22:9 In Hb, the name *Solomon* sounds like "peace."   [B] 22:14 Lit *100,000 talents of gold and 1,000,000 talents of silver*

Moriah, where Abraham had offered Isaac (see Gen 22).

22:5 David knew that Solomon was too **young and inexperienced** to pull off the upcoming building project on his own. This suggests that David spent his remaining days preparing his son to be a leader. Dads, take note.

22:9 Solomon's **name** would be a daily reminder of God's promise. "Solomon" is related to *shalom*, the Hebrew word for peace.

22:11-16 His father's hope that God would grant him **insight and understanding** (22:12) obviously had a significant effect on Solomon. Later, when God asked him what he would like most, Solomon requested "wisdom and knowledge" (2 Chr 1:7-10). Importantly, David's heart desire for Solomon was the same as God's heart desire for Solomon— that he would **keep** and **follow** the ways of the Lord (1 Chr 22:12-13). This should be the deepest desire of all Christian parents for their children.

David's final encouragement for Solomon echoed God's words to Joshua that had been uttered long ago: **Be strong and courageous. Don't be afraid or discouraged** (22:13; see Josh 1:9). Why did he need to say that? Because the natural human tendency is to be afraid in the face of a huge assignment like the responsibility that was being laid on Solomon. We need to remember that the people of Scripture were just that—people. They were humans with the same fears and emotions we have. Yet the most powerful antidote to fear, whether in their time or ours, is knowledge of the Lord's presence. That's why David concluded with the phrase, **may the LORD be with you** (1 Chr 22:16).

23:1 He essentially made Solomon his coregent.

23:2-32 Temple service was to be accomplished by **the Levites**, whom the Lord had set aside to care for and transport the ark,

the tabernacle, and all its furnishings (23:2; see Num 1:50; Deut 10:8). Once the temple was built, there would no longer be a need **to carry the tabernacle or any of the equipment for its service** (1 Chr 23:26). At that point, then, the Levites were to **assist the descendants of Aaron** (the Levitical family chosen for the priesthood) **with the service of the LORD's temple** (23:28). So while the priests offered sacrifices, the Levites not descended from Aaron were responsible for helping with various work in the temple (23:28-32).

The Levites served as Israel's praise and worship team. Their ministry included standing **every morning** and evening **to give thanks and praise to the LORD** (23:30). We know based on how many psalms David wrote that he placed a high value on worship. He wanted to ensure that there were enough Levites—singers and musicians—to praise the Lord continuously.

a 23:4 1Ch 26:29
b 23:5 1Ch 15:16
c 23:6 1Ch 6:1
d 23:13 Ex 6:20
e Ex 28:1
f Ex 30:6-10
g 23:14 Dt 33:1; Ps 90 title
h 23:24 Nm 10:17,21
i 23:25 1Ch 22:9,18

j 23:26 Nm 4:5,15; 7:9
k 23:29 Lv 24:5-9
l Lv 6:20
m 1Ch 9:31
n Lv 6:14-15; 7:12
o Ex 29:40; 30:13; Lv 19:35-36
p 23:31 Is 1:13-14
q Lv 23:2-4
r 23:32 Nm 1:53; 1Ch 9:27
s Nm 3:6-9,38
t 24:1 Ex 6:23
u 24:2 Lv 10:1-2
v 24:3 1Ch 15:11; 24:6,31
w 24:5-6 1Ch 24:31
x 24:6 2Sm 8:17; 1Ch 18:16; 24:31

officers and judges,[a] [5] four thousand are to be gatekeepers, and four thousand are to praise the LORD with the instruments that I have made for worship."[b]

[6] Then David divided them into divisions according to Levi's sons:[c] Gershom,[A] Kohath, and Merari.

[7] The Gershonites: Ladan and Shimei.

[8] Ladan's sons: Jehiel was the first, then Zetham, and Joel — three.

[9] Shimei's sons: Shelomoth, Haziel, and Haran — three. Those were the heads of the families of Ladan.

[10] Shimei's sons: Jahath, Zizah,[B] Jeush, and Beriah. Those were Shimei's sons — four. [11] Jahath was the first and Zizah was the second; however, Jeush and Beriah did not have many sons, so they became one family[c] and received a single assignment.

[12] Kohath's sons: Amram, Izhar, Hebron, and Uzziel — four.

[13] Amram's sons:[d] Aaron and Moses. Aaron, along with his descendants,[e] was set apart forever to consecrate the most holy things, to burn incense in the presence of the LORD,[f] to minister to him, and to pronounce blessings in his name forever. [14] As for Moses the man of God,[g] his sons were named among the tribe of Levi.

[15] Moses's sons: Gershom and Eliezer.

[16] Gershom's sons: Shebuel was first.

[17] Eliezer's sons were Rehabiah, first; Eliezer did not have any other sons, but Rehabiah's sons were very numerous.

[18] Izhar's sons: Shelomith was first.

[19] Hebron's sons: Jeriah was first, Amariah second, Jahaziel third, and Jekameam fourth.

[20] Uzziel's sons: Micah was first, and Isshiah second.

[21] Merari's sons: Mahli and Mushi. Mahli's sons: Eleazar and Kish. [22] Eleazar died having no sons, only daughters. Their cousins, the sons of Kish, married them.

[23] Mushi's sons: Mahli, Eder, and Jeremoth — three.

[24] These were the descendants of Levi by their ancestral families[D] — the family heads, according to their registration by name in the headcount — twenty years old or more, who worked in the service of the LORD's temple.[h] [25] For David said, "The LORD God of Israel has given rest to his people,[i] and he has come to stay in Jerusalem forever. [26] Also, the Levites no longer need to carry the tabernacle or any of the equipment for its service"[j] — [27] for according to the last words of David, the Levites twenty years old or more were to be counted — [28] "but their duty will be to assist the descendants of Aaron with the service of the LORD's temple, being responsible for the courts and the chambers, the purification of all the holy things, and the work of the service of God's temple — [29] as well as the rows of the Bread of the Presence,[k] the fine flour for the grain offering,[l] the wafers of unleavened bread, the baking,[E,m] the mixing,[n] and all measurements of volume and length.[o] [30] They are also to stand every morning to give thanks and praise to the LORD, and likewise in the evening. [31] Whenever burnt offerings are offered to the LORD on the Sabbaths, New Moons,[p] and appointed festivals, they are to offer them regularly in the LORD's presence according to the number prescribed for them.[q] [32] They are to carry out their responsibilities for the tent of meeting, for the holy place,[r] and for their relatives, the descendants of Aaron,[s] in the service of the LORD's temple."

THE DIVISIONS OF THE PRIESTS

24 The divisions of the descendants of Aaron were as follows: Aaron's sons were Nadab, Abihu, Eleazar, and Ithamar.[t] [2] But Nadab and Abihu died before their father, and they had no sons, so Eleazar and Ithamar served as priests.[u] [3] Together with Zadok[v] from the descendants of Eleazar and Ahimelech from the descendants of Ithamar, David divided them according to the assigned duties of their service. [4] Since more leaders were found among Eleazar's descendants than Ithamar's, they were divided accordingly: sixteen heads of ancestral families[F] were from Eleazar's descendants, and eight heads of ancestral families were from Ithamar's. [5] They[w] were assigned by lot, for there were officers of the sanctuary and officers of God among both Eleazar's and Ithamar's descendants.

[6] The secretary, Shemaiah son of Nethanel, a Levite, recorded them in the presence of the king and the officers, the priest Zadok, Ahimelech[x] son of Abiathar, and the heads of families of the priests and the Levites. One ancestral family[G] was taken for Eleazar, and then one for Ithamar.

[A] 23:6 Lit Gershon   [B] 23:10 LXX, Vg; MT reads Zina   [C] 23:11 Lit a father's house   [D] 23:24 Lit the house of their fathers   [E] 23:29 Lit the griddle   [F] 24:4 Lit house of fathers   [G] 24:6 Lit father's house

7 The first lot fell to Jehoiarib,
the second to Jedaiah,
8 the third to Harim, the fourth
to Seorim,
9 the fifth to Malchijah, the sixth
to Mijamin,
10 the seventh to Hakkoz, the eighth
to Abijah,[a]
11 the ninth to Jeshua, the tenth
to Shecaniah,
12 the eleventh to Eliashib, the twelfth
to Jakim,
13 the thirteenth to Huppah,
the fourteenth to Jeshebeab,
14 the fifteenth to Bilgah, the sixteenth
to Immer,
15 the seventeenth to Hezir,
the eighteenth to Happizzez,
16 the nineteenth to Pethahiah,
the twentieth to Jehezkel,
17 the twenty-first to Jachin,
the twenty-second to Gamul,
18 the twenty-third to Delaiah,
and the twenty-fourth to Maaziah.

19 These had their assigned duties for service when they entered the LORD's temple, according to their regulations, which they received from their ancestor Aaron, as the LORD God of Israel had commanded him.

THE REST OF THE LEVITES

20 As for the rest of Levi's sons:
from Amram's sons: Shubael;
from Shubael's sons: Jehdeiah.
21 From Rehabiah:
from Rehabiah's sons: Isshiah was the
first.
22 From the Izharites: Shelomoth;
from Shelomoth's sons: Jahath.
23 Hebron's[A,b] sons:
Jeriah the first, Amariah the second,
Jahaziel the third, and Jekameam the
fourth.
24 From Uzziel's sons: Micah;
from Micah's sons: Shamir.
25 Micah's brother: Isshiah;
from Isshiah's sons: Zechariah.
26 Merari's sons: Mahli and Mushi,

and from his sons, Jaaziah his son.[B]
27 Merari's sons, by his son Jaaziah:[C]
Shoham, Zaccur, and Ibri.
28 From Mahli: Eleazar, who had no sons.
29 From Kish, from Kish's sons:
Jerahmeel.
30 Mushi's sons: Mahli, Eder, and
Jerimoth.

Those were the descendants of the Levites according to their ancestral families.[D] 31 They also cast lots the same way as their relatives the descendants of Aaron did in the presence of King David, Zadok, Ahimelech, and the heads of the families of the priests and Levites — the family heads and their younger brothers alike.[C]

THE LEVITICAL MUSICIANS

25 David and the officers of the army also set apart some of the sons of Asaph, Heman,[d] and Jeduthun, who were to prophesy[e] accompanied by lyres, harps, and cymbals.[f] This is the list of the men who performed their service: 2 From Asaph's sons: Zaccur, Joseph, Nethaniah, and Asarelah, sons of Asaph, under Asaph's authority, who prophesied under the authority of the king. 3 From Jeduthun:[g] Jeduthun's sons: Gedaliah, Zeri, Jeshaiah, Shimei,[E] Hashabiah, and Mattithiah — six — under the authority of their father Jeduthun, prophesying to the accompaniment of lyres, giving thanks and praise to the LORD. 4 From Heman: Heman's sons: Bukkiah, Mattaniah, Uzziel, Shebuel, Jerimoth, Hananiah, Hanani, Eliathah, Giddalti, Romamti-ezer, Joshbekashah, Mallothi, Hothir, and Mahazioth. 5 All these sons of Heman, the king's seer,[h] were given by the promises of God to exalt him,[F] for God had given Heman fourteen sons and three daughters.

6 All these men were under their own fathers' authority for the music in the LORD's

a 24:10 Neh 12:4; Lk 1:5
b 24:23 1Ch 23:19

c 24:31 1Ch 24:5-6
d 25:1 1Ch 6:33,39
e 2Kg 3:15
f 1Ch 15:16; 25:6
g 25:3 1Ch 16:41-42
h 25:5 1Sm 9:9; 2Sm 24:11;
1Ch 21:9

A 24:23 Some Hb mss, some LXX mss; other Hb mss omit *Hebron's*; 1Ch 23:19   B 24:26 Or *Mushi; Jaaziah's sons: Beno.*   C 24:27 Or *sons, Jaaziah: Beno,*   D 24:30 Lit *the house of their fathers*   E 25:3 One Hb ms, LXX; other Hb mss omit *Shimei*   F 25:5 Lit *by the words of God to lift a horn*

24:19 Each of the different families **had their assigned duties for service when they entered the LORD's temple**. This provided enough priests for the continual, round-the-clock worship of the Lord.
25:1 Notice that **the officers of the army** were involved with David in making these appointments. This close connection between worship and Israel's military campaigns is

obvious as far back as the conquest of Jericho (see Josh 6) when Israel basically defeated the city with praise music, marching around the city walls and blasting trumpets.
25:7 These people weren't just born with musical talent. They had to train and practice to become highly skilled. This was their God-given job, and they did it with excellence.

We are all stewards in God's kingdom. We all have responsibilities and gifts from him. Make the most of yours. One day you'll give an account for how faithful you were to your King's agenda (see Luke 19:11-26). Life is like a coin. You can spend it any way you want. But remember: you only get to spend it once.

a25:8 1Ch 26:13

b26:10 1Ch 16:38
c26:13 1Ch 24:5,31; 25:8

temple, with cymbals, harps, and lyres for the service of God's temple. Asaph, Jeduthun, and Heman were under the king's authority. **7** They numbered 288 together with their relatives who were all trained and skilful in music for the LORD. **8** They cast lots for their duties, young and old alike, teacher as well as pupil.[a]

9 The first lot for Asaph fell to Joseph,
his sons, and his relatives — 12[A]
to Gedaliah the second: him,
his relatives, and his sons — 12
10 the third to Zaccur, his sons,
and his relatives — 12
11 the fourth to Izri,[B] his sons,
and his relatives — 12
12 the fifth to Nethaniah, his sons,
and his relatives — 12
13 the sixth to Bukkiah, his sons,
and his relatives — 12
14 the seventh to Jesarelah, his sons,
and his relatives — 12
15 the eighth to Jeshaiah, his sons,
and his relatives — 12
16 the ninth to Mattaniah, his sons,
and his relatives — 12
17 the tenth to Shimei, his sons,
and his relatives — 12
18 the eleventh to Azarel,[C] his sons,
and his relatives — 12
19 the twelfth to Hashabiah, his sons,
and his relatives — 12
20 the thirteenth to Shubael, his sons,
and his relatives — 12
21 the fourteenth to Mattithiah,
his sons, and his relatives — 12
22 the fifteenth to Jeremoth, his sons,
and his relatives — 12
23 the sixteenth to Hananiah, his sons,
and his relatives — 12
24 the seventeenth to Joshbekashah,
his sons, and his relatives — 12
25 the eighteenth to Hanani, his sons,
and his relatives — 12
26 the nineteenth to Mallothi, his sons,
and his relatives — 12
27 the twentieth to Eliathah, his sons,
and his relatives — 12
28 the twenty-first to Hothir, his sons,
and his relatives — 12
29 the twenty-second to Giddalti,
his sons, and his relatives — 12
30 the twenty-third to Mahazioth,
his sons, and his relatives — 12
31 and the twenty-fourth
to Romamti-ezer, his sons,
and his relatives — 12.

THE LEVITICAL GATEKEEPERS

26 The following were the divisions of the gatekeepers:
From the Korahites: Meshelemiah son of Kore, one of the sons of Asaph. **2** Meshelemiah had sons:
Zechariah the firstborn, Jediael the second,
Zebadiah the third, Jathniel the fourth, **3** Elam the fifth, Jehohanan the sixth, and Eliehoenai the seventh.
4 Obed-edom also had sons:
Shemaiah the firstborn, Jehozabad the second,
Joah the third, Sachar the fourth, Nethanel the fifth, **5** Ammiel the sixth, Issachar the seventh, and Peullethai the eighth,
for God blessed him.
6 Also, to his son Shemaiah were born sons who ruled their ancestral families[D] because they were strong, capable men. **7** Shemaiah's sons: Othni, Rephael, Obed, and Elzabad; his relatives Elihu and Semachiah were also capable men. **8** All of these were among the sons of Obed-edom with their sons and relatives; they were capable men with strength for the work — sixty-two from Obed-edom. **9** Meshelemiah also had sons and relatives who were capable men — eighteen. **10** Hosah,[b] from the Merarites, also had sons: Shimri the first (although he was not the firstborn, his father had appointed him as the first), **11** Hilkiah the second, Tebaliah the third, and Zechariah the fourth. The sons and relatives of Hosah were thirteen in all.

12 These divisions of the gatekeepers, under their leading men, had duties for ministering in the LORD's temple, just as their relatives did. **13** They cast lots for each temple gate according to their ancestral families, young and old alike.[c]
14 The lot for the east gate fell to Shelemiah.[E] They also cast lots for his son

A25:9 LXX; MT lacks *his sons, and his relatives*—12   B25:11 Variant of Zeri   C25:18 Variant of Uzziel   D26:6 Lit *the house of their fathers*, also in v. 13   E26:14 Variant of Meshelemiah

26:1 The gatekeepers served as a security detail.
26:13 That **they cast lots** doesn't mean the assignments were random. The Lord providentially directs all things. As Solomon said, "The lot is cast in the lap, but its every decision is from the Lord" (Prov 16:33).

Zechariah, an insightful counselor, and his lot came out for the north gate. ¹⁵ Obededom's was the south gate, and his sons' lot was for the storehouses; ¹⁶ it was the west gate and the gate of Shallecheth on the ascending highway for Shuppim and Hosah.

There were guards stationed at every watch. ¹⁷ There were six Levites each day[A] on the east, four each day on the north, four each day on the south, and two pair at the storehouses. ¹⁸ As for the court on the west, there were four at the highway and two at the court. ¹⁹ Those were the divisions of the gatekeepers from the descendants of the Korahites and Merarites.

THE LEVITICAL TREASURERS AND OTHER OFFICIALS

²⁰ From the Levites, Ahijah was in charge of the treasuries of God's temple and the treasuries of what had been dedicated.[a] ²¹ From the sons of Ladan, who were the descendants of the Gershonites through Ladan and were the family heads belonging to Ladan the Gershonite: Jehieli. ²² The sons of Jehieli, Zetham and his brother Joel, were in charge of the treasuries of the LORD's temple.

²³ From the Amramites, the Izharites, the Hebronites, and the Uzzielites: ²⁴ Shebuel, a descendant of Moses's son Gershom, was the officer in charge of the treasuries. ²⁵ His relatives through Eliezer: his son Rehabiah, his son Jeshaiah, his son Joram, his son Zichri, and his son Shelomith.[B] ²⁶ This Shelomith and his relatives were in charge of all the treasuries of what had been dedicated by King David,[b] by the family heads who were the commanders of thousands and of hundreds, and by the army commanders. ²⁷ They dedicated part of the plunder from their battles for the repair of the LORD's temple. ²⁸ All that the seer Samuel, Saul son of Kish, Abner son of Ner, and Joab son of Zeruiah had dedicated, along with everything else that had been dedicated, were in the care of Shelomith and his relatives.

²⁹ From the Izrahites: Chenaniah and his sons had duties outside the temple[c,c] as officers and judges[d] over Israel. ³⁰ From the Hebronites: Hashabiah[e] and his relatives, 1,700 capable men, had assigned duties in Israel west of the Jordan for all the work of the LORD and for the service of the king. ³¹ From the Hebronites: Jerijah[f] was the head of the Hebronites, according to the family records of his ancestors. A search was made in the fortieth year of David's reign and strong, capable men were found among them at Jazer[g] in Gilead. ³² There were among Jerijah's relatives 2,700 capable men who were family heads. King David appointed them over the Reubenites, the Gadites, and half the tribe of Manasseh as overseers in every matter relating to God and the king.[h]

DAVID'S SECULAR OFFICIALS

27 This is the list of the Israelites, the family heads, the commanders of thousands and the commanders of hundreds, and their officers who served the king in every matter to do with the divisions that were on rotated military duty each month throughout[D] the year. There were 24,000 in each division:

² Jashobeam son of Zabdiel was in charge of the first division,[i] for the first month; 24,000 were in his division. ³ He was a descendant of Perez and chief of all the army commanders for the first month. ⁴ Dodai the Ahohite was in charge of the division for the second month, and Mikloth was the leader; 24,000 were in his division.

ᵃ 26:20 1Ch 26:24,26; 28:12; Ezr 2:69
ᵇ 26:26 2Sm 8:11; 1Ch 18:7-11

ᶜ 26:29 Neh 11:16
ᵈ 1Ch 23:4
ᵉ 26:30 1Ch 27:17
ᶠ 26:31 1Ch 23:19
ᵍ 1Ch 6:81
ʰ 26:32 2Ch 19:11
ⁱ 27:2-15 2Sm 23:8-30; 1Ch 11:11-31

ᴬ 26:17 LXX; MT omits *each day*   ᴮ 26:25 Or *Shelomoth*, also in vv. 26,28   ᶜ 26:29 *the temple* added for clarity   ᴰ 27:1 Lit *that came in and went out month by month for all months of*

26:16 It's important that **there were guards stationed at every watch** because the temple of the Lord was to function twenty-four hours a day, seven days a week. That the doors didn't close reminds us that worshiping God is full-time work.

27:1-34 God has ordained various forms of government: self-government, family government, church government, and civil government. The latter is a legitimate sphere within God's world—but it has a limited agenda. Jesus legitimized government, and also limited its reach, in one brilliant statement: "Give ... to Caesar the things that are Caesar's, and to God the things that are God's" (Matt 22:21).

The biblical role of civil government is to maintain a safe, just, and righteous environment in which freedom can flourish. So the government is supposed to spend its time and energy removing tyranny from the marketplace and producing harmony in society—in other words, promoting and administering justice, protecting law-abiding citizens, punishing the lawless, and ensuring that fairness operates in such areas as business and racial relationships. Government should work to prevent evil and injustice.

If individuals, families, and churches do their jobs—producing responsible self-government within individual lives—the civil government can focus on what it needs to focus on, rather than having to deal with people who look to the government to do everything for them. If you are expecting the civil government to do for you what God says you are to do for yourself, that is a misuse and misappropriation of government. Plus, if you expect Uncle Sam to do everything for you, you are destined for disappointment anyway. Moreover, whenever we appeal to the civil government first to deal with a church matter like divorce, we rebel against God's decentralized approach to government and ignore the separate spheres of his governments.

ᵃ 27:22 1Ch 28:1
ᵇ 27:23 Gn 15:5
ᶜ 27:24 2Sm 24:1-15; 1Ch 21:1-7
ᵈ 27:28 1Kg 10:27; 2Ch 1:15
ᵉ 27:29 1Ch 5:16
ᶠ 27:31 1Ch 5:10,18-21; 11:38
ᵍ 27:33 2Sm 15:12
ʰ 2Sm 15:32,37
ⁱ 27:34 2Sm 8:18; 1Kg 1:8; 1Ch 11:22-24; 18:17; 27:5-6
ʲ 1Sm 22:20-23; 1Kg 1:7; 2:26-27,35; 1Ch 15:11; 18:16; 24:6

⁵ The third army commander, as chief for the third month, was Benaiah son of the priest Jehoiada; 24,000 were in his division. ⁶ This Benaiah was a mighty man among the Thirty and over the Thirty, and his son Ammizabad was in charge^A of his division.

⁷ The fourth commander, for the fourth month, was Joab's brother Asahel, and his son Zebadiah was commander after him; 24,000 were in his division. ⁸ The fifth, for the fifth month, was the commander Shamhuth the Izrahite; 24,000 were in his division. ⁹ The sixth, for the sixth month, was Ira son of Ikkesh the Tekoite; 24,000 were in his division. ¹⁰ The seventh, for the seventh month, was Helez the Pelonite from the descendants of Ephraim; 24,000 were in his division. ¹¹ The eighth, for the eighth month, was Sibbecai the Hushathite, a Zerahite; 24,000 were in his division. ¹² The ninth, for the ninth month, was Abiezer the Anathothite, a Benjaminite; 24,000 were in his division. ¹³ The tenth, for the tenth month, was Maharai the Netophathite, a Zerahite; 24,000 were in his division. ¹⁴ The eleventh, for the eleventh month, was Benaiah the Pirathonite from the descendants of Ephraim; 24,000 were in his division. ¹⁵ The twelfth, for the twelfth month, was Heldai the Netophathite, of Othniel's family;^B 24,000 were in his division.

¹⁶ The following were in charge of the tribes of Israel:
For the Reubenites, Eliezer son of Zichri was the chief official;
for the Simeonites, Shephatiah son of Maacah;
¹⁷ for the Levites, Hashabiah son of Kemuel; for Aaron, Zadok;
¹⁸ for Judah, Elihu, one of David's brothers; for Issachar, Omri son of Michael;
¹⁹ for Zebulun, Ishmaiah son of Obadiah;
for Naphtali, Jerimoth son of Azriel;
²⁰ for the Ephraimites, Hoshea son of Azaziah;
for half the tribe of Manasseh, Joel son of Pedaiah;
²¹ for half the tribe of Manasseh in Gilead, Iddo son of Zechariah;
for Benjamin, Jaasiel son of Abner;
²² for Dan, Azarel son of Jeroham.
Those were the leaders of the tribes of Israel.ᵃ

²³ David didn't count the men aged twenty or under, for the LORD had said he would make Israel as numerous as the stars of the sky.ᵇ ²⁴ Joab son of Zeruiah began to count them, but he didn't complete it. There was wrath against Israel because of this census,ᶜ and the number was not entered in the Historical Recordᶜ of King David.

²⁵ Azmaveth son of Adiel was in charge of the king's storehouses.
Jonathan son of Uzziah was in charge of the storehouses in the country, in the cities, in the villages, and in the fortresses.
²⁶ Ezri son of Chelub was in charge of those who worked in the fields tilling the soil.
²⁷ Shimei the Ramathite was in charge of the vineyards.
Zabdi the Shiphmite was in charge of the produce of the vineyards for the wine cellars.
²⁸ Baal-hanan the Gederite was in charge of the olive and sycamore treesᵈ in the Judean foothills.ᴰ
Joash was in charge of the stores of olive oil.
²⁹ Shitrai the Sharonite was in charge of the herds that grazed in Sharon,ᵉ while Shaphat son of Adlai was in charge of the herds in the valleys.
³⁰ Obil the Ishmaelite was in charge of the camels.
Jehdeiah the Meronothite was in charge of the donkeys.
³¹ Jaziz the Hagriteᶠ was in charge of the flocks.
All these were officials in charge of King David's property.

³² David's uncle Jonathan was a counselor; he was a man of understanding and a scribe. Jehiel son of Hachmoni attendedᴱ the king's sons. ³³ Ahithophelᵍ was the king's counselor. Hushaiʰ the Archite was the king's friend. ³⁴ After Ahithophel came Jehoiada son of Benaiah,ⁱ then Abiathar.ʲ

^A 27:6 LXX; MT omits in charge   ^B 27:15 Lit belonging to Othniel   ᶜ 27:24 LXX; MT reads the number of the Historical Record   ᴰ 27:28 Or the Shephelah   ᴱ 27:32 Lit was with

Joab was the commander of the king's army.[a]

DAVID COMMISSIONS SOLOMON TO BUILD THE TEMPLE

28 David assembled all the leaders of Israel in Jerusalem:[b] the leaders of the tribes, the leaders of the divisions in the king's service, the commanders of thousands and the commanders of hundreds, and the officials in charge of all the property and cattle of the king and his sons, along with the court officials, the fighting men,[c] and all the best soldiers. **2** Then King David rose to his feet and said, "Listen to me, my brothers and my people. It was in my heart to build a house as a resting place for the ark of the LORD's covenant[d] and as a footstool[e] for our God. I had made preparations to build, **3** but God said to me, 'You are not to build a house for my name because you are a man of war and have shed blood.'[f]

4 "Yet the LORD God of Israel chose me out of all my father's family[g] to be king over Israel forever.[h] For he chose Judah as leader,[i] and from the house of Judah, my father's family, and from my father's sons,[j] he was pleased to make me king over all Israel. **5** And out of all my sons[k] — for the LORD has given me many sons — he has chosen my son Solomon to sit on the throne of the LORD's kingdom over Israel.[l] **6** He said to me,[m] 'Your son Solomon is the one who is to build my house and my courts, for I have chosen him to be my son, and I will be his father. **7** I will establish his kingdom forever if he perseveres in keeping my commands and my ordinances as he is doing today.'[n]

8 "So now in the sight of all Israel, the assembly of the LORD, and in the hearing of our God, observe and follow all the commands of the LORD your God so that you may possess this good land and leave it as an inheritance to your descendants forever.

9 "As for you, Solomon my son, know the God of your father, and serve him wholeheartedly and with a willing mind,[o] for the LORD searches every heart and understands the intention of every thought.[p] If you seek him, he will be found by you, but if you abandon him, he will reject you forever.[q] **10** Realize now that the LORD has chosen you to build a house for the sanctuary. Be strong, and do it."[r]

11 Then David gave his son Solomon the plans[s] for the portico[t] of the temple and its buildings, treasuries, upstairs rooms, inner rooms, and a room for the mercy seat.[u] **12** The plans contained everything he had in mind[A,v] for the courts of the LORD's house, all the surrounding chambers, the treasuries[w] of God's house, and the treasuries for what is dedicated. **13** Also included were plans for the divisions of the priests and the Levites; all the work of service in the LORD's house; all the articles of service of the LORD's house; **14** the weight of gold for all the articles for every kind of service; the weight of all the silver articles for every kind of service; **15** the weight of the gold lampstands[x] and their gold lamps, including the weight of each lampstand and its lamps; the weight of each silver lampstand and its lamps, according to the service of each lampstand; **16** the weight of gold for each table for the rows of the Bread of the Presence and the silver for the silver tables; **17** the pure gold for the forks, sprinkling basins, and pitchers; the weight of each gold dish; the weight of each silver bowl; **18** the weight of refined gold for the altar of incense;[y] and the plans for the chariot of[B,z] the gold cherubim that spread out their wings and cover the ark of the LORD's covenant.[aa]

19 David concluded, "By the LORD's hand on me, he enabled me to understand everything in writing, all the details of the plan."[c]

20 Then David said to his son Solomon, "Be strong and courageous,[ab] and do the work. Don't be afraid or discouraged, for the LORD God, my God, is with you. He won't leave you or abandon you[ac] until all the work for the service of the LORD's house is finished. **21** Here are the divisions of the priests and the Levites for all the service of God's house.[ad] Every willing person of any skill[ae] will be at your disposal for the work, and the leaders and all the people are at your every command."

[a] 27:34 1Ch 11:6
[b] 28:1 1Ch 23:2; 27:1-31
[c] 1Ch 11:10-47
[d] 28:2 2Sm 7:1-3; 1Ch 17:1-2; 22:7
[e] Ps 132:7; Is 66:1
[f] 28:3 1Ch 22:8
[g] 28:4 1Sm 16:6-13
[h] 1Ch 17:23,27
[i] Gn 49:8-10; 1Ch 5:2
[j] 1Sm 16:1
[k] 28:5 1Ch 3:1-9; 14:3-7
[l] 1Ch 22:9
[m] 28:6-7 2Sm 7:13-14; 1Ch 22:10
[n] 28:7 1Ch 22:13
[o] 28:9 1Kg 8:61; 1Ch 29:17-19
[p] Gn 6:5; 1Sm 16:7; Ps 139
[q] 28:9 2Ch 15:2; Jr 29:13
[r] 28:10 1Ch 22:13
[s] 28:11 Ex 25:9,40; 1Ch 28:19
[t] 1Kg 6:3
[u] Ex 25:17-22
[v] 28:12 1Ch 28:19
[w] 1Ch 26:20,22,24,26; Ezr 2:69
[x] 28:15 Ex 25:31-39
[y] 28:18 Ex 30:1-10
[z] Ps 18:10
[aa] Ex 25:18-22; 1Kg 8:6-7; 2Ch 5:7-8
[ab] 28:20 Jos 1:6-7; 1Ch 22:13; 2Ch 32:7
[ac] Dt 31:6; Jos 1:5,9; Heb 13:5
[ad] 28:21 1Ch 28:13
[ae] Ex 35:25-35; 36:1-2

A **28:12** Or *he received from the Spirit*   B **28:18** Or *chariot, that is* ; Ps 18:10; Ezk 1:5,15   C **28:19** Hb obscure

---

28:4-7 Notice how many times David said God "chose" him, his tribe, and his son in this passage. This was his way of telling his hearers, "This family's leadership over you is God's doing. Get on board."

28:8 Don't miss the emphasis here on the condition for success in God's kingdom: obedience to God and his Word.

28:10 Be strong, and do it did not mean Solomon was to work in his own strength but in dependence on the Lord. The temple would be the greatest achievement of Solomon's reign and would require every ounce of his ability and dependence on God.

a 29:1 1Ch 22:5
b 1Ch 29:19
c 29:2 1Ch 22:3-5
d Ex 28:18
e 29:4 1Ch 22:14
f 1Kg 9:28
g 29:6 1Ch 27:1; 28:1
h 1Ch 27:25-31
i 29:7 Ezr 2:69; Neh 7:70
j 29:8 1Ch 23:8

k 29:9 1Kg 8:61; 1Ch 28:9;
2Co 9:7
l 29:11 Mt 6:13; Rv 5:13
m 29:12 2Ch 1:12
n 2Ch 20:6
o 29:15 Lv 25:23; Heb 11:13
p Jb 14:2,10-12
q 29:17 1Ch 28:9
r Ps 15:2

CONTRIBUTIONS FOR BUILDING THE TEMPLE

29 Then King David said to all the assembly, "My son Solomon — God has chosen him alone — is young and inexperienced. The task is great[a] because the building will not be built for a human but for the LORD God.[b] 2 So to the best of my ability I've made provision for the house of my God:[c] gold for the gold articles, silver for the silver, bronze for the bronze, iron for the iron, and wood for the wood, as well as onyx, stones for mounting,[A] antimony,[B,d] stones of various colors, all kinds of precious stones, and a great quantity of marble. 3 Moreover, because of my delight in the house of my God, I now give my personal treasures of gold and silver for the house of my God over and above all that I've provided for the holy house: 4 100 tons[C,e] of gold (gold of Ophir[f]) and 250 tons[D] of refined silver for overlaying the walls of the buildings, 5 the gold for the gold work and the silver for the silver, for all the work to be done by the craftsmen. Now who will volunteer to consecrate himself to the LORD today?"

6 Then the leaders of the households, the leaders of the tribes of Israel, the commanders of thousands and of hundreds,[g] and the officials in charge of the king's work[h] gave willingly. 7 For the service of God's house they gave 185 tons[E] of gold and 10,000 gold coins,[F,i] 375 tons[G] of silver, 675 tons[H] of bronze, and 4,000 tons[i] of iron. 8 Whoever had precious stones gave them to the treasury of the LORD's house under the care of Jehiel[j] the Gershonite. 9 Then the people rejoiced because of their leaders' willingness to give, for they had given to the LORD wholeheartedly.[k] King David also rejoiced greatly.

DAVID'S PRAYER

10 Then David blessed the LORD in the sight of all the assembly. David said,

May you be blessed, LORD God of our father Israel, from eternity to eternity. 11 Yours, LORD, is the greatness and the power and the glory and the splendor and the majesty, for everything in the heavens and on earth belongs to you. Yours, LORD, is the kingdom, and you are exalted as head over all.[l] 12 Riches and honor come from you, and you are the ruler of everything.[m] Power and might are in your hand, and it is in your hand to make great and to give strength to all.[n] 13 Now therefore, our God, we give you thanks and praise your glorious name.

14 But who am I, and who are my people, that we should be able to give as generously as this? For everything comes from you, and we have given you only what comes from your own hand.[j] 15 For we are aliens and temporary residents in your presence as were all our ancestors.[o] Our days on earth are like a shadow, without hope.[p] 16 LORD our God, all this wealth that we've provided for building you a house for your holy name comes from your hand; everything belongs to you. 17 I know, my God, that you test the heart[q] and that you are pleased with what is right.[r] I have willingly given all these things with an upright heart, and now I have seen your people

---

A 29:2 Or *mosaic*   B 29:2 In Hb, the word *antimony* is similar to "turquoise"; Ex 28:18.   C 29:4 Lit *3,000 talents*   D 29:4 Lit *7,000 talents*
E 29:7 Lit *5,000 talents*   F 29:7 Or *drachmas,* or *darics*   G 29:7 Lit *10,000 talents*   H 29:7 Lit *18,000 talents*   I 29:7 Lit *100,000 talents*   J 29:14 Lit
and from your hand we have given to you

29:1 That **the building [would] not be built for a human but for the LORD** was a reminder that they were not about to erect a skyscraper for the glory of man but a glorious temple for the worship of the living God. And it would be worth the effort.

29:3 King David set the example and gave generously. That's what leaders do.

29:6-9 In response to David's actions, the leaders **gave willingly** and generously (29:6-8). This offering was given so spontaneously and so openhandedly that it provided the necessary funds for God's work to be carried out without David even having to pass the plate. No wonder the king **rejoiced** (29:9).

29:10-19 David recognized some key truths about giving and gratitude that we sing and talk about in church services but don't always understand. David acknowledged that **everything** belongs to the Lord in the first place (29:11). **Riches and honor come from** him (29:12). When we give to God, then, we are only giving back to him a portion of what he has given to us in the first place.

When my children were young, there were times when they would ask for money so they could buy me a birthday present. What they didn't realize was that they *needed* me to *bless* me. Now I was still touched by their desire to give me a gift, because their hearts were in the right place. But you see, I wasn't any better off having received a present that I had paid for. What was meaningful to me was that my kids wanted to bless me out of their hearts of love for me.

Another principle of giving that we need to embrace is in David's acknowledgment that God tests **the heart** (29:17). When it's all said and done, giving is a heart thing. God is looking at the size of our hearts, not our checkbooks. Jesus gave us the best example of this in the story of the widow and her two small coins. He said of her actions, "This poor widow has put more into the treasury than all the others. For they all gave out of their surplus, but she out of her poverty has put in everything she had—all she had to live on" (Mark 12:43-44).

We must approach not only our giving but also all of life from a kingdom perspective, which recognizes that everything we have and are is from God's hand. Like the lights on the dashboard of your car, which show what's going on deep down under the hood, your willingness to give generously indicates whether or not your heart is right.

who are present^A here giving joyfully and^B willingly to you. **¹⁸** LORD God of Abraham, Isaac, and Israel, our ancestors, keep this desire forever in the thoughts of the hearts of your people, and confirm their hearts toward you. **¹⁹** Give my son Solomon an undivided heart to keep and to carry out all your commands, your decrees, and your statutes,^a and to build the building for which I have made provision.^b

²⁰ Then David said to the whole assembly, "Blessed be the LORD your God." So the whole assembly praised the LORD God of their ancestors.^c They knelt low and paid homage to the LORD and the king.^d **²¹** The following day they offered sacrifices to the LORD and burnt offerings to the LORD: a thousand bulls, a thousand rams, and a thousand lambs, along with their drink offerings, and sacrifices in abundance for all Israel.^e **²²** They ate and drank with great joy in the LORD's presence that day.

THE ENTHRONEMENT OF SOLOMON

Then, for a second time,^f they made David's son Solomon king; they anointed him^c as the LORD's ruler,^g and Zadok as the priest. **²³** Solomon sat on the LORD's throne as king in place of his father David. He prospered, and all Israel obeyed him.^h **²⁴** All the leaders and the mighty men, and all of King David's sons as well, pledged their allegiance to King Solomon. **²⁵** The LORD highly exalted Solomon in the sight of all Israel^i and bestowed on him such royal majesty as had not been bestowed on any king over Israel before him.^j

A SUMMARY OF DAVID'S LIFE

²⁶ David son of Jesse was king over all Israel.^k **²⁷** The length of his reign over Israel was forty years; he reigned in Hebron for seven years and in Jerusalem for thirty-three.^l **²⁸** He died at a good old age,^m full of days,^n riches, and honor, and his son Solomon became king in his place. **²⁹** As for the events of King David's reign, from beginning to end, note that they are written in the Events of the Seer Samuel,^o the Events of the Prophet Nathan,^p and the Events of the Seer Gad,^q **³⁰** along with all his reign, his might, and the incidents that affected him and Israel and all the kingdoms of the surrounding lands.

^a 29:19 Ps 72:1
^b 1Ch 29:2
^c 29:20 Jos 22:33
^d Ex 4:31
^e 29:21 1Kg 8:62-63
^f 29:22 1Ch 23:1

^g 29:22 1Kg 1:33-39
^h 29:23 1Kg 2:12
^i 29:25 2Ch 1:1
^j 1Kg 3:13; 2Ch 1:12
^k 29:26 1Ch 18:14
^l 29:27 2Sm 5:4-5; 1Kg 2:11
^m 29:28 Gn 15:15; Ac 13:36
^n 1Ch 23:1
^o 29:29 1Sm 9:9
^p 2Sm 7:2-4; 12:1-7
^q 1Sm 22:5

---

^A **29:17** Lit *found*   ^B **29:17** Or *now with joy I've seen your people who are present here giving*   ^C **29:22** LXX, Tg, Vg; MT omits *him*

29:23 Don't miss the Chronicler's description that **Solomon sat on the LORD's throne as king**. This indicates that although Solomon was the king, he was *God's* king, sitting on *God's* throne in *God's* kingdom. His was a stewardship of massive proportions.

2 CHRONICLES

INTRODUCTION

Author

See discussion in 1 Chronicles.

Historical Background

See discussion in 1 Chronicles.

Message and Purpose

See discussion in 1 Chronicles.

VIDEO · INTRO

www.bhpublishinggroup.com/qr/te/13_00

Outline

SOLOMON'S REQUEST FOR WISDOM

1 Solomon son of David strengthened his hold on his kingdom.[a] The LORD his God was with him and highly exalted him.[b] **2** Then Solomon spoke to all Israel, to the commanders of thousands and of hundreds, to the judges, and to every leader in all Israel — the family heads.[c] **3** Solomon and the whole assembly with him went to the high place that was in Gibeon[d] because God's tent of meeting, which the LORD's servant Moses had made[e] in the wilderness, was there. **4** Now David had brought the ark of God from Kiriath-jearim to the place[A] he had set up for it, because he had pitched a tent for it in Jerusalem,[f] **5** but he put[B] the bronze altar, which Bezalel son of Uri, son of Hur, had made,[g] in front of the LORD's tabernacle. Solomon and the assembly inquired of him[c] there. **6** Solomon offered sacrifices there in the LORD's presence on the bronze altar at the tent of meeting; he offered a thousand burnt offerings on it.[h]

7 That night[i] God appeared to Solomon and said to him: "Ask. What should I give you?"

8 And Solomon said to God: "You have shown great and faithful love to my father David, and you have made me king in his place.[j] **9** LORD God, let your promise to my father David now come true.[k] For you have made me king over a people as numerous as the dust of the earth.[l] **10** Now grant me wisdom and knowledge so that I may lead these people,[m] for who can judge this great people of yours?"

11 God said to Solomon, "Since this was in your heart, and you have not requested riches, wealth, or glory, or for the life of those who hate you, and you have not even requested long life, but you have requested for yourself wisdom and knowledge that you may judge my people over whom I have made you king, **12** wisdom and knowledge are given to you. I will also give you riches, wealth, and glory, unlike what was given to the kings who were before you, or will be given to those after you."[n] **13** So Solomon went to Jerusalem from[D] the high place that was in Gibeon in front of the tent of meeting, and he reigned over Israel.

SOLOMON'S HORSES AND WEALTH

14 Solomon[o] accumulated 1,400 chariots and 12,000 horsemen,[p] which he stationed in the chariot cities[q] and with the king in Jerusalem. **15** The king made silver and gold as common in Jerusalem as stones, and he made cedar as abundant as sycamore in the Judean foothills. **16** Solomon's horses came from Egypt and Kue.[E] The king's traders would get them from Kue at the going price. **17** A chariot could be imported from Egypt for fifteen pounds[F] of silver and a horse for nearly four pounds.[G] In the same way, they exported them to all the kings of the Hittites and to the kings of Aram through their agents.

SOLOMON'S LETTER TO HIRAM

2 Solomon decided to build a temple for the name of the LORD and a royal palace for himself,[r] **2** so he assigned 70,000 men as porters, 80,000 men as stonecutters in the mountains, and 3,600 as supervisors over them.[s]

3 Then Solomon sent word to King Hiram[H,t] of Tyre:[u]

Do for me what you did for my father David. You sent him cedars to build him a house to live in.[v] **4** Now I am building a temple for the name of the LORD my God in order to dedicate it to him for burning fragrant incense before him,[w] for displaying the rows of the Bread

---

[a] 1:1 1Kg 2:12,46
[b] 1Ch 29:25
[c] 1:2 1Ch 28:1
[d] 1:3 1Kg 3:4
[e] Ex 36:8-38
[f] 1:4 1Ch 13:1-14; 15:25-16:1
[g] 1:5 Ex 31:2-11; 38:1-7
[h] 1:6 1Kg 3:4
[i] 1:7-13 1Kg 3:5-15
[j] 1:8 1Ch 28:5
[k] 1:9 2Sm 7:12-16
[l] Gn 13:16; 22:17
[m] 1:10 1Sm 18:16; 2Sm 5:2

[n] 1:12 1Ch 29:25; 2Ch 9:22
[o] 1:14-17 1Kg 10:26-29; 2Ch 9:25-28
[p] 1:14 1Kg 4:26
[q] 1Kg 9:19
[r] 2:1 1Kg 5:5; 2Ch 2:12
[s] 2:2 1Kg 5:15-16; 9:23; 2Ch 2:18; 8:10
[t] 2:3 2Sm 5:11; 1Kg 5:1-2
[u] 2:3-10 1Kg 5:2-6,10-11
[v] 2:3 1Ch 14:1
[w] 2:4 Ex 30:7

[A] 1:4 Vg; MT omits *the place*   [B] 1:5 Some Hb mss, Tg, Syr; other Hb mss, LXX, Vg read *but there was*   [C] 1:5 Or *it*   [D] 1:13 LXX, Vg; MT reads *to*
[E] 1:16 = Cilicia   [F] 1:17 Lit *600 shekels*   [G] 1:17 Lit *150 shekels*   [H] 2:3 Some Hb mss, LXX, Syr, Vg; other Hb mss read *Huram*; 2Sm 5:11; 1Kg 5:1-2

1:1 Ancient kings often **strengthened [their] hold on [the] kingdom** by eliminating disloyal people in the court and addressing threats to their reign—even if such a purge involved getting rid of family members. Solomon was no exception (see 1 Kgs 1–2).

1:2-6 Solomon quickly established his worthiness to rule by calling **every leader in all Israel** to accompany him to the **tabernacle** to offer **sacrifices** (1:2, 5-6). This inclusion is an indication of the Chronicler's concern for the proper worship of God by his people, which was always the prerequisite for receiving God's blessing. This matter was especially relevant in the Chronicler's day, hundreds of years after Solomon's time, when the people

had returned from Babylon and were trying to put the nation and their lives back together. **1:10-12** Sadly, Solomon began to abandon his God-given **wisdom** as the years passed and came to a bitter end (1:10; see 1 Kgs 11:1-43). Even his great **wealth** and **glory** (2 Chr 1:12) became a source of frustration to him as he explained in great detail in the book of Ecclesiastes. Solomon's life, then, is a sobering reminder of the fleeting nature of fame, wealth, and power when they are not used for the glory of God.

Examples of this truth abound. Consider the legendary boxer Muhammad Ali. In his prime, Ali was easily the most famous athlete on earth. Later in life, however, Ali stated the

futility of fame and power in a *Sports Illustrated* article. He famously said of his career, "I had the world, and it wasn't nothing."

Each of us has a choice regarding whether we will use God's gifts for his glory or for our own. Keep this in mind: your personal glory has a limited shelf life.

2:1-2 These workers were the foreign men living in Israel (2:17-18).

2:3-10 Solomon traded with **King Hiram** for the materials needed for construction (2:3, 10). He also requested a skilled craftsman to lead the work of adorning and beautifying the temple and also asked for the different kinds of wood and materials to be used in the construction (2:7-9).

a 2:4 Ex 25:30
b Ex 29:38-42
c Nm 28:9-10
d 2:5 Ex 15:11; 1Ch 16:25
e 2:6 1Kg 8:27; 2Ch 6:18
f 2:7 Ex 31:3-5; 2Ch 2:13-14
g 1Ch 22:14-16; 28:21
h 2:8 1Kg 10:11-12
i 2:8-9 2Ch 9:10-11
j 2:11 1Kg 10:9; 2Ch 9:8
k 2:12 Ps 33:6; 102:25
l 1Kg 5:7
m 2Ch 2:1
n 2:13-14 1Kg 7:14

o 2:15 2Ch 2:10
p 2:16 1Kg 5:8-9
q 2:17 2Sm 24:1-9; 1Ch 21:1-5
r 2:18 1Kg 5:15-16; 2Ch 2:2
s 3:1-4 1Kg 6:1-3
t 3:1 Gn 22:2
u 3:7 1Kg 6:20-22
v 1Kg 6:29-35

of the Presence continuously,[a] and for sacrificing burnt offerings for the morning and the evening,[b] the Sabbaths[c] and the New Moons, and the appointed festivals of the LORD our God. This is ordained for Israel permanently. [5] The temple that I am building will be great, for our God is greater than any of the gods.[d] [6] But who is able to build a temple for him, since even heaven and the highest heaven cannot contain him?[e] Who am I then that I should build a temple for him except as a place to burn incense before him? [7] Therefore, send me an artisan who is skilled in engraving to work with gold, silver, bronze, and iron, and with purple, crimson, and blue yarn. He will work with the artisans who are with me in Judah and Jerusalem,[f] appointed by my father David.[g] [8] Also, send me cedar, cypress, and algum[A,h] logs from Lebanon, for I know that your servants know how to cut the trees of Lebanon. Note that my servants will be with your servants[i] to prepare logs for me in abundance because the temple I am building will be great and wondrous. [10] I will give your servants, the woodcutters who cut the trees, one hundred thousand bushels[B] of wheat flour, one hundred thousand bushels of barley, one hundred ten thousand gallons[C] of wine, and one hundred ten thousand gallons of oil.

HIRAM'S REPLY

[11] Then King Hiram of Tyre wrote a letter[D] and sent it to Solomon:

Because the LORD loves his people, he set you over them as king.[J]

[12] Hiram also said:

Blessed be the LORD God of Israel, who made the heavens and the earth![k] He gave King David a wise son with insight and understanding,[l] who will build a temple for the LORD and a royal palace for himself.[m] [13] I have now sent Huram-abi,[E] a skillful man who has understanding.[n] [14] He is the son of a woman from the daughters of Dan.

His father is a man of Tyre. He knows how to work with gold, silver, bronze, iron, stone, and wood, with purple, blue, crimson yarn, and fine linen. He knows how to do all kinds of engraving and to execute any design that may be given him. I have sent him to be with your artisans and the artisans of my lord, your father David. [15] Now, let my lord send the wheat, barley, oil, and wine to his servants as promised.[o] [16] We will cut logs from Lebanon, as many as you need, and bring them to you as rafts by sea to Joppa. You can then take them up to Jerusalem.[p]

SOLOMON'S WORKFORCE

[17] Solomon took a census of all the resident alien men in the land of Israel, after the census that his father David had conducted,[q] and the total was 153,600. [18] Solomon made 70,000 of them porters, 80,000 stonecutters in the mountains, and 3,600 supervisors to make the people work.[r]

BUILDING THE TEMPLE

3 Then Solomon began[s] to build the LORD's temple in Jerusalem on Mount Moriah[t] where the LORD[F] had appeared to his father David, at the site David had prepared on the threshing floor of Ornan[G] the Jebusite. [2] He began to build on the second day of the second month in the fourth year of his reign. [3] These are Solomon's foundations[H] for building God's temple: the length[I] was ninety feet,[J] and the width thirty feet.[K] [4] The portico, which was across the front extending across the width of the temple, was thirty feet wide; its height was thirty feet;[L] he overlaid its inner surface with pure gold. [5] The larger room[M] he paneled with cypress wood, overlaid with fine gold, and decorated with palm trees and chains. [6] He adorned the temple with precious stones for beauty, and the gold was the gold of Parvaim. [7] He overlaid the temple — the beams, the thresholds, its walls and doors — with gold,[u] and he carved cherubim on the walls.[v]

A 2:8 = almug in 1Kg 10:11-12   B 2:10 Lit *20,000 cors*   C 2:10 Lit *20,000 baths*   D 2:11 Lit *Tyre said in writing*   E 2:13 Lit *Huram my father*   F 3:1 LXX; Tg reads *the angel of the LORD*; MT reads *he*   G 3:1 = Araunah in 2Sm 24:16-24   H 3:3 Tg reads *The measurements which Solomon decreed*   I 3:3 Lit *length* —*cubits in the former measure*—   J 3:3 Lit *60 cubits*   K 3:3 Lit *20 cubits*, also in vv. 4,8,11,13   L 3:4 LXX, Syr; MT reads *120 cubits*   M 3:5 Lit *The house*

2:12 Hiram's response, **Blessed be the LORD God of Israel, who made the heavens and the earth,** was most likely a courtesy response to Solomon and didn't necessarily reflect Hiram's personal faith.
2:13-14 This craftsman was a half-Israelite, which must have given him some advantage

in working with Solomon's **artisans** and in understanding Israel's culture (2:14).
2:17-18 That the job of the **supervisors** was **to make the people work** makes it clear that these thousands of foreign laborers were far from volunteers. In fact, the increasing harshness with which Solomon extracted what he

needed, even from his own people, became one of the major issues that led to the secession of Israel's ten northern tribes after his death (see 10:1-4).
3:1 This rise in Jerusalem is the place **where the LORD had appeared to . . . David** (see 1 Chr 21:1—22:1), confirming the Lord's will

THE MOST HOLY PLACE

8 Then he made the most holy place; its length corresponded to the width of the temple, 30 feet, and its width was 30 feet.[a] He overlaid it with forty-five thousand pounds[A] of fine gold. **9** The weight of the nails was twenty ounces[B] of gold, and he overlaid the ceiling with gold.

10 He made[b] two cherubim of sculptured work, for the most holy place, and he overlaid them with gold. **11** The overall length of the wings of the cherubim was 30 feet: the wing of one was 7 1/2 feet,[c] touching the wall of the room; its other wing was 7 1/2 feet, touching the wing of the other cherub. **12** The wing of the other[D] cherub was 7 1/2 feet, touching the wall of the room; its other wing was 7 1/2 feet, reaching the wing of the other cherub. **13** The wingspan of these cherubim was 30 feet. They stood on their feet and faced the larger room.[E]

14 He made the curtain of blue, purple, and crimson yarn and fine linen, and he wove cherubim into it.[c]

THE BRONZE PILLARS

15 In front of the temple[d] he made two pillars, each 27 feet[f] high. The capital on top of each was 7 1/2 feet high. **16** He had made chainwork in the inner sanctuary and also put it on top of the pillars.[e] He made a hundred pomegranates and fastened them into the chainwork. **17** Then he set up the pillars in front of the sanctuary, one on the right and one on the left. He named the one on the right Jachin[G] and the one on the left Boaz.[H]

THE ALTAR, RESERVOIR, AND BASINS

4 He made a bronze altar[f] 30 feet[i] long, 30 feet wide, and 15 feet[j] high. **2** Then he made the cast metal basin,[K,g] 15 feet from brim to brim, perfectly round. It was 7 1/2 feet[L] high and 45 feet[M] in circumference. **3** The likeness of oxen[N] was below it, completely encircling it, ten every half yard,[o] completely surrounding the basin. The oxen were cast in two rows when the basin was cast. **4** It stood on twelve oxen, three facing north, three facing west, three facing south, and three facing east. The basin was on top of them and all their hindquarters were toward the center. **5** The basin was three inches[p] thick, and its rim was fashioned like the brim of a cup or a lily blossom. It could hold eleven thousand gallons.[Q]

6 He made ten basins for washing and he put five on the right and five on the left.[h] The parts of the burnt offering were rinsed in them,[i] but the basin was used by the priests for washing.

THE LAMPSTANDS, TABLES, AND COURTS

7 He made the ten gold lampstands according to their specifications and put them in the sanctuary, five on the right and five on the left.[j] **8** He made ten tables and placed them in the sanctuary, five on the right and five on the left.[k] He also made a hundred gold bowls.

9 He made the courtyard[l] of the priests and the large court, and doors for the court. He overlaid the doors with bronze. **10** He put the basin on the right side, toward the southeast.[m] **11** Then Huram[R,n] made[o] the pots, the shovels, and the bowls.

COMPLETION OF THE BRONZE FURNISHINGS

So Huram finished doing the work that he was doing for King Solomon in God's temple: **12** two pillars; the bowls and the capitals on top of the two pillars; the two gratings for covering both bowls of the capitals that were on top of the pillars; **13** the four hundred pomegranates for the two gratings (two rows of pomegranates for each grating covering both capitals' bowls on top of the pillars[p]). **14** He also made the water carts[s,q] and the basins on the water carts. **15** The one basin and the twelve oxen underneath it, **16** the pots, the shovels, the forks, and all their utensils — Huram-abi[T,r] made them for King Solomon for the LORD's temple. All these were made of polished bronze. **17** The king had them cast in clay molds in the Jordan Valley between Succoth and Zeredah. **18** Solomon made all these utensils in such great abundance that the weight of the bronze was not determined.

---

a 3:8 1Kg 6:16
b 3:10-13 1Kg 6:23-28
c 3:14 Ex 26:31
d 3:15-17 1Kg 7:15-22; 2Kg 25:17; Jr 52:21-23
e 3:16 1Kg 6:21; 7:17
f 4:1 Ex 27:1-2; 2Kg 16:14
g 4:2-5 1Kg 7:23-26; Ezk 47:1-12; Rv 22:1

h 4:6 1Kg 7:38-39
i Ezk 40:38
j 4:7 Ex 37:17-24; 1Kg 7:49
k 4:8 1Kg 7:48
l 4:9 1Kg 6:36
m 4:10 1Kg 7:39
n 4:11 1Kg 7:13,40,45
o 4:11-5:1 1Kg 7:40-51
p 4:13 1Kg 7:20
q 4:14 1Kg 7:27-37
r 4:16 1Kg 7:14; 2Ch 2:13

[A] 3:8 Lit *600 talents*　[B] 3:9 Lit *50 shekels*　[C] 3:11 Lit *five cubits*, also in vv. 12,15　[D] 3:12 Syr, Vg; MT reads *the one*　[E] 3:13 Lit *the house*　[F] 3:15 Syr reads *18 cubits* (27 feet); Hb reads *35 cubits* (52 1/2 feet)　[G] 3:17 = He Will Establish　[H] 3:17 = Strength Is in Him　[I] 4:1 Lit *20 cubits*　[J] 4:1 Lit *10 cubits*, also in v. 2　[K] 4:2 Lit *sea*　[L] 4:2 Lit *five cubits*　[M] 4:2 Lit *30 cubits*　[N] 4:3 = gourds in 1Kg 7:24　[O] 4:3 Lit *10 per cubit*　[P] 4:5 Lit *a handbreadth*　[Q] 4:5 Text emended; MT reads *3,000 baths* in 1Kg 7:26　[R] 4:11 = Hiram in 1Kg 7:13,40,45　[S] 4:14 Lit *the stands*　[T] 4:16 Lit *Huram my father*

---

that this was his chosen site. It was also the place where Abraham had offered Isaac in obedience to God (see Gen 22:2).

3:8 The most holy place was also known as the holy of holies. The room contained the ark of the covenant with its lid, or mercy seat. The high priest would enter that room once a year, on the Day of Atonement, to offer a sacrifice for the people's sins. Notice it was shaped like a cube.

a 4:19 Lv 24:5-9
b 4:20 Ex 25:31-40;
2Ch 4:7
c 5:2-14 1Kg 8:1-11
d 5:2 2Ch 1:4

e 5:7 2Ch 3:10
f 5:9 1Kg 8:8
g 5:10 Dt 10:2-5; Heb 9:4
h 5:11 1Ch 24:1-5
i 5:12 1Ch 13:8; 15:16,24
j 2Ch 5:13
k 1Ch 25:1-4
l 5:13 1Ch 16:42
m 1Ch 16:34; 2Ch 7:3
n Ex 40:34-35; Lv 16:2; Nm
9:15-16
o 5:14 Ex 13:21-22; 40:34-
38; Dt 4:11; 5:22; 31:14-15;
2Ch 7:1-3
p 6:1-42 1Kg 8:12-53
q 6:1 Ex 20:21; Dt 4:11; 5:22

COMPLETION OF THE GOLD FURNISHINGS

19 Solomon also made all the equipment in God's temple: the gold altar; the tables on which to put the Bread of the Presence;*a* **20** the lampstands and their lamps of pure gold to burn in front of the inner sanctuary according to specifications;*b* **21** of purest gold; **22** the wick trimmers, sprinkling basins, ladles,^ and firepans — of purest gold; and the entryway to the temple, its inner doors to the most holy place, and the doors of the temple sanctuary — of gold.

5 So all the work Solomon did for the LORD's temple was completed. Then Solomon brought the consecrated things of his father David — the silver, the gold, and all the utensils — and put them in the treasuries of God's temple.

PREPARATIONS FOR THE TEMPLE DEDICATION

2 At that time*c* Solomon assembled at Jerusalem the elders of Israel — all the tribal heads, the ancestral chiefs of the Israelites — in order to bring the ark of the covenant of the LORD up from the city of David,*d* that is, Zion. **3** So all the men of Israel were assembled in the king's presence at the festival; this was in the seventh month.^B

4 All the elders of Israel came, and the Levites picked up the ark. **5** They brought up the ark, the tent of meeting, and the holy utensils that were in the tent. The priests and the Levites brought them up. **6** King Solomon and the entire congregation of Israel who had gathered around him were in front of the ark sacrificing sheep, goats, and cattle that could not be counted or numbered because there were so many. **7** The priests brought the ark of the LORD's covenant to its place, into the inner sanctuary of the temple, to the most

holy place, beneath the wings of the cherubim.*e* **8** And the cherubim spread their wings over the place of the ark so that the cherubim formed a cover above the ark and its poles. **9** The poles were so long that their ends were seen from the holy place*c,f* in front of the inner sanctuary, but they were not seen from outside; they are still there today. **10** Nothing was in the ark except the two tablets that Moses had put in it at Horeb,*D,g* where the LORD had made a covenant with the Israelites when they came out of Egypt.

11 Now all the priests who were present had consecrated themselves regardless of their divisions.*h* When the priests came out of the holy place, **12** the Levitical singers dressed in fine linen and carrying cymbals, harps, and lyres*i* were standing east of the altar, and with them were 120 priests blowing trumpets.*j* The Levitical singers were descendants of Asaph, Heman, and Jeduthun and their sons*k* and relatives. **13** The trumpeters and singers joined together to praise and thank the LORD with one voice. They raised their voices, accompanied by trumpets, cymbals, and musical instruments,*l* in praise to the LORD:

> For he is good;
> his faithful love endures forever.*m*

The temple, the LORD's temple, was filled with a cloud.*n* **14** And because of the cloud, the priests were not able to continue ministering, for the glory of the LORD filled God's temple.*o*

SOLOMON'S DEDICATION OF THE TEMPLE

6 Then Solomon said:*p*
The LORD said he would dwell
in total darkness,*q*
2 but I have built an exalted temple
for you,
a place for your residence forever.

^ 4:22 Or *dishes*, or *spoons*; lit *palms*   ^B 5:3 = Tishri (September–October)   ^c 5:9 Some Hb mss, LXX; other Hb mss read *the ark*; 1Kg 8:8   ^D 5:10 = Sinai

5:1 The treasures **David** had previously dedicated for the temple, when combined with those of Solomon, were so great that there was a surplus.

5:2-3 The transport of **the ark** to its new home (5:2) occurred during the **festival** in **the seventh month**, which was the Festival of Shelters (or Tabernacles or Booths). This helps explain why **all the men of Israel were assembled in** Jerusalem at the time (5:3). The Festival of Shelters was one of Israel's three pilgrim festivals (along with Passover and Pentecost); during it, all men were required to make their pilgrimage to Jerusalem. For that holiday, the people built temporary booths to live in for one week, commemorating the nation's exo-

dus from Egypt when the Israelites became wanderers living in temporary dwellings as the Lord cared for them (see Lev 23:34-43).

5:7 Would the ark stay in its new location? Well, we know the ark was removed at least once, much later in Judah's history, probably during the debauched reign of Manasseh when he defiled the temple by setting up an idol in it. The ark couldn't have been in the temple at that time because Manasseh's godly grandson, Josiah, had to order the ark to be brought back to the temple and left there during his restoration (see the note on 35:1-3).

5:11 The priesthood had twenty-four **divisions**, which rotated the duties the men were

required to perform. The priestly divisions were legitimate in order to get the work of the temple accomplished, but they were irrelevant in this situation in which God himself was the unified focus.

These men with legitimate differences were headed toward the same goal line. We in the church should follow their example.

5:13 The phrase rendered **faithful love** here comes from the great Hebrew word that is variously translated in Bible versions as "lovingkindness," "loyal love," or "mercy." This is the word for God's enduring love for Israel; it's a reminder of the covenant he made with the nation at Mount Sinai.

[a] 6:5-9 2Sm 7:1-13
[b] 6:6 2Ch 12:13
[c] 1Ch 28:4
[d] 6:7 2Sm 7:2-3; 1Ch 22:7

[e] 6:11 2Ch 5:7,10
[f] 6:13 Ex 9:29,33; Ezr 9:5;
Neh 8:4
[g] 1Kg 8:54
[h] 6:14 Ex 15:11; Dt 3:24
[i] Dt 7:9

⯈ KINGDOM LIVING ⯇
COMMUNITY

A Culture's Independence from God

In 2 Chronicles 6, King Solomon had just finished building God's temple in Jerusalem and offered a prayer of dedication. In it, Solomon affirmed that he wanted to lead his people the way God wanted him to lead. And after the prayer, God's glory filled the temple. The people offered sacrifices and held a feast. Later that night, the Lord appeared to Solomon and told him that if the people ever rejected his ways but later repented, he would hear their prayers.

God will deal with a nation that turns its back on him. If a culture wants to be free of God, he will let it have that freedom. But freedom from God brings about dire consequences. Unbelievers do not normally turn to God when things get rough, although we have seen that happen when our nation faces national disasters such as those caused by weather or terrorism. Yet this Scripture isn't addressing secular individuals: it is addressing God's people, who are called by his name.

God's covenant people are the ones who are supposed to pray for their nation. In the Old Testament, his covenant people were the Jews. In the New Testament, the covenant people are those who make up the church—the multi-ethnic body of believers who have accepted Jesus Christ as Lord and Savior. God will pay attention to our prayers when we approach him humbly, repent of our own sins, seek his face, and turn toward him. This is the biblical model of how to begin to positively influence the culture.

FOR THE NEXT COMMUNITY
KINGDOM LIVING LESSON SEE PAGE 493.

³ Then the king turned and blessed the entire congregation of Israel while they were standing. ⁴ He said:
Blessed be the Lord God of Israel!
He spoke directly to my father David,
and he has fulfilled the promise
by his power.
He said,
⁵ "Since the day I brought
my people Israel
out of the land of Egypt,[a]
I have not chosen a city to build
a temple in
among any of the tribes of Israel,
so that my name would be there,
and I have not chosen a man
to be ruler over my people Israel.
⁶ But I have chosen Jerusalem
so that my name will be there,[b]
and I have chosen David
to be over my people Israel."[c]

⁷ My father David had his heart set
on building a temple for the name
of the Lord, the God of Israel.[d]
⁸ However, the Lord said
to my father David,
"Since it was your desire to build
a temple for my name,
you have done well to have this desire.
⁹ Yet, you are not the one to build
the temple,
but your son, your own offspring,

will build the temple for my name."
¹⁰ So the Lord has fulfilled
what he promised.
I have taken the place
of my father David
and I sit on the throne of Israel,
as the Lord promised.
I have built the temple for the name
of the Lord, the God of Israel.
¹¹ I have put the ark there,
where the Lord's covenant is
that he made with the Israelites.[e]

SOLOMON'S PRAYER

¹² Then Solomon stood before the altar of the Lord in front of the entire congregation of Israel and spread out his hands. ¹³ For Solomon had made a bronze platform 7 ¹/₂ feet[A] long, 7 ¹/₂ feet wide, and 4 ¹/₂ feet[B] high and put it in the court. He stood on it,[f] knelt down in front of the entire congregation of Israel, and spread out his hands toward heaven.[g] ¹⁴ He said:
Lord God of Israel,
there is no God like you
in heaven or on earth,[h]
who keeps his gracious covenant
with your servants who walk
before you
with all their heart.[i]
¹⁵ You have kept what you promised
to your servant, my father David.
You spoke directly to him,

a 6:15 1Ch 22:9-10
b 6:16 1Kg 2:4; 2Ch 7:18
c 6:18 2Ch 2:6
d 6:20 Dt 12:11

e 6:26 1Kg 8:35
f 6:28 Jos 2:7; Jdg 16:2-3

and you fulfilled your promise
  by your power,
as it is today.*a*

16 Therefore, LORD God of Israel,
keep what you promised
to your servant, my father David:
"You will never fail to have a man
to sit before me on the throne
  of Israel,*b*
if only your sons guard their way
  to walk in my Law
as you have walked before me."

17 Now, LORD God of Israel,
  please confirm
what you promised
  to your servant David.

18 But will God indeed live on earth
  with humans?
Even heaven, the highest heaven,
  cannot contain you,*c*
much less this temple I have built.

19 Listen*A* to your servant's prayer
  and his petition,
LORD my God,
so that you may hear the cry
  and the prayer
that your servant prays before you,

20 so that your eyes watch over
    this temple
day and night,
toward the place where you said
you would put your name;*d*
and so that you may hear the prayer
your servant prays toward this place.

21 Hear the petitions of your servant
and your people Israel,
which they pray toward this place.
May you hear in your dwelling place
  in heaven.
May you hear and forgive.

22 If a man sins against his neighbor
and is forced to take an oath*B*
and he comes to take an oath
before your altar in this temple,

23 may you hear in heaven and act.
May you judge your servants,
condemning the wicked man
  by bringing

what he has done on his own head
and providing justice
  for the righteous
by rewarding him according to
  his righteousness.

24 If your people Israel are defeated
  before an enemy,
because they have sinned
  against you,
and they return to you and praise
  your name,
and they pray and plead for mercy
before you in this temple,

25 may you hear in heaven
and forgive the sin
  of your people Israel.
May you restore them to the land
you gave them and their ancestors.

26 When the skies are shut and there is
    no rain
because they have sinned
    against you,
and they pray toward this place
and praise your name,
and they turn from their sins
because you are afflicting*c,e* them,

27 may you hear in heaven
and forgive the sin of your servants
and your people Israel,
so that you may teach them
  the good way
they should walk in.
May you send rain on your land
that you gave your people
  for an inheritance.

28 When there is famine in the land,
when there is pestilence,
when there is blight or mildew,
    locust or grasshopper,
when their enemies besiege them
in the land and its cities,*D,E,f*
when there is any plague or illness,

29 every prayer or petition
that any person or that
    all your people Israel may have —
they each know their own affliction*F*
  and suffering —

A 6:19 Lit *Turn*   *B* 6:22 Lit *and he lifts a curse against him to curse him*   *C* 6:26 LXX, Vg; MT reads *answering*; 1Kg 8:35   *D* 6:28 Lit *land of its gates*
E 6:28 Lit *if his* (Israel's) *enemies besiege him in the land of his gates*; Jos 2:7; Jdg 16:2-3   *F* 6:29 Lit *plague*

6:16 God's promise to **David** and his successors could only be enjoyed by those kings who adhered to the Lord. As the rest of 2 Chronicles makes clear, many of David's heirs failed at this and proved unworthy of the promise's blessing. But God's promises can never fail. One day the perfect

and divine Son of David, Jesus Christ, will reign on David's throne forever (see Luke 1:32-33).
6:18 God is independent of the universe. He is our Creator and sustainer. So how can humans expect him to dwell in a temple? The answer is found in the reality that ours is not a

God who is aloof from his creation and takes no interest in human affairs. He is not only transcendent (that is, independent of the physical universe), but he is also *immanent*— that is, he is present within his creation while remaining distinct from it.

as they spread out their hands
   toward this temple,
30 may you hear in heaven,
   your dwelling place,
and may you forgive
   and give to everyone[A]
according to all their ways,
   since you know each heart,
for you alone know the human heart,[a]
31 so that they may fear you
   and walk in your ways
all the days they live on the land
you gave our ancestors.

32 Even for the foreigner who is not of
   your people Israel
but has come from a distant land
because of your great name
and your strong hand
   and outstretched arm:[b]
when he comes and prays
   toward this temple,
33 may you hear in heaven in your
   dwelling place,
and do all the foreigner asks you.
Then all the peoples of the earth
   will know your name,
to fear you as your people Israel do
and know that this temple
   I have built
bears your name.[c]

34 When your people go out
   to fight against their enemies,
wherever you send them,
and they pray to you
in the direction of this city
   you have chosen[d]
and the temple that I have built
   for your name,
35 may you hear their prayer
   and petition in heaven
and uphold their cause.

36 When they sin against you —
   for there is no one
   who does not sin[e] —
and you are angry with them
and hand them over to the enemy,
and their captors deport them
to a distant or nearby country,
37 and when they come to their senses

in the land where they were deported
and repent and petition you
   in their captors' land,
saying: "We have sinned
   and done wrong;
we have been wicked,"
38 and when they return to you with all
   their mind and all their heart
in the land of their captivity
   where they were taken captive,
and when they pray in the direction
   of their land
that you gave their ancestors,
and the city you have chosen,
and toward the temple I have built
   for your name,
39 may you hear their prayer
   and petitions in heaven,
your dwelling place,
and uphold their cause.[B]
May you forgive your people
who sinned against you.

40 Now, my God,
please let your eyes be open
and your ears attentive
to the prayer of this place.[f]
41 Now therefore:[g]

Arise, LORD God, come
   to your resting place,
you and your powerful ark.
May your priests, LORD God,
   be clothed with salvation,
and may your faithful people rejoice
   in goodness.
42 LORD God, do not reject
   your anointed one;[c]
remember the promises
   to your servant David.[h]

THE DEDICATION CEREMONIES

7 When Solomon finished praying,[i]
fire descended from heaven and consumed the burnt offering and the sacrifices,[j] and the glory of the LORD filled the temple. ² The priests were not able to enter the LORD's temple because the glory of the LORD filled the temple of the LORD. ³ All the Israelites were watching when the fire descended and the glory of the LORD came on the temple. They bowed down on the

[a] 6:30 1Sm 16:7; 1Ch 28:9
[b] 6:32 Is 56:6-8; Zch 8:20-23; 14:16-21
[c] 6:33 2Ch 7:14
[d] 6:34 Dt 12:11
[e] 6:36 Jb 15:14-16; Jms 3:2; 1Jn 1:8-10
[f] 6:40 2Ch 7:15; Neh 1:6,11; Ps 17:1
[g] 6:41-42 Ps 132:8-10
[h] 6:42 1Ch 16:8-22; Ps 105:1-15; Is 55:3
[i] 7:1-10 1Kg 8:54
[j] 7:1 Gn 15:7-17; Lv 9:24; Jdg 6:21-24; 1Kg 18:24,38

[A] 6:30 Lit give for the man   [B] 6:39 Lit and do their judgment, or justice   [C] 6:42 Some Hb mss, LXX; other Hb mss read ones; Ps 132:10

7:1-3 Tragically, Ezekiel the prophet would witness the departure of the **glory** cloud during a time of great apostasy on the part of Judah (see Ezek 10:18). But importantly, in Ezekiel's vision of a new temple he saw the glory of God returning too (see Ezek 43:4-5).

The arrival and departure of God's glory from his house points to an important lesson for modern believers. We get all worked up about what is happening in the White House or the Supreme Court without giving much thought to what is happening,

or not happening, in God's church. We must understand that if God doesn't see the church getting things right, it doesn't matter whom we elect to the White House. Judgment and healing start with the household of God.

*7:3 1Ch 16:41; 2Ch 5:13; 20:21; Ezr 3:11; Ps 106:1; Jr 33:11
*b 7:4-5 1Kg 8:62-63
*c 7:6 1Ch 15:16-21; 16:42; 23:5; 2Ch 29:26-30; Neh 12:36
*d 7:7 2Ch 4:1
*e 7:7-10 1Kg 8:64-66
*f 7:7 Lv 7:30-31
*g 7:9 Lv 23:36
*h 7:11-22 1Kg 9:1-9

*i 7:12 Dt 12:5,11
*j 7:13 2Ch 6:26-28
*k 7:14 2Ch 6:37-39
*l 7:15 2Ch 6:20,40
*m 7:16 2Ch 7:12
*n 7:18 2Ch 6:16
*o 7:19 Lv 26:14; Dt 28:15
*p 7:20 Lv 26:33; Dt 29:28; 1Kg 14:15
*q Dt 28:37
*r 7:21-22 Dt 29:24-25

pavement with their faces to the ground. They worshiped and praised the LORD:

For he is good,
for his faithful love endures forever.*a*

4 The king and all the people were offering sacrifices in the LORD's presence.*b* **5** King Solomon offered a sacrifice of twenty-two thousand cattle and one hundred twenty thousand sheep and goats. In this manner the king and all the people dedicated God's temple. **6** The priests and the Levites were standing at their stations. The Levites had the musical instruments of the LORD, which King David had made to give thanks to the LORD — "for his faithful love endures forever" — when he offered praise with them.*c* Across from the Levites, the priests were blowing trumpets, and all the people were standing. **7** Since the bronze altar that Solomon had made*d* could not accommodate the burnt offering, the grain offering, and the fat of the fellowship offerings, Solomon first consecrated the middle of the courtyard*e* that was in front of the LORD's temple and then offered the burnt offerings and the fat of the fellowship offerings there.*f*

8 So Solomon and all Israel with him — a very great assembly, from the entrance to Hamath*A* to the Brook of Egypt — observed the festival at that time for seven days. **9** On the eighth day*B* they held a sacred assembly,*g* for the dedication of the altar lasted seven days and the festival seven days. **10** On the twenty-third day of the seventh month he sent the people home,*c* rejoicing and with happy hearts for the goodness the LORD had done for David, for Solomon, and for his people Israel.

11 So Solomon finished the LORD's temple and the royal palace. Everything that had entered Solomon's heart to do for the LORD's temple and for his own palace succeeded.*h*

THE LORD'S RESPONSE

12 Then the LORD appeared to Solomon at night and said to him:

I have heard your prayer and have chosen this place for myself as a temple of sacrifice.*i* **13** If I shut the sky so there is no rain, or if I command the grasshopper to consume the land, or if I send pestilence on my people,*j* **14** and my people, who bear my name, humble themselves, pray and seek my face, and turn from their evil ways, then I will hear from heaven, forgive their sin, and heal their land.*k* **15** My eyes will now be open and my ears attentive to prayer from this place.*l* **16** And I have now chosen and consecrated this temple so that my name may be there forever; my eyes and my heart will be there at all times.*m*

17 As for you, if you walk before me as your father David walked, doing everything I have commanded you, and if you keep my statutes and ordinances, **18** I will establish your royal throne, as I promised your father David: You will never fail to have a man ruling in Israel.*n*

19 However, if you turn away and abandon my statutes and my commands that I have set before you and if you go and serve other gods and bow in worship to them,*o* **20** then I will uproot Israel from the soil that I gave them, and this temple that I have sanctified for my name I will banish from my presence;*p* I will make it an object of scorn and ridicule among all the peoples.*q* **21** As for this temple, which was exalted, everyone who passes by will be appalled and will say:*r* Why did the LORD do this to this land and this temple? **22** Then they will say: Because

---

*A 7:8 Or from Lebo-hamath   *B 7:9 = the day after the festival, or the 15th day   *C 7:10 Lit people to their tents

---

7:13-14 In this hallmark passage, God calls his people to **pray** (7:14). Prayer enacts God's hand in history like nothing else because prayer is humanity's relational communication with God.

Several key elements in verse 14 determine whether a prayer will prove effective. The first is found in the words **my people, who bear my name**. This is a reference to God's covenant people. We can approach God through our new-covenant relationship with his Son.

The second element of prayer that moves God is the heart attitude of those who seek him. God desires those who **humble themselves** (7:14). Humility includes the idea of

dependency—the recognition that without the Lord, we can do nothing (see John 15:5). Prayer, in fact, is by its nature an admission of our weakness and need. Many Christians don't pray because they are too proud.

A third element related to prayer's effectiveness is God's call to **seek [his] face** (2 Chr 7:14). This means much more than saying "thank you for this food" or reciting "now I lay me down to sleep." Prayer that moves God comes from a recognition that sin turns his face away from us and turns us away from him. The good news is that God invites us to seek his face. He is open to us.

The fourth element of effective prayer is for God's people to **turn from their evil ways** (2 Chr 7:14). The idea here is of turning away from something that displeases God and turning toward something that pleases him. We must turn from anything that is contrary to his will.

7:22 Many years later, when the inhabitants of Jerusalem were uprooted from their land and sent into exile in Babylon, the people would ask, "How could such a calamity fall on us? Aren't we God's people, the object of his favor?" The explanation for God's judgment should have been clear to them.

they abandoned the LORD God of their ancestors who brought them out of the land of Egypt. They clung to other gods and bowed in worship to them and served them. Because of this, he brought all this ruin on them.

SOLOMON'S LATER BUILDING PROJECTS

8 At the end of twenty years[a] during which Solomon had built the LORD's temple and his own palace — [2] Solomon had rebuilt the cities Hiram[A] gave him and settled Israelites there — [3] Solomon went to Hamath-zobah and seized it. [4] He built Tadmor in the wilderness along with all the storage cities that he built in Hamath. [5] He built Upper Beth-horon and Lower Beth-horon[b] — fortified cities with walls, gates, and bars[c] — [6] Baalath, all the storage cities that belonged to Solomon, all the chariot cities, the cavalry cities, and everything Solomon desired to build in Jerusalem, Lebanon, or anywhere else in the land of his dominion. [7] As for all the peoples who remained of the Hethites, Amorites, Perizzites, Hivites, and Jebusites, who were not from Israel[d] — [8] their descendants who remained in the land after them, those the Israelites had not completely destroyed — Solomon imposed forced labor on them; it is this way today.[e] [9] But Solomon did not consign the Israelites to be slaves for his work; they were soldiers, commanders of his captains, and commanders of his chariots and his cavalry. [10] These were King Solomon's deputies: 250 who supervised the people.

[11] Solomon brought the daughter of Pharaoh from the city of David to the house he had built for her,[f] for he said, "My wife must not live in the house[B] of King David of Israel because the places the ark of the LORD has come into are holy."

PUBLIC WORSHIP ESTABLISHED AT THE TEMPLE

[12] At that time[g] Solomon offered burnt offerings to the LORD on the LORD's altar he had made in front of the portico.[h] [13] He followed the daily requirement[i] for offerings according to the commandment of Moses[j] for Sabbaths, New Moons, and the three annual appointed festivals: the Festival of Unleavened Bread, the Festival of Weeks, and the Festival of Shelters.[k] [14] According to the ordinances of his father David, he appointed the divisions of the priests over their service,[l] of the Levites over their responsibilities to offer praise and to minister before the priests following the daily requirement,[m] and of the gatekeepers by their divisions with respect to each temple gate,[n] for this had been the command of David, the man of God.[o] [15] They did not turn aside from the king's command regarding the priests and the Levites concerning any matter or concerning the treasuries.[p] [16] All of Solomon's work was carried out from the day the foundation was laid for the LORD's temple until it was finished. So the LORD's temple was completed.

SOLOMON'S FLEET

[17] At that time[q] Solomon went to Ezion-geber and to Eloth[r] on the seashore in the land of Edom. [18] So Hiram[c] sent ships to him by his servants along with crews of experienced seamen. They went with Solomon's servants to Ophir, took from there seventeen tons[D] of gold, and delivered it to King Solomon.[s]

THE QUEEN OF SHEBA

9 The queen of Sheba heard of Solomon's fame,[t] so she came to test Solomon with difficult questions at Jerusalem with a very large entourage, with camels bearing spices, gold in abundance, and precious stones. She came to Solomon and spoke with him about everything that was on her mind. [2] So Solomon answered all her questions; nothing was too difficult for Solomon to explain to her. [3] When the queen of Sheba observed Solomon's wisdom, the palace he had built, [4] the food at his table, his servants' residence, his attendants' service and their attire, his cupbearers and their attire, and the burnt offerings he offered at the LORD's temple, it took her breath away.

[a] 8:1-10 1Kg 9:10-23
[b] 8:5 1Ch 7:24
[c] 2Ch 14:7
[d] 8:7 Gn 15:18-21
[e] 8:8 1Kg 4:6; 9:21
[f] 8:11 1Kg 3:1; 7:8; 9:24
[g] 8:12-13 1Kg 9:25
[h] 8:12 2Ch 4:1

[i] 8:13 Ex 29:38-42
[j] Nm 28:3
[k] Ex 23:14-17
[l] 8:14 1Ch 24:1-3
[m] 1Ch 25:1
[n] 1Ch 26:1,13
[o] Neh 12:24,36
[p] 8:15 1Ch 26:20-28
[q] 8:17-18 1Kg 9:26-28
[r] 8:17 2Kg 14:22
[s] 8:18 2Ch 9:10,13
[t] 9:1-12 1Kg 10:1-13; Mt 12:42; Lk 11:31

[A] 8:2 = the king of Tyre   [B] 8:11 LXX reads *city*   [C] 8:18 Lit *Huram*   [D] 8:18 Lit *450 talents*

8:3-6 Solomon's desire to extend his kingdom into foreign lands is evident by his conquest of **Hamath-zobah**, a city in modern-day Syria that was almost three hundred miles north of Jerusalem (8:3). His **storage cities** (8:4, 6) in the north and south of his territory also give us a sense of the reach of his empire.
8:11 Solomon accommodated his wives' worship of their false gods, while also trying to remain true to the Lord—which was a losing battle. We see a glimpse of this struggle in Solomon's concern for **the places** connected with the holy **ark**. David's palace was erected at one of these locations, so Solomon built a separate palace for his Egyptian wife, lest her pagan origin and ways defile David's palace.
8:17-18 Solomon owned a fleet of commercial ships that brought precious metals, spices, and beautiful woods to Jerusalem. Trips to such places as **Ophir**, which may have been as far away as east Africa or India, allowed Solomon to tap into incredible resources to enrich his kingdom.
9:1 **The queen** may have led the Sabean peoples of southwestern Arabia.

a 9:7 1Kg 10:8
b 9:8 1Ch 28:5; 29:23
c Dt 7:8; 2Ch 2:11
d 9:10 2Ch 8:18
e 9:13-24 1Kg 10:14-25
f 9:16 1Kg 7:2-5

g 9:21 2Ch 20:36-37
h 9:22 1Kg 3:13; 2Ch 1:12
i 9:25-28 Dt 17:16; 1Kg
10:26-29; 2Ch 1:14-17
j 9:25 1Kg 4:26
k 9:26 Gn 15:18; 1Kg
4:21,24
l 9:29-31 1Kg 11:41-43
m 9:29 1Ch 29:29; 2Ch
12:15; 13:22
n 9:31 1Kg 2:10
o 10:1-19 1Kg 12:1-20

⁵ She said to the king, "The report I heard in my own country about your words and about your wisdom is true. ⁶ But I didn't believe their reports until I came and saw with my own eyes. Indeed, I was not even told half of your great wisdom! You far exceed the report I heard. ⁷ How happy are your men.[A,a] How happy are these servants of yours, who always stand in your presence hearing your wisdom. ⁸ Blessed be the LORD your God! He delighted in you and put you on his throne as king for the LORD your God.[b] Because your God loved Israel enough to establish them forever, he has set you over them as king to carry out justice and righteousness."[c]

⁹ Then she gave the king four and a half tons[B] of gold, a great quantity of spices, and precious stones. There never were such spices as those the queen of Sheba gave to King Solomon. ¹⁰ In addition, Hiram's servants and Solomon's servants who brought gold from Ophir[d] also brought algum wood and precious stones. ¹¹ The king made the algum wood into walkways for the LORD's temple and for the king's palace and into lyres and harps for the singers. Never before had anything like them been seen in the land of Judah.

¹² King Solomon gave the queen of Sheba her every desire, whatever she asked — far more than she had brought the king. Then she, along with her servants, returned to her own country.

SOLOMON'S WEALTH

¹³ The weight of gold that came to Solomon[e] annually was twenty-five tons,[c] ¹⁴ besides what was brought by the merchants and traders. All the Arabian kings and governors of the land also brought gold and silver to Solomon.

¹⁵ King Solomon made two hundred large shields of hammered gold; 15 pounds[D] of hammered gold went into each shield. ¹⁶ He made three hundred small shields of hammered gold; 7 ½ pounds[E] of gold went into each shield. The king put them in the House of the Forest of Lebanon.[f]

¹⁷ The king also made a large ivory throne and overlaid it with pure gold. ¹⁸ The throne had six steps; there was a footstool covered in gold for the throne, armrests on either side of the seat, and two lions standing beside the armrests. ¹⁹ Twelve lions were standing there on the six steps, one at each end. Nothing like it had ever been made in any other kingdom.

²⁰ All of King Solomon's drinking cups were gold, and all the utensils of the House of the Forest of Lebanon were pure gold. There was no silver, since it was considered as nothing in Solomon's time, ²¹ for the king's ships kept going to Tarshish[g] with Hiram's servants, and once every three years the ships of Tarshish would arrive bearing gold, silver, ivory, apes, and peacocks.[F]

²² King Solomon surpassed all the kings of the world in riches and wisdom.[h] ²³ All the kings of the world wanted an audience with Solomon to hear the wisdom God had put in his heart. ²⁴ Each of them would bring his own gift — items[G] of silver and gold, clothing, weapons,[H,I] spices, and horses and mules — as an annual tribute.

²⁵ Solomon[i] had four thousand stalls for horses and chariots, and twelve thousand horsemen.[j] He stationed them in the chariot cities and with the king in Jerusalem. ²⁶ He ruled over all the kings from the Euphrates River to the land of the Philistines and as far as the border of Egypt.[k] ²⁷ The king made silver as common in Jerusalem as stones, and he made cedar as abundant as sycamore in the Judean foothills. ²⁸ They were bringing horses for Solomon from Egypt and from all the countries.

SOLOMON'S DEATH

²⁹ The remaining events[l] of Solomon's reign, from beginning to end, are written in the Events of the Prophet Nathan, the Prophecy of Ahijah the Shilonite, and the Visions of the Seer Iddo concerning Jeroboam son of Nebat.[m] ³⁰ Solomon reigned in Jerusalem over all Israel for forty years. ³¹ Solomon rested with his fathers and was buried in the city of his father David.[n] His son Rehoboam became king in his place.

THE KINGDOM DIVIDED

10 Then Rehoboam went to Shechem,[o] for all Israel had gone to Shechem to make him king. ² When Jeroboam son of Nebat heard about it — for he was in

---

A 9:7 LXX, Old Lat read wives; 1Kg 10:8   B 9:9 Lit 120 talents   C 9:13 Lit 666 talents   D 9:15 Lit 600 (shekels)   E 9:16 Lit 300 (shekels)   F 9:21 Or baboons   G 9:24 Or vessels, or weapons   H 9:24 LXX reads resin   I 9:24 Or fragrant balsam

---

9:22-24 This provides an apt summary of the state of affairs during the heyday of Solomon's reign.
9:29 It's safe to say that no one in Israel could have foreseen, at the time, that Solomon's death would end Israel's golden age begun under David, pave the way for a bitter division of the nation, and open the floodgates of idolatry. Solomon did not live to see the damage done by his departure from the Lord (see 1 Kgs 11:1-13), but his descendants did.
10:1-3 Rehoboam was the only one of what must have been the many sons of Solomon to be named in Scripture (10:1). Immediately after

Egypt where he had fled from King Solomon's presence — Jeroboam returned from Egypt.ᵃ ³ So they summoned him. Then Jeroboam and all Israel came and spoke to Rehoboam: ⁴ "Your father made our yoke harsh. Therefore, lighten your father's harsh service and the heavy yoke he put on us, and we will serve you."

⁵ Rehoboam replied, "Return to me in three days." So the people left.

⁶ Then King Rehoboam consulted with the elders who had attended his father Solomon when he was alive, asking, "How do you advise me to respond to this people?"

⁷ They replied, "If you will be kind to this people and please them by speaking kind words to them, they will be your servants forever."

⁸ But he rejected the advice of the elders who had advised him, and he consulted with the young men who had grown up with him, the ones attending him. ⁹ He asked them, "What message do you advise we send back to this people who said to me, 'Lighten the yoke your father put on us'?"

¹⁰ Then the young men who had grown up with him told him, "This is what you should say to the people who said to you, 'Your father made our yoke heavy, but you, make it lighter on us!' This is what you should say to them: 'My little finger is thicker than my father's waist! ¹¹ Now therefore, my father burdened you with a heavy yoke, but I will add to your yoke; my father disciplined you with whips, but I, with barbed whips.'"ᴬ

¹² So Jeroboam and all the people came to Rehoboam on the third day, just as the king had ordered, saying, "Return to me on the third day." ¹³ Then the king answered them harshly. King Rehoboam rejected the elders' advice ¹⁴ and spoke to them according to the young men's advice, saying, "My father made your yoke heavy,ᴮ,ᵇ but I will add to it; my father disciplined you with whips, but I, with barbed whips."

¹⁵ The king did not listen to the people because the turn of events came from God,ᶜ in order that the LORD might carry out his word that he had spoken through Ahijah the Shilonite to Jeroboam son of Nebat.ᵈ

¹⁶ Whenᵉ all Israel sawᶜ,ᶠ that the king had not listened to them, the people answered the king:

What portion do we have in David?
We have no inheritance in the son
  of Jesse.
Israel, each to your tent;
David, look after
  your own house now!

So all Israel went to their tents. ¹⁷ But as for the Israelites living in the cities of Judah, Rehoboam reigned over them.

¹⁸ Then King Rehoboam sent Hadoram,ᴰ,ᵍ who was in charge of the forced labor, but the Israelites stoned him to death. However, King Rehoboam managed to get into his chariot to flee to Jerusalem. ¹⁹ Israel is in rebellion against the house of David until today.

REHOBOAM IN JERUSALEM

11 When Rehoboam arrived in Jerusalem,ʰ he mobilized the house of Judah and Benjamin — one hundred eighty thousand fit young soldiers — to fight against Israel to restore the reign to Rehoboam. ² But the word of the LORD came to Shemaiah,ⁱ the man of God: ³ "Say to Rehoboam son of Solomon, king of Judah, to all Israel in Judah and Benjamin, and to the rest of the people: ⁴ 'This is what the LORD says: You are not to march up and fight against your brothers.ʲ Each of you return home, for this incident has come from me.'"ᵏ

ᵃ10:2 1Kg 11:40
ᵇ10:14 1Kg 12:14
ᶜ10:15 2Ch 25:16-20
ᵈ1Kg 11:29-39
ᵉ10:16-17 2Sm 20:1-2
ᶠ10:16 1Kg 12:16
ᵍ10:18 1Kg 4:6; 5:14; 12:18
ʰ11:1-4 1Kg 12:21-24
ⁱ11:2 2Ch 12:5-7,15
ʲ11:4 2Ch 28:8-11
ᵏ2Ch 10:15

ᴬ10:11 Lit with scorpions, also in v. 14   ᴮ10:14 Some Hb mss, LXX; other Hb mss read I will make your yoke heavy; 1Kg 12:14   ᶜ10:16 Some Hb mss, LXX; other Hb mss omit saw; 1Kg 12:16   ᴰ10:18 = Adoram in 1Kg 12:18

introducing him, the Chronicler also introduces **Jeroboam**, one of Solomon's officials (10:2; see 1 Kgs 11:26-28). Previously Jeroboam had rebelled against Solomon, possibly over the king's harsh labor practices. Solomon had tried to kill Jeroboam, who fled to Egypt (see 1 Kgs 11:40). But with Solomon dead, Jeroboam felt it was safe to return to Israel (2 Chr 10:2). His stature among the people is obvious from the fact that **they summoned him** to lead them in bringing their complaints to Rehoboam (10:3). **10:4** The statement sounds very much like a loyalty oath conditioned on Rehoboam's willingness to act on their concerns. **10:7** The **kind words** the elders advised the king to give may indicate something stronger than mere gentle comments; it may suggest

that they wanted him to make an alliance with the people in which Rehoboam would commit himself to the asked-for reforms. **10:8-11** The young men's poor advice was designed not only to reject the people's demands but also to serve notice that Rehoboam and his crew were in charge (10:10). The **barbed whips** (10:11) with which they threatened the people were particularly vicious, something like those used to flog Jesus before his crucifixion. **10:15** You might wonder how Rehoboam could be such a fool as to follow advice destined to split the kingdom. "Destined" is actually an appropriate word here because the Chronicler put all these events in perspective when he said they **came from God,**

who had sovereignly decreed that judgment was to fall on Solomon's house because of his departure from the Lord (see 1 Kgs 11:26-40). **10:16-19** Thus, the united kingdom of Israel divided into two parts. Rehoboam's kingdom, located in the south, was called **Judah** (10:17). Until the fall of Judah many years later, the name **Israel** would no longer designate the chosen nation as a whole; it referred only to the northern kingdom consisting of ten tribes (10:19).

It's helpful to recall at this point that the Chronicler is not interested in the events or kings of Israel since his focus is on Jerusalem, the temple, and the Davidic kingdom. **11:1** The two tribes left to Rehoboam were **Judah and Benjamin.**

a 11:5 2Ch 8:2-6; 11:23
b 11:14 Nm 35:2-5
c 2Ch 13:9
d 11:15 Ex 34:16-17
e Lv 17:7
f 1Kg 12:25-33; 13:33
g 11:17 2Ch 12:1
h 11:18 1Sm 16:6
i 11:20 2Ch 13:2
j 11:21 Dt 17:17
k 11:22 Dt 21:15-17

l 12:1 2Ch 11:17; 12:13
m 12:2 1Kg 11:40
n 1Kg 14:25
o 12:3 2Ch 16:8; Nah 3:9
p 12:4 2Ch 11:5-12
q 12:5 2Ch 11:2
r Dt 28:15,25; 2Ch 15:2
s 12:6 Ex 9:27; Dn 9:14
t 12:7 1Kg 21:29
u 2Ch 34:25-27; Ps 78:38
v 12:8 Dt 28:47-48
w 12:9-11 1Kg 14:25-28
x 12:9 2Ch 12:2
y 2Ch 9:15-16

So they listened to what the LORD said and turned back from going against Jeroboam.

JUDAH'S KING REHOBOAM

5 Rehoboam stayed in Jerusalem, and he fortified cities[A,a] in Judah. **6** He built up Bethlehem, Etam, Tekoa, **7** Beth-zur, Soco, Adullam, **8** Gath, Mareshah, Ziph, **9** Adoraim, Lachish, Azekah, **10** Zorah, Aijalon, and Hebron, which are fortified cities in Judah and in Benjamin. **11** He strengthened their fortifications and put leaders in them with supplies of food, oil, and wine. **12** He also put large shields and spears in each and every city to make them very strong. So Judah and Benjamin were his.

13 The priests and Levites from all their regions throughout Israel took their stand with Rehoboam, **14** for the Levites left their pasturelands and their possessions[b] and went to Judah and Jerusalem, because Jeroboam and his sons refused to let them serve as priests of the LORD.[c] **15** Jeroboam appointed his own priests for the high places,[d] the goat-demons,[e] and the golden calves he had made.[f] **16** Those from every tribe of Israel who had determined in their hearts to seek the LORD their God followed the Levites to Jerusalem to sacrifice to the LORD, the God of their ancestors. **17** So they strengthened the kingdom of Judah and supported Rehoboam son of Solomon for three years,[g] because they walked in the ways of David and Solomon for three years.

18 Rehoboam married Mahalath, daughter of David's son Jerimoth and of Abihail daughter of Jesse's son Eliab.[h] **19** She bore sons to him: Jeush, Shemariah, and Zaham. **20** After her, he married Maacah daughter[B,i] of Absalom. She bore Abijah, Attai, Ziza, and Shelomith to him. **21** Rehoboam loved Maacah daughter of Absalom more than all his wives and concubines. He acquired eighteen wives[j] and sixty concubines and was the father of twenty-eight sons and sixty daughters.

22 Rehoboam appointed Abijah son of Maacah as chief, leader among his brothers, intending to make him king.[k]

23 Rehoboam also showed discernment by dispersing some of his sons to all the regions of Judah and Benjamin and to all the fortified cities. He gave them plenty of provisions and sought many wives for them.

SHISHAK'S INVASION

12 When Rehoboam had established his sovereignty and royal power,[l] he abandoned the law of the LORD — he and all Israel with him. **2** Because they were unfaithful to the LORD, in the fifth year of King Rehoboam, King Shishak[m] of Egypt went to war against Jerusalem[n] **3** with 1,200 chariots, 60,000 cavalrymen, and countless people who came with him from Egypt — Libyans,[o] Sukkiim, and Cushites. **4** He captured the fortified cities[p] of Judah and came as far as Jerusalem.

5 Then the prophet Shemaiah[q] went to Rehoboam and the leaders of Judah who were gathered at Jerusalem because of Shishak. He said to them: "This is what the LORD says: 'You have abandoned me; therefore, I have abandoned you to Shishak.'"[r]

6 So the leaders of Israel and the king humbled themselves and said, "The LORD is righteous."[s]

7 When the LORD saw that they had humbled themselves, the LORD's message came to Shemaiah: "They have humbled themselves; I will not destroy them but will grant them a little deliverance.[t] My wrath will not be poured out on Jerusalem through Shishak.[u] **8** However, they will become his servants so that they may recognize the difference between serving me and serving the kingdoms of other lands."[v]

9 So King Shishak of Egypt went to war[w] against Jerusalem.[x] He seized the treasuries of the LORD's temple and the treasuries of the royal palace. He took everything. He took the gold shields that Solomon had made.[y] **10** King Rehoboam made bronze shields to replace them and committed them into the care of the captains of the guards[c] who protected the entrance to the king's palace. **11** Whenever the king entered the LORD's temple, the guards would carry

---

A 11:5 Lit *he built cities for a fortress*   B 11:20 Possibly *granddaughter*, also in v. 21; 2Ch 13:2   c 12:10 Lit *the runners*

11:13-14 The southern kingdom was strengthened by the defection of the **priests and Levites from** the northern kingdom to Jerusalem because they wanted to worship the Lord in the true way.
11:15-16 Jeroboam feared that pilgrimages to the temple in Jerusalem would give the northern tribes incentive to go back to King Rehoboam. As a result of his defen-

sive countermeasures, **those from every tribe of Israel who had determined in their hearts to seek the LORD** moved to Judah (11:16).
11:17 Godly refugees added to Judah's strength. Unfortunately, though, Rehoboam's good situation only lasted **three years** (11:17). While he showed some initial discernment in his rule (11:23), it didn't last long.

12:1 With his throne secure and his military position strong, Rehoboam became spiritually careless. Don't let something similar happen to you.
12:2-4 When God brought the pharaoh **Shishak** against Judah, Rehoboam's **fortified cities** in which he had come to trust were overrun (12:2, 4).

the shields and take them back to the armory.[A] [12] When Rehoboam humbled himself, the LORD's anger turned away from him, and he did not destroy him completely.[a] Besides that, conditions were good in Judah.[b]

REHOBOAM'S LAST DAYS

[13] King Rehoboam[c] established his royal power in Jerusalem. Rehoboam was forty-one years old when he became king, and he reigned seventeen years in Jerusalem, the city the LORD had chosen from all the tribes of Israel to put his name.[d] Rehoboam's mother's name was Naamah the Ammonite. [14] Rehoboam did what was evil, because he did not determine in his heart to seek the LORD.[e]

[15] The events[f] of Rehoboam's reign, from beginning to end, are written in the Events of the Prophet Shemaiah[g] and of the Seer Iddo concerning genealogies.[h] There was war between Rehoboam and Jeroboam throughout their reigns. [16] Rehoboam rested with his fathers and was buried in the city of David. His son Abijah[B,i] became king in his place.

JUDAH'S KING ABIJAH

13 In the eighteenth year[j] of Israel's King Jeroboam, Abijah[B] became king over Judah, [2] and he reigned three years in Jerusalem. His mother's name was Micaiah[C,k] daughter of Uriel; she was from Gibeah.

There was war between Abijah and Jeroboam. [3] Abijah set his army of warriors in order with four hundred thousand fit young men. Jeroboam arranged his mighty army of eight hundred thousand fit young men in battle formation against him. [4] Then Abijah stood on Mount Zemaraim,[l] which is in the hill country of Ephraim, and said, "Jeroboam and all Israel, hear me. [5] Don't you know that the LORD God of Israel gave the kingship over Israel to David and his descendants forever[m] by a covenant of salt?[n] [6] But Jeroboam son of Nebat, a servant of Solomon son of David, rose up and rebelled against his lord.[o] [7] Then worthless and wicked men gathered around him to resist Rehoboam son of Solomon when Rehoboam was young, inexperienced, and unable to assert himself against them.

[8] "And now you are saying you can assert yourselves against the LORD's kingdom, which is in the hand of one of David's sons. You are a vast number and have with you the golden calves that Jeroboam made for you as gods.[D,p] [9] Didn't you banish the priests of the LORD, the descendants of Aaron and the Levites, and make your own priests like the peoples of other lands do?[q] Whoever comes to ordain himself[r] with a young bull and seven rams may become a priest[s] of what are not gods.[r]

[10] "But as for us, the LORD is our God. We have not abandoned him; the priests ministering to the LORD are descendants of Aaron, and the Levites serve at their tasks. [11] They offer a burnt offering and fragrant incense to the LORD every morning and every evening,[u] and they set the rows of the Bread of the Presence on the ceremonially clean table.[v] They light the lamps of the gold lampstand every evening. We are carrying out the requirements of the LORD our God, while you have abandoned him.[w] [12] Look, God and his priests are with us at our head. The trumpets are ready to sound the charge against you. Israelites, don't fight against the LORD God of your ancestors, for you will not succeed."[x]

[13] Now Jeroboam had sent an ambush[y] around to advance from behind them. So they were in front of Judah, and the ambush was behind them. [14] Judah turned and discovered that the battle was in front of them and behind them, so they cried out to the LORD.[z] Then the priests blew the trumpets, [15] and the men of Judah raised the battle cry. When the men of Judah raised the battle cry, God routed Jeroboam and all Israel before Abijah and Judah.[aa] [16] So the Israelites fled before Judah, and God handed them over to them.[ab] [17] Then Abijah and his people struck them with a mighty blow, and five hundred thousand fit young men of Israel were killed. [18] The Israelites were subdued at that time. The Judahites succeeded because they depended on the LORD, the God of their ancestors.

[19] Abijah pursued Jeroboam and captured some cities from him: Bethel, Jeshanah, and

---

[a] 12:12 2Ch 12:6-7
[b] 2Ch 19:3
[c] 12:13-14 1Kg 14:21-22
[d] 12:13 Dt 12:5; 1Kg 9:3
[e] 12:14 2Ch 19:3
[f] 12:15-16 1Kg 14:29-31
[g] 12:15 2Ch 12:5
[h] 2Ch 9:29; 13:22
[i] 12:16 1Kg 14:31-15:8
[j] 13:1-2 1Kg 15:1-2,7
[k] 13:2 1Kg 15:2; 2Ch 11:20,22
[l] 13:4 Jos 18:22
[m] 13:5 2Sm 7:12-16
[n] Lv 2:13; Nm 18:19
[o] 13:6 1Kg 11:26

[p] 13:8 1Kg 12:28
[q] 13:9 2Ch 11:14
[r] Ex 29:29-33
[s] 1Kg 13:33
[t] Jr 2:11; 5:7
[u] 13:11 Ex 29:38; 2Ch 2:4
[v] Ex 25:30; Lv 24:5-9
[w] Ex 25:31-40
[x] 13:12 Nm 10:8-9
[y] 13:13 Jos 8:4-9
[z] 13:14 2Ch 14:11
[aa] 13:15 2Ch 14:12
[ab] 13:16 2Ch 16:8

[A] 12:11 Lit *the chamber of the runners*   [B] 12:16; 13:1 = Abijam in 1Kg 14:31–15:8   [C] 13:2 LXX, Syr, Arabic read *Maacah*; 1Kg 15:2; 2Ch 11:22   [D] 13:8 Or *God*; 1Kg 12:28

12:12-16 Rehoboam's reign was a sad mixture of good and evil—of what might have been and what actually was. Nevertheless, the summary of his reign was that **Rehoboam . . . did not determine in his heart to seek the LORD** (12:14). And that is a tragic way to be remembered.

13:8-11 Israel's army was being led by the **golden calves** Jeroboam had made and the false **priests** he had ordained (13:8-9) while Judah's leader was **the LORD** (13:10). Abijah's nation was still faithfully led in worship by the priests and Levites offering sacrifices at the temple in Jerusalem as instructed long ago (13:11).

13:12 Abijah rightly equated an attack on Judah to a **fight against the LORD**.
13:14-15 Clearly God heard this cry for help because **God routed Jeroboam and all Israel** (13:15).

a 13:20 1Sm 25:38
b 1Kg 14:20
c 13:22 2Ch 24:27
d 1Kg 15:7; 2Ch 9:29; 12:15
e 14:1 1Kg 15:8
f 14:2-3 1Kg 15:11-12
g 14:3 Ex 34:13; Dt 7:5
h 14:5 2Ch 34:4,7
i 14:6 2Ch 11:5
j 2Ch 15:15
k 14:7 2Ch 8:5
l 14:8 2Ch 13:3

m 14:10 2Ch 11:8
n 14:11 2Ch 13:14
o 2Ch 13:18
p 14:12 2Ch 13:15
q 14:13 Gn 10:19
r 14:14 2Ch 17:10
s 15:1 2Ch 20:14; 24:20
t 15:2 2Ch 20:17
u Dt 4:29; 2Ch 15:15; Jr 29:13-14
v 1Ch 28:9
w 15:3 1Kg 12:28-33
x Lv 10:8-11; 2Ch 17:9

Ephron,[A] along with their surrounding villages. 20 Jeroboam no longer retained his power[B] during Abijah's reign; ultimately, the LORD struck him[a] and he died.[b]

21 However, Abijah grew strong, acquired fourteen wives, and fathered twenty-two sons and sixteen daughters. 22 The rest of the events of Abijah's reign, along with his ways and his sayings, are written in the Writing[c] of the Prophet Iddo.[d]

14 1 Abijah rested with his fathers and was buried in the city of David. His son Asa became king in his place.[e] During his reign the land experienced peace for ten years.

JUDAH'S KING ASA

2 Asa did what was good and right[f] in the sight of the LORD his God. 3 He removed the pagan altars and the high places. He shattered their sacred pillars and chopped down their Asherah poles.[g] 4 He told the people of Judah to seek the LORD God of their ancestors and to carry out the instruction and the commands. 5 He also removed the high places and the shrines[c] from all the cities of Judah,[h] and the kingdom experienced peace under him.

6 Because the land experienced peace, Asa built fortified cities in Judah.[i] No one made war with him in those days because the LORD gave him rest.[j] 7 So he said to the people of Judah, "Let's build these cities and surround them with walls and towers, with doors and bars.[k] The land is still ours because we sought the LORD our God. We sought him and he gave us rest on every side." So they built and succeeded.

THE CUSHITE INVASION

8 Asa had an army of three hundred thousand from Judah bearing large shields and spears,[l] and two hundred eighty thousand from Benjamin bearing regular shields and drawing the bow. All these were valiant warriors. 9 Then Zerah the Cushite came against them with an army of one million men and three hundred[D] chariots. They came as far as Mareshah. 10 So Asa marched out against him and lined up in battle formation in Zephathah Valley at Mareshah.[m]

11 Then Asa cried out to the LORD his God:[n] "LORD, there is no one besides you to help the mighty and those without strength. Help us, LORD our God, for we depend on you,[o] and in your name we have come against this large army. LORD, you are our God. Do not let a mere mortal hinder you."

12 So the LORD routed the Cushites before Asa and before Judah,[p] and the Cushites fled. 13 Then Asa and the people who were with him pursued them as far as Gerar.[q] The Cushites fell until they had no survivors, for they were crushed before the LORD and his army. So the people of Judah carried off a great supply of loot. 14 Then they attacked all the cities around Gerar because the terror of the LORD was on them.[r] They also plundered all the cities, since there was a great deal of plunder in them. 15 They also attacked the tents of the herdsmen and captured many sheep and camels. Then they returned to Jerusalem.

REVIVAL UNDER ASA

15 The Spirit of God came on Azariah son of Oded.[s] 2 So he went out to meet Asa and said to him, "Asa and all Judah and Benjamin, hear me. The LORD is with you[t] when you are with him. If you seek him, he will be found by you,[u] but if you abandon him, he will abandon you.[v] 3 For many years Israel has been without the true God,[w] without a teaching priest, and without instruction,[x] 4 but when they

---

A 13:19 Alt Hb tradition reads Ephrain   B 13:20 Lit He did not restrain the power of Jeroboam   C 14:5 Or incense altars   D 14:9 Syr, Arabic read 30,000

14:2-7 King Asa was deliberate about destroying idol worship in Judah and fortifying his territory against future attack (14:3-5).

14:6 While erecting defensive fortifications against enemy attack is good and wise, **peace** and safety ultimately come from **the LORD**.

14:9 **Mareshah** was located about twenty-five miles southwest of Jerusalem.

15:3-6 Likely this is a reference to the period of the judges. So what was it about this era of Israel's history that caused God to deliver distress? **For many years Israel [had] been without the true God, without a teaching priest, and without instruction** (15:3).

The lack of "the true God" does not mean that God had withdrawn himself from Israel. Even in the days of the judges there was reli-

gious activity happening there. But while people were offering sacrifices to God, they were not practicing the kind of authentic religion that pleased him or produced the right kind of response from him.

That Israel was "without a teaching priest" (15:3) indicates that without a faithful teacher of spiritual truth, God's people became confused about the nature of God and mixed their true beliefs with the false ones of the surrounding peoples. The priests, then, were doing an inadequate job of providing a divine viewpoint through which the people could interpret all of life and make God-honoring decisions. There was a systemic spiritual failure at the heart of Israel's spiritual leadership that kept the people ill-informed about their responsibility before God.

The third problem follows as a natural consequence of the first two. Since the people lacked faithful teaching about the one true God, they were essentially left "without instruction" (15:3). And since the divine rules weren't being applied, the people made up their own. One repeated phrase from the book of Judges illustrates this problem perfectly: "everyone did whatever seemed right to him" (Judg 17:6; 21:25).

For God's kingdom people to experience lives that please him and demonstrate his glory in the world, they need knowledge of his kingdom agenda as expressed through his Word. Today, the vehicle through which God teaches his Word and builds up his people is the church of Jesus Christ.

a 15:7 Jos 1:7,9

b 15:8 2Ch 13:19
c 2Ch 4:1; 8:12
d 15:9 2Ch 11:16
e 15:11 2Ch 14:13-15
f 15:12 2Ch 23:16
g 15:13 Ex 22:20; Dt 13:6-9;
17:2-7
h 15:15 2Ch 15:2
i 2Ch 14:6-7
j 15:16-18 1Kg 15:13-15
k 15:16 1Kg 15:2; 2Ch 11:22
l 2Ch 14:2-5

⇀ KINGDOM LIVING ↽
COMMUNITY
Keeping Chaos out of the Culture

In 2 Chronicles 15, we see that Israel's culture deteriorated for a number of reasons. First, they had turned from seeking the one true God. Second, they no longer had teaching priests. The third missing ingredient in Israel was God's law. When a culture has a false view of God built on bad information, God begins to remove the restraint of his law, and evil grows unbridled. Even sinners who respect God somewhat won't do certain things. But once God is removed from or marginalized in a culture, then the standard for a society is gone and God becomes that nation's worst enemy and nightmare. That's what had happened in Israel.

When the rule of God's law is missing, chaos replaces community. You cannot have order and structure in a society without God. Men become enslaved by the very freedom they seek. We have ungodly people in our culture who don't want any divine standard to which they must be held accountable. But when God leaves a society, hope goes with him.

As long as you have God, you have hope. He's the one thing you can count on. If God is still in the picture, and as long as his kingdom agenda is still on the table, it's not over. Even if circumstances collapse, God will keep the culture in place. As long as God is front and center in a culture, life, family, or church, there's hope. But when he is removed, his favor, protection, power, and peace are removed too.

FOR THE NEXT COMMUNITY
KINGDOM LIVING LESSON SEE PAGE 557.

APPLICATION QUESTIONS
READ 2 CHRONICLES 15:3,5-6

– What's your initial reaction to these verses? Why?
– How do you see the cultural symptoms described in these verses reflected in our society today?

prophet, he took courage and removed the abhorrent idols from the whole land of Judah and Benjamin and from the cities he had captured in the hill country of Ephraim.*b* He renovated the altar of the LORD that was in front of the portico of the LORD's temple.*c* **9** Then he gathered all Judah and Benjamin, as well as those from the tribes of Ephraim, Manasseh, and Simeon who were residing among them, for they had defected to him from Israel in great numbers when they saw that the LORD his God was with him.*g*

10 They were gathered in Jerusalem in the third month of the fifteenth year of Asa's reign. **11** At that time they sacrificed to the LORD seven hundred cattle and seven thousand sheep and goats from all the plunder they had brought.*e* **12** Then they entered into a covenant to seek the LORD God of their ancestors with all their heart and all their soul.*f* **13** Whoever would not seek the LORD God of Israel would be put to death, young or old,*B* man or woman.*g* **14** They took an oath to the LORD in a loud voice, with shouting, with trumpets, and with rams' horns. **15** All Judah rejoiced over the oath, for they had sworn it with all their mind. They had sought him with all their heart, and he was found by them.*h* So the LORD gave them rest on every side.*i*

16 King Asa*j* also removed Maacah, his grandmother,*c,k* from being queen mother because she had made an obscene image of Asherah. Asa chopped down her obscene image, then crushed it and burned it in the Kidron Valley.*l* **17** The high places were not taken away from Israel; nevertheless, Asa was wholeheartedly devoted his entire life.*D* **18** He brought his father's consecrated gifts and his own consecrated gifts into God's temple: silver, gold, and utensils.

19 There was no war until the thirty-fifth year of Asa's reign.

turned to the LORD God of Israel in their distress and sought him, he was found by them. **5** In those times there was no peace for those who went about their daily activities because the residents of the lands had many conflicts. **6** Nation was crushed by nation and city by city, for God troubled them with every possible distress. **7** But as for you, be strong; don't give up,*A* for your work has a reward."*a*

8 When Asa heard these words and the prophecy of Azariah son of Oded the

A 15:7 Lit *don't let your hands drop*   *B* 15:13 Or *insignificant or great*   *C* 15:16 Lit *mother*; 1Kg 15:2; 2Ch 11:22   *D* 15:17 Lit *wholehearted all his days*

15:7 These words recall the Lord's admonition to Joshua to be courageous in taking the promised land (see Josh 1:6-9). As Paul would tell the church in Corinth many years later: "be steadfast, immovable, always excelling in the Lord's work, knowing that your labor in the Lord is not in vain" (1 Cor 15:58).
15:9 **When they saw that the LORD his God was with** Asa, many people from the idolatrous northern kingdom of Israel **defected to him**. This suggests that those whose hearts are devoted to the Lord recognize godly spiritual leadership and initiative when they see it.

[a]16:1-6 1Kg 15:17-22
[b]16:7 1Kg 16:1; 2Ch 19:2
[c]2Ch 14:11
[d]16:8 2Ch 12:3
[e]2Ch 14:9-13
[f]16:9 Gn 6:8; Ps 33:18; 34:15; Pr 15:3; Zch 4:10; 1Pt 3:12
[g]2Ch 15:17
[h]16:11-14 1Kg 15:23-24
[i]16:14 Gn 50:2; Jn 12:7; 19:39-40
[j]2Ch 21:19
[k]17:1 1Kg 15:24
[l]17:2 2Ch 11:5
[m]2Ch 15:8
[n]17:4 1Kg 12:28
[o]17:5 2Ch 18:1
[p]17:6 2Ch 14:2-3
[q]2Ch 15:17

ASA'S TREATY WITH ARAM

16 In the thirty-sixth year of Asa,[a] Israel's King Baasha went to war against Judah. He built Ramah in order to keep anyone from leaving or coming to King Asa of Judah. 2 So Asa brought out the silver and gold from the treasuries of the LORD's temple and the royal palace and sent it to Aram's King Ben-hadad, who lived in Damascus, saying, 3 "There's a treaty between me and you, between my father and your father. Look, I have sent you silver and gold. Go break your treaty with Israel's King Baasha so that he will withdraw from me."

4 Ben-hadad listened to King Asa and sent the commanders of his armies to the cities of Israel. They attacked Ijon, Dan, Abel-maim,[A] and all the storage cities[B] of Naphtali. 5 When Baasha heard about it, he quit building Ramah and stopped his work. 6 Then King Asa brought all Judah, and they carried away the stones of Ramah and the timbers Baasha had built it with. Then he built Geba and Mizpah with them.

HANANI'S REBUKE OF ASA

7 At that time, the seer Hanani[b] came to King Asa of Judah and said to him, "Because you depended on the king of Aram and have not depended on the LORD your God,[c] the army of the king of Aram has escaped from you. 8 Were not the Cushites and Libyans a vast army with many chariots and horsemen?[d] When you depended on the LORD, he handed them over to you.[e] 9 For the eyes of the LORD roam throughout the earth[f] to show himself strong for those who are wholeheartedly devoted to him.[g] You have been foolish in this matter. Therefore, you will have wars from now on." 10 Asa was enraged with the seer and put him in prison[C] because of his anger over this. And Asa mistreated some of the people at that time.

ASA'S DEATH

11 Note that the events[h] of Asa's reign, from beginning to end, are written in the Book of the Kings of Judah and Israel. 12 In the thirty-ninth year of his reign, Asa developed a disease in his feet, and his disease became increasingly severe. Yet even in his disease he didn't seek the LORD but only the physicians. 13 Asa rested with his fathers; he died in the forty-first year of his reign. 14 He was buried in his own tomb that he had made for himself in the city of David. They laid him out in a coffin that was full of spices and various mixtures of prepared ointments;[i] then they made a great fire in his honor.[j]

JUDAH'S KING JEHOSHAPHAT

17 His son Jehoshaphat became king in his place[k] and strengthened himself against Israel. 2 He stationed troops in every fortified city of Judah[l] and set garrisons in the land of Judah and in the cities of Ephraim that his father Asa had captured.[m]

3 Now the LORD was with Jehoshaphat because he walked in the former ways of his father David.[D] He did not seek the Baals 4 but sought the God of his father and walked by his commands, not according to the practices of Israel.[n] 5 So the LORD established the kingdom in his hand. Then all Judah brought him tribute, and he had riches and honor in abundance.[o] 6 His mind rejoiced in the LORD's ways, and he again[p] removed the high places and Asherah poles from Judah.[q]

JEHOSHAPHAT'S EDUCATIONAL PLAN

7 In the third year of his reign, Jehoshaphat sent his officials — Ben-hail,[E] Obadiah, Zechariah, Nethanel, and Micaiah — to

[A]16:4 *Abel-beth-maacah* in 1Kg 15:20 [B]16:4 = all Chinnereth in 1Kg 15:20 [C]16:10 Lit *the house of stocks* [D]17:3 Some Hb mss, LXX omit *David* [E]17:7 = Son of Power

16:1-6 Things changed for Asa in the final years of his reign—or, more precisely, he changed in his attitudes and actions during those last years. Despite having sought God's deliverance from the Cushite forces years earlier, Asa panicked and failed to rely on the Lord when **Israel's King Baasha went to war against Judah** (16:1). Perhaps Asa had become complacent during his two decades of peace and spiritual prosperity. But whatever the reason for Asa's lack of trust, he bribed the pagan king **Ben-hadad** of Aram (which is modern-day Syria) to break his treaty with Israel and attack them so that Baasha would withdraw from threatening Judah (16:2-5). Asa used **silver and gold** from the temple's **treasuries** to pay the bribe, which must have been offensive to the Lord (16:2).

16:7-9 Asa's scheme in 16:1-6 had been a military success but a spiritual failure, a reminder that earthly victory is worthless when it comes at the expense of divine favor.

16:10 Instead of falling on his face in repentance before the Lord at this word, Asa reacted like a typical ancient ruler whose actions were called into question.

16:12 This **disease** was probably gout, that left him with severe pain. But apparently Asa had become so hardened by that time that **he didn't seek the LORD** for healing **but only the physicians**. Doing the same is a temptation for us today. We should be grateful for the blessings of doctors and modern medicine. But, ultimately, all healing comes from the Lord. So visit your physician and take your medication. But, first, pray.

16:13-14 The Chronicler's audience lived a generation or so after Israel's return from the Babylonian captivity, which had been a crushing blow that fell because the people and their leaders failed to seek the Lord's agenda. His choice of events to record from the lives of kings like Asa (who often got things right, though not always) was offered purposefully. It reminded God's people of the importance of *complete* faithfulness to him.

17:3-6 This man believed the words written by his great-great-great-grandfather David: "Take delight in the Lord, and he will give you your heart's desires" (Ps 37:4). Therefore, **the LORD established the kingdom in his hand** (2 Chr 17:5).

17:7-9 Jehoshaphat took steps to ensure that God's people did not flounder in ignorance

teach in the cities of Judah.[a] [8] The Levites with them were Shemaiah, Nethaniah, Zebadiah,[A] Asahel, Shemiramoth, Jehonathan, Adonijah, Tobijah, and Tob-adonijah; the priests, Elishama and Jehoram, were with these Levites. [9] They taught throughout Judah, having the book of the LORD's instruction with them.[b] They went throughout the towns of Judah and taught the people.

[10] The terror of the LORD was on all the kingdoms of the lands that surrounded Judah,[c] so they didn't fight against Jehoshaphat. [11] Some of the Philistines also brought gifts and silver as tribute to Jehoshaphat, and the Arabs brought him flocks: 7,700 rams and 7,700 male goats.[d]

JEHOSHAPHAT'S MILITARY MIGHT

[12] Jehoshaphat grew stronger and stronger. He built fortresses[e] and storage cities in Judah [13] and carried out great works in the towns of Judah. He had fighting men, valiant warriors, in Jerusalem. [14] These are their numbers according to their ancestral families.[B] For Judah, the commanders of thousands:

Adnah the commander and three hundred thousand valiant warriors with him;

[15]   next to him, Jehohanan the commander and two hundred eighty thousand with him;

[16]   next to him, Amasiah son of Zichri, the volunteer[f] of the LORD, and two hundred thousand valiant warriors with him;

[17]   from Benjamin, Eliada, a valiant warrior, and two hundred thousand with him armed with bow and shield;

[18]   next to him, Jehozabad and one hundred eighty thousand with him equipped for war.

[19] These were the ones who served the king, besides those he stationed in the fortified cities throughout all Judah.[g]

JEHOSHAPHAT'S ALLIANCE WITH AHAB

18 Now Jehoshaphat[h] had riches and honor in abundance,[i] and he made an alliance with Ahab through marriage.[C,j] [2] Then after some years, he went down to visit Ahab in Samaria. Ahab sacrificed many sheep, goats, and cattle for him and for the people who were with him. Then he persuaded him to attack Ramoth-gilead, [3] for Israel's King Ahab asked Judah's King Jehoshaphat, "Will you go with me to Ramoth-gilead?"

He replied to him, "I am as you are, my people as your people; we will be with you in the battle." [4] But Jehoshaphat said to the king of Israel, "First, please ask what the LORD's will is."

[5] So the king of Israel gathered the prophets, four hundred men, and asked them, "Should we go to Ramoth-gilead for war or should I refrain?"

They replied, "March up, and God will hand it over to the king."

[6] But Jehoshaphat asked, "Isn't there a prophet of the LORD here anymore? Let's ask him."[k]

[7] The king of Israel said to Jehoshaphat, "There is still one man who can inquire of the LORD, but I hate him because he never prophesies good about me, but only disaster. He is Micaiah son of Imlah."

"The king shouldn't say that," Jehoshaphat replied.

[8] So the king of Israel called an officer and said, "Hurry and get Micaiah son of Imlah!"

[9] Now the king of Israel and King Jehoshaphat of Judah, clothed in royal attire, were each sitting on his own throne. They were sitting on the threshing floor

[a]17:7 2Ch 15:3; 35:3
[b]17:9 Dt 6:4-9; 17:18; 28:58,61; 29:21; 30:10; 31:24,26; Jos 1:8; 8:31,34; 23:6; 24:26
[c]17:10 2Ch 14:14
[d]17:11 2Ch 9:14; 26:8
[e]17:12 2Ch 27:4
[f]17:16 Jdg 5:2,9; 1Ch 29:9

[g]17:19 2Ch 17:2
[h]18:1-34 1Kg 22:1-35
[i]18:1 2Ch 17:5
[j]1Kg 3:1; 2Kg 8:18; Ezr 9:14
[k]18:6 2Kg 3:11

[A]17:8 Some Hb mss, Syr, Tg, Arabic read *Zechariah*   [B]17:14 Lit *the house of their fathers*   [C]18:1 Lit *made himself a son-in-law to Ahab*; 1Kg 3:1; Ezr 9:14

---

of God's Word; he essentially protected them from confusion and idolatry. Today, this same responsibility is laid on church leaders for the good of their congregations and on parents for the good of their children.

17:10-13 Jehoshaphat had a clear sense of his kingdom priorities and created an environment in which the ministry of God's Word could flourish. As a result of God's Word being honored among the people, God honored Jehoshaphat's kingdom. **The terror of the LORD** fell on the surrounding nations, and they paid **tribute to Jehoshaphat** (17:10-11). This testified to what God told his people in an earlier generation: "Those who honor me I will honor" (1 Sam 2:30).

18:1-3 For all his good points, Jehoshaphat did make some questionable choices. He made alliances—marital, military, and commercial—with the northern kingdom of Israel, one of which almost cost him his life. Possibly the most glaring was **an alliance** he made with wicked King **Ahab** of Israel when his son married Ahab's daughter (18:1; see 21:6).

Another time Ahab was engaged in fierce warfare with the Arameans (Syrians) and needed Jehoshaphat's help to take the strategic city of **Ramoth-gilead** (18:2-3), situated about fifty miles northeast of Jerusalem on the east side of the Jordan River. Ahab won Jehoshaphat's pledge to fight alongside Israel.

18:5-27 Ahab's **four hundred** false **prophets** desired only to flatter their master, predicting a favorable outcome for an upcoming battle (18:5, 9-11). But the faithful prophet **Micaiah** explained that Ahab was under God's judgment, and God was planning his defeat (18:7-8, 12-17). Amazingly, **a lying spirit** volunteered to **entice** Ahab to attack the Arameans (18:21). Though God was not the author of the lie, he permitted the lying spirit to do his work to bring about Ahab's **disaster** (18:18-22). Later, in a similar way, God would permit a "messenger of Satan" to torment Paul in order to humble the apostle and cause him to depend more on the Lord (2 Cor 12:7-10). The main difference between the two instances is

[a] 18:9 Ru 4:1
[b] 18:13 Nm 22:35,38; 24:13
[c] 18:16 Nm 27:16-17; Ezk 34:5-8; Mt 9:36; Mk 6:34
[d] 18:18 Is 6:1-5; Dn 7:9-10
[e] 18:20-21 Dt 13:1-5; 1Sm 16:14; Jr 27:9-10; Ezk 14:9; 2Th 2:9-12

[f] 18:24 1Kg 20:30
[g] 18:25 2Ch 18:8
[h] 2Ch 34:8
[i] 18:26 2Ch 16:10
[j] 18:27 Mc 1:2
[k] 18:29 2Ch 35:22
[l] 18:31 2Ch 13:14-15
[m] 18:33 2Ch 35:23

at the entrance to Samaria's gate,[a] and all the prophets were prophesying in front of them. **10** Then Zedekiah son of Chenaanah made iron horns and said, "This is what the LORD says: 'You will gore the Arameans with these until they are finished off.'" **11** And all the prophets were prophesying the same, saying, "March up to Ramoth-gilead and succeed, for the LORD will hand it over to the king."

MICAIAH'S MESSAGE OF DEFEAT

12 The messenger who went to call Micaiah instructed him, "Look, the words of the prophets are unanimously favorable for the king. So let your words be like theirs, and speak favorably." **13** But Micaiah said, "As the LORD lives, I will say whatever my God says."[A,b] **14** So he went to the king, and the king asked him, "Micaiah, should we go to Ramoth-gilead for war, or should I[B] refrain?"

Micaiah said, "March up and succeed, for they will be handed over to you."

15 But the king said to him, "How many times must I make you swear not to tell me anything but the truth in the name of the LORD?"

16 So Micaiah said:

I saw all Israel scattered on the hills
like sheep without a shepherd.[c]
And the LORD said,
"They have no master;
let each return home in peace."

17 So the king of Israel said to Jehoshaphat, "Didn't I tell you he never prophesies good about me, but only disaster?" **18** Then Micaiah said, "Therefore, hear the word of the LORD. I saw the LORD sitting on his throne, and the whole heavenly army was standing at his right hand and at his left hand.[d] **19** And the LORD said, 'Who will entice King Ahab of Israel to march up and fall at Ramoth-gilead?' So one was saying this and another was saying that. **20** Then[e] a spirit came forward, stood before the LORD, and said, 'I will entice him.'

"The LORD asked him, 'How?'

21 "So he said, 'I will go and become a lying spirit in the mouth of all his prophets.'

"Then he said, 'You will entice him and also prevail. Go and do that.'

22 "Now, you see, the LORD has put a lying spirit into the mouth of[c] these prophets of yours, and the LORD has pronounced disaster against you."

23 Then Zedekiah son of Chenaanah came up, hit Micaiah on the cheek, and demanded, "Which way did the spirit from the LORD leave me to speak to you?"

24 Micaiah replied, "You will soon see when you go to hide in an inner chamber on that day."[f]

25 Then the king of Israel ordered, "Take Micaiah and return him[g] to Amon, the governor of the city,[h] and to Joash, the king's son, **26** and say, 'This is what the king says: Put this guy in prison[i] and feed him only a little bread and water[D] until I come back safely.'"

27 But Micaiah said, "If you ever return safely, the LORD has not spoken through me." Then he said, "Listen, all you people!"[j]

AHAB'S DEATH

28 Then the king of Israel and Judah's King Jehoshaphat went up to Ramoth-gilead. **29** But the king of Israel said to Jehoshaphat, "I will disguise myself and go into battle, but you wear your royal attire." So the king of Israel disguised himself, and they went into battle.[k] **30** Now the king of Aram had ordered his chariot commanders, "Do not fight with anyone at all[E] except the king of Israel." **31** When the chariot commanders saw Jehoshaphat, they shouted, "He must be the king of Israel!" So they turned to attack him, but Jehoshaphat cried out[l] and the LORD helped him. God drew them away from him. **32** When the chariot commanders saw that he was not the king of Israel, they turned back from pursuing him.

33 But a man drew his bow without taking special aim and struck the king of Israel through the joints of his armor. So he said to the charioteer, "Turn around and take me out of the battle,[F] for I am badly wounded!"[m] **34** The battle raged throughout that day, and the king of Israel propped himself up in his chariot facing the Arameans until evening. Then he died at sunset.

[A] 18:13 LXX, Vg add *to me*; 1Kg 22:14   [B] 18:14 LXX reads *we*; 1Kg 22:15   [C] 18:22 Some Hb mss, LXX, Syr, Vg add *all*; 1Kg 22:23   [D] 18:26 Lit *him on bread of oppression and water of oppression*   [E] 18:30 Lit *with small or with great*   [F] 18:33 LXX, Vg; MT reads *camp*

---

that Paul learned from the experience; Ahab pressed on in his arrogance.
18:29 Ahab may have thought he could fool God and prevent the prophecy's fulfillment.

18:33-34 The disguised king was killed when an enemy archer **drew his bow without taking special aim** (18:33). Of course, nothing is random in a universe governed by an

omniscient (all-knowing) and omnipotent (all-powerful) God. The divinely directed arrow struck Ahab at a weak point in **his armor**, and **he died**.

JEHU'S REBUKE OF JEHOSHAPHAT

19 King Jehoshaphat of Judah returned to his home in Jerusalem in peace. **2** Then Jehu[a] son of the seer Hanani went out to confront him[A] and said to King Jehoshaphat, "Do you help the wicked and love those who hate the LORD?[b] Because of this, the LORD's wrath is on you.[c] **3** However, some good is found in you, for you have eradicated the Asherah poles from the land and have decided to seek God."[d]

JEHOSHAPHAT'S REFORMS

4 Jehoshaphat lived in Jerusalem, and once again he went out among the people from Beer-sheba to the hill country of Ephraim and brought them back to the LORD, the God of their ancestors.[e] **5** He appointed judges in all the fortified cities of the land of Judah, city by city.[f] **6** Then he said to the judges, "Consider what you are doing, for you do not judge for a mere mortal, but for the LORD, who is with you in the matter of judgment.[g] **7** And now, may the terror of the LORD be on you. Watch what you do, for there is no injustice or partiality or taking bribes with the LORD our God."[h]

8 Jehoshaphat also appointed in Jerusalem some of the Levites and priests and some of the Israelite family heads for deciding the LORD's will and for settling disputes of the residents of[B] Jerusalem. **9** He commanded them, saying, "In the fear of the LORD, with integrity, and wholeheartedly, you are to do the following: **10** For every dispute that comes to you from your brothers who dwell in their cities — whether it regards differences of bloodguilt, law, commandment, statutes, or judgments[i] — you are to warn them, so they will not incur guilt before the LORD and wrath will not come on you and your brothers.[j] Do this, and you will not incur guilt.

11 "Note that Amariah, the chief priest, is over you in all matters related to the LORD,

and Zebadiah son of Ishmael, the ruler of the house of Judah, in all matters related to the king, and the Levites are officers in your presence. Be strong; may the LORD be with those who do what is good."[k]

WAR AGAINST EASTERN ENEMIES

20 After this, the Moabites and Ammonites, together with some of the Meunites,[c,l] came to fight against Jehoshaphat. **2** People came and told Jehoshaphat, "A vast number from beyond the Dead Sea and from Edom[D] has come to fight against you; they are already in Hazazon-tamar"[m] (that is, En-gedi). **3** Jehoshaphat was afraid, and he resolved[n] to seek the LORD. Then he proclaimed a fast[o] for all Judah, **4** who gathered to seek the LORD. They even came from all the cities of Judah to seek him.

JEHOSHAPHAT'S PRAYER

5 Then Jehoshaphat stood in the assembly of Judah and Jerusalem in the LORD's temple before the new courtyard. **6** He said:

LORD, God of our ancestors, are you not the God who is in heaven,[p] and do you not rule over all the kingdoms of the nations?[q] Power and might are in your hand, and no one can stand against you. **7** Are you not our God who drove out the inhabitants of this land before your people Israel[r] and who gave it forever to the descendants of Abraham[s] your friend? **8** They have lived in the land and have built you a sanctuary in it for your name and have said, **9** "If disaster comes on us — sword or judgment, pestilence or famine[t] — we will stand before this temple and before you, for your name is in this temple.[u] We will cry out to you because of our distress, and you will hear and deliver."

10 Now here are the Ammonites, Moabites, and the inhabitants of Mount

a 19:2 1Kg 16:1; 2Ch 20:34
b 2Ch 18:1,3
c 2Ch 24:18
d 19:3 2Ch 12:14; 17:4,6
e 19:4 2Ch 15:8-13
f 19:5 Dt 16:18-20
g 19:6 Lv 19:15; Dt 1:17
h 19:7 Gn 18:25; Dt 10:17-18; 32:4
i 19:10 Dt 17:8
j 2Ch 19:2

k 19:11 1Ch 28:20
l 20:1 2Ch 26:7
m 20:2 Gn 14:7
n 20:3 2Ch 19:3
o 1Sm 7:6; Ezr 8:21
p 20:6 Dt 4:39
q 1Ch 29:11
r 20:7 Ps 135:10-12
s Is 41:8
t 20:9 2Ch 6:28-30
u 2Ch 6:20

A 19:2 Lit to his face   B 19:8 LXX, Vg; MT reads disputes and they returned to   C 20:1 LXX; MT reads Ammonites; 2Ch 26:7   D 20:2 Some Hb mss, Old Lat; other Hb mss read Aram

19:1-3 Jehoshaphat did not escape a stern rebuke from the Lord for his foolish decision to side with Ahab. Though the prophet praised the king for opposing idolatry in the land (19:3), he chastised him for helping **wicked** Ahab and loving **those who hate the LORD** (19:2).

19:5-7 Though we do not live in Old Testament Judah, our civil government today is accountable to God to do good too—to act with justice and righteousness (see Rom 13:3-4). The church's responsibility with regard to civil government is to make sure that the state

doesn't lose sight of the truth that God rules and that there is a moral standard by which the political realm must operate. The church is to exercise a prophetic role of being a voice for God and his righteous standards. Our government is in desperate need of leaders who can inject righteousness and justice into our political bloodstream, for a society can never rise above the quality of its leadership.

20:3-12 Jehoshaphat knew what to do because he was familiar with King Solomon's prayer given over a century earlier at the temple dedication (see 6:28-30). He even referred to

that prayer in his own intercession (20:8-9) because his crisis was exactly the kind of disaster Solomon had prayed about. Jehoshaphat knew that God keeps his promises.

This is a powerful example for Christians of how to respond to crises and prevail in God's strength. Though Christians can still be overwhelmed by a crisis situation just like people of the world can, we have the option of looking to the Lord for his intervention and deliverance when we don't know what to do—as Jehoshaphat did when he faced his enemies.

a 20:10 2Ch 20:1,22
b Nm 20:14-21; Dt 2:4-9
c 20:12 Jdg 11:27
d Ps 25:15; 121:1-2
e 20:14 2Ch 15:1; 24:20
f 20:15 Ex 14:13; 2Ch 32:7-8
g 1Sm 17:47; 2Ch 13:15;
14:12
h 20:17 Ex 14:13-14
i Jos 1:9
j 2Ch 15:2
k 20:18 2Ch 7:3
l 20:19 Ex 6:18; 1Ch 9:19
m 20:20 Is 7:9

n 20:21 1Ch 16:29; Ps 29:2
o 1Ch 16:34; 2Ch 5:13; 7:3;
Ps 118:1,29; 136:1
p 20:22 2Ch 13:13
q 20:23 Ezk 38:21; Hg 2:22;
Zch 14:13
r Jdg 7:22; 1Sm 14:20
s 20:29 2Ch 14:14; 17:10

Seir.*a* You did not let Israel invade them when Israel came out of the land of Egypt, but Israel turned away from them and did not destroy them.*b* **11** Look how they repay us by coming to drive us out of your possession that you gave us as an inheritance. **12** Our God, will you not judge them?*c* For we are powerless before this vast number that comes to fight against us. We do not know what to do, but we look to you.*A,d*

GOD'S ANSWER

13 All Judah was standing before the LORD with their dependents, their wives, and their children. **14** In the middle of the congregation, the Spirit of the LORD came on*e* Jahaziel (son of Zechariah, son of Benaiah, son of Jeiel, son of Mattaniah, a Levite from Asaph's descendants), **15** and he said, "Listen carefully, all Judah and you inhabitants of Jerusalem, and King Jehoshaphat. This is what the LORD says: 'Do not be afraid or discouraged because of this vast number,*f* for the battle is not yours, but God's.*g* **16** Tomorrow, go down against them. You will see them coming up the Ascent of Ziz, and you will find them at the end of the valley facing the Wilderness of Jeruel. **17** You do not have to fight this battle. Position yourselves, stand still, and see the salvation of the LORD.*h* He is with you, Judah and Jerusalem. Do not be afraid or discouraged.*i* Tomorrow, go out to face them, for the LORD is with you.' "*j*

18 Then Jehoshaphat knelt low with his face to the ground, and all Judah and the inhabitants of Jerusalem fell down before the LORD to worship him.*k* **19** Then the Levites from the sons of the Kohathites and the Korahites*l* stood up to praise the LORD God of Israel shouting loudly.

VICTORY AND PLUNDER

20 In the morning they got up early and went out to the wilderness of Tekoa. As they were about to go out, Jehoshaphat stood and said, "Hear me, Judah and you inhabitants of Jerusalem. Believe in the LORD your God, and you will be established;*m* believe in his prophets, and you will succeed."

⊸ HOPE WORDS ⊸

Heaven rules in spite of the situation you face. The problem is not yours. The battle is the Lord's.

21 Then he consulted with the people and appointed some to sing for the LORD and some to praise the splendor of his holiness.*n* When they went out in front of the armed forces, they kept singing:*B*

Give thanks to the LORD,
for his faithful love endures forever.*o*

22 The moment they began their shouts and praises, the LORD set an ambush*p* against the Ammonites, Moabites, and the inhabitants of Mount Seir who came to fight against Judah, and they were defeated. **23** The Ammonites and Moabites turned against the inhabitants of Mount Seir and completely annihilated them.*q* When they had finished with the inhabitants of Seir, they helped destroy each other.*r*

24 When Judah came to a place overlooking the wilderness, they looked for the large army, but there were only corpses lying on the ground; nobody had escaped. **25** Then Jehoshaphat and his people went to gather the plunder. They found among them*c* an abundance of goods on the bodies*D* and valuable items. So they stripped them until nobody could carry any more. They were gathering the plunder for three days because there was so much. **26** They assembled in the Valley of Beracah*E* on the fourth day, for there they blessed the LORD. Therefore, that place is still called the Valley of Beracah today. **27** Then all the men of Judah and Jerusalem turned back with Jehoshaphat their leader, returning joyfully to Jerusalem, for the LORD enabled them to rejoice over their enemies. **28** So they came into Jerusalem to the LORD's temple with harps, lyres, and trumpets. **29** The terror of God*s* was on all the kingdoms of the lands when they heard that the LORD had fought against the enemies of Israel. **30** Then Jehoshaphat's kingdom

---

A **20:12** Lit *but on you our eyes*   *B* **20:21** Lit *saying*   *C* **20:25** LXX reads *found cattle*   *D* **20:25** Some Hb mss, Old Lat, Vg read *goods, garments*
E **20:26** = *Blessing*

20:15-17 In other words, in verse 15 the Lord was telling his people, "I've got this." In fact, even though the king's forces would have to face the enemy, they wouldn't have to fire a single arrow (20:16-17).

20:18 Ultimately, Jehoshaphat and his people would win the upcoming battle because they were willing to be on their faces before God. **20:20-30** The moral of this story is that Jehoshaphat trusted in his divine King for a supernatural deliverance. You may not be a

king facing a national military crisis, but you are just as dependent on spiritual intervention for earthly living as he was. Will you look to the Lord as your deliverer when you don't know what to do? Or will you trust in your own ingenuity and in human strength? Don't

was quiet, for his God gave him rest on
every side.[a]

SUMMARY OF JEHOSHAPHAT'S REIGN

31 Jehoshaphat became king over Judah.[b] He
was thirty-five years old when he became
king, and he reigned twenty-five years in
Jerusalem. His mother's name was Azubah
daughter of Shilhi. 32 He walked in the ways
of Asa his father; he did not turn away from
it but did what was right in the LORD's sight.
33 However, the high places were not tak-
en away;[c] the people had not yet set their
hearts on the God of their ancestors.[d]
34 The rest of the events of Jehoshaphat's
reign from beginning to end are written in
the Events of Jehu[e] son of Hanani, which
is recorded in the Book of Israel's Kings.[f]

JEHOSHAPHAT'S FLEET OF SHIPS

35 After this,[g] Judah's King Jehoshaphat
made an alliance with Israel's King Ahaziah,
who was guilty of wrongdoing. 36 Jehoshaphat formed an alliance with him to make
ships to go to Tarshish,[h] and they made the
ships in Ezion-geber. 37 Then Eliezer son of
Dodavahu of Mareshah prophesied against
Jehoshaphat, saying, "Because you formed
an alliance with Ahaziah, the LORD has broken up what you have made." So the ships
were wrecked and were not able to go to
Tarshish.

JEHORAM BECOMES KING OVER JUDAH

21 Jehoshaphat rested with his fathers
and was buried with his fathers in
the city of David. His son Jehoram[A] became
king in his place.[i] 2 He had brothers, sons
of Jehoshaphat: Azariah, Jehiel, Zechariah, Azariah, Michael, and Shephatiah; all
these were the sons of King Jehoshaphat of
Judah.[B] 3 Their father had given them many
gifts of silver, gold, and valuable things,
along with fortified cities[j] in Judah, but
he gave the kingdom to Jehoram because
he was the firstborn. 4 When Jehoram
had established himself over his father's
kingdom, he strengthened his position by
killing with the sword all his brothers as
well as some of the princes of Israel.

JUDAH'S KING JEHORAM

5 Jehoram[k] was thirty-two years old when
he became king, and he reigned eight
years in Jerusalem. 6 He walked in the
ways of the kings of Israel, as the house
of Ahab had done,[l] for Ahab's daughter
was his wife.[m] He did what was evil in the
LORD's sight, 7 but for the sake of the covenant the LORD had made with David, he
was unwilling to destroy the house of David since the LORD had promised[n] to give
a lamp[o] to David and to his sons forever.
8 During Jehoram's reign, Edom rebelled
against Judah's control and appointed
their own king. 9 So Jehoram crossed into
Edom with his commanders and all his
chariots. Then at night he set out to attack the Edomites who had surrounded
him and the chariot commanders. 10 And
now Edom is still in rebellion against Judah's control today. Libnah also rebelled
at that time against his control because he
had abandoned the LORD, the God of his
ancestors. 11 Jehoram also built high places[p] in the hills[C] of Judah, and he caused
the inhabitants of Jerusalem to prostitute
themselves,[q] and he led Judah astray.

ELIJAH'S LETTER TO JEHORAM

12 Then a letter came to Jehoram from the
prophet Elijah, saying:

This is what the LORD, the God of your
ancestor David says: "Because you
have not walked in the ways of your
father Jehoshaphat[r] or in the ways of
King Asa of Judah[s] 13 but have walked
in the ways of the kings of Israel,[t] have
caused Judah and the inhabitants of
Jerusalem to prostitute themselves
like the house of Ahab[u] prostituted itself, and also have killed your
brothers,[v] your father's family, who
were better than you, 14 the LORD is
now about to strike your people, your
sons, your wives, and all your possessions with a horrible affliction. 15 You

[a] 20:30 2Ch 14:6-7; 15:15
[b] 20:31-34 1Kg 22:41-45
[c] 20:33 2Ch 17:6
[d] 2Ch 19:3
[e] 20:34 2Ch 19:2
[f] 1Kg 16:1,7
[g] 20:35-37 1Kg 22:48-49
[h] 20:36 2Ch 9:21
[i] 21:1 1Kg 22:50
[j] 21:3 2Ch 11:5
[k] 21:5-10 2Kg 8:17-22
[l] 21:6 1Kg 12:28-30
[m] 2Ch 18:1
[n] 21:7 2Sm 7:12-17; 1Kg 11:13
[o] 1Kg 11:36; 15:4
[p] 21:11 1Kg 11:7
[q] Lv 20:5
[r] 21:12 2Ch 17:3-4
[s] 2Ch 14:2-5
[t] 21:13 2Ch 21:6
[u] 1Kg 16:31-33
[v] 2Ch 21:4

[A] 21:1 = Joram [B] 21:2 Some Hb mss, LXX, Syr, Vg, Arabic; other Hb mss read *Israel* [C] 21:11 Some Hb mss, LXX, Vg read *cities*

forget: a key lesson in this story is the power of praise (20:21-22).

20:35-37 This effort was another case of light trying to join forces with darkness. Notice that it didn't end well.

21:4-6 Jehoram's biography reads like those of the evil kings of Israel, and that is not by coincidence. Jehoram had married King **Ahab's daughter** (21:6). His treachery was plain from the outset.

21:7 In spite of Jehoram's wickedness, God's promise to the house of **David** remained. Yet while God allowed Jehoram to retain his throne, that didn't mean things would go well for him—just the opposite, in fact. Importantly, a day is coming when the perfect son of David—Jesus Christ—will inherit the throne and reign **forever**.

21:10 The Chronicler doesn't leave us to guess at the reason Jehoram was plagued with rebellions during his reign.

21:11 Jehoram **built high places**—locations on top of hills or mountains for worshiping pagan gods—and **led Judah astray**. This is a sobering reminder that we should never underestimate the power of a leader to take people into ungodliness.

21:12 This **Elijah** was the same one who stared down King Ahab, faced off against 450 false prophets, and called down fire on Mount Carmel (see 1 Kgs 18:20-40).

*a*21:15 2Ch 21:18-19
*b*21:16 2Ch 17:11; 22:1
*c*2Ch 33:11
*d*21:17 2Ch 25:23
*e*21:19 2Ch 16:14
*f*21:20 2Kg 8:17,24
*g*Jr 22:18,28
*h*2Ch 24:25
*i*22:1 2Ch 21:16
*j*22:2-6 2Kg 8:24-29

*k*22:7 2Ch 10:15
*l*2Kg 9:21
*m*2Kg 9:6-7
*n*22:8 2Kg 10:11-14
*o*22:9 2Kg 9:27-28
*p*2Ch 17:4
*q*22:10-12 2Kg 11:1-3
*r*23:1-21 2Kg 11:4-20

yourself will be struck with many illnesses, including a disease of the intestines, until your intestines come out day after day because of the disease."*a*

JEHORAM'S LAST DAYS

16 The LORD roused the spirit of the Philistines and the Arabs*b* who lived near the Cushites to attack Jehoram.*c* **17** So they went to war against Judah and invaded it. They carried off all the possessions found in the king's palace and also his sons and wives; not a son was left to him except Jehoahaz,*A,d* his youngest son.

18 After all these things, the LORD afflicted him in his intestines with an incurable disease. **19** This continued day after day until two full years passed. Then his intestines came out because of his disease, and he died from severe*B* illnesses. But his people did not hold a fire in his honor like the fire in honor of his fathers.*e*

20 Jehoram*f* was thirty-two years old when he became king; he reigned eight years in Jerusalem. He died to no one's regret*C,g* and was buried in the city of David but not in the tombs of the kings.*h*

JUDAH'S KING AHAZIAH

22 Then the inhabitants of Jerusalem made Ahaziah, his youngest son, king in his place, because the troops that had come with the Arabs*i* to the camp had killed all the older sons.*D* So Ahaziah son of Jehoram became king of Judah. **2** Ahaziah*j* was twenty-two*E* years old when he became king, and he reigned one year in Jerusalem. His mother's name was Athaliah, granddaughter*F* of Omri.

3 He walked in the ways of the house of Ahab, for his mother gave him evil advice. **4** So he did what was evil in the LORD's sight like the house of Ahab, for they were his advisers after the death of his father, to his destruction. **5** He also followed their advice and went with Joram*G* son of Israel's King

Ahab to fight against King Hazael of Aram, in Ramoth-gilead. The Arameans*H* wounded Joram, **6** so he returned to Jezreel to recover from the wounds they inflicted on him in Ramoth-gilead*i* when he fought against King Hazael of Aram. Then Judah's King Ahaziah*j* son of Jehoram went down to Jezreel to visit Joram son of Ahab since Joram was ill.

7 Ahaziah's downfall came from God when he went to Joram.*k* When Ahaziah arrived, he went out with Joram to meet Jehu son of Nimshi,*l* whom the LORD had anointed to destroy the house of Ahab.*m* **8** So when Jehu executed judgment on the house of Ahab,*n* he found the rulers of Judah and the sons of Ahaziah's brothers who were serving Ahaziah, and he killed them. **9** Then Jehu looked for Ahaziah,*o* and Jehu's soldiers captured him (he was hiding in Samaria). So they brought Ahaziah to Jehu, and they killed him. The soldiers buried him, for they said, "He is the grandson of Jehoshaphat who sought the LORD with all his heart."*p* So no one from the house of Ahaziah had the strength to rule the kingdom.

ATHALIAH USURPS THE THRONE

10 When*q* Athaliah, Ahaziah's mother, saw that her son was dead, she proceeded to annihilate all the royal heirs*k* of the house of Judah. **11** Jehoshabeath,*L* the king's daughter, rescued Joash son of Ahaziah from the king's sons who were being killed and put him and the one who nursed him in a bedroom. Now Jehoshabeath was the daughter of King Jehoram and the wife of the priest Jehoiada. Since she was Ahaziah's sister, she hid Joash from Athaliah so that she did not kill him. **12** While Athaliah reigned over the land, he was hiding with them in God's temple six years.

ATHALIAH OVERTHROWN

23 Then, in the seventh year,*r* Jehoiada summoned his courage and took the commanders of hundreds into a covenant

*A*21:17 LXX, Syr, Tg read *Ahaziah*   *B*21:19 Lit *evil*   *C*21:20 Lit *He walked in no desirability*   *D*22:1 Lit *the former ones*   *E*22:2 Some LXX mss, Syr; MT reads *42*; 2Kg 8:26   *F*22:2 Lit *daughter*   *G*22:5 = Jehoram   *H*22:5 Lit *Rammites*   *I*22:6 Lit *in Ramah*   *J*22:6 Some Hb mss, LXX, Syr, Vg; other Hb mss read *Azariah*   *K*22:10 Lit *seed*   *L*22:11 = Jehosheba; 2Kg 11:2

21:19-20 Considering his reign of sin, it comes as no surprise that the people of Judah did not **honor** Jehoram at his end (21:19). Rather, he **died to no one's regret**—was buried and forgotten (21:20).

22:1-4 Ahaziah was Jehoram's only surviving son (22:1). Importantly, he was part of the house of Ahab, and the curse on that wicked family continued as Ahaziah followed **evil advice** from **his mother** and **did what was evil in the LORD's sight like the house of Ahab** (22:3-4).

22:5-9 Ahaziah followed the king of Israel into a disastrous battle that ultimately cost Ahaziah his life—but not from battle wounds (22:5-6). As a grandson of Ahab, Ahaziah was under God's judgment that decreed the eradication of Ahab's entire line. Therefore, he was killed by **Jehu . . . whom the LORD had anointed to destroy the house of Ahab** (22:7; see 2 Kgs 9:1-10:17).

22:10 The evil queen mother **Athaliah** (daughter of Ahab, wife of Jehoram, and mother of

Ahaziah) flew into action when she heard her son was dead. **She proceeded to annihilate all the royal heirs of the house of Judah**, so she could usurp the throne.

22:11-12 God still had some faithful people in Judah, even during this brutal period. Two of these people were **Jehoshabeath** (Ahaziah's sister) and her husband **the priest Jehoiada**. Jehoshabeath rescued her infant nephew and hid him in the temple for **six years** while Athaliah **reigned**. Mean-

with him: Azariah son of Jeroham, Ishmael son of Jehohanan, Azariah son of Obed, Maaseiah son of Adaiah, and Elishaphat son of Zichri. **2** They made a circuit throughout Judah. They gathered the Levites from all the cities of Judah and the family heads of Israel, and they came to Jerusalem.

3 Then the whole assembly made a covenant with the king in God's temple. Jehoiada said to them, "Here is the king's son! He will reign, just as the LORD promised[a] concerning David's sons. **4** This is what you are to do: a third of you, priests and Levites who are coming on duty on the Sabbath,[b] are to be gatekeepers. **5** A third are to be at the king's palace, and a third are to be at the Foundation Gate, and all the troops will be in the courtyards of the LORD's temple. **6** No one is to enter the LORD's temple but the priests and those Levites who serve;[c] they may enter because they are holy, but all the people are to obey the requirement of the LORD. **7** Completely surround the king with weapons in hand. Anyone who enters the temple is to be put to death. Be with the king in all his daily tasks."[A]

8 So the commanders of hundreds did everything the priest Jehoiada commanded. They each brought their men — those coming on duty on the Sabbath and those going off duty on the Sabbath — for the priest Jehoiada did not release the divisions.[d] **9** The priest Jehoiada gave to the commanders of hundreds King David's spears, shields, and quivers[B] that were in God's temple. **10** Then he stationed all the troops with their weapons in hand surrounding the king — from the right side of the temple to the left side, by the altar and by the temple.

11 They brought out the king's son, put the crown on him, gave him the testimony,[e] and made him king. Jehoiada and his sons anointed him and cried, "Long live the king!"[f] **12** When Athaliah heard the noise from the troops, the guards, and those praising the king, she went to the troops in the LORD's temple. **13** As she looked, there was the king standing by his pillar[c] at the entrance. The commanders and the trumpeters were by the king, and all the people of the land were rejoicing and blowing trumpets[g] while the singers with musical instruments were

leading the praise. Athaliah tore her clothes and screamed, "Treason! Treason!"

14 Then the priest Jehoiada sent out the commanders of hundreds, those in charge of the army, saying, "Take her out between the ranks, and put anyone who follows her to death by the sword," for the priest had said, "Don't put her to death in the LORD's temple." **15** So they arrested her, and she went by the entrance of the Horse Gate[h] to the king's palace, where they put her to death.

JEHOIADA'S REFORMS

16 Then Jehoiada made a covenant between himself, the king, and the people that they would be the LORD's people. **17** So all the people went to the temple of Baal and tore it down. They smashed its altars and images and killed Mattan, the priest of Baal, at the altars.[i]

18 Then Jehoiada put the oversight of the LORD's temple into the hands of the Levitical priests,[j] whom David had appointed[k] over the LORD's temple, to offer burnt offerings to the LORD as it is written in the law of Moses,[l] with rejoicing and song ordained by[D] David. **19** He stationed gatekeepers[m] at the gates of the LORD's temple so that nothing unclean could enter for any reason. **20** Then he took with him the commanders of hundreds, the nobles, the governors of the people, and all the people of the land and brought the king down from the LORD's temple. They entered the king's palace through the Upper Gate and seated the king on the throne of the kingdom. **21** All the people of the land rejoiced, and the city was quiet, for they had put Athaliah to death by the sword.

JUDAH'S KING JOASH

24 Joash[n] was seven years old when he became king, and he reigned forty years in Jerusalem. His mother's name was Zibiah; she was from Beer-sheba. **2** Throughout the time of the priest Jehoiada, Joash did what was right in the LORD's sight.[o] **3** Jehoiada acquired two wives for him, and he was the father of sons and daughters.

REPAIRING THE TEMPLE

4 Afterward,[p] Joash took it to heart to renovate[q] the LORD's temple. **5** So he gathered

[a] 23:3 2Ch 21:7
[b] 23:4 1Ch 9:25
[c] 23:6 1Ch 23:28-32
[d] 23:8 1Ch 24:1
[e] 23:11 Ex 25:16,21; 31:18
[f] 1Sm 10:24
[g] 23:13 Nm 10:7-10

[h] 23:15 Neh 3:28; Jr 31:40
[i] 23:17 Dt 13:6-9; 1Kg 18:40
[j] 23:18 2Ch 5:5
[k] 1Ch 23:6,25-31
[l] 2Kg 14:6; 2Ch 17:9; Ezr 7:6; Neh 8:1
[m] 23:19 1Ch 9:22
[n] 24:1-2 2Kg 11:21; 12:1-2
[o] 24:2 2Ch 26:4-5
[p] 24:4-12 2Kg 12:4-12
[q] 24:4 2Ch 24:7

[A] 23:7 Lit *king when he comes in and when he goes out*   [B] 23:9 Or *spears and large and small shields*   [C] 23:13 LXX reads *post*   [D] 23:18 Lit *song on the hands of*

---

while, Jehoiada bided his time and waited for an opportunity to oppose Athaliah effectively.
23:12-14 Athaliah's cry of **treason** must have sounded ridiculous to those who remembered how she had murdered her way to the

throne (23:13). In his ironic providence, the Lord saw to it that Athaliah's life fulfilled the spiritual principle of "sowing and reaping." What she had sown, she reaped as the death blow fell. We do well to remember that "God is not mocked" (Gal 6:7).

23:16-19 The priest **Jehoiada** set about restoring the proper worship of God in Judah.
24:4 For the first part of Joash's reign, Jehoiada apparently provided godly influence. Joash commanded the renovation of **the LORD's temple**, which had fallen to disrepair.

[a] 24:5 Ex 30:12-16; 2Ch 34:9-10; Neh 10:32; Mt 17:24
[b] 24:6 Nm 1:50
[c] 24:9 2Ch 36:22
[d] 24:12 2Kg 22:4-6

[e] 24:16 2Ch 21:20; 24:25
[f] 24:18 Ex 34:12-14
[g] 24:19 Jr 7:25
[l] Neh 9:30; Ps 81:8-11; Jr 11:6-8
[j] 24:20 Jdg 6:34; 1Ch 12:18
[k] Nm 14:41
[l] 2Ch 15:2
[m] 24:21 Neh 9:26; Mt 23:35; Lk 11:51
[n] 24:22 Gn 9:5
[o] 24:23 2Kg 12:17
[p] 24:24 2Ch 16:7-8
[q] 2Ch 24:20
[r] 24:25-27 2Kg 12:19-21
[s] 24:25 2Ch 24:16

the priests and Levites and said, "Go out to the cities of Judah and collect silver from all Israel to repair the temple of your God as needed year by year,[a] and do it quickly." However, the Levites did not hurry. [6] So the king called Jehoiada the high priest and said, "Why haven't you required the Levites to bring from Judah and Jerusalem the tax imposed by the LORD's servant Moses and the assembly of Israel for the tent[b] of the testimony? [7] For the sons of that wicked Athaliah broke into the LORD's temple and even used the sacred things of the LORD's temple for the Baals."

[8] At the king's command a chest was made and placed outside the gate of the LORD's temple. [9] Then a proclamation[c] was issued in Judah and Jerusalem that the tax God's servant Moses imposed on Israel in the wilderness be brought to the LORD. [10] All the leaders and all the people rejoiced, brought the tax, and put it in the chest until it was full. [11] Whenever the chest was brought by the Levites to the king's overseers, and when they saw that there was a large amount of silver, the king's secretary and the high priest's deputy came and emptied the chest, picked it up, and returned it to its place. They did this daily and gathered the silver in abundance. [12] Then the king and Jehoiada gave it to those in charge of the labor on the LORD's temple, who were hiring stonecutters and carpenters to renovate the LORD's temple, also blacksmiths and coppersmiths to repair the LORD's temple.[d]

[13] The workmen did their work, and through them the repairs progressed. They restored God's temple to its specifications and reinforced it. [14] When they finished, they presented the rest of the silver to the king and Jehoiada, who made articles for the LORD's temple with it — articles for ministry and for making burnt offerings, and ladles[A] and articles of gold and silver. They regularly offered burnt offerings in the LORD's temple throughout Jehoiada's life.

JOASH'S APOSTASY

[15] Jehoiada died when he was old and full of days; he was 130 years old at his death. [16] He was buried in the city of David with the kings[e] because he had done what was good in Israel with respect to God and his temple.

[17] However, after Jehoiada died, the rulers of Judah came and paid homage to the king. Then the king listened to them, [18] and they abandoned the temple of the LORD, the God of their ancestors, and served the Asherah poles and the idols.[f] So there was wrath[g] against Judah and Jerusalem for this guilt of theirs. [19] Nevertheless, he sent them prophets[h] to bring them back to the LORD; they admonished them, but the people would not listen.[i]

[20] The Spirit of God enveloped[B,j] Zechariah son of Jehoiada the priest. He stood above the people and said to them, "This is what God says, 'Why are you transgressing the LORD's commands so that you do not prosper?[k] Because you have abandoned the LORD, he has abandoned you.'"[l] [21] But they conspired against him and stoned him at the king's command in the courtyard of the LORD's temple.[m] [22] King Joash didn't remember the kindness that Zechariah's father Jehoiada had extended to him, but killed his son. While he was dying, he said, "May the LORD see and demand[n] an account."

ARAMEAN INVASION OF JUDAH

[23] At the turn of the year, an Aramean army attacked Joash.[o] They entered Judah and Jerusalem and destroyed all the leaders of the people among them and sent all the plunder to the king of Damascus. [24] Although the Aramean army came with only a few men, the LORD handed over[p] a vast army to them because the people of Judah had abandoned[q] the LORD, the God of their ancestors. So they executed judgment on Joash.

JOASH ASSASSINATED

[25] When[r] the Arameans saw that Joash had many wounds, they left him. His servants conspired against him, and killed him on his bed, because he had shed the blood of the sons of the priest Jehoiada. So he died, and they buried him in the city of David, but they did not bury him in the tombs of the kings.[s] [26] Those who conspired against him were Zabad, son of the Ammonite woman Shimeath, and Jehozabad, son of the

[A] 24:14 Or *dishes*, or *spoons*; lit *palms*   [B] 24:20 Lit *clothed*

24:15-18 Joash's reign and the worship of God stayed on course as long as Jehoiada lived. But when **Jehoiada died,** Joash did a spiritual 180 (24:17). This tells us that even though Joash had witnessed the devastation and judgment that false worship had brought on Judah, his heart was never fully devoted to the Lord. And, unfortunately, with Jehoiada gone, the vacuum of influence over him was filled by men who steered Joash toward idolatry.
24:20-22 Shockingly, the king put to death the son of the faithful priest who had preserved Joash's own life and placed him on the throne (24:22; see 22:11–23:21). Silencing the Lord's prophet wouldn't prevent the fulfillment of his words.
24:23-27 Once again, the Bible shows that what goes around comes around.

Moabite woman Shimrith.[A,a] [27] The accounts concerning his sons, the many divine pronouncements about him, and the restoration[b] of God's temple are recorded in the Writing[c] of the Book of the Kings. His son Amaziah became king in his place.

JUDAH'S KING AMAZIAH

25 Amaziah[d] became king when he was twenty-five years old, and he reigned twenty-nine years in Jerusalem. His mother's name was Jehoaddan; she was from Jerusalem. [2] He did what was right in the LORD's sight but not wholeheartedly.[e]

[3] As soon as the kingdom was firmly in his grasp,[B] he executed his servants who had killed his father the king. [4] However, he did not put their children to death, because — as it is written in the Law, in the book of Moses,[f] where the LORD commanded — "Fathers are not to die because of children, and children are not to die because of fathers, but each one will die for his own sin."[g]

AMAZIAH'S CAMPAIGN AGAINST EDOM

[5] Then Amaziah gathered Judah and assembled them according to ancestral families,[c] according to commanders of thousands, and according to commanders of hundreds. He numbered those twenty years old or more[h] for all Judah and Benjamin. He found there to be three hundred thousand fit young men who could serve in the army, bearing spear and shield.[i] [6] Then for 7,500 pounds[D] of silver he hired one hundred thousand valiant warriors from Israel.

[7] However, a man of God[j] came to him and said, "King, do not let Israel's army go with you, for the LORD is not with Israel — all the Ephraimites. [8] But if you go with them, do it! Be strong for battle! But God will make you stumble before the enemy,[k] for God has the power to help[l] or to make one stumble."

[9] Then Amaziah said to the man of God, "What should I do about the 7,500 pounds of silver I gave to Israel's division?"

The man of God replied, "The LORD is able to give you much more than this."

[10] So Amaziah released the division that came to him from Ephraim to go home. But they got very angry with Judah and returned home in a fierce rage.

[11] Amaziah strengthened his position and led his people to the Salt Valley. He struck down ten thousand Seirites,[E] [12] and the Judahites captured ten thousand alive. They took them to the top of a cliff where they threw them off, and all of them were dashed to pieces.

[13] As for the men of the division that Amaziah sent back so they would not go with him into battle, they raided the cities of Judah from Samaria to Beth-horon, struck down three thousand of their people, and took a great deal of plunder.

[14] After Amaziah came from the attack on the Edomites, he brought the gods of the Seirites and set them up as his gods. He worshiped before them and burned incense to them.[m] [15] So the LORD's anger was against Amaziah, and he sent a prophet to him, who said, "Why have you sought a people's gods that could not rescue their own people from you?"[n]

[16] While he was still speaking to him, the king asked, "Have we made you the king's counselor? Stop, why should you lose your life?"

So the prophet stopped, but he said, "I know that God intends to destroy you, because you have done this and have not listened to my advice."

AMAZIAH'S WAR WITH ISRAEL'S KING JEHOASH

[17] King Amaziah of Judah took counsel[o] and sent word to Jehoash[f] son of Jehoahaz, son of Jehu, king of Israel, and challenged him: "Come, let's meet face to face."

a 24:26 2Kg 12:21
b 24:27 2Ch 24:12
c 2Ch 13:22
d 25:1-4 2Kg 14:2-6
e 25:2 2Kg 25:14
f 25:4 2Ch 17:9; 23:18
g Dt 24:16; Jr 31:30; Ezk 18:4,20
h 25:5 Nm 1:3
i 2Ch 26:13
j 25:7 2Kg 4:9
k 25:8 Ps 64:7-8
l 2Ch 14:11; 20:6
m 25:14 2Ch 28:23
n 25:15 2Ch 25:11-12
o 25:17-24 2Kg 14:8-14

25:3-4 This was an unusual example of Amaziah's obedience to the law. He put the conspirators to death, but not their children, because that's what the Mosaic law had stipulated.

25:5-8 Amaziah raised a large army from the men of Judah for battle (25:5). But he wanted even more troops. So **he hired one hundred thousand** Israelite **warriors** (25:6). But this move displeased God, who had rejected the idolatrous northern kingdom and sent an unnamed prophet to Amaziah, declaring, **the LORD is not with Israel—all the Ephraimites** (25:7). Ephraim

was a leading tribe of the northern kingdom, so the name was often used to speak of Israel as a whole. The prophet warned the king that if the warriors of Israel joined them, God would cause his forces to **stumble** (25:8).

25:9 **The LORD is able to give you much more than this**, the prophet said. That's a good promise to remember. God doesn't need Satan's help to bless you.

25:10-13 In other words, the Israelite soldiers were so ticked off at not getting a crack at some serious plunder that they ransacked

several towns in **Judah** and slaughtered **three thousand** people (25:13).

25:14-16 The king's decision is inexplicable (25:14), and the utter absurdity of Amaziah's actions is evident in the stinging logic of the prophet's question: **Why have you sought a people's gods that could not rescue their own people from you?** (25:15). His query reveals the stark truth about idolatry: it's insanity. The prophet's parting words foretold the king's earned doom (25:16).

25:17-19 Amaziah apparently traded the wise counsel of God's prophets for foolish **counsel**

a 25:18 Jdg 9:8-15
b 25:19 2Ch 26:16; 32:25
c 25:23 2Ch 21:17; 22:1
d 2Kg 14:13
e 25:24 1Ch 26:15
f 25:25-28 2Kg 14:17-20
g 25:28 2Kg 14:20
h 26:1-2 2Kg 14:21-22

i 26:2 1Kg 9:26; 2Kg
14:22; 16:6
j 26:3-4 2Kg 15:2-3
k 26:5 2Ch 24:2
l Dn 1:17
m 2Ch 15:2
n 26:6 Is 14:29
o 26:8 2Ch 17:11
p 26:9 2Ch 25:23
q Neh 2:13,15; 3:13
r 26:10 Gn 26:18-21
s 26:13 2Ch 25:5

[18] King Jehoash of Israel sent word to King Amaziah of Judah, saying, "The thistle in Lebanon sent a message to the cedar in Lebanon, saying, 'Give your daughter to my son as a wife.' Then a wild animal in Lebanon passed by and trampled the thistle.[a] [19] You have said, 'Look, I[A] have defeated Edom,' and you have become overconfident[B,b] that you will get glory. Now stay at home. Why stir up such trouble so that you fall and Judah with you?"

[20] But Amaziah would not listen, for this turn of events was from God in order to hand them over to their enemies because they went after the gods of Edom. [21] So King Jehoash of Israel advanced. He and King Amaziah of Judah met face to face at Beth-shemesh that belonged to Judah. [22] Judah was routed before Israel, and each man fled to his own tent. [23] King Jehoash of Israel captured Judah's King Amaziah son of Joash, son of Jehoahaz,[C,c] at Beth-shemesh. Then Jehoash took him to Jerusalem and broke down two hundred yards[D] of Jerusalem's wall from the Ephraim Gate to the Corner Gate.[E,d] [24] He took all the gold, silver, all the utensils that were found with Obed-edom[e] in God's temple, the treasures of the king's palace, and the hostages. Then he returned to Samaria.

AMAZIAH'S DEATH

[25] Judah's King Amaziah[f] son of Joash lived fifteen years after the death of Israel's King Jehoash son of Jehoahaz. [26] The rest of the events of Amaziah's reign, from beginning to end, are written in the Book of the Kings of Judah and Israel.

[27] From the time Amaziah turned from following the LORD, a conspiracy was formed against him in Jerusalem, and he fled to Lachish. However, men were sent after him to Lachish, and they put him to death there. [28] They carried him back on horses and buried him with his fathers in the city of Judah.[F,g]

JUDAH'S KING UZZIAH

26 All the people[h] of Judah took Uzziah,[G] who was sixteen years old, and made him king in place of his father Amaziah. [2] After Amaziah the king rested with his fathers, Uzziah rebuilt Eloth[H,i] and restored it to Judah.

[3] Uzziah was sixteen years old[j] when he became king, and he reigned fifty-two years in Jerusalem. His mother's name was Jecoliah; she was from Jerusalem. [4] He did what was right in the LORD's sight just as his father Amaziah had done. [5] He sought God[k] throughout the lifetime of Zechariah, the teacher of the fear[I,l] of God. During the time that he sought the LORD, God gave him success.[m]

UZZIAH'S EXPLOITS

[6] Uzziah went out to wage war against the Philistines,[n] and he tore down the wall of Gath, the wall of Jabneh, and the wall of Ashdod. Then he built cities in the vicinity of Ashdod and among the Philistines. [7] God helped him against the Philistines, the Arabs that live in Gur-baal, and the Meunites. [8] The Ammonites[J] paid tribute to Uzziah,[o] and his fame spread as far as the entrance of Egypt, for God made him very powerful. [9] Uzziah built towers in Jerusalem at the Corner Gate,[p] the Valley Gate,[q] and the corner buttress, and he fortified them. [10] Since he had many cattle both in the Judean foothills[K] and the plain, he built towers in the desert and dug many wells.[r] And since he was a lover of the soil, he had farmers and vinedressers in the hills and in the fertile lands.[L]

[11] Uzziah had an army equipped for combat that went out to war by division according to their assignments, as recorded by Jeiel the court secretary and Maaseiah the officer under the authority of Hananiah, one of the king's commanders. [12] The total number of family heads was 2,600 valiant warriors. [13] Under their authority was an army of 307,500 equipped for combat, a powerful force to help the king against the enemy.[s] [14] Uzziah provided the entire army with shields, spears, helmets, armor, bows, and slingstones. [15] He made skillfully designed devices in Jerusalem to shoot arrows and catapult large stones for use on

[A] 25:19 Some LXX mss, Old Lat, Tg, Vg; MT reads *you*   [B] 25:19 Lit *and your heart has lifted you*   [C] 25:23 = Ahaziah in 2Kg 14:13   [D] 25:23 Lit *400 cubits*   [E] 25:23 Some Hb mss; other Hb mss read *to Happoneh*   [F] 25:28 Some Hb mss read *city of David*   [G] 26:1 = Azariah in 2Kg 14:21   [H] 26:2 LXX, Syr, Vg read *Elath*   [I] 26:5 Some Hb mss, LXX, Syr, Tg, Arabic; other Hb mss, Vg read *visions*   [J] 26:8 LXX reads *Meunites*   [K] 26:10 Or *the Shephelah*   [L] 26:10 Or *in Carmel*

that advised him to challenge Israel to a fight (25:17). **King Jehoash of Israel** tried to warn Amaziah to back off for his own good. While Amaziah had **defeated Edom**, he had become too big for his britches. Jehoash urged the upstart king of Judah to **stay at home** (25:18-19).

25:20-24 A spiritual reality was working the downfall of the king in his earthly stupidity (25:20). The Lord let the stubborn and overconfident king of Judah go into battle and get thrashed (25:21-24).

26:1 The reference to Uzziah's installation on the throne is a little unusual, in that apparently his father Amaziah was not involved in naming his successor.

26:5 Like his grandfather Joash (who'd been counseled by Jehoiada), Uzziah followed the Lord as long as his mentor **Zechariah** was alive. It's not certain that Uzziah's pride and punishment coincided exactly with

the towers and on the corners. So his fame spread even to distant places, for he was wondrously helped until he became strong.

UZZIAH'S DISEASE

16 But when he became strong, he grew arrogant,[a] and it led to his own destruction. He acted unfaithfully against the LORD his God by going into the LORD's sanctuary to burn incense on the incense altar.[b] **17** The priest Azariah,[c] along with eighty brave priests of the LORD, went in after him. **18** They took their stand[d] against King Uzziah and said, "Uzziah, you have no right to offer incense to the LORD[e] — only the consecrated priests, the descendants of Aaron, have the right to offer incense.[f] Leave the sanctuary, for you have acted unfaithfully! You will not receive honor from the LORD God."

19 Uzziah, with a firepan in his hand to offer incense, was enraged. But when he became enraged with the priests, in the presence of the priests in the LORD's temple beside the altar of incense, a skin disease[g] broke out on his forehead. **20** Then Azariah the chief priest and all the priests turned to him and saw that he was diseased on his forehead. They rushed him out of there. He himself also hurried to get out because the LORD had afflicted him. **21** So King Uzziah was diseased to the time of his death.[h] He lived in quarantine[A,i] with a serious skin disease and was excluded from access to the LORD's temple, while his son Jotham was over the king's household governing the people of the land.

22 Now the prophet Isaiah[j] son of Amoz wrote about the rest of the events of Uzziah's reign, from beginning to end. **23** Uzziah rested with his fathers, and he was buried with his fathers in the burial ground of the kings' cemetery,[k] for they said, "He has a skin disease." His son Jotham became king in his place.

JUDAH'S KING JOTHAM

27 Jotham was twenty-five years old[l] when he became king, and he reigned sixteen years in Jerusalem.[m] His mother's name was Jerushah daughter of Zadok. **2** He did what was right in the LORD's sight just as his father Uzziah had done. In addition, he didn't enter the LORD's sanctuary,[n] but the people still behaved corruptly. **3** Jotham built the Upper Gate of the LORD's temple, and he built extensively on the wall of Ophel.[o] **4** He also built cities in the hill country of Judah and fortresses and towers in the forests.[p] **5** He waged war against the king of the Ammonites. He overpowered the Ammonites, and that year they gave him 7,500 pounds[B] of silver, 50,000 bushels[c] of wheat, and 50,000 bushels of barley. They paid him the same in the second and third years. **6** So Jotham strengthened his position because he did not waver in obeying[D] the LORD his God.[q] **7** As for the rest of the events[r] of Jotham's reign, along with all his wars and his ways, note that they are written in the Book of the Kings of Israel and Judah. **8** He was twenty-five years old when he became king, and he reigned sixteen years in Jerusalem. **9** Jotham rested with his fathers and was buried in the city of David. His son Ahaz became king in his place.

JUDAH'S KING AHAZ

28 Ahaz was twenty years old[s] when he became king, and he reigned sixteen years in Jerusalem. He did not do what was right in the LORD's sight[t] like his ancestor David, **2** for he walked in the ways of the kings of Israel[u] and made cast images of the Baals.[v] **3** He burned incense in Ben Hinnom Valley[w] and burned his

[a]26:16 Dt 32:15; 2Ch 25:19
[b]1Kg 13:1-4
[c]26:17 1Ch 6:10
[d]26:18 2Ch 19:2
[e]Nm 16:39-40
[f]Ex 30:7-8
[g]26:19 2Kg 5:25-27
[h]26:21-23 2Kg 15:5-7
[i]26:21 Lv 13:46
[j]26:22 Is 1:1
[k]26:23 2Ch 21:20

[l]27:1-3 2Kg 15:33-35
[m]27:1 2Ch 27:8
[n]27:2 2Ch 26:16-18
[o]27:3 2Ch 33:14; Neh 3:26-27
[p]27:4 2Ch 11:5
[q]27:6 2Ch 26:5
[r]27:7-9 2Kg 15:36-38
[s]28:1-6 2Kg 16:2-4
[t]28:1 2Ch 27:2
[u]28:2 2Ch 22:3
[v]Ex 34:17
[w]28:3 Jos 15:8; 18:16; 2Kg 23:10; Jr 7:29-34; 19:2-6

[A]26:21 Lit *in a house of exemption from duty*   [B]27:5 Lit *100 talents*   [C]27:5 Lit *10,000 cors*   [D]27:6 Lit *he established his ways before*

Zechariah's death, but that may have been the case.

26:16 Uzziah's story took a wrong turn when he allowed his power, fame, and prosperity to make him **arrogant**. At first glance, his sin may seem relatively minor compared to the murders, idolatry, and gross immorality of which several other kings of Judah were guilty. However, by usurping the role of the priest **to burn incense** in the temple, Uzziah committed an act of great unfaithfulness to the Lord.

26:17-18 The priests' actions took tremendous courage considering that the king could have executed them with a word.

26:19-23 Uzziah could have humbled himself when he heard the priests concerns, honoring God and winning their respect. Instead, **he became enraged**. But before the king could unleash his anger, God afflicted him with **a skin disease** (26:19). This required that he live **in quarantine** until the day of his death (26:21). In other words, because of his arrogant violation of God's law, Uzziah spent the rest of his days in isolation. (Keep yourself humble before the Lord. Pride will be your undoing.)

27:1 Uzziah's son **Jotham** got a head start on ruling since he had to assume the reins of leadership during the years his father Uzziah was unable to govern.

27:2 The statement about the **sanctuary** is an obvious reference to Uzziah's sin, but it appears that Jotham learned from his dad's error. This is another instance of the Chronicler using a historical incident to emphasize his message that faithful kings (and the nation under them) would prosper while faithless kings would lead the people into ruin.

28:1-4 Not only did Jotham fail to influence the people to obey the Lord (even though he personally obeyed), but it seems he failed to influence his son as well. **Ahaz** was so thoroughly corrupted by defection from the Lord and idolatry (28:2, 4) that he actually sacrificed **his children** by burning them

a 28:3 Lv 18:21; 2Kg 16:3;
2Ch 33:6
b 2Ch 33:2
c 28:4 2Ch 28:25
d 28:5 2Ch 24:24
e 28:8 2Ch 11:4
f 28:9 Is 47:6
g Ezr 9:6; Rv 18:5
h 28:11 2Ch 28:8

i 28:15 2Ch 28:12
j 2Kg 6:22; Pr 25:21-22
k Dt 34:3
l 28:16 2Kg 16:7
m 28:17 Ob 10-14
n 28:18 Ezk 16:57
o 28:20 1Ch 5:26
p 2Ch 28:16
q 28:23 Jr 44:17-18
r 28:24 2Kg 16:17
s 2Ch 29:7
t 2Ch 30:14; 33:3-5

children in[A,a] the fire, imitating the detestable practices of the nations the LORD had dispossessed before the Israelites.[b] ⁴ He sacrificed and burned incense on the high places,[c] on the hills, and under every green tree.

⁵ So the LORD his God handed Ahaz over[d] to the king of Aram. He attacked him and took many captives to Damascus.

Ahaz was also handed over to the king of Israel, who struck him with great force: ⁶ Pekah son of Remaliah killed one hundred twenty thousand in Judah in one day — all brave men — because they had abandoned the LORD God of their ancestors. ⁷ An Ephraimite warrior named Zichri killed the king's son Maaseiah, Azrikam governor of the palace, and Elkanah who was second to the king. ⁸ Then the Israelites took two hundred thousand captives from their brothers — women, sons, and daughters.[e] They also took a great deal of plunder from them and brought it to Samaria.

⁹ A prophet of the LORD named Oded was there. He went out to meet the army that came to Samaria and said to them, "Look, the LORD God of your ancestors handed them over to you because of his wrath against Judah,[f] but you slaughtered them in a rage that has reached heaven.[g] ¹⁰ Now you plan to reduce the people of Judah and Jerusalem, male and female, to slavery. Are you not also guilty before the LORD your God? ¹¹ Listen to me and return the captives you took from your brothers,[h] for the LORD's burning anger is on you."

¹² So some men who were leaders of the Ephraimites — Azariah son of Jehohanan, Berechiah son of Meshillemoth, Jehizkiah son of Shallum, and Amasa son of Hadlai — stood in opposition to those coming from the war. ¹³ They said to them, "You must not bring the captives here, for you plan to bring guilt on us from the LORD to add to our sins and our guilt. For we have much guilt, and burning anger is on Israel."

¹⁴ The army left the captives and the plunder in the presence of the officers and the congregation. ¹⁵ Then the men who were designated by name[i] took charge of the captives and provided clothes for their naked ones from the plunder. They clothed them, gave them sandals, food and drink,[j] dressed their wounds, and provided donkeys for all the feeble. The Israelites brought them to Jericho, the City of Palms,[k] among their brothers. Then they returned to Samaria.

¹⁶ At that time King Ahaz asked the king of Assyria for help.[l] ¹⁷ The Edomites came again, attacked Judah, and took captives.[m] ¹⁸ The Philistines also raided the cities of the Judean foothills[B] and the Negev of Judah.[n] They captured and occupied Bethshemesh, Aijalon, and Gederoth, as well as Soco, Timnah, and Gimzo with their surrounding villages. ¹⁹ For the LORD humbled Judah because of King Ahaz of Judah,[c] who threw off restraint in Judah and was unfaithful to the LORD. ²⁰ Then King Tiglathpileser[D,o] of Assyria came against Ahaz; he oppressed him and did not give him support.[p] ²¹ Although Ahaz plundered the LORD's temple and the palace of the king and of the rulers and gave the plunder to the king of Assyria, it did not help him.

²² At the time of his distress, King Ahaz himself became more unfaithful to the LORD. ²³ He sacrificed to the gods of Damascus which had defeated him; he said, "Since the gods of the kings of Aram are helping them, I will sacrifice to them so that they will help me."[q] But they were the downfall of him and of all Israel.

²⁴ Then Ahaz gathered up the utensils of God's temple, cut them into pieces,[r] shut the doors of the LORD's temple,[s] and made himself altars on every street corner in Jerusalem.[t] ²⁵ He made high places in every

[A] 28:3 LXX, Syr, Tg read *and passed his children through*   [B] 28:18 Or *the Shephelah*   [C] 28:19 Some Hb mss; other Hb mss read *Israel*   [D] 28:20 Text emended; MT reads *Tilgath-pilneser*; 1Ch 5:6,26

in the **detestable practices of the nations** (27:3)! This sad story highlights where idolatry leads. As we've seen throughout 2 Chronicles, the worship of false gods leads to godless living: wickedness, treachery, and violence.

King Ahaz was notable for another reason, too. About midway through his reign, the northern kingdom of Israel fell to the Assyrians in 722 BC. God had given Israel over to its sin until, finally, his judgment fell on the nation. Ominously, one of the indictments issued against Ahaz was that **he walked in the ways of the kings of Israel** (28:2).

28:9-11 Here the story takes an unusual turn. Not everyone in the northern kingdom had turned away from the Lord, because a **prophet of the LORD named Oded** met the Israelite army returning from its victory over Ahaz (28:9). When Oded saw all the captives straggling along behind the troops, he raised a strong protest. His speech was a passionate plea not to make the suffering of Judah worse by reducing **the people of Judah and Jerusalem . . . to slavery** (28:10). He commanded them to release the **captives** to avoid the **LORD's burning anger** (28:11).

28:12-15 Within this turn of events is the ultimate irony: unfaithful Israel listened to the voice of the Lord, while Judah did not—even though its kings were in the line of faithful David.

28:22-23 Idolatry is blinding, a fact highlighted in the next moves of Ahaz. He became **more unfaithful to the LORD** and **sacrificed to the gods of Damascus which had defeated him**. Ahaz rationalized that **since the gods of the kings of Aram** helped them, these same gods would also help him if he worshiped them (28:23). He didn't understand that each catastrophe he suffered was punishment from the hand of his own God as a result of his disobedience. The idols that he looked to for deliverance were his **downfall** (28:23).

city of Judah to offer incense to other gods, and he angered the Lord, the God of his ancestors.

AHAZ'S DEATH

26 As for the rest of his deeds[a] and all his ways, from beginning to end, they are written in the Book of the Kings of Judah and Israel. **27** Ahaz rested with his fathers and was buried in the city, in Jerusalem, but they did not bring him into the tombs of the kings of Israel. His son Hezekiah became king in his place.

JUDAH'S KING HEZEKIAH

29 Hezekiah was twenty-five years old[b] when he became king, and he reigned twenty-nine years in Jerusalem. His mother's name was Abijah[A] daughter of Zechariah. **2** He did what was right in the Lord's sight[c] just as his ancestor David had done.

3 In the first year of his reign, in the first month, he opened the doors of the Lord's temple and repaired them.[d] **4** Then he brought in the priests and Levites and gathered them in the eastern public square.[e] **5** He said to them, "Hear me, Levites. Consecrate yourselves[f] now and consecrate the temple of the Lord, the God of your ancestors. Remove everything impure from the holy place. **6** For our fathers were unfaithful and did what is evil in the sight of the Lord our God. They abandoned him, turned their faces away from the Lord's dwelling place, and turned their backs on him.[B,g] **7** They also closed the doors of the portico, extinguished the lamps, did not burn incense, and did not offer burnt offerings in the holy place of the God of Israel. **8** Therefore, the wrath of the Lord was on Judah and Jerusalem, and he made them an object of terror, horror, and mockery,[c,h] as you see with your own eyes. **9** Our fathers fell by the sword, and our sons, our daughters, and

our wives are in captivity because of this.[i] **10** It is in my heart now to make a covenant with the Lord, the God of Israel[j] so that his burning anger may turn away from us. **11** My sons, don't be negligent now, for the Lord has chosen you to stand in his presence, to serve him, and to be his ministers and burners of incense."[k]

CLEANSING THE TEMPLE

12 Then the Levites stood up:

> Mahath[l] son of Amasai and Joel son of Azariah from the Kohathites;
> Kish son of Abdi and Azariah son of Jehallelel from the Merarites;[m]
> Joah son of Zimmah and Eden son of Joah from the Gershonites;

13 Shimri and Jeuel from the Elizaphanites;

> Zechariah and Mattaniah from the Asaphites;

14 Jehiel[D] and Shimei from the Hemanites;

> Shemaiah and Uzziel from the Jeduthunites.

15 They gathered their brothers together, consecrated themselves,[n] and went according to the king's command by the words of the Lord[o] to cleanse the Lord's temple.[p] **16** The priests went to the entrance of the Lord's temple to cleanse it. They took all the unclean things they found in the Lord's sanctuary to the courtyard of the Lord's temple. Then the Levites received them and took them outside to the Kidron Valley.[q] **17** They began the consecration on the first day of the first month, and on the eighth day of the month they came to the portico of the Lord's temple. They consecrated the Lord's temple for eight days, and on the sixteenth day of the first month they finished. **18** Then they went inside to King Hezekiah and said, "We have cleansed the whole temple of the Lord, the altar of

[a] 28:26-27 2Kg 16:19-20
[b] 29:1-2 2Kg 18:2-3
[c] 29:2 2Ch 28:1; 34:2
[d] 29:3 2Ch 28:24; 29:7
[e] 29:4 Ezr 10:9; Neh 8:1
[f] 29:5 2Ch 29:15,34; 35:6
[g] 29:6 Ezk 8:16
[h] 29:8 Dt 28:25; Jr 25:18

[i] 29:9 2Ch 28:5-8,17
[j] 29:10 2Ch 23:16
[k] 29:11 Nm 3:6; 8:6
[l] 29:12 2Ch 31:13
[m] Nm 3:19-20
[n] 29:15 2Ch 29:5
[o] 2Ch 30:12
[p] 1Ch 23:28
[q] 29:16 2Ch 15:16

[A] 29:1 = Abi in 2Kg 18:2　[B] 29:6 Lit *and they gave the back of the neck*　[C] 29:8 Lit *hissing*　[D] 29:14 Alt Hb tradition reads *Jehuel*

28:27 That he was refused burial with the other kings is a final statement of his complete unfitness to be identified with the Davidic **kings** before him.

29:1-2 Had the man's son followed in his footsteps, Ahaz could have served as the poster boy for bad fathers. But, remarkably, his son pulled off one of the greatest revivals in Judah's history. The most important thing that the Chronicler could say about **Hezekiah** was that **he did what was right in the Lord's sight just as his ancestor David had done** (29:2). This king was worthy of comparison to David!

29:3-7 Having witnessed firsthand his father's reign, Hezekiah acknowledged the wickedness done by past kings who'd committed evil in God's sight and turned their backs on him (28:6-7). And so, his reforms began in the house of the Lord. He realized that if Judah was going to turn around, they would have to start by worshiping God as he had commanded.

29:8-9 As a teenager and young adult, Hezekiah must have watched in horror as Judah's enemies battered the nation in wars while unspeakable idolatries were practiced in Jerusalem. Hezekiah knew the reason for

these disasters: **the wrath of the Lord was on** his nation (29:8).

29:11 The Levites had an opportunity to reverse the damage done in the past.

29:12-19 For sixteen days, the Levites purified the temple and everything associated with it. When they were done, they were able to report to Hezekiah that they had **cleansed the whole temple of the Lord, the altar of burnt offering and all its utensils, and the table for the rows of the Bread of the Presence and all its utensils** (29:18). In other words, everything was ready for the service of reconsecration and worship.

a 29:19 2Ch 28:24
b 29:22 Lv 4:18
c 29:23 Lv 4:15
d 29:24 Lv 4:26
e 29:25 1Ch 15:16; 25:6
f 2Ch 8:14
g 2Sm 24:11
h 2Sm 7:2; 1Ch 29:29
i 29:26 1Ch 23:5
j 2Ch 5:12

k 29:29 2Ch 20:18
l 29:31 Ex 35:5,22; Ezr 1:4,6; 3:5
m 29:34 2Ch 35:11
n Ps 32:11; 64:10
o 2Ch 30:3
p 29:35 Lv 3:16
q Nm 15:5-10
r 30:1 Ex 12:1-28; 13:1-10
s 30:2 Nm 9:6-14; 2Ch 30:13,15
t 30:3 2Ch 29:34

burnt offering and all its utensils, and the table for the rows of the Bread of the Presence and all its utensils. [19] We have set up and consecrated all the utensils that King Ahaz rejected during his reign[a] when he became unfaithful. They are in front of the altar of the LORD."

RENEWAL OF TEMPLE WORSHIP

[20] King Hezekiah got up early, gathered the city officials, and went to the LORD's temple. [21] They brought seven bulls, seven rams, seven lambs, and seven male goats as a sin offering for the kingdom, for the sanctuary, and for Judah. Then he told the descendants of Aaron, the priests, to offer them on the altar of the LORD. [22] So they slaughtered the bulls, and the priests received the blood and splattered it on the altar.[b] They slaughtered the rams and splattered the blood on the altar. They slaughtered the lambs and splattered the blood on the altar. [23] Then they brought the goats for the sin offering right into the presence of the king and the congregation, who laid their hands on them.[c] [24] The priests slaughtered the goats and put their blood on the altar for a sin offering, to make atonement for all Israel,[d] for the king said that the burnt offering and sin offering were for all Israel.

[25] Hezekiah stationed the Levites in the LORD's temple with cymbals, harps, and lyres[e] according to the command of David,[f] Gad the king's seer,[g] and the prophet Nathan.[h] For the command was from the LORD through his prophets. [26] The Levites stood with the instruments of David,[i] and the priests with the trumpets.[j]

[27] Then Hezekiah ordered that the burnt offering be offered on the altar. When the burnt offerings began, the song of the LORD and the trumpets began, accompanied by the instruments of King David of Israel. [28] The whole assembly was worshiping, singing the song, and blowing the trumpets — all this continued until the burnt offering was completed. [29] When the burnt offerings were completed, the king and all those present with him bowed down and worshiped.[k] [30] Then King Hezekiah and the officials told the Levites to sing praise to the LORD in the words of David and of the seer Asaph. So they sang praises with rejoicing and knelt low and worshiped.

[31] Hezekiah concluded, "Now you are consecrated[A] to the LORD. Come near and bring sacrifices and thank offerings to the LORD's temple." So the congregation brought sacrifices and thank offerings, and all those with willing hearts[l] brought burnt offerings. [32] The number of burnt offerings the congregation brought was seventy bulls, one hundred rams, and two hundred lambs; all these were for a burnt offering to the LORD. [33] Six hundred bulls and three thousand sheep and goats were consecrated.

[34] However, since there were not enough priests, they weren't able to skin all the burnt offerings, so their Levite brothers helped them[m] until the work was finished and until the priests consecrated themselves. For the Levites were more conscientious[B,n] to consecrate themselves than the priests were.[o] [35] Furthermore, the burnt offerings were abundant, along with the fat of the fellowship offerings[p] and with the drink offerings[q] for the burnt offering.

So the service of the LORD's temple was established. [36] Then Hezekiah and all the people rejoiced over how God had prepared the people, for it had come about suddenly.

CELEBRATION OF THE PASSOVER

30 Then Hezekiah sent word throughout all Israel and Judah, and he also wrote letters to Ephraim and Manasseh to come to the LORD's temple in Jerusalem to observe the Passover of the LORD, the God of Israel.[r] [2] For the king and his officials and the entire congregation in Jerusalem decided to observe the Passover of the LORD in the second month,[s] [3] because they were not able to observe it at the appropriate time. Not enough of the priests had consecrated themselves,[t] and the people hadn't been gathered together in Jerusalem. [4] The proposal pleased the king and the congregation, [5] so they affirmed

---

A 29:31 Lit *Now you have filled your hands*   B 29:34 Lit *upright of heart*; Ps 32:11; 64:10

29:31-36 Incredibly, Hezekiah accomplished all of this in just one month, after the temple had been padlocked for years.
30:1 The **Passover** invitation went out not only to Judah, the southern kingdom, but also to those in the northern kingdom of Israel, referred to here as **Ephraim and Manasseh.** This is a reference to those who had not been taken captive by the Assyrians.

30:8-9 **Return to** God (30:9), and he will return to you is a principle also seen in Zechariah 1:3.
30:21-26 **The Festival of Unleavened Bread** that followed the Passover was such a big event in Judah that it took many thousands of animals to provide for all the worshipers (30:22-24). They even took the unprecedented step of extending the festival for another **seven days** (30:23). Through their

enthusiasm the people were saying, in effect, "We haven't worshiped like this in our whole lives. This is tremendous!"
31:1-8 The spiritual celebration was followed by the best of all outcomes in Judah—a spiritual revival that included still another purge of false worship, restoration of the giving of the people (ch. 31), and a miraculous deliverance from the armies of the dreaded Assyrians (ch. 32).

the proposal and spread the message throughout all Israel, from Beer-sheba to Dan,[a] to come to observe the Passover of the LORD, the God of Israel in Jerusalem, for they hadn't observed it often,[A] as prescribed.[B]

[6] So the couriers[b] went throughout Israel and Judah with letters from the hand of the king and his officials, and according to the king's command, saying, "Israelites, return to the LORD, the God of Abraham, Isaac, and Israel so that he may return to those of you who remain, who have escaped the grasp of the kings of Assyria.[c] [7] Don't be like your fathers and your brothers who were unfaithful to the LORD, the God of their ancestors[d] so that he made them an object of horror[e] as you yourselves see. [8] Don't become obstinate[C,f] now like your fathers did. Give your allegiance[D] to the LORD, and come to his sanctuary that he has consecrated forever. Serve the LORD your God so that he may turn his burning anger away from you,[g] [9] for when you return to the LORD, your brothers and your sons will receive mercy in the presence of their captors and will return to this land.[h] For the LORD your God is gracious and merciful;[i] he will not turn his face away from you if you return to him."

[10] The couriers traveled from city to city in the land of Ephraim and Manasseh as far as Zebulun, but the inhabitants[E] laughed at them and mocked them.[j] [11] But some from Asher, Manasseh, and Zebulun humbled themselves and came to Jerusalem.[k] [12] Also, the power of God was at work in Judah to unite them[F] to carry out the command of the king and his officials by the word of the LORD.

[13] A very large assembly of people was gathered in Jerusalem to observe the Festival of Unleavened Bread in the second month. [14] They proceeded to take away the altars that were in Jerusalem,[l] and they took away the incense altars and threw them into the Kidron Valley.[m] [15] They slaughtered the Passover lamb[n] on the fourteenth day of the second month. The priests and Levites were ashamed, and they consecrated themselves and brought burnt offerings to the LORD's temple. [16] They stood at their prescribed posts,[o] according to the law of Moses, the man of God. The priests splattered the blood received from the Levites, [17] for there were many in the assembly who had

not consecrated themselves, and so the Levites were in charge of slaughtering the Passover lambs for every unclean person to consecrate the lambs to the LORD.[p] [18] A large number of the people — many from Ephraim, Manasseh, Issachar, and Zebulun — were ritually unclean, yet they had eaten the Passover[q] contrary to what was written.[r] But Hezekiah had interceded for them, saying, "May the good LORD provide atonement on behalf of [19] whoever sets his whole heart on seeking God,[s] the LORD, the God of his ancestors, even though not according to the purification rules of the sanctuary." [20] So the LORD heard Hezekiah and healed the people.[t] [21] The Israelites who were present in Jerusalem observed the Festival of Unleavened Bread seven days with great joy,[u] and the Levites and the priests praised the LORD day after day with loud instruments. [22] Then Hezekiah encouraged[G,v] all the Levites who performed skillfully before the LORD. They ate at the appointed festival for seven days, sacrificing fellowship offerings and giving thanks to the LORD, the God of their ancestors.[w]

[23] The whole congregation decided to observe[x] seven more days, so they observed seven days with joy, [24] for King Hezekiah of Judah contributed one thousand bulls and seven thousand sheep for the congregation. Also, the officials contributed one thousand bulls and ten thousand sheep for the congregation,[y] and many priests consecrated themselves.[z] [25] Then the whole assembly of Judah with the priests and Levites, the whole assembly that came from Israel, the resident aliens who came from the land of Israel, and those who were living in Judah, rejoiced. [26] There was great rejoicing in Jerusalem, for nothing like this was known since the days of Solomon son of David, the king of Israel.[aa] [27] Then the priests and the Levites[ab] stood to bless the people,[ac] and God heard them, and their prayer came into his holy dwelling place[ad] in heaven.

REMOVAL OF IDOLATRY

31 When all this was completed, all Israel who had attended went out to the cities of Judah and broke up the sacred pillars, chopped down the Asherah poles, and tore down the high places and altars[ae] throughout Judah and Benjamin,

[a] 30:5 Jdg 20:1
[b] 30:6 Est 8:14; Jb 9:25; Jr 51:31
[c] 2Ch 28:20
[d] 30:7 Ezk 20:13
[e] 2Ch 29:8
[f] 30:8 Ex 32:9
[g] 2Ch 29:10
[h] 30:9 Dt 30:2-3
[i] Ex 34:6-7; Mc 7:18
[j] 30:10 2Ch 36:16
[k] 30:11 2Ch 30:18,21,25
[l] 30:14 2Ch 28:24
[m] 2Ch 29:16
[n] 30:15 2Ch 30:2-3
[o] 30:16 2Ch 35:10,15

[p] 30:17 2Ch 29:34
[q] 30:18 Nm 9:10
[r] Ex 12:43-49
[s] 30:19 2Ch 19:3
[t] 30:20 Ps 41:4; Hs 14:4
[u] 30:21 Ex 12:15; 13:6
[v] 30:22 2Ch 32:6
[w] Ezr 10:11
[x] 30:23 1Kg 8:65
[y] 30:24 2Ch 35:7-8
[z] 2Ch 29:34; 30:3
[aa] 30:26 2Ch 7:8-10
[ab] 30:27 2Ch 23:18
[ac] Nm 6:23-27
[ad] Dt 26:15; Ps 68:5
[ae] 31:1 2Kg 18:4

[A] 30:5 Or *in great numbers*   [B] 30:5 Lit *often, according to what is written*   [C] 30:8 Lit *Don't stiffen your neck*   [D] 30:8 Lit *hand*   [E] 30:10 Lit *but they*
[F] 30:12 Lit *to give them one heart*   [G] 30:22 Lit *spoke to the heart of*

a 31:2 1Ch 23:6-23; 24:1-19
b 1Ch 23:28-31
c 31:3 2Ch 35:7
d Nm 28
e 31:4 Nm 18:8
f 31:5 Neh 13:12
g 31:6 Lv 27:30; Dt 14:28
h 31:10 1Ch 6:8-9
i Mal 3:10
j 31:11 1Kg 6:5
k 31:12 2Ch 35:9

l 31:14 1Ch 26:26-28
m 31:15 2Ch 29:12
n Jos 21:9-19
o 31:16 1Ch 23:3
p Ezr 3:4
q 31:17 1Ch 23:24
r 31:19 Lv 25:34; Nm 35:2-5
s 2Ch 31:12-15
t 31:20 2Kg 20:3; 22:2
u 32:1 2Kg 18:13; Is 36:1

as well as in Ephraim and Manasseh, to the last one.[A] Then all the Israelites returned to their cities, each to his own possession.

OFFERINGS FOR LEVITES

2 Hezekiah reestablished the divisions[a] of the priests and Levites for the burnt offerings and fellowship offerings, for ministry, for giving thanks, and for praise in the gates of the camp of the LORD,[b] each division corresponding to his service among the priests and Levites. **3** The king contributed[B] from his own possessions[c] for the regular morning and evening burnt offerings, the burnt offerings of the Sabbaths, of the New Moons, and of the appointed feasts, as written in the law of the LORD.[d] **4** He told the people who lived in Jerusalem to give a contribution[e] for the priests and Levites so that they could devote their energy to the law of the LORD. **5** When the word spread, the Israelites gave liberally of the best of the grain, new wine, fresh oil, honey, and of all the produce of the field, and they brought in an abundance, a tenth[f] of everything. **6** As for the Israelites and Judahites who lived in the cities of Judah, they also brought a tenth of the herds and flocks, and a tenth of the dedicated things that were consecrated to the LORD their God.[g] They gathered them into large piles. **7** In the third month they began building up the piles, and they finished in the seventh month. **8** When Hezekiah and his officials came and viewed the piles, they blessed the LORD and his people Israel.

9 Hezekiah asked the priests and Levites about the piles. **10** The chief priest Azariah, of the household of Zadok,[h] answered him, "Since they began bringing the offering to the LORD's temple, we eat and are satisfied and there is plenty left over because the LORD has blessed his people; this abundance is what is left over."[i]

11 Hezekiah told them to prepare chambers[j] in the LORD's temple, and they prepared them. **12** The offering, the tenth, and the dedicated things were brought faithfully. Conaniah the Levite was the officer in charge of them, and his brother Shimei was second.[k] **13** Jehiel, Azariah, Nahath,

Asahel, Jerimoth, Jozabad, Eliel, Ismachiah, Mahath, and Benaiah were deputies under the authority of Conaniah and his brother Shimei by appointment of King Hezekiah and of Azariah the chief official of God's temple.

14 Kore son of Imnah the Levite, the keeper of the East Gate, was over the freewill offerings to God to distribute the contribution to the LORD and the consecrated things.[l] **15** Eden,[m] Miniamin, Jeshua, Shemaiah, Amariah, and Shecaniah in the cities of the priests[n] were to distribute it faithfully under his authority to their brothers by divisions, whether large or small. **16** In addition, they distributed it to males registered by genealogy three[C,o] years old and above; to all who would enter the LORD's temple for their daily duty,[p] for their service in their responsibilities according to their divisions. **17** They distributed also to those recorded by genealogy of the priests by their ancestral families and the Levites twenty years old and above,[q] by their responsibilities in their divisions; **18** to those registered by genealogy — with all their dependents, wives, sons, and daughters — of the whole assembly (for they had faithfully consecrated themselves as holy); **19** and to the descendants of Aaron, the priests, in the common fields of their cities,[r] in each and every city. There were men who were registered by name[s] to distribute a portion to every male among the priests and to every Levite recorded by genealogy.

20 Hezekiah did this throughout all Judah. He did what was good and upright and true before the LORD his God.[t] **21** He was diligent in every deed that he began in the service of God's temple, in the instruction and the commands, in order to seek his God, and he prospered.

SENNACHERIB'S INVASION

32 After these faithful deeds, King Sennacherib of Assyria came and entered Judah. He laid siege to the fortified cities and intended[D] to break into them.[u] **2** Hezekiah saw that Sennacherib had come and that he planned[E] war on Jerusalem, **3** so he consulted with his

---

[A] 31:1 Lit *Manasseh, until finishing*   [B] 31:3 Lit *The king's portion*   [C] 31:16 *Or 30*; 1Ch 23:3   [D] 32:1 Lit *said to himself*   [E] 32:2 Lit *that his face was for*

31:9-21 King Hezekiah provided for the proper oversight and use of the people's gifts, making sure that the priests, Levites, and their families were provided for.

32:1-8 The events of chapter 31 are intimately linked with what happened next in Hezekiah's reign, because the threat from Assyria came **after these faithful deeds** on Hezekiah's part (32:1). The army of the Assyrian King **Sennacherib** invaded Judah and proceeded to conquer a number of towns on its march toward Jerusalem. Hezekiah did the wisest things he could do in the face of this terrifying threat: He prepared to defend the city (32:2-6) while hoping in the Lord (32:7-8).

officials and his warriors about stopping up the water of the springs that were outside the city, and they helped him. [4] Many people gathered and stopped up all the springs[a] and the stream that flowed through the land;[b] they said, "Why should the kings of Assyria come and find abundant water?" [5] Then Hezekiah strengthened his position by rebuilding the entire broken-down wall[c] and heightening the towers and the other outside wall.[d] He repaired the supporting terraces[e] of the city of David, and made an abundance of weapons and shields.

[6] He set military commanders over the people and gathered the people in the square of the city gate. Then he encouraged them,[A,f] saying, [7] "Be strong and courageous![g] Don't be afraid or discouraged before the king of Assyria or before the large army that is with him, for there are more with us than with him."[h] [8] He has only human strength,[B] but we have the LORD our God to help us and to fight our battles."[i] So the people relied on the words of King Hezekiah of Judah.

SENNACHERIB'S SERVANT'S SPEECH

[9] After this,[j] while King Sennacherib of Assyria with all his armed forces besieged[c] Lachish, he sent his servants to Jerusalem against King Hezekiah of Judah and against all those of Judah who were in Jerusalem, saying, [10] "This is what King Sennacherib of Assyria says: 'What are you relying on that you remain in Jerusalem under siege? [11] Isn't Hezekiah misleading you to give you over to death by famine and thirst when he says, "The LORD our God will keep us from the grasp of the king of Assyria"? [12] Didn't Hezekiah himself remove his high places and his altars[k] and say to Judah and Jerusalem, "You must worship before one altar, and you must burn incense on it"?

[13] " 'Don't you know[l] what I and my fathers have done to all the peoples of the lands? Have any of the national gods of the lands been able to rescue their land from my power? [14] Who among all the gods of these nations that my predecessors completely destroyed was able to

rescue his people from my power, that your God should be able to deliver you from my power?[m] [15] So now,[n] don't let Hezekiah deceive you, and don't let him mislead you like this. Don't believe him, for no god of any nation or kingdom has been able to rescue his people from my power or the power of my fathers. How much less will your God rescue you from my power!' "

[16] His servants said more against the LORD God and against his servant Hezekiah. [17] He also wrote letters to mock the LORD, the God of Israel, saying against him:

Just like the national gods of the lands
that did not rescue their people from
my power, so Hezekiah's God will not
rescue his people from my power.[o]

[18] Then they called out loudly in Hebrew[D] to the people of Jerusalem, who were on the wall, to frighten and discourage them in order that he might capture the city. [19] They spoke against the God of Jerusalem like they had spoken against the gods of the peoples of the earth, which were made by human hands.

DELIVERANCE FROM SENNACHERIB

[20] King Hezekiah and the prophet Isaiah son of Amoz prayed about this and cried out to heaven,[p] [21] and the LORD sent an angel who annihilated every valiant warrior, leader, and commander in the camp of the king of Assyria. So the king of Assyria returned in disgrace to his land. He went to the temple of his god, and there some of his own children struck him down with the sword.[q] [22] So the LORD saved Hezekiah and the inhabitants of Jerusalem from the power of King Sennacherib of Assyria and from the power of all others. He gave them rest[E,r] on every side. [23] Many were bringing an offering to the LORD to Jerusalem and valuable gifts to King Hezekiah of Judah, and he was exalted in the eyes of all the nations after that.[s]

HEZEKIAH'S ILLNESS AND PRIDE

[24] In those days Hezekiah became sick to the point of death, so he prayed to the

[a]32:4 2Kg 20:20
[b]2Ch 32:30
[c]32:5 2Ch 25:23
[d]2Kg 25:4
[e]2Sm 5:9; 1Kg 9:15
[f]32:6 2Ch 30:22
[g]32:7 Dt 31:6; Jos 1:6-9; 10:25; 1Ch 22:13; Ps 31:24
[h]2Kg 6:16; 1Jn 4:4
[i]32:8 2Ch 20:17; Is 31:3; Jr 17:5
[j]32:9-12 2Kg 18:17-22; Is 36:2-7
[k]32:12 2Ch 31:1
[l]32:13-14 2Kg 18:33-35; Is 36:18-20

[m]32:14 Is 10:9-11
[n]32:15-18 2Kg 18:28-30; Is 36:13-15
[o]32:17 2Ch 32:14
[p]32:20 2Kg 19:15; Is 37:15-16
[q]32:21 2Kg 19:35-37; Is 37:36-38
[r]32:22 Ps 23:2
[s]32:23 2Sm 8:10; 2Ch 9:23-24

[A]32:6 Lit he spoke to their hearts   [B]32:8 Lit With him an arm of flesh   [C]32:9 Lit with his dominion was against   [D]32:18 Lit Judahite   [E]32:22 Lit He led them; Ps 23:2

32:9-19 Assyria's spokesman went to great lengths to dishearten the people by mocking and insulting the true God. He explained what the Assyrians had done to the other nations, whose gods had failed to protect them. Why

should the God of puny Judah be any different (32:13-15)?
32:20 This is the great **prophet Isaiah** whose prophecies are recorded in the biblical book that bears his name.

32:25 It appears that when Hezekiah was exalted, it became a source of temptation to succumb to pride. This means that while God had answered Hezekiah's prayer, Hezekiah was ungrateful. He thought more highly

[a] 32:24 2Kg 20:1-3,8-11; Is 38:1-3,7-8
[b] 32:25 2Ch 26:16; 32:31
[c] 2Ch 24:18
[d] 32:26 Jr 26:18-19
[e] 2Kg 20:18-19; Is 39:7-8
[f] 32:30 1Kg 1:33
[g] 2Kg 20:20
[h] 32:31 2Kg 20:12; Is 39:1
[i] 2Ch 32:24
[j] Dt 8:2; 13:3
[k] 32:32-33 2Kg 20:20-21
[l] 32:32 Is 36:1-39:8
[m] 2Kg 18:9-20:19

[n] 33:1-9 2Kg 21:1-9
[o] 33:2 2Ch 28:3
[p] 33:3 2Kg 18:4; 2Ch 31:1
[q] 33:4 2Ch 28:24
[r] 2Ch 7:16
[s] 33:5 2Ch 4:9
[t] 33:6 2Kg 16:3; 2Ch 28:3
[u] Lv 19:31; 20:27; 2Kg 23:24
[v] 33:7-8 1Kg 9:1-9
[w] 33:7 Dt 16:21
[x] 2Kg 21:7
[y] Dt 12:5; 1Kg 11:32
[z] 33:8 2Kg 21:8
[aa] 2Sm 7:10
[ab] 33:10 2Kg 21:10-16

LORD, and he spoke to him and gave him a miraculous sign.[a] 25 However, because his heart was proud,[b] Hezekiah didn't respond according to the benefit that had come to him. So there was wrath on him, Judah, and Jerusalem.[c] 26 Then Hezekiah humbled himself for the pride of his heart — he and the inhabitants of Jerusalem — so the LORD's wrath didn't come[d] on them during Hezekiah's lifetime.[e]

HEZEKIAH'S WEALTH AND WORKS

27 Hezekiah had abundant riches and glory, and he made himself treasuries for silver, gold, precious stones, spices, shields, and every desirable item. 28 He made warehouses for the harvest of grain, new wine, and fresh oil, and stalls for all kinds of cattle, and pens for flocks. 29 He made cities for himself, and he acquired vast numbers of flocks and herds, for God gave him abundant possessions.

30 This same Hezekiah blocked the outlet of the water of the Upper Gihon[f] and channeled it smoothly downward and westward to the city of David.[g] Hezekiah succeeded in everything he did. 31 When the ambassadors of Babylon's rulers[h] were sent[A] to him to inquire about the miraculous sign[i] that happened in the land, God left him to test him and discover what was in his heart.[j]

HEZEKIAH'S DEATH

32 As for the rest of the events[k] of Hezekiah's reign and his deeds of faithful love, note that they are written in the Visions of the Prophet Isaiah son of Amoz,[l] and in the Book of the Kings of Judah and Israel.[m] 33 Hezekiah rested with his fathers and was buried on the ascent to the tombs of David's descendants. All Judah and the inhabitants of Jerusalem paid him honor at his death. His son Manasseh became king in his place.

JUDAH'S KING MANASSEH

33 Manasseh was twelve years old[n] when he became king, and he reigned fifty-five years in Jerusalem. 2 He did what was evil in the LORD's sight, imitating the detestable practices of the nations that the LORD had dispossessed before the Israelites.[o] 3 He rebuilt the high places that his father Hezekiah had torn down[p] and reestablished the altars for the Baals. He made Asherah poles, and he bowed in worship to all the stars in the sky and served them. 4 He built altars[q] in the LORD's temple, where the LORD had said, "Jerusalem is where my name will remain forever."[r] 5 He built altars to all the stars in the sky in both courtyards[s] of the LORD's temple. 6 He passed his sons through the fire in Ben Hinnom Valley.[t] He practiced witchcraft, divination, and sorcery, and consulted mediums and spiritists.[u] He did a huge amount of evil in the LORD's sight, angering him.

7 Manasseh[v] set up a carved image of the idol, which he had made, in God's temple[w] that God had spoken about to David and his son Solomon: "I will establish my name forever[B,x] in this temple and in Jerusalem, which I have chosen out of all the tribes of Israel.[y] 8 I will never again remove the feet of the Israelites from the land where I stationed your[C,z] ancestors,[aa] if only they will be careful to do all I have commanded them through Moses — all the law, statutes, and judgments." 9 So Manasseh caused Judah and the inhabitants of Jerusalem to stray so that they did worse evil than the nations the LORD had destroyed before the Israelites.

MANASSEH'S REPENTANCE

10 The LORD spoke to Manasseh and his people, but they didn't listen.[ab] 11 So he brought against them the military commanders of the king of Assyria. They

[A] 32:31 LXX, Tg, Vg; MT reads *of Babylon sent*   [B] 33:7 LXX, Syr, Tg, Vg; 2Kg 21:7; MT reads *name for Elom*   [C] 33:8 LXX, Syr, Vg read *land I gave to their*; 2Kg 21:8

of himself than he should have. So, the Lord disciplined him—and the people.

32:26 The mention of the Lord's **wrath** here is an ominous note that bad times were still coming.

33:1-3 The ultimate low point of Judah's kings who departed from the Lord seems to have been reached with the long reign of **Manasseh**. And it is evident from the beginning that Manasseh either learned nothing from his godly father, or quickly rejected it once he became king (33:1-2). His actions were a complete reversal of Hezekiah's

reforms. In fact, the Chronicler reports that Manasseh **rebuilt the high places that his father Hezekiah had torn down and reestablished the altars for the Baals** (33:3).

33:4-8 It seems there was no form of degrading worship that Manasseh did not embrace and promote. But these abominations weren't enough for Manasseh. He also desecrated God's temple, erecting **a carved image of the idol, which he had made,** right there in it (33:7).

33:9 God had kicked the Canaanites out of the land because of their wickedness. Now his

people, recipients of that land, were worse than the Canaanites!

33:10-13 Rather than allowing Manasseh to remain on his throne and afflict the nation further, God disciplined the wicked king. Manasseh was captured by the Assyrians and taken like an animal to **Babylon** (33:11). Finally, in great **distress**, Manasseh **sought** the Lord's **favor** and humbled himself (33:12). The Lord was moved by Manasseh's humility, answered his prayer, and returned him to Jerusalem. **So Manasseh came to know that the LORD is God** (33:13).

captured Manasseh with hooks, bound him with bronze shackles, and took him to Babylon.[a] **12** When he was in distress, he sought the favor of the LORD his God and earnestly humbled himself[b] before the God of his ancestors. **13** He prayed to him, and the LORD was receptive to his prayer. He granted his request[c] and brought him back to Jerusalem, to his kingdom. So Manasseh came to know that the LORD is God.[d]

14 After this, he built the outer wall of the city of David from west of Gihon[e] in the valley to the entrance of the Fish Gate;[f] he brought it around the Ophel,[g] and he heightened it considerably. He also placed military commanders in all the fortified cities of Judah.

15 He removed the foreign gods and the idol[h] from the LORD's temple, along with all the altars that he had built on the mountain of the LORD's temple and in Jerusalem, and he threw them outside the city. **16** He built[A] the altar of the LORD and offered fellowship and thank offerings on it. Then he told Judah to serve the LORD, the God of Israel. **17** However, the people still sacrificed at the high places,[i] but only to the LORD their God.

MANASSEH'S DEATH

18 The rest of the events[j] of Manasseh's reign, along with his prayer[k] to his God and the words of the seers who spoke to him in the name of the LORD, the God of Israel, are written in the Events of Israel's Kings. **19** His prayer and how God was receptive to his prayer, and all his sin and unfaithfulness and the sites where he built high places and set up Asherah poles and carved images before he humbled himself, they are written in the Events of Hozai. **20** Manasseh rested with his fathers, and he was buried in his own house. His son Amon became king in his place.

JUDAH'S KING AMON

21 Amon was twenty-two years old when he became king, and he reigned two years in Jerusalem. **22** He did what was evil in

the LORD's sight, just as his father Manasseh had done.[l] Amon sacrificed to all the carved images that his father Manasseh had made, and he served them. **23** But he did not humble himself before the LORD like his father Manasseh humbled himself;[m] instead, Amon increased his guilt.

24 So his servants conspired against him and put him to death[n] in his own house. **25** The common people[B] killed all who had conspired against King Amon, and they made his son Josiah king in his place.

JUDAH'S KING JOSIAH

34 Josiah was eight years old[o] when he became king, and he reigned thirty-one years in Jerusalem. **2** He did what was right in the LORD's sight and walked in the ways of his ancestor David;[p] he did not turn aside to the right or the left.

JOSIAH'S REFORM

3 In the eighth year of his reign, while he was still a youth, Josiah began to seek the God of his ancestor David,[q] and in the twelfth year he began to cleanse Judah and Jerusalem of the high places, the Asherah poles, the carved images,[r] and the cast images. **4** Then in his presence the altars of the Baals were torn down, and he chopped down the shrines[c] that were above them. He shattered the Asherah poles, the carved images, and the cast images, crushed them to dust, and scattered[s] them over the graves of those who had sacrificed to them.[t] **5** He burned the bones of the priests on their altars.[u] So he cleansed Judah and Jerusalem. **6** He did the same in the cities[v] of Manasseh, Ephraim, and Simeon, and as far as Naphtali and on their surrounding mountain shrines.[D] **7** He tore down the altars, and he smashed the Asherah poles and the carved images to powder. He chopped down all the shrines throughout the land of Israel and returned to Jerusalem.[w]

JOSIAH'S REPAIR OF THE TEMPLE

8 In the eighteenth year of his reign,[x] in order to cleanse the land and the temple,

a33:11 2Ch 36:6
b33:12 2Ch 32:26
c33:13 Ezr 8:23
d Dn 4:32
e33:14 1Kg 1:33; 2Ch 32:30
f Neh 3:3
g2Ch 27:3
h33:15 2Ch 33:3-7
i33:17 2Ch 32:12
j33:18-25 2Kg 21:17-24
k33:18 2Ch 33:12-13

l33:22 2Ch 33:2
m33:23 2Ch 33:12,19
n33:24 2Ch 25:27
o34:1-2 2Kg 22:1-2
p34:2 2Ch 29:2
q34:3 1Ch 28:9; 2Ch 11:16; 14:4; 15:12
r2Ch 33:22
s34:4 Ex 32:20
t2Kg 23:6
u34:5 2Kg 23:5,8,16,20
v34:6 2Kg 23:15,19
w34:7 2Ch 31:1
x34:8-12 2Kg 22:3-7

A33:16 Some Hb mss, Syr, Tg, Arabic; other Hb mss, LXX, Vg read *restored*   B33:25 Lit *The people of the land*   C34:4 Lit *incense altars*, also in v. 7
D34:6 One Hb tradition reads *Naphtali with their swords*; alt Hb tradition, Syr, Vg read *Naphtali, the ruins all around*; Hb obscure

---

33:14-17 Upon his restoration, Manasseh tried to undo the evils he'd done. In the end, though, his reforms were limited.

34:1-2 At **eight**, Josiah could hardly be ready to rule. But he obviously had a heart for the Lord, a key fact with which the Chronicler sought to encourage his readers after the

Babylonian captivity. Josiah **did what was right in the LORD's sight and walked in the ways of his ancestor David**. He also merited this praise, which could be said about few other kings of Judah: **He did not turn aside to the right or the left** (34:2).

34:3-7 Josiah's heart for God manifested itself at the age of sixteen when he began **to seek** the Lord in earnest (34:3). And when he was just twenty, he undertook a purge of all false worship and false worshipers that extended all the way north into the territory of Israel (34:5-6; see 1 Kgs 13:1-3).

a 34:8 2Ch 18:25
b 34:9 2Ch 34:14; 35:8
c 2Ch 30:10,18
d 34:12 1Ch 25:1
e 34:14 Dt 31:24-26
f 34:15-32 2Kg 22:8–23:3

g 34:18 Dt 17:18-20
h 34:19 Jos 7:6
i 34:21 2Ch 29:8
j 34:24 2Ch 36:15-21
k Dt 28:15-68
l 34:25 2Ch 33:3
m 34:27-28 1Kg 21:29; 2Ch 12:6-7; 32:26
n 34:28 Is 57:1-2

Josiah sent Shaphan son of Azaliah, along with Maaseiah the governor[a] of the city and the court historian Joah son of Joahaz, to repair the temple of the LORD his God. [9] So they went to the high priest Hilkiah[b] and gave him the silver brought into God's temple. The Levites and the doorkeepers had collected it from Manasseh, Ephraim,[c] and from the entire remnant of Israel, and from all Judah, Benjamin, and the inhabitants of Jerusalem. [10] They gave it to those doing the work — those who oversaw the LORD's temple. They gave it to the workmen who were working in the LORD's temple, to repair and restore the temple; [11] they gave it to the carpenters and builders and also used it to buy quarried stone and timbers — for joining and making beams — for the buildings that Judah's kings had destroyed.

[12] The men were doing the work with integrity. Their overseers were Jahath and Obadiah, Levites from the Merarites, and Zechariah and Meshullam from the Kohathites as supervisors. The Levites were all skilled with musical instruments.[d] [13] They were also over the porters and were supervising all those doing the work task by task. Some of the Levites were secretaries, officers, and gatekeepers.

THE RECOVERY OF THE BOOK OF THE LAW

[14] When they brought out the silver that had been deposited in the LORD's temple, the priest Hilkiah found the book of the law of the LORD written by the hand of Moses.[e] [15] Consequently,[f] Hilkiah told the court secretary Shaphan, "I have found the book of the law in the LORD's temple," and he gave the book to Shaphan.

[16] Shaphan took the book to the king, and also reported, "Your servants are doing all that was placed in their hands. [17] They have emptied out the silver that was found in the LORD's temple and have given it to the overseers and to those doing the work." [18] Then the court secretary Shaphan told the king, "The priest Hilkiah

gave me a book," and Shaphan read from it in the presence of the king.[g]

[19] When the king heard the words of the law, he tore his clothes.[h] [20] Then he commanded Hilkiah, Ahikam son of Shaphan, Abdon son of Micah, the court secretary Shaphan, and the king's servant Asaiah, [21] "Go and inquire of the LORD for me and for those remaining in Israel and Judah, concerning the words of the book that was found. For great is the LORD's wrath that is poured out on us[i] because our ancestors have not kept the word of the LORD in order to do everything written in this book."

HULDAH'S PROPHECY OF JUDGMENT

[22] So Hilkiah and those the king had designated[A] went to the prophetess Huldah, the wife of Shallum son of Tokhath, son of Hasrah, keeper of the wardrobe. She lived in Jerusalem in the Second District. They spoke with her about this.

[23] She said to them, "This is what the LORD God of Israel says: Say to the man who sent you to me, [24] 'This is what the LORD says: I am about to bring disaster on this place and on its inhabitants,[j] fulfilling[B] all the curses written in the book that they read in the presence of the king of Judah,[k] [25] because they have abandoned me[l] and burned incense to other gods so as to anger me with all the works of their hands. My wrath will be poured out on this place, and it will not be quenched.' [26] Say this to the king of Judah who sent you to inquire of the LORD: 'This is what the LORD God of Israel says: As for the words that you heard, [27] because[m] your heart was tender and you humbled yourself before God when you heard his words against this place and against its inhabitants, and because you humbled yourself before me, and you tore your clothes and wept before me, I myself have heard' — this is the LORD's declaration. [28] 'I will indeed gather you to your fathers, and you will be gathered to your grave in peace. Your eyes will not see all the disaster that I am bringing on this place and on its inhabitants.' "[n]

Then they reported to the king.

[A] 34:22 LXX; MT omits *designated*   [B] 34:24 *fulfilling* supplied for clarity

---

34:14-18 The book of God's law, **written by the hand of Moses**, had been tossed aside in some closet in the temple! Imagine Josiah's shock when Shaphan told him, "Guess what we found" (34:16, 18).
34:19 Tearing one's **clothes** was a symbolic act indicating great grief and mourning.

The king realized how far God's people had fallen from him and how much wrath they deserved.
34:29-31 How would you have responded to Huldah's dire predictions (34:22-28)? Would you have been relieved? Would you have thought, "At least I won't have to live through

it?" Nothing like that was on Josiah's mind. The king read **the book of the covenant** in the hearing of **all the people** (34:30). Then he led a **covenant** renewal ceremony in which king and people pledged themselves **to follow the holy LORD** (34:31).

AFFIRMATION OF THE COVENANT BY JOSIAH AND THE PEOPLE

29 So the king sent messengers and gathered all the elders of Judah and Jerusalem. **30** The king went up to the LORD's temple with all the men of Judah and the inhabitants of Jerusalem, as well as the priests and the Levites — all the people from the oldest to the youngest. He read in their hearing all the words of the book of the covenant that had been found in the LORD's temple.[a] **31** Then the king stood at his post[b] and made a covenant in the LORD's presence[c] to follow the LORD and to keep his commands, his decrees, and his statutes with all his heart and with all his soul[d] in order to carry out the words of the covenant written in this book.[e] **32** He had all those present in Jerusalem and Benjamin agree[A] to it. So all the inhabitants of Jerusalem carried out the covenant of God, the God of their ancestors. **33** So Josiah removed everything that was detestable from all the lands belonging to the Israelites,[f] and he required all who were present in Israel to serve the LORD their God. Throughout his reign they did not turn aside from following the LORD, the God of their ancestors.

JOSIAH'S PASSOVER OBSERVANCE

35 Josiah observed the LORD's Passover[g] and slaughtered the Passover lambs on the fourteenth day of the first month.[h] **2** He appointed the priests to their responsibilities and encouraged them to serve in the LORD's temple.[i] **3** He said to the Levites who taught all Israel[j] the holy things of the LORD, "Put the holy ark in the temple built by Solomon son of David king of Israel. Since you do not have to carry it on your shoulders,[k] now serve the LORD your God and his people Israel. **4** "Organize your ancestral families[B] by your divisions[l] according to the written instruction of King David of Israel and that of his son Solomon.[m] **5** Serve in the holy place by the groupings of the ancestral families[C] for your brothers, the lay people,[D] and according to the division of the Levites by family.[n] **6** Slaughter the Passover lambs,[o] consecrate yourselves,[p] and make

preparations for your brothers to carry out the word of the LORD through Moses." **7** Then Josiah donated thirty thousand sheep, lambs, and young goats, plus three thousand cattle from his own possessions, for the Passover sacrifices for all the lay people who were present. **8** His officials also donated willingly for the people, the priests, and the Levites. Hilkiah, Zechariah, and Jehiel, chief officials of God's temple, gave twenty-six hundred Passover sacrifices and three hundred cattle for the priests. **9** Conaniah[q] and his brothers Shemaiah and Nethanel, and Hashabiah, Jeiel, and Jozabad, officers of the Levites, donated five thousand Passover sacrifices for the Levites, plus five hundred cattle. **10** So the service was established; the priests stood at their posts and the Levites in their divisions according to the king's command.[r] **11** Then they slaughtered the Passover lambs, and while the Levites were skinning the animals,[s] the priests splattered the blood[E] they had been given.[F] **12** They removed the burnt offerings so that they might be given to the groupings of the ancestral families[G] of the lay people to offer to the LORD, according to what is written in the book of Moses; they did the same with the cattle. **13** They roasted the Passover lambs with fire according to regulation.[f] They boiled the holy sacrifices in pots, kettles, and bowls; and they quickly brought them to the lay people. **14** Afterward, they made preparations for themselves and for the priests, since the priests, the descendants of Aaron, were busy offering up burnt offerings and fat until night. So the Levites made preparations for themselves and for the priests, the descendants of Aaron. **15** The singers, the descendants of Asaph, were at their stations according to the command of David, Asaph, Heman, and Jeduthun the king's seer.[u] Also, the gatekeepers were at each temple gate.[v] None of them left their tasks because their Levite brothers had made preparations for them. **16** So all the service of the LORD was established that day for observing the Passover and for offering burnt offerings on

a 34:30 Neh 8:1-3
b 34:31 2Kg 11:14; 2Ch 30:16
c 2Ch 23:16; 29:10
d Dt 6:4-6
e Ex 24:3-8; Jos 24:14-28
f 34:33 2Ch 34:3-7
g 35:1 2Kg 23:21
h Ex 12:6; Nm 9:3
i 35:2 2Ch 29:11
j 35:3 2Ch 17:8-9; Neh 8:7
k 1Ch 23:26
l 35:4 1Ch 9:10-13
m 2Ch 8:14
n 35:5 Ezr 6:18
o 35:6 2Ch 35:1,11
p 2Ch 29:5

q 35:9 2Ch 31:12-13
r 35:10 2Ch 35:5
s 35:11 2Ch 29:34
t 35:13 Ex 12:8-9
u 35:15 1Ch 25:1
v 1Ch 26:12-19

A 34:32 Lit *take a stand.*   B 35:4 Lit *the house of your fathers*   C 35:5 Lit *the house of the fathers*   D 35:5 Lit *the sons of the people,* also in vv. 7,12,13
E 35:11 LXX, Vg, Tg; MT omits *blood*   F 35:11 Lit *splattered from their hand*   G 35:12 Lit *house of fathers*

35:1-3 The temple wasn't the only thing that had fallen into neglect when Josiah came to the throne. It had been many years since Judah had observed the **Passover** (35:1). Josiah made elaborate preparations to correct this problem, including his order to replace **the holy ark** in the holy of holies (35:3) after it had obviously been removed from the temple. 35:18 This evaluation is at once both wonderful and tragic. It is wonderful because it demonstrates the intense repentance and devotion to the Lord of this young king. He was going to ensure that God was honored by the nation on his watch. But it is also tragic that the worship of God had been so neglected.

a 35:17 2Ch 30:21
b 35:18-19 2Kg 23:22-23
c 35:20-25 2Kg 23:29-30a
d 35:20 Jr 46:2
e Is 10:9
f 35:21 Jdg 11:12; 2Ch 25:19
g 35:22 2Ch 18:29
h Jdg 5:19
i 35:23 2Ch 18:33
j 35:24 Zch 12:11
k 35:25 Jr 22:10; Lm 4:20

l 35:26-27 2Kg 23:28
m 36:1-4 2Kg 23:30b-34
n 36:4 Jr 22:10-12
o 36:5 2Kg 23:36-37; Jr 22:13-18
p 36:6 2Kg 24:1
q 2Ch 33:11
r Jr 22:18-19
s 36:7 2Kg 24:1-4; Jr 22:13-19; 25:1-9; Dn 1:1; Hab 1:6
t 36:8 2Kg 24:5-6
u 36:9-10 2Kg 24:8-17

the altar of the Lord, according to the command of King Josiah. [17] The Israelites who were present in Judah also observed the Passover at that time and the Festival of Unleavened Bread for seven days.[a] [18] No Passover had been observed[b] like it in Israel since the days of the prophet Samuel. None of the kings of Israel ever observed a Passover like the one that Josiah observed with the priests, the Levites, all Judah, the Israelites who were present in Judah, and the inhabitants of Jerusalem. [19] In the eighteenth year of Josiah's reign, this Passover was observed.

JOSIAH'S LAST DEEDS AND DEATH

[20] After all this[c] that Josiah had prepared for the temple, King Neco of Egypt[d] marched up to fight at Carchemish[e] by the Euphrates, and Josiah went out to confront him. [21] But Neco sent messengers to him, saying, "What is the issue between you and me, king of Judah?[f] I have not come against you today[A] but I am fighting another dynasty.[g] God told me to hurry. Stop opposing God who is with me; don't make him destroy you!"

[22] But Josiah did not turn away from him; instead, in order to fight with him he disguised himself.[c,g] He did not listen to Neco's words from the mouth of God, but went to the Valley of Megiddo[h] to fight. [23] The archers shot King Josiah, and he said to his servants, "Take me away, for I am severely wounded!"[i] [24] So his servants took him out of the war chariot, carried him in his second chariot, and brought him to Jerusalem. Then he died, and they buried him in the tomb of his fathers. All Judah and Jerusalem mourned[j] for Josiah. [25] Jeremiah chanted a dirge[k] over Josiah, and all the male and female singers still speak of Josiah in their dirges today. They established them as a statute for Israel, and indeed they are written in the Dirges.

[26] The rest of the events[l] of Josiah's reign, along with his deeds of faithful love according to what is written in the law of the Lord, [27] and his words, from beginning to end, are written in the Book of the Kings of Israel and Judah.

JUDAH'S KING JEHOAHAZ

36 Then[m] the common people[D] took Jehoahaz son of Josiah and made him king in Jerusalem in place of his father.

[2] Jehoahaz[E] was twenty-three years old when he became king, and he reigned three months in Jerusalem. [3] The king of Egypt deposed him in Jerusalem and fined the land seventy-five hundred pounds[F] of silver and seventy-five pounds[G] of gold.

JUDAH'S KING JEHOIAKIM

[4] Then King Neco of Egypt made Jehoahaz's brother Eliakim king over Judah and Jerusalem and changed Eliakim's name to Jehoiakim. But Neco took his brother Jehoahaz and brought him to Egypt.[n]

[5] Jehoiakim was twenty-five years old when he became king, and he reigned eleven years in Jerusalem. He did what was evil in the sight of the Lord his God.[o] [6] Now King Nebuchadnezzar of Babylon attacked him[p] and bound him in bronze[q] shackles to take him to Babylon.[r] [7] Also Nebuchadnezzar took some of the articles of the Lord's temple to Babylon and put them in his temple in Babylon.[s]

[8] The rest of the deeds of Jehoiakim,[t] the detestable actions he committed, and what was found against him, are written in the Book of Israel's Kings. His son Jehoiachin became king in his place.

JUDAH'S KING JEHOIACHIN

[9] Jehoiachin was eighteen[H] years old[u] when he became king, and he reigned three months and ten days in Jerusalem. He did what was evil in the Lord's sight.

[A] 35:21 LXX, Syr, Tg, Vg; MT reads *Not against you, you today*   [B] 35:21 Lit *house*   [C] 35:22 LXX reads *he was determined*   [D] 36:1 Lit *the people of the land*   [E] 36:2 = Joahaz, also in v. 4   [F] 36:3 Lit *100 talents*   [G] 36:3 Lit *one talent*   [H] 36:9 Some Hb mss, LXX; 2Kg 24:8; other Hb mss read *eight*

35:20-27 Although Josiah was a godly king, God's plan to spare him from seeing the destruction of Judah involved his death.

36:2-3 The text does not explain why Neco came to Jerusalem and **deposed** the king after he'd had only **three months** on the throne, but Neco's control was obvious in that he imposed taxes on the land and installed another son of Josiah as king.

36:4-6 When he placed Jehoahaz's brother **Eliakim** on Judah's throne, **Neco** changed the new king's name to **Jehoiakim**, perhaps to demonstrate again that Egypt was now in charge in Judah. **Jehoahaz** was carried off to Egypt, no doubt to be paraded as Neco's prize and then either imprisoned or worse (36:4). Jehoiakim would be the first of four puppet kings who reigned in Judah before the exile to Babylon.

Throughout his reign, Jehoiakim was a puppet whose strings were being pulled by Judah's oppressors—first Egypt, and then Babylon when Nebuchadnezzar drove out the Egyptians in 605 BC and took control of Judah. We learn in 2 Kings 24:1 that Jehoiakim rebelled against the king of Babylon. As a result, **Nebuchadnezzar** took Jehoiakim to **Babylon** (2 Chr 36:6).

36:9-10 Jehoiakim's son **Jehoiachin** did not fare well at all, due to his **evil** choices (36:9). **Nebuchadnezzar** carried him off **to Babylon** too and made his brother **Zedekiah** king (36:10).

10 In the spring[A,a] Nebuchadnezzar sent for him and brought him to Babylon along with the valuable articles of the LORD's temple. Then he made Jehoiachin's brother Zedekiah king over Judah and Jerusalem.[b]

JUDAH'S KING ZEDEKIAH

11 Zedekiah was twenty-one years old[c] when he became king, and he reigned eleven years in Jerusalem. **12** He did what was evil in the sight of the LORD his God and did not humble himself[d] before the prophet Jeremiah at the LORD's command.[e] **13** He also rebelled against[f] King Nebuchadnezzar who had made him swear allegiance by God. He became obstinate[B,g] and hardened his heart against returning to the LORD, the God of Israel. **14** All the leaders of the priests and the people multiplied their unfaithful deeds, imitating all the detestable practices of the nations, and they defiled the LORD's temple that he had consecrated in Jerusalem.

THE DESTRUCTION OF JERUSALEM

15 But the LORD, the God of their ancestors sent word against them by the hand of his messengers, sending them time and time again,[h] for he had compassion on his people and on his dwelling place. **16** But they kept ridiculing God's messengers,[i] despising his words,[j] and scoffing at his prophets, until the LORD's wrath was so stirred up against his people that there was no remedy.[k] **17** So he brought up against them the king of the Chaldeans,[l] who killed their fit young men with the sword in the house of their sanctuary. He had no pity on young men or young women, elderly or aged; he handed them all over to him. **18** He took everything to Babylon — all the articles of God's temple, large and small, the treasures of the LORD's temple, and the treasures of the king and his officials. **19** Then the Chaldeans burned God's temple.[m] They tore down Jerusalem's wall, burned all its palaces, and destroyed all its valuable articles.

20 He deported those who escaped from the sword to Babylon, and they became servants to him and his sons until the rise of the Persian[c] kingdom.[n] **21** This fulfilled the word of the LORD through Jeremiah,[o] and the land enjoyed its Sabbath rest all the days of the desolation[p] until seventy years were fulfilled.

THE DECREE OF CYRUS

22 In the first year of King Cyrus of Persia,[q] in order to fulfill the word of the LORD spoken through[D] Jeremiah,[r] the LORD roused the spirit of King Cyrus[s] of Persia to issue a proclamation throughout his entire kingdom and also to put it in writing:

23 This is what King Cyrus of Persia says: The LORD, the God of the heavens, has given me all the kingdoms of the earth and has appointed me to build him a temple at Jerusalem in Judah. Any of his people among you may go up, and may the LORD his God be with him.

a 36:10 2Sm 11:1
b Jr 37:1
c 36:11-13 2Kg 24:18-20; Jr 52:1-3
d 36:12 2Ch 33:23
e Jr 21:3-7
f 36:13 Ezk 17:15
g 2Ch 30:8
h 36:15 Jr 7:13; 25:3,11-12
i 36:16 2Ch 30:10; Jr 5:12-13
j Pr 1:24-32
k Ezr 5:12
l 36:17 2Kg 25:1-7; Jr 52:4-11
m 36:19-20 2Kg 25:9-11; Jr 52:13-15
n 36:20 Jr 27:7
o 36:21 Jr 25:11-12; 29:10
p Lv 25:4; 26:33
q 36:22-23 Ezr 1:1-3
r 36:22 Jr 25:11-14; 27:22; 29:10-14; 33:7-10
s Is 44:28; 45:1

A 36:10 Lit *At the return of the year*   B 36:13 Lit *He stiffened his neck*   C 36:20 LXX reads *Median*   D 36:22 Lit *LORD by the mouth of*

36:11-14 Judah's royal puppet show had one final act, and it lasted a long time. **Zedekiah** was the fourth and last of the pitiful puppet kings who did their part to lead Judah into destruction (36:11-12). **36:15** The grace of God is truly amazing. In spite of their centuries of unfaithfulness, the Lord **time and time again** sent **messengers** to warn both the king and people to repent. Why? Because **he had compassion**. God's love is unfathomable.

36:21 In addition to all their other sins, the people had failed to observe the **Sabbath rest** of the land. The law had commanded that the land must lie fallow every seventh year (see Lev 25:1-7). Thus, God gave the people one year of captivity for every Sabbath rest the land had missed: **seventy years**.
36:22-23 Judah's story would've closed on this tragic note were it not for this very important word of hope and future restoration.

(The Chronicler's readers had already witnessed the fulfillment of the promise that God would raise up **King Cyrus of Persia**—the Persians eventually defeated the Babylonians.) Cyrus would have mercy on God's people and be the human instrument of their restoration to the land of Israel (36:22). In 539 BC, he issued a decree that said the Lord had **appointed** him **to build [God] a temple at Jerusalem**. Moreover, God's people were free to return to their land (36:23).

EZRA

INTRODUCTION

Author

THOUGH THE BOOKS OF EZRA and Nehemiah are separate writings in English Bibles, they were regarded as a single book in the Hebrew Bible and were not separated in Hebrew Bibles until the fifteenth century. The early Christian theologian Origen separated Ezra to Nehemiah into two books, and Jerome followed suit with the Latin translation of the Bible, the Vulgate.

Ezra is an anonymous work, but ancient Jewish sources attribute them to Ezra. Some scholars believe the book was written by the Chronicler, the author of 1–2 Chronicles, because 2 Chronicles 36:22-23 and much of Ezra 1:1-3 are identical. Thus, Ezra may have authored both 1–2 Chronicles and Ezra.

Historical Background

Ezra was a priest and scribe sent by Artaxerxes the Persian king to Jerusalem in 458 BC (that is, in "the seventh year of King Artaxerxes," Ezra 7:7) to appoint magistrates and judges and to teach God's law in Israel (see Ezra 7:1-28).

Message and Purpose

The book of Ezra is about spiritual restoration. It deals with the restoration of the temple by Israel's people after their return from Babylonian captivity, which had been a result of their persistent disobedience and idolatry. God had made a kingdom promise to them that if they would return to him, he would bring them back to their land.

Ezra the priest led the second group of exiles back to Israel. He focused on reestablishing the temple and its sacrificial system, making it clear that the worship of God's people would only be effective if they dedicated themselves to obeying God's law. He challenged them that if they would get serious with the Lord, they would experience his covenantal blessings. But this required Israel to stop compromising with God's enemies and to turn from idolatry. Israel needed to be a people separated to God to experience his blessings and be restored to his kingdom promises.

The message of Ezra is that when we depart from God, we lose our experience of him. But when we return to him, he will restore us to fellowship with him.

VIDEO INTRO

www.bhpublishinggroup.com/qr/te/15_00

Outline

THE DECREE OF CYRUS

1 In[a] the first year of King Cyrus of Persia, in order to fulfill the word of the LORD spoken through Jeremiah,[b] the LORD roused the spirit[c] of King Cyrus to issue a proclamation throughout his entire kingdom and to put it in writing:

2 This is what King Cyrus of Persia says: "The LORD, the God of the heavens, has given me all the kingdoms of the earth and has appointed me to build him a house at Jerusalem in Judah.[d] 3 Any of his people among you, may his God be with him, and may he go to Jerusalem in Judah and build the house of the LORD, the God of Israel,[e] the God who is in Jerusalem. 4 Let every survivor,[f] wherever he resides, be assisted by the men of that region with silver, gold, goods, and livestock, along with a freewill offering for the house of God in Jerusalem."

RETURN FROM EXILE

5 So the family heads of Judah and Benjamin, along with the priests and Levites — everyone whose spirit God had roused[g] — prepared to go up and rebuild the LORD's house in Jerusalem. 6 All their neighbors supported them[A,h] with silver articles, gold, goods, livestock, and valuables, in addition to all that was given as a freewill offering. 7 King Cyrus also brought out the articles of the LORD's house that Nebuchadnezzar had taken from Jerusalem and had placed in the house of his gods.[i] 8 King Cyrus of Persia had them brought out under the supervision of Mithredath the treasurer, who counted them out to Sheshbazzar the prince of Judah.[j] 9 This was the inventory:

30 gold basins, 1,000 silver basins,
29 silver knives, 10 30 gold bowls,
410 various[B] silver bowls,
and 1,000 other articles.

11 The gold and silver articles totaled 5,400. Sheshbazzar brought all of them when the exiles went up from Babylon to Jerusalem.

THE EXILES WHO RETURNED

2 These[k] now are the people of the province who came from those captive exiles King Nebuchadnezzar of Babylon[c] had deported to Babylon.[l] They returned to Jerusalem and Judah, each to his own town. 2 They came with Zerubbabel,[m] Jeshua,[n] Nehemiah, Seraiah,[o] Reelaiah, Mordecai, Bilshan, Mispar, Bigvai, Rehum, and Baanah.

The number of the Israelite men included[D]

3	Parosh's descendants[p]	2,172
4	Shephatiah's descendants	372
5	Arah's descendants	775
6	Pahath-moab's descendants: Jeshua's and Joab's descendants	2,812
7	Elam's descendants	1,254
8	Zattu's descendants	945
9	Zaccai's descendants	760
10	Bani's descendants	642
11	Bebai's descendants	623
12	Azgad's descendants	1,222
13	Adonikam's descendants[q]	666
14	Bigvai's descendants	2,056
15	Adin's descendants	454
16	Ater's descendants: of Hezekiah	98
17	Bezai's descendants	323

a1:1 2Ch 36:22-23
b Jr 25:12; 29:10-14
c Ezr 7:27
d1:2-3 Is 44:28; 45:1,13; Dn 9:17
e1:3 Dn 6:26
f1:4 Neh 1:2; Is 10:20-22
g1:5 Ezr 1:1
h1:6 Ezr 6:22
i1:7 2Ch 36:7,10,18; Dn 1:2; 5:2-3
j1:8 Ezr 5:14,16
k2:1-70 Neh 7:6-73
l2:1 2Ch 36:17-20
m2:2 1Ch 3:19; Ezr 3:2; Hg 1:1; Zch 4:6
n Hg 1:1; Zch 3:1-10
o Neh 12:1
p2:3 Ezr 8:3; 10:25; Neh 3:25
q2:13 Ezr 8:13

A1:6 Lit strengthened their hands   B1:10 Or similar   C2:1 Nebuchadnezzar reigned 605–562 BC   D2:2 Lit the men of the people of Israel

1:1 Ezra begins where 2 Chronicles ends (see 2 Chr 36:22-23). **Jeremiah** had prophesied that the Jews would return to the promised land when the seventy years of exile that God had decreed for them were fulfilled (see Jer 29:10). Furthermore, the prophet Isaiah had mentioned **Cyrus** by name, announcing that he would release the Jews and send them home (see Isa 44:28–45:13). These things were foretold far in advance of Cyrus's appearance on the world scene.
1:3-4 Many Jews who had prospered in Persia after its conquest of Babylon decided to stay put, but others returned to their homeland. Many see this event as a second exodus of sorts, since in it God's people again were given permission to leave their land of bondage for the promised land and were richly supplied for the journey by the gifts of **the men of that region** (1:4).
1:5 During the days of moral decay in Jerusalem before the exile, the spiritual and

civil leaders were the prime culprits behind the problems. But in Ezra's day, the leaders aligned themselves with God's agenda. His kingdom had become their priority. If we are to see lasting change in our churches and culture, we need leaders who will allow the same.
1:7 These **articles** were holy, consecrated to the Lord, and it had been an abomination to house them in a pagan temple.
1:8 **Sheshbazzar the prince of Judah** seems to be the leader King Cyrus designated for the return and temple rebuilding. However, Zerubbabel is the generally acknowledged leader. Sheshbazzar is only mentioned three other times in Ezra (1:11; 5:14, 16), so it's possible he died soon after arriving in Jerusalem and was succeeded by Zerubbabel. In any case, the former was the one in charge of taking the temple articles back to Jerusalem (1:11).

1:9-11 Though the numbers listed in verses 9-10 do not add up to the **5,400** in verse 11, it is possible that the first list includes only the larger and more important items.
2:2 These are the leaders of this early return.
2:3-64 This list was meant to confirm that the returnees were true Israelites. Many consider it to be tedious reading, but Ezra 2 would have been an encouragement to the original readers, who were decades removed from this first return in 539 BC and were part of the second return under Ezra. It would have been a blessing to them to read the names of their families and ancestors among those who were willing to leave the safety and the known of Persia to trek back to Israel, to the unknown, and to rebuild the temple out of devotion to the Lord. The reminder of their ancestors' commitment, in fact, would inspire Ezra's readers to renew their own faithfulness to the Mosaic law, as happened in Ezra 9–10.

a 2:21 Mc 5:2; Mt 2:1,6
b 2:26 Jr 31:15; Mt 2:18
c 2:28 Gn 12:8; Jos 7:2; 8:9
d 2:34 Jos 4:19; 5:13; 6:1-25
e 2:41 1Ch 25:1; 2Ch 5:12; 35:15
f 2:42 1Ch 9:17-32; Neh 12:25-26
g 2:43 Ezr 8:20
h 2:55 Neh 11:3

18	Jorah's descendants	112
19	Hashum's descendants	223
20	Gibbar's descendants	95
21	Bethlehem's*a* people	123
22	Netophah's men	56
23	Anathoth's men	128
24	Azmaveth's people	42
25	Kiriatharim's, Chephirah's, and Beeroth's people	743
26	Ramah's*b* and Geba's people	621
27	Michmas's men	122
28	Bethel's and Ai's*c* men	223
29	Nebo's people	52
30	Magbish's people	156
31	the other Elam's people	1,254
32	Harim's people	320
33	Lod's, Hadid's, and Ono's people	725
34	Jericho's*d* people	345
35	Senaah's people	3,630

36 The priests included Jedaiah's descendants of the house of Jeshua 973
37 Immer's descendants 1,052
38 Pashhur's descendants 1,247
39 and Harim's descendants 1,017

40 The Levites included Jeshua's and Kadmiel's descendants from Hodaviah's descendants 74

41 The singers included Asaph's*e* descendants 128

42 The gatekeepers'*f* descendants included Shallum's descendants, Ater's descendants, Talmon's descendants, Akkub's descendants, Hatita's descendants, Shobai's descendants, in all 139

43 The temple servants*g* included Ziha's descendants, Hasupha's descendants, Tabbaoth's descendants, **44** Keros's descendants, Siaha's descendants, Padon's descendants, **45** Lebanah's descendants, Hagabah's descendants, Akkub's descendants, **46** Hagab's descendants, Shalmai's*A* descendants, Hanan's descendants,

47 Giddel's descendants, Gahar's descendants, Reaiah's descendants, **48** Rezin's descendants, Nekoda's descendants, Gazzam's descendants, **49** Uzza's descendants, Paseah's descendants, Besai's descendants, **50** Asnah's descendants, Meunim's*B* descendants, Nephusim's*C* descendants, **51** Bakbuk's descendants, Hakupha's descendants, Harhur's descendants, **52** Bazluth's descendants, Mehida's descendants, Harsha's descendants, **53** Barkos's descendants, Sisera's descendants, Temah's descendants, **54** Neziah's descendants, and Hatipha's descendants.

55 The descendants of Solomon's servants*h* included Sotai's descendants, Hassophereth's descendants, Peruda's descendants, **56** Jaalah's descendants, Darkon's descendants, Giddel's descendants, **57** Shephatiah's descendants, Hattil's descendants, Pochereth-hazzebaim's descendants, and Ami's descendants. **58** All the temple servants and the descendants of Solomon's servants 392.

59 The following are those who came from Tel-melah, Tel-harsha, Cherub, Addan, and Immer but were unable to prove that their ancestral families*D* and their lineage were Israelite: **60** Delaiah's descendants, Tobiah's descendants, Nekoda's descendants 652 **61** and from the descendants of the priests: the descendants of Hobaiah, the descendants of Hakkoz, the descendants of Barzillai — who had taken a wife from the daughters of Barzillai the Gileadite and who bore their name. **62** These searched for their entries in the genealogical records, but they could not be found, so they were disqualified from the priesthood. **63** The

A 2:46 Alt Hb tradition reads *Shamlai's*   *B* 2:50 Alt Hb tradition reads *Meinim's*   *C* 2:50 Alt Hb tradition reads *Nephisim's*   *D* 2:59 Lit *that the house of their fathers*

governor[a] ordered them not to eat the most holy things until there was a priest who could consult the Urim and Thummim.[b]

64 The whole combined assembly numbered 42,360
65 not including their 7,337 male and female servants, and their 200 male and female singers.[c]
66 They had 736 horses, 245 mules,
67 435 camels, and 6,720 donkeys.

GIFTS FOR THE WORK

68 After they arrived at the LORD's house in Jerusalem, some of the family heads gave freewill offerings[d] for the house of God in order to have it rebuilt on its original site. 69 Based on what they could give, they gave 61,000 gold coins,[A] 6,250 pounds[B] of silver, and 100 priestly garments to the treasury[e] for the project. 70 The priests, Levites, singers, gatekeepers, temple servants, and some of the people settled in their towns, and the rest of Israel settled in their towns.[f]

SACRIFICE RESTORED

3 When the seventh month arrived,[g] and the Israelites were in their towns, the people gathered as one in Jerusalem.[h] 2 Jeshua son of Jozadak and his brothers the priests along with Zerubbabel son of Shealtiel[i] and his brothers began to build the altar of Israel's God in order to offer burnt offerings on it, as it is written in the law of Moses, the man of God.[j] 3 They set up the altar on its foundation and offered burnt offerings for the morning and evening on it to the LORD even though they feared the surrounding peoples.[k] 4 They celebrated the Festival of Shelters as prescribed, and offered burnt offerings each day, based on the number specified by ordinance for each festival day.[l] 5 After that, they offered the regular burnt offering and the offerings for the beginning of each month[c,m] and for all the LORD's appointed holy occasions, as well as the freewill offerings brought to[D] the LORD.

6 On the first day of the seventh month they began to offer burnt offerings to the LORD,[n] even though the foundation of the LORD's temple had not yet been laid. 7 They gave money to the stonecutters and artisans, and gave food, drink, and oil to the people of Sidon and Tyre, so they would bring cedar wood from Lebanon to Joppa by sea,[o] according to the authorization given them by King Cyrus of Persia.[p]

REBUILDING THE TEMPLE

8 In the second month of the second year after they arrived at God's house in Jerusalem, Zerubbabel son of Shealtiel, Jeshua son of Jozadak,[q] and the rest of their brothers, including the priests, the Levites, and all who had returned to Jerusalem from the captivity, began to build. They appointed the Levites who were twenty years old or more to supervise the work on the LORD's house.[r] 9 Jeshua with his sons and brothers, Kadmiel with his sons, and the sons of Judah[E] and of Henadad, with their sons and brothers, the Levites,[s] joined together to supervise those working on the house of God.

TEMPLE FOUNDATION COMPLETED

10 When the builders had laid the foundation of the LORD's temple, the priests, dressed in their robes and holding trumpets, and the Levites descended from Asaph,[t] holding cymbals, took their positions to praise the LORD, as King David of Israel had instructed.[u] 11 They sang with praise and thanksgiving to the LORD: "For he is good; his faithful love to Israel endures forever."[v] Then all the people gave a great shout of praise to the LORD because the foundation of the LORD's house had been laid.[w] 12 But many of the older priests, Levites, and family heads, who had seen the first

[a]2:63 Ezr 6:7; Neh 5:14; Hg 1:1
[b]Ex 28:30; Lv 8:8; Nm 27:21; Neh 7:65
[c]2:65 2Ch 35:25
[d]2:68 Nm 15:3; Ezr 1:4
[e]2:69 Ezr 8:33-34
[f]2:70 1Ch 9:2; Neh 11:3
[g]3:1 Lv 23:23-43; Nm 29:1-38
[h]Neh 7:73–8:1
[i]3:2 Ezr 3:8; 5:2; Hg 1:1; 2:21,23
[j]Ex 27:1-8
[k]3:3 Ezr 4:4
[l]3:4 Lv 23:33-43; Nm 29:12-38; Neh 8:13-18; Zch 14:16

[m]3:5 Nm 28:11-14; 1Sm 20:5
[n]3:6 Lv 23:23-25; Nm 29:1-6
[o]3:7 1Kg 5:1-11; 2Ch 2:3-16
[p]Ezr 1:2; 6:3-5
[q]3:8 Ezr 4:3; 5:2; Hg 1:1
[r]1Ch 23:4,24
[s]3:9 Ezr 2:40
[t]3:10 Ezr 2:41
[u]1Ch 6:31; 25:1,6; 2Ch 29:25-26; Neh 12:24,45
[v]3:11 1Ch 16:34; 2Ch 5:13; 7:3; Neh 12:31
[w]Hg 2:18; Zch 4:9

[A]2:69 Or drachmas, or darics   [B]2:69 Lit 5,000 minas   [C]3:5 Lit for the new moons   [D]3:5 Lit well as those of everyone making a freewill offering to
[E]3:9 Or Hodaviah; Neh 7:43; 1 Esdras 5:58

3:2 **Jeshua** was a descendant of Aaron, and **Zerubbabel** was in David's line; thus, the people were guided by authorized leaders.

Since it was the Jews' failure to worship the Lord and serve him only that had led to the destruction of the temple and the Babylonian exile, the returnees knew that the temple had to have priority. And even before it was rebuilt, **the altar** itself was. These returnees wanted to make sure they were faithful to the Mosaic covenant so that they might worship God rightly—unlike their ancestors.

3:3 In other words, they had come to embrace an important lesson: we are to fear God more than man.

3:4 During **the Festival of Shelters** the people were to erect temporary booths to remind them of how their ancestors had lived during their trek through the wilderness after leaving Egypt. For these Israelites who had returned from Babylon to Jerusalem in a second exodus, this celebration was a reminder of God's provision.

3:10 The temple's **foundation** was begun seventy years after Nebuchadnezzar's first

deportation of Jews to Babylon in 605 BC. Some scholars count the beginning of work on the temple as the end of the seventy-year Babylonian exile, while others begin the count with the destruction of Jerusalem and the final deportation to Babylon in 586 BC, ending with the completion of the temple in 515 BC.

3:12-13 While it was a joy to be building God's temple again, those who remembered what once had been knew their efforts could not achieve the structure's former glory.

a 3:12 Hg 2:3
b 3:13 Ps 126:5-6
c 4:1 Neh 2:19-20
d Ezr 1:11; 2:1
e 4:2 2Kg 17:24,27-32;
    19:37; Is 37:38
f 4:3 Neh 2:20
g Ezr 1:1-4
h 4:4 Ezr 3:3
i 4:5 Neh 6:12-13; 13:2
    Ezr 5:5; 6:1
k 4:6 Est 1:1; Dn 9:1
    Ezr 3:3
m 4:7 Ezr 7:1; Neh 2:1
n Dn 1:4; 2:4
o 4:8-9 Ezr 4:17,23-24

p 4:9 Neh 1:1; Est 1:2;
    Dn 8:2
q 4:10 2Kg 17:24
r 4:10-11 Ezr 4:16-17,20
s 4:13 Ezr 4:16,21; Neh 1:3
    Ezr 4:20; 7:24
u 4:15 Ezr 5:17; 6:1

temple, wept loudly when they saw the foundation of this temple,*a* but many others shouted joyfully. **13** The people could not distinguish the sound of the joyful shouting from that of the*A* weeping,*b* because the people were shouting so loudly. And the sound was heard far away.

OPPOSITION TO REBUILDING THE TEMPLE

4 When the enemies of Judah and Benjamin*c* heard that the returned exiles*B,d* were building a temple for the Lord, the God of Israel, **2** they approached Zerubbabel and the family heads and said to them, "Let us build with you, for we also worship your God and have been sacrificing to him*c* since the time King Esar-haddon of Assyria brought us here."*e*

3 But Zerubbabel, Jeshua, and the other heads of Israel's families answered them, "You may have no part with us in building a house for our God,*f* since we alone will build it for the Lord, the God of Israel, as King Cyrus, the king of Persia has commanded us."*g* **4** Then the people who were already in the land*D* discouraged*E* the people of Judah and made them afraid*h* to build. **5** They also bribed officials to act against them to frustrate their plans*i* throughout the reign of King Cyrus of Persia and until the reign of King Darius of Persia.*j*

OPPOSITION TO REBUILDING THE CITY

6 At the beginning of the reign of Ahasuerus,*k* the people who were already in the land*i* wrote an accusation against the residents of Judah and Jerusalem. **7** During the time of King Artaxerxes of Persia,*m* Bishlam, Mithredath, Tabeel and the rest of his colleagues wrote to King Artaxerxes. The letter was written in Aramaic*n* and translated.*F*

8 Rehum the chief deputy and Shimshai the scribe*o* wrote a letter to King Artaxerxes concerning Jerusalem as follows:

9 From Rehum*G* the chief deputy, Shimshai the scribe, and the rest of their colleagues — the judges and magistrates*H* from Tripolis, Persia, Erech, Babylon, Susa*p* (that is, the people of Elam),*i* **10** and the rest of the peoples whom the great and illustrious Ashurbanipal*j* deported and settled in the cities of Samaria*q* and the region west of the Euphrates River.*r*

11 This is the text of the letter they sent to him:

To King Artaxerxes from your servants, the men from the region west of the Euphrates River:

12 Let it be known to the king that the Jews who came from you have returned to us at Jerusalem. They are rebuilding that rebellious and evil city, finishing its walls, and repairing its foundations. **13** Let it now be known to the king that if that city is rebuilt and its walls are finished,*s* they will not pay tribute, duty, or land tax,*t* and the royal revenue*i* will suffer. **14** Since we have taken an oath of loyalty to the king,*k* and it is not right for us to witness his dishonor, we have sent to inform the king **15** that a search should be made in your fathers' record books.*u* In these record books you will discover and verify that the city is a rebellious city, harmful to kings and provinces. There have been revolts in it since ancient times. That is why this city was destroyed. **16** We advise the king that if this city is rebuilt and its walls are finished, you will not have any possession west of the Euphrates.

ARTAXERXES'S REPLY

17 The king sent a reply to his chief deputy Rehum, Shimshai the scribe, and the rest of their colleagues living in Samaria and elsewhere in the region west of the Euphrates River:
Greetings.

A 3:13 Lit *the people*   *B* 4:1 Lit *the sons of the exile*   *C* 4:2 Alt Hb tradition reads *have not been sacrificing*   *D* 4:4 Lit *people of the land*, also in v. 6
E 4:4 Lit *weakened the hands of*   *F* 4:7 Ezr 4:8–6:18 is written in Aramaic.   *G* 4:9 Lit *Then Rehum*   *H* 4:9 Or *ambassadors*   *i* 4:9,13 Aramaic obscure
J 4:10 Lit *Osnappar*   *K* 4:14 Lit *have eaten the salt of the palace*

4:1-5 "The surrounding peoples" (3:3) who didn't want to see the Jews rebuild the temple soon made their presence felt. They first tried to fake friendship with the returnees (4:1-2). But **Zerubbabel** and the other leaders shut this tactic down with a blunt, "Thanks, but no thanks" (4:3). Rebuffed, the locals thus **discouraged the people** from building and **bribed officials** to **frustrate**

the work (4:4-5). (Clearly, they were no friends of the Jews.)
4:6 Reference to Judah's enemies led Ezra to insert a parenthetical account about other trouble (4:6-23) that probably happened before Nehemiah returned and completed rebuilding Jerusalem's walls. Here the issue was the rebuilding of Jerusalem proper, with the opposition beginning in the reign of the

Persian king **Ahasuerus**. The **people who were already in the land** were the descendants of the foreigners whom the Assyrians had imported into Samaria after the fall of the northern kingdom of Israel in 722 BC (see 4:10; cf. 4:2). They were pagans who intermarried with the remaining Jews and mixed the worship of the Lord with their idolatry.

18 The letter you sent us has been translated and read[A,a] in my presence. **19** I issued a decree and a search was conducted. It was discovered that this city has had uprisings against kings since ancient times, and there have been rebellions and revolts in it. **20** Powerful kings have also ruled over Jerusalem and exercised authority over the whole region west of the Euphrates River, and tribute, duty, and land tax were paid to them. **21** Therefore, issue an order for these men to stop, so that this city will not be rebuilt until a further decree has been pronounced by me.[b] **22** See that you not neglect this matter. Otherwise, the damage will increase and the royal interests[B] will suffer.

23 As soon as the text of King Artaxerxes's letter was read to Rehum, Shimshai the scribe, and their colleagues,[c] they immediately went to the Jews in Jerusalem and forcibly stopped them.

REBUILDING OF THE TEMPLE RESUMED

24 Now the construction of God's house in Jerusalem had stopped and remained at a standstill until the second year of the reign of King Darius of Persia.[d] **5 1** But when the prophets Haggai and Zechariah son of Iddo[e] prophesied to the Jews who were in Judah and Jerusalem, in the name of the God of Israel who was over them, **2** Zerubbabel son of Shealtiel and Jeshua son of Jozadak[f] began to rebuild God's house in Jerusalem. The prophets of God[g] were with them, helping them. **3** At that time Tattenai the governor of the region west of the Euphrates River, Shethar-bozenai, and their colleagues[h] came to the Jews and asked, "Who gave you the order to rebuild this temple and finish this structure?"[C,i] **4** They also asked them, "What are the names of the workers[D] who are constructing this building?" **5** But God was watching[E] over[j] the Jewish elders. These men wouldn't stop them until a report was sent to Darius, so that they could receive written instructions about this matter.

THE LETTER TO DARIUS

6 This is the text of the letter that Tattenai the governor of the region west of the Euphrates River, Shethar-bozenai, and their colleagues, the officials in the region, sent to King Darius. **7** They sent him a report, written as follows:

To King Darius:

All greetings.

8 Let it be known to the king that we went to the house of the great God in the province of Judah. It is being built with cut[F] stones, and its beams are being set in the walls. This work is being done diligently and succeeding through the people's efforts.[k] **9** So we questioned the elders and asked, "Who gave you the order to rebuild this temple and finish this structure?" **10** We also asked them for their names, so that we could write down the names of their leaders for your information.

11 This is the reply they gave us:

We are the servants of the God of the heavens and earth, and we are rebuilding the temple that was built many years ago, which a great king of Israel built and finished.[l] **12** But since our fathers angered the God of the heavens, he handed them over to King Nebuchadnezzar of Babylon, the Chaldean, who destroyed this temple and deported the people to Babylon.[m] **13** However, in the first year of King Cyrus of Babylon, he issued a decree

a 4:18 Neh 8:8
b 4:21 Neh 2:5,7-8
c 4:23 Ezr 4:8-10,17
d 4:24 Ezr 4:1-5; Hg 1:1,14
e 5:1 Ezr 6:14; Hg 1:1; Zch 1:1
f 5:2 Ezr 3:2,8,10
g Ezr 6:14
h 5:3 Ezr 6:6,13
i Ezr 1:1-4; 5:9,13; 6:3

j 5:5 Ezr 7:6,9,28; 8:18,22,31
k 5:8 Ezr 6:3-4
l 5:11 1Kg 6:1,37-38
m 5:12 2Ch 36:19-20

A 4:18 Or *been read clearly*   B 4:22 Lit *the kings*   C 5:3 Or *finish its furnishings*, also in v. 9   D 5:4 One Aramaic ms, LXX, Syr; MT reads *Then we told them exactly what the names of the men were*   E 5:5 Lit *But the eye of their God was*   F 5:8 Or *huge*

4:21-22 The Jews' enemies knew that if they could neutralize the construction, they could neutralize the temple, the walls, the city, and the community. And if they were successful in all this, the impact of God's people would be neutralized. In other words, the enemies had an anti-kingdom agenda, and it was successful for a while.

4:24 This verse jumps backward in time, picking up the narrative where Ezra left off at 4:5. Here we learn that the temple work was stopped **until** 520 BC. As much as eighteen years had passed.

5:1-2 Haggai and Zechariah, also featured in the biblical books titled with their names, called God's people back to the work on his house (5:1). Thus, the spiritual and civil leaders were renewed in their desire to finish the work God had given.

5:3-5 Tattenai was taking **names** so he could report the Jewish leaders to King Darius (5:5).

5:8 The regional governor was not making any particular claims about **the great God**. To acknowledge that certain gods had control over certain lands and peoples was a belief very common in the ancient world.

5:11 The Jewish leaders identified themselves as **servants of the God of the heavens and earth**. What a person does flows from who he or she is.

5:12 In other words, the Babylonian king hadn't defeated them because his gods were more powerful. Rather, the God of Judah had delivered them into Nebuchadnezzar's hands because of their disobedience.

5:13-15 The Jewish people in Jerusalem pointed out that far from acting as rebels, they were acting under the orders of an earlier Persian ruler, **Cyrus**.

[a] 5:13 2Ch 36:22-23;
Ezr 1:1-4
[b] 5:14 2Ch 36:7,10,18; Ezr
1:7; Dn 5:2-3
[c] Ezr 1:8,11
[d] 5:15 Ezr 6:5
[e] 5:16 Ezr 3:10
[f] Ezr 5:1-5
[g] 5:17 2Ch 36:22-23;
Ezr 1:1-4
[h] Ezr 6:1-12
[i] 6:1 Ezr 5:17
[j] Ezr 4:15
[k] 6:2 Dn 9:1; Ac 2:9
[l] 6:3 2Ch 36:22-23; Ezr
1:1-4
[m] 1Kg 6:2
[n] 6:4 1Kg 6:36; Ezr 5:8
[o] Ezr 3:7

[p] 6:5 Ezr 1:7
[q] 6:6 Ezr 5:3,6; 6:13
[r] 6:7 Neh 5:14; Hg 1:1
[s] 6:8 Ezr 7:20
[t] 6:9 Ezr 7:17,20-22
[u] 6:10 Ezr 7:23; 1Tm 2:1-2
[v] 6:11 Est 2:23; 9:14
[w] 6:12 Dt 12:5; 2Ch 6:2

to rebuild the house of God.[a] [14] He also took from the temple in Babylon the gold and silver articles of God's house that Nebuchadnezzar had taken from the temple in Jerusalem and carried them to the temple in Babylon.[b] He released them from the temple in Babylon to a man named Sheshbazzar, the governor by the appointment of King Cyrus.[c] [15] Cyrus told him, "Take these articles, put them in the temple in Jerusalem, and let the house of God be rebuilt on its original site."[d] [16] Then this same Sheshbazzar came and laid the foundation of God's house in Jerusalem.[e] It has been under construction from that time until now,[f] but it has not been completed.

[17] So if it pleases the king, let a search of the royal archives[A] in Babylon be conducted to see if it is true that a decree was issued by King Cyrus to rebuild the house of God in Jerusalem.[g] Let the king's decision regarding this matter be sent to us.[h]

DARIUS'S SEARCH

6 King Darius gave the order, and they searched[i] in the library of Babylon in the archives.[B,j] [2] But it was in the fortress of Ecbatana in the province of Media[k] that a scroll was found with this record written on it:
[3] In the first year of King Cyrus, he issued a decree[l] concerning the house of God in Jerusalem:

Let the house be rebuilt as a place for offering sacrifices, and let its original foundations be retained.[c] Its height is to be ninety feet[D] and its width ninety feet,[m] [4] with three layers of cut[E] stones and one of timber.[n] The cost is to be paid from the royal treasury.[F,o] [5] The gold and silver articles of God's house that Nebuchadnezzar took from the temple in Jerusalem and carried to Babylon must also be returned. They

are to be brought to the temple in Jerusalem where they belong[G] and put into the house of God.[p]

DARIUS'S DECREE

[6] Therefore, you must stay away from that place, Tattenai governor of the region west of the Euphrates River, Shethar-bozenai, and your[H] colleagues, the officials in the region.[q] [7] Leave the construction of the house of God alone. Let the governor[r] and elders of the Jews rebuild this house of God on its original site.

[8] I hereby issue a decree concerning what you are to do, so that the elders of the Jews can rebuild the house of God:

The cost is to be paid in full to these men out of the royal revenues[s] from the taxes of the region west of the Euphrates River, so that the work will not stop. [9] Whatever is needed — young bulls, rams, and lambs for burnt offerings to the God of the heavens, or wheat, salt, wine, and oil, as requested by the priests in Jerusalem — let it be given to them every day without fail,[t] [10] so that they can offer sacrifices of pleasing aroma to the God of the heavens and pray for the life of the king and his sons.[u]

[11] I also issue a decree concerning any man who interferes with this directive:

Let a beam be torn from his house and raised up; he will be impaled on it, and his house will be made into a garbage dump because of this offense.[v] [12] May the God who caused his name to dwell there[w] overthrow any king or people who dares[I] to harm or interfere with this house of God in Jerusalem. I, Darius, have issued the decree. Let it be carried out diligently.

[13] Then Tattenai governor of the region west of the Euphrates River, Shethar-boz-

---

[A] 5:17 Lit *treasure house*   [B] 6:1 Lit *Babylon where the treasures were stored*   [C] 6:3 Lit *be brought forth*   [D] 6:3 Lit *60 cubits*   [E] 6:4 Or *huge*   [F] 6:4 Lit *the king's house*   [G] 6:5 Lit *Jerusalem, to its place*,   [H] 6:6 Lit *their*   [I] 6:12 Lit *who stretches out its hand*

5:17 Royal documents were carefully recorded and preserved, so the Jews were confident that they were on solid ground.
6:1-5 That the needed **scroll was found** set in motion a chain of events that led to the temple's completion (6:2).
6:6-9 Thus, **Tattenai** (6:6) was ordered to leave the Jews alone *and* to give them all

the funds they needed from his own coffers. This statement is a reminder that God knows how to take the resources of the wicked to accomplish the work of his kingdom.
6:10 It's doubtful that Darius was a true believer in Israel's God, but clearly he was happy to have the Jews **pray** on his behalf.

6:11-12 This account of God's provision through a threat of royal protection had to be a great encouragement to Ezra's readers; it was evidence of the unending faithfulness of their God.

enai, and their colleagues[a] diligently carried out what King Darius had decreed. [14] So the Jewish elders continued successfully with the building under the prophesying of Haggai the prophet and Zechariah son of Iddo.[b] They finished the building according to the command of the God of Israel and the decrees of Cyrus,[c] Darius, and King Artaxerxes[d] of Persia. [15] This house was completed on the third day of the month of Adar[e] in the sixth year of the reign of King Darius.

TEMPLE DEDICATION AND THE PASSOVER

[16] Then the Israelites, including the priests, the Levites, and the rest of the exiles, celebrated the dedication of the house of God with joy. [17] For the dedication of God's house they offered one hundred bulls, two hundred rams, and four hundred lambs, as well as twelve male goats[f] as a sin offering for all Israel — one for each Israelite tribe. [18] They also appointed the priests by their divisions and the Levites by their groups to the service of God in Jerusalem, according to what is written in the book of Moses.[g]

[19] The exiles[h] observed the Passover[i] on the fourteenth day of the first month. [20] All of the priests and Levites were ceremonially clean, because they had purified themselves. They killed the Passover lamb for themselves, their priestly brothers, and all the exiles.[j] [21] The Israelites who had returned from exile[k] ate it, together with all who had separated themselves from the uncleanness of the Gentiles of the land[A,l] in order to worship the LORD, the God of

Israel. [22] They observed the Festival of Unleavened Bread for seven days[m] with joy, because the LORD had made them joyful, having changed the Assyrian king's attitude toward them, so that he supported them[B] in the work on the house of the God of Israel.[n]

EZRA'S ARRIVAL

7 After these events, during the reign of King Artaxerxes[o] of Persia, Ezra — Seraiah's[p] son, Azariah's son, Hilkiah's[q] son, [2] Shallum's son, Zadok's[r] son, Ahitub's son, [3] Amariah's son, Azariah's son, Meraioth's son, [4] Zerahiah's son, Uzzi's son, Bukki's son, [5] Abishua's son, Phinehas's son, Eleazar's son, the chief priest Aaron's son[s] [6] — came up from Babylon. He was a scribe skilled in the law of Moses,[t] which the LORD, the God of Israel, had given. The king had granted him everything he requested[u] because the hand of the LORD his God was on him.[v] [7] Some of the Israelites, priests, Levites, singers, gatekeepers, and temple servants[w] accompanied him to Jerusalem in the seventh year of King Artaxerxes.

[8] Ezra[c] came to Jerusalem in the fifth month, during the seventh year of the king. [9] He began the journey from Babylon on the first day of the first month[x] and arrived in Jerusalem on the first day of the fifth month[y] since the gracious hand of his God was on him.[z] [10] Now Ezra had determined in his heart to study the law of the

[a]6:13 Ezr 5:3,6; 6:6
[b]6:14 Ezr 5:1; Hg 1:1; Zch 1:1
[c]Ezr 1:1-4; 6:3-5
[d]Ezr 7:12-26
[e]6:15 Est 3:7
[f]6:16-17 2Ch 7:4-5
[g]6:18 Ex 29; Nm 18; 1Ch 24
[h]6:19 Ezr 1:11; 2:1
[i]Ex 12:1-11; Nm 28:16
[j]6:20 2Ch 30:15-17
[k]6:21 Ezr 1:11; 2:1
[l]Ezr 9:11; Neh 10:28

[m]6:22 Ex 12:14-20; Dt 16:3-8
[n]Ezr 6:8-12
[o]7:1 Ezr 4:7; 6:14; Neh 2:1
[p]2Kg 25:18-21; Jr 52:24-27
[q]2Kg 22:4; 23:4
[r]7:2 1Sm 8:17; 1Kg 1:7-8; 2:35
[s]7:1-5 1Ch 6:3-15
[t]7:6 Ezr 7:11-12,21
[u]Neh 2:4-8
[v]Ezr 7:28; 8:22; Neh 2:8,18
[w]7:7 Ezr 2:1-58; Neh 7:6-60
[x]7:9 Ezr 8:15,21,31
[y]Ezr 8:32
[z]Ezr 7:28; 8:18,31; Neh 2:8,18

A6:21 Lit land to them   B6:22 Lit strengthened their hands   C7:8 LXX, Syr, Vg read They

---

6:14-15 Notice the importance of **the prophesying of Haggai the prophet and Zechariah** to the success of the work (6:14). Allowing God's word to lead the way was necessary to keep the workers from becoming discouraged or losing focus. These prophets faithfully reminded the people of the urgency and importance of their work in God's eyes. Thus, the temple was completed in the spring of 515 BC, twenty-one years after the work had begun (6:15).
6:22 The **Festival of Unleavened Bread** reminded the Jews to separate themselves from sin and defilement by removing all leaven (that is, yeast) from their bread and even their houses.
7:1-5 Chapter 7 leaps ahead several decades to the second return under Ezra himself. **During the reign of King Artaxerxes of Persia, Ezra** — the book's namesake — came to Jerusalem in 458 BC (7:1). His genealogy is provided to establish his priestly pedigree and to show that he descended from Aaron (7:1-5).
7:6 Ezra's expertise **in the law of Moses** would become vital to the next events recorded

because though God's people were out of Babylon, there was still a lot of Babylon (that is, idolatry and immorality) in God's people. Ezra's primary ministry in Judah would be resolving this.
     That **the hand of the LORD his God was on him** is the explanation for Ezra's success. In fact, this idea is the key to all that happened in the return of God's people from exile and the rebuilding of the temple, from the first return under Zerubbabel to Nehemiah's building of the wall around Jerusalem. God's "hand" being on this process is mentioned numerous times in Ezra (7:6, 9, 28; 8:18, 22) and twice in Nehemiah (see 2:8, 18). So while pagan kings from Cyrus to Artaxerxes had given the Jews all the protection, royal authority, and financial aid they needed, God was the true King behind these human thrones. He arranged events to fulfill his agenda for Israel.
7:10 Ezra was the total package. First, he studied God's law. The Word of God is supremely authoritative because its author is the King

of creation. If the divine Ruler of the universe has something to communicate to you, you can bet it's important. Ezra, accepting this, was determined to know God's Word through and through.
     Second, he obeyed it. Ezra wasn't content to be a mere academic, studying the Bible while failing to let it affect his beliefs, character, and actions. God wants his Word to guide our decision-making and to set the agenda for our lives, too. Merely knowing it is insufficient; we must live in submission to it.
     Third, Ezra taught God's Word to others. It's good and right to study and obey Scripture. But we must also share it with others so that they in turn can understand and obey it. Only then will our families, churches, and communities be transformed.
     Ezra is a reminder of the importance of godly human leadership within the church. A good leader is someone who knows the way, goes the way, and shows the way, as Ezra did.

[a] 7:10 Neh 8:1-8
[b] 7:12 Ezk 26:7; Dn 2:37
[c] 7:13 Ezr 1:3
[d] 7:14 Est 1:14
[e] 7:15 Hg 2:8
[f] Dt 12:5-6; 2Ch 6:2
[g] 7:16 Ex 3:22; Ezr 1:6
[h] 7:17 Nm 15:1-14; Ezr 6:9
[i] 7:19 Ezr 8:33
[j] 7:20 Ezr 6:4,8; 7:22-23
[k] 7:21 Ezr 4:10; 7:25

[l] 7:21 Ezr 6:8
[m] 7:23 Ezr 6:10
[n] 7:25 Ezr 7:10; Neh 8:1-3,8
[o] 7:26 Ezr 6:11
[p] 7:27 Ezr 6:22
[q] Is 60:7,13
[r] 7:28 Ezr 9:9
[s] Ezr 7:6; 8:18
[t] Ezr 8:1-14,16
[u] 8:1 Ezr 7:7
[v] 8:3 1Ch 3:22
[w] Ezr 2:3; 10:25

LORD, obey it, and teach[a] its statutes and ordinances in Israel.

LETTER FROM ARTAXERXES

[11] This is the text of the letter King Artaxerxes gave to Ezra the priest and scribe, an expert in matters of the LORD's commands and statutes for Israel:[A]

[12] Artaxerxes, king of kings,[b] to Ezra the priest, an expert in the law of the God of the heavens:

Greetings.

[13] I issue a decree that any of the Israelites in my kingdom, including their priests and Levites, who want to go to Jerusalem, may go with you.[c] [14] You are sent by the king and his seven counselors[d] to evaluate Judah and Jerusalem according to the law of your God, which is in your possession. [15] You are also to bring the silver and gold the king and his counselors have willingly given to the God of Israel,[e] whose dwelling is in Jerusalem,[f] [16] and all the silver and gold you receive throughout the province of Babylon, together with the freewill offerings given by the people and the priests to the house of their God in Jerusalem.[g] [17] Then you are to be diligent to buy with this money bulls, rams, and lambs, along with their grain and drink offerings, and offer them on the altar at the house of your God in Jerusalem.[h] [18] You may do whatever seems best to you and your brothers with the rest of the silver and gold, according to the will of your God. [19] Deliver to the God of Jerusalem all the articles given to you for the service of the house of your God.[i] [20] You may use the royal treasury[B] to pay for anything else needed for the house of your God.[j]

[21] I, King Artaxerxes, issue a decree to all the treasurers in the region west of the Euphrates River:[k]

Whatever Ezra the priest, an expert in the law of the God of the heavens, asks of you must be provided in full,[l] [22] up to 7,500 pounds[c] of silver, 500 bushels[D] of wheat, 550 gallons[E] of wine, 550 gallons of oil, and salt without limit.[F] [23] Whatever is commanded by the God of heaven must be done diligently for the house of the God of the heavens, so that wrath will not fall on the realm of the king and his sons.[m] [24] Be advised that you do not have authority to impose tribute, duty, and land tax on any priests, Levites, singers, doorkeepers, temple servants, or other servants of this house of God.

[25] And you, Ezra, according to[G] God's wisdom that you possess, appoint magistrates and judges to judge all the people in the region west of the Euphrates who know the laws of your God and to teach anyone who does not know them.[n] [26] Anyone who does not keep the law of your God and the law of the king, let the appropriate judgment be executed against him, whether death, banishment, confiscation of property, or imprisonment.[o]

[27] Blessed be the LORD, the God of our fathers, who has put it into the king's mind[p] to glorify the house of the LORD in Jerusalem,[q] [28] and who has shown favor to me before the king,[r] his counselors, and all his powerful officers. So I took courage because I was strengthened by the hand of the LORD my God,[H,s] and I gathered Israelite leaders to return with me.[t]

THOSE RETURNING WITH EZRA

[8] These are the family heads and the genealogical records of those who returned with me from Babylon during the reign of King Artaxerxes:[u]

[2]   Gershom,
      from Phinehas's descendants;
      Daniel, from Ithamar's descendants;
      Hattush, from David's descendants,
[3]   who was of
      Shecaniah's descendants;[v]
   Zechariah,
      from Parosh's[w] descendants,

[A] 7:11 Ezr 7:12-26 is written in Aramaic.   [B] 7:20 Lit *the king's house*   [C] 7:22 Lit *100 talents*   [D] 7:22 Lit *100 cors*   [E] 7:22 Lit *100 baths*   [F] 7:22 Lit *without instruction*   [G] 7:25 Lit *to your*   [H] 7:28 Lit *because the hand of the LORD my God was on me*

7:23 Though we have no reason to think Artaxerxes was a true follower of the Lord, he recognized the power of **the God of the heavens**. He probably believed in multiple gods but clearly wanted, like Darius (see 6:10), to experience the favor of the God of Israel. Thus, he called for obedience to God, **so that wrath [would] not fall on [his] realm**. 7:27 Ezra knew praise was the only appropriate response to God's sovereign provision. 7:28 When you know your God and experience his powerful work in your life, you will have the confidence and courage to fulfill the ministry he has given you too. 8:1-14 Ezra's was a much smaller group of returnees than the earlier one led by Zerubbabel and Jeshua (2:1-67).

and 150 men[A] with him
  who were registered
  by genealogy;
4 Eliehoenai son of Zerahiah
  from Pahath-moab's descendants,[a]
  and 200 men with him;
5 Shecaniah[B] son of Jahaziel
  from Zattu's descendants,
  and 300 men with him;
6 Ebed son of Jonathan
  from Adin's descendants,[b]
  and 50 men with him;
7 Jeshaiah son of Athaliah
  from Elam's descendants,
  and 70 men with him;
8 Zebadiah son of Michael
  from Shephatiah's descendants,
  and 80 men with him;
9 Obadiah son of Jehiel
  from Joab's descendants,
  and 218 men with him;
10 Shelomith[c] son of Josiphiah
  from Bani's descendants,
  and 160 men with him;
11 Zechariah son of Bebai
  from Bebai's descendants,
  and 28 men with him;
12 Johanan son of Hakkatan
  from Azgad's descendants,
  and 110 men with him;
13 these are the last ones,
  from Adonikam's descendants,[c]
  and their names are
  Eliphelet, Jeuel, and Shemaiah,
  and 60 men with them;
14 Uthai and Zaccur[D]
  from Bigvai's descendants,
  and 70 men with them.

15 I gathered them at the river[E] that flows to Ahava,[d] and we camped there for three days. I searched among the people and priests, but found no Levites[e] there. 16 Then I summoned the leaders: Eliezer, Ariel, Shemaiah, Elnathan, Jarib, Elnathan, Nathan, Zechariah, and Meshullam,[f] as well as the teachers Joiarib and Elnathan. 17 I

sent them to Iddo, the leader at Casiphia, with a message for[F] him and his brothers, the temple servants[g] at Casiphia, that they should bring us ministers for the house of our God. 18 Since the gracious hand of our God was on us,[h] they brought us Sherebiah[i] — a man of insight from the descendants of Mahli, a descendant of Levi son of Israel — along with his sons and brothers, 18 men, 19 plus Hashabiah,[j] along with Jeshaiah, from the descendants of Merari, and his brothers and their sons, 20 men. 20 There were also 220 of the temple servants,[k] who had been appointed by David and the leaders for the work of the Levites. All were identified by name.

PREPARING TO RETURN

21 I proclaimed a fast[l] by the Ahava River,[G] so that we might humble ourselves before our God and ask him for a safe journey for us, our dependents, and all our possessions. 22 I did this because I was ashamed to ask the king for infantry and cavalry to protect us from enemies during the journey, since we had told him, "The hand of our God is gracious to all who seek him, but his fierce anger is against all who abandon him."[m] 23 So we fasted and pleaded with our God about this, and he was receptive to our prayer.

24 I selected twelve of the leading priests, along with Sherebiah,[n] Hashabiah, and ten of their brothers. 25 I weighed out to them the silver, the gold, and the articles — the contribution for the house of our God that the king, his counselors, his leaders, and all the Israelites who were present had offered. 26 I weighed out to them 24 tons[H] of silver, silver articles weighing 7,500 pounds,[I] 7,500 pounds of gold, 27 twenty gold bowls worth a thousand gold coins,[J] and two articles of fine gleaming bronze, as valuable as gold.[o] 28 Then I said to them, "You are holy to the LORD, and the articles are holy. The silver and gold are a freewill offering[p] to the LORD God of your fathers.

[a]8:4 Ezr 2:6
[b]8:6 Ezr 2:15; Neh 7:20
[c]8:13 Ezr 2:13
[d]8:15 Ezr 8:21,31
[e]Ezr 2:40; 7:7
[f]8:16 Ezr 10:15

[g]8:17 Ezr 2:43; Neh 7:46
[h]8:18 Ezr 7:6
[i]Ezr 8:24; Neh 8:7
[j]8:19 Neh 12:24
[k]8:20 Ezr 2:43; 7:7
[l]8:21 Is 58:3-8
[m]8:22 Dt 31:6,17
[n]8:24 Neh 10:9,11
[o]8:25-27 Ezr 7:15-20
[p]8:28 Ezr 1:4; 2:68-69

[A]8:3 Or *males*; also in vv. 4-14   [B]8:5 LXX, 1 Esdras 8:32; MT reads *the descendants of Shecaniah*   [C]8:10 Some LXX mss, 1 Esdras 8:36; MT reads *the descendants of Shelomith*   [D]8:14 Alt Hb tradition, some LXX mss read *Zabud*   [E]8:15 Or *canal*   [F]8:17 Lit *Casiphia, and I put in their mouth the words to speak to*   [G]8:21 Or *Canal*, also in v. 31   [H]8:26 Lit *650 talents*   [I]8:26 Lit *100 talents*   [J]8:27 Or *1,000 drachmas*, or *1,000 darics*

8:15-17 When the group assembled for the hazardous 900-mile journey to Jerusalem initially, Ezra discovered there were **no Levites** among the returnees (8:15). This was a concern, since Levites would be needed to do the work of the Lord at the temple and to help teach the law of Moses to the people. The exiles would desperately need to understand God's Word if they were to be successful in their resettlement.

8:21 Fasting communicates to God that we are willing to go without a basic necessity for a period because we recognize our need for him is even greater. When we need to experience God more deeply or need his answer in a significant way, fasting is a tangible expression of our dependence on him. Though fasting certainly doesn't twist God's arm to respond as we want, it demonstrates to him (and to us) that we

are serious about living according to his perspective.
8:24-30 This wise move put Ezra above suspicion and delegated participation in the mission to those who would have rightful responsibility for the **holy** articles once in **Jerusalem** (8:28-30). Leaders of God's people must be above reproach and call others to fulfill their own ministerial duties.

a 8:29-30 Neh 13:4-5,9
b 8:31 Ezr 7:9; Neh 2:18
c Ezr 8:21-22
d 8:32 Neh 2:11
e 8:33 Neh 11:16
f 8:35 Ezr 2:1; 6:16
g Lv 1:3-15; 2Ch 29:24,27,31-35
h 8:36 Ezr 7:21,25
i Ezr 7:21-24
j 9:1 Ezk 5:10-12
k Dt 12:29-31; Ezr 9:11
l Gn 15:18; Lv 24:30; Dt 7:1

m 9:2 Dt 14:2
n Dt 7:1-4; Ezr 9:12; Neh 13:1-3,23
o Neh 13:28
p 9:3 2Kg 18:37-19:2; Neh 1:4; Dn 9:3
q 9:4 Ezr 10:3; Is 66:2,5
r Ezr 2:1; 6:16
s Ex 29:38-39
t 9:5 Ex 9:29; Dn 6:10
u 9:6-15 Neh 1:5-11; Dn 9:4-19
v 9:6 Jr 51:9; Rv 18:5
w 9:7 Neh 9:30,36; Dn 9:7
x 9:8 Is 10:20-22
y Is 10:23
z 1Sm 14:29
aa 9:9 Neh 9:36
ab 2Kg 25:28; Ezr 6:22
ac Ezr 1:4; 7:12-20

29 Guard them carefully until you weigh them out in the chambers of the LORD's house before the leading priests, Levites, and heads of the Israelite families in Jerusalem." **30** So the priests and Levites took charge of the silver, the gold, and the articles that had been weighed out, to bring them to the house of our God in Jerusalem.[a]

ARRIVAL IN JERUSALEM

31 We set out from the Ahava River on the twelfth day of the first month to go to Jerusalem. We were strengthened by our God,[A,b] and he kept us from the grasp of the enemy and from ambush along the way.[c] **32** So we arrived at Jerusalem and rested there for three days.[d] **33** On the fourth day the silver, the gold, and the articles were weighed out in the house of our God into the care of the priest Meremoth son of Uriah. Eleazar son of Phinehas was with him. The Levites Jozabad[e] son of Jeshua and Noadiah son of Binnui were also with them. **34** Everything was verified by number and weight, and the total weight was recorded at that time.

35 The exiles who had returned from the captivity[f] offered burnt offerings to the God of Israel: twelve bulls for all Israel, ninety-six rams, and seventy-seven lambs, along with twelve male goats as a sin offering. All this was a burnt offering for the LORD.[g] **36** They also delivered the king's edicts to the royal satraps and governors of the region west of the Euphrates,[h] so that they would support the people and the house of God.[i]

ISRAEL'S INTERMARRIAGE

9 After these things had been done, the leaders approached me and said: "The people of Israel, the priests, and the Levites have not separated themselves[j] from the surrounding peoples whose detestable practices[k] are like those of the Canaanites, Hethites, Perizzites, Jebusites, Ammonites, Moabites, Egyptians, and Amorites.[l]

2 Indeed, the Israelite men[B] have taken some of their daughters as wives for themselves and their sons, so that the holy seed[m] has become mixed with the surrounding peoples.[n] The leaders[c] and officials have taken the lead in this unfaithfulness!"[o] **3** When I heard this report, I tore my tunic and robe, pulled out some of the hair from my head and beard, and sat down devastated.[p]

EZRA'S CONFESSION

4 Everyone who trembled at the words of the God of Israel[q] gathered around me, because of the unfaithfulness of the exiles,[r] while I sat devastated until the evening offering.[s] **5** At the evening offering, I got up from my time of humiliation, with my tunic and robe torn. Then I fell on my knees and spread out my hands to the LORD my God.[t] **6** And I said:[u]

My God, I am ashamed and embarrassed to lift my face toward you, my God, because our iniquities are higher than our heads and our guilt is as high as the heavens.[v] **7** Our guilt has been terrible from the days of our fathers until the present. Because of our iniquities we have been handed over, along with our kings and priests, to the surrounding kings, and to the sword, captivity, plundering, and open shame,[w] as it is today. **8** But now, for a brief moment, grace has come from the LORD our God to preserve a remnant[x] for us and give us a stake[y] in his holy place. Even in our slavery, God has given us a little relief and light to our eyes.[z] **9** Though we are slaves,[aa] our God has not abandoned us in our slavery. He has extended grace to us in the presence of the Persian kings,[ab] giving us relief, so that we can rebuild the house of our God and repair its ruins,[ac] to give us a wall in Judah and Jerusalem.

10 Now, our God, what can we say in light of[D] this? For we have abandoned

---

A 8:31 Lit *The hand of our God was on us*   B 9:2 Lit *they*   C 9:2 Lit *hand of the leaders*   D 9:10 Lit *say after*

8:31 In other words, God had responded with divine deliverance to the people's humble fasting and prayer (see 8:21-23).

9:1-2 After the exodus from Egypt and before Israel entered the promised land, Moses had commanded them not to intermarry with the people groups listed in verse 1 (see Deut 7:1-3). Why? "Because they will turn your sons away from me to worship other gods. Then the Lord's anger will burn against you, and he will swiftly destroy you" (Deut 7:4). The Israelites of Ezra's day, then, were walking a

path that would send them right back into divine judgment.

9:3-4 Ezra himself wasn't guilty of the sin in view, so why was he so concerned? The answer is that Ezra had a right understanding of the *corporate* aspect of being a part of the people of God.

Think of it this way. A faithful offensive lineman may perform a well-executed block. But if the rest of the offensive line collapses and the quarterback is sacked, the faithful football player is still on the losing end of

things because he is part of a *team*. God calls his church a *body*—composed of many parts but functioning as one unit (see 1 Cor 12:12-31). We as the church are not merely to look after ourselves but to practice the "one anothers" of Scripture (see John 15:12; Gal 6:2; Eph 4:32; 1 Thess 5:11). God doesn't want Lone Ranger Christians. Our spiritual vitality and growth only come as we serve the Lord *together*.

9:8-9 In light of God's abundant grace, there was no excuse for this sin of intermarrying with the unrighteous nations surrounding them.

the commands [11] you gave through your servants the prophets, saying: "The land you are entering to possess is an impure land. The surrounding peoples have filled it from end to end with their uncleanness by their impurity and detestable practices.[a] [12] So do not give your daughters to their sons in marriage or take their daughters for your sons.[b] Never pursue their welfare or prosperity,[c] so that you will be strong, eat the good things of the land, and leave it as an inheritance to your sons forever." [13] After all that has happened to us because of our evil deeds and terrible guilt — though you, our God, have punished us less than our iniquities deserve and have allowed us to survive[A,d] — [14] should we break your commands again and intermarry with the peoples who commit these detestable practices?[e] Wouldn't you become so angry with us that you would destroy us, leaving neither remnant nor survivor?[f] [15] LORD God of Israel, you are righteous, for we survive as a remnant[g] today. Here we are before you with our guilt, though no one can stand in your presence because of this.[h]

SENDING AWAY FOREIGN WIVES

10 While Ezra prayed and confessed, weeping and falling facedown[i] before the house of God, an extremely large assembly of Israelite men, women, and children gathered around him. The people also wept bitterly.[j] [2] Then Shecaniah son of Jehiel,[k] an Elamite, responded to Ezra: "We have been unfaithful to our God by marrying foreign women from the surrounding peoples,[l] but there is still hope for Israel in spite of this. [3] Let us therefore make a covenant before our God[m] to send away all the foreign wives and their children, according to the counsel of my lord and of those who tremble at the command of our God.[n] Let it be done according to the law. [4] Get up, for this matter is your responsibility,[o]

and we support you. Be strong and take action!"[p]

[5] Then Ezra got up and made the leading priests, Levites, and all Israel take an oath to do what had been said; so they took the oath.[q] [6] Ezra then went from the house of God and walked to the chamber of Jehohanan son of Eliashib, where he spent the night.[B] He did not eat food or drink water, because he was mourning over the unfaithfulness of the exiles.[r]

[7] They circulated a proclamation throughout Judah and Jerusalem that all the exiles should gather at Jerusalem. [8] Whoever did not come within three days would forfeit all his possessions,[c] according to the decision of the leaders and elders, and would be excluded[s] from the assembly of the exiles.

[9] So all the men of Judah and Benjamin gathered in Jerusalem within the three days. On the twentieth day of the ninth month, all the people sat in the square at the house of God,[t] trembling because of this matter and because of the heavy rain. [10] Then the priest Ezra stood up and said to them, "You have been unfaithful by marrying foreign women, adding to Israel's guilt.[u] [11] Therefore, make a confession to the LORD, the God of your fathers, and do his will. Separate yourselves from the surrounding peoples and your foreign wives."

[12] Then all the assembly responded loudly: "Yes, we will do as you say! [13] But there are many people, and it is the rainy season. We don't have the stamina to stay out in the open. This isn't something that can be done in a day or two, for we have rebelled terribly in this matter. [14] Let our leaders represent the entire assembly. Then let all those in our towns who have married foreign women come at appointed times, together with the elders and judges of each town, in order to avert the fierce anger of our God[v] concerning[D] this matter." [15] Only Jonathan son of Asahel and Jahzeiah son of Tikvah opposed this, with Meshullam[w] and Shabbethai the Levite supporting them.

[a] 9:10-11 Dt 12:29-31; Ezr 9:1
[b] 9:12 Dt 7:1-4; Ezr 9:2; Neh 13:23-28
[c] Dt 7:3; 23:6
[d] 9:13 Is 10:20-22
[e] 9:14 Ezr 9:1-2; Neh 13:23-28
[f] Dt 29:26-28
[g] 9:15 Neh 1:3
[h] Ps 130:3
[i] 10:1 Ezr 9:3,5; Neh 1:4; Dn 9:3-4,20
[j] Ezr 3:12-13
[k] 10:2 Ezr 10:26
[l] Ezr 9:1-2; 10:18,44; Neh 13:23-28
[m] 10:3 2Ch 34:31
[n] Ezr 9:4
[o] 10:4 Ezr 7:25-26

[p] 10:4 Jos 1:6-9
[q] 10:5 Neh 10:29-30; 13:25
[r] 10:6 Dt 9:18-19
[s] 10:7-8 Ezr 7:26
[t] 10:9 Neh 8:1
[u] 10:10 Ezr 9:1-2; Neh 13:23-27
[v] 10:14 2Ch 29:10; 30:8
[w] 10:15 Ezr 8:16

[A] 9:13 Lit and gave us a remnant like this   [B] 10:6 1 Esdras 9:2, Syr; MT, Vg read he went   [C] 10:8 Lit would set apart all his possessions for destruction   [D] 10:14 Some Hb mss, LXX, Vg; other Hb mss read until

10:2-3 The seriousness of the situation is indicated in Shecaniah's use of the word **covenant** to describe the people's earnestness. A *covenant* is a promise that binds the parties to its fulfillment. The people had determined **to send away all the foreign wives and their children** (10:3). This drastic step was necessary to maintain the purity of the restored Israelite community and to avert further spiritual corruption that would bring God's judgment again.

Importantly, the church should not see these events as prescribing a principle for marriages today in which a Christian is married to an unbeliever. Clearly a believer is to marry another believer—one who is "in the Lord" (1 Cor 7:39). But if a person becomes a believer *after* he or she is already married to an unbeliever, Paul gives biblical counsel about such situations in 1 Corinthians 7:12-16.

*a*10:19 Lv 5:14–6:7
*b*10:20 1Ch 24:14
*c*10:21 1Ch 24:8
*d*10:22 1Ch 9:12
*e*10:23 Ezr 2:40
*f*10:24 Ezr 2:41
*g*Ezr 2:42
*h*10:25-43 Ezr 2:3-35; Neh 7:8-38
*i*10:25 Ezr 2:3

*j*10:26 Ezr 2:7; 10:2
*k*10:27 Ezr 2:8
*l*10:28 Ezr 2:11
*m*10:29 Ezr 2:10
*n*10:30 Ezr 2:6
*o*10:31 Ezr 2:32
*p*10:33 Ezr 2:19
*q*10:34 Ezr 2:10
*r*10:43 Ezr 2:29
*s*10:44 Ezr 10:18-43
*t*Neh 13:24

16 The exiles did what had been proposed. The priest Ezra selected men[A] who were family heads, all identified by name, to represent[B] their ancestral families.[C] They convened on the first day of the tenth month to investigate the matter, **17** and by the first day of the first month they had dealt with all the men who had married foreign women.

THOSE MARRIED TO FOREIGN WIVES

18 The following were found to have married foreign women from the descendants of the priests:

from the descendants of Jeshua son of Jozadak and his brothers: Maaseiah, Eliezer, Jarib, and Gedaliah. **19** They pledged[D] to send their wives away, and being guilty, they offered a ram from the flock for their guilt;[a]

20 Hanani and Zebadiah from Immer's[b] descendants;
21 Maaseiah, Elijah, Shemaiah, Jehiel, and Uzziah from Harim's[c] descendants;
22 Elioenai, Maaseiah, Ishmael, Nethanel, Jozabad, and Elasah from Pashhur's[d] descendants.
23 The Levites:[e] Jozabad, Shimei, Kelaiah (that is Kelita), Pethahiah, Judah, and Eliezer.
24 The singers:[f] Eliashib. The gatekeepers:[g] Shallum, Telem, and Uri.
25 The Israelites:[h] Parosh's descendants:[i] Ramiah, Izziah, Malchijah, Mijamin, Eleazar, Malchijah,[E] and Benaiah;

26 Elam's descendants:[j] Mattaniah, Zechariah, Jehiel, Abdi, Jeremoth, and Elijah;
27 Zattu's descendants:[k] Elioenai, Eliashib, Mattaniah, Jeremoth, Zabad, and Aziza;
28 Bebai's descendants:[l] Jehohanan, Hananiah, Zabbai, and Athlai;
29 Bani's descendants:[m] Meshullam, Malluch, Adaiah, Jashub, Sheal, and Jeremoth;
30 Pahath-moab's descendants:[n] Adna, Chelal, Benaiah, Maaseiah, Mattaniah, Bezalel, Binnui, and Manasseh;
31 Harim's descendants:[o] Eliezer, Isshijah, Malchijah, Shemaiah, Shimeon, **32** Benjamin, Malluch, and Shemariah;
33 Hashum's descendants:[p] Mattenai, Mattattah, Zabad, Eliphelet, Jeremai, Manasseh, and Shimei;

34 Bani's descendants:[q] Maadai, Amram, Uel, **35** Benaiah, Bedeiah, Cheluhi, **36** Vaniah, Meremoth, Eliashib, **37** Mattaniah, Mattenai, Jaasu, **38** Bani, Binnui, Shimei, **39** Shelemiah, Nathan, Adaiah, **40** Machnadebai, Shashai, Sharai, **41** Azarel, Shelemiah, Shemariah, **42** Shallum, Amariah, and Joseph;

43 Nebo's descendants:[r] Jeiel, Mattithiah, Zabad, Zebina, Jaddai, Joel, and Benaiah.
44 All of these[s] had married foreign women, and some of the wives had given birth to children.[t]

A10:16 1 Esdras 9:16, Syr; MT, Vg read *priest and men were selected*   B10:16 Lit *name, for*   C10:16 Lit *the house of their fathers*   D10:19 Lit *gave their hand*   E10:25 Some LXX mss, 1 Esdras 9:26 read *Hashabiah*

10:16-17 This process took three months to implement fully.
10:18-44 The Israelite men who had entered into such marriages had flouted the Mosaic law's prohibition against unholy unions (see Deut 7:1-4). And sadly, nearly one-quarter of the offenders were priests and Levites who knew God's Word better than anyone. Only when these leaders had dealt with their sin could the whole assembly move forward in establishing themselves in their land under God's blessing.

NEHEMIAH

INTRODUCTION

Author

THOUGH THE BOOK OF NEHEMIAH is recognized as an anonymous work, it claims to convey "the words of Nehemiah son of Hacaliah" (1:1). This combined with the frequent first-person perspective make clear that much of the content goes back to Nehemiah himself. Thus, we are justified in attributing authorship to him.

Historical Background

Nehemiah was the cupbearer to Artaxerxes the Persian king (see Neh 1:11). Thirteen years after Ezra, in about 445 BC (or "the twentieth year of King Artaxerxes," Neh 2:1), Nehemiah was sent to Jerusalem to rebuild the walls (see Neh 2:1-8) to address the failure of God's people to reestablish what God had intended with regard to their physical, social, political, economic, and family life.

Message and Purpose

Nehemiah led the third return of exiled Jews back to the land of Israel. As cupbearer to the king of Persia, he held an important administrative post in the government. When he received word that the people who had already returned to Jerusalem were in distress, he was greatly disturbed. But, he believed God's promise that when his people repent and return to him, he would restore their land.

Based on God's Word, Nehemiah began a program of what we could call today community development among God's people. With the blessing and help of a pagan king, Nehemiah returned home to rebuild the walls of Jerusalem, the city of God. This demonstrates that even the secular world is subject to God when his people operate according to his kingdom promises and authority.

Nehemiah also provides a study in great leadership. In a mere fifty-two days, Nehemiah led the people, amid opposition, to rebuild Jerusalem's walls. He also called for the development of solid families, for the temple to be the center of life, for the people to live under the covenant promises of God, and for them to become a righteous and just community. The book of Nehemiah is about making wrong things right.

VIDEO   INTRO

www.bhpublishinggroup.com/qr/te/16_00

Outline

a 1:1 Neh 10:1
b Zch 7:1
c Ezr 7:1,8; Neh 2:1
d Est 1:2; Dn 8:2
e 1:2 Neh 7:2
f Ezr 9:8,15; Is 10:20-22
g Ezr 1:11
h 1:3 Ezr 2:1; Neh 11:3
i Ezr 4:12-13,16; Neh 2:13
j 1:4 Ezr 9:3; 10:1; Ps 35:13;
Dn 9:3; Lk 2:37; Ac 13:3
k Ezr 1:2; Neh 2:4
l 1:5-11 Dn 9:4-19
m 1:5 Dt 6:5; 7:9-11;
Rm 8:28
n Dn 9:4
o 1:6 2Ch 6:40
p Ps 88:1-2; 2Tm 1:3
q Dn 9:5,8,20
r 1:7 2Ch 29:6; Dn 9:5-6,11

s 1:8 Dt 4:25-27; 28:64;
Dn 9:7
t 1:9 Dt 30:1-5
u 1:10 Dt 9:29; Dn 9:15
v 1:11 2Ch 6:40
w Gn 24:12
x Neh 2:1
y Gn 40:20
z 2:1 Ezr 7:1,8; Neh 1:1
aa 2:1-2 Pr 15:13
ab 2:3 Ezr 4:12,21; Neh 1:3

1 The words of Nehemiah[a] son of Hacaliah:

NEWS FROM JERUSALEM

During the month of Chislev[b] in the twentieth year,[c] when I was in the fortress city of Susa,[d] 2 Hanani,[e] one of my brothers, arrived with men from Judah, and I questioned them about Jerusalem and the Jewish remnant[f] that had survived the exile.[g] 3 They said to me, "The remnant in the province,[h] who survived the exile, are in great trouble and disgrace. Jerusalem's wall has been broken down, and its gates have been burned."[i]

NEHEMIAH'S PRAYER

4 When I heard these words, I sat down and wept. I mourned for a number of days, fasting and praying[j] before the God of the heavens.[k] 5 I said,[l]

Lord, the God of the heavens, the great and awe-inspiring God who keeps his gracious covenant with those who love him[m] and keep his commands,[n] 6 let your eyes be open and your ears be attentive[o] to hear your servant's prayer that I now pray to you day and night[p] for your servants, the Israelites. I confess the sins[A] we have committed against you. Both I and my father's family have sinned.[q] 7 We have acted corruptly toward you and have not kept the commands, statutes, and ordinances you gave your servant Moses.[r] 8 Please remember what you commanded your servant Moses: "If you are unfaithful, I will scatter you among the peoples.[s] 9 But if you return to me and carefully observe my commands, even though your exiles were banished to the farthest horizon,[B] I will gather them from there and bring them to the place where I chose to have my name dwell."[t] 10 They are your servants and your people. You redeemed them by your great power and strong hand.[u] 11 Please, Lord, let your ear be attentive[v] to the prayer of your servant and to that of your servants who delight to revere your name. Give your servant success today,[w] and grant him compassion in the presence of this man.[C,x]

At the time, I was the king's cupbearer.[y]

NEHEMIAH SENT TO JERUSALEM

2 During the month of Nisan in the twentieth year of King Artaxerxes,[z] when wine was set before him, I took the wine and gave it to the king. I had never been sad in his presence,[2] so the king said to me, "Why are you[D] sad, when you aren't sick? This is nothing but sadness of heart."[aa]

I was overwhelmed with fear 3 and replied to the king, "May the king live forever! Why should I[E] not be sad when the city where my ancestors are buried lies in ruins and its gates have been destroyed by fire?"[ab]

4 Then the king asked me, "What is your request?"

A 1:6 Lit sins of the Israelites   B 1:9 Lit skies   C 1:11 = the king   D 2:2 Lit "Why is your face   E 2:3 Lit my face

---

1:1 Nehemiah, a Jew living in Persia, "was the king's cupbearer" (1:11). More than just a food taster, the cupbearer served as chief of staff. **1:3** Those in his homeland were experiencing insecurity galore because the **broken** wall was a sign of degradation galore. The people who had returned to Jerusalem had made no progress in reestablishing what God had intended with regard to their physical, social, political, economic, and family life. **1:4-5** Nehemiah immediately went to God with his concerns for his people. You can always tell how seriously people believe that only God can make a difference—by how they pray.

While most of us would have jumped in and said, "Fix this problem, Lord," Nehemiah's opening in verse 5 reminds us that we should start off reminding ourselves of who our God is and what he can do! We tend to magnify our problems, when we should magnify God instead. If we rightly see him for who he is, we'll never see our problems as too much for him to handle. **1:6-7** Nehemiah included himself in Israel's sin problem (1:7) because he knew he was in a representative position. A real man says, "I identify with this problem; I own it."

Deterioration—whether in personal life, family life, or society—can be traced back to sin. And one of the great failures in our culture is the failure of the church to acknowledge its own sin. The Bible says, "the time has come for judgment to begin with God's household" (1 Pet 4:17). Only then can we address the unrighteous. **1:9** No matter what mess you've created, no matter how far you've gone, God is in the gathering business. If you are faithful, he will turn circumstances around. No matter how bad things get, God will honor his word. **1:10** The word *servants* here is a good reminder that God obligated himself to the believing world, so the believing world could get things done for the nonbelieving world. **1:11** The **man** referenced here was the king. That Nehemiah intended to ask his help tells us that he saw his own place as being in a strategic position.

Perhaps you work for a major organization, but you have not interpreted your "cupbearing" as an opportunity to make a difference for the glory of God. If we are going to rebuild our communities, we need to "kingdomize"

our skills. For instance, any person who uses a computer and then takes time to teach a brother to use that skill so that he can become employed and take care of his family has kingdomized a skill. Ask the Lord to show you how to use your job situation to make a kingdom difference.

2:3 Nehemiah spoke frankly: **Why should I not be sad when the city where my ancestors are buried lies in ruins?** He did not identify Jerusalem specifically because he was being shrewd. (In Ezra 4 King Artaxerxes had thought that if Jerusalem were rebuilt his people might stop paying taxes.) Nehemiah avoided the political issue by appealing to the king on a personal level. **2:4** Nehemiah was talking to **the king** of Persia, even as he prayed to **the God of the heavens**, a reminder that there is *a* king, and there is *the* King. We want to give up when our careers and marriages are not going right because we are looking at *a* king and not *the* King. But I don't care what you are facing; if you will bring *the* King to bear it, it does not matter how big *a* king—a boss, a rival, a mess—is.

When our church was meeting at a school, we received a letter stating that we could not

So I prayed to the God of the heavens[a] [5] and answered the king, "If it pleases the king, and if your servant has found favor with you, send me to Judah and to the city where my ancestors are buried,[A,b] so that I may rebuild it."[c]

[6] The king, with the queen seated beside him, asked me, "How long will your journey take, and when will you return?" So I gave him a definite time,[d] and it pleased the king to send me.

[7] I also said to the king: "If it pleases the king, let me have letters written to the governors of the region west of the Euphrates River,[e] so that they will grant me safe passage until I reach Judah.[f] And let me have a letter written to Asaph, keeper of the king's forest, so that he will give me timber to rebuild the gates of the temple's fortress,[g] the city wall, and the home where I will live."[B,h] The king granted my requests, for the gracious hand of my God was on me.[i]

[9] I went to the governors of the region west of the Euphrates and gave them the king's letters.[j] The king had also sent officers of the infantry and cavalry with me. [10] When Sanballat the Horonite[k] and Tobiah the Ammonite official heard that someone had come to pursue the prosperity of the Israelites, they were greatly displeased.[l]

PREPARING TO REBUILD THE WALLS

[11] After I arrived in Jerusalem and had been there three days,[m] [12] I got up at night and took a few men with me. I didn't tell anyone what my God had laid on my heart to do for Jerusalem. The only animal I took[c] was the one I was riding. [13] I went out at night through the Valley Gate toward the Serpent's[D] Well and the Dung Gate,[n] and I inspected the walls of Jerusalem that had been broken down and its gates that had been destroyed by fire.[o] [14] I went on to the Fountain Gate[p] and the King's Pool,[q] but farther down it became too narrow for my animal to go through. [15] So I went up at night by way of the valley and inspected the wall. Then heading back, I entered through the Valley Gate[r] and returned. [16] The officials did not know where I had gone or what I was doing, for I had not yet told the Jews, priests, nobles, officials, or the rest of those who would be doing the work. [17] So I said to them, "You see the trouble we are in. Jerusalem lies in ruins and its gates have been burned.[s] Come, let's rebuild Jerusalem's wall,[t] so that we will no longer be a disgrace." [18] I told them how the gracious hand of my God had been on me,[u] and what the king had said to me.

They said, "Let's start rebuilding," and their hands were strengthened[E] to do this good work.

[19] When Sanballat the Horonite, Tobiah the Ammonite official,[v] and Geshem the Arab[w] heard about this, they mocked and despised us, and said, "What is this you're doing? Are you rebelling against the king?"

[20] I gave them this reply, "The God of the heavens is the one who will grant us success. We, his servants, will start building, but you have no share, right, or historic claim in Jerusalem."[x]

REBUILDING THE WALLS

3 The high priest Eliashib[y] and his fellow priests began rebuilding the Sheep Gate.[z] They dedicated it and installed its doors. After building the wall to the Tower of the Hundred and the Tower of Hananel,[aa]

---

[a] 2:4 Neh 1:4
[b] 2:5 Neh 1:3
[c] Ezr 4:21; Dn 9:18
[d] 2:6 Neh 13:6
[e] 2:7 Ezr 4:8-9; 8:36
[f] Ezr 8:22
[g] 2:8 Neh 7:2
[h] Ezr 3:7
[i] Ezr 7:6; Neh 2:18
[j] 2:9 Ezr 8:36
[k] 2:10 Jos 16:3,5; 18:13
[l] Neh 4:7
[m] 2:11 Ezr 8:32
[n] 2:13 Neh 3:13

[o] 2:13 Ezr 4:12; Neh 1:3
[p] 2:14 Neh 3:15; 12:37
[q] 2Kg 18:17; 20:20
[r] 2:15 Neh 3:13
[s] 2:17 Ezr 4:12; Neh 1:3; 2:3
[t] Neh 2:5
[u] 2:18 Ezr 7:9; Neh 2:8
[v] 2:19 Neh 4:7
[w] Neh 6:1,6
[x] 2:19-20 Ezr 4:3-4
[y] 3:1 Neh 12:10; 13:4,7,28
[z] Neh 3:32; 12:39; Jn 5:2
[aa] Neh 12:39; Zch 14:10

[A] 2:5 Lit *city, the house of the graves of my fathers,*   [B] 2:8 Lit *enter*   [C] 2:12 Lit *animal with me*   [D] 2:13 Or *Dragon's*   [E] 2:18 Lit *they put their hands*

---

meet there any longer because three members of the school board were upset by our presence. We called the congregation to pray. We asked for a meeting with the board. Even on the drive to the meeting, we prayed, "Lord, this is bigger than we are. Give us the right words to say, and reverse the decision." There were supposed to be ten board members at the gathering, but only seven showed. The head of the committee thus said, "Since they aren't here, we'll render a decision without them." As a result, the vote went in our favor. We were blessed that day because we appealed to the God of heaven.

2:8 The Bible says, "the earth is the Lord's, and all that is in it" (1 Cor 10:26), so it's a simple matter for God to dispense wealth and resources when doing so will accomplish his divine agenda. He always provides for his will.

2:10 The mention of **Sanballat** and **Tobiah** is a reminder that whenever you are going to do something right, enemies will show up. Satan has an agenda. But remember, "our struggle is not against flesh and blood, but against . . . evil" (Eph 6:12). If you are spending most of your time fighting another person, you are not fighting the problem. The other person is only a tool, a pawn in a spiritual battle.

2:11-15 Similarly, sometimes a family head has to inspect the walls, to look at what is tearing down a home and to ruminate on how the matter can be addressed. With this job comes the tough task of asking, "Am I contributing to this problem? Am I doing what God wants, or what I want?"

2:17 Nehemiah's words, **Come, let's rebuild Jerusalem's wall, so that we will no longer be**

a disgrace suggest that the people of God are sometimes an embarrassment, though we are supposed to be the people of God.

2:19 In other words, they suggested this work of building the wall was a political issue.

3:1 The **rebuilding** work in this passage is a reminder that there is hope for a broken-down life, a broken-down family, a broken-down church, and even a broken-down community when God gets a good person with a good plan going about his kingdom agenda. These people had been living in Jerusalem for years, but they just never linked up to deal with the wall issue. Nehemiah unified them around a common purpose, and suddenly things were getting done.

Don't miss that the **priests** were leading the way in the effort by **rebuilding the Sheep Gate**. What would come through this gate

a 3:2 Ezr 2:34; Neh 7:36
b Neh 12:10
c 3:3 Neh 12:39; Zph 1:10
d Neh 6:1; 7:1
e 3:4 Ezr 8:33
f Ezr 10:15; Neh 3:30;
   6:17-18
g 3:5 Neh 3:27; Am 1:1
h 3:6 Neh 12:39
i 3:7 Jos 9:3
j 2Kg 25:23; Jr 40:5-12
k Neh 2:7-8; 5:14
l Neh 2:7,9
m 3:8 Neh 3:31,32
n 2Ch 32:5; Neh 12:38
o 3:10 Neh 3:23,28

p 3:11 2Ch 26:9; Neh 12:38
q 3:13 Neh 2:13
r 3:14 Jr 6:1
s Neh 2:13
t 3:15 Neh 2:14; 12:37
u Is 8:6; Jn 9:7
v 2Kg 25:4
w Neh 12:37

x 3:16 Jos 15:58; 1Ch 2:45
y 1Kg 2:10; Ac 2:29
z 2Kg 20:20; Is 22:9-11
aa 2Sm 23:8-39
ab 3:17 Ezr 2:40; Neh 7:43
ac 1Sm 23:1-5
ad 3:19 2Ch 26:9

they dedicated it. [2] The men of Jericho[a] built next to Eliashib,[b] and next to them Zaccur son of Imri built.

FISH GATE

[3] The sons of Hassenaah built the Fish Gate.[c] They built it with beams and installed its doors, bolts, and bars.[d] [4] Next to them Meremoth[e] son of Uriah, son of Hakkoz, made repairs. Beside them Meshullam[f] son of Berechiah, son of Meshezabel, made repairs. Next to them Zadok son of Baana made repairs. [5] Beside them the Tekoites[g] made repairs, but their nobles did not lift a finger to help[A] their supervisors.

OLD GATE, BROAD WALL, AND TOWER OF THE OVENS

[6] Joiada son of Paseah and Meshullam son of Besodeiah repaired the Old[B] Gate.[h] They built it with beams and installed its doors, bolts, and bars. [7] Next to them the repairs were done by Melatiah the Gibeonite, Jadon the Meronothite, and the men of Gibeon[i] and Mizpah, who were under the authority[c,j] of the governor[k] of the region west of the Euphrates River.[l] [8] After him Uzziel son of Harhaiah, the goldsmith,[m] made repairs, and next to him Hananiah son of the perfumer made repairs. They restored Jerusalem as far as the Broad Wall.[n]

[9] Next to them Rephaiah son of Hur, ruler of half the district of Jerusalem, made repairs. [10] After them Jedaiah son of Harumaph made repairs across from his house.[o] Next to him Hattush the son of Hashabneiah made repairs. [11] Malchijah son of Harim and Hasshub son

of Pahath-moab made repairs to another section, as well as to the Tower of the Ovens.[p] [12] Beside him Shallum son of Hallohesh, ruler of half the district of Jerusalem, made repairs — he and his daughters.

VALLEY GATE, DUNG GATE, AND FOUNTAIN GATE

[13] Hanun and the inhabitants of Zanoah repaired the Valley Gate. They rebuilt it and installed its doors, bolts, and bars, and repaired five hundred yards[D] of the wall to the Dung Gate.[q] [14] Malchijah son of Rechab, ruler of the district of Beth-haccherem,[r] repaired the Dung Gate.[s] He rebuilt it and installed its doors, bolts, and bars.

[15] Shallun[E] son of Col-hozeh, ruler of the district of Mizpah, repaired the Fountain Gate.[t] He rebuilt it and roofed it. Then he installed its doors, bolts, and bars. He also made repairs to the wall of the Pool of Shelah[u] near the king's garden,[v] as far as the stairs that descend from the city of David.[w]

[16] After him Nehemiah son of Azbuk, ruler of half the district of Beth-zur,[x] made repairs up to a point opposite the tombs of David,[y] as far as the artificial pool[z] and the House of the Warriors.[aa] [17] Next to him the Levites[ab] made repairs under Rehum son of Bani. Beside him Hashabiah, ruler of half the district of Keilah,[ac] made repairs for his district. [18] After him their fellow Levites made repairs under Binnui[F] son of Henadad, ruler of half the district of Keilah. [19] Next to him Ezer son of Jeshua, ruler of Mizpah, made repairs to another section opposite the ascent to the armory at the Angle.[ad]

[A] 3:5 Lit *not bring their neck to the work of*   [B] 3:6 Or *Jeshanah*   [C] 3:7 Or *Mizpah, the seat*   [D] 3:13 Lit *1,000 cubits*   [E] 3:15 Some Hb mss, Syr read *Shallum*   [F] 3:18 Some Hb mss, Syr, LXX; Neh 3:24; other Hb mss, Vg read *Bavvai*

---

once it was back in repair? The sheep that would be sacrificed in the temple.

The mention here of these men brings me to an important point. Whenever people decide they are going to rebuild the community, they must be aware that the most important institution in a community is the church. The values that must be operating in an area in order for it to survive and for businesses to stay within it, have to be set forth by a moral agency. Churches based on the Word of God can begin to turn a dilapidated community around when they operate biblically. **3:2 The men of Jericho** were commuters, meaning that there is a place in a local church family for people who commute a long distance to attend. However, people tend to move away from communities where the spiritual needs are greatest. So while it's okay to commute to your church, make sure you let your godly presence and the strengths

that God has given you be felt in your local community where the walls are torn down and the gates are burned.

3:5 Nehemiah called out those who chose to be lazy. Could his charge against them be said of you?

3:8 These men may not have been used to such physical labor, but they were willing to use their time and energy to make a difference in the community. Similarly, when there is a common agenda, you have to take some of your time and energy and get busy to meet the greater need.

3:9 Even the **ruler of half the district of Jerusalem** made **repairs**. Some people have the idea that a church is blessed because they joined it, but you are the privileged one when you are granted membership, by the grace of God, in his church. It is not because of who we are but because of the cross of Christ and his grace that we are let in.

3:12 God has called women in his kingdom to have strategic positions of responsibility that must be acknowledged and respected. The strengths of godly women are not to be ignored but utilized.

3:13-27 This massive project was handled in much the same way that you would eat an elephant: in manageable sections. The people in Jerusalem for 150 years had been saying, "The job's too big. All the walls are down!" And this is just the kind of thing many people today say at the thought of addressing their broken marriages, kids, and communities. But to do that is to look at the whole elephant rather than at the small bite on your fork. Taking on the whole world *is* too big, so focus on one thing at a time. When you do, what you thought would take centuries to address might well be accomplished in days.

THE ANGLE, WATER GATE, AND TOWER ON THE OPHEL

20 After him Baruch son of Zabbai[A] diligently repaired another section, from the Angle to the door of the house of the high priest Eliashib.[a] **21** Beside him Meremoth[b] son of Uriah, son of Hakkoz, made repairs to another section, from the door of Eliashib's[c] house to the end of his house. **22** And next to him the priests from the surrounding area made repairs.

23 After them Benjamin and Hasshub made repairs opposite their house. Beside them Azariah son of Maaseiah, son of Ananiah, made repairs beside his house. **24** After him Binnui[d] son of Henadad made repairs to another section, from the house of Azariah to the Angle and the corner. **25** Palal son of Uzai made repairs opposite the Angle and tower that juts out from the king's upper palace,[B,e] by the courtyard of the guard.[f] Beside him Pedaiah son of Parosh **26** and the temple servants[g] living on Ophel[h] made repairs opposite the Water Gate[i] toward the east and the tower that juts out. **27** Next to him the Tekoites[j] made repairs to another section from a point opposite the great tower that juts out, as far as the wall of Ophel.[k]

HORSE GATE, INSPECTION GATE, AND SHEEP GATE

28 Each of the priests made repairs above the Horse Gate,[l] each opposite his own house. **29** After them Zadok son of Immer made repairs opposite his house. And beside him Shemaiah son of Shecaniah, guard of the East Gate, made repairs. **30** Next to him Hananiah son of Shelemiah and Hanun the sixth son of Zalaph made repairs to another section.

After them Meshullam son of Berechiah made repairs opposite his room. **31** Next to him Malchijah, one of the goldsmiths,[m] made repairs to the house of the temple servants[n] and the merchants, opposite the Inspection[c] Gate, and as far as the upstairs room on the corner. **32** The goldsmiths[o] and merchants made repairs between the upstairs room on the corner and the Sheep Gate.[p]

PROGRESS IN SPITE OF OPPOSITION

4 When Sanballat[q] heard that we were rebuilding the wall,[r] he became furious. He mocked the Jews[s] **2** before his colleagues and the powerful men[D] of Samaria,[t] and said, "What are these pathetic Jews doing? Can they restore it by themselves? Will they offer sacrifices? Will they ever finish it? Can they bring these burnt stones[u] back to life from the mounds of rubble?"[v] **3** Then Tobiah the Ammonite,[w] who was beside him, said, "Indeed, even if a fox[x] climbed up what they are building, he would break down their stone wall!"

4 Listen, our God, for we are despised. Make their insults return on their own heads and let them be taken as plunder to a land of captivity. **5** Do not cover their guilt or let their sin be erased from your sight, because they have angered[E] the builders.[y]

6 So we rebuilt the wall until the entire wall was joined together up to half its height, for the people had the will to keep working.[z]

7 When Sanballat, Tobiah, and the Arabs,[aa] Ammonites, and Ashdodites heard that the repair to the walls of Jerusalem was progressing and that the gaps were being closed,[ab] they became furious.[ac] **8** They all plotted together to come and fight against Jerusalem and throw it into confusion. **9** So we prayed to our God and stationed a guard because of them day and night.

10 In Judah, it was said:[F]
The strength of the laborer fails,
since there is so much rubble.
We will never be able
to rebuild the wall.

[a] 3:20 Neh 3:1; 12:10
[b] 3:21 Ezr 8:33
[c] Neh 3:1
[d] 3:24 Ezr 8:33
[e] 3:25 Neh 12:37
[f] Jr 32:2
[g] 3:26 Ezr 2:43,55–58; 7:7
[h] Ezr 8:20; Neh 11:21
[i] Neh 8:1
[j] 3:27 Neh 3:5; Am 1:1
[k] Neh 11:21
[l] 3:28 2Ch 23:15
[m] 3:31 Neh 3:8
[n] Neh 7:46–56

[o] 3:32 Neh 3:8,21
[p] Neh 3:1; Jn 5:2
[q] 4:1 Neh 2:10,19; 4:7
[r] Neh 2:17,19
[s] Neh 2:19
[t] 4:2 Ezr 4:9–10
[u] 2Ch 26:19
[v] 2Ch 26:19; Neh 1:3
[w] 4:3 Neh 2:10,19; 6:1,14
[x] Lm 5:18
[y] 4:4–5 Neh 6:14; Jr 18:23
[z] 4:6 Neh 2:20; 6:1,15
[aa] 4:7 Neh 2:19
[ab] Neh 4:2–3
[ac] Neh 2:10

[A] 3:20 Alt Hb tradition, Vg read *Zaccai*; Ezr 2:9   [B] 3:25 Or *and the upper tower that juts out from the palace*   [C] 3:31 Or *Muster*   [D] 4:2 Or *the army*
[E] 4:5 Or *provoked you in front of*   [F] 4:10 Lit *Judah said*

3:29-32 After them . . . And beside him . . . Next to him are all phrases suggesting solidarity and even quality control (3:29-30). God wants you to use your spiritual gift to link up with other Christians and accomplish his divine agenda.

4:1 Sanballat knew that the prospering of the **Jews** would be a threat to his own status.

4:2-3 The last thing the builders needed was someone sitting on the sidelines calling out criticisms. But their enemies' tactics are a reminder that when you take a right stand, you are going to be criticized. Some men, then, need to be criticized for being home with their families too much. Some women need to be criticized for prioritizing marriage. Some teenagers need to be criticized for having high moral standards.

4:4-5 The Lord says, "Vengeance belongs to me; I will repay" (Deut 32:35). When you do the repaying, then, you cancel out divine benefits that you may have otherwise received from God.

4:6 That **the people had the will to keep working** means it was in their hearts and minds to persevere. The greatest task that God has in people's lives is changing our minds to trust that with his help we can do anything.

4:9 The people's actions here are a reminder that the way you know whether you prayed in faith is by what you do after taking a matter to God. You can't say, "I'm praying that God gives me a job," without going job hunting in the meantime. When you pray, you are trusting God so much that you feel confident that you *can* do something. Prayer is the preamble to action.

[a]4:14 Neh 2:16
[b]Dt 1:29; Ezr 3:3; 4:4
[c]2Sm 10:12
[d]4:16 2Ch 18:33
[e]4:19 Neh 2:16
[f]Neh 3:1-32
[g]4:20 Nm 10:1-9; Dt 1:30

[h]5:3 Hg 1:5-11
[i]5:4 Ezr 4:13; 7:24
[j]5:2-4 Dt 15:7-8
[k]5:5 Lv 25:39-43
[l]Ex 21:7-11
[m]5:6 Ex 11:8; Eph 4:26-27
[n]5:7 Ex 22:25; Dt 23:19-20
[o]5:8 Ex 21:8; Lv 25:39-42
[p]Jr 8:9
[q]5:9 Lv 25:36
[r]2Sm 12:14; Neh 4:4
[s]5:11 Neh 10:37

11 And our enemies said, "They won't realize it[A] until we're among them and can kill them and stop the work." 12 When the Jews who lived nearby arrived, they said to us time and again,[B] "Everywhere you turn, they attack[C] us." 13 So I stationed people behind the lowest sections of the wall, at the vulnerable areas. I stationed them by families with their swords, spears, and bows. 14 After I made an inspection, I stood up and said to the nobles, the officials, and the rest of the people,[a] "Don't be afraid of them.[b] Remember the great and awe-inspiring Lord, and fight for your countrymen, your sons and daughters, your wives and homes."[c]

SWORD AND TROWEL

15 When our enemies heard that we knew their scheme and that God had frustrated it, every one of us returned to his own work on the wall. 16 From that day on, half of my men did the work while the other half held spears, shields, bows, and armor.[d] The officers supported all the people of Judah, 17 who were rebuilding the wall. The laborers who carried the loads worked with one hand and held a weapon with the other. 18 Each of the builders had his sword strapped around his waist while he was building, and the trumpeter was beside me. 19 Then I said to the nobles, the officials, and the rest of the people:[e] "The work is enormous and spread out, and we are separated far from one another along the wall.[f] 20 Wherever you hear the trumpet sound, rally to us there. Our God will fight for us!"[g] 21 So we continued the work, while half of the men were holding spears from daybreak until the stars came out. 22 At that time, I also said to the people, "Let everyone and his servant spend the night inside Jerusalem, so that they can stand guard by night and work by day." 23 And I, my brothers, my servants, and the men of the guard with me never took off our clothes. Each carried his weapon, even when washing.[D]

SOCIAL INJUSTICE

5 There was a widespread outcry from the people and their wives against their Jewish countrymen. 2 Some were saying, "We, our sons, and our daughters are numerous. Let us get grain so that we can eat and live." 3 Others were saying, "We are mortgaging our fields, vineyards, and homes to get grain during the famine."[h] 4 Still others were saying, "We have borrowed money to pay the king's tax[i] on our fields and vineyards.[j] 5 We and our children are just like our countrymen and their children, yet we are subjecting our sons and daughters to slavery.[k] Some of our daughters are already enslaved,[l] but we are powerless[E] because our fields and vineyards belong to others."

6 I became extremely angry[m] when I heard their outcry and these complaints. 7 After seriously considering the matter, I accused the nobles and officials, saying to them, "Each of you is charging his countrymen interest."[n] So I called a large assembly against them 8 and said, "We have done our best to buy back our Jewish countrymen who were sold to foreigners, but now you sell your own countrymen, and we have to buy them back."[o] They remained silent and could not say a word.[p] 9 Then I said, "What you are doing isn't right. Shouldn't you walk in the fear of our God[q] and not invite the reproach of our foreign enemies?[r] 10 Even I, as well as my brothers and my servants, have been lending them money and grain. Please, let us stop charging this interest.[F] 11 Return their fields, vineyards, olive groves, and houses to them immediately, along with the percentage[G] of the money, grain, new wine, and fresh oil[s] that you have been assessing them."

[A]4:11 Lit *won't know or see* [B]4:12 Lit *us 10 times* [C]4:12 Or *again from every place, "You must return to* [D]4:23 Lit *Each his weapon the water* [E]5:5 Lit *but there is not the power in our hand* [F]5:10 Or *us forgive these debts* [G]5:11 Lit *hundred*

4:14 The people of God need a shared vision: we too are brothers and sisters in arms, facing a common enemy in the spiritual battle of the cosmos.

4:15-23 These men were dependent on God. But since God had given them weapons, they trusted him to use those means he'd provided to do whatever fighting needed to be done. To use available means without prayer is to be self-sufficient. To pray and not use available means is to be irresponsible. Prudence utilizes the resources that God has given to maximize our ability to do what God has called us to do.

5:1-5 Families were involved in corporate activity and therefore didn't have the time for agricultural development. Facing growing debt and government taxation, they were forced to seek help. Profiteering Jews seized the opportunity to make money off misfortunes by charging exorbitant interest rates on loans made to their Jewish brothers. It's unbiblical to charge interest to profit off someone's distress.

5:9 They weren't walking **in the fear of . . . God**, and it stained God's reputation in the eyes of outsiders. Understand that when you are not doing what is right, it makes God look bad. Your job is to make God look good through everything you do.

5:11 In essence, Nehemiah told them to give back what they'd stolen with interest. This highlights a spiritual principle. If you have done sloppy work for someone, go to them, apologize, and make it up to them. This is the principle of restitution, and it applies to romantic relationships as well. If you have ignored your spouse for five years, go apologize and say, "I want to spend the next five years making it up to you." If you follow up on that promise, you will have the Lord's blessing.

12 They responded: "We will return these
things and require nothing more from
them.[a] We will do as you say."
So I summoned the priests and made
everyone take an oath[b] to do this. 13 I also
shook the folds of my robe and said, "May
God likewise shake from his house and
property everyone who doesn't keep this
promise. May he be shaken out[c] and have
nothing!"
The whole assembly said, "Amen," and
they praised the LORD. Then the people did
as they had promised.[d]

GOOD AND BAD GOVERNORS

14 Furthermore, from the day King Artaxerxes[e] appointed me to be their governor
in the land of Judah — from the twentieth
year until his thirty-second year, twelve
years[f] — I and my associates never ate
from the food allotted to the governor.
15 The governors[g] who preceded me had
heavily burdened the people, taking from
them food and wine as well as a pound[A] of
silver. Their subordinates also oppressed
the people, but because of the fear of God,
I didn't do this.[h] 16 Instead, I devoted myself
to the construction of this wall,[i] and all my
subordinates were gathered there for the
work. We didn't buy any land.[j]
17 There were 150 Jews and officials, as
well as guests from the surrounding nations at my table.[k] 18 Each[B] day, one ox, six
choice sheep, and some fowl were prepared for me. An abundance of all kinds
of wine was provided every ten days.[l] But I
didn't demand the food allotted to the governor, because the burden on the people
was so heavy.
19 Remember me favorably, my God, for
all that I have done for this people.[m]

ATTEMPTS TO DISCOURAGE THE BUILDERS

6 When Sanballat, Tobiah, Geshem the
Arab, and the rest of our enemies[n]
heard that I had rebuilt the wall and that
no gap was left in it[o] — though at that time
I had not installed the doors in the city
gates[p] — 2 Sanballat and Geshem[q] sent
me a message: "Come, let's meet together in the villages of[C] the Ono Valley."[r] They
were planning to harm me.
3 So I sent messengers to them, saying,
"I am doing important work and cannot
come down. Why should the work cease
while I leave it and go down to you?" 4 Four
times they sent me the same proposal, and
I gave them the same reply.
5 Sanballat[s] sent me this same message
a fifth time by his aide, who had an open
letter in his hand. 6 In it was written:

> It is reported among the nations —
> and Geshem[D,t] agrees — that you and
> the Jews plan to rebel. This is the rea-
> son you are building the wall. Accord-
> ing to these reports, you are to become
> their king 7 and have even set up the
> prophets in Jerusalem to proclaim on
> your behalf: "There is a king in Judah."[u]
> These rumors will be heard by the
> king. So come, let's confer together.

8 Then I replied to him, "There is nothing to these rumors you are spreading; you
are inventing them in your own mind."[v]
9 For they were all trying to intimidate[w] us,
saying, "They will drop their hands from[E]
the work,[x] and it will never be finished."
But now, my God, strengthen my hands.[y]

ATTEMPTS TO INTIMIDATE NEHEMIAH

10 I went to the house of Shemaiah son of
Delaiah, son of Mehetabel, who was restricted to his house. He said:

> Let's meet at the house of God,
> inside the temple.
> Let's shut the temple doors
> because they're coming to kill you.
> They're coming to kill you tonight![F]

11 But I said, "Should a man like me run
away? How can someone like me enter the
temple and live?[z] I will not go." 12 I realized
that God had not sent him, because of the
prophecy he spoke against me. Tobiah and
Sanballat[aa] had hired him. 13 He was hired,
so that I would be intimidated,[ab] do as he
suggested, sin, and get a bad reputation, in
order that they could discredit me.

[a] 5:12 Neh 10:31
[b] Ezr 10:5
[c] 5:13 Ac 18:6
[d] Ezr 10:4-5; Neh 13:25
[e] 5:14 Ezr 4:7; 7:1
[f] Neh 13:6
[g] 5:15 Ezr 5:3,14; Hg 1:1
[h] Lv 25:36
[i] 5:16 Neh 4:1; 6:1; 2Th 3:7-10
[j] Neh 5:3,7,11
[k] 5:17 1Kg 4:27; 18:19
[l] 5:18 1Kg 4:22-23
[m] 5:19 Neh 13:14,22,31
[n] 6:1 Neh 2:10,19
[o] Neh 4:6-7
[p] Neh 3:1
[q] 6:2 Neh 2:10
[r] 6:2 1Ch 8:12
[s] 6:5 Neh 2:10
[t] 6:6 Neh 2:19
[u] 6:7 Zch 9:9
[v] 6:8 Jb 13:4; Ps 52:2
[w] 6:9 Ezr 3:3
[x] Ezr 4:4
[y] Neh 5:19; 13:22; Ps 138:3
[z] 6:10-11 Nm 18:7
[aa] 6:12 Neh 2:10; 6:1
[ab] 6:13 Ezr 3:3

[A] 5:15 Lit *40 shekels* [B] 5:18 Lit *And that which was prepared each* [C] 6:2 Or *together at Kephirim in* [D] 6:6 Lit *Gashmu* [E] 6:9 Or *will give up on*
[F] 6:10 Or *by night*

5:19 I love Nehemiah's prayer, **Remember me favorably, my God.** It should make you ask, how is God going to remember me? If God is not well pleased with you, you are a failure. So live in such a way that on judgment day Jesus Christ stands and says, "Well done, good and faithful servant" (Matt 25:21).

6:9 When you know you are doing what God wants you to do, but you are ready to quit, you need to go to God. If you are feeling pressure to walk away from a standard or to make compromises because you are worried about what everybody else thinks, you have to say, "I only care what God thinks." The majority must not be allowed to rule you: God rules.

6:10-14 **Shemaiah** made false claims, and many people misuse the name of the Lord as he did. Please, be careful whom you listen to. Religious terminology does not guarantee legitimacy.

a 6:14 Neh 13:29
b Rv 2:20
c 6:15 Neh 4:1,7; 6:1
d Ezr 6:15
e 6:16 Neh 2:10; 6:1
f Ezr 3:3
g Ex 14:25
h 6:17 Neh 6:1; 13:4-5,7-8
i 6:18 Ezr 10:5
j Neh 3:4,30
k 6:19 Neh 6:9,13
l 7:1 Neh 6:1
m Ezr 2:40-42; Neh 7:43-45
n 7:2 Neh 1:2
o Neh 3:9,12
p Neh 10:23
q Neh 2:8
r 1Kg 18:3; Neh 5:9,15
s 7:3 Neh 4:13,16,22-23
t 7:4 Neh 11:1
u 7:5 Pr 2:6
v 7:5-73 Ezr 2:1-70

w 7:6 2Ch 36:20
x Ezr 2:1
y 7:7 Hg 1:1
z Ezr 2:2; 5:2; Zch 3:3,8
aa 7:8 Ezr 2:3; 8:3; 10:25; Neh 3:25
ab 7:18 Ezr 2:13; 8:13
ac 7:20 Ezr 2:15; 8:6
ad 7:26 Ezr 2:21; Mc 5:2
ae 2Sm 23:28; 2Kg 25:23; Ezr 2:22
af 7:27 Ezr 2:23; Neh 11:32; Jr 1:1
ag 7:32 Gn 12:8; Jos 7:2; Ezr 2:28
ah 7:36 Jos 6:1; Ezr 2:34; Neh 3:2
ai 7:37 1Ch 8:12; Ezr 2:33; Ac 9:32
aj 7:39 1Ch 24:7; Ezr 2:36

14 My God, remember[a] Tobiah and Sanballat for what they have done, and also the prophetess Noadiah[b] and the other prophets who wanted to intimidate me.

THE WALL COMPLETED

15 The wall was completed[c] in fifty-two days, on the twenty-fifth day of the month Elul.[d] **16** When all our enemies[e] heard this, all the surrounding nations were intimidated[f] and lost their confidence,[A] for they realized that this task had been accomplished by our God.[g]

17 During those days, the nobles of Judah sent many letters to Tobiah,[h] and Tobiah's letters came to them. **18** For many in Judah were bound by oath[i] to him, since he was a son-in-law of Shecaniah son of Arah, and his son Jehohanan had married the daughter of Meshullam[j] son of Berechiah. **19** These nobles kept mentioning Tobiah's good deeds to me, and they reported my words to him. And Tobiah sent letters to intimidate[k] me.

THE EXILES RETURN

7 When the wall had been rebuilt and I had the doors installed,[l] the gatekeepers,[m] singers, and Levites were appointed. **2** Then I put my brother Hanani[n] in charge of Jerusalem,[o] along with Hananiah,[p] commander of the fortress,[q] because he was a faithful man who feared God[r] more than most. **3** I said to them, "Do not open the gates of Jerusalem until the sun is hot, and let the doors be shut and securely fastened while the guards are on duty. Station the citizens of Jerusalem as guards, some at their posts and some at their homes."[s]

4 The city was large and spacious, but there were few people in it, and no houses had been built yet.[t] **5** Then my God put it into my mind[u] to assemble the nobles, the officials, and the people to be registered by genealogy. I found the genealogical record of those who came back first, and I found the following written in it:[v]

6 These are the people of the province who went up among the captive exiles deported by King Nebuchadnezzar[w] of Babylon. Each of them returned to Jerusalem and Judah, to his own town.[x] **7** They came with Zerubbabel,[y] Jeshua,[z] Nehemiah, Azariah, Raamiah, Nahamani, Mordecai, Bilshan, Mispereth, Bigvai, Nehum, and Baanah.

The number of the Israelite men included[B]

8	Parosh's descendants[aa]	2,172
9	Shephatiah's descendants	372
10	Arah's descendants	652
11	Pahath-moab's descendants: Jeshua's and Joab's descendants	2,818
12	Elam's descendants	1,254
13	Zattu's descendants	845
14	Zaccai's descendants	760
15	Binnui's descendants	648
16	Bebai's descendants	628
17	Azgad's descendants	2,322
18	Adonikam's descendants[ab]	667
19	Bigvai's descendants	2,067
20	Adin's descendants[ac]	655
21	Ater's descendants: of Hezekiah	98
22	Hashum's descendants	328
23	Bezai's descendants	324
24	Hariph's descendants	112
25	Gibeon's[c] descendants	95
26	Bethlehem's[ad] and Netophah's[ae] men	188
27	Anathoth's[af] men	128
28	Beth-azmaveth's men	42
29	Kiriath-jearim's, Chephirah's, and Beeroth's men	743
30	Ramah's and Geba's men	621
31	Michmas's men	122
32	Bethel's and Ai's men[ag]	123
33	the other Nebo's men	52
34	the other Elam's people	1,254
35	Harim's people	320
36	Jericho's people[ah]	345
37	Lod's, Hadid's, and Ono's[ai] people	721
38	Senaah's people	3,930.

39 The priests included Jedaiah's[aj] descendants of the house of Jeshua — 973

40 Immer's descendants — 1,052

A 6:16 Lit and fell greatly in their eyes   B 7:7 Lit the men of the people of Israel   C 7:25 = Gibbar's in Ezr 2:20

7:1-2 If a leader wants to keep something going in the right direction, he will need to enlist the help of people who are capable. Any workers appointed within the church must be living in submission to the Lord.
7:3 This is a reminder that the church must be ever vigilant as well. Later, Paul would warn the Ephesians elders that "savage wolves" would come in among them and "distort

the truth to lure the disciples into following them" (Acts 20:29-30). The pastors and elders of local churches are to protect God's people by teaching what is faithful to God's Word and exposing what deviates from it.
7:4-69 Nehemiah had restructured the community and provided protection and security and welfare, but **there were few people** actually living in Jerusalem (7:4). Nehemiah

wanted a census of the people so he could bring families back into the city. **God put it into [his] mind** to do this (7:5), a reminder that when you have a dynamic prayer life and an obedient life, the Spirit of God will move your heart to accomplish his will. Nehemiah **found the genealogical record of those who came back first** from exile (7:5); this was exactly what he needed.

41 Pashhur's descendants   1,247
42 Harim's descendants   1,017.

43 The Levites[a] included
Jeshua's descendants: of Kadmiel
Hodevah's descendants   74.

44 The singers[b] included
Asaph's descendants   148.

45 The gatekeepers[c] included
Shallum's descendants,
Ater's descendants,
Talmon's descendants,
Akkub's descendants,
Hatita's descendants,
Shobai's descendants   138.

46 The temple servants[d] included
Ziha's descendants,
Hasupha's descendants,
Tabbaoth's descendants,
47 Keros's descendants,
Sia's descendants,
Padon's descendants,
48 Lebanah's descendants,
Hagabah's descendants,
Shalmai's descendants,
49 Hanan's descendants,
Giddel's descendants,
Gahar's descendants,
50 Reaiah's descendants,
Rezin's descendants,
Nekoda's descendants,
51 Gazzam's descendants,
Uzza's descendants,
Paseah's descendants,
52 Besai's descendants,
Meunim's descendants,
Nephishesim's[A] descendants,
53 Bakbuk's descendants,
Hakupha's descendants,
Harhur's descendants,
54 Bazlith's descendants,
Mehida's descendants,
Harsha's descendants,
55 Barkos's descendants,
Sisera's descendants,
Temah's descendants,
56 Neziah's descendants,
Hatipha's descendants.

57 The descendants of Solomon's servants[e] included

Sotai's descendants,
Sophereth's descendants,
Perida's descendants,
58 Jaala's descendants,
Darkon's descendants,
Giddel's descendants,
59 Shephatiah's descendants,
Hattil's descendants,
Pochereth-hazzebaim's descendants,
Amon's descendants.

60 All the temple servants
and the descendants of Solomon's
servants[f]   392.

61 The following[g] are those who came from Tel-melah, Tel-harsha, Cherub, Addon, and Immer, but were unable to prove that their ancestral families[B] and their lineage were Israelite:
62 Delaiah's descendants,
Tobiah's descendants,
and Nekoda's descendants   642
63 and from the priests: the descendants of Hobaiah, the descendants of Hakkoz, and the descendants of Barzillai — who had taken a wife from the daughters of Barzillai the Gileadite and who bore their name. 64 These searched for their entries in the genealogical records, but they could not be found, so they were disqualified from the priesthood. 65 The governor[h] ordered them not to eat the most holy things until there was a priest who could consult the Urim and Thummim.[i]
66 The whole combined assembly
numbered   42,360
67 not including their 7,337 male
and female servants,
as well as their 245 male
and female singers.
68 They had 736 horses, 245 mules,[c]
69 435 camels, and 6,720 donkeys.[j]

70 Some of the family heads contributed to the project. The governor gave 1,000 gold coins,[D] 50 bowls, and 530 priestly garments to the treasury. 71 Some of the family heads gave 20,000 gold coins and 2,200 silver minas to the treasury for the project. 72 The rest of the people gave 20,000 gold coins, 2,000 silver minas, and 67 priestly garments. 73 The priests, Levites, gatekeepers, temple singers, some of the people,

[a] 7:43 Ezr 2:40; 7:7; 8:15; Neh 13:30
[b] 7:44 1Ch 15:16; Ezr 2:41-43
[c] 7:45 1Ch 9:17-27
[d] 7:46 Neh 11:21
[e] 7:57 1Kg 9:21; Ezr 2:55

[f] 7:60 Ezr 2:58
[g] 7:61-62 Ezr 2:59-60
[h] 7:65 Ezr 2:63; 5:14
[i] Ex 28:30; Lv 8:8; Ezr 2:63
[j] 7:69-72 Ezr 2:64-70

A 7:52 Alt Hb tradition reads *Nephushesim's*   B 7:61 Lit *the house of their fathers*   C 7:68 Some Hb mss, LXX; Ezr 2:66; other Hb mss omit v. 68   D 7:70 Or *drachmas*, or *darics*; also in vv. 71,72

7:70-72 God never ordains things that he does not fund. The funding problems our local churches face often come down to management: we as believers must remember that all we have is his and give generously.

a 7:73 1Ch 9:2; Ezr 2:70;
Neh 7:6
b Lv 23:23–43; Ezr 3:1
c 8:1 Ezr 3:1
d Neh 3:26; 8:16
e Ezr 7:6,11–12; Neh 8:9,13
f 2Ch 34:14; Neh 8:7–9,13–14,18
g 8:2 Lv 23:23; Nm 29:1–6; Neh 6:15
h Ezr 7:1–5
i Neh 8:7,18
j 8:3 Neh 3:26
k Dt 28:61; 2Ch 17:9; 25:4; 34:14–15
l 8:4 2Ch 6:13
m 8:6 1Tm 2:8
n Neh 5:13
o 2Ch 20:18
p 8:7 Neh 9:4–5
q Ezr 8:15,18–19; Neh 7:43
r Lv 10:11; Mal 2:6,8

s 8:9 Neh 5:14–15
t Ezr 7:1–6
u Nm 29:1–6
v Ezr 3:12–13; 10:1,6
w 8:10 2Sm 6:19; Est 9:22
x Nm 29:1–6
y Dt 16:11,14–15
z 8:11 Ps 46:10
aa Nm 29:1–6
ab 8:12 Est 9:22
ac 8:13 Neh 10:28–29
ad Ezr 7:6; Neh 8:1,9
ae 8:14 Jn 7:2
af 8:14–15 Lv 23:4,34–42
ag 8:16 Dt 22:8
ah Neh 3:26; 8:1; 12:37
ai 2Ch 25:23

temple servants, and all Israel settled in their towns.[a]

PUBLIC READING OF THE LAW

8 When the seventh month[b] came and the Israelites had settled in their towns, [1] all the people gathered together[c] at the square in front of the Water Gate.[d] They asked the scribe Ezra[e] to bring the book of the law of Moses[f] that the LORD had given Israel. [2] On the first day of the seventh month,[g] the priest Ezra[h] brought the law[i] before the assembly of men, women, and all who could listen with understanding. [3] While he was facing the square in front of the Water Gate,[j] he read out of it from daybreak until noon before the men, the women, and those who could understand. All the people listened attentively[A] to the book of the law.[k] [4] The scribe Ezra stood on a high wooden platform[l] made for this purpose. Mattithiah, Shema, Anaiah, Uriah, Hilkiah, and Maaseiah stood beside him on his right; to his left were Pedaiah, Mishael, Malchijah, Hashum, Hash-baddanah, Zechariah, and Meshullam. [5] Ezra opened the book in full view of all the people, since he was elevated above everyone. As he opened it, all the people stood up. [6] Ezra blessed the LORD, the great God, and with their hands uplifted[m] all the people said, "Amen, Amen!"[n] Then they knelt low and worshiped the LORD with their faces to the ground.[o]

[7] Jeshua, Bani, Sherebiah, Jamin, Akkub, Shabbethai, Hodiah, Maaseiah, Kelita, Azariah, Jozabad, Hanan, and Pelaiah,[p] who were Levites, [B,q] explained the law[r] to the people as they stood in their places. [8] They read out of the book of the law of God, translating and giving the meaning so that the people could understand what

was read. [9] Nehemiah the governor,[s] Ezra the priest and scribe,[t] and the Levites who were instructing the people said to all of them, "This day[u] is holy to the LORD your God. Do not mourn or weep."[v] For all the people were weeping as they heard the words of the law. [10] Then he said to them, "Go and eat what is rich, drink what is sweet, and send portions to those who have nothing prepared,[w] since today[x] is holy to our Lord. Do not grieve, because the joy of the LORD is your strength."[C,y] [11] And the Levites quieted all the people, saying, "Be still,[z] since today[aa] is holy. Don't grieve." [12] Then all the people began to eat and drink, send portions, and have a great celebration,[ab] because they had understood the words that were explained to them.

FESTIVAL OF SHELTERS OBSERVED

[13] On the second day, the family heads of all the people, along with the priests and Levites,[ac] assembled before the scribe Ezra[ad] to study the words of the law. [14] They found written in the law how the LORD had commanded through Moses that the Israelites should dwell in shelters during the festival of the seventh month.[ae] [15] So they proclaimed and spread this news throughout their towns and in Jerusalem, saying, "Go out to the hill country and bring back branches of olive, wild olive, myrtle, palm, and other leafy trees to make shelters, just as it is written."[af] [16] The people went out, brought back branches, and made shelters for themselves on each of their rooftops[ag] and courtyards, the court of the house of God, the square by the Water Gate,[ah] and the square by the Ephraim Gate.[ai] [17] The

---

[A] 8:3 Lit *The ears of all the people listened*   [B] 8:7 Vg, 1 Esdras 9:48; MT reads *Pelaiah and the Levites*   [C] 8:10 Or *stronghold*

8:1 Ezra had been preaching among the Jews (Ezra 7:10) for fourteen years, creating a spiritual environment, softening the ground with truth, and orienting the people toward a standard. That, in fact, was why Nehemiah had found the people open to the possibility for rebuilding the wall.
8:3 From daybreak until noon is six hours, and the people **listened attentively** the whole time. Should you find yourself saying "I can't pay attention to the Word of God for six hours at a time, consider whether you can watch TV for six hours. Or hang out with your friends. You *can* do what you *want* to do. You can do it because, once you perceive a benefit from a thing, "long" becomes "short." The Judahites perceived the value of the Word of God.
8:5 When Ezra opened the book, **all the people stood** without being asked because they

understood that God was speaking through it. The Word of God is worthy of your reverence.
8:8 Translating and giving the meaning is what we call exposition. It is not enough to hear Scripture read if you don't **understand** it.
8:9 They cried when it dawned on them that because of their refusal to hear the Word of God previously, they had gone nearly a 150 years without progress.
8:10 What you focus on governs how you feel. The reason why many of us stay grieved for so *long* is because we stay focused on what is so *wrong*. Rather than finding our chief **joy** in the Lord, we turn on the TV to escape. We enter into illegitimate relationships to escape. We get involved with drugs or alcohol to escape. If your focus is properly situated on the Lord, however, he will give you his joy; and his joy will give you **strength**.

8:11 In other words, the people were to remember that God was still on the throne, and he was still taking care of business.
8:13 The men, **the family heads**, agreed that they had better take their rightful position. They understood that if **the law** of God does not flow through the leadership of the family, it won't get passed down to the kids. Thus, they set about the task of studying Scripture.
8:14–18 The **shelters** represented the temporary housing the Israelites erected during their wilderness wanderings. The rejoicing was not over the structures, but over the renewed obedience to the Word of God, which had been neglected. For this one week a year they were to be physically reminded that there was a time when they had nothing, and God had taken care of them.

whole community that had returned from exile[a] made shelters and lived in them. The Israelites had not celebrated like this from the days of Joshua son of Nun until that day.[b] And there was tremendous joy.[c] [18] Ezra[A] read out of the book of the law of God[d] every day, from the first day to the last. The Israelites celebrated the festival for seven days, and on the eighth day there was an assembly, according to the ordinance.[e]

NATIONAL CONFESSION OF SIN

9 On the twenty-fourth day of this month[f] the Israelites assembled; they were fasting, wearing sackcloth, and had put dust on their heads.[g] [2] Those of Israelite descent separated themselves from all foreigners,[h] and they stood[i] and confessed their sins and the iniquities of their fathers.[j] [3] While they stood in their places,[k] they read from the book of the law of the LORD their God for a fourth of the day and spent another fourth of the day[l] in confession[m] and worship of the LORD their God. [4] Jeshua, Bani, Kadmiel, Shebaniah, Bunni, Sherebiah, Bani, and Chenani stood on the raised platform built for the Levites[n] and cried out loudly to the LORD their God. [5] Then the Levites — Jeshua, Kadmiel, Bani, Hashabneiah, Sherebiah, Hodiah, Shebaniah, and Pethahiah[o] — said, "Stand up. Blessed be the LORD your God from everlasting to everlasting."[p]

Blessed be your glorious name,[q]
and may it be exalted above
all blessing and praise.
[6]   You,[B] LORD, are the only God.[C,r]
You created the heavens,
the highest heavens with all
their stars,
the earth and all that is on it,
the seas and all that is in them.
You give life to all of them,[s]
and all the stars of heaven worship
you.[t]
[7]   You, the LORD,
are the God who chose Abram
and brought him out of Ur
of the Chaldeans,[u]
and changed his name to Abraham.[v]
[8]   You found his heart faithful
in your sight,[w]

and made a covenant with him
to give the land of the Canaanites,
Hethites, Amorites, Perizzites,
Jebusites, and Girgashites —
to give it to his descendants.[x]
You have fulfilled your promise,
for you are righteous.

[9]   You saw the oppression
of our ancestors in Egypt[y]
and heard their cry at the Red Sea.
[10]   You performed signs and wonders
against Pharaoh,
all his officials, and all the people
of his land,[z]
for you knew how arrogantly
they treated our ancestors.
You made a name for yourself
that endures to this day.
[11]   You divided the sea before them,
and they crossed through it
on dry ground.[aa]
You hurled their pursuers
into the depths
like a stone into raging water.[ab]
[12]   You led them with a pillar of cloud
by day,
and with a pillar of fire by night,
to illuminate the way
they should go.[ac]
[13]   You came down on Mount Sinai,[ad]
and spoke to them from heaven.
You gave them impartial ordinances,
reliable instructions,
and good statutes and commands.
[14]   You revealed your holy Sabbath
to them,
and gave them commands, statutes,
and instruction
through your servant Moses.[ae]
[15]   You provided bread from heaven[af]
for their hunger;
you brought them water
from the rock[ag] for their thirst.
You told them to go in and possess
the land
you had sworn[D] to give them.[ah]

[16]   But our ancestors
acted arrogantly;
they became stiff-necked
and did not listen
to your commands.

[a] 8:17 Ezr 1:11; Neh 7:6
[b] 2Ch 7:9; Ezr 3:4
[c] 2Ch 30:21
[d] 8:18 Neh 8:1,3
[e] Lv 23:34-36
[f] 9:1 Neh 7:73; 8:2
[g] 1Sm 4:12; Neh 1:4; Dn 9:3
[h] 9:2 Ezr 6:21; 10:11; Neh 13:3
[i] Neh 8:5
[j] Neh 1:6; Dn 9:4,20
[k] 9:3 Neh 8:5,7
[l] Neh 8:3
[m] Neh 1:6
[n] 9:4 Neh 8:4
[o] 9:4-5 Neh 8:7
[p] 9:5 1Ch 16:36; Ps 41:13; 106:48
[q] 1Ch 29:13
[r] 9:6 Dt 6:4
[s] 2Kg 19:15
[t] Ps 89:5-7; Lk 2:13
[u] 9:7 Gn 11:28,31
[v] Gn 17:5
[w] 9:8 Gn 15:6; 22:15-18

[x] 9:8 Gn 15:18-21
[y] 9:9 Ex 3:7; 14:10-14,31
[z] 9:10 Ex 3:20; 10:1
[aa] 9:11 Ex 14:21-22
[ab] Ex 14:26-28
[ac] 9:12 Dt 1:32-33
[ad] 9:13 Ex 19:20
[ae] 9:13-14 Ex 20:1-17
[af] 9:15 Ex 16:4
[ag] Ex 17:6
[ah] Dt 1:8,21

[A] 8:18 Some Hb mss, Syr read *They*   [B] 9:6 LXX reads *And Ezra said: You*   [C] 9:6 Lit *are alone*   [D] 9:15 Lit *lifted your hand*

9:5-15 The Levites began to teach the people their history with God. There were some young people in this group who had not been taught the Word of God, and their fathers had not told them how God chose them and brought them out of the land of Egypt! Maybe some of the fathers didn't even know their own history. Thus, the Levites educated a new generation of fathers and leaders who could then teach their children the plan of God. Similarly, we need a new generation of Christian teachers to enter the classroom to convey such truths to our children.

a 9:16–17 Dt 1:26–33
b 9:17 Nm 14:4
c Ex 34:6; Ps 86:15; 103:8
d 9:17–18 Ex 32:4
e 9:19 Ex 16:4; 17:6
f 9:20 Nm 11:17; Neh 9:30
g Ex 16:14–15
h Ex 17:6
i 9:21 Dt 2:7; 29:5
j Dt 8:4
k 9:22 Nm 21:21–35
l 9:23 Gn 15:5; 22:17

m 9:24 Jos 11:23
n 9:25 Dt 6:11; 11:11–12
o 9:26 1Kg 14:9
p 1Kg 18:4; 19:10
q 9:26–28 Jdg 2:6–3:6

17 They refused to listen
and did not remember
your wonders
you performed among them.[a]
They became stiff-necked
and appointed a leader
to return to their slavery in Egypt.[A,b]
But you are a forgiving God,
gracious and compassionate,
slow to anger and abounding
in faithful love,[c]
and you did not abandon them.

18 Even after they had cast an image
of a calf
for themselves and said,
"This is your god who brought you
out of Egypt,"[d]
and they had committed
terrible blasphemies,

19 you did not abandon them
in the wilderness
because of your great compassion.
During the day the pillar of cloud
never turned away from them,
guiding them on their journey.
And during the night the pillar of fire
illuminated the way they should go.[e]

20 You sent your good Spirit[f]
to instruct them.
You did not withhold your manna[g]
from their mouths,
and you gave them water
for their thirst.[h]

21 You provided for them
in the wilderness forty years,[i]
and they lacked nothing.
Their clothes did not wear out,
and their feet did not swell.[j]

22 You gave them kingdoms
and peoples
and established boundaries for
them.
They took possession
of the land of King Sihon[B]
of Heshbon
and of the land of King Og
of Bashan.[k]

23 You multiplied their descendants
like the stars of the sky[l]
and brought them to the land

you told their ancestors to go in
and possess.

24 So their descendants went in
and possessed the land:
You subdued the Canaanites
who inhabited the land
before them
and handed their kings
and the surrounding peoples
over to them,[m]
to do as they pleased with them.

25 They captured fortified cities
and fertile land
and took possession of
well-supplied houses,
cisterns cut out of rock, vineyards,
olive groves, and fruit trees
in abundance.[n]
They ate, were filled,
became prosperous, and delighted
in your great goodness.

26 But they were disobedient
and rebelled against you.
They flung your law
behind their backs[o]
and killed your prophets[p]
who warned them
in order to turn them back to you.
They committed
terrible blasphemies.

27 So you handed them over
to their enemies,
who oppressed them.
In their time of distress,
they cried out to you,
and you heard from heaven.
In your abundant compassion
you gave them deliverers,
who rescued them
from the power of their enemies.

28 But as soon as they had relief,
they again did what was evil
in your sight.
So you abandoned them
to the power of their enemies,
who dominated them.
When they cried out to you again,
you heard from heaven and rescued
them
many times in your compassion.[q]

A 9:17 Some Hb mss, LXX; other Hb mss read in their rebellion   B 9:22 One Hb ms, LXX; other Hb mss, Vg read of Sihon, even the land of the king

9:17 We reflect God's character when we do not abandon our young people who sometimes refuse to listen. Rather, we must be **gracious and compassionate** as he is.
9:26–31 Over and over God **rescued** his people, but they quickly forgot him and returned to their sin (9:27-28).

Teaching sobering truths like these is often frustrating, which is why teachers— the capacity in which the Levites served in this chapter—need both an aptness for teaching accompanied by the power of the Holy Spirit as well as the courage to persevere.

10:28–29 The **gatekeepers** could remind people every time they left the city that they had an obligation to come back and rebuild it. **Temple servants** could tell the Jews every Sabbath day to honor God and his agenda for the sake of their families.

29 You warned them to turn back
    to your law,
but they acted arrogantly
and would not obey your commands.
They sinned against
    your ordinances,
which a person will live by
    if he does them.*a*
They stubbornly resisted,*A*
stiffened their necks, and would not
    obey.

30 You were patient with them
    for many years,
and your Spirit warned them
    through your prophets,*b*
but they would not listen.
Therefore, you handed them over
    to the surrounding peoples.*c*

31 However,
    in your abundant compassion,
you did not destroy them
    or abandon them,*d*
for you are a gracious
    and compassionate God.*e*

32 So now, our God — the great, mighty,
    and awe-inspiring God who keeps
    his gracious covenant*f* —
do not view lightly all the hardships
    that have afflicted us,
our kings and leaders,
our priests and prophets,
our ancestors and all your people,
from the days of the Assyrian kings*g*
    until today.

33 You are righteous concerning all
    that has happened to us,
because you have acted faithfully,
while we have acted wickedly.*h*

34 Our kings, leaders, priests,
    and ancestors
did not obey your law
or listen to your commands
and warnings you gave them.

35 When they were in their kingdom,
    with your abundant goodness that
    you gave them,
and in the spacious and fertile land
    you set before them,*i*
they would not serve you or turn
    from their wicked ways.

36 Here we are today,
    slaves in the land you gave
    our ancestors
so that they could enjoy its fruit
    and its goodness.
Here we are — slaves in it!*j*

37 Its abundant harvest goes
    to the kings
you have set over us,
because of our sins.
They rule over our bodies
and our livestock as they please.*k*
We are in great distress.

ISRAEL'S VOW OF FAITHFULNESS

38 In view of all this, we are making a binding agreement*l* in writing on a sealed document containing the names of our leaders, Levites, and priests.*m*

10 Those whose seals were on the document were
    the governor Nehemiah*n*
        son of Hacaliah, and Zedekiah,
2 Seraiah,*o* Azariah, Jeremiah,
3 Pashhur,*p* Amariah, Malchijah,
4 Hattush, Shebaniah, Malluch,
5 Harim, Meremoth, Obadiah,
6 Daniel, Ginnethon, Baruch,
7 Meshullam, Abijah, Mijamin,
8 Maaziah, Bilgai, and Shemaiah.
    These were the priests.

9 The Levites*q* were
    Jeshua son of Azaniah,
    Binnui of the sons of Henadad,
        Kadmiel,
10 and their brothers
    Shebaniah, Hodiah, Kelita, Pelaiah,
        Hanan,
11 Mica, Rehob, Hashabiah,
12 Zaccur, Sherebiah, Shebaniah,
13 Hodiah, Bani, and Beninu.

14 The heads of the people*r* were
    Parosh, Pahath-moab, Elam,
        Zattu, Bani,
15 Bunni, Azgad, Bebai,
16 Adonijah, Bigvai, Adin,*s*
17 Ater, Hezekiah, Azzur,
18 Hodiah, Hashum, Bezai,
19 Hariph, Anathoth, Nebai,
20 Magpiash, Meshullam, Hezir,
21 Meshezabel, Zadok, Jaddua,
22 Pelatiah, Hanan, Anaiah,
23 Hoshea, Hananiah,*t* Hasshub,
24 Hallohesh, Pilha, Shobek,
25 Rehum, Hashabnah, Maaseiah,
26 Ahijah, Hanan, Anan,
27 Malluch, Harim, Baanah.

28 The rest of the people — the priests, Levites, gatekeepers, singers, and temple servants, along with their wives, sons, and daughters, everyone who is able

a **9:29** Lv 18:5; Dt 30:16
b **9:30** 2Kg 17:13-18; Neh 9:20; Dn 9:6; 1Pt 1:10-12
c Jr 16:10-13
d **9:31** Jr 4:27
e Neh 9:17
f **9:32** Neh 1:5; Dn 9:4
g 2Kg 15:19; 17:3-6
h **9:33** Dn 9:7-8,14
i **9:35** Neh 9:25
j **9:35-36** Dt 28:47-48
k **9:37** Dt 28:33,51
l **9:38** 2Ch 23:16
m Neh 10:1-39
n **10:1** Neh 5:14; 8:9; 12:26
o **10:2-8** Neh 12:1-7,11-21
p **10:3** 1Ch 9:12
q **10:9-13** Neh 8:7; 9:4-5; 12:8-9
r **10:14-27** Ezr 2:1-61; Neh 7:6-63
s **10:16** Ezr 8:6
t **10:23** Neh 7:2

A **9:29** Lit *They gave a stubborn shoulder*

a 10:28 Neh 8:2-3
b Neh 9:2; 13:3
c 10:29 Ezr 10:5; Neh 5:12
d Neh 8:1
e 10:30 Ex 34:16; Neh 13:23
f 10:31 Neh 13:16
g Ex 23:10-11; Lv 25:1-7
h Dt 15:1-3
i 10:32 Ex 30:11-16; Mt 17:24
j 10:33 Lv 24:5-9
k Nm 10:10
l Nm 28:2–29:39
m 10:34 Lv 16:8; Neh 11:1
n Lv 6:12-13; Neh 13:31

o 10:35 Lv 26:1-10; Nm 18:12-13
p 10:36 Ex 13:2,12-13
q 10:37 Lv 23:17; Nm 15:20-21; Ezk 44:30
r Nm 18:12-13
s Lv 27:30
t 10:38 Nm 18:26
u Neh 13:12-13
v 10:39 Dt 12:6,11
w Neh 13:10-11
x 11:1 Neh 7:4
y Neh 10:34
z Neh 11:18; Is 48:2; Rv 11:2; 21:2
aa Ezr 2:70; Neh 7:73
ab 11:2 Jdg 5:9
ac 11:3 1Ch 9:2-34
ad Neh 7:73; 11:20

to understand[a] and who has separated themselves from the surrounding peoples[b] to obey the law of God — 29 join with their noble brothers and commit themselves with a sworn oath[A,c] to follow the law of God given through God's servant Moses[d] and to obey carefully all the commands, ordinances, and statutes of the LORD our Lord.

DETAILS OF THE VOW

30 We will not give our daughters in marriage to the surrounding peoples and will not take their daughters as wives for our sons.[e]

31 When the surrounding peoples bring merchandise or any kind of grain to sell on the Sabbath day, we will not buy from them on the Sabbath or a holy day.[f] We will also leave the land uncultivated in the seventh year[g] and will cancel every debt.[h]

32 We will impose the following commands on ourselves:

To give an eighth of an ounce of silver[B] yearly for the service of the house of our God:[i] 33 the bread displayed before the LORD,[C,j] the daily grain offering, the regular burnt offering, the Sabbath and New Moon offerings,[k] the appointed festivals, the holy things, the sin offerings to atone for Israel,[l] and for all the work of the house of our God.

34 We have cast lots[m] among the priests, Levites, and people for the donation of wood by our ancestral families[D] at the appointed times each year. They are to bring the wood to our God's house to burn on the altar of the LORD our God,[n] as it is written in the law.

35 We will bring the firstfruits of our land and of every fruit tree to the LORD's house year by year.[o] 36 We will also bring the firstborn of our sons and our livestock, as prescribed by the law, and will bring the firstborn of our herds and flocks to the house of our God,[p] to the priests who serve in our God's house. 37 We will bring a loaf from our first batch of dough[q] to the priests at the storerooms of the house of our God. We will also bring the firstfruits of our grain offerings, of every fruit tree, and of the new wine and fresh oil.[r] A tenth of our land's produce belongs to the Levites, for the Levites are to collect the one-tenth offering in all our agricultural towns.[s] 38 A priest from Aaron's descendants is to accompany the Levites when they collect the tenth,[t] and the Levites are to take a tenth of this offering to the storerooms of the treasury in the house of our God.[u] 39 For the Israelites and the Levites are to bring the contributions of grain, new wine, and fresh oil to the storerooms where the articles of the sanctuary are kept[v] and where the priests who minister are, along with the gatekeepers and singers. We will not neglect the house of our God.[w]

RESETTLING JERUSALEM

11 Now the leaders of the people stayed in Jerusalem,[x] and the rest of the people cast lots[y] for one out of ten to come and live in Jerusalem, the holy city,[z] while the other nine-tenths remained in their towns.[aa] 2 The people blessed all the men who volunteered[ab] to live in Jerusalem.

3 These are the heads of the province who stayed in Jerusalem[ac] (but in the villages of Judah each lived on his own property in their towns[ad] — the Israelites,

---

[A] 10:29 Lit *and enter in a curse and in an oath*   [B] 10:32 Lit *give one-third of a shekel*   [C] 10:33 Lit *rows of bread*   [D] 10:34 Lit *the house of our fathers*

10:30 King Solomon had brought wicked idolatrous ideas into his life and into the nation by marrying women who did not worship the Lord. The people now, by contrast, would honor God by obeying his commands.

10:32 The people realized that God had richly blessed them with all the resources they needed, and they could use a portion of it to improve God's **house**. Likewise, God has provided his people with all the money and talents needed to rebuild our churches and our communities. We have the gospel of Christ and the power of the Holy Spirit. He will bless our submission to his program,

but we must step out in obedience and give in order to access those blessings.

11:1-2 God calls for redevelopment in this story. Our church adopted a local apartment complex. We needed to get someone to invade the premises, exert a godly influence there, and duplicate themselves. Consistent with the example presented here, nine people who didn't go were tasked with supporting the one who did.

In Jeremiah 29:7 God said, "Pursue the well-being of the city I have deported you to. Pray to the Lord on its behalf, for when it thrives, you will thrive." Within that state-

ment is the idea that a believer has the ability to impact the pagan environment where he lives. Pornography, crime, and drugs are destroying our kids. So what can you do? In asking God to show you how to build a stable context for life, you will help build a strong family. You can impact your city for Christ.

11:3-36 There is a high degree of organization in this list. In your house, your business, or your world—seek organization. God does not work in the midst of disorder. As 1 Corinthians 14:40 says, "everything is to be done decently and in order." You cannot give chaos to God and say, "Bless it."

priests, Levites, temple servants, and descendants of Solomon's servants[a] — [4] while some of the descendants of Judah and Benjamin settled in Jerusalem):

Judah's[b] descendants:

Athaiah son of Uzziah, son of Zechariah, son of Amariah, son of Shephatiah, son of Mahalalel, of Perez's descendants; [5] and Maaseiah son of Baruch, son of Col-hozeh, son of Hazaiah, son of Adaiah, son of Joiarib, son of Zechariah, a descendant of the Shilonite. [6] The total number of Perez's descendants, who settled in Jerusalem, was 468 capable men.

[7] These were Benjamin's descendants:

Sallu son of Meshullam, son of Joed, son of Pedaiah, son of Kolaiah, son of Maaseiah, son of Ithiel, son of Jeshaiah, [8] and after him Gabbai and Sallai: 928. [9] Joel son of Zichri was the officer over them, and Judah son of Hassenuah was second in command over the city.

[10] The priests:

Jedaiah son of Joiarib, Jachin, and [11] Seraiah son of Hilkiah, son of Meshullam, son of Zadok, son of Meraioth, son of Ahitub, the chief official of God's temple, [12] and their relatives who did the work at the temple: 822. Adaiah son of Jeroham, son of Pelaliah, son of Amzi, son of Zechariah, son of Pashhur, son of Malchijah [13] and his relatives, the heads of families: 242. Amashsai son of Azarel, son of Ahzai, son of Meshillemoth, son of Immer, [14] and their relatives, capable men: 128. Zabdiel son of Haggedolim, was their chief.

[15] The Levites:

Shemaiah son of Hasshub, son of Azrikam, son of Hashabiah, son of Bunni; [16] and Shabbethai and Jozabad, from the heads of the Levites, who supervised the work outside the house of God; [17] Mattaniah son of Mica, son of Zabdi, son of Asaph, the one[A] who began the thanksgiving in prayer;[c] Bakbukiah, second among his relatives; and Abda son of Shammua, son

of Galal, son of Jeduthun.[d] [18] All the Levites in the holy city:[e] 284.

[19] The gatekeepers:

Akkub, Talmon, and their relatives, who guarded the city gates: 172.

[20] The rest of Israel, the priests, and the Levites were in all the villages of Judah, each on his own inherited property.[f] [21] The temple servants lived on Ophel;[g] Ziha and Gishpa supervised the temple servants.

THE LEVITES AND PRIESTS

[22] The leader of the Levites in Jerusalem was Uzzi son of Bani, son of Hashabiah, son of Mattaniah, son of Mica, of the descendants of Asaph, who were singers for the service of God's house. [23] There was, in fact, a command of the king regarding them, and an ordinance regulating the singers'[h] daily tasks. [24] Pethahiah son of Meshezabel, of the descendants of Zerah[i] son of Judah, was the king's[j] agent[B] in every matter concerning the people.

[25] As for the farming settlements with their fields:

Some of Judah's descendants lived
   in Kiriath-arba[k]
and Dibon and their surrounding
   villages,[l] and Jekabzeel and
   its settlements;
[26] in Jeshua, Moladah,[m] Beth-pelet,
[27] Hazar-shual, and Beer-sheba[n]
   and its surrounding villages;
[28] in Ziklag[o] and Meconah
   and its surrounding villages;
[29] in En-rimmon, Zorah,[p]
   Jarmuth,[q] and
[30] Zanoah[r] and Adullam
   with their settlements;
   in Lachish[s] with its
   fields and Azekah[t]
   and its surrounding villages.
So they settled from Beer-sheba[u]
   to Hinnom Valley.[v]

[31] Benjamin's descendants:
   from Geba,[c,w] Michmash,[x] Aija,
   and Bethel[y]
   and its surrounding villages,
[32] Anathoth,[z] Nob,[aa] Ananiah,
[33] Hazor,[ab] Ramah,[ac] Gittaim,[ad]
[34] Hadid, Zeboim,[ae] Neballat,
[35] Lod, and Ono,[af] in Craftsmen's Valley.
[36] Some of the Judean divisions
   of Levites were in Benjamin.

[a] 11:3 Neh 7:39–43,46–60
[b] 11:4-19 1Ch 9:3-21
[c] 11:17 1Ch 6:31,39; 2Ch 5:12

[d] 11:17 1Ch 16:42
[e] 11:18 Neh 11:1; Rv 21:2
[f] 11:20 Nm 36:3; Neh 11:3
[g] 11:21 Neh 3:26
[h] 11:22-23 1Ch 15:16; Neh 7:44
[i] 11:24 Gn 38:30; 1Ch 2:43
[j] Neh 2:1; 5:14
[k] 11:25 Jos 14:15
[l] Jos 3:9,17
[m] 11:26 Jos 15:26-28
[n] 11:27 2Sm 17:11
[o] 11:28 1Sm 27:6
[p] 11:29 Jos 15:33
[q] Jos 10:5
[r] 11:30 Jos 15:34-35
[s] Jos 10:3; 15:39
[t] Jos 10:10
[u] Jos 15:27
[v] 2Kg 23:10
[w] 11:31 Jos 21:17
[x] 1Sm 13:2
[y] Jos 12:9
[z] 11:32 Jos 21:18; Jr 1:1
[aa] 1Sm 21:1; 22:9
[ab] 11:33 Jos 11:1
[ac] Jos 18:25
[ad] 2Sm 4:3
[ae] 11:34 1Sm 13:18
[af] 11:35 1Ch 8:12; Ac 9:32

[A] 11:17 Lit *the head*   [B] 11:24 Lit *was at the king's hand*   [C] 11:31 Or *descendants from Geba lived in*

[a] 12:1-7 Neh 12:12-21 [b] 12:1 Ezr 2:1-2; 7:7 [c] Ezr 3:2 [d] 12:4 Neh 12:16; Zch 1:1 [e] 1Ch 24:10 [f] 12:6 1Ch 24:7 [g] 12:7 Ezr 2:2; 3:2 [h] 12:8 Neh 11:17 [i] 12:10 Neh 3:20

[j] 12:23 1Ch 9:14-22 [k] 12:24 1Ch 16:4; 23:30; 2Ch 29:25 [l] 12:25 Neh 11:17 [m] 1Ch 26:15,17; Ezr 2:42; Neh 11:19 [n] 12:26 Neh 5:14; 10:1 [o] Neh 8:1-2,9 [p] 12:27 Ezr 6:16 [q] 1Ch 15:16 [r] 12:28 1Ch 2:54; 9:16 [s] 12:30 Neh 13:22,30

12 These[a] are the priests and Levites[b]
who went up with Zerubbabel[c] son
of Shealtiel and with Jeshua:
Seraiah, Jeremiah, Ezra,
2 Amariah, Malluch, Hattush,
3 Shecaniah, Rehum, Meremoth,
4 Iddo,[d] Ginnethoi, Abijah,[e]
5 Mijamin, Maadiah, Bilgah,
6 Shemaiah, Joiarib, Jedaiah,[f]
7 Sallu, Amok, Hilkiah, Jedaiah.
These were the heads of the priests and
their relatives in the days of Jeshua.[g]

8 The Levites:
Jeshua, Binnui, Kadmiel,
Sherebiah, Judah, and Mattaniah[h] —
he and his relatives were in charge
of the songs of praise.
9 Bakbukiah, Unni,[A] and their relatives
stood opposite them in the services.
10 Jeshua fathered Joiakim,
Joiakim fathered Eliashib,
Eliashib[i] fathered Joiada,
11 Joiada fathered Jonathan,
and Jonathan fathered Jaddua.[B]

12 In the days of Joiakim, the heads of the
priestly families were

Meraiah	of Seraiah,
Hananiah	of Jeremiah,
13 Meshullam	of Ezra,
Jehohanan	of Amariah,
14 Jonathan	of Malluchi,
Joseph	of Shebaniah,
15 Adna	of Harim,
Helkai	of Meraioth,
16 Zechariah	of Iddo,
Meshullam	of Ginnethon,
17 Zichri	of Abijah,
Piltai	of Moadiah, of Miniamin,
18 Shammua	of Bilgah,
Jehonathan	of Shemaiah,
19 Mattenai	of Joiarib,
Uzzi	of Jedaiah,
20 Kallai	of Sallai,
Eber	of Amok,
21 Hashabiah	of Hilkiah,
and Nethanel	of Jedaiah.

22 In the days of Eliashib, Joiada, Johanan, and Jaddua, the heads of the families
of the Levites and priests were recorded
while Darius the Persian ruled. 23 Levi's descendants, the family heads, were recorded in the Book of the Historical Events[j]
during the days of Johanan son of Eliashib.
24 The heads of the Levites — Hashabiah,
Sherebiah, and Jeshua son of Kadmiel,
along with their relatives opposite them
— gave praise and thanks, division by
division, as David the man of God had
prescribed.[k] 25 This included Mattaniah,[l]
Bakbukiah, and Obadiah. Meshullam, Talmon, and Akkub were gatekeepers who
guarded the storerooms at the city gates.[m]
26 These served in the days of Joiakim son
of Jeshua, son of Jozadak, and in the days
of Nehemiah the governor[n] and Ezra the
priest and scribe.[o]

DEDICATION OF THE WALL

27 At the dedication of the wall[p] of Jerusalem, they sent for the Levites wherever
they lived and brought them to Jerusalem
to celebrate the joyous dedication with
thanksgiving and singing accompanied by
cymbals, harps, and lyres.[q] 28 The singers
gathered from the region around Jerusalem, from the settlements of the Netophathites,[r] 29 from Beth-gilgal, and from the
fields of Geba and Azmaveth, for they had
built settlements for themselves around
Jerusalem. 30 After the priests and Levites
had purified themselves, they purified the
people, the city gates, and the wall.[s]
31 Then I brought the leaders of Judah
up on top of the wall, and I appointed two
large processions that gave thanks. One

[A] 12:9 Alt Hb tradition reads *Unno* [B] 12:10-11 These men were high priests.

12:1-26 In recording the names of **the priests and Levites who went up with Zerubbabel** (12:1), Nehemiah was saying to the returnees, "Look, you have a hundred-year legacy." Everyone stands on someone's shoulders; many someones enabled you to be where you are.

12:27-29 The people prepared to celebrate **with thanksgiving and singing** (12:27) because everybody knew that God was behind their success in erecting the structure. Something is wrong with the fan who can sit still in his seat when his team scores the winning goal with one second left on the clock. How can we not praise God for all he has done on our behalf?

That **they sent for the Levites wherever they lived** (12:27) shows that they got religion back at the center of the nation's life. This detail is important, because if you want heaven to intervene in your earthly circumstances, God's kingdom agenda must become your focus.

12:30 **After the priests and Levites had purified themselves, they purified the people, the city gates, and the wall.** God is absolutely holy—set apart and separate from sinners. He doesn't tolerate wickedness. When we come before his presence, then, we must conform to his agenda. That means we confess our sins before him and walk by grace in righteousness.

My dog gets dirty and wants to come into my house, but to do that he must conform to my agenda. Since this is our Father's world, and we are dirty sinful people, each of us must be made clean to worship God. If you are a Christian, Jesus Christ sanctified you. You are set apart for God.

12:31-42 There were two choirs on the wall; one went to the right and the other to the left. Thus, they were stationed in such a way that they got a panoramic view of what God had done and could reflect on their unity in the flow of movement as they all converged on the house of God.

went to the right on the wall, toward the Dung Gate.[a] **32** Hoshaiah and half the leaders of Judah followed, **33** along with Azariah, Ezra, Meshullam, **34** Judah, Benjamin, Shemaiah, Jeremiah, **35** and some of the priests' sons with trumpets, and Zechariah son of Jonathan, son of Shemaiah, son of Mattaniah, son of Micaiah, son of Zaccur, son of Asaph followed **36** as well as his relatives — Shemaiah, Azarel, Milalai, Gilalai, Maai, Nethanel, Judah, and Hanani, with the musical instruments of David, the man of God.[b] Ezra the scribe[c] went in front of them. **37** At the Fountain Gate[d] they climbed the steps of the city of David[e] on the ascent of the wall and went above the house of David to the Water Gate[f] on the east.

38 The second thanksgiving procession went to the left, and I followed it with half the people along the top of the wall, past the Tower of the Ovens[g] to the Broad Wall,[h] **39** above the Ephraim Gate,[i] and by the Old Gate,[j] the Fish Gate,[k] the Tower of Hananel, and the Tower of the Hundred, to the Sheep Gate.[l] They stopped at the Gate of the Guard.[m] **40** The two thanksgiving processions stood in the house of God. So did I and half of the officials accompanying me, **41** as well as the priests:

Eliakim, Maaseiah, Miniamin,
Micaiah, Elioenai, Zechariah,
and Hananiah, with trumpets;

42 and Maaseiah, Shemaiah, Eleazar, Uzzi, Jehohanan, Malchijah, Elam, and Ezer.

Then the singers sang, with Jezrahiah as the leader. **43** On that day they offered great sacrifices and rejoiced because God had given them great joy.[n] The women and children also celebrated, and Jerusalem's rejoicing was heard far away.[o]

SUPPORT OF THE LEVITES' MINISTRY

44 On that same day men were placed in charge of the rooms[p] that housed the supplies, contributions, firstfruits, and tenths.[q] The legally required portions for the priests and Levites[r] were gathered from the village fields, because Judah was grateful to the priests and Levites who were serving.[s] **45** They performed the service of their God and the service of purification, along with the singers and gatekeepers,[t] as David and his son Solomon had prescribed.[u] **46** For long ago, in the days of David and Asaph,[v] there were heads[A] of the singers and songs of praise and thanksgiving to God.[w] **47** So in the days of Zerubbabel[x] and Nehemiah,[y] all Israel contributed the daily portions[z] for the singers and gatekeepers. They also set aside daily portions for the Levites, and the Levites set aside daily portions[aa] for Aaron's descendants.

NEHEMIAH'S FURTHER REFORMS

13 At that time[ab] the book of Moses[ac] was read publicly to[B] the people.[ad] The command was found written in it that no Ammonite or Moabite[ae] should ever enter the assembly of God,[af] **2** because they did not meet the Israelites with food and water. Instead, they hired Balaam against them to curse them,[ag] but our God turned the curse into a blessing.[ah] **3** When they heard the law, they separated all those of mixed descent[ai] from Israel.

4 Now before this, the priest Eliashib[aj] had been put in charge of the storerooms of the house of our God.[ak] He was a relative[c] of Tobiah[al] **5** and had prepared a large room for him where they had previously stored the grain offerings, the frankincense, the articles, and the tenths of grain, new wine, and fresh oil[am] prescribed for the Levites, singers, and gatekeepers, along with the contributions for the priests.[an] **6** While all this was happening, I was not in Jerusalem, because I had returned to King Artaxerxes[ao] of Babylon[ap] in the

---

[a] 12:31 Neh 2:13
[b] 12:36 1Ch 15:16,19-21; 2Ch 8:14; Neh 12:24
[c] Neh 8:1,4
[d] 12:37 Neh 2:14
[e] Neh 3:15
[f] Neh 3:26; 8:1
[g] 12:38 Neh 3:11
[h] Neh 3:8
[i] 12:39 2Kg 14:13; Neh 8:16
[j] Neh 3:6
[k] Neh 3:3
[l] Neh 3:1; Jn 5:2
[m] Neh 3:25
[n] 12:43 Ezr 6:16-17,22
[o] Ezr 3:13
[p] 12:44 Neh 13:4,13
[q] 12:44 Neh 10:37-39
[r] Neh 7:39-43
[s] Dt 18:8
[t] 12:45 Neh 7:44-45
[u] 2Ch 8:14
[v] 12:46 2Ch 29:30
[w] 1Ch 9:33
[x] 12:47 Neh 7:7; Hg 1:1
[y] Neh 1:1; 5:14
[z] Neh 11:23
[aa] Nm 18:21
[ab] 13:1 Neh 12:27
[ac] Dt 28:61; Neh 8:1-3
[ad] Neh 9:3
[ae] Neh 13:23
[af] Dt 23:3
[ag] 13:2 Nm 22:2-11; 23:7; 24:10; Dt 23:3-5
[ah] Dt 23:4-5
[ai] 13:3 Dt 23:3,6
[aj] 13:4 Neh 12:10,22-23
[ak] Neh 12:44
[al] Neh 2:10; 6:14
[am] 13:5 Neh 12:44
[an] Nm 13:21-32; Dt 14:28-29; 26:12-15
[ao] 13:6 Neh 2:1-8
[ap] Ezr 5:13

[A] 12:46 Alt Hb tradition reads *there was a head*   [B] 13:1 Lit *read in the ears of*   [C] 13:4 Or *an associate*

12:43 Joy is a spiritual tranquility provided by God. When Paul was locked up in chains he said, "Rejoice in the Lord always. I will say it again: Rejoice!" (Phil 4:4). Joy is not circumstantially determined but divinely determined.

12:44-47 When the people got right with God, they prioritized things. They brought in the **contributions** and **tenths** (12:44). If modern believers really understood what the church is and the impact that we could make, there would be no problem getting Christians to serve and give and invest in eternal things.

Our thinking must be conformed to the divine perspective so that our actions follow.

Too many Christians are trying to live in two kingdoms. They are trying to serve God and serve the world order at the same time, and you can't do that. We have a desperate need for people who will put God's kingdom first. **13:4-5** The issue here was letting family relations control spiritual decisions. Eliashib **was a relative of Tobiah** (13:4), archenemy of God. Nehemiah wouldn't even let Tobiah help build the wall (2:20), yet Eliashib had let him take up an apartment in the temple! As

a priest, Eliashib should have been setting the spiritual temperature for the rest of the people. His actions here are a reminder that regardless of your love for your family, they are never to have such an influence on you that you make spiritually foolish choices.

Jesus said, "If anyone comes to me and does not hate his own father and mother, wife and children, brothers and sisters . . . he cannot be my disciple" (Luke 14:26). So if a family member wants you to disobey God, then you have to make a choice. Jesus said, "I did not come to bring peace, but a sword" (Matt 10:34).

a 13:6 Neh 2:1; 5:14
b Neh 1:11; 2:6
c 13:9 1Ch 23:28; 2Ch 29:5; Neh 13:30
d Neh 12:44
e 13:10 Dt 12:19; Neh 12:44,47
f 2Ch 29:5
g 13:11 Neh 10:37-39; Mal 3:10
h Neh 12:44-45
i 13:12 Neh 10:37-38
j 13:13 Neh 7:2; Ac 6:1-5; 1Co 4:2
k Neh 12:47
l 13:14 Neh 5:19; 13:31
m 13:15 Ex 20:8-11; Dt 5:12-15

n 13:16 Neh 10:31
o 13:17 Ex 20:8-11
p 13:18 Ezr 9:10-11,13; Jr 17:21-23
q 13:19 Lv 23:32
r Neh 7:1,3; Jr 17:21-22
s 13:22 Neh 12:30; 13:30
t Ex 20:8
u Neh 5:19; 13:14,31
v Neh 1:5; 9:17,27,31
w 13:23 Dt 23:3; Ezr 9:1-2; Neh 13:1-3; Mal 2:11
x 13:24 Est 1:22; 8:9
y 13:25 Ezr 9:3; Is 50:6
z Ezr 10:5
aa Ezr 9:1-2; Neh 10:30

thirty-second year of his reign.*a* It was only later that I asked the king for a leave of absence*b* 7 so I could return to Jerusalem. Then I discovered the evil that Eliashib had done on behalf of Tobiah by providing him a room in the courts of God's house. 8 I was greatly displeased and threw all of Tobiah's household possessions out of the room. 9 I ordered that the rooms be purified,*c* and I had the articles of the house of God restored there, along with the grain offering and frankincense.*d* 10 I also found out that because the portions for the Levites had not been given,*e* each of the Levites and the singers performing the service had gone back to his own field.*f* 11 Therefore, I rebuked the officials, asking, "Why has the house of God been neglected?"*g* I gathered the Levites and singers together and stationed them at their posts.*h* 12 Then all Judah brought a tenth of the grain, new wine, and fresh oil into the storehouses.*i* 13 I appointed as treasurers over the storehouses the priest Shelemiah, the scribe Zadok, and Pedaiah of the Levites, with Hanan son of Zaccur, son of Mattaniah to assist them, because they were considered trustworthy.*j* They were responsible for the distribution to their colleagues.*k*

14 Remember me for this, my God, and don't erase the deeds of faithful love I have done for the house of my God and for its services.*l*

15 At that time I saw people in Judah treading winepresses on the Sabbath. They were also bringing in stores of grain and loading them on donkeys, along with wine, grapes, and figs. All kinds of goods were being brought to Jerusalem on the Sabbath day. So I warned them against selling food on that day.*m* 16 The Tyrians living there were importing fish and all kinds of merchandise and selling them on the Sabbath to the people of Judah in Jerusalem.*n*

17 I rebuked the nobles of Judah and said to them: "What is this evil you are doing — profaning the Sabbath day?*o* 18 Didn't your ancestors do the same, so that our God brought all this disaster on us and on this city?*p* And now you are rekindling his anger against Israel by profaning the Sabbath!"

19 When shadows began to fall on the city gates of Jerusalem just before the Sabbath, I gave orders that the city gates be closed and not opened until after the Sabbath.*q* I posted some of my men at the gates, so that no goods could enter during the Sabbath day.*r* 20 Once or twice the merchants and those who sell all kinds of goods camped outside Jerusalem, 21 but I warned them, "Why are you camping in front of the wall? If you do it again, I'll use force^A against you." After that they did not come again on the Sabbath. 22 Then I instructed the Levites to purify themselves*s* and guard the city gates in order to keep the Sabbath day holy.*t*

Remember me for this also, my God,*u* and look on me with compassion according to the abundance of your faithful love.*v*

23 In those days I also saw Jews who had married women from Ashdod, Ammon, and Moab.*w* 24 Half of their children spoke the language of Ashdod or the language of one of the other peoples but could not speak Hebrew.^B,*x* 25 I rebuked them, cursed them, beat some of their men, and pulled out their hair.*y* I forced them to take an oath*z* before God and said, "You must not give your daughters in marriage to their sons or take their daughters as wives for your sons or yourselves!*aa* 26 Didn't King Solomon of Israel sin in matters like this? There was not a king like him among many nations. He was loved by his God,

---

^A 13:21 Lit *again, I will send a hand*   ^B 13:24 Lit *Judahite*

13:7-8 In throwing **all of Tobiah's household possessions out** (13:8), Nehemiah made an autocratic decision to cut off a family relationship because it violated the premises of God. If people are rebelling against the principles of God, it's your business to love them enough to turn them around.

13:10-12 The problem presented in verse 10 was a compromise of ministry. The things that mattered to people were put first, and the things of God were put last. Thus, **the portions for the Levites had not been given** (13:10). And as the ministry went downhill, so the spiritual temperature of the people cooled. In Malachi 3:8, the prophet asked, "Will a man rob God?" And indeed, since the

people had stolen from God in the matter of the Levites, their lives were cursed. Believers are to "seek first the kingdom of God and his righteousness" (Matt 6:33).

13:14 When Nehemiah asked God to **remember** him, he was asking for help to accomplish God's kingdom agenda in his community.

13:22 You ought to use the first day of the week, our **Sabbath**, to remind yourself, "I ate last week. My roof is still over my head. I've got clothing." Making time for intentional reflection on the grace of God in your life will result in more consistent obedience and thankfulness.

13:23-24 The **children** mentioned here had not been taught the language in which God's law was written (13:24). In marrying women

who didn't worship and obey the one true God, the men had committed immorality. For this, their children suffered.

13:25-28 I rebuked them, cursed them, beat some of their men, and pulled out their hair (13:25) is one way of saying that Nehemiah went off on them.

To keep yourself from compromising in terms of sexual purity in particular, contemplate the significant damage a breach in standards would do to the cause of Christ, to the respect received from your children, and to your relationship with your spouse (current or future). Satan is actively looking for opportunities to bring you down. He studies your game film. He knows your weaknesses.

and God made him king over all Israel, yet foreign women drew him into sin.[a] [27] Why then should we hear about you doing all this terrible evil and acting unfaithfully against our God by marrying foreign women?"[b] [28] Even one of the sons of Jehoiada, son of the high priest Eliashib,[c] had become a son-in-law to Sanballat the Horonite.[d] So I drove him away from me.[e]

[29] Remember them, my God, for defiling the priesthood as well as the covenant of the priesthood and the Levites.[f]

[30] So I purified them from everything foreign[g] and assigned specific duties to each of the priests and Levites.[h] [31] I also arranged for the donation of wood at the appointed times and for the firstfruits.[i] Remember me, my God, with favor.[j]

[a] 13:26 1Kg 3:13; 11:1-10
[b] 13:27 Ezr 9:1-2
[c] 13:28 Neh 12:10,22-23
[d] Neh 2:10; 4:1; 6:1
[e] Lv 21:10,13-15

[f] 13:29 Neh 6:14; Mal 2:4-8
[g] 13:30 Neh 10:30
[h] Neh 12:44-47
[i] 13:31 Neh 10:34-36
[j] Neh 5:19; 13:14,22

13:28-31 Nehemiah invited God to remember that although **one of the sons of Jehoiada** had compromised (13:28), Nehemiah had not. Surely, then, God would remember him **with favor** at the day of judgment (13:31).

You too can live your life from God's perspective, so that you may hear those joyous words, "well done" (Matt 25:21).

ESTHER

INTRODUCTION

Author

THE AUTHOR OF THE BOOK of Esther is unknown. The book itself names no writer, and no reliable tradition exists identifying one.

Historical Background

In 587 BC, Jerusalem fell to King Nebuchadnezzar who carried many of the people of Judah into exile in Babylon (see 2 Chr 36:15-21). In 539 BC, Cyrus the Great, the ruler of the Medo-Persian Empire, conquered Babylon and issued a decree permitting exiled people, including the Jews, to return to their homelands (see 2 Chr 36:22-23). Though many Jews returned, others continued to live throughout the Medo-Persian Empire. The events of the book of Esther took place during the reign of King Ahasuerus (Xerxes I); he ruled the empire from 486 to 465 BC. His son, Artaxerxes I, would later send both Ezra and Nehemiah to Jerusalem (see Ezra 7:11-28; Neh 2:1-8).

Message and Purpose

Esther is unique because it is the only book in Scripture that does not mention the name of God directly. This is because God wanted to use the book to show how his providence (that is, his invisible hand) works behind the scenes to bring about his purposes in history. So even though God is not on the front page of Esther, his fingerprints are all throughout the book.

Esther's dramatic story unfolds with the people of God, the Jews, living in Persia because of their sin. Through a series of circumstances, the young Jewish woman for whom the book is named is selected as the new queen because of her natural beauty and personality. And yet, her people are threatened with annihilation due to an evil man named Haman. But God, working behind the scenes, brings about his people's deliverance when Esther decides to risk her life to speak up for them to the king and declares, "If I perish, I perish" (Esth 4:16).

This book demonstrates that though his methods vary, God is in control. His kingdom promises and purposes cannot be thwarted.

www.bhpublishinggroup.com/qr/te/17_00

Outline

I. Setting the Stage: A New Queen and a Foiled Assassination (1:1–2:23)
II. The Tension Builds: A Threatened Disaster (3:1–5:14)
III. Climax: The God of Reversals (6:1–10:3)

VASHTI ANGERS THE KING

1 These events took place during the days of Ahasuerus,[a] who ruled 127 provinces[b] from India to Cush. [2] In those days King Ahasuerus reigned from his royal throne[c] in the fortress at Susa.[d] [3] He held a feast[e] in the third year of his reign for all his officials and staff, the army of Persia and Media,[f] the nobles,[g] and the officials from the provinces. [4] He displayed the glorious wealth of his kingdom and the magnificent splendor of his greatness[h] for a total of 180 days.

[5] At the end of this time, the king held a week-long banquet[i] in the garden courtyard[j] of the royal palace[k] for all the people, from the greatest to the least,[l] who were present in the fortress of Susa.[m] [6] White and violet linen hangings were fastened with fine white and purple linen cords to silver rods on marble[A] columns. Gold and silver couches[n] were arranged on a mosaic pavement of red feldspar,[B] marble, mother-of-pearl, and precious stones.

[7] Drinks were served in an array of gold goblets,[o] each with a different design. Royal wine flowed freely, according to the king's bounty.[p] [8] The drinking was according to royal decree: "There are no restrictions." The king had ordered every wine steward in his household to serve whatever each person wanted. [9] Queen Vashti also gave a feast for the women of King Ahasuerus's palace.

[10] On the seventh day, when the king was feeling good from the wine,[q] Ahasuerus commanded Mehuman, Biztha, Harbona,[r] Bigtha, Abagtha, Zethar, and Carkas — the seven eunuchs[s] who personally served him — [11] to bring Queen Vashti before him with her royal crown. He wanted to show off her beauty to the people and the officials, because she was very beautiful.[t] [12] But Queen Vashti refused to come at the king's command that was delivered by his eunuchs. The king became furious and his anger burned within him.[u]

THE KING'S DECREE

[13] The king consulted the wise men[v] who understood the times,[c,w] for it was his normal procedure to confer with experts in law and justice. [14] The most trusted ones[D] were Carshena, Shethar, Admatha, Tarshish, Meres, Marsena, and Memucan. They were the seven officials[x] of Persia and Media[y] who had personal access to the king[z] and occupied the highest positions in the kingdom.[aa] [15] The king asked, "According to the law, what should be done with Queen Vashti, since she refused to obey King Ahasuerus's command that was delivered by the eunuchs?"

[16] Memucan said in the presence of the king and his officials, "Queen Vashti has wronged not only the king, but all the officials and the peoples who are in every one of King Ahasuerus's provinces.[ab] [17] For the queen's action will become public knowledge to all the women and cause them to despise their husbands and say, 'King Ahasuerus ordered Queen Vashti brought before him, but she did not come.' [18] Before this day is over, the noble women of Persia and Media who hear about the queen's act will say the same thing to all the king's officials, resulting in more contempt and fury. [19] "If it meets the king's approval, he should personally issue a royal decree. Let it be recorded in the laws of Persia and Media, so that it cannot be revoked:[ac] Vashti is not to enter King Ahasuerus's presence, and her royal position is to be given to another woman who is more worthy than she.[ad] [20] The decree the king issues will be heard throughout his vast kingdom,[ae] so all women will honor their husbands,[af] from the greatest to the least."[ag]

[21] The king and his counselors approved the proposal, and he followed Memucan's advice. [22] He sent letters to all the royal provinces, to each province in its own script and to each ethnic group in its own language,[ah] that every man should be master of his own house and speak in the language of his own people.

a 1:1 Ezr 4:6; Dn 9:1
b Est 8:9; 9:30
c 1:2 1Kg 1:46
d Ezr 4:9; Neh 1:1; Dn 8:2
e 1:3 Gn 40:20; 1Kg 3:15; Est 2:18
f Dn 5:28
g Est 6:9; Dn 1:3
h 1:4 Dn 4:28-30
i 1:5 Est 2:18
j 2Kg 21:18; Est 7:7-8
k Est 2:8
l Est 1:20
m Ezr 4:9
n 1:6 Est 7:8; Ezk 23:41; Am 6:4
o 1:7 Dn 5:1-3
p Est 2:18
q 1:10 2Sm 13:28
r Est 7:9
s 2Kg 20:18; Est 2:21; 6:14; Mt 19:12
t 1:11 Est 2:7
u 1:12 Est 7:7; Pr 19:12
v 1:13 Jr 10:7; Dn 2:2,12; Mt 2:1
w 1Ch 12:32
x 1:14 Ezr 7:14
y Dn 5:28
z 2Kg 25:19
aa Dn 2:48-49
ab 1:16 Est 1:1,3,5; 9:30
ac 1:19 Est 8:8; Dn 6:8,15
ad Est 2:2,4,17
ae 1:20 Est 1:1; 8:9
af Est 1:10-12; Eph 5:22,24,33; Col 3:18; 1Tm 2:12; 1Pt 3:1
ag Est 1:5
ah 1:22 Neh 13:24; Est 3:12; 8:9

A 1:6 Or alabaster   B 1:6 Or of porphyry   C 1:13 Or understood propitious times   D 1:14 Lit Those near him

---

1:2 **Susa** was located in what is now southwest Iran. **Ahasuerus** was king of the Medo-Persian Empire, and his name is most likely a title (like "president" or "czar") for Xerxes I, who ruled from 486–465 BC.

Importantly, the first Medo-Persian king, Cyrus the Great, had issued a decree in 539 BC permitting the Jews to return to their homeland and rebuild the temple (see 2 Chr 36:22-23). By the time Ahasuerus came to power, many Jews had returned to Jerusalem. Many others had not.

1:10-12 Intoxicated, **Ahasueras** wanted to show off his **very beautiful** queen to his drunken friends. When **Queen Vashti refused** the **king's command**, he went from **feeling good** to being **furious.**

1:13-15 **The king consulted ... experts in law and justice** (1:13) because what had happened wasn't considered a mere marital dispute but a legal matter. Ahasuerus needed counsel about what he should do with Vashti **according to the law** (1:15).

1:16-18 In other words, Memucan said, "She's gotten us all in hot water with our wives, King!"

1:19 That **a royal decree** could not be **revoked** is a government detail that will prove important as the story of Esther unfolds.

1:21-22 This suggestion (1:19-20) was all the king needed to hear. His queen had disrespected him in public, his advisors were in a state of panic, and he needed a plan to prevent things from getting out of hand.

a 2:1 Est 1:3,10
b Est 1:12; 7:10
c Est 1:10–12,16-21
d 2:2 1Kg 1:2
e 2:3 Gn 41:34
f Neh 1:1; Est 1:1; Dn 8:2
g Est 1:10
h Est 2:8–9,12-13
i 2:4 Est 2:17
j Est 1:19
k 2:5 Ezr 2:2; Est 2:15; 3:2
l 2Sm 6:5-13
m 1Sm 9:1
n 2:6 2Kg 24:10-15; 2Ch
36:10; Jr 24:1; 29:1-2
o 2:7 Est 9:29

p 2:14 1Kg 11:3; Dn 5:2
q Est 4:11
r 2:15 Est 9:29
s Est 5:2,8
t 2:16 Est 1:2

THE SEARCH FOR A NEW QUEEN

2 Some time later,[a] when King Ahasuerus's rage[b] had cooled down, he remembered Vashti, what she had done, and what was decided against her.[c] 2 The king's personal attendants suggested, "Let a search be made for beautiful young virgins for the king.[d] 3 Let the king appoint commissioners[e] in each province of his kingdom, so that they may gather all the beautiful young virgins to the harem at the fortress of Susa.[f] Put them under the supervision of Hegai, the king's eunuch,[g] keeper of the women,[h] and give them the required beauty treatments. 4 Then the young woman who pleases the king[i] will become queen instead of Vashti."[j] This suggestion pleased the king, and he did accordingly.

5 In the fortress of Susa, there was a Jewish man named Mordecai[k] son of Jair, son of Shimei,[l] son of Kish,[m] a Benjaminite. 6 He had been taken into exile from Jerusalem with the other captives when King Nebuchadnezzar of Babylon took King Jeconiah of Judah into exile.[n] 7 Mordecai was the legal guardian of his cousin[A] Hadassah (that is, Esther), because she had no father or mother. The young woman had a beautiful figure and was extremely good-looking. When her father and mother died, Mordecai had adopted her as his own daughter.[o]

8 When the king's command and edict became public knowledge and when many young women were gathered at the fortress of Susa under Hegai's supervision, Esther was taken to the palace, into the supervision of Hegai, keeper of the women. 9 The young woman pleased him and gained his favor so that he accelerated the process of the beauty treatments

and the special diet that she received. He assigned seven hand-picked female servants to her from the palace and transferred her and her servants to the harem's best quarters.

10 Esther did not reveal her ethnicity or her family background, because Mordecai had ordered her not to make them known. 11 Every day Mordecai took a walk in front of the harem's courtyard to learn how Esther was doing and to see what was happening to her.

12 During the year before each young woman's turn to go to King Ahasuerus, the harem regulation required her to receive beauty treatments with oil of myrrh for six months and then with perfumes and cosmetics for another six months. 13 When the young woman would go to the king, she was given whatever she requested to take with her from the harem to the palace. 14 She would go in the evening, and in the morning she would return to a second harem under the supervision of the king's eunuch Shaashgaz, keeper of the concubines.[p] She never went to the king again, unless he desired her and summoned her by name.[q]

ESTHER BECOMES QUEEN

15 Esther was the daughter of Abihail,[r] the uncle of Mordecai who had adopted her as his own daughter. When her turn came to go to the king, she did not ask for anything except what Hegai, the king's eunuch, keeper of the women, suggested. Esther gained favor in the eyes of everyone who saw her.[s]

16 She was taken to King Ahasuerus in the palace in the tenth month, the month Tebeth, in the seventh year of his reign.[t]

[A] 2:7 Lit *uncle's daughter*

2:2-4 Everything to this point appeared to have nothing to do with the people of God. An arrogant, Gentile king threw a six-month bash, got drunk, had marital problems, and sent a search party to find him a new beautiful bride. Yet these events started a chain reaction that would lead to the potential destruction of God's people, followed by an amazing eleventh-hour deliverance through his providence. *Providence* is the miraculous and mysterious way that God weaves events together behind the scenes so that his sovereignty over the world is carried out. Though the book of Esther never mentions the name of God, his breathtaking providence in her life and on behalf of his people is unquestionable. **2:7** These details about Esther's looks are important because Esther and Mordecai only entered the picture of events related to the

palace because of her beauty—something outside of their control. Yet that would give them important roles to play in upcoming events regarding the entire Jewish people. God can use every detail of our lives. **2:10** Apparently, Mordecai didn't think she could become queen otherwise because of existing attitudes against the Jews in the empire. **2:12-13** Verse 12 speaks of **each young woman's turn to go to King Ahasuerus**. This was not merely an opportunity to say hello. The phrase was a euphemism for sleeping with the king, as 2:14 makes clear. **2:14** Though this kind of behavior may have been acceptable in the Gentile world, it was considered scandalous among God's people. A man and woman were only to engage in a "one flesh" union when they had come together as husband and wife (Gen 2:24). Furthermore, the

people of Israel were not to marry unbelievers (see Deut 7:3). But sometimes God allows things to happen of which he doesn't approve in order to accomplish his greater purpose. **2:15** Every woman was allowed to take whatever she wished "from the harem to the palace" (see 2:13). But Esther only took what **the king's eunuch … suggested**. In other words, she turned down an opportunity to pile up material things for herself. And as a result, she set herself apart, and people took notice—including the king. **2:16-18** Though much in Esther's story was happening that was inconsistent with God's character, the Jews were his covenant people, and he had promised to cover them. So Esther **won more favor and approval** than the other women, and the king **placed the royal crown on her head** (2:17).

[17] The king loved Esther more than all the other women. She won more favor and approval from him than did any of the other virgins. He placed the royal crown on her head and made her queen in place of Vashti.[a] [18] The king held a great banquet for all his officials and staff.[b] It was Esther's banquet. He freed his provinces from tax payments and gave gifts worthy of the king's bounty.[c]

MORDECAI SAVES THE KING

[19] When the virgins[d] were gathered a second time, Mordecai was sitting at the King's Gate.[e] [20] (Esther had not revealed her family background or her ethnicity, as Mordecai had directed. She obeyed Mordecai's orders, as she always had while he raised her.)

[21] During those days while Mordecai was sitting at the King's Gate, Bigthan and Teresh, two of the king's eunuchs[f] who guarded the entrance, became infuriated and planned to assassinate[A] King Ahasuerus. [22] When Mordecai learned of the plot, he reported it to Queen Esther, and she told the king on Mordecai's behalf.[g] [23] When the report was investigated and verified, both men were hanged on the gallows.[h] This event was recorded in the Historical Record in the king's presence.

HAMAN'S PLAN TO KILL THE JEWS

3 After all this took place, King Ahasuerus honored Haman, son of Hammedatha the Agagite.[i] He promoted him in rank and gave him a higher position than all the other officials.[j] [2] The entire royal staff at the King's Gate[k] bowed down and paid homage to Haman, because the king had commanded this to be done for him. But Mordecai would not bow down or pay homage.[l] [3] The members of the royal staff at the King's Gate asked Mordecai, "Why are you disobeying the king's command?" [4] When they had warned him day after day[m] and he still would not listen to them, they told Haman in order to see if Mordecai's actions would be tolerated, since he had told them he was a Jew.

[5] When Haman saw that Mordecai was not bowing down or paying him homage, he was filled with rage.[n] [6] And when he learned of Mordecai's ethnic identity, it seemed repugnant to Haman to do away with[B] Mordecai alone. He planned to destroy all of Mordecai's people, the Jews,[o] throughout Ahasuerus's kingdom.[p]

[7] In the first month, the month of Nisan, in King Ahasuerus's twelfth year,[q] the Pur — that is, the lot — was cast before Haman for each day in each month, and it fell on the twelfth month,[r] the month Adar.[s] [8] Then Haman informed King Ahasuerus, "There is one ethnic group, scattered throughout the peoples in every province of your kingdom,[t] keeping themselves separate. Their laws are different from everyone else's and they do not obey the king's laws.[u] It is not in the king's best interest to tolerate them.[v] [9] If the king approves, let an order be drawn up authorizing their destruction, and I will pay 375 tons of silver to[C] the officials for deposit in the royal treasury."[w]

[10] The king removed his signet ring[x] from his finger and gave it to Haman son of Hammedatha the Agagite, the enemy of the Jewish people.[y] [11] Then the king told Haman, "The money and people are given to you to do with as you see fit."

[12] The royal scribes were summoned[z] on the thirteenth day of the first month, and the order was written exactly as Haman commanded. It was intended for the royal satraps,[aa] the governors of each of the

[a] 2:17 Est 1:10-11; 2:4
[b] 2:18 Est 1:3
[c] Est 1:7
[d] 2:19 Est 2:12-14
[e] Est 5:13
[f] 2:21 Est 1:10,12; 2:3,14
[g] 2:22 Est 6:2-3
[h] 2:23 Gn 40:19,22; Est 5:14; 7:9-10
[i] 3:1 Ex 17:8-16; 1Sm 15:20
[j] Est 1:3,21; 2:18
[k] 3:2 Est 2:19,21
[l] Est 5:9

[m] 3:4 Gn 39:10
[n] 3:5 Est 1:12; 2:21; 7:7; Dn 3:19
[o] 3:6 Est 6:10
[p] Est 9:24; Ps 83:2-4
[q] 3:7 Est 1:2; 2:16
[r] Est 9:24-28
[s] Ezr 6:15
[t] 3:8 Est 1;1; 8:11,17; 9:2
[u] Jr 29:7; Ac 16:20-21
[v] Ezr 4:12-15
[w] 3:9 Est 4:7
[x] 3:10 Gn 41:42; Est 8:2,8,10; Hg 2:23
[y] Est 7:6; 9:10
[z] 3:12 Est 8:9
[aa] Ezr 8:36

[A] 2:21 Lit and they sought to stretch out a hand against   [B] 3:6 Lit to stretch out a hand against   [C] 3:9 Lit will weigh 10,000 silver talents on the hands of

2:19 That **Mordecai was sitting at the King's Gate** indicates he worked for the king in some capacity.
2:22-23 The last piece of information in verse 22 is important because it tells us Esther gave her cousin credit for uncovering the scheme. The **event was recorded in the Historical Record**, making Mordecai an official hero—though for a time he would go unrewarded (2:23).
This lapse in his receiving affirmation is a reminder that though God may often seem absent in your life, he *is* at work. Trust him where you are because he is doing something bigger than you can imagine.

3:1 Importantly, **Haman** was a descendant of Agag, leader of the Amalekites, an ancient enemy of Israel. The Amalekites had opposed Israel from the beginning, when they had departed from Egypt under Moses (see Exod 17:8-16), so Ahasuerus's new right-hand man would have hated Jews. Moreover, Mordecai was a "son of Kish, a Benjaminite" (Esth 2:5). It was King Saul, son of Kish (1 Sam 9:1-3), who had failed to execute King Agag (see 1 Sam 15:3, 8-9).
3:2 **Mordecai** knew that to give honor to an enemy of God's people was unacceptable (the see the note on 3:1).
3:5-6 Shockingly, genocide was the only thing that would satisfy Haman's hatred.

3:7 Casting **the Pur—that is, the lot**, was like rolling dice. Haman was determining when he would carry out his wicked plan. The lot **fell on the twelfth month, the month Adar** (see 3:13). Haman was probably hoping for a closer date, but as Proverbs says, "The lot is cast into the lap, but its every decision is from the Lord" (Prov 16:33). Thus, God sovereignly provided an eleven-month window of grace to his people. Even when Satan rolls the dice, God loads them.
3:9 Clearly, Haman was no pauper. And he was willing to spend his own resources to wipe out the Jews.
3:10-11 In other words, a wicked man with a vendetta held in his hand the authority to kill God's people.

a 3:12 Est 1:22; 8:9
b 1Kg 21:8
c Est 8:10
d 3:13 2Ch 30:6; Est 8:14
e Est 8:11-13; 9:10
f 3:14-15 Est 8:13-14
g 3:15 Est 7:1; 8:15
h 4:1 Est 3:7-15
i 2Sm 1:11; 3:31; Ezr 9:3
j Is 58:5; Dn 9:3
k Ex 11:6
l 4:2 Est 2:19; 3:2
m 4:3 Est 3:12-15
n Est 8:17; Is 58:5; Dn 9:3; Jnh 3:5-6
o 4:4 Est 7:6

p 4:7 Est 3:9-15
q 4:8 Est 7:3-4
r 4:11 Est 5:1
s Dn 2:9,12-13
t Est 5:2; 8:4
u Est 2:14
v 4:14 Gn 50:20
w Gn 45:5-7

provinces, and the officials of each ethnic group and written for each province in its own script and to each ethnic group in its own language.*a* It was written in the name of King Ahasuerus*b* and sealed with the royal signet ring.*c* [13] Letters were sent by couriers*d* to each of the royal provinces telling the officials to destroy, kill, and annihilate all the Jewish people — young and old, women and children — and plunder their possessions on a single day,*e* the thirteenth day of Adar, the twelfth month.^A [14] A copy of the text, issued as law throughout every province, was distributed to all the peoples so that they might get ready for that day. [15] The couriers left, spurred on by royal command, and the law was issued in the fortress of Susa.*f* The king and Haman sat down to drink, while the city of Susa was in confusion.*g*

MORDECAI APPEALS TO ESTHER

4 When Mordecai learned all that had occurred,*h* he tore his clothes,*i* put on sackcloth and ashes,*j* went into the middle of the city, and cried loudly and bitterly.*k* [2] He went only as far as the King's Gate,*l* since the law prohibited anyone wearing sackcloth from entering the King's Gate. [3] There was great mourning among the Jewish people in every province where the king's command and edict*m* came. They fasted, wept, and lamented, and many lay in sackcloth and ashes.*n*

[4] Esther's female servants and her eunuchs came and reported the news to her, and the queen was overcome with fear.*o* She sent clothes for Mordecai to wear so that he would take off his sackcloth, but he did not accept them. [5] Esther summoned Hathach, one of the king's eunuchs who attended her, and dispatched him to Mordecai to learn what he was doing and why.^B [6] So Hathach went out to Mordecai in the city square in front of the King's Gate. [7] Mordecai told him everything that had happened as well as the exact amount of money Haman had promised to pay the royal treasury for the slaughter of the Jews.*p*

[8] Mordecai also gave him a copy of the written decree issued in Susa ordering their destruction, so that Hathach might show it to Esther, explain it to her, and command her to approach the king, implore his favor, and plead with him personally for her people.*q* [9] Hathach came and repeated Mordecai's response to Esther.

[10] Esther spoke to Hathach and commanded him to tell Mordecai, [11] "All the royal officials and the people of the royal provinces know that one law applies to every man or woman who approaches the king in the inner courtyard*r* and who has not been summoned — the death penalty — *s* unless the king extends the gold scepter, allowing that person to live.*t* I have not been summoned to appear before the king*u* for the last^C thirty days." [12] Esther's response was reported to Mordecai.

[13] Mordecai told the messenger to reply to Esther, "Don't think that you will escape the fate of all the Jews because you are in the king's palace. [14] If you keep silent at this time, relief and deliverance will come to the Jewish people from another place,*v* but you and your father's family will be destroyed. Who knows, perhaps you have come to your royal position for such a time as this."*w*

---

^A 3:13 LXX adds the text of Ahasuerus's letter here.   ^B 4:5 Lit *what is this and why is this*   ^C 4:11 Lit *king these*

3:15 That **the king and Haman sat down to drink, while the city . . . was in confusion** is an ominous insight suggesting that there seemed to be no stopping the madness. Nevertheless, God was at work behind the scenes.
4:4-5 Uninformed of the king's command, Esther didn't understand what was troubling her cousin. At his urging, however, she **was overcome with fear** (4:4).
4:8 Previously, Mordecai had warned Esther to keep her ethnic identity under wraps, possibly because of an anti-Semitic atmosphere (2:10). But now he insisted that she go public. The time had come for God to use

her for her ultimate purpose. Esther had been providentially positioned to leverage influence for God's kingdom purposes. Know that however God blesses you, he does it so that you may be a blessing to others.
4:11 Five years had passed since Esther's wedding, and apparently the honeymoon was over. And it appears that in that time Esther had forgotten that she had not climbed the ladder of success by herself; she had been placed on top by the goodness of God. We are what we are by the grace of God. Extraordinary experiences and opportunities that we are granted are not merely for our sake, but for the sake of God's kingdom agenda. When

we lose sight of that, we miss God's kingdom program in history and become useless to him. Esther needed a reminder of who had placed her in the palace.
4:14 We as Christians need to keep our theology straight, too: God is sovereign and will accomplish his program with or without us. He certainly desires to use you. Yet no one is indispensable. If you refuse to obey him, he will still carry out his agenda through someone else, and you will have missed an opportunity to serve his kingdom purposes.
You have been called to God's kingdom **for such a time as this.** Will you accept your role in the mission?

15 Esther sent this reply to Mordecai:
16 "Go and assemble all the Jews who can
be found in Susa and fast for me. Don't eat
or drink for three days,[a] night or day. I and
my female servants will also fast[b] in the
same way. After that, I will go to the king
even if it is against the law.[c] If I perish, I
perish."[d] **17** So Mordecai went and did everything Esther had commanded him.

ESTHER APPROACHES THE KING

5 On the third day,[e] Esther dressed in her
royal clothing and stood in the inner
courtroom[f] of the palace facing it. The king
was sitting on his royal throne in the royal
courtroom,[A] facing its entrance. **2** As soon
as the king saw Queen Esther standing in
the courtyard, she gained favor in his eyes.
The king extended the gold scepter in his
hand toward Esther, and she approached
and touched the tip of the scepter.[g]
3 "What is it, Queen Esther?" the king
asked her. "Whatever you want, even to
half the kingdom, will be given to you."[h]
4 "If it pleases the king," Esther replied,
"may the king and Haman come today to
the banquet[i] I have prepared for them."
5 The king said, "Hurry, and get Haman
so we can do as Esther has requested." So
the king and Haman went to the banquet
Esther had prepared.
6 While drinking the[B] wine,[j] the king
asked Esther, "Whatever you ask will be
given to you. Whatever you want, even to
half the kingdom, will be done."
7 Esther answered, "This is my petition
and my request: **8** If I have found favor in
the eyes of the king, and if it pleases the

king to grant my petition and perform my
request,[k] may the king and Haman come
to the banquet I will prepare for them.[l] Tomorrow I will do what the king has asked."
9 That day Haman left full of joy and
in good spirits.[C,m] But when Haman saw
Mordecai at the King's Gate, and Mordecai didn't rise or tremble in fear at his
presence, Haman was filled with rage toward Mordecai.[n] **10** Yet Haman controlled
himself and went home. He sent for his
friends and his wife Zeresh[o] to join him.
11 Then Haman described for them his glorious wealth and his many sons. He told
them all how the king had honored him
and promoted him in rank over the oth-
er officials and the royal staff.[p] **12** "What's
more," Haman added, "Queen Esther invited no one but me to join the king at the
banquet she had prepared. I am invited
again tomorrow to join her with the king.
13 Still, none of this satisfies me since I see
Mordecai the Jew sitting at the King's Gate
all the time."
14 His wife Zeresh and all his friends told
him, "Have them build a gallows seventy-five feet[D] tall.[q] Ask the king in the morning to hang Mordecai on it. Then go to the
banquet with the king and enjoy yourself."
The advice pleased Haman, so he had the
gallows constructed.[r]

MORDECAI HONORED BY THE KING

6 That night sleep escaped[s] the king, so
he ordered the book recording daily
events to be brought and read to the king.
2 They found the written report of how Mordecai had informed on Bigthana and Teresh,

---

a 4:16 Est 5:1; Jl 1:14
b Est 9:31
c Est 5:1-2
d Gn 43:14
e 5:1 Est 4:16
f Est 4:11
g 5:2 Est 8:4
h 5:3 Est 7:2; Mk 6:23
i 5:4 Est 1:3,5; 2:18
j 5:6 Est 1:7-8,10; 7:1-2

k 5:8 Est 7:3; 8:5
l Est 6:14
m 5:9 1Kg 8:66; 2Ch 7:10; Pr 15:15
n Est 2:19; 3:2,5
o 5:10 Est 6:13
p 5:11 Est 3:1
q 5:14 Est 6:4; 7:9-10
r Est 6:13
s 6:1 Dn 6:18

---

^A 5:1 Lit *house*   ^B 5:6 Lit *During the banquet of*   ^C 5:9 Lit *left rejoicing and good of heart*   ^D 5:14 Lit *50 cubits*

4:15-17 Sometimes doing the right thing
requires a risky step of faith. Shadrach,
Meshach, and Abednego were commanded
to bow down before an idol (Dan 3:1-30).
Daniel was told to pray to no one but a
human king (Dan 6:1-24). Yet these men, like
this brave queen, all chose to trust God and
take risks. Whether or not they lived to see
another day was God's problem. So what risk
of faith is God calling you to make? Are you
willing to obey God's Word even if it might
cost you? Don't let the time you have been
given pass you by.
5:1-2 "For three days" prior to this (4:16),
Esther had been willing to sacrifice her
physical craving for food in order to
heighten her spiritual awareness because
she needed divine insight to know how to
proceed. And indeed we see here that the
unseen, sovereign God was at work on her
behalf: Esther **gained favor in [the king's]
eyes** (5:2).

5:3 Miraculously, in place of the threat of
death, God granted an open door to Esther
to set her plan in motion.
5:7-8 Why was Esther hesitant to follow
through on what Mordecai had asked her to do
(see 4:8)? Had she gotten cold feet? Regardless,
the wheels of God's providence were turning.
5:9 Haman already hated Mordecai, but this
latest show of defiance **filled [him] with
rage**. He probably thought, "Doesn't this
Jew realize how important I am? The king
and queen can have nothing better than to spend
time with me!"
5:10-14 Haman informed his friends and his
wife about all of his good fortune (5:11-12).
Nevertheless, **none of this** satisfied him
because **Mordecai the Jew** was still breathing
(5:13). But he was so **pleased** with their **advice**
that he immediately started construction on
the **gallows** for Mordecai (5:14).
6:1 On this very night when Haman thought
himself on top of the world, God's people

needed heaven to intervene in history. And
even though he should've been sleeping like a
baby, the king had insomnia for a theological
reason: "A king's heart is like channeled water
in the Lord's hand: He directs it wherever he
chooses" (Prov 21:1). God knows how to keep
people awake at night in order to accomplish
his sovereign program. Thus, the king had
someone read to him **the book recording
daily events**. In other words, he wanted the
most boring book in his possession to be read
to make him sleepy.
6:2 As Haman was plotting Mordecai's
death, the king's sleepless night was filled
with a bedtime story about how **Mordecai**
had saved his life five years prior. Sometimes
we think, "God should act right now in my
circumstances!" But we must recognize that
God is weaving a whole series of people and
events together in history to achieve his kingdom goals. God's kingdom is bigger than you,
and his timing is always perfect.

^a 6:1-2 Est 2:21-23
^b 6:3 Est 10:2-3; Dn 2:48
^c 6:4 Est 5:14
^d 6:6 Est 3:8-9
^e 6:8-9 Gn 41:42-43
^f 6:8 1Kg 1:33
^g 6:9 Est 5:11
^h 6:10 Est 3:6

ⁱ 6:12 Est 5:9,13
^j 2Sm 15:30
^k 6:13 Est 5:10,14
^l Dt 32:10; Zch 2:8
^m 6:14 Est 1:10-11
ⁿ Est 5:7-8
^o 7:1 Gn 40:20
^p 7:2 Est 5:6
^q Est 5:3,6
^r 7:3 Est 2:17; 5:8
^s Est 4:12-14
^t 7:4 Est 3:9,13; 4:7
^u Est 3:13; 8:11; 9:5-10
^v Dt 28:48,68
^w 7:5 Est 3:5-6,8-9
^x 7:6 Est 3:10
^y Est 4:4
^z 7:7 Est 1:12; Pr 20:2
^{aa} Est 1:5-6

two of the king's eunuchs who guarded the entrance, when they planned to assassinate King Ahasuerus.^a ³ The king inquired, "What honor and special recognition have been given to Mordecai for this act?"^b

The king's personal attendants replied, "Nothing has been done for him."

⁴ The king asked, "Who is in the court?" Now Haman was just entering the outer court of the palace to ask the king to hang Mordecai on the gallows he had prepared for him.^c

⁵ The king's attendants answered him, "Haman is there, standing in the court."

"Have him enter," the king ordered. ⁶ Haman entered, and the king asked him, "What should be done for the man the king wants to honor?"^d

Haman thought to himself, "Who is it the king would want to honor more than me?" ⁷ Haman told the king, "For the man the king wants to honor: ⁸ Have them bring a royal garment that the king himself has worn^e and a horse the king himself has ridden,^f which has a royal crown on its head. ⁹ Put the garment and the horse under the charge of one of the king's most noble officials.^g Have them clothe the man the king wants to honor, parade him on the horse through the city square, and proclaim before him, 'This is what is done for the man the king wants to honor.'"

¹⁰ The king told Haman, "Hurry, and do just as you proposed. Take a garment and a horse for Mordecai the Jew,^h who is sitting at the King's Gate. Do not leave out anything you have suggested."

¹¹ So Haman took the garment and the horse. He clothed Mordecai and paraded him through the city square, crying out before him, "This is what is done for the man the king wants to honor."

¹² Then Mordecai returned to the King's Gate,ⁱ but Haman hurried off for home, mournful and with his head covered.^j ¹³ Haman told his wife Zeresh and all his friends^k everything that had happened. His advisers and his wife Zeresh said to him, "Since Mordecai is Jewish, and you have begun to fall before him, you won't overcome him, because your downfall is certain."^l ¹⁴ While they were still speaking with him, the king's eunuchs^m arrived and rushed Haman to the banquet Esther had prepared.ⁿ

HAMAN IS EXECUTED

7 The king and Haman came to feast^{A,o} with Esther the queen. ² Once again, on the second day while drinking wine,^p the king asked Esther, "Queen Esther, whatever you ask will be given to you. Whatever you seek, even to half the kingdom, will be done."^q

³ Queen Esther answered, "If I have found favor in your eyes, Your Majesty, and if the king is pleased,^r spare my life; this is my request. And spare my people; this is my desire.^s ⁴ For my people and I have been sold^t to destruction, death, and extermination.^u If we had merely been sold as male and female slaves,^v I would have kept silent. Indeed, the trouble wouldn't be worth burdening the king."

⁵ King Ahasuerus spoke up and asked Queen Esther, "Who is this, and where is the one who would devise such a scheme?"^{B,w}

⁶ Esther answered, "The adversary and enemy^x is this evil Haman."

Haman stood terrified^y before the king and queen. ⁷ The king arose in anger^z and went from where they were drinking wine to the palace garden.^{C,aa} Haman remained to beg Queen Esther for his life because he realized the king was planning something

---

^A7:1 Lit *drink*   ^B7:5 Lit *who would fill his heart to do this*   ^C7:7 Lit *the garden of the house*, also in v. 8

6:4-5 Who could possibly be available to help the king rectify his oversight at that early hour of the morning? It just so happened that **Haman was . . . entering the outer court . . . to ask the king to hang Mordecai** (6:4). The providence of God was at work.

6:7-9 These actions would publicly position their recipient for a leadership role in the kingdom of Persia.

6:10-11 Imagine the look on Haman's face when he heard the king's words. Everything good he had intended for himself was done to Mordecai, his nemesis! And Haman himself had to lead around the Jewish man whom he hated, as he shouted to the crowds, **This is what is done for the man the king wants to honor** (6:11). This scene is a reminder that "with God all things are possible" (Matt 19:26).

When circumstances look their bleakest, God can connect what doesn't seem connectable. He can cause roads to intersect that look like they could never meet.

6:13 As far as Haman's wife and friends were concerned, what had happened was really bad luck that wouldn't end well.

7:1-2 This **feast** probably wasn't as enjoyable for Haman as the previous one. He was likely nursing a headache after the morning's embarrassment. Worse, before Haman could even eat, the king asked Esther to make her request.

7:3-4 This time, Esther was ready to speak up. But, more to the point, God was ready for her to do so. He wanted everything to occur in exactly the right sequence. It appears, that as Paul would later be restrained by the Holy Spirit (see Acts 16:6-7), so Esther had been

restrained until the stage was set. Esther's spiritual antennae were poised to follow divine leading: Is your spiritual receiver tuned to pick up heaven's signals?

7:5-6 In an instant, Haman went from favored dinner guest to public enemy number one.

7:7-8 Realizing that he had been duped by Haman into authorizing the destruction of his own queen, Ahasuerus was hot. When he stepped out, Haman started **to beg Queen Esther for his life** (7:7). When **the king returned**, he misunderstood Haman's groveling position, thinking that he was trying to assault Esther. That the servants **covered Haman's face** (7:8) tells us he didn't even have an opportunity to explain his actions. The divine Judge was passing sentence on the enemy of his people, and no defense could be given.

exclaimed, "Would he actually violate the queen while I am in the house?" As soon as the statement left the king's mouth, they covered Haman's face.[c]

9 Harbona, one of the king's eunuchs,[d] said: "There is a gallows seventy-five feet[B] tall at Haman's house that he made for Mordecai,[e] who gave the report that saved[C] the king."[f]

The king said, "Hang him on it."

10 They hanged Haman on the gallows he had prepared for Mordecai.[g] Then the king's anger subsided.[h]

ESTHER INTERVENES FOR THE JEWS

8 That same day King Ahasuerus awarded Queen Esther the estate[i] of Haman, the enemy of the Jews.[j] Mordecai entered the king's presence because Esther had revealed her relationship to Mordecai.[k] **2** The king removed his signet ring he had recovered from Haman[l] and gave it to Mordecai, and Esther put him in charge of Haman's estate.

3 Then Esther addressed the king again.[m] She fell at his feet, wept, and begged[n] him to revoke the evil of Haman the Agagite[o] and his plot he had devised against the Jews.[p] **4** The king extended the gold scepter[q] toward Esther, so she got up and stood before the king.

5 She said, "If it pleases the king and I have found favor before him, if the matter seems right to the king and I am pleasing in his eyes,[r] let a royal edict be written. Let it revoke the documents the scheming Haman son of Hammedatha the Agagite wrote to destroy the Jews who are in all the king's provinces.[s] **6** For how could I bear to see the disaster that would come on my people?[t] How could I bear to see the destruction of my relatives?"[u]

7 King Ahasuerus said to Esther the queen and to Mordecai the Jew, "Look, I have given Haman's estate to Esther,[v] and he was hanged on the gallows because he attacked[D] the Jews.[w] **8** Write in the king's name whatever pleases you[x] concerning the Jews, and seal it with the royal signet ring.[y] A document written in the king's name and sealed with the royal signet ring cannot be revoked."[z]

[a] 7:7 Est 6:13
[b] 7:8 Est 1:6
[c] Est 6:12; Jb 9:24

[d] 7:9 Est 1:12
[e] Est 5:14
[f] Est 2:21-23; 6:1-2
[g] 7:10 Est 5:14; Ps 7:16; 94:23; Pr 11:5,6; Dn 6:24
[h] Est 1:12; 2:1
[i] 8:1 Est 3:9; 5:11
[j] Est 3:10; 7:6
[k] Est 2:7,10
[l] 8:2 Est 3:10,12
[m] 8:3 Est 7:3-4,6
[n] Est 7:7
[o] Ex 17:8-16; Est 3:1
[p] Est 3:5-6,8-15
[q] 8:4 Est 4:11; 5:2
[r] 8:5 Est 2:17; 5:8; 7:3
[s] Est 3:13-14
[t] 8:6 Est 4:13-14; 7:3-4
[u] Est 3:13
[v] 8:7 Est 3:9; 5:11; 8:1; Pr 13:22
[w] Est 7:9-10
[x] 8:8 Est 3:11
[y] Est 3:10,12; 8:2; Hg 2:23
[z] Est 1:19; Dn 6:8,12
[aa] 8:9 Est 3:7,12

terrible for him.[a] **8** Just as the king returned from the palace garden to the banquet hall,[A] Haman was falling on the couch[b] where Esther was reclining. The king

---

[A] **7:8** Or *the house of wine*   [B] **7:9** Lit *50 cubits*   [C] **7:9** Lit *who spoke good for*   [D] **8:7** Lit *stretched out his hand against*

7:10 The apparent power of God's enemies is meaningless. When he moves against them, they will fall by their own wicked designs. As Proverbs 28:10 says, "the one who leads the upright into an evil way will fall into his own pit." **8:1-2** The Lord is a God of reversals. Following Esther's intervention, there came a *financial* reversal. Suddenly, everything that Haman owned belonged to the woman who had bravely called him out (Esth 8:1). This highlights the truth of Proverbs 13:22: "the sinner's wealth is stored up for the righteous." Then there was a *political* reversal as the authority that Haman once held was granted to his rival (Esth 8:2). No matter how powerful the people and circumstances aligned against you may seem, they have nothing unless God grants it to them. And if he grants it to them, he can take it away in an instant. **8:8-10** Just as Haman had been given the authority to write orders in the king's name and seal them with **the royal signet ring** (8:8; see 3:12), so now Esther and Mordecai were authorized to do the same.

^a8:9 Est 3:12
^bEzr 8:36
^cEst 1:1; 3:13; 9:30
^dNeh 13:24; Est 1:22; 3:12
^e8:10 Est 3:12-13
^f1Kg 4:26,28
^g8:11 Est 3:13; 9:10
^h8:12 Est 3:7
ⁱ8:13 Est 3:14
^j8:14 Est 3:15
^k8:15 Gn 41:42; Est 5:11; Dn 5:29
^lEst 3:15
^m8:16 Ezr 4:1-3; Ps 97:11
ⁿ8:17 Est 4:3
^oDt 11:25; Est 9:3

^p9:1 Est 8:7-8,10
^qEst 3:7; 8:12
^rEst 3:10; 7:6; 8:1
^s2Sm 22:41; Est 3:5
^t9:2 Est 1:1; 8:9; 9:30
^uEst 8:17
^vEst 3:12,14; 8:13,17
^w9:3 Est 3:12; 8:9
^xEst 8:17
^y9:4 Est 10:2-3
^z2Sm 3:1; 1Ch 11:9
^{aa}9:5 Est 3:13
^{ab}9:6 Est 1:2; 3:15; 8:14
^{ac}9:10 Est 5:11
^{ad}Est 3:10; 7:6; 8:1
^{ae}Est 3:13; 8:11
^{af}9:12 Est 5:6; 7:2; 8:8
^{ag}9:13 Est 8:12; 9:1
^{ah}Est 8:11
^{ai}Est 5:11
^{aj}Est 7:9-10

9 On the twenty-third day of the third month^{aa} — that is, the month Sivan — the royal scribes were summoned. Everything was written exactly as Mordecai^a commanded for the Jews, to the satraps,^b the governors, and the officials of the 127 provinces from India to Cush.^c The edict was written for each province in its own script, for each ethnic group in its own language,^d and to the Jews in their own script and language.

10 Mordecai wrote in King Ahasuerus's name and sealed the edicts with the royal signet ring. He sent the documents by mounted couriers,^e who rode fast horses^f bred in the royal stables. **11** The king's edict gave the Jews in each and every city the right to assemble and defend themselves, to destroy, kill, and annihilate every ethnic and provincial army hostile to them, including women and children, and to take their possessions as spoils of war.^g **12** This would take place on a single day throughout all the provinces of King Ahasuerus, on the thirteenth day of the twelfth month, the month Adar.^h

13 A copy of the text, issued as law throughout every province, was distributed to all the peoplesⁱ so the Jews could be ready to avenge themselves against their enemies on that day. **14** The couriers rode out in haste on their royal horses at the king's urgent command. The law was also issued in the fortress of Susa.^j

15 Mordecai went from the king's presence clothed in royal purple and white, with a great gold crown and a purple robe of fine linen.^k The city of Susa shouted and rejoiced,^l **16** and the Jews celebrated^A with gladness, joy, and honor.^m **17** In every province and every city, wherever the king's command and his law reached, joy and rejoicing took place among the Jews. There was a celebration and a holiday.^{B,n} And many of the ethnic groups of the land professed themselves to be Jews because fear of the Jews^o had overcome them.

VICTORIES OF THE JEWS

9 The king's command and law^p went into effect on the thirteenth day of the twelfth month,^q the month Adar. On the day when the Jews' enemies^r had hoped to overpower them, just the opposite happened. The Jews overpowered those who hated them.^s **2** In each of King Ahasuerus's provinces^t the Jews assembled in their cities to attack those who intended to harm them.^c Not a single person could withstand them; fear of them^u fell on every nationality.^v

3 All the officials of the provinces, the satraps, the governors, and the royal civil administrators^{D,w} aided the Jews because they feared Mordecai.^x **4** For Mordecai exercised great power in the palace,^y and his fame spread throughout the provinces as he became more and more powerful.^z

5 The Jews put all their enemies to the sword, killing and destroying them.^{aa} They did what they pleased to those who hated them. **6** In the fortress of Susa^{ab} the Jews killed and destroyed five hundred men, **7** including Parshandatha, Dalphon, Aspatha, **8** Poratha, Adalia, Aridatha, **9** Parmashta, Arisai, Aridai, and Vaizatha. **10** They killed these ten sons^{ac} of Haman son of Hammedatha, the enemy of the Jews.^{ad} However, they did not seize^E any plunder.^{ae}

11 On that day the number of people killed in the fortress of Susa was reported to the king. **12** The king said to Queen Esther, "In the fortress of Susa the Jews have killed and destroyed five hundred men, including Haman's ten sons. What have they done in the rest of the royal provinces? Whatever you ask will be given to you. Whatever you seek will also be done."^{af}

13 Esther answered, "If it pleases the king, may the Jews who are in Susa also have tomorrow^{ag} to carry out today's law,^{ah} and may the bodies of Haman's ten sons^{ai} be hung on the gallows."^{aj} **14** The king gave the orders for this to be done, so a law was

---

^A8:16 Lit *had light* ^B8:17 Lit *good day* ^C9:2 Lit *cities to send out a hand against the seekers of their evil* ^D9:3 Lit *and those who do the king's work*; Est 3:9 ^E9:10 Lit *not put their hands on*, also in vv. 15,16

8:11-14 The laws of Persia and Media could not be revoked (see 1:19), so the decree Haman had written remained in force. But that didn't mean the Jewish people had to take it lying down. If anyone sought to harm them, the new decree gave them authority to fight back **against their enemies** (8:13).

8:15-16 Here we see an *emotional* reversal. The mourning of the Jews (4:3) had turned to celebration.

8:17 That **many of the ethnic groups of the land professed themselves to be Jews** means

many sinners got saved. To profess oneself to be a Jew was to come under the Jewish covenant. To do this, one had to accept the Jewish God. Unbelievers had seen the deliverance and favor that God had bestowed on his people, and they wanted his covenant protection too. Here, then, we have a *spiritual* reversal.

9:1 On the day when the Jews' enemies had planned to exterminate them, the Jews were prepared to defend themselves—thanks to God's intervention on their behalf through the brave queen.

9:5-10 God had provided the Jews with supernatural deliverance from those who hated them, but his people still had to fight. They couldn't merely sit back and do nothing. The same is true for Christians. We are called to spiritual battle (see 2 Cor 10:3-5; Eph 6:10-18). Yes, God is our Savior and our Deliverer. But he demands we wage spiritual warfare.

9:13 Displaying the corpses **of Haman's ten sons** would serve as a public warning.

announced in Susa, and they hung the bodies of Haman's ten sons. **15** The Jews in Susa assembled again on the fourteenth day of the month of Adar[a] and killed three hundred men in Susa, but they did not seize any plunder.[b]

16 The rest of the Jews in the royal provinces assembled, defended themselves, and gained relief from their enemies. They killed seventy-five thousand[A] of those who hated them,[c] but they did not seize any plunder. **17** They fought on the thirteenth day of the month of Adar and rested on the fourteenth, and it became a day of feasting and rejoicing.

18 But the Jews in Susa had assembled on the thirteenth and the fourteenth days of the month. They rested on the fifteenth day of the month, and it became a day of feasting and rejoicing.[d] **19** This explains why the rural Jews who live in villages observe the fourteenth day of the month of Adar as a time of rejoicing and feasting. It is a holiday when they send gifts to one another.[e]

20 Mordecai[f] recorded these events and sent letters to all the Jews in all of King Ahasuerus's provinces, both near and far. **21** He ordered[g] them to celebrate the fourteenth and fifteenth days of the month of Adar every year **22** because during those days the Jews gained relief from[h] their enemies. That was the month when their sorrow was turned into rejoicing and their mourning into a holiday.[i] They were to be days of feasting,[j] rejoicing, and of sending gifts to one another and to the poor.

23 So the Jews agreed to continue the practice they had begun, as Mordecai had written them to do. **24** For Haman son of Hammedatha the Agagite, the enemy of all the Jews,[k] had plotted against the Jews to destroy them. He cast the Pur — that is, the lot — to crush and destroy them.[l] **25** But when the matter was brought before the king,[m] he commanded by letter that the evil plan Haman had devised against the Jews return on his own head[n] and that he should be hanged with his sons on the gallows.[o] **26** For this

reason these days are called Purim, from the word Pur.[p] Because of all the instructions in this letter as well as what they had witnessed and what had happened to them, **27** the Jews bound themselves, their descendants, and all who joined[q] with them to a commitment that they would not fail to celebrate these two days each and every year according to the written instructions and according to the time appointed. **28** These days are remembered and celebrated by every generation, family, province, and city, so that these days of Purim will not lose their significance in Jewish life[B] and their memory will not fade from their descendants.[r]

29 Queen Esther, daughter of Abihail,[s] along with Mordecai the Jew,[t] wrote this second letter with full authority[u] to confirm the letter about Purim. **30** He sent letters with assurances of peace and security[c] to all the Jews who were in the 127 provinces of the kingdom of Ahasuerus, **31** in order to confirm these days of Purim at their proper time just as Mordecai the Jew and Esther the queen had established them and just as they had committed themselves and their descendants to the practices of fasting[v] and lamentation.[w] **32** So Esther's command confirmed these customs of Purim, which were then written into the record.

MORDECAI'S FAME

10 King Ahasuerus imposed a tax throughout the land[x] even to the farthest shores.[D,y] **2** All of his powerful and magnificent accomplishments[z] and the detailed account of Mordecai's great rank with which the king had honored him,[aa] have they not been written in the Book of the Historical Events of the Kings of Media and Persia?[ab] **3** Mordecai the Jew was second only to King Ahasuerus.[ac] He was famous among the Jews and highly esteemed by many of his relatives.[ad] He continued to pursue prosperity for his people and to speak for the well-being of all his descendants.[ae]

[a] 9:15 Est 9:1
[b] Est 8:11
[c] 9:16 Lv 26:7-8; Est 9:5
[d] 9:18 Est 8:16-17
[e] 9:19 Neh 8:10,12; Est 9:22
[f] 9:20 Est 8:15
[g] 9:21 Est 8:15; 9:3-4
[h] 9:22 Est 4:14
[i] Ps 30:11
[j] Est 8:17
[k] 9:24 Est 3:1,10; 7:6
[l] Est 3:6-7
[m] 9:25 Est 7:3-6
[n] Ps 7:16
[o] Est 5:14; 7:9-10; 9:13-14

[p] 9:26 Est 3:7
[q] 9:27 Est 8:17; Is 56:3,6; Zch 2:11
[r] 9:28 Jos 4:6-7; 1Co 11:24-25
[s] 9:29 Est 2:7,15
[t] Est 3:4-6; 5:13
[u] Est 8:8; Dn 6:8
[v] 9:31 Est 4:16
[w] Est 4:1-3
[x] 10:1 Est 1:1; 8:9
[y] Is 11:11; 24:15
[z] 10:2 Est 1:4
[aa] Est 8:15
[ab] Est 2:23; 6:1-2
[ac] 10:3 Gn 41:40-43; 2Ch 28:7; Est 8:15; Dn 5:7
[ad] Est 8:16-17
[ae] Neh 2:10

[A] 9:16 Some LXX mss read 10,107; other LXX mss read 15,000   [B] 9:28 LXX reads will be celebrated into all times   [C] 9:30 Or of peace and faithfulness
[D] 10:1 Or imposed forced labor on the land and the coasts of the sea

9:23-28 The Jews called their new holiday **Purim, from the word Pur** (9:26). The term *Pur* refers to **the lot** that Haman had **cast** (like rolling dice) to determine when he would **destroy** the Jews (9:24; see 3:7). Haman had looked to chance to fulfill his wicked desires.

The people of God knew that their deliverance had not come by chance but by the providential hand of God; thus, they co-opted the term and used it to magnify God.

10:2-3 Mordecai had been **honored** by the king and was **famous**, yet he knew that

what had happened was not merely for his sake but for the sake of God's kingdom. Therefore, from that day on, he continued **to speak for the well-being of** his people (10:3). May the people of God do the same today.

JOB

INTRODUCTION

Author

THE AUTHOR OF THE BOOK OF JOB is unknown but was likely an Israelite because of his frequent use of God's covenant name, Yahweh (rendered, "the LORD").

Historical Background

Job's story is set in the patriarchal period at a time when wealth was determined by the quantity of livestock and servants one owned. As with other Old Testament patriarchs, Job performed priestly duties for his family (1:5) and lived to a very old age (42:16). The events take place in the country of Uz (1:1), which was located in the northern Arabian Peninsula. The date of the writing is unknown, but Jewish tradition places it during the time of Moses.

Message and Purpose

This book is critical to Scripture because it deals with one of the hardest realities of life: God often seems silent when we are doing our best to please him and yet are experiencing suffering. The question of *why* comes up again and again in life, even as it did for Job, one of the godliest people in the Bible, who had no explanation for why he was suffering so terribly.

In Job, God is engaged in a dialogue with the devil over Job and the pain God allows to come into Job's life. Ultimately, the book reveals God's kingdom authority over life circumstances since not even the devil can do his dirty work without divine permission. As the book unfolds, God reveals things about himself that overwhelm Job. By the end, Job has to repent and bow before God's wisdom—a wisdom that he cannot understand but that he knows is best because he trusts God.

One of the key truths to grasp from the book of Job is that we must trust God even when we cannot understand him, even when he is thoroughly confusing to us. The central statement in the book is one of Job's closing comments to God: "I had heard reports about you, but now my eyes have seen you" (42:5).

www.bhpublishinggroup.com/qr/te/18_00

Outline

JOB AND HIS FAMILY

1 There was a man in the country of Uz[a] named Job.[b] He was a man of complete integrity,[c] who feared God and turned away from evil.[d] **2** He had seven sons and three daughters.[e] **3** His estate included seven thousand sheep and goats, three thousand camels, five hundred yoke of oxen, five hundred female donkeys,[f] and a very large number of servants. Job was the greatest man among all the people of the east.[g]

4 His sons used to take turns having banquets at their homes. They would send an invitation to their three sisters to eat and drink with them. **5** Whenever a round of banqueting was over, Job would send for his children and purify them, rising early in the morning to offer burnt offerings for[A] all of them. For Job thought, "Perhaps my children have sinned, having cursed God in their hearts."[h] This was Job's regular practice.

SATAN'S FIRST TEST OF JOB

6 One day the sons of God[i] came to present themselves before the LORD, and Satan[B] also came with them. **7** The LORD asked Satan, "Where have you come from?"

"From roaming through the earth,"[j] Satan answered him, "and walking around on it."

8 Then the LORD said to Satan, "Have you considered my servant Job? No one else on earth is like him, a man of perfect integrity,[k] who fears God and turns away from evil."[l]

9 Satan answered the LORD, "Does Job fear God for nothing? **10** Haven't you placed a hedge around[m] him, his household, and everything he owns? You have blessed the work of his hands, and his possessions have increased in the land. **11** But stretch out your hand and strike[n] everything he owns, and he will surely curse you to your face."

⊷ HOPE WORDS ⊶

Nothing comes to you that does not pass through God's fingers first.

12 "Very well," the LORD told Satan, "everything he owns is in your power. However, do not lay a hand on Job himself." So Satan left the LORD's presence.

13 One day when Job's sons and daughters were eating and drinking wine in their oldest brother's house, **14** a messenger came to Job and reported: "While the oxen were plowing and the donkeys grazing nearby, **15** the Sabeans[o] swooped down and took them away. They struck down the servants with the sword, and I alone have escaped to tell you!"

16 He was still speaking when another messenger came and reported: "God's fire fell from heaven.[p] It burned the sheep and the servants and devoured them, and I alone have escaped to tell you!"

17 That messenger was still speaking when yet another came and reported: "The Chaldeans formed three bands, made a raid on the camels, and took them away. They struck down the servants with the sword, and I alone have escaped to tell you!"

18 He was still speaking when another messenger came and reported: "Your sons and daughters were eating and drinking wine in their oldest brother's house. **19** Suddenly a powerful wind swept in from the desert and struck the four corners of the house. It collapsed on the young people so that they died, and I alone have escaped to tell you!"

[a] 1:1 Jr 25:20; Lm 4:21
[b] Ezk 14:14,20; Jms 5:11
[c] Jb 2:3; 8:20; 9:20-22
[d] Jb 28:28; Pr 3:7
[e] 1:2 Jb 42:13
[f] 1:3 Jb 42:12
[g] 1Kg 4:30; Is 11:14; Jr 49:28; Ezk 25:4,10
[h] 1:5 Jb 42:8
[i] 1:6 Gn 6:2,4; Jb 2:1; 38:7
[j] 1:7 Pt 5:8
[k] 1:8 Ps 25:21; Pr 29:10
[l] 28:28; Pr 3:7; 13:19; 14:16; 16:6,17
[m] 1:10 Ps 34:7

[n] 1:11 Jb 2:5; 4:5; 5:19
[o] 1:15 Gn 10:7; Jb 6:19; Is 45:14
[p] 1:16 Gn 19:24; 1Kg 18:38; 2Kg 1:10-14

[A] 1:5 Lit *for the number of*   [B] 1:6 Or *the adversary*

1:1 Job was not perfect. Nevertheless, as a person of **integrity**, he practiced fairness and justice in all his dealings. That he **feared God** means he took God seriously and lived to honor him. In a modern context, Job wouldn't act one way at church and another way in the marketplace.

1:5 Job served as the spiritual leader and priest of his family and was clearly a godly man. So, if you consider Job's story as a whole with your own preconceived ideas of what's fair, or with the kind of rigid thinking which says that if A happens, then B must always follow, you'll lose your mind trying to figure out this book. Job's friends, in fact, brought this kind of thinking to the table, and it left them room for only one conclusion: "Job, you must be a

big-time sinner, because look at all the terrible things that have happened to you." Faulty thinking leads to wrong conclusions.

1:6 Up to this point, God in his wisdom has decided not to completely ban **Satan** from his presence. That will happen on a future day when he will be judged and thrown into the lake of fire (Rev 20:10).

Up to the moment of his personal sin, Satan was the "shining morning star" (Isa 14:12). It seems he was God's angel in charge. But he got tired of worshiping God and wanted to be his own god and run his own show. Therefore, every time you try to run your own life and be your own boss, you are saying in essence, "Satan, I agree with you. I too want to ascend to heaven and call my own shots."

1:7 No doubt he'd been looking for someone to "devour" (see 1 Pet 5:8).

1:8 For his own reasons, God goaded Satan into finding out what he already knew personally—that Job's faith was not superficial or based only on his blessings.

1:9-11 Satan was convinced that Job was only in the righteous living game for the blessings. That he only loved God because the money was coming in, his property was extensive, and his family was intact.

1:12 This divine restriction tells us this wouldn't be a battle between equals. God drew the line where Satan had to stop; he maintained authority over the evil one. In his grace, God limits our trials. God's goal was to purify and sanctify Job, not to take him out.

[a] 1:20 Gn 37:29,34; Jos 7:6; Jb 2:12
[b] Jr 7:29; Ezk 7:18; Mc 1:16
[c] 1:21 Jb 3:10-11; 10:17-18; Jr 20:17-18
[d] Ps 139:13,15
[e] Jb 38:1; Ps 113:2; 118:26
[f] 1:22 Jb 2:10
[g] 2:1 Gn 6:2,4; Jb 1:6; 38:7
[h] 2:3 Jb 6:29
[i] Jb 1:1,8; 28:28; Pr 3:7
[j] 2:5 Jb 1:11; 4:5; 19:21
[k] 2:7 Dt 28:27,35
[l] 2:8 2Sm 13:19; Jb 42:6
[m] 2:11 Gn 36:34; 1Ch 1:45; Jb 42:9
[n] Gn 25:2; Jb 8:1; 18:1
[o] Jb 42:11; Ps 69:20; Jr 16:5 2Sm 13:36
[q] Jos 7:6; Lm 2:10; Ezk 27:30
[r] 2:13 Gn 50:10; Ezk 3:15; 45:21
[s] Jb 34:5; Jb 16:6; Ps 39:2
[t] 3:3 Jb 5:7; Pr 23:25; Is 7:14

HOPE WORDS

It's easy to praise God in the sunshine, but your breakthrough comes when you praise him in the dark.

20 Then Job stood up, tore[a] his robe, and shaved[b] his head. He fell to the ground and worshiped, **21** saying:

Naked I came
　from my mother's womb,[c]
and naked I will leave this life.[A,d]
The LORD gives, and the LORD
　takes away.
Blessed be the name of the LORD.[e]

22 Throughout all this Job did not sin or blame God for anything.[B,f]

SATAN'S SECOND TEST OF JOB

2 One day the sons of God[g] came again to present themselves before the LORD, and Satan also came with them to present himself before the LORD. **2** The LORD asked Satan, "Where have you come from?"

"From roaming through the earth," Satan answered him, "and walking around on it."

3 Then the LORD said to Satan, "Have you considered my servant Job? No one else on earth is like him, a man of perfect integrity,[h] who fears God and turns away from evil.[i] He still retains his integrity, even though you incited me against him, to destroy him for no good reason."

4 "Skin for skin!" Satan answered the LORD. "A man will give up everything he owns in exchange for his life. **5** But stretch out your hand and strike[j] his flesh and bones, and he will surely curse you to your face."

6 "Very well," the LORD told Satan, "he is in your power; only spare his life." **7** So Satan left the LORD's presence and infected Job with terrible boils from the soles of his feet to the top of his head.[k] **8** Then Job took a piece of broken pottery to scrape himself while he sat among the ashes.[l]

9 His wife said to him, "Are you still holding on to your integrity? Curse God and die!"

10 "You speak as a foolish woman speaks," he told her. "Should we accept only good from God and not adversity?" Throughout all this Job did not sin in what he said.[C]

JOB'S THREE FRIENDS

11 Now when Job's three friends — Eliphaz the Temanite,[m] Bildad the Shuhite,[n] and Zophar the Naamathite — heard about all this adversity that had happened to him, each of them came from his home. They met together to go and sympathize with him and comfort[o] him. **12** When they looked from a distance, they could barely recognize him. They wept aloud,[p] and each man tore his robe and threw dust into the air and on his head.[q] **13** Then they sat on the ground with him seven days and nights,[r] but no one spoke a word to him because they saw that his suffering[s] was very intense.

JOB'S OPENING SPEECH

3 After this, Job began to speak and cursed the day he was born. **2** He said:

3　May the day I was born perish,
　　and the night that said,
　　"A boy is conceived."[t]
4　If only that day had turned
　　to darkness!
　　May God above not care about it,
　　or light shine on it.

[A] 1:21 Lit *will return there*; Ps 139:13,15　[B] 1:22 Lit *or ascribe blame to God*　[C] 2:10 Lit *sin with his lips*

1:20 Don't miss that Job **fell to the ground and worshiped** after his losses. He knew where to turn when everything fell apart.

1:21 We enter the world **naked** (with nothing), and the only way we won't go to the grave naked is if someone else dresses us for it. The point is we won't take anything with us.

Don't miss that amid the loss of his children and his property, Job confessed that everything he had was from **the LORD**; therefore, God had the right to take it away. It's easy to worship God when everything's smooth. But what we truly believe, whom we really love, is made apparent when the bottom falls out.

2:9-10 At this point, Job's helpmate became a hurt-mate. In verse 9 she urged him to do the very thing Satan wanted. Yet even after he lost his health and had to sit on the garbage heap scraping his sores, Job still understood something we need to grasp. He replied to his wife, **Should we accept only good from God and not adversity?** (2:10). Job knew that the Lord was not Santa Claus whose sole purpose is to give us what we want and never to cause us discomfort. God is sovereign.

As much as we might wish otherwise, trials are inevitable. It's not a question of *if* a believer will suffer but *when* (see John 16:33; Jas 1:2). And those around us will too. Death, disease, pain, loss, and grief don't come with easy explanations. Yet we, like Job, must be convinced of these essential truths: God is sovereign over all things, and God is good. At times he allows Satan to test us. But the good news is that the devil is on a short leash; he can only bring against us what has already passed through God's hands.

2:13 Sometimes the best comfort you can provide is your quiet presence. Remember to "weep with those who weep" (Rom 12:15).

3:1-16 Job felt so low that he wished he had perished at birth. At least then, he reasoned, he **would be at rest** (3:13). That Job railed against his existence is a reminder that being a believer doesn't necessarily mean you will never have times of doubt. God, however, is big enough to handle your doubts and will deal with them as long as you keep the lines of communication with him open. Nevertheless, you need to guard against letting doubts descend into denial of his sovereignty.

5 May darkness and gloom[a]
      reclaim it,
   and a cloud settle over it.
   May what darkens the day terrify it.
6 If only darkness had taken
      that night away!
   May it not appear[A] among the days
      of the year
   or be listed in the calendar.[B]
7 Yes, may that night be barren;
   may no joyful shout[b] be heard in it.
8 Let those who curse days
      condemn[c] it,
   those who are ready
      to rouse Leviathan.[d]
9 May its morning stars grow dark.
   May it wait for daylight
      but have none;
   may it not see the breaking[c]
      of dawn.
10 For that night did not shut
   the doors of my mother's womb,
   and hide sorrow from my eyes.

11 Why was I not stillborn;
   why didn't I die as I came
      from the womb?[e]
12 Why did the knees receive me,
   and why were there breasts for me
      to nurse?[f]
13 Now I would certainly
      be lying down in peace;
   I would be asleep.[g]
   Then I would be at rest[h]
14 with the kings and counselors[i]
      of the earth,
   who rebuilt ruined cities
      for themselves,
15 or with princes who had gold,
   who filled their houses[j]
      with silver.
16 Or why was I not hidden
      like a miscarried child,[k]
   like infants who never
      see daylight?
17 There the wicked[l] cease
      to make trouble,
   and there the weary find rest.
18 The captives are completely
      at rest;[m]
   they do not hear a taskmaster's
      voice.[n]

19 Both small and great are there,
   and the slave is set free
      from his master.[o]
20 Why is light given to one burdened
      with grief,
   and life to those whose existence
      is bitter,[p]
21 who wait for death,[q]
      but it does not come,
   and search for it more than
      for hidden treasure,
22 who are filled with much joy
   and are glad when they reach
      the grave?[r]
23 Why is life given to a man
      whose path is hidden,[s]
   whom God has hedged in?
24 I sigh when food[t] is put
      before me,[D]
   and my groans pour out like water.[u]
25 For the thing I feared
      has overtaken me,
   and what I dreaded has happened
      to me.[v]
26 I cannot relax or be calm;
   I have no rest,[w] for turmoil has come.

FIRST SERIES OF SPEECHES

ELIPHAZ SPEAKS

4 Then Eliphaz the Temanite replied:
² Should anyone try to speak
      with you
   when you are exhausted?
   Yet who can keep from speaking?
3 Indeed, you have instructed many
   and have strengthened[x] weak hands.
4 Your words have steadied the one
      who was stumbling
   and braced the knees
      that were buckling.[y]
5 But now that this has happened
      to you,
   you have become exhausted.
   It strikes[z] you, and you
      are dismayed.
6 Isn't your piety your confidence,
   and the integrity of your life[E]
      your hope?[aa]
7 Consider: Who has perished
      when he was innocent?

[a] 3:5 Jb 10:21-22; 12:22; 28:3
[b] 3:7 Jb 20:5; Ps 63:5
[c] 3:8 Nm 22:11,17; Jb 5:3; Pr 11:26
[d] Jb 41; Ps 74:14; 104:26
[e] 3:10-11 Jb 1:21; 10:17-18; Jr 20:17-18
[f] 3:12 Sg 8:1; Is 66:12; Jl 2:16
[g] 3:13 Ps 13:3; Jr 51:39,57; Mt 8:24
[h] Jb 17:16; Dn 12:13; Rv 14:13
[i] 3:14 Is 14:9; Jr 51:57; Ezk 32:29
[j] 3:15 Jb 17:13; 30:23; Ec 12:5
[k] 3:16 Nm 12:12; Ps 58:8; Ec 6:3
[l] 3:17 Jb 9:22; 11:20; 18:5
[m] 3:18 Pr 1:33; Jr 30:10; 46:27
[n] Ex 3:7; 5:10,13-14; Jb 39:7

[o] 3:19 Jb 9:22; Ec 9:2-3; Is 14:9-10
[p] 3:20 Jb 23:2; Ps 71:20; Lm 1:4
[q] 3:21 1Kg 19:4; Jb 7:15; Jnh 4:3
[r] 3:22 Jb 5:26; 10:19; 17:1
[s] 3:23 Jb 19:8; Lm 3:9; Hs 2:6
[t] 3:24 Jb 6:7; 33:20; Ps 102:4
[u] Ps 6:6; 22:1,14; 32:3
[v] 3:25 Jb 9:28; 13:11; 30:15
[w] 3:26 Jb 30:17; Pr 25:2; Ec 2:23
[x] 4:3 Jb 26:2; Is 35:3; Heb 12:12
[y] 4:4 Dt 3:28; Jb 16:15; Is 41:10
[z] 4:5 Jb 5:19; 6:7; 19:21
[aa] 4:6 Jb 11:18; Ps 119:116; Jr 17:7

[A] 3:6 LXX, Syr, Tg, Vg; MT reads *rejoice*   [B] 3:6 Lit *or enter the number of months*   [C] 3:9 Lit *the eyelids*   [D] 3:24 Or *My sighing serves as my food*
[E] 4:6 Lit *ways*

3:23 Notice that Job didn't say, "Look at what Satan has done to me!" He didn't understand why terrible things had happened to him, but he knew they had come from the hand of his sovereign **God**.

4:7 In general, Eliphaz argued that Job must be suffering because he'd sinned. In Eliphaz's mind, that was the only explanation for all that had happened, since he had a rigid belief in the teaching of retribution. That is, he believed the good guys *always* win, and the bad guys *always* lose. This is why Eliphaz asked, **Who has perished when he was innocent?**

But while it's true that we reap what we sow (see Gal 6:7-9), it's also true that *at*

a 4:7 Jb 8:20; Ps 37:25; Pr 12:21
b 4:8 Jb 5:7; 15:35; Is 59:4
c Ps 7:15; Pr 22:8; Hs 8:7
d 4:9 2Sm 22:26; Jb 37:10; Is 30:33
e Ex 15:8-10; Ps 18:15; 2Th 2:8
f 4:10 Ps 10:9; 17:12; 22:13,21
g Jb 29:17; Ps 3:7; 58:6
h 4:11 Ps 59:11; Pr 20:8,20; Is 33:3
i 4:12 Jb 13:1; 33:16; 36:10,15
j 4:13 Jb 7:14; 20:8; 33:15
k Gn 2:21; 15:12; Jb 33:15
l 4:14 Jb 21:6; Ps 55:5; 119:120
m 4:17 Jb 15:14; 25:4; Pr 20:9
n 4:18 Jb 15:15; 21:22; 25:5
o 4:19 Jb 10:9; 33:6; Is 64:8
p 4:20 Jb 14:2; 20:7; Ps 90:5-6

q 4:21 Jb 36:12; Pr 5:23; 10:21
r 5:1 Jb 15:15; Ps 89:5-7; Dn 4:17
s 5:2 Pr 12:16; 14:18; 19:19
t 5:4 Jb 31:21; Pr 22:22; Is 29:21
u 5:7 Jb 4:8; 15:35; Is 59:4
v 5:8 Jb 13:18; 23:4; Lm 3:59
w 5:9 Jb 9:10; 37:5; Ps 71:19
x Jb 42:5; Ps 40:5; 72:18
y 5:10 Jb 36:27-28; 38:26-28; Jr 14:22
z 5:11 1Sm 2:7; Ps 113:6-7; Mt 5:4
aa 5:13 Ps 9:15-16; Is 29:14; 1Co 3:19
ab 5:14 Dt 28:29; Jb 12:25; Is 59:10
ac 5:15 Ps 55:21; 59:7
ad 5:16 Ps 63:11; 107:42; Rm 3:19

Where have the honest[A]
been destroyed?[a]

8 In my experience,
those who plow injustice
and those who sow trouble[b] reap
the same.[c]

9 They perish at a single blast[d]
from God
and come to an end by the breath
of his nostrils.[e]

10 The lion may roar and the fierce
lion[f] growl,
but the teeth of young lions
are broken.[g]

11 The strong lion dies if it catches
no prey,
and the cubs of the lioness
are scattered.[h]

12 A word was brought to me
in secret;
my ears caught a whisper of it.[i]

13 Among unsettling thoughts
from visions in the night,[j]
when deep sleep[k] comes
over men,

14 fear and trembling came over me[l]
and made all my bones shake.

15 I felt a draft[B] on my face,
and the hair on my body stood up.

16 A figure stood there,
but I could not recognize
its appearance;
a form loomed before my eyes.
I heard a whispering voice:

17 "Can a mortal be righteous
before God?
Can a man be more pure
than his Maker?"[m]

18 If God puts no trust in his servants
and he charges his angels
with foolishness,[C,n]

19 how much more those who dwell
in clay houses,[o]
whose foundation is in the dust,
who are crushed like a moth!

20 They are smashed to pieces
from dawn to dusk;
they perish forever
while no one notices.[p]

21 Are their tent cords not pulled up?
They die without wisdom.[q]

5 Call out! Will anyone answer you?
Which of the holy ones[r] will you
turn to?

2 For anger kills a fool,
and jealousy slays the gullible.[s]

3 I have seen a fool taking root,
but I immediately pronounced
a curse on his home.

4 His children are far from safety.
They are crushed at the city gate,[t]
with no one to rescue them.

5 The hungry consume his harvest,
even taking it out of the thorns.[D]
The thirsty[E] pant
for his children's wealth.

6 For distress does not grow
out of the soil,
and trouble does not sprout
from the ground.

7 But humans are born for trouble[u]
as surely as sparks fly upward.

8 However, if I were you,
I would appeal to God
and would present my case to him.[v]

9 He does great[w]
and unsearchable things,
wonders without number.[x]

10 He gives rain to the earth
and sends water to the fields.[y]

11 He sets the lowly on high,
and mourners are lifted to safety.[z]

12 He frustrates the schemes
of the crafty
so that they[F] achieve no success.

13 He traps the wise in their craftiness
so that the plans of the deceptive
are quickly brought to an end.[aa]

14 They encounter darkness by day,
and they grope at noon
as if it were night.[ab]

15 He saves the needy
from their sharp words[G,ac]
and from the clutches
of the powerful.

16 So the poor have hope,
and injustice shuts its mouth.[ad]

A 4:7 Or the upright, or those with integrity   B 4:15 Or a spirit   C 4:18 Or error; Hb obscure   D 5:5 Hb obscure   E 5:5 Aq, Sym, Syr, Vg; MT reads snares   F 5:12 Lit their hands   G 5:15 Lit from the sword of their mouth; Ps 55:21; 59:7

---

the end of history good will triumph over evil. So reaping good is not always the case in history. Neither is everything that happens to us the result of some sin we have committed (though sometimes it is). Life is too complex for that. To say that wherever there is suffering, you're seeing the result

of someone sowing sin is wrong. Sometimes God permits suffering for his glorious purposes (see John 9:1-3). And Jesus is the perfect example of someone who suffered though he was sinless; he's even the example to follow when we suffer unjustly (see 1 Pet 2:19-23).

4:8-9 Eliphaz was a strict believer in cause and effect, and his theology didn't allow for exceptions (see the note on 4:7). His attitude is summed up in this claim: **In my experience, those who plow injustice and those who sow trouble reap the same** (4:8).

17 See how happy is the person whom
   God corrects;
so do not reject the discipline
   of the Almighty.
18 For he wounds but he
   also bandages;
he strikes, but his hands also heal.[a]
19 He will rescue you
   from six calamities;
no harm will touch you in seven.
20 In famine he will redeem you
   from death,
and in battle, from the power
   of the sword.[b]
21 You will be safe from slander[A]
and not fear destruction
   when it comes.[c]
22 You will laugh at destruction
   and hunger
and not fear the land's wild
   creatures.
23 For you will have a covenant
   with the stones of the field,
and the wild animals will be at peace
   with you.[d]
24 You will know that your tent
   is secure,[e]
and nothing will be missing
   when you inspect your home.
25 You will also know
   that your offspring will be many
and your descendants like the grass
   of the earth.
26 You will approach the grave[f]
   in full vigor,[g]
as a stack of sheaves is gathered
   in its season.

27 We have investigated this,
   and it is true!
Hear it and understand it
   for yourself.

JOB'S REPLY TO ELIPHAZ

6 Then Job answered:
2 If only my grief could be weighed
   and my devastation[h] placed with it
   on the scales.[i]
3 For then it would outweigh the sand
   of the seas!
That is why my words are rash.

4 Surely the arrows of the Almighty
   have pierced[B] me;
my spirit drinks their poison.
God's terrors are arrayed
   against me.[j]
5 Does a wild donkey bray
   over fresh grass
or an ox low over its fodder?
6 Is bland food eaten without salt?
Is there flavor in an egg white?[C]
7 I refuse to touch them;
they are like contaminated food.[k]

8 If only my request would be granted
   and God would provide what
   I hope for:
9 that he would decide to crush me,
   to unleash his power and cut me off!
10 It would still bring me comfort,
   and I would leap for joy
   in unrelenting pain
that I have not denied[D] the words
   of the Holy One.[l]

11 What strength do I have,
   that I should continue to hope?
What is my future, that I should
   be patient?
12 Is my strength that of stone,
   or my flesh made of bronze?
13 Since I cannot help myself,
   the hope for success
   has been banished from me.

14 A despairing man should receive
   loyalty from his friends,[E,m]
even if he abandons the fear
   of the Almighty.
15 My brothers are as treacherous
   as a wadi,
as seasonal streams that overflow
16 and become darkened[F]
   because of ice,
and the snow melts into them.
17 The wadis evaporate
   in warm weather;
they disappear from their channels
   in hot weather.
18 Caravans turn away
   from their routes,
go up into the desert, and perish.

[a] 5:18 Dt 32:39; 1Sm 2:6; Hs 6:1
[b] 5:20 Ps 33:19; 37:19; 144:10
[c] 5:21 Ps 27:5; 31:20; 91:5
[d] 5:23 Ps 91:12; Ezk 34:25; Hs 2:18
[e] 5:24 Jb 8:6; 12:6; 21:9
[f] 5:26 Jb 3:22; 10:19; 17:1
[g] Gn 15:15; 25:8; Jb 21:23
[h] 6:2 Jb 30:13; Ps 57:1; Pr 19:13
[i] Jb 31:6; Dn 5:27; Mc 6:11

[j] 6:4 Jb 30:15; Ps 38:2; 88:16
[k] 6:7 Jb 3:24; 33:20; Ps 107:18
[l] 6:10 Jb 22:22; 23:12; Ps 119:102
[m] 6:14 Jb 19:21; Ps 38:11; Pr 17:17

[A] 5:21 Lit *be hidden from the whip of the tongue*   [B] 6:4 Lit *Almighty are in*   [C] 6:6 Hb obscure   [D] 6:10 Lit *hidden*   [E] 6:14 Lit *To the despairing his friend loyalty*   [F] 6:16 Or *turbid*

5:17 Eliphaz felt that Job might as well admit to his sin and **not reject the discipline of the Almighty**.
6:2-4 Job denied Eliphaz's charges of wrongdoing, saying in effect that his extreme pain gave him a right to moan (6:2-3). He felt like

God was using him for target practice, firing his **arrows** of judgment at him, though he could not imagine why (6:4).
6:14-17 Instead of helping, Eliphaz had only added to Job's misery by his accusations. And judging by Job's reference to his **friends** and

brothers (6:14-15), Job evidently anticipated that he was going to be attacked by Bildad and Zophar too. His friends had thus become like **streams** of water that **evaporate in warm weather** (6:15, 17); they were all talk and no comfort.

[a]6:20 Jr 14:3; Jl 1:11; Am 4:8
[b]6:26 Jb 8:2; 15:2; 16:3
[c]6:27 Jl 3:3; Nah 3:10; 2Pt 2:3
[d]6:28 Jb 24:25; 27:4; 34:6
[e]6:29 Jb 2:3
[f]6:30 Jb 12:11; 27:4
[g]7:1 Jb 14:14; Is 40:2
[h]7:3 Jb 30:17; Ps 6:6; 42:3
[i]7:5 Dt 28:35; Ps 38:5; Is 1:6
[j]7:6 Jb 14:19; 17:15; 19:10
[k]7:7 Jb 9:25; Ps 78:39; Jms 4:14
[l]7:8 Jb 7:21; 20:9; Ps 37:36
[m]7:9 Jb 11:8; 14:13; 17:13,16
[n]7:10 Jb 8:18; 20:9; Ps 103:16
[o]7:12 Jb 26:12; Ps 74:13
[p]Ps 148:7; Is 27:1; Ezk 32:2
[q]7:14 Jb 4:13; 20:8; 33:15
[r]7:15 1Kg 19:4; Jb 3:21; Jnh 4:3
[s]7:16 Jb 7:19; 10:20; Ps 39:13
[t]7:17 Ps 8:4; 144:3; Heb 2:6
[u]7:18 Ps 17:3; 73:14; 139:23

19 The caravans of Tema look
for these streams.
The traveling merchants of Sheba
hope for them.
20 They are ashamed because
they had been confident
of finding water.
When they arrive there,
they are disappointed.[a]
21 So this is what you have
now become to me.[A]
When you see something dreadful,
you are afraid.
22 Have I ever said:
"Give me something"
or "Pay a bribe for me
from your wealth"
23 or "Deliver me
from the enemy's hand"
or "Redeem me from the hand
of the ruthless"?

24 Teach me, and I will be silent.
Help me understand
what I did wrong.
25 How painful honest words can be!
But what does your rebuke prove?
26 Do you think that you can disprove
my words
or that a despairing man's words are
mere wind?[b]
27 No doubt you would cast lots
for a fatherless child
and negotiate a price to sell
your friend.[c]

28 But now, please look at me;
I will not lie to your face.[d]
29 Reconsider; don't be unjust.
Reconsider; my righteousness[e]
is still the issue.
30 Is there injustice on my tongue
or can my palate not taste disaster?[f]

7 Isn't each person consigned
to forced labor[g] on earth?
Are not his days like those
of a hired worker?
2 Like a slave he longs for shade;
like a hired worker he waits
for his pay.
3 So I have been made to inherit
months of futility,
and troubled nights
have been assigned to me.[h]
4 When I lie down I think,
"When will I get up?"
But the evening drags on endlessly,
and I toss and turn until dawn.
5 My flesh is clothed with maggots
and encrusted with dirt.[B]
My skin forms scabs[C]
and then oozes.[i]

6 My days pass more swiftly
than a weaver's shuttle;
they come to an end without hope.[j]
7 Remember that my life is
but a breath.
My eye will never again see
anything good.[k]
8 The eye of anyone who looks on me
will no longer see me.
Your eyes will look for me, but I
will be gone.[l]
9 As a cloud fades away and vanishes,
so the one who goes down to Sheol[m]
will never rise again.
10 He will never return to his house;
his hometown will no longer
remember[D] him.[n]

11 Therefore I will not restrain
my mouth.
I will speak in the anguish
of my spirit;
I will complain in the bitterness
of my soul.
12 Am I the sea[E,o] or a sea monster,[p]
that you keep me under guard?
13 When I say, "My bed will comfort me,
and my couch will ease
my complaint,"
14 then you frighten me with dreams,
and terrify me with visions,[q]
15 so that I prefer strangling[F] —
death rather than life in this body.[G,r]
16 I give up! I will not live forever.
Leave me alone,[s] for my days are
a breath.[H]

17 What is a mere human,
that you think so highly of him
and pay so much attention to him?[t]
18 You inspect him every morning,
and put him to the test
every moment.[u]
19 Will you ever look away from me,
or leave me alone long enough
to swallow?[I]

[A]6:21 Alt Hb tradition reads *So you have now become nothing* [B]7:5 Or *and dirty scabs* [C]7:5 Lit *skin hardens* [D]7:10 Lit *know* [E]7:12 Or *the sea god* [F]7:15 Or *suffocation* [G]7:15 Lit *than my bones* [H]7:16 Or *are futile* [I]7:19 Lit *swallow my saliva?*

6:28 Job wanted Eliphaz to remember that he really was dealing with a man of integrity.
7:1-5 Job's grief led him to lament the **futility** and emptiness of life (7:3).

20 If I have sinned, what have I done
    to you,
Watcher of humanity?
Why have you made me your target,[a]
so that I have become a burden
    to you?[A]
21 Why not forgive my sin
and pardon my iniquity?[b]
For soon I will lie down in the grave.[c]
You will eagerly seek me, but I
    will be gone.[d]

BILDAD SPEAKS

8 Then Bildad the Shuhite replied:
2 How long will you go on saying
    these things?
Your words[e] are a blast of wind.[f]
3 Does God pervert justice?[g]
Does the Almighty pervert
    what is right?[h]
4 Since your children sinned
    against him,
he gave them over to their rebellion.
5 But if you earnestly seek[i] God
and ask the Almighty for mercy,[j]
6 if you are pure and upright,
then he will move even now
    on your behalf
and restore the home where
    your righteousness dwells.[k]
7 Then, even if your beginnings
    were modest,
your final days will be
    full of prosperity.[l]

8 For ask the previous generation,
and pay attention to what
    their fathers discovered,[m]
9 since we were born only yesterday
    and know nothing.
Our days on earth are but a shadow.[n]
10 Will they not teach you and tell you
and speak from
    their understanding?
11 Does papyrus grow where there is
    no marsh?
Do reeds flourish without water?
12 While still uncut shoots,

they would dry up quicker than
    any other plant.
13 Such is the destiny[B] of all
    who forget God;
the hope of the godless[o] will perish.
14 His source of confidence
    is fragile;[c]
what he trusts in is a spider's web.[p]
15 He leans on his web, but it doesn't
    stand firm.
He grabs it, but it does not hold up.
16 He is a well-watered plant
    in the sunshine;
his shoots spread out
    over his garden.
17 His roots are intertwined
    around a pile of rocks.
He looks for a home
    among the stones.
18 If he is uprooted[D] from his place,
it will deny knowing him, saying,
    "I never saw you."[q]
19 Surely this is the joy of his way
    of life;
yet others will sprout
    from the dust.
20 Look, God does not reject a person
    of integrity,
and he will not support[E] evildoers.[r]
21 He will yet fill your mouth
    with laughter
and your lips with a shout of joy.[s]
22 Your enemies will be clothed
    with shame;[t]
the tent[u] of the wicked
    will no longer exist.

JOB'S REPLY TO BILDAD

9 Then Job answered:
2 Yes, I know what you've said is true,
but how can a person be justified
    before God?[v]
3 If one wanted to take[w] him to court,
he could not answer God[F] once
    in a thousand times.[x]
4 God is wise[y] and all-powerful.
Who has opposed him
    and come out unharmed?

[a] 7:20 Jb 16:12; Lm 3:12
[b] 7:21 Jb 11:6; 13:23; 15:5
[c] Jb 17:16; 20:11; Is 26:19
[d] Jb 3:13; 7:8; Ps 37:36
[e] 8:2 Jb 11:2; Pr 10:19; Ec 5:3
[f] Jb 6:26; 15:2; 16:3
[g] 8:3 2Ch 19:6; Jb 34:12; Ps 9:16
[h] Gn 18:25; Jb 34:17; Rm 3:5
[i] 8:5 Ps 63:1; 78:34; Is 26:9
[j] Jb 9:15; 33:24; Ps 30:8
[k] 8:6 Jb 22:23; 42:10; Pr 3:33
[l] 8:7 Jb 36:11; 42:10,12; Jms 5:11
[m] 8:8 Dt 4:32; 32:7; Jb 15:18
[n] 8:9 Ps 102:11; 144:4; Ec 6:12

[o] 8:13 Jb 13:16; 15:34; 27:8
[p] 8:14-15 Jb 27:18; Is 59:5; Mt 7:26-27
[q] 8:18 Jb 7:10; 20:7; Ps 37:36
[r] 8:20 Gn 18:25; Jb 36:6; 2Pt 2:9
[s] 8:21 Jb 33:26; Ps 27:6; 47:5
[t] 8:22 Ps 35:26; 109:29; 132:18
[u] Jb 18:6,14; Ps 52:5; Pr 14:11
[v] 9:2 Jb 25:4; Ps 143:2; Rm 3:20
[w] 9:3 Jb 13:19; 33:13; 40:2
[x] Jb 9:14; 37:19; 40:2
[y] 9:4 Jb 11:6; 12:13; 36:5

[A] 7:20 Alt Hb tradition, LXX; MT, Vg read *myself*   [B] 8:13 Lit *Such are the ways*   [C] 8:14 Or *cut off*; Hb obscure   [D] 8:18 Or *destroyed*   [E] 8:20 Lit *grasp the hand of*   [F] 9:3 Or *court, God would not answer him*

8:4 Unlike Eliphaz, who at least started out gently with Job, Bildad lacked discretion and mercy. He said, **Since your children sinned against [God], he gave them over to their rebellion**. But Bildad had no personal knowledge that Job's children had sinned; he simply assumed it since it fit with his cause-and-effect theology. Be warned: if you go around offering this sort of harsh counsel to those who are suffering, you need to repent.

8:5-7 Bildad told Job that life would be better for him again if Job would just **ask the Almighty for mercy** and start living right (8:5-6). He thought that was the only way God would stop afflicting Job and restore him to a life that was **full of prosperity** (8:7). But Job wasn't suffering because he'd committed some crime.
8:20 The implication here is that if God had rejected him, Job must have lacked **integrity**.

As is often the case when such proverbial statements are made in the Bible, there is truth in this verse. Nevertheless, we can't build a rigid system that allows no exceptions based on one proverb.
9:2 Importantly, the question, **how can a person be justified before God?** is one the Bible answers. If humans are to be justified, God must do it himself (see Rom 3:23-24).

*a*9:5 Jdg 5:5; Ps 18:7;
Mc 1:4
*b*9:7 Is 13:10; Ezk 32:8;
Jl 2:10,31
*c*9:8 Ps 104:2-3; Is 40:22;
44:24
*d*9:9 Jb 38:31-32; Is 40:26;
Am 5:8
*e*9:10 Jb 5:9; Ps 40:5; 72:18
*f*9:11 Jb 23:8-9; 35:14
*g*9:12 Jb 11:10; Is 45:9;
Rm 9:20
*h*9:13 Jb 26:12; Ps 89:10;
Is 51:9
*i*9:15 Jb 8:5; 10:15
*j*9:17 Jb 30:22; Ps 83:15;
Jnh 1:4
*k*9:19 Jb 9:4; Is 28:2; 40:26

*l*9:19 Jr 49:19; 50:44
*m*9:20 Jb 9:28; 40:8;
Is 50:9
*n*9:21 Jb 7:16; 10:1
*o*9:22 Jb 3:19; Ec 9:2-3;
Is 14:3-11
*p*9:24 Jb 12:6,17; Is 29:14;
44:25
*q*9:25 2Sm 18:19-33; 1Kg
1:5; Est 3:13,15
*r*9:25 Jb 7:7; Ps 78:39; Jms 4:14
*s*9:26 Jb 39:29; Is 18:2;
Hab 1:8
*t*9:28 Jb 3:25; 13:11; 31:23
*u*9:29 Jb 10:14; Jl 3:21; Nah 1:3
*v*9:29 Jb 9:20; 40:8;
Is 50:9
*w*9:32 Jb 41:13; Ps 143:2;
Ec 6:10

5 He removes mountains
　　without their knowledge,
　overturning them
　　in his anger.*a*
6 He shakes the earth from its place
　so that its pillars tremble.
7 He commands the sun not to shine
　and seals off the stars.*b*
8 He alone stretches out
　　the heavens*c*
　and treads on the waves of the sea.*A*
9 He makes the stars: the Bear,*B* Orion,
　the Pleiades,*d* and the constellations*c*
　　of the southern sky.
10 He does great
　　and unsearchable things,
　wonders without number.*e*
11 If he passed by me,
　　I wouldn't see him;*f*
　if he went by,
　　I wouldn't recognize him.
12 If he snatches something,
　　who can stop*b* him?
　Who can ask him, "What are
　　you doing?"*g*
13 God does not hold back his anger;
　Rahab's*h* assistants cringe in fear
　　beneath him!

14 How then can I answer him
　or choose my arguments
　　against him?
15 Even if I were in the right,
　　I could not answer.
　I could only beg my Judge for mercy.*i*
16 If I summoned him
　　and he answered me,
　I do not believe he would
　　pay attention to what I said.
17 He batters me with a whirlwind*j*
　and multiplies my wounds
　　without cause.
18 He doesn't let me catch my breath
　but fills me with bitter experiences.
19 If it is a matter of strength, look,
　　he is the powerful one!*k*

If it is a matter of justice, who can
　summon*l* him?*E*
20 Even if I were in the right,
　my own mouth would
　　condemn me;*m*
　if I were blameless, my mouth would
　　declare me guilty.

21 Though I am blameless,
　I no longer care about myself;
　I renounce my life.*n*
22 It is all the same. Therefore I say,
　"He destroys both the blameless
　　and the wicked."*o*
23 When catastrophe*F* brings
　　sudden death,
　he mocks the despair
　　of the innocent.
24 The earth*G* is handed over
　　to the wicked;
　he blindfolds*H* its judges.*p*
　If it isn't he, then who is it?

25 My days fly by faster
　　than a runner;*l,q*
　they flee without seeing any good.*r*
26 They sweep by like boats made
　　of papyrus,
　like an eagle swooping down
　　on its prey.*s*
27 If I said, "I will forget my complaint,
　change my expression, and smile,"
28 I would still live in terror of all
　　my pains.*t*
　I know you will not acquit me.*u*
29 Since I will be found guilty,*v*
　why should I struggle in vain?
30 If I wash myself with snow,
　and cleanse my hands with lye,
31 then you dip me in a pit of mud,
　and my own clothes despise me!

32 For he is not a man like me, that I can
　　answer him,*w*
　that we can take each other
　　to court.

*A*9:8 Or *and walks on the back of the sea god*　*B*9:9 Or *Aldebaran*　*C*9:9 Or *chambers*　*D*9:12 Or *dissuade*　*E*9:19 LXX; MT reads *me*　*F*9:23 Or *whip*;
Hb obscure　*G*9:24 Or *land*　*H*9:24 Lit *covers the faces of*　*I*9:25 = a royal messenger

9:5-9 Job's observations about God display his majesty to us. The God of the Bible **removes mountains, shakes the earth, stretches out the heavens**, and **makes the stars**. He is the holy Creator who holds us in the palm of his hand. **9:15-16** By this point, Job was so distraught that he believed that, **even if [he] were in the right**, God wouldn't **pay attention**.
　We have to remember that sometimes God is silent. But don't count his silence as neglect. When God gives us the silent treatment, it's not because he's in a bad mood or careless.

It's always because he's trying to teach us something we wouldn't otherwise learn. We must trust our God who knows what we don't know, who can do what we can't do, and who never fails.
9:32-33 Job realized he could not defend himself before God: **He is not a man like me, that I can answer him** (9:32). Thus, Job wished there was someone to mediate between them (9:33). A *mediator* is someone who can stand between two parties who are at odds with each other and bring them together.

To effectively mediate between sinners and a holy God, someone would have to be like God and like humans—knowing how God feels and thinks and how we feel and think, too. The mediator Job wished for would have had to understand Job so he could accurately represent him. Yet he must be as great as God himself to accurately represent God. In time, this perfect Mediator who could stand between humanity and God would come in the person of Jesus Christ (see 1 Tim 2:5).

33 There is no mediator between us,
  to lay his hand on both of us.
34 Let him take his rod away from me
  so his terror will no longer
    frighten me.[a]
35 Then I would speak and not
    fear him.
  But that is not the case; I am
    on my own.

10 I am disgusted with my life.[b]
  I will give vent to my complaint
and speak in the bitterness
    of my soul.
2 I will say to God,
  "Do not declare me guilty!
  Let me know why
    you prosecute me.
3 Is it good for you to oppress,
  to reject the work of your hands,[c]
  and favor[A] the plans of the wicked?[d]
4 Do you have eyes of flesh,
  or do you see as a human sees?
5 Are your days like those of a human,
  or your years like those of a man,[e]
6 that you look for my iniquity[f]
  and search for my sin,
7 even though you know that
    I am not wicked
  and that there is no one
    who can rescue
      from your power?[g]

8 "Your hands shaped me
    and formed me.[h]
  Will you now turn and destroy me?
9 Please remember that you
    formed me like clay.
  Will you now return me to dust?[i]
10 Did you not pour me out like milk
  and curdle me like cheese?
11 You clothed me with skin and flesh,
  and wove me together with bones
    and tendons.[j]
12 You gave me life and faithful love,
  and your care has guarded my life.

13 "Yet you concealed these thoughts
    in your heart;

I know that this was
    your hidden plan:[B]
14 if I sin, you would notice,[c]
  and would not acquit me
    of my iniquity.[k]
15 If I am wicked, woe to me!
  And even if I am righteous, I cannot
    lift up my head.
  I am filled with shame[l]
  and have drunk deeply of[D]
    my affliction.[m]
16 If I am proud,[E] you hunt me
    like a lion
  and again display
    your miraculous power against me.[n]
17 You produce new witnesses[F]
    against me
  and multiply your anger toward me.
  Hardships assault me,
    wave after wave.[G]

18 "Why did you bring me out of
    the womb?[o]
  I should have died and never
    been seen.
19 I wish[H] I had never existed
  but had been carried from the womb
    to the grave.[P]
20 Are my days not few? Stop it![I]
  Leave me alone, so that I can smile
    a little
21 before I go to a land of darkness
    and gloom,[q]
  never to return.
22 It is a land of blackness
    like the deepest darkness,
  gloomy and chaotic,
  where even the light is
    like[J] the darkness."

ZOPHAR SPEAKS

11 Then Zophar the Naamathite replied:
  2 Should this abundance of words[r]
    go unanswered
  and such a talker[K] be acquitted?
3 Should your babbling put others
    to silence,
  so that you can keep on ridiculing
  with no one to humiliate you?

A 10:3 Lit shine on   B 10:13 Lit was with you   C 10:14 Lit notice me   D 10:15 Or and look at   E 10:16 Lit If he lifts up   F 10:17 Or You bring fresh troops
G 10:17 Lit Changes and a host are with me   H 10:19 Lit As if   I 10:20 Alt Hb tradition reads Will he not leave my few days alone?
J 10:22 Lit chaotic, and shines as   K 11:2 Lit a man of lips

10:20-21 Job's words reveal that he'd fallen into a deep emotional pit. But sadly, there was no one to lift him out. He needed brothers to give him biblical insight and help him think clearly. He needed believers to walk with him and put their arms around him while he suffered. 11:3-12 It's obvious Zophar never took a class on winning friends and influencing people. He was completely insensitive to Job's situation. He accused Job of **babbling** on (11:3), and he also implied that Job was **worthless** and **stupid** (11:11-12).

  What's interesting is that Zophar shared Job's longing for a hearing before God, but for a different reason. Job was sure God would vindicate him if he could just present his case. Zophar said the opposite would happen; God was letting Job off easy, so if Job were to go to court with God he would surely be condemned (11:5-6). He felt Job should be thankful things weren't as bad as they could be.

a 9:34 Jb 6:4; 13:21; Ps 39:10
b 10:1 Jb 7:16; 9:21; Ps 95:10; 119:158; 139:21; Ezk 6:9; 20:43; 36:31
c 10:3 Ps 128:2
d Ps 1:1; Jb 21:16; 22:18
e 10:5 Jb 36:26; Ps 90:4; 2Pt 3:8
f 10:6 Jb 13:23,26; 14:17; 22:5
g 10:7 Dt 32:39; Is 43:13
h 10:8 Gn 2:7,8,19; Ps 34:15; 94:9; Is 29:16; 43:1,7,21; 44:2,21,24; 45:9,11; 49:5; 64:8; Jr 1:5; 18:6; Zch 12:1
i 10:9 Gn 2:7; Jb 4:19; 34:15
j 10:11 Ps 139:13
k 10:14 Ex 34:7; Jb 7:21; Am 3:2
l 10:15 Hab 2:16
m Jb 9:15; Ps 25:18; Is 3:11
n 10:16 Jb 5:9; Is 38:13; Lm 3:10
o 10:18 Jb 1:21; 10:18-19; Jr 20:17-18
p 10:19 Jb 3:22; 5:26; 17:1
q 10:21 Jb 3:5;12:22; 28:3
r 11:2 Jb 8:2; Pr 10:19; Ec 5:3

[a]11:4 Dt 32:2; Pr 4:2; Is 29:24
[b]11:6 Jb 28:12; 38:36; Ec 7:23,25
[c]Ezr 9:13; Ps 103:10
[d]11:7 Ec 3:11; 8:17; Rm 11:33
[e]11:8 Dt 30:12-13; Ps 139:8-9; Am 9:2-3
[f]11:10 Jb 9:12; 23:13; Rv 3:7
[g]11:11 Jb 34:25; Ps 10:14
[h]11:15 Jb 22:26; Ps 119:6; 1Jn 3:21

[i]11:17 Jb 17:12; Ps 37:6; Is 58:8,10
[j]11:18 Jb 4:6; Ps 119:116; Jr 17:7
[k]Jb 24:23; Ps 4:8; Pr 3:24
[l]11:19 Ps 45:12; Pr 19:6; 29:26
[m]11:20 Jb 3:17; 9:22; 18:5
[n]Jb 8:13; Pr 10:28; 11:7
[o]12:3 Jb 13:2; 15:9; 16:2
[p]12:4 Jb 30:1,9; Jr 20:7; Lm 3:14
[q]12:5 Ps 123:4; Am 6:1
[r]12:6 Jb 5:24; 8:6; 21:9
[s]Ps 73:11; Jr 12:1; Mt 5:45
[t]12:7 Jb 35:11; Mt 6:26
[u]12:9 Ru 1:13; Jb 19:21; Is 41:20
[v]12:10 Gn 2:7; Jb 27:3; 33:4

4 You have said, "My teaching[a]
  is sound,
and I am pure in your sight."
5 But if only God would speak
and open his lips against you!
6 He would show you the secrets
  of wisdom,[b]
for true wisdom has two sides.
Know then that God has chosen
  to overlook some of your iniquity.[c]

7 Can you fathom the depths of God
or discover the limits
  of the Almighty?[d]
8 They are higher than the heavens
  — what can you do?
They are deeper than Sheol —
  what can you know?[e]
9 Their measure is longer
  than the earth
and wider than the sea.

10 If he passes by and throws
  someone in prison
or convenes a court, who can
  stop him?[f]
11 Surely he knows which people
  are worthless.
If he sees iniquity, will he not
  take note of it?[g]
12 But a stupid person
  will gain understanding
as soon as a wild donkey is born
  a human!

13 As for you, if you redirect your heart
and spread out your hands to him
  in prayer —
14 if there is iniquity in your hand,
  remove it,
and don't allow injustice to dwell
  in your tents —
15 then you will hold your head high,
  free from fault.
You will be firmly established
  and unafraid.[h]
16 For you will forget your suffering,
recalling it only as water
  that has flowed by.
17 Your life will be brighter
  than noonday;

its darkness[A] will be
  like the morning.[i]
18 You will be confident, because
  there is hope.[j]
You will look carefully about
  and lie down in safety.[k]
19 You will lie down with no one to
  frighten you,
and many will seek your favor.[l]
20 But the sight of the wicked[m] will fail.
Their way of escape will be cut off,
and their only hope
  is their last breath.[n]

JOB'S REPLY TO ZOPHAR

12 Then Job answered:
2 No doubt you are the people,
and wisdom will die with you!
3 But I also have a mind like you;
I am not inferior to you.
Who doesn't know the things
  you are talking about?[B,o]

4 I am a laughingstock to my[C] friends,
by calling on God, who answers me.[D]
The righteous and upright man is
  a laughingstock.[p]
5 The one who is at ease[q]
holds calamity in contempt
and thinks it is prepared for those
  whose feet are slipping.
6 The tents of robbers are safe,[r]
and those who trouble God
  are secure;
God holds them in his hands.[E,s]

7 But ask the animals, and they will
  instruct you;
ask the birds of the sky, and they will
  tell you.[t]
8 Or speak to the earth, and it will
  instruct you;
let the fish of the sea inform you.
9 Which of all these does not know
that the hand of the LORD
  has done this?[u]
10 The life of every living thing is
  in his hand,
as well as the breath
  of all mankind.[v]

[A]11:17 Text emended; MT reads *noonday; you are dark, you*   [B]12:3 Lit *With whom are not such things as these?*   [C]12:4 Lit *his*   [D]12:4 Lit *him*
[E]12:6 Or *secure; to those who bring their god in their hands*

11:13-14 Like a good preacher, Zophar had three points in his message to Job concerning the steps he needed to take. First, Job needed to **redirect [his] heart** to God; Job needed to stop living in sin and conduct his life in a righteous way. Second, he needed to **spread out** [his] hands to [God] in prayer, which is probably a reference to a prayer of repentance (11:13). Third, Job needed to get rid of any **iniquity** he was practicing and not allow any **injustice** to be found **in his tents**—that is, in his life (11:14). These are great steps for someone who needs to deal with sin to follow, but all of them were based on Zophar's false assumption that Job was under God's discipline due to sin. Good prescription, bad diagnosis. **12:2** Translation? Zophar, your head is too big; do you think you're God's gift of wisdom?

11 Doesn't the ear test words
    as the palate tastes food?
12 Wisdom is found with the elderly,
    and understanding comes
       with long life.^a

13 Wisdom and strength belong to God;
    counsel and understanding are his.^b
14 Whatever he tears down cannot
    be rebuilt;
    whoever he imprisons cannot
    be released.^c
15 When he withholds water,
    everything dries up,
    and when he releases it, it destroys
    the land.^d
16 True wisdom and power belong
    to him.
    The deceived and the deceiver
    are his.
17 He leads counselors away barefoot
    and makes judges go mad.^e
18 He releases the bonds^A put on
    by kings^f
    and fastens a belt
    around their waists.
19 He leads priests away barefoot
    and overthrows
    established leaders.^g
20 He deprives trusted advisers
    of speech
    and takes away the elders'
    good judgment.
21 He pours out contempt on nobles
    and disarms^B the strong.
22 He reveals mysteries
    from the darkness
    and brings the deepest darkness
    into the light.^h
23 He makes nations great,
    then destroys them;
    he enlarges nations,ⁱ
    then leads them away.
24 He deprives the world's leaders
    of reason,

and makes them wander
    in a trackless wasteland.^j
25 They grope around in darkness
    without light;
    he makes them stagger like a
    drunkard.^k

13 Look, my eyes have seen all this;
    my earsⁱ have heard
    and understood it.
2 Everything you know, I also know;
    I am not inferior to you.^m
3 Yet I prefer to speak to the Almighty
    and argue my case before God.ⁿ
4 You use lies like plaster;
    you are all worthless healers.^o
5 If only you would shut up
    and let that be your wisdom!

6 Hear now my argument,
    and listen to my defense.^c
7 Would you testify unjustly
    on God's behalf
    or speak deceitfully for him?
8 Would you show partiality^p to him
    or argue the case in his defense?
9 Would it go well if he examined you?
    Could you deceive him
    as you would deceive a man?^q
10 Surely he would rebuke you
    if you secretly showed partiality.
11 Would God's majesty
    not terrify you?^r
    Would his dread not fall on you?
12 Your memorable sayings
    are proverbs of ash;^s
    your defenses are made of clay.

13 Be quiet,^D and I will speak.
    Let whatever comes happen to me.
14 I will put^E myself at risk^F
    and take my life in my own hands.
15 Even if he kills me, I will hope in him.^G
    I will still defend^t my ways
    before him.

^a 12:12 Jb 12:20; 32:7,9; Ps 119:100
^b 12:13 Jb 9:4; 36:5; 38:36
^c 12:14 Jb 11:10; Is 22:22; Rv 3:7
^d 12:15 Is 41:18; 42:15; 44:3,27
^e 12:17 Jb 9:24; Is 29:14; 44:25
^f 12:18 Jb 12:21; Is 45:1
^g 12:19 Is 40:23; Lk 1:52
^h 12:22 Ps 90:8; Dn 2:22; 1Co 4:5
ⁱ 12:23 Ex 34:24; Is 9:3; 26:15

^j 12:24 Ps 107:40; Dn 4:33
^k 12:25 Dt 28:29; Jb 5:14; Is 59:10
^l 13:1 Jb 4:12; 33:16; 36:10,15
^m 13:2 Jb 12:3; 15:9; 16:2
ⁿ 13:3 Jb 5:8; 23:4; 40:2
^o 13:4 Jb 16:2; Ps 69:20; Ec 4:1
^p 13:8 Dt 10:17; Jb 32:21; 34:19
^q 13:9 Ps 44:21; Pr 18:17; Jr 17:10
^r 13:11 Ex 15:16; Jb 31:23; Is 2:10
^s 13:12 1Sm 24:13; Pr 26:7,9; Is 44:20
^t 13:15 Jb 13:3; 15:3; 23:7

---

^A 12:18 Text emended; MT reads *discipline*   ^B 12:21 Lit *and loosens the belt of*   ^C 13:6 Lit *to the claims of my lips*   ^D 13:13 Lit *quiet before me*
^E 13:14 LXX; MT reads *Why do I put*   ^F 13:14 Lit *I take my flesh in my teeth*   ^G 13:15 Some Hb mss read *I will be without hope*

12:17-23 Counselors, kings, priests, leaders, advisers, nobles—none in humanity can compare to God (12:17-21). The Creator **makes nations great, then destroys them** (12:23). Whatever Job's struggles, he knew his God was glorious and almighty.
13:1-2 In saying, **My eyes have seen all this; my ears have ... understood it** (13:1), Job was sure he could hold his own and more with Eliphaz, Bildad, and Zophar in a theological discussion. He wanted those boys to know they had nothing on him when it came to knowing and understanding God or how life works.

13:4 What Job understood about God allowed him to see that his friends were just whitewashing over the facts with false assumptions about what a terrible sinner he was.
13:5 Eliphaz, Bildad, and Zophar had been at their best when they quietly wept with Job (2:12-13). In Job's advice is a truth that Solomon would write many years later: "Even a fool is considered wise when he keeps silent—discerning, when he seals his lips" (Prov 17:28).
13:15 Consider Job's famous declaration: **Even if [God] kills me, I will hope in him.**

Other than Jesus himself, Job is the classic biblical example of someone who endured the devil's assaults and yet remained faithful to God. Satan took everything Job had, but Job refused to curse God or abandon his faith. This is the kind of resolute faith we need. A faith that perseveres. The only way to lay claim to such a faith is to take advantage of what God provides—to put on the "full armor of God" (see Eph 6:13-18).

a13:16 Jb 8:13; 15:34; 27:8
b13:18 Jb 5:8; 23:4; Lm 3:59
c13:21 Jb 6:4; 9:34; Ps 39:10
d13:22 Jb 9:16; 14:15; Jr 33:3
e13:23 Jb 7:21; 10:6,14; Is 43:25
f13:24 Jb 19:11; 33:10; Lm 2:5
g13:28 Ps 102:26; Is 50:9; 51:8
h14:1 Jb 5:7; 15:35; Is 59:4
i14:2 Ps 103:15-16; Is 40:6-7; Jms 1:10-11
j14:3 Jb 22:4; Ps 143:2; 144:3

k14:5 Jb 21:21; Ps 39:4; 90:12
l14:6 Jb 7:16; 10:20; Ps 39:13
m14:9 Jb 29:19; Ps 1:3; Jr 17:8
n14:12 Is 51:6; Rv 20:11; 21:1
o14:13 Jb 11:8; 17:16; Am 9:2
p Jb 16:9; 19:11; Ps 30:5
q14:14 Jb 6:8; 13:13; 35:14
r Jb 7:1; Is 40:2
s14:15 Jb 9:16; 10:3; 13:22
t14:16 Jb 10:6; 31:4; 34:21
u Jb 10:14; 33:11; Ps 130:3

16 Yes, this will result
    in my deliverance,
for no godless person[a] can appear
    before him.
17 Pay close attention to my words;
    let my declaration ring in your ears.
18 Now then, I have prepared my case;[b]
    I know that I am right.
19 Can anyone indict me?
    If so, I will be silent and die.

20 Only grant these two things
        to me, God,
    so that I will not have to hide
        from your presence:
21 remove your hand from me,
    and do not let your terror
        frighten me.[c]
22 Then call, and I will answer,[d]
    or I will speak, and you can respond
        to me.
23 How many iniquities[e] and sins
        have I committed?[A]
    Reveal to me my transgression
        and sin.
24 Why do you hide your face
    and consider me your enemy?[f]
25 Will you frighten a wind-driven leaf?
    Will you chase after dry straw?
26 For you record bitter accusations
        against me
    and make me inherit the iniquities
        of my youth.
27 You put my feet in the stocks
    and stand watch over all my paths,
    setting a limit for the soles[B]
        of my feet.

28 A person wears out
        like something rotten,
    like a moth-eaten garment.[g]

14 Anyone born of woman
    is short of days and full of trouble.[h]
2 He blossoms like a flower,
        then withers;[i]
    he flees like a shadow
        and does not last.
3 Do you really take notice of one
        like this?
    Will you bring me into judgment
        against you?[C,j]
4 Who can produce something pure
        from what is impure?
    No one!

5 Since a person's days
        are determined
    and the number of his months
        depends on you,
    and since you have set[D] limits
        he cannot pass,[k]
6 look away from him and let him rest
    so that he can enjoy his day
        like a hired worker.[l]

7 There is hope for a tree:
    If it is cut down, it will sprout again,
    and its shoots will not die.
8 If its roots grow old in the ground
    and its stump starts to die in the soil,
9 the scent of water makes it thrive
    and produce twigs like a sapling.[m]
10 But a person dies and fades away;
    he breathes his last — where is he?
11 As water disappears from a lake
    and a river becomes parched
        and dry,
12 so people lie down never
        to rise again.
    They will not wake up
    until the heavens are no more;[n]
    they will not stir from their sleep.

13 If only you would hide me in Sheol[o]
    and conceal me
        until your anger[p] passes.
    If only you would appoint a time
        for me
    and then remember me.
14 When a person dies, will he
        come back to life?
    If so, I would wait[q] all the days
        of my struggle[r]
    until my relief comes.
15 You would call, and I would
        answer you.
    You would long for the work
        of your hands.[s]
16 For then you would count
        my steps[t]
    but would not take note[u] of my sin.
17 My rebellion would be sealed up
        in a bag,
    and you would cover over
        my iniquity.

18 But as a mountain collapses
        and crumbles
    and a rock is dislodged
        from its place,

A13:23 Lit *sins are to me*   B13:27 Lit *paths. You mark a line around the roots*   C14:3 LXX, Syr, Vg read *him*   D14:5 Lit *set his*

13:22-23 God didn't show up for the court scene Job attempted to create.
14:1 Truly, life *is* short and filled with grief. But God is not indifferent to these facts; he himself has entered into our suffering (see 1 Pet 2:24).

19 as water wears away stones
and torrents wash away the soil
from the land,
so you destroy a man's hope.[a]

20 You completely overpower him,
and he passes on;
you change his appearance
and send him away.

21 If his sons receive honor,
he does not know it;
if they become insignificant,
he is unaware of it.[b]

22 He feels only the pain
of his own body
and mourns only for himself.

SECOND SERIES OF SPEECHES

ELIPHAZ SPEAKS

15 Then Eliphaz the Temanite replied:
2 Does a wise man answer
with empty[A] counsel[c]
or fill himself[B]
with the hot east wind?

3 Should he argue[d] with useless talk
or with words that serve
no good purpose?

4 But you even undermine the fear
of God
and hinder meditation before him.

5 Your iniquity[e] teaches you what to say,
and you choose the language
of the crafty.

6 Your own mouth condemns you, not I;
your own lips testify against you.[f]

7 Were you the first human ever born,
or were you brought forth
before the hills?[g]

8 Do you listen in on the council
of God,
or have a monopoly on wisdom?[h]

9 What do you know that we don't?
What do you understand that
is not clear to us?

10 Both the gray-haired and the elderly
are with us—
older than your father.

11 Are God's consolations not enough
for you,
even the words that deal gently
with you?

12 Why has your heart misled you,
and why do your eyes flash

13 as you turn your anger[c] against God
and allow such words to leave
your mouth?

14 What is a mere human, that he
should be pure,[i]
or one born of a woman, that he
should be righteous?

15 If God puts no trust in his holy ones[j]
and the heavens are not pure
in his sight,[k]

16 how much less one who is revolting
and corrupt,[l]
who drinks injustice[m] like water?

17 Listen to me and I will inform you.
I will describe what I have seen,

18 what the wise have declared and
not concealed,
that came from their ancestors,[n]

19 to whom alone the land was given
when no foreigner passed
among them.

20 A wicked person writhes in pain
all his days,
throughout the number of
years reserved for the ruthless.

21 Dreadful sounds fill his ears;
when he is at peace, a robber
attacks him.

22 He doesn't believe he will return
from darkness;
he is destined for the sword.[o]

23 He wanders about for food, asking,
"Where is it?"
He knows the day of darkness is
at hand.

24 Trouble[p] and distress terrify him,
overwhelming him like a king
prepared for battle.

25 For he has stretched out his hand[q]
against God

[a] 14:19 Jb 7:6; 17:15; 19:10
[b] 14:21 Jb 21:21; Ec 9:5; Is 63:16
[c] 15:2 Jb 2:10; 6:26; 27:12
[d] 15:3 Jb 13:3,15; 23:7
[e] 15:5 Jb 13:23,26; 14:17; 22:5
[f] 15:6 2Sm 1:16; Jb 9:20; Lk 19:22
[g] 15:7 Jb 38:21; Ps 90:2; Pr 8:25
[h] 15:8 Jr 23:18; Rm 11:34; 1Co 2:11

[i] 15:14 Jb 4:17; 25:4; Pr 20:9
[j] 15:15 Jb 5:1; Ps 89:5-7; Dn 4:17
[k] Jb 4:18; 21:22; 25:5
[l] 15:16 Ps 14:3; 53:3
[m] Jb 34:7; Ps 14:3
[n] 15:18 Dt 4:32; 32:7; Jb 8:8
[o] 15:22 Dt 32:41-42; Jb 19:29; Is 66:16
[p] 15:24 1Sm 22:2; Jb 36:19; Ps 107:6,13,19,28
[q] 15:25 Is 5:25; 9:16,20; Jr 21:5

[A] 15:2 Lit windy; Jb 16:3   [B] 15:2 Lit his belly   [C] 15:13 Or spirit

---

15:2 Job's three accusers must have huddled together before the second round of speeches and said, "Well, we tried the kid gloves approach, and it didn't work. It's time for the gloves to come off. We're going bare-knuckle." They were ticked that Job hadn't just thrown in the towel, admitted their superior wisdom, and begged God and them for forgiveness. Thus, there's a distinct lack of sympathy here. Eliphaz essentially said Job was just a windbag.

15:4-6 Eliphaz falsely claimed that Job's own words proved he didn't really fear God and was nothing but a hardened sinner!
15:11 Ironically, Eliphaz called his own speech **God's consolations** that Job should appreciate because Eliphaz had spoken **words that [dealt] gently** with him. It's possible to become so convinced of your own wisdom that, if it's ever called into question, you simply buckle down and defend yourself

rather than reevaluating your words. That's the warning sign that you're arrogant and unteachable.
15:21-35 Eliphaz spelled out in great detail the terrible, well-deserved things that happen to wicked people like Job. He saved his cruelest punch for the end, clearly implying that Job had lost his children and everything else because he was **godless** and was getting what he deserved (15:34-35).

a15:28 Jb 3:14; Ps 109:10; Is 5:9
b15:30 Jb 4:9; 22:20; 2Th 2:8
c15:33 Is 18:5; Jr 31:29-30; Ezk 18:2
d15:34 Jb 8:13; 13:16; 27:8
e15:35 Jb 4:8; 5:7; Is 59:4
f Jb 32:19; 37:1; Pr 20:27,30
gPs 7:14; Is 59:4; Hs 10:13
h16:2 Jb 13:4; Ps 69:20; Ec 4:1
i16:3 Jb 15:2

j16:5 Dt 3:28; Jb 4:4; Is 41:10
k16:9 Gn 49:23; Jb 30:21; Ps 55:3
l16:10 1Kg 22:24; Lm 3:30; Mc 5:1
m16:12 Jb 7:20; Lm 3:12
n16:14 Jb 30:14; Jl 2:7
o16:15 Jb 30:19; Ps 7:5; 75:10
p16:16 Ps 44:19; 107:10; Jr 13:16
q16:17 Is 53:9; 59:6; Jnh 3:8
r16:18 Gn 4:10; Is 26:21; Ezk 24:7-8
s16:19 Jb 22:12; Rm 1:9; 1Th 2:5

and has arrogantly opposed
   the Almighty.
26 He rushes headlong at him
   with his thick, studded shields.
27 Though his face is covered with fat[A]
   and his waistline bulges with it,
28 he will dwell in ruined cities,
   in abandoned houses destined
      to become piles of rubble.[a]
29 He will no longer be rich; his wealth
      will not endure.
   His possessions[B] will not increase
      in the land.
30 He will not escape
      from the darkness;
   flames will wither his shoots,
   and by the breath of God's mouth,
      he will depart.[b]
31 Let him not put trust
      in worthless things, being
      led astray,
   for what he gets in exchange
      will prove worthless.
32 It will be accomplished
      before his time,
   and his branch will not flourish.
33 He will be like a vine that drops
      its unripe grapes[c]
   and like an olive tree that sheds
      its blossoms.
34 For the company of the godless[d]
      will have no children,
   and fire will consume the tents
      of those who offer bribes.
35 They conceive trouble[e]
      and give birth to evil;
   their womb[f] prepares deception.[g]

JOB'S REPLY TO ELIPHAZ

16 Then Job answered:
   2 I have heard many things
      like these.
   You are all miserable comforters.[h]
3 Is there no end
      to your empty[c,j] words?
   What provokes you that you
      continue testifying?
4 If you were in my place I could
      also talk like you.
   I could string words together
      against you
   and shake my head at you.
5 Instead, I would encourage you
      with my mouth,

and the consolation from my lips
   would bring relief.[j]
6 If I speak, my suffering
      is not relieved,
   and if I hold back, does any of it
      leave me?
7 Surely he[D] has now exhausted me.
   You have devastated
      my entire family.
8 You have shriveled me up[E]—
      it has become a witness;
   my frailty rises up against me
      and testifies to my face.
9 His anger tears at me,
      and he harasses[k] me.
   He gnashes his teeth at me.
   My enemy pierces me
      with his eyes.
10 They open their mouths against me
   and strike my cheeks
      with contempt;[l]
   they join themselves together
      against me.
11 God hands me over to the unjust;[F]
   he throws me to the wicked.
12 I was at ease, but he shattered me;
   he seized me by the scruff
      of the neck
   and smashed me to pieces.
   He set me up as his target;[m]
13 his archers[G] surround me.
   He pierces my kidneys
      without mercy
   and pours my bile on the ground.
14 He breaks through my defenses
      again and again;[H]
   he charges at me like a warrior.[n]
15 I have sewn sackcloth over my skin;
   I have buried my strength[I]
      in the dust.[o]
16 My face has grown red
      with weeping,
   and darkness[p] covers my eyes,
17 although my hands are free
      from violence[q]
   and my prayer is pure.
18 Earth, do not cover my blood;
   may my cry for help find
      no resting place.[r]
19 Even now my witness is in heaven,
   and my advocate is in the heights![s]

A15:27 Lit with his fat   B15:29 Text emended; MT reads Their gain   C16:3 Lit windy; Jb 15:2   D16:7 Or it   E16:8 Or have seized me; Hb obscure
F16:11 LXX, Vg; MT reads to a boy   G16:13 Or arrows   H16:14 Lit through me, breach on breach   I16:15 Lit horn

16:7-11 Though his friends had an atrocious bedside manner, God was the one who had **devastated [Job's] entire family** (16:7-8). And if that was not bad enough, Job said, **God** was also handing him **over to the unjust** and throwing him **to the wicked** (16:11)—a message that I'm sure his friends got.

20 My friends scoff at me
   as I weep before God.
21 I wish that someone might argue
      for a man with God[a]
   just as anyone[A] would for a friend.
22 For only a few years will pass
   before I go the way of no return.

17 My spirit is broken.
   My days are extinguished.
   A graveyard[b] awaits me.
2 Surely mockers surround[B] me,
   and my eyes must gaze
      at their rebellion.[c]

3 Accept my pledge! Put up security
      for me.[d]
   Who else will be my sponsor?[c]
4 You have closed their minds
      to understanding,
   therefore you will not honor them.
5 If a man denounces his friends
      for a price,
   the eyes of his children will fail.

6 He has made me an object of scorn
      to the people;
   I have become a man people
      spit at.[D,e]
7 My eyes have grown dim from grief,
   and my whole body has become
      but a shadow.
8 The upright are appalled[f] at this,
   and the innocent are roused
      against the godless.
9 Yet the righteous person will hold
      to his way,
   and the one whose hands are clean[g]
      will grow stronger.
10 But come back and try again,
      all of you.[E]
   I will not find a wise man
      among you.

11 My days have slipped by;
   my plans have been ruined,
   even the things dear to my heart.
12 They turned night into day
   and made light seem near in the face
      of darkness.[h]
13 If I await Sheol as my home,
   spread out my bed in darkness,

14 and say to corruption, "You are
      my father,"
   and to the maggot, "My mother"
      or "My sister,"
15 where then is my hope?[j]
   Who can see any hope for me?
16 Will it go down to the gates of Sheol,[k]
   or will we descend together
      to the dust?

BILDAD SPEAKS

18 Then Bildad the Shuhite[l] replied:
   2 How long until you stop talking?
   Show some sense, and then
      we can talk.
3 Why are we regarded as cattle,
   as stupid in your sight?
4 You who tear yourself in anger[F] —
   should the earth be abandoned
      on your account,
   or a rock be removed
      from its place?

5 Yes, the light[m] of the wicked[n]
      is extinguished;
   the flame of his fire does not glow.
6 The light in his tent grows dark,[o]
   and the lamp beside him is put out.
7 His powerful stride is shortened,
   and his own schemes trip him up.[p]
8 For his own feet lead him into a net,
   and he strays into its mesh.
9 A trap catches him by the heel;
   a noose seizes him.
10 A rope lies hidden for him
      on the ground,
   and a snare waits for him
      along the path.
11 Terrors frighten him on every side[q]
   and harass him at every step.
12 His strength is depleted;
   disaster lies ready for him
      to stumble.[G]
13 Parts of his skin are eaten away;
   death's firstborn consumes
      his limbs.
14 He is ripped from the security
      of his tent
   and marched away to the king
      of terrors.
15 Nothing he owned remains
   in his tent.

a 16:21 Jb 31:35; Ec 6:10; Is 45:9
b 17:1 Jb 3:22; 5:26; 10:19
c 17:2 Ps 22:7; 119:51; Jr 20:7
d 17:3 Gn 43:9; Ps 119:122; Pr 6:1
e 17:6 Nm 12:14; Is 50:6; Mt 27:30
f 17:8 Jb 18:20; 21:5; Dn 4:19
g 17:9 2Sm 22:21; Jb 22:30; Ps 24:4
h 17:12 Jb 11:17; Ps 37:6; Is 58:8,10
i 17:14 Jb 3:15; 30:23; Ec 12:5
j 17:15 Jb 7:6; 14:19; 19:10
k 17:16 Jb 7:9; 11:8; 14:13
l 18:1 Jb 2:11; 8:1; 25:1
m 18:5 Jb 21:17; Pr 13:9; 24:20
n Jb 3:17; 9:22; 11:20
o 18:6 Jb 8:22; 18:14; Ps 52:5
p 18:7 Jb 5:13; Pr 4:12
q 18:11 Jb 20:25; 27:20; Jr 6:25

A 16:21 Lit *a son of man*   **B** 17:2 Lit *are with*   **C** 17:3 Or *Who is there that will shake hands with me?*   **D** 17:6 Lit *become a spitting to the faces*
E 17:10 Some Hb mss, LXX, Vg; other Hb mss read *them*   **F** 18:4 Lit *He who tears himself in his anger*   **G** 18:12 Or *disaster hungers for him*

17:1-15 In this chapter, Job fell into further despair as the realization that God wasn't going to just step in and end his grief hit.

18:12-19 According to Bildad, the way you can spot a wicked sinner is that **his strength is depleted** (18:12), **parts of his skin are eaten away** (18:13), he's lost everything (18:15), and

he has no children or **survivor** (18:19), thus leaving little mystery about just which person Bildad had in mind.

a 18:15 Gn 19:24; Ps 11:6; Ezk 38:22

b 18:16 Is 5:24; Hs 9:16; Am 2:9

c 18:17 Ps 34:16; 109:13,15; Pr 10:7

d 18:19 Gn 21:23; Is 14:22; Lm 2:22

e 18:20 Jr 2:12; Ezk 27:35; 32:10

f 18:21 Jb 21:28; Jr 9:3; 1Th 4:5

g 19:3 Gn 31:7; Nm 14:22; Pr 25:8

h 19:5 Ps 35:26; 38:16; 55:12

i 19:6 Jb 27:2; Lm 3:5; Ezk 12:13

j 19:7 Jb 30:20; Lm 3:8; Hab 1:2

k 19:8 Jb 3:23; Lm 3:9; Hs 2:6

l 19:3 29:3; 30:26; Is 59:9

m 19:10 Dt 28:63; Jb 24:20; Ps 52:5

n 19:11 Jb 16:9; 21:17; 40:11

o Jb 13:24; 33:10; Lm 2:5

p 19:12 Ps 27:3; Is 29:3; Jr 50:29

q 19:13 Ps 31:11; 38:11; 88:8,18

r 19:15 Gn 31:15; Ps 69:8; Mt 10:36

s 19:18 2Kg 2:23; Jb 29:8

t 19:19 Jb 30:10; Ps 89:38; Am 5:10

u Ps 41:9; 55:11-12; Jn 13:18

v 19:21 Jb 6:14; Ps 38:11; Pr 17:17

w Ru 1:13; Jb 12:9; Is 41:20

x Jb 1:11; 2:5; 6:7

y 19:25 Jb 16:19; Pr 23:11; Jr 50:34

Burning sulfur*a* is scattered
   over his home.
16 His roots below dry up,
   and his branches above wither away.*b*
17 All memory*c* of him perishes
   from the earth;
   he has no name anywhere.*A*
18 He is driven from light to darkness
   and chased
   from the inhabited world.
19 He has no children or descendants
   among his people,
   no survivor where he used to live.*d*
20 Those in the west are appalled*e*
   at his fate,
   while those in the east tremble
   in horror.
21 Indeed, such is the dwelling of the
   unjust man,
   and this is the place of the one
   who does not know God.*f*

JOB'S REPLY TO BILDAD

19 Then Job answered:
2 How long will you torment me
   and crush me with words?
3 You have humiliated me ten times now,
   and you mistreat*B* me without shame.*g*
4 Even if it is true that I have sinned,
   my mistake concerns only*c* me.
5 If you really want to appear
   superior*h* to me
   and would use my disgrace
   as evidence against me,
6 then understand that it is God
   who has wronged me
   and caught me in his net.*i*

7 I cry out: "Violence!"
   but get no response;*j*
   I call for help, but there is no justice.
8 He has blocked*k* my way so that
   I cannot pass through;
   he has veiled my paths
   with darkness.*l*
9 He has stripped me of my honor
   and removed the crown
   from my head.
10 He tears me down on every side
   so that I am ruined.*D*
   He uproots my hope like a tree.*m*

11 His anger*n* burns against me,
   and he regards me as one of
   his enemies.*o*
12 His troops advance together;
   they construct a ramp*E* against me
   and camp*p* around my tent.
13 He has removed my brothers
   from me;
   my acquaintances
   have abandoned me.*q*
14 My relatives stop coming by,
   and my close friends
   have forgotten me.
15 My house guests*F*
   and female servants regard me
   as a stranger;
   I am a foreigner in their sight.*r*
16 I call for my servant, but he
   does not answer,
   even if I beg him
   with my own mouth.
17 My breath is offensive to my wife,
   and my own family*G*
   finds me repulsive.
18 Even young boys scorn me.
   When I stand up, they mock me.*s*
19 All of my best friends*H*
   despise me,*t*
   and those I love have turned
   against me.*u*
20 My skin and my flesh cling
   to my bones;
   I have escaped with only the skin
   of my teeth.

21 Have mercy on me, my friends,*v*
   have mercy,
   for God's hand*w* has struck me.*x*
22 Why do you persecute me
   as God does?
   Will you never get enough
   of my flesh?

23 I wish that my words
   were written down,
   that they were recorded on a scroll
24 or were inscribed in stone forever
   by an iron stylus and lead!
25 But I know that my Redeemer
   lives,*I,y*

A 18:17 Or *name in the streets*   *B* 19:3 Hb obscure   *C* 19:4 Lit *mistake lives with*   *D* 19:10 Lit *gone*   *E* 19:12 Lit *they raise up their way*   *F* 19:15 Or *The resident aliens in my household*   *G* 19:17 Lit *and the sons of my belly*   *H* 19:19 Lit *of the men of my council*   *I* 19:25 Or *know my living Redeemer*

19:3 The **ten times** Job said his friends had **humiliated** him is a Hebrew expression meaning "often."
19:4 This is another way of saying, "Who invited you to pass judgment? I didn't ask for you three to come."

19:6-7 We might expect a lightning bolt to strike Job at these accusations. But God is gracious.
19:25-27 Hymns and songs of faith have been written from these verses. And what's most amazing about Job's statement of faith here

is that he seemed to expect a bodily resurrection (19:26). If so, this would be the earliest evidence of this doctrine in Scripture. Certainly Job was confident that death would not end his existence, a truth the rest of the Bible affirms.

and at the end he will stand
   on the dust.[a]
26 Even after my skin
   has been destroyed,[A]
   yet I will see God in[B] my flesh.[b]
27 I will see him myself;
   my eyes will look at him, and not
   as a stranger.[c]
   My heart longs[D] within me.[c]

28 If you say, "How will we pursue him,
   since the root of the problem lies
   with him?"[E]
29 then be afraid of the sword,
   because wrath brings punishment
   by the sword,[d]
   so that you may know there is
   a judgment.

ZOPHAR SPEAKS

20 Then Zophar the Naamathite[e] replied:
2 This is why my unsettling thoughts
   compel me to answer,
   because I am upset![F]
3 I have heard a rebuke
   that insults me,
   and my understanding[G]
   makes me reply.[f]

4 Don't you know that
   ever since antiquity,
   from the time a human was placed
   on earth,
5 the joy of the wicked has been brief
   and the happiness of the godless
   has lasted only a moment?[g]
6 Though his arrogance
   reaches heaven,
   and his head touches the clouds,[h]
7 he will vanish forever
   like his own dung.
   Those who know[H] him will ask,
   "Where is he?"[i]
8 He will fly away like a dream
   and never be found;
   he will be chased away like a vision
   in the night.[j]
9 The eye that saw him will see him
   no more,[k]

and his household will no longer
   see him.[i]
10 His children will beg from[i] the poor,
   for his own hands must give back
   his wealth.
11 His frame may be full of
   youthful vigor,
   but it will lie down with him
   in dust.[m]

12 Though evil tastes sweet
   in his mouth
   and he conceals it under his tongue,
13 though he cherishes it and will not
   let it go
   but keeps it in his mouth,[n]
14 yet the food in his stomach turns
   into cobras' venom inside him.
15 He swallows wealth but must
   vomit it up;
   God will force it from his stomach.
16 He will suck the poison of cobras;
   a viper's fangs[j] will kill him.[o]
17 He will not enjoy the streams,
   the rivers flowing with honey
   and curds.[p]
18 He must return the fruit of his labor
   without consuming it;
   he doesn't enjoy the profits
   from his trading.
19 For he oppressed and abandoned
   the poor;
   he seized a house he did not build.[q]

20 Because his appetite
   is never satisfied,[K]
   he does not let anything
   he desires escape.
21 Nothing is left for him to consume;[r]
   therefore, his prosperity
   will not last.
22 At the height of his success[L]
   distress will come to him;[s]
   the full weight of misery[M]
   will crush him.
23 When he fills his stomach,
   God will send his burning anger
   against him,
   raining[r] it down on him
   while he is eating.[N]

[a]19:25 Is 44:6; 48:12; Rv 1:17-18
[b]19:26 Ps 17:15; Is 6:1; 1Co 13:12
[c]19:27 Ps 73:26; 84:2; 119:81
[d]19:29 Jb 15:22; Is 66:16; Ezk 32:10
[e]20:1 Jb 2:11; 11:1; 42:9
[f]20:3 Jb 19:3; 32:18; Ac 2:20
[g]20:5 Jb 8:12-13; Ps 37:35-36; 92:7
[h]20:6 Gn 11:4; Is 14:13-14; Ob 3-4
[i]20:7 Jb 4:20; Ps 90:5-6; Jms 4:14
[j]20:8 Ps 73:20; 90:5; Is 29:7
[k]20:9 Jb 7:8,21; Ps 37:36

[i]20:9 Jb 7:10; 8:18; Ps 103:16
[m]20:11 Jb 7:21; 17:16; Ps 7:5
[n]20:12-13 Ps 10:7; Pr 9:17; 20:17
[o]20:16 Dt 32:33; Pr 23:32; Is 59:5
[p]20:17 Dt 32:13; Jb 29:6; Ps 36:8
[q]20:19 Dt 28:30; Is 5:8; Mc 2:2
[r]20:20-21 Jb 15:29; Pr 17:1; Ec 5:13
[s]20:22 Jdg 2:15; Jb 21:17; Zph 1:17
[t]20:23 Gn 19:24; Ps 11:6; Ezk 38:22

[A]19:26 Lit *skin which they destroyed*, or *skin they destroyed in this way*   [B]19:26 Or *apart from*   [C]19:27 Or *not a stranger*   [D]19:27 Lit *My kidneys grow faint*   [E]19:28 Some Hb mss, LXX, Vg; other Hb mss read *me*   [F]20:2 Lit *because of my feeling within me*   [G]20:3 Lit *and a spirit from my understanding*   [H]20:7 Lit *have seen*   [I]20:10 Or *children must compensate*   [J]20:16 Lit *tongue*   [K]20:20 Lit *Because he does not know ease in his stomach*   [L]20:22 Lit *In the fullness of his excess*   [M]20:22 Some Hb mss, LXX, Vg; other Hb mss read *the hand of everyone in misery*   [N]20:23 Text emended; MT reads *him, against his flesh*

20:4-5 Zophar's logic here is an early attempt to answer one of the most puzzling questions God's people have ever faced: Why do the wicked prosper and the righteous suffer? Zophar was partly correct in saying that the wicked only last for a season and eventually face God's judgment. But that season can seem awfully long to oppressed onlookers when a wicked person enjoys a life of wealth and ease. That, in fact, is why we have to keep a kingdom perspective.

a 20:25 Jb 18:11; 27:20; Jr 6:25
b 20:26 Jb 15:34; Ps 21:9; 50:3
c 20:27 Jb 13:23,26; 15:5; 22:5
d Dt 4:26; Jb 16:18-19; Ps 50:4
e 20:29 Jb 27:13; 31:2; Ps 17:14
f 21:4 Jb 7:11; 10:1; 27:13
g 21:5 Jb 17:8; 18:20; Dn 4:19
h Jdg 18:19; Jb 29:9; 40:4
i 21:6 Jb 4:14; Ps 55:5; 119:120
j 21:9 Jb 5:24; 8:6; 12:6
k Jb 9:34; Ps 73:5

l 21:12 Jb 30:31; Ps 81:2; 150:4
m 21:13 Jb 36:11; Ps 37:7; 73:12
n 21:14 Jb 22:17; Ps 95:10; Pr 1:29
o 21:15 Ex 5:2; Jb 34:9; Mal 3:14
p 21:16 Jb 22:18; Ps 1:1; Pr 1:10
q 21:17 Jb 18:5; Pr 13:9; 24:20
r 21:18 Ps 1:4; 35:5; Is 17:13
s 21:19 Ex 20:5; Jr 31:29; Lm 5:7
t 21:20 Ps 75:8; Is 51:17; Jr 25:15
u 21:21 Jb 14:21; Ec 9:5; Is 63:16
v Jb 14:5; Ps 39:4; 90:12
w 21:22 Is 40:13-14; Rm 11:34; 1Co 2:16
x 21:25 1Sm 1:10; Jb 7:11; 10:1

24 If he flees from an iron weapon,
an arrow from a bronze bow
will pierce him.
25 He pulls it out of his back,
the flashing tip out of his liver.^A
Terrors come over him.*a*
26 Total darkness is reserved
for his treasures.
A fire unfanned by human hands
will consume*b* him;
it will feed on what is left in his tent.
27 The heavens will expose
his iniquity,*c*
and the earth will rise up
against him.*d*
28 The possessions in his house
will be removed,
flowing away on the day
of God's anger.
29 This is the wicked person's lot*e*
from God,
the inheritance God ordained
for him.

JOB'S REPLY TO ZOPHAR

21 Then Job answered:
² Pay close attention to my words;
let this be the consolation you offer.
3 Bear with me while I speak;
then after I have spoken, you may
continue mocking.

4 As for me, is my complaint*f*
against a human being?
Then why shouldn't I be impatient?
5 Look at me and shudder;*g*
put your hand over your mouth.*h*
6 When I think about it, I am terrified
and my body trembles*i* in horror.
7 Why do the wicked continue to live,
growing old and becoming
powerful?
8 Their children are established
while they are still alive,^B
and their descendants,
before their eyes.
9 Their homes are secure
and free of fear;*j*
no rod from God strikes them.*k*
10 Their bulls breed without fail;

their cows calve
and do not miscarry.
11 They let their little ones run
around like lambs;
their children skip about,
12 singing to the tambourine and lyre
and rejoicing at the sound
of the flute.*l*
13 They spend*c* their days
in prosperity*m*
and go down to Sheol in peace.
14 Yet they say to God, "Leave us alone!
We don't want to know your ways.*n*
15 Who is the Almighty, that we
should serve him,
and what will we gain by pleading
with him?"*o*
16 But their prosperity is not
of their own doing.
The counsel of the wicked is far
from me!*p*

17 How often is the lamp*q* of the wicked
put out?
Does disaster^D come on them?
Does he apportion destruction
in his anger?
18 Are they like straw before the wind,
like chaff*r* a storm sweeps away?
19 God reserves a person's punishment
for his children.*s*
Let God repay the person himself,
so that he may know it.
20 Let his own eyes see his demise;
let him drink from
the Almighty's wrath!*t*
21 For what does he care
about his family once he is dead,*u*
when the number of his months
has run out?*v*
22 Can anyone teach God knowledge,*w*
since he judges the exalted ones?^E
23 One person dies in excellent health,^F
completely secure^G and at ease.
24 His body is^H well fed,^I
and his bones are full of marrow.^J
25 Yet another person dies
with a bitter*x* soul,
having never tasted prosperity.

---

^A 20:25 Or *gallbladder*   ^B 21:8 Lit *established before them with them*   ^C 21:13 Alt Hb tradition reads *fully enjoy*   ^D 21:17 Lit *their disaster*
^E 21:22 Probably angels   ^F 21:23 Lit *in bone of his perfection*   ^G 21:23 Text emended; MT reads *health, all at ease*   ^H 21:24 Or *His sides are*;
Hb obscure   ^I 21:24 Lit *is full of milk*   ^J 21:24 Lit *and the marrow of his bones is watered*

20:26, 29 Zophar finished by saying Job, God's got an **inheritance** waiting for you (20:29), but it's **a fire** that will **consume** you (20:26).
21:7-18 Job's complaint that wicked people often prosper reminds me of a similar point that would be made centuries later by the

psalmist (see Ps 73:1-14). But as soon as the latter stepped into God's house, his perspective changed drastically (see Ps 73:15-28). Suddenly, he saw things clearly. He realized that evil people who pay no attention to God have one foot in the grave and the other on

a banana peel. Job wasn't quite to that point of peaceful clarity yet.
21:14-15 This is the attitude of those who live for the moment but not for eternity. These are people who care nothing for their Creator's agenda. They have their own.

26 But they both lie in the dust,
and worms cover them.[a]

27 I know your thoughts very well,
the schemes by which you would
wrong me.
28 For you say, "Where now is
the nobleman's house?"
and "Where are the tents[b]
the wicked lived in?"
29 Have you never consulted
those who travel the roads?
Don't you accept their reports?[A]
30 Indeed, the evil person is spared
from the day of disaster,
rescued from the day of wrath.
31 Who would denounce his behavior
to his face?
Who would repay[c] him for what
he has done?
32 He is carried to the grave,
and someone keeps watch over
his tomb.
33 The dirt on his grave is[B] sweet to him.
Everyone follows behind him,
and those who go before him are
without number.

34 So how can you offer me
such futile comfort?
Your answers are deceptive.

THIRD SERIES OF SPEECHES

ELIPHAZ SPEAKS

22 Then Eliphaz the Temanite replied:
2 Can a man be of any use to God?
Can even a wise man be of use
to him?
3 Does it delight the Almighty if you
are righteous?
Does he profit if you perfect
your behavior?[d]

4 Does he correct you and take you
to court
because of your piety?[e]
5 Isn't your wickedness abundant
and aren't your iniquities endless?
6 For you took collateral[f]
from your brothers without cause,
stripping off their clothes
and leaving them naked.

7 You gave no water to the thirsty
and withheld food
from the famished,[g]
8 while the land belonged
to a powerful man
and an influential man lived on it.
9 You sent widows away
empty-handed,
and the strength of the fatherless[h]
was[c] crushed.
10 Therefore snares surround you,
and sudden dread terrifies[i] you,
11 or darkness, so you cannot see,
and a flood of water covers you.[j]

12 Isn't God as high as the heavens?
And look at the highest stars —
how lofty they are!
13 Yet you say, "What does
God know?
Can he judge
through total darkness?[k]
14 Clouds[l] veil him so that
he cannot see,
as he walks on the circle of the sky."
15 Will you continue
on the ancient path
that wicked men have walked?
16 They were snatched away
before their time,
and their foundations[m]
were washed away by a river.
17 They were the ones who said to God,
"Leave us alone!"
and "What can the Almighty do
to us?"[D,n]
18 But it was he who filled their houses
with good things.
The counsel of the wicked is
far from me!
19 The righteous see this and rejoice;
the innocent mock them, saying,[o]
20 "Surely our opponents
are destroyed,
and fire has consumed
what they left behind."[p]

21 Come to terms with God and be
at peace;[q]
in this way[E] good will come to you.
22 Receive instruction from his mouth,[r]
and place his sayings[s]
in your heart.

[a]21:26 Jb 20:11; Ec 9:2-3;
Is 14:11
[b]21:28 Jb 8:22; 18:21;
Ps 55:15
[c]21:31 Dt 7:10; Jb 34:11;
Ps 62:12
[d]22:2-3 Jb 35:7; Ps 16:2;
Lk 17:10
[e]22:4 Jb 14:3; Ps 143:2
[f]22:6 Ex 22:26; Dt 24:6,17;
Ezk 18:12

[g]22:7 Jb 31:17; Is 58:7;
Mt 25:42
[h]22:9 Jb 24:3; Is 10:2;
Ezk 22:7
[i]22:10 Jb 3:25; 23:15; 31:23
[j]22:11 Jb 38:34; Ps 69:1-2;
Lm 3:54
[k]22:13 Ps 73:11; Is 29:15;
Ezk 8:12
[l]22:14 2Sm 22:12; Jb
26:8; 37:11
[m]22:16 Jb 4:19; Lm 4:11;
Ezk 30:4
[n]22:17 Jb 21:14; Ps 95:10;
107:42
[o]22:19 Ps 52:6; 58:10; Pr
1:26-27
[p]22:20 Jb 1:16; 4:9; 15:30
[q]22:21 Ps 119:165; Pr 3:2;
Is 27:5
[r]22:22 Dt 8:3; Pr 2:6;
Mal 2:7
[s]Jb 6:10; 23:12; Ps 119:102

[A]21:29 Lit signs   [B]21:33 Lit The clods of the wadi are   [C]22:9 LXX, Syr, Vg, Tg read you have   [D]22:17 LXX, Syr; MT reads them   [E]22:21 Lit peace; by them

22:2-3 This is actually good theology. God does not need you or me. We need him, but God is sufficient, complete within himself. He does not need anything in his created order to make him feel better about being God.
22:5-10 If such charges against Job had been true (22:5-9), it was no wonder Eliphaz was convinced that Job was suffering justly. He was simply getting the sentence a righteous and holy God had handed down (22:10).

a 22:23 Is 31:6; 55:7;
Mal 3:7
b 22:24 1Kg 9:28; Jb 28:16;
Is 13:12
c 22:26 Jb 27:10; Ps 37:4;
Is 55:2
d Jb 11:15; 27:10; Is 58:14
e 22:27 Jb 33:26; Ps 50:14;
Is 58:9
f 22:28 Pr 4:18; Is 60:3;
Dn 12:3
g 22:29 Ps 18:27; Mt 23:12;
1Pt 5:5
h 22:30 2Sm 22:21; Jb 17:9;
Ps 24:4
i 23:2 Jb 7:11; 10:1; 21:4
j 23:4 Jb 5:8; 13:18; 35:14
k 23:6 Jb 13:19; 33:13;
Is 45:9
l 23:7 Jb 13:3,15; 15:3
m Gn 18:25; Is 33:22;
Jr 11:20
n 23:8 Jb 9:11; 35:14

o 23:10 Ps 17:3; 66:10;
1Pt 1:7
p 23:11 Jb 17:9; Ps 17:5;
44:18
q 23:12 Jb 6:10; 22:22; Ps
119:102-103,111
r 23:13 Ps 115:3; Is 14:27;
Dn 4:35
s 23:15 Jb 4:14; 22:10; 23:15
t 23:16 Dt 20:3; Is 7:4;
Jr 51:46
u 23:17 Jb 19:8; 29:3; 30:26
v 24:1 Ec 9:12; Is 2:12;
Ac 1:7
w 24:3 Dt 27:19; Jb 22:9;
31:21
x 24:4 Jdg 5:6; Pr 28:28;
Am 2:7

23 If you return*a* to the Almighty,
you will be renewed.
If you banish injustice
from your tent
24 and consign your gold to the dust,
the gold of Ophir*b* to the stones
in the wadis,
25 the Almighty will be your gold
and your finest silver.
26 Then you will delight*c* in
the Almighty
and lift up your face to God.*d*
27 You will pray to him, and he will
hear you,*e*
and you will fulfill your vows.
28 When you make a decision, it will be
carried out,*A*
and light will shine on your ways.*f*
29 When others are humiliated
and you say, "Lift them up,"
God will save the humble.*B,g*
30 He will even rescue the guilty one,
who will be rescued by the purity
of your hands.*h*

JOB'S REPLY TO ELIPHAZ

23 Then Job answered:
² Today also my complaint is bitter.*C,i*
His*D* hand is heavy
despite my groaning.
3 If only I knew how to find him,
so that I could go to his throne.
4 I would plead my case before him*j*
and fill my mouth with arguments.
5 I would learn how*E* he would
answer me;
and understand what he would say
to me.
6 Would he prosecute*k* me forcefully?
No, he would certainly pay attention
to me.
7 Then an upright man could reason*l*
with him,
and I would escape
from my Judge*F,m* forever.

8 If I go east, he is not there,
and if I go west, I cannot
perceive him.*n*
9 When he is at work to the north,
I cannot see him;

when he turns south, I cannot
find him.
10 Yet he knows the way I have taken;*G*
when he has tested me,*o*
I will emerge as pure gold.
11 My feet have followed in his tracks;
I have kept to his way*p* and not
turned aside.
12 I have not departed
from the commands
from his lips;
I have treasured*H* the words*q*
from his mouth
more than my daily food.

13 But he is unchangeable; who can
oppose him?
He does what he desires.*r*
14 He will certainly accomplish
what he has decreed for me,
and he has many more things
like these in mind.*I*
15 Therefore I am terrified*s*
in his presence;
when I consider this, I am afraid
of him.
16 God has made my heart faint;*t*
the Almighty has terrified me.
17 Yet I am not destroyed*J*
by the darkness,*u*
by the thick darkness that covers
my face.

24 Why does the Almighty
not reserve times for judgment?*v*
Why do those who know him
never see his days?
² The wicked displace
boundary markers.
They steal a flock and provide
pasture for it.
3 They drive away the donkeys owned
by the fatherless*w*
and take the widow's ox
as collateral.
4 They push the needy off the road;
the poor of the land are forced
into hiding.*x*
5 Like wild donkeys in the wilderness,
the poor go out to their task
of foraging for food;

A 22:28 Lit *out for you* *B* 22:29 Lit *bowed of eyes* *C* 23:2 Syr, Tg, Vg; MT reads *rebellion* *D* 23:2 LXX, Syr; MT reads *My* *E* 23:5 Lit *the words*
F 23:7 Or *judgment* *G* 23:10 Lit *way with me* *H* 23:12 LXX, Vg read *treasured in my bosom* *I* 23:14 Lit *these with him* *J* 23:17 Or *silenced*

23:3-10 Job maintained that if a trial were held in heaven's court, God would pay attention to his **case** and declare him not guilty (23:4-7). The problem, Job had decided, was that he didn't know where to find God (23:8-9). Yet even though he was frustrated in his desire to get a hearing, Job was confident that God knew his heart. He was sure that when God had **tested** him, he would **emerge as pure gold** (23:10). Like Job, you may not be able to figure out where God is, but he knows where you are. We worship him because of what we know that *he* knows.

23:12 Job's attitude toward God's **commands** is a sobering reminder that believers who aren't regularly feeding on God's Word are malnourished. It's not enough just to be under the teaching of the Bible weekly in church. We also need to be in the Word daily.

the desert provides nourishment
   for their children.
6 They gather their fodder in the field
   and glean the vineyards
     of the wicked.
7 Without clothing, they spend
    the night naked,
   having no covering against the cold.[a]
8 Drenched by mountain rains,
   they huddle against[A] the rocks,
    shelterless.
9 The fatherless infant is snatched
    from the breast;
   the nursing child of the poor
    is seized as collateral.[B]
10 Without clothing,
    they wander about naked.
   They carry sheaves but go hungry.[b]
11 They crush olives in their presses;[c]
   they tread the winepresses,
    but go thirsty.
12 From the city, men[D] groan;
   the mortally wounded cry for help,
   yet God pays no attention
    to this crime.[c]

13 The wicked are those who rebel
    against the light.
   They do not recognize its ways
   or stay on its paths.
14 The murderer rises at dawn
   to kill the poor and needy,
   and by night he becomes a thief.
15 The adulterer's eye watches
    for twilight,
   thinking, "No eye will see me,"
   and he covers his face.
16 In the dark they break[E] into houses;
   by day they lock themselves in,[F]
   never experiencing the light.
17 For the morning is like darkness
    to them.
   Surely they are familiar
    with the terrors of darkness!

18 They float[G] on the surface
    of the water.
   Their section of the land is cursed,
   so that they never go
    to their vineyards.
19 As dry ground and heat snatch away
    the melted snow,
   so Sheol[d] steals those
    who have sinned.

20 The womb forgets them;
   worms feed on them;
   they are remembered[e] no more.
   So injustice is broken like a tree.
21 They prey on[H] the childless woman
    who is unable to conceive,
   and do not deal kindly
    with the widow.
22 Yet God drags away[I] the mighty
    by his power;
   when he rises up, they have
    no assurance of life.
23 He gives them a sense of security,
    so they can rely on it,[f]
   but his eyes[g] watch over their ways.
24 They are exalted for a moment,
    then gone;
   they are brought low and shrivel up
    like everything else.[j]
   They wither like heads of grain.[h]

25 If this is not true, then who
    can prove me a liar[i]
   and show that my speech
    is worthless?

BILDAD SPEAKS

25 Then Bildad the Shuhite replied:
2 Dominion and dread[j] belong
    to him,
   the one who establishes harmony
    in his heights.
3 Can his troops be numbered?
   Does his light not shine
    on everyone?
4 How can a human be justified
    before God?[k]
   How can one born of woman
    be pure?[l]
5 If even the moon does not shine
   and the stars are not pure
    in his sight,[m]
6 how much less a human, who is
    a maggot,
   a son of man,[K] who is a worm![n]

JOB'S REPLY TO BILDAD

26 Then Job answered:
2 How you have helped[o]
    the powerless
   and delivered the arm that is weak!
3 How you have counseled
    the unwise[p]
   and abundantly provided insight!

[a]24:7 Ex 22:26-27; Dt 24:12-13; Jb 22:6
[b]24:10 Dt 24:19; 2Tm 2:6; Jms 5:4
[c]24:12 Jb 1:22; Ps 69:26
[d]24:19 Jb 7:9; Ps 9:17; Pr 27:20
[e]24:20 Jb 18:17; Pr 10:7; Jr 11:19
[f]24:23 Jb 11:18; Ps 4:8; Pr 3:24
[g]Ps 11:4; Pr 15:3; Jr 16:17
[h]24:24 Jb 14:21; Ps 37:10; 106:43
[i]24:25 Jb 6:28; 27:4; 34:6
[j]25:2 2Ch 20:29; Jb 13:11; Ps 36:1
[k]25:4 Jb 9:2; Ps 143:2; Rm 3:20
[l]Jb 4:17; 15:14; Pr 20:9
[m]25:5 Jb 4:18; 15:15; 21:22
[n]25:6 Ps 8:4; 22:6; Is 41:14
[o]26:2 Jb 4:3; Is 35:3; Heb 12:12
[p]26:3 Jb 11:6; Ps 73:24; Jms 1:5

[A]24:8 Lit *they embrace*   [B]24:9 Text emended; MT reads *breast; they seize collateral against the poor*   [C]24:11 Lit *olives between their rows*
[D]24:12 One Hb ms, Syr read *the dying*   [E]24:16 Lit *dig*   [F]24:16 Lit *they seal for themselves*   [G]24:18 Lit *are insignificant*   [H]24:21 LXX, Tg read *They harm*   [I]24:22 Or *God prolongs the life of*   [J]24:24 LXX reads *like a mallow plant in the heat*   [K]25:6 Or *a mere mortal*

24:13-16 Murderers, thieves, and adulterers just seem to have their way. Things are not, however, always what they seem. The physical darkness on which they often rely to cover their deeds is like light to God (see Ps 139:12).

a 26:5 Ps 88:10; Is 26:14,19; Rv 20:13
b 26:6 Ps 30:3,9; Pr 1:12; Is 5:14
c Jb 28:22; Pr 27:20; Rv 9:11
d Ps 139:8; Pr 15:11; Heb 4:13
e 26:8 Jb 37:11; 38:9; Pr 30:4
f 26:10 Ps 104:9; Pr 8:27,29; Jr 5:22
g 26:11 2Sm 22:16; Ps 18:15; 104:7
h 26:12 Is 51:15; Jr 31:35
i Jb 9:13; Ps 89:10; Is 51:9
j 26:13 Jb 41; Ps 33:6; Is 27:1
k 27:2 Jb 19:6; 34:5
l Ex 1:14; Ru 1:20; Jb 3:20
m 27:3 Gn 2:7; Jb 12:10; 33:4
n 27:5 Jb 2:3,9; 31:6; Pr 11:3

o 27:6 Ac 24:16; 1Co 4:4; Rv 9:11
p 27:8 Jb 17:8; 20:5; 36:13
q Jb 8:13; Mt 16:26; Lk 12:20
r 27:10 Jb 22:26; Ps 37:4; Is 55:2
s 27:12 Jb 2:10; 15:2
t 27:13 Jb 20:29; 31:2; Ps 17:14
u 27:15 Jb 18:19; Ps 78:64; Jr 22:10
v 27:17 Pr 13:22; 28:8; Ec 2:26
w 27:18 Jb 4:19; Is 1:8; Jnh 4:5
x 27:20 Jb 18:11; 20:25; Jr 6:25
y Jb 21:18; Ps 83:15; Is 29:6

4 With whom did you speak
    these words?
Whose breath came out of your mouth?

5 The departed spirits tremble
beneath the waters and all that
    inhabit them.*a*

6 Sheol*b* is naked before God,
and Abaddon*c* has no covering.*d*

7 He stretches the northern skies
    over empty space;
he hangs the earth on nothing.

8 He wraps up the water in his clouds,
yet the clouds do not burst
    beneath its weight.*e*

9 He obscures the view of his throne,
    spreading his cloud over it.

10 He laid out the horizon
    on the surface of the waters*f*
at the boundary between light
    and darkness.

11 The pillars that hold up
    the sky tremble,
astounded at his rebuke.*g*

12 By his power he stirred*h* the sea,
and by his understanding
    he crushed Rahab.*i*

13 By his breath the heavens gained
    their beauty;
his hand pierced
    the fleeing serpent.*A,j*

14 These are but the fringes of his ways;
how faint is the word we hear
    of him!
Who can understand
    his mighty thunder?

27

Job continued his discourse, saying:
2 As God lives, who has
    deprived me of justice,*k*
and the Almighty who has
    made me bitter,*l*

3 as long as my breath is still in me
and the breath from God remains
    in my nostrils,*m*

4 my lips will not speak unjustly,
and my tongue will not utter deceit.

5 I will never affirm that you are right.
I will maintain my integrity*B,n*
    until I die.

6 I will cling to my righteousness
and never let it go.

My conscience*o* will not accuse me
    as long as I live!

7 May my enemy be like the wicked
and my opponent like the unjust.

8 For what hope does
    the godless person*p* have when he
    is cut off,
when God takes away his life?*q*

9 Will God hear his cry
when distress comes on him?

10 Will he delight*r* in the Almighty?
Will he call on God at all times?

11 I will teach you about God's power.
I will not conceal what the Almighty
    has planned.*C*

12 All of you have seen this for yourselves,
why do you keep up this empty talk?*s*

13 This is a wicked man's lot*t* from God,
the inheritance the ruthless receive
    from the Almighty.

14 Even if his children increase,
    they are destined for the sword;
his descendants will never
    have enough food.

15 Those who survive him
    will be buried by the plague,
yet their widows will not weep
    for them.*u*

16 Though he piles up silver like dust
and heaps up fine clothing
    like clay —

17 he may heap it up, but the righteous
    will wear it,
and the innocent will divide up
    his silver.*v*

18 The house he built is
    like a moth's cocoon
or a shelter set up by a watchman.*w*

19 He lies down wealthy, but will do so
    no more;
when he opens his eyes, it is gone.

20 Terrors overtake him like a flood;*x*
a storm*y* wind sweeps him away
    at night.

21 An east wind picks him up,
    and he is gone;
it carries him away from his place.

22 It blasts at him without mercy,
while he flees desperately
    from its force.

A 26:13 = Leviathan   *B* 27:5 Lit *will not remove my integrity from me*   *C* 27:11 Lit *what is with the Almighty*

26:7-14 All the fantastic truths Job listed are summed up in the statement, **These are but the fringes of [God's] ways** (26:14). As much as we know about the majesty of God from observing his creation, we've only scratched the surface.

27:8 This is the sobering fate of the wicked: hopelessness.
27:13-23 While the wicked may prosper in this life, an eternal judgment is coming. A lifetime of eighty to ninety years is certainly lengthy. But, in light of eternity, it's a blip on the radar screen. Here and gone. If you won't live for God's agenda in this life, you'll be forced to bow to his agenda in the afterlife—an agenda of everlasting punishment.

23 It claps[a] its hands at him
  and scoffs at him from its place.

A HYMN TO WISDOM

28 Surely there is a mine for silver
     and a place where gold is refined.
2 Iron is taken from the ground,
  and copper is smelted from ore.
3 A miner puts an end to the darkness;
  he probes[A] the deepest recesses
  for ore in the gloomy darkness.
4 He cuts a shaft far
      from human habitation,
  in places unknown to those
      who walk above ground.
  Suspended far away from people,
  the miners swing back and forth.
5 Food may come from the earth,
  but below the surface the earth
      is transformed as by fire.
6 Its rocks are a source of lapis lazuli,[b]
  containing flecks of gold.
7 No bird of prey knows that path;
  no falcon's eye has seen it.
8 Proud beasts have never walked
      on it;
  no lion has ever prowled over it.
9 The miner uses a flint tool
  and turns up ore from the root
      of the mountains.
10 He cuts out channels in the rocks,
   and his eyes spot every treasure.
11 He dams up the streams
       from flowing[B]
   so that he may bring to light
       what is hidden.

12 But where can wisdom[c] be found,
   and where is understanding
       located?
13 No one can know its value,[c]
   since it cannot be found in the land
       of the living.
14 The ocean depths say, "It's not in me,"
   while the sea declares, "I don't
       have it."[d]
15 Gold cannot be exchanged for it,
   and silver cannot be weighed out
       for its price.
16 Wisdom cannot be valued
   in the gold of Ophir,[e]

in precious onyx or lapis lazuli.[f]
17 Gold and glass do not compare
       with it,
   and articles of fine gold
       cannot be exchanged for it.[g]
18 Coral and quartz are not
       worth mentioning.
   The price of wisdom
       is beyond pearls.
19 Topaz from Cush cannot compare
       with it,
   and it cannot be valued in pure gold.

20 Where then does wisdom
       come from,
   and where is understanding located?
21 It is hidden from the eyes
       of every living thing
   and concealed from the birds
       of the sky.
22 Abaddon and Death[h] say,
   "We have heard news of it
       with our ears."
23 But God understands the way
       to wisdom,
   and he knows its location.
24 For he looks to the ends of the earth
   and sees everything
       under the heavens.
25 When God fixed the weight
       of the wind
   and distributed the water
       by measure,[i]
26 when he established a limit[D]
       for the rain[j]
   and a path for the lightning,
27 he considered wisdom
       and evaluated it;
   he established it and examined it.
28 He said to mankind,
   "The fear of the Lord —
       that is wisdom.
   And to turn from evil
       is understanding."[k]

JOB'S FINAL CLAIM OF INNOCENCE

29 Job continued his discourse, saying:
2 If only I could be as in months
       gone by,
   in the days when God
       watched over me,

[a]27:23 Nm 24:10; Jb 34:37; Lm 2:15
[b]28:6 Ex 24:10; Ezk 1:26; Rv 21:19
[c]28:12 Jb 28:20; Pr 16:16; Ec 7:23,25
[d]28:14 Dt 30:11-13; Ps 92:5; Rm 11:33
[e]28:16 1Kg 9:28; 10:11; Jb 22:24

[f]28:16 Pr 3:14-16; 8:10-11; 16:16
[g]28:17 Ps 119:72; Pr 8:19; 20:15
[h]28:22 Jb 25:6; Ps 49:14; Pr 27:20
[i]28:25 Ps 135:7; Pr 30:4; Is 40:12
[j]28:26 Jb 5:10; 37:6; 38:25
[k]28:28 Dt 4:6; Pr 1:7; 9:10

[A]28:3 Lit probes all   [B]28:11 LXX, Vg read He explores the sources of the streams   [C]28:13 LXX reads way   [D]28:26 Or decree

---

28:1-28 This chapter sounds like it came straight out of the book of Proverbs. In fact, it sounds like King Solomon was reading Job when he wrote Proverbs 1:7 and 9:10. To have **wisdom** and **understanding**, to know how to live well in a world gone bad, you have to **fear** the Lord (Job 28:28). That is, you have to

take God seriously and embrace his kingdom agenda for your life—even when you don't know where it will lead. The good news is that God knows.
29:1-25 If you want to be a kingdom man—a man who humbly aligns his life under God's authority—pay attention to the details of

Job's life. In verses 2-5 Job was not saying that his faith was a dead thing of the past. Rather, he was looking back to happier times. The entire book of Job, in fact, shows that he never lost faith in God. A kingdom man won't. Job recalled the respect he had earned for his godly reputation (29:7-11). When he took

a 29:3 Jb 11:17; Ps 18:28;
119:105
b 29:4 Ps 25:14; 55:14;
Pr 3:32
c 29:6 Dt 32:13; Jb 20:17;
Ps 81:16
d 29:7 Dt 25:7; 2Sm
15:2; 2Ch 32:6; Ps 69:12;
Am 5:10
e 29:9 Jdg 18:19; Jb 21:5;
40:4
f 29:10 Ps 22:15; Ezk 3:26
g 29:12 Ex 22:22; Dt 24:17;
27:19; Jb 6:27; 31:21; Ps
10:14; 72:12; Pr 21:13
h 29:14 Ps 132:9; Is 59:17;
Eph 6:14
i 29:15 Is 35:6; 42:7,16;
Mt 11:5

j 29:17 Jb 4:10; Ps 3:7; 58:6
k 29:19 Jb 14:9; Ps 1:3;
Ezk 31:7
l 29:20 Gn 49:24; Is
40:31; 41:1
m 29:22 Dt 32:2
n 30:1 Jb 12:4; Jr 20:7;
Lm 3:14
o 30:4 Jb 12:4; Jr 20:7;
Lm 3:14

3   when his lamp shone
      above my head,
    and I walked through darkness
      by his light!*a*
4   I would be as I was in the days
      of my youth
    when God's friendship*b* rested
      on my tent,
5   when the Almighty was still with me
    and my children were around me,
6   when my feet were bathed in curds
    and the rock*c* poured out streams
      of oil for me!

7   When I went out to the city gate*d*
    and took my seat
      in the town square,
8   the young men saw me
      and withdrew,
    while older men stood to their feet.
9   City officials stopped talking
    and covered their mouths
      with their hands.*e*
10 The noblemen's voices were hushed,
    and their tongues stuck to the roof
      of their mouths.*f*
11 When they heard me,
      they blessed me,
    and when they saw me,
      they spoke well of me.*A*
12 For I rescued the poor who cried out
      for help,
    and the fatherless child who had
      no one to support him.*g*
13 The dying blessed me,
    and I made the widow's heart
      rejoice.
14 I clothed myself in righteousness,*h*
    and it enveloped me;
    my just decisions were like a robe
      and a turban.
15 I was eyes to the blind
    and feet to the lame.*i*
16 I was a father to the needy,
    and I examined the case
      of the stranger.

17 I shattered the fangs of the unjust*j*
    and snatched the prey
      from his teeth.
18 So I thought, "I will die in my own nest
    and multiply my days as the sand.*B*
19 My roots will have access to water,*k*
    and the dew will rest
      on my branches all night.
20 My whole being will be refreshed
      within me,
    and my bow will be renewed
      in my hand."*l*
21 Men listened to me with expectation,
    waiting silently for my advice.
22 After a word from me they did not
      speak again;
    my speech settled on them
      like dew.*m*
23 They waited for me as for the rain
    and opened their mouths as for
      spring showers.
24 If I smiled at them, they couldn't
      believe it;
    they were thrilled at*c* the light
      of my countenance.
25 I directed their course and presided
      as chief.
    I lived as a king among his troops,
    like one who comforts
      those who mourn.

30 But now they mock*n* me,
    men younger than I am,
    whose fathers I would have refused
      to put
    with my sheep dogs.
2   What use to me was the strength
      of their hands?
    Their vigor had left them.
3   Emaciated from poverty and hunger,
    they gnawed the dry land,
    the desolate wasteland by night.
4   They plucked mallow*D,o*
      among the shrubs,

A **29:11** Lit *When an ear heard, it called me blessed, and when an eye saw, it testified for me*   *B* **29:18** Or *as the phoenix*   *c* **29:24** Lit *they did not cast down*   *D* **30:4** Or *saltwort*

---

his **seat in the town square**, everyone took notice (29:7-9). Young men stepped aside when Mr. Job showed up. The older men said, "Quiet! Job has something to say." **City officials** and noblemen **spoke well of** him (29:9-11). Job didn't demand this respect by puffing out his chest; he earned it by his conduct and character. He influenced his neighborhood for the better. When a kingdom man shows up, a higher standard enters the scene.

Importantly, Job was well known for practicing mercy and justice (29:12-17). He was

a successful businessman who also cared for **the poor, the fatherless, the dying, the widow, the blind, the lame, the needy,** and **the stranger** (29:12-13, 15-16). When **the unjust** attempted to sink **fangs** into the innocent, Job busted their chops (29:17). A kingdom man hurts with people who hurt and helps those who need help. He is an advocate for the weak, because his God is the same (see Ps 68:5).

Finally, Job blessed those around him with his wisdom (Job 29:21-25). When he opened

his mouth, **men listened to [him] with expectation** (29:21). Wisdom is the ability to apply God's truth to the practical issues of day-to-day life. The only way to do that is to regularly spend time with God and know his mind on matters. The counsel of a kingdom man is like fresh water to the thirsty.

30:1 Those who'd formerly respected and listened to Job made fun of him because of the calamities that had come upon him. This group included not only his associates but the rabble of society.

and the roots of the broom tree were
their food.
5 They were banished
from human society;
people shouted at them
as if they were thieves.
6 They are living on the slopes
of the wadis,
among the rocks and in holes
in the ground.
7 They bray among the shrubs;
they huddle beneath the thistles.
8 Foolish[a] men, without even a name.
They were forced to leave the land.

9 Now I am mocked by their songs;[b]
I have become an object of scorn
to them.
10 They despise me and keep
their distance from me;[c]
they do not hesitate to spit[d]
in my face.
11 Because God has loosened
my[A] bowstring and oppressed me,
they have cast off restraint
in my presence.[e]
12 The rabble[B] rise up at my right;
they trap[c] my feet
and construct their siege ramp[D]
against me.[f]
13 They tear up my path;
they contribute to my destruction,[g]
without anyone to help them.
14 They advance as through
a gaping breach;
they keep rolling in through
the ruins.[h]
15 Terrors[i] are turned loose against me;
they chase my dignity away
like the wind,
and my prosperity has passed by
like a cloud.

16 Now my life is poured out
before me,
and days of suffering[j]
have seized me.
17 Night pierces my bones,
but my gnawing pains never rest.[k]
18 My clothing is distorted
with great force;
he chokes me by the neck
of my garment.[B]
19 He throws me into the mud,
and I have become like dust
and ashes.[l]

∽ HOPE WORDS ∽

*When God is silent, he is
not still. He does some of his
best work in the dark.*

20 I cry out to you for help, but you
do not answer me;[m]
when I stand up, you merely look
at me.
21 You have turned against me
with cruelty;
you harass[n] me
with your strong hand.
22 You lift me up on the wind
and make me ride it;
you scatter me in the storm.[o]
23 Yes, I know that you will lead me
to death —
the place[p] appointed
for all who live.

24 Yet no one would stretch out
his hand
against a ruined person[E]
when he cries out to him for help
because of his distress.[q]
25 Have I not wept for those
who have fallen
on hard times?
Has my soul not grieved
for the needy?[r]
26 But when I hoped for good,
evil came;
when I looked for light,
darkness[s] came.
27 I am churning within[F]
and cannot rest;
days of suffering confront me.
28 I walk about blackened, but not
by the sun.[G]
I stood in the assembly
and cried out for help.
29 I have become a brother
to jackals
and a companion of ostriches.
30 My skin blackens
and flakes off,[H]
and my bones burn
with fever.[t]
31 My lyre is used for mourning
and my flute for the sound
of weeping.[u]

[a]30:8 Pr 26:7,12; Ec 7:5; Is 32:5-6
[b]30:9 Jb 12:4; 30:1; Lm 3:14
[c]30:10 Jb 19:19; Ps 89:38; Am 5:10
[d]Nm 12:14; Is 50:6; Mt 26:67
[e]30:11 Jb 12:18; 29:20; Ps 32:9
[f]30:12 Jb 16:10; 19:12; Ps 140:4-5
[g]30:13 Jb 6:2; Ps 57:1; Pr 19:13
[h]30:14 Jb 16:14; Jl 2:7
[i]30:15 Jb 18:11; 27:20; Ps 73:19
[j]30:16 Jb 10:15; 30:27; 36:21
[k]30:17 Jb 33:19; Ps 6:2; 38:3
[l]30:19 Jb 16:15; Ps 7:5; 75:10

[m]30:20 Jb 19:7; Ps 18:41; 88:13-14
[n]30:21 Gn 49:23; Jb 16:9; Ps 55:3
[o]30:22 Jb 9:17; Ps 83:15; Jnh 1:4
[p]30:23 Jb 3:15; 17:13; Ec 12:5
[q]30:24 Jb 12:5; 31:29; Pr 24:22
[r]30:25 Jb 5:15; 24:4,14; 31:19
[s]30:26 Jb 19:8; Is 59:9; Lm 3:2
[t]30:30 Ps 102:3; Lm 4:8; 5:10
[u]30:31 Is 24:8; Ezk 26:13; Mt 11:17

[A]30:11 Alt Hb tradition, LXX, Vg read *his*   [B]30:12,18 Hb obscure   [C]30:12 Lit *stretch out*   [D]30:12 Lit *and raise up their destructive paths*
[E]30:24 Lit *a heap of ruins*   [F]30:27 Lit *My bowels boil*   [G]30:28 Or *walk in sunless gloom*   [H]30:30 Lit *blackens away from me*

a 31:1 Pr 4:25; Is 33:15;
2Pt 2:14
b Ex 22:6; Pr 17:24; Mt 5:28
c 31:2 Jb 20:29; 27:13;
Ps 17:14
d 31:4 Jb 14:16; 34:21;
Pr 5:21
e 31:6 Jb 6:2; Dn 5:27;
Mc 6:11
f Jb 2:3,9; 27:5; Pr 11:3
g 31:7 Nm 15:39; Jb 23:11;
Ps 7:3
h 31:8 Lv 26:16; Dt 28:30;
Jb 20:18
i 31:11 Gn 38:24; Lv 20:10;
Dt 22:22,24
j 31:12 Jb 26:6; 28:22; Pr
6:27–29
k 31:15 Ps 119:73; 139:13;
Jr 1:5

l 31:16 Jb 22:9; 24:3,21;
29:13
m 31:19 Ex 22:26; Jb 22:6
n 31:21 Jb 5:4; Pr 22:22;
Is 29:21
o 31:23 Jb 13:11; 22:10;
23:15
p 31:24 Ps 52:7; Mt 6:19;
Mk 10:24
q 31:26 Dt 4:19; 17:3;
Ezk 8:16

31 I have made a covenant
with my eyes.*a*
How then could I look
at a young woman?*A,b*
2 For what portion*c* would I have
from God above,
or what inheritance
from the Almighty on high?
3 Doesn't disaster come to the unjust
and misfortune to evildoers?
4 Does he not see my ways
and number all my steps?*d*

5 If I have walked in falsehood
or my foot has rushed to deceit,
6 let God weigh me on
accurate scales,*e*
and he will recognize my integrity.*f*

7 If my step has turned from the way,
my heart has followed my eyes,
or impurity has stained my hands,*g*
8 let someone else eat
what I have sown,
and let my crops be uprooted.*h*

9 If my heart has gone astray over a
woman
or I have lurked at my
neighbor's door,
10 let my own wife grind grain
for another man,
and let other men sleep with*B* her.
11 For that would be a disgrace;
it would be an iniquity
deserving punishment.*i*
12 For it is a fire that consumes down
to Abaddon;
it would destroy
my entire harvest.*j*

13 If I have dismissed the case
of my male or female servants
when they made a complaint
against me,
14 what could I do when God stands up
to judge?
How should I answer him
when he calls me to account?
15 Did not the one who made me
in the womb also make them?
Did not the same God form us both
in the womb?*k*

16 If I have refused the wishes
of the poor
or let the widow's*l* eyes go blind,
17 if I have eaten my few crumbs alone
without letting the fatherless
eat any of it —
18 for from my youth, I raised him
as his father,
and since the day I was born*c*
I guided the widow —
19 if I have seen anyone dying for lack
of clothing
or a needy person without a cloak,*m*
20 if he*D* did not bless me
while warming himself
with the fleece from my sheep,
21 if I ever cast my vote*E*
against a fatherless child
when I saw that I had support
in the city gate,*n*
22 then let my shoulder blade fall
from my back,
and let my arm be pulled
from its socket.
23 For disaster from God terrifies me,
and because of his majesty
I could not do these things.*o*

24 If I placed my confidence in gold
or called fine gold my trust,*p*
25 if I have rejoiced because my wealth
is great
or because my own hand
has acquired so much,
26 if I have gazed at the sun
when it was shining
or at the moon moving in splendor,*q*
27 so that my heart was secretly enticed
and I threw them a kiss,*F*
28 this would also be an iniquity
deserving punishment,
for I would have denied God above.

29 Have I rejoiced over
my enemy's distress,
or become excited when trouble
came his way?
30 I have not allowed my mouth to sin
by asking for his life with a curse.
31 Haven't the members
of my household said,
"Who is there who has not
had enough to eat at Job's table?"

A 31:1 Or *a virgin*   *B* 31:10 Lit *men kneel down over*   *C* 31:18 Lit *and from my mother's womb*   *D* 31:20 Lit *his loins*   *E* 31:21 Lit *I raise my hand*
F 31:27 Lit *and my hand kissed my mouth*

31:1-34 Job knew that righteousness begins in the heart and mind; therefore, he had **made a covenant with [his] eyes,** so that he might not **look at a young woman** (31:1). If you want to be a godly man, few things are more important—especially in today's culture—than guarding your eyes. Job didn't have to face the temptation of pornography. But he certainly knew what lust was and was confronted with that temptation. So he made a sacred agreement with his eyes to honor God and the women around him.

32 No stranger had to spend the night
    on the street,
for I opened my door to the traveler.
33 Have I covered my transgressions[a]
    as others do[A]
by hiding my iniquity in my heart[b]
34 because I greatly feared the crowds
and because the contempt
    of the clans terrified me,
so I grew silent and would not
    go outside?

35 If only I had someone to hear
    my case![c]
Here is my signature;
    let the Almighty answer me.
Let my Opponent compose
    his indictment.
36 I would surely carry it on my shoulder
and wear it like a crown.[d]
37 I would give him an account of all
    my steps;
I would approach him like a prince.

38 If my land cries out against me
and its furrows join in weeping,
39 if I have consumed its produce
    without payment
or shown contempt for its tenants,[B]
40 then let thorns[e] grow
    instead of wheat
and stinkweed[f] instead of barley.

The words of Job are concluded.

ELIHU'S ANGRY RESPONSE

32 So these three men quit answering
Job, because he was righteous in
his own eyes.[g] **2** Then Elihu son of Barachel
the Buzite[h] from the family of Ram became
angry. He was angry at Job because he had
justified[i] himself rather than God. **3** He was
also angry at Job's three friends because
they had failed to refute him and yet had
condemned him.[c] **4** Now Elihu had waited to speak to Job
because they were all older than he. **5** But
when he saw that the three men could not
answer Job, he became angry.
    6 So Elihu son of Barachel the Buzite re-
plied:

I am young in years,
    while you are old;
therefore I was timid and afraid
    to tell[j] you what I know.
7 I thought that age should speak
and maturity should teach wisdom.

8 But it is the spirit in a person—
the breath[k] from the Almighty—
that gives anyone understanding.
9 It is not only the old who are wise
or the elderly who understand
    how to judge.
10 Therefore I say, "Listen to me.
I too will declare what I know."
11 Look, I waited for your conclusions;
I listened to your insights
as you sought for words.
12 I paid close attention to you.
Yet no one proved Job wrong;
not one of you refuted
    his arguments.
13 So do not claim,
    "We have found wisdom;
let God deal with him, not man."
14 But Job has not directed
    his argument to me,
and I will not respond to him
    with your arguments.

15 Job's friends are dismayed and can
    no longer answer;
words have left them.
16 Should I continue to wait now that
    they are silent,
now that they stand there
    and no longer answer?
17 I too will answer;[D]
yes, I will tell what I know.
18 For I am full of words,
and my spirit[E] compels
    me to speak.[l]
19 My heart[F] is like unvented wine;
it is about to burst
    like new wineskins.[m]
20 I must speak so that I can find relief;
I must open my lips and respond.
21 I will be partial to no one,[n]
and I will not give anyone
    an undeserved title.
22 For I do not know how to give
    such titles;
otherwise, my Maker
    would remove me in an instant.

ELIHU CONFRONTS JOB

33 But now, Job, pay attention
    to my speech,
and listen to all my words.
2 I am going to open my mouth;
my tongue will form words
    on my palate.
3 My words come from
    my upright[o] heart,

[a]31:33 Jb 7:21; 22:5; 33:9
[b]Ps 32:3-5; Pr 28:13; 1Jn 1:8-10
[c]31:35 Jb 16:21; Ec 6:10; Is 45:9
[d]31:36 Pr 4:9; 12:4; 17:6
[e]31:40 Gn 3:18; Is 34:13; Hs 9:6
[f]Pr 24:31; Is 5:2; Hs 10:4
[g]32:1 Jb 10:7; 33:9; 34:5-6
[h]32:2 Gn 22:21; Jr 25:23
[i]Jb 33:32; Jr 3:11; Ezk 16:51-52
[j]32:6 Jb 15:17; 36:2

[k]32:8 Gn 2:7; Jb 33:4; Is 42:5
[l]32:18 Jb 19:3; 32:18; Ac 4:20
[m]32:19 Jb 15:35; 37:1; Pr 20:27,30
[n]32:21 Dt 10:17; Jb 13:8; 34:19
[o]33:3 1Kg 9:4; Ps 25:21; 119:7

[A]31:33 Or as Adam [B]31:39 Lit or caused the breath of its tenants to breathe out [C]32:3 Alt Hb tradition reads condemned God [D]32:17 Lit answer my part [E]32:18 Lit and the spirit of my belly [F]32:19 Lit belly

a 33:4 Jb 27:2; 32:8; 35:13
b Gn 2:7; Jb 27:3; Is 30:33
c 33:5 Jb 23:4; 32:14; 37:19
d 1Sm 17:16; Ps 2:2; Jr
46:4,14
e 33:6 Jb 4:19; 10:9; 13:12
f 33:7 Jb 20:25; Ps 55:4;
88:15
g 33:9 Jb 9:21; 11:4; 34:6
h 33:10 Jb 13:24; 19:11;
Lm 2:5
i 33:11 Jb 10:14; 14:16;
Ps 130:3
j 33:12 Jb 4:17; 9:2; 15:14
k 33:13 Jb 9:3; 13:19; 40:2
l 33:15 Jb 4:13; 7:14; 20:8
m Gn 2:21; 15:12; Jb 4:13
n 33:16 Jb 4:12; 13:1;
36:10,15
o 33:18 Jb 33:28,30; 36:16;
Ps 30:9

p 33:19 Jb 7:13; Ps 41:3;
Hs 7:14
q Jb 30:17; Ps 6:2; 38:3
r 33:20 Jb 3:24; 6:7; Ps
102:4
s 33:23 Ex 23:20,23; Ps
34:7; Is 63:9
t 33:24 Ex 30:12; Ps 49:7;
Pr 21:18
u 33:25 Dt 7:4; 2Kg 5:14;
Jb 20:11
v 33:26 Gn 33:10; Ps 11:7;
17:15
w Ps 23:3; 51:12; 1Jn 1:9
x 33:30 Ps 56:13; Jn 1:4,9

and my lips speak with sincerity
what they know.
4 The Spirit of God has made me,
and the breath of the Almighty*a*
gives me life.*b*
5 Refute me if you can.
Prepare*c* your case against me;
take your stand.*d*
6 I am just like you before God;
I was also pinched off
from a piece of clay.*e*
7 Fear*f* of me should not terrify you;
no pressure from me should weigh
you down.

8 Surely you have spoken
in my hearing,
and I have heard these very[A] words:
9 "I am pure, without transgression;
I am clean and have no iniquity.*g*
10 But he finds reasons to oppose me;
he regards me as his enemy.*h*
11 He puts my feet in the stocks;
he stands watch*i* over all my paths."

12 But I tell you that you are wrong
in this matter,
since God is greater than man.*j*
13 Why do you take*k* him to court
for not answering anything
a person asks?[B]
14 For God speaks time and again,
but a person may not notice it.
15 In a dream, a vision*l* in the night,
when deep sleep comes
over people*m*
as they slumber on their beds,
16 he uncovers their ears*n*
and terrifies them[C] with warnings,
17 in order to turn a person
from his actions
and suppress the pride of a person.
18 God spares his soul from the Pit,*o*
his life from crossing the river
of death.[D]

19 A person may be disciplined
on his bed*p* with pain
and constant distress in his bones,*q*
20 so that he detests bread,
and his soul despises his
favorite food.*r*
21 His flesh wastes away to nothing,[E]
and his unseen bones stick out.
22 He draws near to the Pit,
and his life to the executioners.
23 If there is an angel*s* on his side,
one mediator out of a thousand,
to tell a person what is right for him[F]
24 and to be gracious to him and say,
"Spare him from going down
to the Pit;
I have found a ransom,"*t*
25 then his flesh will be healthier[G] than
in his youth,
and he will return to the days
of his youthful vigor.*u*
26 He will pray to God, and God
will delight in him.
That person will see his face*v*
with a shout of joy,
and God will restore
his righteousness to him.*w*
27 He will look at men and say,
"I have sinned and perverted
what was right;
yet I did not get what I deserved.[H]
28 He redeemed my soul
from going down to the Pit,
and I will continue to see the light."
29 God certainly does all these things
two or three times to a person
30 in order to turn him back
from the Pit,
so he may shine with the light
of life.*x*
31 Pay attention, Job, and listen to me.
Be quiet, and I will speak.
32 But if you have something to say,[I]
answer me;
speak, for I would like to justify you.

[A] 33:8 Lit *heard a sound of*   [B] 33:13 Lit *court, for he does not answer all his words*   [C] 33:16 LXX; MT reads *and seals*   [D] 33:18 Or *from perishing by the sword*   [E] 33:21 Lit *away from sight*   [F] 33:23 Or *to vouch for a person's uprightness*   [G] 33:25 Hb obscure   [H] 33:27 Lit *and the same was not to me*   [I] 33:32 Lit *If there are words*

32:2-3 Like a good theatrical drama, the book of Job has a surprise twist near its end: the appearance of a fourth visitor, **Elihu.** We're not left in doubt regarding how he felt about the discussion he'd overheard.
33:5 Elihu challenged Job, **Refute me if you can.** He was confident that what he was about to say was "the truth, the whole truth, and nothing but the truth" that Job wouldn't be able to contradict.
33:8-13 Elihu had been taking notes. He thus said, in effect, "Job, here's what you've been

saying. You are innocent before God, but despite this he has attacked you without cause and treated you like his enemy" (33:8-11). **But I tell you that you are wrong in this matter, since God is greater than man** (33:12). In other words, Elihu countered that God didn't owe Job an explanation for what he was enduring because God is transcendent. Elihu said in essence, "Let's not forget who is the Creator and who is the creature here" (33:13). 33:19 Critically, not all suffering is punishment for personal sin. For example, the holy Son of

God willingly suffered—the righteous for the unrighteous—to bring us to God (see 1 Pet 3:18). And the author of Hebrews encouraged his readers to endure suffering as the Lord's loving discipline (see Heb 12:5-11). Perhaps, in fact, Elihu had this idea in mind when he said, **A person may be disciplined on his bed with pain**—not because God is judging him for his sin, but because he is refining him for his glorious purposes and helping him avoid future evil.

33 If not, then listen to me;
　　be quiet, and I will teach
　　　you wisdom.

34

Then Elihu continued,[A] saying:
2 Hear my words, you wise ones,
　　and listen to me,
　　　you knowledgeable ones.
3 Doesn't the ear test words
　　as the palate tastes food?
4 Let us judge for ourselves
　　　what is right;
　　let us decide together what is good.
5 For Job has declared, "I am righteous,
　　yet God has deprived me of justice.[a]
6 Would I lie about my case?[b]
　　My wound[B] is incurable,
　　　though I am without transgression."
7 What man is like Job?
　　He drinks derision[c] like water.
8 He keeps company with evildoers
　　and walks with wicked men.
9 For he has said,
　　"A man gains nothing
　　when he becomes God's friend."[d]

10 Therefore listen to me, you men
　　　of understanding.
　　It is impossible for God to do wrong,
　　and for the Almighty to act unjustly.[e]
11 For he repays[f] a person according to
　　　his deeds,
　　and he gives him what his conduct
　　　deserves.[c]
12 Indeed, it is true that God does not
　　　act wickedly
　　and the Almighty does not
　　　pervert justice.[g]
13 Who gave him authority
　　　over the earth?
　　Who put him in charge of
　　　the entire world?[h]
14 If he put his mind to it
　　and withdrew the spirit[i] and breath
　　　he gave,
15 every living thing
　　　would perish together
　　and mankind would return
　　　to the dust.[j]

16 If you have understanding, hear this;
　　listen to what I have to say.
17 Could one who hates justice
　　　govern the world?
　　Will you condemn the mighty
　　　Righteous One,[k]

18 who says to a king,
　　"Worthless man!"
　　and to nobles, "Wicked men!"?[l]
19 God is not partial[m] to princes
　　and does not favor the rich
　　　over the poor,
　　for they are all the work
　　　of his hands.
20 They die suddenly in the middle
　　　of the night;
　　people shudder, then pass away.
　　Even the mighty are removed
　　　without effort.

21 For his eyes watch over
　　　a man's ways,
　　and he observes all his steps.[n]
22 There is no darkness,
　　　no deep darkness,
　　where evildoers can hide.[o]
23 God does not need to examine
　　　a person further,
　　that one should[D] approach him
　　　in court.
24 He shatters the mighty
　　　without an investigation
　　and sets others in their place.[p]
25 Therefore, he recognizes
　　　their deeds[q]
　　and overthrows them by night,
　　　and they are crushed.
26 In full view of the public,[E]
　　he strikes them for their wickedness,
27 because they turned aside
　　　from following him
　　and did not understand any
　　　of his ways
28 but caused the poor to cry out
　　　to him,
　　and he heard the outcry
　　　of the needy.[r]
29 But when God is silent,
　　　who can declare him guilty?
　　When he hides his face, who can
　　　see him?
　　Yet he watches over both individuals
　　　and nations,
30 so that godless men should not rule
　　or ensnare the people.

31 Suppose someone says to God,
　　"I have endured my punishment;
　　I will no longer act wickedly.
32 Teach me what I cannot see;
　　if I have done wrong, I won't
　　　do it again."

34:5 Jb 10:7; 27:2; 33:9
[b]34:6 Jb 6:28; 24:25; 27:4
[c]34:7 Jb 15:16; Pr 19:28
[d]34:9 Ex 5:2; Jb 21:15;
Mal 3:14
[e]34:10 Dt 32:4; Ps 92:15;
Rm 9:14
[f]34:11 Dt 7:10; Jb 21:31;
Is 59:18
[g]34:12 2Ch 19:6; Jb 8:3;
Ps 9:16
[h]34:13 Jb 38:4; Ps 50:12; Is
40:12-14
[i]34:14 Ps 104:29; Ec
3:19; 12:7
[j]34:15 Gn 2:7; Jb 4:19; 10:9
[k]34:17 Gn 18:25; 2Sm 23:3;
Rm 3:5

[l]34:18 Ex 22:28; Jb 12:21;
Ps 107:40
[m]34:19 Dt 10:17; Jb 13:8;
32:21
[n]34:21 Jb 14:16; 31:4;
Pr 5:21
[o]34:22 Ps 139:12; Am 9:2-
3; Heb 4:13
[p]34:24 Jb 12:19; Ps 2:9;
Dn 2:21
[q]34:25 Jb 11:11; Ps 10:14
[r]34:28 Ex 3:7; 22:23;
Jms 5:4

[A]34:1 Lit answered [B]34:6 Lit arrow [C]34:11 Lit and like a path of a man, he causes him to find [D]34:23 Some emend to God has not appointed a time for man to [E]34:26 Lit In a place of spectators

---

34:10 The Lord can do all things—except evil. To do so would be contrary to God's character.

a 34:35 Jb 35:16; 38:2; 42:3
b 34:37 Nm 24:10; Jb 27:23; Lm 2:15
c Jb 16:4; 35:16; Ezk 35:13
d 35:3 Jb 9:29; 21:15; 34:9
e 35:7 Jb 22:3; 41:11; Rm 11:35
f 35:9 Ex 2:23; Jb 24:12; 34:28
g 35:10 Dt 32:6; Is 51:13; Jr 2:8
h Ps 42:8; 77:6; Ac 16:25
i 35:11 Jb 12:7; Mt 6:26
j 35:12 Pr 1:28; Is 1:15; Zch 7:13

k 35:14 Jb 13:18; 23:4; 31:13
l Jb 6:8; 13:13; 14:14
m 35:16 Jb 15:2; 21:22; 34:35
n 36:5 Jb 9:4; 12:13; 38:36
o 36:6 Gn 18:25; Jb 8:20; 2Pt 2:9
p 36:10 Jb 4:12; 13:1; 33:16
q 36:11 Jb 21:13; 22:2; Is 1:19
r 36:12 Jb 4:21; 33:18; Hs 4:6

33 Should God repay you on your terms
when you have rejected his?
You must choose, not I!
So declare what you know.

34 Reasonable men will say to me,
along with the wise men
who hear me,

35 "Job speaks without knowledge;[a]
his words are without insight."

36 If only Job were tested to the limit,
because his answers are like those
of wicked men.

37 For he adds rebellion to his sin;
he scornfully claps[b] in our presence,
while multiplying[c] his words
against God.

35

Then Elihu continued, saying:
2 Do you think it is just
when you say,
"I am righteous before God"?

3 For you ask, "What does
it profit you,[A]
and what benefit comes to me,
if I do not sin?"[d]

4 I will answer you
and your friends with you.

5 Look at the heavens and see;
gaze at the clouds high above you.

6 If you sin, how does it affect God?
If you multiply your transgressions,
what does it do to him?

7 If you are righteous, what do you
give him,
or what does he receive
from your hand?[e]

8 Your wickedness affects a person
like yourself,
and your righteousness, a
son of man.[B]

9 People cry out because of
severe oppression;
they shout for help because of
the power of the mighty.[f]

10 But no one asks, "Where is God
my Maker,[g]
who provides us with songs
in the night,[h]

11 who gives us more understanding
than the animals of the earth
and makes us wiser than the birds
of the sky?"[i]

12 There they cry out,
but he does not answer,
because of the pride of evil people.[j]

13 Indeed, God does not listen
to empty cries,
and the Almighty does not take note
of it —

14 how much less when[c] you complain[D]
that you do not see him,
that your case[k] is before him
and you are waiting[l] for him.

15 But now, because God's anger
does not punish
and he does not pay attention
to transgression,[E]

16 Job opens his mouth in vain
and multiplies words
without knowledge.[m]

36

Then Elihu continued, saying:
2 Be patient with me a little longer,
and I will inform you,
for there is still more to be said
on God's behalf.

3 I will get my knowledge from a
distant place
and ascribe justice to my Maker.

4 Indeed, my words are not false;
one who has complete knowledge is
with you.

5 Yes, God is mighty, but he despises
no one;
he understands all things.[F,n]

6 He does not keep the wicked alive,[o]
but he gives justice to the oppressed.

7 He does not withdraw his gaze
from the righteous,
but he seats them forever
with enthroned kings,
and they are exalted.

8 If people are bound with chains
and trapped by the cords
of affliction,

9 God tells them what they have done
and how arrogantly
they have transgressed.

10 He opens their ears[p] to correction
and tells them to repent
from iniquity.

11 If they listen and serve him,
they will end their days
in prosperity
and their years in happiness.[q]

12 But if they do not listen,
they will cross the river of death[G]
and die without knowledge.[r]

A 35:3 Some emend to *me* B 35:8 Or *a mere mortal* C 35:14 Or *how then can* D 35:14 Lit *say* E 35:15 LXX, Vg; MT reads *folly*, or *arrogance*; Hb obscure F 36:5 Lit *he is mighty in strength of heart* G 36:12 Or *will perish by the sword*

35:8-9 How we live and respond to adversity influences others.

13 Those who have a godless heart
  harbor anger;
  even when God binds them,
  they do not cry for help.
14 They die in their youth;
  their life ends among
  male cult prostitutes.[a]
15 God rescues the afflicted by
  their affliction;
  he instructs them by their torment.
16 Indeed, he lured you from the jaws[A]
  of distress
  to a spacious and unconfined place.
  Your table was spread
  with choice food.
17 Yet now you are obsessed
  with the judgment due
  the wicked;
  judgment and justice
  have seized you.
18 Be careful that no one lures you
  with riches;[B]
  do not let a large ransom[C]
  lead you astray.[b]
19 Can your wealth[D] or all
  your physical exertion
  keep you from distress?[c]
20 Do not long for the night
  when nations will disappear
  from their places.
21 Be careful that you do not turn
  to iniquity,
  for that is why you have been tested
  by[E] affliction.
22 Look, God shows himself exalted
  by his power.
  Who is a teacher like him?
23 Who has appointed his way for him,
  and who has declared, "You have
  done wrong"?[d]
24 Remember that you should praise
  his work,
  which people have sung about.[e]
25 All mankind has seen it;
  people have looked at it
  from a distance.[f]
26 Yes, God is exalted
  beyond our knowledge;[g]
  the number of his years
  cannot be counted.[h]
27 For he makes waterdrops
  evaporate;[F]
  they distill the rain into its[G] mist,[i]

28 which the clouds pour out
  and shower abundantly
  on mankind.
29 Can anyone understand
  how the clouds spread out
  or how the thunder roars
  from God's pavilion?[j]
30 See how he spreads his lightning[k]
  around him
  and covers the depths of the sea.
31 For he judges the nations
  with these;
  he gives food in abundance.[l]
32 He covers his hands with lightning
  and commands it to hit its mark.
33 The[H] thunder declares his presence;[l]
  the cattle also,
  the approaching storm.

37 My heart[m] pounds at this
  and leaps from my chest.[J]
2 Just listen to his thunderous voice
  and the rumbling that comes
  from his mouth.
3 He lets it loose beneath
  the entire sky;
  his lightning to the ends[n]
  of the earth.
4 Then there comes a roaring sound;
  God thunders[o]
  with his majestic voice.
  He does not restrain the lightning
  when his rumbling voice is heard.
5 God thunders wondrously
  with his voice;
  he does great things that
  we cannot comprehend.
6 For he says to the snow,[p]
  "Fall to the earth,"
  and the torrential rains,
  his mighty torrential rains,
7 serve as his sign to all mankind,
  so that all men may know his work.
8 The wild animals enter their lairs
  and stay in their dens.[q]
9 The windstorm comes
  from its chamber,
  and the cold
  from the driving north winds.
10 Ice is formed by the breath of God,[r]
  and watery expanses are frozen.
11 He saturates clouds with moisture;[s]
  he scatters his lightning
  through them.

[a] 36:14 Dt 23:17; 1Kg 14:24;
22:46
[b] 36:18 1Sm 12:3; Ps 26:10;
Am 5:12
[c] 36:19 1Sm 22:2; Jb 15:24;
Ps 107:6,13,19,28
[d] 36:23 Jb 34:10,13; Is
40:13-14; Rm 11:34
[e] 36:24 Ps 92:5; 104:33;
Rv 15:3
[f] 36:25 Ps 19:3; Rm 1:19-
20; Heb 11:13
[g] 36:26 Jb 9:10; 37:5,23;
Ec 8:17
[h] Ps 90:2; 102:24,27;
Heb 1:12
[i] 36:27 Gn 2:6; Jb 28:28;
Ps 147:8

[j] 36:29 Jb 26:14; 37:16; Ps
105:39
[k] 36:30 2Sm 22:15; Jb
38:28; Ps 18:14
[l] 36:31 Jb 37:13; Ps 136:25;
Ac 14:17
[m] 37:1 Jb 15:35; 32:19; Pr
20:27,30
[n] 37:3 Jb 38:13; Is 11:12;
Ezk 7:2
[o] 37:4 Jb 40:9; Ps 18:3; 29:3
[p] 37:6 Jb 6:16; 24:19; 38:22
[q] 37:8 Jb 38:40; Ps 104:22;
Am 3:4
[r] 37:10 2Sm 22:21; Jb 4:9;
Is 30:33
[s] 37:11 Jb 26:8; 36:29; 38:9

[A] 36:16 Lit *from a mouth of narrowness* [B] 36:18 Or *you into mockery* [C] 36:18 Or *bribe* [D] 36:19 Or *cry for help* [E] 36:21 Or *for you have preferred this to*
[F] 36:27 Lit *he draws in waterdrops* [G] 36:27 Or *his* [H] 36:33 Lit *His*, or *Its* [I] 36:33 Lit *thunder announces concerning him* or *it* [J] 37:1 Lit *from its place*

36:21 Elihu reminded Job that sometimes we are **tested by affliction** (36:21). Whatever God intends to teach you through your trials, it is always for your benefit and his glory.

a 37:19 Jb 9:3,14; 40:2;
    Jms 1:5
b 37:22 Ex 15:11; Dt 7:21;
    Hab 3:2

c 37:24 Pr 3:7; 26:5,12,16;
    28:11
d 38:1 2Kg 2:11; Jb 40:6;
    Ezk 13:11,13
e 38:2 Jb 34:35; 35:16; 42:3
f 38:3 2Sm 11:7; Jb 40:7;
    42:4
g 38:4 Ps 89:11; 102:25;
    104:5
h 38:7 Gn 6:2,4; Jb 1:6; 2:1
i 38:9 2Sm 22:10; Jb 22:13;
    37:11

12 They swirl about,
    turning round and round
        at his direction,
    accomplishing everything
        he commands them
    over the surface
        of the inhabited world.
13 He causes this to happen
        for punishment,
    for his land, or for his faithful love.

14 Listen to this, Job.
    Stop and consider God's wonders.
15 Do you know how God directs
        his clouds
    or makes their lightning flash?
16 Do you understand
        how the clouds float,
    those wonderful works of him
        who has perfect knowledge?
17 You whose clothes get hot
    when the south wind brings calm
        to the land,
18 can you help God spread out
        the skies
    as hard as a cast metal mirror?
19 Teach us what we should say
        to him;*a*
    we cannot prepare our case
        because of our darkness.
20 Should he be told that I want
        to speak?
    Can a man speak
        when he is confused?
21 Now no one can even look at the sun
    when it is in the skies,
    after a wind has swept through and
        cleared the clouds away.*A*
22 Yet out of the north he comes,
        shrouded in a golden glow;
    awesome*b* majesty surrounds him.
23 The Almighty — we cannot
        reach him —
    he is exalted in power!
    He will not violate justice and
        abundant righteousness,

24 therefore, men fear him.
    He does not look favorably on any
        who are wise*c* in heart.

THE LORD SPEAKS

38 Then the LORD answered Job from
    the whirlwind.*d* He said:
2   Who is this who obscures
        my counsel
    with ignorant words?*e*
3   Get ready to answer me like a man;
    when I question*f* you,
        you will inform me.
4   Where were you when I established*g*
        the earth?
    Tell me, if you have*B* understanding.
5   Who fixed its dimensions?
        Certainly you know!
    Who stretched a measuring line
        across it?
6   What supports its foundations?
    Or who laid its cornerstone
7   while the morning stars
        sang together
    and all the sons of God*h* shouted
        for joy?

8   Who enclosed the sea behind doors
    when it burst from the womb,
9   when I made the clouds its garment
    and total darkness its blanket,*c,i*
10 when I determined its boundaries*D*
    and put its bars and doors in place,
11 when I declared: "You may come
        this far, but no farther;
    your proud waves stop here"?

12 Have you ever in your life
        commanded the morning
    or assigned the dawn its place,
13 so it may seize the edges of the earth
    and shake the wicked out of it?
14 The earth is changed as clay is
        by a seal;
    its hills stand out like the folds of
        a garment.

A 37:21 Lit *and cleaned them*   *B* 38:4 Lit *know*   *C* 38:9 Lit *swaddling clothes*   *D* 38:10 Lit *I broke my statute on it*

37:15-20 Elihu's questions to Job about how God works his wonders seem to foreshadow God's own coming questions in chapters 38–41.

38:1 That **the LORD answered Job from the whirlwind** means God took over and revealed his awesome sovereignty and power, leaving Job flat on the ground.

38:4 Don't miss the imbalance of power in the divine confrontation. One night I encountered a cockroach in my kitchen. Only this was no ordinary roach. When I moved toward him, he didn't skitter; he didn't run. He sat there as if

to say, "*This* is *my* place." I couldn't believe it when the thing wouldn't budge. And that stubborn posture meant he clearly didn't understand who I was, and thus I squashed that boy flat. Now, what that insect did to me is what autonomous man often does to God. He gets "roachy" on God, digging in his heels or swaggering around like he is someone, like he has power. But it's suicide to get in God's face, because only he has *ultimate* power.

38:5–39:30 God knew Job wouldn't be able to answer his questions. That was the whole point. He'd wanted his day in court, and it

couldn't have been fun to find himself under cross-examination.

In a sense, God's questions were an answer to Job's accusations—not that God needed to defend himself or his actions. But as Job pressed God time and again to tell him why he was suffering and why God was punishing him for no reason (at least no reason as far as Job was concerned), Job's attitude became sinful as he began to see his troubles as God's grossly unfair attack on him. So God humbled Job and helped him see how truly ignorant he was of God's sovereign ways.

15 Light^A is withheld from the wicked,
   and the arm raised in violence
      is broken.

16 Have you traveled to the sources
      of the sea
   or walked in the depths of the oceans?

17 Have the gates^a of death
      been revealed to you?
   Have you seen the gates
      of deep darkness?

18 Have you comprehended the extent
      of the earth?
   Tell me, if you know all this.

19 Where is the road to the home
      of light?
   Do you know where darkness lives,

20 so you can lead it back to its border?
   Are you familiar with the paths
      to its home?

21 Don't you know? You were
      already born;^b
   you have lived so long!^B

22 Have you entered the place
      where the snow is stored?
   Or have you seen the storehouses
      of hail,^c

23 which I hold in reserve for times
      of trouble,
   for the day of warfare and battle?^d

24 What road leads to the place
      where light is dispersed?^c
   Where is the source of the east wind
      that spreads across the earth?

25 Who cuts a channel
      for the flooding rain
   or clears the way for lightning,

26 to bring rain on an uninhabited land,
   on a desert with no human life,^D

27 to satisfy the parched wasteland
   and cause the grass to sprout?^e

28 Does the rain have a father?
   Who fathered the drops of dew?^f

29 Whose womb did the ice come from?
   Who gave birth to the frost
      of heaven

30 when water becomes as hard
      as stone,^E
   and the surface of the watery depths
      is frozen?^g

31 Can you fasten the chains
      of the Pleiades
   or loosen the belt of Orion?

32 Can you bring out the constellations^F
      in their season
   and lead the Bear^G and her cubs?^h

33 Do you know the laws^i of heaven?
   Can you impose its^H authority
      on earth?

34 Can you command^i the clouds
   so that a flood of water covers you?^j

35 Can you send out lightning^k bolts,
      and they go?
   Do they report to you: "Here we are"?

36 Who put wisdom^i in the heart^J
   or gave the mind understanding?

37 Who has the wisdom to number
      the clouds?
   Or who can tilt the water jars
      of heaven

38 when the dust hardens like cast metal
   and the clods of dirt stick together?

39 Can you hunt prey for a lioness
   or satisfy the appetite
      of young lions^m

40 when they crouch in their dens
   and lie in wait within their lairs?

41 Who provides the raven's food^n
   when its young cry out to God
   and wander about for lack of food?

39 Do you know when
      mountain goats give birth?
   Have you watched the deer in labor?

2 Can you count the months
      they are pregnant^k
   so you can know the time
      they give birth?

3 They crouch down to give birth
      to their young;
   they deliver their newborn.^L

4 Their offspring are healthy
      and grow up in the open field.
   They leave and do not return.^M

5 Who set the wild donkey free?
   Who released the swift donkey
      from its harness?

6 I made the desert^o its home,
   and the salty^p wasteland
      its dwelling.

7 It scoffs at the noise of the village
   and never hears the shouts
      of a driver.^q

8 It roams the mountains
      for its pastureland,
   searching for anything green.

---

^a 38:17 Ps 9:13; 107:18; Is 38:10
^b 38:21 Jb 15:7; Ps 90:2; Pr 8:25
^c 38:22 Ex 9:18; Ps 105:32; Is 28:17
^d 38:23 Jos 10:11; Is 30:30; Rv 16:21
^e 38:27 Gn 1:11; 2Sm 23:4; Ps 107:35
^f 38:28 Jb 5:10; Ps 147:8; Jr 14:22
^g 38:29-30 Jb 37:10; Ps 147:16-17
^h 38:31-32 Jb 9:9; Is 40:26; Am 5:8
^i 38:33 Jr 31:35; 33:25
^j 38:34 Jb 22:11; Ps 69:1-2; Lm 3:54
^k 38:35 Ex 19:16; Ps 18:14; 97:4
^l 38:36 Jb 28:12,18,20; Ps 51:6; Ec 2:26
^m 38:39 Ps 104:21; 145:15-16
^n 38:41 1Kg 17:4,6; Ps 147:9; Lk 12:24
^o 39:6 Jb 24:5; 38:26; Jr 2:24
^p Dt 29:23; Ps 107:34; Jr 17:6
^q 39:7 Ex 3:7; 5:10,13-14; Jb 3:18

---

^A 38:15 Lit Their light   ^B 38:21 Lit born; the number of your days is great   ^C 38:24 Or where lightning is distributed   ^D 38:26 Lit no man in it
^E 38:30 Lit water hides itself as the stone   ^F 38:32 Or Mazzaroth; Hb obscure   ^G 38:32 Or lead Aldebaran   ^H 38:33 Or God's   ^i 38:34 Lit lift up your
voice to   ^J 38:36 Or the inner self; Ps 51:6   ^K 39:2 Lit months they fulfill   ^L 39:3 Or they send away their labor pains   ^M 39:4 Lit return to them

a 39:10 Nm 23:22; 24:8; Dt 33:17
b 39:13 Ps 104:17; Jr 8:7; Zch 5:9
c 39:17 Jb 35:11; 38:36
d 39:27 Jr 49:16; Ob 4; Hab 2:9
e 39:29 Jb 9:26; Hab 1:8
f 39:30 Ezk 39:17; Mt 24:28; Lk 17:37
g 40:4 Ezr 9:6; Jb 29:9; 42:6
h 40:5 Jb 9:3,15; 33:14; Ps 62:11
i 40:6 Jb 38:1; Jr 30:23; Ezk 13:11,13
j 40:7 2Sm 11:7; Jb 38:3; 42:4
k 40:8 Jb 9:20,28; Ps 37:33; Is 50:9
l Jb 32:2; Ps 51:4; Rm 3:4
m 40:10 Ps 93:1; 96:6; 104:1

9 Would the wild ox be willing
　to serve you?
Would it spend the night
　by your feeding trough?
10 Can you hold the wild ox*a*
　to a furrow by its harness?
Will it plow the valleys behind you?
11 Can you depend on it because
　its strength is great?
Would you leave it to do
　your hard work?
12 Can you trust the wild ox to harvest
　your grain
and bring it to your threshing floor?

13 The wings of the ostrich flap joyfully,
but are her feathers and plumage
　like the stork's?*A,b*
14 She abandons her eggs
　on the ground
and lets them be warmed in the sand.
15 She forgets that a foot
　may crush them
or that some wild animal
　may trample them.
16 She treats her young harshly, as if
　they were not her own,
with no fear that her labor
　may have been in vain.
17 For God has deprived her of wisdom;
he has not endowed her
　with understanding.*c*
18 When she proudly*A* spreads
　her wings,
she laughs at the horse and its rider.

19 Do you give strength to the horse?
Do you adorn his neck
　with a mane?*A*
20 Do you make him leap like a locust?
His proud snorting
　fills one with terror.
21 He paws*B* in the valley and rejoices
　in his strength;
he charges into battle.*c*
22 He laughs at fear, since he is afraid
　of nothing;
he does not run from the sword.
23 A quiver rattles at his side,
along with a flashing spear
　and a javelin.
24 He charges ahead*D*
　with trembling rage;

he cannot stand still
　at the trumpet's sound.
25 When the trumpet blasts,
　he snorts defiantly.*E*
He smells the battle from a distance;
he hears the officers' shouts
　and the battle cry.

26 Does the hawk take flight
　by your understanding
and spread its wings to the south?
27 Does the eagle soar
　at your command
and make its nest*d* on high?
28 It lives on a cliff where it spends
　the night;
its stronghold is on a rocky crag.
29 From there it searches for prey;*e*
its eyes penetrate the distance.
30 Its brood gulps down blood,
and where the slain are, it is there.*f*

40 The LORD answered Job:
2 Will the one who contends
　with the Almighty correct him?
Let him who argues with God
　give an answer.*f*

3 Then Job answered the LORD:
4 I am so insignificant. How can I
　answer you?*g*
I place my hand over my mouth.
5 I have spoken once,
　and I will not reply;
twice, but now I can add nothing.*h*

6 Then the LORD answered Job from the whirlwind:*i*
7 Get ready to answer me like a man;
When I question*j* you, you will
　inform me.
8 Would you really challenge
　my justice?
Would you declare me guilty*k*
　to justify yourself?*l*
9 Do you have an arm like God's?
Can you thunder with a voice
　like his?

10 Adorn yourself with majesty*m*
　and splendor,
and clothe yourself with honor
　and glory.

A 39:13,18,19 Hb obscure　　*B* 39:21 LXX, Syr; MT reads *They dig*　　*c* 39:21 Lit *he goes out to meet the weaponry*　　*D* 39:24 Lit *He swallowed the ground*
E 39:25 Lit *he says, "Aha!"*　　*f* 40:2 Lit *God respond to it*

40:4-5 Job responded to God the only way a frail human should, with humility.
40:8 It's one thing to scold God for his handling of our affairs when we can't see or hear him. It's another thing to confront God to his face. Yet all of us will stand before him face to face one day like Job did. Job was moved to repentance. Will you shake your fist at God? Or bow your head in humility?

11 Pour out your raging anger;[a]
   look on every proud person
      and humiliate him.[b]
12 Look on every proud person
      and humble him;[c]
   trample the wicked
      where they stand.[A]
13 Hide them together in the dust;
   imprison them in the grave.[B]
14 Then I will confess to you
   that your own right hand[d]
      can deliver you.[e]

15 Look at Behemoth,
   which I made along with you.
   He eats grass like cattle.
16 Look at the strength of his back[c]
   and the power in the muscles
      of his belly.
17 He stiffens his tail like a cedar tree;
   the tendons of his thighs are woven
      firmly together.
18 His bones are bronze tubes;
   his limbs are like iron rods.
19 He is the foremost of God's works;[f]
   only his Maker can draw the sword
      against him.
20 The hills yield food for him,
   while all sorts of wild animals
      play there.
21 He lies under the lotus plants,
   hiding in the protection[D]
      of marshy reeds.
22 Lotus plants cover him
      with their shade;
   the willows by the brook
      surround him.
23 Though the river rages,
      Behemoth is unafraid;
   he remains confident, even if
      the Jordan surges up to his mouth.
24 Can anyone capture him
      while he looks on,[E]
   or pierce his nose with snares?

41 Can you pull in Leviathan[g]
      with a hook[h]
   or tie his tongue down with a rope?
2 Can you put a cord[F]
      through his nose
   or pierce his jaw with a hook?[i]
3 Will he beg you for mercy
   or speak softly to you?

4 Will he make a covenant with you
   so that you can take him
      as a slave forever?[J]
5 Can you play with him like a bird
   or put him on a leash[G] for your girls?
6 Will traders bargain for him
   or divide him
      among the merchants?
7 Can you fill his hide with harpoons
   or his head with fishing spears?
8 Lay a[H] hand on him.
   You will remember the battle
      and never repeat it!
9 Any hope of capturing him
      proves false.
   Does a person not collapse
      at the very sight of him?
10 No one is ferocious enough
      to rouse Leviathan;[k]
   who then can stand against me?
11 Who confronted me, that I
      should repay him?
   Everything under heaven belongs
      to me.[l]
12 I cannot be silent about his limbs,
   his power,
      and his graceful proportions.
13 Who can strip off
      his outer covering?
   Who can penetrate his double layer
      of armor?[i,m]
14 Who can open his jaws,[j]
   surrounded by
      those terrifying teeth?
15 His pride is in his rows of scales,
   closely sealed together.
16 One scale is so close to another[K]
   that no air can pass between them.
17 They are joined to one another,
   so closely connected[L] they cannot
      be separated.
18 His snorting[M] flashes with light,
   while his eyes are like the rays[N]
      of dawn.
19 Flaming torches shoot
      from his mouth;
   fiery sparks fly out!
20 Smoke billows from his nostrils[n]
   as from a boiling pot
      or burning reeds.
21 His breath sets coals ablaze,
   and flames pour out of his mouth.

[a] 40:11 Jb 14:13; 19:11; 21:17
[b] Is 2:11; Ezk 21:26; Dn 4:37
[c] 40:12 Ps 18:27; Is 13:11; 63:3
[d] 40:14 Ps 17:7; 20:6; 108:6
[e] Ps 3:8; 49:7; 62:2
[f] 40:19 Jb 26:14; Pr 8:22
[g] 41:1 Jb 3:8; Ps 104:26; Is 27:1
[h] Is 19:8; Hab 1:15
[i] 41:2 2Kg 19:28; Jb 40:24; Is 37:29

[j] 41:4 Ex 21:6; Dt 15:17; 1Sm 27:12
[k] 41:10 Jb 3:8; Jr 50:44
[l] 41:11 Ps 24:1; Rm 11:35; 1Co 10:26
[m] 41:13 Jr 46:4; 51:3
[n] 41:20 2Sm 22:9; Jb 39:20; Ps 18:8

[A] 40:12 Lit wicked in their place   [B] 40:13 Lit together; bind their faces in the hidden place   [C] 40:16 Or waist   [D] 40:21 Lit plants, in the hiding place
[E] 40:24 Lit capture it in its eyes   [F] 41:2 Lit reed   [G] 41:5 Lit or bind him   [H] 41:8 Lit your   [I] 41:13 LXX; MT reads double bridle   [J] 41:14 Lit open the
doors of his face   [K] 41:16 Lit One by one they approach   [L] 41:17 Lit another; they cling together and   [M] 41:18 Or sneezing   [N] 41:18 Lit eyelids

---

40:15–41:34 The Lord directed Job's attention to **Behemoth** and **Leviathan** (40:15; 41:1). Clearly these beasts were the epitome of strength, ferocity, and terror in Job's day. Yet, they were also objects of God's creative power and wisdom. Humanity cannot comprehend all the intricacies of such creatures. How much less, then, can we comprehend the mysteries of God's providential dealings?

a 41:29 2Ch 30:10; Jb 39:7,18; Hab 1:10
b 41:30 Is 41:15; Am 1:3
c 42:2 Gn 18:14; Jr 23:20; Mt 19:26
d 42:3 Jb 34:35; 35:16; 38:2
e Ps 40:5; 131:1; 139:6
f 42:4 Jb 38:3; 40:7
g 42:5 Jb 19:27; Ps 123:1-2; 141:8
h 42:8 Gn 20:17; Nm 23:1; 1Jn 5:16

22 Strength resides in his neck,
and dismay dances before him.
23 The folds of his flesh
are joined together,
solid as metal^A and immovable.
24 His heart is as hard as a rock,
as hard as a lower millstone!
25 When Leviathan rises, the mighty^B
are terrified;
they withdraw because of
his thrashing.
26 The sword that reaches him
will have no effect,
nor will a spear, dart, or arrow.
27 He regards iron as straw,
and bronze as rotten wood.
28 No arrow can make him flee;
slingstones become like stubble
to him.
29 A club is regarded as stubble,
and he laughs^a at the sound
of a javelin.
30 His undersides are
jagged potsherds,
spreading the mud
like a threshing sledge.^b
31 He makes the depths seethe
like a cauldron;
he makes the sea
like an ointment jar.
32 He leaves a shining wake
behind him;^c
one would think the deep had
gray hair!
33 He has no equal on earth —
a creature devoid of fear!
34 He surveys everything
that is haughty;
he is king over all
the proud beasts.^D

Video Devotional

"I HAVE A PLAN FOR YOU"

God has a good plan for you and it is filled with both a future and a hope.

JOB REPLIES TO THE LORD

42 Then Job replied to the LORD:
2 I^E know that you can do anything
and no plan of yours
can be thwarted.^c
3 You asked, "Who is this who conceals
my counsel with ignorance?"^d
Surely I spoke about things I did not
understand,
things too wondrous for me
to^f know.^e
4 You said, "Listen now, and I will speak.
When I question^f you, you will
inform me."
5 I had heard reports about you,
but now my eyes^g have seen you.
6 Therefore, I reject my words and am
sorry for them;
I am dust and ashes.^G,H

7 After the LORD had finished speaking^I
to Job, he said to Eliphaz the Temanite: "I
am angry with you and your two friends,
for you have not spoken the truth about
me, as my servant Job has. 8 Now take seven
bulls and seven rams, go to my servant
Job, and offer a burnt offering for yourselves. Then my servant Job will pray for
you.^h I will surely accept his prayer and
not deal with you as your folly deserves.
For you have not spoken the truth about
me, as my servant Job has." 9 Then Eliphaz the Temanite, Bildad the Shuhite,
and Zophar the Naamathite went and did
as the LORD had told them, and the LORD
accepted Job's prayer.

GOD RESTORES JOB

10 After Job had prayed for his friends, the
LORD restored his fortunes and doubled

A 41:23 Lit *together, hard on him*   B 41:25 Or *the divine beings*   C 41:32 Lit *a path*   D 41:34 Lit *the children of pride*   E 42:2 Alt Hb tradition reads *You*
F 42:3 Lit *me, and I did not*   G 42:6 LXX reads *I despise myself and melt; I consider myself dust and ashes*   H 42:6 Lit *I reject and I relent, concerning dust and ashes*   I 42:7 Lit *speaking these words*

42:2-6 Job was a righteous man. But even when righteous men are confronted with God's holiness and glory, the response can't be casual. Thus, Job confessed that he had spoken in ignorance of whom he was deal-ing with.

Job was filled with genuine sorrow over the things he had said about God's fairness and the accusations he had made against God's character (42:6). While he had not committed the blatant sins that his friends accused him of, in the end, God's greatness had exposed his pride and presumption.

God sometimes allows us to go through painful and even prolonged suffering to give us a fresh vision of him that goes far beyond what we could have otherwise

experienced. So in the midst of your trials, pray for deliverance. But pray also that God would use your circumstances to allow you to see him, understand him, and worship him as never before.

42:7 What a frightening statement to hear from God! Eliphaz and his pals had tried to defend God and his justice, but in the process they argued that all suffering was the direct result of sin—which wasn't true then and still isn't true today. They had been wrong about Job and—even worse—had been wrong about God. They had, in fact, misrepresented God. Their failure brings to my mind the words of James: "Not many should become teachers, my brothers, because you know that we will receive a

stricter judgment" (Jas 3:1). It's no small thing to teach about God what is false.

42:8 In other words, the man they had con-demned as a sinner was going to be their intermediary. The one who cried out for a "mediator" (9:33) was going to become one.

Importantly, that Job had **spoken the truth about** God, and they had not doesn't mean that every word they spoke was a flat-out lie, or that every word Job uttered was spot-on. Rather, Job's friends had made erroneous statements about the character and works of God and had also made false charges against Job.

42:10 In an amazing display of divine grace, God blessed the later part of Job's life more than the first.

his previous possessions.[a] ¹¹ All his brothers, sisters, and former acquaintances[b] came to him and dined with him in his house. They sympathized with him and comforted him concerning all the adversity the Lord had brought on him. Each one gave him a piece of silver[A,c] and a gold earring.[d]

¹² So the Lord blessed the last part of Job's life more than the first. He owned fourteen thousand sheep and goats, six thousand camels, one thousand yoke of oxen, and one thousand female donkeys. ¹³ He also had seven sons and three daughters. ¹⁴ He named his first daughter Jemimah, his second Keziah, and his third Keren-happuch.[e] ¹⁵ No women as beautiful as Job's daughters could be found in all the land, and their father granted them an inheritance with their brothers.

¹⁶ Job lived 140 years after this and saw his children and their children to the fourth generation. ¹⁷ Then Job died, old and full of days.[f]

[a] 42:10 Ps 14:7; Is 40:2; Mt 5:44
[b] 42:11 Jb 2:11; 19:13
[c] Gn 33:19; Jos 24:32
[d] Gn 24:22; 35:4; Hs 2:13

[e] 42:14 Ps 45:8; Sg 2:14; Jr 4:30
[f] 42:17 Gn 25:8; 35:29; 1Ch 29:28

[A] 42:11 Lit *a qesitah*; the value of this currency is unknown

---

42:11 Notice that they comforted him regarding the adversity that *the Lord* had brought upon him—not that *Satan* had brought upon him. Thus, remember that whatever part the devil plays in your suffering, know that he can only afflict you with trials that have first passed through the hands of an all-wise, all-powerful, and all-loving God.

PSALMS

INTRODUCTION

Author

THE BOOK OF PSALMS HAS no single author. King David authored a large number of the one hundred and fifty psalms—almost half. Seventy-three psalms explicitly bear the designation "a psalm of David." Other authors include Asaph (Pss 50; 73–83), the sons of Korah (Pss 42–49; 84–85; 87), Solomon (Pss 72; 127), Moses (Ps 90), Heman the Ezrahite (Ps 88), and Ethan the Ezrahite (Ps 89). Many other psalms are anonymous.

Historical Background

Psalms is a collection of one hundred and fifty works of Hebrew poetry. Our English word *psalms* comes from the Greek word *psalmoi* ("songs"), which is the title of the collection in the Septuagint, the Greek translation of the Old Testament. Given the likely indications of authorship, the psalms were composed from the time of Moses in the fifteenth century BC to some time after the exile in the sixth century BC. Many of the psalms include titles with a variety of information, such as the psalm's historical context or liturgical use in worship. Psalms is divided into five parts: Book I (Pss 1–41), Book II (Pss 42–72), Book III (Pss 73–89), Book IV (Pss 90–106), and Book V (Pss 107–150).

Message and Purpose

Psalms is actually five books of prayers and praises brought together as one. Each was written to be sung in worship to God. The Psalms cover every possible circumstance that life could ever throw at us, which is why there are one hundred and fifty of them. They cover the ins and outs and the ups and downs of life—touching on physical, financial, emotional, and spiritual needs.

The psalms were written so the people of God could communicate with him in the midst of all of the circumstances of life. They will shape your ability to talk with God and will teach you about his character, attributes, and kingdom purposes in history. Through using the Psalms, you can even talk with God in the very words of Scripture, singing and praying his Word back to him. So, in the same way that you would pick up a hymnal to sing praises to God, pick up the book of Psalms. It will enhance your prayer life, your praise life, and your approach-to-problems life, in the context of God-centered worship.

www.bhpublishinggroup.com/qr/te/19_00

Outline

 a 1:1 Ps 26:4-5; Pr 4:14-15
b 1:2 Jos 1:8; Ps 40:8; 119:14-16
c 1:3 Rv 22:2
d Ps 92:12-14; Jr 17:8
e Dt 5:33
f 1:4 Jb 21:18; Ps 35:5; Hs 13:3
g 1:5 Ps 5:5; 9:16; 76:7; Jr 25:31
h 1:6 Jb 34:21; Ps 37:18; Nah 1:7; Jn 10:14; 2Tm 2:19
i Pr 21:12; Jn 3:16

j 2:1-2 Ac 4:25-26
k 2:1 Is 17:12-13
l Ps 83:2-3
m 2:2 Jr 49:19; 50:44
n 1Sm 2:10; 12:3,5; 2Sm 22:51; Ps 18:50; 20:6; 28:8
o 2:3 Is 58:6; Jr 5:5; Nah 1:13
p 2:4 Ps 37:13; 59:8
q 2:5 Ps 90:7
r 2:6 Ps 48:2; Is 24:23
s 2:7 Mt 3:17; Lk 3:22; Ac 13:33; Heb 1:5; 5:5

APPLICATION QUESTIONS

READ PSALM 1:1-6

- Of what sinful patterns or behaviors do you have a hard time letting go?
- What spiritual disciplines or biblical commands have you resisted in recent months? Why?

BOOK I (PSALMS 1-41)

THE TWO WAYS

1 How happy is the one who does not
walk in the advice of the wicked
or stand in the pathway with sinners
or sit in the company of mockers!*a*

2 Instead, his delight is in the
LORD's instruction,
and he meditates on it day and night.*b*

3 He is like a tree planted
beside flowing streams[A]
that bears its fruit in its season*c*
and whose leaf does not wither.*d*
Whatever he does prospers.*e*

4 The wicked are not like this;
instead, they are like chaff
that the wind blows away.*f*

5 Therefore the wicked will not stand
up in the judgment,*g*
nor sinners in the assembly
of the righteous.

6 For the LORD watches over the way
of the righteous,*h*
but the way of the wicked
leads to ruin.*i*

HOPE WORDS

There are two answers to every question—God's answer and everyone else's. And when those two disagree, everyone else is wrong.

CORONATION OF THE SON

2 Why*j* do the nations rage*k*
and the peoples plot in vain?*l*

2 The kings of the earth take
their stand,*m*
and the rulers conspire together
against the LORD
and his Anointed One:[B],*n*

3 "Let's tear off their chains
and throw their ropes off of us."*o*

4 The one enthroned[C] in heaven
laughs;
the Lord ridicules them.*p*

5 Then he speaks to them
in his anger
and terrifies them in his wrath:*q*

6 "I have installed my king
on Zion, my holy mountain."*r*

7 I will declare the LORD's decree.
He said to me, "You are my Son;[D]
today I have become your Father.*s*

8 Ask of me,
and I will make the nations
your inheritance

[A] **1:3** Or *beside irrigation channels*   [B] **2:2** Or *anointed one*   [C] **2:4** Lit *who sits*   [D] **2:7** Or *son*, also in v. 12

1:1 The word translated **happy** can also be rendered "blessed." To be blessed by God is to be happy. First, the happy person **does not walk in the advice of the wicked**. The fastest way to miss your blessing is to take counsel from those with no regard for God's view on life. Second, he or she does not **stand in the pathway with sinners**. Don't hang out with people who will influence you toward sin and away from God. Third, he or she does not **sit in the company of mockers**. Mockers make light of serious things. The one who is regularly influenced by people with little regard for God finds himself or herself increasingly comfortable with human viewpoints and misses blessings. **1:2** To **delight** in something is to find pleasure in it. The blessed individual finds this in God's Word, meditating **on it day and night**. To meditate on something is to recall, ponder, and interact with it in the mind. When we meditate on God's Word, we mentally chew on it until it becomes part of us. When we meditate on the Word, we think about how it connects to life. We ask ourselves, "How does the Word speak to the circumstances I'm facing?"

1:3 The blessed person **is like a tree planted beside flowing streams**. Such trees are not easily swayed; they hold their ground. That the tree **bears its fruit in its season** indicates that the blessed person is productive, maximizing his or her potential. Importantly, the fruit exists for the benefit of others. Thus, you know that you're blessed when you are being a blessing. **1:4-6** In the ancient process of winnowing, the kernel of grain was separated from the husk. While the kernel fell to the threshing floor to be collected, the worthless husk and other parts—**the chaff**—blew away (1:4). While the righteous who live by God's Word produce things of eternal value (see 1:3), **the wicked** and their useless deeds won't last (1:5-6).
2:1-3 The raging of the nations is **in vain**. While a coalition of world powers could threaten humanity, they pose no threat to the God of the universe. At the height of David's power as king, many nations submitted to Israel and paid tribute, and they desired to **tear off their chains** and be free from David's domination (2:3). But to stand against King David was to stand against God, which is ultimately futile.

How much more is this true of Jesus Christ, the Son of David, the true **Anointed One** (2:2)? To reject the Son is to reject the Father (see 1 John 2:23). Rulers conspired against Jesus and crucified him, yet this was all part of God's plan (see Acts 4:25-28) that he might bring salvation to sinners. In the end, their plot proved futile; even death could not hold him.
2:4-6 In spite of the rebellion of the nations on earth, God remains **enthroned in heaven** and chuckles at the ridiculous rebels and **ridicules them** (2:4). No one who fails to submit to the Lord's authority will escape his **anger** and **wrath** (2:5).
2:7-8 The Davidic king was considered God's "son" when anointed and installed on his throne (see 2 Sam 7:12-14). But Psalm 2:7 is even truer of Jesus, the heir to the Davidic throne and the only one who can truly be called the Son of God. Though David possessed a great kingdom and ruled the nations because of the victories God gave him, only King Jesus will receive all **the nations** as his **inheritance** when he reigns in the millennium (2:8).

[a] 2:8 Jos 23:4; Ps 111:6
[b] 2:8-9 Ps 89:23; Rv 2:26-27; 12:5; 19:15
[c] 2:11 Heb 12:28
[d] 2:12 Jn 3:18
[e] 2Th 1:7-8
[f] Ps 5:11; 34:8,22
[g] 3:title 2Sm 15:13-17
[h] 3:1 2Sm 15:12; Ps 69:4
[i] 3:2 Ps 22:7-8; 71:11
[j] 3:3 Gn 15:1; Dt 33:29; Ps 5:12; 18:2; 28:7; 119:114
[k] Ps 62:7
[l] Ps 110:7
[m] 3:4 Ps 2:6; 43:3; 48:1
[n] 3:5 Lv 26:6; Ps 4:8; Pr 3:24
[o] 3:6 Ps 23:4; 27:3; 118:10-13

[p] 3:7 Ps 7:6
[q] Jb 16:10; Mc 5:1
[r] Ps 58:6
[s] 3:8 Jnh 2:9; Ps 7:10; 19:1
[t] Dt 26:15
[u] 4:title Ps 6 title; Is 38:20; Hab 3:19
[v] 4:1 Ps 7:8; 26:1; 35:24
[w] 25:17; 107:6,13
[x] 4:2 Ps 69:7-10,19-20
[y] Ps 12:2
[z] 4:4 Eph 4:26
[aa] Ps 77:6; 119:55
[ab] 4:5 Dt 33:19; Ps 51:19
[ac] Ps 37:3,5; 62:8

and the ends of the earth
  your possession.[a]

9 You will break them
  with an iron scepter;
  you will shatter them like pottery."[b]

10 So now, kings, be wise;
  receive instruction, you judges
    of the earth.

11 Serve the LORD with reverential awe
  and rejoice with trembling.[c]

12 Pay homage to[A] the Son or he
    will be angry
  and you will perish
    in your rebellion,[B,d]
  for his anger may ignite
    at any moment.[e]
  All who take refuge in him
    are happy.[f]

CONFIDENCE IN TROUBLED TIMES

3 A psalm of David when he fled from his son Absalom.[g]

1 LORD, how my foes increase!
  There are many who attack me.[h]

2 Many say about me,
  "There is no help for him
    in God."[i]   Selah

3 But you, LORD, are a shield
    around me,[j]
  my glory,[k] and the one who lifts up
    my head.[l]

4 I cry aloud to the LORD,
  and he answers me
    from his holy mountain.[m]   Selah

5 I lie down and sleep;
  I wake again because the LORD
    sustains me.[n]

6 I will not be afraid of thousands
    of people
  who have taken their stand
    against me on every side.[o]

7 Rise up, LORD![p]
  Save me, my God!
  You strike all my enemies
    on the cheek;[q]
  you break the teeth
    of the wicked.[r]

8 Salvation belongs to the LORD;[s]
  may your blessing be
    on your people.[t]   Selah

⟶ HOPE WORDS ⟵

*It could be that you don't have
an answer, but God does.*

A NIGHT PRAYER

4 For the choir director: with stringed instruments.[u] A psalm of David.

1 Answer me when I call,
  God, who vindicates me.[C,v]
  You freed me from affliction;[w]
  be gracious to me and hear
    my prayer.

2 How long, exalted ones,[D]
  will my honor be insulted?[x]
  How long will you love
    what is worthless[y]
  and pursue a lie?   Selah

3 Know that the LORD
    has set apart
  the faithful for himself;
  the LORD will hear when I call
    to him.

4 Be angry[E] and do not sin;[z]
  on your bed, reflect in your heart
    and be still.[aa]   Selah

5 Offer sacrifices in righteousness[F,ab]
  and trust in the LORD.[ac]

6 Many are asking, "Who can show us
  anything good?"

[A] 2:12 Lit *Kiss*   [B] 2:12 Lit *perish in the way*   [C] 4:1 Or *God of my righteousness*   [D] 4:2 Lit *long, sons of a man*   [E] 4:4 Or *Tremble*   [F] 4:5 Or *Offer right sacrifices*

2:9 No nation—however powerful—will be able to stand against Jesus when he comes in power. Rebellion against the kingdom reign of the Messiah is pointless; it is the rebellion of an ant against an elephant.
2:10-12 God calls them to **serve** him (2:11). To continue in prideful revolt is a fool's errand that will result in defeat. In Hebrew, to **pay homage** is literally "to kiss" the Son—that is, to submit to his authority and rule. King Jesus is not only to be obeyed but worshiped just as the Father is worshiped (see Phil 2:10-11). So why should the nations **perish in [their] rebellion**? They can escape the Son's anger against sin by taking **refuge**

in him. Those who do so are **happy** and blessed (Ps 2:12). The church is to model this satisfaction that will be universal in the millennial kingdom.
3:3-4 Though he recognized the danger of his situation, David's focus was not ultimately on his enemies but on God—which is a lesson for us all. He cried to the Lord whose earthly throne was on Zion, **his holy mountain** (that is, Jerusalem), where the temple would be built (3:4).
3:5-6 David had a great sense of peace from God in spite of his difficulties. When our circumstances overwhelm us, we are called to look to this same source of peace.

After all, what you look at will affect how you feel.
3:7 To **strike** one's **enemies on the cheek** was an insult intended to bring them to their senses and place them into submission—in this case, both to God and to David.
4:1 David expresses his dependency on the Lord because he is the source of righteousness, the One who vindicated him.
4:2-5 David warns the "sons of a man" (the literal rendering of the CSB's **exalted ones**) to take God seriously; this is what Scripture calls "fearing God." They should tremble before God and not allow their anger to cause them to sin against God's anointed king.

Let the light of your face shine
   on us, LORD.[a]

7 You have put more joy in my heart
   than they have when their grain
   and new wine abound.[b]
8 I will both lie down and sleep
   in peace,[c]
   for you alone, LORD, make me live
   in safety.[d]

THE REFUGE OF THE RIGHTEOUS

5 *For the choir director: with the flutes.*
A psalm of David.

1 Listen to my words, LORD;
   consider my sighing.[e]
2 Pay attention to the sound
      of my cry,[f]
   my King and my God,[g]
   for I pray to you.

3 In the morning,[h] LORD, you hear
      my voice;
   in the morning I plead my case
   to you[i] and watch expectantly.

4 For you are not a God who delights
      in wickedness;
   evil cannot dwell with you.[j]
5 The boastful cannot stand
      in your sight;[k]
   you hate all evildoers.[l]
6 You destroy those who tell lies;[m]
   the LORD abhors
      violent and treacherous people.[n]

7 But I enter your house
   by the abundance
      of your faithful love;[o]
   I bow down toward your holy temple
   in reverential awe of you.[p]
8 LORD, lead me
      in your righteousness[q]
   because of my adversaries;
   make your way straight before me.[r]

9 For there is nothing reliable in what
      they say;[s]
   destruction is within them;
   their throat is an open grave;
   they flatter with their tongues.[t]
10 Punish them, God;
   let them fall by their own schemes.[u]
   Drive them out[v] because of
      their many crimes,
   for they rebel against you.[w]

11 But let all who take refuge in you
      rejoice;[x]
   let them shout for joy forever.
   May you shelter them,[y]
   and may those who love your name
      boast about you.[z]
12 For you, LORD, bless the righteous one;
   you surround him with favor
      like a shield.[aa]

A PRAYER FOR MERCY

6 *For the choir director: with stringed*
instruments, according to Sheminith.[ab]
A psalm of David.

1 LORD, do not rebuke me
      in your anger;
   do not discipline me in your wrath.[ac]
2 Be gracious to me, LORD,
      for I am weak;[A,ad]
   heal me,[ae] LORD, for my bones
      are shaking;[af]
3 my whole being is shaken
      with terror.[ag]
   And you, LORD — how long?[ah]

4 Turn, LORD! Rescue me;
   save me because of your faithful love.[ai]
5 For there is no remembrance of you
      in death;
   who can thank you in Sheol?[aj]

6 I am weary from my groaning;[ak]
   with my tears I dampen my bed
   and drench my couch every night.[al]

[a] 4:6 Nm 6:25; Ps 80:3
[b] 4:7 Is 9:3
[c] 4:8 Ps 3:5
[d] Lv 25:18; Dt 12:10; Jr 32:37; Ezk 34:25
[e] 5:1 Ps 38:9
[f] 5:2 Ps 28:2
[g] Ps 84:3
[h] 5:3 Ps 88:13
[i] Jb 13:18; 23:4; Ps 50:21
[j] 5:4 Ps 92:15
[k] 5:5 Ps 1:5; 73:3; 75:4
[l] Jb 8:20; Ps 11:5; 45:7
[m] 5:6 Rv 21:8
[n] Ps 55:23
[o] 5:7 Ps 69:13; 86:5,15; 106:45; Is 63:7
[p] Ps 138:2
[q] 5:8 Ps 27:11
[r] Pr 4:11

[s] 5:9 Ps 52:2
[t] Ps 12:3; Pr 26:28; Rm 3:13
[u] 5:10 Ps 9:16; 35:8; 141:10
[v] Mt 13:41-42
[w] Pr 17:11
[x] 5:11 Ps 2:12; 64:10
[y] Ps 31:20; 61:4
[z] Ps 9:2
[aa] 5:12 Gn 15:1; Dt 33:29; Ps 3:3; 18:2; 28:7; 119:114
[ab] 6:title 1Ch 15:21; Ps 12 title
[ac] 6:1 Ps 38:1; Jr 10:24
[ad] 6:2 Ps 142:6
[ae] Ps 41:4; Jr 17:14
[af] Jb 4:14
[ag] 6:3 Jb 9:28; Jn 12:27
[ah] Nm 14:27; Ps 13:1-2; 35:17; 79:5; 80:4
[ai] 6:4 Ps 31:16; 109:26
[aj] 6:4-5 Ps 30:9; 88:10-12; 115:17; Ec 9:10; Is 38:18
[ak] 6:6 Ps 69:3; 119:28
[al] Ps 42:3; 102:9

[A] 6:2 Or *sick*

4:7-8 God provides **joy** and **peace** in our suffering. We, in turn, are able to share what we receive with others.
5:3 The more dangerous, difficult, and desperate the circumstances, the more urgent it is to begin each day seeking God's intervention and watching **expectantly** for him to answer.
5:4-6 David extols God's separateness from evil and his hatred of sin because he wants to appeal to God's righteousness for God to act on his behalf.
5:7 Faithful love is a translation of the Hebrew word *hesed*, which refers to God's loyal affection

for those under his covenant. It was because of this love that David was able to enter the Lord's presence to worship him.
5:8-10 Just as God would reverse the actions of Haman against God's people and cause his wicked plot to fall on his own head (see Esth 3–8), David asks that the plots of his enemies would cause their own downfall because they were actually scheming against God.
6:1 To receive mercy is to avoid getting the punishment that you deserve for your sin. Like a son appealing to his father, David asks for relief from earned **rebuke**.

6:2-3 In his pain, David does not run *from* God; he runs *to* God. We too can go to God for mercy and understanding, even in the context of our sin and failure, because of his loyal love and our covenant relationship with him through Jesus Christ (see 1 John 1:5-9).
6:4-5 David asks that God **rescue** him before he descends to the grave (**Sheol**), for then it would be too late. He wants people to see him praise God and to know that God hears and delivers.
6:6-7 David was engulfed in sorrow because of his sins, the actions of his enemies, and the possibility of an untimely death.

a 6:7 Jb 17:7; Ps 31:9; 88:9
b 6:8 Ps 18:6; 34:6; 40:1
c 6:9 Ps 28:6
d Ps 3:4; 66:19-20
e 6:10 Ex 23:27
f Ps 71:13
g 7:1 Ps 11:1; 31:1; 71:1
h Ps 31:15
i 7:2 Ps 57:4; Is 5:29
j 7:3 1Sm 24:11
k 7:4 Ps 55:20
l 1Sm 24:11; 26:18
m 7:5 Am 2:7
n 7:3-5 Jb 31:5-40
o 7:6 Ps 3:7; 17:13
p Ps 59:4
q Jr 15:3
r 7:7 Ps 22:27
s Ps 68:18
t 7:8 Ps 96:13; 98:9
u Ps 26:1; 35:24; 43:1

v 7:9 Ps 94:23
w Is 9:7
x Heb 4:12
y 7:10 2Sm 22:3; Ps 18:2; 144:2
z Ps 36:10
aa 7:11 Ps 9:4; Is 11:4
ab 7:12 Nm 22:23; Dt 32:41
ac Ps 37:14
ad 7:13 Ps 18:14; 45:5; 64:7; 144:6
ae 7:14 Jb 15:35; Is 59:4; Jms 1:15
af 7:15 Ps 9:15; 57:6; Pr 26:27; 28:10
ag 7:16 1Sm 25:39; 1Kg 2:33; Est 9:25
ah 7:17 Ps 9:2; 71:15-16
ai 8:title Pss 81; 84 titles
aj 8:1 Is 12:4
ak Ps 113:4; 148:13
al 8:2 Mt 21:16

7 My eyes are swollen from grief;*a*
   they grow old because of all
      my enemies.

8 Depart from me, all evildoers,
   for the LORD has heard the sound
      of my weeping.*b*
9 The LORD has heard my plea for help;*c*
   the LORD accepts my prayer.*d*
10 All my enemies will be ashamed
   and shake with terror;
   they will turn back*e* and suddenly
      be disgraced.*f*

PRAYER FOR JUSTICE

7 *A Shiggaion of David, which he sang to*
the LORD concerning the words of Cush,
a Benjaminite.

1 LORD my God, I seek refuge in you;*g*
   save me from all my pursuers
      and rescue me*h*
2 or they*A* will tear me like a lion,
   ripping me apart with no one
      to rescue me.*i*

3 LORD my God, if I have done this,
   if there is injustice on my hands,*j*
4 if I have done harm to one at peace
      with me*k*
   or have plundered*B* my adversary
      without cause,*l*
5 may an enemy pursue
      and overtake me;
   may he trample me to the ground*m*
   and leave my honor
      in the dust.*n*   *Selah*

6 Rise up, LORD, in your anger;
   lift yourself up against the fury
      of my adversaries;*o*
   awake for me;*C,p*
   you have ordained a judgment.*q*
7 Let the assembly of peoples gather
      around you;*r*
   take your seat on high over it.*s*
8 The LORD judges the peoples;*t*
   vindicate me, LORD,
   according to my righteousness
   and my integrity.*u*

9 Let the evil of the wicked come
      to an end,*v*
   but establish the righteous.*w*
   The one who examines the thoughts
      and emotions*D*
   is a righteous God.*x*
10 My shield is with God,*y*
   who saves the upright in heart.*z*
11 God is a righteous judge
   and a God who shows his wrath
      every day.*aa*

12 If anyone does not repent,
   he will sharpen his sword;*ab*
   he has strung his bow
      and made it ready.*ac*
13 He has prepared
      his deadly weapons;
   he tips his arrows with fire.*ad*

14 See, the wicked one is pregnant
      with evil,
   conceives trouble, and gives birth
      to deceit.*ae*
15 He dug a pit and hollowed it out
   but fell into the hole he had made.*af*
16 His trouble comes back
      on his own head;
   his own violence comes down
      on top of his head.*ag*

17 I will thank the LORD
   for his righteousness;
   I will sing about the name of the
      LORD Most High.*ah*

GOD'S GLORY, HUMAN DIGNITY

8 *For the choir director: on the Gittith.*ai
A psalm of David.

1 LORD, our Lord,
   how magnificent is your name
      throughout the earth!*aj

You have covered the heavens
   with your majesty.*E,ak*
2 From the mouths of infants and
      nursing babies,*al*
   you have established a stronghold*F*
   on account of your adversaries

A 7:2 Lit *he*   *B* 7:4 Or *me and have spared*   *C* 7:6 LXX reads *awake, Lord my God*   *D* 7:9 Lit *examines hearts and kidneys*   *E* 8:1 Lit *earth, which has set your splendor upon the heavens*   *F* 8:2 LXX reads *established praise*

6:8-10 David declares his separation from **all evildoers**, confident that the Lord had **heard [his] plea for help** (6:8-9). Thus, he looked forward to how God would act on his behalf (6:10).
7:1-2 **Like a lion** chasing its prey, David's enemies (likely King Saul's men) hunted him.
7:3-5 David affirms his integrity. He was confident that he had acted uprightly. It was his enemies who were guilty.

7:11 Not all judgment is reserved for the future. On a daily basis, God carries out judgment on the wicked though they don't expect it.
7:12-16 God is ready, like a warrior with **sword, bow**, and **arrows**, to execute judgment on **anyone** who **does not repent** (7:12-13). He routinely causes the wicked schemes of man to result in their own downfall (7:15-16).

Therefore, we must pursue righteousness, or repent when we have failed, so that God can operate on our behalf and we can avoid such ends.
7:17 To sing **about the name** is to sing about God's character and glory. How can we not give voice to God's praise?

in order to silence the enemy
and the avenger.

3 When I observe your heavens,
the work of your fingers,
the moon and the stars,
which you set in place,[a]
4 what is a human being
that you remember him,
a son of man[A] that you look
after him?[b]
5 You made him little less than God[B,C]
and crowned him with glory
and honor.
6 You made him ruler over the works
of your hands;
you put everything under his feet:[c]
7 all the sheep and oxen,
as well as the animals in the wild,
8 the birds of the sky,
and the fish of the sea
that pass through the currents
of the seas.[d]

9 LORD, our Lord,
how magnificent is your name
throughout the earth!

CELEBRATION OF GOD'S JUSTICE

9 For the choir director: according to
Muth-labben. A psalm of David.
1 I will thank the LORD with all my heart;
I will declare all
your wondrous works.[e]
2 I will rejoice and boast about you;[f]
I will sing about your name,
Most High.[g]

3 When my enemies retreat,
they stumble and perish before you.[h]
4 For you have upheld my just cause;[i]
you are seated on your throne
as a righteous judge.[j]

5 You have rebuked the nations:[k]
You have destroyed the wicked;[l]
you have erased their name forever
and ever.[m]
6 The enemy has come to eternal ruin.
You have uprooted the cities,
and the very memory of them
has perished.[n]

7 But the LORD sits enthroned
forever;[o]
he has established his throne
for judgment.[p]
8 And he judges the world
with righteousness;
he executes judgment on the nations
with fairness.[q]
9 The LORD is a refuge
for the persecuted,
a refuge in times of trouble.[r]
10 Those who know your name
trust in you
because you have not abandoned
those who seek you, LORD.[s]

11 Sing to the LORD, who dwells
in Zion;[t]
proclaim his deeds
among the nations.[u]
12 For the one who seeks
an accounting
for bloodshed remembers them;[v]
he does not forget the cry
of the oppressed.[w]

13 Be gracious to me, LORD;
consider my affliction at the hands
of those who hate me.[x]
Lift me up from the gates of death,[y]
14 so that I may declare
all your praises.
I will rejoice in your salvation[z]
within the gates of Daughter Zion.

[a] 8:3 Ps 33:6; 136:9
[b] 8:4 Jb 7:17-18; Ps 144:3
[c] 8:4-6 1Co 15:27; Eph 1:22; Heb 2:5-8
[d] 8:7-8 Gn 1:26,28
[e] 9:1 1Ch 16:9,24; Ps 26:7; 96:3; 105:2
[f] 9:2 Ps 5:11
[g] 9:3 Ps 7:17; 92:1
[h] 9:3 Lv 26:37; Ps 27:2; 92:9
[i] 9:4 1Kg 8:45,49,59; 2Ch 6:35,39
[j] Ps 7:11
[k] 9:5 Is 17:3
[l] Ps 68:2
[m] Zch 13:2
[n] 9:6 Ps 34:16
[o] 9:7 Ps 29:10; 102:12; Lm 5:19
[p] Ps 89:14
[q] 9:8 Ps 96:13; 98:9; Rv 19:11
[r] 9:9 Ps 14:6; Is 14:32
[s] 9:10 Ps 37:28; 94:14
[t] 9:11 Ps 76:2
[u] 1Ch 16:8; Ps 105:1
[v] 9:12 Gn 9:5
[w] Ps 12:5; Pr 22:22-23
[x] 9:13 Ps 69:14
[y] Ps 30:3; 86:13
[z] 9:14 1Sm 2:1

[A] 8:4 Or a mere mortal [B] 8:5 LXX reads angels [C] 8:5 Or heavenly beings; Hb Elohim

8:3-4 The immensity of the night sky causes David to realize just how small he and the rest of humanity are: **What is a human being that you remember him?** (8:4). The modern person tends to be full of himself or herself because God is so small in his or her eyes. But when we see God as he truly is (massive!), we understand how truly miniscule we are.
8:5-8 Though humankind is small in light of who God is, nevertheless, the Creator made them only a **little less than God and crowned [them] with glory and honor** (8:5). This means that though we are reduced in size in comparison to God, we are increased in significance in relationship to him.
After Satan rebelled, God created Adam and Eve to have dominion over the earth. He made humankind **ruler over the works of [God's]**

hands and **put everything under [people's] feet** (8:6) with the idea that humans would rule on God's behalf. Through us he intended to establish a kingdom that would defeat Satan's. And though Adam and Eve and the rest of us fell into sin, God's kingdom program is fulfilled in Jesus Christ, the God-Man (see Heb 2:6-9).
Jesus defeated Satan and provided redemption for humanity through his atoning death on the cross (see Heb 2:14-17). Ultimately, Christ will reign in his millennial kingdom, subjecting all creation to the kingdom of God (see 1 Cor 15:24-28) and vanquishing Satan once and for all (see Rev 20:1-3, 7-10). Until then, Christ's followers are called to exercise authority on earth in his name and model his kingdom rule (see Matt 28:19-20).

9:1-2 Regardless of his own power and fame, David chooses to **boast** in God alone.
9:7-10 God is the true, eternal King who rules over all. As a result, **he executes judgment on the nations**, acting **with fairness** on behalf of the oppressed and the afflicted (9:8). He is the champion of those who are **persecuted**, providing a secure **refuge** for **those who seek** him (9:9-10).
9:11-12 God **remembers** his people. Therefore, his people should remember to glorify him for his deliverance.
9:13-14 Notice the words **so that** in verse 14. David wants to give verbal witness to God's **salvation** so all Jerusalem would hear and join him in worship.

a 9:15 Ps 7:15; 57:6; Pr 28:10
b 9:16 Is 56:1
c Ps 3:7; Is 11:4
d 9:17 Ps 31:17; 49:14; 55:15
e Jb 8:13; Ps 50:22
f 9:18 Ps 12:5; 72:4
g 9:19 Ps 82:8; 110:6
h 9:20 Ps 14:5
i Ps 62:9
j 10:1 Ps 22:1; 35:22; 38:21; 71:12
k Jb 13:24; Ps 44:24; 88:14
l 10:2 Ps 7:15-16
m 10:3 Ps 49:6
n 2Pt 2:3
o 10:4 Ps 14:1; 53:1

p 10:5 Ps 52:7
q 10:6 Ps 49:11; Rv 18:7
r 10:7 Ps 73:8; 140:3; Rm 3:13-14
s 10:8 Ps 59:3
t Ps 64:4; 94:6
u 10:8-10 Ps 17:11-12; Pr 28:15
v 10:11 Jb 22:13; Ps 59:3
w 10:12 Mc 5:9
x Ps 9:12
y 10:13 Ps 73:11
z 10:14 Ps 33:13-15
aa Ps 68:5; 146:9
ab 10:15 Ps 37:17
ac Ps 89:32
ad 10:16 Ex 15:18; Ps 29:10; Rv 11:15
ae Dt 8:20

15 The nations have fallen into the pit
　　they made;
their foot is caught in the net
　　they have concealed.*a*
16 The LORD has made himself known;
he has executed justice,*b*
snaring the wicked
by the work of their hands.*c*
　　　　　　Higgaion. Selah

17 The wicked will return to Sheol*d* —
all the nations that forget God.*e*
18 For the needy will not always
　　be forgotten;
the hope of the oppressed^A
　　will not perish forever.*f*

19 Rise up, LORD! Do not let
　　mere humans prevail;
let the nations be judged
　　in your presence.*g*
20 Put terror in them, LORD;*h*
let the nations know they are
　　only humans.*i*
　　　　　　　　Selah

― HOPE WORDS ―

*God is often closest when he
seems the furthest away.*

NEED FOR GOD'S JUSTICE

10 LORD,*B,C* why do you stand
　　so far away?*j*
Why do you hide in times
　　of trouble?*k*
2　In arrogance the wicked
　　relentlessly pursue
　　their victims;
let them be caught in the schemes
　　they have devised.*l*

3　For the wicked one boasts about
　　his own cravings;*m*
the one who is greedy curses^D
　　and despises the LORD.*n*
4　In all his scheming,
　　the wicked person
　　arrogantly thinks,^E
　　"There's no accountability,
　　since there's no God."*o*

5　His ways are always secure;^F
your lofty judgments have no effect
　　on him;^G
he scoffs at all his adversaries.*p*
6　He says to himself, "I will never
　　be moved —
from generation to generation
　　without calamity."*q*
7　Cursing, deceit, and violence
　　fill his mouth;
trouble and malice are
　　under his tongue.*r*
8　He waits in ambush
　　near settlements;*s*
he kills the innocent in secret places.
His eyes are on the lookout
　　for the helpless;*t*
9　he lurks in secret like a lion
　　in a thicket.
He lurks in order to seize a victim;
he seizes a victim and drags him
　　in his net.
10　So he is oppressed and beaten down;
helpless people fall because of the
　　wicked one's strength.*u*
11　He says to himself,
　　"God has forgotten;
he hides his face and will
　　never see."*v*

12　Rise up, LORD God! Lift up
　　your hand.*w*
Do not forget the oppressed.*x*
13　Why has the wicked person
　　despised God?
He says to himself, "You will not
　　demand an account."*y*
14　But you yourself have seen trouble
　　and grief,
observing it in order to take
　　the matter into your hands.*z*
The helpless one entrusts himself
　　to you;
you are a helper of the fatherless.*aa*
15　Break the arm of the wicked,
　　evil person,*ab*
until you look for his wickedness,
but it can't be found.*ac*
16　The LORD is King forever and ever;*ad*
the nations will perish
　　from his land.*ae*

^A 9:18 Alt Hb tradition reads *humble* ^B 10:1 Some Hb mss, LXX connect Pss 9–10. ^C 10:1 Together Pss 9–10 form a partial acrostic.
^D 10:3 Or *he blesses the greedy* ^E 10:4 Lit *wicked according to the height of his nose* ^F 10:5 Or *prosperous* ^G 10:5 Lit *judgments are away from in front of him*

9:19-20 David calls on God to strike fear in the hearts of the nations (9:19). Whatever power they thought they possessed, they needed a reminder of their own mortality. After all, **they are only humans** subject to the God who created them (9:20).
10:1-18 **LORD, why do you stand so far away?** and **Why do you hide in times of trouble?** are questions that struggling believers have asked through the ages (10:1). But the question we should be asking is, "*When* will God take action?" (10:14-18).

¹⁷ LORD, you have heard the desire
    of the humble;
you will strengthen their hearts.
You will listen carefully,^a
¹⁸ doing justice for the fatherless
    and the oppressed
so that mere humans from the earth
    may terrify them no more.^b

REFUGE IN THE LORD

11 *For the choir director. Of David.*
I have taken refuge in the LORD.^c
How can you say to me,
"Escape to the mountains^A like a bird!^d
² For look, the wicked string bows;
they put their arrows on bowstrings
to shoot from the shadows
    at the upright in heart.^e
³ When the foundations
    are destroyed,
what can the righteous do?"^f

⁴ The LORD is in his holy temple;^g
the LORD—his throne is in heaven.^h
His eyes watch;
his gaze^B examines everyone.^c
⁵ The LORD examines the righteous,
but he hates the wicked
and^D those who love violence.ⁱ
⁶ Let him rain burning coals^E
    and sulfur on the wicked;
let a scorching wind be the portion
    in their cup.^j
⁷ For the LORD is righteous; he loves
    righteous deeds.
The upright will see his face.^k

OPPRESSION BY THE WICKED

12 *For the choir director: according to*
Sheminith.^I *A psalm of David.*

¹ Help, LORD, for no
    faithful one remains;
the loyal have disappeared
    from the human race.^{F,m}

² They lie to one another;
they speak with flattering lips
    and deceptive hearts.ⁿ
³ May the LORD cut off
    all flattering lips
and the tongue
    that speaks boastfully.^o
⁴ They say, "Through our tongues
    we have power;
our lips are our own — who can be
    our master?"^p

⁵ "Because of the devastation
    of the needy
and the groaning of the poor,
I will now rise up,"
    says the LORD.
"I will provide safety for the one
    who longs for it."^q

⁶ The words of the LORD
    are pure words,
like silver refined
    in an earthen furnace,
purified seven times.^r

⁷ You, LORD, will guard us;^G
you will protect us^H
    from this generation forever.^s
⁸ The wicked prowl^I all around,
and what is worthless is exalted
    by the human race.^t

A PLEA FOR DELIVERANCE

13 *For the choir director. A psalm of David.*
How long, LORD? Will you
    forget me forever?
How long will you hide your face
    from me?^u
² How long will I store up
    anxious concerns^J within me,
agony in my mind every day?
How long will my enemy
    dominate me?^v

^a 10:17 2Ch 7:14; Ps 34:15
^b 10:18 Ex 22:22-24; Dt 10:18
^c 11:1 Ps 7:1; 31:1; 71:1
^d Ps 121:1
^e 11:2 Ps 37:14; 64:4
^f 11:3 Ps 82:5
^g 11:4 Ps 27:4; Hab 2:20
^h Ps 103:19; Is 66:1; Ac 7:49
ⁱ 11:4-5 Ps 33:13-15
^j 11:6 Ezk 38:22
^k 11:7 Ps 17:15; Rv 22:4
^l 12:title 1Ch 15:21; Ps 6 title
^m 12:1 Ps 14:2-3; 53:2-3; Mc 7:2

ⁿ 12:2 Ps 41:6; 144:8; Jr 9:8
^o 12:3 Ps 5:9
^p 12:4 Ps 73:8-9
^q 12:5 Ps 9:18; 72:4
^r 12:6 Ps 18:30; 119:140; Pr 30:5
^s 12:7 Ps 37:28; 97:10
^t 12:8 Ps 4:2; 119:37
^u 13:1 Jb 13:24; Ps 44:24; 89:46
^v 13:2 Ps 6:3; 38:6; 42:9

---

^A 11:1 Lit *your mountain*   ^B 11:4 Lit *eyelids*   ^C 11:4 Or *examines the descendants of Adam*   ^D 11:5 Or *righteous and the wicked, and he hates*
^E 11:6 Sym; MT reads *rain snares, fire*   ^F 12:1 Or *the descendants of Adam*, also in v. 8   ^G 12:7 Some Hb mss, LXX, Jer; other Hb mss read *them*
^H 12:7 Some Hb mss, LXX; other Hb mss read *him*   ^I 12:8 Lit *walk about*   ^J 13:2 Or *up counsels*

Because we know God's character and his past actions, we can have confidence that he will bring justice at the right time. This should encourage us to pray in faith. Even when we see nothing happening, we can be certain that God doesn't miss a thing and has set the timer for when he will intervene.

11:3 The people were afraid that the proliferation of evil and lawlessness in society might cause the nation to crumble.

11:4-7 David's eternal perspective is revealed here. He knows that God is sovereign, ruling from heaven over the affairs of people. He sees the deeds done on earth, **hates the wicked**, and will punish them (11:5-6). A scorching judgment *will* fall on evildoers—in God's appointed time.

In contrast to this fate, **the upright will see [God's] face**. Since he **is righteous**, the Lord **loves** those who perform **righteous deeds** (11:7). Those who follow him will ultimately experience his presence and enjoy his blessings.

12:1-3 The absence of the righteous had created a void that had been filled by corruption. Hypocrisy ruled the day. Thus, David appeals to God to address the problem: to **cut off all flattering lips** (12:3).

12:5 Final deliverance and justice will take place in God's eternal kingdom; nevertheless, there are moments in history when he brings his sovereignty to bear and rights wrongs committed on earth.

12:6 David confesses confidence in the perfection of God's words.

13:1-2 David feels forsaken by God and wrestles with thoughts of abandonment. This is a common human experience. When we encounter trying circumstances over an extended period, we can feel abandoned by God and assume that evil is winning.

a 13:3 Ezr 9:8; Ps 19:8;
Pr 29:13
b 13:4 Ps 89:42
c 13:5 Ps 52:8
d Ps 9:14
e 13:6 Ps 119:17; 142:7
f 14:1 Ps 10:4; 53:1
g 14:2 Ps 33:13-15
h 14:1-3 Ps 12:1; 53:1-3; Mc
7:2; Rm 3:10-12
i 14:4 Ps 27:2; Mc 3:3
j Is 64:7

k 14:5 Ps 53:5
l 14:6 Ezr 4:5
m Ps 9:9; 94:22
n 14:7 Ps 53:6
o 15:1 Ps 61:4
p Ps 43:3
q 15:1-2 Ps 24:3-5; Is
33:14-16
r 15:3 Pr 10:18
s Pr 3:29
t 15:4 Gn 14:17-24; Ps
119:63
u Lv 5:4; Dt 23:21-23
v 15:5 Lv 25:35-38; Dt 33:19
w Ex 23:18; Dt 16:19
x Ps 16:8; 112:6
y 16:title Pss 56-60 titles
z 16:1 Ps 94:22
aa 16:2 Ps 73:25

∽ HOPE WORDS ∽

When God delays, he always delays for a greater purpose.

3 Consider me and answer,
    LORD my God.
  Restore brightness to my eyes;*a*
    otherwise, I will sleep in death.
4 My enemy will say,
    "I have triumphed over him,"
  and my foes will rejoice
    because I am shaken.*b*

5 But I have trusted in your faithful love;*c*
    my heart will rejoice in
    your deliverance.*d*
6 I will sing to the LORD
    because he has treated
    me generously.*e*

A PORTRAIT OF SINNERS

14 *For the choir director. Of David.*
  The fool says in his heart,
    "There's no God."*f*
  They are corrupt; they do vile deeds.
    There is no one who does good.
2 The LORD looks down from heaven
    on the human race[A],*g*
  to see if there is one who is wise,
    one who seeks God.
3 All have turned away;
    all alike have become corrupt.
  There is no one who does good,
    not even one.*h*

4 Will evildoers never understand?
  They consume my people
    as they consume bread;*i*
  they do not call on the LORD.*j*

5 Then[B] they will be filled with dread,
  for God is with those
    who are*c* righteous.*k*
6 You sinners frustrate the plans
    of the oppressed,*l*
  but the LORD is his refuge.*m*

7 Oh, that Israel's deliverance
    would come from Zion!
  When the LORD restores the fortunes
    of his people,*D*
  let Jacob rejoice, let Israel be glad.*n*

A DESCRIPTION OF THE GODLY

15 *A psalm of David.*
  LORD, who can dwell in your tent?*o*
  Who can live on your holy mountain?*p*

2 The one who lives blamelessly,
    practices righteousness,
  and acknowledges the truth
    in his heart*q* —
3 who does not slander with his tongue,*r*
  who does not harm his friend
    or discredit his neighbor,*s*
4 who despises the one rejected
    by the LORD[E]
  but honors those who fear the LORD,*t*
  who keeps his word whatever the cost,*u*
5 who does not lend his silver
    at interest*v*
  or take a bribe
    against the innocent*w* —
  the one who does these things
    will never be shaken.*x*

CONFIDENCE IN THE LORD

16 *A Miktam of David.*
  Protect me, God, for I take refuge
    in you.*z*
2 I[F] said to the LORD, "You are my Lord;
  I have nothing good besides you."[G],*aa*

A 14:2 Or *the descendants of Adam* B 14:5 Or *There* C 14:5 Lit *with the generation of the* D 14:7 Or *restores his captive people* E 15:4 Lit *in his eyes the rejected is despised* F 16:2 Some Hb mss, LXX, Syr, Jer; other Hb mss read *You* G 16:2 Or *"Lord, my good; there is none besides you."*

13:3-4 As powerful as David was, as mighty as his army, he realizes that defeat is certain without God's intervention. Do you see things similarly? Do you recognize that your spiritual defeat is sure without the aid of God's strengthening hand?

13:5 David has confidence in the Lord's **faithful love**—his commitment to his covenant, to his people, and to his king. Regardless of the actions of his enemy, then, David is determined to **rejoice**. Likewise, we should live with expectation in the goodness of God as we wait for him to move in our own situations.

14:1-3 These verses are quoted by Paul in Romans 3:10-12 when he makes his case for the sinfulness of humanity. Elsewhere he says, "All have sinned and fall short of the glory of God"; therefore, our only hope is the grace of God and "the redemption that is in Christ Jesus" (Rom 3:23-24).

14:4-6 David is amazed that the wicked think they can devour God's people and experience no consequences. They are unaware that God will overwhelm them. They don't realize that **God is with those who are righteous** (14:5), and to attack God's people is to attack him. Though for a time **sinners frustrate the plans of the oppressed**, they will not prevail (14:6). So take heart, you who follow the Lord. He keeps track of injustices, and he will bring about your deliverance at the right time.

14:7 Ultimately, this will take place when Jesus Christ rules from David's throne in his millennial kingdom. On that day, God will establish justice and joy universally and comprehensively. In the meantime, God's people are to model his rule in a sinful world.

15:1-5 One cannot simply profess to love God but must actually walk before him in integrity (15:2-3). To have access to God, one's life must reflect devotion to the two great commandments: love for God and love for people (see Mark 12:28-31).

16:1-2 David uses three different Hebrew names for God (*Elohim, Yahweh,* and *Adonai*) to appeal to God's sovereignty for protection.

His claim, **I have nothing good besides you** (16:2), should make us ask whether we can make this same declaration. Believers need to understand that we only have one *source*: God. Everything else is a *resource*.

3 As for the holy people who are
    in the land,[a]
they are the noble ones.
All my delight is in them.
4 The sorrows of those who take
    another god
for themselves will multiply;
I will not pour out
    their drink offerings of blood,
and I will not speak their names
    with my lips.[b]

5 LORD, you are my portion[A]
and my cup of blessing;
you hold my future.[c]
6 The boundary lines have fallen for me
in pleasant places;
indeed, I have a beautiful inheritance.[d]

7 I will bless the LORD who counsels me[e] —
even at night when my thoughts
    trouble me.[B,f]
8 I always let the LORD guide me.[c]
Because he is at my right hand,
I will not be shaken.[g]

9 Therefore my heart is glad
and my whole being rejoices;
my body also rests securely.[h]
10 For you will not abandon me to Sheol;[i]
you will not allow your faithful one
    to see decay.[j]
11 You reveal the path of life to me;
in your presence is abundant joy;[k]
at your right hand are
    eternal pleasures.[l]

A PRAYER FOR PROTECTION

17 *A prayer of David.*

LORD, hear a just cause;[m]
pay attention to my cry;
listen to my prayer —
from lips free of deceit.[n]

2 Let my vindication come from you,
for you see what is right.[o]
3 You have tested my heart;[p]
you have examined me at night.
You have tried me and found
    nothing evil;[q]
I have determined that my mouth
    will not sin.[D]
4 Concerning what people do:
by the words from your lips
I have avoided the ways
    of the violent.[r]
5 My steps are on your paths;
my feet have not slipped.[s]

6 I call on you, God,
because you will answer me;[t]
listen closely to me; hear what I say.
7 Display the wonders
    of your faithful love,[u]
Savior of all who seek refuge[v]
from those who rebel
    against your right hand.[E]
8 Protect me as the pupil of your eye;[w]
hide me in the shadow
    of your wings[x]
9 from[F] the wicked
    who treat me violently,[G]
my deadly enemies
    who surround me.[y]

10 They are uncaring;[H,z]
their mouths speak arrogantly.[aa]
11 They advance against me;[I]
    now they surround me.[ab]
They are determined[J]
to throw me to the ground.[ac]
12 They are[K] like a lion eager to tear,
like a young lion
    lurking in ambush.[ad]

13 Rise up, LORD!
Confront him; bring him down.[ae]

[a] 16:3 Dt 7:6; 14:2; 26:19
[b] 16:4 Ex 23:13; Jos 23:7
[c] 16:5 Nm 18:20; Ps 119:57; Lm 3:24
[d] 16:6 Jr 3:19
[e] 16:7 Ps 73:24
[f] Ps 77:6
[g] 16:8 Ps 15:5; 112:6
[h] 16:9 Ps 4:7-8; 13:5
[i] 16:10 Ps 49:10; 86:13
[j] Jb 33:18,28; Ps 30:3; 103:4; Ac 13:35
[k] 16:11 Ps 21:6
[l] 16:8-11 Ac 2:25-28
[m] 17:1 Ps 9:4
[n] Jb 27:4; Ps 34:13; 1Pt 3:10

[o] 17:2 Ps 26:1; 43:1
[p] 17:3 Ps 66:10; Zch 13:9
[q] Jb 23:10; Ps 26:2
[r] 17:4 Pr 4:14-15
[s] 17:5 Jb 23:11
[t] 17:6 Ps 86:7
[u] 17:7 Ps 85:7
[v] Ps 7:1
[w] 17:8 Pr 7:2
[x] Ps 36:7; 57:1; 63:7; 91:1,4
[y] 17:9 Ps 18:48
[z] 17:10 Ps 119:70
[aa] Ps 31:18
[ab] 17:11 Ps 88:17
[ac] Ps 37:14; 62:4
[ad] 17:12 Ps 7:2; 10:9
[ae] 17:13 Ps 55:23

[A] 16:5 Or *allotted portion* [B] 16:7 Or *at night my heart instructs me* [C] 16:8 Lit *I place the LORD in front of me always* [D] 17:3 Or *evil; my mouth will not sin* [E] 17:7 Or *love, you who save with your right hand those seeking refuge from adversaries* [F] 17:9 Lit *from the presence of* [G] 17:9 Or *who plunder me* [H] 17:10 Lit *have closed up their fat* [I] 17:11 Vg; MT reads *Our steps* [J] 17:11 Lit *They set their eyes* [K] 17:12 Lit *He is*

16:4 Not only does idolatry rob God of his glory, but it also brings inevitable grief to those who practice it. An idol is any person, place, thing, or thought that you look to as your source instead of God.
16:5-6 The Levites were the only Israelite tribe that received no portion in the promised land. Instead, since they received the privilege of serving God in the tabernacle and temple, the Lord himself was to be their inheritance (see Num 18:20; Josh 18:7). Likewise, in spite of all that he had received from God, David sees the Lord himself as his **portion** (Ps 16:5). He had great joy in knowing that God—not his possessions—was his true **inheritance**

(16:6). Whatever material blessings the Lord grants are not your inheritance either. They are merely bonuses.
16:10 **Sheol** refers to the place of the dead. If what is stated in this verse was the case for King David, how much more is it true of the great Son of David, Jesus Christ? Both Peter and Paul applied this passage to the Messiah, whom God raised to life (see Acts 2:24-28; 13:35).
16:11 Both in history and in eternity, there is unfathomable joy in God's presence. Believers must make living in God's presence and anticipating an eternal future with him a way of life.

17:1 In other words, he had no unaddressed sin in his life that would block God's answers to prayer.
17:8 The Lord's protection of his people is described in beautiful imagery. As one is zealous to shield his own **eye** from danger, so God shelters his servants. As a mother bird lovingly protects her chicks, so the Lord overshadows his own.
17:13-15 Though the judgment on evildoers might be delayed, it would come (17:13-14). In the meantime, David chooses to find his ultimate satisfaction in the **presence** of God (17:15).

a 17:13 Ps 7:12
b 17:14 Ps 73:3-7
c 17:15 Ps 11:7; Rv 22:4
d Ps 16:11; 21:6; 73:28
e 18:title 2Sm 22
f 18:2 Ps 62:7; 94:22
g Gn 15:1; Dt 33:29; Ps 3:3;
   5:12; 28:7; 119:114
h 1Sm 2:1,10; Lk 1:69
i 18:3 Ps 48:1; 96:4; 145:3
j Ps 138:7
k 18:4 Ps 124:4
l 18:5 Ps 116:3

m 18:6 Ps 3:4
n Ps 34:15
o 18:7 Is 13:13; Hg 2:6
p 18:8 Ps 21:9; 50:3
q 18:9 Ps 144:5; Is 64:1
r 18:10 Ps 104:3
s 18:11 Ps 97:2
t 18:12 Ps 50:2; Is 60:3
u 18:13 Ps 29:3; 104:7
v 18:14 Ps 144:6
w 18:15 Ex 15:8; Ps 106:9;
   Nah 1:4
x 18:16 Ps 144:7
y 18:17 Ps 35:10; 59:1; 142:6
z 18:18 Ps 55:22; 59:16

With your sword, save me
   from the wicked.*a*
14 With your hand, LORD, save me
   from men,
from men of the world
whose portion is in this life:
You fill their bellies with what
   you have in store;
their sons are satisfied,
and they leave their surplus
   to their children.*b*

15 But I will see your face
   in righteousness;*c*
when I awake, I will be satisfied
   with your presence.*A,d*

⟳ HOPE WORDS ⟳

*Sometimes God lets you hit rock
bottom so that you will discover
that he is the Rock at the bottom.*

PRAISE FOR DELIVERANCE

18 *For the choir director. Of the servant of
the LORD, David, who spoke the words
of this song to the LORD on the day the LORD
rescued him from the grasp of all his enemies
and from the power of Saul.*e* He said:*

1 I love you, LORD, my strength.
2 The LORD is my rock,
my fortress, and my deliverer,*f*
my God, my rock where I seek refuge,
my shield*g* and the horn
   of my salvation,*h*
my stronghold.
3 I called to the LORD, who is
   worthy of praise,*i*
and I was saved from my enemies.*j*

4 The ropes of death were wrapped
   around me;
the torrents of destruction
   terrified me.*k*
5 The ropes of Sheol entangled me;
the snares of death confronted me.*l*

6 I called to the LORD in my distress,
and I cried to my God for help.
From his temple he heard my voice,*m*
and my cry to him reached his ears.*n*

7 Then the earth shook and quaked;
the foundations of the mountains
   trembled;*o*
they shook because he burned
   with anger.
8 Smoke rose from his nostrils,
and consuming fire came
   from his mouth;
coals were set ablaze by it.*B,p*
9 He bent the heavens
   and came down,*q*
total darkness beneath his feet.
10 He rode on a cherub and flew,
soaring on the wings of the wind.*r*
11 He made darkness his hiding place,
dark storm clouds his canopy
   around him.*s*
12 From the radiance of his presence,*t*
his clouds swept onward with hail
   and blazing coals.
13 The LORD thundered from*c* heaven;
the Most High made
   his voice heard.*D,u*
14 He shot his arrows
   and scattered them;
he hurled*E* lightning bolts
   and routed them.*v*
15 The depths of the sea became visible,
the foundations of the world
   were exposed,
at your rebuke, LORD,
at the blast of the breath
   of your nostrils.*w*

16 He reached down from on high
and took hold of me;
he pulled me out of deep water.*x*
17 He rescued me
   from my powerful enemy
and from those who hated me,
for they were too strong for me.*y*
18 They confronted me in the day
   of my calamity,
but the LORD was my support.*z*

A 17:15 Lit *form*   *B* 18:8 Or *him*   *C* 18:13 Some Hb mss, LXX, Tg, Jer; other Hb mss read *in*   *D* 18:13 Some Hb mss read *voice, with hail and blazing coals*   *E* 18:14 Or *multiplied*

18:1-3 As the king of Israel, divinely installed on the throne, David had a legal relationship with God. But the relationship was also one of love: **I love you, LORD, my strength** (18:1). And because the love was reciprocated, David is confident in God as his source of deliverance and **salvation** (18:2). Interestingly, this psalm is also found in 2 Samuel 22.

18:4-6 Sometimes we can be wrapped up by our negative circumstances and surrounded by hopelessness, but this state simply gives God the unique opportunity to demonstrate that he alone is God—the only solution to our problems. We need only ask for his aid. **18:7-19** Since David and God shared an intimate relationship, God **delighted in** him

and orchestrated a massive intervention via creation to deliver David from his **powerful enemy** (18:16-19). Too many believers don't experience close fellowship with God. As a result of the distance, they don't get to see God work on their behalf in a dramatic way.

19 He brought me out
  to a spacious place;[a]
he rescued me because he delighted
  in me.[b]

20 The Lord rewarded me
  according to my righteousness;[c]
he repaid me
  according to the cleanness
  of my hands.[d]

21 For I have kept the ways of the Lord
  and have not turned from my God
  to wickedness.[e]

22 Indeed, I let all his ordinances
  guide me[A]
and have not disregarded
  his statutes.[f]

23 I was blameless toward him[g]
  and kept myself from my iniquity.

24 So the Lord repaid me
  according to my righteousness,[h]
  according to the cleanness
  of my hands in his sight.[i]

25 With the faithful
  you prove yourself faithful,
  with the blameless
  you prove yourself blameless,

26 with the pure
  you prove yourself pure;
  but with the crooked
  you prove yourself shrewd.[j]

27 For you rescue
  an oppressed people,[k]
but you humble those
  with haughty eyes.[l]

28 Lord, you light my lamp;
  my God illuminates my darkness.[m]

29 With you I can attack a barricade,[B]
  and with my God I can leap over
  a wall.[n]

— ⌇ HOPE WORDS ⌇ —

Your commitment in the dark is
the key to your victory in the light.

30 God — his way is perfect;[o]
  the word of the Lord is pure.[p]

He is a shield to all who take refuge
  in him.[q]

31 For who is God besides the Lord?[r]
And who is a rock? Only our God.[s]

32 God — he clothes me with strength[t]
  and makes my way perfect.

33 He makes my feet like the feet
  of a deer[u]
and sets me securely
  on the heights.[C,v]

34 He trains my hands for war;[w]
  my arms can bend a bow of bronze.[x]

35 You have given me the shield
  of your salvation;
your right hand upholds me,[y]
  and your humility exalts me.

36 You make a spacious place beneath
  me for my steps,[z]
  and my ankles do not give way.[aa]

37 I pursue my enemies
  and overtake them;
I do not turn back until they are
  wiped out.[ab]

38 I crush them, and they cannot
  get up;
they fall beneath my feet.[ac]

39 You have clothed me with strength
  for battle;[ad]
you subdue my adversaries
  beneath me.[ae]

40 You have made my enemies retreat
  before me;[D,af]
I annihilate those who hate me.[ag]

41 They cry for help, but there is no one
  to save them[ah] —
they cry to the Lord, but he does not
  answer them.[ai]

42 I pulverize them like dust
  before the wind;[aj]
I trample them[E] like mud
  in the streets.[ak]

43 You have freed me from the feuds
  among the people;
you have appointed me the head
  of nations;[al]
a people I had not known
  serve me.[am]

44 Foreigners submit to me cringing;
  as soon as they hear they obey me.[an]

[a] 18:19 Ps 31:8; 118:5
[b] Ps 41:11
[c] 18:20 Ps 7:8
[d] Ps 24:4
[e] 18:21 Jb 23:11; Ps 119:101
[f] 18:22 Lv 18:4-5
[g] 18:23 Dt 18:13; Ps 37:18; 119:1
[h] 18:24 2Ch 6:23
[i] Ps 24:4
[j] 18:25-26 Mt 16:27; Rv 22:12
[k] 18:27 Ps 72:12
[l] Ps 138:6
[m] 18:28 Ps 112:4; Is 42:16
[n] 18:29 Mt 19:26; Php 4:13
[o] 18:30 Dt 32:4
[p] Ps 19:7

[q] 18:30 Ps 91:4; 144:2
[r] 18:31 Dt 32:39; 1Sm 2:2; Ps 86:8
[s] Ps 62:2
[t] 18:32 Is 45:5
[u] 18:33 Hab 3:19
[v] Dt 32:13; Is 58:14
[w] 18:34 Ps 144:1
[x] Jb 29:20
[y] 18:35 Ps 89:21
[z] 18:36 Ps 31:8; 118:5
[aa] Ps 66:9; Pr 4:12
[ab] 18:37 Ps 44:5
[ac] 18:38 Ps 36:12
[ad] 18:39 1Sm 2:4
[ae] 1Ch 17:10; Ps 81:14
[af] 18:40 Ex 23:27
[ag] Dt 7:10
[ah] 18:41 Ps 50:22
[ai] Mc 3:4
[aj] 18:42 2Kg 13:7
[ak] Is 10:6; Mc 7:10
[al] 18:43 2Sm 8:1-14
[am] Is 55:5
[an] 18:44 Dt 33:29; Ps 66:3

[A] 18:22 Lit *Indeed, all his ordinances have been in front of me* [B] 18:29 Or *a ridge*, or *raiders* [C] 18:33 Or *on my high places* [D] 18:40 Or *You gave me the necks of my enemies* [E] 18:42 Some Hb mss, LXX, Syr, Tg; other Hb mss read *I poured them out*

18:20-24 God rewarded David **according to [his] righteousness** (18:20, 24). Our faithfulness and obedience to God brings rewards, including victory over our circumstances. Never underestimate the blessings that result from being **blameless toward** God (18:23).

18:29 David knew that with God on his side, he could defeat any enemy and advance against any opposition. That should be our mindset as well.

18:41 David cried for help (18:6); the Lord heard and saved (18:7-19). David's enemies **cry for help, but there is no one to save them**.

a 18:45 Mc 7:17
b 18:46 Ps 62:2,6
c 18:47 2Sm 4:8; Ps 94:1
d Ps 47:3; 144:2
e 18:48 Ps 59:1; 140:1
f 18:49 Rm 15:9
g 18:50 Ps 144:10
h 2Sm 7:12-13; Ps 89:4,29
i 19:1 Gn 1:6
j Ps 50:6; Rm 1:19-20
k 19:4 Rm 10:18
l Is 40:22

m 19:6 Ec 1:5
n 19:7 Ps 111:7
o Ps 93:5; 119:130
p 19:8 Ps 119:14
q Ps 13:3
r 19:9 Ps 111:10
s Ps 119:30
t 19:10 Ps 119:72,127
u Ps 119:103
v 19:11 Pr 29:18

45 Foreigners lose heart
and come trembling
    from their fortifications.*a*

46 The LORD lives — blessed be my rock!
The God of my salvation is exalted.*b*

47 God — he grants me vengeance*c*
and subdues peoples under me.*d*

48 He frees me from my enemies.
You exalt me above my adversaries;
you rescue me from violent men.*e*

49 Therefore I will give thanks to you
    among the nations, LORD;
I will sing praises about your name.*f*

50 He gives great victories to his king;*g*
he shows loyalty to his anointed,
to David
    and his descendants forever.*h*

THE WITNESS OF CREATION AND SCRIPTURE

19 *For the choir director. A psalm of David.*

The heavens declare the glory
    of God,
and the expanse*i* proclaims
    the work of his hands.*j*

2 Day after day they pour out speech;
night after night
    they communicate knowledge.*A*

3 There is no speech; there are
    no words;
their voice is not heard.

4 Their message*B* has gone out
    to the whole earth,
and their words to the ends
    of the world.*k*

In the heavens he has pitched a tent
    for the sun.*l*

◦ **HOPE WORDS** ◦

*Nature preaches a sermon
of God's glory.*

5 It is like a bridegroom coming from
    his home;
it rejoices like an athlete
    running a course.

6 It rises from one end of the heavens
and circles to their other end;*m*
nothing is hidden from its heat.

7 The instruction of the LORD
    is perfect,
renewing one's life;*n*
the testimony of the LORD
    is trustworthy,
making the inexperienced wise.*o*

8 The precepts of the LORD are right,
making the heart glad;*p*
the command of the LORD is radiant,
making the eyes light up.*q*

9 The fear of the LORD is pure,
enduring forever;*r*
the ordinances of the LORD
    are reliable
and altogether righteous.*s*

10 They are more desirable
    than gold —
than an abundance of pure gold;*t*
and sweeter than honey
dripping from a honeycomb.*u*

11 In addition, your servant is warned
    by them,
and in keeping them there is
    an abundant reward.*v*

A 19:2 Or *Day to day pours out speech, and night to night communicates knowledge*   *B* 19:4 LXX, Sym, Syr, Vg; MT reads *line*

18:46 David praises God for delivering him from his enemies—proof that he was the living God and not a lifeless idol.
18:50 Remembering his covenant with David to give him a royal dynasty (see 2 Sam 7:11-16), God showed **loyalty to** his **anointed** king and to **his descendants**; this blessing would even impact the Gentiles.
19:1 Divine revelation takes two forms. *Special* revelation consists of the written and living Word of God. In it God reveals in detail who he is, what he has done, and what he requires. Only through the special revelation of Scripture can we know the gospel of Jesus Christ.
  General revelation consists of that which all people everywhere can know about God even if they have no access to Scripture. For instance, our moral conscience lets us know that we are accountable to our Creator (see Rom 2:14-16). Similarly, creation itself testifies to the existence of the One who made all things for his glory (see Rom 1:19-21).

The heavens declare [God's] glory by confirming that an omnipotent deity exists and has made things that are marvelous in scale and complexity.
19:2-6 God's existence is inextricably clear from the world he has made. **The sun** serves as a supreme example (19:4) of this truth. This masterpiece dominates the skies for all to see. **Nothing is hidden from its heat** (19:6). Without the sun, in fact, we would cease to exist; thus, it cannot be hanging in the heavens by chance. The Creator is greater than his creation. Atheistic evolution, then, is the worldview of a fool. Every watch demands a watchmaker.
19:7-10 After opening with the idea of general revelation, David moves to the topic of special revelation: the Word of God as recorded in Scripture (see the note on 19:1). First, Scripture **is perfect**; it lacks nothing. Everything you need to know to be what God expects you to be, in fact, has been revealed there. Second, the Bible **is trustworthy**; it's reliable (19:7). We are

enabled to make good and wise choices that reflect a divine perspective just from reading and trusting it. Third, **the precepts of the LORD**, Scripture's divine principles, lead a person down the right path. They point out the road we ought to take and promise us blessing for taking it. Fourth, the commandments of God are eye-opening (19:8). They illuminate dark situations so that we know how to proceed. Fifth, **the fear of the LORD is pure, enduring forever**. God reveals himself without contamination or flaw. His Word is unchanging and always relevant. Sixth, **the ordinances of the LORD are reliable and altogether righteous** (19:9). *Ordinances* are judgments or verdicts delivered from a judge's bench. We can be assured that anything that comes from the supreme Judge of the earth is right and true. Seventh, the teachings of Scripture **are more desirable than gold** (19:10). The Bible is more valuable than anything the world has to offer because it can provide what the world doesn't have.

12 Who perceives
his unintentional sins?
Cleanse me from my hidden faults.[a]
13 Moreover, keep your servant
from willful sins;[b]
do not let them rule me.[c]
Then I will be blameless
and cleansed
from blatant rebellion.[d]
14 May the words of my mouth
and the meditation of my heart
be acceptable to you,[e]
LORD, my rock and my Redeemer.[f]

DELIVERANCE IN BATTLE

20 *For the choir director. A psalm of David.*

1 May the LORD answer you in a day
of trouble;[g]
may the name of Jacob's God
protect you.[h]
2 May he send you help
from the sanctuary
and sustain you from Zion.[i]
3 May he remember all your offerings
and accept your burnt offering.[j]
Selah

4 May he give you what
your heart desires[k]
and fulfill your whole purpose.[l]
5 Let us shout for joy at your victory[m]
and lift the banner in the name
of our God.[n]
May the LORD fulfill
all your requests.[o]

6 Now I know that the LORD
gives victory to his anointed;[p]
he will answer him
from his holy heaven
with mighty victories
from his right hand.[q]
7 Some take pride in chariots,
and others in horses,
but we take pride in the name of the
LORD our God.[r]
8 They collapse and fall,
but we rise and stand firm.[s]
9 LORD, give victory to the king![t]
May he[A] answer us on the day
that we call.

THE KING'S VICTORY

21 *For the choir director. A psalm of David.*

LORD, the king finds joy
in your strength.
How greatly he rejoices
in your victory![u]
2 You have given him
his heart's desire[v]
and have not denied the request
of his lips.[w] *Selah*
3 For you meet him
with rich blessings;
you place a crown of pure gold
on his head.[x]
4 He asked you for life, and you gave it
to him —
length of days forever and ever.[y]
5 His glory is great
through your victory;
you confer majesty and splendor
on him.[z]
6 You give him blessings forever;[aa]
you cheer him with joy
in your presence.[ab]
7 For the king relies on the LORD;
through the faithful love
of the Most High
he is not shaken.[ac]

8 Your hand will capture
all your enemies;
your right hand will seize
those who hate you.[ad]
9 You will make them burn
like a fiery furnace
when you appear;
the LORD will engulf them
in his wrath,
and fire will devour them.[ae]
10 You will wipe their progeny
from the earth

[a] 19:12 Ps 90:8
[b] 19:13 Nm 15:30
[c] Gn 4:7
[d] Ps 51:7; Ezk 36:25
[e] 19:14 Ps 104:34
[f] Ps 78:35
[g] 20:1 Ps 50:15; 77:2; 102:2
[h] Ps 46:7,11
[i] 20:2 Ps 3:4; 110:2; 128:5
[j] 20:3 Ps 119:108
[k] 20:4 Ps 21:2; 145:19
[l] Ps 138:8
[m] 20:5 Ps 21:1
[n] Is 13:2
[o] Ps 21:2; 1Pt 3:12
[p] 20:6 Ps 18:50
[q] Ps 44:3; 98:1; 118:15
[r] 20:7 Ps 33:17; Is 31:1
[s] 20:8 Is 2:11,17; Mc 7:8
[t] 20:9 Ps 18:50
[u] 21:1 Ps 28:7-8; 59:16-17
[v] 21:2 Ps 20:4; 145:19
[w] Ps 20:5; 1Pt 3:12
[x] 21:3 2Sm 12:30; 1Ch 20:2
[y] 21:4 Ps 61:6; 91:16
[z] 21:5 Ps 8:5; 96:6
[aa] 21:6 1Ch 17:27
[ab] Ps 16:11
[ac] 21:7 Ps 10:6; 16:8
[ad] 21:8 Ex 15:6; Is 10:10
[ae] 21:9 Ps 50:3; 97:3; Mal 4:1

[A] 20:9 Or *LORD, save. May the king*

19:12-13 **Hidden faults** are those no one but God sees. **Willful sins** are wrongs that we actually plan.

20:4-5 The worshipers ask that God would grant the king's **desires** and **fulfill** his battle plans (20:4). They joyfully anticipate **victory** as the king raises **the banner in the name of [their] God** (20:5). David's victory would be seen as God's victory.

20:6 That the Lord would act with **his right hand** indicates that he would demonstrate his great power and strength.

20:7-8 Gentile kings trusted in their military might and boasted in their armaments. But the boast of David and his people was this: **We take pride in the name of the LORD** (20:7). Regardless of the size of the respective armies of Israel and their enemies, David knew that victory comes ultimately from God. Therefore, he trusted in the Lord's character, reputation, and sovereignty—and expected a great **collapse** of his enemy (20:8). As we face the conflicts of life, we too can be certain that our God is big enough to deal with them. The greater our focus *on* God, the greater our confidence *in* God.

21:6-7 What was the key to David's state of blessing? **The faithful love** (Hebrew, *hesed*), or covenant faithfulness, **of the Most High**.

a 21:10 1Kg 13:34; Ps 37:28; Is 14:20
b 21:11 Ps 2:1-3; 7:15-16; 10:2
c 21:12 Ps 7:12
d 21:13 Ps 59:16; 81:1
e 22:1 Mt 27:46; Mk 15:34
f Ps 10:1
g Ps 32:3; 38:8
h 22:2 Ps 42:3; 88:1
i 22:3 Ps 99:3
j 22:4 Ps 107:6
k 22:5 Ps 25:2; 31:1; 71:1; Is 49:23
l 22:6 Jb 25:6
m Ps 109:25; Is 53:3
n 22:7 Mt 27:39; Mk 15:29; Lk 23:35

o 22:8 Mt 27:43
p 22:9 Ps 71:6
q 22:10 Is 46:3; 49:1; Gl 1:15
r 22:11 2Kg 14:26; Ps 71:12; Is 63:5
s 22:12 Ps 68:30; Am 4:1
t 22:13 Ps 10:9; 17:12
u 22:14 Jb 30:16
v Jb 4:14; Ps 6:2; 32:3
w Nah 2:10
x 22:15 Ps 38:10
y Lm 4:4
z Ps 104:29
aa 22:16 Ps 59:6,14
ab Jn 20:25
ac 22:17 Lk 23:35
ad 22:18 Mt 27:35; Lk 23:34; Jn 19:24
ae 22:19 Ps 10:1
af Ps 70:5
ag 22:20 Jr 39:18
ah 22:21 Ps 35:17; 2Tm 4:17

and their offspring
from the human race.[A,a]
11 Though they intend to harm[B] you
and devise a wicked plan,
they will not prevail.[b]
12 Instead, you will put them to flight
when you ready your bowstrings
to shoot at them.[c]

13 Be exalted, Lord, in your strength;
we will sing and praise your might.[d]

FROM SUFFERING TO PRAISE

22 *For the choir director: according to "The Deer of the Dawn." A psalm of David.*

1 My God, my God, why have you
abandoned me?[e]
Why are you so far
from my deliverance[f]
and from my words of groaning?[g]
2 My God, I cry by day, but you
do not answer,
by night, yet I have no rest.[h]
3 But you are holy,
enthroned on the praises of Israel.[i]
4 Our fathers trusted in you;
they trusted, and you rescued them.[j]
5 They cried to you and were set free;
they trusted in you
and were not disgraced.[k]

⌐ HOPE WORDS ⌐

*Faith is acting like something
is so even when it is not so,
in order that it might be so
simply because God said so.*

6 But I am a worm and not a man,[l]
scorned by mankind and despised
by people.[m]
7 Everyone who sees me mocks me;
they sneer[c] and shake their heads:[n]
8 "He relies on[D] the Lord;
let him save him;

let the Lord[E] rescue him,
since he takes pleasure in him."[o]

9 It was you who brought me out
of the womb,
making me secure
at my mother's breast.[p]
10 I was given over to you at birth;[F]
you have been my God
from my mother's womb.[q]
11 Don't be far from me,
because distress is near
and there's no one to help.[r]

12 Many bulls surround me;
strong ones of Bashan encircle me.[s]
13 They open their mouths
against me —
lions, mauling and roaring.[t]
14 I am poured out like water,[u]
and all my bones are disjointed;[v]
my heart is like wax,
melting within me.[w]
15 My strength is dried up
like baked clay;[x]
my tongue sticks to the roof
of my mouth.[y]
You put me into the dust of death.[z]
16 For dogs have surrounded me;[aa]
a gang of evildoers has closed in
on me;
they pierced[G] my hands and my feet.[ab]
17 I can count all my bones;
people[H] look and stare at me.[ac]
18 They divided my garments
among themselves,
and they cast lots for my clothing.[ad]

19 But you, Lord, don't be far away.[ae]
My strength, come quickly
to help me.[af]
20 Rescue my life from the sword,[ag]
my only life[I] from the power
of these dogs.
21 Save me from the lion's mouth,[ah]
from the horns of wild oxen.

[A] 21:10 Or *the descendants of Adam*   [B] 21:11 Lit *they stretch out harm against*   [C] 22:7 Lit *separate with the lip*   [D] 22:8 Or *Rely on*   [E] 22:8 Lit *let him*   [F] 22:10 Lit *was cast on you from the womb*   [G] 22:16 Some Hb mss, LXX, Syr; other Hb mss read *me; like a lion*   [H] 22:17 Lit *they*
[I] 22:20 Lit *my only one*

22:1 It was this deep sense of being divinely **abandoned** that Jesus would experience and express on the cross (see Matt 27:46). Though these words were true of King David, they were fulfilled truly and fully in the Messiah, David's Son.
22:4-5 This history lesson serves as a reminder to David—and to us—to continue to trust the Lord in spite of circumstances.

22:8 These would be the very words used to taunt Jesus as he hung on the cross (see Matt 27:43).
22:9-10 Remember to rehearse your history of trusting in God's protection and provision as David did. It will help you trust in him today and tomorrow.
22:16, 18 The piercing of David's **hands** and **feet** and the casting of **lots** for his **clothing**

are not elaborated on in Scripture but proved prophetic in that they were fulfilled in Jesus's suffering (see Matt 27:35; cp. Isa 53:5; Zech 12:10).
22:20-21 Don't miss the exclamation, **You answered me!** (22:21). In the midst of his despair and petitions, David knows that God has heard his prayers. Therefore he celebrates.

You answered me![A]

22 I will proclaim your name
    to my brothers and sisters;
I will praise you in the assembly.[a]

23 You who fear the LORD, praise him![b]
All you descendants of Jacob,
    honor him!
All you descendants of Israel,
    revere him![c]

24 For he has not despised
    or abhorred
the torment of the oppressed.[d]
He did not hide his face from him[e]
but listened when he cried to him
    for help.[f]

25 I will give praise
    in the great assembly
because of you;[g]
I will fulfill my vows
before those who fear you.[B,h]

26 The humble will eat and be satisfied;[i]
those who seek the LORD
    will praise him.
May your hearts live forever![j]

27 All the ends of the earth
    will remember
and turn to the LORD.
All the families of the nations
will bow down before you,[k]

28 for kingship belongs to the LORD;
he rules the nations.[l]

29 All who prosper on earth will eat
    and bow down;
all those who go down to the dust
will kneel before him —
even the one who cannot preserve
    his life.[m]

30 Their descendants will serve him;

the next generation will be told
    about the Lord.[n]

31 They will come and declare
    his righteousness;
to a people yet to be born
they will declare what he has done.[o]

THE GOOD SHEPHERD

23 *A psalm of David.*
The LORD is my shepherd;[p]
I have what I need.[q]

2 He lets me lie down
    in green pastures;[r]
he leads me beside quiet waters.[s]

3 He renews my life;
he leads me along the right paths[c]
    for his name's sake.[t]

4 Even when I go
    through the darkest valley,[D]
I fear no danger,
for you are with me;[u]
your rod and your staff —
    they comfort me.[v]

⮜ HOPE WORDS ⮞

*Keep your eye on the Shepherd,
and you will make it
through the valley.*

---

5 You prepare a table before me
    in the presence of my enemies;
you anoint my head with oil;[w]
    my cup overflows.[x]

6 Only goodness and faithful love
    will pursue me
all the days of my life,[y]

[a] 22:22 Ps 40:10; Heb 2:12
[b] 22:23 Rv 19:5
[c] Ps 135:20
[d] 22:24 Ps 69:33
[e] Ezk 39:29
[f] Ps 28:2
[g] 22:25 Ps 35:18; 40:9-10
[h] Ps 61:8
[i] 22:26 Ps 107:9
[j] Ps 40:16; 69:32
[k] 22:27 Ps 2:8; 86:9
[l] 22:28 1Ch 16:31; 2Ch 20:6; Mal 1:14; Rv 15:3
[m] 22:29 Is 45:23; Rm 14:11; Php 2:10

[n] 22:30 Ps 102:18,28
[o] 22:31 Ps 71:18; 78:6
[p] 23:1 Gn 48:15; Ps 78:52; Jr 31:10; Ezk 34:11-13; Jn 10:11
[q] Ps 34:9-10; Php 4:19
[r] 23:2 Ps 65:11-13; Ezk 34:14
[s] Ps 36:8
[t] 23:3 Ps 5:8; Pr 4:11
[u] 23:4 Is 43:2
[v] Mc 7:14
[w] 23:5 Ps 92:10
[x] Ps 16:5
[y] 23:6 Ps 25:7; 109:21

[A] 22:21 Or *oxen you rescued me*   [B] 22:25 Lit *him*   [C] 23:3 Or *me in paths of righteousness*   [D] 23:4 Or *the valley of the shadow of death*

22:22-23 Those who have experienced the goodness of God can't help but worship him and exhort others to do the same.
22:27-28 Though he was chosen by God to serve as king, David recognizes that ultimately **kingship belongs to the LORD**. All **the nations** will one day submit to the kingdom of God when the Messiah comes to reign (22:28).
23:1 David started out as a **shepherd** (see 1 Sam 16:11-12; 17:15, 34-37), so he describes his relationship to God in those terms. Some Christians have trusted God to save them for eternity, but they don't have much confidence that he can provide for them in history. David's beautiful, poetic testimony can help instill in us the confidence that he can.
23:2 God met David's *spiritual* needs. The cares and struggles of this world can leave us exhausted. Such times are opportunities

to realize our dependence on the Lord for spiritual refreshment.
23:3 God met David's *directional* needs. Sheep are prone to wander and become lost; they need guidance. Many cars today have navigational systems to warn you to return to the right road when you deviate. Through his Word and his Spirit, God leads us along the right paths in life—and reroutes us when we foolishly become wayward. Why? **For his name's sake**—that is, so that others can hear us say, "My God has brought me here."
23:4 God met David's *emotional* needs. He provides **comfort** with his **rod** (used to beat wild animals that attack the sheep) and his **staff** (used to guide the sheep and pull them back from harm). When life takes you **through the darkest valley**, receive consolation in knowing that your divine Shepherd has power in one hand and grace in the other.

23:5 God met David's *physical* needs. God fed him when he hungered and anointed him **with oil** when he needed healing. God's provision never runs dry. That's why David's **cup overflow[ed]**.
23:6 God met David's *eternal* needs. Shepherds often have sheepdogs that keep the sheep from wandering. The divine Shepherd has two sheepdogs named **goodness and faithful love**. Sometimes they bark and nip at you when you wander from the fold. But they do so with the intent of driving you back into fellowship with your Shepherd, so that you may eternally **dwell in the house of the LORD**.
Our Lord Jesus Christ lays down his life for his sheep (see John 10:11), and through his wounds we are healed (see 1 Pet 2:24). If you have gone astray, return to him (1 Pet 2:25). He will welcome you.

a 23:6 Ps 27:4-6
b 24:1 Dt 10:14; Ps 89:11; 1Co 10:26
c 24:2 Ps 104:5; Pr 8:29
d 24:3 Ps 15:1
e 24:4 Jb 22:30; Ps 73:1; Mt 5:8
f Ps 31:6; 119:37
g 24:5 Ps 115:13
h Ps 65:5
i 24:6 Ps 27:8
j 24:7 Ps 118:19-20; Is 26:2
k 24:8 Ex 15:3; Ps 76:3-6
l 24:10 Is 24:23
m 25:1 Ps 38:15; 86:4
n 25:2 Ps 31:1; 71:1

o 25:2 Ps 13:4; 41:11
p 25:3 Is 49:23
q Pr 2:22; Is 21:2
r 25:4 Ex 33:13; Ps 27:11; 86:11
s 25:5 Jn 16:13
t Ex 15:2
u Ps 40:1
v 25:6 Ps 98:3; 103:17
w 25:7 Jb 13:26
x Ps 51:1
y Neh 13:22
z 25:8 Ps 100:5; Nah 1:7
aa Ps 32:8
ab 25:9 Ps 23:3
ac Ex 18:20; Ps 86:11
ad 25:10 Ps 40:11; 103:17-18
ae 25:11 Jb 7:21; Ps 103:3; Jr 31:34

and I will dwell in[A] the house
  of the Lord
as long as I live.[B,a]

THE KING OF GLORY

24 *A psalm of David.*

The earth and everything in it,
the world and its inhabitants,
belong to the Lord;[b]
2 for he laid its foundation
  on the seas
and established it on the rivers.[c]

3 Who may ascend the mountain
  of the Lord?
Who may stand in his holy place?[d]
4 The one who has clean hands
  and a pure heart,[e]
who has not appealed
  to[c] what is false,[f]
and who has not sworn deceitfully.
5 He will receive blessing
  from the Lord,[g]
and righteousness[D] from the God
  of his salvation.[h]
6 Such is the generation of those
  who inquire of him,
who seek the face of the God
  of Jacob.[E,i]   *Selah*

7 Lift up your heads, you gates!
Rise up, ancient doors!
Then the King of glory will come in.[j]
8 Who is this King of glory?
The Lord, strong and mighty,
the Lord, mighty in battle.[k]
9 Lift up your heads, you gates!
Rise up, ancient doors!
Then the King of glory will come in.
10 Who is he, this King of glory?
The Lord of Armies,
he is the King of glory.[l]   *Selah*

DEPENDENCE ON THE LORD

25 *Of David.*

Lord, I appeal to you.[F,m]
2 My God, I trust in you.
Do not let me be disgraced;[n]

do not let my enemies gloat
  over me.[o]
3 No one who waits for you
  will be disgraced;[p]
those who act treacherously
  without cause
will be disgraced.[q]

4 Make your ways known
  to me, Lord;
teach me your paths.[r]
5 Guide me in your truth
  and teach me,[s]
for you are the God
  of my salvation;[t]
I wait for you all day long.[u]
6 Remember, Lord, your compassion
and your faithful love,
for they have existed
  from antiquity.[G,v]
7 Do not remember the sins
  of my youth[w]
or my acts of rebellion;[x]
in keeping with your faithful love,
  remember me
because of your goodness, Lord.[y]

⮑ HOPE WORDS ⮐

*Truth is fundamentally
God-based knowledge.*

---

8 The Lord is good and upright;[z]
therefore he shows sinners
  the way.[aa]
9 He leads the humble in what
  is right[ab]
and teaches them his way.[ac]
10 All the Lord's ways show
  faithful love and truth
to those who keep his covenant
  and decrees.[ad]
11 Lord, for the sake of your name,
forgive my iniquity, for
  it is immense.[ae]

A 23:6 LXX, Sym, Syr, Tg, Vg, Jer; MT reads *will return to*   B 23:6 Lit *Lord for length of days*; traditionally *Lord forever*   C 24:4 Lit *not lifted up his soul to*   D 24:5 Or *vindication*   E 24:6 LXX; some Hb mss, Syr read *seek your face, God of Jacob*; some Hb mss read *seek your face, Jacob*   F 25:1 Or *To you, Lord, I lift up my soul*   G 25:6 Or *everlasting*

24:4 To have **clean hands and a pure heart** is to have a life that is clean inside and out. **24:7-10** King David calls for the **gates** of the holy city of Jerusalem to be opened for the triumphal procession of **the King of glory**, the Lord Almighty (24:7). The historical context of this psalm may have been David's return from battle with the ark of the covenant, which was considered the Lord's

throne (see, e.g., Exod 25:22; 1 Sam 4:4; Isa 37:16). Above it was the divine **King**—the **Lord of Armies**—who was **mighty in battle** (Ps 24:8, 10) and gave victory to Israel. The Messiah too will one day defeat his enemies in the tribulation and establish his millennial kingdom. **25:6-7** David appeals to God based on the loyal, loving relationship they shared. The

greater his intimacy with God, the greater his dependence on God. The greater his dependence on God, the greater the expectation for intervention and deliverance. This is why our covenant relationship with Christ is so critical. **25:11** David asks God to **forgive [his] iniquity**, which could block the flow of covenant blessings.

Glory

YEARS AGO, MY LIFE WAS turned upside down and inside out because of some depressing news: basketball legend Michael Jordan was retiring. (That's enough to ruin any day.) He was the man who had taken pro-basketball to another level. The media would show clips of "Michael Magic," how he would go up high with only moments left on the clock and hit the shot to win the game. It was impossible for anyone to stop him when he decided that the ball belonged to him. Nothing compared to watching him run down the court, leave the floor, hang in midair, and dunk the ball. The commentator would say, "Ladies and gentlemen, there's living proof that men can fly."

Regardless of which team anyone cheered for, everyone wanted to see Mike. Chicago Bulls' games were always sold out. Do you know why? Because Michael had glory. He had a unique ability to do things that even the best in the game found amazing. That's what glory looks like.

Glory is the result of demonstrating extraordinary quality. It is a by-product created from showing everyone else something truly remarkable. In the case of God, glory comes as a result of not just God showing what he can do but showing who he is. The attributes of God are glorious. Everything that makes him who he is compels all of creation not just to see his glory but to give him praise.

Through his creation, his works, his Word, and his Spirit, God shows us that more than any other, he is worthy of our admiration. He is the "King of glory" (PS 24:7), and we should be captivated by his presence above all others. When he's trying to get our attention, we should never turn away. One of the many amazing aspects of Jesus's life is the fact that the Son made it possible for us to see the Father. And when we truly see God for who he is, we will never feel the need to look elsewhere.

a 25:12 Ps 31:19
b Ps 37:23
c 25:13 Ps 37:11; 69:36
d 25:14 Jn 7:17; 1Co 2:9
e 25:15 Ps 31:4; 124:7
f 25:16 Ps 70:5; 73:14
g 25:17 Lm 1:20
h Jr 10:19
i 25:18 Ps 31:7
j Rm 11:27; 1Jn 3:5
k 25:19 Ps 3:1
l Ps 9:13
m 25:20 Ps 17:8; 31:15
n Ps 86:2
o 25:21 Ps 41:12
p 25:22 Ps 34:22; 130:8
q 26:1 2Kg 20:3; Ps 7:8

r 26:2 Ps 7:9; 17:3; 139:23
s 26:3 Ps 40:10; 86:11
t 26:4-5 Ps 1:1; Pr 4:14-15
u 26:6 Ps 73:13
v Ps 43:4
w 26:7 Jnh 2:9
x Ps 9:1
y 26:8 Ps 27:4
z 26:9 Ps 28:3
aa 26:10 Ex 23:8; Dt 16:19; Ps 15:5
ab 26:11 Jb 31:6; Ps 7:8
ac 26:12 Ps 27:11
ad Ps 35:18; 40:9-10
27:1 Is 60:20; Mc 7:8
af Ps 28:8; 118:6
ag 27:2 Ps 14:4
ah Ps 9:3

12 Who is this person who fears
the LORD?[a]
He will show him the way
he should choose.[b]
13 He will live a good life,
and his descendants will inherit
the land.[A,c]
14 The secret counsel of the LORD
is for those who fear him,
and he reveals his covenant to them.[d]
15 My eyes are always on the LORD,
for he will pull my feet
out of the net.[e]

16 Turn to me and be gracious to me,
for I am alone and afflicted.[f]
17 The distresses of my heart
increase;[B,g]
bring me out of my sufferings.[h]
18 Consider my affliction and trouble,[i]
and forgive all my sins.[j]
19 Consider my enemies;
they are numerous,[k]
and they hate me violently.[l]
20 Guard me and rescue me;[m]
do not let me be put to shame,
for I take refuge in you.[n]
21 May integrity and what is right
watch over me,
for I wait for you.[o]

22 God, redeem Israel, from all
its distresses.[p]

PRAYER FOR VINDICATION
26 *Of David.*
Vindicate me, LORD,
because I have lived with integrity
and have trusted in the LORD
without wavering.[q]

2 Test me, LORD, and try me;
examine my heart and mind.[r]
3 For your faithful love guides me,[c]
and I live by your truth.[s]

4 I do not sit with the worthless
or associate with hypocrites.
5 I hate a crowd of evildoers,
and I do not sit with the wicked.[t]
6 I wash my hands in innocence[u]
and go around your altar, LORD,[v]
7 raising my voice in thanksgiving[w]
and telling about
your wondrous works.[x]

8 LORD, I love the house
where you dwell,
the place where your glory resides.[y]
9 Do not destroy me
along with sinners,
or my life along with men
of bloodshed[z]
10 in whose hands are evil schemes
and whose right hands are filled
with bribes.[aa]

11 But I live with integrity;
redeem me and be gracious
to me.[ab]
12 My foot stands on level ground;[ac]
I will bless the LORD
in the assemblies.[ad]

MY STRONGHOLD
27 *Of David.*
The LORD is my light
and my salvation —
whom should I fear?[ae]
The LORD is the stronghold
of my life —
whom should I dread?[af]
2 When evildoers came against me
to devour my flesh,[ag]
my foes and my enemies stumbled
and fell.[ah]
3 Though an army deploys
against me,

A 25:13 Or *earth*   B 25:17 Or *Relieve the distresses of my heart*   C 26:3 Lit *love is in front of my eyes*

25:12-14 To fear God is to take him seriously. This disposition toward God is reflected by our obedience to him. God rewards **those who fear** him with his inside information— **secret counsel** that is particular to the person and his individual experience of God's **covenant** (25:14).
25:22 The king doesn't want God to rescue him alone but the whole congregation of **Israel**. His request is a reminder that as we pray for ourselves, we ought to look to the needs of fellow believers. Let's ask God to

work through our requests so that he might benefit others as well.
26:3-5 David validates his integrity by pointing to his life and his actions.
26:6-8 To **wash [his] hands** is to metaphorically cleanse his life of evil deeds. David also offers the appropriate sacrifices at the **altar** to atone for sin (26:6). This enables him to attend public worship, where God's **glory** was manifested, so that he could give thanks and proclaim God's **wondrous works** (26:7-8). We are called to do the same: confess our sins to God, celebrate

the atoning sacrifice of Christ through Communion, and join together corporately with God's people to worship God for who he is, what he has done, and what we are trusting him to do.
26:9-12 The king concludes with his desire to separate himself from evildoers (26:9-10), **live with integrity** (26:11), and **bless the LORD in the assemblies** of God's people (26:12). These are key steps for us to take, too.
27:1-3 As his **light**, God illuminates the darkness that surrounds David. As his **salvation** (27:1), God delivers him physically and spiritually.

[a]27:3 Ps 3:6
[b]27:4 Ps 23:6; 26:8
[c]Ps 93:5
[d]Mal 3:1
[e]27:5 Ps 31:20; 91:1; Is 25:4
[f]27:6 Ps 3:3
[g]Ps 54:6; 116:17
[h]Eph 5:19
[i]27:7 Ps 4:3; 30:10
[j]27:8 Ps 24:6; 105:4
[k]27:9 Ps 69:17; 102:2; 143:7
[l]Ps 6:1
[m]Ps 40:17
[n]27:9-10 Ps 37:28; 94:14
[o]27:11 Ps 25:4; 26:12

[p]27:12 Ps 35:11; 41:2; Mt 26:59-60
[q]27:13 Ex 33:19; Ps 116:9; 142:5
[r]27:14 Jos 1:6
[s]Ps 37:34; 130:5
[t]28:1 Ps 83:1
[u]Ps 88:4; 143:7
[v]28:2 Ps 28:2; 134:2; 141:2; 1Tm 2:8
[w]28:3 Ps 26:9-10
[x]28:4 Jr 50:29; Rv 18:6; 22:12
[y]28:5 Jb 34:26-28; Is 5:12
[z]28:6 Ps 31:22
[aa]28:7 Gn 15:1; Dt 33:29; Ps 3:3; 5:12; 18:2; 119:114
[ab]Ps 59:17; 69:30

HOPE WORDS

You may not be in an ideal situation, but you have an ideal God.

my heart will not be afraid;
though a war breaks out against me,
I will still be confident.[a]

4 I have asked one thing
from the LORD;
it is what I desire:
to dwell in the house of the LORD
all the days of my life,[b]
gazing on the beauty of the LORD[c]
and seeking him in his temple.[d]
5 For he will conceal me in his shelter
in the day of adversity;
he will hide me under the cover
of his tent;
he will set me high on a rock.[e]
6 Then my head will be high
above my enemies around me;[f]
I will offer sacrifices in his tent
with shouts of joy.[g]
I will sing and make music
to the LORD.[h]

7 LORD, hear my voice when I call;
be gracious to me and answer me.[i]
8 My heart says this about you:
"Seek[A] his face."
LORD, I will seek your face.[j]
9 Do not hide your face from me;[k]
do not turn your servant away
in anger.[l]
You have been my helper;[m]
do not leave me or abandon me,
God of my salvation.
10 Even if my father and mother
abandon me,
the LORD cares for me.[n]

11 Because of my adversaries,
show me your way, LORD,
and lead me on a level path.[o]
12 Do not give me over to the will
of my foes,

for false witnesses rise up
against me,
breathing violence.[p]
13 I am certain that I will see the
LORD's goodness
in the land of the living.[q]
14 Wait for the LORD;
be strong, and let your heart
be courageous.[r]
Wait for the LORD.[s]

MY STRENGTH

28

Of David.

LORD, I call to you;
my rock, do not be deaf to me.[t]
If you remain silent to me,
I will be like those going down
to the Pit.[u]
2 Listen to the sound of my pleading
when I cry to you for help,
when I lift up my hands
toward your holy sanctuary.[v]

3 Do not drag me away
with the wicked,
with the evildoers,
who speak in friendly ways
with their neighbors
while malice is in their hearts.[w]
4 Repay them according to what
they have done —
according to the evil of their deeds.
Repay them according to the work
of their hands;
give them back what they deserve.[x]
5 Because they do not consider
what the LORD has done
or the work of his hands,
he will tear them down and not
rebuild them.[y]

6 Blessed be the LORD,
for he has heard the sound
of my pleading.[z]
7 The LORD is my strength
and my shield;
my heart trusts in him,
and I am helped.[aa]
Therefore my heart celebrates,
and I give thanks to him
with my song.[ab]

[A]27:8 The command is pl in Hb

27:8 To **seek [the] face** of God is to pursue God's presence in order to experience his favor and fellowship.
27:10 If everyone were to abandon him—even his **father and mother**—he would not be left void of care. God would fill the gap.

27:14 *Waiting* on God does not mean being passive; rather, it is an active engagement of life's challenges within the revealed will of God as we hope for his deliverance.
28:5 People devote themselves to wickedness because they fail to **consider . . . the work of**

[God's] hands. They are without excuse and incur his wrath (see Rom 1:18-23).

[a] 28:8 Ps 20:6; 27:1
[b] 28:9 Ps 33:12; Is 40:11
[c] 29:1-2 1Ch 16:28-29; Ps 96:7-9
[d] 29:3 Jb 37:4-5; Ps 18:13; 104:7
[e] 29:4 Ps 68:33
[f] 29:5 Ps 104:16
[g] 29:6 Ps 114:4,6
[h] Dt 3:8-9
[i] 29:7 Dt 4:12,33
[j] 29:8 Nm 13:26
[k] 29:9 Jb 39:1-3
Is 24:1,3
[m] 29:10 Ps 9:7; 10:17

[n] 29:11 Ps 28:8; 68:35
[o] Php 4:7
[p] 30:1 Ps 3:3
[q] Ps 25:2; 35:19
[r] 30:2 Ps 88:13
[s] 30:3 Ps 86:13
[t] Ps 28:1; 88:4; 143:7
[u] 30:4 Ps 50:5; 149:1
[v] 30:5 Ps 103:9; Is 54:7-8; 2Co 4:17
[w] 30:6 Ps 10:6; 62:2,6
[x] 30:7 Ps 20:8
[y] Ps 104:29
[z] 30:8 Ps 119:58
[aa] 30:9 Ps 6:5; 88:10-12
[ab] 30:10 Ps 4:1; 27:7
[ac] 30:11 Ec 3:4; Is 61:10; Jr 31:13

8 The LORD is the strength of his people;[A]
  he is a stronghold of salvation
    for his anointed.[a]
9 Save your people,
    bless your possession,
  shepherd them, and carry
    them forever.[b]

THE VOICE OF THE LORD

29 A psalm of David.

  Ascribe to the LORD,
    you heavenly beings,[B]
  ascribe to the LORD glory and strength.
2 Ascribe to the LORD the glory due
    his name;
  worship the LORD
  in the splendor of his holiness.[C,c]

3 The voice of the LORD is
    above the waters.
  The God of glory thunders —
    the LORD, above the vast water,[d]
4 the voice of the LORD in power,
  the voice of the LORD in splendor.[e]
5 The voice of the LORD
    breaks the cedars;
  the LORD shatters the cedars
    of Lebanon.[f]
6 He makes Lebanon skip like a calf,[g]
  and Sirion, like a young wild ox.[h]
7 The voice of the LORD flashes
    flames of fire.[i]
8 The voice of the LORD shakes
    the wilderness;
  the LORD shakes the wilderness
    of Kadesh.[j]
9 The voice of the LORD
    makes the deer give birth[D,k]
  and strips the woodlands bare.[l]

  In his temple all cry, "Glory!"

10 The LORD sits enthroned over the flood;
   the LORD sits enthroned,
     King forever.[m]

11 The LORD gives his people strength;[n]
   the LORD blesses his people
     with peace.[o]

JOY IN THE MORNING

30 A psalm; a dedication song for the house. Of David.

1 I will exalt you, LORD,
  because you have lifted me up[p]
  and have not allowed my enemies
    to triumph over me.[q]
2 LORD my God,
  I cried to you for help, and you
    healed me.[r]
3 LORD, you brought me up
    from Sheol;[s]
  you spared me from among those
  going down[E] to the Pit.[t]

4 Sing to the LORD, you his faithful ones,
  and praise his holy name.[u]
5 For his anger lasts only a moment,
  but his favor, a lifetime.
  Weeping may stay overnight,
  but there is joy in the morning.[v]

6 When I was secure, I said,
  "I will never be shaken."[w]
7 LORD, when you showed your favor,
  you made me stand
    like a strong mountain;[x]
  when you hid your face,
    I was terrified.[y]
8 LORD, I called to you;
  I sought favor from my Lord:[z]
9 "What gain is there in my death,
  if I go down to the Pit?
  Will the dust praise you?
  Will it proclaim your truth?[aa]
10 LORD, listen and be gracious to me;
   LORD, be my helper."[ab]

11 You turned my lament into dancing;
   you removed my sackcloth
   and clothed me with gladness,[ac]

[A] 28:8 Some Hb mss, LXX, Syr; other Hb mss read *strength for them*   [B] 29:1 Or *you sons of gods*, or *you sons of mighty ones*   [C] 29:2 Or *in holy attire*, or *in holy appearance*   [D] 29:9 Or *the oaks shake*   [E] 30:3 Some Hb mss, LXX, Theod, Orig, Syr; other Hb mss, Aq, Sym, Tg, Jer read *from going down*

28:9 David was the king, the shepherd of God's sheep. Yet he knew that the Lord is the ultimate **shepherd**, both for him personally and for Israel.

29:2 Worship is not merely something created beings do for God; it is something we rightly owe him.

29:3-9 As Psalm 19:1 says, "The heavens declare the glory of God." And in this passage we see that creation testifies to the majesty of the Creator in a thunderstorm. We must remember that such a spectacular display is

not the work of so-called Mother Nature, but of Father God. And we must give the Lord the exaltation he deserves.

29:10-11 God has used his creation to judge wickedness, as at **the flood** (see Gen 7:11-24), and to deliver his people, as at the Red Sea (see Exod 14:15-31).

30:2-3 David had apparently suffered from a serious physical ailment, but God **healed** him and rescued him **from Sheol**, the grave.

30:5 God's **anger** with his children is temporary. He is eager to reverse course and bring

blessing. God does not enjoy bringing discipline but prefers to shower us with his grace.

30:6 In other words, he had become proud and independent from God. God hates pride. It was the sin of Satan. Therefore, a prideful heart will always drive him away. "God resists the proud but gives grace to the humble" (1 Pet 5:5).

30:11-12 When we experience the deliverance of God in whatever form it takes—spiritual, physical, emotional, relational, or financial—let our testimony be the same as David's: **LORD my God, I will praise you forever** (30:12).

Getting Back What You Have Lost

A MAN FRANTICALLY RUSHED INTO HIS house and told his wife that they had a major problem. Calmly she asked, "What is it?"

"There is water in the carburetor of the car," he replied. "It won't run."

"Water is in the carburetor?" She paused to think about that statement because she knew her husband always took their car to the shop if it needed to be worked on.

"Honey," she said, softly, "I didn't know you knew what a carburetor is. How are you sure that there is water in it?"

A look of helplessness drifted over her husband's face. "Because the car is in the swimming pool," he said. "So, I guess there's water in the carburetor."

This man's situation made him feel hopeless. After all, car ownership doesn't sink much lower than when the vehicle is at the bottom of a pool. Maybe you've never experienced something as drastic as what I have just described, but I would imagine that you have experienced your own time of hopelessness. A time when you felt like giving up—maybe on a situation, a job, a relationship . . . or even on yourself.

If you have been there, or if you are there right now, I point you to the message of Easter: no matter how hopeless things may appear (and nothing can be more hopeless than the Son of God dying on a cross!), God can give back what is lost. When you hope in him, he can turn things around. Remember: "Weeping may stay overnight, but there is joy in the morning" (PS 30:5).

As believers, we have a tremendous reason to hope: God loves us, and he has done everything in his awesome power to make that love available at any time and place. He went so far as to put his Son on the cross so that he could give us hope. All we have to do is ask him to give us the hope we need. He understands the pressures that we feel and knows exactly what we need.

If you are struggling with a situation that seems hopeless, know that you are not alone. Christ, your Savior, is right beside you. As you pray to him, open your heart to his Word. Nothing you face is beyond his ability to heal and restore. Therefore, never give up.

Sometimes our breakthroughs are delayed because God is waiting to see if we will turn to him or if we will keep trying to fix things ourselves—to somehow drive our cars right back out of the pool. But when we put our hope in God, he will move in our lives in mighty ways. So trust him. The same God that raised Jesus from the dead can help you too.

a 30:12 Ps 44:8; 108:1
b 31:1 Ps 25:2
c 31:2 Ps 71:1-2
d 31:3 Ps 18:2; 71:3
e 31:3 Ps 23:3; 25:11
f 31:4 Ps 25:15; 46:1
g 31:5 Lk 23:46
h Ps 25:5
i 31:6 Ps 26:5; Jnh 2:8
j 31:7 Ps 10:14
k 31:8 Dt 32:30
l Jb 36:16
m 31:9 Ps 69:17
n Ps 6:7; 63:1
o 31:10 Ps 102:3
p 32:3; 38:3

q 31:11 Jb 19:13; Ps 38:11; 88:8,18
r 31:12 Ps 88:5; Ec 9:5
s 31:13 Jr 20:10
t Ps 41:7; Mt 27:1
u 31:14 Ps 140:6
v 31:15 Jb 14:5; 24:1
w Ps 59:1
x 31:16 Nm 6:25
y Ps 6:4; 119:135
z 31:17 Ps 25:2-3,20
aa Ps 94:17; 115:17
ab 31:18 Ps 120:2
ac 1Sm 2:3; Ps 94:4
ad 31:19 Ps 5:11; 23:5
ae 31:20 Ps 27:5; 32:7
af 31:21 Ps 28:6
ag 31:22 Ps 88:5; Is 38:11-12
ah Ps 66:19; 145:19

12 so that I can sing to you and not
be silent.
LORD my God, I will praise
you forever.*a*

A PLEA FOR PROTECTION

31 *For the choir director. A psalm of David.*

LORD, I seek refuge in you;
let me never be disgraced.*b*
Save me by your righteousness.

2 Listen closely to me;
rescue me quickly.
Be a rock of refuge for me,
a mountain fortress to save me.*c*

3 For you are my rock
and my fortress;*d*
you lead and guide me
for your name's sake.*e*

4 You will free me from the net
that is secretly set for me,
for you are my refuge.*f*

5 Into your hand I entrust my spirit;*g*
you have redeemed me,^A LORD,
God of truth.*h*

6 I^B hate those who are devoted
to worthless idols,
but I trust in the LORD.*i*

7 I will rejoice and be glad
in your faithful love
because you have seen
my affliction.
You know the troubles of my soul*j*

8 and have not handed me over
to the enemy.*k*
You have set my feet
in a spacious place.*l*

9 Be gracious to me, LORD,
because I am in distress;*m*
my eyes are worn out
from frustration —
my whole being^c as well.*n*

10 Indeed, my life is consumed
with grief
and my years with groaning;*o*
my strength has failed
because of my iniquity,^D
and my bones waste away.*p*

11 I am ridiculed by all my adversaries
and even by my neighbors.

I am dreaded by my acquaintances;
those who see me in the street
run from me.*q*

12 I am forgotten: gone from memory
like a dead person —
like broken pottery.*r*

13 I have heard the gossip of many;
terror is on every side.*s*
When they conspired against me,
they plotted to take my life.*t*

14 But I trust in you, LORD;
I say, "You are my God."*u*

15 The course of my life is
in your power;*v*
rescue me from the power
of my enemies
and from my persecutors.*w*

16 Make your face shine on
your servant;*x*
save me by your faithful love.*y*

17 LORD, do not let me be disgraced
when I call on you.*z*
Let the wicked be disgraced;
let them be quiet^E,F in Sheol.*aa*

18 Let lying lips*ab*
that arrogantly speak
against the righteous
in proud contempt be silenced.*ac*

19 How great is your goodness
that you have stored up for those
who fear you
and accomplished in the sight
of everyone^G
for those who take
refuge in you.*ad*

20 You hide them in the protection
of your presence;
you conceal them in a shelter
from human schemes,
from quarrelsome tongues.*ae*

21 Blessed be the LORD,
for he has wondrously shown
his faithful love to me
in a city under siege.*af*

22 In my alarm I said,
"I am cut off from your sight."*ag*
But you heard the sound
of my pleading
when I cried to you for help.*ah*

---

^A 31:5 Or *spirit. Redeem me*   ^B 31:6 One Hb ms, LXX, Syr, Vg, Jer read *You*   ^C 31:9 Lit *my soul and my belly*   ^D 31:10 LXX, Syr, Sym read *affliction*
^E 31:17 LXX reads *brought down*   ^F 31:17 Or *them wail*   ^G 31:19 Or *of the descendants of Adam*

31:2 Such a stronghold would be impregnable to enemy attack. There is no safer shelter than living under the Lord's covenant covering.
31:5 Like Jesus on the cross, David confessed to God, **Into your hand I entrust my spirit** (see Luke 23:46).

31:9-14 Let David's transparency before God be an example to you. When you have been wounded by life, take these divinely inspired prayers and make them your own.
31:19 God has piled (**stored up**) his **goodness** high and is ready to dispense it to

those who take him seriously, honor him, and look to him with expectation. "What no eye has seen, no ear has heard, and no human heart has conceived—God has prepared these things for those who love him" (1 Cor 2:9).

23 Love the LORD, all his faithful ones.[a]
The LORD protects the loyal,
but fully repays the arrogant.[b]
24 Be strong, and let your heart
be courageous,
all you who put your hope
in the LORD.[c]

THE JOY OF FORGIVENESS

32 *Of David. A Maskil.*

How joyful is the one
whose transgression is forgiven,
whose sin is covered![d]
2 How joyful is a person whom
the LORD does not charge
with iniquity[e]
and in whose spirit is no deceit![f]

3 When I kept silent, my bones
became brittle
from my groaning all day long.[g]
4 For day and night your hand
was heavy on me;[h]
my strength was drained[A]
as in the summer's heat.[i]   *Selah*
5 Then I acknowledged my sin to you
and did not conceal my iniquity.
I said, "I will confess
my transgressions to the LORD,"
and you forgave the guilt of my sin.[j]
Selah

6 Therefore let everyone
who is faithful pray to you
immediately.[B,k]
When great floodwaters come,
they will not reach him.[l]
7 You are my hiding place;[m]
you protect me from trouble.[n]
You surround me with joyful shouts
of deliverance.   *Selah*

8 I will instruct you and show you
the way to go;[o]

with my eye on you,
I will give counsel.[p]
9 Do not be like a horse or mule,
without understanding,
that must be controlled with bit
and bridle
or else it will not come near you.[q]

10 Many pains come to the wicked,[r]
but the one who trusts in the LORD
will have faithful love
surrounding him.[s]
11 Be glad in the LORD and rejoice,
you righteous ones;
shout for joy,
all you upright in heart.[t]

PRAISE TO THE CREATOR

33 Rejoice in the LORD,
you righteous ones;
praise from the upright is beautiful.[u]
2 Praise the LORD with the lyre;
make music to him
with a ten-stringed harp.[v]
3 Sing a new song to him;[w]
play skillfully on the strings,
with a joyful shout.[x]

4 For the word of the LORD is right,
and all his work is trustworthy.[y]
5 He loves righteousness and justice;[z]
the earth is full of the LORD's
unfailing love.[aa]

6 The heavens were made by the word
of the LORD,[ab]
and all the stars, by the breath
of his mouth.[ac]
7 He gathers the water of the sea
into a heap;[C]
he puts the depths into storehouses.[ad]
8 Let the whole earth fear the LORD;
let all the inhabitants of the world
stand in awe of him.[ae]

[a] 31:23 Ps 30:4
[b] Ps 94:2
[c] 31:24 Ps 27:14
[d] 32:1 Ps 85:2
[e] 32:1-2 Rm 4:7-8
[f] 32:2 Jn 1:47
[g] 32:3 Ps 31:10; 38:8
[h] 32:4 Jb 23:2; Ps 38:2
[i] Ps 22:15; 39:10
[j] 32:5 Lv 26:40; Ps 38:18; Pr 28:13; 1Jn 1:9
[k] 32:6 Is 55:6
[l] Ps 124:4-5; Is 43:2
[m] 32:7 Pr 3:21; 91:1
[n] Ps 121:7
[o] 32:8 Ps 25:8,12

[p] 32:8 Ps 33:18; 73:24
[q] 32:9 Pr 26:3; Jms 3:3
[r] 32:10 Pr 13:21; Rm 2:9
[s] Ps 5:12
[t] 32:11 Ps 64:10; 68:3; 97:12
[u] 33:1 Ps 32:11; 147:1; Php 4:4
[v] 33:2 Ps 92:3; 144:9
[w] 33:3 Ps 40:3; 96:1; Is 42:10
[x] Ps 150:4
[y] 33:4 Ps 19:8
[z] 33:5 Ps 11:7; 37:28
[aa] Ps 119:64
[ab] 33:6 Heb 11:3; 2Pt 3:5
[ac] Jb 26:13; Ps 104:30
[ad] 33:7 Ex 15:8; Jos 3:13; Ps 78:13
[ae] 33:8 Ps 67:7; 96:9

[A] 32:4 Hb obscure   [B] 32:6 Lit *you at a time of finding*   [C] 33:7 LXX, Tg, Syr, Vg, Jer read *sea as in a bottle*

31:23-24 David exhorts his fellow worshipers—including you and me—to **love** God, **be strong** and **courageous**, and **put [their] hope** in him. God is worthy of this because of who he is and the support he promises to all who look to him. Let this psalm challenge you to know God's character so you can appeal to it when you need him most.
32:1-2 The apostle Paul writes, "All have sinned and fall short of the glory of God" (Rom 3:23). David knew this to be true—particularly about himself. That's why he could affirm the blessedness of forgiveness from God.
32:3-5 When David left his sins of adultery and murder unaddressed, it took its toll on him,

physically and emotionally (32:3-4). His problem was not medical, though, but theological: God's **hand was heavy on** him (32:4). Thus, David emphasizes the relationship among unaddressed sin, physical and emotional well-being, and loss of fellowship with God. When he **acknowledged [his] sin**, God granted forgiveness and removed David's **guilt** (32:5).
32:9 Such animals are stubborn; they must be made to do what they don't want to do. Similarly, humans don't naturally confess their sins and repent of them. Nevertheless, we must see the incentives for doing so: receiving forgiveness from God, intimacy with God, and joy in God.

32:10-11 When you have sinned and the call for repentance comes, don't hold back. Confess your sins specifically, agree with what God says about them, appeal to his grace and mercy for forgiveness, and anticipate the return of the **joy** of your salvation (32:11).
33:5 Righteousness and justice are regularly linked in Scripture. They combine the vertical righteous standing before God and the horizontal just treatment of our neighbors. They are coupled together here because they must not be separate but operate simultaneously.
33:8-9 The Lord merely speaks, and things happen. He simply declares a thing to be, and it is. Such sovereign, creative power should

a 33:9 Gn 1:3; Ps 147:15,18; 148:5
b 33:10 Ps 2:1-3; Is 8:10; 19:3
c 33:11 Ps 139:17; Pr 19:21; Is 55:8
d 33:12 Ex 19:5; Dt 7:6; Ps 144:15
e 33:13 Jb 28:24; Ps 11:4; 14:2; 53:2
f 33:14 Ps 102:19
g 33:15 Jb 34:21
h 33:16 Ps 44:6; 60:11
i 33:17 Ps 20:7; 147:10; Hs 1:7
j 33:18 Jb 36:7; Ps 34:15; 1Pt 3:12
k 33:19 Jb 5:20; Ps 37:19; 56:13
l 33:20 Ps 130:6; Is 8:17
m Gn 15:1; Dt 33:29; Ps 3:3; 5:12; 18:2; 28:7; 115:9-11
n 33:21 Ps 13:5; 28:7; Jn 16:22
o Zph 3:12
p 33:22 Ps 130:7; 147:11

q 34:title 1Sm 21:10-15
r 34:1 Ps 71:6; Eph 5:20
s 34:2 Ps 44:8; Jr 9:24; 1Co 1:31
t Ps 69:32
u 34:3 Lk 1:46
v Ps 69:30
w 34:4 Ps 34:6,17,19
x 34:5 Is 60:5
y Ps 25:3
z 34:6 Ps 34:4
aa 34:7 Ps 91:11; Heb 1:14
ab 34:8 1Pt 2:3
ac Ps 2:12
ad 34:9 Ps 23:1
ae 34:10 Jb 4:10-11
af Ps 84:11
ag 34:11 Ps 66:16; 111:10
ah 34:12 Ec 3:13; 6:6
ai 34:13 Ps 39:1; 141:3; Pr 13:3; Jms 1:26
aj 34:14 Ps 37:27; Is 1:16-17
ak Rm 14:19; Heb 12:14

9 For he spoke, and it came
    into being;
he commanded, and it came
    into existence.*a*

10 The LORD frustrates the counsel
    of the nations;
he thwarts the plans
    of the peoples.*b*

11 The counsel of the LORD
    stands forever,
the plans of his heart
    from generation to generation.*c*

12 Happy is the nation whose God
    is the LORD —
the people he has chosen to be
    his own possession!*d*

13 The LORD looks down
    from heaven;
he observes everyone.*e*

14 He gazes on all the inhabitants
    of the earth
from his dwelling place.*f*

15 He forms the hearts of them all;
he considers all their works.*g*

16 A king is not saved by
    a large army;
a warrior will not be rescued
    by great strength.*h*

17 The horse is a false hope for safety;
it provides no escape by
    its great power.*i*

18 But look, the LORD keeps his eye on
    those who fear him —
those who depend on
    his faithful love*j*

19 to rescue them from death
and to keep them alive in famine.*k*

20 We wait for the LORD;*l*
he is our help and shield.*m*

21 For our hearts rejoice in him*n*
because we trust in
    his holy name.*o*

22 May your faithful love rest
    on us, LORD,
for we put our hope in you.*p*

THE LORD DELIVERS THE RIGHTEOUS

34 *Concerning David, when he pretended to be insane in the presence of Abimelech,*q *who drove him out, and he departed.*

1 I will bless the LORD at all times;
his praise will always be on my lips.*r*

2 I will boast in the LORD;*s*
the humble will hear and be glad.*t*

3 Proclaim the LORD's greatness
    with me;*u*
let us exalt his name together.*v*

4 I sought the LORD, and he answered me
and rescued me from all my fears.*w*

5 Those who look to him are*A* radiant
    with joy;*x*
their faces will never be ashamed.*y*

6 This poor man cried, and the LORD
    heard him
and saved him from all his troubles.*z*

7 The angel of the LORD encamps
    around those who fear him,
    and rescues them.*aa*

8 Taste and see that the LORD is good.*ab*
How happy is the person who
    takes refuge in him!*ac*

9 You who are his holy ones,
    fear the LORD,
for those who fear him
    lack nothing.*ad*

10 Young lions*B* lack food
    and go hungry,*ae*
but those who seek the LORD
    will not lack any good thing.*af*

11 Come, children, listen to me;
I will teach you the fear
    of the LORD.*ag*

12 Who is someone who desires life,
loving a long life to enjoy
    what is good?*ah*

13 Keep your tongue from evil
and your lips
    from deceitful speech.*ai*

14 Turn away from evil and do
    what is good;*aj*
seek peace and pursue it.*ak*

A 34:5 Some Hb mss, LXX, Aq, Syr, Jer read *Look to him and be*   *B* 34:10 LXX, Syr, Vg read *The rich*

cause everyone everywhere to **fear** and **stand in awe of him** (33:8).
33:10 The **counsel** and **plans** of menacing **nations** may strike fear into the hearts of humans, but they are nothing before God— just a mere "drop in a bucket" (Isa 40:15). **He thwarts** them.
33:20 To **wait for the LORD** is not to be idle. It is to refuse to step out of his will to address your situation.

34:3 In other words, he says, "Don't make me praise God by myself. Let's together make him appear as big as he truly is."
34:4 Faith expressed in prayer is God's antidote for fear (see Phil 4:6-7).
34:6 Though David was a mighty warrior, he was at the mercy of King Achish on this particular occasion. He was a mere **poor man** who could only cry to God. Your weakness is not a liability when the Lord is your God.

34:7 **The angel of the LORD** is the preincarnate Christ.
34:10 What are we called to do in our need? **Seek the LORD.** "Seek first the kingdom of God and his righteousness, and all these things will be provided for you" (Matt 6:33).
34:12-14 If you want **to enjoy what is good** (34:12), then **do what is good** (34:14).

Experiencing God Fully

MANY OLD FOOTBALL AND BASEBALL stadiums have been torn down, and new ones built in their places. The older ones were okay, but they lacked modern improvements and technology. Moreover, many of these older stadiums included seating areas with obstructed views: a beam or a post would block a fan's full visual participation in the sporting event. In fact, oftentimes, if a fan was seated in one of these seats behind a column, he would have to ask another person what had just happened. He'd have to get secondhand information because he couldn't see things for himself. He could hear the noise and excitement, but the column kept him from being a full participant in the activities.

You may spend time in a similar stadium called church. You get there early, try your best to get a good seat, participate enthusiastically in worship, listen attentively to the sermon, but then go home feeling empty. You went hoping to experience God, but somehow, it seemed as though you were just going through the motions. You sensed that others around you were getting more out of the service than you did, but you couldn't pinpoint why.

Let me say that most of us have been there before. It might be safe to say that we tend to mistake an emotional or inspirational experience with an encounter with God. We convince ourselves that if we sing loudly enough, memorize the right Scriptures, and give enough money when the plate comes by, God will slide up beside us and say, "Well done, my good and faithful servant." And when that doesn't happen, it is easy to become disillusioned. But the problem with this kind of thinking is that experiencing God is so much more than an emotional pick-me-up at the end of a church service.

David writes in Psalm 34:7, "The angel of the LORD encamps around those who fear him." The first thing you should know is that the angel of the Lord is no ordinary angel. Throughout the Old Testament, he was worshiped by many and did things that only God can do. He is, in fact, the preincarnate Son of God, our Deliverer. You should also notice in this verse that he is always near "those who fear him." Jesus's protection and presence are very real, and they aren't dependent on loud singing or on how many notes were taken during a sermon. Experiencing God has a lot more to do with fearing him than with boisterous church activity.

But another truth to consider is that just like those fans in the stadium who couldn't see the activity on the field because they were sitting behind columns, many of us come to church trying to experience God while failing to remove our own obstacle called *sin*. We show up, Bible in hand, paying little mind to the truth that we failed to read it all week. We sing a little louder on Sunday to make up for the fact that we lived like pagans Monday through Saturday. Isaiah 59:2 warns, "Your iniquities are separating you from your God, and your sins have hidden his face from you so that he does not listen." Understand that it is impossible to enjoy the fullness of God and benefit from his blessings if we are separated from him. Yet because we fail to deal with our sin, we short-circuit any chance of experiencing God's mercy and love. Thus, we get used to sitting behind columns and leaving empty-handed.

Reverence toward God includes repentance of our sin. It means letting our sins go. We don't hold onto them, nor do we hide them in a closet. God wants you to truly experience him, and he's only going to allow that if you have given him your whole heart.

[a] 34:15 Jb 36:7; Ps 33:18; 1Pt 3:12
[b] 34:12-16 1Pt 3:10-12
[c] 34:16 Am 9:4
[d] 34:17 Ps 145:19
[e] 34:18 Ps 51:17; 147:3; Is 61:1
[f] 34:19 Ps 71:20; 2Tm 3:11-12
[g] 34:20 Jn 19:33,36
[h] 34:21 Ps 94:23; 140:11; Pr 24:16
[i] 34:22 Ps 37:40; Rm 8:33-34
[j] 35:1 Ex 14:25; Is 49:25
[k] 35:2 Ps 5:12; 91:4
[l] 35:3 Ps 13:5; 40:17
[m] 35:4 Ps 40:14; 70:2; 129:5
[n] 35:5 Jb 21:18; Ps 83:13; Is 29:5

[o] 35:6 Ps 73:18; Jr 23:12
[p] 35:7 Ps 140:5
[q] 35:8 Jb 18:8; Ps 7:15
[r] 35:9 Ps 9:14; 13:5
[s] 35:10 Ex 15:11; Ps 86:8; Mc 7:18
[t] Ps 72:12; 82:4
[u] 35:11 Ps 27:12; Pr 19:5,9
[v] 35:12 Ps 38:20; 109:5; Jr 18:20
[w] 35:13 Ps 69:10-11
[x] 35:14 Ps 38:6
[y] 35:15 Jb 30:1,8,12; Ob 12
[z] 35:16 Jb 16:9; Ps 37:12; Lm 2:16
[aa] 35:17 Ps 13:1; Hab 1:13
[ab] Ps 22:20-21
[ac] 35:18 Ps 22:22,25; 40:9-10; Heb 2:12

15 The eyes of the LORD are
    on the righteous,
  and his ears are open to their cry
    for help.[a]
16 The face of the LORD is set
  against those who do what is evil,[b]
  to remove[A] all memory of them
    from the earth.[c]
17 The righteous[B] cry out,
    and the LORD hears,
  and rescues them from all
    their troubles.[d]
18 The LORD is near the brokenhearted;
  he saves those crushed in spirit.[e]

19 One who is righteous has
    many adversities,
  but the LORD rescues him
    from them all.[f]
20 He protects all his bones;
  not one of them is broken.[g]
21 Evil brings death to the wicked,
  and those who hate the righteous
    will be punished.[h]
22 The LORD redeems the life
    of his servants,
  and all who take refuge in him
    will not be punished.[i]

PRAYER FOR VICTORY

35 *Of David.*
  Oppose my opponents, LORD;
  fight those who fight me.[j]
2 Take your shields —
    large and small —
  and come to my aid.[k]
3 Draw the spear and javelin
    against my pursuers,
  and assure me: "I am
    your deliverance."[l]

4 Let those who intend
    to take my life
  be disgraced and humiliated;
  let those who plan to harm me
  be turned back and ashamed.[m]
5 Let them be like chaff in the wind,
  with the angel of the LORD
    driving them away.[n]

6 Let their way be dark and slippery,
  with the angel of the LORD
    pursuing them.[o]
7 They hid their net for me without cause;
  they dug a pit for me without cause.[p]
8 Let ruin come on him unexpectedly,
  and let the net that he hid
    ensnare him;
  let him fall into it — to his ruin.[q]

9 Then I will rejoice in the LORD;
  I will delight in his deliverance.[r]
10 All my bones will say,
  "LORD, who is like you,[s]
  rescuing the poor from one
    too strong for him,
  the poor or the needy from one
    who robs him?"[t]

11 Malicious witnesses come forward;
  they question me about things
    I do not know.[u]
12 They repay me evil for good,
  making me desolate.[v]
13 Yet when they were sick,
  my clothing was sackcloth;
  I humbled myself with fasting,
  and my prayer was genuine.[C,w]
14 I went about mourning as if
    for my friend or brother;
  I was bowed down with grief,
  like one mourning for a mother.[x]
15 But when I stumbled, they gathered
    in glee;
  they gathered against me.
  Assailants I did not know
  tore at me and did not stop.[y]
16 With godless mockery[D]
  they gnashed their teeth at me.[z]

17 Lord, how long will you look on?[aa]
  Rescue me from their ravages;
  rescue my precious life
    from the young lions.[ab]
18 I will praise you in the great assembly;
  I will exalt you
    among many people.[ac]
19 Do not let my deceitful enemies
  rejoice over me;

[A] 34:16 Or *cut off*   [B] 34:17 Lit *They*   [C] 35:13 Lit *prayer returned to my chest*   [D] 35:16 Hb obscure

---

34:15-18 The righteous, those who trust the Lord and submit to his kingdom agenda, receive his full attention. His **eyes** see them, **his ears** hear them, he **rescues them from ... troubles**, and he grants them his presence (34:15, 17-18). As it turns out, **those who do what is evil** also receive God's attention. But, in their case, he sets his **face** against them in order to wipe their **memory ... from the earth**

(34:16). How would you prefer that God take notice of you?
34:19 You haven't seen trouble until you become a Christian because that's when the devil puts his bull's-eye on you; yet the Lord has the ability to rescue, no matter the situation. David learned that truth firsthand.
34:20 This promise found ultimate fulfillment when Jesus went to the cross (see John 19:33-36).

35:1-10 David's prayer is an appeal for God's intervention against his enemies who were persecuting him. He wants God to act as a warrior.
35:19-21 These **enemies** were the kind of people who make false accusations against those living **peacefully** with others (35:19-20).

do not let those who hate me
   without cause[a]
wink at me maliciously.[b]

20 For they do not speak
   in friendly ways,
but contrive fraudulent schemes[A]
against those who live peacefully
   in the land.[c]

21 They open their mouths wide
   against me and say,
"Aha, aha! We saw it!"[B,d]

22 You saw it, Lord; do not be silent.
Lord, do not be far from me.[e]

23 Wake up and rise to my defense,
   to my cause, my God
   and my Lord![f]

24 Vindicate me, Lord my God,
   in keeping with
     your righteousness,
and do not let them
   rejoice over me.[g]

25 Do not let them say in their hearts,
   "Aha! Just what we wanted."
Do not let them say,
   "We have swallowed him up!"[h]

26 Let those who rejoice
   at my misfortune
be disgraced and humiliated;
let those who exalt themselves
   over me
be clothed with shame
   and reproach.[i]

27 Let those who want
   my vindication
shout for joy and be glad;
let them continually say,
   "The Lord be exalted.
He takes pleasure in
   his servant's well-being."[j]

28 And my tongue will proclaim
   your righteousness,
your praise all day long.[k]

HUMAN WICKEDNESS AND GOD'S LOVE

36 For the choir director. Of David, the
Lord's servant.

1 An oracle within my heart
concerning the transgression of the
   wicked person:
Dread of God has no effect on him.[c,j]

2 For with his flattering opinion
   of himself,
he does not discover and hate
   his iniquity.[m]

3 The words from his mouth
   are malicious and deceptive;[n]
he has stopped acting wisely
   and doing good.[o]

4 Even on his bed he makes
   malicious plans.[p]
He sets himself on a path
   that is not good,
and he does not reject evil.[q]

5 Lord, your faithful love reaches
   to heaven,
your faithfulness to the clouds.[r]

6 Your righteousness is
   like the highest mountains,
your judgments
   like the deepest sea.[s]
Lord, you preserve people
   and animals.[t]

7 How priceless your
   faithful love is, God!
People take refuge in the shadow
   of your wings.[u]

8 They are filled from the abundance
   of your house.
You let them drink from
   your refreshing stream.[v]

9 For the wellspring of life is
   with you.[w]
By means of your light we see light.[x]

10 Spread your faithful love over those
   who know you,

[a] 35:19 Ps 38:19; Jn 15:25
[b] Ps 13:4; 30:1; 38:16
[c] 35:20 Ps 55:21; Jr 9:8; Mc 6:12
[d] 35:21 Jb 16:10; Ps 22:13; 40:15; 70:3
[e] 35:22 Ps 10:1; 22:11; 28:1
[f] 35:23 Ps 7:6; 44:23; 59:4
[g] 35:24 Ps 26:1; 43:1
[h] 35:25 Ps 124:3; Lm 2:16
[i] 35:26 Jb 8:22; Ps 40:14; 109:29
[j] 35:27 Ps 40:16; 70:4
[k] 35:28 Ps 71:8,15,24

[l] 36:1 Rm 3:18
[m] 36:2 Dt 29:19; Ps 10:3; 49:18
[n] 36:3 Ps 10:7
[o] Jr 4:22
[p] 36:4 Pr 4:16
[q] Ps 10:7; Is 65:2
[r] 36:5 Ps 57:10; 103:11; 108:4
[s] 36:6 Ps 71:19
[t] Ps 104:14-15
[u] 36:7 Ru 2:12; Ps 17:8; 57:1; 91:4
[v] 36:8 Ps 46:4; 65:4; Jr 31:12-14
[w] 36:9 Jn 4:10,14
[x] Jn 1:9; Ac 26:18

[A] 35:20 Lit *but devise fraudulent words*   [B] 35:21 Lit *Our eyes saw!*   [C] 36:1 Lit *There is no dread of God in front of his eyes*

35:22 Regardless of the lies people spread, God knows the truth.

35:25-26 He pictures his enemies as beasts that wanted to growl, **We have swallowed him up!** (35:25). And since their actions were so shameful, David longs for God to clothe them **with shame** (35:26).

35:28 Don't fail to give God the praise he is due when he comes through for you.

36:1-2 David points to two reasons why **the wicked person** turns to ungodliness: **Dread of God has no effect on him**, and he has a **flattering opinion of himself**. In other words, he has a low view of God and a high view of self.

36:5-6 Where does David turn to find relief from the wickedness that surrounds him? He meditates on God, comparing his **faithful love, faithfulness, righteousness,** and **judgments** to the grandest aspects of the created world.

36:7-8 As the king of Israel, David was a wealthy man. But the most **priceless** treasure to which he had access was the **faithful love** of **God** (36:7). Those who look to God as their source will experience **the abundance of** his provision and be satisfied (36:8).

37:1-2 Don't fret over **evildoers**, for they are temporary and will **wither quickly like grass** under a hot sun.

37:4 You can expect God's movement in your life when your thinking and **desires** match his. He desires to bless you more than you want to be blessed.

37:7-15 Our focus should be on God and not on the wicked. We are to **wait expectantly for him** (37:7). Notice that we are not to merely wait but to wait with expectation—confident that he will respond when our "trust" and "delight" are "in him" (37:3-5). Remember: vengeance belongs to God; he will repay (Deut 32:35). The Lord knows that the **wicked** person's **day is coming** when he will fall by his own schemes (Ps 37:12-15). But those who look to and submit to God

a 36:10 Pr 11:6; Jr 22:16
b 36:11 Ps 38:16; 119:122
c 36:12 Ps 1:5; 140:10;
  Is 26:14
d 37:1 Ps 73:3; Pr 3:31;
  23:17; 24:19
e 37:2 Ps 92:7; 129:6;
  Jms 1:11
f 37:3 Ps 62:8
g Pr 2:21
h 37:4 Ps 21:2; 145:19;
  Is 58:14
i 37:5 Ps 55:22; Pr 16:3;
  1Pt 5:7
j 37:6 Ps 97:11; Is 58:8,10
k 37:7 Ps 40:1; Lm 3:26
l Jr 12:1
m 37:8 Eph 4:31; Col 3:8

n 37:9 Pr 2:21; Is 57:13;
  60:21
o 37:10 Jb 7:10; 24:24; Ps
  35:35-36
p 37:11 Mt 5:5
q Ps 72:7
r 37:12 Ps 31:13,20; 35:16
s 37:13 Ps 2:4; 59:8;
  Hab 1:10
t 1Sm 26:10
u 37:14 Ps 11:2; Lm 2:4
v 37:15 1Sm 2:4; Ps 46:9
w 37:16 Pr 15:16; 16:8
x 37:17 Ps 10:15
y Ps 145:14
z 37:18 Ps 1:6
aa 37:19 Jb 5:20; Ps 33:19
ab 37:20 Ps 68:2; Hs 13:3

and your righteousness
    over the upright in heart.[a]

11 Do not let the foot of the arrogant
    come near me
or the hand of the wicked
    drive me away.[b]

12 There! The evildoers have fallen.
    They have been thrown down
and cannot rise.[c]

INSTRUCTION IN WISDOM

37 *Of David.*

Do not be agitated by evildoers;
do not envy those who do wrong.[d]

2 For they wither quickly like grass
and wilt like tender green plants.[e]

3 Trust in the LORD and do
    what is good;[f]
dwell in the land and live securely.[A,g]

4 Take delight in the LORD,
and he will give you
    your heart's desires.[h]

⟿ HOPE WORDS ⟿

*Don't worry about locating
your purpose if you are
seeking after God because your
purpose will locate you.*

---

5 Commit your way to the LORD;
trust in him, and he will act,[i]
6 making your righteousness shine
    like the dawn,
your justice like the noonday.[j]

7 Be silent before the LORD and wait
    expectantly for him;[k]
do not be agitated by one
    who prospers in his way,
by the person who carries out
    evil plans.[l]

8 Refrain from anger and give up
    your rage;
do not be agitated — it can only
    bring harm.[m]
9 For evildoers will be destroyed,

but those who put their hope
    in the LORD
will inherit the land.[n]

10 A little while, and the wicked person
    will be no more;
though you look for him, he will not
    be there.[o]

11 But the humble will inherit the land[p]
and will enjoy abundant prosperity.[q]

12 The wicked person schemes
    against the righteous
and gnashes his teeth at him.[r]
13 The Lord laughs at him[s]
because he sees that his day
    is coming.[t]

14 The wicked have drawn the sword
    and strung the[B] bow
to bring down the poor and needy
and to slaughter those whose way
    is upright.[u]
15 Their swords will enter
    their own hearts,
and their bows will be broken.[v]

16 The little that the righteous person
    has is better
than the abundance
    of many wicked people.[w]
17 For the arms of the wicked
    will be broken,[x]
but the LORD supports the righteous.[y]

18 The LORD watches over
    the blameless all their days,
and their inheritance
    will last forever.[z]
19 They will not be disgraced in times
    of adversity;
they will be satisfied in days
    of hunger.[aa]

20 But the wicked will perish;
the LORD's enemies, like the glory
    of the pastures,
will fade away —
they will fade away like smoke.[ab]

21 The wicked person borrows
    and does not repay,

A 37:3 Or *and cultivate faithfulness,* or *and befriend faithfulness*   B 37:14 Lit *their*

---

will experience provision and peace (37:9, 11)—and will receive their duly allotted inheritance (see Matt 5:5). **37:16-26** No matter how much the wicked acquire, eventually they will **be broken** and **destroyed** (37:17, 22). No matter how little the righteous have, however, the Lord **supports** and **watches over** them (37:17-18). **Their inheritance will last forever** (37:18). God will keep their blessings secure until the time is right to dispense them—sometimes in history but mostly in eternity. He is a loving Father to his people. Even when they fall, he holds them **with his hand** in a gentle but firm grip (37:24). God's **children** will not be **abandoned**. Instead, he is **generous** to them so that they, in turn, **are a blessing** to others (37:25-26).

but the righteous one is gracious
and giving.[a]

22 Those who are blessed by the Lord
will inherit the land,
but those cursed by him
will be destroyed.[b]

23 A person's steps are established
by the Lord,
and he takes pleasure in his way.[c]

24 Though he falls, he will not
be overwhelmed,
because the Lord supports him with
his hand.[d]

25 I have been young and now I am old,
yet I have not seen
the righteous abandoned
or his children begging for bread.[e]

26 He is always generous,
always lending,
and his children are a blessing.[f]

27 Turn away from evil, do what is good,
and settle permanently.[g]

28 For the Lord loves justice
and will not abandon
his faithful ones.[h]
They are kept safe forever,
but the children of the wicked
will be destroyed.[i]

29 The righteous will inherit the land
and dwell in it permanently.[j]

30 The mouth of the righteous
utters wisdom;
his tongue speaks what is just.[k]

31 The instruction of his God is in his heart;
his steps do not falter.[l]

32 The wicked one lies in wait
for the righteous
and intends to kill him;[m]

33 the Lord will not leave him
in the power of the wicked one
or allow him to be condemned
when he is judged.[n]

34 Wait for the Lord and keep his way,
and he will exalt you to inherit
the land.
You will watch when the wicked
are destroyed.[o]

35 I have seen
a wicked, violent person

well-rooted,[A] like
a flourishing native tree.[p]

36 Then I[B] passed by and noticed
he was gone;
I searched for him, but he could not
be found.[q]

37 Watch the blameless and observe
the upright,
for the person of peace will have
a future.[C,r]

38 But transgressors will all be eliminated;
the future of the wicked
will be destroyed.[s]

39 The salvation of the righteous is
from the Lord,
their refuge in a time of distress.[t]

40 The Lord helps and delivers them;
he will deliver them from the wicked
and will save them
because they take refuge in him.[u]

PRAYER OF A SUFFERING SINNER

38 *A psalm of David to bring
remembrance.*[v]

Lord, do not punish me in your anger
or discipline me in your wrath.[w]

2 For your arrows have sunk into me,
and your hand has pressed down
on me.[x]

3 There is no soundness in my body
because of your indignation;
there is no health[D] in my bones
because of my sin.[y]

4 For my iniquities have flooded
over my head;
they are a burden too heavy for me
to bear.[z]

5 My wounds are foul and festering
because of my foolishness.[aa]

6 I am bent over and brought very low;
all day long I go around
in mourning.[ab]

7 For my insides are full of
burning pain,
and there is no soundness
in my body.[ac]

8 I am faint and severely crushed;
I groan because of the anguish
of my heart.[ad]

9 Lord, my every desire is in front
of you;
my sighing is not hidden from you.[ae]

[a] 37:21 Ps 112:5,9
[b] 37:22 Pr 3:33
[c] 37:23 1Sm 2:9; Ps 66:9
[d] 37:24 Ps 145:14; Pr 24:16; Mc 7:8
[e] 37:25 Is 41:17
[f] 37:26 Dt 15:8; Ps 112:5,9; Mt 5:42
[g] 37:27 Ps 34:14; 102:28
[h] 37:28 Dt 31:6; Heb 13:5
[i] Ps 21:10; Pr 2:22
[j] 37:29 Pr 2:21; Is 60:21
[k] 37:30 Ps 49:3; 119:13; Pr 10:13
[l] 37:31 Dt 6:6; Ps 40:8; 119:11
[m] 37:32 Ps 10:8; 17:11
[n] 37:33 Ps 34:22; 109:31; 2Pt 2:9
[o] 37:34 Ps 27:14; 52:5-6; 91:8

[p] 37:35 Jb 5:3; Jr 12:2
[q] 37:36 Jb 20:5
[r] 37:37 Is 57:1-2
[s] 37:38 Ps 1:4-6; Pr 2:22
[t] 37:39 Ps 3:8; 9:9; 62:1
[u] 37:40 Ps 22:4; 34:22; 54:4
[v] 38:title Ps 70 title
[w] 38:1 Ps 6:1
[x] 38:2 Jb 6:4; Ps 32:4
[y] 38:3 Jb 33:19; Ps 31:10; 102:10
[z] 38:4 Ezr 9:6; Ps 40:12
[aa] 38:5 Is 1:6
[ab] 38:6 Ps 35:14
[ac] 38:7 Ps 38:3; Lm 1:13
[ad] 38:8 Jb 3:24; Ps 6:6; 32:3; Lm 2:11
[ae] 38:9 Ps 10:17

Video Devotional

"ORCHESTRAT-ED EVENTS"

www.bhpublishinggroup.com/qr/te/19-37

God uses detours and intersections to take you from where you are to where he wants you to be.

[A] 37:35 Hb obscure   [B] 37:36 LXX, Syr, Vg, Jer; MT reads *he*   [C] 37:37 Or *posterity*, also in v. 38   [D] 38:3 Hb *shalom*

38:2-8 David was experiencing the chastisement of God, which was affecting him physically, spiritually, and emotionally.

a 38:10 Ps 6:7; 69:3; 88:9
b 38:11 Jb 19:13-20; Ps
31:11; 88:18
c 38:12 Ps 35:4,20; 54:3;
140:5
d 38:13 Ps 39:2,9
e 38:14 Jb 23:4
f 38:15 Ps 17:6; 39:7
g 38:16 Ps 13:4; 35:26
h 38:17 Ps 13:2; 35:15
i 38:18 Ps 32:5; 2Co 7:9-10
j 38:19 Ps 18:17; 35:19
k 38:20 Ps 35:12; 109:5;
3Jn 11
l 38:21 Ps 22:19; 35:22
m 38:22 Ps 40:13,17
n 39:1 Ps 34:13; Jms 3:5-12
o 39:2 Jb 40:4; Ps 38:13

p 39:3 Ps 32:4; Jr 20:9;
Lk 24:32
q 39:4 Ps 78:39; 90:12;
103:14
r 39:5 Ps 62:9; 89:47; 144:4
s 39:6 Ps 49:10; Ec 2:18-19;
Lk 12:20; 1Co 7:31
t 39:7 Ps 38:15
u 39:8 Ps 44:13; 79:4;
119:22
v 39:9 Ps 39:2
w 39:10 Jb 9:34; 13:21;
Ps 32:4
x 39:11 Is 50:9
y 39:5
z 39:12 Ps 35:22
aa 1Ch 29:15; Heb 11:13;
1Pt 2:11
ab 39:13 Jb 7:19; 10:20-21;
Ps 102:24

10 My heart races, my strength
leaves me,
and even the light of my eyes
has faded.[A],[a]
11 My loved ones and friends
stand back from my affliction,
and my relatives stand at a distance.[b]
12 Those who intend to kill me set traps,
and those who want to harm me
threaten to destroy me;
they plot treachery all day long.[c]
13 I am like a deaf person; I do not hear.
I am like a speechless person
who does not open his mouth.[d]
14 I am like a man who does not hear
and has no arguments in his mouth.[e]
15 For I put my hope in you, Lord;
you will answer me, my Lord,
my God.[f]
16 For I said, "Don't let them rejoice
over me —
those who are arrogant toward me
when I stumble."[g]
17 For I am about to fall,
and my pain is constantly with me.[h]
18 So I confess my iniquity;
I am anxious because of my sin.[i]
19 But my enemies are vigorous
and powerful;[B]
many hate me for no reason.[j]
20 Those who repay evil for good
attack me for pursuing good.[k]

21 Lord, do not abandon me;
my God, do not be far from me.[l]
22 Hurry to help me,
my Lord, my salvation.[m]

THE FLEETING NATURE OF LIFE

39 *For the choir director, for Jeduthun.
A psalm of David.*

1 I said, "I will guard my ways
so that I may not sin with my tongue;
I will guard my mouth with a muzzle
as long as the wicked are
in my presence."[n]
2 I was speechless and quiet;
I kept silent, even from speaking good,
and my pain intensified.[o]

3 My heart grew hot within me;
as I mused, a fire burned.[p]
I spoke with my tongue:
4 "Lord, make me
aware of my end
and the number of my days
so that I will know how short-lived
I am.[q]
5 In fact, you have made my days just
inches long,
and my life span is as nothing
to you.
Yes, every human being stands as
only a vapor.[r] *Selah*
6 Yes, a person goes about
like a mere shadow.
Indeed, they rush around in vain,
gathering possessions
without knowing
who will get them.[s]

7 "Now, Lord, what do I wait for?
My hope is in you.[t]
8 Rescue me from all
my transgressions;
do not make me the taunt
of fools.[u]
9 I am speechless; I do not open
my mouth
because of what you have done.[v]
10 Remove your torment from me.
Because of the force of your hand
I am finished.[w]
11 You discipline a person
with punishment for iniquity,
consuming like a moth
what is precious to him;[x]
yes, every human being is only
a vapor.[y] *Selah*

12 "Hear my prayer, Lord,
and listen to my cry for help;
do not be silent at my tears.[z]
For I am here with you
as an alien,
a temporary resident like all
my ancestors.[aa]
13 Turn your angry gaze from me
so that I may be cheered up
before I die and am gone."[ab]

[A] 38:10 Or *and the light of my eyes — even that is not with me* [B] 38:19 Or *numerous*

38:15-20 David recognized that his **sin** had led to his suffering and that his enemies were too **powerful** for him (38:18-19). Only God could deal with both problems. David was helpless to help himself.
38:21-22 In your moments of need, remember that God is your Savior, too. He does not merely provide you with salvation; he *is* your salvation.

39:1-3 David resolves not to sin through his words (39:1). The book of Proverbs contains much wisdom about how to do this, which is necessary help since James reminds us how hard it is to control the tongue (see Jas 3:1-12). Since David did not want to say anything he would regret, he **kept silent**. In the long run, however, he took his silence too far; it only

intensified his **pain** and anguish (Ps 39:2-3). We can sin not just with our words but also with our silence. Knowing when to speak and when to withhold something requires wisdom.
39:12 David asks that God would **not be silent**—as David had been earlier when he should have spoken (see 39:2, 9).

THANKSGIVING AND A CRY FOR HELP

40
For the choir director. A psalm of David.

1 I waited patiently for the Lord,
and he turned to me and heard
my cry for help.[a]

2 He brought me up from a desolate[A] pit,
out of the muddy clay,[b]
and set my feet on a rock,
making my steps secure.[c]

3 He put a new song in my mouth,
a hymn of praise to our God.[d]
Many will see and fear,
and they will trust in the Lord.[e]

4 How happy is anyone
who has put his trust in the Lord
and has not turned to the proud
or to those who run after lies![f]

5 Lord my God, you have done
many things —
your wondrous works
and your plans for us;
none can compare with you.
If I were to report and speak of them,
they are more than can be told.[g]

6 You do not delight in sacrifice
and offering;
you open my ears to listen.[B]
You do not ask for
a whole burnt offering
or a sin offering.[h]

7 Then I said, "See, I have come;
in the scroll it is written about me.[i]

8 I delight to do your will, my God,[j]
and your instruction is deep
within me."[k]

9 I proclaim righteousness
in the great assembly;
see, I do not keep
my mouth closed[c] —
as you know, Lord.[l]

10 I did not hide your righteousness
in my heart;
I spoke about your faithfulness
and salvation;
I did not conceal your constant love
and truth
from the great assembly.[m]

11 Lord, you do not[D] withhold
your compassion from me.
Your constant love and truth
will always guard me.[n]

12 For troubles without number
have surrounded me;
my iniquities have overtaken me;
I am unable to see.
They are more than the hairs
of my head,
and my courage leaves me.[o]

13 Lord, be pleased to rescue me;
hurry to help me, Lord.[p]

14 Let those who intend to take my life
be disgraced and confounded.
Let those who wish me harm
be turned back and humiliated.[q]

15 Let those who say to me, "Aha, aha!"
be appalled because of
their shame.[r]

16 Let all who seek you rejoice
and be glad in you;
let those who love your salvation
continually say,
"The Lord is great!"[s]

17 I am oppressed and needy;
may the Lord think of me.
You are my helper and my deliverer;
my God, do not delay.[t]

VICTORY IN SPITE OF BETRAYAL

41
For the choir director. A psalm of David.

Happy is one who is considerate
of the poor;
the Lord will save him in a day
of adversity.[u]

2 The Lord will keep him
and preserve him;
he will be blessed in the land.[v]
You will not give him over
to the desire of his enemies.[w]

3 The Lord will sustain him
on his sickbed;
you will heal him on the bed
where he lies.[x]

4 I said, "Lord, be gracious to me;
heal me, for I have sinned
against you."[y]

[a] 40:1 Ps 27:14; 34:15; 37:7
[b] 40:2 Ps 69:2,14
[c] Ps 27:5; 37:23
[d] 40:3 Ps 33:3
[e] Dt 13:11
[f] 40:4 Jb 23:11; Ps 84:12
[g] 40:5 Jb 5:9; Ps 71:15; 139:17-18
[h] 40:6 1Sm 15:22; Ps 51:16; Am 5:22
[i] 40:7 Lk 24:44
[j] 40:8 Ps 119:16,24; Jn 4:34
[k] 40:6-8 Ps 119:11; Heb 10:5-9
[l] 40:9 Ps 22:22,25
[m] 40:10 Ac 20:20

[n] 40:11 Ps 36:5; 57:3; 61:7
[o] 40:12 Ps 38:4; 65:3
[p] 40:13 Ps 70:1
[q] 40:14 Ps 35:4,26; 63:9; 70:2
[r] 40:15 Ps 35:21,25; 70:3
[s] 40:16 Ps 35:27; 70:4
[t] 40:17 Ps 86:1; 109:22
[u] 41:1 Ps 82:3-4; Pr 14:21
[v] 41:2 Ps 37:22,28
[w] Ps 27:12
[x] 41:3 Jr 17:14
[y] 41:4 Ps 6:2; 51:4

[A] 40:2 Or *watery* [B] 40:6 Lit *you hollow out ears for me* [C] 40:9 Lit *not restrain my lips* [D] 40:11 Or *Lord, do not*

40:5 David's psalms arose out of his deep experiences of God, and he desired that others would have rich experiences of him too. We ought to keep track of the **wondrous works** that God has accomplished in our lives, so that—like David—we are able to testify confidently that **they are more than can be told**.

40:6-8 The author of Hebrews applies these verses to Jesus Christ, who came to fulfill the Father's purposes (see Heb 10:5-7).

Many people want personal guidance directly from the Lord, yet they skip the guidance available in his revealed Word, in his **instruction** (Ps 40:8). You cannot be led in God's personal will for your life if you neglect his revealed will in Scripture.

41:1-3 God takes note of demonstrations of kindness and causes the blessings of mercy to boomerang back to the merciful. He rewards them with protection, security, and restoration (41:2-3; see Jas 1:27; 2:13).

a 41:5 Ps 38:12
b 41:6 Ps 12:2; 62:4; Pr 26:24-26
c 41:7 Ps 56:5
d 41:8 Ps 71:10-11
e 41:9 Jb 19:19; Ps 55:12-13; Jn 13:18
f 41:10 Ps 9:13
g 41:11 Ps 37:23
h Ps 25:2
i 41:12 Ps 37:17
j Ps 21:6
k 41:13 Ps 72:18-19; 89:52
l 42:1 Ps 84:2; 119:131

m 42:2 Ps 63:1
n 42:3 Ps 79:10; 115:2
o 42:4 Ps 62:8
p 55:14; 100:4
q 42:5 Ps 38:6; 43:5; Mt 26:38
r 42:6 Ps 61:2; Jnh 2:7
s 42:7 Ps 69:1-2; Jnh 2:3
t 42:8 Jb 35:10; Ps 77:6
u 42:9 Ps 18:2; 31:3
v Ps 43:2
w 42:10 Jl 2:17

5 My enemies speak maliciously
about me:
"When will he die
and be forgotten?"[a]
6 When one of them comes to visit,
he speaks deceitfully;
he stores up evil in his heart;
he goes out and talks.[b]
7 All who hate me whisper together
about me;
they plan to harm me.[c]
8 "Something awful has
overwhelmed him,[A]
and he won't rise again from where
he lies!"[d]
9 Even my friend[B] in whom I trusted,
one who ate my bread,
has raised his heel against me.[e]

10 But you, LORD, be gracious to me
and raise me up;
then I will repay them.[f]
11 By this I know that you delight
in me:[g]
my enemy does not shout
in triumph over me.[h]
12 You supported me because of
my integrity[i]
and set me in your presence forever.[j]

13 Blessed be the LORD God of Israel,
from everlasting to everlasting.
Amen and amen.[k]

BOOK II (PSALMS 42–72)

LONGING FOR GOD

42 *For the choir director. A* Maskil *of the sons of Korah.*

1 As a deer longs for
flowing streams,
so I long for you, God.[l]
2 I thirst for God, the living God.

When can I come and appear
before God?[m]
3 My tears have been my food
day and night,
while all day long
people say to me,
"Where is your God?"[n]
4 I remember this as I pour out
my heart:[o]
how I walked with many,
leading the festive procession
to the house of God,
with joyful and thankful shouts.[p]

5 Why, my soul, are you so dejected?
Why are you in such turmoil?
Put your hope in God, for I will
still praise him,
my Savior and my God.[q]
6 I[c] am deeply depressed;
therefore I remember you
from the land of Jordan
and the peaks of Hermon,
from Mount Mizar.[r]
7 Deep calls to deep in the roar
of your waterfalls;
all your breakers and your billows
have swept over me.[s]
8 The LORD will send his faithful love
by day;[t]
his song will be with me
in the night —
a prayer to the God of my life.

9 I will say to God, my rock,[u]
"Why have you forgotten me?
Why must I go about in sorrow
because of
the enemy's oppression?"[v]
10 My adversaries taunt me,
as if crushing my bones,
while all day long they say to me,
"Where is your God?"[w]

A 41:8 Lit *"A thing of worthlessness has been poured into him* B 41:9 Lit *Even a man of my peace* C 42:5-6 Some Hb mss, LXX, Syr; other Hb mss read *him, the salvation of his presence.* [6]*My God, I*

41:9 Perhaps this is a reference to Ahithophel, David's counselor, who betrayed him by joining Absalom's conspiracy (see 2 Sam 15:12; 16:20–17:4). According to the New Testament, though, the passage was ultimately fulfilled when Judas betrayed his Master, the Son of David (see John 13:18-30).

42:3-5 Sometimes it feels like God has taken a long-distance trip and not informed us when he'll return (42:3). The first thing to do in such circumstances is to draw from past experiences with God. The psalmist recalls times when he celebrated with God's people (42:4). The second thing the psalmist does is to counsel himself with the truth. He asks himself why he is **so dejected** and filled with turmoil (42:5). Then he urges himself, in spite of the darkness, **Put your hope in God** (42:5).

Keep track of those times when God has come through for you. It's important to have a history with God so that during the bad times, you can remember the good times to help you persevere. In addition, remember what you know to be true about God. He is faithful and worth hoping in. To hope is to expectantly wait for God to act. Just because you can't see God working doesn't mean he's inactive.

42:6-8 The psalmist's emotional life is like a seesaw; he's up and then down. His trying circumstances are like **breakers** sweeping over him (42:7): he pictures himself being rocked by an enormous wave, only to be overrun by another as soon as it passes. But again he prays for and hopes in God's **faithful love**. Like a child frightened **in the night** by a thunderstorm, he longs for his Father's presence—not to stop the storm but to remind him that he isn't alone (42:8).

42:9 The truth is that God hadn't **forgotten** the psalmist, but sometimes life does feel this way. The apostle Paul reminds us that "all things work together for the good of those who love God" (Rom 8:28). Notice he doesn't say that all things *are* good, but that all things *work together for* good. Right now the pieces of your life may seem unrelated and purposeless. But God is up to something: he's conforming you "to the image of his Son" (see Rom 8:29).

11 Why, my soul, are you so dejected?
    Why are you in such turmoil?
    Put your hope in God, for I will
        still praise him,
    my Savior and my God.[a]

43

[A] Vindicate me, God,
    and champion my cause
    against an unfaithful nation;
    rescue me from the deceitful
        and unjust person.[b]

2 For you are the God of my refuge.
    Why have you rejected me?
    Why must I go about in sorrow
    because of the enemy's oppression?[c]

3 Send your light and your truth;
        let them lead me.[d]
    Let them bring me
        to your holy mountain,
    to your dwelling place.[e]

4 Then I will come to the altar
        of God,
    to God, my greatest joy.[f]
    I will praise you with the lyre,
    God, my God.[g]

5 Why, my soul, are you so dejected?
    Why are you in such turmoil?
    Put your hope in God, for I will
        still praise him,
    my Savior and my God.[h]

ISRAEL'S COMPLAINT

44

For the choir director. A Maskil *of the sons of Korah.*

1 God, we have heard with our ears —
    our ancestors have told us —
    the work you accomplished
        in their days,
    in days long ago:[i]
2 In order to plant them,
    you displaced the nations
        by your hand;
    in order to settle them,
    you brought disaster on
        the peoples.[j]

3 For they did not take the land
        by their sword —
    their arm did not
        bring them victory —
    but by your right hand, your arm,
    and the light of your face,[k]
    because you were favorable
        toward them.[l]

4 You are my King, my God,
    who ordains[B] victories for Jacob.[m]
5 Through you we drive back our foes;
    through your name we trample
        our enemies.[n]
6 For I do not trust in my bow,
    and my sword does not
        bring me victory.[o]
7 But you give us victory over our foes
    and let those who hate us be disgraced.[p]
8 We boast in God all day long;
    we will praise your name forever.[q]
    Selah

9 But you have rejected
        and humiliated us;
    you do not march out
        with our armies.[r]
10 You make us retreat from the foe,
    and those who hate us
    have taken plunder for themselves.[s]
11 You hand us over to be eaten
        like sheep
    and scatter us among the nations.[t]
12 You sell your people for nothing;
    you make no profit
        from selling them.[u]
13 You make us an object of reproach
        to our neighbors,
    a source of mockery and ridicule
        to those around us.[v]
14 You make us a joke
        among the nations,
    a laughingstock[c]
        among the peoples.[w]
15 My disgrace is before me
        all day long,
    and shame has covered my face,[x]

---

[a] 42:11 Ps 43:5; Mt 26:38
[b] 43:1 Ps 5:6; 26:1; 35:24
[c] 43:2 Ps 42:9; 88:14
[d] 43:3 Ps 36:9
[e] Ps 2:6; 46:4; 84:1
[f] 43:4 Ps 26:6
[g] Ps 33:2; 57:8
[h] 43:5 Ps 42:5,11
[i] 44:1 Dt 32:7; Ps 78:3
[j] 44:2 2Sm 7:10; Ps 78:55; 80:8
[k] 44:3 Nm 6:25
[l] Dt 7:7-8; Ps 77:15; Hs 1:7
[m] 44:4 Ps 42:8; 74:12
[n] 44:5 Ps 60:12; 108:13; Zch 10:5
[o] 44:6 1Sm 17:47; Ps 33:16
[p] 44:7 Ps 35:4; 53:5
[q] 44:8 Ps 30:12; 34:2
[r] 44:9 Ps 60:1,10; 74:1; 108:11
[s] 44:10 Lv 26:17; Dt 28:25; Jos 7:8,12
[t] 44:11 Lv 26:33; Dt 4:27; 28:64; Ps 106:27
[u] 44:12 Dt 32:30; Jdg 2:14; 3:8; Is 52:3-4
[v] 44:13 Dt 28:37; Ps 79:4
[w] 44:14 Jb 17:6; Ps 109:25; Jr 24:9
[x] 44:15 2Ch 32:21; Ps 69:7

[A] Ps 43 Many Hb mss connect Pss 42 and 43 [B] 44:4 LXX, Syr, Aq; MT reads *King, God; ordain* [C] 44:14 Lit *shaking of the head*

42:11 The psalmist returns to his earlier refrain: **Put your hope in God**. Even in the dark, then, continue to hope in God. When he doesn't change your situation, keep pursuing him. He is faithful. "Weeping may stay overnight, but there is joy in the morning" (30:5). 43:3 He calls on the Lord to **send [his] light and ... truth**—that is, divine understanding and revelation—to guide him back to God's temple. 43:5 Like the psalmist, we often have to talk to ourselves in the midst of our despair. We need to remind ourselves that God is worthy

of our trust and that we should expect him to answer in a way that will give us a new reason to give fresh praise.
44:1-3 The psalmist bears witness to what he and his fellow Israelites had heard from their **ancestors** about the **work** that God **accomplished** on their behalf **long ago** (44:1). He had **displaced** other **nations** and instead planted Israel's family in the land he had promised to Abraham, Isaac, and Jacob (44:2). None of this happened as a result of their own strength, but because God gave them **victory** (44:3).

44:4-8 Because of what God had done in the past, the psalmist and those with him could trust their divine **King** to provide continuing **victories** for them (44:4). Though they would have to battle their **enemies**, the psalmist knew that success didn't ultimately come from his **bow** or his **sword** (44:5-6). **Victory** comes from the Lord, in whom they could rightly **boast** (44:7-8).
44:9 Just as victory is ultimately from the Lord, so is defeat.

[a]44:16 Ps 8:2; 74:10
[b]44:17 Ps 119:61,153
[c]44:18 Jb 23:11; Ps 37:31; 119:51,157
[d]44:19 Jb 30:29; Jr 9:11
[e]44:20 Dt 6:14; Jb 11:13
[f]44:21 Ps 139:1-2; Jr 17:10; Heb 4:13
[g]44:22 Is 53:7; Jr 12:3; Rm 8:36
[h]44:23 Ps 7:6; 35:23; 78:65
[i]44:24 Jb 13:24; Ps 88:14
[j]44:25 Ps 119:25
[k]44:26 Ps 25:22
[l]45:title Pss 60; 69; 80 titles
[m]45:1 Ezr 7:6
[n]45:2 Lk 4:22
[o]45:2 Ps 21:6
[p]45:3 Is 49:2; Rv 1:16; 19:15
[q]45:4 Ps 65:5; 98:1
[r]45:5 Dt 23:14; Ps 18:14
[s]45:6-7 Heb 1:8-9
[t]45:6 Ps 93:2
[u]45:7 Ps 33:5
[v]45:8 Sg 4:14; Jn 19:39
[w]45:9 Sg 6:8
[x]1Kg 9:28; 10:11
[y]45:10 Ru 1:16-17
[z]45:11 Eph 5:33
[aa]45:12 Ps 68:29; 72:10-11; Is 49:23

16 because of the taunts[A] of the scorner
and reviler,
because of the enemy
and avenger.[a]

17 All this has happened to us,
but we have not forgotten you
or betrayed your covenant.[b]
18 Our hearts have not turned back;
our steps have not strayed
from your path.[c]
19 But you have crushed us in a haunt
of jackals
and have covered us
with deepest darkness.[d]
20 If we had forgotten the name
of our God
and spread out our hands
to a foreign god,[e]
21 wouldn't God have found this out,
since he knows the secrets
of the heart?[f]
22 Because of you we are being put
to death all day long;
we are counted as sheep
to be slaughtered.[g]

23 Wake up, LORD!
Why are you sleeping?
Get up! Don't reject us forever![h]
24 Why do you hide
and forget our affliction
and oppression?[i]
25 For we have sunk down to the dust;
our bodies cling to the ground.[j]
26 Rise up! Help us!
Redeem us because of
your faithful love.[k]

A ROYAL WEDDING SONG

45

For the choir director: according to "The Lilies."[l] *A Maskil of the sons of Korah. A love song.*

1 My heart is moved by a noble theme
as I recite my verses to the king;
my tongue is the pen
of a skillful writer.[m]
2 You are the most handsome of men;[B]
grace flows from your lips.[n]
Therefore God
has blessed you forever.[o]
3 Mighty warrior, strap your sword
at your side.
In your majesty and splendor[p] —
4 in your splendor ride triumphantly
in the cause of truth, humility,
and justice.
May your right hand show
your awe-inspiring acts.[q]
5 Your sharpened arrows pierce
the hearts of the king's enemies;
the peoples fall under you.[r]

6 Your throne,[s] God, is[C] forever
and ever;
the scepter of your kingdom is
a scepter of justice.[t]
7 You love righteousness
and hate wickedness;[u]
therefore God, your God,
has anointed you with the oil
of joy
more than your companions.
8 Myrrh, aloes, and cassia perfume
all your garments;
from ivory palaces harps
bring you joy.[v]
9 Kings' daughters are
among your honored women;[w]
the queen, adorned with gold
from Ophir,
stands at your right hand.[x]

10 Listen, daughter, pay attention
and consider:
forget your people
and your father's house,[y]
11 and the king will desire
your beauty.
Bow down to him,
for he is your lord.[z]
12 The daughter of Tyre,
the wealthy people,
will seek your favor with gifts.[aa]

13 In her chamber, the royal daughter
is all glorious,

[A]44:16 Lit *voice* [B]45:2 Or *of the descendants of Adam* [C]45:6 Or *Your divine throne is*, or *Your throne is God's*

44:22 Paul quotes this passage in Romans 8:36 to emphasize the fact that Christians can expect to face suffering and persecution.
44:26 When you experience unjust suffering and it seems that God has abandoned you, don't cease trusting him. Remember what he has done in the past, understand that suffering is part of the experience of God's people on this fallen earth, and trust him to deliver you according to his faithfulness.

45:6-7 As God's representative, the king would have a **throne** that would last **forever** (45:6), which is an allusion to God's covenant with David (see 2 Sam 7:11-16). The king was just in the administration of his kingdom, loving **righteousness** and hating **wickedness** (45:7). Hebrews 1:8-9 applies these verses to the Son of God, Jesus Christ. He will rule in his millennial kingdom with perfect justice and righteousness. And he fulfills God's covenant with David. By virtue of his resurrection from the dead, he will ever live to sit on David's throne.
45:13-17 This will ultimately be fulfilled at the marriage of the Lamb when the great King, the Lord Jesus Christ, is united forever with his bride, the church (see Rev 19:6-9). In the meantime, like the bride who forsakes her family to be with the king, believers are to forsake the world now that we are promised to Christ (see Luke 14:26-33).

her clothing embroidered
with gold.[a]

14 In colorful garments she is led
to the king;
after her, the virgins,
her companions, are brought
to you.[b]

15 They are led in with gladness
and rejoicing;
they enter the king's palace.[c]

16 Your sons will succeed
your ancestors;
you will make them princes
throughout the land.[d]

17 I will cause your name
to be remembered
for all generations;
therefore the peoples will praise you
forever and ever.[e]

GOD OUR REFUGE

46 For the choir director. A song of
the sons of Korah. According to
Alamoth.[f]

1 God is our refuge and strength,
a helper who is always found
in times of trouble.[g]

2 Therefore we will not be afraid,
though the earth trembles
and the mountains topple
into the depths of the seas,[h]

3 though its water roars
and foams
and the mountains quake
with its turmoil.[i]   *Selah*

4 There is a river—
its streams delight the city of God,
the holy dwelling place
of the Most High.[j]

5 God is within her;
she will not be toppled.
God will help her
when the morning dawns.[k]

6 Nations rage, kingdoms topple;
the earth melts when he lifts
his voice.[l]

7 The LORD of Armies is with us;
the God of Jacob is
our stronghold.[m]   *Selah*

8 Come, see the works of the LORD,
who brings devastation
on the earth.[n]

9 He makes wars cease
throughout the earth.
He shatters bows and cuts spears
to pieces;
he sets wagons ablaze.[o]

10 "Stop your fighting, and know that
I am God,
exalted among the nations,
exalted on the earth."[p]

11 The LORD of Armies is with us;
the God of Jacob is
our stronghold.[q]   *Selah*

HOPE WORDS

*The chaos around you shouldn't
override the calm within you.*

GOD OUR KING

47 For the choir director. A psalm of the
sons of Korah.

1 Clap your hands, all you peoples;[r]
shout to God with a jubilant cry.[s]

2 For the LORD, the Most High,
is awe-inspiring,
a great King over the whole earth.[t]

3 He subdues peoples under us
and nations under our feet.[u]

4 He chooses for us our inheritance—
the pride of Jacob,
whom he loves.[v]   *Selah*

5 God ascends among shouts of joy,
the LORD, with the sound of trumpets.[w]

6 Sing praise to God, sing praise;
sing praise to our King, sing praise![x]

7 Sing a song of wisdom,[A]
for God is King of the whole earth.[y]

[a] 45:13 Ex 39:2-3; Rv 19:7-8
[b] 45:14 Ezk 16:18; 26:16
[c] 45:15 Jr 22:4
[d] 45:16 1Pt 2:9; Rv 1:6; 5:10
[e] 45:17 Mal 1:11
[f] 46:title 1Ch 15:20
[g] 46:1 Ps 9:9; 62:7-8
[h] 46:2 Ps 18:7; 82:5
[i] 46:3 Ps 93:3-4; Jr 5:22
[j] 46:4 Ps 43:3; Rv 22:1-2
[k] 46:5 Is 12:6; Zch 2:10-11
[l] 46:6 Ps 2:1; Jr 25:30

[m] 46:7 Ps 9:9; Jl 3:16
[n] 46:8 Ps 66:5
[o] 46:9 Ps 76:3; Is 2:4; Mc 4:3
[p] 46:10 Ps 100:3; Is 2:11,17
[q] 46:11 Ps 9:9; Jl 3:16
[r] 47:1 Is 55:12
[s] Ps 95:1
[t] 47:2 Dt 7:21; Neh 1:5; Mal 1:14
[u] 47:3 Ps 2:8; 18:47
[v] 47:4 Am 8:7; Nah 2:2
[w] 47:5 2Sm 6:15; Ps 68:18; 98:6
[x] 47:6 Ps 68:4; 89:18
[y] 47:7 Zch 14:9; 1Co 14:15

[A] 47:7 Or *Sing a* maskil

46:1-3 The Lord is a place of security for his people. He is never too busy but always available. The psalmist imagines terrible conditions on earth: earthquakes that topple mountains and cause tsunamis (46:2-3). Yet even if the worst things happen, **we will not be afraid**, for God is still near to help (46:2).
46:4-7 When the Messiah returns to reign in Jerusalem, **the city of God**, the Creator will be intimately accessible to his people

(46:4). God, in the person of the Messiah, will have his throne **within her** (46:5). It will be an Eden-like environment with **a river** in the midst of the city (46:4). No enemies, however strong, will harm it for **the LORD of Armies** is the **stronghold** of his people (46:6-7).
46:8-11 The psalmist encourages and comforts God's people with the knowledge that God would fight their battles and defend them against their enemies (46:8-9). They did

not need to worry or strive when faced with challenges or difficulties. The same is true for us. Remember that the Lord is with his people. He is **our stronghold**—our security and strength (46:11).
47:3-4 God is to be feared specifically because he had subdued nations **under the feet** of his people (47:3). He did this when he chose Israel as his special people (47:4), brought them into the promised land, and drove out Canaan's inhabitants before them.

a 47:8 1Ch 16:31; Ps 22:28; 97:2
b 47:9 Ps 102:22
c Ps 72:11; Is 49:7,23
d 48:1 Ps 2:6; Mc 4:1; Zch 8:3
e 48:2 Mt 5:35
f 48:3 Ps 46:7; 50:2
g 48:4 2Sm 10:6-19
h 48:5 Ex 15:15
i 48:6 Is 13:8; Hs 13:13
j 48:7 1Kg 22:48; Jr 18:17; Ezk 27:26
k 48:8 Ps 87:5; Is 2:2; Mc 4:1
l 48:9 Ps 26:3; 40:10
m 48:10 Ps 113:3; Mal 1:11
n Ps 45:4

o 48:11 Ps 97:8
p 48:12-13 Ps 78:5-7; 122:7
q 48:14 Ps 23:3-4; Is 58:11
r 49:1 Ps 78:1; Mc 1:2
s 49:2 Ps 62:9
t 49:3 Ps 37:30
u 49:4 Nm 12:8; Mt 13:35
v 49:5 Ps 23:4; 27:1
w 49:6 Jb 31:24; Ps 52:7; Pr 11:28
x 49:7 Jb 36:18-19; Mt 25:8-9
y 49:8 Mt 16:26
z 49:9 Jb 33:28; Ps 16:10
aa 49:10 Ec 2:16
ab Ps 39:6; Ec 2:18-19; Lk 12:20

8 God reigns over the nations;
God is seated on his holy throne.[a]
9 The nobles of the peoples
have assembled
with the people of the God
of Abraham.[b]
For the leaders[A] of the earth
belong to God;
he is greatly exalted.[c]

ZION EXALTED

48 *A song. A psalm of the sons of Korah.*
The LORD is great and
highly praised
in the city of our God.[d]
His holy mountain,
2 rising splendidly,
is the joy of the whole earth.
Mount Zion — the summit
of Zaphon —
is the city of the great King.[e]
3 God is known as a stronghold
in its citadels.[f]

4 Look! The kings assembled;
they advanced together.[g]
5 They looked and froze with fear;
they fled in terror.[h]
6 Trembling seized them there,
agony like that of a woman in labor,[i]
7 as you wrecked the ships of Tarshish
with the east wind.[j]

8 Just as we heard, so we have seen
in the city of the LORD of Armies,
in the city of our God;
God will establish it forever.[k]   *Selah*

9 God, within your temple,
we contemplate your faithful love.[l]
10 Like your name, God, so your praise
reaches to the ends of the earth;[m]
your right hand is filled
with justice.[n]

11 Mount Zion is glad.
Judah's villages[B] rejoice
because of your judgments.[o]

12 Go around Zion, encircle it;
count its towers,
13 note its ramparts; tour its citadels
so that you can tell
a future generation:[p]
14 "This God, our God
forever and ever —
he will always lead us."[C,q]

MISPLACED TRUST IN WEALTH

49 *For the choir director. A psalm of the sons of Korah.*
1 Hear this, all you peoples;
listen, all who inhabit the world,[r]
2 both low and high,
rich and poor together.[s]
3 My mouth speaks wisdom;
my heart's meditation
brings understanding.[t]
4 I turn my ear to a proverb;
I explain my riddle with a lyre.[u]

5 Why should I fear in times
of trouble?
The iniquity of my foes surrounds me.[v]
6 They trust in their wealth
and boast of their abundant riches.[w]
7 Yet these cannot redeem a person[D]
or pay his ransom to God[x] —
8 since the price of redeeming him is
too costly,
one should forever stop trying[E,y] —
9 so that he may live forever
and not see the Pit.[z]

10 For one can see that the wise die;
the foolish and stupid also
pass away.[aa]
Then they leave their wealth
to others.[ab]

[A] 47:9 Lit *shields*   [B] 48:11 Lit *daughters*   [C] 48:14 Some Hb mss, LXX; other Hb mss read *over death*   [D] 49:7 Or *Certainly he cannot redeem himself,* or *Yet he cannot redeem a brother*   [E] 49:8 Or *costly, it will cease forever*

47:8-9 As Paul testifies in Philippians 2:10-11, one day "every knee will bow . . . and every tongue will confess that Jesus Christ is Lord, to the glory of God the Father." God's people are to put into practice now what will eventually be true worldwide: submission to God's kingdom agenda, the visible manifestation of the comprehensive rule of God over every area of life. Those who do not bow voluntarily to Christ and his kingdom now will be forced to do so mandatorily later.
48:1-2 Mount Zion is a reference to Jerusalem. It was there where God dwelled among his people Israel, and in it Solomon constructed

God's temple. The city was **holy** because God was in its midst (48:1).
48:4-8 According to the psalmist, the enemies of God's people were defeated, not because of the strength of Israel's army, but because of the strength of Israel's God. Their enemies **froze with fear** and their **ships** were **wrecked** (48:5, 7). **The LORD of Armies** of angels is her defender. Though God would allow Jerusalem to be decimated by Babylon as a result of Israel's sins, he would also **establish it forever** (48:8). The Lord Jesus will rule from Jerusalem during his millennial kingdom. Then, in the new creation, God will dwell with his people forever in the new Jerusalem (see Rev 21:1-27).

48:14 The psalmist exhorts his audience to be confident that **God . . . will always lead** his people. Indeed, the same God who made those who first read this passage secure will eternally keep believers who trust him. Nothing "will be able to separate us from the love of God that is in Christ Jesus our Lord" (Rom 8:39).
49:6-9 Though earthly treasure can buy great material possessions, it cannot buy redemption of one's soul from death (49:7). Wealth cannot acquire salvation because the cost is just too high (49:8). Only one thing can redeem sinful humanity **so that [we] may live forever** (49:9): the precious blood of Jesus Christ.

11 Their graves are
    their permanent homes,[A]
their dwellings from generation
    to generation,
though they have named estates
    after themselves.[a]
12 But despite his assets,[B] mankind
    will not last;
he is like the animals that perish.[b]

13 This is the way of those
    who are arrogant,
and of their followers,
who approve of
    their words.[C,c]   *Selah*
14 Like sheep they are headed
    for Sheol;
Death will shepherd them.
The upright will rule over them
    in the morning,[d]
and their form will waste away
    in Sheol,[D]
    far from their lofty abode.[e]
15 But God will redeem me
from the power of Sheol,
    for he will take me.[f]   *Selah*

16 Do not be afraid when a person
    gets rich,
when the wealth[E]
    of his house increases.[g]
17 For when he dies, he will take
    nothing at all;
his wealth will not follow
    him down.[h]
18 Though he blesses himself
    during his lifetime —
and you are acclaimed
    when you do well
    for yourself[i] —
19 he will go to the generation
    of his fathers;
they will never see the light.[j]
20 Mankind, with his assets
but without understanding,
    is like the animals that perish.[k]

GOD AS JUDGE

50 *A psalm of Asaph.*[l]
The Mighty One, God,[F]
    the LORD, speaks;
he summons the earth
from the rising of the sun
    to its setting.[m]
2 From Zion, the perfection of beauty,
    God appears in radiance.[G,n]
3 Our God is coming; he will not
    be silent!
Devouring fire precedes him,
    and a storm rages around him.[o]
4 On high, he summons heaven
    and earth
in order to judge his people:[p]
5 "Gather my faithful ones to me,
those who made a covenant with me
    by sacrifice."[q]
6 The heavens proclaim
    his righteousness,[r]
for God is the Judge.[s]   *Selah*

7 "Listen, my people, and I will speak;
I will testify against you, Israel.
I am God, your God.[t]
8 I do not rebuke you for your sacrifices
or for your burnt offerings,
    which are continually before me.[u]
9 I will not take a bull
    from your household
or male goats from your pens,[v]
10 for every animal of the forest
    is mine,
the cattle on a thousand hills.
11 I know every bird of the mountains,
and the creatures of the field
    are mine.[w]
12 If I were hungry, I would not tell you,
for the world and everything in it
    is mine.[x]
13 Do I eat the flesh of bulls
or drink the blood of goats?[y]
14 Sacrifice a thank offering to God,[z]
and pay your vows
    to the Most High.[aa]

[a]49:11 Ps 5:9; 10:6
[b]49:12 Ec 3:19
[c]49:13 Ps 31:23; Pr 16:18; 21:24
[d]49:14 Rv 2:26
[e]Jb 24:19; Ps 9:17
[f]49:15 Ps 16:10; 56:13; Hs 13:14
[g]49:16 Ps 37:7
[h]49:17 Jb 27:19; Ps 17:14; 1Tm 6:7
[i]49:18 Dt 29:19; Ps 10:3,6
[j]49:19 Gn 15:15; Jb 33:30; Ps 56:13
[k]49:20 Ec 3:19

[l]50:title 1Ch 16:5,7
[m]50:1 Jos 22:22; Ps 113:3
[n]50:2 Dt 33:2; Ps 48:2; Lm 2:15
[o]50:3 Ps 18:12-13; 97:3
[p]50:4 Dt 4:26; 31:28; 32:1; Is 1:2
[q]50:5 Ex 24:4-8; 2Ch 6:11
[r]50:6 Ps 89:5; 97:6
[s]Ps 75:7; 96:13
[t]50:7 Dt 31:21; Ps 81:8
[u]50:8 1Sm 15:22; Ps 40:6; 51:16
[v]50:9 Ps 69:31
[w]50:10-11 Ex 19:5; Ps 104:24
[x]50:12 Dt 10:14; Ps 24:1; 1Co 10:26
[y]50:13 Is 1:11
[z]50:14 Lv 7:12; Ps 107:22; 116:17
[aa]Dt 23:21; Ps 76:11

[A]49:11 LXX, Syr, Tg; MT reads *Their inner thought is that their houses are eternal*   [B]49:12 Or *honor*   [C]49:13 Lit *and after them with their mouth they were pleased*   [D]49:14 Hb obscure   [E]49:16 Or *glory*, also in v. 17   [F]50:1 Or *The God of gods*   [G]50:2 Or *God shines forth*

49:12, 15 It is foolish to think that the possessions and property we amass in this life will cause our names or reputations to endure. Yet, for those who trust in God, there is hope of eternal life—regardless of the balance of your bank account.
49:16-20 No matter how much money they accumulate, those who lack spiritual **understanding** will be **like the animals that perish** (49:18-20). This is both a reminder and an encouragement to pursue righteousness above riches. Your life will soon end. The

riches you have deposited in heaven will prove far more important in the long run than whatever riches you deposited on earth (see Matt 6:19-21). Prioritize the spiritual over the material.
50:1-6 The psalmist, Asaph, sets forth God's credentials as the Creator. Therefore, his **covenant** people are to listen to him and heed his words (50:5-6).
50:7-15 The Lord warns his people not to let their worship consist of merely outward religious actions—making **sacrifices** and

burnt offerings (50:8). He owns **the cattle on a thousand hills**; therefore, he doesn't *need* his people to provide them to him (50:9-12). What God desires in his followers is inward devotion that is reflected in expressing thanks to God and paying **vows** to him (50:14). He urges people to **call on [him] in a day of trouble**, with the result that he would rescue them and they would **honor** him with praise (50:15). Genuine acts of worship and obedience bring God great glory.

a 50:15 Ps 20:1; 59:16; 77:2
b 50:16 Is 29:13
c 50:17 Pr 5:12; 12:1
d 50:18 Rm 1:32; 1Tm 5:22
e 50:19 Ps 10:7; 36:3; 52:2
f 50:20 Jb 19:18; Mt 10:21
g 50:21 Is 42:14; 57:11
h Ps 90:8
i 50:22 Jb 8:13; Ps 9:17
j 50:23 Ps 85:13; 91:16;
Gl 6:16
k 51:title 2Sm 12:1

l 51:1 Is 43:25; Ac 3:19
m 51:2 Is 1:16; Jr 33:8;
1Jn 1:7,9
n 51:3 Ps 32:5; Pr 28:13;
Is 59:12
o 51:4 Ps 41:4
p Rm 3:4
q 51:5 Jb 15:14; Ps 58:3; Rm
5:12-13
r 51:6 Jb 38:36; Pr 2:6;
Ec 2:26
s 51:7 Lv 14:4,49; Nm 19:18;
Is 1:18
t 51:8 Ps 35:10; Is 38:13
u 51:9 Jr 16:17
v 51:10 Ps 24:4; Mt 5:8;
Jms 4:8
w 51:11 2Kg 13:23; Is 63:10-
11; Jr 7:15

15 Call on me in a day of trouble;
   I will rescue you,
      and you will honor me."*a*

16 But God says to the wicked:
   "What right do you have to recite
      my statutes
   and to take my covenant on your lips?*b*
17 You hate instruction
   and fling my words behind you.*c*
18 When you see a thief,
   you make friends with him,
   and you associate with adulterers.*d*
19 You unleash your mouth for evil
   and harness your tongue for deceit.*e*
20 You sit, maligning your brother,
   slandering your mother's son.*f*
21 You have done these things,
      and I kept silent;
   you thought I was just like you.*g*
   But I will rebuke you
   and lay out the case before you.*A,h*

22 "Understand this,
      you who forget God,
   or I will tear you apart,
   and there will be no one to
      rescue you.*i*
23 Whoever sacrifices a thank offering
      honors me,
   and whoever orders his conduct,
   I will show him the salvation
      of God."*j*

A PRAYER FOR RESTORATION

51 *For the choir director. A psalm of David,
   when the prophet Nathan came to him
after he had gone to Bathsheba.*k

1 Be gracious to me, God,
   according to your faithful love;

according to your abundant
      compassion,
   blot out my rebellion.*l*
2 Completely wash away my guilt
   and cleanse me from my sin.*m*
3 For I am conscious of my rebellion,
   and my sin is always before me.*n*
4 Against you — you alone —
      I have sinned
   and done this evil in your sight.*o*
   So you are right
      when you pass sentence;
   you are blameless when you judge.*p*
5 Indeed, I was guilty
      when I was born;
   I was sinful when my mother
      conceived me.*q*

6 Surely you desire integrity
      in the inner self,
   and you teach me wisdom
      deep within.*r*
7 Purify me with hyssop,
      and I will be clean;
   wash me, and I will be
      whiter than snow.*s*
8 Let me hear joy and gladness;
   let the bones you have crushed
      rejoice.*t*
9 Turn your face away*B* from my sins
   and blot out all my guilt.*u*

10 God, create a clean heart for me
   and renew a steadfast*C* spirit
      within me.*v*
11 Do not banish me
      from your presence
   or take your Holy Spirit from me.*w*
12 Restore the joy of your salvation
      to me,

A 50:21 Lit *lay it out before your eyes*   *B* 51:9 Lit *Hide your face*   *C* 51:10 Or *right*

50:16-21 The wicked, past and present, are condemned for their hypocrisy. They make a pretense of reciting God's **statutes** and **covenant**, but they don't truly care (50:16). And though they assemble with those who love the Lord, they don't take his word into their hearts. They even mistake God's patience for his approval. When he keeps **silent** and doesn't immediately bring retribution, they think he is just like them (50:21). They will one day learn the error of their ways.
50:22-23 Hypocrites are admonished to change their actions before it's too late (50:22). They need to re-examine themselves and understand that God withholds his judgment to allow repentance. Those who repent of their sins and turn to God in faith can have hope because he abundantly pardons, providing **salvation** (50:23).
51:1-3 David wants God to **blot out** his sin from his memory. Of course, God can't forget,

but David wants his sin erased in the sense that God would not relate to him based on his rebellious actions. The king longs for the Lord's supernatural cleansing because he is unable to wash himself and escape the guilt of his wickedness (51:2). He is tormented by the remembrance of what he had done (51:3)—an indication of his heart's sensitivity toward God.
51:4-6 Though David had clearly wronged Bathsheba and Uriah, he understands that ultimately he had **sinned** against God **alone** (51:4). He recognizes that God is the perfect righteous standard by which our actions are judged; therefore, all sin violates his character. All evaluations of right and wrong must be consistent with the standards that he himself has revealed. David knows that he was born, like all humans, with a sin nature: **I was sinful when my mother conceived me** (51:5). David needed

a radical transformation of his **inner self** so that he might learn **wisdom** and adopt God's perspective on all things (51:6). We need the same.
51:7 This plant had been dipped into the Passover lamb's blood when it was applied to the Israelites' doorframes (see Exod 12:21-23).
51:10-13 In requesting that God give him **a clean heart** and not take away the **Holy Spirit from** him (51:10-11), the king was not concerned about losing salvation. He was not speaking of the indwelling of the Spirit, since the Spirit did not indwell Old Testament believers as he does New Testament believers. At issue here is David's desire to fulfill the royal calling God had placed on his life. When he was anointed as king, "the Spirit of the Lord came powerfully on David" (1 Sam 16:13). He did not want to lose God's calling and empowerment like his predecessor Saul

and sustain me by giving me
a willing spirit.[a]

13 Then I will teach the rebellious
your ways,
and sinners will return to you.[b]

14 Save me from the guilt of bloodshed,
God[c] —
God of my salvation —
and my tongue will sing
of your righteousness.[d]

15 Lord, open my lips,
and my mouth will declare
your praise.[e]

16 You do not want a sacrifice,
or I would give it;
you are not pleased
with a burnt offering.[f]

17 The sacrifice pleasing to God is[A]
a broken spirit.
You will not despise a broken
and humbled heart, God.[g]

18 In your good pleasure, cause Zion
to prosper;
build the walls of Jerusalem.[h]

19 Then you will delight
in righteous sacrifices,
whole burnt offerings;
then bulls will be offered
on your altar.[i]

GOD JUDGES THE PROUD

52 *For the choir director. A Maskil of David. When Doeg the Edomite went and reported to Saul, telling him, "David went to Ahimelech's house."*[j]

1 Why boast about evil,
you hero![k]
God's faithful love is constant.[l]

2 Like a sharpened razor,
your tongue devises destruction,
working treachery.[m]

3 You love evil instead of good,
lying instead of
speaking truthfully.[n]   *Selah*

4 You love any words that destroy,
you treacherous tongue![o]

5 This is why God will bring
you down forever.
He will take you, ripping you out of
your tent;
he will uproot you from the land
of the living.[p]   *Selah*

6 The righteous will see and fear,
and they will derisively say
about that hero,[B,q]

7 "Here is the man
who would not make God his refuge,
but trusted in the abundance
of his riches,
taking refuge
in his destructive behavior."[r]

8 But I am like a flourishing olive tree
in the house of God;[s]
I trust in God's faithful love
forever and ever.[t]

9 I will praise you forever for what
you have done.
In the presence
of your faithful people,
I will put my hope in your name,
for it is good.[u]

A PORTRAIT OF SINNERS

53 *For the choir director: on Mahalath.*[v] *A Maskil of David.*

1 The fool says in his heart,
"There's no God."
They are corrupt, and they do
vile deeds.
There is no one who does good.[w]

2 God looks down from heaven
on the human race[c]
to see if there is one who is wise,
one who seeks God.[x]

3 All have turned away;
all alike have become corrupt.
There is no one who does good,
not even one.[y]

[a] 51:12 Ps 13:5
[b] 51:13 Ex 33:13; Ps 25:4; Jr 2:33
[c] 51:14 Ps 26:9
[d] Ps 35:28; 71:15
[e] 51:15 Ex 4:15; Ps 9:14
[f] 51:16 1Sm 15:22; Ps 40:6
[g] 51:17 Ps 34:18
[h] 51:18 Ps 69:35; 102:16; 147:2
[i] 51:19 Ps 4:5; 66:13,15; Mal 3:3
[j] 52:title 1Sm 22:9
[k] 52:1 Ps 94:4
[l] Ps 40:10-11; 138:2
[m] 52:2 Ps 5:9; 50:19; 59:7
[n] 52:3 Ps 58:3; Jr 9:4-5
[o] 52:4 Ps 10:7; Pr 17:4
[p] 52:5 Ps 27:13; Pr 2:22
[q] 52:6 Jb 22:19-20; Ps 37:34
[r] 52:7 Ps 10:6; 49:6; Pr 11:28
[s] 52:8 Ps 1:3; 128:3; Jr 11:16
[t] Ps 143:8
[u] 52:9 Ps 30:12; 54:6
[v] 53:title Ps 88 title
[w] 53:1 Ps 10:4; 14:1
[x] 53:2 Ps 33:13-15
[y] 53:2-3 Rm 3:10-12

[A] 51:17 Lit *The sacrifices of God are*   [B] 52:6 Lit *about him*   [C] 53:2 Or *the descendants of Adam*

had (see 1 Sam 16:14). He thus asks God to return to him **the joy of [his] salvation** so that he would be energized to turn other **sinners** to the Lord in repentance, faith, and obedience (51:12-13).

52:1-4 Doeg, sarcastically called a **hero** here, had told Saul that David had received assistance from Ahimelech the priest. Doeg's actions resulted in the execution of Ahimelech, as well as many other priests and their families (52:1; see 1 Sam 21:1-9; 22:9-23). David contrasts Doeg's character with the Lord's. Whereas the Lord demonstrates

faithful love, this wicked man only loves **evil** and **words that destroy** (Ps 52:1, 3-4).

52:5-7 David is certain that God will judge the wicked, including Doeg, with eternal damnation. He would **bring** the man **down forever** (52:5). His wickedness, then, was only temporary. Since he made **his destructive behavior** his **refuge** instead of God (52:7), Doeg's acts would come crashing down on his own head. **52:8** When you face the wickedness of the world, keep looking to God. You, like David, can be firmly rooted in his truth, thriving in spite of the wicked.

53:1-3 The apostle Paul quotes from these verses in his letter to the Romans as he argues for the universal sinfulness of humanity (see Rom 3:10-12).

The reason people believe **there's no God** is that they are corrupt and commit vile deeds (Ps 53:1). By disbelieving in God and his standards of righteousness, they assume they have absolved themselves of accountability for their actions. Such people do not seek God, so they feel free to become **corrupt** (53:2-3). Nevertheless, God is well aware of their sin; the omniscient Creator sees everything (53:2).

a 53:4 Ps 27:2; Mc 3:3
b Is 64:7
c 53:5 Lv 26:36
d Jr 8:1-2
e Ps 44:7
f 53:6 Ps 14:7; Is 52:7-9; Jr 30:18-19
g 54:title 1Sm 23:19; 26:1
h 54:1 Ps 6:1; 7:8; 35:24; 43:1
i 54:2 Ps 5:1; 17:6; 55:1
j 54:3 Ps 86:14; 143:3; Is 25:5
k 54:4 Ps 118:7; Is 41:10
l 54:5 Ps 94:23; 143:12
m 54:6 Nm 15:3; Ps 116:17
n Ps 52:9
o 54:7 Ps 59:10; 92:11

p 55:1 Lm 3:56
q 55:1-2 Ps 4:1; 5:1-2; 54:2
r 55:2 Ps 64:1; 142:2
s 55:3 2Sm 16:7-8; Ps 71:11
t 55:4 Ps 38:8
u 55:4-5 Ps 18:4-5; 116:3
v 55:6 Jb 3:13
w 55:7 Jr 9:2
x 55:8 Is 4:6; 25:4
y 55:9 Gn 10:25; 11:7
z 55:9-10 Jr 6:7; Hab 1:3
aa 55:11 Ps 5:9; 10:7
ab 55:12-13 Jb 19:13,19; Ps 41:9; 88:18

⁴ Will evildoers never understand?
They consume my people
    as they consume bread;[a]
they do not call on God.[b]
⁵ Then they will be filled
    with dread —
dread like no other[c] —
because God will scatter
the bones of those who besiege you.[d]
You will put them to shame,
for God has rejected them.[e]

⁶ Oh, that Israel's deliverance
    would come from Zion!
When God restores the fortunes
    of his people,[A]
let Jacob rejoice, let Israel be glad.[f]

PRAYER FOR DELIVERANCE

54 *For the choir director: with stringed instruments. A* Maskil *of David. When the Ziphites went and said to Saul, "Is David not hiding among us?"[g]*

¹ God, save me by your name,
and vindicate me by your might![h]
² God, hear my prayer;
listen to the words
    from my mouth.[i]
³ For strangers rise up against me,
and violent men intend to kill me.
They do not let God
    guide them.[B,j]   *Selah*

⁴ God is my helper;
the Lord is the sustainer of my life.[C,k]
⁵ He will repay my adversaries
    for their evil.
Because of your faithfulness,
    annihilate them.[l]

⁶ I will sacrifice a freewill offering
    to you.[m]
I will praise your name, LORD,
because it is good.[n]
⁷ For he has rescued me
    from every trouble,
and my eye has looked down on
    my enemies.[o]

BETRAYAL BY A FRIEND

55 *For the choir director: with stringed instruments. A* Maskil *of David.*

¹ God, listen to my prayer
and do not hide from my plea
    for help.[p]
² Pay attention to me and answer me.[q]
I am restless and in turmoil
    with my complaint,[r]
³ because of the enemy's words,[D]
because of the pressure[E]
    of the wicked.
For they bring down disaster on me
and harass me in anger.[s]

⁴ My heart shudders within me;[t]
terrors of death sweep over me.
⁵ Fear and trembling grip me;
horror has overwhelmed me.[u]
⁶ I said, "If only I had wings
    like a dove!
I would fly away and find rest.[v]
⁷ How far away I would flee;
I would stay in the wilderness.[w]
               Selah
⁸ I would hurry to my shelter
from the raging wind
    and the storm."[x]

⁹ Lord, confuse[F] and confound
    their speech,[G,y]
for I see violence and strife
    in the city;
¹⁰ day and night they make the rounds
    on its walls.
Crime and trouble are within it;[z]
¹¹ destruction is inside it;
oppression and deceit never leave
    its marketplace.[aa]
¹² Now it is not an enemy
    who insults me —
otherwise I could bear it;
it is not a foe who rises up
    against me —
otherwise I could hide from him.
¹³ But it is you, a man who is my peer,
my companion and good friend![ab]

[A] 53:6 Or *restores his captive people*   [B] 54:3 Lit *They do not set God in front of them*   [C] 54:4 Or *is with those who sustain my life*   [D] 55:3 Lit *voice*   [E] 55:3 Or *threat,* or *oppression*   [F] 55:9 Or *destroy*   [G] 55:9 Lit *and divide their tongue*

53:6 God will bring his **deliverance** to his people, restoring their **fortunes** during the millennial kingdom of the Lord Jesus Christ. **54:1-3** Here David pleads with God for deliverance from the Ziphites, the **violent men** who sought to **kill** him without provocation (54:3). The heading of this psalm refers to the time when David was hiding in the Judean wilderness of Ziph. Some of the locals reported this

to Saul and sought to hand him over to the king (see 1 Sam 23:15-29).
    God's **name** (54:1) represents his character and reputation. David thus appealed to God's attributes of righteousness and faithfulness for protection from those who hated him.
54:6-7 David knew the goodness of God by experience, and over time we can too.

Though we can be certain that we will know hardships in this life, we can also be confident in the God who is able to deliver us from them all.
55:9 David asks the Lord to interfere with his enemies' ability to communicate with one another, just as the Lord had confused the speech of those building the tower in Babylon (see Gen 11:1-9).

14 We used to have close fellowship;
we walked with the crowd
  into the house of God.[a]

15 Let death take them by surprise;[b]
let them go down to Sheol alive,
because evil is in their homes
  and within them.[c]

16 But I call to God,
and the LORD will save me.[d]

17 I complain and groan morning,
  noon, and night,[e]
and he hears my voice.[f]

18 Though many are against me,
he will redeem me
  from my battle unharmed.[g]

19 God, the one enthroned
  from long ago,[h]
will hear and will humiliate them
                              Selah

because they do not change
and do not fear God.[i]

20 My friend[j] acts violently
against those at peace with him;[k]
he violates his covenant.[l]

21 His buttery words are smooth,
but war is in his heart.
His words are softer than oil,
but they are drawn swords.[m]

⊷ HOPE WORDS ⊷

*The level of your worry reflects
the size of your faith.*

---

22 Cast your burden on the LORD,
and he will sustain you;[n]
he will never allow the righteous
  to be shaken.[o]

23 God, you will bring them down
to the Pit of destruction;[p]
men of bloodshed
  and treachery

will not live out half their days.[q]
But I will trust in you.[r]

A CALL FOR GOD'S PROTECTION

56 *For the choir director: according to
"A Silent Dove Far Away." A Miktam
of David. When the Philistines seized him in
Gath.*[s]

1 Be gracious to me, God, for a man is
    trampling me;
he fights and oppresses me all day
  long.

2 My adversaries trample me all day,
for many arrogantly fight
    against me.[A,t]

3 When I am afraid,
I will trust in you.[u]

4 In God, whose word I praise,
in God I trust; I will not be afraid.
What can mere mortals do to me?[v]

5 They twist my words all day long;
all their thoughts against me
  are evil.[w]

6 They stir up strife,[B] they lurk;
they watch my steps
while they wait to take my life.[x]

7 Will they escape in spite of such sin?
God, bring down the nations
    in wrath.[y]

8 You yourself have recorded
    my wanderings.[c]
Put my tears in your bottle.
Are they not in your book?[z]

9 Then my enemies will retreat
    on the day when I call.[aa]
This I know: God is for me.[ab]

10 In God, whose word I praise,
in the LORD, whose word I praise,

11 in God I trust; I will not be afraid.
What can mere humans do to me?[ac]

12 I am obligated by vows[D] to you, God;
I will make my thank offerings
    to you.[ad]

---

[a] 55:14 Ps 42:4
[b] 55:15 Pr 6:15; Is 47:11; 1Th 5:3
[c] Nm 16:30,33
[d] 55:16 Ps 119:46
[e] 55:17 Ps 92:2
[f] Ps 64:1; 142:2
[g] 55:18 Ps 56:2; 103:4
[h] 55:19 Ps 93:2
[i] Dt 33:27
[j] 55:20 Ps 55:13
[k] Ps 7:4
[l] Ps 89:34
[m] 55:21 Ps 12:2; 28:3
[n] 55:22 1Pt 5:7
[o] Ps 37:24; 112:6
[p] 55:23 Is 38:17; Ezk 28:8
[q] 55:23 Ps 5:6
[r] Ps 56:3
[s] 56:title 1Sm 21:10-11; 22:1
[t] 56:1-2 Ps 35:1; 57:3
[u] 56:3 Ps 112:7; Pr 29:25; Is 12:2
[v] 56:4 Ps 27:1; 118:6; Heb 13:6
[w] 56:5 Ps 41:7; 2Pt 3:16
[x] 56:6 Ps 10:8-10; 59:3
[y] 56:7 Ezk 17:15; Rm 2:3
[z] 56:8 2Kg 20:5; Ps 139:3; Mal 3:16
[aa] 56:9 Ps 9:3
[ab] Ps 118:6; Rm 8:31
[ac] 56:10-11 Ps 112:7; Pr 29:25; Is 12:2
[ad] 56:12 Ps 50:14

[A] 56:2 Or *many fight against me, O exalted one,* or *many fight against me from the heights* [B] 56:6 Or *They attack* [C] 56:8 Or *misery* [D] 56:12 Lit *On me the vows*

55:16-17 David pleads with God for deliverance, crying out to him around the clock. He doesn't utter a calm, respectable prayer; instead, he complains and groans (55:17), being emotionally honest with God. Be authentic with him when your life is in turmoil. He already knows your thoughts and anxieties, so there's no point trying to hide them from him. **55:20-21** The Lord knew about David's **friend** who broke **covenant** with him (55:20). Such

actions do not go unnoticed by the God who is always faithful to his own covenant. **55:22** Place on God's shoulders that which is weighing you down as you wait for him to intervene in your circumstances. **56:3-4** In the midst of his fears, David utters a prayer that all of God's children would do well to remember: **When I am afraid, I will trust in you . . . . What can mere mortals do to me?** He compared the

size of his enemies to the size of his trustworthy God. Adopting such a perspective will transform how you face negative circumstances. **56:8-9** Tears do not escape God's notice. Your God is aware of the details of your suffering. And in the person of his Son, he took on humanity and suffered for you. Thus, believers can **know** for certain: **God is for me** (56:9).

a 56:13 Jb 33:30; Ps 116:8-9
b 57:title 1Sm 22:1; 24:1-3
c 57:1 Ru 2:12; Ps 17:8; 91:1,4
d 57:2 Ps 138:8
e 57:3 Ps 56:1-2
f Ps 25:10; 40:11
g 57:4 Ps 58:6; 64:3; Pr 30:14
h 57:5 Ps 108:5; 113:4
i 57:6 Ps 9:15; 35:8; Pr 28:10
j 57:7 Ps 59:17; 112:7
k 57:8 Jdg 5:12; Ps 33:2; 81:2
l 57:9 2Sm 22:50; Ps 9:11; 18:49

m 57:10 Ps 36:5; 103:11; Lm 3:22-23
n 57:11 Ps 113:4
o 57:7-11 Ps 108:1-5
p 58:1 Ps 82:2
q 58:2 Ps 94:20; Is 10:1; Mal 3:15
r 58:3 Ps 51:5; Is 48:8
s 58:4 Dt 32:33; Ps 140:3
t 58:5 Ec 10:11; Jr 8:17
u 58:6 Jb 4:10; 29:17; Ps 3:7 Ezk 21:7
v 58:7 Jos 7:5; Ps 112:10;
w 58:8 Jb 3:16; Ec 6:3
x 58:9 Jb 27:21; Pr 10:25; Ec 7:6
y 58:10 Jb 22:19
z Ps 68:23; Jr 11:20; 20:12

13 For you rescued me from death,
even my feet from stumbling,
to walk before God in the light
of life.*a*

PRAISE FOR GOD'S PROTECTION

57 *For the choir director: "Do Not Destroy."*
A Miktam of David. When he fled
*before Saul into the cave.*b*

1 Be gracious to me, God, be gracious
to me,
for I take refuge in you.
I will seek refuge in the shadow
of your wings
until danger passes.*c*
2 I call to God Most High,
to God who fulfills his purpose
for me.*A,d*
3 He reaches down from heaven
and saves me,
challenging the one
who tramples me.*e*   Selah
God sends his faithful love
and truth.*f*
4 I am surrounded by lions;
I lie down among devouring lions —
people whose teeth are spears
and arrows,
whose tongues are sharp swords.*g*
5 God, be exalted
above the heavens;
let your glory be over
the whole earth.*h*
6 They prepared a net for my steps;
I was despondent.
They dug a pit ahead of me,
but they fell into it!*i*   Selah
7 My heart is confident, God, my heart
is confident.
I will sing; I will sing praises.*j*
8 Wake up, my soul!
Wake up, harp and lyre!
I will wake up the dawn.*k*
9 I will praise you, Lord,
among the peoples;
I will sing praises to you
among the nations.*l*
10 For your faithful love is as high as
the heavens;

your faithfulness reaches
the clouds.*m*
11 God, be exalted above the heavens;*n*
let your glory be
over the whole earth.*o*

A CRY AGAINST INJUSTICE

58 *For the choir director: "Do Not Destroy."*
A Miktam of David.

1 Do you really speak righteously,
you mighty ones?*B*
Do you judge people fairly?*p*
2 No, you practice injustice
in your hearts;
with your hands
you weigh out violence
in the land.*q*
3 The wicked go astray
from the womb;
liars wander about from birth.*r*
4 They have venom like the venom
of a snake,
like the deaf cobra that stops up
its ears,*s*
5 that does not listen to the sound
of the charmers
who skillfully weave spells.*t*
6 God, knock the teeth
out of their mouths;
LORD, tear out
the young lions' fangs.*u*
7 May they vanish like water
that flows by;
may they aim
their blunted arrows.*C,v*
8 Like a slug that moves along
in slime,
like a woman's miscarried child,
may they not see the sun.*w*
9 Before your pots can feel the heat of
the thorns —
whether green or burning —
he will sweep them away.*D,x*
10 The righteous one will rejoice
when he sees the retribution;*y*
he will wash his feet in the blood
of the wicked.*z*

A 57:2 Or *who avenges me*   *B* 58:1 Or *Can you really speak righteousness in silence?*   *C* 58:7 Hb obscure   *D* 58:9 Or *thorns, he will sweep it away, whether raw or cooking*

57:4-6 This is likely a reference to his being pursued by Saul, who desperately wanted to strike David down.
57:7-11 Having experienced God's deliverance in the past and looking expectantly for his deliverance in the future, David was dominated by a desire to glorify God. This is the disposition

we should cultivate. Whatever trying circumstances have come our way, we ought to seek to magnify God in and through them.
58:1-5 Mighty ones here refers to unrighteous justices (58:1). Human leaders are supposed to act as God's intermediaries, ruling on his behalf and expressing his own attributes of

righteousness and justice. But these leaders had failed in their accountability before God. David thus compares them to venomous snakes (58:4-5).
58:6 David pleads with God to execute divine judgment on evil people, rendering them as powerless as defanged lions.

11 Then people will say,
  "Yes, there is a reward
      for the righteous!
  There is a God who judges on earth!"[a]

GOD OUR STRONGHOLD

59 *For the choir director: "Do Not Destroy."*
A Miktam of David. When Saul sent
agents to watch the house and kill him.[b]

1 Rescue me from my enemies,
      my God;[c]
  protect me from those who rise up
      against me.[d]
2 Rescue me from those
      who practice sin,
  and save me from men of bloodshed.[e]
3 Because look, LORD, they set
      an ambush for me.[f]
  Powerful men attack me,
  but not because of any sin
      or rebellion of mine.[g]
4 For no fault of mine,
      they run and take up a position.
  Awake to help me, and take notice.[h]
5 LORD God of Armies, you are the
      God of Israel.
  Rise up to punish all the nations;
  do not show favor
      to any wicked traitors.[i]   *Selah*

6 They return at evening,
      snarling like dogs
  and prowling around the city.[j]
7 Look, they spew from their mouths —
  sharp words from[A] their lips.[k]
  "For who," they say, "will hear?"[l]
8 But you laugh at them, LORD;
  you ridicule all the nations.[m]
9 I will keep watch for you,
      my[B] strength,
  because God is my stronghold.[n]
10 My faithful God[C] will come
      to meet me;
  God will let me look down on
      my adversaries.[o]

11 Do not kill them; otherwise,
      my people will forget.

By your power, make them
      homeless wanderers[p]
  and bring them down,
  Lord, our shield.[q]
12 For the sin of their mouths and the
      words of their lips,
  let them be caught in their pride.
  They utter curses and lies.[r]
13 Consume them in rage;
  consume them until
      they are gone.[s]
  Then people will know
      throughout[D] the earth
  that God rules over Jacob.[t]   *Selah*

14 And they return at evening,
      snarling like dogs
  and prowling around the city.[u]
15 They scavenge for food;
  they growl if they are not satisfied.[v]

16 But I will sing of your strength
  and will joyfully proclaim
  your faithful love in the morning.[w]
  For you have been a stronghold
      for me,
  a refuge in my day of trouble.[x]
17 To you, my strength, I sing praises,
  because God is my stronghold —
  my faithful God.[y]

PRAYER IN DIFFICULT TIMES

60 *For the choir director: according to*
"The Lily of Testimony."[z] *A Miktam*
of David for teaching. When he fought with
Aram-naharaim and Aram-zobah, and Joab
returned and struck Edom in Salt Valley,
killing twelve thousand.[aa]

1 God, you have rejected us;
  you have broken us down;
  you have been angry. Restore us![E,ab]
2 You have shaken the land
      and split it open.
  Heal its fissures, for it shudders.[ac]
3 You have made your people
      suffer hardship;
  you have given us wine to drink
  that made us stagger.[ad]

[a] 58:11 Ps 9:8; 67:4; 75:7
[b] 59:title 1Sm 19:11
[c] 59:1 Ps 143:9
[d] 2Sm 22:18; Ps 18:17; 91:14
[e] 59:2 Ps 5:6; 17:7
[f] 59:3 Pr 1:11,18
[g] 1Sm 20:1; 24:11
[h] 59:4 Ps 7:3–4; 69:4
[i] 59:5 Jr 18:23
[j] 59:6 Ps 22:16
[k] 59:7 Ps 52:2; 57:4; 64:3
[l] Ps 73:11
[m] 59:8 Ps 2:4; 37:13
[n] 59:9 Ps 28:8; Jr 16:19
[o] 59:10 Ps 54:7

[p] 59:11 Hs 9:17
[q] Gn 15:1; Dt 33:29; 2Sm 22:3,31; Ps 3:3; 5:12; 18:2; 28:7; 119:114
[r] 59:12 Ps 10:7; Pr 12:13
[s] 59:13 Ps 104:35
[t] Ps 83:18
[u] 59:14 Ps 22:16
[v] 59:15 Jb 15:23; Ps 109:10
[w] 59:16 Ps 5:3; 88:13; 92:2
[x] Is 25:4; Nah 1:7
[y] 59:17 Ps 28:8; Jr 16:19
[z] 60:title Pss 45; 69; 80 titles
[aa] 1Ch 18:3,12
[ab] 60:1 Ps 44:9,23; 79:5
[ac] 60:2 Ps 18:7
[ad] 60:3 Is 51:17–23; Jr 25:15-17

[A] 59:7 Lit *swords are on*   [B] 59:9 Some Hb mss, LXX, Vg, Tg; other Hb mss read *his*   [C] 59:10 Alt Hb tradition reads *My God in his faithful love*
[D] 59:13 Lit *know to the ends of*   [E] 60:1 Or *Turn back to us*

58:11 The judgment of God against evil **is a reward for the righteous**. The day will finally come when the Lord will set *all* things right. All sin will be punished, either in the cross of Christ, or at the final judgment.
59:3–4 David was in danger solely because Saul was consumed by jealousy.
59:9-10 It's easy to be consumed with fear and anxiety when confronted with dreadful

circumstances. To whom will you look when you are faced with a problem that's too powerful for you? Look to the omnipotent "Lord God of Armies" (59:5). He alone can override your negative circumstances so that "all things work together for the good of those who love God, who are called according to his purpose" (Rom 8:28).
59:16 This is a good way to begin your day—looking to God's faithful love to provide you

with strength to make it through the next twenty-four hours.
60:1-3 David prays for a reprieve from **hardship** that God had brought on his people when he was **angry** with them (60:1, 3). Since God was responsible for the damage, only he could **restore** the nation from its brokenness (60:1).

a 60:4 Is 5:26; 11:12; 13:2
b 60:5 Ps 17:7; 20:6; 138:7
c 60:6 Gn 12:6; 33:18
d Gn 33:17
e 60:7 Dt 33:17; Jos 13:31
f Gn 49:10
g 60:8 2Sm 8:2
h 2Sm 8:14
i 2Sm 8:1
j 60:9 Jr 1:18
k 60:10 Ps 44:9
l 60:11 Ps 146:3
m 60:12 Nm 24:18; Ps 44:5; 118:15-16
n 60:5-12 Ps 108:6-13
o 61:1 Ps 17:1; 88:2; 142:6
p 61:2 Ps 88:4
q Ps 27:5
r 61:3 Pr 18:10
s 61:4 Ru 2:12; Ps 17:8; 91:4

t 61:5 Jb 22:27; Ps 56:12
u Mal 4:2
v 61:6 Ps 21:4
w 61:7 Ps 41:12
x Ps 40:11
y 61:8 Ps 7:17; 9:2; 18:49
z Ps 65:1; 116:14,18
aa 62:title Ps 39 title
ab 62:1 Ps 33:20; 37:39
ac 62:1-2 Dt 32:15; 2Sm 22:47
ad 62:2 Ps 37:24; 55:22
ae 62:3 Is 30:13
af 62:4 Ps 4:2; 55:21
ag 62:5 Ps 71:5
ah 62:6 Ps 89:26; 95:1
ai Ps 16:8; 21:7
aj 62:7 Ps 18:2
ak 62:8 Ps 91:2; 118:8-9

⁴ You have given a signal flag to those
      who fear you,
  so that they can flee
      before the archers.^A,a   *Selah*
⁵ Save with your right hand,
      and answer me,
  so that those you love
      may be rescued.^b

⁶ God has spoken in his sanctuary:^B
  "I will celebrate!
  I will divide up Shechem.^c
  I will apportion the Valley
      of Succoth.^d
⁷ Gilead is mine, Manasseh is mine,
  and Ephraim is my helmet;^e
  Judah is my scepter.^f
⁸ Moab is my washbasin.^g
  I throw my sandal on Edom;^h
  I shout in triumph over Philistia."^i

⁹ Who will bring me to the fortified city?
  Who will lead me to Edom?^j
¹⁰ God, haven't you rejected us?
  God, you do not march out
      with our armies.^k
¹¹ Give us aid against the foe,
  for human help is worthless.^l
¹² With God we will perform valiantly;^m
  he will trample our foes.^n

SECURITY IN GOD

61 *For the choir director: on stringed instruments. Of David.*

¹ God, hear my cry;
  pay attention to my prayer.^o
² I call to you from the ends of the earth
  when my heart is without strength.^p
  Lead me to a rock that is
      high above me,^q
³ for you have been a refuge for me,
  a strong tower^r in the face
      of the enemy.
⁴ I will dwell in your tent forever
  and take refuge under the shelter
      of your wings.^s   *Selah*

⁵ God, you have heard my vows;^t
  you have given a heritage
  to those who fear your name.^u
⁶ Add days to the king's life;
  may his years span many generations.^v
⁷ May he sit enthroned
      before God forever.^w
  Appoint faithful love and truth
      to guard him.^x
⁸ Then I will continually sing
      of your name,^y
  fulfilling my vows day by day.^z

TRUST IN GOD ALONE

62 *For the choir director: according to Jeduthun.^aa A psalm of David.*

¹ I am at rest in God alone;
  my salvation comes from him.^ab
² He alone is my rock and my salvation,^ac
  my stronghold;
      I will never be shaken.^ad

³ How long will you threaten a man?
  Will all of you attack^c
  as if he were a leaning wall
  or a tottering fence?^ae
⁴ They only plan to bring him down
  from his high position.
  They take pleasure in lying;
  they bless with their mouths,
  but they curse inwardly.^af   *Selah*

⁵ Rest in God alone, my soul,
  for my hope comes from him.^ag
⁶ He alone is my rock
      and my salvation,^ah
  my stronghold; I will not be shaken.^ai
⁷ My salvation and glory
      depend on God, my strong rock.
  My refuge is in God.^aj
⁸ Trust in him at all times, you people;
  pour out your hearts before him.
  God is our refuge.^ak   *Selah*

⁹ Common people are only a vapor;
  important people, an illusion.

---

^A 60:4 Or *can rally before the archers*, or *can rally because of the truth*   ^B 60:6 Or *has promised by his holy nature*   ^C 62:3 Some Hb mss read *you be struck down*

60:7 Judah is David's tribe, and the Lord calls it his **scepter**. In other words, it is the tribe from which future kings would come.
60:8 Moab, Edom, and **Philistia** were neighboring lands with which Israel was regularly contending. To **throw [a] sandal** at someone is to treat them with contempt.
60:11-12 Only the Lord can provide deliverance. Without him, we cannot succeed; with him, we cannot fail.
61:4 The only wise position from which to operate in life is under the divine covering—

an unassailable place of safety from elements and enemies.
61:5-7 To those who fear [his] name, God gives **a heritage,** a promised inheritance (61:5). The specific heritage he had promised to David was a royal dynasty. So David prays that he might prolong his **life** and let his sons remain **enthroned before God forever** (61:6-7) in accordance with God's covenant promise to him (see 2 Sam 7:11-16). Ultimately God will fulfill this prayer in the Lord Jesus Christ, the Son of David who will reign on David's throne forever.

62:3 David marvels at the attempt of his enemies to oppose him in light of his confidence in God. Did they really think that the king who had God as his stronghold would be as easy to topple as **a tottering fence?** The righteous God would take note of such scheming against his anointed king.
62:8 Believers have every reason to **trust** God as their ever-present **refuge.** Do you?
62:9-10 Life is transitory; therefore, David tells us not to put our trust in sinful actions (**oppression** and **robbery**) as a means of providing

Together on a scale,
they weigh less than[A] a vapor.[a]
10 Place no trust in oppression,
or false hope in robbery.
If wealth increases,
don't set your heart on it.[b]

11 God has spoken once;
I have heard this twice:
strength belongs to God,[c]
12 and faithful love belongs
to you, Lord.
For you repay each according to
his works.[d]

PRAISE GOD WHO SATISFIES

63 *A psalm of David. When he was in the Wilderness of Judah.[e]*

1 God, you are my God; I eagerly
seek you.
I thirst for you;
my body faints for you
in a land that is dry, desolate,
and without water.[f]
2 So I gaze on you in the sanctuary
to see your strength
and your glory.[g]

3 My lips will glorify you
because your faithful love is better
than life.[h]
4 So I will bless you as long as I live;
at your name, I will lift up
my hands.[i]
5 You satisfy me as with rich food;[B][j]
my mouth will praise you
with joyful lips.[k]

6 When I think of you as I lie
on my bed,
I meditate on you
during the night watches[l]
7 because you are my helper;[m]
I will rejoice in the shadow
of your wings.[n]

8 I follow close to you;
your right hand holds on to me.[o]

9 But those who intend to destroy
my life
will go into the depths of the earth.[p]
10 They will be given over to the power
of the sword;[q]
they will become a meal for jackals.
11 But the king will rejoice in God;[r]
all who swear by him will boast,
for the mouths of liars will be shut.[s]

PROTECTION FROM EVILDOERS

64 *For the choir director. A psalm of David.*

1 God, hear my voice when I am
in anguish.[t]
Protect my life from the terror
of the enemy.[u]
2 Hide me from the scheming
of wicked people,[v]
from the mob of evildoers,[w]
3 who sharpen their tongues
like swords
and aim bitter words like arrows,[x]
4 shooting from concealed places
at the blameless.
They shoot at him suddenly
and are not afraid.[y]
5 They adopt[C] an evil plan;
they talk about hiding traps
and say,
"Who will see them?"[D][z]
6 They devise crimes and say,
"We have perfected a secret plan."[aa]
The inner man and the heart
are mysterious.

7 But God will shoot them
with arrows;
suddenly, they will be wounded.[ab]
8 They will be made to stumble;
their own tongues work
against them.

[a] 62:9 Ps 39:5-6,11; Is 40:17
[b] 62:10 Jb 31:24-25; Mk 4:19; 1Tm 6:10,17-19
[c] 62:11 Jb 40:5
[d] 62:12 Mt 16:27; Rm 2:6; Rv 22:12
[e] 63:title 2Sm 16:14; 17:2,29
[f] 63:1 Ps 42:2; Is 26:9
[g] 63:2 Jb 19:26-27; Ps 17:15; 27:4
[h] 63:3 Ps 69:16
[i] 63:4 Ps 28:2; 143:6; Lm 3:41
[j] 63:5 Ps 36:8
[k] Ps 71:23
[l] 63:6 Ps 77:6; 119:148
[m] 63:7 Ps 27:9; 40:17
[n] Ps 17:8; 36:7; 57:1
[o] 63:8 Ps 18:35
[p] 63:9 Ps 55:15; Ezk 26:20; 31:14-18
[q] 63:10 Jr 18:21; Ezk 35:5
[r] 63:11 Ps 21:1
[s] Ps 107:42; Rm 3:19
[t] 64:1 Ps 55:2
[u] Ps 140:1
[v] 64:2 Ps 35:20; 37:12
[w] Ps 22:16; 26:5
[x] 64:3 Ps 52:2; 57:4; Pr 25:18
[y] 64:4 Ps 10:8; 11:2
[z] 64:5 Ps 35:7; 140:5; 141:9
[aa] 64:6 Ps 21:11; 83:3
[ab] 64:7 Ps 7:13; 45:5; 144:6

[A] 62:9 Lit *they go up more than*　[B] 63:5 Lit *with fat and fatness*　[C] 64:5 Or *They strengthen themselves with*　[D] 64:5 Or *it*

---

ourselves with security. For riches are as transitory as life itself. **Wealth** cannot deliver you (62:10). Don't look to the material to do what only the spiritual can do.
62:11-12 Because of his **faithful love**, God has compassion on his people. And because of his strength, he has the power to demonstrate that compassion to them. So all people should take heed: God will **repay each according to his works** (62:12). Let the believer have confidence; let the unbeliever beware.
63:5 When you, like David, realize that God's faithfulness is more important than life-sus-

taining necessities such as **food** and water, you too will **praise [him] with joyful lips**. Such genuine worship will sustain you in your own wilderness experiences.
63:6-8 David's musings should make you ask where to put your focus during your times of suffering. To whom do you first turn for help?
63:9-11 Even though David is in the wilderness, chased from his throne by Absalom and hunted like an animal, he is certain of his enemies' defeat. This was not self-confidence but God-confidence. No matter the negative circumstances you face, then, put

your confidence in the One whose love for you is "better than life" (63:3).
64:4 The blameless are those innocent of wrongdoing.
64:5-6 The wicked encourage one another in their plans to carry out injustice. They don't realize that God hears and sees everything.
64:7-8 Though wicked schemers aim their words like arrows at the innocent (64:4), God himself would launch his own **arrows** and cause their **tongues** to **work against them**. Their evil deeds would return like a boomerang; the destruction they planned for others would be their own downfall.

a 64:8 Jr 18:16; 48:27;
 Lm 2:15
b 64:9 Ps 40:3
c 64:10 Ps 32:11; 68:3;
 97:11-12
d 65:1 Ps 50:14; 116:18
e 65:2 Ps 86:9; Is 2:2-4;
 66:23
f 65:3 Ps 38:14; 40:12; 79:9
g 65:4 Ps 27:4; 84:4
h 65:5 Dt 10:21; 2Sm 7:23;
 Ps 46:8
i 65:6 Ps 93:1; Am 4:13
j 65:7 Ps 107:29; Is 17:13;
 Mt 8:26
k 65:8 Ps 2:8; 139:9; Is
 24:16
l 65:9 Ps 104:13; 147:8;
 Is 45:8
m 65:10 Dt 3:22; Ps 72:6;
 147:8
n 65:11 Ps 104:28; 147:14
o 65:12 Jb 38:26-27; Is
 55:12; Jl 2:22
p 65:13 Ps 72:16; 144:13;
 Is 30:23
q Is 44:23
r 66:1 Ps 98:4; 100:1
s 66:1-2 1Ch 16:29; Ps
 48:10
t 66:3 Ps 18:44; 47:2; 145:6
u 66:4 Ps 72:11; Is 66:23;
 Zph 2:11
v 66:5 Ps 46:8
w 66:6 Ex 14:21; Ps 106:9
x Ex 15:1-21
y 66:7 Ps 14:2; 33:13-14;
 Pr 15:3
z Ps 140:8
aa 66:8 Ps 98:4

All who see them will shake
  their heads.[a]
9 Then everyone will fear
  and will tell about God's work,
  for they will understand
  what he has done.[b]

10 The righteous one rejoices in the LORD
  and takes refuge in him;
  all those who are upright in heart
  will offer praise.[c]

GOD'S CARE FOR THE EARTH

65 *For the choir director. A psalm of David. A song.*

1 Praise is rightfully yours,[A]
  God, in Zion;
  vows to you will be fulfilled.[d]
2 All humanity will come to you,
  the one who hears prayer.[e]
3 Iniquities overwhelm me;
  only you can atone for
    our rebellions.[f]

4 How happy is the one you choose
  and bring near to live in your courts!
  We will be satisfied
    with the goodness of your house,
  the holiness of your temple.[B,g]

5 You answer us in righteousness,
  with awe-inspiring works,
  God of our salvation,
  the hope of all the ends of the earth
  and of the distant seas.[h]
6 You establish the mountains
    by your power;
  you are robed with strength.[i]
7 You silence the roar of the seas,
  the roar of their waves,
  and the tumult of the nations.[j]
8 Those who live far away are awed
    by your signs;
  you make east and west shout for joy.[k]

9 You visit the earth
    and water it abundantly,

enriching it greatly.
God's stream is filled with water,
for you prepare the earth in this way,
  providing people with grain.[l]
10 You soften it with showers and bless
    its growth,
  soaking its furrows and leveling
    its ridges.[m]
11 You crown the year
    with your goodness;
  your carts overflow with plenty.[C,n]
12 The wilderness pastures overflow,
  and the hills are robed with joy.[o]
13 The pastures are clothed with flocks
  and the valleys covered with grain.[p]
  They shout in triumph; indeed,
    they sing.[q]

PRAISE FOR GOD'S MIGHTY ACTS

66 *For the choir director. A song. A psalm.*
  Let the whole earth shout joyfully
    to God![r]
2 Sing about the glory of his name;
  make his praise glorious.[s]
3 Say to God, "How awe-inspiring
  are your works!
  Your enemies will cringe before you
  because of your great strength.[t]
4 The whole earth will worship you
  and sing praise to you.
  They will sing praise
    to your name."[u]   *Selah*

5 Come and see the wonders of God;[v]
  his acts for humanity[D]
  are awe-inspiring.
6 He turned the sea into dry land,
  and they crossed the river on foot.[w]
  There we rejoiced in him.[x]
7 He rules forever by his might;
  he keeps his eye on the nations.[y]
  The rebellious should not
    exalt themselves.[z]   *Selah*

8 Bless our God, you peoples;
  let the sound of his praise
  be heard.[aa]

[A] 65:1 Or *Praise is silence to you,* or *Praise awaits you*   [B] 65:4 Or *house, your holy temple*   [C] 65:11 Lit *your paths drip with fat*   [D] 66:5 Or *for the descendants of Adam*

65:3-4 If David experienced the joy of forgiven sins, even though he had to continue to offer the required sacrifices every year, how much more joy can we experience through Jesus Christ? The sacrifices offered by priests in the temple could not atone for sins once and for all. But when Jesus offered himself as the one perfect sacrifice for sins, he brought eternal forgiveness and sanctification to those who trust in him (see Heb 10:11-18). **65:6-8** The Lord's **power** and **strength** are demonstrated in his sovereignty over cre-

ation. **Mountains** and **seas** bow to his will (65:6-7). His supernatural activity causes people to fear, rejoice, and enter fellowship with him (65:8). **65:9-13** Just as creation displays fruitfulness when it receives God's blessings, the same is true for us. When we turn to God in repentance and faith—whether as new believers or as those who have stepped out of fellowship with God because of sin—we can know the blessing of Christ's atoning work and live a life of fruitfulness (see 1 John 1:9).

66:5-7 The psalmist rehearses **the wonders of God** sovereignly demonstrated when **he turned the sea into dry land** for his people (66:5-6)—both at the Red Sea during the exodus (see Exod 14:15-31) and at the Jordan River as they entered the promised land (see Josh 3:1-17). **The rebellious**—like Pharaoh who spurned God's commands—**should not exalt themselves** (66:7). Even as God supernaturally used the waters to deliver his people, he also used them to vanquish Pharaoh's army.

⁹ He keeps us alive^A
and does not allow our feet to slip.^a

¹⁰ For you, God, tested us;
you refined us as silver is refined.^b

¹¹ You lured us into a trap;
you placed burdens on our backs.^c

¹² You let men ride over our heads;
we went through fire and water,
but you brought us out to abundance.^{B,d}

¹³ I will enter your house
with burnt offerings;
I will pay you my vows^e

¹⁴ that my lips promised
and my mouth spoke
during my distress.^f

¹⁵ I will offer you fattened sheep
as burnt offerings,
with the fragrant smoke of rams;
I will sacrifice bulls
with goats.^g   *Selah*

¹⁶ Come and listen, all who fear God,
and I will tell what he has done
for me.^h

¹⁷ I cried out to him with my mouth,
and praise was on my tongue.ⁱ

¹⁸ If I had been aware of malice
in my heart,
the Lord would not have listened.^j

¹⁹ However, God has listened;
he has paid attention to the sound
of my prayer.^k

²⁰ Blessed be God!
He has not turned away my prayer
or turned his faithful love from me.^l

ALL WILL PRAISE GOD

67 *For the choir director: with stringed instruments. A psalm. A song.*

¹ May God be gracious to us and bless us;
may he make his face shine
upon us^m   *Selah*

² so that your way may be known
on earth,
your salvation among all nations.ⁿ

³ Let the peoples praise you, God;
let all the peoples praise you.^o

⁴ Let the nations rejoice and shout
for joy,
for you judge the peoples
with fairness
and lead the nations on earth.^p *Selah*

⁵ Let the peoples praise you, God,
let all the peoples praise you.^q

⁶ The earth has produced its harvest;
God, our God, blesses us.^r

⁷ God will bless us,
and all the ends of the earth
will fear him.^s

GOD'S MAJESTIC POWER

68 *For the choir director. A psalm of David. A song.*

¹ God arises. His enemies scatter,
and those who hate him flee
from his presence.^t

² As smoke is blown away,
so you blow them away.
As wax melts before the fire,
so the wicked are destroyed
before God.^u

³ But the righteous are glad;
they rejoice before God
and celebrate with joy.^v

⁴ Sing to God! Sing praises
to his name.
Exalt him who rides
on the clouds^C—
his name is the LORD^D—
and celebrate before him.^w

⁵ God in his holy dwelling is
a father of the fatherless
and a champion of widows.^x

^a 66:9 Ps 94:18; 121:3
^b 66:10 Jb 23:10; Ps 17:3; Is 48:10
^c 66:11 Lm 1:13; Ezk 12:13; 17:20
^d 66:12 Ps 18:19; Is 43:2
^e 66:13 Ps 22:25; 116:14; Ec 5:4
^f 66:14 Ps 18:6
^g 66:15 Nm 6:14; Ps 51:19
^h 66:16 Ps 9:1; 34:11; 71:15,24
ⁱ 66:17 Ps 35:28
^j 66:18 Jb 36:21; Jn 9:31
^k 66:19 Ps 116:1-2
^l 66:20 Ps 22:24; 68:35
^m 67:1 Nm 6:25; Ps 4:6; 80:3,7,19

ⁿ 67:2 Ps 98:2; Is 52:10; Ti 2:11
^o 67:3 Ps 45:17; 66:4; 117:1
^p 67:4 Ps 96:10,13; 100:1-2; Is 11:4
^q 67:5 Ps 45:17; 66:8; 117:1
^r 67:6 Lv 26:4; Ps 85:12; Ezk 34:27; Hs 2:22
^s 67:7 1Kg 8:43; 2Ch 6:33; Ps 33:8
^t 68:1 Nm 10:35; Ps 7:6; Ezk 30:26
^u 68:2 Ps 37:20; Hs 13:3
^v 68:3 Ps 32:11; 40:16; 64:10
^w 68:4 Dt 33:26; Ps 7:17; 66:4; Is 19:1
^x 68:5 Dt 24:17,19; Ps 146:9

^A66:9 Lit *He sets our soul in life*   ^B66:12 Or *a place of satisfaction*   ^C68:4 Or *rides through the desert*   ^D68:4 Hb *Yah*

66:10-12 God let his people experience hardship and oppression. In all such things, though, our sovereign God works "for the good of those who love" him (see Rom 8:28). He tests us so that we may be **refined** as **silver** (Ps 66:10). He will permit you to encounter negative circumstances so that he can reveal to you his comfort and power.
66:16-20 Come and listen. The psalmist concludes by sharing his praise with the congregation for God's answer to his prayer. He confesses that this deliverance would not have happened if he had clung to sin in his **heart** (66:18). The principle is clear: honesty and openness before God are essential.

Confession and repentance are necessary if our prayers are not to be hindered (see 1 Pet 3:7). But when we address our personal sin, we open the door to experiencing the **faithful love** of God (Ps 66:20).
67:1-2 The author has a missional reason for his request in verse 1. He desires the Lord's favor **so that [his] way may be known on earth [and his] salvation among nations** (67:2). When God delivers his people and showers them with blessings, his goal is that he would receive glory and that other people would experience salvation and discipleship.
God wants all people everywhere to know him, and this should be our desire as well. He

does not bless you merely for your own sake. He blesses you so that you may be a blessing to others, leading them to put their faith in Jesus Christ, to glorify God, and to live their lives in joyful obedience to him.
67:7 God does not **bless** you so that you can kick back, enjoy your blessings, and be self-absorbed. He blesses you so that you will make his priorities your own. He blesses you so that you will give him public praise and use his blessings in such a way that others will see him for who he is and be compelled to take him seriously.
68:1-3 When God executes justice on the earth, his people rightly **celebrate** (68:3).

a 68:6 Ps 107:14; 113:9;
146:7
b 68:7-8 Ex 19:16-18; Jdg
5:4-5
c 68:9 Lv 26:4; Ezk 34:26
d 68:10 Ps 74:19; 78:20;
107:9
e 68:11 1Sm 18:6-7
f 68:12 Jos 10:16; Jdg 5:30
g 68:13 Gn 49:14; Jdg 5:16
h 68:14 Jos 10:10; Jdg 9:48
i 68:15 Ps 36:6
j 68:16 Ps 48:1-2; 132:13-14;
Is 2:2-4

k 68:17 Hab 3:8
l Dt 33:2
m 68:18 Dt 21:10; Ps 7:7;
Eph 4:8
n 68:19 Ps 55:22; Is 46:3-4
o 68:20 Dt 32:39; Ps 49:15;
56:13
p 68:21 Ps 110:6; Hab 3:13
q 68:22 Nm 21:33; Am
9:1-4
r 68:23 1Kg 21:19; 22:38;
Jr 15:3
s 68:24 Ps 42:4; Is 60:11
t 68:25 Ex 15:20; Jdg 11:34;
1Sm 18:6
u 68:26 Ps 22:25; 26:12
v 68:27 Jdg 5:14,18; 1Sm
9:21

6 God provides homes for those
   who are deserted.
He leads out the prisoners
   to prosperity,[A]
but the rebellious live
   in a scorched land.[a]

7 God, when you went out
   before your people,
when you marched
   through the desert,   *Selah*
8 the earth trembled and the skies
   poured rain
before God, the God of Sinai,[B]
before God, the God of Israel.[b]
9 You, God, showered
   abundant rain;
you revived your inheritance
   when it languished.[c]
10 Your people settled in it;
God, you provided for the poor
   by your goodness.[d]

11 The Lord gave the command;
a great company of women brought
   the good news:[e]
12 "The kings of the armies flee —
   they flee!"
She who stays at home divides
   the spoil.[f]
13 While[C] you lie among
   the sheep pens,[D]
the wings of a dove are covered
   with silver,
and its feathers
   with glistening gold.[g]
14 When the Almighty scattered kings
   in the land,
it snowed on Zalmon.[E,h]

15 Mount Bashan is
   God's towering mountain;
Mount Bashan is a mountain
   of many peaks.[i]
16 Why gaze with envy,
   you mountain peaks,
at the mountain God desired
   for his abode?
The Lord will dwell there forever![j]

17 God's chariots are tens of thousands,
   thousands and thousands;[k]
the Lord is among them
   in the sanctuary[F]
as he was at Sinai.[l]
18 You ascended to the heights,
   taking away captives;
you received gifts from[G] people,
   even from the rebellious,
so that the Lord God
   might dwell there.[H,m]

19 Blessed be the Lord!
Day after day he bears our burdens;
God is our salvation.[n]   *Selah*
20 Our God is a God of salvation,
and escape from death belongs
   to the Lord my Lord.[o]
21 Surely God crushes the heads
   of his enemies,
the hairy brow of one who goes on
   in his guilty acts.[p]
22 The Lord said,
"I will bring them back
   from Bashan;
I will bring them back
   from the depths of the sea[q]
23 so that your foot may wade[I]
   in blood
and your dogs' tongues may have
   their share
from the enemies."[r]
24 People have seen
   your procession, God,
the procession of my God,
   my King, in the sanctuary.[s]
25 Singers lead the way,
   with musicians following;
among them are young women
   playing tambourines.[t]
26 Bless God in the assemblies;
bless the Lord from the fountain
   of Israel.[u]
27 There is Benjamin, the youngest,
   leading them,
the rulers of Judah
   in their assembly,[j]
the rulers of Zebulun, the rulers
   of Naphtali.[v]

[A] 68:6 Or *prisoners with joyous music*; Hb uncertain   [B] 68:8 Or *God, this one of Sinai*   [C] 68:13 Or *If*   [D] 68:13 Or *the campfires*, or *the saddlebags*;
Hb obscure   [E] 68:14 Or *Black Mountain*   [F] 68:17 Or *in holiness*, also in v. 24   [G] 68:18 Lit *among*   [H] 68:18 Or *even those rebelling against the Lord
God's living there*; Hb obscure   [I] 68:23 LXX, Syr read *dip*   [j] 68:27 Hb obscure

68:7-14 David reminds the people of how the
Lord led their ancestors in the **desert** after
the exodus from Egypt (68:7). At **Sinai** he
gave them his law, and he refreshed them in
the wilderness (68:8-9). When they entered
the promised land, God gave them victory.
The kings of the armies fled and were scat-

tered (68:12, 14). Then he blessed them with
the **spoil** taken from their defeated enemies
(68:12-13).
68:18 Paul quotes this verse in Ephesians 4:7-
8, emphasizing that when Christ victoriously
rose from the dead and ascended to heaven,
he rescued those who were captive to Satan

and gave them spiritual gifts so that they
could serve him and others in his church.
68:24-25 David describes a victory parade as the
Lord, the **King**, triumphantly entered his **sanctuary** with singers and **musicians**. This perhaps
describes a procession in which the ark of the
covenant was carried into the tabernacle.

28 Your God has decreed your strength.
Show your strength, God,
you who have acted on our behalf.[a]

29 Because of your temple
at Jerusalem,
kings will bring tribute to you.[b]

30 Rebuke the beast in the reeds,
the herd of bulls with the calves
of the peoples.[c]
Trample underfoot those with bars
of silver.[A]
Scatter the peoples
who take pleasure in war.[d]

31 Ambassadors will come[B]
from Egypt;
Cush will stretch out its hands
to God.[e]

32 Sing to God, you kingdoms
of the earth;
sing praise to the Lord,[f]   *Selah*

33 to him who rides in the ancient,
highest heavens.[g]
Look, he thunders
with his powerful voice![h]

34 Ascribe power to God.
His majesty is over Israel,
his power is among the clouds.[i]

35 God, you are awe-inspiring
in your sanctuaries.
The God of Israel gives power
and strength to his people.
Blessed be God![j]

A PLEA FOR RESCUE

69 *For the choir director: according to*
"The Lilies."[k] Of David.

1 Save me, God,
for the water has risen to my neck.[l]

2 I have sunk in deep mud,
and there is no footing;
I have come into deep water,
and a flood sweeps over me.[m]

3 I am weary from my crying;
my throat is parched.
My eyes fail, looking for my God.[n]

4 Those who hate me without cause
are more numerous than the hairs
of my head;
my deceitful enemies, who would
destroy me,
are powerful.[o]
Though I did not steal, I must repay.[p]

> ~ **HOPE WORDS** ~
>
> *Sometimes God allows something*
> *in your life that only he can fix*
> *so that you will get to see that*
> *he is the One who can fix it.*

5 God, you know my foolishness,
and my guilty acts are not hidden
from you.[q]

6 Do not let those who put their hope
in you
be disgraced because of me,
Lord GOD of Armies;
do not let those who seek you
be humiliated because of me,
God of Israel.[r]

7 For I have endured insults
because of you,
and shame has covered my face.[s]

8 I have become a stranger
to my brothers
and a foreigner
to my mother's sons[t]

9 because zeal for your house
has consumed me,[u]
and the insults of those
who insult you
have fallen on me.[v]

10 I mourned and fasted,
but it brought me insults.[w]

11 I wore sackcloth as my clothing,
and I was a joke to them.

12 Those who sit at the city gate
talk about me,
and drunkards make up songs
about me.[x]

13 But as for me, LORD,
my prayer to you is for a time
of favor.
In your abundant, faithful love, God,
answer me with
your sure salvation.[y]

14 Rescue me from the miry mud;
don't let me sink.
Let me be rescued from those
who hate me
and from the deep water.[z]

[a] 68:28 Ps 44:4; Is 26:12
[b] 68:29 Ps 72:10; Is 18:7; Hg 2:7
[c] 68:30 Ps 22:12
[d] Ps 18:42; 89:10
[e] 68:31 Is 45:14; Zph 3:10
[f] 68:32 Ps 67:4; 102:22
[g] 68:33 Dt 33:26
[h] Ps 29:3-5; 46:6; Is 30:30
[i] 68:34 Ps 29:1; 150:1
[j] 68:35 Dt 10:21; Ps 29:11; Is 40:29
[k] 69:title Pss 45; 60; 80 titles
[l] 69:1 Jb 22:11; Ps 32:6; Jnh 2:5
[m] 69:2 Ps 40:2; 124:4; Jnh 2:3
[n] 69:3 Ps 6:6; 38:10; 119:82,123
[o] 69:4 Ps 38:19
[p] Lv 6:2-5; Ps 35:19; Jn 15:25
[q] 69:5 Ps 38:5; 44:21
[r] 69:6 Ps 25:2-3
[s] 69:7 Ps 44:15; Is 50:6; Jr 51:51
[t] 69:8 Jb 19:13-14; Ps 31:11; 38:11
[u] 69:9 Jn 2:17
[v] Ps 89:50; Rm 15:3
[w] 69:10 Ps 35:13; 109:24-25
[x] 69:11-12 Jb 17:6; 30:9; Ps 44:14; Jr 24:9
[y] 69:13 Ps 109:4; Is 49:8; 2Co 6:2
[z] 69:14 Ps 144:7

[A] 68:30 Or *peoples, trampling on those who take pleasure in silver,* or *peoples, trampling on the bars of silver,* or *peoples, who trample each other for bars of silver*   [B] 68:31 Or *They bring red cloth,* or *They bring bronze*

69:7 In this case, David was suffering for righteous reasons, which is the only kind of suffering God wants us to undergo. "For it is better to suffer for doing good, if that should be God's will, than for doing evil" (1 Pet 3:17).
69:9 Like David, Jesus was **consumed** with **zeal** for God's **house**, demonstrating this when he cleansed the temple (see John 2:17).

[a] 69:15 Nm 16:33; Ps 55:23
[b] 69:16 Ps 25:16; 109:21
[c] 69:17 Ps 27:9; 102:2
[d] 69:18 Ps 119:134
[e] 69:19 Jr 15:15
[f] 69:20 Ps 142:4; Is 63:5
[g] 69:21 Mt 27:34,48; Jn 19:29
[h] 69:22 Ps 35:4-8; Rm 11:9-10; 1Th 5:3
[i] 69:23 Is 6:10; Ezk 29:7; Dn 5:6
[j] 69:24 Ps 79:6; Ezk 21:31; Zph 3:8
[k] 69:25 Mt 23:38; Lk 13:35; Ac 1:20
[l] 69:26 2Ch 28:9; Is 53:4; Zch 1:15
[m] 69:27 Neh 4:5; Ps 109:14

[n] 69:28 Ex 32:32; Dn 12:1; Rv 3:5
[o] 69:29 Ps 20:1; 70:5
[p] 69:30 Ps 100:4; 107:22
[q] 69:31 Ps 50:13-14; 51:16
[r] 69:32 Ps 22:26; 34:2
[s] 69:33 Ps 12:5; 68:6; 146:7
[t] 69:34 Ps 96:11; Is 44:23; 49:13
[u] 69:35 Ps 147:2; Is 44:26
[v] 69:36 Ps 102:28; Is 65:9
[w] 70:title Ps 38 title
[x] 70:1 Ps 38:22
[y] 70:2-3 Ps 35:25; 40:14-15
[z] 70:4 Ps 35:27; 77:13
[aa] 70:5 Ps 40:17; 141:1

15 Don't let the floodwaters
    sweep over me
or the deep swallow me up;
don't let the Pit close its mouth
    over me.[a]
16 Answer me, LORD,
for your faithful love is good.
In keeping with
    your abundant compassion,
turn to me.[b]
17 Don't hide your face
    from your servant,
for I am in distress.
Answer me quickly![c]
18 Come near to me and redeem me;
ransom me because of
    my enemies.[d]

19 You know the insults I endure —
my shame and disgrace.
You are aware of all my adversaries.[e]
20 Insults have broken my heart,
and I am in despair.
I waited for sympathy,
but there was none;
for comforters, but found no one.[f]
21 Instead, they gave me gall
    for my food,
and for my thirst
they gave me vinegar to drink.[g]

22 Let their table set before them be
    a snare,
and let it be a trap for their allies.[h]
23 Let their eyes grow too dim to see,
and let their hips continually quake.[i]
24 Pour out your rage on them,
and let your burning anger
    overtake them.[j]
25 Make their fortification desolate;
may no one live in their tents.[k]
26 For they persecute the one
    you struck
and talk about the pain of those
    you wounded.[l]
27 Charge them with crime on top
    of crime;
do not let them share
    in your righteousness.[m]
28 Let them be erased from the book
    of life

and not be recorded
    with the righteous.[n]
29 But as for me — poor and in pain —
let your salvation protect me, God.[o]
30 I will praise God's name
    with song
and exalt him with thanksgiving.[p]
31 That will please the LORD more than
    an ox,
more than a bull with horns
    and hooves.[q]
32 The humble will see it and rejoice.
You who seek God, take heart![r]
33 For the LORD listens to the needy
and does not despise
his own who are prisoners.[s]

34 Let heaven and earth praise him,
the seas and everything that moves
    in them,[t]
35 for God will save Zion
and build up[A] the cities of Judah.
They will live there
    and possess it.[u]
36 The descendants of his servants
    will inherit it,
and those who love his name
    will live in it.[v]

A CALL FOR DELIVERANCE

70 *For the choir director. Of David. To bring remembrance.*[w]

1 God, hurry to rescue me.
LORD, hurry to help me![x]

2 Let those who seek to kill me
be disgraced and confounded;
let those who wish me harm
be turned back and humiliated.
3 Let those who say, "Aha, aha! "
retreat because of their shame.[y]

4 Let all who seek you rejoice
    and be glad in you;
let those who love your salvation
continually say, "God is great! "[z]
5 I am oppressed and needy;
hurry to me, God.
You are my help and my deliverer;
LORD, do not delay.[aa]

[A] 69:35 Or *and rebuild*

69:15-18 Such helpless feelings are common to the human experience—regardless of the specific circumstances. So when you are suffering and don't know what to pray, let David's prayer here be your own. **69:20-21** Those who could've comforted David instead spitefully offered him bitter **food** and **drink** (69:21). This was fulfilled as prophecy when Jesus was offered vinegar to quench his thirst on the cross (see Matt 27:34; Luke 23:36; John 19:28-30). **69:22-28** David repeatedly prays that the wickedness of his enemies would turn against them. Notice, however, that David does not seek to avenge himself against his enemies but leaves vengeance to God. **70:4-5** Even in the midst of trouble, David cares about God's glorification and the saints' edification. Those who know and have experienced the greatness of God should declare, **God is great!** (70:4).

You Don't Walk This Road Alone

GOD LONGS FOR A DEEP and abiding relationship with you. Because he is dependable, he wants you to depend on him. If you are healthy, it is highly likely that you won't be going to the doctor's office anytime soon. This is because everything within your body seems to be working and doing what it is supposed to do. But when you become sick—and especially if that sickness continues for a long time—chances are that you will make an appointment to visit your doctor. You will choose to enter into your doctor's presence. You will choose to relocate your focus and your thoughts to the one you know can help you through the sickness.

Sometimes God allows troubles or trials in your life to get your focus back onto him, the Great Physician. He sees how you may have drifted from him, and he desires to bring you back into close intimacy with him. God knows how much you need him in order to live a victorious life, and he doesn't want you to walk this road alone. He is with you, even when you forget that he is. He longs to be close to you—not only because he loves you and desires a relationship with you, but also because he knows that without him you will face an enemy who will be able to defeat you. God's presence and proximity are your protection.

Are you in a situation that wants to eat you alive? Are you finding yourself with less hope every day? Do you feel anxious, worried, or in emotional turmoil—or even just alone? If so, then I want to remind you that Jesus is with you right now. And therefore his power and grace are too. And what his power and grace will do is comfort you.

Friend, sometimes God calls us to walk through valleys. I can't promise you a life without wind, clouds, and turmoil. But I can promise you that you don't have to walk through the valley alone. If you will cast your eyes on Jesus Christ, he will meet you where you are. So keep walking. Don't say that you can't make it, because God will make it with you. You don't walk this road alone.

[a] 71:1 Ps 25:20
[b] 71:2 Ps 17:6
[c] 71:1-3 Ps 31:1-3
[d] 71:4 Ps 140:1,4
[e] 71:5 Ps 39:7; Jr 17:13
[f] 71:6 Ps 22:9-10
[g] Ps 34:1
[h] 71:7 Ps 61:3; 62:7; 91:2,9
71:8 Ps 35:28; 63:5
[i] 71:9 Ps 27:9; 71:18; Is 46:3-4
[k] 71:10 Ps 31:13; 56:6; 83:3
71:11 Ps 3:2
[m] 71:12 Ps 22:19; 38:21-22; 40:13
[n] 71:13 Ps 71:24

[o] 71:14 Ps 84:4; 130:7; 147:11
[p] 71:15 Ps 35:28; 40:5; 96:2
[q] 71:16 Ps 51:14; 106:2
[r] 71:17 Dt 4:5; 6:7
[s] 71:18 Is 46:4
[t] Ps 22:30-31; 78:4,6
[u] 71:19 Ex 15:11; Dt 3:24; Ps 86:8
[v] 71:20 Ps 60:3
[w] Ps 85:6
[x] Hs 6:1-2
[y] 71:21 Ps 86:17; Is 12:1; 49:13
[z] 71:22 Ps 33:2; 81:2; 92:1-3
[aa] 71:23 Ps 34:22; 55:18
[ab] 71:24 Ps 35:28; 71:13
[ac] 72:title Ps 127 title
[ad] 72:1 1Kg 3:9; 1Ch 22:12-13; Ps 24:5
[ae] 72:2 Is 9:7; 11:2-5; 32:1

GOD'S HELP IN OLD AGE

71 Lord, I seek refuge in you;
　　let me never be disgraced.[a]

2 In your justice, rescue
　　and deliver me;
listen closely to me and save me.[b]

3 Be a rock of refuge for me,
　　where I can always go.
Give the command to save me,
　　for you are my rock and fortress.[c]

4 Deliver me, my God, from the power
　　of the wicked,
from the grasp of the unjust
　　and oppressive.[d]

5 For you are my hope, Lord God,
　　my confidence from my youth.[e]

6 I have leaned on you from birth;
　　you took me from
　　　my mother's womb.[f]
My praise is always about you.[g]

7 I am like a miraculous sign
　　to many,
and you are my strong refuge.[h]

8 My mouth is full of praise
　　and honor to you all day long.[i]

～ HOPE WORDS ～

*Hope is confident expectation
that God is going to do
what he says he will do.*

9 Don't discard me in my old age.
　　As my strength fails,
　　do not abandon me.[j]

10 For my enemies talk about me,
　　and those who spy on me
　　　plot together,[k]

11 saying, "God has abandoned him;
　　chase him and catch him,
　　for there is no one to rescue him."[l]

12 God, do not be far from me;
　　my God, hurry to help me.[m]

13 May my adversaries be disgraced
　　and destroyed;
may those who intend to harm me
　　be covered with disgrace
　　and humiliation.[n]

14 But I will hope continually
　　and will praise you more and more.[o]

15 My mouth will tell
　　about your righteousness
and your salvation all day long,
　　though I cannot sum them up.[p]

16 I come because of the mighty acts
　　of the Lord God;
I will proclaim your righteousness,
　　yours alone.[q]

17 God, you have taught me
　　from my youth,
and I still proclaim your
　　wondrous works.[r]

18 Even while I am old and gray,
　　God, do not abandon me,[s]
while I proclaim your power
　　to another generation,
your strength to all who are to come.[t]

19 Your righteousness reaches
　　the heights, God,
you who have done great things;
　　God, who is like you?[u]

20 You caused me to experience
　　many troubles and misfortunes,[v]
but you will revive me again.[w]
You will bring me up again,
　　even from the depths of the earth.[x]

21 You will increase my honor
　　and comfort me once again.[y]

22 Therefore, I will praise you
　　with a harp
for your faithfulness, my God;
　　I will sing to you with a lyre,
　　Holy One of Israel.[z]

23 My lips will shout for joy
　　when I sing praise to you
because you have redeemed me.[aa]

24 Therefore, my tongue will proclaim
　　your righteousness all day long,
for those who intend to harm me
　　will be disgraced and confounded.[ab]

A PRAYER FOR THE KING

72 Of Solomon.[ac]
　　God, give your justice to the king
and your righteousness
　　to the king's son.[ad]

2 He will judge your people
　　with righteousness
and your afflicted ones with justice.[ae]

71:5 Never underestimate the staying power of faith when children are taught to know and love the Lord from an early age.

71:17-24 The psalmist emphasizes the longevity of his discipleship. He had learned from God in his **youth** and is **still** proclaiming his **wondrous works** (71:17). Therefore, he prays that God would not **abandon** him when he is **old and gray**. He longs to see **another generation** know and serve the Lord (71:18). Though God had brought **many troubles and misfortunes** into the psalmist's life to strengthen, correct, and develop him (71:20-21; see Heb 12:4-11; Jas 1:1-12), he was confident that God would restore him. Therefore, his mouth would be filled with **praise** as he anticipated the disgrace of those who meant him **harm** (Ps 71:22-24). We can look to God with this same confidence regarding the trials he brings into our lives.

3 May the mountains
bring well-being[A] to the people
and the hills, righteousness.[a]
4 May he vindicate the afflicted
among the people,
help the poor,
and crush the oppressor.[b]

5 May they fear you[B] while the
sun endures
and as long as the moon,
throughout all generations.[c]
6 May the king be like rain that falls
on the cut grass,
like spring showers that water
the earth.[d]
7 May the righteous[c] flourish
in his days
and well-being abound
until the moon is no more.[e]

8 May he rule from sea to sea
and from the Euphrates
to the ends of the earth.[f]
9 May desert tribes kneel before him
and his enemies lick the dust.[g]
10 May the kings of Tarshish
and the coasts and islands
bring tribute,
the kings of Sheba and Seba
offer gifts.[h]
11 Let all kings bow in homage to him,
all nations serve him.[i]

12 For he will rescue the poor
who cry out
and the afflicted who have
no helper.[j]
13 He will have pity on the poor
and helpless
and save the lives of the poor.[k]
14 He will redeem them
from oppression and violence,
for their lives are[D] precious[E]
in his sight.[l]

15 May he live long!
May gold from Sheba be given
to him.
May prayer be offered
for him continually,
and may he be blessed all day long.[m]
16 May there be plenty of grain
in the land;
may it wave on the tops
of the mountains.
May its crops be like Lebanon.
May people flourish in the cities
like the grass of the field.[n]
17 May his name endure forever;
as long as the sun shines,
may his fame increase.
May all nations be blessed by him
and call him blessed.[o]

18 Blessed be the LORD God, the God
of Israel,
who alone does wonders.[p]
19 Blessed be his glorious name
forever;
the whole earth is filled
with his glory.[q]
Amen and amen.
20 The prayers of David son of Jesse
are concluded.[r]

BOOK III (PSALMS 73–89)

GOD'S WAYS VINDICATED

73 *A psalm of Asaph.*[s]
God is indeed good to Israel,
to the pure in heart.[t]
2 But as for me, my feet
almost slipped;
my steps nearly went astray.[u]
3 For I envied the arrogant;
I saw the prosperity of the wicked.[v]

4 They have an easy time
until they die,[F]
and their bodies are well fed.[G,w]

---

[a] 72:3 Is 11:9; 52:7; 55:12
[b] 72:4 Ps 109:31; Is 11:4
[c] 72:5 Ps 89:36-37
[d] 72:6 Dt 32:2; 2Sm 23:3-4; Hs 6:3
[e] 72:7 Ps 37:11; Is 2:4; 60:21
[f] 72:8 Gn 15:18; Ex 23:31; Zch 9:10
[g] 72:9 Ps 22:29; Is 49:23; Mc 7:17
[h] 72:10 1Kg 10:22; 2Ch 9:21; Is 60:6
[i] 72:11 Ps 86:9; 138:4; Is 49:23
[j] 72:12 Jb 29:12-17
[k] 72:13 Pr 19:17; 28:8
[l] 72:14 Ps 69:18; 116:15
[m] 72:15 Is 60:6
[n] 72:16 Jb 5:25; Ps 104:16
[o] 72:17 Gn 12:2-3; 22:18; Ps 89:36
[p] 72:18 Jb 9:10; Ps 86:10; 136:4
[q] 72:19 Nm 14:21; Is 6:3
[r] 72:20 2Sm 23:1
[s] 73:title 1Ch 16:5,7
[t] 73:1 Ps 24:4; 51:10; Mt 5:8
[u] 73:2 Ps 17:5; 66:9; 94:18
[v] 73:3 Ps 37:1; Pr 23:17; 24:1
[w] 73:4 Jb 21:23-24

[A] 72:3 Or *peace*, also in v. 7   [B] 72:5 LXX reads *May he continue*   [C] 72:7 Some Hb mss, LXX, Syr, Jer read *May righteousness*   [D] 72:14 Lit *their blood is*
[E] 72:14 Or *valuable*   [F] 73:4 Lit *For there are no pangs to their death*   [G] 73:4 Lit *fat*

72:5-7 Solomon longs to have a kingdom in which the people fear God forever, to be a **king** who brings life to **the earth**, and to cause **the righteous** to **flourish** under his rule. Thus, he anticipated the reign of the Messiah, for these things will only be true when the Son of God reigns eternally—beginning with his millennial kingdom. **72:8-11** Solomon desires to see his kingdom stretch to **the ends of the earth**, as his **enemies lick the dust** (72:8-9). This is an allusion to the curse on the serpent; it would "eat dust" all of its days (see Gen 3:14). Those who follow

the devil's ways share his fate. Meanwhile **the kings of** the world will **bring tribute** and **bow in homage** to the king (Ps 72:10-11). This is a prophecy that will be fulfilled in the future reign of Christ when "the kings of the earth will bring their glory" into the new Jerusalem (Rev 21:24). **72:12-17** The Messiah's universal reign will be characterized by justice for the **poor** and **afflicted**, as he rescues them from **oppression and violence** (72:12-14). Solomon prays that **all nations** would **be blessed by him** (72:17). God had promised Abraham that all the peoples of the earth would be blessed

through him (Gen 12:3). And indeed, through the "seed" of Abraham, Jesus Christ, all those who put faith in him are blessed with justification from sin (see Gal 3:7-9, 16). **73:1-5** Asaph begins the psalm with a declaration of the goodness of God to his people (73:1). Yet in spite of this divine reality, he confesses that he had almost departed from the right path (73:2). Why? Because he **envied the arrogant** and **saw the prosperity of the wicked** (73:3). Asaph was feeling conflict between his theology and his experience. More than a few Christians have been tempted to think similarly.

[a] 73:5 Jb 21:4
[b] 73:6 Ps 37:35; Pr 16:29; 21:24
[c] 73:7 Jb 15:27; Jr 5:28
[d] 73:8 Ps 17:10; 2Pt 2:18; Jd 16
[e] 73:9 Rv 13:6
[f] 73:10 Jb 15:16
[g] 73:11 Jb 22:13; Ps 10:4,11; Is 29:15
[h] 73:12 Ps 49:6; 52:7; Jr 49:31
[i] 73:13 Ps 26:6; Mt 27:24
[j] 73:14 Jb 33:19; Ps 38:6; 118:18
[k] 73:15 Ps 44:17; 89:33
[l] 73:16 Ec 8:17
[m] 73:17 Jb 8:13; Ps 37:38
[n] 73:18 Ps 35:6,8
[o] 73:19 Nm 16:21; Jb 18:11; Is 47:11
[p] 73:20 Ps 35:23; 59:5; 78:65
[q] 73:21 Ps 109:22
[r] 73:22 Jb 11:12; Ps 92:6
[s] 73:23 Ps 63:8
[t] 73:24 Ps 49:15; Is 58:11
[u] 73:25 Ps 16:2; Php 3:8
[v] 73:26 Ps 16:5; 38:10; 84:2
[w] 73:27 1Ch 5:25; Ps 37:20
[x] 73:28 Ps 40:5; 118:17
[y] 74:title 1Ch 16:5,7
[z] 74:1 Ex 32:11; Ps 60:1,10; 108:11
[aa] 74:2 Is 63:17; Jr 10:16; 51:19
[ab] Is 8:18
[ac] 74:3 Ps 79:1; Is 61:4

5 They are not in trouble like others;
they are not afflicted
like most people.[a]
6 Therefore, pride is their necklace,
and violence covers them
like a garment.[b]
7 Their eyes bulge out from fatness;
the imaginations of their hearts
run wild.[c]
8 They mock,
and they speak maliciously;
they arrogantly
threaten oppression.[d]
9 They set their mouths
against heaven,
and their tongues strut
across the earth.[e]
10 Therefore his people turn to them[A]
and drink in their
overflowing words.[B,f]
11 The wicked say,
"How can God know?
Does the Most High
know everything?"[g]
12 Look at them — the wicked!
They are always at ease,
and they increase their wealth.[h]

13 Did I purify my heart
and wash my hands in innocence
for nothing?[i]
14 For I am afflicted all day long
and punished every morning.[j]
15 If I had decided to say
these things aloud,
I would have betrayed your people.[C,k]
16 When I tried to understand all this,
it seemed hopeless[D,l]
17 until I entered God's sanctuary.
Then I understood their destiny.[m]
18 Indeed, you put them
in slippery places;
you make them fall into ruin.[n]
19 How suddenly they become
a desolation!
They come to an end, swept away
by terrors.[o]
20 Like one waking from a dream,
Lord, when arising, you will despise
their image.[p]

21 When I became embittered
and my innermost being[E]
was wounded,[q]
22 I was stupid and didn't understand;
I was an unthinking animal
toward you.[r]
23 Yet I am always with you;
you hold my right hand.[s]
24 You guide me with your counsel,
and afterward you will take me up
in glory.[F,t]
25 Who do I have in heaven but you?
And I desire nothing on earth
but you.[u]
26 My flesh and my heart may fail,
but God is the strength[G] of my heart,
my portion forever.[v]
27 Those far from you
will certainly perish;
you destroy all who are
unfaithful to you.[w]
28 But as for me, God's presence is
my good.
I have made the Lord God
my refuge,
so I can tell about all you do.[x]

PRAYER FOR ISRAEL

74 *A Maskil of Asaph.*[y]
Why have you
rejected us forever, God?
Why does your anger burn
against the sheep of your pasture?[z]
2 Remember your congregation,
which you purchased long ago
and redeemed as the tribe
for your own possession.[aa]
Remember Mount Zion
where you dwell.[ab]
3 Make your way[H]
to the perpetual ruins,
to all that the enemy has destroyed
in the sanctuary.[ac]

[A] 73:10 Lit *turn here* [B] 73:10 Lit *and waters of fullness are drained by them* [C] 73:15 Lit *betrayed the generation of your sons* [D] 73:16 Lit *it was trouble in my eyes* [E] 73:21 Lit *my kidneys* [F] 73:24 *Or will receive me with honor* [G] 73:26 Lit *rock* [H] 74:3 Lit *Lift up your steps*

73:6-12 By their lives the arrogant proclaim, "Hey, followers of God, why are you wasting your time? I care nothing about him. I live as I please. And I'm doing just fine."

73:12-14 Notice that Asaph didn't hide his feelings from God. He was honest about his confusion and frustration. When you are upset and feel that God has let you down, bring your struggles to him in prayer. He's not afraid of your concerns; he's not troubled by your disappointments. It is far better to pour out your anger and anxieties to God through prayer than to bury them inside and turn to sin (which Asaph almost did; see 73:2).

73:17-20 Asaph's **until** indicates the turning point. When he entered the presence of God, he experienced a fresh vision of his glory and gained an eternal perspective regarding the wicked.

73:27-28 Asaph began this psalm with, "But as for me, my feet almost slipped" (73:2). He finishes with, **But as for me, God's presence is my good** (73:28). So what happened in between verses 2 and 28? He encountered God in worship. In the presence of God, he found the truth, hope, and strength he needed. As a result, he wants nothing more than to **tell** others **about** God (73:28). Let life's confusion drive you to God, not away from him.

74:3 Asaph calls on God to intervene because of the destruction that Babylon had wrought on **the sanctuary**.

4 Your adversaries roared
in the meeting place
where you met with us.[A]
They set up their emblems as signs.[a]
5 It was like men in a thicket of trees,
wielding axes,[b]
6 then smashing all the carvings
with hatchets and picks.[c]
7 They set your sanctuary on fire;
they utterly[B] desecrated
the dwelling place of your name.[d]
8 They said in their hearts,
"Let us oppress them relentlessly."
They burned every place
throughout the land
where God met with us.[C,e]
9 There are no signs for us to see.
There is no longer a prophet.
And none of us knows how long
this will last.[f]
10 God, how long will the enemy mock?
Will the foe insult
your name forever?[g]
11 Why do you hold back your hand?
Stretch out[D] your right hand
and destroy them![h]

12 God my King is from ancient times,
performing saving acts on the earth.[i]
13 You divided the sea
with your strength;
you smashed the heads
of the sea monsters in the water;[j]
14 you crushed the heads of Leviathan;
you fed him to the creatures
of the desert.[k]
15 You opened up springs and streams;[l]
you dried up ever-flowing rivers.[m]
16 The day is yours, also the night;
you established the moon
and the sun.[n]
17 You set all the boundaries of the earth;
you made summer and winter.[o]

18 Remember this: the enemy
has mocked the LORD,
and a foolish people has insulted
your name.[p]
19 Do not give to beasts the life
of your dove;[E]
do not forget the lives
of your poor people forever.[q]

20 Consider the covenant,[r]
for the dark places of the land
are full of violence.[s]
21 Do not let the oppressed turn away
in shame;
let the poor and needy
praise your name.[t]
22 Rise up, God,
champion your cause![u]
Remember the insults
that fools bring against you
all day long.[v]
23 Do not forget the clamor
of your adversaries,
the tumult of your opponents
that goes up constantly.[w]

GOD JUDGES THE WICKED

75 For the choir director: "Do Not Destroy."
A psalm of Asaph.[x] A song.

1 We give thanks to you, God;
we give thanks to you,
for your name is near.
People tell about
your wondrous works.[y]

2 "When I choose a time,
I will judge fairly.[z]
3 When the earth and all
its inhabitants shake,
I am the one who steadies
its pillars.[aa]   *Selah*

4 I say to the boastful,
'Do not boast,'
and to the wicked, 'Do not lift up
your horn.[ab]
5 Do not lift up your horn
against heaven[F]
or speak arrogantly.' "[ac]

6 Exaltation does not come
from the east, the west,
or the desert,
7 for God is the Judge:
He brings down one
and exalts another.[ad]
8 For there is a cup in the LORD's hand,
full of wine blended with spices,
and he pours from it.
All the wicked of the earth
will drink,
draining it to the dregs.[ae]

[a] 74:4 Nm 2:2; Lm 2:6-7
[b] 74:5 Jr 46:22
[c] 74:6 Lm 2:2
[d] 74:7 2Kg 25:9; Ps 79:1
[e] 74:8 Ps 83:4
[f] 74:9 1Sm 3:1; Lm 2:9; Ezk 7:26
[g] 74:10 Ps 79:12; 89:51
[h] 74:11 Ps 59:13; Lm 2:3
[i] 74:12 Ps 47:6-8; 95:3; Jr 10:10
[j] 74:13 Ex 14:21; Is 51:9; Ezk 32:2
[k] 74:14 Jb 41:1; Ps 104:26; Is 27:1
[l] 74:15 Ps 104:10-11
[m] Is 42:15; 44:27
[n] 74:16 Gn 1:14-18; Ps 104:19
[o] 74:17 Gn 8:22; Jb 38:10-11; Pr 8:29; Jr 5:22
[p] 74:18 Ps 14:1; 53:1; 89:51
[q] 74:19 Ps 9:18; 68:10
[r] 74:20 Dt 4:31; Ps 106:45
[s] Ezk 7:23
[t] 74:21 Ps 9:9; 103:6; Is 41:7
[u] 74:22 Ps 9:19; 82:8
[v] Ps 79:12
[w] 74:23 Ps 65:7
[x] 75:title 1Ch 16:5,7
[y] 75:1 Dt 4:7; Ps 26:7; 145:18
[z] 75:2 Ps 9:8; 96:10
[aa] 75:3 1Sm 2:8; Ps 46:6; Is 24:19
[ab] 75:4 Pr 27:1; Jr 9:23
[ac] 75:5 1Sm 2:3; Ps 94:4
[ad] 75:6-7 1Sm 2:7-8; Ps 50:6; Lk 1:52-53
[ae] 75:8 Is 51:17,22; Jr 25:15-17

[A] 74:4 Lit *in your meeting place*   [B] 74:7 Lit *they to the ground*   [C] 74:8 Lit *every meeting place of God in the land*   [D] 74:11 Lit *From your bosom*
[E] 74:19 One Hb ms, LXX, Syr read *life that praises you*   [F] 75:5 Lit *horn to the height*

74:12-23 When we pray for intervention in our circumstances, we too should desire to see God vindicated and glorified. So whatever assistance we need, let us be motivated to see God's name lifted high in praise.
75:2-5 Here God speaks.
75:6-7 No one escapes the righteous gaze of **the Judge** (75:7); therefore, no one will escape his condemnation of pride. "God resists the proud but gives grace to the humble" (1 Pet 5:5).

a 75:9 Ps 9:2; 18:49; 81:1
b 75:10 Jr 48:25
c Ps 89:17; 92:10; 148:14
d 76:title 1Ch 16:5,7
e 76:1 Jr 10:6; Mal 1:11
f 76:2 Gn 14:18; Ps 9:11
g 76:3 Ps 46:9; Is 2:4;
    Jr 49:35
h 76:4 Is 14:25; Nah 2:13
i 76:5 Jr 51:39
j 76:6 Ex 13:1,21
k 76:7 Ps 1:5; 130:3; Nah 1:6
l 76:8 2Ch 20:29-30; Ps
    33:8; Hab 2:20
m 76:9 Ps 9:7-8; Is 3:13-15
n 76:10 Ex 9:16; Rm 9:17
o 76:11 Ps 50:14

p 76:11 Ps 68:29; Is 18:7
q 76:12 Dn 4:37
r 77:title 1Ch 16:5,7
s 77:1 Ps 3:4; 142:1
t 77:2 Gn 37:35; Jb 11:13;
    Jr 31:15
u 77:3 Ps 42:5,11; 43:5;
    55:17; 143:4
v 77:4 Ps 39:9
w 77:5 Dt 32:7; Ps 143:5
x 77:6 Ps 4:4; 42:8
y 77:7 Ps 44:9,23; 74:1; Lm
    2:7; 3:31
z 77:8 Ps 33:11; 85:5; 89:49
aa 77:9 Ps 25:6; 40:11;
    Is 49:15
ab 77:10 Ps 31:22; 73:14
ac 77:11 Ps 105:5; 143:5
ad 77:12 Ps 9:11; 90:16;
    145:5
ae 77:13 Ex 15:11; Ps 71:19;
    86:8

9 As for me, I will tell
   about him forever;
   I will sing praise to the God
   of Jacob.[a]

10 "I will cut off all the horns
   of the wicked,[b]
   but the horns of the righteous
   will be lifted up."[c]

GOD, THE POWERFUL JUDGE

76 *For the choir director: with stringed instruments. A psalm of Asaph.[d] A song.*

1 God is known in Judah;
   his name is great in Israel.[e]
2 His tent is in Salem,
   his dwelling place in Zion.[f]
3 There he shatters the bow's
   flaming arrows,
   the shield, the sword,
   and the weapons of war.[g]   *Selah*

4 You are resplendent and majestic
   coming down from the mountains
   of prey.[h]
5 The brave-hearted
   have been plundered;
   they have slipped
   into their final sleep.
   None of the warriors was able to lift
   a hand.[i]
6 At your rebuke, God of Jacob,
   both chariot and horse lay still.[j]

7 And you — you are to be feared.[A]
   When you are angry,
   who can stand before you?[k]
8 From heaven
   you pronounced judgment.
   The earth feared and grew quiet[l]
9 when God rose up to judge
   and to save all the lowly
   of the earth.[m]   *Selah*
10 Even human wrath will praise you;
   you will clothe yourself
   with the wrath that remains.[B,n]

11 Make and keep your vows
   to the LORD your God;[o]
   let all who are around him
   bring tribute

12 He humbles the spirit of leaders;
   he is feared by the kings
   of the earth.[q]

CONFIDENCE IN A TIME OF CRISIS

77 *For the choir director: according to Jeduthun. Of Asaph.[r] A psalm.*

1 I cry aloud to God,
   aloud to God, and he
   will hear me.[s]
2 I sought the Lord in my day
   of trouble.
   My hands were continually lifted up
   all night long;
   I refused to be comforted.[t]
3 I think of God; I groan;
   I meditate; my spirit
   becomes weak.[u]   *Selah*

4 You have kept me from closing
   my eyes;
   I am troubled and cannot speak.[v]
5 I consider days of old,
   years long past.[w]
6 At night I remember my music;
   I meditate in my heart,
   and my spirit ponders.[x]
7 "Will the Lord reject forever
   and never again show favor?[y]
8 Has his faithful love ceased forever?
   Is his promise at an end
   for all generations?[z]
9 Has God forgotten to be gracious?
   Has he in anger
   withheld his compassion?"[aa] *Selah*

10 So I say, "I am grieved
   that the right hand of the Most High
   has changed."[B,ab]
11 I will remember the LORD's works;
   yes, I will remember
   your ancient wonders.[ac]
12 I will reflect on all you have done
   and meditate on your actions.[ad]

13 God, your way is holy.
   What god is great like God?[ae]
14 You are the God
   who works wonders;

[A] 76:7 Or *are awe-inspiring*   [B] 76:10; 77:10 Hb obscure   [C] 76:11 Or *tribute with awe*

75:10 An animal's **horns** represent power. Thus, God will act in a way that's consistent with his just and righteous character, vanquishing those who exalt themselves but establishing those who submit to his kingdom rule and authority.

76:5-6 Notice how little effort it takes on God's part to defeat the enemies of his people: A mere **rebuke** can do the job (76:6). **76:11** Believers are exhorted to fear **the awe-inspiring** God—that is, to take him seriously—by keeping their **vows** and maintaining their commitment to him. He invites

us to fear and enjoy him now so that we may experience his blessings. Those who do not will experience his judgment.
77:13-15 For comfort and assurance, Asaph turns to recalling and meditating on the **holy** God's deliverances in the past (77:13). We should do the same.

you revealed your strength
   among the peoples.[a]
15 With power you redeemed
   your people,
the descendants of Jacob
   and Joseph.[b]   *Selah*

16 The water saw you, God.
The water saw you; it trembled.
Even the depths shook.[c]
17 The clouds poured down water.
The storm clouds thundered;
your arrows flashed back and forth.[d]
18 The sound of your thunder was
   in the whirlwind;
lightning lit up the world.[e]
The earth shook and quaked.[f]
19 Your way went through the sea
and your path through
   the vast water,
but your footprints were unseen.[g]
20 You led your people like a flock[h]
by the hand of Moses and Aaron.[i]

LESSONS FROM ISRAEL'S PAST
78 A Maskil *of Asaph.*[j]
My people, hear my instruction;
listen to the words
   from my mouth.[k]
2 I will declare wise sayings;
I will speak mysteries
   from the past[l] —
3 things we have heard and known
and that our fathers
   have passed down to us.[m]
4 We will not hide them
   from their children,
but will tell a future generation
the praiseworthy acts of the LORD,
his might, and the wondrous works
he has performed.[n]
5 He established a testimony in Jacob
and set up a law in Israel,
which he commanded our fathers
to teach to their children[o]
6 so that a future generation —
children yet to be born —
   might know.
They were to rise and tell
   their children[p]

7 so that they might
   put their confidence in God
and not forget God's works,
but keep his commands.[q]
8 Then they would not be
   like their fathers,
a stubborn and rebellious
   generation,
a generation whose heart
   was not loyal
and whose spirit was not faithful
   to God.[r]

9 The Ephraimite archers
   turned back
on the day of battle.[s]
10 They did not keep God's covenant
and refused to live by his law.[t]
11 They forgot what he had done,
the wondrous works
   he had shown them.[u]
12 He worked wonders in the sight of
   their fathers
in the land of Egypt, the territory
   of Zoan.[v]
13 He split the sea
   and brought them across;
the water stood firm like a wall.[w]
14 He led them with a cloud by day
and with a fiery light
   throughout the night.[x]
15 He split rocks in the wilderness
and gave them drink as abundant
   as the depths.[y]
16 He brought streams out of the stone
and made water flow down
   like rivers.[z]

17 But they continued to sin
   against him,
rebelling in the desert
   against the Most High.[aa]
18 They deliberately[A] tested God,
demanding the food they craved.[ab]
19 They spoke against God, saying,
"Is God able to provide food
   in the wilderness?
20 Look! He struck the rock and water
   gushed out;
torrents overflowed.[ac]

---

[a] 77:14 Ps 72:18; 106:8
[b] 77:15 Ex 6:6; Dt 9:29; Ps 74:2
[c] 77:16 Ps 114:3; Hab 3:8,10
[d] 77:17 Ps 18:14; Hab 3:11; Zch 9:14
[e] 77:16-18 Ps 29:3,9; 97:4
[f] 77:18 2Sm 22:8; Ps 18:7; Is 13:13
[g] 77:19 Is 43:16
[h] 77:20 Ps 78:52; 80:1
[i] Ps 105:26; Is 63:11-13
[j] 78:title 1Ch 16:5,7
[k] 78:1 Pr 5:7; 7:24; Is 55:3
[l] 78:2 Ps 49:4; Pr 1:6; Mt 13:35
[m] 78:3 Ps 44:1
[n] 78:4 Dt 6:7; 11:19; Ps 145:4
[o] 78:5 Ps 19:7; 81:5; 147:19
[p] 78:6 Ps 11:19; Ps 22:31; 102:18

---

[q] 78:7 Dt 6:12; Ps 103:2; Pr 3:1
[r] 78:8 Dt 31:27; 2Kg 17:14; 2Ch 30:7
[s] 78:9 Ps 44:10
[t] 78:10 1Kg 11:11; 2Kg 17:15; Jr 32:23
[u] 78:11 Ps 106:13
[v] 78:12 Ex 7–12; Ps 78:43
[w] 78:13 Ex 14:21; 15:8; Ps 136:13
[x] 78:14 Ex 13:21; Nm 14:14; Ps 105:39
[y] 78:15 Ex 17:6; Nm 20:8-13; Is 48:21
[z] 78:16 Ps 105:41; 114:8
[aa] 78:17 Dt 9:22; Is 63:10; Heb 3:16
[ab] 78:18 Ex 17:2,7; Ps 106:14; 1Co 10:5-10
[ac] 78:20 Nm 20:11

[A] 78:18 Lit *in their heart*

77:16-20 By recalling this great redemption of Israel by God's hand, Asaph encourages himself that God would again come to the aid of his people. His delayed response does not mean abandonment. His footprints of grace from yesterday give us the power to trust him today.
78:1-2 Asaph invites those with spiritual understanding to hear the **instruction** and **wise sayings** that he was about to share. Those without spiritual perception would not be able to interpret and apply the truths; they would remain **mysteries** from their view. Similarly, those who were without spiritual insight and unwilling to receive it would be unable to understand Jesus's parables (see Matt 13:10-17).
78:5-8 Asaph wants to challenge his own generation **to teach . . . their children** not to be like their ancestors who were **stubborn and rebellious** (78:8). We too must learn from the past, imitating the faithful and avoiding the foolishness of the wicked, if we are to experience the goodness of God.
78:9-20 The significant tribe of Ephraim mentioned in verse 9 was often used as shorthand for the entire northern kingdom of Israel.

[a] 78:19-20 Ex 16:3; Nm 11:4; 21:5
[b] 78:21 Nm 11:1
[c] 78:22 Dt 1:23; 9:23; Heb 3:18
[d] 78:23 Gn 7:11; Mal 3:10
[e] 78:24 Ex 16:4,31; Jn 6:31
[f] 78:25 Ex 16:3
[g] 78:26 Nm 11:31
[h] 78:27-28 Ex 16:13; Ps 105:40
[i] 78:29 Nm 11:4,34
[j] 78:30-31 Nm 11:33-34; Jb 20:23
[k] 78:32 Nm 14:16-17
[l] 78:33 Nm 14:29,35
[m] 78:34 Nm 21:7; Ps 63:1; Hs 5:15
[n] 78:35 Is 44:6,8
[o] 78:36 Is 29:13; 57:11; Ezk 33:31

[p] 78:37 Ps 51:10; 78:8; Ac 8:21
[q] 78:38 Nm 14:18-20; Dt 4:31; Is 12:1
[r] 78:39 Dt 31:27; Ps 107:11
[s] 78:41 Ps 95:8-9
[t] Dt 9:7-8,22; Ps 106:29; Zch 8:14
[u] 78:42 Jdg 8:34; Ps 44:3; 106:10
[v] 78:43 Ex 4:21; 7:3; Ps 105:27
[w] 78:44 Ex 7:14-25; Ps 105:29
[x] 78:45 Ex 8:17; Ps 105:31
[y] Ex 8:3-6; Ps 105:30
[z] 78:46 Ex 10:14-15; Ps 105:34
[aa] 78:47-48 Ex 9:23-24; Ps 105:32
[ab] 78:49 Ex 12:13,23; 2Sm 24:16
[ac] 78:50 Ex 12:29-30
[ad] 78:51 Ex 13:15; Ps 105:36
[ae] Ps 105:23,27

But can he also provide bread
    or furnish meat for his people?"[a]
21 Therefore, the LORD heard
        and became furious;
    then fire broke out against Jacob,
    and anger flared up against Israel[b]
22 because they did not believe God
    or rely on his salvation.[c]
23 He gave a command
        to the clouds above
    and opened the doors of heaven.[d]
24 He rained manna for them to eat;
    he gave them grain from heaven.[e]
25 People[A] ate the bread of angels.[B]
    He sent them an abundant supply
        of food.[f]
26 He made the east wind blow
        in the skies
    and drove the south wind
        by his might.[g]
27 He rained meat on them like dust,
    and winged birds like the sand
        of the seas.
28 He made them fall in the camp,
    all around the tents.[h]
29 The people ate and were
        completely satisfied,
    for he gave them what they craved.[i]
30 Before they had turned from
        what they craved,
    while the food was still
        in their mouths,
31 God's anger flared up against them,
    and he killed some of their best men.
    He struck down Israel's fit
        young men.[j]

32 Despite all this, they kept sinning
    and did not believe
        his wondrous works.[k]
33 He made their days end in futility,
    their years in sudden disaster.[l]
34 When he killed some of them,
    the rest began to seek him;
    they repented
        and searched for God.[m]
35 They remembered that God was
        their rock,
    the Most High God, their Redeemer.[n]
36 But they deceived him
        with their mouths,
    they lied to him with their tongues,[o]
37 their hearts were insincere
        toward him,

and they were unfaithful
    to his covenant.[p]
38 Yet he was compassionate;
    he atoned for their iniquity
    and did not destroy them.
    He often turned his anger aside
    and did not unleash[C] all his wrath.[q]
39 He remembered that they were
        only flesh,
    a wind that passes
        and does not return.[r]
40 How often they rebelled
        against him
    in the wilderness
    and grieved him in the desert.
41 They constantly tested God[s]
    and provoked the Holy One
        of Israel.[t]
42 They did not remember
        his power shown
    on the day he redeemed them
        from the foe,[u]
43 when he performed
        his miraculous signs in Egypt
    and his wonders in the territory
        of Zoan.[v]
44 He turned their rivers into blood,
    and they could not drink
        from their streams.[w]
45 He sent among them swarms
        of flies,[x]
    which fed on them,
    and frogs, which devastated them.[y]
46 He gave their crops to the caterpillar
    and the fruit of their labor
        to the locust.[z]
47 He killed their vines with hail
    and their sycamore fig trees
        with a flood.
48 He handed over their livestock
        to hail
    and their cattle to lightning bolts.[aa]
49 He sent his burning anger
        against them:
    fury, indignation, and calamity —
    a band of deadly messengers.[D,ab]
50 He cleared a path for his anger.
    He did not spare them from death
    but delivered their lives
        to the plague.[ac]
51 He struck all the firstborn[ad] in Egypt,
    the first progeny of the tents
        of Ham.[ae]

[A] 78:25 Lit *Man*   [B] 78:25 Lit *mighty ones*   [C] 78:38 Or *stir up*   [D] 78:49 Or *angels*

78:34-37 When God judged them, some of the people made a pretense of repenting (78:34). But they **were insincere**, confessing with their mouths but demonstrating with their lives that they were still **unfaithful to his covenant** (78:37).
78:42-51 Asaph recalls the plagues that the Lord brought upon **Egypt** (78:43-51)—all of which the people of the exodus had failed to **remember** (78:42).

52 He led his people out like sheep
and guided them like a flock
in the wilderness.[a]
53 He led them safely,
and they were not afraid;
but the sea covered their enemies.[b]
54 He brought them to his holy territory,
to the mountain
his right hand acquired.[c]
55 He drove out nations before them.[d]
He apportioned their inheritance
by lot
and settled the tribes of Israel
in their tents.[e]

56 But they rebelliously tested
the Most High God,
for they did not keep his decrees.[f]
57 They treacherously turned away
like their fathers;
they became warped
like a faulty bow.[g]
58 They enraged him
with their high places
and provoked his jealousy
with their carved images.[h]
59 God heard and became furious;
he completely rejected Israel.[i]
60 He abandoned the tabernacle at Shiloh,
the tent where he resided
among mankind.[j]
61 He gave up his strength to captivity
and his splendor to the hand of a foe.[k]
62 He surrendered his people
to the sword
because he was enraged
with his heritage.[l]
63 Fire consumed
his chosen young men,
and his young women
had no wedding songs.[A,m]
64 His priests fell by the sword,
and the widows could not lament.[n]

65 The Lord awoke as if from sleep,
like a warrior from the effects
of wine.[o]
66 He beat back his foes;
he gave them lasting disgrace.[p]

67 He rejected the tent of Joseph
and did not choose the tribe
of Ephraim.
68 He chose instead the tribe of Judah,
Mount Zion, which he loved.[q]
69 He built his sanctuary like the heights,
like the earth that
he established forever.[r]
70 He chose David his servant
and took him from the sheep pens;[s]
71 he brought him from tending ewes
to be shepherd
over his people Jacob —
over Israel, his inheritance.[t]
72 He shepherded them
with a pure heart
and guided them
with his skillful hands.[u]

FAITH AMID CONFUSION

79 A psalm of Asaph.[v]
God, the nations have invaded
your inheritance,
desecrated your holy temple,
and turned Jerusalem into ruins.[w]
2 They gave the corpses of your servants
to the birds of the sky for food,
the flesh of your faithful ones
to the beasts of the earth.[x]
3 They poured out their blood
like water all around Jerusalem,
and there was no one to bury them.[y]
4 We have become an object of reproach
to our neighbors,
a source of mockery and ridicule
to those around us.[z]

5 How long, Lord? Will you
be angry forever?
Will your jealousy keep burning
like fire?[aa]
6 Pour out your wrath on the nations
that don't acknowledge you,
on the kingdoms that don't call on
your name,[ab]
7 for they have devoured Jacob
and devastated his homeland.[ac]
8 Do not hold past iniquities[B]
against us;

[a] 78:52 Ex 15:22; Ps 77:20
[b] 78:53 Ex 14; 15:19; Jos 24:7; Ps 106:11
[c] 78:54 Ex 15:17; Ps 74:2
[d] 78:55 Jos 11:16-23; Ps 44:2
[e] Jos 13:7; 23:4; Ps 135:12
[f] 78:56 Jdg 2:11-13
[g] 78:57 Ezk 20:27-28; Hs 7:16
[h] 78:58 Jdg 2:12; 1Kg 3:2; Ezk 20:28
[i] 78:59 Dt 32:19; Ps 106:40; Am 6:8
[j] 78:60 Jr 7:12,14; 26:6
[k] 78:61 1Sm 4:17
[l] 78:62 Jdg 20:21; 1Sm 4:10
[m] 78:63 Jr 7:34; 16:9; Lm 2:21
[n] 78:64 Jb 27:15; Ezk 24:23
[o] 78:65 Ps 73:20; 121:4; Is 42:13
[p] 78:66 1Sm 5:6; Ps 40:14

[q] 78:67-68 Ps 87:2
[r] 78:69 1Kg 6
[s] 78:70 1Sm 16:11-13
[t] 78:71 Ps 28:9; Is 40:11
[u] 78:72 1Kg 9:4; Ps 101:2
[v] 79:title 1Ch 16:5,7
[w] 79:1 Jr 26:18; Lm 1:10; Mc 3:12
[x] 79:2 Dt 28:26; Jr 7:33; 16:4
[y] 79:3 Jr 14:16; 16:4; 22:19
[z] 79:4 Ps 44:13-14; 80:6; Dn 9:16
[aa] 79:5 Ps 74:10; 78:58; 80:4
[ab] 79:6 Ps 14:4; Jr 10:25
[ac] 79:7 Ps 53:4

[A] 78:63 Lit *virgins were not praised* [B] 79:8 Or *hold the sins of past generations*

78:67-72 Ultimately, God would choose **the tribe of Judah** and the house of **David** for the messianic line (78:68, 70; see 2 Sam 7:11-16). Thus, the one who shepherded **sheep** (David) would **shepherd** God's **people** in fulfillment of his kingdom purpose (78:70-71). This shepherding role, however, would ultimately be fulfilled by Jesus Christ, the good shepherd (see John 10:1-30).

God's people today need to be students of history. Knowing how God has acted in the past can influence how we respond in the future. Divine sovereignty and human responsibility go hand in hand.
79:1-4 Asaph laments over the city of **Jerusalem**. God's **holy temple** had been **invaded** and **desecrated** (79:1). Many of the people had been killed and left unburied, their bodies

devoured by scavengers (79:2-3). As a result, God's people were an object of scorn among the nations (79:4).
79:8-9 When you need God's intervention, and have dealt with your own sin, appeal to God's glory. As Scripture shows, it's a trusted way to get God's attention.

a 79:8 Ps 142:6; Is 64:9
b 79:9 1Ch 16:35; Ps 85:4
c Ps 25:11; 106:8; Jr 14:7
d 79:10 Ps 42:3,10; 115:2
e Dt 32:43; Ps 94:1-2;
    Jr 46:10
f 79:11 Ps 102:20
g 79:12 Lv 26:21,28
h Ps 74:10,18,22
i 79:13 Ps 74:1; 100:3
j Ps 89:1; Is 43:21
k 80:title Pss 45; 60;
    69 titles
l 1Ch 16:5,7
m 80:1 Ezk 34:11,16,31
n Ps 99:1
o Dt 33:2; Ps 94:1
p 80:2 Nm 2:17-24
q Ps 35:23; 106:47; 118:25
r 80:3 Nm 6:25
s Ps 60:1; 85:4; Lm 5:21
t 80:4 Ps 74:10; 79:5; 85:5
u 80:5 Ps 102:9; Is 30:20;
    Hs 9:4

v 80:6 Ps 44:13; 79:4
w 80:7 Ps 60:1; Lm 5:21
x 80:8 Jr 2:21; 32:41
y 80:9 Am 9:15
z 80:10 Ezk 17:22-24
aa 80:11 Ex 23:31; Dt 11:24;
    Ps 72:8
ab 80:12 Ps 89:40; Is 5:5
ac 80:13 Jr 5:6
ad 80:14 Ps 6:4; 90:13
ae 80:14-15 Is 63:15
af 80:16 Ps 39:11; 76:6;
    Is 33:12
ag 80:17 Ps 89:21
ah 80:18 Ps 71:20; 85:6
ai 80:19 Ps 60:1; 85:4;
    Lm 5:21
aj Mal 1:9
ak 81:title 1Ch 16:5,7; Pss
    8; 84 titles
al 81:1 Ps 59:16; 95:1-2;
    98:4

let your compassion come
    to us quickly,
for we have become very weak.[a]

9 God of our salvation, help us[b] —
for the glory of your name.
Rescue us and atone for our sins,
for your name's sake.[c]

10 Why should the nations ask,
"Where is their God?"[d]
Before our eyes,
let vengeance for the shed blood
    of your servants
be known among the nations.[e]

11 Let the groans of the prisoners
    reach you;
according to your great power,
preserve those condemned to die.[f]

12 Pay back sevenfold to our neighbors[g]
the reproach they have hurled
at you, Lord.[h]

13 Then we, your people, the sheep
    of your pasture,[i]
will thank you forever;
we will declare your praise
to generation after generation.[j]

A PRAYER FOR RESTORATION

80 *For the choir director: according to
"The Lilies."[k] A testimony of Asaph.[l]
A psalm.*

1 Listen, Shepherd of Israel,
who leads Joseph like a flock;[m]
you who sit enthroned
    between the cherubim,[n]
shine[o] [2] on Ephraim,
Benjamin, and Manasseh.[p]
Rally your power and come
    to save us.[q]

3 Restore us, God;
make your face shine on us,[r]
so that we may be saved.[s]

4 LORD God of Armies,
how long will you be angry
with your people's prayers?[t]

5 You fed them the bread of tears
and gave them a full measure[A]
of tears to drink.[u]

6 You put us at odds
    with our neighbors;
our enemies mock us.[v]

7 Restore us, God of Armies;
make your face shine on us, so
    that we may be saved.[w]

8 You dug up a vine from Egypt;
you drove out the nations
    and planted it.[x]

9 You cleared a place for it;
it took root and filled the land.[y]

10 The mountains were covered
    by its shade,
and the mighty cedars[B]
    with its branches.[z]

11 It sent out sprouts toward the Sea[C]
and shoots toward the River.[D,aa]

12 Why have you broken down its walls
so that all who pass by pick its fruit?[ab]

13 Boars from the forest tear at it
and creatures of the field feed on it.[ac]

14 Return, God of Armies.[ad]
Look down from heaven and see;
take care of this vine,

15 the root[E] your right hand planted,
the son[F] that you made strong
    for yourself.[ae]

16 It was cut down and burned;
they[G] perish at the rebuke
    of your countenance.[af]

17 Let your hand be with the man
    at your right hand,
with the son of man
you have made strong for yourself.[ag]

18 Then we will not turn away
    from you;
revive us, and we will call
    on your name.[ah]

19 Restore us, LORD, God of Armies;[ai]
make your face shine on us, so
    that we may be saved.[aj]

A CALL TO OBEDIENCE

81 *For the choir director: on the Gittith. Of
Asaph.[ak]*

1 Sing for joy to God our strength;
shout in triumph to the God
    of Jacob.[al]

A 80:5 Lit *a one-third measure*   B 80:10 Lit *the cedars of God*   C 80:11 = the Mediterranean   D 80:11 = the Euphrates   E 80:15 Hb obscure
F 80:15 Or *shoot*   G 80:16 Or *may they*

79:12 In the Bible, the number *seven* denotes completeness. Thus, a request that God **pay back sevenfold** means that Asaph wants his nation's invaders to experience complete **reproach** for what they'd done.
80:1 **You who sit enthroned between the cherubim** is a reference to God's presence above the ark of the covenant.

80:3 The request that God would **make [his] face shine on** them is a request for him to allow his favor and blessing, which had been blocked because of their sin, to return.
80:8-13 When God delivered his people from **Egypt**, he transplanted them in the land he had promised (80:8-9). For a time, Israel flourished (80:10-11). But then God removed their

protection so that they were oppressed by enemies; they became like an untended vine whose **fruit** could be devoured by animals (80:12-13).
80:17 The request that God rescue his people through **the man at [his] right hand**, the **son of man**, is a reference to the messianic Deliverer.

² Lift up a song — play the tambourine,
the melodious lyre, and the harp.[a]
³ Blow the horn on the day of
our feasts[A]
during the new moon[b]
and during the full moon.
⁴ For this is a statute for Israel,
an ordinance of the God of Jacob.[c]
⁵ He set it up as a decree for Joseph
when he went throughout[B] the land
of Egypt.[d]

I heard an unfamiliar language:
⁶ "I relieved his shoulder
from the burden;
his hands were freed from carrying
the basket.[e]
⁷ You called out in distress,
and I rescued you;
I answered you
from the thundercloud.[f]
I tested you at the Waters
of Meribah.[g]   Selah
⁸ Listen, my people, and I will
admonish you.
Israel, if you would only listen
to me![h]
⁹ There must not be a strange god
among you;
you must not bow down
to a foreign god.[i]
¹⁰ I am the LORD your God,
who brought you up from the land
of Egypt.[j]
Open your mouth wide, and I will
fill it.[k]

¹¹ "But my people did not listen
to my voice;
Israel did not obey me.[l]
¹² So I gave them over
to their stubborn hearts
to follow their own plans.[m]
¹³ If only my people would listen to me
and Israel would follow my ways,[n]

¹⁴ I would quickly subdue their enemies
and turn my hand against their foes."[o]
¹⁵ Those who hate the LORD
would cower to him;[p]
their doom would last forever.[q]
¹⁶ But he would feed Israel[c]
with the best wheat.
"I would satisfy you with honey
from the rock."[r]

A PLEA FOR RIGHTEOUS JUDGMENT

82 A psalm of Asaph.[s]

God stands in the divine assembly;
he pronounces judgment
among the gods:[D,t]
² "How long will you judge unjustly
and show partiality to the wicked?[u]
                                    Selah
³ Provide justice for the needy
and the fatherless;
uphold the rights of the oppressed
and the destitute.[v]
⁴ Rescue the poor and needy;
save them from the power of
the wicked."[w]

⁵ They do not know or understand;
they wander in darkness.[x]
All the foundations of the earth
are shaken.[y]

⁶ I said, "You are gods;[z]
you are all sons of the Most High.[aa]
⁷ However, you will die like humans
and fall like any other ruler."[ab]

⁸ Rise up, God, judge the earth,
for all the nations belong to you.[ac]

PRAYER AGAINST ENEMIES

83 A song. A psalm of Asaph.[ad]

God, do not keep silent.
Do not be deaf, God; do not be quiet.[ae]
² See how your enemies
make an uproar;

[a] 81:2 Ps 33:2; 71:22; 92:3
[b] 81:3 Lv 23:24; Nm 10:10; 29:1
[c] 81:4 1Ch 16:17; Ps 105:10
[d] 81:5 Ps 78:5; 122:4
[e] 81:6 Is 9:4; 10:27
[f] 81:7 Ex 14:24; 20:18-20
[g] Ex 17:1-7; Nm 20:2-13
[h] 81:8 Ps 50:7
[i] 81:9 Ex 20:3-5; 22:20; 34:14
[j] 81:10 Ex 20:2; Dt 5:6
[k] Ps 78:25; 107:9
[l] 81:11 Jr 7:24; 13:10
[m] 81:13 Dt 5:29; Is 48:18
[n] 81:14 Ps 18:47; 47:3; Am 1:8
[p] 81:15 Ps 18:44; 66:3
[q] Dt 32:35
[r] 81:16 Nm 18:12; Dt 32:13-14; Ps 147:14
[s] 82:title 1Ch 16:5,7
[t] 82:1 Jb 21:22; Ps 7:8; 58:11
[u] 82:2 Dt 1:17; Pr 18:5; Mal 2:9
[v] 82:3 Dt 24:17; Is 11:4; Jr 22:16
[w] 82:4 Jb 29:12; Pr 24:11
[x] 82:5 Pr 2:13; Is 44:18
[y] Ps 11:3
[z] 82:6 Jn 10:34
[aa] Ps 82:1; Lk 6:35
[ab] 82:7 Ps 49:12
[ac] 82:8 Ps 58:11; 96:13
[ad] 83:title 1Ch 16:5,7
[ae] 83:1 Ps 28:1; 39:12; Is 62:1

[A] 81:3 Lit *feast*   [B] 81:5 Or *went out against*   [C] 81:16 Lit *him*   [D] 82:1 Or *the heavenly beings*, or *the earthly rulers*; Hb *elohim*

81:9-10 One of the quickest ways to sever fellowship with God is to appeal to false gods in time of need. There is only one true God. Loyalty to him is critical if we are to receive all that he wants us to have.

81:11-12 When his people didn't submit to him, God let them follow their own **stubborn hearts**—a dead-end end street.

81:13-16 Obedience brings blessing, a reversal of fortune, and supernatural provision (see Exod 17:6). The same is true today. If we want God to reverse our circumstances, we need to place ourselves in a position of submission to his will and kingdom authority.

82:1-2 In the divine assembly, which is the assembly of the angels, God **pronounces judgment among the gods** (82:1). In this context, "gods" is a way of referring to human rulers, those who are made in God's image and are charged with the responsibility of mirroring God's character and judgments. But the particular leaders in view had ruled **unjustly** and favored **the wicked** (82:2). They hadn't represented God's way. The courts had failed to exercise justice and righteousness for the poor (see Deut 24:17; Isa 11:4; Jer 22:16).

82:6-8 Though these rulers, these **gods** (see the note on 82:1-2), were **sons of the Most**

High (82:6), they were not behaving as sons of God. (This verse was quoted by Jesus when the Jewish religious leaders wanted to stone him for declaring himself to be the Son of God; see John 10:34-38.) The rulers had failed to exercise justice and righteousness on God's behalf. As a result, they would **die** (Ps 82:7).

83:1-4 Asaph could appeal to God for help because of Israel's covenant relationship to him. Their enemies were his **enemies** (83:2). Therefore, the battle was his.

There are two principles here for believers to remember. First, every battle is spiritual at

a 83:2 Ps 2:1; Is 17:12
b 83:3 Jb 5:12-13; Ps 37:12; 64:2
c 83:4 Ps 41:5; Jr 11:19
d 83:5 Ps 2:2
e 83:6 Gn 25:12-16; Ps 137:7
f 1Ch 5:10; 2Ch 20:10
g 83:7 Jos 13:5; 1Sm 15:2
h 1Sm 4:1; Ezk 27:3
i 83:8 2Kg 15:19
j 83:9 Nm 31:7; Jdg 7:1-24
k Jdg 4:7; 5:21
l 83:10 Jr 9:22; 16:4; 25:33
m 83:11 Jdg 7:25; 8:3
n Jdg 8:5-21
o 83:12 2Ch 20:11
p 83:13 Jb 21:18; Ps 1:4; Is 17:13
q 83:14 Is 9:18; 10:16-19
r 83:15 Jb 9:17; Ps 58:9

s 83:16 Ps 35:26; 109:29; 132:18
t 83:17 Ps 35:4; 70:2
u 83:18 Ps 97:9
v 84:title Pss 8; 81 titles
w 84:1 Ps 43:3; 132:5
x 84:2 Ps 42:1-2; 63:1
y 84:3 Ps 5:2; 43:4
z 84:4 Ps 65:4
aa 84:5 Ps 119:2; 122:1
ab 84:6 Ezk 34:26; Jl 2:23
ac 84:7 Pr 4:18; Is 40:31
ad 84:8 Ps 39:12; 54:2; 86:6

those who hate you
　　have acted arrogantly.[A,a]
3 They devise clever schemes
　　against your people;
　　they conspire against
　　　your treasured ones.[b]
4 They say, "Come, let us
　　wipe them out as a nation
　　so that Israel's name will no longer
　　be remembered."[c]
5 For they have conspired
　　with one mind;
　　they form an alliance[B] against you[d] —
6 the tents of Edom
　　and the Ishmaelites,[e]
　　Moab and the Hagrites,[f]
7 Gebal, Ammon, and Amalek,[g]
　　Philistia with the inhabitants
　　　of Tyre.[h]
8 Even Assyria has joined them;
　　they lend support[c] to the sons
　　　of Lot.[D,i]　　　　Selah

9 Deal with them as you did
　　with Midian,[j]
　　as you did with Sisera
　　and Jabin at the Kishon River.[k]
10 They were destroyed at En-dor;
　　they became manure
　　　for the ground.[l]
11 Make their nobles like Oreb
　　and Zeeb,[m]
　　and all their tribal leaders like Zebah
　　and Zalmunna,[n]
12 who said, "Let us seize
　　God's pastures for ourselves."[o]
13 Make them like tumbleweed,
　　my God,
　　like straw before the wind.[p]
14 As fire burns a forest,
　　as a flame blazes
　　　through mountains,[q]
15 so pursue them with your tempest
　　and terrify them with your storm.[r]

16 Cover their faces with shame
　　so that they will seek
　　　your name, LORD.[s]
17 Let them be put to shame
　　and terrified forever;
　　let them perish in disgrace.[t]
18 May they know that you alone —
　　whose name is the LORD —
　　are the Most High
　　over the whole earth.[u]

LONGING FOR GOD'S HOUSE

84 *For the choir director: on the* Gittith.[v]
A psalm of the sons of Korah.

1 How lovely is your dwelling place,
　LORD of Armies.[w]
2 I long and yearn
　　for the courts of the LORD;
　　my heart and flesh cry out
　　　for[E] the living God.[x]

3 Even a sparrow finds a home,
　and a swallow, a nest for herself
　where she places her young —
　near your altars, LORD of Armies,
　my King and my God.[y]
4 How happy are those who reside
　　in your house,
　　who praise you continually.[z]　　Selah

5 Happy are the people
　　whose strength is in you,
　　whose hearts are set
　　　on pilgrimage.[aa]
6 As they pass through the Valley
　　of Baca,[F]
　　they make it a source
　　　of spring water;
　　even the autumn rain will cover it
　　　with blessings.[G,ab]
7 They go from strength to strength;
　　each appears before God in Zion.[ac]

8 LORD God of Armies, hear my prayer;
　　listen, God of Jacob.[ad]　　Selah

A 83:2 Lit *have lifted their head*　　B 83:5 Lit *they cut a covenant*　　C 83:8 Lit *they are an arm*　　D 83:8 = Moab and Ammon　　E 84:2 Or *flesh shout for joy to*　　F 84:6 Or *Valley of Tears*　　G 84:6 Or *pools*

root—even if there are other physical, emotional, financial, or political components involved. Second, when you're involved in a righteous spiritual battle, you should verbally transfer the fight to the Lord's hands. If you are operating under his covenant and kingdom rule, ask him for help according to his covenantal, faithful love.

83:5-8 Israel's enemies included their own relatives. **Edom** descended from Jacob's brother Esau. **The Ishmaelites** were descended from Abraham. **Moab** and **Ammon** were descendants of Abraham's nephew **Lot**.

83:9-12 Asaph prays earnestly that God would **deal with** Israel's present enemies just as he had dealt with their past enemies. Each of those Asaph names had oppressed Israel during the days of the Judges (see Judg 4:1-24; 6:1–8:21). They sought to subdue God's people and take the land he had given them, saying, **Let us seize God's pastures for ourselves** (Ps 83:12). This, however, was pure foolishness. Though the Lord at times judged Israel by giving its land to others, the land was never *taken* from him. One may as well try to seize a cub from a mother grizzly.

84:1-4 The psalmist expresses his longing to be in **the courts** of the Lord's **dwelling place**, his **house** (84:1-2, 4)—references to the temple. Ultimately, his desire was to be in God's presence, which should be the longing of all those who love God.

84:5-7 The psalmist affirms that blessings come to those who find their **strength** in God alone (84:5). He recharges their spiritual batteries so that **they go from strength to strength** (84:7). Prioritizing God's presence through his Word is a means of finding spiritual refreshment and vigor.

⁹ Consider our shield,^A God;^a
  look on the face
    of your anointed one.^b

¹⁰ Better a day in your courts
  than a thousand anywhere else.
  I would rather stand at the threshold
    of the house of my God
  than live in the tents
    of wicked people.^c
¹¹ For the LORD God is a sun
  and shield.^d
  The LORD grants favor and honor;
  he does not withhold the good
  from those who live with integrity.^e
¹² Happy is the person who trusts
    in you,
  LORD of Armies!^f

RESTORATION OF FAVOR

85 *For the choir director. A psalm of the sons of Korah.*

¹ LORD, you showed favor
    to your land;^g
  you restored the fortunes of Jacob.^{B,h}
² You forgave your people's guilt;
  you covered all their sin.ⁱ   *Selah*
³ You withdrew all your fury;
  you turned from
    your burning anger.^j

⁴ Return to us, God of our salvation,
  and abandon your displeasure
    with us.^k
⁵ Will you be angry with us forever?
  Will you prolong your anger for all
    generations?^l
⁶ Will you not revive us again
  so that your people may rejoice
    in you?^m
⁷ Show us your faithful love, LORD,
  and give us your salvation.ⁿ

⁸ I will listen to what God will say;
  surely the LORD will declare peace
  to his people, his faithful ones,
  and not let them go back
    to foolish ways.^o

⁹ His salvation is very near
    those who fear him,
  so that glory may dwell in our land.^p

¹⁰ Faithful love and truth
    will join together;
  righteousness and peace
    will embrace.^q
¹¹ Truth will spring up from the earth,
  and righteousness will look
    down from heaven.^r
¹² Also, the LORD will provide
    what is good,
  and our land will yield its crops.^s
¹³ Righteousness will go before him
  to prepare the way for his steps.^t

LAMENT AND PETITION

86 *A prayer of David.*

  Listen, LORD, and answer me,
  for I am poor and needy.^u
² Protect my life, for I am faithful.^v
  You are my God; save your servant
    who trusts in you.^w
³ Be gracious to me, Lord,
  for I call to you all day long.^x
⁴ Bring joy to your servant's life,
  because I appeal to you, Lord.^y

⁵ For you, Lord, are kind and ready
    to forgive,^z
  abounding in faithful love to all
    who call on you.^{aa}
⁶ LORD, hear my prayer;
  listen to my plea for mercy.^{ab}
⁷ I call on you in the day of my distress,
  for you will answer me.^{ac}

⁸ Lord, there is no one like you
    among the gods,
  and there are no works like yours.^{ad}
⁹ All the nations you have made
  will come and bow down
    before you, Lord,
  and will honor your name.^{ae}
¹⁰ For you are great
    and perform wonders;
  you alone are God.^{af}

^a84:9 Ps 3:3; 115:9-11
^b1Sm 2:10; 2Ch 6:42; Ps 132:17
^c84:10 Ps 27:4
^d84:11 Ps 3:3; 5:12; 18:2; 28:7; 119:114; Is 60:19-20; Rv 21:23
^ePr 2:7
^f84:12 Ps 40:4
^g85:1 Ps 106:4
^hDt 30:3; Ps 14:7; Jr 29:14
ⁱ85:2 1Kg 8:34; Ps 32:1,5
^j85:3 Ps 78:38; 106:23; Jnh 3:9
^k85:4 Ps 27:9; 79:9; 80:3,7
^l85:5 Ps 74:1; 79:5; 80:4
^m85:6 Ps 71:20; 80:18; 149:2
ⁿ85:7 Ps 69:13; 119:41
^o85:8 Hg 2:9; Zch 9:10

^p85:9 Is 46:13; Zch 2:5; Jn 1:14
^q85:10 Ps 72:3; 89:14
^r85:11 Is 45:8
^s85:12 Ps 65:12-13; 67:6; Ezk 34:27
^t85:13 Ps 89:14; Is 40:3,10; 58:8
^u86:1 Ps 17:6; 31:2; 70:5
^v86:2 1Sm 2:9; Ps 37:28
^wPs 109:26
^x86:3 Ps 25:5; 88:9
^y86:4 Ps 25:1; 43:5
^z86:5 Ps 130:4
^{aa}Ps 103:8; 145:8
^{ab}86:6 Ps 55:1-2
^{ac}86:7 Gn 35:3; Ps 17:6; 20:1
^{ad}86:8 Ex 15:11; Dt 3:24; Ps 89:6
^{ae}86:9 Ps 22:7; Is 66:24; Rv 15:4
^{af}86:10 2Kg 19:15; Ps 72:18; 83:18; Jr 10:6

---

^A84:9 = the king   ^B85:1 Or *restored Jacob from captivity*

84:10 In other words, the psalmist would rather be found serving God than serving self. **84:12** God is the all-powerful One who commands hosts of angelic forces.

85:1-3 The psalmist remembered God's love and **favor** that he had shown to his people by restoring them to their homeland from their Babylonian captivity (85:1). Such a restoration was possible because God **forgave . . . their sin** and removed his **anger** in response to their repentance (85:2-3).

85:6 Our prayers ought to be similarly God-centered, asking for God's intervention so that we might give him public praise. **85:8-13** Deliverance is available to those who take God seriously. Such **faithful ones** (85:8) will experience the fullness of God as he brings **faithful love and truth** together and causes **righteousness and peace** to combine in their lives (85:10). The coupling of these blessings will ultimately be established by the Messiah in his earthly

kingdom rule. **Earth** and **heaven** (85:11) will be united when Jesus Christ comes to reign as King.

86:1-5 David affirms his need for God (**I am poor and needy**), his submission to God (**I am faithful**), and his dependence on God (**your servant . . . trusts in you**). He is confident of God's character and knows the Lord is **kind and ready to forgive** (86:5). Likewise, in your times of need, deal with any known sin in your life and appeal to God's character.

a 86:11 Ps 25:4-5; 26:3
b 86:12 Ps 111:1
c 86:13 Ps 30:3; Ezk 26:20
d 86:14 Ps 54:3
e 86:15 Ex 34:6; Nm 14:18;
Neh 9:17
f 86:16 Ps 25:16; 68:35
g 86:17 Ps 112:10; 132:18
h 87:1 Ps 78:69; Is 28:16
i 87:2 Ps 78:67-68
j 87:3 Ps 48:8
k 87:4 Is 19:23-25; 56:6-7;
Zch 2:10-12

l 87:5 Ps 48:8; Is 2:2
m 87:6 Is 4:3; Ezk 13:9
n 87:7 Ps 46:4; 68:25
o 88:title 1Kg 4:31; 1Ch 2:6
p 88:1 Ps 22:2; 86:3; Lk 18:7
q 88:2 Ps 18:6; 31:2; 86:1
r 88:3 Ps 16:10; 116:3
s 88:4 Ps 28:1; 143:7
t Ps 61:2
u 88:5 Ps 31:12
v Ps 31:22; Is 53:8
w 88:6 Ps 69:15; 86:13;
Ezk 26:20
x 88:7 Ps 32:4; 39:10
y Ps 42:7
z 88:8 Jb 19:13-22; Ps 31:11

11 Teach me your way, LORD,
and I will live by your truth.
Give me an undivided mind to fear
your name.*a*

12 I will praise you with all my heart,
Lord my God,
and will honor
your name forever.*b*

13 For your faithful love
for me is great,
and you rescue my life
from the depths of Sheol.*c*

14 God, arrogant people
have attacked me;
a gang of ruthless men intends
to kill me.
They do not let you guide them.[A]*d*

15 But you, Lord, are a compassionate
and gracious God,
slow to anger and abounding
in faithful love and truth.*e*

16 Turn to me and be gracious to me.
Give your strength
to your servant;
save the son
of your female servant.*f*

17 Show me a sign of your goodness;
my enemies will see and be put
to shame
because you, LORD, have helped
and comforted me.*g*

ZION, THE CITY OF GOD

87 *A psalm of the sons of Korah. A song.*
The city he founded[B] is
on the holy mountains.*h*

2 The LORD loves Zion's city gates
more than all the dwellings
of Jacob.*i*

3 Glorious things are said about you,
city of God.*j*   *Selah*

4 "I will make a record of those
who know me:
Rahab, Babylon, Philistia, Tyre,
and Cush —
each one was born there."*k*

5 And it will be said of Zion,
"This one and that one were born
in her."
The Most High himself
will establish her.*l*

6 When he registers the peoples,
the LORD will record,
"This one was born there."*m*   *Selah*

7 Singers and dancers[C] alike will say,[D]
"My whole source of joy
is[E] in you."*n*

A CRY OF DESPERATION

88 *A song. A psalm of the sons of Korah.*
For the choir director: according to
Mahalath Leannoth. *A Maskil of Heman the*
Ezrahite.[o]

1 LORD, God of my salvation,
I cry out before you day and night.*p*

2 May my prayer reach
your presence;
listen to my cry.*q*

3 For I have had enough troubles,
and my life is near Sheol.*r*

4 I am counted among those
going down to the Pit.*s*
I am like a man
without strength,*t*

5 abandoned[F] among the dead.
I am like the slain lying
in the grave,*u*
whom you no longer remember,
and who are cut off
from your care.[G],*v*

6 You have put me in the lowest part
of the Pit,
in the darkest places,
in the depths.*w*

7 Your wrath weighs heavily on me;*x*
you have overwhelmed me with all
your waves.*y*   *Selah*

8 You have distanced my friends
from me;
you have made me repulsive
to them.*z*
I am shut in and cannot go out.

[A] 86:14 Lit *They do not set you in front of them*   [B] 87:1 Lit *His foundation*   [C] 87:7 Or *musicians*   [D] 87:7 Or *As they dance they will sing*   [E] 87:7 Lit *"All my springs, are*   [F] 88:5 Or *set free*   [G] 88:5 Or *hand*

86:11-13 David asks the Lord to **teach** him so that he could have an **undivided mind** to follow him—rather than trying to pursue two conflicting ways to **live** (86:11). This kind of single-minded devotion to God leads to obedience (**I will live by your truth**) and worship (**I will praise you**).
86:14 The prideful person lives life from his own limited, distorted viewpoint. The hum-

ble person, by contrast, lives life from God's heavenly, righteous viewpoint.
86:15 David appeals to God's righteous character that he revealed to Moses (see Exod 34:6). This God of compassion, grace, faithful love, and truth was available to Moses. He was available to David. And he's available to you.
87:4 When Christ returns to rule on earth from Jerusalem, people from all the nations

will come to worship him—including those who were previously enemies of God and his people: **Rahab** (that is, Egypt), **Babylon, Philistia, Tyre, and Cush**.
87:7 Celebration, typified by **singers and dancers**, will characterize the Messiah's kingdom rule from Jerusalem. The testimony of God's people in that day will be, **My whole source of joy is in you**. Where else could joy be found?

9 My eyes are worn out from crying.[a]
LORD, I cry out to you all day long;[b]
I spread out my hands to you.[c]

10 Do you work wonders for the dead?
Do departed spirits rise up
to praise you?[d] *Selah*

11 Will your faithful love be declared
in the grave,
your faithfulness in Abaddon?[e]

12 Will your wonders be known in
the darkness
or your righteousness in the land
of oblivion?[f]

13 But I call to you for help, LORD;
in the morning my prayer
meets you.[g]

14 LORD, why do you reject me?[h]
Why do you hide your face
from me?[i]

15 From my youth,
I have been suffering and near
death.
I suffer your horrors;
I am desperate.[j]

16 Your wrath sweeps over me;
your terrors destroy me.[k]

17 They surround me like water
all day long;
they close in on me from every side.[l]

18 You have distanced loved one
and neighbor from me;
darkness is my only friend.[A,m]

PERPLEXITY ABOUT GOD'S PROMISES

89 A Maskil *of Ethan the Ezrahite.*[n]

I will sing about the LORD's
faithful love forever;[o]
I will proclaim your faithfulness
to all generations
with my mouth.[p]

2 For I will declare,
"Faithful love is built up forever;
you establish your faithfulness
in the heavens."[q]

3 The LORD said,
"I have made a covenant
with my chosen one;
I have sworn an oath to David
my servant:

4 'I will establish your offspring forever
and build up your throne
for all generations.'"[r] *Selah*

5 LORD, the heavens praise
your wonders[s] —
your faithfulness also —
in the assembly of the holy ones.[t]

6 For who in the skies can compare
with the LORD?
Who among the heavenly beings[B] is
like the LORD?[u]

7 God is greatly feared in the council
of the holy ones,
more awe-inspiring than[c]
all who surround him.[v]

8 LORD God of Armies,
who is strong like you, LORD?[w]
Your faithfulness surrounds you.

9 You rule the raging sea;
when its waves surge,
you still them.[x]

10 You crushed Rahab like one
who is slain;[y]
you scattered your enemies
with your powerful arm.[z]

11 The heavens are yours; the earth
also is yours.
The world and everything in it —
you founded them.[aa]

12 North and south —
you created them.[ab]
Tabor and Hermon shout for joy
at your name.[ac]

13 You have a mighty arm;
your hand is powerful;
your right hand is lifted high.[ad]

14 Righteousness and justice are
the foundation
of your throne;[ae]
faithful love and truth
go before you.[af]

[a] 88:9 Ps 6:7; 31:9
[b] Ps 86:3
[c] Ps 143:6
[d] 88:10 Ps 6:5; 30:9
[e] 88:11 Jb 26:6; Pr 15:11; 27:20
[f] 88:12 Ec 9:5
[g] 88:13 Ps 5:3; 119:147
[h] 88:14 Ps 43:2
[i] Jb 13:24; Ps 10:1; 13:1
[j] 88:15 Jb 31:23
[k] 88:16 Jb 6:4; 9:34
[l] 88:17 Ps 22:12,16; 118:10-12
[m] 88:18 Jb 19:13; Ps 31:11; 38:11
[n] 89:title 1Kg 4:31; 1Ch 2:6
[o] 89:1 Ps 101:1
[p] Ps 92:2; 119:90

[q] 89:2 Ps 36:5
[r] 89:3-4 2Sm 7:8-16; 1Ch 17:7-14; Jr 33:17-21
[s] 89:5 Ps 19:1; 97:6
[t] Ps 149:1
[u] 89:6 Ps 86:8; 113:5
[v] 89:7 Ps 89:5; 96:4
[w] 89:8 Ex 15:11; 2Sm 7:22
[x] 89:9 Jb 38:11; Ps 104:9; Mt 8:23-27
[y] 89:10 Is 30:7; 51:9-10
[z] Ps 68:1; 92:9
[aa] 89:11 1Ch 29:11; Ps 24:1
[ab] 89:12 Jb 26:7
[ac] Ps 133:3; Jr 46:18
[ad] 89:13 Ps 98:1; 118:16
[ae] 89:14 Ps 97:2
[af] Ps 85:13

[A] 88:18 Or *from me, my friends. Oh darkness!* [B] 89:6 Or *the angels,* or *the sons of the mighty* [C] 89:7 Or *ones, revered by*

88:10-12 Heman wants God's deliverance so that he can declare his glory on this side of the grave.
88:13-18 Sometimes we must pray through affliction and uncertainty. When God appears unresponsive and our feelings lead us to despair, our faith in God's character and past actions must push us forward.
89:3-4 This was not fulfilled by an eternal succession of Davidic kings but by one Davidic King who lives forever, the resurrected Lord Jesus Christ (see 2 Sam 7:1-19; Acts 2:29-36). He will reign from David's throne in Jerusalem in his millennial kingdom (see Rev 20:4). Though the sons of David would prove unfaithful in their role as kings, this Son of David will never fail.

[a] 89:15 Ps 98:6
[b] Nm 6:25; Ps 56:13; 1Jn 1:7
[c] 89:16 Ps 20:5; 105:3
[d] 89:17 Ps 28:8
[e] Ps 148:14
[f] 89:18 Ps 84:9
[g] 89:19 2Sm 17:10; 1Kg 11:34; Ps 78:70
[h] 89:20 1Sm 16:13; Ps 47:9; Ac 13:22
[i] 89:21 Ps 18:35; 80:17
[j] 89:22 2Sm 7:10
[k] 89:23 2Sm 7:9; Ps 2:9
[l] 89:24 Ps 21:7; 132:17
[m] 89:25 Ps 72:8
[n] 89:26 2Sm 7:14; 1Ch 22:10
[o] 2Sm 22:47; Ps 18:2
[p] 89:27 Ex 4:22; Jr 31:9; Col 1:15
[q] 89:28 2Ch 13:5; Ps 105:8
[r] 89:29 Is 9:7; Jr 33:17
[s] 89:30 2Sm 7:14; 1Kg 2:4

[t] 89:31 1Sm 12:15
[u] 89:32 Jb 9:34
[v] 89:33 2Sm 7:15
[w] 89:34 Lv 26:44; Jdg 2:1
[x] 89:35 Am 4:2
[y] 89:36 Ps 72:5,17
[z] 89:37 Jb 16:19; Lk 1:33
[aa] 89:38 1Ch 28:9; Ps 44:9
[ab] 89:39 Ps 74:7; Lm 2:7; 5:16
[ac] 89:40 Ps 80:12; Lm 2:2,5
[ad] 89:41 Jr 30:16
[ae] Ps 44:13; 79:4
[af] 89:42 Ps 13:4; 80:6
[ag] 89:43 Ps 44:10
[ah] 89:44 Ezk 28:7
[ai] 89:45 Is 54:4; Ezk 7:18; Ob 10

15 Happy are the people who know
   the joyful shout;[a]
   LORD, they walk in the light
   from your face.[b]
16 They rejoice in your name
   all day long,
   and they are exalted
   by your righteousness.[c]
17 For you are
   their magnificent strength;[d]
   by your favor our horn is exalted.[e]
18 Surely our shield[A]
   belongs to the LORD,
   our king to the Holy One of Israel.[f]

19 You once spoke in a vision
   to your faithful ones
   and said: "I have granted help
   to a warrior;
   I have exalted one chosen[B]
   from the people.[g]
20 I have found David my servant;
   I have anointed him
   with my sacred oil.[h]
21 My hand will always be with him,
   and my arm will strengthen him.[i]
22 The enemy will not oppress[c] him;
   the wicked will not afflict him.[j]
23 I will crush his foes before him
   and strike those who hate him.[k]
24 My faithfulness and love will be
   with him,
   and through my name
   his horn will be exalted.[l]
25 I will extend his power to the sea
   and his right hand to the rivers.[m]
26 He will call to me, 'You are
   my Father,[n]
   my God, the rock of my salvation.'[o]
27 I will also make him my firstborn,
   greatest of the kings of the earth.[p]
28 I will always preserve
   my faithful love for him,
   and my covenant with him
   will endure.[q]
29 I will establish his line forever,
   his throne as long as heaven lasts.[D,r]
30 If his sons abandon my instruction
   and do not live by my ordinances,[s]

31 if they dishonor my statutes
   and do not keep my commands,[t]
32 then I will call their rebellion
   to account with the rod,
   their iniquity with blows.[u]
33 But I will not withdraw
   my faithful love from him
   or betray my faithfulness.[v]
34 I will not violate my covenant
   or change what my lips have said.[w]
35 Once and for all
   I have sworn an oath by my holiness;
   I will not lie to David.[x]
36 His offspring will continue forever,
   his throne like the sun before me,[y]
37 like the moon, established forever,
   a faithful witness in the sky."[z] *Selah*

38 But you have spurned
   and rejected him;
   you have become enraged
   with your anointed.[aa]
39 You have repudiated the covenant
   with your servant;
   you have completely dishonored
   his crown.[E,ab]
40 You have broken down all his walls;
   you have reduced his fortified cities
   to ruins.[ac]
41 All who pass by plunder him;[ad]
   he has become an object of ridicule
   to his neighbors.[ae]
42 You have lifted high the right hand
   of his foes;
   you have made all
   his enemies rejoice.[af]
43 You have also turned back
   his sharp sword
   and have not let him stand
   in battle.[ag]
44 You have made his splendor[F] cease
   and have overturned his throne.[ah]
45 You have shortened the days
   of his youth;
   you have covered him
   with shame.[ai] *Selah*

46 How long, LORD?
   Will you hide forever?

[A] 89:18 = the king   [B] 89:19 Or *exalted a young man*   [C] 89:22 Or *not exact tribute from*   [D] 89:29 Lit *as days of heaven*   [E] 89:39 Lit *have dishonored his crown to the ground*   [F] 89:44 Hb obscure

89:15-16 Those who **walk in the light from [God's] face** live in intimate fellowship with him (89:15). Thus, they **rejoice** in him (89:16). **89:20-29** The **covenant with** David would be kept **forever** through his seed, the Messiah (89:28-29). God will give this King his strength, **faithfulness**, and **power** (89:21, 24-25). The Messiah's kingdom will be universal and unconquerable.

89:30-37 In spite of the failure of the Davidic kings, the Lord assured David that **his offspring [would] continue forever** (89:36). Ultimately, his promises would be kept through Jesus Christ. The sinfulness of humanity can't prevent God from accomplishing his sovereign goals. **89:38-45** The reason the writer is anxious to affirm God's faithfulness to his uncondi-

tional covenant promise in this psalm is that it seemed that God had cast off the Davidic line. One after another of David's sons had been unfaithful—until finally God allowed Jerusalem to be overrun and David's **throne** to be overthrown, too (89:38-40, 44). The sins of the kings and the people had resulted in **shame** (89:45). Had God's judgment trumped his promises?

Will your anger keep burning
    like fire?[a]
47 Remember how short my life is.
Have you created everyone
    for nothing?[b]
48 What courageous person can live
and never see death?
Who can save himself
    from the power of Sheol?[c]   *Selah*
49 Lord, where are the former acts
    of your faithful love
that you swore to David
    in your faithfulness?[d]
50 Remember, Lord, the ridicule
    against your servants —
in my heart I carry abuse from all
    the peoples —
51 how your enemies
    have ridiculed, Lord,
how they have ridiculed every step
    of your anointed.[e]

52 Blessed be the Lord forever.
Amen and amen.[f]

BOOK IV (PSALMS 90–106)

ETERNAL GOD AND MORTAL MAN

90 *A prayer of Moses, the man of God.*
    Lord, you have been our refuge[A]
in every generation.[g]
2 Before the mountains were born,
before you gave birth to the earth
    and the world,
from eternity to eternity,
    you are God.[h]

3 You return mankind to the dust,
saying, "Return,
    descendants of Adam."[i]
4 For in your sight a thousand years
are like yesterday that passes by,
like a few hours of the night.[j]
5 You end their lives;[B] they sleep.[k]
They are like grass that grows
    in the morning —
6 in the morning it sprouts and grows;
by evening it withers and dries up.[l]

7 For we are consumed by your anger;
we are terrified by your wrath.[m]

8 You have set our iniquities
    before you,
our secret sins in the light
    of your presence.[n]
9 For all our days ebb away
under your wrath;
we end our years like a sigh.[o]
10 Our lives last[c] seventy years
or, if we are strong, eighty years.
Even the best of them are[D] struggle
    and sorrow;
indeed, they pass quickly and we
    fly away.[D]
11 Who understands the power
    of your anger?
Your wrath matches the fear that
    is due you.[q]
12 Teach us to number our days carefully
so that we may develop wisdom
    in our hearts.[E,r]

13 Lord — how long?
Turn and have compassion
    on your servants.[s]
14 Satisfy us in the morning
    with your faithful love
so that we may shout with joy
    and be glad all our days.[t]
15 Make us rejoice for as many days
    as you have humbled us,
for as many years as
    we have seen adversity.[u]
16 Let your work be seen
    by your servants,
and your splendor
    by their children.[v]
17 Let the favor of the Lord our God be
    on us;
establish for us the work
    of our hands —
establish the work of our hands![w]

THE PROTECTION OF THE MOST HIGH

91 The one who lives
    under the protection
    of the Most High
dwells in the shadow of the Almighty.[x]

2 I will say[F] concerning the Lord, who
    is my refuge and my fortress,
my God in whom I trust:[y]

---

[a]89:46 Ps 6:3; 13:1; 35:17; 79:5
[b]89:47 Ps 39:6-7; 90:5-6,9-10
[c]89:48 Ps 16:10; 22:29
[d]89:49 2Sm 7:15; Jr 30:9; Ezk 34:23
[e]89:50-51 Ps 69:9; 74:10,18,22
[f]89:52 Ps 41:13; 72:19-20; 106:48
[g]90:1 Ps 71:3
[h]90:2 Jb 36:26; Ps 102:27; Pr 8:25
[i]90:3 Gn 3:19; Ec 12:7
[j]90:4 2Pt 3:8
[k]90:5 Jb 14:12
[l]90:5-6 Jb 14:1-2; Ps 37:2; 103:15-16
[m]90:7 Ps 39:11

[n]90:8 Ps 19:12; Ec 12:14
[o]90:9 Ps 78:33
[p]90:10 Jb 20:8; Ps 78:39
[q]90:11 Ps 76:7
[r]90:12 Dt 32:29; Ps 39:4
[s]90:13 Dt 32:36; Ps 135:14
[t]90:14 Ps 36:8; 65:4; 103:5
[u]90:15 Ps 86:4; 92:4
[v]90:16 Ps 96:6; Is 35:2
[w]90:17 Ps 27:4; Is 26:12
[x]91:1 Ps 27:5; 32:7; 121:5
[y]91:2 Ps 18:2; 61:4; 62:7-8

[A]90:1 Some Hb mss, LXX; other Hb mss read *dwelling place*   [B]90:5 Or *You overwhelm them*; Hb obscure   [C]90:10 Lit *The days of our years in them*   [D]90:10 LXX, Tg, Syr, Vg read *Even their span is*; Hb obscure   [E]90:12 Or *develop a heart of wisdom*   [F]91:1-2 LXX, Syr, Jer read [2]*Almighty, saying,* or [2]*Almighty, he will say*

90:1-2 Since this psalm was authored by **Moses**, it is the oldest of all the psalms.
90:5-9 The transitory nature of humanity's existence is due to sin. Death is God's righteous judgment against man's rebellion (see Gen 3:22-24; Rom 6:23).

90:12 Ask the Lord to make the brevity of life sink in to your soul so that you are convicted to make godly choices during your short stay on earth. Life is like a coin. You can spend it any way you wish, but you can only spend it once.

90:17 A meaningful life in which God **establish[es] the work of our hands** comes through wisdom, and wisdom comes from submitting all we are to God for the brief time he gives us.

a 91:3 Ps 124:7; 141:9;
Ec 9:12
b 91:4 Ps 57:1; 63:7
c Ps 5:12
d 91:5 Ps 58:7; 76:3
e 91:5-6 Jb 5:19-23
f 91:7 2Ch 20:9
g 91:8 Ps 37:34; 58:10
h 91:9 Ps 18:2; 62:7-8
i Ps 121:5
j 91:10 Pr 12:21
k 91:11 Ps 34:7
l 91:11-12 Mt 4:6; Lk
4:10-11
m 91:13 Lk 10:19
n 91:14 Ps 9:10; 37:40;
107:41

o 91:15 2Sm 22:20; Ps
18:19; 50:15
p 91:16 Dt 4:40; Ps 21:4
q Ps 50:23
r 92:1 Ps 135:3; 147:1
s 92:2 Ps 59:16; 89:1; Lm
3:22-23
t 92:3 Ps 33:2
u 92:4 Ps 40:5; 143:5
v 92:5 Ps 139:17; Is 55:8-9
w 92:6 Ps 73:22
x 92:7 Ps 90:5-6
y 92:8 Ps 93:4
z 92:9 Ps 37:20; 68:1
aa 92:10 Ps 89:17,24; 112:9
ab Ps 45:7
ac 92:11 Ps 37:34; 54:7
ad 92:12 Ps 1:3; Is 61:3;
Jr 17:8
ae 92:13 Is 60:21

3 He himself will rescue you
   from the bird trap,*a*
from the destructive plague.
4 He will cover you with his feathers;
   you will take refuge
   under his wings.*b*
His faithfulness will be
   a protective shield.*c*
5 You will not fear the terror
   of the night,
   the arrow that flies by day,*d*
6 the plague that stalks in darkness,
   or the pestilence that ravages
   at noon.*e*
7 Though a thousand fall at your side
   and ten thousand at your right hand,
   the pestilence will not reach you.*f*
8 You will only see it with your eyes
   and witness the punishment
   of the wicked.*g*

9 Because you have made the LORD
   — my refuge,*h*
   the Most High —
   your dwelling place,*i*
10 no harm will come to you;
   no plague will come
   near your tent.*j*
11 For he will give his angels orders
   concerning you,
   to protect you in all your ways.*k*
12 They will support you
   with their hands
   so that you will not strike your foot
   against a stone.*l*
13 You will tread on the lion
   and the cobra;
   you will trample the young lion
   and the serpent.*m*

14 Because he has his heart set on me,
   I will deliver him;
   I will protect him because he knows
   my name.*n*
15 When he calls out to me,
   I will answer him;
   I will be with him in trouble.

I will rescue him
   and give him honor.*o*
16 I will satisfy him with a long life*p*
   and show him my salvation.*q*

GOD'S LOVE AND FAITHFULNESS

92 *A psalm. A song for the Sabbath day.*
   It is good to give thanks
   to the LORD,
   to sing praise to your name,
   Most High,*r*
2 to declare your faithful love
   in the morning
   and your faithfulness at night,*s*
3 with a ten-stringed harp*A*
   and the music of a lyre.*t*

4 For you have made me rejoice, LORD,
   by what you have done;
   I will shout for joy
   because of the works of your hands.*u*
5 How magnificent are
   your works, LORD,
   how profound your thoughts!*v*
6 A stupid person does not know,
   a fool does not understand this:*w*
7 though the wicked sprout like grass
   and all evildoers flourish,
   they will be eternally destroyed.*x*
8 But you, LORD, are exalted forever.*y*
9 For indeed, LORD, your enemies —
   indeed, your enemies will perish;
   all evildoers will be scattered.*z*
10 You have lifted up my horn*aa*
   like that of a wild ox;
   I have been anointed*B* with
   the finest oil.*ab*
11 My eyes look at my enemies;
   when evildoers rise against me,
   my ears hear them.*ac*
12 The righteous thrive like a palm tree
   and grow like a cedar tree
   in Lebanon.*ad*
13 Planted in the house of the LORD,
   they thrive in the courts of
   our God.*ae*

A 92:3 Or *ten-stringed instrument and a harp*   *B* 92:10 Syr reads *you have anointed me*

91:5-8 God covers his own with his faithfulness 24-7, thus providing them with a shield of protection. Knowledge of this should produce confident trust in God. Regardless of the dangers we might face, those who experience the covering that God provides will be cared for. **91:9-13** The one who makes God his or her **refuge** will not experience **harm** because the Lord has commissioned **his angels** to watch over him or her (91:9-11). This tells us that believers have angels divinely assigned to protect and strengthen them from spiritual

dangers—which are depicted here as wild beasts (91:13). Only in eternity will we know how many dangers, toils, and snares angels have protected us from (see Heb 1:14).

When he tempted Jesus in the wilderness, the devil appealed to Psalm 91:11-12, urging Jesus to throw himself from the temple (see Matt 4:5-6) and demonstrating how Scripture can be twisted for selfish purposes. The psalmist wants God's people to understand how he cares for them—not how they can manipulate God to do their bidding.

92:4 One reason there is so little genuine worship among God's people today is that we don't keep track of and call to mind all of God's past deeds.

92:5-15 This psalm gives praise to the eternal perspective of the righteous as opposed to the short-lived perspective of **the wicked** (92:5-9). God causes **the righteous** to **thrive** even in their **old age** (92:12-14). As a result, they **declare** the greatness of God (92:15). Knowing the goodness of God gives rise to the adoration of God.

14 They will still bear fruit in old age,
healthy and green,[a]

15 to declare: "The LORD is just;
he is my rock,
and there is no unrighteousness
in him."[b]

GOD'S ETERNAL REIGN

93

The LORD reigns! He is robed
in majesty;
the LORD is robed,
enveloped in strength.
The world is firmly established;
it cannot be shaken.[c]

2 Your throne has been established
from the beginning;[A]
you are from eternity.[d]

3 The floods have lifted up, LORD,
the floods have lifted up
their voice;
the floods lift up
their pounding waves.[e]

4 Greater than the roar of a
huge torrent —
the mighty breakers of the sea —
the LORD on high is majestic.[f]

5 LORD, your testimonies
are completely reliable;[g]
holiness adorns your house
for all the days to come.[h]

THE JUST JUDGE

94

LORD, God of vengeance —
God of vengeance, shine![i]

2 Rise up, Judge of the earth;
repay the proud what they deserve.[j]

3 LORD, how long will the wicked —
how long will
the wicked celebrate?[k]

4 They pour out arrogant words;
all the evildoers boast.[l]

5 LORD, they crush your people;
they oppress your heritage.[m]

6 They kill the widow and
the resident alien
and murder the fatherless.[n]

7 They say, "The LORD doesn't see it.
The God of Jacob
doesn't pay attention."[o]

8 Pay attention, you stupid people!
Fools, when will you be wise?[p]

9 Can the one who shaped the ear
not hear,
the one who formed the eye
not see?[q]

10 The one who instructs nations,
the one who teaches
mankind knowledge —
does he not discipline?[r]

11 The LORD knows the thoughts
of mankind;
they are futile.[s]

12 LORD, how happy is anyone
you discipline
and teach from your law[t]

13 to give him relief
from troubled times
until a pit is dug for the wicked.[u]

14 The LORD will not leave his people
or abandon his heritage,[v]

15 for the administration of justice will
again be righteous,
and all the upright in heart
will follow[B] it.[w]

16 Who stands up for me
against the wicked?
Who takes a stand for me
against evildoers?[x]

17 If the LORD had not been my helper,
I would soon rest in the silence
of death.[y]

18 If I say, "My foot is slipping,"
your faithful love
will support me, LORD.[z]

19 When I am filled with cares,
your comfort brings me joy.[aa]

20 Can a corrupt throne be your ally,
a throne that makes evil laws?[ab]

21 They band together against the life
of the righteous

[a] 92:14 Is 37:31; 46:4
[b] 92:15 Dt 32:4; Ps 18:2; 94:22
[c] 93:1 1Ch 16:30-31; Ps 96:10; 97:1
[d] 93:2 Ps 9:7; 90:2; 103:19
[e] 93:3 Ps 96:11; 98:7-8
[f] 93:4 Ps 65:7; 89:9; Ezk 43:2
[g] 93:5 Ps 19:7
[h] Ps 29:2; 96:9
[i] 94:1 2Sm 22:48; Ps 18:47-48; Jr 46:10
[j] 94:2 Ps 7:6; 28:4; 98:9
[k] 94:3 Ps 74:10; Rv 6:10
[l] 94:4 1Sm 2:3; Ps 31:18
[m] 94:5 Is 3:15
[n] 94:6 Dt 27:19; Is 10:2

[o] 94:7 Jb 22:13; Ps 10:11
[p] 94:8 Ps 92:6
[q] 94:9 Ex 4:11; Pr 20:12
[r] 94:10 Jb 35:11; Is 28:26
[s] 94:11 Ps 139:2; Is 66:18; 1Co 3:20
[t] 94:12 Ps 25:5,9; 71:17; Is 48:17
[u] 94:13 Ps 7:15; 9:15; Pr 26:27
[v] 94:14 1Sm 12:22; Rm 11:2
[w] 94:15 Ps 36:10; 64:10; 97:11
[x] 94:16 Ps 59:2
[y] 94:17 Ps 124:1-2
[z] 94:18 Ps 18:35; 66:9; 121:3
[aa] 94:19 Is 57:18; 66:13
[ab] 94:20 Ps 50:16; 58:2

[A] 93:2 Lit *from then*   [B] 94:15 Or *heart will support* ; lit *heart after*

93:2 Unlike his creation, which had a start date, God himself is **from eternity**.
93:5 God's Word is without fault and cannot fail. His authoritative written truth reflects his authoritative rule. Since God is sovereign and in a class by himself, whatever he says should be received with delight and obeyed without delay.
94:2-3 Observe that the concerns of God's people today are the same as the concerns of God's people in the past.

94:12-15 The writer finds consolation in reminding himself that the Lord uses **the wicked** as a chastening rod. In other words, evildoers do not have free reign, but God puts them to work to **discipline** his own and accomplish his purposes for them (94:12-13). He will not allow the wicked to escape **justice** (94:13-15).
Believers today can also find comfort in knowing that our God uses the wicked to fulfill his plans. If we receive his discipline,

we will grow spiritually and become more faithful followers of the living God.
94:19 When you are dominated by worry, amp up your confidence in God so that he can relieve the pressure and anxiety you're experiencing.
94:21-23 Rather than growing frustrated by what you see in the headlines, maintain a divine perspective on life. Take the long view of things. The judgment of God will come in time.

a 94:21 2Kg 21:16; Ps 106:38; Jr 26:15
b 94:22 2Sm 22:3; Ps 46:1,7; 62:2,6
c 94:23 Ps 73:27; 94:23; 101:5,8
d 95:1 Jb 38:7; Ps 81:1; 98:4,6
e 95:2 Ps 100:4; Jnh 2:9
f 95:3 Dt 10:17; Ps 47:2; 96:4
g 95:4 Ps 135:6
h 95:5 Gn 1:9-10; Ps 146:6; Jnh 1:9
i 95:6 Ps 96:9; 100:3; Is 17:7
j 95:7 Ps 79:13
k Heb 3:7-11,15; 4:7
l 95:8 Ex 17:7; Dt 6:16
m 95:9 Nm 14:22; Ps 78:18

n 95:10 Dt 9:7; Ac 13:18; Heb 3:10,17
o 95:11 Nm 14:23,28-30; Dt 12:9
p 96:1 1Ch 16:23; Ps 98:1; Is 42:10
q 96:2 Is 25:9; 52:7
r 96:3 1Ch 16:9,24; Ps 145:12
s 96:4 1Ch 16:25; Ps 47:2; 95:3
t 96:5 1Ch 16:27; Jr 10:11
u 96:6 Ps 104:1
v 96:7 1Ch 16:28-29; Ps 29:1
w 96:8 Ps 79:9
x Ps 100:4
y 96:8-9 Ps 29:2
z 96:9 Ps 33:8; 114:7
aa 96:10 Ps 93:1; 97:1
ab 1Ch 16:30
ac Ps 9:8; 67:4; 98:9

and condemn the innocent
to death.[a]

22 But the LORD is my refuge;
my God is the rock
of my protection.[b]

23 He will pay them back for their sins
and destroy them for their evil.
The LORD our God
will destroy them.[c]

WORSHIP AND WARNING

95 Come, let us shout joyfully
to the LORD,
shout triumphantly to the rock
of our salvation![d]

2 Let us enter his presence
with thanksgiving;
let us shout triumphantly to him
in song.[e]

3 For the LORD is a great God,
a great King above all gods.[f]

4 The depths of the earth are
in his hand,
and the mountain peaks are his.[g]

5 The sea is his; he made it.
His hands formed the dry land.[h]

6 Come, let us worship and bow down;
let us kneel before the LORD
our Maker.[i]

7 For he is our God,
and we are the people of his pasture,
the sheep under his care.[A,j]

Today, if you hear his voice:[k]

8 Do not harden your hearts
as at Meribah,
as on that day at Massah
in the wilderness[l]

9 where your fathers tested me;
they tried me, though they had seen
what I did.[m]

10 For forty years I was disgusted
with that generation;

I said, "They are a people
whose hearts go astray;
they do not know my ways."[n]

11 So I swore in my anger,
"They will not enter my rest."[o]

KING OF THE EARTH

96 Sing a new song to the LORD;
let the whole earth sing
to the LORD.[p]

2 Sing to the LORD, bless his name;
proclaim his salvation from day
to day.[q]

3 Declare his glory among the nations,
his wondrous works
among all peoples.[r]

4 For the LORD is great and is
highly praised;
he is feared above all gods.[s]

5 For all the gods of the peoples
are idols,
but the LORD made the heavens.[t]

6 Splendor and majesty are before him;
strength and beauty are
in his sanctuary.[u]

7 Ascribe to the LORD, you families
of the peoples,
ascribe to the LORD glory
and strength.[v]

8 Ascribe to the LORD the glory
of his name;[w]
bring an offering and enter
his courts.[x]

9 Worship the LORD in the splendor
of his holiness;[y]
let the whole earth tremble
before him.[z]

10 Say among the nations:
"The LORD reigns.[aa]
The world is firmly established;
it cannot be shaken.[ab]
He judges the peoples fairly."[ac]

A 95:7 Lit *sheep of his hand*

95:2 When peoples in the ancient world came into the presence of kings to whom they were subjected, they would bring gifts. When we **enter** our King's **presence**, the gift we bring is **thanksgiving** (95:2) for who he is, what he has done, and what we are trusting him to do.
95:8-11 At **Meribah** ("Quarreling") and **Massah** ("Testing") after the exodus, Israel complained to God, demanding water (95:8; see Exod 17:1-7). Then they continued to test God and eventually refused to enter the promised land (Ps 95:9). Therefore, God gave them their wish, swearing, **They will not enter my rest**

(95:11)—that is, they would not experience the blessings that come through a right relationship with him. As a result, **that generation** would spend **forty years** in the wilderness and die there (95:10), and their children would enter the land instead (see Num 14:11-38).
  The author of Hebrews quotes Psalm 95 to warn believers not to miss out on God's "rest"—his blessings and favor—by following a path of unbelief and disobedience (see Heb 4:7-13).
96:4-6 Since only **the LORD** is God, only he should be **praised** and **feared** (96:4). So-called **gods** are mere **idols** conjured up by human

imagination (96:5). While God revealed his **splendor and majesty . . . strength and beauty** in his temple in Jerusalem (96:6), false gods reveal nothing but their inadequacy.
96:7 This is a reminder that God is not the God of Israel only but also the God of the Gentiles. One day every person will bow to Jesus Christ and confess that he is Lord to the glory of God (see Phil 2:10-11).
96:10-13 Just as the psalmist lived in expectation of the coming of the King, so believers today should do the same. May his return motivate our conduct, and may we live in expectation of his intervention in our lives.

11 Let the heavens be glad
and the earth rejoice;
let the sea and all
that fills it resound.[a]

12 Let the fields and everything
in them celebrate.
Then all the trees of the forest
will shout for joy[b]

13 before the LORD, for he is coming —
for he is coming to judge the earth.
He will judge the world
with righteousness
and the peoples
with his faithfulness.[c]

THE MAJESTIC KING

97 The LORD reigns! Let the earth rejoice;
let the many coasts and islands
be glad.[d]

2 Clouds and total darkness
surround him;
righteousness and justice are
the foundation of his throne.[e]

3 Fire goes before him
and burns up his foes on every side.[f]

4 His lightning lights up the world;
the earth sees and trembles.[g]

5 The mountains melt like wax
at the presence of the LORD —
at the presence of the Lord
of the whole earth.[h]

∽ HOPE WORDS ∽
*Let God rule your world if you
want him to rock your world.*

---

6 The heavens proclaim
his righteousness;[i]
all the peoples see his glory.[j]

7 All who serve carved images,
those who boast in idols, will be
put to shame.[k]
All the gods[A] must worship him.[l]

8 Zion hears and is glad,
Judah's villages[B] rejoice
because of your judgments, LORD.[m]

9 For you, LORD,
are the Most High over
the whole earth;
you are exalted above all the gods.[n]

10 You who love the LORD, hate evil![o]
He protects the lives
of his faithful ones;[p]
he rescues them from the power of
the wicked.[q]

11 Light dawns[C,D] for the righteous,
gladness for the upright in heart.[r]

12 Be glad in the LORD,
you righteous ones,
and give thanks to his holy name.[E,S]

PRAISE THE KING

98 *A psalm.*
Sing a new song to the LORD,[t]
for he has performed wonders;
his right hand and holy arm
have won him victory.[u]

2 The LORD has made his victory
known;
he has revealed his righteousness
in the sight of the nations.[v]

3 He has remembered his love
and faithfulness to the house
of Israel;
all the ends of the earth
have seen our God's victory.[w]

4 Let the whole earth shout
to the LORD;
be jubilant, shout for joy, and sing.[x]

5 Sing to the LORD with the lyre,
with the lyre and melodious song.[y]

6 With trumpets and the blast
of the ram's horn
shout triumphantly
in the presence of the LORD, our King.[z]

7 Let the sea and all that fills it,
the world and those who live in it,
resound.[aa]

[a] 96:11 1Ch 16:31-32; Ps 69:34; 98:7
[b] 96:12 Is 35:1; 55:12-13
[c] 96:13 Ps 98:9; Rv 19:11
[d] 97:1 Ps 93:1; 96:10
[e] 97:2 Dt 4:11; 5:20; Ps 18:11
[f] 97:3 Ps 18:8; 50:3
[g] 97:4 Ex 19:16; Ps 77:18
[h] 97:5 Neh 1:5; Mc 1:4
[i] 97:6 Ps 50:6
[j] Is 40:5; 66:18
[k] 97:7 Is 44:9,11; Jr 10:14; 50:2
[l] Heb 1:6
[m] 97:8 Ps 48:11; Zph 3:14
[n] 97:9 1Ch 16:25; Ps 95:3; 96:4
[o] 97:10 Am 5:15
[p] Ps 145:20
[q] Ps 37:40
[r] 97:11 Ps 112:4; Pr 4:18
[s] 97:12 Ps 30:4; 32:11
[t] 98:1 Ps 33:3
[u] Ex 15:6; Is 52:10
[v] 98:2 Is 56:1; 62:2
[w] 98:3 Ps 22:27; Is 52:10
[x] 98:4 Ps 66:1; 100:1; Is 44:23
[y] 98:5 Ps 51:3; Is 51:3
[z] 98:6 Nm 10:10; 2Ch 15:14
[aa] 98:7 1Ch 16:31-32; Ps 93:1; 97:1

[A] 97:7 LXX, Syr read *All his angels*; Heb 1:6   [B] 97:8 Lit *daughters*   [C] 97:11 One Hb ms, LXX, some ancient versions read *rises to shine*; Ps 112:4
[D] 97:11 Lit *Light is sown*   [E] 97:12 Lit *to the memory of his holiness*

97:1 All people (not merely Israel) should rejoice over the reality of God's kingdom rule.
97:4-5 Since creation itself reacts so violently to **the presence of the LORD** (97:5), people should consider what destruction awaits those who oppose him.
97:6 When the Lord returns to rule the earth, **the heavens** will **proclaim his righteousness**

and **all the peoples** will **see his glory**. There will be no hiding it, nor will there be any hiding from it.
97:7 Idolaters **will be put to shame** as they are confronted with the reality that the images in which they placed their trust are worthless.
97:10 In light of God's sovereign rule and judgment of the wicked, those **who love** him

must **hate evil** and obey him. They must learn to see things from God's perspective.
98:1 The phrase **sing a new song** is a reminder that there are always fresh reasons to worship God.
98:7-8 Creation itself is invited to **shout . . . for joy** over the glory of its Creator. How much more should we give him praise?

[a] 98:8 Ps 89:12; Is 55:12
[b] 98:9 Ps 9:8; 67:4; 96:13
[c] 99:1 Ex 25:22; 1Sm 4:4; Ezk 11:22
[d] Ps 33:8
[e] 99:2 Ps 48:1; 113:4

[f] 99:3 Ps 111:9
[g] Is 6:3
[h] 99:4 Ps 33:5; 103:6; Jr 23:5
[i] 99:5 Ps 132:7
[j] Is 6:3
[k] 99:6 Ex 24:6-8; Lv 8:1-30; 1Sm 12:18
[m] 99:7 Nm 12:5; 14:14; Dt 31:15-18
[n] 99:8 Ps 78:38
[o] Jr 46:28
[p] 99:9 Ps 2:6; 48:1; Ezk 20:40
[q] 100:1 Ps 66:1; 98:4
[r] 100:1-2 Ps 95:1-2; 98:4-6
[s] 100:3 Dt 32:6; Ps 95:6
[t] Ps 79:13; 95:7
[u] 100:4-5 Ps 119:90; 136:1; Lm 3:22-23
[v] 100:4 Ps 75:1; 116:17

❧ Questions & Answers ❧

Q How can the Psalms teach us to pray and praise better?

A The Psalms are like a school of prayer. The beautiful thing about them is that they give the panoramic view of prayer and praise. They cover everything: when nothing is wrong, and when everything is wrong. The Psalms provide abundant examples of people struggling with how to pray and praise in their circumstances. They're broad in subject matter, covering virtually any situation that you could face. So work your way through the Psalms. You can do this progressively, from beginning to end. Or you can read them based on specific subject matter, finding psalms that match your circumstances. If you are losing hope right now, read Psalm 42. If you need to praise God, read Psalm 100. If you need to be reminded that God can meet your needs, read Psalm 23. There is a psalm for every circumstance.

FOR THE NEXT Q&A, SEE PAGE 692.

8 Let the rivers clap their hands;
  let the mountains shout together
      for joy[a]
9 before the Lord,
  for he is coming to judge
      the earth.
  He will judge the world righteously
      and the peoples fairly.[b]

THE KING IS HOLY

99 The Lord reigns! Let
      the peoples tremble.
  He is enthroned
      between the cherubim.[c]
  Let the earth quake.[d]
2 The Lord is great in Zion;
  he is exalted above all the peoples.[e]

3 Let them praise your great
  and awe-inspiring name.[f]
  He is holy.[g]

4 The mighty King loves justice.
  You have established fairness;
  you have administered justice
  and righteousness in Jacob.[h]
5 Exalt the Lord our God;
  bow in worship at his footstool.[i]
  He is holy.[j]

6 Moses and Aaron were
      among his priests;[k]
  Samuel also was among
      those calling on his name.
  They called to the Lord
      and he answered them.[l]
7 He spoke to them in a pillar of cloud;[m]
  they kept his decrees
      and the statutes he gave them.
8 Lord our God, you answered them.
  You were a forgiving God to them,[n]
  but an avenger of their sinful actions.[o]

9 Exalt the Lord our God;
  bow in worship at his holy mountain,
  for the Lord our God is holy.[p]

BE THANKFUL

100 *A psalm of thanksgiving.*
      Let the whole earth shout
      triumphantly to the Lord![q]
2 Serve the Lord with gladness;
  come before him with joyful songs.[r]
3 Acknowledge that the Lord is God.
  He made us, and we are his[A,s]—
  his people, the sheep of his pasture.[t]
4 Enter his gates with thanksgiving[u]
  and his courts with praise.
  Give thanks to him and bless
      his name.[v]
5 For the Lord is good, and his
      faithful love endures forever;
  his faithfulness,
      through all generations.

[A] 100:3 Alt Hb tradition, some Hb mss, LXX, Syr, Vg read *and not we ourselves*

98:9 Now is the time to receive the Lord as King. For when he comes, he will **judge the earth**. Therefore, all peoples are encouraged not to delay. When the Messiah comes to rule on earth with his rod of iron in his kingdom, *it will be too late to join him.* "Now is the acceptable time; now is the day of salvation!" (2 Cor 6:2).
99:5 This posture of humility and acknowledgement of his regal authority should be matched by an inward bowing of the heart.
99:6-8 The psalmist recalls God's deeds among Israel's forefathers: **Moses, Aaron,** and **Samuel,** ordinary men with an extraordinary God (99:6). God's people sinned, these men prayed, and God forgave them (99:8). Thus, God is to be praised for raising up these men to mediate for his people. And he is to be praised for not giving his people what their sins deserved. Though he **is holy** and is **an avenger** of sin (98:8-9), he shows mercy.
  For believers today, God has provided the perfect "mediator" (see 1 Tim 2:5) and the ultimate means to forgive sins. Through Jesus Christ and his atoning death on the cross, God exalts both his holiness and his mercy.

100:1 In the Bible, people are to engage in worship with a sense of excitement. You can't worship the Lord without your emotions. It is no mere intellectual exercise. Worship is *all that we are* responding to *all that he is.*
100:3 The Lord is God is a translation of the Hebrew phrase, "Yahweh is Elohim." *Yahweh* is the name of God revealed in his covenant relationship with his people. *Elohim* speaks of power; he is the One who created the heavens and the earth. Thus, the powerful God wants a relationship with you and should be given recognition.

A VOW OF INTEGRITY

101 *A psalm of David.*

I will sing of faithful love
   and justice;
I will sing praise to you, LORD.[a]

2 I will pay attention to the way
   of integrity.
When will you come to me?
I will live with a heart of integrity
   in my house.[b]

3 I will not let anything worthless
   guide me.[A]
I hate the practice of transgression;
it will not cling to me.[c]

4 A devious heart will be far from me;
I will not be involved with[B] evil.[d]

5 I will destroy anyone
who secretly slanders his neighbor;[e]
I cannot tolerate anyone
with haughty eyes
   or an arrogant heart.[f]

6 My eyes favor the faithful
   of the land
so that they may sit down with me.
The one who follows the way
   of integrity
may serve me.[g]

7 No one who acts deceitfully
will live in my palace;
the one who tells lies
will not be retained here
   to guide me.[C,h]

8 Every morning I will destroy
all the wicked of the land,
wiping out all evildoers
   from the LORD's city.[i]

AFFLICTION IN LIGHT OF ETERNITY

102 *A prayer of a suffering person who
is weak and pours out his lament
before the LORD.[j]*

1 LORD, hear my prayer;
let my cry for help come
   before you.[k]

2 Do not hide your face from me
   in my day of trouble.
Listen closely to me;
answer me quickly when I call.[l]

3 For my days vanish like smoke,
and my bones burn like a furnace.[m]

4 My heart is suffering,
   withered like grass;[n]
I even forget to eat my food.[o]

5 Because of the sound
   of my groaning,
my flesh sticks to my bones.[p]

6 I am like an eagle owl,
like a little owl among the ruins.[q]

7 I stay awake;[r]
I am like a solitary bird on a roof.

8 My enemies taunt me
   all day long;
they ridicule and use my name
   as a curse.[s]

9 I eat ashes like bread
and mingle my drinks
   with tears[t]

10 because of your indignation
   and wrath;
for you have picked me up
   and thrown me aside.[u]

11 My days are like
   a lengthening shadow,
and I wither away like grass.[v]

12 But you, LORD,
   are enthroned forever;[w]
your fame endures
   to all generations.[x]

13 You will rise up
   and have compassion on Zion,
for it is time to show favor
   to her —
the appointed time has come.[y]

14 For your servants take delight
   in its stones
and favor its dust.[z]

15 Then the nations will fear the name
   of the LORD,
and all the kings of the earth
   your glory,[aa]

16 for the LORD will rebuild Zion;
he will appear in his glory.[ab]

17 He will pay attention to the prayer
   of the destitute
and will not despise their prayer.[ac]

[a] 101:1 Ps 89:1; 145:7
[b] 101:2 1Kg 9:4; Ps 119:1
[c] 101:3 Dt 15:9; Ps 40:4
[d] 101:4 Pr 3:32; 14:2
[e] 101:5 Ps 50:20
[f] Ps 18:27; Is 5:15
[g] 101:6 Ps 119:1; Pr 11:20
[h] 101:7 Ps 31:18; 52:3; 63:11
[i] 101:8 Ps 119:119; Jr 21:12
[j] 102:title Ps 142:2
[k] 102:1 Ps 18:6; 39:12; 61:1
[l] 102:2 Ps 27:9; 31:2; 69:17

[m] 102:3 Jb 30:30; Ps 31:10; Lm 1:13
[n] 102:4 Ps 37:2
[o] Ezr 10:6; Jb 33:20
[p] 102:5 Jb 19:20; Lm 4:8
[q] 102:6 Is 34:11; Zph 2:14
[r] 102:7 Ps 77:4
[s] 102:8 Ps 31:11; 69:19
[t] 102:9 Ps 42:3; 80:5
[u] 102:10 Jb 30:22
[v] 102:11 Jb 8:9; Ps 109:23
[w] 102:12 Ps 9:7; Lm 5:19
[x] Ps 135:13
[y] 102:13 Is 60:10; Zch 1:12
[z] 102:14 Neh 4:2; Lm 4:1
[aa] 102:15 Ps 138:4; Is 60:3
[ab] 102:16 Ps 147:2; Is 60:1-2
[ac] 102:17 Ps 22:24w

[A] 101:3 Lit *I will not put a worthless thing in front of my eyes*   [B] 101:4 Lit *not know*   [C] 101:7 Lit *be established in front of my eyes*

101:1-5 King David devotes himself to the Lord through the use of his repeated vow **I will.**

He understood that the quality of his character and leadership had a direct influence on the nation. Whether in the church or in society, leadership based on justice and righteousness is a crucial factor in the well-being of those being governed and led.
101:6-7 King David would only have people serving in his administration who displayed **faithful** character and a commitment to God (101:6). Those known for deceit and **lies** would be shown the door (101:7).
102:1-7 When you are suffering and desperate for God's intervention, let these biblical laments guide you in your prayers. When you don't know what to say, use the inspired words of this psalm.
102:8-11 Jerusalem had fallen to the Babylonians and lay in ruins. The psalmist and all of God's people were dealing with the consequences of idolatry.
102:12-17 In the midst of his despair, this man expresses his confidence in the reign of God (**you . . . are enthroned forever**), hope in the covenant faithfulness of God (**you will . . . have compassion on Zion**), and trust in the future victory of God (**the nations will fear the name**) (102:12-13, 15). Therefore, the psalmist continues to pray.

a 102:18 Dt 31:19; Ps 22:30-31; 78:6
b 102:19 Ps 14:2; 33:13; 53:2
c 102:20 Ps 79:11
d 102:21 Ps 22:22
e 102:22 Ps 22:27; 86:9; Zch 8:20-23
f 102:23 Ps 39:5; 89:45
g 102:24 Jb 36:26; Ps 90:2
h 102:25 Neh 9:6; Ps 96:5; Heb 1:10-12
i 102:26 Is 34:4; 51:6; Mt 24:35
j 102:27 Mal 3:6; Jms 1:17
k 102:28 Ps 69:36; 89:4; 112:2
l 103:1 Ps 30:4; 97:12; 104:1
m 103:2 Dt 6:12; 8:11

n 103:3 Is 43:25
o Jr 30:17
p 103:4 Ps 49:15
q Ps 5:12
r 103:5 Ps 107:9
s Is 40:31
t 103:6 Ps 147:7
u 103:7 Ex 33:13
v Ps 78:11; 99:7
w 103:8 Ex 34:6; Nm 14:18; Neh 9:17
x 103:9 Is 57:16; Jr 3:12; Mc 7:19
y 103:10 Ezr 9:13; Lm 3:22
z 103:11 Ps 36:5; 57:10
aa 103:12 Is 43:25; Mc 7:19
ab 103:13 Mal 3:17
ac 103:14 Gn 3:19; Ps 78:39
ad 103:15 Jb 14:2; 1Pt 1:24
ae 103:15-16 Is 40:6-7

18 This will be written
  for a later generation,
and a people who have not yet
  been created will praise the LORD:[a]
19 He looked down from
  his holy heights —
the LORD gazed out from heaven
  to earth[b] —
20 to hear a prisoner's groaning,
to set free those condemned to die,[A,c]
21 so that they might declare
the name of the LORD in Zion
and his praise in Jerusalem,[d]
22 when peoples and kingdoms
  are assembled
to serve the LORD.[e]

23 He has broken my[B] strength
  in midcourse;
he has shortened my days.[f]
24 I say: "My God, do not take me
in the middle of my life![c]
Your years continue
  through all generations.[g]
25 Long ago you established the earth,
and the heavens are the work
  of your hands.[h]
26 They will perish, but you will endure;
all of them will wear out like clothing.
You will change them like a garment,
and they will pass away.[i]
27 But you are the same,
and your years will never end.[j]
28 Your servants' children
  will dwell securely,
and their offspring will be
  established before you."[k]

THE FORGIVING GOD

103 *Of David.*

My soul, bless the LORD,
and all that is within me, bless
  his holy name.[l]
2 My soul, bless the LORD,
and do not forget all his benefits.[m]

3 He forgives all your iniquity;[n]
he heals all your diseases.[o]
4 He redeems your life from the Pit;[p]
he crowns you with faithful love
  and compassion.[q]
5 He satisfies you[D] with good things;[r]
your youth is renewed
  like the eagle.[s]

6 The LORD executes acts
  of righteousness
and justice for all the oppressed.[t]
7 He revealed his ways to Moses,[u]
his deeds to the people of Israel.[v]
8 The LORD is compassionate
  and gracious,
slow to anger and abounding
  in faithful love.[w]
9 He will not always accuse us
or be angry forever.[x]
10 He has not dealt with us as
  our sins deserve
or repaid us according to
  our iniquities.[y]

11 For as high as the heavens are above
  the earth,
so great is his faithful love
toward those who fear him.[z]
12 As far as the east is from the west,
so far has he removed
our transgressions from us.[aa]
13 As a father has compassion
  on his children,
so the LORD has compassion
  on those who fear him.[ab]
14 For he knows what we are made of,
remembering that we are dust.[ac]

15 As for man, his days are
  like grass —
he blooms like a flower of the field;[ad]
16 when the wind passes over it,
  it vanishes,
and its place is no longer known.[E,ae]

A 102:20 Lit *free sons of death*   B 102:23 Some Hb mss, LXX read *his*   C 102:24 Lit *my days*   D 103:5 Lit *satisfies your ornament*; Hb obscure   E 103:16 Lit *place no longer knows it*

102:25-27 The author of Hebrews quotes and applies these verses to Jesus Christ (see Heb 1:10-12). Sharing in the divine nature of God the Father, God the Son is likewise everlasting: "Jesus Christ is the same yesterday, today, and forever" (Heb 13:8).
103:3-5 The benefits God provides that David highlights include spiritual and physical blessings. There are countless reasons to praise God and express our gratitude to him. But since sinful humans are prone to forget to do so, we must bring the benefits of God continually to our minds.

103:8 David describes God's character just as God himself had revealed it to Moses (see Exod 34:6).
103:11-13 How **great is [God's] faithful love** toward those who take him seriously? It's **as high as the heavens are above the earth** (103:11)—that is, beyond our comprehension. How far does he remove his people's **transgressions** from them? **As far as the east is from the west** (103:12)—that is, forgiven sins are never to be seen again. If this was true when Israel offered God-ordained animal sacrifices that could not, in an ultimate sense,

take away sin (see Heb 10:4, 11), how much more is it true of the once-for-all atoning sacrifice of Jesus Christ (see Heb 10:14-18)? David illustrates God's kindness toward those who fear him by picturing **a father** having **compassion on his children** (Ps 103:13).
103:14-18 David underscores the ongoing benefits of God's loyal love for his people by highlighting the weak and temporary nature of man's life. As children of Adam, we are **made of . . . dust** (103:14; see Gen 2:7). The **days** of our lives are like those of **a flower** that blooms for a moment and then **vanishes** (Ps 103:15-16).

17 But from eternity to eternity
the LORD's faithful love is toward
  those who fear him,
and his righteousness
  toward the grandchildren[a]
18 of those who keep his covenant,
who remember to observe
  his precepts.[b]
19 The LORD has established his throne
  in heaven,
and his kingdom rules over all.[c]

20 Bless the LORD,
all his angels of great strength,
who do his word,
obedient to his command.[d]
21 Bless the LORD, all his armies,
his servants who do his will.[e]
22 Bless the LORD, all his works
in all the places where he rules.[f]
My soul, bless the LORD!

GOD THE CREATOR

104
My soul, bless the LORD!
LORD my God, you are
  very great;
you are clothed with majesty
  and splendor.[g]
2 He wraps himself in light as if
  it were a robe,
spreading out the sky like a canopy,[h]
3 laying the beams of his palace
on the waters above,[i]
making the clouds his chariot,[j]
walking on the wings of the wind,[k]
4 and making the winds
  his messengers,[A]
flames of fire his servants.[l]

5 He established the earth
  on its foundations;
it will never be shaken.[m]
6 You covered it with the deep
as if it were a garment;
the water stood
  above the mountains.[n]
7 At your rebuke the water fled;
at the sound of your thunder
  they hurried away[o] —
8 mountains rose and valleys sank[B] —
to the place you established
  for them.[p]

9 You set a boundary
  they cannot cross;
they will never cover
  the earth again.[q]

10 He causes the springs to gush
  into the valleys;
they flow between the mountains.[r]
11 They supply water
  for every wild beast;
the wild donkeys quench
  their thirst.[s]
12 The birds of the sky live
  beside the springs;
they make their voices heard
  among the foliage.[t]
13 He waters the mountains
  from his palace;
the earth is satisfied by the fruit
  of your labor.[u]

14 He causes grass to grow
  for the livestock
and provides crops for man
  to cultivate,
producing food from the earth,[v]
15 wine that makes
  human hearts glad —
making his face shine with oil —
and bread that sustains
  human hearts.[w]

16 The trees of the LORD flourish,[c]
the cedars of Lebanon
  that he planted.[x]
17 There the birds make their nests;
storks make their homes
  in the pine trees.[y]
18 The high mountains are
  for the wild goats;
the cliffs are a refuge for hyraxes.[z]
19 He made the moon to mark
  the[D] festivals;[E]
the sun knows when to set.[aa]
20 You bring darkness,
  and it becomes night,
when all the forest animals stir.[ab]
21 The young lions roar for their prey
and seek their food from God.[ac]
22 The sun rises; they go back
and lie down in their dens.[ad]

[a] 103:17 Ex 20:6; Dt 5:10; Ps 25:6
[b] 103:18 Dt 7:9; Ps 25:10
[c] 103:19 Ps 11:4; 47:2
[d] 103:20 Ps 29:1; 148:2
[e] 103:21 1Kg 22:19; Neh 9:6
[f] 103:22 Ps 145:10
[g] 104:1 Ps 93:1; 103:22
[h] 104:2 Jb 9:8; Is 40:22
[i] 104:3 Am 9:6
[j] Is 19:1
[k] Ps 18:10
[l] 104:4 Ps 148:8; Heb 1:7
[m] 104:5 Jb 38:4; Ps 24:2; 93:1; 96:10
[n] 104:6 Gn 7:19
[o] 104:7 Ps 18:15; 106:9
[p] 104:8 Ps 65:6; Am 4:13

[q] 104:9 Jb 26:10; 38:10-11; Jr 5:22
[r] 104:10 Ps 107:35; Is 41:18
[s] 104:11 Jb 39:5
[t] 104:12 Mt 8:20
[u] 104:13 Dt 5:10; Ps 65:9
[v] 104:14 Jb 28:5; Ps 147:8
[w] 104:15 Gn 18:5; Ps 141:5
[x] 104:16 Nm 24:6
[y] 104:17 Lv 11:19
[z] 104:18 Lv 11:5; Pr 30:26
[aa] 104:19 Gn 1:14; Ps 19:6; 74:16
[ab] 104:20 Is 45:17
[ac] 104:21 Jb 38:39
[ad] 104:22 Jb 37:8

[A] 104:4 Or *angels*   [B] 104:7-8 Or *away. They flowed over the mountains and went down valleys*   [C] 104:16 Lit *are satisfied*   [D] 104:19 Lit *moon for*
[E] 104:19 Or *the appointed times*

By contrast, **the LORD's faithful love** is **from eternity to eternity** for those **who remember to observe his precepts** (103:17-18).
103:20-22 This psalm's review of God's faithfulness toward his people causes David to

erupt like a volcano with praise. May the same be true of all believers.
104:1-3 Here the elements of nature are described as the Lord's clothing, **his palace**, and **his chariot**. He is the all-powerful

Creator, and the whole universe exists to serve his purposes.
104:10-18 The earth is suitable for all kinds of life because God made it so.

a 104:23 Gn 3:19
b 104:24 Pr 3:19; Jr 10:12;
51:15
c 104:25 Gn 1:21; Ps 69:34
d 104:26 Jb 41:1; Ps 74:14;
Is 27:1
e 104:27 Ps 136:25; 145:15;
147:9
f 104:28 Ps 145:16
g 104:29 Jb 10:9; Ps 90:3
h 104:30 Jb 33:4
i 104:31 Ps 72:17
j 104:32 Ex 19:18; Ps 144:5
k 104:33 Ps 63:4; 146:2
l 104:34 Ps 19:14
m 104:35 Ps 37:10; 59:13
n 105:1 Ps 9:11; Is 12:4

o 105:2 Ps 96:3
p 105:3 Ps 33:21
q 105:4 Ps 27:8; 63:2
r 105:5 Ps 77:11; 119:13
s 105:6 Ps 135:4
t 105:7 Is 26:9
u 105:8 Dt 7:9; Ps 106:45;
Lk 1:42
v 105:9 Gn 12:7; 22:16-18
w 105:10 Gn 28:13-15
x 105:11 Gn 13:15; 15:18;
Ps 78:55
y 105:12 Gn 34:30; Dt 7:7
z 105:13 Dt 26:5
aa 105:14 Gn 12:17; 20:3,7
ab 105:15 Gn 20:6-7; 26:11
ac 105:1-15 1Ch 16:8-22
ad 105:16 Gn 41:54; Lv
26:26; Ezk 4:16
ae 105:17 Gn 37:28-36;
45:5; Ac 7:9
af 105:18 Gn 39:20
ag 105:19 Gn 40:20-21
ah 105:20 Gn 41:14

23 Man goes out to his work
and to his labor until evening.[a]

24 How countless are
your works, LORD!
In wisdom you have made them all;
the earth is full of your creatures.[A,b]

25 Here is the sea, vast and wide,
teeming with creatures
beyond number —
living things both large and small.[c]

26 There the ships move about,
and Leviathan, which you formed
to play there.[d]

27 All of them wait for you
to give them their food
at the right time.[e]

28 When you give it to them,
they gather it;
when you open your hand,
they are satisfied with good things.[f]

29 When you hide your face,
they are terrified;
when you take away their breath,
they die and return to the dust.[g]

30 When you send your breath,[B]
they are created,
and you renew the surface
of the ground.[h]

31 May the glory of the LORD
endure forever;
may the LORD rejoice in his works.[i]

32 He looks at the earth,
and it trembles;
he touches the mountains,
and they pour out smoke.[j]

33 I will sing to the LORD all my life;
I will sing praise to my God
while I live.[k]

34 May my meditation be pleasing
to him;
I will rejoice in the LORD.[l]

35 May sinners vanish from the earth
and wicked people be no more.[m]
My soul, bless the LORD!
Hallelujah!

GOD'S FAITHFULNESS TO HIS PEOPLE

105

Give thanks to the LORD, call on
his name;
proclaim his deeds
among the peoples.[n]

2 Sing to him, sing praise to him;
tell about all his wondrous works![o]

3 Honor his holy name;
let the hearts of those who seek the
LORD rejoice.[p]

4 Seek the LORD and his strength;
seek his face always.[q]

5 Remember the wondrous works
he has done,
his wonders, and the judgments
he has pronounced,[C,r]

6 you offspring of Abraham
his servant,
Jacob's descendants —
his chosen ones.[s]

7 He is the LORD our God;
his judgments govern
the whole earth.[t]

8 He remembers his covenant forever,
the promise he ordained
for a thousand generations[u] —

9 the covenant he made
with Abraham,
swore[D] to Isaac,[v]

10 and confirmed to Jacob as a decree
and to Israel
as a permanent covenant:[w]

11 "I will give the land of Canaan to you
as your inherited portion."[x]

12 When they were few in number,
very few indeed,
and resident aliens in Canaan,[y]

13 wandering from nation to nation
and from one kingdom to another,[z]

14 he allowed no one to oppress them;
he rebuked kings on their behalf:[aa]

15 "Do not touch my anointed ones,[ab]
or harm my prophets."[ac]

16 He called down famine
against the land
and destroyed
the entire food supply.[ad]

17 He had sent a man ahead of them —
Joseph, who was sold as a slave.[ae]

18 They hurt his feet with shackles;
his neck was put in an iron collar.[af]

19 Until the time his prediction
came true,
the word of the LORD tested him.[ag]

20 The king sent for him
and released him;
the ruler of peoples set him free.[ah]

[A] 104:24 Lit *possessions* [B] 104:30 Or *Spirit* [C] 105:5 Lit *judgments of his mouth* [D] 105:9 Lit *and his oath*

104:35 Whether through the judgment of God or through faith in Jesus Christ, one day this will be so.
105:4-5 In light of what God has done, his people should **seek his face always** (105:4).
105:12-41 The point of this section is that Israel's story is one that involved the constant supernatural provision and protection of God.

21 He made him master
  of his household,
  ruler over all his possessions[a] —

22 binding[A] his officials at will
  and instructing his elders.[b]

23 Then Israel went to Egypt;
  Jacob lived as an alien in the land
  of Ham.[B,c]

24 The LORD[C] made his people
  very fruitful;
  he made them more numerous
  than their foes,[d]

25 whose hearts he turned to hate
  his people
  and to deal deceptively
  with his servants.[e]

26 He sent Moses his servant,
  and Aaron, whom he had chosen.[f]

27 They performed
  his miraculous signs among them,
  and wonders in the land of Ham.[g]

28 He sent darkness,
  and it became dark —
  for did they not defy
  his commands?[h]

29 He turned their water into blood
  and caused their fish to die.[i]

30 Their land was overrun with frogs,
  even in their royal chambers.[j]

31 He spoke, and insects came[k] —
  gnats throughout their country.[l]

32 He gave them hail for rain,
  and lightning throughout
  their land.[m]

33 He struck their vines and fig trees
  and shattered the trees
  of their territory.[n]

34 He spoke, and locusts came —
  young locusts without number.

35 They devoured all the vegetation
  in their land
  and consumed the produce
  of their land.[o]

36 He struck all the firstborn
  in their land,
  all their first progeny.[p]

37 Then he brought Israel out
  with silver and gold,
  and no one among
  his tribes stumbled.[q]

38 Egypt was glad when they left,
  for the dread of Israel[D] had fallen
  on them.[r]

39 He spread a cloud as a covering
  and gave a fire to light up the night.[s]

40 They asked, and he brought quail
  and satisfied them with bread
  from heaven.[t]

41 He opened a rock, and water
  gushed out;
  it flowed like a stream in the desert.[u]

42 For he remembered
  his holy promise
  to Abraham his servant.[v]

43 He brought his people out
  with rejoicing,
  his chosen ones with shouts of joy.[w]

44 He gave them the lands
  of the nations,
  and they inherited
  what other peoples had worked for.[x]

45 All this happened
  so that they might keep his statutes
  and obey his instructions.[y]
  Hallelujah!

ISRAEL'S UNFAITHFULNESS TO GOD

106 Hallelujah!
  Give thanks to the LORD,
  for he is good;
  his faithful love endures forever.[z]

2 Who can declare
  the LORD's mighty acts
  or proclaim all the praise due him?[aa]

3 How happy are those
  who uphold justice,
  who practice righteousness
  at all times.[ab]

4 Remember me, LORD,
  when you show favor
  to your people.[ac]
  Come to me with your salvation

5 so that I may enjoy the prosperity
  of your chosen ones,
  rejoice in the joy of your nation,
  and boast about your heritage.[ad]

6 Both we and our fathers have sinned;
  we have done wrong
  and have acted wickedly.[ae]

[a]105:21 Gn 41:40-43
[b]105:22 Gn 41:44
[c]105:23 Gn 46:6; Ac 7:15; 13:17
[d]105:24 Ex 1:7,9; Dt 26:5
[e]105:25 Ex 1:8-14; Ac 7:19
[f]105:26 Ex 3:10; 4:12,14
[g]105:27 Ex 7:3; 11:9-10; Ps 78:43-51
[h]105:28 Ex 10:21-23; Ps 99:7
[i]105:29 Ex 7:20-21
[j]105:30 Ex 8:3,6
[k]105:31 Ex 8:21
[l]Ex 8:16-17
[m]105:32-33 Ex 9:23-25
[n]105:33 Ps 78:47
[o]105:34-35 Ex 10:12-15
[p]105:36 Ex 12:29; 13:15; Ps 78:51
[q]105:37 Ex 12:35-36

[r]105:38 Ex 12:33; 15:16
[s]105:39 Ex 13:21; Neh 9:12; Ps 78:14
[t]105:40 Ex 16:15; Ps 78:24
[u]105:41 Ex 17:6; Nm 20:11; Ps 78:15
[v]105:42 Ex 2:24
[w]105:43 Ex 15:1; Ps 106:12
[x]105:44 Jos 24:13; Ps 78:55
[y]105:45 Dt 4:1,40; Ps 78:7
[z]106:1 1Ch 16:34,41; Ps 100:5
[aa]106:2 Ps 145:4,12; 150:2
[ab]106:3 Ps 15:2
[ac]106:4 Ps 119:132
[ad]106:5 Dt 32:9; Ps 105:6,43
[ae]106:6 Lv 26:40; Jr 3:25; 14:20

[A]105:22 LXX, Syr, Vg read *teaching*   [B]105:23 = Egypt, also in v. 27   [C]105:24 Lit *He*   [D]105:38 Lit *them*

105:45 What was the reason for the Lord's remarkable deeds on behalf of Israel? That they **might keep his statutes and obey his instructions**. Similarly, God saves us so that we will love and obey him. We are not delivered from sin and death so that we can go

our own way. We are rescued for reverence; we are saved to serve.
106:1-2 The psalmist exhorts God's people to thank God because his **faithful love** is everlasting. Thus, it's impossible to **praise** him enough and truly give him his **due**.

106:6-12 The psalmist acknowledges that Israel had **sinned** in his day as the nation's ancestors had (106:6). In spite of their lack of faith, God delivered them (Ps 106:9-10). As a result, **they believed his promises and sang his praise** (106:12).

[a]106:7 Ex 14:10-12; Ps 78:17
[b]106:8 Ex 9:16; Ezk 20:9
[c]106:9 Ps 18:15; 104:7; Is 63:11-13
[d]106:10 Ex 14:30; Ps 107:2
[e]106:11 Ex 14:27-28; 15:5; Ps 78:53
[f]106:12 Ex 14:31; 15:1-21; Ps 105:43
[g]106:13 Ex 15:24; 15:1-21; 107:11
[h]106:14 Nm 11:4; Ps 78:18
[i]106:15 Nm 11:31; Ps 78:29
[j]106:16 Nm 16:1-3
[k]106:17 Nm 16:31-32; Dt 11:6
[l]106:18 Nm 16:35
[m]106:19 Ex 32:4; Dt 9:8; Ac 7:41
[n]106:20 Jr 2:11; Rm 1:23
[o]106:21 Dt 10:21; Ps 78:11

[p]106:22 Ps 105:27
[q]106:23 Ex 32:10; Dt 9:14; Ezk 20:8
[r]106:24 Nm 14:31; Dt 9:23; Heb 3:19
[s]106:25 Nm 14:2; Dt 1:27
[t]106:26 Nm 14:28-35; Ezk 20:15; Heb 3:11
[u]106:27 Lv 26:33; Dt 4:27; Ps 44:11
[v]106:28 Nm 25:3; Dt 4:3; Hs 9:10
[w]106:29 Nm 25:4
[x]106:30 Nm 25:7-8
[y]106:31 Gn 15:6; Nm 25:10-13
[z]106:32 Nm 20:2-13; Ps 81:7
[aa]106:33 Ps 78:40; Is 63:10
[ab]106:34 Dt 7:2,16; Jdg 1:21,27-36

7 Our fathers in Egypt did not grasp
the significance of
   your wondrous works
or remember your many acts
   of faithful love;
instead, they rebelled by the sea —
   the Red Sea.[a]
8 Yet he saved them for
   his name's sake,
to make his power known.[b]
9 He rebuked the Red Sea,
   and it dried up;
he led them through the depths
   as through a desert.[c]
10 He saved them from the power
   of the adversary;
he redeemed them from the power
   of the enemy.[d]
11 Water covered their foes;
   not one of them remained.[e]
12 Then they believed his promises
   and sang his praise.[f]

13 They soon forgot his works
   and would not wait
   for his counsel.[g]
14 They were seized with craving
   in the wilderness
   and tested God in the desert.[h]
15 He gave them what they asked for,
   but sent a wasting disease
   among them.[i]
16 In the camp they were envious
   of Moses
   and of Aaron, the LORD's holy one.[j]
17 The earth opened up
   and swallowed Dathan;
   it covered the assembly of Abiram.[k]
18 Fire blazed throughout
   their assembly;
   flames consumed the wicked.[l]

19 At Horeb they made a calf
   and worshiped
   the cast metal image.[m]
20 They exchanged their glory[A,B]
   for the image of a grass-eating ox.[n]
21 They forgot God their Savior,
   who did great things in Egypt,[o]

22 wondrous works in the land
   of Ham,[c]
awe-inspiring acts at the Red Sea.[p]
23 So he said he would have
   destroyed them —
if Moses his chosen one
had not stood before him
   in the breach
to turn his wrath away
   from destroying them.[q]

24 They despised the pleasant land
and did not believe his promise.[r]
25 They grumbled in their tents
and did not listen to the LORD.[s]
26 So he raised his hand against them
   with an oath
that he would make them fall
   in the desert[t]
27 and would disperse
   their descendants[D]
among the nations,
scattering them
   throughout the lands.[u]

28 They aligned themselves with Baal
   of Peor
and ate sacrifices offered
   to lifeless gods.[E,v]
29 They angered the LORD
   with their deeds,
and a plague broke out
   against them.[w]
30 But Phinehas stood up
   and intervened,
and the plague was stopped.[x]
31 It was credited to him
   as righteousness
throughout all generations
   to come.[y]

32 They angered the LORD at the Waters
   of Meribah,
and Moses suffered[F]
   because of them;[z]
33 for they embittered his spirit,[G]
   and he spoke rashly with his lips.[aa]

34 They did not destroy the peoples
   as the LORD had commanded them[ab]

[A]106:20 Alt Hb tradition reads *his glory*, or *my glory*   [B]106:20 = God   [C]106:22 = Egypt   [D]106:27 Syr; MT reads *would make their descendants fall*   [E]106:28 Lit *sacrifices for dead ones*   [F]106:32 Lit *and it was evil for Moses*   [G]106:33 Some Hb mss, LXX, Syr, Jer; other Hb mss read *they rebelled against his Spirit*

106:14-33 But their belief only lasted a little while. They **tested God** on numerous occasions, and he punished them severely (106:14-20). If not for the intercession of **Moses**, God **would have destroyed them** (106:23; see Exod 32). Eventually, they refused to enter the promised **land**, so he sentenced them to die in the **desert** (Ps 106:24-26). In spite of all this, they did not repent (106:28-33). **106:34-45** When Israel entered the promised land, they did not **destroy** all of their enemies as God had **commanded** (106:34). Instead, they **served [the] idols** of the nations, committing horrific acts (106:36-38). Therefore, the Lord let their enemies oppress them (106:41-42). The only thing that prevented Israel from being completely wiped out was **the abundance of [God's] faithful love** (106:45).

35 but mingled with the nations
and adopted their ways.[a]
36 They served their idols,
which became a snare to them.[b]
37 They sacrificed their sons
and daughters to demons.[c]
38 They shed innocent blood —
the blood of their sons
and daughters
whom they sacrificed to the idols
of Canaan;
so the land became polluted
with blood.[d]
39 They defiled themselves
by their actions
and prostituted themselves
by their deeds.[e]

40 Therefore the LORD's anger burned
against his people,
and he abhorred
his own inheritance.[f]
41 He handed them over to the nations;
those who hated them
ruled over them.[g]
42 Their enemies oppressed them,
and they were subdued
under their power.[h]
43 He rescued them many times,
but they continued
to rebel deliberately
and were beaten down
by their iniquity.[i]

44 When he heard their cry,
he took note of their distress,[j]
45 remembered his covenant
with them,
and relented according to
the abundance
of his faithful love.[k]
46 He caused them to be pitied
before all their captors.[l]

47 Save us, LORD our God,
and gather us from the nations,
so that we may give thanks
to your holy name
and rejoice in your praise.[m]

48 Blessed be the LORD God
of Israel,
from everlasting to everlasting.[n]
Let all the people say, "Amen!"
Hallelujah![o]

BOOK V (PSALMS 107–150)

THANKSGIVING FOR GOD'S DELIVERANCE

107 Give thanks to the LORD,
for he is good;
his faithful love endures forever.[p]
2 Let the redeemed
of the LORD proclaim
that he has redeemed them
from the power of the foe[q]
3 and has gathered them
from the lands —
from the east and the west,
from the north and the south.[r]

4 Some[A] wandered
in the desolate wilderness,
finding no way to a city
where they could live.[s]
5 They were hungry and thirsty;
their spirits failed[B] within them.[t]
6 Then they cried out to the LORD
in their trouble;
he rescued them
from their distress.[u]
7 He led them by the right path
to go to a city where they could live.[v]
8 Let them give thanks to the LORD
for his faithful love
and his wondrous works for
all humanity.[w]
9 For he has satisfied the thirsty
and filled the hungry
with good things.[x]

10 Others sat in darkness
and gloom[C] —
prisoners in cruel chains[y] —
11 because they rebelled
against God's commands
and despised the counsel
of the Most High.[z]
12 He broke their spirits[D]
with hard labor;
they stumbled, and there was no one
to help.[aa]
13 Then they cried out to the LORD
in their trouble;
he saved them from their distress.[ab]
14 He brought them out of darkness
and gloom
and broke their chains apart.[ac]
15 Let them give thanks to the LORD
for his faithful love

[a] 106:35 Jdg 3:5-6
[b] 106:36 Dt 7:16; Jdg 2:12
[c] 106:37 Lv 17:7; Dt 32:17
[d] 106:38 Nm 35:33; Is 24:5
[e] 106:39 Lv 18:24; Ezk 20:18,30-31
[f] 106:40 Dt 32:19; Ps 78:59
[g] 106:41 Jdg 2:14; Neh 9:27
[h] 106:42 Jdg 4:3; 10:12
[i] 106:43 Jdg 2:16-18; Ps 81:12
[j] 106:44 Jdg 3:3; 6:7; 10:10
[k] 106:45 Lv 26:42; Ps 105:8
[l] 106:46 1Kg 8:50; 2Ch 30:9; Ezr 9:9
[m] 106:47 Ps 107:3; 147:2
[n] 106:48 Ps 41:13; 72:18; 89:52
[o] 106:47-48 1Ch 16:35-36

[p] 107:1 1Ch 16:34; Ps 100:5; 106:1
[q] 107:2 Ps 78:42; 106:10
[r] 107:3 Is 11:12; 43:5; Ezk 20:34
[s] 107:4 Nm 14:33; 32:13
[t] 107:5 Ps 77:3
[u] 107:6 Ps 106:44
[v] 107:7 Jr 31:9
[w] 107:8 Ps 75:1
[x] 107:9 Ps 22:26; 34:10; Lk 1:53
[y] 107:10 Ps 102:20; Is 42:7; Lk 1:79
[z] 107:11 2Ch 36:16; Ps 78:40; 106:7
[aa] 107:12 Ex 6:9; Dt 26:6; Is 14:3
[ab] 107:13 Ex 2:23-25
[ac] 107:14 Jr 2:20

[A] 107:4 Lit *They*, also in vv. 10,23   [B] 107:5 Lit *their soul fainted*   [C] 107:10 Or *the shadow of death*, also in v. 14   [D] 107:12 Lit *hearts*

107:1-3 This psalm exhorts God's people to **give thanks** to him for his gracious act of redeeming his people from Babylonian exile and gathering them back in the land (107:1). That regathering was only partial, however. It will be permanently fulfilled in the Messiah's millennial-kingdom reign.
107:10-12 The psalmist recalls the Babylonian captivity when God's people were carried off to **hard labor** as a result of their rebellion (107:12).

[a] 107:15 Ps 75:1
[b] 107:16 Is 45:1-2
[c] 107:17 Jr 30:14-15
[d] 107:18 Jb 33:20
[e] 107:19 Nm 21:7-9
[f] 107:20 Jb 33:28,30; Ps 30:3
[g] 107:21 Ps 75:1
[h] 107:22 Ps 9:11; 105:43; 116:17
[i] 107:23 Is 42:10
[j] 107:24 Is 33:21
[k] 107:25 Ps 93:3-4; Ezk 26:19
[l] 107:26 Ps 22:14; 119:28
[m] 107:27 Jb 12:25; Is 29:9
[n] 107:28 Jnh 1:14; Mk 4:39
[o] 107:29 Ps 89:9; Mt 8:26; Lk 8:24
[p] 107:30 Ex 15:13; Ps 78:72

[q] 107:31 Ps 75:1
[r] 107:32 Ps 22:22,25
[s] 107:33 Is 42:15; 50:2
[t] 107:34 Gn 19:24-28; Dt 29:23
[u] 107:35 Is 35:6-7; 41:18
[v] 107:36 Ps 60:9; 146:7
[w] 107:37 Is 65:21; Am 9:14
[x] 107:38 Gn 12:2; Ex 1:7
[y] Dt 7:14
[z] 107:39 Ps 44:25
[aa] 107:40 Jb 12:21
[ab] Jb 12:24
[ac] 107:41 1Sm 2:8; Ps 113:7-8
[ad] Jb 21:11
[ae] 107:42 Jb 22:19; Ps 64:10
[af] Jb 5:16
[ag] 107:43 Ps 64:9; Hs 14:9
[ah] 108:1 Ps 59:17; 112:7
[ai] 108:2 Jdg 5:12; Ps 33:2; 81:2

and his wondrous works for
all humanity.[a]

16 For he has broken down
the bronze gates
and cut through the iron bars.[b]

17 Fools suffered affliction
because of their rebellious ways
and their iniquities.[c]

18 They loathed all food
and came near the gates of death.[d]

19 Then they cried out to the LORD
in their trouble;
he saved them from their distress.[e]

20 He sent his word and healed them;
he rescued them from the Pit.[f]

21 Let them give thanks to the LORD
for his faithful love
and his wondrous works for
all humanity.[g]

22 Let them offer sacrifices
of thanksgiving
and announce his works
with shouts of joy.[h]

23 Others went to sea in ships,
conducting trade on the vast water.[i]

24 They saw the LORD's works,
his wondrous works in the deep.[j]

25 He spoke and raised a stormy wind
that stirred up the waves of the sea.[A,k]

26 Rising up to the sky, sinking down
to the depths,
their courage[B] melting away
in anguish,[l]

27 they reeled and staggered
like a drunkard,
and all their skill was useless.[m]

28 Then they cried out to the LORD
in their trouble,
and he brought them
out of their distress.[n]

29 He stilled the storm to a whisper,
and the waves of the sea[C]
were hushed.[o]

30 They rejoiced when the waves[D]
grew quiet.
Then he guided them to the harbor
they longed for.[D]

31 Let them give thanks to the LORD
for his faithful love

and his wondrous works for
all humanity.[q]

32 Let them exalt him in the assembly
of the people
and praise him in the council
of the elders.[r]

33 He turns rivers into desert,
springs into thirsty ground,[s]

34 and fruitful land
into salty wasteland,
because of the wickedness
of its inhabitants.[t]

35 He turns a desert into a pool,
dry land into springs.[u]

36 He causes the hungry
to settle there,
and they establish a city
where they can live.[v]

37 They sow fields and plant vineyards
that yield a fruitful harvest.[w]

38 He blesses them,
and they multiply greatly;[x]
he does not let
their livestock decrease.[y]

39 When they are diminished
and are humbled
by cruel oppression and sorrow,[z]

40 he pours contempt on nobles[aa]
and makes them wander
in a trackless wasteland.[ab]

41 But he lifts the needy out of
their suffering[ac]
and makes their families multiply
like flocks.[ad]

42 The upright see it and rejoice,[ae]
and all injustice shuts its mouth.[af]

43 Let whoever is wise pay attention
to these things
and consider the LORD's acts
of faithful love.[ag]

A PLEA FOR VICTORY

108

A song. A psalm of David.

My heart is confident, God;
I will sing; I will sing praises
with the whole of my being.[E,ah]

2 Wake up, harp and lyre!
I will wake up the dawn.[ai]

[A] 107:25 Lit *of it*   [B] 107:26 Lit *souls*   [C] 107:29 Lit *of them*   [D] 107:30 Lit *when they*   [E] 108:1 Lit *praises, even my glory*

107:23-32 When those on **ships** encountered the ferocity of **stormy wind** and **waves**, they **cried out** to God, and **he stilled the storm** (107:23-29) and took them where they needed to go. What should people do in light of such glorious deeds? By now, the readers of the psalm know that they should **give thanks to [God] for his faithful love** and **exalt him** (107:31-32). When God delivers us from the overwhelming circumstances of life, we should respond with great praise.
107:33-37 The Lord's power over creation results in **wasteland** becoming **fruitful** (107:34).

Thirsty ground is satisfied so that **hungry** people can be satisfied (107:33, 36).
107:39-42 Whether the opposition is nature or humanity, nothing stands in the way of the sovereign God.

3 I will praise you, LORD,
    among the peoples;
I will sing praises to you
    among the nations. [a]
4 For your faithful love is higher
    than the heavens,
and your faithfulness reaches to
    the clouds. [b]
5 God, be exalted above the heavens, [c]
and let your glory be over
    the whole earth. [d]
6 Save with your right hand
    and answer me
so that those you love
    may be rescued. [e]

7 God has spoken in his sanctuary: [A]
"I will celebrate!
I will divide up Shechem. [f]
I will apportion the Valley
    of Succoth. [g]
8 Gilead is mine, Manasseh is mine,
and Ephraim is my helmet; [h]
Judah is my scepter. [i]
9 Moab is my washbasin; [j]
I throw my sandal on Edom. [k]
I shout in triumph over Philistia." [l]

10 Who will bring me
    to the fortified city?
Who will lead me to Edom? [m]
11 God, haven't you rejected us?
God, you do not march out
    with our armies. [n]
12 Give us aid against the foe,
for human help is worthless. [o]
13 With God we will
    perform valiantly; [p]
he will trample our foes. [q]

PRAYER AGAINST AN ENEMY

109

For the choir director. A psalm of David.

1 God of my praise, do not be silent. [r]

2 For wicked and deceitful mouths
    open against me;
they speak against me
    with lying tongues. [s]
3 They surround me
    with hateful words
and attack me without cause. [t]

4 In return for my love
    they accuse me,
but I continue to pray. [B,u]
5 They repay me evil for good,
and hatred for my love. [v]

6 Set a wicked person over him;
let an accuser [c] stand
    at his right hand. [w]
7 When he is judged, let him
    be found guilty,
and let his prayer be counted as sin. [x]
8 Let his days be few;
let another take over his position. [y]
9 Let his children be fatherless
and his wife a widow. [z]
10 Let his children wander as beggars,
searching for food far [D]
    from their demolished homes. [aa]
11 Let a creditor seize all he has;
let strangers plunder what he has
    worked for. [ab]
12 Let no one show him kindness,
and let no one be gracious
    to his fatherless children. [ac]
13 Let the line of his descendants
    be cut off;
let their name be blotted out
    in the next generation. [ad]
14 Let the iniquity of his fathers
be remembered before the LORD, [ae]
and do not let his mother's sin
    be blotted out. [af]
15 Let their sins [E] always remain
    before the LORD,
and let him remove [F] all memory
    of them from the earth. [ag]

16 For he did not think
    to show kindness,
but pursued the suffering, needy,
    and brokenhearted
in order to put them to death. [ah]
17 He loved cursing — let it fall on him;
he took no delight in blessing —
    let it be far from him. [ai]
18 He wore cursing like his coat —
let it enter his body like water
and go into his bones like oil. [aj]
19 Let it be like a robe he wraps
    around himself,
like a belt he always wears. [ak]

[a] 108:3 2Sm 22:50; Ps 9:11; 18:49
[b] 108:4 Ps 36:5; 103:11; Lm 3:22-23
[c] 108:5 Ps 113:4
[d] 108:1-5 Ps 57:7-11
[e] 108:6 Ps 17:7; 20:6; 138:7
[f] 108:7 Gn 12:6; 33:18
[g] Gn 33:17
[h] 108:8 Dt 33:17; Jos 13:31
[i] Gn 49:10
[j] 108:9 2Sm 8:2
[k] 2Sm 8:14
[l] 2Sm 8:1
[m] 108:10 Jr 1:18
[n] 108:11 Ps 44:9
[o] 108:12 Ps 146:3
[p] 108:13 Nm 24:18; Ps 44:5; 118:15-16
[q] 108:6-13 Ps 60:5-12
[r] 109:1 Ps 28:1; 83:1
[s] 109:2 Ps 10:7; 52:4; 120:2
[t] 109:3 Ps 35:7; 69:4; Jn 15:25
[u] 109:4 Ps 69:13
[v] 109:5 Ps 35:12; 38:20
[w] 109:6 Zch 3:1
[x] 109:7 Ps 1:5; Pr 28:9
[y] 109:8 Ps 55:23; Ac 1:20
[z] 109:9 Ex 22:24
[aa] 109:10 Jb 30:5-8; Ps 59:15
[ab] 109:11 Dt 28:43-44; Lm 5:2
[ac] 109:12 Jb 5:4
[ad] 109:13 Jb 18:17,19; Ps 9:5; Pr 10:7
[ae] 109:14 Ex 20:5; Nm 14:18
[af] Neh 4:5; Jr 18:23
[ag] 109:15 Ps 34:16; 90:8; Jr 16:17
[ah] 109:16 Ps 34:18; 94:6
[ai] 109:17 Pr 14:14; Ezk 35:6; Mt 7:2
[aj] 109:18 Nm 5:22
[ak] 109:19 Ps 73:26

[A] **108:7** Or *has promised by his holy nature* [B] **109:4** Lit *but I, prayer* [C] **109:6** Or *adversary* [D] **109:10** LXX reads *beggars, driven far*
[E] **109:15** Lit *Let them* [F] **109:15** Or *cut off*

108:12-13 Without God we are impotent to achieve anything. **With God we will perform valiantly** (108:13).
109:5-15 David does not seek vengeance himself but calls for divine vengeance. He trusts in the One who declares, "Vengeance belongs to me; I will repay" (Deut 32:35).
109:16-20 David did not ask God to take vengeance on his persecutor merely for his own sake, but because the wicked man lived and acted contrary to God's righteous character.

[a]109:20 Ps 54:5; 94:23; Is 3:11
[b]109:21 Ps 79:9; 106:8
[c]Ps 69:16
[d]109:22 Ps 40:17; 86:1
[e]Ps 143:4
[f]109:23 Ps 102:11
[g]109:24 Jb 16:8; Ps 35:13
[h]109:25 Ps 22:6-7; 69:19
[i]109:26 Ps 119:86
[j]109:27 Jb 37:7
[k]109:28 2Sm 16:11-12; Is 65:14
[l]109:29 Jb 8:22; Ps 35:26; 132:18
[m]109:30 Ps 22:22,25; 35:18; 111:1
[n]109:31 Ps 16:8; 110:5; 121:5

[o]110:1 Mt 22:44; Mk 12:36; Lk 20:42-43; Ac 2:34-35; 1Co 15:25; Heb 1:13
[p]110:2 Ps 45:6; Ezk 19:14
[q]110:3 Jdg 5:2
[r]1Ch 16:29; Ps 96:9
[s]110:4 Gn 14:18; Heb 5:6,10; 7:17,21
[t]110:5 Ps 16:8; 68:14
[u]110:6 Is 66:24; Rv 19:17-18
[v]Ps 68:21
[w]110:7 Jdg 7:5-6
[x]Ps 27:6
[y]111:1 Ps 35:18; 149:1
[z]111:2 Ps 92:5; 143:5

20 Let this be the LORD's payment
to my accusers,
to those who speak evil against me.[a]

21 But you, LORD, my Lord,
deal kindly with me
for your name's sake;[b]
because your faithful love is good,
rescue me.[c]
22 For I am suffering and needy;[d]
my heart is wounded within me.[e]
23 I fade away
like a lengthening shadow;[f]
I am shaken off like a locust.
24 My knees are weak from fasting,
and my body is emaciated.[A,g]
25 I have become an object of ridicule
to my accusers;[B]
when they see me, they shake
their heads in scorn.[h]

26 Help me, LORD my God;
save me according to
your faithful love[i]
27 so they may know that this is
your hand
and that you, LORD, have done it.[j]
28 Though they curse, you will bless.
When they rise up, they will be
put to shame,
but your servant will rejoice.[k]
29 My accusers will be clothed
with disgrace;
they will wear their shame
like a cloak.[l]
30 I will fervently thank the LORD
with my mouth;
I will praise him in the presence
of many.[m]
31 For he stands at the right hand of
the needy
to save him from those who would
condemn him.[n]

THE PRIESTLY KING

110

A psalm of David.

This is the declaration of the LORD
to my Lord:
"Sit at my right hand
until I make your enemies
your footstool."[o]
2 The LORD will extend
your mighty scepter from Zion.
Rule[C] over
your surrounding[D] enemies.[p]
3 Your people will volunteer
on your day of battle.[E,q]
In holy splendor, from the womb
of the dawn,
the dew
of your youth belongs to you.[F,r]
4 The LORD has sworn an oath
and will not take it back:
"You are a priest forever
according to the pattern
of Melchizedek."[s]

5 The Lord is at your right hand;
he will crush kings on the day
of his anger.[t]
6 He will judge the nations,
heaping up corpses;[u]
he will crush leaders
over the entire world.[v]
7 He will drink from the brook
by the road;[w]
therefore, he will lift up his head.[x]

PRAISE FOR THE LORD'S WORKS

111

Hallelujah![G]
I will praise the LORD with all
my heart
in the assembly of the upright
and in the congregation.[y]

2 The LORD's works are great,
studied by all who delight in them.[z]

[A]109:24 Lit *denied from fat* [B]109:25 Lit *to them* [C]110:2 One Hb ms, LXX, Tg read *You will rule* [D]110:2 Lit *Rule in the midst of your* [E]110:3 Lit *power* [F]110:3 Hb obscure [G]111:1 The lines of this poem form an acrostic.

109:26-27 Don't miss that David wants his enemies to know that his deliverance is from the **hand** of God, so that he would receive the glory (109:27).

109:30-31 David is confident of God's character; therefore, he anticipates God's intervention. The God who helps **the needy** (109:31) would help David in time of need—and he will do the same for us.

110:1 David describes a conversation that he was permitted to hear. **The LORD** (Yahweh) spoke to David's **Lord**—that is, to the Messiah. Thus, David overhears God the Father speaking to God the Son, telling him, **Sit at my right hand until I make your enemies your footstool**. To sit at the right hand of a king was a position of privilege and authority. The Father vows to put all of the Son's enemies under his feet. This is an indicator that the promise spoken in the beginning, in which the seed of the woman would vanquish the serpent—"he will strike your head"—will be fulfilled (see Gen 3:15).

Jesus himself claimed that this verse spoke of the Messiah and proved that the Messiah was David's Lord, not merely his descendant (see Matt 22:41-46). The New Testament authors clearly see this verse fulfilled in Jesus, applying it to him numerous times (e.g., Acts 2:34-36; 1 Cor 15:25; Eph 1:20; Heb 1:13). Upon his resurrection and ascension, the Son took his seat at the right hand of God the Father.

110:4 Just as **Melchizedek** was both a king and a priest (see Gen 14:18), so the Messiah would occupy both offices. Moreover, Melchizedek blessed Abraham, and Abraham paid a tithe to Melchizedek (see Gen 14:19-20). According to the author of Hebrews, this shows that Melchizedek's priesthood is superior to the priesthood of the Levites who would descend from Abraham (see Heb 7:1-10). Thus, Jesus—a priest "according to the pattern of Melchizedek"—is superior to the Levitical priests. He has offered a perfect sacrifice to atone for sin, and he lives forever to intercede for us by virtue of his resurrection.

111:1 To declare **hallelujah** is to bestow praise and honor on the Lord.

3 All that he does is splendid
   and majestic;[a]
his righteousness endures forever.[b]
4 He has caused his wondrous works
   to be remembered.[c]
The LORD is gracious
   and compassionate.[d]
5 He has provided food for those
   who fear him;[e]
he remembers
   his covenant forever.[f]
6 He has shown his people the power
   of his works
by giving them the inheritance
   of the nations.[g]
7 The works of his hands are truth
   and justice;
all his instructions are trustworthy.[h]
8 They are established forever
   and ever,
enacted in truth and in uprightness.[i]
9 He has sent redemption
   to his people.[j]
He has ordained
   his covenant forever.
His name is holy and awe-inspiring.[k]

10 The fear of the LORD is the beginning
   of wisdom;[l]
all who follow his instructions[A] have
   good insight.[m]
His praise endures forever.[n]

THE TRAITS OF THE RIGHTEOUS

112 Hallelujah![B]
   Happy is the person who fears
   the LORD,
taking great delight
   in his commands.[o]

2 His descendants will be powerful
   in the land;
the generation of the upright
   will be blessed.[p]
3 Wealth and riches are in his house,[q]
and his righteousness
   endures forever.[r]
4 Light shines in the darkness
   for the upright.[s]
He is gracious, compassionate,
   and righteous.[t]

5 Good will come to the one
   who lends generously
and conducts his business fairly.[u]
6 He will never be shaken.[v]
The righteous one will be
   remembered forever.[w]
7 He will not fear bad news;
his heart is confident,
   trusting in the LORD.[x]
8 His heart is assured; he will not fear.[y]
In the end he will look in triumph
   on his foes.[z]
9 He distributes freely to the poor;
his righteousness endures forever.[aa]
His horn will be exalted in honor.[ab]

10 The wicked one will see it
   and be angry;
he will gnash his teeth in despair.[ac]
The desire of the wicked
   leads to ruin.[ad]

PRAISE TO THE MERCIFUL GOD

113 Hallelujah!
   Give praise, servants
   of the LORD;
praise the name of the LORD.[ae]
2 Let the name of the LORD be blessed
both now and forever.[af]
3 From the rising of the sun
   to its setting,
let the name of the LORD
   be praised.[ag]

4 The LORD is exalted above
   all the nations,[ah]
his glory above the heavens.[ai]
5 Who is like the LORD our God —
   the one enthroned on high,[aj]
6 who stoops down to look
on the heavens and the earth?[ak]
7 He raises the poor from the dust
and lifts the needy
   from the trash heap[al]
8 in order to seat them with nobles —
with the nobles of his people.[am]
9 He gives the childless woman
   a household,
making her the joyful mother
   of children.[an]
Hallelujah!

[a] 111:3 Ps 145:5
[b] Ps 112:3,9; 119:142
[c] 111:4 Ps 78:4
[d] Ps 103:8; 145:8
[e] 111:5 Mt 6:31-33
[f] Ps 105:8
[g] 111:6 Dt 4:38; 32:8; Ps 78:55
[h] 111:7 Ps 19:7; 93:5
[i] 111:8 Ps 119:160; Is 40:8; Mt 5:18
[j] 111:9 Lk 1:68
[k] Ps 99:3; Lk 1:49
[l] 111:10 Pr 1:7; 9:10
[m] Ps 119:98
[n] Ps 44:8; 145:2
[o] 112:1 Ps 1:2; 119:16; 128:1
[p] 112:2 Ps 102:28
[q] 112:3 Pr 3:16; 8:18
[r] Ps 111:3
[s] 112:4 Ps 97:11
[t] Ex 34:6; Neh 9:17; Ps 116:5

[u] 112:5 Ps 15:5; 37:26
[v] 112:6 Ps 55:22
[w] Pr 10:7
[x] 112:7 Ps 56:4; 57:7; Pr 1:33
[y] 112:8 Ps 27:1; 56:11
[z] Ps 54:7; 59:10
[aa] 112:9 2Co 9:9
[ab] Ps 75:10; 89:17
[ac] 112:10 Jb 16:9; Ps 35:16
[ad] Pr 10:28; 11:7
[ae] 113:1 Ps 34:22; 69:36; 135:1
[af] 113:2 Ps 115:18; 145:21
[ag] 113:3 Mal 1:11
[ah] 113:4 Ps 99:2
[ai] Ps 57:5,11; 148:13
[aj] 113:5 Ex 15:11; Ps 89:6
[ak] 113:6 Ps 11:4; 138:6
[al] 113:7 1Sm 2:8; Ps 107:41
[am] 113:8 Jb 36:7
[an] 113:9 1Sm 2:5; Ps 68:6

[A] 111:10 Lit *follow them*   [B] 112:1 The lines of this poem form an acrostic.

111:9 The Lord **is holy and awe-inspiring**. He's in a class by himself.
111:10 The psalmist concludes by describing the disposition that should characterize all true worshipers: **the fear of the LORD**. To take God seriously in this way is the foundation of **wisdom**. To be wise is to have a

clear understanding of how to obey God's commands in specific situations.
112:1 Fearing God is about how you live and not merely what you say.
112:5-10 In short, the righteous will prosper and the wicked will perish (see 1:1-6).

113:1-3 **Give praise . . . praise the name of the LORD . . . . let the name of the LORD be praised** is a threefold call reminding us of the obligation God's people have to continually extol his greatness.
113:5-9 The Lord is transcendent, yet he is also intimately involved with his creation.

ᵃ114:1 Ex 13:3; Ps 81:5
ᵇ114:2 Ex 15:17; Ps 78:68-69
ᶜ114:3 Ex 14:21; Ps 77:16
ᵈJos 3:13-16
ᵉ114:4 Ex 19:18; Ps 29:6
ᶠ114:5 Hab 3:8
ᵍ114:6 Hab 3:10
ʰ114:7 Ps 96:9
ⁱ114:8 Ex 17:6; Nm 20:11; Dt 8:15
ʲ115:1 Ezk 36:22; Dn 9:18-19
ᵏ115:2 Ps 42:3,10; 79:10
ˡ115:3 Ps 135:6; Dn 4:35
ᵐ115:4 2Kg 19:18; Is 37:19
ⁿ115:5-6 Is 46:7
ᵒ115:7 Jr 10:5
ᵖHab 2:18
ۊ115:4-8 Ps 135:15-18

ʳ115:9 Ps 118:2
ˢGn 15:1; Dt 33:29; Ps 3:3; 5:12; 18:2; 28:7; 33:20; 119:114
ᵗ115:10 Ps 118:3; 135:19
ᵘ115:10-11 Ps 33:20
ᵛ115:11 Ps 22:23; 118:4
ʷ115:12 Ps 98:3
ˣ115:13 Rv 11:18; 19:5
ʸ115:14 Dt 1:11
ᶻ115:15 Ps 121:2; 124:8; 134:3
ᵃᵃ115:16 Ps 89:11
ᵃᵇ115:17 Ps 6:5; 31:17; 88:10-12
ᵃᶜ115:18 Ps 113:2; Dn 2:20
ᵃᵈ116:1 Ps 18:1; 66:19
ᵃᵉ116:2 Ps 17:6; 40:1

GOD'S DELIVERANCE OF ISRAEL

114 When Israel came
out of Egypt —
the house of Jacob from a people
who spoke a foreign language[a] —
2 Judah became his sanctuary,
Israel, his dominion.[b]

3 The sea looked and fled;[c]
the Jordan turned back.[d]
4 The mountains skipped like rams,
the hills, like lambs.[e]
5 Why was it, sea, that you fled?
Jordan, that you turned back?[f]
6 Mountains, that you skipped
like rams?
Hills, like lambs?[g]

7 Tremble, earth, at the presence
of the Lord,
at the presence
of the God of Jacob,[h]
8 who turned the rock into a pool,
the flint into a spring.[i]

GLORY TO GOD ALONE

115 Not to us, Lord, not to us,
but to your name give glory
because of your faithful love,
because of your truth.[j]
2 Why should the nations say,
"Where is their God?"[k]
3 Our God is in heaven
and does whatever he pleases.[l]

4 Their idols are silver and gold,
made by human hands.[m]
5 They have mouths
but cannot speak,
eyes, but cannot see.
6 They have ears but cannot hear,
noses, but cannot smell.[n]
7 They have hands but cannot feel,
feet, but cannot walk.[o]
They cannot make a sound
with their throats.[p]
8 Those who make them are[A] just
like them,
as are all who trust in them.[q]

9 Israel,[B] trust in the Lord![r]
He is their help and shield.[s]
10 House of Aaron, trust in the Lord![t]
He is their help and shield.[u]
11 You who fear the Lord,
trust in the Lord![v]
He is their help and shield.
12 The Lord remembers us
and will bless us.
He will bless the house of Israel;
he will bless the house of Aaron;[w]
13 he will bless those who fear
the Lord —
small and great alike.[x]

14 May the Lord add to your numbers,
both yours and your children's.[y]
15 May you be blessed by the Lord,
the Maker of heaven and earth.[z]
16 The heavens are the Lord's,[c]
but the earth he has given
to the human race.[aa]
17 It is not the dead who praise
the Lord,
nor any of those descending
into the silence of death.[ab]
18 But we will bless the Lord,
both now and forever.[ac]
Hallelujah!

∾ **HOPE WORDS** ∾

*Justice is getting what
you deserve. Mercy is not
getting what you deserve.*

THANKS TO GOD FOR DELIVERANCE

116 I love the Lord
because he has heard
my appeal for mercy.[ad]
2 Because he has turned
his ear to me,
I will call out to him as long as
I live.[ae]

3 The ropes of death were wrapped
around me,

[A]115:8 Or *May those who make them become*   [B]115:9 Some Hb mss, LXX, Syr read *House of Israel*   [C]115:16 Lit *the Lord's heavens*

114:3-8 If even creation is moved by God's power, how can weak and sinful humans do less than give him honor? A holy dread and awe of our Creator should be the response of those who know the awesome might of God. **115:1** Believers who have a correct perception of God and a correct perception of themselves know that God alone deserves **glory**, not **us**. **115:2-3** The nations in the ancient world had idols, visual representations of the gods they

worshiped. Thus, when they looked at Israel— for whom idolatry was forbidden (see Exod 20:4-5)—they asked, **Where is their God?** (Ps 115:2). The psalmist answered: **Our God is in heaven and does whatever he pleases** (115:3). In other words, the Lord is not a finite idol but a limitless, transcendent God with the sovereign power to accomplish his will. **115:4-8** The point here is that idols are completely impotent. Verse 8 makes it clear that

you become like that which you worship—so be sure you worship the one true God. **115:17-18** In verse 17 the psalmist is not denying life after death. He is simply saying that submitting to God in praise, faith, and obedience is something we are called to do now. We cannot wait until later. After death, it is too late to make this decision. Only if we **bless** God **now** will we be able to bless him **forever** (115:18).

and the torments of Sheol
   overcame me;
I encountered trouble
   and sorrow.[a]

4 Then I called on the name
   of the LORD:
"LORD, save me!"[b]

5 The LORD is gracious and righteous;
   our God is compassionate.[c]
6 The LORD guards the inexperienced;
   I was helpless, and he saved me.[d]
7 Return to your rest, my soul,
   for the LORD has been good to you.[e]
8 For you, LORD, rescued me
   from death,
my eyes from tears,
   my feet from stumbling.[f]
9 I will walk before the LORD
   in the land of the living.[g]
10 I believed, even when I said,
   "I am severely oppressed."[h]
11 In my alarm I said,
   "Everyone is a liar."[i]

12 How can I repay the LORD
   for all the good he has done
     for me?[j]
13 I will take the cup of salvation
   and call on the name of the LORD.[k]
14 I will fulfill my vows to the LORD
   in the presence of all his people.[l]

15 The death of his faithful ones
   is valuable in the LORD's sight.[m]
16 LORD, I am indeed your servant;
I am your servant, the son
   of your female servant.
You have loosened my bonds.[n]

17 I will offer you a sacrifice
   of thanksgiving
and call on the name of the LORD.[o]
18 I will fulfill my vows to the LORD
   in the presence of all his people,[p]

19 in the courts of the LORD's house —
   within you, Jerusalem.[q]
Hallelujah!

UNIVERSAL CALL TO PRAISE

117 Praise the LORD, all nations!
   Glorify him, all peoples![r]
2 For his faithful love to us is great;
   the LORD's faithfulness
     endures forever.[s]
Hallelujah!

THANKSGIVING FOR VICTORY

118 Give thanks to the LORD,
   for he is good;
his faithful love endures forever.[t]
2 Let Israel say,
   "His faithful love endures forever."[u]
3 Let the house of Aaron say,
   "His faithful love endures forever."[v]
4 Let those who fear the LORD say,
   "His faithful love endures forever."[w]

5 I called to the LORD in distress;[x]
   the LORD answered me
and put me in a spacious place.[A,y]
6 The LORD is for me;
   I will not be afraid.
What can a mere mortal do to me?[z]
7 The LORD is my helper,
Therefore, I will look in triumph
   on those who hate me.[aa]

8 It is better to take refuge in the LORD
   than to trust in humanity.[ab]
9 It is better to take refuge in the LORD
   than to trust in nobles.[ac]

10 All the nations surrounded me;
   in the name of the LORD
     I destroyed them.[ad]
11 They surrounded me, yes,
   they surrounded me;
in the name of the LORD
   I destroyed them.[ae]

[a] 116:3 Ps 18:4-5
[b] 116:4 Ps 18:6; 118:5
[c] 116:5 Ex 34:6; Neh 9:17; Ps 112:4
[d] 116:6 Ps 19:7; 79:8; 142:6
[e] 116:7 Ps 13:6; Jr 6:16
[f] 116:8 Ps 49:15; 56:13
[g] 116:9 Ps 27:13
[h] 116:10 2Co 4:13
[i] 116:11 Ps 31:22; 62:9; Rm 3:4
[j] 116:12 2Ch 32:25; 1Th 3:9
[k] 116:13 Ps 16:5; 105:1
[l] 116:14 Ps 22:25; 50:14
[m] 116:15 Ps 72:14
[n] 116:16 Jb 12:18; Ps 86:16; 107:14
[o] 116:17 Lv 7:12; Ps 50:14
[p] 116:18 Ps 22:25; 50:14

[q] 116:19 Ps 96:8; 102:21
[r] 117:1 Rm 15:11
[s] 117:2 Ps 100:5; 103:11; 146:6
[t] 118:1 2Ch 5:13; Ezr 3:11; Ps 100:5
[u] 118:2 Ps 115:9
[v] 118:3 Ps 115:10; 135:19
[w] 118:4 Ps 22:23; 115:11
[x] 118:5 Ps 18:6; 120:1
[y] Ps 18:19
[z] 118:6 Ps 56:4,11; Heb 13:6
[aa] 118:7 Ps 54:4,7; 59:10
[ab] 118:8 Ps 40:4; 108:12; Jr 17:5
[ac] 118:9 Ps 146:3
[ad] 118:10 Ps 3:6; 88:17
[ae] 118:11 Ps 18:40

[A] 118:5 Or *answered me with freedom*

116:12-14 In light of the Lord's goodness to him, the psalmist contemplates what he could give back to God (116:12). He mentions two things. First, he would **take the cup of salvation** (his blessings and deliverance) that God had graciously given him and **call on [his] name** (116:13). In other words, he would continue to worship and depend on the God who saves. Why would we turn anywhere but to the One who has proven that he can deliver? Second, the psalmist would **fulfill [his] vows to the LORD** (116:14). Obedience is the only appropriate response when God has come through for us.
116:15 God finds great pleasure and joy in fellowship with his children, who go to be with him eternally at death because of their personal relationship with him.
117:1 Paul quotes this verse in Romans 15:11, emphasizing the truth that through the sacrifice of Jesus Christ, the Gentiles can glorify God for his mercy (see Rom 15:7-11). Because of the gospel, Jews and Gentiles are able to come together to worship God for his great salvation.
118:1-4 The psalmist calls on **Israel** (all God's people), **the house of Aaron** (all the priests), and **those who fear the LORD** (all who take him seriously) to **give thanks** to him. Why? Because **his faithful love endures forever**. Notice the repetition. The biblical writers weren't able to emphasize important truths with bold typeface or italics like we do today; instead, they used repetition for emphasis. If there's one thing the psalmist wanted us to know, it is this: for those who come under God's covenant covering, his loyal, covenantal love lasts forever. It doesn't get any better than that.
118:6 The apostle Paul conveyed the same idea this way: "If God is for us, who is against us?" (Rom 8:31).
118:10-14 Victory is found only in God—as the quote from the victory song of God's deliverance at the Red Sea also highlights (118:14; see Exod 15:2).

a 118:12 Dt 1:44
b Ps 58:9; Nah 1:10
c 118:13 Ps 140:4
d 118:14 Ex 15:2; Ps 27:1;
Is 12:2
e 118:15 Ex 15:6; Lk 1:51
f 118:16 Ps 89:13
g 118:17 Ps 73:28; Hab 1:12
h 118:18 Ps 86:13; Jr 30:11;
2Co 6:9
i 118:19 Is 26:2
j 118:20 Ps 24:3-6; Rv 22:14
k 118:21 Ps 116:1
l 118:22 Lk 20:17; Ac 4:11;
1Pt 2:4,7
m 118:23 Mt 21:42; Mk
12:11
n 118:24 Ps 31:7
o 118:25 Neh 2:20; Ps
122:6-7
p 118:25-26 Mt 21:9; Mk
11:9-10; Lk 13:35; Jn 12:13
q 118:26 Ps 129:8

r 118:27 Ex 27:2; Ps 18:28;
1Pt 2:9
s 118:28 Is 25:1
t 118:29 2Ch 5:13; Ezr 3:11;
Ps 100:5
u 119:1 Ps 101:6; Pr 11:20
v Ps 128:1; Mc 4:2
w 119:2 Ps 25:10;
119:10,22,168
x Dt 4:29; 10:12; 11:13;
13:3; 30:2
y 119:3 1Jn 3:9; 5:18
z 119:4 Dt 4:13; Neh 9:13;
Ps 19:8
aa 119:5 Dt 12:1; 2Ch 7:17;
Pr 4:26
ab 119:6 Jb 22:26; Ps 119:80
ac 119:7 Ps 119:62,106
ad 119:8 Ps 38:21; 71:9,18
ae 119:9 2Sm 22:31; Ps 12:6;
19:9-10; 119:140; Pr 20:11;
30:5; Php 4:8

12 They surrounded me like bees;[a]
they were extinguished like a fire
    among thorns;
in the name of the LORD
    I destroyed them.[b]
13 They[A] pushed me hard
    to make me fall,
but the LORD helped me.[c]
14 The LORD is my strength and my song;
he has become my salvation.[d]

15 There are shouts of joy and victory
in the tents of the righteous:
"The LORD's right hand
    performs valiantly![e]
16 The LORD's right hand is raised.
The LORD's right hand
    performs valiantly!"[f]
17 I will not die, but I will live
and proclaim what the LORD
    has done.[g]
18 The LORD disciplined me severely
but did not give me over to death.[h]

19 Open the gates of righteousness
    for me;
I will enter through them
and give thanks to the LORD.[i]
20 This is the LORD's gate;
the righteous will enter through it.[j]
21 I will give thanks to you
because you have answered me
and have become my salvation.[k]
22 The stone that the builders rejected
has become the cornerstone.[l]
23 This came from the LORD;
it is wondrous in our sight.[m]
24 This is the day the LORD has made;
let us rejoice and be glad in it.[n]

25 LORD, save us!
LORD, please grant us success![o]
26 He who comes in the name
of the LORD is blessed.[p]
From the house of the LORD
    we bless you.[q]
27 The LORD is God and has given us
    light.

Bind the festival sacrifice with cords
to the horns of the altar.[r]
28 You are my God, and I will give
    you thanks.
You are my God; I will exalt you.[s]
29 Give thanks to the LORD,
    for he is good;
his faithful love endures forever.[t]

DELIGHT IN GOD'S WORD

א Aleph

119 How[B] happy are those whose
way is blameless,[u]
who walk according to the LORD's
    instruction![v]
2 Happy are those who keep
    his decrees[w]
and seek him with all their heart.[x]
3 They do nothing wrong;[y]
they walk in his ways.
4 You have commanded
    that your precepts[z]
be diligently kept.
5 If only my ways were committed
to keeping your statutes![aa]
6 Then I would not be ashamed[ab]
when I think about
    all your commands.
7 I will praise you
    with an upright heart[ac]
when I learn
    your righteous judgments.
8 I will keep your statutes;
never abandon me.[ad]

ב Beth

9 How can a young man keep his way
    pure?
By keeping your[c] word.[ae]

[A] 118:13 Lit *You*   [B] 119:1 The stanzas of this poem form an acrostic.   [C] 119:9 Or *keeping it according to your*

118:21 How do you respond to answered prayer? Do you give vocal acknowledgement to God and glorify him so that others may be encouraged to trust him? Or do you take his blessings and provision for granted?
118:22-26 The psalmist uses a building metaphor to teach an important truth. **The builders rejected** a **stone** that God had selected. In his sovereign providence, he ensured that this particular stone would **become the cornerstone** of a figurative building of

his design; it would be the stone on which everything else would be aligned (118:22). This imagery is fulfilled in Jesus Christ (see Luke 20:17). He is the Messiah sent by God to his people (Ps 118:26; see Matt 21:9). But Israel's religious leaders rejected him and had him put to death. Nonetheless, God vindicated him, raising him from the dead to be the Lord of all.
Psalm 119 The longest chapter in the Psalter (and the longest in the Bible), this is an acros-

tic psalm. Each of its twenty-two stanzas is introduced by a different letter of the Hebrew alphabet, presented in sequence. The entire psalm is an appreciation for, celebration of, and dependency on the Word of God to enable us to properly negotiate the twists and turns of life.
119:1-2 The Hebrew word translated here as **happy** can also mean "blessed." Those **who walk**—that is, live their lives—according to God's Word are blessed (and happy)!

10 I have sought you
　　with all my heart;[a]
　don't let me wander
　　from your commands.[b]

11 I have treasured your word
　　in my heart[c]
　so that I may not sin against you.

12 LORD, may you be blessed;
　teach me your statutes.[d]

13 With my lips I proclaim
　all the judgments from your mouth.[e]

14 I rejoice in the way revealed by
　　your decrees[f]
　as much as in all riches.

15 I will meditate on your precepts[g]
　and think about your ways.[h]

16 I will delight in your statutes;[i]
　I will not forget your word.

ג Gimel

17 Deal generously with your servant[j]
　so that I might live;
　then I will keep your word.

18 Open my eyes so that
　　I may contemplate
　wondrous things
　　from your instruction.

19 I am a resident alien on earth;[k]
　do not hide your commands
　　from me.

20 I am continually overcome
　with longing for your judgments.[l]

21 You rebuke the arrogant,
　the ones under a curse,[m]
　who wander from your commands.[n]

22 Take insult and contempt away
　　from me,[o]
　for I have kept your decrees.

23 Though princes sit together
　　speaking against me,[p]
　your servant will think
　　about your statutes;[q]

24 your decrees are my delight
　and my counselors.[r]

ד Daleth

25 My life is down in the dust;[s]
　give me life[t] through your word.

26 I told you about my life,
　and you answered me;
　teach me your statutes.[u]

27 Help me understand
　the meaning of your precepts

so that I can meditate on
　　your wonders.[v]

28 I am weary[A] from grief;
　strengthen me through your word.[w]

29 Keep me from the way of deceit
　and graciously give me
　　your instruction.

30 I have chosen the way of truth;
　I have set your ordinances
　　before me.[x]

31 I cling to your decrees;
　LORD, do not put me to shame.[y]

32 I pursue the way of your commands,
　for you broaden
　　my understanding.[B,z]

ה He

33 Teach me, LORD, the meaning[c]
　　of your statutes,
　and I will always keep them.[D,aa]

34 Help me understand
　　your instruction,
　and I will obey it
　and follow it with all my heart.[ac]

35 Help me stay on the path
　　of your commands,[ad]
　for I take pleasure in it.[ae]

36 Turn my heart to your decrees[af]
　and not to dishonest profit.[ag]

37 Turn my eyes
　from looking at what is worthless;[ah]
　give me life in your ways.[E,ai]

38 Confirm what you said
　　to your servant,[aj]
　for it produces reverence for you.

39 Turn away the disgrace I dread;[ak]
　indeed, your judgments are good.

40 How I long for your precepts![al]
　Give me life through
　　your righteousness.

ו Waw

41 Let your faithful love
　　come to me, LORD,[am]
　your salvation, as you promised.[an]

42 Then I can answer the one
　　who taunts me,[ao]
　for I trust in your word.

43 Never take the word of truth
　　from my mouth,
　for I hope in your judgments.[ap]

44 I will always obey your instruction,
　forever and ever.[aq]

[a] 119:10 Ps 119:2
[b] Ps 119:21,118
[c] 119:11 Ps 37:31; 40:8; Lk 2:19,51
[d] 119:12 Ps 119:26,64,108, 124,135,171
[e] 119:13 Ps 40:9; 119:72
[f] 119:14 Ps 119:111,162; Pr 3:13-15; 8:10-11,18-19
[g] 119:15 Ps 1:2; 119:23,48, 78,97,148
[h] Ps 25:4; 27:11; Is 58:2
[i] 119:16 Ps 1:2; 119:24,47, 70,77,92,143,174
[j] 119:17 Ps 13:6; 119:144
[k] 119:19 1Ch 29:15; Ps 39:12; 119:54; Heb 11:13
[l] 119:20 Ps 42:1-2; 63:1; 84:2; 119:40,131
[m] 119:21 Dt 27:26
[n] Ps 119:10,118
[o] 119:22 Ps 39:8; 119:39
[p] 119:23 Ps 119:161
[q] Ps 119:15,27-28
[r] 119:24 Ps 119:16; Rm 7:22
[s] 119:25 Ps 44:25
[t] Ps 119:37,40,88,93,107, 149,154,156,159
[u] 119:26 Ps 25:4; 86:11; 119:12,26,64,68,124,135,171

[v] 119:27 Ps 105:2; 119:15,73,125; 145:5
[w] 119:28 1Pt 5:10
[x] 119:30 Ps 16:8
[y] 119:31 Ps 119:116
[z] 119:32 1Kg 4:29; 2Co 6:11,13
[aa] 119:33 Ps 119:112; Mt 10:22; Heb 3:6; Rv 2:26
[ab] 119:34 Ps 119:125,144,169
[ac] 1Ch 22:12; Ps 119:2,69
[ad] 119:35 Ps 25:4; Is 40:14
[ae] Ps 119:16
[af] 119:36 1Kg 8:58
[ag] Ezk 33:31; Mk 7:21,22; Lk 12:15; Heb 13:5
[ah] 119:37 Is 33:15
[ai] Ps 119:25
[aj] 119:38 2Sm 7:25
[ak] 119:39 Ps 119:22
[al] 119:40 Ps 119:20
[am] 119:41 Ps 119:77
[an] Ps 119:58,76,116,170
[ao] 119:42 Ps 102:8; Pr 27:11
[ap] 119:43 Ps 119:49,74,81, 114,147
[aq] 119:44 Ps 119:33

[A] 119:28 Or *I weep*　[B] 119:32 Lit *you enlarge my heart*　[C] 119:33 Lit *way*　[D] 119:33 Or *will keep it as my reward*　[E] 119:37 Some Hb mss, Tg read *word*

119:11 By treasuring the principles of Scripture in our hearts, we train ourselves to love God's ways.
119:24 There is no better counsel for life than what we find in Scripture.

119:33-40 The psalmist desires a life of value, not one of **disgrace** (119:39). Devotion to the Word can provide such a life.

119:44-48 He vows to always **obey [God's] instruction** and declare it without shame. Do you?

a 119:45 Pr 4:12
b Ps 119:94,155
c 119:46 Mt 10:18; Ac 26:1,2
d 119:47 Ps 119:16,97,127,159
e 119:48 Ps 63:4
f Ps 119:15
g 119:50 Rm 15:4
h 119:51 Jb 23:11; Ps 44:18
i 119:53 Ezr 9:3; Neh 13:25; Ps 119:158
j Ps 89:30
k 119:55 Ps 63:6
l Ps 42:8; 92:2; Is 26:9; Ac 16:25
m 119:56 Ps 119:22,69,100
n 119:57 Ps 16:5; Lm 3:24
o 119:58 1Kg 13:6
p Ps 41:4; 56:1; 57:1
q 119:59 Lk 15:17
r 119:61 Jb 36:8; Ps 140:5
s Ps 119:83,141,153,176

t 119:62 Ps 119:55
u Ps 119:7
v 119:63 Ps 101:6
w 119:64 Ps 33:5
x Ps 119:12
y 119:66 Php 1:9-10
z 119:67 Ps 119:71,75; Jr 31:18-19; Heb 12:5-11
aa 119:68 Ps 100:5; 106:1; 107:1
ab Ps 125:4
ac 119:69 Jb 13:4; Ps 109:2
ad Ps 119:56
ae 119:70 Ps 17:10
af Ps 119:16
ag 119:71 Ps 119:67,75
ah 119:72 Ps 19:10; 119:127; Pr 8:10,11,19
ai 119:73 Jb 10:8; 31:15; Ps 100:3; 139:15-16
aj Ps 119:34
ak 119:74 Ps 34:2; 107:42
al Ps 119:43
am 119:75 Ps 119:138; Heb 12:10
an 119:77 Ps 119:41
ao Ps 119:16

45 I will walk freely in an open place[a]
because I study your precepts.[b]
46 I will speak of your decrees
before kings
and not be ashamed.[c]
47 I delight in your commands,
which I love.[d]
48 I will lift up my hands[e]
to your commands,
which I love,
and will meditate on your statutes.[f]

ז Zayin

49 Remember your word
to your servant;
you have given me hope through it.
50 This is my comfort in my affliction:[g]
Your promise has given me life.
51 The arrogant constantly ridicule me,
but I do not turn away
from your instruction.[h]
52 LORD, I remember your judgments
from long ago
and find comfort.
53 Rage seizes me[i] because of
the wicked
who reject your instruction.[j]
54 Your statutes are the theme of
my song
during my earthly life.[A]
55 LORD, I remember your name[k]
in the night,[l]
and I obey your instruction.
56 This is my practice:
I obey your precepts.[m]

ח Cheth

57 The LORD is my portion;[B,n]
I have promised to keep
your words.
58 I have sought your favor[o] with all
my heart;
be gracious to me[p] according to
your promise.
59 I thought about my ways[q]
and turned my steps back
to your decrees.
60 I hurried, not hesitating
to keep your commands.
61 Though the ropes of the wicked[r]
were wrapped around me,
I did not forget your instruction.[s]

62 I rise at midnight to thank you[t]
for your righteous judgments.[u]
63 I am a friend to all who fear you,[v]
to those who keep your precepts.
64 LORD, the earth is filled with
your faithful love;[w]
teach me your statutes.[x]

ט Teth

65 LORD, you have treated
your servant well,
just as you promised.
66 Teach me good judgment
and discernment,[y]
for I rely on your commands.
67 Before I was afflicted I went astray,[z]
but now I keep your word.
68 You are good,[aa] and you do
what is good;[ab]
teach me your statutes.
69 The arrogant have smeared me
with lies,[ac]
but I obey your precepts with all
my heart.[ad]
70 Their hearts are hard
and insensitive,[ae]
but I delight in your instruction.[af]
71 It was good for me to be afflicted[ag]
so that I could learn your statutes.
72 Instruction from your lips[ah] is better
for me
than thousands of gold
and silver pieces.

י Yod

73 Your hands made me
and formed me;[ai]
give me understanding
so that I can learn your commands.[aj]
74 Those who fear you will see me
and rejoice,[ak]
for I put my hope in your word.[al]
75 I know, LORD, that your judgments
are just
and that you have afflicted me
fairly.[am]
76 May your faithful love comfort me
as you promised your servant.
77 May your compassion
come to me[an]
so that I may live,
for your instruction is my delight.[ao]

[A] 119:54 Lit *song in the house of my sojourning*　　[B] 119:57 Lit *You are my portion*, LORD

119:49-50 Biblical **hope** is not mere wishful thinking (119:49). It is a confident expectation about the future based on the character of God and his promises.
119:60-61 The psalmist was surrounded by wickedness, as if **ropes** were **wrapped** around

him (119:61). Nevertheless, he was committed to keeping the Lord's **commands** (119:60). Obedience was a priority.
119:62 This man's gratefulness for Scripture was so profound that he woke **at midnight** to thank God for it!

119:71 It appears that previously the psalmist got off track spiritually (see 119:67), but the Word corrected him. This brings to mind Proverbs 3:12: "The Lord disciplines the one he loves, just as a father disciplines the son in whom he delights."

78 Let the arrogant be put to shame[a]
for slandering me with lies;
I will meditate on your precepts.
79 Let those who fear you,
those who know your decrees,
turn to me.
80 May my heart be blameless
regarding your statutes[b]
so that I will not be put to shame.

כ Kaph

81 I long for your salvation;[c]
I put my hope in your word.[d]
82 My eyes grow weary
looking for what
you have promised;[e]
I ask, "When will you
comfort me?"
83 Though I have become
like a wineskin dried by smoke,
I do not forget your statutes.
84 How many days must
your servant wait?
When will you execute judgment
on my persecutors?[f]
85 The arrogant have dug pits for me;[g]
they violate your instruction.
86 All your commands are true;
people persecute me with lies —
help me![h]
87 They almost ended my life on earth,
but I did not abandon your precepts.
88 Give me life in accordance with
your faithful love,
and I will obey the decree
you have spoken.

ל Lamed

89 LORD, your word is forever;[i]
it is firmly fixed in heaven.
90 Your faithfulness is
for all generations;[j]
you established the earth,
and it stands firm.[k]
91 Your judgments stand firm today,[l]
for all things are your servants.[m]
92 If your instruction had not been
my delight,
I would have died in my affliction.[n]
93 I will never forget your precepts,
for you have given me life
through them.[o]

94 I am yours; save me,[p]
for I have studied your precepts.[q]
95 The wicked hope to destroy me,[r]
but I contemplate your decrees.
96 I have seen a limit to all perfection,
but your command is without limit.

מ Mem

97 How I love your instruction![s]
It is my meditation all day long.[t]
98 Your commands make me wiser
than my enemies,[u]
for they are always with me.
99 I have more insight than
all my teachers
because your decrees are
my meditation.[v]
100 I understand more than the elders[w]
because I obey your precepts.[x]
101 I have kept my feet
from every evil path[y]
to follow your word.
102 I have not turned from your judgments,[z]
for you yourself have instructed me.
103 How sweet your word is[aa]
to my taste —
sweeter than honey in my mouth.
104 I gain understanding
from your precepts;[ab]
therefore I hate every false way.[ac]

נ Nun

105 Your word is a lamp for my feet[ad]
and a light on my path.
106 I have solemnly sworn[ae]
to keep your righteous judgments.
107 I am severely afflicted;
LORD, give me life according
to your word.[af]
108 LORD, please accept
my freewill offerings of praise,[ag]
and teach me your judgments.[ah]
109 My life is constantly in danger,[A]
yet I do not forget
your instruction.[ai]
110 The wicked have set a trap for me,[aj]
but I have not wandered
from your precepts.[ak]
111 I have your decrees
as a heritage forever;
indeed, they are the joy
of my heart.[al]

[a] 119:78 Jr 50:32
[b] 119:80 Ps 119:1
[c] 119:81 Ps 84:2
[d] Ps 119:43
[e] 119:82 Ps 69:3; 119:123; Is 38:14
[f] 119:84 Rv 6:10
[g] 119:85 Ps 35:7; 57:6; Jr 18:22
[h] 119:86 Ps 35:19; 109:26; 119:78
[i] 119:89 Ps 89:2; 119:160; Is 40:8; Mt 24:35; 1Pt 1:25
[j] 119:90 Ps 89:1-2
[k] Ps 148:6; Ec 1:4
[l] 119:91 Jr 31:35
[m] Ps 104:2-4
[n] 119:92 Ps 119:16,50
[o] 119:93 Ps 119:16,25
[p] 119:94 Ps 119:146
[q] Ps 119:45
[r] 119:95 Ps 40:14
[s] 119:97 Ps 119:47,127,163,165
[t] Ps 1:2; 119:15
[u] 119:98 Dt 4:6; Ps 119:130
[v] 119:99 Ps 119:15
[w] 119:100 Jb 32:7-9
[x] Ps 119:56
[y] 119:101 Pr 1:15
[z] 119:102 Dt 17:20; Jos 23:6; 1Kg 15:5
[aa] 119:103 Ps 19:10; Pr 8:11; 24:13-14
[ab] 119:104 Ps 119:130
[ac] Ps 119:128
[ad] 119:105 Pr 6:23
[ae] 119:106 Neh 10:29
[af] 119:107 Ps 119:25,50
[ag] 119:108 Hs 14:2; Heb 13:15
[ah] Ps 119:12
[ai] 119:109 Ps 119:16
[aj] 119:110 Ps 140:5; 141:9
[ak] Ps 119:10
[al] 119:111 Ps 119:14,162

[A] 119:109 Lit *in my hand*

119:78, 80 The psalmist trusts God to bring **shame** on **the arrogant** and, simultaneously, to keep him from **shame** through a **heart** that is **blameless.**
119:84 The psalmist wonders how long he must wait for deliverance.

119:89-91 Scripture will never change; it remains relevant to all people in every culture throughout history.
119:97-100 By devouring God's commands, the psalmist has become **wiser** (i.e., he had more insight for right living and decision-

making) than his **enemies, teachers,** and **elders** (119:98-100).
119:105 The word is a source of light to guide the believer through life. It's **a lamp** directing our **feet** in a dark world.

a 119:112 Ps 119:33,36
b 119:113 1Kg 18:21; Jms 1:8; 4:8
c Ps 119:47
d 119:114 Gn 15:1; Dt 33:29; Ps 3:3; 28:7; 115:9-11; 144:2; Pr 2:7
e Ps 119:74
f 119:115 Ps 6:8; 139:19; Mt 4:10
g Ps 119:22
h 119:116 Ps 54:4
i Ps 25:20; 31:1; Rm 9:33; Php 1:20
j 119:117 Pr 29:25
k Ps 119:15
l 119:118 Ps 119:10,21
m 119:119 Is 1:25; Ezk 22:18-19
n Ps 119:47
o 119:120 Jb 4:14; Hab 3:16
p 119:121 Jb 29:14
q 119:122 Ps 119:134
r 119:123 Ps 119:82
s 119:124 Ps 51:1; 109:26; 119:88,149,159
t 119:125 Ps 116:16
u Ps 119:27
v 119:126 Jr 18:23
w 119:127 Ps 9:10; 119:47
x 119:128 Ps 19:8
y Ps 119:104
z 119:129 Ps 119:18
aa Ps 119:22
ab 119:130 Pr 6:23
ac Ps 19:7
ad 119:131 Ps 42:1
ae 119:132 Ps 25:16
af 119:133 Ps 17:5
ag Ps 19:13; Rm 6:12
ah 119:134 Ps 142:6; Lk 1:74
ai 119:135 Nm 6:25; Ps 31:16; 80:3,7,19
aj Ps 119:12
ak 119:136 Jr 9:1; 14:17; Lm 3:48
al 119:137 Neh 9:33; Ps 129:4; 145:17; Lm 1:18
am 119:138 Ps 19:7-9; 119:86,90,144,172
an 119:139 Ps 69:9; Jn 2:17
ao 119:140 Ps 12:6; 19:9
ap Ps 119:47
aq 119:141 Ps 22:6
ar Ps 119:61
as 119:142 Ps 119:151,160
at 119:143 Ps 119:24
au 119:144 Ps 19:9

112 I am resolved to obey your statutes
to the very end.[A,a]

ס Samek

113 I hate those who are
double-minded,[b]
but I love your instruction.[c]
114 You are my shelter and my shield;[d]
I put my hope in your word.[e]
115 Depart from me,[f] you evil ones,
so that I may obey
my God's commands.[g]
116 Sustain me as you promised,[h]
and I will live;
do not let me be ashamed
of my hope.[i]
117 Sustain me so that I can be safe[j]
and always be concerned about
your statutes.[k]
118 You reject all who stray
from your statutes,[l]
for their deceit is a lie.
119 You remove all the wicked on earth
as if they were[B] dross from metal;[m]
therefore, I love your decrees.[n]
120 I tremble[c] in awe of you;[o]
I fear your judgments.

ע Ayin

121 I have done what is just and right;[p]
do not leave me to my oppressors.
122 Guarantee your servant's
well-being;[q]
do not let the arrogant
oppress me.
123 My eyes grow weary[r] looking for
your salvation
and for your righteous promise.
124 Deal with your servant based on
your faithful love;[s]
teach me your statutes.
125 I am your servant;[t]
give me understanding[u]
so that I may know your decrees.
126 It is time for the LORD to act,[v]
for they have violated
your instruction.
127 Since I love your commands[w]
more than gold,
even the purest gold,

128 I carefully follow all your precepts[x]
and hate every false way.[y]

פ Pe

129 Your decrees are wondrous;[z]
therefore I obey them.[aa]
130 The revelation of your words[ab]
brings light
and gives understanding
to the inexperienced.[ac]
131 I open my mouth and pant[ad]
because I long for your commands.
132 Turn to me and be gracious to me,[ae]
as is your practice toward those
who love your name.
133 Make my steps steady
through your promise;[af]
don't let any sin dominate me.[ag]
134 Redeem me
from human oppression,[ah]
and I will keep your precepts.
135 Make your face shine on
your servant,[ai]
and teach me your statutes.[aj]
136 My eyes pour out streams of tears[ak]
because people do not follow
your instruction.

צ Tsade

137 You are righteous, LORD,[al]
and your judgments are just.
138 The decrees you issue are righteous
and altogether trustworthy.[am]
139 My anger overwhelms me
because my foes forget
your words.[an]
140 Your word is completely pure,[ao]
and your servant loves it.[ap]
141 I am insignificant and despised,[aq]
but I do not forget your precepts.[ar]
142 Your righteousness is
an everlasting righteousness,
and your instruction is true.[as]
143 Trouble and distress
have overtaken me,
but your commands are
my delight.[at]
144 Your decrees are righteous forever.[au]
Give me understanding,
and I will live.

[A] 119:112 Or *statutes; the reward is eternal*   [B] 119:119 Some Hb mss, DSS, LXX, Aq, Sym, Jer read *All the wicked of the earth you count as*   [C] 119:120 Lit *My flesh shudders*

119:112 The psalmist was **resolved to obey [the Lord's] statutes** so that he could live without stumbling.

119:113-120 The psalmist's devotion to Scripture is not half-hearted; rather, his entire **hope** is in the **word** (119:114). He is aware of what happens to those who **stray from [God's] statutes**: God rejects them and

removes them from the **earth** (119:118-119). Therefore, with deep reverence for the Lord's word, the psalmist confesses, **I tremble in awe of you** (119:120).

119:127 Indeed, nothing is of greater worth than the word.

119:136 This man loves the **instruction** of the Lord so much that he sobbed when others

disobeyed it, a fact that should prompt us to ask how we respond to the world's rejection of God's Word.

119:137 The Lord is **righteous**; he is the standard of what is right.

119:142 Though the standards of this sinful world are constantly in flux, God's **righteousness is . . . everlasting.**

ק Qoph

145 I call with all my heart;
    answer me, LORD.
    I will obey your statutes.[a]

146 I call to you; save me,
    and I will keep your decrees.[b]

147 I rise before dawn and cry out
        for help;[c]
    I put my hope in your word.

148 I am awake through each watch
        of the night
    to meditate on your promise.[d]

149 In keeping with your faithful love,
        hear my voice.
    LORD, give me life in keeping with
        your justice.[e]

150 Those who pursue evil plans[A,f]
        come near;
    they are far from your instruction.

151 You are near, LORD,[g]
    and all your commands are true.[h]

152 Long ago I learned from
        your decrees
    that you have established
        them forever.[i]

ר Resh

153 Consider my affliction
        and rescue me,[j]
    for I have not forgotten
        your instruction.[k]

154 Champion my cause
        and redeem me;[l]
    give me life as you promised.

155 Salvation is far from the wicked
    because they do not study
        your statutes.[m]

156 Your compassions are many, LORD;[n]
    give me life according to
        your judgments.

157 My persecutors and foes are many.[o]
    I have not turned
        from your decrees.[p]

158 I have seen the disloyal[q]
        and feel disgust[r]
    because they do not keep your word.

159 Consider how I love your precepts;
    LORD, give me life according to
        your faithful love.[s]

160 The entirety of your word is truth,
    each of your righteous judgments
        endures forever.[t]

שׂ Sin / שׁ Shin

161 Princes have persecuted me
        without cause,
    but my heart fears only your word.[u]

162 I rejoice over your promise[v]
    like one who finds vast treasure.

163 I hate and abhor falsehood,[w]
    but I love your instruction.[x]

164 I praise you seven times a day
    for your righteous judgments.[y]

165 Abundant peace belongs to those[z]
    who love your instruction;
    nothing makes them stumble.[aa]

166 LORD, I hope for your salvation[ab]
    and carry out your commands.

167 I obey your decrees
    and love them greatly.[ac]

168 I obey your precepts and decrees,
    for all my ways are before you.[ad]

ת Taw

169 Let my cry reach you, LORD;[ae]
    give me understanding according to
        your word.[af]

170 Let my plea reach you;[ag]
    rescue me according to
        your promise.[ah]

171 My lips pour out praise,[ai]
    for you teach me your statutes.[aj]

172 My tongue sings about your promise,[ak]
    for all your commands are righteous.[al]

173 May your hand be ready
        to help me,[am]
    for I have chosen your precepts.[an]

174 I long for your salvation, LORD,
    and your instruction is my delight.[ao]

175 Let me live, and I will praise you;[ap]
    may your judgments help me.

176 I wander like a lost sheep;[aq]
    seek your servant,[ar]
    for I do not forget your commands.[as]

A CRY FOR TRUTH AND PEACE

120
A song of ascents.
    In my distress I called to the LORD,
    and he answered me.[at]

2 "LORD, rescue me from lying lips
    and a deceitful tongue."[au]

3 What will he give you,
    and what will he do to you,
    you deceitful tongue?[av]

[a] 119:145 Ps 119:10,55
[b] 119:146 Ps 3:7
[c] 119:147 Ps 5:3
[d] 119:148 Ps 119:15
[e] 119:149 Ps 119:25,124
[f] 119:150 Ps 6:17,18; 12:20; 14:22; 24:8
[g] 119:151 Ps 34:18; 145:18; Is 50:8
[h] Ps 119:142
[i] 119:152 Ps 119:89; Lk 21:33
[j] 119:153 Ps 119:50; Lm 5:1
[k] Ps 119:16; Hs 4:6
[l] 119:154 1Sm 24:15; Ps 35:1; Mc 7:9
[m] 119:155 Ps 119:45,94
[n] 119:156 2Sm 24:14
[o] 119:157 Ps 7:1
[p] Ps 119:51
[q] 119:158 Pr 14:14
[r] Ps 139:21
[s] 119:159 Ps 119:25,47
[t] 119:160 Ps 119:89,142,152

[u] 119:161 Ps 119:23,120
[v] 119:162 Ps 119:14,111
[w] 119:163 Ps 119:104,128; Pr 13:5
[x] Ps 119:47
[y] 119:164 Ps 119:7,160
[z] 119:165 Pr 3:1-2; Is 26:3; 32:17
[aa] Pr 3:23; Is 63:13
[ab] 119:166 Gn 49:18; Ps 119:81,174
[ac] 119:167 Ps 119:47,129
[ad] 119:168 Ps 139:3; Pr 5:21
[ae] 119:169 Ps 18:6; 102:1; 140:6
[af] Ps 119:144
[ag] 119:170 Ps 28:2; 130:2; 143:1
[ah] Ps 22:20; 59:1
[ai] 119:171 Ps 51:15; 63:3
[aj] Ps 119:12
[ak] 119:172 Ps 51:14
[al] Ps 119:138
[am] 119:173 Ps 37:24; 73:23
[an] Jos 24:22
[ao] 119:174 Ps 119:16,24,166
[ap] 119:175 Ps 119:25
[aq] 119:176 Is 53:6; Jr 50:6
[ar] Mt 18:12; Lk 15:4
[as] Ps 119:16
[at] 120:1 Ps 18:6; Jnh 2:2
[au] 120:2 Pr 12:22
[av] 120:3 Zph 3:13

[A] 119:150 Some Hb mss, LXX, Sym, Jer read *who maliciously persecute me*

119:153-160 Why such confidence that God would deliver him from his troubles? He knows that **the wicked** who reject God's **statutes** do not experience deliverance because **salvation is far from** them (119:155). Deliverance comes to those who hope in God and in his Word.

119:161-168 There is great joy in loving and keeping the Word of God. Those who do so experience **abundant peace** and **nothing makes them stumble** (119:165). **119:171-172** What does the follower of God do when he needs help in the midst of

trouble? His **lips pour out praise** and his **tongue sings**.
119:175 What will the psalmist do if God lets him **live**? **Praise** him more! May it be so with us.

[a] 120:4 Pr 25:18,22
[b] 120:5 Ezk 27:13
[c] Sg 1:5; Ezk 27:21
[d] 120:6 Ps 35:20
[e] 120:7 Ps 109:4
[f] 121:1 Ps 87:1; 123:1
[g] 121:2 Ps 115:15; 124:8
[h] 121:3 Ps 41:2; 66:9; 127:1
[i] 121:4 Dt 33:29
[j] 121:5 Ps 16:8; 91:1,4
[k] 121:6 Is 49:10; Rv 7:16
[l] 121:7 Ps 41:2; 91:10-12
[m] 121:8 Dt 28:6
[n] 122:1 Is 2:3; Mc 4:2; Zch 8:21
[o] 122:2 Ps 9:14; Jr 7:2

[p] 122:3 Neh 4:6; Ps 147:2
[q] 122:4 Is 2:3; Mc 4:2
[r] 1Ch 22:13
[s] 122:5 Dt 17:8; 2Ch 19:8
[t] 122:6 Ps 51:18; Jr 29:7
[u] 122:7 Ps 48:3
[v] 122:8 1Sm 25:6; Ps 85:8
[w] 122:9 Neh 2:10; Est 10:3
[x] 123:1 Ps 2:4; 121:1; 141:8
[y] 123:2 Ps 25:15
[z] 123:3 Neh 4:4; Ps 4:1; 119:22
[aa] 123:4 Is 32:9,11; Am 6:1
[ab] 124:1-2 Ps 94:17
[ac] 124:2 Ps 129:1

4 A warrior's sharp arrows
with burning charcoal![A],[a]

5 What misery that I have stayed
in Meshech,[B],[b]
that I have lived among the tents
of Kedar![C],[c]

6 I have dwelt too long
with those who hate peace.[d]

7 I am for peace; but when I speak,
they are for war.[e]

THE LORD OUR PROTECTOR

121
A song of ascents.
I lift my eyes
toward the mountains.
Where will my help come from?[f]

2 My help comes from the LORD,
the Maker of heaven and earth.[g]

3 He will not allow your foot to slip;
your Protector will not slumber.[h]

4 Indeed, the Protector of Israel
does not slumber or sleep.[i]

5 The LORD protects you;
the LORD is a shelter right
by your side.[D],[j]

6 The sun will not strike you by day
or the moon by night.[k]

7 The LORD will protect you
from all harm;
he will protect your life.[l]

8 The LORD will protect your coming
and going
both now and forever.[m]

A PRAYER FOR JERUSALEM

122
A song of ascents. Of David.
I rejoiced with those who said
to me,
"Let us go to the house of the LORD."[n]

2 Our feet were standing
within your gates, Jerusalem[o] —

3 Jerusalem, built as a city should be,
solidly united,[p]

4 where the tribes, the LORD's tribes,
go up
to give thanks to the name of the LORD.[q]
(This is an ordinance for Israel.[r])

5 There, thrones for judgment are placed,
thrones of the house of David.[s]

6 Pray for the well-being[E] of Jerusalem:
"May those who love you be secure;[t]

7 may there be peace within your walls,
security within your fortresses."[u]

8 Because of my brothers and friends,
I will say, "May peace be in you."[F],[v]

9 Because of the house of the LORD
our God,
I will pursue your prosperity.[w]

LOOKING FOR GOD'S FAVOR

123
A song of ascents.
I lift my eyes to you,
the one enthroned in heaven.[x]

2 Like a servant's eyes
on his master's hand,
like a servant girl's eyes
on her mistress's hand,
so our eyes are on the LORD our God
until he shows us favor.[y]

3 Show us favor, LORD, show us favor,
for we've had more than enough
contempt.[z]

4 We've had more than enough
scorn from the arrogant
and contempt from the proud.[aa]

THE LORD IS ON OUR SIDE

124
A song of ascents. Of David.
If the LORD had not been
on our side —
let Israel say —

2 If the LORD had not been on our side[ab]
when people attacked us,[ac]

3 then they would have swallowed us alive

[A] 120:4 Lit *with coals of the broom bush*   [B] 120:5 = a people far to the north of Palestine   [C] 120:5 = a nomadic people of the desert to the southeast
[D] 121:5 Lit *is your shelter at your right hand*   [E] 122:6 Or *peace*   [F] 122:8 = Jerusalem

120:5-7 **Meshech** is a reference to a people who lived far to the north of Israel, while **Kedar** referred to a people who lived to the southeast (120:5). Likely, then, this was his poetic way of saying that he was surrounded by those who were not God's people.
121:1-2 The psalmist considers **the mountains** of Israel, mighty towers of rock (121:1). But he knows the greatest protection doesn't come from the mountains—but from the One who created them.
121:3 The Lord is the **Protector** of his people. There is no safer place in the universe than being where God wants you to be.

121:5-8 **The LORD is a shelter** (121:5). He protects from all manner of evil, physical and spiritual. Submit yourself to God's kingdom, then, and receive the blessings of his covenental covering.
122:3-5 God had given the twelve **tribes** of **Israel** an **ordinance** to obey. They were to appear before him in Jerusalem at the annual festivals that he had established for them so that they might **give** him **thanks** (122:4; see Deut 16:16-17). Not only was Jerusalem the location of the Lord's tabernacle, it was the city of the king, the location of the **thrones of the house of David**

(122:5)—from whose family the Messiah would come.
122:6-8 The prayer in view here will ultimately be answered under the Messiah's kingdom rule.
123:3 Though their enemies had shown them **contempt**, they were confident that God could reverse their circumstances. Thus, the psalmist prays repeatedly, **Show us favor**. If the Lord grants you favor, no one can stand against you.
124:1-8 To encourage the people of God to trust in his faithfulness in their present circumstances, David recalls God's deliverance in the past. If not for divine intervention at

in their burning anger against us.[a]

4 Then the water would have
   engulfed us;
the torrent would have swept over us;

5 the raging water would have swept
   over us.[b]

6 Blessed be the LORD,
who has not let us be ripped apart
   by their teeth.[c]

7 We have escaped like a bird
   from the hunter's net;
the net is torn, and we have escaped.[d]

8 Our help is in the name of the LORD,
the Maker of heaven and earth.[e]

ISRAEL'S STABILITY

125

A song of ascents.

Those who trust in the LORD are
   like Mount Zion.
It cannot be shaken;
   it remains forever.[f]

2 The mountains surround Jerusalem
and the LORD surrounds his people,
both now and forever.[g]

3 The scepter of the wicked
   will not remain
over the land allotted to the righteous,
so that the righteous will not apply
   their hands to injustice.[h]

4 Do what is good, LORD, to the good,
to those whose hearts are upright.[i]

5 But as for those who turn aside
   to crooked ways,
the LORD will banish them
   with the evildoers.[j]

Peace be with Israel.[k]

ZION'S RESTORATION

126

A song of ascents.

When the LORD restored
   the fortunes of Zion,[A]
we were like those who dream.[l]

2 Our mouths were filled
   with laughter then,[m]
and our tongues with shouts of joy.[n]
Then they said among the nations,
"The LORD has done great things
   for them."[o]

3 The LORD had done great things for us;
we were joyful.[p]

4 Restore our fortunes,[B] LORD,
like watercourses in the Negev.[q]

> ❧ **KINGDOM LIVING** ❧
> COMMUNITY
> *Our Shifting Culture*

A while ago, a crack appeared in one of our bedroom walls. Knowing that repairing it was out of my wheelhouse, I called in a professional who quickly replaced the plaster around the crack and repainted the wall. We thought all was well. But we were wrong. Not long after that, the crack reappeared. And this time, the crack brought along his posse. Before we knew it, a multitude of cracks lined the wall, looking like a city subway map.

I called the professional back and kindly let him know that he didn't quite fix our wall. He offered to fill and repaint again free of charge, and I thought our problem was solved. Wrong again. A couple months later, the cracks reappeared, bringing their aunts, uncles, cousins, nieces, and nephews too.

This time I decided to call a different professional because I was hopeful for a different outcome. The man came to our home, assessed the situation, and then proceeded to tell me that the problem I was facing was not a surface issue. Unfortunately, the cracks in the wall were due to a much deeper problem. We were experiencing a shifting foundation. He told us that until we stabilized it, we would forever be repairing cracks.

What a perfect metaphor for the condition of American culture today. Until we stabilize our nation's spiritual foundation, no number of programs, government grants, or elections will be able to repair the cracks in our cultural walls. We cannot expect to fix the White House if we can't even fix the church house. We, as the body of Christ, must come together across racial, economic, and denominational lines to repair our foundation so we can go and be the salt and light Jesus Christ created us to be in the culture.

FOR THE NEXT COMMUNITY
KINGDOM LIVING LESSON SEE PAGE 882.

---

[a] 124:3 Ps 35:25; 56:1; Pr 1:12
[b] 124:4-5 Jb 22:11; Ps 32:6; 69:2
[c] 124:6 Ps 27:2; Pr 30:14
[d] 124:7 Ps 91:3
[e] 124:8 Ps 115:15; 121:2
[f] 125:1 Ps 46:5
[g] 125:2 Zch 2:5
[h] 125:3 Ps 89:22; Is 14:5
[i] 125:4 Ps 7:10; 119:68
[j] 125:5 Ps 92:7,9; 94:4
[k] 125:4-5 Ps 128:5-6
[l] 126:1 Ps 85:1; Jr 29:14
[m] 126:2 Jb 8:21
[n] Ps 51:14
[o] Ps 71:19

[p] 126:3 Is 25:9
[q] 126:4 Is 35:6; 43:19

[A] 126:1 Or *LORD returned those of Zion who had been captives*   [B] 126:4 Or *Return our captives*

---

the Red Sea, Israel would have been slaughtered by Pharaoh's army and drowned in the **raging water** (124:2-5). But God had enabled his people to escape from their captors **like a bird** from a trapper's snare (124:7).

Take note of times when God delivers you from adversity. You'll need to recall these times

of blessing to give you confidence in God's faithfulness and power for future troubles.

125:3 The ultimate display of God's protection will appear when the Messiah comes to reign as King from Jerusalem in his millennial kingdom. In that day, **the scepter of the wicked will not remain**.

126:1-2 The psalmist recalls the joy that God's people experienced when he **restored [their] fortunes** upon their return after exile (126:1). 126:4-6 Thinking of **watercourses in the Negev**, which were streams that overflowed south of Israel during the rainy season, the psalmist longs for an overflow of God's blessing so that people

a 126:5 Jr 31:9
b 126:6 Is 35:10; 51:11
c 127:1 Ps 78:69
d Ps 121:4
e 127:2 Ps 3:5; 4:8; Pr 3:24

❧ Questions & Answers ❧

Q Why do you consider the family to be the backbone of a civil society? What are some of the key threats to the family that we face in our culture?

A The family is critical because it is the first institution established by God. He gave to the family the responsibility to rule over creation. So the family is not everything, but it's the foundation meant to serve as the basis of replicating God's kingdom program in history. For this reason, the attack on the family is great. Satan waited until Adam got married before he let all hell break loose because he was targeting God's program, not merely an individual.

We live in a day when "family" has been redefined. Many people are not operating within their divinely prescribed roles, and the gifts and callings of family members are not being maximized. The culture is setting priorities, and children are being taught more by the culture than by their parents. This upside-down redefinition and dumbing down of the family has put the whole culture in crisis. You can't have a strong nation when it is dominated by weak families.

FOR THE NEXT Q&A, SEE PAGE 693.

5 Those who sow in tears
  will reap with shouts of joy.*a*
6 Though one goes along weeping,
  carrying the bag of seed,
  he will surely come back
    with shouts of joy,
  carrying his sheaves.*b*

THE BLESSING OF THE LORD

127

A song of ascents. Of Solomon.

Unless the LORD builds a house,
its builders labor over it in vain;*c*
unless the LORD watches over a city,
the watchman stays alert in vain.*d*

2 In vain you get up early
    and stay up late,
  working hard to have enough food—
  yes, he gives sleep to the one he loves.*A,e*

❧ KINGDOM LIVING ❧
PERSONAL
All of Life According to the Kingdom Agenda

My favorite chapter in the Bible is Psalm 128. In it are all of the elements of living according to the kingdom agenda. It begins with the personal life. So if your personal life is out of balance, you can assume it will affect the rest of life. But if your personal life is in alignment with God's kingdom plan, you can look for his blessing and favor in the other spheres too.

The progression of this blessing is laid out beautifully in the chapter. We read about the blessing that comes from personal responsibility or self-government: "How happy [or "blessed"] is everyone who fears the LORD, who walks in his ways! You will surely eat what your hands have worked for. You will be happy, and it will go well for you" (Ps 128:1-2).

Then the blessing moves to the family: "Your wife will be like a fruitful vine within your house, your children, like young olive trees around your table" (128:3). When your family lives according to the principles of God's Word and his perspective, spouses and children flourish.

Next in line is the church: "May the LORD bless you from Zion" (128:5). Zion was the place of worship where the temple was located. The church—the spiritual community—is blessed when God's people operate the way they should, since it is the New Testament expression of Zion (see Heb 12:22-24).

What happens when the individual, the family, and the church get it right? The government of the nation experiences blessing "so that you will see the prosperity of Jerusalem all the days of your life and will see your children's children!" (Ps 128:5-6).

When people govern themselves under God's kingdom rule, there will be peace and blessing in personal lives, the family, the church, and the community. Not only that, but there will also be a godly legacy and inheritance to pass on to future generations.

FOR THE NEXT PERSONAL
KINGDOM LIVING LESSON SEE PAGE 707.

A 127:2 Or *yes, he gives such things to his loved ones while they sleep*

---

might experience restoration and have their sorrow turned to **joy** (126:4-5). Don't become complacent in your expectations. God is "able to do above and beyond all that we ask or think" (Eph 3:20). He can turn our sorrow into blessing.

127:1-2 Even seeking to build a home and a family apart from God is a waste, because no matter how diligently you apply yourself, your human efforts are limited without God to back them. What we need in our households is his involvement and blessing—combined with our faithful labor. No matter how many books on marriage and parenting you read, or how much advice you receive, all falls short unless your foundation is built on God.

[a] 127:3 Dt 7:13; Ps 113:9
[b] 127:4 Ps 120:4
[c] 127:5 Ps 128:2-3
[d] Jl 2:26-27
[e] 128:1 Ps 112:1; 119:1,3

[f] 128:2 Is 3:10
[g] Ec 8:12
[h] 128:3 Ps 52:8; Ezk 19:10
[i] 128:4 Ps 115:13
[j] 128:5 Ps 20:2; 134:3; 135:21
[k] 128:6 Ps 125:5; Pr 17:6

Questions & Answers

Q Christian parents, and particularly fathers, are tasked with the responsibility of raising their children to know the Lord and be educated in the Bible. What advice would you give to fathers to help them take up this responsibility and pass on their faith to their children?

A The simplest way for fathers to lead their families spiritually involves what happens around the table. Psalm 128:3 says that "your children" will be like "young olive trees around your table." This is because the table is not just for eating meals; it's also the place for leading spiritually—through praying for your children, blessing them, guiding them in devotions, correcting them, teaching them life principles, and finding out whether they are fulfilling their daily responsibilities at home and school. Spend as many hours as you can at the family table with your children, using those times as opportunities to make spiritual impact.

FOR THE NEXT Q&A, SEE PAGE 702.

APPLICATION QUESTIONS

READ PSALM 128:1-6

- How has your family contributed to God's kingdom agenda in your neighborhood or community?
- How has your family contributed to God's kingdom agenda as part of your local church?
- How do the members of your family contribute to one another's spiritual growth and development?
- How have you intentionally demonstrated love and respect for your spouse this week?
- To what degree are you able to accept advice and correction from your spouse? Explain.
- What boundaries or guidelines have you and your spouse determined in order to align your family with God's kingdom agenda?
- Do you embrace or resist God's desired alignment for your family?
- What steps can you take to further support your spouse's role and responsibilities in your home?

3 Sons are indeed a heritage
    from the LORD,
  offspring, a reward.[a]
4 Like arrows in the hand of a warrior
  are the sons born in one's youth.[b]
5 Happy is the man who has filled
    his quiver with them.[c]
  They will never be put to shame
  when they speak with their enemies
    at the city gate.[d]

BLESSINGS FOR THOSE WHO FEAR GOD

128 *A song of ascents.*
How happy is everyone
  who fears the LORD,
  who walks in his ways![e]

2 You will surely eat
  what your hands have worked for.[f]
  You will be happy,
  and it will go well for you.[g]
3 Your wife will be like a fruitful vine
  within your house,
  your children, like young olive trees
  around your table.[h]
4 In this very way
  the man who fears the LORD
  will be blessed.[i]

5 May the LORD bless you
    from Zion,
  so that you will see the prosperity
    of Jerusalem
  all the days of your life[j]
6 and will see your children's
    children!

  Peace be with Israel.[k]

127:3-4 Children are to be valued as a gift from the Lord and, thus, receive care and training. Indeed, they are **like arrows** (127:4). But if they are to hit their targets—that is, to fulfill their kingdom purposes—parents must shape them and aim them correctly. Boys and girls must be raised to know the Lord, gaining experiential knowledge of God through watching their parents live in dependence on him.

128:1-2 The first covenantal sphere through which God works is the *individual*. God's goal is that every person learns to take him seriously and to govern himself or herself under divine rule. We must be willing to embrace commitment and accountability. The Lord will bless those who do so in their fortune (**you will surely eat what your hands have worked for**), their feelings (**you will be happy**), and their future (**it will go well for you**) (128:2).

128:3-4 The next sphere is the *family*, which God created to be the foundation of civilization. Societal breakdown in the United States doesn't begin with the White House; it begins in *your* house! Since God designed men to be godly leaders in their homes, he addresses them. To **the man who fears the LORD** (128:4), he says, **Your wife will be like a fruitful vine . . . your children, like young olive trees around your table** (128:3).

When a husband takes God seriously, becomes a servant leader in his home, and loves his wife sacrificially as Christ loved the church (see Eph 5:25), he encourages his wife to be the fruitful helper God wants her to be (see Gen 2:20-23). Furthermore, such a man is diligent to gather his children around the table to teach them wisdom, a habit that will result in productive citizens.

128:5-6 The third sphere through which God accomplishes his kingdom purposes is the *church*. The name **Zion** (128:5) was used in the Old Testament to describe either the city of Jerusalem or the holy temple within it. But in the New Testament, the church is the temple

a 129:1-2 Jr 1:19; 20:11
b 129:3 Mc 3:12
c 129:4 Ps 2:3
d 129:5 Ps 35:4; 70:3; 71:13
e 129:6 2Kg 19:26; Is 37:27
f 129:7 Ps 79:12
g 129:8 Ru 2:4; Ps 118:26
i 130:1 Ps 69:2; Lm 3:55
j 130:2 2Ch 6:40; Ps 28:6;
140:6
j 130:3 Ps 76:7; Mal 3:2;
Rv 6:17

k 130:4 1Kg 8:39-40; Ps
86:5; Jr 33:8-9
l 130:5 Ps 33:20; 119:74,81
m 130:6 Ps 63:6; 119:147
n 130:7 Ps 131:3
o Ps 111:9
p 130:8 Lk 1:68; Ti 2:14
q 131:1 Ps 101:5; Rm 12:16
r Jb 42:3; Ps 139:6
s 131:2 Mt 18:3; 1Co 14:20
t 131:3 Ps 130:7
u 132:1 2Sm 16:12

PROTECTION OF THE OPPRESSED

129 *A song of ascents.*

Since my youth they have often
attacked me —
let Israel say —
2 Since my youth they have often
attacked me,
but they have not prevailed
against me.*a*
3 Plowmen plowed over my back;
they made their furrows long.*b*
4 The LORD is righteous;
he has cut the ropes of the wicked.*c*

5 Let all who hate Zion
be driven back in disgrace.*d*
6 Let them be like grass
on the rooftops,
which withers before it grows up*A,e*
7 and can't even fill the hands
of the reaper
or the arms of the one
who binds sheaves.*f*
8 Then none who pass by will say,
"May the LORD's blessing be on you.
We bless you in the name of the LORD."*g*

AWAITING REDEMPTION

130 *A song of ascents.*

Out of the depths I call
to you, LORD!*h*
2 Lord, listen to my voice;
let your ears be attentive
to my cry for help.*i*

3 LORD, if you kept an account
of iniquities,
Lord, who could stand?*j*

4 But with you there is forgiveness,
so that you may be revered.*k*
5 I wait for the LORD; I wait
and put my hope in his word.*l*
6 I wait for the LORD
more than watchmen
for the morning —
more than watchmen for the morning.*m*

7 Israel, put your hope in the LORD.*n*
For there is faithful love
with the LORD,
and with him is redemption
in abundance.*o*
8 And he will redeem Israel
from all its iniquities.*p*

A CHILDLIKE SPIRIT

131 *A song of ascents. Of David.*

LORD, my heart is not proud;
my eyes are not haughty.*q*
I do not get involved with things
too great or too wondrous for me.*r*
2 Instead, I have calmed
and quieted my soul
like a weaned child with its mother;
my soul is like a weaned child.*s*

3 Israel, put your hope in the LORD,
both now and forever.*t*

DAVID AND ZION CHOSEN

132 *A song of ascents.*

LORD, remember David
and all the hardships he endured,*u*
2 and how he swore an oath
to the LORD,

A 129:6 Or *it can be pulled out*

of God (see 2 Cor 6:16; Eph 2:21), and Christians are said to come to worship at "Mount Zion" (Heb 12:22). Thus, Zion refers to the church, God's people.

If you've been born again by placing faith in Jesus, you're not an only child but part of a family that calls God "our Father" (Matt 6:9). Thus, in the New Testament, taking an active part in a local church is an expected part of the Christian experience. The church is like an embassy operating with God's kingdom authority in a foreign land. It is where the rules of eternity operate at a location in history. We gather together to hear from heaven so that we may live out heaven's viewpoint in the world.

The final sphere is *society*. The psalmist concludes with a desire to see **prosperity [in] Jerusalem** and **peace [in] Israel** (Ps 128:5-6). He desires well-being for the capital and country where God's people dwelled. Frequently, we expect our own country to be made better from the top down though politics, but God wants to see societies trans-

formed from the bottom up. When God's kingdom agenda is a priority in individuals who are committed to families that are committed to churches that are committed to making a difference in their communities, society is transformed for the better.

129:1-4 The psalmist invites God's people to testify to his mighty deliverance. From the beginning of the nation (Israel's **youth**), they were oppressed, but their enemies had **not prevailed against** them (129:2). They had suffered greatly, as if someone had **plowed over** their backs (129:3). Yet because **the LORD is righteous**, he brings justice to his people and thwarts the intentions of **the wicked** (129:4).

129:5 The name **Zion** is frequently used in the Old Testament to speak of the city of Jerusalem or God's holy temple within it.

130:3 The psalmist realizes his desperate situation as his sin is juxtaposed with God's holiness: **If you kept an account of iniquities, Lord who could stand?** When our sin is measured against God's righteousness, we fall

short of God's glory (Rom 3:23) and deserve death (Rom 6:23).

130:4 But—praise God—that's not where it ends, because **with [God] there is forgiveness.** The Lord made forgiveness possible through the atoning sacrifices he required of Israel. But ultimately these sacrifices are fulfilled in Jesus Christ. By faith in his death on the cross, "we have redemption, the forgiveness of sins" (Col 1:14). God extends such grace not so that it will lead to indulgence but **so that [he] may be revered** and taken seriously.

131:1 David understands who he is in light of who God is. Knowing that God alone is exalted and that God hates pride (even in a human king), David rejects a desire to be **proud** or **haughty.**

131:3 David encourages Israel to **hope in the LORD** with the same confidence that he had. Our visible trust, demonstrated in our submission to God's will, should encourage others to do likewise and find rest in him.

making a vow to the Mighty One
of Jacob:[a]

3 "I will not enter my house
or get into my bed,
4 I will not allow my eyes to sleep
or my eyelids to slumber[b]
5 until I find a place for the LORD,
a dwelling for the Mighty One
of Jacob."[c]

6 We heard of the ark in Ephrathah;[A,d]
we found it in the fields of Jaar.[B,e]
7 Let us go to his dwelling place;
let us worship at his footstool.[f]
8 Rise up, LORD, come to
your resting place,
you and your powerful ark.[g]
9 May your priests be clothed
with righteousness,
and may your faithful people shout
for joy.[h]
10 For the sake of your servant David,
do not reject your anointed one.[C,i]

11 The LORD swore an oath to David,
a promise he will not abandon:
"I will set one of your offspring[D]
on your throne.[j]
12 If your sons keep my covenant
and my decrees
that I will teach them,
their sons will also sit on
your throne forever."[k]

13 For the LORD has chosen Zion;
he has desired it for his home:[l]
14 "This is my resting place forever;
I will make my home here
because I have desired it.[m]
15 I will abundantly bless its food;
I will satisfy its needy with bread.[n]
16 I will clothe its priests
with salvation,
and its faithful people will shout
for joy.[o]

17 There I will make a horn grow
for David;[p]
I have prepared a lamp for
my anointed one.[q]
18 I will clothe his enemies
with shame,[r]
but the crown he wears[E]
will be glorious."[s]

LIVING IN HARMONY

133

A song of ascents. Of David.
How good and pleasant it is
when brothers live together
in harmony![t]
2 It is like fine oil on the head,
running down on the beard,
running down Aaron's beard
onto his robes.[u]
3 It is like the dew of Hermon[F]
falling on the mountains of Zion.[v]
For there the LORD has appointed
the blessing —
life forevermore.[w]

CALL TO EVENING WORSHIP

134

A song of ascents.
Now bless the LORD,
all you servants of the LORD
who stand in the LORD's house
at night![x]
2 Lift up your hands in the holy place
and bless the LORD![y]

3 May the LORD,
Maker of heaven and earth,
bless you from Zion.[z]

THE LORD IS GREAT

135

Hallelujah!
Praise the name of the LORD.
Give praise, you servants
of the LORD[aa]
2 who stand in the house of the LORD,
in the courts of the house
of our God.[ab]

[a] 132:2 Gn 49:24; Is 49:26; 60:16
[b] 132:3-4 Pr 6:4
[c] 132:5 1Ch 22:7; Ac 7:46
[d] 132:6 Gn 35:19; Ru 4:11; 1Sm 17:12; Mc 5:2
[e] 1Sm 7:1
[f] 132:7 1Ch 28:2; Ps 99:5
[g] 132:8 2Ch 6:41; Ps 68:1; 78:61
[h] 132:9 Jb 29:14; Ps 149:5
[i] 132:10 2Ch 6:42
[j] 132:11 2Sm 7:12-16; Ps 89:3; Ac 2:30
[k] 132:12 1Kg 8:25; Lk 1:32
[l] 132:13 Ps 68:16; 78:68
[m] 132:14 Mt 23:21
[n] 132:15 Ps 107:9; 147:14
[o] 132:16 2Ch 6:41
[p] 132:17 2Sm 23:5; Lk 1:69
[q] 1Kg 11:36
[r] 132:18 Jb 8:22
[s] Ps 21:3
[t] 133:1 Gn 13:8; Heb 13:1
[u] 133:2 Ex 30:25,30; Lv 8:12
[v] 133:3 Ps 48:1-2; Mc 5:7
[w] Ps 21:4
[x] 134:1 1Ch 9:23-27; Ps 135:1-2
[y] 134:2 Ps 28:2; 63:2; 1Tm 2:8
[z] 134:3 Ps 115:15; 128:5
[aa] 135:1 Ps 113:1; 134:1
[ab] 135:2 Ps 92:13; 116:19

[A] 132:6 = Bethlehem   [B] 132:6 = Kiriath-jearim   [C] 132:10 = the king   [D] 132:11 Lit *set the fruit of your belly*   [E] 132:18 Lit *but on him his crown*
[F] 133:3 The tallest mountain in the region, noted for its abundant precipitation

---

132:6-8 The people remember when Israel brought the ark from **the fields of Jaar** (that is, Kiriath-jearim, 132:6). The Philistines had captured it, endured God's wrath, and returned it (see 1 Sam 5:1–7:1). The people long to go to God's **dwelling place** on earth (the temple) and **worship at his footstool** (the **ark**) (Ps 132:7-8).
132:11-12 The Lord had promised that David's descendants would **sit on [his] throne forever** (132:12). But rather than through a perpetual succession of Davidic kings, this promise would be fulfilled in the resurrected Son of David who lives forever.

132:17-18 The Lord vows to be faithful to his promise to David. His **anointed one** will be a source of power and light (132:17). He will vanquish **his enemies** and reign in glory (132:18). Believers today hope in this same Anointed One, and we long for his kingdom (see Luke 1:32-33; Acts 2:30). "Come, Lord Jesus!" (Rev 22:20).
133:1 When believers come together in peace, love, and unity, it reflects the attitude of Christ (see Phil 2:1-5).
133:3 The atmospheric moisture from Mount **Hermon** fell **on the mountains of Zion,**

bringing refreshment and productivity to the land. Similarly, unity among the people of God frees him to rain down **blessing** on them.
134:1-2 Through Jesus Christ, believers have been made priests to one another (see 1 Pet 2:9; Rev 1:6). Therefore, these words apply to Christians everywhere. We are called to bless God and serve one another.

a 135:3 Ps 100:5; 147:1
b 135:4 Ex 19:5; Dt 7:6-7;
10:15
c 135:5 Ps 95:3; 97:9
d 135:6 Ps 115:3; Is 45:7;
Lm 3:37-38; Dn 4:35
e 135:7 Jb 28:25-26; Jr
10:13; 51:16
f 135:8 Ex 12:12; Ps 78:51;
105:36
g 135:9 Dt 6:22; Ps 78:43
h 135:10 Ps 44:2; 136:17-22
i 135:11 Nm 21:21-35
j 135:12 Dt 29:8; Ps 78:55
k 135:13 Ex 3:15; Ps 102:12
l 135:14 Dt 32:36; Ps 90:13;
106:46
m 135:15 2Kg 19:18; Is 37:19
n 135:16 Hab 2:18
o 135:16-17 Is 46:7
p 135:15-18 Ps 115:4-11

q 135:19 Ps 115:9; 118:2
r Ps 115:10; 118:3
s 135:20 Ps 22:23; 115:11;
118:4
t 135:21 Ps 128:5
u Ps 132:13-14
v 136:1 Ps 106:1; 107:1; 118:1
w 136:2-3 Dt 10:17
x 136:4 Jb 9:10; Ps 72:18
y 136:5 Pr 3:19; Jr 10:12;
51:15
z 136:6 Ps 24:2
aa 136:7 Ps 74:16
ab 136:8-9 Gn 1:16
ac 136:10 Ex 12:29; Ps
78:51; 135:8
ad 136:12 Ex 6:1; Dt 4:34
ae 136:13 Ex 14:21; Ps
66:6; 78:13
af 136:14 Ex 14:21-22;
Ps 106:9
ag 136:15 Ex 14:27; Ps
78:53; 106:11
ah 136:16 Dt 8:15; Ps 78:52

3 Praise the LORD, for the LORD is good;
sing praise to his name,
for it is delightful.*a*
4 For the LORD has chosen Jacob
for himself,
Israel as his treasured possession.*b*
5 For I know that the LORD is great;
our Lord is greater than all gods.*c*
6 The LORD does whatever he pleases
in heaven and on earth,
in the seas and all the depths.*d*
7 He causes the clouds to rise
from the ends of the earth.
He makes lightning for the rain
and brings the wind
from his storehouses.*e*
8 He struck down the firstborn of Egypt,
both people and animals.*f*
9 He sent signs and wonders
against you, Egypt,
against Pharaoh and all
his officials.*g*
10 He struck down many nations
and slaughtered mighty kings:*h*
11 Sihon king of the Amorites,
Og king of Bashan,
and all the kings of Canaan.*i*
12 He gave their land as an inheritance,
an inheritance to his people Israel.*j*

13 LORD, your name endures forever,
your reputation, LORD,
through all generations.*k*
14 For the LORD will vindicate
his people
and have compassion
on his servants.*l*

15 The idols of the nations are of silver
and gold,
made by human hands.*m*
16 They have mouths
but cannot speak,*n*
eyes, but cannot see.
17 They have ears but cannot hear;
indeed, there is no breath
in their mouths.*o*
18 Those who make them are just
like them,
as are all who trust in them.*p*

19 House of Israel, bless the LORD!*q*
House of Aaron, bless the LORD!*r*
20 House of Levi, bless the LORD!
You who revere the LORD,
bless the LORD!*s*
21 Blessed be the LORD from Zion;*t*
he dwells in Jerusalem.*u*
Hallelujah!

GOD'S LOVE IS ETERNAL

136

1 Give thanks to the LORD,
for he is good.*v*
His faithful love endures forever.
2 Give thanks to the God of gods.
His faithful love endures forever.
3 Give thanks to the Lord of lords.*w*
His faithful love endures forever.
4 He alone does great wonders.*x*
His faithful love endures forever.
5 He made the heavens skillfully.*y*
His faithful love endures forever.
6 He spread the land on the waters.*z*
His faithful love endures forever.
7 He made the great lights:*aa*
His faithful love endures forever.
8 the sun to rule by day,
His faithful love endures forever.
9 the moon and stars to rule
by night.*ab*
His faithful love endures forever.
10 He struck the firstborn
of the Egyptians*ac*
His faithful love endures forever.
11 and brought Israel out from among
them
His faithful love endures forever.
12 with a strong hand
and outstretched arm.*ad*
His faithful love endures forever.
13 He divided the Red Sea*ae*
His faithful love endures forever.
14 and led Israel through,*af*
His faithful love endures forever.
15 but hurled Pharaoh
and his army into the Red Sea.*ag*
His faithful love endures forever.
16 He led his people in the wilderness.*ah*
His faithful love endures forever.
17 He struck down great kings
His faithful love endures forever.
18 and slaughtered famous kings —
His faithful love endures forever.

135:15-18 Though the Lord is the Creator of heaven and earth, **silver and gold** idols are **made by human hands** (135:15). They are lifeless (135:15-17) and—unlike the living God who saves—cannot act on behalf of those who worship them. **Those who make them are just like them** (135:18). This is the powerful principle that you become like what you worship. If you look to what is lifeless and empty as your source, your life will reflect it.

135:19-20 The psalmist concludes with a call to all God's people (**Israel**) and all those who serve as priests and ministers in the temple (the houses of **Aaron** and **Levi**) to **bless the LORD.**

136:1-26 This psalm celebrates the *faithful love* (Hebrew, *hesed*) of God, his steadfast and never failing love toward his covenant people. It includes a beautiful line repeated throughout: *His faithful love endures forever.* Probably after the priest sang each verse, the entire congregation would respond by singing this refrain.

19 Sihon king of the Amorites
His faithful love endures forever.

20 and Og king of Bashan —
His faithful love endures forever.

21 and gave their land as
an inheritance,
His faithful love endures forever.

22 an inheritance to Israel his servant.[a]
His faithful love endures forever.

23 He remembered us
in our humiliation[b]
His faithful love endures forever.

24 and rescued us from our foes.[c]
His faithful love endures forever.

25 He gives food to every creature.[d]
His faithful love endures forever.

26 Give thanks to the God of heaven![e]
His faithful love endures forever.

LAMENT OF THE EXILES

137 By the rivers of Babylon —
there we sat down and wept
when we remembered Zion.[f]

2 There we hung up our lyres
on the poplar trees,[g]

3 for our captors there asked us
for songs,
and our tormentors, for rejoicing:
"Sing us one of the songs of Zion."[h]

4 How can we sing the LORD's song
on foreign soil?[i]

5 If I forget you, Jerusalem,
may my right hand forget its skill.[j]

6 May my tongue stick to the roof
of my mouth
if I do not remember you,
if I do not exalt Jerusalem
as my greatest joy![k]

7 Remember, LORD,
what the Edomites said
that day[A] at Jerusalem:
"Destroy it! Destroy it
down to its foundations!"[l]

8 Daughter Babylon,
doomed to destruction,
happy is the one who pays you back
what you have done to us.[m]

9 Happy is he who takes
your little ones
and dashes them against the rocks.[n]

A THANKFUL HEART

138 *Of David.*
I will give you thanks
with all my heart;[o]
I will sing your praise
before the heavenly beings.[B,p]

2 I will bow down
toward your holy temple
and give thanks to your name
for your constant love and truth.
You have exalted your name
and your promise above
everything else.[c,q]

3 On the day I called, you answered me;
you increased strength within me.[D,r]

4 All the kings on earth
will give you thanks, LORD,
when they hear
what you have promised.[E,s]

5 They will sing of the LORD's ways,
for the LORD's glory is great.[t]

6 Though the LORD is exalted,
he takes note of the humble;
but he knows the haughty
from a distance.[u]

7 If I walk into the thick of danger,
you will preserve my life
from the anger of my enemies.[v]
You will extend your hand;
your right hand will save me.[w]

8 The LORD will fulfill his purpose
for me.[x]
LORD, your faithful love
endures forever;
do not abandon the work
of your hands.[y]

THE ALL-KNOWING, EVER-PRESENT GOD

139 *For the choir director. A psalm of David.*

1 LORD, you have searched me
and known me.[z]

[a]136:17-22 Nm 21:21-35; Ps 135:10-12
[b]136:23 Ps 106:45
[c]136:24 Ps 107:2
[d]136:25 Ps 104:27; 145:15
[e]136:26 Neh 1:5
[f]137:1 Ezk 1:1,3
[g]137:2 Jb 30:31; Ezk 26:13
[h]137:3 Ps 80:6
[i]137:4 Neh 12:46
[j]137:5 Is 65:11
[k]137:6 Jb 29:10; Ps 22:15; Ezk 3:26
[l]137:7 Is 34:5-6; Ezk 35:2; Ob 10-14
[m]137:8 Jr 50:1-46; 51:1-64

[n]137:9 2Kg 8:12; Is 13:16; Nah 3:10
[o]138:1 Ps 111:1
[p]Ps 82:1,6-7; 95:3; 96:5
[q]138:2 1Kg 8:29; Ps 5:7; 28:2
[r]138:3 Ps 28:7; 46:1
[s]138:4 Ps 72:11; 102:15
[t]138:5 Ps 21:5; 145:7
[u]138:6 Ps 113:4-7; Pr 3:34; Jms 4:6
[v]138:7 Ps 23:4
[w]Ps 20:6; 60:5
[x]138:8 Ps 57:2; Php 1:6
[y]Jb 10:3; Ps 100:3
[z]139:1 Ps 17:3; 44:21; Jr 12:3

[A]137:7 The day Jerusalem fell to the Babylonians in 586 BC   [B]138:1 Or *before the gods,* or *before judges,* or *before kings*; Hb *elohim*   [C]138:2 Or *You have exalted your promise above all your name*   [D]138:3 Hb obscure   [E]138:4 Lit *hear the words of your mouth*

137:1-6 The psalmist recalls the deep sorrow the exiles experienced during their Babylonian captivity.
137:7-9 The psalmist longs for God's vengeance against **the Edomites** who cheered Jerusalem's **destruction** and against **Babylon** who carried out the violence (137:7-8). His prayer against the **little ones** (137:9) reflected a desire that his enemy would have no descendants.

138:6 God gives attention to **the humble** but rejects the proud (i.e., those who believe they can live their lives independently of him). (See Jas 4:6.)
138:7-8 We too can be brutally honest with God. Even while you praise him, you can ask him not to let you down—particularly in times of crises—knowing that he will answer for your good and his glory.

139:1-4 David contemplates the staggering omniscience of God. Not only does the Lord know everything about the universe, he has also **searched** and **known** his servant (139:1). God knows every last detail about you, too. Nothing escapes his knowledge.

[a]139:2 2Kg 19:27; Is 66:18; Mt 9:4
[b]139:3 Jb 14:16; 31:4
[c]139:4 Heb 4:13
[d]139:5 Jb 9:33; Ps 125:2
[e]139:6 Jb 42:3; Rm 11:33
[f]139:7 Jr 23:24
[g]139:8 Am 9:2-4
[h]Jb 26:6; Is 14:11
[i]139:9-10 Ps 23:2-3
[j]139:11 Jb 22:13-14
[k]139:12 Jb 34:22; Dn 2:22
[l]139:13 Jb 10:11; Ps 119:73
[m]139:14 Ps 40:5

[n]139:15 Jb 10:8-10; Ps 63:9; Ec 11:5
[o]139:16 Jb 14:5
[p]139:17-18 Ps 40:5; 92:5
[q]139:18 Ps 3:5
[r]139:19 Ps 5:6; 6:8; Is 11:4
[s]139:20 Ex 20:7; Jd 15
[t]139:21-22 Ps 26:5; 31:16
[u]139:23 Jb 31:6; Ps 26:2
[v]139:24 Ps 16:11

2 You know when I sit down and when
  I stand up;
you understand my thoughts
  from far away.[a]
3 You observe my travels and my rest;
you are aware of all my ways.[b]
4 Before a word is on my tongue,
you know all about it, LORD.[c]
5 You have encircled me;
you have placed your hand on me.[d]
6 This wondrous knowledge is
  beyond me.
It is lofty; I am unable to reach it.[e]

7 Where can I go to escape
  your Spirit?
Where can I flee
  from your presence?[f]
8 If I go up to heaven, you are there;[g]
if I make my bed in Sheol,
  you are there.[h]
9 If I live at the eastern horizon
or settle at the western limits,[A]
10 even there your hand will lead me;
your right hand will hold on to me.[i]
11 If I say, "Surely the darkness
  will hide me,
and the light around me
  will be night"[j] —
12 even the darkness is not dark to you.
The night shines like the day;
darkness and light are
  alike to you.[k]

13 For it was you who created
  my inward parts;[B]
you knit me together
  in my mother's womb.[l]
14 I will praise you
because I have been remarkably
  and wondrously made.[C,D]
Your works are wondrous,
and I know this very well.[m]

15 My bones were not hidden from you
when I was made in secret,
when I was formed in the depths
  of the earth.[n]
16 Your eyes saw me when
  I was formless;
all my days were written
  in your book and planned
before a single one of them began.[o]
17 God, how precious[E]
  your thoughts are to me;
how vast their sum is!
18 If I counted them,
they would outnumber the grains
  of sand;[p]
when I wake up,[F] I am still with you.[q]

19 God, if only you would kill
  the wicked —
you bloodthirsty men, stay away
  from me[r] —
20 who invoke you deceitfully.
Your enemies swear by you falsely.[s]
21 LORD, don't I hate those
  who hate you,
and detest those who rebel
  against you?
22 I hate them with extreme hatred;
I consider them my enemies.[t]

23 Search me, God, and know my heart;
test me and know my concerns.[u]
24 See if there is any offensive[G] way
  in me;
lead me in the everlasting way.[v]

[A]139:9 Lit *I take up the wings of the dawn; I dwell at the end of the sea*   [B]139:13 Lit *my kidneys*   [C]139:14 DSS, some LXX mss, Syr, Jer read *because you are remarkable and wonderful*   [D]139:14 Hb obscure   [E]139:17 Or *difficult*   [F]139:18 Some Hb mss read *I come to an end*   [G]139:24 Or *idolatrous*

139:5-6 When we comprehend that God can do the incomprehensible, it should cause us to be overwhelmed with worship for him. **139:7-9** Not only is the Lord omniscient, but he is also omnipresent. God is everywhere. He inhabits the universe from top to bottom. **139:10-12** Believer, no matter where you are, God's **right hand will hold on to** you (139:10). So regardless of the circumstances you face, call on the intimate God in your day of distress. He is right by your side. **139:13-14** In spite of popular opinion, we are not the products of evolution. David affirms that God had not only created him, but he had actually **knit [him] together** (139:13). You, too, are a work of art that God put together

by hand. You have been **wondrously made** (139:14). So no matter the circumstances surrounding your conception, your existence is intentional. You are not a mistake, for God makes no mistakes. You are created in the image of God (see Gen 1:27) with purpose and meaning. This truth is to be the foundation for a person's self-worth and self-esteem. **139:15-16** David was **not hidden** from God even when he was in his mother's womb, described poetically in verse 15. This truth is why abortion is so horribly wrong. Divinely-given human life exists from the moment of conception. God didn't merely see an embryo or fetus in the womb; he saw *David* (**Your eyes saw me**, 139:16).

All my days were written in your book and planned before a single one of them began (139:16). The Lord similarly knew all of your days from beginning to end. Your existence is no accident. You are part of the divine plan. **139:19-22** Because of David's deep love for the Lord, he hated everything that was in opposition to him (139:21). Thus, he prays for God's judgment on **the wicked** (139:19) in accordance with his holy character. **139:23-24** Like David, we do not fully know ourselves either. So let us pray that God's Spirit would help us understand ourselves rightly so that we can repent where necessary and enjoy intimate fellowship with him as he leads us **in the everlasting way** (139:24).

PRAYER FOR RESCUE

140 *For the choir director. A psalm of David.*

1 Rescue me, LORD, from evil men.
  Keep me safe from violent men[a]
2 who plan evil in their hearts.
  They stir up wars all day long.[b]
3 They make their tongues
    as sharp as a snake's bite;
  viper's venom is under
      their lips.[c]   *Selah*

4 Protect me, LORD,
    from the power of the wicked.[d]
  Keep me safe from violent men
  who plan to make me stumble.[A,e]
5 The proud hide a trap with ropes
      for me;
  they spread a net along the path
  and set snares for me.[f]   *Selah*

6 I say to the LORD, "You are my God."
  Listen, LORD, to my cry for help.[g]
7 LORD, my Lord, my strong Savior,
  you shield my head on the day
      of battle.[h]
8 LORD, do not grant the desires
      of the wicked;
  do not let them achieve their goals.
  Otherwise, they will
      become proud.[i]   *Selah*

9 When those who surround me
      rise up,[B]
  may the trouble their lips cause
      overwhelm them.[j]
10 Let hot coals fall on them.
  Let them be thrown into the fire,
  into the abyss, never again
      to rise.[k]
11 Do not let a slanderer stay
      in the land.
  Let evil relentlessly[c] hunt down
      a violent man.[l]

12 I[D] know that the LORD upholds
  the just cause of the poor,
  justice for the needy.[m]

13 Surely the righteous will praise
      your name;
  the upright will live in
      your presence.[n]

PROTECTION FROM SIN AND SINNERS

141 *A psalm of David.*

  LORD, I call on you; hurry
      to help me.
  Listen to my voice when I call
      on you.[o]
2 May my prayer be set before you
      as incense,[p]
  the raising of my hands
      as the evening offering.[q]

3 LORD, set up a guard for my mouth;
  keep watch at the door of my lips.[r]
4 Do not let my heart turn
      to any evil thing
  or perform wicked acts
  with men who commit sin.
  Do not let me feast
      on their delicacies.[s]
5 Let the righteous one strike me —
  it is an act of faithful love;
  let him rebuke me —
  it is oil for my head;
  let me[E] not refuse it.[t]
  Even now my prayer is against
  the evil acts of the wicked.[F,u]
6 When their rulers[G]
      will be thrown off
  the sides of a cliff,
  the people[H] will listen to my words,
  for they are pleasing.[v]

7 As when one plows and breaks up
      the soil,
  turning up rocks,
  so our[I] bones have been scattered
  at the mouth of Sheol.[w]

8 But my eyes look to you, LORD, my
      Lord.
  I seek refuge in you; do not
      let me die.[J,x]

[a] 140:1 Ps 18:48; 71:4
[b] 140:2 Ps 36:4; 56:6; Pr 6:14
[c] 140:3 Ps 58:4; Rm 3:13; Jms 3:8
[d] 140:4 Ps 71:4
[e] Ps 36:11
[f] 140:5 Ps 35:7; 141:9; 142:3
[g] 140:6 Ps 31:14; 130:2
[h] 140:7 Ps 28:7; 118:14
[i] 140:8 Ps 10:2-3
[j] 140:9 Ps 7:16; Pr 18:7
[k] 140:10 Ps 11:6; 36:12
[l] 140:11 Ps 34:21
[m] 140:12 1Kg 8:45,49; Ps 9:4; 82:3

[n] 140:13 Ps 11:7; 64:10
[o] 141:1 Ps 22:19; 38:22; 70:5
[p] 141:2 Ex 30:8
[q] Lk 1:10; Rv 5:8; 8:3-4
[r] 141:3 Ps 34:13; 39:1; Pr 13:3; Mc 7:5
[s] 141:4 Ps 119:36; Pr 23:6; Is 32:6
[t] 141:5 Ec 7:5; Gl 6:1
[u] Ps 109:4
[v] 141:6 2Ch 25:12
[w] 141:7 Ps 53:5; 88:3-5
[x] 141:8 Ps 7:1; 57:1; 144:2

[A] 140:4 Lit *to trip up my steps*   [B] 140:9 Lit *Head of those who surround me*   [C] 140:11 Hb obscure   [D] 140:12 Alt Hb tradition reads *You*
[E] 141:5 Lit *my head*   [F] 141:5 Lit *of them*   [G] 141:6 Or *judges*   [H] 141:6 Lit *cliff, and they*   [I] 141:7 DSS reads *my* ; some LXX mss, Syr read *their*
[J] 141:8 Or *not pour out my life*

140:1-5 David appeals to the Lord to defend him against **violent men** who were stirring up trouble for him (140:1).
140:7 As the king, David no doubt had the best armor. But ultimately he knew that God himself was his **shield**—especially when it came to maintaining peace of mind.
140:12 God will intervene on behalf of the downtrodden—either in this life or in the life to come. One day, God will set all things right.
141:1-2 David describes his **prayer** in terms of priestly sacrifices: **incense** or an **offering** burned for the Lord (141:2). He considered his entreaty (141:1) an act of worship.
141:4 David did not want to be lured into sin by the **delicacies** of the wicked—that is, by anything that would appeal to his sinful desires and draw him away from the Lord. Similarly, believers today are exhorted to beware of the desires of the world: "the lust of the flesh, the lust of the eyes, and the pride in one's possessions" (1 John 2:16). Indulging in such "delicacies" does not ultimately satisfy our spiritual hunger. It causes us to lose fellowship with God.
141:5 David welcomes the loving **rebuke** of the **righteous**. Do you?

[a] 141:9 Ps 38:12; 140:5
[b] 141:10 Ps 7:15; 35:8; 57:6
[c] 142:title 1Sm 22:1; 24:3
[d] 142:1 Ps 3:4; 77:1
[e] Ps 30:8
[f] 142:2 Ps 77:2; 102 title
[g] 142:3 Ps 77:3; 143:4
[h] Ps 140:5
[i] 142:4 Ps 69:20; Jr 25:35
[j] 142:5 Ps 16:5; 27:13
[k] 142:6 Ps 79:8; 116:6
[l] Ps 18:17
[m] 142:7 Ps 13:6; 143:11
[n] 143:1 Ps 71:2; 140:6
[o] 143:2 Jb 14:3
[p] Jb 15:14; Ps 130:3; Rm 3:23

[q] 143:3 Ps 88:3-6; Lm 3:6
[r] 143:4 Ps 77:3; 142:3
[s] 143:5 Ps 77:5,10-12
[t] 143:6 Jb 11:13; Ps 42:2; 63:1
[u] 143:7 Ps 69:17; 102:2
[v] Ps 28:1; 88:4
[w] 143:8 Ps 90:14
[x] Ps 25:1,4
[y] 143:9 Ps 31:15; 59:1; 142:6
[z] 143:10 Ps 25:4-5; 31:14; 63:1; 86:2; 119:12
[aa] Ps 23:3
[ab] 143:11 Ps 25:11; 71:20
[ac] 143:12 Ps 54:5; 116:16
[ad] 144:1 1Sm 2:2; Ps 18:2; 19:14; 92:15; 95:1; Is 26:4
[ae] Ps 18:34

9 Protect me from the trap
   they have set for me,
   and from the snares of evildoers.[a]
10 Let the wicked fall
   into their own nets,
   while I pass by safely.[b]

A CRY OF DISTRESS

142 *A Maskil of David. When he was in the cave.[c] A prayer.*

1 I cry aloud to the LORD;[d]
  I plead aloud to the LORD for mercy.[e]
2 I pour out my complaint before him;
  I reveal my trouble to him.[f]
3 Although my spirit is weak within me,
  you know my way.[g]

  Along this path I travel
  they have hidden a trap for me.[h]
4 Look to the right and see:[A]
  no one stands up for me;
  there is no refuge for me;
  no one cares about me.[i]
5 I cry to you, LORD;
  I say, "You are my shelter,
  my portion in the land of the living."[j]
6 Listen to my cry,
  for I am very weak.[k]
  Rescue me from those
     who pursue me,
  for they are too strong for me.[l]
7 Free me from prison
  so that I can praise your name.
  The righteous will gather around me
  because you deal generously with me.[m]

A CRY FOR HELP

143 *A psalm of David.*

  LORD, hear my prayer.
  In your faithfulness listen to my plea,
  and in your righteousness
     answer me.[n]
2 Do not bring your servant
   into judgment,[o]
  for no one alive is righteous
   in your sight.[p]

3 For the enemy has pursued me,
  crushing me to the ground,
  making me live in darkness
  like those long dead.[q]
4 My spirit is weak within me;
  my heart is overcome with dismay.[r]

5 I remember the days of old;
  I meditate on all you have done;
  I reflect on the work of your hands.[s]
6 I spread out my hands to you;
  I am like parched land
     before you.[t]   *Selah*

7 Answer me quickly, LORD;
  my spirit fails.[u]
  Don't hide your face from me,
  or I will be like those
  going down to the Pit.[v]
8 Let me experience
  your faithful love in the morning,
  for I trust in you.[w]
  Reveal to me the way I should go
  because I appeal to you.[x]
9 Rescue me from my enemies, LORD;
  I come to you for protection.[B,y]
10 Teach me to do your will,
   for you are my God.[z]
   May your gracious Spirit
   lead me on level ground.[aa]

11 For your name's sake, LORD,
   let me live.
   In your righteousness deliver me
     from trouble,[ab]
12 and in your faithful love
     destroy my enemies.
   Wipe out all those who attack me,
   for I am your servant.[ac]

A KING'S PRAYER

144 *Of David.*

  Blessed be the LORD, my rock[ad]
  who trains my hands for battle
  and my fingers for warfare.[ae]
2 He is my faithful love
   and my fortress,

[A] 142:4 DSS, LXX, Syr, Vg, Tg read *I look to the right and I see*   [B] 143:9 One Hb ms, LXX; some Hb mss read *I cover myself to you*

142:1-3 If you have assumed that all prayer should be dignified and employ only theological jargon in your petitions to God, you have not understood prayer rightly. Let David be your model. He approaches God honestly, pleading emotionally for deliverance. As a troubled child depends on his or her daddy, go to your heavenly Father in your turmoil and open your heart to him.
142:4-7 David asks for God to **free** him from the **prison** of his circumstances. Notice the purpose for this request: **so that I can praise your name**.

It means David longs for deliverance in part so that he would have another reason to worship. He concludes with confidence that God would **deal generously with** him. As a result, **the righteous [would] gather around** him (142:7). Through divine intervention, then, the man who was alone (142:4) would be alone no longer.
143:5-6 David finds solace and hope in remembering former **days**, when he had experienced God's mighty works (143:5). He longs for God's intervention to restore his spiritually thirsty soul (143:6).

143:8-10 It wasn't enough to be saved from his troubles. David wanted fellowship with God and his direction and guidance as he obeyed God's commands.
143:11-12 When we come under God's covenant covering and submit to his will, we can have confidence that he will work for our good and his glory.
144:1-2 David's descriptions of God show us two things. First, he considers God the definitive source of security. The Lord is a **rock, fortress, stronghold, deliverer, shield,**

my stronghold and my deliverer.
He is my shield,[a] and I take refuge
in him;[b]
he subdues my people[A]
under me.[c]

3 LORD, what is a human that you care
for him,
a son of man[B] that you think
of him?[d]

4 A human is like a breath;
his days are like a passing shadow.[e]

5 LORD, part your heavens
and come down.[f]
Touch the mountains,
and they will smoke.[g]

6 Flash your lightning and scatter
the foe;[C]
shoot your arrows
and rout them.[h]

7 Reach down[D] from on high;[i]
rescue me from deep water,
and set me free
from the grasp of foreigners[j]

8 whose mouths speak lies,
whose right hands
are deceptive.[k]

9 God, I will sing a new song to you;
I will play on a ten-stringed harp
for you[l] —

10 the one who gives victory
to kings,
who frees his servant David
from the deadly sword.[m]

11 Set me free and rescue me
from foreigners[n]
whose mouths speak lies,
whose right hands
are deceptive.[o]

12 Then our sons will be like plants
nurtured in their youth,
our daughters, like corner pillars
that are carved
in the palace style.[p]

13 Our storehouses will be full,
supplying all kinds
of produce;[q]
our flocks will increase
by thousands
and tens of thousands in
our open fields.[r]

14 Our cattle will be well fed.[E]
There will be no breach
in the walls,
no going into captivity,[F]
and no cry of lament in
our public squares.[s]

15 Happy are the people with
such blessings.
Happy are the people whose God is
the LORD.[t]

PRAISING GOD'S GREATNESS

145 *A hymn of David.*

I[G] exalt you, my God the King,
and bless your name
forever and ever.[u]

2 I will bless you every day;
I will praise your name
forever and ever.[v]

3 The LORD is great
and is highly praised;[w]
his greatness is unsearchable.[x]

4 One generation will declare
your works to the next
and will proclaim
your mighty acts.[y]

5 I[H] will speak of your splendor and
glorious majesty
and[I] your wondrous works.[z]

6 They will proclaim the power
of your awe-inspiring acts,
and I will declare
your greatness.[J,aa]

7 They will give a testimony
of your great goodness

---

[a]144:2 Dt 33:29; Ps 3:3;
28:7; 115:9-11; Pr 2:7
[b]2Sm 22:3; Ps 18:2; 71:1-3;
91:4; 144:2; Pr 30:5
[c]Ps 18:39,47
[d]144:3 Jb 7:17; Ps 8:4;
Heb 2:6
[e]144:4 Ps 102:11; 109:23
[f]145:5 2Sm 22:10; Ps
18:9-10
[g]Ps 104:32
[h]144:6 Ps 18:14; Hab 3:11;
Zch 9:14
[i]144:7 Ps 18:16
[j]Ps 69:14
[k]144:8 Ps 12:2; 41:6;
106:26
[l]144:9 Ps 33:2-3; 40:3
[m]144:10 Ps 18:50
[n]144:11 Ps 69:14
[o]Ps 12:2; 41:6; 106:26

[p]144:12 Ps 92:12-14; 128:3
[q]144:13 Ps 107:37-38
[r]Pr 3:9-10
[s]144:14 Is 24:11; Jr 14:2
[t]144:15 Ps 33:12
[u]145:1 Ps 30:1; 34:1; 99:5,9
[v]145:2 Ps 146:2
[w]145:3 Ps 48:1; 147:5
[x]Jb 5:9; 9:10; Is 40:28
[y]145:4 Ps 22:30-31
[z]145:5 Ps 119:27
[aa]145:6 Dt 10:21; Ps 106:2

[A]144:2 Some Hb mss, DSS, Aq, Syr, Tg, Jer read *subdues peoples* ; 2Sm 22:48; Ps 18:47   [B]144:3 Or *a mere mortal*   [C]144:6 Lit *scatter them*
[D]144:7 Lit *down your hands*   [E]144:14 Or *will bear heavy loads,* or *will be pregnant*   [F]144:14 Or *be no plague, no miscarriage*   [G]145:1 The lines of
this poem form an acrostic.   [H]145:5 LXX, Syr read *They*   [I]145:5 LXX, Syr read *and they will tell of*   [J]145:6 Alt Hb tradition,
Jer read *great deeds*

---

and **refuge**. To put this in football terminology, we would say that God is the ultimate defensive line. No opposition can break through. No other source of protection is as reliable.

Second, David expresses the depth of his personal relationship with the Lord through his repeated use of the pronoun **my** before these descriptions. Not only is God a fortress, he is *David's* fortress. Are you appropriating the divine King's power in your life?

144:3-4 David is overwhelmed that God would **care** for **human** beings in general and him in particular (144:3; see also 8:4). What amazing grace that God would condescend to enter into intimate fellowship with humanity! And how (even more) amazing is it that the divine Son of God would take on human nature so that he might redeem us (see Heb 2:1-18)?
144:10 In the end, the size of a king's army is irrelevant. The size of his God is what matters.

As David testifies elsewhere, chariots and horses, symbols of ancient military power, are no match for the Lord (see 20:7).
145:4 Are you committed to exalting God so that his kingdom expands? Do you regularly teach your children about the Lord? Do you share the gospel and your own personal testimony with unbelievers in your circle of influence? Are you discipling others so that the church may mature in Christ?

[a] 145:7 Is 63:7
[b] 145:8 Ex 34:6; Ps 86:5,15; 103:8
[c] 145:9 Ac 14:17
[d] Ps 100:5
[e] 145:10 Ps 19:1; 103:22

[f] 145:11 Jr 14:21
[g] 145:12 Ps 105:1; 145:5
[h] 145:13 Ps 10:16; 2Pt 1:11
[i] Ps 103:8
[j] 145:14 Ps 37:24; 146:8
[k] 145:15 Ps 104:27; 136:25
[l] 145:16 Ps 104:28
[m] 145:17 Ps 116:5
[n] 145:18 Dt 4:7; Ps 34:18; Jn 4:23-24
[o] 145:19 Ps 10:17; 21:2; 37:4
[p] 145:20 Ps 31:23; 97:10
[q] 145:21 Ps 65:2; 150:6
[r] 146:1 Ps 103:1
[s] 146:2 Ps 63:4; 104:33
[t] 146:3 Ps 60:11; 108:12; 118:8-9
[u] 146:4 Gn 2:7; 3:19

❧ Questions & Answers ❧

Q How did you pass on your love for Scripture and commitment to its authority in your family? What are some practical ways that moms and dads can teach their children to love and obey Scripture?

A Parents can get the *Kingdom Family Devotional* and walk their kids through its applicational truths. They should also pray with their children daily and bring a divine perspective to their decision-making so that their kids are bombarded with Scripture. Deuteronomy 6:7-9 says, "Repeat [God's words] to your children. Talk about them when you sit in your house and when you walk along the road, when you lie down and when you get up. Bind them as a sign on your hand and let them be a symbol on your forehead. Write them on the doorposts of your house and on your city gates."

In our home, we have Scripture everywhere. When our children were young, we had devotions regularly at the dinner table, and we worshiped together as a family. We regularly asked, "What does God say about this decision?" Our children were like little balls inside a pinball machine, regularly bumping into the Word of God. Even if kids don't always abide by the Word (which none of us do), running into it so often makes it a part of their orientation.

FOR THE NEXT Q&A, SEE PAGE 728.

and will joyfully sing
    of your righteousness.[a]

8   The LORD is gracious
        and compassionate,
    slow to anger and great
        in faithful love.[b]
9   The LORD is good to everyone;[c]
    his compassion rests
        on all he has made.[d]
10 All you have made
        will thank you, LORD;
    the[A] faithful will bless you.[e]

11 They will speak of the glory
        of your kingdom
    and will declare your might,[f]
12 informing all people
        of your mighty acts
    and of the glorious splendor
        of your[g] kingdom.[g]
13 Your kingdom is
        an everlasting kingdom;
    your rule is for all generations.[h]
    The LORD is faithful in all his words
    and gracious in all his actions.[c,i]

14 The LORD helps all who fall;
    he raises up all who are oppressed.[D,j]
15 All eyes look to you,
    and you give them their food at the
        proper time.[k]
16 You open your hand
    and satisfy the desire
        of every living thing.[l]

17 The LORD is righteous in all his ways
    and faithful in all his acts.[m]
18 The LORD is near all who call out
        to him,
    all who call out to him
        with integrity.[n]
19 He fulfills the desires of those
        who fear him;
    he hears their cry for help
        and saves them.[o]
20 The LORD guards all those
        who love him,
    but he destroys all the wicked.[p]
21 My mouth will declare
        the LORD's praise;
    let every living thing
    bless his holy name forever
        and ever.[q]

THE GOD OF COMPASSION

146 Hallelujah!
    My soul, praise the LORD.[r]
2   I will praise the LORD all my life;
    I will sing to my God as long as I live.[s]

3   Do not trust in nobles,
    in a son of man,[E] who cannot save.[t]
4   When his breath[F] leaves him,
    he returns to the ground;
    on that day his plans die.[u]

[A] 145:10 Lit *your*   [B] 145:12 LXX, Syr, Jer; MT reads *his*   [C] 145:13 One Hb ms, DSS, LXX, Syr; some Hb mss omit *The LORD is faithful in all his words and gracious in all his actions.*   [D] 145:14 Lit *bowed down*   [E] 146:3 Or *a mere mortal*   [F] 146:4 Or *spirit*

145:8 David recites what God himself had revealed to Moses (see Exod 34:6).
145:13 Since God's rule will endure forever, God's people ought to proclaim it and urge everyone everywhere to submit to the King.

145:14-20 David extols the gracious provision of God, who **helps** the **oppressed** and provides **food** for all humanity (145:14-15). He hears those **who call out to him with integrity** (145:18). He delivers **those who fear him** (145:19). He **guards**

all those who love him (145:20). Thus, we see a clear picture of what God expects of us if he is to act on our behalf: we are to pray to him with integrity, live as those who take him seriously, and love him with all that we are.

5 Happy is the one whose help is
    the God of Jacob,
  whose hope is in the LORD his God,[a]
6 the Maker of heaven and earth,
    the sea and everything in them.[b]
  He remains faithful forever,[c]
7 executing justice for the exploited
    and giving food to the hungry.[d]
  The LORD frees prisoners.[e]
8 The LORD opens the eyes of
    the blind.[f]
  The LORD raises up those
    who are oppressed.[A,g]
  The LORD loves the righteous.[h]
9 The LORD protects resident aliens
  and helps the fatherless
    and the widow,[i]
  but he frustrates the ways
    of the wicked.[j]

10 The LORD reigns forever;
  Zion, your God reigns
    for all generations.[k]
  Hallelujah!

GOD RESTORES JERUSALEM

147
Hallelujah!
  How good it is to sing
    to our God,
for praise is pleasant and lovely.[l]

2 The LORD rebuilds Jerusalem;[m]
  he gathers Israel's exiled people.[n]
3 He heals the brokenhearted
  and bandages their wounds.[o]
4 He counts the number of the stars;
  he gives names to all of them.[p]
5 Our Lord is great, vast in power;
  his understanding is infinite.[B,q]
6 The LORD helps the oppressed
  but brings the wicked
    to the ground.[r]

7 Sing to the LORD with thanksgiving;
  play the lyre to our God,[s]
8 who covers the sky with clouds,
  prepares rain for the earth,

and causes grass to grow
    on the hills.[t]
9 He provides the animals
    with their food,
  and the young ravens,
    what they cry for.[u]
10 He is not impressed by the strength
    of a horse;
  he does not value the power
    of a warrior.[C,v]
11 The LORD values
    those who fear him,
  those who put their hope
    in his faithful love.[w]

12 Exalt the LORD, Jerusalem;
  praise your God, Zion![x]
13 For he strengthens the bars
    of your city gates
  and blesses your children
    within you.[y]
14 He endows your territory
    with prosperity;[D,z]
  he satisfies you
    with the finest wheat.[aa]

15 He sends his command
    throughout the earth;
  his word runs swiftly.[ab]
16 He spreads snow like wool;
  he scatters frost like ashes;[ac]
17 he throws his hailstones
    like crumbs.
  Who can withstand his cold?[ad]
18 He sends his word
    and melts them;
  he unleashes his winds,[E]
    and the water flows.[ae]

19 He declares his word to Jacob,
  his statutes and judgments
    to Israel.[af]
20 He has not done this
    for every nation;
  they do not know his judgments.[ag]
  Hallelujah!

---

[a] 146:5 Ps 144:15; Jr 17:7
[b] 146:6 Ps 115:15; Ac 14:15
[c] Ps 117:2
[d] 146:7 Ps 103:6; 107:9
[e] Is 61:1
[f] 146:8 Mt 9:27-30; Jn 9:7
[g] Ps 145:15
[h] Ps 11:7
[i] 146:9 Ex 22:22-23; Dt 10:18
[j] Ps 147:6
[k] 146:10 Ex 15:18; Ps 10:16
[l] 147:1 Ps 33:1; 135:3
[m] 147:2 Ps 51:18; 102:16
[n] Dt 30:3; Ezk 39:28
[o] 147:3 Ps 34:18; Is 61:1
[p] 147:4 Gn 15:5; Is 40:26
[q] 147:5 Ps 48:1; Is 40:28
[r] 147:6 Ps 146:8-9
[s] 147:7 Ps 33:2; 95:1-2

[t] 147:8 Jb 5:10; 38:27; Ps 104:14
[u] 147:9 Jb 38:41; Ps 104:27-28
[v] 147:10 Ps 33:17
[w] 147:11 Ps 33:18; 149:4
[x] 147:12 Ps 99:5,9
[y] 147:13 Neh 7:3
[z] 147:14 Is 54:13
[aa] Dt 32:14; Ps 81:16
[ab] 147:15 Ps 104:4
[ac] 147:16 Jb 37:6; 38:29
[ad] 147:17 Jb 37:9-10
[ae] 147:18 Ps 33:9; 107:20
[af] 147:19 Dt 33:2-4; Mal 4:4
[ag] 147:20 Dt 4:7,32-34

[A] 146:8 Lit *bowed down* [B] 147:5 Lit *understanding has no number* [C] 147:10 Lit *the legs of the man* [D] 147:14 Or *peace* [E] 147:18 Or *breath*

146:5-6 The person who looks to the Lord—**the Maker of heaven and earth**—as his **help** is **happy** or blessed (the Hebrew word can be translated either way), because the Lord has no limitations and is eternally trustworthy.
146:7-9 There is no category of abused, broken, burdened, or underprivileged people on whom the Lord does not have compassion. The same should be true of God's people; the church is called to emulate its Savior and care for the downtrodden, renewing their hope and lightening their loads.

146:10 The psalmist concludes with an affirmation that **the LORD reigns forever**. No matter how difficult your trials, they will not last forever. But God's kingdom will.
147:7-9 God (not Mother Nature) sends **rain** and **causes grass to grow** (147:8). All **animals** receive their sustenance from the Lord's gracious hand (147:9). This is God's common grace upon all of his creation.
147:10-14 What impresses God? What does he value? He cherishes **those who fear him** and **hope in his faithful love** (147:11). So, if

you humbly submit to his kingdom agenda and live in dependence on him, you can rest assured that God will be crazy about you. He loves to bless his people (147:12-14).
147:15-19 The psalmist exalts God for his word. For by his **word** he exercises control over the elements of nature (147:15-18). But, even more, he is to be praised for the word that he revealed specifically to his people (147:19). God's new covenant people should similarly exalt him for the special revelation of both the written Word and the living Word, our Lord Jesus Christ.

[a]148:1 Ps 69:34; Mt 21:9
[b]148:2 Ps 103:20-21
[c]148:3 1Co 15:41
[d]148:4 Gn 1:7; Dt 10:14;
1Kg 8:27
[e]148:5 Ps 33:6,9
[f]148:6 Jr 31:35-36;
33:20,25
[g]148:7 Gn 1:2,21; Ps 74:13
[h]148:8 Ps 18:12; 103:20;
147:16
[i]148:9 Is 44:23; 49:13;
55:12
[j]148:10 Is 43:20; Hs 2:18
[k]148:11 Ps 102:15
[l]148:11-12 Rv 7:9
[m]148:13 Ps 8:1; 113:4;
Is 12:4
[n]148:14 Dt 10:21; Jr 17:14;
Eph 2:17
[o]149:1 Ps 33:3
[p]Ps 35:18; 89:5

[q]149:2 Ps 95:6; Zch 9:9
[r]149:3 Ps 30:11; 81:2
[s]149:4 Ps 147:11; Rm 8:8;
1Co 1:21
[t]Ps 35:27; Is 61:3
[u]149:5 Jb 35:10; Ps 132:16
[v]149:6 Ps 66:17; Heb 4:12
[w]149:7 Ezk 25:16-17;
Mc 5:15
[x]149:8 Jb 36:8
[y]149:9 Ps 148:14; Ezk
28:26
[z]150:1 Gn 1:6; Ps 11:4; 19:1
[aa]150:2 Ps 145:12
[ab]Dt 3:24
[ac]150:3 Ps 98:6
[ad]Ps 33:2
[ae]150:4 Ps 149:3
[af]Jb 21:12; Ps 45:8
[ag]150:5 2Sm 6:5; 1Ch 13:8
[ah]150:6 Ps 145:21

CREATION'S PRAISE OF THE LORD

148 Hallelujah!
Praise the LORD from the heavens;
praise him in the heights.[a]

2 Praise him, all his angels;
praise him, all his heavenly armies.[b]

3 Praise him, sun and moon;
praise him, all you shining stars.[c]

4 Praise him, highest heavens,
and you waters above the heavens.[d]

5 Let them praise the name of the LORD,
for he commanded,
and they were created.[e]

6 He set them in position
forever and ever;
he gave an order that will never
pass away.[f]

7 Praise the LORD from the earth,
all sea monsters and ocean depths,[g]

8 lightning[A] and hail, snow and cloud,
stormy wind that executes
his command,[h]

9 mountains and all hills,
fruit trees and all cedars,[i]

10 wild animals and all cattle,
creatures that crawl
and flying birds,[j]

11 kings of the earth and all peoples,
princes and all judges of the earth,[k]

12 young men as well as young women,
old and young together.[l]

13 Let them praise the name of the LORD,
for his name alone is exalted.
His majesty covers heaven and earth.[m]

14 He has raised up a horn for his people,
resulting in praise to all
his faithful ones,
to the Israelites, the people
close to him.[n]
Hallelujah!

PRAISE FOR GOD'S TRIUMPH

149 Hallelujah!
Sing to the LORD a new song,[o]
his praise in the assembly
of the faithful.[p]

2 Let Israel celebrate its Maker;
let the children of Zion rejoice
in their King.[q]

3 Let them praise his name with dancing
and make music to him
with tambourine and lyre.[r]

4 For the LORD takes pleasure
in his people;[s]
he adorns the humble with salvation.[t]

5 Let the faithful celebrate
in triumphal glory;
let them shout for joy on their beds.[u]

6 Let the exaltation of God be
in their mouths[B]
and a double-edged sword
in their hands,[v]

7 inflicting vengeance on the nations
and punishment on the peoples,[w]

8 binding their kings with chains
and their dignitaries
with iron shackles,[x]

9 carrying out the judgment
decreed against them.
This honor is for all his faithful people.[y]
Hallelujah!

PRAISE THE LORD

150 Hallelujah!
Praise God in his sanctuary.
Praise him in his mighty expanse.[z]

2 Praise him for his powerful acts;[aa]
praise him
for his abundant greatness.[ab]

3 Praise him with trumpet blast;[ac]
praise him with harp and lyre.[ad]

4 Praise him with tambourine
and dance;[ae]
praise him with strings and flute.[af]

5 Praise him
with resounding cymbals;
praise him with clashing cymbals.[ag]

6 Let everything that breathes
praise the LORD.[ah]
Hallelujah!

[A]148:8 Or *fire*   [B]149:6 Lit *throat*

148:1-13 The Maker deserves the worship of all he has made.
148:14 God demonstrated faithfulness to **the Israelites**, the people of Abraham. And through them, he blessed all peoples of the earth (see Gen 12:3; Gal 3:7-18).
149:6-9 In other words, praise is to be accompanied by action. They were to honor God

with their lips and also wage war against wickedness. The Lord honored his people by letting them carry out his own **judgment**, based on his word, against evildoers (149:9).
150:1-6 The psalmist gives a final doxological call for **praise** to **God**—both **in his sanctuary** (the tabernacle or temple) and **in his mighty expanse** (heaven)—for his

abundant greatness (that is, for who he is) and **for his powerful acts** (what he has done) (150:1-2). **Everything that breathes** is to render praise. Thus, the Psalter ends with a call to worship (150:6).

PROVERBS

INTRODUCTION

Author

SOLOMON IS CREDITED WITH THE proverbs of chapters 1–29 of this book. Scripture attests to Solomon's wisdom and that he was a collector of wise sayings (see 1 Kgs 3:5-14; 4:29-34; 5:7, 12; 10:1-3, 23-24). Proverbs 1–24 may have been written down during his reign, while chapters 25–29 contain Solomon's proverbs collected later by King Hezekiah. The final two chapters are credited to Agur and Lemuel, about whom we know nothing. An editor was inspired to collect all of these sayings into the book we now have.

Historical Background

Solomon's reign as king represented the peak of prosperity for the nation of Israel. This period witnessed the greatest extent of the nation's territory and saw peace and international trade (see 1 Kgs 4:20-25; 10:21-29). Solomon was likely familiar with the ancient wisdom tradition in Egypt, but through God's inspiration and gift of great wisdom, he composed superior sayings. While he addressed his teachings to his son(s), they are applicable to all people.

Message and Purpose

Proverbs is one of the most neglected books in the Bible, yet it is a key piece of Scripture. It is a book about wisdom—the ability to take biblical truth and apply it to life's realities. It contrasts the person who does this with the fool, the person who refuses to live by God's standards. According to Proverbs, you become wise when you apply God's principles to your practical decision-making. And when you do, you can live life the way God meant it to be lived.

Life is full of choices. We've all made good choices and bad choices, wise ones and foolish ones. The good news is that with insight from the book of Proverbs in mind, you can begin applying its wisdom to all the scenarios of your life. Proverbs covers everything from parenting, marriage, money, and friends, to how to relate to God. If you will use the wisdom of Proverbs as you make future decisions, then, it will save you time, grief, regret, and even money so that you can experience the benefits of kingdom living here and now.

www.bhpublishinggroup.com/qr/te/20_00

Outline

a 1:1 1Kg 4:32; Pr 10:1; 25:1;
Ec 12:9
b 1:3 Pr 2:9
c 1:4 Pr 8:5
d Pr 2:11; 3:21
e 1:5 Pr 9:9; 16:21,23
f 1:6 Nm 12:8; Jdg 14:12; Ps
49:4; Hab 2:6
g 1:7 Jb 28:28; Ps 111:10; Pr
9:10; 15:33
h Eph 5:17
i 1:8 Pr 6:20; 31:1

j 1:9 Pr 4:9
k Gn 41:42; Pr 6:21; Dn
5:29
l 1:10 Pr 16:29
m Ps 141:4
n 1:11 Pr 12:6; Jr 5:26
o Ps 10:8
p 1:12 Ps 124:3
q Ps 28:1
r 1:13 Pr 24:4
s 1:15 Ps 1:1; Pr 4:14
t Ps 119:101; Pr 16:19
u 1:16 Pr 6:17-18; Is 59:7;
Rm 3:15
v 1:19 Pr 15:27; Ezk 22:27;
Hab 2:6-12
w 1:20 Pr 8:1-3; 9:3

THE PURPOSE OF PROVERBS

1 The proverbs of Solomon[a]
    son of David, king of Israel:
2 For learning wisdom and discipline;
   for understanding
      insightful sayings;
3 for receiving prudent instruction
   in righteousness, justice,
      and integrity;[b]
4 for teaching shrewdness
   to the inexperienced,[A,c]
   knowledge and discretion[d]
      to a young man —
5 let a wise person listen
   and increase learning,[e]
   and let a discerning person
      obtain guidance —
6 for understanding a proverb
   or a parable,[B]
   the words of the wise,
      and their riddles.[f]

APPLICATION QUESTIONS

READ PROVERBS 1:7

– Do you experience fear at the thought of
  submitting your life entirely to the authority
  of God's kingdom agenda? Explain.
– How is fear currently influencing your relationship with God?
– When have you recently experienced the fear
  of the Lord?

---

7 The fear of the LORD
   is the beginning of knowledge;[g]
   fools despise wisdom
      and discipline.[h]

AVOID THE PATH OF THE VIOLENT

8 Listen, my son,
   to your father's instruction,
   and don't reject
      your mother's teaching,[i]

9 for they will be a garland[j] of favor
      on your head
   and pendants[c] around your neck.[k]
10 My son, if sinners entice you,[l]
   don't be persuaded.[m]
11 If they say — "Come with us!
   Let's set an ambush[n]
      and kill someone.[D]
   Let's attack some innocent person[o]
      just for fun![E]
12 Let's swallow them alive,[p]
      like Sheol,
   whole, like those who go down
      to the Pit.[q]
13 We'll find all kinds
      of valuable property
   and fill our houses with plunder.[r]
14 Throw in your lot with us,
   and we'll all share the loot"[F] —
15 my son, don't travel that road
      with them[s]
   or set foot on their path,[t]
16 because their feet run toward evil
   and they hurry to shed blood.[u]
17 It is useless to spread a net
   where any bird can see it,
18 but they set an ambush
      to kill themselves;[G]
   they attack their own lives.
19 Such are the paths of all who make
      profit dishonestly;[v]
   it takes the lives of those
      who receive it.[H]

WISDOM'S PLEA

20 Wisdom calls out in the street;
   she makes her voice heard
      in the public squares.[w]
21 She cries out above[I] the commotion;
   she speaks at the entrance
      of the city gates:
22 "How long, inexperienced ones,
   will you love ignorance?

[A] 1:4 Or *simple,* or *gullible*   [B] 1:6 Or *an enigma*   [C] 1:9 Lit *chains*   [D] 1:11 Lit *Let's ambush for blood*   [E] 1:11 Lit *person for no reason*   [F] 1:14 Lit *us; one bag will be for all of us*   [G] 1:18 Lit *they ambush for their blood*   [H] 1:19 Lit *takes the life of its masters*   [I] 1:21 Lit *at the head of*

1:2-6 To be **wise** is to take God's perspective and turn it into functional application (1:5-6). It's spiritual understanding applied to earthly living; it's the God-given ability to make good decisions.

1:7 To have true **knowledge** is to perceive the right nature of a thing. Proverbs teaches that all true wisdom and knowledge is rooted in God and his Word, and it urges us to cultivate a fear of God (take him seriously) through a relationship with him.

Fools are self-centered people who live without regard to wisdom and moral values. A fool rejects God's perspective and substitutes his own.

1:8-9 Instruction on how to be wise begins in the home. Parents have the responsibility to teach their children to know God, to see the world from his perspective, and to live in accordance with his agenda. And children have the responsibility to listen. While that doesn't go down too well with a lot of kids today, especially when they reach the age at which they are confident they know more than their parents and think they can do better, Solomon says listening to your parents' advice is like adorning yourself with gold.

1:10-16 Don't let **sinners entice you** (1:10). To put this passage in modern terms, if you don't want to be a drug addict, don't hang out with drug addicts. If you don't want to be a gang

member, don't let gang members be your running buddies. "Bad company corrupts good morals" (1 Cor 15:33).

1:17-19 We as parents must know our kids' companions. If they are going out with friends, find out where they'll be. When they tell you they're just going to hang out, ask them where they'll be hanging out—in case you want to join them. You have a right to know what they're up to, and you're responsible for knowing. Make sure your kids understand this: when foolish people look for trouble, they are simply setting a trap for themselves.

1:20-21 There are only two answers to any issue: God's answer and everybody else's. And everybody else is wrong. **Wisdom** is crying

How long will you mockers[a]
   enjoy mocking
and you fools hate knowledge?[b]
23 If you respond to my warning,[A,c]
   then I will pour out my spirit
      on you[d]
   and teach you my words.
24 Since I called out and you refused,[e]
   extended my hand and no one
      paid attention,[f]
25 since you neglected all my counsel[g]
   and did not accept my correction,

26 I, in turn, will laugh at
   your calamity.[h]
I will mock when terror
   strikes you,
27 when terror strikes you like a storm
and your calamity comes
   like a whirlwind,
when trouble and stress
   overcome you.
28 Then they will call me,
   but I won't answer;
they will search for me, but won't
   find me.[i]
29 Because they hated knowledge,
   didn't choose to fear the LORD,[j]
30 were not interested in my counsel,
   and rejected all my correction,[k]
31 they will eat the fruit of their way[l]
   and be glutted with
      their own schemes.[m]
32 For the apostasy
   of the inexperienced
      will kill them,[n]
and the complacency of fools
   will destroy them.
33 But whoever listens to me
   will live securely
and be undisturbed by the dread
   of danger."[o]

WISDOM'S WORTH

2 My son, if you accept my words[p]
   and store up my commands
      within you,
2 listening closely[B] to wisdom
   and directing your heart
      to understanding;
3 furthermore, if you call out
   to insight
and lift your voice to understanding,
4 if you seek it like silver
   and search for it like hidden treasure,[q]
5 then you will understand the fear
   of the LORD
   and discover the knowledge of God.
6 For the LORD gives wisdom;
   from his mouth come knowledge
      and understanding.[r]
7 He stores up success[c] for the upright;
He is a shield for those who live
   with integrity[s]

[a]1:22 Ps 1:1
[b]Jb 21:14; Pr 1:29; 5:12
[c]1:23 Pr 3:11; 15:5,31-32
[d]Jl 2:28
[e]1:24 Is 65:12; 66:4; Jr 7:13; Zch 7:11
[f]Is 65:2; Rm 10:21
[g]1:25 Ps 107:11; Lk 7:30

[h]1:26 Ps 2:4
[i]1:28 1Sm 8:18
[j]1:29 Pr 1:7
[k]1:30 Pr 5:12; 15:5
[l]1:31 Jr 6:19
[m]Pr 14:14; 28:19
[n]1:32 Jr 2:19
[o]1:33 Ps 112:7-8; Pr 3:24-26
[p]2:1 Pr 4:10
[q]2:4 Jb 3:21; Mt 13:44
[r]2:6 Jb 32:8
[s]2:7 Ps 84:11; Pr 10:9; 20:7; 28:18; 30:5

A1:23 Lit *you turn back to my reprimand*   B2:2 Lit *you, stretching out your ear*   C2:7 Or *resourcefulness*

---

out for someone to pay attention to truth. Are you listening?
1:26 You do *not* want to hear God declare to you, **I . . . will laugh at your calamity**. So remember Galatians 6:7: "Don't be deceived: God is not mocked. For whatever a person sows he will also reap."

1:29-31 In other words, a fool will be stuffed with his own stupidity to his own detriment. **2:1-5** Godly wisdom doesn't just fall into your lap. It requires diligent pursuit. Finding it requires digging into God's Word the way a miner digs for **silver** and other **hidden treasure** (2:4).

2:6-19 Many people rise early to exercise because they're serious about getting in shape, but they're too tired to rise early to spend time in God's Word. Others set aside time for their favorite TV show, but God can't get a slot on their schedules. The Lord is the one who **gives wisdom** (2:6). You can't

[a] 2:8 1Sm 2:9; Ps 66:9
[b] 2:11 Pr 4:6; 6:22
[c] 2:11-13 Ps 82:5; Pr 15:19;
16:17; Jn 3:19,20
[d] 2:14 Pr 10:23
[e] 2:15 Ps 125:5; Pr 21:8
[f] Pr 3:32; 14:2
[g] 2:16 Pr 9:13-18
[h] Pr 5:3,20; 6:24; 7:5,21;
23:27
[i] 2:17 Mal 2:14-15
[j] 2:18 Pr 7:27; 9:18; 21:16
[k] 2:16-19 Ps 16:11; Pr 5:6;
7:5,21-27; 23:27-28; Ec 7:26
[l] 2:20 Heb 6:12

[m] 2:21 Pr 10:30; Mt 5:5-6
[n] 2:22 Ps 37:38
[o] Dt 28:63; Ps 52:5
[p] 3:1 Dt 30:16
[q] 3:2 Ps 91:16; Pr 3:16; 4:10;
9:11; 10:27
[r] 3:1-2 Pr 4:1-4; 6:20-23;
7:1-3
[s] 3:3 Pr 1:9; 6:21; 7:3;
2Co 3:3
[t] 3:4 Dt 4:6; 1Sm 2:26; Lk
2:52; Rm 14:18
[u] 3:5 Ps 37:3,5
[v] Jr 9:23
[w] 3:6 Pr 11:5

> ### ⤳ HOPE WORDS ⤳
> *God can accomplish in a*
> *moment what would take*
> *years on your own. Seek him*
> *and his path. Watch him open*
> *the doors to your destiny.*

8 so that he may guard the paths
of justice
and protect the way
of his faithful followers.[a]
9 Then you will understand
righteousness, justice,
and integrity — every good path.
10 For wisdom will enter your heart,
and knowledge will delight you.
11 Discretion will watch over you,
and understanding will guard you.[b]
12 It will rescue you from the way
of evil —
from anyone who says
perverse things,
13 from those who abandon
the right paths
to walk in ways of darkness,[c]
14 from those who enjoy doing evil[d]
and celebrate perversion,
15 whose paths are crooked,[e]
and whose ways are devious.[f]
16 It will rescue you
from a forbidden woman,[g]
from a wayward woman
with her flattering talk,[h]
17 who abandons the companion
of her youth[i]
and forgets the covenant of her God;
18 for her house sinks down to death
and her ways to the land
of the departed spirits.[j]
19 None return who go to her;
none reach the paths of life.[k]
20 So follow the way of the good,[l]
and keep to the paths
of the righteous.

21 For the upright will inhabit the land,
and those of integrity will remain
in it;[m]
22 but the wicked will be cut off
from the land,[n]
and the treacherous ripped
out of it.[o]

> ### ⤳ HOPE WORDS ⤳
> *A person who is serious about*
> *fulfilling his purpose will learn*
> *to view all of life through the*
> *grid of God's intentions.*

TRUST THE LORD

3 My son, don't forget my teaching,
but let your heart keep
my commands;[p]
2 for they will bring you
many days, a full life,[A,q]
and well-being.[r]
3 Never let loyalty and faithfulness
leave you.
Tie them around your neck;
write them on the tablet
of your heart.[s]
4 Then you will find favor
and high regard
with God and people.[t]

APPLICATION QUESTIONS

READ PROVERBS 3:5-6

– Why is trust necessary to live according to
God's kingdom agenda?
– What are some of the crooked areas in your
life that need to be straightened out?
– How do you currently plan to address those
areas?

---

5 Trust in the LORD with all your heart,[u]
and do not rely on
your own understanding;[v]
6 in all your ways know him,
and he will make your paths straight.[w]

[A] **3:2** Lit *days, years of life*

---

obtain it anywhere else. So how eager are
you to have **discretion** and **understanding
. . . guard you** and **rescue you from the way
of evil**? (2:11-12). How desperate are you to
be protected from **those . . . whose paths are
crooked**? (2:14-15). If you are not spiritually
hungry, ask God to give you a new spiritual
appetite (see Ps 42:1; Matt 5:6).
2:20 Smart hikers know to stick to the trail.
God has prepared a spiritual path from which
we shouldn't deviate.

2:22 Those who reject God's wisdom in order
to pursue wickedness and foolishness may
seem to flourish for a while, but eventually
they'll be pulled up like weeds.
3:5-6 The Hebrew word for **trust** means to
lie down on—to put your entire weight on
something. When you go to sleep, you lie
down on your bed because you believe it
is strong enough to hold you. **With all your
heart** means entirely, without exception. So
in essence God says, "Trust me completely;

I can sustain you. Your own understanding
won't support you."
   In all your ways know him is an umbrella
statement covering anything having to do
with your life. Pleasing God in all things is to
become your goal. Know God in all your ways
by prayerfully consulting his Word.
   When you rely on God in all you do, **he will
make your paths straight.** God can remove
obstacles and even cut a path through the
woods.

7 Don't be wise in your own eyes;[a]
  fear the LORD and turn away
    from evil.[b]
8 This will be healing for your body[A,c]
  and strengthening for your bones.[d]
9 Honor the LORD
    with your possessions
  and with the first produce
    of your entire harvest;[e]
10 then your barns will be
    completely filled,
  and your vats will overflow
    with new wine.[f]
11 Do not despise
    the LORD's instruction, my son,
  and do not loathe his discipline;[g]
12 for the LORD disciplines the one
    he loves,
  just as a father disciplines the son in
    whom he delights.[h]

WISDOM BRINGS HAPPINESS

13 Happy is a man who finds wisdom[i]
  and who acquires understanding,
14 for she is more profitable than silver,
  and her revenue is better than gold.[j]
15 She is more precious than jewels;[k]
  nothing you desire can equal her.[l]
16 Long life[B] is in her right hand;
  in her left, riches and honor.[m]
17 Her ways are pleasant,[n]
  and all her paths, peaceful.
18 She is a tree of life[o] to those
    who embrace her,
  and those who hold on to her
    are happy.

19 The LORD founded the earth
    by wisdom[p]
  and established the heavens
    by understanding.
20 By his knowledge the watery depths
    broke open,[q]
  and the clouds dripped with dew.[r]

21 Maintain sound wisdom
    and discretion.
  My son, don't lose sight of them.[s]

22 They will be life for you[c,t]
  and adornment[D] for your neck.
23 Then you will go safely on your way;
  your foot will not stumble.[u]
24 When you lie[E] down, you will not
    be afraid;[v]
  you will lie down, and your sleep
    will be pleasant.
25 Don't fear sudden danger
  or the ruin of the wicked
    when it comes,[w]
26 for the LORD will be your confidence[F]
  and will keep your foot from a snare.[x]

TREAT OTHERS FAIRLY

27 When it is in your power,[G]
  don't withhold good[y] from the one
    to whom it belongs.
28 Don't say to your neighbor,
    "Go away! Come back later.
  I'll give it tomorrow" —
    when it is there with you.[z]
29 Don't plan any harm
    against your neighbor,[aa]
  for he trusts you and lives near you.
30 Don't accuse anyone
    without cause,[ab]
  when he has done you no harm.
31 Don't envy a violent man[ac]
  or choose any of his ways;
32 for the devious are detestable
    to the LORD,
  but he is a friend[H] to the upright.[ad]
33 The LORD's curse is on the household
    of the wicked,[ae]
  but he blesses the home
    of the righteous;
34 He mocks those who mock,
  but gives grace to the humble.[af]
35 The wise will inherit honor,
  but he holds up fools to dishonor.[I]

A FATHER'S EXAMPLE

4 Listen, sons, to a father's discipline,[ag]
  and pay attention so that
    you may gain understanding,
2 for I am giving you good instruction.[ah]
  Don't abandon my teaching.

[a] 3:7 Pr 26:5,12; 28:11,26; Rm 12:16
[b] Jb 1:1; 28:28; Ps 37:27; Pr 16:6
[c] 3:8 Pr 4:22
[d] Jb 21:24
[e] 3:9 Ex 23:19; Lv 23:9–14; Dt 26:2
[f] 3:10 Dt 28:8; Mal 3:10
[g] 3:11 Pr 5:11–13; 15:5,31–33
[h] 3:12 Dt 8:5; Jb 5:17–18; Pr 13:24; Heb 12:5–7
[i] 3:13 Pr 8:32,34
[j] 3:14 Jb 28:15–19; Pr 8:10,19; 16:16; 22:1
[k] 3:15 Jb 28:18
[l] Pr 8:11; 20:15
[m] 3:16 Pr 8:18; 21:21; 22:4
[n] 3:17 Mt 11:19
[o] 3:18 Gn 2:9; Pr 11:30; 13:12; 15:4; Rv 2:7
[p] 3:19 Ps 104:24; Pr 8:27
[q] 3:20 Gn 7:11
[r] 3:21 Pr 4:21

[t] 3:22 Pr 4:22
[u] 3:23 Ps 91:12; Pr 4:12
[v] 3:24 Jb 11:19; Ps 3:5; Pr 6:22
[w] 3:25 Jb 5:21; Ps 91:5; 1Pt 3:14
[x] 3:26 1Sm 2:9
[y] 3:27 Gl 6:10
[z] 3:28 Lv 19:13; Dt 24:15
[aa] 3:29 Pr 6:14; 14:22
[ab] 3:30 Pr 24:28; Rm 12:18
[ac] 3:31 Ps 37:1; Pr 23:17; 24:1,19
[ad] 3:32 Ps 25:14; Pr 11:20; 12:22; 15:8–9
[ae] 3:33 Zch 5:3–4; Mal 2:2
[af] 3:34 Jms 4:6; 1Pt 5:5
[ag] 4:1 Ps 34:11; Pr 1:8
[ah] 4:2 Jb 11:4

[A] 3:8 Lit navel   [B] 3:16 Lit Length of days   [C] 3:22 Or be your throat   [D] 3:22 Or grace   [E] 3:24 LXX reads sit   [F] 3:26 Or be at your side   [G] 3:27 Lit in the power of your hands   [H] 3:32 Or confidential counsel   [I] 3:35 Or but haughty fools dishonor, or but fools exalt dishonor

---

3:7 You can't just talk about trusting the Lord without walking the talk.
3:9 Giving to the work of the Lord and honoring him with how you spend your money is crucial because it's a tangible expression of your faith. It demonstrates how much you value him.
3:11-12 Godly parents don't withhold loving discipline from their children. The more you love, in fact, the more you correct what is wrong and train in what is right.

3:19-20 In other words, **wisdom** is part of the fabric of the universe. Reject wisdom, and you're rejecting the reason for your existence.
3:21-26 Exercise sound, biblical judgment in your day-to-day life, and God himself **will be your confidence** and watch over you (3:26).
3:27-30 These admonitions, at their core, are really just another way of saying, "Love your neighbor as yourself" (Lev 19:18; Mark 12:31). Treat others the way you want to be treated.

Love God and love your neighbor; you can't have one without the other.
3:31-32 When we see evil people prosper, we're tempted to **envy** them (3:31). But we need to wear our spiritual spectacles so that we get the complete picture. God detests the **devious**, but **he is a friend to the upright** (3:32). Which would you rather be?
4:1-4 Solomon shows the progression of godly instruction and obedience from one

a 4:4 Pr 3:1-2; 6:20-23;
7:1-2
b 4:5 Pr 16:16
c 4:6 2Th 2:10
d 4:7 Pr 16:16
e 4:8 1Sm 2:30
f 4:9 Pr 1:9; 16:31
g 4:10 Pr 2:1
h Pr 3:2
i 4:11 1Sm 12:23
j 4:12 Jb 18:7; Ps 18:36
k Pr 3:23
l 4:13 Pr 3:18
m 4:14 Ps 1:1; Pr 1:15
n 4:16 Ps 36:4; Mc 2:1

o 4:18 2Sm 23:4
p 4:19 Is 59:9-10; Jr 23:12;
Jn 12:35
q Pr 24:16; Jn 11:10
r 4:20 Pr 5:1
s 4:21 Pr 3:21
t 4:23 Mt 15:19; Mk 7:18-23
u 4:24 Pr 6:12
v 4:25 Heb 12:2
w 4:26 Pr 5:6,21; Heb 12:13
x 4:27 Dt 5:32-33; 28:13-14;
Jos 1:7; 23:6; 1Kg 15:5
y 5:1 Pr 4:20; 22:17
z 5:2 Mal 2:7
aa 5:4 Pr 5:8-11; 6:32-33;
Ec 7:26

3 When I was a son with my father,
tender and precious to my mother,
4 he taught me and said:
"Your heart must hold on
to my words.
Keep my commands and live.[a]
5 Get wisdom, get understanding;[b]
don't forget or turn away
from the words from my mouth.
6 Don't abandon wisdom, and she will
watch over you;
love her,[c] and she will guard you.
7 Wisdom is supreme —
so get wisdom.
And whatever else you get,
get understanding.[d]
8 Cherish her, and she will exalt you;
if you embrace her, she will
honor you.[e]
9 She will place a garland of favor
on your head;
she will give you a crown of beauty."[f]

TWO WAYS OF LIFE

10 Listen, my son. Accept my words,[g]
and you will live many years.[h]
11 I am teaching you the way
of wisdom;
I am guiding you on straight paths.[i]
12 When you walk, your steps will not
be hindered;[j]
when you run, you will not stumble.[k]
13 Hold on to instruction; don't let go.[l]
Guard it, for it is your life.
14 Keep off the path of the wicked;[m]
don't proceed on the way
of evil ones.
15 Avoid it; don't travel on it.
Turn away from it, and pass it by.
16 For they can't sleep
unless they have done what is evil;
they are robbed of sleep
unless they make someone stumble.[n]
17 They eat the bread of wickedness
and drink the wine of violence.

18 The path of the righteous is
like the light of dawn,[o]
shining brighter and brighter
until midday.
19 But the way of the wicked is
like the darkest gloom;[p]
they don't know what makes
them stumble.[q]

THE STRAIGHT PATH

20 My son, pay attention to my words;
listen closely to my sayings.[r]
21 Don't lose sight of them;[s]
keep them within your heart.
22 For they are life to those
who find them,
and health to one's whole body.
23 Guard your heart above all else,[A]
for it is the source of life.[t]
24 Don't let your mouth
speak dishonestly,[u]
and don't let your lips talk deviously.
25 Let your eyes look forward;
fix your gaze[B] straight ahead.[v]
26 Carefully consider the path[C]
for your feet,[w]
and all your ways
will be established.
27 Don't turn to the right or to the left;[x]
keep your feet away from evil.

AVOID SEDUCTION

5 My son, pay attention
to my wisdom;
listen closely[D] to my understanding[y]
2 so that you may maintain discretion
and your lips safeguard
knowledge.[z]
3 Though the lips
of the forbidden woman
drip honey
and her words are[E]
smoother than oil,
4 in the end she's as bitter
as wormwood[aa]

[A] 4:23 Or *heart with all diligence*   [B] 4:25 Lit *eyelids*   [C] 4:26 Or *Clear a path*   [D] 5:1 Lit *wisdom; stretch out your ear*   [E] 5:3 Lit *her palate is*

---

generation to the next. Parents are to be the dominant moral influencers and instructors of children.

4:5-7 Remember when cereal boxes came with prizes inside? They were at the bottom of the box, and your mom wouldn't let you shove your hand in to search for them. If you wanted the prizes, you had to eat your way to them. Similarly, if you want the rest of your life to be better than the part you've already lived, wisdom is there for the taking. But you must earnestly pursue it.

4:10 Accepting godly wisdom from one's parents can help you **live** longer, and I never

met anyone who didn't want to live a few extra years!

4:14-15 When you see the highway leading to hell, turn your car the other way.

4:17 Just as Jesus considered obeying God to be his "food" (see John 4:34), those who reject God feast on a diet of **wickedness.**

4:20 The repetitiveness of Solomon's call for his son to **pay attention** and **listen** is intentional. It's a reminder that parents can't offer their children wise instructions one time and suppose their job is done—mission accomplished. Instructing our children is an ongoing responsibility.

5:1-14 Whether the temptation up for discussion is fornication, adultery, or pornography, fathers must warn their sons that though the promise made by such things is sweet, following such a path leads **to death** (5:3-6). **Keep your way far from her** (5:8) is a reminder not to walk near the edge of the cliff. Sexual indiscretion will affect your wealth (e.g., alimony payments), your health (e.g., sexually transmitted diseases), and your reputation (5:10, 14). The man who lets his untamed sexual desires lead the way is repeatedly shown by Solomon to be a fool who is walking to his own funeral (5:7-14).

and as sharp as
a double-edged sword.[a]

5 Her feet go down to death;
her steps head straight for Sheol.[b]

6 She doesn't consider the path of life;
she doesn't know that her ways
are unstable.

7 So now, sons, listen to me,
and don't turn away from the words
from my mouth.[c]

8 Keep your way far from her.
Don't go near the door of her house.[d]

9 Otherwise, you will give up
your vitality to others
and your years to someone cruel;

10 strangers will drain your resources,
and your hard-earned pay will end
up in a foreigner's house.

11 At the end of your life, you will lament
when your physical body
has been consumed,

12 and you will say,
"How I hated discipline,
and how my heart
despised correction.[e]

13 I didn't obey my teachers
or listen closely[A] to my instructors.

14 I am on the verge of complete ruin
before the entire community."

ENJOY MARRIAGE

15 Drink water from your own cistern,
water flowing from your own well.[f]

16 Should your springs flow
in the streets,
streams in the public squares?[g]

17 They should be for you alone
and not for you to share
with strangers.

18 Let your fountain be blessed,
and take pleasure in the wife
of your youth.[h]

19 A loving deer, a graceful doe[B] —
let her breasts always satisfy you;[i]
be lost in her love forever.

20 Why, my son, would you
lose yourself
with a forbidden woman
or embrace a wayward woman?[j]

21 For a man's ways are before
the LORD's eyes,[k]
and he considers all his paths.[l]

22 A wicked man's iniquities will
trap him;[m]
he will become tangled in the ropes
of his own sin.[n]

23 He will die because there is
no discipline,[o]
and be lost because of
his great stupidity.

FINANCIAL ENTANGLEMENTS

6 My son, if you have put up security
for your neighbor[c]
or entered into an agreement
with[D] a stranger,[p]

2 you have been snared by the words
of your mouth
trapped by the words from your mouth.

3 Do this, then, my son,
and free yourself,
for you have put yourself
in your neighbor's power:
Go, humble yourself, and plead
with your neighbor.

4 Don't give sleep to your eyes
or slumber to your eyelids.[q]

5 Escape like a gazelle from a hunter,[E]
like a bird from a hunter's trap.[E,r]

LAZINESS

6 Go to the ant,[s] you slacker![t]
Observe its ways and become wise.

7 Without leader, administrator,
or ruler,

8 it prepares its provisions in summer;
it gathers its food during harvest.[u]

9 How long will you stay in bed,
you slacker?
When will you get up from your sleep?

10 A little sleep, a little slumber,
a little folding of the arms to rest,

11 and your poverty will come like
a robber,
your need, like a bandit.[v]

THE MALICIOUS MAN

12 A worthless person,[w] a wicked man
goes around speaking dishonestly,[x]

a 5:4 Ps 55:21; 57:4
b 5:5 Pr 7:27; 9:18
c 5:7 Pr 7:24
d 5:8 Pr 2:18; 7:8; 9:14
e 5:12 Ps 107:11; Pr 1:7,28–31; 12:1; 13:18
f 5:15 Sg 4:12,15
g 5:16 Pr 7:12
h 5:18 Ec 9:9; Mal 2:14
i 5:19 Sg 4:5
j 5:20 Pr 2:16

k 5:21 Jb 14:16; Ps 119:168; Hs 7:2; Heb 4:13
l Pr 4:25–26
m 5:22 Nm 32:23; Ps 7:15–16
n Pr 11:6
o 5:23 Jb 4:21
p 6:1 Pr 11:15; 17:18; 20:16; 22:26; 27:13
q 6:4 Ps 132:4
r 6:5 Ps 91:3; 124:7
s 6:6 Pr 30:24–25
t Pr 10:26; 13:4; 20:4; 26:16
u 6:8 Pr 10:5; 30:25
v 6:10–11 Pr 20:13; 24:33–34; 26:14; Ec 4:5
w 6:12 1Sm 25:25; Pr 16:27; 19:28
x Pr 4:24

A 5:13 Lit or turn my ear   B 5:19 Or graceful mountain goat   C 6:1 Or friend   D 6:1 Lit or slapped hands for   E 6:5 Lit hand

---

5:15-19 Many think the Bible is negative about sex, but it's difficult to reach that conclusion after reading passages like this one as well as Song of Songs. In fact, God invented sex! Under the covering of God's covenant, in the environment of a lifelong marriage commitment between a husband and wife, sex is a good gift of God intended to be enjoyed (5:19).

5:20-21 Make no mistake: nothing is truly done "in secret." We live under the gaze of an omnipresent God. You may think no one sees what you do in the dark. You might be good at covering your tracks. But God sees all.

6:1-5 To **put up security for your neighbor** (6:1) is like being a cosigner for someone else's debts. If the borrower defaults, guess

who's left holding the bag? Don't trap yourself into assuming another person's financial obligations (6:2-5).

6:6-11 Laziness has no place among God's people. See 10:4; 12:24; 18:9.

6:12-15 In Proverbs, the foolish individual is always ultimately overtaken by the consequences of his own actions.

[a] 6:13 Ps 35:19; Pr 10:10; 16:30
[b] 6:14 Pr 3:29; Mc 2:1
[c] Pr 6:19; 16:27-28; 28:25
[d] 6:15 2Ch 36:16; Pr 24:22; 29:1; Is 30:13-14; Jr 19:11
[e] 6:17 Ps 18:27; Pr 21:4; 30:13
[f] Ps 31:18; 120:2; Pr 12:22; 17:7
[g] Dt 19:10; Pr 1:16; Is 1:15; 59:7
[h] 6:18 Gn 6:5
[i] Pr 1:16
[j] 6:19 Ex 20:16; Ps 27:12; Pr 12:17; 14:5,25
[k] Pr 6:14; 16:27-28; 28:25
[l] 6:20 Pr 1:8; 31:1
[m] 6:21 Pr 1:9; 3:3; 7:3
[n] 6:23 Ps 119:105
[o] Pr 3:1-2; 4:4; 7:2; 19:16
[p] 6:24 Pr 7:5
[q] 6:25 Mt 5:28
[r] Sg 4:9

[s] 6:26 Pr 2:18-19; 7:21-23,27; 23:27-28; Ezk 13:18
[t] 6:29 Pr 16:5
[u] 6:30 Jr 49:9; Ob 5
[v] 6:31 Ex 22:1-4; Ps 79:12
[w] 6:32 Pr 7:22-23
[x] 6:34 Pr 27:4; Sg 8:6
[y] 7:1 Pr 2:1
[z] 7:2 Pr 3:1-2; 4:4; 6:23; 19:16
[aa] Dt 32:10; Ps 17:8; Zch 2:8
[ab] 7:3 Dt 11:18; Pr 3:3; 6:21
[ac] 7:4 Sg 4:9
[ad] 7:5 Pr 5:3,20; 6:24; 7:21
[ae] 7:6 Jdg 5:28; Sg 2:9

13 winking[a] his eyes, signaling
with his feet,
and gesturing with his fingers.
14 He always plots evil[b] with perversity
in his heart;
he stirs up trouble.[c]
15 Therefore calamity
will strike him suddenly;
he will be shattered instantly,
beyond recovery.[d]

WHAT THE LORD HATES

16 The LORD hates six things;
in fact, seven are detestable to him:
17 arrogant eyes,[e] a lying tongue,[f]
hands that shed innocent blood,[g]
18 a heart that plots wicked schemes,[h]
feet eager to run to evil,[i]
19 a lying witness who gives
false testimony,[j]
and one who stirs up trouble
among brothers.[k]

WARNING AGAINST ADULTERY

20 My son, keep
your father's command,
and don't reject
your mother's teaching.[l]
21 Always bind them
to your heart;
tie them around your neck.[m]
22 When you walk here and there,
they will guide you;
when you lie down, they will
watch over you;
when you wake up, they will
talk to you.
23 For a command is a lamp,
teaching is a light,[n]
and corrective discipline is the way
to life.[o]
24 They will protect you
from an evil woman,[A]
from the flattering[B] tongue of
a wayward woman.[p]
25 Don't lust in your heart
for her beauty[q]
or let her captivate you
with her eyelashes.[r]

26 For a prostitute's fee is only a loaf
of bread,[c]
but the wife of another man[D] goes
after a precious life.[s]
27 Can a man embrace fire
and his clothes not be burned?
28 Can a man walk on burning coals
without scorching his feet?
29 So it is with the one who sleeps with
another man's wife;
no one who touches her
will go unpunished.[t]
30 People don't despise the thief
if he steals
to satisfy himself when he is hungry.[u]
31 Still, if caught, he must pay
seven times as much;[v]
he must give up all the wealth
in his house.
32 The one who commits adultery[E]
lacks sense;
whoever does so destroys himself.[w]
33 He will get a beating[F] and dishonor,
and his disgrace will
never be removed.
34 For jealousy enrages a husband,[x]
and he will show no mercy
when he takes revenge.
35 He will not be appeased by anything
or be persuaded by lavish bribes.

7 My son, obey my words,
and treasure my commands.[y]
2 Keep my commands and live,[z]
and guard my instructions
as you would the pupil of your eye.[aa]
3 Tie them to your fingers;
write them on the tablet
of your heart.[ab]
4 Say to wisdom, "You are my sister,"[ac]
and call understanding your relative.
5 She will keep you
from a forbidden woman,
a wayward woman with
her flattering talk.[ad]

A STORY OF SEDUCTION

6 At the window of my house
I looked through my lattice.[ae]

[A] 6:24 LXX reads *from a married woman*   [B] 6:24 Lit *smooth*   [C] 6:26 Or *On account of a prostitute, one is left with only a loaf of bread*   [D] 6:26 Lit *but a wife of a man*   [E] 6:32 Lit *commits adultery with a woman*   [F] 6:33 Or *plague*

6:16-19 God **hates** all sin. But these things that are particularly **detestable to him** have to do with how we relate to others (6:16). Pride, or **arrogant eyes** (6:17), is first on God's list. It's the sin that led Satan to rebel against God and set up a rival kingdom (see Isa 14:12-14). Pride is typically the headwaters of other sins. When we think too highly of ourselves, we are tempted to commit the other six things

that are detestable to God, stirring up **trouble among brothers** (Prov 6:19). This is no minor matter because God responds to the unity of his people.
6:20-23 Dads must not assume they can have "the talk" one time with their boys and then forget the whole thing. Your son needs ongoing warning and exhortation if he is to avoid giving in to the sexual corruption that

everyone around him is indulging in.
6:27-29 This is the Galatians 6:7 principle at work, a reminder that you reap what you sow. If you adopt a baby dragon for a pet, don't be shocked when it grows up to eat you.
7:3 This is a reminder that the Israelites were commanded to make God's Word an inextricable part of their everyday lives (Deut 6:4-9).
7:6-27 Sexual immorality is personified as

⁷ I saw among the inexperienced,^A
I noticed among the youths,
a young man lacking sense.
⁸ Crossing the street near her corner,
he strolled down the road
to her house
⁹ at twilight, in the evening,
in the dark of the night.^a
¹⁰ A woman came to meet him
dressed like a prostitute,^b
having a hidden agenda.^B
¹¹ She is loud and defiant;^c
her feet do not stay at home.^d
¹² Now in the street, now in the squares,^e
she lurks at every corner.^f
¹³ She grabs him and kisses him;
she brazenly says^C to him,
¹⁴ "I've made fellowship offerings;
today I've fulfilled my vows.^g
¹⁵ So I came out to meet you,
to search for you, and I've found you.
¹⁶ I've spread coverings on my bed^h —
richly colored linen from Egypt.ⁱ
¹⁷ I've perfumed my bed
with myrrh, aloes, and cinnamon.^j
¹⁸ Come, let's drink deeply
of lovemaking until morning.^k
Let's feast on each other's love!
¹⁹ My husband isn't home;
he went on a long journey.
²⁰ He took a bag of silver with him
and will come home at the time
of the full moon."
²¹ She seduces him
with her persistent pleading;
she lures with her flattering^D talk.
²² He follows her impulsively
like an ox going to the slaughter,
like a deer bounding toward a trap^E
²³ until an arrow pierces its^F liver,^l
like a bird darting into a snare^m —
he doesn't know it will cost him
his life.

²⁴ Now, sons, listen to me,
and pay attention to the words
from my mouth.
²⁵ Don't let your heart turn aside
to her ways;
don't stray onto her paths.ⁿ

²⁶ For she has brought many
down to death;
her victims are countless.^G
²⁷ Her house is the road to Sheol,
descending to the chambers
of death.^o

WISDOM'S APPEAL

⁸ Doesn't wisdom^p call out?
Doesn't understanding make
her voice heard?
² At the heights overlooking
the road,
at the crossroads, she takes
her stand.
³ Beside the gates^q leading
into the city,
at the main entrance, she cries out:
⁴ "People, I call out to you;
my cry is to the children of Adam.
⁵ Learn to be shrewd,
you who are inexperienced;
develop common sense,
you who are foolish.
⁶ Listen, for I speak of noble things,
and what my lips say is right.
⁷ For my mouth tells the truth,^r
and wickedness is detestable
to my lips.
⁸ All the words from my mouth
are righteous;
none of them are deceptive
or perverse.^s
⁹ All of them are clear
to the perceptive,^t
and right to those
who discover knowledge.
¹⁰ Accept my instruction
instead of silver,
and knowledge rather
than pure gold.^u
¹¹ For wisdom is better than jewels,^v
and nothing desirable
can equal it.^w
¹² I, wisdom, share a home
with shrewdness
and have knowledge and discretion.^x
¹³ To fear the LORD is to hate evil.^y
I hate arrogant pride, evil conduct,
and perverse speech.

^a 7:9 Jb 24:15
^b 7:10 Gn 38:14-15
^c 7:11 Pr 9:13
^d 1Tm 5:13
^e 7:12 Pr 5:16; 9:14
^f Pr 23:28
^g 7:14 Lv 7:11-18; Dt 23:18; Ps 56:12
^h 7:16 Pr 31:22
ⁱ Ezk 27:7
^j 7:17 Ex 30:23; Ps 45:8
^k 7:18 Sg 5:1
^l 7:21-23 Pr 2:16-19; 5:3-6; 23:27-28
^m 7:23 Ec 9:12
ⁿ 7:25 Pr 5:8

^o 7:27 Pr 2:18; 5:5; 9:18; 1Co 6:9; Rv 22:15
^p 8:1-3 Pr 1:20-21; 9:3,13-15
^q 8:3 Jb 29:7
^r 8:7 Ps 37:30
^s 8:8 Dt 32:5; Pr 2:15; Php 2:15
^t 8:9 Pr 14:6
^u 8:10 Pr 3:14-15; 8:19; 16:16
^v 8:11 Jb 28:12-19
^w Pr 3:15; 20:15
^x 8:12 Pr 1:4
^y 8:13 Pr 16:6

^A 7:7 Or simple, or gullible, or naive   ^B 7:10 Or prostitute with a guarded heart   ^C 7:13 Lit she makes her face strong and says   ^D 7:21 Lit smooth   ^E 7:22 Text emended; MT reads like a shackle to the discipline of a fool; Hb obscure   ^F 7:23 Or his   ^G 7:26 Or and powerful men are all her victims

a woman on the prowl. In every corner of our culture, in fact, immorality is poised to entrap new victims. But the one who impulsively pursues a woman who is not his wife—whether she is single, married to another, or beckoning from a digital screen—**doesn't know** intuitively that **it will cost him his life** (7:23). He must be warned.

8:1-4 Wisdom takes her message out into the open and offers her gift to everyone because her agenda is God's agenda. Therefore she stands in the middle of the street and calls out, freely offering a spiritual view of life.

Parent, God has given you the responsibility to instill wisdom in your children, and there are lots of noises competing for their attention. So since wisdom doesn't whisper or mumble, make sure you don't either. Your children need to hear you.

a 8:14 Ec 7:19
b 8:15 2Ch 1:10; Dn 2:21; Rm 13:1
c 8:17 1Sm 2:30; Jn 14:21
d Pr 1:28; 2:4-5; Jms 1:5
e 8:18 Pr 3:16
f Ps 112:3; Mt 6:33
g 8:19 Jb 28:15; Pr 3:14; 8:10; 16:16
h 8:22 Gn 1:1; Jb 28:26-28; Ps 104:24
i 8:23 Jn 1:1-3; 17:5
j 8:24 Gn 1:2; Pr 3:20
k 8:25 Ps 90:2
l 8:27 Pr 3:19
m Jb 26:10
n 8:29 Jb 38:8-11; Ps 104:9
o Jb 38:4-5; Ps 104:5
p 8:30 Jb 28:20-27; 38-39; Pr 3:19-20; Jr 10:12; 51:15; Zch 13:7; Jn 1:2-3

q 8:31 Jb 38:4-7
r Heb 2:6-8
s 8:32 Ps 119:1-2; 128:1; Lk 11:28
t 8:33 Pr 4:1
u 8:34 Pr 3:13
v 8:35 Pr 4:4,22; 7:2; 9:11; 12:28; Jn 17:3
w Pr 3:4; 12:2; 13:13; 18:22
x 8:36 Pr 15:32
y Pr 11:19; 21:6
z 9:1 Pr 14:1; Eph 2:20-22; 1Pt 2:5
aa 9:2 Mt 22:4
ab Sg 8:2
ac Lk 14:17
ad 9:3 Ps 68:11; Mt 22:3
ae Pr 8:2-3; 9:14-15; Mt 10:27
af 9:4 Pr 6:32
ag 9:5 Is 55:1; Jn 6:27,51
ah 9:8 Pr 15:12; Mt 7:6
ai Ps 141:5
aj 9:9 Pr 1:5; 16:21,23

14 I possess good advice
  and sound wisdom;[A]
I have understanding and strength.[a]
15 It is by me that kings reign[b]
  and rulers enact just law;
16 by me, princes lead,
  as do nobles
  and all righteous judges.[B]
17 I love those who love me,[c]
  and those who search for me
    find me.[d]
18 With me are riches and honor,[e]
  lasting wealth and righteousness.[f]
19 My fruit is better than solid gold,
  and my harvest than pure silver.[g]
20 I walk in the ways of righteousness,
  along the paths of justice,
21 giving wealth as an inheritance
    to those who love me,
  and filling their treasuries.

22 "The LORD acquired[c] me
  at the beginning of his creation,[D]
  before his works of long ago.[h]
23 I was formed[E] before ancient times,
  from the beginning,
    before the earth began.[i]
24 I was born
  when there were no watery depths[j]
  and no springs filled with water.
25 Before the mountains
    were established,
  prior to the hills,[k] I was
    given birth —
26 before he made the land, the fields,
  or the first soil on earth.
27 I was there when he established
    the heavens,[l]
  when he laid out the horizon
    on the surface of the ocean,[m]
28 when he placed the skies above,
  when the fountains of the ocean
    gushed out,
29 when he set a limit for the sea
  so that the waters would not violate
    his command,[n]
  when he laid out the foundations
    of the earth.[o]
30 I was a skilled craftsman[F]
    beside him.[p]

31 I was his[G] delight every day,
  always rejoicing before him.
  I was rejoicing in
    his inhabited world,[q]
  delighting in the children of Adam.[r]

32 "And now, sons, listen to me;
  those who keep my ways are happy.[s]
33 Listen to instruction and be wise;[t]
  don't ignore it.
34 Anyone who listens to me is happy,[u]
  watching at my doors every day,
  waiting by the posts of my doorway.
35 For the one who finds me finds life[v]
  and obtains favor from the LORD,[w]
36 but the one who misses me[H]
  harms himself;[x]
  all who hate me love death."[y]

WISDOM VERSUS FOOLISHNESS

9 Wisdom has built her house;[z]
  she has carved out her seven pillars.
2 She has prepared her meat;[aa]
  she has mixed her wine;[ab]
  she has also set her table.[ac]
3 She has sent out
  her female servants;[ad]
  she calls out from the highest points
    of the city:[ae]
4 "Whoever is inexperienced,
  enter here!"
  To the one who lacks sense,[af]
  she says,
5 "Come, eat my bread,[ag]
  and drink the wine I have mixed.
6 Leave inexperience behind,
  and you will live;
  pursue the way of understanding.
7 The one who corrects a mocker
  will bring abuse on himself;
  the one who rebukes the wicked
    will get hurt.[I]
8 Don't rebuke a mocker, or he will
    hate you;[ah]
  rebuke the wise, and he will
    love you.[ai]
9 Instruct the wise, and he will be
    wiser still;
  teach the righteous, and he will
    learn more.[aj]

A 8:14 Or resourcefulness   B 8:16 Some Hb mss, LXX read nobles who judge the earth   C 8:22 Or possessed, or made   D 8:22 Lit way
E 8:23 Or consecrated   F 8:30 Or a confidant, or a child, or was constantly   G 8:30 LXX; MT omits his   H 8:36 Or who sins against me
I 9:7 Lit man: his blemish

8:17 **Love** Wisdom, and she will **love** you; **search** for her, and you'll **find** her. If you heed God's "seek and find" commands, he always promises to deliver what you're looking for (see Jer 29:13; Matt 7:7-8).
8:22-30 Wisdom is woven into creation; therefore, you can't escape the consequences of rejecting it. God accomplished his glorious work with wisdom, so why attempt your own work without it?
9:1-6 Wisdom has prepared a mind-blowing banquet of blessing for those who will accept her invitation (9:1-5), and rejecting her offer is like rejecting the only source of food. We desperately need God's wisdom, so we need to RSVP immediately and partake of the feast offered.
9:7-9 The difference between **a mocker** (9:7) and **the wise** lies in an individual's willingness to be corrected.

HOPE WORDS

*Wisdom is the willingness
and ability to apply spiritual
truths to life's realities.*

10 "The fear of the LORD is
   the beginning of wisdom,[a]
   and the knowledge of the Holy One[b]
   is understanding.
11 For by me your days will be many,
   and years will be added to your life.
12 If you are wise, you are wise
   for your own benefit;[c]
   if you mock, you alone will bear
   the consequences."

13 Folly is a rowdy woman;[d]
   she is gullible and knows nothing.[e]
14 She sits by the doorway of her house,
   on a seat at the highest point
   of the city,
15 calling to those who pass by,
   who go straight ahead on their paths:[f]
16 "Whoever is inexperienced,
   enter here!"
   To the one who lacks sense, she says,
17 "Stolen water is sweet,
   and bread eaten secretly is tasty!"[g]
18 But he doesn't know
   that the departed spirits are there,[h]
   that her guests are in the depths
   of Sheol.[i]

A COLLECTION OF SOLOMON'S PROVERBS

10 Solomon's proverbs:[j]
   A wise son brings joy to his father,
   but a foolish son, heartache
   to his mother.[k]

2 Ill-gotten gains do not
   profit anyone,
   but righteousness rescues
   from death.[l]

3 The LORD will not let the righteous
   go hungry,[m]
   but he denies the wicked
   what they crave.[n]

4 Idle hands make one poor,
   but diligent hands bring riches.[o]

5 The son who gathers
   during summer is prudent;
   the son who sleeps during harvest
   is disgraceful.[p]

6 Blessings are on the head
   of the righteous,
   but the mouth of the wicked
   conceals violence.[q]

7 The remembrance of the righteous
   is a blessing,
   but the name of the wicked will rot.[r]

8 A wise heart accepts commands,[s]
   but foolish lips will be destroyed.

9 The one who lives with integrity
   lives securely,[t]
   but whoever perverts his ways
   will be found out.[u]

10 A sly wink of the eye[v] causes grief,
   and foolish lips will be destroyed.

11 The mouth of the righteous is
   a fountain of life,[w]
   but the mouth of the wicked
   conceals violence.[x]

12 Hatred stirs up conflicts,
   but love covers all offenses.[y]

13 Wisdom is found on the lips
   of the discerning,

[a] 9:10 Jb 28:28; Ps 111:10; Pr 1:7; 15:33
[b] Pr 30:3; Hs 11:12; Rv 16:5
[c] 9:12 Jb 22:2
[d] 9:13 Pr 7:11
[e] Pr 5:6
[f] 9:14-15 Pr 7:11-12; 9:3-4
[g] 9:17 Pr 20:17
[h] 9:18 Pr 2:18; 21:16
[i] Pr 5:5; 7:27
[j] 10:1 Pr 1:1
[k] Pr 15:20; 17:25; 23:24-25; 29:3,15

[l] 10:2 Pr 11:4,18; 12:28; 21:6; Ezk 7:19; Lk 12:19-20
[m] 10:3 Ps 37:25; Mt 6:33
[n] Ps 112:10
[o] 10:4 Pr 12:24,27; 13:4,11; 19:15; 21:5
[p] 10:5 Pr 6:6-11; 30:25
[q] 10:6 Pr 10:11
[r] 10:7 Ps 9:5-6; 112:6
[s] 10:8 Mt 7:24
[t] 10:9 Ps 23:4; Pr 2:7; 3:23; 19:1; 20:7; 28:6,18; Is 33:15-16
[u] Pr 26:26; Mt 10:26; 1Tm 5:25
[v] 10:10 Ps 35:19; Pr 6:13; 16:30
[w] 10:11 Ps 37:30; Pr 13:14; 14:27; 16:22
[x] Pr 10:6
[y] 10:12 Pr 17:9; Jms 5:20; 1Pt 4:8

9:10 Wisdom, the ability to understand the divine perspective and apply it to life, comes from God. If you're going to become wise, you have to get to know God through his Word and take him seriously.
9:11 If you accept Wisdom's banquet invitation (9:1-5), she'll keep you from dying an untimely death through foolishness.
9:13-18 There's another party going on, distracting people from the pursuit of wisdom. The devil has a banquet prepared too, hosted by **Folly** (9:13). Her meal may be **sweet** and **tasty** (9:17), but it'll kill you (9:18).
10:1 Since Proverbs is an essential manual that helps parents teach their children wisdom, it's

not surprising that this first proverb speaks to how the presence or absence of wisdom in a child's heart affects his relationship to his parents. From the beginning, teach your children a divine perspective of life so they're equipped to make decisions that glorify God.
10:6 In God's economy, **blessings** come on those who seek to live in conformity to God's character.
10:9 The one who acts honestly and honorably, even when no one is watching, receives divine protection. No such safety net exists for the one who **perverts his ways**.
10:11 That **the mouth of the righteous is a fountain of life, but the mouth of the wicked**

conceals violence is a reminder that growing up in Christ means using our tongues to refresh others. That, however, goes against the natural perversity of the human heart and requires the power of the Holy Spirit. With his help, we *can* control our tongues.
10:12 The Bible doesn't command us to like one another; it commands us to "love one another" (John 13:34). In the Bible, love is not a giddy feeling or butterflies in the stomach. Biblical **love** is measured in sacrificing for the good of others.
10:13-14 It's amazing how much the Bible says about our speech. If you want to do a study that will challenge and change you, explore what God's Word says about your words.

a 10:13 Pr 19:29; 26:3
b 10:14 Pr 10:8; 12:13;
13:3; 18:7
c 10:15 Ps 52:7; Pr 18:11
d 10:16 Pr 11:19
e 10:17 Pr 5:12-13,22-23;
6:23; 13:13-14
f 10:18 Pr 11:13
g 10:19 Pr 17:27-28; Jms
1:19; 3:2
h 10:20 Pr 8:19; 10:32
i 10:21 Hs 4:6
j 10:22 Gn 24:35; 26:12; Dt
8:18; Jms 1:17
k Mt 6:31-32
l 10:23 Pr 2:14; 15:21
m 10:24 Pr 1:26-27; Is 66:4;
Heb 10:27

n 10:24 Ps 37:4; 145:19; Pr
11:23; Mt 5:6; 1Jn 5:14-15
o 10:25 Jb 21:18; Is 29:5-7
p Ps 15:5; Pr 10:30; 12:3,7;
Mt 7:24-27
q 10:26 Pr 26:6
r 10:27 Pr 3:2
s Jb 15:32-33; Pr 14:26-27;
15:16; 19:23
t 10:28 Pr 11:23; 23:18;
Jr 29:11
u Jb 8:13; 14:9; Pr 11:7;
Ezk 37:11
v 10:29 Pr 13:6; 21:15
w 10:30 Ps 21:7; 37:29;
125:1; Pr 2:21-22; 12:3
x 10:31 Ps 37:30
y Ps 37:38; 120:2-4
z 10:32 Ec 10:12
aa Pr 2:12; 10:20; 15:28
ab 11:1 Dt 25:13-16; Pr
20:10,23; Mc 6:10-11
ac Lv 19:36; Pr 16:11; Ezk
45:10
ad 11:2 Pr 15:33; 18:12;
22:4; 29:23

but a rod is for the back of the one
who lacks sense.*a*

14 The wise store up knowledge,
but the mouth of the fool
hastens destruction.*b*

15 The wealth of the rich is
his fortified city;*c*
the poverty of the poor is
their destruction.

16 The reward of the righteous is life;
the wages of the wicked
is punishment.*d*

17 The one who follows instruction is
on the path to life,
but the one who rejects correction
goes astray.*e*

18 The one who conceals hatred has
lying lips,
and whoever spreads slander is
a fool.*f*

19 When there are many words,
sin is unavoidable,
but the one who controls his lips
is prudent.*g*

20 The tongue of the righteous is
pure silver;
the heart of the wicked is
of little value.*h*

21 The lips of the righteous feed many,
but fools die for lack of sense.*i*

22 The LORD's blessing enriches,*j*
and he adds no painful effort to it.*^,k*

23 As shameful conduct is pleasure
for a fool,*l*
so wisdom is for a person
of understanding.

24 What the wicked dreads will come
to him,*m*

but what the righteous desire
will be given to them.*n*

25 When the whirlwind passes,
the wicked are no more,*o*
but the righteous
are secure forever.*p*

26 Like vinegar to the teeth and smoke
to the eyes,*q*
so the slacker is to the one
who sends him on an errand.

27 The fear of the LORD
prolongs life,*B,r*
but the years of the wicked
are cut short.*s*

28 The hope of the righteous is joy,*t*
but the expectation of the wicked
will perish.*u*

29 The way of the LORD is a stronghold
for the honorable,
but destruction awaits
the malicious.*v*

30 The righteous will never be shaken,
but the wicked will not remain
on the earth.*w*

31 The mouth of the righteous
produces wisdom,*x*
but a perverse tongue will be
cut out.*y*

32 The lips of the righteous know
what is appropriate,*z*
but the mouth of the wicked,
only what is perverse.*aa*

11 Dishonest scales are detestable
to the LORD,*ab*
but an accurate weight is
his delight.*ac*

2 When arrogance comes,
disgrace follows,
but with humility comes wisdom.*ad*

^*A*10:22 Or *and painful effort adds nothing to it*   *B*10:27 Lit LORD *adds to days*

10:18 The person whose heart is filled with hatred experiences a Catch-22. Either he **conceals** his **hatred** and is a liar, or he **spreads [his] slander** and is **a fool**.
10:20 The tongue of the righteous is valuable to those around him because it builds them up and dispenses God's viewpoint like riches.
10:22 A **blessing** in this instance is a God-given capacity to enjoy his goodness. Money and good health are certainly nice things to

have, but they are not necessarily blessings in the biblical sense. Many people have such things but don't enjoy them and aren't blessed by them. They have no sense of God's peace or satisfaction in their hearts; thus, even "good" things can become a source of unhappiness or discontentment. When God pours out his goodness to you, he gives you joy and peace and satisfaction with it, regardless of your particular situation.

10:23 What's a telltale sign of a fool? **Shameful conduct is pleasure** to him. Evil has stopped being evil for the one who rejects God. It moves under the heading of entertainment.
10:32 You can tell the difference between **the righteous** and **the wicked** simply by listening to them talk. Jesus said, "The mouth speaks from the overflow of the heart" (Matt 12:34).
11:1 The Lord hates dishonesty in the marketplace.

3 The integrity of the upright
    guides them,[a]
but the perversity of the treacherous
    destroys them.[b]

4 Wealth is not profitable on a day
    of wrath,
but righteousness rescues
    from death.[c]

5 The righteousness of the blameless
    clears his path,
but the wicked person will fall
    because of his wickedness.

6 The righteousness of the upright
    rescues them,
but the treacherous are trapped
    by their own desires.[d]

7 When the wicked person dies,
    his expectation comes to nothing,
and hope placed in wealth[A,B]
    vanishes.[e]

8 The righteous one is rescued
    from trouble;
in his place, the wicked
    one goes in.[f]

9 With his mouth the ungodly
    destroys his neighbor,
but through knowledge
    the righteous are rescued.

10 When the righteous thrive,
    a city rejoices;[g]
when the wicked die, there is
    joyful shouting.

11 A city is built up by the blessing
    of the upright,[h]
but it is torn down by the mouth
    of the wicked.[i]

12 Whoever shows contempt
    for his neighbor lacks sense,
but a person with understanding
    keeps silent.[j]

13 A gossip goes around revealing
    a secret,
but a trustworthy person keeps
    a confidence.[k]

14 Without guidance, a people will fall,
but with many counselors
    there is deliverance.[l]

15 If someone puts up security
    for a stranger,
he will suffer for it,[m]
but the one who hates
    such agreements is protected.

16 A gracious woman gains honor,
but violent[c] people gain only riches.

17 A kind man benefits himself,[n]
but a cruel person brings ruin
    on himself.[o]

18 The wicked person earns
    an empty wage,
but the one who sows righteousness,
    a true reward.[p]

19 Genuine righteousness
    leads to life,[q]
but pursuing evil leads to death.[r]

20 Those with twisted minds
    are detestable to the LORD,
but those with blameless conduct
    are his delight.[s]

21 Be assured[D] that a wicked person
    will not go unpunished,[t]
but the offspring of the righteous
    will escape.

22 A beautiful woman who rejects
    good sense
is like a gold ring in a pig's snout.[u]

23 The desire of the righteous
    turns out well,[v]
but the hope of the wicked
    leads to wrath.[w]

[a] 11:3 Pr 13:6
[b] Pr 11:17-19; 19:3
[c] 11:4 Gn 7:1; Pr 10:2; 11:28; 12:28; Zph 1:18
[d] 11:6 Ps 7:15-16; Pr 5:22; Ec 10:8
[e] 11:7 Jb 8:13; Pr 10:28; 24:14
[f] 11:8 Pr 21:18
[g] 11:10 Pr 28:12
[h] 11:11 Pr 14:34
[i] 14:1; 29:4
[j] 11:12 Pr 14:21

[k] 11:13 Lv 19:16; Pr 10:18; 20:19; 1Tm 5:13
[l] 11:14 Pr 15:22; 20:18; 24:6
[m] 11:15 Pr 6:1-2; 17:18; 22:26
[n] 11:17 Mt 5:7; 25:34-36
[o] Pr 11:3
[p] 11:18 Pr 10:2-3; Hs 10:12; Gl 6:8-9; Jms 3:18
[q] 11:19 Pr 10:16-17; 19:23
[r] Rm 6:23; Jms 1:15
[s] 11:20 1Ch 29:17; Ps 119:1; Pr 3:32; 12:22; 13:6; 15:8-9,26
[t] 11:21 Pr 16:5
[u] 11:22 Gn 24:47
[v] 11:23 Ps 37:4-5; Pr 10:24; Jr 29:11
[w] Pr 10:28; 11:7; Rm 2:8-9

[A] 11:7 LXX reads *hope of the ungodly*   [B] 11:7 Or *strength*   [C] 11:16 Or *ruthless*   [D] 11:21 Lit *Hand to hand*

11:10 At a wicked man's death, people don't even grieve; they celebrate. Worse, such a person is consigned to a joyless eternity separated from God. There is no fulfillment in hell, no dreams, only bitter regrets.
11:11 God's kingdom agenda is to be lived out by Christians as they interact with their world. We must align our lives with his game plan as we love God, love our neighbors, and influence our society.

11:13 If someone prefers spilling the beans in **gossip**, they don't deserve your **confidence**.
11:14 Don't be a Lone Ranger Christian. Don't think you can succeed apart from the help of a community of believers in a local church. Instead, seek **guidance** from those who will speak the divine viewpoint into your life.
11:15 See 6:1-5.
11:16-21 These verses are examples that describe the practical outcomes of two

opposing mindsets: righteousness and wickedness.
11:22 Nothing is more attractive than a wise woman who makes God's agenda her own (see 31:10-31). But, if a physically beautiful woman **rejects good sense**, at heart she's no more attractive than **a pig's snout**. Put lipstick on a pig, and it's still a pig.
11:23 See 11:4-9.

[a] 11:24 Ps 112:9; Pr 11:25; 21:26
[b] Pr 13:7; 22:16; 28:27
[c] 11:25 Pr 3:9-10; 2Co 9:6-11
[d] Mt 5:7; 10:42
[e] 11:26 Pr 24:24
[f] Gn 42:6
[g] 11:27 Php 4:8
[h] Est 7:10; Ps 7:15-16
[i] 11:28 Ps 49:6
[j] Ps 1:3; 92:12; Pr 11:4; 14:11; Jr 17:8
[k] 11:29 Pr 15:27
[l] Ec 5:16
[m] 11:30 Pr 3:18
[n] 11:31 Dt 32:25; Pr 13:21; 1Pt 4:18
[o] 12:1 Pr 3:11; 5:11-13; 15:5,31-32
[p] 12:2 Pr 8:35

[q] 12:2 Pr 14:17; 24:8
[r] 12:3 Ps 16:8; 21:7; Pr 10:30
[s] 12:4 Pr 18:22; 19:14; 31:10
[t] Pr 14:30
[u] 12:6 Pr 1:11
[v] Pr 14:2
[w] 12:7 Jb 34:25
[x] Ps 103:17-18; Pr 10:25; Mt 7:24-27
[y] 12:9 Pr 11:24; 13:7; Rm 12:3
[z] 12:10 Dt 25:4; Pr 27:23; Jnh 4:11
[aa] 12:11 Pr 24:27
[ab] Pr 28:19

24 One person gives freely,
yet gains more;[a]
another withholds what is right,
only to become poor.[b]

25 A generous person
will be enriched,[c]
and the one who gives a drink
of water
will receive water.[d]

26 People will curse[e] anyone
who hoards grain,
but a blessing will come to the one
who sells it.[f]

27 The one who searches
for what is good[g] seeks favor,
but if someone looks for trouble,
it will come to him.[h]

28 Anyone trusting in his riches
will fall,[i]
but the righteous will flourish
like foliage.[j]

29 The one who brings ruin
on his household[k]
will inherit the wind,[l]
and a fool will be a slave
to someone whose heart is wise.

30 The fruit of the righteous is a tree
of life,[m]
and a wise person
captivates people.

31 If the righteous will be repaid
on earth,
how much more the wicked
and sinful.[n]

12 Whoever loves discipline
loves knowledge,
but one who hates correction
is stupid.[o]

2 One who is good obtains favor
from the LORD,[p]

but he condemns a person
who schemes.[q]

3 No one can be made secure
by wickedness,
but the root of the righteous
is immovable.[r]

4 A wife of noble character[A] is
her husband's crown,[s]
but a wife who causes shame
is like rottenness
in his bones.[t]

5 The thoughts of the righteous
are just,
but guidance from the wicked
is deceitful.

6 The words of the wicked are
a deadly ambush,[u]
but the speech of the upright
rescues them.[v]

7 The wicked are overthrown
and perish,[w]
but the house of the righteous
will stand.[x]

8 A man is praised for his insight,
but a twisted mind is despised.

9 Better to be disregarded, yet have
a servant,
than to act important but have
no food.[y]

10 The righteous cares about
his animal's health,[z]
but even the merciful acts
of the wicked are cruel.

11 The one who works his land
will have plenty of food,[aa]
but whoever chases fantasies
lacks sense.[ab]

12 The wicked desire what evil people
have caught,[B]

[A] 12:4 Or *A wife of quality,* or *A wife of good character*   [B] 12:12 Or *desire a stronghold of evil*

11:24-26 Giving reveals who comes first in our lives (see 3:9). When we use our money and resources to promote God's agenda—building up the saints, spreading the gospel, helping those in need—he promises blessing, which is the capacity to enjoy and extend his goodness (see 10:22).
11:28 As Solomon has said, "Trust in the Lord with all your heart" (3:5). Nothing else can support you. See 30:7-9.

12:1 See 3:11-12; 9:7-9.
12:4 That **a wife of noble character is her husband's crown** foreshadows the book's closing praise of a capable wife (31:10-31). By contrast, a shameful wife makes her husband miserable.
12:5 At conversion, the Christian receives a new mind: "the mind of Christ" (1 Cor 2:16), but too many believers slump into their old way of thinking. Righteous living can only proceed from righteous thinking.

12:6 See 10:11, 18-21, 31-32.
12:7 This proverb calls to mind Jesus's parable of the two builders in Matthew 7:24-27. Let everything you do be built on a foundation of trusting in God's view of things as revealed in his Word.
12:10 A Christian who is committed to God's rule knows that animals are part of God's creation and deserve our compassionate care.

but the root of the righteous
is productive.

13 By rebellious speech an evil person
is trapped,[a]
but a righteous person escapes
from trouble.[b]

14 A person will be satisfied with good
by the fruit of his mouth,[c]
and the work of a person's hands
will reward him.[d]

15 A fool's way is right
in his own eyes,[e]
but whoever listens to counsel
is wise.

16 A fool's displeasure is known
at once,
but whoever ignores an insult
is sensible.[f]

17 Whoever speaks the truth declares
what is right,
but a false witness speaks deceit.[g]

18 There is one who speaks rashly,
like a piercing sword;[h]
but the tongue of the wise
brings healing.[i]

19 Truthful lips endure forever,
but a lying tongue, only a moment.[j]

20 Deceit is in the hearts of those
who plot evil,
but those who promote peace
have joy.[k]

21 No disaster overcomes
the righteous,[l]
but the wicked are full of misery.

22 Lying lips are detestable
to the LORD,[m]
but faithful people
are his delight.[n]

23 A shrewd person
conceals knowledge,
but a foolish heart
publicizes stupidity.[o]

24 The diligent hand will rule,
but laziness will lead to
forced labor.[p]

25 Anxiety in a person's heart
weighs it down,
but a good word cheers it up.[q]

26 A righteous person is careful
in dealing with his neighbor,[A]
but the ways of the wicked
lead them astray.[r]

27 A lazy hunter doesn't roast
his game,[s]
but to a diligent person, his wealth
is precious.[t]

28 There is life in the path
of righteousness,
and in its path there is no death.[B,u]

13 A wise son responds to his
father's discipline,
but a mocker doesn't listen
to rebuke.

2 From the fruit of his mouth,
a person will enjoy good things,[v]
but treacherous people have
an appetite for violence.[w]

3 The one who guards his mouth
protects his life;[x]
the one who opens his lips invites
his own ruin.[y]

4 The slacker craves, yet has nothing,
but the diligent is fully satisfied.[z]

5 The righteous hate lying,
but the wicked bring
disgust and shame.

[a] 12:13 Pr 10:14; 13:3; 18:7
[b] Pr 21:23; 29:6
[c] 12:14 Pr 13:2; 18:20
[d] Pr 1:31; 28:19; Is 3:10
[e] 12:15 Pr 16:2; 21:2
[f] 12:16 Pr 11:13; 12:23; 17:9; 29:11
[g] 12:17 Pr 6:19; 14:5,25
[h] 12:18 Ps 57:4
[i] Pr 4:22; 15:4
[j] 12:19 Ps 52:4-5; Pr 19:9
[k] 12:20 Pr 14:22
[l] 12:21 Ps 91:10; 1Pt 3:13
[m] 12:22 Rv 22:15
[n] Pr 3:32; 11:20; 15:8-9,26

[o] 12:23 Pr 11:13; 12:16; 13:16; 15:2
[p] 12:24 Pr 10:4; 13:4; 19:15
[q] 12:25 Ps 94:19; Pr 15:13; 16:24; Mt 6:25-34
[r] 12:26 Pr 14:22
[s] 12:27 Pr 19:15,24; 26:15
[t] Pr 10:4; 13:4
[u] 12:28 Pr 10:2; 13:14; 14:27
[v] 13:2 Pr 12:14
[w] Pr 1:10-12,31; 18:20-21; Is 32:6-8
[x] 13:3 Pr 18:21; 21:23; Jms 3:2
[y] Pr 10:14; 12:13; 18:7
[z] 13:4 Pr 10:4; 12:24,27; 19:15

[A] 12:26 Or *person guides his neighbor*   [B] 12:28 Or *righteousness, but the crooked way leads to death*

12:13-14 Jesus told his listeners that they would be judged by their own words (see Matt 12:37). **12:15** The fool's underlying problem is he can't see that his spiritual eyesight is blurred. As a result, he never **listens to counsel**. He just listens to himself tell himself that he's okay. **12:16, 18** Remember what James says about the tongue: it's "a restless evil, full of deadly poison" (Jas 3:8). This is the principle at work behind the **fool's displeasure** (Prov 12:16) when he **speaks rashly** (at 12:18). It's a reminder

that when we are quick to speak—often out of anger—good results rarely follow. We must engage our minds before we speak. **12:22** When he prayed to the Father, Jesus said, "Your word is truth" (John 17:17), and he told his disciples, "I am the way, the truth, and the life" (John 14:6). Lying, then, is contrary to God's own character and behavior. **12:25** Throughout Scripture, we're called by God to practice the "one anothers" (see Rom 12:10; Gal 6:2; Eph 4:32; Col 3:9; 1 Thess

4:18; Heb 10:24). A practical way to love and bless one another is to offer a **good word** that **cheers** the heart of a struggling believer. **12:27** See 6:6-11; 10:2-5; 12:24; 18:9; 26:13-16. **13:1** Parents have significantly more experience than their kids, and **wise** kids know it. Teenagers who want to grow in wisdom will humbly receive instruction and admonishment from their moms and dads. **13:2-3** See 10:11, 13-14, 32; 11:13; 12:13-14. **13:5** See 12:22.

a 13:6 Pr 10:29; 11:3
b 13:7 Pr 11:24; Lk 12:20-21;
1Tm 6:17-19; Rv 3:17-18
c Lk 12:33; 2Co 6:10;
Jms 2:5
d 13:8 Jb 2:4; Pr 10:15
e 13:9 Pr 4:18
f Jb 18:5-6; Pr 20:20; 24:20
g 13:10 Pr 17:19
h 13:11 Pr 10:2; 20:21; 23:5
i Pr 10:4; 21:5-6
j 13:12 Pr 11:30; 15:4
k 13:13 Nm 15:31; 2Ch 36:16
l Pr 3:1-2; 4:4; 6:23
m 13:14 Pr 10:11; 14:27
n Ps 18:5; 116:3
o 13:15 Pr 3:4

p 13:16 Pr 12:23; 15:2;
Ec 10:3
q 13:17 Pr 25:13
r 13:18 Pr 5:12-14; 12:1;
15:31-33
s 13:19 Pr 16:22; 29:27
t 13:21 Ps 32:10; Pr 11:31;
13:13
u 13:22 Jb 27:13-17; Pr 28:8;
Ec 2:26
v 13:24 Pr 19:18; 22:15;
23:13-14; 29:15,17
w Dt 8:5; Pr 3:12; Heb
12:5-7
x 13:25 Pr 10:3

6 Righteousness guards people
   of integrity,[A]
but wickedness undermines
   the sinner.[a]

7 One person pretends to be rich
   but has nothing;[b]
another pretends to be poor but has
   abundant wealth.[c]

8 Riches are a ransom
   for a person's life,[d]
but a poor person hears no threat.

9 The light of the righteous
   shines brightly,[e]
but the lamp of the wicked is put out.[f]

10 Arrogance leads to nothing but strife,[g]
but wisdom is gained by those
   who take advice.

11 Wealth obtained by fraud
   will dwindle,[h]
but whoever earns it through labor[B]
   will multiply it.[i]

12 Hope delayed makes the heart sick,
but desire fulfilled is a tree of life.[j]

13 The one who has contempt
   for instruction will pay
   the penalty,[k]
but the one who respects
   a command will be rewarded.[l]

14 A wise person's instruction is
   a fountain of life,[m]
turning people away
   from the snares of death.[n]

15 Good sense wins favor,[o]
but the way of the treacherous
   never changes.[C]

16 Every sensible person
   acts knowledgeably,
but a fool displays his stupidity.[p]

17 A wicked envoy falls into trouble,
but a trustworthy courier
   brings healing.[q]

18 Poverty and disgrace come to those
   who ignore discipline,
but the one who accepts correction
   will be honored.[r]

19 Desire fulfilled is sweet
   to the taste,
but to turn from evil is detestable
   to fools.[s]

20 The one who walks with the wise
   will become wise,
but a companion of fools
   will suffer harm.

21 Disaster pursues sinners,
but good rewards the righteous.[t]

22 A good man leaves an inheritance
   to his[D] grandchildren,
but the sinner's wealth is stored up
   for the righteous.[u]

23 The uncultivated field of the poor
   yields abundant food,
but without justice, it is swept away.

24 The one who will not use the rod
   hates his son,[v]
but the one who loves him
   disciplines him diligently.[w]

25 A righteous person eats
   until he is satisfied,
but the stomach of the wicked
   is empty.[x]

[A] 13:6 Lit *guards integrity of way*   [B] 13:11 Lit *whoever gathers upon his hand*   [C] 13:15 LXX, Syr, Tg read *treacherous will perish*   [D] 13:22 Or *inheritance: his*

13:7 See 12:9.
13:9 The Lord expects his people to live under his rule and let his glory shine through their good works (see Matt 5:14-16). **But the lamp of the wicked** will be snuffed out (Prov 13:9).
13:10 **Arrogance** is another word for pride. It's Satan's sin of choice (see Isa 14:13-14) and is number one on God's hate list (Prov 6:16-17).
13:11 See 10:2.
13:13 See 1:22-33.
13:17 That a **trustworthy** person bears **healing** news reminds me of Isaiah 52:7: "How beautiful on the mountains are the feet of the herald . . . who brings news of good things."
13:18 See 1:22-33; 3:11-12; 9:7-9; 10:17; 25:11-12; 29:1.

13:20 Spend time with wise people, and you will learn from them. Hang out with fools, and their corrupt moral values will rub off on you so that you **suffer harm**. You see, fools don't offer correction. So if your thinking is self-centered and your decisions lack good judgment, a fool will simply make you feel good about the path you're already on.
13:22 God has a way of transferring the resources of the wicked to be used and developed for kingdom purposes. For example, after God judged Egypt with plagues, he told the Israelites to ask their Egyptian neighbors for silver and gold (see Exod 11:1-2). God then had the Israelites take that

wealth and build a tabernacle where they could worship him. Later, he told Israel to take the land of Canaan, then inhabited by unrighteous people, and do his kingdom business within it (see Ps 105:43-45). God knows how to make theological transactions in favor of the righteous to accomplish his purposes.
13:24 This verse is not a license for abuse. A **rod** refers to any reasonable discipline inflicting sufficient pain that discourages the bad and encourages the good. When our children become teenagers, for instance, appropriate discipline may be the loss of a privilege—that can certainly be painful.

14

Every wise woman builds
　　her house,[a]
but a foolish one tears it down
　　with her own hands.[b]

2　Whoever lives with integrity
　　fears the LORD,[c]
but the one who is devious
　　in his ways despises him.[d]

3　The proud speech of a fool brings
　　a rod of discipline,[A]
but the lips of the wise
　　protect them.[e]

4　Where there are no oxen, the
　　feeding trough is empty,[B]
but an abundant harvest comes
　　through the strength of an ox.

5　An honest witness
　　does not deceive,
but a dishonest witness utters lies.[f]

6　A mocker seeks wisdom
　　and doesn't find it,
but knowledge comes easily
　　to the perceptive.

7　Stay away from a foolish person;
you will gain no knowledge
　　from his speech.[g]

8　The sensible person's wisdom is
　　to consider his way,
but the stupidity of fools
　　deceives them.

9　Fools mock at making reparation,[c]
but there is goodwill
　　among the upright.

10　The heart knows its own bitterness,
and no outsider shares in its joy.

11　The house of the wicked
　　will be destroyed,

but the tent of the upright
　　will flourish.[h]

12　There is a way that seems right
　　to a person,[i]
but its end is the way to death.[j]

13　Even in laughter a heart
　　may be sad,
and joy may end in grief.[k]

14　The disloyal one will get
　　what his conduct deserves,
and a good one,
　　what his deeds deserve.[l]

15　The inexperienced one
　　believes anything,[m]
but the sensible one watches[D]
　　his steps.

16　A wise person is cautious and turns
　　from evil,[n]
but a fool is easily angered
　　and is careless.[E]

17　A quick-tempered person
　　acts foolishly,
and one who schemes is hated.[o]

18　The inexperienced inherit
　　foolishness,
but the sensible are crowned
　　with knowledge.

19　The evil bow before those
　　who are good,
and the wicked, at the gates
　　of the righteous.

20　A poor person is hated even
　　by his neighbor,[p]
but there are many who love
　　the rich.[q]

21　The one who despises
　　his neighbor sins,[r]

[a] 14:1 Ru 4:11; Pr 9:1; 24:3; 31:10-27
[b] Pr 11:11; 29:4
[c] 14:2 Pr 19:1; 28:6
[d] Pr 2:15
[e] 14:3 Pr 12:6
[f] 14:5 Ex 20:16; 23:1; Pr 6:19; 12:17; 14:25
[g] 14:7 Pr 2:15
[h] 14:11 Pr 10:25; 11:28; 12:7; Mt 7:24-27
[i] 14:12 Pr 12:15; 16:25
[j] Pr 5:4; Rm 6:21
[k] 14:13 Ec 2:1-2; Lk 6:25
[l] 14:14 Pr 1:31; 12:14; 18:20; 28:19
[m] 14:15 Eph 4:14; Jms 1:5-8
[n] 14:16 Jb 28:28; Ps 34:14; Pr 3:7; 22:3
[o] 14:17 Pr 12:2; 24:8
[p] 14:20 Pr 19:7
[q] Pr 19:4
[r] 14:21 Pr 11:12

[A] 14:3 Some emend to *In the mouth of a fool is a rod for his back*　[B] 14:4 Or *clean*　[C] 14:9 Or *at guilt offerings*　[D] 14:15 Lit *the prudent understands*
[E] 14:16 Or *and falls*

14:4 Use your resources wisely. Invest your money in that from which you can expect **an abundant harvest**.
14:11 See 12:7.
14:12 In the book of Judges, Israel was in a dark and disastrous period because "everyone did whatever seemed right to him" (Judg 21:25). This highlights the problem with worldly, human wisdom: it *seems right*! And without comparison to the divine perspective, it looks pretty good. Human strategies and philosophies about life, in fact, have a bunch of people convinced because they appeal to our own self-centered notions of what's best. But those who won't seek God's opinion regarding the right path will pay a high price in the end. Rely solely on human logic to chart the course of your life, and it will lead you on a path to hell.
14:16-17 See 29:11.
14:18-19 These verses highlight the truth that the wise will ultimately be **crowned** for their godly deeds (14:18). Joseph is a prime biblical example of this principle. His jealous brothers sold him as a slave. He was unjustly accused of adultery and thrown in prison. Yet, through it all, he maintained his integrity and "the Lord was with Joseph" (see Gen 37:26-28; 39:2, 6-21). In the end, he was elevated to prominence, and his wicked brothers bowed before him (see Gen 42:6)—just as he had dreamed they would (see Gen 37:5-11).

a 14:21 Ps 41:1
b 14:22 Pr 6:14-15; 12:26
c Pr 12:20
d 14:23 Pr 21:5
e 14:25 Pr 6:19; 12:17; 14:5
f 14:26 Pr 29:25
g 14:27 Pr 13:14; 16:22; 19:23
h 14:29 Pr 16:32; 19:11; Ec 7:9; Jms 1:19
i 14:30 Pr 3:8; 4:22; 16:24
j Pr 12:4; 27:4; Jms 3:16
k 14:31 Pr 17:5; 21:13; Mt 25:40; 1Jn 3:17
l Pr 3:9; 14:21; 19:17; 22:2
m 14:32 Pr 17:15; 73:24; Pr 24:16; 2Co 1:9; 5:8; 2Tm 4:18
n Pr 10:25

o 14:33 Pr 15:14; 18:15; Ec 7:9
p 14:34 Pr 11:11
q 14:35 Pr 22:29; Mt 24:45-47; 25:21
r 15:1 Jdg 8:1-3; Pr 25:15; Ec 10:4
s 1Sm 25:10-13; 1Kg 12:13-16
t 15:2 Pr 12:23; 13:16; 15:28
u 15:3 2Ch 16:9; Jb 31:4; Zch 4:10; Heb 4:13
v 15:4 Pr 11:30; 13:12
w 15:5 Pr 3:11; 12:1; 15:31-33
x 15:8 Pr 21:27; 28:9; Ec 5:1; Is 1:11; Jr 6:20; Mc 6:7
y Pr 15:29
z 15:9 Pr 3:32; 11:20; 12:22; 1Tm 6:11

but whoever shows kindness
　　to the poor will be happy.*a*

22 Don't those who plan evil go astray?*b*
　But those who plan good find loyalty
　　and faithfulness.*c*

23 There is profit in all hard work,
　but endless talk^A leads only
　　to poverty.*d*

24 The crown of the wise is
　　their wealth,
　but the foolishness of fools
　　produces foolishness.

25 A truthful witness rescues lives,
　but one who utters lies is deceitful.*e*

26 In the fear of the LORD one has
　　strong confidence
　and his children have a refuge.*f*

27 The fear of the LORD is a fountain
　　of life,
　turning people away
　　from the snares of death.*g*

28 A large population is a king's splendor,
　but a shortage of people is
　　a ruler's devastation.

29 A patient person shows great
　　understanding,*h*
　but a quick-tempered one
　　promotes foolishness.

30 A tranquil heart is life to the body,*i*
　but jealousy is rottenness
　　to the bones.*j*

31 The one who oppresses the poor
　　person insults his Maker,*k*
　but one who is kind to the needy
　　honors him.*l*

32 The wicked one is thrown down
　　by his own sin,*m*
　but the righteous one has a refuge
　　in his death.*n*

33 Wisdom resides in the heart
　　of the discerning;*o*
　she is known^B even among fools.

34 Righteousness exalts a nation,
　but sin is a disgrace to any people.*p*

35 A king favors a prudent servant,*q*
　but his anger falls on
　　a disgraceful one.

15 A gentle answer turns away anger,*r*
　but a harsh word stirs up wrath.*s*

2 The tongue of the wise
　　makes knowledge attractive,
　but the mouth of fools
　　blurts out foolishness.*t*

3 The eyes of the LORD
　　are everywhere,
　observing the wicked and the good.*u*

4 The tongue that heals is a tree of life,*v*
　but a devious tongue^C
　　breaks the spirit.

5 A fool despises
　　his father's discipline,
　but a person who accepts correction
　　is sensible.*w*

6 The house of the righteous
　　has great wealth,
　but trouble accompanies the income
　　of the wicked.

7 The lips of the wise
　　broadcast knowledge,
　but not so the heart of fools.

8 The sacrifice of the wicked
　　is detestable to the LORD,*x*
　but the prayer of the upright is
　　his delight.*y*

9 The LORD detests the way
　　of the wicked,
　but he loves the one
　　who pursues righteousness.*z*

---

^A 14:23 Lit *but word of lips*　　^B 14:33 LXX reads *unknown*　　^C 15:4 Lit *but crookedness in it*

14:28-35 God's Word forms the standard not only for personal righteousness but also for national obedience (14:34). There are principles God has established that will benefit a society if they are followed—even if the leaders themselves don't know God. As Paul later urged Timothy to pray for governmental leaders "so that we may lead a tranquil and

quiet life in all godliness and dignity" (1 Tim 2:1-2), so we should pray for leaders to be sensitive to God's way of doing things.

Pray that your leaders will be **patient** (Prov 14:29), content and not power-hungry (14:30), **kind to the poor** (14:31), **righteous** (14:32), wise (14:33), and will surround themselves with wise administrators (14:35). When biblical principles

infiltrate society, their restraining influence is felt as an expression of God's grace that he makes available to all. See 16:10-15; 19:12.
15:4 See 10:11, 13-14, 18-21, 31-32; 11:12-13; 12:13-14, 16-22; 16:21-24; 25:11-12.
15:5 See 1:8-9; 4:10-13; 13:1.
15:8-9 Neither an evil person's life nor religion has value.

10 Discipline is harsh for the one
     who leaves the path;
the one who hates correction
     will die.

11 Sheol and Abaddon lie open
     before the LORD[a] —
how much more, human hearts.[b]

12 A mocker doesn't love one
     who corrects him;[c]
he will not consult the wise.

13 A joyful heart makes a face cheerful,
but a sad heart produces
     a broken spirit.[d]

14 A discerning mind
     seeks knowledge,[e]
but the mouth of fools feeds
     on foolishness.[f]

15 All the days of the oppressed
     are miserable,
but a cheerful heart has
     a continual feast.

16 Better a little with the fear
     of the LORD
than great treasure with turmoil.[g]

17 Better a meal of vegetables
     where there is love
than a fattened ox[h] with hatred.[i]

18 A hot-tempered person
     stirs up conflict,[j]
but one slow to anger[k] calms strife.

19 A slacker's way is like
     a thorny hedge,
but the path of the upright is
     a highway.[l]

20 A wise son brings joy to his father,
but a foolish man despises
     his mother.[m]

21 Foolishness brings joy to one
     without sense,
but a person with understanding
     walks a straight path.[n]

22 Plans fail when there is no counsel,
but with many advisers
     they succeed.[o]

23 A person takes joy in giving
     an answer;[A]
and a timely word — how good
     that is![p]

24 For the prudent the path of life
     leads upward,
so that he may avoid going down
     to Sheol.

25 The LORD tears apart the house
     of the proud,
but he protects
     the widow's territory.[q]

26 The LORD detests the plans of the
     one who is evil,
but pleasant words are pure.[r]

27 The one who profits dishonestly[s]
     troubles his household,
but the one who hates bribes
     will live.[t]

28 The mind of the righteous person
     thinks before answering,[u]
but the mouth of the wicked
     blurts out evil things.[v]

29 The LORD is far from the wicked,[w]
but he hears the prayer
     of the righteous.[x]

30 Bright eyes cheer the heart;
good news strengthens[B] the bones.[y]

31 One who[c] listens
     to life-giving rebukes[z]
will be at home among the wise.

32 Anyone who ignores discipline
     despises himself,[aa]
but whoever listens to correction
     acquires good sense.[D,ab]

33 The fear of the LORD is what
     wisdom teaches,
and humility comes before honor.[ac]

---

[a] 15:11 Jb 26:6; Ps 139:8
[b] 1Sm 16:7; 2Ch 6:30; Ps 44:21; Ac 1:24
[c] 15:12 Pr 9:8; Am 5:10
[d] 15:13 Pr 12:25; 14:30; 15:30; 17:22; 18:14
[e] 15:14 Pr 14:33; 18:15
[f] Mt 12:34
[g] 15:16 Ps 37:16; Pr 16:8; Ec 4:6; 1Tm 6:6
[h] 15:17 Mt 22:4; Lk 15:23
[i] Pr 16:19; 17:1
[j] 15:18 Pr 16:28; 26:21; 29:22
[k] Pr 14:29
[l] 15:19 Pr 16:17,31; 22:5-6
[m] 15:20 Pr 10:1; 23:24-25; 29:3,15
[n] 15:21 Pr 4:11,25; 10:23; Eph 5:15

[o] 15:22 Pr 8:14-16; 11:14; 24:6
[p] 15:23 Pr 25:11; Is 50:4
[q] 15:25 Ps 68:5; 146:9
[r] 15:26 Pr 11:20; 15:8-9; 16:24
[s] 15:27 Pr 1:19; Jr 17:11
[t] Ex 23:8; Dt 16:19; Ps 15:5; Pr 17:23; 28:16
[u] 15:28 Pr 18:13; 1Pt 3:15
[v] Pr 15:2
[w] 15:29 Ps 18:41; Pr 28:9
[x] Ps 145:18-19; Pr 15:8
[y] 15:30 Pr 14:30; 15:13; 17:22
[z] 15:31 Pr 3:11
[aa] 15:32 Pr 12:1
[ab] Pr 3:11; 5:12-14
[ac] 15:33 Pr 18:12; 22:4; 29:23

[A] **15:23** Lit *in an answer of his mouth*   [B] **15:30** Lit *makes fat*   [C] **15:31** Lit *An ear that*   [D] **15:32** Lit *acquires a heart*

15:10 See 1:22-33; 3:11-12; 9:7-9; 10:17; 25:11-12; 29:1.
15:15 See 12:25; 17:22.
15:16-17 See 19:1; 22:1-5.
15:18 See 29:11.
15:20 See 10:1.
15:22 See 11:14; 20:18.

15:24 There are two ways to live, two paths to take. Each has a very different destination. See 2:20-22.
15:26-27 To hate is not necessarily a sin. It depends on the object of your hatred. **The Lord detests the plans of the one who is evil**

(15:26). So God's people ought to hate evil too—such as **bribes** that cause the wicked to profit **dishonestly** (15:27).
15:28 See 12:16, 18.
15:29 Prayer is like a heavenly key in the hand of the righteous.

a 16:1 Pr 16:9; 19:21
b 16:2 1Sm 16:7; Pr 17:3;
    19:21; 21:2
c 16:3 Ps 37:4-5
d 16:4 Ex 9:16; Rm 9:21-22
e 16:5 2Ch 32:25; Pr 6:16-
    17; 8:13
f Ps 101:5; Pr 11:21; 16:18
g 16:6 Dn 4:27; Lk 11:41
h Jb 28:28; Pr 3:7; 14:16
i 16:7 2Ch 17:10
j 16:8 Ps 37:16; Pr 15:16-17;
    16:19; 28:6

k 16:9 Ps 37:23; Pr 16:1;
    19:21; 20:24; Jr 10:23
l 16:10 2Sm 14:17,20;
    1Kg 3:28
m 2Sm 23:2-3; Pr 18:14-15
n 16:11 Lv 19:36; Pr 11:1; Ezk
    45:10; Mc 6:11
o 16:12 Pr 31:3-5
p Ps 101; Pr 25:5
q 16:14 Ec 10:4
r 16:16 Pr 3:14; 8:10,19; 22:1
s 16:17 Is 35:8
t Pr 2:11-13; 15:19
u 16:18 Pr 11:2; 16:5; 18:12;
    29:23; Dn 4:37; Ob 3-4

16

1 The reflections of the heart
   belong to mankind,
but the answer of the tongue is
   from the LORD.*a*

2 All a person's ways seem right
   to him,
but the LORD weighs motives.*A,b*

3 Commit your activities to the LORD,
and your plans will be established.*c*

APPLICATION QUESTIONS

READ PROVERBS 16:4

— How have your recent actions and attitudes
  reflected God's sovereignty over your life?
— In what areas of life are you attempting to
  operate by your own rules?

---

4 The LORD has prepared everything
   for his purpose —
even the wicked for the day
   of disaster.*d*

5 Everyone with a proud heart is
   detestable to the LORD;*e*
be assured,*B* he will not
   go unpunished.*f*

6 Iniquity is atoned for by loyalty
   and faithfulness,*g*
and one turns from evil by the fear
   of the LORD.*h*

7 When a person's ways please
   the LORD,
he makes even his enemies to be
   at peace with him.*i*

8 Better a little with righteousness
than great income
   with injustice.*j*

9 A person's heart plans his way,
but the LORD determines his steps.*k*

10 God's verdict is on the lips
    of a king;*C,l*
his mouth should not give
    an unfair judgment.*m*

11 Honest balances and scales are
    the LORD's;
all the weights in the bag are
    his concern.*n*

12 Wicked behavior is detestable
    to kings,*o*
since a throne is established
    through righteousness.*p*

13 Righteous lips are a king's delight,
and he loves one
    who speaks honestly.

14 A king's fury is a messenger
    of death,
but a wise person appeases it.*q*

15 When a king's face lights up,
    there is life;
his favor is like a cloud
    with spring rain.

16 Get wisdom —
how much better it is than gold!
And get understanding —
    it is preferable to silver.*r*

17 The highway of the upright*s*
    avoids evil;
the one who guards his way protects
    his life.*t*

18 Pride comes before destruction,
and an arrogant spirit before a fall.*u*

A 16:2 Lit *spirits*   *B* 16:5 Lit *hand to hand*   *C* 16:10 Or *A divination is on the lips of a king*

16:2 See 21:2.
16:3 If you truly **commit your activities to the
LORD**, it means your will is in submission to
his. When that happens, you're inviting his
will to be done "on earth as it is in heaven"
(Matt 6:10-11).
16:4 God exercises his prerogative to do
whatever he pleases with his creation. Why?
Because "the earth and everything in it, the
world and its inhabitants, belong to the Lord"
(Ps 24:1).
   Suppose you came into my home and
told me you didn't like how I had arranged
and decorated everything. I would have one
response for you: "When you start buying
the furniture and paying the bills, we can
entertain your viewpoint. But as long as I'm

spending the money, your viewpoint carries
no clout in my house."
   When we start creating planets and giving
life, perhaps then we can start dictating how
God ought to run the universe. But unless we
get that divine clout, we cannot exercise that
divine prerogative. It always belongs to God,
and he does whatever he chooses. This teaching does not just appear as a fleeting thought
in the Bible, but as an overwhelming doctrine
(see, e.g., Job 42:2; Ps 115:3; Eph 1:11). Not even
evil and unrighteousness can escape the
all-controlling hand of the God who has even
made wicked people for his own purposes.
16:5 See 6:16-17.
16:7 When you align yourself under God's
program, it leads to blessing. Most of those

blessings are reserved for eternity, but God
can cause the most extraordinary things to
happen in history when our **ways please**
him.
16:9 See 16:1, 4.
16:10-15 Rightly administered, government
"is God's servant for your good" (Rom 13:4),
so followers of God ought to "submit to the
governing authorities" (Rom 13:1). As servants
of the true King, human kings should render
righteous judgments and hate wickedness.
When human government is unrighteous, it
is the responsibility of God's people to inter-
pose themselves to defend innocent victims
and to stand up in obedience to God (e.g.,
Exod 1:16-20; Esth 4; Dan 3; Acts 4:18-20).
16:17 See 2:11; 12:28.

*God has your tomorrow covered
even though you haven't been
there yet. He's got the plan.*

19 Better to be lowly of spirit
   with the humble[A,a]
than to divide plunder with the proud.[b]

20 The one who understands a matter
   finds success,[c]
and the one who trusts in the LORD
   will be happy.[d]

21 Anyone with a wise heart
   is called discerning,
and pleasant speech[B]
   increases learning.[e]

22 Insight is a fountain of life[f]
   for its possessor,
but the discipline of fools is folly.

23 The heart of a wise person instructs
   his mouth;
it adds learning to his speech.[C,g]

24 Pleasant words are a honeycomb:[h]
   sweet to the taste[D] and health
   to the body.[E,J]

25 There is a way that seems right
   to a person,
but its end is the way to death.[J]

26 A worker's appetite works for him
   because his hunger[F] urges him on.

27 A worthless person digs up evil,
   and his speech is like
   a scorching fire.[k]

28 A contrary person spreads conflict,
   and a gossip separates close friends.[l]

29 A violent person lures his neighbor,[m]
   leading him on a path that is
   not good.[n]

30 The one who narrows his eyes
   is planning deceptions;
the one who compresses his lips
   brings about evil.[o]

31 Gray hair is a glorious crown;[p]
   it is found in the ways
   of righteousness.[q]

32 Patience is better than power,
   and controlling one's emotions,[G]
   than capturing a city.[r]

33 The lot is cast into the lap,
   but its every decision is
   from the LORD.[s]

17 Better a dry crust with peace
   than a house full of feasting
   with strife.[t]

2 A prudent servant will rule over
   a disgraceful son
and share an inheritance
   among brothers.

3 A crucible for silver, and a smelter
   for gold,[u]
and the LORD is the tester of hearts.[v]

4 A wicked person listens to
   malicious talk;[H]
a liar pays attention to
   a destructive tongue.

5 The one who mocks the poor insults
   his Maker,[w]
and one who rejoices over calamity
   will not go unpunished.[x]

6 Grandchildren are the crown
   of the elderly,
and the pride of children is
   their fathers.

[a] 16:19 Pr 29:23; Is 57:15
[b] Ex 15:9; Ps 37:16; Pr 1:13-14; 15:16-17; 16:8
[c] 16:20 Pr 19:8
[d] Ps 2:12; 34:8; 40:4; 84:12; 146:5; Jr 17:7
[e] 16:21 Pr 1:5; 9:9; 16:23
[f] 16:22 Pr 10:11; 13:14; 14:27
[g] 16:23 Ps 37:30; Pr 1:5; 9:9; Mt 12:34
[h] 16:24 Ps 19:10; Pr 15:26
[i] Pr 4:22; 15:30; 25:13
[j] 16:25 Pr 14:12; 24:20
[k] 16:27 Pr 6:12; 19:28; 26:23; Jms 3:6
[l] 16:28 Pr 6:14,19; 17:9; 26:20-21; 28:25

[m] 16:29 Pr 1:10
[n] 1Sm 12:23; Ps 36:4; Pr 28:10
[o] 16:30 Ps 35:19; Pr 6:12-14; 10:10
[p] 16:31 Lv 19:32; Pr 4:9; 20:29
[q] Pr 3:1-2
[r] 16:32 Pr 25:15,28; 29:11
[s] 16:33 Pr 16:1; 19:21; 21:31
[t] 17:1 Pr 15:17; 21:9,19; 25:24
[u] 17:3 Pr 27:21
[v] 1Ch 29:17; Ps 26:2; Pr 16:2; 21:2; Is 48:10; Jr 17:10; Mal 3:3
[w] 17:5 Pr 14:31; 21:13
[x] Jb 31:29; Pr 24:17; Lm 1:21-22; Ezk 25:6-7; 35:15; Ob 12

[A] 16:19 Alt Hb tradition reads *afflicted*   [B] 16:21 Lit *and sweetness of lips*   [C] 16:23 Lit *learning upon his lips*   [D] 16:24 Lit *throat*   [E] 16:24 Lit *bones*
[F] 16:26 Lit *mouth*   [G] 16:32 Lit *and ruling over one's spirit*   [H] 17:4 Lit *to lips of iniquity*

16:20 See 3:13, 18; 29:18.
16:27-30 Whether by deceiving (16:30), spreading **conflict** (16:28), or performing violence (16:29), wicked men cause harm to others. If you don't want to become like them, keep your distance!
16:31 Young people who embrace foolishness typically despise the elderly as being out of touch and easily dismiss them. But they do so

to their own peril. God's viewpoint is clear: you are to "honor the old" out of the fear of the Lord (Lev 19:32).
16:32 See 29:11.
17:2 If you embrace wisdom, God can miraculously reverse your circumstances.
17:4 See 10:11, 13-14, 18-21, 31-32; 11:12-13; 12:13-14, 16-22; 16:21-24; 25:11-12.

17:5 God cares for the poor (see Lev 19:10; Ps 35:10) and expects the same from his people (see Ps 41:1; Jas 2:1-7).
17:6 This verse strikes a special chord with me. Now I don't claim the title **elderly**, but I can testify that **grandchildren are the crown** of those in their senior years. What a blessing when God lets you enjoy the children of your own children in whom you've invested!

a 17:8 Ex 23:8; Is 1:23;
Am 5:12
b Pr 18:16; 19:6; 21:14
c 17:9 Pr 10:12; Jms 5:20;
1Pt 4:8
d Lv 19:16; Pr 11:13; 16:28
e 17:11 Ps 78:49
f 17:12 2Sm 17:8; Hs 13:8
g 17:13 Ps 35:12; 109:5
h 2Sm 12:10
i 17:14 Pr 20:3; 25:8
j 17:15 Ex 23:7; Pr 17:26;
18:5; 24:23-24; Is 5:23
k 17:16 Pr 4:5,7; 18:15; 23:23
l 17:17 Ru 1:16; Pr 18:24;
27:10

m 17:18 Pr 6:1-5; 11:15;
22:26
n 17:19 Pr 29:22
o 17:20 Jr 23:36
p 17:21 Pr 10:1; 17:25; 19:13;
23:24-25
q 17:22 Ps 22:15; Pr 14:30;
15:13; 18:14
r 17:23 Pr 17:8
s Dt 16:19; Ps 15:5; Pr 18:5;
Mc 3:11; 7:3
t 17:24 Ec 2:14
u 17:25 Pr 10:1; 17:21; 19:13
v 17:26 Pr 17:15; 18:5;
24:23-24
w 17:27 Pr 10:19; Jms
1:19; 3:2

7 Eloquent words are not appropriate
on a fool's lips;
how much worse are lies for a ruler.

8 A bribe*a* seems like a magic stone
to its owner;
wherever he turns, he succeeds.*b*

9 Whoever conceals an offense
promotes love,*c*
but whoever gossips about it
separates friends.*d*

10 A rebuke cuts into
a perceptive person
more than a hundred lashes
into a fool.

11 An evil person desires only rebellion;
a cruel messenger^A,e^ will be sent
against him.

12 Better for a person to meet a bear
robbed of her cubs*f*
than a fool in his foolishness.

13 If anyone returns evil for good,*g*
evil will never depart
from his house.*h*

14 To start a conflict is to release
a flood;
stop the dispute before it breaks out.*i*

15 Acquitting the guilty
and condemning the just*j*—
both are detestable to the Lord.

16 Why does a fool have money
in his hand
with no intention
of buying wisdom?*k*

17 A friend loves at all times,*l*
and a brother is born for
a difficult time.

18 One without sense enters
an agreement^B^
and puts up security
for his friend.*m*

19 One who loves to offend
loves strife;*n*
one who builds a high threshold
invites injury.

20 One with a twisted mind
will not succeed,
and one with deceitful speech
will fall into ruin.*o*

21 A man fathers a fool
to his own sorrow;
the father of a fool has no joy.*p*

22 A joyful heart is good medicine,
but a broken spirit dries up
the bones.*q*

23 A wicked person secretly takes
a bribe*r*
to subvert the course
of justice.*s*

24 Wisdom is the focus
of the perceptive,
but a fool's eyes*t* roam to the ends
of the earth.

25 A foolish son is grief to his father
and bitterness to the one
who bore him.*u*

26 It is certainly not good to fine
an innocent person
or to beat a noble
for his honesty.^C,v^

27 The one who has knowledge
restrains his words,*w*
and one who keeps a cool head^D^
is a person of understanding.

^A^17:11 Or *a merciless angel*   ^B^17:18 Lit *sense slaps hands*   ^C^17:26 Or *noble unfairly*   ^D^17:27 Lit *spirit*

17:8 See 15:27.
17:9 Whoever conceals an offense doesn't mean to excuse sin; rather, it means a person isn't out to destroy you by using your transparency against you. A godly friend wants to lift you out of the mud—not leave you in it. **17:12** How dangerous is it to pal around with foolish people? Solomon says you're better off facing a grizzly **bear** mama who's been **robbed of her cubs.**
17:14 It only takes one harsh word to open the floodgates of **conflict.** "Don't give the devil an opportunity" (Eph 4:26-27) to hinder

God's work among his people. **Stop a dispute** before it starts. See Proverbs 29:11.
17:15 See 16:10-13.
17:17 When do you need **a friend** the most? Not when you're on top. A true friend stays with you when you're heading downhill, when times are rough. Sometimes you don't know who your friends are, in fact, until you're in trouble.
Too many of us are Lone Ranger Christians. We're trying to make it by ourselves when God's plan is for us to grow, serve, and love in community. You can't fulfill the "one another"

commands of Scripture by yourself (see, e.g., John 15:12; Gal 6:2; Eph 4:32; 1 Thess 5:11).
17:18 See 6:1-5.
17:19 See 17:14; 29:11.
17:21 See 10:1.
17:22 Speak "the truth in love" (see Eph 4:15) because God has given us the ability to turn **a broken spirit** into **a joyful heart** with our words. See Proverbs 12:25.
17:23 See 15:27.
17:24 The chief desire **of the perceptive** is to apply the divine viewpoint to every area of life.
17:27 See 17:14; 29:11.

28 Even a fool is considered wise
  when he keeps silent —
discerning, when he seals
  his lips.[a]

18 One who isolates himself pursues
  selfish desires;
he rebels against all sound wisdom.

2 A fool does not delight
  in understanding,
but only wants to show off
  his opinions.[A,b]

3 When a wicked person comes,
  contempt also comes,
and along with dishonor, derision.

4 The words of a person's mouth
  are deep waters,[c]
a flowing river, a fountain
  of wisdom.[B]

5 It is not good to show partiality
  to the guilty,[d]
denying an innocent
  person justice.[e]

6 A fool's lips lead to strife,
  and his mouth provokes
  a beating.[f]

7 A fool's mouth is his devastation,
  and his lips are a trap for his life.[g]

8 A gossip's words are
  like choice food
that goes down
  to one's innermost being.[C,h]

9 The one who is lazy in his work
  is brother to a vandal.[D,i]

10 The name of the Lord is
  a strong tower;[j]
the righteous run to it
  and are protected.[E,k]

11 The wealth of the rich is
  his fortified city;
in his imagination it is
  like a high wall.[l]

12 Before his downfall a person's heart
  is proud,[m]
but humility comes
  before honor.[n]

13 The one who gives an answer
  before he listens —
this is foolishness and disgrace
  for him.[o]

14 A person's spirit can
  endure sickness,
but who can survive
  a broken spirit?[p]

15 The mind of the discerning
  acquires knowledge,
and the ear of the wise
  seeks it.[q]

16 A person's gift opens doors[F]
  for him
and brings him before the great.[r]

17 The first to state his case
  seems right
until another comes
  and cross-examines him.[s]

18 Casting the lot[t] ends quarrels
and separates powerful opponents.

19 An offended brother is
  harder to reach[G]
than a fortified city,
and quarrels are like the bars
  of a fortress.

20 From the fruit of a person's mouth
  his stomach is satisfied;
he is filled with the product
  of his lips.[u]

[a] 17:28 Jb 13:5; Pr 10:19
[b] 18:2 Pr 12:23; 13:16; Ec 10:3
[c] 18:4 Pr 20:5
[d] 18:5 Lv 19:15; Dt 1:17; 24:17; Ps 15:5; 82:2; Pr 24:23-24; 28:21
[e] Pr 17:15
[f] 18:6 Pr 19:29
[g] 18:7 Ps 64:8; 140:9; Pr 10:14; 12:13; 13:3; Ec 10:12
[h] 18:8 Pr 26:22
[i] 18:9 Pr 28:24
[j] 18:10 Ps 18:2; 61:3; 91:2; 144:2
[k] Pr 29:25

[l] 18:11 Pr 10:15
[m] 18:12 Pr 16:18
[n] Pr 11:2; 15:33; 29:23
[o] 18:13 Pr 15:28
[p] 18:14 Pr 15:13; 17:22
[q] 18:15 Pr 14:33; 15:14
[r] 18:16 Gn 32:20; 1Sm 25:27; Pr 17:8; 19:6; 21:14
[s] 18:17 1Kg 3:16-28
[t] 18:18 Pr 16:33
[u] 18:20 Pr 1:31; 12:14; 14:14

[A] 18:2 Lit to uncover his heart [B] 18:4 Or waters; a fountain of wisdom is a flowing river [C] 18:8 Lit to the chambers of the belly [D] 18:9 Lit master of destruction [E] 18:10 Lit raised high [F] 18:16 Lit gift makes room [G] 18:19 LXX, Syr, Tg, Vg read is stronger

---

17:28 There is a time when we must speak (see 17:22). On the other hand, the one who opens his mouth too much (usually to hear himself talk) is likely to stick his foot in it (see 10:19).
18:1 See 11:14; 17:17.
18:2 See 10:19; 17:28.
18:4 See 16:21-24; 17:22.
18:5 See 16:10-11.
18:9 This indicates that to accept a paycheck without accomplishing the work agreed upon is stealing.

18:11 The rich man thinks his **wealth** is **his fortified city**. But Solomon, who had more riches than he could ever want, knew the only sure refuge in times of tribulation is the Lord.
18:13 See 12:18.
18:14 See 17:22.
18:16 Solomon has condemned bribes—evil gifts that pervert justice (15:27; 17:23). But that's not what he's talking about here. He's simply acknowledging the fact that expres-

sions of kindness can **open doors** that are otherwise closed.
18:17 When hearing a **case**, we should always be determined to hear both sides of a dispute before we come to any conclusions about the matter.
18:18 **Casting the lot** was a practice similar to rolling dice to discern God's will. Today God gives believers his indwelling Holy Spirit to guide us.
18:20-21 See 10:11, 13-14, 18-21, 31-32; 11:12-13; 12:13-14, 16-22; 16:21-24; 25:11-12.

[a] 18:21 Pr 13:2; Mt 12:37; 15:11,18-20; Jms 3:8
[b] 18:22 Pr 12:4; 19:14; 31:10-31
[c] Pr 8:35
[d] 18:23 Pr 19:7
[e] Jms 2:6
[f] 18:24 Pr 17:17; 27:10; Jn 15:13
[g] 19:1 Ps 26:11; 37:16; Pr 10:9; 14:2; 20:7; 28:6

[h] 19:2 Rm 10:2
[i] Pr 21:5; 28:20; 29:20
[j] 19:3 Is 8:21
[k] 19:4 Pr 14:20; 19:6
[l] 19:5 Dt 19:16-19; Pr 19:9; 21:28
[m] Pr 6:19
[n] 19:6 Pr 29:26
[o] Pr 14:20; 17:8; 19:4
[p] 19:7 Ps 38:11
[q] Pr 18:23
[r] 19:8 Pr 16:20
[s] 19:9 Pr 19:5; 21:28
[t] 19:10 Pr 17:7; 26:1
[u] Pr 30:22; Ec 10:6-7
[v] 19:11 Pr 14:29
[w] Pr 11:13; 17:9
[x] 19:12 Pr 16:14
[y] Ps 133:3; Pr 20:2; 28:15; Hs 14:5; Mc 5:7

www.bhpublishinggroup.com/qr/te/20-19

Questions & Answers

Q The Bible has much to say about how we talk to one another, whether the issue is lying, bitterness, slander, anger, or foul language. Why is this matter of how we speak so important that it is repeatedly addressed in Scripture?

A Scripture has much to say about our speech because "death and life are in the power of the tongue" (Prov 18:21). What the tongue says reflects the heart. So when our words toward another person are bitter, it's because our hearts are bitter. What comes out of our mouths represents the overflow of our hearts. Therefore, we must be concerned about where our words are coming from—not merely what they are conveying. When we notice that our tongues are not what they ought to be, that's an invitation to get our hearts right with God. Only then can we truly address our language problem. A heart filled with love for God and people will be reflected in how we talk to others.

FOR THE NEXT Q&A, SEE PAGE 831.

Video Devotional

"DIVINE INTERVENTION"

When things look like they are out of your control, they are simply out of your control. God can intervene to reverse your situation. He is sovereign.

21 Death and life are in the power
    of the tongue,
    and those who love it will eat its fruit.[a]

22 A man who finds a wife finds
    a good thing[b]
    and obtains favor from the LORD.[c]

23 The poor person pleads,[d]
    but the rich one answers roughly.[e]

24 One with many friends may be harmed,[A]
    but there is a friend who stays closer
    than a brother.[f]

19 Better a poor person who lives
    with integrity[g]
    than someone who has deceitful lips
    and is a fool.

2 Even zeal is not good
    without knowledge,[h]
    and the one who acts hastily[B] sins.[i]

3 A person's own foolishness leads
    him astray,
    yet his heart rages against the LORD.[j]

4 Wealth attracts many friends,[k]
    but a poor person is separated
    from his friend.

5 A false witness will not
    go unpunished,[l]
    and one who utters lies
    will not escape.[m]

6 Many seek a ruler's favor,[n]
    and everyone is a friend of one
    who gives gifts.[o]

7 All the brothers of a poor person
    hate him;[p]
    how much more do his friends
    keep their distance from him!
    He may pursue them with words,[q]
    but they are not there.[C]

8 The one who acquires good sense[D]
    loves himself;
    one who safeguards understanding
    finds success.[r]

9 A false witness will not
    go unpunished,
    and one who utters lies perishes.[s]

10 Luxury is not appropriate
    for a fool[t]—
    how much less for a slave to rule
    over princes![u]

11 A person's insight gives
    him patience,[v]
    and his virtue is to overlook
    an offense.[w]

12 A king's rage is like the roaring
    of a lion,[x]
    but his favor is like dew on the grass.[y]

[A] 18:24 Some LXX mss, Syr, Tg, Vg read *friends must be friendly*   [B] 19:2 Lit *who is hasty with feet*   [C] 19:7 Hb uncertain   [D] 19:8 Lit *acquires a heart*

18:22 God gave Eve to Adam as a "helper"—a complement (see Gen 2:18). When a kingdom man finds a kingdom woman for **a wife**, he **obtains favor**.

18:24 Solomon isn't saying it's bad to have a lot of **friends**. But if everyone is your friend, something may be wrong. Everybody wants to be your friend when times are good for you—especially if you're wealthy (see 19:4). But if you make these hangers-on your constant and only source of companionship, you're not choosing wisely.

19:5 See 12:19, 22; 25:18-19.

19:7 But remember 19:1.

19:8 By contrast, the person who indulges in foolish living isn't doing himself any favors. In reality, he hates himself because foolishness leads to ruin and, perhaps, an early grave (see 4:10-13).

19:11 See 29:11.

19:12 When government is acting justly, the only person who needs to fear **a king's rage** is the one who does wrong (see Rom 13:4).

13 A foolish son is his father's ruin,[a]
    and a wife's nagging is
        an endless dripping.[b]

14 A house and wealth are inherited
        from fathers,[c]
    but a prudent wife is
        from the LORD.

15 Laziness induces deep sleep,
    and a lazy person will go hungry.[d]

16 The one who keeps commands
        preserves himself;[e]
    one who disregards[A] his ways
        will die.[f]

17 Kindness to the poor is a loan
        to the LORD,[g]
    and he will give a reward
        to the lender.[B,h]

18 Discipline your son
        while there is hope;
    don't set your heart on being
        the cause of his death.[C,i]

19 A person with intense anger bears
        the penalty;
    if you rescue him, you'll have to do
        it again.[j]

20 Listen to counsel
        and receive instruction
    so that you may be wise
        later in life.[D,k]

21 Many plans are in a person's heart,
    but the LORD's decree will prevail.[l]

22 What is desirable in a person is
        his fidelity;
    better to be a poor person
        than a liar.[m]

23 The fear of the LORD leads to life;
    one will sleep at night[E]
        without danger.[n]

24 The slacker buries his hand
        in the bowl;
    he doesn't even bring it back
        to his mouth![o]

25 Strike a mocker, and the inexperienced
        learn a lesson;[p]
    rebuke the discerning,
        and he gains knowledge.[q]

26 The one who plunders his father
        and evicts his mother
    is a disgraceful and shameful son.

27 If you stop listening to correction,
        my son,
    you will stray from the words
        of knowledge.

28 A worthless witness mocks justice,
    and a wicked mouth
        swallows iniquity.[r]

29 Judgments are prepared
        for mockers,
    and beatings for the backs of fools.[s]

20 Wine is a mocker,[t] beer is a brawler;
    whoever goes astray[F]
    because of them is not wise.

2 A king's terrible wrath is
        like the roaring of a lion;
    anyone who provokes him
        endangers himself.[u]

3 Honor belongs to the person
        who ends a dispute,[v]
    but any fool can get himself
        into a quarrel.[w]

[a] 19:13 Pr 10:1; 17:25; 28:7
[b] Pr 21:9,19; 27:15
[c] 19:14 2Co 12:14
[d] 19:15 Pr 6:9-11; 10:4; 13:4; 21:25
[e] 19:16 Lk 10:28
[f] Pr 3:1-2; 4:4; 13:13
[g] 19:17 Dt 15:7-10; Pr 14:31; 28:27; Ec 11:1-2; Mt 10:42; 25:40; 2Co 9:6-8; Heb 6:10
[h] Lk 6:38
[i] 19:18 Pr 13:24; 23:13-14; 29:17
[j] 19:19 Pr 22:24-25; 29:22
[k] 19:20 Pr 12:1; 15:5,31-32
[l] 19:21 Ps 33:10-11; Pr 16:1,9,33; 21:31; Is 14:26-27
[m] 19:22 Pr 19:1; 28:6
[n] 19:23 Pr 14:26-27
[o] 19:24 Pr 12:27; 20:4; 26:14-15
[p] 19:25 Pr 21:11
[q] Pr 9:8
[r] 19:28 Jb 15:16; 34:7
[s] 19:29 Pr 10:13; 18:6; 26:3
[t] 20:1 Gn 9:21; Pr 23:29-30; Is 28:7; Hs 4:11
[u] 20:2 Nm 16:38; Est 4:11; Pr 8:36; 19:12; 28:15; Hab 2:10
[v] 20:3 Pr 17:14
[w] Pr 15:18; 18:6; 22:10

[A] 19:16 Or *despises*, or *treats lightly*   [B] 19:17 Lit *to him*   [C] 19:18 Lit *don't lift up your soul to his death*   [D] 19:20 Lit *in your end*   [E] 19:23 Lit *will spend the night satisfied*   [F] 20:1 Or *whoever staggers*

19:15 See 10:4-5; 13:25.
19:16 See 2:20-22; 11:4-10, 16-21; 12:28; 14:12; 15:24.
19:18 If you fail to **discipline your son** in the home, he'll pay for his lack of self-control outside the home—maybe even by his death. Don't hate your child by neglecting to intervene in his life. See 13:24.
19:20 See 1:22-33; 3:11-12; 9:7-9; 10:17.
19:21 We can plan our schedules as much as we want, but only what God has declared is guaranteed to take place. God did not create us and redeem us to live a plotless, purposeless existence. And that's good news! I don't

know many people who are content to live and die and have on their tombstone, "Joe was here." We were made for greater things than to occupy space on the planet. God has a calling for you and me, and the beauty of it is that our callings are tailor-made for each of us. In the same way that we have unique fingerprints and DNA, we all have unique callings. Don't settle for a paycheck, a house, and two cars. That may be the American dream, but God has a dream for you that is bigger. **The LORD's decree will prevail**, so seek him and his calling for your life.
19:22 See 19:1.

19:24 See 26:13-16.
19:26 Young people need to know that their parents have a God-ordained role. A child's first obligation is to his parent—not his buddies.
19:29 See 1:22-33.
20:1 Alcohol consumption is not completely condemned in the Bible. Wine is often featured in the Old and New Testaments during times of celebration. It was also a common beverage because of the lack of water purification systems in ancient times. Drunkenness, however, is condemned soundly in Scripture.
20:2 See 19:12.

a 20:4 Pr 24:27,30-34
b 20:5 Pr 18:4
c 20:6 Ps 53:2-3; Pr 28:20;
Ec 7:28; Lk 18:8
d 20:7 Pr 2:7,20-21; 10:9;
13:6
e Ps 37:26; 112:2
f 20:8 Pr 20:26; 25:5;
Mt 25:32
g 20:9 1Kg 8:46; Jb 15:15-
16; Ps 14:2-3; Ec 7:20; Rm
3:9-12; 1Jn 1:8
h 20:10 Dt 25:14-15; Pr 11:1;
20:23; Mc 6:10-11
i 20:11 Pr 21:8; Mt 7:16
j 20:12 Ex 4:11; Ps 94:9; Pr
22:2; 29:13
k 20:13 Pr 6:10-11; 19:15;
24:33-34

l 20:15 Pr 3:15; 8:11
m 20:16 Dt 24:12-13; Pr
6:1-5; 11:15; 27:13
n 20:17 Pr 9:17
o 20:18 Pr 11:14; 15:22
p Pr 24:6; Lk 14:31
q 20:19 Lv 19:16; Pr 11:13
r Pr 13:3
s 20:20 Ex 21:17; Pr 24:20;
30:11
t Jb 18:5
u 20:21 Pr 21:5; 23:5; 28:22;
Lk 15:11-13
v 20:22 Pr 24:29; Mt 5:39;
Rm 12:17,19; 1Th 5:15;
1Pt 3:9
w Ps 27:14
x Ps 37:7-9
y 20:23 Pr 20:10; Mc 6:11
z Pr 11:1
aa 20:24 Pr 16:9,33; 19:21

4 The slacker does not plow
    during planting season;[A]
at harvest time he looks,[B]
    and there is nothing.[a]

5 Counsel in a person's heart is
    deep water;[b]
but a person of understanding
    draws it out.

6 Many a person proclaims
    his own loyalty,
but who can find
    a trustworthy person?[c]

7 A righteous person acts
    with integrity;[d]
his children who come after him
    will be happy.[e]

8 A king sitting on a throne to judge
separates out all evil
    with his eyes.[f]

9 Who can say, "I have kept
    my heart pure;
I am cleansed from my sin"?[g]

10 Differing weights
    and varying measures[c] —
both are detestable to the LORD.[h]

11 Even a young man is known
    by his actions —
by whether his behavior is pure
    and upright.[i]

12 The hearing ear
    and the seeing eye —
the LORD made them both.[j]

13 Don't love sleep, or you will
    become poor;
open your eyes, and you'll have
    enough to eat.[k]

14 "It's worthless, it's worthless!"
    the buyer says,
but after he is on his way, he gloats.

15 There is gold and a multitude
    of jewels,
but knowledgeable lips are
    a rare treasure.[l]

16 Take his garment,
for he has put up security
    for a stranger;
get collateral if it is for foreigners.[m]

17 Food gained by fraud is sweet
    to a person,[n]
but afterward his mouth is full
    of gravel.

18 Finalize plans with counsel,[o]
and wage war with sound guidance.[p]

19 The one who reveals secrets is
    a constant gossip;[q]
avoid someone with a big mouth.[r]

20 Whoever curses his father
    or mother[s] —
his lamp will go out in deep darkness.[t]

21 An inheritance gained prematurely
will not be blessed ultimately.[u]

22 Don't say, "I will avenge this evil!"[v]
Wait on the LORD,[w] and he will
    rescue you.[x]

23 Differing weights[D] are detestable
    to the LORD,[y]
and dishonest scales[z] are unfair.

24 Even a courageous person's steps
    are determined by the LORD,[aa]
so how can anyone understand
    his own way?

[A] 20:4 Lit *plow in winter* [B] 20:4 Lit *inquires* [C] 20:10 Lit *Stone and stone, measure and measure* [D] 20:23 Lit *A stone and a stone*

20:4 See 10:4-5.
20:7 Know that the choices you make every day—both small and large—affect your kids. What legacy do you want to leave them?
20:9 Solomon's rhetorical question is a reminder that his exhortations in Proverbs regarding righteousness are not blind to the reality of human sinfulness. Ultimately, no one is righteous but one (see Luke 18:19; Rom 3:10). But by trusting in the righteousness of Jesus Christ and being led by the Holy Spirit, we can pursue lives in alignment with God's standards.
20:10 See 11:1.

20:11 A reputation is cultivated over time.
20:13-14 Use Proverbs' observations about how the world works and the influence of the Holy Spirit to help you make sensible decisions. The lazy person loves **sleep** and thus goes hungry, so **open your eyes** if you don't want to be **poor** (20:13). Similarly, don't believe everything you hear. If someone is trying to work a deal to his own advantage, he may say something that doesn't match reality. Be discerning (20:14).
20:15 See 8:5-21.
20:17 Indulging in sin, however **sweet**, leads to unpleasant consequences.

20:18 Don't engage in an activity without doing wise planning by obtaining **sound guidance**. If you seek no advice but your own, the results will be as limited as the input. See 11:14.
20:19 See 11:12-13; 17:9; 26:20.
20:21 This proverb brings to mind Jesus's parable of the Prodigal Son (see Luke 15:11-32). When someone unskilled at financial management acquires money quickly, he's likely to lose it quickly too.
20:22 Moses and Paul agree that the best course of action is leaving vengeance in the hands of God (see Deut 32:35; Rom 12:19).
20:24 See 16:1, 4.

25 It is a trap for anyone to dedicate
    something rashly
and later to reconsider his vows.[a]

26 A wise king separates out
    the wicked[b]
and drives the threshing wheel[c]
    over them.

27 The LORD's lamp sheds light on
    a person's life,[A]
searching the innermost parts.[B,d]

28 Loyalty and faithfulness guard a king;
through loyalty he maintains
    his throne.

29 The glory of young men is
    their strength,
and the splendor of old men is
    gray hair.[e]

30 Lashes and wounds purge away
    evil,[f]
and beatings cleanse
    the innermost parts.[c]

21 A king's heart is like
    channeled water
in the LORD's hand:
He directs it wherever he chooses.[g]

2 All a person's ways seem right
    to him,
but the LORD weighs hearts.[h]

3 Doing what is righteous and just
is more acceptable to the LORD
    than sacrifice.[i]

4 The lamp that guides the wicked —
haughty eyes and an arrogant heart[j]
    — is sin.

5 The plans of the diligent
    certainly lead to profit,
but anyone who is reckless
    certainly becomes poor.[k]

6 Making a fortune
    through a lying tongue
is a vanishing mist,[D] a pursuit
    of death.[E,F,l]

7 The violence of the wicked
    sweeps them away
because they refuse to act justly.

8 A guilty one's conduct is crooked,[m]
but the behavior of the innocent
    is upright.[n]

9 Better to live on the corner
    of a roof
than to share a house
    with a nagging wife.[o]

10 A wicked person desires evil;
he has no consideration[G]
    for his neighbor.[p]

11 When a mocker is punished,
    the inexperienced become wiser;
when one teaches a wise man,
    he acquires knowledge.[q]

12 The Righteous One[H] considers
    the house of the wicked;
he brings the wicked to ruin.

13 The one who shuts his ears
    to the cry of the poor
will himself also call out
    and not be answered.[r]

14 A secret gift soothes anger,
and a covert bribe, fierce rage.[s]

15 Justice executed is a joy
    to the righteous
but a terror to those
    who practice iniquity.[t]

16 The person who strays from the way
    of prudence
will come to rest in the assembly of
    the departed spirits.[u]

[a] 20:25 Nm 30:2; Dt 23:21; Ec 5:4-6
[b] 20:26 Pr 20:8
[c] Is 28:27
[d] 20:27 Ps 139:23; Pr 20:30; 1Co 2:11
[e] 20:29 Lv 19:32; Pr 16:31
[f] 20:30 Is 53:5
[g] 21:1 Ezr 6:22
[h] 21:2 Pr 12:15; 16:2; 17:3; 24:12; Lk 16:15
[i] 21:3 1Sm 15:22; Pr 15:8; Hs 6:6; Mc 6:7-8; Mt 9:13
[j] 21:4 Ps 101:5; Pr 6:16-17; 30:13
[k] 21:5 Pr 10:4; 14:23; 21:20; 28:22
[l] 21:6 Pr 8:36; 13:11; 20:21
[m] 21:8 Pr 2:15
[n] Pr 20:11
[o] 21:9 Pr 15:16-17; 17:1; 21:19; 25:24
[p] 21:10 Pr 14:21
[q] 21:11 Pr 19:25
[r] 21:13 Pr 14:31; 17:5; Mt 18:30-34; Jms 2:13; 1Jn 3:17
[s] 21:14 Pr 17:8; 18:16; 19:6
[t] 21:15 Pr 10:29; Rm 13:3
[u] 21:16 Ps 49:14; Pr 2:18; 9:18

[A] 20:27 Lit breath [B] 20:27 Lit the chambers of the belly [C] 20:30 Lit beatings the chambers of the belly [D] 21:6 Or a breath blown away
[E] 21:6 Some Hb mss, LXX, Vg read a snare of death [F] 21:6 Lit is vanity, ones seeking death [G] 21:10 Or favor [H] 21:12 Or righteous one

---

20:25 Don't make a rash commitment to the Lord and later change your mind.
20:29 See 16:31.
20:30 Governments are ordained by God to punish criminals (see Rom 13:4). Just rulers therefore protect their citizens and chastise wrongdoers.
21:1 Psalm 22:28 declares that "kingship belongs to the LORD; he rules the nations." No matter how powerful the rulers of this world are, they cannot prevent God from fulfilling his purposes—whether they acknowledge him or not.
21:2 We don't always know why we do what we do, and at times we can fool ourselves into thinking that our reasons are God's reasons. The Lord looks right through to the very center of who we are, and he knows exactly what drives us.
21:3 Remember the example of King Saul (see 1 Sam 15:1-29).
21:4 See 6:16-17; 13:10; 27:1.
21:5-7 God expects us to earn through honest and **diligent** labor (21:5), not through **lying** (21:6) or **violence** (21:7). This is a kingdom standard.
21:8 Whether we embrace our own agenda or God's agenda will be revealed by either **behavior**.
21:14 See 18:16.
21:16 See 2:20-22; 11:4-10, 21; 12:28; 14:12; 15:24.

Give, Save, Spend

DO YOU START OUT EACH day singing, "I owe, I owe, so off to work I go?" It is no secret that many of us are drowning in a sea of debt. Taking on debt has become a way of life in our culture. It's the newest addiction. But as a result, instead of living for the future, we end up paying for the past.

Scripture tells us that it is not good for believers to live in debt. Proverbs 22:7 says, "The borrower is a slave to the lender." In fact, God tells us in Luke 16:10-11 that if a man or woman is not able to properly handle the money that God gives, he or she gets cut off from receiving other blessings from him too.

Debt is not just about money. I don't want you to miss that. Debt is about your spiritual connection to God. That's why I want to give you three words for living a life without debt: give, save, spend. They are three simple words, but if you will put them into practice they can restore your financial situation into the way it was intended to be.

First, *give*. Proverbs 3:9-10 says, "Honor the LORD with your possessions and with the first produce of your entire harvest; then your barns will be completely filled." Now, you may be saying that you don't see how you can give to God when you can't even pay all of your bills. But God says that if you will give to him—honor him—he will make sure you have enough for what you need.

When I was in seminary and Lois and I had young children, we tried to take care of our family with only $900 a month. Even though the amount we had was small, we always gave $90 to God first as a way of saying that we were trusting him as our source. We weren't just giving a tithe. We were acknowledging ownership by stating who really owned the $900. Even though things were tight, God was faithful to provide for us at all times.

Next, *save*. A portion of every dollar that you earn should go into savings. Egypt was able not only to survive a seven-year famine at the time of Joseph, but they were also able to feed people in other lands. This is because Joseph instructed the Egyptians to set aside—to save—a portion of every harvest during the seven years leading up to the drought (SEE GEN 41:28-57). Life has a way of surprising us with unexpected expenses. But if you'll make saving your money a practice, you will be prepared for what is in store.

Last, *spend*. But spend wisely. Plan your spending. Draw up, agree upon, and stick to a family or personal budget. You can play hard, but play smart. God tells us in Proverbs 21:5, "The plans of the diligent certainly lead to profit, but anyone who is reckless certainly becomes poor." There is nothing wrong with spending money or enjoying blessings in life. It just needs to be done with wisdom and restraint.

Live by these three words—give, save, spend—and experience God restoring your financial situation.

a 21:17 Ec 2:1–3,10–11
b 21:18 Pr 11:8; Is 43:3

c 21:19 Pr 21:9
d 21:20 Jb 20:15,18; Ps 112:3; Pr 10:4; 28:20; Mt 25:1–13
e 21:21 Pr 3:16; 8:18; 15:9; Mt 5:6; 6:33
f 21:22 2Sm 5:6–9; Pr 14:26; 24:5; Ec 7:19; 9:14–18
g 21:23 Pr 12:13; 13:3; Jms 3:2
h 21:24 Ps 1:1; Pr 1:22; 21:11
i 21:25 Pr 10:4; 12:24; 13:4; 19:15,24
j 21:26 Ps 37:26; Pr 11:24–25
k 21:27 Pr 15:8; 28:9; Is 66:3
l 21:28 Pr 19:5,9
m 21:29 Pr 7:13
n 21:30 Is 8:9–10; 1Co 3:19–20

KINGDOM LIVING
FAMILY
Training Your Child According to His or Her Bent

Proverbs 22:6 gives an important statement regarding a child's spiritual development: "Start a youth out on his way; even when he grows old he will not depart from it." A proverb is not a promise but a truism, conveying this: "If you will do something, this is the result you can normally expect."

Let me show you how this works with Proverbs 22:6. The Hebrew word translated "start out" derives from a term referring to the palate. A Hebrew mother would chew her baby's food to soften it and then put the food in the baby's mouth. The presence of the food would excite the child's palate, and the child would begin eating and then swallow the nourishment.

Child training, therefore, involves making our teaching palatable so that our children can digest and benefit from it. This doesn't mean soft-pedaling the truth or only saying what our kids want to hear. The idea of making our teaching palatable really comes through in the middle phrase of Proverbs 22:6. The writer said we are to start a child out "on his way." Another translation is "according to his way"—that is, according to each child's unique personality or bent.

In essence, the Bible is saying to parents, "Don't try to come up with a standard approach to apply to all your children. Since each child is different and has a unique temperament, the way you interact with and train your children should differ from child to child." Kingdom parents seeking to raise kingdom kids will look to identify each of their children's strengths and spiritual gifts, and then focus on the development and encouragement of those. They will also impart a kingdom worldview into daily conversations and also to the devotions shared around the table.

FOR THE NEXT FAMILY
KINGDOM LIVING LESSON SEE PAGE 1086.

whoever loves wine and oil will not
get rich.*a*

18 The wicked are a ransom
for the righteous,
and the treacherous, for[A] the upright.*b*

19 Better to live in a wilderness
than with a nagging
and hot-tempered wife.*c*

20 Precious treasure and oil are
in the dwelling of a wise person,
but a fool consumes them.[B]*d*

21 The one who pursues righteousness
and faithful love
will find life, righteousness, and honor.*e*

22 A wise person went up against a city
of warriors
and brought down its secure fortress.*f*

23 The one who guards his mouth
and tongue
keeps himself out of trouble.*g*

24 The arrogant and proud person,
named "Mocker,"
acts with excessive arrogance.*h*

25 A slacker's craving will kill him
because his hands refuse to work.*i*

26 He is filled with craving[C] all day long,
but the righteous give and don't
hold back.*j*

27 The sacrifice of a wicked person
is detestable—
how much more so
when he brings it with ulterior motives!*k*

28 A lying witness will perish,*l*
but the one who listens
will speak successfully.

29 A wicked person puts on a bold face,*m*
but the upright one considers
his way.

30 No wisdom, no understanding,
and no counsel
will prevail against the LORD.*n*

17 The one who loves pleasure
will become poor;

[A] 21:18 Or *in place of*   [B] 21:20 Lit *it*   [C] 21:26 Lit *He craves a craving*

21:19 See 12:4.
21:23 See 10:11, 13–14, 18–21, 31–32; 11:12–13; 12:13–14, 16–22; 16:21–24; 25:11–12.
21:25-26 See 10:4–5.
21:27 We are to worship God because he

deserves it—not simply because we selfishly want something from him.
21:28 See 12:17, 19, 22; 25:18–19.

21:29 A **bold face** doesn't replace sound decision-making. A confident attitude that's not informed by wisdom will lead to disaster.
21:30 Try to be wise without bowing to God, and you will lose.

*a*21:31 Ps 20:7; 33:17;
108:10-13; Is 31:1
b Jr 3:23; 1Co 15:57
c 22:1 Pr 10:7; 8:10; Ec 7:1
d 22:2 Jb 31:13,15; Pr 29:13
e 22:3 Pr 14:16; 27:12; Is
26:20
f 22:4 Pr 15:33; 21:21; 29:23
g 22:5 Pr 7:23; 15:19
h 22:6 Eph 6:4
i 22:7 Pr 18:23; Jms 2:6
j Dt 28:12-13
k 22:8 Jb 4:8; Hs 10:13-14
l 22:9 Pr 19:17; 2Co 9:6
m Lk 14:13-14
o 22:10 Gn 21:9-10
p Pr 26:20

q 22:11 Pr 16:13
r 22:13 Pr 26:13
s 22:14 Pr 2:16-19;
7:5,21,27; 23:27-28; Ec 7:26
t 22:15 Pr 13:24; 23:13-14;
29:15
u 22:16 Pr 11:24; 22:7; 28:27
c 22:17 Pr 5:1

31 A horse is prepared for the day
of battle,[a]
but victory comes from the LORD.[b]

22 A good name is to be chosen
over great wealth;
favor is better than silver and gold.[c]

2 Rich and poor have this in common:[A]
the LORD makes them all.[d]

APPLICATION QUESTIONS

READ PROVERBS 22:6

– How committed are you to disciplining your
children in order to raise them in the way they
should go?

3 A sensible person sees danger
and takes cover,
but the inexperienced keep going
and are punished.[e]

4 Humility, the fear of the LORD,
results in wealth, honor, and life.[f]

5 There are thorns and snares
on the way of the crooked;[g]
the one who guards himself stays
far from them.

6 Start a youth out on his way;[h]
even when he grows old he will
not depart from it.

7 The rich rule over the poor,[i]
and the borrower is a slave
to the lender.[j]

8 The one who sows injustice
will reap disaster,[k]
and the rod of his fury
will be destroyed.

9 A generous person[B] will be blessed,[l]
for he shares his food with the poor.[m]

10 Drive out a mocker,[o] and conflict
goes too;
then quarreling and dishonor
will cease.[p]

11 The one who loves a pure heart
and gracious lips — the king is
his friend.[q]

12 The LORD's eyes keep watch
over knowledge,
but he overthrows the words
of the treacherous.

13 The slacker says,
"There's a lion outside!
I'll be killed in the public square! "[r]

14 The mouth of the forbidden woman
is a deep pit;
a man cursed by the LORD will fall
into it.[s]

15 Foolishness is bound to the heart
of a youth;
a rod of discipline will separate it
from him.[t]

16 Oppressing the poor to enrich oneself,
and giving to the rich — both lead
only to poverty.[u]

WORDS OF THE WISE

17 Listen closely,[c] pay attention
to the words of the wise,[v]
and apply your mind
to my knowledge.

18 For it is pleasing if you keep them
within you
and if they are[D] constantly
on your lips.

19 I have instructed you today —
even you —
so that your confidence may be
in the LORD.

[A]22:2 Lit *poor meet*   [B]22:9 Lit *Good of eye*   [C]22:17 Lit *Stretch out your ear*   [D]22:18 Or *you; let them be,* or *you, so that they are*

22:2 The Lord has made both the **rich** man and the **poor** one, and both are accountable to him for how they live.
22:6 Another way to translate **on his way** is "according to his way"—that is, according to each child's unique personality or bent. The way you deal with each child under your authority, then, should differ so that every one benefits from the kind of training most likely to leave a positive impact.
22:7 Avoid excessive debt. Learn sound financial principles and live within your means.
22:8-11 If you plant tomatoes, you won't get pumpkins. You harvest what you plant; you reap what you sow. Sow **injustice** and reap **disaster** (22:8); sow generosity and reap a blessing (22:9). Mocking lips reap **conflict** (22:10); **gracious lips** reap the king's attention (22:11).
22:13 In other words, **the slacker** makes excuses to avoid working.
22:14 See 5:1-23; 6:20–7:27.
22:15 Solomon is talking about willful **foolishness**—not just childish silliness. Many kids who are now reaching adulthood were never disciplined by their parents. Unfortunately, since they didn't receive loving discipline at home, society is forced to correct them through the police and the government.
22:19 Receiving wise instruction is essential **so that your confidence may be in the LORD**—not in people. A disciple of Jesus Christ is one for whom regular interaction with the Word of God is as necessary and desirable as obtaining food for the body. Scripture equips us to live the Christian life. Our minds, which are constantly bombarded with the world's unbiblical ideas, need to be renewed so our lives can be transformed (see Rom 12:2). When you try to change your actions without changing your thinking, you only do a temporary, patchwork job. If you want to fix what you do, you must first fix how you think about what you do. A transformed mind comes through the study and application of the Word of God.

20 Haven't I written for you
    thirty sayings[A]
about counsel and knowledge,
21 in order to teach you true
    and reliable words,
so that you may give
    a dependable report[B,a]
to those who sent you?[b]

22 Don't rob a poor person
    because he is poor,
and don't crush the oppressed[c] at
    the city gate,[d]
23 for the LORD will
    champion their cause[e]
and will plunder those
    who plunder them.

24 Don't make friends
    with an angry person,[c]
and don't be a companion
    of a hot-tempered one,[f]
25 or you will learn his ways[g]
and entangle yourself in a snare.

26 Don't be one of those
    who enter agreements,[D]
who put up security for loans.[h]
27 If you have nothing with which
    to pay,
even your bed will be taken
    from under you.[i]

28 Don't move
    an ancient boundary marker
that your fathers set up.[j]

29 Do you see a person skilled
    in his work?
He will stand in the presence
    of kings.
He will not stand in the presence
    of the unknown.[k]

23 When you sit down to dine
    with a ruler,
consider carefully what[E] is
    before you,

2 and put a knife to your throat
    if you have a big[F] appetite;
3 don't desire his choice food,[l]
    for that food is deceptive.

4 Don't wear yourself out to get rich;[m]
    because you know better, stop!
5 As soon as your eyes fly to it,
    it disappears,[n]
for it makes wings for itself
    and flies like an eagle to the sky.

6 Don't eat a stingy person's bread,[G,o]
    and don't desire his choice food,[p]
7 for it's like someone calculating
    inwardly.[H,q]
"Eat and drink," he says to you,
    but his heart is not with you.[r]
8 You will vomit the little you've eaten
    and waste your pleasant words.

9 Don't speak to[I] a fool,
    for he will despise the insight
    of your words.[s]

10 Don't move
    an ancient boundary marker,[t]
and don't encroach on the fields
    of the fatherless,
11 for their Redeemer is strong,[u]
and he will champion their cause
    against you.[v]

12 Apply yourself to discipline
and listen to words of knowledge.

13 Don't withhold discipline
    from a youth;
if you punish him with a rod,
    he will not die.[w]
14 Punish him with a rod,
and you will rescue his life
    from Sheol.[x]

15 My son, if your heart is wise,
    my heart will indeed rejoice.[y]
16 My innermost being will celebrate
    when your lips say what is right.[z]

[a] 22:21 Lk 1:3-4
[b] Pr 10:26; 25:13
[c] 22:22 Ex 23:6; Jb 31:16; Zch 7:10; Mal 3:5
[d] Ru 4:11; Pr 24:7; Zch 8:16
[e] 22:23 1Sm 25:39; Ps 12:5; 35:10; 68:5; 140:12; Pr 23:10-11; Is 3:13-15
[f] 22:24 Pr 15:18; 19:19
[g] 22:25 1Co 15:33
[h] 22:26 Pr 6:1-5; 11:15; 17:18
[i] 22:27 Ex 22:26; Pr 20:16
[j] 22:28 Dt 19:14; 27:17; Jb 24:2; Pr 23:10; Hs 5:10
[k] 22:29 Gn 41:46; 1Kg 10:8; Pr 14:35

[l] 23:3 Gn 27:4; Pr 23:6; Dn 1:8
[m] 23:4 Pr 15:27; 28:20; Mt 6:19; 1Tm 6:9-10; Heb 13:5
[n] 23:5 Pr 27:24
[o] 23:6 Dt 15:9; Pr 28:22; Mt 6:23
[p] Pr 23:3
[q] 23:7 Mt 6:21; Lk 12:34
[r] Pr 26:24-25
[s] 23:9 Mt 7:6
[t] 23:10 Pr 22:28
[u] 23:11 Jr 50:34
[v] Pr 22:22-23
[w] 23:13 Pr 13:24; 19:18; 22:15
[x] 23:14 1Co 5:5
[y] 23:15 Pr 10:1; 15:20; 23:24-25; 29:3
[z] 23:16 Pr 8:6

[A] 22:20 Text emended; one Hb tradition reads *you previously*; alt Hb tradition reads *you excellent things*; LXX, Syr, Vg read *you three times*   [B] 22:21 Lit *give dependable words*   [C] 22:24 Lit *with a master of anger*   [D] 22:26 Lit *Don't be among hand slappers*   [E] 23:1 Or *who*   [F] 23:2 Lit *you are the master of an*   [G] 23:6 Lit *eat bread of an evil eye*   [H] 23:7 LXX reads *it is like someone swallowing a hair in the throat*   [I] 23:9 Lit *in the ears of*

22:22-23 See 17:5.
22:26-27 See 6:1-5.
22:28 To **move an ancient boundary marker** was an attempt to acquire land dishonestly.
22:29 Since they represent the Lord Jesus Christ, Christians should be known as those who work with excellence at whatever they do (see Col 3:23). "Good enough" doesn't cut it.

23:1-3 Beware of indebting yourself to the rich and powerful. Their extravagant gifts are often motivated by a desire to get more from you than they give.
23:6-8 Like the rich man (see 23:1-3), the **stingy** man may also have ulterior motives for his gifts. Be discerning.
23:9 See 9:7-9.

23:12 A Christian who suffers from spiritual Alzheimer's loses the ability to apply a spiritual mind to his daily interactions. He or she forgets how to think in terms of God's kingdom agenda and defaults to a secular way of thinking. We must continuously transform our thought patterns and discipline our minds to focus on the realm of the Spirit.
23:13-14 See 13:24; 22:15; 29:15, 17.

[a]23:17 Ps 37:1; Pr 24:1,19
[b]Pr 28:14
[c]23:18 Ps 9:18; Pr 10:28; 24:14; Jr 29:11
[d]23:20 Pr 20:1; 23:29-30; Is 5:22; Mt 24:49; Lk 21:34; Rm 13:13; Eph 5:18
[e]Pr 28:7
[f]23:21 Pr 6:10-11
[g]23:22 Pr 1:8; 15:20; Eph 6:1
[h]23:23 Pr 4:5,7; 16:16; 18:15; Mt 13:44
[i]23:24 Pr 10:1; 23:15; 29:3
[j]23:25 Pr 27:11
[k]23:27 Pr 22:14
[l]23:28 Pr 6:26; 7:12,22-23; Ec 7:26
[m]23:29 Pr 23:35
[n]23:30 Is 5:11,22

[o]23:31 Eph 5:18
[p]Sg 7:9
[q]23:33 Is 28:7
[r]23:35 Pr 23:29; Jr 5:3
[s]Is 56:12
[t]24:1 Ps 37:1; Pr 23:17; 24:19
[u]Ps 1:1; Pr 1:15
[v]24:2 Ps 10:7
[w]24:3 Pr 14:1
[x]24:5 Pr 21:22
[y]24:6 Pr 11:14; 15:22; 20:18
[z]24:7 Pr 14:6; 17:16,24
[aa]Jb 5:4; Ps 127:5
[ab]24:8 Rm 1:30

17 Don't let your heart envy sinners;[a]
   instead, always fear the LORD.[b]
18 For then you will have a future,
   and your hope will not be dashed.[c]

19 Listen, my son, and be wise;
   keep your mind on the right course.
20 Don't associate with those
      who drink too much wine[d]
   or with those who gorge themselves
      on meat.[e]
21 For the drunkard and the glutton
      will become poor,
   and grogginess will clothe them
      in rags.[f]

22 Listen to your father who gave
      you life,
   and don't despise your mother
      when[A] she is old.[g]
23 Buy — and do not sell — truth,
   wisdom, instruction,
      and understanding.[h]
24 The father of a righteous son
      will rejoice greatly,
   and one who fathers a wise son
      will delight in him.[i]
25 Let your father and mother
      have joy,[j]
   and let her who gave birth to you
      rejoice.

26 My son, give me your heart,
   and let your eyes observe my ways.
27 For a prostitute is a deep pit,[k]
   and a wayward woman is
      a narrow well;
28 indeed, she sets an ambush
      like a robber[l]
   and increases the number
      of unfaithful people.

29 Who has woe? Who has sorrow?
   Who has conflicts?
      Who has complaints?
   Who has wounds for no reason?[m]
   Who has red eyes?
30 Those who linger over wine;
   those who go looking
      for mixed wine.[n]

31 Don't gaze at wine because it is red,[o]
   because it gleams in the cup
   and goes down smoothly.[p]
32 In the end it bites like a snake
   and stings like a viper.
33 Your eyes will see strange things,
   and you will say absurd things.[B,q]
34 You'll be like someone sleeping
      out at sea
   or lying down on the top
      of a ship's mast.
35 "They struck me, but[c] I feel no pain!
   They beat me, but I didn't know it![r]
   When will I wake up?
   I'll look for another drink."[s]

24 Don't envy the evil[t]
   or desire to be with them,[u]
2 for their hearts plan violence,
   and their words stir up trouble.[v]

3 A house is built by wisdom,[w]
   and it is established
      by understanding;
4 by knowledge the rooms are filled
   with every precious
      and beautiful treasure.

5 A wise warrior is better
      than a strong one,[D]
   and a man of knowledge than one
      of strength;[E,x]
6 for you should wage war
      with sound guidance —
   victory comes
      with many counselors.[y]

7 Wisdom is inaccessible to[F] a fool;[z]
   he does not open his mouth
      at the city gate.[aa]

8 The one who plots evil[ab]
   will be called a schemer.
9 A foolish scheme is sin,
   and a mocker is detestable to people.

10 If you do nothing in a difficult time,
   your strength is limited.
11 Rescue those being taken off
      to death,

[A]23:22 Or *because*   [B]23:33 Or *will speak perversities,* or *inverted things*   [C]23:35 LXX, Syr, Tg, Vg read *me," you will say, "but*   [D]24:5 LXX, Syr; MT reads *is in strength*   [E]24:5 LXX, Syr, Tg; MT reads *knowledge exerts strength*   [F]24:7 Lit *is too high for*

23:17-18 See 3:31-35; 24:1-2.
23:26-28 See 5:1-23; 6:20-7:27.
24:1-2 Choosing friends will lead us down either the wise or the foolish path. The people in our lives can encourage wise, kingdom living or be a stumbling block to it.
24:3-4 If your family is built upon **wisdom**, **understanding**, and **knowledge**, your home

will be filled with **beautiful treasure** regardless of your income. Such a family is prepared to extend God's kingdom rule into the world.
24:5-6 See 11:14; 20:18.
24:7 At **the city gate** leaders gathered to discuss important matters. The **fool** has nothing to offer; thus, he has no business there.

24:11-12 One example of how the principle in verse 11 can be applied regards the wickedness of abortion. For Christians to say, **But we didn't know about this** (24:12) is to be like the priest and Levite in Jesus's parable of the good Samaritan who essentially stuck their heads in the sand to avoid helping their neighbor (see Luke 10:25-37). God will **repay**

and save those stumbling
   toward slaughter.[a]
12 If you say, "But we didn't know
   about this,"
won't he who weighs hearts[b]
   consider it?
Won't he who protects
   your life[c] know?
Won't he repay a person
   according to his work?[d]

13 Eat honey,[e] my son, for it is good,
and the honeycomb is sweet
   to your palate;[f]
14 realize that wisdom is the same
   for you.[g]
If you find it, you will have a future,
and your hope will never fade.[h]

15 Don't set an ambush, you
   wicked one,
at the camp of the righteous man;[i]
don't destroy his dwelling.
16 Though a righteous person falls
   seven times,
he will get up,[j]
but the wicked will stumble
   into ruin.[k]

17 Don't gloat when your enemy falls,
and don't let your heart rejoice
   when he stumbles,[l]
18 or the LORD will see, be displeased,
and turn his wrath away from him.

19 Don't be agitated by evildoers,
and don't envy the wicked.[m]
20 For the evil have no future;[n]
the lamp of the wicked will be
   put out.[o]

21 My son, fear the LORD, as well as
   the king,[p]
and don't associate with rebels,[A]
22 for destruction will come suddenly
   from them;
who knows what distress these two
   can bring?

23 These sayings also belong to the wise:[q]

It is not good to show partiality
   in judgment.[r]

24 Whoever says to the guilty,
   "You are innocent"[s] —
peoples will curse him,[t] and nations
   will denounce him;
25 but it will go well with those
   who convict the guilty,
and a generous blessing will come
   to them.

26 He who gives an honest answer
gives a kiss on the lips.

27 Complete your outdoor work,
   and prepare your field;[u]
afterward, build your house.

28 Don't testify against your neighbor
   without cause.[v]
Don't deceive with your lips.
29 Don't say, "I'll do to him what he did
   to me;
I'll repay the man for what
   he has done."[w]

30 I went by the field of a slacker
and by the vineyard of one
   lacking sense.
31 Thistles had come up everywhere,
weeds covered the ground,[x]
and the stone wall was ruined.
32 I saw, and took it to heart;
I looked, and received instruction:
33 a little sleep, a little slumber,
a little folding of the arms
   to rest,
34 and your poverty will come
   like a robber,
and your need, like a bandit.[y]

HEZEKIAH'S COLLECTION

25 These too are proverbs
   of Solomon,[z]
which the men of King Hezekiah[aa]
   of Judah copied.

2 It is the glory of God to conceal
   a matter[ab]
and the glory of kings to investigate
   a matter.
3 As the heavens are high
   and the earth is deep,
so the hearts of kings cannot
   be investigated.

[a] 24:11 Ps 82:4; Is 58:6-7
[b] 24:12 1Sm 16:7; Ps 44:21; Pr 21:2
[c] Ps 121:3-8
[d] Jb 34:11; Ps 62:12
[e] 24:13 Pr 25:16
[f] Sg 5:1
[g] 24:14 Ps 19:10; 119:103
[h] Pr 10:28; 23:18; Jr 29:11
[i] 24:15 Pr 10:9-10
[j] 24:16 Jb 5:19; Ps 37:24
[k] Pr 14:32; 29:16
[l] 24:17 Ps 35:15,19; Pr 17:5; Ob 12; Mc 7:8
[m] 24:19 Ps 37:1; Pr 23:17; 24:1
[n] 24:20 Ps 37:38; Pr 14:11; 16:25
[o] Jb 18:5; 21:17; Pr 13:9; 20:20
[p] 24:21 Mt 22:21; Rm 13:1-7; 1Pt 2:13-14,17
[q] 24:23 Pr 1:6; 22:17
[r] Dt 1:17; 16:19; Pr 18:5; 28:21

[s] 24:24 Pr 17:15
[t] Pr 11:26
[u] 24:27 Pr 20:4
[v] 24:28 Ex 20:16; Pr 25:18
[w] 24:29 Dt 32:35; Pr 20:22; Mt 5:39; Rm 12:17,19
[x] 24:31 Gn 3:18; Pr 20:4
[y] 24:34 Pr 6:10-11; 20:13
[z] 25:1 Pr 1:1
[aa] 2Kg 18-20
[ab] 25:2 Dt 29:29; Rm 11:33

[A] 24:21 Or *those given to change*

---

a person according to his work (Prov 24:12), so do what you can to help fight such wickedness and love those around you.
24:16 The foolish and wicked are stumbling through life without hope. God's people

stumble too, but he helps them up—often with the aid of the godly people we have gathered around us.
24:17-18 As Jesus said, "Love your enemies and pray for those who persecute you" (Matt 5:44).

24:19-20 See 3:31-35; 24:1-2.
24:28-29 See 12:17, 19, 22; 24:17-18; 25:18-19.

*25:4 Ezk 22:18; Mal 3:2–3
*2Tm 2:21
*25:5 Pr 20:8,26
*Pr 16:12
*25:7 Lk 14:7–11
*25:8 Pr 17:14; Mt 5:25;
1Co 6:7
*25:9 Pr 17:9; Mt 18:15
*25:11 Pr 8:10; 15:23; 16:16
*25:12 Pr 15:31
*25:13 Pr 13:17; 16:24;
25:25
*25:14 Jd 12

*25:15 Pr 15:1; 16:14,32;
Ec 10:4
*25:16 Jdg 14:8; 1Sm
14:25
*Pr 25:27
*25:18 Ex 20:16; Pr 24:28
*Ps 57:4; Pr 12:18
*25:19 2Kg 18:21
*25:20 Rm 12:15
*25:21 Ex 23:4–5; 2Kg
6:22; 2Ch 28:15; Mt 5:44;
Rm 12:20
*25:22 Mt 6:4
*25:24 Pr 15:17; 17:1;
21:9,19
*25:25 Pr 15:30
*25:26 Dt 13:6–8; Gl 2:4–5

4 Remove impurities from silver,*
and material will be produced^
for a silversmith. ^,*
5 Remove the wicked
from the king's presence,*
and his throne will be established
in righteousness.*

6 Don't boast about yourself
before the king,
and don't stand in the place
of the great;
7 for it is better for him to say to you,
"Come up here!"
than to demote you in plain view
of a noble. *,*

8 Don't take a matter to court hastily.*
Otherwise, what will
you do afterward
if your opponent* humiliates you?
9 Make your case with your opponent
without revealing another's secret;*
10 otherwise, the one who hears
will disgrace you,
and you'll never live it down.*

11 A word spoken at the right time
is like gold apples in silver settings.*
12 A wise correction to a receptive ear*
is like a gold ring or an ornament
of gold.

13 To those who send him,
a trustworthy envoy
is like the coolness of snow
on a harvest day;
he refreshes the life of his masters.*

14 The one who boasts about a gift
that does not exist
is like clouds and wind
without rain.*
15 A ruler can be persuaded
through patience,

and a gentle tongue can break
a bone.*
16 If you find honey,* eat only
what you need;
otherwise, you'll get sick from it
and vomit.*
17 Seldom set foot
in your neighbor's house;
otherwise, he'll get sick of you
and hate you.

18 A person giving false testimony
against his neighbor*
is like a club, a sword,
or a sharp arrow.*
19 Trusting an unreliable person in a
difficult time
is like a rotten tooth
or a faltering foot.*
20 Singing songs to a troubled heart
is like taking off clothing
on a cold day
or like pouring vinegar on soda.^,*
21 If your enemy is hungry, give him
food to eat,
and if he is thirsty, give him water
to drink;*
22 for you will heap burning coals
on his head,
and the LORD will reward you.*
23 The north wind produces rain,
and a backbiting tongue,
angry looks.
24 Better to live on the corner
of a roof
than to share a house
with a nagging wife.*
25 Good news from a distant land
is like cold water
to a parched throat.^,*
26 A righteous person who yields
to the wicked*

^25:4 Lit *will come out* ; Ex 32:24   ^25:4 Or *and a vessel will be produced by a silversmith*   ^25:7 Lit *you before a noble whom your eyes see*
^25:8 Or *neighbor*, also in v. 9   ^25:10 Lit *and your evil report will not turn back*   ^25:20 Lit *natron,* or *sodium carbonate*
^25:25 Or *a weary person*

25:5 This implies that just government requires just officials.
25:6-7 Jesus told a parable that similarly condemns pride and praises humility (see Luke 14:7-11), so let the Lord exalt you.
25:8-10 Don't be quick to sue someone. Make every effort to settle out of court.
25:13 Few things are as highly valued as being **trustworthy**. Employers want employees whom they can trust to work diligently and with integrity. People want friends whom they can confide in without risk of betrayal.

Add trustworthiness to your character, then, and watch your usefulness to God expand.
25:15 This proverb reminds us of Jesus's parable of the Persistent Widow (see Luke 18:1-8).
25:17 If you darken your neighbor's door too often, you'll wear out your welcome. Don't be a high-maintenance friend.
25:18-19 To what does Solomon compare an unreliable person? A **club**, **a sword**, **a sharp arrow**, **a rotten tooth**, and a **faltering foot**. In other words, a person whose words are **false** inevitably brings harm to others.

25:20 If we want to bless others with our words, we need to discern not only *what* is appropriate to say but also *when* it's appropriate to say it.
25:21-22 Paul drew on this passage in Romans 12:19-21 to remind believers to conquer evil with good. Do good to those who hate you and leave their judgment to God.
25:23-28 These verses graphically demonstrate that our actions can either bless others or wear them out.

is like a muddied spring
   or a polluted well.[a]
27 It is not good to eat too much honey[b]
   or to seek glory after glory.[A,c]
28 A person who does not control
   his temper[d]
is like a city whose wall
   is broken down.[e]

26

Like snow in summer and rain
   at harvest,[f]
honor is inappropriate for a fool.[g]
2 Like a flitting sparrow
   or a fluttering swallow,[h]
an undeserved curse goes nowhere.[i]
3 A whip for the horse, a bridle
   for the donkey,[j]
and a rod for the backs of fools.[k]
4 Don't answer a fool according to
   his foolishness[l]
or you'll be like him yourself.
5 Answer a fool according to
   his foolishness[m]
or he'll become wise
   in his own eyes.[n]
6 The one who sends a message
   by a fool's hand[o]
cuts off his own feet
   and drinks violence.[p]
7 A proverb in the mouth of a fool
is like lame legs that hang limp.
8 Giving honor to a fool
is like binding a stone in a sling.
9 A proverb in the mouth of a fool
is like a stick with thorns,
brandished by[B] the hand
   of a drunkard.
10 The one who hires a fool
   or who hires those passing by
is like an archer
   who wounds everyone.
11 As a dog returns to its vomit,
so also a fool repeats
   his foolishness.[q]
12 Do you see a person who is wise
   in his own eyes?[r]

There is more hope for a fool
   than for him.[s]
13 The slacker says, "There's a lion
   in the road —
a lion in the public square!"[t]
14 A door turns on its hinges,
and a slacker, on his bed.[u]
15 The slacker buries his hand
   in the bowl;
he is too weary to bring it
   to his mouth![v]
16 In his own eyes, a slacker is wiser[w]
than seven who can answer sensibly.

17 A person who is passing by and
   meddles in a quarrel that's not his
is like one who grabs a dog
   by the ears.
18 Like a madman who throws
   flaming darts and deadly arrows,[x]
19 so is the person who deceives
   his neighbor
and says, "I was only joking!"

20 Without wood, fire goes out;
without a gossip, conflict dies down.[y]
21 As charcoal for embers and wood
   for fire,
so is a quarrelsome person
   for kindling strife.[z]
22 A gossip's words are like choice food
that goes down to
   one's innermost being.[C,aa]

23 Smooth[D] lips with an evil heart
are like glaze on an earthen vessel.[ab]
24 A hateful person disguises himself
   with his speech
and harbors deceit within.
25 When he speaks graciously,
   don't believe him,
for there are seven detestable things
   in his heart.[ac]
26 Though his hatred is concealed
   by deception,

---

[a] 25:26 Ezk 32:2; 34:18-19
[b] 25:27 Pr 25:16
[c] Pr 27:2
[d] 25:28 Pr 16:32; 29:11
[e] Neh 1:3
[f] 26:1 1Sm 12:17
[g] Pr 17:7; 19:10
[h] 26:2 Pr 27:8
[i] Nm 23:8; Dt 23:5; 2Sm 16:12
[j] 26:3 Ps 32:9
[k] Pr 10:13; 19:29
[l] 26:4 Pr 23:9; 29:9; Mt 7:6; Lk 23:9
[m] 26:5 Mt 16:1-4; 21:24-27
[n] Pr 26:12; 28:11; Rm 12:16
[o] 26:6 Pr 10:26; 25:13
[p] Pr 13:2
[q] 26:11 2Pt 2:22
[r] 26:12 Pr 3:7; 26:5; Rm 12:16

[s] 26:12 Pr 29:20
[t] 26:13 Pr 22:13
[u] 26:14 Pr 6:9-10; 19:15
[v] 26:15 Pr 12:27; 19:24
[w] 26:16 Pr 26:5,12; 28:11
[x] 26:18 Is 50:11
[y] 26:20 Pr 16:28; 22:10
[z] 26:21 Pr 15:18
[aa] 26:22 Pr 18:8
[ab] 26:23 Mt 23:27; Lk 11:39
[ac] 26:25 Ps 28:3

[A] 25:27 Lit seek their glory, glory   [B] 26:9 Lit thorn that goes up into   [C] 26:22 Lit to the chambers of the belly   [D] 26:23 LXX; MT reads Burning

---

26:4-5 Sometimes, when dealing with a fool, the best policy is to ignore him so that you don't entangle yourself in his ways (26:4). At other times, the wiser choice may be to respond to the fool using his own argument to demonstrate how silly he is (26:5). Paul followed the latter course in 2 Corinthians (see 2 Cor 11:16-27).

26:6-12 Given all this, why would anyone choose the fool's way? Yet young people do so every day. Parents, love your children enough to teach them—and model for them—that life lived from the divine

point-of-view will bring them blessing and joy.

26:13 Some of Solomon's descriptions of the lazy man are quite humorous, but there's nothing funny about Paul's prescription for the lazy in God's kingdom: "If anyone isn't willing to work, he should not eat" (2 Thess 3:10).

26:17 Solomon isn't talking about someone who's trying to bring reconciliation to those at odds with each other. He's talking about a busybody who's sticking his nose where it doesn't belong.

26:18-19 Don't assume you can manipulate the feelings of others, claim you were **only joking**, and escape the consequence of people hating you for it in the end.

26:20-22 Some people love to gossip and quarrel like they're eating **choice food** (26:22). But gossip and quarreling are sins that plague our world and, unfortunately, many churches. Both serve as **wood** for the **fire** of conflict (26:20-21). Some have started gossip fires that burned up another's reputation entirely. When gossip is eliminated, conflict is snuffed out. See 11:13; 17:9.

his evil will be revealed
in the assembly.
27 The one who digs a pit will fall
into it,
and whoever rolls a stone —
it will come back on him.[a]
28 A lying tongue hates
those it crushes,
and a flattering mouth causes ruin.

27 Don't boast about tomorrow,
for you don't know what a day
might bring.[b]

2 Let another praise you, and not
your own mouth —
a stranger, and not your own lips.[c]

3 A stone is heavy and sand, a burden,
but aggravation from a fool
outweighs them both.

4 Fury is cruel, and anger a flood,
but who can withstand jealousy?[d]

5 Better an open reprimand
than concealed love.[e]

6 The wounds of a friend
are trustworthy,[f]
but the kisses of an enemy
are excessive.[g]

7 A person who is full tramples
on a honeycomb,[h]
but to a hungry person,
any bitter thing is sweet.

8 Anyone wandering from his home
is like a bird wandering from its nest.[i]

9 Oil[j] and incense bring joy
to the heart,
and the sweetness of a friend
is better than self-counsel.[A]

10 Don't abandon your friend
or your father's friend,[k]
and don't go to your brother's house
in your time of calamity;
better a neighbor nearby
than a brother far away.[l]

11 Be wise, my son, and bring
my heart joy,[m]
so that I can answer anyone
who taunts me.[n]

12 A sensible person sees danger
and takes cover;
the inexperienced keep going
and are punished.[o]

13 Take his garment,
for he has put up security for a stranger;
get collateral if it is for foreigners.[B,p]

14 If one blesses his neighbor
with a loud voice early
in the morning,
it will be counted as a curse to him.

15 An endless dripping on a rainy day
and a nagging wife are alike;[q]
16 the one who controls her controls
the wind
and grasps oil with his right hand.

17 Iron sharpens iron,
and one person sharpens another.[C]

18 Whoever tends a fig tree[r] will eat
its fruit,[s]
and whoever looks after his master
will be honored.

19 As water reflects the face,
so the heart reflects the person.

20 Sheol and Abaddon[t] are
never satisfied,[u]

[a] 26:27 Est 7:10; Jb 4:8; Pr 28:10; Dn 6:24; Mt 26:52 [b] 27:1 Lk 12:19-20; Jms 4:13-14 [c] 27:2 Pr 25:27; 2Co 10:12,18; 12:11 [d] 27:4 Pr 6:34 [e] 27:5 Pr 28:23 [f] 27:6 Ps 141:5 [g] Lk 22:48 [h] 27:7 Pr 25:16 [i] 27:8 Pr 26:2 [j] 27:9 Ps 23:5
[k] 27:10 2Sm 10:2 [l] Pr 17:17 [m] 27:11 Pr 10:1; 23:24-25; 29:3 [n] Ps 119:42; 127:5 [o] 27:12 Pr 22:3 [p] 27:13 Pr 6:1-5; 11:15; 20:16 [q] 27:15 Pr 19:13 [r] 27:18 Am 7:14 [s] Sg 8:12; 1Co 3:8; 9:7; 2Tm 2:6 [t] 27:20 Jb 26:6; Pr 15:11 [u] Pr 30:15-16; Hab 2:5

[A] 27:9 LXX reads *heart, but the soul is torn up by affliction* [B] 27:13 Lit *a foreign woman* [C] 27:17 Lit *and a man sharpens his friend's face*

27:2 See 25:6-7.
27:4 Solomon says **jealousy** is more relentless than anger. Don't foolishly make yourself its target (see 6:32-35).
27:6 Better the friend who will, with love, wound us for our good, than someone who excessively kisses up to us and never tells it like it is. After all, didn't Judas betray Jesus with a kiss? A true friend corrects you when you're wrong. A legitimate friend will never absolve you of the evil you do.
27:8 The **wandering** man Solomon describes is not merely out for a stroll. He's wandering away from responsibility and into trouble.
27:11 See 10:1.
27:12 Avoid **danger** and punishment; be sensible and take cover within God's covenant and agenda.
27:13 See 6:1-5.
27:14 Being a morning person can be a blessing—unless you force it on others until they curse you!
27:15-16 The **nagging wife** needs to spend some time with the "wife of noble character" described in 31:10-31.
27:17 We need friends who will challenge and sharpen our thinking, help us make good decisions, and help us hone our spiritual lives until they are razor-sharp. Good friends work to rub off dull edges and make each other better. That's why we need ministries and churches that are full of men and women talking about more than work, the weather, and sports.
27:19 What's in your **heart reflects** who you are.
27:20 Just as the grave is never satisfied but always claims more corpses, so also the greedy person never has enough. The cure for the cycle is a heart that regularly expresses gratitude to God.

and people's eyes are
never satisfied.[a]

21 A crucible refines silver, a smelter
refines gold,
and a person refines his praise.[b]

22 Though you grind a fool
in a mortar with a pestle
along with grain,
you will not separate his foolishness
from him.[c]

23 Know well the condition
of your flock,[d]
and pay attention to your herds,

24 for wealth is not forever;[e]
not even a crown lasts for all time.

25 When hay is removed
and new growth appears
and the grain from the hills
is gathered in,

26 lambs will provide your clothing,
and goats, the price of a field;

27 there will be enough goat's milk
for your food —
food for your household
and nourishment for your
female servants.[f]

28 The wicked flee when no one
is pursuing them,[g]
but the righteous are as bold as a lion.[h]

2 When a land is in rebellion, it has
many rulers,[i]
but with a discerning
and knowledgeable person,
it endures.

3 A destitute leader[A] who oppresses
the poor
is like a driving rain that leaves
no food.[j]

4 Those who reject the law
praise the wicked,[k]
but those who keep the law pit
themselves against them.[l]

5 The evil do not understand justice,[m]
but those who seek the LORD
understand everything.[n]

6 Better the poor person who lives
with integrity[o]
than the rich one who distorts right
and wrong.[B,p]

7 A discerning son keeps the law,
but a companion of gluttons
humiliates his father.[q]

8 Whoever increases his wealth
through excessive interest[r]
collects it for one who is kind
to the poor.[s]

9 Anyone who turns his ear
away from hearing the law —
even his prayer is detestable.[t]

10 The one who leads the upright
into an evil way
will fall into his own pit,[u]
but the blameless will inherit
what is good.[v]

11 A rich person is wise in
his own eyes,
but a poor one who has discernment
sees through him.

12 When the righteous triumph,
there is great rejoicing,[c]
but when the wicked come
to power,
people hide.[w]

13 The one who conceals his sins
will not prosper,[x]
but whoever confesses
and renounces them
will find mercy.[y]

14 Happy is the one who is always
reverent,[z]
but one who hardens his heart falls
into trouble.[aa]

[a] 27:20 Ec 1:8; 4:8
[b] 27:21 Pr 16:2; 17:3
[c] 27:22 Pr 23:35; 26:11; Jr 5:3
[d] 27:23 Ezk 34:12; Jn 10:3,14; Ac 20:28
[e] 27:24 Lk 16:9
[f] 27:27 Pr 31:15
[g] 28:1 Lv 26:17; Ps 53:5
[h] Eph 6:19-20
[i] 28:2 1Kg 16:8-28; 2Kg 15:8-15
[j] 28:3 Ex 9:25
[k] 28:4 Rm 1:32
[l] 1Kg 18:18; Neh 13:11,15; Mt 3:7; 14:4; Eph 5:11
[m] 28:5 Ps 92:6
[n] Ps 119:100; Jn 7:17; 1Co 2:15; Jms 1:5; 1Jn 2:20,27
[o] 28:6 Pr 19:1; 20:7
[p] Pr 16:8,19; 19:22; Is 5:20
[q] 28:7 Dt 21:20; Pr 17:25; 23:20; 29:3
[r] 28:8 Ex 22:25; Lv 25:36
[s] Jb 27:17; Pr 13:22; Ec 2:26; Ezk 18:13,17
[t] 28:9 Ps 109:7; Pr 15:8,29; 21:27
[u] 28:10 Ps 7:15; Pr 16:29; 26:27; Mt 18:6
[v] Mt 5:6
[w] 28:12 Pr 11:10; 28:28; 29:2; Ec 10:5-6
[x] 28:13 Jb 31:33; Ps 32:3
[y] Ps 32:5; Jms 5:16; 1Jn 1:9
[z] 28:14 2Ch 19:7; Pr 23:17
[aa] Ps 95:8

[A]28:3 LXX reads A wicked man   [B]28:6 Lit who twists two ways   [C]28:12 Lit glory

---

27:21-22 When an honorable man is placed in the **crucible** of life, the godliness stored up in his heart will be seen, and people will **praise** him (27:21). Likewise, when hard times **grind a fool**, you'll see the **foolishness** that was within him all along (27:22).

28:1 A **wicked** person has a guilty conscience and is always looking over his shoulder. The **righteous** can live with godly boldness.

28:6 See 19:1; 22:1-5.
28:9 See 15:8-9; 21:2-3.
28:11 Solomon speaks to the self-deception to which we are all prone. The person who is **wise in his own eyes**, which is an easy trap to fall into—especially when the person fooling himself has all the outward markings of success—can be completely *without* wisdom. The **discernment** spoken of here is

a valuable tool because the Holy Spirit helps us see things clearly.
28:12 See 14:28-35; 16:10-15.
28:13-14 "Confess your sins," James says, so that "you may be healed" (Jas 5:16). Solomon agrees (Prov 28:13). But the one who **hardens his heart** against God—like Pharaoh (see Exod 8:15, 32; 9:34)—**falls into trouble** (Prov 28:14).

[a] 28:15 Ex 1:14; Pr 29:2; Mt 2:16
[b] Pr 19:12; 1Pt 5:8
[c] 28:16 1Kg 12:1-19; Ps 15:5; Pr 15:27
[d] 28:17 Gn 4:14; 9:6; Ex 21:14
[e] Nm 35:31
[f] 28:18 Pr 2:7; 10:9; 20:7
[g] 28:19 Pr 24:27
[h] Pr 1:31; 12:11,14; 14:14
[i] 28:20 Pr 10:6; Mt 25:21
[j] Pr 20:21; 28:22; 1Tm 6:9
[k] 28:21 Pr 18:5; 24:23
[l] Ezk 13:19
[m] 28:22 Pr 13:11; 20:21; 21:5; 22:16
[n] 28:23 Pr 27:5-6
[o] Pr 26:28; 29:5
[p] 28:24 Pr 19:26
[q] Pr 30:20; Mk 7:11
[r] Pr 18:9
[s] 28:25 Pr 15:18
[t] Ps 37:3-5; Pr 3:5-6; Jr 17:7-8
[u] 28:26 Pr 3:5-7
[v] 28:27 Pr 11:24; 19:17; 22:16
[w] 28:28 Pr 28:12; 29:2
[x] 29:1 Pr 1:24-31; 6:14-15
[y] 29:2 Ex 2:23; Est 8:15; Pr 11:10; 28:12,28
[z] 29:3 Pr 10:1; 15:20; 23:24-25; 27:11; 28:7
[aa] Pr 5:9-10; 6:26; Lk 15:13,30
[ab] 29:4 2Ch 9:8; Pr 29:14
[ac] Pr 17:23
[ad] 29:5 Pr 26:28; 27:6; 28:23
[ae] 29:6 Pr 12:13; 18:7; Ec 9:12
[af] Ex 15:1

15 A wicked ruler over a helpless people[a]
is like a roaring lion
   or a charging bear.[b]

16 A leader who lacks understanding
is very oppressive,
but one who hates dishonest profit
prolongs his life.[c]

17 Someone burdened by bloodguilt[A]
will be a fugitive until death.[d]
Let no one help him.[e]

18 The one who lives with integrity
   will be helped,
but one who distorts right
   and wrong[B]
will suddenly fall.[f]

19 The one who works his land
will have plenty of food,[g]
but whoever chases fantasies
will have his fill of poverty.[h]

20 A faithful person will have
   many blessings,[i]
but one in a hurry to get rich[j]
will not go unpunished.

21 It is not good to show partiality[k] —
yet even a courageous person may
   sin for a piece of bread.[l]

22 A greedy one[C] is in a hurry
   for wealth;
he doesn't know that poverty
   will come to him.[m]

23 One who rebukes a person
   will later find more favor[n]
than one who flatters[D]
   with his tongue.[o]

24 The one who robs his father
   or mother[p]
and says, "That's no sin,"[q]
is a companion to a person
   who destroys.[r]

25 A greedy person stirs up conflict,[s]
but whoever trusts in the LORD
   will prosper.[t]

26 The one who trusts in himself[E] is
   a fool,
but one who walks in wisdom
   will be safe.[u]

27 The one who gives to the poor
will not be in need,
but one who turns his eyes away[F]
will receive many curses.[v]

28 When the wicked come to power,
people hide,
but when they are destroyed,
the righteous flourish.[w]

29 One who becomes stiff-necked,
   after many reprimands
will be shattered instantly —
beyond recovery.[x]

2 When the righteous flourish,
   the people rejoice,
but when the wicked rule,
   people groan.[y]

3 A man who loves wisdom brings joy
   to his father,[z]
but one who consorts
   with prostitutes
   destroys his wealth.[aa]

4 By justice a king brings stability
   to a land,[ab]
but a person who demands
   "contributions"[G]
demolishes it.[ac]

5 A person who flatters[H]
   his neighbor
spreads a net for his feet.[ad]

6 An evil person is caught by sin,[ae]
but the righteous one sings
   and rejoices.[af]

[A] 28:17 Lit *the blood of a person*   [B] 28:18 Lit *who is twisted regarding two ways*   [C] 28:22 Lit *A man with an evil eye*   [D] 28:23 Lit *is smooth*   [E] 28:26 Lit *his heart*   [F] 28:27 Lit *who shuts his eyes*   [G] 29:4 The Hb word for *contributions* usually refers to offerings in worship.   [H] 29:5 Lit *is smooth on*

28:17-18 Your treatment of others will either bless you or curse you.
28:19 See 6:6-11; 10:2-5; 12:24; 18:9; 26:13-16.
28:20 The typical route to wealth is to earn it little-by-little, through honest labor. Participating in a get-rich-quick scheme is the fastest route to ruin.
28:21 Some people can be bought cheaply, but bribes are wicked. See 15:27.

28:23 A loving rebuke is always better than empty flattery.
28:24 See 19:26.
28:26 If we trust God, we're kept safe from the pitfalls the world and the devil put in our paths. And while this is no guarantee that misfortune won't befall us Christians, it is a promise that God will watch over us no matter our circumstances.

29:1 Falling into ruin because of your own foolishness is pitiful, but how much worse is it to fall into ruin *after* you've received many warnings to change your course? See 1:22-33; 3:11-12; 9:7-9; 10:17; 25:11-12.
29:3 See 5:1-23; 6:20-7:27.
29:4 See 14:28-35; 16:10-15.
29:6 **Sin** promises freedom and then enslaves the one **caught by** it.

7 The righteous person knows
　　the rights[A] of the poor,[a]
but the wicked one does not
　　understand these concerns.

8 Mockers inflame a city,[b]
but the wise turn away anger.

9 If a wise person goes to court
　　with a fool,
there will be ranting and raving
　　but no resolution.[B,C]

10 Bloodthirsty men hate
　　an honest person,[d]
but the upright care about him.[c]

11 A fool gives full vent to his anger,[D,e]
but a wise person holds it
　　in check.[f]

12 If a ruler listens to lies,[g]
all his officials will be wicked.

13 The poor and the oppressor
　　have this in common:[E]
the LORD gives light to the eyes
　　of both.[h]

14 A king who judges the poor
　　with fairness —
his throne will be
　　established forever.[i]

15 A rod of correction
　　imparts wisdom,[j]
but a youth left to himself[F]
is a disgrace to his mother.[k]

16 When the wicked increase,
　　rebellion increases,
but the righteous will see
　　their downfall.[l]

17 Discipline your child,[m] and
　　it will bring you peace of mind
　　and give you delight.

18 Without revelation[G,n] people
　　run wild,[o]
but one who follows
　　divine instruction will be happy.[p]

> ⌁ **HOPE WORDS** ⌁
>
> *The only way you will be able
> to see life with clear vision is
> when you view all of life from
> a kingdom perspective.*

19 A servant cannot be disciplined
　　by words;
though he understands,
　　he doesn't respond.[q]

20 Do you see someone who speaks
　　too soon?[r]
There is more hope for a fool
　　than for him.[s]

21 A servant pampered from his youth
will become arrogant[H] later on.

22 An angry person stirs up conflict,
and a hot-tempered one[I]
　　increases rebellion.[t]

23 A person's pride will humble him,[u]
but a humble spirit will gain honor.[v]

24 To be a thief's partner is
　　to hate oneself;
he hears the curse but
　　will not testify.[w]

25 The fear of mankind is a snare,[x]
but the one who trusts in the LORD
　　is protected.[J,y]

26 Many desire a ruler's favor,[z]
but a person receives justice
　　from the LORD.[aa]

[a] 29:7 Jb 29:16; Ps 41:1
[b] 29:8 Pr 11:11; 26:21; 29:22
[c] 29:9 Pr 26:4
[d] 29:10 Gn 4:5-8; 1Jn 3:12
[e] 29:11 Pr 12:16
[f] Pr 16:32; 25:28
[g] 29:12 1Kg 22:8,21-23
[h] 29:13 Pr 22:2
[i] 29:14 Ps 72:4; Pr 16:12; 25:5; Is 11:4
[j] 29:15 Pr 13:24; 22:15
[k] Pr 10:1; 17:25
[l] 29:16 Ps 37:34,36; 58:10; 91:8; 92:11
[m] 29:17 Pr 13:24

[n] 29:18 1Sm 3:1; Ps 74:9; Am 8:11-12
[o] Ex 32:25
[p] Ps 119:2; Pr 8:32; Jn 13:17; Jms 1:25
[q] 29:19 Mt 18:17
[r] 29:20 Lv 5:4; Jdg 11:30-31,34; Pr 10:19; 17:27; 19:2; 20:25
[s] Pr 26:12
[t] 29:22 Pr 15:18; 26:21; 28:25
[u] 29:23 2Sm 22:28; Mt 23:12; Jms 4:6
[v] Pr 11:2; 15:33; 18:12; 22:4
[w] 29:24 Lv 5:1
[x] 29:25 Gn 12:12; 20:2; 1Sm 13:11; Lk 12:4; Jn 12:42-43
[y] Pr 14:27; 18:10
[z] 29:26 Pr 16:15; 19:6
[aa] Is 49:4; 1Co 4:4-5

[A] 29:7 Lit *justice*　[B] 29:9 Lit *rest*　[C] 29:10 Or *person, and seek the life of the upright*　[D] 29:11 Lit *spirit*　[E] 29:13 Lit *oppressor meet*　[F] 29:15 Lit *youth sent away*　[G] 29:18 Lit *vision*　[H] 29:21 Hb obscure　[I] 29:22 Lit *a master of rage*　[J] 29:25 Lit *raised high*

29:9 Avoid a dispute with **a fool**. He'll rant and rave, but you'll go nowhere except in circles.
29:10 Our attitude toward people operating with honesty and integrity reveals the condition of our own hearts.
29:11 A wise man guards his mouth, knowing that he can bring endless grief upon himself if he doesn't.
29:15-17 It's easy to wimp out, be passive, and withhold discipline. But doing so will

eventually bring you sorrow and disgrace. So if you don't want to see your children join the ranks of the rebellious, discipline them for their own good, for eventually the wicked will experience **downfall** (29:16). See 13:24; 22:15.
29:18 Without the wisdom God's Word gives, people are prone to throw off all restraint. This, in fact, is a description of our culture today: people are running into walls and

down blind alleys for lack of truth. The remedy to the problem is found in hearing and receiving biblical instruction.
29:23 See 6:16-17; 13:10; 27:1.
29:25 If you live your life as a people-pleaser, you're not pleasing the Lord. You're stuck in a trap.
29:26 Though rulers are responsible to administer justice in the world, ultimately **justice** comes from a sovereign God.

[a] 29:27 Pr 29:10; Mt 10:22;
Jn 15:18; 1Jn 3:13
[b] 30:1 Nm 24:3; Pr 31:1;
Nah 1:1; Hab 1:1; Zch 9:1;
Mal 1:1
[c] 30:2 1Kg 3:7
[d] 30:3 Pr 9:10
[e] 30:4 Jn 3:13; Eph 4:9-10
[f] Jb 26:8; 38:9
[g] Jb 38:4-5; Ps 93:1; 119:90;
Is 45:18
[h] Mt 11:27; Rv 19:12-13
[i] 30:5 Ps 12:6; 18:30
[j] Ps 3:3
[k] 30:6 Dt 4:2; 12:32; Rv
22:18
[l] Dt 18:22
[m] 30:8 Jb 23:12; Mt 6:11;
Php 4:11-12

[n] 30:9 Dt 6:10-12; 8:11-14
[o] Jos 24:27; Jb 31:28
[p] Ex 5:2
[q] Ex 20:5; Eph 4:28
[r] Lv 19:11-12
[s] 30:10 Ec 7:21
[t] 30:11 Ex 21:17; Pr 20:20
[u] 30:12 Pr 16:2; Lk 18:11
[v] 30:14 Ps 57:4
[w] Jb 29:17
[x] Ps 14:4
[y] 30:15 Pr 6:16; 30:18,21,29
[z] 30:16 Pr 27:20; Hab 2:5
[aa] Gn 30:1
[ab] 30:17 Gn 9:22
[ac] Dt 28:26

27 An unjust person is detestable
    to the righteous,
and one whose way is upright
    is detestable to the wicked.[a]

THE WORDS OF AGUR

30
The words of Agur son of Jakeh.
    The pronouncement.[A,b]

The man's oration to Ithiel, to Ithiel
    and Ucal:[B]

2 I am more stupid than
    any other person,[c]
and I lack a human's ability
    to understand.[c]
3 I have not gained wisdom,
and I have no knowledge
    of the Holy One.[d]
4 Who has gone up to heaven
    and come down?[e]
Who has gathered the wind
    in his hands?
Who has bound up the waters
    in a cloak?[f]
Who has established all the ends
    of the earth?[g]
What is his name,
and what is the name of his son —
    if you know?[h]
5 Every word of God is pure;[D,i]
he is a shield to those
    who take refuge in him.[j]
6 Don't add to his words,[k]
or he will rebuke you,
    and you will be proved a liar.[l]

7 Two things I ask of you;
    don't deny them to me before I die:
8 Keep falsehood and deceitful words
    far from me.
Give me neither poverty
    nor wealth;
feed me with the food I need.[m]

9 Otherwise, I might have too much[n]
and deny you,[o] saying,
    "Who is the LORD?"[p]
or I might have nothing and steal,[q]
    profaning[E] the name of my God.[r]

10 Don't slander a servant to his master
or he will curse you,[s] and you will
    become guilty.

11 There is a generation that curses
    its father
and does not bless its mother.[t]
12 There is a generation that is pure
    in its own eyes,[u]
yet is not washed from its filth.
13 There is a generation —
how haughty its eyes
    and pretentious its looks.[F]
14 There is a generation whose teeth
    are swords,[v]
whose fangs are knives,[w]
devouring the oppressed
    from the land[x]
and the needy from among mankind.

15 The leech has two daughters:
    "Give, Give!"
Three things[y] are never satisfied;
    four never say, "Enough!":
16 Sheol;[z] a childless womb;[aa]
earth, which is never satisfied
    with water;
and fire, which never says, "Enough!"

17 As for the eye that ridicules
    a father[ab]
and despises obedience to a mother,
may ravens of the valley pluck it out
    and young vultures eat it.[ac]

18 Three things are too wondrous
    for me;
four I can't understand:

[A] 30:1 Or son of Jakeh from Massa; Pr 31:1   [B] 30:1 Hb uncertain. Sometimes read with different word division as oration: I am weary, God, I am weary, God, and I am exhausted, or oration: I am not God, I am not God, that I should prevail. LXX reads My son, fear my words and when you have received them repent. The man says these things to the believers in God, and I pause.   [C] 30:2 Lit I am more stupid than a man   [D] 30:5 Lit refined
[E] 30:9 Lit grabbing   [F] 30:13 Lit and its eyelids lifted up

---

29:27 **The righteous** and **the wicked** are like oil and water; they don't mix. Each naturally hates the actions of the other.
30:1 We don't know anything about either **Agur** or King Lemuel (see 31:1), but the inclusion of their words in Proverbs is an example of the way the Holy Spirit oversaw and superintended the inspiration of Scripture.
30:2-3 Agur's attitude toward himself is similar to Paul's personal declaration that he was the chief of all sinners (see 1 Tim 1:15). Indeed, the one who spends much time with a holy God comes to see just how sinful his own heart is.

30:5-6 God has weighed and examined **every word** of the Bible to get just the ones he wanted. Our job is to believe and obey his Word, not to put our own words on par with his.
30:8-9 We need to keep material things in their proper perspective and ask God to meet our needs so we can keep our focus where it ought to be.
30:10 It's easy to play fast and loose with our words when it comes to deriding others. Instead, develop a habit of praising good works so that others may be encouraged and

so you may give glory to the God who stands behind the good works.
30:11-14 Sadly, the **generation** Solomon describes could be the young people of our own time. Kids need fathers who are kingdom-minded men—men who make it a priority to spend time with their children, teach them the ways of the Lord, discipline them with love, and model godliness.
30:15-16 See 27:20.
30:17 See 20:20.
30:18-20 **An eagle**, **a snake**, and **a ship** leave no long-term trace of their journeys (30:19).

19   the way of an eagle in the sky,
      the way of a snake on a rock,
      the way of a ship at sea,
      and the way of a man
         with a young woman.

20   This is the way of an adulteress:
      she eats and wipes her mouth
      and says, "I've done nothing wrong."[a]

21   The earth trembles
         under three things;
      it cannot bear up under four:
22   a servant when he becomes king,[b]
      a fool when he is stuffed with food,
23   an unloved woman
         when she marries,[c]
      and a servant girl when she ousts
         her queen.

24   Four things on earth are small,
      yet they are extremely wise:
25   ants are not a strong people,
      yet they store up their food
         in the summer;[d]
26   hyraxes are not a mighty people,
      yet they make their homes
         in the cliffs;[e]
27   locusts have no king,
      yet all of them march in ranks;[f]
28   a lizard[A] can be caught
         in your hands,
      yet it lives in kings' palaces.

29   Three things are stately in their stride;
      four are stately in their walk:
30   a lion, which is mightiest
         among beasts
      and doesn't retreat before anything;
31   a strutting rooster;[B] a goat;
      and a king at the head of his army.[c]

32   If you have been foolish
         by exalting yourself

or if you've been scheming,
put your hand over your mouth.[g]
33   For the churning of milk
         produces butter,
      and twisting a nose draws blood,
      and stirring up anger
         produces strife.[h]

THE WORDS OF LEMUEL

31 The words of King Lemuel,
      a pronouncement[D,i] that
      his mother taught him:

2   What should I say, my son?
     What, son of my womb?[j]
     What, son of my vows?
3   Don't spend your energy[k]
        on women
     or your efforts on those
        who destroy kings.[l]
4   It is not for kings, Lemuel,
     it is not for kings[m] to drink wine[n]
     or for rulers to desire beer.
5   Otherwise, he will drink,
     forget what is decreed,[o]
     and pervert justice for all
        the oppressed.[E,p]
6   Give beer to one who is dying
     and wine to one whose life is bitter.[q]
7   Let him drink so that he can forget
        his poverty
     and remember his trouble no more.[r]
8   Speak up[F] for those who have
        no voice,[G,s]
     for the justice of all
        who are dispossessed.[H]
9   Speak up, judge righteously,[t]
     and defend the cause of
        the oppressed and needy.[u]

IN PRAISE OF A WIFE OF NOBLE CHARACTER

10   Who can find a wife
         of noble character?[I,v]

[a]30:20 Pr 28:24; 1Jn 1:8
[b]30:22 Pr 19:10; Ec 10:7
[c]30:23 Gn 29:30-31; Dt 21:15
[d]30:25 Pr 6:6-8
[e]30:26 Lv 11:5; Ps 104:18
[f]30:27 Jl 2:7-8

[g]30:32 Jb 21:5; Mc 7:16
[h]30:33 Pr 10:12; 29:22
[i]31:1 Pr 30:1
[j]31:2 Is 49:15
[k]31:3 Pr 5:9
[l]Dt 17:17; 1Kg 11:1; Neh 13:26
[m]31:4 1Kg 16:9; 20:16; Ec 10:17
[n]Pr 20:1
[o]31:5 Hs 4:11
[p]Ps 72:1-2; Is 28:7
[q]31:6 Jb 3:20
[r]31:7 Ps 104:15
[s]31:8 Dt 29:12-17
[t]31:9 Lv 19:15; Dt 1:16
[u]Is 1:17; Jr 22:16
[v]31:10 Ru 3:11; Pr 12:4; 18:22; 19:14

[A]30:28 Or *spider*   [B]30:31 Or *a greyhound*   [C]30:31 LXX reads *king addressing his people*   [D]31:1 Or *of Lemuel, king of Massa,* or *of King Lemuel, a burden*   [E]31:5 Lit *sons of affliction*   [F]31:8 Lit *Open your mouth,* also in v. 9   [G]31:8 Lit *who are mute*   [H]31:8 Lit *all the sons of passing away*
[I]31:10 Or *a wife of quality,* or *a capable wife*

Similarly, the **adulteress** assumes she leaves no lasting trace of her liaisons and thus feels no guilt (30:20). But an omniscient God is always watching.
30:21-23 These verses describe people no one wants to encounter. Be a blessing to others— not the kind of person others hope to avoid.
30:24-28 Your size and personal power are irrelevant. God is immense and can accomplish mind-blowing things through you!
30:29-31 If these **beasts** are **stately** (30:29-30), how much more grand is a mighty **king at the head of his army** (30:31)? And if a mag-

nificent human king deserves our awe, what should our response be to the divine King who reigns from heaven with the earth as his footstool (see Isa 66:1)?
30:32 Sometimes the best solution is just to stop talking.
31:1-2 To kids, **King Lemuel** would say, "Listen to your mama." To mothers he would say, "Keep doing what you're doing; teach them the way they should go; your faithful deeds do not go unnoticed."
31:3-9 A kingdom man doesn't spend all his **energy** playing the field (31:3). Instead he

finds a godly woman (see 31:10-31), marries her, and cherishes her. He also doesn't waste all his time on drinking **wine** and **beer** so that his head is fogged and he forgets to do **justice** (31:4-5). Rather, he speaks up **for those who have no voice** (31:8) and defends **the cause of the oppressed** (31:9). A kingdom man goes into battle as God's soldier to serve others.
31:10-12 You can marry a pretty woman. You can marry a rich woman. But many a man has been disappointed when he discovered that the elegance he saw on the outside didn't match what was on the inside. So marry a wise

a 31:14 1Kg 10:22
b 31:15 Pr 20:13
c 27:27; Lk 12:42
d 31:16 Mt 21:33
e 31:17 Pr 31:25
f 31:18 Mt 25:8
g 31:19 Pr 31:13
h 31:20 Dt 15:11; Pr 22:9;
31:9; Rm 12:13; Eph 4:28

i 31:22 Pr 7:16
j Gn 41:42; Rv 19:8,14
k Jdg 8:26; Lk 16:19
l 31:23 Ru 4:1-2; Pr 24:7;
31:31
m 31:25 Pr 31:17
n 1Tm 2:9-10
o Pr 31:21
p 31:27 Pr 31:15
q 31:29 Pr 12:4; 31:10;
Sg 6:8-9
r 31:30 1Pt 3:3-4

She is far more precious
  than jewels.[A]

11 The heart of her husband trusts
  in her,
and he will not lack anything good.

12 She rewards him with good, not evil,
all the days of her life.

13 She selects wool and flax
and works with willing hands.

14 She is like the merchant ships,
bringing her food from far away.[a]

15 She rises while it is still night[b]
and provides food for her household
and portions[B] for
  her female servants.[c]

16 She evaluates a field and buys it;
she plants a vineyard
  with her earnings.[c,d]

17 She draws on her strength[D]
and reveals that her arms
  are strong.[e]

18 She sees that her profits are good,
and her lamp never goes out
  at night.[f]

19 She extends her hands
  to the spinning staff,
and her hands hold the spindle.[g]

20 Her hands reach[E] out to the poor,
and she extends her hands
  to the needy.[h]

21 She is not afraid for her household
  when it snows,
for all in her household
  are doubly clothed.[F]

22 She makes her own bed coverings;[i]
her clothing is fine linen[j]
  and purple.[k]

23 Her husband is known
  at the city gates,
where he sits among the elders
  of the land.[l]

24 She makes and sells
  linen garments;
she delivers belts[G]
  to the merchants.

25 Strength[m] and honor are
  her clothing,[n]
and she can laugh at the time
  to come.[o]

26 Her mouth speaks wisdom,
and loving instruction[H] is
  on her tongue.

27 She watches over the activities
  of her household[p]
and is never idle.[I]

28 Her children rise up
  and call her blessed;
her husband also praises her:

29 "Many women[J] have done
  noble deeds,
but you surpass them all!"[q]

30 Charm is deceptive and beauty
  is fleeting,[r]
but a woman who fears the LORD
  will be praised.

31 Give her the reward of her labor,[K]
and let her works praise her
  at the city gates.

[A] 31:10 Vv. 10-31 form an acrostic.   [B] 31:15 Or *tasks*   [C] 31:16 Or *vineyard by her own labors*   [D] 31:17 Lit *She wraps strength around her like a belt*
[E] 31:20 Lit *Her hand reaches*   [F] 31:21 LXX, Vg; MT reads *are dressed in scarlet*   [G] 31:24 Or *sashes*   [H] 31:26 Or *and the teaching of kindness*
[I] 31:27 Lit *and does not eat the bread of idleness*   [J] 31:29 Lit *daughters*   [K] 31:31 Lit *the fruit of her hands*

---

woman of noble character who loves God, and don't let her go. An excellent woman is one who knows how to grab heaven and apply it to earth so life becomes better for everyone under her influence.

31:13-27 God has given a woman the unique responsibility of watching **over the activities of her household** (31:27). The word *household* shows up three times in this section (31:15, 21, 27), indicating the attention a woman of excellence gives to her family's needs. She understands the central place that the home plays in the kingdom of God. And while the husband's role is to be the head of the home, the wife is the chief operating officer—the internal home manager. She **is never idle** (31:27). Rather than bored, she's industrious.

What we have here is a person with business acumen (31:14). She spends money wisely and uses it in the best way to get maximum yield for the benefit of her family. That's what's happening when **she evaluates a field and buys it** and **plants a vineyard with her earnings** (31:16). When Paul encourages women to be "workers at home" (Titus 2:5) and to "manage their households" (1 Tim 5:14), he doesn't mean they have to stay inside the four walls of a house. He means that everything a woman does outside the home complements what goes on inside it.

The woman does have an outside ministry: **she extends her hands to the needy** (Prov 31:20). In other words, she's not engaging on social media all day. She's not gossiping. Instead, she's helping the less fortunate. So she's busy making money, making a difference, and investing in others.

When she does speak, she **speaks wisdom, and loving instruction is on her tongue** (31:26). She has the ability to use the right words at the right time as she encounters real-life situations. **Her husband** benefits from the fact that he's married to such a rare lady (31:23).

31:30 The reason this woman was wise, the reason she could prioritize her family, the reason she had everything in order, is because she took God seriously. She had a divine worldview. The marketplace didn't control her; her friends didn't control her; the television didn't control her. God controlled her.

31:31 The reason we forget to praise women of excellence in our marriages and communities is that we get used to them. We take them for granted. But offering **praise** is like watering a flower, thus allowing its buds to open up. So praise the godly women in your life and watch them blossom.

ECCLESIASTES

INTRODUCTION

Author

THE AUTHOR STATES THAT HE is "son of David" and "king over Israel in Jerusalem" (1:1, 12). He was also an explorer and a teacher of proverbs (12:9). Solomon, then, is the likely author. Many scholars think the book was written too late in Israel's history to come from Solomon, so they date it to at least five hundred years after him. However, strong evidence attests that the book does indeed come from Solomon's time.

For example, the book displays knowledge of literature from Mesopotamia and Egypt. Solomon had close contact with Egypt, and his empire stretched to the Euphrates River. Therefore, it makes sense that he would have known and reflected upon such texts. Moreover, it is unlikely that a Jew writing five hundred or more years later, when Egyptian and Mesopotamian glory was finished and when Israel was a backwater nation, would have had access to such texts or been so familiar with them. Importantly, the book shows no similarities with the Greek philosophy that flourished five hundred years after Solomon. Thus, the traditional view that Solomon is the author is best.

Historical Background

Ecclesiastes is identified as part of the wisdom literature of the Bible. Ancient Egypt and Babylon produced their own wisdom writings as well. Books like Proverbs and Ecclesiastes help readers grapple with the practical and philosophical issues of life. Ecclesiastes goes further though, engaging the question of the "futility" of life lived "under the sun" (1:2-3).

Message and Purpose

Ecclesiastes is one of my favorite books in the Old Testament because it deals with what life is all about and shows how real the Bible is. It was written by a very

wealthy and wise man who described life as a puzzle he couldn't quite put together despite his vast riches and wisdom. So he went on a pilgrimage to find out the meaning of life, taking his readers along on his binges of the pleasures of the flesh, the accumulation of wealth, and the reality of death. He discovered that living independently of God was "a pursuit of the wind" (1:14, 17; 2:11, 17; 4:4; 6:9), or what Solomon calls "absolute futility" (1:2; 12:8).

This book is a big deal because in it we find a man who made huge mistakes that would eventually split his entire kingdom. It's important for us to grab hold of this book and learn from Solomon's mistakes as we build our families and apply God's kingdom principles to our lives today. That, in fact, was what Solomon wanted his readers to do because he finishes the book by talking about the importance of getting God into the picture early in life (12:1-7).

www.bhpublishinggroup.com/qr/te/21_00

Outline

[a] 1:1 Ec 1:12; 7:27; 12:8-10
[b] 1Kg 2:12; Pr 1:1
[c] 1:2 Ps 39:5-6; 62:9; 144:4;
Ec 12:8; Rm 8:20
[d] 1:3 Ec 2:11,22; 3:9; 5:16
[e] 1:4 Ps 104:5; 119:90;
1Jn 2:17
[f] 1:5 Ps 19:6
[g] 1:6 Ec 11:5; Jn 3:8
[h] 1:8 Pr 27:20; Ec 4:8
[i] 1:11 Dt 9:14; Ec 2:16; 9:5
[j] 1:12 Ec 1:1; 7:27; 12:8-10

[k] 1:13 Ec 1:17
[l] 1Kg 4:29-34; Ec 3:10-11;
7:25; 8:17
[m] Gn 3:19; Ec 2:23,26;
3:10; 4:8
[n] 1:14 Pr 27:16; Ec 2:11,17;
4:4; 6:9
[o] 1:15 Ec 7:13
[p] 1:16 1Kg 3:12; 4:30; 10:23;
Ec 2:9
[q] 1:17 Ec 1:13
[r] Ec 2:12; 7:25
[s] Ec 2:11,17; 4:4,6,16; 6:9
[t] 1:18 Ec 2:23; 12:12
[u] 2:1 Ec 7:4; 8:15; Lk 12:19
[v] 2:2 Pr 14:13; Ec 7:3,6
[w] 2:3 Ps 104:15; Ec 10:19
[x] Ec 7:25
[y] Ec 2:24; 3:12,13; 5:18; 8:15
[z] 2:4 1Kg 7:1-12
[aa] Sg 8:11
[ab] 2:5 Sg 4:16

EVERYTHING IS FUTILE

1 The words of the Teacher,[A,a] son of David, king in Jerusalem.[b] 2 "Absolute futility," says the Teacher. "Absolute futility. Everything is futile."[c]

3 What does a person gain for all his efforts
that he labors at under the sun?[d]

4 A generation goes and a generation comes,
but the earth remains forever.[e]

5 The sun rises and the sun sets;
panting, it returns to the place[f] where it rises.

6 Gusting to the south,
turning to the north,
turning, turning, goes the wind,[g]
and the wind returns in its cycles.

7 All the streams flow to the sea,
yet the sea is never full;
to the place where the streams flow,
there they flow again.

8 All things[B] are wearisome,
more than anyone can say.
The eye is not satisfied by seeing[h]
or the ear filled with hearing.

9 What has been is what will be,
and what has been done is
what will be done;
there is nothing new under the sun.

10 Can one say about anything,
"Look, this is new"?
It has already existed in the ages
before us.

11 There is no remembrance of those
who[C] came before;[i]
and of those who will come after
there will also be no remembrance
by those who follow them.

THE LIMITATIONS OF WISDOM

12 I, the Teacher,[j] have been[D] king over Israel in Jerusalem. 13 I applied my mind to examine[k] and explore through wisdom all that is done under heaven.[l] God has given people[E] this miserable task to keep them occupied.[m] 14 I have seen all the things that are done under the sun and have found everything to be futile, a pursuit of the wind.[F,n]

15 What is crooked cannot
be straightened;[o]
what is lacking cannot be counted.

16 I said to myself, "See, I have amassed wisdom far beyond all those who were over Jerusalem before me,[p] and my mind has thoroughly grasped[G] wisdom and knowledge." 17 I applied my mind to know wisdom and knowledge,[q] madness and folly;[r] I learned that this too is a pursuit of the wind.[s]

18 For with much wisdom is
much sorrow;[t]
as knowledge increases,
grief increases.

THE EMPTINESS OF PLEASURE

2 I said to myself, "Go ahead, I will test you with pleasure;[u] enjoy what is good." But it turned out to be futile. 2 I said about laughter,[v] "It is madness," and about pleasure, "What does this accomplish?" 3 I explored with my mind the pull of wine[w] on my body — my mind still guiding me with wisdom — and how to grasp folly,[x] until I could see what is good for people to do under heaven[H] during the few days of their lives.[y]

THE EMPTINESS OF POSSESSIONS

4 I increased my achievements. I built houses[z] and planted vineyards[aa] for myself. 5 I made gardens[ab] and parks for myself and planted every kind of fruit tree in them. 6 I constructed reservoirs for myself from which to irrigate a grove of

---

[A] 1:1 Or of Qoheleth, or of the Leader of the Assembly   [B] 1:8 Or words   [C] 1:11 Or of the things that   [D] 1:12 Or Teacher, was   [E] 1:13 Or given the descendants of Adam   [F] 1:14 Or a feeding on wind, or an affliction of spirit; also in v. 17   [G] 1:16 Or discerned   [H] 2:3 Two Hb mss, LXX, Syr read the sun

---

1:1 In Ecclesiastes we're reading about King Solomon's perspective on his life experiences after he had both strayed from and returned to the Lord. The sum of his thoughts in this book is that a life disconnected from God is not much of a life at all. It's a saccharin existence, a sugary substitute for the real deal. Without God, life is empty.

1:2-3 **Everything is futile** (1:2). *Everything* is empty and meaningless—from a merely human perspective. The phrase **under the sun** (1:3), which occurs often in Ecclesiastes, is a reference to living from an earthly perspective because "under the sun" is where people work, play, and raise their families.

1:10 Throughout the ages, manufacturers continue to work with the same raw materials—they just reconfigure them.

1:11 No one wants to be forgotten, which is why a popular fundraising strategy is to invite people to donate to a project so it can be named after them. But the cold reality is this: everyone is forgotten eventually.

2:1-3 It seems Solomon looked at his empire and experiences and said, "There's got to be more than this." And what we'll see in the chapters to come is that if you look for the meaning of life *in life*, you'll never find it. Nevertheless, Solomon began a tour of discovery, testing himself **with pleasure**. But though he explored how to satisfy himself with fun, **it turned out to be futile** (2:1). It wasn't any more fulfilling than an amusement park ride, which is exciting for two minutes, and then over. He was like a kid who gets every toy he wants for his birthday—only to be bored after a week. Entertainment was nice while it lasted, but it didn't provide permanent meaning.

2:4-10 Have you ever gotten depressed and gone shopping? It appears Solomon knew the feeling.

flourishing trees.[a] [7] I acquired male and female servants and had slaves who were born in my house.[b] I also owned livestock — large herds and flocks — more than all who were before me in Jerusalem.[c] [8] I also amassed silver and gold for myself, and the treasure of kings and provinces.[d] I gathered male and female singers for myself,[e] and many concubines, the delights of men.[A,B] [9] So I became great and surpassed all who were before me in Jerusalem;[f] my wisdom also remained with me. [10] All that my eyes desired, I did not deny them.[g] I did not refuse myself any pleasure, for I took pleasure in all my struggles. This was my reward for all my struggles.[h] [11] When I considered all that I had accomplished[c] and what I had labored to achieve, I found everything to be futile and a pursuit of the wind.[D,i] There was nothing to be gained under the sun.[j]

THE RELATIVE VALUE OF WISDOM

[12] Then I turned to consider wisdom,[k] madness, and folly, for what will the king's successor[E] be like? He[F] will do what has already been done.[i] [13] And I realized that there is an advantage to wisdom over folly, like the advantage of light over darkness.[m]

[14]   The wise person has eyes
        in his head,
    but the fool walks in darkness.[n]

Yet I also knew that one fate comes to them both.[o] [15] So I said to myself, "What happens to the fool will also happen to me. Why then have I been overly wise?"[p] And I said to myself that this is also futile. [16] For, just like the fool, there is no lasting remembrance of the wise,[q] since in the days to come both will be forgotten. How is it that the wise person dies just like the fool? [17] Therefore, I hated life because the work that was done under the sun was distressing to me. For everything is futile and a pursuit of the wind.

THE EMPTINESS OF WORK

[18] I hated all my work that I labored at under the sun[r] because I must leave it to the one who comes after me.[s] [19] And who knows whether he will be wise or a fool?[t] Yet he will take over all my work that I labored at skillfully under the sun. This too is futile. [20] So I began to give myself over[G] to despair concerning all my work that I had labored at under the sun. [21] When there is a person whose work was done with wisdom, knowledge, and skill,[u] and he must give his portion to a person who has not worked for it, this too is futile and a great wrong. [22] For what does a person get with all his work and all his efforts[v] that he labors at under the sun? [23] For all his days are filled with grief, and his occupation is sorrowful;[w] even at night, his mind does not rest.[x] This too is futile.

[24] There is nothing better for a person than to eat, drink, and enjoy[H,i] his work.[y] I have seen that even this is from God's hand,[z] [25] because who can eat and who can enjoy life[j] apart from him?[k] [26] For to the person who is pleasing in his sight, he gives wisdom, knowledge, and joy;[aa] but to the sinner he gives the task of gathering and accumulating in order to give to the one who is pleasing in God's sight.[ab] This too is futile and a pursuit of the wind.[ac]

THE MYSTERY OF TIME

3 There is an occasion for everything, and a time for every activity under heaven:[ad]

[2]   a time to give birth and a time
        to die;[ae]
    a time to plant and a time
        to uproot;[L]

[a] 2:6 Neh 2:14; 3:15-16
[b] 2:7 Gn 14:14; 15:3
[c] 1Kg 4:23
[d] 2:8 1Kg 9:28; 10:10,14,21
[e] 2Sm 19:35
[f] 2:9 1Ch 29:25; Ec 1:16
[g] 2:10 Ec 6:2
[h] Ec 3:22; 5:18; 9:9
[i] 2:11 Ec 1:14; 2:22-23
[j] Ec 1:3; 3:9; 5:16
[k] 2:12 Ec 1:17
[l] Ec 1:9-10; 3:15
[m] 2:13 Ec 7:11-12,19; 9:18; 10:10
[n] 2:14 Pr 2:10-13; 1Jn 2:11
[o] Ps 49:10; Ec 3:19; 6:6; 7:2; 9:2-3
[p] 2:15 Ec 6:8,11; 7:16
[q] 2:16 Dt 32:26; 2Sm 18:18; Ec 1:11; 9:5

[r] 2:18 Ec 1:3; 2:11
[s] Ps 39:6; 49:10; Pr 13:22
[t] 2:19 Ezk 18:9-10
[u] 2:21 Ec 4:4
[v] 2:22 Ec 1:3; 2:11
[w] 2:23 Jb 5:7; 14:1
[x] Ps 127:2
[y] 2:24 Ec 2:3; 3:12-13,22; 5:18; 6:12; 8:15; 9:7; Is 56:12; Lk 12:19; 1Co 15:32; 1Tm 6:17
[z] Ec 3:13
[aa] 2:26 Jb 32:8; Pr 2:6
[ab] Jb 27:16-17; Pr 13:22; 28:8
[ac] Ec 1:14
[ad] 3:1 Ec 3:17; 8:6
[ae] 3:2 Jb 14:5; Heb 9:27

[A] 2:8 LXX, Theod, Syr read *and male cupbearers and female cupbearers*; Aq, Tg, Vg read *a cup and cups*; Hb obscure   [B] 2:8 Or *many treasures that people delight in*   [C] 2:11 Lit *all my works that my hands had done*   [D] 2:11 Or *a feeding on wind*, or *an affliction of spirit*; also in vv. 17,26
[E] 2:12 Lit *the man who comes after the king*   [F] 2:12 Some Hb mss read *They*   [G] 2:20 Lit *And I turned to cause my heart*   [H] 2:24 Syr, Tg; MT reads *There is no good in a person who eats and drinks and enjoys*   [I] 2:24 Lit *and his soul sees good*   [J] 2:25 LXX, Theod, Syr read *can drink*
[K] 2:25 Some Hb mss, LXX, Syr read *me*   [L] 3:2 Lit *uproot what is planted*

2:11 Solomon had it all, but that left him empty.

2:15-16 In other words, the king was bothered that a dead dummy and a dead genius share the same basic fate: they end up in a grave.

2:24 At this point, we see a ray of light in the king's musings. Solomon comes to a refrain that he'll repeat throughout the book: **There is nothing better for a person than to eat, drink, and enjoy his work. . . .this is from God's hand**. He has spoken about the depressing realities of life, but here he begins interjecting God strategically along the way.

God doesn't mind your enjoyment of legitimate pleasures. He isn't upset that you like your job, food, possessions, or relationships; in fact, these are gifts from him. The problem comes when you look for *meaning* in these things—because at that point you're trying to find in them something that they weren't designed to provide.

3:1-9 Life can become miserably predictable. The same old you, wearing the same old clothes, driving the same old car, working the same old job, eating the same old food, returning to the same old house, watching the same old shows, and climbing into the same old bed—day in and day out—gets old. That frustration with routine reflects Solomon's mood here. He's not merely saying there's a time for everything, including life's joys and sorrows. He's saying, "We're trapped." Like hamsters running on a wheel, our legs do a lot of running, but they finish right where we started.

[a] 3:4 Rm 12:15
[b] Ex 15:20
[c] 3:5 2Kg 3:19,25; Is 5:2
[d] 1Co 7:5
[e] 3:7 Am 5:13; 1Co 14:26-32
[f] 3:8 Mt 5:9; 10:34
[g] 3:9 Ec 1:3
[h] 3:10 Ec 1:13; 2:26
[i] 3:11 Gn 1:31
[j] Jb 5:9; Ec 7:23; 8:17;
Rm 11:33
[k] 3:13 Ec 2:24; 5:19
[l] 3:14 Rv 22:18-19
[m] Ex 7:5; Ezk 36:23
[n] 3:15 Ec 1:9; 6:10

[o] 3:16 Ec 4:1; 5:8; 8:9
[p] 3:17 Ec 11:9; Mt 16:27; Rm
2:6-10; 2Th 1:6-9
[q] Ec 3:1
[r] 3:18 Ps 49:12,20; 73:22
[s] 3:19 Ec 9:12
[t] 3:20 Gn 3:19; Ec 12:7
[u] 3:22 Ec 2:24
[v] Ec 2:18; 6:12; 8:7; 10:14
[w] 4:1 Jb 35:9; Ec 3:16; 5:8
[x] 4:2 Jb 3:11-26
[y] 4:3 Ec 6:3; Lk 23:29
[z] 4:4 1Sm 18:9; Ec 2:21; Ac
13:45; 2Co 12:20
[aa] Ec 1:14
[ab] 4:5 Pr 6:10; 24:33
[ac] Is 9:20
[ad] 4:6 Pr 15:16-17

∽ HOPE WORDS ∽

Time doesn't heal. God heals, in time.

3 a time to kill and a time to heal;
a time to tear down and a time
to build;
4 a time to weep and a time to laugh;[a]
a time to mourn and a time
to dance;[b]
5 a time to throw stones and a time
to gather stones;[c]
a time to embrace and a time
to avoid embracing;[d]
6 a time to search and a time to count
as lost;
a time to keep and a time
to throw away;
7 a time to tear and a time to sew;
a time to be silent and a time
to speak;[e]
8 a time to love and a time to hate;
a time for war and a time for peace.[f]

9 What does the worker gain from his struggles?[g] 10 I have seen the task that God has given the children of Adam to keep them occupied.[h] 11 He has made everything appropriate[A] in its time.[i] He has also put eternity in their hearts,[B] but no one can discover the work God has done from beginning to end.[j] 12 I know that there is nothing better for them than to rejoice and enjoy the[C] good life. 13 It is also the gift of God whenever anyone eats, drinks, and enjoys all his efforts.[k] 14 I know that everything God does will last forever; there is no adding to it or taking from it.[l] God works so that people will be in awe of him.[m] 15 Whatever is, has already been,[n] and whatever will be, already is. However, God seeks justice for the persecuted.[D]

THE MYSTERY OF INJUSTICE AND DEATH

16 I also observed under the sun: there is wickedness at the place of judgment and there is wickedness at the place of righteousness.[o] 17 I said to myself, "God will judge the righteous and the wicked,[p] since there is a time for every activity and every work."[q] 18 I said to myself, "This happens so that God may test the children of Adam and they may see for themselves that they are like animals."[r] 19 For the fate of the children of Adam and the fate of animals is the same.[s] As one dies, so dies the other; they all have the same breath. People have no advantage over animals since everything is futile. 20 All are going to the same place; all come from dust, and all return to dust.[t] 21 Who knows if the spirits of the children of Adam go upward and the spirits of animals go downward to the earth? 22 I have seen that there is nothing better than for a person to enjoy his activities[u] because that is his reward. For who can enable him to see what will happen after he dies?[E,v]

4 Again, I observed all the acts of oppression being done under the sun.[w] Look at the tears of those who are oppressed; they have no one to comfort them. Power is with those who oppress them; they have no one to comfort them. 2 So I commended the dead,[x] who have already died, more than the living, who are still alive. 3 But better than either of them is the one who has not yet existed,[y] who has not seen the evil activity that is done under the sun.

THE LONELINESS OF WEALTH

4 I saw that all labor and all skillful work is due to one person's jealousy of another.[z] This too is futile and a pursuit of the wind.[F,aa]
5 The fool folds his arms[ab]
and consumes his own flesh.[ac]
6 Better one handful with rest
than two handfuls with effort and a
pursuit of the wind.[ad]

[A] 3:11 Or beautiful   [B] 3:11 Or has put a sense of past and future into their minds, or has placed ignorance in their hearts   [C] 3:12 Lit his   [D] 3:15 Lit God seeks what is pursued   [E] 3:22 Lit after him   [F] 4:4 Or a feeding on wind, or an affliction of spirit; also in vv. 6,16

3:10-11 Solomon is saying that God has created time in such a way that it cannot bring fulfillment. Rather, it reveals a vacuum in the human heart that can only be filled by the transcendent—by him. Humanity is in tension: we live in the routine of time, but our hearts are designed to long for something eternal.
3:12-13 Appropriate pleasures are a gift of God; enjoy them. Just don't expect to discover ultimate meaning in these things. God has intentionally created dissatisfaction in life to drive us to him.

3:16-17 Indeed, miscarriages of justice are frequent in the world (3:16). The wicked prosper; the righteous suffer. As a result, life seems unfair. Nevertheless, God will see that justice is done (3:17).
3:22 Solomon encourages the responsible enjoyment of the life God has granted.
4:1-3 If we're honest with ourselves, most of us have felt the same way at one time or another. Cruelty and coercion are realities even today: political corruption, racial discrimination, religious persecution, sex

trafficking, domestic violence, child abuse, and the list goes on. Evil is everywhere, and its existence leads to skepticism. But God is good, and humanity's story isn't over.
4:4 In other words, it's a dog-eat-dog world.
4:5 This means that if you refuse to work, you'll go hungry.
4:6 In other words, it's better to earn only what you need and get rest, than to be a miserable workaholic keeping up with the Joneses.

7 Again, I saw futility under the sun: **8** There is a person without a companion,^A without even a son or brother, and though there is no end to all his struggles, his eyes are still not content with riches.^a "Who am I struggling for," he asks, "and depriving myself of good things?" This too is futile and a miserable task.

APPLICATION QUESTIONS

READ ECCLESIASTES 4:12

– How have others strengthened your efforts to faithfully follow God's kingdom agenda?

9 Two are better than one because they have a good reward for their efforts. **10** For if either falls, his companion can lift him up; but pity the one who falls without another to lift him up. **11** Also, if two lie down together, they can keep warm; but how can one person alone keep warm?^b **12** And if someone overpowers one person, two can resist him. A cord of three strands is not easily broken.

13 Better is a poor but wise youth than an old but foolish king who no longer pays attention to warnings.^c **14** For he came from prison to be king,^d even though he was born poor in his kingdom. **15** I saw all the living, who move about under the sun, follow^B a second youth who succeeds him. **16** There is no limit to all the people who were before them, yet those who come later will not rejoice in him. This too is futile and a pursuit of the wind.^e

CAUTION IN GOD'S PRESENCE

5 Guard your steps when you go to the house of God. Better to approach in obedience than to offer the sacrifice as fools do,^f for they ignorantly do wrong. **2** Do not be hasty to speak, and do not be impulsive to make a speech before God.

God is in heaven and you are on earth, so let your words be few.^g **3** Just as dreams accompany much labor, so also a fool's voice comes with many words.^h **4** When you make a vow to God,^i don't delay fulfilling it, because he does not delight in fools. Fulfill what you vow. **5** Better that you do not vow than that you vow and not fulfill it.^j **6** Do not let your mouth bring guilt on you,^k and do not say in the presence of the messenger that it was a mistake.^l Why should God be angry with your words and destroy the work of your hands? **7** For many dreams bring futility, so do many words.^m Therefore, fear God.

THE REALITIES OF WEALTH

8 If you see oppression of the poor^n and perversion of justice and righteousness in the province, don't be astonished at the situation,^o because one official protects another official, and higher officials protect them. **9** The profit from the land is taken by all; the king is served by the field.^C,p

10 The one who loves silver is never satisfied with silver, and whoever loves wealth is never satisfied with income. This too is futile. **11** When good things increase, the ones who consume them multiply; what, then, is the profit to the owner, except to gaze at them with his eyes? **12** The sleep of the worker is sweet, whether he eats little or much, but the abundance of the rich permits him no sleep.

13 There is a sickening tragedy I have seen under the sun: wealth kept by its owner to his harm.^q **14** That wealth was lost in a bad venture, so when he fathered a son, he was empty-handed. **15** As he came from his mother's womb, so he will go again, naked as he came;^r he will take nothing for his efforts that he can carry in his hands. **16** This too is a sickening tragedy: exactly as he comes, so he will go. What does the one

^a 4:8 Pr 27:20; Ec 1:8; 5:10
^b 4:11 1Kg 1:1-4
^c 4:13 Ec 9:15
^d 4:14 Gn 41:14,41-43
^e 4:16 Ec 1:14
^f 5:1 1Sm 15:22; Mt 5:23-24
^g 5:2 Pr 10:19; Mt 6:7
^h 5:3 Jb 11:2
^i 5:4 Nm 30:2; Dt 6:13; 23:21-22; Pr 20:25
^j 5:5 Pr 20:25; Mt 5:33-37; Ac 5:4; Jms 5:12
^k 5:6 Jdg 11:30-31,34
^l Nm 15:25
^m 5:7 Ec 6:11
^n 5:8 Ec 4:1
^o 1Pt 4:12
^p 5:9 Pr 27:23-27
^q 5:13 Ec 6:1-2
^r 5:15 Jb 1:21

---

^A 4:8 Lit *person, but there is not a second,*   ^B 4:15 Lit *with*   ^C 5:9 Hb obscure

---

4:8-12 It's better not to be alone; it's best to have someone walking beside you who cares for you. There's obvious power in numbers, so don't cut yourself off from community.
4:13 Don't ever get too self-important to learn. We all know people who've reached the top and yet are fools.
4:16 Solomon is frustrated as he thinks of all the successive generations that populate the earth and realizes again that trying to establish oneself for the long term **is futile**.
5:1-3 This is a reminder that you're a fool if you go to church to tell God what to do. He's up there, and you're down here. Your brain doesn't have as much to offer him as you

might think it does. So be quick to hear from God's divine perspective and slow to speak your mind.
5:4-6 Fulfill what you vow to God (5:4)—or don't vow at all. You want God working for you, not against you. Don't take your spiritual commitment casually, then. You need God's supernatural intervention.
5:8 In a fallen world, those in power often do evil things. But Scripture reminds us that the wicked will not always prosper. A day of reckoning is coming (see Ps 73).
5:10 It's not wrong to have money, but it's wrong to *love* it—to consider the material more important than the spiritual.

5:12 When you hoard, you become a slave to your stuff.
5:14 This is a reminder that poor decisions about money affect the next generation.
5:15-16 In the end, the number of outfits in your closet won't matter. On your deathbed, you won't be bragging about your cars. What's going to matter is the spiritual legacy you left behind for others and the heavenly investments you forwarded ahead. The spiritual must always trump the material. The fool "stores up treasure for himself" but isn't "rich toward God" (see Luke 12:21). It's far better to seek that which lasts forever: the kingdom of God (see Matt 6:33).

a 5:16 Ec 1:3
b Pr 11:29
c 5:17 Ps 127:2
d 5:18 Ec 2:24
e Ec 2:10
f 5:19 2Ch 1:12
g Ec 6:2
h Ec 3:13
i 6:1 Ec 5:13
j 6:2 1Kg 3:13
k Ps 17:14; 73:7
l 6:3 Is 14:20; Jr 8:2; 22:19
m Jb 3:16; Ec 4:3
n 6:7 Pr 16:26
o 6:8 Ec 2:15

p 6:9 Ec 11:9
q Ec 1:14
r 6:10 Gn 2:19; Ec 1:9-10; 3:15
s Jb 9:32; Is 45:9
t 6:11 Pr 10:19; Mt 6:7
u 6:12 Ec 3:22
v 7:1 Pr 22:1; Ezk 36:21
w Ec 4:2
x 7:2 Ps 90:12
y 7:3 Pr 14:13
z 7:5 Pr 13:1
aa 7:6 Ps 58:9; 118:12
ab 7:7 Ec 4:1
ac Dt 16:19; Pr 17:8

gain[a] who struggles for the wind?[b] [17] What is more, he eats in darkness all his days,[c] with much frustration, sickness, and anger.

[18] Here is what I have seen to be good:[d] It is appropriate to eat, drink, and experience good in all the labor one does under the sun during the few days of his life God has given him, because that is his reward.[e] [19] Furthermore, everyone to whom God has given riches and wealth,[f] he has also allowed them to enjoy them, take his reward, and rejoice in his labor.[g] This is a gift of God,[h] [20] for he does not often consider the days of his life because God keeps him occupied with the joy of his heart.

6 Here is a tragedy I have observed under the sun,[i] and it weighs heavily on humanity:[A] [2] God gives a person riches, wealth, and honor[j] so that he lacks nothing of all he desires for himself,[k] but God does not allow him to enjoy them. Instead, a stranger will enjoy them. This is futile and a sickening tragedy. [3] A man may father a hundred children and live many years. No matter how long he lives,[B] if he is not satisfied by good things and does not even have a proper burial,[l] I say that a stillborn child is better off than he.[m] [4] For he comes in futility and he goes in darkness, and his name is shrouded in darkness. [5] Though a stillborn child does not see the sun and is not conscious, it has more rest than he. [6] And if a person lives a thousand years twice, but does not experience happiness, do not both go to the same place?

[7]   All of a person's labor is
     for his stomach,[C,n]
     yet the appetite is never satisfied.

[8] What advantage then does the wise person have over the fool?[o] What advantage is there for the poor person who knows how to conduct himself before others? [9] Better what the eyes see than wandering desire.[p] This too is futile and a pursuit of the wind.[D,q]

[10] Whatever exists was given its name long ago,[E,r] and it is known what mankind is. But he is not able to contend with the one stronger than he.[s] [11] For when there are many words, they increase futility.[t] What is the advantage for mankind? [12] For who knows what is good for anyone in life, in the few days of his futile life that he spends like a shadow?[u] Who can tell anyone what will happen after him under the sun?

WISE SAYINGS

7 A good name is better than
     fine perfume,[v]
     and the day of one's death is better
     than the day of one's birth.[w]
[2]   It is better to go to a house
     of mourning
     than to go to a house of feasting,
     since that is the end of all mankind,
     and the living should take it
     to heart.[x]
[3]   Grief is better than laughter,
     for when a face is sad, a heart
     may be glad.[y]
[4]   The heart of the wise is in a house
     of mourning,
     but the heart of fools is in a house
     of pleasure.
[5]   It is better to listen to rebuke
     from a wise person
     than to listen to the song of fools,[z]
[6]   for like the crackling
     of burning thorns under the pot,[aa]
     so is the laughter of the fool.
     This too is futile.
[7]   Surely, the practice of extortion
     turns a wise person
     into a fool,[ab]
     and a bribe corrupts the mind.[ac]

A 6:1 Or *it is common among men*   B 6:3 Lit *how many years*   C 6:7 Lit *mouth*   D 6:9 Or *a feeding on wind*, or *an affliction of spirit*   E 6:10 Lit *name already*

5:18-20 Maintain a joyful **heart** (5:20) that comes from a spirit of thanksgiving as you benefit from the everyday blessings you enjoy. I might want steak and potatoes tomorrow, but I'm going to thank the Lord that I'm not starving as I settle for pork and beans today. **6:1-2** If you exclude God from your life equation, you may never experience pleasure from your wealth either (see Luke 12:19-20). **6:3-5** How awful to live your life in such a way that you wish you'd never been born! The antidote for that tendency is a day-by-day grateful attitude toward God. Don't wait until retirement to live a thankful life. You may not make it to retirement. **6:9** Be content with what God gives. Kids want toys; adults just want bigger and more

expensive toys. But if you chase after physical pleasures, your soul will become anemic. Pursue what your soul needs to be truly satisfied. **6:10-11** God has appointed a day for each of us to die (see Heb 9:27). You might be late for a lot of events in life, but you won't miss that one! So maximize the days you've been given, not contending with God, but looking to him to punctuate life with his presence. **7:1** Whether it's a woman wearing the latest fragrance or a man wearing cologne, people take notice when a person smells good and ask, "What's that you have on?" It's far better, though, that people take notice of you because of the pleasant scent of your dignity and character. After all, no matter how sweet-smelling your perfume, it can't make up

for a foul-smelling reputation. Work on your character so you'll have a fragrant reputation. **7:2-4** At the funeral home things get real. You're obliged to stare at a casket and admit to yourself, "One day, that's going to be me in there." A visit to a funeral will remind you of what's important and that your days are numbered. It will help you live with an eternal perspective. **7:5-6** Being wise isn't tied to academic accomplishment: a fool can have a PhD. Wisdom is the ability to make spiritually informed decisions. It's applying the divine truth of God's kingdom rule to every area of life. If someone with a divine perspective rebukes you, let him speak into your life so you can become wise. A wise rebuke is far more valuable than a fool singing your praises.

8 The end of a matter is better
   than its beginning;
   a patient spirit is better
   than a proud spirit.[a]
9 Don't let your spirit rush to be angry,
   for anger abides in the heart of fools.[b]
10 Don't say, "Why were the former days
   better than these?"[c]
   since it is not wise of you to ask this.
11 Wisdom is as good as an inheritance
   and an advantage to those who see
   the sun,
12 because wisdom is protection
   as silver is protection;
   but the advantage of knowledge
   is that wisdom preserves the life
   of its owner.[d]
13 Consider the work of God,[e]
   for who can straighten out
   what he has made crooked?[f]

14 In the day of prosperity be joyful,[g] but
in the day of adversity, consider: God has
made the one as well as the other,[h] so that
no one can discover anything that will
come after him.

AVOIDING EXTREMES

15 In my futile life[A] I have seen everything:[i]
someone righteous perishes in spite of
his righteousness,[j] and someone wicked
lives long in spite of his evil.[k] **16** Don't be
excessively righteous, and don't be overly
wise.[l] Why should you destroy yourself?
17 Don't be excessively wicked, and don't
be foolish. Why should you die before your
time?[m] **18** It is good that you grasp the one
and do not let the other slip from your
hand. For the one who fears God will end
up with both of them.
19 Wisdom makes the wise person
   stronger
   than ten rulers of a city.[n]

20 There is certainly no one
   righteous on the earth
   who does good and never sins.[o]

21 Don't pay attention[B] to everything
people say, or you may hear your servant
cursing you,[p] **22** for in your heart you know
that many times you yourself have cursed
others.

WHAT THE TEACHER FOUND

23 I have tested all this by wisdom. I resolved, "I will be wise," but it was beyond me. **24** What exists is beyond reach
and very deep.[q] Who can discover it? **25** I
turned my thoughts to know, explore, and
examine wisdom[r] and an explanation for
things, and to know that wickedness is stupidity and folly is madness. **26** And I find
more bitter than death[s] the woman who
is a trap:[t] her heart a net and her hands
chains. The one who pleases God will escape her, but the sinner will be captured
by her. **27** "Look," says the Teacher, "I have
discovered this by adding one thing to another to find out the explanation, **28** which
my soul continually searches for but does
not find: I found one person in a thousand,
but none of those was a woman.[u] **29** Only
see this: I have discovered that God made
people upright,[v] but they pursued many
schemes."

WISDOM, AUTHORITIES,
AND INEQUITIES

8 Who is like the wise person, and who
   knows the interpretation of a matter?
A person's wisdom brightens his face, and
the sternness of his face is changed.[w]

2 Keep[c] the king's command because of
your oath made before God.[x] **3** Do not be
in a hurry; leave his presence,[y] and don't
persist in a bad cause, since he will do

[a] 7:8 Pr 14:29
[b] 7:9 Pr 14:17; Jms 1:19
[c] 7:10 Jdg 6:13
[d] 7:12 Pr 3:18
[e] 7:13 Ec 3:11
[f] Ec 1:15
[g] 7:14 Ec 3:22
[h] Lm 3:38
[i] 7:15 Ec 6:12; 9:9
[j] Ec 8:14
[k] Ec 8:12-13
[l] 7:16 Ec 2:15; Rm 12:3
[m] 7:17 Jb 22:16; Ps 55:23;
Pr 10:27
[n] 7:19 Ec 9:13-18

[o] 7:20 1Kg 8:46; Rm 3:23
[p] 7:21 Pr 30:10
[q] 7:24 Rm 11:33
[r] 7:25 Ec 1:15,17
[s] 7:26 Pr 5:4
[t] Pr 6:25
[u] 7:28 1Kg 11:3
[v] 7:29 Gn 1:27
[w] 8:1 Dt 28:50
[x] 8:2 Ex 22:11; 2Sm 21:7;
Ezk 17:18
[y] 8:3 Ec 10:4

[A] 7:15 Lit *days*   [B] 7:21 Lit *Don't give your heart*   [C] 8:2 Some Hb mss, LXX, Vg, Tg, Syr; other Hb mss read *I, keep*

7:9 Many people commit foolish mistakes
because they were hasty in their outrage.
7:10 There's nothing wrong with reminiscing
with friends and family, but don't waste all
your time gabbing about and longing for the
good ol' days. If you choose to live in yesterday, you won't make forward progress and
will fail to achieve what God wants you to
be tomorrow.
7:11-12 Whatever financial **inheritance** you
leave behind for your children, make certain that you also leave them a legacy of
wisdom (7:11). Financial security is tenuous,
but wisdom provides the security of God's
perspective.
7:13-15 Deuteronomy 29:29 reminds us that
"the hidden things belong to the Lord." In

the same vein, Solomon invites us to consider God's works and ask ourselves **who can
straighten out what he has made crooked?**
(Eccl 7:13). If you consume yourself with trying to figure out what God doesn't explain,
you'll only get a headache. As sure as we don't
always answer our kids' "why?" questions
because we know it wouldn't be appropriate
to do so or because they wouldn't understand
anyway, God often does not reveal his ways
to us. That he has made the **day of prosperity**
and the **day of adversity** (7:14) is a reminder
that he's sovereign. When things are out of
your control, thank God that they are in his
control. Develop a spiritual viewpoint.
7:16 Solomon is talking about going *beyond*
what God requires. That approach is exactly

what the Pharisees did. They added their
own standards to God's standards, and in
the name of righteousness became self-righteous. Wise in their own eyes.
7:20 We all fall short; everyone **sins**—but that
doesn't give us license to persist in wickedness.
7:29 The book of Genesis explains how
humanity wandered from God, how evil pro-
liferated as a result, and lays the groundwork
for why the world suffers.
8:2-5 The apostle Paul commands Christians
to "submit to the governing authorities"
(Rom 13:1). So, also, Solomon urges us to obey
legitimate governmental authorities and to
be careful how we relate to those authorities
because of the power they exercise over us.

ᵃ 8:4 Jb 9:12; Dn 4:35
ᵇ 8:5 Rm 13:3
ᶜ 8:6 Ec 3:1,17
ᵈ 8:7 Ec 3:22; 6:12; 9:12;
    10:14
ᵉ 8:8 Ps 148:8; Pr 30:4;
    Mk 4:39
ᶠ Jn 10:18; 2Tm 1:10
ᵍ 8:10 Ec 9:5
ʰ 8:11 Rm 2:4; 2Pt 3:9
ⁱ 8:12 Ec 7:15
ʲ Dt 12:25; Ps 37:11; Pr 1:33;
    Is 3:10
ᵏ 8:13 Is 3:11
ˡ Jb 14:2; Ec 6:12
ᵐ 8:14 Ec 7:15
ⁿ Jb 21:7; Ps 73:3; Jr 12:1
ᵒ 8:15 Ec 2:24

ᵖ 8:16 Ec 1:13-14
ᵠ 8:17 Ec 3:11; 7:25-29; 11:5
ʳ 9:1 Dt 33:3
ˢ 9:2 Jb 9:22
ᵗ Ec 2:14
ᵘ 9:3 Ec 1:17
ᵛ 9:5 Ec 2:16
ʷ 9:7 Ec 2:24; 3:13; 5:18;
    8:15
ˣ 9:8 Ps 23:5

whatever he wants. **4** For the king's word is authoritative, and who can say to him, "What are you doing?"ᵃ **5** The one who keeps a command will not experience anything harmful,ᵇ and a wise heart knows the right time and procedure. **6** For every activity there is a right time and procedure,ᶜ even though a person's troubles are heavy on him. **7** Yet no one knows what will happenᵈ because who can tell him what will happen? **8** No one has authority over the windᴬ to restrain it,ᵉ and there is no authority over the day of death;ᶠ no one is discharged during battle, and wickedness will not allow those who practice it to escape. **9** All this I have seen, applying my mind to all the work that is done under the sun, at a time when one person has authority over another to his harm.

10 In such circumstances, I saw the wicked buried. They came and went from the holy place,ᵍ and they were praisedᴮ in the city where they did those things. This too is futile. **11** Because the sentence against an evil act is not carried out quickly,ʰ the heart of people is filled with the desire to commit evil. **12** Although a sinner does evil a hundred times and prolongs his life,ⁱ I also know that it will go well with God-fearing people,ʲ for they are reverent before him. **13** However, it will not go well with the wicked,ᵏ and they will not lengthen their days like a shadow,ˡ for they are not reverent before God.

14 There is a futility that is done on the earth: there are righteous people who get what the actions of the wicked deserve,ᵐ and there are wicked people who get what the actions of the righteous deserve.ⁿ I say that this too is futile. **15** So I commended enjoyment because there is nothing better for a person under the sun than to eat, drink, and enjoy himself,ᵒ for this will accompany him in his labor during the days of his life that God gives him under the sun.

16 When I applied my mind to know wisdomᵖ and to observe the activity that is done on the earth (even though one's eyes do not close in sleep day or night), **17** I observed all the work of God and concluded that a person is unable to discover the work that is done under the sun. Even though a person labors hard to explore it, he cannot find it;ᵠ even if a wise person claims to know it, he is unable to discover it.

ENJOY LIFE DESPITE DEATH

9 Indeed, I took all this to heart and explained it all: The righteous, the wise, and their works are in God's hands.ʳ People don't know whether to expect love or hate. Everything lies ahead of them. **2** Everything is the same for everyone:ˢ There is one fate for the righteous and the wicked,ᵗ for the good and the bad,ᶜ for the clean and the unclean, for the one who sacrifices and the one who does not sacrifice. As it is for the good, so also it is for the sinner; as it is for the one who takes an oath, so also for the one who fears an oath. **3** This is an evil in all that is done under the sun: there is one fate for everyone. In addition, the hearts of people are full of evil, and madness is in their hearts while they live;ᵘ after that they go to the dead. **4** But there is hope for whoever is joinedᴰ with all the living, since a live dog is better than a dead lion. **5** For the living know that they will die, but the dead don't know anything. There is no longer a reward for them because the memory of them is forgotten.ᵛ **6** Their love, their hate, and their envy have already disappeared, and there is no longer a portion for them in all that is done under the sun.

7 Go, eat your bread with pleasure, and drink your wine with a cheerful heart, for God has already accepted your works.ʷ **8** Let your clothes be white all the time, and never let oil be lacking on your head.ˣ

ᴬ 8:8 Or *life-breath*   ᴮ 8:10 Some Hb mss, LXX, Aq, Theod, Sym; other Hb mss read *forgotten*   ᶜ 9:2 LXX, Aq, Syr, Vg; MT omits *and the bad*   ᴰ 9:4 Alt Hb tradition reads *chosen*

8:6 Timing matters. *When* you do something is often as important as *what* you do. Certain comments, for instance, are not appropriate when someone is grieving. And when in mixed company, it's sometimes best to save your thoughts for a private conversation at a later hour.

8:9 The concept of authority is a good thing. God exercises authority over humanity. He ordains rulers to have authority over people. Husbands are called to exercise godly authority in their homes. **Authority** must not be abused.

8:11-13 In other words, if justice doesn't come immediately, some people think it isn't coming at all (8:11). **God-fearing people**, however, know better (8:12). Eternal judgment may be delayed, but it's certain. One day the books will be opened. There will be a day of reckoning to determine the reward for believers and a judgment to punish unbelievers. **It will not go well with the wicked** (8:13).

8:14-17 If the under-the-sun perspective is all you have, you're going to experience frustration and despair when you see all the inequi-ties and injustices in the world. The way the world works is ultimately incomprehensible to man. We need God's perspective.

9:4 This is a reminder that, as far as our earthly existence is concerned, life—even when filled with struggles and disappointments—is preferable to death.

9:7-10 Since you don't know what tomorrow will bring, enjoy the legitimate pleasures of each day, because God "richly provides us with all things to enjoy" (1 Tim 6:17). Don't, however, seek enjoyment independent of him.

⁹ Enjoy life with the wife you love all the days of your fleeting^A life,^a which has been given to you under the sun, all your fleeting days. For that is your portion in life and in your struggle^b under the sun. ¹⁰ Whatever your hands find to do, do with all your strength,^c because there is no work, planning, knowledge, or wisdom^d in Sheol where you are going.

THE LIMITATIONS OF WISDOM

¹¹ Again I saw under the sun that the race is not to the swift,^e or the battle to the strong,^f or bread to the wise, or riches to the discerning, or favor to the skillful; rather, time and chance happen to all of them. ¹² For certainly no one knows his time:^g like fish caught in a cruel net or like birds caught in a trap,^h so people are trapped in an evil time^i as it suddenly falls on them.^j

¹³ I have observed that this also is wisdom under the sun, and it is significant to me: ¹⁴ There was a small city with few men in it. A great king came against it, surrounded it, and built large siege works against it. ¹⁵ Now a poor wise man was found in the city,^k and he delivered the city by his wisdom.^l Yet no one remembered that poor man. ¹⁶ And I said, "Wisdom is better than strength,^m but the wisdom of the poor man is despised, and his words are not heeded."

¹⁷ The calm words of the wise
  are heeded
  more than the shouts of a ruler
    over fools.
¹⁸ Wisdom is better than weapons
    of war,
  but one sinner can destroy
    much good.^n

THE BURDEN OF FOLLY

10 Dead flies make a perfumer's oil
    ferment and stink;^o
  so a little folly outweighs wisdom
    and honor.
² A wise person's heart goes
    to the^B right,
  but a fool's heart to the left.

³ Even when the fool walks
    along the road, his heart
    lacks sense,
  and he shows everyone he is a fool.^p
⁴ If the ruler's anger rises against you,
    don't leave your post,^q
  for calmness puts great offenses
    to rest.^r

⁵ There is an evil I have seen under the sun, an error proceeding from the presence of the ruler:
⁶ The fool is appointed
    to great heights,^s
  but the rich remain
    in lowly positions.
⁷ I have seen slaves on horses,^t
  but princes walking on the ground
    like slaves.^u

⁸ The one who digs a pit may fall
    into it,^v
  and the one who breaks
    through a wall may be bitten
    by a snake.^w
⁹ The one who quarries stones
    may be hurt by them;
  the one who splits logs
    may be endangered by them.
¹⁰ If the ax is dull, and one does not
    sharpen its edge,
  then one must exert more strength;
  however, the advantage of wisdom
    is that it brings success.
¹¹ If the snake bites before
    it is charmed,^x
  then there is no advantage
    for the charmer.^c
¹² The words from the mouth
    of a wise person are gracious,^y
  but the lips of a fool consume him.^z
¹³ The beginning of the words
    from his mouth is folly,
  but the end of his speaking
    is evil madness;
¹⁴ yet the fool multiplies words.
  No one knows what will happen,
  and who can tell anyone
    what will happen after him?^aa

^a 9:9 Ec 6:12; 7:15
^b Ec 2:10
^c 9:10 Rm 12:11; Col 3:23
^d Ec 9:5
^e 9:11 Am 2:14-15
^f 2Ch 20:15
^g 9:12 Ec 8:7
^h Pr 7:23
^i Pr 29:6
^j Lk 21:34-35
^k 9:15 Ec 4:13
^l 2Sm 20:22
^m 9:16 Ec 7:19
^n 9:18 Jos 7:1
^o 10:1 Ex 30:25

^p 10:3 Pr 13:16; 18:2
^q 10:4 Ec 8:3
^r 1Sm 25:24-33; Pr 25:15
^s 10:6 Est 3:1; Pr 28:12; 29:2
^t 10:7 Pr 19:10
^u Est 6:8-10
^v 10:8 Ps 7:15
^w Am 5:19
^x 10:11 Jr 8:17
^y 10:12 Pr 10:32; 22:11; Lk 4:22
^z Pr 18:7
^aa 10:14 Ec 8:7,17

---

^A 9:9 Or *futile*   ^B 10:2 Lit *his*   ^C 10:11 Lit *master of the tongue*

9:11-12 Our existence often looks like a roll of the dice. And regardless of whatever strength, wisdom, riches, or skill a person has, **time and chance happen to all** (9:11). Life appears to be random. **Certainly no one knows his time** (9:12). Yet we must live with an eternal perspective.
10:1 As the author of the book of Proverbs, Solomon had vast experience in thinking about life and composing wise sayings. It's not surprising, then, that as he moves toward

his conclusion to Ecclesiastes, he includes a string of proverbial statements.

What Solomon is saying here is that fools make their **folly** known; there's no hiding it. It only takes a little foolishness, in fact, to contaminate an otherwise sweet reputation and **stink** it up.
10:3 Though a man's wisdom may be unseen or even forgotten by everyone but God (9:15), a fool's actions are visible to all. Whichever

way a wise man goes, in fact, you can count on a fool heading in the opposite direction.
10:8-10 Wisdom doesn't eliminate all negative contingencies (10:8-9); nevertheless, wisdom gives a person an **edge** that you don't want to be without (10:10).
10:12-14 One way to know fools is by how much they talk (10:14). Elsewhere, Solomon reminds us, "When there are many words, sin is unavoidable" (Prov 10:19).

a 10:16 Pr 30:21-22; Is 3:4,12
b 10:17 Pr 31:4; Is 5:11
c 10:19 Ps 104:15
d Ec 7:12
e 10:20 Ex 22:28
f 2Kg 6:12; Lk 12:3
g 11:1 Dt 15:10; Pr 19:17; Mt 10:42; Gl 6:9-10; Heb 6:10
h 11:2 Ps 112:9; Mt 5:42; Lk 6:30; 1Tm 6:18-19

i 11:5 Jb 10:10-11; Ps 139:14-16; Is 55:9; Jn 3:6-8; Rm 11:33
j 11:7 Ec 6:5; 7:11
k 11:8 Ec 12:1
l 11:9 Ec 2:24; 3:12-13,22; 5:18; 8:15; 9:7-9
m 11:10 2Co 7:1; 2Tm 2:22
n 12:1 Ec 11:8

15 The struggles of fools weary them,
for they don't know how to go
to the city.
16 Woe to you, land, when your king is
a youth*a*
and your princes feast in the morning.
17 Blessed are you, land,
when your king is a son of nobles
and your princes feast
at the proper time —
for strength and not
for drunkenness.*b*
18 Because of laziness the roof caves in,
and because of negligent hands
the house leaks.
19 A feast is prepared for laughter,
and wine makes life happy,*c*
and money*A* is the answer
for everything.*d*
20 Do not curse the king
even in your thoughts,*e*
and do not curse a rich person
even in your bedroom,*f*
for a bird of the sky may carry
the message,
and a winged creature may report
the matter.

INVEST IN LIFE

11 Send your bread on the surface
of the water,*g*
for after many days you may find it.
2 Give a portion to seven or even
to eight,*h*
for you don't know what disaster
may happen on earth.
3 If the clouds are full,
they will pour out rain
on the earth;
whether a tree falls to the south
or the north,
the place where the tree falls,
there it will lie.
4 One who watches the wind
will not sow,

and the one who looks at the clouds
will not reap.
5 Just as you don't know the path
of the wind,
or how bones develop in*B* the womb
of a pregnant woman,
so also you don't know the work
of God who makes everything.*i*
6 In the morning sow your seed,
and at evening do not let
your hand rest,
because you don't know
which will succeed,
whether one or the other,
or if both of them will be
equally good.
7 Light is sweet,
and it is pleasing for the eyes to see
the sun.*j*
8 Indeed, if someone lives many years,
let him rejoice in them all,
and let him remember the days
of darkness,*k* since they
will be many.
All that comes is futile.
9 Rejoice, young person,
while you are young,
and let your heart be glad in the days
of your youth.
And walk in the ways of your heart
and in the desire of your eyes;*l*
but know that for all of these things
God will bring you to judgment.
10 Remove sorrow from your heart,
and put away pain from your flesh,*m*
because youth and the prime of life
are fleeting.

THE TWILIGHT OF LIFE

12 So remember your Creator in the
days of your youth:
Before the days of adversity come,
and the years approach
when you will say,*n*
"I have no delight in them";

A 10:19 Lit *silver*   *B* 11:5 Or *know how the life-breath comes to the bones in*

10:16-17 The character of a nation's rulers is crucial since its citizens will inevitably be blessed or suffer as a result of their leadership.
10:18 You don't have to intentionally break something; just fail to take care of it. This can be applied to the physical realm as well as to the spiritual. Neglect your spiritual life, and it will deteriorate.
10:20 Watch the words you say. **Do not curse the king**—even in private. **For a bird of the sky may carry the message, and . . . report the matter**. This advice sounds like Solomon was anticipating our age of YouTube and social media! And indeed, things said in secret often have a way of getting out. Be on guard.

11:1-6 At issue here is the need to practice fiscal responsibility. Give your investments time to grow (11:1) and diversify, **for you don't know what disaster may happen** (11:2). In other words, don't put all your eggs in one basket. Practice occupational responsibility too. **One who watches the wind will not sow** (11:4), meaning that if you procrastinate because of circumstances, you won't accomplish anything. And since you **don't know the work of God who makes everything** (11:5), don't put God in a box based on your limited perspective and framework of thinking (see Isa 55:9). He'll blow up your box every time. Instead, be industrious even

as you trust him. **In the morning sow your seed, and at evening do not let your hand rest** (Eccl 11:6).
11:8-10 Maximize your life while you can because you can't go back and do it over again. Today is the tomorrow that you were looking for yesterday. But remember: **for all of these things God will bring you to judgment** (11:9). You and God are going to talk about your choices one day, so live with the end in view.
12:1-6 The phrase **in the days of your youth** indicates that children should be urged to start looking at the world through the lens of God's Word while they're young (12:1), so

[a] 12:2 Is 5:30; Ezk 32:7-8

[b] 12:3 Gn 27:1; 48:10; 1Sm 3:2
[c] 12:4 Jr 25:10; Rv 18:22
[d] 12:5 Jb 17:13; 30:23
[e] Jr 9:17
[f] 12:6 Zch 4:2-3
[g] 12:7 Gn 2:7; 3:19; Ec 3:21
[h] 12:8 Ec 1:2
[i] 12:9 1Kg 4:32; Pr 1:1
[j] 12:11 Pr 1:6; 22:17
[k] Ezr 9:8; Is 22:23

❧ KINGDOM LIVING ❧
PERSONAL
Fearing God

What happens when you're driving down the highway and see a police car parked by the roadside? You slow down. Why? The officer might not even be looking your way. That car may just be sitting there. But on the side of that car is an authority symbol that gets your attention whenever you see it. In fact, it arrests your attention and will probably cause you to alter your behavior out of healthy fear.

This is not unlike the kind of fear we should show toward God. Yet some of us are speeding down the highway of life, and we don't even slow down when God shows up. There's no fear of God in our hearts. He doesn't even arrest our attention. If that's the case, we need to cultivate the fear of God by spending time getting to know him. As we read his Word, we learn more about our God, who is indeed worthy of all glory, honor, and respect.

A crisis in our lives often brings fear. We become afraid when we don't have the ability to fix our problems. It's a reminder that we are fallible. But God asks us to fear him, not our circumstances. This is because he is greater than our circumstances. God is always faithful and always present in our lives. All he wants is our dependence on him alone. As you face your crisis, if you will begin to seek God and fear him above all else, it will make all the difference in the world. God embraces the seriousness of your pursuit of him and responds with his care, provision, and power.

FOR THE NEXT PERSONAL
KINGDOM LIVING LESSON SEE PAGE 1182.

2   before the sun and the light
        are darkened,[a]
    and the moon and the stars,

and the clouds return
        after[A] the rain;
3   on the day when the guardians
        of the house tremble,
    and the strong men stoop,
    the women who grind grain cease
        because they are few,
    and the ones who watch
        through the windows see dimly,[b]
4   the doors at the street are shut
    while the sound of the mill fades;[c]
    when one rises at the sound of a bird,
    and all the daughters of song
        grow faint.
5   Also, they are afraid of heights
        and dangers on the road;
    the almond tree blossoms,
    the grasshopper loses its spring,[B]
    and the caper berry has no effect;
    for the mere mortal is headed
        to his eternal home,[d]
    and mourners will walk around
        in the street;[e]
6   before the silver cord is snapped,[c]
    and the gold bowl is broken,[f]
    and the jar is shattered at the spring,
    and the wheel is broken into the well;
7   and the dust returns to the earth
        as it once was,
    and the spirit returns to God
        who gave it.[g]

8 "Absolute futility," says the Teacher. "Everything is futile."[h]

THE TEACHER'S OBJECTIVES AND CONCLUSION

9 In addition to the Teacher being a wise man, he constantly taught the people knowledge; he weighed, explored, and arranged many proverbs.[i] 10 The Teacher sought to find delightful sayings and write words of truth accurately. 11 The sayings of the wise are like cattle prods,[j] and those from masters of collections are like firmly embedded nails.[k] The sayings are given by one Shepherd.[D]

[A]12:2 Or *with*   [B]12:5 Or *grasshopper is weighed down,* or *grasshopper drags itself along*   [C]12:6 Alt Hb tradition reads *removed*   [D]12:11 Or *by a shepherd*

sow the seeds of God consciousness into your children. Exhort them to make their Creator—the source and sustainer of life—their reference point.

Solomon uses a variety of metaphors to talk about the aging process and what inevitably follows it (12:2-6). Bones turn brittle; hands tremble; muscles weaken; disease invades. Therefore, before the gloom of old age sets in, adopt a godly perspective. If while you're young you're always "dying to do this" and "dying to do that," one day you'll discover that you're just dying.

12:7 We began as dust, and we return to dust (see Gen 2:7). So if this is all you have to look forward to, it's empty. There's no ultimate meaning in life. To find true meaning, you have to bring God to bear on your life and let him bring perspective and higher purpose into the emptiness.

12:9-11 Solomon **taught the people** in part through these **many proverbs** (12:9). God graciously gave him wisdom so that he might pass it along, and his descriptions and illustrations are vital because they grab our attention, help us understand **truth,** and

emphasize its relevance to our lives (12:10). (Preachers, take note!)

In a sense, Solomon's wise sayings **are like cattle prods** used to motivate an ox; they provoke us to a response. They provide a divine frame of reference and enable us to discern the best choices to make. When accepted, they work **like firmly embedded nails** driven into our hearts and minds (12:11).

Ultimately, **the sayings** we find in this book **are given by one Shepherd** (12:11). The Lord works through them to prick our consciences and apply them to our hearts.

[a] 12:12 1Kg 4:32-33; Jn
21:25
[b] Ec 1:18
[c] 12:13 Pr 1:7; Ec 3:14; 5:7;
7:18; 8:12-13
[d] Ps 97:5; Ac 4:12; Rm 10:12
[e] 12:14 Ec 3:17; 11:9; Rv
20:12

> ∽ **HOPE WORDS** ∽
>
> *Start where you are. Do*
> *what you can. Then watch*
> *God open up the doors.*

[12] But beyond these, my son, be warned: there is no end to the making of many books,[a] and much study wearies the body.[b] [13] When all has been heard, the conclusion of the matter is this: fear God[c] and keep his commands, because this is for all[A] humanity.[d] [14] For God will bring every act to judgment,[e] including every hidden thing, whether good or evil.

[A] 12:13 Or *is the whole duty of*

12:12 There's a seemingly endless supply of resources based on Scripture. That's because the Bible is so deep that theologians can't touch the bottom, but it's so shallow that babies won't drown in it. Nevertheless, me must remember that **much**

study wearies the body. There comes a time when you must put down the books and choose wisely.

12:13-14 The actions of humanity—good and evil—are all on tape. And while you can't erase what's on your tape, you can

create new and better footage. As long as you draw breath, the recorder is still running. Seek God's divine perspective for your day-to-day decisions and make your life count toward the fulfillment of his kingdom agenda.

SONG OF SONGS

INTRODUCTION

Author

THIS BOOK CALLS ITSELF "The Song of Songs, which is Solomon's" (1:1), but the phrasing reflects the ambiguity of the Hebrew words. It could be understood as claiming that King Solomon is the author, or it could indicate that it was written for Solomon. The traditional position of the church is that Solomon authored the book.

Some critical Bible scholars believe Solomon's authorship to be impossible, pointing to words that reflect Greek and Persian influences—which would be problematic because those kingdoms didn't arise for hundreds of years after his death. They claim that these words demonstrate that the book was written after the exile—not during the time of the monarchy of Solomon's day. The evidence to which they point, though, is inconclusive. Other scholars have shown that these words may actually come from other Semitic languages contemporary with Solomon's day, and many words and descriptions in the book actually favor a date during Israel's monarchy. Thus, we are on good ground to believe that 1:1 refers to Solomon as the writer.

It is true that Solomon strayed significantly from the biblical ideal for marriage, having hundreds of wives and concubines (see 1 Kgs 11:3). His sin, however, did not prevent God from graciously using him to reveal divine truth.

Historical Background

Song of Songs is an example of an ancient Near Eastern love song. The closest parallel to it is the Egyptian love poetry that existed during Solomon's time. Given his extensive knowledge, Solomon would have been familiar with such literature (see 1 Kgs 4:29-34).

The various place names mentioned in Song of Songs were located in the northern part of Solomon's kingdom (e.g., Damascus, Shunem, Tirzah, and

Mount Hermon). After the division of the kingdom into north (Israel) and south (Judah), a poem about a king in Jerusalem likely would not have included these locations.

Message and Purpose

Song of Songs is a book that is often misunderstood, misapplied, or simply unread. It is the lover's song, a story about God's love applied to human relationships. God wants that love expressed in romantic relationships; therefore, Solomon is allowed to bring in a man and a woman on their journey to and in their marriage. His telling includes the physical part of their union—which is something that God himself endorses.

The Song of Songs is a very tender, touching—and, yes, sensual—book given to us so that we can understand not only how we can relate to God, but how he wants us to relate to one another within the context of marriage. God doesn't shy away from these matters. So since God gave us this book, let's find out what he has to say about tenderness, care, and love as a reflection of his kingdom relationship with us.

www.bhpublishinggroup.com/qr/te/22_00

Outline

a 1:1 1Kg 4:32
b 1:2 Sg 4:10
c 1:3 Jn 12:3
d Ec 7:1
e 1:4 Hs 11:4
f 1:5 Sg 2:7; 3:5,10; 5:8,16; 8:4
g Ps 120:5; Is 60:7
h Sg 2:14; 4:3; 6:4
i 1:6 Ps 69:8
j Sg 8:11
k 1:7 Sg 3:1-4
l Sg 2:16; 6:3
m Is 13:20; Jr 33:12
n Sg 8:13

o 1:8 Sg 5:9; 6:1
p 1:9 Sg 1:15
q 2Ch 1:16-17
r 1:10 Sg 5:13
s 1:12 Sg 4:14; Mk 14:3; Jn 12:3
t 1:13 Ps 45:8; Jn 19:39
u 1:14 Sg 4:13
v 1Sm 23:29
w 1:15 Sg 4:1
x 1:16 Sg 2:3
y 2:1 Sg 5:13; 7:2; Hs 14:5

1

The Song of Songs, which is
Solomon's.*a*

Woman

2 Oh, that he would kiss me
with the kisses of his mouth!
For your caresses*A* are
more delightful than wine.*b*

3 The fragrance of your perfume
is intoxicating;*c*
your name is perfume poured out.*d*
No wonder young women*B*
adore you.

4 Take me with you*e* — let's hurry.
Oh, that the king would bring*c* me
to his chambers.

Young Women

We will rejoice and be glad in you;
we will celebrate your caresses
more than wine.

Woman

It is only right that they adore you.

5 Daughters of Jerusalem,*f*
I am dark like the tents of Kedar,*g*
yet lovely*h* like the curtains
of Solomon.

6 Do not stare at me because
I am dark,
for the sun has gazed on me.
My mother's sons were angry
with me;*i*
they made me take care
of the vineyards.*j*
I have not taken care of
my own vineyard.

7 Tell me, you whom I love:*k*
Where do you pasture your sheep?*l*
Where do you let them rest
at noon?*m*
Why should I be like one who veils
herself*D*
beside the flocks
of your companions?*n*

Man*E*

8 If you do not know,
most beautiful of women,*o*
follow*F* the tracks of the flock,
and pasture your young goats
near the shepherds' tents.

9 I compare you, my darling,*p*
to a*G* mare
among Pharaoh's chariots.*q*

10 Your cheeks are beautiful
with jewelry,*r*
your neck with its necklace.

11 We will make gold jewelry for you,
accented with silver.

Woman

12 While the king is on his couch,*H*
my perfume*i* releases
its fragrance.*s*

13 The one I love is a sachet of myrrh
to me,*t*
spending the night
between my breasts.

14 The one I love is a cluster
of henna blossoms to me,*u*
in the vineyards of En-gedi.*v*

Man

15 How beautiful you are, my darling.
How very beautiful!
Your eyes are doves.*w*

Woman

16 How handsome you are, my love.*x*
How delightful!
Our bed is verdant;

17 the beams of our house
are cedars,
and our rafters are cypresses.*J*

2

I am a wildflower*K* of Sharon,
a lily*L* of the valleys.*y*

Man

2 Like a lily among thorns,
so is my darling
among the young women.

A 1:2 Or *acts of love*   *B* 1:3 Or *wonder virgins*   *C* 1:4 Or *The king has brought*   *D* 1:7 Or *who wanders*   *E* 1:8 Some understand the young women to be the speakers in this verse.   *F* 1:8 Lit *go out for yourself into*   *G* 1:9 Lit *my*   *H* 1:12 Or *is at his table*   *I* 1:12 Lit *nard*   *J* 1:17 Or *firs*, or *pines*   *K* 2:1 Traditionally *rose*   *L* 2:1 Or *lotus*

1:1 It might seem strange that Solomon (who "had seven hundred wives" and "three hundred" concubines by the end of his life; 1 Kgs 11:3) would author this love poem about a monogamous romance. Nevertheless, God sovereignly used him to give us a divine perspective on the subject.

1:2-4 Name refers to character and reputation. This book is presented as a poetic exchange between a man (**the king**, 1:4) and a woman (the "Shulammite," 6:13), though a few other characters make appearances along the way.

1:5-6 Of special note here is the woman's proud recognition of her color: **I am dark like the tents of Kedar, yet lovely** (1:5). She saw herself as black and beautiful.

1:7 That the woman is not like **one who veils herself**—a reference to a prostitute—is important. She's a woman of dignity, bringing to mind Proverbs 31:30: "Charm is deceptive and beauty is fleeting, but a woman who fears the Lord will be praised."

1:9, 15 The man compares his beloved's loveliness to amazing creatures that God has made. This is a reminder that men have power to build women up with words. So husband, when was the last time you told your wife how beautiful she is?

Woman

3 Like an apricot[A] tree
    among the trees of the forest,
so is my love among the young men.
I delight to sit in his shade,
and his fruit is sweet to my taste.

4 He brought me
    to the banquet hall,[B,a]
and he looked on me with love.[C,b]

5 Sustain me with raisins;
refresh me with apricots,[D]
for I am lovesick.[c]

6 May his left hand be
    under my head,
and his right arm embrace me.[d]

7 Young women of Jerusalem,
    I charge you
by the gazelles and the wild does
    of the field,
do not stir up or awaken love
until the appropriate time.[E,e]

8 Listen! My love is approaching.
Look! Here he comes,
leaping over the mountains,[f]
bounding over the hills.

9 My love is like a gazelle
or a young stag.[g]
See, he is standing
    behind our wall,
gazing through the windows,
peering through the lattice.

10 My love calls to me:

Man

Arise,[h] my darling.
Come away, my beautiful one.

11 For now the winter is past;
the rain has ended and gone away.

12 The blossoms appear
    in the countryside.
The time of singing[F] has come,
and the turtledove's cooing is heard
    in our land.[i]

13 The fig tree ripens its figs;[j]
the blossoming vines give off
    their fragrance.[k]

Arise, my darling.
Come away, my beautiful one.

14 My dove,[l] in the clefts of the rock,[m]
in the crevices of the cliff,
let me see your face,[G]
let me hear your voice;[n]
for your voice is sweet,
and your face is lovely.[o]

Woman[H]

15 Catch the foxes for us[p] —
the little foxes that ruin
    the vineyards —
for our vineyards are in bloom.[q]

Woman

16 My love is mine and I am his;[r]
he feeds among the lilies.

17 Until the day breaks[I]
and the shadows flee,
turn around, my love, and be
    like a gazelle
or a young stag[s]
    on the divided mountains.[J,t]

3 In my bed at night[k]
I sought the one I love;[u]
I sought him, but did not find him.[L,v]

2 I will arise now and go
    about the city,
through the streets
    and the plazas.[w]
I will seek the one I love.
I sought him, but did not find him.

3 The guards who go about the city
    found me.[x]
I asked them, "Have you seen the one
    I love?"

4 I had just passed them
when I found the one I love.
I held on to him and would not
    let him go
until I brought him
    to my mother's house[y] —
to the chamber of the one
    who conceived me.

a 2:4 Sg 1:4
b Ps 20:5
c 2:5 Sg 5:8
d 2:6 Sg 8:3
e 2:7 Sg 3:5; 5:8; 8:4
f 2:8 Is 52:7
g 2:9 Sg 2:17; 8:14
h 2:10 Sg 2:13
i 2:12 Jr 8:7
j 2:13 Mt 24:32
k Sg 7:12

l 2:14 Sg 5:2; 6:9
m Jr 48:28
n Sg 8:13
o Sg 1:5
p 2:15 Ezk 13:4
q Sg 2:13
r 2:16 Sg 6:3; 7:10; 8:6
s 2:17 Sg 2:9
t Sg 4:5-6; 8:14
u 3:1 Sg 1:7
v Sg 5:6
w 3:2 Jr 5:1
x 3:3 Sg 5:7
y 3:4 Sg 8:2

A 2:3 Or apple B 2:4 Lit the house of wine C 2:4 Or and his banner over me is love D 2:5 Or apples E 2:7 Lit until it pleases F 2:12 Or pruning G 2:14 Or form H 2:15 The speaker could be the woman, the man, or both. I 2:17 Lit breathes J 2:17 Or the Bether mountains, or the mountains of spices; Hb obscure K 3:1 Or bed night after night L 3:1 LXX adds I called him, but he did not answer me

---

2:3 That the man is her **apricot tree** suggests that no matter how difficult her circumstances, she trusts that with him there is rest and refreshment.
2:4 **He looked on me with love** can be translated, "His banner over me is love" (see the CSB footnote). Banners are used to promote our allegiance. They advertise what we value. Solomon, then, wants everyone to know the woman is his treasure.

2:6-7 That she longs for **his left hand** to be **under** her **head** and **his right arm** to **embrace** her (2:6) means she desires sexual intimacy with him, but they are not yet married. Therefore, she tells the **young women of Jerusalem** (and herself), **do not...awaken love until the appropriate time** (2:7). The consummation must await the wedding night, when the time will be right.
2:8-9 This man is moving **like a gazelle** because nothing will stand in his way or delay

him (2:9). After all, *she* is waiting at the end of his journey.
2:10-14 Husband, you are to be the spring to your woman's winter. The wife in Psalm 128:3 is "a fruitful vine" within the home. So if you want a summer wife who consistently bears good fruit, don't bring home winter weather!
2:15 This is a vivid way of acknowledging that little things can wreck a relationship. Identify and catch your own **foxes** before it's too late.

a 3:5 Sg 2:7; 5:8; 8:4
b 3:6 Sg 6:10; 8:5
c Sg 4:6,14
d 3:8 Ps 45:3
e Ps 91:5
f 3:10 Sg 1:5
g 3:11 Is 3:16-17; 4:4
h Is 62:5
i 4:1 Sg 1:15; 5:12
j Sg 6:5

k 4:2 Sg 6:6
l 4:3 Jos 2:18
m Sg 6:7
n 4:4 Sg 7:4
o 4:5 Sg 7:3
p 4:6 Sg 2:17
q Sg 3:6; 4:14
r 4:7 Sg 1:15; Eph 5:27
s 4:8 1Kg 4:33
t Is 62:5
u Dt 3:9; 1Ch 5:23
v 4:9 Sg 6:5; 7:5
w Sg 5:1-2
x 4:10 Sg 1:2,4
y 4:11 Pr 5:3
z Ex 3:8,17; Nm 14:8;
16:13-14

5 Young women of Jerusalem,
   I charge you
by the gazelles and the wild does
   of the field,
do not stir up or awaken love
until the appropriate time.[A,a]

Narrator

6 Who is this[b] coming up
   from the wilderness
like columns of smoke,
scented with myrrh and frankincense[c]
from every fragrant powder
   of the merchant?

7 Look! Solomon's bed
surrounded by sixty warriors
from the mighty men of Israel.
8 All of them are skilled with swords
and trained in warfare.
Each has his sword at his side[d]
to guard against the terror
   of the night.[e]

9 King Solomon made a carriage
   for himself
with wood from Lebanon.
10 He made its posts of silver,
its back[B] of gold,
and its seat of purple.
Its interior is inlaid with love[c]
by the young women of Jerusalem.[f]
11 Go out, young women of Zion,[g]
and gaze at King Solomon,
wearing the crown
   his mother placed on him
on the day of his wedding[h] —
the day of his heart's rejoicing.

Man

4 How beautiful you are, my darling.
How very beautiful!
Behind your veil,
your eyes are doves.[i]
Your hair is like a flock of goats
streaming down Mount Gilead.[j]
2 Your teeth are like a flock
   of newly shorn sheep
coming up from washing,
each one bearing twins,

and none has lost its young.[D,k]
3 Your lips are like a scarlet cord,[l]
and your mouth[E] is lovely.
Behind your veil,
your brow[F] is like a slice
   of pomegranate.[m]
4 Your neck is like the tower of David,[n]
constructed in layers.
A thousand shields are hung on it —
all of them shields of warriors.
5 Your breasts are like two fawns,
twins of a gazelle,[o] that feed
   among the lilies.
6 Until the day breaks[G]
and the shadows flee,[p]
I will make my way to the mountain
   of myrrh
and the hill of frankincense.[q]
7 You are absolutely beautiful,[r]
   my darling;
there is no imperfection in you.

8 Come with me from Lebanon,[H,s]
   my bride;[t]
come with me from Lebanon!
Descend from the peak of Amana,
from the summit of Senir
   and Hermon,[u]
from the dens of the lions,
from the mountains of the leopards.
9 You have captured my heart,[v]
   my sister,[w] my bride.
You have captured my heart
with one glance of your eyes,
with one jewel of your necklace.
10 How delightful your caresses are,
   my sister, my bride.
Your caresses are much better
   than wine,[x]
and the fragrance of your perfume
   than any balsam.
11 Your lips drip sweetness like
   the honeycomb, my bride.[y]
Honey and milk[z] are
   under your tongue.
The fragrance of your garments
   is like the fragrance of Lebanon.

12 My sister, my bride, you are
   a locked garden —

[A] 3:5 Lit *until it pleases*   [B] 3:10 Or *base,* or *canopy*   [C] 3:10 Or *leather*   [D] 4:2 Lit *and no one bereaved among them*   [E] 4:3 Or *speech*   [F] 4:3 Or *temple,*
or *cheek,* or *lips*   [G] 4:6 Lit *breathes*   [H] 4:8 In Hb, the word for *Lebanon* is similar to "frankincense" in Sg 4:6,14,15.

3:5 No one should **awaken** sexual desires until they can be legitimately enjoyed in the marriage bed. God created sex, but he means for us to delight in it within the covenant bonds of matrimony.
3:6-11 Solomon's wedding processional is luxurious.

4:1-7 The husband lavishes his new bride with admiration. Her **eyes, hair, teeth, lips,** and **neck** are all described with poetic praise (4:1-4). And though these could have been adored before the wedding day, on the wedding night even her **breasts** receive her husband's praise (4:5-6). This couple is naked and not ashamed.

4:12 That the bride is **a locked garden** means she came to her groom as a virgin. But now, on her wedding night, she is open for her husband's enjoyment (see the note on 5:1).

a locked garden[A]
and a sealed spring.[a]

13 Your branches are a paradise[B]
of pomegranates
with choicest fruits;[b]
henna with nard,

14 nard and saffron, calamus
and cinnamon,[c]
with all the trees of frankincense,[d]
myrrh and aloes,[e]
with all the best spices.

15 You are a garden spring,
a well of flowing water[f]
streaming from Lebanon.

Woman

16 Awaken,[g] north wind;
come, south wind.
Blow on my garden,
and spread the fragrance
of its spices.
Let my love come to his garden
and eat its choicest fruits.[h]

Man

5 I have come to my garden —
my sister, my bride.
I gather[c] my myrrh with my spices.
I eat my honeycomb
with my honey.
I drink my wine with my milk.

Narrator

Eat, friends!
Drink, be intoxicated
with caresses![D,j]

Woman

2 I was sleeping, but my heart
was awake.
A sound! My love was knocking![j]

Man

Open to me, my sister, my darling,
my dove, my perfect one.
For my head is drenched with dew,
my hair with droplets of the night.

Woman

3 I have taken off my clothing.[k]
How can I put it back on?
I have washed my feet.

How can I get them dirty?

4 My love thrust his hand
through the opening,
and my feelings were stirred
for him.

5 I rose to open for my love.
My hands dripped with myrrh,[l]
my fingers with flowing myrrh
on the handles of the bolt.

6 I opened to my love,
but my love had turned
and gone away.
My heart sank[E] because
he had left.[F]
I sought him, but did not find him.[m]
I called him, but he did not answer.

7 The guards who go about the city
found me.[n]
They beat and wounded me;
they took my cloak[G] from me —
the guardians of the walls.[o]

8 Young women of Jerusalem,
I charge you,[p]
if you find my love,
tell him that I am lovesick.[q]

Young Women

9 What makes the one you love better
than another,
most beautiful of women?[r]
What makes him better
than another,
that you would give us this charge?

Woman

10 My love is fit and strong,[H,S]
notable among ten thousand.[t]

11 His head is purest gold.
His hair is wavy[I,u]
and black as a raven.

12 His eyes are like doves[v]
beside flowing streams,
washed in milk
and set like jewels.[J]

13 His cheeks[w] are like beds of spice,
mounds of[K] perfume.
His lips are lilies,
dripping with flowing myrrh.[x]

14 His arms[L] are rods of gold
set[M] with beryl.[y]
His body[N] is an ivory panel
covered with lapis lazuli.[z]

[a] 4:12 1Kg 21:8; Est 8:10; Jb 9:7
[b] 4:13 Sg 7:13
[c] 4:14 Ex 30:23
[d] Sg 4:6
[e] Sg 3:6; Jn 19:39
[f] 4:15 Gn 26:19; Lv 14:5; Jr 2:13
[g] 4:16 Sg 2:7; 3:5; 8:4
[h] Sg 7:13
[i] 5:1 Pr 5:19
[j] 5:2 Sg 2:8
[k] 5:3 Lk 11:7

[l] 5:5 Sg 5:13
[m] 5:6 Sg 3:1-2
[n] 5:7 Sg 3:3
[o] Sg 8:9-10
[p] 5:8 Sg 2:7; 3:5; 8:4
[q] Sg 2:5
[r] 5:9 Sg 1:8; 6:1
[s] 5:10 1Sm 16:12
[t] Ps 45:2
[u] 5:11 Sg 5:2
[v] 5:12 Sg 1:15; 4:1
[w] 5:13 Sg 1:10
[x] Sg 5:5
[y] 5:14 Ex 28:20; 39:13; Ezk 1:16
[z] Ex 24:10

[A] 4:12 Some Hb mss read *locked fountain* [B] 4:13 Or *park*, or *orchard* [C] 5:1 Lit *pluck* [D] 5:1 Or *Drink your fill, lovers* [E] 5:6 Lit *My soul went out*
[F] 5:6 Or *spoken* [G] 5:7 Or *veil*, or *shawl* [H] 5:10 Or *is radiant and ruddy* [I] 5:11 Or *is like palm leaves*; Hb obscure [J] 5:12 Lit *milk sitting in fullness*
[K] 5:13 LXX, Vg read *spice, yielding* [L] 5:14 Lit *hands* [M] 5:14 Lit *filled*; Sg 5:2,12 [N] 5:14 Lit *abdomen*

5:1 Notice the inclusion of a **narrator** here. Who but God could have access to this couple's bedroom? His interruption is a reminder that God himself is pleased that the pair is pleased. Sex is God's gift to married couples.
5:2-6 This passage is a reminder that sometimes the passions of husbands and wives aren't in sync. We do well, then, to remember Paul's words: "Love is patient, love is kind. . . . [It] is not irritable, and does not keep a record of wrongs" (1 Cor 13:4-5).

a 5:15 Sg 7:4-5
b 1Kg 4:33
c 5:16 Sg 4:7
d 6:2 Sg 4:16; 5:1
e Sg 5:13
f Sg 1:7
g Sg 2:1
h 6:3 Sg 2:16; 7:10; 8:6
i 6:4 Nm 2:2-3; Sg 6:10
j 6:5 Sg 4:9
k Sg 4:1
l 6:6 Sg 4:2
m 6:7 Sg 4:3
n 6:8 1Kg 11:3
o 6:9 Sg 2:14; 5:2
p Pr 31:29

q 6:9 Gn 30:13
r 6:10 Sg 3:6; 8:5
s Sg 6:4
t 6:11 Sg 7:12
u 6:13 Jdg 21:21
v Gn 32:2; 2Sm 17:24
w 7:1 Ps 45:13
x 7:3 Sg 4:5
y 7:4 Sg 4:4

15 His legs are alabaster pillars
set on pedestals of pure gold.
His presence is like Lebanon,[a]
as majestic as the cedars.[b]
16 His mouth is sweetness.
He is absolutely desirable.[c]
This is my love, and this is my friend,
young women of Jerusalem.

Young Women

6 Where has your love gone,
most beautiful of women?
Which way has he[A] turned?
We will seek him with you.

Woman

2 My love has gone down
to his garden,[d]
to beds of spice,[e]
to feed in the gardens[f]
and gather lilies.[g]
3 I am my love's and my love is mine;[h]
he feeds among the lilies.

Man

4 You are as beautiful as Tirzah,
my darling,
lovely as Jerusalem,
awe-inspiring as an army
with banners.[i]
5 Turn your eyes away from me,
for they captivate me.[j]
Your hair is like a flock of goats
streaming down from Gilead.[k]
6 Your teeth are like a flock of ewes
coming up from washing,
each one having a twin,
and not one missing.[B,l]
7 Behind your veil,[m]
your brow[c] is like a slice
of pomegranate.
8 There are sixty queens
and eighty concubines[n]
and young women[D]
without number.
9 But my dove,[o] my virtuous one,
is unique;[p]
she is the favorite of her mother,

perfect to the one who gave her birth.
Women see her and declare
her fortunate;[q]
queens and concubines also,
and they sing her praises:

10 Who is this[r] who shines
like the dawn,
as beautiful as the moon,
bright as the sun,
awe-inspiring as an army
with banners?[s]

Woman

11 I came down to the walnut grove
to see the blossoms of the valley,
to see if the vines were budding[t]
and the pomegranates blooming.
12 I didn't know what was happening
to me.
I felt like I was
in a chariot with a nobleman.[E]

Young Women

13 Come back, come back,
Shulammite![F]
Come back, come back, that
we may look at you!

Man

How you gaze at the Shulammite,
as you look at the dance[u]
of the two camps![G,v]

7 How beautiful are
your sandaled feet, princess![H,w]
The curves of your thighs
are like jewelry,
the handiwork of a master.
2 Your navel is a rounded bowl;
it never lacks mixed wine.
Your belly is a mound of wheat
surrounded by lilies.
3 Your breasts are like two fawns,
twins of a gazelle.[x]
4 Your neck is like a tower of ivory,[y]
your eyes like pools in Heshbon
by Bath-rabbim's gate.

A 6:1 Lit *your love*   B 6:6 Lit *and no one bereaved among them*   C 6:7 Or *temple*, or *cheek*, or *lips*   D 6:8 Or *and virgins* ; Sg 1:3   E 6:12 Hb obscure
F 6:13 Or *the perfect one*, or *the peaceable one*   G 6:13 Or *dance of Mahanaim*   H 7:1 Lit *daughter of a nobleman*, or *prince*

5:16 This bridegroom is more than good looking. He is her **friend**, her intimate companion. He's a kingdom man.
6:2-3 This is poetic language signaling that the couple's lovemaking has resumed. In the wife's declaration, **I am my love's and my love is mine** (6:3), she acknowledges that the two of them have "become one" (see Gen 2:24).
The apostle Paul says the mystery of a one-flesh union between a man and a woman is

meant to preview the union of Christ and the church (see Eph 5:29-31). John even describes the final joining together of the Lord Jesus and his people as "the marriage feast of the Lamb" and his bride (see Rev 19:7-9). The beautiful declaration, "I am my love's and my love is mine" (Song 6:3), is but a pale reflection of the more glorious divine declaration, "I will be their God, and they will be my people" (Jer 31:33).

6:11-12 Nature's readiness for spring is an illustration of this wife's readiness for love-making (6:11). Intimacy with her husband is compared to riding **in a chariot with a nobleman** (6:12). She's on cloud nine at the thought.
7:1-8 This passage should make husbands ask, do I affirm my wife? Let your bride know she's your treasure.

Your nose is like the tower
of Lebanon
looking toward Damascus.
5 Your head crowns you[A]
like Mount Carmel,
the hair of your head
like purple cloth —
a king could be held captive[a]
in your tresses.
6 How beautiful you are
and how pleasant,[b]
my love, with such delights!
7 Your stature is like a palm tree;
your breasts are clusters of fruit.
8 I said, "I will climb the palm tree
and take hold of its fruit."[c]
May your breasts be like clusters
of grapes,
and the fragrance of your breath
like apricots.[d]
9 Your mouth[B] is like fine wine[e] —

Woman

flowing smoothly for my love,
gliding past my lips and teeth![c]
10 I am my love's,
and his desire[f] is for me.[g]

11 Come, my love,
let's go to the field;
let's spend the night
among the henna blossoms.[D]
12 Let's go early to the vineyards;
let's see if the vine has budded,
if the blossom has opened,
if the pomegranates are in bloom.[h]
There I will give you my caresses.
13 The mandrakes[i] give off a fragrance,
and at our doors is every delicacy,
both new and old.
I have treasured them up for you,
my love.

8 If only I could treat you
like my brother,[E]
one who nursed
at my mother's breasts,
I would find you in public
and kiss you,
and no one would scorn me.

2 I would lead you, I would take you,
to the house of my mother[j]
who taught me.[F]
I would give you spiced wine
to drink
from the juice of my pomegranate.
3 May his left hand be
under my head,
and his right arm embrace me.[k]
4 Young women of Jerusalem,
I charge you,
do not stir up or awaken love
until the appropriate time.[l]

Young Women

5 Who is this[m] coming up
from the wilderness,
leaning on the one she loves?

Woman

I awakened you under
the apricot tree.[n]
There your mother conceived you;
there she conceived and gave
you birth.
6 Set me as a seal on your heart,
as a seal on your arm.[o]
For love is as strong as death;[p]
jealousy is as unrelenting as Sheol.
Love's flames are fiery flames[q] —
an almighty flame![G]
7 A huge torrent cannot
extinguish love;
rivers cannot sweep it away.
If a man were to give all his wealth[H]
for love,[r]
it would be utterly scorned.

Brothers

8 Our sister is young;
she has no breasts.[s]
What will we do for our sister
on the day she is spoken for?
9 If she is a wall,
we will build a silver barricade
on her.
If she is a door,
we will enclose her
with cedar planks.[t]

[a] 7:5 Sg 4:9
[b] 7:6 Sg 1:15-16
[c] 7:8 Pr 5:19
[d] Sg 2:3
[e] 7:9 Sg 5:16
[f] 7:10 Gn 3:16; 4:7
[g] Sg 2:16; 6:3; 8:6
[h] 7:12 Sg 6:11
[i] 7:13 Gn 30:14-16

[j] 8:2 Sg 3:4
[k] 8:3 Sg 2:6
[l] 8:4 Sg 2:7; 3:5
[m] 8:5 Sg 3:6; 6:10
[n] Sg 2:3
[o] 8:6 Sg 2:16; 6:3; 7:10
[p] Rm 8:38-39; 1Co 13:8
[q] Dt 32:21-22; Pr 6:34; 27:4
[r] 8:7 Pr 6:35
[s] 8:8 Ezk 16:7
[t] 8:9 1Kg 6:15

[A] 7:5 Lit *head upon you is*   [B] 7:9 Lit *palate*   [C] 7:9 LXX, Syr, Vg; MT reads *past lips of sleepers*   [D] 7:11 Or *the villages*   [E] 8:1 Lit *Would that you were like a brother to me*   [F] 8:2 LXX adds *and into the chamber of the one who bore me*   [G] 8:6 Or *the blaze of the LORD*   [H] 8:7 Lit *all the wealth of his house*

7:10-13 In a world in which promiscuity is rampant, our culture needs to be reminded that monogamy is holy, beautiful, and exciting.
8:1 That the Shulammite wishes she could **treat** her husband **like** her **brother** means she wants the freedom to show affection to him in public.

8:6 True love says, "I'm not in this partnership to feel good; I'm here to build a lasting relationship." Only this kind of love is enduring.
8:8-10 Brothers discuss how they can prepare their young **sister** for marriage (8:8), deciding to help her protect herself and to reward her for being **a wall**, that is, steadfast in her commitment to purity (8:9). Let your

daughters know, moms and dads, that you're proud of them when they demand that men respect them. Guide them in setting boundaries. That these brothers are also prepared to **enclose** their sister should she prove willing to compromise with sexual sin (8:9) is a reminder not to give our children more liberty than they can handle.

a 8:11 Ec 2:4
b Mt 21:33
c Is 7:23
d 8:12 Sg 1:6

e 8:13 Sg 1:7
f Sg 2:14
g 8:14 Sg 2:17

Woman

10 I am[A] a wall
and my breasts like towers.
So in his eyes I have become
like one who finds[B] peace.[C]

11 Solomon owned a vineyard
in Baal-hamon.[a]
He leased the vineyard to tenants.[b]
Each was to bring for his fruit
one thousand pieces of silver.[c]

12 I have my own vineyard.[D,d]
The one thousand are for you,
Solomon,

but two hundred for those who take
care of its fruits.

Man

13 You[E] who dwell in the gardens,
companions[e] are listening
for your voice;
let me hear you![f]

Woman

14 Run away with me,[F] my love,
and be like a gazelle
or a young stag
on the mountains of spices.[g]

[A] 8:10 Or *was*   [B] 8:10 Or *brings*   [C] 8:10 In Hb, the word for *peace* sounds similar to Solomon and Shulammite.   [D] 8:12 Lit *My vineyard, which is mine, is before me*; Sg 1:6   [E] 8:13 In Hb, the word for *You* is feminine.   [F] 8:14 Lit *Flee*

8:11-12 As **Solomon** had the prerogative to lease his **vineyard to tenants** (8:11), so his wife had the prerogative to lease her **vineyard**, her body, to him (8:12). She gave herself willingly.

ISAIAH

INTRODUCTION

Author

ACCORDING TO ISAIAH 1:1, the book is the vision of "Isaiah son of Amoz," who ministered in the eighth century BC during the reigns of "Uzziah, Jotham, Ahaz, and Hezekiah"—kings of Judah. Though Isaiah's authorship was accepted for centuries, it has been challenged by modern critical scholars. Many of them argue that Isaiah couldn't have written chapters 40–66, because these chapters detail Judah's defeat by Babylon, their exile, and their return to the land. These scholars believe a prophet in the eighth century couldn't possibly know about future events. And this is true—unless the Creator God who knows the future revealed them to him. Since God can make the future known to his servants, then there is no reason to reject that Isaiah wrote chapters 40–66 and is, therefore, the author of the entire book.

Historical Background

According to Isaiah 6:1, the prophet received his call from God to ministry "in the year that King Uzziah died" (ca. 742 BC). During this glorious vision of the Lord seated on his throne, Isaiah responded to the Lord's question, "Who will go for us?" with, "Here I am. Send me" (6:8).

Uzziah's reign was a prosperous time for Judah, but the nation of Assyria was rising to power. In 722 BC, the northern kingdom of Israel fell to Assyrian domination. Though the Lord would supernaturally protect Judah from Assyrian aggression, another superpower was on the horizon: Babylon. Isaiah would not live to see the Babylonians assail Judah. But he warned sinful Judah that they were coming. Nevertheless, God's judgment would be followed by God's grace, for Isaiah prophesied that the Lord would bring his people back from exile when their punishment was complete.

Message and Purpose

Isaiah, a great prophet to the southern kingdom of Judah, blazed onto the scene to describe the condition of this kingdom that was going down spiritually and headed toward disaster. He calls on the people to repent and get right with God, telling them, "Though yours sins are scarlet, they will be as white as snow" (1:18).

The classic passage in this book is found in chapter 6, describing Isaiah's official call to his prophetic task when he saw the Lord in all of his majestic holiness. That call came in a bad year, when good King Uzziah died. That meant Judah's human hope to set things right was gone, but Isaiah learned that even in times like that the Lord was still on his throne and still in control.

Isaiah is a long book because it deals with two great sweeps of time—the days in which the prophet lived and the time yet to come when the Messiah returns and establishes his kingdom of righteousness. That's why Isaiah 53 is such a precious chapter, telling us of the Messiah, the Suffering Servant, who would bear our sins and someday rule as King. The message of Isaiah to us today is to adjust the way we live so that when the King returns, we can enter into the kingdom full speed ahead because we have prepared ourselves by living according to God's righteous standards.

VIDEO | INTRO

www.bhpublishinggroup.com/qr/te/23_00

Outline

I. The Judgment of God (1:1–39:8)
  A. God's Judgment on Judah (1:1–5:30)
  B. The Commissioning of Isaiah (6:1–13)
  C. The Coming Messiah (7:1–12:6)
  D. God's Judgment on the Nations (13:1–23:18)
  E. Isaiah's Prophecy of the End Times (24:1–27:13)
  F. Woes and Blessings on Israel and Judah (28:1–35:10)
  G. Historical Interlude: Sennacherib and Hezekiah (36:1–39:8)
II. The Blessing of God (40:1–66:24)
  A. God's Deliverance of His People (40:1–48:22)
  B. Salvation through the Servant (49:1–57:21)
  C. God's Restoration of Israel and the World (58:1–66:24)

a 1:1 Pr 29:18; Dn 8:1; Ob 1; Nah 1:1; Hab 2:2-3
b Is 2:1; 13:1
c 2Ch 26:3-5
d 2Kg 15:32-38
e 2Kg 16:1-4
f 2Kg 18:1-8
g Hs 1:1; Mc 1:1
h 1:2 Dt 4:26; 32:1; Is 30:1; Mc 1:2
i Is 30:1
j 1:3 Jr 8:7
k 1:4 Is 13:11
l Is 14:20; Mt 3:7
m Dt 4:31
n Nm 14:11; Dt 31:20; Pr 5:12; Is 5:24
o Is 5:19,24; 10:20; 12:6; 29:19; 30:11-15
p 1:6 Jb 2:7
q Ps 38:3
r 1:7 Lv 26:33; Dt 28:51-52; Is 6:11-12; Jr 44:6
s 1:8 Is 10:32; 37:22; Zch 2:10; 9:9
t 1:9 1Sm 17:45
u Is 10:21-22
v Gn 19:24-25; Is 3:9; 13:19; Rm 9:29
w 1:10 Is 28:14
x Is 3:9; Ezk 16:46-49,55; Rv 11:8
y 1:11 1Sm 15:22; Jr 6:20; Hs 6:6; Am 5:21-24; Mt 23:23; Mk 12:33
z 1:13 Mal 1:10
aa Nm 28:11; 1Ch 23:31
ab Ex 12:16; Lv 23:36
ac Is 13:11
ad 1:15 1Kg 8:22
ae Is 59:2; Jr 7:16; Ezk 8:18; Am 5:23; Hab 1:2; Zch 7:13
af Pr 1:28; Is 59:1-3; Mc 3:4
ag 1:16 Ps 26:6; Is 4:4; 52:11
ah Jr 25:5
ai 1:17 Dt 16:20; 1Kg 3:11; Ps 89:14; Is 10:2; 11:4; Am 5:15; Zch 7:9

1 The vision*a* concerning Judah and Jerusalem that Isaiah*b* son of Amoz saw during the reigns*A,B* of Kings Uzziah,*c* Jotham,*d* Ahaz,*e* and Hezekiah*f* of Judah.*g*

JUDAH ON TRIAL

2 Listen, heavens,
   and pay attention, earth,*h*
for the LORD has spoken:
"I have raised children*c*
   and brought them up,
but they have rebelled against me.*i*
3 The ox knows its owner,
and the donkey its master's
   feeding trough,
but Israel does not know;
my people do not understand."*j*

4 Oh sinful nation,
people weighed down with iniquity,*k*
brood of evildoers,*l*
depraved children!
They have abandoned*m* the LORD;
they have despised*n* the Holy One
   of Israel;*o*
they have turned their backs on him.

5 Why do you want more beatings?
Why do you keep on rebelling?
The whole head is hurt,
and the whole heart is sick.
6 From the sole of the foot
   even to the head,*p*
no spot is uninjured*q* —
wounds, welts, and festering sores
not cleansed, bandaged,
or soothed with oil.

7 Your land is desolate,
your cities burned down;*r*
foreigners devour your fields
right in front of you —
a desolation, like a place demolished
   by foreigners.
8 Daughter Zion*s* is abandoned
like a shelter in a vineyard,
like a shack in a cucumber field,
like a besieged city.

9 If the LORD of Armies*t*
had not left us a few survivors,*u*
we would be like Sodom,
we would resemble Gomorrah.*v*

10 Hear the word of the LORD,*w*
you rulers of Sodom!
Listen to the instruction of our God,
you people of Gomorrah!*x*
11 "What are all your sacrifices to me?"
asks the LORD.
"I have had enough
   of burnt offerings and rams
and the fat of well-fed cattle;
I have no desire for the blood of bulls,
lambs, or male goats.*y*
12 When you come to appear before me,
who requires this from you —
this trampling of my courts?
13 Stop bringing useless offerings.*z*
Your incense is detestable to me.
New Moons and Sabbaths,*aa*
and the calling
   of solemn assemblies*ab* —
I cannot stand iniquity*ac*
   with a festival.
14 I hate your New Moons
   and prescribed festivals.
They have become a burden to me;
I am tired of putting up with them.
15 When you spread out your hands
   in prayer,*ad*
I will refuse to look at you;
even if you offer countless prayers,
I will not listen.*ae*
Your hands are covered with blood.*af*

PURIFICATION OF JERUSALEM

16 "Wash yourselves.
   Cleanse yourselves.*ag*
Remove your evil deeds
   from my sight.
Stop doing evil.*ah*
17 Learn to do what is good.
Pursue justice.*ai*
Correct the oppressor.*D*
Defend the rights of the fatherless.
Plead the widow's cause.

A 1:1 Lit *saw in the days*   *B* 1:1 ca 792–686 BC   *C* 1:2 Or *sons*, also in v. 4   *D* 1:17 Or *Aid the oppressed*

1:5-8 Judah's insistence on rebelling against the Lord was ridiculous in light of the chastisements God had already laid on the people. The nation is pictured as a body so covered with **festering sores** that there's no healthy place to land another blow (1:6)! Nevertheless, she persisted in her sin, even though her enemies were already besieging her cities.
1:9 Isaiah likened Judah to **Sodom** and **Gomorrah**. Their earned fate was the epitome of God's judgment on sinful people.

1:13-15 Hypocritical acts of religious observance make God sick. Judah's citizens did the right things outwardly (1:13-14), but their every act of worship had become abhorrent to God because they performed them with evil hearts (1:15). Judah was a place where injustice and treachery flourished, and the helpless were mistreated by the powerful.
1:17 True repentance, which is the inner resolve to turn from sin and return to God,

would be obvious in the nation's treatment of the weakest members of society. To live out a faith that is valuable to God, then, we must reach out to those who can't help themselves. After all, that's what our heavenly Father did for us. When we were sinners and could do nothing for God, God in Christ became sin for us that we might become the righteousness of God in him (2 Cor 5:21). God wants his children to act like their Father.

18 "Come, let us settle this,"[a]
    says the LORD.
"Though your sins are scarlet,
    they will be as white as snow;[b]
though they are crimson red,
    they will be like wool.
19 If you are willing and obedient,
    you will eat the good things
        of the land.[c]
20 But if you refuse and rebel,
    you will be devoured by the sword."[d]
For the mouth of the LORD
    has spoken.[e]

21 The faithful town —
    what an adulteress[A] she has become!
She was once full of justice.
Righteousness once dwelt in her,
    but now, murderers!
22 Your silver has become dross to be
        discarded,
    your beer[B] is diluted with water.
23 Your rulers are rebels,
    friends of thieves.[f]
They all love graft
    and chase after bribes.[g]
They do not defend the rights
        of the fatherless,
and the widow's case never comes
        before them.[h]

24 Therefore the Lord GOD of Armies,
    the Mighty One of Israel, declares:
"Ah, I will get even with my foes;
I will take revenge
    against my enemies.[i]
25 I will turn my hand against you[j]
    and will burn away
        your dross completely;[C]
I will remove all your impurities.[k]
26 I will restore your judges[l] to what
    they were at first,[D]
and your advisers to what they were
    at the start.[E]
Afterward you will be called
    the Righteous City,[m]
a Faithful Town."

27 Zion will be redeemed by justice,
    those who repent, by righteousness.[n]

28 At the same time both rebels
    and sinners will be broken,
and those who abandon the LORD
    will perish.
29 Indeed, they[F] will be ashamed
    of the sacred trees
you desired,[o]
    and you will be embarrassed
    because of the garden shrines
you have chosen.[p]
30 For you will become like an oak
    whose leaves are withered,
and like a garden without water.[q]
31 The strong one will become tinder,
    and his work a spark;
both will burn together,[r]
    with no one to extinguish
        the flames.[s]

THE CITY OF PEACE

2 The vision that Isaiah[t] son of Amoz
saw concerning Judah and Jerusalem:
2 In[u] the last days[v]
    the mountain of the LORD's house[w]
        will be established
at the top of the mountains
    and will be raised above the hills.
All nations will stream to it,[x]
3 and many peoples will come
    and say,
"Come, let us go up to the mountain
    of the LORD,
to the house of the God of Jacob.[y]
He will teach us about his ways
so that we may walk in his paths."
For instruction will go out of Zion
and the word of the LORD
    from Jerusalem.
4 He will settle disputes
    among the nations
and provide arbitration
    for many peoples.
They will beat their swords
    into plows
and their spears
    into pruning knives.[z]
Nation will not take up the sword
    against nation,
and they will never again train
    for war.[aa]

[a] 1:18 Is 41:1,21; 43:26;
Mc 6:2
[b] Ps 51:7; Is 43:25; 44:22;
Rv 7:14
[c] 1:19-20 Dt 30:15-20
[d] 1:20 Jr 12:12
[e] Is 24:3; 40:5; 58:14;
Mc 4:4
[f] 1:23 Hs 5:10
[g] Ex 23:8; Mc 7:2-6
[h] Ex 22:22; Dt 24:17; Is
10:2; Jr 5:28; Ezk 22:7;
Zch 7:10
[i] 1:24 Is 35:4; 59:18; Jr
46:10
[j] 1:25 Ps 81:14; Is 5:25;
Am 1:8
[k] Ezk 22:20; Mal 3:3
[l] 1:26 Is 60:17; Mt 19:28
[m] Is 33:5; 60:14; 62:1-2;
Zch 8:3
[n] 1:27 Rm 3:26

[o] 1:29 Is 2:8; 57:5; Hs 4:13
[p] Is 65:3; 66:17
[q] 1:30 Ps 1:3; Is 64:6
[r] 1:31 Is 5:24; 9:19; 26:11;
33:11-14
[s] Is 66:24; Mt 3:12; Mk 9:43
[t] 2:1 2Kg 19:2; 20:1; 2Ch
26:22; 32:20; Is 1:1; 13:1
[u] 2:2-4 Mc 4:1-4; Rm 2:20
[v] 2:2 Nm 24:14; Dt 4:30;
Ezk 38:16; Hs 3:5
[w] 2Ch 33:15; Is 27:13; 66:20
[x] Ps 22:27; Is 56:7; Zch
14:10
[y] 2:3 Is 29:23; 45:23; 60:13;
66:18
[z] 2:4 Is 11:6-9; 32:17-18;
Jl 3:10
[aa] Ps 72:3,7; Is 9:7; Hs 2:18;
Zch 9:10

[A] 1:21 Or *prostitute*   [B] 1:22 Or *wine*   [C] 1:25 Lit *dross as with lye*   [D] 1:26 Lit *judges as at the first*   [E] 1:26 Lit *advisers as at the beginning*   [F] 1:29 Some
Hb mss; other Hb mss, Tg read *you*

1:25 Unfortunately, Judah's repentance would only come after the severest of judgment at the hands of the Babylonians. It would **burn** away Judah's **dross** and **impurities**, leaving behind a righteous remnant that would one day enjoy God's favor.

2:1-4 This passage is a prophetic look ahead to the millennial reign of Christ, when God will restore righteous rule to the world. Jewish believers in him will finally live in real peace, as will all the nations (2:4), and they will occupy all of the land God gave to Abraham.

Initially, Jesus was rejected when he presented himself to the Jews as their King. They even cried, "We have no king but Caesar!" (John 19:15), scorning Christ. But God promised David that his Son would rule on his throne forever. Jesus is that Son, and he will one day take the throne in **Jerusalem** (Isa 2:3).

a **2:5** Ps 27:1; 43:3
b **2:6** Dt 31:17; Ps 94:14;
Is 1:4
c Lv 19:26; Dt 18:10-14; 2Kg
21:6; 2Ch 33:6; Jr 27:9;
Mc 5:12
d Jdg 14:3; 1Sm 6:2; 2Kg
1:2-6
e **2:7** Dt 17:17
f **2:8** Is 10:10-11; 19:1-3;
31:7; Jr 2:28
g Is 41:21-29; 44:9-17
h **2:9** Ex 34:7
i **2:10** Rv 6:15
j 1Sm 11:7; 2Ch 14:14; 17:10;
19:7; Is 2:19,21
k 2Th 1:9
l **2:11** Ps 18:27; Is 2:17; Mc
2:3; 2Co 10:5
m **2:12** Mal 4:1
n **2:13** Ps 29:5; Is 14:8;
Hs 14:5
o Ezk 27:6; Zch 11:2
p **2:14** Is 40:4
q **2:15** Is 25:12; Zph 1:16
r **2:16** 1Kg 10:22; Is 23:1,14;
60:9

s **2:17** Mt 25:13
t **2:19** Is 2:10
u Ps 18:7; Is 13:13; 24:1,19-
20; Hg 2:6-7; Heb 12:26
v **2:20** Is 30:22; 31:7
w **2:21** Is 2:10
x **2:22** Ps 39:11; 144:4;
146:3; Jr 17:5; Jms 4:14
y **3:2** 2Kg 24:14; Ezk
17:13-14
z **3:4** Ec 10:16
aa **3:5** Mc 7:3-6

THE DAY OF THE LORD

5 House of Jacob,
come and let us walk
in the LORD's light.*a*
6 For you have abandoned*b* your people,
the house of Jacob,
because they are full of divination
from the East
and of fortune-tellers*c*
like the Philistines.*d*
They are in league^A with foreigners.
7 Their^B,^C land is full of silver and gold,
and there is no limit
to their treasures;
their land is full of horses,
and there is no limit
to their chariots.*e*
8 Their land is full of idols;*f*
they worship the work
of their hands,
what their fingers have made.*g*
9 So humanity is brought low,
and each person is humbled.
Do not forgive them!^h
10 Go into the rocks*i*
and hide in the dust
from the terror of the LORD*j*
and from his majestic splendor.*k*
11 The pride of mankind^D
will be humbled,*l*
and human loftiness
will be brought low;
the LORD alone will be exalted
on that day.

12 For a day belonging to the LORD
of Armies is coming
against all that is proud and lofty,*m*
against all that is lifted up — it will
be humbled —
13 against all the cedars of Lebanon,*n*
lofty and lifted up,
against all the oaks of Bashan,*o*
14 against all the high mountains,*p*
against all the lofty hills,
15 against every high tower,*q*
against every fortified wall,
16 against every ship of Tarshish,*r*
and against every splendid sea vessel.

17 The pride of mankind will be
brought low,
and human loftiness
will be humbled;
the LORD alone will be exalted
on that day.*s*
18 The idols will vanish completely.
19 People will go into caves
in the rocks*t*
and holes in the ground,
away from the terror of the LORD
and from his majestic splendor,
when he rises to terrify the earth.*u*
20 On that day people will throw
their silver and gold idols,*v*
which they made to worship,
to the moles and the bats.
21 They will go into the caves of the rocks
and the crevices in the cliffs,
away from the terror of the LORD
and from his majestic splendor,*w*
when he rises to terrify the earth.
22 Put no more trust in a mere human,
who has only the breath
in his nostrils.*x*
What is he really worth?

JUDAH'S LEADERS JUDGED

3 Note this: The Lord GOD of Armies
is about to remove from Jerusalem
and from Judah
every kind of security:
the entire supply of bread and water,
2 heroes and warriors,*y*
judges and prophets,
fortune-tellers and elders,
3 commanders of fifty and dignitaries,
counselors, cunning magicians,^E
and necromancers.^F
4 "I will make youths their leaders,*z*
and unstable rulers^G will govern them."
5 The people will oppress one another,*aa*
man against man, neighbor
against neighbor;
the young will act arrogantly
toward the old,
and the worthless
toward the honorable.

---

^A **2:6** Or *They teem*, or *They partner*; Hb obscure　　^B **2:7** Lit *Its*　　^C **2:7** = the house of Jacob　　^D **2:11** Lit *Mankind's proud eyes*　　^E **3:3** Or *skilled craftsmen*
^F **3:3** Or *mediums*　　^G **3:4** Or *mischief-makers*

2:7-8 Judah likely concluded its own wealth with **no limit** (2:7) was the fruit of worshiping **idols** (2:8).

2:10-21 The Old Testament prophets wrote not just of things relatively near but also of things further away. It is doubtful that Isaiah even knew he was writing about the last days when Israel's Messiah would return in glory (see Rev 6:15-17). He probably did not see the

long valley between the two mountain peaks of Judah's judgment and the judgments of the tribulation. He just faithfully recorded what the Holy Spirit inspired him to write.

3:1-3 That pagan occultists, whose penalty under the law was death, were included in this list of leaders and counselors trusted by Judah gives a clear picture of how depraved God's people had become.

3:4-7 In other words, Judah would be led by those wholly inadequate to lead. Unfortunately, we see this happening too often in our own times as leaders who know nothing of true leadership rise to power. Governments and school systems alone can't develop wise leaders when homes are lacking God's leadership. We need to teach and live God's Word within our own walls if we want to see godly

6 A man will even seize his brother
   in his father's house, saying:
   "You have a cloak — you be
      our leader!
   This heap of rubble will be
      under your control."
7 On that day he will cry out, saying:
   "I'm not a healer.
   I don't even have food or clothing
      in my house.
   Don't make me the leader
      of the people!"
8 For Jerusalem has stumbled
   and Judah has fallen
   because they have spoken and acted
      against the Lord,[a]
   defying his glorious presence.[b]
9 The look on their faces testifies
      against them,
   and like Sodom,[c] they flaunt their sin;
   they do not conceal it.
   Woe to them,
   for they have brought disaster
      on themselves.[d]
10 Tell the righteous that it will go well
      for them,
   for they will eat the fruit of their labor.
11 Woe to the wicked — it will go badly
      for them,
   for what they have done will be done
      to them.
12 Youths oppress my people,[e]
   and women rule over them.
   My people, your leaders mislead you;
   they confuse the direction
      of your paths.[f]

13 The Lord rises to argue the case
   and stands to judge the people.[g]
14 The Lord brings this charge
   against the elders and leaders
      of his people:[h]
   "You have devastated the vineyard.
   The plunder from the poor is
      in your houses.[i]
15 Why do you crush my people
   and grind the faces of the poor?"

This is the declaration
   of the Lord God of Armies.

JERUSALEM'S WOMEN JUDGED

16 The Lord also says:
   Because the daughters of Zion
      are haughty,[j]
   walking with heads held high
   and seductive eyes,
   prancing along,
   jingling their ankle bracelets,
17   the Lord will put scabs on the heads
   of the daughters of Zion,
   and the Lord will shave
      their foreheads bare.

18 On that day[k] the Lord will strip their finery: ankle bracelets, headbands, crescents,[l] **19** pendants, bracelets, veils, **20** headdresses, ankle jewelry, sashes, perfume bottles, amulets,[m] **21** signet rings, nose rings,[n] **22** festive robes, capes, cloaks, purses, **23** garments, linen clothes, turbans, and shawls.
24   Instead of perfume there will be
      a stench;
   instead of a belt, a rope;
   instead of
      beautifully styled hair,[o] baldness;[p]
   instead of fine clothes, sackcloth;[q]
   instead of beauty, branding.[A]
25   Your men will fall by the sword,
   your warriors in battle.
26   Then her gates[r] will lament
      and mourn;
   deserted, she will sit on the ground.[s]
4 On that day seven women
   will seize one man,[t] saying,
   "We will eat our own bread
   and provide our own clothing.
   Just let us bear your name.
   Take away our disgrace."[u]

ZION'S FUTURE GLORY

2 On that day the Branch[B] of the Lord will be beautiful and glorious,[v] and the fruit of the land[w] will be the pride and glory[x] of Israel's survivors.[y] **3** Whoever remains in

[a] 3:8 Ps 73:9-11
[b] Nm 14:22-23; Is 43:7; 48:11; 59:19
[c] 3:9 Is 1:9-10; 13:19
[d] Rm 6:23
[e] 3:12 Is 3:4
[f] Is 28:14-22
[g] 3:13 Ps 7:6; Hs 4:1
[h] 3:14 Mc 3:1-3
[i] Ezk 18:10-18; 33:15

[j] 3:16 Is 32:9-15; 1Pt 3:3-4
[k] 3:18 Is 27:12
[l] Jdg 8:21,26
[m] 3:20 Ezk 24:17
[n] 3:21 Gn 24:47; Ezk 16:12
[o] 3:24 1Pt 3:3
[p] Is 15:2; 22:12; Ezk 27:31; Am 8:10; Mc 1:16
[q] Gn 37:34; Is 15:3; Jr 48:36-38; Lm 2:10
[r] 3:26 Jr 14:2; Lm 1:4
[s] Jb 2:13; Is 47:1; Lm 2:10
[t] 4:1 Is 3:25
[u] Gn 19:31-32; 30:23; Neh 1:3; Is 54:4; Lk 1:25
[v] 4:2 2Sm 23:4-5; Ps 132:17; Jr 23:5; 33:15; Zch 3:8; 6:12
[w] Ps 72:16; Is 27:6
[x] Is 3:18
[y] Gn 45:7; Jdg 21:17; 2Kg 19:30-31; Is 10:20; 37:31-32; Jl 2:32; Ob 17

[A] 3:24 DSS read *shame*   [B] 4:2 Or *plant*

---

leadership at the helm of our neighborhoods, schools, and government.
3:9 Judah paraded its sin **like Sodom**, whose men flaunted their homosexuality in God's face (see Gen 19). As a result, God's people **brought disaster on themselves.**
3:10 Don't miss the promise of rescue and blessing for **the righteous** amid this chaos.
3:16–4:1 The **daughters of Zion**, elaborately adorned with all manner of jewelry, obviously benefited from the ill-gotten wealth alluded to in 3:14-15 (3:16, 18-23). In response

to their arrogant displays of finery, the Lord decreed, **Instead of perfume there will be a stench . . . instead of beautifully styled hair, baldness; instead of fine clothes, sackcloth; instead of beauty, branding** (3:24). As Judah's men would fall in battle, slaughtered by the Babylonian invasion, Judah's surviving women—the ones not taken away as captives—would go to desperate lengths to try and ease their **disgrace** (4:1).
4:2-6 While Isaiah may have only understood this section as speaking of the nation's

future return from captivity in Babylon, the term **Branch of the Lord** (4:2) is a reference to Christ as the righteous descendant of King David (see 11:1). This will be ultimately fulfilled at Christ's return to reign as the true King of Israel. And just as God's glory was visible to Israel during the exodus, so the visible **glory** of God will be seen over **Mount Zion** (4:5). Despite severe judgment of Judah, God would preserve, restore, and rebuild a remnant of his people according to his promises.

a 4:3 Is 28:5; Rm 11:4-5
b Is 52:1; 62:12
c Ex 32:32; Ps 69:28; 87:6; 139:16; Is 49:16; Ezk 13:9; Mal 3:16; Lk 10:20; Ac 13:48
d 4:4 2Ch 4:6; Ezk 40:38; Zch 13:1
e Is 1:15; 3:13-15
f Is 28:6
g Is 1:31; 9:19; 33:14; Mal 3:2; Mt 3:11; Lk 3:17
h 4:5 Gn 1:1; Is 40:26,28; 41:20; 43:1,7,15; 45:7-8; 65:17-18
i Ex 13:21-22; 14:20; 40:34; Nm 9:15-23
j 4:6 Ps 27:5; Is 25:4; 32:1-2
k 5:1 Ps 80:8; Jr 12:10; Mt 21:33; Lk 20:9
l 5:2 Jr 2:21
m Is 40:31
n Mt 21:19; Mk 11:13; Lk 13:6
o 5:4 Mc 6:3-4; Mt 23:37
p 5:5 Ps 89:40; Jr 5:10
q Ps 80:12

r 5:6 2Ch 36:19-21; Is 7:19-25; 24:1,3; 27:2-6; Jr 25:11
s Gn 3:18; Is 7:23-25; 9:18; 10:17; 27:4; 32:13
t 5:7 Ps 80:8-11
u 5:8 Jr 22:13-17; Mc 2:2; Hab 2:9-12
v 5:9 Am 3:10,15
w 5:11 Lv 10:9; Nm 6:3; Dt 29:6; Jdg 13:4; Is 5:22; 24:9; 28:7; 56:12
x 5:12 Dt 32:4; Jb 34:27; 36:24; Ps 28:5; 44:1; 64:9-10
y Ex 32:16; 34:10; Ps 8:3,6; 19:1; 92:4-5; Is 10:12; 29:23
z 5:13 Is 1:3; 27:11; Hs 4:6; Lk 11:52; 19:42; 1Tm 1:13

Zion and whoever is left in Jerusalem[a] will be called holy[b] — all in Jerusalem written in the book of life[A,c] — [4] when the Lord has washed away the filth[d] of the daughters of Zion and cleansed the bloodguilt[e] from the heart of Jerusalem by a spirit of judgment[f] and a spirit of burning.[g] [5] Then the LORD will create[h] a cloud of smoke by day[i] and a glowing flame of fire by night over the entire site of Mount Zion and over its assemblies. For there will be a canopy over all the glory,[B] [6] and there will be a shelter for shade from heat by day, and a refuge and shelter from storm and rain.[j]

SONG OF THE VINEYARD

5 I will sing about the one I love,
  a song about my loved one's vineyard:[k]
The one I love had a vineyard
  on a very fertile hill.
[2] He broke up the soil, cleared it
    of stones,
and planted it with the finest vines.[l]
He built a tower in the middle of it
and even dug out a winepress there.
He expected[m] it to yield
    good grapes,
but it yielded
    worthless grapes.[n]

[3] So now, residents of Jerusalem
and men of Judah,
please judge between me
and my vineyard.
[4] What more could I have done
  for my vineyard
than I did?[o]
Why, when I expected a yield
  of good grapes,
did it yield worthless grapes?
[5] Now I will tell you
what I am about to do
  to my vineyard:
I will remove its hedge,[p]
and it will be consumed;
I will tear down its wall,[q]
and it will be trampled.

[6] I will make it a wasteland.[r]
It will not be pruned or weeded;
thorns and briers will grow up.[s]
I will also give orders to the clouds
that rain should not fall on it.
[7] For the vineyard of the LORD
  of Armies
is the house of Israel,[t]
and the men[C] of Judah,
the plant he delighted in.
He expected justice
but saw injustice;
he expected righteousness,
but heard cries of despair.

JUDAH'S SINS DENOUNCED

[8] Woe to those who add house
  to house[u]
and join field to field
until there is no more room
and you alone are left in the land.

[9] I heard the LORD of Armies say:
Indeed, many houses[v]
  will become desolate,
grand and lovely ones
  without inhabitants.
[10] For a ten-acre[D] vineyard will yield
only six gallons of wine,[E]
and ten bushels[F] of seed will yield
only one bushel of grain.[G]

[11] Woe to those who rise early
  in the morning
in pursuit of beer,[w]
who linger into the evening,
inflamed by wine.
[12] At their feasts they have lyre, harp,
tambourine, flute, and wine.
They do not perceive
  the LORD's actions,[x]
and they do not see the work
  of his hands.[y]

[13] Therefore my people will go into exile
because they lack knowledge;[z]
her[H] dignitaries are starving,

A 4:3 Lit Jerusalem recorded for life   B 4:5 Or For glory will be a canopy over all   C 5:7 Lit man   D 5:10 Lit ten-yoke   E 5:10 Lit one bath
F 5:10 Lit one homer   G 5:10 Lit yield an ephah   H 5:13 Lit its

---

5:1-7 Jesus would allude to this metaphor (see Matt 21:33-46). In his retelling of the story of the vineyard owner, not only would his servants reject him but they would also kill his son.

5:8-23 Woe to Judah, God said in response to his complete disappointment in his people (5:8). There are two meanings for this terminology in Scripture. One is that of sorrow for what has happened to the unfortunate; the second is a warning of coming disaster. This

woe is of the latter variety; it's followed by five more pronouncements of woe for various sins (5:11, 18, 20-22).

In the midst of these denunciations God made a declaration relevant to our day: **My people will go into exile because they lack knowledge** (5:13). One major reason the people of Judah would be judged and sent into exile, then, was that they didn't know—and hadn't bothered to learn—God's views on life. They simply ignored his Word. God wanted

his entire people to be a light of his knowledge and a reflection of his glory, teaching their neighbors his truth. But instead of influencing the world around them, they had become imitators of the world.

Today the church should be the primary university for the culture. It should be leading the way in educating the masses since it can interject a God-centered perspective, his kingdom agenda, into any discussion. Everything the Bible speaks about, it speaks

and her masses are parched
   with thirst.
14 Therefore Sheol enlarges its throat
and opens wide its enormous jaws,[a]
and down go Zion's dignitaries,
   her masses,
her crowds, and those who celebrate
   in her!
15 Humanity is brought low, each
   person is humbled,
and haughty eyes are humbled.[b]
16 But the LORD of Armies is exalted
   by his justice,[c]
and the holy God[d] shows that he is
   holy through his righteousness.[e]
17 Lambs will graze
as if in[A] their own pastures,[f]
and resident aliens[B] will eat
among the ruins of the rich.

18 Woe to those who drag iniquity
with cords of deceit[g]
and pull sin along with cart ropes,
19 to those who say:
"Let him hurry up and do
   his work quickly
so that we can see it!
Let the plan[h] of the Holy One
   of Israel[i] take place
so that we can know it!"
20 Woe to those who call evil good
and good evil,[j]
who substitute darkness for light
and light for darkness,
who substitute bitter for sweet
and sweet for bitter.
21 Woe to those
   who consider themselves wise
and judge themselves clever.[C,k]
22 Woe to those who are heroes
   at drinking wine,
who are champions at pouring beer,[l]
23 who acquit the guilty for a bribe[m]
and deprive the innocent of justice.

24 Therefore, as a tongue of fire
   consumes straw
and as dry grass shrivels in the flame,
so their roots will become
   like something rotten

and their blossoms will blow away
   like dust,
for they have rejected[n]
the instruction of the LORD of Armies,
and they have despised
the word of the Holy One of Israel.[o]
25 Therefore the LORD's anger burned[p]
   against his people.
He raised his hand against them
   and struck them;
the mountains quaked,[q]
and their corpses were like garbage
   in the streets.
In all this, his anger has
   not turned away,
and his hand is still raised to strike.[r]

26 He raises a signal flag
   for the distant nations[s]
and whistles[t] for them
   from the ends of the earth.
Look — how quickly and swiftly
   they come!
27 None of them grows weary
   or stumbles;[u]
no one slumbers or sleeps.
No belt is loose
and no sandal strap broken.
28 Their arrows are sharpened,
and all their bows strung.
Their horses' hooves are like flint;
their chariot wheels are
   like a whirlwind.
29 Their roaring is like a lion's;[v]
they roar like young lions;[w]
they growl and seize their prey
and carry it off,
and no one can rescue it.
30 On that day they will roar over it,
like the roaring of the sea.
When one looks at the land,
there will be darkness and distress;
light will be obscured by clouds.[D]

ISAIAH'S CALL AND MISSION

6 In the year that King Uzziah[x] died, I saw the Lord[y] seated on a high and lofty[z] throne,[aa] and the hem of his robe filled the temple. **2** Seraphim[E] were standing above him; they each had six wings:[ab] with two

[a]5:14 Pr 30:16; Hab 2:5
[b]5:15 Is 2:9,11,17; 10:33
[c]5:16 Is 33:5,10
[d]Is 6:3
[e]Is 8:13; 29:23; 1Pt 3:15
[f]5:17 Mc 2:12
[g]5:18 Pr 5:22; Is 59:4-8; Jr 23:10-14
[h]5:19 Jb 38:2; 42:3; Ps 33:11; 106:13; 107:11; Pr 19:21; Is 14:26; 19:17; 46:10-11
[i]Is 1:4
[j]5:20 Pr 17:15; Am 5:7; Mal 2:17
[k]5:21 Pr 3:7; Rm 12:16; 1Co 3:18
[l]5:22 Is 5:11
[m]5:23 Ex 23:8; Pr 17:15; Is 1:23; 33:15

[n]5:24 Is 8:6; 30:9,12; Am 2:4; Ac 13:41
[o]Is 5:19; Jr 51:5
[p]5:25 Nm 11:10,33; 32:10-13; Dt 6:15; Jos 7:1; 23:16; 2Kg 13:3; Ps 106:40
[q]Am 1:1; Zch 14:5
[r]Is 9:12,17,21; 10:4; 14:27
[s]5:26 Is 10:5; 11:10,12; 13:2; 18:3
[t]Is 7:18; Zch 10:8
[u]5:27 1Jn 2:10
[v]5:29 Jdg 14:5; Hs 13:8; Jl 1:6; Nah 2:12-13
[w]Rv 9:17
[x]6:1 2Kg 15:1-7; Is 1:1; 14:28
[y]Gn 32:30; Ex 3:1-6; 24:9-10; Jos 5:13-15; 1Kg 22:19; Is 31:3; Jn 1:18; 4:24; 12:41
[z]Is 52:13; 57:15
[aa]Ps 9:7; 11:4; 45:6; Is 66:1; Jr 3:17; Ezk 1:26; 10:1; 43:7
[ab]6:2 Rv 4:8

[A]5:17 Syr reads graze in   [B]5:17 LXX reads sheep   [C]5:21 Lit and clever before their face   [D]5:30 Lit its clouds   [E]6:2 = heavenly beings

about authoritatively. And it speaks to every issue of life. So through all of the church's ministries, people ought to be encountering a God-centered worldview.
6:1 Though he certainly wasn't perfect (see 2 Chr 26:16-21), **Uzziah** had been a good king who had brought Judah a long way back toward God (see 2 Chr 26:3-5). Through

this human king's sad passing, Isaiah was reminded that *the* King was still alive and well.
   Sometimes it takes a tragedy in our lives, or other negative circumstances, for us to truly see God. We may know him as our Savior but not be growing in a day-by-day experience of adopting his perspective of the world and

living in obedience to it. Difficult situations help to shift our focus off the created things and onto the Creator. God is not merely interested in getting us to heaven. He wants us to see and experience him here.
6:2 The **seraphim** who were calling out eternal praise had **six wings**: four were for worship, and two were for working. To me, this indicates

a 6:2 Ezk 1:14
b 6:3 Ex 16:10; 24:16-17; 40:34-35; 1Kg 8:11; Is 35:2; 40:5; 60:1; Ezk 1:28; Lk 9:32
c Nm 14:21; Ps 72:19
d 6:4 Ex 19:8; Hab 3:3-10; Rv 15:8
e 6:5 Ex 33:20; Jdg 13:22; Is 59:3; Jr 9:3-8; Lk 5:8
f Ex 6:12,30
g 6:6 Lv 6:12-13; 17:11
h 6:7 Jr 1:9; Dn 10:16
i Ex 21:30; 30:12-16
j 6:9-10 Mt 13:14-15; Mk 4:12; Lk 8:10; Jn 12:40; Ac 28:26-27
k 6:10 Zch 7:11-12; 1Th 2:16

l 6:11 Ps 79:5; 89:46
m Is 1:7; 27:10
n 6:13 Is 41:8; 43:5; 45:25; 53:10; 59:21; 65:9,23; 66:22
o Is 11:1
p 7:1 Is 1:1
q 2Kg 15:25,37; 16:5
r 7:2 Is 7:13; 9:7; 16:5; 22:9,22; 29:1; 37:35; 38:5; 55:3
s Is 8:12; 9:9
t 7:3 Is 8:3,18
u 2Kg 18:17; Is 36:2
v 7:4 Gn 15:1; Ex 14:13; 20:20; Nm 14:9; Dt 20:3; 31:6; Jos 10:8,25; Is 10:24; 35:4; 41:14
w 7:7 Is 8:10

they covered their faces, with two they covered their feet, and with two they flew.*a* **3** And one called to another:

Holy, holy, holy is the LORD
of Armies;
his glory*b* fills the whole earth.*c*

4 The foundations of the doorways shook*d* at the sound of their voices, and the temple was filled with smoke.

5 Then I said:

Woe is me*e* for I am ruined[A]
because I am a man of unclean lips
and live among a people
of unclean lips,*f*
and because my eyes have seen
the King,
the LORD of Armies.

6 Then one of the seraphim flew to me, and in his hand was a glowing coal that he had taken from the altar*g* with tongs. **7** He touched my mouth*h* with it and said:

Now that this has touched your lips,
your iniquity is removed
and your sin is atoned for.*i*

8 Then I heard the voice of the Lord asking:

Who should I send?
Who will go for us?

I said:

Here I am. Send me.

9 And he replied:

Go! Say to these people:
Keep listening,
but do not understand;*j*
keep looking, but do not perceive.

10 Make the minds[B] of these people dull;
deafen their ears and blind their eyes;
otherwise they might see
with their eyes
and hear with their ears,
understand with their minds,
turn back, and be healed.*k*

11 Then I said, "Until when, Lord?"*l* And he replied:

Until cities lie in ruins
without inhabitants,*m*
houses are without people,
the land is ruined and desolate,
12 and the LORD drives the people
far away,
leaving great emptiness in the land.
13 Though a tenth will remain in the land,
it will be burned again.
Like the terebinth or the oak
that leaves a stump when felled,
the holy seed*n* is the stump.*o*

THE MESSAGE TO AHAZ

7 This took place during the reign of Ahaz, son of Jotham, son of Uzziah king of Judah:*p* Aram's King Rezin and Israel's King Pekah son of Remaliah went to fight against Jerusalem,*q* but they were not able to conquer it.

2 When it became known to the house of David*r* that Aram had occupied Ephraim,[C] the heart of Ahaz*c* and the hearts of his people trembled like trees of a forest shaking in the wind.

3 The LORD said to Isaiah, "Go out with your son Shear-jashub[D,t] to meet Ahaz at the end of the conduit of the upper pool,*u* by the road to the Launderer's Field. **4** Say to him: Calm down and be quiet. Don't be afraid or cowardly*v* because of these two smoldering sticks, the fierce anger of Rezin and Aram, and the son of Remaliah. **5** For Aram, along with Ephraim and the son of Remaliah, has plotted harm against you. They say, **6** 'Let us go up against Judah, terrorize it, and conquer it for ourselves. Then we can install Tabeel's son as king in it.'"

7 This is what the Lord GOD says:

It will not happen; it will not occur.*w*
8 The[E] chief city of Aram is Damascus,
the chief of Damascus is Rezin
(within sixty-five years

[A] 6:5 Or *I must be silent*   [B] 6:10 Lit *heart*   [C] 7:2 Lit *Aram has rested upon Ephraim, his heart*   [D] 7:3 = A Remnant Will Return   [E] 7:8 Lit *For the*

---

that when we prioritize worship over working, our work will be more fruitful.
6:3 The angelic beings who called out these words weren't stuttering; the triple repetition was for emphasis. God is perfect, pure, and righteous. God's holiness, his separateness, is the centerpiece of his character. All of his other attributes flow from it. His wrath against sin, then, is a *holy* wrath. His sovereignty over the universe is a *holy* sovereignty. His love for the world is a *holy* love. If God is anything, he is holy.
6:4 That **the temple was filled with smoke** is a reference to the glory of God.

6:5 The word **ruined** means "coming undone," so Isaiah felt like he was falling apart before a holy God. Despite being a significant prophet dedicated to the service of God, Isaiah fully felt his own inadequacy.
6:11-12 Isaiah wanted to know how long he would have to speak to a spiritually dead nation. Unfortunately, he learned, their defiant state would continue until Judah was destroyed. Isaiah would prophesy to Judah the rest of his life, perishing before the Babylonian captivity.
7:1-2 While the northern kingdom of Israel was still intact, as it was during the early years of

Isaiah's prophecy, the king of Israel and **King Rezin** of Aram (that is, Syria) allied themselves to wage war against Judah, which caused the hearts of Judah's people to tremble in fear. Notice that Isaiah referred to the kingdom of Judah as **the house of David** (7:2). This was a way of telling Isaiah's readers that God had not forgotten or abandoned his promise that a ruler would come from David's line to fulfill all his promises to his people (see 2 Sam 7:1-17).
7:7-8 Not only would the plot against Judah fail, but scheming Israel—here referred to as **Ephraim** (one of the leading tribes there)— would also soon be devastated.

Ephraim will be too shattered to be a people),

9 the chief city of Ephraim is Samaria, and the chief of Samaria is the son of Remaliah. If you do not stand firm in your faith, then you will not stand at all.

THE IMMANUEL PROPHECY

10 Then the LORD spoke again to Ahaz: **11** "Ask for a sign[a] from the LORD your God — it can be as deep as Sheol or as high as heaven." **12** But Ahaz replied, "I will not ask. I will not test the LORD." **13** Isaiah[b] said, "Listen, house of David! Is it not enough for you to try the patience of men? Will you also try the patience of my God?[c] **14** Therefore, the Lord himself will give you[A] a sign: See, the virgin will conceive,[B] have a son, and name him Immanuel.[C,d] **15** By the time he learns to reject what is bad and choose what is good,[e] he will be eating curds[D] and honey.[f] **16** For before the boy knows to reject what is bad and choose what is good, the land of the two kings you dread will be abandoned. **17** The LORD will bring on you, your people, and your father's house such a time as has never been since Ephraim separated from Judah:[g] He will bring the king of Assyria."[h]

18 On that day[i]
the LORD will whistle[j] to flies
at the farthest streams of the Nile
and to bees in the land of Assyria.
19 All of them will come and settle
in the steep ravines, in the clefts
of the rocks,[k]

in all the thornbushes, and in all the water holes.

20 On that day the Lord will use a razor[l] hired from beyond the Euphrates River — the king of Assyria[m] — to shave the hair on your heads, the hair on your legs, and even your beards.

21 On that day
a man will raise a young cow
and two sheep,
22 and from the abundant milk they give
he will eat curds,
for every survivor in the land
will eat curds and honey.[n]

23 And on that day
every place where there were a
thousand vines,
worth a thousand pieces of silver,
will become thorns and briers.[o]
24 A man will go there with bow
and arrows
because the whole land
will be thorns and briers.
25 You will not go to all the hills
that were once tilled with a hoe,
for fear of the thorns and briers.
Those hills will be places for oxen
to graze
and for sheep to trample.

THE COMING ASSYRIAN INVASION

8 Then the LORD said to me, "Take a large piece of parchment[E] and write on it with an ordinary pen:[F,p] Maher-shalal-hash-baz.[G] **2** I have appointed[H] trustworthy

[a] 7:11 2Kg 19:29; Is 37:30; 38:7-8; 55:13
[b] 7:13 Mt 3:3; 12:17
[c] Is 1:14; 43:24; Jr 15:6; 20:9; Mal 2:17
[d] 7:14 Is 8:8,10; Mt 1:23; Lk 1:31
[e] 7:15 Dt 1:39
[f] Ex 3:8; 2Sm 17:29; Is 7:22; 8:15
[g] 7:17 1Kg 12:16
[h] 2Ch 28:20; Is 8:7-8; 10:5-6
[i] 7:18 Is 27:12
[j] Is 5:25
[k] 7:19 Is 2:19; Jr 16:16

[l] 7:20 2Kg 18:13-16; Is 24:1; Ezk 5:1-4
[m] Is 8:7; 11:15; Jr 2:18
[n] 7:22 Is 8:15
[o] 7:23 Is 5:6
[p] 8:1 Is 30:8; Hab 2:2

[A] 7:14 In Hb, the word *you* is pl [B] 7:14 Or *virgin is pregnant, will* [C] 7:14 = God With Us [D] 7:15 Or *sour milk* [E] 8:1 Hb obscure [F] 8:1 Lit *with the pen of a man* [G] 8:1 = Speeding to the Plunder, Hurrying to the Spoil [H] 8:2 Vg; MT, one DSS ms read *I will appoint*; one DSS ms, LXX, Syr, Tg read *Appoint*

7:12-13 Isaiah's angry reaction (7:13) shows that Ahaz's refusal to request a sign validating the prophecy (7:12) was said in mock piety and was the result of his unbelief. Such lack of faith in God would be Ahaz's downfall. After all, "If you do not stand firm in your faith, then you will not stand at all" (7:9). Those are words we all need to hear.

7:14-19 *Immanuel* means "God with us" (7:14). While Isaiah's words would have ultimate fulfillment in Jesus Christ as the Gospel of Matthew makes clear (see Matt 1:22-23), they had a more immediate application too.

The birth prophesied was to be **a sign** to King Ahaz specifically (Isa 7:14), but its lifetime unfolded hundreds of years before the birth of Christ. Thus the child, who was to be a sign that Judah would not be conquered by the Israel-Aram alliance, was most likely the son soon to be born to Isaiah and "the prophetess" (8:3). This son would have the God-given name *Maher-shalal-hash-baz*, which means "Speeding to the

Plunder, Hurrying to the Spoil" (8:1). This child was the sign to Ahaz personally because, **before the boy [knew] to reject what is bad and choose what is good, the land of the two kings** whom Ahaz dreaded would **be abandoned** (7:16). And indeed, this happened about three years later when Aram was crushed by the Assyrians (7:17-19). The name *Immanuel*, when applied to Isaiah's son, indicated that God had not abandoned his promises to the house of David.

"The prophetess," Isaiah's wife, may well have been a virgin when Isaiah made this prophecy to Ahaz. If so, the meaning for the immediate context of 7:14 would then be, "An unmarried young woman who is a virgin now will get married and bear a son"—which was fulfilled when Isaiah married her and she gave birth.

7:20-25 The good news of Judah's escape from conquest by Israel and Aram was tempered by the bad news of God's judgment on Ahaz and Judah's unfaithful people. The prophecy that Isaiah's son would be eating "curds and honey"

(see 7:15) was not encouraging, since these were foods of nomadic people—indicating that Judah would be desolated (see 7:21-25). The king of Assyria, Tiglath-pileser III, got Aram off Judah's back. But then he invaded Judah and exacted a heavy tribute. God called him **a razor hired from beyond the Euphrates River** who would **shave** all the hair off of Judah (7:20). Such was the ultimate humiliation for a Jewish man in that day.

Why was God so angry with Ahaz and Judah? In 2 Kings 16:7-14, we learn that Ahaz begged Tiglath-pileser III to save him from Aram and Israel, and he gave him silver and gold from the Lord's temple as incentive. Not only this, but Ahaz also liked Tiglath-pileser's pagan altar so much that he had one made just like it in Jerusalem!

8:1-10 As happened often in the prophets' writings, assurance was given in the midst of God's pronouncements of judgment. Chapter 8 begins with the prophecy of Judah's

a 8:2 2Kg 16:10-11,15-16
b 8:4 Is 7:16
c Is 7:8-9
d 8:6 Is 7:1
e 8:8 Is 30:28
f Is 7:14; 8:10
g 8:10 Is 14:27
h Is 8:8
i 8:11 Ezk 2:8
j 8:12 Is 7:2; 30:1
k 1Pt 3:14

l 8:13 Nm 20:12
m 1Pt 3:15
n 8:14 Is 4:6; 25:4; Ezk 11:16
o Ps 91:12; Is 26:4
p Lk 2:34; Rm 9:33; 1Pt 2:8
q 8:15 Is 28:13; 59:10; Lk 20:18; Rm 9:32
r 8:16 Is 8:1-2; 29:11-12
s Dn 12:4
t 8:17 Ps 27:14; 33:20; 37:34; 130:5-6; Is 25:9; 30:18; Lm 3:26; Hab 2:3; 1Co 1:7; Php 3:20
u Dt 31:17; Is 1:15; 45:15; 54:8
v 8:18 Heb 2:13
w 8:19 Lv 20:6; 2Kg 21:6; 23:24; Is 19:3; 29:4; 47:12-13
x 1Sm 28:8-11
y 8:20 Is 1:10; Lk 16:29
z 8:22 Is 5:30; 59:9; Jr 13:16; Am 5:18,20; Zph 1:14-15
aa 9:1 Mt 4:15

witnesses — the priest Uriah and Zechariah son of Jeberechiah."[a]

[3] I was then intimate with the prophetess, and she conceived and gave birth to a son. The LORD said to me, "Name him Mahershalal-hash-baz, [4] for before the boy knows how to call 'Father,' or 'Mother,'[b] the wealth of Damascus and the spoils of Samaria will be carried off to the king of Assyria."[c]

[5] The LORD spoke to me again:
[6] Because these people rejected
    the slowly flowing water of Shiloah
    and rejoiced with[A] Rezin
    and the son of Remaliah,[d]
[7] the Lord will certainly bring
    against them
    the mighty rushing water
    of the Euphrates River —
    the king of Assyria and all his glory.
    It will overflow its channels
    and spill over all its banks.
[8] It will pour into Judah,
    flood over it, and sweep through,
    reaching up to the neck;[e]
    and its flooded banks[B]
    will fill your entire land, Immanuel![f]

[9] Band together,[c] peoples,
    and be broken;
    pay attention, all you distant lands;
    prepare for war, and be broken;
    prepare for war, and be broken.
[10] Devise a plan; it will fail.[g]
    Make a prediction;
    it will not happen.
    For God is with us.[D,h]

THE LORD OF ARMIES, THE ONLY REFUGE

[11] For this is what the LORD said to me with great power, to keep[E] me from going the way of this people:[i]
[12] Do not call everything a conspiracy
    these people say is a conspiracy.[j]
    Do not fear what they fear;[k]
    do not be terrified.

[13] You are to regard only the LORD
    of Armies as holy.[l]
    Only he should be feared;[m]
    only he should be held in awe.
[14] He will be a sanctuary;[n]
    but for the two houses of Israel,
    he will be a stone[o] to stumble over
    and a rock to trip over,[p]
    and a trap and a snare
    to the inhabitants of Jerusalem.
[15] Many will stumble over these;[q]
    they will fall and be broken;
    they will be snared and captured.

[16] Bind up the testimony.[r]
    Seal up the instruction[s]
    among my disciples.
[17] I will wait for the LORD,[t]
    who is hiding his face
    from the house of Jacob.[u]
    I will wait for him.

[18] Here I am with the children the LORD has given me[v] to be signs and wonders in Israel from the LORD of Armies who dwells on Mount Zion. [19] When they say to you, "Inquire of the mediums and the spiritists who chirp and mutter,"[w] shouldn't a people inquire of their God?[r] Should they inquire of the dead on behalf of the living?[x] [20] Go to God's instruction and testimony![y] If they do not speak according to this word, there will be no dawn for them.

[21] They will wander through the land, dejected and hungry. When they are famished, they will become enraged, and, looking upward, will curse their king and their God. [22] They will look toward the earth[z] and see only distress, darkness, and the gloom of affliction, and they will be driven into thick darkness.

BIRTH OF THE PRINCE OF PEACE

9 Nevertheless, the gloom of the distressed land will not be like that of the former times when he humbled the land of Zebulun and the land of Naphtali. [aa] But in

---

A 8:6 Or *and rejoiced over*   B 8:8 Lit *its outspread wings*   C 8:9 Or *Raise the war cry,* or *Be shattered*   D 8:10 Hb *Immanuel*   E 8:11 DSS; MT reads *instruct*   F 8:19 Or *gods*

8:1-4 deliverance from Israel and Aram (8:1-4; see the note on 7:14-19). But because this mercy from God did not lead Judah to repentance, the same Assyrian army would pour into Judah like **mighty rushing water** (8:7), reaching up to the nation's **neck** (8:8). In other words, God's people would almost, but not quite, drown because of their sin. Yet Isaiah used the name **Immanuel**, and its meaning, **God is with us** (8:8, 10; see the note on 7:14)—offering reminders that God would not completely abandon his people.

8:14 Paul and Peter apply this text to Jesus Christ (see Rom 9:33; 1 Pet 2:8). The Son of God shares the same divine nature as the Father, so the New Testament writers often read passages of Scripture that originally referred to God and apply them to God the Son.

8:19 Nobody calls the morgue for help when they're in trouble. So why seek counsel from those who have died rather than from the living God?

9:1-2 The reference to **the land of Zebulun and . . . Naphtali** points to the northern kingdom of Israel. At this time, it was already a vassal state of Assyria and headed for destruction because of the people's sins. Yet God would one day **bring honor to** this land, for his Son would live and minister there (9:1). Indeed, there would come a day when **the people walking in darkness** would see **a great light** (9:2); the kingdom of heaven would come near (see Matt 4:15-17).

the future he will bring honor to the way
of the sea, to the land east of the Jordan,
and to Galilee of the nations.

2 The people walking in darkness
have seen a great light;[a]
a light has dawned
on those living in the land
of darkness.[b]
3 You have enlarged the nation
and increased its joy.[A,c]
The people have rejoiced before you
as they rejoice at harvest time
and as they rejoice
when dividing spoils.[d]
4 For you have shattered
their oppressive yoke[e]
and the rod on their shoulders,
the staff of their oppressor,
just as you did on the day of Midian.[f]
5 For every trampling boot of battle
and the bloodied garments of war
will be burned as fuel for the fire.

⌁ HOPE WORDS ⌁

*Peace is not the absence of fear;
it is the presence of God.*

---

6 For a child will be born for us,
a son will be given to us,[g]
and the government will be
on his shoulders.[h]
He will be named
Wonderful Counselor,[i] Mighty God,[j]
Eternal Father,[k] Prince of Peace.[l]
7 The dominion will be vast,
and its prosperity will never end.[m]
He will reign on the throne of David
and over his kingdom,
to establish and sustain it
with justice and righteousness
from now on and forever.
The zeal of the LORD of Armies
will accomplish this.[n]

THE HAND RAISED AGAINST ISRAEL

8 The Lord sent a message
against Jacob;
it came against Israel.
9 All the people —
Ephraim and the inhabitants
of Samaria[o] — will know it.
They will say with pride
and arrogance:
10 "The bricks have fallen,
but we will rebuild with cut stones;
the sycamores have been cut down,
but we will replace them
with cedars."
11 The LORD has raised up
Rezin's adversaries against him
and stirred up his enemies.
12 Aram from the east and Philistia
from the west
have consumed Israel
with open mouths.
In all this, his anger
has not turned away,
and his hand is still raised to strike.[p]

13 The people did not turn to him
who struck them;
they did not seek the LORD
of Armies.
14 So the LORD cut off Israel's head
and tail,[q]
palm branch and reed
in a single day.
15 The head is the elder,
the honored one;[r]
the tail is the prophet,
the one teaching lies.[s]
16 The leaders of the people
mislead them,
and those they mislead
are swallowed up.[B]
17 Therefore the Lord does not rejoice
over[c] Israel's young men
and has no compassion
on its fatherless and widows,
for everyone is a godless evildoer,[t]

[a] 9:2 Mt 4:16; Eph 5:8
[b] Lk 1:79
[c] 9:3 Is 26:15
[d] 1Sm 30:16
[e] 9:4 Is 10:27; 14:25
[f] Jdg 7:25; Is 10:26
[g] 9:6 Is 7:14; 11:1-2; 53:2; Lk 2:11; Jn 3:16
[h] Is 22:22; Mt 28:18; 1Co 15:25
[i] Is 28:29
[j] Dt 10:17; Neh 9:32; Is 10:21
[k] Is 63:16; 64:8
[l] Is 26:3,12; 54:10; 66:12
[m] 9:7 Ps 89:4; Dn 2:44; Lk 1:32-33
[n] Is 37:32; 59:17

[o] 9:9 Ac 1:8
[p] 9:12 Is 5:25
[q] 9:14 Is 19:15
[r] 9:15 Is 3:2-3
[s] Is 28:15; 59:3-4; Jr 23:14,32; Mt 24:24
[t] 9:17 Is 1:4; 10:6; 14:20; 31:2; 32:6

[A] 9:3 Alt Hb tradition reads *have not increased joy*   [B] 9:16 Or *are confused*   [C] 9:17 DSS read *not spare*

9:6 Notice that Isaiah said **a child will be born for us, a son will be** *given* **to us** (emphasis added). This tells us that Jesus had to be *born* as a child to come to us, but he is also the preexistent Son of God who was *given* to us.

Here again we see the "near" and "far" aspects that frequently occur in Old Testament prophecy because Jesus was born two thousand years ago as a child, but **the government** of the universe has yet to be placed **on his shoulders**. This will happen

at his coronation as King of kings in the millennium.

9:7 Some have so spiritualized Christ's kingdom that its sociopolitical features have become little more than an ideology. Our kingdom activity today should be reflective of, and point to, the ultimate kingdom of Jesus Christ in which he will execute justice for the oppressed and rule righteously over his subjects.

9:8-17 Although Isaiah was primarily a prophet to the southern kingdom of Judah,

he also delivered God's message to **Jacob**— that is, to the people of Israel (9:8). They had arrogantly vowed to recover from the calamity that had fallen upon them and come out even stronger (9:9-10). But God had another plan—they'd be destroyed. That he would **cut off Israel's head and tail** means Israel's wicked leaders, the elders and the prophets who led the whole nation astray, would be punished (9:14-16).

[a] 9:18 Ps 83:14; Is 1:7; Nah 1:10; Mal 4:1
[b] 9:19 Is 1:31; 24:6
[c] Mc 7:2,6
[d] 9:20 Is 8:21-22
[e] Dt 28:53-57; Is 49:26
[f] 9:21 2Ch 28:6,8; Is 11:13
[g] Is 5:25
[h] 10:1 Is 5:8; 28:1; 29:1,15; 30:1; 31:1; 33:1; 45:9
[i] 10:2 Ps 35:10; Pr 22:22; Ec 5:8; Is 61:8; Jr 21:12; Ezk 18:12; 22:29
[j] Ex 22:22; Dt 24:17; 27:19; Ps 68:5; 94:6; Is 1:17,23; Jr 22:3; Ezk 22:7; Zch 7:10; Mal 3:5
[k] 10:4 Is 5:25; 9:12,17,21

[l] 10:6 2Kg 21:14; Jr 49:32; Ezk 7:21; 26:12; 29:19
[m] 2Sm 22:43; Ps 18:42; Ezk 26:11; Mc 7:10
[n] 10:9 Ac 1:8
[o] 10:11 2Kg 21:11; 23:24; 2Ch 15:8; 24:18
[p] 10:12 Jr 50:31
[q] 10:13 Jr 15:13; 17:3; 20:5
[r] 2Sm 22:48

and every mouth speaks folly.
In all this, his anger has not turned
   away,
and his hand is still raised to strike.

18 For wickedness burns like a fire[a]
that consumes thorns and briers
and kindles the forest thickets
so that they go up in a column
   of smoke.
19 The land is scorched
by the wrath of the Lord of Armies,
and the people are like fuel
   for the fire.[b]
No one has compassion
   on his brother.[c]
20 They carve meat on the right,
but they are still hungry;[d]
they have eaten on the left,
but they are still not satisfied.
Each one eats the flesh
   of his own arm.[e]
21 Manasseh is with Ephraim,
and Ephraim with Manasseh;
together, both are against Judah.[f]
In all this, his anger has not turned
   away,
and his hand is still raised to strike.[g]

10

Woe[h] to those enacting
   crooked statutes
and writing oppressive laws
2 to keep the poor from getting
   a fair trial
and to deprive the needy
   among my people of justice,[i]
so that widows can be their spoil
and they can plunder the fatherless.[j]
3 What will you do on the day
   of punishment
when devastation comes
   from far away?
Who will you run to for help?
Where will you leave your wealth?
4 There will be nothing to do
except crouch among the prisoners
or fall among the slain.
In all this, his anger has not turned
   away,
and his hand is still raised to strike.[k]

ASSYRIA, THE INSTRUMENT OF WRATH

5 Woe to Assyria, the rod
   of my anger —
the staff in their hands is my wrath.
6 I will send him against
   a godless nation;
I will command him to go
against a people destined
   for my rage,
to take spoils, to plunder,[l]
and to trample them down like clay[m]
   in the streets.
7 But this is not what he intends;
this is not what he plans.
It is his intent to destroy
and to cut off many nations.
8 For he says,
"Aren't all my commanders kings?
9 Isn't Calno like Carchemish?
Isn't Hamath like Arpad?
Isn't Samaria[n] like Damascus?[A]
10 As my hand seized
   the idolatrous kingdoms,
whose idols exceeded
   those of Jerusalem and Samaria,
11 and as I did to Samaria
   and its worthless images
will I not also do to Jerusalem
   and its idols?"[o]

JUDGMENT ON ASSYRIA

12 But when the Lord finishes all his work against Mount Zion and Jerusalem, he will say, "I[B] will punish the king of Assyria for his arrogant acts and the proud look in his eyes."[p] 13 For he said:

I have done this by my own strength
and wisdom, for I am clever.
I abolished the borders of nations
and plundered their treasures;[q]
like a mighty warrior, I subjugated
   the inhabitants.[C]
14 My hand has reached out, as if
   into a nest,
to seize the wealth of the nations.
Like one gathering abandoned eggs,
I gathered the whole earth.
No wing fluttered;
no beak opened or chirped.

[A] 10:9 Cities conquered by Assyria   [B] 10:12 LXX reads *Jerusalem, he*   [C] 10:13 Or *I brought down their kings*

10:1-2 God expects his people to lead the way in caring for the poor and advocating for the oppressed. James tells us "to look after orphans and widows" (Jas 1:27).
10:5-7 This is an example of the mysterious mingling of divine sovereignty and human responsibility that we often see in the Bible. The Assyrian king was a tool in God's righteous hands to chastise his people. But the king wasn't intentionally serving the Lord; he was serving himself. Perhaps the most famous example of this phenomenon is when Joseph told his brothers who had sold him into slavery, "You planned evil against me; God planned it for good to bring about the present result—the survival of many people" (Gen 50:20). Regardless of what wickedness humans have planned, God is always working behind the scenes to accomplish his purposes.
10:8-11 The Assyrians assumed that just as they had marched through and conquered other lands (including Israel), they could easily sweep on south and take **Jerusalem** (10:11). But Judah's day for defeat had not yet come.

15 Does an ax exalt itself
above the one who chops with it?
Does a saw magnify itself
above the one who saws with it?
It would be like a rod waving the one
who lifts^A it!
It would be like a staff lifting the one
who isn't wood!
16 Therefore the Lord GOD of Armies
will inflict an emaciating disease
on the well-fed of Assyria,
and he will kindle a burning fire
under its glory.
17 Israel's Light will become a fire,
and its Holy One, a flame.^a
In one day it will burn and consume
Assyria's thorns and thistles.^b
18 He will completely destroy
the glory of its forests and orchards
as a sickness consumes a person.
19 The remaining trees of its forest
will be so few in number
that a child could count them.

THE REMNANT WILL RETURN

20 On that day the remnant of Israel and
the survivors of the house of Jacob will
no longer depend on the one who struck
them, but they will faithfully depend on
the LORD, the Holy One of Israel.^c
21 The remnant will return,
the remnant of Jacob,
to the Mighty God.
22 Israel, even if your people were
as numerous
as the sand of the sea,
only a remnant of them will return.^d
Destruction has been decreed;
justice overflows.
23 For throughout the land
the Lord GOD of Armies
is carrying out a destruction
that was decreed.

24 Therefore, the Lord GOD of Armies
says this: "My people who dwell in Zion,
do not fear Assyria, though they strike you
with a rod and raise their staff over you as
the Egyptians did. 25 In just a little while
my wrath will be spent and my anger will
turn to their destruction." 26 And the LORD
of Armies will brandish a whip against
him as he did when he struck Midian at
the rock of Oreb;^e and he will raise his staff
over the sea as he did in Egypt.

GOD WILL JUDGE ASSYRIA

27 On that day
his burden will fall
from your shoulders,
and his yoke from your neck.
The yoke will be broken
because your neck will be too
large.^B,f
28 Assyria has come to Aiath
and has gone through Migron,
storing their equipment
at Michmash.
29 They crossed over
at the ford, saying,
"We will spend the night at Geba."
The people of Ramah are trembling;
those at Gibeah of Saul have fled.
30 Cry aloud, daughter of Gallim!
Listen, Laishah!
Anathoth is miserable.
31 Madmenah has fled.
The inhabitants of Gebim
have sought refuge.
32 Today the Assyrians will stand
at Nob,
shaking their fists at the mountain
of Daughter Zion,
the hill of Jerusalem.
33 Look, the Lord GOD of Armies
will chop off the branches
with terrifying power,
and the tall trees will be cut down,
the high trees felled.
34 He is clearing the thickets
of the forest with an ax,
and Lebanon with its majesty
will fall.

REIGN OF THE DAVIDIC KING

11 Then a shoot will grow
from the stump of Jesse,^g
and a branch^h from his roots
will bear fruit.
2 The Spirit of the LORD will rest
on him^i —
a Spirit of wisdom
and understanding,
a Spirit of counsel and strength,
a Spirit of knowledge and of the fear
of the LORD.

^a 10:17 Is 4:5; 5:24; 47:14
^b Gn 3:18; Is 5:6; 7:23-25;
9:18; 27:4; Hs 10:8
^c 10:20 Is 1:4
^d 10:22 2Kg 19:30,31; Ezr
9:8,15; Is 11:11,16; 28:5;
37:31,32; 46:3; Jr 23:3; 31:7;
Rm 9:27-28

^e 10:26 Jdg 7:25
^f 10:27 Gn 27:40; Dt 28:48;
Jr 28:10; 30:8; Lm 1:14
^g 11:1 Is 9:7; 11:10; Ac 13:23
^h Is 14:19; 60:21; Jr 23:5;
33:15; Dn 11:7; Zch 3:8;
6:12
^i 11:2 Is 42:1; 48:16; 61:1;
Mt 3:16; Jn 1:32

---

^A 10:15 Some Hb mss, Syr, Vg read *wave he who lifts*   ^B 10:27 Lit *because of fatness*; Hb obscure

---

10:20-22 Though the northern kingdom of Israel would fall as a result of the **destruction** that God had **decreed** (10:22), he would spare a **remnant**.

10:32-34 The Lord would level the pagan nation of Assyria as if he were **clearing** a **forest with an ax** (10:33-34). The bigger they are, the harder they fall.

11:1-2 Jesse was the father of King David, so God is proclaiming through Isaiah that he hasn't abandoned the Davidic dynasty (11:1). This is a reference to the promised Messiah.

a 11:3 Jn 2:25; 7:24
b 11:4 Ps 72:2,13-14; Is 3:14
c Ps 2:9; Is 49:2; Mal 4:6;
   Rv 1:16; 19:15
d Gn 18:25; Ps 139:19; Ezk
3:18-19; 18:20-24; 33:8-15
e Jb 4:9; Is 30:28,33;
   2Th 2:8
f 11:5 Eph 6:14
g Eph 6:14
h 11:6 Is 65:25; Jr 5:6; Hs
   2:18; 13:6-9
i 11:9 Ps 98:2-3; Is 45:6;
52:10; 66:18-23; Hab 2:14
j 11:10 Is 11:1
k Is 49:22; 62:10; Jn 3:14-
   15; 12:32
l Rm 15:12; Rv 5:5
m Is 14:3; 28:12; 32:17-18
n 11:11 Is 27:12

o 11:11 Is 10:20-22; 37:4,31-
   32; 46:3
p 11:12 Is 56:8; Zph 3:10;
   Zch 10:6
q Rv 7:1; 20:8
r 11:13 Is 9:21; Jr 3:18; Ezk
37:16-17,22; Hs 1:11
s 11:14 Jr 49:28
t Ps 60:8; 83:6
u 11:15 Is 7:20; 8:7; Rv 16:12
v 11:16 Is 19:23; 35:8; 40:3;
   62:10
w Ex 14:26-29
x 12:1 Is 40:1
y 12:2 Ex 15:2; Ps 118:14
z 12:3 Jn 4:10; 7:37-38
aa 12:4 1Ch 16:8; Ps 105:1;
   145:4

3 His delight will be in the fear
    of the LORD.
He will not judge
    by what he sees with his eyes,[a]
he will not execute justice
    by what he hears with his ears,
4 but he will judge
    the poor righteously[b]
and execute justice
    for the oppressed of the land.
He will strike the land
    with a scepter[A] from his mouth,[c]
and he will kill the wicked[d]
    with a command[B] from his lips.[e]
5 Righteousness will be a belt
    around his hips;[f]
faithfulness will be a belt
    around his waist.[g]
6 The wolf will dwell with the lamb,[h]
and the leopard will lie down
    with the goat.
The calf, the young lion,
    and the fattened calf
    will be together,
and a child will lead them.
7 The cow and the bear will graze,
    their young ones
      will lie down together,
and the lion will eat straw like cattle.
8 An infant will play
    beside the cobra's pit,
and a toddler will put his hand
    into a snake's den.
9 They will not harm or
    destroy each other
on my entire holy mountain,
for the land will be as full
of the knowledge of the LORD
as the sea is filled with water.[i]

ISRAEL REGATHERED

10 On that day the root of Jesse[j]
will stand as a banner
    for the peoples.[k]
The nations will look to him for
    guidance,[l]
and his resting place will be glorious.[m]

11 On that day[n] the Lord will extend his
hand a second time to recover the remnant of his people who survive — from
Assyria, Egypt, Pathros, Cush, Elam, Shinar,
Hamath, and the coasts and islands of the
west.[o]
12 He will lift up a banner for the nations
    and gather the dispersed of Israel;[p]
he will collect the scattered of Judah
    from the four corners of the earth.[q]
13 Ephraim's envy will cease;[r]
    Judah's harassing will end.
Ephraim will no longer be envious
    of Judah,
and Judah will not harass Ephraim.
14 But they will swoop down
    on the Philistine flank to the west.
Together they will plunder
    the people of the east.[s]
They will extend their power
    over Edom and Moab,
and the Ammonites will be
    their subjects.[t]
15 The LORD will divide[C,D] the Gulf
    of Suez.[E]
He will wave his hand
    over the Euphrates
    with his mighty wind[u]
and will split it into seven streams,
letting people walk through on foot.
16 There will be a highway
    for the remnant of his people
who will survive from Assyria,[v]
as there was for Israel
when they came up from the land
    of Egypt.[w]

A SONG OF PRAISE

12 On that day you will say:
"I will give thanks to you, LORD,
    although you were angry with me.
Your anger has turned away,
    and you have comforted me.[x]
2 Indeed, God is my salvation;
I will trust him and not be afraid,
for the LORD, the LORD himself,
    is my strength and my song.
He has become my salvation."[y]
3 You will joyfully draw water[z]
    from the springs of salvation,
4 and on that day you will say:
"Give thanks to the LORD;
    proclaim his name!
Make his works known
    among the peoples.[aa]
Declare that his name is exalted.

[A] 11:4 Lit *the rod*   [B] 11:4 Lit *with the breath*   [C] 11:15 Text emended; MT reads *destroy*   [D] 11:15 Or *dry up*   [E] 11:15 Lit *the Sea of Egypt*

11:6-9 Even the animal kingdom will be renewed in Christ's millennial kingdom, and creatures now considered predator and prey will be at peace with one another. **11:11-12** God will initiate a second exodus, bringing the Jews back to Israel from their lands of exile. This is a reference to the reestablished nation appearing in the kingdom age. **11:15-16** God will again part bodies of water so that his people can return easily, just as he dried up the Red Sea when the Israelites departed **Egypt** (11:16).

12:1-6 This is a song of praise for what God will do when Israel meets her King and acknowledges him at his second coming when he establishes his kingdom.

5 Sing to the LORD, for he has done
    glorious things.[a]
Let this be known
    throughout the earth.
6 Cry out and sing, citizen of Zion,
for the Holy One of Israel[b] is
    among you
in his greatness."

A PRONOUNCEMENT AGAINST BABYLON

13 A pronouncement[c] concerning Babylon[d] that Isaiah son of Amoz saw:

2 Lift up a banner
    on a barren mountain.[e]
Call out to them.
Signal with your hand,
    and they will go
through the gates of the nobles.
3 I have commanded
    my consecrated ones;
yes, I have called my warriors,
who celebrate my triumph,
to execute my wrath.[f]
4 Listen, a commotion
    on the mountains,
like that of a mighty people!
Listen, an uproar
    among the kingdoms,
like nations being gathered together!
The LORD of Armies is mobilizing
    an army for war.
5 They are coming from a distant land,
from the farthest horizon —
the LORD and the weapons
    of his wrath —
to destroy the whole country.[A]

6 Wail! For the day of the LORD is near.[g]
It will come as destruction
    from the Almighty.[h]
7 Therefore everyone's hands
    will become weak,
and every man will lose heart.[B]
8 They will be horrified;
pain and agony will seize them;
they will be in anguish like a woman
    in labor.[i]
They will look at each other,
their faces flushed with fear.
9 Look, the day[j] of the LORD
    is coming —

cruel, with rage and burning anger —
to make the earth a desolation
and to destroy its sinners.[k]
10 Indeed, the stars of the sky
    and its constellations[c]
will not give their light.
The sun will be dark when it rises,
and the moon will not shine.[l]
11 I will punish the world for its evil,[m]
and wicked people
    for their iniquities.
I will put an end to the pride
    of the arrogant[n]
and humiliate the insolence
    of tyrants.
12 I will make a human more scarce
    than fine gold,
and mankind more rare
    than the gold of Ophir.[o]
13 Therefore I will make
    the heavens tremble,
and the earth will shake
    from its foundations[p]
at the wrath of the LORD of Armies,
on the day of his burning anger.
14 Like wandering gazelles
and like sheep without a shepherd,[q]
each one will turn to his own people,
each one will flee to his own land.
15 Whoever is found will be stabbed,
and whoever is caught will die
    by the sword.
16 Their children will be dashed
    to pieces before their eyes;[r]
their houses will be looted,
and their wives raped.
17 Look! I am stirring up the Medes
    against them,[s]
who cannot be bought off
    with[D] silver
and who have no desire for gold.
18 Their bows will cut young men
    to pieces.
They will have no compassion
    on offspring;
they will not look with pity
    on children.

19 And Babylon, the jewel
    of the kingdoms,
the glory of the pride
    of the Chaldeans,

[a] 12:5 Ex 15:1; Ps 98:1; Is 24:14; 42:10-11; 44:23
[b] 12:6 Is 1:4
[c] 13:1 Is 14:28; 15:1; 17:1; 19:1; 21:1,11,13; 22:1; 23:1; 30:6
[d] Is 13:19; 14:4; 47:1-15; Jr 24:1; 50:1-51:64; Mt 1:11; Rv 14:8
[e] 13:2 Is 5:26; Jr 50:2
[f] 13:3 Ps 78:21,50; Ezk 5:15; 20:8
[g] 13:6 Is 2:12; 10:3; 13:9; 34:2,8; 61:2; Ezk 30:3; Am 5:18; Zph 1:7
[h] Is 10:25; 14:23; Jl 1:15
[i] 13:8 Is 26:17; Jr 4:31; Jn 16:21
[j] 13:9 Mt 25:13

[k] 13:9 Dt 32:43
[l] 13:10 Is 34:4; Mt 24:29; Mk 13:24-25; Lk 21:26; Rv 8:12
[m] 13:11 Jr 23:2; 36:31; 44:29
[n] Is 2:11; 23:9; Dn 5:22-23
[o] 13:12 1Kg 9:28; Jb 28:16; Ps 45:9
[p] 13:13 Ps 18:7; Is 2:19; 24:1,19-20; Hg 2:6
[q] 13:14 1Kg 22:17; Mt 9:36; Mk 6:34; 1Pt 2:25
[r] 13:16 Ps 137:8-9; Is 13:18; 14:21; Hs 10:14; Nah 3:10
[s] 13:17 Jr 51:11; Dn 5:28

[A] 13:5 Or earth   [B] 13:7 Lit every man's heart will melt   [C] 13:10 Or Orions   [D] 13:17 Lit who have no regard for

---

13:1-22 Babylon was going to be destroyed because of its **pride** (13:1, 19). The mention of **the Medes** (13:17) leads some to believe that Isaiah was describing Babylon's defeat in 539 BC, but the desolation in 13:20-22 does not fit this later conquest because the city of Babylon was not rendered unlivable by the Medes and Persians. More likely, Isaiah was prophesying the sack of Babylon by the Assyrian king, Sennacherib, in 689 BC. He ransacked the great city whose arrogance was an offense to God. Regardless, Babylon stood throughout Scripture for everything that was arrogant, evil, and opposed to God. Thus, the **LORD of Armies**, the name of God that signifies his power (13:4), would bring judgment upon this **jewel of** a kingdom (13:19).

ᵃ 13:19 Gn 19:24; Jr 14:18;
50:40; Am 4:11
ᵇ 13:20 Is 14:23; 34:10-15;
Jr 51:37-43
ᶜ 13:21 Is 34:11-15; Zph
2:14; Rv 18:2
ᵈ 14:1 1Kg 3:26
ᵉ Dt 7:7; Ps 102:13; Zch 1:17
ᶠ Dt 12:10; 2Sm 7:1
ᵍ Dt 14:21,29; Zch 8:22-23;
Eph 2:12-14
ʰ 14:2 Is 9:7; 45:14-25;
49:22-26; 60:9; 61:5;
66:19-24
ⁱ 14:3 Gn 3:16; Is 14:3;
Jr 44:19
ʲ Ex 1:14
ᵏ 14:4 Mc 2:4; Hab 2:6

ˡ 14:8 Ps 104:16; Is 55:12;
Ezk 31:16
ᵐ 14:12 2Pt 1:19; Rv 2:28;
22:16
ⁿ Is 34:4; Lk 10:18; Rv
8:10; 9:1
ᵒ 14:13 Jr 51:53; Ezk 28:2;
Am 9:2
ᵖ Dn 5:22-23; 8:10; 2Th 2:4
ᑫ Ps 48:2
ʳ 14:15 Ps 28:1; Is 38:18; Ezk
28:8; Mt 11:23; Lk 10:15
ˢ 14:17 Jl 1:19-20; 2:3,22;
3:19

will be like Sodom and Gomorrah
when God overthrew them.ᵃ

20 It will never be inhabited
or lived in from generation
to generation;ᵇ
a nomad will not pitch his tent there,
and shepherds will not let
their flocks rest there.

21 But desert creatures
will lie down there,
and owls will fill the houses.
Ostriches will dwell there,
and wild goats will leap about.ᶜ

22 Hyenas will howl in the fortresses,
and jackals, in the luxurious palaces.
Babylon's time is almost up;
her days are almost over.

ISRAEL'S RETURN

14 For the LORD will have compassionᵈ
on Jacob and will choose Israel
again.ᵉ He will settle them on their own
land.ᶠ The resident alien will join them and
be united with the house of Jacob.ᵍ ² The
nations will escort Israel and bring it to
its homeland. Then the house of Israel will
possess them as male and female slaves in
the LORD's land.ʰ They will make captives
of their captors and will rule over their
oppressors.

DOWNFALL OF THE KING OF BABYLON

³ When the LORD gives you rest from your
pain,ⁱ torment, and the hard laborʲ you
were forced to do, ⁴ you will sing this song
of contempt about the king of Babylonᵏ
and say:

How the oppressor
has quieted down,
and how the ragingᴬ
has become quiet!

5 The LORD has broken the staff
of the wicked,
the scepter of the rulers.

6 It struck the peoples in anger
with unceasing blows.
It subdued the nations in rage
with relentless persecution.

7 The whole earth is calm and at rest;
people shout with a ringing cry.

8 Even the cypresses and the cedars
of Lebanon
rejoice over you:ˡ
"Since you have been laid low,
no lumberjack has come against us."

9 Sheol below is eager to greet
your coming,
stirring up the spirits
of the departed for you —
all the rulersᴮ of the earth —
making all the kings of the nations
rise from their thrones.

10 They all respond to you, saying,
"You too have become as weak
as we are;
you have become like us!

11 Your splendor has been
brought down to Sheol,
along with the music of your harps.
Maggots are spread out under you,
and worms cover you."

12 Shining morning star,ᶜ,ᵐ
how you have fallen
from the heavens!ⁿ
You destroyer of nations,
you have been cut down
to the ground.

13 You said to yourself,
"I will ascend to the heavens;ᵒ
I will set up my throne
above the stars of God.ᵖ
I will sit on the mount
of the gods' assembly,
in the remotest parts of the North.ᴰ,ᑫ

14 I will ascend above
the highest clouds;
I will make myself
like the Most High."

15 But you will be brought down
to Sheol
into the deepest regions of the Pit.ʳ

16 Those who see you will stare at you;
they will look closely at you:
"Is this the man who caused
the earth to tremble,
who shook the kingdoms,

17 who turned the world
into a wilderness,ˢ

ᴬ 14:4 DSS; Hb uncertain   ᴮ 14:9 Lit *rams*   ᶜ 14:12 Or *Day Star, son of the dawn*   ᴰ 14:13 Or *of Zaphon*

14:12-14 Here the ruler is described in language that could not be attributed to any mere man. It's best, then, to see Isaiah speaking here of the original fall of Satan and applying it to the king of Babylon. The devil was originally the **shining morning star,** a beautiful angelic being who fell **from** **the heavens** (14:12). He rebelled against God and thus became Satan, God's ultimate adversary. Satan's **I will** statements in these verses describe his rebellion when he tried to usurp God's throne (14:13-14). For this he's destined for eternal punishment (see Matt 25:41). The sentence will be carried out as the last stages of God's prophetic plan are unveiled (see Rev 20:10). Satan's future defeat at the end of the millennium was typified in history by the crushing of Babylon, a symbol of rebellion against God ever since the founding of the city of Babylon (or Babel; see Gen 11:1-9).

⚜ KINGDOM LIVING ⚜
KINGDOM
They Will Rule

When God created Adam and Eve, he said, "They will rule the fish of the sea, the birds of the sky, the livestock, the whole earth, and the creatures that crawl on the earth" (Gen 1:26). Then God told them to "subdue" the earth (Gen 1:28). This is known in theological terms as the *dominion covenant*.

It was impossible for God to forgo having a kingdom that would rule over and defeat the kingdom of Satan. When Jesus Christ sets up his millennial kingdom, it will be the final, triumphant declaration of God's glory. Satan will then be chained up to demonstrate his utter defeat and judgment (see Rev 20:1-3). Yet, until then, God has created people like you and me to harness, and rule, parts of his creation. Every person was created with that divine intent.

Why is it important for you to grasp the unfolding of God's kingdom? Because when God said "they will rule," he made that statement for you. Ruling is *your* commission from God. God stated that he would not rule independently of humans—that humankind's decisions would carry weight regarding what he would or would not do.

He did this for one reason: to demonstrate to the devil that he can do more through a lesser creature—you or me—in manifesting his glory than through the one who was once a "shining morning star" (Isa 14:12). God has a plan for you that is bigger than you.

FOR THE NEXT KINGDOM
KINGDOM LIVING LESSON SEE PAGE 888.

---

who destroyed its cities
and would not release the prisoners
to return home?"
¹⁸ All the kings of the nations
lie in splendor,
each in his own tomb.
¹⁹ But you are thrown out
without a grave,
like a worthless branch,
covered by those slain
with the sword
and dumped into a rocky pit
like a trampled corpse.

²⁰ You will not join them in burial,
because you destroyed your land
and slaughtered your own people.
The offspring of evildoers
will never be mentioned again.ᵃ
²¹ Prepare a place of slaughter
for his sons,
because of the iniquityᵇ
of their fathers.
They will never rise up to possess
a land
or fill the surface of the earth
with cities.

²² "I will rise up against them" — this is the declaration of the LORD of Armies — "and I will cut off from Babylon her reputation, remnant, offspring, and posterity" — this is the LORD's declaration. ²³ "I will make her a swampland and a region for herons,ᴬ and I will sweep her away with the broom of destruction."
This is the declaration of the LORD of Armies.

ASSYRIA WILL BE DESTROYED

²⁴ The LORD of Armies has sworn:
As I have purposed, so it will be;
as I have planned it, so it will happen.ᶜ
²⁵ I will break Assyriaᵈ in my land;
I will tread him down
on my mountain.
Then his yoke will be taken from them,
and his burden will be removed
from their shoulders.
²⁶ This is the planᵉ prepared
for the whole earth,
and this is the hand stretched out
against all the nations.
²⁷ The LORD of Armies himself
has planned it;
therefore, who can stand in its way?
It is his hand that is outstretched,
so who can turn it back?

A PRONOUNCEMENT AGAINST PHILISTIA

²⁸ In the year that King Ahaz died,ᶠ this pronouncement came:ᵍ
²⁹ Don't rejoice, all of you in Philistia,
because the rod of the one
who struck youʰ is broken.
For a viper will come from the rootᴮ
of a snake,
and from its egg comes
a flying serpent.ⁱ

ᵃ 14:20 Jb 18:16,19; Ps 21:10; 37:28; Is 1:4; 31:2
ᵇ 14:21 Is 13:11
ᶜ 14:24 Pr 16:4; Is 46:11; Jr 23:20; 30:24; 51:29; Zch 1:6; Eph 1:11; Rv 17:17
ᵈ 14:25 Is 8:7; 10:5-15,27
ᵉ 14:26 Is 5:19
ᶠ 14:28 2Kg 16:20; 2Ch 28:27; Is 6:1
ᵍ Is 13:1
ʰ 14:29 1Sm 17:50; 18:25-30; 19:8; 23:1-5; 2Sm 5:17-25; 8:1
ⁱ Ex 4:2-3; 7:10-12; Is 30:6

ᴬ 14:23 Or *hedgehogs*; Hb obscure   ᴮ 14:29 Or *stock*

14:24 Anyone who thinks his plans will stand is in for a rude awakening when his agenda bumps up against God's. His agenda always wins.

a 14:30 Ex 4:22
b 14:31 Is 3:26; 24:12; 45:2
c Jos 2:9,24
d Is 41:25; Jr 1:13-14; 4:6;
6:1; 47:2; 50:3,9,41
e 14:32 Ps 87:1,5; 102:16; Is
28:16; 44:28; 54:11
f 15:1-7 Gn 19:31-37; Is
11:14; 25:10; Jr 48:1-38;
Ezk 25:8-11; Am 2:1-3;
Zph 2:8-9
g 15:1 Nm 21:28
h 15:4 Nm 21:28; 32:3;
Jr 48:34
i 15:5 Gn 19:21-22
j 15:6 Nm 32:3,36; Jos 13:27

k 15:7 Is 30:6; Jr 48:36
l 15:9 2Kg 3:22-23
m 2Sm 23:20; 1Ch 11:22
n 16:1 2Kg 3:4
o 2Kg 14:7; Is 42:11
p 16:3 1Kg 18:4
q 16:5 Is 9:6-7; 32:1; 55:4;
Dn 7:14; Mc 4:7; Lk 1:33
r 16:6 Jr 48:29; Am 2:1; Ob
3-4; Zph 2:8,10

30 Then the firstborn[a] of the poor
    will be well fed,
and the impoverished will lie down
    in safety,
but I will kill your root with hunger,
    and your remnant will be slain.
31 Wail, you gates![b] Cry out, city!
    Tremble with fear,[c] all Philistia!
For a cloud of dust is coming
    from the north,[d]
and there is no one missing from
    the invader's ranks.
32 What answer will be
    given to the messengers
    from that nation?
The LORD has founded Zion,[e]
    and his oppressed people
    find refuge in her.

A PRONOUNCEMENT AGAINST MOAB

15 A pronouncement concerning Moab:[f]
    Ar in Moab is devastated,[g]
destroyed in a night.
Kir in Moab is devastated,
destroyed in a night.
2 Dibon went up to its temple
    to weep at its high places.
Moab wails on Nebo and at[A] Medeba.
Every head is shaved;
    every beard is chopped short.
3 In its streets they wear sackcloth;
    on its rooftops
    and in its public squares
    everyone wails,
    falling down and weeping.
4 Heshbon and Elealeh cry out;
    their voices are heard as far away
    as Jahaz.[h]
Therefore the soldiers of Moab
    cry out,
    and they tremble.[B]
5 My heart cries out over Moab,
    whose fugitives flee as far as Zoar,[i]
    to Eglath-shelishiyah;
they go up the Ascent
    of Luhith weeping;
they raise a cry of destruction
    on the road to Horonaim.
6 The Waters of Nimrim[j] are desolate;

the grass is withered, the foliage
    is gone,
and the vegetation has vanished.
7 So they carry their wealth
    and belongings
over the Wadi of the Willows.[k]
8 For their cry echoes
    throughout the territory of Moab.
Their wailing reaches Eglaim;
    their wailing reaches Beer-elim.
9 The Waters of Dibon[c] are full
    of blood,[l]
but I will bring on Dibon[c] even more
    than this —
a lion for those who escape
    from Moab,
and for the survivors in the land.[m]

16 Send lambs to the ruler
    of the land,[n]
from Sela in the desert[o]
to the mountain of Daughter Zion.
2 Like a bird fleeing,
    forced from the nest,
the daughters of Moab
    will be at the fords of the Arnon.

3 Give us counsel and make
    a decision.
Shelter us at noonday
    with shade that is as dark as night.
Hide the refugees;[p]
    do not betray the one who flees.
4 Let my refugees stay with you;
    be a refuge for Moab[D]
    from the aggressor.

When the oppressor has gone,
    destruction has ended,
and marauders have vanished
    from the land,
5 a throne will be established in love,[q]
    and one will sit on it faithfully[E]
    in the tent of David,
judging and pursuing what is right,
    quick to execute justice.

6 We have heard of Moab's pride[r] —
    how very proud he is —

A 15:2 Or *wails over Nebo and over*   B 15:4 Lit *out, he trembles within himself*   C 15:9 DSS, some LXX mss, Vg; MT reads *Dimon*   D 16:4 Or *you;*
Moab — be a refuge for him   E 16:5 Or *continually*

14:31 The Philistines were one of Israel's oldest and fiercest enemies. They were shattered by the Assyrians at the end of the eighth century BC.
15:1-9 The Moabites descended from Moab, the son of Lot, who was the nephew of Abraham (see Gen 11:27; 19:36-37). In spite of this family connection, Moab was one of Israel's

cruelest enemies. The various Moabite cities Isaiah catalogued in 15:1-4 would all be destroyed by an Assyrian invasion.
16:1-4 In desperation, Moabite refugees would **send lambs . . . to the mountain of Daughter Zion** (16:1), a reference to Jerusalem, in hopes they could find asylum there (16:2-4). This plea was answered by a proph-

ecy that **the aggressor**, Sennacherib, would be destroyed himself (16:4). Nevertheless, Moab would be swept into the dustbin of history. It had long arrogantly rejected the Lord, relying on its own power.
16:5 This is an announcement of the coming kingdom of Jesus Christ.

his haughtiness, his pride,
his arrogance,
and his empty boasting.
7 Therefore let Moab wail;
let every one of them
wail for Moab.
You who are completely devastated,
mourn
for the raisin cakes[a]
of Kir-hareseth.[b]
8 For Heshbon's terraced vineyards
and the grapevines of Sibmah
have withered.
The rulers of the nations
have trampled its choice vines
that reached as far as Jazer[c]
and spread to the desert.
Their shoots spread out
and reached the sea.[d]
9 So I join with Jazer
to weep for the vines of Sibmah;
I drench Heshbon and Elealeh
with my tears.
Triumphant shouts
have fallen silent[A]
over your summer fruit
and your harvest.
10 Joy and rejoicing[e]
have been removed
from the orchard;
no one is singing or shouting for joy
in the vineyards.[f]
No one tramples grapes[B]
in the winepresses.
I have put an end to the shouting.
11 Therefore I moan like the sound of
a lyre for Moab,[g]
as does my innermost being
for Kir-heres.
12 When Moab appears
and tires himself out on
the high place[h]
and comes to his sanctuary to pray,
it will do him no good.[i]

13 This is the message that the LORD previously announced about Moab. 14 And now the LORD says, "In three years, as a hired worker counts years,[j] Moab's splendor will become an object of contempt, in spite of a very large population. And those who are left will be few and weak."

A PRONOUNCEMENT AGAINST DAMASCUS

17 A pronouncement[k] concerning Damascus:[l]

Look, Damascus is no longer a city.
It has become a ruined heap.
2 The cities of Aroer are abandoned;
they will be places for flocks.
They will lie down without fear.
3 The fortress disappears
from Ephraim,[m]
and a kingdom from Damascus.
The remnant of Aram will be
like the splendor of the Israelites.
This is the declaration of the LORD
of Armies.

JUDGMENT AGAINST ISRAEL

4 On that day
the splendor of Jacob will fade,
and his healthy body[c]
will become emaciated.[n]
5 It will be as if a reaper had gathered
standing grain —
his arm harvesting the heads
of grain —
and as if one had gleaned heads
of grain
in the Valley of Rephaim.[o]
6 Only gleanings will be left in Israel,[p]
as if an olive tree had been beaten —
two or three olives at the very top
of the tree,
four or five on its fruitful branches.
This is the declaration of the LORD,
the God of Israel.

7 On that day people will look to their Maker and will turn their eyes to the Holy One of Israel.[q] 8 They will not look to the altars[r] they made with their hands or to the Asherahs and shrines[D,s] they made with their fingers.
9 On that day their strong cities will be
like the abandoned woods
and mountaintops
that were abandoned because of
the Israelites;
there will be desolation.
10 For you have forgotten the God
of your salvation,
and you have failed to remember

a 16:7 2Sm 6:19; 1Ch 16:3; Sg 2:5; Hs 3:1
b 2Kg 3:25; Jr 48:31
c 16:8 Nm 21:32; Jos 13:25
d Jr 48:32
e 16:10 Is 24:8; Jr 48:33
f Jdg 9:27; Is 24:7; Am 5:11,17
g 16:11 Is 15:5; 63:15; Jr 48:36; Hs 11:8; Php 2:1
h 16:12 1Kg 18:29
i Is 15:2
j 16:14 Jb 7:1; 14:6; Is 21:16

k 17:1 Is 13:1
l Gn 14:15; 15:2; 2Kg 16:9; Jr 49:23; Am 1:3-5; Zch 9:1; Ac 9:2
m 17:3 Is 7:8,16; 8:4
n 17:4 Is 10:16
o 17:5 2Sm 5:18,22
p 17:6 Dt 4:27; Is 24:13; 27:12; Ob 5; Rm 11:19
q 17:7 Is 1:4
r 17:8 2Ch 34:7; Is 27:9
s Ex 34:13; Dt 7:5; Mc 5:14

A 16:9 Or Battle cries have fallen   B 16:10 Lit wine   C 17:4 Lit and the fat of his flesh   D 17:8 Or incense altars

---

17:1-3 **Damascus** was a major city in Aram (modern-day Syria; 17:1). The city appeared in Isaiah 7, when the kings of Aram and Israel made an ill-fated alliance to ward off the threat posed by the Assyrians. God proph-

esied their ruin then, and this chapter is a restatement of that disaster. Assyria defeated Aram in 732 BC.
17:7 Once the assault against them started, the Israelites would realize that their idols

were powerless to save them, and they would turn to their **Maker**. How much better it is to turn to him before judgment day!

[a]17:10 Dt 6:12; 8:11,14,19;
32:18; Jdg 3:7; 1Sm 12:9; Ps
106:21; Is 8:14; 26:4; 51:13;
Jr 3:21; 13:25; Ezk 22:12;
23:35; Hs 2:13
[b]17:12 Ps 93:1-5; Is 8:9-10;
Lk 21:25
[c]17:13 Is 33:3
[d]Ps 9:5; Is 41:11
[e]Jb 21:18; Ps 1:4; 83:13; Is
29:5; 41:15-16
[f]18:1 2Kg 19:9; Is 20:3-5;
Ezk 30:4-5,9; Zph 2:12;
3:10

[g]18:7 Ps 68:31; Is 45:14;
Zph 3:10; Ac 8:27-38
[h]19:1 Is 13:1
[i]Jr 46:13-26; Ezk 29:1-31:2;
31:18-32:32; Jl 3:19
[j]Ps 18:9-10; 104:3; Mt
26:64; Rv 1:7
[k]Ex 12:12; Jr 43:12; 44:8
[l]Jos 2:11; Is 13:7
[m]19:2 Mk 13:12
[n]Jdg 7:22; 1Sm 14:20; 2Ch
20:23; Mt 10:21,36; Mk
13:8; Lk 21:10
[o]19:3 1Ch 10:13; Is 8:19;
Dn 2:2
[p]19:4 Is 20:4; Jr 46:26;
Ezk 29:19

the rock of your strength;[a]
therefore you will plant
    beautiful plants
and set out cuttings from exotic vines.
11 On the day that you plant,
you will help them to grow,
and in the morning
you will help your seed to sprout,
but the harvest will vanish
on the day of disease
    and incurable pain.

JUDGMENT AGAINST THE NATIONS

12 Ah! The roar of many peoples —
they roar like the roaring of the seas.
The raging of the nations —
they rage like the rumble
    of rushing water.[b]
13 The nations rage like the rumble of a
    huge torrent.[c]
He rebukes them, and they flee
    far away,[d]
driven before the wind like chaff
    on the hills[e]
and like tumbleweeds before a gale.
14 In the evening — sudden terror!
Before morning — it is gone!
This is the fate of those
    who plunder us
and the lot of those who ravage us.

THE LORD'S MESSAGE TO CUSH

18 Woe to the land
    of buzzing insect wings[A]
beyond the rivers of Cush,[f]
2 which sends envoys by sea,
in reed vessels over the water.

Go, swift messengers,
to a nation tall and smooth-skinned,
to a people feared far and near,
a powerful nation
    with a strange language,[B]
whose land is divided by rivers.
3 All you inhabitants of the world
and you who live on the earth,
when a banner is raised
    on the mountains, look!
When a trumpet sounds, listen!

4 For the LORD said to me:
I will quietly look out from my place,

like shimmering heat in sunshine,
like a rain cloud in harvest heat.
5 For before the harvest,
when the blossoming is over
and the blossom becomes
    a ripening grape,
he will cut off the shoots
    with a pruning knife,
and tear away and remove
    the branches.
6 They will all be left for the birds
    of prey on the hills
and for the wild animals
    of the land.
The birds of prey will spend
    the summer feeding on them,
and all the wild animals the winter.

7 At that time a gift will be brought to
the LORD of Armies from[c] a people tall
and smooth-skinned,[g] a people feared far
and near, a powerful nation with a strange
language, whose land is divided by rivers
— to Mount Zion, the place of the name of
the LORD of Armies.

A PRONOUNCEMENT
AGAINST EGYPT

19 A pronouncement[h] concerning Egypt:[i]
    Look, the LORD rides
    on a swift cloud[j]
and is coming to Egypt.
Egypt's idols will tremble
    before him,[k]
and Egypt will lose heart.[D,l]
2 I will provoke Egyptians
    against Egyptians;
each will fight against his brother[m]
and each against his friend,
city against city,
    kingdom against kingdom.[n]
3 Egypt's spirit will be disturbed
    within it,
and I will frustrate its plans.
Then they will inquire of idols,
    ghosts,
and spiritists.[o]
4 I will hand over Egypt
    to harsh masters,[p]
and a strong king will rule it.
This is the declaration
    of the Lord GOD of Armies.

[A]18:1 Or of sailing ships   [B]18:2 Hb obscure   [C]18:7 DSS, LXX, Vg; MT omits from   [D]19:1 Lit Egypt's heart will melt within it

---

18:1 Cush encompassed parts of modern Sudan, Egypt, and Ethiopia, although it is usually identified with the latter.
18:7 This prophecy that the people of Cush would one day come to Jerusalem to worship the Lord is a possible reference to Christ's mil-

lennial kingdom when people of all nations will worship him.
19:1-4 Egypt figures prominently in the story of God's people. By the end of Genesis, Egypt was a source of protection from famine for the descendants of Jacob. By

the beginning of Exodus, Egypt was their enemy and persecutor. At one time it was the greatest power in the ancient world. But by Isaiah's day, Egypt too was threatened by Assyria. King Esarhaddon of Assyria conquered it in 671 BC.

5 The water of the sea will dry up,
and the river will be parched
and dry.
6 The channels will stink;
they will dwindle, and Egypt's canals
will be parched.
Reed and rush will wilt.
7 The reeds by the Nile, by the mouth
of the river,
and all the cultivated areas
of the Nile
will wither, blow away, and vanish.
8 Then the fishermen will mourn.
All those who cast hooks
into the Nile will lament,
and those who spread nets
on the water will give up.
9 Those who work with flax
will be dismayed;[a]
those combing it and weaving linen
will turn pale.[A]
10 Egypt's weavers[B] will be dejected;
all her wage earners
will be demoralized.

11 The princes of Zoan
are complete fools;[b]
Pharaoh's wisest advisers
give stupid advice!
How can you say to Pharaoh,
"I am one[C] of the wise,
a student of eastern[D] kings"?
12 Where then are your wise men?
Let them tell you and reveal
what the LORD of Armies
has planned against Egypt.
13 The princes of Zoan have been fools;
the princes of Memphis
are deceived.[c]
Her tribal chieftains have led
Egypt astray.
14 The LORD has mixed within her
a spirit of confusion.
The leaders have made Egypt
stagger in all she does,
as a drunkard staggers in his vomit.
15 No head or tail, palm or reed,[d]
will be able to do anything for Egypt.

EGYPT WILL KNOW THE LORD

16 On that day Egypt will be like women and will tremble with fear because of the threatening hand of the LORD of Armies when he raises it against them. **17** The land of Judah will terrify Egypt; whenever Judah is mentioned, Egypt will tremble because of what the LORD of Armies has planned[e] against it.

18 On that day five cities in the land of Egypt will speak the language of Canaan and swear loyalty to the LORD of Armies. One of the cities will be called the City of the Sun.[E,F]

19 On that day there will be an altar to the LORD in the center of the land of Egypt and a pillar to the LORD near her border.[f] **20** It will be a sign and witness to the LORD of Armies in the land of Egypt. When they cry out to the LORD because of their oppressors, he will send them a savior and leader, and he will rescue them.[g] **21** The LORD will make himself known to Egypt, and Egypt will know the LORD on that day. They will offer sacrifices and offerings;[h] they will make vows to the LORD and fulfill them. **22** The LORD will strike Egypt, striking and healing. Then they will turn to the LORD and he will be receptive to their prayers and heal them.

23 On that day there will be a highway[i] from Egypt to Assyria. Assyria will go to Egypt, Egypt to Assyria, and Egypt will worship with Assyria. **24** On that day Israel will form a triple alliance with Egypt and Assyria — a blessing within the land. **25** The LORD of Armies will bless them, saying, "Egypt my people, Assyria my handiwork,[j] and Israel my inheritance are blessed."[k]

NO HELP FROM CUSH OR EGYPT

20 In the year that the chief commander,[l] sent by King Sargon of Assyria, came to Ashdod[m] and attacked and captured it — **2** during that time the LORD had spoken through Isaiah[n] son of Amoz, saying, "Go, take off your sackcloth[G] and remove the sandals from your feet," and he did that, going stripped and barefoot[o] — **3** the LORD said, "As my servant Isaiah has gone stripped and barefoot three years as a sign and omen against Egypt and Cush,[p] **4** so the king of Assyria will lead the captives of Egypt[q] and the exiles

[a] 19:9 Pr 7:16; Ezk 27:7
[b] 19:11 Nm 13:22; Ps 78:12,43; Is 30:4
[c] 19:13 Jr 2:16; 46:14,19; Ezk 30:13
[d] 19:15 Is 9:14-16

[e] 19:17 Is 5:19
[f] 19:19 Gn 28:18; Ex 24:4; Jos 22:10,26-27
[g] 19:20 Jdg 3:9,15; 6:7; 10:10
[h] 19:21 Is 56:7; 60:7; Zch 14:16-18
[i] 19:23 Is 11:16; 35:8; 49:11; 62:10
[j] 19:25 Ps 100:3; Is 29:23; 45:11; 60:21; 64:8; Eph 2:10
[k] Dt 9:26,29; 32:9; Ps 28:9; Is 47:6; 63:17
[l] 20:1 2Kg 18:17
[m] 1Sm 5:1
[n] 20:2 Mt 3:3; 12:17
[o] 1Sm 19:24; Mc 1:8
[p] 20:3 Is 8:18
[q] 20:4 Is 19:4

[A] 19:9 DSS, Tg; MT reads *weavers of white cloth* [B] 19:10 Or *foundations* [C] 19:11 Lit *a son* [D] 19:11 Lit *a son of ancient* [E] 19:18 Some Hb mss, DSS, Sym, Tg, Vg, Arabic; other Hb mss read *of Destruction*; LXX reads *of Righteousness* [F] 19:18 = the ancient Egyptian city Heliopolis [G] 20:2 Lit *off the sackcloth from your waist*

19:5-10 The conquest under God's judgment would wreak havoc on a land whose livelihood depended on the Nile River. The Lord would **dry up** Egypt's **water** source (19:5).
19:14 The smartest and brightest are no match for the One who is the source of all wisdom.
19:22 God is always ready to show grace and mercy to those who will repent.

[a] 20:5 2Kg 18:21; Is 30:3-5; 31:1; Ezk 29:6-7
[b] 21:1 Is 13:1
[c] Is 13:20-22; 14:23; 21:9; Jr 51:41-44
[d] 21:2 Is 24:16; 33:1
[e] 21:3 Ps 48:6; Is 13:8; 16:11; 26:17-18; Jr 4:31; 6:24; 22:23; 30:6; 50:43; Mc 4:9-10; 1Th 5:3
[f] 21:4 Dt 28:67
[g] 21:5 Jr 51:39,57; Dn 5:1-4

[h] 21:8 Hab 2:1
[i] 21:9 2Sm 1:19; Is 3:8; 14:12; Jr 51:8; Ezk 32:22; Rv 14:8; 18:2
[j] Is 46:1; Jr 50:2; 51:44
[k] 21:10 Jr 51:33; Mc 4:13
[l] 21:11 Is 21:1
[m] Gn 25:14
[n] Dt 2:8; Ezk 35:2
[o] 21:13 Jr 25:23-24; 49:28
[p] Gn 10:7; Jr 25:23; 49:8; Ezk 27:15
[q] 21:14 Gn 25:15; Jb 6:19
[r] 21:16 Is 16:14
[s] Ps 120:5; Sg 1:5; Is 42:11; 60:7; Jr 2:10; Ezk 27:21

of Cush, young and old alike, stripped and barefoot, with bared buttocks — to Egypt's shame. [5] Those who made Cush their hope and Egypt their boast will be dismayed and ashamed.[a] [6] And the inhabitants of this coastland will say on that day, 'Look, this is what has happened to those we relied on and fled to for help to rescue us from the king of Assyria! Now, how will we escape?'"

A JUDGMENT ON BABYLON

21 A pronouncement[b] concerning the desert by the sea:[c]
Like storms that pass over the Negev, it comes from the desert, from the land of terror.

[2] A troubling vision is declared to me:
"The treacherous one acts treacherously,[d]
and the destroyer destroys.
Advance, Elam! Lay siege, you Medes!
I will put an end to all the groaning."

[3] Therefore I am[A] filled with anguish.
Pain grips me, like the pain of a woman in labor.[e]
I am too perplexed to hear, too dismayed to see.

[4] My heart staggers; horror terrifies me.
He has turned my last glimmer of hope[B]
into sheer terror.[f]

[5] Prepare a table,[g] and spread out a carpet!
Eat and drink!
Rise up, you princes, and oil the shields!

[6] For the Lord has said to me,
"Go, post a lookout;
let him report what he sees.
[7] When he sees riders — pairs of horsemen,
riders on donkeys,
riders on camels —
he must pay close attention."

[8] Then the lookout[c] reported,
"Lord, I stand on the watchtower all day,[h]
and I stay at my post all night.
[9] Look, riders come — horsemen in pairs."
And he answered, saying,
"Babylon has fallen,[i] has fallen.
All the images of her gods have been shattered on the ground."[j]

[10] My people who have been crushed on the threshing floor,[k]
I have declared to you
what I have heard from the LORD of Armies,
the God of Israel.

A PRONOUNCEMENT AGAINST DUMAH

[11] A pronouncement[l] concerning Dumah:[D,m]
One calls to me from Seir,[n]
"Watchman, what is left of the night?
Watchman, what is left of the night?"
[12] The watchman said,
"Morning has come, and also night.
If you want to ask, ask!
Come back again."

A PRONOUNCEMENT AGAINST ARABIA

[13] A pronouncement concerning Arabia:[o]
In the desert[E] brush
you will camp for the night,
you caravans of Dedanites.[p]
[14] Bring water for the thirsty.
The inhabitants of the land of Tema[q]
meet[F] the refugees with food.
[15] For they have fled from swords,
from the drawn sword,
from the bow that is strung,
and from the stress of battle.

[16] For the Lord said this to me: "Within one year,[r] as a hired worker counts years, all the glory of Kedar[s] will be gone. [17] The remaining Kedarite archers will be few in number." For the LORD, the God of Israel, has spoken.

[A] 21:3 Lit *my waist is*, or *my insides are*   [B] 21:4 Lit *my twilight*   [C] 21:8 DSS, Syr; MT reads *Then a lion*   [D] 21:11 Some Hb mss, LXX read *Edom*
[E] 21:13 LXX, Syr, Tg, Vg read *desert at evening*   [F] 21:14 LXX, Syr, Tg, Vg read *meet* as a command

---

20:5-6 Rely on God, and you have nothing to fear—regardless of the outcome. Rely on man, and you have everything to lose—regardless of the promise.
21:9 Some Bible interpreters believe this passage refers to Babylon's defeat by the Assyrian

king, Sennacherib, in 689 BC (see the note on 13:1-22). Others believe it refers to the Persian Empire's conquest of Babylon in 539 BC (see Dan 5).
21:11 There was a **Dumah** in Arabia that was conquered by Assyria in the seventh century BC, but **Seir** was located in Edom.

21:13-14 The desert tribes in **Arabia** would also suffer at the hands of the Assyrians. **Tema** was an oasis whose water would be needed for **thirsty . . . refugees** when Assyria attacked.

A PRONOUNCEMENT AGAINST JERUSALEM

22 A pronouncement[a] concerning the Valley of Vision:[b]
What's the matter with you?
Why have all of you gone up
to the rooftops?[c]
2 The noisy city, the jubilant town,[d]
is filled with celebration.
Your dead did not die by the sword;
they were not killed in battle.
3 All your rulers have fled together,
captured without a bow.
All your fugitives
were captured together;
they had fled far away.
4 Therefore I said,
"Look away from me!
Let me weep bitterly![e]
Do not try to comfort me
about the destruction
of my dear[A] people."
5 For the Lord GOD of Armies
had a day of tumult, trampling,
and confusion[f]
in the Valley of Vision —
people shouting[B] and crying
to the mountains;
6 Elam took up a quiver
with chariots and horsemen,[C]
and Kir[g] uncovered the shield.
7 Your best valleys were full
of chariots,
and horsemen were positioned
at the city gates.
8 He removed the defenses of Judah.

On that day you looked to the weapons
in the House of the Forest.[h] 9 You saw that
there were many breaches in the walls of
the city of David.[i] You collected water
from the lower pool.[j] 10 You counted the
houses of Jerusalem so that you could
tear them down to fortify the wall. 11 You
made a reservoir between the walls[k] for
the water of the ancient pool,[l] but you did
not look to the one who made it, or consider the one who created it long ago.
12 On that day the Lord GOD of Armies
called for weeping,[m] for wailing,
for shaven heads,
and for the wearing of sackcloth.
13 But look: joy and gladness,
butchering of cattle,
slaughtering of sheep and goats,
eating of meat, and drinking
of wine —
"Let us eat and drink, for tomorrow
we die!"[n]
14 The LORD of Armies has
directly revealed to me:[o]
"This iniquity will not be wiped out
for you people as long as you
live."[D,p]
The Lord GOD of Armies has spoken.

A PRONOUNCEMENT AGAINST SHEBNA

15 The Lord GOD of Armies said: "Go to
Shebna,[q] that steward who is in charge
of the palace, and say to him: 16 What are
you doing here? Who authorized you to
carve out a tomb for yourself here, carving your tomb on the height and cutting
a resting place for yourself out of rock?[r]
17 Look, you strong man! The LORD is about
to shake you violently. He will take hold of
you, 18 wind you up into a ball, and sling
you into a wide land.[E] There you will die,
and there your glorious chariots will be
— a disgrace to the house of your lord. 19 I
will remove you from your office; you will
be ousted from your position.
20 "On that day I will call for my servant,
Eliakim son of Hilkiah.[s] 21 I will clothe him
with your robe and tie your sash around
him. I will hand your authority over to him,
and he will be like a father to the inhabitants of Jerusalem and to the house of Judah.[t] 22 I will place the key[u] of the house of

[a] 22:1 Is 13:1
[b] Ps 125:2; Jr 21:13; Jl 3:12,14
[c] Is 15:3
[d] 22:2 Is 23:7; 32:13
[e] 22:4 Is 15:3; 33:7; Jr 9:1; Zch 12:10
[f] 22:5 Is 10:6; 37:3; 63:3
[g] 22:6 2Kg 16:9; Am 1:5; 9:7
[h] 22:8 1Kg 7:2; 10:17
[i] 22:9 Lk 2:4
[j] 2Kg 20:20; Neh 3:16
[k] 22:11 2Kg 25:4; Jr 39:4
[l] 22:11 2Kg 20:20; 2Ch 32:3-4
[m] 22:12 Is 32:11; Jl 1:13; 2:17
[n] 22:13 Is 56:12; 1Co 15:32
[o] 22:14 Is 5:9
[p] 1Sm 3:14; Ezk 24:13
[q] 22:15 2Kg 18:18,26,37; Is 36:3,11,22; 37:2
[r] 22:16 2Sm 18:18; 2Ch 16:14; Mt 27:60
[s] 22:20 2Kg 18:18; Is 36:3,22; 37:2
[t] 22:21 Gn 45:8; Jb 29:16
[u] 22:22 Mt 16:19; Rv 3:7

[A] 22:4 Lit *of the daughter of my* [B] 22:5 Or *Vision — a tearing down of a wall,* or *Vision — Kir raged*; Hb obscure [C] 22:6 Lit *chariots of man*
[D] 22:14 Lit *for you until you die* [E] 22:17-18 Hb obscure

22:1-14 Jerusalem's inhabitants could go **up to the rooftops** of their houses and see the Assyrian army massed against their city and building siege ramps against its wall (22:1). But instead of turning to the Lord in repentance and seeking his protection, the people actually resorted to partying! (22:2, 13). There was a fatalistic tone to the festivities, though, because the people said, **Let us eat and drink, for tomorrow we die!** (22:13). The apostle Paul quotes this verse as an appropriate response to life if there is no resurrection—no hope in God beyond the grave (see 1 Cor 15:32).

In addition to their partying, they scrambled to defend themselves. They tried to **fortify** the **walls** (22:9-10). They stored **water**. But their fatal mistake was not turning to the Lord, **the one who made it** (22:11).

22:15-19 **Shebna** was a high official in Judah (22:15), and he certainly must've been wicked to warrant specific mention! His pride is evident in his plan to have a burial spot in Jerusalem that was so prominent that his name would be remembered for generations (22:16). God hates pride, and his plans for Shebna were the exact opposite of the steward's (22:17-19).

22:20-25 **Eliakim** was a faithful **servant** of the Lord, who would provide wise counsel and a steadying hand in Jerusalem (22:20). God would grant him Shebna's **authority**, and he would serve Jerusalem in godliness (22:21). While Shebna sought glory and was denied, Eliakim sought nothing but would find **honor** (22:23). Nevertheless, he would be unable to prevent Judah's inevitable collapse (22:25). Nations need godly leaders, yet godly leaders alone can't protect citizens who refuse to repent of their wickedness.

a 22:22 Jb 12:14
b 23:1 Is 13:1
c Jos 19:29; 1Kg 5:1;
Jr 25:22; 47:4; Ezk
26:1–27:36; Jl 3:4-8; Am
1:9; Zch 9:2-4
d Gn 10:4; 1Kg 10:22
e Jr 2:10; Ezk 27:6; Ac 11:19
f 23:2 Gn 10:15; Jos 19:28;
Jr 25:22; 27:3; Ezk 27:8;
32:30; Jl 3:4; Zch 9:2
g 23:3 Ezk 27:3-23
h 23:5 Ac 21:7

i 23:11 Ex 14:21; Is 14:26
j 23:12 Is 23:1; Jr 2:10; Ezk
27:6; Ac 4:36; 11:19-20;
13:4; 15:39; 21:3,16; 27:4
k 23:17 Jr 25:11,22
l Ac 21:7

David on his shoulder; what he opens, no one can close; what he closes, no one can open.[a] 23 I will drive him, like a peg, into a firm place. He will be a throne of honor for his father's family. 24 They will hang on him all the glory of his father's family: the descendants and the offshoots — all the small vessels, from bowls to every kind of jar. 25 On that day" — the declaration of the LORD of Armies — "the peg that was driven into a firm place will give way, be cut off, and fall, and the load on it will be destroyed." Indeed, the LORD has spoken.

A PRONOUNCEMENT AGAINST TYRE

23 A pronouncement[b] concerning Tyre:[c]
Wail, ships of Tarshish,[d]
for your haven has been destroyed.
Word has reached them
from the land of Cyprus.[A,e]
2 Mourn, inhabitants of the coastland,
you merchants of Sidon;[f]
your agents have crossed the sea[B]
3 over deep water.
Tyre's revenue was the grain
from Shihor —
the harvest of the Nile.
She was the merchant
among the nations.[g]
4 Be ashamed, Sidon, the stronghold
of the sea,
for the sea has spoken:
"I have not been in labor or given birth.
I have not raised young men
or brought up young women."
5 When the news reaches Egypt,
they will be in anguish
over the news about Tyre.[h]
6 Cross over to Tarshish;
wail, inhabitants of the coastland!
7 Is this your jubilant city,
whose origin was in ancient times,
whose feet have taken her
to reside far away?
8 Who planned this against Tyre,
the bestower of crowns,
whose traders are princes,
whose merchants are
the honored ones of the earth?

9 The LORD of Armies planned it,
to desecrate all its glorious beauty,
to disgrace all the honored ones
of the earth.
10 Overflow[c] your land like the Nile,
daughter of Tarshish;
there is no longer anything
to restrain you.[D]
11 He stretched out his hand
over the sea;[i]
he made kingdoms tremble.
The LORD has commanded
that the Canaanite fortresses
be destroyed.
12 He said,
"You will not celebrate anymore,
ravished young woman,
daughter of Sidon.
Get up and cross over to Cyprus[j] —
even there you will have no rest!"
13 Look at the land of the Chaldeans —
a people who no longer exist.
Assyria destined it
for desert creatures.
They set up their siege towers
and stripped its palaces.
They made it a ruin.
14 Wail, ships of Tarshish,
because your fortress is destroyed!

15 On that day Tyre will be forgotten for seventy years — the life span of one king. At the end of seventy years, what the song says about the prostitute will happen to Tyre:
16 Pick up your lyre,
stroll through the city,
you forgotten prostitute.
Play skillfully,
sing many a song
so that you will be remembered.

17 And at the end of the seventy years,[k] the LORD will restore Tyre[l] and she will go back into business, prostituting herself with all the kingdoms of the world throughout the earth. 18 But her profits and wages will be dedicated to the LORD. They will not be stored or saved, for her profit will go to those who live in the LORD's

---

^A 23:1 Hb *Kittim*   ^B 23:2 DSS; MT reads *Sidon, whom the seafarers have filled*   ^C 23:10 DSS, LXX read *Work*   ^D 23:10 Or *longer any harbor*

23:1-2 In the Bible, **Tyre** is often linked with the city of **Sidon** because they were two major seaports of Phoenicia.
23:8-9 Tyre's **merchants** were considered **the honored ones of the earth** (22:8), but that meant nothing because the Lord had **planned** to **disgrace** them (22:9). This is a sobering reminder that to be honored in the eyes of

people means nothing if you earn God's displeasure.
23:14 Tyre was not actually **destroyed** until several hundred years later, but in God's sight the judgment was as good as done.
23:15 Exactly when Tyre would be **forgotten for seventy years** is unclear. The length suggests the seventy years of the Babylonian

captivity of Judah, but that was much later. Thus, some suggest it refers to a period when Assyria ruled Tyre and limited its trade.
23:18 God knows how to take the wealth of the wicked and use it for kingdom purposes.

presence, to provide them with ample food and sacred clothing.

THE EARTH JUDGED

24 Look, the LORD is stripping
the earth bare
and making it desolate.
He will twist its surface and scatter
its inhabitants:
2 people and priest alike,
servant and master,
female servant and mistress,
buyer and seller,
lender and borrower,
creditor and debtor.
3 The earth will be stripped
completely bare
and will be totally plundered,
for the LORD has spoken
this message.[a]

4 The earth mourns and withers;
the world wastes away and withers;
the exalted people of the earth
waste away.
5 The earth is polluted
by its inhabitants,[b]
for they have transgressed
teachings,
overstepped decrees,
and broken
the permanent covenant.[c]
6 Therefore a curse has consumed
the earth,[d]
and its inhabitants
have become guilty;
the earth's inhabitants
have been burned,
and only a few survive.
7 The new wine mourns;[e]
the vine withers.
All the carousers now groan.
8 The joyful tambourines[f]
have ceased.
The noise of the jubilant
has stopped.
The joyful lyre has ceased.

9 They no longer sing
and drink wine;
beer is bitter to those who drink it.
10 The city of chaos is shattered;[g]
every house is closed to entry.[h]
11 In the streets they cry[A] for wine.
All joy grows dark;
earth's rejoicing goes into exile.
12 Only desolation remains in the city;
its gate has collapsed in ruins.
13 For this is how it will be on earth
among the nations:
like a harvested olive tree,
like a gleaning after a grape harvest.[i]

14 They raise their voices, they sing out;
they proclaim in the west
the majesty of the LORD.
15 Therefore, in the east
honor the LORD!
In the coasts and islands of the west
honor the name of the LORD,
the God of Israel.
16 From the ends of the earth
we hear songs:
The Splendor of the Righteous One.[j]

But I said, "I waste away!
I waste away![B]
Woe is me."
The treacherous act treacherously;
the treacherous deal
very treacherously.[k]

17 Panic, pit, and trap await you[l]
who dwell on the earth.[m]
18 Whoever flees at the sound of panic
will fall into a pit,
and whoever escapes from the pit
will be caught in a trap.
For the windows on high
are opened,[n]
and the foundations of the earth
are shaken.[o]
19 The earth is completely devastated;
the earth is split open;
the earth is violently shaken.

a 24:3 Is 1:20; 6:11
b 24:5 Gn 3:17; 6:5,11-12; Nm 35:33; Is 9:17; 10:6
c Gn 9:16; 17:7; Ex 31:16; Lv 24:8; 2Sm 23:5; Ps 105:10; Is 55:3; 61:8; Jr 32:40; Ezk 16:60
d 24:6 Jos 23:15; Is 34:5; 43:28; Zch 5:3-4
e 24:7 Is 16:10; Jl 1:10,12
f 24:8 Ex 15:20; Jdg 11:34; 1Sm 18:6; Is 30:32; Jr 31:4

g 24:10 Is 34:11
h Is 23:1
i 24:13 Is 17:6
j 24:16 Ex 9:27; Pr 21:12; Ac 3:14; 7:52; 22:14
k Is 21:2; 33:1; Jr 3:20; 5:11
l 24:17 Am 5:19
m 24:17-18 Jr 48:43-44
n 24:18 Gn 7:11
o Ps 18:7; 46:2; Is 2:19,21; 13:13

A 24:11 Lit streets she cries   B 24:16 Hb obscure

24:1-6 Isaiah is referring to something far larger than the judgments of his day. In view here is universal judgment, set in motion directly by God. **The permanent covenant** probably refers to God's universal laws of righteousness that all people are obliged to obey (24:5).
24:7-13 Isaiah pictured a sinful humanity groaning under the weight of God's wrath. All of their joy, festivities, and drinking? Gone.
24:14, 16 These were evidently the righteous praising God for his glory and his

righteous judgment on sin. **They sing** (24:14) because they are spared the wrath of God, which is the best reason of all to sing! Don't miss that their song has one subject: **The Splendor of the Righteous One** (24:16). This great chorus of voices will be heard in Christ's millennial kingdom when he returns to judge and rule the earth for one thousand years.
24:17-22 When the Son of God comes in his fiery wrath to execute his justice, it will be futile to run. The wicked won't escape,

and this group will include both God's earthly enemies and the heavenly ones too: **the LORD will punish the army of the heights in the heights and the kings of the ground on the ground** (24:21). The angelic forces that rebelled with Satan, then, will meet their doom. Moreover, the world's mighty leaders who defy God will be treated as **prisoners** in the great tribulation (24:22). When Jesus comes to take his rightful throne, there will be no doubt about who is earth's rightful King.

*a*24:20 Is 19:14
*b*24:21 Is 27:12
*c*24:22 Rv 20:1-3
*d*Rv 20:2
*e*24:23 Is 2:2-4; 1Co 15:54
*f*25:1 Ex 15:2; Ps 118:28; Is 7:13; 44:17
*g*25:2 Is 17:1; 26:5
*h*Col 3:11
*i*25:4 Mt 11:29
*j*Is 4:6; 32:2

*k*25:6 Is 2:2-4
*l*Is 24:23; Rv 19:9
*m*25:7 2Co 3:15-16; Eph 4:18
*n*25:8 Hs 13:14; 1Co 15:54; Rv 21:4
*o*Is 30:19; 35:10; 51:11; 65:19; Rv 7:17; 21:4
*p*Ps 89:50-51; Is 51:7; 54:4; Mt 5:11; 1Pt 4:14
*q*25:9 Is 35:1-2,10; 66:10
*r*25:10 Nm 24:17; Is 15:1
*s*25:11 Is 2:10-12,15-17; 16:6,14
*t*25:10-12 Is 26:5-6

20 The earth staggers like a drunkard[a]
and sways like a hut.
Earth's rebellion weighs it down,
and it falls, never to rise again.

21 On that day[b] the LORD will punish
the army of the heights in the
heights
and the kings of the ground on the
ground.

22 They will be gathered together
like prisoners in a pit.[c]
They will be confined to a dungeon;[d]
after many days
they will be punished.

23 The moon will be put to shame
and the sun disgraced,
because the LORD of Armies
will reign as king
on Mount Zion in Jerusalem,
and he will display his glory
in the presence of his elders.[e]

SALVATION AND JUDGMENT ON THAT DAY

25 LORD, you are my God;[f]
I will exalt you. I will praise
your name,
for you have accomplished wonders,
plans formed long ago,
with perfect faithfulness.

2 For you have turned the city
into a pile of rocks,[g]
a fortified city, into ruins;
the fortress of barbarians[h] is
no longer a city;
it will never be rebuilt.

3 Therefore, a strong people
will honor you.
The cities of violent nations
will fear you.

4 For you have been a stronghold
for the poor person,
a stronghold for the needy[i]
in his distress,
a refuge from storms and a shade
from heat.[j]
When the breath of the violent
is like a storm against a wall,

5 like heat in a dry land,
you will subdue the uproar
of barbarians.
As the shade of a cloud cools
the heat of the day,
so he will silence the song
of the violent.

6 On this mountain,[A,k]
the LORD of Armies will prepare for
all the peoples a feast of choice
meat,[l]
a feast with aged wine, prime cuts of
choice meat,[B] fine vintage wine.

7 On this mountain
he will destroy the burial shroud,
the shroud over all the peoples,
the sheet covering all the nations;[m]

8 he will destroy death forever.[n]
The Lord GOD will wipe away
the tears
from every face[o]
and remove his people's disgrace[p]
from the whole earth,
for the LORD has spoken.

9 On that day it will be said,
"Look, this is our God;
we have waited for him, and he has
saved us.
This is the LORD; we have waited
for him.
Let us rejoice and be glad
in his salvation."[q]

10 For the LORD's power will rest
on this mountain.

But Moab[r] will be trampled
in his place[c]
as straw is trampled in a dung pile.

11 He will spread out his arms
in the middle of it,
as a swimmer spreads out his arms
to swim.
His pride will be brought low,
along with the trickery of his hands.[s]

12 The high-walled fortress
will be brought down,
thrown to the ground, to the dust.[t]

[A]25:6 = Mount Zion   [B]25:6 Lit *wine, fat full of marrow*   [C]25:10 Or *trampled under him*

25:6-9 Speaking of the millennial kingdom, Isaiah says, **On this mountain, the LORD of Armies will prepare for all the peoples a feast** (25:6). This promise emphasizes both God's care for his people and the worldwide reach of Christ's rule as the Lord of all the earth. This is not the marriage supper of the Lamb (Rev 19), which occurs before the kingdom is established, but a banquet celebrating Christ's victory over all the forces of earth. And it gets even better. God will **destroy death forever** and **wipe away the tears from every face** (25:8). Those are promises you can bank on. And what a joy and privilege it will be to stand among those who declare, **Look, this is our God; we have waited for him, and he has saved us** (25:9)! Those who trust him now will see the vindication of their hope and the fulfillment of God's Word.

25:10-11 That Christ will rule **on this mountain** refers to Jerusalem where his throne will be established. **Moab** is used here probably as a representative of all of God's enemies—none of whom will be able to stand before him. The image of rebellious nations swimming **in a dung pile** (25:10) could not be more graphic. Those who, like Moab, proudly shake their fist at God will experience complete humiliation.

THE SONG OF JUDAH

26 On that day this song will be sung
in the land of Judah:
We have a strong city.
Salvation is established as walls
and ramparts.[a]

2 Open the gates
so a righteous nation can come in —
one that remains faithful.

⤳ HOPE WORDS ⤳

*You cannot expect to have
peace around you if you do
not have peace within you.*

---

3 You will keep the mind that is
dependent on you
in perfect peace,[b]
for it is trusting in you.

4 Trust in the LORD forever,
because in the LORD, the LORD himself,
is an everlasting rock![c]

5 For he has humbled those who live
in lofty places —
an inaccessible city.[d]
He brings it down; he brings it down
to the ground;
he throws it to the dust.

6 Feet trample it,
the feet of the humble,
the steps of the poor.

GOD'S PEOPLE VINDICATED

7 The path of the righteous is level;[e]
you clear a straight path
for the righteous.

8 Yes, LORD, we wait for you
in the path of your judgments.
Our desire is for your name
and renown.[f]

9 I long for you in the night;[g]
yes, my spirit within me
diligently seeks you,
for when your judgments are
in the land,
the inhabitants of the world
will learn righteousness.

10 But if the wicked man is
shown favor,
he does not learn righteousness.
In a righteous land he acts unjustly
and does not see the majesty
of the LORD.

11 LORD, your hand is lifted up
to take action,
but they do not see it.
Let them see your zeal for your people
and be put to shame.
Let fire consume your adversaries.

12 LORD, you will establish peace for us,
for you have also done all our work
for us.

13 LORD our God, lords other than you
have owned[A] us,
but we remember your name alone.[h]

14 The dead do not live;
departed spirits do not rise up.
Indeed, you have punished
and destroyed them;
you have wiped out all memory
of them.[i]

15 You have added to the nation, LORD.[j]
You have added to the nation;
you are honored.
You have expanded all the borders
of the land.[k]

16 LORD, they went to you
in their distress;[l]
they poured out whispered prayers
because your discipline fell on them.[B]

17 As a pregnant woman
about to give birth
writhes and cries out in her pains,[m]
so we were before you, LORD.

18 We became pregnant, we writhed
in pain;
we gave birth to wind.
We have won no victories on earth,
and the earth's inhabitants
have not fallen.

19 Your dead will live; their bodies[c]
will rise.[n]
Awake and sing, you who dwell
in the dust!

[a] 26:1 Is 60:18
[b] 26:3 Is 26:12; 27:5; 57:19; 66:12
[c] 26:4 Ps 73:26; Is 17:10; 30:29; 44:8
[d] 26:5-6 Is 25:10-12
[e] 26:7 Ps 27:11
[f] 26:8 Ex 3:15
[g] 26:9 Ps 77:2; 84:2; 119:20,81

[h] 26:13 Jn 10:25
[i] 26:14 Jb 18:17; Ps 9:6
[j] 26:15 Is 9:3
[k] Is 33:17; 54:2-3
[l] 26:16 Is 37:3; Hs 5:15
[m] 26:17 Is 13:8
[n] 26:19 Is 25:8; Ezk 37:1-14; Dn 12:2; Hs 13:14; Mt 11:5; Lk 7:22; Jn 8:51

[A] 26:13 Or *married*　　[B] 26:16 Hb obscure　　[c] 26:19 Lit *live; my body they*

26:3 Such **peace** is not only valid in the kingdom age, but also for all those who tune their minds to God's spiritual realities.
26:5-7 The reversal of earthly fortunes in Christ's kingdom continues with the picture of the proud and mighty **who live in lofty places** (26:5). They're convinced they're out of reach, only to find themselves trampled by **the feet of the humble** and **the poor** (26:6). By contrast, though God's people may have trials, he will smooth out their **path** (26:7).
26:10-11 It takes a special kind of blindness not to recognize the work of God when it is all around us, but Judah did not turn back to the Lord because they stubbornly refused to give up their evil ways. They would not *want* to be saved from judgment because they didn't *want* to be saved. And so they would fall to God's consuming **fire** (26:11; see Heb 12:29).
26:14 Oppression will never happen again when all evil rulers are **dead**.
26:19 This is a clear promise of resurrection for the righteous.

a 26:20 Is 10:5,25; 13:5;
34:2; 66:14
b 26:21 Mc 1:3
c Is 13:11
d 27:1 Jb 3:8; 41:1,34; Ps
74:14; 104:26
e Is 51:9
f 27:2 Ps 80:8; Is 5:7; Jr 2:21
g 27:4 2Sm 23:6; Is 10:17
h 27:6 Is 37:31
i Is 35:1-2; Hs 14:5-6
j 27:7 Is 10:12,17; 30:31-33;
31:8-9; 37:36-38

k 27:9 Is 13:11
l Rm 11:27
m 27:11 Ps 32:9; 49:20;
Jr 4:22
n Jb 4:17; Ps 95:6; Pr 14:31;
Is 17:7; 29:16; 44:2; 45:9,11;
51:13; 54:5; Hs 8:14
o 27:12 Is 3:18; 7:18,20;
11:11; 24:21; Zch 12:8
p Gn 15:18
q 27:13 Lv 25:9; 1Ch
15:24; Mt 24:31; 1Th 4:16;
Rv 11:15
r 28:1 Is 28:7; Hs 7:5

For you will be covered
with the morning dew,[A]
and the earth will bring out
the departed spirits.

20 Go, my people, enter your rooms
and close your doors behind you.
Hide for a little while until the wrath
has passed.[a]

21 For look, the LORD is coming
from his place[b]
to punish the inhabitants
of the earth for their iniquity.[c]
The earth will reveal the blood shed
on it
and will no longer conceal her slain.

LEVIATHAN SLAIN

27 On that day the LORD with his relentless, large, strong sword will
bring judgment on Leviathan,[d] the fleeing serpent — Leviathan, the twisting
serpent. He will slay the monster that is
in the sea.[e]

THE LORD'S VINEYARD

2 On that day
sing about a desirable vineyard:[f]
3 I am the LORD, who watches over it
to water it regularly.
So that no one disturbs it,
I watch over it night and day.
4 I am not angry.
If only there were thorns and briers[g]
for me to battle,
I would trample them
and burn them to the ground.
5 Or let it take hold of my strength;
let it make peace with me —
make peace with me.
6 In days to come,
Jacob will take root.[h]
Israel will blossom and bloom[i]
and fill the whole world with fruit.

7 Did the LORD strike Israel
as he struck the one
who struck Israel?[j]
Was Israel killed like those killed
by the LORD?

8 You disputed with Israel
by banishing and driving her away.[B]
He removed her
with his severe storm
on the day of the east wind.
9 Therefore Jacob's iniquity[k]
will be atoned for in this way,
and the result of the removal
of his sin will be this:[l]
when he makes all the altar stones
like crushed bits of chalk,
no Asherah poles or incense altars
will remain standing.
10 For the fortified city will be desolate,
pastures deserted and abandoned
like a wilderness.
Calves will graze there,
and there they will spread out
and strip its branches.
11 When its branches dry out,
they will be broken off.
Women will come and make fires
with them,
for they are not a people
with understanding.[m]
Therefore their Maker[n] will not
have compassion on them,
and their Creator will not
be gracious to them.

12 On that day[o]
the LORD will thresh grain
from the Euphrates River
as far as the Wadi of Egypt,[p]
and you Israelites will be gathered
one by one.
13 On that day
a great trumpet[q] will be blown,
and those lost in the land of Assyria
will come,
as well as those dispersed
in the land of Egypt;
and they will worship the LORD
at Jerusalem on the holy mountain.

WOE TO SAMARIA

28 Woe to the majestic crown
of Ephraim's drunkards,[r]
and to the fading flower
of its beautiful splendor,

A 26:19 Lit *For your dew is a dew of lights*   B 27:8 Hb obscure

---

27:1 At Christ's return to defeat his foes and
establish his kingdom, he will strike down
Israel's enemies. They are represented here
by **Leviathan, the fleeing serpent**. There was
a myth in the ancient Near East about this
creature. Isaiah was not endorsing it as fact;
he simply borrowed the imagery to depict
God's enemies.

27:2-6 This description of Israel as the Lord's
vineyard (27:2) in the kingdom contrasts
sharply with the depiction of Israel as a vineyard
in 5:1-7. It highlights the dramatic turn that will
come about for God's people. In Isaiah's day,
Israel was an unfruitful kingdom, producing
worthless grapes. But in the kingdom to come,
redeemed Israel will thrive under God's tending.

28:1-3 Although Isaiah's primary message was
to Judah, God also used him to speak to the
northern kingdom in the last years before its
decimation by the Assyrians. Ephraim was
a common name for the northern nation of
Israel, since it was the most prominent of its
ten tribes.

which is on the summit above
   the rich valley.
Woe to those overcome
   with wine.
2 Look, the Lord has a strong
   and mighty one[a] —
like a devastating hail storm,
like a storm with strong
   flooding water.
He will bring it across the land
   with his hand.
3 The majestic crown
   of Ephraim's drunkards
will be trampled underfoot.
4 The fading flower
   of his beautiful splendor,
which is on the summit
   above the rich valley,
will be like a ripe fig
   before the summer harvest.[b]
Whoever sees it will swallow it
while it is still in his hand.
5 On that day
the LORD of Armies will become
   a crown of beauty
and a diadem of splendor[c]
   to the remnant of his people,
6 a spirit of justice
to the one who sits in judgment,[d]
and strength
to those who repel attacks at the city
   gate.

7 Even these stagger because of wine
and stumble under the influence
   of beer:
priest and prophet stagger
   because of beer,
they are confused by wine.[e]
They stumble because of beer,
they are muddled in their visions,
they stumble in their judgments.
8 Indeed, all their tables are covered
   with vomit;
there is no place without a stench.
9 Who is he trying to teach?
Who is he trying to instruct?
Infants[A] just weaned
   from milk?
Babies[A] removed from the breast?

10 "Law after law, law after law,
line after line, line after line,
a little here, a little there."[B]
11 For he will speak to this people
with stammering speech
and in a foreign language.[f]
12 He had said to them:
"This is the place of rest;
let the weary rest;[g]
this is the place of repose."
But they would not listen.

13 The word of the LORD will come
   to them:
"Law after law, law after law,
line after line, line after line,
a little here, a little there,"
so they go stumbling backward,
to be broken, trapped, and captured.[h]

A DEAL WITH DEATH

14 Therefore hear the word
   of the LORD,[i] you scoffers[j]
who rule this people
   in Jerusalem.
15 For you said, "We have made
   a covenant with Death,
and we have an agreement
   with Sheol;
when the overwhelming
   catastrophe[c] passes through,[k]
it will not touch us,
because we have made falsehood
   our refuge
and have hidden behind treachery."
16 Therefore the Lord GOD said:
"Look, I have laid a stone[l] in Zion,
a tested stone,
a precious cornerstone,
   a sure foundation;[m]
the one who believes
   will be unshakable.[D,n]
17 And I will make justice
   the measuring line
and righteousness
   the mason's level."[o]
Hail will sweep away
   the false refuge,
and water will flood
   your hiding place.

[a]28:2 Is 8:7; 40:10
[b]28:4 Hs 9:10; Mc 7:1; Nah 3:12
[c]28:5 Is 62:3
[d]28:6 1Kg 3:28; Is 11:2; 32:1,15-16; Jn 5:30
[e]28:7 Is 5:11,22; 9:15; 22:13; 56:12; Hs 4:11
[f]28:11-12 Is 5:26-29; 33:19; 1Co 14:21
[g]28:12 Is 11:10; 30:15; 32:17-18; Jr 6:16; Mt 11:28-29
[h]28:13 Is 8:15; Mt 21:44
[i]28:14 Is 1:10; 39:5,8; 66:5
[j]Is 29:20
[k]28:15 Is 8:7-8
[l]28:16 Is 8:14; 26:4
[m]Mt 21:42; Mk 12:10; Lk 20:17; Ac 4:11; 1Co 3:11; Eph 2:20
[n]Rm 9:33; 1Pt 2:6
[o]28:17 2Kg 21:13; Is 5:16; 30:18; 61:8; Am 7:7-9

[A]28:9 Lit *Those*   [B]28:10 Hb obscure, also in v. 13   [C]28:15 Or *whip*; Hb obscure, also in v. 18   [D]28:16 Lit *will not hurry*

28:7-8 Israel's pitiful spiritual leaders were nothing more than drunks.
28:9-13 God turned the mocking of Israel's prophets and priests, who'd been harassing Isaiah (28:9-10), back on them (28:11-13). Isaiah said, in effect, "If you don't want to listen to God's spokesman delivering his message of warning and judgment, then you will hear it from a people whose language you do not know." They would hear it from the Assyrians.
28:14-15 Though the warnings in this chapter were directed against the northern kingdom, the Lord also had a word for Judah, particularly those who ruled **in Jerusalem** (28:14). They had made a very strange boast (28:15). Evidently, and foolishly, these corrupt leaders were affirming their confidence in their alliance with Egypt to save them from the Assyrian invasion. The statement may also reflect their belief in false gods, since **Death** (28:15) was often personified as a god in the pagan religions practiced around them.
28:16 The apostle Paul saw this fulfilled in the Lord Jesus Christ, the **stone in Zion** (Rom 9:33).

a 28:19 2Ch 29:8; Jr 15:4;
     24:9; 29:18
b 28:21 2Sm 5:20; 1Ch 14:11
c Jos 10:10,12; 2Sm 5:25;
     1Ch 14:16
d 28:22 Is 10:22-23; Rm
     9:27-28

e 28:29 Is 9:6; Jr 32:19
f 29:1 2Sm 5:9
g 29:4 Is 8:19
h 29:5 Is 17:13; 41:15-16
i Is 17:14; 30:13; 47:11;
     1Th 5:3
j 29:6 Ex 9:23; 19:16,19;
20:18; 1Sm 2:10; 12:18; Jb
40:9; Ps 77:18; Zch 14:5;
     Rv 4:5; 11:13
k 29:7 Mc 4:11-12; Zch 12:9
l Jb 20:8; Ps 73:20; Is 17:14

18 Your covenant with Death
     will be dissolved,
and your agreement with Sheol
     will not last.
When the overwhelming
     catastrophe passes through,
you will be trampled.
19 Every time it passes through,
it will carry you away;
it will pass through
     every morning —
every day and every night.
Only terror*a* will cause you
to understand the message.^A
20 Indeed, the bed is too short
     to stretch out on,
and its cover too small to wrap up in.
21 For the LORD will rise up as he did
     at Mount Perazim.*b*
He will rise in wrath, as at the Valley
     of Gibeon,*c*
to do his work, his unexpected work,
and to perform his task,
     his unfamiliar task.
22 So now, do not scoff,
or your shackles
     will become stronger.
Indeed, I have heard from the Lord
     GOD of Armies
a decree of destruction
     for the whole land.*d*

GOD'S WONDERFUL ADVICE

23 Listen and hear my voice.
Pay attention and hear what I say.
24 Does the plowman plow every day
     to plant seed?
Does he continuously break up
     and cultivate the soil?
25 When he has leveled its surface,
does he not then scatter black cumin
     and sow cumin?
He plants wheat in rows and barley
     in plots,
with spelt as their border.
26 His God teaches him order;
he instructs him.
27 Certainly black cumin
     is not threshed
with a threshing board,
and a cart wheel is not rolled
     over the cumin.

But black cumin is beaten out
     with a stick,
and cumin with a rod.
28 Bread grain is crushed,
but is not threshed endlessly.
Though the wheel
     of the farmer's cart rumbles,
his horses do not crush it.
29 This also comes from the LORD
     of Armies.
He gives wondrous advice;
he gives great wisdom.*e*

WOE TO JERUSALEM

29 Woe to Ariel,*B* Ariel,
     the city where David camped!*f*
Continue year after year;
let the festivals recur.
2 I will oppress Ariel,
and there will be mourning
     and crying,
and she will be to me like an Ariel.
3 I will camp in a circle around you;
I will besiege you with earth ramps,
and I will set up my siege towers
     against you.
4 You will be brought down;
you will speak from the ground,
and your words will come from low
     in the dust.
Your voice will be like that of a spirit
     from the ground;*g*
your speech will whisper
     from the dust.
5 Your many foes*c* will be like fine dust,*h*
and many of the ruthless,
     like blowing chaff.
Then suddenly, in an instant,*i*
6 you will be punished by the LORD
     of Armies
with thunder, earthquake,
     and loud noise,
storm, tempest, and a flame
     of consuming fire.*j*
7 All the many nations*k*
going out to battle against Ariel —
all the attackers, the siege works
     against her,
and those who oppress her —
will then be like a dream, a vision
     in the night.*l*

---

^A 28:19 Or *The understanding of the message will cause sheer terror*   ^B 29:1 Or *Altar Hearth,* or *Lion of God*; Hb obscure, also in v. 2
                                                       ^c 29:5 Lit *foreigners*

28:18 See the note on 28:14-15.
28:21 The **unfamiliar task** was severe judgment.
29:1-3 Even though the Assyrian army was occupied with the northern kingdom, Judah

was also in the enemy's crosshairs. Sennacherib's army marched to **Ariel**, another name for Jerusalem (29:1-2). The Assyrians besieged it, but it was not yet Judah's time for judgment (29:3). The Assyrian enemy would be

destroyed by God's supernatural intervention (see ch. 37).

8 It will be like a hungry one
   who dreams he is eating,
then wakes and is still hungry;
and like a thirsty one who dreams
   he is drinking,
then wakes and is still thirsty,
   longing for water.
So it will be for all the many nations
who go to battle
   against Mount Zion.

9 Stop and be astonished;
blind yourselves and be blind!
They are drunk,[A] but not with wine;
they stagger,[B] but not with beer.[a]
10 For the LORD has poured out on you
an overwhelming urge to[c] sleep;[b]
he has shut your eyes (the prophets)
and covered your
   heads (the seers).[c]
11 For you the entire vision will be like the
words of a sealed document.[d] If it is giv-
en to one who can read and he is asked to
read it,[D] he will say, "I can't read it, because
it is sealed." 12 And if the document is given
to one who cannot read and he is asked to
read it,[E] he will say, "I can't read."
   13 The Lord said:
These people approach me
   with their speeches[e]
to honor me with lip-service[F] —
yet their hearts are far from me,
and human rules direct their
   worship of me.[G]
14 Therefore, I will again confound
   these people
with wonder after wonder.[f]
The wisdom of their wise
   will vanish,[g]
and the perception
   of their perceptive will be hidden.

15 Woe to those who go
   to great lengths
to hide their plans from the LORD.[h]
They do their works in the dark,
and say, "Who sees us?
   Who knows us?"[i]
16 You have turned things around,
as if the potter were the same
   as the clay.
How can what is made say
   about its maker,
"He didn't make me"?[j]
How can what is formed
say about the one who formed it,
"He doesn't understand
   what he's doing"?

17 Isn't it true that in just
   a little while
Lebanon will become an orchard,
and the orchard will seem
   like a forest?[k]
18 On that day the deaf will hear[l]
the words of a document,
and out of a deep darkness
the eyes of the blind will see.
19 The humble will have joy
after joy in the LORD,
and the poor people will rejoice[m]
in the Holy One of Israel.[n]
20 For the ruthless one will vanish,
the scorner will disappear,[o]
and all those who lie in wait
   with evil intent
will be killed —
21 those who, with their speech,
accuse a person of wrongdoing,
who set a trap for the
   one mediating at the city gate
and without cause deprive
   the righteous of justice.[p]

[a] 29:9 Lk 1:15
[b] 29:10 Ps 69:23; Is 6:9-10; Mc 3:6
[c] Rm 11:8
[d] 29:11 Is 8:16; Dn 12:4,9; Mt 13:11; Rv 5:1
[e] 29:13 Ezk 33:31; Mt 15:8-9; Mk 7:6-7
[f] 29:14 Is 6:9-10; 28:21; 65:7; Hab 1:5
[g] Is 44:25; Jr 8:9; 49:7; 1Co 1:19

[h] 29:15 Ps 10:11,13; Is 28:15; 30:1
[i] Jb 22:13; Is 57:12; Ezk 8:12
[j] 29:16 Rm 9:20
[k] 29:17 Ps 84:6; 107:33,35; Is 32:15
[l] 29:18 Is 35:5; 42:18-19; 43:8; Mt 11:5; Mk 7:37
[m] 29:19 Ps 69:32; Is 49:13
[n] Is 1:4
[o] 29:20 Is 28:14
[p] 29:21 Is 32:7; Am 5:10,12

A 29:9 LXX, Tg, Vg read Be drunk   B 29:9 Tg, Vg read wine; stagger   C 29:10 Lit you a spirit of   D 29:11 Lit If one gives it to one who knows the
document, saying, "Read this, please"   E 29:12 Lit who does not know the document, saying, "Read this, please"   F 29:13 Lit their mouth and honor
me with its lips   G 29:13 Lit their fearing of me is a taught command of men

29:9-11 These verses illustrate a principle of spiritual receptivity and blindness that we see throughout Scripture. When people refuse to listen to God and reject his Word by deliberately closing their ears and eyes to it, God confirms their rebellious decision by sending them blindness and deafness. That's what happened to Pharaoh: He hardened his heart (see Exod 7:22; 8:15, 32); then God hardened it for him (Exod 9:12). The people of Judah blinded themselves, yet God also covered the eyes of the prophets and seers (29:10). This brings to mind the fact that Jesus said on more than one occasion that his teaching was meant to veil spiritual truth from those who had already made up their minds to reject it. The result for Judah was that God's message

was like the words of a sealed document that no one could understand (29:11).
29:13 This is a reminder that prayer and praise have to come from a heart in tune with God to be valid. Years later, these same words of condemnation would be fulfilled by the Jewish religious leaders of Jesus's day (see Matt 15:7-9).
29:17-21 These verses point forward to the kingdom age, which from God's point of view will come in just a little while (29:17). On that day, when Jesus Christ reigns in righteous glory, the deaf will hear and the eyes of the blind will see (29:18). God's kingdom will also be characterized by complete justice for the humble and the poor (29:19).
   Justice will be perfect when God's kingdom fully comes to earth, but we as believers

are not to ignore the importance of justice today as we seek to live out God's kingdom agenda. Biblical justice is not a man-made system ultimately leading to the negation of freedom. Instead, it promotes freedom by emphasizing accountability, equality, and responsibility in providing a spiritual underpinning in the social realms. It is the equitable and impartial application of God's moral law in society.
   Each of the four jurisdictions in God's kingdom—individual, family, church, and state—is called to promote justice and responsibility under God in its own distinct way. His Word is the standard by which the aspects of his law, reflected in truth and righteousness, govern what we do.

[a] 29:22 Is 41:8; 51:2; 63:16
[b] 29:23 2Sm 23:1; Ps 24:6; 76:6; 114:7; Is 2:3
[c] Is 5:16; 8:13
[d] 30:1 Dt 21:18-21; Is 1:2,23; 30:9; 65:2
[e] Is 29:15
[f] 30:2 Is 31:1; Jr 43:7
[g] Is 36:9
[h] 30:3 Is 20:5-6; 36:6; Jr 42:18,22
[i] 30:4 Is 19:11
[j] 30:5 Jr 2:36
[k] 30:6 Is 13:1

[l] 30:6 Dt 8:15
[m] 30:7 Ps 87:4; 89:10; Is 51:9; Ezk 29:3,7
[n] 30:9 Is 30:1
[o] 30:10 1Kg 22:8,13; Jr 6:14; 23:17,26; Ezk 13:8-16; Rm 16:18; 2Tm 4:3-4
[p] 30:11 Is 1:4; 41:14-20; 43:14; 45:11; 48:17; 49:7; 54:5; 55:5; 60:9,14
[q] 30:13 Is 13:11
[r] 30:14 Ps 2:9; Jr 19:10-11

22 Therefore, the Lord who redeemed Abraham[a] says this about the house of Jacob:

Jacob will no longer be ashamed,
and his face will no longer be pale.
23 For when he sees his children,
the work of my hands
within his nation,
they will honor my name,
they will honor the Holy One
of Jacob[b]
and stand in awe of the God of Israel.[c]
24 Those who are confused
will gain understanding,
and those who grumble
will accept instruction.

CONDEMNATION OF THE EGYPTIAN ALLIANCE

30 Woe to the rebellious children![d]
This is the Lord's declaration.
They carry out a plan,[e] but not mine;
they make an alliance,
but against my will,
piling sin on top of sin.
2 Without asking my advice
they set out to go down to Egypt[f]
in order to seek shelter
under Pharaoh's protection
and take refuge in Egypt's shadow.[g]
3 But Pharaoh's protection
will become your shame,
and refuge in Egypt's shadow
your humiliation.[h]
4 For though his[A] princes are at Zoan[i]
and his messengers reach
as far as Hanes,
5 everyone will be ashamed
because of a people who can't help.
They are of no benefit, they are
no help;
they are good for nothing but shame
and disgrace.[j]

6 A pronouncement[k] concerning the animals of the Negev:[B]

Through a land of trouble
and distress,
of lioness and lion,

of viper and flying serpent,[l]
they carry their wealth on the backs
of donkeys
and their treasures on the humps
of camels,
to a people who will not help them.
7 Egypt's help is completely worthless;
therefore, I call her:
Rahab Who Just Sits.[m]

8 Go now, write it on a tablet
in their presence
and inscribe it on a scroll;
it will be for the future,
forever and ever.
9 They are a rebellious people,
deceptive children,[n]
children who do not want to listen
to the Lord's instruction.
10 They say to the seers, "Do not see,"
and to the prophets,
"Do not prophesy the truth to us.
Tell us flattering things.[o]
Prophesy illusions.
11 Get out of the way!
Leave the pathway.
Rid us of the Holy One of Israel."[p]
12 Therefore the Holy One
of Israel says:
"Because you have rejected
this message
and have trusted in oppression
and deceit,
and have depended on them,
13 this iniquity[q] of yours will be
like a crumbling gap,
a bulge in a high wall
whose collapse will come
in an instant — suddenly!
14 Its collapse will be
like the shattering
of a potter's jar,[r] crushed to pieces,
so that not even a fragment
of pottery
will be found among
its shattered remains —
no fragment large enough
to take fire from a hearth
or scoop water from a cistern."

[A] 30:4 Or *Judah's*   [B] 30:6 Or *Southland*

30:1-5 The "pro-Egypt" party was lobbying hard for Judah to reach out **to Egypt** for help (30:1-2), but seeking aid from that place made no sense. Egypt was a fading power by this time, so politically and militarily the Egyptians had nothing to offer Judah. In fact, Egypt itself was headed for defeat at the hands of the Assyrians! Moreover, God had expressly forbidden his people to make alliances with Egypt, or even to go back to that place of their slavery (see Deut 17:16). Relying on Egypt sent a clear signal that Judah was depending on Egypt's gods instead of the true God.

30:10-11 These people, determined to rely on Egypt instead of God, were like people who say, "I've made up my mind; don't confuse me with the facts" (30:10). They didn't want to hear from **the Holy One of Israel** (30:11). Like rebellious children, they had their fingers in their ears.

30:12-14 Though the people of Judah didn't want another message from God, they got one—a powerful word of judgment. Their sin would crumble like a weak wall collapsing **suddenly** (30:13). And as in Humpy Dumpty's case, there would be no way to put the shattered **pieces** of their supposed strength back together again (30:14).

15 For the Lord GOD, the Holy One
        of Israel, has said:
    "You will be delivered by returning
        and resting;
    your strength will lie
        in quiet confidence.
    But you are not willing."
16 You say, "No!
    We will escape on horses" —
    therefore you will escape! —
    and, "We will ride on fast horses" —
    but those who pursue you
        will be faster.[a]
17 One thousand will flee at the threat
        of one,[b]
    at the threat of five you will flee,
    until you remain
    like a solitary pole on a mountaintop
    or a banner on a hill.

THE LORD'S MERCY TO ISRAEL

18 Therefore the LORD is waiting
        to show you mercy,
    and is rising up
        to show you compassion,[c]
    for the LORD is a just God.
    All who wait patiently for him
        are happy.

19 For people will live on Zion in Jerusalem. You will never weep again; he will
show favor to you at the sound of your
outcry; as soon as he hears, he will answer you. 20 The Lord will give you meager bread and water during oppression,[d]
but your Teacher[A] will not hide any longer. Your eyes will see your Teacher, 21 and
whenever you turn to the right or to the
left, your ears will hear this command
behind you: "This is the way. Walk in it."[e]
22 Then you will defile your silver-plated
idols and your gold-plated images. You
will throw them away like menstrual
cloths, and call them filth. 23 Then he will send rain for your seed
that you have sown in the ground, and the
food, the produce of the ground, will be
rich and plentiful. On that day your cattle
will graze in open pastures.[f] 24 The oxen and
donkeys that work the ground will eat salted fodder scattered with winnowing shovel[g] and fork. 25 Streams flowing with water
will be on every high mountain and every
raised hill on the day of great slaughter

when the towers fall. 26 The moonlight will
be as bright as the sunlight, and the sunlight will be seven times brighter[h] — like
the light of seven days — on the day[i] that
the LORD bandages his people's injuries and
heals the wounds he inflicted.[j]

ANNIHILATION OF THE ASSYRIANS

27 Look there! The LORD[B] is coming
        from far away,
    his anger burning and heavy
        with smoke.[c]
    His lips are full of fury,
    and his tongue is like a consuming fire.
28 His breath is like
        an overflowing torrent[k]
    that rises to the neck.[l]
    He comes to sift the nations
        in a sieve of destruction
    and to put a bridle on the jaws
        of the peoples
    to lead them astray.[m]
29 Your singing will be like that
    on the night of a holy festival,
    and your heart will rejoice
    like one who walks to the music
        of a flute,
    going up to the mountain
        of the LORD,
    to the Rock of Israel.[n]
30 And the LORD will make the splendor
        of his voice heard
    and reveal his arm[o] striking in
        angry wrath
    and a flame of consuming fire,
    in driving rain, a torrent,
        and hailstones.
31 Assyria will be shattered
        by the voice of the LORD.
    He will strike with a rod.
32 And every stroke
        of the appointed[D] staff
    that the LORD brings down on him
    will be to the sound of tambourines
        and lyres;
    he will fight against him
        with brandished weapons.
33 Indeed! Topheth has been ready[p]
    for the king for a long time.
    Its funeral pyre is deep and wide,
    with plenty of fire and wood.
    The breath of the LORD,[q]
        like a torrent of burning sulfur,
    kindles it.

a 30:16 Is 31:1,3
b 30:17 Lv 26:36; Dt 28:25;
32:30; Jos 23:10; Pr 28:1
c 30:18 2Pt 3:9
d 30:20 1Kg 22:27; Ps 80:5
e 30:21 Is 35:8-9
f 30:23 Ps 144:13; Is 32:20;
Hs 4:16
g 30:24 Mt 3:12

h 30:26 Is 24:23; 60:19-20;
Rv 21:23; 22:5
i Mt 25:13
j Is 33:24; Jr 33:6; Hs 6:1-2
k 30:28 Is 11:4; 30:33;
2Th 2:8
l Is 8:8
m 2Kg 19:28; Is 37:29
n 30:29 Is 8:14; 26:4
o 30:30 Ex 6:6; Dt 4:34;
Jb 40:9; Is 53:1; Jr 32:17;
Ezk 20:33
p 30:33 2Kg 23:10; Jr
7:31; 19:6
q Is 40:7

A 30:20 Or teachers   B 30:27 Or Look, the name of the LORD   C 30:27 Hb obscure   D 30:32 Some Hb mss read punishing

30:18-26 This is a description of Israel's blessing in the millennial kingdom.
30:20-21 The **Teacher** mentioned here is a reference to the Messiah, Jesus: no human could fulfill this role as perfectly as is described in
verse 21 (see Ps 32:8).

[a] 31:1 Is 30:2,7; 36:6
[b] Dt 17:16; Ps 20:7; 33:17; Is
    2:7; 30:16; 36:9
[c] Is 9:13; 17:7-8; Dn 9:13;
    Am 5:4-8
[d] 31:2 Is 45:7
[e] Nm 23:19; Is 22:14; Jr
    44:29
[f] 31:4 Nm 24:9; Hs 11:10;
    Am 3:8
[g] Is 42:13; Zch 12:8
[h] 31:5 Dt 32:11; Ps 91:4
[i] 31:6 Is 1:5; 59:13
[j] 31:7 Is 2:20; 30:22

[k] 31:8 Is 37:7,36-38
[l] Gn 49:15; Is 14:2
[m] 31:9 Dt 32:31,37
[n] Is 5:26; 13:2; Jr 4:6,21;
    51:12,27
[o] Lv 10:2; Is 10:17; 30:33
[p] 32:1 Ps 72:1-4; Is 9:6-7;
    11:4-5; Jr 23:5; Zch 9:9;
    14:9
[q] 32:2 Is 4:6; 25:4
[r] Is 30:25
[s] 32:3 Is 29:18
[t] 32:4 Is 33:19
[u] 32:5 Ps 107:40; 118:9;
    146:3
[v] 32:6 Is 3:15; 10:2

THE LORD, THE ONLY HELP

31 Woe to those who go down
    to Egypt for help[a]
and who depend on horses!
They trust in the abundance
    of chariots
and in the large number
    of horsemen.[b]
They do not look[c] to the Holy One
    of Israel
and they do not seek the LORD.

2 But he also is wise
    and brings disaster.[d]
He does not go back on what
    he says;[e]
he will rise up against the house
    of the wicked
and against the allies of evildoers.

3 Egyptians are men, not God;
    their horses are flesh, not spirit.
When the LORD raises his hand
    to strike,
the helper will stumble
and the one who is helped will fall;
both will perish together.

4 For this is what the LORD said to me:
As a lion or young lion growls
    over its prey[f]
when a band of shepherds
    is called out against it,
and is not terrified by their shouting
or subdued by their noise,
so the LORD of Armies
    will come down
to fight on Mount Zion
and on its hill.[g]

5 Like hovering birds,
so the LORD of Armies
    will protect Jerusalem[h] —
by protecting it, he will rescue it,
by sparing it, he will deliver it.

6 Return to the one the Israelites have
greatly rebelled against.[i] 7 For on that day,
every one of you will reject the silver and
gold idols that your own hands have sinfully made.[j]

8 Then Assyria will fall,
    but not by human sword;
a sword will devour him,
    but not one made by man.[k]
He will flee from the sword;
    his young men will be put
    to forced labor.[l]

9 His rock[A] will pass away
    because of fear,[m]
and his officers will be afraid
    because of the signal flag.[n]
This is the LORD's declaration — whose
fire is in Zion and whose furnace is in Jerusalem.[o]

THE RIGHTEOUS KINGDOM
ANNOUNCED

32 Indeed, a king will reign righteously,
    and rulers will rule justly.[p]
2 Each will be like a shelter
    from the wind,
a refuge from the rain,[q]
like flowing streams[r] in a dry land
and the shade of a massive rock
    in an arid land.

3 Then the eyes of those who see
    will not be closed,
and the ears of those who hear
    will listen.[s]

4 The reckless mind
    will gain knowledge,
and the stammering tongue[t]
    will speak clearly and fluently.

5 A fool will no longer be called
    a noble,[u]
nor a scoundrel said
    to be important.

6 For a fool speaks foolishness
    and his mind plots iniquity.
He lives in a godless way
and speaks falsely about the LORD.
He leaves the hungry empty
and deprives the thirsty of drink.[v]

7 The scoundrel's weapons
    are destructive;
he hatches plots to destroy
    the needy with lies,
even when the poor person says
    what is right.

[A] 31:9 Perhaps the Assyrian king

31:5 God would **protect Jerusalem**—not
because they deserved his protection—
but because God remained faithful to his
covenant.
31:8 The Assyrians camped at Israel's gates
were no problem for God. He'd take them out
in one night (see ch. 37)—not with the help of
the armies of Judah, but through "the angel
of the Lord" (Isa 37:36).

32:1 Under the rule of heaven on earth,
Christ's administrators will be a protection
for those in need. What a huge contrast to
the way Judah's leaders in Isaiah's day ran
things!
32:3-4 The people who enter the millennial
kingdom will be believers who survived the
great tribulation as well as the saints who
return with Jesus. There will be births in the

kingdom age, and these people will also see
and understand spiritual truth clearly. It
will be an age for which God's people have
longed but have never fully experienced.
True **knowledge** will be universally accepted,
taught, and understood (32:4). Our age has
been marked by spiritual blindness. The
truth is denied and twisted by those who
don't know the Lord.

8 But a noble person plans
  noble things;
he stands up for noble causes.

9 Stand up, you complacent women;[a]
  listen to me.
Pay attention to what I say,
  you overconfident daughters.
10 In a little more than a year
  you overconfident ones
    will shudder,
for the grapes will fail
  and the harvest will not come.
11 Shudder, you complacent ones;
  tremble, you overconfident ones!
Strip yourselves bare[b]
  and put sackcloth
    around your waists.
12 Beat your breasts
  in mourning[c]
for the delightful fields
  and the fruitful vines,[d]
13 for the ground of my people
  growing thorns and briers,[e]
indeed, for every joyous house
  in the jubilant city.
14 For the palace will be deserted,
  the busy city abandoned.
The hill and the watchtower
  will become
barren places forever,
  the joy of wild donkeys,
  and a pasture for flocks,
15 until the Spirit[A] from on high
  is poured out on us.[f]
Then the desert will become
  an orchard,
and the orchard will seem
  like a forest.[g]
16 Then justice will inhabit
  the wilderness,
and righteousness will dwell
  in the orchard.
17 The result of righteousness
  will be peace;[h]
the effect of righteousness
  will be quiet confidence forever.
18 Then my people will dwell
  in a peaceful place,
in safe and secure dwellings.

19 But hail will level the forest,[B,i]
  and the city will sink
    into the depths.[j]
20 You will be happy as you sow seed
  beside abundant water,[k]
  and as you let oxen and donkeys
    range freely.[l]

THE LORD RISES UP

33 Woe, you destroyer
    never destroyed,
  you traitor never betrayed!
When you have finished destroying,
  you will be destroyed.
When you have finished betraying,
  they will betray you.[m]

2 LORD, be gracious to us! We wait
    for you.[n]
Be our strength every morning
  and our salvation in time
    of trouble.[o]
3 The peoples flee
    at the thunderous noise;[p]
  the nations scatter when you rise
    in your majesty.
4 Your spoil will be gathered
    as locusts are gathered;
  people will swarm over it
    like an infestation of locusts.
5 The LORD is exalted, for he dwells
    on high;
  he has filled Zion with justice
    and righteousness.
6 There will be times of security
    for you —
  a storehouse of salvation, wisdom,
    and knowledge.
The fear of the LORD is
  Zion's treasure.[q]

7 Listen! Their warriors cry loudly
    in the streets;
  the messengers of peace
    weep bitterly.[r]
8 The highways are deserted;
  travel has ceased.
An agreement has been broken,[s]
  cities[c] despised,
  and human life disregarded.

a 32:9 Is 47:8; Am 6:1; Zph 2:15
b 32:11 Is 47:2-3
c 32:12 Nah 2:7
d Mk 14:25
e 32:13 Is 5:6; 7:23-25; 9:18; 27:4
f 32:15 Is 11:2; 44:3; 59:21; Ezk 39:29; Jl 2:28
g Is 29:17; 35:1-2
h 32:17 Ps 72:2-3; 85:8; 119:165; Is 2:4; Rm 14:17; Jms 3:18

i 32:19 Is 28:2,17; 30:30
j Is 24:10,12; 26:5; 27:10; 29:4
k 32:20 Nm 24:7; Ec 11:1; Is 30:23-24
l Is 30:24
m 33:1 2Kg 18:14-36; Is 17:14; 21:2
n 33:2 Is 25:9; 26:8
o Ex 15:2; Ps 28:8; Is 12:2; 17:10; 51:5
p 33:3 Is 17:13; 21:15
q 33:6 Is 11:2-3; Ac 9:31
r 33:7 2Kg 18:18,37; Is 36:3,22
s 33:8 2Kg 18:14-17; Is 24:5

A 32:15 Or a wind   B 32:19 Hb obscure   C 33:8 DSS read witnesses

32:9 These **women** dismissed Isaiah's warnings: they thought they would continue in luxury and self-indulgence without interruption (see the note on 3:16–4:1).
32:14 The abandonment of **the busy city** may imply that dozens of other Judean cities would be captured and ransacked by the Assyrians too.

32:15-17 Isaiah turned to the distant future again with further prophecy about the blessedness of the kingdom age.
33:1 Though God was using Assyria to discipline his people, it was a destruction machine that would, in the end, be annihilated itself when God's wrath against his rebellious children had been satisfied. Assyria would

experience the destruction it had wreaked on others.
33:2 This is the cry of those in Judah who were living righteous lives.

a 33:9 Is 3:26; 24:4; 29:2
b 33:10 Ps 12:5; Is 2:19,21
c 33:11 Ps 7:14; Is 26:18; 59:4; Jms 1:15
d 33:13 Is 18:2; Eph 2:17
e 33:14 Is 30:27,30; 66:15; Heb 12:29
f 33:15 Ps 15:2; 24:4; Is 58:6-11
g Ps 119:37
h 33:17 Is 6:5; 24:23; 33:21-22; Zch 9:9
i Is 54:2-3

j 33:19 Dt 28:49-50; Is 28:11; Jr 5:15
k 33:20 Ps 46:5; 125:1-2; Is 32:18
l Is 54:2
m 33:21 Rm 8:31
n Is 41:18; 43:19-20; 48:18; 66:12
o 33:22 Is 1:10; 51:4,7; Jms 4:12
p 2Sm 22:3; 23:5; 2Kg 19:19,34; Is 25:9; 35:4; 38:20
q 33:24 Is 40:2; 44:22; Jr 50:20; Mc 7:18-19; 1Jn 1:7-9
r Is 13:11
s 34:1 Ps 49:1; Is 1:2; 41:1; 43:9; 45:20
t Ps 24:1; Is 6:3; 42:5
u 34:2 Is 13:5; Jr 10:10; 50:13
v Jos 6:21; 1Sm 15:3; Is 11:5; 24:1,6; 43:28
w 34:3 Is 14:21; 18:6; Ezk 39:17; Jl 2:10; Am 4:10; Rv 19:17-19
x Ps 46:2-3

9 The land mourns and withers;*a*
Lebanon is ashamed and wilted.
Sharon is like a desert;
Bashan and Carmel shake off
their leaves.

10 "Now I will rise up,"*b* says the LORD.
"Now I will lift myself up.
Now I will be exalted.

11 You will conceive chaff;*c*
you will give birth to stubble.
Your breath is fire that will
consume you.

12 The peoples will be burned to ashes,
like thorns cut down and burned
in a fire.

13 You who are far off, hear what
I have done;
you who are near,*d* know my strength."

14 The sinners in Zion are afraid;
trembling seizes the ungodly:
"Who among us can dwell
with a consuming fire?*e*
Who among us can dwell
with ever-burning flames?"

15 The one who lives righteously
and speaks rightly,*f*
who refuses profit from extortion,
whose hand never takes a bribe,
who stops his ears from listening
to murderous plots
and shuts his eyes against
evil schemes*g* —

16 he will dwell on the heights;
his refuge will be
the rocky fortresses,
his food provided, his water assured.

17 Your eyes will see the King
in his beauty;*h*
you will see a vast land.*i*

18 Your mind will meditate
on the past terror:
"Where is the accountant?*A*
Where is the tribute collector?*B*
Where is the one who spied out
our defenses?"*C*

19 You will no longer see
the barbarians,

a people whose speech is difficult
to comprehend —
who stammer in a language that is
not understood.*j*

20 Look at Zion, the city
of our festival times.
Your eyes will see Jerusalem,
a peaceful pasture,*k* a tent
that does not wander;
its tent pegs will not be pulled up
nor will any of its cords
be loosened.*l*

21 For the majestic one, our LORD,
will be there,*m*
a place of rivers and broad streams
where ships that are rowed
will not go,
and majestic vessels will not pass.*n*

22 For the LORD is our Judge,
the LORD is our Lawgiver,*o*
the LORD is our King.
He will save us.*p*

23 Your ropes are slack;
they cannot hold the base
of the mast
or spread out the flag.
Then abundant spoil will be divided,
the lame will plunder it,

24 and none there will say, "I am sick."
The people who dwell there
will be forgiven*q* their iniquity.*r*

THE JUDGMENT OF THE NATIONS

34 You nations, come here and listen;
you peoples, pay attention!*s*
Let the earth and all that fills it hear,
the world and all that comes
from it.*t*

2 The LORD is angry with all
the nations,
furious with all their armies.*u*
He will set them apart
for destruction,*v*
giving them over to slaughter.

3 Their slain will be thrown out,
and the stench of their corpses
will rise;*w*
the mountains will flow*D*
with their blood.*x*

A 33:18 Lit *counter*   *B* 33:18 Lit *weigher*   *C* 33:18 Lit *who counts towers*   *D* 34:3 Or *melt*, or *dissolve*

33:22 Notice Isaiah's descriptions of God: **Judge . . . Lawgiver . . . King**. Man was created in the image of God, and God established government; therefore, it stands to reason that human governments should pattern themselves after God's government. In a fallen world, God's kingdom agenda is accomplished through decentralized institutions that recognize and submit to the divine authority of his Word.

When Jesus returns as the last Adam (see 1 Cor 15:45-49), he will do what the first Adam did not do: he will serve as a just and righteous Judge, Lawgiver, and King. Those who submit to his kingdom agenda now will have the privilege of ruling with him in the kingdom. Right now, God is selecting his prime ministers, governors, mayors, city council members, and so forth—faithful people who

will rule with him in his earthly kingdom. Will you be among them?
34:2 All the nations have opposed God and his people, filling up the cup of God's righteous wrath to be poured out in fury against them during the last great rebellion against heaven.

⁴ All^A the stars in the sky^a will dissolve.
The sky will roll up like a scroll,^b
and its stars will all wither
as leaves wither on the vine,
and foliage on the fig tree.^c

THE JUDGMENT OF EDOM

⁵ When my sword has drunk its fill^B,^d
in the heavens,
it will then come down on Edom^e
and on the people I have set apart
for destruction.

⁶ The LORD's sword is covered
with blood.
It drips with fat,
with the blood of lambs and goats,
with the fat of the kidneys of rams.^f
For the LORD has a sacrifice
in Bozrah,^g
a great slaughter in the land of Edom.

⁷ The wild oxen will be struck^c down
with them,
and young bulls with the mighty bulls.
Their land will be soaked with^D blood,
and their soil will be saturated
with fat.

⁸ For the LORD has a day of vengeance,^h
a time of paying back Edom
for its hostility against Zion.

⁹ Edom's streams will be turned
into pitch,
her soil into sulfur;^i
her land will become burning pitch.

¹⁰ It will never go out — day or night.
Its smoke will go up forever.^j
It will be desolate, from generation
to generation;
no one will pass through it forever
and ever.^k

¹¹ Eagle owls^E and herons^F
will possess it,
and long-eared owls and ravens
will dwell there.^l
The LORD will stretch out
a measuring line

and a plumb line over her
for her destruction and chaos.^m

¹² No nobles will be left to proclaim
a king,
and all her princes will come
to nothing.

¹³ Her palaces will be overgrown
with thorns;
her fortified cities, with thistles
and briers.^n
She will become a dwelling for jackals,
an abode^G for ostriches.^o

¹⁴ The desert creatures
will meet hyenas,
and one wild goat will call
to another.
Indeed, the night birds
will stay there
and will find a resting place.

¹⁵ Sand partridges^H will make
their nests there;
they will lay and hatch their eggs
and will gather their broods
under their shadows.
Indeed, the birds of prey
will gather there,
each with its mate.^p

¹⁶ Search and read the scroll
of the LORD:^q
Not one of them will be missing,
none will be lacking its mate,
because he has ordered it
by my^I mouth,
and he will gather them by his Spirit.

¹⁷ He has cast the lot for them;
his hand allotted their portion
with a measuring line.
They will possess it forever;^r
they will dwell in it from generation
to generation.

THE RANSOMED RETURN TO ZION

35 The wilderness and the dry land
will be glad;
the desert will rejoice and blossom
like a wildflower.^J,s

Cross-references

^a 34:4 2Kg 17:16; 21:3,5; 23:4-5
^b Rv 6:12-14
^c Ps 102:25-27; Is 13:10; 51:6; Ezk 32:7-8; Jl 3:15; Mt 24:29; Mk 13:24-25; 2Pt 3:10,12
^d 34:5 Dt 32:41-43; Jr 46:10; Ezk 21:3-5
^e Nm 20:14-21; Is 63:1; Jr 49:7-8,20; Ezk 25:12-14; 35:1-15; Jl 3:19; Am 1:11-12; Ob 1-14; Mal 1:4
^f 34:6 Is 25:6; 30:32; Jr 46:10; 51:40; Ezk 39:17; Zph 1:7-9
^g Gn 36:33; Is 63:1; Jr 49:13,22
^h 34:8 Is 13:6; 35:4; 47:3; 61:2; 63:4
^i 34:9 Gn 19:24; Dt 29:23; Ps 11:6; Is 30:33; Ezk 38:22
^j 34:10 Is 1:31; 66:24; Rv 14:11; 19:3
^k Is 13:20-22; Ezk 29:11; Mal 1:3-4
^l 34:11 Is 13:21-22; 14:23; Zph 2:14

^m 34:11 2Kg 21:13; Is 24:10; Lm 2:8
^n 34:13 Is 32:13
^o Ps 44:19; Is 13:22; Jr 9:11; 10:22; Mal 1:3
^p 34:15 Dt 14:13
^q 34:16 Ps 40:7; 139:16; Is 8:16; 30:8; Dn 7:10; Mal 3:16; Rv 20:12
^r 34:17 Nm 24:18
^s 35:1 Ps 65:12; Is 6:11; 7:21-25; 27:10; 32:15; 41:18-19; 51:3; 55:12-13

Text notes

^A 34:4 DSS read *And the valleys will be split, and all* ^B 34:5 DSS read *sword will appear* ^C 34:7 Or *will go* ^D 34:7 Or *will drink its fill of* ^E 34:11 Or *Pelicans* ^F 34:11 Or *hedgehogs* ^G 34:13 DSS, LXX, Syr, Tg; MT reads *jackals, grass* ^H 34:15 Or *Arrow snakes*, or *Owls* ^I 34:16 Some Hb mss; other Hb mss, DSS, Syr, Tg read *his* ^J 35:1 Or *meadow saffron*; traditionally *rose*

Study notes

34:4 The reference to **the stars** may be literal, in which case Isaiah could be describing the eternal state following the millennium: "The [new Jerusalem] does not need the sun or the moon to shine on it, because the glory of God illuminates it, and its lamp is the Lamb" (Rev 21:23). It's also possible that Isaiah was speaking metaphorically of worldly leaders whose powers will be stripped when Christ returns to defeat Satan.
34:5 Edom was an example of the ungodly nations God would judge and destroy. The

New Testament similarly used Esau, Edom's forefather, as an example of a godless person in order to warn believers: "Make sure that there isn't any immoral or irreverent person like Esau, who sold his birthright in exchange for a single meal" (Heb 12:16).
34:8 Although the Edomites should have supported Israel on its journey through the desert from Egypt to Canaan, they turned against the Israelites and made their journey harder (see Num 20:14-21).

34:10 A similar expression is used of the judgment on those who worship the antichrist during the tribulation: "the smoke of their torment will go up forever and ever" (Rev 14:11).
35:1 After the judgments of the tribulation will follow the joys of Christ's millennial kingdom. This is a promise that is particularly meaningful to anyone who has been to the Holy Land and seen the vast expanses of dry, desert land.

[a] 35:2 Sg 2:1; 5:15; 7:5; Is 33:9
[b] Ex 16:7,10; Lv 9:6,23; Nm 29:6; Is 40:5; Ezk 1:28; 3:23
[c] Ps 45:3-4; 96:6; 104:1; 145:5,12; Is 2:10,19,21; 53:2; 63:1; Ezk 16:14
[d] 35:3 Heb 12:12
[e] 35:4 Is 1:24; 34:8; 47:3; 59:17; 61:2; 63:4
[f] Is 33:22
[g] 35:5 Is 29:18; 32:3-4; 42:7,16,18; 50:4; Mt 11:5; Lk 7:22; Jn 9:6-7
[h] 35:6 Zph 3:19; Mt 11:5; 15:30-31; 21:14; Ac 3:1-8; 8:7; 14:8-10
[i] Ex 4:11; Mk 7:32; 9:25
[j] Is 41:18; 43:19; Jn 7:38-39
[k] 35:7 Is 49:10
[l] Is 13:22; 34:13
[m] 35:8 Is 40:3; 42:16; 43:16,19; 49:11; 51:10; 57:14; 62:10
[n] Is 4:3; 52:1; Mt 7:13-14; 1Pt 1:15-16
[o] Is 52:1; Rv 21:27
[p] Ps 139:24; Is 2:3; 8:11; 30:21; 42:24; 48:17; 58:13
[q] 35:10 Is 51:11

[r] 35:10 Is 65:19; Rm 9:2; Rv 21:4
[s] 36:1-22 2Kg 18:13,17-37; 2Ch 32:1-16,18
[t] 36:2 Jos 15:20,39
[u] Is 7:3
[v] 36:3 Is 22:15,20-21
[w] 36:5 2Kg 18:7
[x] 36:6 Ezk 29:6-7
[y] Is 30:3-7
[z] 36:7 Dt 12:2-5; 2Kg 18:4-5
[aa] 36:9 Is 20:5; 30:2-5,7; 31:3

It will blossom abundantly
and will also rejoice with joy
    and singing.
The glory of Lebanon will be given
    to it,
the splendor of Carmel and Sharon.[a]
They will see the glory of the Lord,[b]
the splendor of our God.[c]
3 Strengthen the weak hands,
    steady the shaking knees![d]
4 Say to the cowardly:
"Be strong; do not fear!
Here is your God;
    vengeance is coming.[e]
God's retribution is coming; he will
    save you."[f]
5 Then the eyes of the blind
    will be opened,
and the ears of the deaf unstopped.[g]
6 Then the lame will leap like a deer,[h]
and the tongue of the mute will sing
    for joy,[i]
for water will gush
    in the wilderness,
and streams in the desert;[j]
7 the parched ground will become
    a pool,
and the thirsty land springs.[k]
In the haunt of jackals,[l] in their lairs,
there will be grass, reeds,
    and papyrus.
8 A road will be there and a way;[m]
it will be called the Holy Way.[n]
The unclean will not travel on it,[o]
but it will be for the one who walks
    the path.[p]
Fools will not wander on it.
9 There will be no lion there,
and no vicious beast will go up on it;
they will not be found there.
But the redeemed will walk on it,
10 and the ransomed of the Lord
    will return[q]
and come to Zion with singing,
crowned with unending joy.

Joy and gladness will overtake them,
and sorrow and sighing will flee.[r]

SENNACHERIB'S INVASION

36 In the fourteenth year of King Hezekiah,[s] King Sennacherib of Assyria attacked all the fortified cities of Judah and captured them. 2 Then the king of Assyria sent his royal spokesman, along with a massive army, from Lachish[t] to King Hezekiah at Jerusalem. The Assyrian stood near the conduit of the upper pool, by the road to the Launderer's Field.[u] 3 Eliakim son of Hilkiah, who was in charge of the palace, Shebna the court secretary,[v] and Joah son of Asaph, the court historian, came out to him.

4 The royal spokesman said to them, "Tell Hezekiah:

The great king, the king of Assyria, says this: What are you relying on?[A] 5 You[B] think mere words are strategy and strength for war. Who are you now relying on that you have rebelled against me?[w] 6 Look, you are relying on Egypt, that splintered reed of a staff[x] that will pierce the hand of anyone who grabs it and leans on it. This is how Pharaoh king of Egypt is to all who rely on him.[y] 7 Suppose you say to me, 'We rely on the Lord our God.' Isn't he the one whose high places and altars Hezekiah has removed, saying to Judah and Jerusalem, 'You are to worship at this altar'?[z]

8 "Now make a deal with my master, the king of Assyria. I'll give you two thousand horses if you're able to supply riders for them! 9 How then can you drive back a single officer among the least of my master's servants? How can you rely on Egypt for chariots and horsemen?[aa] 10 Have I attacked this land to destroy it without the Lord's

---

A 36:4 Lit What is this trust that you trust   B 36:5 Many Hb mss, DSS, 2Kg 18:20; MT reads I

35:3 The author of Hebrews similarly urges his Christian readers (Heb 12:12). God's people throughout the ages need encouragement to persevere in the midst of a sinful world that entices and threatens them. Yet, if you align yourself with the King, you need not fear. Though the gates of hell rise against you, Satan can't prevail against Christ's church (see Matt 16:18). Therefore, look to the Lord. If you focus on his will for you, it will bring you much joy. This, in turn, will strengthen you to keep fighting the good fight, because "the joy of the Lord is your strength" (Neh 8:10).
35:5-10 We experience the joy of the Lord as

we sing to and worship him, but life also contains trials and sadness. In that day, however, we will know **unending joy** (35:10).
36:4-7 Ironically, this man's first reason for demanding Jerusalem's surrender was what Isaiah had been telling his people. Judah's desperate hope that an alliance with **Egypt** would somehow bring victory was absolutely futile (36:6). Next he proceeded to insult **the Lord** by saying that Judah's hope in him was also pointless. After all, hadn't Hezekiah removed his **high places**? (36:7). Of course, these were actually pagan locations for idol worship, and Hezekiah had done the right thing in

destroying them. The Assyrian commander thus revealed his complete ignorance of God.
36:8 The horse and rider comment was the ancient equivalent of saying, "Beating you will be so easy that I'll fight you with one hand tied behind my back."
36:10 Actually, God had sent the Assyrians, wielding them as a rod of anger to chastise his people for their sin (see 10:5-6). But Isaiah made it clear that Assyria had not come on this quest in submission to the Lord. So though God would use Assyria to discipline his people, he would also thrash Assyria for its pride (see 10:12).

approval? The LORD said to me, 'Attack this land and destroy it.'"

11 Then Eliakim, Shebna, and Joah said to the royal spokesman, "Please speak to your servants in Aramaic,[a] since we understand it. Don't speak to us in Hebrew[A] within earshot of the people who are on the wall."

12 But the royal spokesman replied, "Has my master sent me to speak these words to your master and to you, and not to the men who are sitting on the wall, who are destined with you to eat their own excrement and drink their own urine?"

13 Then the royal spokesman stood and called out loudly in Hebrew:

Listen to the words of the great king, the king of Assyria! **14** This is what the king says: "Don't let Hezekiah deceive you,[b] for he cannot rescue you. **15** Don't let Hezekiah persuade you to rely on the LORD, saying, 'The LORD will certainly rescue us! This city will not be handed over to the king of Assyria.'"

16 Don't listen to Hezekiah, for this is what the king of Assyria says: "Make peace[B] with me and surrender to me. Then every one of you may eat from his own vine and his own fig tree[c] and drink water from his own cistern **17** until I come and take you away to a land like your own land — a land of grain and new wine, a land of bread and vineyards. **18** Beware that Hezekiah does not mislead you by saying, 'The LORD will rescue us.'[d] Has any one of the gods of the nations[e] rescued his land from the power of the king of Assyria? **19** Where are the gods of Hamath and Arpad?[f] Where are the gods of Sepharvaim? Have they rescued Samaria from my power?[g] **20** Who

among all the gods of these lands ever rescued his land from my power? So will the LORD rescue Jerusalem from my power?"

21 But they kept silent; they didn't say anything, for the king's command was, "Don't answer him."[h] **22** Then Eliakim son of Hilkiah, who was in charge of the palace, Shebna the court secretary, and Joah son of Asaph, the court historian, came to Hezekiah with their clothes torn and reported to him the words of the royal spokesman.

HEZEKIAH SEEKS ISAIAH'S COUNSEL

37 When King Hezekiah heard their report,[i] he tore his clothes, put on sackcloth,[j] and went to the LORD's temple. **2** He sent Eliakim, who was in charge of the palace, Shebna the court secretary, and the leading priests, who were wearing sackcloth, to the prophet Isaiah son of Amoz. **3** They said to him, "This is what Hezekiah says: 'Today is a day of distress, rebuke, and disgrace.[k] It is as if children have come to the point of birth, and there is no strength to deliver them.[l] **4** Perhaps the LORD your God will hear all the words of the royal spokesman, whom his master the king of Assyria sent to mock the living God,[m] and will rebuke him for the words that the LORD your God has heard. Therefore offer a prayer for the surviving remnant.'"[n]

5 So the servants of King Hezekiah went to Isaiah, **6** who said to them, "Tell your master, 'The LORD says this: Don't be afraid[o] because of the words you have heard, with which the king of Assyria's attendants have blasphemed me.[p] **7** I am about to put a spirit[q] in him and he will hear a rumor and return to his own land, where I will cause him to fall by the sword.'"[r]

[a]36:11 Ezr 4:7; Dn 2:4
[b]36:14 Is 37:10
[c]36:16 1Kg 4:25; Mc 4:4; Zch 3:10
[d]36:18 Is 37:10
[e]1Ch 5:25; Is 37:12
[f]36:19 Is 10:9-11; 37:11-13; Jr 49:23
[g]2Kg 17:6
[h]36:21 Pr 26:4
[i]37:1-35 2Kg 19:1-34
[j]37:1 Gn 37:34; 2Sm 3:31; 1Kg 21:27; Is 3:24
[k]37:3 Is 22:5; 26:16; 33:2; Nah 1:7; Hab 3:16
[l]Is 26:17-18; 66:9; Hs 13:13
[m]37:4 Dt 5:26; 1Sm 17:26,36; Jr 10:10
[n]Is 1:9; 46:3
[o]37:6 Is 7:4; 35:4
[p]Ps 44:7,13-16; Is 52:5; Rm 2:24
[q]37:7 Nm 5:14; Is 19:14; Hs 4:12; Zch 13:2; 2Tm 1:7
[r]Is 37:36-38

[A]36:11 Lit *Judahite*, also in v. 13　　[B]36:16 Lit *a blessing*

36:11-12 Aramaic was a trade language of the day similar to **Hebrew** (36:11). The spokesman didn't want to switch to it because he wanted everyone in Jerusalem—not just the king—to grasp what they were facing.
36:13-16 It's clear that Hezekiah (to his great credit) had been assuring his people of God's ability to deliver them. But Assyria's representative implied that Judah's king was a fool who would get them all killed. Thus, he argued, there was only one sane thing they could do: **Make peace with me and surrender** (36:16). Interestingly, when life becomes hard, these are words that Satan will whisper

to you. But though the "father of lies" (John 8:44) promises peace, he only delivers slavery.
36:18-20 In other words, he said, "No god has been able to stop us, and neither will yours." But Assyria would soon learn the difference between the gods of the nations and the true, living God.
36:22 Tearing one's clothing was a sign of despair.
37:1 When there seems to be no hope, you too should humble yourself before the Lord and seek his face. Hezekiah's actions were an acknowledgment that Judah's only hope lay in the power and promises of God.

37:4 Use of the word **perhaps** in his message to Isaiah was not a sign of doubt in the Lord's ability to hear and answer. Instead, it was a sign of humility, showing that Hezekiah would wait for the divine King's answer instead of assuming he knew what it was.
37:6 Don't be afraid is repeated multiple times throughout Scripture. If you place yourself under the umbrella of God's covenantal protection, you have no need to fear.
37:7 God would judge King Sennacherib for his blasphemy by having him assassinated in **his own land**.

a 37:8 Jos 10:31-32
b Nm 33:20; Jos 10:29
c 37:9 Is 18:1; 20:5
d 37:10 Is 36:14-15
e 37:12 Is 36:18
f 2Kg 17:6; 18:11
g Gn 11:31; 12:1-4; Ac 7:2
h 37:14 Dt 22:17; 1Kg 8:22;
Ezk 2:10
i 37:15 2Ch 32:20
j 37:16 Ex 25:22; Nm 7:89;
1Sm 4:4; 2Sm 6:2; Ps
80:1; 99:1
k Dt 10:17; 2Sm 7:28; Ps
86:10; 90:2; 136:2-3
l 1Kg 8:39; Neh 9:6; Ps 4:8;
83:18; 86:10; Rv 15:4
m 2Ch 36:20; Ps 68:32;
Rv 11:15
n Ex 20:11; Neh 9:6; Ps
146:6; Ac 4:24
o 37:17 2Ch 6:40; Ps 17:6;
Dn 9:18
p Is 42:5; 45:12; Jr 10:12
q Is 37:4
r 37:19 Dt 32:17; 2Ch 13:9;
Jr 2:11; 5:7; 16:20; Hs 8:6;
Ac 19:26; Gl 4:8
s Dt 4:28; 28:36,64; 29:17;
Ezk 20:32
t Is 2:8,20; 17:8; 31:7;
41:24,29; 44:9-20; 46:6

u 37:20 Jos 4:24; 1Kg 8:60;
20:13; Is 45:3,6
v Is 37:16
w 37:22 Lm 2:13; Is 1:8;
3:16-17; 4:4; 52:2; 62:11
x Jb 16:4; Ps 22:7; 109:25; Jr
18:16; Lm 2:15
y 37:23 Ps 74:10,18; Is 37:4;
Gl 6:7
z Is 2:11; 5:15,21
aa Gn 12:3; Ex 23:22
ab 37:24 Ex 14:26-28;
15:4,19; Dt 20:1; Jos 11:4-9;
2Ch 16:8; Ps 68:17
ac 37:25 Dt 11:10; 1Kg 20:10
ad 37:26 Is 40:21,28
ae Is 5:19; 10:5-6; 14:24-26;
22:11; 46:11; Jr 18:11; Ac
2:23; 4:27-28; 1Pt 2:8
af Is 34:13

SENNACHERIB'S LETTER

8 When the royal spokesman heard that the king of Assyria had pulled out of Lachish,*a* he left and found him fighting against Libnah.*b* **9** The king had heard concerning King Tirhakah of Cush,*c* "He has set out to fight against you." So when he heard this, he sent messengers to Hezekiah, saying, **10** "Say this to King Hezekiah of Judah: 'Don't let your God, on whom you rely, deceive you*d* by promising that Jerusalem won't be handed over to the king of Assyria. **11** Look, you have heard what the kings of Assyria have done to all the countries: they completely destroyed them. Will you be rescued? **12** Did the gods of the nations*e* that my predecessors destroyed rescue them — Gozan,*f* Haran,*g* Rezeph, and the Edenites in Telassar? **13** Where is the king of Hamath, the king of Arpad, the king of the city of^A Sepharvaim, Hena, or Ivvah?'"

⟿ HOPE WORDS ⟿

Prayer is relational
communication with God.

HEZEKIAH'S PRAYER

14 Hezekiah took the letter from the messengers' hands, read it, then went up to the Lᴏʀᴅ's temple and spread it out before the Lᴏʀᴅ.*h* **15** Then Hezekiah prayed*i* to the Lᴏʀᴅ:

16 Lᴏʀᴅ of Armies, God of Israel, enthroned between the cherubim,*j* you are God*k* — you alone*l* — of all the kingdoms of the earth.*m* You made the heavens and the earth.*n* **17** Listen closely, Lᴏʀᴅ, and hear;*o* open your eyes, Lᴏʀᴅ, and see.*p* Hear all the words that Sennacherib has sent to mock the living God.*q* **18** Lᴏʀᴅ, it is true that the kings of Assyria have devastated all these countries and their lands. **19** They have thrown their gods into the fire, for they were not gods*r* but made from wood and stone*s* by human hands.*t* So they have destroyed them. **20** Now, Lᴏʀᴅ our God, save us from his power

so that all the kingdoms of the earth may know that you, Lᴏʀᴅ, are God^B,*u* — you alone.*v*

GOD'S ANSWER THROUGH ISAIAH

21 Then Isaiah son of Amoz sent a message to Hezekiah: "The Lᴏʀᴅ, the God of Israel, says, 'Because you prayed to me about King Sennacherib of Assyria, **22** this is the word the Lᴏʀᴅ has spoken against him:

Virgin Daughter Zion*w*
   despises you and scorns you;
Daughter Jerusalem
   shakes her head*x*
behind your back.
23 Who is it you have mocked*y*
   and blasphemed?
Against whom have you raised
   your voice
and lifted your eyes in pride?*z*
Against the Holy One of Israel!*aa*
24 You have mocked the Lord
   through*c* your servants.
You have said, "With my
   many chariots*ab*
I have gone up to the heights
   of the mountains,
to the far recesses of Lebanon.
I cut down its tallest cedars,
   its choice cypress trees.
I came to its distant heights,
   its densest forest.
25 I dug wells and drank water in
   foreign lands.^D
I dried up all the streams
   of Egypt
with the soles of my feet."*ac*
26 Have you not heard?*ad*
I designed it long ago;
I planned it in days gone by.*ae*
I have now brought it to pass,
and you have crushed
   fortified cities*af*
into piles of rubble.
27 Their inhabitants have
   become powerless,
dismayed, and ashamed.
They are plants of the field,
   tender grass,

---

^A 37:13 Or *king of Lair*, ^B 37:20 *are God* supplied for clarity; see v. 16 ^C 37:24 Lit *by the hand of* ^D 37:25 DSS, 2Kg 19:24; MT omits *in foreign lands*

37:8 Libnah was a town about twenty-five miles southwest of Jerusalem.
37:14-19 Hezekiah responded once again in faith by taking the enemy's **letter** to the **temple** (37:14) and offering a tremendous prayer that glorified the Lord as the only Creator and Sovereign of the world. Though Isaiah

had promised deliverance, Hezekiah did not presume upon God's grace.
37:20 The king asked God to judge the Assyrians for the right reason: **save us from his power so that all the kingdoms of the earth may know that you, Lᴏʀᴅ, are God**.

37:23-24 Technically, the king of Assyria had mocked Judah. But, ultimately, he had **mocked the Lord** (37:24), whom Sennacherib thought was no different from the gods of the nations.

grass on the rooftops,
blasted by the east wind.[A]

28 But I know your sitting down,
your going out and your coming in,[a]
and your raging against me.
29 Because your raging against me
and your arrogance have reached
my ears,[b]
I will put my hook in your nose[c]
and my bit in your mouth;[d]
I will make you go back
the way you came.

30 " 'This will be the sign for you:[e] This year you will eat what grows on its own, and in the second year what grows from that. But in the third year sow and reap, plant vineyards and eat their fruit. **31** The surviving remnant of the house of Judah will again take root[f] downward and bear fruit upward. **32** For a remnant[g] will go out from Jerusalem, and survivors from Mount Zion. The zeal of the LORD of Armies will accomplish this.'[h]

33 "Therefore, this is what the LORD says about the king of Assyria:

He will not enter this city,
shoot an arrow here,
come before it with a shield,
or build up a siege ramp against it.
34 He will go back
the way he came,
and he will not enter this city.
This is the LORD's declaration.
35 I will defend this city and rescue it
for my sake[i]
and for the sake of
my servant David."[j]

DEFEAT AND DEATH OF SENNACHERIB

36 Then[k] the angel of the LORD[l] went out and struck down one hundred eighty-five thousand in the camp of the Assyrians. When the people got up the next morning — there were all the dead bodies! **37** So King Sennacherib of Assyria broke camp

and left. He returned home and lived in Nineveh.[m]

38 One day, while he was worshiping in the temple of his god Nisroch, his sons Adrammelech and Sharezer struck him down with the sword and escaped to the land of Ararat.[n] Then his son Esar-haddon[o] became king in his place.

HEZEKIAH'S ILLNESS AND RECOVERY

38 In those days Hezekiah became terminally ill.[p] The prophet Isaiah son of Amoz came and said to him, "This is what the LORD says: 'Set your house in order,[q] for you are about to die; you will not recover.' "[B]

2 Then Hezekiah turned his face to the wall and prayed to the LORD. **3** He said, "Please, LORD, remember how I have walked before you faithfully and wholeheartedly,[r] and have done what pleases you."[C,s] And Hezekiah wept bitterly.

4 Then the word of the LORD came to Isaiah: **5** "Go and tell Hezekiah, 'This is what the LORD God of your ancestor David says: I have heard your prayer; I have seen your tears. Look, I am going to add fifteen years to your life.[D,t] **6** And I will rescue you and this city from the grasp of the king of Assyria; I will defend this city.[u] **7** This is the sign to you[v] from the LORD that he will do what[E] he has promised:[F] **8** I am going to make the sun's shadow that goes down on the stairway of Ahaz go back by ten steps.' "[W] So the sun's shadow[G] went back the ten steps it had descended.

9 A poem by King Hezekiah of Judah after he had been sick and had recovered from his illness:

10 I said: In the prime[H] of my life[x]
I must go to the gates of Sheol;[y]
I am deprived of the rest of my years.
11 I said: I will never see the LORD,
the LORD in the land of the living;[z]
I will not look on humanity
any longer
with the inhabitants of what is
passing away.[I]

[a]**37:28** Ps 139:1
[b]**37:29** Is 10:12
[c]Ezk 19:9; 29:4; 38:4
[d]Is 30:28
[e]**37:30** Ex 3:12; 1Sm 2:34; 1Kg 13:3; Is 7:14; 38:7; Jr 44:29; Lk 2:12
[f]**37:31** Is 27:6
[g]**37:32** Ezr 9:14; Is 10:20-22
[h]2Kg 19:31; Is 9:7; 59:17; Jl 2:18; Zch 1:14
[i]**37:35** Is 43:25; 48:9,11
[j]1Kg 11:13,32-38; 2Kg 20:6; Ezk 34:23
[k]**37:36-38** 2Kg 19:35-37; 2Ch 32:21
[l]**37:36-38** Gn 16:7-11; Ex 3:2; Nm 22:22-35; Jdg 6:11-12; 2Sm 24:16; Ps 34:7
[m]**37:37** Gn 10:11; Jnh 1:2; 3:3; 4:11; Zph 2:13
[n]**37:38** Gn 8:4; Jr 51:27
[o]Ezr 4:2
[p]**38:1-8** 2Kg 20:1-6,9-11; 2Ch 32:24
[q]**38:1** 2Sm 17:23
[r]**38:3** Gn 17:1; 1Kg 2:4; 3:6; 8:23; 2Kg 18:5-6; Ps 26:3
[s]Dt 6:18
[t]**38:5** 2Kg 18:2,13
[u]**38:6** Is 31:5; 37:35
[v]**38:7** Is 37:30
[w]**38:8** Jos 10:12-14
[x]**38:10** Ps 102:24
[y]Ps 107:18
[z]**38:11** Ps 27:13; 116:9

[A]**37:27** DSS; MT reads *rooftops, field before standing grain*   [B]**38:1** Lit *live*   [C]**38:3** Lit *what is good in your eyes*   [D]**38:5** Lit *days*, also in v. 10
[E]**38:7** Lit *this thing*   [F]**38:7** Lit *said*   [G]**38:8** Lit *And the sun*   [H]**38:10** Lit *quiet*   [I]**38:11** Some Hb mss, Tg read *of the world*

37:30-32 God assured Hezekiah that life would continue in Judah despite the momentary Assyrian threat. Crops would be planted and harvested, even though the Assyrians had ravaged much of Judah. By **the third year**, the harvest would be plentiful (37:30).
37:36 Don't miss that **the LORD** destroyed thousands of Assyrian soldiers in their own camp while the people of Judah slept!

37:37-38 Sennacherib was eventually slain by his own **sons** while **worshiping . . . his god**. No matter how devotedly you serve them, idols can't deliver you either.
38:1-6 When **Hezekiah became terminally ill**, which actually happened before Assyria's siege of Jerusalem, God sent **Isaiah** to the king with the announcement of his impending death (38:1). If what happened in this

passage was a faith test, Hezekiah passed. And he got a tremendous bonus. God said, **I will rescue you and this city from the grasp of the king of Assyria; I will defend [Jerusalem]** (38:6).
38:10 The king spoke honestly of his anguish at the prospect of dying at a young age. **Sheol** was the name for the place of the dead.

a 38:12 2Co 5:1,4; 2Pt
1:13-14
b Jb 7:6; Heb 1:12
c Jb 6:9
d Jb 4:20; Ps 73:14
e 38:14 Is 59:11; Ezk 7:16;
Nah 2:7
f Jb 17:3; Ps 119:122
g 38:15 1Kg 21:27
h 1Sm 1:10; Ezk 27:31; Jb
3:20; 7:11; 10:1
i 38:16 Ps 119:71,75
j Ps 39:13
k Ps 119:25
l 38:17 Heb 12:11
m Jb 33:18,30; Ps 103:4;
106:23; Ezk 20:17; Jnh 2:6
n Is 43:25; Jr 31:34; Mc 7:19
o 38:18 Ps 6:5; 30:9; 88:10-
12; 115:17
p 38:19 Dt 6:7; 11:19; Ps
78:5-7
q 38:20 Ps 23:6; 116:17-19
r 38:21-22 2Kg 20:7-8

s 39:1-8 2Kg 20:12-19;
2Ch 32:31
t 39:2 2Kg 18:15-16
u 2Ch 32:25
v 39:5 Is 28:14; Zch 7:4;
8:1,18
w 39:6 2Kg 24:13; 25:13-15;
Jr 20:5
x 39:8 2Ch 32:26
y 40:1 Is 12:1; 49:13; 51:3,12;
52:9; 61:2; 66:13; Jr 31:10-
14; Zph 3:14-17; 2Co 1:4
z 40:2 Is 13:11
aa Lv 26:41,43; Is 27:9

12 My dwelling is plucked up
     and removed from me
   like a shepherd's tent.*a*
  I have rolled up my life
     like a weaver;*b*
  he cuts me off from the loom.*c*
  By nightfall[A] you make an end
     of me.*d*
13 I thought until the morning:
  He will break all my bones
     like a lion.
  By nightfall you make an end of me.
14 I chirp like a swallow or a crane;*e*
  I moan like a dove.*e*
  My eyes grow weak looking upward.
  Lord, I am oppressed; support me.*f*

15 What can I say?
  He has spoken to me,
   and he himself has done it.
  I walk along slowly all my years*g*
   because of the bitterness
     of my soul.*h*
16 Lord, by such things people live,*i*
  and in every one of them my spirit
     finds life;
  you have restored me to health*j*
  and let me live.*k*
17 Indeed, it was for my own well-being
   that I had such intense bitterness;*l*
  but your love has delivered me
   from the Pit of destruction,*m*
  for you have thrown all my sins
     behind your back.*n*
18 For Sheol cannot thank you;
  Death cannot praise you.*o*
  Those who go down to the Pit
   cannot hope for your faithfulness.
19 The living, only the living
     can thank you,
   as I do today;
  a father will make your faithfulness
     known to children.*p*
20 The LORD is ready to save me;
  we will play stringed instruments
   all the days of our lives
     at the house of the LORD.*q*

21 Now Isaiah*r* had said, "Let them take
a lump of pressed figs and apply it to his

infected skin, so that he may recover." 22 And Hezekiah had asked, "What is the sign that I will go up to the LORD's temple?"

HEZEKIAH'S FOLLY

39 At that time*s* Merodach-baladan son of Baladan, king of Babylon, sent letters and a gift to Hezekiah since he heard that he had been sick and had recovered. 2 Hezekiah was pleased with the letters, and he showed the envoys his treasure house — the silver, the gold, the spices, and the precious oil — and all his armory, and everything that was found in his treasuries.*t* There was nothing in his palace and in all his realm that Hezekiah did not show them.*u*

3 Then the prophet Isaiah came to King Hezekiah and asked him, "What did these men say, and where did they come to you from?"

Hezekiah replied, "They came to me from a distant country, from Babylon."

4 Isaiah asked, "What have they seen in your palace?"

Hezekiah answered, "They have seen everything in my palace. There isn't anything in my treasuries that I didn't show them."

5 Then Isaiah said to Hezekiah, "Hear the word of the LORD of Armies:*v* 6 'Look, the days are coming when everything in your palace and all that your fathers have stored up until today will be carried off to Babylon; nothing will be left,' says the LORD.*w* 7 'Some of your descendants — who come from you, whom you father — will be taken away, and they will become eunuchs in the palace of the king of Babylon.'"

8 Then Hezekiah said to Isaiah, "The word of the LORD that you have spoken is good," for he thought: There will be peace and security during my lifetime.*x*

GOD'S PEOPLE COMFORTED

40 "Comfort, comfort my people,"*y* says your God.
2 "Speak tenderly to[B] Jerusalem,
  and announce to her
  that her time of forced labor is over,
  her iniquity*z* has been pardoned,*aa*

[A] 38:12 Lit *From day until night*, also in v. 13   [B] 40:2 Lit *Speak to the heart of*

39:1-2 The visit by representatives of **Merodach-baladan**, son of the king of Babylon (39:1) preceded the siege of chapters 36–37, since it is highly unlikely that these messengers would have been able to enter Jerusalem with the Assyrians surrounding the city. Importantly, Babylon would be the next great world power in the years to come, but in Isa-

iah's day it was another vassal state under Assyria.

39:5-8 The prophesied tragedy must have seemed like a remote prospect to Hezekiah. After all, in his day more than a century before these events, Babylon was just another nation trying desperately to hold back the Assyrians. So, selfishly, Hezekiah breathed a

sigh of relief that this would not be fulfilled in his **lifetime** (39:8).

40:1-2 The prophet looks ahead to the Babylonian captivity of Judah—about a century away—and her eventual return to the land. Many critical Bible scholars believe this dramatic shift—combined with Isaiah's prophecy that Judah would suffer exile in

and she has received
  from the LORD's hand
double for all her sins."[a]

3 A voice of one crying out:
  Prepare the way of the LORD
    in the wilderness;[b]
  make a straight highway for our God
    in the desert.[c]
4 Every valley will be lifted up,
  and every mountain and hill
    will be leveled;
  the uneven ground
    will become smooth
  and the rough places, a plain.[d]
5 And the glory of the LORD
    will appear,[e]
  and all humanity[A] together
    will see it,[f]
  for the mouth of the LORD
    has spoken.[g]

6 A voice was saying, "Cry out!"
  Another said,[B]
    "What should I cry out?"
  "All humanity is grass,[h]
  and all its goodness is like the flower
    of the field.[i]
7 The grass withers, the flowers fade
  when the breath[c] of the LORD blows
    on them;[D]
  indeed, the people are grass.
8 The grass withers, the flowers fade,[j]
  but the word of our God
    remains forever."[k]

9 Zion, herald of good news,
  go up on a high mountain.[l]
  Jerusalem, herald of good news,[m]
  raise your voice loudly.
  Raise it, do not be afraid!

Say to the cities of Judah,
  "Here is your God!"[n]
10 See, the Lord GOD comes
    with strength,
  and his power establishes his rule.[o]
  His wages are with him,[p]
  and his reward accompanies him.
11 He protects his flock
    like a shepherd;[q]
  he gathers the lambs in his arms
  and carries them in the fold
    of his garment.
  He gently leads those that are nursing.

12 Who has measured the waters
    in the hollow of his hand
  or marked off the heavens
    with the span of his hand?[r]
  Who has gathered the dust
    of the earth in a measure
  or weighed the mountains
    on a balance
  and the hills on the scales?
13 Who has directed[E] the Spirit
    of the LORD,
  or who gave him counsel?[s]
14 Who did he consult?
  Who gave him understanding[t]
  and taught him the paths of justice?
  Who taught him knowledge
  and showed him the way
    of understanding?
15 Look, the nations are like a drop
    in a bucket;
  they are considered as a speck
    of dust on the scales;
  he lifts up the islands like fine dust.
16 Lebanon's cedars are not enough
    for fuel,
  or its animals enough
    for a burnt offering.[u]

[a] 40:2 Ex 22:7-8; Jr 16:18; Zch 9:12; Rv 18:6
[b] 40:3 Mal 3:1; 4:5-6
[c] Mt 3:3; Mk 1:3; Lk 3:4; Jn 1:23
[d] 40:4-5 Lk 3:5-6
[e] 40:5 Is 35:2
[f] Is 52:10; Jl 2:28
[g] Is 1:20; 34:16; 58:14
[h] 40:6-8 1Pt 1:24-25
[i] 40:6 Jb 14:2; Ps 102:11; 103:15
[j] 40:8 Jms 1:11
[k] Is 55:11; 59:21; Mk 13:31; Lk 21:33
[l] 40:9 Is 52:7
[m] Is 61:1
[n] 40:9 Is 25:9; 35:2
[o] 40:10 Is 59:16-18
[p] Is 62:11; Rv 22:12
[q] 40:11 Jr 31:10; Ezk 34:12-14,23,31; Mc 5:4; Jn 10:11,14-16
[r] 40:12 Is 48:13; Heb 1:10-12
[s] 40:13 Rm 11:34; 1Co 2:16
[t] 40:14 Jb 21:22; Col 2:3
[u] 40:16 Ps 50:9-11; Mc 6:6-7; Heb 10:5-9

Babylon—points to two different authors for the book. They suggest one author wrote chapters 1–39; then another author wrote chapters 40–66 after Judah's exile. But the most significant evidence given for this argument is that Isaiah couldn't possibly have predicted a future Jewish exile in Babylon, which assumes that God could not supernaturally reveal this to him. If one does not automatically rule out the possibility that God can reveal future events to his servants, then there is no compelling evidence to reject that all sixty-six chapters are the work of Isaiah.

Judah's **forced labor** in the land of captivity would end when the people had experienced the full measure of discipline for their many sins (40:2).

40:3-5 Though God would providentially provide a smooth path for the Jews to return to

Jerusalem from Babylon, the Gospel writers saw this as ultimately fulfilled in John the Baptist (see Matt 3:1-3; Mark 1:1-4; Luke 3:1-6). He would be the **voice . . . crying out** to **prepare the way of the LORD** (40:3). Through his ministry, John would pave the way for the ministry of Jesus and point others to "the Lamb of God, who takes away the sin of the world" (John 1:29).

40:8 To the people of Judah in Isaiah's day, this was a reminder to trust God's promises especially when times are hard. To the Jews in Babylon who read these words years later, this was a reminder of God's never-failing faithfulness to his covenant. And Peter uses it to remind us as Christians of the enduring power of the word of the gospel that we believed (see 1 Pet 1:23-25). Indeed, because **the word of our God**

remains forever, we can't lose the salvation Christ won for us.

40:12-26 Here God asks questions demonstrating his unrivaled sovereignty over the nations. **Who has . . . marked off the heavens with the span of his hand?** (40:12). Answer: no one. God alone spoke the world into existence and **calls all of [the stars] by name** (40:26). **Who has directed the Spirit of the LORD, or who gave him counsel?** (40:13). Answer: no one. The omniscient God possesses all knowledge; he doesn't need to ask advice or consult Google. **With whom will you compare God? . . . Who is [his] equal?** (40:18, 25). Answer: no one. He is the unique, one-and-only Lord of creation. And if humans are not worthy to be compared to him, how much less worthy is an inanimate **idol**? (40:18-20).

[a] 40:17 Is 29:7
[b] 40:18 Ex 8:10; 15:11; 1Sm 2:2; Is 40:25; 46:5; Mc 7:18; Ac 17:29
[c] 40:19 Is 2:20; 30:22; 41:7; 44:10
[d] 40:20 1Sm 5:3; Is 44:9-15; 46:6-7; Jr 10:3-5
[e] 40:21 Ps 19:1; 50:6; Is 37:26; Ac 14:17; Rm 1:19-20
[f] Is 48:13; 51:13
[g] 40:22 Nm 13:33
[h] Jb 9:8; Is 37:16; 42:5; 44:24
[i] Jb 36:29; Ps 18:11; 19:4; 104:2
[j] 40:23 Jb 12:21; Ps 107:40; Is 34:12
[k] 40:24 Ps 1:4; Is 41:2,16; 64:6; Ezk 17:10,24; Nah 1:4
[l] 40:25 Is 46:5; Ac 17:29
[m] 40:26 Is 42:5; 48:12-13

[n] 40:26 Ps 147:4-5
[o] 40:27 Is 7:13; 49:4,14
[p] 40:28 Gn 21:33; Ps 90:2
[q] Ps 147:5; Rm 11:33
[r] 40:31 Jb 17:9; Ps 103:5; 2Co 4:8-10,16; 12:9
[s] Ex 19:4; Dt 32:11; Lk 18:1; 2Co 4:1,16; Gl 6:9; Heb 12:3
[t] 41:1 Is 11:11; Hab 2:20; Zch 2:13
[u] 41:2 Is 41:25; 45:1-3; 46:11; Rv 16:12
[v] Is 42:6

17 All the nations are as nothing
before him;
they are considered by him
as empty nothingness.[a]

18 With whom will you compare God?
What likeness will you set up for
comparison with him?[b]

19 An idol? — something that
a smelter casts
and a metalworker plates with gold
and makes silver chains for?[c]

20 A poor person contributes wood for
a pedestal
that will not rot.[A]
He looks for a skilled craftsman
to set up an idol that will not
fall over.[d]

21 Do you not know?[e]
Have you not heard?
Has it not been declared to you
from the beginning?
Have you not considered
the foundations of the earth?[f]

22 God is enthroned above the circle
of the earth;
its inhabitants are
like grasshoppers.[g]
He stretches out the heavens
like thin cloth[h]
and spreads them out like a tent
to live in.[i]

23 He reduces princes to nothing[j]
and makes judges of the earth like a
wasteland.

24 They are barely planted, barely sown,
their stem hardly takes root
in the ground
when he blows on them
and they wither,
and a whirlwind carries them away
like stubble.[k]

25 "To whom will you compare me,[l]
or who is my equal?"
asks the Holy One.

26 Look up[B] and see!
Who created[m] these?

He brings out the stars by number;
he calls all of them by name.[n]
Because of his great power
and strength,
not one of them is missing.

27 Jacob, why do you say,
and, Israel, why do you assert:
"My way is hidden from the LORD,
and my claim is ignored
by my God"?[o]

~ **HOPE WORDS** ~

*Sometimes we step out in faith
but then let circumstances
pull us under.*

---

28 Do you not know?
Have you not heard?
The LORD is the everlasting God,[p]
the Creator of the whole earth.
He never becomes faint or weary;
there is no limit to his understanding.[q]

29 He gives strength to the faint
and strengthens the powerless.

30 Youths may become faint and weary,
and young men stumble and fall,

31 but those who trust in the LORD
will renew their strength;[r]
they will soar on wings like eagles;[s]
they will run and not
become weary,
they will walk and not faint.

THE LORD VERSUS THE NATIONS' GODS

41 "Be silent before me, coasts and
islands![t]
And let peoples renew
their strength.
Let them approach; let them testify;
let's come together for the trial.

2 Who has stirred up someone
from the east?[u]
In righteousness he calls him to
serve.[C,D,v]

[A] **40:20** Or *who is too poor for such an offering*, or *who chooses mulberry wood as a votive gift*; Hb obscure   [B] **40:26** Lit *Lift up your eyes on high*   [C] **41:2** Or *Righteousness calls him to serve*   [D] **41:2** Lit *to his foot*

40:29 Make no mistake: The words *faint* and *powerless* describe us all. When was the last time you asked him to renew your strength?
40:31 Only **those who trust** God's perspective on their situations **will run and not become weary** as God provides a second wind to make it through challenges. Only those who believe

his Word and submit to it can expect to experience his spiritual power for daily life. You **will walk and not faint** as God changes you, whether or not he changes your situation.
41:2 Who is this **someone from the east** whom God has **stirred up**? This is a reference to Cyrus the Great, the leader of the (then future) Persian Empire that would conquer

Babylon in 539 BC, 150 years into the future. Isaiah does not mention Cyrus by name until 44:28 and 45:1. But at this point, God is hinting at his long-range plan for Judah. It includes raising up a leader to smash the Babylonian Empire, release the Jews from captivity, and permit them to return home (see 2 Chr 36:22-23).

The Lord hands nations over
  to him,[a]
and he subdues kings.
He makes them like dust
    with his sword,
like wind-driven stubble
    with his bow.
3 He pursues them, going on safely,
  hardly touching the path
    with his feet.
4 Who has performed and done this,
  calling the generations
    from the beginning?
I am the Lord, the first
and with the last[b] — I am he."[c]

5 The coasts and islands see
    and are afraid,
  the whole earth trembles.[d]
They approach and arrive.
6 Each one helps the other,
  and says to another, "Take courage!"
7 The craftsman encourages
    the metalworker;[e]
the one who flattens
    with the hammer
encourages the one who strikes
    the anvil,
saying of the soldering, "It is good."
He fastens it with nails so that
    it will not fall over.[f]

8 But you, Israel, my servant,[g]
Jacob, whom I have chosen,[h]
descendant of Abraham,
    my friend[i] —
9 I brought[A] you from the ends
    of the earth
and called you
    from its farthest corners.
I said to you: You are my servant;
I have chosen you; I haven't
    rejected you.[j]
10 Do not fear, for I am with you;[k]
  do not be afraid, for I am your God.[l]
I will strengthen you; I will help you;
I will hold on to you
    with my righteous right hand.[m]

11 Be sure that all who are enraged
    against you
will be ashamed and disgraced;[n]
those who contend with you

will become as nothing
  and will perish.
12 You will look for those who contend
    with you,
but you will not find them.
Those who war against you
will become absolutely nothing.
13 For I am the Lord your God,[o]
who holds your right hand,
who says to you, 'Do not fear,
I will help you.
14 Do not fear, you worm Jacob,[p]
you men[B] of Israel.
I will help you' —
    this is the Lord's declaration.
Your Redeemer[q] is the Holy One
    of Israel.[r]
15 See, I will make you
    into a sharp threshing board,
new, with many teeth.
You will thresh mountains
    and pulverize them
and make hills into chaff.[s]
16 You will winnow them[t]
and a wind will carry them away,
a whirlwind will scatter them.
But you will rejoice in the Lord;
you will boast in the Holy One
    of Israel.

⁓ HOPE WORDS ⁓

*Never let who you are get
in the way of who God is.*

---

17 The poor and the needy seek water,
    but there is none;
their tongues are parched
    with thirst.
I will answer them.[u]
I am the Lord, the God of Israel. I
    will not abandon them.
18 I will open rivers
on the barren heights,[v]
and springs in the middle
    of the plains.
I will turn the desert into a pool
and dry land into springs.[w]
19 I will plant cedars,
acacias, myrtles, and olive trees
    in the wilderness.[x]
I will put juniper trees,

a 41:2 2Ch 36:23; Ezr 1:2
b 41:4 Is 43:10; 44:6; Rv 1:8,17; 22:13
c Is 43:13; 46:4; 48:12
d 41:5 Ps 67:7
e 41:7 Is 40:19
f Is 40:20; 46:7
g 41:8 Is 42:19; 43:10; 44:1-2,21; 45:4; 48:20; 49:3; 54:17; Ezk 28:25; 37:25; Lk 1:54
h Is 42:1; 43:10,20; 44:1-2; 45:4; 49:7; 65:9,15,22
i 2Ch 20:7; Jms 2:23
j 41:9 Is 43:5-7
k 41:10 Gn 26:24; 28:15; Is 43:5; Jr 1:19; 15:20; 42:11
l Ezk 34:31
m Ex 15:6,12; Ps 18:35; 48:10; 63:8; 138:7; 139:10
n 41:11 Is 45:24

o 41:13 Is 43:3
p 41:14 Jb 25:6; Ps 22:6
q Is 43:14; 44:6,24; 47:4; 48:17; 49:7,26; 54:5,8; 59:20; 60:16; 63:16
r Is 1:4
s 41:15 Mc 4:13; Hab 3:12
t 41:16 Jr 51:2
u 41:17 Is 43:20; 44:3; 49:10; 55:1
v 41:18 Is 30:25
w Ps 107:35; Is 35:6-7; 43:19
x 41:19 Is 35:1; 55:13; 60:13

A 41:9 Or *seized*   B 41:14 LXX reads *small number*; DSS read *dead ones*

41:7 The one who trusts an idol needs to nail it down so it won't tip over while he's praying to it. How much better it is to trust in the true God, who has the power to topple empires.

41:11-16 God set Israel apart and promised by covenant to be her protector (41:14). Kingdoms and empires that not only refused to recognize and bow before Israel's God, but also attacked and abused his people, would be tossed into the dustbin of history. They would be ground into dust so fine that **a wind will carry them away** (41:15-16).

a 41:20 Jb 12:9; Is 66:14
b Is 4:5
c 41:22 Is 44:7-8; 45:21; 46:10
d 41:23 Is 42:9; 45:3; Jn 13:19
e 41:24 Ps 115:8; Is 44:9; 1Co 8:4
f 41:25 Jr 50:3
g Is 41:2; 46:11
h Ezr 1:2-4
i 41:27 Is 40:9; 44:28; 52:7; Nah 1:15

j 41:28 Is 46:7
k 42:1-4 Mt 12:18-21
l 42:1 Is 49:3-7; 50:10
m Is 41:8-9; Lk 9:35; 23:35; 1Pt 2:4,6
n Mt 3:17; 17:5; Mk 1:11; Lk 3:22; 2Pt 1:17
o Nm 11:16-17; 1Sm 16:13; Ps 33:6; 139:7; Is 11:2; 40:7; 59:21; Lk 4:18-21
p Is 2:4; 51:4-5
q 42:4 Is 11:11; 24:15; 42:10,12; 49:1; 51:5; 60:9; 66:19
r 42:5 Ps 104:2; Is 40:22
s Ps 136:6; Is 34:1
t Jb 12:10; 33:4; Is 57:16; Dn 5:23; Ac 17:25
u 42:6 Is 5:7,16; 9:7; 11:4-5; 32:1; 41:2; 45:8,13; 51:5-8; 56:1; 60:21; Jr 23:5-6
v Is 41:10,13
w Is 49:8
x Is 49:6
y 42:7 Ac 26:17-18
z Is 35:5; 49:9; 61:1; Heb 2:14-15

elms, and cypress trees together in
the desert,
20 so that all may see and know,
consider and understand,
that the hand of the LORD
has done this,[a]
the Holy One of Israel has created[b] it.

21 "Submit your case," says the LORD.
"Present your arguments,"
says Jacob's King.
22 "Let them come and tell us
what will happen.[c]
Tell us the past events,
so that we may reflect on them
and know the outcome,
or tell us the future.
23 Tell us the coming events,[d]
then we will know that you are gods.
Indeed, do something good or bad,
then we will be in awe[A] when we
see it.
24 Look, you are nothing[e]
and your work is worthless.
Anyone who chooses you
is detestable.

25 "I have stirred up one
from the north,[f] and he has come,
one from the east[g] who invokes
my[B] name.[h]
He will march over rulers as if
they were mud,
like a potter who treads the clay.
26 Who told about this
from the beginning,
so that we might know,
and from times past,
so that we might say, 'He is right'?
No one announced it,
no one told it,
no one heard your words.
27 I was the first to say to Zion,[c]
'Look! Here they are!'
And I gave Jerusalem a herald
with good news.[i]
28 When I look, there is no one;
there is no counselor among them;

when I ask them, they have
nothing to say.[j]
29 Look, all of them are a delusion;[D]
their works are nonexistent;
their images are wind
and emptiness.

THE SERVANT'S MISSION

42 "This[k] is my servant;[l]
I strengthen him,
this is my chosen one;[m] I delight
in him.[n]
I have put my Spirit on him;[o]
he will bring justice[E] to the nations.[p]
2 He will not cry out or shout
or make his voice heard
in the streets.
3 He will not break a bruised reed,
and he will not put out
a smoldering wick;
he will faithfully bring justice.
4 He will not grow weak
or be discouraged
until he has established justice
on earth.
The coasts and islands will wait
for his instruction."[q]

5 This is what God, the LORD, says —
who created the heavens
and stretched them out,[r]
who spread out the earth
and what comes from it,[s]
who gives breath to the people on it
and spirit to those
who walk on it[t] —
6 "I am the LORD. I have called you
for a righteous purpose,[F,u]
and I will hold you by your hand.[v]
I will watch over you, and I
will appoint you
to be a covenant for the people[w]
and a light to the nations,[x]
7 in order to open blind eyes,[y]
to bring out prisoners
from the dungeon,[z]
and those sitting in darkness
from the prison house.

A 41:23 DSS read we may hear   B 41:25 DSS read his   C 41:27 Lit First to Zion   D 41:29 DSS, Syr read are nothing   E 42:1 DSS read his justice
F 42:6 Or you by my righteousness; lit you in righteousness

41:25 God repeated his plan to raise Cyrus to liberate his captive people from Babylon: **I have stirred up one from the north**. Though in 41:2 it is said that Cyrus comes from the *east*, both are correct. Persia lay to the east, but it would attack Babylon from the north. 42:1 King Cyrus of Persia would serve God as the human instrument of freedom to the Jews in bondage. But who is the ultimate preeminent one upon whom God will place his **Spirit**

so that he may bring **justice to the nations**? This is God's Messiah, his Anointed One. The passage, then, is fulfilled in Jesus Christ (see Matt 12:15-21).
42:2-4 Both advents of Christ are in view in these verses. In his earthly ministry, he was humble and lowly, dealing gently with broken and sinful people (42:2-3). But when he comes a second time to defeat his foes and establish his kingdom, Jesus **will not grow**

weak or be discouraged. He will establish **justice on earth** (32:4). For one thousand years, King Jesus will deal swiftly and surely from his throne in Jerusalem.
42:6-8 Jesus Christ would be **a light to the nations** (42:6) so that he might **open blind eyes** (42:7), extending God's offer of salvation to all people. He purchased salvation from sin on the cross so that all who trust in him would have the righteousness God requires.

Bringing Justice to the Bruised Reeds

HAVE YOU EVER BEEN BULLIED? I have. In the sixth grade. At that time, we had a student in our class who had obviously failed a few grades already. Most of us boys were still scrawny, but this guy looked like a prize fighter, towering over us with an intimidating scowl.

Nobody likes bullies. They push you. Shove you. Mock you. Even chase you. I remember being chased all the way back to my house one time. I ran up the steep steps to our home, opened the door, and quickly shut it behind me. I could feel my heart beating in my mouth. Eventually I grew bigger. And after the sixth grade, I don't remember ever experiencing a bully again. But that encounter was enough for me to taste how bitter bullies really are.

It's bad enough to be bullied by someone you don't really know, someone you don't particularly care for. But to be mocked and jeered by those whom you love—that creates a deeper pain, maybe the deepest there is.

Jesus came to bring salvation to his own, yet his own rejected him (SEE JOHN 1:11). They stripped him, robed him in scarlet, stuck a crown of thorns on his head, and knelt before him in mockery. They spat on him. They beat him with a reed—the same reed they had just placed in his right hand (as if it were a scepter) for the purpose of mocking him (SEE MATT 27:27-30).

Importantly, this isn't the first time a reed shows up in the Bible. (Although the CSB translates the original Greek word here as "staff" rather than "reed" in Matthew 27, it's the exact same word that appears in the Greek translation of the following Old Testament passage.) Isaiah speaks of another reed—a bruised reed that stands for those who have been hurt, bullied, and bent. Isaiah's passage also speaks of the Messiah's faithfulness to those who may have been harassed by people. Perhaps by a hurtful mate, a parent, a friend, an employer. By someone that was once trusted. Isaiah says of Jesus, "He will not break a bruised reed, and he will not put out a smoldering wick; he will faithfully bring justice" (ISA 42:3).

How ironic that the one who came to bring justice to bruised human reeds received an unjust beating by a reed. He who would hold the wilted reed in his hand and nurture it back gently to health stood bloodied and mocked by those he came to save. And yet he said nothing in return to their cruelty. They led him as "a sheep to the slaughter" (ACTS 8:32), even though he was the true King.

I can't imagine saying nothing in such a circumstance. Can you? In fact, I can't imagine possessing more power than those doing the bullying and yet refusing to use it. But we must remember that nails didn't hold Christ to the cross. Love did. A love that looked down as he hung on the cross and saw the reed used to mock and hit him. And in that reed, he saw the salvation he was securing for you and me.

a 42:8 Ex 20:3-5; Is 48:11
b 42:9 Is 43:19; 48:3,6;
Rv 21:4
c 42:10 Ps 33:3; 96:1; 98:1;
144:9
d Ps 96:11; 98:7
e 42:11 Is 21:16; 60:7
f Is 16:1
g 42:13 Is 9:7; 26:11; 37:32;
59:17
h 42:14 Ps 50:21; Is 57:11;
62:1; 64:12; 65:6
i Is 13:8
j 42:15 Is 44:27; 50:2;
Nah 1:4-6
k 42:16 Is 29:18; 30:21;
32:3; Jr 31:8-9; Lk 1:78-79
l Eph 5:8
m Is 40:4; Lk 3:5
n Jos 1:5; Ps 94:14; Is 41:17;
Heb 13:5

o 42:17 Ps 97:7; Is 1:29;
44:9,11; 45:16
p 42:18 Is 35:5
q 42:19 Is 41:8-9; 43:10;
44:1-2,21; 45:4; 48:20;
49:3; 54:17; Ezk 28:25;
37:25; Lk 1:54
r 42:20 Rm 2:21-23
s 42:22 Dt 1:39; Jr 2:14; Ezk
34:8; 36:4
t 42:25 Is 29:13; 47:7; 57:1;
Jr 12:11; Hs 7:9

8 I am the LORD. That is my name,
and I will not give my glory
to another[a]
or my praise to idols.
9 The past events
have indeed happened.
Now I declare new events;[b]
I announce them to you
before they occur."

A SONG OF PRAISE

10 Sing a new song to the LORD;[c]
sing his praise from the ends
of the earth,
you who go down to the sea with all
that fills it,[d]
you coasts and islands
with your[A] inhabitants.
11 Let the desert and its cities shout,
the settlements where Kedar dwells
cry aloud.[e]
Let the inhabitants of Sela
sing for joy;[f]
let them cry out
from the mountaintops.
12 Let them give glory to the LORD
and declare his praise in the coasts
and islands.
13 The LORD advances like a warrior;
he stirs up his zeal like a soldier.[g]
He shouts, he roars aloud,
he prevails over his enemies.

14 "I have kept silent from ages past;
I have been quiet
and restrained myself.[h]
But now, I will groan like a woman
in labor,[i]
gasping breathlessly.
15 I will lay waste mountains and hills
and dry up all their vegetation.
I will turn rivers into islands
and dry up marshes.[j]
16 I will lead the blind by a way
they did not know;[k]
I will guide them on paths
they have not known.
I will turn darkness to light in front
of them[l]
and rough places into level ground.[m]
This is what I will do for them,
and I will not abandon them."[n]

17 They will be turned back
and utterly ashamed —
those who trust in an idol
and say to a cast image,
'You are our gods!'[o]

ISRAEL'S BLINDNESS
AND DEAFNESS

18 "Listen, you deaf!
Look, you blind, so that
you may see.[p]
19 Who is blind but my servant,[q]
or deaf like my messenger
I am sending?
Who is blind
like my dedicated one,[B]
or blind like the servant
of the LORD?
20 Though seeing many things,[C]
you pay no attention.
Though his ears are open,
he does not listen."[r]

21 Because of his righteousness,
the LORD was pleased
to magnify his instruction
and make it glorious.
22 But this is a people plundered
and looted,
all of them trapped in holes
or imprisoned in dungeons.
They have become plunder[s]
with no one to rescue them
and loot, with no one saying,
"Give it back!"
23 Who among you will hear this?
Let him listen and obey
in the future.
24 Who gave Jacob to the robber,[D]
and Israel to the plunderers?
Was it not the LORD?
Have we not sinned against him?
They were not willing to walk
in his ways,
and they would not listen
to his instruction.
25 So he poured out his furious anger
and the power of war on Jacob.
It surrounded him with fire,
but he did not know it;
it burned him, but he didn't take it to
heart.[t]

[A] 42:10 Lit *their*   [B] 42:19 Hb obscure   [C] 42:20 Alt Hb tradition reads *You see many things;*   [D] 42:24 Lit *to loot*

42:16 There's only one cure for spiritual blindness: you must go to the One who can turn on the lights. "For God who said, 'Let light shine out of darkness,' has shone in our hearts to give the light of the knowledge of God's glory in the face of Jesus Christ" (2 Cor 4:6).
42:19-20 There was no one so **blind** as God's **servant** Israel (42:19) because in spite of all the privileges Israel had received, in spite of all they had seen, they paid **no attention** (42:20). That is why Israel (and Judah) would suffer such strong judgment. They had a choice between God's rich blessings and exile. They *chose* exile.

RESTORATION OF ISRAEL

43 Now this is what the LORD says —
the one who created you, Jacob,
and the one who formed
you, Israel[a] —
"Do not fear, for I have
redeemed you;[b]
I have called you by your name;
you are mine.[c]
2   I will be with you[d]
when you pass through the waters,[e]
and when you pass
through the rivers,
they will not overwhelm you.
You will not be scorched
when you walk through the fire,[f]
and the flame will not burn you.
3   For I am the LORD your God,[g]
the Holy One of Israel,
and your Savior.[h]
I have given Egypt as a ransom
for you,
Cush and Seba in your place.
4   Because you are precious
in my sight[i]
and honored, and I love you,[j]
I will give people
in exchange for you
and nations instead of your life.
5   Do not fear, for I am with you;
I will bring your descendants
from the east,[k]
and gather you from the west.[l]
6   I will say to the north,
'Give them up!'
and to the south,
'Do not hold them back!'
Bring my sons from far away,[m]
and my daughters from the ends
of the earth[n] —
7   everyone who bears my name
and is created for my glory.
I have formed them;
indeed, I have made them."

8   Bring out a people who are blind,
yet have eyes,[o]
and are deaf, yet have ears.
9   All the nations
are gathered together,
and the peoples are assembled.[p]
Who among them can declare this,[q]
and tell us the former things?
Let them present their witnesses
to vindicate themselves,
so that people may hear and say,
"It is true."
10 "You are my witnesses"[r] —
this is the LORD's declaration —
"and my servant
whom I have chosen,[s]
so that you may know
and believe me
and understand that I am he.[t]
No god was formed before me,
and there will be none after me.[u]
11 I — I am the LORD.
Besides me, there is no Savior.[v]
12 I alone declared, saved,
and proclaimed —
and not some foreign god[A]
among you.
So you are my witnesses" —
this is the LORD's declaration —
"and[B] I am God.[w]
13 Also, from today on I am he alone,
and none can rescue
from my power.[x]
I act, and who can
reverse it?"[y]

GOD'S DELIVERANCE OF REBELLIOUS ISRAEL

14 This is what the LORD, your Redeemer,[z]
the Holy One of Israel[aa] says:
Because of you, I will send an army[c]
to Babylon
and bring all of them as fugitives,[D]
even the Chaldeans[ab] in the ships
in which they rejoice.[E]
15 I am the LORD, your Holy One,
the Creator of Israel, your King.

16 This is what the LORD says —
who makes a way in the sea,
and a path through raging water,[ac]
17 who brings out the chariot
and horse,[ad]
the army
and the mighty one together
(they lie down, they do not
rise again;
they are extinguished, put out
like a wick[ae]) —

---

a 43:1 Is 43:7,15,21; 44:2,21,24
b Is 44:22-23; 48:20
c Gn 32:28; Is 45:3-4
d 43:2 Dt 31:6,8,23; Jos 1:5; 3:7; Jr 1:8; 30:11; 46:28
e Ps 66:12; Is 8:7-8
f Is 29:6; 30:27-29; Dn 3:25,27
g 43:3 Ex 20:2; Is 41:13
h Is 19:20; 43:11; 45:15,21; 49:26; 60:16; 63:8
i 43:4 2Kg 1:13-14; Ps 36:7; 72:14; Pr 3:15; Is 28:16
j Is 63:9
k 43:5 Is 41:8; 61:9
l Is 49:12
m 43:6 2Co 6:18
n Is 45:22
o 43:8 Is 6:9; 42:19; Ezk 12:2
p 43:9 Is 34:1; 41:1
q Is 41:22-23,26

r 43:10 Is 44:8; Ac 1:8
s Is 41:8
t Is 41:4
u Is 44:6,8; 45:5-6
v 43:11 Is 43:3; 45:21; Hs 13:4
w 43:12 Ps 46:10; 50:7; Is 45:22; 46:9
x 43:13 Dt 32:39; Jn 10:28-29
y Jb 9:12; Is 14:27
z 43:14 Jb 19:25; Ps 19:14; 78:35; Pr 23:11; Is 41:14; Jr 50:34
aa Is 1:4
ab Is 23:13
ac 43:16 Ex 14:21-22; Ps 77:19; Is 11:15; 44:27; 50:2; 51:10; 63:11-12
ad 43:17 Ex 15:19
ae Ps 118:12; Is 1:31

A **43:12** Lit *not a foreigner*   B **43:12** Or *that*   C **43:14** *an army* supplied for clarity   D **43:14** Or *will break down all their bars*   E **43:14** Hb obscure

---

43:1-7 God dealt differently with Israel than he did with any other people because of their special, covenantal relationship with him. The promise to give **Egypt as a ransom for** Israel, along with **Cush and Seba** (43:3), evidently refers to Cyrus as the Jews' liberator (see 44:28; 45:1). These nations were examples of God's promise: **I will give people in exchange for you** (43:4). Israel's enemies would be taken down, never to rise again. But God's people had a glorious future because of their glorious, merciful God. These verses teach a principle that is still true today: God adjusts his dealings with people based on their relationship to him.
43:11 Indeed, to look anywhere else for salvation is to look in vain.

a 43:18 Is 65:17; Jr 23:7
b 43:19 Is 42:9; 48:6; 2Co 5:17
c Ex 17:6; Nm 20:11; Dt 8:15; Ps 78:16; Is 35:1,6; 41:18-19; 49:10; 51:3
d 43:20 Is 41:17-18; 48:21
e 43:21 Ps 102:18; Is 42:12; Lk 1:74-75; 1Pt 2:9
f 43:22 Mc 6:3; Mal 1:13; 3:14
g 43:23 Zch 7:5-6; Mal 1:6-8

h 43:24 Ps 95:10; Is 1:14; 7:13; Ezk 6:9; Mal 2:17
i Is 13:11
j 43:25 Is 44:22; 55:7; Jr 50:20; Heb 2:17
k Is 37:35; 48:9,11; Ezk 36:22
l Is 38:17; Jr 31:34; Mk 2:7
m 43:26 Is 1:18; 41:1; 50:8
n 43:27 Is 51:2; Ezk 16:3
o Is 9:15; 28:7; 29:10; Jr 5:31
p 43:28 Is 24:6; 34:5; Jr 24:9; Dn 9:11; Zch 8:13
q 44:1 Is 41:8-9; 42:1; 43:10,20; 45:4; 49:7; 65:9,15,22
r 44:2 Dt 32:15; 33:5,26
s 44:3 Is 32:15; Jl 2:28
t 44:6 Is 41:14; 43:14
u Is 41:4; 43:10; 48:12; Rv 1:8,17; 22:13
v Is 43:11; 44:8; 45:5-6

⇝ HOPE WORDS ⇝

As long as you are too attached to your past, you negate what God wants to do in your future. Learn from yesterday; don't live in it.

18 "Do not remember the past events,
pay no attention to things of old.*a*
19 Look, I am about to do
something new;*b*
even now it is coming.
Do you not see it?
Indeed, I will make a way
in the wilderness,*c*
rivers^A in the desert.
20 Wild animals —
jackals and ostriches — will
honor me,
because I provide water
in the wilderness,
and rivers in the desert,*d*
to give drink to my chosen people.

⇝ HOPE WORDS ⇝

It's one thing to say that God can make a way. It's another thing to see him make a way.

21 The people I formed for myself
will declare my praise.*e*

22 "But, Jacob, you have not called on me,
because, Israel, you have
become weary of me.*f*
23 You have not brought me your sheep
for burnt offerings
or honored me with your sacrifices.*g*
I have not burdened you
with offerings
or wearied you with incense.^B
24 You have not bought me
aromatic cane with silver,
or satisfied me with the fat
of your sacrifices.

But you have burdened me
with your sins;
you have wearied me^h
with your iniquities.*i*
25 "I — I sweep away
your transgressions*j*
for my own sake*k*
and remember your sins no more.*l*
26 Remind me. Let's argue
the case together.*m*
Recount the facts, so that you may
be vindicated.
27 Your first father sinned,*n*
and your mediators have rebelled
against me.*o*
28 So I defiled the officers
of the sanctuary,
and set Jacob apart
for destruction*p*
and Israel for scorn.

SPIRITUAL BLESSING

44 "And now listen,
Jacob my servant,
Israel whom I have chosen.*q*
2 This is the word of the LORD
your Maker, the one
who formed you from the womb:
He will help you.
Do not fear, Jacob my servant,
Jeshurun^C whom I have chosen.*r*
3 For I will pour water on
the thirsty land
and streams on the dry ground;
I will pour out my Spirit*s*
on your descendants
and my blessing on your offspring.
4 They will sprout among^D the grass
like poplars by flowing streams.
5 This one will say, 'I am the LORD's';
another will use the name of Jacob;
still another will write on his hand,
'The LORD's,'
and take on the name of Israel."

NO GOD OTHER THAN THE LORD

6 This is what the LORD, the King of Israel and its Redeemer,*t* the LORD of Armies, says:

I am the first and I am the last.*u*
There is no God but me.*v*

---

^A 43:19 DSS read *paths*　^B 43:23 I.e., with demands for offerings and incense　^C 44:2 = Upright One　^D 44:4 Some Hb mss, DSS, LXX read *as among*

43:18-19 This promise must have reminded Isaiah's readers of the exodus from Egypt, when God saved their forefathers from bondage and led them through the wilderness. But the exodus from Babylon would be even better, since it would restore the Jews to their homeland from which they had been expelled because of their sins.
43:25 God would intervene on behalf of his people not because on their righteousness or their faithfulness to the covenant they'd made with him. (In this, they were complete and total failures.) He would save them **for [his] own sake**.
44:1-5 This national future blessing will be fulfilled completely during Christ's millennial kingdom, when Israel will be delivered from her unbelief.

7 Who, like me, can announce
    the future?
Let him say so and make a case
    before me,[a]
since I have established
    an ancient people.
Let these gods declare[A]
    the coming things,
and what will take place.

8 Do not be startled or afraid.
Have I not told you and declared it
    long ago?
You are my witnesses![b]
Is there any God but me?[c]
There is no other Rock;[d]
    I do not know any.

9 All who make idols are nothing,
and what they treasure
    benefits no one.
Their witnesses do not see
    or know anything,
so they will be put to shame.[e]

10 Who makes a god or casts
    a metal image
that benefits no one?[f]

11 Look, all its worshipers will be
    put to shame,
and the craftsmen are humans.
They all will assemble and stand;
they all will be startled
    and put to shame.

12 The ironworker labors
    over the coals,
shapes the idol with hammers,
and works it with his strong arm.
Also he grows hungry
    and his strength fails;
he doesn't drink water
    and is faint.

13 The woodworker stretches out
    a measuring line,
he outlines it with a stylus;
he shapes it with chisels
and outlines it with a compass.
He makes it according to
    a human form,[g]
like a beautiful person,
to dwell in a temple.

14 He cuts down[B] cedars for his use,
or he takes a cypress or an oak.

He lets it grow strong
    among the trees of the forest.
He plants a laurel, and the rain
    makes it grow.

15 A person can use it for fuel.
He takes some of it
    and warms himself;
also he kindles a fire
    and bakes bread;
he even makes it into a god
    and worships it;
he makes an idol from it
    and bows down to it.

16 He burns half of it in a fire,
and he roasts meat on that half.
He eats the roast and is satisfied.
He warms himself and says, "Ah!
I am warm, I see the blaze."

17 He makes a god or his idol
    with the rest of it.
He bows down to it and worships;
he prays to it,[h] "Save me, for you are
    my god."

18 Such people[c] do not comprehend
and cannot understand,
for he has shut their eyes[D]
    so they cannot see,
and their minds
    so they cannot understand.

19 No one comes to his senses;[E]
no one has the perception
    or insight to say,
"I burned half of it in the fire,
I also baked bread on its coals,
I roasted meat and ate.
Should I make something detestable[j]
    with the rest of it?
Should I bow down to a block
    of wood?"

20 He feeds on[F] ashes.
His deceived mind
    has led him astray,
and he cannot rescue himself,
or say, "Isn't there a lie
    in my right hand?"[j]

21 Remember these things, Jacob,
and Israel, for you are
    my servant;
I formed you, you are my servant;
Israel, you will never be forgotten
    by me.[G,k]

[a] 44:7 Is 41:22,26
[b] 44:8 Is 43:10
[c] Dt 4:35,39; 1Sm 2:2; Is 45:5; Jl 2:27
[d] Is 17:10; 26:4; 30:29
[e] 44:9 Ps 97:7; Is 42:17; 44:11; 45:16
[f] 44:10 Is 41:29; Jr 10:5; Hab 2:18; Ac 19:26
[g] 44:13 Ps 115:5-7

[h] 44:17 1Kg 18:26,28; Is 45:20
[i] 44:19 Dt 27:15; 1Kg 11:5,7; 2Kg 23:13-14
[j] 44:20 Is 57:11; 59:3-4,13; Rm 1:25
[k] 44:21 Is 49:15

[A] 44:7 Lit *declare them* —   [B] 44:14 Lit *To cut down for himself*   [C] 44:18 Lit *They*   [D] 44:18 Or *for their eyes are shut*   [E] 44:19 Lit *No one returns to his heart*   [F] 44:20 Or *He shepherds*   [G] 44:21 DSS, LXX, Tg read *Israel, do not forget me*

44:12-17 Isaiah provides a detailed account of the efforts to make an idol, showing how ludicrous the whole idea of idolatry is.

44:19-20 Some say that pagan practices are simply the efforts of innocent, ignorant people trying their best to worship whoever they believe to be in control. But Isaiah's account leaves us no room to conclude that those practicing idolatry are anything less than rebellious sinners who have allowed themselves to be deceived by the evil one. The apostle Paul adds the helpful insight that when people "suppress the truth" about God, they will believe anything. They are "without excuse" (see Rom 1:18-23).

[a] 44:22 Ps 51:1,9; Is 43:25; Ac 3:19
[b] Is 31:6; 55:7
[c] Is 43:1; 48:20; 1Co 6:20; 1Pt 1:18-19
[d] 44:23 Ps 69:34; 96:11-12; Is 42:10; 49:13
[e] Is 49:3; 61:3
[f] 44:24 Is 41:14; 43:14
[g] Is 44:2
[h] Is 40:22; 42:5; 45:12,18; 51:13
[i] 44:25 2Sm 15:31; Jb 5:12-14; Ps 33:10; Is 29:14; Jr 51:57; 1Co 1:20,27
[j] 44:28 Is 45:1
[k] Eph 1:9
[l] 2Ch 36:22-23; Ezr 1:1; Is 14:32; 45:13; 54:11
[m] 45:1 Is 44:28
[n] Ps 73:23; Is 41:13; 42:6
[o] Jb 12:21; Is 45:5

[p] 45:2 Is 40:4
[q] Ps 107:16
[r] 45:3 Jr 41:8; 50:37
[s] Ex 33:12,17; Is 43:1; 49:1
[t] 45:4 Is 41:8; 42:19
[u] 45:5 Is 45:6,14,18,21; 46:9
[v] Is 44:6,8
[w] 45:6 Ps 102:15; Is 37:20; Mal 1:11
[x] 45:7 Ps 104:20; 105:28
[y] Gn 50:20; 1Sm 16:14; 1Kg 21:21; 22:8; 2Kg 6:33; Jb 2:10; Ps 78:49; Is 13:11; 31:2; 47:11; Jr 1:14; Lm 3:38; Am 3:6
[z] 45:8 Hs 10:12
[aa] Ps 85:11; Is 61:11
[ab] 45:9 Is 29:16; 64:8; Jr 18:6; Rm 9:20-21

22 I have swept away
   your transgressions like a cloud,[a]
and your sins like a mist.
Return to me,[b]
   for I have redeemed you.[c]
23 Rejoice, heavens,[d] for the LORD
   has acted;
shout, depths of the earth.
Break out into singing, mountains,
forest, and every tree in it.
For the LORD has redeemed Jacob,
and glorifies himself through Israel.[e]

RESTORATION OF ISRAEL THROUGH CYRUS

24 This is what the LORD, your Redeemer[f]
who formed you from the womb,[g] says:
   I am the LORD, who made everything;
   who stretched out the heavens
      by myself;[h]
   who alone spread out the earth;
25   who destroys the omens
      of the false prophets
   and makes fools of diviners;
   who confounds the wise
   and makes
      their knowledge foolishness;[i]
26   who confirms the message
      of his servant
   and fulfills the counsel
      of his messengers;
   who says to Jerusalem, "She will
      be inhabited,"
   and to the cities of Judah, "They will
      be rebuilt,"
   and I will restore her ruins;
27   who says to the depths of the sea,
      "Be dry,"
   and I will dry up your rivers;
28   who says to Cyrus,[j] "My shepherd,
   he will fulfill all my pleasure"[k]
   and says to Jerusalem, "She will
      be rebuilt,"[l]
   and of the temple, "Its foundation
      will be laid."

45 The LORD says this to Cyrus,
      his anointed,[m]
whose right hand I have grasped[n]
to subdue nations before him
and disarm[A] kings,[o]
to open doors before him,
and even city gates will not be shut:

2 "I will go before you
   and level the uneven places;[B,p]
I will shatter the bronze doors
   and cut the iron bars in two.[q]
3 I will give you the treasures
      of darkness
   and riches from secret places,[r]
   so that you may know that I am
      the LORD.
I am the God of Israel, who calls you
   by your name.[s]
4 I call you by your name,
   for the sake of my servant Jacob[t]
   and Israel my chosen one.
I give a name to you,
   though you do not know me.
5 I am the LORD, and there is
      no other;[u]
   there is no God but me.[v]
I will strengthen[C] you,
   though you do not know me,

⇝ HOPE WORDS ⇜

If you want to run your own world, go make one. God is in charge of this one.

---

6 so that all may know from the rising
      of the sun to its setting
   that there is no one but me.[w]
I am the LORD, and there is no other.
7 I form light and create darkness,[x]
I make success and create disaster;[y]
I am the LORD, who
   does all these things.

8 "Heavens, sprinkle from above,
and let the skies
   shower righteousness.[z]
Let the earth open up
so that salvation will sprout
and righteousness will spring up
   with it.[aa]
I, the LORD, have created it.

9 "Woe to the one who argues
   with his Maker —
one clay pot among many.[D]
Does clay say to the one forming it,
'What are you making?'[ab]

[A] 45:1 Lit *unloosen the waist of*   [B] 45:2 DSS, LXX read *the mountains*   [C] 45:5 Lit *gird*   [D] 45:9 Lit *a clay pot with clay pots of the ground*

44:28 Cyrus, a Persian king, would rise and defeat the Babylonian Empire, and God announced it more than a century before it happened. Imagine the comfort and hope the book of Isaiah was to later readers exiled in Babylon, when a ruler named Cyrus came to power and challenged Babylon! **45:5-6** Ironically, this unredeemed, idol-worshiping king named Cyrus would do such a work by God's power that all would **know** **from the rising of the sun to its setting that there is no** god but the LORD (45:6). **45:9-13** God gets to decide how the game is played (45:9-12). No one in Israel, then, could question why God did what he did in

Or does your work say,
'He has no hands'?[A]

10 Woe to the one who says
   to his father,
'What are you fathering?'
or to his mother,[B]
'What are you giving birth to?' "

11 This is what the LORD,
the Holy One of Israel[a]
   and its Maker, says:
"Ask me what is to happen
   to[c] my sons,[b]
and instruct me about the work
   of my hands.[c]

12 I made the earth,
and created humans on it.
It was my hands that stretched out
   the heavens,[d]
and I commanded
   everything in them.

13 I have stirred him up
   in righteousness,[e]
and will level all roads
   for him.
He will rebuild my city,[f]
and set my exiles free,[g]
not for a price or a bribe,"
says the LORD of Armies.

GOD ALONE IS THE SAVIOR

14 This is what the LORD says:
"The products of Egypt
   and the merchandise of Cush
and the Sabeans, men of stature,[h]
will come over to you[i]
and will be yours;
they will follow you,
they will come over in chains
and bow down to you.
They will confess[D] to you,
'God is indeed with you,[j] and there is
   no other;
there is no other God.' "

15 Yes, you are a God who hides,[k]
God of Israel, Savior.[l]

16 All of them are put to shame,
   even humiliated;[m]
the makers of idols
   go in humiliation together.

17 Israel will be saved by the LORD
with an everlasting salvation;
you will not be put to shame
   or humiliated
for all eternity.[n]

18 For this is what the LORD says —
the Creator of the heavens,
the God who formed the earth
   and made it,
the one who established it
(he did not create it to be
   a wasteland,
but formed it to be inhabited)[o] —
he says, "I am the LORD,
and there is no other.

19 I have not spoken in secret,[p]
somewhere in a land
   of darkness.
I did not say to the descendants
   of Jacob:
Seek me in a wasteland.[q]
I am the LORD, who
   speaks righteously,[r]
who declares what is right.

20 "Come, gather together,
and approach, you fugitives
   of the nations.
Those who carry their wooden idols
and pray to a god who cannot save[s]
have no knowledge.[t]

21 Speak up and present your case[E,u] —
yes, let them consult each other.
Who predicted this long ago?
Who announced
   from ancient times?
Was it not I, the LORD?
There is no other God but me,
a righteous God and Savior;[v]
there is no one except me.[w]

22 Turn to me and be saved,
all the ends of the earth.
For I am God,
and there is no other.

23 By myself I have sworn;[x]
truth has gone from my mouth,[y]
a word that will not be revoked:
Every knee will bow[z] to me,
every tongue will swear allegiance.

[a] 45:11 Is 1:4
[b] Jr 31:9
[c] Is 19:25; 29:23; 60:21; 64:8
[d] 45:12 Ps 104:2; Is 42:5; 44:24
[e] 45:13 Is 41:2
[f] 2Ch 36:22-23; Is 44:28
[g] Is 52:3
[h] 45:14 Is 18:1; 43:3
[i] Is 14:1-2; 49:23; 54:3
[j] 1Co 14:25
[k] 45:15 Ps 44:24; Is 1:15; 8:17; 57:17
[l] Is 43:3
[m] 45:16 Is 42:17; 44:9

[n] 45:17 Is 49:23; 50:7; 54:4
[o] 45:18 Gn 1:26; Ps 115:16
[p] 45:19 Is 48:16
[q] 2Ch 15:2; Ps 78:34; Jr 29:13-14
[r] Ps 19:8; Is 45:23; 63:1
[s] 45:20 Is 44:17; 46:1,7; Jr 10:5
[t] Is 44:18-19; 48:5-7
[u] 45:21 Is 41:21-23; 43:9
[v] Is 43:3,11
[w] Dt 4:35; 6:4; Mk 12:32
[x] 45:23 Gn 22:16; Is 62:8; Heb 6:13
[y] Is 55:11
[z] Rm 14:11; Php 2:10

[A] 45:9 Or making? Your work has no hands.   [B] 45:10 Lit to a woman   [C] 45:11 Or me the coming things about   [D] 45:14 Lit pray   [E] 45:21 Lit and approach

---

the way he chose to do it. If he wanted to use an unrighteous king like Cyrus to accomplish his righteous purposes, that's what he would do (45:13).

45:14-17 Since the Gentle nations surrounding Israel were also part of God's creation and under his sovereign rule, the Lord spoke of a day when these people would also bow

before God and say to Israel, **God is indeed with you, and there is no other** (45:14). This can only describe conditions during Christ's millennial reign, when he will return in glory and power, purging Israel of her unbelief as she acknowledges her Savior. This will be Israel's true golden age, when the nation **will be saved by the LORD** and **will not be put to shame** (45:17).

45:23 Every knee will bow to me, every tongue will swear allegiance. Paul applies these words to Jesus, demonstrating that he is truly God (see Phil 2:10-11). Thus, all people have two choices: either bow willingly in faith and confess Jesus Christ as the only Savior, or be broken by his wrath and forced to bow as an object of his judgment.

God's Eternal Drama

PROPHECY IS THE UNROLLING OF God's plan, his eternal drama, for the ages. When God gives his names, he defines himself as "I Am." He is always and eternally in the present tense. When you have a puzzle, one of the best ways to see how it fits together is by examining the picture on the box top. If you simply look at the pieces, they don't relate as you stare at them. If you get the view presented on the box, however, you can put the puzzle in order. Prophecy is the Bible's way of providing a big picture about the future.

Prophecy also reveals the character of God. When you see God's overarching program, then you get to know more about God. Isaiah 46:9-10 makes a very personal statement related to God's knowledge and his prophetic program: "Remember what happened long ago, for I am God, and there is no other; I am God, and no one is like me. I declare the end from the beginning, and from long ago what is not yet done, saying: my plan will take place, and I will do all my will."

Prophecy gives you confidence to trust God. If God knows tomorrow already, then you and I can go to sleep tonight without fear. Additionally, Paul argues repeatedly that he got so overwhelmed with thinking about God's character that he couldn't help but worship God whenever he saw his powerful plan unfold.

Prophecy also produces stability during trials. In John 14, Jesus was soon to ascend to heaven. The disciples had been walking with him for three years and were about to be left alone. Their question was this: How will we make it? Jesus responded with these well-known, well-preached, well-worn words: "Don't let your heart be troubled. Believe in God; believe also in me. In my Father's house are many rooms; if not, I would have told you. I am going away to prepare a place for you. If I go away and prepare a place for you, I will come again and take you to myself, so that where I am you may be also" (JN 14:1-3).

Focus on those words, "Don't let your heart be troubled." Prophecy produces calm in the midst of a storm. Jesus goes on to tell the disciples he's going to send a Counselor to take care of his followers—including you and me—while he's away. So what does God want us to do with this information? Paul tells us: "Encourage one another with these words" (1TH 4:18). You see, the point of prophecy is to produce encouragement.

We've made earth too big. We've made Satan too big. We've made people too big. And as a result, they all ruin our day. Prefer to think on heaven, and you'll be okay on earth. A heavenly perspective gives calm in the midst of chaos and trials.

24 It will be said about me,
    'Righteousness and strength
    are found only in the LORD.' "
    All who are enraged against him
    will come to him and be
        put to shame.[a]
25 All the descendants of Israel
    will be justified and find glory
        through the LORD.

THERE IS NO ONE LIKE GOD

46 Bel crouches; Nebo cowers.[b]
    Idols depicting them are
        consigned to beasts and cattle.
    The images you carry are loaded,
    as a burden for the weary animal.
2 The gods cower;
    they crouch together;
    they are not able to rescue
        the burden,
    but they themselves go
        into captivity.[c]

3 "Listen to me, house of Jacob,
    all the remnant of the house of Israel,
    who have been sustained
        from the womb,
    carried along since birth.
4 I will be the same until your old age,[d]
    and I will bear you up when you
        turn gray.
    I have made you,
        and I will carry you;
    I will bear and rescue you.

5 "Who will you compare me
        or make me equal to?
    Who will you measure me with,
        so that we should be
        like each other?[e]
6 Those who pour out their bags
        of gold
    and weigh out silver on scales —
    they hire a goldsmith
        and he makes it into a god.
    Then they kneel and bow down to it.[f]
7 They lift it to their shoulder
        and bear it along;[g]

they set it in its place, and there
    it stands;
it does not budge from its place.[h]
They cry out to it
    but it doesn't answer;
it saves no one from his trouble.

8 "Remember this and be brave;[A]
    take it to heart, you transgressors!
9 Remember what happened
        long ago,[i]
    for I am God, and there is no other;
    I am God, and no one is like me.
10 I declare the end
        from the beginning,
    and from long ago what is
        not yet done,
    saying: my plan will take place,
    and I will do all my will.[j]
11 I call a bird of prey[B] from the east,[k]
    a man for my purpose
        from a far country.
    Yes, I have spoken; so I will also
        bring it about.[l]
    I have planned it; I will also do it.
12 Listen to me, you hardhearted,
    far removed from justice:
13 I am bringing my justice near;[m]
    it is not far away,
    and my salvation will not delay.
    I will put salvation in Zion,
    my splendor in Israel.

THE FALL OF BABYLON

47 "Go down and sit in the dust,[n]
    Virgin Daughter Babylon.[o]
    Sit on the ground without a throne,
    Daughter Chaldea!
    For you will no longer be called
        pampered and spoiled.
2 Take millstones and grind flour;[p]
    remove your veil,
    strip off your skirt, bare your thigh,
    wade through the streams.
3 Your nakedness will be uncovered,
    and your disgrace will be exposed.[q]
    I will take vengeance;
    I will spare no one."[c]

[a] 45:24 Is 41:11
[b] 46:1 Jr 50:2-4; 51:44
[c] 46:2 Jdg 18:17-18,24; 2Sm 5:21; Jr 43:12-13; 48:7; Hs 10:5-6
[d] 46:4 Ps 71:18
[e] 46:5 Is 40:18,25
[f] 46:6 Is 40:19; 41:7; 44:12-17; Jr 10:4
[g] 46:7 Is 45:20; 46:1; Jr 10:5

[h] 46:7 Is 40:20; 41:7
[i] 46:9 Dt 32:7; Is 42:9; 65:17
[j] 46:10 Ps 33:11; Pr 19:21; Is 5:19; 14:24; 25:1; 40:8; Ac 5:39
[k] 46:11 Is 44:28–45:1
[l] Nm 23:19; Is 14:24; 37:26
[m] 46:13 Is 51:5; 61:11; Rm 3:21
[n] 47:1 Is 3:26; Jr 48:18
[o] Ps 137:8; Jr 50:42; 51:33; Zch 2:7
[p] 47:2 Ex 11:5; Jb 31:10; Mt 24:41
[q] 47:3 Jr 13:26; Lm 1:8; Ezk 16:37; Nah 3:5

[A] 46:8 Hb obscure   [B] 46:11 = Cyrus   [C] 47:3 Hb obscure

46:1-4 The Babylonian gods **Bel** and **Nebo**, possibly also known as the god Marduk and his son, were lifeless idols (46:1). They had to be carried on carts because they couldn't do anything for themselves (46:1-2). The true God of Israel, by contrast, carried his people from **womb** to grave (46:3-4). Whom would you prefer to worship and serve? **46:10** There is plenty of mystery in this statement because God's knowledge of the

future includes not only everything that actually happens but also everything that could potentially happen. But since God will accomplish his **will**, discovering and obeying it—through his Word and in the power of his Holy Spirit—should be our chief concern. We are obligated to live righteously, and God will use our obedience to help accomplish his plan. **46:11** The **bird of prey from the east** is a reference to King Cyrus of Persia.

47:1-7 Though God **was angry** with his people and would use Babylon to chastise them, Babylon's goal was domination and cruelty, showing **no mercy** (47:6). So God had already prepared Babylon's punishment: **I will spare no one** (47:3).

[a] 47:4 Is 41:14; 43:14
[b] 47:5 Is 23:2; Jr 8:14; Lm 2:10; 3:2,28
[c] 47:8 Zph 2:15
[d] Rv 18:7
[e] 47:9 Is 47:13; Nah 3:4; Rv 18:23
[f] 47:10 Ps 139:3,11
[g] 47:11 Is 13:6; Jr 51:8,43; Lk 17:27; 1Th 5:3

[h] 47:13 Is 8:19; 44:25; 47:9; Dn 2:2,10
[i] 47:14 Is 5:24; Mal 4:1
[j] Is 10:17; Jr 51:30–32,58
[k] 48:1 Nm 24:7; Dt 33:28; Ps 68:26
[l] Dt 6:13; Is 45:23; 65:16
[m] 48:2 Is 10:20; Jr 7:4; 21:2; Mc 3:11; Rm 2:17
[n] 48:4 Ex 32:9; Dt 31:27; Ezk 2:4; 3:7-9
[o] 48:5 Jr 44:15-18
[p] 48:6 Is 42:9; 43:19

4 The Holy One of Israel is
    our Redeemer;[a]
The Lord of Armies is his name.

5 "Daughter Chaldea,
sit in silence[b] and go into darkness.
For you will no longer be called
    mistress of kingdoms.

6 I was angry with my people;
I profaned my possession,
and I handed them over to you.
You showed them no mercy;
you made your yoke very heavy
    on the elderly.

7 You said, 'I will be the queen forever.'
You did not take these things to heart
or think about their outcome.

8 "So now hear this, lover of luxury,
who sits securely,[c]
who says to herself,
'I am, and there is no one else.
I will never be a widow
or know the loss of children.'[d]

9 These two things will happen to you
suddenly, in one day:
loss of children and widowhood.
They will happen to you
    in their entirety,
in spite of your many sorceries[e]
and the potency of your spells.

10 You were secure in your wickedness;
you said, 'No one sees me.'[f]
Your wisdom and knowledge
led you astray.
You said to yourself,
'I am, and there is no one else.'

11 But disaster will happen to you;
you will not know how to avert it.
And it will fall on you,
but you will be unable to ward it off.[A]
Devastation will happen
    to you suddenly
and unexpectedly.[g]

12 So take your stand with your spells
and your many sorceries,
which you have wearied yourself with
    from your youth.
Perhaps you will be able to succeed;
perhaps you will inspire terror!

13 You are worn out
    with your many consultations.

So let the astrologers stand
    and save you —
those who observe the stars,[h]
those who predict monthly
what will happen to you.

14 Look, they are like stubble;[i]
fire burns them.[j]
They cannot rescue themselves
from the power[B] of the flame.
This is not a coal
    for warming themselves,
or a fire to sit beside!

15 This is what they are to you —
those who have wearied you
and have traded with you
    from your youth;
each wanders on his own way;
no one can save you.

ISRAEL MUST LEAVE BABYLON

48 "Listen to this, house of Jacob —
those who are called
by the name Israel
and have descended from[C] Judah,[k]
who swear by the name of the Lord[l]
and declare the God of Israel,
but not in truth or righteousness.

2 For they are named after the Holy City,
and lean on the God of Israel;[m]
his name is the Lord of Armies.

3 I declared the past events long ago;
they came out of my mouth;
    I proclaimed them.
Suddenly I acted, and they occurred.

4 Because I know that you are stubborn,
and your neck is iron[D]
and your forehead bronze,[n]

5 therefore I declared to you long ago.
I announced it to you
    before it occurred,
so you could not claim, 'My idol
    caused them;
my carved image and cast idol
    control them.'[o]

6 You have heard it. Observe it all.
Will you not acknowledge it?
From now on I will announce
    new things to you,
hidden things that
    you have not known.[p]

7 They have been created now, and not
    long ago;

[A] 47:11 Or to atone for it   [B] 47:14 Lit hand   [C] 48:1 Lit have come from the waters of   [D] 48:4 Lit is an iron sinew

47:10 I am, and there is no one else is a statement of deity reserved for God alone (see 43:10-11; 44:6; 45:21-22). This is a significant insight into why the name *Babylon* became synonymous in Scripture with arrogant humanity rising up in fierce rebellion against God (see Rev 17).

48:3-9 As far back as Deuteronomy, God had told Israel that if they disobeyed him, he would scatter them in judgment and then regather them when their chastisement was complete (see Deut 30:1-5). The things God spoke through Isaiah were **new** in that until

God revealed and named Cyrus as Israel's liberator, the people did not know how God would accomplish their release from captivity (48:6).

you have not heard of them
before today,
so you could not claim, 'I already
knew them!'
8 You have never heard; you have
never known;
for a long time your ears have not
been open.
For I knew that you
were very treacherous,
and were known as a rebel
from birth.[a]
9 I will delay my anger for the sake
of my name,
and I will restrain myself
for your benefit and for my praise,
so that you will not be destroyed.
10 Look, I have refined you,[b] but not
as silver;
I have tested[A] you in the furnace
of affliction.
11 I will act for my own sake,
indeed, my own,[c]
for how can I[B] be defiled?
I will not give my glory to another.[d]

12 "Listen to me, Jacob,
and Israel, the one called by me:
I am he; I am the first,
I am also the last.[e]
13 My own hand founded the earth,
and my right hand spread out
the heavens;[f]
when I summoned them,
they stood up together.
14 All of you, assemble and listen!
Who among the idols[c] has declared
these things?
The LORD loves him;[D]
he will accomplish his will
against Babylon,[g]
and his arm will be against
the Chaldeans.
15 I — I have spoken;
yes, I have called him;[h]
I have brought him,
and he will succeed in his mission.[i]
16 Approach me and listen to this.
From the beginning I have not
spoken in secret;[j]

from the time anything existed,
I was there."
And now the Lord GOD
has sent me and his Spirit.[k]

17 This is what the LORD, your Redeemer,[l]
the Holy One of Israel[m] says:
I am the LORD your God,
who teaches you for your benefit,
who leads you in the way
you should go.
18 If only you had paid attention
to my commands.
Then your peace would have been
like a river,[n]
and your righteousness
like the waves of the sea.[o]
19 Your descendants would have been
as countless as the sand,[p]
and the offspring of your body
like its grains;
their name would not be cut off
or eliminated from my presence.

20 Leave Babylon,
flee from the Chaldeans!
Declare with a shout of joy,
proclaim this,
let it go out to the end of the earth;
announce,
"The LORD has redeemed
his servant[q] Jacob!"
21 They did not thirst
when he led them through the deserts;
he made water flow from the rock
for them;[r]
he split the rock, and water
gushed out.
22 "There is no peace for the wicked,"
says the LORD.[s]

THE SERVANT BRINGS SALVATION

49 Coasts and islands,[E] listen to me;
distant peoples, pay attention.
The LORD called[t] me
before I was born.
He named me while I was
in my mother's womb.[u]
2 He made my words
like a sharp sword;[v]

[a] 48:8 Dt 9:7,24; Ps 58:3; Is 46:8
[b] 48:10 Dt 4:20; 1Kg 8:51; Jr 11:4; Ezk 22:18-22; 1Pt 1:7
[c] 48:11 Is 43:25; Ezk 20:9
[d] Is 42:8
[e] 48:12 Is 41:4; 43:10-13; 46:4; Rv 1:17
[f] 48:13 Ps 102:25; Is 42:5; 45:12,18; Heb 1:10-12
[g] 48:14 Is 13:4-5,17-19; 46:10-11
[h] 48:15 Is 41:2; 45:1-2
[i] Is 53:10
[j] 48:16 Is 45:19

[k] 48:16 Nm 27:18; Ps 51:11; Is 61:1; 63:7,10; Zch 2:9,11
[l] 48:17 Is 41:14; 43:14
[m] Is 1:4
[n] 48:18 Is 32:16-18; 66:12
[o] Dt 5:29; 32:29; Ps 81:13-16; Am 5:24
[p] 48:19 Gn 22:17; Is 10:22; 44:3-4; 54:3; Hs 1:10
[q] 48:20 Is 41:8-9; 42:19; 43:10; 44:1-2,21; 45:4; 49:3; 54:17; Lk 1:54
[r] 48:21 Ex 17:6; Ps 78:15-16
[s] 48:22 Is 57:21
[t] 49:1 Is 44:2,24; 46:3; Jr 1:5
[u] Lk 1:15
[v] 49:2 Is 11:4; Heb 4:12; Rv 1:16; 2:12,16

48:12 God is **the first** and **also the last**. Interestingly, the risen and glorified Lord Jesus Christ makes this same claim: "I am the Alpha and the Omega, the first and the last, the beginning and the end" (Rev 22:13).
48:18 **If only** the Israelites had listened to and obeyed God, the horrors of the Babylonian captivity would not have happened.

What troubles might we be spared should we choose to obey God?
48:22 If you sow wickedness, it is impossible to reap peace.
49:1-7 Though the servant is called **Israel** in verse 3, he can't be the nation itself because the passage says his mission is to bring **Jacob/Israel** back to the Lord (49:5). So what's going

on? He is Christ who confirmed his calling as God's instrument of salvation: **The LORD called me before I was born** (49:1). This tells us that before the foundation of the world, the persons of the Godhead determined the plan of salvation. The Son of God is identified with the people of God because he will succeed where Israel failed.

a 49:2 Is 51:16
b 49:3 Is 41:8-9; 42:1; 49:5-7; 50:10; 52:13; 53:11; Ezk 34:23-24; Zch 3:8; Ac 3:13
c 49:6 Is 42:6; 51:4; Lk 2:32; Ac 13:47; 26:23
d Ac 13:47
e 49:7 Is 41:14; 43:14
f Ps 22:6-8; 69:7-9; Is 53:3
g Is 1:4
h Is 41:8-9; 42:1; 43:10,20; 44:1-2; 45:4; 65:9,15,22
i 49:8 Ps 69:13; 2Co 6:2
j Is 42:6

k 49:9 Is 42:7; 61:1; Lk 4:18
l Is 41:18
m 49:10 Ps 23:2; Is 40:11; Jn 4:10; Rv 7:16-17
n 49:11 Is 40:4
o 49:12 Is 43:5-6
p 49:13 Is 44:23
q Is 40:1
r Is 54:7-10; Mt 11:29
s 49:16 Sg 8:6; Hg 2:23
t 49:18 Is 60:4

he hid me in the shadow
of his hand.*a*
He made me like a sharpened arrow;
he hid me in his quiver.
3 He said to me, "You are my servant,*b*
Israel, in whom I will be glorified."
4 But I myself said: I have labored
in vain,
I have spent my strength for nothing
and futility;
yet my vindication is with the LORD,
and my reward is with my God.
5 And now, says the LORD,
who formed me from the womb
to be his servant,
to bring Jacob back to him
so that Israel might be gathered
to him;
for I am honored in the sight
of the LORD,
and my God is my strength —
6 he says,
"It is not enough for you to be
my servant
raising up the tribes of Jacob
and restoring the protected ones
of Israel.
I will also make you a light
for the nations,*c*
to be my salvation to the ends
of the earth."*d*
7 This is what the LORD,
the Redeemer*e* of Israel,
his Holy One, says
to one who is despised,
to one abhorred by people,*A,f*
to a servant of rulers:
"Kings will see, princes will stand up,
and they*B* will all bow down
because of the LORD, who is faithful,
the Holy One of Israel*g* —
and he has chosen you."*h*

8 This is what the LORD says:
I will answer you in a time of favor,
and I will help you in the day
of salvation.*i*
I will keep you,
and I will appoint you
to be a covenant for the people,*j*

to restore the land,
to make them possess
the desolate inheritances,
9 saying to the prisoners: Come out,*k*
and to those who are in darkness:
Show yourselves.
They will feed along the pathways,
and their pastures will be on all
the barren heights.*l*
10 They will not hunger or thirst,
the scorching heat or sun will not
strike them;
for their compassionate one
will guide them,
and lead them to springs.*m*
11 I will make all my mountains
into a road,
and my highways will be raised up.*n*
12 See, these will come from far away,
from the north and from the west,*C,o*
and from the land of Sinim.*D,E*

13 Shout for joy, you heavens!*p*
Earth, rejoice!
Mountains break into joyful shouts!
For the LORD has comforted
his people,*q*
and will have compassion
on his afflicted ones.*r*

ZION REMEMBERED

14 Zion says, "The LORD
has abandoned me;
the Lord has forgotten me!"
15 "Can a woman forget
her nursing child,
or lack compassion for the child
of her womb?
Even if these forget,
yet I will not forget you.
16 Look, I have inscribed you
on the palms of my hands;*s*
your walls are continually
before me.
17 Your builders*F* hurry;
those who destroy
and devastate you will leave you.
18 Look up, and look around.
They all gather together; they come
to you.*t*

A 49:7 Or *by the nation*   *B* 49:7 Lit *princes and they*   *C* 49:12 Lit *sea*   *D* 49:12 DSS read *of the Syenites*   *E* 49:12 Perhaps modern Aswan in southern Egypt   *F* 49:17 DSS, Aq, Theod, Vg; MT, Syr, Sym read *sons*

The servant's lament, **I have labored in vain** (49:4), could be a reference to Israel's rejection of Christ at his first coming (see John 1:11). This makes sense because God promises the servant, **I will also make you a light for the nations, to be my salvation to the ends of the earth** (49:6). Jesus fulfilled this in his ministry (see Matt 4:14-16). Further-

more, God also said of the servant that he would be **despised** (49:7). But, at his second coming, he will be triumphant, and **all** will **bow** to him (49:7).
49:8-9 This is a reference to Christ's millennial kingdom when the land of Israel will be restored to welcome back Israel's captives and exiles.

49:14-17 Verse 14 was the cry of captives, who were reassured that God's love for his people was greater than a mother's love for her **child** (49:15). Isaiah's later readers in captivity in Babylon would identify with this complaint, but they would also read of God's deliverance as their captors disappeared in a flood of God's judgment (49:17).

As I live" —
    this is the Lord's declaration —
"you will wear all your children[A]
    as jewelry,
and put them on as a bride does.
19 For your waste and desolate places
    and your land marked by ruins —
will now be indeed too small
    for the inhabitants,[a]
and those who swallowed you up
    will be far away.
20 Yet as you listen, the children
    that you have been deprived of
    will say,
'This place is too small for me;
    make room for me so that
    I may settle.'[b]
21 Then you will say within yourself,
'Who fathered these for me?
I was deprived of my children
    and unable to conceive,
exiled and wandering —
but who brought them up?
See, I was left by myself —
but these, where did they
    come from?'"[B]

22 This is what the Lord God says:
Look, I will lift up my hand
    to the nations,
and raise my banner to the peoples.[c]
They will bring your sons
    in their arms,
and your daughters will be carried
    on their shoulders.[d]
23 Kings will be your guardians
and their queens[c]
    your nursing mothers.[e]
They will bow down to you
    with their faces to the ground
and lick the dust at your feet.[f]
Then you will know that I am the
    Lord;[g]
those who put their hope in me
    will not be put to shame.[h]

24 Can the prey be taken from
    a mighty man,
or the captives of a tyrant[D]
    be delivered?
25 For this is what the Lord says:
"Even the captives of a mighty man
    will be taken,

and the prey of a tyrant
    will be delivered;
I will contend with the one
    who contends with you,
and I will save your children.
26 I will make your oppressors eat
    their own flesh,[i]
and they will be drunk
    with their own blood
as with sweet wine.
Then all people will know
that I, the Lord, am your Savior,[j]
and your Redeemer,[k] the Mighty One
    of Jacob."[l]

50 This is what the Lord says:
Where is your mother's
    divorce certificate
that I used to send her away?[m]
Or to which of my creditors
    did I sell you?[n]
Look, you were sold
    for your iniquities,[o]
and your mother was sent away
because of your transgressions.
2 Why was no one there
    when I came?
Why was there no one to answer
    when I called?
Is my arm too weak to redeem?[p]
Or do I have no power to rescue?
Look, I dry up the sea
    by my rebuke;[q]
I turn the rivers into a wilderness;
their fish rot because of lack
    of water
and die of thirst.
3 I dress the heavens in black
and make sackcloth
    their clothing.[r]

THE OBEDIENT SERVANT

4 The Lord God has given me
the tongue of those
    who are instructed[s]
to know how to sustain the weary
    with a word.
He awakens me each morning;
he awakens my ear to listen
    like those being instructed.[t]
5 The Lord God has opened my ear,
and I was not rebellious;
I did not turn back.[u]

[a] 49:19 Is 54:1-2; Zch 10:10
[b] 49:20 Is 54:1-3
[c] 49:22 Is 11:10-12; 18:3; 62:10
[d] Is 14:2; 43:6; 60:4
[e] 49:23 Is 60:3,10-11
[f] Is 14:1-2
[g] Is 41:20; 43:10; 60:16
[h] Ps 25:3; Is 45:17; Jl 2:27

[i] 49:26 Is 9:20
[j] Is 43:3
[k] Is 41:14
[l] Gn 49:24; Ps 132:2,5; Is 60:16
[m] 50:1 Dt 24:1-3; Jr 3:8
[n] Dt 32:30; 2Kg 4:1; Neh 5:5
[o] Is 13:11
[p] 50:2 Gn 18:14; Nm 11:23; Is 59:1
[q] Ex 14:21; Is 43:16; 44:27
[r] 50:3 Rv 6:12
[s] 50:4 Is 8:16; 54:13
[t] Jn 4:34
[u] 50:5 Jn 8:29; 14:31; 15:10; Php 2:8; Heb 5:8

[A] 49:18 Lit all of them   [B] 49:21 Lit where are they   [C] 49:23 Lit princesses   [D] 49:24 DSS, Syr, Vg; MT reads a righteous man

---

49:22-23 In that glorious day, the Gentile nations will help the Jews return to their land (49:22). Furthermore, the nations will **bow down** in humility before Israel and her Messiah (49:23).

49:25 The Lord promises, **I will contend with the one who contends with you.** This brings to mind God's promise to Abraham: "I will curse anyone who treats you with contempt" (Gen 12:3).

50:4-5 God's Servant-Messiah, in contrast to the faithless nation, let his **ear** be **opened** by God (50:5). He was willing to be **instructed** (50:4).

[a] 50:6 Mt 26:67; 27:26; Mk 14:65; 15:19; Lk 22:63; Jn 19:1-5
[b] 50:7 Ezk 3:8-9
[c] 50:8 Is 45:25
[d] 50:9 Rm 8:33-34
[e] Jb 13:28; Is 51:8; Hs 5:12
[f] 50:10 Is 42:1; 49:3-7; 52:13; 53:11; Ezk 34:23-24; Zch 3:8; Ac 3:13
[g] 51:2 Gn 12:1; 15:5; Dt 1:10; Is 29:22; 41:8; 63:16; Ezk 33:24
[h] 51:3 Is 40:1
[i] Gn 2:8; Jl 2:3
[j] Gn 13:10
[k] 51:4 Is 42:6; 49:6
[l] 51:5 Is 46:13; 54:17
[m] Is 40:10
[n] 51:6 Ps 102:25-26; Is 34:4; Mt 24:35; Heb 1:10-12; 2Pt 3:10
[o] Is 45:17; 2Tm 2:10; Heb 5:9
[p] 51:7 Ps 37:31
[q] 51:8 Is 50:9
[r] Is 14:11

6 I gave my back to those who beat me,
and my cheeks to those who tore out
my beard.
I did not hide my face from scorn
and spitting.[a]
7 The Lord God will help me;
therefore I have not
been humiliated;
therefore I have set my face
like flint,[b]
and I know I will not
be put to shame.
8 The one who vindicates me is near;[c]
who will contend with me?
Let us confront each other.[A]
Who has a case against me?[B]
Let him come near me!
9 In truth, the Lord God will help me;
who will condemn me?[d]
Indeed, all of them will wear out
like a garment;
a moth will devour them.[e]
10 Who among you fears the Lord
and listens to his servant?[f]
Who among you walks in darkness,
and has no light?
Let him trust in the name of the
Lord;
let him lean on his God.
11 Look, all you who kindle a fire,
who encircle yourselves
with[c] torches;
walk in the light of your fire
and of the torches you have lit!
This is what you'll get from my hand:
you will lie down in a place
of torment.

SALVATION FOR ZION

51 Listen to me, you
who pursue righteousness,
you who seek the Lord:
Look to the rock from which
you were cut,
and to the quarry from which
you were dug.
2 Look to Abraham your father,
and to Sarah who gave birth to you.

When I called him, he was only one;
I blessed him and made him many.[g]
3 For the Lord will comfort Zion;[h]
he will comfort all her waste places,
and he will make her wilderness
like Eden,[i]
and her desert like the garden
of the Lord.[j]
Joy and gladness will be found
in her,
thanksgiving and melodious song.
4 Pay attention to me, my people,
and listen to me, my nation;
for instruction will come from me,
and my justice for a light
to the nations.[k]
I will bring it about quickly.
5 My righteousness is near,[l]
my salvation appears,
and my arms will bring justice
to the nations.[m]
The coasts and islands will put
their hope in me,
and they will look to my strength.[D]
6 Look up to the heavens,
and look at the earth beneath;
for the heavens will vanish
like smoke,
the earth will wear out
like a garment,
and its inhabitants will die
like gnats.[E,n]
But my salvation will last forever,[o]
and my righteousness will never
be shattered.
7 Listen to me, you who
know righteousness,
the people in whose heart is
my instruction:[p]
do not fear disgrace by men,
and do not be shattered
by their taunts.
8 For moths will devour them
like a garment,[q]
and worms will eat them
like wool.[r]

[A] 50:8 Lit us stand   [B] 50:8 Lit Who is lord of my judgment   [C] 50:11 Syr reads who set ablaze   [D] 51:5 Lit arm   [E] 51:6 Or die in like manner

---

50:6 The Gospel writers affirm that this humiliation was fulfilled in Jesus Christ (see Matt 26:67; 27:30; John 19:1).
50:10 Given the servant's obedience in the midst of great suffering, Isaiah exhorted his readers, everyone who **fears the Lord,** to remain faithful in spite of their suffering. The same exhortation applies to us today. Christians are called to share in Christ's sufferings so that we may share in his joy (see 1 Pet 2:21; 4:13-14).

51:2-3 Although in captivity, the faithful in Babylon were exhorted to remember their heritage by looking back **to Abraham your father, and to Sarah who gave birth to you** (51:2). This would have reminded the Jewish captives that their nation was born out of God's eternal covenant with Abraham, a promise of blessing they could cling to during their present suffering. The promise of future restoration was a reminder that God would remember his covenant (51:3).

51:4 Only when Christ reigns in his millennial kingdom will we see his **justice** shine as **a light to the nations.**
51:5 **The coasts and islands** is a figure of speech for the farthest corners of the world.
51:6 Christ's second coming will also bring about the end of the present **heavens** and **earth,** which **will vanish like smoke** to make way for the new heavens and new earth (cf. 65:17; 66:22).

But my righteousness
   will last forever,
and my salvation for all generations.

9 Wake up, wake up!
Arm of the LORD, clothe yourself
   with strength.
Wake up as in days past,
   as in generations long ago.
Wasn't it you who hacked Rahab
   to pieces,[a]
who pierced the sea monster?[b]

10 Wasn't it you who dried up the sea,[c]
   the waters of the great deep,
who made the sea-bed into a road
for the redeemed to pass over?[d]

11 And the ransomed of the LORD
   will return[e]
and come to Zion with singing,
   crowned with unending joy.
Joy and gladness will overtake them,
and sorrow and sighing will flee.

12 I — I am the one who comforts you.
Who are you that you should
   fear humans who die,[f]
or a son of man who is given up
   like grass?[g]

13 But you have forgotten the LORD,
   your Maker,
who stretched out the heavens
   and laid the foundations
   of the earth.[h]
You are in constant dread
   all day long
because of the fury of the oppressor,
who has set himself to destroy.
But where is the fury
   of the oppressor?[i]

14 The prisoner[A] is soon to be set free;
he will not die and go to the Pit,
and his food will not be lacking.

15 For I am the LORD your God
who stirs up the sea so that
   its waves roar[j] —
his name is the LORD of Armies.

16 I have put my words in your mouth,[k]
and covered you in the shadow
   of my hand,[l]
in order to plant[B] the heavens,
   to found the earth,
and to say to Zion, "You are
   my people."

17 Wake yourself, wake yourself up!
Stand up, Jerusalem,
you who have drunk the cup
   of his fury[m]
from the LORD's hand;
you who have drunk the goblet
   to the dregs —
the cup that causes people to stagger.

18 There is no one to guide her
among all the children
   she has raised;
there is no one to take hold
   of her hand
among all the offspring
   she has brought up.

19 These two things have happened
   to you:[n]
devastation and destruction,
famine and sword.
Who will grieve for you?
How can I[C] comfort you?

20 Your children have fainted;
they lie at the head of every street
like an antelope in a net.
They are full of the LORD's fury,
the rebuke of your God.

21 So listen to this, suffering
and drunken one — but not
   with wine.[o]

22 This is what your Lord says —
   the LORD, even your God,
who defends his people[p] —
"Look, I have removed
   from your hand
the cup that causes staggering;
that goblet, the cup of my fury.
You will never drink it again.

23 I will put it into the hands
   of your tormentors,
who said to you:[q]
Lie down, so we can walk over you.
You made your back like the ground,
and like a street for those who walk
   on it.

52 "Wake up, wake up;
   put on your strength, Zion!
Put on your beautiful garments,[r]
Jerusalem, the Holy City![s]
For the uncircumcised
   and the unclean
   will no longer enter you.[t]

[a] 51:9 Jb 26:12; Ps 89:10; Is 30:7
[b] Ps 74:13; Is 27:1
[c] 51:10 Is 11:15-16; 50:2; 63:11-12
[d] Ex 15:13
[e] 51:11 Is 35:10
[f] 51:12 Ps 118:6; Is 2:22
[g] Is 40:6-7; Jms 1:10-11; 1Pt 1:24
[h] 51:13 Is 44:24; 45:12; Am 9:6; Zch 12:1
[i] Is 49:26
[j] 51:15 Ps 107:25; Jr 31:35
[k] 51:16 Is 59:21
[l] Ex 33:22; Is 49:2

[m] 51:17 Jb 21:20; Is 63:6; Jr 25:15; Mt 20:22; 26:39; Jn 18:1; Rv 14:10
[n] 51:19 Is 47:9
[o] 51:21 Is 29:9
[p] 51:22 Is 3:12-13; 49:25; Jr 50:34
[q] 51:23 Is 49:26; Jr 25:15-17,26,28; Zch 12:2
[r] 52:1 Is 61:3
[s] Neh 11:1; Is 48:2
[t] Is 35:8; Rv 21:27

[A] 51:14 Hb obscure [B] 51:16 Syr reads *to stretch out* [C] 51:19 DSS, LXX, Syr, Vg read *you? Who can*

51:10 This is a reference to the first exodus from Egypt under Moses. Since God had **dried up the sea** so the children of Israel could cross over to the promised land, he could similarly redeem his people again.

51:19-23 Though they had endured **devastation and destruction**, God's judgment had ended (51:19-22). He would turn the tables and bring his fury upon their **tormentors** (51:23).

52:1 The day when **the unclean** will not be allowed in **Jerusalem** can only be when the Servant-Messiah, Jesus Christ, reigns in his millennial kingdom.

[a] 52:3 Is 45:13; 1Pt 1:18
[b] 52:4 Gn 46:6
[c] 52:5 Ezk 36:20; Rm 2:24
[d] 52:6 Is 49:23
[e] 52:7 Nah 1:15; Rm 10:15
[f] Ps 93:1; Is 24:23
[g] 52:8 Is 62:6
[h] 52:9 Is 44:26; 51:3; 61:4
[i] Is 40:1
[j] 52:10 Ps 98:1-3; Is 51:9; 66:18-19
[k] Is 40:5; Lk 3:6

[l] 52:11 Is 48:20; Jr 50:8; Ezk 20:34,41; Zch 2:6,7; 2Co 6:17
[m] 2Co 6:17; 2Tm 2:19
[n] 52:12 Ex 12:11,33; Dt 16:3
[o] Ex 23:23; Dt 1:30; 31:8; Is 45:2
[p] Jos 6:9,13; Is 58:8
[q] 52:13 Is 42:1; 49:3-7; 50:10; 53:11; Ezk 34:23-24; Zch 3:8; Ac 3:13
[r] Php 2:9-11
[s] 52:15 Nm 19:18-21; Ezk 36:25
[t] Rm 15:21; Eph 3:5
[u] 53:1 Is 30:30; 40:10; 48:14; 51:9; 52:10; Lk 1:51; Ac 13:17
[v] Jn 12:38; Rm 10:16
[w] 53:2 Is 11:1
[x] Is 52:14
[y] 53:3 Ps 22:6; Is 49:7; Lk 18:31-33
[z] Mk 8:31; Jn 1:10-11; Heb 4:15

2 Stand up, shake the dust
    off yourself!
Take your seat, Jerusalem.
Remove the bonds[A] from your neck,
captive Daughter Zion."

3 For this is what the LORD says:
"You were sold for nothing,
and you will be redeemed
    without silver."[a]

4 For this is what the Lord GOD says:
"At first my people went down
    to Egypt to reside there,[b]
then Assyria oppressed them
    without cause.[B]

5 So now what have I here" —
    this is the LORD's declaration —
"that my people are taken away
    for nothing?
Its rulers wail" —
    this is the LORD's declaration —
"and my name is continually
    blasphemed all day long.[c]

6 Therefore my people will know
    my name;[d]
therefore they will know on that day
that I am he who says:
Here I am."

7 How beautiful on the mountains
are the feet of the herald,
who proclaims peace,
who brings news of good things,[e]
who proclaims salvation,
who says to Zion, "Your God reigns!"[f]

8 The voices of your watchmen[g] —
they lift up their voices,
shouting for joy together;
for every eye will see
when the LORD returns to Zion.

9 Be joyful, rejoice together,
you ruins of Jerusalem![h]
For the LORD has comforted
    his people;[i]
he has redeemed Jerusalem.

10 The LORD has displayed
    his holy arm
in the sight of all the nations;[j]
all the ends of the earth will see
the salvation of our God.[k]

11 Leave, leave, go out from there![l]
Do not touch anything unclean;
go out from her, purify yourselves,[m]
you who carry the vessels
    of the LORD.

12 For you will not leave in a hurry,[n]
and you will not have to take flight;
because the LORD is going
    before you,[o]
and the God of Israel is
    your rear guard.[p]

THE SERVANT'S SUFFERING AND EXALTATION

13 See, my servant[C,q] will be successful;[D]
he will be raised and lifted up
    and greatly exalted.[r]

14 Just as many were appalled
    at you[E] —
his appearance
    was so disfigured
that he did not look like a man,
and his form did not resemble
    a human being —

15 so he will sprinkle
    many nations.[F,s]
Kings will shut their mouths
    because of him,
for they will see
    what had not been told them,
and they will understand
    what they had not heard.[t]

53 Who has believed
    what we have heard?[G]
And to whom has the arm
    of the LORD[u] been revealed?[v]

2 He grew up before him
    like a young plant[w]
and like a root out of dry ground.
He didn't have an impressive form
or majesty that we should look
    at him,
no appearance that we should
    desire him.[x]

3 He was despised and rejected
    by men,[y]
a man of suffering who knew
    what sickness was.[z]

[A] 52:2 Alt Hb tradition reads *The bonds are removed*   [B] 52:4 Or *them at last*, or *them for nothing*   [C] 52:13 Tg adds *the Messiah*   [D] 52:13 Or *will act wisely*   [E] 52:14 Some Hb mss, Syr, Tg read *him*   [F] 52:15 LXX reads *so many nations will marvel at him*   [G] 53:1 Or *believed our report*

52:5-6 Because of their gross unfaithfulness, God's people—who were supposed to be a light to their pagan neighbors—caused God's **name** to be **continually blasphemed** (52:5). We must live in such a way as to help people grasp God's righteous character.
52:11-12 The warning to the righteous to separate themselves from the unrighteous

could have been addressed to the captives in Babylon, telling them not to stay behind once Cyrus set them free. Or it may be a yet future warning to the faithful in Israel to separate themselves from the ungodly in the kingdom age.
52:13-15 In this section of Isaiah's Servant Songs, we are on holy ground. The following

verses (52:13–53:12) testify to the coming suffering, death, and resurrection of Jesus Christ. His universal recognition as Lord is still future, but in God's eternal plan it is as good as accomplished.
53:1 The great sin of Israel's leaders and people was their failure to recognize their Messiah when he came. A relative few in Israel **believed**.

He was like someone
  people turned away from;[A]
he was despised, and we didn't
  value him.

4 Yet he himself bore our sicknesses,
  and he carried our pains;[a]
but we in turn
  regarded him stricken,
struck down by God,[b] and afflicted.
5 But he was pierced because of
  our rebellion,[c]
crushed because of our iniquities;[d]
punishment[e] for our peace was
  on him,
and we are healed by his wounds.[f]
6 We all went astray like sheep;[g]
we all have turned to our own way;
and the Lord has punished him
for[B] the iniquity[h] of us all.[i]

7 He was oppressed and afflicted,
  yet he did not open his mouth.
Like a lamb led to the slaughter
and like a sheep silent
  before her shearers,
he did not open his mouth.[j]
8 He was taken away because of
  oppression and judgment;
and who considered his fate?[C]
For he was cut off from the land
  of the living;
he was struck because of
  my people's rebellion.
9 He was assigned a grave
  with the wicked,
but he was with a rich man
  at his death,[k]
because he had done no violence
and had not spoken deceitfully.[l]

10 Yet the Lord was pleased[m]
  to crush him severely.[D,n]
When[E] you make him
  a guilt offering,[o]
he will see his seed, he will prolong
  his days,

and by his hand, the Lord's pleasure
  will be accomplished.[p]
11 After his anguish,
he will see light[F] and be satisfied.
By his knowledge,
my righteous[q] servant[r]
  will justify many,[s]
and he will carry their iniquities.
12 Therefore I will give him[G] the many
  as a portion,
and he will receive[H] the mighty as spoil,
because he willingly submitted
  to death,[t]
and was counted among the rebels;[u]
yet he bore the sin of many[v]
and interceded for the rebels.[w]

FUTURE GLORY FOR ISRAEL

54 "Rejoice, childless one,
  who did not give birth;
burst into song and shout,
you who have not been in labor![x]
For the children of the desolate one
  will be more
than the children
  of the married woman,"[y]
says the Lord.
2 "Enlarge the site of your tent,
and let your tent curtains
  be stretched out;[z]
do not hold back;
lengthen your ropes,
and drive your pegs deep.
3 For you will spread out to the right
  and to the left,[aa]
and your descendants
  will dispossess nations
and inhabit the desolate cities.

4 "Do not be afraid, for you will not
  be put to shame;[ab]
don't be humiliated, for you will not
  be disgraced.
For you will forget the shame
  of your youth,
and you will no longer remember
the disgrace of your widowhood.[ac]

[a] 53:4 Mt 8:17; 1Pt 2:21
[b] Ps 69:26
[c] 53:5 Is 53:8; Rm 4:25; 1Co 15:3; Heb 9:28
[d] Is 1:4
[e] Jr 2:30; Zph 3:2; Heb 5:8
[f] 53:5-6 1Pt 2:24-25
[g] 53:6 Mt 18:12
[h] Is 13:11
[i] 2Co 5:21; Col 2:14
[j] 53:7 Jr 11:19; Mt 26:63; 27:12-14; Lk 23:9; Jn 19:9; Ac 8:32-33; 1Pt 2:23
[k] 53:9 Mt 27:57-60
[l] Heb 4:15; 1Pt 2:22; 1Jn 3:5
[m] 53:10 Is 44:28; 55:11
[n] Dt 29:22; Is 17:11
[o] Lv 5:1-19
[p] 53:10 Is 46:10
[q] 53:11 1Jn 2:1
[r] Is 42:1
[s] Ac 13:39; Rm 5:18-19
[t] 53:12 Mt 26:42; Jn 10:14-18; Php 2:6-8
[u] Lk 22:37
[v] Heb 9:28
[w] Lk 23:34; Rm 8:34; Heb 7:25
[x] 54:1 Gl 4:27
[y] 1Sm 2:5; Is 62:4
[z] 54:2 Is 49:19-20
[aa] 54:3 Gn 28:14; Is 43:5-6; 60:3
[ab] 54:4 Is 45:17
[ac] Is 4:1; 25:8; 51:7

[A] 53:3 Lit *And like a hiding of faces from him*   [B] 53:6 Or *has placed on him*; lit *with*   [C] 53:8 Or *and as for his generation, who considered him?*   [D] 53:10 Or *him; he made him sick.*   [E] 53:10 Or *If*   [F] 53:11 DSS, LXX; MT omits *light*   [G] 53:12 Or *him with*   [H] 53:12 Or *receive with*

53:5-6 These verses couldn't more clearly depict what Jesus Christ endured. The use of language is precise regarding the kind of death he would die (**he was pierced**) and the reason for it (**because of our iniquities**) (53:5). He was **punished . . . for the iniquity of us all.** Hundreds of years before it would happen, the prophet testified to the substitutionary atonement of Christ on the cross.
53:7 The Gospel writers testify to Jesus's silence before those who falsely accused

him (see Matt 27:13-14; Mark 14:60-61; 15:4-5; Luke 23:8-9).
53:9 Matthew tells us that "a rich man from Arimathea, named Joseph" asked Pilate for Jesus's body and buried him in his own tomb (Matt 27:57-60). The fulfillment of prophecies like this one is testimony to the divine inspiration and truthfulness of the Bible.
53:10 The Father and Son had been in loving communion from eternity past, yet **the**

Lord was pleased to crush him severely. Why? Because the Son's death as **a guilt offering**—a reference to the Old Testament sacrifices for sin (see Lev 5:14—6:7)—was the only way to bring about our salvation.
53:11 **After his anguish, he will see light** refers to the fact that God the Father raised God the Son from the dead. He is now the resurrected Lord.

a 54:5 Jr 3:14; Hs 2:19
b Is 1:4
c Is 41:14; 43:14
d 54:6 Is 49:14-21; 50:1-2;
62:4
e Mal 2:14
f 54:7 Is 26:20
g 54:8 Dt 31:17-18; Is 8:17
h Ps 100:5; Jr 31:3; 33:11
i 54:9 Gn 9:11
j Ezk 39:29
k 54:10 Nm 25:12; Ezk
34:25; Mal 2:5
l 54:11 Rv 21:19
m 54:13 Jn 6:45

n 54:17 Is 41:8-9; Lk 1:54
o Is 45:24; 46:13
p 55:1 Ps 42:1-2; 63:1;
143:6; Is 41:17; 44:3; Jn
4:14; 7:37; Rv 21:6
q 55:3 Gn 9:16; 17:7; 2Sm
23:5; Is 24:5; 59:21; 61:8
r Ac 13:34

5 Indeed, your husband is
    your Maker[a] —
his name is the LORD of Armies —
and the Holy One of Israel[b] is
    your Redeemer;[c]
he is called the God of the whole earth.
6 For the LORD has called you,
like a wife deserted and wounded
    in spirit,[d]
a wife of one's youth[e]
    when she is rejected,"
says your God.
7 "I deserted you for a brief moment,[f]
but I will take you back
    with abundant compassion.
8 In a surge of anger
I hid my face[g] from you for a moment,
but I will have compassion on you
with everlasting love,"[h]
says the LORD your Redeemer.
9 "For this is like the days[A] of Noah
    to me:
when I swore that the water of Noah
would never flood the earth again,[i]
so I have sworn that I will not
    be angry with you
or rebuke you.[j]
10 Though the mountains move
and the hills shake,
my love will not be removed from you
and my covenant of peace[k] will not
    be shaken,"
says your compassionate LORD.

11 "Poor Jerusalem, storm-tossed,
    and not comforted,
I will set your stones
    in black mortar,[B]
and lay your foundations in lapis
    lazuli.[l]
12 I will make your fortifications[c]
    out of rubies,
your gates out of sparkling stones,
and all your walls out of
    precious stones.
13 Then all your children will be taught
    by the LORD,[m]
their prosperity will be great,

14 and you will be established
on a foundation of righteousness.
You will be far from oppression,
you will certainly not be afraid;
you will be far from terror,
it will certainly not come near you.
15 If anyone attacks you,
it is not from me;
whoever attacks you
will fall before you.
16 Look, I have created
    the craftsman
who blows on the charcoal fire
and produces a weapon suitable
    for its task;
and I have created the destroyer
    to cause havoc.
17 No weapon formed against you
    will succeed,
and you will refute any accusation[D]
raised against you in court.
This is the heritage
    of the LORD's servants,[n]
and their vindication is
    from me."[o]
This is the LORD's declaration.

COME TO THE LORD

55 "Come, everyone who is thirsty,[p]
come to the water;
and you without silver,
come, buy, and eat!
Come, buy wine and milk
without silver and without cost!
2 Why do you spend silver on what
    is not food,
and your wages on what
    does not satisfy?
Listen carefully to me, and eat
    what is good,
and you will enjoy the choicest
    of foods.[E]
3 Pay attention and come to me;
listen, so that you will live.
I will make a permanent covenant
    with you[q]
on the basis of the faithful
    kindnesses of David.[F,r]

[A] 54:9 DSS, Cairo Geniza; MT, LXX read *waters*   [B] 54:11 Lit *in antimony*   [C] 54:12 Lit *suns*; perhaps *shields*; Ps 84:11   [D] 54:17 Lit *refute every tongue*
[E] 55:2 Lit *enjoy fatness*   [F] 55:3 Or *with you, the faithful acts of kindness shown to David*

54:6-7 Israel was **like a wife deserted and wounded in spirit**, but not because her husband was cruel to her (54:6). Israel's husband was the Lord, who had to reject his wife for **a brief moment** because of her sin (54:7). His promise, though, had always been to take her back to cleanse and restore her.
54:8-10 The captives from Judah in Babylon must have wondered more than once if they had gone too far in their sin and alienated God forever, but God assured them of his **everlasting love** (54:8). To illustrate this, God compared their situation to **the days of Noah**, when God judged the earth in his righteous anger (54:9). Yet once the judgment was over, God's anger subsided and he gave Noah the promise that he would never again destroy the whole earth with a flood (see Gen 7:5–9:17). In the same way, God promised that he would never again forsake Israel: **my love**

will not be removed from you (54:10). This refers ultimately to the millennial kingdom.
54:12 The **precious stones** God will use to adorn his holy city are described in detail in Revelation 21:9-27.
55:1 God offers healing and salvation from sin, along with millennial and eternal blessings, **without silver and without cost**. This is a powerful Old Testament affirmation of God's free gift of grace.

a 55:4 Ps 18:43
b Ezk 34:24; 37:24-25; Dn 9:25; Mc 5:2
c 55:5 Is 45:14,22-24; 49:6

d 55:5 Zch 8:22
e Is 1:4
f Is 60:9
g 55:6 Ps 32:6; Am 5:4
h 55:7 Ps 33:10; Is 32:7; 59:7; 65:2
i Is 1:18; 43:25; 44:22
j 55:9 Ps 103:11
k 55:10 2Co 9:10
l 55:11 Is 45:23; 46:10; 53:10
m 55:12 Ps 98:8; Is 44:23

❧ Questions & Answers ❧

Q There have been various attacks on the concepts of the inspiration and inerrancy of the Bible. Why do you consider these to be critical theological doctrines? How important is commitment to these doctrines for your ministry as a pastor?

A It is critical that the Bible be trusted. When you challenge the inerrancy, infallibility, and trustworthiness of the Bible, you are questioning God's voice, which means you are questioning God. The real issue is this: Can a perfect God have an imperfect Word? No! Not if he claims perfection about that Word. The Bible makes clear, "No prophecy ever came by the will of man; instead, men spoke from God as they were carried along by the Holy Spirit" (2 Pet 1:21).

No Scripture resulted from someone merely making something up. The authors of biblical books were moved by God's Spirit to write through their own personalities. The result is verbal, plenary inspiration—that is, the Holy Spirit inspired the entire Bible, down to the very words chosen. God protected the living Word (Jesus) from sin by the virgin birth because he was conceived "from the Holy Spirit" (Matt 1:20). He also protected the written Word (Scripture) from error by the same Holy Spirit.

God can be trusted; therefore, what he's written can be trusted. If what God has written cannot be trusted, then he cannot be trusted either. And if he cannot be trusted, why should we entrust our lives to his kingdom agenda?

FOR THE NEXT Q&A, SEE PAGE 950.

4 Since I have made him a witness
    to the peoples,[a]
  a leader and commander
    for the peoples,[b]
5 so you will summon a nation
    you do not know,[c]
and nations who do not know you
    will run to you.[d]
  For the LORD your God,
    even the Holy One of Israel,[e]
    has glorified you."[f]

6 Seek the LORD while he may be found;
    call to him while he is near.[g]
7 Let the wicked one abandon his way
    and the sinful one his thoughts;[h]
  let him return to the LORD,
    so he may have compassion on him,
  and to our God, for he will
    freely forgive.[i]

➢ HOPE WORDS ➢

Don't focus on the size of your problem. Focus on the size of your God.

8 "For my thoughts are not
    your thoughts,
  and your ways are not my ways."
    This is the LORD's declaration.
9 "For as heaven is higher than earth,[j]
    so my ways are higher than your ways,
  and my thoughts than your thoughts.
10 For just as rain and snow fall
    from heaven
  and do not return there
  without saturating the earth
  and making it germinate and sprout,
  and providing seed to sow
    and food to eat,[k]
11 so my word that comes
    from my mouth
  will not return to me empty,
  but it will accomplish what I please
  and will prosper in what I send it
    to do."[l]

12 You will indeed go out with joy
    and be peacefully guided;
  the mountains and the hills
    will break into singing before you,
  and all the trees of the field will clap
    their hands.[m]
13 Instead of the thornbush, a cypress
    will come up,

55:4-5 These statements are about Jesus the King of Israel, who will rule not only his own people, but also Gentile nations that did **not know** him (55:5). Christ's kingdom reign will extend to every corner of the earth.
55:7-8 Grace does not make sense to us because it does not reflect how people treat one another. But God's perspective is not our perspective. That's why we need the Holy Spirit to enable us to have a heavenly perspective; we need "the mind of Christ" (1 Cor 2:16).
55:10-11 God's Word is always purposeful, and his purposes are always achieved. The Bible can be trusted.
55:13 The **thornbush** and **brier**, which began to plague the world after Adam and Eve sinned (see Gen 3:17-18), will be replaced by plants of beauty and usefulness on the new earth God has promised.

[a] 55:13 Is 35:1-2; 41:19; 60:13
[b] Is 63:12-14; Jr 33:9
[c] 56:1 Gn 18:19; Ps 106:3; Pr 21:3
[d] Ps 98:2; Is 46:13; 51:5; Rm 1:17; 3:21
[e] 56:2 Is 58:13
[f] 56:3 Is 14:1; 56:6
[g] Dt 23:1
[h] 56:5 Is 55:13; Rv 2:17
[i] 56:7 Is 2:2-3

[j] 56:7 Mal 1:11
[k] Jr 7:11; Mt 21:13; Mk 11:17; Lk 19:46
[l] 56:8 Is 11:12; 60:3-11; 66:18-21; Jn 10:16
[m] 56:11 Jr 10:21; 23:1; 50:6; Ezk 34:2
[n] 56:12 Lk 12:19; 1Co 15:32

and instead of the brier, a myrtle
  will come up;[a]
this will stand as a monument for
  the Lord,[b]
an everlasting sign that will not
  be destroyed.

A HOUSE OF PRAYER FOR ALL

56 This is what the Lord says:
Preserve justice and do
  what is right,[c]
for my salvation is coming soon,
and my righteousness will be revealed.[d]
2 Happy is the person who does this,
  the son of man who holds it fast,
who keeps the Sabbath
  without desecrating it,
and keeps his hand from doing
  any evil.[e]

3 No foreigner who has joined himself
  to the Lord
should say,
"The Lord will exclude me
  from his people,"[f]
and the eunuch should not say,
"Look, I am a dried-up tree."[g]
4 For the Lord says this:
"For the eunuchs who keep
  my Sabbaths,
and choose what pleases me,
and hold firmly to my covenant,
5 I will give them, in my house
  and within my walls,
a memorial and a name
better than sons and daughters.
I will give each of them
  an everlasting name
that will never be cut off.[h]
6 As for the foreigners who join
  themselves to the Lord
to minister to him, to
  love the name of the Lord,
and to become his servants —
all who keep the Sabbath
  without desecrating it
and who hold firmly to my covenant —
7 I will bring them
  to my holy mountain[i]

and let them rejoice in my house
  of prayer.
Their burnt offerings and sacrifices
will be acceptable on my altar,[j]
for my house will be called a house
  of prayer
for all nations."[k]
8 This is the declaration
  of the Lord God,
who gathers the dispersed
  of Israel:
"I will gather to them still others
besides those already gathered."[l]

UNRIGHTEOUS LEADERS CONDEMNED

9 All you animals of the field and forest,
  come and eat!
10 Israel's[A] watchmen are blind,
  all of them,
they know nothing;
all of them are mute dogs,
  they cannot bark;
they dream, lie down,
  and love to sleep.
11 These dogs have fierce appetites;
  they never have enough.
And they are shepherds
  who have no discernment;
all of them turn to their own way,
every last one for his own profit.[m]
12 "Come, let me get some wine,
  let's guzzle some beer;
and tomorrow will be like today,
  only far better!"[n]

57 The righteous person perishes,
  and no one takes it to heart;
the faithful are taken away,
with no one realizing
that the righteous person
  is taken away
because of[B] evil.
2 He will enter into peace —
they will rest on their beds[c] —
everyone who lives uprightly.

PAGAN RELIGION DENOUNCED

3 But come here,
  you witch's sons,

[A] 56:10 Or *His*, or *Its*   [B] 57:1 Or *taken away from the presence of*   [C] 57:2 Either *their deathbeds* or *their graves*

56:6-8 Gentiles who believed in the God of Israel and bound themselves to him had a place within his covenant community in the Old Testament dispensation. Here they were assured that they would also share in the kingdom with Israel, including sharing in Israel's regathering to enjoy God's salvation and blessings under Christ's righteous rule. God also promises special blessing and kingdom position to those who maintain their sexual purity (1 Cor 6:9-10).
56:9-12 The joys of God's salvation and his millennial kingdom form a stark contrast to the close of this section (56:9–57:21), in which God turned his attention to the sinfulness of his people in Isaiah's day. Things were so bad that God invited the **animals** to devour them (56:9). The Babylonian destroyers of Judah are probably in view here. The nation's spiritual leaders, who should have been alert **watchmen**, were like **mute dogs** who cared only for themselves and their own appetites (56:10-12).
57:3 This was a stinging rebuke of the people's unfaithfulness to the Lord by worshiping idols. The words highlight the depravity of their idolatrous worship.

offspring of an adulterer
and a prostitute!^A
4 Who are you mocking?
Who are you opening your mouth
and sticking out your tongue at?
Isn't it you, you rebellious children,^a
you offspring of liars,
5 who burn with lust among the oaks,
under every green tree,^b
who slaughter children in the wadis
below the clefts of the rocks?^c
6 Your portion is
among the smooth stones
of the wadi;
indeed, they are your lot.
You have even poured out
a drink offering to them;
you have offered a grain offering;
should I be satisfied with these?
7 You have placed your bed
on a high and lofty mountain;^d
you also went up there
to offer sacrifice.
8 You have set up your memorial
behind the door and doorpost.
For away from me, you stripped,
went up, and made your bed wide,^e
and you have made a bargain^B
for yourself with them.
You have loved their bed;
you have gazed on their genitals.^{C,D}
9 You went to the king with oil
and multiplied your perfumes;
you sent your envoys far away^f
and sent them down even to Sheol.
10 You became weary
on your many journeys,
but you did not say, "It's hopeless!"^g
You found a renewal
of your strength;^E
therefore you did not grow weak.
11 Who was it you dreaded and feared,
so that you lied and didn't
remember me
or take it to heart?
I have kept silent for a long time,
haven't I?^{F,h}
So you do not fear me.
12 I will announce your righteousness,
and your works — they will not
profit you.

13 When you cry out,
let your collection of idols
rescue you!
The wind will carry all of them off,
a breath will take them away.
But whoever takes refuge in me
will inherit the land^i
and possess my holy mountain.^j

HEALING AND PEACE

14 He said,
"Build it up, build it up,
prepare the way,
remove every obstacle
from my people's way."^k
15 For the High and Exalted One,
who lives forever, whose name
is holy,^l says this:
"I live in a high and holy place,
and with the oppressed and lowly
of spirit,^m
to revive the spirit of the lowly
and revive the heart
of the oppressed.^n
16 For I will not accuse you forever,
and I will not always be angry;^o
for then the spirit would grow weak
before me,
even the breath, which I have made.
17 Because of his sinful greed
I was angry,^p
so I struck him; I was angry
and hid;
but he went on turning back
to the desires of his heart.
18 I have seen his ways,
but I will heal him;
I will lead him and restore comfort
to him and his mourners,^q
19 creating words of praise."^{G,r}
The Lord says,
"Peace, peace to the one who is far
or near,^s
and I will heal him.
20 But the wicked are
like the storm-tossed sea,^t
for it cannot be still,
and its water churns up mire
and muck.
21 There is no peace for the wicked,"
says my God.^u

^a 57:4 Is 30:1,9
^b 57:5 2Kg 16:4; Jr 2:20; 3:13
^c 2Kg 23:10; Ps 106:37-38; Jr 7:31; Ezk 16:20-21
^d 57:7 Jr 3:6; Ezk 16:16
^e 57:8 Ezk 23:17-18
^f 57:9 Ezk 16:26-29
^g 57:10 Jr 2:25; 18:12
^h 57:11 Ps 50:21; Is 42:14

^i 57:13 Ps 37:3,9; Is 25:4
^j Is 65:9
^k 57:14 Is 62:10; Jr 18:15
^l 57:15 Lk 1:49
^m Ps 34:18; 51:17; Is 66:2
^n Ps 147:3; Is 61:1-3
^o 57:16 Gn 6:3; Ps 103:9; Jr 3:12
^p 57:17 Is 2:7; 56:11; Jr 6:13
^q 57:18 Is 61:1-3
^r 57:19 Is 6:7; 51:16; 59:21; Heb 13:15
^s Ac 2:39; Eph 2:17
^t 57:20 Ps 107:29
^u 57:21 Is 48:22; 59:8

---

^A 57:3 Lit and she acted as a prostitute   ^B 57:8 Lit you cut   ^C 57:8 Lit hand   ^D 57:8 In Hb, the word "hand" is probably a euphemism for genitals.
^E 57:10 Lit found life of your hand   ^F 57:11 LXX reads And I, when I see you, I pass by   ^G 57:19 Lit creating fruit of the lips

---

57:4 It wasn't enough for the people in Isaiah's day to engage in pagan worship; they also mocked the righteous who remained faithful to God.
57:5 The idolaters fed their sexual depravity with rituals that included every form of moral degeneration. This was combined with the unimaginable horror of sacrificing their **children**, possibly to Molech, the god of the Ammonites who demanded child sacrifice.
57:15 The righteous were encouraged to remember that even though the God of Israel is the **High and Exalted One**, he delights to dwell with **the lowly**. What a wonderful insight into his character.

a 58:2 Ps 119:151; Is 29:13; 57:3; Jms 4:8
b 58:3 Mal 3:14; Lk 18:12
c Is 22:12-13; Zch 7:5-6
d 58:5 Est 4:3; Dn 9:3
e 58:6 Jb 36:8; Ps 107:10; Ec 7:26
f Neh 5:10-12; Is 58:9; Jr 34:8
g 58:7 Jb 31:19-20; Is 58:10; Ezk 18:7,16
h Mt 25:35-36; Lk 3:11
i Dt 22:1-4; Lk 10:31-32

j 58:8 Is 30:26; 33:24; Jr 30:17; 33:6
k Ps 85:13; Is 62:1
l Ex 14:19; Is 52:12
m 58:9 Ps 50:15; Is 55:6; 65:24
n Pr 6:13

o 58:10 Jb 11:17; Ps 37:6; Is 42:16; 58:8
p 58:11 Sg 4:15; Is 27:3; Jr 31:12
q Jn 4:14; 7:38
r 58:12 Ezr 6:14; Neh 4:6; Is 49:8; 61:4; Ezk 36:10
s 1Kg 6:37; Ezr 3:10-12
t 58:13 Ex 31:16-17; 35:2-3; Is 56:2-6; Jr 17:21-27
u Is 55:8

v 58:14 Jb 22:26; Ps 37:4
w Dt 32:13; 33:29; Is 33:16; Hab 3:19

Video Devotional

"BEAUTY IN THE DETOUR"

When life seems pointless or you feel you have taken a wrong turn, keep the faith. Hang in there. God is taking you forward.

TRUE FASTING

58 "Cry out loudly,[A] don't hold back!
Raise your voice like a trumpet.
Tell my people their transgression
and the house of Jacob their sins.

2 They seek me day after day
and delight to know my ways,
like a nation that does what is right
and does not abandon the justice
of their God.
They ask me
for righteous judgments;
they delight in the nearness
of God."[a]

3 "Why have we fasted,
but you have not seen?[b]
We have denied ourselves,
but you haven't noticed!"[B]
"Look, you do as you please
on the day of your fast,
and oppress all your workers.[c]

4 You fast with contention and strife
to strike viciously with your fist.
You cannot fast as you do today,
hoping to make your voice heard
on high.

5 Will the fast I choose be like this:
A day for a person to deny himself,
to bow his head like a reed,
and to spread out sackcloth
and ashes?[d]
Will you call this a fast
and a day acceptable to the LORD?

6 Isn't this the fast I choose:
To break the chains of wickedness,[e]
to untie the ropes of the yoke,
to set the oppressed free,
and to tear off every yoke?[f]

7 Is it not to share your bread
with the hungry,[g]
to bring the poor and homeless
into your house,
to clothe the naked
when you see him,[h]
and not to ignore your own flesh
and blood?[C,i]

8 Then your light will appear
like the dawn,

and your recovery
will come quickly.[j]
Your righteousness will go
before you,[k]
and the LORD's glory will be
your rear guard.[l]

9 At that time, when you call, the LORD
will answer;[m]
when you cry out, he will say,
'Here I am.'
If you get rid of the yoke among you,
the finger-pointing
and malicious speaking,[n]

10 and if you offer yourself[D]
to the hungry,
and satisfy the afflicted one,
then your light will shine
in the darkness,[o]
and your night will be like noonday.

11 The LORD will always lead you,
satisfy you in a parched land,
and strengthen your bones.
You will be like a watered garden[p]
and like a spring whose water
never runs dry.[q]

12 Some of you will rebuild
the ancient ruins;[r]
you will restore the foundations laid
long ago;[s]
you will be called the repairer
of broken walls,
the restorer of streets
where people live.

13 "If you keep from desecrating[E]
the Sabbath,[t]
from doing whatever you want
on my holy day;
if you call the Sabbath a delight,
and the holy day
of the LORD honorable;
if you honor it, not going
your own ways,[u]
seeking your own pleasure,
or talking business;[F,G]

14 then you will delight in the LORD,[v]
and I will make you ride
over the heights of the land,[w]

[A] 58:1 Lit *with throat* [B] 58:3 These are Israel's words to God. [C] 58:7 Lit *not hide yourself from your flesh* [D] 58:10 Some Hb mss, LXX, Syr read *offer your bread* [E] 58:13 Lit *keep your foot from* [F] 58:13 Or *idly* [G] 58:13 Lit *or speak a word*

58:3-4 Israel wondered why God wasn't answering their prayers, but even their fasting was a classic example of empty ritual: **you do as you please on the day of your fast** (58:3).

Importantly, fasting is a spiritual discipline that continues to be proper for believers when we want to make our **voice heard on high** (58:4). When we fast with the proper motivation, our voices *are* heard in

heaven—that is, we come into God's presence in a powerful way. So imagine the voice the church can have in heaven today, if we come together across class, ethnic, and denominational boundaries to collectively fast and call on God to intervene.

58:6-7 James offers similar counsel: "Pure and undefiled religion before God the Father is this: to look after orphans and widows in

their distress and to keep oneself unstained from the world" (Jas 1:27). Kingdom people help others.

59:2 In other words, they—not God—were the problem.

59:9-12 Notice the use of *us* and *we* and *our* here. Like other Old Testament prophets who denounced Israel's sins, Isaiah identified with his people in confessing Israel's sins.

and let you enjoy the heritage
of your father Jacob."
For the mouth of the LORD
has spoken.[a]

SIN AND REDEMPTION

59 Indeed, the LORD's arm is not
too weak to save,[b]
and his ear is not too deaf to hear.
2 But your iniquities[c]
are separating you
from your God,
and your sins have hidden his face
from you[d]
so that he does not listen.[e]
3 For your hands are defiled
with blood
and your fingers, with iniquity;
your lips have spoken lies,
and your tongues mutter injustice.
4 No one makes claims justly;
no one pleads honestly.
They trust in empty
and worthless words;
they conceive trouble and give birth
to iniquity.[f]
5 They hatch viper's eggs
and weave spider's webs.
Whoever eats their eggs will die;
crack one open, and a viper
is hatched.
6 Their webs cannot become clothing,
and they cannot cover themselves
with their works.
Their works are sinful works,
and violent acts are in their hands.
7 Their feet run after evil,[g]
and they rush to shed
innocent blood.[h]
Their thoughts are sinful thoughts;[i]
ruin and wretchedness are
in their paths.
8 They have not known the path
of peace,[j]
and there is no justice in their ways.
They have made their roads crooked;
no one who walks on them
will know peace.[k]

9 Therefore justice is far from us,
and righteousness does not
reach us.
We hope for light,
but there is darkness;

for brightness, but we live
in the night.
10 We grope along a wall like the blind;
we grope like those without eyes.[l]
We stumble at noon as though
it were twilight;
we are like the dead among those
who are healthy.
11 We all growl like bears
and moan like doves.[m]
We hope for justice,
but there is none;
for salvation, but it is far from us.
12 For our transgressions
have multiplied before you,[n]
and our sins testify against us.[o]
For our transgressions are with us,
and we know our iniquities:[p]
13 transgression and deception
against the LORD,
turning away from following
our God,
speaking oppression and revolt,
conceiving and uttering lying words
from the heart.
14 Justice is turned back,
and righteousness stands far off.
For truth has stumbled
in the public square,
and honesty cannot enter.
15 Truth is missing,
and whoever turns from evil
is plundered.

The LORD saw that there was
no justice,
and he was offended.
16 He saw that there was no man —
he was amazed that there was
no one interceding;[q]
so his own arm brought salvation,
and his own righteousness
supported him.
17 He put on righteousness as body
armor,
and a helmet of salvation
on his head;[r]
he put on garments of vengeance
for clothing,
and he wrapped himself in zeal
as in a cloak.[s]
18 So he will repay according to
their deeds:[t]
fury to his enemies,

[a] 58:14 Is 1:20; 40:5
[b] 59:1 Nm 11:23; Is 50:2; Jr 32:17
[c] 59:2 Is 13:11
[d] Dt 31:17-18; 32:20; Is 50:6; Ezk 39:29; Mc 3:4
[e] Dt 3:26; 23:5; Jb 35:13; Is 1:15
[f] 59:4 Jb 15:35; Ps 7:14; Is 33:11
[g] 59:7-8 Rm 3:15-17
[h] 59:7 Pr 1:16; 6:17
[i] Mk 7:21-22
[j] 59:8 Lk 1:79
[k] Is 57:20-21

[l] 59:10 Dt 28:29; Jb 5:14
[m] 59:11 Is 38:14; Ezk 7:16
[n] 59:12 Ezr 9:6
[o] Is 3:9; Jr 14:7; Hs 5:5
[p] Is 13:11
[q] 59:16 Is 41:28; 63:5; Ezk 22:30
[r] 59:17 Eph 6:14,17; 1Th 5:8
[s] Is 9:7; 37:32; Zch 1:14
[t] 59:18 Jr 25:14; Rv 22:12

59:16 Where were the prophets, priests, and kings? Though there were exceptions (such as Isaiah, of course), most leaders had become corrupt. Instead of leading the nation in righteousness, they had led them in wickedness. What, then, would this faithful, covenant-keeping God do? He himself would intercede. **59:18-20** This is a picture of Christ's second coming, when he will crush all of his **enemies** and reign in righteousness (59:18). To the enemies of God, Christ comes as a terrifying conqueror (59:19). But to those **who turn from transgression**, Christ will come as **Redeemer** (59:20).

a 59:19 Ps 113:3
b Is 30:28; 66:12
c 59:20 Is 41:14; 43:14
d 59:20-21 Ezk 18:30-31;
Rm 11:26-27
e 59:21 Jr 31:31-34
f Is 51:16
g 60:1 Is 9:2; 26:19; 30:26;
51:17; 52:2; Eph 5:14
h Is 40:5; 58:8; Mal 4:2
i 60:3 Is 42:6; 49:6; Rv
21:24
j 60:4 Is 49:18-22

k 60:5 Ps 34:5
l Is 61:6
m 60:6 Gn 25:3; Ps 72:10
n Mt 2:11
o 60:7 Gn 25:13
p Is 19:19; 56:7
q Is 60:13; Hg 2:7,9
r 60:8 Hs 11:11
s 60:9 Is 51:5
t Ps 48:7; Is 2:16
u Is 14:2; 43:6; 49:22
v Is 1:4; 60:14
w Is 55:5
x 60:10 Is 14:1-2; 61:5;
Zch 6:15
y Is 49:7,23; Rv 21:24
z Hab 3:2
aa 60:11 Rv 21:25-26

retribution to his foes,
and he will repay the coasts and
islands.
19 They will fear the name of the LORD
in the west
and his glory in the east;[A,a]
for he will come
like a rushing stream[b]
driven by the wind of the LORD.
20 "The Redeemer[c] will come to Zion,
and to those in Jacob who turn
from transgression."[d]
This is the LORD's declaration.

21 "As for me, this is my covenant with
them,"[e] says the LORD: "My Spirit who is on
you, and my words that I have put in your
mouth,[f] will not depart from your mouth,
or from the mouths of your children, or
from the mouths of your children's children, from now on and forever," says the
LORD.

⤳ HOPE WORDS ⤶

*You were made to reflect
God's glory. Shine.*

THE LORD'S GLORY IN ZION

60 Arise, shine, for your light
has come,[g]
and the glory of the LORD shines
over you.[B,h]
2 For look, darkness will
cover the earth,
and total darkness the peoples;
but the LORD will shine over you,
and his glory will appear over you.
3 Nations will come to your light,
and kings
to your shining brightness.[i]
4 Raise your eyes and look around:
they all gather and come to you;
your sons will come from far away,
and your daughters on the hips of
nannies.[j]

5 Then you will see and be radiant,[k]
and your heart will tremble
and rejoice,[c]
because the riches of the sea
will become yours
and the wealth of the nations
will come to you.[l]
6 Caravans of camels will cover
your land[D] —
young camels of Midian
and Ephah —
all of them will come from Sheba.[m]
They will carry gold
and frankincense[n]
and proclaim the praises
of the LORD.
7 All the flocks of Kedar
will be gathered to you;
the rams of Nebaioth will serve you[o]
and go up on my altar
as an acceptable sacrifice.[p]
I will glorify my beautiful house.[q]

8 Who are these who fly
like a cloud,
like doves to their shelters?[r]
9 Yes, the coasts and islands will wait
for me[s]
with the ships of Tarshish
in the lead,[t]
to bring your children
from far away,[u]
their silver and gold with them,
for the honor of the LORD your God,
the Holy One of Israel,[v]
who has glorified you.[w]
10 Foreigners will rebuild your walls,[x]
and their kings will serve you.[y]
Although I struck you in my wrath,
yet I will show mercy to you
with my favor.[z]
11 Your city gates will always
be open;
they will never be shut day or night
so that the wealth of the nations
may be brought into you,[aa]
with their kings being led
in procession.

A 59:19 Lit *sunrise*   B 60:1 = Jerusalem   C 60:5 Lit *expand*   D 60:6 Lit *cover you*

60:1-3 Through God's redeeming power
and his eternal covenant of blessing on
Israel, the nation will experience unending
joy and blessing as the world capital and
centerpiece of Christ's reign. Israel will be
a light to the nations because **the glory of
the LORD** will shine both in her and from
her to the corners of the earth (60:1). God's
light will overcome the **total darkness** that
has covered the world since the fall and

kept countless billions in spiritual darkness (60:2). But in the millennium, entire
nations and their **kings** will be drawn to
Israel to learn the truth about God and his
salvation (60:3). This is necessary because
many people will be born during this one-
thousand-year paradise on earth, and they
will need to learn of Christ.
60:4 Though many Jews have returned to
Israel from many countries in recent times,

most do not believe in Jesus as their Messiah.
Many Bible teachers, then, do not identify
this modern return with the prophecies of
Israel's regathering. More likely, passages
such as this one refer to the reign of Christ
on earth when the Jewish people will embrace
him as Messiah.
60:11 Jerusalem's **gates will always be open** so
that the nations' **kings** may come at all times
to bring gifts and pay homage to Christ.

12 For the nation and the kingdom
that will not serve you will perish;
those nations will be annihilated.[a]
13 The glory of Lebanon will come
to you[b] —
its pine, elm,
and cypress together[c] —
to beautify the place
of my sanctuary,
and I will glorify
my dwelling place.[A]
14 The sons of your oppressors
will come and bow down to you;[d]
all who reviled you
will fall facedown at your feet.[e]
They will call you the City
of the LORD,
Zion of the Holy One of Israel.[f]
15 Instead of your being deserted
and hated,
with no one passing through,[g]
I will make you an object
of eternal pride,[h]
a joy from age to age.
16 You will nurse on the milk
of nations,
and nurse at the breast of kings;[i]
you will know that I, the LORD,
am your Savior[j]
and Redeemer,[k] the Mighty One
of Jacob.[l]

17 I will bring gold instead of bronze;
I will bring silver instead of iron,
bronze instead of wood,
and iron instead of stones.
I will appoint peace
as your government
and righteousness
as your overseers.
18 Violence will never again
be heard of in your land;[m]
devastation and destruction
will be gone from your borders.
You will call your walls Salvation[n]
and your city gates Praise.

19 The sun will no longer be your light
by day,
and the brightness of the moon
will not shine on you.
The LORD will be
your everlasting light,[o]
and your God will be your splendor.
20 Your sun will no longer set,
and your moon will not fade;
for the LORD will be
your everlasting light,
and the days of your sorrow
will be over.[p]
21 All your people will be righteous;[q]
they will possess the land forever;[r]
they are the branch I planted,
the work of my[B] hands,
so that I may be glorified.[s]
22 The least will become a thousand,
the smallest a mighty nation.
I am the LORD;
I will accomplish it quickly
in its time.

MESSIAH'S JUBILEE

61 The Spirit of the Lord GOD is
on me,[t]
because the LORD has anointed me
to bring good news to the poor.[u]
He has sent me to heal[c]
the brokenhearted,
to proclaim liberty to the captives
and freedom to the prisoners;[v]
2 to proclaim the year
of the LORD's favor,[w]
and the day of our God's vengeance;[x]
to comfort[y] all who mourn,
3 to provide for those who mourn
in Zion;
to give them a crown of beauty
instead of ashes,
festive oil instead of mourning,[z]
and splendid clothes
instead of despair.[D]
And they will be called
righteous trees,

---

a 60:12 Zch 14:17-19
b 60:13 Is 35:2
c Is 41:19
d 60:14 Is 14:1-2; Zch 8:23
e Is 49:23; Rv 3:9
f Is 1:26
g 60:15 Is 34:10
h Is 65:18
i 60:16 Is 49:23; 66:11-12
j Is 43:3; 49:26
k Is 41:14; 43:14
l Gn 49:24; Ps 132:2,5; Is 49:26
m 60:18 Is 11:9
n Is 26:1

o 60:19 Zch 14:6-7; Rv 21:23; 22:5
p 60:20 Is 35:10; 65:19; Rv 21:4
q 60:21 Is 52:1
r Ps 37:9; Ezk 37:25
s Is 61:3
t 61:1-2 Is 11:2; 42:1; 48:16; Lk 4:18-19
u 61:1 Lk 7:22
v Is 42:7; 49:9
w 61:2 Is 49:8
x Is 2:12; 13:6; 34:2,8
y Is 40:1
z 61:3 Ps 45:7; Heb 1:9

A 60:13 Lit *glorify the place of my feet*   B 60:21 LXX, DSS read *his*   C 61:1 Lit *bind up*   D 61:3 Lit *a dim spirit*

60:12 We know from Revelation 20:7-9 that Satan will deceive and lead Gentile nations in a brief rebellion at the end of the millennial age, but this uprising will be immediately crushed and the rebels **annihilated**.
61:1-2 When Jesus read Isaiah 61:1-2 in the synagogue in Nazareth and proclaimed, "Today as you listen, this Scripture has been fulfilled," the people knew he was claiming to be the Messiah (see Luke 4:16-21). And they weren't happy about it. After all, Jesus was one of them. Nazareth was his hometown, and he was thought to be the son of the local carpenter (Luke 4:21-22). They wanted a Messiah with might and power. And as Isaiah said about the Servant-Messiah, "He didn't have an impressive form or majesty . . . no appearance that we should desire him" (Isa 53:2). So Jesus wasn't the Messiah, the Anointed One, they were expecting. In fact, they were so enraged with him that they tried to toss him off a cliff (see Luke 4:28-30)!

Nevertheless, Jesus was right. His earthly ministry did fulfill this messianic prophecy— at least part of it. He came **to bring good news**, to **heal**, and to proclaim **freedom** from Satan (61:1). He came **to proclaim the year of the LORD's favor** (61:2). But that's where Jesus stopped when he read from Isaiah (see Luke 4:18-19). At his first advent, he brought salvation. At his second advent, he will bring **the day of our God's vengeance** (61:2). God's judgment awaits the second coming of Christ, when he will crush his enemies and restore Israel to a place of glory.

[a] 61:3 Is 60:21; Jr 17:7-8
[b] 61:4 Is 49:8; 58:12; Ezk 36:33; Am 9:14
[c] 61:5 Is 14:2; 60:10
[d] 61:6 Ex 19:6; Is 66:21; 1Pt 2:5,9
[e] 61:7 Is 54:4
[f] Is 40:2; Zch 9:12
[g] 61:8 Ps 11:7; Is 59:15
[h] Is 24:5; 55:3
[i] 61:10 Is 49:18; 52:1; 59:17
[j] 61:10 Rv 21:2
[k] 61:11 Is 45:23-24; 60:18,21
[l] 62:1 Ps 83:1; Is 64:12; 65:6
[m] Is 1:26; 58:8; 61:11
[n] 62:2 Is 60:3
[o] Is 60:14; Rv 2:17; 3:12
[p] 62:3 Is 28:5; Zch 9:16; 1Th 2:19
[q] 62:4 Is 54:6-7; 60:15,18
[r] Hs 2:19-20
[s] 62:5 Is 65:19
[t] 62:6 Is 52:8; Jr 6:17; Ezk 3:17; 33:7

planted by the LORD
to glorify him.[a]

4 They will rebuild the ancient ruins;[b]
they will restore
the former devastations;
they will renew the ruined cities,
the devastations
of many generations.

5 Strangers will stand and feed
your flocks,
and foreigners will be
your plowmen and vinedressers.[c]

6 But you will be called
the LORD's priests;[d]
they will speak of you as ministers
of our God;
you will eat the wealth
of the nations,
and you will boast in their riches.

7 In place of your shame, you will
have a double portion;[e]
in place of disgrace, they will rejoice
over their share.
So they will possess double
in their land,[f]
and eternal joy will be theirs.

8 For I the LORD love justice;[g]
I hate robbery and injustice;[A]
I will faithfully reward my people
and make a permanent covenant[h]
with them.

9 Their descendants will be known
among the nations,
and their posterity among the peoples.
All who see them will recognize
that they are a people the LORD
has blessed.

10 I rejoice greatly in the LORD,
I exult in my God;
for he has clothed me
with the garments of salvation
and wrapped me in a robe
of righteousness,[i]
as a groom wears a turban

and as a bride adorns herself
with her jewels.[j]

11 For as the earth produces its growth,
and as a garden enables
what is sown to spring up,
so the Lord GOD
will cause righteousness
and praise
to spring up before all the nations.[k]

ZION'S RESTORATION

62 I will not keep silent
because of Zion,
and I will not keep still
because of Jerusalem,[l]
until her righteousness shines
like a bright light[m]
and her salvation,
like a flaming torch.

2 Nations will see your righteousness[n]
and all kings, your glory.
You will be given a new name
that the LORD's mouth
will announce.[o]

3 You will be a glorious crown
in the LORD's hand,
and a royal diadem in the palm
of your God's hand.[p]

4 You will no longer be called Deserted,[q]
and your land will not
be called Desolate;
instead, you will be called
My Delight Is in Her,[B]
and your land Married;[C,r]
for the LORD delights in you,
and your land will be married.

5 For as a young man marries
a young woman,
so your sons will marry you;
and as a groom rejoices
over his bride,
so your God will rejoice over you.[s]

6 Jerusalem,
I have appointed watchmen
on your walls;[t]
they will never be silent, day or night.

[A] 61:8 Some Hb mss, DSS, LXX, Syr, Tg, Vg; other Hb mss read *robbery with a burnt offering*   [B] 62:4 Or *Hephzibah*   [C] 62:4 Or *Beulah*

61:5-6 As the Gentiles enrich and serve Israel, God's people will finally be what they were always meant to be—a nation in which all of the people will be called **the LORD's priests** (61:6; see Exod 19:6), ministering his grace to all the world.
61:7 That Israel will receive **a double portion** of inheritance as the firstborn of the Lord (see Exod 4:22; Deut 21:17) is in contrast to Israel having received "double for all her sins" (Isa 40:2).
61:8 This **permanent covenant** with Israel is a reference to the "new covenant" (see

Jer 31:31-34), which Jesus established when he "poured out" his blood on the cross for the forgiveness of sins (see Luke 22:20; Heb 8:7-13). Israel will live under this when Jesus comes to rule on the throne of David in his millennial kingdom.
61:10 The Lord's Servant-Messiah, Jesus Christ, will give praise to God for his luxurious **garments of salvation** and his **robe of righteousness**. Endowed with these, he will accomplish God's purposes for Israel and for the world.

62:4 This power of God to give a new name to a person or a nation is nothing new (see Gen 17:3-5, 15-16; 32:27-28; Hos 1:4-7). In Isaiah's day, God called Israel **Deserted** (possibly referring specifically to Jerusalem) and **Desolate**. But the day is coming when God will say of Israel **My Delight Is in Her**, and the land will no longer be forlorn. It will be like a bride united with her beloved groom.
62:6-9 These verses are an encouragement to God's people in any age to be persistent in prayer. We're to pray with expectancy,

There is no rest for you,
who remind the LORD.
7 Do not give him rest
until he establishes
and makes Jerusalem
the praise of the earth.[a]

8 The LORD has sworn
with his right hand
and his strong arm:
I will no longer give your grain
to your enemies for food,[b]
and foreigners will not drink
the new wine
for which you have labored.
9 For those who gather grain will eat it
and praise the LORD,
and those who harvest the grapes
will drink the wine
in my holy courts.

10 Go out, go out through the city gates;
prepare a way for the people!
Build it up, build up the highway;[c]
clear away the stones!
Raise a banner for the peoples.[d]
11 Look, the LORD has proclaimed
to the ends of the earth,
"Say to Daughter Zion:[e]
Look, your salvation is coming,
his wages are with him,[f]
and his reward accompanies him."
12 And they will be called[A]
the Holy People,[g]
the LORD's Redeemed;
and you will be called Cared For,
A City Not Deserted.

THE LORD'S DAY OF VENGEANCE

63 Who is this coming from Edom[h]
in crimson-stained garments
from Bozrah —
this one who is splendid in his apparel,
striding in his formidable[B] might?

It is I, proclaiming vindication,[c]
powerful to save.

2 Why are your clothes red,
and your garments like one
who treads a winepress?[i]

3 I trampled the winepress alone,
and no one from the nations was
with me.
I trampled them in my anger
and ground them underfoot
in my fury;
their blood spattered my garments,
and all my clothes were stained.
4 For I planned the day of vengeance,[j]
and the year
of my redemption[D] came.
5 I looked, but there was no one
to help,[k]
and I was amazed that no one assisted;
so my arm accomplished victory
for me,
and my wrath assisted me.
6 I crushed nations in my anger;
I made them drunk with my wrath[l]
and poured out their blood
on the ground.[m]

REMEMBRANCE OF GRACE

7 I will make known
the LORD's faithful love
and the LORD's praiseworthy acts,
because of all the LORD has done
for us —
even the many good things
he has done for the house of Israel,
which he did for them based on
his compassion
and the abundance of
his faithful love.
8 He said, "They are indeed my people,
children who will not be disloyal,"
and he became their Savior.

[a] 62:7 Is 60:18; Jr 33:9; Zph 3:19-20
[b] 62:8 Lv 26:16; Dt 28:31,33; Jdg 6:3-6; Is 1:7; Jr 5:17
[c] 62:10 Is 11:16; 19:23; 35:8; 49:11; 57:14
[d] Is 11:10,12; 49:22
[e] 62:11 Zch 9:9; Mt 21:5
[f] Is 40:10; Rv 22:12
[g] 62:12 Dt 7:6; Is 4:3; 1Pt 2:9
[h] 63:1 Ps 137:7; Is 34:5-6; Ezk 25:12-14; 35:1-15; Ob 1-14; Mal 1:2-5

[i] 63:2 Rv 19:13-15
[j] 63:4 Is 34:8; 61:2; Jr 46:10
[k] 63:5 Is 59:16
[l] 63:6 Is 29:9; 51:17; Jr 51:39
[m] Rv 14:20

[A] 62:12 Lit *will call them*   [B] 63:1 Syr, Vg read *apparel, striding forward in*   [C] 63:1 Or *righteousness*   [D] 63:4 Or *blood retribution*

---

like **watchmen on [the] walls** of a city who are always on alert for whatever news comes (62:6). The immediate context is God's call to his people to pray persistently and expectantly for his salvation and deliverance to come in the person of the Messiah. **There is no rest for you, who remind the LORD** of his promises and ask him to fulfill them (62:6) could be called the Old Testament equivalent of Paul's command to "pray constantly" (1 Thess 5:17). We're even called to wear God out with our prayers: **Do not give him rest** (Isa 62:7). Jesus agreed and told his disciples "to pray always and not give up" (Luke 18:1).

62:12 The new names God gave to his people (62:4-5) are not enough. He has a few more: **the Holy People, the LORD's Redeemed . . . Cared For, A City Not Deserted**. Those are names that guarantee a glorious future.
63:1 **Edom** serves as an example of what will happen to the nations that reject Christ (**Bozrah** was one of its capital cities). See Numbers 20:14-21 for insight into this people group's cruelty.
63:2-6 The nations God will judge at Christ's return are pictured metaphorically as trampled in God's **winepress** until they are **crushed** (63:2, 6). Indeed, when the sins of the nations are ripe, they will be judged in the "winepress of God's wrath" (Rev 14:19). Now

is the day of repentance; now is the time for second chances. In that day, there will be no second chances, and there will be no escape.
63:7-10 Here the focus shifts dramatically to the declarations of God's people as they remember **the many good things he has done for the house of Israel. . . . The angel of his presence saved them**, most notably in the exodus under Moses (63:7,9). But since that was true, the exiles in Babylon might ask, "Why are we in this mess in Babylon?" Isaiah answers on God's behalf: **they rebelled and grieved his Holy Spirit** (63:10)—a statement that Paul echoes in Ephesians 4:30. Therefore, God **fought against them** (63:10).

a 63:9 Jdg 10:16
b Dt 7:7-8
c Dt 1:31; 32:10-12; Is 46:3
d 63:10 Ps 51:11; 78:40;
106:33; Is 48:16; Ac 7:51;
Eph 4:30
e 63:12 Ex 14:21; Ps 74:13
f 63:15 Dt 26:15; Ps 80:14

g 63:16 Is 41:14; 43:14
h 63:17 Is 6:10
i 63:18 Ps 74:3-7; Is 64:11
j 63:19 Dt 28:10; Is 43:7;
65:1
k 64:1 Ex 19:18; Ps 18:9;
144:5
l Jdg 5:5; Ps 68:8; Nah 1:5
m 64:3 Dt 10:21; 2Sm 7:23;
Ps 65:5
n Mc 1:3-4; Hab 3:13
o 64:4 1Co 2:9

9 In all their suffering, he suffered,[A,a]
and the angel of his presence
saved them.
He redeemed them
because of his love
and compassion;[b]
he lifted them up and carried them
all the days of the past.[c]
10 But they rebelled
and grieved his Holy Spirit.[d]
So he became their enemy
and fought against them.
11 Then he[B] remembered the days
of the past,
the days of Moses and his people.
Where is he who brought them
out of the sea
with the shepherds[c] of his flock?
Where is he who put his Holy Spirit
among the flock?
12 He made his glorious strength
available at the right hand of Moses,
divided the water before them[e]
to make an eternal name for himself,
13 and led them through the depths
like a horse in the wilderness,
so that they did not stumble.
14 Like cattle that go down
into the valley,
the Spirit of the LORD gave them[D] rest.
You led your people this way
to make a glorious name
for yourself.

ISRAEL'S PRAYER

15 Look down from heaven and see[f]
from your lofty home —
holy and beautiful.
Where is your zeal and your might?
Your yearning[E] and your compassion
are withheld from me.
16 Yet you are our Father,
even though Abraham does not
know us
and Israel doesn't recognize us.

You, LORD, are our Father;
your name is Our Redeemer[g]
from Ancient Times.
17 Why, LORD, do you make us stray
from your ways?
You harden our hearts so we do not
fear[F] you.[h]
Return, because of your servants,
the tribes of your heritage.
18 Your holy people had a possession[G]
for a little while,
but our enemies have trampled down
your sanctuary.[i]
19 We have become like those
you never ruled,
like those who did not bear
your name.[j]

64 If only you would tear
the heavens open
and come down,[k]
so that mountains would quake
at your presence[l] —
2 just as fire kindles brushwood,
and fire boils water —
to make your name known
to your enemies,
so that nations will tremble
at your presence!
3 When you did awesome works[m]
that we did not expect,
you came down,[n]
and the mountains quaked
at your presence.
4 From ancient times no one has heard,
no one has listened to,
no eye has seen any God except you
who acts on behalf of the one
who waits for him.[o]
5 You welcome the one who joyfully
does what is right;
they remember you in your ways.
But we have sinned, and you
were angry.
How can we be saved if we remain
in our sins?[H]

[A] 63:9 Alt Hb tradition reads *did not suffer*   [B] 63:11 Or *they*   [C] 63:11 LXX, Tg, Syr read *shepherd*   [D] 63:14 Lit *him*   [E] 63:15 Lit *The agitation of your inward parts*   [F] 63:17 Lit *our heart from fearing*   [G] 63:18 Or *Your people possessed your holy place*   [H] 64:5 Lit *angry; in them continually and we will be saved*; Hb obscure

63:11-15 When God came to Moses in the burning bush, he said, "I have observed the misery of my people in Egypt, and have heard them crying out because of their oppressors. I know about their sufferings, and I have come down to rescue them" (Exod 3:7-8). He had done it before; he would do it again.
63:16-17 They asked for deliverance even though they had to admit with embarrassment that they were so sinful that their ancestors **Abraham** and **Israel** (Jacob) would

not **recognize** them (Isa 63:16). That's quite a statement considering what a deceiver Jacob was—until God straightened out his act. God's people had gotten so bad that they had become like Pharaoh, who rejected God's demands to let his people go and hardened his own heart (see Exod 8:32). Eventually, God confirmed Pharaoh's choice and hardened his heart too (Exod 9:12). The people of Israel and Judah rejected the Lord repeatedly. No matter how many times God urged them through his prophets to repent, they pressed on in

their idolatry. So he hardened their **hearts** and judged them through the nations that conquered them (Isa 63:17).
64:4 We need to remember how God has come through in our past circumstances so that we can have faith to call on him in our time of need, for he **acts on behalf of the one who waits for him**. To "wait" for God doesn't mean to sit and do nothing. It means to live faithfully according to the agenda of God's Word as we patiently expect him to answer in his own time and way.

6   All of us have become
        like something unclean,
    and all our righteous acts are
        like a polluted^A garment;^a
    all of us wither like a leaf,^b
    and our iniquities^c carry us away
        like the wind.
7   No one calls on your name,
        striving to take hold of you.
    For you have hidden your face
        from us^d
    and made us melt because of^B,C
        our iniquity.

8   Yet LORD, you are our Father;^e
    we are the clay, and you are our potter;
    we all are the work of your hands.^f
9   LORD, do not be terribly angry
    or remember our iniquity forever.^g
    Please look — all of us are
        your people!
10 Your holy cities have become
        a wilderness;
    Zion has become a wilderness,
    Jerusalem a desolation.^h
11 Our holy and beautiful^D temple,
        where our fathers praised you,
    has been burned down,
    and all that was dear to us lies
        in ruins.^i
12 LORD, after all this, will you
        restrain yourself?
    Will you keep silent and afflict
        us severely?^j

THE LORD'S RESPONSE

65 "I was sought by those
        who did not ask;
    I was found by those
        who did not seek me.
    I said, 'Here I am, here I am,'

to a nation that did not call
    on^E my name.^k
2   I spread out my hands all day long
    to a rebellious people^l
    who walk in the path that is not
        good,
    following their own thoughts.
3   These people continually anger me
        to my face,
    sacrificing in gardens,^m
    burning incense on bricks,
4   sitting among the graves,
    spending nights in secret places,
    eating the meat of pigs,^n
    and putting polluted broth
        in their bowls.^F
5   They say, 'Keep to yourself,
    don't come near me, for I am
        too holy for you!'
    These practices are smoke
        in my nostrils,
    a fire that burns all day long.
6   Look, it is written in front of me:
    I will not keep silent,^o
        but I will repay;^p
    I will repay them fully^G
7   for your iniquities
        and the iniquities^q
    of your^H fathers together,"
    says the LORD.
    "Because they burned incense
        on the mountains
    and reproached me on the hills,^r
    I will reward them fully^I
        for their former deeds."

8 The LORD says this:
    "As the new wine is found in a bunch
        of grapes,
    and one says, 'Don't destroy it,
        for there's some good^J in it,'

Cross-reference column:
^a 64:6 Is 61:10; Php 3:7-9
^b Ps 90:5-6; Is 1:30
^c Is 13:11
^d 64:7 Is 54:8
^e 64:8 Is 63:16
^f Is 29:16; 45:9; Rm 9:20-21
^g 64:9 Is 43:25; 57:17;
   Mc 7:18
^h 64:10 Is 62:4
^i 64:11 2Kg 25:9; Ps 74:5-7;
   Is 63:18; Mt 23:38
^j 64:12 Is 42:14

^k 65:1 Is 63:19; Hs 1:10; Rm
   10:20; Jms 2:7
^l 65:2 Rm 10:21
^m 65:3 Is 1:29; 66:17
^n 65:4 Lv 11:7; Is 66:3,17
^o 65:6 Ps 50:3,21; Is 42:14;
   64:12
^p Jr 16:18
^q 65:7 Is 13:11
^r Ezk 20:27-28; Hs 9:10;
   Zch 8:14; Mal 3:7

---

^A 64:6 Lit *menstrual*   ^B 64:7 LXX, Syr, Vg, Tg read *and delivered us into the hand of*   ^C 64:7 Lit *melt by the hand of*   ^D 64:11 Or *glorious*; Is 60:7
^E 65:1 Or *that was not called by*   ^F 65:3-4 These vv. describe pagan worship.   ^G 65:6 Lit *repay into their lap*   ^H 65:7 LXX, Syr read *for their
iniquities and the iniquities of their*   ^I 65:7 Lit *reward into their lap*   ^J 65:8 Or *there's a blessing*

64:6-7 No amount of worship and prayers for deliverance will help if we continue to live by our own agenda and for our own glory. Therefore, the people had to say, **All of us have become like something unclean, and all our righteous acts are like a polluted garment** (64:6). As the old saying goes, confession is good for the soul.
64:8-12 This was an urgent request for God to make his power manifest to his enemies, remember his people's afflictions, and rescue them before they were beyond recovery. The end of this long prayer is a good example of what it means to remind God that we as his people are frail and sinful humans, and that he needs to intervene because of what he values so much—his people and his Holy Land (64:12).

65:2-7 Though God **spread out [his] hands** to them, his people followed **their own thoughts** (65:2). And, of course, their thoughts led to their actions: **sacrificing in gardens** (practicing idolatry; 65:3), **sitting among the graves** (talking to the dead), and **eating . . . pigs** (rejecting God's holiness laws; 65:4). They **anger me to my face**, God declared (65:3). **I will repay them fully** (65:6-7).
  Our actions too are determined by our thinking. That's why you need to adopt God's thinking about the issues of life. You must be "transformed by the renewing of your mind" (Rom 12:2). By tending to the soil of our minds and sowing our thoughts with the Word of God, we will make it possible to bear good fruit in what we say and in what we do.

65:8-16 Even during judgment God promised to spare his righteous remnant, those who were faithful to him in the midst of perverse generations (65:8-10). The wicked, on the other hand, will not be spared: **you did what was evil in my sight and chose what I did not delight in** (65:12). God then presented a stark contrast between the fate of the wicked and the fate of his **servants**. The wicked would experience hunger, thirst, shame, anguish, lament, cursing, and death (65:13-15). But God's servants will **eat, drink, rejoice**, and **shout for joy** (65:13-14). Given the two options, there's simply no contest. Regardless of the hardships one may face in life by following the Lord, the end result is worth it: **the former troubles will be forgotten** (65:16).

[a] **65:9** Jr 31:36-37
[b] **65:9** Is 41:8
[c] Is 49:8; 60:21; Am 9:11-15
[d] **65:10** Is 33:9; 35:2
[e] Jos 7:26; Hs 2:15
[f] Is 51:1
[g] **65:12** 2Ch 36:15-16; Pr 1:24; Is 41:28; 50:2; 66:4; Jr 7:13
[h] **65:15** Jr 24:9; 25:18; Zch 8:13
[i] Is 62:2
[j] **65:16** Ps 31:5; 2Co 1:20; Rv 3:7,14

[k] **65:17** Is 66:22; 2Pt 3:13; Rv 21:1
[l] **65:19** Is 25:8; 30:19; 35:10; 51:11; Rv 7:17; 21:4
[m] **65:20** Ec 8:12-13; Is 3:11; 22:14
[n] **65:21** Jos 24:13; Is 37:30; Jr 29:5,28; Ezk 28:26; Zph 1:13
[o] **65:22** Ps 92:12-14
[p] **65:23** Dt 28:3-12; Is 55:2
[q] Is 61:9
[r] **65:24** Ps 91:15; Is 55:6; 58:9; Dn 9:20-23; 10:12

so I will act because of my servants
and not destroy them all.
9 I will produce descendants
from Jacob,[a]
and heirs to my mountains
from Judah;
my chosen[b] ones will possess it,
and my servants will dwell there.[c]
10 Sharon will be a pasture for flocks,[d]
and the Valley of Achor a place
for herds to lie down,[e]
for my people who have sought me.[f]
11 But you who abandon the LORD,
who forget my holy mountain,
who prepare a table for Fortune
and fill bowls of mixed wine
for Destiny,[A]
12 I will destine you for the sword,
and all of you will kneel down
to be slaughtered,
because I called
and you did not answer,
I spoke and you did not hear;
you did what was evil in my sight
and chose what I did not
delight in."[g]

13 Therefore, this is what the Lord GOD says:
"My servants will eat,
but you will be hungry;
my servants will drink,
but you will be thirsty;
my servants will rejoice,
but you will be put to shame.
14 My servants will shout for joy
from a glad heart,
but you will cry out
from an anguished heart,
and you will lament out of
a broken spirit.
15 You will leave your name behind
as a curse for my chosen ones,[h]
and the Lord GOD will kill you;
but he will give his servants
another name.[i]
16 Whoever asks for a blessing
in the land
will ask for a blessing by the God
of truth,[j]
and whoever swears in the land
will swear by the God of truth.
For the former troubles
will be forgotten
and hidden from my sight.

HOPE WORDS

Truth is the standard to which all other things must conform because truth is reality in its original form.

A NEW CREATION

17 "For I will create a new heaven
and a new earth;[k]
the past events will not
be remembered or come to mind.
18 Then be glad and rejoice forever
in what I am creating;
for I will create Jerusalem to be a joy
and its people to be a delight.
19 I will rejoice in Jerusalem
and be glad in my people.
The sound of weeping and crying
will no longer be heard in her.[l]
20 In her, a nursing infant
will no longer live
only a few days,[B]
or an old man not live out his days.
Indeed, the one who dies
at a hundred years old
will be mourned as a young man,[C]
and the one who misses
a hundred years
will be considered cursed.[m]
21 People will build houses and live
in them;
they will plant vineyards and eat
their fruit.[n]
22 They will not build and others live
in them;
they will not plant and others eat.
For my people's lives will be
like the lifetime of a tree.[o]
My chosen ones will fully enjoy
the work of their hands.
23 They will not labor without success[p]
or bear children destined
for disaster,
for they will be a people blessed
by the LORD
along with their descendants.[q]
24 Even before they call, I will answer;[r]
while they are still speaking,
I will hear.
25 The wolf and the lamb
will feed together,[D]

[A] **65:11** Pagan gods [B] **65:20** Lit *her, no longer infant of days* [C] **65:20** Lit *the youth of a hundred years will die* [D] **65:25** Lit *as one*

65:17-25 Several of the most well-known characteristics of Christ's kingdom are found in this description of that golden age, including **a new heaven and a new earth** (65:17), the end of **weeping** (65:19), and a redeemed animal kingdom (65:25).

and the lion will eat straw
　　like cattle,[a]
but the serpent's food
　　will be dust![b]
They will not do what is evil
　　or destroy
on my entire holy mountain,"[c]
says the LORD.

FINAL JUDGMENT AND JOYOUS RESTORATION

66 This is what the LORD says:
Heaven[d] is my throne,[e]
and earth is my footstool.[f]
Where could you possibly build a
　　house for me?
And where would my
　　resting place be?[g]

2　My hand made all these things,
　　and so they all came into being.
　　　　This is the LORD's declaration.
I will look favorably on this kind
　　of person:
one who is humble,[h]
　　submissive[A] in spirit,[i]
and trembles at my word.

3　One person slaughters an ox,
　　　　another kills a person;
one person sacrifices a lamb,
　　　　another breaks a dog's neck;
one person offers a grain offering,
　　　　another offers pig's blood;
one person offers incense,
　　　　another praises an idol —
all these have chosen their ways
and delight
　　in their abhorrent practices.[j]

4　So I will choose their punishment,
　　and I will bring on them
　　　　what they dread
because I called
　　and no one answered;
I spoke and they did not listen;
they did what was evil in my sight
and chose what I did
　　not delight in.[k]

5　You who tremble at his word,[l]
　　hear the word of the LORD:[m]
"Your brothers who hate
　　and exclude you
for my name's sake have said,[n]
'Let the LORD be glorified
so that we can see your joy!'
But they will be put to shame."[o]

6　A sound of uproar from the city!
A voice from the temple —
　　the voice of the LORD,
paying back his enemies
　　what they deserve![p]

7　Before Zion was in labor,
　　she gave birth;
before she was in pain, she delivered
　　a boy.

8　Who has heard of such a thing?
Who has seen such things?
Can a land be born in one day
or a nation be delivered
　　in an instant?
Yet as soon as Zion was in labor,
she gave birth to her sons.

9　"Will I bring a baby to the point
　　of birth
and not deliver it?"
says the LORD;
"or will I who deliver,
　　close the womb?"
says your God.

10　Be glad for Jerusalem and rejoice
　　over her,
all who love her.[q]
Rejoice greatly with her,
all who mourn over her —

11　so that you may nurse
　　and be satisfied
from her comforting breast
and drink deeply
　　and delight yourselves
from her glorious breasts.

12　For this is what the LORD says:
I will make peace flow to her
　　like a river,[r]
and the wealth[B] of nations
　　like a flood;[s]
you will nurse and be carried
　　on her hip[t]
and bounced on her lap.

13　As a mother comforts her son,
so I will comfort you,[u]
and you will be comforted
　　in Jerusalem.

14　You will see, you will rejoice,
and you[c] will flourish like grass;[v]
then the LORD's power
　　will be revealed to his servants,
but he will show his wrath
　　against his enemies.

[a] 65:25 Is 11:6-9
[b] Gn 3:14; Mc 7:17
[c] Is 11:9; 27:13; 56:7
[d] 66:1-2 Ac 7:49-50
[e] 66:1 Ps 11:4; Mt 5:34-35; 23:22
[f] 1Ch 28:2; Ps 99:5
[g] 2Sm 7:5; 1Kg 8:27; Jr 23:24
[h] 66:2 Ps 86:1; Pr 16:19; Mt 11:29
[i] Ps 34:18; Mt 5:3; 1Tm 2:11
[j] 66:3 Am 5:21-25
[k] 66:4 2Kg 21:2,6; Is 59:7; 65:12; Jr 7:30
[l] 66:5 Ezr 9:4; 10:3
[m] Is 28:14
[n] Mt 5:10-12; 10:22; Jn 9:34; 15:18-20
[o] Is 26:11; 44:9; 65:13

[p] 66:6 Is 59:18; 65:6; Jl 3:7
[q] 66:10 Ps 122:6; 137:6; Is 65:18
[r] 66:12 Ps 72:3,7; Is 48:18
[s] Is 61:6
[t] Is 60:4-5
[u] 66:13 Ps 86:17; Is 40:1; 49:13; 51:13; 52:9; 2Co 1:3-4
[v] 66:14 Ps 72:16; Pr 11:28; Is 58:11

[A] 66:2 Lit *broken*　　[B] 66:12 Or *glory*　　[C] 66:14 Lit *your bones*

66:6 There will come a time when the grace of God will end and those who reject him will be confirmed in their choices. No one will stand; no one will escape.
66:7 Israel's restoration in the kingdom age will be accomplished so quickly it will be like a woman delivering her baby before she **was in labor**.

a 66:15 Is 33:14; Mal 3:1-2;
2Th 1:7-8; 2Pt 3:7
b Ps 68:17; Is 5:28; Hab 3:8
c 66:16 Gn 6:12; Jr 12:12;
25:31; Ezk 20:48; 21:4-5
d 66:17 Is 65:3-5
e 66:18 Is 45:22-25; Jr 3:17
f 66:19 Gn 10:2,5; 1Kg
10:22; Jr 46:9; Ezk 27:10,13
g 1Ch 16:24; Ps 96:3

h 66:20 Ps 2:6; Is 56:7; Ezk
20:40; Jl 3:17
i 66:21 Ex 19:6; Is 61:6; 1Pt
2:5,9; Rv 1:6
j 66:22 Is 65:17; Heb 12:26-
27; 2Pt 3:13; Rv 21:1
k 66:24 Is 1:2; 5:25; 34:3
l Jb 7:5; Is 14:11
m Mk 9:48
n Dn 12:2

15 Look, the LORD will come
　　with fire[a] —
his chariots are like the whirlwind[b] —
to execute his anger with fury
and his rebuke with flames of fire.
16 For the LORD will execute judgment
on all people[c] with his fiery sword,
and many will be slain by the LORD.

17 "Those who dedicate and purify themselves to enter the groves[d] following their leader,[A] eating meat from pigs, vermin,[B] and rats, will perish together."
　　This is the LORD's declaration.
18 "Knowing[c] their works and their thoughts, I have come to gather all nations and languages;[e] they will come and see my glory. **19** I will establish a sign among them, and I will send survivors from them to the nations — to Tarshish, Put,[D] Lud (who are archers), Tubal, Javan,[f] and the coasts and islands far away — who have not heard about me or seen my glory. And they will proclaim my glory among the nations.[g] **20** They will bring all your brothers from all

the nations as a gift to the LORD on horses and chariots, in litters, and on mules and camels, to my holy mountain Jerusalem,"[h] says the LORD, "just as the Israelites bring an offering in a clean vessel to the house of the LORD. **21** I will also take some of them as priests and Levites,"[i] says the LORD.
22　　"For just as the new heavens
　　　　and the new earth,[j]
which I will make,
will remain before me" —
　　this is the LORD's declaration —
"so your offspring and your name
　　will remain.
23　　All mankind will come
　　　　to worship me
from one New Moon to another
and from one Sabbath to another,"
says the LORD.

24 "As they leave, they will see the dead bodies of those who have rebelled against me;[k] for their worm[l] will never die, their fire will never go out,[m] and they will be a horror to all mankind."[n]

A 66:17 Hb obscure　**B 66:17** Lit *abhorrent things*　**C 66:18** LXX, Syr; MT omits *Knowing*　**D 66:19** LXX; MT reads *Pul*

66:19-20 When Jesus Christ returns to rule the earth, people in the farthest corners of the world will know of his salvation. It appears that believing Jews will go to other **nations** to **proclaim** God's **glory** (66:19), resulting in salvation for Israel's Gentile **brothers** as a gift to the Lord (66:20).

66:22-23 When God makes everything **new** in his eternal kingdom, the old distinctions and divisions won't apply anymore: **All mankind will come to worship**. Knowing that God is building his kingdom today, and that his kingdom will come fully and finally at the return of Christ, the best thing believers can

do is to understand the requirements of his kingdom agenda and get on with the task of fulfilling them.

JEREMIAH

INTRODUCTION

Author

BEFORE HE WAS CALLED AS a prophet of the Lord, Jeremiah was a priest "living in Anathoth in the territory of Benjamin" (1:1). He began prophesying "in the thirteenth year of the reign of" Judah's King Josiah and continued into Judah's exile in Babylon (1:2-3). Thus, Jeremiah's ministry started in about 626 BC and continued for several years after 586 BC. Jeremiah saw the downfall of Judah, the destruction of Jerusalem, and the exile of God's people. Because of the tremendous sorrow this caused him (9:1), he is often referred to as "the weeping prophet."

Historical Background

Jeremiah's ministry began during the reign of King Josiah of Judah. Unlike his wicked father Amon and grandfather Manasseh, Josiah followed the Lord (see 2 Kgs 22:2). He even led the people to renew their covenant with God. He also brought about many reforms in Judah, including repairing the temple, removing pagan idolatry from the land, and observing the Passover. But though Josiah did much good, he could not ultimately overcome the great evils done by the kings who had gone before him—especially Manasseh's. Therefore, God was determined to bring his anger down on Judah and Jerusalem (see 2 Kgs 23:26-27).

Josiah died in a battle with Pharaoh Neco of Egypt in 609 BC. His son Jehoahaz was king for only three months before Neco imprisoned him and made Josiah's son Jehoiakim king in his place. In 605 BC Neco was defeated by the Babylonians, and Judah fell into the hands of Babylon by the next year. When Jehoiakim rebelled against Babylon's King Nebuchadnezzar in about 600 BC, Nebuchadnezzar invaded Judah and besieged Jerusalem. He deposed Jehoiakim in 598 BC, carried his son Jehoiachin into exile in 597 BC, and made Zedekiah—another of Josiah's sons—king of Judah. Then, in 588 BC, Zedekiah rebelled against Babylon. And as a result, Nebuchadnezzar ravaged Jerusalem, destroyed the temple, and carried many of Judah's inhabitants (including Zedekiah) into exile in 587–586 BC.

Message and Purpose

Jeremiah brought a lot of emotion to his prophetic role, earning him the name "the weeping prophet." As judgment was being prepared for the sinful kingdom of Judah through the Babylonian Empire, Jeremiah was called to announce the rightness of that judgment because of Judah's great sin against God. His daunting task was to bring this message of rejection to God's people. But in the midst of that, Jeremiah also issued a call to the people to repent so that their situation might be reversed, and another call to the people who would not be taken into captivity in Babylon to repent so that things would not become worse.

God commanded Jeremiah not to marry as an illustration of the isolation God was feeling from his sinful people. And yet, it is in Jeremiah that God reveals a new kingdom covenant he would make with his people to cleanse them, give them new hearts, and restore them to him. The good news of Jeremiah is that despite our sin, God offers us restoration if we will repent and return to him.

www.bhpublishinggroup.com/qr/te/24_00

Outline

1 The words of Jeremiah,[a] the son of
Hilkiah, one of the priests living in
Anathoth[b] in the territory of Benjamin.
2 The word of the LORD came to him in
the thirteenth year of the reign of Josiah[c]
son of Amon, king of Judah. 3 It also came
throughout the days of Jehoiakim[d] son of
Josiah, king of Judah, until the fifth month
of the eleventh year of Zedekiah[e] son of
Josiah, king of Judah, when the people of
Jerusalem went into exile.

THE CALL OF JEREMIAH

4 The word of the LORD came to me:

5 I chose you before I formed you
in the womb;
I set you apart before you were born.[f]
I appointed you a prophet
to the nations.[g]

6 But I protested, "Oh no, Lord GOD! Look,
I don't know how to speak[h] since I am only
a youth."[i]
7 Then the LORD said to me:

Do not say, "I am only a youth,"[j]
for you will go to everyone
I send you to
and speak whatever I tell you.[k]
8 Do not be afraid of anyone,[l]
for I will be with you to rescue you.[m]
This is the LORD's declaration.

9 Then the LORD reached out his hand,
touched my mouth,[n] and told me:

I have now filled your mouth
with my words.[o]
10 See, I have appointed you today
over nations and kingdoms
to uproot and tear down,
to destroy and demolish,[p]
to build and plant.[q]

TWO VISIONS

11 Then the word of the LORD came to me,
asking, "What do you see, Jeremiah?"[r]
I replied, "I see a branch of an almond
tree."
12 The LORD said to me, "You have seen
correctly, for I watch over[A] my word to accomplish it."[s] 13 Again the word of the LORD
came to me asking, "What do you see?"
And I replied, "I see a boiling pot,[t] its lip
tilted from the north to the south."
14 Then the LORD said to me, "Disaster
will be poured out[B] from the north[u] on all
who live in the land. 15 Indeed, I am about
to summon all the clans and kingdoms of
the north."[v]

This is the LORD's declaration.
They will come, and each king
will set up his throne
at the entrance to Jerusalem's gates.
They will attack
all her surrounding walls
and all the other cities of Judah.

16 "I will pronounce my judgments against
them for all the evil they did when they
abandoned me to burn incense to other
gods and to worship the works of their
own hands.[w]
17 "Now, get ready. Stand up and tell them
everything that I command you. Do not be
intimidated by them[x] or I will cause you
to cower before them. 18 Today, I am the
one who has made you a fortified city,[y]
an iron pillar, and bronze walls[z] against
the whole land — against the kings of Judah, its officials, its priests, and the population. 19 They will fight against you but
never prevail over you,[aa] since I am with
you to rescue you."[ab]
This is the LORD's declaration.

ISRAEL ACCUSED OF APOSTASY

2 The word of the LORD came to me: 2 "Go
and announce directly to Jerusalem
that this is what the LORD says:

I remember the loyalty
of your youth,[ac]
your love as a bride —

[a] **1:1** 2Ch 35:25; 36:12; Ezr 1:1; Dn 9:2; Mt 2:17; 16:14; 27:9
[b] Jos 21:18; 1Kg 2:26; Jr 32:7
[c] **1:2** 2Kg 21:24; 22:1; Jr 25:3; 36:2; Zph 1:1
[d] **1:3** 2Kg 23:34; 24:2; 1Ch 3:15; Jr 22:18; 25:1; 35:1
[e] 2Kg 24:17-20; 1Ch 3:16; Jr 21:1; 27:1; 39:2
[f] **1:5** 1Sm 1:22; Ps 22:9-10; 139:13-16; Is 44:2; 49:1-6; Lk 1:15; Gl 1:15
[g] Jr 25:15-26
[h] **1:6** Ex 4:10; 1Co 2:1-5
[i] 1Kg 3:7
[j] **1:7** 1Tm 4:12
[k] Dt 18:18; Jr 1:17; Ezk 2:7
[l] **1:8** Ezk 2:6
[m] Gn 26:3; 31:3; Ex 3:12; Is 43:2; Jr 15:20
[n] **1:9** Is 6:7
[o] Is 51:16
[p] **1:10** 2Co 10:4-5
[q] Jr 12:14-17; 18:7,9; 19:7; 24:6; 31:28; Col 2:6-7
[r] **1:11** Jr 24:3; Am 8:2; Zch 4:2

[s] **1:12** Jr 31:28; Php 1:6
[t] **1:13** Ezk 24:3
[u] **1:14** Jr 4:6,20; 6:1; 15:12; 47:2; 50:3,9,41; 51:48
[v] **1:15** Jr 25:9
[w] **1:16** Ex 20:3; Is 37:19; 44:15; Ac 7:41
[x] **1:17** Ezk 2:6-7; 1Th 2:2
[y] **1:18-19** Jr 15:20
[z] **1:18** Jr 6:27; Ezk 3:8-9
[aa] **1:19** Ps 129:2
[ab] Jr 1:6
[ac] **2:2** Ezk 16:8,60; Hs 2:15; Rv 2:4

[A] **1:12** In Hb, the word for *almond tree* sounds like the word for *watch over* [B] **1:14** LXX reads *will boil*

1:1 The town of **Anathoth** was located about three miles northeast of Jerusalem.
1:2-3 Jeremiah's ministry covers a period of forty-plus years, beginning **in the thirteenth year of the reign of Josiah** (1:2), the last of the good kings of Judah, and continuing through the destruction of Jerusalem and the people's **exile** into Babylon in 586 BC (1:3). Israel had already been swept away by the Assyrians in 722 BC.
1:5-6 Like Moses before him (see Exod 4:10), Jeremiah **protested** God's call on his life because he didn't **know how to speak** (Jer 1:6). But God delights in demonstrating his great power in human weakness (see 2 Cor 12:9).
1:8-10 Jeremiah's message was not one of complete despair and destruction: after the people had experienced seventy years of exile in Babylon, God was going to bring them back to the land and rebuild his temple. Still, it wouldn't be popular.
1:11-12 The Hebrew words for **almond** and **watch** sound alike in Hebrew. Thus, God would see to it that every word he gave Jeremiah to deliver would blossom and come to pass.
1:13-14 What Jeremiah saw was an unmistakable picture of the **disaster** coming upon Judah when the armies of King Nebuchadnezzar of Babylon would swoop down on Jerusalem. The accuracy of God's Word is amazing. While Babylon was actually east of Judah, its armies invaded **from the north**, following the trade routes that took travelers around the Arabian Desert instead of through it.
1:17 If you have bad news to deliver that people need to hear, there's no use delaying it or dancing around it.
2:2-3 Like the betrayed husband of a wayward bride, God recalls the days when his people were faithful. **Israel** (meaning the entire nation, not merely the northern kingdom) **was holy to the LORD** (2:3). Of all the nations,

how you followed me
in the wilderness,
in a land not sown.

3 Israel was holy to the LORD,[a]
the firstfruits of his harvest.[b]
All who ate of it found
themselves guilty;[c]
disaster came on them."
This is the LORD's declaration.

4 Hear the word of the LORD,
house of Jacob
and all families of the house
of Israel.

5 This is what the LORD says:

What fault did your fathers find
in me[d]
that they went so far from me,
followed worthless idols,[e]
and became worthless themselves?[f]

6 They stopped asking, "Where is
the LORD[g]
who brought us from the land
of Egypt,
who led us through the wilderness,[h]
through a land of deserts
and ravines,
through a land of drought
and darkness,[A]
a land no one traveled through
and where no one lived?"

7 I brought you to a fertile land[i]
to eat its fruit and bounty,
but after you entered, you defiled
my land;[j]
you made
my inheritance[k] detestable.

8 The priests quit asking, "Where is
the LORD?"
The experts in the law no longer
knew me,[l]
and the rulers[m] rebelled against me.
The prophets prophesied by[B] Baal[n]
and followed useless idols.[o]

9 Therefore, I will bring a case
against you again.
This is the LORD's declaration.
I will bring a case
against your children's children.[p]

10 Cross over to the coasts of Cyprus[C,q]
and take a look.
Send someone to Kedar[r]
and consider carefully;
see if there has ever been
anything like this:

11 Has a nation ever exchanged
its gods?[s]
(But they were not gods![t])
Yet my people have exchanged
their[D] Glory
for useless idols.[u]

12 Be appalled at this, heavens;[v]
be shocked and utterly desolated!
This is the LORD's declaration.

13 For my people have committed
a double evil:
They have abandoned me,[w]
the fountain of living water,[x]
and dug cisterns for themselves —
cracked cisterns that cannot
hold water.[y]

CONSEQUENCES OF APOSTASY

14 Is Israel a slave?
Was he born into slavery?[E]
Why else has he become a prey?

15 The young lions have roared
at him;[z]
they have roared loudly.
They have laid waste his land.[aa]
His cities are in ruins,
without inhabitants.

16 The men of Memphis
and Tahpanhes[ab]
have also broken your skull.

17 Have you not brought this
on yourself[ac]
by abandoning the LORD your God
while he was leading you
along the way?

18 Now what will you gain
by traveling along the way
to Egypt[ad]
to drink the water of the Nile?[F]
What will you gain
by traveling along the way
to Assyria[ae]
to drink the water
of the Euphrates?[af]

[a] 2:3 Dt 7:6
[b] Jms 1:18
[c] Gn 12:3; Ps 105:14-15; Is 41:11
[d] 2:5 Is 5:4; Mc 6:3
[e] 2Kg 17:15; Jr 2:25; Hs 2:5
[f] Ps 115:8; Hs 9:10; Rm 1:21
[g] 2:6 Jdg 6:13; Jb 35:10
[h] Dt 8:15; 32:10
[i] 2:7 Ex 3:8; Dt 8:7-10; Jr 4:26
[j] Nm 35:33; Ezk 36:17
[k] Jr 16:18
[l] 2:8 Hs 4:6; Mal 2:7; Lk 11:52
[m] Jr 23:1-4; Ezk 34
[n] Jr 2:23; 9:14
[o] Hab 2:8
[p] 2:9 Ex 20:5; Is 3:13; Mc 6:1-8

[q] 2:10 Gn 10:4; Nm 24:24; Is 23:1,12; Am 6:2; Ac 13:4
[r] Ps 120:5
[s] 2:11 Mc 4:5
[t] Jr 16:20; Gl 4:8
[u] Ps 106:20; Hs 4:7; Rm 1:23; 1Pt 1:18
[v] 2:12 Dt 32:1; Is 1:2; Mc 6:1
[w] 2:13 Jdg 10:13
[x] Ps 36:9; Jr 17:13; Jn 4:10
[y] Is 55:2; Gl 1:6-7
[z] 2:15 Is 5:29
[aa] Is 1:7
[ab] 2:16 Jr 44:1; 46:14,19; Ezk 30:13,16,18
[ac] 2:17 Jr 4:18
[ad] 2:18 Is 30:1-2; 31:1
[ae] Hs 7:11
[af] Is 8:7

[A] 2:6 Or shadow of death   [B] 2:8 = in the name of   [C] 2:10 Lit to the islands of Kittim   [D] 2:11 Alt Hb tradition reads my   [E] 2:14 Lit born of a house
[F] 2:18 Lit of Shihor

Israel was set apart by God to be his chosen people.
2:6-8 God's people had turned away from the One who had delivered them from slavery and taken them to the promised **land** (2:6-7). Everyone who should have known better, in fact, was guilty of this betrayal: the **priests**, **experts in the law**, **rulers**, and **prophets** (2:8). **2:13** In preferring idolatry, the nation made a terrible spiritual trade. Thirsty people trading a flowing fountain for empty holes. It doesn't get much more absurd than that.

2:18 Judah's so-called solution to the problems they'd brought on themselves was not to turn back to the Lord, but to turn to **Egypt** and **Assyria** to fix their mess by playing the game of political intrigue and power brokering.

a 2:19 Is 3:9; Hs 5:5
b Jr 4:18
c 2:20 Lv 26:13; Is 10:27; Nah 1:13
d Dt 12:2; 1Kg 14:23; 2Kg 17:10; Is 57:5; Jr 3:6; Ezk 6:13; Hs 4:13
e Ezk 16:28; Hs 2:5
f 2:21 Gn 49:11; Ps 80:8; Is 5:2
g Is 5:4
h 2:22 Ps 51:2,7; Mal 3:2; Eph 5:26
i Ps 90:8
j 2:23 Jr 2:8; 9:14
k Gn 3:13; 1Sm 15:13; Pr 28:13; Jr 3:13; 1Jn 1:8
l 2:24 Jb 39:5; Hs 8:9
m 2:25 Jr 18:12
n Dt 32:16; Jr 3:13
o 2:26 Jr 2:36; 6:15; 8:9,12; Rm 6:21

p 2:26 Ezr 9:7
q 2:27 2Ch 29:6; Jr 18:17; 32:33; Ezk 8:16
r Jdg 10:9-10; Is 26:16
s 2:28 Dt 32:37-38; Jdg 10:14; Is 45:20
t 2:29 Jr 2:9
u 2:30 Pr 3:11; Is 1:5; 9:13; Jr 5:3; 17:23; 32:33; Am 4:10
v Mt 23:34
w 2:31 Jr 50:12; Hs 2:3
x 2:32 Is 61:10
y Ps 106:21; Jr 13:25; 18:15; Ezk 22:12; 23:35; Hs 8:14
z 2:34 2Kg 21:16; 24:4; Ps 106:38; Jr 19:4; 22:3,17
aa Ex 22:2
ab 2:35 Jb 33:9

19 Your own evil will discipline you;[a]
your own apostasies
will reprimand you.
Recognize[A] how evil and bitter[b] it is
for you to abandon the LORD
your God
and to have no fear of me.
This is the declaration
of the Lord GOD of Armies.

20 For long ago I[B] broke your yoke;[c]
I[B] tore off your chains.
You insisted, "I will not serve!"
On every high hill
and under every green tree[d]
you lay down like a prostitute.[e]

21 I planted you, a choice vine[f]
from the very best seed.
How then could you turn into
a degenerate, foreign vine?[g]

22 Even if you wash with lye
and use a great amount of bleach,[C,h]
the stain of your iniquity is still
in front of me.[i]
This is the Lord GOD's declaration.

23 How can you protest, "I am
not defiled;
I have not followed the Baals"?[j]
Look at your behavior in the valley;
acknowledge what you have done.[k]
You are a swift young camel
twisting and turning on her way,

24 a wild donkey[l] at home[D]
in the wilderness.
She sniffs the wind in the heat
of her desire.
Who can control her passion?
All who look for her will not
become weary;
they will find her
in her mating season.[E]

25 Keep your feet from going bare
and your throat from thirst.
But you say, "It's hopeless;[m]
I love strangers,[n]
and I will continue to follow them."

26 Like the shame of a thief
when he is caught,
so the house of Israel has been
put to shame.[o]

They, their kings, their officials,
their priests, and their prophets[p]

27 say to a tree, "You are my father,"
and to a stone, "You gave birth
to me."
For they have turned their back
to me
and not their face,[q]
yet in their time of disaster[r] they beg,
"Rise up and save us!"

28 But where are your gods you made
for yourself?
Let them rise up and save you[s]
in your time of disaster if they can,
for your gods are as numerous
as your cities, Judah.

JUDGMENT DESERVED

29 Why do you bring a case
against me?[t]
All of you have rebelled against me.
This is the LORD's declaration.

30 I have struck down your children
in vain;
they would not accept discipline.[u]
Your own sword has devoured
your prophets[v]
like a ravaging lion.

31 Evil generation,
pay attention to the word
of the LORD!
Have I been a wilderness to Israel
or a land of dense darkness?[w]
Why do my people claim,
"We will go where we want;[F]
we will no longer come to you"?

32 Can a young woman forget
her jewelry[x]
or a bride her wedding sash?
Yet my people have forgotten me[y]
for countless days.

33 How skillfully you pursue love;
you also teach evil women
your ways.

34 Moreover, your skirts are stained
with the blood of the innocent poor.[z]
You did not catch them breaking
and entering.[aa]
But in spite of all these things

35 you claim, "I am innocent.[ab]
His anger is sure to turn away
from me."
But I will certainly judge you

A 2:19 Lit Know and see   B 2:20 LXX reads you   C 2:22 Lit cleansing agent   D 2:24 Lit donkey taught   E 2:24 Lit her month   F 2:31 Or "We have taken control, or "We can roam

2:23-25 Judah had God for a husband, but said, I love strangers (2:25). God considered her idolatry with foreign gods to be spiritual adultery.

2:27-28 When disaster struck, the people begged God to save them (2:27), but he pointed them to their false gods so they could see whether their idols of wood and stone could help (2:28).

2:35 To deny your sin is to call God a liar (see 1 John 1:10).

because you have said, "I have
not sinned."[a]

36 How unstable you are,[b]
constantly changing your ways!
You will be put to shame by Egypt[c]
just as you were put to shame
by Assyria.

37 Moreover, you will be led out
from here
with your hands on your head[d]
since the LORD has rejected
those you trust;[e]
you will not succeed even with
their help.[A]

WAGES OF APOSTASY

3 If[B] a man divorces his wife
and she leaves him
to marry another,
can he ever return to her?[f]
Wouldn't such a land[c] become
totally defiled?
But you!
You have prostituted yourself
with many partners[g] —
can you return to me?[h]
This is the LORD's declaration.

2 Look to the barren heights[i] and see.
Where have you not been immoral?
You sat waiting for them
beside the highways[j]
like a nomad in the desert.
You have defiled the land
with your prostitution
and wickedness.[k]

3 This is why the showers
haven't come[l] —
why there has been no spring rain.
You have the brazen look[m]
of a prostitute[D]
and refuse to be ashamed.[n]

4 Haven't you recently called to me,
"My Father.[o]
You were my friend in my youth."[p]

5 Will he bear a grudge forever?[q]
Will he be endlessly infuriated?"
This is what you have said,
but you have done the evil things
you are capable of.

UNFAITHFUL ISRAEL, TREACHEROUS JUDAH

6 In the days of King Josiah the LORD asked me, "Have you seen what unfaithful Israel has done? She has ascended every high hill and gone under every green tree to prostitute herself there.[r] **7** I thought, 'After she has done all these things, she will return to me.' But she didn't return, and her treacherous sister Judah[s] saw it. **8** I[E] observed that it was because unfaithful Israel had committed adultery that I had sent her away and had given her a certificate of divorce.[u] Nevertheless, her treacherous sister Judah was not afraid but also went and prostituted herself.[v] **9** Indifferent to[F] her prostitution, she defiled the land and committed adultery with stones[w] and trees.[x] **10** Yet in spite of all this, her treacherous sister Judah didn't return to me with all her heart[y] — only in pretense."

This is the LORD's declaration.

11 The LORD announced to me, "Unfaithful Israel has shown herself more righteous than treacherous Judah.[z] **12** Go, proclaim these words to the north, and say,

'Return, unfaithful Israel.[aa]
This is the LORD's declaration.
I will not look on you
with anger,[G]
for I am unfailing in my love.[ab]
This is the LORD's declaration.
I will not be angry forever.[ac]

13 Only acknowledge
your guilt[ad] —
you have rebelled against the LORD
your God.[ae]
You have scattered your favors
to strangers
under every green tree[af]
and have not obeyed me.
This is the LORD's declaration.

14 " 'Return, you faithless children[ag] —
this is the LORD's declaration — for I am your master,[H,ah] and I will take you,[ai] one from a city and two from a family, and I will bring you to Zion. **15** I will give you shepherds who are loyal to me,[I,aj] and they will shepherd you with knowledge and skill.

---

[a] 2:35 Pr 28:13; 1Jn 1:8,10
[b] 2:36 Jms 1:8
[c] Is 30:3
[d] 2:37 2Sm 13:19
[e] 1Sm 15:23,26; 2Kg 17:20; Jr 7:29
[f] 3:1 Dt 24:1-4
[g] Ezk 16:26,28
[h] Hs 2:7
[i] 3:2 Dt 12:2; Ezk 16:52
[j] Gn 38:14; Pr 7:10-12; Ezk 16:25
[k] Nm 14:33
[l] 3:3 Zch 14:7
[m] Ezk 3:7-8
[n] Jr 6:15; 8:12
[o] 3:4 Ex 4:22; Is 1:2; 64:8; Hs 11:1; Gl 4:6
[p] Ps 71:17; Hs 2:15
[q] 3:5 Lv 19:18; Ps 103:9; Is 57:16; Nah 1:2

[r] 3:6 Jr 2:20
[s] 3:7 Hs 14:1
[t] Ezk 16:46
[u] 3:8 Dt 24:1-4; Is 50:1; Hs 2:2
[v] Ezk 23:11
[w] 3:9 Is 57:6
[x] Dt 28:36; Jr 2:27; Ezk 20:32; Hab 2:19; Rv 9:20
[y] 3:10 Hs 7:14
[z] 3:11 Ezk 16:51-52; 23:11
[aa] 3:12 Pr 28:13
[ab] Ps 86:5; 145:17
[ac] Ps 103:9; Is 57:16; Mc 7:18
[ad] 3:13 Lv 26:40; 1Jn 1:9
[ae] 2Kg 18:20; Is 36:5; Jr 2:29
[af] Dt 12:2; 2Kg 16:4; 2Ch 28:4; Is 57:5; Jr 2:20; 3:6,13; Ezk 20:47
[ag] 3:14 Hs 14:1
[ah] Hs 2:16-17
[ai] Hs 2:19-20
[aj] 3:15 1Sm 13:14; Jr 23:4; Ezk 34:23; Ac 20:28; Eph 4:11

[A] 2:37 Lit *with them* [B] 3:1 One Hb ms, LXX, Syr; other Hb mss read *Saying: If* [C] 3:1 LXX reads *woman* [D] 3:3 Lit *have a prostitute's forehead*
[E] 3:8 One Hb ms, Syr read *She* [F] 3:9 Lit *From the lightness of* [G] 3:12 Lit *not cause my face to fall on you* [H] 3:14 Or *husband* [I] 3:15 Lit *shepherds*
according to my heart

3:1-3 What a picture of Judah's spiritual wickedness! They forsook her position as the Lord's bride to be a **brazen . . . prostitute** (3:3). **3:6-8** The northern kingdom of **Israel** had already been taken into captivity by the Assyrians. When Israel was judged for her spiritual adulteries (3:6), Judah should have taken note and avoided her ways. But **Judah**

proved to be even more **treacherous** than her sister Israel (3:7-8)! **3:10** While Judah made a **pretense** of repenting, God saw right through it. We should take care because it's possible to show up at church on Sunday and sing praises to the Lord—but have a heart that is rock hard.

3:14-18 This is an ideal picture of a united nation (Israel and Judah) returning to the true worship of God; such would be so glorious that even the **ark of the LORD's covenant** would not be missed (3:16). What we see here, then, is a picture of Israel's future repentance when the Messiah, Jesus Christ, returns for his millennial kingdom (3:16-18).

a 3:16 Gn 1:28; Ex 1:12
b Ex 37:1-9; Dt 31:24-29;
1Kg 8:6
c 3:17 Ezk 43:7; Rv 22:1,3
d Is 2:2-4; 43:9; 56:6-7;
66:18; Jr 16:19
e Dt 12:5
f 3:18 Is 11:12-13; Jr 50:4-5;
Ezk 37:15-22; Hs 11:1
g Am 9:15
h 3:19 Dt 32:8-9; Ps 16:6;
Lm 2:15; Ezk 20:6,15
i 3:20 Ex 21:8-9; Is 48:8; Hs
1:2; 5:7; 6:7
j 3:21 Is 17:10
k 3:22 Is 57:18; Hs 5:15–6:3;
14:1-3
l 3:23 Ps 121:1-2
m Ps 3:8; Jr 17:5-8

n 3:25 Jb 8:22; Ezr 9:6
o Is 64:5; Jr 8:14; 14:7,20;
Lm 3:42; 5:16; Dn 9:5
p Ezr 9:7; Ezk 2:3
q 4:1 Zch 1:3
r Jr 7:30; 16:18; 32:34
s 4:2 Dt 6:13; 10:20; Jr 5:2
t Is 65:16
u Hs 2:19
v Gn 26:3-4
w Gn 12:1-3; 18:18; 22:18;
1Co 1:31
x 4:3 Hs 10:12
y Mt 13:7
z 4:4 Gn 17:14; Dt 10:16; Jr
9:25; Rm 2:28-29
aa Is 1:31; Jr 21:12; Am 5:6;
Mal 4:1
ab 4:5 Jr 6:1; Hs 5:8; Jl 2:1;
1Th 4:16-17
ac 4:6 Is 62:10
ad Is 14:31; 41:25; Jr 1:13;
4:20; 6:1; 15:12; 47:2;
50:3,9,41; 51:48; Ezk 26:7

16 When you multiply and increase in the land,*a* in those days — this is the LORD's declaration — no one will say again, "The ark of the LORD's covenant."*b* It will never come to mind, and no one will remember or miss it. Another one will not be made.*A* **17** At that time Jerusalem will be called The LORD's Throne,*c* and all the nations will be gathered to it,*d* to the name of the LORD in Jerusalem.*e* They will cease to follow the stubbornness of their evil hearts. **18** In those days the house of Judah will join with the house of Israel,*f* and they will come together from the land of the north to the land I have given your ancestors to inherit.'*g*

TRUE REPENTANCE

19 I thought, "How I long to make you
　　my sons
　and give you a desirable land,
　the most beautiful inheritance*h*
　　of all the nations."
I thought, "You will call me
　'My Father'
and never turn away from me."
20 However, as a woman may betray
　　her lover,*B*
so you have betrayed*i* me,
　house of Israel.
　This is the LORD's declaration.

21 A sound is heard
　　on the barren heights:
the children of Israel weeping
　and begging for mercy,
for they have perverted their way;
they have forgotten the LORD
　their God.*j*
22 Return, you faithless children.
I will heal your unfaithfulness.*k*
"Here we are, coming to you,
for you are the LORD our God.
23 Surely, falsehood comes
　　from the hills,
commotion from the mountains,*l*
but the salvation of Israel
is only in the LORD our God.*m*
24 From the time of our youth
the shameful one*C* has consumed
what our fathers
　　have worked for —
　their flocks and their herds,
　their sons and their daughters.

25 Let us lie down in our shame;
let our disgrace cover us.*n*
We have sinned against the LORD
　our God,*o*
both we and our fathers,
from the time of our youth
　even to this day.*p*
We have not obeyed the LORD
　our God."

BLESSING OR CURSE

4 If you return,*D* Israel —
　　this is the LORD's declaration —
you will return to me,*q*
if you remove your abhorrent idols*r*
　from my presence
　and do not waver,
2 then you can swear,
　"As the LORD lives,"*s*
in truth,*t* in justice,
　and in righteousness,*u*
then the nations will be blessed*E*
　by him*v*
and will pride themselves in him.*w*

3 For this is what the LORD says to the men of Judah and Jerusalem:
Break up the unplowed ground;*x*
do not sow among the thorns.*y*
4 Circumcise yourselves to the LORD;
remove the foreskin
　of your hearts,*z*
men of Judah and residents
　of Jerusalem.
Otherwise, my wrath will break out
　like fire
and burn with no one
　to extinguish it*aa*
because of your evil deeds.

JUDGMENT FROM THE NORTH

5 Declare in Judah, proclaim in Jerusalem, and say:
Blow the ram's horn
　throughout the land.*ab*
Cry out loudly and say:
Assemble yourselves,
and let's flee to the fortified cities.
6 Lift up a signal flag toward Zion.*ac*
Run for cover! Don't stand still!
For I am bringing disaster
　from the north —
a crushing blow.*ad*

A 3:16 Or *It will no longer be done*　*B* 3:20 Lit *friend*　*C* 3:24 = Baal　*D* 4:1 Or *Repent*　*E* 4:2 Or *will bless themselves*

4:4 While the Jews were circumcised in body, they were not set apart in their **hearts**.
4:5-9 Judah refused to heed warning, so here God makes it clear that he is using Babylon to accomplish his purposes: **I am bringing**

disaster from the north (4:6). The picture he paints of the coming invasion leaves no doubt about the terror in store for Judah. The leaders from every sphere, who should have led the people to the Lord, will be incapable

of leading (4:9). This is a perfect illustration of the chaos that ensues when a nation's leaders are not following God's kingdom agenda.

7 A lion has gone up
 from his thicket;[a]
a destroyer of nations has set out.
He has left his lair
to make your land a waste.
Your cities will be reduced
 to uninhabited ruins.[b]
8 Because of this, put on sackcloth;
mourn and wail,[c]
for the LORD's burning anger[d]
has not turned away from us.

9 "On that day" — this is the LORD's declaration — "the king and the officials will lose their courage. The priests will tremble in fear, and the prophets will be scared speechless."
10 I said, "Oh no, Lord GOD, you have certainly deceived[e] this people and Jerusalem, by announcing, 'You will have peace,'[f] while a sword is at[A] our throats."
11 "At that time it will be said to this people and to Jerusalem, 'A searing wind[g] blows from the barren heights in the wilderness on the way to my dear[B] people. It comes not to winnow or to sift; [C] a wind too strong for this comes at my call.[C] Now I will also pronounce judgments against them.'"[h]
13 Look, he advances like clouds;[i]
his chariots are like a storm.[j]
 His horses are swifter than eagles.[k]
Woe to us, for we are ruined![l]
14 Wash the evil
 from your heart,[m] Jerusalem,
so that you will be delivered.
How long will you harbor
malicious thoughts?[n]
15 For a voice announces from Dan,
proclaiming malice
 from Mount Ephraim.
16 Warn the nations: Look!
Proclaim to Jerusalem:
Those who besiege are coming
from a distant land;[o]
they raise their voices
against the cities of Judah.
17 They have her surrounded[p]
like those who guard a field,

because she has rebelled against me.[q]
 This is the LORD's declaration.
18 Your way and your actions
have brought this on you.[r]
This is your punishment. It is
 very bitter,
because it has reached your heart!

JEREMIAH'S LAMENT

19 My anguish, my anguish![D] I writhe
 in agony!
Oh, the pain in[E] my heart![s]
My heart pounds;
I cannot be silent.
For you, my soul,
have heard the sound
 of the ram's horn —
the shout of battle.
20 Disaster after disaster[t] is reported
because the whole land is destroyed.
Suddenly my tents are destroyed,
my tent curtains, in a moment.
21 How long must I see the signal flag
and hear the sound
 of the ram's horn?

22 "For my people are fools;
they do not know me.
They are foolish children,
without understanding.[u]
They are skilled in doing what is evil,
but they do not know how to do
 what is good."[v]

23 I looked at the earth,
and it was formless and empty.[w]
I looked to the heavens,
and their light was gone.[x]
24 I looked at the mountains,
and they were quaking;[y]
all the hills shook.
25 I looked, and there was no human
 being,[z]
and all the birds of the sky had fled.[aa]
26 I looked, and the fertile field[ab] was
 a wilderness.[ac]
All its cities were torn down
because of the LORD
 and his burning anger.[ad]

[a] 4:7 Ps 10:9; 17:12; Is 5:29; Jr 2:15; 5:6; 25:38; 49:19; 50:17,44
[b] Is 1:7; 6:11
[c] 4:8 Jl 1:13
[d] Nm 25:4; Ps 78:49
[e] 4:10 1Kg 22:22; Ezk 14:9; 2Th 2:11
[f] Jr 6:14; 23:17
[g] 4:11 Ezk 17:10
[h] 4:12 Jr 1:16; Ezk 5:8
[i] 4:13 Rv 1:7
[j] Is 5:28; 66:15
[k] 2Sm 1:23; Jb 9:26; Lm 4:19
[l] Lm 5:16
[m] 4:14 Ps 51:2,7; Is 1:16; Jr 2:22; Ti 3:5; Jms 4:8
[n] Ps 119:113
[o] 4:16 Is 39:3
[p] 4:17 2Kg 25:1-4

[q] 4:17 Is 1:20
[r] 4:18 Ps 107:17; Pr 1:31; Jr 7:3,5; 17:10; 18:11; 23:22; 25:5; 26:3,13; 32:19; Hs 4:9; 12:2; Zch 1:4,6
[s] 4:19 Is 16:11; Hab 3:16; Rm 9:1-2
[t] 4:20 Ezk 7:26
[u] 4:22 Ps 82:5; Is 1:3
[v] Rm 16:19
[w] 4:23 Gn 1:2; Jb 26:7; Is 45:18
[x] Is 5:30; 13:10
[y] 4:24 Jdg 5:5; Ps 46:1-3
[z] 4:25 Gn 2:5
[aa] Zph 1:3
[ab] 4:26 Jr 2:7
[ac] Ps 107:34
[ad] Ps 76:7

[A] 4:10 Lit *sword touches* [B] 4:11 Lit *to the daughter of my* [C] 4:12 Lit *comes for me* [D] 4:19 Lit *My inner parts, my inner parts* [E] 4:19 Lit *the walls of*

4:10 This is Jeremiah's complaint that God had *allowed* the false prophets of Judah to prophesy peace and prosperity when catastrophe was at the door. But we need to remember that God does not deceive or lie. His apparent deception only comes to people who have already welcomed deception and refuse to repent. God's hard work of judgment in this case was a confirming act to the hardhearted, not a con of the innocent.

4:11-13 The Babylonian army would sweep across the land like the harsh desert **wind**, which blew so hard that it parched and cracked the ground (4:11). The advancing horses and chariots of Nebuchadnezzar's hordes would stir up dust **clouds** (4:13).
4:22 The people had become experts at wickedness and novices at righteousness. This is the exact opposite of God's will for his **children**, as Paul writes: "I want you to be wise about

what is good, and yet innocent about what is evil" (Rom 16:19).
4:23-26 Jeremiah describes **the earth** as **formless and empty** (4:23) to compare Judah's situation to the condition of the world before God began shaping and filling it (see Gen 1:2). All that remained was a **wilderness** because of his **burning anger** (Jer 4:26). Creation was being undone.

[a] 4:27 Is 6:11
[b] Neh 9:31; Jr 5:10,18; Rm 11:1-7
[c] 4:28 Jr 8:13; 14:2; Hs 4:3
[d] Ps 105:28; Is 13:10; 50:3; Ezk 30:18
[e] Nm 23:19; Is 46:11; 48:15; Ezk 37:14
[f] 4:29 2Kg 25:4
[g] Is 2:19-21
[h] 4:30 Is 10:3
[i] 2Kg 9:30
[j] Jr 30:14; Lm 1:19
[k] Ezk 23:9-10,22
[l] 4:31 Ps 48:6; Is 13:8; 21:3; 42:14; Jr 6:24; 13:21; 22:23; 30:6; 50:43; Mc 4:9-10; 1Th 5:3
[m] Is 1:15
[n] 5:1 2Ch 16:9
[o] Ps 14:1-3; Ezk 22:30; Rm 3:10
[p] Gn 18:26-32
[q] 5:2 Jr 4:2
[r] Lv 19:12; Is 48:1; Jr 7:9
[s] 5:3 2Ch 16:9; Ps 51:6
[t] Pr 23:35

[u] 5:3 Pr 27:22
[v] Ezk 3:7-9
[w] Hs 11:5
[x] 5:4 Gn 18:19; 2Kg 17:26; 21:22; Ps 95:10; Jr 8:7; Hs 4:6
[y] Mc 3:1
[z] 5:5 Ps 103:7
[aa] Ps 2:3; Jr 2:20
[ab] 5:6 2Kg 17:26; Jr 4:7; 25:38
[ac] Hs 13:7; Rv 13:2
[ad] Is 59:12
[ae] Jr 3:6,8,11-12,22; 14:7; 30:15; Am 5:12
[af] 5:7 Dt 32:21; Jos 23:7; Gl 4:8
[ag] Hs 4:10
[ah] 1Kg 18:24
[ai] 5:8 Ezk 23:20
[aj] Jr 13:27
[ak] Ex 20:14; Ezk 22:11
[al] 5:9 Jr 5:29; 8:10; 9:9
[am] Dt 32:35; Heb 10:30
[an] 5:10 2Kg 24:2
[ao] Jr 4:27

27 For this is what the LORD says:
The whole land will be a desolation,[a]
but I will not finish it off.[b]
28 Because of this, the earth will mourn;[c]
the skies above will grow dark.[d]
I have spoken; I have planned,
and I will not relent or turn back
from it.[e]

29 Every city flees[f]
at the sound of the horseman
and the archer.
They enter the thickets
and climb among the rocks.[g]
Every city is abandoned;
no inhabitant is left.
30 And you, devastated one, what are
you doing[h]
that you dress yourself in scarlet,
that you adorn yourself
with gold jewelry,
that you enhance your eyes
with makeup?[i]
You beautify yourself for nothing.
Your lovers reject you;[j]
they intend to take your life.[k]
31 I hear a cry like a woman in labor,[l]
a cry of anguish like one bearing
her first child.
The cry of Daughter Zion
gasping for breath,
stretching out her hands:[m]
"Woe is me, for my life is weary
because of the murderers!"

THE DEPRAVITY OF JERUSALEM

5 Roam[n] through the streets
of Jerusalem.
Investigate;[A]
search in her squares.
If you find one person,[o]
any who acts justly,
who pursues faithfulness,
then I will forgive her.[p]
2 When they say, "As the LORD lives,"[q]
they are swearing falsely.[r]
3 LORD, don't your eyes
look for faithfulness?[s]
You have struck them, but they felt
no pain.[t]

You finished them off,
but they refused to accept discipline.[u]
They made their faces harder
than rock,[v]
and they refused to return.[w]

4 Then I thought:
They are just the poor;
they have been foolish.
For they don't understand the way
of the LORD,[x]
the justice of their God.[y]
5 I will go to the powerful
and speak to them.
Surely they know the way of the LORD,
the justice of their God.[z]
However, these also had broken
the yoke
and torn off the chains.[aa]
6 Therefore, a lion from the forest
will strike them down.[ab]
A wolf from arid plains
will ravage them.
A leopard[ac] stalks their cities.
Anyone who leaves them
will be torn to pieces
because their rebellious acts
are many,[ad]
their unfaithful deeds numerous.[ae]

7 Why should I forgive you?
Your children have abandoned me
and sworn by those who are
not gods.[af]
I satisfied their needs, yet they
committed adultery;[ag]
they gashed themselves[ah]
at the[B] prostitute's house.
8 They are well-fed,[C] eager[D] stallions,[ai]
each neighing[aj] after
someone else's wife.[ak]
9 Should I not punish them
for these things?[al]
This is the LORD's declaration.
Should I not avenge myself[am]
on such a nation as this?

10 Go up among her vineyard terraces
and destroy them,[an]
but do not finish them off.[ao]

[A] 5:1 Lit See and know   [B] 5:7 Or adultery and trooped to the, or adultery and lodged at the; Hb obscure   [C] 5:8 Lit well-equipped; Hb obscure
[D] 5:8 Lit early-rising; Hb obscure

4:27 Knowing the grief of his prophet, God graciously promises a future hope.
4:31 Like a woman in labor, Judah would cry in anguish when the murderous Babylonians got hold of her. Normally the cries of a woman about to give birth signal that there is joy ahead, but Judah's labor would end in a spiritual miscarriage.

5:1 The Lord gives Jeremiah what would seem like an easy assignment: If you find one person, any who acts justly, who pursues faithfulness, then I will forgive Jerusalem. Now, that's a better deal than God granted to Abraham, who received God's promise that Sodom wouldn't be destroyed if there were ten righteous people in it (see Gen 18:32). But Jeremiah

couldn't dig up even one person in the streets of Jerusalem who followed the Lord. The holy city, then, was worse than Sodom!
5:10-11 The house of Israel and the house of Judah were God's vineyard (see Isa 5:1-7), but the people had become so unfaithful that God decrees its branches are to be cut back severely.

Prune away her shoots,
for they do not belong to the LORD.[a]
11 They, the house of Israel
and the house of Judah,
have dealt very treacherously
with me.[b]
This is the LORD's declaration.
12 They have contradicted the LORD
and insisted, "It won't happen.[A,c]
Harm won't come to us;
we won't see sword or famine."
13 The prophets become only wind,
for the LORD's word is not in them.
This will in fact happen to them.

COMING JUDGMENT

14 Therefore, this is what the Lord GOD of Armies says:

Because you have spoken
this word,
I am going to make my words
become fire in your mouth.[d]
These people are the wood,
and the fire will consume them.[e]
15 I am about to bring a nation
from far away against you,[f]
house of Israel.
This is the LORD's declaration.
It is an established nation,
an ancient nation,
a nation whose language
you do not know
and whose speech
you do not understand.[g]
16 Their quiver is like an open grave;[h]
they are all warriors.
17 They will consume your harvest
and your food.[i]
They will consume your sons
and your daughters.
They will consume your flocks
and your herds.
They will consume your vines
and your fig trees.
With the sword they will destroy
your fortified cities[j] in which
you trust.

18 "But even in those days" — this is the LORD's declaration — "I will not finish you off.[k] 19 When people ask, 'For what offense has the LORD our God done all these things to us?' You will respond to them, 'Just as you abandoned me[l] and served foreign gods in your land, so will you serve strangers in a land that is not yours.'[m]

20 "Declare this in the house of Jacob;
proclaim it in Judah, saying:
21 Hear this,
you foolish and senseless[B] people.[n]
They have eyes, but they don't see.
They have ears, but they don't hear.[o]
22 Do you not fear me?
This is the LORD's declaration.
Do you not tremble before me,
the one who set the sand
as the boundary of the sea,
an enduring barrier that
it cannot cross?[p]
The waves surge, but they
cannot prevail.
They roar but cannot pass over it.
23 But these people have stubborn
and rebellious hearts.[q]
They have turned aside
and have gone away.
24 They have not said to themselves,
'Let's fear the LORD our God,[r]
who gives the seasonal rains,
both autumn and spring,[s]
who guarantees to us
the fixed weeks of the harvest.'
25 Your guilty acts have diverted
these things from you.
Your sins have withheld my bounty
from you,[t]
26 for wicked men live among my people.
They watch like hunters[c]
lying in wait.[D,u]
They set a trap;[v]
they catch men.
27 Like a cage full of birds,
so their houses are full of deceit.[w]
Therefore they have grown powerful
and rich.
28 They have become fat[x] and sleek.
They have also excelled
in evil matters.
They have not taken up cases,
such as the case of the fatherless,
so they might prosper,
and they have not defended
the rights of the needy.[y]
29 Should I not punish them
for these things?
This is the LORD's declaration.
Should I not avenge myself[z]
on such a nation as this?

[a] 5:10 Hs 1:9
[b] 5:11 Is 21:2; 24:16; 48:8; Hs 6:7
[c] 5:12 Is 28:15; Jr 23:17
[d] 5:14 Hs 6:5; Rv 11:5
[e] Zch 12:6
[f] 5:15 Is 10:3; 13:5; 30:27; Jr 4:16
[g] Dt 28:49; Is 28:11; 33:19; 1Co 14:21
[h] 5:16 Ps 5:9; Rm 3:13
[i] 5:17 Lv 26:16; Dt 28:31,33,51
[j] Hs 8:14
[k] 5:18 2Ch 12:12; Jr 4:27; 5:10; 30:11; Ezk 11:13; 20:17; Rm 11:1-5
[l] 5:19 Dt 28:20; 29:24-25; 31:16; Jdg 2:12; 1Sm 8:8; 1Kg 9:8-9; Is 1:4,28; Jr 1:16; 2:13,17,19; 16:11; 17:13
[m] 5:19 Dt 4:27-28; 28:47-48
[n] 5:21 Dt 32:6
[o] Ps 115:5-6; 135:16-17; Is 6:9; 42:20; Ezk 12:2; Mt 13:14; Mk 8:18
[p] 5:22 Jb 26:10; 38:10-11; Ps 104:9; Pr 8:29
[q] 5:23 Dt 21:18,20; Ps 78:8; Is 1:5; Heb 3:12
[r] 5:24 Pr 9:10; Hs 6:1
[s] Dt 11:14; Jl 2:23; Mt 5:45
[t] 5:25 Is 59:2
[u] 5:26 Pr 1:11
[v] Ps 10:9
[w] 5:27 Ps 10:7; 50:19; Is 3:14; 5:18; 30:12; Jr 8:5; Zph 1:9; Ac 13:10; Rm 1:29
[x] 5:28 Dt 32:15
[y] Dt 24:14; Jb 29:16; 30:25; 31:19; Ps 82:3-4; 140:12; Pr 14:31; 31:9; Is 1:23; Zch 7:10; Ac 4:34
[z] 5:29 Jr 5:9; 8:19; Heb 10:30

[A] 5:12 Lit "He does not exist"   [B] 5:21 Lit without heart   [C] 5:26 Lit hunters of birds   [D] 5:26 Hb obscure

5:12-13 The false **prophets** gave the people false hope. Nevertheless, the Babylonian army was going to destroy everyone and everything in Judah.

5:19 **You abandoned me and served foreign gods in your land.** If you choose to serve the devil, God will let you do it. But it won't provide the pleasure and freedom you're expecting.

5:22 To **fear** the Lord is to take him seriously. 5:31 A culture cannot long stand when worship has become corrupted and the worshipers love the corruption.

[a] 5:30 Hs 6:10
[b] 5:31 Jr 6:13; 8:10; 14:14;
20:6; 23:14,25–26,32;
27:10,14–16; 28:15;
29:9,21,31; Lm 2:14;
Zch 13:3
[c] Dt 32:29; Is 10:3
[d] 6:1 Ex 9:19; Is 10:31; Jr 4:6
[e] Jr 4:5; 51:27; Am 3:6
[f] 2Sm 14:2; 2Ch 11:6; 20:20
[g] Jdg 20:38,40; Neh 3:14
[h] Jr 1:13; 4:6,20; 6:22; 15:12;
47:2; 50:3,9,41; 51:48
[i] 6:3 Jr 4:17
[j] 6:4 Jr 51:27; Mc 3:5
[k] 6:6 Dt 20:19–20
[l] Is 30:12; 59:9–15; Jr 22:17;
Ezk 22:7,12,29; Am 3:9;
Hab 1:3
[m] 6:7 Jr 20:8; Am 3:10;
Hab 1:3
[n] 6:8 Ezk 23:18; Hs 9:12
[o] Jr 9:11; 25:9; 29:18; 34:22;
Ezk 30:12

[p] 6:9 Is 10:20; Jr 31:7;
Ezk 9:8; 11:13; Mc 2:12;
Zph 3:13
[q] 6:10 Lv 26:41; Jr 9:26;
Ezk 44:7,9
[r] 1Sm 15:23; Jr 8:9
[s] 6:11 Jr 20:9; Hs 5:10
[t] Jr 9:21
[u] 6:12 Jr 8:10–12
[v] Ex 3:20; Jr 15:6; Ezk 6:14;
14:13; 25:7; Zph 1:4
[w] 6:13 Est 1:20; Jr 8:10;
31:34; 42:1,8; 44:12
[x] Pr 1:19; 15:27; Hab 2:9
[y] Jr 5:31; 8:10; 14:14; 20:6;
23:14,25–26,32; 27:10,14–
16; 28:15; 29:9,21,31; Lm
2:14; Zch 13:3
[z] 6:14 1Ch 12:18; Is 57:19
[aa] 6:15 Jr 3:3; 8:12

30 An appalling, horrible thing
   has taken place in the land.[a]
31 The prophets prophesy falsely,[b]
   and the priests rule
     by their own authority.
   My people love it like this.
   But what will you do at the end
     of it?[c]

THREATENED SIEGE OF JERUSALEM

6 "Run for cover[d]
   out of Jerusalem, Benjaminites.
   Sound the ram's horn[e] in Tekoa;[f]
   raise a smoke signal[g]
     over Beth-haccherem,[A]
   for disaster threatens
     from the north,[h]
   even a crushing blow.
2 Though she is beautiful
     and delicate,
   I will destroy[B] Daughter Zion.
3 Shepherds and their flocks
     will come against her;
   they will pitch their tents
     all around her.[i]
   Each will pasture his own portion.
4 Set them apart for war[j]
     against her;
   rise up, let's attack at noon.
   Woe to us, for the day is passing;
     the evening shadows grow long.
5 Rise up, let's attack by night.
   Let us destroy her fortresses."

6 For this is what the LORD of Armies says:
   Cut down the trees;[k]
   raise a siege ramp
     against Jerusalem.
   This city must be punished.
   There is nothing but oppression
     within her.[l]
7 As a well gushes out its water,
   so she pours out her evil.[c]
   Violence and destruction[m] resound
     in her.
   Sickness and wounds keep coming
     to my attention.
8 Be warned, Jerusalem,
   or I will turn away from you;[n]
   I will make you a desolation,
   a land without inhabitants.[o]

WRATH ON ISRAEL

9 This is what the LORD of Armies says:
   Glean the remnant of Israel[p]
     as thoroughly as a vine.
   Pass your hand once more
     like a grape gatherer
     over the branches.

10 Who can I speak to and give
     such a warning[D]
   that they will listen?
   Look, their ear is uncircumcised,[E,q]
   so they cannot pay attention.
   See, the word of the LORD
     has become contemptible
     to them —
   they find no pleasure in it.[r]
11 But I am full of the LORD's wrath;
   I am tired of holding it back.[s]
   Pour it out on the children
     in the street,[t]
   on the gathering of young men
     as well.
   For both husband and wife
     will be captured,
   the old with the very old.[F]
12 Their houses will be turned over
     to others,[u]
   their fields and wives as well,
   for I will stretch out my hand[v]
   against the inhabitants
     of the land.
   This is the LORD's declaration.
13 For from the least to the greatest
     of them,[w]
   everyone is making
     profit dishonestly.[x]
   From prophet to priest,
   everyone deals falsely.[y]
14 They have treated my people's
     brokenness superficially,
   claiming, "Peace, peace,"[z]
   when there is no peace.
15 Were they ashamed when they acted
     so detestably?
   They weren't at all ashamed.
   They can no longer
     feel humiliation.[aa]
   Therefore, they will fall
     among the fallen.

[A] 6:1 = House of the Vineyard   [B] 6:2 Or silence   [C] 6:7 Or well keeps its water fresh, so she keeps her evil fresh   [D] 6:10 Or and bear witness   [E] 6:10 They are unresponsive to God.   [F] 6:11 Lit with fullness of days

---

6:1-12 Fearsome judgment was so sure that the only hope of escape was to get **out of Jerusalem** (6:1), which meant running into the arms of the Babylonians. Jeremiah would eventually tell King Zedekiah to do just that, in fact—surrender to the Babylonians so that

they might survive (38:17-18). But the king and the people would refuse to listen: **the word of the LORD** had **become contemptible to them** (6:10). They hated God's word, and in rejecting it, they'd run headlong into his **wrath** (6:11).

6:13-14 Those responsible to proclaim God's word and offer sacrifices for sins were leading the way in wickedness! In **claiming, "Peace, peace," when there is no peace** (6:14) they had abdicated their responsibilities and were sugarcoating Judah's situation.

When I punish them,
   they will collapse,[a]
says the LORD.

DISASTER BECAUSE OF DISOBEDIENCE

16 This is what the LORD says:
   Stand by the roadways and look.
   Ask about the ancient paths,[b]
   "Which is the way to what is good?"
   Then take it
   and find rest for yourselves.[c]
   But they protested, "We won't!"
17 I appointed watchmen over you[d]
   and said, "Listen for the sound
     of the ram's horn."
   But they protested, "We won't listen!"

18 Therefore listen, you nations
   and you witnesses,
   learn what the charge is
     against them.
19 Listen, earth!
   I am about to bring disaster
     on these people,
   the fruit of their own plotting,[e]
   for they have paid no attention
     to my words.
   They have rejected my instruction.[f]
20 What use to me is frankincense
     from Sheba[g]
   or sweet cane[h] from a distant land?
   Your burnt offerings
     are not acceptable;
   your sacrifices do not please me.[i]
21 Therefore, this is what
     the LORD says:
   I am going to place stumbling blocks
     before these people;
   fathers and sons together
     will stumble over them;[j]
   friends and neighbors
     will also perish.

A CRUEL NATION FROM THE NORTH

22 This is what the LORD says:
   Look,[k] an army is coming
     from a northern land;[l]
   a great nation will be stirred up
     from the remote regions
     of the earth.[m]
23 They grasp bow and javelin.
   They are cruel and show no mercy.[n]

Their voice roars like the sea,[o]
   and they ride on horses,
   lined up like men in battle formation
     against you, Daughter Zion.

24 We have heard about it,
   and our hands have become weak.
   Distress has seized us —
   pain, like a woman in labor.[p]
25 Don't go out to the fields;
   don't walk on the road.
   For the enemy has a sword;
   terror is on every side.[q]

26 My dear[A] people, dress yourselves
     in sackcloth
   and roll in the dust.[r]
   Mourn as you would for an only son,[s]
   a bitter lament,
   for suddenly the destroyer[t]
     will come on us.[u]

JEREMIAH APPOINTED AS AN EXAMINER

27 I have appointed you to be
     an assayer among my people —
   a refiner[B] —
   so you may know and assay
     their way of life.[v]
28 All are stubborn rebels
     spreading slander.[w]
   They are bronze and iron;
   all of them are corrupt.[x]
29 The bellows blow,
   blasting the lead with fire.
   The refining is completely in vain;
   the evil ones are not separated out.
30 They are called rejected silver,
   for the LORD has rejected them.[y]

FALSE TRUST IN THE TEMPLE

7 This is the word that came to Jeremiah from the LORD: **2** "Stand in the gate of the house of the LORD[z] and there call out this word: 'Hear the word of the LORD, all you people of Judah who enter through these gates to worship the LORD. **3** "This is what the LORD of Armies, the God of Israel, says: Correct your ways and your actions,[aa] and I will allow you to live in this place. **4** Do not trust deceitful words, chanting, "This is the temple of the LORD, the temple of the LORD, the temple of the LORD.""

---

[a] **6:13-15** Jr 8:10-12
[b] **6:16** Is 59:8; Jr 18:15; Jb 24:13; Pr 8:20; 12:28
[c] Mt 11:29
[d] **6:17** Is 21:11; 58:1; Hs 9:8
[e] **6:19** Pr 1:31
[f] Is 5:24; Jr 23:17
[g] **6:20** 1Kg 10:1; Is 60:6
[h] Ex 30:23; Is 43:24; Ezk 27:19
[i] Ps 40:6; Is 1:11; 43:23; 66:3; Hs 9:4; Am 5:21; Mc 6:6; Mal 1:10
[j] **6:21** Is 8:15; Jr 31:9; Ezk 7:19
[k] **6:22-24** Jr 50:41-43
[l] Jr 50:41-43
[m] **6:22** Jr 25:32; 31:8
[n] **6:23** Is 13:18; Jr 50:42; Hab 1:6-17
[o] **6:23** Is 5:30; 17:12
[p] **6:24** Ps 48:6; Is 13:8; 21:3; 42:14; Jr 4:31; 13:21; 22:23; 30:6; 50:43; Mc 4:9-10; 1Th 5:3
[q] **6:25** Ps 31:13; Jr 20:3,10; 49:29
[r] **6:26** Jr 25:34; Ezk 27:30; Mc 1:10
[s] Am 8:10
[t] Ex 12:23; Is 21:2; 54:16; Jr 48:8,15,18,32; 1Co 10:10; Heb 11:28
[u] Is 47:11; Jr 4:20; 15:8
[v] **6:27** 1Ch 29:17; Ps 7:9; Pr 17:3
[w] **6:28** Lv 19:16; Pr 11:13; 20:19; Is 1:23
[x] 2Ch 27:2; Is 1:4
[y] **6:30** 1Sm 15:23,26; Jr 2:37; 7:29
[z] **7:2** Jr 26:2
[aa] **7:3** Jr 4:18; 18:11; 26:13

[A] **6:26** Lit *Daughter of my*   [B] **6:27** Text emended; MT reads *fortress*

6:19-20 As the prophet Samuel had told Israel's first king years before, "To obey is better than sacrifice" (1 Sam 15:22), because when offered from sin-stained hands, offerings to the Lord are detestable.

6:30 God's people **are called rejected silver** because they had become corrupted with impurities and could no longer be refined. **7:4** Judah vainly assumed that the mere presence of the temple in their nation would keep

them safe from judgment. They even chanted about **the temple of the LORD**, showing that it was little more than a good luck charm to them.

a 7:5 Jr 22:3
b 7:6 Dt 19:10,13; 21:8-9;
2Kg 21:16; 24:4; Jr 22:3,17;
26:15; Mt 27:4
c 7:7 Gn 12:7; Jos 1:2;
Jr 30:3
d 7:9 Ex 20:3-17; Lv 19:11-
12; Dt 5:7-21; Ezk 18:5-
9,14-18; 22:6-12; Hs 4:2
e 7:10 Jr 32:34
f 7:11 Is 56:7; Mt 21:13; Mk
11:17; Lk 19:46
g 7:11 Ps 33:13-15; Ezk 8:12;
Am 9:1-4
h 7:12 Dt 12:11; 14:23;
16:6,11
i 7:13 Jr 7:25; 11:7; 25:3;
26:5; 29:19; 32:33; 35:14-
15; 44:4
j Pr 1:24; Is 65:12
k 7:14 Dt 12:5; 1Kg 9:7;
Mk 13:2
l 7:15 Dt 29:28; 2Kg 17
m 7:16 Jr 11:14; 14:11-12; 15:1
n Gn 23:8; Ru 1:16; Jr 27:18
o Ex 32:11-13,20-34; Jr
14:11; 15:1

p 7:18 Jr 44:17-19,25
q 7:19 Jb 35:6
r 7:20 Jr 42:18; Lm 4:11
s Nah 1:6
t 7:21 Dt 12:4-28; Ps 50:13;
Hs 8:13
u 7:22 Hs 6:6
v 7:23 Dt 5:33
w 7:24 Ps 81:11
x Jr 15:6
y 7:25 2Kg 9:7; 17:13; Jr
26:5; 29:19; 35:15; 44:4;
Ezk 38:17; Zch 1:6
z 2Ch 36:15-16; Jr 25:4
aa 7:26 Ex 32:9; Dt 9:6,13;
2Kg 17:14; Jr 17:23; 19:15
ab 1Kg 16:25; 2Kg 21:11

5 Instead, if you really correct your ways and your actions, if you act justly toward one another,[A,a] **6** if you no longer oppress the resident alien, the fatherless, and the widow[b] and no longer shed innocent blood in this place or follow other gods, bringing harm on yourselves, **7** I will allow you to live in this place, the land I gave to your ancestors[c] long ago and forever. **8** But look, you keep trusting in deceitful words that cannot help.

9 " 'Do you steal, murder, commit adultery, swear falsely, burn incense to Baal, and follow other gods that you have not known?[d] **10** Then do you come and stand before me in this house[e] that bears my name and say, "We are rescued, so we can continue doing all these detestable acts"? **11** Has this house, which bears my name, become a den of robbers[f] in your view? Yes, I too have seen it.[g]

This is the LORD's declaration.

SHILOH AS A WARNING

12 " 'But return to my place that was at Shiloh, where I made my name dwell at first.[h] See what I did to it because of the evil of my people Israel. **13** Now, because you have done all these things — this is the LORD's declaration — and because I have spoken to you time and time again[B] but you wouldn't listen,[i] and I have called to you, but you wouldn't answer,[j] **14** what I did to Shiloh I will do to the house that bears my name[k] — the house in which you trust — the place that I gave you and your ancestors. **15** I will banish you from my presence, just as I banished all of your brothers, all the descendants of Ephraim.'[l]

DO NOT PRAY FOR JUDAH

16 "As for you, do not pray for these people.[m] Do not offer a cry or a prayer on their behalf, and do not beg me,[n] for I will not listen to you.[o] **17** Don't you see how they behave in the cities of Judah and in the streets of Jerusalem? **18** The sons gather wood, the fathers light the fire, and the women knead dough to make cakes for the queen of heaven,[C,p] and they pour out drink offerings to other gods so that they provoke me to anger. **19** But are they really provoking me? " [q] This is the LORD's declaration. "Isn't it they themselves being provoked to disgrace?"

20 Therefore, this is what the Lord GOD says: "Look, my anger — my burning wrath — is about to be poured out on this place,[r] on people and animals, on the tree of the field, and on the produce of the land. My wrath will burn and not be quenched."[s]

OBEDIENCE OVER SACRIFICE

21 This is what the LORD of Armies, the God of Israel, says: "Add your burnt offerings to your other sacrifices, and eat the meat yourselves,[t] **22** for when I brought your ancestors out of the land of Egypt, I did not speak with them[u] or command them concerning burnt offering and sacrifice. **23** However, I did give them this command: 'Obey me, and then I will be your God, and you will be my people. Follow every way I command you so that it may go well with you.' [v] **24** Yet they didn't listen or pay attention[w] but followed their own advice and their own stubborn, evil heart. They went backward and not forward.[x] **25** Since the day your ancestors came out of the land of Egypt until today, I have sent all my servants the prophets[y] to you time and time again.[D,z] **26** However, my people wouldn't listen to me or pay attention but became obstinate;[E,aa] they did more evil than their ancestors.[ab]

A LAMENT FOR DISOBEDIENT JUDAH

27 "When you speak all these things to them, they will not listen to you. When you call to them, they will not answer you. **28** Therefore, declare to them, 'This is the nation that would not listen to the LORD their God and would not accept discipline. Truth[F] has perished — it has disappeared from their mouths. **29** Cut off the hair of

---

A 7:5 Lit *justly between a man and his neighbor*   B 7:13 Lit *you rising early and speaking*   C 7:18 = a pagan goddess   D 7:25 Lit *you, each day rising early and sending*   E 7:26 Lit *but stiffened their neck*   F 7:28 Or *Faithfulness*

7:9-11 They were like children playing tag, treating the temple like a base where they would be safe from harm. In essence, God's response was, "Are you serious? You think you can act like that and then come before me for blessing as if I don't know what you're doing?" Jesus took up Jeremiah's words against the people of Israel in his own day; they were also guilty of desecrating God's "house of prayer" (see Matt 21:13). **7:14-15** The Bible doesn't describe what eventually happened to Shiloh, which long housed

the tabernacle, but archaeological evidence suggests the Philistines destroyed it in about 1050 BC. The presence of the tabernacle, then, did not save Shiloh from God's judgment. What happened there, in fact, would happen again in Jeremiah's day: **what I did to Shiloh I will do to the house that bears my name** (7:14). And as he had **banished . . . the descendants of Ephraim** (that is, Israel) through the Assyrians, so God would banish Judah through the Babylonians (7:15).

7:18 **The queen of heaven** was probably the Assyrian-Babylonian goddess Ishtar who represented love and fertility. **7:22-24** The idolatry of God's people was nothing new. All the way back to the exodus from Egypt and their birth as a nation, Israel had been rebellious and stubborn. God had given them one basic command: **Obey me, and then I will be your God, and you will be my people** (7:23). Yet they **followed their own advice** (7:24).

your sacred vow[A,a] and throw it away. Raise up a dirge on the barren heights,[b] for the LORD has rejected and abandoned the generation under his wrath.' [c]

[30] "For the Judeans have done what is evil in my sight." This is the LORD's declaration. "They have set up their abhorrent things[d] in the house that bears my name in order to defile it.[e] [31] They have built the high places of Topheth[B,f] in Ben Hinnom Valley[C,g] in order to burn their sons and daughters in the fire,[h] a thing I did not command; I never entertained the thought.[D]

[32] "Therefore, look, the days are coming"[i] — the LORD's declaration — "when this place will no longer be called Topheth and Ben Hinnom Valley, but the Valley of Slaughter.[j] Topheth will become a cemetery,[E] because there will be no other burial place. [33] The corpses of these people will become food for the birds of the sky and for the wild animals of the land, with no one to scare them away.[k] [34] I will remove from the cities of Judah and the streets of Jerusalem the sound of joy and gladness and the voices of the groom and the bride,[l] for the land will become a desolate waste.[m]

DEATH OVER LIFE

8 "At that time" — this is the LORD's declaration — "the bones of the kings of Judah, the bones of her officials, the bones of the priests, the bones of the prophets, and the bones of the residents of Jerusalem will be brought out of their graves.[n] [2] They will be exposed[o] to the sun, the moon, and all the stars in the sky,[p] which they have loved, served, followed, consulted, and worshiped. Their bones will not be collected and buried but will become like manure on the soil's surface.[q] [3] Death will be chosen over life[r] by all the survivors of this evil family, those who remain wherever I have banished them."[s] This is the declaration of the LORD of Armies.

[4] "You are to say to them: This is what the LORD says:

Do people fall and not get up again?[t]
If they turn away, do they
    not return?
[5] Why have these people
    turned away?

Why is Jerusalem always
    turning away?
They take hold of deceit;[u]
they refuse to return.[v]
[6] I have paid careful attention.
They do not speak what is right.
No one regrets his evil,
asking, 'What have I done?'
Everyone has stayed his course
like a horse rushing into battle.[w]
[7] Even storks in the sky
know their seasons.
Turtledoves, swallows, and cranes[F]
are aware of their migration,
but my people do not know
the requirements of the LORD.[x]

PUNISHMENT FOR JUDAH'S LEADERS

[8] "How can you claim, 'We are wise;
the law of the LORD is with us'?
In fact, the lying pen of scribes[y]
has produced falsehood.
[9] The wise will be put to shame;
they will be dismayed and snared.
They have rejected the word
    of the LORD,[z]
so what wisdom do they really have?
[10] Therefore, I will give[aa] their wives
    to other men,
their fields to new occupants,
for from the least to the greatest,[ab]
everyone is making
    profit dishonestly.
From prophet to priest,
everyone deals falsely.
[11] They have treated the brokenness
of my dear[G] people superficially,
claiming, 'Peace, peace,'
when there is no peace.
[12] Were they ashamed when they acted
    so detestably?
They weren't at all ashamed.
They can no longer feel humiliation.
Therefore, they will fall
    among the fallen.
When I punish them,
    they will collapse,"[ac]
says the LORD.

[13] I will gather them and bring them
    to an end.[H,ad]
This is the LORD's declaration.

[a] 7:29 Nm 6:1-8
[b] 7:29 Jr 3:2,21
[c] Is 2:6
[d] 7:30 Jr 4:1; 16:18; 32:34
[e] 2Kg 23:24
[f] 7:31 2Kg 23:10; Jr 19:6,11-14
[g] Jos 15:8; Jr 19:5; 32:35
[h] Lv 18:21; Dt 12:31; 2Kg 17:17,31; 2Ch 28:3; Jr 19:5; Ezk 16:21; 20:31; 23:25,37,47
[i] 7:32 Jr 16:14; 19:6; 23:5; 48:12; 49:2; 51:47,52
[j] Jr 19:6
[k] 7:33 Dt 28:26; Ps 79:2; Jr 16:4; 19:7; 34:20; Ezk 29:5
[l] 7:34 Jr 16:9; 25:10; 33:11
[m] Lv 26:31,33; Is 64:11; Jr 25:9,11,18; 27:17; 44:2,6,22
[n] 8:1 Jdg 9:37; 23:16; Am 2:1
[o] 8:2 2Sm 21:12-14; Ps 53:5; Ezk 6:5
[p] Dt 4:19; 2Kg 17:16; 21:3; 23:4-5; Ezk 8:16
[q] Ps 83:10; Jr 9:22; 16:4; 25:33
[r] 8:3 Dt 30:11-20; Jb 3:21-22; 7:15-16; Rv 9:6
[s] Jr 23:3,8; 29:14,18; 32:37; Dn 9:7
[t] 8:4 Is 24:20; Jr 25:27; Am 5:2
[u] 8:5 Jr 14:14; 23:26; Zph 3:13
[v] Jr 5:3; Hs 11:5
[w] 8:6 Jb 39:19-25
[x] 8:7 Jb 19:24; Ps 95:10; Is 1:3; Jr 4:22; 5:4
[y] 8:8 Jb 19:24; Ps 45:1; Jr 17:1
[z] 8:9 1Sm 15:23,26
[aa] 8:10-12 Jr 6:13-15
[ab] 8:10 Est 1:20; Jr 6:13; 31:34; 42:1,8; 44:12
[ac] 8:12 Jr 10:15; 49:8; 51:18
[ad] 8:13 Zph 1:2

[A] 7:29 Lit off your consecration   [B] 7:31 Lit of the fireplace   [C] 7:31 A valley south of Jerusalem   [D] 7:31 Lit command, and it did not arise on my heart   [E] 7:32 Lit They will bury in Topheth   [F] 8:7 Hb obscure   [G] 8:11 Lit of the daughter of my, also in vv. 19,21,22   [H] 8:13 Lit Gathering I will end them

7:31 Such horrific crimes against children would not go unpunished.
8:1-3 God's judgment on Judah would be so complete that even the dead wouldn't escape (8:1-2). Things wouldn't be any better for the living, who would prefer **death** to life as captives (8:3).
8:7 Even birds know where to go during various seasons, but the people of Judah had no sense to turn around when they had gone the wrong way. They even lacked the sense to repent of their evil.
8:8 God pointed to the false security of those who thought they were **wise** simply because they had his **law**.

a 8:14 2Kg 7:3-4; Jr 9:15;
21:8-9
b Is 64:5; Jr 3:25; 14:7,20;
Lm 3:42; 5:16; Dn 9:5
c 8:15 Jr 14:19; 33:9
d 8:16 Jdg 5:22; Jr 47:3;
50:11
e 8:17 Nm 21:6-9; Dt 32:24
f Ps 58:4-5; Ec 10:11
g 8:18 Lm 5:17
h 8:19 Ps 99:2; 102:21; Jr
14:9; Jl 3:17,21; Mc 3:11
i Dt 32:21; Jr 2:5

j 8:21 Jr 6:14; 8:11
k 8:22 Gn 37:25; Jr 46:11
l 9:1 Ps 42:3; Jr 13:17; Lm
2:11; Lk 19:41
m 9:2 1Kg 19:9-10
n Jr 23:10; Hs 7:4; Mal 3:5
o Is 24:16; 33:1; Jr 12:1
p 9:3 Jr 4:22
q 9:4 Gn 27:36
r Jr 6:28
s 9:5 Gn 31:7
t 9:6 Gn 27:35-36; 34:13
u Rm 1:17

There will be no grapes on the vine,
no figs on the fig tree,
and even the leaf will wither.
Whatever I have given them
will be lost to them.

GOD'S PEOPLE UNREPENTANT

14 Why are we just sitting here?
Gather together; let us enter
the fortified cities
and perish there,[A]
for the LORD our God
has destroyed[B] us.
He has given us poisoned water
to drink,[a]
because we have sinned
against the LORD.[b]

15 We hoped for peace, but there was
nothing good;
for a time of healing, but there was
only terror.[c]

16 From Dan, the snorting
of horses is heard.
At the sound of the neighing
of mighty steeds,[d]
the whole land quakes.
They come to devour the land
and everything in it,
the city and all its residents.

17 Indeed, I am about to send snakes
among you,
poisonous vipers[e] that cannot
be charmed.[f]
They will bite you.
This is the LORD's declaration.

LAMENT OVER JUDAH

18 My joy has flown away;
grief has settled on me.
My heart is sick.[g]

19 Listen — the cry of my dear people
from a faraway land,
"Is the LORD no longer in Zion,[h]
her King not within her?"
Why have they angered me
with their carved images,
with their worthless foreign idols?[i]

20 Harvest has passed,
summer has ended,
but we have not been saved.

21 I am broken by the brokenness
of my dear people.[j]
I mourn; horror has taken hold
of me.

22 Is there no balm in Gilead?[k]
Is there no physician there?
So why has the healing
of my dear people
not come about?

9 If my head were a flowing spring,
my eyes a fountain of tears,
I would weep day and night[l]
over the slain of my dear[c] people.

2 If only I had a traveler's
lodging place
in the wilderness,[m]
I would abandon my people
and depart from them,
for they are all adulterers,[n]
a solemn assembly
of treacherous people.[o]

3 They bent their tongues
like their bows;
lies and not faithfulness prevail
in the land,
for they proceed from one evil
to another,
and they do not take me
into account.[p]
This is the LORD's declaration.

IMMINENT RUIN AND EXILE

4 Everyone has to be on guard
against his friend.
Don't trust any brother,
for every brother will
certainly deceive,[q]
and every friend spread slander.[r]

5 Each one betrays his friend;[s]
no one tells the truth.
They have taught their tongues
to speak lies;
they wear themselves out
doing wrong.

6 You live in a world
of deception.[D,t]
In their deception they refuse
to know me.[u]
This is the LORD's declaration.

A 8:14 Or there be silenced   B 8:14 Or silenced   C 9:1 Lit slain among the daughter of my   D 9:6 LXX reads Oppression on oppression, deceit on deceit

8:14-16 The people would realize their sin and repent, but it would be too late when the sound of the Babylonians' **horses** coming **from Dan** in the north echoed (8:16).
8:22 Though their suffering was the result of their sin, Jeremiah longed for God to apply healing **balm** to their wounds. May the church of Jesus Christ have the same concern and compassion for the suffering among God's people.
9:1 Jeremiah's declaration here shows why he is known as "the weeping prophet."
9:2 Though he felt compassion for his people (see 9:1), Jeremiah wasn't oblivious to the reason for Judah's judgment. In fact, his righteous soul was offended by their sin, so much so that he wanted to get away from them. They were **a solemn assembly of treacherous** folks.
9:4-6 In a society where lying was commonplace, nobody could trust anyone—not even family.

7 Therefore, this is what the LORD of Armies says:

I am about to refine them
and test them,[a]
for what else can I do
because of my dear[A] people?[B]
8 Their tongues are deadly arrows —
they speak deception.[b]
With his mouth
one speaks peaceably
with his friend,
but inwardly he sets up an ambush.
9 Should I not punish them
for these things?
This is the LORD's declaration.
Should I not avenge myself[c]
on such a nation as this?

10 I will raise weeping and a lament
over the mountains,
a dirge over the wilderness
grazing land,
for they have been so scorched
that no one passes through.
The sound of cattle is
no longer heard.
From the birds of the sky
to the animals,[d]
everything has fled — they have
gone away.
11 I will make Jerusalem a heap
of rubble,[e]
a jackals' den.[f]
I will make the cities of Judah
a desolation,
an uninhabited place.

12 Who is the person wise enough to understand this?[g] Who has the LORD spoken to, that he may explain it? Why is the land destroyed and scorched like a wilderness, so no one can pass through? **13** The LORD said, "It is because they abandoned my instruction,[h] which I set before them, and did not obey my voice or walk according to it. **14** Instead, they followed the stubbornness of their hearts[i] and followed the Baals as their fathers taught them."[j] **15** Therefore, this is what the LORD of Armies, the God of Israel, says: "I am about to feed this people wormwood[k] and give them poisonous water to drink.[l] **16** I will scatter them among the nations[m] that they and their fathers have not known. I

will send a sword after them until I have finished them off."

MOURNING OVER JUDAH

17 This is what the LORD of Armies says:

Consider, and summon the women
who mourn;[n]
send for the skillful women.
18 Let them come quickly to raise
a lament over us
so that our eyes may overflow
with tears,
our eyelids be soaked with weeping.
19 For a sound of lamentation is heard
from Zion:
How devastated we are.
We are greatly ashamed,[o]
for we have abandoned the land;
our dwellings have been torn down.

20 Now hear the word of the LORD,
you women.
Pay attention to[c] the words
from his mouth.
Teach your daughters a lament
and one another a dirge,
21 for Death[p] has climbed
through our windows;
it has entered our fortresses,
cutting off children from the streets,
young men from the squares.

22 "Speak as follows: 'This is what the LORD declares: Human corpses will fall like manure on the surface of the field,[q] like newly cut grain[r] after the reaper with no one to gather it.

BOAST IN THE LORD

23 " 'This is what the LORD says:

The wise person should not boast
in his wisdom;
the strong should not boast
in his strength;
the wealthy should not boast
in his wealth.
24 But the one who boasts should boast
in this:
that he understands
and knows me[s] —
that I am the LORD,
showing faithful love,
justice, and righteousness
on the earth,

---

[a] 9:7 Is 1:25; Jr 6:27
[b] 9:8 Pr 28:3
[c] 9:9 Jr 5:9,29
[d] 9:10 Jr 4:25; 12:4
[e] 9:11 2Kg 19:25; Is 25:2
[f] Jr 10:22; 49:33; 51:37
[g] 9:12 Ps 107:43; Ec 8:1; Hs 14:9
[n] 9:13 2Ch 12:1
[i] 9:14 Dt 29:19; Ps 81:12
[j] Jr 2:8,23
[k] 9:15 Dt 29:18; Jr 23:15; Lm 3:19
[l] Jr 8:14; 23:15
[m] 9:16 Lv 26:33; Dt 4:27; 28:64

[o] 9:17 Ec 12:5; Am 5:16
[o] 9:19 Jr 2:26; 6:15; 8:12
[p] 9:21 Jb 18:13; 28:22; Ps 49:14
[q] 9:22 2Kg 9:30,32,37
[r] Am 2:13; Mc 4:12; Zch 12:6
[s] 9:24 Ps 34:2; 64:10; 105:3; 1Co 1:31; 2Co 10:17

[A] 9:7 Lit *of the daughter of my*   [B] 9:7 LXX, Tg read *because of their evils*   [C] 9:20 Lit *Your ears must receive*

9:23-24 We tend to brag about educational achievements, employment accomplishments, financial successes, and physical prowess. But God says, "If you really want something to shout about, brag that you know me. If you can't talk about that, you don't have much to boast about." To know God (not merely to know *about* God) in intimate fellowship is the most meaningful pursuit of life.

a 9:25 Jr 4:4; Rm 2:28-29
b 9:26 Lv 19:27; Jr 25:23;
49:32; Ezk 44:7,9
c 10:2 Jr 2:23,36
d 10:4 Is 40:19
e Is 41:7
f 10:5 Ps 115:5; 1Co 12:2
g Ps 115:7; Is 46:7
h Is 41:23-24
i 10:3-5 Is 44:9-20
j 10:6 Ex 15:11; 2Sm 7:22;
1Kg 8:23
k Ps 76:1; 86:10; Mal 1:11
l 10:7 Ps 22:28; 47:7-8;
Jr 8:19

m 10:9 Ezk 27:12,25; 38:13
n Dn 10:5
o 10:10 2Ch 15:3
p Dt 5:26; 1Sm 17:26,36;
2Kg 19:4,16
q Ex 15:18; Ps 10:16; 29:10
r 2Sm 22:8; Ps 18:7; Is 13:13
s 10:11 Ps 96:5
t Is 2:18
u 10:12 Jb 38:4; Ps 93:1;
96:10
v Pr 3:19-20; 8:22-29
w Jb 9:8; Ps 104:2; Is 45:12
x 10:13 Jr 5:22; 31:35
y Jb 38:25-30,34-38;
Ps 135:7
z 10:14 Is 40:18-31; 46:1-7
aa Is 41:29
ab Hab 2:19
ac 10:15 Jr 8:12; 51:18
ad 10:16 Gn 2:7-8,19; Ps
94:9; 95:5
ae Dt 4:20; 32:8-9; Ps 74:2
af 10:12-16 Jr 51:15-19

for I delight in these things.
This is the LORD's declaration.

25 " 'Look, the days are coming — this is the LORD's declaration — when I will punish all the circumcised yet uncircumcised:[a] **26** Egypt, Judah, Edom, the Ammonites, Moab, and all the inhabitants of the desert who clip the hair on their temples.[A] All these nations are uncircumcised, and the whole house of Israel is uncircumcised in heart.' "[b]

FALSE GODS CONTRASTED WITH THE CREATOR

10 Hear the word that the LORD has spoken to[B] you, house of Israel. **2** This is what the LORD says:

Do not learn the way of the nations[c]
or be terrified by signs
　　in the heavens,
although the nations are terrified
　　by them,
3　for the customs of the peoples
　　are worthless.
Someone cuts down a tree
　　from the forest;
it is worked by the hands
　　of a craftsman with a chisel.
4　He decorates it with silver and gold.[d]
It is fastened with hammer
　　and nails,[e]
so it won't totter.
5　Like scarecrows
　　in a cucumber patch,
　　their idols cannot speak.[f]
They must be carried[g] because
　　they cannot walk.
Do not fear them for they can do
　　no harm[h] —
and they cannot do any good.[i]

6　LORD, there is no one like you.[j]
You are great;
　　your name is great in power.[k]
7　Who should not fear you,
King of the nations?[l]
It is what you deserve.
For among all the wise people
　　of the nations

and among all their kingdoms,
　　there is no one like you.
8　They are both stupid and foolish,
instructed by worthless idols
made of wood!
9　Beaten silver is brought
　　from Tarshish[m]
and gold from Uphaz.[c,n]
The work of a craftsman
and of a goldsmith's hands
is clothed in blue and purple,
all the work of skilled artisans.
10　But the LORD is the true God;[o]
he is the living God[p]
　　and eternal King.[q]
The earth quakes at his wrath,[r]
and the nations cannot endure
　　his rage.

11 You are to say this to them: "The gods that did not make the heavens[s] and the earth will perish from the earth[t] and from under these heavens."[D]
12　He made the earth by his power,
established the world[u]
　　by his wisdom,[v]
and spread out the heavens
　　by his understanding.[w]
13　When he thunders,[E]
the waters in the heavens
　　are in turmoil,[x]
and he causes the clouds to rise
from the ends of the earth.
He makes lightning for the rain
and brings the wind
　　from his storehouses.[y]

14　Everyone is stupid and ignorant.
Every goldsmith is put to shame
by his carved image,[z]
for his cast images are a lie;[aa]
there is no breath in them.[ab]
15　They are worthless, a work
　　to be mocked.
At the time of their punishment
they will be destroyed.[ac]
16　Jacob's Portion[F] is not like these
because he is the one who formed
　　all things.[ad]
Israel is the tribe of his inheritance;[ae]
the LORD of Armies is his name.[af]

[A] 9:26 Or *who live in distant places*　[B] 10:1 Or *against*　[C] 10:9 Or *Ophir*　[D] 10:11 This is the only Aramaic v. in Jr.　[E] 10:13 Lit *At his giving of the voice*
[F] 10:16 = the LORD

9:25-26 The Jews trusted in the covenant sign of circumcision. They considered it a get-out-of-jail-free card, protecting them from God's wrath. But circumcision was to be an outward sign of an inner reality: a heart that loved God. **10:5** Idols can't even move unless someone carries them. So why would anyone be afraid of them? Idols are to be mocked, not feared!

10:8 Scripture consistently teaches that those who make idols and trust in them "are just like them" (Pss 115:8; 135:18). **10:11** This verse is written in Aramaic, a language similar to Hebrew, and is the only such passage in the book. Aramaic was the trade language of Jeremiah's day. So the verse is probably in this language so that the crafts-

men and goldsmiths who made the idols (10:9, 14) could understand that their **gods** would **perish** (10:8). **10:16** In calling himself **Jacob's Portion**, God undoubtedly encouraged Jeremiah. It was a reminder that he would not wipe out Israel forever.

EXILE AFTER THE SIEGE

17 Gather up your belongings[A]
from the ground,[a]
you who live under siege.

18 For this is what the LORD says:
Look, I am flinging away[b]
the land's residents at this time
and bringing them such distress
that they will feel it.

JEREMIAH GRIEVES

19 Woe to me because of
my brokenness —
I am severely wounded![c]
I exclaimed, "This is
my intense suffering,
but I must bear it."

20 My tent is destroyed;[d]
all my tent cords are snapped.
My sons have departed from me
and are no more.
I have no one to pitch my tent again
or to hang up my curtains.

21 For the shepherds are stupid:
They don't seek the LORD.[e]
Therefore they have not prospered,
and their whole flock is scattered.

22 Listen! A noise — it is coming —
a great commotion[f] from the land
to the north.
The cities of Judah will be
made desolate,
a jackals' den.[g]

23 I know, LORD,
that a person's way of life is not
his own;
no one who walks determines
his own steps.[h]

24 Discipline me, LORD, but with justice —
not in your anger,[i]
or you will reduce me to nothing.

25 Pour out your wrath on the nations
that don't recognize you
and on the families
that don't call on your name,
for they have consumed Jacob;
they have consumed him
and finished him off
and made his homeland desolate.[j]

REMINDER OF THE COVENANT

11 This is the word that came to Jeremiah from the LORD: **2** "Listen to the words of this covenant[k] and tell them to the men of Judah and the residents of Jerusalem. **3** Tell them, 'This is what the LORD, the God of Israel, says: "Let a curse be on the man who does not obey the words of this covenant,[l] **4** which I commanded your ancestors when I brought them out of the land of Egypt,[m] out of the iron furnace."[n] I declared, "Obey me, and do everything that I command you, and you will be my people, and I will be your God,"[o] **5** in order to establish the oath I swore to your ancestors,[p] to give them a land flowing with milk and honey, as it is today.'"

I answered, "Amen, LORD."[q]

6 The LORD said to me, "Proclaim all these words in the cities of Judah and in the streets of Jerusalem: 'Obey the words of this covenant and carry them out.' **7** For I strongly warned your ancestors when I brought them out of the land of Egypt until today, warning them time and time again,[B,r] 'Obey me.' **8** Yet they would not obey or pay attention; each one followed the stubbornness of his evil heart.[s] So I brought on them all the curses of this covenant, because they had not done what I commanded them to do."

9 The LORD said to me, "A conspiracy has been discovered among the men of Judah[t] and the residents of Jerusalem. **10** They have returned to the iniquities of their fathers[u] who refused to obey my words and have followed other gods to worship them.[v] The house of Israel and the house of Judah broke my covenant I made with their ancestors.

11 "Therefore, this is what the LORD says: I am about to bring on them disaster that they cannot escape.[w] They will cry out to me, but I will not hear them. **12** Then the cities of Judah and the residents of Jerusalem will go and cry out to the gods they have been burning incense to, but they certainly will not save them in their time of disaster.[x] **13** Your gods are indeed as numerous as your cities, Judah,[y] and the altars you have set up to Shame[C,z] — altars to burn incense to Baal — as numerous as the streets of Jerusalem.

[a] **10:17** Ezk 12:3
[b] **10:18** 1Sm 25:29
[c] **10:19** Jr 14:17; 30:12; Nah 3:19
[d] **10:20** Jr 4:20
[e] **10:21** 2Ch 16:12; Is 9:13; 31:1
[f] **10:22** Jr 4:29; 6:22-23
[g] Jr 9:11
[h] **10:23** Ps 37:23; Pr 3:5-6; 16:9
[i] **10:24** Ps 6:1; 38:1
[j] **10:25** Ps 79:6-7

[k] **11:2** Dt 29:9
[l] **11:3** Dt 27:26; Gl 3:10
[m] **11:4** Dt 29:25; Jr 7:22; 34:13
[n] Dt 4:20; 1Kg 8:51
[o] Dt 29:13; Jr 24:7; 30:22
[p] **11:5** Gn 26:3; Dt 7:8
[q] Dt 27:15-16
[r] **11:7** 2Ch 36:15; Jr 7:13,25; 25:3; 26:5; 29:19; 32:33; 35:14-15; 44:4
[s] **11:8** Jr 3:17; 7:24; 16:12
[t] **11:9** Ezk 22:25; Hs 6:9
[u] **11:10** Lv 26:39-40; Neh 9:2; Is 65:7
[v] Dt 28:14; Jr 13:10; 35:15
[w] **11:11** Jr 39:4-7; Am 9:1-4
[x] **11:12** Dt 32:35-37
[y] **11:13** Jr 2:28
[z] Jr 3:24; Hs 9:10

10:24 God's **discipline** is for our good, if we are willing to receive it. It may be painful. But for those who are trained by it, "it yields the peaceful fruit of righteousness" (Heb 12:11).
11:2-5 God's message was a restatement of the basic terms of the Mosaic **covenant** (11:2-3).

Obey God and be blessed (11:4), or disobey him and be cursed (11:3).
11:10 In spite of hundreds of years of history showing what happened when the Israelites disobeyed God, the people plunged headlong into idolatry and other sins, bringing to mind the old cliché, like father like son.

11:13 Your gods are indeed as numerous as your cities, Judah is quite an accusation! The people had shoved Baal worship in God's face, so to speak, and he wasn't going to put up with them anymore.

[a] 11:14 Jr 7:16; 14:11
[b] 11:15 Jr 7:1-15
[c] Hg 2:12
[d] 11:16 Ps 52:8; 128:3; Hs 14:6
[e] Ezk 31:12
[f] Ezk 1:24
[g] 11:17 Is 5:2,7; Jr 2:21
[h] 11:19 Ps 44:11,22; Is 53:7; Jr 12:3
[i] Ps 27:13; Is 53:8; Ezk 26:20
[j] 11:20 Jr 9:7; 12:3
[k] Ps 7:9; 17:3; 26:2
[l] Jr 20:12
[m] 11:21 Jr 1:1; 32:7-9
[n] Am 7:13

[o] 11:21-22 Am 7:16-17
[p] 11:23 Jr 23:12
[q] 12:1 Ezr 9:15; Neh 9:8,33; Ps 119:137
[r] Jb 9:14-15; 13:13-28; 23:2-17
[s] Ps 73
[t] 12:2 Ps 1:3; Jr 17:7-8
[u] Ps 28:3; Is 29:13
[v] 12:3 Ps 139; Jr 1:5
[w] Ps 7:9; Jr 11:20
[x] Jr 11:19
[y] 12:4 Is 24:4-7; Jr 4:28; 23:10
[z] Zph 1:3
[aa] Dt 32:20; Jb 22:13; Jr 29:11
[ab] 12:5 Jr 50:44
[ac] 12:6 Jn 1:11
[ad] Jr 11:19

14 "As for you, do not pray for these people. Do not raise up a cry or a prayer on their behalf,[a] for I will not be listening when they call out to me at the time of their disaster.

15 What right does my beloved have
   to be in my house,[b]
having carried out so many
   evil schemes?
Can holy meat[A,C] prevent
   your disaster[B]
so you can celebrate?

16 The LORD named you
   a flourishing olive tree,[d]
beautiful with well-formed fruit.
He has set fire to it,
and its branches are consumed[c,e]
with the sound of a mighty tumult.[f]

17 "The LORD of Armies who planted you[g] has decreed disaster against you, because of the disaster[D] the house of Israel and the house of Judah brought on themselves when they angered me by burning incense to Baal."

18 The LORD informed me, so I knew.
   Then you helped me to see
      their deeds,
19 for I was like a docile[E] lamb led
      to slaughter.[h]
I didn't know that they had
   devised plots against me:
"Let's destroy the tree with its fruit;[F]
let's cut him off from the land
   of the living[i]
so that his name will no longer
   be remembered."

20 But, LORD of Armies,
   who judges righteously,
who tests[J] heart[G] and mind,[k]
let me see your vengeance on them,
for I have presented my case to you.[l]

21 Therefore, here is what the LORD says concerning the people of Anathoth[m] who intend to take your life. They warn, "Do not prophesy in the name of the LORD,[n] or you will certainly die at our hand." 22 Therefore, this is what the LORD of Armies says: "I am about to punish them. The young men will die by the sword; their sons and daughters will die by famine.[o] 23 They will have no remnant, for I will bring disaster on the people of Anathoth[p] in the year of their punishment."

JEREMIAH'S COMPLAINT

12 You will be righteous, LORD,[q]
   even if I bring a case against you.
Yet, I wish to contend with you:[r]
Why does the way of the wicked
   prosper?[s]
Why do all the treacherous live
   at ease?
2 You planted them,[t] and they
   have taken root.
They have grown
   and produced fruit.
You are ever on their lips,[H]
but far from their conscience.[G,u]
3 As for you, LORD, you know me;
   you see me.[v]
You test whether my heart is
   with you.[w]
Drag the wicked away like sheep
   to slaughter[x]
and set them apart for the day
   of killing.
4 How long will the land mourn[y]
and the grass of every field wither?
Because of the evil of its residents,
animals and birds have been
   swept away,[z]
for the people have said,
"He cannot see what our end
   will be."[l,aa]

THE LORD'S RESPONSE

5 If you have raced with runners
and they have worn you out,
how can you compete with horses?
If you stumble[J] in a peaceful land,
what will you do in the thickets
   of the Jordan?[ab]
6 Even your brothers —
   your own father's family —
even they were treacherous
   to you;[ac]
even they have cried out loudly
   after you.[ad]
Do not have confidence in them,
though they speak well of you.

[A] 11:15 = sacrificial meat   [B] 11:15 LXX; MT reads *meat pass from you*   [C] 11:16 Vg; MT reads *broken*   [D] 11:17 Or *evil*   [E] 11:19 Or *pet*   [F] 11:19 Lit *bread*
[G] 11:20; 12:2 Lit *kidneys*   [H] 12:2 Lit *are near in their mouth*   [I] 12:4 LXX reads *see our ways*   [J] 12:5 Or *you are secure*

11:18-23 The reaction to Jeremiah was a classic sinful response: we don't like the message, so let's kill the messenger. Shockingly, the conspirators were **the people of Anathoth**, Jeremiah's home boys (11:21, 23; see 1:1). Their plot would fail.

12:1 Why **wicked** people **prosper** is an age-old question (see Ps 73), but God didn't try to explain himself to Jeremiah because he doesn't have to defend his righteousness or the wisdom of his ways. He's God.

12:5 The point of these rhetorical questions was this: if Jeremiah couldn't handle the present, he'd really have a tough time in the days ahead. There was no one Jeremiah could trust—no one but God.

⁷ I have abandoned my house;[a]
I have deserted my inheritance.
I have handed the love of my life
over to her enemies.
⁸ My inheritance has behaved
toward me
like a lion in the forest.
She has roared against me.
Therefore, I hate her.[b]
⁹ Is my inheritance like a hyena[A] to me?
Are birds of prey circling her?
Go, gather all the wild animals;[c]
bring them to devour her.
¹⁰ Many shepherds have destroyed
my vineyard;
they have trampled my plot of land.[d]
They have turned my desirable plot
into a desolate wasteland.
¹¹ They have made it a desolation.
It mourns, desolate, before me.
All the land is desolate,
but no one takes it to heart.[e]
¹² Over all the barren heights
in the wilderness
the destroyers have come,
for the LORD has a sword
that devours
from one end of the earth
to the other.
No one has peace.[f]
¹³ They have sown wheat
but harvested thorns.[g]
They have exhausted themselves
but have no profit.[h]
Be put to shame by your harvests
because of the LORD's
burning anger.[i]

¹⁴ This is what the LORD says: "Concerning all my evil neighbors who attack the inheritance that I bequeathed to my people, Israel, I am about to uproot them[j] from their land, and I will uproot the house of Judah from them. ¹⁵ After I have uprooted them, I will once again have compassion[k] on them and return each one to his inheritance and to his land. ¹⁶ If they will diligently learn the ways of my people[l] — to

swear by my name, 'As the LORD lives,' just as they taught my people to swear by Baal — they will be built up among my people. ¹⁷ However, if they will not obey, then I will uproot and destroy that nation."[m]
This is the LORD's declaration.

LINEN UNDERWEAR

13 This is what the LORD said to me: "Go and buy yourself a linen undergarment[n] and put it on. ² But do not put it in water." ² So I bought underwear as the LORD instructed me and put it on.

³ Then the word of the LORD came to me a second time: ⁴ "Take the underwear that you bought and are wearing,[c] and go at once to the Euphrates[D] and hide it in a rocky crevice."[o] ⁵ So I went and hid it by the Euphrates, as the LORD commanded me.

⁶ A long time later the LORD said to me, "Go at once to the Euphrates and get the underwear that I commanded you to hide there." ⁷ So I went to the Euphrates and dug up the underwear and got it from the place where I had hidden it, but it was ruined — of no use at all.

⁸ Then the word of the LORD came to me: ⁹ "This is what the LORD says: Just like this I will ruin the great pride of both Judah and Jerusalem.[p] ¹⁰ These evil people, who refuse to listen to me, who follow the stubbornness of their own hearts,[q] and who have followed other gods to serve and bow in worship — they will be like this underwear, of no use at all. ¹¹ Just as underwear clings to one's waist, so I fastened the whole house of Israel and of Judah to me"[r] — this is the LORD's declaration — "so that they might be my people for my fame, praise, and glory,[s] but they would not obey.

THE WINE JARS

¹² "Say this to them: 'This is what the LORD, the God of Israel, says: Every jar should be filled with wine.' Then they will respond to you, 'Don't we know that every jar should be filled with wine?' ¹³ And you will say

[a] 12:7 Ezk 8:1–11:25
[b] 12:8 Hs 9:15; Am 6:8
[c] 12:9 Is 56:9; Jr 7:33
[d] 12:10 Is 63:18
[e] 12:11 Is 42:25
[f] 12:12 2Ch 15:5; Is 48:22; Ezk 13:16
[g] 12:13 Lv 26:16; Dt 28:38; Hs 8:7; Mc 6:15; Hg 1:6
[h] Is 55:2
[i] Jr 4:26; 25:37-38
[j] 12:14 Jr 1:10; 18:7-8
[k] 12:15 Jr 30:18; 31:20; 33:26; 42:12
[l] 12:16 Is 2:2-4; Mc 4:1-5

[m] 12:17 Is 60:12
[n] 13:1 Ex 39:27-29; Lv 16:4; Ezk 44:17-18
[o] 13:4 Jr 51:63
[p] 13:9 Lv 26:19
[q] 13:10 Jr 16:12
[r] 13:11 Dt 4:3-4; 10:20
[s] Dt 26:19; Ezk 16:8-14

[A] 12:9 Hb obscure   [B] 13:1 Lit *around your waist*   [C] 13:4 Lit *wearing around your waist*   [D] 13:4-7 Perhaps a place near Anathoth with the same spelling as the river

---

12:7-12 God uses a variety of illustrations to describe both the wicked nature of his people and the judgment he intends for them. One of the most powerful is his description of the invading Babylonians as **a sword [of the LORD] that devours** so completely that no one can escape (12:12).
13:4 The reference here is probably not to the **Euphrates** River, which would have required

a seven hundred-mile round trip for Jeremiah. More likely, it refers to another place a few miles from the prophet's home of Anathoth. In Hebrew, "Euphrates" is spelled "Perath." The site near Anathoth was spelled the same way.
13:6-11 When Jeremiah returned and **dug up** the garment, **it was ruined—of no use at all** (13:7). Similarly, God's people were like a tattered and rotted undergarment. God wanted

to "wear" his people close to himself, but they—essentially ruined by the filth of their choices—wouldn't have it (13:11).
13:12-14 **Wine**, normally a sign of blessing and meant for refreshment, became a symbol of God's curse on Judah (13:12). The people would stagger around like drunks when the Babylonians came (13:13). They would **smash** into each other in confusion and terror (13:14).

[a] 13:14 Lm 2:2,17,21; 3:43
[b] 13:16 Jos 7:19; 1Sm 6:5;
   Ps 29:1-2
[c] 13:17 Ps 80:1; 95:7; Jr
   23:1-4
[d] 13:18 2Kg 24:12; Jr 22:26
[e] 13:20 Jr 1:13-15; 4:6; 10:22
[f] 13:21 Ps 48:6; Is 13:8; 21:3;
   42:14; Jr 4:31; 6:24; 22:23;
   30:6; 50:43; Mc 4:9-10;
   1Th 5:3
[g] 13:22 Jr 5:6; 30:15
[h] Ezk 16:37-39; Hs 2:3,10;
   Nah 3:5
[i] 13:23 Ec 5:1; Jr 4:22;
   Hs 5:4
[j] 13:24 Jb 13:25; Ps 83:13;
   Is 40:24
[k] 13:25 Ps 106:21; Jr 2:32;
   18:15; Ezk 22:12; 23:35;
   Hs 8:14
[l] Jr 3:23
[m] 13:26 Is 47:2-3; Jr 49:10;
   Nah 3:5
[n] 13:27 Jr 2:23-24; 5:8
[o] Hs 8:5
[p] 14:1 Jr 17:8
[q] 14:2 Is 3:26
[r] 1Sm 5:12
[s] 14:3 Est 6:12; 7:8
[t] 14:4 Jl 1:11
[u] 14:6 Jr 2:24

to them, 'This is what the LORD says: I am about to fill all who live in this land — the kings who reign for David on his throne, the priests, the prophets, and all the residents of Jerusalem — with drunkenness. [14] I will smash them against each other, fathers and sons alike — this is the LORD's declaration. I will allow no mercy, pity, or compassion to keep me from destroying them.'"[a]

THE LORD'S WARNING

15 Listen and pay attention.
Do not be proud,
for the LORD has spoken.
16 Give glory to the LORD your God[b]
before he brings darkness,
before your feet stumble
on the mountains at dusk.
You wait for light,
but he brings darkest gloom[A]
and makes total darkness.
17 But if you will not listen,
my innermost being will weep
in secret
because of your pride.
My eyes will overflow with tears,
for the LORD's flock[c] has been
taken captive.

18 Say to the king
and the queen mother:[d]
Take a humble seat,
for your glorious crowns
have fallen from your heads.
19 The cities of the Negev are under siege;
no one can help them.
All of Judah has been taken
into exile,
taken completely into exile.
20 Look up and see
those coming from the north.[e]
Where is the flock entrusted
to you,
the sheep that were your pride?

THE DESTINY OF JERUSALEM

21 What will you say when he appoints
close friends as leaders over you,
ones you yourself trained?
Won't labor pains seize you,[f]
as they do a woman in labor?
22 And when you ask yourself,
"Why have these things happened
to me?"

it is because of your great guilt[g]
that your skirts have been
stripped off,[h]
your body exposed.[B]
23 Can the Cushite change his skin,
or a leopard his spots?
If so, you might be able to do
what is good,[i]
you who are instructed in evil.
24 I will scatter you[c]
like drifting chaff[j]
before the desert wind.
25 This is your lot,
what I have decreed for you —
this is the LORD's declaration —
because you have forgotten me[k]
and trusted in lies.[l]
26 I will pull your skirts up
over your face
so that your shame might be seen.[m]
27 Your adulteries and
your lustful neighing,[n]
your depraved prostitution
on the hills, in the fields —
I have seen your abhorrent acts.
Woe to you, Jerusalem!
You are unclean —
for how long yet?[o]

THE DROUGHT

14 This is the word of the LORD that came
to Jeremiah concerning the drought:[p]
2 Judah mourns;
her city gates languish.[q]
Her people are on the ground
in mourning;
Jerusalem's cry rises up.[r]
3 Their nobles send their servants[D]
for water.
They go to the cisterns;
they find no water;
their containers return empty.
They are ashamed and humiliated;
they cover their heads.[s]
4 The ground is cracked
since no rain has fallen on the land.
The farmers are ashamed;[t]
they cover their heads.
5 Even the doe in the field
gives birth and abandons her fawn
since there is no grass.
6 Wild donkeys stand
on the barren heights[u]
panting for air like jackals.

[A] 13:16 Or brings a shadow of death   [B] 13:22 Lit your heels have suffered violence   [C] 13:24 Lit them   [D] 14:3 Lit little ones

---

13:18 Jeremiah was told to speak judgment to the eighteen-year-old **king**, Jeconiah (Jehoiachin), and **the queen mother** Nehushta (see 2 Kgs 24:8). They were exhorted to **humble** themselves in light of the coming invasion, but they did not.
13:23 Can the Cushite change his skin, or a leopard his spots? In this Jeremiah was saying that black skin color was as basic to the Cushite/Ethiopian as unrighteous behavior was to the nation of Israel.

Their eyes fail
because there are no green plants.

7 Though our iniquities testify
  against us,
Lord, act for your name's sake.
Indeed, our rebellions[a] are many;
we have sinned against you.[b]

8 Hope of Israel,[c]
its Savior in time of distress,
why are you like a resident alien
  in the land,
like a traveler stopping only
  for the night?

9 Why are you like a helpless man,
like a warrior unable to save?[d]
Yet you are among us, Lord,[e]
and we bear your name.
Don't leave us!

10 This is what the Lord says concerning these people:

Truly they love to wander;[f]
they never rest their feet.
So the Lord does not accept them.
Now he will remember their iniquity
and punish their sins.[g]

FALSE PROPHETS TO BE PUNISHED

11 Then the Lord said to me, "Do not pray for the well-being of these people.[h] 12 If they fast, I will not hear their cry of despair. If they offer burnt offering and grain offering, I will not accept them. Rather, I will finish them off by sword, famine, and plague."[i]

13 And I replied, "Oh no, Lord God! The prophets are telling them, 'You won't see sword or suffer famine. I will certainly give you lasting peace in this place.' "[j]

14 But the Lord said to me, "These prophets are prophesying a lie in my name. I did not send them, nor did I command them or speak to them. They are prophesying to you a false vision, worthless divination, the deceit[k] of their own minds.[l]

15 "Therefore, this is what the Lord says concerning the prophets who prophesy in my name, though I did not send them, and who say, 'There will never be sword or famine in this land.' By sword and famine these prophets will meet their end. 16 The

people they are prophesying to will be thrown into the streets of Jerusalem because of the famine and the sword. There will be no one to bury them[m] — they, their wives, their sons, and their daughters. I will pour out their own evil on them."

JEREMIAH'S REQUEST

17 You are to speak this word to them:

Let my eyes overflow with tears;
day and night may they not stop,[n]
for the virgin daughter of my people
has been destroyed
  by a crushing blow,[o]
an extremely severe wound.[p]

18 If I go out to the field,
look — those slain by the sword!
If I enter the city,
look — those ill[q] from famine!
For both prophet and priest
travel to a land they do not know.

19 Have you completely rejected Judah?
Do you detest[r] Zion?
Why do you strike us
with no hope of healing for us?
We hoped for peace,
but there was nothing good;
for a time of healing,
but there was only terror.[s]

20 We acknowledge
  our wickedness, Lord,
the iniquity of our fathers;[t]
indeed, we have sinned against you.

21 For your name's sake,
  don't despise us.
Don't disdain your glorious throne.[u]
Remember your covenant[v] with us;
do not break it.

22 Can any of the worthless idols
  of the nations[w] bring rain?
Or can the skies alone give showers?
Are you not the Lord our God?
We therefore put our hope in you,[x]
for you have done all these things.

THE LORD'S NEGATIVE RESPONSE

15 Then the Lord said to me: "Even if[y] Moses and[z] Samuel should[aa] stand before me,[ab] my compassions would not reach out to these people. Send them from

[a] 14:7 Jr 2:19; 3:6,22; 5:6
[b] Is 64:5; Jr 3:25; 8:14; 14:20; Lm 3:42; 5:16; Dn 9:5,11
[c] 14:8 Jr 17:13; 50:7
[d] 14:9 Is 59:1
[e] Ex 29:45
[f] 14:10 Jr 5:31; Am 8:12
[g] Hs 8:13
[h] 14:11 Jr 7:16; 11:14; 15:1
[i] 14:12 Jr 5:12
[j] 14:13 Jr 4:10; 6:13-14; 8:10-12
[k] 14:14 Ps 119:118; Jr 8:5; 23:26
[l] Jr 5:31; 20:6; 23:25-26,32; 27:10,14-16; 29:9,21,31

[m] 14:16 Jr 7:33; 9:22
[n] 14:17 Jr 9:1,10; 13:17
[o] Jr 4:6; 6:1
[p] Jr 10:19; 30:12
[q] 14:18 Dt 29:22
[r] 14:19 Lv 26:11,30,43-44
[s] Jr 8:15; 33:9
[t] 14:20 Jr 3:25; 11:10; 16:12-13
[u] 14:21 Dt 32:19; Jr 15:6; 17:12
[v] Lv 26:44; Jdg 2:1; Is 33:8
[w] 14:22 Jr 8:19; 10:8,15; 16:19
[x] Is 8:17; 25:9
[y] 15:1 Ps 99:6; Ezk 14:14
[z] Ex 32:11-14; Ps 106:23
[aa] 1Sm 7:9; 12:23
[ab] Jr 15:19; 35:19

14:7-9 As a result of drought, the people began to cry out to God in their suffering and expressed what sounded like genuine repentance. They admitted that they had been very sinful and rebellious, and called God the **Hope of Israel** and their **Savior** (14:8). 14:10-12 God reacted to his people's apparent confession (see 14:7-9) by saying, in effect, "I

hear what they're saying, but it's all a sham. They are still wandering away from me as fast as **their feet** will carry them (14:10). So I will judge them."
14:20-22 This confession by the people *sounds* like it comes from a broken and contrite group who were ready to return to the Lord who was their true and only hope, but they were just

trying to make a foxhole deal with God so that he would get them out of their mess.
15:1 God chose two of the greatest intercessors in Israel's history, **Moses** and **Samuel**, to illustrate the impossibility of anyone changing his mind about his judgment of Judah. Moses had interceded for Israel after their idolatry with the golden calf (see Exod 32–33).

[a]15:1 Ex 6:1; 8:2; 9:2; 10:27; Jr 50:33
[b]15:2 Jr 14:12; 43:11; Ezk 5:12; Zch 11:9
[c]15:3 Jr 22:19; 49:20–50:45
[d]Is 18:6; Jr 7:33; 19:7
[e]15:4 2Kg 21:1-18; 2Ch 33:1-20
[f]15:5 Lm 1:1-2; Am 5:2
[g]Is 51:19; Nah 3:7
[h]15:6 Dt 32:15
[i]Is 1:14; 7:13; Jr 6:11; 20:9
[j]15:7 Jdg 2:19; 2Kg 17:13; 2Ch 7:14; Neh 9:35; Jr 18:11; 25:5; 35:15
[k]15:8 Gn 22:17; 32:12; 41:49
[l]15:9 Ru 4:15; 1Sm 2:5; Jb 42:13

[m]15:10 Jb 3:1-10
[n]Is 53:3
[o]15:13 Ps 44:12; Is 52:3
[p]15:13-14 Dt 32:22; Jr 17:3-4; Ezk 32:9
[q]15:15 Jr 12:3
[r]Jdg 16:28; Neh 5:19; 13:14,22,31; Ps 106:4; Lk 23:42
[s]Jr 11:20
[t]Ps 69:7-9
[u]15:16 Ezk 3:3
[v]Jr 14:9

my presence, and let them go.[a] **2** If they ask you, 'Where will we go?' tell them: This is what the LORD says:

Those destined for death,[b]
   to death;
those destined for the sword,
   to the sword.
Those destined for famine,
   to famine;
those destined for captivity,
   to captivity.

3 "I will ordain four kinds[A] of judgment for them" — this is the LORD's declaration — "the sword to kill, the dogs to drag away,[c] and the birds of the sky and the wild animals of the land[d] to devour and destroy. **4** I will make them a horror to all the kingdoms of the earth because of Manasseh[e] son of Hezekiah, the king of Judah, for what he did in Jerusalem.

5   Who will have pity on you,
         Jerusalem?[f]
      Who will show sympathy
         toward you?[g]
      Who will turn aside
         to ask about your well-being?
6   You have left me."[h]
         This is the LORD's declaration.
      "You have turned your back,
      so I have stretched out my hand
         against you
      and destroyed you.
      I am tired[i] of showing compassion.
7   I scattered them
         with a winnowing fork
      at the city gates of the land.
      I made them childless; I destroyed
         my people.
      They would not turn
         from their ways.[j]
8   I made their widows
         more numerous
      than the sand of the seas.[k]
      I brought a destroyer at noon
      against the mother of young men.
      I suddenly released on her
      agitation and terrors.
9   The mother of seven grew faint;[l]
      she breathed her last breath.
      Her sun set while it was still day;

she was ashamed and humiliated.
      The rest of them I will give over
         to the sword
      in the presence of their enemies."
         This is the LORD's declaration.

JEREMIAH'S COMPLAINT

10   Woe is me, my mother,
         that you gave birth to me,[m]
      a man who incites dispute
         and conflict
      in all the land.
      I did not lend or borrow,
      yet everyone curses me.[n]

THE LORD'S RESPONSE

11 The LORD said:
      Haven't I set you loose for your
         good?
      Haven't I punished you
      in a time of trouble,
      in a time of distress
         with the enemy?[B]
12   Can anyone smash iron,
      iron from the north, or bronze?
13   I will give up your wealth
      and your treasures as plunder,
      without cost,[o] for all your sins
      in all your borders.
14   Then I will make you serve
         your enemies[c]
      in a land you do not know,
      for my anger will kindle a fire
      that will burn against you.[D]

JEREMIAH'S PRAYER
FOR VENGEANCE

15   You know,[q] LORD;
      remember me and take note
         of me.[r]
      Avenge me against my persecutors.[s]
      In your patience,[D]
         don't take me away.
      Know that I suffer disgrace
         for your honor.[t]
16   Your words were found,
         and I ate them.[u]
      Your words became a delight to me
      and the joy of my heart,
      for I bear your name,[v]
      LORD God of Armies.

[A]15:3 Lit *families*   [B]15:11 Hb obscure   [C]15:14 Some Hb mss, LXX, Syr, Tg; other Hb mss read *you pass through*   [D]15:15 Lit *In the slowness of your anger*

Samuel interceded when they were being threatened by the Philistines (see 1 Sam 7:5-11) and again when the people demanded a human king (see 1 Sam 12:19–25).
15:4 King **Manasseh** of Judah reigned fifty-five years and plunged Judah into the grossest sins imaginable (see 2 Kgs 21:1-16).

15:6 If God becomes **tired of showing compassion** to you, you are without hope! That's why the good news of the gospel is so good. In it, God shows his overflowing compassion. Those who repent of their sin and trust in Jesus have the sure hope of forgiveness and eternal life.

15:10 Jeremiah lamented his birth because he was the object of Judah's scorn, even though he had done nothing wrong and had been faithful in delivering God's message.

17 I never sat with the band of revelers,
and I did not celebrate with them.
Because your hand was on me,
　I sat alone,[a]
for you filled me with indignation.
18 Why has my pain become unending,
my wound incurable,[b]
refusing to be healed?
You truly have become like a mirage
　to me —
water that is not reliable.

JEREMIAH TOLD TO REPENT

19 Therefore, this is what the LORD says:
If you return, I will take you back;
you will stand in my presence.
And if you speak noble words,
rather than worthless ones,
you will be my spokesman.[c]
It is they who must return to you;
you must not return to them.
20 Then I will make you a fortified wall
　of bronze
to this people.
They will fight against you
but will not overcome you,
for I am with you
to save you and rescue you.[d]
　This is the LORD's declaration.
21 I will rescue you from the power
　of evil people
and redeem you from the grasp
　of the ruthless.

NO MARRIAGE FOR JEREMIAH

16 The word of the LORD came to me: **2** "Do not marry or have sons or daughters in this place. **3** For this is what the LORD says concerning sons and daughters born in this place as well as concerning the mothers who bear them and the fathers who father them in this land: **4** They will die from deadly diseases. They will not be mourned or buried but will be like manure on the soil's surface.[e] They

will be finished off by sword and famine. Their corpses will become food for the birds of the sky and for the wild animals of the land.[f]

5 "For this is what the LORD says: Don't enter a house where a mourning feast is taking place.[A] Don't go to lament or sympathize with them, for I have removed my peace from these people as well as my faithful love and compassion." This is the LORD's declaration.[g] **6** "Both great and small will die in this land without burial. No lament will be made for them, nor will anyone cut himself or[h] shave his head for them.[B] **7** Food won't be provided for the mourner[i] to comfort him because of the dead. A consoling drink won't be given him for the loss of his father or mother. **8** Do not enter the house where feasting is taking place to sit with them to eat and drink. **9** For this is what the LORD of Armies, the God of Israel, says: I am about to eliminate from this place, before your very eyes and in your time, the sound of joy and gladness, the voice of the groom and the bride.[j]

ABANDONING THE LORD
AND HIS LAW

10 "When you tell these people all these things, they will say to you, 'Why has the LORD declared all this terrible disaster against us?[k] What is our iniquity? What is our sin that we have committed against the LORD our God?' **11** Then you will answer them, 'Because your fathers abandoned me[l] — this is the LORD's declaration — and followed other gods, served them, and bowed in worship to them.[m] Indeed, they abandoned me and did not keep my instruction. **12** You did more evil than your fathers.[n] Look, each one of you was following the stubbornness of his evil heart, not obeying me. **13** So I will hurl you from this land into a land that you and your fathers

[a] 15:17 2Kg 3:15; Ps 102:7; Is 8:11; Lm 3:28
[b] 15:18 Jr 19:8; 30:12,14,17
[c] 15:19 Ex 4:16
[d] 15:20 Jr 1:8,19; 30:11; 42:11
[e] 16:4 Jr 8:2; 9:22; 25:33
[f] 16:4 Dt 28:26; Is 18:6; Jr 7:33
[g] 16:5 Ps 25:6; 40:11; 69:16
[h] 16:6 Dt 14:1
[i] 16:7 Dt 26:14; Ezk 24:17; Hs 9:4
[j] 16:9 Jr 7:34; 25:10; 33:11
[k] 16:10 Jr 5:19
[l] 16:11 Dt 29:25; Jr 1:16; 2:13,17,19; 5:19; 17:13; 22:9
[m] Dt 29:26
[n] 16:12 Jr 7:26

[A] 16:5 Lit *house of mourning*　[B] 16:6 This custom demonstrated pagan mourning rituals.

15:19 It seems the prophet went too far in his self-pity, because the chapter closes with God telling Jeremiah to repent so that he might continue serving.
15:20-21 The prophet was not to expect to receive the "Citizen of the Year" award from the Jerusalem Chamber of Commerce for his faithful service because if Jeremiah served God faithfully, he would inevitably be hated by those who hated God. God, however, would make him **a fortified wall** against their attacks (15:20). Greater suffering was ahead for Jeremiah; nevertheless, he would endure—not because of his will power—but

because the Lord would **rescue** and **redeem** him (15:21).
　Christian, take note. The power of evil people is not ultimate. It is nothing compared to the strong arm of God. Trust him with all your heart and remember his words: **I am with you to save you and rescue you** (15:20).
16:1-4 Like the prophet Hosea's marriage to the prostitute Gomer (see Hos 1:2-3), Jeremiah's home situation was to be a sign to Judah—a sign of judgment on God's people. The absence of children in Jeremiah's house was a warning that any children born in the land would **die** (Jer 16:3-4).

16:5 Between having no family and not participating in social gatherings, Jeremiah would be a social pariah. The reason for God's command was important, though: He had so given up on this rebellious and hard-hearted people that he had disowned them. He would no longer lament or rejoice with them, so Jeremiah couldn't either.
16:10 In other words, the people were like a child standing over a broken jar with a cookie in each hand, asking his mother, "What cookies?"

a 16:13 Jr 15:14; 17:4; 22:26
b Dt 4:28; 28:36,64
c 16:14 Jr 7:32; 19:6; 23:5;
    48:12; 49:2; 51:47,52
d 16:14-15 Jr 23:7-8
e 16:15 Jr 3:18
    Jr 23:8
g 16:16 Am 4:2; Hab 1:14-15
h 16:17 2Ch 16:9; Jb 34:21;
    Ps 90:8; Pr 5:21; Jr 32:19
i 16:18 Jr 17:18
j 16:19 Ps 37:39; Nah 1:7
k Jr 8:19; 10:8,15; 14:22
l 16:20 Gn 1:26; Jr 2:11
m 16:21 Jr 33:2

n 17:1 Jb 19:24
o Pr 3:3; 7:3; Jr 31:33-34
p 17:2 Dt 16:21; 1Kg 14:23;
    2Kg 17:10
q 17:3 Ps 44:10; Is 10:6;
    42:22-24; Jr 20:5; 49:31-32;
    Ezk 7:21; 26:12; 29:19;
    36:4; Am 3:11; Zph 1:13
r Jr 15:13
s 17:4 Jr 16:13; 22:28;
    Ezk 32:9
t Dt 32:22; Jr 15:14
u 17:5 Ps 146:3
v 2Ch 32:8
w 17:6 Jr 48:6
x Gn 19:24-26; Ps 107:34
y 17:7 Ps 40:4
z 17:8 Ps 1:3; Ezk 17:5-8

are not familiar with.*a* There you will worship other gods*b* both day and night, for I will not grant you grace.'*A*

14 "However, look, the days are coming"*c* — the LORD's declaration — "when it will no longer be said, 'As the LORD lives who brought the Israelites from the land of Egypt,'*d* **15** but rather, 'As the LORD lives who brought the Israelites from the land of the north*e* and from all the other lands where he had banished them.' For I will return them to their land that I gave to their ancestors.*f*

PUNISHMENT OF EXILE

16 "I am about to send for many fishermen"*g* — this is the LORD's declaration — "and they will fish for them. Then I will send for many hunters, and they will hunt them down on every mountain and hill and out of the clefts of the rocks, **17** for my gaze takes in all their ways.*h* They are not concealed from me, and their iniquity is not hidden from my sight. **18** I will first repay them double for their iniquity*i* and sin because they have polluted my land. They have filled my inheritance with the carcasses of their abhorrent and detestable idols."

19   LORD, my strength
          and my stronghold,
     my refuge in a time of distress,*j*
     the nations will come to you
     from the ends of the earth,
          and they will say,
     "Our fathers inherited only lies,
     worthless idols*k* of no benefit
          at all."
20   Can one make gods for himself?
     But they are not gods.*l*
21   "Therefore, I am about
          to inform them,
     and this time I will
          make them know
     my power and my might;
     then they will know that my name
          is the LORD."*m*

THE PERSISTENT SIN OF JUDAH

17 The sin of Judah is inscribed
          with an iron stylus.*n*
     With a diamond point
     it is engraved on the tablet
          of their hearts*o*
     and on the horns of their*B* altars,
2   while their children remember
          their altars
     and their Asherah poles,
          by the green trees
     on the high hills *p* —
3   my mountains in the countryside.
     I will give up your wealth
     and all your treasures as plunder*q*
     because of the sin
          of your high places*c*
     in all your borders.*r*
4   You will, on your own, relinquish
          your inheritance
     that I gave you.
     I will make you serve your enemies
     in a land you do not know,*s*
     for you have set my anger on fire;*t*
     it will burn forever.

CURSE AND BLESSING

5 This is what the LORD says:
     Cursed is the person who trusts
          in mankind.*u*
     He makes human flesh his strength,*v*
     and his heart turns from the LORD.
6   He will be like a juniper
          in the Arabah;*w*
     he cannot see when good comes
     but dwells in the parched places
          in the wilderness,
     in a salt land where no one lives.*x*
7   The person who trusts in the LORD,
     whose confidence indeed is
          the LORD, is blessed.*y*
8   He will be like a tree planted
          by water;*z*
     it sends its roots out toward a stream,
     it doesn't fear when heat comes,
     and its foliage remains green.

A 16:13 Or *compassion*   *B* 17:1 Some Hb mss, Syr, Vg; other Hb mss read *your*   *c* 17:3 Lit *plunder, your high places because of sin*

16:14-15 The defining moment in the history of the Jewish nation was the exodus from Egypt, but God promised that in the future he would be known — not as the One who brought the Israelites out of Egypt — but as the One **who brought the Israelites . . . from all the other lands where he had banished them** (16:15). Though many Jews would eventually return to their homeland from Babylon, this regathering or second exodus will be fully realized when Jesus Christ returns to establish his millennial kingdom. **17:1-4** Judah's people were such hard-hearted idolaters that even **their children** participated

in false worship using **Asherah poles**, idols set up to the Canaanite goddess of fertility (17:2). These evil symbols appeared and disappeared at various times throughout Israel's history. The low point probably came when King Manasseh erected one in the temple, although he later removed it (see 2 Kgs 21:7; 2 Chr 33:15). This was significant because God laid a large part of the blame for Judah's pitiful spiritual condition at Manasseh's feet (Jer 15:4). Nevertheless, the people themselves had set God's **anger on fire** (17:4). That's a blaze you don't want to be caught in.

17:5-8 These verses reveal the stark contrast between two ways of life — either to trust in the strength of humanity and be **cursed**, or to trust in the Lord and be **blessed** (17:5, 7). The picture of a bush in the **Arabah**, the desert portion of Israel, brings to mind the ultimate in dryness and scorching heat; it's **a salt land where no one lives** (17:6). This is probably a reference to the area around the Dead Sea, which is filled with salt and so many other minerals that nothing can survive in it. But the person who trusts in the Lord **will be like a tree planted by water** (17:8), language reminiscent of the blessed man of Psalm 1.

It will not worry in a year
of drought
or cease producing fruit.

THE DECEITFUL HEART

9 The heart is more deceitful
than anything else,[a]
and incurable —
who can understand it?[b]
10 I, the LORD, examine the mind,
I test the heart,[A,c]
to give to each according to
his way,
according to what
his actions deserve.[d]
11 He who makes a fortune unjustly
is like a partridge that hatches eggs
it didn't lay.
In the middle of his life
his riches will abandon him,
so in the end he will be a fool.[e]
12 A glorious throne[f]
on high[g] from the beginning
is the place of our sanctuary.[h]
13 LORD, the hope of Israel,[i]
all who abandon you
will be put to shame.
All who turn away from me
will be written in the dirt,
for they have abandoned
the LORD, the fountain
of living water.[j]

JEREMIAH'S PLEA

14 Heal me, LORD, and I will be healed;
save me, and I will be saved,
for you are my praise.[k]
15 Hear how they keep challenging me,[l]
"Where is the word of the LORD?
Let it come!"
16 But I have not run away from being
your shepherd,
and I have not longed for
the fatal day.[m]
You know my words were spoken
in your presence.
17 Don't become a terror to me.
You are my refuge[n] in the day
of disaster.

18 Let my persecutors be put to shame,[o]
but don't let me be put to shame.
Let them be terrified, but don't
let me be terrified.
Bring on them the day of disaster;[p]
shatter them with total[B] destruction.

OBSERVING THE SABBATH

19 This is what the LORD said to me, "Go
and stand at the People's Gate, through
which the kings of Judah enter and leave,
as well as at all the gates of Jerusalem.
20 Announce to them, 'Hear the word of the
LORD, kings of Judah, all Judah, and all the
residents of Jerusalem who enter through
these gates. 21 This is what the LORD says:
Watch yourselves; do not pick up a load
and bring it in through Jerusalem's gates
on the Sabbath day.[q] 22 Do not carry a load
out of your houses on the Sabbath day or
do any work,[r] but keep the Sabbath day
holy, just as I commanded your ancestors.[s]
23 They wouldn't listen or pay attention but
became obstinate,[t] not listening or accepting discipline.

24 "'However, if you listen to me — this
is the LORD's declaration — and do not
bring loads through the gates of this city
on the Sabbath day, but keep the Sabbath
day holy and do no work on it, 25 kings
and princes will enter through the gates
of this city. They will sit on the throne of
David;[u] they will ride in chariots and on
horses[v] with their officials, the men of
Judah, and the residents of Jerusalem.
This city will be inhabited forever. 26 Then
people will come from the cities of Judah and from the area around Jerusalem,
from the land of Benjamin and from the
Judean foothills, from the hill country
and from the Negev[w] bringing burnt offerings and sacrifices, grain offerings
and frankincense, and thank offerings
to the house of the LORD. 27 But if you do
not listen to me to keep the Sabbath day
holy by not carrying a load while entering the gates of Jerusalem on the Sabbath
day, I will set fire to its gates,[x] and it will
consume the citadels[y] of Jerusalem[z] and
not be extinguished.'"[aa]

[a] 17:9 Gn 6:5
[b] Jr 15:18; Mc 1:9
[c] 17:10 Dt 8:2; Ps 17:3; 26:2
[d] Jr 4:18; 7:3,5; 18:11; 23:22; 25:5; 26:3,13; 32:19; Rm 2:6
[e] 17:11 Lk 12:20
[f] 17:12 Is 6:1-3; Jr 14:21; Ezk 1:26-28
[g] Ps 102:19; Jr 25:30
[h] Ps 68:33-35; Is 60:13
[i] 17:13 Jr 14:8; 50:7
[j] Jr 2:13
[k] 17:14 Ps 22:25; 71:6; 109:1
[l] 17:15 Is 5:19; 2Pt 3:4
[m] 17:16 Am 5:18
[n] 17:17 Ps 46:1; 61:3; 62:7-8

[o] 17:18 Ps 35:4
[p] Ps 35:8
[q] 17:21 Neh 13:15-21; Jn 5:9-12
[r] 17:22 Ex 20:8-10; Dt 5:12-14; Is 56:2-6
[s] Ezk 20:12
[t] 17:23 Jr 7:26
[u] 17:25 Jr 22:2,30; 29:16; 36:30
[v] Jr 22:4
[w] 17:26 Jr 32:44; 33:13
[x] 17:27 Lm 4:11
[y] Jr 49:27; Am 1:14
[z] 2Kg 25:9
[aa] Jr 7:20

A 17:10 Lit kidneys   B 17:18 Lit double

17:10 God examines **the mind** and tests **the heart**, which explains why people testify that when they read the Bible, they feel as if it is looking into the deepest recesses of their minds and hearts. They feel this because God's Word is alive and powerful, constantly probing us. It's a good thing to be probed and exposed by the incision that

God makes in our lives by his Word (see Heb 4:12), because that's when we really deal with deep-rooted sin and begin to grow.
17:18 Jeremiah prayed that his tormenters would be **put to shame**—not out of personal bitterness or revenge but because they had scorned the Lord and his word.

17:24-27 If God's people would keep his **Sabbath** (see Exod 20:8-9), Israel would enjoy untold blessing, peace, and prosperity (Jer 17:24-26). Refusal to obey, however, would result in destruction (17:27).

*a*18:2 Is 29:16; Jr 19:1-2
*b*18:4 Rm 9:21
*c*18:6 Gn 2:7-8; Is 43:1; 64:8
*d*18:7 Jr 1:10; 24:6; 31:28
*e*18:8 2Sm 24:1; Jr 42:10; Jnh 3:10
*f*18:9 Jr 1:10
*g*18:10 Ezk 18:25-29; 33:12-13
*h*18:11 Jr 4:18; 7:3; 35:15
*i*18:12 Is 57:12; Jr 2:25
*j*18:13 Jr 5:30; Hs 6:10

*k*18:15 Jr 2:32; 3:21; 13:25; Ezk 22:12; 23:35; Hs 8:14
*l*Ezk 14:3,4,7; 44:12; Rv 2:14
*m*Jr 6:16
*n*18:16 Dt 28:37; 2Ch 29:8; 30:7; Jr 5:30; 19:8; 25:9,18; 29:18; 42:18; 44:12,22; 50:13; Mc 6:16; Zph 2:15
*o*Lm 2:15
*p*Jr 19:8; 49:17
*q*Jb 2:11; 42:11; Ps 22:7; 69:20; Is 51:19; Jr 15:5; 48:27; Nah 3:7
*r*18:17 Ex 10:13; 14:21; Jb 27:21; 38:24; Ps 48:7; Is 27:8; Jr 13:24
*s*2Ch 29:6; Jr 2:27; 32:33; Ezk 8:16
*t*18:18 Jr 11:19
*u*Jr 2:8,26; 5:31; 6:13; 8:10; 13:13; 23:11,33; Ezk 7:26; Mc 3:11; Zph 3:4
*v*Jr 5:13
*w*18:19 Ps 55:2-3; 142:6
*x*18:20 Ps 35:7; 57:6
*y*18:21 Ps 109:9-20

PARABLE OF THE POTTER

18 This is the word that came to Jeremiah from the LORD: **2** "Go down at once to the potter's house;*a* there I will reveal my words to you." **3** So I went down to the potter's house, and there he was, working away at the wheel.*A* **4** But the jar that he was making from the clay became flawed in the potter's hand, so he made it into another jar, as it seemed right for him to do.*b*

5 The word of the LORD came to me: **6** "House of Israel, can I not treat you as this potter treats his clay?" — this is the LORD's declaration. "Just like clay in the potter's hand, so are you in my hand, house of Israel.*c* **7** At one moment I might announce concerning a nation or a kingdom that I will uproot, tear down, and destroy it.*d* **8** However, if that nation about which I have made the announcement turns from its evil, I will relent concerning the disaster I had planned to do to it.*e* **9** At another time I might announce concerning a nation or a kingdom that I will build and plant it.*f* **10** However, if it does what is evil in my sight by not listening to me, I will relent concerning the good I had said I would do to it.*g* **11** So now, say to the men of Judah and to the residents of Jerusalem, 'This is what the LORD says: Look, I am about to bring harm to you and make plans against you. Turn now, each from your evil way, and correct your ways and your deeds.'*h* **12** But they will say, 'It's hopeless.*i* We will continue to follow our plans, and each of us will continue to act according to the stubbornness of his evil heart.'"

DELUDED ISRAEL

13 Therefore, this is what the LORD says:

Ask among the nations,
who has heard things like these?
Virgin Israel has done
a most horrible thing.*j*
14 Does the snow of Lebanon ever leave
the highland crags?

Or does cold water flowing
from a distance ever fail?
15 Yet my people have forgotten me.*k*
They burn incense to worthless idols
that make them stumble
in their ways*l*
on the ancient roads,*m*
and make them walk on new paths,
not the highway.
16 They have made their land a horror,*n*
a perpetual object of scorn;*B,o*
all who pass by it will be appalled*p*
and shake their heads.*q*
17 I will scatter them before the enemy
like the east wind.*r*
I will show them*C* my back and not
my face*s*
on the day of their calamity.

PLOT AGAINST JEREMIAH

18 Then certain ones said, "Come, let's make plans against Jeremiah,*t* for instruction will never be lost from the priest,*u* or counsel from the wise, or a word from the prophet.*v* Come, let's denounce him*D* and pay no attention to all his words."

19 Pay attention to me, LORD.
Hear what my opponents
are saying!*w*
20 Should good be repaid with evil?
Yet they have dug a pit for me.*x*
Remember how I stood before you
to speak good on their behalf,
to turn your anger from them.
21 Therefore, hand their children
over to famine,*y*
and give them over to the power of
the sword.
Let their wives become childless
and widowed,
their husbands slain
by deadly disease,*E*
their young men struck down
by the sword in battle.
22 Let a cry be heard from their houses
when you suddenly bring raiders
against them,

---

*A*18:3 Lit *pair of stones*   *B*18:16 Lit *hissing*   *C*18:17 LXX, Lat, Syr, Tg; MT reads *will look at them*   *D*18:18 Lit *let's strike him with the tongue*
*E*18:21 Lit *by death*

18:5-10 Just as a potter has freedom to make what he chooses from his clay, so the sovereign Lord has freedom to save or destroy any nation based on its response to his pronouncements. Nineveh comes to mind as an example of God relenting in judgment when the Ninevites humbled themselves with repentance in response to Jonah's preaching (see Jonah 3:5-10). The people of Jesus's day were an example of rejecting God's word—in this case the incarnate

Word—and turning blessing into cursing (see Matt 12:41).
18:13 Judah's rebellion against God was so shocking that even those in **the nations** around her had never heard of such a thing as a people refusing to worship and follow their god.
18:16 God's destruction of Judah would be so complete that any traveler who passed by would be horrified and **shake** his head.
18:18 The prophet's enemies launched a slander campaign against him, hoping to smear

Jeremiah's reputation so that no one would take his message seriously.
18:19-23 Jeremiah had heard God say time and again that Judah was beyond redemption in terms of warding off the coming invasion and captivity. Here he steps back, so to speak, and says, "God, pour out your judgment on my enemies, who are also your enemies. I've done all I can for them. Judge them as their sins deserve."

for they have dug a pit to capture me
and have hidden snares for my feet.[a]
23 But you, LORD, know
all their deadly plots against me.
Do not wipe out their iniquity;[b]
do not blot out their sin before you.
Let them be forced to stumble
before you;
deal with them in the time
of your anger.

THE CLAY JAR

19 This is what the LORD says: "Go, buy a potter's clay[c] jar. Take[A] some of the elders of the people and some of the leading priests[d] 2 and go out to Ben Hinnom Valley[e] near the entrance of the Potsherd Gate. Proclaim there the words I speak to you. 3 Say, 'Hear the word of the LORD, kings of Judah and residents of Jerusalem.[f] This is what the LORD of Armies, the God of Israel, says: I am going to bring such disaster on this place that everyone who hears about it will shudder[B,g] 4 because they have abandoned me[h] and made this a foreign place. They have burned incense in it to other gods that they, their fathers, and the kings of Judah have never known. They have filled this place with the blood of the innocent.[i] 5 They have built high places to Baal on which to burn their children in the fire as burnt offerings to Baal, something I have never commanded or mentioned; I never entertained the thought.[C,j] 6 "Therefore, look, the days are coming[k] — this is the LORD's declaration — when this place will no longer be called Topheth and Ben Hinnom Valley, but Slaughter Valley.[l] 7 I will spoil the plans of Judah and Jerusalem in this place. I will make them fall by the sword before their enemies, by the hand of those who intend to take their life. I will provide their corpses as food for the birds of the sky and for the wild animals of the land.[m] 8 I will make this city desolate, an object of scorn. Everyone who passes by it will be appalled and scoff because of all its wounds.[n] 9 I will make them eat the flesh of their sons and their daughters,

and they will eat each other's flesh in the distressing siege inflicted on them by their enemies who intend to take their life.'[o] 10 "Then you are to shatter the jar in the presence of the people going with you, 11 and you are to proclaim to them, 'This is what the LORD of Armies says: I will shatter these people and this city, like one shatters a potter's jar that can never again be mended. They will bury the dead in Topheth because there is no other place for burials.[p] 12 That is what I will do to this place — this is the declaration of the LORD — and to its residents, making this city like Topheth. 13 The houses of Jerusalem and the houses of the kings of Judah will become impure like that place Topheth — all the houses on whose rooftops they have burned incense to all the stars in the sky[q] and poured out drink offerings to other gods.'"

14 Jeremiah returned from Topheth, where the LORD had sent him to prophesy, stood in the courtyard of the LORD's temple,[r] and proclaimed to all the people, 15 "This is what the LORD of Armies, the God of Israel, says: 'I am about to bring on this city — and on all its cities — every disaster that I spoke against it, for they have become obstinate, not obeying my words.'"[s]

JEREMIAH BEATEN BY PASHHUR

20 Pashhur the priest,[t] the son of Immer[u] and chief official in the temple of the LORD, heard Jeremiah prophesying these things. 2 So Pashhur had the prophet Jeremiah beaten and put him in the stocks[v] at the Upper Benjamin Gate[w] in the LORD's temple. 3 The next day, when Pashhur released Jeremiah from the stocks, Jeremiah said to him, "The LORD does not call you Pashhur, but Terror Is on Every Side,[D] 4 for this is what the LORD says, 'I am about to make you a terror to both yourself and those you love.[x] They will fall by the sword of their enemies before your very eyes.[y] I will hand Judah over to the king of Babylon, and he will deport them to Babylon and put them to the sword. 5 I will give away all the

a 18:22 Ps 140:5; 142:3
b 18:23 Neh 4:5
c 19:1 Jr 18:2
d 2Kg 19:2
e 19:2 2Kg 23:10; 2Ch 28:3; Jr 7:31-32
f 19:3 Jr 17:20
g 1Sm 3:11; 2Kg 21:12
h 19:4 Dt 28:20; 31:16; 1Sm 8:8; 1Kg 11:33; 2Kg 22:17; 2Ch 34:25; Jr 1:16; 5:7
i Dt 19:10; 27:25; 2Kg 21:6,16; 24:4; Is 59:7; Jr 2:34
j 19:5 Jr 7:31; 32:35
k 19:6 Jr 7:32; 16:14; 23:5; 48:12; 49:2; 51:47,52
l Jr 25:34
m 19:7 Dt 28:26; Ps 79:2; Jr 7:33; 15:3; 16:4
n 19:8 Dt 28:37; 2Ch 29:8; 30:7; Jr 5:30; 25:9,18; 29:18; 42:18; 44:12,22; 49:17; 50:13; Mc 1:9; 6:16; Nah 3:19; Zph 2:15

o 19:9 Dt 28:53-57; Lm 4:10; Ezk 5:10
p 19:11 Jr 7:32
q 19:13 Dt 4:19; 2Kg 17:16; 23:4-5; Zph 1:5
r 19:14 2Ch 20:5; Jr 26:2
s 19:15 Jr 7:26
t 20:1 1Ch 9:12; Jr 21:1; 38:1
u 1Ch 24:14; Ezr 2:37-38
v 20:2 Jb 13:27; Jr 29:26; Ac 16:24
w Jr 37:13; 38:7; Zch 14:10
x 20:4 Jr 6:25; 20:10; 46:5
y 2Sm 12:11; Is 1:7; Jr 16:9; 29:21; 39:16; 51:24

A 19:1 Syr, Tg; MT omits Take   B 19:3 Lit about it, his ears will tingle; Hb obscure   C 19:5 Lit mentioned, and it did not arise on my heart
D 20:3 = Magor-missabib

19:1-2 The **jar** became another object lesson of God's determination to break Judah (19:1). **The Potsherd Gate** was so named because it was the passage through which potters took their potsherds (broken pieces of pottery) to be discarded. The **valley** mentioned was where the Judeans had previously sacrificed their children to idols (19:2; see 7:31). So if ever there was an unholy place, this was it.

19:6-7 As a result of Judah's disgusting practices, God said **Ben Hinnom Valley** would be called **Slaughter Valley** (19:6) because the dead bodies of Judah's slain people would pile up and become **food for . . . wild animals** (19:7). **19:9** This chilling prophecy warns that the people would resort to cannibalism as the **siege** by the Babylonians cut off Jerusalem's food supply.

20:1-6 Notice the flogging didn't dampen Jeremiah's commitment to share God's truth. He even told **Pashhur**, the priest who'd so mistreated him, that the Lord had decided on a new name for him: **Terror Is on Every Side** (20:3), a reference to what this man and his family would experience when God handed **Judah over to . . . Babylon** (20:4). Pashhur and his family would be deported in part because

[a] 20:5 Pr 15:6
[b] Dt 28:33; Ezk 23:29
[c] 2Kg 20:17; 21:14; Lm 2:7
[d] 20:6 Jr 34:3; Mc 4:10
[e] Jr 5:31; 14:13-14;
23:25-26,32; 27:10,14-16;
29:9,21,31
[f] 20:7 1Kg 20:20-22; 2Ch
18:20; Jr 15:18
[g] Gn 38:23; Jb 12:4; Ps
44:14; Jr 48:26-27,39; Lm
2:15-17; 3:14
[h] 20:8 Jr 6:7
[i] 20:9 Ex 5:23; Dt 18:20;
Ac 5:40
[j] Jb 32:18-20; Ps 39:3
[k] Jr 6:11; Am 3:8; 1Co 9:16
[l] 20:10 Jr 6:25; 20:3; 46:5
[m] Ps 35:15; 41:9; 56:6
[n] 20:11 Ex 15:3
[o] Mc 3:7
[p] 20:12 Jr 11:20

[q] 20:14 Jb 3:3
[r] 20:16 Gn 19:25
[s] Jr 18:22
[t] 20:17 Jb 3:10-11
[u] 20:18 Jb 3:20; Lm 3:1
[v] 21:1 1Ch 9:12; Neh 11:12;
Jr 38:1
[w] Jr 29:24-29; 37:3;
52:24-27
[x] 21:2 2Kg 24:11; 25:22;
2Ch 36:6-13
[y] 21:4 Jr 32:5; 37:8-10
[z] Is 13:4
[aa] 21:5 1Sm 4:1-5:12;
Lm 2:5

wealth[a] of this city, all its products[b] and valuables. Indeed, I will hand all the treasures of the kings of Judah over to their enemies. They will plunder them, seize them, and carry them off to Babylon.[c] 6 As for you, Pashhur, and all who live in your house, you will go into captivity. You will go to Babylon.[d] There you will die, and there you will be buried, you and all your friends to whom you prophesied lies.' "[e]

JEREMIAH COMPELLED TO PREACH

7 You deceived[f] me, LORD,
and I was deceived.
You seized me and prevailed.
I am a laughingstock all the time;[g]
everyone ridicules me.
8 For whenever I speak, I cry out,
I proclaim, "Violence and destruction!"[h]
so the word of the LORD
has become my
constant disgrace and derision.
9 I say, "I won't mention him
or speak any longer in his name."[i]
But his message becomes
a fire burning in my heart,[j]
shut up in my bones.
I become tired of holding it in,[k]
and I cannot prevail.
10 For I have heard the gossip
of many people,
"Terror is on every side![l]
Report him; let's report him!"
Everyone I trusted[A] watches
for my fall.[m]
"Perhaps he will be deceived
so that we might prevail against him
and take our vengeance on him."
11 But the LORD is with me
like a violent warrior.[n]
Therefore, my persecutors
will stumble and not prevail.
Since they have not succeeded,
they will be utterly shamed,
an everlasting humiliation that will
never be forgotten.[o]
12 LORD of Armies, testing the righteous
and seeing the heart[B] and mind,
let me see your vengeance on them,
for I have presented my case to you.[p]

13 Sing to the LORD!
Praise the LORD,
for he rescues the life of the needy
from evil people.

JEREMIAH'S LAMENT

14 May the day I was born
be cursed.[q]
May the day my mother bore me
never be blessed.
15 May the man be cursed
who brought the news
to my father, saying,
"A male child is born to you,"
bringing him great joy.
16 Let that man be like the cities
the LORD demolished
without compassion.[r]
Let him hear an outcry
in the morning[s]
and a war cry at noontime
17 because he didn't kill me
in the womb[t]
so that my mother might have been
my grave,
her womb eternally pregnant.
18 Why did I come out of the womb
to see only struggle and sorrow,[u]
to end my life in shame?

ZEDEKIAH'S REQUEST DENIED

21 This is the word that came to Jeremiah from the LORD when King Zedekiah sent Pashhur[v] son of Malchijah and the priest Zephaniah[w] son of Maaseiah to Jeremiah, asking, 2 "Inquire of the LORD on our behalf, since King Nebuchadnezzar[C][x] of Babylon is making war against us. Perhaps the LORD will perform for us something like all his past wondrous works so that Nebuchadnezzar will withdraw from us." 3 But Jeremiah answered, "This is what you are to say to Zedekiah: 4 'This is what the LORD, the God of Israel, says: I am about to repel the weapons of war in your hands,[y] those you are using to fight the king of Babylon and the Chaldeans[D] who are besieging you outside the wall, and I will bring them into the center of this city.[z] 5 I myself will fight against you[aa] with an outstretched

---

[A] 20:10 Lit Every man of my peace   [B] 20:12 Lit kidneys   [C] 21:2 Lit Nebuchadrezzar   [D] 21:4 = Babylonians

---

Pashhur had **prophesied lies** of his own—perhaps in an attempt to discredit Jeremiah's message (20:6).
20:11-13 Even though he was probably still in pain from his beating (20:2), Jeremiah found his voice to offer a song of **praise** to **the LORD** (20:13). This calls to mind Paul and Silas praying and singing praises to God in

the Philippian jail after being beaten (see Acts 16:22-25).
20:14-18 This is like the prayers of Job who suffered as much as any person ever has. Jeremiah's emotions are fluctuating in the midst of his distress—as anyone's would.
21:2 King Zedekiah's hope for **wondrous works** was probably a reference to the days

of King Hezekiah, when the Lord supernaturally routed the Assyrians (see 2 Kgs 18–19).
21:5 Instead of delivering the city, God himself would fight against it with **a strong arm**—a metaphorical way of referring to his omnipotent power.

hand and a strong arm,[a] with anger, rage, and intense wrath. [6] I will strike the residents of this city, both people and animals. They will die in a severe plague. [7] Afterward — this is the LORD's declaration — King Zedekiah of Judah, his officers, and the people — those in this city who survive the plague, the sword, and the famine — I will hand over to King Nebuchadnezzar of Babylon,[b] to their enemies, yes, to those who intend to take their lives. He will put them to the sword; he won't spare them or show pity or compassion.'[c]

A WARNING FOR THE PEOPLE

[8] "But tell this people, 'This is what the LORD says: Look, I am setting before you the way of life and the way of death.[d] [9] Whoever stays in this city will die by the sword, famine, and plague, but whoever goes out and surrenders to the Chaldeans who are besieging you will live and will retain his life like the spoils of war.[e] [10] For I have set my face against this city to bring disaster and not good[f] — this is the LORD's declaration. It will be handed over to the king of Babylon, who will burn it.'[g]

[11] "And to the house of the king of Judah say this: 'Hear the word of the LORD! [12] House of David, this is what the LORD says:

Administer justice every morning,
    and rescue the victim of robbery
    from his oppressor,[h]
or my anger will flare up like fire
    and burn unquenchably
    because of your evil deeds.
[13]   Beware! I am against you,[i]
    you who sit above the valley,
    you atop the rocky plateau —
        this is the LORD's declaration —
    you who say, "Who can come down
        against us?[j]
    Who can enter our hiding places?"
[14]   I will punish you according to
        what you have done[k] —
        this is the LORD's declaration.
    I will kindle a fire in your forest[l]
    that will consume everything
        around it.'"[m]

JUDGMENT AGAINST SINFUL KINGS

22 This is what the LORD says: "Go down to the palace of the king of Judah and announce this word there. [2] You are to say, 'Hear the word of the LORD, king of Judah, you who sit on the throne of David[n] — you, your officers, and your people who enter these gates. [3] This is what the LORD says: Administer justice and righteousness.[o] Rescue the victim of robbery from his oppressor.[p] Don't exploit or brutalize the resident alien, the fatherless, or the widow.[q] Don't shed innocent blood in this place. [4] For if you conscientiously carry out this word, then kings sitting on David's throne will enter through the gates of this palace[r] riding on chariots and horses — they, their officers, and their people. [5] But if you do not obey these words, then I swear by myself[s] — this is the LORD's declaration — that this house will become a ruin.'"[t]

[6] For this is what the LORD says concerning the house of the king of Judah:

    "You are like Gilead[u] to me,
    or the summit of Lebanon,
    but I will certainly turn you
        into a wilderness,
    uninhabited cities.
[7]   I will set apart destroyers[v]
        against you,
    each with his weapons.
    They will cut down the choicest
        of your cedars
    and throw them into the fire.

[8] "Many nations will pass by this city and ask one another, 'Why did the LORD do such a thing to this great city?' [9] They will answer, 'Because they abandoned the covenant[w] of the LORD their God and bowed in worship to other gods and served them.'"[x]

A MESSAGE CONCERNING SHALLUM

[10]   Do not weep for the dead;
        do not mourn for him.
    Weep bitterly for the one
        who has gone away,
    for he will never return again
        and see his native land.[y]

[a] 21:5 Dt 5:15; 26:8; 1Kg 8:42; Ps 136:12
[b] 21:7 Jr 37:17; 39:5-9; 52:9
[c] 2Ch 36:17
[d] 21:8 Dt 30:15-19; Pr 12:28; Jr 8:3
[e] 21:9 Jr 38:2; 39:18; 45:5
[f] 21:10 Jr 31:28; 39:16; 44:11,27; Am 9:4
[g] Jr 34:2,22; 37:8; 38:18
[h] 21:12 Dt 28:29; Ec 4:1; Jr 22:3
[i] 21:13 Ezk 13:8
[j] Jr 49:4
[k] 21:14 Is 3:10
[l] Ezk 20:47
[m] Jr 50:32

[n] 22:2 2Sm 3:10; 1Kg 2:12,24,45; Is 9:7; Jr 17:25; 22:30; 29:16; 36:30
[o] 22:3 2Sm 8:15; 1Kg 10:9; 2Ch 9:8; Is 33:5; 59:14; Jr 9:24; 23:5; 33:15; Am 5:7,24
[p] Dt 28:29; Ps 35:10; Ec 4:1; Jr 21:12
[q] Dt 14:29; 24:17,19-21; 27:19; Ps 146:9; Jr 7:6; Ezk 22:7
[r] 22:4 Jr 17:25
[s] 22:5 Gn 22:16; 1Sm 3:14; Ps 89:3,35; Is 45:23; 54:9; Jr 44:26; 49:13
[t] Jr 17:27
[u] 22:6 Sg 4:1; Jr 8:22; 46:11; 50:19; Mc 7:14; Zch 10:10
[v] 22:7 Ex 12:23; 2Sm 24:16; Is 54:16
[w] 22:8-9 Dt 29:24-25; 1Kg 19:10,14
[x] 22:9 Dt 30:17
[y] 22:10 2Sm 12:22-23

21:8-10 God had already decreed that Jerusalem would be handed over to the Babylonians and destroyed. Nevertheless, the people were given a choice about their fate: they could choose **life** or **death** (21:8). Those who held out in Jerusalem would die by God's three familiar forms of judgment: **the sword, famine, and plague**. Those who surrendered to the Babylonians (**Chaldeans**) would save their lives—although they'd be led into captivity (21:9). Because anyone who went over to the enemy was considered a traitor, this was not an easy choice to make.

21:11-14 The kings **of Judah** were the descendants of David, the one through whom Messiah would come. If any kings should have practiced righteousness and **justice**, then, it was the kings of the **house of David** (21:11-12). David was "a man after [God's] own heart" (1 Sam 13:14). But if Zedekiah thought that being David's successor gave him an insider advantage with God, he was sorely mistaken.

Being David's descendant gave one no advantage unless it was accompanied by obedience. The Babylonian siege ramps being built outside the walls of Jerusalem should have driven Zedekiah and his officials to their knees.

22:8-9 Make no mistake: your spiritual commitments have significant consequences for you and for those around you, too.

22:10-30 The actions of Zedekiah's three immediate predecessors, and their corresponding judgment by the Lord, should have

[a] 22:11 2Kg 23:32-35; 1Ch 3:15
[b] 22:13 Mc 3:10
[c] Lv 19:13; Jms 5:4
[d] 22:14 1Kg 6:9,15,18; 7:3,7
[e] 22:15 Jr 22:3
[f] 22:16 Dt 24:14
[g] 22:17 Is 30:12; 59:9-15; Jr 6:6; Ezk 22:7,12,29; Mc 3:11; Hab 1:3
[h] 22:18 2Kg 23:34-24:6; 2Ch 36:4-8
[i] 22:19 Jr 36:30
[j] 22:20 Nm 27:12; Dt 32:49
[k] Jr 3:1
[l] 22:21 Jr 3:25
[m] 22:22 Is 41:11
[n] 22:23 Ps 48:6; Is 13:8; 21:3; 42:14; Jr 4:31; 6:24; 13:21; 30:6; 50:43; Mc 4:9-10; 1Th 5:3
[o] 22:24 2Kg 24:6-17; Jr 37:1; 52:31
[p] Gn 38:18; 1Kg 21:8; Hg 2:23
[q] 22:25 Jr 34:20-21
[r] 22:26 2Kg 24:15
[s] 2Kg 24:8

[11] For this is what the LORD says concerning Shallum[a] son of Josiah, king of Judah, who became king in place of his father Josiah, and who has left this place: "He will never return here again, [12] but he will die in the place where they deported him, never seeing this land again."

A MESSAGE CONCERNING JEHOIAKIM

[13] Woe for the one who builds
his palace
through unrighteousness,[b]
his upstairs rooms
through injustice,
who makes his neighbor serve
without pay
and will not give him his wages,[c]
[14] who says, "I will build myself
a massive palace,
with spacious upstairs rooms."
He will cut windows[A] in it,
and it will be paneled with cedar[d]
and painted bright red.
[15] Are you a king because you excel
in cedar?
Didn't your father eat and drink
and administer justice
and righteousness?[e]
Then it went well with him.
[16] He took up the case of the poor
and needy;[f]
then it went well.
Is this not what it means
to know me?
This is the LORD's declaration.
[17] But you have eyes and a heart
for nothing
except your own dishonest profit,
shedding innocent blood
and committing extortion
and oppression.[g]

[18] Therefore, this is what the LORD says concerning Jehoiakim[h] son of Josiah, king of Judah:

They will not mourn for him, saying,
"Woe, my brother!" or "Woe,
my sister!"
They will not mourn for him, saying,
"Woe, lord! Woe, his majesty!"
[19] He will be buried like a donkey,[i]
dragged off and thrown
outside Jerusalem's gates.
[20] Go up to Lebanon and cry out;
raise your voice in Bashan;
cry out from Abarim,[j]
for all your lovers[B]
have been crushed.[k]
[21] I spoke to you when
you were secure.
You said, "I will not listen."
This has been your way since youth;[l]
indeed, you have never listened
to me.
[22] The wind will take charge of[C] all
your shepherds,
and your lovers will go
into captivity.
Then you will be ashamed
and humiliated[m]
because of all your evil.
[23] You residents of Lebanon,
nestled among the cedars,
how you will groan[D] when pains
come on you,
agony like a woman in labor.[n]

A MESSAGE CONCERNING CONIAH

[24] "As I live" — this is the LORD's declaration — "though you, Coniah[E,o] son of Jehoiakim, the king of Judah, were a signet ring[p] on my right hand, I would tear you from it. [25] In fact, I will hand you over to those you dread,[q] who intend to take your life, to Nebuchadnezzar king of Babylon and the Chaldeans. [26] I will hurl you and the mother who gave birth[r] to you into another land,[s] where neither of you were born, and there you will both die. [27] They will never return to the land they long to return to."

[A] 22:14 Lit my windows [B] 22:20 Or friends, or allies, also in v. 22 [C] 22:22 Lit will shepherd [D] 22:23 LXX, Syr, Vg; MT reads will be pitied
[E] 22:24 = Jehoiachin

served as object lessons for Zedekiah not to follow their destructive and evil ways. That they are addressed here demonstrates that Jeremiah's book does not always follow a neat chronological order.

The third king in Jeremiah's series of messages was Jehoiachin, also known as **Coniah** or Jeconiah (22:24; see Matt 1:11). God's word to this man was filled with judgment and even contempt, calling him **a despised, shattered pot** (Jer 22:28). Coniah was so useless to the Lord that he placed a severe curse on

this king and his family, saying none of Coniah's descendants would sit **on the throne of David** (22:30).

This curse has serious messianic implications, for the Messiah was to come from David's line. And surprisingly, Coniah appears in Jesus's genealogy in Matthew (as Jeconiah; see Matt 1:11). Had Jesus been Joseph's biological son, then, he would have been prevented from sitting on the throne of David by this curse. But of course, Jesus was not conceived by Joseph but by the

Holy Spirit. So since Joseph was Jesus's legal father, but not his biological father, Jesus was not contaminated by the curse on Jeconiah's descendants.

The Messiah, though, still had to have a biological tie to David, which Jesus had—as demonstrated in Luke's genealogy (see Luke 3:23-38). Luke traced Jesus's lineage back to David through Solomon's son Nathan, in what many commentators agree was the genealogical line of Mary, who was Jesus's biological mother.

28 Is this man Coniah
a despised, shattered pot,[a]
a jar no one wants?
Why are he and his descendants
hurled out
and cast into a land
they have not known?
29 Earth, earth, earth,
hear the word of the LORD!

30 This is what the LORD says:
Record this man as childless,[b]
a man who will not be successful
in his lifetime.
None of his descendants
will succeed
in sitting on the throne of David[c]
or ruling again in Judah.

THE LORD AND HIS SHEEP

23 "Woe to the shepherds who destroy and scatter the sheep of my pasture!"[d] This is the LORD's declaration. **2** "Therefore, this is what the LORD, the God of Israel, says about the shepherds who tend my people: You have scattered my flock,[e] banished them, and have not attended to them.[f] I am about to attend to you because of your evil acts" — this is the LORD's declaration. **3** "I will gather the remnant of my flock from all the lands where I have banished them,[g] and I will return them to their grazing land. They will become fruitful and numerous.[h] **4** I will raise up shepherds over them who will tend them.[i] They will no longer be afraid or discouraged, nor will any be missing."[j] This is the LORD's declaration.

THE RIGHTEOUS BRANCH OF DAVID

5 "Look, the days are coming"[k] — this is the LORD's declaration —
"when I will raise up a Righteous
Branch for David.[l]
He will reign wisely as king
and administer justice and
righteousness in the land.[m]
6 In his days Judah will be saved,
and Israel will dwell securely.[n]
This is the name he will be called:
The LORD Is Our Righteousness.[A,o]

7 "Look, the days are coming"[p] — the LORD's declaration — "when it will no longer be said, 'As the LORD lives[q] who brought the Israelites from the land of Egypt,' **8** but, 'As the LORD lives, who brought and led the descendants of the house of Israel from the land of the north and from all the other countries where I[B] had banished them.' They will dwell once more in their own land."[r]

FALSE PROPHETS CONDEMNED

9 Concerning the prophets:
My heart is broken within me,[s]
and all my bones tremble.
I have become like a drunkard,
like a man overcome by wine,
because of the LORD,
because of his holy words.
10 For the land is full of adulterers;[t]
the land mourns[u] because
of the curse,[v]
and the grazing lands
in the wilderness have dried up.
Their way of life[c] has become evil,
and their power is not rightly used
11 because both prophet and priest
are ungodly,[w]
even in my house[x] I have found
their evil.
This is the LORD's declaration.
12 Therefore, their way will seem
like slippery paths in the gloom.[y]
They will be driven away
and fall down there,
for I will bring disaster on them,
the year of their punishment.[z]
This is the LORD's declaration.

13 Among the prophets of Samaria
I saw something disgusting:
They prophesied by Baal
and led my people Israel astray.[aa]
14 Among the prophets
of Jerusalem also
I saw a horrible thing:[ab]
They commit adultery and walk
in lies.
They strengthen the hands
of evildoers,
and none turns his back on evil.
They are all like Sodom[ac] to me;

[a] 22:28 Ps 31:12; Jr 48:38; Hs 8:8
[b] 22:30 1Ch 3:17; Mt 1:12
[c] Jr 36:30
[d] 23:1 Ps 100:3; Ezk 34:2,31; Zch 11:5-7,15-17
[e] 23:2 Jr 10:21; 50:6; Ezk 34:5,12,31
[f] Ps 8:4; Is 23:16; Ezk 34:3
[g] 23:3 Ezk 34:12-13
[h] Gn 1:26-28; 9:1-7; 35:11
[i] 23:4 Ezk 34:23; Mc 5:2-6
[j] Ezk 34:25; Mc 7:14
[k] 23:5 Jr 7:32; 9:25; 16:14; 19:6; 23:5,7; 30:3; 31:27,31; 33:14-16; 48:12; 49:2; 51:47,52
[l] 1Kg 12:16; Is 4:2; 55:3-4; Jr 30:9; 33:15; Ezk 34:23; 37:24-25; Hs 3:5; Zch 3:8; 6:12
[m] 1Ch 18:14; Ps 99:4; Is 9:7; 11:1-9; 33:5; Jr 9:24; 22:15; 33:15
[n] 23:6 Dt 33:12,28; Ps 16:9; Pr 1:33; Jr 33:16
[o] Ps 4:1; Jr 33:16; 1Co 1:30
[p] 23:7 Jr 7:32; 16:14; 19:6; 48:12; 49:2; 51:47,52
[q] Jdg 8:19; 1Sm 14:39,45; 2Sm 4:9; 1Kg 1:29; 2:24; Jr 4:1-2; 5:2; 16:14-15; 38:16; Hs 4:15
[r] 23:8 Jr 16:15
[s] 23:9 Hab 3:16
[t] 23:10 Jr 9:2; Hs 7:4; Mal 3:5
[u] Jr 12:4; Am 1:2; Rm 8:22
[v] Dt 11:29; 27:13; Gl 3:13
[w] 23:11 Jr 6:13; 14:18; Zph 3:4
[x] 1Ch 17:14; 28:6; Is 56:5,7; Jr 11:15; 12:7; Ezk 23:39; Hs 9:15; Hab 1:9; Zch 1:16; Mal 3:10
[y] 23:12 Ps 35:6; 73:18
[z] Jr 11:23; 48:44
[aa] 23:13 Pr 12:26; Is 3:12; Jr 50:6; Mc 3:5
[ab] 23:14 Jr 5:30; Hs 6:10
[ac] Gn 13:10-13; 18:16-19:28; Is 1:10-17

[A] 23:6 = Yahweh-zidkenu [B] 23:8 LXX reads he [C] 23:10 Lit Their manner of running

23:1-2 These **shepherds** were uncaring, faithless leaders of Judah.
23:5 This is a reference to the coming of God's Son, the Messiah, the Lord Jesus Christ. He will rule in righteousness for one thousand years in his millennial kingdom.

23:9-14 The prophets referenced here were the liars who denied Jeremiah's message and lulled the people of Judah into a false security even as the Babylonians marched toward Jerusalem. Just as **the prophets of Samaria** in the northern kingdom **led...Israel astray** (23:13), so the prophets of Judah were so gross in their immorality that the Lord compared them to **Sodom** and **Gomorrah** (23:14; see Gen 19).

a 23:15 Am 5:7; 6:12
b Jr 8:14; 9:15
c 23:16 Jr 14:14; Lm 2:9; Ezk 7:26; 12:24; 13:16; Mc 3:6
d Is 1:20; 40:5; 58:14; 62:2; Jr 9:12; Mc 4:4
e 23:17 Is 5:24
f Jr 4:10
g 23:18 Jb 15:8; Ps 25:14; 89:7
h 23:19 Ps 83:15; Is 29:6; Zch 9:14
i 23:20 Gn 27:45; Is 5:25; 9:12,17,21; 10:4; Jr 2:35
j 23:19-20 Jr 30:23-24
k 23:21 Jr 14:14
l Jos 7:22; 2Sm 18:21; Ps 147:15
m 23:22 Jr 4:18
n 23:23 Ps 139:1-10; Am 9:2-3

o 23:24 Gn 3:8; 4:14; Jb 34:22
p Ps 139:7-12; Am 9:2-4
q 23:25 Jr 5:31; 14:14; 20:6; 23:32; 27:10,14-16; 29:9,21,31
r 23:27 Jdg 3:7; 8:33-34
s 23:30 Dt 18:20; Jr 14:14-15; Ezk 13:8
t 23:32 Dt 18:20
u Is 30:5-6; Jr 2:8,11

Jerusalem's residents are
like Gomorrah.

15 Therefore, this is what the LORD of Armies says concerning the prophets:

I am about to feed them wormwood*a*
and give them poisoned water
to drink,*b*
for from the prophets of Jerusalem
ungodliness^A has spread
throughout the land.

16 This is what the LORD of Armies says: "Do not listen to the words of the prophets who prophesy to you. They are deluding you. They speak visions from their own minds,*c* not from the LORD's mouth.*d* **17** They keep on saying to those who despise me,*e* 'The LORD has spoken: You will have peace.'*f* They have said to everyone who follows the stubbornness of his heart, 'No harm will come to you.'"

18   For who has stood in the council*g*
             of the LORD
     to see and hear his word?
     Who has paid attention to his word
             and obeyed?

19   Look, a storm from the LORD!*h*
     Wrath has gone out,
             a whirling storm.
     It will whirl about the heads
             of the wicked.

20   The LORD's anger will not turn away*i*
             until he has completely fulfilled
             the purposes of his heart.
     In time to come you will
             understand it clearly.*j*

21   I did not send out these prophets,*k*
             yet they ran.*l*
     I did not speak to them,
             yet they prophesied.

22   If they had really stood in my council,
             they would have enabled my people
             to hear my words
     and would have turned them
             from their evil ways
             and their evil deeds.*m*

23 "Am I a God who is only near"*n* — this is the LORD's declaration — "and not a God who is far away? **24** Can a person hide in secret places where I cannot see him?"*o* — the LORD's declaration. "Do I not fill the heavens and the earth?"*p* — the LORD's declaration.

25 "I have heard what the prophets who prophesy a lie in my name have said: 'I had a dream! I had a dream!'*q* **26** How long will this continue in the minds of the prophets prophesying lies, prophets of the deceit of their own minds? **27** Through their dreams that they tell one another, they plan to cause my people to forget my name as their fathers forgot my name through Baal worship.*r* **28** The prophet who has only a dream should recount the dream, but the one who has my word should speak my word truthfully, for what is straw compared to grain?" — this is the LORD's declaration. **29** "Is not my word like fire" — this is the LORD's declaration — "and like a hammer that pulverizes rock? **30** Therefore, take note! I am against the prophets"*s* — the LORD's declaration — "who steal my words from each other. **31** I am against the prophets" — the LORD's declaration — "who use their own tongues to make a declaration. **32** I am against those who prophesy false dreams"*t* — the LORD's declaration — "telling them and leading my people astray with their reckless lies. It was not I who sent or commanded them, and they are of no benefit at all*u* to these people" — this is the LORD's declaration.

THE BURDEN OF THE LORD

33 "Now when these people or a prophet or a priest asks you, 'What is the burden^B of the LORD?' you will respond to them, 'What is the burden? I will throw you away! This is the LORD's declaration.' **34** As for the prophet, priest, or people who say, 'The burden of the LORD,' I will punish that man and his household. **35** This is what each man is to say to his friend and to his brother: 'What has the LORD answered?' or 'What has the LORD spoken?' **36** But no longer refer to^C the burden of the LORD, for each man's word becomes his burden and you pervert the words of the living God, the LORD of Armies, our God. **37** Say to the prophet, 'What has the LORD answered you?' or 'What has the LORD spoken?' **38** But if you say, 'The

---

^A 23:15 Or *pollution* ^B 23:33 The Hb word for *burden* (Ex 23:5; 2Sm 15:33) can also mean "oracle" (Is 13:1; Nah 1:10). ^C 23:36 Or *longer remember*

23:17-29 The prophets' assurances of safety to Judah were diametrically opposed to God's commands to repent (see 25:17-18). If God's Word clearly condemns your actions and someone assures you that **no harm will come to you** (23:17), you'd better find a new counselor. Otherwise, prepare to meet the **wrath** of God (23:19-20). His **word** is **like a hammer that pulverizes rock** (23:29). If you play a game of chicken with God's Word on any matter, there's only one possible outcome for you: getting pulverized.

23:33-40 God was tired of hearing the lying prophets try to authenticate their messages by saying, **The burden of the LORD** (23:34) as if it were a magic formula. God holds His Word in high esteem.

burden of the LORD,' then this is what the LORD says: Because you have said, 'The burden of the LORD,' and I specifically told you not to say, 'The burden of the LORD,' [39] I will surely forget you.[A] I will throw you away from my presence — both you and the city that I gave you and your fathers. [40] I will bring on you everlasting disgrace and humiliation[a] that will never be forgotten."

THE GOOD AND THE BAD FIGS

24 After King Nebuchadnezzar of Babylon had deported Jeconiah[B] son of Jehoiakim king of Judah, the officials of Judah, and the craftsmen and metalsmiths[b] from Jerusalem and had brought them to Babylon, the LORD showed me two baskets of figs[c] placed in front of the temple of the LORD. [2] One basket contained very good figs, like early figs,[d] but the other basket contained very bad figs, so bad they were inedible. [3] The LORD said to me, "What do you see, Jeremiah?"

I said, "Figs! The good figs are very good, but the bad figs are extremely bad, so bad they are inedible."

[4] The word of the LORD came to me: [5] "This is what the LORD, the God of Israel, says: Like these good figs, so I regard as good the exiles from Judah I sent away from this place to the land of the Chaldeans. [6] I will keep my eyes on them for their good[e] and will return them to this land. I will build them up and not demolish them; I will plant them and not uproot them.[f] [7] I will give them a heart to know me,[g] that I am the LORD. They will be my people, and I will be their God because they will return to me with all their heart.[h]

[8] "But as for the bad figs, so bad they are inedible,[i] this is what the LORD says: In this way I will deal with King Zedekiah of Judah, his officials, and the remnant of Jerusalem — those remaining in this land or living in the land of Egypt.[j] [9] I will make them an object of horror[k] and a disaster to all the kingdoms of the earth, an example for disgrace, scorn, ridicule,[l] and cursing, wherever I have banished them.[m] [10] I will send the sword, famine, and plague[n] against them until they have perished from the land I gave to them and their ancestors."

THE SEVENTY-YEAR EXILE

25 This is the word that came to Jeremiah concerning all the people of Judah in the fourth year of Jehoiakim[o] son of Josiah, king of Judah (which was the first year of King Nebuchadnezzar of Babylon). [2] The prophet Jeremiah spoke concerning all the people of Judah and all the residents of Jerusalem as follows: [3] "From the thirteenth year of Josiah son of Amon,[p] king of Judah, until this very day — twenty-three years — the word of the LORD has come to me, and I have spoken to you time and time again,[C,q] but you have not obeyed. [4] The LORD sent all his servants the prophets to you time and time again,[D] but you have not obeyed or even paid attention.[E,r] [5] He announced, 'Turn, each of you, from your evil way of life and from your evil deeds.[s] Live in the land the LORD gave to you and your ancestors long ago and forever.[t] [6] Do not follow other gods to serve them and to bow in worship to them,[u] and do not anger me by the work of your hands.[v] Then I will do you no harm.' [7] "But you have not obeyed me' — this is the LORD's declaration — 'with the result that you have angered me by the work of your hands and brought disaster on yourselves.'

[8] "Therefore, this is what the LORD of Armies says: 'Because you have not obeyed my words, [9] I am going to send for all the families of the north'[w] — this is the LORD's

Cross-references
a 23:40 Ps 78:66; Jr 20:11
b 24:1 2Kg 24:14,16; Jr 29:2
c Am 8:1
d 24:2 Is 28:4; Hs 9:10; Mc 7:1
e 24:6 Am 9:4
f Jr 1:10
g 24:7 Dt 30:6; Jr 31:33; 32:40
h 2Ch 6:38; Jr 29:13
i 24:8 Jr 29:17

j 24:8 Jr 44:1
k 24:9 2Ch 29:8; Jr 15:4; 29:18
l Dt 28:37; 1Kg 9:7; 2Ch 7:20
m Jr 24:9; 42:18; 44:8,12; 49:13
n 24:10 Jr 14:12; 21:9; 29:17-18
o 25:1 Jr 26:1; 2Ch 33:34-24:6; 2Ch 36:4-8; Jr 36:1
p 25:3 Jr 1:2
q 2Ch 36:15; Jr 7:13,25; 11:7; 25:3; 26:5; 29:19; 32:33; 35:14,15; 44:4
r 25:4 Jr 7:25-26
s 25:5 2Kg 17:13; Jr 4:18; 18:11; 35:15; Zch 1:4; Ac 3:26
t Jr 35:15; 40:9; Ezk 36:28; 37:25
u 25:6 Dt 8:19; Jr 13:10
v Dt 31:29; 1Kg 16:7; Jr 44:8
w 25:9 Jr 1:13; 16:16; 43:10

A 23:39 Some Hb mss; other Hb mss, LXX, Syr, Vg read *surely lift you up*   B 24:1 = Jehoiachin   C 25:3 Lit *you; rising early and speaking*   D 25:4 Lit *to you, rising early and sending*   E 25:4 Lit *even inclined your ear to hear*

24:1-10 The **two baskets of figs** couldn't have differed from one another more: there were ripe, edible figs and rotten, disgusting ones (24:1-2). They represented those who had gone into captivity and those who stayed in Judah or fled to Egypt (24:5, 8).

One might think the exiles were the bad figs and the latter were the good figs, but not so. The exiles who went to Babylon actually were **sent away** by the Lord (24:5). They went with his promise of restoration once their hearts had turned fully back to him (24:6-7).

King Zedekiah, Judah's final king, and those with him were **the bad figs** (24:8). They continued to disobey God and would experience his curse (24:9-10). Jeremiah warned Zedekiah to surrender to Nebuchadnezzar, but he wouldn't listen (see 38:14-28). He also advised those who rebelled against Nebuchadnezzar not to flee to Egypt, but they rejected his counsel (see 42:1–44:14). Therefore, God condemned them to be an object of **scorn** (24:9). Those who are determined to act like rotten fruit can't complain when they're treated like rotten fruit.

25:1 The date for this chapter places it even earlier than the previous message, around 604 BC, at the beginning of Nebuchadnezzar's reign. Nevertheless, the topical way the book is arranged makes this message the climax of Jeremiah's warnings to Judah.

25:3-4 God's faithful prophet had been at it for **twenty-three years** (25:3). And I don't know any pastor who would have wanted the flock Jeremiah oversaw. Jeremiah could probably have counted his "converts" on one hand, with fingers left over. Though he'd **spoken . . . time and time again**, most hadn't **even paid attention** (25:3-4).

25:7 The people of Judah had **brought disaster on** themselves. Ignoring God's Word has consequences.

a 25:9 Is 45:1
b Jr 4:7; 18:16; 19:8
c Dt 28:37; 2Ch 29:8; 30:7;
Jr 5:30; 19:8; 25:18; 29:18;
42:18; 44:12,22; 49:17;
50:13; Mc 6:16; Zph 2:15
d 25:10 Jr 7:34; 16:9; 33:11
e 25:11 2Ch 36:21; Is 23:15;
Jr 29:10; Dn 9:2; Zch
1:12; 7:5
f 25:12 Is 13:19
g 25:14 Ps 28:4; Pr
24:12,29; Jr 50:29; Lm 3:64
h 25:15 Jb 21:20; Ps 75:8;
Is 51:17; 63:6; Jr 49:12; Rv
14:8,10; 18:3
i 25:16 Jr 9:16; 24:10; 29:17;
49:37

j 25:23 Lv 19:27; Jr 9:26;
49:32
k 25:26 Jr 51:41
l 25:27 Jr 25:16; Hab 2:16
m 25:29 2Sm 12:11; 1Kg
14:10; 21:21; 2Kg 22:16;
2Ch 34:24; Is 13:11; 31:2;
Jr 4:6; 6:19; 11:23; 21:10;
23:12; 44:11; 45:5
n Dn 9:18
o 25:28-29 Jr 49:12-13

declaration — 'and send for my servant[a] Nebuchadnezzar king of Babylon, and I will bring them against this land, against its residents, and against all these surrounding nations, and I will completely destroy them and make them an example of horror[b] and scorn, and ruins forever.[c] 10 I will eliminate the sound of joy and gladness from them — the voice of the groom and the bride,[d] the sound of the millstones and the light of the lamp. 11 This whole land will become a desolate ruin, and these nations will serve the king of Babylon for seventy years.[e] 12 When the seventy years are completed, I will punish the king of Babylon and that nation' — this is the LORD's declaration — 'the land of the Chaldeans, for their iniquity, and I will make it a ruin forever.[f] 13 I will bring on that land all my words I have spoken against it, all that is written in this book that Jeremiah prophesied against all the nations. 14 For many nations and great kings will enslave them, and I will repay them according to their deeds and the work of their hands.'"[g]

THE CUP OF GOD'S WRATH

15 This is what the LORD, the God of Israel, said to me: "Take this cup of the wine of wrath from my hand and make all the nations to whom I am sending you drink from it.[h] 16 They will drink, stagger,[A] and go out of their minds because of the sword I am sending among them."[i]

17 So I took the cup from the LORD's hand and made all the nations to whom the LORD sent me drink from it.

18 Jerusalem and the other cities of Judah, its kings and its officials, to make them a desolate ruin, an example for scorn and cursing — as it is today;

19 Pharaoh king of Egypt, his officers, his leaders, all his people,
20 and all the mixed peoples; all the kings of the land of Uz; all the kings of the land of the Philistines — Ashkelon, Gaza, Ekron, and the remnant of Ashdod;
21 Edom, Moab, and the Ammonites;
22 all the kings of Tyre, all the kings of Sidon, and the kings of the coasts and islands;
23 Dedan, Tema, Buz, and all those who clip the hair on their temples;[B,j]
24 all the kings of Arabia, and all the kings of the mixed peoples who have settled in the desert;
25 all the kings of Zimri, all the kings of Elam, and all the kings of Media;
26 all the kings of the north, both near and far from one another; that is, all the kingdoms of the world throughout the earth. Finally, the king of Sheshach[C,k] will drink after them.

27 "Then you are to say to them, 'This is what the LORD of Armies, the God of Israel, says: Drink,[l] get drunk, and vomit. Fall down and never get up again, as a result of the sword I am sending among you.' 28 If[D] they refuse to accept the cup from your hand and drink, you are to say to them, 'This is what the LORD of Armies says: You must drink! 29 For I am already bringing disaster[m] on the city that bears my name,[n] so how could you possibly go unpunished? You will not go unpunished, for I am summoning a sword against all the inhabitants of the earth. This is the declaration of the LORD of Armies.'[o]

A 25:16 Or *vomit*   B 25:23 Or *who live in distant places*   C 25:26 = Babylon   D 25:28 Or *When*

25:11-12 The prophet Daniel was probably reading this portion of Jeremiah's prophecy when he realized that "the number of years for the desolation of Jerusalem would be seventy" and prayed for God to restore his people to their land (Dan 9:2-3).

The number *seventy* wasn't chosen out of thin air. Over the years, Israel had failed to obey the law of Sabbath rest for the land, which required it to lie fallow every seventh year (see Lev 25:1-7). The people hadn't failed to do this once or twice — but for 490 years! That equates to a total of seventy missed Sabbath years. God would see to it that his land received its rest — with his people's obedience or without it.
25:15-16 The **cup of the wine of [God's] wrath** (25:15) is a familiar biblical image for the

stored-up judgment of holy God against sin. 25:27-29 An important principle of biblical justice is embedded in this prophecy. One of the sins for which Judah was repeatedly condemned was mistreatment of the poor and defenseless among her people. Social injustices were not merely viewed as secular affronts to communities, but also as a spiritual affront to God (see Zech 7:9-12). God's people were specifically instructed to seek the welfare of the secular city in which they were living and to pray for its well-being so that it would become a better place.

One role of the church today, and of believers who comprise the church, is to execute divine justice on behalf of the oppressed. We are not to mistreat the poor (see Jas 2:15-16)

or have prejudice (see Gal 2:11-14). Rather, the church is commissioned to meet the physical needs of the "have nots" within it and in society.

This is not, however, to be confused with subsidizing irresponsibility, which the Bible strictly prohibits (see Prov 6:9-11; 10:4; 13:18; 24:30-34; 2 Thess 3:10). Even in the biblical practice of gleaning — leaving behind portions of a harvest for the poor to collect — the poor needed to exercise responsibility in gathering what had been left behind (see Lev 23:22). The amount of work that was put forth resulted in the amount of food obtained. The church is to work for conditions under which all people have the same opportunity to provide for themselves and their families.

JUDGMENT ON THE WHOLE WORLD

30 "As for you, you are to prophesy all these things to them, and say to them:

The LORD roars from on high;
he makes his voice heard
    from his holy dwelling.[a]
He roars loudly
    over his grazing land;
he calls out with a shout, like those
    who tread grapes,
against all the inhabitants
    of the earth.

31 The tumult reaches to the ends
    of the earth
because the LORD brings a case
    against[b] the nations.
He enters into judgment
    with all people.[c]
As for the wicked, he hands them over
    to the sword —
    this is the LORD's declaration.

32 "This is what the LORD of Armies says:
Pay attention! Disaster spreads
    from nation to nation.
A huge storm is stirred up
    from the ends of the earth."[d]

33 Those slain by the LORD[e] on that day will be scattered from one end of the earth to the other. They will not be mourned,[f] gathered, or buried. They will be like manure on the soil's surface.

34 Wail, you shepherds, and cry out.
Roll in the dust,[g] you leaders
    of the flock.
Because the days of your slaughter
    have come,[h]
you will fall and become shattered
    like a precious vase.

35 Flight will be impossible
    for the shepherds,
and escape, for the leaders
    of the flock.

36 Hear the sound of the shepherds' cry,
the wail of the leaders of the flock,
for the LORD is destroying
    their pasture.

37 Peaceful grazing land
    will become lifeless
because of the LORD's burning anger.[i]

38 He has left his den like a lion,
for their land has become
    a desolation
because of the sword[A]
    of the oppressor,[j]
because of his burning anger.

JEREMIAH'S SPEECH IN THE TEMPLE

26 At the beginning of the reign of Jehoiakim[k] son of Josiah, king of Judah, this word came from the LORD: **2** "This is what the LORD says: Stand in the courtyard of the LORD's temple and speak all the words I have commanded you to speak to all Judah's cities that are coming to worship there. Do not hold back a word.[l] **3** Perhaps they will listen and turn — each from his evil way of life — so that I might relent[m] concerning the disaster that I plan to do to them because of the evil of their deeds. **4** You are to say to them, 'This is what the LORD says: If you do not listen to me by living according to my instruction that I set before you[n] **5** and by listening to the words of my servants the prophets[o] — whom I have been sending to you time and time again,[B,p] though you did not listen — **6** I will make this temple like Shiloh.[q] I will make this city an example for cursing for all the nations of the earth.' "

JEREMIAH SEIZED

7 The priests, the prophets, and all the people heard Jeremiah speaking these words in the temple of the LORD. **8** When he finished the address the LORD had commanded him to deliver to all the people, immediately the priests, the prophets, and all the people took hold of him, yelling, "You must surely die! **9** How dare you prophesy in the name of the LORD, 'This temple will become like Shiloh and this city will become an uninhabited ruin'! " Then all the people crowded around Jeremiah at the LORD's temple.

10 When the officials of Judah heard about these things, they went from the king's palace to the LORD's temple and sat at the entrance of the New Gate of the LORD's temple.[C,r] **11** Then the priests and prophets

---

[a] 25:30 Dt 26:15; 2Ch 30:27; Jb 37:4; Ps 76:2; Hs 11:10; Jl 3:16; Am 1:2; 3:8
[b] 25:31 Jb 11:5; Jr 2:9; Hs 4:1; 12:3; Mc 6:2
[c] Is 66:16
[d] 25:32 Jr 23:19; 30:23
[e] 25:33 Is 66:16
[f] Jr 16:4
[g] 25:34 Jb 2:8,12; Jr 6:26; Ezk 27:30
[h] Jr 7:32; 19:6
[i] 25:37 Nm 32:14; 2Ch 28:11; Zph 2:2

[j] 25:38 Jr 46:16
[k] 26:1 2Kg 23:34–24:6; 2Ch 36:4-8
[l] 26:2 Dt 4:2; Ec 3:14
[m] 26:3 Ex 32:12,14; Am 7:3,6; Jnh 3:9-10
[n] 26:4 Lv 26:14
[o] 26:5 Jr 25:3-4
[p] Jr 7:13,25; 11:7; 25:3; 29:19; 32:33; 35:14-15; 44:4
[q] 26:6 Jos 18:1,8-10; 21:2; 1Sm 1:3
[r] 26:10 Jr 36:10; Ezk 46:1,3

[A] 25:38 Some Hb mss, LXX, Tg; other Hb mss read *burning* mss read *the New Gate of the LORD*   [B] 26:5 Lit *you, rising early and sending*   [C] 26:10 Many Hb mss, Syr, Tg, Vg; other Hb

---

25:30 Like a lion ready to pounce, God **roars** against nations that dismiss him.

26:1-6 The message recorded here was actually delivered earlier than the previous one, **at the beginning of the reign of Jehoiakim son of Josiah** (26:1), probably in 609–608 BC.

26:7-11 Rather than repenting, **the priests, the prophets, and all the people** were so furious at Jeremiah for his prophecy of doom for the **temple** and Jerusalem that they wanted to kill him (26:7-9). They even dragged him to the temple for a trial! The

city officials gathered at the **New Gate of the LORD's temple**, where the priests and prophets themselves called for the **death** penalty on God's spokesman—another indication of how far Judah had sunk into sin (26:10-11).

a 26:11 Jr 38:4
b 26:13 Jr 4:18; 7:3-5; 18:11
c 26:15 Dt 19:10,13; 21:8-9;
2Kg 21:16; 24:4; Jr 7:6;
22:3,17; Mt 27:4
d 26:17 Ac 5:34
e 26:18 Mc 1:1,14
f 2Kg 16:20; 18:4-21:3; Is
36:1-39:8
g Mc 3:12
h 26:19 2Ch 32:26
i Ex 32:14; 2Sm 24:16

j 26:20 Jos 9:17; 1Sm
6:21; 7:2
k 26:22 Jr 36:12
l 26:24 2Kg 22:12,14; Jr
39:14; 40:5-43:6
m 27:1 2Kg 24:17; Jr 1:3; 21:1
n 27:2 Jr 28:10-13
o Jr 2:20; 5:5; 30:8
p 27:3 Jr 25:21-22
q 27:5 Dt 4:34; 5:15; 7:19;
1Kg 8:42; Ps 136:12; Jr
32:17,21; Ezk 20:33-34
r Is 45:12
s Ps 115:15-16; Dn 4:17
t 27:6 Is 44:28; Jr 25:9
u 2Kg 24:11; 25:22; 2Ch
36:6-13

said to the officials and all the people, "This man deserves the death sentence because he has prophesied against this city, as you have heard with your own ears."[a]

JEREMIAH'S DEFENSE

12 Then Jeremiah said to all the officials and all the people, "The LORD sent me to prophesy all the words that you have heard against this temple and city. **13** So now, correct your ways and deeds,[b] and obey the LORD your God so that he might relent concerning the disaster he had pronounced against you. **14** As for me, here I am in your hands; do to me what you think is good and right. **15** But know for certain that if you put me to death, you will bring innocent blood[c] on yourselves, on this city, and on its residents, for it is certain the LORD has sent me to speak all these things directly to you."

JEREMIAH RELEASED

16 Then the officials and all the people told the priests and prophets, "This man doesn't deserve the death sentence, for he has spoken to us in the name of the LORD our God!"

17 Some of the elders of the land stood up[d] and said to all the assembled people, **18** "Micah the Moreshite[e] prophesied in the days of King Hezekiah of Judah[f] and said to all the people of Judah, 'This is what the LORD of Armies says:

Zion will be plowed like a field,
Jerusalem will become ruins,
and the temple's mountain will be
a high thicket.'[g]

19 Did King Hezekiah of Judah and all the people of Judah put him to death? Did not the king fear the LORD and plead for the LORD's favor,[A,h] and did not the LORD relent concerning the disaster he had pronounced against them?[i] We are about to bring a terrible disaster on ourselves!"

THE PROPHET URIAH

20 Another man was also prophesying in the name of the LORD — Uriah son of Shemaiah from Kiriath-jearim.[j] He prophesied against this city and against this land in words like all those of Jeremiah. **21** King Jehoiakim, all his warriors, and all the officials heard his words, and the king tried to put him to death. When Uriah heard, he fled in fear and went to Egypt. **22** But King Jehoiakim sent men to Egypt: Elnathan son of Achbor[k] and certain other men with him went to Egypt. **23** They brought Uriah out of Egypt and took him to King Jehoiakim, who executed him with the sword and threw his corpse into the burial place of the common people.[B]

24 But Ahikam[l] son of Shaphan supported Jeremiah, so he was not handed over to the people to be put to death.

THE YOKE OF BABYLON

27 At the beginning of the reign of Zedekiah[c] son of Josiah, king of Judah,[m] this word came to Jeremiah from the LORD:[D] **2** This is what the LORD said to me: "Make chains and yoke bars[n] for yourself and put them on your neck.[o] **3** Send word to the king of Edom, the king of Moab, the king of the Ammonites, the king of Tyre, and the king of Sidon[p] through messengers who are coming to King Zedekiah of Judah in Jerusalem. **4** Command them to go to their masters, saying, 'This is what the LORD of Armies, the God of Israel, says: Tell this to your masters: **5** "By my great strength and outstretched arm,[q] I made the earth,[r] and the people, and animals on the face of the earth. I give it to anyone I please.[E,s] **6** So now I have placed all these lands under the authority of my servant[t] Nebuchadnezzar,[u] king of Babylon. I have even given him the wild animals to serve him. **7** All nations will serve him, his son,

---

26:12-15 Remember that when you faithfully proclaim God's truth, it's backed by his authority, not yours. Also, notice that in his approach Jeremiah was not simply bashing his people or giving them no chance to turn away God's wrath: he offered hope (26:13). **26:16** The secular officials and the people did what the nation's spiritual leaders should have done; they recognized and authenticated God's true word spoken by his true prophet and then led the way in repentance. **26:17-19 Some** of the wisest **elders** cited a precedent for listening to, rather than executing, Jeremiah: the case of the prophet

Micah, who brought a similar message during the reign of **Hezekiah** (26:17-18). That **king** listened to God's prophet and led Judah in repentance that delayed judgment (26:19). **26:20-23** This **Uriah** was an otherwise unknown prophet of Jeremiah's time (26:20). Given what happened to him, Jeremiah had plenty of cause to be on edge. **27:1-11** When the kings of five nations sent **messengers** (27:3) to Jerusalem asking Zedekiah to join them in a rebellion against Babylon, Jeremiah was waiting with a stark message of the futility of their plans. He went to the court in Jerusalem with **chains and**

yoke bars hanging around his neck as a warning not to try what they were planning, but to allow **Nebuchadnezzar** to put his yoke on them and take them away to Babylon (27:2-7).

Jeremiah's advice to them came from the Creator of the universe, who held all the nations in his hands and could do with them whatever he pleased (27:4-5). God had decreed that **all** lands would have to submit to **Babylon** until that great kingdom's own time of judgment and collapse came (27:6-7). Any nation that rejected the Lord's command, then, would be devastated by his three-fold messengers of suffering (27:8).

and his grandson until the time for his own land comes, and then many nations and great kings will enslave him.[a]

8 " "As for the nation or kingdom that does not serve King Nebuchadnezzar of Babylon and does not place its neck under the yoke of the king of Babylon, that nation I will punish by sword, famine, and plague — this is the LORD's declaration — until through him I have destroyed it. 9 So you should not listen to your prophets, diviners,[b] dreamers, fortune-tellers,[c] or sorcerers[d] who say to you, 'Don't serve the king of Babylon!' 10 They are prophesying a lie[e] to you so that you will be removed from your land. I will banish you, and you will perish. 11 But as for the nation that will put its neck under the yoke of the king of Babylon and serve him, I will leave it in its own land, and that nation will cultivate[A] it and reside in it. This is the LORD's declaration." '"

WARNING TO ZEDEKIAH

12 I spoke to King Zedekiah of Judah[f] in the same way: "Put your necks under the yoke of the king of Babylon, serve him and his people, and live! 13 Why should you and your people die[g] by the sword, famine, and plague as the LORD has threatened against any nation that does not serve the king of Babylon? 14 Do not listen to the words of the prophets who are telling you, 'Don't serve the king of Babylon,' for they are prophesying a lie to you.[h] 15 'I have not sent them' — this is the LORD's declaration — 'and they are prophesying falsely in my name; therefore, I will banish you, and you will perish — you and the prophets who are prophesying to you.' "

16 Then I spoke to the priests and all these people, saying, "This is what the LORD says: 'Do not listen to the words of your prophets. They are prophesying to you, claiming, "Look, very soon now the articles of the LORD's temple will be brought back from Babylon."[i] They are prophesying a lie to you. 17 Do not listen to them. Serve the king of Babylon and live! Why should

this city become a ruin?[j] 18 If they are indeed prophets and if the word of the LORD is with them, let them intercede with the LORD of Armies not to let the articles that remain in the LORD's temple, in the palace of the king of Judah, and in Jerusalem go to Babylon.' 19 For this is what the LORD of Armies says about the pillars, the basin,[B] the water carts,[k] and the rest of the articles that still remain in this city, 20 those King Nebuchadnezzar of Babylon did not take when he deported Jeconiah[c] son of Jehoiakim, king of Judah, from Jerusalem to Babylon along with all the nobles of Judah[l] and Jerusalem. 21 Yes, this is what the LORD of Armies, the God of Israel, says about the articles that remain in the temple of the LORD, in the palace of the king of Judah, and in Jerusalem: 22 'They will be taken to Babylon and will remain there until I attend to them again.'[m] This is the LORD's declaration. 'Then I will bring them up and restore them to this place.' "[n]

HANANIAH'S FALSE PROPHECY

28 In that same year, at the beginning of the reign of King Zedekiah of Judah,[o] in the fifth month of the fourth year, the prophet Hananiah son of Azzur from Gibeon[p] said to me in the temple of the LORD in the presence of the priests and all the people, 2 "This is what the LORD of Armies, the God of Israel, says: 'I have broken the yoke of the king of Babylon.[q] 3 Within two years I will restore to this place all the articles of the LORD's temple[r] that King Nebuchadnezzar of Babylon took from here and transported to Babylon. 4 And I will restore to this place Jeconiah[c] son of Jehoiakim, king of Judah, and all the exiles from Judah[s] who went to Babylon' — this is the LORD's declaration — 'for I will break the yoke of the king of Babylon.' "

JEREMIAH'S RESPONSE TO HANANIAH

5 The prophet Jeremiah replied to the prophet Hananiah in the presence of the priests and all the people who were

[a] 27:7 Jr 25:12
[b] 27:9 Dt 18:10,14; Jr 14:14; 29:8
[c] Lv 19:26; Dt 18:10,14; 2Ch 33:6
[d] Ex 7:11; Dt 18:10; 2Ch 33:6
[e] 27:10 Jr 5:31; 14:14; 20:6; 23:25-26,32; 27:14-16; 29:9,21,31
[f] 27:12 Jr 28:1; 38:17
[g] 27:13 Ezk 18:31
[h] 27:14 Jr 14:14
[i] 27:16 2Kg 24:13; 2Ch 36:7,10; Jr 28:3
[j] 27:17 Jr 7:34
[k] 27:19 2Kg 25:13,16; Jr 52:17,20
[l] 27:20 Neh 6:17; 13:17; Jr 39:6
[m] 27:22 Jr 29:10; 32:5
[n] Ezr 1:7-11; 5:13-15; 7:19
[o] 28:1 Jr 27:12
[p] Jos 9:3
[q] 28:2 Jr 27:12
[r] 28:3 Jr 27:16
[s] 28:4 2Kg 24:10-17

[A] 27:11 Lit work [B] 27:19 Lit sea [C] 27:20; 28:4 = Jehoiachin

---

27:14-15 Judah's king was putting his hopes in these false prophets who were assuring him Judah would never be taken. Be careful where you put your trust.
27:16-22 When Nebuchadnezzar deported the first exiles from Judah in about 605 BC, including Daniel, he took "some of the vessels" from the temple to Babylon (see Dan 1:1-7). Now it was about sixteen years past that time (judging by the time stamp of Jer 28:1). Those temple **articles** were still in Babylon,

but the false **prophets** boldly predicted that these items would be returned soon (27:16). According to Jeremiah, though, not only would the stolen articles remain in Babylon, but also the items currently in the temple would be carried off (27:17-22).
28:1-4 One of the false prophets who continually preached a prosperity gospel of success and restoration for Judah was **Hananiah** (28:1). He insisted that the nation's trouble with Babylon was just a two-year problem

(28:3). Hananiah even stole Jeremiah's signature phrase: **this is the LORD's declaration** (28:4). Speaking lies is one thing; putting them in the mouth of the Lord is a whole other matter. Such audacity would cost Hananiah his life.
28:5-6 Jeremiah didn't declare, **Amen! May the LORD do that** because Hananiah's words were true but because Jeremiah *wished* that this optimistic message could be true (28:6).

ᵃ 28:6 1Kg 1:36
ᵇ 28:9 Dt 18:20-22
ᶜ 28:10 Jr 27:2

ᵈ 28:14 Dt 28:48
ᵉ Jr 25:11
ᶠ Jr 27:6
ᵍ 28:15 Jr 29:31; Ezk 13:22
ʰ 28:16 Dt 13:5; Is 59:13;
　　Jr 29:32

⚜ KINGDOM LIVING ⚜
COMMUNITY
The Role of Christians in Culture

When we examine deteriorating cultures throughout history, we often find that the people of God withdrew from them. For example, when Christians abandon a community's hub, taking their skills, resources, and moral influence with them, those neighborhoods deteriorate. When Christians leave the public school system, moral values are systematically erased there until they practically become illegal to teach. When Christians vacate the media, spiritual perspective goes with them. When Christians get out of politics, a godly moral framework through which to define and interpret our laws goes with them.

God's people have been called to penetrate society as both salt and light. Christians must offer others hope because no earthly institution can offer real hope for the world. The absence of righteousness in our culture has everything to do with the absence of God's people influencing the culture. When Jesus Christ returns, we will no longer need to worry about transforming our culture because he will set up his kingdom rule. But until that time, we need to reach the world for him.

What is the role of Christians in culture? Jeremiah 29:4-11 illustrates this foundational principle: society is transformed when God's people execute his kingdom agenda in history. The prophet Jeremiah challenged the Jews in Babylonian captivity to regain their spiritual clarity. The Babylonian pagans weren't Israel's greatest problem. Rather, the Jews had become pagans themselves and had failed to remain God's distinct people.

When the church fails to be God's unique people, the entire culture will suffer the effects of our sin. Christians *must* maintain their example of godliness regardless of what secular society values or purports.

FOR THE NEXT COMMUNITY
KINGDOM LIVING LESSON SEE PAGE 1035.

standing in the temple of the Lord. ⁶ The prophet Jeremiah said, "Amen!ᵃ May the Lord do that. May the Lord make the words you have prophesied come true and may he restore the articles of the Lord's temple and all the exiles from Babylon to this place! ⁷ Only listen to this message I am speaking in your hearing and in the hearing of all the people. ⁸ The prophets who preceded you and me from ancient times prophesied war, disaster,ᴬ and plague against many lands and great kingdoms. ⁹ As for the prophet who prophesies peace — only when the word of the prophet comes true will the prophet be recognized as one the Lord has truly sent."ᵇ

HANANIAH BREAKS JEREMIAH'S YOKE

¹⁰ The prophet Hananiah then took the yoke bar from the neck of the prophet Jeremiah and broke it.ᶜ ¹¹ In the presence of all the people Hananiah proclaimed, "This is what the Lord says: 'In this way, within two years I will break the yoke of King Nebuchadnezzar of Babylon from the neck of all the nations.'" The prophet Jeremiah then went on his way.

THE LORD'S WORD AGAINST HANANIAH

¹² After the prophet Hananiah had broken the yoke bar from the neck of the prophet Jeremiah, the word of the Lord came to Jeremiah: ¹³ "Go say to Hananiah, 'This is what the Lord says: You broke a wooden yoke bar, but in its place you will make an iron yoke bar. ¹⁴ For this is what the Lord of Armies, the God of Israel, says: I have put an iron yoke on the neck of all these nations that they might serve King Nebuchadnezzar of Babylon,ᵈ and they will serve him.ᵉ I have even put the wild animals under him.'"ᶠ

¹⁵ The prophet Jeremiah said to the prophet Hananiah, "Listen, Hananiah! The Lord did not send you, but you have led these people to trust in a lie.ᵍ ¹⁶ Therefore, this is what the Lord says: 'I am about to send you off the face of the earth. You will die this year because you have preached rebellion against the Lord.'"ʰ

ᴬ 28:8 Some Hb mss, Vg read *famine*

28:9 Jeremiah stated the test of a true prophet: **only when the word of the prophet comes true will the prophet be recognized as one the Lord has truly sent** (see Deut 18:20-22).

Hananiah's prophecy wouldn't meet the standard.
28:10-17 Hananiah's lying and strutting were pointless. The Lord God, the King of the universe, is sovereign. Any attempt to oppose his agenda will fail. Will you join his kingdom work and experience blessing or oppose him and be put to shame?

17 And the prophet Hananiah died that year in the seventh month.

JEREMIAH'S LETTER TO THE EXILES

29 This is the text of the letter[a] that the prophet Jeremiah sent from Jerusalem to the remaining exiled elders, the priests, the prophets, and all the people Nebuchadnezzar[b] had deported from Jerusalem to Babylon. **2** This was after King Jeconiah,[A,C] the queen mother, the court officials, the officials of Judah and Jerusalem, the craftsmen, and the metalsmiths had left Jerusalem. **3** He sent the letter with Elasah son of Shaphan and Gemariah son of Hilkiah,[d] whom Zedekiah king of Judah sent to Babylon to King Nebuchadnezzar of Babylon. The letter stated:

4 This is what the LORD of Armies, the God of Israel, says to all the exiles I deported from Jerusalem to Babylon: **5** "Build houses and live in them.[e] Plant gardens and eat their produce. **6** Find wives for yourselves, and have sons and daughters. Find wives for your sons and give your daughters to men in marriage so that they may bear sons and daughters. Multiply there; do not decrease.[f] **7** Pursue the well-being[B] of the city I have deported you to. Pray to the LORD on its behalf,[g] for when it thrives, you will thrive."

⌐ HOPE WORDS ⌐

If you can't change it and God has allowed it, then find out how to prosper in it.

8 For this is what the LORD of Armies, the God of Israel, says: "Don't let your prophets who are among you[h] and your diviners deceive you,[i] and don't listen to the dreams you elicit from them, **9** for they are prophesying falsely to you in my name. I have not sent them."[j] This is the LORD's declaration.

10 For this is what the LORD says: "When seventy years for Babylon are complete,[k] I will attend to you and will confirm my promise concerning you to restore you to this place. **11** For I know the plans I have for you"[l] — this is the LORD's declaration — "plans for your well-being, not for disaster, to give you a future and a hope. **12** You will call to me and come and pray to me, and I will listen to you.[m] **13** You will seek me[n] and find me when you search for me with all your heart. **14** I will be found by you" — this is the LORD's declaration — "and I will restore your fortunes[C,o] and gather you from all the nations and places where I banished you" — this is the LORD's declaration. "I will restore you to the place from which I deported you."[p]

15 You have said, "The LORD has raised up prophets for us in Babylon!" **16** But this is what the LORD says concerning the king sitting on David's throne[q] and concerning all the people living in this city — that is, concerning your brothers who did not go with you into exile. **17** This is what the LORD of Armies says: "I am about to send sword, famine, and plague against them,[r] and I will make them like rotten figs that are inedible because they are so bad. **18** I will pursue them with sword, famine, and plague. I will make them a horror to all the kingdoms of the earth — a curse and a desolation, an object of scorn and a disgrace among all the nations[s] where I have banished them.[t] **19** I will do this because they have not listened to my words" — this is the LORD's declaration — "the words that I sent to them with my servants the prophets time and time again.[D,u] And you too have not listened." This is the LORD's declaration.

a 29:1 2Sm 11:14-15; 1Kg 21:8-11
b 2Kg 24:11; 25:22; 2Ch 36:6-13
c 29:2 Jr 24:1; 27:20; 28:4
d 29:3 1Ch 6:13
e 29:5 Jr 29:28
f 29:6 Gn 17:5-6; 35:10-11
g 29:7 Ezr 6:10; 1Tm 2:1-2
h 29:8 Jr 27:9
i Jr 27:15

j 29:9 Jr 5:31; 14:14; 20:6; 23:25-26,32; 27:10,14-16; 29:21,31
k 29:10 Jr 25:12; Dn 9:2
l 29:11 Ps 33:10; Jr 26:3; 36:3
m 29:12 Dt 30:1-10; Jr 3:12
n 29:13 Dt 4:29; 1Ch 28:9; 2Ch 15:2
o 29:14 Jb 42:10; Jr 32:44; 49:39; Ezk 16:53; 39:25; Hs 6:11; Zph 2:7
Dt 30:3; Jr 30:3
q 29:16 Jr 17:25; 22:2,30; 36:30
r 29:17 Jr 14:12; 21:9; 24:10
s 29:18 Dt 28:37; 2Ch 29:8; 30:7; Jr 5:30; 19:8; 25:9,18; 29:18; 42:18; 44:12,22; 49:17; 50:13; Mc 6:16; Zph 2:15
t 29:19 Dt 30:1; Jr 8:3; 16:15
u 29:19 Jr 7:13,25; 11:7; 25:3; 26:5; 32:33; 35:14-15; 44:4

A 29:2 = Jehoiachin   B 29:7 Or peace   C 29:14 Or will end your captivity   D 29:19 Lit prophets, rising up early and sending

---

29:1 As a result of damaging lies spread by false prophets like Hananiah, the exiles had been encouraged to become passive in their captivity, sitting around waiting for a quick release that wasn't coming (see 29:8-9).
29:4 The first thing the exiles needed to learn was that the Babylonians were not to blame for their captivity. In the grand scheme of things, *God* had **deported** them **to Babylon**. Nebuchadnezzar was merely the instrument God used to punish them for their sins.

29:5-6 God wanted his people to establish a kingdom presence in exile. While they were waiting for a better *tomorrow*, they were to be industrious *today*. Earth is not merely a place to wait for a ride to heaven. It's where we live out God's kingdom agenda in history.
29:7 For too many years, Christians have secluded themselves within their churches. We have abandoned the culture to Satan. But God's message is to pursue the good of the culture in which we live—to get busy loving our neighbors.

29:11-14 When we evaluate verse 11 in context, we see that it's God's promise to bless his people in the midst of a pagan culture. This, however, demands more than attending church on Sunday, tapping our feet to the music, hearing a sermon, and saying, "Amen." We must commit our hearts to the Lord 24/7 because when we worship and obey the Lord through our day-to-day walk with him, he's ready to communicate with us and even reverse our circumstances (29:12-14).

In All Things

YOU EXIST FOR GOD. You are his special creation. He made you because he loves you. The reason you are to get up every morning is to fulfill the purpose that God has for your life. And it is a great purpose, a wonderful purpose. In fact, God says in Jeremiah 29:11 that he has good plans for you when you seek him and his will for your life. It's a good plan just for you.

The God who created you for himself has never made any mistakes. There have been no failures or flaws in his plan for you. Yes, there are trials that you may have to endure. But the negative realities that you may be facing, or have faced, will work together for good if you love God, draw near to him, and experience him (SEE RM 8:28). He promises.

God's Word tells us, "In all these things [trials, struggles, emptiness, pain] we are more than conquerors through him who loved us" (RM 8:37). But the most important word in that verse is often overlooked. I must have preached on that verse a hundred times in my first thirty years of preaching, but I never saw its all-important word until three decades had passed. I was studying this passage in relation to my own life when it was as if God took a yellow highlighter and suddenly made one word come alive for me.

You might think that I am going to say "conquerors" is the most important word. Actually, no. The most important word is "in." Because we are often tempted to believe that God has promised to keep us "from" the trials, tests, and pains of life and, then, when he doesn't, we feel let down, discouraged, or defeated. But God never promised to deliver us *from* all things. He has promised that *in* all these things we are more than conquerors. We will receive the benefits and blessings that come only through our deep and meaningful experiences of him.

This powerful principle has warmed my heart, and I want it to warm yours too. Life is too important and too short to miss out on all that God has for you. Don't be confused when God does not deliver you "from" circumstances or situations. That may not be his intention. Rather, know that "in" those trials and troubles, God will cause you to conquer. Victory isn't always found in escape. Sometimes, in fact, the greatest victory comes as a result of living fully and freely within the challenges of life. It is in those times that God is carving out your calling through the chiseling of your character as he shapes you into the strong, patient, caring, and trusting kingdom follower he created you to be.

20 Hear the word of the LORD, all you exiles I have sent from Jerusalem to Babylon.[a] **21** This is what the LORD of Armies, the God of Israel, says about Ahab son of Kolaiah and concerning Zedekiah son of Maaseiah, the ones prophesying a lie to you in my name:[b] "I am about to hand them over to King Nebuchadnezzar of Babylon, and he will kill them before your very eyes. **22** Based on what happens to them, all the exiles of Judah who are in Babylon will create a curse[c] that says, 'May the LORD make you like Zedekiah and Ahab, whom the king of Babylon roasted in the fire!'[d] **23** because they have committed an outrage[e] in Israel by committing adultery with their neighbors' wives and have spoken in my name a lie, which I did not command them. I am he who knows, and I am a witness." This is the LORD's declaration.

24 To Shemaiah the Nehelamite you are to say, **25** "This is what the LORD of Armies, the God of Israel, says: You[A] in your own name have sent out letters to all the people of Jerusalem, to the priest Zephaniah[f] son of Maaseiah, and to all the priests, saying, **26** 'The LORD has appointed you priest in place of the priest Jehoiada to be the chief officer[g] in the temple of the LORD, responsible for every madman[h] who acts like a prophet. You must confine him in the stocks[i] and an iron collar. **27** So now, why have you not rebuked Jeremiah of Anathoth who has been acting like a prophet among you?[j] **28** For he has sent word to us in Babylon, claiming, "The exile will be long. Build houses and settle down. Plant gardens and eat their produce."'"[k] **29** The priest Zephaniah read this letter in the hearing of the prophet Jeremiah.

A MESSAGE ABOUT SHEMAIAH

30 Then the word of the LORD came to Jeremiah: **31** "Send a message to all the exiles, saying, 'This is what the LORD says concerning Shemaiah the Nehelamite. Because Shemaiah prophesied to you, though I did not send him, and made you trust a lie,[l] **32** this is what the LORD says: I am about to punish Shemaiah the Nehelamite and his descendants. There will not be even one of his descendants living among these people,[m] nor will any ever see the good that I will bring to my people — this is the LORD's declaration — for he has preached rebellion against the LORD.'"[n]

RESTORATION FROM CAPTIVITY

30 This is the word that came to Jeremiah from the LORD. **2** "This is what the LORD, the God of Israel, says: Write on a scroll all the words that I have spoken to you,[o] **3** for look, the days are coming" — this is the LORD's declaration — "when I will restore the fortunes[B] of my people Israel and Judah,"[p] says the LORD. "I will restore them to the land I gave to their ancestors and they will possess it."

4 These are the words the LORD spoke to Israel and Judah. **5** This is what the LORD says:

We have heard a cry of terror,
of dread — there is no peace.
6 Ask and see
whether a male can give birth.
Why then do I see every man
with his hands on his stomach
like a woman in labor
and every face turned pale?[q]
7 How awful that day will be![r]
There will be no other like it![s]
It will be a time of trouble for Jacob,
but he will be saved out of it.

8 On that day —
this is the declaration of the LORD
of Armies —

a 29:20 Jr 24:5
b 29:21 Jr 14:14; 29:9
c 29:22 Is 65:15
d Dn 3:6
e 29:23 Gn 34:7; Dt 22:21; Jos 7:15
f 29:25 Jr 21:1; 37:3; 52:24-27
g 29:26 2Ch 31:13; Jr 20:1
h 2Kg 9:11; Hs 9:7
i 2Ch 16:10; Jr 20:2
j 29:27 Jr 1:1
k 29:28 Jr 29:5

l 29:31 Jr 27:10,14-16; 28:15; 29:9,21,23
m 29:32 Jr 17:6
n Jr 28:16
o 30:2 Ex 17:14; 34:1,27; Nm 5:23; Dt 17:18; 27:3; 31:19; Is 30:8; Jr 36:2,28; Ezk 43:11; Hs 8:12; Hab 2:2; 1Co 14:37; Rv 1:11; 10:4; 14:13; 19:9; 21:5
p 30:3 Jr 33:7,11; Ezk 37:15-23; 39:25; Jl 3:1; Am 9:14
q 30:6 Ps 48:6; Is 13:8; 21:3; 42:14; Jr 4:31; 6:24; 13:21; 22:23; 50:43; Mc 4:9-10; 1Th 5:3
r 30:7 Jl 2:11; Zph 1:14
s Dn 12:1

A 29:25 Lit *Because you*   B 30:3 Or *will end the captivity*

29:20-22 Jeremiah's letter punctured the fantasies spread by the false prophets.
29:23 Not only had they spoken lies in God's name, but they had also committed **adultery with their neighbors' wives**—a reminder that wicked theology is often accompanied by a wicked lifestyle.
30:1-3 Some of Jeremiah's prophecies of Judah's restoration occurred in history; others can only be accomplished when Christ returns. For instance, God's promise that **the**

days are coming . . . when [he] will restore the fortunes of . . . Israel and Judah (30:3) looks forward to the end of time, because the northern kingdom of Israel was not impacted by Judah's captivity, having gone into captivity themselves over a century earlier. God prophesied a day when the two kingdoms would again join together as one in the promised land.
30:7 The Hebrew phrase translated **time of trouble** is the same one translated **time of**

12:1 as time of distress. Both passages speak of this time period as worse than any the world has seen: **There will be no other like it** (Jer 30:7); "such as never has occurred since nations came into being" (Dan 12:1). This is a picture of the coming seven-year great tribulation immediately preceding Christ's return. It will be a time of unparalleled suffering for Israel until Jesus appears to judge their enemies and rescue them.

[a] 30:8 Gn 27:40; Jr 2:20; 28:4,11; Ezk 34:27; Nah 1:13

[b] Jr 27:2

[c] Ezk 34:27

[d] 30:9 Is 55:3-5; Ezk 34:23-24; 37:24-25; Hs 3:5; Lk 1:69; Ac 13:23,34

[e] 30:10 Is 41:8; 44:2; 45:4; 48:20; Jr 46:27; Ezk 28:25; 37:25

[f] Lv 26:6; Jr 46:27; Ezk 34:28; 39:26; Mc 4:4; Zph 3:13

[g] 30:11 2Kg 19:34; Is 37:35; Jr 15:20

[h] 30:10-11 Ex 34:7; Jr 46:27-28

[i] 30:12 Jr 10:19; 15:18; 17:9

[j] 30:13 Hs 5:13

[k] 30:14 Jr 4:30; Lm 1:19

[l] Jr 2:30; 5:3; 7:28

[m] Is 13:9

[n] 30:15 Jr 5:6; Am 5:12

[o] 30:16 Jr 10:25

[p] Ezk 39:10; Hab 2:8

[q] 30:17 Is 58:8; Jr 8:22; 33:6

[r] 30:18 Jr 30:3

[s] Jr 12:15; 31:20; 33:26; 42:12

[t] 30:19 Jr 29:6

[u] 30:20 Jdg 10:12; Is 19:20-25

[v] 30:21 Nm 16:5

[w] 30:22 Jr 11:4; 24:7; 31:33

[x] 30:23 Ps 83:15; Is 29:6; Zch 9:14

I will break his yoke from your
  neck[a]
and tear off your chains,[b]
and strangers will never again
  enslave him.[c]

9 They will serve the LORD their God
and David their king,
whom I will raise up for them.[d]

10 As for you, my servant Jacob,[e]
do not be afraid —
  this is the LORD's declaration —
and do not be discouraged, Israel,
for without fail I will save you out of
  a distant place,
your descendants, from the land
  of their captivity!
Jacob will return and have calm
  and quiet
with no one to frighten him.[f]

11 For I will be with you —
  this is the LORD's declaration —
to save you![g]
I will bring destruction
  on all the nations
where I have scattered you;
however, I will not bring destruction
  on you.
I will discipline you justly,
and I will by no means
  leave you unpunished.[h]

HEALING ZION'S WOUNDS

12 For this is what the LORD says:
Your injury is incurable;
  your wound most severe.[i]

13 You have no defender for your case;[j]
There is no remedy for your sores,
  and no healing for you.[A]

14 All your lovers have forgotten you;[k]
they no longer look for you,
for I have struck
  you as an enemy would,
with the discipline[l]
  of someone cruel,[m]
because of your enormous guilt
  and your innumerable sins.

15 Why do you cry out
  about your injury?
Your pain has no cure!
I have done these things to you
because of your enormous guilt
  and your innumerable sins.[n]

16 Nevertheless, all who devoured you
  will be devoured,[o]
and all your adversaries —
  all of them —
will go off into exile.
Those who plunder you
  will be plundered,
and all who raid you will be raided.[p]

17 But I will bring you health[q]
and will heal you of your wounds —
  this is the LORD's declaration —
for they call you Outcast,
Zion whom no one cares about.

RESTORATION OF THE LAND

18 This is what the LORD says:
I will certainly restore the fortunes[B]
  of Jacob's tents[r]
and show compassion[s]
  on his dwellings.
Every city will be rebuilt
  on its mound;
every citadel will stand
  on its proper site.

19 Thanksgiving will come
  out of them,
a sound of rejoicing.
I will multiply them,
  and they will not decrease;[t]
I will honor them, and they will not
  be insignificant.

20 His children will be as in past days;
his congregation will be established
  in my presence.
I will punish all his oppressors.[u]

21 Jacob's leader will be one of them;
his ruler will issue from him.
I will invite him to me, and he will
  approach me,[v]
for who would otherwise
  risk his life to approach me?
This is the LORD's declaration.

22 You will be my people,
and I will be your God.[w]

THE WRATH OF GOD

23 Look, a storm from the LORD![x]
Wrath has gone out,
a churning storm.
It will whirl about the heads
  of the wicked.

24 The LORD's burning anger will not
  turn back

[A] 30:13 Or No one pleads that your sores should be healed. There is no remedy for you.   [B] 30:18 Or certainly end the captivity

---

30:9 Christ, the Messiah from the line of **David their king**, will rescue and restore his people. 30:12,17 Judah's desperate, sinful condition had left the nation with gaping wounds that no one could heal (30:12). Yet, "What is impossible with man is possible with God" (Luke 18:27). The Lord would intervene (Jer 30:17). 30:18–22 Though Israel has been back in their territory since the rebirth of the nation in 1948, most of the Jewish people continue to disbelieve the gospel of Jesus Christ. But when many Jews embrace Jesus as their Messiah during his millennial kingdom (see Rom 11:25-27), God will again gladly identify with Israel (Jer 30:22).

until he has completely fulfilled
the purposes of his heart.
In time to come you will
understand it.[a]

GOD'S RELATIONSHIP WITH HIS PEOPLE

31 "At that time" — this is the LORD's declaration — "I will be the God of all the families of Israel,[b] and they will be my people."

[2] This is what the LORD says:
The people who survived the sword
found favor in the wilderness.[c]
When Israel went to find rest,[d]

[3] the LORD appeared to him[A]
from far away.
I have loved you
with an everlasting love;[e]
therefore, I have continued
to extend faithful love to you.[f]

[4] Again I will build you so that
you will be rebuilt,
Virgin Israel.[g]
You will take up
your tambourines again[h]
and go out in joyful dancing.

[5] You will plant vineyards again[i]
on the mountains of Samaria;
the planters will plant and will enjoy
the fruit.[j]

[6] For there will be a day
when watchmen will call out
in the hill country of Ephraim,
"Come, let's go up to Zion,[k]
to the LORD our God!"

GOD'S PEOPLE BROUGHT HOME

[7] For this is what the LORD says:
Sing with joy for Jacob;
shout for the foremost of the nations!
Proclaim, praise, and say,
"LORD, save your people,[l]
the remnant of Israel!"[m]

[8] Watch! I am going to bring them
from the northern land.
I will gather them
from remote regions
of the earth[n] —
the blind and the lame will be
with them,[o]
along with those who are pregnant
and those about to give birth.

They will return here
as a great assembly![p]

[9] They will come weeping,
but I will bring them back
with consolation.[B,q]
I will lead them to wadis filled
with water,
by a smooth way where
they will not stumble,[r]
for I am Israel's Father,
and Ephraim is my firstborn.[s]

[10] Nations, hear the word
of the LORD,
and tell it among the far off coasts
and islands![t]
Say, "The one who scattered Israel
will gather him.[u]
He will watch over him
as a shepherd guards his flock,

[11] for the LORD has ransomed Jacob
and redeemed him from the power
of one stronger than he."[v]

[12] They will come and shout for joy
on the heights of Zion;[w]
they will be radiant with joy[x]
because of the LORD's goodness,
because of the grain, the new wine,
the fresh oil,[y]
and because of the young
of the flocks and herds.
Their life will be
like an irrigated garden,
and they will no longer grow weak
from hunger.

[13] Then the young women will rejoice
with dancing,
while young and old men
rejoice together.
I will turn their mourning
into joy,[z]
give them consolation,
and bring happiness out of grief.

[14] I will refresh the priests
with an abundance,[c,aa]
and my people will be satisfied
with my goodness.
This is the LORD's declaration.

LAMENT TURNED TO JOY

[15] This is what the LORD says:
A voice was heard in Ramah,[ab]
a lament with bitter weeping —
Rachel weeping for her children,

---

[a] 30:23-24 Jr 23:19-20
[b] 31:1 Jr 30:22
[c] 31:2 Ex 33:12-17
[d] Jos 23:1; 2Sm 7:11; 1Kg 8:56; 1Ch 23:25
[e] 31:3 Is 54:8
[f] Ps 36:10; 109:12
[g] 31:4 Jr 18:13; 31:21; Am 5:2
[h] Ex 15:20; Jdg 11:34; 1Sm 18:6
[i] 31:5 Am 5:11
[j] Lv 19:23,25; Dt 20:6; 28:30
[k] 31:6 Is 2:3
[l] 31:7 Ps 28:9; Hab 3:13; Zch 8:7
[m] Is 10:20; Jr 6:9; Ezk 11:13; Mc 2:12; Zph 3:13
[n] 31:8 Neh 1:9; Is 43:6; Jr 32:37; Ezk 34:13; 37:21; 39:27; Zch 10:8,10
[o] Lv 21:18; Mt 11:5; Lk 14:13

[p] 31:8 Ezk 38:15
[q] 31:9 Jb 15:11
[r] Pr 4:12; Is 63:13; Ezk 36:15
[s] Ex 4:22-23; Dt 32:19; Is 63:16; 64:8; Hs 11:1; Mal 2:10; Jn 8:41
[t] 31:10 Is 40:15; Jr 25:22; 47:4
[u] Dt 30:3; Is 11:12; Ezk 11:17; 20:34,41; 28:25; Mc 4:6; Zph 3:19
[v] 31:11 Is 41:14; 43:1; 44:23; 48:20; 60:16
[w] 31:12 Ps 71:23; 92:4; Is 49:13; Zch 2:10
[x] Ps 34:5; Is 60:5
[y] Nm 18:12; Dt 7:13; Hg 1:11
[z] 31:13 Ps 105:43; Is 35:10; 51:3,11; Lm 5:15
[aa] 31:14 Dt 31:20; Ps 36:8; Is 30:23
[ab] 31:15 Jos 18:25; Jdg 4:5; 1Sm 1:19; 19:18; Jr 40:1

[A] 31:3 LXX; MT reads *me*   [B] 31:9 LXX; MT reads *supplications*   [C] 31:14 Lit *fatness*

31:15-17 Jeremiah depicts **Rachel**, the wife of Jacob (see Gen 29:28), **weeping for her children** (31:15), the people of Israel who had gone into exile. But God promises future joy, for the **children will return. . . . There is hope** (31:16-17). Similarly, Matthew sees "Rachel weeping" at Herod's massacre of the children as he sought to slay the young Jesus (see Matt 2:16-18). But, again, this grief will one day turn to joy when many Jewish people receive their Messiah during his millennial reign (see Rom 11:25-27).

[a]31:15 Mt 2:18
[b]31:17 Jr 5:31; 23:20; 29:11
[c]31:18 Hs 4:16; 10:11
[d]Ps 40:5; Jr 3:22
[e]31:19 Ezk 21:12
[f]Ps 35:4; Ezr 9:6; Is 41:11;
Jr 8:12; 14:3; 22:22; Ezk
36:32

[g]31:20 Is 5:7; Hs 11:1
[h]Jr 12:15; 30:18; 33:26;
42:12; Hs 11:4,8-9
[i]31:21 2Kg 23:17; Ezk 39:15
[j]31:22 Jr 3:14,22; 49:4
[k]31:23 Jb 8:6; Jr 50:7
[l]Ps 2:6; 3:4; 48:1; 99:9

⚜ KINGDOM LIVING ⚜

KINGDOM

The Covenants of the Kingdom

When it comes to the way God governs his kingdom, the word that stands out as the central theme is *covenant*. God administers his kingdom through his covenants.

If you, like me, are a citizen of the United States of America, then you fall underneath a covenantal document called the Constitution. The Constitution is the umbrella document that covers the operations of the "kingdom" called the U.S.A. It's a unique document in that it declares much by way of a proclamation of freedom.

You may hear people who feel they have been treated unjustly say, "I know my rights," appealing to their constitutional rights—particularly the amendments attached to the Constitution. These amendments declare the rights, privileges, and authority one has as an American citizen.

But if you are a Christian, then you are also part of another kingdom—the kingdom of God. And as such, you also have covenantal rights, privileges, and authority. Yet if you do not know those rights, or how to properly exercise them, then you can be illegitimately oppressed simply because you are not operating by the instructions or functioning under the umbrella of God's kingdom covenant.

In the Bible, a *covenant* is a divinely created bond. And, friend, as a believer in Jesus you are situated securely within this divinely created bond. It is a spiritually binding relationship between God and you that is inclusive of certain agreements, conditions, benefits, responsibilities, and effects. God's power, provisions, and authority to you operate under and within his covenants. Understanding each of these in order to live according to them is an important part of living a life under God.

FOR THE NEXT KINGDOM
KINGDOM LIVING LESSON SEE PAGE 1103.

refusing to be comforted
　　for her children
because they are no more.[a]

16 This is what the LORD says:
Keep your voice
　　from weeping
and your eyes from tears,
for the reward for your work
　　will come —
　　　　this is the LORD's declaration —
and your children will return
　　from the enemy's land.
17 There is hope for your future[b] —
　　　　this is the LORD's declaration —
and your children will return
　　to their own territory.
18 I have surely heard
　　Ephraim moaning,
"You disciplined me,
　　and I have been disciplined
like an untrained calf.[c]
Take me back, so that I can return,
for you, LORD, are my God.[d]
19 After my return, I felt regret;
After I was instructed, I struck
　　my thigh in grief.[e]
I was ashamed and humiliated[f]
because I bore the disgrace
　　of my youth."

20 Isn't Ephraim a precious son to me,
　　a delightful child?[g]
Whenever I speak against him,
I certainly still think about him.
Therefore, my inner being yearns
　　for him;
I will truly have compassion
　　on him.[h]
This is the LORD's declaration.

REPENTANCE AND RESTORATION

21 Set up road markers[i] for yourself;
　　establish signposts!
Keep the highway in mind,
　　the way you have traveled.
Return, Virgin Israel!
Return to these cities of yours.
22 How long will you turn
　　　　here and there,
faithless daughter?[j]
For the LORD creates something new
　　in the land[A] —
a female[B] will shelter[C] a man.

23 This is what the LORD of Armies, the God of Israel, says: "When I restore their fortunes,[D] they will once again speak this word in the land of Judah and in its cities: 'May the LORD bless you, righteous settlement,[k] holy mountain.'[l] **24** Judah and all its

---

[A]31:22 Or *new on earth*　[B]31:22 Or *woman*　[C]31:22 Or *female surrounds*, or *female courts*; Hb obscure　[D]31:23 Or *I end their captivity*

cities will live in it together — also farmers and those who move[A] with the flocks — 25 for I satisfy the thirsty person and feed all those who are weak."[a]

26 At this I awoke and looked around. My sleep had been most pleasant to me.

27 "Look, the days are coming" — this is the LORD's declaration — "when I will sow the house of Israel[b] and the house of Judah with the seed of people and the seed of animals. 28 Just as I watched over them to uproot and to tear them down, to demolish and to destroy, and to cause disaster,[c] so will I watch over them to build and to plant them"[d] — this is the LORD's declaration. 29 "In those days, it will never again be said,

'The fathers have eaten sour grapes,
  and the children's teeth are set
    on edge.'[e]

30 Rather, each will die for his own iniquity.[f] Anyone who eats sour grapes — his own teeth will be set on edge.

THE NEW COVENANT

31 "Look, the days are coming"[g] — this is the LORD's declaration — "when I will make a new covenant[h] with the house of Israel and with the house of Judah. 32 This one will not be like the covenant I made with their ancestors on the day I took them by the hand to lead them out of the land of Egypt — my covenant that they broke even though I am their master"[B,i] — the LORD's declaration. 33 "Instead, this is the covenant I will make with the house of Israel after those days" — the LORD's declaration. "I will put my teaching within them and write it on their hearts. I will be their God, and they will be my people. 34 No longer will one teach his neighbor or his brother, saying, 'Know the LORD,'[j] for they will all know me, from the least to the greatest of them"[k] — this is the LORD's declaration. "For I will forgive their iniquity[l] and never again remember their sin.

35 "This is what the LORD says:
The one who gives the sun for light
    by day,
the fixed order of moon and stars
    for light by night,
who stirs up the sea and makes
    its waves roar[m] —
the LORD of Armies is his name:
36 If this fixed order departs
    from before me —
    this is the LORD's declaration —
only then will Israel's descendants
    cease
to be a nation before me forever."[n]

37 "This is what the LORD says:
Only if the heavens above
    can be measured
and the foundations
    of the earth below explored,
will I reject all of Israel's descendants
because of all they have done —
    this is the LORD's declaration.

38 "Look, the days are coming" — the LORD's declaration — "when the city[c] from the Tower of Hananel[o] to the Corner Gate[p] will be rebuilt for the LORD. 39 A measuring line will once again stretch out straight to the hill of Gareb[q] and then turn toward Goah. 40 The whole valley — the corpses, the ashes, and all the fields as far as the Kidron Valley[r] to the corner of the Horse Gate[s] to the east — will be holy to the LORD. It will never be uprooted or demolished again."

JEREMIAH'S LAND PURCHASE

32 This is the word that came to Jeremiah from the LORD in the tenth year of King Zedekiah[t] of Judah, which was the eighteenth year of Nebuchadnezzar.[u] 2 At that time, the army of the king of Babylon was besieging Jerusalem,[v] and the prophet Jeremiah was imprisoned in the guard's courtyard[w] in the palace of the king of Judah. 3 King Zedekiah of Judah had imprisoned him, saying, "Why are

[a] 31:25 Ps 107:9; Is 55:1; Jn 4:14; 6:35; 7:35; Rv 21:6; 22:17
[b] 31:27 Ezk 36:9,11; Hs 2:23
[c] 31:28 Jr 21:10; 39:16; 44:27; Am 9:4
[d] Jr 1:10; 18:7-10; 44:27
[e] 31:29 Ezk 18:2
[f] 31:30 Dt 24:6; Ezk 18:20
[g] 31:31-34 Heb 8:8-12; 10:16-17
[h] 31:31 Ezk 37:26; Hs 2:18; Lk 22:20; 1Co 11:25; 2Co 3:6; Heb 9:15; 12:24
[i] 31:32 Is 54:4; 62:4; Mal 2:11
[j] 31:34 Jdg 2:10; 1Sm 3:7; Hs 2:20
[k] Est 1:20; Jr 6:13; 8:10; 42:1,8; 44:12
[l] Nm 14:19; Ps 103:3; Jr 36:3

[m] 31:35 Ps 46:3; Is 51:15; Jr 5:22
[n] 31:36 Jr 33:18; 35:19
[o] 31:38 Neh 3:1; 12:39
[p] 2Kg 14:13; 2Ch 26:9; Zch 14:10
[q] 31:39 Zch 2:1
[r] 31:40 2Kg 23:4
[s] Neh 3:28
[t] 32:1 2Kg 24:17-20; 2Ch 36:10-12; Jr 27:1-11
[u] Jr 29:1
[v] 32:2 Jr 39:1
[w] Neh 3:25; Jr 33:1; 37:21; 38:6; 39:14

[A]31:24 Tg, Vg, Aq, Sym; MT reads *and they will move*   [B]31:32 Or *husband*   [C]31:38 = Jerusalem

---

31:31-34 This **new covenant** God would make **with the house of Israel and ... Judah** would be unlike the one **made with their ancestors**, a reference to the Mosaic covenant (31:31-32). The blessings of the Mosaic covenant were conditioned on Israel's obedience, and Israel failed to keep its side of the agreement: they **broke** it (32:32). Therefore, God brought down curses on the people.

Israel broke God's law not because there was something wrong with it, but because there was something wrong with their hearts.

The law revealed their sinfulness and their inability to obey faithfully, so God promised a new relationship with him that was so rich and dynamic that God would **write** his teaching **on their hearts** (31:33).

In the Communion ceremony, Christians are told to partake of the cup "in remembrance of" Christ and the new covenant instituted by his atoning death (see 1 Cor 11:25-26). The day is coming when the people of Israel will also collectively follow their Messiah, Jesus Christ (see Jer 31:31).

31:35-37 Only if creation's **fixed order** can be undone **will Israel's descendants cease to be a nation before** him (31:35-36). This covenant is unilateral, depending only on God, and is therefore unbreakable.

32:1-2 This was about a year before Jerusalem fell, though it was already under siege by Babylon.

32:3-5 The clueless Zedekiah couldn't understand why Jeremiah would predict disaster on his own people and king. It never occurred to him that Jeremiah might actually be speaking on behalf of the Lord—serving as a *true* prophet.

[a]32:4 Jr 34:3
[b]32:3-5 Jr 21:3-7; 27:22; 34:2-3; 37:11-14
[c]32:7 1Kg 2:26; Jr 1:1; 11:21,23
[d]Lv 25:24-52; Ru 4:1-7
[e]32:9 Gn 23:16; Zch 11:12
[f]32:10 Jr 32:44
[g]32:12 Jr 36:4-32; 43:3,6; 45:1-2
[h]32:15 Jr 32:43

[i]32:16 Jr 42:4
[j]32:17 2Kg 19:15; 2Ch 2:12; Is 37:16
[k]Dt 4:37; Neh 1:10; Jr 27:5
[l]Gn 18:14; Ex 3:20; 15:11; 34:10; Dt 17:8; Ps 40:5; 78:4; Jr 32:27; Zch 8:6; Mt 17:20; 19:26
[m]32:18 Ex 20:5-6; 34:7; Nm 14:18; Dt 5:9-10; 7:9
[n]Neh 9:32
[o]32:19 Jr 4:18; 17:10
[p]32:20 Ex 1–15; Dt 6:22; Neh 9:10
[q]Is 63:12,14; Dn 9:15
[r]32:21 Ex 7:3; Dt 4:34; 6:22; 26:8; 34:11; Ps 78:43; 135:9
[s]32:22 Ex 3:8,17; Lv 20:24; Nm 13:27; Dt 26:9
[t]32:23 Nm 14:22; Dt 28:45,62; Jos 5:6; Jdg 6:10; 2Kg 18:12; Ps 78:10; 81:11; Is 42:24; Jr 9:13; 32:23; 44:10
[u]Jr 11:8
[v]32:24 2Kg 25:1; Jr 6:6; Ezk 4:2
[w]32:27 Nm 16:22; 27:16
[x]Gn 18:4
[y]32:28 Jr 32:3

you prophesying as you do? You say, 'This is what the LORD says: Look, I am about to hand this city over to Babylon's king, and he will capture it. [4] King Zedekiah of Judah will not escape from the Chaldeans; indeed, he will certainly be handed over to Babylon's king. They will speak face to face[A] and meet eye to eye.[a] [5] He will take Zedekiah to Babylon, where he will stay until I attend to him — this is the LORD's declaration. For you will fight the Chaldeans, but you will not succeed.'"[b]

[6] Jeremiah replied, "The word of the LORD came to me: [7] Watch! Hanamel, the son of your uncle Shallum, is coming to you to say, 'Buy my field in Anathoth[c] for yourself, for you own the right of redemption[d] to buy it.'

[8] "Then, as the LORD had said, my cousin Hanamel came to the guard's courtyard and urged me, 'Please buy my field in Anathoth in the land of Benjamin, for you own the right of inheritance and redemption. Buy it for yourself.' Then I knew that this was the word of the LORD. [9] So I bought the field in Anathoth from my cousin Hanamel, and I weighed out the silver to him[e] — seventeen shekels[B] of silver. [10] I recorded it on a scroll,[f] sealed it, called in witnesses, and weighed out the silver on the scales. [11] I took the purchase agreement — the sealed copy with its terms and conditions and the open copy — [12] and gave the purchase agreement to Baruch[g] son of Neriah, son of Mahseiah. I did this in the sight of my cousin[c] Hanamel, the witnesses who had signed the purchase agreement, and all the Judeans sitting in the guard's courtyard.

[13] "I charged Baruch in their sight, [14] 'This is what the LORD of Armies, the God of Israel, says: Take these scrolls — this purchase agreement with the sealed copy and this open copy — and put them in an earthen storage jar so they will last a long time. [15] For this is what the LORD of Armies, the God of Israel, says: Houses, fields, and vineyards will again be bought in this land.'[h]

[16] "After I had given the purchase agreement to Baruch, son of Neriah, I prayed to the LORD:[i] [17] Oh, Lord GOD! You yourself made the heavens and earth[j] by your great power[k] and with your outstretched arm. Nothing is too difficult for you![l] [18] You show faithful love to thousands but lay the fathers' iniquity on their sons' laps after them,[m] great and mighty God[n] whose name is the LORD of Armies, [19] the one great in counsel and powerful in action. Your eyes are on all the ways of the children of men[D] in order to reward each person according to his ways and as the result of his actions.[o] [20] You performed signs and wonders in the land of Egypt[p] and still do today, both in Israel and among all mankind. You made a name[q] for yourself, as is the case today. [21] You brought your people Israel out of Egypt with signs and wonders, with a strong hand and an outstretched arm, and with great terror.[r] [22] You gave them this land you swore to give to their ancestors, a land flowing with milk and honey.[s] [23] They entered and possessed it, but they did not obey you or live according to your instructions.[t] They failed to perform all you commanded them to do,[u] and so you have brought all this disaster on them. [24] Look! Siege ramps[v] have come against the city to capture it, and the city, as a result of the sword, famine, and plague, has been handed over to the Chaldeans who are fighting against it. What you have spoken has happened. Look, you can see it! [25] Yet you, Lord GOD, have said to me, 'Purchase the field and call in witnesses' — even though the city has been handed over to the Chaldeans!'"

[26] The word of the LORD came to Jeremiah: [27] "Look, I am the LORD, the God over every creature.[w] Is anything too difficult for me?[x] [28] Therefore, this is what the LORD says: I am about to hand this city over to the Chaldeans,[y] to Babylon's king Nebuchadnezzar, and he will capture it. [29] The Chaldeans who are fighting against this city will come and set this city on fire. They will burn it, including the houses where incense has been burned to Baal

---

[A]32:4 Lit *His mouth will speak with his mouth*   [B]32:9 About seven ounces   [C]32:12 Some Hb mss, LXX, Syr; other Hb mss read *uncle*   [D]32:19 Or *Adam*

32:6-15 God told Jeremiah to redeem a plot of his family's land in his hometown of **Anathoth** (32:6-12; see Lev 25:25-28), which was already under Babylonian control. This would be like buying a car that the owner no longer possessed because it had been stolen! Nevertheless, Jeremiah obeyed God—although it seemed to make about as much sense as arranging deck chairs on the sinking *Titanic*.

Then Jeremiah learned what this meant: **Houses, fields, and vineyards will again be bought in this land** (Jer 32:15). God's people would one day return home.
32:17-25 Jeremiah's prayer expresses his faith and confidence in God—and his perplexity at how God was working out his plan. We don't have to understand God's ways to trust him.

32:27 Jeremiah knew that God's rhetorical question, **Is anything too difficult for me?** was not a multiple-choice question. Why, then, did God profess his omnipotence? Because he was about to tell Jeremiah that after Judah's punishment was complete (see 32:28-35), God would do the seemingly impossible. He'd bring the nation back to its land and the people would enjoy prosperity again (see 32:36-44).

on their rooftops and where drink offerings have been poured out to other gods to anger me.[a] 30 From their youth, the Israelites and Judeans have done nothing but what is evil in my sight! They have done nothing but anger me by the work of their hands"[b] — this is the LORD's declaration — 31 "for this city has caused my wrath and fury from the day it was built until now. I will therefore remove it from my presence[c] 32 because of all the evil the Israelites and Judeans have done to anger me — they, their kings,[d] their officials, their priests, and their prophets, the men of Judah, and the residents of Jerusalem. 33 They have turned their backs to me and not their faces.[e] Though I taught them time and time again,[A,f] they do not listen and receive discipline. 34 They have placed their abhorrent things[g] in the house that bears my name and have defiled it. 35 They have built the high places of Baal in Ben Hinnom Valley to sacrifice their sons and daughters in the fire[B] to Molech[h] — something I had not commanded them. I had never entertained the thought[c] that they do this detestable act causing Judah to sin!

36 "Now therefore, this is what the LORD, the God of Israel, says to this city about which you said, 'It has been handed over to Babylon's king through sword, famine, and plague': 37 I will certainly gather them from all the lands where I have banished them in my anger, rage and intense wrath, and I will return them to this place and make them live in safety.[i] 38 They will be my people, and I will be their God.[j] 39 I will give them integrity of heart[k] and action[D] so that they will fear me always, for their good and for the good of their descendants after them.

40 "I will make a permanent covenant with them:[l] I will never turn away from doing good to them, and I will put fear of me in their hearts so they will never again turn away from me.[m] 41 I will take delight in them to do what is good for them, and with all my heart and mind I will faithfully plant them in this land.[n]

42 "For this is what the LORD says: Just as I have brought all this terrible disaster on these people,[o] so am I about to bring on them all the good I am promising them.

43 Fields will be bought in this land about which you are saying,[p] 'It's a desolation[q] without people or animals; it has been handed over to the Chaldeans!' 44 Fields will be purchased, the transaction written on a scroll and sealed,[r] and witnesses will be called on in the land of Benjamin,[s] in the areas surrounding Jerusalem, and in Judah's cities — the cities of the hill country, the cities of the Judean foothills, and the cities of the Negev — because I will restore their fortunes."[E]

This is the LORD's declaration.

ISRAEL'S RESTORATION

33 While he was still confined in the guard's courtyard,[t] the word of the LORD came to Jeremiah a second time: 2 "The LORD who made the earth,[F] the LORD who forms it to establish it,[u] the LORD is his name,[v] says this: 3 Call to me and I will answer you[w] and tell you great and incomprehensible things you do not know.[x] 4 For this is what the LORD, the God of Israel, says concerning the houses of this city and the palaces of Judah's kings, the ones torn down for defense against the assault ramps and the sword:[y] 5 The people coming to fight the Chaldeans will fill the houses with the corpses of their own men that I strike down in my wrath and rage. I have hidden my face[z] from this city because of all their evil. 6 Yet I will certainly bring health[aa] and healing to it and will indeed heal them. I will let them experience the abundance[G] of true peace.[ab] 7 I will restore the fortunes[H] of Judah and of Israel and will rebuild them as in former times.[ac] 8 I will purify them from all the iniquity they have committed against me,[ad] and I will forgive all the iniquities they have committed against me, rebelling against me. 9 This city will bear on my behalf a name of joy, praise, and glory[ae] before all the nations of the earth, who will hear of all the prosperity I will give them. They will tremble with awe because of all the good and all the peace[af] I will bring about for them.

10 "This is what the LORD says: In this place, which you say is a ruin,[ag] without people or animals — that is, in Judah's cities and Jerusalem's streets that are a desolation without people, without inhabitants,

[a] 32:29 Jr 11:17; 44:3,8
[b] 32:30 Jr 25:7
[c] 32:31 2Kg 23:27; 24:3
[d] 32:32 Jr 2:26
[e] 32:33 2Ch 29:6; Jr 2:27; 18:17; Ezk 8:16
[f] Jr 7:13,25; 11:7; 25:3; 26:5; 29:19; 35:14,15; 44:4
[g] 32:34 Jr 4:1; 7:30; Ezk 5:11
[h] 32:35 Lv 18:21; 20:2-5; Dt 18:10; 2Kg 23:10; Jr 7:31; 19:4
[i] 32:37 Dt 12:10; Is 11:12; Jr 23:3; 29:14; 30:10; 31:8-14; Ezk 11:17; 28:26; 34:25,28; 36:24
[j] 32:38 Jr 11:4; 24:7; 30:22; Ezk 11:20; 14:11; 36:28; 37:23
[k] 32:39 Ezk 11:19
[l] 32:40 Gn 17:7,13,19; Is 55:3; 61:8; Jr 50:5; Ezk 16:60; 37:26
[m] Dt 19:20; Is 2:4; 60:18; Jr 3:16; 30:8; 31:34; Ezk 29:16; Jl 2:26-27; Am 9:15; Mc 4:3; Nah 1:15; Zph 3:11; Heb 8:11; 10:17
[n] 32:41 Jr 24:6
[o] 32:42 Jr 31:28

[p] 32:43 Jr 32:15
[q] Jr 33:10
[r] 32:44 Jr 32:10
[s] Jr 17:26
[t] 33:1 Jr 32:2
[u] 33:2 Gn 2:18-19
[v] Ex 6:3
[w] 33:3 Ps 91:15; Jr 29:12
[x] Is 48:6
[y] 33:4 Jr 32:24
[z] 33:5 Dt 31:17; 32:20; Is 54:8
[aa] 33:6 Is 58:8; Jr 8:22; 30:17
[ab] 2Kg 20:19; Est 9:30; Is 39:8
[ac] 33:7 Is 1:26
[ad] 33:8 Ps 51:2; Ezk 36:25; Heb 9:11-14
[ae] 33:9 Dt 26:19; Jr 13:11; Zph 3:19-20
[af] Jr 8:15; 14:19
[ag] 33:10 Jr 32:43

[A] 32:33 Lit them, rising up early and teaching   [B] 32:35 Lit to make their sons and daughters pass through the fire   [C] 32:35 Lit them, and it did not arise on my heart   [D] 32:39 Lit give them one heart and one way   [E] 32:44 Or will end their captivity   [F] 33:2 LXX; MT reads made it   [G] 33:6 Or fragrance; Hb obscure   [H] 33:7 Or will end the captivity, also in v. 11

33:10-11 The thought of a restored people in a restored land where there was **joy and gladness** (33:11) must have been an encouragement to Jeremiah as he heard the clanging of the Babylonians' tools as they built siege ramps against Jerusalem's walls.

a 33:11 Jr 7:34; 16:9; 25:10
b 33:12 Is 65:10; Ezk 34:12-15
c 33:13 Lv 27:32
d Jr 17:26
e 33:14 Jos 21:45; Jr 23:5-6
f 33:15 Is 4:2; Zch 3:8
g 33:16 Dt 33:12
h 33:17 1Kg 2:4; 8:25; 9:5
i 33:18 Jr 31:36; 35:19

j 33:20 Gn 8:22; Is 54:9-10; Jr 31:35-37
k 33:21 2Sm 7:11-16; 2Ch 21:7; Ps 89:3
l Is 61:6; Ezk 45:4-5; Jl 1:9,13
m 33:22 Gn 22:17
n 33:24 Dt 7:6; 14:2
o 33:25 Ps 74:16-17
p 33:26 Jr 12:15; 30:18; 31:20; 33:7; 42:12
q 34:1 2Kg 25:1; Jr 39:1; 52:4
r Jr 1:15
s 34:2 Jr 32:3,28
t 34:3 Jr 32:4; 38:18,23; Ezk 17:18; 1Th 5:3
u Jr 32:4

and without animals — there will be heard again [11] a sound of joy and gladness, the voice of the groom and the bride,[a] and the voice of those saying,

Give thanks to the LORD of Armies,
for the LORD is good;
his faithful love endures forever

as they bring thank offerings to the temple of the LORD. For I will restore the fortunes of the land as in former times, says the LORD.

[12] "This is what the LORD of Armies says: In this desolate place — without people or animals — and in all its cities there will once more be a grazing land where shepherds may rest flocks.[b] [13] The flocks will again pass under the hands of the one who counts them[c] in the cities of the hill country,[d] the cities of the Judean foothills, the cities of the Negev, the land of Benjamin — the areas around Jerusalem and in Judah's cities, says the LORD.

GOD'S COVENANT WITH DAVID

[14] "Look, the days are coming" —
this is the LORD's declaration —
"when I will fulfill the good promise
that I have spoken
concerning the house of Israel
and the house of Judah.[e]
[15] In those days and at that time
I will cause a Righteous Branch[f]
to sprout up for David,
and he will administer justice
and righteousness in the land.
[16] In those days Judah will be saved,
and Jerusalem will dwell securely,[g]
and this is what she will be named:
The LORD Is Our Righteousness.[A]

[17] "For this is what the LORD says: David will never fail to have a man sitting on the throne of the house of Israel.[h] [18] The Levitical priests will never fail to have a man always before me to offer burnt offerings, to burn grain offerings, and to make sacrifices.[i]

[19] The word of the LORD came to Jeremiah: [20] "This is what the LORD says: If you can break my covenant with the day and my covenant with the night so that day and night cease to come at their regular time,[j] [21] then also my covenant with my servant David[k] may be broken. If that could happen, then he would not have a son reigning on his throne and the Levitical priests would not be my ministers.[l] [22] Even as the stars of heaven cannot be counted, and the sand of the sea cannot be measured,[m] so too I will make innumerable the descendants of my servant David and the Levites who minister to me."

[23] The word of the LORD came to Jeremiah: [24] "Have you not noticed what these people have said? They say, 'The LORD has rejected the two families he had chosen.'[n] My people are treated with contempt and no longer regarded as a nation among them. [25] This is what the LORD says: If I do not keep my covenant with the day and with the night, and if I fail to establish the fixed order of heaven and earth,[o] [26] then I might also reject the descendants of Jacob and of my servant David. That is, I would not take rulers from his descendants to rule over the descendants of Abraham, Isaac, and Jacob. But in fact, I will restore their fortunes[B] and have compassion on them."[p]

JEREMIAH'S WORD TO KING ZEDEKIAH

34 This is the word that came to Jeremiah from the LORD when King Nebuchadnezzar of Babylon,[q] his whole army, all the kingdoms of the lands under his control,[r] and all other peoples were fighting against Jerusalem and all its surrounding cities: [2] "This is what the LORD, the God of Israel, says: Go, speak to King Zedekiah of Judah, and tell him, 'This is what the LORD says: I am about to hand this city over to the king of Babylon,[s] and he will burn it. [3] As for you, you will not escape[t] from him but are certain to be captured and handed over to him. You will meet the king of Babylon eye to eye and speak face to face;[c,u] you will go to Babylon.

[4] " 'Yet hear the LORD's word, King Zedekiah of Judah. This is what the LORD says

---

A 33:16 = *Yahweh-zidkenu*   B 33:26 Or *I will end their captivity*   C 34:3 Lit *and his mouth will speak to your mouth*

33:15 The prophets often used tree imagery to speak of the Messiah who rises from the family of **David**. Although God chopped down the Davidic family tree—the royal dynasty of David—because of its sin, a new growth would sprout up from it. The Davidic covenant did not promise an unbroken monarchy; instead, God promised that a righteous king would arise from David's line to rule forever. Jesus fulfilled

this promise, as we see in the New Testament genealogies (see Matt 1:1-16; Luke 3:23-38).

33:17-18 In Old Testament Israel, the offices of king and priest were kept distinct, but the New Testament reveals that they come together in Christ. Jesus is the true heir to the throne of David. He is also the true priest—not a Levitical priest—but a superior one, "a priest forever according to the order of

Melchizedek" (Heb 5:6; 6:20; 7:17; see the notes on Heb 7:1-17).

33:25-26 God has tied himself to his promises; the only way they can fail is if he ceases to be God.

34:2-3 It's interesting that God said Zedekiah would **meet the king of Babylon eye to eye** (34:3), given that when they did meet, Nebuchadnezzar had him blinded (see 52:11).

concerning you: You will not die by the sword; **5** you will die peacefully. There will be a burning ceremony for you just like the burning ceremonies for your ancestors, the kings of old who came before you.[a] "Oh, master!" will be the lament for you, for I have spoken this word. This is the LORD's declaration.'"

6 So the prophet Jeremiah related all these words to King Zedekiah of Judah in Jerusalem **7** while the king of Babylon's army was attacking Jerusalem and all of Judah's remaining cities — that is, Lachish and Azekah,[b] for they were the only ones left of Judah's fortified cities.

THE PEOPLE AND THEIR SLAVES

8 This is the word that came to Jeremiah from the LORD after King Zedekiah made a covenant with all the people who were in Jerusalem to proclaim freedom[c] to them. **9** As a result, each was to let his male and female Hebrew slaves go free, and no one was to enslave his fellow Judean.[d] **10** All the officials and people who entered into covenant to let their male and female slaves go free — in order not to enslave them any longer — obeyed and let them go free. **11** Afterward, however, they changed their minds and took back their male and female slaves they had let go free and forced them to become slaves again.

12 Then the word of the LORD came to Jeremiah from the LORD: **13** "This is what the LORD, the God of Israel, says: I made a covenant[e] with your ancestors when I brought them out of the land of Egypt, out of the place of slavery, saying, **14** 'At the end of seven years, each of you must let his fellow Hebrew who sold himself[A] to you go. He may serve you six years, but then you must let him go free from your service.'[f] But your ancestors did not obey me or pay any attention. **15** Today you repented and did what pleased me, each of you proclaiming freedom for his neighbor. You made a covenant before me[g] at the house that bears my name.[h] **16** But you

have changed your minds[i] and profaned my name.[j] Each has taken back his male and female slaves who had been let go free to go wherever they wanted, and you have again forced them to be your slaves.

17 "Therefore, this is what the LORD says: You have not obeyed me by proclaiming freedom, each for his fellow Hebrew and for his neighbor.[k] I hereby proclaim freedom for you[l] — this is the LORD's declaration — to the sword, to plague, and to famine! I will make you a horror to all the earth's kingdoms.[m] **18** As for those who disobeyed my covenant,[n] not keeping the terms of the covenant they made before me, I will treat them like the calf they cut in two in order to pass between its pieces.[o] **19** The officials of Judah and Jerusalem, the court officials, the priests, and all the people of the land who passed between the pieces of the calf — **20** all these I will hand over to their enemies, to those who intend to take their life. Their corpses will become food for the birds of the sky and for the wild animals of the land.[p] **21** I will hand King Zedekiah of Judah and his officials over to their enemies, to those who intend to take their lives, to the king of Babylon's army that is withdrawing. **22** I am about to give the command — this is the LORD's declaration — and I will bring them back to this city. They will fight against it, capture it, and burn it.[q] I will make Judah's cities a desolation, without inhabitant."[r]

THE RECHABITES' EXAMPLE

35 This is the word that came to Jeremiah from the LORD in the days of Jehoiakim[s] son of Josiah, king of Judah: **2** "Go to the house of the Rechabites, speak to them,[t] and bring them to one of the chambers[u] of the temple of the LORD to offer them a drink of wine."

3 So I took Jaazaniah son of Jeremiah, son of Habazziniah, and his brothers and all his sons — the entire house of the Rechabites — **4** and I brought them into the temple of the LORD to a chamber occupied

[a] 34:5 2Ch 16:14; 21:19
[b] 34:7 Jos 10:3-35
[c] 34:8 Lv 25:10; Is 61:1; Ezk 46:17
[d] 34:9 Lv 25:39
[e] 34:13 Jr 31:32
[f] 34:14 Ex 21:2-6; Dt 15:12-17
[g] 34:15 2Kg 23:3
[h] Jr 7:10-11

[i] 34:16 Jr 34:11
[j] Lv 19:12; 22:32; Pr 30:9; Ezk 20:9,14,22; 36:20-23; 39:7; Am 2:7; Mal 1:11-12
[k] 34:17 Is 9:19; Jr 31:34; Zch 7:9-10; Mal 2:10
[l] Mt 7:2
[m] 2Ch 29:8; Jr 15:4; 24:9; 29:18
[n] 34:18 Jos 7:11; 2Kg 18:12
[o] Gn 15:10,17-18
[p] 34:20 Dt 28:26; Is 18:6; Jr 7:33
[q] 34:22 Jr 21:10; 34:2; 37:8; 38:18
[r] Jr 4:7; 9:11; 33:10; 44:22; 46:19; 48:9; 51:37
[s] 35:1 2Kg 23:34-24:19; 2Ch 36:4-8
[t] 35:2 1Ch 2:55
[u] 1Kg 6:5,8; 1Ch 9:26,33

A 34:14 Or *who was sold*

34:8-16 Desperate for any edge, Zedekiah revived the stipulation that any Jew who was enslaved to a fellow Jew in a form of indentured service was to be freed after six years (34:8-10, 13-14; see Exod 21:2). Yet **afterward** people **changed their minds** and re-enslaved their fellow Jews (Jer 34:11, 16)! Why? Apparently because the Babylonians had suddenly withdrawn from the siege of Jerusalem to deal with the Egyptian army that had marched out to engage them (see 34:21; 37:5). In other words, with things

seemingly back to normal, they saw no need to become so spiritual. But while the people of Judah took the Babylonian withdrawal as a sign that their scheme had manipulated God into turning the tide for them, their false spirituality simply increased the Lord's anger (34:15-16). **34:17-20** God had a bitterly ironic form of **freedom** in store for Judah: **the sword . . . plague . . . famine!** (34:17). All the people had ratified the slave-releasing covenant by passing between the two halves of the sacrificial

animal—so God said **their corpses** would be treated in the same way when the Babylonians returned (34:18-20). As Paul told the Galatians, "God is not mocked. For whatever a person sows he will also reap" (Gal 6:7). **35:1-11** The **Rechabites** were Jewish nomads forced to move to Jerusalem when the Babylonians marched into Judah. They were under a long-standing family covenant not to drink wine. Their **ancestor** had given this command (3:6-10).

a 35:4 Dt 33:1
b 35:6 2Kg 10:15,23
c 35:7 Ex 20:12; Eph 6:2-3
d 35:11 2Kg 24:1-2
e 35:13 Jr 31:18; 32:33
f 35:14 Jr 7:13,25; 11:7; 25:3;
26:5; 29:19; 32:33; 44:4
g 35:15 Jr 18:11
h Jr 7:6

i 35:15 Jr 34:14
j 35:19 Jr 31:36; 33:18
k 36:1 Jr 25:1; 45:1; 46:2
l 36:2 Ps 40:7; Jr 30:2;
36:17,28; Ezk 2:9
m 36:3 2Ch 7:14; Jr 31:34;
33:8; 36:31; Mk 4:12;
Ac 26:18
n 36:4 Jr 32:12-16; 43:3,6;
45:1-2
o 36:5 Jr 32:2; 33:1
p 36:7 1Kg 8:28,45,49; Ps
119:170

by the sons of Hanan son of Igdaliah, a man of God,[a] who had a chamber near the officials' chamber, which was above the chamber of Maaseiah son of Shallum the doorkeeper. [5] I set jars filled with wine and some cups before the sons of the house of the Rechabites and said to them, "Drink wine!"

[6] But they replied, "We do not drink wine, for Jonadab,[b] son of our ancestor Rechab, commanded: 'You and your descendants must never drink wine. [7] You must not build a house or sow seed or plant a vineyard. Those things are not for you. Rather, you must live in tents your whole life, so you may live a long time on the soil where you stay as a resident alien.'[c] [8] We have obeyed Jonadab, son of our ancestor Rechab, in all he commanded us. So we haven't drunk wine our whole life — we, our wives, our sons, and our daughters. [9] We also have not built houses to live in and do not have vineyard, field, or seed. [10] But we have lived in tents and have obeyed and done everything our ancestor Jonadab commanded us. [11] However, when King Nebuchadnezzar of Babylon marched into the land,[d] we said, 'Come, let's go into Jerusalem to get away from the Chaldean and Aramean armies.' So we have been living in Jerusalem."

[12] Then the word of the LORD came to Jeremiah: [13] "This is what the LORD of Armies, the God of Israel, says: Go, say to the men of Judah and the residents of Jerusalem, 'Will you not accept discipline[e] by listening to my words? — this is the LORD's declaration. [14] The words of Jonadab, son of Rechab, have been carried out. He commanded his descendants not to drink wine, and they have not drunk to this day because they have obeyed their ancestor's command. But I have spoken to you time and time again,[A,f] and you have not obeyed me! [15] Time and time again[B] I have sent you all my servants the prophets, proclaiming, "Turn, each one from his evil way,[g] and correct your actions. Stop following other gods to serve them.[h] Live in the land that I gave you and your ancestors." But you did not pay attention or

obey me.[i] [16] Yes, the sons of Jonadab son of Rechab carried out their ancestor's command he gave them, but these people have not obeyed me. [17] Therefore, this is what the LORD, the God of Armies, the God of Israel, says: I will certainly bring on Judah and on all the residents of Jerusalem all the disaster I have pronounced against them because I have spoken to them, but they have not obeyed, and I have called to them, but they did not answer.'"

[18] But to the house of the Rechabites Jeremiah said, "This is what the LORD of Armies, the God of Israel, says: 'Because you have obeyed the command of your ancestor Jonadab and have kept all his commands and have done everything he commanded you, [19] this is what the LORD of Armies, the God of Israel, says: Jonadab son of Rechab will never fail to have a man to stand before me always.'"[j]

JEREMIAH DICTATES A SCROLL

36 In the fourth year of Jehoiakim son of Josiah,[k] king of Judah, this word came to Jeremiah from the LORD: [2] "Take a scroll,[l] and write on it all the words I have spoken to you concerning Israel, Judah, and all the nations from the time I first spoke to you during Josiah's reign until today. [3] Perhaps when the house of Judah hears about all the disaster I am planning to bring on them, each one of them will turn from his evil way. Then I will forgive their iniquity[m] and their sin."

[4] So Jeremiah summoned Baruch[n] son of Neriah. At Jeremiah's dictation,[C] Baruch wrote on a scroll all the words the LORD had spoken to Jeremiah. [5] Then Jeremiah commanded Baruch, "I am restricted;[o] I cannot enter the temple of the LORD, [6] so you must go and read from the scroll — which you wrote at my dictation[D] — the words of the LORD in the hearing of the people at the temple of the LORD on a day of fasting. Read his words in the hearing of all the Judeans who are coming from their cities. [7] Perhaps their petition will come before the LORD,[p] and each one will turn from his evil way, for the anger and fury that the LORD has pronounced against this

---

A 35:14 Lit *you, rising up early and speaking*   B 35:15 Lit *Rising up early and sending*   C 36:4 Lit *From Jeremiah's mouth*   D 36:6 Lit *wrote from my mouth*

35:12-16 That which is true in a small matter is surely true in a similar, more significant one. For generations the Rechabites had remained faithful to their promises, although there was nothing inherently spiritual about living as they did (see 35:8). So if these nomads could be so obedient to a man's words, why could

the people of Judah not bring themselves to obey the word of **God** (35:13)? After all, while we don't know the reasons behind Jonadab's commands, the Rechabites heeded him. Yet God commanded his people for their own good—so they could live and enjoy his blessing—but they **did not pay attention** (35:15-16).

35:17-19 Make no mistake: Rebellion against God has consequences. But so does a life of faithfulness.

36:5 While Jeremiah had been faithful to God's word, the spiritual leaders who rejected it had barred this prophet from God's house of worship!

people are intense." **8** So Baruch son of Neriah did everything the prophet Jeremiah had commanded him. At the LORD's temple he read the LORD's words from the scroll.

BARUCH READS THE SCROLL

9 In the fifth year of Jehoiakim son of Josiah, king of Judah, in the ninth month,*a* all the people of Jerusalem and all those coming in from Judah's cities into Jerusalem proclaimed a fast before the LORD.*b* **10** Then at the LORD's temple, in the chamber of Gemariah son of Shaphan the scribe,*c* in the upper courtyard at the opening of the New Gate*d* of the LORD's temple, in the hearing of all the people, Baruch read Jeremiah's words from the scroll.

11 When Micaiah son of Gemariah, son of Shaphan, heard all the words of the LORD from the scroll, **12** he went down to the scribe's chamber in the king's palace. All the officials were sitting there — Elishama the scribe, Delaiah son of Shemaiah, Elnathan son of Achbor,*e* Gemariah son of Shaphan, Zedekiah son of Hananiah, and all the other officials. **13** Micaiah reported to them all the words he had heard when Baruch read from the scroll in the hearing of the people. **14** Then all the officials sent word to Baruch through Jehudi son of Nethaniah, son of Shelemiah, son of Cushi, saying, "Bring the scroll that you read in the hearing of the people, and come." So Baruch son of Neriah took the scroll and went to them. **15** They said to him, "Sit down and read it in our hearing." So Baruch read it in their hearing.

16 When they had heard all the words, they turned to each other in fear and said to Baruch, "We must surely tell the king all these things." **17** Then they asked Baruch, "Tell us, how did you write all these words? At his dictation?"*A*

18 Baruch said to them, "At his dictation. He recited all these words to me while I was writing on the scroll in ink."

JEHOIAKIM BURNS THE SCROLL

19 The officials said to Baruch, "You and Jeremiah must hide and tell no one where you are." **20** Then, after depositing the scroll in the chamber of Elishama the scribe, the officials came to the king at the courtyard and reported everything in the hearing of the king. **21** The king sent Jehudi to get the scroll, and he took it from the chamber of Elishama the scribe. Jehudi then read it in the hearing of the king and all the officials who were standing by the king. **22** Since it was the ninth month, the king was sitting in his winter quarters*f* with a fire burning in front of him. **23** As soon as Jehudi would read three or four columns, Jehoiakim would cut the scroll*B* with a scribe's knife and throw the columns into the fire in the hearth until the entire scroll was consumed by the fire in the hearth. **24** As they heard all these words, the king and all of his servants did not become terrified*g* or tear their clothes. **25** Even though Elnathan, Delaiah, and Gemariah had urged the king not to burn the scroll, he did not listen to them. **26** Then the king commanded Jerahmeel the king's son, Seraiah son of Azriel, and Shelemiah son of Abdeel to seize the scribe Baruch and the prophet Jeremiah, but the LORD hid them.

JEREMIAH DICTATES ANOTHER SCROLL

27 After the king had burned the scroll and the words Baruch had written at Jeremiah's dictation,*c* the word of the LORD came to Jeremiah: **28** "Take another scroll, and once again write on it the original words that were on the original scroll that King Jehoiakim of Judah burned.*h* **29** You are to proclaim concerning King Jehoiakim of Judah, 'This is what the LORD says: You have burned the scroll, asking, "Why have you written on it that*i* the king of Babylon will certainly come and destroy this land and cause it to be without people or animals?"*j* **30** Therefore, this is what the LORD says concerning King Jehoiakim of Judah: He will have no one to sit on David's throne,*k* and his corpse will be thrown out to be exposed to the heat of day and the frost of night.*l* **31** I will punish him, his descendants, and his officers for their iniquity. I will bring on them, on the residents of Jerusalem, and on the people of Judah all the disaster, which I warned them about but they did not listen.'"

32 Then Jeremiah took another scroll and gave it to Baruch son of Neriah, the

a 36:9 Jr 36:22
b 2Ch 20:3
c 36:10 2Kg 22:3-14; 2Ch 34:8-20; Jr 29:3
d Jr 26:10
e 36:12 Jr 26:22

f 36:22 Am 3:15
g 36:24 Jr 36:16
h 36:28 Ex 34:1
i 36:29 Jr 26:9
j Ps 135:8; Jr 7:20; 21:6; 32:43; 33:10,12; 50:3; 51:62
k 36:30 Jr 17:25; 22:2,30; 29:16
l Gn 31:40; Dt 21:23; 1Kg 13:22-30; 2Kg 9:37; Is 14:19; Jr 26:23

A 36:17 Lit *From his mouth*, also in v. 18   *B* 36:23 Lit *columns, he would tear it*   *C* 36:27 Lit *written from Jeremiah's mouth*

36:19-20 These men knew King Jehoiakim was not likely to be happy about this news condemning Judah, its king, and its people. That's why they told Baruch and Jeremiah to **hide** (36:19) while they approached him about the **scroll** (36:20).

36:23 With these actions the king revealed his lack of concern for God's word and Judah's sin. Yet if you receive an eviction notice, burning it won't keep you from being evicted.

36:30 Jehoiakim's son Jeconiah (Jehoiachin) would rule for only three months before the Babylonians carried him into exile (see 2 Chr 36:8-10).

[a] 36:32 Jr 36:4,18
[b] 37:1 2Kg 24:17; 2Ch 36:10
[c] Ezk 17:12-21
[d] Jr 22:24
[e] 37:2 2Ch 36:12-16
[f] 37:3 Jr 38:1
[g] 2Kg 25:18-21; Jr 21:1;
     29:24-29
[h] 37:4 Jr 32:2-3
[i] 37:5 Ezk 17:15
[j] 37:7 Jr 21:1-2
[k] Lm 4:17
[l] 37:8 Jr 21:10; 34:2,22;
     38:18
[m] 37:10 Jr 21:4-5

[n] 37:12 Jr 32:1-15
[o] 37:13 Jr 38:7; Zch 14:10
[p] 37:15 Jr 38:26
[q] 37:16 Gn 40:15; Is 24:22;
     Zch 9:11
[r] 37:17 Jr 38:14-16
[s] Jr 21:7
[t] 37:19 Jr 28:1-17
[u] 37:20 Jr 38:26
[v] 37:21 Jr 32:2
[w] 38:1 Jr 37:3

scribe, and he wrote on it at Jeremiah's dictation[A] all the words of the scroll that Jehoiakim,[a] Judah's king, had burned in the fire. And many other words like them were added.

JERUSALEM'S LAST DAYS

37 Zedekiah son of Josiah[b] reigned as king in the land of Judah[c] in place of Coniah[B,d] son of Jehoiakim, for King Nebuchadnezzar of Babylon made him king. **2** He and his officers and the people of the land did not obey the words of the LORD[e] that he spoke through the prophet Jeremiah.

3 Nevertheless, King Zedekiah sent Jehucal[f] son of Shelemiah and Zephaniah[g] son of Maaseiah, the priest, to the prophet Jeremiah, requesting, "Please pray to the LORD our God for us!" **4** Jeremiah was going about his daily tasks[c] among the people, for he had not yet been put into the prison.[h] **5** Pharaoh's army had left Egypt,[i] and when the Chaldeans, who were besieging Jerusalem, heard the report, they withdrew from Jerusalem.

6 The word of the LORD came to the prophet Jeremiah: **7** "This is what the LORD, the God of Israel, says: This is what you will say to Judah's king,[j] who is sending you to inquire of me: 'Watch: Pharaoh's army, which has come out to help you,[k] is going to return to its own land of Egypt. **8** The Chaldeans will then return and fight against this city. They will capture it and burn it.[l] **9** This is what the LORD says: Don't deceive yourselves by saying, "The Chaldeans will leave us for good," for they will not leave. **10** Indeed, if you were to strike down the entire Chaldean army that is fighting with you,[m] and there remained among them only the badly wounded[D] men, each in his tent, they would get up and burn this city.'"

JEREMIAH'S IMPRISONMENT

11 When the Chaldean army withdrew from Jerusalem because of Pharaoh's army, **12** Jeremiah started to leave Jerusalem to go to the land of Benjamin to claim his portion there[n] among the people. **13** But when he was at the Benjamin Gate,[o] an officer of the guard was there, whose name was Irijah son of Shelemiah, son of Hananiah, and he apprehended the prophet Jeremiah, saying, "You are defecting to the Chaldeans."

14 "That's a lie," Jeremiah replied. "I am not defecting to the Chaldeans!" Irijah would not listen to him but apprehended Jeremiah and took him to the officials. **15** The officials were angry at Jeremiah and beat him and placed him in jail in the house of Jonathan[p] the scribe, for it had been made into a prison. **16** So Jeremiah went into a cell in the dungeon[q] and stayed there many days.

JEREMIAH SUMMONED BY ZEDEKIAH

17 King Zedekiah later sent for him and received him, and in his house privately asked him, "Is there a word from the LORD?"[r]

"There is," Jeremiah responded. He continued, "You will be handed over to the king of Babylon."[s] **18** Then Jeremiah said to King Zedekiah, "How have I sinned against you or your servants or these people that you have put me in prison? **19** Where are your prophets who prophesied to you, claiming, 'The king of Babylon will not come against you and this land'?[t] **20** So now please listen, my lord the king. May my petition come before you.[u] Don't send me back to the house of Jonathan the scribe, or I will die there."

21 So King Zedekiah gave orders, and Jeremiah was placed in the guard's courtyard.[v] He was given a loaf of bread each day from the bakers' street until all the bread was gone from the city. So Jeremiah remained in the guard's courtyard.

JEREMIAH THROWN INTO A CISTERN

38 Now Shephatiah son of Mattan, Gedaliah son of Pashhur, Jucal[E] son of Shelemiah,[w] and Pashhur son of Malchijah heard the words Jeremiah was

---

[A] 36:32 Lit *it from Jeremiah's mouth*   [B] 37:1 = Jehoiachin   [C] 37:4 Lit *was coming in and going out*   [D] 37:10 Lit *the pierced*   [E] 38:1 = Jehucal in Jr 37:3

37:1-2 Zedekiah was a puppet king put on the throne by **Nebuchadnezzar**. Still, if he had listened to the Lord, he could have prevented disaster.
37:5 There was a deceptive lull in the siege of Jerusalem when the Babylonian army (**the Chaldeans**) temporarily withdrew to fight the armies of Pharaoh coming up from **Egypt**.

37:11-12 When the Babylonian army temporarily withdrew, the pressure on Jerusalem eased, for a while at least. So Jeremiah tried to **leave** the city to go to his home in **the land of Benjamin** on family business (37:12).
37:17 The king seemed to know in his heart that Jeremiah was speaking a true **word from the LORD**, which would explain why he sent

for the prophet to see what God's latest word was.
37:18-20 The false **prophets** who had told Judah that Babylon was no threat were suddenly nowhere to be found, while Jeremiah had fearlessly and faithfully stood his ground (37:19).

speaking to all the people: **2** "This is what the Lord says: 'Whoever stays in this city will die by the sword, famine, and plague,[a] but whoever surrenders to the Chaldeans will live.[b] He will retain his life like the spoils of war and will live.'[c] **3** This is what the Lord says: 'This city will most certainly be handed over to the king of Babylon's army,[d] and he will capture it.'"

4 The officials then said to the king, "This man ought to die, because he is weakening the morale[A] of the warriors who remain in this city and of all the people by speaking to them in this way. This man is not pursuing the welfare of this people, but their harm."[e]

5 King Zedekiah said, "Here he is; he's in your hands since the king can't do anything against you." **6** So they took Jeremiah and dropped him into the cistern of Malchiah the king's son, which was in the guard's courtyard, lowering Jeremiah with ropes. There was no water in the cistern, only mud, and Jeremiah sank in the mud.[f]

7 But Ebed-melech, a Cushite court official in the king's palace, heard Jeremiah had been put into the cistern. While the king was sitting at the Benjamin Gate,[g] **8** Ebed-melech went from the king's palace and spoke to the king: **9** "My lord the king, these men have been evil in all they have done to the prophet Jeremiah. They have dropped him into the cistern where he will die from hunger, because there is no more bread in the city."[h]

10 So the king commanded Ebed-melech, the Cushite, "Take from here thirty men under your authority[B] and pull the prophet Jeremiah up from the cistern before he dies."

11 So Ebed-melech took the men under his authority[c] and went to the king's palace to a place below the storehouse.[D] From there he took old rags and worn-out clothes and lowered them by ropes to Jeremiah in the cistern. **12** Ebed-melech the Cushite called down to Jeremiah, "Place these old rags and clothes between your armpits and the ropes." Jeremiah did this. **13** They pulled him up with the ropes and lifted him out of the cistern, but he remained in the guard's courtyard.

ZEDEKIAH'S FINAL MEETING WITH JEREMIAH

14 King Zedekiah sent for the prophet Jeremiah and received him at the third entrance of the Lord's temple. The king said to Jeremiah, "I am going to ask you something; don't hide anything from me."

15 Jeremiah replied to Zedekiah, "If I tell you, you will kill me, won't you? Besides, if I give you advice, you won't listen to me anyway."

16 King Zedekiah swore to Jeremiah in private,[i] "As the Lord lives, who has given us this life,[j] I will not kill you or hand you over to these men who intend to take your life."

17 Jeremiah therefore said to Zedekiah, "This is what the Lord, the God of Armies, the God of Israel, says: 'If indeed you surrender to the officials of the king of Babylon,[k] then you will live, this city will not be burned, and you and your household will survive. **18** But if you do not surrender to the officials of the king of Babylon, then this city will be handed over to the Chaldeans.[l] They will burn it, and you yourself will not escape from them.'"

19 But King Zedekiah said to Jeremiah, "I am worried about the Judeans who have defected to the Chaldeans. They may hand me over to the Judeans to abuse me."[m]

20 "They will not hand you over," Jeremiah replied. "Obey the Lord in what I am telling you, so it may go well for you and you can live. **21** But if you refuse to surrender, this is the verdict[E] that the Lord has shown me: **22** 'All the women[F] who remain in the palace of Judah's king will be brought out to the officials of the king of Babylon and will say to you,[G]

"Your trusted friends[H]
    misled[I] you
and overcame you.
Your feet sank into the mire,
    and they deserted you."

23 All your wives and children will be brought out to the Chaldeans.[n] You yourself

[a] 38:2 Jr 14:12; 21:9; 24:10; 27:8; 29:17-18; 32:24,36; 38:2; 42:17,22; 44:13; Ezk 6:11; 12:16
[b] Jr 21:9; 38:17-21
[c] Jr 21:9; 39:18; 45:5
[d] 38:3 Jr 32:3-5
[e] 38:4 Jr 29:11
[f] 38:6 Gn 37:20-24
[g] 38:7 Jr 20:2; Ezk 48:32; Zch 14:10
[h] 38:9 Jr 37:21

[i] 38:16 Jr 37:17
[j] Is 57:16
[k] 38:17 2Kg 24:12; Jr 27:12; 38:2; 39:3
[l] 38:18 Jr 22:25; 32:24-25,28,43; 43:3
[m] 38:19 Jdg 19:25; 1Sm 31:4
[n] 38:23 Jr 39:6; 41:10

A 38:4 Lit *hands*   B 38:10 Lit *men in your hand*   C 38:11 Lit *men in his hand*   D 38:11 Or *treasury*   E 38:21 Or *promise*; lit *word*   F 38:22 Or *wives*   G 38:22 *to you* supplied for clarity   H 38:22 Lit *"The men of your peace*   I 38:22 Or *incited*

38:4 To these men, Jeremiah's words of national demise were treason.
38:5 Zedekiah's sniveling reply is pathetic. After all, he was king.
38:7-13 The bravest of Jeremiah's few friends in the city was **Ebed-melech**, an African (**Cushite**)

who obviously feared God. He courageously approached Zedekiah for permission to rescue Jeremiah from the pit (38:8-13).
38:14-16 The king's vacillation was really on display as he arranged a secret meeting for fear of his own officials. He wanted to hear

what Jeremiah had to say, but he lacked the courage and spiritual commitment to make the right call.
38:17-18 Only by submitting to defeat at the hands of Babylon would the king and the city **survive** (38:17).

a 38:25 Jr 38:4-6
b 38:26 Jr 37:20
c 39:1-7 2Kg 25:1-7; Jr 52:4-11; Ezk 24:1-2
d 39:2 Lm 4:10
e 39:3 2Kg 25:8
f 39:4 Neh 3:15
g Dt 2:8; 2Sm 4:7
h 39:5 Jr 32:4-5; 34:3

i 39:7 Ezk 12:8-13
j 39:8 2Kg 25:9
k 39:9 2Kg 25:8-20; Jr 52:12-30; Dn 2:14
l 39:8-10 2Kg 25:9-12; Jr 52:13-16
m 39:14 Jr 38:28; 40:1-6
n Jr 40:5,7
o 2Kg 22:12
p 39:15 Jr 33:1
q 39:16 Jr 38:1-13
r 39:18 Jr 21:9; 38:2; 45:5

will not escape from them, for you will be seized by the king of Babylon and this city will burn.'"

²⁴ Then Zedekiah warned Jeremiah, "Don't let anyone know about this conversation[A] or you will die. ²⁵ The officials may hear that I have spoken with you[a] and come and demand of you, 'Tell us what you said to the king; don't hide anything from us and we won't kill you. Also, what did the king say to you?' ²⁶ If they do, tell them, 'I was bringing before the king my petition that he not return me to the house of Jonathan to die there.'"[b] ²⁷ All the officials did come to Jeremiah, and they questioned him. He reported the exact words to them the king had commanded, and they quit speaking with him because the conversation[B] had not been overheard. ²⁸ Jeremiah remained in the guard's courtyard until the day Jerusalem was captured, and he was there when it happened.[c]

THE FALL OF JERUSALEM TO BABYLON

39 In the ninth year of King Zedekiah of Judah, in the tenth month, King Nebuchadnezzar of Babylon advanced against Jerusalem with his entire army and laid siege to it.[c] ² In the fourth month of Zedekiah's eleventh year, on the ninth day of the month, the city was broken into.[d] ³ All the officials of the king of Babylon entered and sat at the Middle Gate: Nergal-sharezer, Samgar, Nebusarsechim[D] the chief of staff, Nergal-sharezer the chief soothsayer, and all the rest of the officials of Babylon's king.[e]

⁴ When King Zedekiah of Judah and all the fighting men saw them, they fled. They left the city at night by way of the king's garden[f] through the city gate between the two walls. They left along the route to the Arabah.[g] ⁵ However, the Chaldean army pursued them and overtook Zedekiah in the plains of Jericho. They arrested him and brought him up to Nebuchadnezzar, Babylon's king, at Riblah in the land of Hamath. The king passed sentence on him there.[h]

⁶ At Riblah the king of Babylon slaughtered Zedekiah's sons before his eyes, and he also slaughtered all Judah's nobles. ⁷ Then he blinded Zedekiah and put him in bronze chains to take him to Babylon.[i] ⁸ The Chaldeans next burned down the king's palace and the people's houses and tore down the walls of Jerusalem.[j] ⁹ Nebuzaradan, the captain of the guards,[k] deported the rest of the people to Babylon — those who had remained in the city and those deserters who had defected to him along with the rest of the people who remained. ¹⁰ However, Nebuzaradan, the captain of the guards, left in the land of Judah some of the poor people who owned nothing, and he gave them vineyards and fields at that time.[l]

JEREMIAH FREED BY NEBUCHADNEZZAR

¹¹ Speaking through Nebuzaradan, captain of the guards, King Nebuchadnezzar of Babylon gave orders concerning Jeremiah: ¹² "Take him and look after him. Don't do him any harm, but do for him whatever he says." ¹³ Nebuzaradan, captain of the guards, Nebushazban the chief of staff, Nergal-sharezer the chief soothsayer, and all the captains of Babylon's king ¹⁴ had Jeremiah brought from the guard's courtyard[m] and turned him over to Gedaliah[n] son of Ahikam,[o] son of Shaphan, to take him home. So he settled among his own people.

¹⁵ Now the word of the LORD had come to Jeremiah when he was confined in the guard's courtyard:[p] ¹⁶ "Go tell Ebed-melech the Cushite,[q] 'This is what the LORD of Armies, the God of Israel, says: I am about to fulfill my words for disaster and not for good against this city. They will take place before your eyes on that day. ¹⁷ But I will rescue you on that day — this is the LORD's declaration — and you will not be handed over to the men you dread. ¹⁸ Indeed, I will certainly deliver you so that you do not fall by the sword. Because you have trusted in me, you will retain your life like the spoils of war.[r] This is the LORD's declaration.'"

[A] 38:24 Lit *about these words*   [B] 38:27 Lit *word*   [C] 38:28 Or *captured. This is what happened when Jerusalem was captured:*   [D] 39:3 LXX; MT reads *Samgar-nebu, Sarsechim*

39:1-2 The Babylonians breached Jerusalem's walls and entered the city in 587–586 BC.
39:3 The **officials** of Babylon **sat at the Middle Gate** to demonstrate that they were now in charge and to judge those still in the city who'd resisted them.
39:10 When the southern kingdom fell, only a handful of **poor people** were permitted to

stay behind. Their story unfolds in the chapters to come.
39:11-12 That God had his eye on Jeremiah was apparent in that Nebuchadnezzar, the great conqueror, gave orders for Jeremiah to be treated kindly.
39:13-14 **Gedaliah** had been appointed by the Babylonians as governor of the few people

who were left behind in Judah (see 40:5,7). Gedaliah took Jeremiah back to his **home** (39:14), which must have seemed a little surreal to the prophet with his nation in ruins.
39:16-18 Previously **Ebed-melech** saved Jeremiah's life (39:16; see 38:7-13). In spite of his nation's downfall, his trust in God was rewarded (39:18).

JEREMIAH STAYS IN JUDAH

40 This is the word that came to Jeremiah from the LORD after Nebuzaradan, captain of the guards, released him at Ramah.[a] When he found him, he was bound in chains with all the exiles of Jerusalem and Judah who were being exiled to Babylon. [2] The captain of the guards took Jeremiah and said to him, "The LORD your God decreed this disaster on this place,[b] [3] and the LORD has fulfilled it. He has done just what he decreed. Because you people have sinned against the LORD[c] and have not obeyed him, this thing has happened. [4] Now pay attention: Today I am setting you free from the chains that were on your hands.[d] If it pleases you to come with me to Babylon, come, and I will take care of you. But if it seems wrong to you to come with me to Babylon, go no farther.[A] Look — the whole land is in front of you.[e] Wherever it seems good and right for you to go, go there." [5] When Jeremiah had not yet turned to go, Nebuzaradan said to him,[B] "Return[c] to Gedaliah son of Ahikam, son of Shaphan, whom the king of Babylon has appointed over the cities of Judah, and stay with him among the people or go wherever it seems right for you to go." So the captain of the guards gave him a ration[f] and a gift[g] and released him. [6] Jeremiah therefore went to Gedaliah son of Ahikam at Mizpah,[h] and he stayed with him among the people who remained in the land.

GEDALIAH ADVISES PEACE

[7] All the commanders of the armies that were in the countryside — they and their men — heard that the king of Babylon had appointed Gedaliah son of Ahikam over the land. He had been put in charge of the men, women, and children from among the poorest of the land, who had not been deported to Babylon. [8] So they came to Gedaliah at Mizpah. The commanders included Ishmael[i] son of Nethaniah, Johanan and Jonathan the sons of Kareah, Seraiah son of Tanhumeth, the sons of Ephai the Netophathite, and Jezaniah son of the Maacathite — they and their men. [9] Gedaliah son of Ahikam, son of Shaphan, swore an oath to them and their men, assuring them, "Don't be afraid to serve the Chaldeans. Live in the land and serve the king of Babylon, and it will go well for you.[j] [10] As for me, I am going to live in Mizpah to represent you[D] before the Chaldeans[k] who come to us. As for you, gather wine, summer fruit, and oil, place them in your storage jars, and live in the cities you have captured."

[11] When all the Judeans in Moab[l] and among the Ammonites and in[m] Edom and in all the other lands[n] also heard that the king of Babylon had left a remnant in Judah and had appointed Gedaliah son of Ahikam, son of Shaphan, over them, [12] they all returned from all the places where they had been banished[o] and came to the land of Judah, to Gedaliah at Mizpah, and harvested a great amount of wine and summer fruit.

[13] Meanwhile, Johanan son of Kareah and all the commanders of the armies in the countryside came to Gedaliah at Mizpah [14] and warned him, "Don't you realize that Baalis, king of the Ammonites, has sent Ishmael son of Nethaniah[p] to kill you?" But Gedaliah son of Ahikam would not believe them. [15] Then Johanan son of Kareah suggested to Gedaliah in private at Mizpah, "Let me go kill Ishmael son of Nethaniah. No one will know it. Why should he kill you and allow all of Judah that has gathered around you to scatter and the remnant of Judah to perish?"[q] [16] But Gedaliah son of Ahikam responded to Johanan son of Kareah, "Don't do that! What you're saying about Ishmael is a lie."

[a] 40:1 1Kg 15:17-22; 2Ch 16:1-6
[b] 40:2 Dt 29:24-28
[c] 40:3 Dn 9:10-12
[d] 40:4 Jr 39:12
[e] Gn 20:15
[f] 40:5 2Kg 25:30; Jr 52:34
[g] 2Sm 11:8
[h] 40:6 Jdg 20:1-3; 1Sm 7:5-16; Jr 41:1-16
[i] 40:8 Jr 41:1,9
[j] 40:7-9 2Kg 25:22-24
[k] 40:10 Dt 1:38
[l] 40:11 Nm 22:1
[m] 1Sm 11:1; 12:12
[n] Gn 36:8
[o] 40:12 Jr 23:3,8; 29:14; 32:37
[p] 40:14 Jr 41:10
[q] 40:15 Jr 42:2

[A] 40:4 Lit *Babylon, stop*   [B] 40:5 *Nebuzaradan said to him* supplied for clarity   [C] 40:5 LXX reads *"But if not, run, return*; Hb obscure
[D] 40:10 Lit *to stand*

40:4-5 Under orders from Nebuchadnezzar himself, Nebuzaradan gave Jeremiah the choice to come with him **to Babylon** or stay in Judah (40:4). Jeremiah's desire must have been reflected in his face, because even before he **turned to go** back to his people, the Babylonian advised him to go to the new governor **Gedaliah** for protection and provision (40:5). **40:6 Mizpah** was a town a few miles north of Jerusalem; it became the new administrative center following the capital's total destruction. **40:7-8** Even amid the devastation, rebellion still lingered in some of the Jews left behind.

The commanders of the armies that were in the countryside (40:7) that had survived the Babylonian invasion heard about Gedaliah's appointment. These men and their leaders, most notably **Ishmael** (40:8), who was a relative of King Zedekiah (see 41:1), came to Gedaliah at Mizpah to find out what was going on. **40:9 Serve the king of Babylon, and it will go well for you** is essentially what God had been telling the people of Judah to do for years. **40:11-12** As news of Gedaliah's appointment and kindly attitude toward the survivors in the land spread, Jews who had fled to neighboring lands started pouring into Judah. These refugees helped bring in a great harvest, and things seemed to be looking up. But trouble was brewing.

40:13-14 Ammon was on Nebuchadnezzar's list of places to conquer, so it may be that this plot against Gedaliah was concocted to keep the Babylonians occupied with Judah and to preserve Ammon (40:14). It's also likely that Ishmael and his followers didn't want to submit to the Babylonians. **40:15** Johanan privately offered to **kill Ishmael** to avoid having the Babylonians come down on the people of Judah again.

a 41:2 Jr 52:30
b 41:1-3 2Kg 25:25
c 41:5 Jos 18:1
d 1Kg 16:24
e Dt 14:1
f Lv 19:27-28; 21:5
g 2Kg 25:9
h 41:9 1Kg 15:16-22
i 41:10 Jr 40:14

j 41:11 Jr 40:7-8,13-16
k 41:12 2Sm 2:13
l 41:17 2Sm 19:37-38
m 41:18 2Kg 25:26; Jr 40:5
n 42:1 Jr 40:13; 41:11
o Est 1:20; Jr 6:13; 8:10;
31:34; 42:8; 44:12
p 42:2 Jr 36:7
q 1Sm 7:8; 12:19; Is 37:4;
Jr 42:20
r Lv 26:22

GEDALIAH ASSASSINATED BY ISHMAEL

41 In the seventh month, Ishmael son of Nethaniah, son of Elishama, of the royal family and one of the king's chief officers, came with ten men to Gedaliah son of Ahikam at Mizpah. They ate a meal together there in Mizpah, **2** but then Ishmael son of Nethaniah and the ten men who were with him got up and struck down Gedaliah son of Ahikam, son of Shaphan, with the sword; he killed the one the king of Babylon had appointed in the land.[a] **3** Ishmael also struck down all the Judeans who were with Gedaliah at Mizpah, as well as the Chaldean soldiers who were there.[b]

4 On the day after he had killed Gedaliah, when no one knew yet, **5** eighty men came from Shechem, Shiloh,[c] and Samaria[d] who had shaved their beards,[e] torn their clothes, and gashed themselves, and[f] who were carrying grain and incense offerings to bring to the temple of the LORD.[g] **6** Ishmael son of Nethaniah came out of Mizpah to meet them, weeping as he came. When he encountered them, he said, "Come to Gedaliah son of Ahikam!" **7** But when they came into the city, Ishmael son of Nethaniah and the men with him slaughtered them and threw them into[A] a cistern.

8 However, there were ten men among them who said to Ishmael, "Don't kill us, for we have hidden treasure in the field — wheat, barley, oil, and honey!" So he stopped and did not kill them along with their companions. **9** Now the cistern where Ishmael had thrown all the corpses of the men he had struck down was a large one[B] that King Asa had made in the encounter with King Baasha of Israel.[h] Ishmael son of Nethaniah filled it with the slain.

10 Then Ishmael took captive all the rest of the people of Mizpah including the daughters of the king — all those who remained in Mizpah over whom Nebuzaradan, captain of the guards, had appointed Gedaliah son of Ahikam. Ishmael son of Nethaniah took them captive and set off to cross over to the Ammonites.[i]

THE CAPTIVES RESCUED BY JOHANAN

11 When Johanan son of Kareah and all the commanders of the armies[j] with him heard of all the evil that Ishmael son of Nethaniah had done, **12** they took all their men and went to fight with Ishmael son of Nethaniah. They found him by the great pool in Gibeon.[k] **13** When all the people held by Ishmael saw Johanan son of Kareah and all the commanders of the army with him, they rejoiced. **14** All the people whom Ishmael had taken captive from Mizpah turned around and rejoined Johanan son of Kareah. **15** But Ishmael son of Nethaniah escaped from Johanan with eight men and went to the Ammonites. **16** Johanan son of Kareah and all the commanders of the armies with him then took from Mizpah all the remnant of the people whom he had recovered from Ishmael son of Nethaniah after Ishmael had killed Gedaliah son of Ahikam — men, soldiers, women, children, and court officials whom he brought back from Gibeon. **17** They left, stopping in Geruth Chimham,[l] which is near Bethlehem, in order to make their way into Egypt, **18** away from the Chaldeans. For they feared them because Ishmael son of Nethaniah had struck down Gedaliah son of Ahikam, whom the king of Babylon had appointed over the land.[m]

THE PEOPLE SEEK JEREMIAH'S COUNSEL

42 Then all the commanders of the armies, along with Johanan son of Kareah,[n] Jezaniah son of Hoshaiah, and all the people from the least to the greatest,[o] approached **2** the prophet Jeremiah and said, "May our petition come before you;[p] pray to the LORD your God on our behalf,[q] on behalf of this entire remnant (for few of us remain out of the many,[r] as you can see with your own eyes), **3** that the LORD your God may tell us the way we should go and the thing we should do."

4 So the prophet Jeremiah said to them, "I have heard. I will now pray to the LORD your God according to your words, and I

[A] 41:7 Syr; MT reads *slaughtered them in*   [B] 41:9 LXX; MT reads *down by the hand of Gedaliah*

41:4-5 These **men** were from what had been the northern kingdom of Israel. They had come grieving, hoping to make offerings to the Lord at the **temple**, which had been destroyed by that time (41:5).

41:7, 10 Perhaps in his twisted mind Ishmael thought he was rescuing his people from the "Babylonian collaborator" Gedaliah and his accomplices. Regardless, Ishmael was a brutal murderer who made a difficult situation worse.

41:13-18 If the freed people had returned to Mizpah and resumed their lives, they might have been fine, despite the expected reprisals from Babylon. God had promised them his overseeing care. But they were convinced that the Babylonians would return and slaughter them for Ishmael's deeds, so they decided **to make their way into Egypt** (41:17). Instead of looking north for the next attack from Nebuchadnezzar, or looking south for deliverance from Egypt, they should have been looking up to God for deliverance.

42:1-6 This straggly band of Israelites got together and decided it would be a good idea to get God's rubber stamp of approval

will tell you every word that the LORD answers you; I won't withhold a word from you."[a]

[5] And they said to Jeremiah, "May the LORD be a true and faithful witness against us if we don't act according to every word the LORD your God sends you to tell us.[b] [6] Whether it is pleasant or unpleasant, we will obey the LORD our God to whom we are sending you so that it may go well with us.[c] We will certainly obey the LORD our God!"

JEREMIAH'S ADVICE TO STAY

[7] At the end of ten days, the word of the LORD came to Jeremiah, [8] and he summoned Johanan son of Kareah, all the commanders of the armies who were with him, and all the people from the least to the greatest.

[9] He said to them, "This is what the LORD says, the God of Israel to whom you sent me to bring your petition before him: [10] 'If you will indeed stay in this land, then I will rebuild and not demolish you,[d] and I will plant and not uproot you, because I relent concerning the disaster that I have brought on you.[e] [11] Don't be afraid of the king of Babylon[f] whom you now fear; don't be afraid of him' — this is the LORD's declaration — 'because I am with you to save you[g] and rescue you from him. [12] I will grant you compassion,[h] and he[A] will have compassion on you and allow you to return to your own soil.'

[13] "But if you say, 'We will not stay in this land,'[i] in order to disobey the LORD your God, [14] and if you say, 'No, instead we'll go to the land of Egypt[j] where we will not see war or hear the sound of the ram's horn[k] or hunger for food, and we'll live there,' [15] then hear the word of the LORD, remnant of Judah! This is what the LORD of Armies, the God of Israel,[l] says: 'If you are firmly resolved to go to Egypt[m] and stay there for a while, [16] then the sword[n] you fear will overtake you there in the land of Egypt, and the famine you are worried about will

follow on your heels[B] there to Egypt, and you will die there. [17] All who resolve to go to Egypt to stay there for a while will die by the sword, famine, and plague. They will have no survivor or fugitive from the disaster I will bring on them.'

[18] "For this is what the LORD of Armies, the God of Israel, says: 'Just as my anger and fury were poured out on Jerusalem's residents,[o] so will my fury pour out on you if you go to Egypt. You will become an example for cursing, scorn,[p] execration, and disgrace, and you will never see this place again.' [19] The LORD has spoken concerning you, remnant of Judah: 'Don't go to Egypt.' Know for certain that I have warned you today![q] [20] You have gone astray at the cost of your lives[c] because you are the ones who sent me to the LORD your God, saying, 'Pray to the LORD our God on our behalf, and as for all that the LORD our God says, tell it to us, and we'll act accordingly.' [21] For I have told you today, but you have not obeyed the LORD your God in everything he has sent me to tell you. [22] Now therefore, know for certain that by the sword, famine, and plague you will die in the place where you desired to go to stay for a while."

JEREMIAH'S COUNSEL REJECTED

43 When Jeremiah had finished speaking to all the people all the words of the LORD their God — all these words the LORD their God had sent him to give them — [2] then Azariah[D] son of Hoshaiah,[r] Johanan son of Kareah, and all the other arrogant men responded to Jeremiah, "You are speaking a lie! The LORD our God has not sent you to say, 'You must not go to Egypt to stay there for a while!' [3] Rather, Baruch son of Neriah is inciting you against us to hand us over to the Chaldeans to put us to death or to deport us to Babylon!"

[4] So Johanan son of Kareah, all the commanders of the armies, and all the people failed to obey the LORD's command to stay

[a] 42:4 1Sm 3:17-18
[b] 42:5 Gn 31:50; Jdg 11:10
[c] 42:6 Jr 7:23
[d] 42:10 Jr 24:6
[e] Ex 32:12,14; 2Sm 24:16; Jr 18:8; 26:3,13; Jl 2:13; Jnh 3:10; 4:2
[f] 42:11 Jr 41:18
[g] Rm 8:31
[h] 42:12 Neh 1:11; Jr 12:15; 30:18; 31:20; 33:26
[i] 42:13 Jr 44:16-17
[j] 42:14 Jr 41:17
[k] Jr 4:19,21
[l] 42:15 Is 21:10; Jr 7:3,21; 9:15; 16:9; 19:3,15; 27:4,21; 28:2,14; 29:4,8,21,25
[m] Dt 17:16; Jr 44:12-14
[n] 42:16 Ezk 11:8
[o] 42:18 Jr 7:20
[p] Dt 28:37; 2Ch 29:8; 30:7; Jr 5:30; 18:16; 19:8; 25:9,18; 29:18; 44:12,22; 49:17; 50:13; Mc 6:16; Zph 2:15
[q] 42:19 Ezk 2:5
[r] 43:2 Jr 42:1

for their plans, so they went en masse to Jeremiah with a very pious-sounding request. Jeremiah had heard empty statements like theirs before; nevertheless, he promised to **pray** and tell them **every word** God revealed to him (42:4). In response, the people promised that whether the news was good or bad, they would **certainly obey the LORD** (42:5-6). **42:9-12** If the people would **stay in [their] land,** God promised to **rebuild** and **plant** them after the disaster of Jerusalem's destruction

and the captivity (42:9-10). Now that was quite a deal God was offering: recovery and prosperity in their own land and protection from their feared enemy! All the people had to do was stay home and enjoy God's blessings. **42:13-16 No, instead we'll go to . . . Egypt** (42:14) was the equivalent of saying, "Thanks for your advice, God. But we've got a better plan." **42:20-21** While they'd claimed that they wanted the truth from God, in reality they had no intention of obeying him. Don't presume

to ask for the King's direction in your life if you aren't prepared to follow in obedience. **43:2-4** In their arrogance, the people claimed Jeremiah was a liar (43:2). They even went so far as to accuse Jeremiah's secretary of **inciting** Jeremiah against them **to hand [them] over to the Chaldeans** (43:3). **So Johanan** and his fellow **commanders** (43:4) led the people on a trek down to Egypt—it included Jeremiah and Baruch, who must have been taken against their will (see 43:6).

a 43:5 Jr 40:11-12
b 43:6 Jr 39:10; 40:7
c 43:7-8 Jr 2:16; 44:1; 46:14
d 43:11 Jr 44:13; 46:13-26
e Jr 15:2
f 43:12 Ex 12:12; Is 19:1; Jr 46:25; Ezk 30:13
g Ps 104:2; Is 49:18
h 44:1 Ex 14:2; Nm 33:7; Jr 46:14; Ezk 29:10
i Jr 2:16; 43:7-9; 46:14
j Is 19:13; Jr 2:16; 46:14,19; Ezk 30:13,16; Hs 9:6
k Is 11:11; Ezk 29:14; 30:14

l 44:2 Jos 8:26; Is 5:9; 6:11; Jr 2:15; 4:29; 6:8; 33:10; 34:22; 44:22; 48:9; 51:37; Zph 3:6
m 44:3 Jr 7:19
n 2Kg 22:17; 2Ch 28:25; 34:25; Jr 1:16; 7:9; 19:4,13; 32:29
o 44:4 Jr 7:13,25; 11:7; 25:3; 26:5; 29:19; 32:33; 35:14,15
p 44:6 Jr 7:34
q 44:7 1Sm 15:3; 22:19
r Jr 11:23; 40:15; 44:15; Ezr 9:14
s 44:8 Jr 24:9; 42:18; 44:12; 49:13
t 44:11 Jr 21:10
u 1Sm 20:15; Ps 109:13; Is 10:7; Jr 9:21; 47:4; 51:62; Ob 14
v 44:12 Jr 42:15-18
w Est 1:20; Jr 6:13; 8:10; 31:34; 42:1; 42:8
x Jr 18:16
y Dt 28:37; 2Ch 29:8; 30:7; Jr 5:30; 18:16; 19:8; 25:9,18; 29:18; 42:18; 44:22; 49:17; 50:13; Mc 6:16; Zph 2:15

in the land of Judah. [5] Instead, Johanan son of Kareah and all the commanders of the armies led away the whole remnant of Judah,[a] those who had returned to stay in the land of Judah from all the nations where they had been banished. [6] They led away the men, women, children, king's daughters, and everyone whom Nebuzaradan, captain of the guards, had allowed to remain with Gedaliah son of Ahikam son of Shaphan.[b] They also led the prophet Jeremiah and Baruch son of Neriah away. [7] They went to the land of Egypt because they did not obey the LORD. They went as far as Tahpanhes.[c]

GOD'S SIGN TO THE PEOPLE IN EGYPT

[8] Then the word of the LORD came to Jeremiah at Tahpanhes: [9] "Pick up some large stones and set them in the mortar of the brick pavement that is at the opening of Pharaoh's palace at Tahpanhes. Do this in the sight of the Judean men [10] and tell them, 'This is what the LORD of Armies, the God of Israel, says: I will send for my servant Nebuchadnezzar king of Babylon, and I will place his throne on these stones that I have embedded, and he will pitch his pavilion over them. [11] He will come and strike down the land of Egypt[d] — those destined for death, to death; those destined for captivity, to captivity; and those destined for the sword,[e] to the sword. [12] I[A] will kindle a fire in the temples of Egypt's gods,[f] and he will burn them and take them captive. He will clean the land of Egypt as a shepherd picks lice off[B] his clothes,[g] and he will leave there unscathed. [13] He will smash the sacred pillars of the sun temple[C,D] in the land of Egypt and burn the temples of the Egyptian gods.'"

GOD'S JUDGMENT AGAINST HIS PEOPLE IN EGYPT

44 This is the word that came to Jeremiah for all the Jews living in the land of Egypt — at Migdol,[h] Tahpanhes,[i] Memphis,[j] and in the land of Pathros:[k] [2] "This is what the LORD of Armies, the God of Israel, says: You have seen all the disaster I brought against Jerusalem and all Judah's cities. Look, they are a ruin today without an inhabitant in them[l] [3] because of the evil they committed to anger me,[m] by going and burning incense to serve other gods that they, you, and your fathers did not know.[n] [4] So I sent you all my servants the prophets time and time again,[E,o] saying, 'Don't commit this detestable action that I hate.' [5] But they did not listen or pay attention; they did not turn from their evil or stop burning incense to other gods. [6] So my fierce wrath poured out and burned in Judah's cities and Jerusalem's streets[p] so that they became the desolate ruin they are today.

[7] "So now, this is what the LORD, the God of Armies, the God of Israel, says: Why are you doing such terrible harm to yourselves? You are cutting off man and woman, infant and nursing baby[q] from Judah, leaving yourselves without a remnant.[r] [8] You are angering me by the work of your hands. You are burning incense to other gods in the land of Egypt where you have gone to stay for a while. As a result, you will be cut off and become an example for cursing and insult among all the nations of earth.[s] [9] Have you forgotten the evils of your fathers, the evils of Judah's kings, the evils of their wives, your own evils, and the evils of your wives that were committed in the land of Judah and in the streets of Jerusalem? [10] They have not become humble to this day, and they have not feared or followed my instruction or my statutes that I set before you and your ancestors.

[11] "Therefore, this is what the LORD of Armies, the God of Israel, says: I am about to set my face against you to bring disaster,[t] to cut off all Judah.[u] [12] And I will take away the remnant of Judah,[v] those who have set their face to go to the land of Egypt to stay there. All of them will meet their end in the land of Egypt. They will fall by the sword; they will meet their end by famine. From the least to the greatest,[w] they will die by the sword and by famine. Then they will become an example for cursing, scorn,[x] execration, and disgrace.[y]

[A] 43:12 LXX, Syr, Vg read *He*　　[B] 43:12 Or *will wrap himself in the land of Egypt as a shepherd wraps himself in*　　[C] 43:13 Or *Beth-shemesh*
[D] 43:13 = of Heliopolis　　[E] 44:4 Lit *prophets, rising up early and sending*

43:7 Tahpanhes means "palace of the Negro." **43:8-13** Jeremiah's sign was simple. He **embedded** some stones in the **pavement** leading to **Pharaoh's palace** in northern Egypt (43:9-10). In this place where the people of Judah must have been feeling safe, Jeremiah then prophesied that they would see the Babylonian army invade Egypt to do there what they'd done in Judah (43:10-13). Where Jeremiah had placed the stones, Nebuchadnezzar would set up his headquarters (43:10)! A few hundred miles and a national border would be no problem for God to overcome when he stretched out his hand of judgment.

44:1-6 If you fail to learn from the mistakes of those who failed in the past, be prepared to follow in their footsteps. This seems to be God's message to the people of Judah who had disobediently run off to Egypt. Serving false gods and rejecting God is a sure path to ruin.

13 I will punish those living in the land of Egypt just as I punished Jerusalem by sword, famine, and plague. **14** Then the remnant of Judah — those going to live for a while there in the land of Egypt — will have no fugitive or survivor to return to the land of Judah where they are longing[A] to return to stay,[a] for they will not return except for a few fugitives."

THE PEOPLE'S STUBBORN RESPONSE

15 However, all the men who knew that their wives were burning incense to other gods, all the women standing by — a great assembly — and all the people who were living in the land of Egypt at Pathros answered Jeremiah, **16** "As for the word you spoke to us in the name of the LORD, we are not going to listen to you! **17** Instead, we will do everything we promised:[B] we will burn incense to the queen of heaven[c] and offer drink offerings to her just as we, our fathers, our kings, and our officials did in Judah's cities[b] and in Jerusalem's streets. Then we had enough food, we were well off, and we saw no disaster, **18** but from the time we ceased to burn incense to the queen of heaven and to offer her drink offerings, we have lacked everything, and through sword and famine we have met our end."[c]

19 And the women said,[D] "When we burned incense to the queen of heaven and poured out drink offerings to her, was it apart from our husbands' knowledge[d] that we made sacrificial cakes in her image and poured out drink offerings to her?"

20 But Jeremiah responded to all the people — the men, women, and all the people who were answering him: **21** "As for the incense you burned in Judah's cities[e] and in Jerusalem's streets — you, your fathers, your kings, your officials, and the people of the land — did the LORD not remember them? He brought this to mind. **22** The LORD can no longer bear your evil deeds and the detestable acts you have committed,[f] so your land has become a waste, a desolation, and an example for cursing, without inhabitant, as you see today. **23** Because you burned incense and sinned against

the LORD and didn't obey the LORD[g] and didn't follow his instruction, his statutes, and his testimonies, this disaster has come to you, as you see today."

24 Then Jeremiah said to all the people, including all the women, "Hear the word of the LORD, all you people of Judah who are in the land of Egypt.[h] **25** This is what the LORD of Armies, the God of Israel, says: 'As for you and your wives, you women have spoken with your mouths, and you men fulfilled it by your deeds, saying, "We will keep our vows that we have made to burn incense to the queen of heaven and to pour out drink offerings for her." Go ahead, confirm your vows! Keep your vows!'

26 "Therefore, hear the word of the LORD, all you Judeans who live in the land of Egypt: 'I have sworn by my great name,[i] says the LORD, that my name will never again be invoked by anyone of Judah in all the land of Egypt,[j] saying, "As the Lord GOD lives." **27** I am watching over them for disaster and not for good,[k] and everyone from Judah who is in the land of Egypt will meet his end by sword or famine until they are finished off. **28** Those who escape the sword will return from the land of Egypt to the land of Judah only few in number,[l] and the whole remnant of Judah, the ones going to the land of Egypt to stay there for a while, will know whose word stands, mine or theirs! **29** This will be a sign to you' — this is the LORD's declaration — 'that I will punish you in this place, so you may know that my words of disaster concerning you will certainly come to pass.[m] **30** This is what the LORD says: I am about to hand over Pharaoh Hophra,[n] Egypt's king, to his enemies, to those who intend to take his life, just as I handed over Judah's King Zedekiah[o] to Babylon's King Nebuchadnezzar, who was his enemy, the one who intended to take his life.'"

THE LORD'S MESSAGE TO BARUCH

45 This is the word that the prophet Jeremiah spoke to Baruch son of Neriah[p] when he wrote these words on a scroll at Jeremiah's dictation[E,q] in the

[a] 44:14 Jr 22:26-27
[b] 44:17 Jr 7:18
[c] 44:18 Jr 14:15; 16:4
[d] 44:19 Nm 30:6-7
[e] 44:21 Ezk 8:10-11
[f] 44:22 Is 1:14; 7:13; 43:24; Jr 15:6; Mal 2:17
[g] 44:23 Jr 40:3
[h] 44:24 Jr 43:7
[i] 44:26 Gn 22:16; 1Sm 3:14; Ps 89:3,35; Is 45:23; 54:9; Jr 22:5; 49:13
[j] Ezk 20:39
[k] 44:27 Jr 21:10; 31:28; 39:16; Am 9:4
[l] 44:28 Is 27:12-13
[m] 44:29 Pr 19:21
[n] 44:30 Ezk 29:3; 30:21
[o] Jr 39:5-7
[p] 45:1 Jr 32:12
[q] Jr 36:4,18

44:17-18 The depths of this crowd's depravity became clear when they claimed that their problems began when they **ceased to burn incense to the queen of heaven** (44:18), a pagan goddess. The unspoken assumption was that worshiping the Lord had gotten them nowhere. Serving him instead of their

idols, they foolishly decided, was the reason for their disaster.
44:25 That is, "Have it your way. Worship and plead with the queen of heaven. See where that gets you."
44:30 The leader to whom the Jews fled for protection wouldn't even be able to protect

himself. This was fulfilled in 570–569 BC when **Pharaoh Hophra** was deposed in an army coup and eventually assassinated.
45:1 The events of this chapter are out of sequence historically, since they occurred around 604 BC, years before Judah fell.

a 45:1 Jr 36:1
b 45:3 Ps 6:6
c 45:4 Jr 24:6
d 45:5 Jr 21:9; 38:2; 39:18
e 46:1 Jr 25:15-38
f 46:2 2Kg 23:29
g 2Ch 35:20
h Jr 45:1
i 46:3 Jr 49:14; Ob 1
j 46:4 Jb 41:13; Jr 51:3
k 46:5 Jr 6:25; 20:3-4,10; 49:29
l 46:6 Am 2:14

m 46:6 Dn 11:19
n 46:7 Jr 47:2
o 46:8 Am 8:8
p 46:9 Gn 10:6; Ezk 30:5
q Gn 10:13; 1Ch 1:11
r Is 66:19
s 46:10 Is 34:5-8; Ezk 39:17-20; Zph 1:7
t Zph 1:7
u 46:11 Gn 37:25; Jr 8:22; 51:8
v 46:12 Jr 13:26; Hs 4:7; Nah 3:5
w 46:13 Jr 43:8-13
x 46:14 Jr 2:16; 43:7-9; 44:1

fourth year of Jehoiakim son of Josiah, king of Judah:*a* ² "This is what the Lord, the God of Israel, says to you, Baruch: ³ 'You have said, "Woe is me, because the Lord has added misery to my pain! I am worn out with^ groaning and have found no rest." '*b*

⁴ "This is what you are to say to him: 'This is what the Lord says: "What I have built I am about to demolish, and what I have planted I am about to uproot*c* — the whole land! ⁵ But as for you, do you pursue great things for yourself? Stop pursuing! For I am about to bring disaster on everyone" — this is the Lord's declaration — "but I will grant you your life like the spoils of war*d* wherever you go." ' "

PROPHECIES AGAINST THE NATIONS

46 This is the word of the Lord that came to the prophet Jeremiah about the nations:*e*

PROPHECIES AGAINST EGYPT

² About Egypt and the army of Pharaoh Neco, Egypt's king,*f* which was defeated at Carchemish*g* on the Euphrates River by King Nebuchadnezzar of Babylon in the fourth year of Judah's King Jehoiakim son of Josiah:*h*

³   Deploy small shields*i* and large;
     approach for battle!
⁴   Harness the horses;
     mount the steeds;*B*
     take your positions with helmets on!
     Polish the lances;
     put on armor!*j*
⁵   Why have I seen this?
     They are terrified,
     they are retreating,
     their warriors are crushed,
     they flee headlong,
     they never look back,
     terror is on every side!*k*
     This is the Lord's declaration.
⁶   The swift cannot flee,
     and the warrior cannot escape!*l*

     In the north by the bank
     of the Euphrates River,
     they stumble and fall.*m*

⁷   Who is this, rising like the Nile,*n*
     with waters that churn like rivers?
⁸   Egypt rises like the Nile,*o*
     and its waters churn like rivers.
     He boasts, "I will go up, I will cover
     the earth;
     I will destroy cities
     with their residents."
⁹   Rise up, you cavalry!
     Race furiously, you chariots!
     Let the warriors march out —
     Cush and Put,*p*
     who are able to handle shields,
     and the men of Lud,*q*
     who are able to handle and string
     the bow.*r*
¹⁰   That day belongs to the Lord,
     the God of Armies,
     a day of vengeance to avenge himself
     against his adversaries.
     The sword will devour
     and be satisfied;
     it will drink its fill of their blood,
     because it will be a sacrifice*s*
     to the Lord, the God of Armies,
     in the northern land
     by the Euphrates River.*t*
¹¹   Go up to Gilead and get balm,*u*
     Virgin Daughter Egypt!
     You have multiplied remedies in vain;
     there is no healing for you.
¹²   The nations have heard
     of your dishonor,*v*
     and your cries fill the earth,
     because warrior stumbles
     against warrior
     and together both of them have fallen.

¹³ This is the word the Lord spoke to the prophet Jeremiah about the coming of King Nebuchadnezzar of Babylon to defeat the land of Egypt:*w*

¹⁴   Announce it in Egypt,
     and proclaim it in Migdol!*x*

---

^ 45:3 Lit *I labored in my*   *B* 46:4 Or *mount up, riders*

45:4-5 Apparently, Baruch thought serving alongside a great prophet like Jeremiah would bring him **great things**, like prominence and respect (45:5). But God made it clear to Baruch that his dream of the bright lights would go unfulfilled. Instead, God gave him the best gift he could ask for in the midst of the destruction around him: his **life** (45:5). **46:2-9** The execution of God's wrath against **Egypt** was fulfilled when **the army of Pharaoh**

Neco . . . was defeated . . . by King Nebuchadnezzar of Babylon (46:2). This took place in 605 BC. The Pharaoh had grand plans for Egypt to conquer the world and spread its influence like the Nile River overflowing its banks (46:7-8), but God had other plans. Here he sarcastically urges the Egyptian army to call out its forces and prepare for battle against Nebuchadnezzar (46:3-4, 9). Though Egypt's army did all this, the battle turned into such a rout

that Egypt's panic-stricken warriors stumbled over each other trying to get away (46:5-6). **46:13-19** There is a significant gap in time between the prophecy of Egypt's defeat at Carchemish in 605 BC (46:2) and the events prophesied beginning in 46:13. The latter was a prophecy of Nebuchadnezzar's invasion of Egypt, which occurred in about 568 BC. In between these events, Nebuchadnezzar's father died, so he returned to Babylon to secure

Proclaim it in Memphis
and in Tahpanhes!
Say, "Take positions!
Prepare yourself,
for the sword devours
all around you."[a]

15 Why have your strong ones
been swept away?
Each has not stood,
for the LORD has thrust him down.
16 He continues to stumble.[b]
Indeed, each falls over the other.
They say, "Get up! Let's return
to our people
and to our native land,
away from the oppressor's sword."[c]
17 There they will cry out,
"Pharaoh king of Egypt
was all noise;
he let the opportune moment pass."

18 As I live —
this is the King's declaration;
the LORD of Armies is
his name[d] —
the king of Babylon[A] will come
like Tabor among the mountains
and like Carmel by the sea.
19 Get your bags ready for exile,
inhabitant of Daughter Egypt![e]
For Memphis will become
a desolation,
uninhabited ruins.

20 Egypt is a beautiful young cow,[f]
but a horsefly from the north
is coming against her.[B,g]
21 Even her mercenaries among her
are like stall-fed calves.
They too will turn back;
together they will flee;
they will not take their stand,
for the day of their calamity
is coming on them,
the time of their punishment.[h]
22 Egypt will hiss
like a slithering snake,[c]
for the enemy will come
with an army;
with axes they will come against her
like those who cut trees.[i]

23 They will cut down her forest —
this is the LORD's declaration —
though it is dense,
for they are more numerous
than locusts;
they cannot be counted.[j]
24 Daughter Egypt will be put to shame,
handed over to a northern people.[k]

25 The LORD of Armies, the God of Israel, says, "I am about to punish Amon, god of Thebes,[l] along with Pharaoh, Egypt, her gods, and her kings — Pharaoh and those trusting in him. 26 I will hand them over to those who intend to take their lives[m] — to King Nebuchadnezzar of Babylon and his officers. But after this,[n] Egypt[D] will be inhabited again as in ancient times."
This is the LORD's declaration.

REASSURANCE FOR ISRAEL

27 But you, my servant Jacob,
do not be afraid,[o]
and do not be discouraged, Israel,
for without fail I will save you
from far away,
and your descendants from the land
of their captivity!
Jacob will return and have calm
and quiet
with no one to frighten him.
28 And you, my servant Jacob,
do not be afraid —
this is the LORD's declaration —
for I will be with you.[p]
I will bring destruction
on all the nations
where I have banished you,
but I will not bring destruction
on you.
I will discipline you with justice,
and I will by no means
leave you unpunished.[q]

PROPHECIES AGAINST THE PHILISTINES

47 This is the word of the LORD that came to the prophet Jeremiah about the Philistines[r] before Pharaoh defeated Gaza.[s] 2 This is what the LORD says:

a 46:14 Jr 46:10
b 46:16 Lv 26:36-37
c Jr 50:16
d 46:18 Jr 48:15; 51:57
e 46:19 Jr 48:18
f 46:20 Hs 10:11
g Jr 1:13-14
h 46:21 Jr 50:27,31
i 46:22 Ps 74:5
j 46:23 Jdg 6:5; 7:12
k 46:24 Jr 1:15
l 46:25 Ezk 30:14-16
m 46:26 Jr 44:30; Ezk 32:11
n Ezk 29:8-14
o 46:27 Is 41:8; 44:2; 45:4
p 46:28 Jr 1:8,19; 30:11; 42:11
q 46:27-28 Jr 30:10-11
r 47:1 Jr 25:20
s Am 1:6-7; Zph 2:4

A 46:18 Lit He   B 46:20 Some Hb mss, LXX, Syr; other Hb mss read is coming, coming   C 46:22 Lit Her sound is like a snake as it goes   D 46:26 Lit it

his throne. When he resumed his attack on Egypt, Pharaoh Hophra was king. Now instead of fighting the Babylonians by the Euphrates River, the Egyptians would see them coming against their own land, ravaging as they went. **46:20** Egypt is called **a beautiful young cow**, possibly in reference to the Egyptian bull-god Apis.

46:26 The prophecy against Egypt ends with an intriguing statement: **But after this, Egypt will be inhabited again as in ancient times**. In Isaiah 19, we also learn that Egypt will one day be redeemed and worship the true God (Isa 19:16-22).
47:1-5 The Philistines were longtime enemies of Israel. This prophecy pictures Bab-

ylon as **water . . . rising from the north** that would **overflow the land** (47:2) and **destroy all the Philistines** (47:4). This happened in 604 BC when Nebuchadnezzar's armies destroyed **Ashkelon**, one of Philistia's principal cities (47:5).

[a] 47:2 Jr 1:13; 4:6,20; 6:1;
50:3,9,41; 51:48
[b] Is 8:7-8
[c] 47:3 Jdg 5:22; Jr 8:16;
50:11
[d] Nah 3:2-3
[e] 47:4 Jr 25:22; Jl 3:4; Am
1:8-10
[f] Gn 10:14; Am 9:7
[g] 47:5 Jr 48:37
[h] Jdg 1:18; Jr 25:20
[i] 47:6 Ezk 21:3-5
[j] 47:7 Ezk 14:17
[k] Mc 6:9
[l] 48:1 Gn 19:37; Nm 22:1;
24:17; 25:1; Dt 23:3; 34:5-
6; Jdg 3:30; Ru 1:2; 2Sm
8:2; 1Kg 11:7; 2Kg 1:1; Is
15:1; Ezk 25:8-11; Am 2:1-2;
Zph 2:8-9
[m] Nm 32:3; Jr 48:22
[n] Nm 32:37; Jr 48:23;
Ezk 25:9
[o] 48:2 Jr 48:34,45; 49:3

[p] 48:2 Jr 29:18; Am 1:11
[q] 48:3 Is 15:5; Jr 48:34
[r] Jr 51:54
[s] 48:5 Is 15:5
[t] 48:6 Jr 51:6,45
[u] Is 41:19; Jr 17:6
[v] 48:7 Nm 1:29; Jdg 11:24;
1Kg 11:7,33; 2Kg 23:13; Jr
48:13,45-47
[w] Jr 49:3
[x] 48:8 Jr 6:26; 48:15,18,32
[y] Jos 13:9,17,21
[z] 48:9 Jdg 9:45; Jr 17:6; Ezk
47:11; Zph 2:9
[aa] Jos 8:26; Is 5:9; 6:11;
Jr 2:15; 4:29; 6:8; 33:10;
34:22; 44:2,22; 51:37;
Zph 3:6
[ab] 48:10 1Kg 20:42
[ac] 48:11 Ps 75:8; Zph 1:12
[ad] 48:12 Jr 7:32; 16:14; 19:6;
23:7; 49:2; 51:47,52

Look, water is rising from the north[a]
and becoming an overflowing wadi.
It will overflow the land
and everything in it,[b]
the cities and their inhabitants.
The people will cry out,
and every inhabitant of the land
will wail.

3 At the sound of the stomping hooves
of his stallions,[c]
the rumbling of his chariots,
and the clatter of their wheels,[d]
fathers will not turn back
for their sons.
They will be utterly helpless[A]

4 on account of the day that is coming
to destroy all the Philistines,
to cut off from Tyre and Sidon
every remaining ally.[e]
Indeed, the LORD is about to destroy
the Philistines,
the remnant of the coastland
of Caphtor.[B,f]

5 Baldness[g] is coming to Gaza;
Ashkelon will become silent.[h]
Remnant of their valley,
how long will you gash yourself?

6 Oh, sword of the LORD![i]
How long will you be restless?
Go back to your sheath;
be still; be silent!

7 How can it[c] rest
when the LORD has given it
a command?[j]
He has assigned it[k]
against Ashkelon and the shore
of the sea.

PROPHECIES AGAINST MOAB

48 About Moab,[l] this is what the LORD
of Armies, the God of Israel, says:
Woe to Nebo,[m] because it is
about to be destroyed;
Kiriathaim will be put to shame;[n]
it will be taken captive.
The fortress will be put to shame
and dismayed!

2 There is no longer praise for Moab;
they plan harm against her
in Heshbon:[o]

Come, let's cut her off
from nationhood.
Also, Madmen, you will be silenced;
the sword will follow[p] you.

3 A voice cries out from Horonaim,[q]
"devastation and a crushing blow!"[r]

4 Moab will be shattered;
her little ones will cry out.

5 For on the Ascent to Luhith
they will be weeping continually,[D]
and on the descent to Horonaim
will be heard cries of distress
over the destruction:[s]

6 Flee! Save your lives![t]
Be like a juniper bush[E,u]
in the wilderness.

7 Because you trust in your works
and treasures,
you will be captured also.
Chemosh[v] will go into exile
with his priests and officials.[w]

8 The destroyer[x] will move
against every town;
not one town will escape.
The valley will perish,
and the plain will be annihilated,[y]
as the LORD has said.

9 Make Moab a salt marsh,[F,z]
for she will run away;[G]
her towns will become a desolation,
without inhabitant.[aa]

10 The one who does
the LORD's business deceitfully[H]
is cursed,[ab]
and the one who withholds
his sword from bloodshed is cursed.

11 Moab has been left quiet
since his youth,
settled like wine on its dregs.[ac]
He hasn't been poured
from one container to another
or gone into exile.
So his taste has remained the same,
and his aroma hasn't changed.

12 Therefore look, the days
are coming[ad] —
this is the LORD's declaration —
when I will send pourers to him,
who will pour him out.

[A] 47:3 Lit *Because of weakened hands*   [B] 47:4 Probably Crete   [C] 47:7 LXX, Vg; MT reads *you*   [D] 48:5 Lit *Luhith, weeping goes up with weeping*
[E] 48:6 Or *like Aroer*; Is 17:2; Jr 48:19   [F] 48:9 LXX reads *a sign*; Vg reads *a flower*; Syr, Tg read *a crown*   [G] 48:9 Hb obscure   [H] 48:10 Or *negligently*

48:1 Moab was located east of the Dead Sea between Edom and Ammon. The Moabites should have been allies of Israel, since they were the descendants of Lot and, therefore, of Abraham. But Israel's history showed that the Moabites harassed and attacked the Israelites at various times—especially when they were weak.

48:7 The Moabites trusted in their god **Chemosh**. In his unfaithfulness, Solomon had worshiped this false deity who was abhorrent to the Lord (see 1 Kgs 11:7). This idol was doomed to topple, along with **his priests and officials**.

48:10 The extent of God's anger against the Moabites was such that he even warns her destroyers to be diligent in their work: **The one . . . who withholds his sword from bloodshed is cursed.**

They will empty his containers
and smash his jars.
13 Moab will be put to shame
because of Chemosh,
just as the house of Israel was
put to shame
because of Bethel[a]
that they trusted in.

14 How can you say, "We are warriors —
valiant men for battle"?
15 The destroyer of Moab and its towns
has come up,[A]
and the best of its young men
have gone down to slaughter.
This is the King's declaration;
the LORD of Armies is his name.[b]
16 Moab's calamity is near at hand;
his disaster is rushing swiftly.
17 Mourn for him,
all you surrounding nations,
everyone who knows his name.
Say, "How the mighty scepter[c]
is shattered,
the glorious staff! "

18 Come down from glory;
sit on parched ground,
resident of the daughter of Dibon,[d]
for the destroyer of Moab has come
against you;
he has destroyed your fortresses.
19 Stand by the highway and watch,
resident of Aroer![e]
Ask him who is fleeing or her
who is escaping,[f]
"What happened? "
20 Moab is put to shame,
indeed dismayed.
Wail and cry out![g]
Declare by the Arnon
that Moab is destroyed.

21 "Judgment has come to the land of the plateau[h] — to Holon, Jahzah, Mephaath, 22 Dibon, Nebo, Beth-diblathaim, 23 Kiriathaim, Beth-gamul, Beth-meon,[i] 24 Kerioth,[j] Bozrah, and all the towns of the land of Moab, those far and near. 25 Moab's horn is chopped off;[k] his arm is shattered."[l]
This is the LORD's declaration.

26 "Make him drunk, because he has exalted himself against the LORD.[m] Moab will wallow in his own vomit, and he will also become a laughingstock. 27 Wasn't Israel a laughingstock to you?[n] Was he ever found among thieves? For whenever you speak of him you shake your head."[p]
28 Abandon the towns!
Live in the cliffs,
residents of Moab!
Be like a dove
that nests inside the mouth
of a cave.[q]
29 We have heard of Moab's pride,
great pride, indeed —
his insolence, arrogance, pride,
and haughty heart.
30 I know his outburst.
This is the LORD's declaration.
It is empty.
His boast is empty.
31 Therefore, I will wail over Moab.
I will cry out for Moab, all of it;
he will moan for the men
of Kir-heres.
32 I will weep for you, vine of Sibmah,
with more than the weeping
for Jazer.
Your tendrils have extended
to the sea;
they have reached to the sea
and to Jazer.[B]
The destroyer has fallen
on your summer fruit
and grape harvest.
33 Gladness and celebration are taken
from the fertile field
and from the land of Moab.
I have stopped the flow of wine
from the winepresses;
no one will tread with shouts of joy.
The shouting is not a shout of joy.[r]

34 "There is a cry from Heshbon to Elealeh; they make their voices heard as far as Jahaz[s] — from Zoar to Horonaim and Eglath-shelishiyah — because even the Waters of Nimrim have become desolate. 35 In Moab, I will stop" — this is the LORD's declaration — "the one who offers sacrifices

[a] 48:13 1Kg 12:28-33; 13:1-5; 2Kg 10:29; 23:15; Hs 4:15; Am 3:14; 4:4; 5:5-6
[b] 48:15 Jr 46:18; 51:57
[c] 48:17 Ps 110:2; Ezk 19:11-12,14
[d] 48:18 Jos 13:8-9; Jr 46:19
[e] 48:19 Dt 2:36
[f] 1Sm 4:13,16
[g] 48:20 Is 14:31; Jr 25:34; 47:2; Ezk 21:12
[h] 48:21 Jos 13:17-19
[i] 48:23 Jos 13:17
[j] 48:24 Jr 48:41; Am 2:2
[k] 48:25 Ps 75:10; Lm 2:3; Am 3:14
[l] Jb 38:15; Ps 10:15; 37:17; Ezk 30:21-24

[m] 48:26 Jr 48:42
[n] 48:26-27 Gn 38:23; Jb 12:4; Ps 44:14; Jr 20:7; 48:39; Lm 2:15-17; 3:14
[o] 48:27 Jr 2:26
[p] 2Kg 19:21; Jb 2:11; 16:4; 42:11; Ps 22:7; 64:8; 69:20; 109:25; Is 37:22; 51:19; Jr 15:5; 18:16; Lm 2:15; Nah 3:7
[q] 48:28 Is 2:19-21
[r] 48:31-33 Is 16:7-10
[s] 48:34 Is 15:4-6

[A] 48:15 Or Moab is destroyed; he has come up against its cities   [B] 48:32 Some Hb mss read reached as far as Jazer

---

48:13 The Moabites had failed to learn an important lesson from their cousins in Israel. Moab would be **put to shame because of** their false god **Chemosh, just as the house of Israel was put to shame** for their idolatry at **Bethel** (see 1 Kgs 12:25-33).

48:25 This prophecy picturing the completeness of Moab's destruction uses two familiar Old Testament metaphors for power: **Moab's horn is chopped off; his arm is shattered.**
48:27-28 Israel's downfall was a laughing matter to Moab (48:27); therefore, Moab's people

are warned to flee from their cities and hide in caves to escape God's wrath (48:28).
48:31-32 Don't miss that God says he will **wail**, **cry out**, and **weep** over Moab's fall. It's a reminder that God takes no pleasure in judgment. Nevertheless, his holy character demands it.

a 48:35 Jr 11:12-13; 18:15
b 48:36 Is 15:5
c 48:37-38 Is 15:2-3; Jr 47:5
d 48:37 Lv 19:28; 21:5; Jr 5:7; 41:5; 47:5
e Jr 4:8; 6:26; 49:3
f 48:38 Jr 22:28
g 48:29-39 Is 16:6-11; Zph 2:9-10
h 48:40 Dt 28:49; Jr 49:22
i 48:41 Is 13:8; Jr 49:22
j 48:42 Jr 48:26
k 48:43 Jr 30:5; 49:5
l 48:44 Jr 23:12
m 48:43-44 Is 24:17-18

n 48:45-46 Nm 21:28-29
o 48:47 Jr 49:6,39
p 49:1 Gn 19:38; Dt 2:19; 23:3; Jdg 10:6-7; 1Sm 11:11; 12:12; 1Kg 11:5-7,33; 2Kg 24:2; Neh 2:10; Is 11:14; Jr 40:14; Ezk 21:28-32; 25:2-10; Am 1:13-15; Zph 2:8-9
q 1Kg 11:5,7,33; Zph 1:5
r 49:2 Jr 7:32; 16:14; 19:6; 23:7; 48:12; 51:47,52
s Jr 4:19
t Dt 3:11; 2Sm 11:1; 12:26-29; Ezk 25:5; Am 1:14
u 49:3 Nm 21:21-25,34; Dt 2:24,30; Jos 12:2; Jdg 11:26; Jr 48:2
v Jr 48:37
w Jr 48:7
x 49:5 Jr 48:43-44

on the high place and burns incense to his gods.*a* 36 Therefore, my heart moans like flutes for Moab,*b* and my heart moans like flutes for the people of Kir-heres. And therefore, the wealth he has gained has perished. 37 Indeed, every head is bald and every beard is chopped short.*c* On every hand is a gash*d* and sackcloth*e* around the waist. 38 On all the rooftops of Moab and in her public squares, everyone is mourning because I have shattered Moab like a jar no one wants."*f* This is the LORD's declaration. 39 "How broken it is! They wail! How Moab has turned his back! He is ashamed. Moab will become a laughingstock and a shock to all those around him."*g*

40 For this is what the LORD says:
Look! He will swoop down
    like an eagle
and spread his wings against Moab.*h*
41 The towns have[A] been captured,
and the strongholds seized.
In that day the heart
    of Moab's warriors
will be like the heart of a woman
    with contractions.*i*
42 Moab will be destroyed
    as a people
because he has exalted himself
    against the LORD.*j*
43 Panic,*k* pit, and trap
await you, resident of Moab.
    This is the LORD's declaration.
44 He who flees from the panic will fall
    in the pit,
and he who climbs from the pit
will be captured in the trap,
for I will bring against Moab
the year of their punishment.*l*
    This is the LORD's declaration.*m*

45 Those who flee will stand exhausted
    in Heshbon's shadow
because fire has come out
    from Heshbon
and a flame from within Sihon.
It will devour Moab's forehead
and the skull of the noisemakers.
46 Woe to you, Moab!
The people of Chemosh
    have perished

because your sons have been
    taken captive
and your daughters have gone
    into captivity.*n*
47 Yet, I will restore the fortunes[B]
of Moab in the last days.*o*
This is the LORD's declaration.
The judgment on Moab ends here.

PROPHECIES AGAINST AMMON

49 About the Ammonites,*p* this is what the LORD says:
Does Israel have no sons?
Is he without an heir?
Why then has Milcom[C,D]
    dispossessed Gad*q*
and his people settled in their cities?
2 Therefore look, the days
    are coming*r* —
this is the LORD's declaration —
when I will make the shout
    of battle*s* heard
against Rabbah*t* of the Ammonites.
It will become a desolate mound,
and its surrounding villages will be
    set on fire.
Israel will dispossess
    their dispossessors,
says the LORD.
3 Wail, Heshbon,*u* for Ai is devastated;
cry out, daughters of Rabbah!
Clothe yourselves with sackcloth,*v*
    and lament;
run back and forth
    within your walls,[E]
because Milcom will go into exile
together with his priests
    and officials.*w*
4 Why do you boast
    about your valleys,
your flowing valley,[F]
you faithless daughter —
you who trust in your treasures
and say, "Who can attack me?"
5 Look, I am about to bring terror
    on you*x* —
this is the declaration
of the Lord GOD of Armies —
from all those around you.
You will be banished,
    each person headlong,

[A] 48:41 Or *Kerioth has*   [B] 48:47 Or *will end the captivity*   [C] 49:1 LXX, Syr, Vg; MT reads *Malkam*   [D] 49:1 = Molech   [E] 49:3 Or *sheep pens*
[F] 49:4 Or *about your strength, your ebbing strength*

48:42-44 When you make yourself God's enemy, there is no escape.
48:47 God's declaration, **I will restore the fortunes of Moab in the last days**, is most likely a reference to the millennial kingdom of Christ.

49:1-6 Ammon was Moab's first cousin (see Gen 19:36-38). The reasons for Ammon's judgment largely paralleled those of Moab: mistreatment of Israel, idolatry, and pride (Jer 49:1, 4). The Ammonite god **Milcom** (49:1), also known as Molech, was detestable to the Lord.

His worship included child sacrifice, a horrific practice that Israel sometimes engaged in (see 7:31; Lev 20:1-5; 2 Kgs 23:10). Ammon had **dispossessed** the tribe of **Gad** from their land, but God pronounced that Israel would **dispossess their dispossessors** (Jer 49:2). Yet,

with no one to gather up
    the fugitives.
6 But after that, I will restore
    the fortunes[A] of the Ammonites.[a]
    This is the LORD's declaration.

PROPHECIES AGAINST EDOM

7 About Edom,[b] this is what the LORD of Armies says:

Is there no longer wisdom
    in Teman?[c]
Has counsel perished
    from the prudent?
Has their wisdom rotted away?[d]
8 Run! Turn back! Lie low,
    residents of Dedan,[e]
for I will bring Esau's calamity
    on him[f]
at the time I punish him.[g]
9 If grape harvesters came to you,
    wouldn't they leave
      some gleanings?[h]
Were thieves to come in the night,
they would destroy only
    what they wanted.[i]
10 But I will strip Esau bare;
I will uncover his secret places.[j]
He will try to hide,[k]
    but he will be unable.
His descendants will be destroyed
along with his relatives
    and neighbors.
He will exist no longer.[l]
11 Abandon your fatherless;
    I will preserve them;
let your widows trust in me.[m]

12 For this is what the LORD says: "If those who do not deserve to drink the cup must drink it, can you possibly remain unpunished? You will not remain unpunished, for you must drink it too. 13 For by myself I have sworn"[n] — this is the LORD's declaration — "Bozrah[B] will become a desolation, a disgrace, a ruin, and an example for cursing, and all its surrounding cities will become ruins forever."[o]
14 I have heard an envoy
    from the LORD;
a messenger has been sent
    among the nations:

Assemble yourselves to come
    against her.
Rise up for war!

15 I will certainly make you
    insignificant among the nations,
    despised among humanity.
16 As to the terror you cause,[c]
    your arrogant heart
      has deceived you.
You who live in the clefts of the rock,[D]
you who occupy
    the mountain summit,
though you elevate your nest
    like the eagles,
even from there I will bring you down.
    This is the LORD's declaration.[p]

17 "Edom will become a desolation. Everyone who passes by her will be appalled and scoff because of all her wounds.[q] 18 As when Sodom and Gomorrah were overthrown along with their neighbors,"[r] says the LORD, "no one will live there; no human being will stay in it even temporarily.[s]
19 "Look, it will be like a lion coming from the thickets[E] of the Jordan to the watered grazing land.[t] I will chase Edom away from her land in a flash. I will appoint whoever is chosen for her. For who is like me?[u] Who will issue me a summons?[v] Who is the shepherd who can stand against me?"[w]
20 Therefore, hear the plans that the LORD has drawn up against Edom and the strategies he has devised against the people of Teman:[x] The flock's little lambs will certainly be dragged away,[y] and their grazing land will be made desolate because of them.[z] 21 At the sound of their fall the earth will quake;[aa] the sound of her cry will be heard at the Red Sea.[ab] 22 Look! It will be like an eagle soaring upward, then swooping down and spreading its wings over Bozrah. In that day the hearts of Edom's warriors will be like the heart of a woman with contractions.[ac]

PROPHECIES AGAINST DAMASCUS

23 About Damascus:[ad]
Hamath and Arpad are
    put to shame,[ae]

---

[a] 49:6 Jr 48:47; 49:39
[b] 49:7 Gn 25:30; 32:3; 36:1; Nm 20:18-21; 24:18; Jdg 11:17-18; 2Sm 8:14; 2Kg 8:20-22; Ps 60:8; Is 34:5-8
[c] Gn 36:15; Ezk 25:13; Am 1:12
[d] Ob 8-9
[e] Gn 25:1-3; Ezk 25:13
[f] Gn 25:25,30; 36:1; Ob 8,18
[g] Jr 6:15; 8:12; Ob 8-13
[h] 49:9 Dt 24:21
[i] Ob 5
[j] 49:10 Jr 23:24; Ob 6
[k] Ob 3
[l] Mal 1:3-4
[m] 49:11 Dt 10:18; Ps 68:5; Pr 15:25; Jms 1:27
[n] 49:13 Gn 22:16; 1Sm 3:14; Ps 89:3,35; Is 45:23; 54:9; Jr 22:5; 44:26
[o] 49:12-13 Jr 25:28-29; Am 1:12
[p] 49:14-16 Ob 1-4
[q] 49:17 Dt 28:37; 2Ch 29:8; 30:7; Jr 5:30; 18:16; 19:8; 25:9,18; 29:18; 42:18; 44:12,22; 50:13; Mc 6:16; Zph 2:15
[r] 49:18 Gn 19:24-25
[s] Jr 49:33; 50:40; Zph 2:9
[t] 49:19 Jr 50:44
[u] Mc 7:18
[v] Jb 9:19; Jr 12:5; 50:44; Zch 11:3
[w] 2Ch 20:6; Jb 41:10
[x] 49:20 Is 14:26; 19:12,17; 23:8; Jr 18:11; 49:30; 50:45; 51:12; Mc 2:3
[y] Jr 15:3; 22:19
[z] Jr 9:10; 23:10; 25:30-38
[aa] 49:21 Is 29:6; 64:1; Ezk 26:15; 31:16; 38:19; Mt 28:2; Rv 8:5
[ab] 49:18-21 Jr 50:40,44-46
[ac] 49:22 Jr 48:40-41
[ad] 49:23 Is 17:1; Am 1:3
[ae] 2Kg 18:34

[A] 49:6 Or will end the captivity, also in v. 39   [B] 49:13 = Edom's capital   [C] 49:16 Lit Your horror   [D] 49:16 = Petra   [E] 49:19 Lit pride

---

as in the case of other nations under his wrath, God promises to one day **restore the fortunes of the Ammonites** (49:6; see 46:26; 48:47).
49:7-10 The Edomites were the descendants of Esau, Jacob's brother. The **wisdom in Teman** was well known (Jer 49:7); "Eliphaz the Temanite" was one of the elders who

counseled Job (Job 2:11). But their wisdom failed the Edomites as they fell under God's condemnation.
Jeremiah describes the completeness of Edom's destruction. **Grape harvesters** would typically leave behind **some gleanings**, and even **thieves** would only take **what**

they wanted (Jer 49:9). But Esau would not be so fortunate. **He [would] exist no longer** (49:10).
49:23 Damascus was the capital of Aram (modern Syria), another kingdom in Jeremiah's day that came under God's judgment for warring against his people.

a 49:24 Is 13:8; 42:14; Jr
4:31; 6:24; 22:23; 30:6;
50:43; Mc 4:9-10
b 49:25 Jr 33:9
c 49:26 Jr 50:30
d 49:27 Am 1:4
e 49:28 Gn 25:13; Ps 120:5;
Is 21:16-17; 60:7; Jr 2:10;
Ezk 27:21
f 2Kg 24:11; 25:22; 2Ch
36:6-13
g 49:29 Ps 31:13; Jr 6:25;
20:3-4,10
h 49:31 Jdg 18:7-10; Ps
73:12; Is 47:8; Ezk 38:10-11;
Zph 2:15; Zch 7:7
i 49:32 Is 10:6; Ezk 25:7;
Nah 2:9

j 49:33 Jr 9:11; 10:22; 51:37
k Jr 49:18; 50:40
l 49:34 Jr 27:12; 28:1; 29:3
m 49:35 Is 22:6
n 49:37 Jr 9:16
o 49:39 Jr 48:47; 49:6
p 50:1 Is 13:1
q 50:2 Ps 60:4; Is 5:26; 18:3

for they have heard a bad report
    and are agitated,
like^A the anxious sea that cannot
    be calmed.

24 Damascus has become weak;
    she has turned to run;
panic has gripped her.
Distress and labor pains
    have seized her
like a woman in labor.^a

25 How can the city of praise
    not be abandoned,^b
the town that brings me joy?

26 Therefore, her young men will fall
    in her public squares;
all the warriors will perish
    in that day.
This is the declaration of the LORD
    of Armies.^c

27 I will set fire to the wall of Damascus;
it will consume Ben-hadad's citadels.^d

PROPHECIES AGAINST KEDAR
AND HAZOR

28 About Kedar^e and the kingdoms of Hazor, which King Nebuchadnezzar^f of Babylon defeated, this is what the LORD says:
Rise up, attack Kedar,
and destroy the people of the east!

29 They will take their tents
    and their flocks
along with their tent curtains
    and all their equipment.
They will take their camels
    for themselves.
They will call out to them,
"Terror is on every side!"^g

30 Run! Escape quickly! Lie low,
    residents of Hazor —
    this is the LORD's declaration —
for King Nebuchadnezzar of Babylon
    has drawn up a plan against you;
he has devised a strategy against you.

31 Rise up, attack a nation at ease,
    one living in security.
    This is the LORD's declaration.
They have no doors, not even
    a gate bar;
they live alone.^h

32 Their camels will become plunder,
and their massive herds of cattle
    will become spoil.^i

I will scatter them to the wind
    in every direction,
those who clip the hair on
    their temples;
I will bring calamity on them
    across all their borders.
    This is the LORD's declaration.

33 Hazor will become a jackals' den,^j
    a desolation forever.
No one will live there;
no human being will stay in it even
    temporarily.^k

PROPHECIES AGAINST ELAM

34 This is the word of the LORD that came to
the prophet Jeremiah about Elam^B at the
beginning of the reign of King Zedekiah
of Judah.^l 35 This is what the LORD of Armies says:
I am about to shatter Elam's bow,^m
    the source^c of their might.

36 I will bring the four winds
    against Elam
from the four corners of the heavens,
    and I will scatter them
    to all these winds.
There will not be a nation
to which Elam's banished ones
    will not go.

37 I will devastate Elam
    before their enemies,
before those who intend to take
    their lives.
I will bring disaster on them,
    my burning anger.
    This is the LORD's declaration.
I will send the sword after them^n
    until I finish them off.

38 I will set my throne in Elam,
    and I will destroy the king
    and officials from there.
    This is the LORD's declaration.

39 Yet, in the last days,
I will restore the fortunes of Elam.^o
    This is the LORD's declaration.

PROPHECIES AGAINST BABYLON

50 This is the word the LORD spoke
about Babylon,^p the land of the
Chaldeans, through the prophet Jeremiah:

2 Announce to the nations;
    proclaim and raise up a signal flag;^q

^A 49:23 Lit *in*   ^B 49:34 = modern Iran   ^C 49:35 Lit *first*

49:28-33 Kedar and **Hazor** were nomadic
tribes of Arabia, which also experienced
the fury of **Nebuchadnezzar** (49:28). That
they didn't live in a walled city (49:31) made
them easier prey. The devastation would be
so great in their territory that **no one** would
live there (49:33).
49:34-37 Elam was a kingdom east of Babylon in modern-day Iran (49:34). Since God's
judgments against the nations were often
described in terms appropriate to each country and Elam's soldiers were well known as
archers, God would **shatter Elam's bow** in
which they trusted (49:35).

proclaim, and hide nothing.
Say, "Babylon is captured;
Bel[a] is put to shame;
Marduk is terrified."
Her idols are put to shame;
her false gods, devastated.

3 For a nation from the north
will attack her;[b]
it will make her land desolate.
No one will be living in it —
both people and animals
will escape.[A,C]

4 In those days and at that time —
this is the LORD's declaration —
the Israelites and Judeans
will come together,[d]
weeping as they come,
and will seek the LORD their God.[e]

5 They will ask about Zion,
turning their faces to this road.
They will come and join themselves[B]
to the LORD
in a permanent covenant[f] that will
never be forgotten.

6 My people were lost sheep;[g]
their shepherds led them astray,[h]
guiding them the wrong way
in the mountains.[i]
They wandered from mountain
to hill;
they forgot their resting place.

7 Whoever found them devoured them.
Their adversaries said,
"We're not guilty;
instead, they have sinned
against the LORD,
their righteous grazing land,[j]
the hope of their ancestors,[k]
the LORD."

8 Escape from Babylon;[l]
depart from the Chaldeans' land.
Be like the rams that lead the flock.

9 For I will soon stir up and bring
against Babylon[m]
an assembly of great nations
from the north country.

They will line up in battle formation
against her;[n]
from there she will be captured.
Their arrows will be
like a skilled[c] warrior
who does not return empty-handed.

10 The Chaldeans will
become plunder;
all Babylon's plunderers will be
fully satisfied.
This is the LORD's declaration.

11 Because you rejoice,
because you celebrate —
you who plundered
my inheritance —
because you frolic like a young cow
treading grain
and neigh like stallions,[o]

12 your mother[p] will be
utterly humiliated;
she who bore you will be
put to shame.
Look! She will lag behind
all[D] the nations —
an arid wilderness, a desert.[q]

13 Because of the LORD's wrath,
she will not be inhabited;
she will become a desolation,
every bit of her.
Everyone who passes
through Babylon
will be appalled
and scoff because of all her wounds.[r]

14 Line up in battle formation
around Babylon,
all you archers!
Shoot at her! Do not spare
an arrow,
for she has sinned against the LORD.

15 Raise a war cry against her
on every side!
She has thrown up her hands
in surrender;
her defense towers have fallen;
her walls are demolished.[s]
Since this is the LORD's vengeance,[t]
take your vengeance on her;
as she has done, do the same to her.

---

a 50:2 Is 46:1; Jr 51:44
b 50:3 Is 41:25; Jr 1:13–15;
6:1,22; 47:2; 50:9,41; 51:48
c Ps 135:8; Jr 7:20; 21:6;
32:43; 33:10,12; 36:29;
51:62
d 50:4 Is 11:12–13; Jr 3:18;
Ezk 37:15–22; Hs 11:1
e 2Ch 11:16; 15:4; Hs 3:5
f 50:5 Gn 9:16; 17:7,13,19;
Is 55:3; 61:8; Jr 32:40; Ezk
16:60; 37:26
g 50:6 Is 53:6
h Jr 23:2,13
i Ezk 34:6
j 50:7 Jr 31:23; 40:2–3
k Jr 14:8; 17:13
l 50:8 Jr 51:6; Rv 18:4
m 50:9 Jr 51:1,11,29,35

n 50:9 Jr 6:23; 50:14,42;
51:27
o 50:11 Jdg 5:22; Jr 8:16;
47:3
p 50:12 Jr 2:31; 51:47;
Hs 2:4–5
q Jr 51:43
r 50:13 Dt 28:37; 2Ch
29:8; 30:7; Jr 5:30; 18:16;
19:8; 25:9,18; 29:18; 42:18;
44:12,22; 49:17; Mc 6:16;
Zph 2:15
s 50:15 Jr 51:58
t Jr 46:10

A 50:3 Lit *escape; they will walk*   B 50:5 LXX; MT reads *Come and join yourselves*   C 50:9 Some Hb mss, LXX, Syr; other Hb mss read *bereaving*
D 50:12 Lit *Look! The last of*

50:1–3 Though God used **Babylon** to carry out his punishment of his people and the nations, Babylon was not a righteous servant of the Lord (50:1–2). It just wanted to vanquish and dominate others for the sake of its own pride and power.
The initial descriptions of judgment reflect the familiar prophetic technique of blending the immediate with the far-off, since the great devastation outlined in 50:2–3 did not

happen when the Medes and Persians conquered the city and killed King Belshazzar (see Dan 5:30–31). There is a future destruction of Babylon in Revelation 17–18 during the end of the tribulation, when this proud empire that came to stand for the worst in resistance to the Lord will be crushed. This may be what is in view here in Jeremiah.
50:4–6 The prophecy that **the Israelites and Judeans will come together, weeping as they**

come, and will seek the LORD their God (50:4) awaits Christ's return in the millennium. At that time, his **lost sheep** (50:6) will recognize and bow before him as Savior and Messiah.
50:10–16 God was angered at Babylon's joy and arrogance while plundering Judah, his **inheritance** (50:11). Therefore, God's judgment against Babylon would not be satisfied until **every bit of her** had become desolate (50:13).

a 50:16 Jr 46:16
b Is 13:14
c 50:17 Jr 2:15; 4:7
d 2Kg 24:10-12; 25:1-7
e 50:18 Is 10:12
f 50:19 Jr 22:6; 23:3; 33:12; Ezk 34:14
g Is 33:9; Mc 7:14; Nah 1:4
h 50:20 Nm 14:20; Jr 31:34; 36:3
i Jr 39:10; 52:16; Zph 3:12
j 50:21 1Kg 9:4; 2Kg 21:8; 2Ch 7:17
k 50:22 Jr 51:54-56
l 50:23 Jr 51:41

m 50:24 Jr 51:31; Dn 5:30-31
n 50:25 Is 13:5
o 50:27 Is 10:3; Jr 46:21; Ezk 21:25,29; Hs 5:9; Mc 7:4; 2Pt 2:9
p 50:28 2Kg 18:16; 23:4; 24:13; Jr 51:11
q 50:29 Ps 28:4; Pr 24:12,29; Jr 25:14; 50:29; 51:24; Lm 3:64
r Ps 71:22; Is 1:4; 37:23; Jr 51:5
s 50:30 Jr 49:26

16 Cut off the sower from Babylon
as well as him who wields the sickle
at harvest time.
Because of the oppressor's sword,[a]
each will turn to his own people,[b]
each will flee to his own land.

THE RETURN OF GOD'S PEOPLE

17 Israel is a stray lamb,
chased by lions.[c]
The first who devoured him was
the king of Assyria;
the last who crushed his bones
was King Nebuchadnezzar
of Babylon.[d]

18 Therefore, this is what the LORD of Armies, the God of Israel, says: I am about to punish the king of Babylon[e] and his land just as I punished the king of Assyria.
19 I will return Israel
to his grazing land,[f]
and he will feed on Carmel
and Bashan;
he will be satisfied
in the hill country of Ephraim
and of Gilead.[g]
20 In those days and at that time —
this is the LORD's declaration —
one will search for Israel's iniquity,
but there will be none,
and for Judah's sins,
but they will not be found,
for I will forgive[h] those I leave
as a remnant.[i]

THE INVASION OF BABYLON

21 Attack the land of Merathaim,
and those living in Pekod.
Put them to the sword;
completely destroy them —
this is the LORD's declaration —
do everything I have
commanded you.[j]
22 The sound of war is in the land[k] —
a crushing blow!
23 How the hammer
of the whole earth
is cut down and smashed!
What a horror Babylon has become
among the nations![l]

24 Babylon, I laid a trap for you,
and you were caught,[m]
but you did not even know it.
You were found and captured
because you pitted yourself
against the LORD.
25 The LORD opened his armory
and brought out his weapons
of wrath,[n]
because it is a task of the Lord GOD
of Armies
in the land of the Chaldeans.
26 Come against her
from the most distant places.[A]
Open her granaries;
pile her up like mounds of grain
and completely destroy her.
Leave her no survivors.
27 Put all her young bulls to the sword;
let them go down to the slaughter.
Woe to them because their day
has come,
the time of their punishment.[o]

THE HUMILIATION OF BABYLON

28 There is a voice of fugitives
and refugees
from the land of Babylon.
The voice announces in Zion
the vengeance of the LORD
our God,
the vengeance for his temple.[p]
29 Summon the archers to Babylon,
all who string the bow;
camp all around her;
let none escape.
Repay her according to her deeds;[q]
just as she has done, do the same
to her,
for she has acted arrogantly
against the LORD,
against the Holy One of Israel.[r]
30 Therefore, her young men will fall
in her public squares;
all the warriors will perish
in that day.
This is the LORD's declaration.[s]
31 Look, I am against you,
you arrogant one —
this is the declaration of
the Lord GOD of Armies —

A 50:26 Lit from the end

for your day has come,
the time when I will punish you.
³² The arrogant will stumble and fall[a]
with no one to pick him up.
I will set fire to his cities,
and it will consume everything
around him.[b]

THE DESOLATION OF BABYLON

³³ This is what the LORD of Armies says:
Israelites and Judeans alike
have been oppressed.
All their captors hold them fast;[c]
they refuse to release them.
³⁴ Their Redeemer is strong;
the LORD of Armies is his name.
He will fervently
champion their cause[d]
so that he might bring rest
to the earth
but turmoil to those who live
in Babylon.[e]
³⁵ A sword is over the Chaldeans —
this is the LORD's declaration —
against those who live in Babylon,
against her officials, and against
her sages.
³⁶ A sword is against the diviners,
and they will act foolishly.
A sword is
against her heroic warriors,
and they will be terrified.
³⁷ A sword is against his horses
and chariots
and against all the foreigners
among them,[f]
and they will be like women.[g]
A sword is against her treasuries,
and they will be plundered.
³⁸ A drought will come on her waters,
and they will be dried up.
For it is a land of carved images,
and they go mad because of
terrifying things.[A,h]

³⁹ Therefore, desert creatures[B] will live
with hyenas,
and ostriches will also live in her.
It will never again be inhabited
or lived in through all generations.[i]
⁴⁰ Just as God demolished Sodom
and Gomorrah
and their neighboring towns[j] —
this is the LORD's declaration —

so no one will live there;
no human being will stay in it even
temporarily
as a temporary resident.[k]

THE CONQUEST OF BABYLON

⁴¹ Look! A people comes
from the north.[l]
A great nation and many kings
will be stirred up
from the remote regions
of the earth.[m]
⁴² They grasp bow and javelin.
They are cruel and show no mercy.
Their voice roars like the sea,[n]
and they ride on horses,
lined up like men in battle formation
against you, Daughter Babylon.
⁴³ The king of Babylon has heard
about them;
his hands have become weak.
Distress has seized him —
pain, like a woman in labor.[o]

⁴⁴ "Look, it will be like a lion coming
from the thickets[C,p] of the Jordan to the
watered grazing land. I will chase Babylon[D] away from her land in a flash. I will
appoint whoever is chosen for her. For
who is like me? Who will issue me a summons? Who is the shepherd who can stand
against me?"
⁴⁵ Therefore, hear the plans that the LORD
has drawn up against Babylon and the
strategies he has devised against the land
of the Chaldeans:[q] Certainly the flock's little lambs will be dragged away; certainly
the grazing land will be made desolate because of them. ⁴⁶ At the sound of Babylon's
conquest the earth will quake; a cry will be
heard among the nations.[r]

GOD'S JUDGMENT ON BABYLON

51 This is what the LORD says:
I am about to rouse the spirit of a
destroyer[E] against Babylon[s]
and against the population
of Leb-qamai.[F,G]
² I will send strangers to Babylon
who will scatter her and strip
her land bare,[t]
for they will come against her
from every side in the day
of disaster.

[a] 50:32 Ps 27:2; Pr 24:16-17; Is 3:8; 8:15; 31:3
[b] Jr 21:14
[c] 50:33 2Ch 28:11; 30:9; Is 14:17; 61:1; Jr 13:17
[d] 50:34 1Sm 24:15; Pr 23:11; Is 47:4; Jr 51:36
[e] Mc 4:10
[f] 50:37 Ex 12:38; Neh 13:1-3; Jr 25:20
[g] Jr 51:30
[h] 50:38 Ex 15:16; 23:27; Jb 20:25
[i] 50:39 Is 13:20-21; 34:13-14
[j] 50:40 Gn 19:24-25

[k] 50:40 Jr 49:18-21,33
[l] 50:41-43 Jr 6:22-24; 49:24
[m] 50:41 Jr 6:22; 25:32; 31:8
[n] 50:42 Is 5:30; 17:12
[o] 50:43 Ps 48:6; Is 13:8; 21:3; 42:14; Jr 4:31; 6:24; 13:21; 22:23; 30:6; 49:24; Mc 4:9-10; 1Th 5:3
[p] 50:44 Ps 10:9; 17:12; Is 5:29; Jr 2:15; 5:6; 12:5; 25:38; 50:17; Zch 11:3
[q] 50:45 Jr 51:29
[r] 50:44-46 Jr 49:19-21
[s] 51:1 Jr 4:11-12; 50:9
[t] 51:2 Jr 15:7; Mt 3:12

[A] 50:38 Or of dreaded gods   [B] 50:39 Or desert demons   [C] 50:44 Lit pride   [D] 50:44 Lit them   [E] 51:1 Or to stir up a destructive wind   [F] 51:1 Lit heart of my adversaries   [G] 51:1 = Chaldeans

50:41-46 The chapter ends with a prophecy that seems to point to the final destruction of a rebuilt Babylon in the end time. If verse 46 is yet future, it could refer to the wailing of Revelation 18:9-19, which ends with this cry of horror at Babylon's complete destruction: "Woe, woe, the great city . . . for in a single hour she was destroyed" (Rev 18:19).

a 51:3 Jb 41:13; Jr 46:4
b 51:4 Jr 51:47,52
c 51:5 Ps 78:41; Is 37:23; Jr 50:29
d 51:6 Jr 50:8; Rv 18:4
e Jr 48:6; 51:45
f Ps 28:4; 137:8; Is 66:6
g 51:7 Rv 17:4
h Rv 14:8; 18:3
i Jr 25:16
j 51:8 Jr 8:22; 46:11
k 51:9 Is 13:14
l Rv 18:5
m 51:10 Ps 37:6
n Jr 50:28
o 51:11 Is 5:28; Jr 50:9,14,29; 51:3
p Jr 50:28
q 51:12 Ps 60:4; Is 5:26; 18:3

r 51:12 Is 14:26; 19:12,17; 23:8; Jr 18:11; 49:20,30; 50:45; Mc 2:3
s 51:13 Rv 17:1
t 51:15 Jb 38:4; Ps 93:1; 96:10
u Pr 3:19-20; 8:22-29
v Jb 9:8; Ps 104:2; Is 45:12
w 51:16 Jr 5:22; 31:35
x Jb 38:25-30,34-38; Ps 135:7
y 51:17 Is 40:18-31; 46:1-7
z Is 41:29
aa Hab 2:19
ab 51:18 Jr 10:3,8
ac Jr 6:15; 10:15; 49:8
ad 51:19 Gn 2:7-8,19; Ps 95:5; Is 43:1
ae Dt 4:20; 32:8-9; Ps 74:2; 78:71; Is 63:17; Mc 7:18; Eph 1:18
af 51:15-19 Jr 10:12-16

3 Don't let the archer string his bow;
don't let him put on[A] his armor.[a]
Don't spare her young men;
completely destroy her entire army!

4 Those who were slain will fall
   in the land of the Chaldeans,
those who were pierced through,
   in her streets.[b]

5 For Israel and Judah are not
   left widowed
by their God, the LORD of Armies,
though their land is full of guilt
against the Holy One of Israel.[c]

6 Leave Babylon;[d]
save your lives, each of you![e]
Don't perish because of her guilt.
For this is the time
   of the LORD's vengeance —
he will pay her what she deserves.[f]

7 Babylon was a gold cup
   in the LORD's hand,[g]
making the whole earth drunk.
The nations drank her wine;[h]
therefore, the nations go mad.[i]

8 Suddenly Babylon fell
   and was shattered.
Wail for her;
get balm[j] for her wound —
perhaps she can be healed.

9 We tried to heal Babylon,
but she could not be healed.
Abandon her!
Let each of us go to his own land,[k]
for her judgment extends to the sky
and reaches as far as the clouds.[l]

10 The LORD has brought about
   our vindication;[m]
come, let's tell in Zion
what the LORD our God
   has accomplished.[n]

11 Sharpen the arrows![o]
Fill the quivers![B]
The LORD has roused the spirit
of the kings of the Medes
because his plan is aimed at Babylon
to destroy her,
for it is the LORD's vengeance,
vengeance for his temple.[p]

12 Raise up a signal flag[q]

against the walls of Babylon;
fortify the watch post;
set the watchmen in place;
prepare the ambush.
For the LORD has both planned
   and accomplished
what he has threatened
against those who live in Babylon.[r]

13 You who reside
   by abundant water,[s]
rich in treasures,
your end has come,
your life thread is cut.

14 The LORD of Armies has sworn by himself:
I will fill you up with men
   as with locusts,
and they will sing the victory song
   over you.

15 He made the earth by his power,
established the world[t]
   by his wisdom,[u]
and spread out the heavens
   by his understanding.[v]

16 When he thunders,[c]
the waters in the heavens are
   tumultuous,[w]
and he causes the clouds
to rise from the ends
   of the earth.
He makes lightning for the rain
and brings the wind
   from his storehouses.[x]

17 Everyone is stupid
   and ignorant.
Every goldsmith is put to shame
   by his carved image,[y]
for his cast images are a lie;[z]
there is no breath in them.[aa]

18 They are worthless,[ab] a work
   to be mocked.
At the time of their punishment
   they will be destroyed.[ac]

19 Jacob's Portion[D] is not like these
because he is the one who formed
   all things.[ad]
Israel is the tribe
   of his inheritance;[ae]
the LORD of Armies is
   his name.[af]

A 51:3 Hb obscure   B 51:11 Or *Grasp the shields!*   C 51:16 Lit *At his giving of the voice*   D 51:19 = The LORD

51:6-9 The warning to **leave Babylon** and avoid **her guilt** contains end-time imagery reflected in the book of Revelation. God proclaims that he will pour his wrath on Babylon during the tribulation: "Come out of her, my people, so that you will not share in her sins or receive any of her plagues" (Rev 18:4; see also Jer 51:45-46). According to Jeremiah, Babylon's destruction **extends to the sky** (51:9). This reference to the sky is picked up by the apostle John in his recorded vision of an "angel" flying through the air, announcing, "Babylon the Great has fallen" (Rev 14:8). **51:17-18** No idol can deliver those under God's wrath.

20 You are my war club,
my weapons of war.
With you I will smash nations;
with you I will bring kingdoms
to ruin.
21 With you I will smash the horse
and its rider;
with you I will smash the chariot
and its rider.
22 With you I will smash man
and woman;[a]
with you I will smash the old man
and the youth;
with you I will smash the young man
and the young woman.
23 With you I will smash the shepherd
and his flock;
with you I will smash the farmer
and his ox-team.[A]
With you I will smash governors
and officials.

24 "Before your very eyes, I will repay
Babylon and all the residents of Chaldea
for all their evil they have done in Zion."[b]
This is the LORD's declaration.
25 Look, I am against you,
devastating mountain.
This is the LORD's declaration.
You devastate the whole earth.
I will stretch out my hand
against you,[c]
roll you down from the cliffs,
and turn you into
a charred mountain.
26 No one will be able to retrieve
a cornerstone
or a foundation stone from you,
because you will become
desolate forever.
This is the LORD's declaration.

27 Raise a signal flag[d] in the land;
blow a ram's horn
among the nations;[e]
set apart the nations against her.[f]
Summon kingdoms against her —
Ararat, Minni, and Ashkenaz.
Appoint a marshal against her;
bring up horses like a swarm[B]
of locusts.
28 Set apart the nations for battle
against her —
the kings of Media,

her governors and all her officials,
and all the lands they rule.
29 The earth quakes[g] and trembles
because the LORD's intentions
against Babylon stand:
to make the land of Babylon
a desolation, without
inhabitant.
30 Babylon's warriors have
stopped fighting;[h]
they sit in their strongholds.
Their might is exhausted;
they have become like women.
Babylon's homes have been
set ablaze,
her gate bars are shattered.[i]
31 Messenger races
to meet messenger,[j]
and herald to meet herald,
to announce to the king of Babylon
that his city has been captured
from end to end.[k]
32 The fords have been seized,[l]
the marshes set on fire,
and the fighting men are terrified.

33 For this is what the LORD of Armies,
the God of Israel, says:
Daughter Babylon is
like a threshing floor
at the time it is trampled.[m]
In just a little while her harvest time
will come.[n]

34 "King Nebuchadnezzar of Babylon
has devoured me;
he has crushed me.
He has set me aside
like an empty dish;
he has swallowed me
like a sea monster;[o]
he filled his belly with my delicacies;
he has vomited me out.[c]
35 Let the violence done to me
and my family be done
to Babylon,"
says the inhabitant of Zion.
"Let my blood be on the inhabitants
of Chaldea,"
says Jerusalem.

36 Therefore, this is what the LORD says:
I am about to champion your cause[p]
and take vengeance on your behalf;

a 51:22 2Ch 36:17; Is 13:15-18
b 51:24 2Sm 12:11; Is 1:7; Jr 16:9; 20:4; 29:21; 39:16; 50:15,29
c 51:25 Jr 15:6; Ezk 6:14; 25:7
d 51:27 Ps 60:4; Is 5:26; 18:3
e Jr 4:5; 6:1
f Jr 6:4; 22:7; 50:9

g 51:29 Ps 18:7; Is 13:13; Jr 50:46
h 51:30 Jr 50:37
i Lm 2:9; Nah 3:13
j 51:31 2Ch 30:6
k Jr 50:24
l 51:32 Jdg 12:5
m 51:33 Is 21:10
n Is 17:5; Jl 3:13; Rv 14:15
o 51:34 Ps 74:13; Is 27:1; Ezk 29:3
p 51:36 1Sm 24:15; Pr 23:11; Jr 50:34

A 51:23 Lit yoke   B 51:27 Hb obscure   C 51:34 Lit has rinsed me off

51:20-23 The reference to God's **war club** that he used to **smash** nations could refer to King Cyrus of Persia, who was Babylon's conqueror. Just as the Lord used Nebuchadnezzar as his hammer

of judgment against other lands, so he would use Cyrus to route the Babylonians. While God uses pagan powers to accomplish his will, he still holds them responsible for their sins.

51:34-35 The city of **Jerusalem** (51:35) is pictured as the spokesperson for God's people, lamenting the devastation that **Nebuchadnezzar** brought upon the inhabitants of Judah (51:34).

[a] 51:36 Ex 14:16–15:21
[b] 51:37 2Ch 29:8; Jr 18:16;
19:8
[c] Jr 4:7; 9:11; 33:10; 34:22;
44:2,22; 46:19; 48:9; 49:33
[d] 51:39 Jr 51:57
[e] 51:40 Is 34:6; Ezk 39:18
[f] 51:41 Jr 25:26
[g] Jr 25:26
[h] Jr 33:9; 49:25
[i] Jr 50:23
[j] 51:42 Is 8:7-8
[k] 51:43 Jr 50:12
[l] 51:44 Is 46:1; Jr 50:2
[m] Jb 20:15
[n] Is 2:2; Mc 4:1
[o] 51:45 Jr 51:6
[p] Jr 48:6; 51:6
[q] 51:47 Jr 7:32; 16:14; 19:6;
23:7; 48:12; 49:2; 51:52
[r] Jr 50:2
[s] Jr 50:12

[t] 51:48 Is 44:23; 49:13
[u] Is 41:25; Jr 4:6,20; 6:1;
15:12; 47:2; 50:3,9,41
[v] 51:50 Jr 44:28
[w] 51:51 Ps 44:15
[x] Lm 1:10
[y] 51:53 Gn 11:4; Is 14:12-14;
Jr 49:16
[z] 51:54 Jr 50:22
[aa] Jr 4:6; 6:1; 14:17; 48:3;
Zph 1:10

I will dry up her sea[a]
and make her fountain run dry.
37 Babylon will become a heap
of rubble,
a jackals' den,
a desolation and an object of scorn,[b]
without inhabitant.[c]
38 They will roar together
like young lions;
they will growl like lion cubs.
39 While they are flushed with heat,
I will serve them a feast,
and I will make them drunk so that
they celebrate.[A,d]
Then they will fall asleep forever
and never wake up.
This is the LORD's declaration.
40 I will bring them down like lambs
to the slaughter,
like rams together with male goats.[e]

41 How Sheshach[B,f] has been captured,[g]
the praise[h] of the whole earth seized.
What a horror Babylon has become
among the nations![i]
42 The sea has risen over Babylon;[j]
she is covered
with its tumultuous waves.
43 Her cities have become a desolation,[k]
an arid desert,
a land where no one lives,
where no human being even
passes through.
44 I will punish Bel[l] in Babylon.
I will make him vomit
what he swallowed.[m]
The nations will no longer stream
to him;[n]
even Babylon's wall will fall.

45 Come out from among her,
my people![o]
Save your lives, each of you,[p]
from the LORD's burning anger.
46 May you not become cowardly
and fearful
when the report is proclaimed
in the land,
for the report will come one year,
and then another the next year.
There will be violence in the land
with ruler against ruler.
47 Therefore, look, the days are coming[q]
when I will punish
Babylon's carved images.[r]
Her entire land will suffer shame,
and all her slain will lie fallen
within her.[s]

48 Heaven and earth and everything
in them
will shout for joy[t] over Babylon
because the destroyers
from the north[u]
will come against her.
This is the LORD's declaration.

49 Babylon must fall because of
the slain of Israel,
even as the slain of the
whole earth fell
because of Babylon.
50 You who have escaped the sword,[v]
go and do not stand still!
Remember the LORD from far away,
and let Jerusalem come
to your mind.

51 We are ashamed
because we have heard insults.[w]
Humiliation covers our faces
because foreigners have entered
the holy places of the LORD's temple.[x]

52 Therefore, look, the days
are coming —
this is the LORD's declaration —
when I will punish
her carved images,
and the wounded will groan
throughout her land.
53 Even if Babylon should ascend
to the heavens[y]
and fortify her tall fortresses,
destroyers will come against her
from me.
This is the LORD's declaration.

54 The sound of a cry from Babylon![z]
The sound of terrible destruction[aa]
from the land of the Chaldeans!
55 For the LORD is going
to devastate Babylon;
he will silence her mighty voice.
Their waves roar like a huge torrent;
the tumult of their voice resounds,
56 for a destroyer is coming
against her,
against Babylon.
Her warriors will be captured,
their bows shattered,
for the LORD is a God of retribution;
he will certainly repay.
57 I will make her princes
and sages drunk,
along with her governors, officials,
and warriors.

[A]51:39 LXX reads *pass out*　[B]51:41 = Babylon

Then they will fall asleep forever
and never wake up.[a]
This is the King's declaration;
the LORD of Armies is his name.[b]

58 This is what the LORD of Armies says:
Babylon's thick walls will be
totally demolished,[c]
and her high gates set ablaze.
The peoples will have labored
for nothing;[d]
the nations will weary themselves
only to feed the fire.

59 This is what the prophet Jeremiah commanded Seraiah son of Neriah son of Mahseiah,[e] the quartermaster, when he went to Babylon with King Zedekiah of Judah in the fourth year of Zedekiah's reign. **60** Jeremiah wrote on one scroll about all the disaster that would come to Babylon;[f] all these words were written against Babylon.

61 Jeremiah told Seraiah, "When you get to Babylon, see that you read all these words aloud. **62** Say, 'LORD, you have threatened to cut off[g] this place so that no one will live in it — people or animals.[h] Indeed, it will remain desolate forever.' **63** When you have finished reading this scroll, tie a stone to it and throw it into the middle of the Euphrates River.[i] **64** Then say, 'In the same way, Babylon will sink and never rise again because of the disaster I am bringing on her. They will grow weary.'"
The words of Jeremiah end here.

THE FALL OF JERUSALEM

52 Zedekiah was twenty-one years old when he became king, and he reigned eleven years in Jerusalem. His mother's name was Hamutal daughter of Jeremiah; she was from Libnah. **2** Zedekiah did what was evil in the LORD's sight just as Jehoiakim had done.[j] **3** Because of the LORD's anger, it came to the point in Jerusalem and Judah that he finally banished them from his presence. Then Zedekiah rebelled against the king of Babylon.[k]

4 In the ninth year of Zedekiah's reign, on the tenth day of the tenth month, King Nebuchadnezzar of Babylon advanced against Jerusalem with his entire army. They laid siege to the city and built a siege wall against it all around. **5** The city was under siege until King Zedekiah's eleventh year.

6 By the ninth day of the fourth month the famine was so severe in the city that the common people had no food. **7** Then the city was broken into, and all the warriors fled. They left the city at night by way of the city gate between the two walls near the king's garden, though the Chaldeans surrounded the city. They made their way along the route to the Arabah.[l] **8** The Chaldean army pursued the king and overtook Zedekiah in the plains of Jericho. Zedekiah's entire army left him and scattered. **9** The Chaldeans seized the king and brought him to the king of Babylon at Riblah in the land of Hamath, and he passed sentence on him.

10 At Riblah the king of Babylon slaughtered Zedekiah's sons before his eyes, and he also slaughtered the Judean commanders. **11** Then he blinded Zedekiah and bound him with bronze chains. The king of Babylon brought Zedekiah to Babylon, where he kept him in custody[A] until his dying day.[m]

12 On the tenth day of the fifth month — which was the nineteenth year of King Nebuchadnezzar, king of Babylon — Nebuzaradan, the captain of the guards, entered Jerusalem as the representative

---

[a] 51:57 Jr 51:39
[b] Jr 46:18; 48:15
[c] 51:58 Jr 50:15
[d] Hab 2:13
[e] 51:59 Jr 32:12
[f] 51:60 Jr 36:2
[g] 51:62 1Sm 20:15; Ps 109:13; Is 10:7; Jr 9:21; 44:11; 47:4; Ob 14
[h] Ps 135:8; Jr 7:20; 21:6; 32:43; 33:10,12; 36:29; 50:3
[i] 51:63 Jr 19:10-11; Rv 18:21

[j] 52:2 2Kg 23:34–24:6; 2Ch 36:4-8
[k] 52:1-3 2Kg 24:18-20; 2Ch 36:11-13
[l] 52:7 Dt 2:8
[m] 52:4-11 2Kg 25:1-7; Jr 39:1-7

[A] 52:11 Lit *in a house of guards*

51:63-64 Such a prophecy hardly seemed possible at the time—except for those with eyes of faith to trust God's sovereign promises.
52:1-34 This chapter is a historical supplement added about twenty-five years later as a further confirmation that Jeremiah's prophecies did come to pass.

The fate of King Jehoiachin is explained in verses 31-34. In God's providence, **King Evil-merodach**, Nebuchadnezzar's son, **pardoned King Jehoiachin of Judah and released him** (52:31). Then he set Jehoiachin's **throne above the thrones of the kings who were with him in Babylon** (52:32). Jehoiachin had reigned only three months in Jerusalem before being deposed by Nebuchadnezzar (see 2 Kgs 24:8-12), but he was on the throne long enough to be identified as a king who did evil before the Lord.

So why did Jehoiachin receive such favor from the Babylonians—and ultimately, from God?

The explanation may lie in two realities that have to do with the purpose of the book of Jeremiah and the certainty of both God's judgments and promises. The long life of Jehoiachin in exile had to be a reminder to his fellow exiles that God was executing his fierce judgment on his people. But at the same time, Jehoiachin's long survival in Babylon and his restoration to a place of honor also served to remind the exiles that God had not completely abandoned them and would one day restore them to their land.

Despite his unfaithfulness, Jehoiachin was, after all, a Davidic king, a symbol of hope to the people of Judah that God had a future of blessing for them. And even though Jehoiachin himself was judged and cursed by having no descendant "on the throne of David" (see Jer 22:30), the Davidic line through whom Jesus would come did not end.

To bypass the curse on Jehoiachin, the last of Solomon's descendants, the line of succession transferred to David's son Nathan. The importance of this can be seen in the genealogy of Jesus through Mary, whose ancestors were of Nathan's line (see Luke 3:31). Thus the messianic line was preserved and Jesus's claim to the throne of David legitimized.

The subsequent generations of Israelites who would read the book of Jeremiah would find, even amid its judgments, the hope of fulfillment of God's ultimate promise—the coming of David's greater son, the Lord Jesus Christ, to bring together all of God's promises to his people.

[a] 52:13-14 2Ch 36:19
[b] 52:12-16 2Kg 25:8-12; Jr 39:8-10
[c] 52:17 1Kg 7:23,27
[d] 52:19 Ex 25:29; 37:16; Nm 4:7
[e] 52:22 1Kg 7:16-20,41-42; 2Ch 4:12-13

[f] 52:17-27 2Kg 25:13-21
[g] 52:28 2Kg 24:12-16
[h] 52:31-34 2Kg 25:27-30

of[A] the king of Babylon. [13] He burned the LORD's temple, the king's palace, all the houses of Jerusalem; he burned down all the great houses. [14] The whole Chaldean army with the captain of the guards tore down all the walls surrounding Jerusalem.[a] [15] Nebuzaradan, the captain of the guards, deported some of the poorest of the people, as well as the rest of the people who remained in the city, the deserters who had defected to the king of Babylon, and the rest of the craftsmen. [16] But Nebuzaradan, the captain of the guards, left some of the poorest of the land to be vine-dressers and farmers.[b]

[17] Now the Chaldeans broke into pieces the bronze pillars for the LORD's temple and the water carts and the bronze basin[B] that were in the LORD's temple,[c] and they carried all the bronze to Babylon. [18] They also took the pots, shovels, wick trimmers, sprinkling basins, dishes, and all the bronze articles used in the temple service. [19] The captain of the guards took away the bowls, firepans, sprinkling basins, pots, lampstands, pans, and drink offering bowls[d] — whatever was gold or silver.

[20] As for the two pillars, the one basin, with the twelve bronze oxen under it, and the water carts[c] that King Solomon had made for the LORD's temple, the weight of the bronze of all these articles was beyond measure. [21] One pillar was 27 feet[D] tall, had a circumference of 18 feet,[E] was hollow — four fingers thick — [22] and had a bronze capital on top of it.[e] One capital, encircled by bronze grating and pomegranates, stood 7 ½ feet[F] high. The second pillar was the same, with pomegranates. [23] Each capital had ninety-six pomegranates all around it. All the pomegranates around the grating numbered one hundred.

[24] The captain of the guards also took away Seraiah the chief priest, Zephaniah the priest of the second rank, and the three doorkeepers. [25] From the city he took a court official[G] who had been appointed over the warriors; seven trusted royal aides[H] found in the city; the secretary of the commander of the army, who enlisted the people of the land for military duty; and sixty men from the common people[I] who were found within the city. [26] Nebuzaradan, the captain of the guards, took them and brought them to the king of Babylon at Riblah. [27] The king of Babylon put them to death at Riblah in the land of Hamath. So Judah went into exile from its land.[f]

[28] These are the people Nebuchadnezzar deported:[g] in the seventh year, 3,023 Jews; [29] in his eighteenth year,[J] 832 people from Jerusalem; [30] in Nebuchadnezzar's twenty-third year, Nebuzaradan, the captain of the guards, deported 745 Jews. Altogether, 4,600 people were deported.

JEHOIACHIN PARDONED

[31] On the twenty-fifth day of the twelfth month of the thirty-seventh year of the exile of Judah's King Jehoiachin, King Evil-merodach of Babylon, in the first year of his reign, pardoned King Jehoiachin of Judah and released him from prison. [32] He spoke kindly to him and set his throne above the thrones of the kings who were with him in Babylon. [33] So Jehoiachin changed his prison clothes, and he dined regularly in the presence of the king of Babylon for the rest of his life. [34] As for his allowance, a regular allowance was given to him by the king of Babylon, a portion for each day until the day of his death, for the rest of his life.[h]

[A] 52:12 Lit *Jerusalem; he stood before*   [B] 52:17 Lit *sea*   [C] 52:20 LXX, Syr; MT reads *oxen under the water carts*   [D] 52:21 Lit *18 cubits*   [E] 52:21 Lit *12 cubits*   [F] 52:22 Lit *five cubits*   [G] 52:25 Or *a eunuch*   [H] 52:25 Lit *seven men who look on the king's face*   [I] 52:25 Lit *the people of the land*   [J] 52:29 Some Hb mss, Syr add *he deported*

LAMENTATIONS

INTRODUCTION

Author

THOUGH THE AUTHOR'S NAME IS not listed anywhere in the book, ancient Jewish tradition holds that the prophet Jeremiah wrote Lamentations.

Historical Background

As the title of the book suggests, it is about pain and suffering—but not without hope in God. Jeremiah wrote in light of the fall of Jerusalem to the Babylonians in 587–586 BC. He includes references to the siege of Jerusalem (2:20-22; 3:5, 7), the devastation of the city (2:3-5; 4:11; 5:18), and the exile of the people (1:1, 4-5, 18; 2:9, 14; 3:2, 19; 4:22; 5:2). These events were cause for great sorrow, so Jeremiah has often been called "the weeping prophet."

The five chapters in the book are five poems of lament. Each one, except chapter 5, is an "alphabetic acrostic"—that means it is broken into twenty-two verses or stanzas that begin with the twenty-two letters of the Hebrew alphabet, in alphabetical order.

Message and Purpose

This is a sad book written by "the weeping prophet" during a sad time. The Babylonians had attacked Jerusalem and brought an end to the southern kingdom of Judah. Many of the people had been taken into captivity, while others had fled.

Lamentations is a poetic expression of the pain of sin's consequences. What we hear and read in it reflect the tears of the prophet who saw destruction all around him. Yet in the middle of all the pain and sorrow, Jeremiah highlights the faithfulness of God. First, there was God's faithfulness in warning that if his people departed from him, he would bring judgment on them. But Lamentations is also about hope (3:21-23), because God's mercies are seen even in the midst of judgment. If his people will return to him in repentance, God will return to them and limit, or even reverse, the consequences of their disobedience.

Lamentations is a reminder of God's covenantal Kingdom sanctions—namely, that sin brings pain and tears, but God is always ready to show mercy when we repent and return to him.

www.bhpublishinggroup.com/qr/te/25_00

Outline

I. The Devastation and Lament of Jerusalem (1:1-22)
II. God's Judgment on Jerusalem (2:1-22)
III. Words of Anguish, Words of Hope (3:1-66)
IV. The Devastated People of Jerusalem (4:1-22)
V. The Prayer of Judah's People (5:1-22)

*a*1:1 Lm 3:28
*b*Lm 1:17
*c*Ex 22:22; Dt 10:18; 24:19-21; Is 1:17; 47:8-9
*d*1:2 Ps 6:6
*e*Jr 3:1; 22:20-22
*f*1:3 Dt 28:65; Ps 116:7
*g*1:4 2Sm 5:7; Ps 20:2; Jr 51:35
*h*Dt 16:16; 2Ch 8:13; Ps 84:5; Is 1:11-17
*i*1:5 Dt 28:13,44
*j*Jb 3:26; 12:6; Jr 12:1
*k*1:6 Ezk 27:10
*l*Lm 2:1,4,8; 4:22
*m*Jr 39:4-7

*n*1:7 Is 58:7; Lm 3:19
*o*1:9 Jr 13:22,26; Nah 3:5
*p*Dt 28:43
*q*1:10 Dt 23:3; Neh 13:1-3; Ezk 44:9
*r*1:11 Jr 38:9; 52:6
*s*Lm 1:19; 2:20; 4:10
*t*1:12 Ps 89:41; Jr 22:8
*u*Am 5:18

LAMENT OVER JERUSALEM

א Aleph

1 How[A] she sits alone,[a]
the city[b] once crowded with people!
She who was great
　among the nations
has become like a widow.[c]
The princess among the provinces
has been put to forced labor.

ב Beth

2 She weeps bitterly
　during the night,[d]
with tears on her cheeks.
There is no one to offer her comfort,
not one from all her lovers.[B,e]
All her friends have betrayed her;
they have become her enemies.

ג Gimel

3 Judah has gone into exile
following[c] affliction
　and harsh slavery;
she lives among the nations
but finds no place to rest.[f]
All her pursuers have overtaken her
in narrow places.

ד Daleth

4 The roads to Zion[g] mourn,
for no one comes
　to the appointed festivals.[h]
All her gates are deserted;
her priests groan,
her young women grieve,
and she herself is bitter.

ה He

5 Her adversaries have become
　her masters;[i]
her enemies are at ease,[j]
for the LORD has made her suffer
because of her many transgressions.
Her children have gone away
as captives before the adversary.

ו Waw

6 All the splendor[k] has vanished
from Daughter Zion.[l]
Her leaders are like stags
that find no pasture;
they stumble away exhausted
before the hunter.[m]

ז Zayin

7 During the days of her affliction
　and homelessness[n]
Jerusalem remembers all
　her precious belongings
that were hers in days of old.
When her people fell
　into the adversary's hand,
she had no one to help.
The adversaries looked at her,
laughing over her downfall.

ח Cheth

8 Jerusalem has sinned grievously;
therefore, she has become an object
　of scorn.[D]
All who honored her now despise her,
for they have seen her nakedness.
She herself groans and turns away.

ט Teth

9 Her uncleanness stains her skirts.[o]
She never considered her end.
Her downfall was astonishing;[p]
there was no one to comfort her.
LORD, look on my affliction,
for the enemy boasts.

י Yod

10 The adversary has seized
all her precious belongings.
She has even seen the nations
enter her sanctuary —
those you had forbidden
to enter your assembly.[q]

כ Kaph

11 All her people groan
while they search for bread.[r]
They have traded
　their precious belongings for food
in order to stay alive.[s]
LORD, look and see
how I have become despised.

ל Lamed

12 Is this nothing to you, all you
　who pass by?[t]
Look and see!
Is there any pain like mine,
which was dealt out to me,
which the LORD made me suffer
on the day of his burning anger?[u]

[A]1:1 The stanzas in Lm 1–4 form an acrostic.　[B]1:2 = Jerusalem's political allies　[C]1:3 Or *because of*　[D]1:8 Or *become impure*

1:2 Judah's false gods and political allies, **her lovers**, were unwilling to help Judah as they were dragged away in chains to Babylon. **1:8-9** God's people had turned from the well-lighted way of his Word to follow evil down a dark, back street. And now the city is like a discarded lady of the night whose lovers have tired of her and pushed her aside. **1:12-21** From this point throughout the rest of the chapter, the pronouns **me, mine, I,** and **my** help personify the city of Jerusalem and give her a voice. The city calls to the nations around her for some measure of pity over her astonishing destruction.

מ Mem

13 He sent fire from on high[a]
    into my bones;
he made it descend.[A,b]
He spread a net for my feet[c]
and turned me back.
He made me desolate,
sick all day long.

נ Nun

14 My transgressions
    have been formed into a yoke,[B,C,d]
fastened together by his hand;
they have been placed on my neck,
and the Lord has broken my strength.
He has handed me over
to those I cannot withstand.

ס Samek

15 The Lord has rejected[e]
all the mighty men within me.
He has summoned an army[D]
    against me
to crush my young warriors.
The Lord has trampled
    Virgin Daughter Judah[f]
like grapes in a winepress.[g]

ע Ayin

16 I weep because of these things;
my eyes flow[E] with tears.[h]
For there is no one nearby
    to comfort me,[i]
no one to keep me alive.
My children are desolate
because the enemy has prevailed.

פ Pe

17 Zion stretches out her hands;
there is no one to comfort her.
The LORD has issued a decree
    against Jacob
that his neighbors should be
    his adversaries.
Jerusalem has become
something impure[j] among them.

צ Tsade

18 The LORD is just,
for I have rebelled
    against his command.[k]

Listen, all you people;
look at my pain.
My young women and young men
have gone into captivity.[l]

ק Qoph

19 I called to my lovers,[m]
but they betrayed me.
My priests and elders
perished in the city
while searching for food
to keep themselves alive.[n]

ר Resh

20 LORD, see how I am in distress.
I am churning within;[o]
my heart is broken,[F]
for I have been very rebellious.
Outside, the sword takes
    the children;
inside, there is death.[p]

ש Shin

21 People have heard me groaning,[q]
but there is no one to comfort me.
All my enemies have heard
    of my misfortune;
they are glad that
    you have caused it.[r]
Bring on the day
    you have announced,
so that they may become like me.[s]

ת Taw

22 Let all their wickedness come
    before you,
and deal with them
as you have dealt with me
because of all my transgressions.[t]
For my groans are many,
and I am sick at heart.

JUDGMENT ON JERUSALEM

א Aleph

2 How the Lord has overshadowed
Daughter Zion with his anger!
He has thrown down Israel's glory
from heaven to earth.
He did not acknowledge
    his footstool[u]
in the day of his anger.[v]

---

[a] 1:13 Gn 19:24; Hs 8:14; Am 1:4–2:5
[b] 1Kg 18:38; 2Kg 1:10,12; Jb 30:30; Jr 20:9
[c] Ps 35:7; Is 51:20; Ezk 12:13; Hs 7:12
[d] 1:14 Gn 27:40; Lv 26:13; Dt 28:48; 2Ch 10:3–11; Is 9:4; Jr 27:2,6–11
[e] 1:15 Ps 119:118
[f] Lm 2:2,5
[g] Is 63:1–6; Jl 3:12–15; Rv 14:17–20; 19:15
[h] 1:16 Jr 9:1,18; Lm 2:11,18; 3:48–49
[i] Is 40:1
[j] 1:17 Lv 15:19–20; Ezk 7:19–20; 18:6
[k] 1:18 Neh 9:33

[l] 1:18 Dt 28:41; 2Ch 29:9; Ezr 9:7; Jr 48:46
[m] 1:19 Lm 1:2
[n] Lm 1:11
[o] 1:20 Jb 30:27
[p] Dt 32:25; Ezk 7:15
[q] 1:21 Lm 1:4,8
[r] Lm 2:15–17
[s] Is 62:8–63:6; Ezk 38–39; Jl 3:1–3; Mc 7:8–13; Zch 14:1–9
[t] 1:22 Lm 4:21–22
[u] 2:1 1Ch 28:2; Ps 99:5; 132:7
[v] Jb 20:28; Ps 110:5; Zph 2:2–3

[A] 1:13 DSS, LXX; MT reads *bones, and it prevailed against them*   [B] 1:14 Some Hb mss, LXX read *He kept watch over my transgressions*   [C] 1:14 Or *The yoke of my transgressions is bound*; Hb obscure   [D] 1:15 Or *has announced an appointed time*   [E] 1:16 Lit *my eye, my eye flows*   [F] 1:20 Lit *is turned within me*

1:14 This word picture is the fulfillment of Jeremiah's "yoke of . . . Babylon" prophecy (see Jer 27:1–12), warning King Zedekiah that the people of Judah would serve Nebuchadnezzar and have their necks "under the yoke of the king of Babylon" (Jer 27:8).

1:18 Don't miss that Jerusalem acknowledges that her sad circumstances are the result of her rebellion **against** God's **command**. Everything that had come upon her was deserved. **2:1-5** With great grief, Jeremiah describes the total ruin of Jerusalem by the Babylo-

nians. But the invaders are barely mentioned because the point is that God **overshadowed . . . swallowed up . . . demolished . . . cut off . . . and destroyed** Judah as a result of his **burning anger** (2:3) against his people.

a 2:2 Jb 16:13; Lm 3:43;
Ezk 8:18
b Is 2:12,15
c Ps 89:39; Is 43:28; 47:6
d 2:3 Ps 75:5,10; Jr 48:25
e Ex 6:6; Dt 4:34
f Dt 4:24; Heb 12:29
g 2:4 Ps 7:12; Lm 3:12
h 1Kg 20:6; Ezk 24:16,21,25
i 2:5 Is 29:2
j 2:6 Ps 74:4
k 2:7 Ps 89:39

l 2:8 2Kg 21:13; Is 28:17;
34:11,17
m 2:9 Neh 1:3; Jr 14:2
n Ezk 7:26; Mc 3:6
o 2:10 Gn 37:34; Jos 7:6;
Neh 9:1; Jb 2:12-13; Ezk
27:30
p Jb 10:15; Is 58:5
q 2:11 Ps 69:3; Jr 9:1; 14:17;
Lm 3:48-49
r Ps 22:14; Jr 4:19
s Lm 3:48
t Jr 44:7
u 2:12 Dt 28:51; Hs 2:8-9;
7:14

ב Beth

2 Without compassion[a] the Lord
 has swallowed up
 all the dwellings of Jacob.
In his wrath he has demolished
 the fortified cities[b]
 of Daughter Judah.
He brought them to the ground
 and defiled the kingdom
 and its leaders.[c]

ג Gimel

3 He has cut off every horn[d] of Israel
 in his burning anger
and withdrawn his right hand[e]
 in the presence of the enemy.
He has blazed against Jacob
 like a flaming fire
 that consumes everything.[f]

ד Daleth

4 He has strung his bow
 like an enemy;[g]
his right hand is positioned
 like an adversary.
He has killed everyone who was the
 delight to the eye,[h]
pouring out his wrath like fire
 on the tent of Daughter Zion.

ה He

5 The Lord is like an enemy;
 he has swallowed up Israel.
He swallowed up all its palaces
 and destroyed its fortified cities.
He has multiplied mourning
 and lamentation
 within Daughter Judah.[i]

ו Waw

6 He has wrecked his temple[A]
 as if it were merely a shack in a
 field,[B]
destroying his place of meeting.[j]
The LORD has abolished
 appointed festivals and Sabbaths
 in Zion.
He has despised king and priest
 in his fierce anger.

ז Zayin

7 The Lord has rejected his altar,
 repudiated his sanctuary;[k]
he has handed the walls
 of her palaces

over to the enemy.
They have raised a shout
 in the house of the LORD
as on the day
 of an appointed festival.

ח Cheth

8 The LORD determined to destroy
 the wall of Daughter Zion.
He stretched out a measuring line[l]
 and did not restrain himself
 from destroying.
He made the ramparts
 and walls grieve;
together they waste away.

ט Teth

9 Zion's gates have fallen
 to the ground;[m]
he has destroyed and shattered
 the bars on her gates.
Her king and her leaders live
 among the nations,
instruction[c] is no more,
and even her prophets receive
 no vision from the LORD.[n]

י Yod

10 The elders of Daughter Zion
 sit on the ground in silence.
They have thrown dust
 on their heads[o]
and put on sackcloth.
The young women of Jerusalem
 have bowed their heads
 to the ground.[p]

כ Kaph

11 My eyes are worn out
 from weeping;[q]
I am churning within.
My heart is poured out in grief[D,r]
because of the destruction
 of my dear people,[s]
because infants and nursing
 babies faint
 in the streets of the city.[t]

ל Lamed

12 They cry out to their mothers,
 "Where is the grain and wine? "[u]
as they faint like the wounded
 in the streets of the city,
as their life pours out
 in the arms of their mothers.

A 2:6 Lit booth   B 2:6 Lit it were a garden   C 2:9 Or the law   D 2:11 Lit My liver is poured out on the ground

2:6 Though his temple was the place he had chosen for his name, God had warned, "I will banish [the temple] from my presence" if Israel
turned to other gods (2 Chr 7:16, 19-20).
2:10 These were symbolic acts of great grief (see Neh 9:1; Job 16:15).

מ Mem

13 What can I say on your behalf?
What can I compare you to,
    Daughter Jerusalem?
What can I liken you to,
so that I may console you,
    Virgin Daughter Zion?
For your ruin is as vast as the sea.
Who can heal you?[a]

נ Nun

14 Your prophets saw visions for you
that were empty and deceptive;[A,b]
they did not reveal your iniquity
and so restore your fortunes.[c]
They saw pronouncements for you
that were empty and misleading.

ס Samek

15 All who pass by
scornfully clap their hands[d] at you.
They hiss[e] and shake their heads[f]
at Daughter Jerusalem:
Is this the city that was called
the perfection of beauty,[g]
the joy of the whole earth?[h]

פ Pe

16 All your enemies
open their mouths against you.[i]
They hiss and gnash their teeth,[j]
saying, "We have swallowed her up.[k]
This is the day we have waited for!
We have lived to see it."

ע Ayin

17 The LORD has done what he planned;
he has accomplished his decree,
which he ordained in days of old.
He has demolished
    without compassion,[l]
letting the enemy gloat over you
and exalting the horn
    of your adversaries.

צ Tsade

18 The hearts of the people cry out
    to the Lord.
Wall of Daughter Zion,[m]
let your tears run down like a river

day and night.[n]
Give yourself no relief
and your[B] eyes no rest.

ק Qoph

19 Arise, cry out in the night
from the first watch of the night.
Pour out your heart like water
before the Lord's presence.[o]
Lift up your hands to him
for the lives of your children
who are fainting from hunger
at the head of every street.[p]

ר Resh

20 LORD, look and consider
to whom you have done this.
Should women eat
    their own children,[q]
the infants they have nurtured?[c]
Should priests and prophets
be killed in the Lord's sanctuary?

שׁ Shin

21 Both young and old
are lying on the ground in the streets.
My young women and young men
have fallen by the sword.
You have killed them in the day
    of your anger,
slaughtering without compassion.[r]

ת Taw

22 You summon those who terrorize
        me[D] on every side,[s]
as if for an appointed festival day;
on the day of the LORD's anger
no one escaped or survived.
My enemy has destroyed
those I nurtured[E] and reared.

HOPE THROUGH GOD'S MERCY

א Aleph

3 **1** I am the man who has seen affliction
under the rod of God's wrath.
2 He has driven me away
    and forced me to walk
in darkness instead of light.[t]
3 Yes, he repeatedly turns his hand
against me all day long.

[a] 2:13 Nah 3:19
[b] 2:14 Jr 5:12-13; 23:9-40; 28:1-4; 29:29-32; Ezk 13:8-16
[c] Dt 30:1-3; Jr 29:11-14; 30:1-3
[d] 2:15 Nm 24:10; Ezk 25:6
[e] 1Kg 9:8; Jr 19:8
[f] Ps 22:7; 109:25; Mk 15:29
[g] Ps 50:2
[h] Ps 48:2
[i] 2:16 Dt 28:37; Jb 16:10; Ps 22:13; Lm 3:46
[j] Jb 16:9; Ps 35:16; 37:12
[k] Lm 2:2,5,8
[l] 2:17 Lm 2:2,21; 3:43; Ezk 7:8-9
[m] 2:18 Lm 2:8

[n] 2:18 Jr 4:31; 14:17
[o] 2:19 Ps 42:4; 62:8; 77:2; 84:2; 142:2
[p] Is 51:20
[q] 2:20 Lv 26:27-29; Dt 28:53-57; 2Kg 6:24-31; Jr 19:9; Lm 4:10
[r] 2:21 Lm 2:2,17; 3:43
[s] 2:22 Ps 31:13; Jr 6:25; 20:10
[t] 3:2 Jb 12:25; Am 5:18,20

[A] 2:14 Or insipid   [B] 2:18 Lit and the daughter of your   [C] 2:20 Or infants in a healthy condition; Hb obscure   [D] 2:22 Or terrors   [E] 2:22 Or I bore healthy; Hb obscure

---

2:14 Examples of these false **prophets** from Jeremiah's day include Pashhur, Hananiah, Ahab, Zedekiah, and Shemaiah (see Jer 20:1-6; 28:1-17; 29:21-32).
2:17 This is a reminder that the Babylonians were merely the weapons in God's hand used to accomplish what he had **ordained**. Centuries before, when he'd established

his covenant with Israel, he'd threatened judgment for their disobedience (see Deut 28:15-68). Then, after years of observing their idolatry, he specifically warned that he would use the Babylonians to punish his people (see 2 Kgs 20:17-18; Hab 1:6).
2:19 When God is your biggest problem (see the note on 2:17), he is also your only hope.

His holiness is unchanging. So when it confronts you, you must do the adjusting.
3:1 In addition to the pain of witnessing Jerusalem's destruction, Jeremiah had physical and emotional scars from decades of prophetic ministry to people who'd refused to listen.

*a*3:4 Jb 13:28; Ps 32:3; 38:3; 49:14; Mc 3:1-3
*b*Ps 51:8; Is 38:13
*c*3:5 Jb 19:8,12
*d*Lm 3:19
*e*3:6 Jb 10:20-22; Ps 88:6; 143:3
*f*3:7 Jb 19:8
*g*3:8 Jb 30:20; Ps 22:2; Is 59:2; Lm 3:44
*h*3:9 Jb 13:27; 23:12; Is 63:17; Hs 2:6
*i*Jb 19:8; Ps 23:3; Pr 2:15; 3:6,17; 4:11
*j*3:10 Hs 13:7-8
*k*3:12 Ps 7:12; Lm 2:4
*l*3:13 Jb 16:13; Pr 7:23
*m*3:14 Jb 12:4; Jr 20:7; Lm 1:7
*n*Jb 30:9; Ps 69:12
*o*3:15 Jr 9:15; 23:15
*p*3:16 Ps 3:7; 58:6; Pr 20:17
*q*3:17 Ps 88:15; Lm 3:31

*r*3:19 Is 58:7; Lm 1:7
*s*Dt 29:18; Jr 9:15; 23:15
*t*3:20 Ps 42:5-6,11; 43:5; 44:25
*u*3:21 Jb 13:15; Ps 33:22; 71:14; 130:5; Mc 7:7
*v*3:22 Ps 89:1; 103:17; Is 63:7
*w*3:23 Ps 36:5; 89:1-8; 100:5
*x*3:24 Nm 18:20; Ps 73:26; 142:5; Jr 10:16
*y*3:25 Ps 25:3; 50:4-31; 49:23
*z*3:26 Ps 37:7; 130:5,7; 1Th 5:10; 2Tm 4:8; 2Pt 3:14
*aa*Ps 37:39; 119:81; Is 46:13
*ab*3:27 Jr 27:11; Lm 1:14
*ac*3:28 Jr 15:17
*ad*3:29 Nm 22:31; Jos 7:6; 1Sm 25:23
*ae*3:30 Is 50:6; Mt 5:39; Lk 6:29

ב Beth

4 He has worn away my flesh and skin;*a*
   he has broken my bones.*b*
5 He has laid siege against me,*c*
   encircling me with bitterness
    and hardship.*d*
6 He has made me dwell in darkness
   like those who have been dead
    for ages.*e*

ג Gimel

7 He has walled me in
   so I cannot get out;*f*
  he has weighed me down
    with chains.
8 Even when I cry out and plead
   for help,
  he blocks out my prayer.*g*
9 He has walled in my ways
   with blocks of stone;*h*
  he has made my paths crooked.*i*

ד Daleth

10 He is^A a bear waiting in ambush,
   a lion in hiding.*j*
11 He forced me off my way
   and tore me to pieces;
  he left me desolate.
12 He strung his bow*k*
   and set me as the target
    for his arrow.

ה He

13 He pierced my kidneys
   with shafts from his quiver.*l*
14 I am a laughingstock*m*
   to all my people,*B*
  mocked by their songs*n* all day long.
15 He filled me with bitterness,
   satiated me with wormwood.*o*

ו Waw

16 He ground my teeth with gravel*p*
   and made me cower*c* in the dust.
17 I have been deprived*D* of peace;*q*
   I have forgotten what prosperity is.

18 Then I thought, "My future^E is lost,
   as well as my hope from the LORD."

ז Zayin

19 Remember^F my affliction
   and my homelessness,*r*
  the wormwood and the poison.*s*
20 I continually remember them
   and have become depressed.^G,*t*
21 Yet I call this to mind,
   and therefore I have hope:*u*

ח Cheth

22 Because of the LORD's faithful love*v*
   we do not perish,^H
  for his mercies never end.
23 They are new every morning;
   great is your faithfulness!*w*
24 I say, "The LORD is my portion,*x*
   therefore I will put my hope in him."

ט Teth

25 The LORD is good to those who wait*y*
   for him,
  to the person who seeks him.
26 It is good to wait quietly*z*
   for salvation from the LORD.*aa*
27 It is good for a man to bear
   the yoke*ab*
  while he is still young.

י Yod

28 Let him sit alone and be silent,*ac*
   for God has disciplined^I him.
29 Let him put his mouth
   in the dust*ad* —
  perhaps there is still hope.
30 Let him offer his cheek
   to the one who would strike him;*ae*
  let him be filled with disgrace.

כ Kaph

31 For the Lord
   will not reject us forever.
32 Even if he causes suffering,
   he will show compassion

---

^A3:10 Lit *is to me*   ^B3:14 Some Hb mss, LXX, Vg; other Hb mss, Syr read *all peoples*   ^C3:16 Or *and trampled me*   ^D3:17 Syr, Vg; MT reads *You deprived my soul*   ^E3:18 Or *splendor*   ^F3:19 Or *I remember*   ^G3:20 Alt Hb tradition reads *and you cause me to collapse*   ^H3:22 One Hb mss, Syr, Tg read *The LORD's faithful love, indeed, does not perish*   ^I3:28 Lit *has laid a burden on*

3:20 Jeremiah's depression brings us to the low point of the book, but it also leads us to a springboard for Jeremiah's great testimony of God's faithfulness: verses 21-23.
3:21-23 In 3:18 Jeremiah confessed that his "hope" was lost, but in 3:21 he declares, **I have hope.** So where did he find hope in the midst of his affliction? Hope actually returned when he took control of his mind and turned his thoughts in a Godward direction: **I call this to mind . . . Because of the LORD's faithful**

love we do not perish, for his mercies never end. They are new every morning. So while the prophet didn't deny his pain, yet he was assured that despair never has the last word when God is our hope.

God could be merciful even in Jeremiah's day because he knew what he would do through his Son. Jesus Christ satisfied God's wrath against sin so that he can deal with us in mercy—which is exactly what we need. When you're guilty, throw yourself on his mercy.

3:24 God's mercies are real, but they are only mine if I appropriate them, as Jeremiah did. Remember: putting your hope in God isn't passive—it's active.
3:25-30 Those who hope in God **wait for him** (3:25-26), seek him, and receive his discipline willingly.
3:31-32 Jeremiah knew of God's covenant love; he knew God would not **reject** his people **forever** (3:31). Though God **causes suffering** if necessary, **he will show compassion**

according to the abundance of his
  faithful love.[a]

33 For he does not enjoy
  bringing affliction[b]
  or suffering on mankind.

ל **Lamed**

34 Crushing all the prisoners
  of the land[A]
  beneath one's feet,
35 denying justice to a man[c]
  in the presence of the Most High,
36 or subverting a person in his
  lawsuit[d] —
  the Lord does not approve
  of these things.

מ **Mem**

37 Who is there who speaks
  and it happens,
  unless the Lord has ordained it?[e]
38 Do not both adversity and good
  come from the mouth
  of the Most High?[f]
39 Why should any living
  person complain,
  any man, because of the punishment
  for his sins?

נ **Nun**

40 Let us examine and probe our ways,
  and turn back to the LORD.[g]
41 Let us lift up our hearts and our hands[h]
  to God in heaven:
42 "We have sinned and rebelled;
  you have not forgiven.[i]

ס **Samek**

43 "You have covered yourself in anger
  and pursued us;
  you have killed without compassion.[j]
44 You have covered yourself
  with a cloud
  so that no prayer can get through.[k]
45 You have made us disgusting filth
  among the peoples.[l]

פ **Pe**

46 "All our enemies
  open their mouths against us.[m]
47 We have experienced panic
  and pitfall,[n]
  devastation and destruction."

48 My eyes flow with streams of tears
  because of the destruction
  of my dear people.

ע **Ayin**

49 My eyes overflow unceasingly,
  without end,[o]
50 until the LORD looks down
  from heaven and sees.[p]
51 My eyes bring me grief
  because of the fate of all the women
  in my city.

צ **Tsade**

52 For no reason, my enemies[B]
  hunted me like a bird.[q]
53 They smothered my life in[c] a pit[r]
  and threw stones on me.
54 Water flooded over my head,[s]
  and I thought, "I'm going to die!"[t]

ק **Qoph**

55 I called on your name, LORD,
  from the depths of the pit.
56 You heard my plea:
  Do not ignore my cry for relief.
57 You came near whenever I called
  you;
  you said, "Do not be afraid."

ר **Resh**

58 You championed my cause, Lord;[u]
  you redeemed my life.[v]
59 LORD, you saw the wrong done to me;
  judge my case.
60 You saw all their vengefulness,
  all their plots against me.[w]

שׂ **Sin** / שׁ **Shin**

61 LORD, you heard their insults,[x]
  all their plots against me.
62 The slander[D] and murmuring
  of my opponents
  attack me all day long.
63 When they sit and when
  they rise, look,
  I am mocked by their songs.[y]

ת **Taw**

64 You will pay them back
  what they deserve, LORD,
  according to the work
  of their hands.[z]

[a] 3:32 Ps 106:43-45; Ac 14:22; 2Co 4:17; Heb 12:6
[b] 3:33 Heb 12:10-11
[c] 3:35 Ex 23:6; Dt 16:19; 24:17; Mal 3:5
[d] 3:36 Ex 23:2-3
[e] 3:37 Ps 33:9-11
[f] 3:38 Gn 50:20; 1Sm 16:14; Jb 2:10; Ps 78:49; Is 45:7; Jr 1:14; 32:42; Am 3:6
[g] 3:40 Ps 119:5; 139:23-24
[h] 3:41 Ps 25:1
[i] 3:42 Dt 29:20; 2Kg 24:4; Jr 5:7
[j] 3:43 Lm 2:2,17,21; Ezk 7:8-9; 8:18
[k] 3:44 Lm 3:8
[l] 3:45 1Co 4:13
[m] 3:46 Lm 2:16
[n] 3:47 Is 24:17; Jr 48:43

[o] 3:48-49 Jr 9:1,18; Lm 1:16; 2:11
[p] 3:50 Ps 14:2; 102:19
[q] 3:52 Ps 35:7
[r] 3:53 Gn 37:20-29; Jr 38:6-13
[s] 3:54 Ps 42:7; 69:1-2; Jnh 2:3,5
[t] Ezk 37:11
[u] 3:58 Ps 43:1; Pr 23:11; Jr 50:34
[v] Ps 103:4; 119:154
[w] 3:60 Jr 11:19
[x] 3:61 Lm 5:1
[y] 3:63 Jb 30:9; Ps 69:12; Lm 3:14
[z] 3:64 Ps 28:4; Rm 2:6; Rv 20:12-13

[A]3:34 Or *earth* [B]3:52 Or *Those who were my enemies for no reason* [C]3:53 Or *They ended my life in*; Hb obscure [D]3:62 Lit *lips*

---

according to the abundance of his faithful love (3:32).
3:34-36 God did **not approve of** the injustices of the Babylonians (3:36), but he used them for his purposes—to punish his people for their sins.

3:40-42 God's people are to hope in his mercy by examining their **ways** (3:40), confessing their sins, and turning back to him.
3:53-58 Jeremiah's reference to being tossed in **a pit** by his enemies and almost

drowning acknowledges a low point of his life, the moment he thought he would **die** (3:53-54 see Jer 38:1-6). But when he called on the Lord from its **depths**, God answered (Lam 3:55-58).

a 3:65 Is 6:10
b 3:66 Ps 8:3
c 4:1 Ezk 7:19-20
d 4:2 Is 62:3; Zch 9:16
e 4:3 Jb 39:13-18
f 4:4 Ps 22:15
g 4:5 Jdg 8:26; Est 8:15
h 4:6 Gn 18–19; Is 3:9;
Jr 23:14
i 4:8 Jb 30:30; Lm 5:10
j 4:10 Dt 28:53; 2Kg 6:9
k Jr 8:11,21; Lm 2:11; 3:48
l 4:11 Lm 2:3-4
m 4:12 2Sm 5:6-8; Ps
48:1-5
n 4:13 Ps 106:38-39; Ezk
22:1-5
o 4:14 Dt 28:29; Is 59:10;
Zph 1:17
p Lv 21:11

65 You will give them a heart
    filled with anguish. A,a
May your curse be on them!
66 You will pursue them in anger
    and destroy them
    under your heavens. B,b

TERRORS OF THE BESIEGED CITY

א Aleph

4 How the gold has become tarnished,
  the fine gold become dull!
The stones of the temple c lie scattered
  at the head of every street. c

ב Beth

2 Zion's precious children —
  once worth their weight
    in pure gold d —
how they are regarded as clay jars,
the work of a potter's hands!

ג Gimel

3 Even jackals offer their breasts
  to nurse their young,
but my dear people
  have become cruel
like ostriches e in the wilderness.

ד Daleth

4 The nursing baby's tongue
  clings to the roof of his mouth
    from thirst. f
Infants beg for food,
  but no one gives them any.

ה He

5 Those who used to eat delicacies
  are destitute in the streets;
those who were reared
  in purple garments g
huddle in trash heaps.

ו Waw

6 The punishment of my dear people
  is greater than that of Sodom, h
which was overthrown in an instant
without a hand laid on it.

ז Zayin

7 Her dignitaries were brighter
    than snow,
  whiter than milk;

their bodies D were more ruddy
  than coral,
their appearance like lapis lazuli.

ח Cheth

8 Now they appear darker than soot; i
  they are not recognized
    in the streets.
Their skin has shriveled
  on their bones;
it has become dry like wood.

ט Teth

9 Those slain by the sword are
    better off
  than those slain by hunger,
who waste away, pierced with pain
because the fields lack produce.

י Yod

10 The hands of compassionate women
  have cooked their own children; j
they became their food
  during the destruction
    of my dear people. k

כ Kaph

11 The LORD has exhausted his wrath,
  poured out his burning anger;
he has ignited a fire in Zion,
and it has consumed
  her foundations. l

ל Lamed

12 The kings of the earth
  and all the world's inhabitants
    did not believe
that an enemy or adversary
could enter Jerusalem's gates. m

מ Mem

13 Yet it happened because of the sins
    of her prophets
and the iniquities of her priests,
who shed the blood of the righteous
    within her. n

נ Nun

14 Blind, they stumbled in the streets, o
  defiled by this blood, p
so that no one dared
  to touch their garments.

A 3:65 Or them an obstinate heart; Hb obscure   B 3:66 Lit under the LORD's heavens   C 4:1 Or The sacred gems   D 4:7 Lit bones

---

4:1-5 Jeremiah describes the scene of Jerusalem's earned downfall by employing a series of graphic illustrations contrasting the people's former health, security, and comforts of life with their pitiful condition after the enemy finished with them.

4:10 Intense hunger during the city's long siege by the Babylonian army turned normal human emotions into twisted attempts at survival. Not only did Jerusalem's little ones languish in hunger and thirst that their parents couldn't satisfy,

but also some families actually engaged in the horrific practice of cannibalism on their **children**!

ס Samek

15 "Stay away! Unclean!"
people shouted at them.
"Away, away! Don't touch us!"[a]
So they wandered aimlessly.[b]
It was said among the nations,
"They can stay here no longer."

פ Pe

16 The LORD himself
has scattered them;
he no longer watches over them.
The priests are not respected;
the elders find no favor.

ע Ayin

17 All the while our eyes were failing
as we looked in vain for help;[c]
we watched from our towers
for a nation that would not save us.

צ Tsade

18 Our steps were closely followed
so that we could not walk
in our streets.
Our end approached;[d] our time
ran out.
Our end had come!

ק Qoph

19 Those who chased us were swifter
than eagles in the sky;[e]
they relentlessly pursued us
over the mountains
and ambushed us
in the wilderness.

ר Resh

20 The LORD's anointed, the breath
of our life,[A,f]
was captured in their traps.
We had said about him,
"We will live under his protection
among the nations."

ש Sin

21 So rejoice and be glad,
Daughter Edom,[g]
you resident of the land of Uz![h]
Yet the cup[i] will pass to you as well;
you will get drunk
and expose yourself.

ת Taw

22 Daughter Zion, your punishment
is complete;
he will not lengthen your exile.[B]
But he will punish your iniquity,
Daughter Edom,
and will expose your sins.[j]

PRAYER FOR RESTORATION

5 LORD, remember what has happened
to us.
Look, and see our disgrace![k]
2 Our inheritance
has been turned over to strangers,
our houses to foreigners.
3 We have become
orphans, fatherless;
our mothers are widows.
4 We must pay for the water we drink;
our wood comes at a price.
5 We are closely pursued;
we are tired, and no one
offers us rest.
6 We made a treaty with[c] Egypt
and with Assyria,
to get enough food.[l]
7 Our fathers sinned;
they no longer exist,
but we bear their punishment.
8 Slaves rule over us;[m]
no one rescues us from them.
9 We secure our food at the risk
of our lives
because of the sword
in the wilderness.
10 Our skin is as hot[D] as an oven[n]
from the ravages of hunger.
11 Women have been raped in Zion,
virgins in the cities of Judah.
12 Princes have been hung up
by their hands;
elders are shown no respect.[o]
13 Young men labor at millstones;[p]
boys stumble under loads of wood.
14 The elders have left the city gate,
the young men, their music.[q]
15 Joy has left our hearts;[r]
our dancing has turned
to mourning.
16 The crown has fallen
from our head.[s]
Woe to us, for we have sinned.[t]

[a] 4:15 Lv 13:45-46
[b] Gn 4:12
[c] 4:17 Jr 37:7-8
[d] 4:18 Ezk 7:2-12; Am 8:2
[e] 4:19 Jr 4:13; Hab 1:8
[f] 4:20 Gn 2:7; 2Kg 25:7
[g] 4:21 Ezk 35:15; Ob 12
[h] Jr 25:20
[i] Is 51:17; Jr 25:15-16; Hab 2:16
[j] 4:22 Ps 137:7; Ezk 25:12-14; Jl 3:19
[k] 5:1 Ps 74:18,22; 89:50-51
[l] 5:6 Hs 12:1
[m] 5:8 Pr 30:21-23; Ec 10:7
[n] 5:10 Lm 4:8
[o] 5:12 Lm 4:16
[p] 5:13 Ex 11:5; Jdg 16:21; Is 47:2
[q] 5:14 Is 24:8
[r] 5:15 Am 8:10
[s] 5:16 Jb 19:9; Is 28:3; Jr 13:18
[t] Jr 8:14; 14:20; Dn 9:11

[A] 4:20 Lit *nostrils*   [B] 4:22 Or *not deport you again*   [C] 5:6 Lit *We gave the hand to*   [D] 5:10 Or *black*; Hb obscure

---

4:20 King Zedekiah, a Davidic king, should have been the example to his people of godliness and justice; however, he repeatedly refused to listen to God through Jeremiah—leading to his capture at the city's fall.

5:6-8 The real tragedy of Judah's foreign alliances was that in turning to nations like **Egypt** and **Assyria** for help, their **fathers** had disobeyed God and put his people at the mercy of the ungodly (5:6-7). Our choices, too, will impact those who come after us.

5:15-16 How tragic that it took such intense suffering for the people to utter the confession God had been waiting to hear: **Woe to us, for we have sinned** (5:16).

[a] 5:17 Ps 69:23; Ec 12:3
[b] 5:18 Is 13:19-22; 34:11-15
[c] 5:19 Ps 9:7; 45:6; 102:12; Ezk 43:7; Heb 1:8; Rv 4:9-10; 5:13

[d] 5:20 Ps 13:1
[e] 5:21 Jr 15:19; 31:18

17 Because of this, our heart is sick;
because of these, our eyes grow dim:[a]
18 because of Mount Zion,
which lies desolate
and has jackals prowling in it.[b]
19 You, LORD, are enthroned forever;
your throne endures
from generation to generation.[c]

20 Why do you continually forget us,[d]
abandon us for our entire lives?
21 LORD, bring us back to yourself,
so we may return;[e]
renew our days as in former times,
22 unless you have completely
rejected us
and are intensely angry with us.

5:20-22 Verse 20 is a plea for God to remember his covenant. And importantly, the only way God would turn away from his people forever was if he **completely rejected** them (5:22). That, however, would have required God to be unfaithful to his promises. And since that could never happen (see 3:23). the book of Lamentations ends with hope that God will bring them back and **renew** them (5:21).

EZEKIEL

INTRODUCTION

Author

THE WRITER OF THE BOOK bearing his name is Ezekiel son of Buzi. This priest, along with thousands of other residents of Judah, had been deported to Babylon. He began prophesying when he was thirty years old (1:1-3). Some critical scholars have rejected the claim that the historical prophet Ezekiel could have served as the author of the entire book. However, the book is written with a unified and consistent style. It is reasonable, then, to accept Ezekiel as the author.

Historical Background

In 598–597 BC, King Nebuchadnezzar deported ten thousand people from Judah to Babylon (see 2 Kgs 24:10-14), including Ezekiel. Judah's King Jehoiachin was taken to Babylon as well (2 Kgs 24:15). It was during "the fifth year of King Jehoiachin's exile" (593 BC), when Ezekiel was thirty, that the word of the Lord first came to him in Babylon (Ezek 1:1-3). The prophet's messages were intended primarily for the Jewish exiles there. Interestingly, many of Ezekiel's prophetic oracles included date references (e.g., 8:1; 20:1; 24:1; 26:1). The last date is found in 29:17; it refers to "the twenty-seventh year" of Jehoiachin's exile (571 BC). Thus, Ezekiel's prophetic ministry lasted at least twenty-two years.

Message and Purpose

The book of Ezekiel records the prophet's message to the people of the southern kingdom of Judah, now incarcerated in Babylon because of their rebellion against God. The theme of the book is the glory of God, which departed from the temple in Jerusalem because of the people's sin. Thus, his manifest presence was no longer in their midst.

Ezekiel also prophesied, in chapters 40–48, of a coming restoration. The regathering of God's people would occur with the coming of the Messiah to establish his kingdom, which we know as the future one-thousand-year reign of Jesus Christ called the millennial kingdom.

The prophet wanted God's people to know that as bad as things were during their captivity, God still had a plan and would keep his covenant promises despite their rebellion and the consequences they were enduring. Ezekiel thus called on the people to have faith in God even in the discipline of captivity.

He also foretold that the glory of God would return when the Messiah reigns. We learn from this book that God's glorification is his greatest purpose. And when we too live for his kingdom purposes, his glory—his manifest presence—is made real to us and to the world.

VIDEO   INTRO

www.bhpublishinggroup.com/qr/te/26_00

Outline

I. God's Appearance to and Commissioning of Ezekiel (1:1–3:27)
  A. Ezekiel's Vision of God (1:1-28)
  B. God's Call and Commission to Ezekiel (2:1–3:27)

II. Prophecies against Judah (4:1–24:27)
  A. The Necessity of Judah's Judgment and Exile (4:1–11:25)
  B. The Hopelessness of Judah's False Optimism (12:1–19:14)
  C. The History of Judah's Sins (20:1–24:27)

III. Prophecies against Gentile Nations (25:1–32:32)

IV. Prophecies of Israel's Restoration (33:1–39:29)

V. Prophecies of Israel in the Millennial Kingdom (40:1–48:35)
  A. The New Temple (40:1–43:27)
  B. The New Worship (44:1–46:24)
  C. The New Land (47:1–48:35)

a 1:1 Ezk 3:15,23;
10:15,20,22
b Mt 3:16; Mk 1:10; Lk 3:21;
Jn 1:51; Ac 7:56; 10:11; Rv
4:1; 19:11
c Ex 24:10; Nm 12:6; Ezk
8:3; 11:24; 40:2
d 1:2 2Kg 24:8,12,15,17;
25:27,29
e 1:3 Gn 15:1; 1Sm 15:10;
2Sm 7:4; 1Kg 6:11; 21:17;
Is 38:4; Jr 1:2; Jnh 1:1; Hg
1:1; Zch 1:1
f Ezk 24:24
g Gn 11:28
h 1Kg 18:46; 2Kg 3:15; 1Ch
28:19; Ezk 3:14-22; 37:1;
40:1; Ezr 7:6,28
i 1:4 2Kg 2:1; Jb 38:1; 40:6;
Ps 77:18; Is 66:15; Nah 1:3
j Ezk 1:27; 8:2
k 1:5 Ezk 10:14,21; Rv 4:6-8
l 1:7 Dn 10:6; Rv 1:15
m 1:8 Ezk 1:17; 10:11
n Ezk 10:8,21
o 1:9 Ezk 10:22
p 1:10 Rv 4:7
q Ezk 10:14-21
r 1:11 Is 6:2; Ezk 1:23
s 1:12 Ezk 10:11,22
t Ezk 1:20
u 1:13 Ps 104:4; Rv 4:5
v 1:14 Zch 4:10
w Mt 24:27; Lk 17:24

x 1:16 Ezk 10:9-11
y Dn 10:6
z 1:18 Ezk 10:12; Rv 4:6,8
aa 1:19-21 Ezk 10:16-17,19
ab 1:22 Ezk 10:1
ac Gn 1:6-8
ad Rv 4:6
ae 1:24 Ezk 43:2; Rv 1:15;
19:6
af Ezk 10:5
ag Dn 10:6
ah 1:26 Ezk 10:1
ai Is 6:1; Ezk 24:10
aj 1:27 Ezk 1:4; 8:2

I In the thirtieth year, in the fourth month, on the fifth day of the month, while I was among the exiles by the Chebar Canal,[a] the heavens were opened[b] and I saw visions of God.[c] 2 On the fifth day of the month — it was the fifth year of King Jehoiachin's exile[d] — 3 the word of the LORD came[e] directly to the priest Ezekiel[f] son of Buzi, in the land of the Chaldeans[g] by the Chebar Canal. The LORD's hand was on him there.[h]

VISION OF THE LORD'S GLORY

4 I looked, and there was a whirlwind[i] coming from the north, a huge cloud with fire flashing back and forth and brilliant light all around it. In the center of the fire, there was a gleam like amber.[j] 5 The likeness of four living creatures came from it,[k] and this was their appearance: They looked something like a human, 6 but each of them had four faces and four wings. 7 Their legs were straight, and the soles of their feet were like the hooves of a calf, sparkling like the gleam of polished bronze.[l] 8 They had human hands under their wings on their four sides.[m] All four of them had faces and wings.[n] 9 Their wings were touching. The creatures did not turn as they moved; each one went straight ahead.[o] 10 Their faces looked something like the face of a human,[p] and each of the four had the face of a lion on the right, the face of an ox on the left, and the face of an eagle.[q] 11 That is what their faces were like. Their wings were spread upward; each had two wings touching that of another and two wings covering its body.[r] 12 Each creature went straight ahead.[s] Wherever the Spirit[A] wanted to go, they went without turning as they moved.[t]

13 The likeness of the living creatures was like the appearance of blazing coals of fire or like torches.[u] Fire was moving back and forth between the living creatures; it was bright, with lightning coming out of it. 14 The creatures were darting back and forth[v] like flashes of lightning.[w]

15 When I looked at the living creatures, there was one wheel on the ground beside each of the four-faced creatures. 16 The appearance of the wheels[x] and their craftsmanship was like the gleam of beryl,[y] and all four had the same likeness. Their appearance and craftsmanship was like a wheel within a wheel. 17 When they moved, they went in any of the four directions, without turning as they moved. 18 Their rims were tall and awe-inspiring. Each of their four rims were full of eyes[z] all around. 19 When the living creatures moved,[aa] the wheels moved beside them, and when the creatures rose from the earth, the wheels also rose. 20 Wherever the Spirit wanted to go, the creatures went in the direction the Spirit was moving. The wheels rose alongside them, for the spirit of the living creatures was in the wheels. 21 When the creatures moved, the wheels moved; when the creatures stopped, the wheels stopped; and when the creatures rose from the earth, the wheels rose alongside them, for the spirit of the living creatures was in the wheels.

22 Over the heads of the living creatures[ab] the likeness of an expanse[ac] was spread out. It gleamed like awe-inspiring crystal,[ad] 23 and under the expanse their wings extended one toward another. They each also had two wings covering their bodies. 24 When they moved, I heard the sound of their wings like the roar of a huge torrent,[ae] like the voice of the Almighty,[af] and a sound of tumult like the noise of an army.[ag] When they stopped, they lowered their wings.

25 A voice came from above the expanse over their heads; when they stopped, they lowered their wings. 26 Something like a throne with the appearance of lapis lazuli was above the expanse over their heads.[ah] On the throne, high above, was someone who looked like a human.[ai] 27 From what seemed to be his waist up, I saw a gleam like amber, with what looked like fire enclosing it all around.[aj] From what seemed to be his waist down, I also saw what

A 1:12 Or spirit, also in v. 20

1:1 Ezekiel's reference to **the thirtieth year** most likely reveals his age, which was the point at which a man from the tribe of Levi could become a priest (see Num 4:2-3, 22-23, 29-30). As one of the earliest captives taken from Jerusalem to Babylon by Nebuchadnezzar in 598–597 BC, Ezekiel was **among the first exiles** of Judah.
1:5-14 Bearers of God's throne and protectors of his glory, these angelic beings

minister in God's holy presence (see also Isa 6:1-3).
1:15-21 That the **rims** of the wheels were **full of eyes** (1:18) suggests the all-seeing omniscience of God. What becomes clear in the rest of this chapter is that the angelic beings were below God's throne, which was not a stationary object but a moving platform—like a chariot—that moved **wherever the Spirit wanted to go** (1:20). Israel's

all-knowing, all-present God could follow his people wherever they went; indeed, his presence is inescapable.
1:22 The **expanse** mentioned is translated from the same Hebrew word used in Genesis 1:6 to describe God's creation of the sky. Throughout this vision Ezekiel used terms like this one in an attempt to find adequate language to describe what he was seeing.

looked like fire. There was a brilliant light all around him. **28** The appearance of the brilliant light all around was like that of a rainbow in a cloud on a rainy day.[a] This was the appearance of the likeness of the LORD's glory.[b] When I saw it, I fell facedown and heard a voice speaking.[c]

MISSION TO REBELLIOUS ISRAEL

2 He said to me, "Son of man, stand up on your feet[d] and I will speak with you." **2** As he spoke to me, the Spirit entered me and set me on my feet,[e] and I listened to the one who was speaking to me. **3** He said to me, "Son of man, I am sending you to the Israelites, to[A] the rebellious pagans who have rebelled against me. The Israelites and their ancestors have transgressed against me to this day.[f] **4** The descendants are obstinate[B] and hardhearted.[g] I am sending you to them, and you must say to them, 'This is what the Lord GOD says.' **5** Whether they listen or refuse to listen[h] — for they are a rebellious house — they will know that a prophet has been among them.[i]

6 "But you, son of man, do not be afraid of them and do not be afraid of their words,[j] even though briers and thorns are beside you and you live among scorpions.[k] Don't be afraid of their words or discouraged by the look on their faces, for they are a rebellious house. **7** Speak my words to them whether they listen or refuse to listen,[l] for they are rebellious.

8 "And you, son of man, listen to what I tell you: Do not be rebellious like that rebellious house. Open your mouth and eat what I am giving you."[m] **9** So I looked and saw a hand reaching out to me,[n] and there was a written scroll in it.[o] **10** When he unrolled it before me, it was written on the front and back; words of lamentation, mourning, and woe were written on it.

3 He said to me: "Son of man, eat what you find here. Eat this scroll,[p] then go and speak to the house of Israel." **2** So I opened my mouth, and he fed me the scroll. **3** "Son of man," he said to me, "feed your stomach and fill your belly with this scroll I am giving you." So I ate it,[q] and it was as sweet as honey in my mouth.[r]

4 Then he said to me: "Son of man, go to the house of Israel and speak my words to them. **5** For you are not being sent to a people of unintelligible speech or a difficult language but to the house of Israel — **6** not to the many peoples of unintelligible speech or a difficult language, whose words you cannot understand. No doubt, if I sent you to them, they would listen to you.[s] **7** But the house of Israel will not want to listen to you because they do not want to listen to me.[t] For the whole house of Israel is hardheaded and hardhearted. **8** Look, I have made your face as hard as their faces and your forehead as hard as their foreheads.[u] **9** I have made your forehead like a diamond, harder than flint. Don't be afraid of them or discouraged by the look on their faces, though they are a rebellious house."

10 Next he said to me: "Son of man, listen carefully to all my words that I speak to you and take them to heart. **11** Go to your people, the exiles, and speak to them. Tell them, 'This is what the Lord GOD says,' whether they listen or refuse to listen."[v]

12 The Spirit then lifted me up,[w] and I heard a loud rumbling sound behind me — bless the glory of the LORD in his place! — **13** with the[c] sound of the living creatures' wings brushing against each other[x] and the sound of the wheels beside them,[y] a loud rumbling sound. **14** The Spirit lifted me up and took me away. I left in bitterness and in an angry spirit, and the LORD's hand was on me powerfully.[z] **15** I

[a] 1:28 Gn 9:13; Rv 4:3; 10:1
[b] Ex 24:16; Ezk 8:4; 11:22-23; 43:4-5
[c] Gn 17:3; Ezk 3:23; Dn 8:17; Rv 1:17
[d] 2:1 Dn 10:11
[e] 2:2 Ezk 3:24; Dn 8:18
[f] 2:3 Ezk 20:18,30
[g] 2:4 Ezk 3:7
[h] 2:5 Ezk 3:11,27
[i] Ezk 33:33
[j] 2:6 Jr 1:8,17; Ezk 3:9
[k] 2Sm 23:6; Ezk 28:24; Mc 7:4
[l] 2:7 Jr 1:7,17
[m] 2:8 Jr 15:16; Ezk 3:3; Rv 10:9
[n] 2:9 Ezk 8:3
[o] Jr 36:2; Ezk 3:1

[p] 3:1 Ezk 2:8-9
[q] 3:3 Jr 15:16
[r] Ps 19:10; 119:103; Rv 10:9-10
[s] 3:6 Mt 11:21,23
[t] 3:7 Jn 15:20
[u] 3:8 Jr 1:18; 5:3
[v] 3:11 Ezk 2:5,7
[w] 3:12 Ezk 8:3; Ac 8:39
[x] 3:13 Ezk 1:24
[y] Ezk 1:15; 10:16-17
[z] 3:14 2Kg 3:15

2:1-2 Ezekiel's humility before God was appropriate, but God had work for him to do; therefore, **the Spirit** enabled the prophet to **stand up** so he could hear what God wanted to tell him. **2:4-7** The compound name **Lord GOD** (2:4) or Adonai Yahweh, was one of Ezekiel's favorite titles for God. He used it over two hundred times. It's a powerful combination that emphasizes God's sovereign authority and covenant-keeping faithfulness: these are two themes of the prophet's ministry.

Ezekiel's job was not to be *successful* as humans define success; rather, he was to be faithful in declaring God's message **whether** the people would **listen or refuse to listen** (2:5, 7).

3:3 Ezekiel was to digest the Word of God—to read it and make it a part of himself. The initial sweetness of the **scroll** indicates that even though a specific message from God can be hard to hear, nevertheless it is still welcome to the believer who appropriates it.

3:4-6 God confirmed Israel's rebellious nature to Ezekiel by saying that if he were sent to a foreign people whose **language** differed from his own, they would believe him and repent! But not **Israel** (or in Ezekiel's case specifically, the surviving kingdom of Judah); they didn't want to hear from Ezekiel because they didn't want to hear from God (see 3:7).

3:7-9 The people to whom Ezekiel was being sent were **hardheaded and hardhearted**, so God told Ezekiel that he was going to make him just as tough so he could speak to them without being **discouraged**.

3:14-15 Why did Ezekiel leave that glorious vision **in bitterness and in an angry spirit** (3:14)? Because the sin of Judah's people angered him as much as it angered the Lord. True spirituality is manifested when we feel the way God feels about unrighteousness. The prophet was so overwhelmed by all that had happened and the gravity of his message that he could do little more than sit and reflect for a whole week.

a 3:15 Jb 2:13; Ps 137:1
b 3:16 Jr 42:7
c 3:17 Is 52:8; 56:10; 62:6; Jr 6:17; Ezk 33:7-9
d 2Ch 19:10; Is 58:1
e 3:18-19 Ezk 33:3,6,8-9
f 3:19 Ezk 14:14,20; Ac 18:6; 1Tm 4:16
g 3:20 Ezk 18:24
h Jr 6:21
i 3:22 Ezk 8:4
j Ac 9:6
k 3:23 Ezk 1:28; Ac 7:55
l Ezk 1:1
m 3:24 Ezk 2:2
n 3:25 Ezk 4:8

o 3:26 Ps 22:15
p Lk 1:20,22
q 3:27 Ezk 24:27; 33:22
r 4:2 Jr 6:6; Ezk 21:22
s 4:3 Is 8:18; 20:3; Ezk 12:6,11; 24:24-27
t 4:5 Nm 14:34
u 4:8 Ezk 3:25

came to the exiles at Tel-abib, who were living by the Chebar Canal, and I sat there among them stunned for seven days.*a*

EZEKIEL AS A WATCHMAN

[16] Now at the end of seven days the word of the Lord came to me:*b* [17] "Son of man, I have made you a watchman over the house of Israel.*c* When you hear a word from my mouth, give them a warning from me.*d* [18] If I say to the wicked person,*e* 'You will surely die,' but you do not warn him — you don't speak out to warn him about his wicked way in order to save his life — that wicked person will die for his iniquity. Yet I will hold you responsible for his blood. [19] But if you warn a wicked person and he does not turn from his wickedness or his wicked way, he will die for his iniquity, but you will have rescued yourself.*f* [20] Now if a righteous person turns from his righteousness and acts unjustly,*g* and I put a stumbling block in front of him, he will die.*h* If you did not warn him, he will die because of his sin, and the righteous acts he did will not be remembered. Yet I will hold you responsible for his blood. [21] But if you warn the righteous person that he should not sin, and he does not sin, he will indeed live because he listened to your warning, and you will have rescued yourself."

[22] The hand of the Lord was on me there, and he said to me, "Get up, go out to the plain,*i* and I will speak with you there."*j* [23] So I got up and went out to the plain. The Lord's glory was present there,*k* like the glory I had seen by the Chebar Canal,*l* and I fell facedown. [24] The Spirit entered me and set me on my feet.*m* He spoke with me and said: "Go, shut yourself inside your house. [25] As for you, son of man, they will put ropes on you*n* and bind you with them so you cannot go out among them. [26] I will

make your tongue stick to the roof of your mouth,*o* and you will be mute*p* and unable to be a mediator for*A* them, for they are a rebellious house. [27] But when I speak with you, I will open your mouth,*q* and you will say to them, 'This is what the Lord God says.' Let the one who listens, listen, and let the one who refuses, refuse — for they are a rebellious house.

JERUSALEM'S SIEGE DRAMATIZED

4 "Now you, son of man, take a brick, set it in front of you, and draw the city of Jerusalem on it. [2] Then lay siege against it:*r* Construct a siege wall, build a ramp, pitch military camps, and place battering rams against it on all sides. [3] Take an iron plate and set it up as an iron wall between yourself and the city. Face it so that it is under siege, and besiege it. This will be a sign for the house of Israel.*s*

[4] "Then lie down on your left side and place the iniquity*B* of the house of Israel on it. You will bear their iniquity for the number of days you lie on your side. [5] For I have assigned you the years of their iniquity according to the number of days you lie down, 390 days; so you will bear the iniquity of the house of Israel.*t* [6] When you have completed these days, lie down again, but on your right side, and bear the iniquity of the house of Judah. I have assigned you forty days, a day for each year. [7] Face the siege of Jerusalem with your arm bared, and prophesy against it. [8] Be aware that I will put cords on you so you cannot turn from side to side until you have finished the days of your siege.*u*

[9] "Also take wheat, barley, beans, lentils, millet, and spelt. Put them in a single container and make them into bread for yourself. You are to eat it during the number of days you lie on your side, 390 days. [10] The food you eat each day will weigh eight

---

A 3:26 Or *to rebuke*   *B* 4:4 Or *punishment*

3:17-21 The prophet's commission as **a watchman over the house of Israel** (3:17) involved a two-fold principle: the individual's responsibility to turn from his own sin and the responsibility of God's spokesman to deliver his message faithfully. Believers in Jesus Christ bear the responsibility to proclaim the good news so that sinners may believe, be saved, and follow him in godliness. After all, how can we keep silent when we know how people can escape the wrath of God?

3:26 That Ezekiel's **tongue** would **stick to the roof of [his] mouth** suggested that he wouldn't have anything to say to the rebellious Israelites unless it was the message God had given him.

3:27 Whether the people heard and repented, or rejected and plunged into ruin, the prophet was only to say, **This is what the Lord God says**, letting the chips fall where they might. In fact, this should be the posture of every preacher.

4:1-2 The exiles observing this knew what these devices meant, but they must have been in disbelief to think that the holy city would ever come under such a devastating attack (after all, the actual fall of Jerusalem was still about six years away). **Jerusalem** was the place of God's presence and, presumably, his protection. But it was exactly that kind of thinking that Ezekiel had to dislodge from the people's minds. Their sins had doomed Jerusalem.

4:4-7 God had the northern kingdom of Israel in mind when he told Ezekiel to lie on his **left side**; it had been destroyed long before by the Assyrians in 722 BC, so the **390** referred to the years of Israel's **iniquity according to the number of days** God told Ezekiel to face north (4:4-5). Ezekiel was to lie on his **right side** facing south toward **Jerusalem** to **bear the iniquity of the house of Judah,** which in this interpretation had accumulated **forty** years of sin before its judgment (4:6-7).

4:10-11 The meager size of the daily loaves, **eight ounces,** and ration of water, **a sixth of a gallon,** symbolized the extreme scarcity that the people of Jerusalem would experience during the coming Babylonian siege (see 4:16).

ounces;[A] you will eat it at set times.[B] [11] You will also drink a ration of water, a sixth of a gallon,[C] which you will drink at set times. [12] You will eat it as you would a barley cake and bake it over dried human excrement in their sight." [13] The LORD said, "This is how the Israelites will eat their bread — ceremonially unclean — among the nations where I will banish them."[a]

[14] But I said, "Oh, Lord GOD, I have never been defiled. From my youth until now I have not eaten anything that died naturally or was mauled by wild beasts.[b] And impure meat has never entered my mouth."[c]

[15] He replied to me, "Look, I will let you use cow dung instead of human excrement, and you can make your bread over that." [16] He said to me, "Son of man, I am going to cut off the supply of bread in Jerusalem.[d] They will anxiously eat food they have weighed out and in dread drink rationed water[e] [17] for lack of bread and water. Everyone will be devastated and waste away because of their iniquity.[f]

EZEKIEL DRAMATIZES JERUSALEM'S FALL

5 "Now you, son of man, take a sharp sword,[g] use it as you would a barber's razor, and shave your head and beard. Then take a set of scales and divide the hair. [2] You are to burn a third of it in the city when the days of the siege have ended;[h] you are to take a third and slash it with the sword all around the city; and you are to scatter a third to the wind, for I will draw a sword to chase after them. [3] But you are to take a few strands from the hair and secure them in the folds of your robe.[i] [4] Take some more of them, throw them into the fire, and burn them in it.[j] A fire will spread from it to the whole house of Israel.

[5] "This is what the Lord GOD says: I have set this Jerusalem in the center of the nations, with countries all around her. [6] She has rebelled against my ordinances with more wickedness than the nations, and

against my statutes more than the countries that surround her. For her people have rejected my ordinances and have not walked in my statutes.

[7] "Therefore, this is what the Lord GOD says: Because you have been more insubordinate than the nations around you[k] — you have not walked in my statutes or kept my ordinances; you have not even kept the ordinances of the nations around you — [8] therefore, this is what the Lord GOD says: See, I myself am against you, Jerusalem, and I will execute judgments within you in the sight of the nations. [9] Because of all your detestable practices, I will do to you what I have never done before and what I will never do again.[l] [10] As a result, fathers will eat their sons[m] within Jerusalem,[D] and sons will eat their fathers. I will execute judgments against you and scatter all your survivors to every direction of the wind.

[11] "Therefore, as I live" — this is the declaration of the Lord GOD — "I will withdraw and show you no pity, because you have defiled my sanctuary[n] with all your abhorrent acts and detestable practices.[o] Yes, I will not spare you. [12] A third of your people will die by plague and be consumed by famine within you;[p] a third will fall by the sword all around you; and I will scatter a third to every direction of the wind, and I will draw a sword to chase after them.[q] [13] When my anger is spent and I have vented my wrath on them, I will be appeased.[r] Then after I have spent my wrath on them, they will know that I, the LORD, have spoken in my jealousy.[s]

[14] "I will make you a ruin and a disgrace among the nations around you, in the sight of everyone who passes by. [15] So you[E] will be a disgrace and a taunt, a warning and a horror, to the nations around you when I execute judgments against you in anger,[t] wrath, and furious rebukes. I, the LORD, have spoken. [16] When I shoot deadly arrows of famine at them, arrows for destruction that I will send to

[a] 4:13 Dn 1:8; Hs 9:3
[b] 4:14 Lv 17:15; 22:8; Ezk 44:31
[c] Ac 10:14
[d] 4:16 Lv 26:26; Ezk 5:16; 14:13
[e] Ezk 12:19
[f] 4:17 Lv 26:39; Ezk 24:23; 33:10
[g] 5:1 Lv 21:5; Is 7:20; Ezk 44:20
[h] 5:2 Ezk 4:2-8
[i] 5:3 Jr 40:6; 52:16
[j] 5:4 Jr 44:14

[k] 5:7 Jr 2:10-11
[l] 5:9 Dn 9:12; Am 3:2
[m] 5:10 Lv 26:29; Dt 28:53-57; Jr 19:9
[n] 5:11 Jr 7:9-11; Ezk 8:5-6,16
[o] Ezk 7:20; 11:18,21
[p] 5:12 Jr 15:2; 21:9; Ezk 5:17; 6:11-12
[q] Jr 15:2; 43:10-11; 44:27
[r] 5:13 Is 1:24
[s] Ezk 36:5-6; 38:19
[t] 5:15 Ps 79:3-10; Ezk 22:4

[A] 4:10 Lit 20 shekels [B] 4:10 Lit from time to time, also in v. 11 [C] 4:11 Lit hin [D] 5:10 Lit you [E] 5:15 DSS, LXX, Syr, Tg, Vg; MT reads she

---

4:14-17 Ezekiel's life had been dedicated to keeping God's laws, including his dietary restrictions. While he was allowed to use an alternate fuel, the point of his actions remained: Jerusalem's inhabitants would be reduced to taking desperate survival measures that they would never have imagined in their worst nightmares.

5:1-4 Each pile symbolized a judgment against Jerusalem and its people: fire, violence, and scattering.

5:5-6 God had **set . . . Jerusalem in the center of the nations** as a city on a hill, populated by his chosen people, to be a witness to his holiness by their love and devotion to him. But Israel had **rebelled**.

5:9-10 The principle at work here is this: The greater the sin, the greater the consequence.

5:12 In this verse, God provides the interpretation of the symbolic acts Ezekiel performed with the three parts of his hair (see 5:2). The few hairs hidden in the prophet's robe (see

5:3) had represented a righteous remnant preserved from immediate judgment. (Both 5:4 and the final verses of this chapter argue against their total safety.) Likely, God chose to deliver some so they would be a witness to the awfulness of Judah's sin and the righteousness of God's judgment, as indicated in 6:8-10.

5:14-17 Notice the repetition of the phrase **I, the LORD, have spoken** among the terrifying judgments cataloged here (5:15, 17). It's a reminder that these are the pronouncements

[a] 5:17 Lv 26:6; Dt 32:23-25
[b] 6:2 Ezk 36:1
[c] 6:3-4 Lv 26:30
[d] 6:8 Jr 44:14,28; Ezk 7:16
[e] 6:9 Dt 4:29
[f] Ps 78:40
[g] Ezk 20:43; 36:31

[h] 6:11 Ezk 21:14,17; 25:6
[i] Ezk 5:12
[j] 6:12 Ezk 5:13
[k] 6:13 Ezk 6:4-7
[l] Is 57:5-7; Jr 2:20; Ezk 20:28; Hs 4:13
[m] 6:14 Is 5:25
[n] 7:2 Am 8:2,10
[o] 7:4 Ezk 5:11
[p] Ezk 11:21

destroy you, inhabitants of Jerusalem, I will intensify the famine against you and cut off your supply of bread. [17] I will send famine and dangerous animals against you. They will leave you childless. Plague and bloodshed will sweep through you, and I will bring a sword against you. I, the LORD, have spoken."[a]

PROPHECY AGAINST ISRAEL'S IDOLATRY

6 The word of the LORD came to me: [2] "Son of man, face the mountains of Israel[b] and prophesy against them. [3] You are to say: Mountains of Israel, hear the word of the Lord GOD! This is what the Lord GOD says to the mountains and the hills, to the ravines and the valleys: I am about to bring a sword against you, and I will destroy your high places.[c] [4] Your altars will be desolated and your shrines[A] smashed. I will throw down your slain in front of your idols. [5] I will lay the corpses of the Israelites in front of their idols and scatter your bones around your altars. [6] Wherever you live the cities will be in ruins and the high places will be desolate, so that your altars will lie in ruins and be desecrated,[B] your idols smashed and obliterated, your shrines cut down, and what you have made wiped out. [7] The slain will fall among you, and you will know that I am the LORD.

[8] "Yet I will leave a remnant when you are scattered among the nations, for throughout the countries there will be some of you who will escape the sword.[d] [9] Then your survivors will remember me among the nations where they are taken captive,[e] how I was crushed by their promiscuous hearts that turned away from me and by their eyes that lusted after their idols.[f] They will loathe themselves because of the evil things they did,[g] their detestable actions of every kind. [10] And they will know that I am the LORD; I did not threaten to bring this disaster on them without a reason.

LAMENT OVER THE FALL OF JERUSALEM

[11] "This is what the Lord GOD says: Clap your hands, stamp your feet,[h] and cry out over all the evil and detestable practices of the house of Israel, who will fall by the sword, famine, and plague.[i] [12] The one who is far off will die by plague; the one who is near will fall by the sword; and the one who remains and is spared[c] will die of famine. In this way I will exhaust my wrath on them.[j] [13] You will all know that I am the LORD when their slain lie among their idols around their altars,[k] on every high hill,[l] on all the mountaintops, and under every green tree and every leafy oak — the places where they offered pleasing aromas to all their idols. [14] I will stretch out my hand against them,[m] and wherever they live I will make the land a desolate waste, from the wilderness to Diblah.[D] Then they will know that I am the LORD."

ANNOUNCEMENT OF THE END

7 The word of the LORD came to me: [2] "Son of man, this is what the Lord GOD says to the land of Israel:
An end! The end has come
   on the four corners of the earth.[n]
[3]   The end is now upon you;
   I will send my anger against you
   and judge you according to
      your ways.
   I will punish you for all
      your detestable practices.
[4]   I will not look on you with pity
      or spare you,[o]
   but I will punish you
      for your ways[p]

[A] 6:4 Or incense altars, also in v. 6   [B] 6:6 Hb obscure   [C] 6:12 Or besieged   [D] 6:14 Some Hb mss, some LXX mss read Riblah; 2Kg 23:33; Jr 39:5

---

of Israel's perfectly just and holy God whose righteous standards had been dragged through the dirt by the same people who had promised to uphold them in loving obedience. We must never extol the love of God at the expense of his just wrath against sin.
6:2 Ezekiel often used the name **Israel** to refer to the chosen nation, even though the northern kingdom known by that name was long gone.
6:3-4 These **mountains** and **hills** were the places where idolatry was flourishing among the people of Judah. The **high places** were worship centers believed to bring the worshiper closer to the false gods to whom they were offering sacrifices (6:3). Though a few

good kings had tried to eradicate such things, by Ezekiel's day, idol worship at these pagan **shrines** was active (6:4) to the point that God was ready to take action.
6:7 **You will know that I am the LORD** is a phrase that appears over sixty times in Ezekiel. By using the name "Lord" (Yahweh), the name of his covenant faithfulness, God was reminding his faithless people that he was no mere offended deity. He was a grieved, loving husband whose fidelity to his covenant promises had been met by his people's blatant unfaithfulness.
6:9 An idol is any person, place, thing, or thought that you look to as your source.

6:11 **Clap your hands** and **stamp your feet** were instructions that were to be carried out as signs of derision against **the house of Israel** for all of the people's sins.
6:14 Some Old Testament manuscripts have "Riblah" in place of **Diblah** (see the CSB footnote); the former was a northern city in the land of Israel. To date, there is no record of a city named "Diblah," and the letters *d* and *r* in Hebrew are very similar, so a scribe could easily have substituted one for the other. The reading "Riblah" fits the context, giving the meaning, "from the south [the wilderness] to the north [Riblah]," the entire land.

and for your detestable practices
  within you.
Then you will know that I am
  the Lord."[a]

⁵ This is what the Lord God says:
Look, one disaster after another
  is coming![b]
⁶ An end has come; the end has come!
It has awakened against you.
Look, it is coming!
⁷ Doom[A] has come on you,[c]
  inhabitants of the land.
The time has come; the day is near.
There will be panic
  on the mountains
and not celebration.[d]

⁸ I will pour out my wrath on you
  very soon;[e]
I will exhaust my anger against you
and judge you
  according to your ways.
I will punish you for all your
  detestable practices.
⁹ I will not look on you with pity
  or spare you.
I will punish you for your ways
and for your detestable practices
  within you.
Then you will know
that it is I, the Lord, who strikes.

¹⁰ Here is the day! Here it comes!
Doom is on its way.[f]
The rod has blossomed;[g]
arrogance has bloomed.[h]
¹¹ Violence has grown into a rod
  of wickedness.[i]
None of them will remain:
none of that crowd,
none of their wealth,
and none of the eminent[B]
  among them.

¹² The time has come; the day
  has arrived.
Let the buyer not rejoice[j]
and the seller not mourn,
for wrath is on her whole crowd.[k]
¹³ The seller will certainly not return
to what was sold

as long as he and the buyer
  remain alive.[c]
For the vision concerning
  her whole crowd
will not be revoked,
and because of the iniquity
  of each one,
none will preserve his life.

¹⁴ They have blown the trumpet[l]
and prepared everything,
but no one goes to war,
for my wrath is on her whole crowd.
¹⁵ The sword is on the outside;[m]
plague and famine are on the inside.
Whoever is in the field will die
  by the sword,
and famine and plague will devour
whoever is in the city.

¹⁶ The survivors among them
  will escape[n]
and live on the mountains.
Like doves of the valley,
all of them will moan,
each over his own iniquity.
¹⁷ All their hands will become weak,[o]
and all their knees will run
  with urine.[D]
¹⁸ They will put on sackcloth,
and horror will overwhelm them.
Shame will cover all their faces,
and all their heads will be bald.[p]

¹⁹ They will throw their silver
  into the streets,
and their gold will seem like
  something filthy.[q]
Their silver and gold will be unable
  to save them
in the day of the Lord's wrath.[r]
They will not satisfy their appetites
or fill their stomachs,
for these were the stumbling blocks[s]
that brought about their iniquity.

²⁰ He appointed his beautiful ornaments
  for majesty,
but[E] they made
  their detestable images
  from them,
their abhorrent things.[t]

[a] 7:4 Ezk 6:7,14
[b] 7:5 2Kg 21:12-13
[c] 7:7 Ezk 7:10
[d] Jl 2:1-2; Am 5:18-20; Zph 1:14-15
[e] 7:8 Ezk 20:8,21
[f] 7:10 Ezk 7:7
[g] Nm 17:8
[h] Is 10:5; Mt 24:32-33
[i] 7:11 Ps 73:8; 125:3
[j] 7:12 Pr 20:14
[k] Is 24:2

[l] 7:14 Nm 10:9
[m] 7:15 Jr 14:18; Ezk 6:11-12
[n] 7:16 Ezk 6:8; 14:22
[o] 7:17 Is 13:7; Ezk 21:7
[p] 7:18 Is 15:2-3; Am 8:10
[q] 7:19 Is 2:20; 30:22
[r] Pr 11:4; Zph 1:18
[s] Ezk 14:3
[t] 7:20 Jr 7:30; Ezk 16:17

[A] 7:7 Or A leash; Hb obscure, also in v. 10   [B] 7:11 Some Hb mss, Syr, Vg read and no rest   [C] 7:13 Lit sold, while still in life is their life   [D] 7:17 Lit knees
will go water   [E] 7:20 Or They turned their beautiful ornaments into objects of pride, and

---

7:10-11 As when Jeremiah spoke of an almond tree in bloom (Jer 1:11-12) to illustrate coming judgment, so here the message was the same—except that in this case the blossom was Judah's **arrogance** producing the vio-

lence that would come upon the people to punish them.
7:15-16 For the people of Judah who'd piled up sins against God, there was simply no place to go to escape his wrath.

7:17-18 This pictures a people shaking so hard in terror that they literally wet themselves and try in vain to show some repentance by wearing **sackcloth** and shaving their heads **bald**.

[a] 7:21 2Kg 24:13
[b] 7:23 Jr 27:2
[c] Ezk 8:17; 9:9
[d] 7:24 Ezk 21:31; 28:7
[e] 2Ch 7:20; Ezk 24:21
[f] 7:26 Is 47:11; Jr 4:20
[g] Ezk 21:7
[h] Jr 21:2; 37:17
[i] Ps 74:9; Mc 3:6
[j] 7:27 Mt 7:2

[k] 8:1 Ezk 14:1; 20:1
[l] Ezk 1:3
[m] 8:2 Ezk 1:27
[n] Ezk 1:4,27
[o] 8:3 Ezk 11:1,24; 40:2;
     2Co 12:1-4
[p] Ex 20:4; Dt 32:16
[q] 8:4 Ezk 9:3
[r] Ezk 1:28; 3:22-23
[s] 8:6 Ezk 5:11; 8:9,17;
     23:4-5
[t] 8:10 Ex 20:4; Dt 4:16-18;
     Rm 1:23

Therefore, I have made these
into something filthy to them.
21 I will hand these things over
to foreigners as plunder[a]
and to the wicked of the earth
as spoil,
and they will profane them.
22 I will turn my face from them
as they profane my treasured place.
Violent men will enter it
and profane it.

23 Forge the chain,[b]
for the land is filled with crimes
of bloodshed,
and the city is filled with violence.[c]
24 So I will bring the most evil
of nations[d]
to take possession of their houses.
I will put an end to the pride
of the strong,
and their sacred places
will be profaned.[e]
25 Anguish is coming!
They will look for peace,
but there will be none.
26 Disaster after disaster
will come,[f]
and there will be rumor
after rumor.[g]
Then they will look for a vision
from a prophet,[h]
but instruction will perish
from the priests
and counsel from the elders.[i]
27 The king will mourn;
the prince will be clothed
in grief;
and the hands of the people
of the land will tremble.
I will deal with them according to
their own conduct,
and I will judge them
by their own standards.[j]
Then they will know that I am
the Lord.

VISIONARY JOURNEY TO JERUSALEM

8 In the sixth year, in the sixth month, on the fifth day of the month, I was sitting in my house and the elders of Judah were sitting in front of me,[k] and there the hand of the Lord God came down on me.[l] 2 I looked, and there was someone who looked like a man.[A] From what seemed to be his waist down was fire, and from his waist up was something that looked bright,[m] like the gleam of amber.[n] 3 He stretched out what appeared to be a hand and took me by the hair of my head. Then the Spirit lifted me up between earth and heaven and carried me in visions of God[o] to Jerusalem, to the entrance of the inner gate that faces north, where the offensive statue that provokes jealousy[p] was located. 4 I saw the glory of the God of Israel[q] there, like the vision I had seen in the plain.[r]

PAGAN PRACTICES IN THE TEMPLE

5 The Lord said to me, "Son of man, look toward the north." I looked to the north, and there was this offensive statue north of the Altar Gate, at the entrance. 6 He said to me, "Son of man, do you see what they are doing here — more detestable acts that the house of Israel is committing[s] — so that I must depart from my sanctuary? You will see even more detestable acts." 7 Then he brought me to the entrance of the court, and when I looked there was a hole in the wall. 8 He said to me, "Son of man, dig through the wall." So I dug through the wall and discovered a doorway. 9 He said to me, "Go in and see the detestable, wicked acts they are committing here."

10 I went in and looked, and there engraved all around the wall was every kind of abhorrent thing — crawling creatures and beasts — as well as all the idols of the house of Israel.[t] 11 Seventy elders from the house of Israel were standing before them,

7:22 In other words, God would allow the Babylonian invaders to **profane** his holy temple. At this revelation, the exiles listening to Ezekiel in Babylon and the recipients of his prophecies back in Jerusalem knew the full horrors of God's coming judgment.
7:26-27 Though the people would listen frantically to all kinds of rumors coming out of Babylon and other places that spoke of rescue or relief, they would all prove false (7:26). Nothing would hold back God's hand until his sinful people had learned that he alone is God (7:27).

8:1 **The elders of Judah** were no doubt there to seek a word from the Lord.
8:3-6 Ezekiel must have been appalled at the sight of this pagan **statue** (perhaps an Asherah pole used in sexually degrading worship) defiling God's temple, where **the glory of the God of Israel** alone was to reside (8:3-4). But this scene marked only the beginning of Judah's **detestable** practices that caused God to ask Ezekiel essentially, "Do you understand now why I have to leave my temple? And you haven't seen anything yet!" (8:5-6).

8:7-11 Ezekiel got the inside scoop on what Judah's religious leaders were doing behind closed doors (8:7-9). **Seventy elders** were worshiping images of **every kind of abhorrent thing ... as well as all the idols of the house of Israel.** One of these men Ezekiel recognized: **Jaazaniah son of Shaphan** (8:10-11). Judah's secret sins on earth were an open scandal in heaven.
8:12 The men were offering incense in idolatrous worship, without any fear or remorse because they had concluded that God had **abandoned the land** and no longer saw or cared what they did.

with Jaazaniah son of Shaphan[a] standing among them. Each had a firepan in his hand, and a fragrant cloud of incense was rising up. **12** He said to me, "Son of man, do you see what the elders of the house of Israel are doing in the darkness, each at the shrine of his idol? For they are saying, 'The LORD does not see us. The LORD has abandoned the land.'"[b] **13** Again he said to me, "You will see even more detestable acts that they are committing."

14 Then he brought me to the entrance of the north gate of the LORD's house, and I saw women sitting there weeping for Tammuz. **15** And he said to me, "Do you see this, son of man? You will see even more detestable acts than these."

16 So he brought me to the inner court of the LORD's house, and there were about twenty-five men at the entrance of the LORD's temple, between the portico and the altar,[c] with their backs to the LORD's temple and their faces turned to the east.[d] They were bowing to the east in worship of the sun.[e] **17** And he said to me, "Do you see this, son of man? Is it not enough for the house of Judah to commit the detestable acts they are doing here, that they must also fill the land with violence[f] and repeatedly anger me,[g] even putting the branch to their nose?[A] **18** Therefore I will respond with wrath.[h] I will not show pity or spare them.[i] Though they call loudly in my hearing,[j] I will not listen to them."

VISION OF SLAUGHTER IN JERUSALEM

9 Then he called loudly in my hearing, "Come near, executioners of the city, each of you with a destructive weapon in his hand." **2** And I saw six men coming from the direction of the Upper Gate,[k] which faces north, each with a war club in his hand. There was another man among them, clothed in linen,[l] carrying writing equipment. They came and stood beside the bronze altar.

3 Then the glory of the God of Israel[m] rose from above the cherub where it had been, to the threshold of the temple. He called to the man clothed in linen and carrying writing equipment. **4** "Pass throughout the city of Jerusalem," the LORD said to him, "and put a mark on the foreheads[n] of the men who sigh and groan[o] over all the detestable practices committed in it."

5 He spoke to the others in my hearing: "Pass through the city after him and start killing; do not show pity or spare them![p] **6** Slaughter the old men, the young men and women, as well as the children and older women,[q] but do not come near anyone who has the mark.[r] Begin at my sanctuary."[s] So they began with the elders who were in front of the temple. **7** Then he said to them, "Defile the temple and fill the courts with the slain.[t] Go!" So they went out killing people in the city.

8 While they were killing, I was left alone. And I fell facedown and cried out, "Oh, Lord GOD![u] Are you going to destroy the entire remnant of Israel when you pour out your wrath on Jerusalem?"

9 He answered me, "The iniquity of the house of Israel and Judah is extremely great; the land is full of bloodshed,[v] and the city full of perversity. For they say, 'The LORD has abandoned the land;[w] he does not see.'[x] **10** But as for me, I will not show pity or spare them.[y] I will bring their conduct down on their own heads."[z]

11 Then the man clothed in linen and carrying writing equipment reported back, "I have done all that you commanded me."

---

[a] 8:11 Nm 11:16,25; Lk 10:1
[b] 8:12 Ps 14:1; Is 29:15; Ezk 9:9
[c] 8:16 Jl 2:17
[d] Jr 2:27; 32:33
[e] Dt 4:19; 17:3
[f] 8:17 Ezk 7:11,23; 9:9
[g] Jr 7:18-19
[h] 8:18 Ezk 5:13
[i] Ezk 5:11
[j] Mc 3:4
[k] 9:2 2Kg 15:35; Jr 20:2
[l] 9:2 Lv 16:4
[m] 9:3 Ezk 10:4,18; 11:22-23
[n] 9:4 Rv 7:2-3; 9:4; 14:1
[o] Ps 119:53,136; Jr 13:17
[p] 9:5 Ezk 5:11
[q] 9:6 2Ch 36:17
[r] Rv 9:4
[s] Jr 25:29
[t] 9:7 Ezk 7:20-22
[u] 9:8 Ezk 11:13
[v] 9:9 2Kg 21:16
[w] Ezk 8:12
[x] Is 29:15
[y] 9:10 Ezk 5:11; 7:4; 8:18
[z] Ezk 11:21

[A] 8:17 Alt Hb tradition reads *my nose*

8:14-15 Tammuz was the Babylonian god believed to provide vegetation (8:14). His worship included all manner of immorality, yet these women of Judah were worshiping this degrading deity instead of the God of Israel who provided them with all the bounty of their land.

8:16-17 The twenty-five men the prophet saw must have been priests, based on their location **between the portico and the altar**. They were standing in that holy place, not interceding with God for the people, but **with . . . their faces turned to the east . . . bowing . . . in worship of the sun** (8:16). This is exactly the kind of thing Paul describes when writing to the church in Rome: "They exchanged the truth of God for a lie, and worshiped and served what has been cre-

ated instead of the Creator" (Rom 1:25). Such things always result in degradation and the deterioration of the culture (see Rom 1:18-32).

9:1 That God **called loudly** suggests urgency. It was time for Jerusalem's **executioners** to line up for duty.

9:3 God's people had turned their backs on him, and in response he was turning his back on them—literally leaving the city. Believers today can forfeit God's active presence operating in their lives when they live with unaddressed sin (see 1 John 1:5-9).

9:4 Those to be marked were the righteous remnant, the ones who shared God's view of sin. God has always had his faithful ones, even when the majority of people are at their worst (see 1 Kgs 19:18).

9:5-6 We're not told how many righteous people were marked, but everyone else in Jerusalem was to be consigned to death—young and old, male and female, without **pity** (9:5; for more on God's lack of pity on them, see 9:10).

9:7 Corpses in the house of God would **defile** it, but it had already been defiled by the idols and the false worship. The carnage would illustrate that truth.

9:9 God's people had grown so spiritually calloused that they thought he had **abandoned the land**, which in their warped minds meant they could do anything they wanted without fear of reprisal. In one way, though, they were right: God's presence was in the process of departing from Jerusalem—but not because he no longer cared.

a 10:1 Ezk 1:22,26
b 10:2 Ezk 1:13; Rv 8:5
c 10:3 1Kg 8:10-11
d Ezk 8:3,16
e 10:4 Ezk 9:3; 10:18; 11:22-23; 43:2-5; 44:4
f Ex 40:34-35; Is 6:1-4; Rv 15:8
g Ezk 1:28; Hg 2:7
h 10:8 Ezk 1:8
i 10:9 Ezk 1:15-17
j Dn 10:6
k 10:11 Ezk 1:17
l 10:12 Rv 4:6,8
m Ezk 1:18

n 10:14 Ezk 1:6,10; 10:21
o 10:15 Ezk 1:3,5
p 10:17 Ezk 1:21
q 10:18 Ezk 10:4
r Ps 18:10
s 10:19 Ezk 11:22
t 10:20 Ezk 1:5,22,26; 10:15
u Ezk 1:1
v 10:21 Ezk 1:6,8; 10:14; 41:18-19
w 10:22 Ezk 1:10
x 11:1 Ezk 3:12,14; 8:3
y 11:2 Gn 6:5; Ps 36:4; Pr 14:2; Mc 2:1
z 11:3 Jr 29:28; Am 3:15; Zph 1:13
aa Jr 1:13; Ezk 24:3,6

GOD'S GLORY LEAVES THE TEMPLE

10 Then I looked, and there above the expanse over the heads[a] of the cherubim was something like a throne with the appearance of lapis lazuli. [2] The LORD spoke to the man clothed in linen and said, "Go inside the wheelwork beneath the cherubim. Fill your hands with blazing coals from among the cherubim and scatter them over the city."[b] So he went in as I watched.

[3] Now the cherubim were standing to the south of the temple when the man went in, and the cloud[c] filled the inner court.[d] [4] Then the glory of the LORD rose from above the cherub to the threshold of the temple.[e] The temple was filled with the cloud,[f] and the court was filled with the brightness of the LORD's glory.[g] [5] The sound of the cherubim's wings could be heard as far as the outer court; it was like the voice of God Almighty when he speaks.

[6] After the LORD commanded the man clothed in linen, saying, "Take fire from inside the wheelwork, from among the cherubim," the man went in and stood beside a wheel. [7] Then the cherub reached out his hand to the fire that was among them. He took some and put it into the hands of the man clothed in linen, who took it and went out. [8] The cherubim appeared to have the form of human hands under their wings.[h]

[9] I looked, and there were four wheels beside the cherubim,[i] one wheel beside each cherub. The luster of the wheels was like the gleam of beryl.[j] [10] In appearance, all four looked alike, like a wheel within a wheel. [11] When they moved, they would go in any of the four directions,[k] without pivoting as they moved. But wherever the head faced, they would go in that direction, without pivoting as they went. [12] Their entire bodies,[l] including their backs, hands, wings, and the wheels that the four of them had, were full of eyes all around.[m] [13] As I listened the wheels were called "the wheelwork." [14] Each one had

four faces:[n] one was the face of a cherub, the second the face of a man, the third the face of a lion, and the fourth the face of an eagle.

[15] The cherubim ascended; these were the living creatures I had seen by the Chebar Canal.[o] [16] When the cherubim moved, the wheels moved beside them, and when they lifted their wings to rise from the earth, even then the wheels did not veer away from them. [17] When the cherubim stopped,[p] the wheels stood still, and when they ascended, the wheels ascended with them, for the spirit of the living creatures was in them.

[18] Then the glory of the LORD moved away from the threshold of the temple[q] and stopped above the cherubim.[r] [19] The cherubim lifted their wings and ascended from the earth right before my eyes;[s] the wheels were beside them as they went. The glory of the God of Israel was above them, and it stopped at the entrance to the eastern gate of the LORD's house.

[20] These were the living creatures I had seen[t] beneath the God of Israel by the Chebar Canal,[u] and I recognized that they were cherubim. [21] Each had four faces and each had four wings,[v] with what looked something like human hands under their wings. [22] Their faces looked like the same faces I had seen[w] by the Chebar Canal. Each creature went straight ahead.

VISION OF ISRAEL'S CORRUPT LEADERS

11 The Spirit then lifted me up[x] and brought me to the eastern gate of the LORD's house, which faces east, and at the gate's entrance were twenty-five men. Among them I saw Jaazaniah son of Azzur, and Pelatiah son of Benaiah, leaders of the people. [2] The LORD[A] said to me, "Son of man, these are the men who plot evil[y] and give wicked advice in this city. [3] They are saying, 'Isn't the time near to build houses?[B,z] The city is the pot,[aa] and we are the

---

A 11:2 Lit He   B 11:3 Or "The time is not near to build houses."

10:2 God ordered the angelic figure to scoop his hands full of **blazing coals** from the altar in the temple and **scatter them over** Jerusalem. Indeed, Jerusalem would be cleansed by destruction as the Babylonians burned everything to the ground.

10:12 These cherubim were the same "living creatures" he'd seen by the Chebar Canal in chapter 1 (10:20). That the bodies of all these figures are described as **full of eyes all around** suggests God's all-seeing omniscience.

10:13 **The wheels** are also called **the wheelwork**, as if spinning in readiness to carry God's presence and glory on his chariot-throne out of the temple and away from Jerusalem.

10:15-16 As Ezekiel watched, no doubt in anguish, the **cherubim ascended** and **the wheels moved beside them** as God's chariot-throne lifted up from the temple and prepared to depart. This was terrible news for the nation: the absence of God's presence leaves his people in a hopeless situation.

11:1 Likely these **twenty-five men** were the same ones who were earlier worshiping the sun in the temple (see 8:16).

11:2-4 These men compared Jerusalem to a strong iron **pot** that would keep its people, **the meat** in the pot, safe from the fire (11:3). That kind of blind arrogance aroused God's righteous anger, and he thundered, **Prophesy against them . . . son of man!** (11:4). In Ezekiel, we see God regularly use the expression "son of man" as a term for the frailty of mankind in contrast to God.

meat.' **4** Therefore, prophesy against them. Prophesy, son of man!'"

5 Then the Spirit of the LORD came on me, and he told me, "You are to say, 'This is what the LORD says: That is what you are thinking, house of Israel; and I know the thoughts that arise in your mind.[a] **6** You have multiplied your slain in this city,[b] filling its streets with them.

7 "'Therefore, this is what the Lord GOD says: The slain you have put within it are the meat,[c] and the city is the pot, but I[A] will take you out of it.[d] **8** You fear the sword,[e] so I will bring the sword against you.[f] This is the declaration of the Lord GOD. **9** I will take you out of the city and hand you over to foreigners; I will execute judgments against you.[g] **10** You will fall by the sword,[h] and I will judge you at the border of Israel.[i] Then you will know that I am the LORD. **11** The city will not be a pot for you,[j] and you will not be the meat within it. I will judge you at the border of Israel, **12** so you will know that I am the LORD, whose statutes you have not followed and whose ordinances you have not practiced. Instead, you have acted according to the ordinances of the nations around you.'"[k]

13 Now while I was prophesying, Pelatiah son of Benaiah died.[l] Then I fell facedown and cried out loudly, "Oh, Lord GOD![m] You are bringing the remnant of Israel to an end!'"

PROMISE OF ISRAEL'S RESTORATION

14 The word of the LORD came to me again: **15** "Son of man, your own relatives, those who have the right to redeem your property,[B,C] along with the entire house of Israel — all of them — are those to whom the residents of Jerusalem have said, 'You are far from the LORD; this land has been given to us as a possession.'

16 "Therefore say, 'This is what the Lord GOD says: Though I sent them far away among the nations and scattered them among the countries, yet for a little while I have been a sanctuary for them[n] in the countries where they have gone.'

17 "Therefore say, 'This is what the Lord GOD says: I will gather you from the peoples[o] and assemble you from the countries where you have been scattered, and I will give you the land of Israel.'

18 "When they arrive there, they will remove all its[p] abhorrent acts[q] and detestable practices from it. **19** I will give them integrity of[D] heart[r] and put a new spirit within them; I will remove their heart of stone[s] from their bodies[E] and give them a heart of flesh,[t] **20** so that they will follow my statutes,[u] keep my ordinances, and practice them. They will be my people, and I will be their God.[v] **21** But as for those whose hearts pursue their desire for abhorrent acts and detestable practices, I will bring their conduct down on their own heads."[w] This is the declaration of the Lord GOD.

GOD'S GLORY LEAVES JERUSALEM

22 Then the cherubim, with the wheels beside them, lifted their wings,[x] and the glory of the God of Israel was above them. **23** The glory of the LORD[y] rose up from within the city and stopped on the mountain[z] east of the city.[F,aa] **24** The Spirit lifted me up[ab] and brought me to Chaldea and to the exiles in a vision from the Spirit of God. After the vision I had seen left me, **25** I spoke to the exiles about all the things the LORD had shown me.

[a] 11:5 Jr 17:10; Ezk 2:2
[b] 11:6 Ezk 7:23; 22:2-6,9,12,27
[c] 11:7 Ezk 24:3-13; Mc 3:2-3
[d] Ezk 11:9
[e] 11:8 Pr 10:24; Is 66:4
[f] Jb 3:25; Is 24:17-18
[g] 11:9 Ezk 5:8
[h] 11:10 Jr 39:6; 52:9-10
[i] 2Kg 14:25
[j] 11:11 Ezk 11:3,7
[k] 11:12 Ezk 8:10,14,16
[l] 11:13 Ac 5:5
[m] Ezk 9:8

[n] 11:16 Is 8:14
[o] 11:17 Ezk 20:34,41-42; 28:25
[p] 11:18 Ezk 37:23
[q] Ezk 5:11
[r] 11:19 Jr 32:39
[s] Zch 7:12
[t] Ps 51:10; Jr 31:33; Ezk 36:26; 2Co 3:3
[u] 11:20 Ps 105:45; Ezk 36:27
[v] Ezk 36:28
[w] 11:21 Ezk 9:10
[x] 11:22 Ezk 10:19
[y] 11:23 Ezk 8:4
[z] Zch 14:4
[aa] 11:22-23 Ezk 10:4
[ab] 11:24 Ezk 8:3

[A] 11:7 Some Hb mss, LXX, Syr, Tg, Vg; other Hb mss read *he relatives*   [B] 11:15 LXX, Syr read *your relatives, your fellow exiles*   [C] 11:15 Or *own brothers, your*   [D] 11:19 Lit *give them one*   [E] 11:19 Lit *flesh*   [F] 11:23 = the Mount of Olives

11:7-8 Verse 7 is a counter word play on the leaders' prior claim in 11:3 regarding the safety of their city. God said he would reverse the leaders' imagery of the safe **pot**, dumping Jerusalem's people out of it (11:7) and bringing **the sword** of the Babylonians against them (11:8).
11:9-10 God uses evil people, places, and things to judge the sin and rebellion among his own people. This particular prophecy was fulfilled when those captured in Jerusalem by Nebuchadnezzar's army were brought to him at his army headquarters in Riblah in northern Israel to be either executed or sent into exile (see 2 Kgs 25:18-21).
11:13 Pelatiah was one of the twenty-five evil leaders in 11:1.

11:15 Selfishly, **the residents of Jerusalem** scoffed at the relatives of the exiles in Babylon who still lived among them. Though the **relatives** had **the right to redeem [the] property** of their exiled families, the wicked people of Jerusalem told them that the **land [had] been given to [them] as a possession**. They were using geography to determine God's favor.
11:16-20 This prophecy has a near and a far fulfillment, which is true of many Old Testament prophecies. God did reassemble his people from the **countries where [they had] been scattered**, and he has given them **the land of Israel** again today (11:16-17). But, importantly, they do not have the **new spirit** that God said he would give them, replacing **their heart of stone** with **a heart of flesh** (11:19). These

promises await the time when Israel collectively recognizes Jesus Christ as their Messiah (see Zech 12:10) and Christ establishes his millennial kingdom with his throne in Jerusalem.
11:22-23 The departure of God's glory had happened once before at the tabernacle, in the days of Eli the priest when the ark of the covenant was captured and Eli was judged for failing to restrain his two evil sons, Hophni and Phinehas (1 Sam 3–4). In recognition of God's judgment, Phinehas's wife named her son "Ichabod," which means, "no glory." Maybe no one thought such a thing would ever happen again. Regardless, the warning of Ichabod even applies to the church: when it abandons Christ, its lampstand is removed (see Rev 2:5).

EZEKIEL DRAMATIZES THE EXILE

12 The word of the LORD came to me: **2** "Son of man, you are living among a rebellious house.*a* They have eyes to see but do not see, and ears to hear but do not hear,*b* for they are a rebellious house.*c*

3 "Now you, son of man, get your bags ready for exile and go into exile in their sight during the day. You will go into exile from your place to another place while they watch; perhaps they will understand, though they are a rebellious house. **4** During the day, bring out your bags like an exile's bags while they look on. Then in the evening go out in their sight like those going into exile. **5** As they watch, dig through the wall and take the bags out through it. **6** And while they look on, lift the bags to your shoulder and take them out in the dark; cover your face so that you cannot see the land. For I have made you a sign to the house of Israel."*d*

7 So I did just as I was commanded. In the daytime I brought out my bags like an exile's bags. In the evening I dug through the wall by hand; I took them out in the dark, carrying them on my shoulder in their sight.

8 In the morning the word of the LORD came to me: **9** "Son of man, hasn't the house of Israel, that rebellious house,*e* asked you, 'What are you doing?'*f* **10** Say to them, 'This is what the Lord GOD says: This pronouncement concerns the prince*A* in Jerusalem and the whole house of Israel living there.'*B* **11** You are to say, 'I am a sign for you. Just as I have done, it will be done to them; they will go into exile,*g* into captivity.' **12** The prince who is among*h* them will lift his bags to his shoulder in the dark and go out. They*C* will dig through the wall to bring him out through it. He will cover his face so he cannot see the land with his eyes. **13** But I will spread my net over him, and he will be caught in my snare. I will bring him to Babylon, the land of the

Chaldeans, yet he will not see it,*i* and he will die there. **14** I will also scatter all the attendants who surround him and all his troops to every direction of the wind,*j* and I will draw a sword to chase after them. **15** They will know that I am the LORD*k* when I disperse them among the nations and scatter them among the countries.*l* **16** But I will spare a few of them from the sword,*m* famine, and plague, so that among the nations where they go they can tell about all their detestable practices. Then they will know that I am the LORD."

EZEKIEL DRAMATIZES ISRAEL'S ANXIETY

17 The word of the LORD came to me: **18** "Son of man, eat your bread with*n* trembling and drink your water with anxious shaking. **19** Then say to the people of the land, 'This is what the Lord GOD says about the residents of Jerusalem in the land of Israel: They will eat their bread with anxiety and drink their water in dread, for their*D,E* land will be stripped of everything*o* in it because of the violence of all who live there. **20** The inhabited cities will be destroyed, and the land will become dreadful. Then you will know that I am the LORD.'"

A DECEPTIVE PROVERB STOPPED

21 Again the word of the LORD came to me: **22** "Son of man, what is this proverb you people have about the land of Israel,*p* which goes, 'The days keep passing by,*q* and every vision fails'? **23** Therefore say to them, 'This is what the Lord GOD says: I will put a stop to this proverb, and they will not use it again in Israel.'*r* But say to them, 'The days have arrived,*s* as well as the fulfillment of every vision. **24** For there will no longer be any false vision or flattering divination*t* within the house of Israel. **25** But I, the LORD, will speak whatever message I will speak, and it will be done.*u* It will no longer be delayed.*v* For in your

A 12:10 = King Zedekiah　*B* 12:10 Lit *Israel among them*　*C* 12:12 LXX, Syr read *He*　*D* 12:19 Lit *its*　*E* 12:19 = Jerusalem's

12:4-6 Covering his **face** (12:6) symbolized that **those going into exile** (12:4-5) would never see the land of Israel again. Seventy years would pass before the Jews would be allowed to go home.
12:12-14 This **prince** is a reference to Zedekiah, the puppet king whom Nebuchadnezzar had placed on Jerusalem's throne (12:12). Indeed, he tried to escape the city at night, but the Babylonians overtook him and brought him to Nebuchadnezzar, who killed Zedekiah's sons before his eyes and then gouged them out so that he never saw

Babylon even though he was taken there (12:13; see 2 Kgs 25:1-7).
12:15 This is a sobering reminder that if people will not respond to God voluntarily, they will be forced to do so by his judgment.
12:17-19 Ezekiel's display of nervousness reinforced the word the Lord had delivered earlier (see 4:16). Indeed, the people would **eat their bread with anxiety and drink their water in dread** as God **stripped** the land bare and destroyed cities because of the inhabitants' **violence** (12:19). This was the only way these spiritually blind and deaf rebels could

be brought to see and understand that the Lord alone was their God.
12:21-25 Judah's people had a **proverb** that basically said, "Ezekiel keeps insisting doom is coming, but nothing has happened yet!" (12:22). To this God replied, **I will put a stop to this proverb. . . . For in your days, rebellious house, I will . . . bring it to pass** (12:23-25). In other words, he'd heard enough of their nonsense. Every word he had spoken would happen—not in the distant future—but in their lifetime.

days, rebellious house, I will speak a message and bring it to pass. This is the declaration of the Lord GOD.'"

26 The word of the LORD came to me: **27** "Son of man, notice that the house of Israel is saying, 'The vision that he sees concerns many years from now;[a] he prophesies about distant times.' **28** Therefore say to them, 'This is what the Lord GOD says: None of my words will be delayed any longer. The message I speak will be fulfilled. This is the declaration of the Lord GOD.'"

ISRAEL'S FALSE PROPHETS CONDEMNED

13 The word of the LORD came to me: **2** "Son of man, prophesy against the prophets of Israel who[b] are prophesying. Say to those who prophesy out of their own imagination,[c] 'Hear the word of the LORD! **3** This is what the Lord GOD says: Woe to the foolish prophets who follow their own spirit and have seen nothing. **4** Your prophets, Israel, are like jackals among ruins. **5** You did not go up to the gaps[d] or restore the wall around the house of Israel so that it might stand in battle on the day of the LORD. **6** They saw false visions and their divinations were a lie.[e] They claimed, "This is the LORD's declaration," when the LORD did not send them,[f] yet they wait for the fulfillment of their message. **7** Didn't you see a false vision and speak a lying divination when you proclaimed, "This is the LORD's declaration," even though I had not spoken?

8 "'Therefore, this is what the Lord GOD says: You have spoken falsely and had lying visions; that's why you discover that I am against you. This is the declaration of the Lord GOD. **9** My hand will be against the prophets who see false visions and speak lying divinations.[g] They will not be present in the council of my people or be recorded in the register of the house of Israel, and they will not enter the land of Israel. Then you will know that I am the Lord GOD.

10 "'Since they have led my people astray by saying, "Peace,"[h] when there is no peace, and since when a flimsy wall is being built, they plaster it with whitewash,[i] **11** therefore, tell those plastering it with whitewash that it will fall. Torrential rain will come,[j] and I will send hailstones plunging[A] down, and a whirlwind will be released. **12** When the wall has fallen, will you not be asked, "Where's the whitewash you plastered on it?"

13 "'So this is what the Lord GOD says: I will release a whirlwind in my wrath. Torrential rain will come in my anger, and hailstones will fall in destructive fury. **14** I will demolish the wall you plastered with whitewash and knock it to the ground so that its foundation is exposed.[k] The city will fall, and you will be destroyed within it. Then you will know that I am the LORD. **15** After I exhaust my wrath against the wall and against those who plaster it with whitewash, I will say to you, "The wall is no more and neither are those who plastered it — **16** those prophets of Israel who prophesied to Jerusalem and saw a vision of peace for her when there was no peace."[l] This is the declaration of the Lord GOD.'

17 "Now you, son of man, face[B] the women among your people who prophesy[m] out of their own imagination, and prophesy against them.[n] **18** Say, 'This is what the Lord GOD says: Woe to the women who sew magic bands on the wrist of every hand and who make veils for the heads of people of every size in order to ensnare lives. Will you ensnare the lives of my people but preserve your own?' **19** You profane me among my people for handfuls of barley[p] and scraps of bread; you put those to death who should not die and spare those who

---

[a] 12:27 Ezk 12:22; Dn 10:14
[b] 13:2 Ezk 22:25,28
[c] Jr 23:16,26
[d] 13:5 Ps 106:23; Ezk 22:30
[e] 13:6 Ezk 22:28
[f] Jr 14:14; 23:21; 28:15
[g] 13:9 Jr 20:3-6; 28:15-17
[h] 13:10 Jr 6:14; 8:11; 14:13; Mc 3:5
[i] Ezk 22:28; Mt 23:27; Ac 23:3
[j] 13:11 Ezk 38:22; Mt 7:27
[k] 13:14 1Co 3:10-15
[l] 13:16 Jr 6:14; 8:11
[m] 13:17 Jdg 4:4; 2Kg 22:14; Ac 21:9
[n] Ezk 13:2
[o] 13:18 2Pt 2:14
[p] 13:19 Pr 28:21; Mc 3:5

[A] 13:11 One Hb ms, LXX, Vg; other Hb mss read *and you, hailstones, will plunge*   [B] 13:17 Lit *set your face*

12:27 Sometimes, when people see no divine judgment looming on the horizon, they assume all is well. But the fact that God does not immediately punish us for our sins doesn't mean he takes no notice of them or isn't offended by them. The reason that judgment is delayed is that God is giving people time to repent and put their faith in his Son. Nevertheless, death can take anyone at any time. We must urge people not to think that they have years to "get right with God." Our message should be the same as Paul's message: "Now is the day of salvation!" (2 Cor 6:2).

13:2-3 The prophetic office was Judah's last hope for a true word from God. After all, the civil leaders were mostly corrupt, and the priests were worshiping the sun in God's temple (8:16). The prophets should have stepped into the gap; instead, they proclaimed visions from the Lord though they had actually **seen nothing** (13:3).

13:10-12 Some prophets led the people astray, making a false promise of **peace** when there was **no peace** to be found. They uttered deception, covering up their **flimsy** position before God by whitewashing over the truth with lies, the way a poor builder

would try to hide his defective work (13:10). But God would expose their lies, leaving the people to wonder, too late, what happened to all the false prophets' glowing promises (13:11-12).

13:17-18 In this case Judah's prophetesses were like sorceresses or spiritists. They used pagan occult objects such as **magic bands** to trick the gullible into believing they warded off evil spirits or brought good luck. If God's people were where they should have been spiritually, these sorceresses would have been executed for their evil (see Deut 18:20-22).

a 13:21 Ps 91:3; 124:7
b 13:22 Jr 28:15
c Jr 23:14
d 13:23 Mc 3:5-6
e 14:1 Ezk 8:1; 20:1
    Ezk 33:31-32
g 14:3 Ezk 7:19
    Ezk 20:3,31
i 14:6 1Sm 7:3; Neh 1:9;
    Is 2:20; 30:22; 55:6-7;
    Ezk 18:30

j 14:8 Is 65:15; Jr 44:11; Ezk
    5:15; 15:7
k 14:9 Jdg 9:23; 1Sm 16:14;
1Kg 22:23; Jr 20:7; 2Th 2:11
    Jr 6:14-15; 14:15
m 14:11 Ezk 11:18; 37:23
    Ezk 36:28
n 14:13 Lv 26:26; Is 3:1;
    Ezk 4:16
p 14:14 Jr 15:1
    q Gn 6:8
r Ezk 28:3; Dn 1:6
s Jb 1:1,5; 42:8-9
t 14:15 Lv 26:22; Nm 21:6;
    2Kg 17:25; Ezk 5:17
u 14:16 Gn 19:29; Ezk 18:20
v 14:17 Lv 26:25; Ezk 5:12;
    21:3-4
w Ezk 25:13; Zph 1:3

should not live, when you lie to my people, who listen to lies.

20 "'Therefore, this is what the Lord God says: I am against your magic bands with which you ensnare people like birds, and I will tear them from your arms. I will free the people you have ensnared like birds. 21 I will also tear off your veils and rescue my people from your hands,*a* so that they will no longer be prey in your hands. Then you will know that I am the Lord. 22 Because you have disheartened the righteous person with lies (when I intended no distress),*b* and because you have supported^ the wicked*c* person so that he does not turn from his evil way to save his life, 23 therefore you will no longer see false visions or practice divination.*d* I will rescue my people from your hands. Then you will know that I am the Lord.'"

IDOLATROUS ELDERS PUNISHED

14 Some of the elders of Israel came*e* to me and sat down in front of me.*f* 2 Then the word of the Lord came to me: 3 "Son of man, these men have set up idols in their hearts and have put their sinful stumbling blocks in front of themselves.*g* Should I actually let them inquire of me?*h*

4 "Therefore, speak to them and tell them, 'This is what the Lord God says: When anyone from the house of Israel sets up idols in his heart and puts his sinful stumbling block in front of himself, and then comes to the prophet, I, the Lord, will answer him appropriately.*B* I will answer him according to his many idols, 5 so that I may take hold of the house of Israel by their hearts. They are all estranged from me because of their idols.'

6 "Therefore, say to the house of Israel, 'This is what the Lord God says: Repent and turn away*i* from your idols; turn your faces away from all your detestable things. 7 For when anyone from the house of Israel or from the aliens who reside in Israel separates himself from me, setting up idols in

his heart and putting his sinful stumbling block in front of himself, and then comes to the prophet to inquire of me, I, the Lord, will answer him myself. 8 I will turn against that one and make him a sign and a proverb; I will cut him off from among my people.*j* Then you will know that I am the Lord.

9 "'But if the prophet is deceived and speaks a message, it was I, the Lord, who deceived that prophet.*k* I will stretch out my hand against him and destroy him from among my people Israel.*l* 10 They will bear their punishment — the punishment of the one who inquires will be the same as that of the prophet — 11 in order that the house of Israel may no longer stray from following me and no longer defile themselves*m* with all their transgressions. Then they will be my people and I will be their God.*n* This is the declaration of the Lord God.'"

FOUR DEVASTATING JUDGMENTS

12 The word of the Lord came to me: 13 "Son of man, suppose a land sins against me by acting faithlessly, and I stretch out my hand against it to cut off its supply of bread,*o* to send famine through it, and to wipe out both man and animal from it. 14 Even if these three men*p* — Noah,*q* Daniel,*r* and Job*s* — were in it, they would rescue only themselves by their righteousness." This is the declaration of the Lord God.

15 "Suppose I allow dangerous animals*t* to pass through the land and depopulate it so that it becomes desolate, with no one passing through it for fear of the animals. 16 Even if these three men were in it, as I live" — the declaration of the Lord God — "they could not rescue their sons or daughters. They alone would be rescued, but the land would be desolate.*u*

17 "Or suppose I bring a sword*v* against that land and say, 'Let a sword pass through it,' so that I wipe out both man and animal from it.*w* 18 Even if these three men were in

---

^ 13:22 Lit *strengthened the hand of*   B 14:4 Alt Hb tradition reads *him who comes*

14:4 Anyone who would inquire of God while secretly worshiping idols would indeed get an answer from him, but not the answer desired. God's answer would be a word of judgment.

14:6 God has essentially the same message for people today. Unbelievers are urged to turn from their idols to trust in Jesus. And even Christians are urged to guard themselves from idols (1 John 5:21). This is the only way to experience true blessing from God, in fact. Since God is a jealous God, there is no

room for competing deities (see Exod 20:5; 34:14; Jas 4:5).

14:8 God would make the idolater an example to others so that they understood what would happen to those who make a pretense of following God but whose hearts are far from him. There are many people today who follow the same path, and it remains a dangerous route.

14:12-20 Could such a faithless nation as Judah be spared through intercessory prayer? As it turned out, **even if . . . Noah, Daniel, and**

Job . . . were in it, they would rescue only themselves by their righteousness (14:14). They were three of the greatest examples of faith and godly favor; nevertheless, their righteousness could not protect such a wicked land.

Contrast this with the Lord Jesus Christ. He alone is able to save all sinners by his own righteousness. Anyone who trusts in Christ as his sin-bearer, in fact, is granted a righteousness that is not his own—"the righteousness from God based on faith" (Phil 3:9).

it, as I live" — the declaration of the Lord GOD — "they could not rescue their sons or daughters, but they alone would be rescued. **19** "Or suppose I send a plague into that land[a] and pour out my wrath on it with bloodshed to wipe out both man and animal from it. **20** Even if Noah, Daniel, and Job were in it, as I live" — the declaration of the Lord GOD — "they could not rescue their son or daughter. They would rescue only themselves by their righteousness. **21** "For this is what the Lord GOD says: How much worse will it be when I send my four[b] devastating judgments against Jerusalem — sword, famine, dangerous animals, and plague — in order to wipe out both man and animal from it! **22** Even so, there will be survivors left in it, sons and daughters who will be brought out. Indeed, they will come out to you, and you will observe their conduct and actions.[c] Then you will be consoled about the devastation I have brought on Jerusalem, about all I have brought on it. **23** They will bring you consolation when you see their conduct and actions, and you will know that it was not without cause that I have done what I did to it."[d] This is the declaration of the Lord GOD.

PARABLE OF THE USELESS VINE

15 Then the word of the LORD came to me: **2** "Son of man, how does the wood of the vine,[e] that branch among the trees of the forest, compare to any other wood? **3** Can wood be taken from it to make something useful? Or can anyone make a peg from it to hang things on? **4** In fact, it is put into the fire as fuel.[f] The fire devours both of its ends, and the middle is charred. Can it be useful for anything? **5** Even when it was whole it could not be made into a useful object. How much less can it ever be made into anything useful when the fire has devoured it and it is charred!"

6 Therefore, this is what the Lord GOD says, "Like the wood of the vine among the trees of the forest, which I have given to the fire as fuel, so I will give up the residents of Jerusalem. **7** I will turn against them.[g] They may have escaped from the fire, but it will still consume them.[h] And you will know that I am the LORD when I turn against them. **8** I will make the land desolate because they have acted unfaithfully." This is the declaration of the Lord GOD.

PARABLE OF GOD'S ADULTEROUS WIFE

16 The word of the LORD came to me again: **2** "Son of man, confront Jerusalem with her detestable practices.[i] **3** You are to say, 'This is what the Lord GOD says to Jerusalem: Your origin and your birth were in the land of the Canaanites. Your father was an Amorite and your mother a Hethite.[j] **4** As for your birth, your umbilical cord wasn't cut on the day you were born,[k] and you weren't washed clean[A] with water. You were not rubbed with salt or wrapped in cloths.[l] **5** No one cared enough about you to do even one of these things out of compassion for you. But you were thrown out into the open field because you were despised on the day you were born.

6 " 'I passed by you and saw you thrashing around in your blood, and I said to you as you lay in your blood, "Live!" Yes, I said to you as you lay in your blood, "Live!"[B] **7** I made you thrive[c] like plants of the field.[m] You grew up and matured and became very beautiful.[D] Your breasts were formed and your hair grew, but you were stark naked.

8 " 'Then I passed by you and saw you, and you were indeed at the age for love. So I spread the edge of my garment over you and covered your nakedness.[n] I pledged myself to you,[o] entered into a covenant with you — this is the declaration of the Lord GOD — and you became

[right margin references]
[a] 14:19 2Sm 24:15; Ezk 38:22
[b] 14:21 Ezk 5:17; 33:27; Am 4:6-10; Rv 6:8
[c] 14:22 Ezk 6:8; 12:16; 20:43; 36:20
[d] 14:23 Jr 22:8-9
[e] 15:2 Ps 80:8-16; Is 5:1-7; Hs 10:1
[f] 15:4 Jn 15:6

[g] 15:7 Ezk 14:8
[h] Is 24:18
[i] 16:2 Is 58:1; Ezk 20:4; 22:2
[j] 16:3 Dt 7:1; Jdg 3:5; 1Kg 9:20-21; Ezk 16:45
[k] 16:4 Hs 2:3
[l] Lk 2:12
[m] 16:7 Ex 1:7
[n] 16:8 Ru 3:9; Jr 2:2
[o] Gn 22:16-18

<hr>

[A] 16:4 Hb obscure   [B] 16:6 Some Hb mss, LXX, Syr omit *Yes, I said to you as you lay in your blood, "Live!"*   [C] 16:7 LXX reads *Thrive; I made you*
[D] 16:7 Or *matured and developed the loveliest of ornaments*

<hr>

14:21 These **four devastating judgments** foreshadow the four horsemen that God will unleash on an unbelieving world during the great tribulation (see Rev 6:1-8).
14:22-23 Judah would have **survivors** who would be taken to Babylon so Ezekiel and the other exiles could **be consoled about the devastation . . . on Jerusalem** (14:22). The consolation, however, wasn't based on the righteousness of these survivors. Rather, the people exiled previously would see the newcomers' unrighteous **conduct** and know that

it was not without cause that God brought destruction on Jerusalem (14:23).
15:1-8 God did not create **the wood of the vine** to be made into furniture or some other useful item requiring strength (15:2-3). Its job was to hold the fruit it was designed to produce, and then become **fuel** (15:4-5). So while **the residents of Jerusalem** had **escaped** the **fire** of Babylon when the enemy first came in 597 BC, the reprieve was only temporary. Fire would still **consume them** when God brought down the final curtain

of judgment (15:6-8). They were good for nothing else.
16:3 Amorites and Hethites were two pagan peoples in the promised land whose practices the Jews had adopted.
16:6-8 God himself took pity on the **thrashing** baby, the Jewish people, and selected her as his own, providing her with everything necessary to mature into a woman of beauty (16:6-7). Then, when Jerusalem became of marriageable age, God pledged his protection and provision, and she became his beloved (16:8).

[a]16:8 Ex 19:5; 24:7-8
[b]16:11-12 Gn 24:22,47
[c]16:13 Dt 32:13-14; Ps 45:13-14
[d]16:14 Lm 2:15
[e]16:15 Is 57:8; Jr 2:20
[f]Pr 7:8-13
[g]16:17 Ex 12:35; 32:2-4
[h]16:19 Hs 2:8
[i]16:20 Jr 7:31; 19:5; Ezk 23:37
[j]16:21 Lv 18:21; Dt 18:10; 2Kg 17:17; Ezk 20:31
[k]16:22 Jr 2:2

[l]16:24 Jr 11:13
[m]16:25 Pr 9:14
[n]16:26 Ezk 23:19-20
[o]16:27 Ezk 16:57
[p]16:28 2Kg 16:7,10-18; 2Ch 28:16,20-23; Jr 2:18,36
[q]16:29 Ezk 23:14-16
[r]16:31 Is 52:3
[s]16:36 Jr 2:34
[t]16:37 Jr 13:22,26; Ezk 23:9,22

mine.[a] [9]I washed you with water, rinsed off your blood, and anointed you with oil. [10]I clothed you in embroidered cloth and provided you with fine leather[A] sandals. I also wrapped you in fine linen and covered you with silk. [11]I adorned you with jewelry, putting bracelets on your wrists and a necklace around your neck. [12]I put a ring in your nose,[b] earrings on your ears, and a beautiful crown on your head. [13]So you were adorned with gold and silver,[c] and your clothing was made of fine linen, silk, and embroidered cloth. You ate fine flour, honey, and oil. You became extremely beautiful and attained royalty. [14]Your fame spread among the nations because of your beauty, for it was perfect through my splendor,[d] which I had bestowed on you. This is the declaration of the Lord GOD.

[15]"But you trusted in your beauty and acted like a prostitute because of your fame.[e] You lavished your sexual favors on everyone who passed by.[f] Your beauty became his.[A] [16]You took some of your clothing and made colorful high places for yourself, and you engaged in prostitution on them. These places should not have been built, and this should never have happened![A] [17]You also took your beautiful jewelry made from the gold and silver I had given you,[g] and you made male images so that you could engage in prostitution with them. [18]Then you took your embroidered clothing to cover them and set my oil and incense before them. [19]The food that I gave you — the fine flour, oil, and honey that I fed you — you set it before them as a pleasing aroma.[h] That is what happened. This is the declaration of the Lord GOD.

[20]"'You even took your sons and daughters you bore to me and sacrificed them to these images as food.[i] Wasn't your prostitution enough? [21]You slaughtered my children and gave them up when you passed them through the fire[j] to the images. [22]In all your detestable practices and acts of prostitution, you did not remember the days of your youth[k] when you were stark naked and thrashing around in your blood.

[23]"Then after all your evil — Woe, woe to you! — the declaration of the Lord GOD — [24]you built yourself a mound and made yourself an elevated place in every square.[l] [25]You built your elevated place at the head of every street[m] and turned your beauty into a detestable thing. You spread your legs to everyone who passed by and increased your prostitution. [26]You engaged in promiscuous acts with Egyptian men, your well-endowed neighbors, and increased your prostitution[n] to anger me.

[27]"Therefore, I stretched out my hand against you and reduced your provisions. I gave you over to the desire of those who hate you, the Philistine women,[o] who were embarrassed by your indecent conduct. [28]Then you engaged in prostitution with the Assyrian men because you were not satisfied.[p] Even though you did this with them, you were still not satisfied. [29]So you extended your prostitution to Chaldea,[q] the land of merchants, but you were not even satisfied with this!

[30]"'How your heart was inflamed with lust[B] — the declaration of the Lord GOD — when you did all these things, the acts of a brazen prostitute, [31]building your mound at the head of every street and making your elevated place in every square. But you were unlike a prostitute because you scorned payment.[r] [32]You adulterous wife, who receives strangers instead of her husband! [33]Men give gifts to all prostitutes, but you gave gifts to all your lovers. You bribed them to come to you from all around for your sexual favors. [34]So you were the opposite of other women in your acts of prostitution; no one solicited you. When you paid a fee instead of one being paid to you, you were the opposite.

[35]"Therefore, you prostitute, hear the word of the LORD! [36]This is what the Lord GOD says: Because your lust was poured out and your nakedness exposed by your acts of prostitution with your lovers, and because of all your detestable idols and the blood of your children that you gave to them,[s] [37]I am therefore going to gather all the lovers you pleased[t] — all those

---

[A]16:10,15,16 Hb obscure   [B]16:30 Or *was sick*

16:15 Shockingly, the Lord's bride let her looks and fame go to her head and turned from her Provider to **prostitute** herself to idols in the most degrading ways possible! Jerusalem's idolatry is described in terms of adultery, which is why Ezekiel 16:5-34 contains sexually graphic imagery to depict the nation's sins.
16:20-22 Offering her **sons and daughters** as sacrifices to idols was a particular outrage to

God, for his bride who had been left to die in infancy was now killing the **children** he had given her (16:20-21).
16:26 The reference to the nation's dalliances with **Egyptian men** in particular (see also the Assyrians and Babylonians ["Chaldea"] in 16:28-29) may refer to the Israelites' foreign alliances as well as their searching for new pagan gods to worship.

16:27 Even the pagan nations were **embarrassed by** the depths of Jerusalem's **indecent conduct**!
16:36-41 The irony of Jerusalem's prostitution with her pagan lovers is that they, unlike the spiritual husband she'd scorned had done throughout her history, would not rally to her defense because they cared nothing for her. They would be her executioners!

you loved as well as all those you hated. I will gather them against you from all around and expose your nakedness[a] to them so they see you completely naked. [38] I will judge you the way adulteresses and those who shed blood are judged.[b] Then I will bring about the shedding of your blood in jealous wrath.[c] [39] I will hand you over to them, and they will demolish your mounds and tear down your elevated places. They will strip off your clothes,[d] take your beautiful jewelry, and leave you stark naked. [40] They will bring a mob against you[e] to stone you and to cut you to pieces with their swords. [41] They will burn your houses and execute judgments against you in the sight of many women. I will stop you from being a prostitute,[f] and you will never again pay fees for lovers. [42] So I will satisfy my wrath against you,[g] and my jealousy will turn away from you. Then I will be calm and no longer angry. [43] Because you did not remember the days[h] of your youth but enraged me with all these things, I will also bring your conduct down on your own head.[i] This is the declaration of the Lord God. Haven't you committed depravity in addition to all your detestable practices?

[44] "Look, everyone who uses proverbs will quote this proverb about you: "Like mother, like daughter." [45] You are the daughter of your mother, who despised her husband and children. You are the sister of your sisters,[j] who despised their husbands and children. Your mother was a Hethite and your father an Amorite.[k] [46] Your older sister was Samaria,[l] who lived with her daughters to the north of you, and your younger sister was Sodom, who lived with her daughters to the south of you. [47] Didn't you walk in their ways and do their detestable practices? It was only a short time before all your ways were more corrupt than theirs.[m]

[48] "As I live — the declaration of the Lord God — your sister Sodom and her daughters have not behaved as you and your daughters have.[n] [49] Now this was the iniquity of your sister Sodom: She and her daughters had pride, plenty of food,[o] and comfortable security, but didn't support[A] the poor and needy. [50] They were haughty and did detestable acts before me, so I removed them when I saw this.[B,p] [51] But Samaria did not commit even half your sins. You have multiplied your detestable practices beyond theirs and made your sisters appear righteous by all the detestable acts you have committed. [52] You must also bear your disgrace, since you have helped your sisters out.[C] For they appear more righteous than you because of your sins, which you committed more detestably than they did. So you also, be ashamed and bear your disgrace, since you have made your sisters appear righteous.

[53] "I will restore their fortunes,[q] the fortunes of Sodom and her daughters and those of Samaria and her daughters. I will also restore[D] your fortunes among them,[r] [54] so you will bear your disgrace and be ashamed of all you did when you comforted them.[s] [55] As for your sisters, Sodom and her daughters and Samaria and her daughters will return to their former state. You and your daughters will also return to your former state. [56] Didn't you treat your sister Sodom as an object of scorn when you were proud, [57] before your wickedness was exposed? It was like the time you were scorned by the daughters of Aram[E,t] and all those around her, and by the daughters of the Philistines — those who treated you with contempt from every side. [58] You yourself must bear the consequences of your depravity and detestable practices[u] — this is the Lord's declaration.

[59] "For this is what the Lord God says: I will deal with you according to what you have done, since you have despised the oath by breaking the covenant.[v] [60] But I will remember the covenant I made with you in the days of your youth, and I will

[a] 16:37 Is 47:3
[b] 16:38 Ezk 23:45
[c] Gn 9:6; Ezk 23:25
[d] 16:39 Ezk 23:26; Hs 2:3
[e] 16:40 Ezk 23:47
[f] 16:41 Ezk 23:48
[g] 16:42 Ezk 5:13; 21:17
[h] 16:43 Ps 78:42
[i] Ezk 11:21; 22:31
[j] 16:45 Ezk 23:2
[k] Ezk 16:31
[l] 16:46 Ezk 23:4,33
[m] 16:47 Ezk 5:6

[n] 16:48 Mt 10:15; 11:23-24
[o] 16:49 Gn 13:10
[p] 16:50 Gn 18:20-21
[q] 16:53 Is 1:9
[r] Jr 20:16
[s] 16:54 Ezk 14:22-23
[t] 16:57 2Kg 16:5-7
[u] 16:58 Ezk 23:49
[v] 16:59 Ezk 17:19

16:43 It's important to remember that God's people had brought judgment on themselves. So many terrible, sad things happened because they had forgotten what he had done for them.

16:48-52 Sodom was legendary for its sin, revealed here to be a lack of concern for the poor along with its detestable acts (homosexuality, rape, and violence) (16:48-50). Samaria, the capital of the northern kingdom of Israel, had long since been destroyed for its idolatry, but even its people did not commit even half the sins of Jerusalem (16:51). Both of these wicked cities, in fact, appeared more righteous than Jerusalem (16:52). This is an incredible statement of the extent of the city's sin, which was committed despite its people having the greatest of spiritual advantages—including the temple and the manifest presence of God.

16:59-63 The oath Israel made refers to the Mosaic covenant (16:59), the only one established by oath. The covenant made . . . in the days of your youth refers to the Abrahamic covenant, and the permanent covenant speaks of the new covenant of Jeremiah 31:31-34, which also includes believers in Christ (Ezek 16:60). In his millennial kingdom Jesus will rule over all, and Israel will be fully redeemed and will know the Lord as they experience the new covenant nationally (16:62).

[a]16:60 Is 55:3; Jr 32:38-41
[b]16:61 Ezk 6:9
[c]16:62 Hs 2:19-20
[d]16:63 Ezk 36:31-32
[e]Rm 3:19
[f]17:2 Ezk 20:49; 24:3
[g]17:3 Jr 48:40
[h]Ezk 17:12
[i]17:5 Dt 8:7-9
[j]Is 44:4
[k]17:6 Ezk 17:14
[l]17:7 Ezk 31:4

[m]17:9 2Kg 25:7
[n]17:10 Gn 41:6; 2Kg 19:26; Ezk 19:12; Hs 13:15; Jnh 4:8
[o]17:12 Ezk 2:3-5; 12:9-11
[p]2Kg 24:11-15
[q]17:13 2Kg 24:17
[r]2Ch 36:13
[s]17:14 Ezk 29:14
[t]17:15 2Kg 24:20; 2Ch 36:13
[u]Dt 17:16
[v]17:16 Ezk 12:13
[w]17:17 Jr 37:5,7
[x]17:18 1Ch 29:24

establish a permanent covenant with you.[a] [61] Then you will remember your ways[b] and be ashamed when you[A] receive your older and younger sisters. I will give them to you as daughters, but not because of your covenant. [62] I will establish my covenant with you,[c] and you will know that I am the LORD, [63] so that when I make atonement for all you have done, you will remember and be ashamed,[d] and never open your mouth again because of your disgrace.[e] This is the declaration of the Lord GOD.' "

PARABLE OF THE EAGLES

17 The word of the LORD came to me: [2] "Son of man, pose a riddle and speak a parable to the house of Israel.[f] [3] You are to say, 'This is what the Lord GOD says: A huge eagle with powerful wings,[g] long feathers, and full plumage of many colors came to Lebanon and took the top of the cedar.[h] [4] He plucked off its topmost shoot, brought it to the land of merchants, and set it in a city of traders. [5] Then he took some of the land's seed and put it in a fertile field;[i] he set it like a willow,[j] a plant[B] by abundant water. [6] It sprouted and became a spreading vine, low in height with its branches turned toward him,[k] yet its roots stayed under it. So it became a vine, produced branches, and sent out shoots.

[7] " 'But there was another huge eagle with powerful wings and thick plumage. And this vine bent its roots toward him! It stretched out its branches to him from the plot where it was planted,[l] so that he might water it. [8] It had been planted in a good field by abundant water in order to produce branches, bear fruit, and become a splendid vine.'

[9] "You are to say, 'This is what the Lord GOD says: Will it flourish? Will he not tear out its roots[m] and strip off its fruit so that it shrivels? All its fresh leaves will wither! Great strength and many people will not be needed to pull it from its roots. [10] Even though it is planted, will it flourish? Won't it wither completely when the east wind strikes it?[n] It will wither on the plot where it sprouted.' "

[11] The word of the LORD came to me: [12] "Now say to that rebellious house,[o] 'Don't you know what these things mean?' Tell them, 'The king of Babylon came to Jerusalem, took its king and officials,[p] and brought them back with him to Babylon. [13] He took one of the royal family[q] and made a covenant with him, putting him under oath.[r] Then he took away the leading men of the land, [14] so that the kingdom would be humble and not exalt itself[s] but would keep his covenant in order to endure. [15] However, this king revolted against him[t] by sending his ambassadors to Egypt so they might give him horses and a large army.[u] Will he flourish? Will the one who does such things escape? Can he break a covenant and still escape?

[16] " 'As I live — this is the declaration of the Lord GOD — he will die in Babylon, in the land of the king who put him on the throne,[v] whose oath he despised and whose covenant he broke. [17] Pharaoh with his mighty army and vast company will not help him in battle,[w] when ramps are built and siege walls constructed to destroy many lives. [18] He despised the oath by breaking the covenant. He did all these things even though he gave his hand in pledge.[x] He will not escape!

[19] " 'Therefore, this is what the Lord GOD says: As I live, I will bring down on his head my oath that he despised and my covenant that he broke. [20] I will spread my net over

[A]16:61 Some LXX mss, Syr read I [B]17:5 Hb obscure

17:3-21 The **huge eagle** who **came to Lebanon** and **plucked off its topmost shoot** to take it to another land was Nebuchadnezzar, which means that Lebanon stood for Jerusalem (17:3-4; cf. 17:11-12). This referred to the king's first invasion of Judah in 597 BC when he took King Jehoiachin, the "topmost shoot," to Babylon and installed Zedekiah in his place.

Nebuchadnezzar left Judah intact, though weakened (17:5-6; explained in 17:13-14). They were humbled by Babylon with their **branches turned toward** Nebuchadnezzar in subjugation (17:6). When Nebuchadnezzar put Zedekiah on the throne in Jerusalem, he also put **him under oath** to be faithful to his Babylonian overlord (17:13). Nebuchadnezzar further weakened Judah by taking away **the leading men of the land**, but the **kingdom** of

Judah would survive if Zedekiah would **keep his covenant** (17:13-14).

Zedekiah, however, wouldn't think twice about breaking his promise to Nebuchadnezzar. Instead of keeping his pact with Babylon, **this vine** [Zedekiah] **bent its roots toward** the other **huge eagle** in Ezekiel's parable—that is, he revolted by going to the king of Egypt for military help in breaking Babylon's grip (17:7-8; explained in 17:15).

Go back to 17:5-6 to recall how Nebuchadnezzar planted Zedekiah in Jerusalem as a vine whose branches were bent toward him—which was God's will and part of his judgment on his people. This was stated again in 17:8 to reinforce the futility of Zedekiah's revolt, which failed completely because he found no aid in **Egypt**. The **king**, acting foolishly,

had broken his **covenant** and would find no **escape** (17:15). **Pharaoh** would provide no help when Jerusalem was attacked (17:17).

The parable continued with the ruin of Zedekiah (17:9-10; explained in 17:16, 18-21). Nebuchadnezzar would **tear out [his] roots** (17:9), using the imagery of Zedekiah and Jerusalem as a vine. Zedekiah would **wither completely** (17:10): he would **die in Babylon** (17:16). Why? Because **he despised the oath by breaking the covenant** (17:18). Now, that's a statement that we need to read carefully. God hates covenant-breakers, even those who made a covenant with a pagan king! In 17:19-21 Ezekiel provides a detailed prophecy of what happened to Zedekiah and his army when they tried to escape out the back gate as the Babylonians broke into Jerusalem (see 2 Kgs 25:1-10).

him,[a] and he will be caught in my snare.[b] I will bring him to Babylon and execute judgment on him there for the treachery he committed against me.[c] **21** All the fugitives[A] among his troops will fall by the sword, and those who survive will be scattered to every direction of the wind.[d] Then you will know that I, the LORD, have spoken.

22 "This is what the Lord GOD says:

I will take a sprig
from the lofty top of the cedar
    and plant it.[e]
I will pluck a tender sprig
from its topmost shoots,
and I will plant it
on a high towering mountain.
23 I will plant it on Israel's
    high mountain[f]
so that it may bear branches,
    produce fruit,
and become a majestic cedar.
Birds of every kind will nest under it,[g]
taking shelter in the shade
    of its branches.
24 Then all the trees of the field
    will know
that I am the LORD.
I bring down the tall tree,
and make the low tree tall.[h]
I cause the green tree to wither
and make the withered tree thrive.[i]
I, the LORD, have spoken
and I will do it.' "[j]

PERSONAL RESPONSIBILITY FOR SIN

18 The word of the LORD came to me: **2** "What do you mean by using this proverb concerning the land of Israel:

'The fathers eat sour grapes,[k]
and the children's teeth are set
    on edge'?[l]

3 As I live" — this is the declaration of the Lord GOD — "you will no longer use this proverb in Israel.[m] **4** Look, every life belongs to me.[n] The life of the father is like the life of the son — both belong to me. The person who sins is the one who will die.[o]

5 "Suppose a man is righteous and does what is just and right: **6** He does not eat at the mountain shrines[B,p] or look to the idols of the house of Israel. He does not defile his neighbor's wife[q] or approach a woman during her menstrual impurity.[r] **7** He doesn't oppress anyone[s] but returns his collateral to the debtor.[t] He does not commit robbery, but gives his bread to the hungry[u] and covers the naked with clothing. **8** He doesn't lend at interest or for profit[v] but keeps his hand from injustice and carries out true justice between men.[w] **9** He follows my statutes and keeps my ordinances, acting faithfully. Such a person is righteous; he will certainly live."[x] This is the declaration of the Lord GOD.

10 "But suppose the man has a violent son, who sheds blood[y] and does any of these things, **11** though the father has done none of them. Indeed, when the son eats at the mountain shrines and defiles his neighbor's wife, **12** and when he oppresses the poor and needy, commits robbery, and does not return collateral, and when he looks to the idols, commits detestable acts,[z] **13** and lends at interest or for profit, will he live? He will not live! Since he has committed all these detestable acts, he will certainly die. His death will be his own fault.[C,aa]

14 "Now suppose he has a son who sees all the sins his father has committed, and though he sees them, he does not do likewise. **15** He does not eat at the mountain shrines or look to the idols of the house of Israel. He does not defile his neighbor's wife. **16** He doesn't oppress anyone, hold collateral, or commit robbery. He gives his bread to the hungry and covers the naked with clothing. **17** He keeps his hand from harming the poor, not taking interest or profit on a loan. He practices my ordinances and follows my statutes. Such a person will not die for his father's iniquity. He will certainly live.

18 "As for his father, he will die for his own iniquity because he practiced fraud, robbed his brother, and did among his people what was not good.[ab] **19** But you may ask, 'Why doesn't the son suffer punishment for the father's iniquity?'[ac] Since the son has done what is just and right, carefully observing all my statutes, he will certainly live. **20** The person who sins is the one who will die.[ad] A son won't suffer punishment for the father's iniquity, and a father won't suffer punishment for the son's iniquity.[ae] The righteousness of the righteous person will be on him,[af] and the wickedness of the wicked person will be on him.[ag]

[a] 17:20 Ezk 12:13
[b] 2Kg 25:5-6; Jr 39:5
[c] Ezk 20:35-36
[d] 17:21 Ezk 5:10
[e] 17:22 Ps 2:6
[f] 17:23 Ezk 20:40
[g] Dn 4:12
[h] 17:24 Is 40:4
[i] Am 9:11
[j] Nm 14:35; Ps 33:9; Is 46:11; 55:11; Ezk 17:24; 22:14; 24:14; 36:36; 37:14
[k] 18:2 Lm 5:7
[l] Jr 31:29
[m] 18:3 Ezk 12:23
[n] 18:4 Nm 16:22; 27:16
[o] Dt 24:16; Ezk 18:20; Rm 6:23
[p] 18:6 Ezk 22:9
[q] Ex 20:17-18; Lv 20:10
[r] Lv 18:19-20
[s] 18:7 Ex 22:21

[t] 18:7 Dt 24:12-13
[u] Mt 25:35-40
[v] 18:8 Ex 22:25; Lv 25:35-37
[w] Zch 8:16
[x] 18:9 Am 5:4
[y] 18:10 Nm 35:31
[z] 18:12 Ezk 8:6,17
[aa] 18:13 Lv 20:9,11
[ab] 18:18 Ezk 3:18
[ac] 18:19 Ex 20:5
[ad] 18:20 Ezk 18:4
[ae] Dt 24:16; Jn 9:2
[af] Is 3:10-11
[ag] Rm 2:6-9

[A] 17:21 Some Hb mss, LXX, Syr, Tg read *choice men*   [B] 18:6 Lit *the mountains*, also in vv. 11,15   [C] 18:13 Lit *His blood will be on him*

17:22 The phrase **tender sprig** alludes to another prophecy regarding the Messiah: "A shoot will grow from the stump of Jesse, and a branch from his roots will bear fruit" (Isa 11:1).

18:2 The idea behind the saying was that those in the land under Babylon's heel were suffering not because they had sinned, but because their parents had. It was so well known that Jeremiah, who also wrote to the Jews in exile, quoted it (see Jer 31:29-30). They were confusing the cumulative effects of sin with each person's responsibility for his or her personal sins.

a 18:21 Ezk 33:12,19
b 18:22 Ezk 33:16
c Ps 18:20-24
d 18:23 Ezk 33:11
e 18:24 Ezk 3:20; 33:18
f 2Pt 2:20
g 18:25 Ezk 18:29; 33:17,20
h 18:30 Ezk 7:3,8; 33:20
i 18:31 Jr 32:39

j 19:1 Ezk 26:17; 27:2
k 19:3 2Kg 23:31-32
l 19:4-5 2Kg 23:34
m 19:6 Jr 22:13-17
n 19:8 2Kg 24:2,11
o 19:9 2Ch 36:6
p Ezk 6:2

21 "But if the wicked person turns from all the sins he has committed,[a] keeps all my statutes, and does what is just and right, he will certainly live; he will not die. **22** None of the transgressions he has committed will be held against him.[b] He will live because of the righteousness he has practiced.[c] **23** Do I take any pleasure in the death of the wicked?"[d] This is the declaration of the Lord God. "Instead, don't I take pleasure when he turns from his ways and lives? **24** But when a righteous person turns from his righteousness[e] and acts unjustly, committing the same detestable acts that the wicked do, will he live? None of the righteous acts he did will be remembered.[f] He will die because of the treachery he has engaged in and the sin he has committed.

25 "But you say, 'The Lord's way isn't fair.'[g] Now listen, house of Israel: Is it my way that is unfair? Instead, isn't it your ways that are unfair? **26** When a righteous person turns from his righteousness and acts unjustly, he will die for this. He will die because of the injustice he has committed. **27** But if a wicked person turns from the wickedness he has committed and does what is just and right, he will preserve his life. **28** He will certainly live because he thought it over and turned from all the transgressions he had committed; he will not die. **29** But the house of Israel says, 'The Lord's way isn't fair.' Is it my ways that are unfair, house of Israel? Instead, isn't it your ways that are unfair?

30 "Therefore, house of Israel, I will judge each one of you according to his ways."[h] This is the declaration of the Lord God. "Repent and turn from all your rebellious acts, so they will not become a sinful stumbling block to you. **31** Throw off all the transgressions you have committed, and get yourselves a new heart and a new spirit.[i] Why should you die, house of Israel? **32** For I take no pleasure in anyone's death."

This is the declaration of the Lord God. "So repent and live!

A LAMENT FOR ISRAEL'S PRINCES

19 "As for you, take up a lament for the princes of Israel,[j] **2** and say:

What was your mother? A lioness!
She lay down among the lions;
she reared her cubs
among the young lions.
3   She brought up one of her cubs,
and he became a young lion.[k]
After he learned to tear prey,
he devoured people.
4   When the nations heard about him,
he was caught in their pit.
Then they led him away with hooks
to the land of Egypt.[l]

5   When she saw that she waited
in vain,
that her hope was lost,
she took another of her cubs
and made him a young lion.
6   He prowled among the lions,[m]
and he became a young lion.
After he learned to tear prey,
he devoured people.
7   He devastated their strongholds[A]
and destroyed their cities.
The land and everything
in it shuddered
at the sound of his roaring.
8   Then the nations from
the surrounding provinces
set out against him.[n]
They spread their net over him;
he was caught in their pit.
9   They put a wooden yoke on him[B]
with hooks[o]
and led him away to the king
of Babylon.
They brought him into the fortresses
so his roar could no longer be heard
on the mountains of Israel.[p]

_A19:7 Tg, Aq; MT reads *knew their widows*   _B19:9 Or *put him in a cage*

18:21-24 This chapter is not teaching that salvation is attained through works. The actions in view here were practiced out of the outflow of hearts that were or were not in right standing before God.

18:25-30 Judah had the common (and wrong) view that God weighed actions and if the good outweighed the bad, a person was okay in his sight. But God proved that salvation was a matter of where you end up, not where you start. That's why he told Judah in essence, "If you repent I will judge you based on your repentance, not your wickedness." That's good news. But he also reversed it and said, "If you don't repent, I will judge you on your wickedness, not how good you were before you turned to wickedness."

18:31-32 Ultimately, the only way to be saved is by getting **a new heart** (18:31). And the only way to get that is to **repent**, trust Jesus Christ, and receive a transformed heart through the work of the Holy Spirit (18:32; see 36:26-27; cf. Jer 31:31-34).

19:1 A **lament** was normally a dirge or funeral song honoring someone who had died, although the three kings alluded to in this chapter deserved none.

19:2-4 The **lioness** (19:2) represented Israel, the nation that had produced so many great kings. But the first one referenced here is generally agreed to be Jehoahaz, an evil king who came to the throne in Jerusalem after the early death of his father, good King Josiah (see 2 Kgs 23:31-32). Jehoahaz **devoured people** through his bad decisions during his three-month reign, but he was captured by Pharaoh Neco (Ezek 19:3-4; see 2 Kgs 23:33).

19:5-9 The second cub was another bad king, Jehoiachin (19:5). He also reigned just three months in Jerusalem, causing great suffering, before Nebuchadnezzar captured him and took him to Babylon (see 2 Kgs 23:34–24:6). Jehoiachin never returned home, **so his roar could no longer be heard** in **Israel** (Ezek 19:9).

10 Your mother was like a vine
　　in your vineyard,[A,a]
　planted by the water;
　it was fruitful and full of branches[b]
　because of abundant water.
11 It had strong branches, fit for
　　the scepters of rulers;
　its height towered
　　among the clouds.[B]
So it was conspicuous for its height
　as well as its many branches.
12 But it was uprooted in fury,[c]
　thrown to the ground,
　and the east wind dried up its fruit.
　Its strong branches were torn off
　　and dried up;[d]
　fire consumed them.
13 Now it is planted in the wilderness,[e]
　in a dry and thirsty land.
14 Fire has gone out from its
　　main branch[c]
　and has devoured its fruit,
　so that it no longer has
　　a strong branch,
　a scepter for ruling.[f]
This is a lament and should be used as a
lament."

ISRAEL'S REBELLION

20 In the seventh year, in the fifth month, on the tenth day of the month, some of Israel's elders came to inquire of the Lord,[g] and they sat down in front of me. **2** Then the word of the Lord came to me: **3** "Son of man, speak with the elders of Israel and tell them, 'This is what the Lord God says: Are you coming to inquire of me? As I live, I will not let you inquire of me.[h] This is the declaration of the Lord God.'

4 "Will you pass judgment against them, will you pass judgment, son of man? Explain the detestable practices of their fathers to them.[i] **5** Say to them, 'This is what the Lord God says: On the day I chose Israel, I swore an oath[D,j] to the descendants of Jacob's house and made myself known

to them in the land of Egypt. I swore to them, saying, "I am the Lord your God."[k] **6** On that day I swore[E] to them that I would bring them out[l] of the land of Egypt into a land I had searched out for them, a land flowing with milk and honey,[m] the most beautiful of all lands.[n] **7** I also said to them, "Throw away, each of you, the abhorrent things that you prize,[F] and do not defile yourselves with the idols of Egypt.[o] I am the Lord your God."[p]

8 "'But they rebelled against me and were unwilling to listen to me. None of them threw away the abhorrent things that they prized,[G] and they did not abandon the idols of Egypt. So I considered pouring out my wrath on them,[q] exhausting my anger against them within the land of Egypt. **9** But I acted for the sake of my name,[r] so that it would not be profaned in the eyes of the nations they were living among, in whose sight I had made myself known to Israel by bringing them out of Egypt. **10** "'So I brought them out of the land of Egypt and led them into the wilderness.[s] **11** Then I gave them my statutes and explained my ordinances to them — the person who does them will live by them.[t] **12** I also gave them my Sabbaths to serve as a sign between me and them,[u] so that they would know that I am the Lord who consecrates them.

13 "'But the house of Israel rebelled against me in the wilderness.[v] They did not follow my statutes and they rejected my ordinances — the person who does them will live by them.[w] They also completely profaned my Sabbaths.[x] So I considered pouring out my wrath on them in the wilderness to put an end to them.[y] **14** But I acted for the sake of my name, so that it would not be profaned in the eyes of the nations in whose sight I had brought them out. **15** However, I swore to them[z] in the wilderness that I would not bring them into the land I had given them — the most beautiful of all lands, flowing with milk

[a]19:10 Ps 80:8-11
[b]Dt 8:7-9
[c]19:12 Jr 31:28
[d]Hs 13:15
[e]19:13 2Kg 24:12-16; Hs 2:3
[f]19:14 Lm 2:5
[g]20:1 Ezk 8:1,11-12; 14:1
[h]20:3 Ezk 14:3
[i]20:4 Ezk 16:2; 22:2
[j]20:5 Ex 6:6-8

[k]20:5 Ex 6:2-3
[l]20:6 Jr 32:22
[m]Ex 3:8
[n]Ps 16:6; 48:2; 50:2; Jr 3:19
[o]20:7 Lv 18:3
[p]Ex 20:2
[q]20:8 Ezk 5:13; 7:8
[r]20:9 Ezk 36:21-22
[s]20:10 Ex 13:18,20
[t]20:11 Lv 18:5; Rm 10:5; Gl 3:12
[u]20:12 Ex 31:13
[v]20:13 Nm 14:11-12,22
[w]Lv 18:5
[x]Ezk 22:8; 23:38; 44:24
[y]Ex 32:10; Dt 9:8
[z]20:15 Nm 14:28-30

[A]19:10 Some Hb mss; other Hb mss read *blood*　　[B]19:11 Or *thick foliage*　　[C]19:14 Lit *from the branch of its parts*　　[D]20:5 Lit *I lifted my hand*
[E]20:6 Lit *lifted my hand*, also in vv. 15,23,28,42　　[F]20:7 Lit *things of your eyes*　　[G]20:8 Lit *things of their eyes*

19:10-14 The third king is King Zedekiah. Nebuchadnezzar left him on the throne and left Jerusalem intact, still **planted** in the holy land to flourish if the king would only keep his covenant (19:10-11). But when Zedekiah broke his word, the Babylonian army **uprooted** Jerusalem **in fury** as **fire consumed** the holy city (19:12; see 2 Kgs 24:18-20). Its people were deported to **a . . . thirsty land** (Ezek 19:13), and with the Babylonian exile, the last Davidic king was removed from the throne. There

was **no longer . . . a strong branch, a scepter for ruling** (19:14). Nevertheless, they will be restored in Jesus Christ when he comes to rule on his millennial throne. He is "the Son of David" (Matt 1:1), "the King of Israel" (John 1:49), and "the Lion from the tribe of Judah, the Root of David" (Rev 5:5).
20:1-3 This happened in 591 BC, about the seventh year of Zedekiah's doomed rule in Jerusalem. The inquiry made by the **elders** (20:1) isn't recorded, but judging from the response

to it they had come wanting good news from God without having a willingness to follow him. God flatly refused to let the elders **inquire** of him because of their sins and those of Judah's people, whom they represented.
20:5 The reference to God choosing Israel during the days of Moses was not a denial of his choice of Abraham and his descendants to be his people. It was a recognition that Israel was born as a nation when God sent Moses to lead them out of **the land of Egypt**.

a 20:16 Ezk 11:21; 14:3-7
b 20:17 Ezk 11:13
c 20:18 Mt 15:1-3
d 20:19 Dt 5:32-33
e 20:20 Jr 17:22
f 20:21 Nm 21:5; 25:1-3
g 20:23 Lv 26:33

h 20:24 Ezk 6:9
i 20:25 Ps 81:12; Rm
    1:21-25,28
j 20:26 Lv 18:21
k Ezk 6:7
l 20:27 Rm 2:24
m 20:28 Ezk 6:13
n 20:30 Jdg 2:19; Jr 7:26;
    16:12
o 20:31 Ezk 16:20
p 20:32 Dt 4:28; 2Kg 19:18;
    Rv 9:20
q Ezk 11:5
r 20:33 Jr 21:5
s 20:34 Jr 31:8; Ezk 36:24;
    37:21
t Ex 6:6; Dt 4:34
u 20:35 Ezk 19:13
v 20:36 Nm 14:21-23,28
w 20:37 Lv 27:32; Jr 33:13

⇨ Questions & Answers ⇦

Q In your pastoral work, what do you see as the biggest barriers to an individual prioritizing God's kingdom in his or her life?

A One of the great pressures that people face is to conform—whether to peer groups, to a work environment, or to educational instruction. We desire acceptance, recognition, and being valued—and oftentimes this comes through adapting to the culture. So I think the pressure to conform in order to receive value and acceptance is a dominant reason why Christians often limit their pursuit of spiritual growth.

FOR THE NEXT Q&A, SEE PAGE 1006.

and honey — **16** because they rejected my ordinances, profaned my Sabbaths, and did not follow my statutes. For their hearts went after their idols.[a] **17** Yet I spared them from destruction and did not bring them to an end in the wilderness.[b]

18 " 'Then I said to their children in the wilderness, "Don't follow the statutes of your fathers, defile yourselves with their idols, or keep their ordinances.[c] **19** I am the LORD your God. Follow my statutes, keep my ordinances, and practice them.[d] **20** Keep my Sabbaths holy,[e] and they will be a sign between me and you, so you may know that I am the LORD your God."

21 " 'But the children rebelled against me.[f] They did not follow my statutes or carefully keep my ordinances — the person who does them will live by them. They also profaned my Sabbaths. So I considered pouring out my wrath on them and exhausting my anger against them in the wilderness. **22** But I withheld my hand and acted for the sake of my name, so that it would not be profaned in the eyes of the nations in whose sight I brought them out. **23** However, I swore to them in the wilderness that I would disperse them among the nations and scatter them among the countries.[g] **24** For they did not practice my ordinances but rejected my statutes and profaned my Sabbaths, and their eyes

were fixed[h] on their fathers' idols. **25** I also gave them statutes that were not good and ordinances[i] they could not live by. **26** When they sacrificed every firstborn in the fire,[A,j] I defiled them through their gifts in order to devastate them so they would know that I am the LORD.'[k]

27 "Therefore, son of man, speak to the house of Israel, and tell them, 'This is what the Lord GOD says: In this way also your fathers blasphemed me by[l] committing treachery against me: **28** When I brought them into the land that I swore to give them and they saw any high hill or leafy tree,[m] they offered their sacrifices and presented their offensive offerings there. They also sent up their pleasing aromas and poured out their drink offerings there. **29** So I asked them, "What is this high place you are going to?" And it is still called Bamah[B] today.'

30 "Therefore say to the house of Israel, 'This is what the Lord GOD says: Are you defiling yourselves the way your fathers did,[n] and prostituting yourselves with their abhorrent things? **31** When you offer your gifts, sacrificing your children in the fire,[C,o] you still continue to defile yourselves with all your idols today. So should I let you inquire of me, house of Israel? As I live — this is the declaration of the Lord GOD — I will not let you inquire of me!

ISRAEL'S RESTORATION

32 " 'When you say, "Let us be like the nations, like the clans of other countries, serving wood and stone,"[p] what you have in mind will never happen.[q] **33** As I live — the declaration of the Lord GOD — I will reign over you with a strong hand, an outstretched arm,[r] and outpoured wrath. **34** I will bring you from the peoples and gather you from the countries where you were scattered,[s] with a strong hand, an outstretched arm,[t] and outpoured wrath. **35** I will lead you into the wilderness of the peoples[u] and enter into judgment with you there face to face. **36** Just as I entered into judgment with your fathers in the wilderness of the land of Egypt,[v] so I will enter into judgment with you. This is the declaration of the Lord GOD. **37** I will make you pass under the rod[w] and will bring you into

---

A **20:26** Lit *they made every firstborn pass through the fire*   B **20:29** = High Place   C **20:31** Lit *gifts, making your children pass through the fire*

20:22 Though God's people cared nothing for his glory, God himself is always zealous for it. **20:33-44** The language in these verses cannot be matched to the return from exile in Babylon, or to any era in Israel's history. This gathering, then, is yet in the future, when God reclaims Israel **from the countries where [they were] scattered** (20:34). Israel will then be led **into the wilderness** for the purpose of **judgment**, as God did after the exodus from **Egypt** (20:35-36). But this time all the rebels will be weeded out and only true believers will enter the land, which is a picture of Israel's purging in the tribulation and their worship of the Messiah, Jesus, in his millennial kingdom (20:44).

the bond of the covenant. **38** I will purge you of those who rebel and transgress against me.*a* I will bring them out of the land where they live as foreign residents, but they will not enter the land of Israel. Then you will know that I am the LORD.

39 " 'As for you, house of Israel, this is what the Lord GOD says: Go and serve your idols, each of you. But afterward you will surely listen to me, and you will no longer defile my holy name with your gifts and idols.*b* **40** For on my holy mountain, Israel's high mountain — the declaration of the Lord GOD — there the entire house of Israel, all of them,*c* will serve me in the land. There I will accept them and will require your contributions and choicest gifts,*d* all your holy offerings. **41** When I bring you from the peoples and gather you from the countries where you have been scattered, I will accept you as a pleasing aroma. And I will demonstrate my holiness through you in the sight of the nations.*e* **42** When I lead you into the land of Israel, the land I swore to give your fathers, you will know that I am the LORD.*f* **43** There you will remember your ways and all your deeds by which you have defiled yourself,*g* and you will loathe yourselves for all the evil things you have done.*h* **44** You will know that I am the LORD,*i* house of Israel, when I have dealt with you for the sake of my name*j* rather than according to your evil ways and corrupt acts. This is the declaration of the Lord GOD.' "

FIRE IN THE SOUTH

45 The word of the LORD came to me: **46** "Son of man, face the south and preach against it. Prophesy against the forest land in the Negev,*k* **47** and say to the forest there, 'Hear the word of the LORD! This is what the Lord GOD says: I am about to ignite a fire in you, and it will devour every green tree and every dry tree in you. The blazing flame will not be extinguished, and every face from the south to the north will be scorched by it. **48** Then all people will see that I, the LORD, have kindled it.*l* It will not be extinguished.' "

49 Then I said, "Oh, Lord GOD, they are saying of me, 'Isn't he just composing parables?' "*m*

GOD'S SWORD OF JUDGMENT

21 The word of the LORD came to me again: **2** "Son of man, face*n* Jerusalem and preach against the sanctuaries. Prophesy against the land of Israel, **3** and say to it, 'This is what the LORD says: I am against you.*o* I will draw my sword from its sheath and cut off from you both the righteous and the wicked. **4** Since I will cut off*A* both the righteous and the wicked, my sword will therefore come out of its sheath against all people from the south to the north.*p* **5** So all people will know that I, the LORD, have taken my sword from its sheath — it will not be sheathed again.'*q*

6 "But you, son of man, groan! Groan bitterly with a broken heart*B* right before their eyes. **7** And when they ask you, 'Why are you groaning?' then say, 'Because of the news that is coming.' Every heart will melt, and every hand will become weak. Every spirit will be discouraged, and all knees will run with urine.*c* Yes, it is coming and it will happen. This is the declaration of the Lord GOD.' "

8 The word of the LORD came to me: **9** "Son of man, prophesy, 'This is what the Lord says!' You are to proclaim,

'A sword!*5* A sword is sharpened
  and also polished.*r*
10 It is sharpened for slaughter,
  polished to flash like lightning!
  Should we rejoice?
  The scepter of my son,
  the sword despises every tree.*D*
11 The sword is given to be polished,
  to be grasped in the hand.
  It is sharpened, and it is polished,
  to be put in the hand of the slayer.'*u*

12 "Cry out and wail, son of man, for it is against my people. It is against all the princes of Israel! They are given over to the sword with my people. Therefore strike your thigh in grief.*v* **13** Surely it will be a trial! And what if the sword despises even the scepter? The scepter will not continue."*D* This is the declaration of the Lord GOD.

14 "So you, son of man, prophesy and clap your hands together:*w*

Let the sword strike two times,
  even three.

a 20:38 Ezk 34:17-22
b 20:39 Is 1:13-15; Ezk 23:38-39
c 20:40 Ezk 37:22,24
d Is 60:7; Ezk 43:27
e 20:41 Is 5:16; Ezk 28:25; 2Co 6:17
f 20:42 Ezk 36:23; 38:23
g 20:43 Ezk 6:9; 16:61,63
n Ezk 36:31
i 20:44 Ezk 24:24
j Ezk 36:22
k 20:46 Ezk 21:2
l 20:48 Jr 21:14
m 20:49 Ezk 17:2

n 21:2 Ezk 20:46
o 21:3 Ezk 5:8
p 21:4 Ezk 7:2; 20:47
q 21:5 Ezk 21:30
r 21:7 Ezk 7:26
s 21:9 Dt 32:41
t Jr 46:4
u 21:11 Ezk 21:19
v 21:12 Jr 31:19
w 21:14 Nm 24:10

A 21:4 Lit *off from you*   *B* 21:6 Lit *insides,* or *waist*   *C* 21:7 Lit *knees will go water*   *D* 21:10,13 Hb obscure

20:46-48 Even though the Babylonians would come from the north, the destructive **fire** they would **ignite** would burn from south (**the Negev**) to north.

20:49 In other words, the people said of Ezekiel, "He's merely making up stories. All is well."

21:12-13 Ezekiel was told to **cry out and wail** for the extent of this judgment that would leave no one on the throne of David in Jerusalem. Though his lineage would survive the slaughter, his descendants—with the exception of Jesus, the Messiah—would never again rule as the nation's kings.

[a] 21:15 Ezk 32:20
[b] Ezk 21:28
[c] 21:17 Ezk 5:13
[d] 21:20 Jr 49:2
[e] 21:22 Ezk 4:2; 26:9
[f] 21:23 Ezk 17:16,18
[g] 21:25 2Kg 24:20
[h] Ezk 21:29

[i] 21:26 Ezk 17:24; Lk 1:52
[j] 21:27 Jr 23:5-6
[k] 21:28 Is 31:8; Jr 12:12;
    46:10,14
[l] 21:29 Ezk 13:6-9; 22:28
[m] 21:30 Jr 47:6-7
[n] 21:31 Ezk 22:20-21
[o] 21:32 Ezk 25:10
[p] 22:2 Ezk 16:2; 20:4

It is a sword for massacre,
a sword for great massacre —
it surrounds[A] them!
15 I have appointed a sword[a]
    for slaughter[B]
at all their gates,
so that their hearts may melt
and many may stumble.
Yes! It is ready to flash
    like lightning;[b]
it is drawn[B] for slaughter.
16 Slash to the right;
turn to the left —
wherever your blade is directed.
17 I also will clap my hands together, and I will satisfy my wrath.[c] I, the LORD, have spoken."

18 The word of the LORD came to me: 19 "Now you, son of man, mark out two roads that the sword of Babylon's king can take. Both of them should originate from the same land. And make a signpost at the fork in the road to each city. 20 Mark out a road that the sword can take to Rabbah of the Ammonites[d] and to Judah into fortified Jerusalem. 21 For the king of Babylon stands at the split in the road, at the fork of the two roads, to practice divination: he shakes the arrows, consults the idols, and observes the liver. 22 The answer marked[c] Jerusalem appears in his right hand, indicating that he should set up battering rams,[e] give the order to[D] slaughter, raise a battle cry, set battering rams against the gates, build a ramp, and construct a siege wall. 23 It will seem like false divination to those who have sworn an oath to the Babylonians,[E,f] but it will draw attention to their guilt so that they will be captured. 24 "Therefore, this is what the Lord GOD says: Because you have drawn attention to your guilt, exposing your transgressions, so that your sins are revealed in all your actions — since you have done this, you will be captured by them. 25 And you, profane and wicked prince of Israel,[F,g] the day has come[h] for your punishment.[G]

26 "This is what the Lord GOD says:
Remove the turban, and take off
    the crown.

Things will not remain as they are;[H]
exalt the lowly and bring down
    the exalted.[i]
27 A ruin, a ruin,
I will make it a ruin!
Yet this will not happen
until he comes;[j]
I have given the judgment to him.[i]

28 "Now you, son of man, prophesy, and say, 'This is what the Lord GOD says concerning the Ammonites and their contempt.' You are to proclaim,
'A sword! A sword
is drawn for slaughter,
polished to consume,[k] to flash
    like lightning.
29 While they offer false visions[l]
and lying divinations about you,
the time has come to put you
to the necks of the profane
    wicked ones;
the day has come
for final punishment.

30 "'Return it to its sheath![m]

"'I will judge you'
in the place
    where you were created,
in the land of your origin.
31 I will pour out my indignation
    on you;
I will blow the fire of my fury
    on you.[n]
I will hand you over to brutal men,
skilled at destruction.
32 You will be fuel for the fire.
Your blood will be spilled
    within the land.
You will not be remembered,[o]
for I, the LORD, have spoken.'"

INDICTMENT OF SINFUL JERUSALEM

22 The word of the LORD came to me: 2 "As for you, son of man, will you pass judgment? Will you pass judgment against the city of blood? Then explain all her detestable practices to her.[p] 3 You are to say, 'This is what the Lord GOD says: A

[A] 21:14 Or penetrates [B] 21:15 Hb obscure [C] 21:22 Lit The divination for [D] 21:22 Lit rams, open the mouth in [E] 21:23 Lit them
[F] 21:25 = King Zedekiah [G] 21:25 Lit come in the time of the punishment of the end, also in v. 29 [H] 21:26 Lit This not this [I] 21:27 Or comes to whom
it rightfully belongs, and I will give it to him [J] 21:30 = the Ammonites

21:18-22 The Ammonites, whose capital was **Rabbah** (think modern-day Jordan with its capital of Amman) had also rebelled against Babylon. Nebuchadnezzar reached a crossroads and had to decide whether to attack Jerusalem or Rabbah (21:19-20). He consulted all of his pagan objects and

rites, but God intervened and led him to **Jerusalem** where he set up his siege ramps (21:21-22).
21:23 Even as Babylon was building siege works, some in Jerusalem thought Nebuchadnezzar's actions were the result of **false divination** and would fail.

21:28 Ammon was the first on a list of nations that were to be judged for their mistreatment of Israel, with God indicating it would be invaded and destroyed by "the people of the east" (see 25:1-5).

city that sheds blood[a] within her walls so that her time of judgment has come and who makes idols for herself so that she is defiled! **4** You are guilty of the blood you have shed,[b] and you are defiled from the idols you have made. You have brought your judgment[A] days near and have come to your years of punishment.[B] Therefore, I have made you a disgrace to the nations and a mockery to all the lands. **5** Those who are near and those far away from you will mock you, you infamous one full of turmoil.

6 " 'Look, every prince of Israel[c] within you has used his strength to shed blood. **7** Father and mother are treated with contempt,[d] and the resident alien is exploited within you. The fatherless and widow are oppressed in you.[e] **8** You despise my holy things and profane my Sabbaths.[f] **9** There are men within you who slander in order to shed blood.[g] People who live in you eat at the mountain shrines;[c] they commit depraved acts within you. **10** Men within you have sexual intercourse with their father's wife and violate women during their menstrual impurity.[h] **11** One man within you commits a detestable act with his neighbor's wife;[i] another defiles his daughter-in-law with depravity; and yet another violates his sister, his father's daughter.[j] **12** People who live in you accept bribes in order to shed blood.[k] You take interest and profit on a loan and brutally extort your neighbors.[l] You have forgotten me.[m] This is the declaration of the Lord God.

13 " 'Now look, I clap my hands together against the dishonest profit you have made[n] and against the blood shed among you. **14** Will your courage endure[o] or your hands be strong in the days when I deal with you? I, the Lord, have spoken, and I will act.[p] **15** I will disperse you among the nations and scatter you among the countries;[q] I will purge your uncleanness.[r] **16** You[D] will be profaned in the sight of the nations. Then you will know that I am the Lord.' "[s]

JERUSALEM AS GOD'S FURNACE

17 The word of the Lord came to me: **18** "Son of man, the house of Israel has become merely dross to me.[t] All of them are copper, tin, iron, and lead inside the furnace;[u] they are just dross from silver. **19** Therefore, this is what the Lord God says: Because all of you have become dross, I am about to gather you into Jerusalem. **20** Just as one gathers silver, copper, iron, lead, and tin into the furnace to blow fire[v] on them and melt them, so I will gather you in my anger and wrath, put you inside, and melt you. **21** Yes, I will gather you together and blow on you with the fire of my fury, and you will be melted within the city. **22** As silver is melted inside a furnace, so you will be melted inside the city. Then you will know that I, the Lord, have poured out my wrath on you."[w]

INDICTMENT OF A SINFUL LAND

23 The word of the Lord came to me: **24** "Son of man, say to her, 'You are a land that has not been cleansed,[x] that has not received rain in the day of indignation.' **25** The conspiracy of her prophets[y] within her is[E] like a roaring lion tearing its prey: they devour people, seize wealth and valuables, and multiply the widows within her. **26** Her priests do violence to my instruction and profane my holy things.[z] They make no distinction between the holy and the common, and they do not explain the difference between the clean and the unclean.[aa] They close their eyes to my Sabbaths, and I am profaned among them.

27 "Her officials within her are like wolves tearing their prey, shedding blood, and destroying lives in order to make profit dishonestly. **28** Her prophets plaster for them with whitewash by seeing false visions and lying divinations,[ab] saying, 'This is what the Lord God says,' when the Lord has not spoken. **29** The people of the land have practiced extortion and committed robbery.[ac] They have oppressed the poor and needy and unlawfully exploited the resident alien. **30** I searched for a man

[a] 22:3 Ezk 22:6,27; 23:37,45
[b] 22:4 2Kg 21:16
[c] 22:6 Is 1:23
[d] 22:7 Ex 20:12; Lv 20:9; Dt 27:16
[e] Ex 22:22
[f] 22:8 Lv 19:30; Ezk 20:13
[g] 22:9 Lv 19:16
[h] 22:10 Lv 18:7-8,19
[i] 22:11 Ezk 20:17; Ezk 18:11
[j] Lv 18:9,15; 20:17
[k] 22:12 Ex 23:8
[l] Lv 19:13; 25:36; Dt 23:19
[m] Ezk 23:35
[n] 22:13 Ezk 21:14,17
[o] 22:14 Ezk 21:7
[p] Ezk 17:24
[q] 22:15 Dt 4:27; Ezk 12:15
[r] Ezk 23:27,48
[s] 22:16 Ps 83:18; Ezk 6:7

[t] 22:18 Ps 119:119; Is 1:22
[u] Pr 17:3
[v] 22:20 Is 1:25
[w] 22:22 Ezk 20:8,33
[x] 22:24 Ezk 24:13
[y] 22:25 Jr 11:9; Hs 6:9
[z] 22:26 1Sm 2:12-17,22
[aa] Lv 10:10
[ab] 22:28 Ezk 13:10-15
[ac] 22:29 Ezk 9:9; 22:7

[A] **22:4** *judgment* supplied for clarity   [B] **22:4** *punishment* supplied for clarity   [C] **22:9** Lit *the mountains*   [D] **22:16** One Hb ms, LXX, Syr, Vg read *I*
[E] **22:24-25** LXX reads *indignation*, **25** *whose princes within her are*

22:4 The violence in the city was sin against one's fellow man, against others made in the image of God.

22:13 To **clap** one's **hands** was a sign of derision.

22:19 Dross is scum that is scraped away after metal is refined.

22:21-22 The Babylonians would burn the Israelites in **the fire of [God's] fury** (22:21). Then his sinful people would know that he is **the Lord** as his **wrath** was **poured out on** them (22:22).

How much better it is for God to confirm his sovereignty in our lives by blessing our obedience than by punishing our disobedience!

22:25-29 Here we get a picture of a society in complete chaos and breakdown. Every sphere of authority in God's kingdom program—from the religious leaders, to the civil government, and even the family unit—was failing in its responsibility to carry out God's kingdom agenda.

22:30-31 The principle of representation allows God to hold back his judgment if he has sufficient intermediaries whose righteousness can be credited to the benefit of the unrighteous. When such representatives are absent and the people do not repent, then judgment falls (see Gen 18:22-33; 1 Cor 7:13-14).

*a*22:30 Ezk 13:5
b Ex 32:11–14; Ps 106:23
*c*22:31 Ezk 7:3,8–9; 9:10
*d*23:2 Ezk 16:46
*e*23:3 Lv 17:7; Jr 3:9
*f*23:5 2Kg 15:19; 16:7; 17:3;
Ezk 16:28; Hs 5:13; 8:9–10
*g*23:8 Ex 32:4; 1Kg 12:28;
2Kg 10:29; 17:16
*h*23:9 Ezk 16:37; 23:22
*i*23:11 Jr 3:8–11; Ezk 16:51

*j*23:12 2Kg 16:7–20
*k*23:14 Ezk 8:10
l Ezk 16:29
*m*23:16 Is 57:9
*n*23:17 2Kg 24:17
*o*23:18 Ps 78:59; 106:40;
Jr 12:8
*p*23:21 Ezk 16:26
*q*23:23 Jr 50:21

among them who would repair the wall*a* and stand in the gap before me on behalf of the land so that I might not destroy it,*b* but I found no one. **31** So I have poured out my indignation on them and consumed them with the fire of my fury. I have brought their conduct down on their own heads."*c* This is the declaration of the Lord God.

THE TWO IMMORAL SISTERS

23 The word of the Lord came to me again: **2** "Son of man, there were two women,*d* daughters of the same mother, **3** who acted like prostitutes in Egypt,*e* behaving promiscuously in their youth. Their breasts were fondled there, and their virgin nipples caressed. **4** The older one was named Oholah,*A* and her sister was Oholibah.*B* They became mine and gave birth to sons and daughters. As for their names, Oholah represents Samaria and Oholibah represents Jerusalem.

5 "Oholah acted like a prostitute even though she was mine. She lusted after her lovers, the Assyrians:*f* warriors **6** dressed in blue, governors and prefects, all of them desirable young men, horsemen riding on steeds. **7** She offered her sexual favors to them; all of them were the elite of Assyria. She defiled herself with all those she lusted after and with all their idols. **8** She didn't give up her promiscuity that began in Egypt,*g* when men slept with her in her youth, caressed her virgin nipples, and poured out their lust on her. **9** Therefore, I handed her over to her lovers,*h* the Assyrians she lusted for. **10** They exposed her nakedness, seized her sons and daughters, and killed her with the sword. Since they executed judgment against her, she became notorious among women.

11 "Now her sister Oholibah saw this, but she was even more depraved in her lust than Oholah, and made her promiscuous acts worse than those of her sister.*i* **12** She lusted after the Assyrians:*j* governors and prefects, warriors splendidly dressed, horsemen riding on steeds, all of them desirable young men. **13** And I saw that she had defiled herself; both of them had taken the same path. **14** But she increased her promiscuity when she saw male figures carved on the wall,*k* images of the Chaldeans, engraved in bright red,*l* **15** wearing belts on their waists and flowing turbans on their heads; all of them looked like officers, a depiction of the Babylonians in Chaldea, their native land. **16** At the sight of them*C* she lusted after them and sent messengers to them in Chaldea.*m* **17** Then the Babylonians came to her,*n* to the bed of love, and defiled her with their lust. But after she was defiled by them, she turned away from them in disgust. **18** When she flaunted her promiscuity and exposed her nakedness, I turned away from her in disgust just as I turned away from her sister.*o* **19** Yet she multiplied her acts of promiscuity, remembering the days of her youth when she acted like a prostitute in the land of Egypt **20** and lusted after their lovers, whose sexual members*D* were like those of donkeys and whose emission was like that of stallions. **21** So you revisited the depravity of your youth, when the Egyptians caressed your nipples to enjoy your youthful breasts.*p*

22 "Therefore, Oholibah, this is what the Lord God says: I am going to incite your lovers against you, those you turned away from in disgust. I will bring them against you from every side: **23** the Babylonians and all the Chaldeans; Pekod, Shoa, and Koa;*q* and all the Assyrians with them — desirable young men, all of them governors and prefects, officers and administrators, all of them riding on steeds. **24** They will come against you with an assembly of peoples and with weapons, chariots, and*E* wagons. They will set themselves against you

*A*23:4 = Her Tent   *B*23:4 = My Tent Is in Her   *C*23:16 Lit *of her eyes*   *D*23:20 Lit *whose flesh*   *E*23:24 LXX reads *peoples, from the north, chariots and*; Hb obscure

23:2-4 Together these sisters represented the entire nation of Israel, which spent its youth **in Egypt** where its people first succumbed to idol worship (23:3). **Samaria** was the capital of the northern kingdom of Israel (which by this time had been destroyed), and **Jerusalem** was the capital of the southern kingdom of Judah (23:4). Their sexual promiscuity was metaphorical for their spiritual adultery against the Lord.
23:5-10 **Oholah** (Samaria) sought out **the Assyrians** (23:5) as the rulers of the northern kingdom prostituted themselves to that

pagan nation. Because God's people did not give up their **promiscuity** (23:8), God handed them over to the Assyrians to be oppressed and eventually **killed** by them. Israel was destroyed in 722 BC (23:10).
23:11-13 Oholibah's lusting **after the Assyrians** (23:12) probably refers to the actions of King Ahaz of Judah, who sought an alliance with Assyria to beat back an invasion from Israel (the northern kingdom) and Aram (see 2 Kgs 16). In doing so, he made Judah a vassal state of Assyria for the next century.

23:14-21 King Jehoiakim turned to the **Babylonians** and willingly made Judah its vassal state (23:14-17), but when Babylon proved to be a harsh taskmaster, God's nation came full circle and turned to **Egypt** for aid. Thus she **revisited the depravity of** **[her] youth** and turned to the country that had originally enslaved her (23:19-21). But her attempt to be rescued by Egypt proved futile. Only God could provide the help needed.
23:22 God sometimes uses the unrighteous to judge his people (see Hab 1:12-13).

on every side with large and small shields and helmets. I will delegate judgment to them, and they will judge you by their own standards. **25** When I vent my jealous rage on you,[a] they will deal with you in wrath. They will cut off your nose and ears, and the rest of you[A] will fall by the sword. They will seize your sons and daughters, and the rest of you will be consumed by fire. **26** They will strip off your clothes and take your beautiful jewelry.[b] **27** So I will put an end to your depravity and sexual immorality, which began in the land of Egypt, and you will not look longingly at them or remember Egypt anymore.

28 "For this is what the Lord GOD says: I am going to hand you over to those you hate, to those you turned away from in disgust. **29** They will treat you with hatred, take all you have worked for, and leave you stark naked,[c] so that the shame of your debauchery will be exposed, both your depravity and promiscuity. **30** These things will be done to you because you acted like a prostitute with the nations,[d] defiling yourself with their idols. **31** You have followed the path of your sister, so I will put her cup in your hand."[e]

32 This is what the Lord GOD says:

"You will drink your sister's cup,[f]
    which is deep and wide.
You will be an object of[B] ridicule
    and scorn,
    for it holds so much.[g]
33 You will be filled with drunkenness
    and grief,
with a cup of devastation
    and desolation,
    the cup of your sister Samaria.
34 You will drink it and drain it;
    then you will gnaw its broken pieces,
    and tear your breasts.
For I have spoken."
    This is the declaration
    of the Lord GOD.

35 Therefore, this is what the Lord GOD says: "Because you have forgotten me[h] and cast me behind your back,[i] you must bear the consequences of your indecency and promiscuity."

36 Then the LORD said to me: "Son of man, will you pass judgment against Oholah and Oholibah?[j] Then declare their detestable practices to them.[k] **37** For they have committed adultery, and blood is on their hands; they have committed adultery with their idols. And the children they bore to me they have sacrificed in the fire[c] as food for the idols.[l] **38** They also did this to me: they defiled my sanctuary[m] on that same day and profaned my Sabbaths.[n] **39** On the same day they slaughtered their children for their idols, they entered my sanctuary to profane it.[o] Yes, that is what they did inside my house.

40 "In addition, they sent for men who came from far away when a messenger was dispatched to them. And look how they came! You bathed, painted your eyes,[p] and adorned yourself with jewelry for them.[q] **41** You sat on a luxurious couch with a table spread before it,[r] on which you had set my incense and oil. **42** The sound of a carefree crowd was there. Drunkards[D] from the desert were brought in, along with common men. They put bracelets on the women's hands and beautiful tiaras on their heads. **43** Then I said concerning this woman worn out by adultery: Will they[E] now have illicit sex with her, even her? **44** Yet they had sex with her as one does with a prostitute. This is how they had sex with Oholah and Oholibah, those depraved women. **45** But righteous men will judge them the way adulteresses[s] and those who shed blood are judged, for they are adulteresses and blood is on their hands.

46 "This is what the Lord GOD says: Summon[F] an assembly against them and consign them to terror and plunder.[t] **47** The assembly will stone them and cut them down with their swords.[u] They will kill their sons and daughters and burn their houses. **48** So I will put an end to depravity in the land, and all the women will be admonished not to imitate your depraved

[a] 23:25 Ex 34:14; Ezk 5:13; 8:17-18; Zph 1:18
[b] 23:26 Ezk 16:39
[c] 23:29 Ezk 16:7,22,39
[d] 23:30 Ezk 6:9
[e] 23:31 2Kg 21:13; Jr 7:14-15
[f] 23:32 Ps 75:8; Is 51:17; Jr 25:15; Lm 4:21; Hab 2:16; Zch 12:2; Mt 20:22; 26:39; Rv 14:10
[g] Ezk 22:4-5
[h] 23:35 Is 17:10; Jr 3:21; Ezk 22:12; Hs 8:14; 13:6
[i] 1Kg 14:9; Jr 2:27; 32:33

[j] 23:36 Jr 1:10; Ezk 20:4; 22:2
[k] Is 58:1; Ezk 16:2; Mc 3:8
[l] 23:37 Ezk 16:20-21; 20:26,31
[m] 23:38 2Kg 21:4,7
[n] Ezk 20:13
[o] 23:39 Jr 7:9-11
[p] 23:40 2Kg 9:30; Jr 4:30
[q] Is 3:18-23; Ezk 16:13-16
[r] 23:41 Is 57:7
[s] 23:45 Ezk 16:38
[t] 23:46 Jr 15:4; 24:9; 29:18
[u] 23:47 Lv 20:10; Ezk 16:40

[A] 23:25 Or *and your descendants*   [B] 23:32 Or *It will bring*   [C] 23:37 Lit *have made pass through the fire*   [D] 23:42 Or *Sabeans*   [E] 23:43 Or *They will*   [F] 23:46 Or *I will summon*

23:25-26 In other words, Jerusalem's enemies would inflict punishment similar to the mutilation that was often carried out in that part of the ancient world against a prostitute to ruin her beauty. When the Babylonians were finished with Jerusalem, she would no longer be attractive to anyone.
23:30-34 The **cup** in view here is that of God's wrath.

23:35 The leaders and people of Jerusalem would pay the price for their betrayal of their covenant God.
23:36-39 Our theology matters. Worship and obedience to the true God will result in righteousness and justice, but worship and obedience to idols will result in the worst kinds of immorality and violence against the helpless.

23:45 **Righteous men** is probably a reference to God's prophets like Ezekiel.
23:47 Stoning was the penalty for adultery. Everything mentioned here would happen when both Samaria and Jerusalem fell to invaders.

a 23:49 Is 59:18; Ezk
7:4,9; 9:10
b 24:2 2Kg 25:1
c 24:3 Ezk 17:2; 20:49
d Jr 1:13-14; Ezk 11:3,7,11
e 24:6 Ezk 22:2-3,27
f 24:7 Lv 17:13-14; Dt
12:16,24
g 24:8 Is 26:21
h 24:9 Hab 2:12

i 24:11 Ezk 22:15; 23:27
j 24:13 Ezk 5:13; 8:18
k 24:14 Ezk 17:24
l Ezk 18:30; 36:19
m 24:16 1Kg 20:6; Pr 5:18;
Ec 9:9; Sg 7:10
n Jr 16:5; 22:10
o 24:17 Lv 21:10-12
p Jr 16:7; Hs 9:4

behavior. [49] They will punish you for your depravity,[a] and you will bear the consequences for your sins of idolatry. Then you will know that I am the Lord GOD."

PARABLE OF THE BOILING POT

24 The word of the LORD came to me in the ninth year, in the tenth month, on the tenth day of the month: [2] "Son of man, write down today's date, this very day. The king of Babylon has laid siege to Jerusalem this very day.[b] [3] Now speak a parable[c] to the rebellious house. Tell them, 'This is what the Lord GOD says:

Put the pot[d] on the fire —
put it on,
and then pour water into it!
[4] Place the pieces of meat in it,
every good piece —
thigh and shoulder.
Fill it with choice bones.
[5] Take the choicest of the flock
and also pile up the fuel[A] under it.
Bring it to a boil
and cook the bones in it.

[6] "Therefore, this is what the Lord GOD says:

Woe to the city of bloodshed,[e]
the pot that has corrosion inside it,
and its corrosion has not come out
of it!
Empty it piece by piece;
lots should not be cast for its contents.
[7] For the blood she shed[B] is still
within her.
She put it out on the bare rock;
she didn't pour it on the ground
to cover it with dust.[f]
[8] In order to stir up wrath
and take vengeance,[g]
I have put her blood
on the bare rock,
so that it would not be covered.

[9] "Therefore, this is what the Lord GOD says:

Woe to the city of bloodshed![h]

I myself will make the pile
of kindling large.
[10] Pile on the logs and kindle the fire!
Cook the meat well
and mix in the spices![C,D]
Let the bones be burned!
[11] Set the empty pot on its coals
so that it becomes hot
and its copper glows.
Then its impurity will melt inside it;
its corrosion will be consumed.[i]
[12] It has frustrated every effort;[E]
its thick corrosion will not come off.
Into the fire with its corrosion!
[13] Because of the depravity
of your uncleanness —
since I tried to purify you,
but you would not be purified
from your uncleanness —
you will not be pure again
until I have satisfied my wrath
on you.[j]
[14] I, the LORD, have spoken.
It is coming, and I will do it![k]
I will not refrain, I will not show pity,
and I will not relent.
I[F] will judge you
according to your ways and deeds.[l]
This is the declaration
of the Lord GOD.' "

THE DEATH OF EZEKIEL'S WIFE: A SIGN

[15] Then the word of the LORD came to me: [16] "Son of man, I am about to take the delight of your eyes[m] away from you with a fatal blow. But you must not lament or weep or let your tears flow.[n] [17] Groan quietly; do not observe mourning rites for the dead.[o] Put on your turban and strap your sandals on your feet; do not cover your mustache or eat the bread of mourners."[G,p] [18] I spoke to the people in the morning, and my wife died in the evening. The next morning I did just as I was commanded. [19] Then the people asked me, "Won't you tell us what these things you are doing mean for us?"

A 24:5 Lit *bones* B 24:7 Lit *For her blood* C 24:10 Some Hb mss read *well; remove the broth*; LXX reads *fire so that the meat may be cooked and the broth may be reduced* D 24:10 Or *and stir the broth* E 24:12 Hb obscure F 24:14 Some Hb mss, LXX, Syr, Tg, Vg; other Hb mss read *They*
G 24:17 Lit *men*, also in v. 22

24:1 This date was the same as is recorded in 2 Kings 25:1. It occurred in 588 BC when King Nebuchadnezzar and his army came against Jerusalem to begin the final siege.
24:3-14 Some of Jerusalem's leaders had given their people false assurance by using the imagery of Jerusalem as a strong **pot** inside which their inhabitants were safe, like **meat** (24:3-4; see 11:3). But Jerusalem was really a

rusty pot that was about to be set on fire and brought to a boil by the Babylonians, consuming everyone and everything in it.
24:16 This is a reference to Ezekiel's wife. It was a hard command, and Ezekiel had little time to prepare for the blow.
24:19-24 The people were surprised by Ezekiel's lack of outward mourning and wanted to know what it meant—sensing it was a pro-

phetic message to them (24:19). Indeed, the prophet's message was of overwhelming loss for his fellow exiles, who were about to lose their beloved city and many loved ones when Jerusalem was destroyed. But the exiles, like Ezekiel, would be unable to grieve because of the draining effect of God's judgment (23:20-24).

20 So I answered them: "The word of the LORD came to me: **21** Say to the house of Israel, 'This is what the Lord GOD says: I am about to desecrate my sanctuary, the pride of your power, the delight of your eyes, and the desire of your heart. Also, the sons and daughters you left behind will fall by the sword.[a] **22** Then you will do just as I have done: You will not cover your mustache or eat the bread of mourners. **23** Your turbans will remain on your heads and your sandals on your feet. You will not lament or weep[b] but will waste away[c] because of your iniquities and will groan to one another. **24** Now Ezekiel will be a sign for you.[d] You will do everything that he has done. When this happens, you will know that I am the Lord GOD.'

25 "As for you, son of man, know that on that day I will take from them their stronghold — their pride and joy, the delight of their eyes, and the longing of their hearts — as well as their sons and daughters. **26** On that day a fugitive will come to you and report the news.[e] **27** On that day your mouth will be opened to talk with him; you will speak and no longer be mute.[f] So you will be a sign for them, and they will know that I am the LORD."

PROPHECIES AGAINST THE NATIONS
JUDGMENT AGAINST AMMON

25 Then the word of the LORD came to me: **2** "Son of man, face the Ammonites and prophesy against them.[g] **3** Say to the Ammonites, 'Hear the word of the Lord GOD: This is what the Lord GOD says: Because you said, "Aha!"[h] about my sanctuary when it was desecrated, about the land of Israel when it was laid waste, and about the house of Judah when they went into exile, **4** therefore I am about to give you to the people of the east as a possession. They will set up their encampments and pitch their tents among you. They will eat your fruit and drink your milk. **5** I will make Rabbah a pasture[i] for camels and Ammon a resting place for sheep. Then you will know that I am the LORD.

6 " 'For this is what the Lord GOD says: Because you clapped your hands,[j] stamped your feet, and rejoiced over the land of Israel with wholehearted contempt, **7** therefore I am about to stretch out my hand against you[k] and give you as plunder to the nations. I will cut you off from the peoples and eliminate you from the countries. I will destroy you, and you will know that I am the LORD.

JUDGMENT AGAINST MOAB

8 " 'This is what the Lord GOD says: Because Moab and Seir said,[l] "Look, the house of Judah is like all the other nations." **9** Therefore I am about to expose Moab's flank beginning with its[A] frontier cities, the splendor of the land: Beth-jeshimoth, Baal-meon,[m] and Kiriathaim. **10** I will give it along with Ammon to the people of the east as a possession, so that Ammon will not be remembered among the nations. **11** So I will execute judgments against Moab, and they will know that I am the LORD.

JUDGMENT AGAINST EDOM

12 " 'This is what the Lord GOD says: Because Edom acted vengefully against the house of Judah[n] and incurred grievous guilt by taking revenge on them, **13** therefore this is what the Lord GOD says: I will stretch out my hand against Edom and cut off both man and animal from it. I will make it a wasteland; they will fall by the sword from Teman to Dedan. **14** I will take my vengeance[o] on Edom through my people Israel, and they will deal with Edom according to my anger and wrath. So they will know my vengeance. This is the declaration of the Lord GOD.

JUDGMENT AGAINST PHILISTIA

15 " 'This is what the Lord GOD says: Because the Philistines acted in vengeance and took revenge with deep contempt,[p] destroying because of their perpetual

a 24:21 Jr 6:11; 16:3-4; Ezk 23:25,47
b 24:23 Jb 27:15; Ps 78:64
c Lv 26:39
d 24:24 Ezk 4:3; Lk 11:29-30
e 24:26 Ezk 33:21-22
f 24:27 Ezk 3:26-27
g 25:2 Jr 49:1-6
h 25:3 Ezk 21:28; 26:2
i 25:5 Jr 49:2; Ezk 21:20
j 25:6 Jb 27:23; Nah 3:19
k 25:7 Zph 1:4
l 25:8 Is 15:1; Jr 48:1; Am 2:1-2
m 25:9 Jr 48:23
n 25:12 2Ch 28:17; Ps 137:7; Jr 49:7-22
o 25:14 Is 11:14
p 25:15 Is 14:29-31

A 25:9 Lit *with the cities, with its*

24:27 When the news of the disaster came, Ezekiel's **mouth** would be **opened to talk with** the messenger. He had previously been forbidden to speak except what God told him to say (see 3:25-27).
25:1-7 The sin of the **Ammonites** was gloating over the fall of Jerusalem and the destruction of the temple (25:2-3). Therefore, their own land would be invaded and Ammon too would fall (25:4-7). The judgment on Ammon was pronounced in 21:28-32.

25:8-10 Moab's people were close relatives of the Ammonites, since their two ancestors were the sons of Lot's incestuous relationships with his daughters (see Gen 19:30-38). Moab's sin was treating **the house of Judah**, representing all of God's chosen people, **like all the other nations** (25:8). Moab acted on that mistaken idea by becoming a perpetual enemy of Israel. God would judge Moab by turning over their land to the same **people of the east** who were going to conquer Ammon (25:10; see 25:4).

25:12-14 Edom was mentioned in 16:57 as one of the peoples who despised the Israelites. The Edomites refused to allow Israel to cross their land after leaving Egypt, and because they also **acted vengefully against the house of Judah** by trying to help bring about its downfall during the years of Babylon's invasions, God decreed Edom's downfall (see the book of Obadiah).
25:15-17 These longtime enemies of God's people lived along the Mediterranean Coast.

a 25:16 Jr 25:20; 47:1-7
b 1Sm 30:14; Zph 2:5
c 25:17 Ps 9:16
d 26:2 2Sm 5:11; Jl 3:4
e Ezk 25:3
f 26:3 Is 23:3; Ezk 26:17; 28:2; Am 1:9; Zch 9:2; Mt 11:22
g 26:5 Ezk 25:7; 29:19
h 26:6 Ezk 16:46,53; 26:8
i 26:7 Jr 52:32; Dn 2:37,47
j 26:8 Ezk 21:22

k 26:11 Hab 1:8
l 26:12 Ezk 27:3-27
m 26:13 Is 23:16; 24:8-9; Am 6:5
n 26:14 Is 14:27
o 26:15 Jr 49:21
p 26:16 Jnh 3:6
q Ezk 27:35
r 26:17 Ezk 27:2,32; 28:12
s 26:18 Ezk 26:15

hatred, **16** therefore this is what the Lord GOD says: I am about to stretch out my hand against the Philistines,[a] cutting off the Cherethites and wiping out what remains of the coastal peoples.[A,B] **17** I will execute severe vengeance against them with furious rebukes. They will know that I am the LORD[c] when I take my vengeance on them.' "

THE DOWNFALL OF TYRE

26 In the eleventh year, on the first day of the month, the word of the LORD came to me: **2** "Son of man, because Tyre[d] said about Jerusalem, 'Aha![e] The gateway to the peoples is shattered. She has been turned over to me.[B] I will be filled now that she lies in ruins,' **3** therefore this is what the Lord GOD says: See, I am against you, Tyre![f] I will raise up many nations against you, just as the sea raises its waves. **4** They will destroy the walls of Tyre and demolish her towers. I will scrape the soil from her and turn her into a bare rock. **5** She will become a place in the sea to spread nets, for I have spoken." This is the declaration of the Lord GOD. "She will become plunder for the nations,[g] **6** and her villages on the mainland will be slaughtered by the sword.[h] Then they will know that I am the LORD."

7 For this is what the Lord GOD says: "See, I am about to bring King Nebuchadnezzar[c] of Babylon, king of kings,[i] against Tyre from the north with horses, chariots, cavalry, and a huge assembly of troops. **8** He will slaughter your villages on the mainland with the sword. He will set up siege works,[j] build a ramp, and raise a wall of shields against you. **9** He will direct the blows of his battering rams against your walls and tear down your towers with his iron tools. **10** His horses will be so numerous that their dust will cover you. When he enters your gates as an army entering a breached city,

your walls will shake from the noise of cavalry, wagons, and chariots. **11** He will trample all your streets with the hooves of his horses.[k] He will slaughter your people with the sword, and your mighty pillars will fall to the ground. **12** They will take your wealth as spoil and plunder your merchandise.[l] They will also demolish your walls and tear down your beautiful homes. Then they will throw your stones, timber, and soil into the water. **13** I will put an end to the noise of your songs,[m] and the sound of your lyres will no longer be heard. **14** I will turn you into a bare rock, and you will be a place to spread nets. You will never be rebuilt, for I, the LORD, have spoken."[n] This is the declaration of the Lord GOD.

15 This is what the Lord GOD says to Tyre: "Won't the coasts and islands quake at the sound of your downfall,[o] when the wounded groan and slaughter occurs within you? **16** All the princes of the sea will descend from their thrones,[p] remove their robes, and strip off their embroidered garments. They will clothe themselves with trembling; they will sit on the ground, tremble continually, and be appalled[q] at you. **17** Then they will lament[r] for you and say of you,

'How you have perished,
    city of renown,
you who were populated
    from the seas![D]
She who was powerful on the sea,
    she and all of her inhabitants
    inflicted their terror.[E]
18 Now the coastlands tremble[s]
    on the day of your downfall;
the islands in the sea
    are alarmed by your demise.' "

19 For this is what the Lord GOD says: "When I make you a ruined city like other deserted cities, when I raise up the deep against you so that the mighty waters

A 25:16 Lit the seacoast   B 26:2 Or It has swung open for me   C 26:7 Lit Nebuchadrezzar   D 26:17 Some LXX mss read 'How you were destroyed from the seas, city of renown!   E 26:17 Lit and all her inhabitants who put their terror on all her inhabitants; Hb obscure

The conflict started with the conquest of the promised land when the Israelites failed to dislodge the Philistines. David defeated them repeatedly during his reign—starting with his battle against Goliath—but the Philistines had for generations **acted in vengeance** on Israel **because of their perpetual hatred** of God's people (25:15). **Cherethites** is a synonym for Philistines (25:16-17).
26:1 The date of the prophecy places it just before Jerusalem's fall, which makes God's condemnation of the Mediterranean coastal city of Tyre timely.

26:2-6 Tyre's joy at Jerusalem's downfall was prompted by greed (26:2; see 25:3). With Judah out of the way, the lucrative overland trade routes between Mesopotamia and Egypt were open. Tyre hoped to control them as it controlled the sea trade routes. But because Tyre rejoiced over the fall of the people, God would **raise up many nations against** Tyre that would crash into it like sea waves (26:3-4). The city's defense would become **a bare rock** on which fishermen would **spread nets** to dry, and **her villages on the mainland [would] be slaughtered** (26:5-6).

26:7-14 History tells us **King Nebuchadnezzar of Babylon** besieged Tyre for thirteen years, and although the island fortress survived, he destroyed all the mainland parts (26:7-11).

The nouns changed to the plural in 26:12-14, possibly referring to later forces that came against Tyre, most notably Alexander the Great in 332 BC. He used the rubble from the destroyed mainland city to build a causeway to the island fortress, destroying it too. The ancient site of Tyre has never been **rebuilt**, as the Lord said (26:14).

cover you, **20** then I will bring you down to be with those who descend to the Pit,[a] to the people of antiquity. I will make you dwell in the underworld[A] like[B] the ancient ruins, with those who descend to the Pit, so that you will no longer be inhabited or display your splendor[c] in the land of the living.[b] **21** I will make you an object of horror, and you will no longer exist.[c] You will be sought but will never be found again." This is the declaration of the Lord God.

THE SINKING OF TYRE

27 The word of the Lord came to me: **2** "Now, son of man, lament for Tyre.[d] **3** Say to Tyre, who is located at the entrance of the sea, merchant of the peoples[e] to many coasts and islands, 'This is what the Lord God says:

Tyre, you declared,
"I am perfect in beauty."
4   Your realm was in the heart
        of the sea;
    your builders perfected your beauty.
5   They constructed all your planking
        with pine trees from Senir.[f]
    They took a cedar from Lebanon
        to make a mast for you.
6   They made your oars of oaks
        from Bashan.
    They made your deck
        of cypress wood
    from the coasts of Cyprus,[g]
        inlaid with ivory.
7   Your sail was made of
    fine embroidered linen from Egypt,
        and served as your banner.
    Your awning was of blue
        and purple fabric
    from the coasts of Elishah.
8   The inhabitants of Sidon and Arvad[h]
        were your rowers.
    Your wise men were
        within you, Tyre;
    they were your captains.
9   The elders of Gebal and its wise men[i]
        were within you,
            repairing your leaks.

    " 'All the ships of the sea
        and their sailors
    came to you to barter
        for your goods.

10   Men of Persia, Lud, and Put[j]
    were in your army, serving
        as your warriors.
    They hung shields and helmets
        in you;
    they gave you splendor.
11   Men of Arvad and Helech
    were stationed on your walls
        all around,
    and Gammadites were
        in your towers.
    They hung their shields[D] all around
        your walls;
    they perfected your beauty.

12 " 'Tarshish[k] was your trading partner because of your abundant wealth of every kind. They exchanged silver, iron, tin, and lead for your merchandise. **13** Javan, Tubal, and Meshech[l] were your merchants. They exchanged slaves[E] and bronze utensils for your goods. **14** Those from Beth-togarmah[m] exchanged horses, war horses, and mules for your merchandise. **15** Men of Dedan[F,n] were also your merchants; many coasts and islands were your regular markets. They brought back ivory tusks[o] and ebony as your payment. **16** Aram[G] was your trading partner because of your numerous products. They exchanged turquoise,[H] purple and embroidered cloth, fine linen, coral,[H] and rubies[H] for your merchandise. **17** Judah and the land of Israel were your merchants. They exchanged wheat from Minnith,[p] meal,[I] honey, oil, and balm, for your goods. **18** Damascus was also your trading partner because of your numerous products and your abundant wealth of every kind, trading in wine from Helbon and white wool.[J] **19** Vedan[K] and Javan from Uzal[H,q] dealt in your merchandise; wrought iron, cassia,[r] and aromatic cane were exchanged for your goods. **20** Dedan[s] was your merchant in saddlecloths for riding. **21** Arabia and all the princes of Kedar were your business partners, trading with you in lambs, rams, and goats. **22** The merchants of Sheba[t] and Raamah traded with you. For your merchandise they exchanged the best of all spices and all kinds of precious stones as well as gold.[u] **23** Haran, Canneh, Eden,[v] the merchants of Sheba, Asshur,[w] and Chilmad traded

[a] 26:20 Jb 33:28; Ps 28:1; 30:3; Is 14:15; Ezk 28:8; 31:14; 32:18-30
[b] Jr 33:9; Zch 2:8
[c] 26:21 Ezk 27:36; 28:19
[d] 27:2 Ezk 28:12; 32:2
[e] 27:3 Is 23:2
[f] 27:5 Dt 3:9
[g] 27:6-7 Gn 10:4; 1Ch 1:7
[h] 27:8 Gn 10:18
[i] 27:9 1Kg 5:18

[j] 27:10 Ezk 30:5; 38:5
[k] 27:12 Gn 10:4; Ezk 38:13
[l] 27:13 Gn 10:2; Ezk 38:2; 39:1
[m] 27:14 Gn 10:3; Ezk 38:6
[n] 27:15 Ezk 38:13
[o] 1Kg 10:22
[p] 27:17 Jdg 11:33
[q] 27:19 Gn 10:27
[r] Ex 30:24
[s] 27:20 Ezk 38:13
[t] 27:22 Gn 10:7; Ezk 38:13
[u] 1Kg 10:1-2; Rv 18:12
[v] 27:23 2Kg 19:12; Is 37:12
[w] Gn 25:3

[A] 26:20 Lit *the lower parts of the earth*   [B] 26:20 Some Hb mss, LXX; other Hb mss, Syr read *in*   [C] 26:20 LXX reads *or appear*   [D] 27:11 Or *quivers*; Hb obscure   [E] 27:13 Lit *souls of men*   [F] 27:15 LXX reads *Rhodes*   [G] 27:16 Some Hb mss, Aq, Syr read *Edom*   [H] 27:16,19 Hb obscure   [I] 27:17 Or *resin*; Hb obscure   [J] 27:18 Or *and wool from Zahar*   [K] 27:19 Or *Dan*

26:20 God confirmed the completeness of Tyre's judgment, saying its people had descended **to the Pit**, the place of death which people in the ancient world feared as the place of no return. While there was a city of Tyre in Jesus's day, it was a greatly weakened place.
27:1-9 The first part of God's **lament** for Tyre (27:2) describes the city's former greatness by comparing the city to its beautiful ships.

a 27:25 1Kg 10:22; 22:48; Is 2:16
b 27:26 Ezk 26:19
c 27:28 Ezk 26:10,15
d 27:30 Rv 18:17-19
e 27:32 Ezk 26:17

f 27:35 Ezk 26:15-16
g 27:36 1Kg 9:8; Jr 19:8; Zph 2:15
h Ezk 26:21; 28:19
i 28:2 Is 14:14; Ac 12:22-23; 2Th 2:4
j 28:3 Dn 1:20; 2:20-23,28; 5:11-12
k 28:4 Ezk 27:33; Zch 9:2-3
l 28:7 Ezk 30:11; 31:12; 32:12
m 28:8 Ezk 26:20
n 28:10 Ezk 31:18; 32:30
o Ezk 30:12

with you. ²⁴ They were your merchants in choice garments, cloaks of blue and em-broidered materials, and multicolored carpets,^ which were bound and secured with cords in your marketplace. ²⁵ Ships of Tarshish*a* were the carriers for your goods.

" 'So you became full
and heavily loaded*B*
in the heart of the sea.

²⁶ Your rowers have brought you
onto the high seas,*b*
but the east wind has wrecked you
in the heart of the sea.

²⁷ Your wealth, merchandise, and goods,
your sailors and captains,
those who repair your leaks,
those who barter for your goods,
and all the warriors on board,
with all the other people within you,
sink into the heart of the sea
on the day of your downfall.

²⁸ " 'The countryside shakes
at the sound of your sailors' cries.*c*

²⁹ All the oarsmen
disembark from their ships.
The sailors and all the captains
of the sea
stand on the shore.

³⁰ Because of you, they raise their voices
and cry out bitterly.
They throw dust on their heads;*d*
they roll in ashes.

³¹ They shave their heads
because of you
and wrap themselves in sackcloth.
They weep over you
with deep anguish
and bitter mourning.

³² " 'In their wailing they lament
for you,*e*
mourning over you:
"Who was like Tyre,
silenced^ in the middle of the sea?

³³ When your merchandise
was unloaded from the seas,
you satisfied many peoples.
You enriched the kings of the earth
with your abundant wealth
and goods.

³⁴ Now you are wrecked by the sea
in the depths of the waters;

your goods and the people
within you
have gone down.

³⁵ All the inhabitants of the coasts
and islands
are appalled*f* at you.
Their kings shudder with fear;
their faces are contorted.

³⁶ Those who trade among the peoples
scoff*c,g* at you;
you have become an object of horror
and will never exist again." ' "*h*

THE FALL OF TYRE'S RULER

28 The word of the LORD came to me: ² "Son of man, say to the ruler of Tyre, 'This is what the Lord GOD says: Your*D* heart is proud, and you have said, "I am a god;*i* I sit in the seat of gods in the heart of the sea." Yet you are a man and not a god, though you have regarded your heart as that of a god. ³ Yes, you are wiser than Daniel;*j* no secret is hidden from you! ⁴ By your wisdom and understanding you have acquired wealth for yourself. You have ac-quired gold and silver for your treasuries.*k* ⁵ By your great skill in trading you have in-creased your wealth, but your heart has become proud because of your wealth.

⁶ " 'Therefore, this is what the Lord GOD says:
Because you regard your heart
as that of a god,

⁷ I am about to bring strangers
against you,
ruthless men from the nations.
They will draw their swords
against your magnificent wisdom
and will pierce your splendor.*l*

⁸ They will bring you down to the Pit,*m*
and you will die a violent death
in the heart of the sea.

⁹ Will you still say, "I am a god,"
in the presence of those
who slay*E* you?
Yet you will be only a man, not a god,
in the hands of those who kill you.

¹⁰ You will die the death
of the uncircumcised*n*
at the hands of strangers.*o*
For I have spoken.
This is the declaration
of the Lord GOD.' "

^27:24,32 Hb obscure   ^B 27:25 Or *and very glorious*   ^C 27:36 Lit *hiss*   ^D 28:2 Lit *Because your*   ^E 28:9 Some Hb mss, LXX, Syr, Vg; other Hb mss read *of the one who kills*

27:26 It's at this point in the chapter that God's lament begins to sound like one. Everything Tyre was known for would all come crashing down when God's **east wind** of judgment blew.
28:3-5 This king thought he was **wiser than Daniel** the prophet (28:3) because he had gained so much wealth for his kingdom by great skill in trading.

A LAMENT FOR TYRE'S KING

11 The word of the LORD came to me: **12** "Son of man, lament[a] for the king of Tyre and say to him, 'This is what the Lord GOD says:

You were the seal[A] of perfection,[B]
full of wisdom and perfect
    in beauty.[b]
13 You were in Eden,[c] the garden
    of God.
Every kind of precious stone
    covered you:
carnelian, topaz, and diamond,[B]
beryl, onyx, and jasper,
lapis lazuli, turquoise[c] and emerald.[D]
Your mountings and settings
    were crafted in gold;[d]
they were prepared on the day
    you were created.
14 You were an anointed
    guardian cherub,[e]
for[E] I had appointed you.
You were on the holy mountain
    of God;
you walked among the fiery stones.
15 From the day you were created
you were blameless in your ways
until wickedness was found in you.
16 Through the abundance
    of your trade,
you were filled with violence,
    and you sinned.
So I expelled you in disgrace
from the mountain of God,
and banished you, guardian cherub,[F]
from among the fiery stones.
17 Your heart became proud because of
    your beauty;[f]
For the sake of your splendor
you corrupted your wisdom.
So I threw you down to the ground;[G]
I made you a spectacle before kings.
18 You profaned your sanctuaries
by the magnitude of your iniquities
in your dishonest trade.
So I made fire come
    from within you,

and it consumed you.[g]
I reduced you to ashes
    on the ground
in the sight of everyone
    watching you.
19 All those who know you
    among the peoples
are appalled at you.
You have become an object of horror
and will never exist again.' "[h]

A PROPHECY AGAINST SIDON

20 The word of the LORD came to me: **21** "Son of man, face Sidon[i] and prophesy against it. **22** You are to say, 'This is what the Lord GOD says:

Look! I am against you, Sidon,[j]
and I will display my glory
    within you.
They will know that I am the LORD
when I execute judgments
    against her[k]
and demonstrate my holiness
    through her.
23 I will send a plague against her[l]
and bloodshed in her streets;
the slain will fall within her,
while the sword is against her[H]
    on every side.
Then they will know that
    I am the LORD.

24 " 'The house of Israel will no longer be hurt by[i] prickly briers or painful thorns[m] from all their neighbors who treat them with contempt. Then they will know that I am the Lord GOD.

25 " 'This is what the Lord GOD says: When I gather the house of Israel[n] from the peoples where they are scattered, I will demonstrate my holiness through them in the sight of the nations, and they will live in their own land, which I gave to my servant Jacob. **26** They will live there securely,[o] build houses, and plant vineyards.[p] They will live securely when I execute

---

^a 28:12 Ezk 27:2
^b Ezk 27:3
^c 28:13 Gn 2:8; Ezk 31:9,16,18; 36:35
^d Ex 39:10-13
^e 28:14 Ex 25:18-22
^f 28:17 Ezk 28:2

^g 28:18 Ezk 19:14
^h 28:19 Ezk 26:21; 27:36
ⁱ 28:21 Gn 10:19; Is 23:2; Jl 3:4
^j 28:22 Ezk 26:3; Zch 9:2; Mt 11:22
^k Ezk 30:19
^l 28:23 Ezk 38:22
^m 28:24 Nm 33:55
ⁿ 28:25 Ps 106:47; Ezk 20:41; 34:13
^o 28:26 Jr 23:6; Ezk 34:25,28; 38:8
^p Jr 32:15; Ezk 11:3

---

^A 28:12 Or *sealer*   ^B 28:12,13 Hb obscure   ^C 28:13 Or *malachite, or garnet*   ^D 28:13 Or *beryl*   ^E 28:14 Or *With an anointed guardian cherub*
^F 28:16 Or *and the guardian cherub banished you*   ^G 28:17 Or *earth*   ^H 28:23 Or *within her by the sword*   ^I 28:24 Lit *longer have*

28:12-19 These verses cannot be applied to any human ruler alone—especially one whom God had just taken pains to condemn as a mere man who had divine pretensions (see 28:2). The being we're introduced to in these verses, then, is the power behind this king: Lucifer's pride led him to rebel against God and become Satan.

Originally, Lucifer was **an anointed guardian cherub**. And as God's glory blazed in eternity past, Lucifer was right in the middle of it (28:14). He was assigned to lead the angelic

host in the worship and service of Yahweh. So how could **wickedness** be found in this exalted angel (28:15)? Because God gave this perfect being the right of choice—that is, to serve him by choice, not simply by mandate. God was not going to force Lucifer to worship him, because God wants willing worship. Lucifer exercised his choice to rebel against God and tried to usurp his rule. As a result of his rebellion, he was **expelled . . . in disgrace** from heaven and thrown down to the earth because of his pride (28:16-17).

One day this enemy of God and humanity will be judged and "thrown into the lake of fire and sulfur . . . tormented . . . forever" (Rev 20:10). Hell was created for Satan and the angels who joined him in rebellion (see Matt 25:41). People also go to hell when they choose to join Satan in his rebellion against God by refusing to accept God's means of salvation: Christ (see John 3:18-21).
28:20-23 Sidon's sins are not listed, probably because it was so closely identified with Tyre.

^a 28:26 Ezk 25:11
^b 29:2 Is 19:1–17; Jr 46:2–26; Ezk 30–32
^c 29:3 Ps 74:13; Is 27:1; Ezk 32:2
^d 29:4 Jb 41:2; Ezk 38:4
^e 29:5 Ezk 32:4–6
^f Jr 8:2; 25:33
^g Ezk 39:4
^h 29:7 2Kg 18:21; Is 36:6

ⁱ 29:8 Ezk 14:17
^j 29:9 Ezk 30:7–8
^k 29:11 Ezk 32:13
^l 29:12 Ezk 30:7
^m Ezk 12:15; 30:15,23,26
ⁿ 29:13 Is 19:22–23
^o 29:16 Is 20:5; 30:1–3; Ezk 17:15
^p 29:18 Ezk 26:7–12

judgments^a against all their neighbors who treat them with contempt. Then they will know that I am the LORD their God.'"

A PROPHECY OF EGYPT'S RUIN

29 In the tenth year, in the tenth month on the twelfth day of the month, the word of the LORD came to me: ² "Son of man, face Pharaoh king of Egypt and prophesy against him and against all of Egypt.^b ³ Speak to him and say, 'This is what the Lord GOD says:

Look, I am against you, Pharaoh
   king of Egypt,
the great monster^{A,C} lying
   in the middle of his Nile,
who says, "My Nile is my own;
I made it for myself."
⁴ I will put hooks in your jaws^d
and make the fish of your streams
   cling to your scales.
I will haul you up
   from the middle of your Nile,
and all the fish of your streams
   will cling to your scales.
⁵ I will leave you in the desert,^e
you and all the fish of your streams.
You will fall on the open ground
and will not be taken away
   or gathered for burial.^f
I have given you
   to the wild creatures of the earth
   and the birds of the sky as food.^g

⁶ " 'Then all the inhabitants of Egypt
   will know that I am the LORD,
for they^B have been a staff
   made of reed
   to the house of Israel.
⁷ When Israel grasped you
   by the hand,
you splintered,^h tearing all
   their shoulders;
when they leaned on you,
you shattered and made all
   their hips unsteady.^C

⁸ "'Therefore, this is what the Lord GOD says: I am going to bring a swordⁱ against you and cut off both man and animal from you. ⁹ The land of Egypt will be a desolate ruin.^j Then they will know that I am the LORD. Because you^D said, "The Nile is my own; I made it," ¹⁰ therefore, I am against you and your Nile. I will turn the land of Egypt into ruins, a desolate waste from Migdol to Syene, as far as the border of Cush. ¹¹ No human foot will pass through it, and no animal foot will pass through it.^k It will be uninhabited for forty years. ¹² I will make the land of Egypt a desolation among^E desolate lands, and its cities will be a desolation among^F ruined cities^l for forty years. I will disperse the Egyptians among the nations and scatter them throughout the lands.^m

¹³ "'For this is what the Lord GOD says: At the end of forty years I will gather the Egyptians from the peoples where they were dispersed.ⁿ ¹⁴ I will restore the fortunes of Egypt and bring them back to the land of Pathros, the land of their origin. There they will be a lowly kingdom. ¹⁵ Egypt will be the lowliest of kingdoms and will never again exalt itself over the nations. I will make them so small they cannot rule over the nations. ¹⁶ It will never again be an object of trust^o for the house of Israel, drawing attention to their iniquity of turning to the Egyptians. Then they will know that I am the Lord GOD.'"

BABYLON RECEIVES EGYPT AS COMPENSATION

¹⁷ In the twenty-seventh year, in the first month, on the first day of the month, the word of the LORD came to me: ¹⁸ "Son of man, King Nebuchadnezzar of Babylon made his army labor strenuously against Tyre.^p Every head was made bald and every shoulder chafed, but he and his army received no compensation from Tyre for the labor he expended against it. ¹⁹ Therefore,

---

^A 29:3 Or *crocodile*   ^B 29:6 LXX, Syr, Vg read *you*   ^C 29:7 LXX, Syr, Vg; MT reads *and you caused their hips to stand*   ^D 29:9 LXX, Syr, Vg; MT reads *he*   ^E 29:12 Or *Egypt the most desolate of*   ^F 29:12 Or *be the most desolate of*

29:1-3 This **word of the LORD** to Ezekiel came almost a year after Nebuchadnezzar's siege of Jerusalem began (29:1). **Pharaoh** was another **king** who considered himself to be a god and the master of the **Nile** River (28:2-3).
29:4-9 When Zedekiah reached out to Egypt for help in his attempt to break his word to Nebuchadnezzar and throw off Babylon's rule, Pharaoh Hophra said he would assist. But Zedekiah was leaning on a useless ally (see 29:6-7). Hophra's half-hearted attempt didn't help, and he withdrew, leaving Zedekiah and

Judah to face Nebuchadnezzar's wrath. Egypt would be judged for this and dragged away from her place of safety, leaving the nation abandoned **in the desert** (29:4-5). Its false promises of support for Israel led it to become a **desolate ruin** (29:7-9).
29:17-20 The **twenty-seventh year** is in view in these verses—a time after the other events Ezekiel described. It is included here because of its logical connection to the previous events discussed. Nebuchadnezzar's long siege of Tyre had been financially unprofit-

able. His army had fought so long that the men had become **bald** from wearing their helmets and **chafed** from their armor (29:18). So God decided to **give . . . Egypt to King Nebuchadnezzar** both as judgment against the land of Israel's original enslavement and as Nebuchadnezzar's **pay** since **he labored for** the Lord (29:19-20). This is an amazing statement of how God's work intertwines with human events as he raises up and puts down rulers. God is sovereign over nations and their leaders (see Prov 21:1).

this is what the Lord God says: I am going to give the land of Egypt to King Nebuchadnezzar of Babylon,[a] and he will carry off its wealth, seizing its spoil and taking its plunder. This will be his army's compensation. [20] I have given him the land of Egypt as the pay he labored for, since they worked for me." This is the declaration of the Lord God. [21] "In that day I will cause a horn to sprout[b] for the house of Israel, and I will enable you to speak out[c] among them. Then they will know that I am the Lord."

EGYPT'S DOOM

30 The word of the Lord came to me: [2] "Son of man, prophesy and say, 'This is what the Lord God says:

Wail,[d] "Woe because of that day!"

[3] For a day is near;
a day belonging to the Lord is near.[e]
It will be a day of clouds,[f]
a time of doom[A] for the nations.

[4] A sword will come against Egypt,
and there will be anguish in Cush
when the slain fall in Egypt,
and its wealth is taken away,
and its foundations are demolished.

[5] Cush, Put, and Lud,[g]
and all the various foreign troops,[B]
plus Libya[C] and the men
of the covenant land
will fall by the sword
along with them.

[6] This is what the Lord says:
Those who support Egypt will fall,
and its proud strength will collapse.
From Migdol to Syene
they will fall within it by the sword.
This is the declaration
of the Lord God.

[7] They will be desolate
among[D] desolate lands,
and their cities will lie
among ruined[E] cities.[h]

[8] They will know that I am the Lord
when I set fire to Egypt[i]
and all its allies are shattered.

[9] On that day, messengers will go out from me in ships[j] to terrify confident Cush. Anguish will come over them on the day of Egypt's doom.[f] For indeed it is coming.

[10] "This is what the Lord God says:
I will put an end to the hordes[G]
of Egypt
by the hand of King Nebuchadnezzar
of Babylon.

[11] He along with his people,
ruthless men from the nations,
will be brought in to destroy
the land.
They will draw their swords
against Egypt
and fill the land with the slain.[k]

[12] I will make the streams dry
and sell the land to evil men.[l]
I will bring desolation
on the land and everything in it
by the hands of foreigners.
I, the Lord, have spoken.

[13] "This is what the Lord God says:
I will destroy the idols and put an end
to the false gods in Memphis.[m]
There will no longer be
a prince from the land of Egypt.
And I will instill fear in that land.

[14] I will make Pathros[n] desolate,
set fire to Zoan,
and execute judgments on Thebes.

[15] I will pour out my wrath
on Pelusium,
the stronghold of Egypt,
and will wipe out the hordes
of Thebes.

[16] I will set fire to Egypt;
Pelusium will writhe in anguish,
Thebes will be breached,

[a] 29:19 Ezk 30:10,24-25; 32:11
[b] 29:21 1Sm 2:10; Ps 92:10; 132:17
[c] Ezk 3:27; 24:27; 33:22
[d] 30:2 Is 13:6; Ezk 21:12; Jl 1:11,13
[e] 30:3 Jl 2:1; Ob 15
[f] Ezk 32:7; 34:12
[g] 30:5 Jr 46:9
[h] 30:7 Ezk 29:12

[i] 30:8 Ezk 22:31
[j] 30:9 Is 18:1-2
[k] 30:11 Ezk 28:7; 31:12
[l] 30:12 Is 19:4
[m] 30:13 Jr 43:12-13
[n] 30:14 Jr 44:1,15; Ezk 29:14

[A] 30:3 of doom supplied for clarity   [B] 30:5 Or all Arabia   [C] 30:5 Lit Cub; Hb obscure   [D] 30:7 Or be the most desolate of   [E] 30:7 Or will be the most ruined of   [F] 30:9 Lit of Egypt   [G] 30:10 Or pomp, or wealth, also in v. 15

29:21 It's not likely that this refers to Ezekiel speaking, since he would have been about eighty-three years old by this time and Israel's restoration to the land was decades into the future. It could mean that when his prophecies came to pass, the people of Israel would see that he had faithfully declared God's word to them.

30:4 Cush encompassed what is now southern Egypt, Sudan, and northern Ethiopia.

30:6-9 Egypt's allies were in trouble, too. **From Migdol to Syene,** the far northern to the far southern borders of Egypt, those who supported the nation would also **fall within**

it by the sword, because the Lord declared it (30:6). Be careful with whom you ally yourself. **30:13-19 Memphis** was an important religious center with many temples and idols (30:13). According to Jeremiah 44:1, there were also Jews from Judah living there. They had fled to Memphis in an attempt to escape Nebuchadnezzar's assault on Jerusalem, despite Jeremiah's clear warning not to leave the land (see Jer 42:19-22). Now they, the "men of the covenant land," would be caught up in Egypt's disastrous judgment (see Ezek 30:5).

Thebes (30:14-16) was Egypt's longtime capital; it had been destroyed by the Assyrians in

663 BC, but was later rebuilt. Its **hordes** of people were wiped out when the city was breached by the Babylonians, a destruction also prophesied by Jeremiah (30:15; see Jer 46:25, where the focus was on judging the god of Thebes).

Tehaphnehes was the location of one of Pharaoh's palaces, a symbol of Egypt's **proud strength** that God would bring to an end (Ezek 30:18). Given all the devastation, Egypt also would have to bow in acknowledgement that God alone is Lord (30:19).

a 30:18 Ezk 34:12
b 30:21 Ps 10:15; 37:17
c 30:23 Ezk 29:12
d 30:24 Zph 2:12

e 31:1 Ezk 30:20
f 31:3 Is 10:33–34; Ezk 17:3–4,22; 31:16
g 31:5 Dn 4:11
h Ezk 17:5
i 31:6 Ezk 17:23; Dn 4:12,21; Mt 13:32
j 31:8 Gn 2:8; Is 51:3; Ezk 28:13

and Memphis will face foes
   in broad daylight.^A

17 The young men of On^B
   and Pi-beseth
will fall by the sword,
   and those cities^C will go
   into captivity.

18 The day will be dark^D
   in Tehaphnehes,
when I break the yoke
   of Egypt there
and its proud strength
comes to an end in the city.
A cloud^a will cover Tehaphnehes,^E
and its surrounding villages will go
   into captivity.

19 So I will execute judgments
   against Egypt,
and they will know that I am the
   LORD.' "

PHARAOH'S POWER BROKEN

20 In the eleventh year, in the first month, on the seventh day of the month, the word of the LORD came to me: 21 "Son of man, I have broken the arm^b of Pharaoh king of Egypt. Look, it has not been bandaged — no medicine has been applied and no splint put on to bandage it so that it can grow strong enough to handle a sword. 22 Therefore, this is what the Lord GOD says: Look! I am against Pharaoh king of Egypt. I will break his arms, both the strong one and the one already broken, and will make the sword fall from his hand. 23 I will disperse the Egyptians among the nations and scatter them among the countries.^c 24 I will strengthen the arms of Babylon's king and place my sword^d in his hand. But I will break the arms of Pharaoh, and he will groan before him as a mortally wounded man. 25 I will strengthen the arms of Babylon's king, but Pharaoh's arms will fall. They will know that I am the LORD when I place my sword in the hand of Babylon's king and he wields it against the land of Egypt. 26 When I disperse the Egyptians among the nations and scatter them among the countries, they will know that I am the LORD."

DOWNFALL OF EGYPT AND ASSYRIA

31 In the eleventh year,^e in the third month, on the first day of the month, the word of the LORD came to me: 2 "Son of man, say to Pharaoh king of Egypt and to his hordes,

'Who are you like in your greatness?
3 Think of Assyria, a cedar
      in Lebanon,^f
   with beautiful branches
      and shady foliage
   and of lofty height.
   Its top was among the clouds.^F
4 The waters caused it to grow;
   the underground springs
      made it tall,
   directing their rivers all around
   the place where the tree was planted
   and sending their channels
   to all the trees of the field.
5 Therefore the cedar became greater
      in height
   than all the trees of the field.^g
   Its branches multiplied,
   and its boughs grew long
   as it spread them out
   because of the abundant water.^h
6 All the birds of the sky
   nested in its branches,^i
   and all the animals of the field
   gave birth beneath its boughs;
   all the great nations lived
      in its shade.
7 It was beautiful in its size,
      in the length of its limbs,
   for its roots extended
      to abundant water.
8 The cedars in God's garden
      could not eclipse it;^j
   the pine trees couldn't compare
      with its branches,
   nor could the plane trees match
      its boughs.
   No tree in the garden of God
   could compare with it in beauty.
9 I made it beautiful with its
      many limbs,
   and all the trees of Eden,
   which were in God's garden,
      envied it.

---

^A 30:16 Or *foes daily*   ^B 30:17 LXX, Vg; MT reads *iniquity*   ^C 30:17 Or *and the women*; lit *and they*   ^D 30:18 Some Hb mss, LXX, Syr, Tg, Vg; other Hb mss read *will withhold*   ^E 30:18 Or *Egypt*   ^F 31:3 Or *thick foliage*, also in vv. 10,14

30:21-26 The imagery of broken and strengthened arms once more draws attention to the outworking of God's sovereign will and control in and through human events and rulers.

31:1-9 The reference to **Assyria** (31:3) would remind Hophra not only that the Assyrians had once defeated his kingdom, but also that they themselves had been crushed by the Babylonians under Nebuchadnezzar in 609 BC—the same nation and king whom God was going to use to topple Egypt.

The Assyrian Empire dominated the ancient world from the ninth to the seventh centuries BC before it was conquered by Babylon. From God's perspective, Pharaoh Hophra fancied himself the next great thing in world leaders (a reminder of how little things have changed), but this ruler was in for a rude awakening. God had brought down mightier thrones than his.

10 " 'Therefore, this is what the Lord GOD says: Since it[A] towered high in stature and set its top among the clouds, and it[B] grew proud[a] on account of its height, **11** I determined to hand it over to a ruler of nations;[b] he would surely deal with it. I banished it because of its wickedness. **12** Foreigners, ruthless men from the nations,[c] cut it down and left it lying. Its limbs fell on the mountains and in every valley; its boughs lay broken in all the earth's ravines. All the peoples of the earth left its shade and abandoned it. **13** All the birds of the sky nested on its fallen trunk, and all the animals of the field were among its boughs. **14** This happened so that no trees planted beside water would become great in height and set their tops among the clouds, and so that no other well-watered trees would reach them in height. For they have all been consigned to death, to the underworld, among the people[c] who descend to the Pit.[d]

15 " 'This is what the Lord GOD says: I caused grieving on the day the cedar went down to Sheol.[e] I closed off the underground deep because of it:[D] I held back the rivers of the deep, and its abundant water was restrained. I made Lebanon mourn on account of it, and all the trees of the field fainted because of it. **16** I made the nations quake at the sound of its downfall, when I threw it down to Sheol to be with those who descend to the Pit. Then all the trees of Eden,[f] the choice and best of Lebanon, all the well-watered trees, were comforted[g] in the underworld. **17** They too descended with it to Sheol, to those slain by the sword. As its allies[E,F] they had lived in its shade among the nations.

18 " 'Who then are you like in glory and greatness among Eden's trees? You also will be brought down to the underworld to be with the trees of Eden. You will lie among the uncircumcised with those slain by the sword.[h] This is Pharaoh and all his hordes. This is the declaration of the Lord GOD.' "

A LAMENT FOR PHARAOH

32 In the twelfth year, in the twelfth month, on the first day of the month, the word of the LORD came to me: **2** "Son of man, lament[i] for Pharaoh king of Egypt and say to him,

'You compare yourself to a lion
   of the nations,
but[G] you are like a monster[H,j]
   in the seas.
You thrash about in your rivers,
churn up the waters with your feet,
and muddy the[i] rivers.

3 " 'This is what the Lord GOD says:
I will spread my net over you[k]
with an assembly of many peoples,
and they[J] will haul you up in my net.
4 I will abandon you on the land
and throw you onto the open field.
I will cause all the birds of the sky
to settle on you
and let the wild creatures
   of the entire earth
eat their fill of you.[l]
5 I will put your flesh
   on the mountains[m]
and fill the valleys with your carcass.
6 I will drench the land
with the flow of your blood,
even to the mountains;
the ravines will be filled
   with your gore.

7 " 'When I snuff you out,
I will cover the heavens
and darken their stars.
I will cover the sun with a cloud,[n]
and the moon will not give its light.
8 I will darken all the shining lights
in the heavens over you,
and will bring darkness
   on your land.
This is the declaration
   of the Lord GOD.

9 " 'I will trouble the hearts
   of many peoples,

[a] 31:10 Ezk 28:17; Dn 5:20
[b] 31:11 Ezk 30:10-11; Dn 5:18-19
[c] 31:12 Ezk 28:7; 32:12
[d] 31:14 Ezk 26:20
[e] 31:15 Ezk 32:22-23
[f] 31:16 Ezk 26:15; 27:28; Hg 2:7
[g] Ezk 32:31
[h] 31:18 Ezk 28:10; 32:19,21

[i] 32:2 Ezk 19:1; 27:2; 28:12
[j] Is 27:1
[k] 32:3 Ezk 12:13
[l] 32:4 Ezk 29:3-5
[m] 32:5 Ezk 31:12
[n] 32:7 Jl 2:2,31; 3:15; Am 8:9; Mt 24:29; Rv 6:12; 8:12

[A] 31:10 Syr, Vg; MT, LXX read *you*   [B] 31:10 Lit *its heart*   [C] 31:14 Or *the descendants of Adam*   [D] 31:15 Or *I covered it with the underground deep*
[E] 31:17 LXX, Syr read *offspring*   [F] 31:17 Lit *arm*   [G] 32:2 Or *'Lion of the nations, you are destroyed;*   [H] 32:2 Or *crocodile*   [I] 32:2 Lit *their*   [J] 32:3 LXX, Vg read *I*

31:10-14 Assyria's **stature** as top dog among the nations caused it to grow **proud** (31:10). In this context, that refers to puffing oneself up in God's sight instead of humbly bowing before him and acknowledging him as the one true God. The Babylonians left them lying in ruins as an object lesson to other nations not to exalt themselves Assyria had done (31:11-14).

31:16-17 The idea of other nations (represented by **trees**), who were already in **Sheol** (the grave or **underworld**) being **comforted** by Assyria's fall may mean that they were "relieved," so to speak, that even the great Assyria could be taken down and suffer the same fate they had. **32:1** Ezekiel dated this prophecy to March of 585 BC. This was about a year and seven months after the fall of Jerusalem, and two

months after the news of the disaster reached the exiles in Babylon.
32:6-8 The mention of **blood** flowing through the land of Egypt and thick **darkness** covering it suggests two of the exodus plagues when God judged Egypt the first time.
32:9-10 Egypt's fall would have a shattering effect on the other Gentile nations. What happened to Egypt could happen to them.

a 32:10 Ezk 27:35
b Ezk 26:16
c 32:12 Ezk 28:7; 31:12
d 32:13 Ezk 29:11
e 32:15 Ex 7:5
f 32:16 2Sm 1:17; 2Ch
35:25; Jr 9:17; Ezk 26:17

g 32:18 Ezk 26:20
h 32:20 Ezk 21:15
i 32:21 Is 14:9-11; Ezk
31:15-18
j 32:24 Gn 10:22

when I bring about your destruction
among the nations,
in countries you have not known.
10 I will cause many peoples
to be appalled at you,
and their kings will shudder
with fear because of you[a]
when I brandish my sword
in front of them.
On the day of your downfall
each of them will tremble
every moment[b] for his life.

11 " 'For this is what the Lord God says:
The sword of Babylon's king
will come against you!
12 I will make your hordes fall
by the swords of warriors,
all of them ruthless men
from the nations.[c]
They will ravage Egypt's pride,
and all its hordes will be destroyed.
13 I will slaughter all its cattle
that are beside many waters.
No human foot
will churn them again,
and no cattle hooves
will disturb them.[d]
14 Then I will let their waters settle
and will make their rivers flow
like oil.
This is the declaration
of the Lord God.
15 When I make the land of Egypt
a desolation,
so that it is emptied of everything
in it,
when I strike down all
who live there,
then they will know that
I am the Lord.[e]

16 " 'The daughters of the nations will
chant that lament.[f] They will chant it over
Egypt and all its hordes. This is the declaration of the Lord God.' "

EGYPT IN SHEOL

17 In the twelfth year,[A] on the fifteenth day
of the month, the word of the Lord came
to me: 18 "Son of man, wail over the hordes
of Egypt and bring Egypt and the daughters of mighty nations down to the underworld,[B] to be with those who descend to
the Pit:[g]
19 Who do you surpass in loveliness?
Go down and be laid to rest
with the uncircumcised!
20 They will fall among those slain
by the sword.
A sword is appointed![h]
They drag her and all
her hordes away.
21 Warrior leaders will speak
from the middle of Sheol
about him[c] and his allies:
'They have come down;
the uncircumcised lie
slain by the sword.'[i]

22 "Assyria is there with
her whole assembly;
her graves are all around her.
All of them are slain, fallen
by the sword.
23 Her graves are set
in the deepest regions
of the Pit,
and her assembly is all around
her burial place.
All of them are slain, fallen
by the sword—
those who once spread terror
in the land of the living.

24 "Elam[j] is there
with all her hordes
around her grave.
All of them are slain, fallen
by the sword—
those who went down
to the underworld uncircumcised,
who once spread their terror
in the land of the living.
They bear their disgrace
with those who descend to the Pit.
25 Among the slain
they prepare a bed for Elam
with all her hordes.
Her graves are all around her.
All of them are uncircumcised,
slain by the sword,

A 32:17 LXX reads year, in the first month,   B 32:18 Lit the lower parts of the earth, also in v. 24   C 32:21 Either Pharaoh or Egypt

They would **tremble** at the thought of this
possibility for the rest of their lives (32:10).
32:13-15 Even the animals in Egypt would suffer as the land was decimated (32:13). The Nile
and its streams would be placid and **flow like
oil**, instead of being churned up and muddied
by humans and animals moving through them
(32:14-15).

32:18-20 This prophecy against Egypt views
the nation's demise from the perspective of
the **underworld**. Using poetry, God depicts
Egypt's arrival there, where it finds itself
among many other ungodly nations that
had already gone down **to the Pit** (32:18).
There Egypt would discover that it was no
better than any other nation that defied God.

The term **uncircumcised** always described a
death of shame in such contexts (32:19).
32:21 Those nations already in the grave
would mock Egypt, saying in effect, "Well,
look who's come to join the rest of us lowly
warriors to lie here shamed in the afterlife!
If it isn't mighty Egypt, who thought he was
better than everyone else!"

although their terror
    was once spread
in the land of the living.
They bear their disgrace
with those who descend to the Pit.
They are placed among the slain.

26 "Meshech and Tubal[A,a] are there,
with all their hordes.
Their graves are all around them.
All of them are uncircumcised,
    slain by the sword,
although their terror was
    once spread
in the land of the living.

27 They do not lie down
with the fallen warriors
    of the uncircumcised,[B]
who went down to Sheol
with their weapons of war,
whose swords were placed
    under their heads[c]
and their shields[D]
rested on their bones,
although the terror
    of these warriors
was once in the land
    of the living.

28 But you will be shattered
and will lie down
    among the uncircumcised,
with those slain by the sword.[b]

29 "Edom[c] is there, her kings and all
    her princes,
who, despite their strength,
    have been placed
among those slain by the sword.
They lie down
    with the uncircumcised,
with those who descend to the Pit.

30 All the leaders of the north[d]
and all the Sidonians[e] are there.
They went down in shame
    with the slain,
despite the terror
    their strength inspired.
They lie down uncircumcised
with those slain by the sword.
They bear their disgrace
with those who descend
    to the Pit.

31 "Pharaoh will see them
and be comforted[f] over all
    his hordes —
Pharaoh and his whole army,
slain by the sword."
    This is the declaration
    of the Lord GOD.

32 "For I will spread my[E] terror
in the land of the living,
so Pharaoh and all his hordes
will be laid to rest
    among the uncircumcised,
with those slain by the sword."
    This is the declaration
    of the Lord GOD.

EZEKIEL AS ISRAEL'S WATCHMAN

33 The word of the LORD came to me: 2 "Son of man, speak to your people and tell them, 'Suppose I bring the sword against a land, and the people of that land select a man from among them, appointing him as their watchman. 3 And suppose he sees the sword coming against the land and blows his trumpet[g] to warn the people. 4 Then, if anyone hears the sound of the trumpet but ignores the warning,[h] and the sword comes and takes him away, his death will be his own fault.[F] 5 Since he heard the sound of the trumpet but ignored the warning, his death is his own fault.[G] If he had taken warning, he would have saved his life. 6 However, suppose the watchman sees the sword coming but doesn't blow the trumpet, so that the people aren't warned, and the sword comes and takes away their lives. Then they have been taken away because of their iniquity, but I will hold the watchman accountable for their blood.'

7 "As for you, son of man, I have made you a watchman for the house of Israel.[i] When you hear a word from my mouth, give them a warning from me. 8 If I say to the wicked, 'Wicked one, you will surely die,'[j] but you do not speak out to warn him about his way, that wicked person will die for his iniquity, yet I will hold you responsible for his blood. 9 But if you warn a wicked person to turn from his way and he doesn't turn from it, he will die for his iniquity, but you will have rescued yourself.

[a] 32:26 Gn 10:2; Ezk 27:13; 38:2-3
[b] 32:28 Is 14:18
[c] 32:29 Ezk 25:12-14
[d] 32:30 Ezk 38:6,15; 39:2
[e] Ezk 28:21-23

[f] 32:31 Ezk 31:16-18
[g] 33:3 Nm 10:9
[h] 33:4 Zch 1:4
[i] 33:7 Ezk 3:17-19
[j] 33:8 Ezk 18:4

[A] 32:26 Lit Meshech-tubal   [B] 32:27 LXX reads of antiquity   [C] 32:27 Or Do they not . . . heads?   [D] 32:27 Emended; MT reads iniquities
[E] 32:32 Alt Hb tradition, LXX, Syr read his   [F] 33:4 Lit his blood will be on his head   [G] 33:5 Lit his blood will be on him

---

32:31 When **Pharaoh** Hophra and the **hordes** of his armies reached the grave, he would be able to take some perverse comfort from the fact that at least he and his army weren't the only ones to die in the same humiliating defeat that these other nations had suffered.
33:7-9 God stressed the personal responsibility of both the **watchman** (Ezekiel) and those who heard his message of repentance that was to follow. Similarly, it is the role of spiritual leaders today to warn God's people of his just judgment against sin and call them to repentance. Leaders who fail to fully carry out this sacred duty are accountable.

[a] 33:10 Lv 26:39; Ezk 4:17; 24:23
[b] Ezk 37:11
[c] 33:11 Ezk 18:23,30-32; Hs 11:8; 1Tm 2:4; 2Pt 3:9
[d] 33:13 Ezk 3:20; 18:24,26
[e] 33:15 Lv 18:5; Dt 5:33; 1Kg 3:14; Ezk 20:11
[f] 33:16 Is 1:18; 43:25; Ezk 18:21-22
[g] 33:17 Ezk 18:25-30
[h] 33:22 Ezk 3:26-27; 24:26-27
[i] 33:24 Is 51:2
[j] Gn 15:7; 28:4
[k] Ezk 36:2
[l] 33:25 Lv 19:26
[m] 33:26 Ezk 18:6,10-11,15
[n] 33:27 Ezk 5:12
[o] 33:28 Ezk 35:3
[p] Ezk 7:24
[q] Ezk 6:2

10 "Now as for you, son of man, say to the house of Israel, 'You have said this: "Our transgressions and our sins are heavy on us, and we are wasting away because of them![a] How then can we survive?" '[b] 11 Tell them, 'As I live — this is the declaration of the Lord GOD — I take no pleasure in the death of the wicked, but rather that the wicked person should turn from his way and live.[c] Repent, repent of your evil ways! Why will you die, house of Israel?'

12 "Now, son of man, say to your people, 'The righteousness of the righteous person will not save him on the day of his transgression; neither will the wickedness of the wicked person cause him to stumble on the day he turns from his wickedness. The righteous person won't be able to survive by his righteousness on the day he sins. 13 When I tell the righteous person that he will surely live, but he trusts in his righteousness and acts unjustly, then none of his righteousness will be remembered, and he will die because of the injustice he has committed.[d]

14 " 'So when I tell the wicked person, "You will surely die," but he repents of his sin and does what is just and right — 15 he returns collateral, makes restitution for what he has stolen, and walks in the statutes of life[e] without committing injustice — he will certainly live; he will not die. 16 None of the sins he committed will be held[A] against him. He has done what is just and right; he will certainly live.[f]

17 " 'But your people say, "The Lord's way isn't fair,"[g] even though it is their own way that isn't fair. 18 When a righteous person turns from his righteousness and commits injustice, he will die for it. 19 But if a wicked person turns from his wickedness and does what is just and right, he will live because of it. 20 Yet you say, "The Lord's way isn't fair." I will judge each of you according to his ways, house of Israel.' "

THE NEWS OF JERUSALEM'S FALL

21 In the twelfth year of our exile, in the tenth month, on the fifth day of the month, a fugitive from Jerusalem came to me and reported, "The city has been taken!" 22 Now the hand of the LORD had been on me the evening before the fugitive arrived, and he opened my mouth before the man came to me in the morning. So my mouth was opened and I was no longer mute.[h]

ISRAEL'S CONTINUED REBELLION

23 Then the word of the LORD came to me: 24 "Son of man, those who live in the[B] ruins in the land of Israel are saying, 'Abraham was only one person,[i] yet he received possession of the land.[j] But we are many; surely the land has been given to us as a possession.'[k] 25 Therefore say to them, 'This is what the Lord GOD says: You eat meat with blood in it,[l] look to your idols, and shed blood. Should you then receive possession of the land? 26 You have relied on your swords, you have committed detestable acts, and each of you has defiled his neighbor's wife. Should you then receive possession of the land?'[m]

27 "Tell them this: 'This is what the Lord GOD says: As surely as I live, those who are in the ruins will fall by the sword, those in the open field I have given to wild animals to be devoured, and those in the strongholds and caves will die by plague.[n] 28 I will make the land a desolate waste,[o] and its proud strength will come to an end.[p] The mountains of Israel[q] will become desolate, with no one passing through. 29 They will know that I am the LORD when I make the land a desolate waste because of all the detestable acts they have committed.'

[A] 33:16 Lit *remembered* [B] 33:24 Lit *these*

33:10-11 For the first time, they acknowledged that it was because of their **transgressions** that they were **wasting away** (33:10). In response, God told Ezekiel to give them words of comfort (33:11).

33:12-16 God's declaration that a person is **righteous**—in right standing before him—is always based on faith that expresses itself in right actions. What we do advertises what we really believe.

33:17 One way we know the Israelites of Ezekiel's day needed his preaching of personal responsibility was that they were still blaming God for being unfair in the way he dealt with them. This was the height of blasphemy, an instance of the creature accusing the Creator.

33:21 Jerusalem was destroyed and the temple burned in August 586 BC, but news of that didn't reach the exile community in Babylon until January 585 BC, when a survivor **reported** it.

33:22 The prophet had known something major was coming, since the Lord had **opened** his **mouth** the **evening before**. For some time, he'd been kept **mute** unless conveying a specific word from the Lord.

33:24 Those who'd narrowly escaped death at the hands of the Babylonians were claiming to be a righteous remnant, the true sons and daughters of **Abraham** to whom God had given **the land** by an eternal covenant based on his faith. Their argument sounded like this: "Sure, things are bad for us now, but we're 'naming and claiming' our inheritance."

33:25-29 To those mentioned in 33:24 who assumed they'd inherit the land by default, God essentially said, "You have broken my covenant, relied on yourselves instead of on me, and committed detestable acts. And then you appeal to me on the grounds of my covenant with righteous Abraham? I don't think so." (33:25-26). In time, the same disasters that took down the other people of Jerusalem would catch up to them (33:27-29).

30 "As for you, son of man, your people are talking about you near the city walls and in the doorways of their houses. One person speaks to another, each saying to his brother, 'Come and hear what the message is that comes from the LORD!' **31** So my people come to you in crowds,^A^ sit in front of you, and hear your words, but they don't obey them. Their mouths go on passionately, but their hearts pursue dishonest profit. **32** Yes, to them you are like a singer of passionate songs who has a beautiful voice and plays skillfully on an instrument. They hear your words, but they don't obey them. **33** Yet when all this comes true^a^ — and it definitely will — then they will know that a prophet has been among them."

THE SHEPHERDS AND GOD'S FLOCK

34 The word of the LORD came to me: **2** "Son of man, prophesy against the shepherds of Israel. Prophesy, and say to them, 'This is what the Lord GOD says to the shepherds: Woe to the shepherds of Israel, who have been feeding themselves!^b^ Shouldn't the shepherds feed their flock? **3** You eat the fat, wear the wool, and butcher the fattened animals, but you do not tend the flock.^c^ **4** You have not strengthened the weak, healed the sick, bandaged the injured, brought back the strays, or sought the lost.^d^ Instead, you have ruled them with violence and cruelty. **5** They were scattered for lack of a shepherd;^e^ they became food for all the wild animals^f^ when they were scattered. **6** My flock went astray on all the mountains and every high hill.^g^ My flock was scattered over the whole face of the earth, and there was no one searching or seeking for them.

7 "'Therefore, you shepherds, hear the word of the LORD. **8** As I live — this is the declaration of the Lord GOD — because my flock, lacking a shepherd, has become prey and food for every wild animal, and because my shepherds do not search for my flock, and because the shepherds feed themselves rather than my flock, **9** therefore, you shepherds, hear the word of the LORD!

10 "'This is what the Lord GOD says: Look, I am against the shepherds.^h^ I will demand my flock from them^B^ and prevent them from shepherding the flock. The shepherds will no longer feed themselves, for I will rescue my flock from their mouths so that they will not be food for them.

11 "'For this is what the Lord GOD says: See, I myself will search for my flock and look for them. **12** As a shepherd looks for his sheep on the day he is among his scattered flock, so I will look for my flock. I will rescue them from all the places where they have been scattered^i^ on a day of clouds and total darkness. **13** I will bring them out from the peoples, gather them from the countries, and bring them to their own soil. I will shepherd them on the mountains of Israel, in the ravines, and in all the inhabited places of the land. **14** I will tend them in good pasture, and their grazing place will be on Israel's lofty mountains. There they will lie down in a good grazing place; they will feed in rich pasture on the mountains of Israel. **15** I will tend my flock and let them lie down.^j^ This is the declaration of the Lord GOD. **16** I will seek the lost,^k^ bring back the strays, bandage the injured,^l^ and strengthen the weak, but I will destroy^C^ the fat and the strong. I will shepherd them with justice.

17 "'As for you, my flock, the Lord GOD says this: Look, I am going to judge between one sheep and another, between the rams and goats.^m^ **18** Isn't it enough for you to feed on the good pasture? Must you also trample the rest of the pasture with your feet? Or isn't it enough that you drink the clear water? Must you also muddy the rest with your feet? **19** Yet my flock has to feed on what your feet have trampled, and drink what your feet have muddied.

^a^ 33:33 Jr 28:9; Ezk 33:29
^b^ 34:2 Jr 23:1
^c^ 34:3 Pr 27:23
^d^ 34:4 Zch 11:16; Lk 15:4
^e^ 34:5 Nm 27:17; 1Kg 22:17; Jr 10:21; 23:2; 50:6; Mt 9:36
^f^ Ezk 34:28
^g^ 34:6 1Pt 2:25

^h^ 34:10 Jr 21:13; Ezk 5:8; 13:8
^i^ 34:12 Jr 23:3
^j^ 34:15 Ps 23:1-2
^k^ 34:16 Ps 119:176; Lk 19:10
^l^ Ps 147:3; Is 30:26; Hs 6:1
^m^ 34:17 Mt 25:31-33

---

^A^**33:31** Lit *you like the coming of a people*   ^B^**34:10** Lit *their hand*   ^C^**34:16** Some Hb mss, LXX, Syr, Vg read *watch over*

33:30-33 In contrast to the obstinate refusal of those back in Judah to pay any attention to Ezekiel's messages, his "congregation" of fellow exiles in Babylon had grown large. Nevertheless, they didn't **obey** what he taught (33:31-32). Yet a day of reckoning was coming, probably referring to the day when all people will stand before God to be judged by him (33:33).

34:3-4 Shepherds are to care for their sheep, but the nation's leaders preferred to feed themselves rather than to **tend the flock** (34:3). Their sin was not mere neglect. They

also treated the weakest members of society **with . . . cruelty** (34:4).

34:5-6 When government and religious leaders fail to fulfill their God-ordained calling in his kingdom program to uphold justice, keep the peace, and punish evil, then chaos, loss of freedom, and tyranny follow. That, in fact, is exactly what happened in Israel. The bad kings, false prophets, and faithless priests had failed to carry out God's agenda, and the people suffered.

34:10 This warning applies to church leaders today (see Acts 20:28-35).

34:11-16 These promises of God's care were not fulfilled completely when the people returned from exile in Babylon. These verses describe Israel in Christ's millennial kingdom when Israel is fully regathered and restored under its good shepherd.

34:17 Before Christ establishes his kingdom, a judgment must be held to separate the righteous from the wicked—that is, the sheep from the goats (Matt 25:31-46)—because these two groups will still exist in that day as they did in Ezekiel's.

*34:23 Ps 78:70-71; Jn 10:11,16
*34:24 Jr 30:9; Ezk 37:24
*34:25 Ezk 37:26
*Is 11:6-9
*Ezk 28:26
*34:26 Ps 2:6; 15:1; 133:3; Is 27:13; Jr 31:23
*Dt 11:13-14; 28:12
*34:27 Lv 26:13; Is 52:2-3; Jr 30:8
*34:29 Ezk 36:3,6,15
*34:30 Ex 6:7; Lv 26:12; Dt 29:13; Jr 30:22; 31:33; Ezk 11:20; 36:28; 37:23,27; Zch 8:8; 2Co 6:16; Heb 8:10; Rv 21:3
*34:31 Ps 100:3; Jr 23:1
*35:2 Ezk 25:12-14

*35:3 Ezk 6:14
*35:5 Ps 137:7; Ezk 25:15
*Ezk 7:2; 21:25,29
*35:6 Is 63:2-6; Ezk 16:38; 32:6
*35:7 Ezk 33:28
*35:8 Ezk 31:12; 32:4-5
*35:10 Ps 48:1-3; Ezk 48:35
*35:13 Jr 48:26,42; Ob 12; Zph 2:8

20 " 'Therefore, this is what the Lord God says to them: See, I myself will judge between the fat sheep and the lean sheep. 21 Since you have pushed with flank and shoulder and butted all the weak ones with your horns until you scattered them all over, 22 I will save my flock. They will no longer be prey, and I will judge between one sheep and another. 23 I will establish over them one shepherd, my servant David, and he will shepherd them. He will tend them himself and will be their shepherd. *24 I, the Lord, will be their God, and my servant David* will be a prince among them. I, the Lord, have spoken.

25 " 'I will make a covenant of peace* with them and eliminate dangerous creatures* from the land, so that they may live securely* in the wilderness and sleep in the forest. 26 I will make them and the area around my hill* a blessing: I will send down showers in their season;* they will be showers of blessing. 27 The trees of the field will yield their fruit, and the land will yield its produce; my flock will be secure in their land. They will know that I am the Lord when I break the bars of their yoke and rescue them from the power of those who enslave them.* 28 They will no longer be prey for the nations, and the wild creatures of the earth will not consume them. They will live securely, and no one will frighten them. 29 I will establish for them a place renowned for its agriculture,^ and they will no longer be victims of famine in the land. They will no longer endure the insults of the nations.* 30 Then they will know that I, the Lord their God, am with them, and that they, the house of Israel, are my people.* This is the declaration of the Lord God. 31 You are my flock, the human flock of my pasture, and I am your God. This is the declaration of the Lord God.' "*

A PROPHECY AGAINST EDOM

35 The word of the Lord came to me: 2 "Son of man, face Mount Seir* and prophesy against it. 3 Say to it, 'This is what the Lord God says:

Look! I am against you, Mount Seir. I will stretch out my hand against you and make you a desolate waste.*
4 I will turn your cities into ruins, and you will become a desolation. Then you will know that I am the Lord.

5 " 'Because you maintained a perpetual hatred* and gave the Israelites over to the power of the sword in the time of their disaster, the time of final punishment,* 6 therefore, as I live — this is the declaration of the Lord God — I will destine you for bloodshed, and it will pursue you. Since you did not hate bloodshed, it will pursue you.* 7 I will make Mount Seir a desolate waste and will cut off from it those who come and go.* 8 I will fill its mountains with the slain;* those slain by the sword will fall on your hills, in your valleys, and in all your ravines. 9 I will make you a perpetual desolation; your cities will not be inhabited. Then you will know that I am the Lord.

10 " 'Because you said, "These two nations and two lands will be mine, and we will possess them" — though the Lord was there* — 11 therefore, as I live — this is the declaration of the Lord God — I will treat you according to the anger and jealousy you showed in your hatred of them. I will make myself known among them^B when I judge you. 12 Then you will know that I, the Lord, have heard all the blasphemies you uttered against the mountains of Israel, saying, "They are desolate. They have been given to us to devour!" 13 You boasted against me* with your mouth, and spoke many words against me. I heard it myself!

14 " 'This is what the Lord God says: While the whole world rejoices, I will make you a desolation. 15 Just as you rejoiced over the inheritance of the house of Israel because it became a desolation, I will deal the same way with you: you will become a desolation, Mount Seir, and so will all Edom in its entirety. Then they will know that I am the Lord.'

^34:29 LXX, Syr read *a plant of peace*   ^B35:11 LXX reads *you*

34:23 Jesus Christ, the Son of **David**, will be Israel's perfect **shepherd**. As David was a faithful shepherd (see 1 Sam 17:34-37), so the Lord Jesus will be even more so (see John 10:11-18).
34:25-31 These verses echo other Old Testament prophecies that speak of Israel's safety in the land from both dangerous animals and human enemies. The land itself will also be perpetually productive during the kingdom age. Most important of all, the people of Israel will recognize their true Messiah, their shepherd.
35:1-4 Even though the Edomites and Israelites were closely related (they were the descendants of Esau and Jacob, the sons of Isaac, respectively), **Mount Seir**, the range south of the Dead Sea where the Edomites lived, was under God's judgment.
35:10-15 One reason Edom would come under God's wrath was that, when the **two nations** (Israel and Judah) fell, Edom greedily desired to take their **two lands** for themselves, even though they were promised to the Jews (35:10). Since Edom **rejoiced** when Israel was made **a desolation**, God would make Edom one (35:14-15).

God Is in Charge

WHEN I WAS IN COLLEGE, and later in seminary, professors usually handed out course syllabi on the first day of class. Each syllabus presented an outline of the course, with enough detail to let me know what the professor expected of me and where the course was going. It gave the highlights of a class without providing every detail of every upcoming lecture or assignment. Those came as the semester unfolded.

Another thing the syllabus did was let my classmates and me know who was in charge of the class. Clearly, the professor had the authority to choose the assignments and the reading we would do. There may have been some choice in topic for a paper, or some optional readings, but basically we did what the instructor wanted.

Bible prophecy functions somewhat like a course syllabus. God doesn't give us every detail of his program, but he gives us enough so we can know where history is going and what he expects of us. Just as important is the fact that the Bible lets us know whose classroom we are in. History is "his story"— it's God's story, the outworking of God's plan for the ages. He is in charge.

That truth ought to comfort you. It certainly comforts me. With all of the uncertainty in our world today, it is good to know that God is in charge. Though God has revealed to us some of what will happen in the days ahead, he has not given us the details for everything.

Our job is to know him and his Word so intimately that even when we walk through times of darkness and unknowns, we take courage in our relationship with him. One of the greatest ways to experience peace in your life is to relinquish your thoughts of trying to control things. Though history often seems out of control, it is not. Rather, it is simply out of *your* control. Ultimately, this is God's universe; he is in charge. You can try to intervene, but he will have the final say.

Studying prophecy helps us to let go of our will and to allow his will to unfold without a fight. Surrendering to the sovereignty of God will usher in a level of satisfying contentment that you may have never experienced before.

a36:1 Ezk 6:2
b36:2 Ezk 25:3; 26:2
c Dt 32:13
d36:3 Ezk 35:13
e36:4 Ezk 34:8,28
f36:5 Dt 4:24
g Ezk 35:10,15
h36:6 Ps 74:10; 123:3-4
i36:7 Ezk 20:5
j36:8 Ezk 17:23
k36:9 Lv 26:9
l36:10 Ezk 37:21-22
m36:11 Jr 33:12
n36:11 Is 51:3
o36:12 Ob 17
p36:13 Nm 13:32
q36:15 Ezk 34:29
r36:17 Jr 2:7
s Lv 15:19
t36:18 Ezk 16:36; 22:3
u36:19 Dt 28:64; Ezk 22:15
v Rm 2:6
w36:20 Is 52:5; Rm 2:24
x36:21 Is 48:9; Ezk 20:44
y36:22 Dt 9:5
z Ps 115:1; Is 43:25; 48:11;
Ezk 20:9; Dn 9:18-19

RESTORATION OF ISRAEL'S MOUNTAINS

36 "Son of man, prophesy to the mountains of Israel and say, 'Mountains of Israel, hear the word of the LORD.[a] [2] This is what the Lord GOD says: Because the enemy has said about you, "Aha![b] The ancient heights[c] have become our possession,"'[3] therefore, prophesy and say: 'This is what the Lord GOD says: Because they have made you desolate and have trampled you from every side, so that you became a possession for the rest of the nations and an object of people's gossip and slander,[d] [4] therefore, mountains of Israel, hear the word of the Lord GOD. This is what the Lord GOD says to the mountains and hills, to the ravines and valleys, to the desolate ruins and abandoned cities, which have become plunder[e] and a mockery to the rest of the nations all around.

[5] "'This is what the Lord GOD says: Certainly in my burning zeal I speak against the rest of the nations and all of Edom,[f] who took[A] my land as their own possession with wholehearted rejoicing and utter contempt[g] so that its pastureland became[B] plunder. [6] Therefore, prophesy concerning the land of Israel and say to the mountains and hills, to the ravines and valleys: This is what the Lord GOD says: Look, I speak in my burning zeal[h] because you have endured the insults of the nations. [7] Therefore, this is what the Lord GOD says: I swear[c] that the nations all around you will endure their own insults.[i]

[8] "'You, mountains of Israel, will produce your branches[j] and bear your fruit for my people Israel, since their arrival is near. [9] Look! I am on your side; I will turn toward you,[k] and you will be tilled and sown. [10] I will fill you with people, with the whole house of Israel in its entirety.[l] The cities will be inhabited and the ruins rebuilt. [11] I will fill you with people and animals,[m] and they will increase and be fruitful. I will make you inhabited as you once were and make you better off than you were before. Then you will know that I am the LORD.[n] [12] I will cause people, my people Israel, to walk on you; they will possess you,[o] and you will be their inheritance. You will no longer deprive them of their children.

[13] "'This is what the Lord GOD says: Because some are saying to you, "You devour people and deprive your nation of children,"[p] [14] therefore, you will no longer devour people and deprive your nation of children.[D] This is the declaration of the Lord GOD. [15] I will no longer allow the insults of the nations to be heard against you, and you will not have to endure the reproach of the peoples anymore;[q] you will no longer cause your nation to stumble.[E] This is the declaration of the Lord GOD.'"

RESTORATION OF ISRAEL'S PEOPLE

[16] The word of the LORD came to me: [17] "Son of man, while the house of Israel lived in their land, they defiled it with their conduct and actions.[r] Their behavior before me was like menstrual impurity.[s] [18] So I poured out my wrath[t] on them because of the blood they had shed on the land, and because they had defiled it with their idols. [19] I dispersed them among the nations, and they were scattered among the countries.[u] I judged them according to their conduct and actions.[v] [20] When they came to the nations where they went, they profaned my holy name,[w] because it was said about them, 'These are the people of the LORD, yet they had to leave his land in exile.' [21] Then I had concern for my holy name,[x] which the house of Israel profaned among the nations where they went.

[22] "Therefore, say to the house of Israel, 'This is what the Lord GOD says: It is not for your sake that I will act,[y] house of Israel, but for my holy name,[z] which you

---

[A]36:5 Lit gave [B]36:5 Or contempt, to empty it of; Hb obscure [C]36:7 Lit lift up my hand [D]36:14 Alt Hb tradition reads and cause your nation to stumble [E]36:15 Some Hb mss, Tg read no longer bereave your nation of children

---

36:6 In the prophets, God's *zeal* (or "jealousy") speaks of his exclusive covenant love for Israel and determination to act on his people's behalf (e.g., Isa 42:13; 63:15; Zech 1:14; 8:2).
36:13-15 In the kingdom age, God will take away Israel's reproach when the Messiah rules the nations. Israel's enemies had a saying: **You devour people and deprive your nation of children** (36:13), an insult that God said would no longer **be heard against** his people because there would no longer be any truth in it (36:15).

36:23 This restoration is a further promise of blessing in the millennial kingdom, when Israel's rejection of the Messiah will end and Jesus Christ will reign on the Davidic throne in Jerusalem. This will include Israel's spiritual restoration.
36:27 That God will put his **Spirit within** his people is a description of the "new covenant" (see Jer 31:31-34) that was inaugurated with the death of Jesus Christ and that will be applied to Israel when he returns and his people confess him.

36:31 When Israel experiences God's grace in Christ, its people **will loathe** their sins and realize that God has saved them because of his grace and mercy.
36:35 Israel's inward cleansing will be accompanied by the restoration of the land to a beauty and fruitfulness that will make the land **like the garden of Eden.** Israel's splendor in the kingdom will be such that everyone will know God has fulfilled all his promises to his covenant people.

profaned among the nations where you went. **23** I will honor the holiness of my great name, which has been profaned among the nations — the name you have profaned among them. The nations will know that I am the Lord — this is the declaration of the Lord God — when I demonstrate my holiness through you in their sight.[a]

24 "For I will take you from the nations and gather you from all the countries, and will bring you into your own land.[b] **25** I will also sprinkle clean water on you, and you will be clean.[c] I will cleanse you from all your impurities and all your idols.[d] **26** I will give you a new heart and put a new spirit within you;[e] I will remove your heart of stone[A] and give you a heart of flesh.[f] **27** I will place my Spirit within you[g] and cause you to follow my statutes and carefully observe my ordinances.[h] **28** You will live in the land that I gave your fathers;[i] you will be my people, and I will be your God.[j] **29** I will save you from all your uncleanness. I will summon the grain and make it plentiful, and I will not bring famine on you.[k] **30** I will also make the fruit of the trees and the produce of the field plentiful, so that you will no longer experience reproach among the nations on account of famine.

31 "You will remember your evil ways and your deeds that were not good,[l] and you will loathe yourselves for your iniquities and detestable practices.[m] **32** It is not for your sake that I will act[n] — this is the declaration of the Lord God — let this be known to you. Be ashamed and humiliated because of your ways, house of Israel!

33 "This is what the Lord God says: On the day I cleanse you from all your iniquities, I will cause the cities to be inhabited, and the ruins will be rebuilt.[o] **34** The desolate land will be cultivated instead of lying desolate in the sight of everyone who passes by. **35** They will say, "This land that was desolate has become like the garden of Eden.[p] The cities that were once ruined, desolate, and demolished are now fortified and inhabited." **36** Then

the nations that remain around you will know that I, the Lord, have rebuilt what was demolished and have replanted what was desolate. I, the Lord, have spoken and I will do it.[q]

37 "This is what the Lord God says: I will respond to the house of Israel and do this for them:[r] I will multiply them in number like a flock.[s] **38** So the ruined cities will be filled with a flock of people, just as Jerusalem[s] is filled with a flock of sheep for sacrifice[c] during its appointed festivals. Then they will know that I am the Lord.'"

THE VALLEY OF DRY BONES

37 The hand of the Lord was on me,[t] and he brought me out by his Spirit[u] and set me down in the middle of the valley; it was full of bones. **2** He led me all around them. There were a great many of them on the surface of the valley, and they were very dry. **3** Then he said to me, "Son of man, can these bones live?"

I replied, "Lord God, only you know."[v]

4 He said to me, "Prophesy concerning these bones and say to them: Dry bones, hear the word of the Lord! **5** This is what the Lord God says to these bones: I will cause breath to enter you, and you will live.[w] **6** I will put tendons on you, make flesh grow on you, and cover you with skin. I will put breath in you so that you come to life. Then you will know that I am the Lord."[x]

7 So I prophesied as I had been commanded. While I was prophesying, there was a noise, a rattling sound, and the bones came together, bone to bone. **8** As I looked, tendons appeared on them, flesh grew, and skin covered them, but there was no breath in them. **9** He said to me, "Prophesy to the breath,[D] prophesy, son of man. Say to it: This is what the Lord God says: Breath, come from the four winds and breathe into these slain so that they may live!"[y] **10** So I prophesied as he commanded me; the breath entered them,[z] and they came to life and stood on their feet, a vast army.

11 Then he said to me, "Son of man, these bones are the whole house of Israel.[aa] Look

[a] 36:23 Ezk 20:41; 38:23; 39:7,25
[b] 36:24 Ezk 34:13; 37:21
[c] 36:25 Ps 51:7; Heb 9:13,19; 10:22
[d] Jr 33:8
[e] 36:26 Ezk 18:31; Jl 2:28
[f] Dt 30:6; Ezk 11:19; 2Co 3:3
[g] 36:27 Ezk 37:14
[h] Jr 24:7; 31:33; 32:40
[i] 36:28 Ezk 37:23-25
[j] Ezk 34:30
[k] 36:29-30 Ezk 34:27,29
[l] 36:31 Ezk 16:61-63
[m] Ezk 6:9; 20:43
[n] 36:32 Dt 9:5
[o] 36:33 Ezk 36:10
[p] 36:35 Is 51:3; Jl 2:3

[q] 36:36 Ezk 17:24
[r] 36:37 Ezk 14:3
[s] 36:38 2Ch 35:7-9
[t] 37:1 Ezk 1:3
[u] Ezk 8:3; 11:24
[v] 37:3 Dt 32:39; 1Sm 2:6
[w] 37:5 Gn 2:7; Ps 104:29-30
[x] 37:6 Jl 2:27; 3:17
[y] 37:9 Ps 104:30
[z] 37:10 Rv 11:11
[aa] 37:11 Ezk 36:10

[A] 36:26 Lit *stone from your flesh*   [B] 36:37 Lit *flock of people*   [C] 36:38 Lit *as the consecrated flock, as the flock of Jerusalem*   [D] 37:9 Or *wind*, or *spirit*, also in v. 10

37:2-3 Ezekiel may have been reluctant to speak more confidently given that Israel was in ruins and the bones of Jerusalem's people were still lying in the city's rubble.

37:4-14 How would God revive the disconnected, lifeless bones of Israel? Through word and Spirit. As Ezekiel spoke as instructed, God caused the bones to begin knitting themselves together with flesh (37:7-8). But the

word had to be accompanied by the giving of the Spirit for **breath** to enter these bodies (37:9-10), providing a classic illustration of spiritual revival.

Chapter 36 had already revealed that Israel's receiving of the Spirit of God will occur in the kingdom when Jesus Christ returns and God's chosen people are given a new heart as promised in the new covenant. In that day,

God said, **I will put my Spirit in you**, and Israel will be settled in their land (37:14). The dry bones will become a new nation.

Similarly, the Word and the Spirit bring spiritual revival to God's church today. When one or both are absent, then God's people have no living experience of his reality in their midst (see 2 Cor 3:17-18).

a 37:11 Ps 141:7
b Eph 2:12
c Is 49:14; Lm 3:54
d 37:12 Is 26:19; 66:14; Hs 13:14; Rm 11:15
e 37:13 Jn 5:28-29; 1Co 15:21-22; Rv 20:4-5
f 37:14 Ezk 36:27
g Ezk 17:24
h 37:16 Nm 17:2-3
i 2Ch 11:11-17
j 37:17 Is 11:13; Hs 1:11
k 37:18 Ezk 12:9; 24:19
l 37:20 Ezk 12:3
m 37:21 Ezk 36:24
n 37:22 Jr 3:18
o Ezk 34:23-24

p 37:23 Ezk 36:25
q Ezk 36:28-29
r Rm 11:26
s Ezk 36:38
t 37:24 Ezk 34:23-24; Jn 10:16
u Ezk 36:27
v 37:25 Is 60:21
w Jn 12:34
x 37:26 Is 54:10; Ezk 34:25
y Is 55:3; Jr 32:40; Ezk 16:60; Heb 13:20
z 37:27 Jn 1:14
aa Ezk 36:28
ab 37:28 Ezk 20:12
ac 38:2 Gn 10:2; Ezk 39:1; Rv 20:8
ad Ezk 27:13
ae 38:4 2Kg 19:28; Ezk 29:4
af Dn 11:40
ag 38:5 Ezk 27:10
ah 38:6 Gn 10:2
ai Gn 10:3

how they say, 'Our bones are dried up,*a* and our hope has perished;*b* we are cut off.'*c* **12** Therefore, prophesy and say to them: 'This is what the Lord God says: I am going to open your graves and bring you up from them,*d* my people, and lead you into the land of Israel. **13** You will know that I am the Lord, my people, when I open your graves and bring you up from them.*e* **14** I will put my Spirit in you,*f* and you will live, and I will settle you in your own land. Then you will know that I am the Lord. I have spoken, and I will do it.*g* This is the declaration of the Lord.' "

THE REUNIFICATION OF ISRAEL

15 The word of the Lord came to me: **16** "Son of man, take a single stick and write on it:*h* Belonging to Judah and the Israelites associated with him. Then take another stick and write on it: Belonging to Joseph — the stick of Ephraim — and all the house of Israel associated with him.*i* **17** Then join them together into a single stick so that they become one in your hand.*j* **18** When your people ask you, 'Won't you explain to us what you mean by these things?'*k* — **19** tell them, 'This is what the Lord God says: I am going to take the stick of Joseph, which is in the hand of Ephraim, and the tribes of Israel associated with him, and put them together with the stick of Judah. I will make them into a single stick so that they become one in my hand.'

20 "When the sticks you have written on are in your hand and in full view of the people,*l* **21** tell them, 'This is what the Lord God says: I am going to take the Israelites out of the nations where they have gone.*m* I will gather them from all around and bring them into their own land. **22** I will make them one nation in the land,*n* on the mountains of Israel, and one king will rule over all of them.*o* They will no longer be two nations and will no longer be divided into two kingdoms. **23** They will

not defile themselves anymore with their idols,*p* their abhorrent things, and all their transgressions.*q* I will save them from all their apostasies by which^A they sinned,*r* and I will cleanse them. Then they will be my people, and I will be their God.*s* **24** My servant David will be king over them, and there will be one shepherd for all of them.*t* They will follow my ordinances, and keep my statutes and obey them.*u*

25 "They will live in the land that I gave to my servant Jacob,*v* where your fathers lived. They will live in it forever with their children and grandchildren, and my servant David will be their prince forever.*w* **26** I will make a covenant of peace with them;*x* it will be a permanent covenant*y* with them. I will establish and multiply them and will set my sanctuary among them forever. **27** My dwelling place will be with them;*z* I will be their God, and they will be my people.*aa* **28** When my sanctuary is among them forever, the nations will know that I, the Lord, sanctify Israel.' "*ab*

THE DEFEAT OF GOG

38 The word of the Lord came to me: **2** "Son of man, face Gog, of the land of Magog,*ac* the chief prince of^B Meshech and Tubal.*ad* Prophesy against him **3** and say, 'This is what the Lord God says: Look, I am against you, Gog, chief prince of Meshech and Tubal. **4** I will turn you around, put hooks in your jaws,*ae* and bring you out with all your army, including horses and riders,*af* who are all splendidly dressed, a huge assembly armed with large and small shields, all of them brandishing swords. **5** Persia,*ag* Cush, and Put are with them, all of them with shields and helmets; **6** Gomer*ah* with all its troops; and Beth-togarmah*ai* from the remotest parts of the north along with all its troops — many peoples are with you.

7 " 'Be prepared and get yourself ready, you and your whole assembly that has

---

^A **37:23** Some Hb mss, LXX, Sym; other Hb mss read *their settlements where* ^B **38:2** Or *the prince of Rosh,*

37:15-17 **Judah** was the dominant tribe in the southern kingdom, while **Ephraim**, whose patriarch was one of Joseph's sons, was the largest tribe in the northern kingdom (37:16). The future of Israel would be one of unity, not division (37:17).

37:22 The **one king** in view here is Jesus Christ, when he returns to reign.

37:26 The mention of the **sanctuary** anticipates the prophecy of the rebuilt temple in chapters 40–43.

38:1-6 **Gog** is a person, and the ancient Jewish historian Josephus identified **Magog** as the

land from which the Scythians descended in an area now occupied by Russia and several other nations of the former Soviet Union. Gog was called **the chief prince of Meshech and Tubal** (38:2), areas located in modern-day Turkey. Ezekiel named these and other nations because God is going to draw them into battle against Israel at a strategic time in history, when his and Israel's enemies will be massed against Israel (38:4). The armies aligned against Israel will include **Persia** and **Cush** (38:5-6).

38:7-9 Some identify this attack with one at the end of the millennium (see Rev 20:7-9),

but the details between the passages are vastly different, and in the latter case these names are probably used symbolically of God's worldwide enemies. The best choice for Ezekiel's battle seems to be around the middle of the tribulation, when Israel is **regathered** and is living in peace (Ezek 38:8), but this peace may be that of the false covenant of peace with the antichrist (see Dan 9:27; Matt 24:15-22), which he will violate. Israel at this point has not recognized the Messiah, and has more purging to undergo. Thus, Gog's **troops** will mass against Israel (Ezek 38:9).

been mobilized around you; you will be their guard. [8] After a long time you will be summoned. In the last years you will enter a land that has been restored from war[A] and regathered from many peoples to the mountains of Israel, which had long been a ruin.[a] They were brought out from the peoples, and all of them now live securely. [9] You, all of your troops, and many peoples with you will advance, coming like a thunderstorm; you will be like a cloud covering the land.

[10] " 'This is what the Lord God says: On that day, thoughts will arise in your mind, and you will devise an evil plan. [11] You will say, "I will advance against a land of open villages; I will come against a tranquil people who are living securely,[b] all of them living without walls and without bars or gates"[c] — [12] in order to seize spoil and carry off plunder,[d] to turn your hand against ruins now inhabited and against a people gathered from the nations, who have been acquiring cattle and possessions and who live at the center of the world. [13] Sheba[e] and Dedan[f] and the merchants of Tarshish[g] with all its rulers[B] will ask you, "Have you come to seize spoil? Have you mobilized your assembly to carry off plunder, to make off with silver and gold, to take cattle and possessions, to seize plenty of spoil?" '

[14] "Therefore prophesy, son of man, and say to Gog, 'This is what the Lord God says: On that day when my people Israel are dwelling securely,[h] will you not know this [15] and come from your place in the remotest parts of the north[i] — you and many peoples with you, who are all riding horses — a huge assembly, a powerful army? [16] You will advance against my people Israel like a cloud covering the land. It will happen in the last days, Gog, that I will bring you against my land so that the nations may know me, when I show myself holy through you in their sight.[j]

[17] " 'This is what the Lord God says: Are you the one I spoke about in former times through my servants, the prophets of Israel, who for years prophesied in those times that I would bring you against them? [18] Now on that day, the day when Gog comes against the land of Israel — this is the declaration of the Lord God — my wrath will flare up.[c] [19] I swear in my zeal and fiery rage:[k] On that day there will be a great earthquake in the land of Israel. [20] The fish of the sea, the birds of the sky, the animals of the field, every creature that crawls on the ground, and every human being on the face of the earth will tremble before me. The mountains will be demolished, the cliffs will collapse, and every wall will fall to the ground. [21] I will call for a sword against him on all my mountains — this is the declaration of the Lord God — and every man's sword will be against his brother.[l] [22] I will execute judgment on him with plague and bloodshed. I will pour out torrential rain, hailstones, fire, and burning sulfur on him, as well as his troops and the many peoples who are with him.[m] [23] I will display my greatness and holiness, and will reveal myself in the sight of many nations.[n] Then they will know that I am the Lord.'

THE DISPOSAL OF GOG

39 "As for you, son of man, prophesy against Gog and say, 'This is what the Lord God says: Look, I am against you, Gog, chief prince of[D] Meshech and Tubal.[o] [2] I will turn you around, drive you on,[p] and lead you up from the remotest parts of the north. I will bring you against the mountains of Israel. [3] Then I will knock your bow from your left hand and make your arrows drop from your right hand. [4] You, all your troops, and the peoples who are with you will fall on the mountains of Israel. I will give you as food to every kind of predatory bird and to the wild animals. [5] You will fall on the open field,[q] for I have spoken. This is the declaration of the Lord God.

[6] " 'I will send fire against Magog[r] and those who live securely on the coasts and islands. Then they will know that I am the Lord. [7] So I will make my holy name known among my people Israel and will no longer allow it to be profaned. Then

---

[a] 38:8 Ezk 36:8-11
[b] 38:11 Jdg 18:7
[c] Jr 49:31
[d] 38:12 Is 10:6; Ezk 29:19
[e] 38:13 Ezk 27:22
[f] Ezk 27:20
[g] Ezk 27:12
[h] 38:14 Jr 23:6
[i] 38:15 Ezk 39:2
[j] 38:16 Ezk 28:22

[k] 38:19 Ezk 36:6
[l] 38:21 Ezk 14:17
[m] 38:22 Rv 16:18-21
[n] 38:23 Ezk 37:28
[o] 39:1 Ezk 38:2-3
[p] 39:2 Ezk 38:4
[q] 39:5 Ezk 32:4
[r] 39:6 Am 1:4,7,10

[A] 38:8 Lit *from the sword*   [B] 38:13 Lit *young lions,* or *villages*   [C] 38:18 Lit *up in my anger*   [D] 39:1 Or *Gog, prince of Rosh,*

38:10-16 Gog will think this is his own plan; therefore, he will be confident of success because he assumes Israel will be easy pickings for spoil (38:10-13). But Gog and his allies do not know that God is gathering them to his land for another purpose entirely. Gog won't know that he and his massive army are heading straight into God's trap, **so that the**

nations may know who the true God is when he shows himself **holy** to the whole world (38:14-16).
38:17-23 When Gog and his armies reach Israel, God's **wrath will flare**. In his **fiery rage**, he will send a **great earthquake** to Israel that will make every living creature **tremble** and will demolish natural and manmade objects

(38:18-20). Gog's troops will be so panicked that they will begin killing each other, and the slaughter will be helped along by other God-sent disasters (38:21-22). Gog's invasion will be crushed as the world watches God display his **holiness**, leaving no doubt to the unbelieving world during the tribulation that he alone is God (38:23).

^a39:7 Ezk 36:20-23
^b39:10 Is 14:2; 33:1
^c39:12 Dt 21:23
^d39:13 Jr 33:9; Zph 3:19-20
^eEzk 28:22
^f39:17 Rv 19:17-18

^g39:19 Rv 19:21
^h39:21 Ezk 36:23; 38:16,23
ⁱ39:23 Ezk 36:18-20,23
^j39:25 Is 27:12-13; Jr 33:7;
Ezk 34:13
^kEzk 36:10; 37:21-22;
Hs 1:11
^l39:26 Ezk 16:53-54,63
^m39:27 Ezk 20:41; 38:23
ⁿ39:29 Ezk 36:27; 37:14;
Jl 2:28

the nations will know that I am the Lord, the Holy One in Israel.^a ⁸ Yes, it is coming, and it will happen. This is the declaration of the Lord God. This is the day I have spoken about.

⁹ " 'Then the inhabitants of Israel's cities will go out, kindle fires, and burn the weapons — the small and large shields, the bows and arrows, the clubs and spears. For seven years they will use them to make fires. ¹⁰ They will not gather wood from the countryside or cut it down from the forests, for they will use the weapons to make fires. They will take the loot from those who looted them and plunder those who plundered them.^b This is the declaration of the Lord God.

¹¹ " 'Now on that day I will give Gog a burial place there in Israel — the Travelers' Valley^A east of the Sea. It will block those who travel through, for Gog and all his hordes will be buried there. So it will be called Hordes of Gog^B Valley. ¹² The house of Israel will spend seven months burying them in order to cleanse the land.^c ¹³ All the people of the land will bury them and their fame will spread^d on the day I display my glory.^e This is the declaration of the Lord God.

¹⁴ " 'They will appoint men on a full-time basis to pass through the land and bury the invaders^c who remain on the surface of the ground, in order to cleanse it. They will make their search at the end of the seven months. ¹⁵ When they pass through the land and one of them sees a human bone, he will set up a marker next to it until the buriers have buried it in Hordes of Gog Valley. ¹⁶ There will even be a city named Hamonah^D there. So they will cleanse the land.'

¹⁷ "Son of man, this is what the Lord God says: Tell every kind of bird and all the wild animals, 'Assemble and come! Gather from all around to my sacrificial feast that I am slaughtering for you, a great feast on the mountains of Israel;^f you will eat flesh and drink blood. ¹⁸ You will eat the flesh of mighty men and drink the blood of the earth's princes: rams, lambs, male goats, and all the fattened bulls of Bashan. ¹⁹ You will eat fat until you are satisfied^g and drink blood until you are drunk, at my sacrificial feast that I have prepared for you. ²⁰ At my table you will eat your fill of horses and riders, of mighty men and all the warriors. This is the declaration of the Lord God.'

ISRAEL'S RESTORATION TO GOD

²¹ "I will display my glory among the nations,^h and all the nations will see the judgment I have executed and the hand I have laid on them. ²² From that day forward the house of Israel will know that I am the Lord their God. ²³ And the nations will know that the house of Israel went into exile on account of their iniquity, because they dealt unfaithfully with me.ⁱ Therefore, I hid my face from them and handed them over to their enemies, so that they all fell by the sword. ²⁴ I dealt with them according to their uncleanness and transgressions, and I hid my face from them.

²⁵ "So this is what the Lord God says: Now I will restore the fortunes of Jacob^j and have compassion on the whole house of Israel,^k and I will be jealous for my holy name. ²⁶ They will feel remorse for^{E,F} their disgrace^l and all the unfaithfulness they committed against me, when they live securely in their land with no one to frighten them. ²⁷ When I bring them back from the peoples and gather them from the countries of their enemies, I will demonstrate my holiness through them in the sight of many nations.^m ²⁸ They will know that I am the Lord their God when I regather them to their own land after having exiled them among the nations. I will leave none of them behind.^G ²⁹ I will no longer hide my face from them, for I will pour out my Spirit on the house of Israel."ⁿ This is the declaration of the Lord God.

---

^A39:11 Hb obscure   ^B39:11 = Hamon-gog, also in v. 15   ^C39:14 Or *basis, some to pass through the land, and with them some to bury those*   ^D39:16 In Hb, *Hamonah* is related to the word "horde."   ^E39:26 Some emend to *will forget*   ^F39:26 Lit *will bear*   ^G39:28 Lit *behind there any longer*

39:9-13 Many commentators have a hard time seeing a literal burning of the **weapons**, which would suggest they are like ancient wooden weapons that could be easily burned (37:9). But this is what the text says, and 37:10 is even clearer, stating that during this period of **seven years** Israel would not need any other source of firewood. The burial time for Gog's troops also suggests

the extent of the slaughter—**seven months** of burials **in order to cleanse the land** as the surrounding nations hear of the great victory God gave Israel and see his **glory** on display (39:12-13).

39:14-20 The importance of burying every bone so as not to defile the land with unburied corpses will lead to a **full-time** cadre of men searching for remains for **seven months,**

during which they will find so many that the gravediggers will live in their own city until the job is done (39:14-16). God will also announce a feast to the creatures of Israel to fatten themselves on the corpses of Gog's troops, which is a reversal of God's usual **sacrificial feast** in which people eat the flesh of animals. This time, God will prepare the meal (39:17-20).

THE NEW TEMPLE

40 In the twenty-fifth year of our exile, at the beginning of the year, on the tenth day of the month in the fourteenth year after Jerusalem had been captured,[a] on that very day the LORD's hand was on me,[b] and he brought me there. **2** In visions of God[c] he took me to the land of Israel and set me down on a very high mountain.[d] On its southern slope was a structure resembling a city. **3** He brought me there, and I saw a man whose appearance was like bronze,[e] with a linen cord and a measuring rod in his hand.[f] He was standing by the city gate. **4** He spoke to me: "Son of man, look with your eyes, listen with your ears,[g] and pay attention to everything I am going to show you, for you have been brought here so that I might show it to you. Report everything you see to the house of Israel."[h]

THE WALL AND OUTER GATES

5 Now there was a wall surrounding the outside of the temple.[i] The measuring rod in the man's hand was six units of twenty-one inches;[A] each unit was the standard length plus three inches.[B] He measured the thickness of the wall structure; it was 10½ feet,[c] and its height was the same. **6** Then he came to the gate that faced east and climbed its steps.[j] He measured the threshold of the gate; it was 10½ feet deep — one threshold was 10½ feet deep. **7** Each recess was 10½ feet long and 10½ feet deep, and there was a space of 8¾ feet[D] between the recesses. The inner threshold of the gate on the temple side next to the gate's portico was 10½ feet. **8** Next he measured the gate's portico; **9** it[E] was 14 feet,[F] and its jambs were 3½ feet.[G] The gate's portico was on the temple side. **10** There were three recesses on each side of the east gate, each with the same measurements, and the jambs on either side also had the same measurements. **11** Then he measured the width of the gate's entrance; it was 17½ feet,[H] while the

width[I] of the gate was 22¾ feet.[J] **12** There was a barrier of 21 inches[K] in front of the recesses on both sides, and the recesses on each side were 10½ feet[L] square. **13** Then he measured the gate from the roof of one recess to the roof of the opposite one; the distance was 43¾ feet.[M] The openings of the recesses faced each other. **14** Next, he measured the porch — 105 feet.[N,O] **15** The distance from the front of the gate at the entrance to the front of the gate's portico on the inside was 87½ feet.[P] **16** The recesses and their jambs had beveled windows all around the inside of the gate.[k] The porticoes also had windows all around on the inside. Each jamb was decorated with palm trees.[l]

17 Then he brought me into the outer court,[m] and there were chambers and a paved surface laid out all around the court.[n] Thirty chambers faced the pavement, **18** which flanked the courtyard's gates and corresponded to the length of the gates; this was the lower pavement. **19** Then he measured the distance from the front of the lower gate to the exterior front of the inner court; it was 175 feet.[o] This was the east; next the north is described.

20 He measured the gate of the outer court facing north, both its length and width. **21** Its three recesses on each side, its jambs, and its portico had the same measurements as the first gate: 87½ feet long and 43¾ feet wide. **22** Its windows, portico, and palm trees had the same measurements as those of the gate that faced east. Seven steps led up to the gate, and its portico was ahead of them. **23** The inner court had a gate facing the north gate, like the one on the east. He measured the distance from gate to gate; it was 175 feet.

24 He brought me to the south side, and there was also a gate on the south. He measured its jambs and portico; they had the same measurements as the others. **25** Both the gate and its portico had windows all around, like the other windows. It was 87½ feet long and 43¾ feet wide. **26** Its

[a] 40:1 2Kg 25:1-7; Jr 39:1-9; 52:4-11; Ezk 33:21
[b] Ezk 1:3; 3:14,22; 37:1
[c] 40:2 Ezk 1:1; 8:3; Dn 7:1,7
[d] Is 2:2-3; Ezk 17:23; 20:40; 37:22; Mc 4:1; Rv 21:10
[e] 40:3 Ezk 1:7; Dn 10:6;
[f] Ezk 47:3; Zch 2:1-2; Rv 11:1; 21:15
[g] 40:4 Ezk 2:1,3,6,8; 44:5
[h] Ezk 43:10
[i] 40:5 Is 26:1; Ezk 42:20
[j] 40:6 Ezk 43:1

[k] 40:16 1Kg 6:4; Ezk 41:16,26
[l] 1Kg 6:29,32,35; 2Ch 3:5; Ezk 41:18-20,25-26
[m] 40:17 Ezk 10:5; 42:1; 46:21; Rv 11:2
[n] 2Kg 23:11; 1Ch 9:26; 23:28; 2Ch 31:11

[A] 40:5 = a long cubit   [B] 40:5 Lit *six cubits by the cubit and a handbreadth*   [C] 40:5 Lit *was one rod,* also in v. 7   [D] 40:7 Lit *five cubits,* also in v. 30
[E] 40:8-9 Some Hb mss, Syr, Vg; other Hb mss read *gate facing the temple side; it was one rod.* **9** *Then he measured the gate's portico; it*
[F] 40:9 Lit *eight cubits*   [G] 40:9 Lit *two cubits*   [H] 40:11 Lit *10 cubits*   [I] 40:11 Lit *length*   [J] 40:11 Lit *13 cubits*   [K] 40:12 Lit *one cubit,* also in v. 42
[L] 40:12 Lit *six cubits*   [M] 40:13 Lit *25 cubits,* also in vv. 21,25,29,33,36   [N] 40:14 MT adds *To the jamb of the court, the gate was all around*;
Hb obscure   [O] 40:14 Lit *60 cubits*   [P] 40:15 Lit *50 cubits,* also in vv. 21,25,29,33,36   [Q] 40:19 Lit *100 cubits,* also in vv. 23,27,47

40:1-2 The information given in verse 1 places the next prophecy in 573 BC. The **Jerusalem** revealed to the prophet, however, was a far different version than Ezekiel would have seen in his own day after the Babylonian conquest. **40:3** The figure of brilliant appearance was no doubt an angel.

40:5-16 The future revealed to Ezekiel includes a rebuilt **temple** where God's people will worship him in spirit and in truth under the rule of Christ. This millennial temple will serve in the midst of God's people as a visible symbol of the new covenant he promised to establish.

40:17-18 The **thirty chambers** are rooms which might be used for storage or for meeting places when the people celebrate their feasts (40:17).

a 40:35 Ezk 47:2
b 40:38 2Ch 4:6
c 40:39 Lv 1:3-4; 4:2-3
d Lv 5:1-6

e 40:42 Ex 20:25
f 40:44 1Ch 6:31-32; 16:41-43; 25:1-7
g 40:45 1Ch 9:23; Ps 134:1
h 40:46 1Kg 2:35
i Lv 6:12-13; Ezk 43:19; 44:15
j 40:47 Ezk 43:13-17
k 40:49 1Kg 6:3
l 1Kg 7:15-22; 2Ch 3:17; Jr 52:17-23; Rv 3:12
m 41:1 Ezk 40:2-3,17

stairway had seven steps, and its portico was ahead of them. It had palm trees on its jambs, one on each side. **27** The inner court had a gate on the south. He measured from gate to gate on the south; it was 175 feet.

THE INNER GATES

28 Then he brought me to the inner court through the south gate. When he measured the south gate, it had the same measurements as the others. **29** Its recesses, jambs, and portico had the same measurements as the others. Both it and its portico had windows all around. It was 87 1/2 feet long and 43 3/4 feet wide. **30** (There were porticoes all around, 43 3/4 feet long and 8 3/4 feet wide.^) **31** Its portico faced the outer court, and its jambs were decorated with palm trees. Its stairway had eight steps.

32 Then he brought me to the inner court on the east side. When he measured the gate, it had the same measurements as the others. **33** Its recesses, jambs, and portico had the same measurements as the others. Both it and its portico had windows all around. It was 87 1/2 feet long and 43 3/4 feet wide. **34** Its portico faced the outer court, and its jambs were decorated with palm trees on each side. Its stairway had eight steps.

35 Then he brought me to the north gate.^a When he measured it, it had the same measurements as the others, **36** as did its recesses, jambs, and portico. It also had windows all around. It was 87 1/2 feet long and 43 3/4 feet wide. **37** Its portico^B faced the outer court, and its jambs were decorated with palm trees on each side. Its stairway had eight steps.

ROOMS FOR PREPARING SACRIFICES

38 There was a chamber whose door opened into the gate's portico.^c The burnt offering was to be washed there.^b **39** Inside the gate's portico there were two tables on each side, on which to slaughter the burnt offering, sin offering,^c and guilt offering.^d **40** Outside, as one approaches the entrance of the north gate, there were two tables on one side and two more tables on the other side of the gate's portico. **41** So there were four tables inside the gate and four outside, eight tables in all on which the slaughtering was to be done. **42** There were also four tables of cut stone for the burnt offering,^e each 31 1/2 inches^D long, 31 1/2 inches wide, and 21 inches high. The utensils used to slaughter the burnt offerings and other sacrifices were placed on them. **43** There were three-inch^E hooks^f fastened all around the inside of the room, and the flesh of the offering was to be laid on the tables.

ROOMS FOR SINGERS AND PRIESTS

44 Outside the inner gate, within the inner court, there were chambers for the singers:^G,f one^H beside the north gate, facing south, and another beside the south^i gate, facing north. **45** Then the man said to me: "This chamber that faces south is for the priests who keep charge of the temple.^g **46** The chamber that faces north is for the priests who keep charge of the altar. These are the sons of Zadok,^h the ones from the sons of Levi who may approach the LORD to serve him."^i **47** Next he measured the court. It was square, 175 feet long and 175 feet wide. The altar^j was in front of the temple.

48 Then he brought me to the portico of the temple and measured the jambs of the portico; they were 8 3/4 feet thick on each side. The width of the gate was 24 1/2 feet,^J and the side walls of the gate were^k 5 1/4 feet^L wide on each side. **49** The portico was 35 feet^M across and 21^N feet^O deep, and 10 steps led^P up to it.^k There were pillars by the jambs, one on each side.^l

INSIDE THE TEMPLE

41 Next he brought me into the great hall and measured the jambs;^m on each side the width of the jamb was 10 1/2 feet.^Q,R **2** The width of the entrance was 17 1/2 feet,^s and the side walls of the

A 40:30 Some Hb mss, LXX omit v. 30   B 40:37 LXX; MT reads jambs   C 40:38 Text emended; MT reads door was by the jambs, at the gates   D 40:42 Lit one and a half cubits   E 40:43 Lit one handbreadth   F 40:43 Or ledges   G 40:44 LXX reads were two chambers   H 40:44 LXX; MT reads singers, which was   I 40:44 LXX; MT reads east   J 40:48 Lit 14 cubits   K 40:48 LXX; MT omits 24 1/2 feet, and the side walls of the gate were   L 40:48 Lit three cubits   M 40:49 Lit 20 cubits   N 40:49 LXX; MT reads 19 1/4   O 40:49 Lit 12 cubits   P 40:49 MT reads and it was on steps that they would go   Q 41:1 LXX; MT reads jambs; they were 10 1/2 feet wide on each side — the width of the tabernacle   R 41:1 Lit six cubits, also in vv. 3,5   S 41:2 Lit 10 cubits

40:41-43 That animal sacrifices will be resumed in the millennial kingdom does not imply a reversion to the Levitical sacrificial system. After all, such sacrifices could never ultimately take away sins (see Heb 10:4, 11) and were fulfilled in Christ's once-for-all atoning death on the cross (Heb 10:12-18). These offerings, however, will be offered not to cover sins, but as memorials to and reminders of the sacrifice of the Messiah that took away sin forever (see Acts 21:26). They will serve to commemorate what he did, just as the Lord's Supper does today. **41:4** Ezekiel was barred from this smaller room because it was **the most holy place**: the holy of holies.

entrance were 8 ¾ feet[A] wide on each side. He also measured the length of the great hall, 70 feet,[B] and the width, 35 feet.[C,a] **3** He went inside the next room and measured the jambs at the entrance;[b] they were 3 ½ feet[D] wide. The entrance was 10 ½ feet wide, and the width of the entrance's side walls on each side[E] was 12 ¼ feet.[F] **4** He then measured the length of the room adjacent to the great hall, 35 feet, and the width, 35 feet.[C] And he said to me, "This is the most holy place."[d]

OUTSIDE THE TEMPLE

5 Then he measured the wall of the temple; it was 10 ½ feet thick. The width of the side rooms all around the temple was 7 feet.[G,e] **6** The side rooms were arranged one above another in three stories of thirty rooms each.[H] There were ledges on the wall of the temple all around to serve as supports for the side rooms, so that the supports would not be in the temple wall itself.[f] **7** The side rooms surrounding the temple widened at each successive story, for the structure surrounding the temple went up by stages. This was the reason for the temple's broadness as it rose. And so, one would go up from the lowest story to the highest by means of the middle one.[i,g]

8 I saw that the temple had a raised platform surrounding it; this foundation for the side rooms was 10 ½ feet high.[j,h] **9** The thickness of the outer wall of the side rooms was 8 ¾ feet. The free space between the side rooms of the temple **10** and the outer chambers was 35 feet wide all around the temple.[i] **11** The side rooms opened into the free space, one entrance toward the north and another to the south. The area of free space was 8 ¾ feet wide all around.

12 Now the building that faced the temple yard toward the west was 122 ½ feet[K] wide. The wall of the building was 8 ¾ feet thick on all sides, and the building's length was 157 ½ feet.[L]

13 Then the man measured the temple; it was 175 feet[M] long.[J] In addition, the temple yard and the building, including its walls, were 175 feet long. **14** The width of the front of the temple along with the temple yard to the east was 175 feet. **15** Next he measured the length of the building facing the temple yard to the west, with its galleries[N] on each side;[k] it was 175 feet.

INTERIOR WOODEN STRUCTURES

The interior of the great hall and the porticoes of the court — **16** the thresholds, the beveled windows,[l] and the balconies all around with their three levels opposite the threshold — were overlaid with wood on all sides.[m] They were paneled from the ground to the windows (but the windows were covered), **17** reaching to the top of the entrance, and as far as the inner temple and on the outside. On every wall all around, on the inside and outside, was a pattern **18** carved with cherubim and palm trees.[n] There was a palm tree between each pair of cherubim.[o] Each cherub had two faces: **19** a human face turned toward the palm tree on one side,[p] and a lion's face turned toward it on the other. They were carved throughout the temple on all sides. **20** Cherubim and palm trees were carved from the ground to the top of the entrance and on the wall of the great hall.

21 The doorposts of the great hall were square,[q] and the front of the sanctuary had the same appearance. **22** The altar was[o] made of wood, 5 ¼ feet[p] high and 3 ½ feet long.[q] It had corners, and its length[R] and sides were of wood.[r] The man told me, "This is the table that stands before the LORD."[s]

23 The great hall and the sanctuary each had a double door,[t] **24** and each of the doors had two swinging panels.[u] There were two panels for one door and two for the other. **25** Cherubim and palm trees were carved on the doors of the great hall like those carved on the walls. There was a wooden canopy[i,v] outside, in front of the portico. **26** There were beveled windows and palm trees on both sides,[w] on the side walls of the portico, the side rooms of the temple, and the canopies.[i]

[a] 41:2 1Kg 6:2,17
[b] 41:3 Ezk 40:16
[c] 41:4 1Kg 6:20
[d] 1Kg 6:16
[e] 41:5 1Kg 6:5-10
[f] 41:6 1Kg 6:6
[g] 41:7 1Kg 6:8
[h] 41:8 Ezk 40:5
[i] 41:10 Ezk 40:17
[j] 41:13 Ezk 40:47

[k] 41:15 Ezk 42:3,5
[l] 41:16 1Kg 6:4; Ezk 40:16,25
[m] 1Kg 6:15
[n] 41:18 1Kg 6:29
[o] 2Ch 3:5; Ezk 40:16
[p] 41:19 Ezk 1:10; 10:14
[q] 41:21 1Kg 6:33; Ezk 40:9,14,16; 41:1
[r] 41:22 Ex 30:1-3; 1Kg 6:20; Rv 8:3
[s] Ex 25:23,30; Lv 24:6; Ezk 23:41; 44:16; Mal 1:7,12
[t] 41:23 1Kg 6:31-35
[u] 41:24 1Kg 6:34
[v] 41:25 1Kg 7:6
[w] 41:26 Ezk 40:16

[A] 41:2 Lit *five cubits*, also in vv. 9,11,12　[B] 41:2 Lit *40 cubits*　[C] 41:2 Lit *20 cubits*, also in vv. 4,10　[D] 41:3 Lit *two cubits*, also in v. 22　[E] 41:3 LXX; MT reads *width of the entrance*　[F] 41:3 Lit *seven cubits*　[G] 41:5 Lit *four cubits*　[H] 41:6 Lit *another three and thirty times*　[I] 41:7,25,26 Hb obscure　[J] 41:8 Lit *a full rod of six cubits of a joint*; Hb obscure　[K] 41:12 Lit *70 cubits*　[L] 41:12 Lit *90 cubits*　[M] 41:13 Lit *100 cubits*　[N] 41:15 Or *ledges*　[O] 41:21-22 Or *and in front of the sanctuary was something that looked like* [22]*an altar*　[P] 41:22 Lit *three cubits*　[Q] 41:22 LXX reads *long and 3 ½ feet wide*　[R] 41:22 LXX reads *base*

41:12 This large building west of the temple was left unexplained except for its dimensions. **41:20** The **carved** figures represent the guardians of God's presence, as Ezekiel had seen in his initial vision. The **palm trees** stand for God's blessing and fruitfulness. **41:22** This may be the **altar** of incense or the **table** that holds the Bread of the Presence— both of which were in the original tabernacle (see Exod 30:1-3; 25:23-30).

[a] 42:1 Ezk 40:17,28,48; 41:1
[b] 42:2 Ezk 41:12; 42:10,13
[c] 42:2 Ezk 41:13
[d] 42:3 Ezk 40:17
[e] Ezk 41:15-16
[f] 42:4 Ezk 46:19
[g] 42:6 Ezk 41:6
[h] 42:8 Ezk 41:13-14
[i] 42:9 Ezk 44:5; 46:19
[j] 42:10 Ezk 42:1
[k] 42:11 Ezk 42:4

[l] 42:13 Lv 10:3; Dt 21:5;
  Ezk 40:46
[m] Ex 29:31; Lv 7:6;
  10:13-14,17
[n] Lv 6:25,29; 14:13; Nm
  18:9-10
[o] 42:14 Ex 29:4-9; Lv
  8:7,13; Is 61:10; Zch 3:4-5
[p] Ezk 44:19
[q] 42:15 Ezk 40:6; 43:1
[r] 42:20 Is 60:18; Ezk 40:5;
  Zch 2:5
[s] Ezk 45:2; Rv 21:16
[t] Ezk 22:26; 44:23; 48:15
[u] 43:1 Ezk 10:19; 40:6;
  42:15; 44:1
[v] 43:2 Is 6:3; Ezk 1:28; 3:23;
  10:18-19
[w] Ezk 11:22-23
[x] Ezk 1:24; Rv 1:15
[y] Ezk 1:28; 10:4; Rv 18:1
[z] 43:3 Ezk 1:4-28
[aa] Jr 1:10; Ezk 9:1
[ab] Ezk 1:3
[ac] Ezk 1:28; 3:23

THE PRIESTS' CHAMBERS

42 Then the man led me out by way of the north gate into the outer court.[a] He brought me to the group of chambers opposite the temple yard and opposite the building[b] to the north. [2] Along the length of the chambers, which was 175 feet,[A,C] there was an entrance on the north; the width was 87 ½ feet.[B] [3] Opposite the 35 foot space[c] belonging to the inner court and opposite the paved surface[d] belonging to the outer court, the structure rose gallery by gallery[e] in three tiers. [4] In front of the chambers was a walkway toward the inside,[f] 17 ½ feet[D] wide and 175 feet long,[E] and their entrances were on the north. [5] The upper chambers were narrower because the galleries took away more space from them than from the lower and middle stories of the building. [6] For they were arranged in three stories and had no pillars like the pillars of the courts;[g] therefore the upper chambers were set back from the ground more than the lower and middle stories. [7] A wall on the outside ran in front of the chambers, parallel to them, toward the outer court; it was 87 ½ feet long. [8] For the chambers on the outer court were 87 ½ feet long, while those facing the great hall were 175 feet long.[h] [9] At the base of these chambers there was an entryway on the east side as one enters them from the outer court.[i] [10] In the thickness of the wall of the court toward the south,[F] there were chambers facing the temple yard[j] and the western building, [11] with a passageway in front of them, just like the chambers that faced north.[k] Their length and width, as well as all their exits, measurements, and entrances, were identical. [12] The entrance at the beginning of the passageway, the way in front of the corresponding[G] wall as one enters on the east side, was similar to the entrances of the chambers that were on the south side.

[13] Then the man said to me, "The northern and southern chambers that face the courtyard are the holy chambers where the priests who approach the LORD will eat[l] the most holy offerings.[m] There they will deposit the most holy offerings — the grain offerings, sin offerings, and guilt offerings — for the place is holy.[n] [14] Once the priests have entered, they are not to go out from the holy area to the outer court until they have removed the clothes they minister in, for these are holy.[o] They are to put on other clothes before they approach the public area."[p]

OUTSIDE DIMENSIONS OF THE TEMPLE COMPLEX

[15] When he finished measuring inside the temple complex, he led me out by way of the gate that faced east and measured all around the complex.[q] [16] He measured the east side with a measuring rod; it was 875 feet[H] by the measuring rod.[I] [17] He[J] measured the north side; it was 875 feet by the measuring rod. [18] He[K] measured the south side; it was 875 feet by the measuring rod. [19] Then he turned to the west side and measured 875 feet by the measuring rod. [20] He measured the temple complex on all four sides. It had a wall all around it,[r] 875 feet long and 875 feet[s] wide, to separate the holy from the common.[t]

RETURN OF THE LORD'S GLORY

43 He led me to the gate,[u] the one that faces east, [2] and I saw the glory of the God of Israel[v] coming from the east.[w] His voice sounded like the roar of a huge torrent,[x] and the earth shone with his glory.[y] [3] The vision I saw[z] was like the one I had seen when he[L] came to destroy the city,[aa] and like the ones I had seen by the Chebar Canal.[ab] I fell facedown.[ac] [4] The glory of the LORD entered the temple by

---

[A] 42:2 Lit *100 cubits*, also in vv. 4,8   [B] 42:2 Lit *50 cubits*, also in v. 7   [C] 42:3 Lit *20 cubits*   [D] 42:4 Lit *10 cubits*   [E] 42:4 LXX, Syr; MT reads *wide, a way of one cubit*   [F] 42:10 LXX; MT reads *east*   [G] 42:12 Or *protective*; Hb obscure   [H] 42:16 Lit *500 in rods*, also in vv. 17,18,19   [I] 42:16 Lit *rod all around*, also in vv. 17,18,19   [J] 42:17 LXX reads *Then he turned to the north and*   [K] 42:18 LXX reads *Then he turned to the south and*   [L] 43:3 Some Hb mss, Theod, Vg; other Hb mss, LXX, Syr read *I*

42:13-14 These rooms will serve as **holy chambers where the priests who approach the LORD will eat the most holy offerings** they have deposited from the sacrifices the people bring (42:13). The law of Moses made provision for the priests to eat a portion of the Israelites' offerings as part of their means of support, and this will be the case again in the millennial temple. A second purpose for

these rooms is to give the priests a place to change out of their holy garments and into their street clothes before leaving the **holy area** of the temple (42:14). This will keep the special garments within the temple.

42:20 The last phrase emphasized what Ezekiel's vision of the temple—and in truth his entire prophecy was all about—preserving the holiness of God. The temple's design

limited access to the holy areas, yet there was also access to God through his appointed representatives. Jesus Christ ministers today in the heavenly sanctuary and will do so forever as our eternal high priest.

43:4-5 Ezekiel 43 is one of the most exciting chapters in the Bible. Here we see the departed **glory** of God coming back into his house in an awesome display of majesty!

way of the gate that faced east.[a] **5** Then the Spirit lifted me up[b] and brought me to the inner court, and the glory of the LORD filled the temple.[c]

6 While the man was standing beside me, I heard someone speaking to me from the temple.[d] **7** He said to me: "Son of man, this is the place of my throne and the place for the soles of my feet,[e] where I will dwell among the Israelites forever.[f] The house of Israel and their kings will no longer defile my holy name by their religious prostitution and by the corpses[A,g] of their kings at their high places.[B,h] **8** Whenever they placed their threshold next to my threshold and their doorposts beside my doorposts, with only a wall between me and them, they were defiling my holy name by the detestable acts they committed.[i] So I destroyed them in my anger. **9** Now let them remove their prostitution and the corpses[j] of their kings far from me, and I will dwell among them forever.[k]

10 "As for you, son of man, describe the temple to the house of Israel,[l] so that they may be ashamed of their iniquities.[m] Let them measure its pattern,[n] **11** and they will be ashamed of all that they have done. Reveal[c] the design of the temple to them — its layout with its exits and entrances[o] — its complete design along with all its statutes, design specifications, and laws. Write it down in their sight[p] so that they may observe its complete design and all its statutes and may carry them out.[q] **12** This is the law of the temple: All its surrounding territory on top of the mountain[r] will be especially holy. Yes, this is the law of the temple.

THE ALTAR

13 "These are the measurements of the altar[s] in units of length (each unit being the standard length plus three inches):[D,t] The gutter is 21 inches[E] deep and 21 inches wide, with a rim of nine inches[F] around its edge. This is the base[G] of the altar. **14** The distance from the gutter on the ground to the lower ledge is 3 ½ feet,[H] and the width of the ledge is 21 inches. There are 7 feet[I]

from the small ledge to the large ledge, whose width is also 21 inches. **15** The altar hearth[J] is 7 feet high, and four horns[U] project upward from the hearth. **16** The hearth is square, 21 feet[K] long by 21 feet wide.[V] **17** The ledge is 24 ½ feet[L] long by 24 ½ feet wide, with four equal sides.[W] The rim all around it is 10 ½ inches,[M] and its gutter is 21 inches all around it. The altar's steps face east."[X]

18 Then he said to me: "Son of man,[y] this is what the Lord GOD says: These are the statutes for the altar on the day it is constructed, so that burnt offerings[z] may be sacrificed on it and blood may be splattered on it:[aa] **19** You are to give a bull from the herd[ab] as a sin offering[ac] to the Levitical priests who are from the offspring of Zadok,[ad] who approach me in order to serve me."[ae] This is the declaration of the Lord GOD. **20** "You are to take some of its blood and apply it to the four horns[af] of the altar, the four corners of the ledge, and all around the rim. In this way you will purify the altar and make atonement for it.[ag] **21** Then you are to take away the bull for the sin offering, and it must be burned outside the sanctuary in the place appointed for the temple.[ah]

22 "On the second day you are to present an unblemished male goat as a sin offering. They will purify the altar just as they did with the bull. **23** When you have finished the purification, you are to present a young, unblemished bull[ai] and an unblemished ram from the flock.[aj] **24** You are to present them before the LORD; the priests will throw salt on them and sacrifice them as a burnt offering to the LORD.[ak] **25** You will offer a goat for a sin offering each day for seven days.[al] A young bull and a ram from the flock, both unblemished, are also to be offered. **26** For seven days the priests are to make atonement for the altar and cleanse it. In this way they will consecrate it[N] **27** and complete the days of purification. Then on the eighth day[am] and afterward, the priests will offer your burnt offerings and fellowship offerings on the altar, and I will accept you."[an] This is the declaration of the Lord GOD.

[a] 43:4 Ezk 10:19
[b] 43:5 Ezk 3:14; 2Co 12:2-4
[c] Ezk 10:4
[d] 43:6 Ezk 1:26
[e] 43:7 Ps 47:8
[f] Ezk 37:26-28
[g] Lv 26:30; Ezk 6:5,13
[h] Ezk 6:3-5
[i] 43:8 Ezk 8:3
[j] 43:9 Ezk 18:30
[k] Ezk 37:26-28
[l] 43:10 Ezk 40:4
[m] Ezk 16:61-63
[n] Ezk 28:12
[o] 43:11 Ezk 44:5
[p] Ezk 12:3
[q] Ezk 11:20
[r] 43:12 Ezk 40:2
[s] 43:13 Ex 27:1-8; 2Ch 4:1
[t] Ezk 40:5

[u] 43:15 Ex 27:2; Lv 9:9; 1Kg 1:50; Ps 118:27
[v] 43:16 Ex 27:1
[w] 43:17 Ex 20:26
[x] Ezk 40:6
[y] 43:18 Ezk 2:1
[z] Ex 40:29
[aa] Lv 1:5,11; Heb 9:21-22
[ab] 43:19 Lv 4:3
[ac] Ezk 45:19; Heb 7:27
[ad] 1Kg 2:35; Ezk 40:46
[ae] Nm 16:5
[af] 43:20 Lv 8:15; 9:9
[ag] Lv 16:19
[ah] 43:21 Ex 29:14; Lv 4:12; Heb 13:11
[ai] 43:23 Ex 29:1,10; Ezk 45:18
[aj] Ex 29:1
[ak] 43:24 Lv 2:13; Nm 18:19; Mk 9:49-50; Col 4:6
[al] 43:25 Ex 29:35-37; Lv 8:33
[am] 43:27 Lv 9:1
[an] Ezk 20:40

43:8 Political leaders and systems must never be allowed to make themselves equal to God, nor should God's people allow politics and political parties to compete with the kingdom of God.

43:10-12 God told Ezekiel to **describe the temple to the house of Israel** (43:10) to remind them of the shameful acts they committed that caused the magnificent temple of Solomon to be destroyed and to motivate them to obedience in the future.

a 44:2 Ezk 43:2-4
b 44:3 Gn 31:54; Ex 24:9-11
c Ezk 46:2,8-10
d 44:4 Is 6:3; Ezk 3:23; 43:5
e Ezk 1:28; 43:3
f 44:5 Dt 32:46; Ezk 40:4
g Dt 12:32; Ezk 43:10-11
h 44:6 Ezk 2:5-7; 3:9
i Ezk 45:9; 1Pt 4:3
j 44:7 Lv 22:25
k Lv 26:41; Dt 10:16; Jr 4:4; 9:26
l 44:8 Lv 22:2; Nm 18:7

m 44:10 2Kg 23:8-9
n Nm 18:23
o 44:11 1Ch 26:1-19
p 2Ch 29:34; 30:17
q Nm 16:9
r 44:12 Ps 106:26
s 44:13 2Kg 23:9
t 44:14 Nm 18:4; 1Ch 23:28-32
u 44:15 Ezk 40:46
v 44:16 Nm 18:5,7-8

THE PRINCE'S PRIVILEGE

44 The man then brought me back toward the sanctuary's outer gate that faced east, and it was closed. [2] The LORD said to me: "This gate will remain closed. It will not be opened, and no one will enter through it, because the LORD, the God of Israel, has entered through it.[a] Therefore it will remain closed. [3] The prince himself will sit in the gate to eat a meal before the LORD.[b] He is to enter by way of the portico[c] of the gate and go out the same way."

[4] Then the man brought me by way of the north gate to the front of the temple. I looked, and the glory of the LORD filled his temple.[d] And I fell facedown.[e] [5] The LORD said to me: "Son of man, pay attention;[f] look with your eyes and listen with your ears to everything I tell you about all the statutes and laws of the LORD's temple.[g] Take careful note of the entrance of the temple along with all the exits of the sanctuary.

THE LEVITES' DUTIES AND PRIVILEGES

[6] "Say to the rebellious people,[h] the house of Israel, 'This is what the Lord GOD says: I have had enough[i] of all your detestable practices, house of Israel. [7] When you brought in foreigners,[j] uncircumcised in both heart and flesh,[k] to occupy my sanctuary, you defiled my temple while you offered my food — the fat and the blood. You[A] broke my covenant by all your detestable practices. [8] You have not kept charge of my holy things[l] but have appointed others to keep charge of my sanctuary for you.'

[9] "This is what the Lord GOD says: No foreigner, uncircumcised in heart and flesh, may enter my sanctuary, not even a foreigner who is among the Israelites. [10] Surely the Levites who wandered away from me when Israel went astray, and who strayed from me after their idols,[m] will bear the consequences of their iniquity.[n] [11] Yet they will occupy my sanctuary, serving as guards at the temple gates[o] and ministering at the temple. They will slaughter the burnt offerings[p] and other sacrifices for the people and will stand before them to serve them.[q] [12] Because they ministered to the house of Israel before their idols and became a sinful stumbling block to them, therefore I swore an oath[B] against them"[r] — this is the declaration of the Lord GOD — "that they would bear the consequences of their iniquity. [13] They must not approach me to serve me as priests[s] or come near any of my holy things or the most holy things. They will bear their disgrace and the consequences of the detestable acts they committed. [14] Yet I will make them responsible for the duties of the temple[t] — for all its work and everything done in it.

THE PRIESTS' DUTIES AND PRIVILEGES

[15] "But the Levitical priests descended from Zadok,[u] who kept charge of my sanctuary when the Israelites went astray from me, will approach me to serve me. They will stand before me to offer me fat and blood." This is the declaration of the Lord GOD. [16] "They are the ones who may enter my sanctuary[v] and approach my table to serve

---

[A] 44:7 LXX, Syr, Vg; MT reads *They*   [B] 44:12 Lit *I lifted my hand*

44:1-3 There will be one gate leading into the millennial Jerusalem through which Israel's worshipers will not come. Ezekiel had seen God's glory come back into the temple through the **gate that faced east,** which God ordered to be **closed** and **remain closed** because his glory and holy presence had **entered through it** (44:1-2). But **the prince himself** will be allowed to enter here (see also 46:2) **to eat a meal before the LORD,** possibly the fellowship offerings (44:3).

There is some debate about this prince's identity. One suggestion is that he is Christ himself, the only one worthy to enter a gate that God sanctified by his holy presence. But elsewhere in Ezekiel this prince is said to offer a sin offering for himself (see 45:22), have children (see 46:16), and possess an allotment of land (see 46:18)—all of which are inappropriate descriptions of Christ. In 34:24, God himself said, speaking of the kingdom age, "I, the Lord, will be their God,

and my servant David will be a prince among them." God repeated this prophecy later by saying, "My servant David will be king over them . . . and [he] will be their prince forever" (37:24-25). Based on these passages, the prince Ezekiel mentions is none other than the resurrected King David, leading God's people again in a role under the lordship of the Messiah. There is a lot to commend this view, since David was a type of Christ and Jesus was called the Son of David.

44:5-6 God told Ezekiel to pay close attention to his holy laws regarding the **temple** (44:5). Then he could teach them to his fellow exiles and record them for future generations so that they wouldn't commit the same sins as their ancestors and fall under the same judgment (44:6).

44:7-8 One of the sins practiced in the land was bringing **foreigners, uncircumcised in both heart and flesh,** into the temple for the wrong reasons (44:7). These were not

Gentiles who wanted to sincerely worship the God of Israel but idolaters who corrupted God's worship and his people. Yet the Israelites gave these people **charge of [his] sanctuary** (44:8)!

44:10-14 During the days of Israel's apostasy, these men who were supposed to be guardians of God's holiness and who handled his holy things also **strayed** into idolatry (44:10). As a result of their sin, they will have a diminished role in the millennial age, **serving as guards at the temple gates and ministering at the temple** in lesser roles (44:11-12). No longer will they be **priests** or handle **any of [the] holy things** as part of their reduced temple assignments (44:13-14).

44:15-16 **Zadok** was chief priest during Solomon's reign; he'd remained faithful to God while the Israelites were turning away from him (44:15). His descendants will be honored by their appointment to **serve** God in the priestly role in the millennial temple (44:16).

me.[a] They will keep my mandate. **17** When they enter the gates of the inner court they are to wear linen garments;[b] they must not have on them anything made of wool when they minister at the gates of the inner court and within it. **18** They are to wear linen turbans on their heads and linen undergarments around their waists.[c] They are not to put on anything that makes them sweat. **19** Before they go out to the outer court,[A] to the people, they must take off the clothes they have been ministering in, leave them in the holy chambers, and dress in other clothes[d] so that they do not transmit holiness to the people through their clothes.[e]

20 "They may not shave their heads[f] or let their hair grow long,[g] but are to carefully trim their hair. **21** No priest may drink wine before he enters the inner court.[h] **22** He is not to marry a widow or a divorced woman, but may marry only a virgin from the offspring of the house of Israel,[i] or a widow who is the widow of a priest. **23** They are to teach my people the difference between the holy and the common, and explain to them the difference between the clean and the unclean.[j]

24 "In a dispute, they will officiate as judges and decide the case according to my ordinances.[k] They are to observe my laws and statutes regarding all my appointed festivals, and keep my Sabbaths holy.[l] **25** A priest may not come near a dead person so that he becomes defiled.[m] However, he may defile himself for a father, a mother, a son, a daughter, a brother, or an unmarried sister. **26** After he is cleansed, he is to count off seven days for himself.[n] **27** On the day he goes into the sanctuary, into the inner court[o] to minister in the sanctuary, he is to present his sin offering." This is the declaration of the Lord GOD.

28 "This will be their inheritance: I am their inheritance.[p] You are to give them no possession in Israel: I am their possession. **29** They will eat the grain offering, the sin offering,[q] and the guilt offering.

Everything in Israel that is permanently dedicated to the LORD will belong to them.[r] **30** The best of all the firstfruits of every kind and contribution of every kind from all your gifts will belong to the priests.[s] You are to give your first batch of dough to the priest[t] so that a blessing may rest on your homes.[u] **31** The priests may not eat any bird or animal that died naturally or was mauled by wild beasts.[v]

THE SACRED PORTION OF THE LAND

45 "When you divide the land by lot as an inheritance,[w] set aside a donation to the LORD, a holy portion of the land,[x] 8 1/3 miles[B] long and 6 2/3 miles[C] wide. This entire region will be holy. **2** In this area there will be a square section[D] for the sanctuary, 875 by 875 feet,[E,y] with 87 1/2 feet[F] of open space all around it. **3** From this holy portion,[G] you will measure off an area 8 1/3 miles long and 3 1/3 miles[H] wide, in which the sanctuary, the most holy place,[z] will stand.[I] **4** It will be a holy area of the land to be used by the priests who minister in the sanctuary, who approach to serve the LORD.[aa] It will be a place for their houses, as well as a holy area for the sanctuary. **5** There will be another area 8 1/3 miles long and 3 1/3 miles wide for the Levites who minister in the temple;[ab] it will be their possession for towns to live in.[J]

6 "As the property of the city, set aside an area 1 2/3 miles[k] wide and 8 1/3 miles long, adjacent to the holy donation of land.[ac] It will be for the whole house of Israel. **7** And the prince will have the area on each side of the holy donation of land and the city's property, adjacent to the holy donation and the city's property, stretching to the west on the west side and to the east on the east side.[ad] Its length will correspond to one of the tribal portions from the western boundary to the eastern boundary. **8** This will be his land as a possession in Israel. My princes will no longer oppress my people[ae] but give the rest of the land to the house of Israel according to their tribes.

[a] 44:16 Ezk 41:22
[b] 44:17 Ex 28:42-43; 39:27-29
[c] 44:18 Ex 28:40
[d] 44:19 Ezk 42:14
[e] Lv 6:27
[f] 44:20 Lv 21:5
[g] Nm 6:5
[h] 44:21 Lv 10:9
[i] 44:22 Lv 21:7,13-14
[j] 44:23 Lv 10:10; Ezk 22:26
[k] 44:24 Dt 17:8-9; 2Ch 19:8
[l] Ezk 20:20; 22:26
[m] 44:25 Lv 21:1-4
[n] 44:26 Nm 19:11-19
[o] 44:27 Lv 5:3,6
[p] 44:28 Nm 18:20; Dt 18:2; Jos 13:33
[q] 44:29 Nm 18:9,14; Jos 13:14
[r] 44:29 Lv 27:21,28
[s] 44:30 Nm 18:8-13; Neh 10:35-37
[t] Nm 15:20-21
[u] Mal 3:10
[v] 44:31 Lv 22:8
[w] 45:1 Ezk 47:21; 48:29
[x] Ezk 48:8-9
[y] 45:2 Ezk 42:20
[z] 45:3 Ezk 43:12
[aa] 45:4 Ezk 48:10-11
[ab] 45:5 Ezk 48:13
[ac] 45:6 Ezk 48:15-18
[ad] 45:7 Ezk 48:21
[ae] 45:8 Ezk 19:7; 22:27

[A] 44:19 Some Hb mss, LXX, Syr, Vg; other Hb mss read *court, to the outer court*   [B] 45:1 Lit *25,000 cubits*, also in vv. 3,5,6   [C] 45:1 LXX reads *20,000 cubits*; MT reads *10,000 cubits*   [D] 45:2 Lit *square all around*   [E] 45:2 Lit *500 by 500 cubits*   [F] 45:2 Lit *50 cubits*   [G] 45:3 Lit *this measured portion*   [H] 45:3 Lit *10,000 cubits*, also in v. 5   [I] 45:3 Lit *be*   [J] 45:5 LXX; MT, Syr, Tg, Vg read *possession—20 chambers*   [K] 45:6 Lit *5,000 cubits*

44:17-23 The priests of the millennial kingdom will follow Mosaic regulations such as wearing linen garments when they minister, changing their clothes before going back among the people, not adopting the common signs of mourning, not drinking wine before they go in to do their priestly duties, and not marrying women who have previously been married. Such regulations set priests apart to serve God, demonstrating that they were wholly his in every area of their lives.
44:25 The priests will be allowed to mourn the death of a close relative, although death will be a rare occurrence in Christ's kingdom.
45:1-5 God gave directions on how Jerusalem and the area will be arranged in the kingdom, both as a place for the millennial temple and as places of residence for the priests and Levites close to it. They are to **set aside a donation to the LORD, a holy portion of the land** (45:1) for the obvious reason that it will contain God's holy house and servants (45:4-5).

a 45:9 Ezk 44:6
b Jr 22:3
c 45:10 Lv 19:36; Dt 25:15
d 45:12 Ex 30:13; Lv 27:25
e 45:15 Lv 1:4; 6:30

f 45:19 Ezk 43:20
g 45:20 Lv 4:2; 5:17
h 45:21 Ex 12:18; Lv 23:4-8;
    Nm 28:16-17; Dt 16:1
i 45:25 Lv 23:33-43; Dt
    16:13-15
j 46:1 Ex 20:9-10

9 "This is what the Lord God says: You have gone too far,[A,a] princes of Israel! Put away violence and oppression and do what is just and right.[b] Put an end to your evictions of my people." This is the declaration of the Lord God. **10** "You are to have honest scales, an honest dry measure,[B] and an honest liquid measure.[C,c] **11** The dry measure[D] and the liquid measure[E] will be uniform, with the liquid measure containing 5 ½ gallons[F] and the dry measure holding half a bushel.[F] Their measurement will be a tenth of the standard larger capacity measure.[G] **12** The shekel[H] will weigh twenty gerahs.[d] Your mina will equal sixty shekels.

THE PEOPLE'S CONTRIBUTION TO THE SACRIFICES

13 "This is the contribution you are to offer: Three quarts[I] from five bushels[J] of wheat and[K] three quarts from five bushels of barley. **14** The quota of oil in liquid measures[L] will be one percent of every[M] cor. The cor equals ten liquid measures or one standard larger capacity measure,[N] since ten liquid measures equal one standard larger capacity measure. **15** And the quota from the flock is one animal out of every two hundred from the well-watered pastures of Israel. These are for the grain offerings, burnt offerings, and fellowship offerings, to make atonement for the people."[e] This is the declaration of the Lord God. **16** "All the people of the land must take part in this contribution for the prince in Israel. **17** Then the burnt offerings, grain offerings, and drink offerings for the festivals, New Moons, and Sabbaths — for all the appointed times of the house of Israel — will be the prince's responsibility. He will provide the sin offerings, grain offerings, burnt offerings, and fellowship offerings to make atonement on behalf of the house of Israel.

18 "This is what the Lord God says: In the first month, on the first day of the month, you are to take a young, unblemished bull and purify the sanctuary. **19** The priest is to take some of the blood from the sin offering and apply it to the temple doorposts, the four corners of the altar's ledge, and the doorposts of the gate of the inner court.[f] **20** You are to do the same thing on the seventh day of the month for everyone who sins unintentionally or through ignorance.[g] In this way you will make atonement for the temple.

21 "In the first month, on the fourteenth day of the month, you are to celebrate the Passover, a festival of seven days during which unleavened bread will be eaten.[h] **22** On that day the prince will provide a bull as a sin offering on behalf of himself and all the people of the land. **23** During the seven days of the festival, he will provide seven bulls and seven rams without blemish as a burnt offering to the Lord on each of the seven days, along with a male goat each day for a sin offering. **24** He will also provide a grain offering of half a bushel[O] per bull and half a bushel per ram, along with a gallon[P] of oil for every half bushel. **25** At the festival that begins on the fifteenth day of the seventh month,[Q,i] he will provide the same things for seven days — the same sin offerings, burnt offerings, grain offerings, and oil.

SACRIFICES AT APPOINTED TIMES

46 "This is what the Lord God says: The gate of the inner court that faces east is to be closed during the six days of work, but it will be opened on the Sabbath day[j] and opened on the day of the New Moon. **2** The prince should enter from the outside by way of the gate's portico and stand at the gate's doorpost while the priests sacrifice his burnt offerings and fellowship offerings. He will bow in worship at the gate's threshold and then depart, but the gate is not to be closed until evening. **3** The people of the land will also bow in worship before the Lord at the

---

A 45:9 Lit *Enough of you*   B 45:10 Lit *an honest ephah*   C 45:10 Lit *and an honest bath*   D 45:11 Lit *The ephah*   E 45:11 Lit *the bath*   F 45:11 Lit *one-tenth of a homer*   G 45:11 Lit *be based on the homer*   H 45:12 A shekel is about two-fifths of an ounce of silver   I 45:13 Lit *One-sixth of an ephah*   J 45:13 Lit *a homer*   K 45:13 LXX, Vg; MT reads *and you are to give*   L 45:14 Lit *oil, the bath, the oil*   M 45:14 Lit *be a tenth of the bath from the*   N 45:14 Lit *10 baths, a homer*   O 45:24 Lit *an ephah*   P 45:24 Lit *a hin*   Q 45:25 = the Festival of Shelters

---

45:8-12 God turned his attention from the nation's future, righteous prince to the present, unrighteous **princes** who were in exile with Ezekiel (45:8). His rebuke of their evil that led to Judah's downfall was stinging: **You have gone too far, princes of Israel!** These coldhearted leaders had used **violence** and **oppression** to fuel their greed, using dishonest business prac-

tices to cheat their people (45:9-10). But God warned them to start using honest measures and reminded them what these were (45:11-12). Even in exile, the Israelite community needed leaders, and God wanted Israel's to know that he was watching and would weigh their actions. **45:21** In the millennial age, observances such as **Passover** will not be held to provide

an animal sacrifice to cover the people's sins for another year; they will be a celebration of Christ's once-for-all sacrifice for sin.
46:1-11 God's instructions for Israel's worship in the millennial temple continue here. Ezekiel was still in his visionary state as he received these commands (see 40:1-2).

entrance of that gate on the Sabbaths and New Moons.

4 "The burnt offering that the prince presents to the LORD[a] on the Sabbath day is to be six unblemished lambs[b] and an unblemished ram. **5** The grain offering will be half a bushel[A] with the ram,[c] and the grain offering with the lambs will be whatever he wants to give, as well as a gallon[B] of oil for every half bushel. **6** On the day of the New Moon, the burnt offering is to be a young, unblemished bull, as well as six lambs and a ram without blemish. **7** He will provide a grain offering of half a bushel with the bull, half a bushel with the ram, and whatever he can afford with the lambs, together with a gallon of oil for every half bushel. **8** When the prince enters,[d] he is to go in by way of the gate's portico and go out the same way.

9 "When the people of the land come before the LORD at the appointed times,[c,e] whoever enters by way of the north gate to worship is to go out by way of the south gate, and whoever enters by way of the south gate is to go out by way of the north gate. No one may return through the gate by which he entered, but is to go out by the opposite gate. **10** When the people enter, the prince will enter with them, and when they leave, he will leave. **11** At the festivals and appointed times, the grain offering will be half a bushel with the bull, half a bushel with the ram, and whatever he wants to give with the lambs, along with a gallon of oil for every half bushel.

12 "When the prince makes a freewill offering, whether a burnt offering or a fellowship offering as a freewill offering to the LORD,[f] the gate that faces east is to be opened for him. He is to offer his burnt offering or fellowship offering just as he does on the Sabbath day. Then he will go out, and the gate is to be closed after he leaves.

13 "You are to offer an unblemished year-old male lamb as a daily burnt offering to the LORD; you will offer it every morning.[g] **14** You are also to prepare a grain offering every morning along with it: three quarts,[D] with one-third of a gallon[E] of oil to moisten the fine flour — a grain offering to the LORD. This is a permanent statute to be observed regularly. **15** They will offer the lamb, the grain offering, and the oil every morning as a regular burnt offering.

TRANSFER OF ROYAL LANDS

16 "This is what the Lord GOD says: If the prince gives a gift to each of his sons as their inheritance, it will belong to his sons. It will become their property by inheritance. **17** But if he gives a gift from his inheritance to one of his servants, it will belong to that servant until the year of freedom,[h] when it will revert to the prince. His inheritance belongs only to his sons; it is theirs. **18** The prince must not take any of the people's inheritance, evicting them from their property.[i] He is to provide an inheritance for his sons from his own property, so that none of my people will be displaced from his own property."

THE TEMPLE KITCHENS

19 Then he brought me through the entrance[j] that was at the side of the gate, into the priests' holy chambers, which faced north. I saw a place there at the far western end. **20** He said to me, "This is the place where the priests will boil the guilt offering and the sin offering,[k] and where they will bake the grain offering,[l] so that they do not bring them into the outer court and transmit holiness to the people." **21** Next he brought me into the outer court and led me past its four corners. There was a separate court in each of its corners. **22** In the four corners of the outer court there were enclosed[f] courts, 70 feet[G] long by 52½ feet[H] wide. All four corner areas had the same dimensions. **23** There was a stone wall[i] around the inside of them, around the four of them, with ovens built at the base of the walls on all sides. **24** He said to me: "These are the kitchens where those who minister at the temple will cook the people's sacrifices."

[a] 46:4 Ezk 45:17
[b] Nm 28:9
[c] 46:5 Nm 28:12; Ezk 45:24
[d] 46:8 Ezk 44:3
[e] 46:9 Ex 23:14-17
[f] 46:12 Lv 23:38
[g] 46:13 Ex 29:38

[h] 46:17 Lv 25:10
[i] 46:18 Ezk 45:8-9
[j] 46:19 Ezk 42:9
[k] 46:20 2Ch 35:13; Ezk 44:29
[l] Lv 2:4-7

[A] 46:5 Lit *an ephah*, also in vv. 7,11 [B] 46:5 Lit *a hin*, also in vv. 7,11 [C] 46:9 Or *the festivals* [D] 46:14 Lit *one-sixth of an ephah* [E] 46:14 Lit *one-third of a hin* [F] 46:22 Hb obscure [G] 46:22 Lit *40 cubits* [H] 46:22 Lit *30 cubits* [I] 46:23 Or *a row*

46:12 By definition there is no set time for this **offering**, so the regulations for keeping the eastern gate closed will be set aside so that this leader can bring an offering expressing his love for God.

46:16-17 Remarkably, even in the kingdom age the ownership of the new land of Israel will be governed by the ancient law of the Year of Jubilee (see Lev 25:8-13).

46:18 Unlike the evil princes of Ezekiel's day (see 45:8-9), the righteous **prince** of the millennial age will never take the people's land by force.

46:19-24 These **kitchens** will be in distinct parts of the temple complex, keeping the priests separate from the people as they eat their sacrificial portions that have been made holy before the Lord (46:24). When the Israelites brought fellowship offerings to God at the temple, they were allowed to eat a part of them with their families and friends in a joyful meal. It will be that way again in the kingdom temple.

God Holds the Victory

W E'VE LEARNED A LOT ABOUT the earth by going out into space and looking back at our planet. Science has gained insight into weather patterns, the location of natural resources, and other good things that we might not have known if we had stayed on the ground. Studying prophecy is like traveling in space. Prophecy takes us beyond the limitations of our time-and-space-bound world and circumstances and lets us see the bigger picture. This should result in a drastic change in how we view the temporary versus how we view the eternal.

The Greek general Alexander the Great is reported to have said that Megiddo, which will one day be the scene for the battle of Armageddon, is the most natural battlefield in the world. He was talking about a plain that stretches for many miles, allowing for the movement of vast armies. It's here that Satan, the antichrist, and the false prophet will gather their armies for a last stand against God that will accomplish his purpose of judgment against them.

When heaven opened to give him a glimpse of such things, John saw an awesome sight: "There was a white horse. Its rider is called Faithful and True" (REV 19:11). This image of a conqueror riding a white horse was something that many in New Testament times could have readily related to. When a victorious Roman general returned from battle with his captives and the spoils, he rode through Rome in a victory parade—mounted on a white horse. A white horse was a symbol of victory in that day. The Bible powerfully presents Jesus Christ as returning to earth for his day of conquest, for the day when he lays claim to the ultimate and final victory in history.

Even while Satan is making what appear to be unsolvable messes all around the world, he is actually accomplishing God's program—driving things toward their promised conclusion. He is a puppet on God's string. On Satan's best day, he is helping achieve the program of God. Don't ever forget that.

God has promised that he holds the victory. He has told us who will ultimately rule over all. So what appears to be chaos in our world today will all change when Jesus's feet touch down on the Mount of Olives. The mountain will divide all the way down to the Dead Sea. In fact, Ezekiel 47:1-10 says that when this happens, the Dead Sea will become a place of life instead of a place where nothing can live because of the high salt content. Nature itself will respond and come alive at the return of Christ (SEE RM 8:19-22).

When Jesus enters the final battle, things will change in a hurry. Everything that has happened until that point in history will culminate in a climactic conclusion ushering in the completeness of Christ's rule. Until then, you are to press on. And to do so knowing that "all things" are working "together for the good of those who love God, who are called according to his purpose" (RM 8:28).

THE LIFE-GIVING RIVER

47 Then he brought me back to the entrance of the temple and there was water flowing from under the threshold of the temple toward the east, for the temple faced east. The water was coming down from under the south side of the threshold of the temple, south of the altar.[a] **2** Next he brought me out by way of the north gate and led me around the outside to the outer gate that faced east; there the water was trickling from the south side. **3** As the man went out east with a measuring line in his hand,[b] he measured off a third of a mile[A] and led me through the water. It came up to my ankles. **4** Then he measured off a third of a mile and led me through the water. It came up to my knees. He measured off another third of a mile and led me through the water. It came up to my waist. **5** Again he measured off a third of a mile, and it was a river that I could not cross on foot. For the water had risen; it was deep enough to swim in, a river that could not be crossed on foot.

6 He asked me, "Do you see this, son of man?" Then he led me back to the bank of the river. **7** When I had returned, I saw a very large number of trees along both sides of the riverbank.[c] **8** He said to me, "This water flows out to the eastern region and goes down to the Arabah. When it enters the sea, the sea of foul water,[B,c] the water of the sea becomes fresh.[d] **9** Every kind of living creature that swarms will live wherever the river flows,[D] and there will be a huge number of fish because this water goes there. Since the water will become fresh, there will be life everywhere the river goes. **10** Fishermen will stand beside it from En-gedi to En-eglaim.[E] These will become places where nets are spread out to dry. Their fish will consist of many different kinds, like the fish of the Mediterranean Sea.[e] **11** Yet its swamps and marshes will not be healed; they will be left for salt. **12** All kinds of trees providing food will grow along both banks of the river. Their leaves will not wither, and their fruit will not fail.[f] Each month they will bear fresh fruit because the water comes from the sanctuary. Their fruit will be used for food and their leaves for medicine."[g]

THE BORDERS OF THE LAND

13 This is what the Lord GOD says: "This is[F] the border you will use to divide the land[h] as an inheritance for the twelve tribes of Israel. Joseph will receive two shares.[i] **14** You will inherit it in equal portions, since I swore[G] to give it to your ancestors.[j] So this land will fall to you as an inheritance.

15 This is to be the border of the land: On the north side[k] it will extend from the Mediterranean Sea by way of Hethlon and Lebo-hamath to Zedad,[H] **16** Berothah, and Sibraim (which is between the border of Damascus and the border of Hamath), as far as Hazer-hatticon, which is on the border of Hauran. **17** So the border will run from the sea to Hazar-enon at the border[l] of Damascus, with the territory of Hamath to the north. This will be the northern side.

18 On the east side it will run between Hauran and Damascus, along the Jordan between Gilead and the land of Israel; you will measure from the

---

Cross references (right margin):

[a] 47:1 Ps 46:4; Zch 14:8; Rv 22:1
[b] 47:3 Ezk 40:3
[c] 47:7 Rv 22:2
[d] 47:8 Ex 15:26; 2Kg 2:21
[e] 47:10 Nm 34:3; Ezk 48:28
[f] 47:12 Ps 1:3
[g] Rv 22:2
[h] 47:13 Nm 34:2-12
[i] Gn 48:15-16
[j] 47:14 Dt 1:8; Ezk 20:6
[k] 47:15 Nm 34:7-9; Ezk 48:1
[l] 47:17 Nm 34:9

[A] 47:3 Lit 1,000 cubits, also in vv. 4,5   [B] 47:8 Or enters the sea, being brought out to the sea; Hb obscure   [C] 47:8 = the Dead Sea   [D] 47:9 LXX, Vg; MT reads the two rivers flow   [E] 47:10 Two springs near the Dead Sea   [F] 47:13 Tg, Vg; Syr reads The valley of   [G] 47:14 Lit lifted my hand   [H] 47:15 LXX; MT reads and Lebo to Zedad, Hamath; Ezk 48:1

47:1-12 In Scripture, water is often tied to life and to the work of the Holy Spirit (see John 7:37-39), so the river that will flow from the millennial temple is further evidence that the Spirit of God has returned to his house. It's another way of testifying to God's people that he is in the place and that his blessing is flowing from him to the entire land.

There's a kingdom lesson here for us today because the church is supposed to model the kingdom of God. We are supposed to be a living illustration of the flowing, deepening, and growing life that happens when the Holy Spirit manifests his growing presence in a community of believers (see Eph 2:19-22).

The reason our culture is drying up is that there's no spiritual water flowing out of the sanctuary into the world. But we aren't going to get the water flowing down the streets of our communities, bringing life where there is death, until it begins to flow down the aisles of our churches. If God's presence doesn't show up among his people, how will it show up in our neighborhoods, in the nation, and in the world?

47:13-20 The borders outlined here are similar to those originally given to Moses (see Num 34:1-12), but Israel never fully occupied them at any time in their history.

The division of the land to the twelve tribes of Israel includes the note that **Joseph will receive two shares** (Ezek 47:13), which is a reference to his two sons, Ephraim and Manasseh. There are different listings of the tribes throughout the Old Testament, depending on the reason for the listings. And that's the case even here in the millennium age, because the subject is the land allotments. The tribe of Levi did not have a portion of the land given to them since they were set apart to the Lord. He was to be their inheritance.

That doesn't mean, of course, that the Levites didn't have homes or anything to pass on to their descendants. They were provided for in Israel's history, and Ezekiel's vision showed that they would have residences within the temple complex during the kingdom age, too. So there was no need to list them with the tribes. That takes care of one of the tribes that Ephraim and Manasseh replaced. But the other one was Joseph himself. This brings us to twelve allotments in chapter 48, with the other ten of Jacob's sons being named.

a 47:19 Nm 34:5; 1Kg 8:65;
Is 27:12
b Ezk 48:28
c 47:21 Ezk 45:1
d 47:22 Ac 11:18; 15:9; Eph
2:12-14; 3:6; Col 3:11

e 48:8-9 Ezk 45:1-5
f 48:11 Ezk 44:10,15
g 48:13 Ezk 45:1
h 48:14 Lv 25:34; 27:28
i 48:15 Ezk 45:6
j 48:19 Ezk 45:6
k 48:21 Ezk 34:24; 45:7

northern border to the eastern sea.[A] This will be the eastern side.

[19] On the south side it will run from Tamar to the Waters of Meribath-kadesh,[B] and on to the Brook of Egypt[a] as far as the Mediterranean Sea.[b] This will be the southern side.

[20] On the west side the Mediterranean Sea will be the border, from the southern border up to a point opposite Lebo-hamath. This will be the western side.

[21] "You are to divide this land among yourselves according to the tribes of Israel.[c] [22] You will allot it as an inheritance for yourselves and for the aliens residing among you,[d] who have fathered children among you. You will treat them[c] like native-born Israelites; along with you, they will be allotted an inheritance among the tribes of Israel. [23] In whatever tribe the alien resides, you will assign his inheritance there." This will the declaration of the Lord GOD.

THE TRIBAL ALLOTMENTS

48 "Now these are the names of the tribes:

From the northern end, along the road of Hethlon, to Lebo-hamath as far as Hazar-enon, at the northern border of Damascus, alongside Hamath and extending from the eastern side to the sea, will be Dan — one portion.
[2] Next to the territory of Dan, from the east side to the west, will be Asher — one portion.
[3] Next to the territory of Asher, from the east side to the west, will be Naphtali — one portion.
[4] Next to the territory of Naphtali, from the east side to the west, will be Manasseh — one portion.
[5] Next to the territory of Manasseh, from the east side to the west, will be Ephraim — one portion.
[6] Next to the territory of Ephraim, from the east side to the west, will be Reuben — one portion.
[7] Next to the territory of Reuben, from the east side to the west, will be Judah — one portion.

[8] "Next to the territory of Judah, from the east side to the west, will be the portion you donate to the LORD, 8 1/3 miles[D] wide, and as long as one of the tribal portions from the east side to the west.[e] The sanctuary will be in the middle of it.
[9] "The special portion you donate to the LORD will be 8 1/3 miles long and 3 1/3 miles[E] wide. [10] This holy donation will be set apart for the priests alone. It will be 8 1/3 miles long on the northern side, 3 1/3 miles wide on the western side, 3 1/3 miles wide on the eastern side, and 8 1/3 miles long on the southern side. The LORD's sanctuary will be in the middle of it. [11] It is for the consecrated priests, the sons of Zadok, who kept my charge[f] and did not go astray as the Levites did when the Israelites went astray. [12] It will be a special donation for them out of the holy donation of the land, a most holy place adjacent to the territory of the Levites.
[13] "Next to the territory of the priests, the Levites will have an area 8 1/3 miles long and 3 1/3 miles wide. The total length will be 8 1/3 miles and the width 3 1/3 miles.[g] [14] They must not sell or exchange any of it, and they must not transfer this choice part of the land, for it is holy to the LORD.[h]
[15] "The remaining area, 1 2/3 miles[F] wide and 8 1/3 miles long, will be for common use by the city,[i] for both residential and open space. The city will be in the middle of it. [16] These are the city's measurements:
1 1/2 miles[G] on the north side;
1 1/2 miles on the south side;
1 1/2 miles on the east side;
and 1 1/2 miles on the west side.
[17] The city's open space will extend:
425 feet[H] to the north,
425 feet to the south,
425 feet to the east,
and 425 feet to the west.

[18] "The remainder of the length alongside the holy donation will be 3 1/3 miles to the east and 3 1/3 miles to the west. It will run alongside the holy donation. Its produce will be food for the workers of the city. [19] The city's workers from all the tribes of Israel will cultivate it.[j] [20] The entire donation will be 8 1/3 miles by 8 1/3 miles; you are to set apart the holy donation along with the city property as a square area.
[21] "The remaining area on both sides of the holy donation and the city property will belong to the prince.[k] He will own the land adjacent to the tribal portions, next to the 8 1/3 miles of the donation as far as the

---

[A] 47:18 = the Dead Sea   [B] 47:19 = Kadesh-barnea   [C] 47:22 Lit *They will be to you*   [D] 48:8 Lit *25,000 cubits*, also in vv. 9,10,13,15,20,21
[E] 48:9 Lit *10,000 cubits*, also in vv. 10,13,18   [F] 48:15 Lit *5,000 cubits*   [G] 48:16 Lit *4,500 cubits*, also in vv. 30,32,33,34   [H] 48:17 Lit *250 cubits*

eastern border and[A] next to the 8 ⅓ miles of the donation as far as the western border. The holy donation and the sanctuary of the temple will be in the middle of it. **22** Except for the Levitical property and the city property in the middle of the area belonging to the prince, the area between the territory of Judah and that of Benjamin will belong to the prince.[a]

23 "As for the rest of the tribes:
From the east side to the west, will be Benjamin — one portion.
24 Next to the territory of Benjamin, from the east side to the west, will be Simeon — one portion.
25 Next to the territory of Simeon, from the east side to the west, will be Issachar — one portion.
26 Next to the territory of Issachar, from the east side to the west, will be Zebulun — one portion.
27 Next to the territory of Zebulun, from the east side to the west, will be Gad — one portion.
28 Next to the territory of Gad toward the south side, the border will run from Tamar to the Waters[b] of Meribath-kadesh, to the Brook of Egypt, and out to the Mediterranean Sea. **29** This is the land you are to allot as an inheritance to Israel's tribes,[c] and these will be their portions." This is the declaration of the Lord GOD.

THE NEW CITY

30 "These are the exits of the city:
On the north side, which measures 1 ½ miles, **31** there will be three gates facing north, the gates of the city being named for the tribes of Israel: one, the gate of Reuben; one, the gate of Judah; and one, the gate of Levi.
32 On the east side, which is 1 ½ miles, there will be three gates: one, the gate of Joseph; one, the gate of Benjamin; and one, the gate of Dan.
33 On the south side, which measures 1 ½ miles, there will be three gates: one, the gate of Simeon; one, the gate of Issachar; and one, the gate of Zebulun.
34 On the west side, which is 1 ½ miles, there will be three gates: one, the gate of Gad; one, the gate of Asher; and one, the gate of Naphtali.
35 The perimeter of the city will be six miles,[B] and the name of the city from that day on will be, The LORD Is There."[d]

a 48:22 Jos 18:21-28
b 48:28 2Ch 20:2

c 48:29 Ezk 47:13-20
d 48:35 Is 12:6; 14:32; 24:23; Jr 3:17; 8:19; 14:9; Ezk 35:10; Jl 3:21; Zch 2:10; Rv 21:3; 22:3

[A] 48:21 Lit *border, and to the west,*　　[B] 48:35 Lit *18,000 cubits*

47:22 Even the aliens residing among the Israelites in the kingdom, a reference to Gentiles who believed in and worshiped the Messiah, will have special privileges. Aliens who wanted to follow the God of Israel were always allowed to live among his people and were treated kindly by them, but these people will also be **allotted an inheritance among the tribes of Israel**.

48:35 The most important thing Ezekiel could say about the city under the perfect, righteous rule of its rightful King was the new name it will bear: **The LORD Is There.** The holy city had become unholy and doomed to destruction, and God's glory had departed. But in the glorious future, it will be restored when King Jesus returns to claim his rightful place and establish his millennial kingdom reign.

DANIEL

INTRODUCTION

Author

UNTIL MODERN TIMES, IT WAS broadly accepted that Daniel authored the book that bears his name. Modern critical scholars, however, usually reject that the historical Daniel wrote it—as they do in the cases of a number of other prophetic biblical books. This is mostly based on a denial of the possibility of predictive prophecy. Yet, unless one assumes that God is unable to reveal the future to his prophets, then there is no good reason to deny the traditional view that Daniel wrote the book. Moreover, the discovery of a portion of a Daniel manuscript among the Dead Sea Scrolls testifies to an older date of writing than most critical scholars are willing to affirm. Thus, it is likely that Daniel wrote the book sometime after the end of the Babylonian captivity in the sixth century BC.

Daniel claims to have received visions from God, which he subsequently recorded (e.g., 2:19; 7:2; 8:1; 10:7). In Matthew 24:15, Jesus attributes the prophecy about the "abomination of desolation" (Dan 9:27; 11:31; 12:11) to Daniel. This confirms that our Lord believes the historical Daniel authored the book.

Historical Background

King Nebuchadnezzar of Babylon besieged Judah three times: once in 605 BC, again in 597 BC, and again in 586 BC. During the last of these, he destroyed Jerusalem and razed the temple. But it was after the first invasion that Daniel and his friends were taken to Babylon in captivity (1:1-7). Daniel's service to Nebuchadnezzar began after his arrival there and continued into the reign of Cyrus, the Medo-Persian king who defeated the Babylonians (1:21; 10:1).

Message and Purpose

The book of Daniel is about how God's people are to live during the times of the Gentiles. Daniel was one of the first exiles to Babylon, where the Jews fell under Gentile domination because of their sin and rebellion against God.

Daniel's book is designed to teach how the entire period of Gentile rule—from Daniel's day to the second coming of the Messiah to set up his kingdom—should be viewed. God used the nations to bring judgment and discipline on Israel. In his own life, Daniel also illustrated how the people of God were to live, showing what faithfulness to God and his kingdom agenda looked like even when undergoing his discipline.

This book includes prophecy, as well as prayer, apocalyptic visions, and insight into spiritual warfare—all of which teach that God's people are under his sovereignty even when circumstances on earth do not appear to be in their favor. Daniel shows that the God of heaven rules on earth, even when earth seems to be out of control.

Outline

DANIEL'S CAPTIVITY IN BABYLON

1 In the third year of the reign of King Jehoiakim[a] of Judah, King Nebuchadnezzar[A,b] of Babylon came to Jerusalem and laid siege to it. **2** The Lord handed King Jehoiakim of Judah over to him, along with some of the vessels from the house of God.[c] Nebuchadnezzar carried them to the land of Babylon,[B,d] to the house of his god,[c] and put the vessels in the treasury of his god.

3 The king ordered Ashpenaz, his chief eunuch,[D] to bring some of the Israelites from the royal family[e] and from the nobility — **4** young men without any physical defect, good-looking, suitable for instruction in all wisdom,[f] knowledgeable, perceptive, and capable of serving in the king's palace.[g] He was to teach them the Chaldean language[h] and literature. **5** The king assigned them daily provisions from the royal food and from the wine that he drank.[i] They were to be trained for three years, and at the end of that time they were to attend the king.[E,j] **6** Among them, from the Judahites, were Daniel,[k] Hananiah, Mishael, and Azariah. **7** The chief eunuch gave them names; he gave the name Belteshazzar to Daniel, Shadrach to Hananiah, Meshach to Mishael, and Abednego to Azariah.[l]

FAITHFULNESS IN BABYLON

8 Daniel determined that he would not defile himself with the king's food[m] or with the wine he drank. So he asked permission from the chief eunuch not to defile himself.[n] **9** God had granted Daniel kindness and compassion from the chief eunuch,[o] **10** yet he said to Daniel, "I fear my lord the king, who assigned your food and drink. What if he sees your faces looking thinner than the other young men your age? You would endanger my life[F] with the king."

11 So Daniel said to the guard whom the chief eunuch had assigned to Daniel, Hananiah, Mishael, and Azariah, **12** "Please test your servants for ten days. Let us be given vegetables to eat and water to drink. **13** Then examine our appearance and the appearance of the young men who are eating the king's food, and deal with your servants based on what you see." **14** He agreed with them about this and tested them for ten days. **15** At the end of ten days they looked better and healthier[G] than all the young men who were eating the king's food.[p] **16** So the guard continued to remove their food and the wine they were to drink and gave them vegetables.

FAITHFULNESS REWARDED

17 God gave these four young men knowledge and understanding[q] in every kind of literature and wisdom. Daniel also understood visions and dreams[r] of every kind. **18** At the end of the time that the king had said to present them, the chief eunuch presented them to Nebuchadnezzar. **19** The king interviewed them, and among all of them, no one was found equal to Daniel, Hananiah, Mishael, and Azariah.[s] So they began to attend the king. **20** In every matter of wisdom and understanding that the king consulted them about, he found them ten times[H,t] better than all the magicians and mediums[u] in his entire kingdom. **21** Daniel remained there until the first year of King Cyrus.[v]

NEBUCHADNEZZAR'S DREAM

2 In the second year of his reign, Nebuchadnezzar had dreams[w] that troubled him, and sleep deserted him.[x] **2** So the king gave orders to summon the magicians,

[a] 1:1 2Kg 24:1-2; 2Ch 36:5-6
[b] Jr 25:1; 52:12,28-30
[c] 1:2 2Kg 24:13; 2Ch 36:7-10; Ezr 5:14; Jr 27:19-22; Dn 5:2
[d] Gn 10:10; 11:2; Is 11:11; Zch 5:11
[e] 1:3 2Kg 20:18; 24:15; Is 39:7; Dn 1:9
[f] 1:4 Dn 9:22
[g] Is 39:7
[h] Jr 5:15
[i] 1:5 2Kg 25:30; Dn 11:26
[j] Gn 41:46; 1Sm 16:22
[k] 1:6 Ezk 14:14,20; 28:3
[l] 1:7 2Kg 23:34; 24:17; Dn 4:8,19; 5:12; 10:1
[m] 1:8 Pr 23:1-2
[n] Lv 3:17; 11:47; Ps 141:4; Ezk 4:13; Hs 9:3; Ac 10:11-15
[o] 1:9 Gn 39:21; 1Kg 8:50; Jb 5:15; Ps 106:46; Pr 16:7; Ac 7:10

[p] 1:15 Ex 23:25
[q] 1:17 Jb 32:8; Ac 7:22; Jms 1:5
[r] 1Kg 3:10-12; Dn 2:19,30; 4:18-19; 7:1
[s] 1:18-19 Gn 41:37-39
[t] 1:20 Gn 31:7; Nm 14:22; Jb 19:3
[u] Pr 3:13-18; Dn 5:11-12
[v] 1:21 Ezr 1:1-2; Is 45:1; Dn 6:28; 10:1
[w] 2:1 Gn 40:5-8; Dn 4:5; 5:9
[x] Gn 41:1,8; Est 6:1; Dn 6:18

[A] 1:1 Or Nebuchadrezzar   [B] 1:2 Lit Shinar   [C] 1:2 Or gods   [D] 1:3 Or his eunuchs   [E] 1:5 Lit to stand before the king   [F] 1:10 Lit would make my head guilty   [G] 1:15 Lit fatter of flesh   [H] 1:20 Lit hands

---

1:1 Nebuchadnezzar's invasion of Judah in 605 BC was the first of his three invasions and deportations that ended in the nation's exile. The destruction of **Jerusalem** began what Jesus called "the times of the Gentiles" (Luke 21:24). This period will continue until he returns.
1:2 Taking **vessels** from the temple showed dominance over Judah.
1:3-6 Daniel and his three friends were perhaps teenagers at the time. Daniel was a person of exceptional character and capability. The royal plan was to train him and the others to be Nebuchadnezzar's court advisers (1:4). But along the way, Daniel would face a crisis of worldview and truth that would pit him against the most powerful human king and kingdom on earth.

1:7 Daniel, whose name means, "God is My Judge," was to be called **Belteshazzar**—"Bel Protect Him." Every aspect of Daniel's re-education was designed to remind him that he needed to operate from a Babylonian worldview. In the integrity of his heart, however, he knew that he served only one true King and maintained the worldview of his kingdom.
1:8 Daniel's decision was made to avoid violating the law of Moses regarding the foods the Jews were not to eat (see Lev 11), especially food that was offered to idols (see Exod 34:15).
1:14-16 Israel had disobeyed God and suffered for it in exile, but this story tells us that God stood ready to bless his people when they obeyed and trusted him. We too live in a fallen

world, and we're called to be good citizens in it. Often, though, being good citizens requires rejecting the world's way of doing things and honoring God instead.
1:17-21 In terms of ability, these **four young men** (1:17) stood head and shoulders above all of the so-called wise men of Babylon. That's because their allegiance was to a heavenly King.
2:1 With this introduction to chapter 2, faithful readers of the Old Testament will recall an earlier biblical story—that of Pharaoh and Joseph—in which a pagan ruler had troubling **dreams** and turned to a spokesman of the one true God for counsel (Gen 41:1-45).
2:2 Chaldeans in this instance were influential Babylonian wise men.

a 2:2 Dt 18:10,11; 2Ch 33:6;
Is 47:9,12
b 2:4 Ezr 4:7; Is 36:11
c 1Kg 1:31; Dn 3:9; 5:10;
6:6,21
d 2:5 Ezr 6:11; Dn 3:29
e 2:6 Dn 5:7,16
f 2:9 Is 41:23
g 2:10 Dn 5:11-16
h 2:11 Ex 29:45; Is 57:15
i 2:12 Ps 76:10; Dn 2:24;
3:13,19
j 2:14 Gn 37:36

k 2:15 Dn 3:22
l 2:18 Mt 18:19
m Jr 33:3
n Mal 3:18
o 2:19 Nm 12:6; Jb 33:15-16;
Am 3:7
p 2:20 1Ch 29:10; Ps 72:18;
Lk 1:68
q Jb 12:13; Is 28:29
r 2:21 1Ch 29:11-12; Dn
4:17; Rm 13:1
s Jb 12:16-22
t 2:22 Jb 12:22; Ps 139:12; Jr
23:24; Am 4:13; Heb 4:13
u Jn 1:4-5; 1Tm 6:16; Jms
1:17; 1Jn 1:5
v 2:23 Gn 31:42; Ex 3:15; Dt
26:7; 1Ch 12:17; 29:18
w Dn 1:17-18
x 2:24 Dn 2:14-15
y Ac 27:24
z 2:25 Ezr 4:1; 6:16,19-20;
10:7,16; Dn 5:13

mediums, sorcerers, and Chaldeans^A,a^ to tell the king his dreams. When they came and stood before the king, ^3^ he said to them, "I have had a dream and am anxious to understand it."

^4^ The Chaldeans spoke to the king (Aramaic^B,b^ begins here): "May the king live forever.^c^ Tell your servants the dream, and we will give the interpretation."

^5^ The king replied to the Chaldeans, "My word is final: If you don't tell me the dream and its interpretation, you will be torn limb from limb,^c^ and your houses will be made a garbage dump.^d^ ^6^ But if you make the dream and its interpretation known to me, you'll receive gifts, a reward, and great honor from me.^e^ So make the dream and its interpretation known to me."

^7^ They answered a second time, "May the king tell the dream to his servants, and we will have known the interpretation."

^8^ The king replied, "I know for certain you are trying to gain some time, because you see that my word is final. ^9^ If you don't tell me the dream, there is one decree for you.^f^ You have conspired to tell me something false or fraudulent until the situation changes. So tell me the dream and I will know you can give me its interpretation."

^10^ The Chaldeans answered the king, "No one on earth can make known what the king requests.^g^ Consequently, no king, however great and powerful, has ever asked anything like this of any magician, medium, or Chaldean. ^11^ What the king is asking is so difficult that no one can make it known to him except the gods, whose dwelling is not with mortals."^h^ ^12^ Because of this, the king became violently angry^i^ and gave orders to destroy all the wise men of Babylon. ^13^ The decree was issued that the wise men were to be executed, and they searched for Daniel and his friends, to execute them.

^14^ Then Daniel responded with tact and discretion to Arioch, the captain of the king's guard,^D,j^ who had gone out to execute the wise men of Babylon. ^15^ He asked Arioch, the king's officer, "Why is the decree from the king so harsh?"^E,k^ Then Arioch explained the situation to Daniel. ^16^ So Daniel went and asked the king to give him some time, so that he could give the king the interpretation.

^17^ Then Daniel went to his house and told his friends Hananiah, Mishael, and Azariah about the matter, ^18^ urging them to ask the God of the heavens^l^ for mercy^m^ concerning this mystery, so Daniel and his friends would not be destroyed with the rest of Babylon's wise men.^n^ ^19^ The mystery was then revealed to Daniel in a vision^o^ at night, and Daniel praised the God of the heavens ^20^ and declared:

> May the name of God
> be praised forever and ever,^p^
> for wisdom^q^ and power belong
> to him.
> ^21^ He changes the times
> and seasons;
> he removes kings
> and establishes kings.^r^
> He gives wisdom to the wise
> and knowledge to those
> who have understanding.^s^
> ^22^ He reveals the deep
> and hidden things;
> he knows what is
> in the darkness,^t^
> and light dwells with him.^u^
> ^23^ I offer thanks and praise to you,
> God of my fathers,^v^
> because you have given me
> wisdom and power.
> And now you have let me know
> what we asked of you,
> for you have let us know^w^
> the king's mystery.^F^

^24^ Therefore Daniel went to Arioch,^x^ whom the king had assigned to destroy the wise men of Babylon. He came and said to him, "Don't destroy the wise men of Babylon! Bring me before the king, and I will give him the interpretation."^y^ ^25^ Then Arioch quickly brought Daniel before the king and said to him, "I have found a man among the Judean exiles^z^ who can let the king know the interpretation."

2:4 The parenthetical note that **Aramaic begins here** refers to the fact that Daniel 2:4–7:28 was written in Aramaic rather than Hebrew.

2:5 This was the kind of outrageous demand ancient kings could make—illustrating the fury they could generate if their whims weren't met.

2:10-11 As diplomatically as they could, they informed the king that he was crazy: **No one on earth can make known what the king requests. . . . No one can make it known to him except the gods**. Now, they were partly correct because no one on earth could make it known. There is one in heaven, however, who can do anything. The Chaldeans were

right to look for a divine answer, but there is only one capable deity.

2:19 Before Daniel went public with the information divinely provided, he first **praised . . . God**. Why? Because when we're experiencing chaos, we need to remind ourselves that there's a God in heaven who reigns over the confusion on earth—and give him thanks.

²⁶ The king said in reply to Daniel, whose name was Belteshazzar,[a] "Are you able to tell me the dream I had and its interpretation?"[b] ²⁷ Daniel answered the king: "No wise man, medium, magician, or diviner[c] is able to make known to the king the mystery he asked about. ²⁸ But there is a God in heaven who reveals mysteries, and he has let King Nebuchadnezzar know what will happen in the last days.[d] Your dream and the visions that came into your mind as you lay in bed[e] were these: ²⁹ Your Majesty, while you were in your bed, thoughts came to your mind about what will happen in the future.[A,f] The revealer of mysteries[g] has let you know what will happen. ³⁰ As for me, this mystery has been revealed to me,[h] not because I have more wisdom than anyone living, but in order that the interpretation might be made known to the king, and that you may understand the thoughts of your mind.[i]

THE DREAM'S INTERPRETATION

³¹ "Your Majesty, as you were watching, suddenly a colossal statue appeared. That statue, tall and dazzling, was standing in front of you, and its appearance was terrifying. ³² The head of the statue was pure gold, its chest and arms were silver, its stomach and thighs were bronze, ³³ its legs were iron, and its feet were partly iron and partly fired clay. ³⁴ As you were watching, a stone broke off without a hand touching it,[B,j] struck the statue[k] on its feet of iron and fired clay, and crushed them.[l] ³⁵ Then the iron, the fired clay, the bronze, the silver, and the gold were shattered and became like chaff[m] from the summer threshing floors. The wind carried them away, and not a trace of them could be found. But the stone that struck the statue became a great mountain and filled[n] the whole earth.

³⁶ "This was the dream; now we will tell the king its interpretation. ³⁷ Your Majesty, you are king of kings.[o] The God of the heavens has given you sovereignty, power,[p] strength, and glory. ³⁸ Wherever people live — or wild animals, or birds of the sky — he has handed them over to you and made you ruler over them all.[q] You are the head of gold.

³⁹ "After you, there will arise another kingdom, inferior to yours, and then another, a third kingdom, of bronze, which will rule the whole earth.[r] ⁴⁰ A fourth kingdom will be as strong as iron; for iron crushes and shatters everything, and like iron that smashes, it will crush and smash all the others.[C,s] ⁴¹ You saw the feet and toes, partly of a potter's fired clay and partly of iron — it will be a divided kingdom, though some of the strength of iron will be in it. You saw the iron mixed with clay, ⁴² and that the toes of the feet were partly iron and partly fired clay — part of the kingdom will be strong, and part will be brittle. ⁴³ You saw the iron mixed with clay — the peoples will mix with one another[D] but will not hold together, just as iron does not mix with fired clay.

⁴⁴ "In the days of those kings, the God of the heavens will set up a kingdom that will never be destroyed,[t] and this kingdom will not be left to another people. It will crush all these kingdoms[u] and bring them to an end, but will itself endure forever. ⁴⁵ You saw a stone[v] break off from the mountain without a hand touching it,[E,w] and it crushed the iron, bronze, fired clay, silver, and gold. The great God has told the king what will happen in the future.[x] The dream is certain, and its interpretation reliable."

[a] 2:26 Dn 1:7; 5:12
[b] Dn 5:16
[c] 2:27 Dn 1:20; 4:7; 5:7,11
[d] 2:28 Is 2:2; Dn 10:14; Hs 3:5; Mc 4:1
[e] Dn 4:5; 7:15
[f] 2:29 Rv 1:1
[g] Jb 12:20-22; Dn 2:45
[h] 2:30 Eph 3:3
[i] Gn 41:16; Ec 3:18; Am 4:13; Ac 3:12
[j] 2:34 Jb 34:20; Lm 4:6; Dn 8:25; 2Co 5:1
[k] Mt 21:44; Lk 20:18
[l] Ps 2:9; Is 60:12
[m] 2:35 Ps 1:4; Is 17:13; 41:15-16; Hs 13:3

[n] 2:35 Is 2:2; Mc 4:1
[o] 2:37 Is 47:5; Jr 27:6-7; Ezk 26:7
[p] Pr 8:15
[q] 2:38 Dn 5:10; Jr 27:6; 28:14; Dn 4:21
[r] 2:39 Dn 5:28,31; 7:6
[s] 2:40 Dn 7:7,23
[t] 2:44 Ps 145:13; Ezk 37:25; Dn 4:3; 6:26; 7:14; Lk 1:33
[u] Ps 2:9; Mt 21:44
[v] 2:45 Is 28:16
[w] Dn 2:34
[x] Jr 32:18-19; Dn 2:29; Mal 1:11

[A] 2:29 Lit happen after this, also in v. 45   [B] 2:34 Lit off not by hands   [C] 2:40 Lit all these   [D] 2:43 Lit another in the seed of men   [E] 2:45 Lit mountain, not by hands

2:27-30 Daniel didn't fail to give glory to **God** for the revelation (2:28). He also confessed that the **mystery** was *not* **revealed to** him because he had **more wisdom than anyone living** (2:30), which indicates that even though Daniel was the only person on earth who knew the answer, he was humble. Indeed, God hadn't revealed the truth to Daniel to show how smart Daniel was; he'd revealed it so that the king would glorify God (see 2:45-47). **2:36-38** After explaining what *the king alone* knew—the basic details of the **dream**, Daniel explained what *no one* knew—the dream's **interpretation** (2:36). Nebuchadnezzar was the **head of gold** because as far as earthly powers were concerned, he was currently **king of kings** (2:37-38). This power, however, had

not originated with Nebuchadnezzar. On the contrary, **the God of the heavens**—the God of Israel—had granted the king of Babylon **power** (2:37). **2:39** The kingdom illustrated by a "chest and arms" of "silver" (2:32) was the Medo-Persian Empire that overthrew Babylon decades later when Daniel was serving the Babylonian king named Belshazzar (see 5:13-31). The **third kingdom** was Greece under Alexander the Great, who destroyed it (2:39). **2:40-43** In view here is the Roman Empire, **as strong as iron**, which crushed Greece. It was still in power when Jesus was born. But though Rome's might was unmatched and it would **smash all the** other empires, it had a flaw, a weakness (2:40). From God's perspec-

tive, the thing that distinguished Rome was that its **feet** and **toes** were comprised of **iron** and **clay** (20:41), a mixture of two substances that **will not hold together** (2:42-43). And indeed, the Roman Empire fell not by military conquest but by decay from within as immorality collided with Rome's governmental structures to weaken the kingdom. **2:44-45** This kingdom's reign will be fulfilled when Christ returns to set up his millennial rule. He is the "stone broke off without a hand touching it" (2:34), which means he is from God, and Jesus is called a stone throughout Scripture (e.g., 1 Pet 2:4-8). In Nebuchadnezzar's dream the stone became a **mountain** (Dan 2:45)—that is, a kingdom—that will **endure forever** (2:44).

a 2:46 Mt 8:2; Ac 10:25;
14:13; Rv 19:10; 22:8
b 2:47 Dt 10:17; Ps 136:2-3;
1Tm 6:15; Rv 17:14; 19:16
c Am 3:7
d 2:48 Gn 41:41; Dn
3:1,12,30
e 2:49 Dn 1:17; 3:12
f Est 2:19,21; Am 5:15
g 3:1 1Kg 12:28; Is 46:6;
Jr 16:20; Hs 2:8; 8:4;
Hab 2:19
h Gn 11:2; Dn 2:48-49
i 3:2 Ezr 8:36; Dn 2:48;
6:1-7
j 3:5 Gn 4:21; 1Ch 6:31;
25:6; Jb 21:12; 30:31; Ps
33:2; 71:22; 81:2; 149:3;
150:4; Is 5:12
k Dn 2:46
l 3:6 Jr 29:22; Mt 13:42,50;
Rv 9:2

m 3:8 Dn 2:2,4-5,10
n Ezr 4:12-16; Est 3:8-9;
Dn 6:12,24
o 3:10 Dn 4:6; 6:26
p 3:12 Dn 1:7
q Dn 6:13
r 3:13 Dn 2:12
s 3:14 Jr 50:2
t 3:15 Ex 5:20; 2Kg 18:35;
Is 36:18
u 3:17 Ps 10:4; 14:1; 53:1; Hs
13:4; Heb 11:6
v 1Sm 17:37; Jb 5:19; Jr
15:20-21; 2Co 1:10
w 3:18 Heb 11:25
x Jos 24:15

NEBUCHADNEZZAR'S RESPONSE

46 Then King Nebuchadnezzar fell face-down, worshiped Daniel, and gave orders to present an offering and incense to him.[a] **47** The king said to Daniel, "Your God is indeed God of gods, Lord of kings,[b] and a revealer of mysteries,[c] since you were able to reveal this mystery." **48** Then the king promoted Daniel and gave him many generous gifts. He made him ruler over the entire province of Babylon and chief governor over all the wise men of Babylon.[d] **49** At Daniel's request, the king appointed Shadrach, Meshach, and Abednego[e] to manage the province of Babylon. But Daniel remained at the king's court.[f]

NEBUCHADNEZZAR'S GOLD STATUE

3 King Nebuchadnezzar made a gold statue,[g] ninety feet high and nine feet wide.[A] He set it up on the plain of Dura in the province of Babylon.[h] **2** King Nebuchadnezzar sent word to assemble the satraps, prefects, governors, advisers, treasurers, judges, magistrates, and all the rulers[i] of the provinces to attend the dedication of the statue King Nebuchadnezzar had set up. **3** So the satraps, prefects, governors, advisers, treasurers, judges, magistrates, and all the rulers of the provinces assembled for the dedication of the statue the king had set up. Then they stood before the statue Nebuchadnezzar had set up.

4 A herald loudly proclaimed, "People of every nation and language, you are commanded: **5** When you hear the sound of the horn, flute, zither,[B] lyre,[C] harp, drum,[D] and every kind of music,[j] you are to fall facedown and worship[k] the gold statue that King Nebuchadnezzar has set up. **6** But whoever does not fall down and worship will immediately be thrown into a furnace of blazing fire."[l]

7 Therefore, when all the people heard the sound of the horn, flute, zither, lyre, harp, and every kind of music, people of every nation and language fell down and worshiped the gold statue that King Nebuchadnezzar had set up.

THE FURNACE OF BLAZING FIRE

8 Some Chaldeans[m] took this occasion to come forward and maliciously accuse[E,n] the Jews. **9** They said to King Nebuchadnezzar, "May the king live forever. **10** You as king have issued a decree[o] that everyone who hears the sound of the horn, flute, zither, lyre, harp, drum, and every kind of music must fall down and worship the gold statue. **11** Whoever does not fall down and worship will be thrown into a furnace of blazing fire. **12** There are some Jews you have appointed to manage the province of Babylon: Shadrach, Meshach, and Abednego.[p] These men have ignored you,[q] the king; they do not serve your gods or worship the gold statue you have set up."

13 Then in a furious rage[r] Nebuchadnezzar gave orders to bring in Shadrach, Meshach, and Abednego. So these men were brought before the king. **14** Nebuchadnezzar asked them, "Shadrach, Meshach, and Abednego, is it true that you don't serve my gods or worship the gold statue[s] I have set up? **15** Now if you're ready, when you hear the sound of the horn, flute, zither, lyre, harp, drum, and every kind of music, fall down and worship the statue I made. But if you don't worship it, you will immediately be thrown into a furnace of blazing fire — and who is the god who can rescue you from my power?"[t]

16 Shadrach, Meshach, and Abednego replied to the king, "Nebuchadnezzar, we don't need to give you an answer to this question. **17** If the God we serve exists,[u] then he can rescue[v] us from the furnace of blazing fire, and he can[f] rescue us from the power of you, the king. **18** But even if he does not rescue us,[G] we want you as king to know that we will not serve[w] your gods[x] or worship the gold statue you set up."

A 3:1 Lit statue, its height sixty cubits, its width six cubits   B 3:5 Or lyre   C 3:5 Or sambuke   D 3:5 Or pipe   E 3:8 Lit and eat the pieces of   F 3:17 Or If the God whom we serve is willing to save us from the furnace of blazing fire, then he will   G 3:18 Lit But if not

---

2:47 The greatest king on earth was made to confess the dominance of the true God through the ministry of a servant.
2:48 Like Joseph before him (Gen 41:37-45), Daniel went from the bottom to the top—which is a reminder that God knows how to grant authority to those who submit themselves to his authority.
3:8-12 Shadrach, Meshach, and Abednego knew the king was demanding they do the very thing that had led to Judah's ejection from their homeland—commit idolatry. Their actions in this passage illustrate a kingdom response common to our era and culture: protest through civil disobedience. This involves deliberate personal resistance to a government decree that violates God's standards.
3:14-15 It's surprising that the king gave the accused an opportunity to answer the charges against them. That he did may indicate the esteem he had for them. Nevertheless, he would only accept one response: complete capitulation.
3:16-18 These three preferred death over unfaithfulness to God and had no doubt prepared themselves for the possibility of this day far in advance.

Walk by Faith; Don't Just Talk by Faith

A LITTLE BIRD WAS FLYING SOUTH for the winter, but the air became so cold that it began to freeze and could not get to a warmer climate. After some time, the bird collapsed in a large field where a herd of cows grazed. Eventually, a cow came by and dropped manure on the freezing bird. At first, the bird was very upset until it felt how warm the manure was. Before too long, it began to thaw out and became so excited that it started singing with joy. Just then, a cat happened to be passing by and heard the bird's joyful song. He followed it to the pile of manure and started digging until he discovered the little bird and promptly ate it.

There are a number of lessons we can learn from this story. First, not everybody who drops manure on you is your enemy. Second, not everybody who digs you out is your friend. And third, when you're in manure, it's best to keep your mouth shut.

If we live long enough, each of us will find ourselves in a situation that seems much worse than we can bear. In fact, we can feel as if we've been buried under a pile of manure. However, if our expectations are set on Jesus Christ and his providential care, we will not stumble at the thought of going through times of trial. In fact, we'll have his hope to comfort us even in what appear to be hopeless situations.

I love the account in Daniel 3: King Nebuchadnezzar "commanded some of the best soldiers in his army to tie up Shadrach, Meshach, and Abednego and throw them into the furnace of blazing fire" (DN 3:20). These Jewish men were in a bad situation. It doesn't get much worse than being thrown into a fiery furnace—unless, of course, you are bound first and then thrown into a fiery furnace. Nevertheless, these three young men put their faith in God and gained a tremendous victory.

After their divine rescue, we read, "Then King Nebuchadnezzar jumped up in alarm. He said to his advisers, 'Didn't we throw three men, bound, into the fire?' 'Yes, of course, Your Majesty,' they replied to the king. He exclaimed, 'Look! I see four men, not tied, walking around in the fire unharmed; and the fourth looks like a son of the gods" (DN 3:24-25).

God honored the faith of these three young men by delivering them from the furnace, even while they were still in it. He can do the same for you when you live as a faith-walker, rather than as a mere faith-talker.

a 3:19 Est 7:7
b 3:22 Dn 2:15
c 3:24 Dn 4:19
d 3:25 Ps 91:3-9; Is 43:2
e Mt 14:33; Mk 1:1; Lk 1:35;
Jn 3:18; Ac 9:20
f 3:26 Dn 4:2
g 3:27 Heb 11:34
h Dt 29:5
i 3:28 Heb 1:14
j Ps 34:7; Is 37:36; Ac
5:19; 12:7
k Ps 22:4-5; Is 12:2; 26:3-4;
Jr 17:7
l 3:29 Dn 4:6

m 3:29 Dn 3:4,7; 4:1; 5:19;
6:25; 7:14; Rv 5:9; 7:9;
10:11; 11:9; 13:7; 14:6; 17:15
n Ezr 6:11; Dn 2:5
o 3:30 Dn 2:48-49
p 4:1 Dn 6:25
q 2Pt 1:2
r 4:2 Dn 6:27; Jn 4:48; Ac
2:22; 2Co 12:12; Heb 2:4
s 4:3 Ps 105:27; Is 25:1
t Ps 145:13; Dn 2:44; 4:34;
7:14,27; 2Pt 1:11
u Is 9:7; Dn 6:26; 1Pt 5:11;
Rv 1:6; 5:13
v 4:4 Ps 30:6; Is 47:7-8
w 4:5 Dn 2:28; 7:15
x 4:6 Dn 3:10,29
y Gn 41:8; Dn 2:12
z 4:7 Dn 2:2
aa 4:8 Dn 1:7
ab Gn 41:38; Dn 2:11
ac 4:9 Dn 5:11
ad Ezk 28:3

19 Then Nebuchadnezzar was filled with rage,[a] and the expression on his face changed toward Shadrach, Meshach, and Abednego. He gave orders to heat the furnace seven times more than was customary, **20** and he commanded some of the best soldiers in his army to tie up Shadrach, Meshach, and Abednego and throw them into the furnace of blazing fire. **21** So these men, in their trousers, robes, head coverings,[A] and other clothes, were tied up and thrown into the furnace of blazing fire. **22** Since the king's command was so urgent[B,b] and the furnace extremely hot, the raging flames[c] killed those men who carried Shadrach, Meshach, and Abednego up. **23** And these three men, Shadrach, Meshach, and Abednego fell, bound, into the furnace of blazing fire.

DELIVERED FROM THE FIRE

24 Then King Nebuchadnezzar jumped up in alarm.[c] He said to his advisers, "Didn't we throw three men, bound, into the fire?"

"Yes, of course, Your Majesty," they replied to the king.

25 He exclaimed, "Look! I see four men, not tied, walking around in the fire unharmed;[d] and the fourth looks like a son of the gods."[D,e]

26 Nebuchadnezzar then approached the door of the furnace of blazing fire and called: "Shadrach, Meshach, and Abednego, you servants of the Most High God — come out!" So Shadrach, Meshach, and Abednego came out of the fire.[f] **27** When the satraps, prefects, governors, and the king's advisers gathered around, they saw that the fire had no effect[g] on[E] the bodies of these men: not a hair of their heads was singed, their robes were unaffected, and there was no smell of fire on them.[h] **28** Nebuchadnezzar exclaimed, "Praise to the God of Shadrach, Meshach, and Abednego! He sent his angel[F,i] and rescued his servants who trusted in him.[j] They violated the king's command and risked their lives rather than serve or worship any god except their own God.[k] **29** Therefore I issue a decree[l] that anyone of any people,

nation, or language[m] who says anything offensive against the God of Shadrach, Meshach, and Abednego will be torn limb from limb and his house made a garbage dump.[n] For there is no other god who is able to deliver like this." **30** Then the king rewarded Shadrach, Meshach, and Abednego in the province of Babylon.[o]

NEBUCHADNEZZAR'S PROCLAMATION

4 King Nebuchadnezzar,

To those of every people, nation, and language, who live on the whole earth:[p]

May your prosperity increase.[q] **2** I am pleased to tell you about the miracles and wonders[r] the Most High God has done for me.

3 How great are his miracles,
    and how mighty his wonders![s]
  His kingdom is an eternal kingdom,[t]
    and his dominion is from generation
    to generation.[u]

THE DREAM

4 I, Nebuchadnezzar, was at ease in my house and flourishing in my palace.[v] **5** I had a dream, and it frightened me; while in my bed, the images and visions in my mind alarmed me.[w] **6** So I issued a decree[x] to bring all the wise men of Babylon to me in order that they might make the dream's interpretation known to me.[y] **7** When the magicians, mediums, Chaldeans, and diviners came in, I told them the dream, but they could not make its interpretation known to me.[z]

8 Finally Daniel, named Belteshazzar[aa] after the name of my god — and a spirit of the holy gods is in him[ab] — came before me. I told him the dream: **9** "Belteshazzar, head of the magicians, because I know that you have the spirit of the holy gods[ac] and that no mystery puzzles you,[ad] explain to me the visions of my dream that I saw, and its interpretation. **10** In the visions of my mind as I was lying in bed, I saw this:

A 3:21 The identity of these articles of clothing is uncertain.   B 3:22 Or *harsh*   C 3:22 Lit *the flame of the fire*   D 3:25 Or *of a divine being*   E 3:27 Lit *fire had not overcome*   F 3:28 Or *messenger*

3:22 The radiant heat was so great that the men carrying the protestors were **killed**. No doubt wearing flammable clothing (see 3:21), the faithful Hebrews had no hope—unless hope itself intervened.
3:25 That the **fourth** man in the fire looked like **a son of the gods** suggests that he was either the preincarnate Christ or an angel.

4:1-3 The Most High God (4:2; see 3:26), or the variation "the Most High," appears thirteen times in Daniel. It refers to God's ability to overrule man's kingdoms and his superiority over all so-called gods. As Nebuchadnezzar is about to explain, he learned this the hard way.
4:5-8 It's strange that Nebuchadnezzar asked his wise men for help instead of seeking out

Daniel first—given Daniel's past experience with dreams (see 2:31-45). But apparently, Nebuchadnezzar was a slow learner. He had **named** Daniel **Belteshazzar** after the name of his Babylonian god Bel. The man clung to his pagan idols (4:8).

There was a tree in the middle
of the earth,
and it was very tall.
11 The tree grew large and strong;
its top reached to the sky,[a]
and it was visible to the ends
of the[A] earth.
12 Its leaves were beautiful, its fruit
was abundant,
and on it was food for all.[b]
Wild animals found shelter under it,
the birds of the sky[c] lived in its branches,
and every creature was fed from it.[d]

13 "As I was lying in my bed, I also saw in
the visions of my mind a watcher, a holy
one,[B,e] coming down from heaven.[f] 14 He
called out loudly:
Cut down the tree and chop off
its branches;
strip off its leaves and scatter its fruit.
Let the animals flee from under it,
and the birds from its branches.[g]
15 But leave the stump with its roots
in the ground[h]
and with a band of iron and bronze
around it
in the tender grass of the field.
Let him be drenched with dew
from the sky
and share the plants of the earth[i]
with the animals.
16 Let his mind be changed from that
of a human,
and let him be given the mind
of an animal
for seven periods of time.[c,D,j]
17 This word is by decree of the watchers,
and the decision is by command
from the holy ones.
This is so that the living will know
that the Most High is ruler
over human kingdoms.
He gives them to anyone he wants
and sets the lowliest of people
over them.[k]
18 This is the dream that I, King Nebuchadnezzar, had. Now, Belteshazzar, tell me the
interpretation, because none of the wise
men of my kingdom can make the interpretation known to me.[l] But you can, because you have a spirit of the holy gods."

THE DREAM INTERPRETED

19 Then Daniel, whose name is Belteshazzar, was stunned for a moment, and his
thoughts alarmed him. The king said, "Belteshazzar, don't let the dream or its interpretation alarm you."
Belteshazzar answered, "My lord, may
the dream apply to those who hate you, and
its interpretation to your enemies![m] 20 The
tree you saw, which grew large and strong,
whose top reached to the sky and was visible to the whole earth, 21 and whose leaves
were beautiful and its fruit abundant
— and on it was food for all, under it the
wild animals lived, and in its branches the
birds of the sky lived — 22 that tree is you,
Your Majesty. For you have become great
and strong: your greatness has grown and
even reaches the sky, and your dominion
extends to the ends of the earth.[n]
23 "The king saw a watcher, a holy one,
coming down from heaven and saying,
'Cut down the tree and destroy it, but leave
the stump with its roots in the ground and
with a band of iron and bronze around it
in the tender grass of the field. Let him be
drenched with dew from the sky and share
food with the wild animals for seven periods of time.' 24 This is the interpretation,
Your Majesty, and this is the decree of the
Most High that has been issued against my
lord the king:[o] 25 You will be driven away
from people to live with the wild animals.
You will feed on grass like cattle[p] and be
drenched with dew from the sky for sev-
en periods of time, until you acknowledge
that the Most High is ruler over human
kingdoms, and he gives them to anyone he
wants.[q] 26 As for the command to leave the
tree's stump with its roots, your kingdom
will be restored[E] to you as soon as you acknowledge that Heaven[F] rules.[r] 27 Therefore,
may my advice seem good to you my king.
Separate yourself from your sins by doing
what is right,[s] and from your injustices by
showing mercy to the needy.[t] Perhaps there
will be an extension of your prosperity."[u]

THE SENTENCE EXECUTED

28 All this happened to King Nebuchadnezzar.[v] 29 At the end of twelve months, as
he was walking on the roof of the royal

[a] 4:11 Gn 11:4
[b] 4:12 Gn 2:9; Rv 22:2
[c] Ezk 17:23; Mt 13:32; Lk 13:9
[d] Ezk 31:3–6
[e] 4:13 Dt 33:2; Ps 89:7; Zch 14:5; Jd 14
[f] Rv 10:1; 18:1; 20:1
[g] 4:14 Ezk 31:10-14
[h] 4:15 Jb 14:7-9
[i] Gn 3:18
[j] 4:16 Dn 7:25
[k] 4:17 1Sm 2:8; Ps 9:16; Jr 27:5-7; Dn 5:21
[l] 4:18 Gn 41:8; Dn 5:8

[m] 4:19 2Sm 18:32
[n] 4:22 Jr 27:6-8; Ezk 31:3
[o] 4:24 Jb 40:11-12; Ps 107:40
[p] 4:25 Ps 106:20; Jr 27:5
[q] Ps 83:18; Dn 5:21
[r] 4:26 Dn 2:37
[s] 4:27 Pr 28:13; Ac 8:22
[t] Ps 41:1-3; Is 58:6-7; Ezk 18:7
[u] Jr 18:8; Jn 3:10
[v] 4:28 Nm 23:19; Zch 1:6

4:15 The pronoun in **let him be drenched with dew** suggests the "tree" was actually a man.
4:16 He was to be driven mad and **given the mind of an animal for** seven years
4:27 The last word in Daniel's visit was his heartfelt plea for Nebuchadnezzar, who was

both the "tree" and the "stump" in the dream (4:14-15), to repent and throw himself on the mercy of God. But interestingly, there was no response from the king at all.
4:29-30 God's extension of grace, that lasted **twelve months**, did not move the king to

repent (4:29). If anything, the delay probably made him think he had dodged the bullet. One day he looked out from his palace and exclaimed, **Is this not Babylon the Great that I have built . . . by my vast power and for my majestic glory?** (4:30). In other words, he

palace in Babylon, 30 the king exclaimed,
"Is this not Babylon the Great that I have
built to be a royal residence by my vast
power and for my majestic glory?"[a]
31 While the words were still in the king's
mouth, a voice came from heaven: "King
Nebuchadnezzar, to you it is declared that
the kingdom has departed from you.[b]
32 You will be driven away from people to
live with the wild animals, and you will
feed on grass like cattle for seven periods
of time, until you acknowledge that the
Most High is ruler over human kingdoms,
and he gives them to anyone he wants."
33 At that moment the message against
Nebuchadnezzar was fulfilled. He was
driven away from people. He ate grass
like cattle, and his body was drenched with
dew from the sky, until his hair grew like
eagles' feathers and his nails like birds'
claws.[c]

NEBUCHADNEZZAR'S PRAISE

34 But at the end of those days, I, Nebuchadnezzar, looked up to heaven, and my sanity
returned to me. Then I praised the Most
High and honored and glorified him who
lives forever:[d]

For his dominion is
an everlasting dominion,
and his kingdom is from generation
to generation.[e]
35 All the inhabitants of the earth
are counted as nothing,[f]
and he does what he wants[g]
with the army of heaven
and the inhabitants of the earth.
There is no one who can block
his hand
or say to him,
"What have you done?"[h]

36 At that time my sanity returned to me,
and my majesty and splendor returned
to me for the glory of my kingdom. My
advisers and my nobles sought me out, I
was reestablished over my kingdom, and
even more greatness came to me.[i] 37 Now
I, Nebuchadnezzar, praise, exalt, and glorify the King of the heavens, because all his
works are true and his ways are just.[j] He is
able to humble[k] those who walk in pride.[l]

BELSHAZZAR'S FEAST

5 King Belshazzar[m] held a great feast for
a thousand of his nobles and drank
wine in their presence. 2 Under the influence of[A] the wine, Belshazzar gave orders
to bring in the gold and silver vessels[n] that
his predecessor[B] Nebuchadnezzar had tak-
en from the temple in Jerusalem, so that
the king and his nobles, wives, and concubines could drink from them. 3 So they
brought in the gold[C] vessels that had been
taken from the temple, the house of God
in Jerusalem,[o] and the king and his nobles,
wives, and concubines drank from them.
4 They drank the wine and praised their
gods made of gold and silver, bronze, iron,
wood, and stone.[p]

THE HANDWRITING ON THE WALL

5 At that moment the fingers of a man's
hand appeared and began writing on the
plaster of the king's palace wall next to the
lampstand. As the king watched the hand[D]
that was writing, 6 his face turned pale,[E]
and his thoughts so terrified him that he
soiled himself[F] and his knees knocked together. 7 The king shouted to bring in the
mediums, Chaldeans, and diviners. He said
to these wise men of Babylon, "Whoever
reads this inscription and gives me its interpretation will be clothed in purple, have
a gold chain around his neck,[q] and have
the third highest position in the kingdom."
8 So all the king's wise men came in, but
none could read the inscription or make
its interpretation known to him. 9 Then

[a] 4:30 Is 24:23; Ezk 26:20; 28:22; 38:23; 39:13,21; Hab 2:4; 1Co 4:7
[b] 4:31 Lk 12:20
[c] 4:32-33 Dn 5:21
[d] 4:34 Dn 6:26; 12:7; Rv 4:10
[e] Ps 145:13; Jr 10:10; Mc 4:7
[f] 4:35 Is 40:15-17
[g] Jb 9:12; 42:2; Ps 115:3; 135:6; Rm 9:20; Eph 1:11
[h] Is 40:17; 43:13; 45:9; Rm 9:20
[i] 4:36 2Ch 33:12-13; Pr 22:4
[j] 4:37 Dt 32:4; Ps 33:4; Rv 15:3
[k] Ex 18:11; Jb 40:11-12
[l] 2Sm 22:28; Ps 18:27; Pr 16:18; 29:23; Rm 12:16; Jms 4:6; 1Pt 5:5
[m] 5:1 Dn 7:1; 8:1
[n] 5:2 1Kg 7:51; 2Kg 24:13; 2Ch 36:7,10; Ezr 5:14; 6:5; Jr 52:19; Dn 1:2
[o] 5:3 1Ch 22:2; Ezr 1:4; 2:68; 3:8; 4:24; 5:2,16-17; 6:3,12; Neh 6:10; Ps 42:4; Mt 12:4; Heb 10:21
[p] 5:4 Is 46:6
[q] 5:7 Gn 41:42

[A] 5:2 Or *When he tasted* [B] 5:2 Or *father*, or *grandfather* [C] 5:3 Theod, Vg add *and silver* [D] 5:5 Lit *part of the hand* [E] 5:5-6 Lit *writing*, [6] *the king's brightness changed* [F] 5:6 Lit *that the knots of his loins were loosed*

congratulated himself for the splendor of all he surveyed.

4:33 Nebuchadnezzar was struck with a form of madness that caused him to behave and live like an animal—quite the humbling circumstance for the world leader of his day. This story is a reminder that the farther a government drifts from God and seeks to become its own god, the more it sets itself up for heavenly political action.

4:34-37 God decreed that Nebuchadnezzar would have to acknowledge that "Heaven rules" (see 4:26). In the end, that's exactly what he did (4:34-35). Nebuchadnezzar's last recorded words in the Bible are these: **[God] is able to humble those who walk in pride** (4:37). That's a truth we all need to embrace and live in accordance with. Remember, pride still comes before a fall (see Prov 16:18).

5:1-4 These events occurred in 539 BC, the year—the very night, in fact—that the great Babylonian kingdom founded by Nebuchadnezzar fell to a coalition of the Medes and the Persians. **Nebuchadnezzar** is called Belshazzar's **predecessor**, which some translations render as "father" since the ancient world often used this term to refer to a man's ancestors (5:2). In truth, Belshazzar was probably Nebuchadnezzar's grandson.

Assuming Belshazzar knew of Nebuchadnezzar's humiliation at the hands of God (see ch. 4), he certainly hadn't learned from it. Rather, he showed his contempt for God's holy vessels by treating them like bar mugs (5:2-4).

5:5-8 The Lord began to write about Belshazzar's doom on the **palace wall**, and the king literally lost control of his bowels out of fear (5:5-6). Like Nebuchadnezzar before him, though, the king promised reward to anyone who could interpret the **inscription** (5:7). But his so-called wise men were fools (5:8).

King Belshazzar became even more terrified, his face turned pale,[A] and his nobles were bewildered.[a]

10 Because of the outcry of the king and his nobles, the queen[B] came to the banquet hall. "May the king live forever," she said. "Don't let your thoughts terrify you or your face be pale.[C,D] **11** There is a man in your kingdom who has a spirit of the holy gods in him.[c] In the days of your predecessor he was found to have insight, intelligence, and wisdom like the wisdom of the gods. Your predecessor, King Nebuchadnezzar, appointed him chief of the magicians, mediums, Chaldeans, and diviners. Your own predecessor, the king, **12** did this because Daniel, the one the king named Belteshazzar, was found to have an extraordinary spirit, knowledge and intelligence, and the ability to interpret dreams, explain riddles, and solve problems.[d] Therefore, summon Daniel, and he will give the interpretation."

DANIEL BEFORE THE KING

13 Then Daniel was brought before the king. The king said to him, "Are you Daniel, one of the Judean exiles that my predecessor the king brought from Judah?[e] **14** I've heard that you have a spirit of the gods in you, and that insight, intelligence, and extraordinary wisdom are found in you. **15** Now the wise men and mediums were brought before me to read this inscription and make its interpretation known to me, but they could not give its interpretation. **16** However, I have heard about you that you can give interpretations and solve problems. Therefore, if you can read this inscription and give me its interpretation, you will be clothed in purple, have a gold chain around your neck, and have the third highest position in the kingdom."[f]

17 Then Daniel answered the king, "You may keep your gifts and give your rewards to someone else;[g] however, I will read the inscription for the king and make the interpretation known to him. **18** Your Majesty, the Most High God gave sovereignty,[h] greatness, glory, and majesty to your predecessor Nebuchadnezzar.[i] **19** Because of the greatness he gave him, all peoples, nations, and languages[j] were terrified and fearful of him. He killed anyone he wanted and kept alive anyone he wanted; he exalted anyone he wanted and humbled anyone he wanted. **20** But when his heart was exalted and his spirit became arrogant,[k] he was deposed from his royal throne and his glory was taken from him.[l] **21** He was driven away from people,[m] his mind was like an animal's, he lived with the wild donkeys,[n] he was fed grass like cattle, and his body was drenched with dew from the sky until he acknowledged that the Most High God is ruler over human kingdoms and sets anyone he wants over them.[o]

22 "But you his successor, Belshazzar, have not humbled your heart,[p] even though you knew all this. **23** Instead, you have exalted yourself against the Lord of the heavens. The vessels from his house were brought to you, and as you and your nobles, wives, and concubines drank wine from them,[q] you praised the gods made of silver and gold, bronze, iron, wood, and stone, which do not see or hear or understand.[r] But you have not glorified the God who holds your life-breath in his hand and who controls the whole course of your life.[D,s] **24** Therefore, he sent the hand, and this writing was inscribed.

THE INSCRIPTION'S INTERPRETATION

25 "This is the writing that was inscribed: MENE, MENE, TEKEL, and PARSIN. **26** This is the interpretation of the message:
'Mene'[E] means that God has numbered[F] the days of your kingdom and brought it to an end.[t]
27 'Tekel'[G] means that you have been weighed[H] on the balance and found deficient.
28 'Peres'[I,J] means that your kingdom has been divided and given to the Medes and Persians."[K]

29 Then Belshazzar gave an order, and they clothed Daniel in purple, placed a gold chain around his neck,[u] and issued

[a] 5:9 Dn 2:1; 5:6; 7:28
[b] 5:10 1Kg 21:5
[c] 5:11 Dn 4:8-9,18
[d] 5:12 Gn 41:11-15; Dn 6:3
[e] 5:13 Dn 1:3-4; 2:25
[f] 5:16 Gn 40:8; Dn 5:7,29
[g] 5:17 2Kg 5:15-16
[h] 5:18 Dn 4:2

[i] 5:18 Jr 27:5-7
[j] 5:19 Dn 2:12-13; 3:6
[k] 5:20 Ex 9:17; Is 15:25; Pr 16:18; Is 57:15; Jr 48:29; Dn 4:30-31
[l] Jr 13:18
[m] 5:21 Ex 9:17; Jb 15:25
[n] Jb 39:5-8
[o] Dn 4:30-31
[p] 5:22 Ex 10:3; 2Ch 33:23; 36:12
[q] 5:23 Jr 51:39,57
[r] 2:12; 37:23; Jr 50:29; Dn 5:3-4
[s] Ps 31:15
[t] 5:26 Is 13:17-19; Dn 2:44; 6:26; Hs 1:4
[u] 5:29 Dn 5:7,16

[A] 5:9 Lit *his brightness changed on him* [B] 5:10 Perhaps the queen mother [C] 5:10 Lit *your brightness change* [D] 5:23 Lit *and all your ways belong to him* [E] 5:26 Or *a mina* [F] 5:26 The Aramaic word for *numbered* sounds like *mene*. [G] 5:27 Or *a shekel* [H] 5:27 The Aramaic word for *weighed* sounds like *tekel*. [I] 5:28 Or *half a shekel* [J] 5:28 In Aramaic, the word *peres* is the sg form of "parsin" in v. 25. [K] 5:28 The Aramaic word for *divided* and *Persians* sounds like *peres*.

5:22-24 The underlying problem leading to the writing on the wall was that rather than repenting of the very things that had gotten his predecessor in trouble, Belshazzar had simply shaken his fist in God's face.

5:25-30 This story is so famous that the expression, "He can see the writing on the wall," has become a proverb meaning that a person can see what's coming in his future, that he understands his fate. And while it was too late for Belshazzar to change course, it's not too late for you. If you have a heart filled with pride, turn to the Lord in repentance, for "God resists the proud, but gives grace to the humble (Jas 4:6).

a 5:31 Dn 6:1; 9:1; 11:1
b 6:2 Dn 2:48-49; 5:16,29
c Ezr 4:22; Est 7:4
d 6:3 Dn 5:12,14; 9:23
e Gn 41:40; Est 10:3
f 6:4 Gn 43:18; Jdg 14:4; Jr 20:10; Dn 3:8; Lk 20:20
g Dn 6:22; Lk 20:26; 23:14; Php 2:15; 1Pt 2:12; 3:16
h 6:5 Ac 24:13-16,20-21
i 6:6 Neh 2:3; Dn 2:4; 5:10; 6:21
j 6:7 Dn 3:2,27
k Ps 10:9; Dn 3:6; 6:16
l 6:8 Est 3:12; 8:10; Is 10:1
m Est 1:9; 8:8; Dn 6:12,15
n 6:9 Ps 118:9; 146:3

o 6:10 1Kg 8:44-49; Ps 5:7; Jnh 2:4
p Ps 34:1; Dn 9:4-19; Php 4:6; 1Th 5:17-18
q 6:11 Ps 37:32-33; Dn 6:6
r 6:12 Dn 3:8-12; Ac 16:19-21
s Est 1:19; Dn 6:8,15
t 6:13 Est 3:8; Dn 3:12; Ac 5:29
u 6:14 Mk 6:26
v 6:15 Est 8:8; Ps 94:20,21; Dn 6:8,12
w 6:16 2Sm 3:39; Jr 38:5; Dn 6:7
x Jb 5:19; Ps 37:39-40; Is 41:10; 2Co 1:10
y 6:17 Lm 3:53; Mt 27:66
z 6:18 2Sm 12:16,17
aa Est 6:1; Ps 77:4; Dn 2:1

a proclamation concerning him that he should be the third ruler in the kingdom.

30 That very night Belshazzar the king of the Chaldeans was killed, **31** and Darius the Mede*a* received the kingdom at the age of sixty-two.

THE PLOT AGAINST DANIEL

6 Darius decided*A* to appoint 120 satraps over the kingdom, stationed throughout the realm, **2** and over them three administrators, including Daniel.*b* These satraps would be accountable to them so that the king would not be defrauded.*c* **3** Daniel*B* distinguished himself above the administrators and satraps because he had an extraordinary spirit,*d* so the king planned to set him over the whole realm.*e* **4** The administrators and satraps, therefore, kept trying to find a charge against Daniel*f* regarding the kingdom. But they could find no charge or corruption,*g* for he was trustworthy, and no negligence or corruption was found in him. **5** Then these men said, "We will never find any charge against this Daniel unless we find something against him concerning the law of his God."*h*

6 So the administrators and satraps went together to the king and said to him, "May King Darius live forever.*i* **7** All the administrators of the kingdom,*j* the prefects, satraps, advisers, and governors have agreed that the king should establish an ordinance and enforce an edict that for thirty days, anyone who petitions any god or man except you, the king, will be thrown into the lions' den.*k* **8** Therefore, Your Majesty, establish the edict*l* and sign the document so that, as a law of the Medes and Persians, it is irrevocable and cannot be changed."*m* **9** So King Darius signed the written edict.*n*

DANIEL IN THE LIONS' DEN

10 When Daniel learned that the document had been signed, he went into his house. The windows in its upstairs room opened toward Jerusalem,*o* and three times a day he got down on his knees, prayed, and gave thanks to his God,*p* just as he had done before. **11** Then these men went as a group and found*q* Daniel petitioning and imploring his God. **12** So they approached the king*r* and asked about his edict: "Didn't you sign an edict that for thirty days any person who petitions any god or man except you, the king, will be thrown into the lions' den?"

The king answered, "As a law of the Medes and Persians, the order stands*c* and is irrevocable."*s*

13 Then they replied to the king, "Daniel, one of the Judean exiles, has ignored you,*t* the king, and the edict you signed, for he prays three times a day." **14** As soon as the king heard this, he was very displeased; he set his mind on rescuing Daniel*u* and made every effort until sundown to deliver him.

15 Then these men went together to the king and said to him, "You know, Your Majesty, that it is a law of the Medes and Persians that no edict or ordinance the king establishes can be changed."*v*

16 So the king gave the order, and they brought Daniel and threw him into the lions' den.*w* The king said to Daniel, "May your God, whom you continually serve,*x* rescue you!" **17** A stone was brought and placed over the mouth of the den.*y* The king sealed it with his own signet ring and with the signet rings of his nobles, so that nothing in regard to Daniel could be changed. **18** Then the king went to his palace and spent the night fasting.*z* No diversions*b* were brought to him, and he could not sleep.*aa*

DANIEL RELEASED

19 At the first light of dawn the king got up and hurried to the lions' den. **20** When he reached the den, he cried out in anguish to Daniel. "Daniel, servant of the living God,"

A 6:1 Lit It was pleasing before Darius   *B* 6:3 Lit Now this Daniel   *c* 6:12 Lit the word is certain   *D* 6:18 Aramaic obscure

---

6:1-3 Daniel, whose government work extended past the Babylonian period and into the days of **Darius** (6:1), was a godly and capable leader because his first allegiance was to his heavenly King. He wasn't primarily serving human rulers, but serving God (see Col 3:23).
6:4-5 The other government officials hated Daniel—not because he was evil—but because he was good. This is often the response of the wicked toward the righteous. Why did Cain murder Abel? "Because [Cain's] deeds were evil, and his brother's were righteous" (1 John 3:12).

The officials tried **to find a charge against Daniel** (Dan 6:4), but he had been serving in the government for almost forty years by this point, and his ethical record was spotless. So what was plan B? They tried to **find something against him concerning the law of his God** (6:5). Consider yourself blessed if the only thing your enemies can say about you is that you're too faithful to God.
6:10 Notice that Daniel didn't make a big deal out of his opposition to the unfair edict or flaunt his prayers. He simply went home and prayed **just as he had done**

before, with his windows **opened**. No earthly commands could prevent him from fulfilling his heavenly duties. His attitude was the same as that of the apostles many years later: "We must obey God rather than people" (Acts 5:29).
6:12-14 When the men informed on Daniel, the king immediately realized he'd been set up (6:13-14). He'd been duped into executing his best administrator!

the king said,[A] "has your God, whom you continually serve, been able to rescue you[a] from the lions?"

[21] Then Daniel spoke with the king: "May the king live forever. [22] My God sent his angel[b] and shut the lions' mouths; and they haven't harmed me, for I was found innocent before him. And also before you, Your Majesty, I have not done harm."

[23] The king was overjoyed and gave orders to take Daniel out of the den. When Daniel was brought up from the den, he was found to be unharmed, for he trusted in his God.[c] [24] The king then gave the command, and those men who had maliciously accused Daniel[B,d] were brought and thrown into the lions' den — they, their children, and their wives.[e] They had not reached the bottom of the den before the lions overpowered them and crushed all their bones.

⟾ HOPE WORDS ⟾

The kingdom agenda is the visible manifestation of God's comprehensive rule over every area of life.

DARIUS HONORS GOD

[25] Then King Darius wrote to those of every people, nation, and language who live on the whole earth: "May your prosperity abound.[f] [26] I issue a decree[g] that in all my royal dominion, people must tremble in fear before the God of Daniel:[h]

For he is the living God,
and he endures forever;
his kingdom will never be destroyed,[i]
and his dominion has no end.
[27]   He rescues and delivers;
he performs signs and wonders

in the heavens and on the earth,[j]
for he has rescued Daniel
from the power of the lions."

[28] So Daniel prospered[k] during the reign of Darius and[c] the reign of Cyrus the Persian.[l]

APPLICATION QUESTIONS

READ DANIEL 7:1-14

– Which images are emphasized most in Daniel's vision?

– How do verses 13-14 enhance your understanding of God's kingdom?

– How have you intentionally served Jesus in recent days?

DANIEL'S VISION OF THE FOUR BEASTS

7 In the first year of King Belshazzar of Babylon, Daniel had a dream with visions in his mind[m] as he was lying in his bed. He wrote down the dream,[n] and here is the summary[D] of his account. [2] Daniel said, "In my vision at night I was watching, and suddenly the four winds of heaven[o] stirred up the great sea. [3] Four huge beasts[p] came up from the sea,[q] each different from the other.

[4] "The first was like a lion[r] but had eagle's wings. I continued watching until its wings were torn off. It was lifted up from the ground, set on its feet like a man, and given a human mind.

[5] "Suddenly, another beast appeared, a second one, that looked like a bear.[s] It was raised up on one side, with three ribs in its mouth between its teeth. It was told, 'Get up! Gorge yourself on flesh.'

[6] "After this, while I was watching, suddenly another beast appeared. It was like a leopard[t] with four wings of a bird on its back. It had four heads,[u] and it was given dominion.

[a] 6:20 Gn 18:14; Nm 11:23; Jr 32:17; Dn 3:17
[b] 6:22 Nm 20:16; Is 63:9; Dn 3:28; Ac 12:11; Heb 1:14
[c] 6:23 1Ch 5:20; 2Ch 20:20; Ps 118:8-9; Is 26:3; Dn 3:17-18
[d] 6:24 Dn 3:8; 6:12-13
[e] Dt 24:16; 2Kg 14:6; Est 9:10
[f] 6:25 Ezr 4:17; 1Pt 1:2
[g] 6:26 Ezr 6:8-12; 7:13,21; Dn 3:29; 4:6
[h] Dn 5:19
[i] Ps 93:1-2; Dn 2:44; 7:14; Mal 3:6

[j] 6:27 Dn 4:2-3
[k] 6:28 Dn 1:21
[l] 2Ch 36:22-23; Dn 10:1
[m] 7:1 Jb 33:14-16; Dn 1:17; 2:1; 4:5-9; Jl 2:28
[n] Jr 36:4,32
[o] 7:2 Ezk 37:9; Zch 2:6; Rv 7:1
[p] 7:3 Dn 7:17
[q] Rv 13:1; 17:8
[r] 7:4 Jr 4:7; 25:9; Rv 13:2
[s] 7:5 Rv 13:2
[t] 7:6 Hab 1:8; Rv 13:2
[u] Dn 8:22

[A] 6:20 Lit *said to Daniel*   [B] 6:24 Lit *had eaten his pieces*   [C] 6:28 Or *Darius, even*   [D] 7:1 Lit *beginning*

6:24 This gruesome judgment was typical of the vengeance taken by kings in the ancient world.

6:26-27 Darius's **decree** honoring the true God is a theological gem that sounds like it could have been written by one of the psalmists. As Nebuchadnezzar had (see 3:29; 4:3, 34-35), this Gentile ruler gave glory to **the living God** (6:26) who **rescues and delivers**. (6:27). The Jewish people may have been in exile, but God had not abandoned them; moreover, he was determined to receive praise from their captors.

7:1 Events in Daniel are not always presented in chronological order. **Belshazzar** was dethroned at the end of chapter 5.

7:2-3 An interesting shift in perspective is on display here. In Nebuchadnezzar's dream, these same four kingdoms were represented by a glorious, awe-inspiring statue (see 2:31). But in Daniel's, these Gentile kingdoms were **huge beasts** coming **up from the sea** (7:3), bent on dominion.

7:4 The first beast represents Babylon. That its **wings were torn off** is perhaps a reference to God reducing Nebuchadnezzar to madness until he learned to humbly give God glory (see 4:28-37).

7:5 The **second** beast represents the Medo-Persian Empire. The **bear** was likely **raised up on one side** because the Persians defeated the Medes and absorbed them into

the empire. Combined, their forces were able to defeat Babylon.

The **three ribs** in the bear's **mouth** symbolize the three great enemies that Persia defeated in its conquest: Egypt, Assyria, and Babylon. All of them were gobbled up by the Medo-Persian Empire, which ruled for some two hundred years.

7:6 The Greek Empire established by Alexander the Great is represented by the third beast—a speedy **leopard**. The Greeks under Alexander defeated the Medo-Persians in a matter of a few months in 334 BC. The **four heads** Daniel saw refer to the four kingdoms into which Alexander's domain was split after his death.

a 7:7 Dn 7:19,23
b Dn 7:20,24; Rv 12:3; 13:1
c 7:8 Dn 7:11,20–26; 8:9
d Rv 13:5–6
e 7:9 Mt 19:28; Rv 20:4
f Mk 9:3
g Is 1:18; Rv 1:14
h Ezk 1:13,26
i Ezk 10:2,6
j 7:10 Dt 33:2; 1Kg 22:19;
        Rv 5:11
k Ps 96:11–13; Rv 9:16
l Dn 7:26
m Dn 12:1; Rv 20:11–15
n 7:11 Dn 7:26; Rv 19:20;
        20:10
o 7:12 Ps 75:6–7; Dn 2:21

p 7:13 Mt 16:27–28; 24:30;
        Lk 21:27; Ac 7:56; Rv
        1:7,13; 14:14
q Mt 26:64; Mk 13:26;
        14:62
r 7:14 Jn 3:35; 1Co 15:27;
        Eph 1:20–22; Php 2:9; Rv
        1:6; 11:15
s Ps 72:11; 102:22; Rv 10:11
t Dn 3:14,17–18,28; 6:17,21;
        7:27
u Heb 12:28
v 7:15 Dn 4:19; 7:1,28
w 7:16 Zch 1:9,19; Rv 5:5;
        7:13–14
x Dn 7:3

y 7:18 Ps 149:5–9; Is 60:12–
        14; Rv 2:26–27; 11:15; 22:5
z 7:19 Dn 7:7–8
aa 7:20 Rv 12:3
ab Dn 7:8; 2Th 2:9–10
ac 7:21 Rv 11:7; 13:7
ad 7:22 Dn 7:10; 1Co 6:2–3

7 "After this, while I was watching in the night visions, suddenly a fourth beast[a] appeared, frightening and dreadful, and incredibly strong, with large iron teeth. It devoured and crushed, and it trampled with its feet whatever was left. It was different from all the beasts before it, and it had ten horns.[b] 8 "While I was considering the horns, suddenly another horn,[c] a little one, came up among them, and three of the first horns were uprooted before it. And suddenly in this horn there were eyes like the eyes of a human and a mouth that was speaking arrogantly.[d]

THE ANCIENT OF DAYS AND THE SON OF MAN

9 "As I kept watching,
    thrones were set in place,[e]
    and the Ancient of Days
        took his seat.
His clothing was white
    like snow,[f]
and the hair of his head
    like whitest wool.[g]
His throne was flaming fire;[h]
    its wheels were blazing fire.[i]
10   A river of fire was flowing,
    coming out from his presence.
Thousands upon thousands[j]
        served him;
    ten thousand times ten thousand[k]
        stood before him.
The court was convened,[l]
    and the books were opened.[m]

11 "I watched, then, because of the sound of the arrogant words the horn was speaking. As I continued watching, the beast was killed and its body destroyed and given over to the burning fire.[n] 12 As for the rest of the beasts, their dominion was removed, but an extension of life was granted to them for a certain period of time.[o] 13 I continued watching in the night visions,

and suddenly one like a son of man[p]
    was coming with the clouds
        of heaven.[q]
He approached the Ancient of Days
    and was escorted before him.
14   He was given dominion,[r]
    and glory, and a kingdom;
    so that those of every people,
        nation, and language[s]
    should serve[t] him.
His dominion is
    an everlasting[u] dominion
    that will not pass away,
and his kingdom is one
    that will not be destroyed.

INTERPRETATION OF THE VISION

15 "As for me, Daniel, my spirit was deeply distressed within me,[A] and the visions in my mind terrified me.[v] 16 I approached one of those who were standing by and asked him[w] to clarify all this. So he let me know the interpretation of these things:[x] 17 'These huge beasts, four in number, are four kings who will rise from the earth. 18 But the holy ones of the Most High will receive the kingdom and possess it forever, yes, forever and ever.'[y]

19 "Then I wanted to be clear about the fourth beast,[z] the one different from all the others, extremely terrifying, with iron teeth and bronze claws, devouring, crushing, and trampling with its feet whatever was left. 20 I also wanted to know about the ten horns[aa] on its head and about the other horn that came up, before which three fell — the horn that had eyes, and a mouth that spoke arrogantly,[ab] and that looked bigger than the others. 21 As I was watching, this horn waged war[ac] against the holy ones and was prevailing over them 22 until the Ancient of Days arrived and a judgment[ad] was given in favor of the holy ones of the Most High, for the time had come, and the holy ones took possession of the kingdom.

7:7-8 The **fourth beast** corresponds to the Roman Empire. God gave Daniel a much more complete picture of it than received in Nebuchadnezzar's day because the Roman Empire will appear in history again, except in a different form—during the great tribulation. This beast was **frightening**, and out of it came **ten horns** (7:7)—that is, ten kings or kingdoms. Daniel noticed that **a little** horn appeared **among** them. The keys to identifying this figure are its **eyes of a human and a mouth ... speaking arrogantly** (7:8). This figure is the antichrist, called "a beast" in Revelation 13:1. He is the final world ruler whose reign

of terror during the tribulation will bring to completion the times of the Gentiles.
7:9-14 There is hope for God's people in every age because **the Ancient of Days** (7:9) and the **son of man** (7:13), God the Father and God the Son, have everything under control. Jesus applied this passage to himself during his ministry (7:13; see Matt 26:64; Mark 14:62; Luke 21:27), and the tribulation chaos will end when he returns in glory with his saints and consigns all of his enemies to **the burning fire** (Dan 7:11).
That the Ancient of Days presented the Son with **an everlasting dominion** (7:14) is

a prophetic picture of God the Father handing over the kingdoms of this world for the Lord Jesus Christ to rule in fulfillment of the dominion mandate given to man (see Ps 8:3-8).
7:19-20 The Roman Empire, **the fourth beast**, did not fade away into history as did the other three kingdoms (7:19). The angel revealed to Daniel that in fact a future form of the Roman Empire would emerge, characterized by **ten horns** (7:20). These "horns" were representative of "ten kings" who would "rise from this kingdom" (7:24). The **other horn** is the antichrist (7:20).

23 "This is what he said: 'The fourth beast will be a fourth kingdom on the earth, different from all the other kingdoms. It will devour the whole earth, trample it down, and crush it. **24** The ten horns[a] are ten kings who will rise from this kingdom. Another king, different from the previous ones, will rise after them and subdue three kings. **25** He will speak words against the Most High[b] and oppress[A] the holy ones[c] of the Most High. He will intend to change religious festivals[B] and laws,[d] and the holy ones will be handed over to him for a time, times, and half a time.[C,e] **26** But the court will convene,[f] and his dominion will be taken away, to be completely destroyed forever.[g] **27** The kingdom, dominion, and greatness of the kingdoms under all of heaven will be given to the people, the holy ones of the Most High. His kingdom will be an everlasting kingdom,[h] and all rulers will serve and obey him.'

28 "This is the end of the account. As for me, Daniel, my thoughts terrified me greatly,[i] and my face turned pale,[D] but I kept the matter to myself."[j]

THE VISION OF A RAM AND A GOAT

8 In the third year of King Belshazzar's[k] reign, a vision appeared to me, Daniel, after the one that had appeared to me earlier.[l] **2** I saw the vision, and as I watched, I was in the fortress city of Susa,[m] in the province of Elam.[n] I saw in the vision that I was beside the Ulai Canal. **3** I looked up,[E] and there was a ram[o] standing beside the canal. He had two horns. The two horns were long, but one was longer than the other, and the longer one came up last. **4** I saw the ram charging to the west, the north, and the south.[p] No animal could stand against him, and there was no rescue from his power. He did whatever he wanted[q] and became great.

5 As I was observing, a male goat appeared, coming from the west across the surface of the entire earth without touching the ground. The goat had a conspicuous horn[f] between his eyes.[r] **6** He came toward the two-horned ram I had seen standing beside the canal and rushed at him with savage fury. **7** I saw him approaching the ram, and infuriated with him, he struck the ram, breaking his two horns, and the ram was not strong enough to stand against him. The goat threw him to the ground and trampled him, and there was no one to rescue the ram from his power. **8** Then the male goat acted even more arrogantly,[s] but when he became powerful, the large horn was broken.[t] Four conspicuous horns came up in its place, pointing toward the four winds of heaven.[u]

THE LITTLE HORN

9 From one of them a little horn[v] emerged and grew extensively toward the south and the east and toward the beautiful land.[G,w] **10** It grew as high as the heavenly army, made some of the army and some of the stars[H] fall to the earth,[x] and trampled them.[y] **11** It acted arrogantly[z] even against the Prince of the heavenly army;[aa] it revoked his regular sacrifice[ab] and overthrew the place of his sanctuary. **12** In the rebellion, the army was given up, together with the regular sacrifice. The horn threw truth to the ground and was successful[ac] in what it did.

[a] 7:24 Dn 7:7; Rv 17:12
[b] 7:25 Dn 11:36; Rv 13:1-6
[c] Rv 13:7; 18:24
[d] Dn 2:21
[e] Dn 12:7; Rv 11:2; 12:14
[f] 7:26 Dn 7:10
[g] Rv 17:14; 19:20
[h] 7:27 Ps 145:13; Is 9:7; Lk 1:33; Rv 11:15; 22:5
[i] 7:28 Dn 4:19
[j] Lk 2:19,51
[k] 8:1 Dn 5:1
[l] Dn 7:1
[m] 8:2 Ezr 4:9; Neh 1:1; Est 1:2; 2:8
[n] Gn 10:22; 14:1; Is 11:11; Jr 25:25; Ezk 33:24
[o] 8:3 Dn 8:20

[p] 8:4 Dt 33:17; 1Kg 22:11; Ezk 34:21
[q] Dn 11:3
[r] 8:5 Dn 8:21
[s] 8:8 2Ch 26:16; Dn 5:20
[t] Dn 8:22
[u] Dn 7:2; Rv 7:1
[v] 8:9 Dn 7:8; 8:23
[w] Ps 48:2; Dn 11:16,41
[x] 8:10 Is 14:13; Jr 48:26; Rv 12:4
[y] Dn 7:7
[z] 8:11 2Kg 19:22-23; 2Ch 32:15-17; Is 37:23; Dn 11:36-37
[aa] Ezk 46:14; Dn 11:31; 12:11
[ab] 8:12 Is 59:14; Dn 11:36

[A] **7:25** Lit *wear out*   [B] **7:25** Lit *change times*   [C] **7:25** Or *for three and a half years*   [D] **7:28** Lit *my brightness changed on me*   [E] **8:3** Lit *I lifted my eyes and looked*   [F] **8:5** Lit *a horn of a vision*   [G] **8:9** = Israel   [H] **8:10** Or *some of the army, that is, some of the stars*

7:27 In spite of the trials to come, God reigns over his creation and will end rebellion once and for all. Daily we can rejoice because we know how the story ends.

8:1-8 Biblical critics, who dismiss the possibility of predictive prophecy, insist that this must have been written in the second century BC rather than in the sixth. But for believers, the incredible accuracy of this passage's historical fulfillment is just further evidence of the inspiration and inerrancy of God's Word.

The fortress city of Susa (8:2) was in the eastern part of the Medo-Persian Empire. The **ram**, its leader, was charging with no other power able to stop him (8:3-4). But then **a male goat appeared, coming from the west . . . without touching the ground**, a detail symbolizing lightning speed of movement and conquest. This goat had

great power—**a conspicuous horn** (8:5). As Daniel watched, the goat smashed the ram to the ground and became the new world power (8:6-7). This is another picture of the Greek Empire under Alexander the Great, the "third king/kingdom" of the earlier visions in the book (cf. 2:39; 7:6). But at the height of its power, the goat's **large horn was broken**, and out of it came **four** other **horns** (8:8). Indeed, when Alexander died, his kingdom was divided among four men.

8:9-11 This figure sounds like the little horn of 7:8 and 7:24-26 (the antichrist), but given the details here (and those later in Daniel), this appears to be a picture of the brutal and infamous Seleucid ruler Antiochus IV. Also called Epiphanes, he was one of the four rulers who emerged from the divided Greek Empire after Alexander's death.

8:12-14 Antiochus Epiphanes (see the note on 8:9-11) invaded Israel with the purpose of "Hellenizing" the Jews, trying to force them to accept Greek dress, customs, and religion. He stopped the sacrifices from **168–165 BC—2,300 evenings and mornings** or 1,150 days (8:13-14). He also desecrated the temple in Jerusalem by erecting a statue of the Greek god Zeus and sacrificing a pig on the altar.

Eventually a band of Jews led by Judas Maccabeus defeated the Seleucid forces and cleansed the temple (as described in the Jewish book of 1 Maccabees). Its rededication is still celebrated by Jews today during the Jewish festival of Hanukkah (meaning, "dedication"). Antiochus IV appears here not only because he was a prominent figure in Israel's prophetic future, but also because he was also a mirror image of the still future little horn of Daniel 7, the antichrist.

a 8:13 Dn 4:13,23; 1Pt 1:12
b Ps 74:10; 79:5; Is 6:11; Dn 12:6,8; Rv 6:10
c Is 63:18; Jr 12:10; Lk 21:24; Heb 10:29; Rv 11:2
d 8:15 Dn 7:13; 10:16,18
e 8:16 Dn 9:21; Lk 1:19,26
f 8:17 Ezk 1:28; 44:4; Dn 2:46; Rv 1:17
g Dn 11:35,40
h 8:18 Dn 10:9; Lk 9:32
i Ezk 2:2; Dn 10:10,16,18
j 8:19 Mt 13:7
k 8:20 Dn 8:3
l 8:24 Dn 11:36; 12:7

m 8:24 Dn 7:27
n 8:25 Jb 34:20; Dn 2:34,45
o 8:26 Ezk 12:27; Dn 12:4,9; Rv 10:4; 22:10
p 8:27 Dn 7:28; 8:17; Hab 3:16
q Dn 2:48
r 9:1 Dn 5:31; 6:1; 11:1
s 9:2 2Ch 36:21; Ezr 1:1; Jr 25:11-12; 29:10; Zch 7:5
t 9:3 Neh 1:4; Jb 2:8; Is 61:3; Lk 10:13
u 9:4 Dt 7:21; Neh 9:32
v Dt 7:9
w 1Jn 4:20
x Dt 7:9; Neh 1:5
y 9:5 1Kg 8:48; Neh 9:33; Ps 106:6; Is 64:5-7; Jr 14:7
z Lm 1:18,20
aa Ps 119:176; Is 53:6; Dn 9:11

13 Then I heard a holy one speaking,*a* and another holy one said to the speaker, "How long will the events of this vision last*b* — the regular sacrifice, the rebellion that makes desolate, and the giving over of the sanctuary and of the army to be trampled?"*c* **14** He said to me,*A* "For 2,300 evenings and mornings; then the sanctuary will be restored."

INTERPRETATION OF THE VISION

15 While I, Daniel, was watching the vision and trying to understand it, there stood before me someone who appeared to be a man.*d* **16** I heard a human voice calling from the middle of the Ulai: "Gabriel,*e* explain the vision to this man."

17 So he approached where I was standing; when he came near, I was terrified and fell facedown.*f* "Son of man," he said to me, "understand that the vision refers to the time of the end."*g* **18** While he was speaking to me, I fell into a deep sleep,*h* with my face to the ground. Then he touched me, made me stand up,*i* **19** and said, "I am here to tell you what will happen at the conclusion of the time of wrath, because it refers to the appointed time of the end.*j* **20** The two-horned ram*k* that you saw represents the kings of Media and Persia. **21** The shaggy goat represents the king of Greece, and the large horn between his eyes represents the first king.*B* **22** The four horns that took the place of the broken horn represent four kingdoms. They will rise from that nation, but without its power.

23 Near the end of their kingdoms, when the rebels have reached the full measure of their sin,*c* a ruthless*D* king, skilled in intrigue,*E* will come to the throne.

24 His power will be great, but it will not be his own. He will cause outrageous destruction*l* and succeed in whatever he does.

He will destroy the powerful along with the holy people.*m*

25 He will cause deceit to prosper through his cunning and by his influence, and in his own mind he will exalt himself. He will destroy many in a time of peace; he will even stand against the Prince of princes. Yet he will be broken — not by human hands.*n*

26 The vision of the evenings and the mornings that has been told is true. Now you are to seal up the vision*o* because it refers to many days in the future."

27 I, Daniel, was overcome and lay sick for days.*p* Then I got up and went about the king's business.*q* I was greatly disturbed by the vision and could not understand it.

DANIEL'S PRAYER

9 In the first year of Darius,*r* the son of Ahasuerus, a Mede by birth, who was made king over the Chaldean kingdom — **2** in the first year of his reign, I, Daniel, understood from the books according to the word of the LORD to the prophet Jeremiah that the number of years for the desolation of Jerusalem would be seventy.*s* **3** So I turned my attention to the Lord God to seek him by prayer and petitions, with fasting, sackcloth, and ashes.*t* **4** I prayed to the LORD my God and confessed:

Ah, Lord — the great and awe-inspiring God*u* who keeps his gracious covenant*v* with those who love him*w* and keep his commands*x* — **5** we have sinned,*y* done wrong, acted wickedly, rebelled,*z* and turned away from your commands and ordinances.*aa*

A 8:14 LXX, Theod, Syr, Vg read *him*   *B* 8:21 = Alexander the Great   *C* 8:23 Lit *have become complete*   *D* 8:23 Lit *strong of face*   *E* 8:23 Lit *king, and understanding riddles*

8:16 **Gabriel** appears again in the Gospel of Luke, where he announces to the priest Zechariah the coming of John the Baptist, and to Mary the coming of Jesus Christ (Luke 1:19, 26). 8:17 Humans in Scripture are frequently filled with awe and fear when knowingly in the presence of angels (see, e.g., Dan 10:8-9; Luke 1:12; Rev 19:10; 22:8). 8:19-27 This is the span of time opening with the entry of the times of the Gentiles and ending with Christ's second coming (8:19). **The two-horned ram . . . represents the kings**

of Media and Persia, while the **shaggy goat** represents **the king of Greece** (Alexander the Great). Theirs are the second and third empires revealed in the book of Daniel (8:20-21). The **four horns** (8:22) represent the four leaders, including Antiochus Epiphanes (see the notes on 8:9-14), who divided Alexander's kingdom. Antiochus's demonic reign is prophesied again in 8:23-26 and mirrors the coming antichrist. 9:2 The Lord had revealed to **Jeremiah** (which Jeremiah subsequently communicated to the Jewish exiles), "When seventy years for Bab-

ylon are complete, I . . . will confirm my promise concerning you to restore you to this place" (Jer 29:10; cf. Jer 25:11-12). In other words, God's people would soon be returning to their land! 9:3-19 Like Nehemiah after him would do (Neh 1:4-11), Daniel immediately **prayed to the LORD** on behalf of the people (Dan 9:3-4). Though he knew what God had said, Daniel wasn't going to presume on God's promise. Rather, he decided to *ask* God to forgive the wickedness of his people and deliver them (9:5-19).

⁶ We have not listened to your servants the prophets,[a] who spoke in your name to our kings, leaders, fathers, and all the people of the land.

⁷ Lord, righteousness belongs to you,[b] but this day public shame belongs to us: the men of Judah, the residents of Jerusalem, and all Israel — those who are near and those who are far, in all the countries where you have banished them because of the disloyalty they have shown toward you. **⁸** LORD, public shame[c] belongs to us, our kings, our leaders, and our fathers, because we have sinned against you.[d] **⁹** Compassion and forgiveness belong to the Lord our God, though we have rebelled against him **¹⁰** and have not obeyed the LORD our God by following his instructions that he set before us through his servants[e] the prophets.

¹¹ All Israel has broken your law and turned away,[f] refusing to obey you. The promised curse[A] written in the law of Moses,[g] the servant of God, has been poured out on us because we have sinned against him. **¹²** He has carried out his words[h] that he spoke against us and against our rulers[B,i] by bringing on us a disaster that is so great that nothing like what has been done to Jerusalem has ever been done[j] under all of heaven. **¹³** Just as it is written in the law of Moses,[k] all this disaster has come on us, yet we have not sought the favor of[l] the LORD our God by turning from our iniquities and paying attention to your truth.[m] **¹⁴** So the LORD kept the disaster in mind and brought it on us, for the LORD our God is righteous in all he has done. But we have not obeyed him.

¹⁵ Now, Lord our God, who brought your people out of the land of Egypt with a strong hand[n] and made your name renowned[o] as it is this day, we have sinned, we have acted wickedly. **¹⁶** Lord, in keeping with all your righteous acts, may your anger and wrath[p] turn away from your city Jerusalem, your holy mountain;[q] for because of our sins and the iniquities of our fathers, Jerusalem and your people have become an object of ridicule to all those around us.

¹⁷ Therefore, our God, hear the prayer and the petitions of your servant. Make your face shine[r] on your desolate sanctuary[s] for the Lord's sake. **¹⁸** Listen closely,[c] my God, and hear. Open your eyes and see our desolations and the city that bears your name. For we are not presenting our petitions before you based on our righteous acts, but based on your abundant compassion. **¹⁹** Lord, hear! Lord, forgive! Lord, listen and act! My God, for your own sake, do not delay,[t] because your city and your people bear your name.

THE SEVENTY WEEKS OF YEARS

²⁰ While I was speaking, praying, confessing my sin and the sin of my people Israel,[u] and presenting my petition before the LORD my God concerning the holy mountain of my God — **²¹** while I was praying, Gabriel,[v] the man I had seen in the first vision,[w] reached me in my extreme weariness, about the time of the evening offering.[x] **²²** He gave me this explanation: "Daniel, I've come now to give you understanding.[y] **²³** At the beginning of your petitions an answer went out, and I have come to give it, for you are treasured by God.[D,z] So consider the message and understand the vision:[aa]

24   Seventy weeks are decreed[ab]
          about your people
              and your holy city —
          to bring the rebellion to an end,
          to put a stop to sin,
          to atone for iniquity,
          to bring in
              everlasting righteousness,[ac]
          to seal up vision and prophecy,
          and to anoint the most holy place.
25   Know and understand this:
          From the issuing of the decree
          to restore and rebuild Jerusalem[ad]

---

[a] 9:6 2Ch 36:16; Jr 44:4-5
[b] 9:7 Jr 23:6; 33:16; Dn 9:18
[c] 9:8 Ps 37:1-2
[d] Ps 78:56-64
[e] 9:10 2Kg 17:13-15; 18:12
[f] 9:11 Is 1:3-4; Jr 8:5-10
[g] Dt 28:15-68; 29:16–30:20; Lk 2:22
[h] 9:12 Is 44:26; Jr 44:2-6; Lm 2:17; Zch 1:6
[i] Jb 12:17; Ps 82:2-7; 148:11
[j] Lm 1:12; 2:13; Ezk 5:9
[k] 9:13 Lv 26:14-45; Dt 28:15-68; Dn 9:11
[l] Jb 36:13; Is 9:13; Jr 2:30; 5:3; Mal 1:9
[m] Jr 31:18
[n] 9:15 Dt 5:15
[o] Neh 9:10; Jr 32:20
[p] 9:16 Jr 32:31-32

[q] 9:16 Ps 87:1-3; Dn 9:20; Jl 3:17; Zch 8:3
[r] 9:17 Nm 6:25; Ps 31:17; 67:2
[s] Lm 5:18
[t] 9:19 Ps 44:23; 74:10-11
[u] 9:20 Ps 145:18; Is 58:9; Dn 9:3; 10:12
[v] 9:21 Dn 8:16; Lk 1:19,26
[w] Dn 8:1,15
[x] Ex 29:39; 1Kg 18:36; Ezr 9:4
[y] 9:22 Dn 8:16; 10:21; Zch 1:9
[z] 9:23 Dn 10:11,19
[aa] Mt 24:15
[ab] 9:24 Lv 25:8; Nm 14:34; Ezk 4:5-6
[ac] Is 51:6,8; 56:1; Jr 23:5-6; Rm 3:21-22
[ad] 9:25 Ezr 4:24; 6:1-15; Neh 2:1-8; 3:1

[A] 9:11 Lit *The curse and the oath*   [B] 9:12 Lit *against rulers who ruled us*   [C] 9:18 Lit *Stretch out your ear*   [D] 9:23 *by God* added for clarity

---

9:24 Seventy weeks is literally "seventy sevens" in Hebrew. In context, Daniel had just been praying with regard to the seventy *years* that Israel would be in captivity according to Jeremiah's prophecy. So, "seventy sevens" means seventy times seven years, or 490 years.

During this time period God would bring an **end** to the **rebellion** of Israel, **put a stop to sin** in Israel through the new covenant, **atone for iniquity** through his Son Jesus Christ, and **bring in everlasting righteousness** through the millennial reign of Christ. That's a pretty incredible to-do list!

9:25 The reference to **the decree** is most likely to 444 BC, when Persian King Artaxerxes sent Nehemiah to begin rebuilding the walls in Jerusalem (see Neh 2:1-8). From that point until **an Anointed One** came, there would be **seven weeks and sixty-two weeks**. Since the "weeks" are periods of seven years, that's

[a]**9:25** Mt 1:17; Jn 1:41; 4:25
[b]**9:26** Is 53:8; Mk 9:12; Lk 24:26
[c]Mt 24:2; Mk 13:2; Lk 19:43-44
[d]Nah 1:8

[e]**9:27** Dn 11:31; Mt 24:15; Mk 13:14; Lk 21:20
[f]Is 7:7-8; Mt 4:5
[g]Is 10:23; 28:22
[h]**10:1** Dn 1:21; 6:28
[i]Dn 1:7
[j]Dn 1:17; 2:21
[k]**10:2** Ezr 9:4-5; Neh 1:4
[l]**10:3** Dn 6:18; Am 6:6; Mt 6:17
[m]**10:4** Ezk 1:3; Dn 8:2
[n]**10:5** Ezk 9:2; Dn 12:6-7
[o]Rv 1:13; 15:6
[p]Jr 10:9
[q]**10:6** Rv 1:14; 2:18; 19:12
[r]Rv 19:6
[s]**10:7** 2Kg 6:17-20
[t]Ac 9:7
[u]Ezk 12:18
[v]**10:8** Gn 32:24
[w]Dn 7:28; 8:27; Hab 3:16
[x]**10:9** Gn 15:12; Jb 4:13; Dn 8:18

Questions & Answers

Q Why is prayer so critical?

A Prayer is critical because we are engaged in invisible, spiritual warfare. We are called to "pray at all times in the Spirit" (Eph 6:18) because Satan and his demons are trying to block God coming through for you, like the demons who tried to block the answer to Daniel's prayer (see Dan 10:10-13). You can't see this spiritual warfare, but it is very real, and we can only override it through our contact and communication with the living God. You need spiritual forces at work on your behalf, God's angels operating for you. If you are going to engage in spiritual warfare and request intervention from God, then you need a spiritual communication device. Prayer is our direct line to God.

FOR THE NEXT Q&A, SEE PAGE 1089.

until an Anointed One,[a] the ruler,[A]
will be seven weeks
and sixty-two weeks.
It will be rebuilt with a plaza
and a moat,
but in difficult times.
26 After those sixty-two weeks
the Anointed One will be cut off[b]
and will have nothing.
The people of the coming ruler
will destroy the city[c]
and the sanctuary.[B]
The[C] end will come with a flood,[d]
and until the end there will be[D] war;
desolations are decreed.
27 He will make a firm covenant[E]
with many for one week,
but in the middle of the week
he will put a stop to sacrifice
and offering.
And the abomination of desolation[e]
will be on a wing[f] of the temple[F,G]
until the decreed destruction[g]
is poured out on the desolator."

VISION OF A GLORIOUS ONE

10 In the third year of King Cyrus of
Persia,[h] a message was revealed to
Daniel, who was named Belteshazzar.[i] The
message was true and was about a great
conflict. He understood the message and
had understanding of the vision.[j]
2 In those days I, Daniel, was mourning
for three full weeks.[k] 3 I didn't eat any rich
food,[l] no meat or wine entered my mouth,
and I didn't put any oil on my body until
the three weeks were over. 4 On the twenty-fourth day of the first month,[H] as I was
standing on the bank of the great river,[m]
the Tigris, 5 I looked up, and there was a
man dressed in linen,[n] with a belt of gold[o]
from Uphaz[I,p] around his waist. 6 His body
was like beryl,[J] his face like the brilliance
of lightning, his eyes like flaming torches,[q] his arms and feet like the gleam of polished bronze, and the sound of his words
like the sound of a multitude.[r]
7 Only I, Daniel, saw the vision.[s] The men
who were with me did not see it,[t] but a
great terror fell on them,[u] and they ran and
hid. 8 I was left alone, looking at this great
vision.[v] No strength was left in me; my face
grew deathly pale,[K,w] and I was powerless.
9 I heard the words he said, and when I
heard them I fell into a deep sleep,[L,x] with
my face to the ground.

[A]**9:25** Or *until an anointed one, a prince* [B]**9:26** MT; Theod, some mss read *The city and the sanctuary will be destroyed when the ruler comes.* [C]**9:26** Lit *Its*, or *His* [D]**9:26** Or *end of a* [E]**9:27** Or *will enforce a covenant* [F]**9:27** LXX; MT reads *of abominations* [G]**9:27** Or *And the desolator will be on the wing of abominations*, or *And the desolator will come on the wings of monsters* (or *of horror*); Hb obscure [H]**10:4** = Nisan (March–April) [I]**10:5** Some Hb mss read *Ophir* [J]**10:6** The identity of this stone is uncertain. [K]**10:8** Lit *my splendor was turned on me to ruin* [L]**10:9** Lit *a sleep on my face*

a total of sixty-nine (seven plus sixty-two) times seven years, or 483 years.

During the first "seven weeks" (or "seven sevens")—forty-nine years—Jerusalem was rebuilt. Nehemiah experienced these **difficult times** when his enemies wished to put an end to the work (see Neh 4:1-23; 6:1-14).

After the next time segment, the "sixty-two weeks" (434 years), the "Anointed One" would appear. This is the translation of the Hebrew word *Messiah*—in Greek, *Christ*. So from the decree to rebuild Jerusalem (444 BC) to the coming of the Messiah would be 49 plus 434, equaling 483 years. However, we must keep in mind that these are *prophetic* years, not necessarily our modern *calendar* years. Nevertheless, if we compare Daniel's three and a half years (see 9:27) with the 1,260 days of Revelation 11:3 (also Rev 12:6) and the forty-two months of Revelation 11:2 (also Rev 13:5), we see that all three are talking about the same time period—the last half of the seven-year great tribulation period. Forty-two months of 1,260 days works out to thirty days per month. That results in a *prophetic* year of 360 days. When the calculations are made, 483 prophetic years from 444 BC causes us to arrive at AD 33, the year of Christ's crucifixion and resurrection.

9:26 **The Anointed One will be cut off** refers to the crucifixion of Christ. But clearly there is a break between Daniel's sixty-ninth and seventieth weeks that continues even today. The interlude is the church age, which Daniel did not foresee. **The coming ruler** is the antichrist, who will arise at the beginning of Daniel's seventieth week (the tribulation) to wreak havoc.

9:27 The antichrist will be a world leader pretending to bring peace to Israel. But **in the middle of the week**—halfway through the tribulation—he will set himself up as a god in Israel's temple, demanding worship and finally revealing himself as the wicked beast that he is (see Rev 13:4-8). At the end of the tribulation, the Lord will pour out his judgment on this **desolator**.

ANGELIC CONFLICT

10 Suddenly, a hand touched me and set me shaking on my hands and knees. **11** He said to me, "Daniel, you are a man treasured by God.[A,a] Understand the words that I'm saying to you. Stand on your feet,[b] for I have now been sent to you."[c] After he said this to me, I stood trembling.

12 "Don't be afraid,[d] Daniel," he said to me, "for from the first day that you purposed to understand and to humble yourself before your God,[e] your prayers were heard. I have come because of your prayers.[f] **13** But the prince of the kingdom of Persia opposed me for twenty-one days. Then Michael,[g] one of the chief princes, came to help me after I had been left there with the kings of Persia.[h] **14** Now I have come to help you understand what will happen to your people in the last days,[i] for the vision refers to those days."[j]

15 While he was saying these words to me, I turned my face toward the ground and was speechless.[k] **16** Suddenly one with human likeness[l] touched my lips.[m] I opened my mouth and said to the one standing in front of me, "My lord, because of the vision, anguish overwhelms me and I am powerless.[n] **17** How can someone like me,[o] your servant,[B] speak with someone like you, my lord? Now I have no strength, and there is no breath in me."

18 Then the one with a human appearance touched me again and strengthened me.[p] **19** He said, "Don't be afraid,[q] you who are[c] treasured by God.[r] Peace to you; be very strong!"[s]

As he spoke to me, I was strengthened and said, "Let my lord speak, for you have strengthened me."[t]

20 He said, "Do you know why I've come to you? I must return at once to fight against the prince of Persia, and when I leave, the prince of Greece will come.[u] **21** However, I will tell you what is recorded in the book of truth. (No one has the courage to support me against those princes

except Michael,[v] your prince. **11** In the first year of Darius the Mede,[W] I stood up to strengthen and protect him.) **2** Now I will tell you the truth.[x]

PROPHECIES ABOUT PERSIA AND GREECE

"Three more kings will arise in Persia, and the fourth will be far richer than the others. By the power he gains through his riches, he will stir up everyone against the kingdom of Greece.[y] **3** Then a warrior king will arise; he will rule a vast realm and do whatever he wants.[z] **4** But as soon as he is established, his kingdom will be broken up and divided to the four winds of heaven,[aa] but not to his descendants; it will not be the same kingdom that he ruled, because his kingdom will be uprooted and will go to others besides them.[ab]

KINGS OF THE SOUTH AND THE NORTH

5 "The king of the South[ac] will grow powerful, but one of his commanders will grow more powerful and will rule a kingdom greater than his. **6** After some years they will form an alliance, and the daughter of the king of the South will go to the king of the North[ad] to seal the agreement. She will not retain power, and his strength will not endure. She will be given up, together with her entourage, her father,[D] and the one who supported her during those times. **7** In the place of the king of the South, one from her family[E] will rise up, come against the army, and enter the fortress of the king of the North. He will take action against them and triumph. **8** He will take even their gods captive to Egypt, with their metal images and their precious articles of silver and gold.[ae] For some years he will stay away from the king of the North, **9** who will enter the kingdom of the king of the South and then return to his own land.

10 "His sons will mobilize for war and assemble a large number of armed forces. They will advance, sweeping through like a flood,[F,af] and will again wage war as

[a] 10:11 Dn 9:23; 10:19
[b] Ezk 2:2; Dn 8:18
[c] Heb 11:14
[d] 10:12 Is 41:10,14; Dn 10:19
[e] Dn 9:2-23; 10:2-3
[f] Ac 10:30-31
[g] 10:13 Dn 10:21; 12:1; Jd 9; Rv 12:7
[h] Dn 7:17; 8:21
[i] 10:14 Dt 31:29; Dn 2:28
[j] Dn 8:26; 12:4,9
[k] 10:15 Ezk 3:26; 24:27; Lk 1:20
[l] 10:16 Dn 8:15
[m] Is 6:7; Jr 1:9
[n] Dn 7:15,28; 8:17,27; 10:8-9
[o] 10:17 Ex 24:10-11; Is 6:1-5
[p] 10:18 Is 35:3-4
[q] 10:19 Jdg 6:23; Is 43:1; Dn 10:12
[r] Dn 9:23; 10:11
[s] Jos 1:6-7,9; Is 35:4
[t] Ps 138:2; 2Co 12:9
[u] 10:20 Dn 8:21; 11:2

[v] 10:21 Dn 10:13; Rv 12:7
[W] 11:1 Dn 5:31; 9:1
[x] 11:2 Dn 8:26; 10:1,21
[y] Dn 8:21; 10:20
[z] 11:3 Dn 5:19; 8:4; 11:16,36
[aa] 11:4 Jr 49:36; Ezk 37:9; Dn 7:2; 8:8; Zch 2:6; 6:5; Rv 7:1
[ab] Jr 12:15,17; 18:7
[ac] 11:5 Dn 11:9,11,14,25,40
[ad] 11:6 Dn 11:13,15,40
[ae] 11:8 Is 37:19; 46:1-2; Jr 43:12-13
[af] 11:10 Is 8:8; Jr 46:7-8; 51:42; Dn 11:26,40

[A] **10:11** *by God* added for clarity, also in v. 19   [B] **10:17** Lit *Can I, a servant of my lord*   [C] **10:19** Lit *afraid, man*   [D] **11:6** Some Hb mss, Theod read *the child*; Syr, Vg read *her children*   [E] **11:7** Lit *from the shoot of her roots*   [F] **11:10** Lit *advance and overflow and pass through*

10:12-13 Here we are given insight into the warfare that takes place in the spiritual realm. A figure called **the prince of the kingdom of Persia** opposed the angel sent to help Daniel for the full period during which Daniel had been fasting and praying (see 10:2-3)! This was clearly a high-ranking demon assigned to the nation of Persia to represent the devil's king-

dom and fight against God's. We learn in Jude 9 that **Michael** is an "archangel" (Dan 10:13). **10:20** The angel's words indicate that the demons of Satan's kingdom are always at war against God's kingdom and servants. It's this warfare that you can't see—the war in the spiritual realm—that you must be prepared to wage (see Eph 6:10-18).

11:4-6 After Alexander the Great died, his empire was **divided** into four (11:4). The Ptolemies of Egypt and the Seleucids of Syria, who rose to power through this arrangement, were called **the king of the South** and **the king of the North** (11:5-6) by Daniel. The terms refer to their geographical locations in relation to Israel.

a 11:13 Dn 4:16; 12:7
b 11:15 Jr 6:6; Ezk 4:2; 17:17
c 11:16 Dn 5:19; 11:3,36
d Dn 8:9; 11:41
e 11:17 2Kg 12:17; Ezk 4:3,7
f 11:18 Gn 10:5; Is 66:19; Jr 2:10; 31:10; Zph 2:11
g Hs 12:14
h 11:19 Ps 27:2; Jr 46:6
i Jb 20:8; Ps 37:36; Ezk 26:21
j 11:20 2Kg 23:35
k 11:21 Is 53:3
l Dn 8:25; 11:24

m 11:24 Nm 13:20; Neh 9:25; Ezk 34:14
n 11:26 Dn 1:5,8,13,15
o 11:27 Ps 12:2; Jr 9:3-5; 41:1-3
p Dn 8:19; 11:35,40; Hab 2:3
q 11:30 Gn 10:4; Nm 24:24; 1Ch 1:7; Is 23:1,12; Jr 2:10
r 11:31 Dn 8:11-13; 12:11
s Dn 9:27; 12:11; Mt 24:15; Mk 13:14
t 11:32 Mc 5:7-9; Zch 9:13-16; 10:3-6
u 11:33 Mal 2:7
v Mt 24:9; Jn 16:2; Heb 11:36-38
w 11:34 Dn 11:21,32; Mt 7:15; Ac 20:29-30; Rm 16:18
x 11:35 Dt 8:16; Pr 17:3; Dn 12:10; Zch 13:9; Mal 3:2-3
y Dn 12:10

far as his fortress. **11** Infuriated, the king of the South will march out to fight with the king of the North, who will raise a large army, but they will be handed over to his enemy. **12** When the army is carried off, he will become arrogant and cause tens of thousands to fall, but he will not triumph. **13** The king of the North will again raise a multitude larger than the first. After some years^A,a he will advance with a great army and many supplies.

14 "In those times many will rise up against the king of the South. Violent ones among your own people will assert themselves to fulfill a vision, but they will fail. **15** Then the king of the North will come, build up a siege ramp,^b and capture a well-fortified city. The forces of the South will not stand; even their select troops will not be able to resist. **16** The king of the North who comes against him will do whatever he wants,^c and no one can oppose him. He will establish himself in the beautiful land^B,d with total destruction in his hand. **17** He will resolve^e to come with the force of his whole kingdom and will reach an agreement with him.^C He will give him a daughter in marriage^D to destroy it,^E but she will not stand with him or support him. **18** Then he will turn his attention to the coasts and islands^F,f and capture many. But a commander will put an end to his taunting; instead, he will turn his taunts against him.^g **19** He will turn his attention back to the fortresses of his own land, but he will stumble, fall,^h and be no more.^i

20 "In his place one will arise who will send out a tax collector^j for the glory of the kingdom; but within a few days he will be broken, though not in anger^G or in battle.

21 "In his place a despised^k person will arise; royal honors will not be given to him, but he will come during a time of peace^H,i and seize the kingdom by intrigue. **22** A flood of forces will be swept away before him; they will be broken, as well as the covenant prince. **23** After an alliance is made with him, he will act deceitfully. He will rise to power with a small nation.^i

24 During a time of peace,^i he will come into the richest parts of the province^m and do what his fathers and predecessors never did. He will lavish plunder, loot, and wealth on his followers, and he will make plans against fortified cities, but only for a time.

25 "With a large army he will stir up his power and his courage against the king of the South. The king of the South will prepare for battle with an extremely large and powerful army, but he will not succeed, because plots will be made against him. **26** Those who eat his provisions^n will destroy him; his army will be swept away, and many will fall slain. **27** The two kings, whose hearts are bent on evil, will speak lies^o at the same table but to no avail, for still the end will come at the appointed time.^p **28** The king of the North will return to his land with great wealth, but his heart will be set against the holy covenant;^K he will take action, then return to his own land.

29 "At the appointed time he will come again to the South, but this time^L will not be like the first. **30** Ships of Kittim^M,q will come against him, and being intimidated, he will withdraw. Then he will rage against the holy covenant and take action. On his return, he will favor those who abandon the holy covenant. **31** His forces will rise up and desecrate the temple fortress. They will abolish the regular sacrifice^r and set up the abomination of desolation.^s **32** With flattery he will corrupt those who act wickedly toward the covenant, but the people who know their God will be strong and take action.^t **33** Those who have insight among the people^u will give understanding to many, yet they will fall by the sword and flame,^v and be captured and plundered for a time. **34** When they fall, they will be helped by some, but many others will join them insincerely.^w **35** Some of those who have insight will fall so that they may be refined,^x purified, and cleansed^y until the time of the end, for it will still come at the appointed time.

---

^A 11:13 Lit *At the end of the times* ^B 11:16 = Israel ^C 11:17 = the king of the South ^D 11:17 Lit *him the daughter of women*
^E 11:17 Perhaps the kingdom ^F 11:18 of the Mediterranean ^G 11:20 Or *not openly* ^H 11:21 Or *come without warning* ^I 11:23 Or *a few people*
^J 11:24 Or *Without warning* ^K 11:28 Or *the Jewish people and religion* ^L 11:29 Lit *but the last* ^M 11:30 = the Romans

---

11:21 The **despised person** refers to the great enemy of the Jews, Antiochus Epiphanes (see the notes on 8:9-14).
11:29-33 When the Romans opposed him on a second attempt to invade Egypt, Antiochus withdrew in humiliation and took out his rage on the Jews on his way back to Syria (11:29-30). It was then that he set up his own **abomination of desolation** (11:31; cf. 9:27), and thousands of faithful Jews who resisted him were martyred (11:33). **But the people who know their God will be strong and take action** (11:32). Life's circumstances would not keep them down.

36 "Then the king will do whatever he wants.[a] He will exalt and magnify himself above every god,[b] and he will say outrageous things against the God of gods.[c] He will be successful until the time of wrath is completed,[d] because what has been decreed will be accomplished. **37** He will not show regard for the gods[A] of his fathers, the god desired by women, or for any other god,[e] because he will magnify himself above all. **38** Instead, he will honor a god of fortresses — a god his fathers did not know — with gold, silver, precious stones, and riches. **39** He will deal with the strongest fortresses with the help of a foreign god. He will greatly honor those who acknowledge him,[B] making them rulers over many and distributing land as a reward.

40 "At the time of the end, the king of the South will engage him in battle, but the king of the North will storm against him[f] with chariots, horsemen, and many ships. He will invade countries and sweep through them like a flood.[g] **41** He will also invade the beautiful land,[h] and many will fall. But these will escape from his power: Edom, Moab, and the prominent people[c] of the Ammonites.[i] **42** He will extend his power against the countries, and not even the land of Egypt will escape. **43** He will get control over the hidden treasures of gold and silver and over all the riches of Egypt. The Libyans and Cushites will also be in submission.[D,j] **44** But reports from the east[k] and the north will terrify him, and he will go out with great fury to annihilate and completely destroy many. **45** He will pitch his royal tents between the sea and[E] the beautiful holy mountain,[l] but he will meet his end with no one to help him.

12 At that time Michael,[m] the great prince who stands watch over your people, will rise up. There will be a time of distress[n]

such as never has occurred[o] since nations came into being until that time.[p] But at that time all your people who are found written in the book[q] will escape.[r]

2 Many who sleep in the dust[s] of the earth will awake, some to eternal life,[t] and some to disgrace and eternal contempt.[u]

3 Those who have insight will shine like the bright expanse of the heavens,[v] and those who lead many to righteousness,[w] like the stars forever and ever.

4 "But you, Daniel, keep these words secret[x] and seal the book[y] until the time of the end.[z] Many will roam about,[aa] and knowledge will increase."[F]

5 Then I, Daniel, looked, and two others were standing there, one on this bank of the river and one on the other. **6** One of them said to the man dressed in linen,[ab] who was above the water of the river,[ac] "How long until the end[ad] of these wondrous things?" **7** Then I heard the man dressed in linen, who was above the water of the river. He raised both his hands[G,ae] toward heaven and swore by him who lives eternally[af] that it would be for a time, times, and half a time.[ag] When the power of the holy people is shattered, all these things will be completed.

8 I heard but did not understand. So I asked, "My lord, what will be the outcome of these things?"[ah]

9 He said, "Go on your way, Daniel, for the words are secret[ai] and sealed until the time of the end.[aj] **10** Many will be purified,[ak] cleansed, and refined,[al] but the wicked will act wickedly;[am] none of the wicked will understand, but those who have insight will understand.[an] **11** From

[a] 11:36 Dn 5:19; 11:3,16
[b] Is 14:13; Dn 5:20; 8:11,25; 2Th 2:4
[c] Rv 13:5-6
[d] Is 10:25; 26:20; Dn 8:19
[e] 11:37 1Co 8:5-6
[f] 11:40 Is 5:28; Jr 4:13
[g] Dn 11:10,26; Zch 9:14
[h] 11:41 Is 11:14; Dn 8:9; 11:16
[i] Jr 48:47; 49:6
[j] 11:43 2Ch 12:3; Ezk 30:4; Nah 3:9
[k] 11:44 Rv 16:12
[l] 11:45 Is 11:9; 27:13; 65:25; 66:20; Dn 9:16,20
[m] 12:1 Dn 10:13,21; Jd 9; Rv 12:7
[n] Mt 24:21; Mk 13:19

[o] 12:1 Jr 30:7; Ezk 5:9; Dn 9:12
[p] Rv 16:18
[q] Dn 7:10; 10:21; Rv 20:12
[r] Php 4:3; Rv 20:12; 21:27
[s] 12:2 Is 26:19; Ezk 37:12-14
[t] Mt 25:46; Jn 5:28-29
[u] Is 66:24
[v] 12:3 Gn 1:6; Ps 19:1; Jn 5:35
[w] Is 53:11; Dn 11:33
[x] 12:4 Dn 8:26; 12:9; Rv 10:4
[y] Is 8:16; Jr 32:9-12; Rv 22:10
[z] Dn 8:17; 12:9,13
[aa] 2Ch 16:9; Jr 5:1; Am 8:12
[ab] 12:6 Ezk 9:2; Dn 10:5
[ac] Dn 8:16
[ad] Dn 8:13; Mt 24:3; Mk 13:4
[ae] 12:7 Ezk 20:5; Rv 10:5-6
[af] Dn 4:34
[ag] Dn 7:25; Rv 11:2; 12:14
[ah] 12:8 1Th 5:10; 2Pt 3:10-14
[ai] 12:9 Rv 10:4
[aj] Dn 12:4
[ak] 12:10 Zch 13:9; Ac 1:6-7; 2Th 2:7-12
[al] Dn 11:35
[am] Is 32:6-7; Rv 22:11
[an] Dn 12:3; Hs 14:9; Jn 7:17; 8:47

[A] 11:37 Or God   [B] 11:39 Or those he acknowledges   [C] 11:41 Lit the first   [D] 11:43 Lit Cushites at his steps   [E] 11:45 Or the seas at   [F] 12:4 LXX reads and the earth will be filled with unrighteousness   [G] 12:7 Lit raised his right and his left

---

11:36 The change in focus of this prophecy may not be readily apparent, but it is clear from what follows that the angel stops talking about Antiochus at this point. Here the antichrist himself steps onto the scene as the seventieth "week" of seven years in the prophecy in Daniel 9 is unfolded and the seven years of the tribulation to come are discussed. The antichrist's true character as a monstrous beast is revealed: he will desire to be worshiped personally.

11:37-45 The antichrist's world reign in the tribulation will not be without opposition, as these verses describe. The attack against him by **the king of the South** and **the king of the North** (11:40) almost certainly refers to a larger coalition of forces than simply Egypt and Syria, as was the case in the days of Antiochus. That this conflict results in the antichrist meeting **his end** (11:45), which happens when Jesus Christ returns and defeats him, suggests this battle occurs near the end of the tribulation.

12:2 Those Jews who believe in Jesus the Messiah will be resurrected at the beginning of Christ's millennial kingdom to enjoy the eternal benefits of God's covenant promises to his people.

12:11 The second half of the tribulation would be **1,290 days**. This equals three-and-a-half prophetic years, 1,260 days, plus an extra thirty days (see the discussion of prophetic years in the note on 9:25). This, then, could be the time between the announcement that

a 12:11 Dn 9:27
b Dn 11:31; Mt 24:15; Mk 13:14
c 12:12 Is 30:18

d 12:13 Is 57:2; Rv 14:13

the time the daily sacrifice is abolished and the abomination of desolation*a* is set up,*b* there will be 1,290 days. **12** Happy is the one who waits*c* for and reaches 1,335 days. **13** But as for you, go on your way to the end;*A* you will rest, and then you will stand to receive*d* your allotted inheritance at the end of the days."

A **12:13** LXX omits *to the end*

the abomination of desolation (12:11) is going to be **set up** and its actual erection, or it could allow for the cleansing of the temple after this sacrilege is removed.

12:12 This number extends the time after the tribulation for another forty-five days, yet those who persevere to the end of this period are clearly blessed. Some Bible scholars suggest this extra time could allow for the gathering and judgment of the Gentile nations (see Matt 25:31-46).

12:13 These final words from heaven are for Daniel personally. A kingdom man like him will certainly not lose his reward.

HOSEA

INTRODUCTION

Author

HOSEA EXERCISED HIS PROPHETIC MINISTRY during the reigns of several kings (1:1), indicating that his career spanned at least forty years. It began sometime during the reign of Jeroboam II of Israel, who ruled the northern kingdom as coregent with his father Jehoash from 793 to 782 BC. Then he ruled independently until 753 BC. Hosea's ministry ended during the reign of Hezekiah, who ruled the southern kingdom of Judah from 716 to 685 BC.

Of all the prophetic books, Hosea is perhaps the most autobiographical. His own marriage and family form a vital part of his unique message. Though Hosea did not neglect Judah in his prophecy, his messages were primarily directed toward the northern kingdom of Israel, often spoken of as "Ephraim" and represented by the royal city of Samaria. Hosea likely lived and worked in or around Samaria and probably moved to Jerusalem by the time Samaria fell to the Assyrians in 722 BC.

Historical Background

During the reign of Jeroboam II, the northern kingdom experienced a time of general affluence, military strength, and national stability. The economy was strong, and the mood was optimistic—at least among the upper class. During a time of Assyrian weakness (the time of the prophet Jonah), Israel and Judah expanded. But after Jeroboam's death in 753 BC, Israel experienced anarchy, going through six kings in thirty years—four of whom were assassinated: Zechariah, Shallum, Pekahiah, and Pekah. Assyria gained power at this time, so Israel's days were numbered. God would use Assyria to punish Israel for their sins against him, as Hosea made clear.

Message and Purpose

Hosea is a book of six cycles that involve sin, salvation, judgment, and restoration. It is set against the backdrop of a covenantal marriage between Hosea and his wife Gomer, who broke that covenant. God used their relationship to illustrate the fact that Israel, the people with whom he had entered into a sacred covenant, had also broken faith by committing spiritual adultery with false gods. Their actions broke God's heart.

Israel's sin brought judgment, just as Hosea's wife suffered for her waywardness. But this book also demonstrates God's heart for forgiveness and reconciliation as Hosea was told to welcome his wife back even though she had been unfaithful to him. Through his prophet's actions, then, God was saying to Israel, "I will welcome you back if you will re-covenant yourselves to me." Under God's kingdom plan, he would forgive his people's sins and restore their relationship.

Hosea teaches that God will not allow his people to become unfaithful to him without consequences. Just as a husband and wife expect faithfulness from one another in marriage, God expects the full-time commitment of his people.

Outline

I. God's Tenacious Love (1:1–3:5)
II. The Charge against Israel and Their Leaders (4:1–5:15)
III. Israel's Wickedness and God's Call to Repentance (6:1–7:16)
IV. Idolatry and Exile (8:1–10:15)
V. God's Compassion and Judgment (11:1–14:9)

VIDEO | INTRO

www.bhpublishinggroup.com/qr/te/28_00

[a] 1:1 2Ch 26:1-23; Is 1:1; Am 1:1
[b] 2Kg 15:5; 2Ch 27:1-9
[c] 2Kg 16:1-20; 2Ch 28:1-27; Is 1:1; 7:1-17; Mc 1:1
[d] 2Kg 18:1-20:21; 2Ch 29:1-32:33; Mc 1:1
[e] 2Kg 13:13; 14:23-29; Am 1:1
[f] 1:2 Hs 3:1
[g] 1:3 Ezk 23:4
[h] 1:4 Hs 2:22
[i] 2Kg 9:24-10:11
[j] 2Kg 9:7; 10:30; 15:10
[k] 1:5 Gn 49:24; Jb 29:20; Jr 49:35
[l] Jos 17:16; Jdg 6:33
[m] 1:7 Is 30:18
[n] Jr 25:5-6; Zch 9:9-10
[o] Ps 44:3-7

[p] 1:9 Ex 6:7; Lv 26:12; Jr 7:23; 11:4; 30:22; Ezk 36:28
[q] 1:10 Gn 22:17; Jr 33:22
[r] Rm 9:25-27
[s] 1:11 Jr 23:5-6; 50:4-5; Ezk 37:18-25; Hs 3:5
[t] Jr 30:21; Hs 3:5
[u] Ezk 36:9-11
[v] 2:2 Ezk 23:45
[w] Is 50:1
[x] Jr 3:1,9,13
[y] 2:3 Ezk 16:7,22,39
[z] Is 32:13-14; Hs 13:15
[aa] Jr 14:3; Am 8:11-13
[ab] 2:4 Jr 13:14
[ac] 2:5 Is 1:21; Hs 3:1
[ad] Jr 2:25
[ae] Jr 44:17-18

1

The word of the Lord that came to Hosea son of Beeri during the reigns of Uzziah,[a] Jotham,[b] Ahaz,[c] and Hezekiah,[d] kings of Judah, and of Jeroboam[e] son of Jehoash, king of Israel.

HOSEA'S MARRIAGE AND CHILDREN

2 When the Lord first spoke to Hosea, he said this to him:

Go and marry a woman of
promiscuity,[f]
and have children of promiscuity,
for the land is committing
blatant acts of promiscuity
by abandoning the Lord.

3 So he went and married Gomer daughter of Diblaim, and she conceived and bore him a son.[g] **4** Then the Lord said to him:

Name him Jezreel,[A,h]
for in a little while
I will bring the bloodshed of Jezreel[i]
on the house of Jehu[j]
and put an end to the kingdom
of the house of Israel.
5 On that day I will break the bow
of Israel[k]
in the Valley of Jezreel.[l]

6 She conceived again and gave birth to a daughter, and the Lord said to him:

Name her Lo-ruhamah,[B]
for I will no longer have compassion
on the house of Israel.
I will certainly take them away.
7 But I will have compassion
on the house of Judah,[m]
and I will deliver them by
the Lord their God.[n]
I will not deliver them
by bow, sword, or war,
or by horses and cavalry.[o]

8 After Gomer had weaned Lo-ruhamah, she conceived and gave birth to a son. **9** Then the Lord said:

Name him Lo-ammi,[c]

for you are not my people,
and I will not be your God.[D,p]
10 Yet the number of the Israelites
will be like the sand of the sea,[q]
which cannot be measured
or counted.
And in the place where they were told:
You are not my people,
they will be called:
Sons of the living God.[r]
11 And the Judeans and the Israelites
will be gathered together.[s]
They will appoint for themselves
a single ruler[t]
and go up from[E] the land.
For the day of Jezreel[u] will be great.

2

Call[F] your brothers: My People
and your sisters: Compassion.

ISRAEL'S ADULTERY REBUKED

2 Rebuke your mother; rebuke her.[v]
For she is not my wife and I am not
her husband.[w]
Let her remove
the promiscuous look
from her face[x]
and her adultery
from between her breasts.
3 Otherwise, I will strip her naked[y]
and expose her as she was
on the day of her birth.
I will make her like a desert[z]
and like a parched land,
and I will let her die of thirst.[aa]
4 I will have no compassion
on her children[ab]
because they are the children
of promiscuity.
5 Yes, their mother is promiscuous;
she conceived them
and acted shamefully.[ac]
For she thought, "I will follow
my lovers,[ad]
the men who give me my food
and water,
my wool and flax, my oil
and drink."[ae]

[A] 1:4 = God Sows   [B] 1:6 = No Compassion   [C] 1:9 = Not My People   [D] 1:9 Lit *not be yours*   [E] 1:11 Or *and flourish in*; Hb obscure   [F] 2:1 Lit *Say to*

1:1 The name **Hosea** comes from the Hebrew verb meaning "to save or deliver." Hosea's message is an offer of salvation and deliverance to those in Israel and Judah who would receive it.

1:2 Given the Lord's stance toward sexual immorality, adultery, and prostitution (Exod 20:14; Lev 19:29; 1 Cor 6:12-19), this is a shocking command. But there was a reason for God's directive: **the land is committing blatant acts of promiscuity by abandoning the Lord.** People needed to see things from God's perspective.

1:4 **Jezreel** is a term symbolic of the judgment that would come upon Israel. Just as **Jehu** put the family members of the house of Ahab to death in Jezreel (see 2 Kgs 10:1-17), God was going to **put an end to the kingdom of the house of Israel.**

1:6 **Lo-ruhamah** means "No Compassion." It indicated that God would **no longer have compassion on the house of Israel** because of their sin.

1:9 After delivering Israel from slavery in Egypt, God had made a covenant with them.

He promised that if they would keep his commands, they would be his own special "possession" (Exod 19:5). But Israel had forgotten that the blessings under God's covenant were conditioned on their obedience.

1:10 Don't overlook this message of hope. Hosea looks to a future day when the number of Israelites will be countless. **They will be called: Sons of the living God.**

2:2 The **mother** in view here is Israel's leadership.

6 Therefore, this is what I will do:
I will block her[A] way[a] with thorns;[b]
I will enclose her with a wall,
so that she cannot find her paths.[c]

7 She will pursue her lovers
but not catch them;[d]
she will look for them
but not find them.
Then she will think,
"I will go back
to my former husband,[e]
for then it was better for me
than now."[f]

8 She does not recognize[g]
that it is I who gave her the grain,[h]
the new wine, and the fresh oil.
I lavished silver and gold on her,
which they used for Baal.

9 Therefore, I will take back my grain
in its time[i]
and my new wine in its season;
I will take away my wool and linen,
which were to cover her nakedness.

10 Now I will expose her shame[j]
in the sight of her lovers,
and no one will rescue her
from my power.

11 I will put an end to all
her celebrations:[k]
her feasts,[l] New Moons,[m]
and Sabbaths —
all her festivals.

12 I will devastate her vines
and fig trees.[n]
She thinks that these are her wages
that her lovers have given her.
I will turn them into a thicket,[o]
and the wild animals will eat them.[p]

13 And I will punish her for the days
of the Baals,[q]
to which she burned incense.[r]
She put on her rings and her jewelry[s]
and followed her lovers,
but she forgot me.[t]
This is the LORD's declaration.

ISRAEL'S ADULTERY FORGIVEN

14 Therefore, I am going
to persuade her,
lead her to the wilderness,[u]
and speak tenderly to her.[B]

15 There I will give her vineyards
back to her[v]
and make the Valley of Achor[c,w]
into a gateway of hope.
There she will respond as she did
in the days of her youth,[x]
as in the day she came out
of the land of Egypt.

16 In that day —
this is the LORD's declaration —
you will call me, "My husband,"[y]
and no longer call me, "My Baal."[D]

17 For I will remove the names of the Baals
from her mouth;
they will no longer be remembered
by their names.

18 On that day I will make a covenant
for them
with the wild animals, the birds
of the sky,
and the creatures that crawl
on the ground.[z]
I will shatter bow, sword,
and weapons of war in the land[E,aa]
and will enable the people
to rest securely.[ab]

19 I will take you to be my wife forever.[ac]
I will take you to be my wife
in righteousness,
justice, love, and compassion.[ad]

20 I will take you to be my wife
in faithfulness,
and you will know the LORD.[ae]

21 On that day I will respond[af] —
this is the LORD's declaration.
I will respond to the sky,
and it will respond to the earth.

22 The earth will respond to the grain,[ag]
the new wine, and the fresh oil,
and they will respond to Jezreel.

23 I will sow her[F] in the land for myself,[ah]
and I will have compassion[ai]
on Lo-ruhamah;
I will say to Lo-ammi:[aj]
You are my people,[ak]
and he will say, "You are my God."

WAITING FOR RESTORATION

3 Then the LORD said to me, "Go again;
show love to a woman who is loved by
another man and is an adulteress,[al] just as

[a] 2:6 Jb 19:8
[b] Hs 9:6; 10:8
[c] Jr 18:15
[d] 2:7 Hs 5:13
[e] Jr 2:2; 3:1; Ezk 16:8; 23:4
[f] Jr 14:22; Hs 13:6
[g] 2:8 Is 1:3
[h] Ezk 16:19
[i] 2:9 Hs 8:7; 9:2
[j] 2:10 Ezk 16:37
[k] 2:11 Jr 7:34; 16:9
[l] Hs 3:4; Am 5:21; 8:10
[m] Is 1:13-14
[n] 2:12 Jr 5:17; 8:13
[o] Ps 80:12; Is 5:5; 7:23
[p] Is 32:13-15
[q] 2:13 Hs 4:13; 11:2
[r] Jr 7:9
[s] Ezk 16:12,17; 23:40
[t] Hs 4:6; 8:14; 13:6
[u] 2:14 Ezk 20:33-38

[v] 2:15 Ezk 28:25-26
[w] Jos 7:26
[x] Jr 2:1-3
[y] 2:16 Is 54:5
[z] 2:18 Jb 5:23; Is 11:6-9; Ezk 34:25
[aa] Ezk 39:1-10
[ab] Ezk 34:25
[ac] 2:19 Is 62:4-5
[ad] Is 1:27; 54:6-8
[ae] 2:20 Hs 6:6; 13:4
[af] 2:21 Is 55:10; Zch 8:12; Mal 3:10-11
[ag] 2:22 Jr 31:12; Jl 2:19
[ah] 2:23 Jr 31:37
[ai] Hs 1:6
[aj] Hs 1:9
[ak] Hs 2:1; Rm 9:25
[al] 3:1 Hs 1:2

[A] 2:6 LXX, Syr; MT reads *your*   [B] 2:14 Lit *speak to her heart*   [C] 2:15 = Trouble   [D] 2:16 Or *My Master*   [E] 2:18 Or *war on the earth*   [F] 2:23 = Israel

---

2:8-9 By following after **Baal** (2:8), Israel had thanked and worshiped the wrong god. Thus, the Lord would end their plentiful harvests. **2:14-16** God poetically expresses abiding love and compassion toward his people through Hosea. He stands ready to forgive. He'll restore their fortunes and take them back to the days when they were first married—when **she came out of the land of Egypt** (2:15)—and rejoiced in the God who saved them. Israel will come to their senses, repent, and call the Lord, **My husband** (2:16). **2:23** Don't ever think you can't experience a reversal of fortune. God delights in welcoming back his wayward children (consider the parable of the Prodigal Son; Luke 15:11-32). **3:1-3** In this action is a picture of the unfailing, persistent love of God. Moreover, it is what God does for us through Jesus, who bought us with his own blood: "He gave himself for us to redeem us from all lawlessness and to cleanse

a 3:1 2Sm 6:19; 1Ch 16:3;
Sg 2:5
b 3:2 Ru 4:10
c 3:4 Hs 13:10-11
d Dn 9:27; 11:31; 12:11;
Hs 2:11
e Hs 10:1-2
f Ex 28:4-12; 1Sm 23:9-12
g Gn 31:19,34; Jdg 17:5;
18:14,17
h 3:5 Jr 50:4-5
i Is 11:1-10; Jr 23:5-6; 33:15-
16; Ezk 34:24; Rm 11:23
j Jr 31:9
k 4:1 Hs 5:1
l Hs 12:2; Mc 6:2
m Is 59:4; Jr 7:28
n Hs 6:6
o Hs 5:4
p 4:2 Hs 10:4
q Hs 7:3; 10:13; 11:12
r Hs 6:9
s Hs 7:1
t Hs 7:4
u Hs 6:8; 12:14
v 4:3 Is 24:4; 33:9
w Jr 4:25
x Gn 1:20-25
y 4:4 Ezk 3:26; Am 5:10,13
z Dt 17:12-13
aa 4:5 Ezk 14:3; Hs 5:5
ab Hs 2:2,5
ac 4:6 Is 5:13
ad Mal 2:7-8
ae Zch 11:8-9,15-17

af 4:6 Hs 2:13; 8:14; 13:6
ag 4:7 Hs 10:1; 13:6
ah Hab 2:16
ai 4:8 Hs 10:13
aj Is 56:11; Mc 3:11
ak 4:9 Is 24:2; Jr 5:31
al Hs 8:13; 9:9
am 4:10 Lv 26:26; Is 65:13;
Mc 6:14
an Hs 7:4
ao Hs 9:17
ap 4:11 Hs 5:4
aq Is 5:12; 28:7
ar 4:12 Is 44:19; Jr 2:27
as Hs 5:4
at Hs 9:1
au 4:13 Jr 3:6
av Hs 2:13; 11:2
aw Jr 2:20
ax 4:14 Hs 4:18; 7:4

the LORD loves the Israelites though they turn to other gods and love raisin cakes."*a* ² So I bought her for fifteen shekels of silver and five bushels of barley.*A,B,b* ³ I said to her, "You are to live with me many days. You must not be promiscuous or belong to any man, and I will act the same way toward you." ⁴ For the Israelites must live many days without king or prince,*c* without sacrifice*d* or sacred pillar,*e* and without ephod*f* or household idols.*g* ⁵ Afterward, the people of Israel will return*h* and seek the LORD their God and David their king.*i* They will come with awe to the LORD*j* and to his goodness in the last days.

GOD'S CASE AGAINST ISRAEL

4 Hear the word of the LORD,*k*
   people of Israel,
for the LORD has a case*l*
   against the inhabitants of the land:
There is no truth,*m* no faithful love,*n*
and no knowledge of God*o*
   in the land!
² Cursing,*p* lying,*q* murder,*r* stealing,*s*
and adultery*t* are rampant;
one act of bloodshed
   follows another.*u*
³ For this reason the land mourns,*v*
and everyone who lives
   in it languishes,
along with the wild animals*w*
   and the birds of the sky;
even the fish of the sea disappear.*x*
⁴ But let no one dispute;*y*
   let no one argue,
for my case is against you priests.*C,D,z*
⁵ You will stumble by day;*aa*
the prophet will also stumble
   with you by night.
And I will destroy your mother.*ab*
⁶ My people are destroyed for lack
   of knowledge.*ac*
Because you have
   rejected knowledge,*ad*
I will reject you*ae* from serving
   as my priest.

Since you have forgotten the law
   of your God,*af*
I will also forget your sons.
⁷ The more they multiplied,*ag*
the more they sinned against me.
I*E* will change their*F* honor
   into disgrace.*ah*
⁸ They feed on the sin*G* of my people;*ai*
they have an appetite
   for their iniquity.*aj*
⁹ The same judgment will happen
to both people and priests.*ak*
I will punish them for their ways*al*
and repay them for their deeds.
¹⁰ They will eat but not be satisfied;*am*
they will be promiscuous*an*
   but not multiply.
For they have abandoned
   their devotion to the LORD.*ao*
¹¹ Promiscuity,*ap* wine, and new wine
take away one's understanding.*aq*

¹² My people consult
   their wooden idols,*ar*
and their divining rods inform them.
For a spirit of promiscuity
   leads them astray;*as*
they act promiscuously*at*
in disobedience to*H* their God.
¹³ They sacrifice
   on the mountaintops,*au*
and they burn offerings
   on the hills,*av*
and under oaks, poplars,
   and terebinths,*aw*
because their shade is pleasant.
And so your daughters
   act promiscuously
and your daughters-in-law
   commit adultery.
¹⁴ I will not punish
   your daughters
when they act promiscuously
or your daughters-in-law
when they commit adultery,
for the men themselves go off
   with prostitutes*ax*

A 3:2 LXX reads *barley and a measure of wine*   *B* 3:2 Lit *silver, a homer of barley, and a lethek of barley*   *C* 4:4 Text emended; MT reads *argue, and your people are like those contending with a priest*   *D* 4:4 Hb obscure   *E* 4:7 Alt Hb tradition, Syr, Tg read *They*   *F* 4:7 Alt Hb tradition reads *my*   *G* 4:8 Or *sin offerings*   *H* 4:12 Lit *promiscuously from under*

---

for himself a people for his own possession, eager to do good works" (Titus 2:14).
4:1-2 When regard for God doesn't cross the minds of a nation on a daily basis, it's not surprising that the Ten Commandments are also completely ignored.
4:3 See Rom 8:20-21.
4:6 When leaders pursue their own selfish agenda, people almost inevitably follow.

4:7-13 God had commanded humanity to "be fruitful and multiply" (see Gen 1:28; 9:7). He'd **multiplied** the people of Israel (Hos 4:7; Exod 1:7) and promised to multiply them further (see Lev 26:9), but there was a condition for this blessing from God: their obedience (Deut 30:16). Thus, God would **repay them for their deeds** (Hos 4:9): **they would be promiscuous but not multiply**

(4:10). Nations surrounding Israel engaged in cult prostitution (4:14), committing sexual immorality as "worship" so the gods would bless them with children. Israel had become infected with this fertility religion (4:12-13), but it would not provide what they wanted. The blessing of children comes from God alone (see Ps 127:3).

and make sacrifices
    with cult prostitutes.[a]
People without discernment
    are doomed.[b]

WARNINGS FOR ISRAEL AND JUDAH

15 Israel, if you act promiscuously,
    don't let Judah become guilty!
Do not go to Gilgal[c]
    or make a pilgrimage to Beth-aven,[A,d]
and do not swear an oath:
    As the Lᴏʀᴅ lives![e]
16 For Israel is as obstinate
    as a stubborn cow.[f]
Can the Lᴏʀᴅ now shepherd them
    like a lamb in an open meadow?[g]
17 Ephraim is attached to idols;[h]
    leave him alone![i]
18 When their drinking is over,
    they turn to promiscuity.
Israel's leaders[B] fervently
    love disgrace.[c]
19 A wind with its wings will
    carry them off,[D,j]
and they will be ashamed
    of their sacrifices.

5 Hear this, priests![k]
Pay attention, house of Israel!
Listen, royal house!
For the judgment applies to you
because you have been a snare
    at Mizpah[l]
and a net spread out on Tabor.
2 Rebels[m] are deeply involved
    in slaughter;[n]
I will be a punishment
    for all of them.[c]
3 I know Ephraim,[o]
    and Israel is not hidden from me.
For now, Ephraim,[p]
    you have acted promiscuously;
Israel is defiled.
4 Their actions do not allow them
    to return to their God,[q]
for a spirit of promiscuity
    is among them,[r]
and they do not know the Lᴏʀᴅ.[s]
5 Israel's arrogance testifies
    against them.[E,t]

6 They go with their flocks and herds
    to seek the Lᴏʀᴅ[w]
but do not find him;[x]
he has withdrawn from them.[y]
7 They betrayed the Lᴏʀᴅ;[z]
indeed, they gave birth
    to illegitimate children.[aa]
Now the New Moon[ab]
    will devour them
along with their fields.[ac]

8 Blow the horn in Gibeah,[ad]
the trumpet in Ramah;[ae]
raise the war cry in Beth-aven:[af]
Look behind you,[F] Benjamin![ag]
9 Ephraim will become
    a desolation[ah]
on the day of punishment;[ai]
I announce what is certain
    among the tribes of Israel.[aj]
10 The princes of Judah are like those
    who move boundary markers;[ak]
I will pour out my fury[al] on them
    like water.[am]
11 Ephraim is oppressed,
    crushed in judgment,[an]
for he is determined to follow
    what is worthless.[G]
12 So I am like rot to Ephraim[ao]
and like decay to the house of Judah.
13 When Ephraim saw his sickness
    and Judah his wound,
Ephraim went to Assyria[ap]
    and sent a delegation
    to the great king.[H,aq]
But he cannot cure you or heal
    your wound.[ar]
14 For I am like a lion to Ephraim[as]
and like a young lion to the house
    of Judah.
Yes, I will tear them to pieces
    and depart.[at]
I will carry them off,
    and no one can rescue them.[au]
15 I will depart and return to my place
until they recognize their guilt
    and seek my face;[av]

Both Israel and Ephraim stumble
because of their iniquity;[u]
even Judah will stumble with them.[v]

[a] 4:14 Dt 23:17
[b] Hs 5:4
[c] 4:15 Hs 9:15; 12:1
[d] 1Kg 12:28-29; Hs 5:8; 10:5,8
[e] Jr 5:2; 44:26
[f] 4:16 Ps 78:8
[g] Is 5:17; 7:25
[h] 4:17 Hs 13:2
[i] Ps 81:12; Hs 4:4
[j] 4:19 Hs 12:1; 13:5
[k] 5:1 Hs 4:1
[l] Hs 9:8
[m] 5:2 Hs 9:15
[n] Hs 4:2; 6:9
[o] 5:3 Hs 6:4; 7:1; Am 3:2; 5:12
[p] Hs 6:10
[q] 5:4 Hs 4:11
[r] Hs 4:12
[s] Hs 4:6,11,14
[t] 5:5 Hs 7:10

[u] 5:5 Hs 4:5
[v] Ezk 23:31-35
[w] 5:6 Hs 8:13; Mc 6:6-7
[x] Is 1:15; Jr 14:12
[y] Ezk 8:6
[z] 5:7 Is 48:8; Hs 6:7
[aa] Hs 2:4
[ab] Hs 2:11
[ac] Is 1:14
[ad] 5:8 Hs 9:9; 10:9
[ae] Is 10:29; Jr 31:15
[af] Hs 4:15
[ag] Jdg 5:14
[ah] 5:9 Is 28:1-4; Hs 9:11-17
[ai] Is 37:3
[aj] Is 46:10; Zch 1:6
[ak] 5:10 Dt 27:17
[al] Ezk 7:8
[am] Ps 32:6; 93:3-4
[an] 5:11 Hs 9:16
[ao] 5:12 Ps 39:11; Is 51:8
[ap] 5:13 Hs 7:11; 8:9; 12:1
[aq] Hs 10:6
[ar] Hs 14:3
[as] 5:14 Hs 7:2; Hs 13:7; Am 3:4
[at] Ps 50:22
[au] Mc 5:8
[av] 5:15 Is 64:7-9; Jr 3:13-14

[A] 4:15 = House of Wickedness   [B] 4:18 Lit *Her shields*; Ps 47:9; 89:18   [C] 4:18; 5:2 Hb obscure   [D] 4:19 Lit *wind will bind it in its wings*   [E] 5:5 Lit *against his face*   [F] 5:8 Or *We will follow you*   [G] 5:11 Or *follow a command*; Hb obscure   [H] 5:13 Or *to King Yareb*

4:15-16 Gilgal was one of Israel's centers of false religion, so here Hosea exhorts **Judah** not to follow the example of Israel (4:15), who was like **a stubborn cow** (4:16).
4:17 Ephraim was one of Joseph's sons (Gen 41:52), and the tribe called by his name lived within the northern kingdom of Israel.

4:18 Be open to the conviction of the Holy Spirit so that you don't develop a stubborn spirit and fail to experience shame when you should.
5:4 You can't have fellowship with God while walking in darkness. If you want to return to God and know his favor, you have to forsake

the disobedience that led you away from him in the first place.
5:15 God's favor, blessings, and fellowship are only accessible when we submit to the road of repentance.

[a] 5:15 Ps 50:15; 78:34; Jr
2:27; Hs 3:5
[b] 6:1 Jr 50:4-5
[c] Hs 5:14
[d] Hs 14:4
[e] Is 30:26
[f] 6:2 Ps 30:5
[g] Dt 32:39
[h] 6:3 Is 2:3; Mc 4:2
[i] Ps 19:6; Mc 5:2
[j] Jl 2:23
[k] 6:4 Hs 7:1; 11:8
[l] Ps 78:34-37
[m] 6:5 1Sm 15:32-33; Jr
1:10,18; 5:14
[n] 6:6 Hs 4:1
[o] Mt 9:13; 12:7
[p] 6:7 Hs 8:1
[q] Hs 5:7

[r] 6:8 Hs 12:11
[s] Hs 4:2
[t] 6:9 Hs 7:1
[u] Jr 7:9-10; Hs 4:2
[v] Ezk 22:9; 23:27; Hs 2:10
[w] 6:10 Jr 5:30-31; 23:14
[x] Hs 5:3
[y] 6:11 Jr 51:33; Jl 3:13
[z] Zph 2:7
[aa] 7:1 Ezk 24:13; Hs 6:4;
7:13; 11:8
[ab] Hs 5:3
[ac] Hs 8:5-6; 10:5,7; 13:16
[ad] Hs 4:2
[ae] Hs 6:9
[af] 7:2 Ps 25:7; Jr 14:10; 17:1;
Am 8:7
[ag] Jr 2:19; 4:18; Hs 4:9
[ah] 7:3 Jr 28:1-4; Mc 7:3
[ai] Hs 4:2; 11:12
[aj] 7:4 Jr 9:2; 23:10
[ak] 7:5 Is 28:1,7-8

they will search for me
   in their distress.[a]

A CALL TO REPENTANCE

6 Come, let us return to the LORD.[b]
For he has torn us,[c]
   and he will heal us;[d]
he has wounded us,
   and he will bind up our wounds.[e]
2 He will revive us after two days,[f]
   and on the third day
     he will raise us up
so we can live in his presence.[g]
3 Let us strive to know the LORD.[h]
His appearance is as sure as
   the dawn.[i]
He will come to us like the rain,[j]
like the spring showers that water
   the land.

∼ HOPE WORDS ∼

*God is more interested in
devotion than duty.*

THE LORD'S FIRST LAMENT

4 What am I going to do
   with you, Ephraim?[k]
What am I going to do
   with you, Judah?
Your love is like the morning mist[l]
and like the early dew that vanishes.
5 This is why I have used
   the prophets
to cut them down;[A,m]
I have killed them with the words
   from my mouth.
My judgment strikes like lightning.[B]
6 For I desire faithful love
   and not sacrifice,
the knowledge of God[n] rather than
   burnt offerings.[o]

7 But they, like Adam,[C] have violated
   the covenant;[p]
there they have betrayed me.[q]

8 Gilead is a city of evildoers,[r]
tracked with bloody footprints.[s]
9 Like raiders who wait in ambush
   for someone,[t]
a band of priests murders
   on the road to Shechem.[u]
They commit atrocities.[v]
10 I have seen something horrible[w]
   in the house of Israel:
Ephraim's promiscuity is there;[x]
Israel is defiled.
11 A harvest is also appointed
   for you, Judah.[y]

When I[D] return my people
   from captivity,[z]

7 1 when I heal Israel,[aa]
the iniquity of Ephraim[ab]
   and the crimes of Samaria[ac]
will be exposed.
For they practice fraud;[ad]
a thief breaks in;
a raiding party pillages outside.[ae]
2 But they never consider
   that I remember all their evil.[af]
Now their actions are
   all around them;[ag]
they are right in front of my face.

ISRAEL'S CORRUPTION

3 They please the king with their evil,[ah]
the princes with their lies.[ai]
4 All of them commit adultery;[aj]
they are like an oven heated
   by a baker
who stops stirring the fire
from the kneading of the dough
   until it is leavened.
5 On the day of our king,
the princes are sick with the heat
   of wine[ak] —
there is a conspiracy with traitors.[E]
6 For they — their hearts
   like an oven —
draw him into their oven.
Their anger smolders all night;
in the morning it blazes
   like a flaming fire.

[A] 6:5 Or *have cut down the prophets*   [B] 6:5 LXX, Syr, Tg; MT reads *Your judgments go out as light*   [C] 6:7 Or *they, as at Adam*, or *they, like men*,   [D] 6:11 Or *you, Judah, when I*   [E] 7:5 Lit *wine — he stretches out his hand to scorners*; Hb obscure

---

6:1-3 Hosea reminds the people that God is always ready to receive and forgive. Sometimes, though, the prophets provided more insight into spiritual matters than they could've realized. Verses 2 and 3 are supremely true of Christ, whom God "raised on the third day according to the Scriptures" (1 Cor 15:4).
6:4-5 God sounds like an exasperated parent who loves his children but is grieved by their behavior (6:4). He had sent his **prophets** to chastise them and urge them to repent (6:5).
6:6 This is not a rejection of the sacrificial system. After all, God instituted it. Rather, God is telling Israel, "Don't think you can live as you please, reject my word, and then come offer a sacrifice to make everything okay." God's grace doesn't grant us freedom to do whatever we choose.
6:7–7:2 Israel wasn't merely naughty. What God saw was **horrible**: promiscuity, fraud, theft, and pillaging (6:10; 7:1). Nothing can be hidden from an omniscient (all-knowing) and omnipresent (everywhere-present) God. Whatever they did was done **right in front of [his] face** (7:2).
7:3 The sin of rulers can be even more devastating than that of most because their unrighteous actions distress and influence the people of the nation.

7 All of them are as hot as an oven,[a]
and they consume their rulers.[b]
All their kings fall;
not one of them calls on me.[A]

8 Ephraim has allowed himself
to get mixed up with the nations.
Ephraim is unturned bread
baked on a griddle.
9 Foreigners consume his strength,[c]
but he does not notice.[d]
Even his hair is streaked with gray,
but he does not notice.
10 Israel's arrogance testifies
against them,[B,e]
yet they do not return to the LORD
their God,[f]
and for all this, they do not seek him.

11 So Ephraim has become like a silly,
senseless dove;[g]
they call to Egypt,[h] and they go
to Assyria.[i]
12 As they are going, I will spread
my net over them;[j]
I will bring them down like birds
of the sky.
I will discipline them in accordance
with the news that reaches[C]
their assembly.

THE LORD'S SECOND LAMENT

13 Woe to them,[k] for they fled from me;[l]
destruction to them,
for they rebelled against me!
Though I want to redeem them,[m]
they speak lies against me.
14 They do not cry to me
from their hearts;
rather, they wail on their beds.
They slash themselves[D,n] for grain
and new wine;[o]
they turn away from me.
15 I trained and strengthened
their arms,[p]
but they plot evil against me.[q]
16 They turn, but not to what is above;[E]
they are like a faulty bow.[r]
Their leaders will fall by the sword
because of their insolent tongue.[s]
They will be ridiculed for this
in the land of Egypt.[t]

ISRAEL'S FALSE HOPES

8 Put the horn to your mouth![u]
One like an eagle comes
against the house of the LORD,[v]
because they transgress
my covenant[w]
and rebel against my law.[x]
2 Israel cries out to me,[y]
"My God, we know you!"
3 Israel has rejected what is good;[z]
an enemy will pursue him.

4 They have installed kings,[aa]
but not through me.
They have appointed leaders,
but without my approval.
They make their silver and gold[ab]
into idols for themselves
for their own destruction.[F]
5 Your calf-idol[G,ac]
is rejected, Samaria.[ad]
My anger burns against them.
How long will they be incapable
of innocence?[ae]
6 For this thing is from Israel —
a craftsman made it,[af]
and it is not God.
The calf of Samaria will be smashed
to bits!

7 Indeed, they sow the wind[ag]
and reap the whirlwind.[ah]
There is no standing grain;
what sprouts fails to yield flour.[ai]
Even if they did,
foreigners would swallow it up.
8 Israel is swallowed up![aj]
Now they are among the nations
like discarded pottery.[ak]
9 For they have gone up to Assyria[al]
like a wild donkey going off
on its own.
Ephraim has paid for love.[am]

[a]7:7 Ps 21:9
[b]Hs 13:10
[c]7:9 Is 1:7
[d]Hs 4:6
[e]7:10 Hs 5:5
[f]Hs 5:4
[g]7:11 Hs 4:6,11,14; 5:4
[h]Hs 8:13; 9:3,6
[i]Hs 5:13; 8:9; 12:1
[j]7:12 Ezk 12:13
[k]7:13 Hs 9:12
[l]Jr 14:10; Hs 9:17
[m]Jr 51:9; Hs 7:1; Mt 23:37
[n]7:14 1Kg 18:28
[o]Am 2:8
[p]7:15 Hs 11:3
[q]Nah 1:9
[r]7:16 Ps 78:57
[s]7:16 Ps 12:3-4; 17:10; Dn 7:25; Mal 3:13-14
[t]Ezk 23:32
[u]8:1 Hs 5:8
[v]Dt 28:49
[w]Hs 6:7
[x]Hs 4:6; 8:12
[y]8:2 Hs 7:14
[z]8:3 Hs 3:5
[aa]8:4 Hs 13:10-11
[ab]Hs 2:8; 13:1-2
[ac]8:5 Hs 10:5; 13:2
[ad]1Kg 12:28-29; Hs 7:1
[ae]Ps 19:13; Jr 13:27
[af]8:6 Hs 13:2
[ag]8:7 Hs 10:13
[ah]Is 66:15; Nah 1:3
[ai]Hs 2:9
[aj]8:8 Jr 51:34
[ak]Jr 25:34; Hs 13:15
[al]8:9 Hs 7:11
[am]Ezk 16:33

[A]7:3-7 These vv. may refer to a king's assassination; Hb obscure. [B]7:10 Lit *against his face* [C]7:12 Lit *news to* [D]7:14 Some Hb mss, LXX; other Hb mss read *They stay* [E]7:16 Some emend to *turn to what is useless* [F]8:4 Lit *themselves that it might be cut off* [G]8:5 Lit *calf*

7:8-9 **Ephraim** had gotten involved with foreign nations and didn't realize they were getting burned.
7:11-12 Ephraim is pictured flitting over to **Egypt** and then fluttering over to **Assyria** (7:11), looking for a safe place to land. But the Lord would bring him down.
7:13-15 You can sense the anguish God experienced from his people's rejection of him: **They fled from me . . . They rebelled against me . . . . They do not cry to me from their hearts . . . . They plot evil against me**. Though he **trained and strengthened** them, they slashed themselves (7:14-15)—probably in a pagan ritual pleading for divine help (see 1 Kgs 18:27-29).
7:16 If you look for counsel or aid from anywhere other than the heavenly realm, you're wasting your time. You will only **fall** and **be ridiculed**.
8:2-3 There's little point in crying, **My God, [I] know you!** when all your actions prove the opposite.
8:4 Israel put their hopes in earthly things that couldn't save them. Today people are tempted to pursue the same poor bargains—trusting in money, power, the government, technology, etc., rather than trusting in the God who inhabits eternity.

a 8:10 Jr 42:2
b Is 10:8
c 8:11 Hs 10:1; 12:11
d 8:12 Hs 4:6
e 8:13 Hs 5:6; 9:4
f Jr 6:20; 7:21
g Hs 7:2; Lk 12:2; 1Co 4:5
h Hs 4:9; 9:7
i Hs 9:3,6
j 8:14 Hs 2:13; 4:6; 13:6
k Is 9:9-10
l Jr 17:27
m 9:1 Is 22:12-13; Hs 10:5
n Hs 4:12
o Hs 7:14
p 9:2 Hs 2:9
q 9:3 Hs 7:16; 8:13
r Ezk 4:13
s Hs 11:7
t 9:4 Nm 15:5,7,10

u 9:4 Nm 19:11-14; Dt
26:12-14; Jr 16:5-7
v 9:5 Is 10:3; Jr 5:31
w Hs 2:11; Jl 1:13
x 9:6 Is 19:13; Jr 2:16; 44:1;
46:14,19; Ezk 30:13,16
y Is 5:6; 7:23; Hs 10:8
z 9:7 Is 10:3; Jr 10:15;
Mc 7:4
aa Is 34:8; Jr 16:18; 25:14
ab Lm 2:14
ac Is 44:25
ad Ezk 14:9-10
ae 9:8 Pr 29:5-6; Hs 5:1
af 9:9 Is 31:6
ag Jdg 19-21; Hs 5:8; 10:9
ah Hs 7:2; 8:13
ai 9:10 Mc 7:1
aj Jr 24:2
ak Nm 25:1-9
al Jr 11:13; Hs 4:18
am Ezk 20:8

10 Even though they hire lovers
   among the nations,
I will now round them up,
and they will begin to decrease
   in number*a*
under the burden of the king
   and leaders.*b*

11 When Ephraim multiplied his altars
   for sin,*c*
they became his altars for sinning.

12 Though I were to write out for him
ten thousand points
   of my instruction,*d*
they would be^A regarded
   as something strange.

13 Though they offer sacrificial gifts^B,*e*
and eat the flesh,*f*
the LORD does not accept them.
Now he will remember their guilt*g*
and punish their sins;*h*
they will return to Egypt.*i*

14 Israel has forgotten his Maker*j*
   and built palaces;*k*
Judah has also multiplied
   fortified cities.
I will send fire on their cities,*l*
and it will consume their citadels.

THE COMING EXILE

9 Israel, do not rejoice jubilantly
   as the nations do,*m*
for you have acted promiscuously,*n*
   leaving your God.
You love the wages of a prostitute
on every grain-threshing floor.*o*

2 Threshing floor and wine vat
   will not sustain them,*p*
and the new wine will fail them.

3 They will not stay in the land
   of the LORD.
Instead, Ephraim will return to Egypt,*q*
and they will eat unclean food*r*
   in Assyria.*s*

4 They will not pour out
   their wine offerings to the LORD,*t*

and their sacrifices
   will not please him.
Their food will be like the bread
   of mourners;
all who eat it become defiled.*u*
For their bread will be
   for their appetites alone;
it will not enter the house
   of the LORD.

5 What will you do on a festival day,*v*
on the day of the LORD's feast?*w*

6 For even if they flee
   from devastation,
Egypt will gather them,
   and Memphis will bury them.*x*
Thistles will take possession
   of their precious silver;
thorns will invade their tents.*y*

7 The days of punishment have come;*z*
the days of retribution have come.*aa*
Let Israel recognize it!
The prophet is a fool,*ab*
and the inspired man is insane,*ac*
because of the magnitude
of your iniquity and hostility.*ad*

8 Ephraim's watchman is with my God.
Yet the prophet encounters
   a bird trap
on all his pathways.*ae*
Hostility is in the house of his God!

9 They have deeply
   corrupted themselves*af*
as in the days of Gibeah.*ag*
He will remember their iniquity;
he will punish their sins.*ah*

EPHRAIM BEREAVED OF OFFSPRING

10 I discovered Israel
like grapes in the wilderness.*ai*
I saw your fathers
like the first fruit of the fig tree
   in its first season.*aj*
But they went to Baal-peor,*ak*
consecrated themselves to Shame,*c,al*
and became abhorrent,*am*
like the thing they loved.

^A 8:12 Or *Though I wrote out . . . instruction, they are*   ^B 8:13 Hb obscure   ^c 9:10 = Baal

8:12 Indeed, the person who refuses to listen to reason is determined to do what he wants no matter what anyone says. Many are set in their ways and consider God's words in Scripture **strange**.

8:14 **Israel** had **forgotten his Maker**, but God doesn't forget to punish.

9:1 The reference to prostitution **on every grain-threshing floor** was another way of saying that Israel was participating in the Canaanite fertility rites, a sexual type of worship committed in the presence of an idol—glaring evidence of departure from God's covenant.

9:3 Expulsion from the land is what happened to the previous occupants because of their sins (see Exod 23:24-33), and it is what was prophesied to happen to Israel if they followed in those footsteps (see Deut 4:25-27). Israel abandoned the covenant lifestyle, with all of its blessings, in favor of a promiscuous lifestyle identical to that of the surrounding nations. They wanted to be *like* everyone else; as a result, they would be *with* everyone else.

9:7 God repeatedly sent prophets to warn his people, but Israel considered **the prophet** a **fool** and **insane**. If you're faithful to God's Word, be prepared for people to think you're crazy too.

9:8 **Watchman** is a biblical term for prophet (Jer 6:17; Ezek 3:17).

9:10 That Israel **became abhorrent, like the thing they loved** is a principle you can take to the bank. You will become like that which you worship (see Ps 115:4-8)—whether an idol or Jesus Christ.

11 Ephraim's glory will fly away
  like a bird:[a]
no birth, no pregnancy,
  no conception.[b]
12 Even if they raise children,
  I will bereave them of each one.
Yes, woe to them when I depart
  from them![c]
13 I have seen Ephraim like Tyre,[d]
  planted in a meadow,
so Ephraim will bring out
  his children
  to the executioner.
14 Give them, LORD —
  What should you give?
Give them a womb that miscarries
  and breasts that are dry![e]
15 All their evil appears at Gilgal,[f]
  for there I began to hate them.
I will drive them from my house
  because of their evil,
  wicked actions.[g]
I will no longer love them;
  all their leaders are rebellious.[h]
16 Ephraim[i] is struck down;
  their roots are withered;
  they cannot bear fruit.[j]
Even if they bear children,
  I will kill the precious offspring
  of their wombs.[k]
17 My God will reject them
  because they have not listened
  to him;[l]
they will become wanderers
  among the nations.[m]

THE VINE AND THE CALF

10 Israel is a lush[A] vine;[n]
  it yields fruit for itself.
The more his fruit increased,
  the more he increased the altars.[o]
The better his land produced,
  the better they made
  the sacred pillars.[p]
2 Their hearts are devious;[B,q]
  now they must bear their guilt.[r]
The LORD will break down
  their altars[s]
  and demolish their sacred pillars.

3 In fact, they are now saying,
  "We have no king!
For we do not fear the LORD.[t]
  What can a king do for us?"
4 They speak mere words,
  taking false oaths
  while making covenants.[u]
So lawsuits break out
  like poisonous weeds in the furrows
  of a field.[v]

5 The residents of Samaria[w]
  will have anxiety
over the calf[x] of Beth-aven.[y]
Indeed, its idolatrous priests
  rejoiced over it;
the people will mourn over it,
  over its glory.[z]
It will certainly go into exile.
6 The calf itself will be taken
  to Assyria[aa]
as an offering to the great king.[C,ab]
Ephraim will experience shame;[ac]
Israel will be ashamed
  of its counsel.[ad]
7 Samaria's king will disappear[D,ae]
  like foam[E] on the surface
  of the water.
8 The high places[af] of Aven,
  the sin of Israel,[ag]
will be destroyed;
thorns and thistles will grow
  over their altars.[ah]
They will say to the mountains,[ai]
  "Cover us!"
and to the hills, "Fall on us!"[aj]

ISRAEL'S DEFEAT BECAUSE OF SIN

9 Israel, you have sinned
  since the days of Gibeah;[ak]
they have taken their stand there.
Will not war against the unjust
  overtake them in Gibeah?
10 I will discipline[al] them
  at my discretion;[am]
nations will be gathered
  against them
to put them in bondage[F]
  for their double iniquity.[an]

[a] 9:11 Hs 4:7; 10:4
[b] Hs 4:10
[c] 9:12 Hs 7:13
[d] 9:13 Ezk 27:3-4
[e] 9:14 Gn 49:25
[f] 9:15 Hs 4:15; 12:11
[g] Hs 4:9; 7:2; 12:2
[h] Hs 5:2
[i] 9:16 Hs 5:11
[j] Hs 8:7
[k] Ezk 24:21
[l] 9:17 Hs 4:10
[m] Hs 7:13
[n] 10:1 Is 5:1-7; Ezk 15:1-6
[o] Hs 8:11; 12:11
[p] 1Kg 14:23; Hs 3:4
[q] 10:2 1Kg 18:21; Zph 1:5
[r] Hs 13:16
[s] Mc 5:13

[t] 10:3 Ps 12:4; Is 5:19
[u] 10:4 Ezk 17:13-19; Hs 4:2
[v] Dt 31:16-17; 2Kg 17:3-4
[w] 10:5 Hs 7:1
[x] Hs 8:5-6
[y] Hs 4:15; 5:8
[z] Hs 9:11
[aa] 10:6 Hs 11:5
[ab] Hs 5:13
[ac] Hs 4:7
[ad] Is 30:3; Jr 7:24
[ae] 10:7 Hs 13:11
[af] 10:8 Dt 12:2; Hs 4:13
[ag] 1Kg 12:28-30; 13:34
[ah] Is 32:13; Hs 9:6
[ai] Lk 23:30; Rv 6:16
[aj] Rv 6:16
[ak] 10:9 Hs 5:8; 9:9
[al] 10:10 Hs 4:9
[am] Ezk 5:13
[an] Jdg 19–21; 1Kg 12:28-30

[A] 10:1 Or *ravaged*   [B] 10:2 Or *divided*   [C] 10:6 Or *to King Yareb*   [D] 10:7 Or *will be cut off*   [E] 10:7 Or *a stick*   [F] 10:10 LXX, Syr, Vg read *against them when they are disciplined*

9:14 The people had sought fertility from lifeless idols, but they would lose their children.
9:17 Turning away from the King and kingdom principles leaves you with some of the world—but all of nothing.
10:9-10 As proof of Israel's sin heritage, Hosea first calls Israel to remember **the days of Gibeah** (10:9; see Judg 19:1-30; 20:1-10). The gang rape and murder of a Levite's concubine there is Hosea's historical point of reference. God did not allow the perverted men to go unpunished then, and he will not allow Israel to go unpunished either (Hos 10:10).

10:11 Sometimes calves were permitted to walk on grain stalks, separating the grain from the chaff. The calf could then eat freely without doing any real labor. But God says such easy days are over. In response to Israel's sin, he will now **yoke** them for hard **plowing.**

a 10:11 Jr 5:11; Hs 4:16
b Jr 28:14
c Ps 66:12
d 10:12 Pr 11:18
e Jr 4:3
f Hs 4:1; 12:6
g Hs 6:3
h Is 44:3; 45:8
i 10:13 Jb 4:8; Gl 6:7
j Hs 4:2; 7:3; 11:12
k Ps 33:16
l 10:14 Is 17:3
m Hs 13:16
n 10:15 Hs 4:15; 10:5
o 11:1 Dt 4:37; 7:6-8; 10:14-
15; Ps 78:68; Is 41:8; Am
3:2; Mal 1:2
p Ex 4:22-23; Dt 32:5-6,18-
20; Ps 103:13; Jr 3:19; Hs
1:10; Mt 2:15
q 11:2 2Kg 17:13-15
r Hs 2:13; 4:13
s Is 65:7; Jr 18:15

t 11:3 Hs 7:15
u Dt 1:31; 32:10-11
v Ex 15:26
w 11:4 Jr 31:2-3
x Hs 10:11
y Ex 16:32
z 11:5 Hs 7:16; 8:13; 9:3;
10:6
aa Hs 7:16
ab 11:6 Hs 13:16
ac Lm 2:9
ad Hs 4:16-17
ae 11:7 Jr 8:5
af 11:8 Hs 6:4; 7:1
ag Gn 14:8; Dt 29:23
ah Gn 14:2; 19:1-29; Dt
29:23
ai 11:9 Dt 13:17
aj Jr 26:3; 30:11
ak Is 5:24; 12:6; 41:14,16
al 11:10 Hs 3:5; 6:1-3
am Is 31:4; Jl 3:16; Am 1:2
an Is 66:2-5
ao 11:11 Is 60:8; Hs 7:11
ap Is 11:11

11 Ephraim is a well-trained calf*a*
that loves to thresh,
but I will place a yoke on*A* her
fine neck.*b*
I will harness Ephraim;*c*
Judah will plow;
Jacob will do the final plowing.
12 Sow righteousness for yourselves*d*
and reap faithful love;
break up your unplowed ground.*e*
It is time to seek the LORD*f*
until he comes*g*
and sends righteousness
on you like the rain.*h*

13 You have plowed wickedness
and reaped injustice;*i*
you have eaten the fruit of lies.*j*
Because you have trusted
in your own way*B*
and in your large number
of soldiers,*k*
14 the roar of battle will rise
against your people,
and all your fortifications
will be demolished*l*
in a day of war,
like Shalman's destruction
of Beth-arbel.
Mothers will be dashed to pieces
along with their children.*m*
15 So it will be done to you, Bethel,*n*
because of your extreme evil.
At dawn the king of Israel will be
totally destroyed.

THE LORD'S LOVE FOR ISRAEL

11 When Israel was a child,
I loved him,*o*
and out of Egypt I called my son.*p*
2 Israel called to the Egyptians*q*
even as Israel was leaving them.*c*
They kept sacrificing
to the Baals*r*
and burning offerings to idols.*s*

3 It was I who taught Ephraim
to walk,*t*
taking them*D* by the hand,*E,u*
but they never knew
that I healed them.*v*
4 I led them with human cords,
with ropes of love.*w*
To them I was like one
who eases the yoke from their jaws;*x*
I bent down to give them food.*y*
5 Israel will not return to the land
of Egypt
and Assyria will be his king,*z*
because they refused to repent.*aa*
6 A sword will whirl
through his cities;*ab*
it will destroy and devour the bars
of his gates,*F,ac*
because of their schemes.*ad*
7 My people are bent on turning
from me.*ae*
Though they call to him on high,
he will not exalt them at all.

8 How can I give you up, Ephraim?*af*
How can I surrender you, Israel?
How can I make you like Admah?*ag*
How can I treat you like Zeboiim?*ah*
I have had a change of heart;
my compassion is stirred!
9 I will not vent the full fury of my anger;*ai*
I will not turn back
to destroy Ephraim.*aj*
For I am God and not man,
the Holy One among you;*ak*
I will not come in rage.*G*
10 They will follow the LORD;*al*
he will roar like a lion.*am*
When he roars,
his children will come trembling
from the west.*an*
11 They will be roused like birds
from Egypt
and like doves*ao* from the land
of Assyria.*ap*

A 10:11 Lit *will pass over* *B* 10:13 LXX reads *your chariots* *C* 11:2 Lit *They called to them; thus they went from before them* *D* 11:3 LXX, Syr, Vg; MT
reads *him* *E* 11:3 Lit *them on his arms* *F* 11:6 Or *devour his empty talkers*, or *devour his limbs*; Hb obscure *G* 11:9 Or *come into any city*; Hb obscure

11:1 Israel's childhood refers to their journey into Egypt in obedience to God when they were less than a hundred people (see Gen 46:3-27). They arrived in Egypt as a family with the promise from God of becoming a great nation.
Out of Egypt I called my son was another point of history taught to all Jewish children; it's a reference to the exodus when God brought his people out of slavery. When he wrote his Gospel, Matthew saw this as ultimately fulfilled in Jesus Christ—God's true Son who also came out of Egypt (see Matt 2:15).

11:6-7 Punishment and captivity were unavoidable (11:6)—not because God has a bad temper, but because his **people** were **bent on turning from** him (11:7). Holy justice would have to be carried out.
11:8 The average Bible reader probably cruises right past **Admah** and **Zeboiim** without recognizing the names; however, most readers recognize the names of their sister cities, Sodom and Gomorrah. Yet, the Lord actually destroyed all four places in his anger over their wickedness (see Deut 29:23). The thought of such destruction coming upon

God's beloved people makes his heart ache and stirs up his **compassion**. Thus, the Lord declares, **I have had a change of heart**. God's grace on sinners is a result of his own unmerited kindness and love.
11:9 **For I am God and not man** is a reminder that his ways are higher than ours (see Isa 55:8-9).
11:10 Elsewhere Hosea compares God to a lion who would attack Israel for their sins (see 5:14; 13:7). Here the comparison is positive. He will **roar like a lion** calling his cubs, and they **will come trembling** in submission.

Then I will settle them
in their homes.[a]
This is the LORD's declaration.
12 Ephraim surrounds me with lies,[b]
the house of Israel, with deceit.
Judah still wanders with God
and is faithful to the holy ones.[A]

GOD'S CASE AGAINST JACOB'S HEIRS

12 Ephraim chases[B] the wind[c]
and pursues the east wind.[d]
He continually multiplies lies
and violence.
He makes a covenant with Assyria,[e]
and olive oil is carried to Egypt.[f]

2 The LORD also has a dispute
with Judah.
He is about to punish Jacob
according to his conduct;[g]
he will repay him based on his actions.
3 In the womb he grasped
his brother's heel,[h]
and as an adult he wrestled
with God.[i]
4 Jacob struggled with the angel
and prevailed;
he wept and sought his favor.[j]
He found him at Bethel,[k]
and there he spoke with him.[c,l]
5 The LORD is the God of Armies;
the LORD is his name.[m]
6 But you must return to your God.[n]
Maintain love and justice,[o]
and always put your hope in God.[p]

7 A merchant loves to extort[q]
with dishonest scales in his hands.[r]
8 But Ephraim thinks,
"How rich I have become;[s]
I made it all myself.
In all my earnings,
no one can find any iniquity in me[t]
that I can be punished for!"[D]

JUDGMENT ON APOSTATE ISRAEL

9 I have been the LORD your God
ever since[E] the land of Egypt.[u]
I will make you live in tents again,[v]
as in the festival days.

10 I will speak through the prophets[w]
and grant many visions;
I will give parables
through the prophets.[x]
11 Since Gilead is full of evil,[y]
they will certainly come to nothing.
They sacrifice bulls in Gilgal;[z]
even their altars will be
like piles of rocks[aa]
on the furrows of a field.

FURTHER INDICTMENT
OF JACOB'S HEIRS

12 Jacob fled to the territory
of Aram.[ab]
Israel worked to earn a wife;[ac]
he tended flocks for a wife.[ad]
13 The LORD brought Israel from Egypt
by a prophet,[ae]
and Israel was tended by a prophet.

14 Ephraim has provoked bitter anger,[af]
so his Lord will leave his bloodguilt
on him[ag]
and repay him for his contempt.[ah]

13 When Ephraim spoke,[ai]
there was trembling;
he was exalted in Israel.[aj]
But he incurred guilt through Baal[ak]
and died.

2 Now they continue to sin
and make themselves a cast image,[al]
idols skillfully made
from their silver,[am]
all of them the work of craftsmen.[an]
People say about them,
"Let the men who sacrifice[F] kiss
the calves."[ao]
3 Therefore, they will be
like the morning mist,[ap]
like the early dew that vanishes,
like chaff blown
from a threshing floor,[aq]
or like smoke from a window.[ar]

DEATH AND RESURRECTION

4 I have been the LORD your God[as]
ever since[G] the land of Egypt;

[a]11:11 Ezk 34:27-28
[b]11:12 Hs 4:2; 7:3
[c]12:1 Jr 22:22; Hs 4:19
[d]Gn 41:6; Ezk 17:10
[e]Hs 5:13; 7:11; 8:9
[f]2Kg 17:4
[g]12:1 Hs 4:9; 7:2
[h]12:3 Gn 25:26; 27:36
[i]Gn 32:24-28
[j]12:4 Gn 32:26
[k]Gn 28:13-15; 35:10-15
[l]Gn 28:10-22; 35:1-14
[m]12:5 Ex 3:15
[n]12:6 Hs 6:1-3; 10:12
[o]Hs 6:6
[p]Mc 7:7
[q]12:7 Hs 7:14
[r]Pr 11:1; Am 8:5; Mc 6:11
[s]12:8 Ps 62:10; Hs 13:6
[t]Hs 4:8; 14:1; Am 3:15; 6:4-6
[u]12:9 Hs 11:1; 13:3
[v]Lv 23:42

[w]12:10 Jr 7:25
[x]Ezk 17:2; 20:49
[y]12:11 Hs 6:8
[z]Hs 4:15; 9:15
[aa]Hs 8:11; 10:1-2
[ab]12:12 Gn 28:5
[ac]Gn 29:20
[ad]Gn 29:1-20
[ae]12:13 Ex 14:19-22; Is 63:11-14
[af]12:14 2Kg 17:7-18
[ag]Ezk 18:10-13
[ah]Dn 11:18; Mc 6:16
[ai]13:1 Jb 29:21-22
[aj]Jdg 8:1; 12:1
[ak]Hs 2:8-17; 11:2
[al]13:2 Is 46:6; Jr 10:4; Hs 2:8
[am]Is 44:17-20
[an]Hs 8:6
[ao]Hs 8:5-6; 10:5
[ap]13:3 Hs 6:4
[aq]Ps 1:4; Is 17:13; Dn 2:35
[ar]Ps 68:2
[as]13:4 Hs 12:9

[A]11:12 Hb obscure   [B]12:1 Or grazes on, or tends   [C]12:4 LXX, Syr; MT reads us   [D]12:8 Lit iniquity which is sin   [E]12:9 LXX reads God who brought you out of   [F]13:2 Or "Those who make human sacrifices   [G]13:4 DSS, LXX read God who brought you out of

12:1 Israel repeatedly pursued alliances with foreign nations, leading to idolatry and further failure to rely on the Lord.
12:3-5 As Judah's forefather Jacob had wrestled with God and sought his favor (12:3-4), so Judah must also look to God for his blessing and not to foreign nations or false gods.

12:6 to maintain love and justice, and always put your hope in God is solid advice. God stands ready to receive those who make God's agenda of love and justice their own.
13:1 When Ephraim spoke, there was trembling is another way of saying they enjoyed great respect. Idolatry and rejection of the

living God, however, had since ruined them. This is what sin does to a person. No matter an individual's strength, ability, social status, or economic capability, moral degeneration and foolishness are cancers that quickly eat away at character.

ᵃ 13:4 Ex 20:3; 2Kg 18:35
ᵇ Is 43:11; 45:21-22
ᶜ 13:5 Dt 32:10
ᵈ 13:6 Dt 8:12,14; 32:13-15;
Jr 5:7
ᵉ Hs 7:14
ᶠ Hs 2:13; 4:6; 8:14
ᵍ 13:7 Hs 5:14
ʰ Jr 5:6
ⁱ 13:8 Ps 50:22
ʲ 13:9 Jr 2:17,19; Hs 6:1-2;
Mal 1:12-13
ᵏ 13:10 2Kg 17:4; Hs 8:4
ˡ Hs 7:7
ᵐ 13:11 1Sm 8:7
ⁿ 1Kg 14:7-10; Hs 10:7
ᵒ 13:12 Dt 32:34-35; Jb
14:17; Rm 2:5
ᵖ 13:13 Mc 4:9-10
ᑫ Dt 32:6; Hs 5:4
ʳ Is 37:3; 66:9
ˢ 13:14 Hs 6:1-2
ᵗ 1Co 15:55
ᵘ Jr 20:16; 31:35-37
ᵛ 13:15 Gn 49:22; Hs 10:1
ʷ Gn 41:6; Jr 4:11-12; Ezk
17:10; 19:12

ˣ 13:15 Jr 51:36
ʸ Jr 20:5
ᶻ 13:16 Hs 7:1
ᵃᵃ Hs 10:2
ᵃᵇ Hs 7:14
ᵃᶜ Hs 11:6
ᵃᵈ Hs 10:14
ᵃᵉ 2Kg 15:16
ᵃᶠ 14:1 Hs 6:1; 10:12; 12:6
ᵃᵍ Hs 4:8; 5:5; 9:7
ᵃʰ 14:2 Mc 7:18-19
ᵃⁱ Heb 13:15
ᵃʲ 14:3 Hs 5:13
ᵃᵏ Is 31:1
ᵃˡ Hs 4:12
ᵃᵐ Hs 8:6; 13:2
ᵃⁿ Ps 68:5
ᵃᵒ 14:4 Is 57:18; Hs 6:1
ᵃᵖ Zph 3:17
ᵃᑫ Is 12:1
ᵃʳ 14:5 Is 26:19
ᵃˢ Sg 2:1; Mt 6:28
ᵃᵗ Is 35:2
ᵃᵘ 14:6 Jr 11:16
ᵃᵛ Sg 4:11

you know no God but me,ᵃ
and no Savior exists besides me.ᵇ

5 I knewᴬ you in the wilderness,ᶜ
in the land of drought.
6 When they had pasture,
they became satisfied;ᵈ
they were satisfied,
and their hearts became proud.ᵉ
Therefore they forgot me.ᶠ
7 So I will be like a lionᵍ to them;
I will lurk like a leopardʰ on the path.
8 I will attack them
like a bear robbed of her cubs
and tear open the rib cage
over their hearts.
I will devour them there
like a lioness,ⁱ
like a wild beast that would rip
them open.
9 I will destroy you, Israel;
you have no help but me.ᴮ,ʲ

10 Where now is your king,ᶜ,ᵏ
that he may save you in all
your cities,
and theᴰ rulers ᴱ,ˡ you
demanded, saying,
"Give me a king and leaders"?
11 I give you a king in my angerᵐ
and take away a king in my wrath.ⁿ
12 Ephraim's guilt is preserved;
his sin is stored up.ᵒ
13 Labor pains come on him.ᵖ
He is not a wise son;ᑫ
when the time comes,
he will not be born.ᶠ,ʳ

14 I will ransom them from the power
of Sheol.
I will redeemᴳ them from death.ˢ
Death, where are your barbs?
Sheol, where is your sting?ᵗ
Compassion is hidden
from my eyes.ᵘ

THE COMING JUDGMENT

15 Although he flourishes
among his brothers,ᴴ,ᵛ
an east wind will come,ʷ

a wind from the LORD rising up
from the desert.
His water source will fail,
and his spring will run dry.ˣ
The windⁱ will plunder the treasuryʸ
of every precious item.

16 Samariaᶻ will bear her guiltᵃᵃ
because she has rebelled
against her God.ᵃᵇ
They will fall by the sword;ᵃᶜ
their children will be dashed
to pieces,ᵃᵈ
and their pregnant women
ripped open.ᵃᵉ

A PLEA TO REPENT

14 Israel, return to the LORD
your God,ᵃᶠ
for you have stumbled
in your iniquity.ᵃᵍ
2 Take words of repentance with youᵃʰ
and return to the LORD.
Say to him: "Forgive all our iniquity
and accept what is good,
so that we may repay you
with praiseʲ from ourᵏ lips.ᵃⁱ
3 Assyria will not save us,ᵃʲ
we will not ride on horses,ᵃᵏ
and we will no longer proclaim,
'Our gods!'ᵃˡ
to the work of our hands.ᵃᵐ
For the fatherless
receives compassion in you."ᵃⁿ

A PROMISE OF RESTORATION

4 I will heal their apostasy;ᵃᵒ
I will freely love them,ᵃᵖ
for my anger will have turned
from him.ᵃᑫ
5 I will be like the dew to Israel;ᵃʳ
he will blossom like the lilyᵃˢ
and take root like
the cedars of Lebanon.ᵃᵗ
6 His new branches will spread,
and his splendor will be
like the olive tree,ᵃᵘ
his fragrance, like
the forest of Lebanon.ᵃᵛ

ᴬ 13:5 LXX, Syr read *fed*   ᴮ 13:9 LXX reads *At your destruction, Israel, who will help you?*   ᶜ 13:10 LXX, Syr, Vg; MT reads *I will be your king*
ᴰ 13:10 Lit *your*   ᴱ 13:10 Or *judges*   ᶠ 13:13 Lit *he will not present himself at the opening of the womb for sons*   ᴳ 13:14 Or *Should I ransom . . . ? Should
I redeem . . . ?*   ᴴ 13:15 Or *among reeds*   ⁱ 13:15 Probably the Assyrian king   ʲ 14:2 LXX reads *with the fruit*   ᵏ 14:2 Lit *repay the bulls of our*

13:6 When you become **satisfied**, you are tempted to take the credit for yourself as Israel did. Then your heart becomes **proud**, and you forget God. Therefore, you must constantly nurture a humble heart that looks to God's Word and power as your source of strength and sustenance.

13:14 The apostle Paul quotes from this text to demonstrate God's victory over death and the law through the resurrection power of Jesus Christ (see 1 Cor 15:54-57).
14:1-3 What's the only appropriate response to God's anger against sin? **Repentance**— that is, **return to the LORD** (14:1-2). Do an

about-face; change your ways. Plead with him to **forgive** your sin and **praise** him (14:2), knowing that no one saves but him (14:3).

7 The people will return and live
　　beneath his shade.[a]
　　They will grow grain[b]
　　and blossom like the vine.
　　His renown will be like the wine
　　　of Lebanon.

8 Ephraim, why should I[A] have
　　anything more
　　to do with idols?[c]
　　It is I who answer and watch
　　over him.

I am like a flourishing pine tree;[d]
your fruit comes from me.[e]

9 Let whoever is wise[f] understand
　　these things,
　　and whoever is insightful
　　　recognize them.
　　For the ways of the LORD
　　　are right,[g]
　　and the righteous walk in them,[h]
　　but the rebellious stumble
　　in them.[i]

[a] 14:7 Ezk 17:23
[b] Hs 2:21-22
[c] 14:8 Jb 34:32

[d] 14:8 Is 41:19
[e] Ezk 17:13
[f] 14:9 Ps 107:43; Jr 9:12
[g] Ps 111:7-8; Zph 3:5
[h] Is 26:7
[i] Is 1:28

[A] 14:8 LXX reads *he*

14:9 Since the Lord's ways are **right**, you need to transform your thoughts to match his. A kingdom mind views life from the divine viewpoint (found in his Word) and lives accordingly. In fact, having a kingdom mindset is the difference between **the righteous** who **walk** in God's ways and **the rebellious** who **stumble in them**.

JOEL

INTRODUCTION

Author

THE OLD TESTAMENT INCLUDES A number of people named Joel (see 1 Sam 8:2; 1 Chr 4:35; 6:33; 11:38; 15:7; Ezra 10:43; Neh 11:9), but none of these can be identified with the author of this book. Unfortunately, we know nothing about Joel other than his father's name, Pethuel (Joel 1:1).

Historical Background

It is impossible to determine the exact date of Joel's book. He does not introduce his prophetic work by mentioning who was on the throne in Israel or Judah at the time, unlike many other Old Testament prophets (see Isaiah, Jeremiah, Daniel, Hosea, Amos, Micah, Zephaniah, Haggai, and Zechariah). And Joel also doesn't indicate the specific sins of the people. He doesn't explicitly say what behavior needed changing. Rather, he was concerned mainly with motivating repentance by proclaiming the coming "day of the LORD" (Joel 1:15).

Message and Purpose

The prophet Joel speaks to God's people about their desperate need of repentance in order to experience restoration. They were under judgment because they continually rebelled against God, leading to exile and all manner of other repercussions. Joel's message was that it was no longer business as usual because of a catastrophic event they were facing, called the day of the Lord. This phrase refers to a time of judgment that precedes restoration, a time when God recalibrates to make right what is wrong. With the day of the Lord looming before the nation of Israel, Joel told the people to cease all normal activity. He urged them to call a solemn assembly to get right before God so he would remove the locusts that were ravaging the land—a sign of his judgment.

If the people would repent, Joel had a powerful message of blessing from God. Not only would he remove the locusts, he would restore the years the locusts had eaten. Joel wanted the people of God (then and now) to know that God is holy, demands repentance, and will judge. But when repentance occurs, he can restore what rebellion has destroyed and turn cursing into kingdom blessing.

VIDEO · INTRO

www.bhpublishinggroup.com/qr/te/29_00

Outline

I. The Foreshadow of Devastation (1:1-20)
II. The Day of the Lord and the Call to Repentance (2:1-32)
III. Judgment on the Nations and Blessing on Israel (3:1-21)

1

The word of the LORD that came[a] to Joel son of Pethuel:

A PLAGUE OF LOCUSTS

2   Hear this,[b] you elders;
    listen, all you inhabitants of the land.
    Has anything like this
       ever happened in your days[c]
    or in the days of your ancestors?
3   Tell your children about it,[d]
    and let your children tell their children,
    and their children the next generation.
4   What the devouring locust[e] has left,
    the swarming locust has eaten;
    what the swarming locust has left,
    the young locust[f] has eaten;
    and what the young locust has left,
    the destroying locust[g] has eaten.

5   Wake up, you drunkards,[h] and weep;
    wail, all you wine drinkers,
    because of the sweet wine,
    for it has been taken
       from your mouth.
6   For a nation has invaded my land,[i]
    powerful and without number;
    its teeth are the teeth of a lion,
    and it has the fangs of a lioness.[j]
7   It has devastated my grapevine
    and splintered my fig tree.
    It has stripped off its bark
       and thrown it away;
    its branches have turned white.
8   Grieve like a young woman dressed
       in sackcloth,[k]
    mourning for the husband
       of her youth.
9   Grain and drink offerings have been
       cut off[l]
    from the house of the LORD;
    the priests, who are ministers
       of the LORD, mourn.[m]
10 The fields are destroyed;[n]
    the land grieves;
    indeed, the grain is destroyed;
    the new wine is dried up;[o]
    and the fresh oil fails.[p]
11 Be ashamed, you farmers,[q]
    wail, you vinedressers,[A]

over the wheat and the barley,
    because the harvest of the field
       has perished.[r]
12 The grapevine is dried up,[s]
    and the fig tree is withered;
    the pomegranate,[t] the date palm,[u]
       and the apple[v] —
    all the trees of the orchard —
       have withered.
    Indeed, human joy has dried up.[w]

13 Dress in sackcloth and lament,[x]
       you priests;[y]
    wail,[z] you ministers of the altar.
    Come and spend the night
       in sackcloth,[aa]
    you ministers of my God,
    because grain and drink offerings
    are withheld from the house
       of your God.
14 Announce a sacred fast;[ab]
    proclaim an assembly!
    Gather the elders[ac]
    and all the residents of the land
    at the house of the LORD your God,[ad]
    and cry out to the LORD.[ae]

THE DAY OF THE LORD

15 Woe because of that day![af]
    For the day of the LORD is near
    and will come as devastation
       from the Almighty.[ag]
16 Hasn't the food been cut off
    before our eyes,[ah]
    joy and gladness[ai]
    from the house of our God?
17 The seeds lie shriveled
       in their casings.[B,aj]
    The storehouses are in ruin,
    and the granaries are broken down,
    because the grain has withered away.
18 How the animals groan![ak]
    The herds of cattle wander
       in confusion
    since they have no pasture.
    Even the flocks of sheep and goats
       suffer punishment.
19 I call to you, LORD,[al]
    for fire has consumed

a 1:1 Hs 1:1; Mc 1:1; Zph 1:1
b 1:2 Hs 4:1; 5:1
c Dt 4:32; Jr 2:10; Mk 2:12
d 1:3 Ex 10:2; Jos 4:22;
   Ps 78:4
e 1:4 Ex 10:4; Jl 2:25;
   Am 4:9
f Ps 105:34; Nah 3:15-16
g Ps 78:46; Is 33:4
h 1:5 Jl 3:3
i 1:6 Jl 2:2,11,25
j Rv 9:7-8
k 1:8 Is 22:12; Jr 4:8; 6:26
l 1:9 Hs 9:4; Jl 2:14
m Hs 10:5; Jl 2:17
n 1:10 Is 24:4
o Hs 9:2
p Dt 28:51; Hs 2:8-13;
   Hg 1:11
q 1:11 Jr 14:4; 51:23; Am
   5:16

r 1:11 Is 17:11; Jr 9:12
s 1:12 Hab 3:17
t Hg 2:19
u Sg 7:8
v Sg 2:3
w Is 16:10; 24:11
x 1:13 Jr 4:8; Ezk 7:18
y Jl 2:17
z Jr 9:10
aa 1Kg 21:27
ab 1:14 Jl 2:15-16
ac Jl 1:2
ad 2Ch 20:3; Neh 9:1; Jr
   36:6,9
ae Jnh 3:8
af 1:15 Jr 30:7; Am 5:16
ag Is 13:6,9; Ezk 30:2-3; Jl
   2:1-2,11,31
ah 1:16 Is 3:7
ai Is 16:10; Jr 48:33
aj 1:17 Is 17:10-11
ak 1:18 1Kg 18:5; Jr 12:4;
   14:5-6; Hs 4:3
al 1:19 Ps 50:15; Mc 7:7

A 1:11 Or *The farmers are dismayed, the vinedressers wail*   B 1:17 Or *clods*; Hb obscure

---

1:1 The word of the LORD that came to Joel. The words that follow, then, have their source in God. Joel didn't seek this message. He was called by God—not vice versa. The King came to a servant and commanded the servant to comply.
1:4 Massive **locust** swarms had stripped the land bare. A foreign army couldn't have left the country more devastated.
1:7 The **grapevine** and the **fig tree** were two principle producers of food for the land.

1:8 Sackcloth was a rough and scratchy fabric.
1:12 For an agrarian culture like Joel's, it's not surprising that **human joy ... dried up** in the aftermath of the locust calamity.
1:13-14 Joel calls everyone to **lament**, gather at **the house of the LORD**, and **cry out to** him. The locust destruction was bad, but something worse was coming. Their work was only a prelude.

1:15 The phrase **day of the LORD** also occurs in many other prophetic books of the Old Testament (see Isa 13:6, 9; Ezek 13:5; Amos 5:18, 20; Obad 15; Zeph 1:7, 14). It often refers to a time of God's judgment in history on the sins of Israel or of other nations. It can also refer to the ultimate day of the Lord, when his judgment will be carried out on unbelievers at the end of time (see 1 Thess 5:1-5).

[a] 1:19 Jr 9:10; Am 7:4
[b] 1:20 Ps 104:21; 147:9
[c] 1Kg 17:7; 18:5
[d] 2:1 Jr 4:5; 51:27; Jl 2:15
[e] Jl 1:15; 2:11,31; 3:14
[f] 2:2 Jl 2:31; Zph 1:15
[g] Is 60:2; Zph 1:15
[h] Jl 1:6; 2:11,25
[i] Lm 1:12; Dn 9:12; 12:1; Jl 1:2
[j] Ex 10:14
[k] 2:3 Ps 97:3; Is 9:18-19
[l] Gn 2:8-15; Ezk 36:35
[m] Ex 10:5,15; Ps 105:34-35
[n] 2:4 Rv 9:7
[o] 2:5 Rv 9:9
[p] Is 5:24; 30:30
[q] 2:6 Is 13:8; Nah 2:10
[r] 2:7 Pr 30:27

[s] 2:9 Ex 10:6
[t] Jr 9:21
[u] 2:10 Ps 18:7; Nah 1:5
[v] Is 13:10; 34:4; Jr 4:23; Ezk 32:7-8; Mt 24:29; Rv 8:12
[w] Jl 3:15
[x] 2:11 Ps 46:6; Is 13:4
[y] Jl 2:25
[z] Jr 50:34; Rv 18:8
[aa] Jl 1:15; 2:31; 3:14
[ab] Ezk 22:14
[ac] 2:12 1Kg 8:35-40; 2Ch 7:14
[ad] Est 4:3
[ae] 2:13 Ps 51:17; Is 57:15
[af] Jr 41:5
[ag] Ex 34:6; Nm 14:18; 1Ch 21:15; Neh 9:17; Ps 86:15; 103:8; 145:8; Jr 18:8; Jnh 4:2
[ah] 2:14 Jnh 3:9
[ai] Hg 2:19
[aj] Jl 1:9,13
[ak] 2:15 Jl 2:1
[al] 2Kg 10:20
[am] 2:16 1Sm 16:5; 2Ch 29:5
[an] 2:15-16 2Ch 20:3; Neh 9:1; Jr 36:6,9
[ao] 2:16 Ps 19:5

the pastures of the wilderness,[a]
and flames have devoured
all the trees of the orchard.
20 Even the wild animals cry out to[A] you,[b]
for the river beds are dried up,[c]
and fire has consumed
the pastures of the wilderness.

2 Blow the horn in Zion;[d]
sound the alarm on my holy mountain!
Let all the residents
of the land tremble,
for the day of the LORD is coming;[e]
in fact, it is near —
2 a day of darkness and gloom,[f]
a day of clouds and total darkness,[g]
like the dawn spreading
over the mountains;
a great and strong people[h] appears,
such as never existed in ages past[i]
and never will again
in all the generations to come.[j]

3 A fire devours in front of them,[k]
and behind them a flame blazes.
The land in front of them
is like the garden of Eden,[l]
but behind them,
it is like a desert wasteland;[m]
there is no escape from them.
4 Their appearance is like that of horses,[n]
and they gallop like war horses.
5 They bound on the tops
of the mountains.
Their sound is like the sound of chariots,[o]
like the sound of fiery flames
consuming stubble,[p]
like a mighty army deployed for war.

6 Nations writhe in horror before them;[q]
all faces turn pale.
7 They attack as warriors attack;
they scale walls as men of war do.
Each goes on his own path,[r]
and they do not change their course.
8 They do not push each other;
each proceeds on his own path.
They dodge the arrows, never stopping.

9 They storm the city;
they run on the wall;
they climb into the houses;[s]
they enter through the windows
like thieves.[t]
10 The earth quakes before them;[u]
the sky shakes.
The sun and moon grow dark,[v]
and the stars cease their shining.[w]
11 The LORD makes his voice heard[x]
in the presence of his army.[y]
His camp is very large;
those who carry out his command
are powerful.[z]
Indeed, the day of the LORD
is terrible and dreadful[aa] —
who can endure it?[ab]

GOD'S CALL FOR REPENTANCE

12 Even now —
this is the LORD's declaration —
turn to me with all your heart,[ac]
with fasting, weeping, and mourning.[ad]
13 Tear your hearts,[ae]
not just your clothes,[af]
and return to the LORD your God.
For he is gracious and compassionate,
slow to anger,
abounding in faithful love,
and he relents
from sending disaster.[ag]
14 Who knows? He may turn and relent[ah]
and leave a blessing behind him,[ai]
so you can offer grain and wine
to the LORD your God.[aj]

15 Blow the horn in Zion![ak]
Announce a sacred fast;[al]
proclaim an assembly.
16 Gather the people;
sanctify the congregation;[am]
assemble the aged;[B,an]
gather the infants,
even babies nursing at the breast.
Let the groom leave his bedroom,[ao]
and the bride
her honeymoon chamber.

[A] 1:20 Or *animals pant for*; Hb obscure   [B] 2:16 Or *elders*

2:3-9 Who are these determined invaders? This could be either a metaphorical description of the locusts from chapter 1 or a human army. Either way, they ravage the land (2:3), make a deafening noise (2:5), and horrify those in their path (2:6). Their approach is comprehensive—all areas are covered; all exits are sealed; no escapes are left (2:7-9). **2:10-11** That **the earth quakes . . . the sky shakes . . . . The sun and moon grow dark** and

the stars cease their shining (2:10) means this is ultimately the work of God. The power of heaven was about to be unleashed on the earthly realm. It's *his* **army** in view, ready to bring *his* judgment (2:11). **2:12** In other words, God says through his prophet, repent! To repent is to change one's mind in order to reverse direction. When you realize you've taken the wrong road, the only right response is to turn around and go the other way. Such a spiritual turnaround

requires an outward manifestation of actions that matches the inward attitude, including **mourning**. **2:13-14** If you've held to prolonged unrighteous attitudes against God, you've made him your enemy. But don't run from him because he's also your only hope. **He relents from sending disaster** (2:13) and is the only source of true **blessing** (2:14). **2:16-17** Crucial to genuine repentance is heartfelt prayer.

17 Let the priests,[a] the LORD's ministers,
  weep between the portico
    and the altar.[b]
  Let them say:
  "Have pity on your people, LORD,[c]
  and do not make your inheritance
    a disgrace,[d]
  an object of scorn among the nations.
  Why should it be said
    among the peoples,
  'Where is their God?'"[e]

GOD'S RESPONSE TO HIS PEOPLE

18 Then the LORD became jealous for his
  land[f] and spared his people.[g] 19 The LORD
  answered his people:
  Look, I am about to send you
  grain, new wine, and fresh oil.[h]
  You will be satiated with them,
  and I will no longer make you
  a disgrace among the nations.[i]

20 I will drive the northerner far from you[j]
  and banish him to a dry
    and desolate land,
  his front ranks into the Dead Sea,[k]
  and his rear guard
    into the Mediterranean Sea.[l]
  His stench will rise;
  yes, his rotten smell will rise,[m]
  for he has done astonishing things.

21 Don't be afraid, land;[n]
  rejoice and be glad,
  for the LORD has done
    astonishing things.[o]
22 Don't be afraid, wild animals,
  for the wilderness pastures
    have turned green,[p]
  the trees bear their fruit,
  and the fig tree and grapevine yield
    their riches.
23 Children of Zion,[q] rejoice and be glad
  in the LORD your God,[r]
  because he gives you the autumn rain
  for your vindication.[A,s]
  He sends showers for you,
  both autumn and spring rain[t]
    as before.

24 The threshing floors will be full
    of grain,[u]
  and the vats will overflow
  with new wine and fresh oil.
25 I will repay you for the years
  that the swarming locust ate,[v]
  the young locust, the destroying locust,
  and the devouring locust —
  my great army that I sent against you.
26 You will have plenty to eat
    and be satisfied.[w]
  You will praise the name of the
    LORD your God,[x]
  who has dealt wondrously with you.[y]
  My people will never again be put
    to shame.[z]
27 You will know that I am present
    in Israel[aa]
  and that I am the LORD your God,
  and there is no other.[ab]
  My people will never again be put
    to shame.[ac]

GOD'S PROMISE OF HIS SPIRIT

28 After this[ad]
  I will pour out my Spirit[ae]
    on all humanity;[af]
  then your sons and your daughters
    will prophesy,
  your old men will have dreams,
  and your young men will see visions.
29 I will even pour out my Spirit
  on the male and female slaves
    in those days.[ag]
30 I will display wonders
  in the heavens and on the earth:[ah]
  blood, fire, and columns of smoke.
31 The sun will be turned to darkness
  and the moon to blood[ai]
  before the great and terrible day
    of the LORD comes.[aj]
32 Then everyone who calls
  on the name of the LORD will be saved,[ak]
  for there will be an escape
  for those on Mount Zion
    and in Jerusalem,
  as the LORD promised,[al]
  among the survivors the LORD calls.

[a] 2:17 Jl 1:9
[b] Hs 10:5; Jl 1:13
[c] Is 37:20; Am 7:2,5
[d] Ps 44:13; 74:10
[e] Ps 42:3,10; 79:10; 115:2
[f] 2:18 Ezk 36:5,6; Zch 1:14; 8:2
[g] Is 60:10; 63:9,15
[h] 2:19 Jr 31:12; Hs 2:21-22
[i] Ezk 34:29; 36:15
[j] 2:20 Jr 1:14-15
[k] Zch 14:8
[l] Dt 11:24
[m] Is 34:3; Am 4:10
[n] 2:21 Jl 1:10
[o] Ps 126:2-3
[p] 2:22 Ps 65:12; Jr 9:10; Jl 1:19
[q] 2:23 Ps 149:2
[r] Is 12:2-6
[s] Dt 11:13-15
[t] Hs 6:3; Zch 10:1

[u] 2:24 Lv 26:10; Am 9:13; Mal 3:10
[v] 2:25 Jl 1:4-7; 2:2-11
[w] 2:26 Dt 11:15; Is 62:9
[x] Ps 113:1; 135:1; 148:5,13
[y] Ps 126:2; Is 25:1
[z] Is 45:17
[aa] 2:27 Jl 3:17,21
[ab] Dt 4:35,39; 1Kg 8:60; Is 45:5-6
[ac] Is 49:23
[ad] 2:28-32 Ac 2:17-21
[ae] 2:28 Is 32:15; 44:3; Ezk 39:29
[af] Is 40:5; 49:26
[ag] 2:29 1Co 12:13
[ah] 2:30 Lk 21:11,25-26
[ai] 2:31 Is 13:9-10; 34:4; Mt 24:29; Mk 13:24
[aj] Zph 1:14-16; Mal 4:1,5
[ak] 2:32 Rm 10:13
[al] Ob 17

A 2:23 Or righteousness

2:18 In view here is not the kind of sinful jealousy or envy that God condemns in us (as
in Rom 13:13; 2 Cor 12:20; Gal 5:20). Instead,
this is the **jealous[y]** of a faithful husband
who prizes his bride and won't let anyone
harm her.
2:20 The description of **the northerner** here
seems to indicate that those described in
2:2-9 were people and not locusts. Therefore,
this is likely a reference to an eschatological

event when God will protect Israel from invading armies (see, e.g., Dan 11:36-45).
2:28-32 Peter quotes this passage in his great
sermon delivered on the first Pentecost following Christ's ascension (see Acts 2:17-21).
It's a fitting mention in Acts because there the
Lord began to fulfill this promise to **pour out
[his] Spirit on all humanity** (Joel 2:28). Moses
had desired that God might do such a thing
(see Num 11:29). And indeed, on Pentecost,

the initial fulfillment began among the Jews
and then spread as Gentiles were brought
into the church (see Acts 10:44-48).
  The Holy Spirit isn't reserved for the Jews
only or for a select group of believers. There
are no second-class Christians who receive
only partial membership in the church. God's
Spirit is available to all who receive Christ as
their Savior.

a 3:1 Jr 32:44; 33:7,11; Ezk 39:25
b 3:2 Is 66:18; Mc 4:12
c Jl 3:12,14
d Is 66:16; Jr 25:31
e Jr 50:17; Ezk 34:6
f Ezk 35:10; 36:1-5
g 3:3 Ob 11; Nah 3:10
h Am 2:6
i 3:4 Am 1:9; Zch 9:2-4
j Am 1:6-8; Zch 9:5-7
k Ps 28:4
l 3:5 1Kg 20:6; 2Ch 36:19; Lm 1:10-11
m 3:6 Is 66:19; Ezk 27:13
n 3:7 Zch 9:13
o 3:8 Is 14:2; 60:14
p Jb 1:15; Ps 72:10; Ezk 38:13
q 3:9 Jr 51:27-28
r Jr 6:4; Mc 3:5
s Is 8:9-10; Jr 46:3-4; Zch 14:2-3
t 3:10 Is 2:4; Mc 4:3
u 3:11 Ezk 38:15-16
v Is 13:3

w 3:12 Ps 7:6; 98:9; Is 3:13
x 3:13 Jr 51:33; Hs 6:11
y Is 63:3; Lm 1:15
z Gn 18:20; Rv 19:14-16
aa 3:14 Is 34:2-8
ab Jl 1:15; 2:1,11
ac 3:15 Jl 2:10,31
ad 3:16 Hs 11:10; Am 1:2
ae Jr 25:30; Am 1:2
af Ezk 38:19; Jl 2:10; Hg 2:6
ag Ps 46:1; 62:8; Pr 14:26
ah Jr 16:19; Nah 1:7
ai 3:17 Ex 6:7; 29:46; Ezk 20:20
aj Is 11:9; 56:7; Ezk 20:40
ak Is 4:3; Ob 17
al Is 52:1; Nah 1:15
am 3:18 Am 9:13
an Ex 3:8
ao Is 30:25; 35:6
ap Ezk 47:1-12
aq Nm 25:1; Ezk 47:8
ar 3:19 Ob 10
as 3:20 Ezk 37:25; Am 9:15
at 3:21 Is 4:4

JUDGMENT OF THE NATIONS

3 Yes, in those days and at that time,
　　when I restore the fortunes of Judah
　　　and Jerusalem,*a*
2　I will gather all the nations*b*
　　and take them to the Valley
　　　of Jehoshaphat.*A,C*
　I will enter into judgment
　　with them there*d*
　because of my people,
　　my inheritance Israel.
　The nations have scattered
　　the Israelites
　　in foreign countries*e*
　and divided up my land.*f*
3　They cast lots for my people;*g*
　　they bartered a boy for a prostitute
　　and sold a girl for wine to drink.*h*

4 And also: Tyre,*i* Sidon, and all the territories of Philistia*j* — what are you to me? Are you paying me back or trying to get even with me? I will quickly bring retribution on your heads.*k* 5 For you took my silver and gold and carried my finest treasures*l* to your temples. 6 You sold the people of Judah and Jerusalem to the Greeks*m* to remove them far from their own territory. 7 Look, I am about to rouse them up from the place where you sold them;*n* I will bring retribution on your heads. 8 I will sell your sons and daughters to the people of Judah,*o* and they will sell them to the Sabeans,*B,p* to a distant nation, for the LORD has spoken.

9　Proclaim this among the nations:*q*
　　Prepare for holy war;*r*
　　rouse the warriors;*s*
　　let all the men of war advance
　　　and attack!
10　Beat your plows into swords
　　and your pruning knives into spears.*t*
　　Let even the weakling say, "I am
　　　a warrior."
11　Come quickly,*c* all
　　　you surrounding nations;
　　gather yourselves.*u*
　　Bring down
　　　your warriors there, LORD.*v*

12　Let the nations be roused
　　and come to the Valley
　　　of Jehoshaphat,
　　for there I will sit down

　to judge all
　　the surrounding nations.*w*
13　Swing the sickle
　　because the harvest is ripe.*x*
　Come and trample the grapes
　　because the winepress is full;*y*
　the wine vats overflow
　　because the wickedness
　　　of the nations is extreme.*z*

14　Multitudes, multitudes*aa*
　　in the valley of decision!
　For the day of the LORD is near*ab*
　　in the valley of decision.
15　The sun and moon will grow dark,
　　and the stars will cease
　　　their shining.*ac*
16　The LORD will roar from Zion*ad*
　　and make his voice heard
　　　from Jerusalem;*ae*
　heaven and earth will shake.*af*
　But the LORD will be a refuge
　　for his people,*ag*
　a stronghold for the Israelites.*ah*

ISRAEL BLESSED

17　Then you will know
　　that I am the LORD your God,*ai*
　who dwells in Zion, my holy mountain.*aj*
　Jerusalem will be holy,*ak*
　and foreigners will never
　　overrun it again.*al*
18　In that day
　　the mountains will drip
　　　with sweet wine,*am*
　and the hills will flow with milk.*an*
　All the streams of Judah will flow
　　with water,*ao*
　and a spring will issue
　　from the LORD's house,*ap*
　watering the Valley of Acacias.*D,aq*
19　Egypt will become desolate,
　　and Edom a desert wasteland,
　because of the violence done
　　to the people of Judah*ar*
　in whose land they shed
　　innocent blood.
20　But Judah will be inhabited forever,*as*
　　and Jerusalem from generation
　　　to generation.
21　I will pardon their bloodguilt,*E,at*
　　which I have not pardoned,
　　for the LORD dwells in Zion.

---

^A 3:2 = The LORD Will Judge　　^B 3:8 Probably the south Arabian kingdom of Sheba (modern Yemen)　　^C 3:11 LXX, Syr, Tg read *Gather yourselves and come*; Hb obscure　　^D 3:18 Or *Shittim*　　^E 3:21 LXX, Syr read *I will avenge their blood*

3:12-14 Since there's no known **Valley of Jehoshaphat** (3:12) and it's also referred to as **the valley of decision** (3:14), it's likely the site of the end-time battle of Armageddon (see Rev 16:16), meaning "hill or mount of Megiddo." Megiddo was the site of many significant battles (e.g., Judg 5:19; 2 Kgs 9:27; 23:29-30).
3:19-20 The day of the Lord will bring judgment and destruction on God's enemies but blessing and deliverance for his people.

AMOS

INTRODUCTION

Author

AMOS WAS NOT A PROPHET by vocation; he was a sheep breeder (1:1). God took him from the flock and commanded him to prophesy against Israel (7:14). Thus, he ministered to the northern kingdom, even though Amos himself was from Judah. His hometown was Tekoa, a village located about ten miles south of Jerusalem (1:1). Tekoa was in the hill country, a rugged area that required its citizens to be just as rugged in order to make the land work for them. According to 2 Chronicles 11:5-11, Tekoa was fortified by Rehoboam, king of Judah, as a defense city for Jerusalem. Amos prophesied in the eighth century BC, during the reigns of King Uzziah (792–740 BC) of Judah and King Jeroboam II (793–753 BC) of Israel.

Historical Background

The time period during the reigns of Uzziah and Jeroboam II was one of prosperity and military success for both Israel and Judah. Samaria, the capital city of Israel, for instance, experienced wealth and luxury; however, this was accompanied by idolatry and moral decline. As a result, Amos cried out against Samaria's wickedness and self-indulgence (Amos 3:9; 4:1; 6:1; 8:14). Though its leaders experienced prosperity, the poor were exploited (2:6; 3:10; 4:1; 5:11; 8:4-6). It was against this nation—bereft of righteousness and full of corruption and idolatry—that Amos was sent to prophesy, "Let justice flow like water, and righteousness, like an unfailing stream" (5:24).

Message and Purpose

The prophecy of Amos was delivered to the people in the northern kingdom of Israel who appeared to be experiencing kingdom blessings. But God had a message for them: prosperity does not imply kingdom blessing when it is mixed with rebellion against him. Amos's readers were actually living under God's displeasure because they enjoyed the benefits of prosperity while ignoring the disenfranchised among them. They celebrated their affluence while being unjust to those who didn't enjoy the same economic and social status.

Amos was very direct in telling the people they could not enjoy kingdom benefits without living kingdom lives. God expects his people to be a blessing; we should not simply use his blessings for selfish indulgence. The people needed to learn that living under God's kingdom rule was to be done in an obedient and generous way.

Amos also prophesied about the day when a restored remnant of Israel would be the means through whom God would bring blessing to all people. Amos shows how God uses those living under his kingdom plan to accomplish his promises of blessing.

www.bhpublishinggroup.com/qr/te/30_00

Outline

a 1:1 2Kg 3:4; Am 7:14-15
b 2Sm 14:2; Jr 6:1
c 2Kg 15:1-7; 2Ch 26:1-23;
Is 1:1; Hs 1:1
d 2Kg 14:23-29
e Zch 14:5
f 1:2 Is 42:13; Jr 25:30; Jl
3:16; Am 3:8
g Is 24:4-7; Jr 12:4; 23:10; Jl
1:10,18-19
h Am 9:3
i 1:3 Is 17:1-3
j Pr 30:15-29; Am 2:1,4,6
k 1:4 2Kg 8:11-15;
13:3,22,24
l 1:5 Gn 22:17; Neh 1:3; Lm
2:9; Hs 11:6; Nah 3:13
m 2Kg 16:9; Am 9:7
n 1:6 Jr 47:1,4-5; Ezk
25:15-17

o 1:8 2Ch 26:6; Am 3:9;
Zch 9:6
p Jr 47:5; Zph 2:4
q Is 14:29-31; Ezk 25:16
r 1:9 Is 23; Ezk 26:1-28:19
s 1Kg 5:1,12; 9:11-14
t 1:10 Zch 9:4
u 1:11 Jr 49:8-22; Ezk
25:12-14
v Nm 20:14; Dt 2:4; 23:7;
Ob 10-14
w Gn 37:33; Ps 7:2; Hs 5:14
x 1:12 Jr 49:7,20
y 1:13 Jr 49:1-6; Ezk 25:1-7;
Zph 2:8-11

1 The words of Amos, who was one of the sheep breeders[A],[a] from Tekoa[b] — what he saw regarding Israel in the days of King Uzziah[c] of Judah and Jeroboam[d] son of Jehoash, king of Israel, two years before the earthquake.[e]

2 He said:

The LORD roars[f] from Zion
and makes his voice heard
    from Jerusalem;
the pastures
    of the shepherds mourn,[B],[g]
and the summit of Carmel[h] withers.

JUDGMENT ON ISRAEL'S NEIGHBORS

3 The LORD says:

I will not relent
    from punishing Damascus[i]
for three crimes, even four,[j]
because they threshed Gilead
    with iron sledges.
4 Therefore, I will send fire
    against Hazael's palace,
and it will consume
    Ben-hadad's[k] citadels.
5 I will break down the gates[C],[l]
    of Damascus.
I will cut off the ruler
    from the Valley of Aven,
and the one who wields the scepter
    from Beth-eden.
The people of Aram will be exiled
    to Kir.[m]
The LORD has spoken.

6 The LORD says:

I will not relent from punishing Gaza[n]
for three crimes, even four,
because they exiled
    a whole community,
handing them over to Edom.
7 Therefore, I will send fire
    against the walls of Gaza,

and it will consume
    its citadels.
8 I will cut off the ruler from Ashdod,[o]
and the one who wields the scepter
    from Ashkelon.[p]
I will also turn my hand
    against Ekron,
and the remainder of the Philistines[q]
    will perish.
The Lord GOD has spoken.

9 The LORD says:

I will not relent
    from punishing Tyre[r]
for three crimes, even four,
because they handed over
    a whole community of exiles
    to Edom
and broke[D] a treaty of brotherhood.[s]
10 Therefore, I will send fire[t]
    against the walls of Tyre,
and it will consume its citadels.

11 The LORD says:

I will not relent
    from punishing Edom[u]
for three crimes, even four,
because he pursued his brother
    with the sword.[v]
He stifled his compassion,
his anger tore at him[w] continually,
and he harbored
    his rage incessantly.
12 Therefore, I will send fire
    against Teman,[x]
and it will consume the citadels
    of Bozrah.

13 The LORD says:

I will not relent from punishing
    the Ammonites[y]
for three crimes, even four,
because they ripped open

[A] 1:1 Or *the shepherds*   [B] 1:2 Or *dry up*   [C] 1:5 Lit *gate bars*   [D] 1:9 Lit *and did not remember*

1:1 Apparently, this particular **earthquake** was so significant that people knew exactly what Amos was referring to. And **two years** before it, God had decided to shake things up with the power of his word.

1:3 Each vision begins with, **I will not relent from punishing _____ for three crimes, even four** (1:3, 6, 9, 11, 13; 2:1, 4, 6). Bible scholars debate what this expression means. Some think the numbers are to be added together, totaling seven, the number of completion. Thus, these nations had "maxed out" on their sins. Wickedness had reached its full measure, and they were ripe for judgment.

    Damascus was the capital of Aram (modern Syria), which bordered Israel. Their sin concerned their treatment of **Gilead**, a city

in northern Israel. Damascus was about to experience the kingdom principle of reaping what you sow (see Gal 6:7).

1:6-8 Gaza, Ashdod, Ashkelon, and **Ekron** were major Philistine cities along the Mediterranean Coast. The Philistine armies had raided communities, captured the people, and sold them as slaves **to Edom** (1:6). God condemns kidnapping and selling humans into slavery (see Exod 21:16). Moreover, he promised to curse those who cursed his people (see Gen 12:3). Thus, **fire** would descend on the Philistines (Amos 1:7).

1:9-10 King David and Hiram, a former king of **Tyre,** had established a peaceful working trade relationship between their two countries (see 2 Sam 5:11), but Tyre eventually broke the treaty

through war with Israel and turning their captives over to enemies. So, as with Gaza, Tyre's **walls** would be consumed (Amos 1:10).

1:11-12 Edom's people were the descendants of Esau, Jacob's brother. Their major cites— **Teman** and **Bozrah**—would be destroyed for their cruelty (1:12).

1:13-15 The Ammonites were also related to the Israelites. They were descendants of Lot, Abraham's nephew. The Ammonites had a long history of fighting against Israel (see Judg 10:9) and Judah (2 Chr 20:1-25). **They** even **ripped open the pregnant women of Gilead in order to enlarge their territory** (1:13)! Thus, Ammon's capital city of **Rabbah** would be destroyed, and their leaders would be carried **into exile** (1:14-15).

the pregnant women of Gilead[a]
in order to enlarge their territory.[b]

14 Therefore, I will set fire to the walls
of Rabbah,[c]
and it will consume its citadels.
There will be shouting on the day
of battle[d]
and a violent wind on the day
of the storm.[e]

15 Their king and his princes
will go into exile together.[f]
The Lord has spoken.

2 The Lord says:
I will not relent
from punishing Moab[g]
for three crimes, even four,
because he burned the bones
of the king of Edom to lime.[h]

2 Therefore, I will send fire
against Moab,
and it will consume the citadels
of Kerioth.[i]
Moab will die with a tumult,[j]
with shouting and the sound
of the ram's horn.

3 I will cut off the judge[k] from the land
and kill all its officials[l] with him.
The Lord has spoken.

JUDGMENT ON JUDAH

4 The Lord says:
I will not relent
from punishing Judah[m]
for three crimes, even four,
because they have rejected
the instruction of the Lord[n]
and have not kept his statutes.[o]
The lies[p] that
their ancestors followed[q]
have led them astray.

5 Therefore, I will send fire[r]
against Judah,
and it will consume the citadels
of Jerusalem.

JUDGMENT ON ISRAEL

6 The Lord says:
I will not relent from punishing Israel[s]
for three crimes, even four,
because they sell a righteous person
for silver

and a needy person for a pair
of sandals.[t]

7 They trample the heads of the poor[u]
on the dust of the ground
and obstruct the path of the needy.[v]
A man and his father
have sexual relations
with the same girl,[w]
profaning my holy name.[x]

8 They stretch out beside
every altar[y]
on garments taken as collateral,[z]
and in the house of their God
they drink wine obtained
through fines.[aa]

9 Yet I destroyed the Amorite[ab]
as Israel advanced;
his height[ac] was like the cedars,
and he was as sturdy as the oaks;
I destroyed his fruit[ad] above
and his roots beneath.

10 And I brought you from the land
of Egypt[ae]
and led you forty years
in the wilderness[af]
in order to possess the land
of the Amorite.[ag]

11 I raised up some of your sons
as prophets[ah]
and some of your young men
as Nazirites.[ai]
Is this not the case, Israelites?
This is the Lord's declaration.

12 But you made the Nazirites
drink wine
and commanded the prophets,
"Do not prophesy."[aj]

13 Look, I am about to crush[A] you
in your place[ak]
as a wagon crushes when full
of grain.

14 Escape will fail the swift,[al]
the strong one will not
maintain his strength,[am]
and the warrior will not save his life.

15 The archer will not stand
his ground,[an]
the one who is swift of foot
will not save himself,
and the one riding a horse will not
save his life.[ao]

[a] 1:13 2Kg 8:12; 15:16; Hs 13:16
[b] Is 5:8; Ezk 35:10
[c] 1:14 1Ch 20:1; Jr 49:2
[d] Ezk 21:22; Am 2:2
[e] Is 29:6; 30:30
[f] 1:15 Jr 49:3
[g] 2:1 Is 15–16; Jr 48; Ezk 25:8–11
[h] Lv 20:14; 21:9
[i] 2:2 Jr 48:24,41
[j] Jr 48:45
[k] 2:3 Ps 2:10; 141:6
[l] Jb 12:21; Is 40:23
[m] 2:4 2Kg 17:19; Hs 2:12; Am 3:2
[n] Jdg 2:17–20; 2Kg 22:11–17; Jr 6:19; 8:9
[o] Jr 44:10; Ezk 5:7
[p] Is 9:15–16; Jr 11:10–13; 23:14,21–22
[q] Jr 9:14; 16:11–12; Ezk 20:18,24,30
[r] 2:5 Jr 17:27; 21:10
[s] 2:6 2Kg 18:12

[t] 2:6 Dt 16:18–20; Am 5:12; 8:6
[u] 2:7 Am 5:11; 8:4; Mc 2:2,9
[v] Jb 24:4
[w] Hs 4:14
[x] Lv 18:21; Pr 30:9; Ezk 36:20–23
[y] 2:8 Am 3:14
[z] Ex 22:26
[aa] Am 4:1; 6:6
[ab] 2:9 Jos 10:12
[ac] Nm 13:28–33
[ad] Ezk 17:9; Mal 4:1
[ae] 2:10 Ex 20:2; Am 3:1; 9:7
[af] Dt 2:7
[ag] Nm 21:25
[ah] 2:11 Dt 18:18–19; Jr 1:4–5; Am 7:14–15
[ai] Nm 6:1–21; Jdg 13:2–5; 1Sm 1:11
[aj] 2:12 Jr 11:21; Am 7:13,16
[ak] 2:13 Jl 3:13
[al] 2:14 Is 30:16–17
[am] Jr 9:23
[an] 2:15 Jr 51:56; Ezk 39:3
[ao] Is 31:3

[A] 2:13 Or *hinder*; Hb obscure

2:1-3 The Moabites too were descendants of Lot. Interpreters are uncertain why Moab **burned the bones of the king of Edom to lime** (2:1), but some believe they used this lime to make plaster for their walls. In any case, it was a severe act of violence. Thus, the same **fire**

(2:2) that God was sending against the rest of Israel's neighbors (1:4, 7, 10, 12, 14) would **consume** Moab (2:2).
2:4-5 That Amos turned his prophetic arsenal in Judah's direction reminds us that God does not show partiality.

2:6-16 Since Israel wanted to act like those who don't know God, they would be treated like those who don't know God. If anyone should have known better than to do the kind of things listed here, it was those who had received God's holy Word.

*a*2:16 Jdg 4:17
*b*3:1 Am 2:10
*c*3:2 Ex 19:5-6; Dt 4:32-37
*d*Jr 14:10; Ezk 20:36; Dn 9:12
*e*3:3 Lv 26:23-24
*f*3:4 Ps 104:21; Hs 5:14; 11:10
*g*3:6 Jr 4:5,19,21; 6:1; Hs 5:8; Zph 1:16
*h*Nm 10:9; Jr 4:19; Jl 2:1
*i*Is 14:24-27; 45:7
*j*Lm 3:37-39
*k*3:7 Gn 18:17; Jr 23:18,22; Jnh 1:2
*l*3:8 Am 1:2
*m*Jnh 1:1-3; 3:1-3
*n*Jr 6:10-11; 20:9
*o*3:9 1Sm 5:1; Am 1:8
*p*Am 4:1; 6:1
*q*Am 5:11; 6:8
*r*3:10 Ps 14:3; Jr 4:22; Am 5:7; 6:12
*s*Hab 2:8-10; Zph 1:9; Zch 5:3-4

*t*3:11 Am 6:14
*u*Am 2:14
*v*2Kg 17:5-6; 18:9-12
*w*3:12 1Sm 17:34-37
*x*Ps 132:3
*y*Est 1:6; 7:8; Am 6:4
*z*3:13 Ezk 2:7
*aa*3:14 Hs 10:5-8,14-15; Am 4:4; 5:5-6; 7:10,13
*ab*Lv 8:15; 16:18-19; 1Kg 1:50-51; 2:28; Ps 118:27
*ac*Hs 10:1-2
*ad*3:15 Jr 36:22
*ae*Jdg 3:20
*af*1Kg 22:39; 2Ch 9:17; Am 6:4
*ag*Am 2:5; 6:11
*ah*4:1 Ps 22:12; Ezk 39:18
*ai*Ex 23:3,6; Lv 19:15; 25:35; Dt 15:4-11; Am 5:11; 8:6
*aj*Am 2:8; 6:6
*ak*4:2 Am 6:8; 8:7
*al*Ps 89:35
*am*Is 37:29; Ezk 38:4
*an*2Kg 19:28; 2Ch 33:10-11
*ao*4:3 Jr 52:7

16 Even the most courageous
    of the warriors
will flee naked on that day*a* —
    this is the LORD's declaration.

GOD'S REASONS FOR PUNISHING ISRAEL

3 Listen to this message that the LORD has spoken against you, Israelites, against the entire clan that I brought from the land of Egypt:*b*
2 I have known only you*c*
    out of all the clans of the earth;
therefore, I will punish you for all
    your iniquities.*d*
3 Can two walk together*e*
    without agreeing to meet?
4 Does a lion roar*f* in the forest
    when it has no prey?
Does a young lion growl from its lair
    unless it has captured something?
5 Does a bird land in a trap on the ground
    if there is no bait for it?
Does a trap spring from the ground
    when it has caught nothing?
6 If a ram's horn*g* is blown in a city,
    aren't people afraid?*h*
If a disaster*i* occurs in a city,
    hasn't the LORD done it?*j*
7 Indeed, the Lord GOD does nothing
without revealing his counsel
to his servants the prophets.*k*
8 A lion has roared;*l*
    who will not fear?
The Lord GOD has spoken;*m*
    who will not prophesy?*n*

9 Proclaim on the citadels in Ashdod*o*
and on the citadels in the land
    of Egypt:
Assemble on the mountains
    of Samaria,*p*
and see the great turmoil in the city
and the acts of oppression within it.*q*
10 The people are incapable
    of doing right*r* —
    this is the LORD's declaration —
those who store up violence
    and destruction*s*
in their citadels.

11 Therefore, the Lord GOD says:
An enemy*t* will surround the land;
he will destroy*u* your strongholds
and plunder your citadels.*v*

12 The LORD says:
As the shepherd snatches two legs
or a piece of an ear
from the lion's mouth,*w*
so the Israelites who live in Samaria
will be rescued
with only the corner of a bed*x*
or the*A* cushion*B* of a couch.*C,y*

13 Listen and testify*z* against the house
    of Jacob —
    this is the declaration
    of the Lord GOD,
    the God of Armies.
14 I will punish the altars of Bethel*aa*
on the day I punish Israel
    for its crimes;
the horns of the altar*ab* will be cut off
and fall to the ground.*ac*
15 I will demolish the winter house*ad*
and the summer house;*ae*
the houses inlaid with ivory*af*
    will be destroyed,
and the great houses*ag* will come
    to an end.
This is the LORD's declaration.

SOCIAL AND SPIRITUAL CORRUPTION

4 Listen to this message, you cows
    of Bashan*ah*
who are on the hill of Samaria,
women who oppress the poor
and crush the needy,*ai*
who say to their husbands,
    "Bring us something to drink."*aj*

2 The Lord GOD has sworn*ak* by his ho-
    liness:*al*
Look, the days are coming*D*
when you will be taken away
    with hooks,*am*
every last one of you with fishhooks.*an*
3 You will go through breaches
    in the wall,*ao*

---

*A*3:12 Or *Israelites will be rescued, those who sit in Samaria on a corner of a bed or a*   *B*3:12 Hb obscure   *C*3:12 LXX, Aq, Sym, Theod, Syr, Tg, Vg read *or in Damascus*   *D*4:2 Lit *coming on you*

3:1-2 Israel's relationship to God makes their wicked behavior astounding. Their rejection of the God who saved them couldn't go unpunished.

3:3-6 The point here is that when disaster comes upon Israel, they can rest assured that it is the Lord's judgment on their sin.

3:10-11 **The people** had persisted in sin for so long that it became second nature to them. Since **violence and destruction** were what they understood (3:10), violence and destruction were what they would get (3:11). This prophecy came to pass when the Assyrians captured Samaria in 722 BC

and carried the people into captivity (see 2 Kgs 17:6).

4:1 What a contrast these lazy, demanding **women** were to the "wife of noble character" in Proverbs 31: she feared the Lord, served her family, and ministered to the poor (see Prov 31:10-31).

each woman straight ahead,
and you will be driven along
  toward Harmon.
    This is the LORD's declaration.

4   Come to Bethel and rebel;
rebel even more at Gilgal!*a*
Bring your sacrifices
  every morning,*b*
your tenths every three days.
5   Offer leavened bread as
  a thank offering,*c*
and loudly proclaim
  your freewill offerings,*d*
for that is what you Israelites
  love to do!*e*
    This is the declaration
    of the Lord GOD.

GOD'S DISCIPLINE AND ISRAEL'S APOSTASY

6   I gave you absolutely nothing
  to eat^A,*f*
in all your cities,
a shortage of food in all
  your communities,
yet you did not return to me.*g*
    This is the LORD's declaration.

7   I also withheld the rain from you*h*
while there were still three months
  until harvest.
I sent rain on one city
but no rain on another.*i*
One field received rain
while a field with no rain withered.*j*
8   Two or three cities staggered
to another city to drink water*k*
but were not satisfied,*l*
yet you did not return*m* to me.
    This is the LORD's declaration.

9   I struck you with blight and mildew;*n*
the locust devoured*o*
your many gardens and vineyards,
your fig trees and olive trees,*p*
yet you did not return to me.*q*
    This is the LORD's declaration.

10   I sent plagues like those of Egypt;*r*
I killed your young men
  with the sword,*s*

along with your captured horses.*t*
I caused the stench of your camp
to fill your nostrils,*u*
yet you did not return to me.*v*
    This is the LORD's declaration.

11   I overthrew some of you
as I^B overthrew Sodom
  and Gomorrah,*w*
and you were like a burning stick
snatched from a fire,*x*
yet you did not return to me*y* —
    This is the LORD's declaration.

12   Therefore, Israel, that is what
  I will do to you,
and since I will do that to you,
Israel, prepare to meet your God!*z*
13   He is here:
the one who forms
  the mountains,*aa*
creates the wind,*ab*
and reveals his thoughts to man,*ac*
the one who makes the dawn
  out of darkness
and strides on the heights
  of the earth.*ad*
The LORD, the God of Armies,
  is his name.*ae*

LAMENTATION FOR ISRAEL

5 Listen to this message that I am singing for you, a lament,*af* house of Israel:
2   She has fallen;
Virgin Israel*ag* will never rise again.*ah*
She lies abandoned on her land
with no one to raise her up.*ai*
3 For the Lord GOD says:
The city that marches out
  a thousand strong
will have only a hundred left,*aj*
and the one that marches out
  a hundred strong
will have only ten left*ak* in the house
  of Israel.

SEEK GOD AND LIVE

4 For the LORD says to the house of Israel:
Seek me and live!*al*
5   Do not seek Bethel*am*
or go to Gilgal*an*
or journey to Beer-sheba,*ao*

---

a 4:4 Am 5:5
b Am 5:21-22
c 4:5 Lv 7:12
d Lv 22:18-21
e Jr 7:9-10; Hs 9:1,10
f 4:6 Is 3:1; Jr 14:18
g Is 9:13; Jr 5:3; Hg 2:17
h 4:7 Jr 3:1-3; 5:23-25
i Ex 9:4,26; 10:22-23
j Lv 26:18-19; Jl 1:10-12
k 4:8 1Kg 18:5; Jr 14:4
l Ezk 4:16; Hg 1:6
m Jr 3:7
n 4:9 Dt 28:22; Hg 2:17
o Jl 1:4; Am 7:1-2
p Dt 28:38-42; Jl 1:4-7,12
q Jr 3:10
r 4:10 Ex 11:4-5; Dt 28:27,60
s Jr 11:22; 18:21; 48:15

t 4:10 2Kg 13:3,7
u Is 34:3
v Is 9:13
w 4:11 Gn 19:24-25
x Zch 3:1-2
y Is 9:13
z 4:12 Is 32:11; 64:2; Jr 5:22
aa 4:13 Jb 38:4-7; Ps 65:6; Is 40:12
ab Ps 135:7
ac Ps 139:2; Dn 2:30
ad Mc 1:3
ae Am 5:8-9,27; 9:5-6
af 5:1 Jr 7:29; 9:10,17; Ezk 19:1
ag 5:2 Jr 14:17; 31:4,21
ah Am 8:14
ai Is 51:18
aj 5:3 Is 6:13
ak Am 6:9
al 5:4 Dt 4:29; 32:46-47
am 5:5 1Kg 12:28-29
an 1Sm 7:16; 11:14
ao Gn 21:31-33

---

^A 4:6 Lit *you cleanness of teeth*   ^B 4:11 Lit *God*

4:4-5 When the nation split into northern and southern kingdoms, King Jeroboam of Israel built an altar at **Bethel** (4:4) and made two golden calves for the people to worship in order to prevent them from traveling to the temple in Judah (see 1 Kgs 12:25-33). This was in direct violation of the Mosaic law. Amos sarcastically encourages his audience to continue in the idolatry they love so that they can see where devotion to false gods ends. 4:6-12 Israel had been given chance after chance to repent, disciplined in various ways designed to correct their bad behavior (4:6-11). Now, the gloves were coming off (4:12). 5:2 Israel had turned away from the only one who could have helped them.

^a5:6 Is 55:3,6-7
^bDt 4:24; 32:22; Heb 12:29
^cIs 33:14; 66:24; Jr 4:4
^d5:7 Am 6:12
^e5:8 Jb 9:9; 38:31
^fGn 1:2-3; Jb 38:12
^gAm 8:9
^hPs 104:6-9; Jr 10:13
ⁱJb 36:27-30
^jAm 4:13; 9:5-6
^k5:9 Is 29:5
^lMc 5:11
^m5:10 Is 29:21
ⁿIs 59:15
^o5:11 Am 3:9; 8:6; Jms 1:27
^pAm 3:15; 6:11
^qDt 28:30; Mc 6:15; Zph 1:13
^r5:12 Is 1:23; 5:23
^sAm 2:6-7

^t5:13 Ec 3:7; Hs 4:4
^u5:14 Is 48:1-2
^v5:15 Rm 12:9
^wIs 1:17
^xJl 2:14
^yMc 3:5,7-8
^z5:16 Jr 9:10,18-20; Am 8:3
^{aa}Jl 1:11
^{ab}Jr 9:17
^{ac}5:17 Is 16:10; Jr 48:33
^{ad}Ex 12:12
^{ae}5:18 Is 5:19; Jl 1:15; 2:1,11,31
^{af}Is 5:30
^{ag}5:19 Jb 20:24; Is 24:17; Jr 15:2-3
^{ah}5:20 Is 13:10; Zph 1:15
^{ai}Jl 2:2; Zph 1:15

for Gilgal will certainly go
　　into exile,
and Bethel will come to nothing.
6 Seek the LORD^a and live,
　　or he will spread like fire^b
　　throughout the house of Joseph;
it will consume everything
　　with no one at Bethel
　　to extinguish it.^c
7 Those who turn justice
　　into wormwood^d
also throw righteousness
　　to the ground.

8 The one who made the Pleiades
　　and Orion,^e
who turns darkness^A into dawn^f
and darkens day into night,^g
who summons the water
　　of the sea^h
and pours it out over the surface
　　of the earthⁱ —
the LORD is his name.^j
9 He brings destruction^B
　　on the strong,^{C,k}
and it falls on the fortress.^l

10 They hate the one who convicts
　　the guilty^m
　　at the city gate,
and they despiseⁿ the one
　　who speaks with integrity.
11 Therefore, because you trample on
　　the poor^o
and exact a grain tax from him,
you will never live in the houses
　　of cut stone^p
you have built;
you will never drink the wine
from the lush vineyards
you have planted.^q
12 For I know your crimes
　　are many
and your sins innumerable.
They oppress the righteous,^r
　　take a bribe,
and deprive the poor of justice^s
　　at the city gates.

13 Therefore, those who have insight
　　will keep silent^{D,t}
at such a time,
for the days are evil.

14 Pursue good and not evil
so that you may live,
and the LORD, the God of Armies,
will be with you
as you have claimed.^u
15 Hate evil and love good;^v
establish justice
　　in the city gate.^w
Perhaps the LORD, the God
　　of Armies, will be gracious^x
to the remnant of Joseph.^y

16 Therefore the LORD, the God of Armies,
the Lord, says:
There will be wailing in all
　　the public squares;^z
they will cry out in anguish^E in all
　　the streets.
The farmer will be called on
　　to mourn,^{aa}
and professional mourners^{F,ab}
　　to wail.
17 There will be wailing in all
　　the vineyards,^{ac}
for I will pass among you.^{ad}
The LORD has spoken.

THE DAY OF THE LORD

18 Woe to you who long for the day
　　of the LORD!^{ae}
What will the day of the LORD
　　be for you?
It will be darkness and not light.^{af}
19 It will be like a man who flees
　　from a lion^{ag}
only to have a bear confront him.
He goes home and rests his hand
　　against the wall
only to have a snake bite him.
20 Won't the day of the LORD
be darkness rather than light,^{ah}
even gloom without any brightness
　　in it?^{ai}

^A5:8 Or turns the shadow of death　^B5:9 Hb obscure　^C5:9 Or stronghold　^D5:13 Or who are prudent will perish　^E5:16 Lit will say, "Alas! Alas!"
^F5:16 Lit and those skilled in lamentation

5:6 Jesus put **seek the LORD and live** this way: "Seek first the kingdom of God and his righteousness" (Matt 6:33). This, in fact, is the only path to blessing.

Seeking God and his kingdom is not a one-day-a-week activity. It's a daily attempt to adopt God's perspective on life as revealed in his Word. And it includes living out that perspective. **5:14-17** God's promise was plain for all who would hear: **Pursue good and not evil so** **that you may live, and the LORD . . . will be with you** (5:14). Since Israel wouldn't listen, their future would include **wailing**, cries of **anguish**, and mourning (5:16-17). **5:18-19** The **day of the LORD** is a theme that occurs in many of the prophetic books; frequently, it refers to times in history when God carried out acts of judgment. The phrase also describes the day of God's ultimate judgment at the end of history (see

1 Thess 5:1-5). While some Israelites looked forward to the day when God's vengeance would be unleashed on the pagan nations, Israel themselves had become a pagan nation! Thus, the thing they anticipated would not be a day of **light** and blessing but a day of **darkness** and judgment (5:18). Its arrival would be akin to narrowly escaping the jaws of a **lion** only to be mauled by a **bear** (5:19).

[a] 5:21 Is 1:11-16; 66:3; Am 6:8
[b] Lv 26:31; Jr 14:12; Hs 5:6

[c] 5:22 Mc 6:6-7
[d] Jr 14:12
[e] Lv 7:11-15
[f] 5:23 Is 5:12
[g] 5:21-24 Mc 6:6-8
[h] 5:25 Dt 32:17; Jos 24:14; Neh 9:18-21; Ac 7:42-43
[i] 5:26 Is 44:12-20
[j] 5:25-27 2Kg 17:5-6; Ac 7:42-43
[k] 5:27 Am 4:13
[l] 6:1 Is 32:9-11; Zph 1:12
[m] 6:2 Gn 10:10; Is 10:9
[n] 1Kg 8:65; 2Kg 18:34; Is 10:9
[o] 1Sm 5:8; 2Ch 26:6
[p] 6:3 Am 9:10
[q] Am 3:10

⮞ KINGDOM LIVING ⮜
COMMUNITY
Biblical Justice and the Poor

Repeatedly throughout Scripture, God reveals himself as a defender and deliverer. The Israelites' exodus out of Egypt dramatically portrays God's execution of biblical justice on behalf of a group of oppressed people. Later, when God gave his laws to Israel, he reminded them of this deliverance. He said, "You must not exploit a resident alien or oppress him, since you were resident aliens in the land of Egypt" (Exod 22:21).

God regularly tied either a presence or an absence of biblical justice to a presence or absence of his blessing. For example, Israel's worship was rejected because of an absence of justice in society (see Amos 5:21-24). The Israelites were taken into captivity and held in bondage because of their rebellion against God. He had repeatedly told them to turn from their sin and practice justice and righteousness, to pay back what was stolen, and to secure every pledge (see Ezek 33:10-33).

The destruction of Sodom and Gomorrah, as another example, is often attributed solely to the blatant practice of homosexuality; however, God also links his wrath to their lack of concern for "the poor" (Ezek 16:49). The prophets of the Old Testament regularly condemned the people for their social injustices as well. These social condemnations were not merely viewed as secular affronts to communities but also a spiritual affront to God (see Zech 7:9-12).

Believers are to execute divine justice on behalf of the defenseless, poor, and oppressed; and they are to influence the culture to do the same. Scripture relates biblical justice distinctly to these groups as a primary concern because they most represent the helpless in society and bear the brunt of injustices.

FOR THE NEXT COMMUNITY
KINGDOM LIVING LESSON SEE PAGE 1053.

21 I hate, I despise, your feasts![a]
    I can't stand the stench
    of your solemn assemblies.[b]

⬳ HOPE WORDS ⬲
Be careful never to be doing so much for God that you miss him in the process.

22 Even if you offer me
    your burnt offerings
        and grain offerings,[c]
    I will not accept them;[d]
    I will have no regard
    for your fellowship offerings
        of fattened cattle.[e]
23 Take away from me the noise
        of your songs!
    I will not listen to the music
        of your harps.[f]
24 But let justice flow like water,
    and righteousness,
        like an unfailing stream.[g]

25 "House of Israel, was it sacrifices and grain offerings that you presented to me during the forty years in the wilderness?[h] 26 But you have taken up[A] Sakkuth your king and Kaiwan your star god,[B] images you have made for yourselves.[i] 27 So I will send you into exile beyond Damascus."[j] The Lord, the God of Armies, is his name.[k] He has spoken.

WOE TO THE COMPLACENT

6 Woe to those who are at ease in Zion[l]
    and to those who feel secure
        on the hill of Samaria —
    the notable people in this first
        of the nations,
    those the house of Israel
        comes to.
2   Cross over to Calneh[m] and see;
    go from there to great Hamath;[n]
    then go down to Gath[o]
        of the Philistines.
    Are you better than
        these kingdoms?
    Is their territory larger
        than yours?
3   You dismiss any thought
        of the evil day[p]
    and bring in a reign of violence.[q]

[A] 5:26 Or *you will lift up*   [B] 5:26 LXX reads *taken up the tent of Molech and the star of your god Rephan*; Ac 7:43

5:21-24 God hated the religious practices of Israel and refused to accept them (5:21-23). Why? Because **justice** was absent from Israelite society (5:24). This is a reminder that you can't worship God on Sunday and despise your neighbor on Monday. You can't

read your Bible in private and then oppress your brother in public.

Martin Luther King Jr. underscored the connection between having faith in God and doing works of righteousness when he quoted Amos 5:24 in his "I Have a Dream" speech.

6:2 Israel had done everything they could to look just like everyone else. Therefore, they would be carried into captivity by the same instrument of God's power (Assyria) that had destroyed all these other places.

a 6:4 Am 3:15
b Am 3:12
c Ezk 34:2-3
d 6:5 Am 5:23; 8:10
e 1Ch 15:16
f 6:6 Am 2:8; 4:1
g Jr 8:21; Lm 2:11
h 6:7 Am 7:11,17
i 1Kg 20:16-21; Dn 5:4-6,30
j 6:8 Gn 22:16; Jr 22:5; 51:14
k Lv 26:30; Dt 32:19; Ps
106:40
l Am 3:10-11
m Hs 11:6
n 6:9 Am 5:3
o 6:10 1Sm 31:12; 2Ch
16:14; Jr 34:5
p Is 48:1; Jr 44:26; Hs 4:15
q 6:11 Am 1:1; 9:9
r 6:12 1Kg 21:7-13; Is
59:13-14
s Is 5:20; Am 5:7; Rv 8:11

t 6:13 Jb 8:14-15; Ps 2:2-4;
Lk 12:19-20
u Ps 75:4; Is 28:14-15
v 6:14 Am 3:11
w Nm 34:7-8; 2Kg 14:25
x 7:1 Ex 10:12-15; Dt
28:38,42; Jl 1:4
y 7:2 Ex 10:15
z Jr 14:7,20-21; Ezk 9:8;
11:13
aa Is 37:4; Jr 42:2
ab 7:3 Jr 26:19; Hs 11:8
ac 7:4 Am 1:3-2:5
ad 7:5 Ps 85:4; Jl 2:17
ae 7:6 Ps 106:45; Jnh 3:10
af 7:8 Jr 1:11; Am 8:2
ag Is 28:17; 34:11; Lm 2:8
ah Am 8:2
ai 7:9 2Kg 17:9-13; Hs 10:8
aj Lv 26:31; Is 63:18; Jr 51:51

4 They lie on beds inlaid with ivory,*a*
sprawled out on their couches,*b*
and dine on lambs from the flock*c*
and calves from the stall.
5 They improvise songs*A* to the sound
of the harp*d*
and invent*8* their own
musical instruments like David.*e*
6 They drink wine by the bowlful*f*
and anoint themselves
with the finest oils
but do not grieve over the ruin
of Joseph.*g*
7 Therefore, they will now go
into exile
as the first of the captives,*h*
and the feasting*i* of those
who sprawl out
will come to an end.

ISRAEL'S PRIDE JUDGED

8 The Lord God has sworn by himself*j* —
this is the declaration of the Lord, the God
of Armies:
I loathe Jacob's pride*k*
and hate his citadels,*l*
so I will hand over the city*m*
and everything in it.

9 And if there are ten men left in one
house, they will die.*n* **10** A close relative*c*
and burner*D,o* will remove his corpse*E* from
the house. He will call to someone in the
inner recesses of the house, "Any more
with you?"
That person will reply, "None."
Then he will say, "Silence, because the
Lord's name must not be invoked."*p*
11 For the Lord commands:
The large house will be smashed
to pieces,
and the small house to rubble.*q*

12 Do horses gallop on the cliffs?
Does anyone plow there with oxen?*F*
Yet you have turned justice
into poison*r*
and the fruit of righteousness
into wormwood*s* —

13 you who rejoice over Lo-debar*t*
and say, "Didn't we capture Karnaim
for ourselves by our own strength?"*u*
14 But look, I am raising up a nation
against you, house of Israel*v* —
this is the declaration of the Lord,
the God of Armies —
and they will oppress you
from the entrance of Hamath*G,W*
to the Brook of the Arabah.*H*

FIRST VISION: LOCUSTS

7 The Lord God showed me this: He
was forming a swarm of locusts*x* at
the time the spring crop first began to
sprout — after the cutting of the king's
hay. **2** When the locusts finished eating the
vegetation of the land,*y* I said, "Lord God,
please forgive!*z* How will Jacob survive
since he is so small?"*aa*
3 The Lord relented concerning this.*ab* "It
will not happen," he said.

SECOND VISION: FIRE

4 The Lord God showed me this: The Lord
God was calling for a judgment by fire.*ac*
It consumed the great deep and devoured
the land. **5** Then I said, "Lord God, please
stop!*ad* How will Jacob survive since he is
so small?"
6 The Lord relented concerning this.*ae*
"This will not happen either," said the
Lord God.

THIRD VISION: A PLUMB LINE

7 He showed me this: The Lord was standing there by a vertical wall with a plumb
line in his hand. **8** The Lord asked me,
"What do you see, Amos?"*af*
I replied, "A plumb line."
Then the Lord said, "I am setting a plumb
line among my people Israel;*ag* I will no
longer spare them:*ah*
9 Isaac's high places*ai* will be deserted,
and Israel's sanctuaries
will be in ruins;*aj*
I will rise up
against the house of Jeroboam
with a sword."

A 6:5 Hb obscure   *B* 6:5 Or *compose on*   *C* 6:10 Lit *His uncle*   *D* 6:10 A burner of incense, a memorial fire, or a body; Hb obscure
E 6:10 Lit *remove bones*   *F* 6:12 Some emend to *plow the sea*   *G* 6:14 Or *from Lebo-hamath*   *H* 6:14 Probably the Valley of Zared at the southeast
end of the Dead Sea

6:4-6 This enjoyment of luxury was clearly
at the expense of the poor (see 2:7; 4:1; 5:11).
6:8 God hates all sin, but he especially hates
pride. That was the sin of Satan, who wanted
to be like God (see Isa 14:12-14). It's not surprising, then, for God to say, **I loathe Jacob's
pride.** God's people are to reflect his character—not the devil's.

7:1-3 In response to Amos's prayers, **the Lord
relented** (7:3, 6). Just as he did with Abraham
(Gen 18:16-33), God shared his plans with
a kingdom man. And just as Abraham did,
Amos—this kingdom man—interceded so
that God might be merciful.
7:7-8 By holding a plumb line, one could
determine whether a wall was vertically

straight. When the Lord told Amos, **I am setting a plumb line among my people Israel,**
he was implying that Israel was morally
crooked (7:8).

AMAZIAH'S OPPOSITION

10 Amaziah the priest[a] of Bethel sent word to King Jeroboam of Israel, saying, "Amos has conspired against you[b] right here in the house of Israel. The land cannot endure all his words, **11** for Amos has said this: 'Jeroboam will die by the sword, and Israel will certainly go into exile from its homeland.'"[c]

12 Then Amaziah said to Amos, "Go away, you seer![d] Flee to the land of Judah. Earn your living[A] and give your prophecies there, **13** but don't ever prophesy[e] at Bethel again, for it is the king's sanctuary[f] and a royal temple."

14 So Amos answered Amaziah, "I was[B] not a prophet or the son of a prophet;[c,g] rather, I was[B] a herdsman,[h] and I took care of sycamore figs. **15** But the LORD took me from following the flock[i] and said to me, 'Go, prophesy to my people Israel.'"[j]

16 Now hear the word of the LORD. You say:

Do not prophesy[k] against Israel;
do not preach[l] against the house
of Isaac.

17 Therefore, this is what the LORD says:

Your wife will be a prostitute
in the city,[m]
your sons and daughters will fall
by the sword,[n]
and your land will be divided up
with a measuring line.
You yourself will die on pagan[D] soil,[o]
and Israel will certainly go
into exile[p]
from its homeland.

FOURTH VISION: A BASKET OF SUMMER FRUIT

8 The Lord GOD showed me this: a basket of summer fruit. **2** He asked me, "What do you see, Amos?"[q]

I replied, "A basket of summer fruit."[E,r]

The LORD said to me, "The end has come for my people Israel;[s] I will no longer spare them.[r] **3** In that day the temple[F] songs[u] will become wailing"[V] — this is the Lord GOD's declaration. "Many dead bodies, thrown everywhere! Silence!"[x]

4 Hear this, you who trample
on the needy[y]

and do away with the poor
of the land,[z]
5 asking, "When will the New Moon
be over
so we may sell grain,[aa]
and the Sabbath,
so we may market wheat?[ab]
We can reduce the measure
while increasing the price[G]
and cheat with dishonest scales.[ac]
6 We can buy the poor with silver
and the needy for a pair of sandals[ad]
and even sell the chaff!"

7 The LORD has sworn[ae] by the Pride of Jacob:[H,af]

I will never forget all their deeds.[ag]
8 Because of this,
won't the land quake[ah]
and all who dwell in it mourn?[ai]
All of it will rise like the Nile;[aj]
it will surge and then subside
like the Nile in Egypt.[ak]

9 And in that day —
this is the declaration
of the Lord GOD —
I will make the sun go down at noon;[al]
I will darken the land
in the daytime.[am]
10 I will turn your feasts
into mourning[an]
and all your songs
into lamentation;[ao]
I will cause everyone[i]
to wear sackcloth[ap]
and every head to be shaved.[aq]
I will make that grief
like mourning for an only son[ar]
and its outcome like a bitter day.

11 Look, the days are coming —
this is the declaration
of the Lord GOD —
when I will send a famine
through the land:
not a famine of bread or a thirst
for water,
but of hearing the words
of the LORD.[as]
12 People will stagger from sea to sea
and roam from north to east

[a] 7:10 1Kg 12:31-32; 13:33
[b] Jr 26:8-11; 38:4
[c] 7:11 Am 5:27
[d] 7:12 Mt 8:34
[e] 7:13 Am 2:12; Ac 4:18
[f] 1Kg 12:29; Am 7:9
[g] 7:14 2Kg 2:3; 4:38;
2Ch 19:2
[h] Am 1:1
[i] 7:15 2Sm 7:8
[j] Jr 1:7; Ezk 2:3-4
[k] 7:16 Am 2:12
[l] Mc 2:6
[m] 7:17 Hs 4:13-14
[n] Jr 14:16
[o] 2Kg 17:6; Ezk 4:13; Hs 9:3
[p] Jr 36:29-31
[q] 8:2 Am 7:8
[r] Jr 24:3
[s] Ezk 7:2-3,6
[t] Am 7:8
[u] 8:3 Am 5:23; 6:4-5
[v] Am 5:16
[w] Is 34:3; Jr 33:5; Nah 3:3
[x] Am 6:10
[y] 8:4 Am 2:7; 5:11-12

[z] 8:4 Is 10:2
[aa] 8:5 Nm 28:11; 2Kg 4:23
[ab] Ex 31:13-17
[ac] Dt 25:13-15; Pr 20:23;
Hs 12:7
[ad] 8:6 Am 2:6
[ae] 8:7 Am 4:2; 6:8
[af] Dt 33:26,29; Ps 47:4
[ag] Ps 10:11; Hs 7:2; 8:13
[ah] 8:8 Ps 18:7; 60:2; Is 5:25;
Am 1:1
[ai] Hs 4:3
[aj] Jr 46:7-8
[ak] Am 9:5
[al] 8:9 Is 13:10; Ezk 32:7;
Jl 2:10,31
[am] Is 59:9-10; Am 4:13; 5:8;
Mt 27:45
[an] 8:10 Jb 20:23; Am 5:21
[ao] Lm 5:15; Hs 2:11; Jms 4:9
[ap] Ezk 7:18
[aq] Is 22:12; Jr 48:37;
Ezk 7:18
[ar] Zch 12:10-14
[as] 8:9-11 Mc 3:6-7

[A] 7:12 Lit *Eat bread*   [B] 7:14 Or *am*   [C] 7:14 = a prophet's disciple or a member of a prophetic guild   [D] 7:17 Lit *unclean*   [E] 8:2 In Hb the word for *summer fruit* sounds like the word for *end*.   [F] 8:3 Or *palace*   [G] 8:5 Lit *reduce the ephah and make the shekel great*   [H] 8:7 = the LORD or the promised land   [I] 8:10 Lit *every waist*

7:12-13 No doubt under the king's orders Amaziah commanded Amos to quit preaching and take his prophecies to **Judah** instead (7:12). But Amos knew whose agenda he was called to follow. Like the apostles, he was to "obey God rather than people" (Acts 5:29).

8:1-3 The **basket of summer fruit** represents the completion of a full cycle from growth to harvest to consumption. Sinful Israel was ripe for judgment (8:2-3).

a 8:12 Ezk 20:3,31
b 8:13 Lm 1:18; 2:21
c 8:13 Is 41:17; Hs 2:3
d 8:14 Hs 8:5
e 1Kg 12:28-29
f Am 5:5
g Am 5:2; Jr 25:27
h 9:1 Am 3:14
i Zph 2:14
j Jos 5:13-15; Am 7:9,17
k Jr 11:11
l 9:2 Ps 139:8
m Jr 51:53; Ob 4
n 9:3 Jb 34:22; Ps 139:9-10
o Jnh 2:2-6
p Is 27:1
q 9:4 Lv 26:33
r 9:2-4 Jb 34:21-22; Ps
139:7-12; Jr 23:24
s 9:4 Jr 21:10; 44:27
t 9:5 Ps 104:32; 144:5;
Is 64:1
u Am 8:8
v 9:6 Ps 104:3,13

w 9:6 Ps 102:25; Is 48:13;
51:13
x Ps 104:6
y Am 4:13; 5:8-9
z 9:7 2Ch 14:9,12; Is 20:4;
43:3
aa Dt 2:23; Jr 47:4
ab 2Kg 16:9; Is 22:6
ac 9:8 Am 9:4
ad Am 3:12
ae Jr 5:10; 30:11; 31:35-36;
Jl 2:32
af 9:9 Is 30:28; Lk 22:31
ag 9:10 Is 33:14; Zch 13:8
ah Jr 5:12; 23:17; Am 6:3
ai 9:11 Lv 23:42-43; 2Sm
11:11; 1Kg 20:12; Is 4:6
aj 2Sm 7:11-16; Jr 23:5; Ezk
34:23-24; Zch 9:9-10; Lk
1:32; Rv 5:5
ak Is 44:26
al Is 63:11; Jr 46:26
am 9:12 Ezk 36:5; Ob 21
an 9:11-12 Is 43:6-7; Mal
1:11; Ac 15:15-18
ao 9:13 Lv 26:5

seeking the word of the LORD,*a*
but they will not find it.

13 In that day
    the beautiful young women,*b*
    the young men also, will faint
        from thirst.*c*
14 Those who swear by the guilt
        of Samaria*d*
    and say, "As your god lives, Dan,"*e*
    or, "As the way^AB
        of Beer-sheba lives"*f* —
    they will fall, never to rise again.*g*

FIFTH VISION: THE LORD BESIDE THE ALTAR

9 I saw the Lord standing beside the altar,*h* and he said:
    Strike the capitals of the pillars*i*
    so that the thresholds shake;
    knock them down on the heads
        of all the people.
    Then I will kill the rest of them
        with the sword.*j*
    None of those who flee
        will get away;*k*
    none of the fugitives will escape.
2 If they dig down to Sheol,*l*
    from there my hand will take them;
    if they climb up to heaven,*m*
    from there I will bring them down.
3 If they hide
    on the top of Carmel,
    from there I will track them down*n*
        and seize them;
    if they conceal themselves
    from my sight on the sea floor,*o*
    from there I will command
        the sea serpent to bite them.*p*
4 And if they are driven
    by their enemies into captivity,*q*
    from there I will command
        the sword to kill them.*r*
    I will keep my eye on them
    for harm and not for good.*s*

5 The Lord, the GOD of Armies —
    he touches the earth;*t*
    it melts, and all who dwell
        in it mourn;
    all of it rises like the Nile
    and subsides like the Nile of Egypt.*u*
6 He builds his upper chambers
    in the heavens*v*

and lays the foundation of his vault
    on the earth.*w*
He summons the water of the sea
    and pours it out over the surface
        of the earth.*x*
The LORD is his name.*y*

ANNOUNCEMENT OF JUDGMENT

7 Israelites, are you not
    like the Cushites to me?*z*
    This is the LORD's declaration.
    Didn't I bring Israel from the land
        of Egypt,
    the Philistines from Caphtor,*C,aa*
    and the Arameans from Kir?*ab*
8 Look, the eyes of the Lord GOD
    are on the sinful kingdom,*ac*
    and I will obliterate it
    from the face of the earth.*ad*
    However, I will not totally destroy
    the house of Jacob*ae* —
        this is the LORD's declaration —
9 for I am about to give the command,
    and I will shake the house of Israel*af*
        among all the nations,
    as one shakes a sieve,
    but not a pebble will fall
        to the ground.
10 All the sinners among my people*ag*
    who say:
    "Disaster will never overtake^D
    or confront us,"*ah*
    will die by the sword.

ANNOUNCEMENT OF RESTORATION

11 In that day
    I will restore the fallen shelter*ai*
        of David:*aj*
    I will repair its gaps,
    restore its ruins,*ak*
    and rebuild it as in the days of old,*al*
12 so that they may possess
    the remnant of Edom*am*
    and all the nations
    that bear my name^E,an —
        this is the declaration of the LORD;
        he will do this.

13 Look, the days are coming —
    this is the LORD's declaration —
    when the plowman will overtake
        the reaper*ao*
    and the one who treads grapes,

9:1-3 There will be no hiding or escaping from God's wrath when it comes.
9:7 **The Cushites** or Ethiopians were descended from Cush, the son of Ham, the son of Noah

(see Gen 9:18; 10:6). This verse, therefore, is another reminder of how strong the Jewish-African link was in biblical times (see the notes on Gen 9:18–10:1-32).

9:11 **The fallen shelter of David** is a reference to the Davidic monarchy. In the future millennial kingdom, Jesus Christ will sit on David's throne.

the sower of seed.
The mountains will drip
with sweet wine,
and all the hills will flow
with it.[a]
14 I will restore the fortunes
of my people Israel.[A,b]
They will rebuild and occupy
ruined cities,[c]

plant vineyards and drink
their wine,
make gardens and eat
their produce.[d]
15 I will plant them on their land,
and they will never again
be uprooted
from the land I have given them.[e]
The Lord your God has spoken.

[a] 9:13 Jl 2:24; 3:18
[b] 9:14 Dt 30:3; Jr 31:23; 32:42-44
[c] Jr 30:18; 33:10-11

[d] 9:14 Is 65:21; Jr 31:5
[e] 9:15 2Sm 7:10; Jr 24:6

[A] 9:14 Or restore my people Israel from captivity

9:15 In the millennial kingdom, God will restore Israel to their land, never to be removed again. Amos seals his prophecy with the following words to guarantee their truthfulness: **The Lord your God has spoken**.

OBADIAH

INTRODUCTION

Author

NOTHING IS KNOWN ABOUT OBADIAH. His common Hebrew name means "servant of the Lord."

Historical Background

Scholars are uncertain when Obadiah was written. The most likely option is that it was penned shortly after the final destruction of Jerusalem by the Babylonians in 586 BC. Verses 10-14 mention Edom's participation in the downfall and plundering of Jerusalem (see also Ezek 35:15).

Message and Purpose

Obadiah, the shortest book in the Old Testament, is a prophetic condemnation of Edom for their treatment of the people of Judah. Theirs was a conflict dating back to the twins in Rebekah's womb, who were their patriarchs. The Edomites were descendants of her elder son Esau, and the people of Judah were the descendants of Jacob.

Just as there was conflict in the womb between Jacob and Esau (see Gen 25:21-26), there was conflict between their peoples. The Edomites had closed their borders and their hearts to the people of Israel as they are on their way to the promised land. They also reveled in the judgment and destruction of Judah years later by the Babylonians, picking off some stragglers and returning others to their captors. They even looted Jerusalem after its fall.

God's judgment against Edom, therefore, was harsh: the nation would be destroyed with no possibility of recovery. It tells us God is opposed to piling additional troubles on those who are suffering, even if they are being disciplined by him. Obadiah, in fact, teaches the vital lesson that God's treatment of us is based in part on the way we treat others in his kingdom family.

VIDEO INTRO

www.bhpublishinggroup.com/qr/te/31_00

Outline

I. The Judgment against Edom (1-9)
II. Edom's Sins against Judah (10-14)
III. The Day of the Lord (15-21)

The vision of Obadiah.

EDOM'S CERTAIN JUDGMENT

This is what the Lord God has said about Edom:[a]

We have heard a message
from the Lord;[b]
an envoy has been sent[c]
among the nations:
"Rise up,[d] and let us go to war
against her."[A]

2 Look, I will make you insignificant[e]
among the nations;
you will be deeply despised.

3 Your arrogant heart
has deceived you,[f]
you who live in clefts of the rock[B,C,g]
in your home on the heights,
who say to yourself,
"Who can bring me down
to the ground?"[h]

4 Though you seem to soar[D]
like an eagle[i]
and make your nest
among the stars,[j]
even from there I will
bring you down.
This is the Lord's declaration.

5 If thieves came to you,[k]
if marauders by night —
how ravaged you would be! —
wouldn't they steal only
what they wanted?
If grape pickers came to you,
wouldn't they leave some grapes?[l]

6 How Esau will be pillaged,[m]
his hidden treasures searched out![n]

7 Everyone who has a treaty with you[o]
will drive you to the border;
everyone at peace with you
will deceive and conquer you.
Those who eat your bread[p]
will set[E] a trap for you.
He will be unaware of it.[q]

8 In that day —
this is the Lord's declaration —

will I not eliminate the wise ones
of Edom[r]
and those who understand
from the hill country of Esau?

9 Teman,[F,s] your warriors[t]
will be terrified
so that everyone
from the hill country of Esau
will be destroyed by slaughter.[u]

EDOM'S SINS AGAINST JUDAH

10 You will be covered with shame
and destroyed forever
because of violence done
to your brother Jacob.[v]

11 On the day you stood aloof,[w]
on the day strangers captured
his wealth,[G]
while foreigners entered
his city gate
and cast lots for Jerusalem,[x]
you were just like one of them.[y]

12 Do not[H] gloat over your brother[z]
in the day of his calamity;
do not rejoice over the people
of Judah[aa]
in the day of their destruction;
do not boastfully mock[I,ab]
in the day of distress.[ac]

13 Do not enter my people's city gate
in the day of their disaster.[ad]
Yes, you — do not gloat
over their misery
in the day of their disaster,
and do not appropriate
their possessions[ae]
in the day of their disaster.

14 Do not stand at the crossroads[J,af]
to cut off their fugitives,
and do not hand over their survivors
in the day of distress.

JUDGMENT OF THE NATIONS

15 For the day of the Lord[ag] is near,
against all the nations.[ah]
As you have done,[ai] it will be done
to you;

[a] 1 Gn 25:30; Ps 137:7; Is 21:11-12; 34:1-17; 63:1-6; Ezk 25:12-14; Am 1:11-12; Mal 1:2-5
[b] 1-4 Jr 49:14-16
[c] 1 Is 18:2; 30:4
[d] Jr 6:4-5
[e] 2 Nm 24:18; Is 23:9
[f] 3 Is 16:6
[g] 2Kg 14:7; 2Ch 25:12
[h] Is 14:13-15
[i] 4 Jb 20:6-7; Hab 2:9
[j] Is 14:12-15
[k] 5 Jr 49:9
[l] Lv 19:10; 25:5,11
[m] 6 Jr 49:10
[n] Mal 1:2-3
[o] 7 Ps 55:20; Jr 30:14; Am 1:9
[p] Ps 41:9
[q] Jr 49:7

[r] 8 Jb 4:1; 5:12-14
[s] 9 Gn 36:11; 1Ch 1:45; Jb 2:11; Hab 3:3
[t] Jr 49:22
[u] Is 34:5-8; 63:1-3; Jr 49:7,20; Ezk 25:13; Am 1:12; Ob 5
[v] 10 Ezk 25:12-14; Jl 3:19; Am 1:11
[w] 11 Ps 83:5-6; 137:7; Am 1:6,9
[x] Jl 3:3; Nah 3:10
[y] 2Ch 21:17; Ezk 35:10
[z] 12 Mc 4:11; 7:10
[aa] Ps 83:1-6; 137:7-9; Lm 4:21-22; Ezk 35:15; 36:5
[ab] Ps 31:18; Ezk 35:12
[ac] Gn 35:3; Ps 50:15; Jr 16:19
[ad] 13 Ezk 35:5
[ae] Ezk 35:10; 36:2-3
[af] 14 Is 16:3-4
[ag] 15 Jl 1:15; 2:1,11,31; Am 5:18,20
[ah] Is 13:6; Jl 3:14; Zph 1:7,14
[ai] Jr 50:29; 51:56

[A] 1 = Edom [B] 3 Or in Sela; probably = Petra [C] 3 Probably Petra [D] 4 Or to build high [E] 7 Some LXX mss, Sym, Tg, Vg; MT reads They will set your bread as [F] 9 = a region or city in Edom [G] 11 Or forces [H] 12-14 Or You should not throughout vv. 12-14 [I] 12 Lit not make your mouth big [J] 14 Hb obscure

1 **Edom** was a hostile neighbor on Judah's southeast border and fought with Israel and Judah on a number of occasions (e.g., 1 Sam 14:47; 1 Kgs 11:15-17; 2 Chr 20:22; 21:8-11).
2-3 The Edomites apparently thought they were big stuff, because here God vows to make them **insignificant** (v. 2). Pride is the chief sin, the one that led Satan to rebel against God (see Ezek 28:17). While we puff out our chests like we're somebody, God isn't impressed.

7 International **peace** negotiations are fragile and untrustworthy for a nation that rejects the Lord.
8-9 Notice Obadiah doesn't encourage Edom to repent to avoid God's judgment. The just Judge of the nations had rendered a verdict with no appeal.
10 Since the Edomites had descended from Esau, the **brother** of Jacob, Scripture refers to their nations as brothers. But there was bad

blood in the family (see, e.g., 1 Sam 14:47-48; 2 Sam 8:13-14; 1 Kgs 11:14-22).
11-12 In a day of **calamity**, Esau's descendants offered neither help nor compassion to **the people of Judah** (v. 12). They could have blessed Israel and been blessed by God (see Gen 12:3); instead, they chose to **gloat . . . rejoice** and **mock** (v. 12). Bad idea.
15 **As you have done, it will be done to you** brings to mind the guy we've all known who

a 15 Jr 50:15; Ezk 35:11
b 16 Jr 49:12
c Is 51:22-23
d 17 Is 4:2-3
e 16-17 Is 66:20; Jl 2:32
f 17 Is 14:1-2; Am 9:11-15
g Ezk 36:2-5
h 18 Is 5:24; 9:18-19; Am 1:12; Zch 12:6
i Jr 11:23

j 19 Is 11:14
k Am 9:11-12
l Is 11:14
m Jr 31:5; 32:44
n 20 1Kg 17:9-10; Lk 4:26
o Jr 32:44; 33:13
p 21 Neh 9:27; Is 4:5; 18:7; 24:23; Dn 2:44; Mc 4:7
q Ps 22:28; 47:7-9; 67:4; Zch 14:9

what you deserve will return
on your own head.*a*

16 As you have drunk
on my holy mountain,*b*
so all the nations will
drink continually.*c*
They will drink and gulp down
and be as though they had
never been.

17 But there will be a deliverance
on Mount Zion,*d*
and it will be holy;*e*
the house of Jacob will dispossess*f*
those who dispossessed them.*A,g*

18 Then the house of Jacob will be
a blazing fire,*h*
and the house of Joseph,
a burning flame,
but the house of Esau
will be stubble;
Jacob*B* will set them on fire
and consume Edom.*c*
Therefore no survivor will remain*i*

of the house of Esau,
for the LORD has spoken.

FUTURE BLESSING FOR ISRAEL

19 People from the Negev will possess*j*
the hill country of Esau;*k*
those from the Judean foothills
will possess
the land of the Philistines.*l*
They*D* will possess
the territories of Ephraim
and Samaria,*m*
while Benjamin will possess Gilead.

20 The exiles of the Israelites who are
in Halah*E*
and who are among the Canaanites
as far as Zarephath*n*
as well as the exiles of Jerusalem
who are in Sepharad
will possess the cities of the Negev.*o*

21 Saviors*F* will ascend Mount Zion*p*
to rule over the hill country of Esau,
but the kingdom will be the LORD's.*q*

A 17 DSS, LXX, Syr, Vg, Tg; MT reads *Jacob will possess its inheritance* *B* 18 Lit *they* *C* 18 Lit *them* *D* 19 = The house of Jacob *E* 20 Or *of this host of the Israelites*; Hb obscure *F* 21 Or *Those who have been delivered*

---

got what he had coming to him. Here God tells Edom they will receive exactly what they had dealt to others. And this is what all humanity deserves: just retribution for sins. But that's what makes God's grace so amazing. Grace means giving someone what they *don't* deserve. And as believers in Jesus

Christ, that's what we receive. But for those, like Edom, who oppose God's agenda, **what they deserve will return on** their **own head.** **16** The Bible often uses the metaphor of drinking to speak of God's judgment and wrath (e.g., Job 21:20; Isa 51:17; Jer 49:12-13; Rev 14:10).

17 The day of the Lord will bring judgment to God's enemies but **deliverance** to his people, reversing fortunes.

21 Though people possess lands, earth's kingdoms are really **the LORD's.**

JONAH

INTRODUCTION

Author

THE BOOK OF JONAH IS anonymous. But if Jonah did not write it, he was presumably the source of the story.

Historical Background

Jonah son of Amittai was an eighth-century-BC prophet from Gath-hepher in the land of Zebulun (1:1; see 2 Kgs 14:25). According to 2 Kings 14:23-25, he predicted that King Jeroboam II (793–753 BC) of the northern kingdom would restore Israel's northern border.

The city of Nineveh, to which Jonah preached, was a major city of the Assyrian Empire; it was located in northeastern Mesopotamia on the east bank of the Tigris River (about 220 miles north of modern Baghdad, Iraq). Longtime enemies of Israel, the Assyrians were cruel in battle. Ancient Assyrian artwork, in fact, depicts horrific scenes of their treatment of those whom they conquered, and Israel would eventually fall to Assyria in 722 BC. During the days of King Sennacherib of Assyria, his palace was located in Nineveh (see 2 Kgs 19:36). The prophet Nahum prophesied the eventual destruction of Nineveh (Nah 3:7), which was overthrown by the Medes and Chaldeans in 612 BC.

Message and Purpose

Jonah ministered during the reign of King Jeroboam II. He was called by God to go to the wicked city of Nineveh and tell the people to repent. While it's easy to miss the concern of this book by focusing on Jonah, it is really about the character of God. It begins with God and ends with God. He is the one who initiates all the action.

The message of the book for Israel related to what was happening to Jonah. That message was that God loves all people, Jews and Gentiles. Though Israel's sins put them in the same scenario for judgment that the Ninevites were in, Jonah showed the Israelites that God's love is for all who repent. The book of Jonah, in fact, is a message of grace because God gave the Ninevites a forty-day window in which to repent. It reveals to us the heart of God to see people across all racial, social, class, and cultural lines repent and be saved. And our hearts should reflect the same desire. Jonah was a reluctant prophet God used to teach us the kingdom perspective God's people are to have toward all humankind.

VIDEO INTRO

www.bhpublishinggroup.com/qr/te/32_00

Outline

I.   The Prophet's Rebellion (1:1-17)
II. The Prophet's Prayer (2:1-10)
III. The Prophet's Preaching (3:1-10)
IV. The Prophet's Anger (4:1-11)

a 1:1 2Kg 14:25; Jnh 3:1;
Mt 12:39–41; 16:4; Lk
11:29–30,32
b 1:2 Nm 22:20; Dt 10:11;
Jos 7:10
c Jnh 3:2-3; 4:11
d Gn 10:11; 2Kg 19:36; Is
37:37; Nah 1:1; Zph 2:13
e Dt 15:9; 24:15; 2Kg 23:17;
Is 58:1
f Jnh 3:8
g Gn 18:20; Hs 7:2
h 1:3 Is 23:1,6,10; Jr 10:9
i Gn 4:16; Ps 139:7,9-10
j Jnh 2:6
k 2Ch 2:16; Ezr 3:7; Ac 9:36,43
l 1:4 1Sm 18:11; 20:33; Is
22:17; Jr 22:26-28
m Ps 107:25–28; 135:7
n 1:5 1Kg 18:26
o Ac 27:18-19,38
p Gn 2:21; 15:12; Jdg 4:21;
Dn 8:18; 10:9; 1Th 5:6
q 1:6 Ps 107:28
r 2Sm 12:22; Am 5:15; Jnh 3:9
s 1:7 Jos 7:14-18; 1Sm 10:20-21;
14:41-42; Pr 16:33; Ac 1:23-26
t Nm 32:23; Pr 16:33
u 1:8 Jos 7:19; 1Sm 14:43
v Gn 47:3; 1Sm 30:13
w 1:9 Gn 14:13; 39:14; Ex
1:15; 2:13; 1Sm 4:6
x 2Kg 17:25,28,32-33
y Gn 24:3,7; Ezr 1:2; Neh
1:4; Ps 136:26; Dn 2:18
z Neh 9:6; Ps 95:5; 146:6
aa 1:10 Jnh 1:3

ab 1:12 2Sm 24:17; 1Ch 21:17
ac 1:14 Ps 107:28
ad Ps 51:18; 115:3; 135:6; Pr
21:1; Is 55:11; Lm 3:37-39;
Dn 4:34-35; Mt 11:25
ae 1:15 Ps 65:7; 93:3-4;
107:29
af 1:16 Is 59:19; Mc 7:17; Zph
2:11; Mal 1:14; Lk 8:22-25
ag Ps 50:14; 66:13-14; 76:11;
116:17-18
ah 1:17 Gn 9:2; Nm 11:22;
1Kg 4:33; Ps 8:8
ai Mt 12:40; 16:4; Lk 11:29-
30; Jn 11:6,14
aj 2:1 Jb 13:15; Ps 130:1-2;
Lm 3:53-56
ak 2:2 1Sm 30:6; Ps 18:4-6;
22:24; 120:1
al Ps 18:5-6; 86:13; 88:1-7;
Is 28:15; 38:18
am Ps 34:7
an 2:3 Ps 69:1-2,14-15; Lm 3:54
ao Neh 9:11

JONAH'S FLIGHT

1 The word of the LORD came to Jonah son of Amittai:*a* 2 "Get up!*b* Go to the great city*c* of Nineveh*d* and preach against it*e* because their evil*f* has come up before me."*g* 3 Jonah got up to flee to Tarshish*h* from the LORD's presence.*i* He went down*j* to Joppa*k* and found a ship going to Tarshish. He paid the fare and went down into it to go with them to Tarshish from the LORD's presence.

4 But the LORD threw*l* a great wind onto the sea,*m* and such a great storm arose on the sea that the ship threatened to break apart. 5 The sailors were afraid, and each cried out to his god.*n* They threw the ship's cargo into the sea to lighten the load.*o* Meanwhile, Jonah had gone down to the lowest part of the vessel and had stretched out and fallen into a deep sleep.*p*

6 The captain approached him and said, "What are you doing sound asleep? Get up! Call to your god.^A,*q* Maybe this god will consider us,*r* and we won't perish."

7 "Come on!" the sailors said to each other. "Let's cast lots.*s* Then we'll know who is to blame for this trouble we're in." So they cast lots, and the lot singled out Jonah.*t* 8 Then they said to him, "Tell us who is to blame for this trouble we're in.*u* What is your business,*v* and where are you from? What is your country, and what people are you from?"

9 He answered them, "I'm a Hebrew.*w* I worship^B the LORD,*x* the God of the heavens,*y* who made the sea*z* and the dry land."

10 Then the men were seized by a great fear and said to him, "What is this you've done?" The men knew he was fleeing from the LORD's presence*aa* because he had told them. 11 So they said to him, "What should

we do to you so that the sea will calm down for us?" For the sea was getting worse and worse.

12 He answered them, "Pick me up and throw me into the sea so that it will calm down for you, for I know that I'm to blame*ab* for this great storm that is against you." 13 Nevertheless, the men rowed hard to get back to dry land, but they couldn't because the sea was raging against them more and more.

14 So they called out to the LORD:*ac* "Please, LORD, don't let us perish because of this man's life, and don't charge us with innocent blood! For you, LORD, have done just as you pleased."*ad* 15 Then they picked up Jonah and threw him into the sea, and the sea stopped its raging.*ae* 16 The men were seized by great fear of the LORD,*af* and they offered a sacrifice to the LORD and made vows.*ag*

17 The LORD appointed a great fish*ah* to swallow Jonah, and Jonah was in the belly of the fish three days and three nights.*ai*

～ HOPE WORDS ～

When it is out of control, it is simply out of your control.

JONAH'S PRAYER

2 Jonah prayed to the LORD his God from the belly of the fish:*aj*
2 I called to the LORD in my distress,*ak*
　　and he answered me.
I cried out for help
　　from deep inside^C Sheol;*al*
you heard my voice.*am*
3 You threw me into the depths,*an*
　　into the heart of the seas,*ao*

---

^A 1:6 Or *God*　^B 1:9 Or *fear*　^C 2:2 Lit *from the stomach of*

1:1-2 In the eighth century BC, God reached down into the school of the prophets—which included Jonah, Amos, and Hosea in the northern kingdom of Israel—and told Jonah to **go to the great city of Nineveh**.

1:3 Why did Jonah head in the opposite direction from his assignment? First, the Ninevites were a violent people: they would torture you, kill you, put your corpse on display, and later paint pictures to document their atrocities. Second, Jonah didn't want to preach to these people because he was afraid they might actually repent and be forgiven! Nineveh was a major Assyrian city; if Assyrian citizens were to escape God's judgment, they could eventually conquer Israel.

1:4 If you're a Christian and rebelling against God, he's coming after you. And one of the ways he does so is through circumstances.

The negative circumstances in your life may be a **storm** with your name on it.

1:6 Notice the irony of this pagan sailor telling the preacher to pray! When Jonah wouldn't respond to discipline, the Lord rebuked him through an unbeliever.

1:7 Casting lots was a practice like rolling dice. See Proverbs 16:33.

1:11-13 The problem that was causing their trouble was spiritual, not merely meteorological or social. And the same is true for many of your problems. Often solutions have to be based on a spiritual perspective.

1:14, 16 These sailors, who earlier were praying to their false gods (see 1:5), suddenly **called out to the LORD** (1:14) . . . **offered a sacrifice** to him, and **made vows** (1:16). That means the Lord used Jonah's disobedience to make these sinning sailors pray to him. Even

in our rebellion, then, God can accomplish his work. Ultimately, you don't determine what God accomplishes; you only determine where you fit in the plan.

1:17 God sent a whale-a-gram to trap his fleeing prophet. When you're running from a particular aspect of your calling, God will send circumstances, and they will find you.

2:1 When the storm threatened destruction, when sinners criticized him, Jonah remained rebellious. But when he was swallowed by a fish, **Jonah prayed**. Some of us don't get right with God until circumstances are so adverse that they swallow us whole either. Let's repent and pray before we find ourselves in such desperate straits.

2:3 Ultimately, it wasn't the sailors but God who was responsible for tossing the prophet overboard.

and the current[A] overcame me.
All your breakers and your billows
swept over me.[a]

4 But I said, "I have been banished[b]
from your sight,[c]
yet I will look once more[B]
toward your holy temple.[d]

5 The water engulfed me up
to the neck;[C,e]
the watery depths overcame me;
seaweed was wrapped
around my head.[f]

6 I sank to the foundations
of the mountains,[g]
the earth's gates shut
behind me forever![h]
Then you raised my life[i] from the Pit,
LORD my God![j]

7 As my life was fading away,[k]
I remembered the LORD,[l]
and my prayer came to you,[m]
to your holy temple.[n]

8 Those who cherish worthless idols[o]
abandon their faithful love,[p]

9 but as for me, I will sacrifice[q] to you
with a voice of thanksgiving.[r]
I will fulfill[s] what I have vowed.
Salvation[D] belongs to the LORD."[t]

10 Then the LORD commanded the fish,[u]
and it vomited Jonah onto dry land.

JONAH'S PREACHING

3 The word of the LORD came to Jonah
a second time:[v] 2 "Get up! Go to the
great city of Nineveh[w] and preach[x] the
message that I tell you." 3 Jonah got up and
went to Nineveh according to the LORD's
command.

Now Nineveh was an extremely great
city,[E,y] a three-day walk. 4 Jonah set out
on the first day of his walk in the city and
proclaimed,[z] "In forty days Nineveh will be
demolished!" 5 Then the people of Nineveh
believed God. They proclaimed a fast[aa] and
dressed in sackcloth — from the greatest
of them to the least.

6 When word reached the king of Nineveh, he got up from his throne, took off his
royal robe, put on sackcloth,[ab] and sat in ashes. 7 Then he issued a decree[ac] in Nineveh:
By order of the king and his nobles: No
person or animal, herd or flock, is to
taste anything at all. They must not eat
or drink water. 8 Furthermore, both people and animals must be covered with
sackcloth, and everyone must call out
earnestly to God.[ad] Each must turn from
his evil ways[ae] and from his wrongdoing.[F] 9 Who knows?[af] God may turn and
relent; he may turn from his burning
anger so that we will not perish.[ag]

10 God saw their actions — that they had
turned from their evil ways[ah] — so God relented from the disaster[ai] he had threatened them with. And he did not do it.

JONAH'S ANGER

4 Jonah was greatly displeased and
became furious.[aj] 2 He prayed to the
LORD:[ak] "Please, LORD, isn't this what I
thought while I was still in my own country? That's why I fled toward Tarshish in the

[a]2:3 Ps 42:7
[b]2:4 Lv 21:7
[c]Ps 31:22-23; Jr 7:15
[d]1Kg 8:38; 2Ch 6:38; Ps 5:7; 138:2
[e]2:5 Ps 69:1-2; 105:18; Pr 23:2; Lm 3:54
[f]Ps 18:4-5
[g]2:6 Ps 116:3
[h]Jb 38:10; Ps 9:13; Is 38:10; Mt 16:18
[i]Jb 33:28; Ps 16:10; 30:3; Is 38:17
[j]Ps 30:3; 86:13
[k]2:7 Ps 142:3
[l]2Sm 14:11; Ps 77:10-11; 143:5
[m]2Ch 30:27; Ps 18:6
[n]Ps 11:4; 65:4; 88:2; Mc 1:2; Hab 2:20
[o]2:8 2Kg 17:15; Ps 31:6; Jr 16:18
[p]Ps 31:6
[q]2:9 Ps 50:14,23; Jr 33:11; Hs 14:2
[r]Ps 26:7
[s]Jb 22:27; Ps 22:25; 116:14,18; Ec 5:4-5
[t]Ps 3:8; Is 12:2; 45:17; Rv 7:10
[u]2:10 Jnh 1:17
[v]3:1 Jnh 1:1
[w]3:2 Zph 2:13-15
[x]Jr 1:17; Ezk 2:7
[y]3:3 Gn 10:11-12; Jnh 1:2; 4:11
[z]3:4 2Kg 18:26-28; Mt 12:41; Lk 11:32
[aa]3:5 Dn 9:3; Jl 1:14
[ab]3:6 1Kg 21:27; Est 4:1-4; Jr 6:26; Ezk 27:30-31
[ac]3:7 2Ch 20:3; Ezr 8:21
[ad]3:8 Ps 130:1; Jnh 1:6,14
[ae]Is 1:16-19; 55:6-7; Jr 18:11
[af]3:9 2Sm 12:22; Jl 2:14
[ag]Jr 18:7-8
[ah]3:10 1Kg 21:27-29; 2Kg 17:13; 2Ch 7:14; Jr 18:11; 31:18
[ai]Ex 32:14; Am 7:3,6
[aj]4:1 Jnh 4:9; Mt 20:15; Lk 15:28
[ak]4:2 Jr 20:7

[A]2:3 Lit river [B]2:4 LXX reads said, "Indeed, will I look . . . ? [C]2:5 Or me, threatening my life [D]2:9 Or Deliverance [E]3:3 Or was a great city to God [F]3:8 Or injustice, or violence

2:6 Have you ever been in a **Pit**, so to speak? Are you there now? If so, there's good news: The Pit is not a bad place to be if it gets you back in the will of God. When a visit to that place is what it takes to nudge you back on track spiritually, you can thank God for it.
2:7-9 When my son was young, I told him to empty the trash. He told me that he didn't feel like it, but I assured him I could change the way he felt. And I did. Likewise, God changed the way Jonah felt because God loved him enough to do so. As a result, Jonah remembered that **salvation belongs to the LORD**; therefore, he was ready to **fulfill** what he had previously **vowed** (2:9).
2:10–3:1-3 Jonah was given a second chance to make a right decision. Valuable time and energy had been wasted, though, and the prophet was no doubt stinky and sticky from his ordeal. When God calls you to obedience, you need to understand this: he's not going to change his character or his Word. We are

the ones who have to adjust. It's best to do things his way from the start.
In Matthew's Gospel, we learn that the unbelieving scribes and Pharisees were demanding a sign from Jesus. He told them that they would be given "the sign of the prophet Jonah" (Matt 12:38-39). "For as Jonah was in the belly of the huge fish three days and three nights, so the Son of Man will be in the heart of the earth three days and three nights" (Matt 12:40; see Jonah 1:17).
When Jonah came out of the fish, he carried a message of repentance to Nineveh. God would show compassion on Nineveh through the symbolic death and resurrection of a prophet. But in Jesus Christ he showed mercy on you and me by the actual death and resurrection of the Son of God. Indeed, then, "something greater than Jonah is here" (Matt 12:41).
3:4-5 **In forty days Nineveh will be demol-ished!** is a summary of Jonah's two-part ser-mon (3:4). Nineveh would be judged for their

sin, but the Ninevites had a forty-day window to repent. To repent is to give God the oppor-tunity to limit or reverse his judgment. And when repentance happens, you have revival: as people turn, so God turns. And if you're still alive, there's still time to repent.
Jonah almost missed the privilege of par-ticipating in this great evangelistic event (3:5) because he didn't like what God told him to do. So remember: if you run from God's will, you might miss out on one of the most sig-nificant moves of God in your life.
3:10 God never changes, but he can adjust to the changes in humans. While he doesn't change his holy standards, he will alter his intended outcome. In this case, repentance produced something for his grace and mercy to respond to. God has enough grace and mercy for everyone—including people whom you have given up on. So remember, he can get through when you can't.
4:2-3 In short, Jonah didn't want to see God's grace fall on a wicked people. He knew God's

The God of Second Chances

HAS GOD EVER SAID SOMETHING to you, or asked you to do something, that you didn't like or didn't want to do? You knew you heard him clearly, but you also knew that you weren't really into his request, demand, or expectation. In fact, to you it seemed like God was making a request that revealed that he had lost his mind. Of course you would never come right out and say that, but the thought crossed your own.

If this has ever happened to you, then take comfort in knowing that you are in good company. The greatest evangelist ever to walk this planet had a similar response. I say that he is the greatest evangelist because at no other time in the history of humankind has one man preached one sermon, and an entire city—from king to commoner to cow—responded and turned their lives around. I am talking about Jonah.

God had told Jonah to go to the Ninevites and tell them that he was going to judge them if they didn't straighten up. One thing to keep in mind about the Ninevites is that they were a very violent group of people. They would just as soon kill you and put your dead body on display then ask you what you had come to see them about. So it's not entirely surprising that Jonah didn't want to go to them.

Not only was he scared of them, though. He was also scared that they might repent and then God, in his mercy, would forgive them. Jonah wanted to see them judged. Jonah didn't want to give them the opportunity to turn from their wicked ways and receive forgiveness from the Lord. So Jonah set out in the opposite direction from where God had told him to go. Jonah thought he could somehow hide from God, the Creator of the universe.

But no location is too far out of the reach of God's call on your life. God knew exactly where Jonah was and sent a tumultuous storm into the heart of the sea where he was sailing. This wreaked havoc on the boat and the sailors cried out for help, eventually tossing Jonah overboard in an attempt to save their own lives. Thus, Jonah wound up in the belly of a great fish that would eventually transport him right back to where God wanted him to go. Jonah got a second chance to obey God, and after his nightmare in the sea, he chose obedience.

If you, like Jonah, have strayed from the direction and path that God had once revealed to you, I encourage you to cry out to him today. Don't wait until God has to maneuver your circumstances to get you where he wants you to go. Rather, call out to God wherever you are right now. He can hear you. He can reach you where you are. He longs to bring you back in line with his purpose and plan for you. Ask him to do this before he has to intervene in a more drastic way like he did with Jonah.

first place.[a] I knew that you are a gracious and compassionate God,[b] slow to anger, abounding in faithful love, and one who relents from sending disaster.[c] **3** And now, LORD, take my life from me,[d] for it is better for me to die than to live."[e]

4 The LORD asked, "Is it right for you to be angry?"

5 Jonah left the city and found a place east of it.[f] He made himself a shelter there and sat in its shade to see what would happen to the city. **6** Then the LORD God appointed a plant, and it grew over Jonah to provide shade for his head to rescue him from his trouble.[A] Jonah was greatly pleased with the plant. **7** When dawn came the next day, God appointed a worm that attacked the plant, and it withered.[g]

8 As the sun was rising, God appointed a scorching east wind.[h] The sun beat down on Jonah's head[i] so much that he almost fainted, and he wanted to die. He said, "It's better for me to die than to live."[j]

9 Then God asked Jonah, "Is it right for you to be angry about the plant?"

"Yes, it's right!" he replied. "I'm angry enough to die!"

10 So the LORD said, "You cared about the plant, which you did not labor over and did not grow. It appeared in a night and perished in a night. **11** But may I not care about the great city of Nineveh,[k] which has more than a hundred and twenty thousand people who cannot distinguish between their right and their left,[l] as well as many animals?"[m]

[a]4:2 Jnh 1:3
[b]Ex 34:6; Nm 14:18; Ps 86:5,15; Jl 2:13
[c]Neh 9:17
[d]4:3 1Kg 19:4; Jb 6:8-9
[e]Jb 7:15-16; Ec 7:1
[f]4:5 1Kg 19:9,13
[g]4:7 Jl 1:12

[h]4:8 Ezk 19:12; Hs 13:15
[i]Ps 121:6; Is 49:10
[j]Jnh 4:3
[k]4:11 Jnh 3:10
[l]Dt 1:39; Is 7:16
[m]Ps 36:6

^A4:6 Or *disaster*, or *evil*

---

character, and he knew that if Nineveh genuinely repented, God would forgive them.

All of us need a God who will reverse his decision of judgment, but we are often so unlike God that we are unwilling to reverse our own judgmental decisions. Are there people in your life whose salvation would make you angry? Would it disappoint you to learn that a certain person had become a Christian? Think about it. How would you fare before God if he were as angry and unrelenting as you?

4:4 This is a question we should ask ourselves more often. In every case, we must determine whether our anger is legitimate or illegitimate.

4:5 No doubt he was rooting for the Ninevites' zeal to fade so that God would pull a Sodom and Gomorrah on them (see Gen 19:24-25, 28).

4:6-8 Even as God worked on behalf of his heart (4:6), Jonah couldn't see God: he simply saw negative circumstances that infuriated him (4:7-8). That speaks to his spiritual immaturity.

When you're having a bad day, do you ever ask yourself if the things happening to you might be God's sovereign appointments designed for your good? Perhaps that irritating coworker is meant to serve as a divine appointment to help you grow in love for others.

4:10-11 In other words, while Jonah was miserable over the loss of a twenty-four hour *plant*

he'd had absolutely nothing to do with, he was willing to watch thousands of *people* created in God's image die and go to hell. And though Jonah liked it when God cared for him and provided him with shade from the heat, when God wanted to care for sinners who couldn't **distinguish between their right and their left**—that is, young children—Jonah got bent out of shape. God's prophet may have had God's words, but he didn't have God's heart.

Do you have God's heart for others? After all, if not for God's providential work in your life, you would never have come to Christ. So will you be transformed by the grace of God and serve as his instrument of grace?

MICAH

INTRODUCTION

Author

MICAH WAS A NATIVE OF MORESHETH, a small town on the border of the city of Gath (1:1, 14). He ministered to both the northern kingdom of Israel and the southern kingdom of Judah, prophesying the destruction of Samaria (1:5-7) and Jerusalem (1:8-16). He also foresaw the birth of the Messiah in Bethlehem (5:2). Micah ministered "in the days of Jotham, Ahaz, and Hezekiah, kings of Judah" (1:1). And since he saw Samaria's future judgment, which occurred in 722 BC, the likely time period for his ministry is between 730 and 690 BC.

Historical Background

In Micah's day, the kingdoms of Judah and Israel were in the midst of positive economic changes. New wealth in the cities, primarily because of a long period of peace, allowed the rich to expand their wealth to the detriment of the lower class. This led to privileges being extended to one group while they were being denied to the other. With more wealth, people had the wherewithal to indulge other appetites—which sometimes manifested themselves in sin and moral degradation. In both kingdoms, the greater the wealth, the greater the distance there was between the people and their God. Micah called Israel and Judah to repent and turn back to the Lord.

Message and Purpose

The message of Micah is that God is displeased with social injustice, declining morality, and living without a view to the Messiah's kingdom reign. Micah wanted his own people in the southern kingdom of Judah to know that God was just as upset with them as he

was with the rebellious northern kingdom of Israel. He condemned the social inequities of his day that did not reflect God's kingdom principles that they were to be living out until the Messiah came. Those in power were practicing bribery, confiscating the fields of the people, oppressing the poor, and abusing women and children. They were disregarding the Mosaic law and its protections for the vulnerable. Personal holiness was also absent as the people lived in decadence.

Micah directly connects the Messiah's reign with the everyday living of his people. God would not ignore the people's insensitivity, unrighteousness, and oppression. There is to be a direct connection between our faith and our social concerns. Micah's message is that the spiritual must not become disconnected from the social. When the spiritual is applied to the social in righteous ways, God blesses.

VIDEO INTRO

www.bhpublishinggroup.com/qr/te/33_00

Outline

I. The Approaching Punishment of Israel and Judah (1:1–2:13)
II. Punishment of Leaders and False Prophets (3:1-12)
III. The Coming Kingdom and King (4:1–5:15)
IV. The Lawsuit against Judah (6:1-16)
V. Spiritual Ruin, Renewal, and Restoration (7:1-20)

1

The word of the LORD that came[a] to Micah[b] the Moreshite[c] — what he saw regarding Samaria and Jerusalem in the days of Jotham,[d] Ahaz,[e] and Hezekiah,[f] kings of Judah.

COMING JUDGMENT ON ISRAEL

2 Listen, all you peoples;[g]
pay attention, earth[A] and everyone
in it![h]
The Lord GOD will be a witness
against you,[i]
the Lord, from his holy temple.[j]
3 Look, the LORD is leaving his place[k]
and coming down to trample
the heights[B] of the earth.[l]
4 The mountains will melt
beneath him,
and the valleys will split apart,
like wax near a fire,[m]
like water cascading down
a mountainside.
5 All this will happen because of
Jacob's rebellion
and the sins of the house of Israel.
What is the rebellion of Jacob?
Isn't it Samaria?[n]
And what is the high place of Judah?[o]
Isn't it Jerusalem?
6 Therefore, I will make Samaria
a heap of ruins[p] in the countryside,
a planting area[q] for a vineyard.
I will roll her stones[r] into the valley
and expose her foundations.[s]
7 All her carved images
will be smashed[t] to pieces;
all her wages[u] will be burned
in the fire,
and I will destroy all her idols.
Since she collected the wages
of a prostitute,[v]
they will be used again
for a prostitute.

MICAH'S LAMENT

8 Because of this I will lament and wail;
I will walk barefoot and naked.[w]
I will howl like the jackals[x]
and mourn like ostriches.[C]

9 For her wound is incurable[y]
and has reached even Judah;[z]
it has approached my
people's city gate,[aa]
as far as Jerusalem.
10 Don't announce it in Gath,[ab]
don't weep at all.
Roll in the dust in Beth-leaphrah.
11 Depart in shameful nakedness,[ac]
you residents of Shaphir;
the residents of Zaanan[ad] will not
come out.
Beth-ezel is lamenting;
its support[D] is taken from you.
12 Though the residents of Maroth
anxiously wait for something good,[ae]
disaster has come from the LORD[af]
to the gate of Jerusalem.
13 Harness the horses to the chariot,
you residents of Lachish.[ag]
This was the beginning of sin
for Daughter Zion
because Israel's acts of rebellion[ah]
can be traced to you.
14 Therefore, send farewell gifts[ai]
to Moresheth-gath;
the houses of Achzib[aj] are
a deception[ak]
to the kings of Israel.
15 I will again bring a conqueror
against you who live in Mareshah.[al]
The nobility[E] of Israel will come
to Adullam.[am]
16 Shave yourselves bald and cut off
your hair[an]
in sorrow for your precious children;
make yourselves as bald as an eagle,
for they have been taken from you
into exile.[ao]

OPPRESSORS JUDGED

2

Woe to those who dream
up wickedness
and prepare evil plans[ap]
on their beds!
At morning light[aq] they
accomplish it
because the power is in their hands.[ar]

---

[a]1:1 Hs 1:1; Jl 1:1; Zph 1:1
[b]2Ch 29:5-11; 32:24-26; Jr 26:18
[c]Mc 1:14
[d]2Kg 15:5,32-38; 2Ch 27:1-9; Is 1:1; Hs 1:1
[e]2Kg 16:1-20; 2Ch 28:1-27; Is 7:1-12
[f]2Kg 18:1-20; 2Ch 29:1-31
[g]1:2 1Kg 22:28; 2Ch 18:27; Jr 6:19; 22:29
[h]Ps 24:1; Is 34:1; Jr 47:2
[i]1Sm 12:5-6; Ps 50:7; Jr 42:5; Mal 3:5
[j]Ps 11:4; Hab 2:20
[k]1:3 Is 26:21
[l]Am 4:13
[m]1:4 Ps 97:5; Is 64:1-2; Nah 1:5
[n]1:5 Is 7:9; Am 8:14
[o]2Ch 34:3-4
[p]1:6 Mc 3:12
[q]Jr 31:5; Am 5:11
[r]Lm 4:1
[s]Ezk 13:14
[t]1:7 Dt 9:21; 2Ch 34:7
[u]Dt 23:18
[v]Dt 23:18
[w]1:8 Is 20:2-4; 32:11
[x]Is 13:21-22

[y]1:9 Is 3:26; Jr 30:12,15
[z]2Kg 18:13-16; 19:31-37; Is 8:7-8
[aa]Mc 1:12
[ab]1:10 2Sm 1:20
[ac]1:11 Ezk 23:29
[ad]Jos 15:37
[ae]1:12 Is 59:9-11; Jr 14:19
[af]Jdg 2:15; 2Kg 17:7; 21:12; Is 45:7; Mc 2:3
[ag]1:13 Jos 10:3; 2Kg 14:19; Is 36:2
[ah]Mc 1:5
[ai]1:14 2Kg 16:8
[aj]Jos 15:44
[ak]Jr 15:18
[al]1:15 Jos 15:44
[am]Jos 12:15; 15:35; 1Sm 22:1; 2Sm 23:13
[an]1:16 Jb 1:20; Is 22:12; Jr 7:29
[ao]2Kg 17:6; Am 7:11,17 Nah 1:11
[ap]2:1 Ps 36:4; Is 32:7; Nah 1:11
[aq]Hs 7:6-7
[ar]Gn 31:29; Dt 28:32; Pr 3:27

[A]1:2 Or land [B]1:3 Or high places [C]1:8 Or eagle owls; lit daughters of the desert [D]1:11 Lit its standing place; Hb obscure [E]1:15 Lit glory

---

1:1 Moresheth lay southwest of Jerusalem and was by no means a significant place. The calling of Micah, in fact, is proof that a kingdom man can be found anywhere. 1:3-5 The idolatry of **Samaria** and **Jerusalem** (1:5)—the capital cities of the northern and southern kingdoms—had become so great that God was coming down to the **earth** to address it (1:3-4).

1:7 In the days of Moses, Israel had entered into a covenant with the Lord. Through his prophets, God often spoke of it as a marriage covenant. Thus, when Israel engaged in idolatry, worshiping **images** and aligning themselves with the gods of pagan nations, God considered it spiritual "adultery" (see Jer 13:27; Ezek 23:37). That's why Micah says that Samaria **collected the wages of a prostitute**.

Yet all their wealth would be carried off by another idol-worshiping nation. 1:11-15 Micah grieves over the Judean towns that would be laid waste—including his hometown of **Moresheth-gath** (1:14). 2:1-3 God has plans (2:3) for those who carry out injustice (2:1-2). Plans to take them down.

a 2:2 Jr 22:17; Am 8:4
b Is 5:8
c 1Kg 21:1-15
d Ex 20:17; Is 5:8
e 2:3 Dt 28:48; Jr 18:11
f Jr 8:3; Am 3:1-2
g Lm 1:14; 5:5
h Is 2:11-12
i Am 5:13
j 2:4 Hab 2:6
k Jr 9:10,17-21; Mc 1:8
l Is 6:11; 24:3; Jr 4:13
m Jr 6:12; 8:10
n 2:5 Nm 34:13,16-29; Jos 18:4,10
o 2:6 Is 30:10; Am 2:12; 7:16
p Is 29:10; Mc 3:6
q Mc 6:16
r 2:7 Is 50:2; 59:1
s Ps 119:65,68,116; Jr 15:16
t Is 15:2; 84:11
u 2:8 Jr 12:8
v Mc 3:2-3; 7:2-3
w Ps 120:6-7
x 2:9 Jr 10:20
y Ezk 39:21; Hab 2:14
z 2:10 Dt 3:19-20; 12:8-10
aa Ps 106:38
ab Lv 18:25-28
ac 2:11 Jr 5:13,31

ad 2:11 Is 28:7
ae Is 30:10-11
af 2:12 Mc 4:6-7
ag 2Kg 19:31; Mc 5:7-8; 7:18
ah Is 23:3; Ezk 36:35-38
ai 3:1 Is 1:10; Mc 3:9
aj Ps 82:1-5; Jr 5:5
ak 3:2 Ps 53:4; Ezk 22:27; Mc 2:8; 7:2-3
al 3:3 Ps 14:4; 27:2; Zph 3:3
am Ezk 11:3,6-7
an 3:4 Ps 18:41; Pr 1:28; Is 1:15; Jr 11:11
ao Dt 31:17; Is 59:2

2 They covet fields*a* and seize them;*b*
they also take houses.
They deprive a man of his home,*c*
a person of his inheritance.*d*

3 Therefore, the LORD says:
I am now planning*e* a disaster
against this nation;*f*
you cannot free your necks from it.*g*
Then you will not walk so proudly*h*
because it will be an evil time.*i*

4 In that day one will take up*j* a taunt
against you
and lament mournfully,*k* saying,
"We are totally ruined!*l*
He measures out the allotted land
of my people.
How he removes it from me!
He allots our fields*m* to traitors."

5 Therefore, there will be no one
in the assembly of the LORD
to divide the land by casting lots.^A,*n*

GOD'S WORD REJECTED

6 "Quit your preaching,"*o*
they^B preach.
"They should not preach these things;*p*
shame will not overtake us."^C,*q*

7 House of Jacob, should it be asked,
"Is the Spirit of the LORD impatient?*r*
Are these the things he does?"
Don't my words bring good*s*
to the one who walks uprightly?*t*

8 But recently my people have risen up
like an enemy:*u*
You strip off the splendid robe*v*
from those who are
passing through confidently,*w*
like those returning from war.

9 You force*x* the women of my people
out of their comfortable homes,
and you take my blessing^D,*y*
from their children forever.

10 Get up and leave,
for this is not your place of rest*z*
because defilement*aa*
brings destruction —
a grievous destruction!*ab*

11 If a man comes
and utters empty lies*ac* —

"I will preach to you about wine
and beer"*ad* —
he would be just the preacher
for this people!*ae*

THE REMNANT REGATHERED

12 I will indeed gather*af* all
of you, Jacob;
I will collect the remnant of Israel.*ag*
I will bring them together like sheep
in a pen,
like a flock in the middle
of its pasture.
It will be noisy with people.*ah*

13 One who breaks open the way
will advance before them;
they will break out, pass
through the city gate,
and leave by it.
Their King will pass through
before them,
the LORD as their leader.

UNJUST LEADERS JUDGED

3 Then I said, "Now listen,*ai*
leaders of Jacob,
you rulers of the house of Israel.
Aren't you supposed to know
what is just?*aj*

2 You hate good and love evil.
You tear off people's skin*ak*
and strip their flesh
from their bones.

3 You eat the flesh*al* of my people
after you strip their skin
from them
and break their bones.
You chop them up*am*
like flesh for the cooking pot,
like meat in a cauldron."

4 Then they will cry out*an* to the LORD,
but he will not answer them.
He will hide his face from them
at that time*ao*
because of the crimes
they have committed.

FALSE PROPHETS JUDGED

5 This is what the LORD says
concerning the prophets

---

^A 2:5 Lit LORD *stretching the measuring line by lot*   ^B 2:6 = the prophets   ^C 2:6 Text emended; MT reads *things. Shame will not depart*
^D 2:9 Perhaps *the land*

2:6 When a kingdom man speaks God's truth, the unrighteous don't want to hear it (see the response to Stephen in Acts 7:57). Micah's audience insisted no judgment would **overtake** them.
2:12 Like a faithful shepherd, God would gather his **sheep**—just as the good shepherd Jesus Christ would one day (see John 10:11-18).

3:1-3 Micah compares these **leaders** (3:1) with cannibals. Instead of protecting the people they are supposed to lead, they devour them (3:3)!
3:5 That these false **prophets proclaim . . . peace when they have food to sink their teeth into but declare war against the one who puts nothing in their mouths** means

you could guarantee a good word from them by filling their stomachs or pockets. If you were poor with nothing to offer, however, the prophets only had harsh words for you. This state of affairs would make it hard for the poor to trust God, and it would give the rich a false sense of security.

who lead my people astray,[a]
who proclaim[b] peace
when they have food to sink
    their teeth into
but declare war against the one
who puts nothing in their mouths.

6 Therefore, it will be
    night[c] for you —
without visions;
it will grow dark for you —
without divination.[d]
The sun will set[e] on these prophets,
and the daylight will turn black
    over them.

7 Then the seers will be ashamed[f]
and the diviners disappointed.[g]
They will all cover their mouths[A,h]
because there will be no answer
    from God.[i]

8 As for me, however, I am filled
    with power[j]
by the Spirit of the LORD,
with justice and courage,
to proclaim to Jacob his rebellion
and to Israel his sin.[k]

ZION'S DESTRUCTION

9 Listen to this, leaders of the house
    of Jacob,[l]
you rulers of the house of Israel,
who abhor justice[m]
and pervert everything
    that is right,

10 who build Zion with bloodshed[n]
and Jerusalem with injustice.

11 Her leaders issue rulings
    for a bribe,[o]
her priests teach for payment,[p]
and her prophets practice divination
    for silver.
Yet they lean on the LORD, saying,
"Isn't the LORD[q] among us?
No disaster will overtake us."

12 Therefore, because of you,
Zion will be plowed like a field,
Jerusalem will become ruins,[r]
and the temple's mountain[s]
will be a high thicket.[t]

THE LORD'S RULE
FROM RESTORED ZION

4 In the last days[u]
the mountain of the LORD's house[v]
will be established
at the top of the mountains
and will be raised above the hills.
Peoples will stream to it,[w]

2 and many nations will come
    and say,[x]
"Come, let us go up to the mountain
    of the LORD,[y]
to the house of the God of Jacob.
He will teach us about his ways[z]
so we may walk in his paths."
For instruction will go out of Zion[aa]
and the word of the LORD
    from Jerusalem.

3 He will settle disputes
    among many peoples[ab]
and provide arbitration
    for strong nations
that are far away.
They will beat their swords
    into plows
and their spears
    into pruning knives.
Nation will not take up the sword
    against nation,
and they will never again train
    for war.

4 But each person will sit
    under his grapevine[ac]
and under his fig tree
with no one to frighten him.[ad]
For the mouth of the LORD[ae]
    of Armies
has spoken.

5 Though all the peoples each walk
in the name of their gods,[af]
we will walk[ag] in the name of the
    LORD our God
forever and ever.[ah]

6 On that day —
    this is the LORD's declaration —
I will assemble the lame
and gather the scattered,[ai]
those I have injured.

[a] 3:5 Is 3:12; 9:15-16; Jr 14:14-15
[b] Jr 6:14
[c] 3:6 Is 8:20-22; 29:10-12
[d] Dt 18:10; Jos 13:22
[e] Is 59:10
[f] 3:7 Zch 13:4
[g] Is 44:25; 47:12-14
[h] Lv 13:45; Lm 4:13-15; Ezk 24:17,22; Mc 7:16
[i] 1Sm 28:6; Is 29:9-12; Mc 3:4
[j] 3:8 Is 61:1-2; Jr 1:18
[k] Is 58:1
[l] 3:9 Mc 3:1
[m] Ps 58:1-2; Is 1:23
[n] 3:10 Jr 22:13,17; Hab 2:12
[o] 3:11 Is 1:23; Mc 7:3
[p] Jr 6:13
[q] Is 48:2
[r] 3:12 Jr 9:11
[s] Mc 4:1
[t] Jr 26:18

[u] 4:1-3 Is 2:2-4; Dn 2:28; 10:14; Hs 3:5; Mc 5:10
[v] 4:1 Ezk 43:12; Mc 3:12; Zch 8:3
[w] Ps 22:27; 86:9; Jr 3:17
[x] 4:2 Zch 2:11; 14:16
[y] Is 56:6-7; Jr 31:6
[z] Ps 25:8-9,12; Is 54:13
[aa] Is 42:1-4; Zch 14:8-9
[ab] 4:3 Is 11:3-5
[ac] 4:4 1Kg 4:25; Zch 3:10
[ad] Lv 26:6; Jr 30:10
[ae] Is 1:20; 40:5
[af] 4:5 2Kg 17:29
[ag] Zch 10:12
[ah] Jos 24:15; Is 26:8,13
[ai] 4:6 Is 35:6; Jr 31:8; Mc 2:12; Zph 3:19

[A] 3:7 Lit mustache

3:6 The punishment for giving false light (that is, spiritual insight that deviates from God's truth) is experiencing darkness.
3:8 A kingdom man like Micah relies on the Spirit's **power** (not his own) and is willing to speak boldly, calling **sin** what it is.
3:9-12 Micah condemns all three levels of spiritual leadership in Israel: **leaders . . . priests . . . and prophets** (3:9, 11). They were corrupt; nonetheless, they assumed God was

on their side and concluded that **no disaster** would **overtake [them]** (3:11). They couldn't be more misguided: **Jerusalem** would **become ruins** (3:12).
4:1-2 The restored kingdom coming to **Jerusalem** (4:2) is the future millennial kingdom of the Messiah. When it is established, the nations will go there—not so they can merely know about God—but so that they may be taught to **walk in his paths** (4:2).

Doing so is what it means to be kingdom people.
4:3-4 Christ's millennial kingdom will bring the peace and security humanity dreams of.
4:5 Though they may be surrounded by idolatrous people who **walk in the name of their gods**, kingdom men and women **walk in the name of the LORD**. They wear their commitment to God on their sleeves each day.

[a] 4:7 Mc 5:7-8; 7:18; Mt 11:5; Lk 14:21
[b] Is 24:23
[c] 4:8 Ps 48:3,12; 61:3
[d] Is 1:26; Zch 9:10
[e] 4:9 Jr 8:19
[f] Is 3:1-3
[g] 4:10 Mc 5:3
[h] 2Kg 20:18; Hs 2:14
[i] Is 43:14; 45:13; Mc 7:8-12
[j] Is 48:20; 52:9-12
[k] 4:11 Is 5:25-30; 17:12-14
[l] 4:12 Ps 147:19-20
[m] 4:13 Is 41:15
[n] Jr 51:20-23
[o] Is 60:9
[p] 5:1 1Kg 22:24; Jb 16:10; Lm 3:30

[q] 5:2 Gn 35:19; Ru 4:11; 1Sm 17:12; Mt 2:6
[r] Is 11:1; Lk 2:4
[s] 2Ch 7:18; Is 11:1; Jr 30:21; Zch 9:9; Mt 2:6
[t] Ps 74:2; 102:25; Pr 8:22-23; Hab 1:12
[u] 5:3 Hs 11:8; Mc 4:10; 7:13
[v] Mc 4:9-10
[w] Is 10:20-22; Mc 5:7-8
[x] Mc 4:6-7
[y] 5:4 Is 40:11; 49:9; Ezk 34:13-15,23-24; Mc 7:14
[z] Is 45:22; 52:10
[aa] 5:5 Is 9:6
[ab] Is 8:7-8; 10:24-27
[ac] 5:6 Nah 2:11-13; Zph 2:13
[ad] Gn 10:8-12
[ae] Is 14:25; 37:36-37
[af] 5:7 Is 10:21; Mc 2:12; 4:7; 7:18
[ag] Dt 32:2; 2Sm 17:12; Ps 110:3; Hs 14:5
[ah] Ps 72:6; Is 44:3
[ai] 5:8 Gn 49:9; Nm 24:9

7 I will make the lame into a remnant,[a]
those far removed
  into a strong nation.
Then the LORD will reign over them[b]
  in Mount Zion
from this time on and forever.
8 And you, watchtower for the flock,[c]
fortified hill[A] of Daughter Zion,
the former rule[d] will come to you;
sovereignty will come
  to Daughter Jerusalem.

FROM EXILE TO VICTORY

9 Now, why are you shouting loudly?[e]
Is there no king with you?
Has your counselor perished[f]
so that anguish grips you
  like a woman in labor?
10 Writhe and cry out,[B,g] Daughter Zion,
like a woman in labor,
for now you will leave the city[h]
and camp in the open fields.
You will go to Babylon;
there you will be rescued;[i]
there the LORD will redeem you[j]
from the grasp of your enemies!
11 Many nations have now assembled
  against you;[k]
they say, "Let her be defiled,
and let us feast our eyes on Zion."
12 But they do not know
  the LORD's intentions[l]
or understand his plan,
that he has gathered them
like sheaves to the threshing floor.
13 Rise and thresh,[m] Daughter Zion,
for I will make your horns iron
and your hooves bronze
so you can crush many peoples.[n]
Then you[C] will set apart
  their plunder[o]
for the LORD,
their wealth for the Lord of the
  whole earth.

FROM DEFEATED RULER
TO CONQUERING KING

5 Now, daughter who is under attack,
you slash yourself in grief;
a siege is set against us!
They are striking the judge[p] of Israel
on the cheek with a rod.

2 Bethlehem Ephrathah,[q]
you are small among the clans
  of Judah;
one will come from you[r]
to be ruler over Israel for me.[s]
His origin[D] is from antiquity,[t]
from ancient times.
3 Therefore, Israel will be abandoned[u]
  until the time
when she who is in labor[v]
  has given birth;
then the rest of the ruler's brothers[w]
  will return
to the people of Israel.[x]
4 He will stand and shepherd them[y]
in the strength of the LORD,
in the majestic name of the LORD
  his God.
They will live securely,
for then his greatness will extend
to the ends of the earth.[z]
5 He will be their peace.[aa]
When Assyria invades our land,[ab]
  when it marches
  against our fortresses,
we will raise against it
  seven shepherds,
even eight leaders of men.
6 They will shepherd[ac] the land
  of Assyria with the sword,
the land of Nimrod[ad]
  with a drawn blade.[E]
So he will rescue us[ae] from Assyria
when it invades our land,
when it marches
  against our territory.

THE GLORIOUS AND PURIFIED
REMNANT

7 Then the remnant of Jacob[af]
will be among many peoples
like dew from the LORD,[ag]
like showers on the grass,[ah]
which do not wait for anyone
or linger for mankind.
8 Then the remnant of Jacob
will be among the nations,
  among many peoples,
like a lion among animals
  of the forest,[ai]
like a young lion among flocks
  of sheep,

[A] 4:8 Or flock, Ophel   [B] 4:10 Hb obscure   [C] 4:13 LXX, Syr, Tg; MT reads I   [D] 5:2 Lit His going out   [E] 5:6 Aq, Vg; MT, Sym read Nimrod at its gateways

4:9-13 **Like a woman in labor,** the people of Judah would **cry out** in pain when **Babylon** carried them away (4:9-10). Yet the Lord would rescue them from their **enemies** (4:10). The plunderer would become the plundered (4:12).

5:2 Hundreds of years later, God ensured the fulfillment of this prophecy through a Roman census that took Joseph and his pregnant bride Mary to his ancestral home of Bethlehem. There Mary gave birth to the One who would one day rule the world (see Luke 2:1-7).

Clearly, this would be no ordinary king: **His origin is from antiquity, from ancient times** (Mic 5:2). Micah thus affirms this King's pre-existence. Conceived by the Holy Spirit in the womb of a virgin, this King is the Son of God (see Luke 1:26-37).

which tramples[a] and tears[b]
    as it passes through,
and there is no one to rescue them.[c]
9 Your hand will be lifted up
    against your adversaries,[d]
and all your enemies will be destroyed.

10 In that day—
    this is the LORD's declaration—
I will remove your horses from you[e]
and wreck your chariots.
11 I will remove the cities of your land[f]
and tear down all your fortresses.[g]
12 I will remove sorceries
    from your hands,[h]
and you will not have
    any more fortune-tellers.
13 I will remove your carved images[i]
and sacred pillars from you
so that you will no longer worship
the work of your hands.
14 I will pull up the Asherah poles[j]
    from among you[k]
and demolish your cities.[A]
15 I will take vengeance in anger
    and wrath[l]
against the nations that have not
    obeyed me.

GOD'S LAWSUIT AGAINST JUDAH

6 Now listen to what the LORD is saying:
Rise, plead your case
    before the mountains,
and let the hills hear
    your complaint.[B]
2 Listen to the LORD's lawsuit,[m]
you mountains
    and enduring foundations
    of the earth,[n]
because the LORD has a case
    against his people,[o]
and he will argue it against Israel.
3 My people,[p] what have I done
    to you,[q]
or how have I wearied you?[r]
Testify against me!
4 Indeed, I brought you up[s]
    from the land of Egypt
and redeemed you[t] from that place
    of slavery.[u]
I sent Moses,[v] Aaron, and Miriam[w]
    ahead of you.
5 My people,
    remember what King
    Balak of Moab[x] proposed,
what Balaam son of Beor
    answered him,[y]
and what happened from
    the Acacia Grove[C,z] to Gilgal[aa]

[a] 5:8 Ps 44:5; Is 41:15-16; Mc 4:13; Zch 10:5
[b] Hs 5:14
[c] Ps 50:22
[d] 5:9 Ps 10:12; 21:8; Is 26:11

[e] 5:10 Dt 17:16; Is 2:7; Hs 14:3
[f] 5:11 Is 1:7; 6:11
[g] Is 2:12-17; Hs 10:14; Am 5:9
[h] 5:12 Dt 18:10-12; Is 2:6; 8:19
[i] 5:13 Is 2:18,20; 17:8; Ezk 6:9
[j] 5:14 Dt 16:21
[k] Ex 34:13; Is 27:9
[l] 5:15 Is 1:24; 65:12
[m] 6:2 Is 3:13; Jr 2:9
[n] 2Sm 22:16; Ps 104:5
[o] 6:3 Ps 50:7
[p] Jr 2:5
[q] Is 43:22-23
[s] 6:4 Ex 12:51; 20:2
[t] Dt 7:8
[u] Ex 20:2
[v] Ps 77:20
[w] Ex 15:20
[x] 6:5 Nm 22:5-6
[y] Nm 22-24
[z] Nm 25:1; Jos 2:1; 3:1
[aa] Jos 4:19; 5:9-10

A 5:14 Or *shrines*   B 6:1 Lit *voice*   C 6:5 Or *from Shittim*

6:2-3 Before all of creation, the Lord presents his lawsuit regarding his people's infidelity. His point is solid. God is not at fault for his people's choices: they are.
6:4-5 The Lord's argument goes to the core of his relationship with Israel. First, he says,

I brought you up from the land of Egypt and redeemed you from that place of slavery (6:4). The exodus was the most significant event in the history of Israel. Second, God gave Israel great leaders, including **Moses, Aaron, and Miriam** (6:4). Third, God provided protection

in the nation's journey to the promised land when he intervened in the matter of **King Balak of Moab** and **Balaam son of Beor** (6:5). Balak wanted Balaam to pronounce a curse upon Israel. Instead, God commanded Balaam to pronounce a blessing (see Num 22-24).

a 6:5 1Sm 12:7; Ps 103:6;
Is 1:27
b 6:6 Ps 40:6-8
c Ps 51:16-17
d 6:7 Ps 50:9; Is 40:16
e Lv 18:21; 20:1-5; Jr 7:31
f 6:8 Dt 30:15
g Dt 10:12
h Is 56:1; Jr 22:3; Mt 23:23
i Hs 6:6
j Is 57:15; 66:2
k 6:10 Jr 5:26-27; Am 3:10
l Ezk 45:9-10; Am 8:5
m 6:11 Lv 19:36; Hs 12:7
n 6:12 Is 1:23; 5:7; Am 6:3-
4; Mc 2:1-2
o Jr 9:2-6,8; Hs 7:13;
Am 2:4
p Is 3:8

q 6:13 Mc 1:9
r Is 1:7; 6:11
s 6:14 Is 9:20
t Is 30:6
u 6:15 Dt 28:38-40; Jr 12:13
v Am 5:11; Zph 1:13
w 6:16 1Kg 16:25-34; 2Kg
21:3; 2Ch 21:6,13; Jr 7:24
x Jr 18:16
y Jr 19:8; 25:9,18; 29:18
z Ps 44:13; Jr 51:51; Hs 12:14
aa 7:1 Is 24:13
ab Is 28:4; Hs 9:10
ac 7:2 Is 57:1
ad 1Kg 19:10
ae Is 59:7; Mc 3:10
af Jr 5:26; Hs 5:1
ag 7:3 Pr 4:16-17
ah Am 5:12; Mc 3:11

so that you may acknowledge
the LORD's righteous acts.[a]

6 What should I bring
before the LORD[b]
when I come to bow before God
on high?
Should I come before him
with burnt offerings,[c]
with year-old calves?

7 Would the LORD be pleased
with thousands of rams[d]
or with ten thousand streams of oil?
Should I give my firstborn
for my transgression,[e]
the offspring of my body
for my own sin?

APPLICATION QUESTIONS

READ MICAH 6:8

– How have you recently obeyed God's requirements in this verse?

8 Mankind, he has told each of you
what is good[f]
and what it is the LORD requires
of you:[g]
to act justly,[h]
to love faithfulness,[i]
and to walk humbly with your God.[j]

VERDICT OF JUDGMENT

9 The voice of the LORD calls out
to the city[A]
(and it is wise to fear your name):
"Pay attention to the rod
and the one who ordained it.[B]

10 Are there still[C] the treasures
of wickedness[k]
and the accursed short measure[l]
in the house of the wicked?

11 Can I excuse wicked scales
or bags of deceptive weights?[m]

12 For the wealthy of the city are full
of violence,[n]
and its residents speak lies;[o]
the tongues in their mouths
are deceitful.[p]

13 "As a result, I have begun to strike
you severely,[D,q]
bringing desolation because of
your sins.[r]

14 You will eat but not be satisfied,[s]
for there will be hunger within you.
What you acquire, you cannot save,[t]
and what you do save,
I will give to the sword.[C]

15 You will sow but not reap;[u]
you will press olives
but not anoint yourself with oil;
and you will tread grapes
but not drink the wine.[v]

16 The statutes of Omri
and all the practices
of Ahab's house
have been observed;
you have followed their policies.[w]
Therefore, I will make you
a desolate place[x]
and the city's[E] residents an object
of contempt;[F,y]
you will bear the scorn
of my people."[G,z]

ISRAEL'S MORAL DECLINE

7 How sad for me!
For I am like one who —
when the summer fruit
has been gathered
after the gleaning
of the grape harvest[aa] —
finds no grape cluster to eat,
no early fig, which I crave.[ab]

2 Faithful people have vanished
from the land;[ac]
there is no one upright
among the people.[ad]
All of them wait in ambush
to shed blood;[ae]
they hunt each other with a net.[af]

3 Both hands are good[ag]
at accomplishing evil:
the official and the judge demand
a bribe;[ah]
when the powerful man
communicates his evil desire,
they plot it together.

A 6:9 = Jerusalem   B 6:9 Or *attention, you tribe. Who has ordained it?*; Hb obscure   C 6:10,14 Hb obscure   D 6:13 LXX, Aq, Theod, Syr, Vg;
MT reads *I have made you sick by striking you down*   E 6:16 Lit *and its*   F 6:16 Lit *residents a hissing*   G 6:16 LXX reads *of the peoples*

6:8 What God wants is your love and obedience. He's a personal God and expects
a personal relationship. He also expects
you to love your neighbors by doing them
good and ministering to their needs. The
answer to what it is that **the LORD requires**
is simple. Every person is **to act justly, to
love faithfulness, and to walk humbly**

with . . . God. Religion becomes authentic
when it demonstrates itself in the equitable application of biblical truth in order to
meet the needs of people in God's name
(see Jas 1:27).
6:14 It's possible to get everything you
want—but not be **satisfied**. True satisfaction
is found in God.

6:16 **Omri** and **Ahab** were two wicked kings
who ruled over the northern kingdom.
7:1-2 Micah laments the problem he sees.
**Faithful people have vanished from the land;
there is no one upright** (7:2).

4 The best of them is like a brier;[a]
the most upright is worse
than a hedge of thorns.[b]
The day of your watchmen,
the day of your punishment,
is coming;[c]
at this time their panic is here.[d]

5 Do not rely on a friend;[e]
don't trust in a close companion.
Seal your mouth
from the woman who lies
in your arms.

6 Surely a son considers his father
a fool,[f]
a daughter opposes her mother,
and a daughter-in-law is
against her mother-in-law;
a man's enemies are the men
of his own household.

7 But I will look to the LORD;[g]
I will wait for the God
of my salvation.[h]
My God will hear me.[i]

ZION'S VINDICATION

8 Do not rejoice over me,[j] my enemy!
Though I have fallen, I will stand up;[k]
though I sit in darkness,
the LORD will be my light.[l]

9 Because I have sinned against him,
I must endure the LORD's rage
until he champions my cause[m]
and establishes justice for me.[n]
He will bring me into the light;[o]
I will see his salvation.[A,p]

10 Then my enemy will see,
and she will be covered with shame,
the one who said to me,
"Where is the LORD your God?"[q]
My eyes will look at her in triumph;
at that time she will be trampled
like mud in the streets.[r]

11 A day will come for rebuilding
your walls;[s]
on that day your boundary
will be extended.[t]

12 On that day people will come to you[u]
from Assyria and the cities of Egypt,
even from Egypt to the Euphrates River

and from sea to sea
and mountain to mountain.

13 Then the earth will become
a wasteland[v]
because of its inhabitants
and as a result of their actions.[w]

MICAH'S PRAYER ANSWERED

14 Shepherd your people[x]
with your staff,[y]
the flock that is your possession.
They live alone[z] in a woodland
surrounded by pastures.
Let them graze in Bashan
and Gilead[aa]
as in ancient times.[ab]

15 I will perform miracles for them[B]
as in the days of your exodus
from the land of Egypt.[ac]

16 Nations will see and be ashamed
of[C] all their power.
They will put their hands
over their mouths,[ad]
and their ears will become deaf.

17 They will lick the dust like a snake;[ae]
they will come trembling out of
their hiding places[af]
like reptiles slithering
on the ground.[ag]
They will tremble in the presence
of the LORD our God;[ah]
they will stand in awe of you.

18 Who is a God like you,[ai]
forgiving iniquity and passing
over rebellion[aj]
for the remnant of his inheritance?[ak]
He does not hold on
to his anger forever[al]
because he delights in faithful love.[am]

19 He will again have compassion
on us;
he will vanquish our iniquities.[an]
You will cast all our[D] sins
into the depths of the sea.[ao]

20 You will show loyalty to Jacob[ap]
and faithful love to Abraham,
as you swore to our fathers[aq]
from days long ago.

---

[a] 7:4 Ezk 2:6; 28:24
[b] Nah 1:10
[c] Is 10:3; Hs 9:7
[d] Is 22:5
[e] 7:5 Jr 9:4
[f] 7:6 Mt 10:21,35-36;
Lk 12:53
[g] 7:7 Hab 2:1
[h] Ps 130:5; Is 25:9
[i] Ps 4:3
[j] 7:8 Ob 12
[k] Am 9:11
[l] Ps 27:1; Is 9:2
[m] 7:9 Jr 50:34
[n] Jb 23:3-7; Lm 3:58
[o] Ps 37:6; Is 42:7,16
[p] Is 46:13; 56:1
[q] 7:10 Ps 42:3,10; 79:10;
115:2; Jl 2:17
[r] Ps 18:42; Zch 10:5
[s] 7:11 Is 54:11; Am 9:11
[t] Zph 2:2
[u] 7:12 Is 19:23-25; 60:4,9

[v] 7:13 Jr 25:11; Mc 6:13
[w] Is 3:10-11; Mc 3:4
[x] 7:14 Ps 95:7; Is 40:11;
49:10; Mc 5:4
[y] Lv 27:32; Ps 23:4
[z] Nm 23:9; Dt 33:28
[aa] Jr 50:19
[ab] Am 9:11
[ac] 7:15 Ex 3:20; 34:10; Ps
78:11-16
[ad] 7:16 Mc 3:7
[ae] 7:17 Ps 72:9; Is 49:23
[af] Ps 18:45
[ag] Dt 32:24
[ah] Is 25:3; 59:19
[ai] 7:18 Ex 15:11; Ps 71:19;
Is 40:18
[aj] Ex 34:7,9; Is 43:25;
Rm 3:25
[ak] Mc 2:12; 4:7; 5:7-8
[al] Ps 103:8-9,13
[am] Jr 32:41
[an] 7:19 Jr 50:20
[ao] 7:18-19 Ps 103:9-12; Is
38:17; 43:25; Jr 31:34
[ap] 7:20 Gn 24:27; 32:10
[aq] Dt 7:8,12

[A] 7:9 Or *righteousness*   [B] 7:15 = Israel   [C] 7:16 Or *ashamed in spite of*   [D] 7:19 Some Hb mss, LXX, Syr, Vg; other Hb mss read *their*

7:7 Need hope? **Look to the LORD.**
7:8-10 Micah gives voice to Jerusalem who confesses, **I have sinned** and **I must endure the LORD's rage**. But, in the end, Zion will be established again and **will see his salvation** (7:9). Then the enemies of God and of his people will be put to **shame** (7:10).

7:11 Though their fall was certain, Jerusalem's **walls** would be rebuilt.
7:14 Micah's compassion and care are seen in his request to God: **Shepherd your people with your staff.** Elsewhere Scripture testifies to the loving care of God for his people in terms of a shepherd and his sheep (see Ps 23).

7:19 The Lord is a covenant-keeping God who **will cast all our sins into the depths of the sea.** What a beautiful picture: our sins completely removed forever! The suffering and death of the sinless Son of God on our behalf made this possible.
7:20 Israel *will* see all of the promises of **Abraham**, Isaac, and **Jacob** fulfilled.

NAHUM

INTRODUCTION

Author

THE AUTHOR OF THE BOOK OF NAHUM is the only person with that name in the Old Testament. Except for the name of his hometown of Elkosh (1:1), nothing certain is known about him.

Historical Background

Nahum's prophetic book is a declaration of judgment on the Assyrian city of Nineveh, which was located about twenty miles north of the modern Iraqi capital of Baghdad. The Ninevites had responded with repentance when Jonah preached to them many years prior, but by the time of Nahum's book, their leaders had returned to wickedness.

Two events help determine the earliest and latest possible dates for the composition of Nahum's writing. The first is the capture and downfall of Thebes in about 663 BC. The second is Nineveh's ultimate destruction, which occurred in 612 BC. Nahum's emphasis on the seemingly recent fall of Thebes (3:8) favors a date shortly after 663 BC, during the reign of wicked King Manasseh (686–642 BC) or his evil son Amon (642–640 BC). This likely coincided with the reign of the cruel Assyrian king named Ashurbanipal (ca. 668–627 BC); if so, Assyria was at the height of its power.

Message and Purpose

The book of Nahum is God's announcement of judgment on the kingdom of Assyria, specifically on its capital city, Nineveh. God had used the Assyrians as the agents of judgment against his people for their rebellion and disobedience: Assyria had destroyed the northern kingdom of Israel and carried its inhabitants into captivity. But through Nahum, God was declaring that the cruel, evil Assyrian Empire would fall, too.

The book also has a second purpose. The prophet wanted to assure God's people that he would restore them according to his kingdom promises if they would repent and return to him. Though God had allowed Israel's painful, crushing defeat because of their sin, he would not let his people's sins cancel out his promises.

Nahum's name means "to console" or "consolation." And through this prophet, God was consoling his people in the midst of their painful judgment and also letting Nineveh know that he would not ignore their evil. Nahum informs us that God is loving, yet he is also just. We must not allow one aspect of his character to cancel out the others in our minds.

VIDEO   INTRO

www.bhpublishinggroup.com/qr/te/34_00

Outline

I. The Declaration of Judgment (1:1-15)
II. The Power of Judgment (2:1-13)
III. The Finality of Judgment (3:1-19)

1

The pronouncement[a] concerning Nineveh.[b] The book of the vision of Nahum the Elkoshite.

GOD'S VENGEANCE

2 The Lord is a jealous
    and avenging God;
the Lord takes vengeance
    and is fierce in[A] wrath.
The Lord takes vengeance
    against his foes;[c]
he is furious with his enemies.[d]
3 The Lord is slow to anger but great
    in power;
the Lord will never leave
    the guilty unpunished.[e]
His path is in the whirlwind
    and storm,[f]
and clouds are the dust
    beneath his feet.[g]
4 He rebukes the sea and dries it up,
    and he makes all the rivers run dry.[h]
Bashan and Carmel wither;[i]
    even the flower of Lebanon withers.
5 The mountains quake before him,
    and the hills melt;
the earth trembles[B,C]
    at his presence —
    the world and all who live in it.[j]
6 Who can withstand his indignation?
Who can endure his burning anger?[k]
His wrath is poured out like fire;[l]
    even rocks are shattered before him.

DESTRUCTION OF NINEVEH

7 The Lord is good,
    a stronghold in a day of distress;
he cares for those who take refuge[m]
    in him.
8 But he will completely
    destroy Nineveh[D]
with an overwhelming flood,[n]
    and he will chase his enemies
    into darkness.

9 Whatever you[E] plot against the Lord,
    he will bring it
    to complete destruction;[o]
oppression will not rise up
    a second time.
10 For they will be consumed
    like entangled thorns,[p]
like the drink of a drunkard
    and like straw that is fully dry.[F]
11 One has gone out from you,[G]
    who plots evil against the Lord,
    and is a wicked counselor.

PROMISE OF JUDAH'S DELIVERANCE

12 This is what the Lord says:
    Though they are strong[H]
        and numerous,
    they will still be mowed down,
    and he[i] will pass away.
    Though I have punished you,[J,q]
    I will punish you no longer.[r]
13 For I will now break off his yoke
        from you
    and tear off your shackles.

THE ASSYRIAN KING'S DEMISE

14 The Lord has issued an order concerning you:
    There will be no offspring
    to carry on your name.[K,s]
    I will eliminate the carved idol
        and cast image
    from the house of your gods;[t]
    I will prepare your grave,
    for you are contemptible.

15 Look to the mountains —
    the feet of the herald,[u]
    who proclaims peace.
    Celebrate your festivals, Judah;
    fulfill your vows.
    For the wicked one will never again
    march through you;
    he will be entirely wiped out.

[a] 1:1 Is 13:1; 30:6; Jr 18:18; Ezk 12:10; Hab 1:1; Zch 9:1; 12:1; Mal 1:1
[b] Jnh 3:3-4; 4:11; Nah 2:8; Zph 2:13
[c] 1:2 Dt 32:35, 41,43; Ps 94:1; 149:7; Is 1:24; 59:17; Jr 5:9,29; 9:9; 46:10; 50:15; 51:6,11,36; Ezk 25:14-17; Mc 5:15; 2Th 1:8; Heb 10:30
[d] Dt 6:15; Ps 94:1; Is 63:1-6; Jr 46:10; 50:28-29; Mc 5:15; Zph 1:18
[e] 1:3 Ex 34:6-7; Nm 14:18
[f] Pr 1:27; 10:25; Is 66:15; Jr 4:13; Hs 8:7
[g] Dt 33:26; Ps 68:4; 104:3; Mt 24:30; 26:64
[h] 1:4 2Sm 22:16; Ps 106:9; Is 50:2; Mt 8:26
[i] Is 33:9; Jr 50:19
[j] 1:5 Jdg 5:5; Ps 18:7; 46:2-3; 97:5; Is 54:10; 64:1,3; Jr 4:24; Am 8:8; Mc 1:4
[k] 1:6 Ps 7:11; 69:24; 78:49; Jl 2:11; Mal 3:2
[l] Ps 21:9; Is 9:19; 30:30; Jr 4:4; Lm 4:11; Ezk 22:20; Zph 1:18
[m] 1:7 2Sm 22:3; Ps 17:7; 34:8
[n] 1:8 Nah 2:6

[o] 1:9 Ps 2:1-4
[p] 1:10 Mal 4:1
[q] 1:12 Is 10:5-34
[r] Ps 30:5; 103:9; Is 54:8
[s] 1:14 Lv 20:3; 1Sm 24:21; Ps 89:4; Is 48:19; 66:22
[t] Dt 27:15; Jdg 18:14
[u] 1:15 Is 52:7; 61:1; Rm 10:15

[A] 1:2 Lit *is a master of*   [B] 1:5 Some emend to *earth is laid waste*   [C] 1:5 Lit *lifts*   [D] 1:8 Lit *her place*   [E] 1:9 = Nineveh   [F] 1:10 Hb obscure   [G] 1:11 Possibly Nineveh   [H] 1:12 Lit *intact*   [i] 1:12 Either the king of Assyria or his army   [J] 1:12 = Judah   [K] 1:14 Lit *It will not be sown from your name any longer*

1:1 This was not the first time one of Israel's prophets delivered God's message to **Nineveh**. Jonah had warned that God would destroy it, and the Ninevites repented. But by the time of Nahum, the people and their leaders had returned to wickedness.
1:2 In view here is not the kind of wicked jealousy or envy that the Bible condemns in sinners (e.g., Rom 13:13; 2 Cor 12:20; Gal 5:20 -21). Rather, this is the jealousy of a husband who sees some chump brazenly hitting on his wife and wants to protect her.

As Israel's husband, the Lord would tolerate no rival gods or nations that abused his people.
1:7 That **the Lord is good** is no contradiction of God's righteous wrath against sin—unless you assume *good* means "weak" or "apathetic." Since he's good, he must also address evil; he can't let it go unanswered.
1:9 It's hard to imagine anyone plotting against an all-knowing, all-powerful being. Yet to reject God's word and mistreat his people is to **plot against** him.
1:10 Since the Assyrians had besieged Israel and Judah (see 2 Kgs 17–19), the Assyrians would **be consumed**.

1:12 Here the Lord promises to deliver Judah from the hand of Assyria. The divine lawn mower was ready: **they** would **be mowed down**.
1:14 The Lord's threat directed toward the Assyrian king shows how weak he really was in the grand scheme of things. The Lord himself would **prepare** his **grave**.
1:15 **Look to the mountains—the feet of the herald, who proclaims peace** is language similar to Isaiah 40:9 and 52:7. Nahum 1:15 and Isaiah 52:7 are quoted in Romans 10:15.

a 2:1 Ezk 29:12-13; 30:23,26
b Pr 24:5; Am 2:14
c 2:2 Ps 47:4; Am 6:8; 8:7
d Is 24:1,3
e Ps 80:12-15; Jr 12:10
f 2:3 Ezk 23:14
g 2Kg 2:11; 6:17; Is 66:15
h 2:6 Nah 1:8
i 2:7 Is 38:14; 59:11
j Is 32:12
k 2:9 Ezk 38:13
l 2Ch 32:27; 36:10; Dn 11:8;
Nah 3:3

m 2:10 Dt 20:8; Jos 7:5; Is
13:7; 19:1; Ezk 21:7,15
n Is 35:3
o Ps 69:23
p Is 21:3; Jl 2:6
q 2:11 Is 2:15; 5:26-29; Jr
4:7; 5:6; 50:17; 51:38; Jl 1:6;
Am 3:12
r Lv 26:6; Dt 28:26; Jr 7:33
s 2:12 Jb 38:39-40
t 2:13 Jr 21:13; 23:30-32;
50:31; 51:25; Ezk 5:8; 13:8;
21:3; 26:3; 28:22; 29:3,10;
38:3; 39:1; Nah 3:5
u Is 31:8; Jr 46:10
v Rv 18:22-23
w 3:1 Ezk 7:23; 9:9; 22:2-3;
24:6,9; Hab 2:12
x Nah 2:9
y 3:2 Jdg 5:22; Jb 39:24;
Jr 47:3
z 3:3 Lv 26:30; Ps 110:6; Is
66:24; Jr 41:9; Ezk 6:5
aa Nah 2:9
ab 3:4 2Kg 9:22; Pr 7:10-23;
Ezk 16:15; 23:1-21; Rv
17:3-6

ATTACK AGAINST NINEVEH

2 One who scatters is coming up
　　against you.[a]
Man the fortifications!
Watch the road!
Brace[A] yourself!
Summon all your strength![b]

2 For the LORD will restore the majesty
　　of Jacob,[c]
yes,[B] the majesty of Israel,
though ravagers
　　have ravaged them[d]
and ruined their vine branches.[e]

3 The shields of his[c] warriors
　　are dyed red;
the valiant men are dressed
　　in scarlet.[f]
The fittings of the chariot flash
　　like fire[g]
on the day
　　of its battle preparations,
and the spears are brandished.

4 The chariots dash madly
　　through the streets;
they rush around in the plazas.
They look like torches;
they dart back and forth
　　like lightning.

5 He gives orders to his officers;
they stumble as they advance.
They race to its wall;
the protective shield is set
　　in place.

6 The river gates are opened,
and the palace erodes away.[h]

7 Beauty[D] is stripped;[E]
she is carried away;
her ladies-in-waiting moan
like the sound of doves[i]
and beat their breasts.[j]

8 Nineveh has been like a pool
　　of water
from her first days,[E]
but they are fleeing.
"Stop! Stop!" they cry,
but no one turns back.

9 "Plunder the silver!
　　Plunder the gold!"[k]
There is no end to the treasure,
an abundance
　　of every precious thing.[l]

10 Desolation, decimation, devastation!
Hearts melt,[m]
knees tremble,[n]
insides churn,[o]
every face grows pale![p]

11 Where is the lions' lair,[q]
or the feeding ground
　　of the young lions,
where the lion and lioness prowled,
and the lion's cub,
with nothing to frighten
　　them away?[r]

12 The lion mauled whatever
　　its cubs needed
and strangled prey
　　for its lionesses.
It filled up its dens with the kill,
and its lairs with mauled prey.[s]

13 Beware, I am against you.[t]
　　This is the declaration of the LORD
　　of Armies.
I will make your chariots go up
　　in smoke,[F]
and the sword will devour
　　your young lions.[u]
I will cut off your prey
　　from the earth,
and the sound of your messengers
will never be heard again.[v]

NINEVEH'S DOWNFALL

3 Woe to the city of blood,[w]
totally deceitful,
full of plunder,
never without prey.[x]

2 The crack of the whip
and rumble of the wheel,
galloping horse
and jolting chariot![y]

3 Charging horseman,
flashing sword,
shining spear;
heaps of slain,
mounds of corpses,[z]
dead bodies without end[aa] —
they stumble over their dead.

4 Because of the
　　continual prostitution
　　of the prostitute,
the attractive mistress of sorcery,
who treats nations
　　and clans like merchandise
by her prostitution and sorcery,[ab]

A 2:1 Lit *Strengthen*　　B 2:2 Or *like*　　C 2:3 = the army commander attacking Nineveh　　D 2:7 Text emended; MT reads *Huzzab*　　E 2:7,8 Hb obscure
F 2:13 Lit *will burn her chariots in smoke*

2:1-6 Nahum taunts Nineveh like the Assyrians used to taunt other nations (see 2 Kgs 18:30-35): **Man the fortifications! . . . Summon all your strength!** (Nah 2:1). He eggs them on with sarcasm, knowing full well that none of those actions will do them any good. They're like a ninety-eight-pound weakling facing a heavyweight boxer. Israel's champion has no equal.

5 I am against you.[a]
   This is the declaration of the LORD
      of Armies.
   I will lift your skirts
      over your face
   and display your nakedness
      to nations,
   your shame to kingdoms.[b]
6 I will throw filth on you
   and treat you with contempt;[c]
   I will make a spectacle of you.
7 Then all who see you will recoil
      from you, saying,[d]
   "Nineveh is devastated;
   who will show sympathy
      to her?"
   Where can I find anyone
      to comfort you?

8 Are you better than Thebes[A,e]
   that sat along the Nile
   with water surrounding her,
   whose rampart was the sea,
   the river[B,c] her wall?
9 Cush and Egypt were
      her endless source of strength;
   Put and Libya were
      among her[D] allies.
10 Yet she became an exile;
   she went into captivity.
   Her children were also dashed
      to pieces[f]
   at the head of every street.
   They cast lots for her dignitaries,[g]
   and all her nobles were bound
      in chains.
11 You[E] also will become drunk;
   you will hide.[F]
   You also will seek refuge
      from the enemy.

12 All your fortresses are fig trees
   with figs that ripened first;
   when shaken, they fall —
   right into the mouth of the eater!

13 Look, your troops are like women
      among you;
   your land's city gates
   are wide open to your enemies.
   Fire will devour the bars of your gates.

14 Draw water for the siege;
   strengthen your fortresses.
   Step into the clay and tread
      the mortar;
   take hold of the brick-mold!
15 The fire will devour you there;
   the sword will cut you down.
   It will devour you
      like the young locust.[h]
   Multiply yourselves
      like the young locust;
   multiply like the swarming locust!
16 You have made your merchants[i]
   more numerous than the stars
      of the sky.
   The young locust strips[G] the land
   and flies away.
17 Your court officials are
      like the swarming locust,
   and your scribes like clouds of locusts,
   which settle on the walls
      on a cold day;
   when the sun rises, they take off,
   and no one knows where they are.

18 King of Assyria,
      your shepherds slumber;[j]
   your officers sleep.
   Your people are scattered
      across the mountains[k]
   with no one to gather
      them together.[l]
19 There is no remedy for your injury;
   your wound is severe.[m]
   All who hear the news about you
   will clap their hands
      because of you,[n]
   for who has not experienced
   your constant cruelty?

[a] 3:5 Nah 2:13
[b] Is 47:3; Jr 13:22,26; Ezk 16:37; 23:29
[c] 3:6 Ps 107:40; Is 16:14; Dn 12:2; Mc 6:16; Mal 2:3
[d] 3:7 Dt 28:25,37; 2Ch 29:8; 30:7; Ps 31:11; Is 66:24; Jr 15:4; 24:9; 50:23
[e] 3:8 Jr 46:25; Ezk 30:14-16
[f] 3:10 2Kg 8:12; Is 13:16; Hs 10:14
[g] Ob 11

[h] 3:15 Jl 1:4
[i] 3:16 Ezk 16:29; 17:4; 27:3,13,20,23-24; Zph 1:11; Rv 18:3,11,15,23
[j] 3:18 Jr 23:1-2; 50:6
[k] Ezk 34:6
[l] 1Kg 22:17
[m] 3:19 Jr 10:19; 14:17; 30:12
[n] Ps 47:1; 98:8; Lm 2:15; Ezk 22:13

[A] 3:8 Hb No-amon   [B] 3:8 LXX, Syr, Vg read water   [C] 3:8 Lit sea from sea   [D] 3:9 Lit your   [E] 3:11 = Nineveh   [F] 3:11 Or will be overcome
[G] 3:16 Or sheds its skin

3:5 As Assyria had exhibited cruelty and brought shame upon the nations, God would **shame** them before the **kingdoms** of the world. Judgment may seem slow in com-ing, but it always comes. What goes around comes around. 3:19 Here the defeated king of Assyria is addressed by the prophet of God. Indeed, Assyria's destruction came in 612 BC. A life of wickedness and injustice will lead to calamity and judgment.

HABAKKUK

INTRODUCTION

Author

HABAKKUK WAS A PROPHET (1:1); otherwise, nothing is known about him. Though most prophets spoke to the people on behalf of God, Habakkuk spoke to God on behalf of the people.

Historical Background

The northern kingdom of Israel fell to the Assyrians in 722 BC. These conquerors subsequently fell to the Babylonians in 612 BC. The Babylonians, or "Chaldeans" (1:6), would also eventually bring Jerusalem and the whole southern kingdom of Judah to ruin.

In 609 BC, King Josiah of Judah was killed in battle by Pharaoh Neco of Egypt, and Judah came under Egyptian control. Neco was subsequently defeated by the Babylonians four years later, and Judah fell into the hands of Babylon by 604 BC. Jehoiakim, the king whom Neco had placed on Judah's throne, rebelled against Babylon in about 600 BC. In response, Nebuchadnezzar the Babylonian king besieged Jerusalem. He deposed Jehoiakim in 598 BC and carried his son Jehoiachin into exile the next year. But that was not the end of Judah's misery. Zedekiah, Judah's final king, also rebelled against Babylon in 588 BC. As a result, Nebuchadnezzar descended on Jerusalem with a vengeance, ravaged the city, destroyed the temple, and carried many of Judah's inhabitants (including Zedekiah) into exile in 587–586 BC.

Habakkuk probably wrote in 609–605 BC, after the death of King Josiah but before Judah fell under Babylonian control.

Message and Purpose

Habakkuk was a perplexed prophet who lived in the last days of the southern kingdom of Judah, before the Babylonians invaded it and took the people into captivity. The prophet struggled because God used the evil Babylonians to judge his people; in other words, he used the clearly unrighteous to judge the more righteous, and Habakkuk wrestled with whether God was fair for doing so. While we all struggle with this issue at times, the book of Habakkuk serves as an invitation to look at the "who" when we don't understand the "why." It prompts us to trust God's sovereignty over his kingdom purposes even when we don't comprehend them.

Habakkuk invites us to draw near to God even when we don't get all of our questions answered—and even when it seems that God is working against us! The book teaches that we can take our stand and praise God even when we don't grasp what he's doing. Habakkuk encourages us both with his doxology at the end of the book (3:16-19) and with his declaration, "The righteous one will live by his faith" (2:4).

VIDEO | INTRO

www.bhpublishinggroup.com/qr/te/35_00

Outline

I. Habakkuk's Dialogue with God (1:1–2:20)
   A. Habakkuk's First Question (1:1-4)
   B. God's First Response (1:5-11)
   C. Habakkuk's Second Question (1:12–2:1)
   D. God's Second Response (2:2-20)
II. Habakkuk's Prayer (3:1-19)

1

The pronouncement[a] that the prophet Habakkuk saw.[b]

HABAKKUK'S FIRST PRAYER

2　How long,[c] LORD, must I call
　　for help[d]
　and you do not listen
　or cry out to you about violence[e]
　and you do not save?
3　Why do you force me to look
　　at injustice?[f]
　Why do you tolerate[A] wrongdoing?
　Oppression and violence are right
　　in front of me.
　Strife is ongoing,
　　and conflict escalates.
4　This is why the law is ineffective
　and justice never emerges.
　For the wicked restrict[g]
　　the righteous;
　therefore, justice[h]
　　comes out perverted.

GOD'S FIRST ANSWER

5　Look at the nations[B,i] and observe[j]—
　be utterly astounded![k]
　For I am doing something
　　in your days
　that you will not believe[l]
　when you hear about it.[m]
6　Look! I am raising up[n]
　　the Chaldeans,[c]
　that bitter,[o] impetuous nation
　that marches across
　　the earth's open spaces
　to seize territories not its own.
7　They are fierce[p] and terrifying;
　their views of justice
　　and sovereignty
　stem from themselves.
8　Their horses are swifter[q]
　　than leopards[r]
　and more fierce[p] than wolves
　　of the night.
　Their horsemen charge ahead;
　their horsemen come
　　from distant lands.
　They fly like eagles,
　　swooping to devour.[s]

9　All of them come to do violence;
　their faces[t] are set
　　in determination.[E]
　They gather[u] prisoners like sand.[v]
10　They mock[w] kings,
　and rulers are a joke to them.
　They laugh[x] at every fortress
　and build siege ramps
　　to capture[y] it.
11　Then they sweep[z] by like the wind
　and pass through.
　They are guilty;[F] their strength
　　is their god.

HABAKKUK'S SECOND PRAYER

12　Are you not from eternity,
　　LORD my God?[aa]
　My Holy One,[ab] you[G] will not die.
　LORD, you appointed them
　　to execute judgment;
　my Rock,[ac] you destined them
　　to punish us.
13　Your eyes[ad] are too pure[ae] to look
　　on evil,
　and you cannot
　　tolerate wrongdoing.
　So why do you tolerate those
　　who are treacherous?[af]
　Why are you silent
　while one[H] who is wicked
　　swallows up
　one[I] who is more righteous
　　than himself?
14　You have made mankind
　like the fish of the sea,[ag]
　like marine creatures that have
　　no ruler.
15　The Chaldeans pull them all up
　　with a hook,
　catch them in their dragnet,[ah]
　and gather them in their fishing net;
　that is why they are glad and rejoice.
16　That is why they sacrifice
　　to their dragnet
　and burn incense
　　to their fishing net,
　for by these things their portion
　　is rich
　and their food plentiful.[ai]

[a] 1:1 Is 13:1; 30:6; Jr 18:18; Ezk 12:10; Hab 1:1; Zch 9:1; 12:1; Mal 1:1
[b] Nm 24:4; Jb 19:26; Is 13:1
[c] 1:2 Ps 4:2; 6:3; 13:1
[d] Jb 19:7; Ps 5:2; Lm 3:8
[e] Jr 6:7; Ezk 7:11,23; 8:17; 12:19; 45:9; Mc 6:12; Hab 1:9; 2:8,17
[f] 1:3 Jb 4:8; Ps 5:5; Is 5:7
[g] 1:4 Jdg 20:43; Ps 22:12
[h] Ex 23:6
[i] 1:5 Ps 2:1
[j] Gn 15:5
[k] Gn 43:33; Ps 48:5; Ec 5:8
[l] Gn 15:6
[m] Ac 13:41
[n] 1:6 Ru 4:5
[o] Jdg 18:25
[p] 1:7 Sg 6:4,10
[q] 1:8 2Sm 1:23
[r] Is 11:6; Jr 5:6; 13:23; Hs 13:7
[s] Dt 28:49

[t] 1:9 Gn 48:11
[u] Dt 11:14
[v] Jos 11:4
[w] 1:10 2Kg 2:23
[x] 2Ch 30:10
[y] Nm 21:32
[z] 1:11 Is 8:8
[aa] 1:12 1Ch 29:10; Ps 90:2; 93:2; 103:17; Mc 5:2
[ab] Is 1:4
[ac] Dt 32:4; Ps 18:2
[ad] 1:13 2Ch 6:20; 16:9
[ae] Ex 25:11; Ps 12:6; 19:9; 51:10; Pr 22:11; Ezk 36:25
[af] Jdg 9:23
[ag] 1:14 Ec 9:12
[ah] 1:15 2Kg 19:28; 2Ch 33:11; Is 37:29; Jr 16:16; Ezk 19:4,9; 29:4; 38:4; Am 4:2
[ai] 1:16 Dt 8:17; Is 10:13; 37:24-25

[A] 1:3 Lit observe, also in v. 13　[B] 1:5 DSS, LXX, Syr read Look, you treacherous people　[C] 1:6 = the Babylonians　[D] 1:8 Or and quicker　[E] 1:9 Hb obscure　[F] 1:11 Or wind, and transgress and incur guilt　[G] 1:12 Alt Hb tradition reads we　[H] 1:13 = Babylon　[I] 1:13 = Judah

---

1:2-3 Ever felt alone in standing for justice, while God seemed indifferent? This happens when we forget that God alone can see the whole picture, and he's working out his sovereign plan in the midst of the chaos. When you realize he is omniscient (all knowing), omnipotent (all powerful), and holy (perfectly righteous in all he does), then you'll realize he knows how to run things better than you do.

1:4 In order for laws to have teeth, there needs to be some form of enforcement behind them.
1:6 *Chaldeans* is another name for the Babylonians. God would use them to punish the wickedness of Judah.
1:13-17 Habakkuk wondered how God could be **silent** while a **wicked** people swallowed those who were **more righteous** (1:13). Sure,

Judah was bad, but **the Chaldeans** were even worse! All the nations were like **fish** in their **net**, just waiting to be slaughtered (1:14-17). Habakkuk couldn't comprehend that God, who is righteous, gives free reign to an evil nation that doesn't give him glory.

a 2:1 1Ch 9:27; 2Ch 8:14; Is 21:6-9
b Ps 85:8
c 2:2 1Sm 3:1; Ps 89:19; Pr 29:18; Is 1:1
d 2:3 Gn 18:14; 21:2; 2Kg 4:16-17; Dn 8:19; 11:27,29,35
e Dn 10:1,14; 11:35; Heb 10:36-37; 2Pt 3:9; Rv 22:10
f 2:4 Rm 1:17; Gl 3:11
g 2:5 Pr 27:20; 30:15-16; Is 5:14
h Is 13:4; 43:9; 66:18; Jr 3:17; Hs 10:10; Jl 3:2,11; Zph 3:8; Zch 12:3; 14:2; Mt 25:32
i 2:6 Is 14:4; Mc 2:4
j 1Kg 18:21; Ps 82:2; Pr 1:22; Jr 4:14,21; 23:26; 31:22; Hs 8:5
k Dt 24:10-13
l 2:7 2Kg 21:14; Is 42:22,24; Jr 49:32
m 2:8 Is 10:13; Ezk 36:4
n Zph 3:8
o Jr 6:7; Ezk 7:11,23; 8:17; 12:19; 45:9; Mc 6:12; Hab 1:2-3,9; 2:17
p Is 33:1; Jr 25:12,14; Hab 2:17; Rv 13:10
q 2:9 Pr 1:9; 15:27; Jr 6:13; 8:10; Ezk 22:27
r Pr 11:28; Jr 22:13; 49:16; Ob 4; Rv 18:7
s 2:11 Lk 19:40
t 2:12 Ezk 22:2-3; Mc 3:10
u 2:13 Jr 51:58
v 2:14 Nm 14:21; Ps 33:5; 72:19; 119:64; Is 6:3; 11:9; Jr 23:24

17 Will they therefore empty their net
and continually slaughter nations
without mercy?

HABAKKUK WAITS FOR GOD'S RESPONSE

2 I will stand at my guard post
and station myself
on the lookout tower.*a*
I will watch to see what he will say
to me*b*
and what I should^A reply
about my complaint.

GOD'S SECOND ANSWER

2 The LORD answered me:
Write down this vision;*c*
clearly inscribe it on tablets
so one may easily read it.^B

3 For the vision is yet
for the appointed time;*d*
it testifies about the end
and will not lie.
Though it delays, wait for it,
since it will certainly come and not
be late.*e*

∾ HOPE WORDS ∾

*Faith is the means to access
all that God has stored up
for you in his grace.*

4 Look, his ego is inflated;*c*
he is without integrity.
But the righteous one will live
by his faith.^D,*f*
5 Moreover, wine^E betrays;
an arrogant man is never at rest.^F
He enlarges his appetite like Sheol,
and like Death he is never satisfied.*g*
He gathers all the nations
to himself;*h*
he collects all the peoples
for himself.

THE FIVE WOE ORACLES

6 Won't all of these take up a taunt
against him,*i*
with mockery and riddles about him?
They will say:

Woe to him who amasses
what is not his —
how much longer?*j* —
and loads himself with goods
taken in pledge.*k*
7 Won't your creditors suddenly arise,
and those who disturb you wake up?
Then you will become spoil for them.*l*
8 Since you have plundered
many nations,*m*
all the peoples who remain
will plunder you*n* —
because of human bloodshed
and violence*o* against lands, cities,
and all who live in them.*p*

9 Woe to him who dishonestly makes
wealth for his house^G,*q*
to place his nest on high,
to escape the grasp of disaster!*r*
10 You have planned shame
for your house
by wiping out many peoples
and sinning against your own self.
11 For the stones will cry out^s
from the wall,
and the rafters will answer them
from the woodwork.

12 Woe to him who builds a city
with bloodshed
and founds a town with injustice!*t*
13 Is it not from the LORD of Armies
that the peoples labor only to fuel
the fire
and countries exhaust themselves
for nothing?*u*
14 For the earth will be filled
with the knowledge
of the LORD's glory,
as the water covers the sea.*v*

---

^A 2:1 Syr reads *what he will*   ^B 2:2 Lit *one who reads in it may run*   ^C 2:4 Hb obscure   ^D 2:4 Or *faithfulness*   ^E 2:5 DSS read *wealth*   ^F 2:5 Or *man does not endure*; Hb obscure   ^G 2:9 Or *dynasty*

2:1 In Habakkuk's mind, it wasn't fair that God was using an ally of Satan to judge the people of his kingdom. **2:2-3** Though God is the Creator and Judge of the universe, he takes the time to respond to his servant and let him in on what he's doing. History would be a witness to God's revelation, which is why the prophet was to **write** it **down** (2:2). The Babylonians would surely invade at **the appointed time** (2:3).

2:4 Indeed, the Babylonian king was **without integrity. But**—and this is what Habakkuk and all those who follow God need to know above all else—**the righteous one will live by his faith.** So, Habakkuk did not get a ten-point answer to his concerns or receive a long, drawn-out discussion of God's ways. God simply told him in essence, "Trust me and follow my instructions." God has everything under control. God's agenda may be mysterious, but everything he does will bring him glory and is ultimately for the good of his people (see Rom 8:28).

2:7-8 God would use the wicked Babylonians to punish Judah, but they too would be judged. The one who had **plundered many nations** would be plundered (2:8).

2:12-20 God has a track record of consistency, and persistent sin always brings his judgment. Even the wicked who escape it in this earthly life will face it in eternity. All human sin will either be judged in hell or at the cross of Christ.

15 Woe to him who gives
   his neighbors drink,
   pouring out your wrath[A]
   and even making them drunk,
   in order to look at their nakedness!
16 You will be filled with disgrace
   instead of glory.
   You also — drink,
   and expose your uncircumcision![B]
   The cup in the LORD's right hand
   will come around to you,
   and utter disgrace will cover
   your glory.[a]
17 For your violence against Lebanon
   will overwhelm you;
   the destruction of animals
   will terrify you[c]
   because of your human bloodshed
   and violence
   against lands, cities, and all who live
   in them.

18 What use is a carved idol
   after its craftsman carves it?
   It is only a cast image, a teacher
   of lies.
   For the one who crafts its shape
   trusts in it
   and makes idols that cannot speak.
19 Woe to him who says to wood:
   Wake up!
   or to mute stone: Come alive!
   Can it teach?
   Look! It may be plated with gold
   and silver,
   yet there is no breath[b] in it at all.

20 But the LORD is in his holy temple;[c]
   let the whole earth
   be silent in his presence.[d]

HABAKKUK'S THIRD PRAYER

3 A prayer of the prophet Habakkuk. According to *Shigionoth*.[D,e]
2 LORD, I have heard the report
   about you;
   LORD, I stand in awe of your deeds.[f]
   Revive your work in these years;
   make it known in these years.
   In your wrath remember mercy![g]

3 God comes from Teman,
   the Holy One
   from Mount Paran.[h]   *Selah*
   His splendor covers the heavens,
   and the earth is full of his praise.[i]
4 His brilliance is like light;
   rays are flashing from his hand.
   This is where his power is hidden.
5 Plague goes before him,
   and pestilence follows
   in his steps.
6 He stands and shakes[E] the earth;[j]
   he looks and startles the nations.
   The age-old mountains
   break apart;
   the ancient hills sink down.[k]
   His pathways are ancient.[l]
7 I see the tents of Cushan[F]
   in distress;
   the tent curtains of the land
   of Midian tremble.
8 Are you angry at the rivers, LORD?
   Is your wrath against the rivers?
   Or is your rage against the sea
   when you ride on your horses,
   your victorious chariot?[m]
9 You took the sheath from your bow;
   the arrows are ready[G] to be used
   with an oath.[H,n]   *Selah*
   You split the earth with rivers.
10 The mountains see you
   and shudder;[o]
   a downpour of water sweeps by.
   The deep roars with its voice[p]
   and lifts its waves[i] high.
11 Sun and moon stand still
   in their lofty residence,[q]
   at the flash of your flying arrows,
   at the brightness
   of your shining spear.
12 You march across the earth
   with indignation;
   you trample down the nations
   in wrath.[r]
13 You come out to save your people,[s]
   to save your anointed.[J]
   You crush the leader of the house
   of the wicked
   and strip him from foot[k]
   to neck.   *Selah*

[a] 2:15-16 Rv 14:8-10
[b] 2:19 Ex 32:4; Dt 27:15; Jdg 17:4; Is 30:22; 40:18-20; 44:9-20; Jr 10:14
[c] 2:20 Ps 11:4
[d] Zph 1:7; Zch 2:13
[e] 3:1 Ps 7 title
[f] 3:2 Ps 44:1; 64:9; 77:12; 90:16; 92:4; 111:3; 143:5
[g] Is 60:10

[h] 3:3 Dt 33:2; Jdg 5:4-5
[i] 1Ch 29:11; Jb 37:22; Ps 48:10; 72:19; 148:13; Is 42:10
[j] 3:6 Jb 9:6; Is 13:13; 24:19; Jl 2:10; 3:16; Hg 2:6,21; Heb 12:26
[k] Mc 1:4; Zch 14:4
[l] Jr 6:16; 18:15
[m] 3:8 Ps 68:17
[n] 3:9 Dt 32:40-43
[o] 3:10 Ps 77:16
[p] Ex 19:18; Ps 77:16
[q] 3:11 Jos 10:12-13
[r] 3:12 Ps 60:12; 68:30; 108:13; Is 25:10; 63:3; Mc 1:3
[s] 3:13 Dt 33:29; Jdg 2:18; Ps 28:9; Jr 15:20; Ezk 37:23; Zch 8:7; 9:16; Mt 1:21

[A]2:15 Or *venom*   [B]2:16 DSS, LXX, Aq, Syr, Vg read *and stagger*   [C]2:17 DSS, LXX, Aq, Syr, Tg, Vg; MT reads *them*   [D]3:1 Perhaps a passionate song with rapid changes of rhythm, or a dirge   [E]3:6 Or *surveys*   [F]3:7 = Midian   [G]3:9 Or *set*   [H]3:9 Hb obscure   [i]3:10 Lit *hands*   [J]3:13 The Davidic king or the nation of Israel   [k]3:13 Lit *foundation*

3:2 With his perspective righted, Habakkuk stands **in awe** of God. As he considers God's **deeds**—what he's done in the past and what he'll do in the future—Habakkuk asks God to **remember mercy** even as he justly pours out his **wrath**. This kind of intercession on behalf of others, in fact, is what godly people do. It's what Moses did (see Exod 32:11-14), and it's what Daniel did (see Dan 9:1-19). So remind God of his promises and plead for mercy. **3:13-16** In time, God will **save** his **people** (3:13). But in the meantime, Habakkuk would have to **quietly wait for the day of distress to come against the** invaders (3:16). Sometimes in the midst of trouble, we too must be patient, trusting God's promises and following his kingdom agenda for us.

*a*3:15 Ps 77:19
*b*3:16 Dn 10:4-9; Rv 1:17
c Is 37:3; Ob 12,14; Nah 1:7

*d*3:18 1Sm 2:1; 1Ch 16:35;
Ps 9:14; 40:16; 73:25; Is
25:9; 61:10
*e*3:19 1Sm 30:6; 1Ch 16:11;
Ps 18:1; 22:19; 28:7-8;
29:11; 105:4; 118:14; Is 12:2;
33:2; 45:24; 49:5; 51:9; Jr
16:19; Eph 6:10
f Ps 18:33
g 2Sm 22:34; Ps 18:33

14 You pierce his head
with his own spears;
his warriors storm out to scatter us,
gloating as if ready to
secretly devour the weak.
15 You tread the sea with your horses,
stirring up the vast water.*a*

HABAKKUK'S CONFIDENCE IN GOD EXPRESSED

16 I heard, and I trembled within;*b*
my lips quivered at the sound.
Rottenness entered my bones;
I trembled where I stood.
Now I must quietly wait for the day
of distress*c*
to come against the people
invading us.

17 Though the fig tree
does not bud
and there is no fruit on the vines,
though the olive crop fails
and the fields produce no food,
though the flocks disappear
from the pen
and there are no herds in the stalls,
18 yet I will celebrate in the LORD;
I will rejoice in the God
of my salvation!*d*
19 The LORD my Lord is my strength;*e*
he makes my feet like those
of a deer*f*
and enables me to walk
on mountain heights!*g*

For the choir director: on *A* stringed instruments.

*A*3:19 Lit *on my*

3:17-18 **Though the fig tree does not bud . . . the flocks disappear . . . yet I will . . . rejoice in the God of my salvation!** In other words, whatever happens to me, I'll praise the God who saves me.

3:19 When you know God's character (who he is) and his works (what he has done), you'll know that you can trust him to give you the **strength** to keep going (i.e., **feet like those of a deer**)—even in the dark (see Isa 40:27-31).

ZEPHANIAH

INTRODUCTION

Author

ZEPHANIAH'S NAME MEANS "Yahweh has hidden or protected." He was a prophet of royal lineage, and his genealogy in 1:1 reaches back four generations to King Hezekiah. (Most other prophets listed only two generations; see Zech 1:1.) Zephaniah prophesied in the days of King Josiah.

Historical Background

King Josiah's father Amon (Zeph 1:1) was a wicked man—so was his grandfather Manasseh. That heritage of wicked kings helps explain the rampant idolatry that plagued the land of Judah when Josiah inherited the throne in 640 BC.

Throughout his reign, Josiah struggled to squelch idolatry. Things were so bad that Judah's priests, along with pagan priests, led worship of Yahweh while also bowing before pagan gods (1:4-6)! It was the public reading of the book of the law that finally helped spawn reforms in the land: false priests were removed, people repented, pagan altars and idols were destroyed (see 2 Kgs 23:1-14). The existence of Judah's idolatrous practices in Zephaniah 1:4-6 implies that Zephaniah probably prophesied before Josiah's reforms began (ca. 621 BC).

Message and Purpose

The theme of Zephaniah is the day of the Lord—a time of darkness, gloom, and pain as God responds to humankind's sin, whether that of unbelievers or that of his people. Nevertheless, the day of the Lord also has a positive side. It is a time of restoration after judgment, like the construction of new buildings in place of the condemned ones that were torn down.

Zephaniah not only wrote about the day of the Lord in his time, but about the day of the Lord yet to come in the seven-year tribulation at the end of history. Then God will judge the world and prepare the nation of Israel for Christ's second coming to establish his millennial kingdom.

Today we experience glimpses of the day of the Lord as he judges us for our sins, with the hope of restoration. Society at large will see it in the days to come as God judges the world for its rejection of Christ. The character of God demands that this day must come, so place yourself in a posture of repentance.

Outline

*a*1:1 2Kg 16:20; 18:1–20:21
*b*2Kg 22:1–23:30; 2Ch 34:1–36:1; Jr 1:2
*c*2Kg 21:18-25
*d*1:2 Gn 6:7; 7:4
*e*1:3 1Kg 14:10; Ezk 14:17
*f*Is 13:9-12; Mt 13:41
*g*1:4 Ex 3:20; Ps 138:7; Ezk 14:9; 25:7,16; Zph 2:13
*h*1Kg 16:30-32
*i*2Kg 23:5
*j*1:5 Jr 19:13; 32:29
*k*Dt 6:13; Is 48:1
*l*1Kg 11:5; 2Kg 23:13; Jr 49:1,3
*m*1:7 Nm 13:30; Jdg 3:19; Hab 2:20; Zch 2:13
*n*Zph 1:14,18; 2:2-3

*o*1:7 Is 34:6; Jr 46:10
*p*Lv 7:11-21; 1Sm 16:5; 2Ch 35:5-13; Jr 22:17
*q*1:9 Zph 1:10; 3:11,16
*r*1Sm 5:5
*s*1:10 2Ch 33:14; Neh 3:3; 12:39
*t*2Kg 22:14; 2Ch 34:22
*u*1:12 Ex 15:8; Is 25:6; Jr 48:11
*v*Mal 2:17
*w*1:13 Dt 28:30; Am 5:11; Mc 6:15
*x*1:14 Is 13:6,9; Jl 1:15; 2:1,11,31; 3:14; Am 5:18,20; Ob 15; Zch 14:1; Mal 4:5

1 The word of the LORD that came to Zephaniah son of Cushi, son of Gedaliah, son of Amariah, son of Hezekiah,*a* in the days of Josiah*b* son of Amon,*c* king of Judah.

THE GREAT DAY OF THE LORD

2 I will completely
   sweep away everything
from the face of the earth*d* —
   this is the LORD's declaration.
3 I will sweep away people
   and animals;*e*
I will sweep away the birds of the sky
   and the fish of the sea,
and the ruins^A along with
   the wicked.*f*
I will cut off mankind
   from the face of the earth.
   This is the LORD's declaration.

4 I will stretch out my hand*g*
   against Judah
and against all the residents
   of Jerusalem.
I will cut off every vestige of Baal*h*
   from this place,
   the names of the pagan priests*i*
along with the priests;
5 those who bow in worship
   on the rooftops*j*
to the stars in the sky;
those who bow and pledge loyalty
   to the LORD*k*
but also pledge loyalty to Milcom;^B,*l*
6 and those who turn back
   from following the LORD,
who do not seek the LORD or inquire
   of him.
7 Be silent in the presence of the Lord
   GOD,*m*
for the day of the LORD is near.*n*

Indeed, the LORD has prepared
   a sacrifice;*o*
he has consecrated his guests.*p*

8 On the day of the LORD's sacrifice
   I will punish the officials,
   the king's sons,
and all who are dressed
   in foreign clothing.
9 On that day*q* I will punish
all who skip over the threshold,^C,*r*
who fill their master's house
   with violence and deceit.

10 On that day —
   this is the LORD's declaration —
there will be an outcry
   from the Fish Gate,*s*
a wailing from the Second District,*t*
and a loud crashing from the hills.
11 Wail, you residents of the Hollow,^D
for all the merchants^E
   will be silenced;
all those loaded with silver
   will be cut off.

12 And at that time I will
   search Jerusalem with lamps
and punish those
   who settle down comfortably,^F,*u*
who say to themselves:
The LORD will not do good or evil.*v*
13 Their wealth will become plunder
and their houses a ruin.
They will build houses but never live
   in them,
plant vineyards but never drink
   their wine.*w*

14 The great day of the LORD is near,*x*
near and rapidly approaching.

---

^A1:3 Perhaps objects connected with idolatry   ^B1:5 Some LXX mss, Syr, Vg; MT, other LXX mss read *their king*   ^C1:9 Hb obscure   ^D1:11 Or *the market district*   ^E1:11 Or *Canaanites*   ^F1:12 Lit *who thicken on their dregs*

1:1 Zephaniah was of Hamitic origin, having descended from the line of Cush. This is implied in the name of his father, **Cushi** (see Gen 10:6). He was also a descendant of King **Hezekiah**. Being of royal blood, he had insider knowledge about how a righteous kingdom should be managed and what happens when unrighteousness runs rampant.
1:2-3 Worldwide judgment will come. God will **sweep away everything from the face of the earth** (1:2)—an insight reminiscent of the time when God spoke similarly to Noah before the flood (see Gen 6:7). This destruction will be comprehensive (Zeph 1:3), and not even a cruise liner could rescue those destined to perish.
1:4-6 The temple was intended to be God's house and was designed to bear his name

alone; therefore, he served notice: **Baal** is being evicted (1:4). Double-minded worshipers would be shown the door (1:4-5)—along with any **who do not seek the LORD** (1:6). Since they wanted to worship the gods they made rather than the God who made them, they would meet the same fate as their idols.
1:7 Scripture frequently speaks of the **day of the LORD**, a time of judgment for God's enemies (1:7-18) and hope for God's people (3:9-20). Sometimes it refers to God's intervention in history (e.g., Joel 2:1-11); at other times, it refers to his intervention at the end of history (e.g., 1 Thess 5:1-5).
1:8 These men were operating by their agenda and not by God's. The Lord does not ride on the backs of politicians; he rides on his own glory and righteousness.

1:10-13 Those who profited from the avarice behind the perverse worship at the temple would be the recipients of the Lord's wrath. From the entry into the business area (**the Fish Gate**) to the business area itself (**the Second District**) to the **wealth** of the business owners, nothing of theirs would be left (1:10-11, 13).
1:14-18 The wrath God unleashed on the Egyptians leading up to the exodus was coming to Judah and their capital, Jerusalem. Back then God had told the Israelites through Moses what would happen if they broke their covenant with him (see Deut 28:15-68). Here, with vivid language, Zephaniah gives terrifying insight into the full scope of the **day of the LORD** (1:14).

Listen, the day of the LORD —
then the warrior's cry is bitter.
15 That day is a day of wrath,
a day of trouble and distress,
a day of destruction and desolation,
a day of darkness[a] and gloom,
a day of clouds and total darkness,[b]
16 a day of trumpet blast
and battle cry
against the fortified cities,
and against the high corner towers.
17 I will bring distress on mankind,
and they will walk like the blind[c]
because they have sinned
against the LORD.
Their blood will be poured out
like dust
and their flesh like dung.
18 Their silver and their gold
will be unable to rescue them
on the day of the LORD's wrath.[d]
The whole earth will be consumed
by the fire of his jealousy,[e]
for he will make a complete,
yes, a horrifying end
of all the inhabitants of the earth.

A CALL TO REPENTANCE

2 Gather yourselves together;
gather together, undesirable[A] nation,
2 before the decree[f] takes effect
and the day passes like chaff,
before the burning
of the LORD's anger[g]
overtakes you,
before the day of the LORD's anger
overtakes you.[h]
3 Seek the LORD,[i] all you humble[j]
of the earth,
who carry out what he commands.
Seek righteousness, seek humility;
perhaps you will be concealed[k]
on the day of the LORD's anger.

JUDGMENT AGAINST THE NATIONS

4 For Gaza will be abandoned,
and Ashkelon will become a ruin.
Ashdod will be driven out at noon,
and Ekron will be uprooted.[l]
5 Woe, inhabitants of the seacoast,
nation of the Cherethites![B,m]

The word of the LORD is
against you,[n]
Canaan, land of the Philistines:
I will destroy you until there is
no one left.[o]
6 The seacoast will
become pasturelands
with caves for shepherds and pens
for sheep.
7 The coastland will belong
to the remnant of the house
of Judah;
they will find pasture there.
They will lie down in the evening
among the houses of Ashkelon,
for the LORD their God will return
to them
and restore their fortunes.[p]

8 I have heard the taunting[q] of Moab
and the insults of the Ammonites,[r]
who have taunted my people
and threatened their territory.
9 Therefore, as I live —
this is the declaration of the LORD
of Armies,
the God of Israel —
Moab will be like Sodom[s]
and the Ammonites
like Gomorrah:[t]
a place overgrown with weeds,
a salt pit, and a perpetual wasteland.
The remnant of my people
will plunder them;
the remainder of my nation
will dispossess them.
10 This is what they get for their pride,
because they have taunted
and acted arrogantly[u]
against the people of the LORD
of Armies.
11 The LORD will be terrifying to them
when he starves all the gods
of the earth.
Then all the distant coasts and
islands of the nations
will bow in worship to him,
each in its own place.

12 You Cushites will also be slain
by my sword.[v]

[a] 1:15 Am 1:14; 5:18-20; Ob 12-14
[b] Ps 97:2; Ezk 34:12; Jl 2:2
[c] 1:17 Lm 4:14
[d] 1:18 Ezk 7:19
[e] Ex 34:14; Dt 29:20; Ps 79:5; Zph 3:8; Zch 1:14; 8:2
[f] 2:2 Jb 23:14; Ps 2:7; 148:6
[g] Nm 25:4; 32:14; Jr 4:8; 12:13; 25:37; 30:24; 51:45
[h] Lm 2:2
[i] 2:3 1Ch 22:19; 2Ch 12:14; 14:4; 15:12-13; 16:12; Ps 34:10; Is 9:13; 51:1; Hs 10:12; Am 5:14; Zph 1:6; Zch 8:21-22
[j] Nm 12:3; Ps 25:9; 37:11; 76:9; Am 8:4
[k] Gn 4:14; Ex 3:6; Ps 17:8
[l] 2:4 Jr 25:20; Am 1:6-8; Zch 9:5-7
[m] 2:5 Ezk 25:16

[n] 2:5 Is 37:22; Jr 16:10; 42:19; Am 3:1
[o] Is 5:9; 6:11; Jr 4:7; 26:9; 33:10; 34:22; 44:22; 46:19; 48:9; Zph 3:6
[p] 2:7 Ps 85:1; Jr 30:18; 48:47; Lm 2:14
[q] 2:8 Ps 42:10; 102:8; 119:42; Mt 27:44; Heb 10:33
[r] Am 1:13
[s] 2:9 Is 1:9; 3:9; 13:19; Jr 23:14; Rm 9:29
[t] Gn 19:24-25
[u] 2:10 Jr 48:42
[v] 2:12 Is 18:1-7

[A] 2:1 Or shameless   [B] 2:5 = Sea Peoples

2:1-3 God has an agenda for nations, cities, families, and individuals; and he holds everyone accountable to it. Even at this point in Judah's history, the divine King offers a call to repentance. They can be like the children of Israel in the exodus generation and accept the Lord's protection, or they can be like the Egyptians of that time and reject the message of judgment to their own destruction.
2:4-5 God the King's judgment was straightforward for the nation of Philistia in general and for four of its cities in particular: **Gaza**, **Ashkelon**, **Ashdod**, and **Ekron**.

2:9 The mere mention of **Sodom** and **Gomorrah** is enough to send chills down your spine in light of the judgment that God brought on them (see Gen 19:1-29).
2:11 All people **will bow** before God in the end (see Phil 2:10-11). Better to do it in the joy of salvation than in the terror of judgment.

*2:13 Nah 2:8; 3:7
*2:15 Is 13:3; 22:2; 23:7;
24:8; 32:13; Zph 3:11
*3:1 Ex 23:21; Dt 9:24; Ps
106:43
*Is 59:3
*3:2 1Sm 15:22
*Jb 5:17
*Pr 3:5
*3:3 Ezk 22:25
*Hab 1:8; Mt 7:15; Ac 20:29
*3:4 Jdg 9:4
*Ezk 22:26
*3:5 Ps 129:4
*Ps 92:15
*Jr 8:12

*3:6 Zph 1:16
*Jr 44:2; Zph 2:5
*3:8 Jr 3:21; Ps 33:20; Is
8:17; 30:18; 64:4
*Ps 69:24; Ezk 21:31; 22:31;
Nah 1:6
*Dt 29:20; Ps 79:5; Zch
1:14; 8:2
*3:9 Dn 12:10
*3:10 Is 18:1-3
*3:11 Gn 2:25; 2Sm 19:5;
Ps 25:3
*Is 1:2
*Jr 48:29
*Is 11:9
*3:12 Is 66:2

13 He will also stretch out his hand
        against the north
and destroy Assyria;
he will make Nineveh a desolate ruin,*
dry as the desert.
14 Herds will lie down in the middle
        of it,
every kind of wild animal.^A
Both eagle owls^B and herons^C
will roost in the capitals of its pillars.
Their calls will sound^D
        from the window,
but devastation^E will be
        on the threshold,
for he will expose the cedar work.^F
15 This is the jubilant^D city
that lives in security,
that thinks to herself:
I exist, and there is no one else.
What a desolation she has become,
a place for wild animals
        to lie down!
Everyone who passes by her
scoffs^G and shakes his fist.

WOE TO OPPRESSIVE JERUSALEM

3 Woe to the city that is rebellious^H,^C
        and defiled,^a
the oppressive city!
2 She has not obeyed;^e
she has not accepted discipline.^f
She has not trusted^g in the LORD;
she has not drawn near to her God.
3 The^I princes within her are
        roaring lions;^h
her judges are wolves of the night,^I
which leave nothing
        for^J the morning.
4 Her prophets are reckless^J —
treacherous men.
Her priests profane the sanctuary;
they do violence to instruction.^k
5 The righteous LORD is in her;^I
he does no wrong.^m
He applies his justice morning
        by morning;
he does not fail at dawn,
yet the one who does wrong
        knows no shame.^n

6 I have cut off nations;
their corner towers^o are destroyed.
I have laid waste their streets,
with no one to pass through.
Their cities lie devastated,
without a person,
        without an inhabitant.^p
7 I thought: You will certainly fear me
        and accept correction.
Then her dwelling place^k
would not be cut off
based on all that I had allocated
        to her.
However, they became more corrupt
in all their actions.
8 Therefore, wait for me^q —
        this is the LORD's declaration —
until the day I rise up for plunder.^L
For my decision is to gather nations,
to assemble kingdoms,
in order to pour out my indignation^r
        on them,
all my burning anger;
for the whole earth
        will be consumed
by the fire of my jealousy.^s

FINAL RESTORATION PROMISED

9 For I will then restore
pure^t speech to the peoples
so that all of them may call
on the name of the LORD
and serve him with a single purpose.^M
10 From beyond the rivers of Cush^u
        my supplicants,
        my dispersed people,
will bring an offering to me.
11 On that day you^N will not be put
        to shame^v
because of everything you have done
in rebelling^w against me.
For then I will remove
from among you your jubilant,^x
        arrogant people,
and you will never again be haughty
on my holy mountain.^y
12 I will leave
a meek and humble people^z
        among you,

---

^A2:14 Lit *every wild animal of a nation*   ^B2:14 Or *the pelicans*   ^C2:14 Or *the hedgehogs*   ^D2:14 Lit *sing*   ^E2:14 LXX, Vg read *ravens*
^F2:14 Hb obscure   ^G2:15 Or *hisses*   ^H3:1 Or *filthy*   ^I3:3 Lit *Her*   ^J3:3 Or *that had nothing to gnaw in*   ^K3:7 LXX, Syr read *her eyes*   ^L3:8 LXX, Syr
read *for a witness*; Vg reads *up forever*   ^M3:9 Lit *with one shoulder*   ^N3:11 = Israel

---

2:13-15 The seat of Assyrian power, **Nineveh**
had thought to herself, **I exist, and there is
no one else** (2:13, 15), but this is God-talk
reserved for the Lord alone (see Isa 46:9).
When infinite power speaks to finite power,
finite power loses the argument.

3:6-7 Jerusalem's God had judged wicked
nations before Jerusalem's eyes (3:6), which
should have made them take notice and **fear**
the Lord. Instead, the people **became more
corrupt** (3:7).
3:11-12 God **will remove ... arrogant people**
(3:11) and **leave a meek and humble people**

(3:12). Satan fell because of pride (see Isa
14:12-15; Ezek 28:17). He wanted the glory
that was God's alone. And he's been leading
humanity in the same direction ever since.
But God "resists the proud, but gives grace to
the humble" (Jas 4:6). There's room for only
one deity, and the role is taken.

and they will take refuge
in the name of the LORD.
13 The remnant[a] of Israel will no longer
do wrong or tell lies;
a deceitful tongue will not be found
in their mouths.
They will pasture and lie down,
with nothing to make them afraid.[b]

14 Sing for joy, Daughter Zion;
shout loudly, Israel!
Be glad and celebrate with all
your heart,
Daughter Jerusalem!
15 The LORD has removed
your punishment;
he has turned back your enemy.
The King of Israel, the LORD,
is among you;
you need no longer fear harm.
16 On that day it will be said
to Jerusalem:
"Do not fear;
Zion, do not let your hands
grow weak.[c]
17 The LORD your God is among you,
a warrior[d] who saves.

He will rejoice over you[e]
with gladness.
He will be quiet[A] in his love.
He will delight in you with singing."[f]

18 I will gather those
who have been driven[g]
from the appointed festivals;
they will be a tribute from you[B]
and a reproach on her.[c]
19 Yes, at that time
I will deal with all who oppress you.
I will save the lame[h] and gather
the outcasts;[i]
I will make those
who were disgraced
throughout the earth
receive praise and fame.
20 At that time I will bring
you[D] back,
yes, at the time I will gather you.
I will give you fame and praise
among all the peoples
of the earth,
when I restore your fortunes[j]
before your eyes.
The LORD has spoken.

[a] 3:13 Gn 45:7; 2Kg 19:31; Jr 23:3
[b] Gn 42:28; Jr 50:19; Ezk 34:14; Mc 4:4; 7:14
[c] 3:16 Jr 6:24; 50:43
[d] 3:17 Jos 1:14; Jb 16:14; Ps 78:65

[e] 3:17 Dt 28:63; 30:9
[f] Ps 30:5
[g] 3:18 Lm 1:4–5; 3:33
[h] 3:19 Ex 14:30
[i] Mc 4:6
[j] 3:20 Jb 42:10; Jr 29:14; Ezk 39:25; Hs 6:11; Jl 3:1

[A] 3:17 LXX, Syr read *He will renew you*   [B] 3:18 = Jerusalem   [C] 3:18 Hb obscure   [D] 3:20 = people of Israel

3:14–15 There is no greater **joy** (3:14) than knowing the sins that condemned you have been forgiven!
3:15 May the church live before the world as if **the King of Israel . . . is among** us.
3:17 If you are God's child, you can know that *God himself* will **rejoice over you** and **with singing**. God doesn't merely save repentant sinners from destruction; he makes them his own.

HAGGAI

INTRODUCTION

Author

THIS BOOK STATES THAT ITS prophecies came from the Lord to the prophet Haggai (1:1, 3).

Historical Background

After years of rejecting the warnings of prophets, Judah was devastated by King Nebuchadnezzar, and Judah's people were taken into captivity to Babylon for seventy years. After that, God graciously allowed them to return home. At the time Haggai wrote, those who'd returned had been back in the promised land for sixteen years. They'd laid the foundation for a new temple, but no further work had been accomplished.

Message and Purpose

The book of Haggai was written to the Jewish remnant that had returned to their homeland after the Babylonian captivity. Unfortunately, they were suffering from spiritual insensitivity and inertia. God had been put on their back burner, and his kingdom priorities had become secondary to their personal priorities. So though the people were supposed to put God first by rebuilding the temple, they were letting it lay in ruins while they built their own houses. At the same time, however, they wanted God to prioritize them.

One of the kingdom principles seen throughout Scripture is that we must seek God's kingdom and glory above all. God will not allow himself to be in second place in the lives of his people. His message through Haggai was that if the people would put his kingdom agenda before their own agenda, then they would have his help. He wanted them to know what Jesus would tell his disciples many years later: "Seek first the kingdom of God and his righteousness, and all these things will be provided for you" (Matt 6:33).

www.bhpublishinggroup.com/qr/te/37_00

Outline

I.   The Wake-Up Call (1:1-11)
II. The People's Response (1:12-15)
III. The Shake-Up Call (2:1-9)
IV. The Lord's Declaration (2:10-23)

COMMAND TO REBUILD THE TEMPLE

1 In the second year of King Darius,[A,a] on the first day of the sixth month, the word of the LORD came through the prophet[b] Haggai to Zerubbabel son of Shealtiel,[c] the governor of Judah, and to Joshua son of Jehozadak, the high priest:[d] 2 "The LORD of Armies says this: These people say: The time has not come for the house of the LORD to be rebuilt."[e] 3 The word of the LORD came through the prophet Haggai: 4 "Is it a time for you yourselves to live in your paneled houses,[f] while this house[B] lies in ruins? " 5 Now, the LORD of Armies says this: "Think carefully[g] about[C] your ways:

6 You have planted much
but harvested little.
You eat
but never have enough
to be satisfied.
You drink
but never have enough to be happy.
You put on clothes
but never have enough to get warm.
The wage earner puts his wages
into a bag with a hole in it."[h]

7 The LORD of Armies says this: "Think carefully about your ways. 8 Go up into the hills, bring down lumber, and build the house; and I will be pleased with it and be glorified," says the LORD. 9 "You expected much, but then it amounted to little. When you brought the harvest to your house, I ruined[D] it. Why? " This is the declaration of the LORD of Armies. "Because my house still lies in ruins, while each of you is busy with his own house.

10 So on your account,[E]
the skies have withheld the dew
and the land its crops.[i]

11 I have summoned a drought
on the fields and the hills,
on the grain, new wine, fresh oil,
and whatever the ground yields,
on man and animal,
and on all that your hands produce."

THE PEOPLE'S RESPONSE

12 Then Zerubbabel[j] son of Shealtiel, the high priest Joshua son of Jehozadak, and the entire remnant of the people[k] obeyed the LORD their God and the words of the prophet Haggai, because the LORD their God had sent him. So the people feared the LORD.[l] 13 Then Haggai, the LORD's messenger, delivered the LORD's message to the people: "I am with you[m] — this is the LORD's declaration." 14 The LORD roused the spirit[n] of Zerubbabel son of Shealtiel, governor of Judah, the spirit of the high priest Joshua son of Jehozadak, and the spirit of all the remnant of the people. They began work on the house of the LORD of Armies, their God, 15 on the twenty-fourth day of the sixth month, in the second year of King Darius.

ENCOURAGEMENT AND PROMISE

2 On the twenty-first day of the seventh month,[o] the word of the LORD came through the prophet Haggai: 2 "Speak to Zerubbabel son of Shealtiel, governor of Judah, to the high priest Joshua son of Jehozadak, and to the remnant of the people: 3 'Who is left among you who saw this house in its former glory? How does it look to you now? Doesn't it seem to you like nothing by comparison?[p] 4 Even so, be strong, Zerubbabel — this is the LORD's declaration.[q] Be strong, Joshua son of Jehozadak, high priest. Be strong, all you

[a] 1:1 Ezr 4:5; Neh 12:22; Dn 9:11; 11:1; Hg 1:15; 2:10; Zch 1:1,7; 7:1
[b] Ezr 5:1; 6:14
[c] 1Ch 3:19; Ezr 3:2,8; 5:2; Neh 12:1; Hg 1:12,14; 2:2,23; Lk 3:27
[d] Hg 1:12,14; 2:2,4; Zch 3:1,8; 6:11
[e] 1:2 Ezr 1:3
[f] 1:4 1Kg 7:7; Jr 22:14
[g] 1:5 Hg 2:15,18
[h] 1:6 Lv 26:20; Dt 28:38-40
[i] 1:10 Lv 26:20; Dt 11:17

[j] 1:12 1Ch 13:9; Ezr 3:8; Neh 12:1; Hg 2:2; Zch 4:6
[k] Is 10:20-21; Jr 41:10; Hg 2:2
[l] Ex 14:31; Dt 4:10; 1Sm 12:18
[m] 1:13 Hg 2:4
[n] 1:14 1Ch 5:26; Ezr 1:1,5; Is 13:17; 14:9; 41:10; 45:13; Jr 51:11
[o] 2:1 Lv 23:33-43; 2Ch 7:8-10
[p] 2:3 1Kg 5:13-16; 6:38; 1Ch 29:1-8; Ezr 3:10-13; Zch 4:10
[q] 2:4 Jos 1:6-9; 1Ch 28:10,20

[A] 1:1 King of Persia reigned 522–486 BC [B] 1:4 = the temple [C] 1:5 Lit Place your heart on, also in v. 7 [D] 1:9 Lit blew on [E] 1:10 Or So above you

---

1:2 The Israelites had been back home for sixteen years, and they'd not rebuilt the temple that the Babylonians destroyed many years earlier. That was a significant decision because it suggested that it wasn't important to have God in their midst; after all, the sanctuary was to be the place of his manifest presence. Not rebuilding the temple was an indicator that they hadn't returned to God. Building it would indicate they had.

1:3-4 That they had time to repair their own houses says their failure to erect the temple wasn't a time problem; it was a priority problem (1:4). People make time for what they think is important. At three o'clock on Sunday afternoon, for instance, everybody makes time to watch football. For

three hours, people will sit and observe a game. Yet most routinely claim they've no time to read the Bible, pray, meditate, or go to church. We know we are repenting and returning when we put God first.

1:5-6 One way to know you've not returned to God fully is if you find yourself living an unsatisfied life. To get our attention, God can make sure our hard work does not satisfy. But if we're following his agenda—seeking first his kingdom (see Matt 6:33)—we can find satisfaction even when we don't have much (see Phil 4:11, 13).

1:9-11 **You expected much, but then it amounted to little** (1:9) is the Lord's way of saying, "You wanted me to give you something, but I blew it away to remind you that

my house still lies in ruins (1:9). You need to get to work on remedying the problem."

Sometimes Christians call the negative circumstances in their lives "bad luck," but don't disconnect God from your mess. If there's calamity in your world, it didn't happen because of impersonal forces operating on the universe.

1:12-13 In this response of obedience, they were becoming what the remnant of God's people should be (1:12). Thus, God assured them of his presence to guide and empower them as they obeyed his word: **I am with you** (1:13).

2:3 This series of questions acknowledges the people's disappointment that the temple they were constructing couldn't compare to the splendor of Solomon's.

a 2:4 Hg 1:13; Zch 8:9
b 2:5 Ex 33:14-17
c 2:6 Hg 2:21
d Is 64:2; Ezk 38:19-20;
Heb 12:26-28
e 2:7 Ex 40:34-35; 1Kg
8:10-11; Is 60:1-13
f 2:9 Mt 12:42
g Is 60:18
h 2:11 Mal 2:7
i 2:12 Jr 11:15
j 2:13 Lv 11:39; 22:4-6; Nm
19:11-13,22

k 2:17 Dt 28:22; 1Kg 8:37;
Am 4:9
l Ps 105:32-33
m 2:18 Hg 1:5,7
n 2:19 Zch 8:9-13
o 2:21 Hg 2:6-7; Ezk
38:19-20
p 2:22 Gn 19:25; Am 4:11
q 2:23 Est 8:8; Jr 22:23-25
r Mt 1:12-13

people of the land — this is the Lord's declaration. Work! For I am with you[a] — the declaration of the Lord of Armies. [5] This is the promise I made to you when you came out of Egypt,[b] and my Spirit is present among you; don't be afraid.'"

[6] For the Lord of Armies says this: "Once more, in a little while, I am going to shake the heavens and the earth,[c] the sea and the dry land.[d] [7] I will shake all the nations so that the treasures of all the nations will come, and I will fill this house with glory,"[e] says the Lord of Armies. [8] "The silver and gold belong to me" — this is the declaration of the Lord of Armies. [9] "The final glory of this house[A] will be greater than the first,"[f] says the Lord of Armies. "I will provide peace in this place"[g] — this is the declaration of the Lord of Armies.

FROM DEPRIVATION TO BLESSING

[10] On the twenty-fourth day of the ninth month, in the second year of Darius, the word of the Lord came to the prophet Haggai: [11] "This is what the Lord of Armies says: Ask the priests for a ruling.[h] [12] If a man is carrying consecrated meat in the fold of his garment, and it touches bread, stew, wine, oil, or any other food, does it become holy?"[i]

The priests answered, "No."

[13] Then Haggai asked, "If someone defiled by contact with a corpse touches any of these, does it become defiled?"[j]

The priests answered, "It becomes defiled."

[14] Then Haggai replied, "So is this people, and so is this nation before me — this is the Lord's declaration. And so is every

work of their hands; even what they offer there is defiled.

[15] "Now from this day on, think carefully: Before one stone was placed on another in the Lord's temple, [16] what state were you in?[B] When someone came to a grain heap of twenty measures, it only amounted to ten; when one came to the winepress to dip fifty measures from the vat, it only amounted to twenty. [17] I struck you — all the work of your hands — with blight, mildew,[k] and hail,[l] but you didn't turn to me — this is the Lord's declaration. [18] "From this day on, think carefully;[m] from the twenty-fourth day of the ninth month, from the day the foundation of the Lord's temple was laid; think carefully. [19] Is there still seed left in the granary? The vine, the fig, the pomegranate, and the olive tree have not yet produced. But from this day on I will bless you."[n]

PROMISE TO ZERUBBABEL

[20] The word of the Lord came to Haggai a second time on the twenty-fourth day of the month: [21] "Speak to Zerubbabel, governor of Judah: I am going to shake the heavens and the earth.[o] [22] I will overturn royal thrones and destroy the power of the Gentile kingdoms.[p] I will overturn chariots and their riders. Horses and their riders will fall, each by his brother's sword. [23] On that day" — this is the declaration of the Lord of Armies — "I will take you, Zerubbabel son of Shealtiel, my servant" — this is the Lord's declaration — "and make you like my signet ring,[q] for I have chosen you."[r] This is the declaration of the Lord of Armies.

[A] 2:9 Or *The glory of this latter house*   [B] 2:16 Hb obscure

---

2:5 God made a **promise** to Israel when he brought them **out of Egypt** that he would bring them to a place of blessing. And indeed he had. They'd since been removed from that place and returned to it, but in spite of all that had happened, God's **Spirit** was still **among** his people. He'd not forgotten them.

2:6-7 Shaking refers to God's intentional interruption of the natural order of things. And in this case, he intended to shake things up to turn things around so that **glory** would come to his **house** (2:7). In chapter 1 God shook things up so that Israel would put him first. And often once we learn to do that, he'll shake things up "once more" to remind us that we are in an unshakable kingdom.

Before you go to church, you iron your clothes because you want to look nice. You

see something crooked and wrinkly and straighten it out. You apply heat and steam to accomplish the desired result. And similarly, God will apply heat to your situation just long enough to straighten your thinking. He wants to look good in you when you represent him.

2:9 The people were advancing God's kingdom program, giving God a central place of worship. Thus, the temple they built would be a precursor to the millennial temple that will stand when the Messiah rules the world from Jerusalem. The restored temple of the future will have a **greater** glory than Solomon's because of the presence of Jesus.

2:12-14 Defilement is transferable, like a contagious disease (2:13). Disobedience by God's

people, then, renders sacrifices unacceptable (2:14). Obedience is necessary for worship to be accepted.

2:15-19 Haggai reminded the people of the economic disaster that came on them because of their disobedience (2:15-17). Since they'd shifted priorities and obeyed, however, God would turn their curses into blessings (2:19).

2:23 **Zerubbabel** was God's appointed leader for the temple rebuilding task and was a prototype of the Messiah as he led the people to do the kingdom work of prioritizing God. Indeed, the true Messiah would come in the Davidic line through Zerubbabel and will ultimately lead the nation from the temple in Jerusalem.

ZECHARIAH

INTRODUCTION

Author

ZECHARIAH, SON OF BERECHIAH AND grandson of Iddo (1:1), was a prophet to the Jewish people who returned home from the Babylonian captivity. Apparently, he was also a priest (see Neh 12:12, 16). He and the prophet Haggai prophesied to Zerubbabel and the other leaders, encouraging them as they rebuilt the temple in Jerusalem (Ezra 5:1-2; 6:14), which was completed in 515–516 BC (Ezra 6:14-15). Zechariah dates the start of his prophetic ministry to "the eighth month, in the second year of Darius" (Zech 1:1), which was 520 BC.

Historical Background

In 538–539 BC, Cyrus the Persian king issued a decree for the Jewish people to rebuild their temple (Ezra 1:1-4). Though their homeland and capital city had been devastated, they began reconstructing the temple in earnest. But opposition from surrounding enemies caused the project to come to a halt (Ezra 4:1-5). In 520 BC, during the reign of Cyrus's successor King Darius, Zechariah began his prophetic ministry and called God's discouraged people to continue the task of rebuilding the temple (Zech 1:1; Ezra 4:24–5:2).

Message and Purpose

Zechariah's prophetic book is filled with eschatological visions and symbols designed to show that God has a plan to bring about his kingdom through his coming Messiah. Zechariah called God's people to be faithful while God demonstrated his faithfulness to them. The Messiah's rule would come, but until then God's people had to prepare themselves for it. Zechariah teaches that while God's promises are sure, the implementation of his kingdom program requires our involvement through repentance and obedience.

Zechariah, whose name means "the Lord remembers," called the people to remember God's promises. He also reassured them that God would establish his rule on earth through the union of the roles of King and priest in the Messiah. And he would exercise these roles not only for Israel, but for the whole world. Thus, although the people had been sent into captivity because of their rebellion, God had not forgotten them and would restore them if they would repent.

Zechariah is also important for its prophetic accuracy, foretelling Jesus's triumphal entry into Jerusalem hundreds of years before it occurred.

www.bhpublishinggroup.com/qr/te/38_00

Outline

I. The Kingdom Is Coming (1:1–8:23)
   A. Kingdom Repentance (1:1-6)
   B. Kingdom Visions (1:7–6:15)
   C. Kingdom Fast (7:1–8:23)
II. The King Is Coming (9:1–14:21)
   A. Judgment on Enemies and the Coming of the Shepherd (9:1–11:17)
   B. The Messiah and His Kingdom (12:1–14:21)

a 1:1 Ezr 4:5,24; 5:5-7; Ezr 6:1,12-15; Neh 12:22; Hg 1:1,15; 2:10; Zch 7:1
b Ezr 5:1; 6:14
c 1:2 Zch 8:14
d 1:3 Neh 1:9; Is 44:22; Jr 3:7,10; 24:7; Am 4:6-11; Mal 3:7
e 1:4 2Ch 30:7,8; Ps 78:8,57
f Dn 9:6,10; Am 3:7
g 2Kg 17:13; 2Ch 7:14; Ezk 33:9,11
h 1:6 Jr 51:12; Lm 2:17; Zch 8:14-15
i 1:8 Rv 6:4

j 1:11 Jos 11:23; Jdg 5:31; Is 14:7
k 1:12 Ps 13:1; 79:5; 89:46; 90:13; Jr 25:11-12; 29:10
l 1:14 Ex 20:5; 34:14; Dt 4:24; 5:9; 6:15; Jos 24:19; Nah 1:2; Zch 8:2
m 1:15 Is 34:2; Nah 1:2
n 1:16 2Kg 21:13; Is 28:17; 34:11; Lm 2:8; Am 7:17
o 1:17 2Ch 6:6; Is 40:1; Zch 2:12
p 1:18 Ezk 43:15,20

A PLEA FOR REPENTANCE

1 In the eighth month, in the second year of Darius,*a* the word of the Lord came to the prophet Zechariah*b* son of Berechiah, son of Iddo: **2** "The Lord was extremely angry with your ancestors.*c* **3** So tell the people, 'This is what the Lord of Armies says: Return to me — this is the declaration of the Lord of Armies — and I will return to you, says the Lord of Armies.*d* **4** Do not be like your ancestors;*e* the earlier prophets proclaimed to them:*f* This is what the Lord of Armies says: Turn from your evil ways and your evil deeds.*g* But they did not listen or pay attention to me — this is the Lord's declaration. **5** Where are your ancestors now? And do the prophets live forever? **6** But didn't my words and my statutes that I commanded my servants the prophets overtake your ancestors?'"

So the people repented and said, "As the Lord of Armies decided to deal with us for our ways and our deeds, so he has dealt with us."*h*

THE NIGHT VISIONS

7 On the twenty-fourth day of the eleventh month, which is the month of Shebat, in the second year of Darius, the word of the Lord came to the prophet Zechariah son of Berechiah, son of Iddo:

FIRST VISION: HORSEMEN

8 I looked out in the night and saw a man riding on a chestnut*A* horse.*i* He was standing among the myrtle trees in the valley.*B* Behind him were chestnut, brown, and white horses. **9** I asked, "What are these, my lord?"

The angel who was talking to me replied, "I will show you what they are."

10 Then the man standing among the myrtle trees explained, "They are the ones the Lord has sent to patrol the earth."

11 They reported to the angel of the Lord standing among the myrtle trees, "We have patrolled the earth, and right now the whole earth is calm and quiet."*j*

12 Then the angel of the Lord responded, "How long, Lord of Armies, will you withhold mercy from Jerusalem and the cities of Judah that you have been angry with these seventy years?"*k* **13** The Lord replied with kind and comforting words to the angel who was speaking with me.

14 So the angel who was speaking with me said, "Proclaim: The Lord of Armies says: I am extremely jealous*l* for Jerusalem and Zion. **15** I am fiercely angry with the nations that are at ease,*m* for I was a little angry, but they made the destruction worse.*c* **16** Therefore, this is what the Lord says: In mercy, I have returned to Jerusalem; my house will be rebuilt within it — this is the declaration of the Lord of Armies — and a measuring line will be stretched out over Jerusalem.*n*

17 "Proclaim further: This is what the Lord of Armies says: My cities will again overflow with prosperity; the Lord will once more comfort Zion and again choose Jerusalem."*o*

SECOND VISION: FOUR HORNS AND CRAFTSMEN

18 Then I looked up and saw four horns.*p* **19** So I asked the angel who was speaking with me, "What are these?"

And he said to me, "These are the horns that scattered Judah, Israel, and Jerusalem." **20** Then the Lord showed me four craftsmen. **21** I asked, "What are they coming to do?"

He replied, "These are the horns that scattered Judah so no one could raise his head. These craftsmen have come to terrify them, to cut off*D* the horns of the

---

A 1:8 Lit *red*   *B* 1:8 Lit *depths*   *C* 1:15 Lit *they helped for evil*   *D* 1:21 Lit *throw down*

1:1 Zechariah reminds his readers that the true King is in heaven when he says **the word of the Lord came to** him. When you're at the end of your rope, what you need more than anything else is the word of the Lord.
1:3 Even today, God calls us to repentance and faith. If we respond to him, we can count on him to show himself mighty on our behalf.
1:4-6 While their **ancestors** thought they could despise God and get away with it, they'd been proven wrong (1:4). As Isaiah says, "People are grass. The grass withers . . . but the word of our God remains forever" (Isa 40:7-8). So don't play chicken with God's Word. There will be only one winner, and it won't be you.

1:8-9 The prophet was given a glimpse into the angelic activity transpiring behind the scenes. It's a reminder that when we think nothing is happening, God is always at work.
1:10-11 The all-knowing God does not need angels to inform him of the state of the earth. Nevertheless, he has created them to serve him and to help humanity (see Heb 1:7, 13-14), and they must report to him. If angels must give an account of their work to the Lord, how much more will the followers of Jesus Christ have to give an account of their service to the King?
1:12-13 The **comforting words** from the Lord no doubt indicate that his anger was complete (1:13). After all, the Lord had promised through the prophet Jeremiah, "When sev-

enty years for Babylon are complete, I will . . . confirm my promise concerning you to restore you to this place" (Jer 29:10). The time of exile had come to an end.
1:14 That **the Lord** was **jealous for Jerusalem** indicates his intense love for his people.
1:16 **I have returned to Jerusalem** can also be rendered as a future verb: "I will return to Jerusalem." The Lord's future return "to Jerusalem" is a reference to the coming of the Messiah to rule on his throne in the millennial kingdom.
1:18-21 God had given a promise regarding the nations of the world and their relationship to his people: "I will bless those who bless you, I will curse anyone who treats you with contempt" (Gen 12:3). Enemy nations experienced the power of God's curse.

nations that raised a horn against the land of Judah to scatter it."

THIRD VISION: SURVEYOR

2 I looked up and saw a man with a measuring line in his hand. [2] I asked, "Where are you going?"

He answered me, "To measure Jerusalem to determine its width and length."

[3] Then the angel who was speaking with me went out, and another angel went out to meet him. [4] He said to him, "Run and tell this young man: Jerusalem will be inhabited without walls because of the number of people and livestock in it."[a] [5] The declaration of the LORD: "I myself will be a wall[b] of fire around it, and I will be the glory within it."

[6] "Listen! Listen! Flee from the land of the north"[c] — this is the LORD's declaration — "for I have scattered you like the four winds of heaven" — this is the LORD's declaration. [7] "Listen, Zion! Escape, you who are living with Daughter Babylon." [8] For the LORD of Armies says this: "In pursuit of his glory, he sent me against the nations plundering you, for whoever touches you touches the pupil[A] of my[B] eye. [9] For look, I am raising my hand against them, and they will become plunder for their own servants.[d] Then you will know that the LORD of Armies has sent me.

[10] "Daughter Zion, shout for joy and be glad, for I am coming to dwell among you" — this is the LORD's declaration. [11] "Many nations will join themselves to the LORD on that day and become my[c] people.[e] I will dwell among you, and you will know that the LORD of Armies has sent me to you. [12] The LORD will take possession of Judah as his portion in the Holy Land, and he will once again choose Jerusalem.[f] [13] Let all people be silent[g] before the LORD, for from his holy dwelling he has roused himself."

FOURTH VISION: HIGH PRIEST AND BRANCH

3 Then he showed me the high priest Joshua[h] standing before the angel of the LORD,[i] with Satan[D,j] standing at his right side to accuse him. [2] The LORD[E] said to Satan: "The LORD rebuke you, Satan! May the LORD who has chosen Jerusalem rebuke you! Isn't this man a burning stick snatched from the fire?"[k]

[3] Now Joshua was dressed with filthy[E] clothes[f] as he stood before the angel.[m] [4] So the angel of the LORD[G] spoke to those[H] standing before him, "Take off his filthy clothes!" Then he said to him, "See, I have removed your iniquity from you,[n] and I will clothe you with festive robes."

[5] Then I said, "Let them put a clean turban[o] on his head." So a clean turban was placed on his head, and they clothed him in garments while the angel of the LORD was standing nearby.

[6] Then the angel of the LORD charged Joshua: [7] "This is what the LORD of Armies says: If you walk in my ways and keep my mandates, you will both rule my house and take care of my courts; I will also grant you access among these who are standing here.

[a] 2:4 Is 49:19; Jr 31:27; Ezk 36:11
[b] 2:5 Is 26:1
[c] 2:6 Jr 6:22; 10:22; 50:9
[d] 2:9 Is 11:15; 19:16
[e] 2:10-11 Ps 47:9; Is 42:6; Mc 4:2
[f] 2:12 2Ch 6:6; Zch 1:17; 3:2
[g] 2:13 Hab 2:20
[h] 3:1 Hg 1:1,12,14; 2:4; Zch 6:11
[i] Gn 16:7-13; 21:17; 22:11-16; 31:11-13
[j] 1Ch 21:1; Jb 1:6-12; Rv 12:10
[k] 3:2 Dt 4:20; Am 4:11
[l] 3:3 Dt 23:13; Is 4:4
[m] Lv 22:3
[n] 3:4 2Sm 24:10; Jb 7:21; Mc 7:18
[o] 3:5 Ex 28:36-38

A 2:8 Or *apple*   B 2:8 Alt Hb tradition; MT reads *his*   C 2:11 LXX, Syr read *his*   D 3:1 Or *the accuser*   E 3:2 Syr reads *The Angel of the LORD*
F 3:3 Probably stained with human excrement   G 3:4 Lit *he*   H 3:4 = the angels

---

2:1-2 Dimensions could be determined by measuring a city's walls. In previous years, Jerusalem had formidable walls to provide defense against enemies. But the fact that the Jews had been exiled was proof that the walls could be—and had been—breached (see 2 Chr 36:19).
2:5 The idea of **a wall of fire** protecting God's people is reminiscent of the pillar of fire God used to protect Moses and the children of Israel as they left Egypt (see Exod 14:24). The Egyptian army was a major earthly superpower, but it was nothing before the God of creation. Similarly, the Lord guarantees the safety of his city in the millennium. He will be their wall of protection.
2:6-9 The Lord exhorts those Jews remaining in Babylon to return to Jerusalem because those who'd plundered Judah would be the object of God's wrath.
2:10-13 Jerusalem will be glorified when the Messiah comes **to dwell** within the city

during his millennial kingdom (2:10). At that time, Gentiles will join with believing Jews to worship the Messiah: **Many nations will join themselves to the LORD . . . and become** his **people** (2:11). Then Israel will be **the Holy Land** it was created to be (2:12). All humanity will submit to the Messiah's authority when he returns to earth (2:13).
3:1 **Satan** is the Hebrew word that means "adversary." It is also used as a proper name to refer to the one known in Scripture as "the evil one" (Matt 6:13; 2 Thess 3:3), "the devil," "the ancient serpent," and "the great dragon" (Rev 12:9). Satan was once a righteous angel, but he rebelled against the Lord and fell from grace (see the note on Isa 14:12-14). He has set up a rival "kingdom" in opposition to God (Matt 12:26). He tempted Adam and Eve to reject God's word (see Gen 3:1-5) and still tempts us today. He seeks to hinder the work of God's kingdom in the world (see Mark 4:15; 1 Thess 2:18).

One of the chief ways Satan opposes God's kingdom is by acting as "the accuser of our brothers and sisters" whom he "accuses . . . before our God day and night" (Rev 12:10).
3:2-7 Though Satan is "a liar and the father of lies" (John 8:44), sometimes—when he points out our sin—his accusations are correct. Enter the redeeming work of Christ on the cross to forgive believers and set them free from slavery to sin. In spite of Satan's continual accusations, Christians have "conquered him by the blood of the Lamb" (Rev 12:10-11). Therefore, we can accomplish the kingdom tasks that God puts before us. In order for him to **grant you access** to his kingdom power and restore you to your kingdom position and purpose, he calls you to repent and walk in his ways and keep his mandates (Zech 3:7). This is the appropriate response to God's grace (see Luke 22:31-32; cf. John 21:15-17).

a 3:8 Is 4:2; 11:1; Jr 23:5; 33:15; Ezk 17:22-24; Zch 6:12
b 3:9 Ps 118:22-23; Is 8:14; 28:16; Dn 2:35,45; Zch 4:10; Rv 5:6
c Zch 4:10
d 3:10 1Kg 4:25; 2Kg 18:31; Mc 4:1-8
e 4:6 Hs 1:7; Hg 2:4-5
f 4:7 Mt 17:20; 21:21; 1Co 13:2
g Is 40:4
h 4:8 Zch 6:9

i 4:9 Ezr 3:8-11; 5:16
j 4:10 Hg 2:3-4
k 2Ch 16:9; Ps 34:15; Pr 15:3; Am 9:8; 1Pt 3:12
l 4:14 Jr 33:17-22
m Rv 11:3-4

n 5:1 Ezk 2:9-10; Rv 5:1; 10:2
o 5:2 Ex 26:15-25; 1Kg 6:3; 1Pt 4:17
p 5:3 Dt 11:26-28; 28:15-68
q 5:4 Ps 147:15; Is 55:11
r Ezr 6:11; Dn 2:5; 3:29

8 "Listen, High Priest Joshua, you and your colleagues sitting before you; indeed, these men are a sign that I am about to bring my servant, the Branch.*a* **9** Notice the stone*b* I have set before Joshua; on that one stone are seven eyes.*c* I will engrave an inscription on it" — this is the declaration of the LORD of Armies — "and I will take away the iniquity of this land in a single day. **10** On that day, each of you will invite his neighbor to sit under his vine and fig tree."*d* This is the declaration of the LORD of Armies.

FIFTH VISION: GOLD LAMPSTAND

4 The angel who was speaking with me then returned and roused me as one awakened out of sleep. **2** He asked me, "What do you see?"

I replied, "I see a solid gold lampstand with a bowl at the top. The lampstand also has seven lamps at the top with seven spouts for each of*A* the lamps. **3** There are also two olive trees beside it, one on the right of the bowl and the other on its left."

4 Then I asked the angel who was speaking with me, "What are these, my lord?"

5 "Don't you know what they are?" replied the angel who was speaking with me.

I said, "No, my lord."

6 So he answered me, "This is the word of the LORD to Zerubbabel: 'Not by strength or by might, but by my Spirit,'*e* says the LORD of Armies. **7** 'What are you, great mountain?*f* Before Zerubbabel you will become a plain.*g* And he will bring out the capstone accompanied by shouts of: Grace, grace to it!'"

8 Then the word of the LORD came to me:*h* **9** "Zerubbabel's hands have laid the foundation of this house,*i* and his hands will complete it. Then you will know that the LORD of Armies has sent me to you. **10** For who despises the day of small things?*j* These seven eyes of the LORD, which scan throughout the whole earth, will rejoice when they see the ceremonial stone*j* in Zerubbabel's hand."*k*

11 I asked him, "What are the two olive trees on the right and left of the lampstand?" **12** And I questioned him further, "What are the two streams*c* of the olive trees, from which the golden oil is pouring through the two golden conduits?"

13 Then he inquired of me, "Don't you know what these are?"

"No, my lord," I replied.

14 "These are the two anointed ones,"*D,l* he said, "who stand by the Lord of the whole earth."*m*

SIXTH VISION: FLYING SCROLL

5 I looked up again and saw a flying scroll.*n* **2** "What do you see?" he asked me.

"I see a flying scroll," I replied, "thirty feet*E* long and fifteen feet*F* wide."*o*

3 Then he said to me, "This is the curse*p* that is going out over the whole land, for everyone who is a thief, contrary to what is written on one side, has gone unpunished,*G* and everyone who swears falsely, contrary to what is written on the other side, has gone unpunished. **4** I will send it out,"*q* — this is the declaration of the LORD of Armies — "and it will enter the house of the thief and the house of the one who swears falsely by my name. It will stay inside his house and destroy it along with its timbers and stones."*r*

A 4:2 Or *seven lips to*   *B* 4:10 Lit *the tin stone*   *C* 4:12 Or *branches*   *D* 4:14 = Joshua and Zerubbabel   *E* 5:2 Lit *20 cubits*   *F* 5:2 Lit *10 cubits*
G 5:3 Or *side, will be removed*

3:8 The Branch (see 6:12) is a messianic reference. God had promised David that a dynasty of kings would descend from him, leading to a King who would have an eternal throne and kingdom (see 2 Sam 7:11-16; 1 Chr 17:10-14). But most of the Davidic kings rebelled against the Lord; therefore, they experienced God's judgment when Judah was carried into exile by Babylon. Nevertheless, God promised, "A shoot will grow from the stump of Jesse [David's father], and a branch from his roots will bear fruit" (Isa 11:1).

4:6 The Jews in Jerusalem had faced much opposition and discouragement (see Ezra 4:1-23); therefore, if **Zerubbabel** were to complete the temple, it would not be the result of mere human strength but through the supernatural empowering of the Holy **Spirit**. Thus, the abundant oil supplying the brilliant lampstand represented the overflowing power of God's Spirit (see Zech 4:2).

As you seek to engage in God's kingdom work in the world, you too should remember that human effort will only get you so far. The empowerment to do the work of God comes only through the Spirit of God.

4:11-14 Kings and priests were anointed in the Old Testament (see Lev 8:10-12; 1 Sam 16:13); therefore, in the days of Zechariah, **the two anointed ones** (4:14) would be Joshua the high priest and Zerubbabel the (Davidic) governor (since Jerusalem was ruled by Persia and could not have their own king). However, the angel also seems to be pointing Zechariah to a yet future time, for these two anointed ones **stand by the Lord of the whole earth** (4:14). In the messianic kingdom, Israel will rebuild the millennial temple (see Ezek 40-48). Then they will fulfill their role as a light to the nations when the Messiah (who is both King and priest) rules all as the Lord of the earth.

5:1-4 The **scroll** represents the judgment of God's Word symbolically covering Israel (5:1-2). The vision indicates that the Lord's judgment is all encompassing and does not allow for any to escape. He *will* deal once and for all with the sinful transgression of his law when the Messiah comes and establishes his kingdom.

5:5-11 When God's judgment comes on the sins of Israel (see 5:1-4), then the nation's wickedness will be removed to the place of destruction: **Shinar** (5:11)—that is, Babylon (see Gen 11:2; Rev 18:2, 21). In the coming kingdom ruled by the Messiah, there will be no room for wickedness.

SEVENTH VISION: WOMAN IN THE BASKET

5 Then the angel who was speaking with me came forward and told me, "Look up and see what this is that is approaching." **6** So I asked, "What is it?"

He responded, "It's a measuring basket[A] that is approaching." And he continued, "This is their iniquity[B] in all the land." **7** Then a lead cover was lifted, and there was a woman[a] sitting inside the basket.[b] **8** "This is Wickedness," he said. He shoved her down into the basket and pushed the lead weight over its opening. **9** Then I looked up and saw two women approaching with the wind in their wings. Their wings were like those of a stork,[c] and they lifted up the basket between earth and sky. **10** So I asked the angel who was speaking with me, "Where are they taking the basket?"

11 "To build a shrine for it in the land of Shinar,"[d] he told me. "When that is ready, the basket will be placed there on its pedestal."

EIGHTH VISION: FOUR CHARIOTS

6 Then I looked up again and saw four chariots coming from between two mountains. The mountains were made of bronze. **2** The first chariot had chestnut[c] horses,[e] the second chariot black horses,[f] **3** the third chariot white horses,[g] and the fourth chariot dappled[h] horses — all strong horses. **4** So I inquired of the angel who was speaking with me, "What are these, my lord?"

5 The angel told me, "These are the four spirits[D,i] of heaven going out after presenting themselves to the Lord of the whole earth. **6** The one with the black horses is going to the land of the north, the white horses are going after them, but the dappled horses are going to the land of the south." **7** As the strong horses went out, they wanted to go patrol the earth, and the LORD said, "Go, patrol the earth." So they patrolled the earth. **8** Then he summoned me saying, "See, those going to the land of the north have pacified my Spirit in the northern land."

CROWNING OF THE BRANCH

9 The word of the LORD came to me:[j] **10** "Take an offering from the exiles, from Heldai, Tobijah, and Jedaiah, who have arrived from Babylon, and go that same day to the house of Josiah son of Zephaniah. **11** Take silver and gold, make a crown,[E] and place it on the head of Joshua son of Jehozadak, the high priest. **12** You are to tell him: This is what the LORD of Armies says: Here is a man whose name is Branch;[k] he will branch out from his place and build the LORD's temple. **13** Yes, he will build the LORD's temple; he will be clothed in splendor[l] and will sit on his throne and rule. There will also be a priest on his throne, and there will be peaceful counsel between the two of them.[m] **14** The crown will reside in the LORD's temple as a memorial to Heldai, Tobijah, Jedaiah, and Hen[F] son of Zephaniah. **15** People who are far off will come and build the LORD's temple, and you will know that the LORD of Armies has sent me to you. This will happen when you fully obey the LORD your God."[n]

DISOBEDIENCE AND FASTING

7 In the fourth year of King Darius,[o] the word of the LORD came to Zechariah on the fourth day of the ninth month, which is Chislev. **2** Now the people of Bethel had sent Sharezer, Regem-melech, and their men to plead for the LORD's favor[p] **3** by asking the priests who were in the house of the LORD of Armies as well as the prophets, "Should we mourn and fast in the fifth month as we have done these many years?"

4 Then the word of the LORD of Armies came to me: **5** "Ask all the people of the land and the priests: When you fasted and lamented in the fifth and in the seventh months for these seventy years, did you really fast for me?[q] **6** When you eat and drink, don't you eat and drink simply for yourselves?[r] **7** Aren't these the words that

a 5:7 Hs 9:15; Rv 17:1
b Lv 19:36; Dt 25:14; Pr 20:10; Ezk 45:10; Am 8:5
c 5:9 Jr 8:7
d 5:11 Gn 11:9
e 6:2 Rv 6:4
f Rv 6:5-6
g 6:3 Rv 6:2; 19:11
h Gn 31:10,12
i 6:5 Jr 49:36; Rv 7:1-3
j 6:9 Zch 4:8
k 6:12 Zch 3:8
l 6:13 1Ch 16:27; 29:25; Ps 96:6
m Ps 45:6-7; 110:1-7; Dn 7:9-14; Heb 1:3,13; Rv 5:6
n 6:15 Dt 28:1
o 7:1 Zch 1:1
p 7:2 Zch 8:21-22
q 7:5 Is 58:1-7
r 7:6 1Co 10:31

A 5:6 Lit *It's an ephah*   B 5:6 One Hb ms, LXX, Syr; other Hb mss read *eye*   C 6:2 Lit *red*   D 6:5 Or *winds*   E 6:11 Lit *crowns*   F 6:14 Probably Josiah

6:1 Mountains carry the idea of strength and power (see Isa 2:2; Dan 2:35). These may represent heaven.

6:7 These spirits **patrol the earth**, keeping watch on the Lord's behalf for anything that opposes the King's agenda. To know that the God of heaven is always watching over his creation is a comfort to the people of God throughout the ages.

6:11-13 The making of the **crown** symbolizes the unification of the office of priest and king (6:11). Joshua prefigured this, but it would ultimately be fulfilled in the Messiah, who will rebuild the temple and rule over his kingdom in the millennium. He will be **a priest on his throne** (6:13).

6:14-15 The crown being **in the LORD's temple** (6:14) was a reminder of their future Messiah and their obligation to **fully obey the LORD** (6:15).

7:2-6 Now that **the people of Bethel** were back in the land and the temple was nearly built, they wanted to know whether this mourning and fasting was still necessary (7:2-3). God's answer makes it clear that they had not asked an innocent question (7:5). They'd just been going through rituals, merely eating and drinking rather than rejoicing in God's deeds and provisions (7:6).

a 7:9 Ex 18:19-23; Zch 8:16
b Jr 7:5-7; Hs 10:12; Mc 6:8
c 7:10 Dt 14:29; 16:11
d Mt 22:39; Jms 3:5-6
e 7:11 Zch 1:4
f Is 6:10
g 7:12 Jr 7:13,24
h 8:2 Zch 1:14
i 8:3 Is 1:26

j 8:8 Is 11:11-12; Mc 2:12-13
k Gn 17:7-8; Dt 26:17-18;
Rv 21:3
l 8:12 Dt 31:7; Jos 1:6;
Is 49:8
m 8:13 Dt 21:23; 2Kg 22:19
Gn 12:2-3
o 8:15 Dt 8:16; Jr 32:40-41;
Ezk 36:11
p 8:17 Mc 2:1
q Dt 10:12-22; Mt 22:39
r Lv 5:4; Nm 30:2; Jr 5:2
s 8:19 2Kg 25:3-4; Jr 39:2

the Lord proclaimed through the earlier prophets when Jerusalem was inhabited and secure,^A along with its surrounding cities, and when the southern region and the Judean foothills were inhabited?"

8 The word of the Lord came to Zechariah: **9** "The Lord of Armies says this: 'Make fair decisions.^a Show faithful love and compassion^b to one another. **10** Do not oppress the widow or the fatherless, the resident alien or the poor,^c and do not plot evil in your hearts against one another.'^d **11** But they refused to pay attention^e and turned a stubborn shoulder; they closed their ears so they could not hear.^f **12** They made their hearts like a rock so as not to obey the law or the words that the Lord of Armies had sent by his Spirit through the earlier prophets.^g Therefore intense anger came from the Lord of Armies. **13** Just as he had called, and they would not listen, so when they called, I would not listen, says the Lord of Armies. **14** I scattered them with a windstorm over all the nations that had not known them, and the land was left desolate behind them, with no one coming or going. They turned a pleasant land into a desolation."

OBEDIENCE AND FEASTING

8 The word of the Lord of Armies came: **2** The Lord of Armies says this: "I am extremely jealous^h for Zion; I am jealous for her with great wrath." **3** The Lord says this: "I will return to Zion and live in Jerusalem. Then Jerusalem will be called the Faithful City;^i the mountain of the Lord of Armies will be called the Holy Mountain." **4** The Lord of Armies says this: "Old men and women will again sit along the streets of Jerusalem, each with a staff in hand because of advanced age. **5** The streets of the city will be filled with boys and girls playing in them." **6** The Lord of Armies says this: "Though it may seem impossible to the remnant of this people in those days,

should it also seem impossible to me?" — this is the declaration of the Lord of Armies. **7** The Lord of Armies says this: "I will save my people from the land of the east and the land of the west.^B **8** I will bring them back^j to live in Jerusalem. They will be my people, and I will be their faithful and righteous God."^k

9 The Lord of Armies says this: "Let your hands be strong, you who now hear these words that the prophets spoke when the foundations were laid for the rebuilding of the temple, the house of the Lord of Armies. **10** For prior to those days neither man nor animal had wages. There was no safety from the enemy for anyone who came or went, for I turned everyone against his neighbor. **11** But now, I will not treat the remnant of this people as in the former days" — this is the declaration of the Lord of Armies. **12** "For they will sow in peace: the vine will yield its fruit, the land will yield its produce, and the skies will yield their dew. I will give the remnant of this people all these things as an inheritance.^l **13** As you have been a curse among the nations,^m house of Judah and house of Israel, so I will save you, and you will be a blessing.^n Don't be afraid; let your hands be strong." **14** For the Lord of Armies says this: "As I resolved to treat you badly when your fathers provoked me to anger, and I did not relent," says the Lord of Armies, **15** "so I have resolved again in these days to do what is good to Jerusalem and the house of Judah.^o Don't be afraid. **16** These are the things you must do: Speak truth to one another; make true and sound decisions within your city gates. **17** Do not plot evil^p in your hearts against your neighbor,^q and do not love perjury,^r for I hate all this" — this is the Lord's declaration.

18 Then the word of the Lord of Armies came to me: **19** The Lord of Armies says this: "The fast of the fourth month,^s the fast of the fifth, the fast of the seventh, and

---

7:9 Biblical **love** isn't a sentimental feeling. To love your neighbor is to righteously desire his or her good and to meet his or her needs in a way that glorifies God.
7:10 Do not oppress the widow or the fatherless, the resident alien or the poor brings to my mind James's teaching to the Christians to whom he was writing: "Pure and undefiled religion before God the Father is this: to look after orphans and widows in their distress" (Jas 1:27). God champions the cause of the weak and oppressed. He expects the same of his people, if they expect to be in fellowship with him.

7:11-12 In other words, the previous generations had not been merely passive but had actively opposed God's law. Nevertheless, you can't mock God and expect no consequences. And the consequences for Israel and Judah had been disastrous.
8:3 The **Jerusalem** that existed prior to the captivity cannot compare with the Jerusalem of the future; they are as different as day and night. Zechariah's vision of the coming messianic kingdom when Jesus Christ will dwell in the midst of the city is a beautiful reminder that through his righteous reign and

protective care, Jerusalem will be a place of faithfulness and security.
8:4-8 A people whose city had been destroyed and who had been oppressed and killed by their enemies will one day see a complete reversal of circumstances for Jerusalem. Those to whom Zechariah was preaching may have thought all this **impossible** (8:6), but "with God all things are possible" (Matt 19:26).
8:16-17 If the people wanted the blessings that their ancestors had lost, they **must do** the kingdom agenda that their ancestors had rejected.

the fast of the tenth[a] will become times of joy, gladness, and cheerful festivals for the house of Judah. Therefore, love truth and peace." **20** The LORD of Armies says this: "Peoples will yet come, the residents of many cities; **21** the residents of one city will go to another, saying: Let's go at once to plead for the LORD's favor and to seek the LORD of Armies. I am also going. **22** Many peoples and strong nations will come to seek the LORD of Armies in Jerusalem and to plead for the LORD's favor."[b] **23** The LORD of Armies says this: "In those days, ten men from nations of every language will grab the robe of a Jewish man tightly, urging: Let us go with you,[c] for we have heard that God is with you."

JUDGMENT OF ZION'S ENEMIES

9 A pronouncement:
The word of the LORD
is against the land of Hadrach,
and Damascus[d] is its resting place —
for the eyes of humanity
and all the tribes of Israel
are on the LORD[A] —
2 and also against Hamath,[e]
which borders it,
as well as Tyre[f] and Sidon,[g]
though they are very shrewd.
3 Tyre has built herself a fortress;
she has heaped up silver like dust
and gold like the dirt of the streets.
4 Listen! The Lord will impoverish her
and cast her wealth into the sea;
she herself will be consumed by fire.[h]
5 Ashkelon will see it and be afraid;
Gaza too, and will writhe
in great pain,
as will Ekron, for her hope will fail.
There will cease to be a king in Gaza,
and Ashkelon will
become uninhabited.

6 A mongrel people will live
in Ashdod,
and I will destroy the pride
of the Philistines.[i]
7 I will remove the blood
from their mouths
and the abhorrent things[j]
from between their teeth.
Then they too will become
a remnant for our God;
they will become like a clan
in Judah
and Ekron like the Jebusites.[k]
8 I will encamp at my house
as a guard,
against those who march
back and forth,
and no oppressor will march
against them again,
for now I have seen
with my own eyes.

THE COMING OF ZION'S KING

9 Rejoice greatly, Daughter Zion!
Shout in triumph,
Daughter Jerusalem!
Look, your King is coming to you;
he is righteous and victorious,[B]
humble and riding on a donkey,
on a colt, the foal of a donkey.[l]
10 I will cut off the chariot
from Ephraim
and the horse from Jerusalem.
The bow of war will be removed,
and he will proclaim peace
to the nations.
His dominion will extend from sea
to sea,
from the Euphrates River
to the ends of the earth.[m]
11 As for you,
because of the blood
of your covenant,[n]

[a] 8:19 2Kg 25:1; Jr 39:1
[b] 8:20-22 Is 2:2-3; Jr 16:19; Mc 4:1-3; Mal 1:11-14
[c] 8:23 Is 4:1
[d] 9:1 Gn 15:2; 1Kg 11:24; Sg 7:4; Is 7:8; Am 1:3
[e] 9:2 2Kg 14:25
[f] Jos 19:29; Is 23:1
[g] Gn 10:15
[h] 9:4 Ezk 26:4-6; 27:27

[i] 9:6 Am 1:6-8; Zph 2:4-6
[j] 9:7 Lv 11:10; Dt 29:17; Dn 11:31
[k] 2Sm 5:6-10; 24:16-25
[l] 9:9 Is 62:11; Mt 21:5; Jn 12:15
[m] 9:10 Ps 72:8; Mc 7:12
[n] 9:11 Heb 10:29; 13:20

[A] 9:1 Or eyes of the LORD are on mankind —   [B] 9:9 Or and has salvation

8:19 Times of fasting honor the Lord and bring joy when they are set in the context of a relationship with him. Moreover, fasting must not be divorced from a life that loves **truth and peace**. To fulfill religious duties while ignoring kingdom principles is to embrace empty ritual rather than kingdom relationship.

8:20-23 At this point Zechariah returns to a vision of the millennial kingdom.

In that day, peoples from all over the world will go to **Jerusalem** to **seek the LORD** due to their supernatural transformation as a result of their acceptance of the Messiah (8:20-22).

9:1-5 Israel and Judah had many enemies throughout their history. In every direction

there were nations wishing for their demise. The prophetic promise of Zechariah is that there will come a time when the enemies of God's people will be permanently removed. That news would have captured the hearts and minds of the former exiles.

9:6-8 Notice that in spite of his judgment on the Philistines, God promised that **they too** would **become a remnant for our God** (9:7). There will one day be "a vast multitude from every nation, tribe, people, and language" worshiping the Lamb (Rev 7:9)—even from among those who were some of the greatest enemies of his people.

9:9 In Zechariah's day, Jerusalem had no king but was ruled over by foreign powers. But in the future, the **righteous and victorious**

Messiah would enter Jerusalem **riding on ... the foal of a donkey**.

This was fulfilled in part when Jesus rode into Jerusalem on a donkey days before he was crucified as an atoning substitute for sinners and rose from the dead (see Matt 21:1-11). When he returns, he will again enter Jerusalem—this time as a triumphant King establishing his kingdom.

9:11-16 According to Isaiah, Jerusalem had received "double for all her sins" (Isa 40:2). But in the days to come, God declares, **I will restore double to you** (Zech 9:12). They will conquer their enemies with the Lord providing defense (9:13-15). In the last days, in fact, God will deliver Israel and cause his people to sparkle **like jewels in a crown** (9:16).

[a] 9:11 Gn 37:24; Jr 38:6
[b] 9:12 Jb 42:10; Is 61:7;
Jr 16:18
[c] 9:13 Dn 8:21; 10:20
[d] 9:14 Ps 83:15
[e] 9:15 Nm 23:24
[f] Ex 27:3
[g] Lv 1:5,11; 3:2
[h] 9:16 Ezk 36:38
[i] Lv 8:9
[j] 10:1 Dt 28:12; Is 30:23;
Jr 51:16
[k] 10:2 Jr 27:9; Mc 3:7

[l] 10:4 Jdg 20:2; 1Sm 14:38;
Ps 118:22; Is 28:16
[m] Jdg 4:21
[n] 2Kg 13:15–17; Rv 6:2
[o] 10:6 Ps 103:12
[p] 10:7 Is 7:8
[q] Ex 4:14; Ps 16:9
[r] 10:8 Is 5:26; 7:18
[s] Ex 13:13; 21:8; 34:20; Jb
5:20; Ps 130:8; Is 51:11;
Mc 6:4
[t] 10:9 Gn 26:12; Ex 23:16;
Ps 126:5
[u] Gn 40:23; Jos 1:13
[v] 10:10 Gn 31:21; Dt 34:1;
Ps 60:7

I will release your prisoners
from the waterless cistern.[a]

12 Return to a stronghold,
you prisoners who have hope;
today I declare that I will restore
double to you.[b]

13 For I will bend Judah as my bow;
I will fill that bow with Ephraim.
I will rouse your sons, Zion,
against your sons, Greece.[A,C]
I will make you
like a warrior's sword.

14 Then the LORD will appear
over them,
and his arrow will fly like lightning.
The Lord GOD will sound
the trumpet
and advance
with the southern storms.[d]

15 The LORD of Armies will
defend them.
They will consume and conquer
with slingstones;
they will drink and be rowdy as if
with wine.[e]
They will be as full as
the sprinkling basin,[f]
like those at the corners of the altar.[g]

16 The LORD their God will save them
on that day
as the flock of his people;[h]
for they are like jewels in a crown,[i]
sparkling over his land.

17 How lovely and beautiful!
Grain will make
the young men flourish,
and new wine, the young women.

THE LORD RESTORES HIS PEOPLE

10 Ask the LORD for rain
in the season of spring rain.
The LORD makes the rain clouds,
and he will give them showers
of rain
and crops in the field for everyone.[j]

2 For the idols speak falsehood,
and the diviners[k] see illusions;
they relate empty dreams
and offer empty comfort.
Therefore the people wander
like sheep;
they suffer affliction because
there is no shepherd.

3 My anger burns
against the shepherds,

so I will punish the leaders.[B]
For the LORD of Armies has tended
his flock,
the house of Judah;
he will make them
like his majestic steed in battle.

4 The cornerstone[l] will come from
Judah.[C]
The tent peg[m] will come from them
and also the battle bow[n] and
every[D] ruler.
Together[5] they will be like warriors
in battle
trampling down the mud
of the streets.
They will fight because the LORD is
with them,
and they will put horsemen
to shame.

6 I will strengthen the house of Judah
and deliver the house of Joseph.[E]
I will restore[F] them
because I have compassion on them,
and they will be
as though I had never
rejected them.[o]
For I am the LORD their God,
and I will answer them.

7 Ephraim[p] will be like a warrior,
and their hearts will be glad as if
with wine.
Their children will see it
and be glad;[q]
their hearts will rejoice in the LORD.

8 I will whistle[r] and gather them
because I have redeemed[s] them;
they will be as numerous as
they once were.

9 Though I sow[t] them
among the nations,
they will remember[u] me
in the distant lands;
they and their children will live
and return.

10 I will bring them back from the land
of Egypt
and gather them from Assyria.
I will bring them to the land
of Gilead[v]
and to Lebanon,
but it will not be enough for them.

11 The LORD[G] will pass through the sea
of distress
and strike the waves of the sea;

[A] 9:13 Lit *Javan*　[B] 10:3 Lit *male goats*　[C] 10:4 Lit *him*　[D] 10:4 Lit *also from him the . . . , from him every*　[E] 10:6 = the northern kingdom
[F] 10:6 Other Hb mss, LXX read *settle*　[G] 10:11 Lit *He*

10:2 That **there is no shepherd** means Judah's leaders had failed to follow God and care for his people.
10:8–12 The Messiah will reunite and restore his people under his kingdom rule, and they will walk in his ways.

all the depths of the Nile
　　will dry up.[a]
The pride of Assyria will be
　　brought down,
and the scepter of Egypt will come
　　to an end.
12 I will strengthen[b] them in the Lord,
　　and they will march[c] in his name —
　　this is the Lord's declaration.

ISRAEL'S SHEPHERDS: GOOD AND BAD

11 Open your gates, Lebanon,
　　and fire will consume your cedars.[d]
2 Wail, cypress,[e] for the cedar
　　has fallen;
　　the glorious trees are destroyed!
Wail, oaks of Bashan,[f]
　　for the stately forest has fallen!
3 Listen to the wail[g] of the shepherds,[h]
　　for their glory is destroyed.
Listen to the roar of young lions,[i]
　　for the thickets of the Jordan[j]
　　are[A] destroyed.

4 The Lord my God says this: "Shepherd the flock intended for slaughter. **5** Those who buy them slaughter them but are not punished.[k] Those who sell them say: Blessed be the Lord because I have become rich! Even their own shepherds have no compassion for them. **6** Indeed, I will no longer have compassion on the inhabitants of the land" — this is the Lord's declaration. "Instead, I will turn everyone over to his neighbor and his king. They will devastate the land, and I will not rescue it from their hand."[l]

7 So I shepherded the flock intended for slaughter, the oppressed of the flock.[B] I took two staffs, calling one Favor[m] and the other Union, and I shepherded the flock. **8** In one month I got rid of three shepherds. I became impatient with them, and they also detested me. **9** Then I said, "I will no longer shepherd you. Let what is dying die, and let what is perishing perish; let

the rest devour each other's flesh." **10** Next I took my staff called Favor and cut it in two, annulling the covenant I had made with all the peoples. **11** It was annulled on that day, and so the oppressed of the flock[c] who were watching me knew that it was the word of the Lord. **12** Then I said to them, "If it seems right to you, give me my wages; but if not, keep them." So they weighed my wages, thirty pieces of silver.[n]

13 "Throw it to the potter,"[D] the Lord said to me — this magnificent price I was valued by them. So I took the thirty pieces of silver and threw it into the house of the Lord, to the potter.[E,o] **14** Then I cut in two my second staff, Union, annulling the brotherhood between Judah and Israel.

15 The Lord also said to me: "Take the equipment of a foolish shepherd. **16** I am about to raise up a shepherd in the land who will not care for those who are perishing, and he will not seek the lost[F] or heal the broken. He will not sustain the healthy,[G] but he will devour the flesh of the fat sheep[p] and tear off their hooves.

17 Woe to the worthless shepherd
　　who deserts the flock![q]
May a sword strike[H] his arm
　　and his right eye!
May his arm wither away
　　and his right eye go
　　completely blind!"

JUDAH'S SECURITY

12 A pronouncement:
　　The word of the Lord
　　concerning Israel.
A declaration of the Lord,
　　who stretched out the heavens,[r]
laid the foundation of the earth,[s]
　　and formed the spirit of man
　　within him.

2 "Look, I will make Jerusalem a cup that causes staggering[t] for the peoples who surround the city. The siege against Jerusalem

[a] 10:11 Gn 8:7; Jos 2:10; 4:23; 1Kg 17:7; Jb 12:15; Ps 74:15; Pr 17:22
[b] 10:12 Zch 10:6
[c] Jos 6:3; Ps 68:7; Jr 46:9
[d] 11:1 Jdg 9:15; 2Kg 19:23; Ps 29:5; Sg 5:15; Is 2:13
[e] 11:2 Is 14:8
[f] Is 2:13; Ezk 27:6
[g] 11:3 Is 15:8; Zph 1:10
[h] Zch 10:2-3
[i] Jb 4:10; Ps 34:10; Is 5:29; Nah 2:11
[j] Jr 49:19
[k] 11:5 Ps 34:22
[l] 11:6 Jr 13:14; Lm 2:2,17,21; Ezk 7:4,9
[m] 11:7 Ps 90:17; Zch 11:10

[n] 11:12 Ex 21:32
[o] 11:13 Mt 26:15; 27:3-10
[p] 11:16 Ezk 34:3-4
[q] 11:17 Jr 23:2
[r] 12:1 Is 45:12; 51:13; Jr 10:12; 51:15
[s] Jb 38:4; Heb 1:10
[t] 12:2 Is 51:22-23; Jr 25:15-16; Rv 16:19

11:7-11 The Lord called Zechariah to stand in for the good shepherd (See 11:4), so the prophet shepherded the flock with **Favor** and **Union** (see 11:7). That the leaders, **three shepherds** (probably representative of prophets, priests, and kings), **detested** the good shepherd (11:7-8) most likely refers prophetically to the rejection of the Messiah at his first coming. Thus, the prophet declares, **I will no longer shepherd you** (11:9). This might refer to the "partial hardening" that would come upon Israel for spurning their Messiah (Rom 11:25).

11:12-14 This literal event in Zechariah's life would also be fulfilled as prophecy when the true good shepherd came. Judas Iscariot, one of Jesus's twelve disciples, agreed to betray him to the chief priests for "thirty pieces of silver" (Matt 26:14-16). When Judas felt remorse after this, he returned the money and hanged himself (Matt 27:1-5). The chief priests "bought the potter's field with" the coins (Matt 27:6-7).

11:15-17 The **worthless shepherd** represented is likely the antichrist (11:17). Everything he'll

do is the opposite of what the good shepherd would do (see John 10:11-16). In the end, the foolish shepherd will be vanquished.

12:1 The Creator of the universe is powerful enough to accomplish all of his will. If he declares something, it's as good as done.

12:2 The image of a **cup** brings to mind other prophetic passages describing the "cup" of the wrath of God (see, e.g., Isa 51:17; Jer 25:15-16). Those who attempt to attack the Messiah's capital city, then, will experience God's fury.

[a] 12:2 Jr 4:16; Ezk 38:8-
9,14-16; Zch 14:2
[b] 12:3 Jl 3:1-2
[c] 12:4 Dt 28:28
[d] Is 37:17; Jr 32:19
[e] 12:6 Jr 5:14; Ob 18
[f] 12:8 2Kg 19:34; 20:6; Is
37:35; 38:6; Zch 9:15
[g] Lv 26:8; Jos 23:10
[h] 12:10 Is 44:3; Ezk 36:27;
39:29; Jl 2:28-29; Zch 4:6;
Ac 2:17
[i] Jr 6:26; Jn 19:37; Rv 1:7
[j] 12:12 2Sm 5:14; Lk 3:31

[k] 12:13 Ex 6:17; Nm 3:18;
1Ch 6:17
[l] 13:1 Ps 36:9; 68:26; Pr
14:27; Jr 2:13; 17:13
[m] Zch 3:1-10
[n] 13:2 Ex 17:14; Dt 12:3;
25:19; 29:20; 32:26; Ps
34:16; 109:15
[o] 13:3 Dt 13:5; 18:20; Jr
14:14-15; 23:14-16,30-31;
27:15-16; Ezk 13:2-4,9,16;
Mc 3:5-6,11
[p] 13:4 1Kg 19:13,19; 2Kg 2:8
[q] 13:5 Am 7:14
[r] 13:6 1Kg 18:28
[s] 13:7 Mt 26:31; Mk 14:27
[t] 13:9 Ps 66:10; Pr 17:3; Is
48:10; Mal 3:3

will also involve Judah.[a] [3] On that day I will make Jerusalem a heavy stone for all the peoples; all who try to lift it will injure themselves severely when all the nations of the earth gather against her.[b] [4] On that day" — this is the LORD's declaration — "I will strike every horse with panic and its rider with madness.[c] I will keep a watchful eye on[d] the house of Judah but strike all the horses of the nations with blindness. [5] Then each of the leaders of Judah will think to himself: The residents of Jerusalem are my strength through the LORD of Armies, their God. [6] On that day I will make the leaders of Judah like a firepot in a woodpile,[e] like a flaming torch among sheaves; they will consume all the peoples around them on the right and the left, while Jerusalem continues to be inhabited on its site, in Jerusalem. [7] The LORD will save the tents of Judah first, so that the glory of David's house and the glory of Jerusalem's residents may not be greater than that of Judah. [8] On that day the LORD will defend the inhabitants of Jerusalem,[f] so that on that day the one who is weakest among them will be like David on that day, and the house of David will be like God, like the angel of the LORD, before them.[g] [9] On that day I will set out to destroy all the nations that come against Jerusalem.

MOURNING FOR THE PIERCED ONE

[10] "Then I will pour out a spirit[A,h] of grace and prayer on the house of David and the residents of Jerusalem, and they will look at[B] me whom they pierced. They will mourn for him as one mourns for an only child and weep bitterly for him as one weeps for a firstborn.[i] [11] On that day the mourning in Jerusalem will be as great as the mourning of Hadad-rimmon in the plain of Megiddo. [12] The land will mourn, every family by itself: the family of David's house by itself and their women by themselves; the family of Nathan's[C,j] house by itself and their women by themselves; [13] the family of Levi's house by itself and their women by themselves; the family of Shimei[D,k] by itself and their women by themselves; [14] all the remaining families, every family by itself, and their women by themselves.

GOD'S PEOPLE CLEANSED

13 "On that day a fountain[l] will be opened for the house of David and for the residents of Jerusalem, to wash away sin and impurity.[m] [2] On that day" — this is the declaration of the LORD of Armies — "I will remove the names of the idols from the land, and they will no longer be remembered.[n] I will banish the prophets[E] and the unclean spirit from the land. [3] If a man still prophesies, his father and his mother who bore him will say to him: You cannot remain alive because you have spoken a lie in the name of the LORD. When he prophesies, his father and his mother who bore him will pierce him through.[o] [4] On that day every prophet will be ashamed of his vision when he prophesies; they will not put on a hairy cloak[p] in order to deceive. [5] He will say: I am not a prophet; I work the land, for a man purchased[F] me as a servant since my youth.[q] [6] If someone asks him: What are these wounds[r] on your chest?[G] — then he will answer: I received the wounds in the house of my friends.

[7]   Sword, awake against my shepherd,
      against the man who is
        my associate —
      this is the declaration of the LORD
      of Armies.
    Strike the shepherd, and the sheep
      will be scattered;[s]
    I will turn my hand
      against the little ones.
[8]   In the whole land —
      this is the LORD's declaration —
    two-thirds[H] will be cut off and die,
      but a third will be left in it.
[9]   I will put this third through the fire;
    I will refine them as silver is refined
      and test them as gold is tested.[t]

[A] 12:10 Or out the Spirit   [B] 12:10 Or to   [C] 12:12 = a son of David   [D] 12:13 = a descendant of Levi   [E] 13:2 = false prophets   [F] 13:5 Or sold
[G] 13:6 Lit wounds between your hands   [H] 13:8 Lit two-thirds in it

12:8 Don't miss that the **weakest** of Jerusalem's inhabitants **will be like David** the warrior king.
12:10 The one **whom they pierced** is a reference to Jesus Christ.
13:1-2 After their repentance (13:1), God will cleanse the nation from their sinfulness, and the land will be purged from its evil and idolatry (13:2).
13:7 The Jews did indeed reject the **shepherd** when he came to them. In fact, on the night

he was betrayed, during his final meal with his disciples, Jesus quoted from this passage and told them, "Tonight all of you will fall away because of me" (Matt 26:31).
13:9 The future tribulation will result in Israel's persecution and ultimate purification when they call on the name of the Lord in repentance and faith. Then God's people will experience his kingdom promises.
14:1-5 Zechariah 14:1 refers to a time of divine judgment and restoration. It will be a time

of judgment for God's enemies and deliverance for his followers—judgment in the tribulation and restoration in the millennial kingdom. **Nations** will **gather** against Israel for their destruction (14:2), but God will use this gathering as the occasion to **fight** for Israel and rescue them (14:3). The Messiah will come to **the Mount of Olives** to judge the nations, and the mountain will **split** and provide a way of escape for those trapped in Jerusalem (14:4-5).

They will call on my name,
and I will answer them.[a]
I will say: They are my people,
and they will say: The LORD is
our God."[b]

THE LORD'S TRIUMPH AND REIGN

14 Look, a day belonging to the LORD is coming[c] when the plunder taken from you will be divided in your presence. [2] I will gather all the nations against Jerusalem for battle.[d] The city will be captured, the houses looted, and the women raped. Half the city will go into exile, but the rest of the people will not be removed from the city.

[3] Then the LORD will go out to fight against those nations as he fights on a day of battle.[e] [4] On that day his feet will stand on the Mount of Olives,[f] which faces Jerusalem on the east. The Mount of Olives will be split in half from east to west, forming a huge valley, so that half the mountain will move to the north and half to the south. [5] You will flee by my mountain valley,[A] for the valley of the mountains will extend to Azal. You will flee as you fled[B] from the earthquake in the days of King Uzziah of Judah.[g] Then the LORD my God will come and all the holy ones[h] with him.[C,i]

[6] On that day there will be no light; the sunlight and moonlight will diminish.[D,E,j] [7] It will be a unique day known only to the LORD,[k] without day or night, but there will be light at evening.

[8] On that day living water will flow out from Jerusalem,[i] half of it toward the eastern sea[F] and the other half toward the western sea,[G] in summer and winter alike. [9] On that day the LORD will become King over the whole earth[m] — the LORD alone, and his name alone.[n] [10] All the land from Geba[o] to Rimmon[p] south of Jerusalem will be changed into a plain. But Jerusalem will be raised up and will remain[H] on its site from the Benjamin Gate[q] to the place of the First Gate,[i] to the Corner Gate,

and from the Tower of Hananel to the royal winepresses.[r] [11] People will live there, and never again will there be a curse of complete destruction. So Jerusalem will dwell in security.

[12] This will be the plague with which the LORD strikes all the people who have warred against Jerusalem: their flesh will rot while they stand on their feet, their eyes will rot in their sockets, and their tongues will rot in their mouths. [13] On that day a great panic from the LORD will be among them, so that each will seize the hand of another, and the hand of one will rise against the other. [14] Judah will also fight at Jerusalem, and the wealth of all the surrounding nations will be collected: gold, silver, and clothing in great abundance.[s] [15] The same plague as the previous one will strike[J] the horses, mules, camels, donkeys, and all the animals that are in those camps.

[16] Then all the survivors from the nations that came against Jerusalem will go up year after year to worship the King, the LORD of Armies, and to celebrate the Festival of Shelters.[t] [17] Should any of the families of the earth not go up to Jerusalem to worship the King, the LORD of Armies, rain will not fall on them. [18] And if the people[K] of Egypt will not go up and enter, then rain will not fall on them; this will be the plague the LORD inflicts on the nations who do not go up to celebrate the Festival of Shelters. [19] This will be the punishment of Egypt and all the nations that do not go up to celebrate the Festival of Shelters.

[20] On that day, the words HOLY TO THE LORD will be on the bells of the horses.[u] The pots in the house of the LORD will be like the sprinkling basins before the altar. [21] Every pot in Jerusalem and in Judah will be holy to the LORD of Armies. All who sacrifice will come and use the pots to cook in. And on that day there will no longer be a Canaanite[L] in the house of the LORD of Armies.

---

[a] 13:9 Ps 20:9; 27:7; 86:7; 102:2; Pr 1:28; Is 58:9; 65:24; Jr 33:3
[b] Ex 6:7; Lv 26:12; Jr 7:23; 11:4; 24:7; 30:22; 31:1,33; 32:38; Ezk 11:20; 14:11; 36:28; 37:23,27; Zch 8:8; 2Co 6:16; Heb 8:10
[c] 14:1 Is 39:6; Jr 7:32; Am 9:13
[d] 14:2 Jl 3:2; Zch 12:2-3
[e] 14:3 Rv 19:11-21
[f] 14:4 Ezk 11:23; Mt 24:3; Ac 1:11-12
[g] 14:5 Am 1:1
[h] Dt 33:2-3; Ps 89:5,7; Dn 7:21; Jd 14
[i] Ps 89:5-7; Mt 25:31
[j] 14:6 Is 13:10; Jl 2:10; 3:15
[k] 14:7 Mt 24:36
[l] 14:8 Ezk 47:7; 47:1-12; Jl 3:18; Rv 8:8-9; 16:3
[m] 14:9 Mt 25:31
[n] Dt 4:35,39; 6:4; Is 45:5
[o] 14:10 2Kg 23:8
[p] Neh 11:29
[q] Jr 37:13

[r] 14:10 Neh 3:1; 12:39; Jr 31:38-40
[s] 14:14 Mc 4:13; Hg 2:7
[t] 14:16 Lv 23:33-36
[u] 14:20 Ex 28:36; 39:30

[A] 14:5 Some Hb mss, LXX, Sym, Tg read *The valley of my mountains will be blocked*   [B] 14:5 LXX reads *It will be blocked as it was blocked*   [C] 14:5 Some Hb mss, LXX, Vg, Tg, Syr; other Hb mss read *you*   [D] 14:6 LXX, Sym, Syr, Tg, Vg read *no light or cold or ice*   [E] 14:6 Lit *no light; the precious ones will congeal*   [F] 14:8 = the Dead Sea   [G] 14:8 = the Mediterranean Sea   [H] 14:10 Or *will be inhabited*   [I] 14:10 Or *the former gate*   [J] 14:15 Lit *be on*   [K] 14:18 Lit *family*   [L] 14:21 Or *merchant*

14:6-19 God will transform the entire environment and topography of Jerusalem (14:6-8, 10-11). **King** Jesus will reign **over the whole earth** from that place (14:9). Those who **warred against Jerusalem** and the Messiah will suffer a plague of judgment (14:12), but **all the survivors from the nations** will come to Jerusalem **to worship**

the King who will reign in prominence and dominance (14:16). They will celebrate **the Festival of Shelters**, and if any nation refuses to celebrate, God will withhold **rain** from them (14:16-19). Though there will be some rebellion in the messianic kingdom before the eternal state is ushered in, the general nature of the kingdom will

involve the exaltation of the Lord. Any open rebellion against Messiah will be quickly crushed.

14:20-21 Knowledge of God's glorious future for his people should motivate believers of every age to endure and obey. Let us joyfully worship the One who will bring history to its divinely ordained conclusion.

MALACHI

INTRODUCTION

Author

WE KNOW NOTHING ABOUT THE author of this book bearing his name other than that Malachi means "my messenger." Since God is the one speaking in the vast majority of the verses, it's clear the book's emphasis is on the message rather than the messenger.

Historical Background

There's nothing in the book to allow us to date it with certainty, but some bits of evidence favor a date after the Babylonian exile. The mention of a governor in 1:8 points to the Persian period when Judah was a province or sub-province of the Persian Empire. In 515 BC, the Jerusalem temple had been rebuilt and worship had been reestablished (1:6-11; 2:1-3; 3:1, 10). But the enthusiasm inspired by the ministries of Haggai and Zechariah had waned. The social and religious problems that Malachi addresses reflect the situation portrayed in Ezra 9 and 10 and Nehemiah 5 and 13. This suggests a date not long before Ezra's return to Judah (ca. 460 BC) or Nehemiah's second term as governor of Judah (Neh 13:6-7; ca. 435 BC).

Message and Purpose

Malachi is the in-your-face prophet who has one simple message: take God seriously. The priests of his day were playing religious games, going through religious motions, and leading God's people to worship casually. Malachi was called to confront God's people with who he really is. When you understand who God is and how much he loves his people, you don't treat him carelessly.

God was insulted by the sloppy worship of Malachi's time: people were bringing him animals for sacrifice they wouldn't serve to their human leaders. They didn't esteem God as the great King that he is. Moreover, they were divorcing without cause because they didn't take God's covenant of marriage seriously, and they were robbing him of the tithes due to him. God's people were acknowledging his name without engaging his person.

As a result, things were falling apart. Locusts were destroying the agriculture. Yet through it all, the people acted as if they'd done nothing wrong. The book of Malachi is a call to all of us that while God is a loving Father, he is not to be taken lightly. His kingdom demands our total allegiance.

www.bhpublishinggroup.com/qr/te/39_00

Outline

I. Introduction (1:1)
II. Taking God's Love Seriously (1:2-5)
III. Taking Worship Seriously (1:6-14)
IV. Taking Covenants Seriously (2:1-9)
V. Taking Marriage Seriously (2:10-16)
VI. Taking God's Justice Seriously (2:17–3:6)
VII. Taking Giving Seriously (3:7-12)
VIII. Taking Reverence for God Seriously (3:13-18)
IX. Taking God's Sovereignty Seriously (4:1-6)

THE LORD'S LOVE FOR ISRAEL

1 A pronouncement:[a]
The word of the LORD[b] to Israel through[c] Malachi.[A]

2 "I have loved you,"[d] says the LORD.

Yet you ask, "How have you loved us?"

"Wasn't Esau Jacob's brother?"[e] This is the LORD's declaration. "Even so, I loved Jacob, **3** but I hated Esau.[f] I turned his mountains into a wasteland, and gave his inheritance to the desert jackals."[g]

4 Though Edom says: "We have been devastated, but we will rebuild[B] the ruins," the LORD of Armies says this: "They may build, but I will demolish. They will be called a wicked country[h] and the people the LORD has cursed[c] forever.[i] **5** Your own eyes will see this, and you yourselves will say, 'The LORD is great, even beyond[D] the borders of Israel.'[j]

DISOBEDIENCE OF THE PRIESTS

6 "A son honors his father, and a servant his master. But if I am a father, where is my honor? And if I am a master, where is your fear of me?[k] says the LORD of Armies to you priests, who despise my name."

Yet you ask: "How have we despised your name?"

7 "By presenting defiled food on my altar."

"How have we defiled you?" you ask.[l]

When you say: "The LORD's table is contemptible."[m]

8 "When you present a blind animal for sacrifice, is it not wrong? And when you present a lame or sick animal, is it not wrong?[n] Bring it to your governor! Would he be pleased with you or show you favor?" asks the LORD of Armies. **9** "And now plead for God's favor. Will he be gracious to us?[o] Since this has come from your hands, will he show any of you favor?"[p] asks the LORD of Armies. **10** "I wish one of you would shut the temple doors,[q] so that you would no longer kindle a useless fire on my altar![r] I am not pleased with you," says the LORD of Armies, "and I will accept[s] no offering from your hands.[t]

11 "My name will be great among the nations,[u] from the rising of the sun to its setting. Incense[E] and pure offerings will be presented in my name in every place because my name will be great among the nations,"[F] says the LORD of Armies.

12 "But you are profaning it[v] when you say: 'The Lord's table is defiled, and its product, its food, is contemptible.' **13** You also say: 'Look, what a nuisance!' And you scorn[G] it,"[H,W] says the LORD of Armies. "You bring stolen,[I,X] lame, or sick animals. You bring this as an offering! Am I to accept that from your hands?" asks the LORD.

14 "The deceiver is cursed who has an acceptable male in his flock and makes a vow but sacrifices a defective animal to the Lord.[y] For I am a great King," says the LORD of Armies, "and my name will be feared among the nations.

WARNING TO THE PRIESTS

2 "Therefore, this decree[z] is for you priests: **2** If you don't listen, and if you don't take it to heart[aa] to honor my name," says the LORD of Armies, "I will send a curse

[a]1:1 Is 13:1; Zch 9:1; 12:1
[b]Hs 1:1; Jl 1:1; Mc 1:1; Zph 1:1
[c]Jr 37:2; Hg 1:1
[d]1:2 Dt 4:37; 7:6-8; 10:14-15; Neh 13:26; Ps 78:68
[e]Gn 25:25-26; 36:19
[f]1:3 Gn 25:23; Rm 9:10-13
[g]Is 34:5-17; Jr 49:7-22; Ezk 35:1-15
[h]1:4 Mal 3:12,15
[i]Is 34:5-17; Jr 49:17-18; Mal 1:14; 2:2; 3:9; 4:6
[j]1:5 Ps 67:1-7; 72:8-11; Ezk 39:7; Zch 12:1-10; Rm 11:11-12
[k]1:6 1Sm 2:30; Dn 5:23; Hg 1:8
[l]1:7 Ezk 22:26
[m]Ezk 41:22; 44:16
[n]1:8 Lv 22:18-25; Dt 15:21; 17:1
[o]1:9 1Sm 13:12; Pr 19:6; Dn 9:13
[p]Nm 6:25-26
[q]1:10 2Ch 28:24
[r]Pr 1:17; Is 1:14
[s]Lv 22:19-21
[t]Is 1:10-17; Jr 6:20; Am 5:21-23; Mc 6:6-8
[u]1:11 Ps 113:3; Is 45:6; 59:19; Mt 8:11
[v]1:12 Lv 22:2; Ezk 13:19; 22:26; 36:20-23; Mal 2:10-11
[w]1:13 1Sm 2:29
[x]2Sm 24:24
[y]1:14 Lv 22:18-25; 27:9-10; Nm 30:2; Dt 23:21-23; Ec 5:4-7
[z]2:1 Nah 1:14
[aa]2:2 Is 42:25; 57:1; Jr 12:11

[A]1:1 = My Messenger   [B]1:4 Or *will return and build*   [C]1:4 Or *LORD is angry with*   [D]1:5 Or *great over*   [E]1:11 Or *Burnt offerings*   [F]1:11 Or *is great . . . are presented . . . is great*   [G]1:13 Lit *blow at*   [H]1:13 Alt Hb tradition reads *me*   [I]1:13 Or *injured*

1:1 Malachi's name means "My Messenger." His message is simple: take God seriously.

1:2-3 **Jacob** and **Esau** were brothers who gave rise to two nations (see Gen 25:23), Israel and Edom. In the Bible, the love/hate contrast has to do with *selection*—choosing something. (In this case, the choice is to service, not personal salvation.) For instance, Jesus tells his followers they cannot be his disciples unless they "hate" their own parents (Luke 14:26). Jesus isn't contradicting the Ten Commandments with that statement (see Exod 20:12). Rather, he's saying that if you have to choose between your family on the one hand and God on the other, you should choose God.

1:6 To **fear** the Lord is to honor him, to take him seriously. Instead, the **priests** despised his **name**—that is, his character and position. They thought little of them.

1:8 Do you want a first-class God while offering second-class worship? Do you give him your leftover time, talents, and treasures after you have little or nothing left? Are you unwilling to be inconvenienced by involvement in the church? Do you avoid sacrificing for fellow believers? You don't have to say you despise the Lord: to convey the same point, all you have to do is give him your leftovers while also asking for his blessings.

1:10 There's nothing impressive about dunking a basketball after you've lowered the rim from ten feet to six, yet Israel had lowered the standard of worship—and they were excited about dunking the worship ball. God, however, wasn't impressed.

1:12-13 The Israelites said **the Lord's table is defiled** and called it a **nuisance** (1:12). Sacrificing those lambs and spilling their blood was a messy, smelly business. But they had forgotten that the sacrificial system was God's gracious means of dealing with their sin so he could give them the provisions of his covenant. They were despising that which was the source of their life and blessing!

Paul dealt with a similar defiling of the Lord's table when some of the Corinthians took Communion in an unworthy way (see 1 Cor 11:20-22, 27-31). So, how do you approach the Lord's Supper? Remember, it's not a matter of merely eating and drinking. Through worshipfully participating in it, "You proclaim the Lord's death until he comes" (1 Cor 11:26).

2:1-9 God's **covenant with Levi** (2:4) is the covenant made with the descendants of Levi who were to perform priestly duties and to care for the tabernacle/temple, under the umbrella of the Mosaic covenant that governed the sacrificial system.

A covenant is no mere contract. It's a spiritually binding relational agreement between God and his people. Covenants are the means by which God administers and governs his kingdom. A divine covenant provides covering. There is protection and provision under it. Through covenants, God works out his kingdom agenda for the benefit of his people. The covenant of Levi **was one of life and peace** (2:5).

But though covenants were intended to bring blessing, they also included sanctions

[a] 2:2 Dt 28:20; Pr 3:33; 28:27; Mal 3:9
[b] 2:3 Hs 4:6-8
[c] Ex 29:14; Lv 16:27
[d] 2:4 Nm 25:11-13; Dt 10:8; 33:8-11; Neh 13:29; Jr 33:17-22
[e] 2:5 1Sm 25:6; Pr 3:2
[f] Mal 1:6
[g] 2:6 Gn 5:22,24; 6:9; Mc 6:8
[h] Is 53:6; Jr 23:22; Ezk 3:19-20

[i] 2:7 2Ch 36:15-16; Hg 1:13
[j] 2:8 Ex 32:8; Dt 31:29; Mal 3:7
[k] Pr 4:16; Is 8:14-15; Hs 14:1
[l] 2:9 Mal 1:6-7
[m] Lv 19:15; Dt 10:17; Ps 82:2; Mt 22:16; 1Tm 5:21; Jms 2:1,9
[n] 2:10 Ex 4:22-23; Is 63:16; Hs 11:1; Mal 1:6; Jn 8:41
[o] Dt 32:6; Is 43:1-7; 64:8
[p] Ex 21:8; Jdg 9:23; Jb 6:15; Is 21:2; Jr 3:20

⇾ KINGDOM LIVING ⇽
FAMILY
Marriage Is a Covenant

A covenant is more than a formal contractual arrangement. Biblically, it's a spiritual and relational bond between God and a person, or people, inclusive of certain agreements, conditions, benefits, and effects. Whenever God wanted to formalize his relationship with his people, he established a covenant. There are a number of these agreements in Scripture: the Abrahamic covenant, the Mosaic covenant, the Davidic covenant, and the new covenant are all formal arrangements that are spiritually binding in a legal capacity between God and a person (or people).

Marriage is another covenant that God established. Therefore, the marriage covenant can never operate to its fullest potential without the ongoing involvement of God. Biblical, spiritual, and theological covenants assume God's integration into every aspect of the relationship in order for a covenant to maximize its purpose.

When the practical realities of God are dismissed from the marital covenantal relationship, it becomes an invitation to the devil to create havoc in the home. This happens because there has been a departure from God's overarching transcendence. Yet, conversely, when the aspects of God's covenant are upheld within a marriage relationship, the marriage then flourishes as a result of the blessings and benefits that come tied to the covenant itself.

One of the surest ways to experience fulfillment in a marriage is for spouses to align under the comprehensive rule of God. What does that mean practically? It occurs when God's thoughts and his Word are brought to bear on every decision and interaction within the marriage and home. It means that God has the final say as ruler and supreme authority, whether that involves emotions, relational approaches, financial decisions, work-related choices, or other things. Let God's viewpoint come to bear in every aspect of your marriage, and you will live out the blessings and benefits of his covenant in your home.

FOR THE NEXT FAMILY
KINGDOM LIVING LESSON SEE PAGE 1101.

among you, and I will curse your blessings.[a] In fact, I have already begun to curse them because you are not taking it to heart. **3** "Look, I am going to rebuke your descendants,[b] and I will spread animal waste[A] over your faces, the waste from your festival sacrifices,[c] and you will be taken away with it. **4** Then you will know that I sent you this decree, so that my covenant with Levi[d] may continue," says the LORD of Armies. **5** "My covenant with him was one of life and peace,[e] and I gave these to him; it called for reverence, and he revered me and stood in awe of my name.[f] **6** True instruction was in his mouth, and nothing wrong was found on his lips. He walked with me[g] in peace and integrity and turned many from iniquity.[h] **7** For the lips of a priest should guard knowledge, and people should desire instruction from his mouth, because he is the messenger of the LORD of Armies.[i]

8 "You, on the other hand, have turned from the way.[j] You have caused many to stumble[k] by your instruction. You have violated[B] the covenant of Levi," says the LORD of Armies. **9** "So I in turn have made you despised[l] and humiliated before all the people because you are not keeping my ways but are showing partiality in your instruction."[m]

JUDAH'S MARITAL UNFAITHFULNESS
10 Don't all of us have one Father?[n] Didn't one God create us?[o] Why then do we act treacherously against one another,[p]

[A] 2:3 Dung or entrails   [B] 2:8 Lit *corrupted*

if the responsibilities and guidelines of the covenant were not followed. Malachi delivers a warning from the Lord to the **priests** who were failing to **honor [his] name** (2:1-2). He declares, **I will send a curse among you** because they did not take **it to heart** (2:2). They ought to have **revered** the Lord, walked with him in **peace** and fairness, **turned many from** sin, and instructed the people (2:5-7). Instead, they had **caused**

many to stumble by [their] instruction. Put simply, they had **violated the covenant of Levi** (2:8). In response, the Lord **despised** them (2:9). The flow of covenantal blessings was hindered, and the hammer of covenantal sanctions was falling.

Under the new covenant, we have a better high priest. The author of Hebrews tells us our mediator, Jesus Christ, can save those who come to God through him (see Heb 7:25).

He's not talking about initial conversion; he's writing to those who are already Christians. He's using the word "save" to speak of deliverance in history. The Levitical priests failed, but the high priest of the new covenant can bring God's promises to you. God has already blessed those who trust in Christ with every spiritual blessing (Eph 1:3). Your relationship to this Mediator grants you access to these benefits.

profaning[a] the covenant of our fathers?[b] [11] Judah has acted treacherously, and a detestable[c] act has been done in Israel and in Jerusalem. For Judah has profaned[d] the LORD's sanctuary,[A,e] which he loves,[f] and has married the daughter of a foreign god.[B,g] [12] May the LORD cut off[h] from the tents of Jacob the man who does this, whoever he may be,[C,i] even if he presents an offering to the LORD of Armies.

∽ HOPE WORDS ∽

Some of our prayers for direction go unanswered because God sees we are not doing anything with what we already know.

---

[13] This is another thing you do. You are covering the LORD's altar with tears, with weeping and groaning,[j] because he no longer respects your offerings or receives them gladly from your hands.[k]

[14] And you ask, "Why?" Because even though the LORD has been a witness[l] between you and the wife of your youth,[m] you have acted treacherously against her. She was your marriage partner[n] and your wife by covenant.[o] [15] Didn't God make them one and give them a portion of spirit? What is the one seeking?[c] Godly offspring. So watch yourselves carefully,[D,p] so that no one acts treacherously against the wife of his[E] youth.

[16] "If he hates[q] and divorces his wife,"[r] says the LORD God of Israel, "he[F] covers his garment with injustice,"[s] says the LORD of Armies. Therefore, watch yourselves carefully,[G] and do not act treacherously.

JUDGMENT AT THE LORD'S COMING

[17] You have wearied the LORD[t] with your words.

Yet you ask, "How have we wearied him?"

When you say, "Everyone who does what is evil is good in the LORD's sight, and he is delighted with them,[u] or else where is the God of justice?"[v]

3 "See, I am going to send my messenger,[w] and he will clear the way before me.[x] Then the Lord you seek[y] will suddenly come to his temple,[z] the Messenger of the covenant you delight in — see, he is coming," says the LORD of Armies. [2] But who can endure the day of his coming? And who will be able to stand when he appears?[aa] For he will be like a refiner's fire[ab] and like launderer's bleach.[H,ac] [3] He will be like a refiner and purifier of silver; he will purify the sons of Levi and refine them like gold and silver.[ad] Then they will present offerings to the LORD in righteousness. [4] And the offerings of Judah and Jerusalem will please the LORD as in days of old[ae] and years gone by.

[5] "I will come to you in judgment, and I will be ready to witness against sorcerers and adulterers; against those who swear falsely; against those who oppress the hired worker, the widow, and the fatherless; and against those who deny justice to the resident alien.[af] They do not fear me,"[ag] says the LORD of Armies. [6] "Because I, the LORD, have not changed,[ah] you descendants of Jacob have not been destroyed.[I,ai]

[a] 2:10 Nm 30:2; Ps 55:20; 89:34; Mal 1:12
[b] 1Kg 8:21
[c] 2:11 Lv 18:22-30; Ezr 9:1-14; Neh 13:4-9
[d] Jr 16:18; Ezk 44:7
[e] Ex 36:1-6; Zph 3:4
[f] Ps 78:68-69
[g] Dt 7:3-4; Ezr 9:1-2,10-14; Neh 13:23-30
[h] 2:12 Ex 12:19; 31:14
[i] Ru 4:10; 1Sm 24:21
[j] 2:13 Ps 6:6-10
[k] 1Kg 8:28-30; Is 56:7
[l] 2:14 Gn 31:50-53; Jdg 11:10; 1Sm 12:5
[m] Pr 2:16-17; 5:18; Is 54:6
[n] Ec 4:10
[o] Ezk 16:8,59-62; Hs 2:16-20
[p] 2:15 Ex 23:13; Jos 23:11
[q] 2:16 Gn 29:31; Dt 21:15-17; 22:13,16; Jdg 15:2; Pr 30:23
[r] Dt 24:1-4
[s] Gn 6:11,13; Ps 73:6; Jr 22:3; Hab 1:2-3

[t] 2:17 Is 43:22-24
[u] Dt 25:16; Mal 3:15
[v] Neh 9:33; Is 40:27
[w] 3:1 Ex 23:20; 33:2; 2Ch 36:15-16
[x] Is 40:3; Mk 1:2; Lk 1:76
[y] Hs 5:6
[z] Ps 24:7-10
[aa] 3:2 Rv 6:17
[ab] Dt 4:24; Is 1:25; Zch 13:9
[ac] Jr 2:22
[ad] 3:3 Ps 12:6; Pr 17:3; Ezk 22:22
[ae] 3:4 Am 9:11
[af] 3:5 Ex 20:14,16; 22:18-24; Dt 18:10; 24:14,17; Jr 5:2,7; 7:6,9
[ag] Dt 10:17-20; Mal 2:5
[ah] 3:6 Nm 23:19; Ps 33:11; 119:89-91; Rm 11:29; Heb 6:17-18; Jms 1:17
[ai] Ps 124; Hs 11:9

[A] 2:11 Or *profaned what is holy to the LORD*   [B] 2:11 = a woman who worshiped a foreign god   [C] 2:12,15 Hb obscure   [D] 2:15 Lit *So guard yourselves in your spirit*   [E] 2:15 Lit *your*   [F] 2:16 Or *The LORD God of Israel says that he hates divorce and the one who*   [G] 2:16 Lit *Therefore, guard yourselves in your spirit*   [H] 3:2 Lit *cleansing agent*   [I] 3:6 Or *Because I, the LORD, do not change, you descendants of Jacob are not destroyed*

2:11 The reference to **the daughter of a foreign god** means Jewish men were marrying non-Jewish women who worshiped pagan deities and brought their foreign gods into **the LORD's sanctuary**.

2:13-14 Since they disregarded the marriage covenant, God wasn't answering their prayers (see 1 Pet 3:7)! Marriage is a spiritual and covenantal matter. When a Christian marries a non-Christian, there will be a clash of gods and covenants. Don't partner with someone who doesn't share your faith because you're going in two different directions (see 2 Cor 6:14-16).

2:15 Happiness is a *benefit* of marriage, not its *purpose*. The purpose of God's covenants is always the expansion of his kingdom in history. Through marriage, in particular, God seeks **godly offspring**. That means that having a child isn't about gaining a "mini-me."

God wants us to have and raise children in the knowledge of the Lord so that his image is spread worldwide for his glory.

2:16 God permits divorce in certain limited cases (for immorality, see Matt 19:9; for abandonment, see 1 Cor 7:15), but it's not what he intended from the beginning (see Matt 19:8). Call it what you like, but getting a "no-fault" divorce and separating for "irreconcilable differences" is not a covenantal option. In God's eyes, it's a treacherous act with spiritual consequences.

3:1 This text is quoted in Mark 1:2 and applied to John the Baptist, who prepared **the way** for Jesus and called people to repent. A **clear** path must be made by cutting down the mountains of human pride to make a humble plain for God's glory to land on.

3:2-5 Just as the **refiner** puts **gold and silver** in the flame to burn off the dross (3:3),

God has to refine and purify his people. He must remove what doesn't belong so they can receive his covenantal benefits. Similarly, the author of Hebrews insists that God disciplines his children for their good (see Heb 12:3-11). The Lord will come **in judgment** against those who demonstrate in a variety of ways that they think they can go to church on Sunday and treat others with injustice and contempt the rest of the week (Mal 3:5).

3:6 In theology, this unchangeableness of God's essential nature and character is called the *immutability* of God. People change, but God is consistent and faithful. He is a "compassionate and gracious God, slow to anger and abounding in faithful love and truth" (Exod 34:6). Therefore, his people receive grace rather than what they deserve.

Turning Things Around

PERHAPS YOU FIND YOURSELF FACING some kind of hardship. You might be saying, "I need God to do something about my unique, special, only-applies-to-me situation." It may feel like no one else in the world can relate to what you're going through, so you're crying out to God to reverse your circumstances.

We've all been there—or will be. Difficulty is no stranger to any of us and yet, when we're in the thick of it, it can feel pretty lonely. Sometimes it even feels like God has abandoned us. But nothing could be further from the truth. In Malachi 3:7 God says, "Return to me, and I will return to you." So if it feels like God is distant, it probably means we're the ones who wandered off.

Maybe you remember how it was before seat belts were required. Back then, you knew when couples were happy because the girl was sitting right up close to her guy. And you could tell when things weren't so great because the girl would sit as far from the guy as their car would allow.

It's the same with God; we want to be close with him, but a distance has formed between us called *consequences*. In other words, by taking our eyes off of him and placing them on our problems, we've moved away from him and toward the very thing that causes us grief. What you're trying to do is reverse the consequences you're facing in your life, but until you have fully submitted yourself to God, the distance between you and him will only grow.

Consider James 4:7: "Submit to God. Resist the devil, and he will flee from you." Notice that the first thing you are commanded to do is submit to God, not to resist the devil. Why is this important? The truth is that while Satan's not scared of you, he is scared of God working through you, which will never happen if you have not placed yourself under his authority.

This reality is why spiritual U-turns are so important. Perhaps you were driving down the highway of life when suddenly you realized that you were going the wrong way. Maybe you weren't paying attention or just made a bad decision about where and when to turn. Regardless, you realize that if you keep going in the same direction, you will never get to where you want to be. You need to take the next available exit, turn the vehicle around, and start driving back in the direction you came. Once you do, you'll start to decrease the distance between you and God and can begin reversing the consequences you face.

Repenting is like taking that exit to get turned around and back on track. You need to identify sin in your life and repent of it. This involves more than just changing your mind about sin: you need to commit to a complete turnaround. This starts with a confession of what you did wrong. In 1 John 1:9, we read, "If we confess our sins, he is faithful and righteous to forgive us our sins and to cleanse us from all unrighteousness." So when you confess, call it what God calls it. It's not a bad habit or a mistake; it's just straight-up sin. Then take the on-ramp back toward God. Think of it like returning home. In Zechariah 1:3 the Lord says, "Return to me . . . and I will return to you."

Until you make changes in behavior regarding your sin, you'll always miss the off-ramp, destining yourself to drive further away from where you want to be. So, repent. Confess. Return. God's Word makes it pretty clear what you have to do if you want to turn your life around and reverse your consequences.

Questions & Answers

Q What role does the command to give a tenth (or tithe) play in good stewardship of all of our resources (including our money)?

A The command to tithe is a command to recognize God's ownership of everything you have. He is your source in life. We see this even at the very beginning when God kept one tree for himself and forbid Adam and Eve from partaking of it. This was to demonstrate that they were not autonomous and had to subject themselves to God. He is responsible for the money and the resources that we have, but he wants to make sure that *we* recognize that he is our source. So he tells his people in essence, "The first tenth of what I give you is not yours; it's mine. I want to see whether *you* recognize it."

FOR THE NEXT Q&A, SEE PAGE 1097.

ROBBING GOD

7 "Since the days of your fathers, you have turned from my statutes; you have not kept them.[a] Return to me,[b] and I will return to you,"[c] says the Lord of Armies.

Yet you ask, "How can we return?"

8 "Will a man rob[d] God? Yet you are robbing me!"

"How do we rob you?" you ask.

"By not making the payments of the tenth and the contributions.[e] **9** You are suffering under a curse, yet[A] you — the whole nation — are still robbing me. **10** Bring the full tenth into the storehouse[f] so that there may be food in my house.[g] Test me in this way,"[h] says the Lord of Armies. "See if I will not open the floodgates of heaven[i] and pour out a blessing for you without measure.[j] **11** I will rebuke the devourer[B,k] for you, so that it will not ruin the produce of your land and your vine in your field will not fail to produce fruit," says the Lord of Armies. **12** "Then all the nations will consider you fortunate, for you will be a delightful land," says the Lord of Armies.

THE RIGHTEOUS AND THE WICKED

13 "Your words against me are harsh,"[l] says the Lord.

Yet you ask, "What have we spoken against you?"

14 You have said: "It is useless to serve God. What have we gained by keeping his requirements[m] and walking mournfully[n] before the Lord of Armies? **15** So now we consider the arrogant[o] to be fortunate.[p] Not only do those who commit wickedness prosper, they even test God[q] and escape."[r]

16 At that time those who feared the Lord spoke to one another. The Lord took notice and listened. So a book of remembrance[s] was written before him for those who feared the Lord and had high regard for his name. **17** "They will be mine," says the Lord of Armies,[t] "my own possession on the day I am preparing. I will have compassion on them as a man has compassion on his son who serves him.[u] **18** So you will again see the difference between

[a] 3:7 Jos 1:7; 23:6; 1Kg 8:58; 2Kg 17:15; Ezr 9:7; Am 2:4; Mal 2:8
[b] Dt 4:30; 30:2; 2Ch 30:6,9; Is 55:7; Jl 2:13; Zch 1:3
[c] 1Kg 8:33; Jr 15:19; 24:7
[d] 3:8 Pr 22:22-23
[e] Lv 7:14,32-33; 27:30-32; Nm 18:8-24; Dt 12:5-19; 14:22-29; 26:12
[f] 3:10 Jos 6:19,24; 1Kg 7:51
[g] 2Ch 31:4-10; Neh 10:34-39; Ezk 44:28-31
[h] Ex 4:1-9; Jdg 6:36-40
[i] Gn 7:11; 8:2; Dt 11:16-17
[j] Dt 28:12; Is 41:18-20; Jl 2:18-32; Am 9:13-15
[k] 3:11 Jl 1:4; 2:25
[l] 3:13 Ps 119:23; Ezk 35:13
[m] 3:14 Lv 8:35; Dt 11:1
[n] Ps 35:14; 38:6
[o] 3:15 Ps 119:21,85; Is 13:11; Jr 43:2
[p] Gn 30:13; Ps 72:17; Pr 31:28
[q] Ps 78:18,41,56; 95:9
[r] Ezk 17:15
[s] 3:16 Ex 32:32; Est 6:1; Dn 12:1
[t] 3:17 Ex 19:5; Dt 7:6; 14:2; 26:18; Ps 135:4
[u] Ps 103:13; Jl 2:18; Zch 11:5-6

[A] 3:9 Or *because*   [B] 3:11 Perhaps locusts

3:8 God commanded the Israelites to tithe—to give a tenth of what he gave to them (Lev 27:30, 32; Num 18:21-24; Deut 12:6; 14:22-23). By giving back to God ten percent of what he'd provided, his people acknowledged his sovereignty, expressed gratitude to him, and demonstrated faith that he would continue to provide. When they did, they came under the cover of his covenant. This practice and purpose of the tithe continued in the New Testament (see Heb 7:4-10), since Jesus continues the priesthood of Melchizedek who received a tithe (see Gen 14:18-20; Heb 5:5).

Your level of spiritual seriousness and development will always show up in your checkbook. Statistics typically report that the average local church is supported by twenty percent of its members and that the average Christian gives less than three percent of his or her income to God. Many Christians, then, suffer from what I call "cirrhosis of the giver."

And while general paralysis sets in when reaching for the wallet or purse to support the ministry of one's church, the disease—amazingly—disappears at the mall. And at the movies. And at restaurants. We cannot accomplish kingdom work when we **rob** (Mal 3:8) the kingdom.

3:10 Those who preach a "prosperity gospel" misuse passages like this one. Understand: God does not promise to give you earthly wealth when you give generously to the kingdom. He's not a slot machine. What is a **blessing** from God, then? It's experiencing, enjoying, and extending the goodness of God in your life. After all, you can have money and not be blessed. You can be wealthy and have no joy or peace.

3:13-15 For this first group, God is like a spare tire—someone to turn to when circumstances go flat. When he bails them out, they put him back in the spiritual trunk. **Your words**

against me are harsh, the Lord tells them. But they don't know what he's talking about (3:13). So he spells it out for them. They have said, **It is useless to serve God** (3:14). They feel they are doing a lot of religious activity for God and getting nothing out of it. The wicked, they believe, are thus better off than they. The way to unlock the door to a new level of experience with God is to pursue a relationship with him—to pursue him for who he is, not just for what we want him to give us.

3:16-17 This second group is described as **those who feared the Lord**. They took God seriously. And don't miss this: **The Lord took notice and listened** (3:16). And how does he respond to their faith? He says, **I will have compassion on them** (3:17). If we examine him honestly and see him as he has truly revealed himself in Scripture, we will find that God is absolutely worthy of all our love and reverence and service.

a 4:2 Ps 37:6; Is 58:8

b 4:4 Dt 4:10,15; 5:2
c 4:5 Mt 11:13-14
d Jl 2:31; Ac 2:20
e 4:6 Lk 1:17

the righteous and the wicked, between one who serves God and one who does not serve him.

THE DAY OF THE LORD

4 "For look, the day is coming, burning like a furnace, when all the arrogant and everyone who commits wickedness will become stubble. The coming day will consume them," says the LORD of Armies, "not leaving them root or branches. ² But for you who fear my name, the sun of righteousness will rise with healing in its wings,ᵃ and you will go out and playfully jump like calves from the stall.ᴬ ³ You will

trample the wicked, for they will be ashes under the soles of your feet on the day I am preparing," says the LORD of Armies.

A FINAL WARNING

4 "Remember the instruction of Moses my servant, the statutes and ordinances I commanded him at Horebᵇ for all Israel. ⁵ Look, I am going to send you the prophet Elijahᶜ before the great and terrible day of the LORD comes.ᵈ ⁶ And he will turn the hearts of fathers to their children and the hearts of children to their fathers.ᵉ Otherwise, I will come and strike the landᴮ with a curse."

ᴬ 4:2 Or like stall-fed calves   ᴮ 4:6 Or earth

4:1 Malachi is talking here about the eschatological day. *Eschatology* is the study of the last things. **The day is coming** refers to the moment when Jesus Christ brings history to a climax (see 1 Thess 5:1-5). When the day of the Lord arrives, it has a two-fold effect: the bringing down of the wicked and the lifting up of the righteous.

The coming day will consume them means that those who do not trust in Jesus Christ

will experience eternal judgment, forever separated from the goodness and grace of God.

4:4 The admonition to **remember the instruction of Moses** is a reminder to remember God's Word. In essence, he says, "Don't give up—because the day is coming when I'm going to break through and separate the righteous from the wicked as promised."

4:5-6 Jesus says this promise was fulfilled in John the Baptist (Matt 11:14). John called people to repentance in order to prepare the way for the Lord. This repentance would not only restore people's relationship to God but also their relationships to one another. The angel Gabriel told Zechariah that his son John would go before the Lord "in the spirit and power of Elijah" (Luke 1:17).

THE
NEW TESTAMENT

MATTHEW

INTRODUCTION

Author

ALTHOUGH THE AUTHOR DIDN'T IDENTIFY himself by name in the text, the title of this Gospel includes the name "Matthew" in the earliest existing manuscripts. In addition, several early church fathers (including Papias, Irenaeus, and Origen) attributed authorship to Matthew. Papias also said that Matthew originally wrote the Gospel in Hebrew (what we have today is in Greek).

Many critical scholars today deny that Matthew is the author. They claim that the Greek Matthew that we have does not look like it was translated from Hebrew. If Papias was wrong about that, they argue, he was probably wrong about who wrote it. But there are other scholars who think Matthew could be a Greek translation from Hebrew. Regardless, it wouldn't necessarily mean Papias was wrong about authorship. The early church unanimously claimed that the apostle Matthew penned the Gospel that bears his name.

There is also internal evidence to support this—that is, evidence within the Gospel itself. Mark 2:14 and Luke 5:27 call the tax collector who became a disciple "Levi." In Matthew 9:9-13, this man is named "Matthew." Also, in 10:3, the apostle Matthew is identified as a tax collector, and it may be that he had two names like Simon/Peter.

Though we can't be absolutely certain, it is best to trust the testimony of the early church and affirm that Matthew wrote this Gospel.

Historical Background

Most—though not all—scholars today think that Matthew used Mark's Gospel as one of his sources when composing his own Gospel. If this is true, Matthew must have been written after Mark. It is likely that Mark's Gospel was written sometime in the AD 50s (see Historical Background in the introduction to Mark's Gospel). Matthew, then, could have been written any time beginning in the mid to late 50s. The church father Irenaeus, who wrote in the late second century, claimed that Matthew wrote his Gospel while Paul and Peter were preaching in Rome. This would have been in the early 60s.

Message and Purpose

Matthew was a tax collector, which means he was unpopular. He left everything to follow Jesus after he concluded that Jesus was the Messiah. Matthew was authorized to write the Gospel that bears his name, and its subject is very simple: it's about the King and his kingdom. Matthew was introducing, especially to Jews, the message that God had sent his King, his Messiah, who would rule as his Regent on earth by offering the kingdom to his people. In this sense Matthew is the culmination of all the Old Testament's anticipation of the Messiah who was to come.

The apostle's concern was giving convincing proof that Jesus was the messianic King whom the Jews were anticipating and whom the world needs so desperately. That's why he began with Jesus's genealogy to establish his lineage through David. Matthew also presented Jesus's kingdom discourses, teaching, and miracles as proof of his messianic claim.

The book leads to a disquieting moment, the crucifixion. If Jesus is the Messiah, how could he be put to death? Thankfully, the scene is followed by the resurrection and the announcement that the King is alive and coming back, and that his kingdom is in this world today. Jesus's Great Commission at the end of Matthew's Gospel (28:18-20) means that the book of Matthew is relevant for us as believers today.

www.bhpublishinggroup.com/qr/te/40_00

Outline

a 1:1-6 Ru 4:18-22; 2Sm
  7:12-16; 1Ch 2:1-15; Lk
  3:32-34
b 1:1 Mk 12:26; Lk 3:4; Ac
  1:20; Php 4:3; Rv 3:5
c Ps 89:3; Is 9:6; Lk 1:32,69
d Gn 22:18; Mt 9:7; Rm
  1:3; Gl 3:16
e 1:2 Gn 29:35; Ps 14:7;
  105:9; Mt 8:11; 22:32;
  Jms 2:21
f 1:3 Gn 38:29-30; 46:12;
  Lk 3:33
g 1:5 Ru 1:4; 2:1; Lk 3:32
h 1:6 1Sm 16:1; 17:12; 2Sm
  11:27; 12:24
i 1:7-8 1Kg 11:43; 14:31;
  15:8,24; 22:50; 2Kg 14:21
j 1:9-10 2Kg 15:5,38; 16:20;
  20:21; 21:18,24
k 1:11 2Kg 24:6,14; Is 5:13; Jr
  27:20; Ezk 1:1; Mt 1:17

l 1:12-13 Gn 10:10; 1Ch
  3:17; Lk 3:27,30
m 1:16 Mt 27:17,22; Lk 2:11;
  Jn 1:45; 4:25
n 1:17 2Kg 24:14; Jr 27:20;
  Dn 9:25-26; Mk 8:29; Ac
  2:31,36,38
o 1:18 Mt 12:46; Lk 1:27,35
p 1:19 Mt 13:17; Mk 10:12;
  Lk 2:36; 1Co 14:35; 2Co
  11:2; Gl 4:27
q Dt 22:20-24; 24:1-4; Mt
  2:7; Lk 16:18; Jn 8:4-5

THE GENEALOGY OF JESUS CHRIST

1 An[a] account[b] of the genealogy of Jesus Christ, the Son of David,[c] the Son of Abraham:[d]

FROM ABRAHAM TO DAVID

2 Abraham fathered[A] Isaac,
Isaac fathered Jacob,
Jacob fathered Judah and his brothers,[e]
3 Judah fathered Perez and Zerah
   by Tamar,
Perez fathered Hezron,
Hezron fathered Aram,[f]
4 Aram fathered Amminadab,
Amminadab fathered Nahshon,
Nahshon fathered Salmon,
5 Salmon fathered Boaz by Rahab,
Boaz fathered Obed by Ruth,
Obed fathered Jesse,[g]
6 and Jesse fathered King David.

FROM DAVID TO THE BABYLONIAN EXILE

David fathered Solomon[B]
   by Uriah's wife,[h]
7 Solomon fathered Rehoboam,
Rehoboam fathered Abijah,
Abijah fathered Asa,[c]
8 Asa[c] fathered Jehoshaphat,
Jehoshaphat fathered Joram,[D]
Joram fathered Uzziah,[i]
9 Uzziah fathered Jotham,
Jotham fathered Ahaz,
Ahaz fathered Hezekiah,
10 Hezekiah fathered Manasseh,
Manasseh fathered Amon,[E]
Amon fathered Josiah,[j]
11 and Josiah fathered Jeconiah
   and his brothers
   at the time of the exile to Babylon.[k]

FROM THE EXILE TO THE CHRIST

12 After the exile to Babylon
Jeconiah fathered Shealtiel,
Shealtiel fathered Zerubbabel,
13 Zerubbabel fathered Abiud,
Abiud fathered Eliakim,
Eliakim fathered Azor,[j]
14 Azor fathered Zadok,
Zadok fathered Achim,
Achim fathered Eliud,
15 Eliud fathered Eleazar,
Eleazar fathered Matthan,
Matthan fathered Jacob,
16 and Jacob fathered Joseph
   the husband of Mary,
who gave birth to Jesus who is called
   the Christ.[m]

17 So all the generations from Abraham to David were fourteen generations; and from David until the exile to Babylon, fourteen generations; and from the exile to Babylon until the Christ, fourteen generations.[n]

THE NATIVITY OF THE CHRIST

18 The birth of Jesus Christ came about this way: After his mother Mary had been engaged[F] to Joseph, it was discovered before they came together that she was pregnant from the Holy Spirit.[o] 19 So her husband Joseph, being a righteous man,[p] and not wanting to disgrace her publicly, decided to divorce her secretly.[q]

20 But after he had considered these things, an angel of the Lord appeared to him in a dream, saying, "Joseph, son of David, don't be afraid to take Mary as your wife, because what has been conceived in

A 1:2 In vv. 2-16 either a son, as here, or a later descendant, as in v. 8   B 1:6 Other mss add King   C 1:7,8 Other mss read Asaph   D 1:8 = Jehoram
E 1:10 Other mss read Amos   F 1:18 Or betrothed

1:1 Jesus had a legitimate legal claim to be the Messiah. He was **the Son of David**, heir to the throne (see 2 Sam 7:12-16; Isa 11:1-10).
1:3-5 The women mentioned in Jesus's line were particularly questionable. **Tamar** (1:3) was a Canaanite who posed as a prostitute. **Rahab** (1:5) was a prostitute. **Ruth** (1:5) was from Moab, a non-Israelite nation that worshiped idols. Moreover, the women were of Hamitic descent. Their mention here is a reminder that Jesus's background is mixed racially, including both Jews and Gentiles and indicating that Jesus's kingdom identity and rule extends to all people.
It blesses me to know that Jesus had black in his blood because this destroys any perception of black inferiority. In Christ we find perfect man and sinless Savior. This knowledge frees blacks from an inferiority com-

plex, and at the same time it frees whites from the superiority myth. In Christ, we all have our heritage. Black people and all others can find historical, cultural, and racial identity in him.
1:11-17 The genealogy in 1:2-16 is that of Jesus's adoptive father, Joseph. The inclusion of **Jeconiah**—also known as Jehoiachin and Coniah (see 1 Chr 3:16; 2 Chr 36:8-9; and Jer 22:24)—signals a problem. Jeconiah would not have a biological descendant sitting on David's throne because of his own sins (Jer 22:30). So, although Joseph had a legal right to the throne, because of Jeremiah's prophecy, it would never happen biologically. Thus, Matthew makes it clear that Joseph is not Jesus's *biological* father but his *adoptive* father. Jesus's genealogy through Mary (see Luke 3:23-38) reveals that Jesus is also

related to David biologically through David's son Nathan (Luke 3:31). Therefore, he can sit on the throne.
1:18-19 In biblical times, a marriage in the Orient included several stages. The engagement was a legal contract, as binding as marriage.
1:20 God has created laws (such as the law of gravity) that govern the universe. When he intervenes in the regular course of events, interrupts those laws, and demonstrates his power over creation, a *miracle* takes place. This would be the most unique birth in history because Mary had never been touched by a man. A virgin would miraculously give birth because of the activity of **the Holy Spirit**. The greatest miracle in human history occurred when God became man, combining full deity and full humanity in one person.

her is from the Holy Spirit.[a] [21] She will give birth to a son, and you are to name him Jesus,[b] because he will save his people from their sins."[c]

[22] Now all this took place to fulfill what was spoken by the Lord through the prophet:

[23] See, the virgin will become pregnant
  and give birth to a son,
  and they will
   name him Immanuel,[A]

which is translated "God is with us."[d]

[24] When Joseph woke up, he did as the Lord's angel had commanded him. He married her[e] [25] but did not have sexual relations with her until she gave birth to a son.[B] And he named him Jesus.[f]

WISE MEN VISIT THE KING

2 After Jesus was born in Bethlehem of Judea in the days of King Herod, wise men from the east arrived in Jerusalem,[g] [2] saying, "Where is he who has been born king of the Jews?[h] For we saw his star at its rising[i] and have come to worship him."[c]

[3] When King Herod heard this, he was deeply disturbed, and all Jerusalem with him. [4] So he assembled all the chief priests and scribes[j] of the people and asked them where the Christ would be born.

[5] "In Bethlehem of Judea," they told him, "because this is what was written by the prophet:

[6] **And you, Bethlehem**, in the land
  of Judah,
 are by no means **least**
  among the rulers of Judah:
 Because out of you will come
  a ruler
 who will shepherd my people
 Israel."[D,k]

[7] Then Herod secretly summoned the wise men and asked them the exact time the star appeared. [8] He sent them to Bethlehem and said, "Go and search carefully for the child. When you find him, report back to me so that I too can go and worship him."[E,l]

[9] After hearing the king, they went on their way. And there it was — the star they had seen at its rising. It led them until it came and stopped above the place where the child was. [10] When they saw the star, they were overwhelmed with joy. [11] Entering the house, they saw the child with Mary his mother, and falling to their knees, they worshiped him.[F] Then they opened their treasures and presented him with gifts: gold, frankincense, and myrrh.[m] [12] And being warned[n] in a dream not to go back to Herod, they returned to their own country by another route.

THE FLIGHT INTO EGYPT

[13] After they were gone, an angel of the Lord appeared to Joseph in a dream, saying, "Get up! Take the child and his mother, flee to Egypt, and stay there until I tell you. For Herod is about to search for the child to kill him."[o] [14] So he got up, took the child and his mother during the night, and escaped to Egypt. [15] He stayed there until Herod's death, so that what was spoken by the Lord through the prophet might be fulfilled: **Out of Egypt I called my Son.**[G,p]

THE MASSACRE OF THE INNOCENTS

[16] Then Herod, when he realized that he had been outwitted by the wise men, flew into a rage. He gave orders to massacre all the boys in and around Bethlehem who

[a]1:20 2Ch 1:1; Mt 13:49; 27:19; Jn 6:20; Rm 1:3
[b]1:21 Lk 1:31; 2:21; Jn 10:25; 1Jn 2:12
[c]Lk 2:11; Jn 1:29; Ac 4:12; 5:31; 13:23,38-39
[d]1:22-23 Is 7:14; Mt 21:1-4; Lk 24:44; Rm 1:2-4
[e]1:24 Mt 1:6; 13:49; Lk 1:1; 19:32; Jd 5
[f]1:25 Gn 4:1,17; Ex 13:2; Jdg 11:39; 1Sm 1:19; Lk 2:7,21
[g]2:1 Gn 25:6; 1Kg 4:30; Lk 1:5; 2:4-7
[h]2:2 Jr 23:5; 30:9; Zch 9:9; Mt 27:11; Lk 19:38; Jn 1:49
[i]Nm 24:17; Rv 22:16
[j]2:4 Mt 16:21; 20:18; 21:15; 27:41; Lk 9:22
[k]2:6 2Sm 5:2; Mc 5:2; Jn 7:42; 21:16

[l]2:7-8 Mk 5:6; Lk 1:7; Ac 13:6; Rv 1:16
[m]2:11 Ps 72:10; Is 60:6; Mt 1:18; 12:46; Mk 5:6
[n]2:12 Mt 27:19; Lk 2:26; Ac 10:22; Heb 8:5; 11:7
[o]2:13 Mt 1:20; 13:49; Mk 11:18; Jms 4:7
[p]2:15 Ex 4:22; Nm 24:8; Hs 11:1

[A]1:23 Is 7:14 [B]1:25 Other mss read *to her firstborn son* [C]2:2 Or *to pay him homage* [D]2:6 Mc 5:2 [E]2:8 Or *and pay him homage* [F]2:11 Or *they paid him homage* [G]2:15 Hs 11:1

1:21 *Jesus* is a Greek name corresponding to the Hebrew name *Joshua,* which means "the Lord saves." Thus, according to the angel, the child's name is to indicate the reason he had come into the world.

1:23 *Immanuel,* Matthew tells us, means **God is with us.** Jesus Christ is incarnate deity. That is the essence of Christmas. All the problems in this world can be traced back to sin, and Jesus Christ entered the world to forgive us for our sins, give us victory over our sins, and give us an eternal home free from sin. That truth is what Christmas is all about. If you miss that, you've missed the point.

2:1-2 According to legend, there were three **wise men**—perhaps from Babylonia or Persia. But while we know they brought three specific gifts, we don't know how many men there were. Moreover, the wise men

weren't present at the nativity. By the time they arrived, Joseph and Mary were living in a house (see 2:11). Jesus was a toddler when the wise men saw him.

2:3 **Herod** the Great wasn't a Jew, but an Idumean whom the Romans had made a ruler of the Jews.

2:4-6 Sadly, while these leaders clearly knew the Scriptures, they never pursued the Savior (see John 5:39-40). They didn't act on what they studied.

2:8 Herod had ulterior motives. He wasn't about to let anyone take away his kingdom.

2:11 These men had traveled an incredible distance for perhaps as long as two years to worship this King, but they knew he was worth the journey. How much are you willing to be inconvenienced to worship the King of kings? How badly do you want him?

2:12-13 Since they had faithfully sought the Savior, the wise men received inside information (2:12). Joseph also—since he had obeyed the Lord's word (1:24-25)—received further help regarding the next steps he should take (2:13). When you obey God's revelation, you get further divine illumination.

2:14-15 In his prophecy, Hosea was talking about Israel, whom God called his "son" and delivered from "Egypt" (see Hos 11:1), but Matthew understood that Israel was a type of God's Son who was yet to come. A *type* is a historical person, institution, or event that prefigures a future corresponding reality. Thus, as God called his son Israel out of **Egypt,** so he would call his true **Son** out (Matt 2:15).

2:16-18 As Israel wept in Jeremiah's day for their children in exile (see Jer 31:15-16), so they wept again in Matthew's day for their

a 2:16 Is 59:7; Mk 10:34; Ac 13:6; 25:3; Rv 12:4

b 2:18 Gn 35:19; Jdg 4:5; Jr 31:15; Ac 8:2; 2Co 7:7

c 2:19 Mt 1:20; 13:49; Lk 1:11; Jd 5

d 2:22 Mt 17:22; Lk 1:5; Ac 27:29; Col 3:21; Heb 8:5

e 2:23 Mk 1:24; Lk 1:26; Jn 1:45-46

f 3:1-12 Mk 1:3-8; Lk 3:2-17; Jn 1:6-8,19-28

g 3:1 Jos 15:61; Jdg 1:16

h 3:2 Dn 2:44; Mt 4:17; 6:10; 10:7; Mk 1:15; Lk 10:9; 11:20; 21:31

i 3:3 Is 40:3; Lk 1:17,76; Jn 1:23

j 3:5-6 Mt 23:37; Mk 1:5; Lk 3:3; Jn 15:22; Ac 19:18

k 3:7 Mt 16:1; 22:23; 23:15; Ac 4:1; 5:17; 23:6

l Mt 12:34; 23:33; Rm 5:9; 1Th 1:10

m 3:8 Mt 3:10; 12:33; 13:8,26; 21:19,34,41,43; Mk 11:14

n 3:9 Lk 3:8; Jn 8:33,39; Ac 13:26; Rm 4:1

o 3:10 Mt 7:19; Lk 13:7,9; Jn 15:2,6

p 3:11 Mk 1:4,8; Jn 1:26; Ac 1:5

q Is 4:4; Jn 1:33; Ac 2:3-4; 11:16; Ti 3:5

r 3:12 Is 30:24; Mt 13:30; Mk 9:43,48; Lk 3:17

s 3:13-17 Mk 1:9-11; Lk 3:21-22; Jn 1:31-34

were two years old and under, in keeping with the time he had learned from the wise men.*a* **17** Then what was spoken through Jeremiah the prophet was fulfilled:

18 A voice was heard in Ramah,
weeping,*A* and great mourning,
Rachel weeping for her children;
and she refused to be consoled,
because they are no more.*B,b*

THE RETURN TO NAZARETH

19 After Herod died, an angel of the Lord appeared in a dream to Joseph in Egypt,*c* **20** saying, "Get up, take the child and his mother, and go to the land of Israel, because those who intended to kill the child are dead." **21** So he got up, took the child and his mother, and entered the land of Israel. **22** But when he heard that Archelaus was ruling over Judea in place of his father Herod, he was afraid to go there. And being warned in a dream, he withdrew to the region of Galilee.*d* **23** Then he went and settled in a town called Nazareth to fulfill what was spoken through the prophets, that he would be called a Nazarene.*e*

THE HERALD OF THE CHRIST

3 In those days John the Baptist came,*f* preaching in the wilderness of Judea*g* **2** and saying, "Repent, because the kingdom of heaven has come near!"*h* **3** For he is the one spoken of through the prophet Isaiah, who said:

A voice of one crying out
in the wilderness:
Prepare the way for the Lord;
make his paths straight!*i*

4 Now John had a camel-hair garment with a leather belt around his waist, and his food was locusts and wild honey. **5** Then people from Jerusalem, all Judea, and all the vicinity of the Jordan were going out to him, **6** and they were baptized by him in the Jordan River, confessing their sins.*j*

7 When he saw many of the Pharisees and Sadducees*k* coming to his baptism, he said to them, "Brood of vipers! Who warned you to flee from the coming wrath?*l* **8** Therefore produce fruit*m* consistent with*D* repentance. **9** And don't presume to say to yourselves, 'We have Abraham as our father.'*n* For I tell you that God is able to raise up children for Abraham from these stones. **10** The ax is already at the root of the trees. Therefore, every tree that doesn't produce good fruit will be cut down and thrown into the fire.*o*

11 "I baptize you with*E* water for repentance,*p* but the one who is coming after me is more powerful than I. I am not worthy to remove*F* his sandals. He himself will baptize you with the Holy Spirit and fire.*q* **12** His winnowing shovel is in his hand, and he will clear his threshing floor and gather his wheat into the barn. But the chaff he will burn with fire that never goes out."*r*

THE BAPTISM OF JESUS

13 Then Jesus came from Galilee to John at the Jordan, to be baptized by him.*s* **14** But John tried to stop him, saying, "I need to be baptized by you, and yet you come to me?" **15** Jesus answered him, "Allow it for now, because this is the way for us to fulfill all

---

A 2:18 Other mss read *Ramah, lamentation, and weeping,*   *B* 2:18 Jr 31:15   *C* 3:3 Is 40:3   *D* 3:8 Lit *fruit worthy of*   *E* 3:11 Or *in*   *F* 3:11 Or *to carry*

---

children who were persecuted in connection to Jesus.

2:23 That Jesus **would be called a Nazarene** is not found in the Old Testament. So likely Matthew was thinking of statements like Isaiah 53:3: "He was despised and rejected by men" (see also Ps 22:6; Isa 49:7), because Nazareth was viewed as a despised community from which no good thing could come (see John 1:46).

3:1 The wilderness (then and now) is a barren place of preparation and development for what God is planning to do.

3:2 Repentance is essential for experiencing the presence and grace of God. It involves changing the mind in order to reverse direction. It is the inner resolve and determination to turn from sin and turn to God.

3:4 John's austere lifestyle, odd wardrobe, and confrontational preaching were reminiscent of another of God's messengers: Elijah (see, e.g., 2 Kgs 1:3-17).

3:6 By **confessing their sins** and being **baptized**, the people were making a public declaration that they had changed their minds and agreed with what God said about their sins.

3:7 Why did John accept other people but not this group? Because, although they were okay with listening to his message, they wanted their lives left alone. Like some people today, they didn't mind attending a church service as long as it didn't affect how they were running their own affairs. They wanted information, but not transformation.

3:8 Genuine **repentance** is confirmed by actions. When I travel, I tell the airline agent, "I'm Tony Evans, and I have a reservation." The agent then asks, "Can I see your proof of identification?" They don't want mere communication that I am who I claim to be; they want authentication. Therefore, they want to see something that verifies what I affirm. Similarly, shouting, "Hallelujah! Amen! Praise the Lord!" is fine but insufficient. Repentance shows up in your hands and feet, not just in your lips. Without the **fruit**, the visible proof

of true heart repentance, judgment is coming (3:10).

3:11 John's declaration corresponds to the promise of the prophets (see Ezek 36:27; Joel 2:28), the confirmation of Jesus (see John 14:16-17; 15:26; Acts 1:4-5), and the fulfillment in the early church (see Acts 2:1-4; 10:44-45).

3:12 A farmer would winnow grain by tossing it in the air. The wind would blow away the **chaff**—the useless husks—while the **wheat** would fall to be gathered up.

3:13-15 Since John's message was about repentance, he considered it inappropriate and inconceivable that he would baptize the Messiah, because Jesus had nothing to repent of. But in his substitutionary death on the cross, Jesus would bear the transgressions of sinners and credit them with his perfect righteousness (see 2 Cor 5:21). As his ministry began, then, he intended to identify with sinful humanity on whose behalf he would perfectly fulfill all the demands of God's law. This baptism would

righteousness." Then John allowed him to be baptized.

16 When Jesus was baptized, he went up immediately from the water. The heavens[a] suddenly opened for him,[A] and he saw the Spirit of God descending like a dove and coming down on him.[b] **17** And a voice from heaven said: "This is my beloved Son, with whom I am well-pleased."[c]

THE TEMPTATION OF JESUS

4 Then[d] Jesus was led up by the Spirit into the wilderness to be tempted by the devil.[e] **2** After he had fasted forty days and forty nights,[f] he was hungry. **3** Then the tempter approached him and said, "If you are the Son of God, tell these stones to become bread."[g]

4 He answered, "It is written: **Man must not live on bread alone but on every word that comes from the mouth of God.**"[B,h]

5 Then the devil took him to the holy city, had him stand on the pinnacle of the temple,[i] **6** and said to him, "If you are the Son of God, throw yourself down. For it is written:

He will give his angels[j] orders concerning you,
and they will support you
with their hands
so that you will not strike
your foot against a stone."[C,k]

7 Jesus told him, "It is also written: **Do not test the Lord your God.**"[D,l]

8 Again, the devil took him to a very high mountain and showed him all the kingdoms of the world and their splendor. **9** And he said to him, "I will give you all these things if you will fall down and worship me."[E]

[a] 3:16 Mt 24:35; Lk 12:33; Ac 17:24; Eph 6:9; Rv 21:10
[A] Is 11:2; Jn 1:32; Ac 7:56; 2Pt 1:17
[c] 3:17 Ps 2:7; Is 42:1; Lk 9:35; Jn 12:28
[d] 4:1-11 Mk 1:12-13; Lk 4:1-13
[e] 4:1 Jos 15:61; Jdg 1:16; Jn 1:6-7; Jms 1:14
[f] 4:2 Ex 34:28; 1Kg 19:8; Jn 9:4
[g] 4:3 Mk 3:11; 5:7; Lk 1:35; 4:41; Jn 1:34,49; Ac 9:20
[h] 4:4 Dt 8:3
[i] 4:5 Neh 11:1,18; Dn 9:24; Mt 27:53
[j] 4:6 Gn 16:7; Mt 13:49; Lk 1:11; Ac 5:19; Rv 14:6
[k] Ps 91:11-12; 1Pt 2:8
[l] 4:7 Dt 6:16; 1Sm 7:3; 1Ch 21:1

^A 3:16 Other mss omit *for him*   ^B 4:4 Dt 8:3   ^C 4:6 Ps 91:11-12   ^D 4:7 Dt 6:16   ^E 4:9 Or *and pay me homage*

also identify Jesus with John and affirm his kingdom message.
3:16-17 Note that all three members of the Trinity appear here, working simultaneously. The Father and the Spirit publicly endorsed the Son for his kingdom mission.
4:1 Notice that the temptation of the Son was God's idea: **Jesus was led up by the Spirit into the wilderness**. This tells us God was not on the defensive in this matter. He was on the offensive, demonstrating the superiority of his Son over Satan.
    Why did God test his Son this way? The Bible describes Jesus as the "second man" or "last Adam" (1 Cor 15:45, 47). The first Adam was tested in the garden, gave in to Satan, and got the human race kicked into the wil-

derness. The last Adam went into the wilderness to defeat Satan so that he can escort us back to the garden.
4:2 To *fast* is to give up a physical craving to fulfill a greater spiritual need. It prioritizes feeding the spirit with prayer and fellowship with God to overcome feeding the stomach.
4:3 Clearly the devil had been watching Jesus go without food. He knows what you're up to, too, and directs his temptations accordingly.
4:4 If Jesus, the living Word, needed to use the written Word (Deut 8:3 in this case) to deal with the enemy of the Word, how much more do you? He gave you the Bible so you could wield it like a sword (see Eph 6:17).
4:5-6 Challenging Jesus to jump to his death doesn't sound like much of a temptation. But

notice that he supported his appeal by quoting (4:6) God's promise of angelic protection in Psalm 91:11-12. Jesus, then, had an opportunity to demonstrate undeniably that he was the Messiah. The problem was that doing so ignored God's plan. It would bypass the cross.
    The devil knows the Bible, and he uses it. If he can't convince you to act independently of God, he'll work through your religion.
4:7 Jesus quoted Deuteronomy 6:16: **Do not test the Lord your God.** In other words, he knew we are never to use disobedience to back God into a corner in order to force him to fulfill his plan.
4:8-9 Satan wants us to bow to him. He'll make intriguing offers to get us to do so, but they're never worth the price.

a 4:10 Dt 6:13; 1Ch 21:1
b 4:11 Mt 26:53; Lk 22:43; Heb 1:14
c 4:12 Mt 14:3; Mk 1:14; Lk 3:20; Jn 3:24
d Lk 4:14; Jn 1:43; 2:11
e 4:13 Mk 1:21; 2:1; Lk 4:23; Jn 2:12; 4:46
f 4:15-16 Is 9:1-2; 42:7; Lk 2:32
g 4:17 Mt 3:2; 5:3,10,19-20; 7:21; 8:11; Mk 1:14
h 4:18-22 Mk 1:16-20; Lk 5:2-11; Jn 1:40-42
i 4:18 Mt 15:29; Mk 7:31; Lk 5:1; Jn 6:1
j 4:23-25 Mk 1:35-39; Lk 4:42-44
k 4:23 Mt 13:54; 24:14; Ac 10:38
l 4:24 Lk 2:2; Ac 15:23; Gl 1:21
m Mt 8:16; 9:32; Mk 5:15; Jn 10:21
n 4:25 Mk 3:7; 5:20; Lk 6:17
o 5:1 Mk 3:13; Lk 9:28; Jn 6:3,15
p 5:2 Ac 8:35; 10:34; 18:14
q 5:3 Is 57:15; 66:2
r Mt 19:14; 25:34; Mk 10:14; Lk 6:20
s 5:4 Is 61:2; Mt 11:29; 21:5; Jn 16:20; Rv 7:17
t 5:5 Ps 37:11; Rm 4:13; Rv 21:7

10 Then Jesus told him, "Go away,[A] Satan! For it is written: **Worship the Lord your God, and serve only him.**"[B,a] **11** Then the devil left him, and angels came and began to serve him.[b]

MINISTRY IN GALILEE

12 When he heard that John had been arrested,[c] he withdrew into Galilee.[d] **13** He left Nazareth and went to live in Capernaum[e] by the sea, in the region of Zebulun and Naphtali. **14** This was to fulfill what was spoken through the prophet Isaiah:

15   Land of Zebulun and land
            of Naphtali,
        along the road by the sea,
            beyond the Jordan,
        Galilee of the Gentiles.
16   The people who live
            in darkness
        have seen a great light,
        and for those living in the land
            of the shadow of death,
        a light has dawned.[C,D,f]

17 From then on Jesus began to preach, "Repent, because the kingdom of heaven[g] has come near."

THE FIRST DISCIPLES

18 As[h] he was walking along the Sea of Galilee,[i] he saw two brothers, Simon (who is called Peter), and his brother Andrew. They were casting a net into the sea — for they were fishermen. **19** "Follow me," he told them, "and I will make you fish for[E] people." **20** Immediately they left their nets and followed him.

21 Going on from there, he saw two other brothers, James the son of Zebedee, and his brother John. They were in a boat with Zebedee their father, preparing their nets, and he called them. **22** Immediately they left the boat and their father and followed him.

TEACHING, PREACHING, AND HEALING

23 Now Jesus began to go all over Galilee,[j] teaching in their synagogues, preaching the good news of the kingdom, and healing every[F] disease and sickness[G] among the people.[k] **24** Then the news about him spread throughout Syria.[l] So they brought to him all those who were afflicted, those suffering from various diseases and intense pains, the demon-possessed, the epileptics, and the paralytics.[m] And he healed them. **25** Large crowds followed him from Galilee, the Decapolis, Jerusalem, Judea, and beyond the Jordan.[n]

THE SERMON ON THE MOUNT

5 When he saw the crowds, he went up on the mountain,[o] and after he sat down, his disciples came to him. **2** Then[H] he began to teach them, saying:[p]

THE BEATITUDES

3   "Blessed are the poor in spirit,[q]
        for the kingdom of heaven[r] is theirs.
4   Blessed are those who mourn,[s]
        for they will be comforted.
5   Blessed are the humble,[t]
        for they will inherit the earth.

A 4:10 Other mss read "Get behind me   B 4:10 Dt 6:13   C 4:16 Lit dawned on them   D 4:15-16 Is 9:1-2   E 4:19 Or you fishers of   F 4:23 Or every kind of   G 4:23 Or physical ailment   H 5:2 Lit Then opening his mouth

4:10 If you're a Christian, you have no obligation to the devil, and you have Jesus's delegated authority against **Satan**. "Resist the devil [with the Word and in obedience to God], and he will flee from you [as he fled from Christ]" (Jas 4:7).
4:11 When the fallen angel left, faithful **angels** came and fulfilled their rightful role: serving Christ and giving him the worship he deserves.
4:17 Jesus preached in continuity with the kingdom message of John: **Repent, because the kingdom of heaven has come near** (see 3:2).
4:19 There's an important principle here. If you're not fishing, you're not following. If your Christian life does not involve evangelizing the lost, you're not functioning like the disciple Jesus intends you to be. Not every believer is called to a full-time Christian vocation, but every believer is called to be a full-time Christian.
4:23 These actions are the hallmarks of Jesus's ministry. **Teaching** involves clearly articulat-

ing the content of the message. **Preaching** includes calling for a response to what is taught. **Healing** consists of a visible demonstration of the power of the message.
5:1-2 Matthew 5–7, delivered on a **mountain**, is known as the Sermon on the Mount. It's Jesus's kingdom manifesto. The first few verses of it are known as the Beatitudes (5:3-10); they set forth the character of kingdom men and women. We could call the Beatitudes antibiotics from God's pharmacy that can aid life transformation. They are a reminder that Jesus is primarily concerned with what's happening on your inside, which should be the basis of what you're showing on the outside.
5:3 To be **poor in spirit** is to be conscious of one's continual dependence on God. Kingdom people recognize their own inadequacy and insufficiency apart from him.
    God's **kingdom** refers to God's rule. If you're "poor in spirit," you'll get to see God's heav-

enly rule in your earthly life. Only by being desperately dependent on God can you become what he created you to be.
5:4 **Blessed are those who mourn** refers to being saddened by the things that sadden God. God grieves over the sin and wretchedness of the world (see Gen 6:5-6). Sin and its consequences surround us, tempting us to become numb. Instead, we must pray that God would give us the emotions of his heart, so that we can experience the encouraging, strengthening comfort of God.
5:5 Some translations render **the humble** as "the meek." It's important to understand that meekness doesn't mean weakness. Consider, for example, the process of breaking a horse. The idea is not to break the horse of its strength or speed; rather, the goal is to break the horse of its self-will. As long as you remain independent and "wild," you will never maximize God's intention for you. To be meek is to learn to submit your will to God's.

6 Blessed are those who hunger and
thirst for righteousness,[a]
for they will be filled.
7 Blessed are the merciful,
for they will be shown mercy.[b]
8 Blessed are the pure in heart,
for they will see God.[c]
9 Blessed are the peacemakers,
for they will be called sons of God.[d]
10 Blessed are those who
are persecuted because
of righteousness,
for the kingdom of heaven[e] is theirs.

11 "You are blessed when they insult you and persecute you and falsely say every kind of evil against you because of me. **12** Be glad and rejoice, because your reward is great in heaven. For that is how they persecuted[f] the prophets who were before you.[g]

BELIEVERS ARE SALT AND LIGHT

13 "You are the salt of the earth. But if the salt should lose its taste, how can it be made salty?[A] It's no longer good for anything but to be thrown out and trampled under people's feet.[h]

14 "You are the light of the world. A city situated on a hill cannot be hidden.[i] **15** No one lights a lamp[j] and puts it under a basket, but rather on a lampstand, and it gives light for all who are in the house.[k] **16** In the same way, let your light shine before others, so that they may see your good works and give glory to your Father in heaven.[l]

CHRIST FULFILLS THE LAW

17 "Don't think that I came to abolish the Law or the Prophets. I did not come to abolish but to fulfill.[m] **18** For truly I tell you, until heaven and earth pass away,

[A]5:13 Or *how can the earth be salted?*

[a]5:6 Is 55:1-2; Jn 4:14; 6:48; 7:37
[b]5:7 Pr 11:17; Mt 18:33; Lk 6:36; 2Tm 1:16
[c]5:8 Ps 24:4; Heb 12:14; 1Jn 3:2; Rv 22:4
[d]5:9 Mt 5:45; Lk 6:35; Rm 8:14; Jms 3:18; 1Jn 3:1
[e]5:10 Mt 19:14; 25:34; Mk 10:14; Lk 6:20; 22:29
[f]5:12 Mt 2:23; 2Tm 3:12
[g]Mt 23:37; Ac 7:52; 1Th 2:15
[h]5:13 Mk 9:50; Lk 14:34
[i]5:14 Pr 4:18; Jn 8:12; Php 2:15
[j]5:15 Jn 5:35; Rv 21:23
[k]Mk 4:21; Lk 8:16; 11:33
[l]5:16 Mt 9:8; Jn 15:8; 1Pt 2:12
[m]5:17 Mt 7:12; Rm 3:31; 10:4; 13:8; Gl 3:24

5:6 Far too many of God's children are spiritually malnourished—not because they don't eat, but because they eat the wrong things. Donuts taste good, but they have no nutritional value. You can't have a donut-level spiritual diet and then wonder why you don't experience God's blessings. To hunger **for righteousness** is to apply the righteous standard of God to your life. You need to be hungry for that which pleases God. If you train your appetite in this way you will be **filled**—you'll be satisfied with divine contentment.

5:7 There's a blessing for those who are **merciful** (that is, who exercise pity rather than just condemnation), because you can bank on the fact that a time is coming when you'll need **mercy**.

5:8 Purity of **heart** involves being authentic before God, so come clean with him about the good, the bad, and the ugly, and you'll see him operating powerfully in your life.

5:9 To be a **peacemaker** is to be a mediator and resolve conflicts between estranged parties. You make peace by identifying the truth, addressing the sin, and constructing a bridge between those who are at odds with one another. Peacemaking can be difficult work. But, if we persevere in it, we **will be**

called sons of God because we will resemble our Daddy. He sent *the* Son of God to be our Mediator, bridging the gap created by our sin and granting us peace with him.

5:10 To be **persecuted because of righteousness** is to be mistreated because you display the kingdom characteristics described in 5:3-9. Some people won't like you for doing so. Persecution may take a variety of forms and come from a variety of sources (your family, an employer, the culture, the government). But in receiving it you'll be in the company of a class of people (see Heb 11) of whom the world is not worthy (Heb 11:38).

5:11-12 Notice that the persecution that brings blessing is directly tied to Jesus. **When they insult you** and tell lies about you **because of** him, **you are blessed** (5:11). Since essentially the same thing happened to the Old Testament **prophets**, you're in good company. But how can you **rejoice** in the midst of the mess? You can remember that **your reward is great in heaven** (5:12), because "the sufferings of this present time are not worth comparing with the glory that is going to be revealed to us" (Rom 8:18).

5:13 Christians are to be **salt** in this decaying world. But if you become too mixed up with

the world and allow its values to affect you, you will lose your uniqueness as a Christian and your ability to make a kingdom difference.

5:14 In Scripture, the world is pictured as a dark place that requires illumination (see John 1:4-5; 3:19). Jesus is "the light of the world" (John 8:12), so he expects his followers to be lights too. We are not to be secret agent saints.

5:15-16 Are you a light among your acquaintances? Are you a light at work and at the gym? Are you a light in your culture and in your community? To hide a light is contradictory to its purpose. **Let your light shine.** You must shine so that people **may see your good works and give glory to your Father in heaven** (5:16). A good work is a righteous and biblically authorized action that is beneficial to others and for which God gets the credit.

5:17 **The Law or the Prophets** is a way of referring to the Old Testament, which was intended to point to Christ. He, in fact, is the theme of the Old Testament Scriptures (see Luke 24:27, 44; John 5:39-40). In order to provide us with righteousness, making us acceptable before God, he had to live a life of complete obedience to God's law.

a 5:18–19 Mt 11:11; 24:35; Lk 16:17; Jms 2:10
b 5:21 Ex 20:13; Dt 5:17
c Mt 19:18; 23:31,35; Mk 10:19; Lk 18:20; Rm 13:9; Jms 2:11
d 5:22 Mt 18:9; Mk 9:43; Jms 3:6; 1Jn 3:15
e 5:25 Pr 25:8; Lk 12:58
f 5:27 Ex 20:14; Dt 5:18
g 5:28 2Sm 11:2; Jb 31:1; Pr 6:25
h 5:29 Mt 18:9; Mk 9:47
i Mt 10:28; 23:15,33; Lk 12:5
j 5:31 Jr 3:1; Mt 19:7; Mk 10:4
k Dt 24:1
l 5:32 Mt 19:9; Mk 10:11; Lk 16:18; Rm 7:3; 1Co 7:11
m 5:33 Lv 19:12; Nm 30:2; Dt 23:21; Mt 23:16
n 5:34–35 Ps 48:2; Is 66:1; Mt 23:22; Ac 7:49; Jms 5:12
o 5:37 Mt 6:13; 13:19,38; Jn 17:15; 2Th 3:3
p 5:38 Ex 21:24; Lv 24:20; Dt 19:21

not the smallest letter[A] or one stroke of a letter will pass away from the law until all things are accomplished. **19** Therefore, whoever breaks one of the least of these commands and teaches others to do the same will be called least in the kingdom of heaven. But whoever does and teaches these commands will be called great in the kingdom of heaven.[a] **20** For I tell you, unless your righteousness surpasses that of the scribes and Pharisees, you will never get into the kingdom of heaven.

APPLICATION QUESTIONS

READ MATTHEW 5:23–24

- How do these verses contribute to your understanding of reconciliation?

MURDER BEGINS IN THE HEART

21 "You have heard that it was said to our ancestors, **Do not murder**,[B,b] and whoever murders will be subject to judgment.[c] **22** But I tell you, everyone who is angry with his brother or sister[c] will be subject to judgment. Whoever insults[D] his brother or sister, will be subject to the court.[E] Whoever says, 'You fool!' will be subject to hellfire.[F,d] **23** So if you are offering your gift on the altar, and there you remember that your brother or sister has something against you, **24** leave your gift there in front of the altar. First go and be reconciled with your brother or sister, and then come and offer your gift. **25** Reach a settlement quickly with your adversary while you're on the way with him to the court, or your adversary will hand you over to the judge, and the judge to[G] the officer, and you will be thrown into prison.[e] **26** Truly I tell you, you will never get out of there until you have paid the last penny.[H]

ADULTERY BEGINS IN THE HEART

27 "You have heard that it was said, **Do not commit adultery**.[I,f] **28** But I tell you, everyone who looks at a woman lustfully has already committed adultery with her in his heart.[g] **29** If your right eye causes you to sin,[h] gouge it out and throw it away. For it is better that you lose one of the parts of your body than for your whole body to be thrown into hell.[i] **30** And if your right hand causes you to sin, cut it off and throw it away. For it is better that you lose one of the parts of your body than for your whole body to go into hell.

DIVORCE PRACTICES CENSURED

31 "It was also said, **Whoever divorces**[j] **his wife must give her a written notice of divorce**.[j,k] **32** But I tell you, everyone who divorces his wife, except in a case of sexual immorality, causes her to commit adultery. And whoever marries a divorced woman commits adultery.[l]

TELL THE TRUTH

33 "Again, you have heard that it was said to our ancestors, **You must not break your oath, but you must keep your oaths to the Lord**.[K,m] **34** But I tell you, don't take an oath at all: either by heaven, because it is God's throne; **35** or by the earth, because it is his footstool; or by Jerusalem, because it is the city of the great King.[n] **36** Do not swear by your head, because you cannot make a single hair white or black. **37** But let your 'yes' mean 'yes,' and your 'no' mean 'no.' Anything more than this is from the evil one.[o]

GO THE SECOND MILE

38 "You have heard that it was said, **An eye for an eye** and **a tooth for a tooth**.[L,p] **39** But

---

A 5:18 Or *not one iota*; *iota* is the smallest letter of the Gk alphabet.   B 5:21 Ex 20:13; Dt 5:17   C 5:22 Other mss add *without a cause*
D 5:22 Lit *Whoever says 'Raca'*; an Aramaic term of abuse that puts someone down, insulting one's intelligence   E 5:22 Lit *Sanhedrin*
F 5:22 Lit *the gehenna of fire*   G 5:25 Other mss read *judge will hand you over to*   H 5:26 Lit *quadrans*, the smallest and least valuable Roman coin, worth 1/64 of a daily wage   I 5:27 Ex 20:14; Dt 5:18   J 5:31 Dt 24:1   K 5:33 Lv 19:12; Nm 30:2; Dt 23:21   L 5:38 Ex 21:24; Lv 24:20; Dt 19:21

5:20 Unless, as a disciple of Jesus, you are committed to growing in righteousness, the heavenly kingdom will not be expressed in your earthly history. **The scribes and Pharisees** were concerned only with external righteousness.

5:21-22 God not only considers our actions but also our thoughts and words. He's concerned with the motives of the heart.

5:23-24 In order to have a healthy vertical relationship—intimacy and fellowship with God—you must maintain your horizontal relationships with others. Make peace with your adversary inasmuch as it depends on you.

5:27-30 Sexual purity involves more than avoiding a physical act. It involves the heart, too. Pornography is a huge stumbling block to moral purity and a clear example of the kind of sin that Jesus warned against (5:28). Jesus calls not for physical mutilation (again, sin is a matter of the heart), but for a radical approach to avoiding sin.

5:32 The Jewish religious leaders had varying understandings of divorce. Some thought one could divorce for any reason. But marriage vows are to be viewed as sacred and permanent.

5:33-37 Jesus didn't deny the legitimacy of all oath-taking. We find oaths in the Old

Testament, such as when covenant relationships were established. So Jesus was warning against careless, profane, and flippant uses of oaths in everyday speech. An oath shouldn't be used to convince someone of the truthfulness of what you're saying; that might only be a cover-up for deception.

5:38-42 The Old Testament principle of **an eye for an eye and a tooth for a tooth** (5:38; see Lev 24:20) was intended to keep justice fair and limited. Punishment was to be in proportion to the crime. But Jesus wanted his followers to develop a spirit of servanthood that would extend beyond what's required and even apply to those who mis-

a 5:39 Lk 6:29-30; Rm 12:17; 1Co 6:7; 1Pt 3:9

b 5:42 Dt 15:8; Lk 6:34
c 5:43 Lv 19:18; Dt 23:6; Lk 10:29
d 5:44 Lk 6:27; 23:34; Ac 7:60; Rm 12:20; 1Co 4:12; 1Pt 2:23
e 5:45 Jb 25:3; Mt 5:9; Lk 6:35; Ac 14:17
f 5:47 Mt 5:37; Mk 6:51; Jn 10:10; Rm 3:1; 2Co 9:1
g 5:48 Gn 17:1; Lv 19:2; Php 3:15; Col 4:12; Jms 1:4; 1Pt 1:15
h 6:1-2 Mt 23:5; Lk 6:24
i 6:4 Jr 17:10; Lk 14:14; Col 3:23-24; Heb 4:13
j 6:5 Mt 6:16; Mk 11:25; Lk 6:24; 18:11
k 6:6 2Kg 4:33; Is 26:20; Mt 6:18

➤ KINGDOM LIVING ❦
FAMILY
God, Our Heavenly Father

Statistics tell us that more than half the couples that get married today will also get divorced. For the African American community, figures are even more sobering. More than seventy percent of our children will grow up in broken homes, usually without a father.

God created us to be a part of a family. We are his children—members of his family—and our home is not broken. You and I are loved unconditionally. God's love for us is eternal. It does not change and will not fade. Regardless of whether you're married, single, divorced, or widowed, God is your heavenly Father, and he has promised never to leave us. This truth should add a tremendous amount of security to your life, especially when you live devoted to him and not to yourself.

Tragically, when couples put their own interests ahead of their vows to God and their love for one another, something is bound to give. And when marriages fall apart, deep feelings of resentment and sorrow flourish. When people don't feel loved, their hearts can be filled with sadness that often leads to anger and hurtful behaviors. How can you help? It all begins with unconditional love—God's love poured into you and poured out to those around you.

FOR THE NEXT FAMILY
KINGDOM LIVING LESSON SEE PAGE 1400.

who asks you, and don't turn away from the one who wants to borrow from you.*b*

LOVE YOUR ENEMIES

43 "You have heard that it was said, **Love your neighbor***B,C* and hate your enemy. **44** But I tell you, love your enemies*C* and pray for those who*D* persecute you,*d* **45** so that you may be*E* children of your Father in heaven. For he causes his sun to rise on the evil and the good, and sends rain on the righteous and the unrighteous.*e* **46** For if you love those who love you, what reward will you have? Don't even the tax collectors do the same? **47** And if you greet only your brothers and sisters, what are you doing out of the ordinary?*F,f* Don't even the Gentiles*G* do the same? **48** Be perfect,*g* therefore, as your heavenly Father is perfect.

HOW TO GIVE

6 "Be careful not to practice your righteousness*H* in front of others to be seen by them. Otherwise, you have no reward with your Father in heaven. **2** So whenever you give to the poor, don't sound a trumpet before you, as the hypocrites do in the synagogues and on the streets, to be applauded by people. Truly I tell you, they have their reward.*h* **3** But when you give to the poor, don't let your left hand know what your right hand is doing, **4** so that your giving may be in secret. And your Father who sees in secret will reward you.*i,j*

HOW TO PRAY

5 "Whenever you pray, you must not be like the hypocrites, because they love to pray standing in the synagogues and on the street corners to be seen by people. Truly I tell you, they have their reward.*j* **6** But when you pray, go into your private room, shut your door, and pray to your Father who is in secret. And your Father who sees in secret will reward you.*j,k* **7** When you pray, don't babble like the Gentiles, since

I tell you, don't resist*A* an evildoer. On the contrary, if anyone slaps you on your right cheek, turn the other to him also.*a* **40** As for the one who wants to sue you and take away your shirt, let him have your coat as well. **41** And if anyone forces you to go one mile, go with him two. **42** Give to the one

A 5:39 Or *don't set yourself against*, or *don't retaliate against who hate you*,   *B* 5:43 Lv 19:18   *C* 5:44 Other mss add *bless those who curse you, do good to those*   *D* 5:44 Or *may become*, or *may show yourselves to be*   *E* 5:47 Or *doing that is superior*; lit *doing more*   *G* 5:47 Other mss read *tax collectors*   *H* 6:1 Other mss read *charitable giving*   *I* 6:4 Other mss read *will himself reward you openly*
J 6:6 Other mss add *openly*

treat them. As Paul says, it means not repaying "evil for evil . . . but conquer[ing] evil with good" (Rom 12:17, 21).
5:43-45 To **love your enemies** (5:44) is to reflect the character of **your Father in heaven** (5:45). There are certain blessings that he gives to all people. **He causes his sun to rise on the evil and the good** (5:45). You don't have to be a Christian to feel the sunshine and to breathe oxygen.

5:48 To **be perfect** as God **is perfect** does not mean to be sinless; rather, it means to love others—in the power of the Holy Spirit—by seeking their best interests as a reflection of God's character. Loving your neighbor doesn't require having warm and fuzzy feelings for him; it means seeking his well-being.
6:2-6 In old western movies, they would create a town that appeared to be full of buildings, but each structure was a façade.

A building might look like a saloon from the front, but there was nothing on the other side of its door. Similarly, **hypocrites** (6:2) are play actors, giving an external appearance of spirituality without an accompanying internal reality.

If, like a hypocrite, you **give** for the applause of people, that's all the **reward** you're going to get. But give and pray **in secret**, and **your Father** will **reward you** (6:3-6).

a 6:7 1Kg 18:26; Ec 5:2
b 6:8 Mt 9:12; Mk 2:17; Lk 5:31; 9:11; 10:42; Ac 2:45
c 6:9-13 Lk 11:1-13
d 6:9 Lk 11:2; 1Co 7:14
e 6:10 Ps 103:20; Mt 3:2; 4:17; 26:42; Lk 22:42; Ac 21:14
f 6:11-12 Pr 30:8; Rm 4:4; Gl 5:3
g 6:13 Mt 26:41; 1Co 10:13; 2Pt 2:9
h 6:5 Mt 5:37; Jn 17:15; 2Th 3:3; 2Tm 4:18
i 6:14 Mk 11:25; Eph 4:32; Col 3:13
j 6:15-16 Is 58:5; Mt 18:35; Jms 2:13
k 6:17 Ru 3:3; 2Sm 12:20; Dn 10:3

l 6:19 Pr 23:4; Heb 13:5
m 6:20 Mt 19:21; Lk 12:33; 18:22; 1Tm 6:19
n 6:23 Mt 4:16; 8:12; 22:13; 25:30; 27:45
o 6:24 Lk 16:13; Gl 1:10; Jms 4:4
p 6:25-33 Lk 12:22-31

they imagine they'll be heard for their many words.[a] 8 Don't be like them, because your Father knows the things you need before you ask him.[b]

APPLICATION QUESTIONS

READ MATTHEW 6:9-13

– What do you like best about Jesus's prayer? Why?
– How does this prayer compare to the way you normally pray?
– How will you intentionally submit to God's will this week?

THE LORD'S PRAYER

9 "Therefore, you should pray like this:[c]
　　Our Father in heaven,
　　your name be honored as holy.[d]
10　Your kingdom come.
　　Your will be done
　　on earth as it is in heaven.[e]
11　Give us today our daily bread.[A]
12　And forgive us our debts,
　　as we also have forgiven our debtors.[f]
13　And do not bring us into[B] temptation,[g]
　　but deliver us from the evil one.[c,h]

14 "For if you forgive others their offenses, your heavenly Father will forgive you as well.[i] 15 But if you don't forgive others,[D] your Father will not forgive your offenses.

HOW TO FAST

16 "Whenever you fast, don't be gloomy like the hypocrites. For they make their faces unattractive[E,j] so that their fasting is obvious to people. Truly I tell you, they have their reward. 17 But when you fast, put oil on your head and wash your face,[k] 18 so that

your fasting isn't obvious to others but to your Father who is in secret. And your Father who sees in secret will reward you.[F]

GOD AND POSSESSIONS

19 "Don't store up for yourselves treasures[G] on earth, where moth and rust destroy and where thieves break in and steal.[l] 20 But store up for yourselves treasures in heaven,[m] where neither moth nor rust destroys, and where thieves don't break in and steal. 21 For where your treasure is, there your heart will be also.

22 "The eye is the lamp of the body. If your eye is healthy, your whole body will be full of light. 23 But if your eye is bad, your whole body will be full of darkness. So if the light within you is darkness, how deep is that darkness!"[n]

24 "No one can serve two masters, since either he will hate one and love the other, or he will be devoted to one and despise the other. You cannot serve both God and money.[o]

APPLICATION QUESTIONS

READ MATTHEW 6:25-34

– What are the main benefits or desirable things mentioned in these verses?
– What do these verses teach about anxiety? What are the main causes of anxiety in your life?
– Identify one change you'll make this week to place God and his kingdom first in your life.

THE CURE FOR ANXIETY

25 "Therefore I tell you:[p] Don't worry about your life, what you will eat or what you will drink; or about your body, what you will

---

[A] 6:11 Or *our necessary bread*, or *our bread for tomorrow*　[B] 6:13 Or *do not cause us to come into*　[C] 6:13 Or *from evil*; some later mss add *For yours is the kingdom and the power and the glory forever. Amen.*　[D] 6:15 Other mss add *their wrongdoing*　[E] 6:16 Or *unrecognizable*, or *disfigured*　[F] 6:18 Other mss add *openly*　[G] 6:19 Or *valuables*

6:9 Some people have had bad fathers and say they can't relate to God as Father, but we are not to measure our heavenly Father by the standard of our earthly ones. Rather, we are to measure our earthly fathers by the standard of our **Father in heaven**—who is perfect. He is the ultimate definition of what a father is. Notice also that he is *our* Father (so you're not the only kid in the family). To honor God as **holy** is to treat him as unique—in a class by himself. He is the Creator of all and the only one deserving of worship.
6:10 Jesus calls his disciples to make a pledge of allegiance to the **kingdom** of God—to God's rule over his creation. When Olympic athletes are awarded gold medals, they don't get to choose the song they hear at the award ceremony. The song played is the national anthem of their country. Similarly, you are called to march to God's tune.

God's **will** is what God wants—when, where, and how he wants it. Those who are part of God's family are to follow God's rules. He's sovereign, and he'll accomplish his purposes with you or without you. The question is, will you get to take part in it?
6:11 Just as the Israelites relied on God to provide manna regularly in the wilderness, so you are to live your life in dependence on God—one day at a time.
6:12 **Forgive us our debts, as we also have forgiven our debtors** relates to sins. When God forgives, he no longer credits sin to your account. And as we have been forgiven by God, so we are to forgive the sins others commit against us.
6:13 Satan is smarter than we are and has centuries of experience ruining human lives. So ask God to keep you from getting into situations that detour you from the kingdom road.

6:14-15 Don't miss that God's forgiveness is conditioned on your forgiveness of others. Jesus isn't talking about salvation here, but about our fellowship with God after we're saved, as a part of our discipleship. To **forgive** is to not hold a grudge, not to seek retribution. Since we all need forgiveness regularly, we must not withhold it.
6:16 If your goal in fasting is for other people to celebrate how spiritual you look, then their approval will be your only **reward**.
6:24 Few things can distract us as effectively as becoming slaves to **money**. Having money is not the problem, though. The danger is when money has *you* and becomes more important to you than spiritual things. God must have your devotion if you are to receive his kingdom direction.
6:25-30 For many of us, the admonition not to **worry about your life** (6:25) sounds just as

a 6:25 Lk 10:41; Php 4:6; 1Pt 5:7

b 6:26 Jb 38:41; Ps 147:9; Mt 10:29-31

c 6:29-30 1Kg 10:4-7; Mt 8:26; 14:31; 16:8

d 6:33 Mk 1:15; Ac 20:25

e Mt 27:19; Lk 7:29; 23:41,47; Jn 5:30; 17:25; Ac 3:14

f 1Kg 3:13; Mt 19:28; Mk 10:29; Lk 18:29; 1Tm 4:8

g 6:34 Mt 6:25; Lk 10:41; Php 4:6; 1Pt 5:7

h 7:1-5 Mk 4:24-25; Lk 6:37-42

i 7:2 Mk 4:24; Lk 6:38; Rm 2:1; 14:10; Jms 2:13

⇒ KINGDOM LIVING ⇐

KINGDOM

Seeking First the Kingdom

God's kingdom is lived out from the perspective of heaven, not earth. That's why Jesus said, "Seek first the kingdom of God and his righteousness, and all these things will be provided for you" (Matt 6:33). Far too many Christians, though, think they can mix a little of God with a lot of the world. They're willing to follow several isolated fragments of what they find in God's Word—going to church for fellowship, giving money when it's convenient, not stealing, and so on—but they're not willing to submit to God's comprehensive plan and purpose for their lives. They're not willing to be part of his kingdom agenda.

That's a big problem. Because when you bring the world into the Word, you're asking God, the King, to bless something that's contrary to his kingdom. He won't do that. In the end, your efforts to keep hold of only a little piece of God actually prevent you from experiencing any part of God because you can't operate in two kingdoms at once.

If you lose sight of the kingdom, God's perspective gets lost and you start focusing on the tangible and temporal things in life. When that happens, your judgment begins to be skewed and your decisions become shortsighted. Rather than living out your destiny and purpose, you may end up with wasted time, effort, energy, and emotions.

But when God's kingdom is prioritized, you get to see heaven both rule and overrule in your life. You will witness God trump circumstances and people that you thought had the last word because only God has the last word. You'll get to experience him at a whole new level as you experience him as King.

FOR THE NEXT KINGDOM
KINGDOM LIVING LESSON SEE PAGE 1128.

---

wear. Isn't life more than food and the body more than clothing?*a* **26** Consider the birds of the sky: They don't sow or reap or gather into barns, yet your heavenly Father feeds them. Aren't you worth more than they?*b* **27** Can any of you add one moment to his life span*A* by worrying? **28** And why do you worry about clothes? Observe how the wildflowers of the field grow: They don't labor or spin thread. **29** Yet I tell you that not even Solomon in all his splendor was adorned like one of these. **30** If that's how God clothes the grass of the field, which is here today and thrown into the furnace tomorrow, won't he do much more for you — you of little faith?*c* **31** So don't worry, saying, 'What will we eat?' or 'What will we drink?' or 'What will we wear?' **32** For the Gentiles eagerly seek all these things, and your heavenly Father knows that you need them. **33** But seek first the kingdom of God*B,d* and his righteousness,*e* and all these things will be provided for you.*f* **34** Therefore don't worry about tomorrow, because tomorrow will worry about itself. Each day has enough trouble*g* of its own.

DO NOT JUDGE

7 "Do not judge, so that you won't be judged.*h* **2** For you will be judged by the same standard with which you judge others, and you will be measured by the same measure you use.*i* **3** Why do you look at the splinter in your brother's eye but

---

A 6:27 Or *add a single cubit to his height*   *B* 6:33 Other mss omit *of God*

---

impossible to obey as "Don't breathe." Worry and anxiety over life are commonplace. But to this Jesus said in effect, "When was the last time you saw a bird with an ulcer?" **Birds** don't worry about where they're going to get their next meal, and yet the **heavenly Father feeds them** (6:26). Flowers don't agonize over looking pretty, but **not even Solomon in all his splendor** could match the beauty in the fields of God's creation (6:28-29)? If God gives this kind of attention to birds and flowers, **won't he do much more for you.** (6:30)? Trust him.

6:33 How do you know if you're putting God's kingdom first? Ask yourself this question: When I need guidance to make decisions, where do I go first? For many Christians, God is like a spare tire. He's the One they run to when all else fails. So, do you seek God's perspective first (through his Word and godly counsel), or do you seek the world's perspective? Kingdom Christians appeal to God's view and his righteous standards first. Do this, and **all these things will be provided for you.** Align yourself with his agenda, and your Daddy will take responsibility for meeting your needs.

6:34 Focusing on living for God's kingdom today is the antidote for **worry**.

7:1 To illegitimately **judge** is to create your own standard of what is acceptable and measure everyone against it, hypocritically critiquing others. Not surprisingly, people who do this typically find no problems with their own behavior. That's because when a sinner creates a standard, he becomes the standard. When my son was eleven years old, he wanted to show me how he could dunk a basketball in the gym. The problem was that he had asked a janitor to lower the rim so that he could dunk it. Those who hypocritically judge others use a standard, but it isn't God's. It's been lowered.

7:3-5 Imagine straining to see a nearly invisible speck while being oblivious to a board protruding from your eyeball! Instead of being judgmental toward others, allow God's standard to be applied to your own life. If you're honest, you'll discover that you fall short. When you've addressed your own sin, you'll be more understanding, compassionate, and righteous in your assessments and better able to help a brother or sister address his or her own sin.

[a] 7:3 Lk 6:41; Jn 8:7-9
[b] 7:6 Pr 9:7-8; 23:9; Mt 15:26

[c] 7:7-11 Lk 11:9-13
[d] 7:7 Mt 18:22; Mk 11:24; Jn 14:13-14; 15:7; 16:24; Jms 1:5; 1Jn 3:22; 5:14
[e] 7:8 Pr 8:17; Is 55:6; Jr 29:12-13
[f] 7:11 Gn 6:5; 8:21
[g] 7:12 Mt 22:40; Lk 6:31; Rm 13:8; Gl 5:14
[h] 7:13-14 Lk 13:23-24
[i] 7:13 Mt 26:8; Mk 14:4; Jn 17:12; Ac 8:20; Rm 9:22; Php 1:28
[j] 7:15 Mt 24:11,24; Mk 13:22; Lk 6:26; Ac 13:6; 2Pt 2:1
[k] Mt 9:36; 10:6,16; 12:11-12; 15:24; 18:12-13
[l] Mc 3:5; 2Tm 3:5
[m] Ezk 22:27; Jn 10:12; Ac 20:29
[n] 7:16-21 Pr 11:30; Mt 12:33; Lk 6:43-44; Jn 4:36; Jms 3:12
[o] 7:16 Mt 13:7; Heb 6:8
[p] 7:19 Jr 11:19; Mt 3:10; Lk 3:9; 13:7; Jn 15:2; Jd 12
[q] 7:20 Mt 7:16; 12:33; Lk 6:44; Jms 3:12
[r] 7:21 Mt 3:2; 18:3; Mk 9:43
[s] Ps 143:10; Pr 16:9; Mt 12:50; Gl 1:4; Eph 1:9; 1Jn 2:17
[t] Hs 8:2; Mt 25:11; Lk 6:46; Rm 2:13; Jms 1:22
[u] 7:22 Mk 3:15; Rv 9:20; 18:2
[v] Nm 24:4; Mt 10:15; Lk 13:25; Jn 11:51; 1Co 13:2

❧ Questions & Answers ❧

Q Why does Jesus's command to "seek first the kingdom of God" (Matt 6:33) accompany his teaching on worry? How does worry impact our ability to seek God first?

A Worry is one of the great distractions of life, and it is more than mere concern. Concern involves controlling how much time and attention you give to an issue. Worry occurs when the issue controls you. And when the issues in our lives are controlling us, then the kingdom goes to the back of the line in terms of our priorities, because we've given our worries too much clout.

Legitimate concern is necessary. But we must control what we think about, how much we think about it, and how we allow it to influence us. When the kingdom is pushed to the background because an issue in your life has assumed control, then that issue has become an idol and a god, thus hindering the true God from meeting the need that is causing you to worry.

FOR THE NEXT Q&A, SEE PAGE 1134.

don't notice the beam of wood in your own eye?[a] [4] Or how can you say to your brother, 'Let me take the splinter out of your eye,' and look, there's a beam of wood in your own eye? [5] Hypocrite! First take the beam of wood out of your eye, and then you will see clearly to take the splinter out of your brother's eye. [6] Don't give what is holy to dogs or toss your pearls before pigs,[b] or they will trample them under their feet, turn, and tear you to pieces.

ASK, SEARCH, KNOCK

[7] "Ask,[c] and it will be given to you.[d] Seek, and you will find. Knock, and the door[A] will be opened to you. [8] For everyone who asks receives, and the one who seeks finds,[e] and to the one who knocks, the door will be opened. [9] Who among you, if his son asks him for bread, will give him a stone? [10] Or if he asks for a fish, will give him a snake? [11] If you then, who are evil,[f] know how to give good gifts to your children, how much more will your Father in heaven give good things to those who ask him. [12] Therefore, whatever you want others to do for you, do also the same for them, for this is the Law and the Prophets.[g]

ENTERING THE KINGDOM

[13] "Enter through the narrow gate.[h] For the gate is wide and the road broad that leads to destruction,[i] and there are many who go through it. [14] How narrow is the gate and difficult the road that leads to life, and few find it.

[15] "Be on your guard against false prophets[j] who come to you in sheep's[k] clothing[l] but inwardly are ravaging wolves.[m] [16] You'll recognize them by their fruit.[n] Are grapes gathered from thornbushes or figs from thistles?[o] [17] In the same way, every good tree produces good fruit, but a bad tree produces bad fruit. [18] A good tree can't produce bad fruit; neither can a bad tree produce good fruit. [19] Every tree that doesn't produce good fruit is cut down and thrown into the fire.[p] [20] So you'll recognize them by their fruit.[q]

[21] "Not everyone who says to me, 'Lord, Lord,' will enter the kingdom of heaven,[r] but only the one who does the will[s] of my Father in heaven.[t] [22] On that day many will say to me, 'Lord, Lord, didn't we prophesy in your name, drive out demons[u] in your name, and do many miracles in your name?'[v]

[A] 7:7 Lit and it

7:6 There are numerous places in the Bible in which God instructs his people to make judgment calls. Here is one of them: **Don't give what is holy to dogs or toss your pearls before pigs**. These are references to those who despise spiritual things, but you can't obey this command unless you can discern who the "dogs" and "pigs" are.

The difference between judgmentalism and doing what Jesus calls us to do here is the standard used. When you sinfully judge, you use your own standard and condemn others. When you obey Jesus's words, you use wisdom, refusing to give what is precious in God's sight to those who refuse to value spiritual things.

7:7-8 Prayer is an earthly request for heavenly intervention. There are three answers to prayer: yes, no, or wait. If you haven't heard yes or no, then you keep asking.

7:12 Within this verse is the Golden Rule. In short, it means to love others: to practice the "one anothers" of Scripture (e.g., John 15:12; Gal 6:2; Eph 4:32; 1 Thess 5:11).

7:13-14 The **broad** road that many people follow, seeking to have a relationship with God, is called religion (7:13). *Religion* is man's attempt to make himself acceptable to a holy God. But the **narrow** gate that **leads to life** is Jesus; he makes us acceptable. **Few** find this road because few are willing to accept God's way to obtain eternal life

(7:14). The only legitimate way to a relationship with God is *his* way: through his Son and his cross.

7:15-18 The lesson here is that you need to examine the evidence of a teacher's life and ministry. Is that person's teaching and doctrine consistent with God's Word? Does his or her lifestyle display holiness and love for the Lord? If either answer is no, don't be deceived.

7:21-23 Someone can call Jesus, **Lord, Lord**, and have a ministry that *appears* to be authentic (7:21-22). Nevertheless, a lack of good fruit will expose them. The King of kings will thus respond, **Depart from me, you lawbreakers!** (7:23). False teachers will experience his judgment.

23 Then I will announce to them, 'I never knew you. **Depart from me, you law-breakers!'**[A,B,a]

THE TWO FOUNDATIONS

24 "Therefore,[b] everyone who hears these words[c] of mine and acts on them will be like a wise man who built his house on the rock. **25** The rain fell, the rivers rose, and the winds blew and pounded that house. Yet it didn't collapse, because its foundation was on the rock. **26** But everyone who hears these words of mine and doesn't act on them will be like a foolish man who built his house on the sand. **27** The rain fell, the rivers rose, the winds blew and pounded that house, and it collapsed. It collapsed with a great crash."

28 When Jesus had finished saying these things,[d] the crowds were astonished at his teaching,[e] **29** because he was teaching them like one who had authority, and not like their scribes.

A MAN CLEANSED

8 When he came down from the mountain, large crowds[f] followed him. **2** Right away[g] a man with leprosy[c] came up and knelt before him,[h] saying, "Lord, if you are willing, you can make me clean." **3** Reaching out his hand, Jesus touched him, saying, "I am willing; be made clean." Immediately his leprosy was cleansed. **4** Then Jesus told him, "See that you don't tell anyone;[i] but go, show yourself to the priest, and offer the gift that Moses commanded, as a testimony to them."[j]

A CENTURION'S FAITH

5 When he entered Capernaum,[k] a centurion came to him, pleading with him, **6** "Lord, my servant is lying at home paralyzed, in terrible agony."

7 He said to him, "Am I to come and heal him?"[D]

8 "Lord," the centurion replied, "I am not worthy to have you come under my roof. But just say the word, and my servant will be healed.[E] **9** For I too am a man under authority, having soldiers under my command.[E] I say to this one, 'Go,' and he goes; and to another, 'Come,' and he comes; and to my servant, 'Do this!' and he does it."

10 Hearing this, Jesus was amazed and said to those following him, "Truly I tell you, I have not found anyone in Israel with so great a faith. **11** I tell you that many will come from east and west to share the banquet[F] with Abraham, Isaac, and Jacob in the kingdom of heaven.[m] **12** But the sons of the kingdom will be thrown into the outer darkness where there will be weeping and gnashing of teeth."[n] **13** Then Jesus told the centurion, "Go. As you have believed,[o] let it be done for you." And his servant was healed that very moment.[G]

HEALINGS AT CAPERNAUM

14 Jesus went into Peter's house[p] and saw his mother-in-law lying in bed with a fever. **15** So he touched her hand, and the fever left her. Then she got up and began to serve him. **16** When evening came, they brought to him many who were demon-possessed. He drove out the spirits[q] with a word and healed all who were sick,[r] **17** so that what was spoken through the prophet Isaiah might be fulfilled:

He himself took our weaknesses and carried our diseases.[H,S]

[a]7:23 Ps 5:5; 6:8; Mt 25:12,41; Lk 13:25-27
[b]7:24-27 Lk 6:47-49; Jms 1:22-25
[c]7:24 Mt 12:36; Mk 4:14; Lk 6:47; 8:21; Jn 1:1; 2:22
[d]7:28 Mt 11:1; 13:53; 19:1; 26:1
[e]Mt 13:54; 22:23; Mk 1:22; 6:2; 11:18; Lk 4:32; Jn 7:46
[f]8:1 Mt 5:1; Lk 3:7
[g]8:2-4 Mk 1:40-44; Lk 5:12-14
[h]8:2 Mt 9:18; 15:25; 18:26; 20:20; Jn 9:38; Ac 10:25
[i]8:4 Mt 9:30; 17:9; Mk 5:43; 7:36; 8:30
[j]Lv 14:3-4,10; Lk 5:14; 17:14
[k]8:5-13 Lk 7:1-10; Jn 4:46-54

[l]8:8 Ps 107:20; Lk 15:19,21
[m]8:11 Is 49:12; 59:19; Mk 1:11; Lk 13:29; Eph 3:6
[n]8:12 Mt 13:42,50; 22:13; 24:51; 25:30; Lk 13:28
[o]8:13 Mt 9:22,29; Jn 4:53
[p]8:14-16 Mk 1:29-34; Lk 4:38-41
[q]8:16 Mk 3:15; 1Tm 4:1; 1Jn 4:1
[r]Mt 4:24; 8:33; Ac 19:12
[s]8:17 Is 53:4; Mt 1:22

[A]7:23 Lit *you who work lawlessness* [B]7:23 Ps 6:8 [C]8:2 Gk *lepros*; a term for various skin diseases, also in v. 3; see Lv 13–14 [D]8:7 Or "I will come and heal him." [E]8:9 Lit *under me* [F]8:11 Lit *recline at the table* [G]8:13 Or *that hour*; lit *very hour* [H]8:17 Is 53:4

7:24-27 I once had a crack in a wall of my house. No matter how many times I had it fixed, the crack came back. Finally, I learned the problem wasn't with the wall; the problem was a shifting foundation. Many of us have "cracks" in our lives—emotional, relational, financial—but we address the symptoms and not the source of the problem. If you want stability in your personal life, your family, your ministry, and your community, you need the strong, sturdy foundation of God's Word—which includes both knowledge of the Bible and applying it to life. Wisdom is the ability and willingness to apply spiritual truth to life's circumstances. Foolishness is unwillingness to do so.

8:2 There's nothing wrong with seeking a doctor's help when you're sick. The problem is in neglecting to seek God's help and treating the doctor as if he's a god.

8:8-9 This Roman officer understood how **authority** works. He had men under his command, and he didn't need to be present for his soldiers to obey his orders—any more than he needed Caesar to visit him personally to get him to jump. A subordinate only needs to know that a superior has issued an order (8:9). The centurion knew that Jesus possessed authority to heal. Therefore, he trusted that Jesus didn't have to be physically present but only **say the word** (8:8).

8:10 What made the centurion's **faith** so **great** was his total confidence in Jesus's word. Great faith comes when we truly understand the greatness of the object of our faith.

8:12 **The sons of the kingdom** refers to unregenerate Jews. Unfaithful believers will lose rewards in Jesus's millennial kingdom rule while faithful believers will be rewarded with rich inheritance. **Outer darkness** and **weeping and gnashing of teeth** are pictures of profound regret due to loss of rewards at the judgment seat of Christ because of their unfaithfulness. The context determines whether this phrase is referring to believers (see 25:29-30) or to unbelievers (see 13:47-50).

8:15 Notice what this woman did as soon as she got up from her sickbed. Likewise, when the Lord ministers to you, it should be reflected in your service to him.

8:16-17 The point here is that Jesus's healing ministry validated prophecy regarding the Messiah. A day is coming when, because of his death on the cross, sickness, pain, and death will be abolished forever (see Isa 53:5; Rev 21:4).

[a] 8:18 Mt 14:22; Mk 4:35;
Lk 8:22; Jn 6:15-17
[b] 8:19-22 Lk 9:57-60
[c] 8:20 Dn 7:14; Mt 9:6;
12:8; 13:41; Mk 8:31
[d] 8:23-27 Mk 4:36-41; Lk
8:22-25; Jn 6:16-21
[e] 8:23 Mt 10:1; 26:56; Mk
3:7; 16:20; Lk 6:13; Jn 12:16
[f] 8:26 Ps 65:7; 89:9; 107:29;
Mt 6:30; Lk 4:39
[g] 8:27 Mk 1:27; Lk 5:9
[h] 8:28-34 Mk 5:1-17; Lk
8:26-37
[i] 8:29 Jdg 11:12; 2Sm 16:10;
Mk 1:24; Lk 4:34; Jn 2:4;
Ac 8:7

[j] 8:34 1Kg 17:18; Lk 5:8;
Ac 16:39
[k] 9:1 Mt 4:13; Mk 5:21
[l] 9:2-8 Mk 2:3-12; Lk
5:18-26
[m] 9:2 Mt 4:24; 8:10,13;
9:22; Lk 7:48; Jn 16:33
[n] 9:3 Mt 26:65; Jn 10:36
[o] 9:4 Mt 12:25; Lk 6:8;
9:47; 11:17
[p] 9:8 Mt 5:16; 15:31; Lk
7:16; 13:13; Jn 15:8; Ac 4:21
[q] 9:9-17 Mk 2:14-22; Lk
5:27-38
[r] 9:9 Mt 10:3; Mk 2:14;
3:18; Lk 6:15; Ac 1:13

THE COST OF FOLLOWING JESUS

18 When Jesus saw a large crowd[A][a] around him, he gave the order to go to the other side of the sea. **19** A scribe approached him and said,[b] "Teacher, I will follow you wherever you go." **20** Jesus told him, "Foxes have dens, and birds of the sky have nests, but the Son of Man[c] has no place to lay his head." **21** "Lord," another of his disciples said, "first let me go bury my father." **22** But Jesus told him, "Follow me, and let the dead bury their own dead."

WIND AND WAVES OBEY JESUS

23 As he got into the boat,[d] his disciples[e] followed him. **24** Suddenly, a violent storm arose on the sea, so that the boat was being swamped by the waves — but Jesus kept sleeping. **25** So the disciples came and woke him up, saying, "Lord, save us! We're going to die!"

26 He said to them, "Why are you afraid, you of little faith?" Then he got up and rebuked the winds and the sea,[f] and there was a great calm.

27 The men were amazed and asked, "What kind of man is this? Even the winds and the sea obey[g] him!"

DEMONS DRIVEN OUT BY JESUS

28 When he had come to the other side,[h] to the region of the Gadarenes,[B] two demon-possessed men met him as they came out of the tombs. They were so violent that no one could pass that way. **29** Suddenly they shouted, "What do you have to do with us,[c] Son of God? Have you come here to torment us before the time?"[i] **30** A long way off from them, a large herd of pigs was feeding. **31** "If you drive us out,"

the demons begged him, "send us into the herd of pigs."

32 "Go!" he told them. So when they had come out, they entered the pigs, and the whole herd rushed down the steep bank into the sea and perished in the water. **33** Then the men who tended them fled. They went into the city and reported everything, especially what had happened to those who were demon-possessed. **34** At that, the whole town went out to meet Jesus. When they saw him, they begged him to leave their region.[j]

THE SON OF MAN FORGIVES AND HEALS

9 So he got into a boat, crossed over, and came to his own town.[k] **2** Just then[l] some men[D] brought to him a paralytic lying on a stretcher. Seeing their faith, Jesus told the paralytic, "Have courage, son, your sins are forgiven."[m]

3 At this, some of the scribes said to themselves, "He's blaspheming!"[n]

4 Perceiving their thoughts,[o] Jesus said, "Why are you thinking evil things in your hearts?[E] **5** For which is easier: to say, 'Your sins are forgiven,' or to say, 'Get up and walk'? **6** But so that you may know that the Son of Man has authority on earth to forgive sins" — then he told the paralytic, "Get up, take your stretcher, and go home." **7** So he got up and went home. **8** When the crowds saw this, they were awestruck[F][G] and gave glory[p] to God, who had given such authority to men.

THE CALL OF MATTHEW

9 As Jesus went on from there,[q] he saw a man named Matthew sitting at the toll booth, and he said to him, "Follow me," and he got up and followed him.[r]

[A] 8:18 Other mss read *saw large crowds*   [B] 8:28 Other mss read *Gergesenes*   [C] 8:29 Other mss add *Jesus*   [D] 9:2 Lit *then they*   [E] 9:4 Or *minds*
[F] 9:8 Other mss read *amazed*   [G] 9:8 Lit *afraid*

8:20 In other words, he asked the would-be disciple, "Are you sure you understand what you're getting yourself into? Will you follow me when there's no Hilton, no Holiday Inn?" Are you committed to Jesus, even when times are hard?

8:21-22 The man's request (8:21) was another way of saying he wanted to receive his inheritance before he committed himself to discipleship. Once his father died and left him sufficient funds, he'd be all in. But Jesus permitted no postponement: **Follow me, and let the dead bury their own dead** (8:22)—that is, let those who are spiritually dead worry about such things. Are you willing to risk discipleship even when it doesn't fit with your economic plans?

8:27 That the disciples were **amazed** at Jesus's lordship over creation suggests they hadn't *fully* known who was in the boat with them. The storms and trials of life are designed to give you a bigger view of God and a more precise understanding of who Jesus is, too. The size of your faith is ultimately tied to the size of your God.

8:29 Demons clearly know that a day of judgment is coming. But they refuse to live in light of it. People do that too (see Rom 1:32).

8:33-34 Did the Gentile herdsmen rejoice that two men had been miraculously set free of their oppression? No. Jesus was responsible for a negative impact on their livelihood. So, sadly, financial loss took priority over spiritual gain.

9:1 Jesus's **own town** was Capernaum (see 4:13).

9:2 By his words, Jesus affirmed his own deity and did what only God could do.

9:5-7 Clearly it was **easier** to claim to be able to forgive sins than to actually heal, but in order to demonstrate his **authority** in the spiritual realm (**to forgive sins**), Jesus also demonstrated his authority in the physical realm (to heal lame legs).

9:9 **Matthew** was also known as Levi (see Mark 2:14). He was a Jewish tax collector and was thus considered a traitor since it was his job to collect taxes from his own people on behalf of the Roman Empire. Moreover, tax collectors would stick their own surcharge onto the tax so that they could make a nice profit off of their fellow Jews.

10 While he was reclining at the table in the house, many tax collectors and sinners came to eat with Jesus and his disciples.[a] **11** When the Pharisees saw this, they asked his disciples, "Why does your teacher eat with tax collectors and sinners?"[b] **12** Now when he heard this, he said, "It is not those who are well who need a doctor, but those who are sick.[c] **13** Go and learn what this means: **I desire mercy and not sacrifice.**[A,d] For I didn't come to call the righteous, but sinners."[B]

A QUESTION ABOUT FASTING

14 Then John's disciples came to him, saying, "Why do we and the Pharisees fast often, but your disciples do not fast?"[e] **15** Jesus said to them, "Can the wedding guests[c] be sad while the groom is with them? The time[D] will come when the groom will be taken away from them, and then they will fast. **16** No one patches an old garment with unshrunk cloth, because the patch pulls away from the garment and makes the tear worse. **17** And no one puts[E] new wine into old wineskins. Otherwise, the skins burst, the wine spills out, and the skins are ruined. No, they put new wine into fresh wineskins, and both are preserved."

A GIRL RESTORED AND A WOMAN HEALED

18 As he was telling them these things,[f] suddenly one of the leaders came and knelt down before him, saying, "My daughter just died,[F] but come and lay your hand on her, and she will live."[g] **19** So Jesus and his disciples got up and followed[h] him.

20 Just then, a woman who had suffered from bleeding for twelve years approached from behind and touched the end of his robe,[i] **21** for she said to herself, "If I can just touch his robe, I'll be made well."[G,j]

22 Jesus turned and saw her. "Have courage, daughter," he said. "Your faith has saved you."[H,k] And the woman was made well from that moment.[I]

23 When Jesus came to the leader's house, he saw the flute players and a crowd lamenting loudly.[l] **24** "Leave," he said, "because the girl is not dead but asleep."[m] And they laughed at him. **25** After the crowd had been put outside, he went in and took her by the hand, and the girl got up.[n] **26** Then news of this spread throughout that whole area.[o]

HEALING THE BLIND

27 As Jesus went on from there, two blind men followed him, calling out, "Have mercy on us, Son of David!"[p] **28** When he entered the house, the blind men approached him, and Jesus said to them, "Do you believe[q] that I can do this?"

They said to him, "Yes, Lord."

29 Then he touched their eyes, saying, "Let it be done for you according to your faith." **30** And their eyes were opened. Then Jesus warned them sternly, "Be sure that no one finds out."[r] **31** But they went out and spread the news about him throughout that whole area.

DRIVING OUT A DEMON

32 Just as they were going out, a demon-possessed man who was unable to speak was brought to him.[s] **33** When the demon had been driven out, the man who had been mute spoke, and the crowds were amazed, saying, "Nothing like this has ever been seen in Israel!" **34** But the Pharisees said, "He drives out demons by the ruler of the demons."[t]

THE LORD OF THE HARVEST

35 Jesus continued going around to all the towns and villages, teaching in their

[a] 9:10 Mt 10:42; 28:19; Lk 14:26; Jn 8:31; 13:35; 15:8; Ac 6:1
[b] 9:11 Mt 11:19; Lk 5:30; 15:2; Gl 2:15
[c] 9:12 Mk 2:17; Lk 5:31
[d] 9:13 Hs 6:6; Mc 6:6-8; Mt 12:7
[e] 9:14 Mt 11:2; 14:12; 15:2; Lk 11:1; 18:12
[f] 9:18-26 Mk 5:22-43; Lk 8:41-56
[g] 9:18 Mt 8:2-3; Mk 5:23
[h] 9:19 Lk 5:11; Jn 8:12
[i] 9:20 Lv 15:25; Nm 15:38; Dt 22:12; Mt 14:36; 23:5
[j] 9:21 Mt 14:36; Mk 3:10; Lk 6:19
[k] 9:22 Mt 15:28; Mk 10:52; Lk 7:50; 17:19; 18:42
[l] 9:23 2Ch 35:25; Jr 9:17; 16:6; Ezk 24:17; Rv 18:22
[m] 9:24 Jn 11:13; Ac 20:10
[n] 9:25 Mk 9:27; Ac 3:7; 9:40-41
[o] 9:26 Mk 4:24; 9:31; 14:1; Mk 1:28; Lk 4:14
[p] 9:27 Mt 1:1; 12:23; 15:22; 20:30-31; Mk 10:47; Lk 18:38-39
[q] 9:28 Mk 11:24; Jn 3:16; Ac 10:43; Rm 10:9; 1Pt 1:8-10
[r] 9:29-30 Mt 8:4,13; 9:22; Mk 8:25; Jn 9:26
[s] 9:32-34 Mt 12:22-24; Lk 11:14-15
[t] 9:34 Mk 3:22; Jn 7:20

[A] 9:13 Hs 6:6   [B] 9:13 Other mss add *to repentance*   [C] 9:15 Lit *the sons of the bridal chamber*   [D] 9:15 Lit *days*   [E] 9:17 Lit *And they do not put*   [F] 9:18 Lit *daughter has now come to the end*   [G] 9:21 Or *be saved*   [H] 9:22 Or *has made you well*   [I] 9:22 Lit *hour*

9:10 Matthew had found grace and refused to keep it to himself because he knew others needed the same. That's why he threw a party at his **house** and invited other **tax collectors and sinners** to it.

9:11 The Pharisees couldn't conceive of upstanding, religious Jews socializing and eating **with tax collectors and sinners**. Tragically, many modern believers turn all of their focus inward to their Christian club and forget the reason Jesus came to earth: to invite new members to the family. When was the last time you connected a sinner to the Savior?

9:13 By quoting Hosea 6:6, Jesus essentially told the Pharisees to go back and study their

Bibles: **I desire mercy and not sacrifice**. The Pharisees offered plenty of religious sacrifices, but their hearts weren't merciful. Similarly, if your praise and worship isn't making you more compassionate toward the lost, you've missed the point of church.

9:15 The kingdom of God had come near because the King of the kingdom—the Messiah—had arrived. A time for fasting would come later when the **groom** (King Jesus) was taken from them. As sure as you don't grieve at a **wedding** feast, you don't fast at a celebration.

9:22 According to Leviticus 15:25-27, the woman's flow of blood would've made her and anything she touched ceremonially unclean.

But instead of uncleanness flowing to Jesus through her touch, healing flowed to her.

9:27 The prophet Isaiah had much to say about the Messiah, God's Servant, the King who was to come. He would be a descendant **of David** (of the "stump of Jesse," Isa 11:1), and he would bring healing (see Isa 42:6-7). These men, recognizing Jesus as the Messiah, knew what Jesus could do.

9:28-29 It's not enough to have faith: that faith must be declared publicly.

9:33 When the Lord drove out the demon, **the man who had been mute** could speak. This tells us that in the realm of God's kingdom, Satan's power is restrained; thus, you want to be living under God's kingdom rule.

[a]9:35 Mt 4:23; Mk 1:15
[b]9:36 Mt 14:14; 15:32; Mk 6:34; 8:2
[c]Nm 27:17; 1Kg 22:17; Ezk 34:5; Zch 10:2
[d]9:37 Mt 10:1; 26:56; Mk 3:7; 16:20; Lk 6:13; Jn 12:16
[e]10:1–4 Mk 3:13-19; 6:13-16
[f]10:1 Mt 9:35; Mk 6:7; Lk 9:1
[g]10:2 Mt 4:18,21; 16:18; Jn 1:42
[h]10:4 Mt 26:14; Lk 22:3; Jn 6:71; 13:2,26
[i]10:5 2Kg 17:24; Lk 9:52; 17:16; Jn 4:9; Ac 8:25
[j]10:6 Ps 119:36; Is 53:6; Jr 50:6; Mt 9:36; 18:12
[k]Ac 2:36; 7:42; Heb 8:8,10
[l]10:7 Mt 3:2-3; 4:17; Lk 10:9
[m]10:8 Mk 3:15; Rv 9:20; 18:2
[n]10:9–15 Mk 6:6–8; Lk 9:3-5; 10:4-12
[o]10:10 Lk 10:7; 1Co 9:14; 1Tm 5:18
[p]10:12 1Sm 25:6; 1Ch 12:18; Ps 122:7-8
[q]10:13 Ps 35:13; Mt 8:8; Ac 16:15
[r]10:14 Neh 5:13; Lk 10:11; Ac 13:51

[s]10:15 Mt 12:36; Ac 17:31; Heb 10:25; 2Pt 2:9; 1Jn 4:17
[t]Mt 11:22,24; 2Pt 2:6; Jd 6-7
[u]10:16 Gn 3:1; Lk 10:3; Rm 16:19; Php 2:15
[v]10:17 Mk 13:9,11; Lk 12:11-12; Ac 5:40; 26:11
[w]10:18 Mt 28:19; Rm 1:5; Gl 1:16
[x]10:19 Ex 4:12; Nm 23:5; Dt 18:18; Mt 6:25
[y]10:20 Ps 51:11; Jn 1:33; Ac 2:4; Rm 8:9; Gl 5:25; Ti 3:5
[z]Lk 12:12; Ac 4:8; 13:9; 2Co 13:3
[aa]10:21 Mc 7:6; Mt 10:35-36; Mt 13:12
[ab]10:22 Mt 24:9; Lk 21:17; Jn 15:18
[ac]Mt 24:13; Mk 13:13; Jn 12:12-13
[ad]10:23 Mt 12:15; Ac 8:1; 9:25; 14:6; 17:10; 15:20
[ae]10:24 Lk 6:40; Jn 13:16; 15:20
[af]10:25 2Kg 1:2; Mt 12:24,27; Mk 3:22; Lk 11:15,18-19
[ag]10:26-33 Lk 12:2-9
[ah]10:26 Mk 4:22; Lk 8:17; 12:2
[ai]10:27 Mt 24:17; Lk 5:19; 12:3; Ac 5:20
[aj]10:28 Is 8:12-13; 51:12-13; Jr 1:8; 1Pt 3:14

synagogues, preaching the good news of the kingdom,[a] and healing every[A] disease and every sickness.[B,C] 36 When he saw the crowds, he felt compassion for them, because they were distressed and dejected,[b] like sheep without a shepherd.[c] 37 Then he said to his disciples,[d] "The harvest is abundant, but the workers are few. 38 Therefore, pray to the Lord of the harvest to send out workers into his harvest."

COMMISSIONING THE TWELVE

10 Summoning his twelve disciples,[e] he gave them authority over unclean spirits, to drive them out and to heal every[A] disease and sickness.[C,f] 2 These are the names of the twelve apostles:[g] First, Simon, who is called Peter, and Andrew his brother; James the son of Zebedee, and John his brother; 3 Philip and Bartholomew; Thomas and Matthew the tax collector; James the son of Alphaeus, and Thaddaeus;[D] 4 Simon the Zealot,[E] and Judas Iscariot, who also betrayed him.[h]

5 Jesus sent out these twelve after giving them instructions: "Don't take the road that leads to the Gentiles, and don't enter any Samaritan[i] town. 6 Instead, go to the lost sheep[j] of the house of Israel.[k] 7 As you go, proclaim: 'The kingdom of heaven has come near.'[l] 8 Heal the sick, raise the dead, cleanse those with leprosy,[F] drive out demons.[m] Freely you received, freely give. 9 Don't acquire gold, silver, or copper for your money-belts.[n] 10 Don't take a traveling bag for the road, or an extra shirt, sandals, or a staff, for the worker[o] is worthy of his food. 11 When you enter any town or village, find out who is worthy, and stay there until you leave. 12 Greet a household when you enter it,[p] 13 and if the household is worthy, let your peace be on it; but if it is unworthy, let your peace return to you.[q] 14 If anyone does not welcome you or listen to your words, shake the dust off your feet[r]

when you leave that house or town. 15 Truly I tell you, it will be more tolerable on the day of judgment[s] for the land of Sodom and Gomorrah than for that town.[t]

PERSECUTIONS PREDICTED

16 "Look, I'm sending you out like sheep among wolves. Therefore be as shrewd as serpents and as innocent as doves.[u] 17 Beware of them, because they will hand you over to local courts[G] and flog you in their synagogues.[v] 18 You will even be brought before governors and kings because of me, to bear witness to them and to the Gentiles.[w] 19 But when they hand you over, don't worry about how or what you are to speak.[x] For you will be given what to say at that hour, 20 because it isn't you speaking, but the Spirit[y] of your Father is speaking through you.[z]

21 "Brother will betray brother to death, and a father his child. Children will rise up against parents and have them put to death.[aa] 22 You will be hated by everyone because of my name.[ab] But the one who endures to the end will be saved.[ac] 23 When they persecute you in one town, flee to another.[ad] For truly I tell you, you will not have gone through the towns of Israel before the Son of Man comes. 24 A disciple[H] is not above his teacher, or a slave above his master.[ae] 25 It is enough for a disciple to become like his teacher and a slave like his master. If they called the head of the house 'Beelzebul,' how much more the members of his household![af]

FEAR GOD

26 "Therefore,[ag] don't be afraid of them, since there is nothing covered that won't be uncovered and nothing hidden that won't be made known.[ah] 27 What I tell you in the dark, speak in the light. What you hear in a whisper,[I] proclaim on the housetops.[ai] 28 Don't fear those who kill the body but are not able to kill the soul;[aj]

[A]9:35, 10:1 Or *every kind of*   [B]9:35 Other mss add *among the people*   [C]9:35; 10:1 Or *physical ailment*   [D]10:3 Other mss read *and Lebbaeus, whose surname was Thaddaeus*   [E]10:4 Lit *the Cananaean*   [F]10:8 Gk *lepros* ; a term for various skin diseases; see Lv 13–14   [G]10:17 Or *sanhedrins*
[H]10:24 Or *student*   [I]10:27 Lit *in the ear*

9:37-38 Jesus called his disciples—including us—to **pray** for the recruitment of kingdom-minded **workers** (9:38).

10:1-2 Jesus gave the Twelve, including Judas, **authority** and power to perform what he himself had been doing (10:1). They had been promoted from disciples to **apostles** (10:2).

10:5-6 Later, through the ministry of the Holy Spirit, the message of Jesus would spread **to the Gentiles** (see, e.g., Acts 1:8; 10:34-48; 11:1-18).

10:8-10 They were not to charge money for their ministry, but they could accept support.

10:14 Shaking **the dust off** in this manner was a sign of disdain for those rejecting God's kingdom.

10:15 The **day of judgment** will be more bearable for the wicked Old Testament towns **of Sodom and Gomorrah than** it will be for those who reject the message of Jesus.

10:16-17 Jesus made clear to the Twelve that persecution from kingdom opponents would accompany message proclamation (10:17), so they were to be **shrewd** but **innocent**—that is, to minister with wisdom and grace (10:16).

10:21-22 This persecution will become especially intense during the tribulation period, about which Jesus would have more to say (see ch. 24).

10:25 If those in the world call Jesus **Beelzebul**, the ruler of demons (Satan), his followers shouldn't expect to receive better treatment.

10:26 No persecution of God's people will remain secret forever. God *will* turn the tables.

10:28-31 There's no need to **fear those who** have temporary power in history (10:28); believers rightly fear God, who has limitless

rather, fear him who is able to destroy both soul and body in hell.[a] 29 Aren't two sparrows sold for a penny?[A] Yet not one of them falls to the ground without your Father's[b] consent.[B] 30 But even the hairs of your head have all been counted.[c] 31 So don't be afraid; you are worth more than many sparrows.[d]

ACKNOWLEDGING CHRIST

32 "Therefore, everyone who will acknowledge me before others, I will also acknowledge him before my Father in heaven.[e] 33 But whoever denies me before others,[f] I will also deny him before my Father in heaven. 34 Don't assume that I came to bring peace on the earth. I did not come to bring peace, but a sword.[g] 35 For I came to turn

a man against his father,
a daughter against her mother,
a daughter-in-law against
    her mother-in-law;

36   and a man's enemies will be
      the members of his household.[C,h]

37 The one who loves a father or mother more than me is not worthy of me;[i] the one who loves a son or daughter more than me is not worthy of me. 38 And whoever doesn't take up his cross and follow me is not worthy of me. 39 Anyone who finds his life will lose it,[j] and anyone who loses his life because of me will find it.[k]

A CUP OF COLD WATER

40 "The one who welcomes you welcomes me,[l] and the one who welcomes me welcomes him who sent me.[m] 41 Anyone who welcomes a prophet[n] because he is a prophet[D] will receive a prophet's reward. And anyone who welcomes a righteous person because he's righteous[E] will receive a righteous person's reward. 42 And whoever gives[o] even a cup of cold water to one of these little ones because he is a disciple,[F,p] truly I tell you, he will never lose his reward."

JOHN THE BAPTIST DOUBTS

11 When Jesus had finished giving instructions to his twelve disciples, he moved on from there to teach and preach in their towns.[q] 2 Now when John heard in prison what the Christ was doing, he sent a message through his disciples[r] 3 and asked him, "Are you the one who is to come, or should we expect someone else?"[s]

4 Jesus replied to them, "Go and report to John what you hear and see: 5 The blind receive their sight, the lame walk, those with leprosy[G] are cleansed, the deaf hear, the dead are raised, and the poor are told the good news,[t] 6 and blessed is the one who isn't offended by me."[u]

7 As these men were leaving, Jesus began to speak to the crowds about John: "What did you go out into the wilderness to see? A reed swaying in the wind?[v] 8 What then did you go out to see? A man dressed in soft clothes? See, those who wear soft clothes are in royal palaces. 9 What then did you go out to see? A prophet? Yes, I tell you, and more than a prophet.[w] 10 This is the one about whom it is written:

See, I am sending my messenger
    ahead of you;
he will prepare your way
    before you.[H,x]

11 "Truly I tell you, among those born of women no one greater than John the Baptist has appeared,[I] but the least in the

[a] 10:28 Mt 5:22; Lk 12:5; Heb 10:31; Jms 4:12
[b] 10:29 Mt 5:16; 11:27; Lk 11:13; Jn 8:42
[c] 10:30 1Sm 14:45; 2Sm 14:11; Lk 21:18; Ac 27:34
[d] 10:31 Mt 6:26; 12:12
[e] 10:32 Lk 12:8; Rm 10:9-10; Rv 3:5
[f] 10:33 Mk 8:38; Lk 9:26; 2Tm 2:12; 2Pt 2:1
[g] 10:34-36 Lk 12:51-53
[h] 10:36 Ps 41:9; 55:12-13; Mc 7:6; Jn 13:18
[i] 10:37-39 Lk 14:25-27
[j] 10:39 Mt 16:25; Mk 8:35; Lk 9:24; 17:33; Jn 12:25
[k] Mt 9:9; Jn 8:12; 12:26; 21:19
[l] 10:40 Mt 18:5; Lk 10:16; Jn 13:20; Gl 4:14
[m] Mk 9:37; Lk 9:48; Jn 12:44
[n] 10:41 1Kg 17:10-15; 18:4; 2Kg 4:8; 3Jn 5-8

[o] 10:42 Mt 25:40; Mk 9:41; Heb 6:10
[p] Mt 28:19; Lk 14:26; Jn 8:31; 13:35; 15:8; Ac 6:1
[q] 11:1 Mt 7:28; 9:35; Lk 23:5
[r] 11:2-19 Lk 7:18-35
[s] 11:3 Ps 118:26; Jn 6:14; 11:27; Heb 10:37
[t] 11:5 Is 35:5; 61:1; Lk 4:18; Jms 2:5
[u] 11:6 Is 8:14-15; Mt 13:21; Jn 6:61; 16:1
[v] 11:7 Mt 3:1; Eph 4:14
[w] 11:9 Mt 14:5; 21:26; Lk 1:76
[x] 11:10 Mal 3:1; Mk 1:2

power in eternity. He's sovereign over the events of your life. Nothing comes to you that hasn't first passed through his fingers. His children are valuable to him (10:29-31).
10:32 The Greek word translated **acknowledge** here can also be rendered as "confess." To confess something is to publicly affirm it—to declare it openly and plainly. Jesus isn't talking about salvation here. His words are set in the context of a discussion about being a disciple (10:24-25). You can be saved but fail to publicly acknowledge your relationship with Jesus. You're not to be a secret agent Christian but a vocal and visible disciple.
10:33 This is not referring to salvation in eternity but deliverance in history. If you're a covert follower of Jesus, there will be negative repercussions; you can expect prayer

requests to be denied in history and loss of kingdom rewards in eternity. Go public with your Christian faith.
10:34-36 Peace on the earth is coming, but not yet (10:34). Association with Jesus can introduce problems in your relationships—even within your own family (10:35-36).
10:38 Your **cross** has to do with your public identification with Jesus. To bear your cross is to endure hardship specifically because you're a visible and verbal follower of him. If you're unwilling to do that, you're unworthy of Christ—that is, your relationship is distant.
10:39 In order to experience the life you're looking for, you must be willing to lose the life you have. This is one of Jesus's paradoxical statements. Give your life over to Christ, and he'll give it back to you. Try to live your life

on your own terms, and you'll **lose** what you think you have.
10:40 A disciple of Jesus Christ is his representative. As Paul would later say, "We are ambassadors for Christ" (2 Cor 5:20).
11:2-3 John had believed that Jesus was the Christ (3:14). But as he languished in prison, he began to have doubts. Wasn't the Christ supposed to separate the "wheat" from "the chaff" (see 3:12)? Jesus's miracles and healings were fine, but when would he judge God's enemies?
11:4-5 Jesus reminded **John** that his healing ministry and his proclamation of **the good news** matched the expectations of the Messiah (see Isa 61:1). His words and deeds validated who he was. The judgment of the wicked would come in the future.

*a*11:14 Mal 4:5; Mt 17:10-13; Mk 9:11-13; Lk 1:17; Jn 1:21
*b*11:15 Mt 13:9; Mk 4:23; Lk 8:8; 14:35; Rv 2:7
*c*11:18 Mt 3:4; Lk 1:15
*d*11:19 Mt 9:10; Lk 7:36; 14:1; Jn 2:1; 12:2
*e*9:11; 18:17; Lk 15:2; 19:7
*f*11:21-24 Lk 10:12-15
*g*11:21 Mk 6:45; Lk 9:10; Jn 12:21
*h*Mt 15:21; Lk 6:17; Ac 12:20
*i*11:22 Ezk 28:2-4; Am 1:9-10; Mt 10:15; 15:21; Mk 3:8
*j*11:23 Is 14:13,15; Mt 4:13
*k*11:25-27 Lk 10:21-22
*l*11:25 Ps 8:2; Lk 22:42; Jn 11:41; 1Co 1:26; 2Co 3:14
*m*11:27 Mt 28:18; Jn 1:18; 7:29; 8:19; 10:15; 17:25-26
*n*11:28 Jr 31:25; Jn 7:37
*o*11:29 Jn 13:15; Eph 4:20; Php 2:5; 1Pt 2:21; 1Jn 2:6
*p*Jr 6:16; Zch 9:9; 2Co 10:1; Php 2:7-8
*q*12:1-8 Mk 2:23-28; Lk 6:1-5
*r*12:1 Mt 10:1; 26:56; Mk 3:7; 16:20; Lk 6:13; Jn 12:16
*s*12:2 Mt 12:10; Lk 13:14; 14:3; Jn 5:10; 7:23; 9:16

kingdom of heaven is greater than he. ¹² From the days of John the Baptist until now, the kingdom of heaven has been suffering violence,^A and the violent have been seizing it by force. ¹³ For all the prophets and the law prophesied until John. ¹⁴ And if you're willing to accept it, he is the Elijah who is to come.*a* ¹⁵ Let anyone who has ears^B listen.*b*

AN UNRESPONSIVE GENERATION

¹⁶ "To what should I compare this generation? It's like children sitting in the marketplaces who call out to other children:

¹⁷ We played the flute for you,
   but you didn't dance;
   we sang a lament,
   but you didn't mourn!^C

¹⁸ For John came neither eating nor drinking, and they say, 'He has a demon!'^C ¹⁹ The Son of Man came eating and drinking, and they say, 'Look, a glutton and a drunkard,*d* a friend of tax collectors and sinners!'^E Yet wisdom is vindicated^D by her deeds."^E ²⁰ Then he proceeded to denounce the towns where most of his miracles were done, because they did not repent: ²¹ "Woe to you, Chorazin!*f* Woe to you, Bethsaida!*g* For if the miracles that were done in you had been done in Tyre and Sidon,*h* they would have repented in sackcloth and ashes long ago. ²² But I tell you, it will be more tolerable for Tyre and Sidon on the day of judgment*i* than for you. ²³ And you, Capernaum, will you be exalted to heaven? No, you will go down to Hades.*j* For if the miracles that were done in you had been done in Sodom, it would have remained until today. ²⁴ But I tell you, it will be more tolerable for the land of Sodom on the day of judgment than for you."

THE SON GIVES KNOWLEDGE AND REST

²⁵ At that time Jesus said,*k* "I praise you, Father, Lord of heaven and earth, because you have hidden these things from the wise and intelligent and revealed them to infants.*l* ²⁶ Yes, Father, because this was your good pleasure.^F ²⁷ All things have been entrusted to me by my Father. No one knows the Son except the Father, and no one knows the Father except the Son and anyone to whom the Son desires^G to reveal him.*m*

²⁸ "Come to me, all of you who are weary and burdened, and I will give you rest.*n* ²⁹ Take up my yoke and learn from me,*o* because I am lowly and humble in heart, and you will find rest for your souls.*p* ³⁰ For my yoke is easy and my burden is light."

⮌ HOPE WORDS ⮌

You can find no rest in life until you find rest in God.

LORD OF THE SABBATH

12 At that time Jesus passed through the grainfields on the Sabbath.*q* His disciples*r* were hungry and began to pick and eat some heads of grain. ² When the Pharisees saw this, they said to him, "See, your disciples are doing what is not lawful^S to do on the Sabbath."

---

^A 11:12 Or *has been forcefully advancing* ^B 11:15 Other mss add *to hear* ^C 11:17 Or *beat your chests in grief* ^D 11:19 Or *declared right* ^E 11:19 Other mss read *children* ^F 11:26 Lit *was well-pleasing in your sight* ^G 11:27 Or *wills*, or *chooses*

11:16-19 Jesus compared the **generation** that was rejecting his message to a group of fussy **children** who were never satisfied (11:16-17). John the Baptist lived an ascetic lifestyle, and they called him **demon**-possessed (11:18). **The Son of Man** ate and drank, and they called him **a glutton and a drunkard**. There's just no pleasing some people, **yet wisdom is vindicated by her deeds** (11:19)—that is, your ability to apply spiritual truth will be demonstrated by what you do. Those who scorned John and Jesus proved that their wisdom tanks were on empty.

11:20-24 Wicked Old Testament cities that incurred God's wrath will find **the day of judgment** more **tolerable** than will those cities that rejected Jesus (11:22, 24). These Galilean cities had heard the word and seen the power of the King of kings, the God-Man. Therefore, their actions would be weightier. The greater the knowledge of God's revelation, the greater the accountability for those who reject it.

11:25-27 Jesus said, in effect, "Thank you, Father, that you keep secrets from people who think they're smart enough to figure out life independent of you." God is happy to hide answers from those who don't think they need him (11:25-26). The answer to life's burdens isn't found via mere human wisdom but through accepting the divine viewpoint. We must become like **infants** who trust their daddy (11:25). And the only way to know and have access to our Father who hides things from self-sufficient people is through knowing and trusting his Son, Jesus Christ (11:27).

11:28 In view here is the invitation to salvation. To **rest** is to put your burdens in God's hands and enjoy his provision of forgiveness and eternal life.

11:29 A **yoke** is a wooden bar harnessed to the necks of a pair of oxen to bring them under submission and enable them to do the work that the farmer has for them. To train younger oxen, farmers would yoke them to older, experienced oxen. When you come to Jesus, he *gives* you rest in terms of your salvation. When you accept the "yoke" of discipleship, you *find* **rest** and experience it in your daily life.

11:30 Jesus didn't say you would no longer have burdens if you hitched to him. He said their weight would decrease. A suitcase packed full may be too heavy to carry. But, if the case has wheels, your burden will become lighter though your circumstances haven't changed. God can put wheels on your burdens so that you can deal with them more easily.

12:1-2 According to the Mosaic law, you couldn't work **on the Sabbath**, but **the Pharisees** had created so many additional regulations and introduced so many scenarios to the way the Sabbath was handled that they considered the disciples' actions equivalent to working in **the grainfields**.

3 He said to them, "Haven't you read
what David did when he and those who
were with him were hungry: 4 how he entered the house of God, and they ate[A] the
bread of the Presence — which is not lawful for him or for those with him to eat,
but only for the priests?[a] 5 Or haven't you
read in the law that on Sabbath days the
priests in the temple violate the Sabbath
and are innocent?[b] 6 I tell you that something greater than the temple is here.[c] 7 If
you had known what this means, **I desire
mercy and not sacrifice**,[B,d] you would not
have condemned the innocent. 8 For the
Son of Man is Lord of the Sabbath."[e]

THE MAN WITH THE SHRIVELED HAND

9 Moving on from there, he entered their
synagogue.[f] 10 There he saw a man who
had a shriveled hand, and in order to accuse him they asked him, "Is it lawful to
heal on the Sabbath?"[g]
11 He replied to them, "Who among you,
if he had a sheep that fell into a pit on the
Sabbath, wouldn't take hold of it and lift
it out?[h] 12 A person is worth far more than
a sheep;[i] so it is lawful to do what is good
on the Sabbath."
13 Then he told the man, "Stretch out
your hand." So he stretched it out, and it
was restored,[j] as good as the other. 14 But
the Pharisees went out and plotted against
him, how they might kill him.[k]

THE SERVANT OF THE LORD

15 Jesus was aware of this and withdrew.
Large crowds[C] followed him, and he
healed them all.[l] 16 He warned them not
to make him known,[m] 17 so that what was
spoken through the prophet Isaiah might
be fulfilled:

18 **Here is my servant
whom I have chosen,
my beloved in whom I delight;
I will put my Spirit on him,
and he will proclaim justice
to the nations.**[n]
19 **He will not argue or shout,
and no one will hear his voice
in the streets.**
20 **He will not break a bruised reed,
and he will not put out
a smoldering wick,
until he has led justice to victory.**[D]
21 **The nations will put their hope
in his name.**[E,o]

A HOUSE DIVIDED

22 Then a demon-possessed man[p] who was
blind and unable to speak was brought to
him. He healed him, so that the man[F] could
both speak and see.[q] 23 All the crowds were
astounded and said, "Could this be the Son
of David?"[r]
24 When the Pharisees heard this, they
said, "This man drives out demons only by
Beelzebul, the ruler of the demons."[s]
25 Knowing their thoughts,[t] he told
them: "Every kingdom divided against itself is headed for destruction, and no city
or house divided against itself will stand.
26 If Satan[u] drives out Satan, he is divided
against himself. How then will his kingdom stand? 27 And if I drive out demons
by Beelzebul, by whom do your sons
drive them out? For this reason they will
be your judges.[v] 28 If I drive out demons
by the Spirit of God, then the kingdom
of God has come upon you.[w] 29 How can
someone enter a strong man's house and
steal his possessions unless he first ties
up[x] the strong man? Then he can plunder
his house. 30 Anyone who is not with me
is against me,[y] and anyone who does not
gather with me scatters. 31 Therefore,[z] I tell
you, people will be forgiven every sin and

[a] 12:4 Ex 25:30; Lv 24:5-9; 1Sm 21:6
[b] 12:5 Nm 28:9-10; 1Ch 9:32; Jn 7:22-23
[c] 12:6 2Ch 6:18; Mal 3:1; Mt 12:41-42
[d] 12:7 Hs 6:6; Mc 6:8; Mt 9:13
[e] 12:8 Mt 8:20; 9:6; 12:32,40
[f] 12:9-14 Mk 3:1-6; Lk 6:6-11
[g] 12:10 Mt 12:2; Lk 13:14; 14:3; Jn 9:16
[h] 12:11 Ex 23:4-5; Dt 22:4; Lk 14:5
[i] 12:12 Mt 6:26; 10:31
[j] 12:13 1Kg 13:4; Mt 8:3; Ac 28:8
[k] 12:14 Mt 26:4; 27:1; Mk 3:6; Lk 6:11; Jn 10:39; 11:53
[l] 12:15 Mt 4:23; 10:23; 19:2; Mk 3:7
[m] 12:16 Mt 8:4; 9:30
[n] 12:18 Mt 3:17; 17:5; Lk 4:18; Jn 3:34
[o] 12:18-21 Is 42:1-4; Jn 10:25
[p] 12:22-24 Lk 11:14-15
[q] 12:22 Mt 4:24; 9:32-34
[r] 12:23 2Ch 1:1; Mt 1:1; Rm 1:3
[s] 12:24 Mt 9:34; 10:25; Mk 3:22
[t] 12:25-29 Mk 3:23-27; Lk 11:17-22
[u] 12:26 Mt 4:1,10; 13:19; Ac 13:10
[v] 12:27 2Kg 2:7; Ac 19:13
[w] 12:28 Lk 17:21; 1Jn 3:8
[x] 12:29 Is 49:24; 53:12
[y] 12:30 Mk 9:40; Lk 9:50; 11:23
[z] 12:31-32 Mk 3:28-30; Lk 12:10

[A] 12:4 Other mss read *he ate* [B] 12:7 Hs 6:6 [C] 12:15 Other mss read *Many* [D] 12:20 Or *until he has successfully put forth justice*
[E] 12:18-21 Is 42:1-4 [F] 12:22 Lit *mute*

12:3-4 To mention **David** was to mention a Jewish hero. When David and his men were running from Saul, he took **the bread of the Presence** from **the house of God**—the tabernacle—for them to eat, even though it was **only for the priests**. Scripture itself, then, testifies that God's laws were never meant to get in the way of taking care of the necessities of life. The Sabbath was for the benefit of man, not for his destruction (see Mark 2:27).

12:5 **Priests** have to do God's work on **the Sabbath**. Should your understanding of the commands of God prevent you from loving and serving God, you're using his commands inappropriately.

12:6 The *only* thing **greater than** God's house is God; therefore, Jesus was letting them know who he was.

12:10 When the Pharisees asked whether it was **lawful to heal on the Sabbath**, they weren't asking an honest question but looking for an opportunity to **accuse** Jesus.

12:11-12 Jesus reasoned that acts of mercy don't dishonor the Sabbath—especially since people are more valuable than animals.

12:16-21 Jesus wasn't seeking public notoriety. He wasn't seeking to be a superstar (12:16). As Matthew says, he wanted to fulfill God's Word as written in Isaiah 42:1-4, demonstrating the Messiah's compassion (12:17-21).

12:24-28 The Pharisees accused Jesus of driving out **demons** by the power of Satan (12:24). Jesus observed how illogical their accusation was: **If Satan drives out Satan, he is divided against himself** (12:26). Satan may be thoroughly evil, but he's more clever than that. He doesn't work against his own plan, and the Pharisees knew it. The only alternative was the truth: Jesus had driven out demons **by the Spirit of God** (12:28).

12:31-32 God revealed the reality of who Jesus is through his mighty words and works. If anyone rejects this demonstration of the Holy Spirit's power and attributes it to the devil, he is rejecting salvation.

*a*12:31 Heb 6:4-6; 10:26; 1Jn 5:16
*b*12:32 Mt 11:19; Mk 2:10; Jn 7:12; 9:24
*c*Mk 10:30; Lk 12:10; 20:34-35; Eph 1:21; Ti 2:12; Heb 6:5
*d*12:33 Mt 7:18-19,23; Lk 6:43-44; Jn 15:4-7
*e*12:34 1Sm 24:13; Mt 3:7; 23:33; Lk 6:45; Eph 4:29
*f*12:35 Mt 13:52; Col 4:6
*g*12:36 Mt 12:41; Jn 5:29; 1Jn 4:17
*h*Lk 16:2; Ac 17:40; Rm 14:12; Heb 13:17; 1Pt 4:5
*i*12:38 Mt 16:1; Mk 8:11-12; Lk 11:16; Jn 2:18; 6:30; 1Co 1:22
*j*12:39 Mk 8:11-12; Lk 11:29-32
*k*Is 57:3; Mt 16:4; Mk 8:38
*l*12:40 Jnh 1:17
*m*Jnh 1:17
*n*12:41 Jr 3:11; Ezk 16:51; Rm 2:27
*o*Jnh 1:2; 3:5
*p*12:42 1Kg 10:1; 2Ch 9:1

*q*12:43-45 Lk 11:24-26
*r*12:45 Heb 6:4; 2Pt 2:20
*s*12:46-50 Mk 3:31-35; Lk 8:19-21
*t*12:46 Mt 13:55; Mk 6:3; Jn 2:12; Ac 1:14; 1Co 9:5; Gl 1:19
*u*12:49 Mt 10:42; 28:19; Lk 14:26; Jn 8:31; 13:35; 15:8; Ac 6:1
*v*12:50 Mt 6:1; 7:21; Jn 15:14; Heb 2:11
*w*13:1-15 Mk 4:1-12; Lk 8:4-10
*x*13:2 Mk 3:9; Lk 5:3
*y*13:3 Mk 13:10,34-36; 15:15; 21:33,45; 22:1; 24:32; Mk 4:2

blasphemy,*a* but the blasphemy against[A] the Spirit will not be forgiven.[B] **32** Whoever speaks a word against the Son of Man,*b* it will be forgiven him; but whoever speaks against the Holy Spirit, it will not be forgiven him, either in this age or in the one to come.*c*

A TREE AND ITS FRUIT

33 "Either make the tree good and its fruit will be good, or make the tree bad[C] and its fruit will be bad; for a tree is known by its fruit.*d* **34** Brood of vipers! How can you speak good things when you are evil? For the mouth speaks from the overflow*e* of the heart. **35** A good person produces good things from his storeroom of good, and an evil person produces evil things from his storeroom of evil.*f* **36** I tell you that on the day of judgment*g* people will have to account*h* for every careless[D] word they speak.[E] **37** For by your words you will be acquitted, and by your words you will be condemned."

THE SIGN OF JONAH

38 Then some of the scribes and Pharisees said to him, "Teacher, we want to see a sign from you."*i*

39 He answered them,*j* "An evil and adulterous generation demands a sign, but no sign will be given to it except the sign of the prophet Jonah.*k* **40** For as Jonah was in the belly of the huge fish[F,*l*] three days and three nights,*m* so the Son of Man will be in the heart of the earth three days and three nights. **41** The men of Nineveh will stand up at the judgment with this generation and condemn it,*n* because they repented at Jonah's preaching; and look — something greater than Jonah is here.*o* **42** The queen of the south*p* will rise up at the judgment with

this generation and condemn it, because she came from the ends of the earth to hear the wisdom of Solomon; and look — something greater than Solomon is here.

AN UNCLEAN SPIRIT'S RETURN

43 "When an unclean spirit comes out of a person, it roams through waterless places looking for rest but doesn't find any.*q* **44** Then it says, 'I'll go back to my house that I came from.' Returning, it finds the house vacant, swept, and put in order. **45** Then it goes and brings with it seven other spirits more evil than itself, and they enter and settle down there. As a result, that person's last condition is worse than the first.*r* That's how it will also be with this evil generation."

TRUE RELATIONSHIPS

46 While he*s* was still speaking with the crowds, his mother and brothers were standing outside wanting to speak to him.*t* **47** Someone told him, "Look, your mother and your brothers are standing outside, wanting to speak to you."[G] **48** He replied to the one who was speaking to him, "Who is my mother and who are my brothers?" **49** Stretching out his hand toward his disciples,*u* he said, "Here are my mother and my brothers! **50** For whoever does the will of my Father in heaven is my brother and sister and mother."*v*

THE PARABLE OF THE SOWER

13 On that day Jesus went out of the house and was sitting by the sea.*w* **2** Such large crowds gathered around him that he got into a boat and sat down, while the whole crowd stood on the shore.*x* **3** Then he told them many things in parables,*y* saying: "Consider the sower who

[A]12:31 Or *of* [B]12:31 Other mss add *people* [C]12:33 Or *decayed*; lit *rotten* [D]12:36 Lit *worthless* [E]12:36 Lit *will speak* [F]12:40 Or *sea creature*; Jnh 1:17 [G]12:47 Other mss omit this v.

12:36 When you open your mouth, you reveal what's deep down inside—whether good or evil. So you've got to watch your mouth. God is tape-recording our words, and we will **have to account for every careless** one. The way to tame your tongue is to address your heart. And the way to address your heart is to devote it to the King's agenda.

12:38 Only spiritually stubborn and blind people request **a sign** in the face of overwhelming evidence.

12:39-40 Jonah was **in the belly of the huge fish three days and three nights.** Jesus would similarly spend **three days and three nights** in the earth (12:40). His resurrection from the dead would be the crowning demonstration that he is the Son of God.

12:41-42 On the day of **judgment**, many Gentiles **will stand** and condemn the wicked generation of Israelites who rejected Jesus. After all, the citizens of **Nineveh** repented at the preaching of **Jonah**, who had no great sign to show. **The queen of the south** traveled far to hear the wisdom of Solomon, who was a mere earthly king. But **something greater** than Jonah and Solomon had arrived (12:42). The heavenly King had come working miraculous signs, so they were without excuse for not repenting and believing in him.

12:43-45 If you try to clean up your life with self-righteousness and religious activity, you'll only make yourself worse. Without submission to the Lord and the presence of the

Holy Spirit to fill the void, you're simply opening yourself to greater demonic influence.

12:46-47 The Gospel of John says Jesus's **brothers** didn't believe in him during his ministry (John 7:1-5), so perhaps they'd come to take him home quietly.

12:48-50 Our blood relationships—whether by family or race—are outweighed by our relationships to other Christians through Jesus's blood. When you trust in Christ, you have a new family. This doesn't mean you ignore your physical family. It means your obedience as a child of your heavenly Father takes priority.

13:3-9 As Jesus explains in 13:18-23, this story illustrates the different ways people respond when they hear the Word of God. It's crucial

✦ KINGDOM LIVING ✦
CHURCH
The Agenda of the Church

Our society is not changing for the good today. Why? Because the church has settled for buildings and programs instead of accessing the authority of the kingdom and the power of the Holy Spirit. We've had church services, but we haven't had transformation. Unless the church becomes Spirit-filled and kingdom-minded, we are not being the church that Christ came to build. In fact, Jesus only mentioned *church* three times in his earthly ministry, and all three times are recorded in the kingdom-focused book of Matthew. The word *kingdom*, by contrast, is found fifty-four times in Matthew alone.

Yet, surprisingly, we often hear more about the church than the kingdom. We plant churches rather than promoting the kingdom. Our seminaries teach our future leaders how to *do* church rather than how to *be* about the kingdom. We ought to focus on both the kingdom and the church because they are interconnected. We can't have church without the kingdom; the kingdom carries out its agenda through the church.

It is high time we become kingdom people representing something bigger than our own individualized preferences. It is time we made God's kingdom our rule and his glory our goal. God didn't establish the church to make us feel good.

The failure to recognize this broader agenda has kept churches ingrown, divided, and fragmented. Until the church begins functioning for the kingdom rather than merely for itself, it cannot have the voice and the comprehensive impact it was created to have in areas such as social justice, race relations, economics, education, and government.

FOR THE NEXT CHURCH
KINGDOM LIVING LESSON SEE P. 1118.

it grew up quickly since the soil wasn't deep. **6** But when the sun came up, it was scorched, and since it had no root, it withered away. **7** Other seed fell among thorns, and the thorns came up and choked it. **8** Still other seed fell on good ground and produced fruit: some a hundred, some sixty, and some thirty times what was sown.[a] **9** Let anyone who has ears[A] listen."[b]

WHY JESUS USED PARABLES

10 Then the disciples[c] came up and asked him, "Why are you speaking to them in parables?"[d]

11 He answered, "Because the secrets of the kingdom of heaven have been given for you to know,[e] but it has not been given to them. **12** For whoever has, more will be given to him, and he will have more than enough; but whoever does not have, even what he has will be taken away from him.[f] **13** That is why I speak to them in parables, because looking they do not see,[g] and hearing they do not listen or understand.[h] **14** Isaiah's prophecy is fulfilled in them, which says:

> You will listen and listen,
> but never understand;
> you will look and look,
> but never perceive.[i]
> **15** For this people's heart
>   has grown callous;
> their ears are hard of hearing,
> and they have shut their eyes;
> otherwise they might see
>   with their eyes,
> and hear with their ears, and
> understand with their hearts,
> and turn back —
> and I would heal them.[B,j]

16 "Blessed are your eyes[k] because they do see, and your ears because they do hear.[l] **17** For truly I tell you, many prophets and righteous people longed to see the things you see but didn't see them, to hear the things you hear but didn't hear them.[m]

THE PARABLE OF THE SOWER EXPLAINED

18 "So listen to the parable of the sower:[n] **19** When anyone hears the word about the kingdom and doesn't understand it, the evil

a 13:8 Gn 26:12; Mt 13:23
b 13:9 Mt 11:15; 13:43; Lk 8:8; 14:35; Rv 2:7,11,17,29; 3:6,13,22
c 13:10 Mt 9:10; Mk 10:10; Lk 6:1; Jn 6:3; Ac 6:1
d Mt 13:35; 15:15; 21:33,45; 22:1; 24:32
e 13:11 Mt 11:25; 19:11; Jn 6:65; 1Co 2:10; Col 1:27; 1Jn 2:20,27
f 13:12 Mt 25:29; Lk 8:18; 19:26; Jn 15:2; Jms 4:6
g 13:13 Dt 29:4; Is 42:19-20; Jr 5:21; Ezk 12:2
h Mt 15:10; 16:12; 17:13; Mk 8:21
i 13:14 Is 6:9; Mk 4:12; Lk 8:10; Jn 12:40; Ac 28:26-27; Rm 11:8
j 13:15 Is 6:10; Mt 15:8; Heb 5:11
k 13:16-17 Lk 10:23-24
l 13:16 Mt 16:17; Jn 20:29
m 13:17 Jn 8:56; Heb 11:13; 1Pt 1:10-12
n 13:18-23 Mk 4:13-20; Lk 8:11-15

went out to sow. **4** As he sowed, some seed fell along the path, and the birds came and devoured them. **5** Other seed fell on rocky ground where it didn't have much soil, and

A 13:9 Other mss add *to hear*   B 13:14-15 Is 6:9-10

that you not only hear Jesus, but have a heart that's willing to receive his words in order to benefit from them.
13:10-12 The secrets of the kingdom refer to those things that were hidden in the Old Testament and are revealed in the New, with the coming of Christ (13:11). When you respond to

the spiritual light you've been given, you'll receive more light—more understanding. But when you reject the light, the opposite happens (13:12).
13:13 Jesus spoke in parables to give understanding to the disciples while also confounding those who refused to believe.

13:18-23 The parable's point is clear: It is the condition of the heart in its openness to receive and respond to God's Word that will determine the Word's effectiveness in a person's life.

*a*13:19 Mt 4:23; 5:37; 6:13
*b*13:20 Is 58:2; Ezk 33:31-
32; Mk 6:20; Jn 5:35
*c*13:21 Mk 4:17; 10:30;
Ac 8:1; 13:50; Rm 8:35;
2Co 12:10
*d*13:22 Rm 12:2; 2Tm 4:10;
1Jn 2:15
*e*Mt 19:23; Mk 10:23; 1Tm
6:9-10; 2Tm 4:10
*f*13:24 Mt 18:23; 20:1; 25:1;
Mk 4:26,30
*g*13:27 Mt 10:24; Col 3:11;
4:1; Rv 1:1
*h*13:31-32 Mk 4:30-32; Lk
13:18-19
*i*13:31 Mt 13:24; 17:20;
Lk 17:6

*j*13:32 Ps 104:12; Ezk 17:23;
31:6; Dn 4:12
*k*13:33 Gn 18:6; Lk 13:21;
Gl 5:9
*l*13:34 Mk 4:34; Jn 10:6;
16:25
*m*13:35 Ps 78:2; Rm
16:25-26; 1Co 2:7; Eph 3:9;
Col 1:26
*n*13:36 Mt 13:3; 15:15;
21:33,45; 22:1; 24:32
*o*13:38 Mt 8:12; Jn 8:44; Ac
13:10; 1Jn 3:10
*p*13:39 Jl 3:13; Heb 9:26;
Rv 14:15
*q*13:40 Mt 24:3; 28:20
*r*13:41 Zph 1:3; Mt 8:20;
18:7; 24:31
*s*13:42 Rv 1:15; 9:2
*t*Mt 8:12; Rv 19:20; 20:10
*u*13:43 Dn 12:3; Mt 11:15;
1Co 15:42

one comes and snatches away what was sown in his heart. This is the one sown along the path.*a* 20 And the one sown on rocky ground — this is one who hears the word and immediately receives it with joy.*b* 21 But he has no root and is short-lived. When distress or persecution*c* comes because of the word, immediately he falls away. 22 Now the one sown among the thorns — this is one who hears the word, but the worries of this age*d* and the deceitfulness^A of wealth*e* choke the word, and it becomes unfruitful. 23 But the one sown on the good ground — this is one who hears and understands the word, who does produce fruit and yields: some a hundred, some sixty, some thirty times what was sown."

THE PARABLE OF THE WHEAT AND THE WEEDS

24 He presented another parable to them: "The kingdom of heaven may be compared to a man who sowed good seed in his field.*f* 25 But while people were sleeping, his enemy came, sowed weeds among the wheat, and left. 26 When the plants sprouted and produced grain, then the weeds also appeared. 27 The landowner's servants*g* came to him and said, 'Master, didn't you sow good seed in your field? Then where did the weeds come from?'

28 "'An enemy did this,' he told them.

"'So, do you want us to go and pull them up?' the servants asked him.

29 "'No,' he said. 'When you pull up the weeds, you might also uproot the wheat with them. 30 Let both grow together until the harvest. At harvest time I'll tell the reapers: Gather the weeds first and tie them in bundles to burn them, but collect the wheat in my barn.'"

THE PARABLES OF THE MUSTARD SEED AND OF THE LEAVEN

31 He*h* presented another parable to them: "The kingdom of heaven*i* is like a mustard seed that a man took and sowed in his field.

32 It's the smallest of all the seeds, but when grown, it's taller than the garden plants and becomes a tree, so that the birds of the sky come and nest in its branches."*j*

33 He told them another parable: "The kingdom of heaven is like leaven^B that a woman took and mixed into fifty pounds^C of flour until all of it was leavened."*k*

USING PARABLES FULFILLS PROPHECY

34 Jesus told the crowds all these things in parables, and he did not tell them anything without a parable,*l* 35 so that what was spoken through the prophet might be fulfilled:

I will open my mouth
  in parables;
I will declare things kept secret
from the foundation
  of the world. ^D,E,m

JESUS INTERPRETS THE PARABLE OF THE WHEAT AND THE WEEDS

36 Then he left the crowds and went into the house. His disciples approached him and said, "Explain to us the parable of the weeds in the field."*n*

37 He replied: "The one who sows the good seed is the Son of Man; 38 the field is the world; and the good seed — these are the children of the kingdom. The weeds are the children of the evil one,*o* 39 and the enemy who sowed them is the devil. The harvest is the end of the age, and the harvesters are angels.*p* 40 Therefore, just as the weeds are gathered and burned in the fire, so it will be at the end of the age.*q* 41 The Son of Man will send out his angels, and they will gather from his kingdom all who cause sin^F and those guilty of lawlessness. ^G,r 42 They will throw them into the blazing furnace*s* where there will be weeping and gnashing of teeth.*t* 43 Then the righteous will shine like the sun in their Father's kingdom. Let anyone who has ears^H listen.*u*

---

^A13:22 Or *pleasure*   ^B13:33 Or *yeast*   ^C13:33 Lit *three sata*; about 40 liters   ^D13:35 Some mss omit *of the world*   ^E13:35 Ps 78:2   ^F13:41 Or *stumbling*   ^G13:41 Or *those who do lawlessness*   ^H13:43 Other mss add *to hear*

13:24-30 Matthew includes Jesus's explanation of this parable in 13:36-43.

13:31-32 Though God's kingdom rule began in a seemingly insignificant way with a few Galilean fishermen and a tax collector, it would grow tremendously with the blessings of God. Christianity would become a significant worldwide movement in spite of its humble beginnings.

13:33 Though **the kingdom** started out small, it will continue to expand and spread throughout the world by the power of the Holy Spirit.

13:34-35 Matthew frequently observes how Jesus's life, words, and deeds fulfilled the Old Testament (e.g., 2:15; 4:14-16; 8:17; 12:17-21). Even his ministry of teaching **in parables** was a fulfillment of Scripture (see Ps 78:2).

13:38-40 Self-righteous religion will grow in the world alongside true Christianity. There will be those who appear to be saved. They use spiritual-sounding language and

get involved in church programs, but their Christianity is only an imitation. They may camouflage themselves among true believers, but God can't be deceived.

13:42 Here **weeping and gnashing of teeth** (cf. 13:50) refers to the profound regret of unbelievers who are cast into hell since they enter eternity without imputed righteousness (see 2 Cor 5:21).

THE PARABLES OF THE HIDDEN TREASURE AND OF THE PRICELESS PEARL

44 "The kingdom of heaven is like treasure, buried in a field, that a man found and reburied. Then in his joy he goes and sells everything he has and buys that field.[a]

45 "Again, the kingdom of heaven is like a merchant in search of fine pearls. **46** When he found one priceless[A] pearl, he went and sold everything he had and bought it.[b]

THE PARABLE OF THE NET

47 "Again, the kingdom of heaven is like a large net thrown into the sea. It collected every kind of fish,[c] **48** and when it was full, they dragged it ashore, sat down, and gathered the good fish into containers, but threw out the worthless ones. **49** So it will be at the end of the age. The angels will go out, separate the evil people from the righteous,[d] **50** and throw them into the blazing furnace, where there will be weeping and gnashing of teeth.[e]

THE STOREHOUSE OF TRUTH

51 "Have you understood all these things?"[B] They answered him, "Yes."

52 "Therefore," he said to them, "every teacher of the law[c] who has become a disciple in the kingdom of heaven is like the owner of a house who brings out of his storeroom treasures new and old."[f]

REJECTION AT NAZARETH

53 When Jesus had finished these parables, he left there. **54** He went to his hometown[g] and began to teach them in their synagogue, so that they were astonished and said, "Where did this man get this wisdom and these miraculous powers?[h] **55** Isn't this the carpenter's son?[i] Isn't his mother called Mary, and his brothers James,[j] Joseph,[D] Simon, and Judas?[k] **56** And his sisters, aren't they all with us? So where does he get all these things?" **57** And they were offended by him.

Jesus said to them, "A prophet is not without honor except in his hometown and in his household."[l] **58** And he did not do many miracles there because of their unbelief.

JOHN THE BAPTIST BEHEADED

14 At that time[m] Herod the tetrarch[n] heard the report about Jesus. **2** "This is John the Baptist," he told his servants. "He has been raised from the dead, and that's why miraculous powers are at work in him."[o]

3 For Herod had arrested John, chained[E] him, and put him in prison on account of Herodias, his brother Philip's wife,[p] **4** since John had been telling him, "It's not lawful[q] for you to have her." **5** Though Herod wanted to kill John, he feared the crowd since they regarded John as a prophet.[r]

6 When Herod's birthday celebration came, Herodias's daughter danced before them[F] and pleased Herod. **7** So he promised with an oath to give her whatever she asked. **8** Prompted by her mother, she answered, "Give me John the Baptist's head here on a platter." **9** Although the king regretted it, he commanded that it be granted because of his oaths and his guests. **10** So he sent orders and had John beheaded in the prison. **11** His head was brought on a platter and given to the girl, who carried it to her mother. **12** Then his disciples came, removed the corpse,[G] buried it, and went and reported to Jesus.

FEEDING OF THE FIVE THOUSAND

13 When Jesus heard about it,[s] he withdrew from there by boat to a remote place to be alone. When the crowds heard this, they followed him on foot from the towns.

[a] 13:44 Is 55:1; Php 3:7-8; Rv 3:18
[b] 13:46 Pr 2:4; Mt 7:6
[c] 13:47 Mt 3:2; 13:44; 22:10
[d] 13:49 Mt 13:39-40; 25:32
[e] 13:50 Mt 8:12; 13:42
[f] 13:52 Mt 12:35; 28:19
[g] 13:54-58 Mk 6:1-6; Lk 4:16-30
[h] 13:54 Mt 2:23; 4:23; 7:28
[i] 13:55 Mt 13:55; Mk 6:3; Lk 3:23; Jn 6:42
[j] Jms 1:1; Jd 1
[k] Mt 12:46; Jn 7:5
[l] 13:57 Jr 11:21; 12:6; Lk 4:24; Jn 4:44
[m] 14:1-12 Mk 6:14-29; Lk 9:7-9
[n] 14:1 Mk 8:15; Lk 3:19; 13:31; 23:7; Ac 4:27; 12:1; 13:1
[o] 14:2 Mt 16:14; Mk 6:14; Lk 9:7
[p] 14:3 Mt 4:12; 11:2; Jn 3:24
[q] 14:4 Lv 18:16; 20:21
[r] 14:5 Mt 11:9; 21:26,46
[s] 14:13-21 Mk 6:32-44; Lk 9:10-17; Jn 6:1-13

[A] 13:46 Or *very precious*   [B] 13:51 Other mss add *Jesus asked them*   [C] 13:52 Or *every scribe*   [D] 13:55 Other mss read *Joses*; Mk 6:3   [E] 14:3 Or *bound*
[F] 14:6 Lit *danced in the middle*   [G] 14:12 Other mss read *body*

13:44-46 Those who discover and recognize the worth of living life under the rule of God will sacrifice anything of earthly value for participation in his kingdom.

13:47-50 Like the parable of the weeds and wheat (13:24-30, 36-43), this illustration describes the final judgment when those who persist in unrepentance and unbelief will be cast into hell. Hell is an uncomfortable topic. But when you're dying of cancer and need drastic medical treatment, the doctor isn't concerned about making you comfortable. He tells you about the plan that might save your life. Sin is worse than cancer. Christians

need to share the truth about Jesus so that unbelievers have a chance to undergo gospel surgery and avoid the blazing furnace of God's judgment.

13:52 All believers are called to be disciples of Jesus and students of the Word. As you grow in understanding the Bible—both *the new* (the teachings of Jesus and the apostles in the New Testament) and *the old* (the law and the prophets of the Old Testament)—you are to help the world know the King and follow his kingdom rule.

13:58 God will choose not to do things that he wants to do when you don't take seriously

what he has to say. Don't be a hindrance to God's work in your life. Believe his Word. Trust his promises. Follow in obedience.

14:1 Herod the tetrarch—also known as Herod Antipas—was the son of Herod the Great, who'd sought to kill the infant Jesus (2:1-18). As we'll see, the apple didn't fall far from the tree.

14:7-8 Herodias couldn't stand to hear John the Baptist call attention to her sin (14:3-5), so she wanted him dead. The rejection of God by unbelievers will often lead them to hate his followers and their righteous lives (see 1 John 3:12-13).

[a]14:14 Mt 4:23; 9:36
[b]14:15 Mt 10:1; 26:56; Mk
3:7; 16:20; Lk 6:13; Jn 12:16
[c]14:19 1Sm 9:13; Mt 26:26;
Mk 8:7; 14:22; Lk 24:30;
Ac 27:35
[d]14:20 Mt 16:9; Mk 6:43;
8:19; Lk 9:17; Jn 6:13
[e]14:22-33 Mk 6:45-51;
Jn 6:15-21
[f]14:23 Lk 6:12; 9:48
[g]14:25 Mt 24:23; Mk 13:35

[h]14:27 Dt 31:6; Is 41:13;
43:1-2; Mt 17:7; Lk 2:10;
Rv 1:17
[i]14:31 Mt 6:30; 8:26; 16:8
[j]14:33 Ps 2:7; Mt 16:16;
26:63; Mk 1:1; Lk 4:41;
Jn 11:4
[k]14:34-36 Mk 6:53-56; Jn
6:24-25
[l]14:34 Mk 6:5; Lk 5:1
[m]14:36 Mt 9:20; Mk 3:10;
Lk 6:19; Ac 5:15
[n]15:1-20 Mk 7:1-23
[o]15:1 Mk 3:22; Jn 1:19
[p]15:2 Mt 10:1; 26:56; Mk
3:7; 16:20; Lk 6:13; Jn 12:16
[q]Lk 11:38; Gl 1:14; Col 2:8;
Heb 11:2

14 When he went ashore,[A] he saw a large crowd, had compassion on them, and healed their sick.[a]

15 When evening came, the disciples[b] approached him and said, "This place is deserted, and it is already late.[B] Send the crowds away so that they can go into the villages and buy food for themselves."

16 "They don't need to go away," Jesus told them. "You give them something to eat."

17 "But we only have five loaves and two fish here," they said to him.

18 "Bring them here to me," he said. **19** Then he commanded the crowds to sit down on the grass. He took the five loaves and the two fish, and looking up to heaven, he blessed them. He broke the loaves and gave them to the disciples, and the disciples gave them to the crowds.[c] **20** Everyone ate and was satisfied. They picked up twelve baskets full of leftover pieces.[d] **21** Now those who ate were about five thousand men, besides women and children.

WALKING ON THE WATER

22 Immediately[e] he[c] made the disciples get into the boat and go ahead of him to the other side, while he dismissed the crowds. **23** After dismissing the crowds, he went up on the mountain by himself to pray. Well into the night, he was there alone.[f] **24** Meanwhile, the boat was already some distance[D] from land,[E] battered by the waves, because the wind was against them. **25** Jesus came toward them walking on the sea[g] very early in the morning.[F] **26** When the disciples saw him walking on the sea, they were terrified. "It's a ghost!" they said, and they cried out in fear.

27 Immediately Jesus spoke to them. "Have courage! It is I. Don't be afraid."[h]

28 "Lord, if it's you," Peter answered him, "command me to come to you on the water."

29 He said, "Come."

And climbing out of the boat, Peter started walking on the water and came toward Jesus. **30** But when he saw the strength of the wind,[G] he was afraid, and beginning to sink he cried out, "Lord, save me!"

31 Immediately Jesus reached out his hand, caught hold of him, and said to him, "You of little faith, why did you doubt?"[i]

32 When they got into the boat, the wind ceased. **33** Then those in the boat worshiped him and said, "Truly you are the Son of God."[j]

MIRACULOUS HEALINGS

34 When they had crossed over,[k] they came to shore at Gennesaret.[l] **35** When the men of that place recognized him, they alerted the whole vicinity and brought to him all who were sick. **36** They begged him that they might only touch the end of his robe, and as many as touched it were healed.[m]

THE TRADITION OF THE ELDERS

15 Then[n] Jesus was approached by Pharisees and scribes from Jerusalem, who asked,[o] **2** "Why do your disciples[p] break the tradition of the elders? For they don't wash their hands when they eat."[H,q]

3 He answered them, "Why do you break God's commandment because of your

---

[A]14:14 Lit *Coming out* (of the boat)   [B]14:15 Lit *and the time* (for the evening meal) *has already passed*   [C]14:22 Other mss read *Jesus*
[D]14:24 Lit *already many stadia*; one *stadion* = 600 feet   [E]14:24 Other mss read *already in the middle of the sea*   [F]14:25 Lit *fourth watch of the night* = 3 to 6 a.m.   [G]14:30 Other mss read *saw the wind*   [H]15:2 Lit *eat bread* = eat a meal

---

14:18-21 "Not enough" can become "more than enough" when two things happen. Bring what little you have to Jesus. Then believe that Jesus can intercede in your situation, bringing abundance out of deficiency. He can demonstrate the supernatural in the midst of your natural problem.

14:22 Don't overlook that Jesus **made the disciples get into the boat and go ahead of him**. They were in God's perfect will and about to enter a perfect storm, indicating that obeying God can sometimes lead to rough sailing.

14:23-24 When the boat was far from shore, they were **battered by the waves, because the wind was against them** (14:24). And where was Jesus? He'd gone up **the mountain by himself to pray** (14:23). Though Jesus was absent from them, he wasn't unmindful of their needs. Paul told the Romans that Jesus intercedes for believers (Rom 8:34). His full-time job is serving as the intercessor between you and God. And he's the perfect one to do

it because he's fully God and fully human. He understands God, and he understands you.

14:25-27 Jesus came to them in an unexpected way so they could understand and experience him as never before. He demonstrated his divine authority over the world that he created (see John 1:3; Col 1:16; Heb 1:2).

14:28-31 Matthew wants readers to know that this miracle was made possible by Jesus's power, not Peter's. Before you look down your nose at Peter, though, keep in mind that he was the only one who got out of the boat to attempt the impossible. The other disciples just stared as he stepped out in faith. Remember, Jesus rebuked him for having *little* faith—not for having *no* faith (14:31).

14:33 Why would Jesus intentionally let his followers go through such a fearful situation? Look at what happened when he saved them. The disciples **worshiped him** and declared, **Truly you are the Son of God!** Jesus wants you

to discover that he's bigger than your fears, and invites you to praise him.

14:36 The power of the kingdom emanated from Jesus Christ. One day that power will rid the universe of pain and death forever (see Rev 21:4).

15:2 This wasn't a matter of proper hygiene. Washing **hands** before meals was a purely ritualistic exercise that had no basis in the Old Testament Scriptures. Nevertheless, they considered it a religious duty signaling spiritual purity.

15:3 Traditions aren't necessarily bad. They typically involve passing on some custom, practice, or belief to subsequent generations. God even provided Israel with many traditions to follow as part of his law and sacrificial system. But the problem with traditions comes in when they invalidate, cover up, camouflage, or negate the Word of God. When you replace Scripture with something of your own invention, you're wasting your time in worship on Sunday.

tradition? **4** For God said:[A] **Honor your father and your mother;**[B,a] and, **Whoever speaks evil of father or mother must be put to death.**[C,b] **5** But you say, 'Whoever tells his father or mother, "Whatever benefit you might have received from me is a gift committed to the temple," **6** he does not have to honor his father.'[D] In this way, you have nullified the word of God[E] because of your tradition. **7** Hypocrites! Isaiah prophesied correctly about you when he said:

8   **This people**[F] **honors me**
          with their lips,
    but their heart is far from me.
9   **They worship me in vain,**
          teaching as doctrines
          human commands."[G,C]

DEFILEMENT IS FROM WITHIN

10 Summoning the crowd, he told them, "Listen and understand: **11** It's not what goes into the mouth that defiles[d] a person, but what comes out of the mouth — this defiles a person."[e]

12 Then the disciples came up and told him, "Do you know that the Pharisees took offense when they heard what you said?" **13** He replied, "Every plant that my heavenly Father didn't plant will be uprooted.[f] **14** Leave them alone! They are blind guides.[H] And if the blind guide the blind, both will fall into a pit."[g]

15 Then Peter said, "Explain this parable to us."[h]

16 "Do you still lack understanding?" he[I] asked. **17** "Don't you realize[J] that whatever goes into the mouth passes into the stomach and is eliminated?[K] **18** But what comes out of the mouth comes from the heart, and this defiles a person.[I] **19** For from the heart come evil thoughts, murders, adulteries, sexual immoralities, thefts, false testimonies,[J] slander.[k] **20** These are the things that defile a person; but eating with unwashed hands does not defile a person."[l]

A GENTILE MOTHER'S FAITH

21 When Jesus left there,[m] he withdrew to the area of Tyre and Sidon.[n] **22** Just then a Canaanite woman from that region came and kept crying out,[L] "Have mercy on me, Lord, Son of David! My daughter is severely tormented by a demon."[o]

23 Jesus did not say a word to her. His disciples[p] approached him and urged him, "Send her away because she's crying out after us."

24 He replied, "I was sent only to the lost sheep of the house of Israel."[q]

25 But she came, knelt before him, and said, "Lord, help me!"

26 He answered, "It isn't right to take the children's bread and throw it to the dogs."[r]

27 "Yes, Lord," she said, "yet even the dogs eat the crumbs that fall from their masters' table."

28 Then Jesus replied to her, "Woman, your faith is great. Let it be done for you as you want." And from that moment[M] her daughter was healed.[s]

HEALING MANY PEOPLE

29 Moving on from there,[t] Jesus passed along the Sea of Galilee.[u] He went up on a mountain and sat there, **30** and large crowds came to him, including the lame, the blind, the crippled, those unable to

[a] 15:4 Ex 20:12; Dt 5:16; Eph 6:2
[b] Ex 21:17; Lv 20:9
[c] 15:8-9 Is 29:13; Ezk 33:31; Col 2:22; Ti 1:14
[d] 15:11 Mt 15:18; Mk 7:15; Ac 21:28; Heb 9:13
[e] Ac 10:14-15; 1Tm 4:3
[f] 15:13 Is 60:21; 61:3; Jn 15:2; 1Co 3:9
[g] 15:14 Mal 2:8; Mt 23:16,24; Lk 6:39
[h] 15:15 Mt 13:36; Mk 7:17

[i] 15:18 Mt 12:34; Jms 3:6
[j] 15:19 Eph 4:31; Col 3:8; 1Tm 6:4
[k] 15:20 Mt 11:18; Mk 7:2,5; 1Co 6:9-10
[m] 15:21-28 Mk 7:24-30
[n] 15:21 Mt 11:21; Mk 7:24
[o] 15:22 Gn 10:15,19; Jdg 1:30-33; Mt 4:24; 9:27
[p] 15:23 Mt 10:1; 26:56; Mk 3:7; 16:20; Lk 6:13; Jn 12:16
[q] 15:24 Mt 10:6,23; Jn 4:22; Rm 15:8
[r] 15:26 Ex 22:31; 2Kg 9:10; Mt 8:2; Php 3:2
[s] 15:28 Mt 9:22; 17:18; Jn 4:52-53
[t] 15:29-31 Mk 7:31-37
[u] 15:29 Mt 9:8; 18:8; Mk 9:43

[A] 15:4 Other mss read *commanded, saying*   [B] 15:4 Ex 20:12; Dt 5:16   [C] 15:4 Ex 21:17; Lv 20:9   [D] 15:6 Other mss read *then he does not have to honor his father or mother*   [E] 15:6 Other mss read *commandment*   [F] 15:8 Other mss add *draw near to me with their mouths, and*   [G] 15:8-9 Is 29:13 LXX   [H] 15:14 Other mss add *for the blind*   [I] 15:16 Other mss read *Jesus*   [J] 15:17 Other mss add *yet*   [K] 15:17 Lit *and goes out into the toilet*   [L] 15:22 Other mss read *and cried out to him*   [M] 15:28 Lit *hour*

15:10-11 We tend to justify our sinful words and actions by pointing to what others did that caused our responses, but our circumstances don't cause our sin. They just provide the context and the opportunity for the sinful desires ruling our hearts to express themselves. Defilement is an internal matter, and external activity can't change a heart.
15:18-19 Jesus spoke of **the heart** to refer to our inner spiritual selves. The heart is where sin and defilement arise. Jesus is a heart specialist. Through a relationship with him, your heart can be transformed so that you love God and people.
15:21 The Old Testament prophets denounced **Tyre and Sidon,** Gentile cities on the Mediterranean Coast, for their wickedness (see Isa 23; Ezek 28; Joel 3:4-8).

15:24 In other words, he'd been **sent** on a mission to the Jews—not to Gentiles like this Canaanite woman. Now, we know from the rest of Matthew (e.g., 8:5-13), and the rest of the Bible (e.g., Rom 1:16), that Jesus brought God's grace to all people, Jew and Gentile alike. But the focus of his earthly ministry was on the descendants of Abraham, Isaac, and Jacob. After his death and resurrection, he would command his disciples to take his message to "all nations" (Matt 28:19) and to "the end of the earth" (Acts 1:8).
15:25 Like Jacob wrestling with God, this Canaanite woman wouldn't *let go* unless Jesus blessed her (see Gen 32:24-26). Remember: when God doesn't answer your prayers about a specific need, it's likely he's

trying to deepen your faith. So be persistent in prayer.
15:26-27 The Greek word for *dogs* typically referred to little house dogs or lapdogs (15:26). So Jesus wasn't insulting the woman but saying he had to feed the Jews first, just as a parent is obliged to feed the children before the house pets. Nevertheless, she wasn't giving up. **Even the dogs eat the crumbs that fall from their masters' table** (15:27)—that is, "Even though the puppies don't eat first, they still get to eat! I'm willing to settle for your leftovers, Jesus." That's desperate humility.
15:28 This Canaanite started with *faith.* Then, by persevering through a series of difficulties intended by God to take her deeper, she ended up with *great faith.*

*a*15:31 Is 29:23; Lk 1:68; Ac 13:17
*b*15:32-39 Mt 14:14-21; Mk 8:1-10
*c*15:33 Mk 8:4; 2Co 11:26; Heb 11:38

*d*15:36 Mt 26:27; Lk 22:17; Jn 6:11,23; Ac 27:35; Rm 14:6; 1Co 10:30
*e*15:39 Mk 3:9; 8:10
*f*16:1-12 Mt 12:38-39; Mk 8:11-21; Lk 12:54-56
*g*16:1 Lk 11:16; 1Co 1:22

☞ KINGDOM LIVING ☜
CHURCH
The Purpose of the Church

One of the premiere purposes of the church is to legislate the values of God's kingdom. By legislate I don't necessarily mean that it's our function to create laws in society. Instead, I mean that the church is called to make things happen in God's kingdom. We Christians are not just passive reflections of God's goodness; we also take an active role in carrying out God's kingdom agenda.

Look at Matthew 16:18, where Jesus first used the word *church*: "On this rock I will build my church, and the gates of Hades will not overpower it." The Greek word translated "church" is *ekklēsia*. In the first century AD, *ekklēsia* was a term used to describe a group of people called out from the general population to serve in a government capacity. If you were part of an *ekklēsia*, you were part of a governing body charged with making laws or guidelines for the benefit of your community.

This has interesting implications for what it means to be a church—an *ekklēsia*—in today's world. When we say we're going to church or that we're members of a church, we're usually referring to a place where we passively encounter positive experiences. We go to church to find encouragement, to be taught, and to experience fellowship. Those are important aspects of church, but more should be involved.

To be part of the church as Jesus defined it is to be part of a spiritual legislative body tasked with enacting heaven's viewpoint in hell's society. In the midst of this world filled with sin, corruption, pain, and death, God has placed an *ekklēsia*—a group of people called out to make a difference and improve the world through the execution of his kingdom agenda. That's the church (see Matt 16:19).

FOR THE NEXT CHURCH
KINGDOM LIVING LESSON SEE PAGE 1140.

speak, and many others. They put them at his feet, and he healed them. **31** So the crowd was amazed when they saw those unable to speak talking, the crippled restored, the lame walking, and the blind seeing,*a* and they gave glory to the God of Israel.

FEEDING OF THE FOUR THOUSAND

32 Jesus called his disciples and said,*b* "I have compassion on the crowd, because they've already stayed with me three days and have nothing to eat. I don't want to send them away hungry, otherwise they might collapse on the way."

33 The disciples said to him, "Where could we get enough bread in this desolate place*c* to feed such a crowd?"

34 "How many loaves do you have?" Jesus asked them.

"Seven," they said, "and a few small fish."

35 After commanding the crowd to sit down on the ground, **36** he took the seven loaves and the fish, gave thanks, broke them, and gave them to the disciples, and the disciples gave them to the crowds.*d* **37** They all ate and were satisfied. They collected the leftover pieces — seven large baskets full. **38** Now there were four thousand men who had eaten, besides women and children. **39** After dismissing the crowds, he got into the boat and went to the region of Magadan.*A,e*

THE LEAVEN OF THE PHARISEES AND THE SADDUCEES

16 The Pharisees and Sadducees approached,*f* and tested him, asking him to show them a sign from heaven.*g* **2** He replied, "When evening comes you say, 'It will be good weather because the sky is red.' **3** And in the morning, 'Today will be stormy because the sky is red and threatening.' You*B* know how to read the appearance of the sky, but you can't read the signs of the times.*C* **4** An evil and adulterous

*A*15:39 Other mss read *Magdala*   *B*16:3 Other mss read *Hypocrites! You*   *C*16:2-3 Other mss omit *When* (v. 2) through end of v. 3

15:36 Notice that the food didn't supernaturally appear in the hands of the crowd. Rather, Jesus used his **disciples** to distribute it. He calls his disciples to be distributors—on his behalf—of the blessings, provisions, power, and message of the kingdom.
16:1 These Jewish religious groups had little in common. They disagreed on significant

theological matters, but their mutual disdain for Jesus brought them together to test him.
16:2-3 These religious men had missed the open and obvious signs that the kingdom of God had appeared in Jesus Christ. If they were really interested in who he was, **the signs of the times** would've convinced them of the truth (16:3).

16:4 As **Jonah** spent three days "in the belly of the fish" (Jonah 1:17), Jesus Christ would spend three days in the belly of the earth (see Matt 12:39-40). So in effect, Jesus said, "You want a sign? I'm going to give you a whopper." Jesus was going to rise from the dead. His resurrection would be the sign of signs, the supreme miracle demonstrating his identity. To reject

APPLICATION QUESTIONS

READH MATTHEW 16:13-20

– What do these verses teach about the church?
– What does Jesus's vision for the church communicate about you as a church member?

---

generation demands a sign, but no sign will be given to it except the sign of[A] Jonah."[a] Then he left them and went away.

[5] The disciples reached the other shore,[B] and they had forgotten to take bread. [6] Then Jesus told them, "Watch out and beware of the leaven[c] of the Pharisees and Sadducees."[b]

[7] They were discussing among themselves, "We didn't bring any bread."

[8] Aware of this, Jesus said, "You of little faith,[c] why are you discussing among yourselves that you do not have bread? [9] Don't you understand yet? Don't you remember the five loaves for the five thousand and how many baskets you collected? [10] Or the seven loaves for the four thousand and how many large baskets you collected?[d] [11] Why is it you don't understand that when I told you, 'Beware of the leaven of the Pharisees and Sadducees,' it wasn't about bread?[e] [12] Then they understood that he had not told them to beware of the leaven in bread, but of the teaching of the Pharisees and Sadducees.[f]

PETER'S CONFESSION OF THE MESSIAH

[13] When Jesus came to the region of Caesarea Philippi,[D,g] he asked his disciples, "Who do people say that the Son of Man is?"[E]

[14] They replied, "Some say John the Baptist; others, Elijah; still others, Jeremiah or one of the prophets."[h]

[15] "But you," he asked them, "who do you say that I am?"

[16] Simon Peter answered, "You are the Messiah, the Son of the living God."[i]

[17] Jesus responded, "Blessed are you, Simon son of Jonah,[F,j] because flesh and blood did not reveal this to you, but my Father in heaven.[k] [18] And I also say to you that you are Peter,[l] and on this rock I will build my church,[l] and the gates of Hades will not overpower it. [19] I will give you the keys of the kingdom of heaven,[m] and whatever you bind on earth will have been bound[G] in heaven, and whatever you loose on earth will have been loosed[H] in heaven." [20] Then he gave the disciples orders to tell no one that he was[i] the Messiah.[n]

[a] 16:4 Mt 4:13; 21:17; Lk 11:29
[b] 16:6 Mt 3:7; 8:15; Lk 12:1; 1Co 5:6-8; Gl 5:9
[c] 16:8 Mt 6:30; 8:26; 14:31; Lk 12:28
[d] 16:9-10 Mt 14:17-21; 15:34-38
[e] 16:11 Mt 3:7; 16:6; Mk 8:15; Lk 12:1

[f] 16:12 Mt 5:20; 17:13; 23:3
[g] 16:13-14 Mk 8:27-29; Lk 9:18-20
[h] 16:14 Mt 14:2; 17:10; Mk 6:15; Lk 9:8; Jn 1:21
[i] 16:16 Mt 1:16; Jn 11:27
[j] 16:17 Jn 1:42; 21:15-17
[k] 1Co 15:50; Gl 1:16; Eph 6:12; Heb 2:14
[l] 16:18 Mt 18:17; Ac 5:11; 7:38; 8:1,3; 9:31; 11:22,26
[m] 16:19 Is 22:22; Mt 18:18; Jn 20:23; Rv 1:18; 3:7
[n] 16:20 Mk 8:30; Lk 9:21

[A] 16:4 Other mss add *the prophet*   [B] 16:5 Lit *disciples went to the other side*   [C] 16:6 Or *yeast*, also in vv. 11,12   [D] 16:13 A town north of Galilee at the base of Mount Hermon   [E] 16:13 Other mss read *that I, the Son of Man, am*   [F] 16:17 Or *son of John*   [G] 16:19 Or *earth will be bound*   [H] 16:19 Or *earth will be loosed*   [I] 16:20 Other mss add *Jesus*

---

what happened on the first Easter is to reject the greatest sign God could provide. As Paul would later tell the Corinthians, Christianity stands or falls with the resurrection of Jesus Christ from the dead (see 1 Cor 15:12-19). Unfortunately, most of the Jewish religious leaders prodding Jesus for a sign would refuse to believe even this (see Matt 28:11-15).

16:8-10 Had they forgotten so quickly how he'd miraculously fed thousands on two occasions (16:9-10; see 14:13-21; 15:32-39)? A lack of food isn't a problem even with the Son of God.

16:11-12 Jesus was metaphorically comparing the **teaching of the Pharisees and Sadducees** to **leaven**, yeast. It permeated and influenced the Jewish people, resulting in unbelief. Watch out, then, for those who pursue self-righteous religion and teach others to do the same. A relationship with God through Christ is what's needed.

16:13 **Caesarea Philippi** was a city about twenty-five miles north of the Sea of Galilee where there was a temple honoring the Roman emperor Caesar Augustus. Perhaps the reverence for a mortal man is what prompted Jesus to ask his followers, **Who do people say that the Son of Man is?**

16:15 The *you* here is plural, so the question was addressed to the entire group.

16:18 Since Peter confessed Jesus as the Christ, Jesus used his name in a play on words.

In Greek, Peter's name is *petros*, which means "stone." But when Jesus said, **On this rock I will build my church**, he used the Greek word *petra*, which was a collection of rocks knitted together to form a larger slab. Jesus's church, then, would be comprised of his unified followers who confess him as the Christ, the Son of the living God, as Peter did.

The Greek word for "church" is *ekklēsia*, a term used to refer to an assembly or gathering of people, especially for legal purposes (see Acts 19:39-41). The church is like an embassy. The U.S. has embassies throughout the world, and the people working at an embassy are to live out the values and laws of the U.S. as they represent their homeland in a foreign country. Each embassy, then, is a little bit of America a long way from home. Similarly, the church of the Lord Jesus is to adopt the agenda of its heavenly King and enact it on earth. Christ's church is a little bit of heaven a long way from home, designed to withstand the authority of hell (its **gates**). Hell's attempt to stop the church's progress in history is thwarted as the church executes heaven's authority on earth.

16:19 What are these **keys of the kingdom of heaven**? They're divinely authorized resources that grant us authority and access (see Isa 22:22). Christians, through the church, have access to heaven's kingdom rule. You're supposed to be regularly utilizing heaven to help you live on earth—not merely visiting church on Sunday mornings. Believers are to study the Bible and gather with the church for a reason: to learn how to access the divine viewpoint and live out God's kingdom rule in their communities. You will never rule your world of relationships, emotions, employment, or finances if you continue to employ the keys the world offers you—or if you're not connected to a local church that possesses and operates with the keys of the kingdom.

Whatever you bind on earth will have been bound in heaven, and whatever you loose on earth will have been loosed in heaven. To *bind* and to *loose* are to restrain and to set free. The church is to use heaven's keys (heaven's viewpoint and spiritual resources on a matter) to operate according to that perspective, and then call on heaven's authority to bind and loose. It's critical to understand that heaven is waiting on the church to act in the matter of permitting and releasing before heaven's authority gets activated in history.

Binding and loosing doesn't imply you can make God do whatever you want. First, it must be in accordance with God's will. You can only bind and loose what "will have been" already bound and loosed in heaven. Second, know that answers to prayer are not for your sole benefit. They're to benefit others, too. God calls his people to be a blessing.

a 16:21-28 Mk 8:31–9:1; Lk 9:22-27

b 16:21 Mt 17:9; 20:18; 27:63; Lk 24:7; Jn 2:19

c 16:23 2Sm 19:22; Rm 8:5,7; Php 2:5; 3:19; Col 3:2

d 16:24 Mt 10:38; Lk 14:27

e 16:25 Mt 10:39; Jn 12:25

f 16:26 Ps 49:7-8; Lk 12:20

g 16:27 Mt 26:64; Mk 8:38; Ac 1:11; 1Th 1:10; 4:16; Rv 1:7

h 16:28 Mt 4:23; 10:23; Ac 20:25

i 17:1-8 Mk 9:2-8; Lk 9:28-36

j 17:1 Mt 26:37; Mk 5:37

k 17:2 Ps 104:2; Dn 7:9; Mt 28:3; 2Co 3:18; Rv 1:16; 10:1

l 17:4 Mk 9:5; Lk 9:33

m 17:5 Is 42:1; Mt 3:17; Mk 1:11; Lk 3:22; Ac 3:22; 2Pt 1:16-18

n 17:6 Mt 10:1; 26:56; Mk 3:7; 16:20; Lk 6:13; Jn 12:16

o 17:7 Dn 8:18; 9:21; 10:10; Mt 14:27

p 17:9-13 Mk 9:9-13

q 17:10 Mal 4:5; Mt 11:14

r 17:11 Mal 4:6; Lk 1:16-17

s 17:12 Mt 14:3,10; 16:21

t 17:14-21 Mk 9:14-29; Lk 9:37-43

HIS DEATH AND RESURRECTION PREDICTED

21 From*a* then on Jesus began to point out to his disciples that it was necessary for him to go to Jerusalem and suffer many things from the elders, chief priests, and scribes, be killed, and be raised the third day.*b* **22** Peter took him aside and began to rebuke him, "Oh no,ᴬ Lord! This will never happen to you!"

23 Jesus turned and told Peter, "Get behind me, Satan! You are a hindrance to me because you're not thinking about God's concernsᴮ but human concerns."ᶜ

TAKE UP YOUR CROSS

24 Then Jesus said to his disciples, "If anyone wants to follow after me, let him deny himself, take up his cross, and follow me.*d* **25** For whoever wants to save his life will lose it, but whoever loses his life because of me will find it.*e* **26** For what will it benefit someone if he gains the whole world yet loses his life? Or what will anyone give in exchange for his life?*f* **27** For the Son of Man is going to come with his angels in the glory of his Father,*g* and then he will reward each according to what he has done. **28** Truly I tell you, there are some standing here who will not taste death until they see the Son of Man coming in his kingdom."ʰ

THE TRANSFIGURATION

17 After six days*i* Jesus took Peter, James, and his brother John and led them up on a high mountain by themselves.*j* **2** He was transfigured in front of them, and his face shone like the sun; his clothes became as white as the light.ᵏ **3** Suddenly, Moses and Elijah appeared to them, talking with him. **4** Then Peter said to Jesus, "Lord, it's good for us to be here. If you want, I will set upᶜ three shelters here: one for you, one for Moses, and one for Elijah."*l*

5 While he was still speaking, suddenly a bright cloud coveredᴰ them, and a voice from the cloud said: "This is my beloved Son, with whom I am well-pleased. Listen to him!"*m* **6** When the disciplesⁿ heard this, they fell facedown and were terrified. **7** Jesus came up, touched them, and said, "Get up; don't be afraid."*o* **8** When they looked up they saw no one except Jesus alone.

9 As they were coming down the mountain, Jesus commanded them,*p* "Don't tell anyone about the vision until the Son of Man is raisedᴱ from the dead."

10 So the disciples asked him, "Why then do the scribes say that Elijah must come first?"*q*

11 "Elijah is comingᶠ and will restore everything," he replied.ᴳ,*r* **12** "But I tell you: Elijah has already come, and they didn't recognize him. On the contrary, they did whatever they pleased to him. In the same way the Son of Man is going to suffer at their hands."*s* **13** Then the disciples understood that he had spoken to them about John the Baptist.

THE POWER OF JESUS OVER A DEMON

14 When they reached the crowd,*t* a man approached and knelt down before him.

ᴬ16:22 Lit *"Mercy to you = "May God have mercy on you*   ᴮ16:23 Lit *about the things of God*   ᶜ17:4 Other mss read *Let's make*
ᴰ17:5 Or *enveloped*; Ex 40:34-35   ᴱ17:9 Other mss read *Man has risen*   ᶠ17:11 Other mss add *first*   ᴳ17:11 Other mss read *Jesus said to them*

16:21 Jesus gave the foundation for the gospel in summary form (see 1 Cor 15:3-4).

16:22-23 Peter's attempt to protect Jesus was the work of the devil (16:22). Any attempt to make Jesus King without the cross (remember Satan's temptations in 4:2-10?) is an attempt to thwart God's plan of salvation. Instead of being a *stone* (see 16:18), Peter had become **a hindrance**, which can also be translated "stumbling block."

You're not thinking about God's concerns but human concerns means Peter's viewpoint was warped (16:23). He was seeing things from a merely human perspective, not a divine one. He had aligned himself with Satan's program without realizing it.

16:24 After explaining his mission (his death and resurrection), Jesus explained the mission of his followers, discipleship: **If anyone wants to follow after me, let him deny himself, take up his cross, and follow me.** People don't typically wake in the morning and say, "I can't wait to deny myself today!" But, in order to experience the lordship and provision of Christ on earth, you must be willing to say "no" to yourself.

16:25-26 If you totally identify with Jesus and live according to his agenda, you'll find the abundant life you never knew was possible (16:25; see John 10:10). What good is it to gain worldly stuff while losing spiritual blessings and the peace that make life worthwhile (Matt 16:26)?

16:27 As sure as Jesus "conquered the world" (John 16:33), **he will reward** those who choose his way.

16:28 This was fulfilled when Peter, James, and John witnessed Jesus's transfiguration (see 17:1-9). They saw his humanity peeled back and got a glimpse of his glorious deity.

17:3 These two eminent Old Testament figures—**Moses and Elijah**—had lived hundreds of years earlier. This scene, then, informs us that those who experience death (e.g., Moses) have cognitive understanding and an ability to communicate. Together, they symbolize all those who make up God's king-dom—those who will be raptured and not see death (like Elijah) and those who will die and go to be with the Lord (like Moses).

Moreover, Moses represented the Law, and Elijah represented the Prophets. Together they represented the complete Old Testament. Along with the disciples, they represent both the Old and New Testaments centered on Jesus.

17:5 God the Father interrupted Peter to give a verbal and visual validation of his one and only Son, the King of kings.

17:9 If the crowds heard about it, the story would likely create confusion and cause them to forcibly make Jesus king. Instead, it was to be part of the kingdom message that the disciples would proclaim, calling sinners to place their faith in the risen King.

17:12-13 Jesus said **Elijah [had] already come** (17:12). In the Gospel of Luke, the angel told John's father Zechariah that his son would go before the Lord "in the spirit and power of Elijah" (Luke 1:17).

15 "Lord," he said, "have mercy on my son, because he has seizures[A] and suffers terribly. He often falls into the fire and often into the water. **16** I brought him to your disciples, but they couldn't heal him."[a]

17 Jesus replied, "You unbelieving and perverse generation, how long will I be with you? How long must I put up with you? Bring him here to me."[b] **18** Then Jesus rebuked the demon,[B] and it[C] came out of him,[C] and from that moment[D] the boy was healed.

19 Then the disciples approached Jesus privately and said, "Why couldn't we drive it out?"

20 "Because of your little faith," he[E] told them. "For truly I tell you, if you have faith the size of[F] a mustard seed, you will tell this mountain, 'Move from here to there,' and it will move.[d] Nothing will be impossible for you."[G,e]

⤳ HOPE WORDS ⤳

Faith doesn't make sense.
It makes miracles.

THE SECOND PREDICTION OF HIS DEATH

22 As[f] they were gathering together[H] in Galilee, Jesus told them, "The Son of Man is about to be betrayed into the hands of men. **23** They will kill him, and on the third day he will be raised up." And they were deeply distressed.

PAYING THE TEMPLE TAX

24 When they came to Capernaum, those who collected the temple tax approached Peter and said, "Doesn't your teacher pay the temple tax?"[g]

25 "Yes," he said.

When he went into the house, Jesus spoke to him first,[i] "What do you think, Simon? From whom do earthly kings collect tariffs or taxes? From their sons or from strangers?"[J,h]

26 "From strangers," he said.[K]

"Then the sons are free," Jesus told him. **27** "But, so we won't offend them, go to the sea, cast in a fishhook, and take the first fish that you catch. When you open its mouth you'll find a coin.[L] Take it and give it to them for me and you."[i]

WHO IS THE GREATEST?

18 At that time[D,J] the disciples[k] came to Jesus and asked, "So who is greatest in the kingdom of heaven?"[l] **2** He called a child and had him stand among them. **3** "Truly I tell you," he said, "unless you turn and become like children,[m] you will never enter the kingdom of heaven.[n] **4** Therefore, whoever humbles himself like this child — this one is the greatest in the kingdom of heaven. **5** And whoever welcomes[M] one child like this in my name welcomes me.

6 "But whoever causes one of these little ones who believe in me to fall away — it would be better for him if a heavy millstone were hung around his neck and he were drowned in the depths of the sea.[o] **7** Woe to the world because of offenses. For offenses will inevitably come, but woe to that person by whom the offense comes.[p] **8** If your hand or your foot causes you to fall away, cut it off and throw it away. It is better for you to enter life maimed or lame than to have two hands or two feet and be thrown into the eternal fire.[q] **9** And if your eye causes you to fall away, gouge it out and throw it away.

[a] 17:16 Mt 10:1; Mk 6:7; Lk 10:17
[b] 17:17 Jn 14:9; 20:27; Php 2:15
[c] 17:18 Zch 3:2; Mt 8:26; Mk 1:25; Lk 4:35; Jd 9
[d] 17:20 Mt 21:21-22; Mk 11:23; Lk 17:6; Jn 11:40; 1Co 13:2
[e] Mk 9:23,29; 13:31
[f] 17:22-23 Mt 16:21; 20:17; Mk 8:31; 9:30-32; Lk 9:44-45
[g] 17:24 Ex 30:13; 38:26; Mk 9:33
[h] 17:25 Mt 22:17,19; Mk 12:14; Rm 13:7
[i] 17:27 Mt 5:29; Jn 6:61
[j] 18:1-5 Mk 9:33-37; Lk 9:46-48
[k] 18:1 Mt 9:10; Mk 10:10; Lk 6:1; Jn 6:3; Ac 6:1
[l] Mt 22:24; Jn 3:35; 13:20
[m] 18:3 Mt 19:14; Mk 10:15; Lk 18:17; 1Co 14:20; 1Pt 2:2
[n] Mt 5:20; 7:21; 19:23-24; Mk 9:47; Jn 3:5
[o] 18:6 Mk 9:42; Lk 17:2; 1Co 8:12
[p] 18:7 Mt 26:24; Lk 17:1; 1Co 11:19
[q] 18:8 Mt 5:30; 25:41; Mk 9:43

[A] 17:15 Lit *he is moonstruck*; thought to be a form of epilepsy   [B] 17:18 Lit *rebuked him*, or *it*   [C] 17:18 Lit *the demon*   [D] 17:18; 18:1 Lit *hour*   [E] 17:20 Other mss read *your unbelief, Jesus*   [F] 17:20 Lit *faith like*   [G] 17:20 Some mss include v. 21: "However, this kind does not come out except by prayer and fasting."   [H] 17:22 Other mss read *were staying*   [I] 17:25 Lit *Jesus anticipated him by saying*   [J] 17:25 Or *foreigners*   [K] 17:26 Other mss read *Peter said to him*   [L] 17:27 Gk *stater*, worth 2 double-drachmas   [M] 18:5 Or *receives*

17:15 We know from the parallel account in Mark's Gospel that the father also said his **son** had a demon, or "spirit" (Mark 9:14-18).
17:16-17 That the disciples **couldn't** cast out the demon wasn't merely a failure of power; it was a failure of faith, a failure to trust in the power of God.
17:20 Have you ever seen **mustard seed[s]**? They're tiny! So apparently, the disciples' faith was microscopic. But with even a small trust in an omnipotent God, the **impossible** becomes possible.
17:22-23 Jesus understood the direction his life would take; he knew his fate. It was no surprise but was under his sovereign control.

17:24 This **tax** was used for the upkeep of **the temple**. If those running things at the temple understood who Jesus was, they wouldn't be asking him to pay it. After all, it was *his* temple.
17:27 Jesus didn't want to enter into unnecessary conflict—and you shouldn't either. Though the government and unbelievers don't recognize Christ or his kingdom, that's no reason to cause needless offense.
18:1 So who is greatest in the kingdom of heaven? That's an unexpected question. Yet, notice that in 18:2-5 Jesus didn't condemn **the disciples** for asking it or for desiring to be great. Instead, he challenged worldly

assumptions about the methods used to become great.
18:2-4 The lesson here is that true greatness comes through humility and a childlike faith that trusts God completely.
18:5 If you want fellowship with Jesus, you need to be in fellowship with the humble.
18:6 To trip up children spiritually is to incur greater judgment. According to Jesus, drowning in the sea with a heavy rock hung around your neck would be preferable!
18:8-9 Jesus wasn't calling for self-mutilation. Rather, people must be willing to avoid eternal judgment at any cost.

a 18:9 Mt 5:22,29; Mk 9:47
b 18:10 Est 1:14; Lk 1:19;
Rv 8:2
c Ps 34:7; 91:11; Heb 1:14
d Mt 6:29; 25:40,45; Lk
15:7,10
e 18:12-14 Lk 15:1-7
f 18:12 Mt 17:25; 21:28
g 18:15 Lv 19:17; Lk 17:3;
Gl 6:1; 2Th 3:15; Jms 5:19;
1Pt 3:1
h 18:16 Nm 35:30; Jn 8:17;
2Co 13:1; 1Tm 5:19; Heb
10:28
i 18:17 Mt 16:18; 1Co 14:4;
Rv 1:4
j Rm 16:17; 1Co 5:9; 6:1-6;
2Th 3:6,14; 2Jn 10
k 18:18 Mt 16:19; Jn 20:23

l 18:21 Lk 17:3-4; Col 3:13
m 18:25 Ex 21:2; Lv 25:39;
2Kg 4:1; Neh 5:5,8; Lk 7:42
n 18:28 Mt 20:2; 22:19; Mk
6:37; 14:5; Lk 7:41; 10:35;
Jn 6:7

It is better for you to enter life with one eye than to have two eyes and be thrown into hellfire.[A,a]

THE PARABLE OF THE LOST SHEEP

10 "See to it that you don't despise one of these little ones,[b] because I tell you that in heaven their angels[c] continually view the face of my Father in heaven.[B,d] **12** What do you think?[e] If someone has a hundred sheep, and one of them goes astray, won't he leave the ninety-nine on the hillside and go and search for the stray?[f] **13** And if he finds it, truly I tell you, he rejoices over that sheep[c] more than over the ninety-nine that did not go astray. **14** In the same way, it is not the will of your Father in heaven that one of these little ones perish.

RESTORING A BROTHER

15 "If your brother sins against you,[D] go and rebuke him in private.[E] If he listens to you, you have won your brother.[g] **16** But if he won't listen, take one or two others with you, so that **by the testimony**[F] **of two or three witnesses every fact may be established.**[G,h] **17** If he doesn't pay attention to them, tell the church.[H,i] If he doesn't pay attention even to the church, let him be like a Gentile and a tax collector to you.[j] **18** Truly I tell you, whatever you bind on earth will have been bound[I] in heaven, and whatever you loose on earth will have been loosed[J] in heaven.[k] **19** Again, truly I tell you, if two of you on earth agree about any matter that you[k] pray for, it will be done for you[L] by my Father in heaven. **20** For where two or three are gathered together in my name, I am there among them."

THE PARABLE OF THE UNFORGIVING SERVANT

21 Then Peter approached him and asked, "Lord, how many times shall I forgive my brother or sister who sins against me? As many as seven times?"[l]

22 "I tell you, not as many as seven," Jesus replied, "but seventy times seven.[M] **23** "For this reason, the kingdom of heaven can be compared to a king who wanted to settle accounts with his servants. **24** When he began to settle accounts, one who owed ten thousand talents[N] was brought before him. **25** Since he did not have the money to pay it back, his master commanded that he, his wife, his children, and everything he had be sold to pay the debt.[m] **26** "At this, the servant fell facedown before him and said, 'Be patient with me, and I will pay you everything.' **27** Then the master of that servant had compassion, released him, and forgave him the loan. **28** "That servant went out and found one of his fellow servants who owed him a hundred denarii.[O,n] He grabbed him, started choking him, and said, 'Pay what you owe!' **29** "At this, his fellow servant fell down[P] and began begging him, 'Be patient with me, and I will pay you back.' **30** But he

---

[A] 18:9 Lit *gehenna of fire* [B] 18:10 Some mss include v. 11: *For the Son of Man has come to save the lost.* [C] 18:13 Lit *over it* [D] 18:15 Other mss omit *against you* [E] 18:15 Lit *him between you and him alone* [F] 18:16 Lit *mouth* [G] 18:16 Dt 19:15 [H] 18:17 Or *congregation* [I] 18:18 Or *earth will be bound* [J] 18:18 Or *earth will be loosed* [K] 18:19 Lit *they* [L] 18:19 Lit *for them* [M] 18:22 Or *but seventy-seven times* [N] 18:24 A talent is worth about 6,000 denarii, or twenty years' wages for a laborer [O] 18:28 A denarius = one day's wage [P] 18:29 Other mss add *at his feet*

18:12-14 God goes to great lengths to rescue us, as Jesus's story about the great love of God illustrates.

18:15 To be a member of a local church is to live under the authority of Jesus Christ in fellowship with and in accountability to other believers. Notice that the matter in view involves a **brother**—a fellow believer. Moreover, the concern is a brother's **sins.** It has nothing to do with a clash of personal preferences. The issue is a violation of God's standards. Such behavior calls for a **rebuke** in **private.** Walk alongside believers going in the wrong direction and help them turn back to God.

18:16 Witnesses help to ensure that the matter isn't a mere personal squabble, a false accusation, or an overreaction—but a refusal to repent over sin. The church is about more than sermons and songs. It's about holiness, grace, and tough love.

18:17 If a sinning saint fails to "listen" (18:16) even to the church, the unrepentant member

is to **be like a Gentile and a tax collector to** them. This is the sober and unfortunate step of excommunication in which the person is no longer considered a member of the congregation and is removed from fellowship. The church is no longer to associate with the person as they would a brother or sister in Christ (see 1 Cor 5:3-5, 9-13; 2 Thess 3:14-15). One of the primary ways this discipline is carried out is around the Communion table. The Lord's Supper is a meal for believers, not unbelievers.

All the while, the church should pray for the straying sinner, holding out hope that the Lord might lead him to repentance. If he rejects his sinful lifestyle, the church should welcome him with forgiveness and an affirmation of love (see 2 Cor 2:5-8).

18:19-20 When a congregation acts in accordance with Scripture to promote God's glory and the good of an erring member, heaven backs up the church.

18:21-22 Jewish rabbis taught that forgiveness need only be extended three times. So **Peter** may have thought he was being generous by suggesting that he **forgive [his] brother or sister seven times** (18:21). By saying, **seventy times seven**, though, Jesus insisted that forgiveness has no limits (18:22).

18:24 A talent was the largest unit of currency. **Ten thousand talents** would be equivalent to an unfathomable amount of money today. If he were telling the story to modern U.S. listeners, Jesus would have said "millions of dollars." The point was the servant owed a debt that was impossible to pay—just like the sin debt we owe to God.

18:28 A hundred denarii represented about a hundred days' wages. The amount was child's play compared to what the demanding man owed the king.

18:29-30 The second servant begged for mercy—just as the first had done (18:29). But this lender was unwilling to show the same compassion he'd been granted and **threw** his fellow servant **into prison** (18:30).

wasn't willing. Instead, he went and threw him into prison until he could pay what was owed. **31** When the other servants saw what had taken place, they were deeply distressed and went and reported to their master everything that had happened. **32** Then, after he had summoned him, his master said to him, 'You wicked servant! I forgave you all that debt because you begged me. **33** Shouldn't you also have had mercy on your fellow servant, as I had mercy on you?' [a] **34** And because he was angry, his master handed him over to the jailers to be tortured until he could pay everything that was owed. **35** So also my heavenly Father will do to you unless every one of you forgives his brother or sister [A] from your [B] heart." [b]

THE QUESTION OF DIVORCE

19 When Jesus had finished saying these things, [c] he departed from Galilee and went to the region of Judea across the Jordan. [d] **2** Large crowds followed him, and he healed them there. [e] **3** Some Pharisees approached him to test him. They asked, "Is it lawful for a man to divorce his wife on any grounds?" [f]

4 "Haven't you read," he replied, "that he who created [c] them in the beginning **made them male and female,** [D,g] **5** and he also said, 'For this reason a man will leave his father and mother and be joined to his wife, and the two will become one flesh'?** [E,h] **6** So they are no longer two, but one flesh. Therefore, what God has joined together, let no one separate."

7 "Why then," they asked him, "did Moses command us to give divorce papers [i] and to send her away?"

8 He told them, "Moses permitted you to divorce your wives because of the hardness of your hearts, but it was not like that from the beginning. **9** I tell you, whoever divorces his wife, except for sexual immorality, and marries another commits adultery." [F,j]

10 His disciples [k] said to him, "If the relationship of a man with his wife is like this, it's better not to marry."

11 He responded, "Not everyone can accept this saying, but only those to whom it has been given. [l] **12** For there are eunuchs who were born that way from their mother's womb, there are eunuchs who were made by men, and there are eunuchs who have made themselves that way because of the kingdom of heaven. The one who is able to accept it should accept it."

BLESSING THE CHILDREN

13 Then children were brought to Jesus for him to place his hands on them and pray, but the disciples rebuked them. [m] **14** Jesus said, "Leave the children alone, and don't try to keep them from coming to me, because the kingdom of heaven belongs to such as these." [G,n] **15** After placing his hands on them, he went on from there.

THE RICH YOUNG RULER

16 Just then someone came up and asked him, [o] "Teacher, what good must I do to have eternal life?" [p]

17 "Why do you ask me about what is good?" [H] he said to him. "There is only one who is good. [i] If you want to enter into life, keep the commandments." [q]

18 "Which ones?" he asked him.

Jesus answered: **Do not murder; do not commit adultery; do not steal; do not bear false witness;** [r] **19** honor your father and your mother; and love your neighbor as yourself.** [J,s]

[a] 18:33 Mt 6:12; Eph 4:32; Col 3:13; 1Jn 4:11
[b] 18:35 Pr 21:13; Mt 6:14; Jms 2:13
[c] 19:1-9 Mk 10:1-12
[d] 19:1 Mt 7:28; Lk 9:51; Jn 10:40
[e] 19:2 Mt 4:23; 12:15
[f] 19:3 Mt 5:31; Jn 8:6
[g] 19:4 Gn 2:18; Mt 21:16
[h] 19:5 Gn 2:24; Mal 2:15; 1Co 6:16; Eph 5:31
[i] 19:7 Dt 24:1-4; Mt 5:31

[j] 19:9 Mt 5:32; Lk 16:18
[k] 19:10 Mt 10:1; 26:56; Mk 3:7; 16:20; Lk 6:13; Jn 12:16
[l] 19:11 Mt 13:11; 1Co 7:7
[m] 19:13-15 Mk 10:13-16; Lk 18:15-17
[n] 19:14 Mt 18:3; 1Pt 2:2
[o] 19:16-29 Mk 10:17-30; Lk 10:25-28; 18:18-30
[p] 19:16 Mk 10:17; Jn 12:25; Ac 13:48
[q] 19:17 Lv 18:5; Neh 9:29; Ezk 20:21
[r] 19:18 Ex 20:13-16; Dt 5:17-20
[s] 19:19 Ex 20:12; Lv 19:18; Dt 5:16; Mt 5:43; 22:39; Gl 5:14; Jms 2:8

[A] 18:35 Other mss add *their trespasses*　[B] 18:35 Lit *his*　[C] 19:4 Other mss read *made*　[D] 19:4 Gn 1:27; 5:2　[E] 19:5 Gn 2:24　[F] 19:9 Other mss add *Also whoever marries a divorced woman commits adultery*; Mt 5:32　[G] 19:14 Lit *heaven is of such ones*　[H] 19:17 Other mss read *"Why do you call me good?"*　[I] 19:17 Other mss read *"No one is good but one—God*　[J] 19:18-19 Ex 20:12-16; Lv 19:18; Dt 5:16-20

18:35 Our debt to God is infinitely greater than our brother's or sister's debt to us. Recognizing that positions us to receive from God the very thing that others desire from us: mercy. **19:4-6** At the dawn of creation, God made one man for one woman, with no escape hatch. The purpose of marriage is to advance *God's* kingdom rule on earth for his glory. It means working together with your spouse for that joint goal. **19:6** God intended marriage as a permanent relationship between one man and one woman. **19:7-8** Moses *permitted* divorce; he did not *command* it. **19:9** If a husband or wife commits adultery (or abandons their mate; see 1 Cor 7:15),

the spouse has a permissible reason for divorce—though this doesn't mean that divorce is *required*. If God's Word gives you permission to divorce, then you have permission to remarry another Christian. According to Jesus, though, if a divorce is illegitimate, it leads to an illegitimate remarriage. To remarry after an unbiblical divorce is to commit **adultery**.

Christian couples should never let the word *divorce* enter into their conversations. They ought to view the marriage bond as sacred, sacrifice as necessary to make it work, and seek godly counsel from the church. **19:14** Jesus doesn't want anyone to stand between him and children. That **the kingdom**

of heaven belongs to such as these implies you have to be willing to humble yourself like a little child to come to Jesus as your Savior and experience his kingdom rule as Lord. **19:17-19** Since the man wanted to **enter into life,** Jesus told him to **keep the commandments** of God. God's laws represent his perfect, holy standard. If a person can perfectly keep the commandments, he will indeed merit eternal life. The problem is that we are all sinners unable to meet the standards of a righteous God (see Rom 3:23). God gave us his laws, in fact, to show us we couldn't keep them and to drive us to the Savior. **19:22** That the man **had many possessions** and was unwilling to part with them for the

[a] 19:21 Lk 12:33; 16:9; Ac
2:45; 4:35; 1Tm 6:18
[b] 19:23 Mt 13:22; Mk 10:23;
1Co 1:26; 1Tm 6:9
[c] 19:24 Mt 12:28; Mk 10:25;
Lk 18:25
[d] 19:26 Gn 18:14; Jb 42:2; Jr
32:17; Zch 8:6; Mk 10:27;
Lk 18:27
[e] 19:28 Is 65:17; 66:22; 2Pt
3:13; Rv 21:1
[f] Ps 45:6; Mt 25:31; Heb
1:8; Rv 3:21; 22:1,3
[g] 19:29 Mt 6:33; Mk 10:29;
Lk 18:29
[h] 19:30 Mt 20:16; 21:31;
Mk 10:31; Lk 13:30
[i] 20:1 Mt 13:24; 21:28,33

[j] 20:8 Lv 19:13; Dt 24:15
[k] 20:12 Jnh 4:8; Lk 12:55;
Jms 1:11
[l] 20:13 Mt 22:12; 26:50
[m] 20:15 Dt 15:9; Pr 23:6;
Mt 6:23; Mk 7:22
[n] 20:16 Mt 19:30; Mk
10:31; Lk 13:30
[o] 20:17-19 Mk 10:32-34; Lk
18:31-33
[p] 20:18 Mt 16:21; 26:66;
Jn 19:7
[q] 20:19 Mt 27:2; Ac 2:23;
3:13; 4:27; 21:11

20 "I have kept all these,"[A] the young man told him. "What do I still lack?"

21 "If you want to be perfect,"[B] Jesus said to him, "go, sell your belongings and give to the poor,[a] and you will have treasure in heaven. Then come, follow me."

22 When the young man heard that, he went away grieving, because he had many possessions.

POSSESSIONS AND THE KINGDOM

23 Jesus said to his disciples, "Truly I tell you, it will be hard for a rich person to enter the kingdom of heaven.[b] **24** Again I tell you, it is easier for a camel to go through the eye of a needle than for a rich person to enter the kingdom of God."[c]

25 When the disciples heard this, they were utterly astonished and asked, "Then who can be saved?"

26 Jesus looked at them and said, "With man this is impossible, but with God all things are possible."[d]

27 Then Peter responded to him, "See, we have left everything and followed you. So what will there be for us?"

28 Jesus said to them, "Truly I tell you, in the renewal of all things,[e] when the Son of Man sits on his glorious throne,[f] you who have followed me will also sit on twelve thrones, judging the twelve tribes of Israel. **29** And everyone who has left houses or brothers or sisters or father or mother[c] or children or fields because of my name will receive a hundred times more and will inherit eternal life.[g] **30** But many who are first will be last, and the last first.[h]

THE PARABLE OF THE VINEYARD WORKERS

20 "For the kingdom of heaven is like a landowner who went out early in the morning to hire workers for his vineyard.[i] **2** After agreeing with the workers on one denarius,[D] he sent them into his vineyard for the day. **3** When he went out about nine in the morning,[E] he saw others standing in the marketplace doing nothing. **4** He said to them, 'You also go into my vineyard, and I'll give you whatever is right.' So off they went. **5** About noon and about three,[F] he went out again and did the same thing. **6** Then about five[G] he went out and found others standing around[H] and said to them, 'Why have you been standing here all day doing nothing?'

7 "'Because no one hired us,' they said to him.

"'You also go into my vineyard,' he told them.[I] **8** When evening came, the owner of the vineyard told his foreman, 'Call the workers and give them their pay,[j] starting with the last and ending with the first.'

9 "When those who were hired about five came, they each received one denarius. **10** So when the first ones came, they assumed they would get more, but they also received a denarius each. **11** When they received it, they began to complain to the landowner: **12** 'These last men put in one hour, and you made them equal to us who bore the burden of the day's work and the burning heat.'[k]

13 "He replied to one of them, 'Friend,[l] I'm doing you no wrong. Didn't you agree with me on a denarius?'[D] **14** Take what's yours and go. I want to give this last man the same as I gave you. **15** Don't I have the right to do what I want with what is mine? Are you jealous[j] because I'm generous?'[K,m] **16** "So the last will be first, and the first last."[L,n]

THE THIRD PREDICTION OF HIS DEATH

17 While going up to Jerusalem,[o] Jesus took the twelve disciples aside privately and said to them on the way, **18** "See, we are going up to Jerusalem. The Son of Man will be handed over to the chief priests and scribes, and they will condemn him to death.[p] **19** They will hand him over to the Gentiles[q] to be mocked, flogged,[M] and crucified, and on the third day he will be raised."[N]

[A] 19:20 Other mss add *from my youth*   [B] 19:21 Or *complete*   [C] 19:29 Other mss add *or wife*   [D] 20:2 A denarius = one day's wage, also in vv. 9,10,13
[E] 20:3 Lit *about the third hour*   [F] 20:5 Lit *about the sixth hour and the ninth hour*   [G] 20:6 Lit *about the eleventh hour,* also in v. 9   [H] 20:6 Other mss
add *doing nothing*   [I] 20:7 Other mss add *'and you'll get whatever is right.'*   [J] 20:15 Lit *Is your eye evil;* an idiom for jealousy or stinginess
[K] 20:15 Lit *good*   [L] 20:16 Other mss add *"For many are called, but few are chosen."*   [M] 20:19 Or *scourged*   [N] 20:19 Other mss read *will rise again*

sake of a neighbor in need, revealed that he was indeed a sinner. And rather than acknowledge his sinfulness and come to Christ for salvation, **he went away**.

19:23 The **rich** often trust in and are attached to their wealth. People who focus on storing up riches in this world easily allow this world to distract them from thoughts of the world to come.

19:28 The **renewal of all things** is a reference to Jesus's millennial reign.

19:29 To **inherit eternal life** is not only to enter eternal life but also to receive its benefits.

19:30 Don't let earthly success or worldly gain prevent you from sacrificing as necessary to serve the Lord in light of the rewards to be received in the world to come.

20:1-15 Through this story Jesus was teaching that God is both fair and generous. We should rejoice when God is gracious toward others and not resent it. While the Jews expected better treatment from God because of their background as God's people, the Gentiles would be objects of his compassion as well.

SUFFERING AND SERVICE

20 Then the mother of Zebedee's sons approached him with her sons.[a] She knelt down to ask him for something.[b] **21** "What do you want?" he asked her.

"Promise,"[A] she said to him, "that these two sons of mine may sit, one on your right and the other on your left, in your kingdom."[c]

22 Jesus answered, "You don't know what you're asking. Are you able to drink the cup that I am about to drink?"[B,d]

"We are able," they said to him.

23 He told them, "You will indeed drink my cup,[c] but to sit at my right and left is not mine to give; instead, it is for those for whom it has been prepared by my Father."[e]

24 When the ten disciples heard this, they became indignant with the two brothers. **25** Jesus called them over and said, "You know that the rulers of the Gentiles lord it over them, and those in high positions act as tyrants over them. **26** It must not be like that among you. On the contrary, whoever wants to become great among you must be your servant,[f] **27** and whoever wants to be first among you must be your slave; **28** just as the Son of Man did not come to be served, but to serve,[g] and to give his life as a ransom for many."[h]

TWO BLIND MEN HEALED

29 As they were leaving Jericho, a large crowd followed him.[i] **30** There were two blind men sitting by the road. When they heard that Jesus was passing by, they cried out, "Lord, have mercy on us, Son of David!" **31** The crowd demanded that they keep quiet, but they cried out all the more, "Lord, have mercy on us, Son of David!"[j]

32 Jesus stopped, called them, and said, "What do you want me to do for you?"

33 "Lord," they said to him, "open our eyes." **34** Moved with compassion, Jesus touched their eyes. Immediately they could see, and they followed him.

THE TRIUMPHAL ENTRY

21 When they approached Jerusalem[k] and came to Bethphage at the Mount of Olives,[l] Jesus then sent two disciples, **2** telling them, "Go into the village ahead of you. At once you will find a donkey tied there with her colt. Untie them and bring them to me. **3** If anyone says anything to you, say that the Lord needs them, and he will send them at once."

4 This took place so that what was spoken through the prophet might be fulfilled:

5 Tell Daughter Zion,
  "See, your King is coming to you,
  gentle, and mounted on a donkey,
  and on a colt,
  the foal of a donkey."[D,m]

6 The disciples went and did just as Jesus directed them. **7** They brought the donkey and its colt; then they laid their clothes on them, and he sat on them. **8** A very large crowd spread their clothes on the road; others were cutting branches from the trees and spreading them on the road. **9** Then the crowds who went ahead of him and those who followed shouted:

Hosanna to the Son of David!
**Blessed is he who comes
  in the name
  of the Lord!**[E]
Hosanna in the highest heaven![n]

10 When he entered Jerusalem, the whole city was in an uproar, saying, "Who is this?" **11** The crowds were saying, "This is the prophet Jesus[o] from Nazareth in Galilee."

[a] 20:20-28 Mk 10:35-45; Lk 22:24-27
[b] 20:20 Mt 4:21; 8:2
[c] 20:21 Mt 16:28; 19:28; 25:31,34; Lk 23:42
[d] 20:22 Is 51:22; Jr 49:12; Mk 14:36
[e] 20:23 Ac 12:2; Rv 1:9
[f] 20:26 Mt 23:11; Mk 9:35
[g] 20:28 Lk 22:27; Jn 13:13-15; 2Co 8:9; Php 2:7
[h] Mt 26:28; 1Tm 2:6; Ti 2:14; Heb 9:28
[i] 20:29-34 Mk 10:46-52; Lk 18:35-43
[j] 20:30-31 Mt 9:27; 21:9; 22:42

[k] 21:1-9 Mk 11:1-10; Lk 19:28-38; Jn 12:12-19
[l] 21:1 Zch 14:4; Mt 24:3; 26:30; Lk 19:29,37; 21:37; Jn 8:1; Ac 1:12
[m] 21:5 Is 62:11; Zch 9:9
[n] 21:9 Ps 118:25; Mt 9:27; 23:39; Lk 2:14
[o] 21:11 Mk 6:15; Lk 7:16; 13:33; 24:19; Jn 1:21; 4:19; 6:14

[A] 20:21 Lit *Say* [B] 20:22 Other mss add *and (or) to be baptized with the baptism which I am baptized?* [C] 20:23 Other mss add *and be baptized with the baptism with which I am baptized.* [D] 21:5 Is 62:11; Zch 9:9 [E] 21:9 Ps 118:25-26

20:21 The seats to the **right** and **left** of a king were reserved for those in positions of special authority. The New Testament describes Jesus sitting at God's "right hand" (see Rom 8:34; Eph 1:20; Col 3:1; Heb 1:3; 8:1; 1 Pet 3:22).
20:22-23 Are you able to drink the cup that I am about to drink? (20:22). By this he meant the suffering he was about to endure. James would be martyred (see Acts 12:1-2), and John would experience exile (see Rev 1:9).
20:25-27 In the dog-eat-dog world of earthly success, you reach greatness by stepping on others. In the kingdom of God, you reach greatness by serving others in love.
Sometimes people think being a Christian means having no aspirations, but Jesus

didn't condemn the aspiration for greatness. Rather, he condemned the worldly method for achieving it. So dream big. Ask God how you can use your skills and talents to make the biggest possible kingdom impact. But realize that when it comes to the people of God, servants—not celebrities—are on top.
20:28 God exalted Jesus and gave him the name above all names, but Jesus attained this greatness by humbling himself as a servant and suffering unto death to save others (see Phil 2:5-11). The Son of God chose the way of sacrificial service, so why would you expect a different path for yourself?
20:30 The cry, **Lord, have mercy on us, Son of David!** indicates that these men recog-

nized his messianic authority, and with that authority came the supernatural right to heal.
20:31-32 Don't let others keep you from crying out to the Lord either (20:31). Pursue him until you hear a word from him, in spite of voices that try to keep you quiet. And when he comes through, follow him in even deeper faith and greater service.
21:9 By calling Jesus the **Son of David**, they weren't merely acknowledging who his ancestor was. They recognized this itinerant preacher from Nazareth as the Messiah, the promised King.

a 21:12-16 Mk 11:15-18; Lk
19:45-47; Jn 2:14-16
b 21:12 Ex 30:13; Lv 1:14;
5:7; 12:8; Dt 14:25
c 21:13 Jr 7:11
d 21:16 Ps 8:2; Mt 11:25;
12:3,5; 19:4; 22:31
e 21:17 Mt 26:6; Mk 11:1; Lk
19:29; 24:50; Jn 11:18
f 21:18-22 Mk 11:12-
14,20-24

g 21:21 Mt 17:20; Lk 17:6;
1Co 13:2; Jms 1:6
h 21:22 Mt 7:7-8; Jn 11:22
i 21:23-27 Mk 11:27-33;
Lk 20:1-8
j 21:23 Ex 2:14; Mt 26:55;
Ac 4:7; 7:27
k 21:25 Mt 13:54; Lk 7:30;
15:18,21; Jn 3:27
l 21:26 Mt 14:5; 21:46; Mk
11:32; 12:12
m Mt 11:9; Mk 6:20
n 21:28 Mt 20:1

CLEANSING THE TEMPLE

12 Jesus went into the temple[A,a] and threw out all those buying and selling. He overturned the tables of the money changers and the chairs of those selling doves.[b] **13** He said to them, "It is written, **my house will be called a house of prayer,**[B] but you are making it **a den of thieves!**"[C,c]

CHILDREN PRAISE JESUS

14 The blind and the lame came to him in the temple, and he healed them. **15** When the chief priests and the scribes saw the wonders that he did and the children shouting in the temple, "*Hosanna* to the Son of David!" they were indignant **16** and said to him, "Do you hear what these children are saying?"

Jesus replied, "Yes, have you never read:

You have prepared[D] **praise**[d]
**from the mouths of infants
and nursing babies?**"[E]

17 Then he left them, went out of the city to Bethany,[e] and spent the night there.

THE BARREN FIG TREE

18 Early in the morning,[f] as he was returning to the city, he was hungry. **19** Seeing a lone fig tree by the road, he went up to it and found nothing on it except leaves. And he said to it, "May no fruit ever come from you again!" At once the fig tree withered. **20** When the disciples saw it, they were amazed and said, "How did the fig tree wither so quickly?"

21 Jesus answered them, "Truly I tell you, if you have faith and do not doubt, you will not only do what was done to the fig tree, but even if you tell this mountain, 'Be lifted up and thrown into the sea,' it will be done.[g] **22** And if you believe, you will receive[h] whatever you ask for in prayer."

THE AUTHORITY OF JESUS CHALLENGED

23 When he entered the temple,[i] the chief priests and the elders of the people came to him as he was teaching and said, "By what authority are you doing these things? Who gave you this authority?"[j]

24 Jesus answered them, "I will also ask you one question, and if you answer it for me, then I will tell you by what authority I do these things. **25** Did John's baptism come from heaven, or was it of human origin?"

They discussed it among themselves, "If we say, 'From heaven,' he will say to us, 'Then why didn't you believe him?'[k] **26** But if we say, 'Of human origin,' we're afraid of the crowd,[l] because everyone considers John to be a prophet."[m] **27** So they answered Jesus, "We don't know."

And he said to them, "Neither will I tell you by what authority I do these things.

THE PARABLE OF THE TWO SONS

28 "What do you think? A man had two sons. He went to the first and said, 'My son, go work in the vineyard today.'[n]

29 "He answered, 'I don't want to,' but later he changed his mind and went. **30** Then the man went to the other and said the same thing. 'I will, sir,' he answered, but he didn't go. **31** Which of the two did his father's will?"

They said, "The first."

Jesus said to them, "Truly I tell you, tax collectors and prostitutes are entering

^A 21:12 Other mss add *of God*   ^B 21:13 Is 56:7   ^C 21:13 Jr 7:11   ^D 21:16 Or *restored*   ^E 21:16 Ps 8:2

21:12-13 In **the temple** in Jerusalem, pilgrims who'd come to offer sacrifices could buy animals from those selling them, as well as exchange currency with the **money changers** (21:12). Instead of a place focused on worship of the one true and living God, the temple had become a place of materialism and commercialism. When the temple was dedicated, Solomon prayed that God would hear the prayers of his people from the temple and forgive, heal, defend, and bless them (2 Chr 6:14-42). Yet some were using God's house to rob the people and reap a financial reward.

Religious materialism often appears among God's people today as a result of prosperity theology. It's easy to find so-called preachers on the radio and television whose essential message is that God exists to bless you, as if the Creator and Ruler of the universe is your personal spiritual Santa Claus. Moreover, they seek their own financial "blessing" from God by using you to foot the bill. It doesn't

matter who a preacher is, if you have to pay for his blessing, his ministry's a racket.

21:15-16 The religious leaders **were indignant** (21:15) because they couldn't believe this Galilean would allow children to hail him as the Messiah. But Jesus once again questioned the Jewish leaders' lack of Bible knowledge. He defended the children's **praise** by insisting that it was a fulfillment of Scripture (21:16; see Ps 8:2).

21:18-19 While the **fig tree** had given the impression of having fruit, it was barren (21:19). This condition was true of Israel. With all the people's religious practices, they gave an appearance of godliness but bore no authentic fruit.

21:22 Jesus wanted the disciples to understand the power of **prayer**. God wants followers of great faith, as opposed to the faithless Jewish leaders.

21:23-27 Jesus put these critics in a catch-22 situation. If they said John's baptism was **from heaven**, the obvious question would

be, **Then why didn't you believe him?** If they said, **of human origin**, they would be in trouble with the crowds who considered **John to be a prophet** (21:25-26). Since they were concerned with appearance more than anything, they were in a no-win situation. So they answered, **We don't know.** They punted the football, so to speak. Jesus had laid the perfect trap. They demonstrated by their response that they weren't really interested in the truth, so he refused to answer their question (21:27).

21:31-32 By answering Jesus's question correctly, the Jewish leaders condemned themselves. The **tax collectors and prostitutes** refused to obey God at first but later repented. The leaders, on the other hand, claimed to follow God but didn't have the actions to back it up. And even when they saw the tax collectors and prostitutes repent and believe, they still didn't **change [their] minds** (21:32). Lips that say, "Amen," mean nothing without hands and feet backing them up.

the kingdom of God before you. **32** For John came to you in the way of righteousness,[a] and you didn't believe him. Tax collectors and prostitutes did believe him; but you, when you saw it, didn't even change your minds then and believe him.

THE PARABLE OF THE VINEYARD OWNER

33 "Listen[b] to another parable:[c] There was a landowner, who planted a vineyard, put a fence around it, dug a winepress in it, and built a watchtower.[d] He leased it to tenant farmers and went away.[e] **34** When the time came to harvest fruit, he sent his servants to the farmers to collect his fruit. **35** The farmers took his servants, beat one, killed another, and stoned a third.[f] **36** Again, he sent other servants, more than the first group, and they did the same to them. **37** Finally, he sent his son to them. 'They will respect my son,' he said.

38 "But when the tenant farmers saw the son, they said to each other, 'This is the heir. Come, let's kill him and take his inheritance.'[g] **39** So they seized him, threw him out of the vineyard, and killed him. **40** Therefore, when the owner of the vineyard comes, what will he do to those farmers?"

41 "He will completely destroy those terrible men," they told him, "and lease his vineyard to other farmers who will give him his fruit at the harvest."[h]

42 Jesus said to them, "Have you never read in the Scriptures:

> **The stone that
> the builders rejected
> has become the cornerstone.**[A]
> **This is what the Lord has done
> and it is wonderful
> in our eyes**?[B,j]

43 Therefore I tell you, the kingdom of God will be taken away from you and given to a people producing its fruit. **44** Whoever falls on this stone will be broken to pieces;[j] but on whomever it falls, it will shatter him."[c]

45 When the chief priests and the Pharisees heard his parables,[k] they knew he was speaking about them. **46** Although they were looking for a way to arrest him, they feared the crowds, because the people regarded him as a prophet.[l]

THE PARABLE OF THE WEDDING BANQUET

22 Once more Jesus spoke to them in parables: **2** "The kingdom of heaven[m] is like a king who gave a wedding banquet for his son.[n] **3** He sent his servants to summon those invited to the banquet,[o] but they didn't want to come. **4** Again, he sent out other servants and said, 'Tell those who are invited: See, I've prepared my dinner; my oxen and fattened cattle have been slaughtered, and everything is ready. Come to the wedding banquet.'[p]

5 "But they paid no attention and went away, one to his own farm, another to his business, **6** while the rest seized his servants, mistreated them, and killed them. **7** The king[D] was enraged, and he sent out his troops, killed those murderers, and burned down their city.

8 "Then he told his servants, 'The banquet is ready, but those who were invited were not worthy.[q] **9** Go then to where the roads exit the city and invite everyone you find to the banquet.'[r] **10** So those servants went out on the roads and gathered everyone they found, both evil and good. The wedding banquet[E] was filled with guests.[F] **11** When the king came in to see the guests, he saw a man there who was not dressed for a wedding.[s] **12** So he said to him, 'Friend,[t] how did you get in here without wedding clothes?' The man was speechless.

13 "Then the king told the attendants, 'Tie him up hand and foot,[G] and throw him into

[a] 21:32 Pr 8:20; Mt 3:8-12; 2Pt 2:21
[b] 21:33-46 Mk 12:1-12; Lk 20:9-19
[c] 21:33 Mt 13:3,34-36; 15:15; 22:1; 24:32
[d] Is 5:1-2; Lk 14:28
[e] Ps 80:8; Sg 8:11-12; Mt 25:14
[f] 21:35 2Ch 24:21; Neh 9:26; Mt 5:12; 23:34,37; Ac 7:52; 1Th 2:15; Heb 11:36-37
[g] 21:38 Ps 2:8; Heb 1:2
[h] 21:41 Mt 8:11; Ac 13:46; 18:6; 28:28
[i] 21:42 Ps 118:22-23; Ac 4:11; Rm 9:33; 1Pt 2:7

[j] 21:44 Is 8:14-15; Rm 9:32-33; 1Pt 2:8
[k] 21:45 Mt 13:3,35; 15:15; 21:33; 22:1; 24:32
[l] 21:46 Mt 26:4; Mk 11:18; Lk 19:47-48; Jn 7:25,30,44
[m] 22:2-14 Lk 14:16-24
[n] 22:2 Mt 13:24; Lk 12:36; Jn 2:2; Rv 19:7
[o] 22:3 Est 6:14; Pr 9:3,5
[p] 22:4 Pr 9:2; Mt 21:36
[q] 22:8 Mt 10:11; Ac 13:46
[r] 22:9 Ezk 21:21; Ob 14
[s] 22:11 Rv 19:8; 22:14
[t] 22:12 Mt 20:13; 26:50

21:40-42 Jesus asked, **What will** the vineyard owner **do to those farmers?** (21:40). There's only one possible answer, and the religious leaders gave it: **He will completely destroy those terrible men** (21:41). Again, the leaders' failure to understand the Bible was actually a fulfillment of the Bible. Jesus claimed that he was **the stone that the builders rejected** (21:42), as described in Psalm 118:22-23. Thus, he was the "son" in the parable—scorned and (soon-to-be) killed—and they were the wicked tenant farmers.

22:5-7 This describes the response of the nation of Israel to God's messianic plan—a response reflected primarily in Israel's leaders. They rejected God's Son and his kingdom (22:5-6). God would bring fiery judgment on them with Rome's destruction of Jerusalem in AD 70. **22:8-10** I understand this image to refer to the millennial reign of Christ.

22:13 Many interpreters see this ejection as a description of final judgment. However, this language of **weeping and gnashing of teeth** is a picture of "sons of the kingdom" losing rewards in the millennial period (see 8:12). While they have accepted an invitation to enter the banquet, the messianic kingdom, those who don't utilize what God has provided and fail to be faithful servants will lose out on full participation in the millennial kingdom. As a result, they will experience profound regret. Many are called to salvation because of their faith in Christ, but few are chosen to rule with him in his millennial reign because of their unfaithfulness (see Luke 19:12-27; 1 Cor 3:12-15; 9:26-27; 2 Tim 2:12).

a 22:14 Mt 20:16; Rv 17:14
b 22:15-22 Mk 12:13-17; Lk 20:20-26
c 22:16 Mk 2:8; 3:6; 8:15
d Jn 3:2; Ac 10:34; 13:10; 18:26
e 22:17 Mk 12:14,16-17; Lk 2:1; 3:1; 20:22,24-25; Jn 19:12,15

f 22:21 Mt 17:25; Rm 13:7
g 22:23-32 Mk 12:18-27; Lk 20:27-38
h 22:23 Mt 3:7; Ac 4:1; 23:8

❧ KINGDOM LIVING ❧
KINGDOM
The Greatest Commands

Jesus said in Matthew 4:4, "Man must not live on bread alone but on every word that comes from the mouth of God." Life itself is tied to biblical authority. If you rebel against it, you're rebelling against life. You need to know God's commandments so you can obey them and live.

In response to this thought, you may be saying, "Tony, the Bible is a big book. It takes a lifetime to understand the Bible! How can I possibly do what you're suggesting?" Well, the Bible is not quite as difficult as you may think. Yes, it's so inexhaustible that theologians do spend lifetimes trying to understand it. Yet it is also so clear that children can grasp it. The Bible has relatively few core teachings. Though it may talk about them in a thousand different ways, the Bible only has a handful of foundational truths.

Exodus 20 contains what Moses literally called "the ten words." We know them as the Ten Commandments. If you understand the Ten Commandments, you will grasp the core of what God expects from you. But even better than that, Jesus summarized the essence of these commands for us in Matthew 22:36-40. A lawyer came to Jesus and asked him a lawyer-type question in verse 36: "Which command in the law is the greatest?"

Jesus told him, "'Love the Lord your God with all your heart, with all your soul, and with all your mind.' . . . The second [command] is like it: 'Love your neighbor as yourself'" (22:37, 39). There you have the very core of how you are to live out God's kingdom agenda. Let love rule and reign supreme in your thoughts, actions, and motives.

FOR THE NEXT KINGDOM
KINGDOM LIVING LESSON SEE PAGE 1144.

the outer darkness, where there will be weeping and gnashing of teeth.'

14 "For many are invited, but few are chosen."*a*

GOD AND CAESAR

15 Then the Pharisees went and plotted how to trap him by what he said.*A,b* **16** So they sent their disciples to him, along with the Herodians.*c* "Teacher," they said, "we know that you are truthful and teach truthfully the way of God. You don't care what anyone thinks nor do you show partiality.*B,d* **17** Tell us, then, what you think. Is it lawful to pay taxes to Caesar*e* or not?"

18 Perceiving their malicious intent, Jesus said, "Why are you testing me, hypocrites? **19** Show me the coin used for the tax." They brought him a denarius.*c* **20** "Whose image and inscription is this?" he asked them.

21 "Caesar's," they said to him.

Then he said to them, "Give, then, to Caesar the things that are Caesar's, and to God the things that are God's."*f* **22** When they heard this, they were amazed. So they left him and went away.

THE SADDUCEES
AND THE RESURRECTION

23 That same day some Sadducees,*g* who say there is no resurrection, came up to him and questioned him:*h* **24** "Teacher, Moses said, **if a man dies, having no children, his brother is to marry his wife and raise up**

A 22:15 Lit *trap him in a word*   *B* 22:16 Lit *don't look on the face of men*   *C* 22:19 A denarius = one day's wage

---

22:15-16 The Pharisees were the conservative religious movement of the day (22:15). **The Herodians** were not a religious group at all, but a political party that supported the dynasty of Herod. The only thing they had in common was their mutual hatred of Jesus. Nevertheless, the groups came to Jesus full of compliments: **You are truthful and teach truthfully. . . . You don't care what anyone thinks nor do you show partiality** (22:16). Hearing such words from such people would raise a few eyebrows. The alert listener would suspect something was up.

22:17 This may seem like an easy question to answer, but the men were attempting to put Jesus in a no-win situation. Israel was under Roman rule, so Jews were required to pay taxes to Rome. To be an advocate for paying taxes, then, would put Jesus at odds with the people who hated being subject to the pagan Romans. But to publicly denounce paying taxes would put him at odds with the Roman authorities.

22:19 A **denarius** was a Roman **coin** that was the equivalent of one day's wage.

22:20-22 This Roman coin had an engraving of the emperor, Tiberius Caesar, on it; thus, Jesus concluded, it made sense to give Caesar what clearly belonged to him. Moreover, since human beings bear God's "image," they naturally belong to God (Gen 1:26-27) and should submit to him.

It's proper to pay taxes to a government for the services it provides. However, everything falls within God's realm. The government may give you highways, but God gives you oxygen. You owe him more than a weekly visit on Sundays. Give him total obedience in honor of the daily benefits he gives you.

22:23-28 The **Sadducees** were a powerful religious sect associated with the high priests and aristocratic families. They rejected many of the theological views of the Pharisees—including belief in the **resurrection** (22:23). Pointing to the law that required a deceased man's brother to marry his wife in order to continue his brother's family line (22:24; see Deut 25:5-6), they proposed a hypothetical scenario in order to make a mockery of the doctrine of the resurrection of the dead. If **seven brothers** had the same woman for a

offspring for his brother.^(A,a) ^25 Now there were seven brothers among us. The first got married and died. Having no offspring, he left his wife to his brother. ^26 The same thing happened to the second also, and the third, and so on to all seven. ^27 Last of all, the woman died. ^28 In the resurrection, then, whose wife will she be of the seven? For they all had married her."^B

^29 Jesus answered them, "You are mistaken, because you don't know the Scriptures or the power of God. ^30 For in the resurrection they neither marry nor are given in marriage but are like^c angels in heaven.^b ^31 Now concerning the resurrection of the dead, haven't you read what was spoken to you by God: ^32 **I am the God of Abraham and the God of Isaac and the God of Jacob**?^(D,c) He^E is not the God of the dead, but of the living."

^33 And when the crowds heard this, they were astonished at his teaching.

APPLICATION QUESTIONS

READ MATTHEW 22:37-39

- How have you demonstrated your love for God this week?
- How have you intentionally sought to love your neighbor this month?

THE PRIMARY COMMANDS

^34 When^d the Pharisees heard that he had silenced the Sadducees, they came together. ^35 And one of them, an expert in the law, asked a question to test him:^e ^36 "Teacher, which command in the law is the greatest?"

^37 He said to him, "**Love the Lord your God with all your heart, with all your soul, and with all your mind.**^(f,f) ^38 This is the greatest and most important^G command. ^39 The second is like it: **Love your neighbor as yourself.**^(H,g) ^40 All the Law and the Prophets depend^i on these two commands."^h

THE QUESTION ABOUT THE CHRIST

^41 While the Pharisees were together, Jesus questioned them,^i ^42 "What do you think about the Messiah? Whose son is he?"

They replied, "David's."

^43 He asked them, "How is it then that David, inspired by the Spirit,^j calls him 'Lord'?:
^44   The Lord declared
         to my Lord,
     'Sit at my right hand
     until I put your enemies
         under your feet'?^(K,L,K)

^45 "If David calls him 'Lord,' how, then, can he be his son?" ^46 No one was able to answer him at all,^M and from that day no one dared to question him anymore.^i

RELIGIOUS HYPOCRITES DENOUNCED

23 Then^m Jesus spoke to the crowds and to his disciples:^n ^2 "The scribes and the Pharisees are seated in the chair of Moses.^o ^3 Therefore do whatever they tell you, and observe it. But don't do what they do, because they don't practice what they teach.^p ^4 They tie up heavy loads that are hard to carry^N and put them on people's shoulders, but they themselves aren't willing to lift a

^a 22:24 Dt 25:5
^b 22:30 Mt 24:38; Lk 17:27
^c 22:32 Ex 3:6; Ac 7:32
^d 22:34-40 Mk 12:28-33; Lk 10:25-28
^e 22:35 Lk 7:30; 10:25; 11:45; 14:3
^f 22:37 Dt 6:5; Lk 10:27
^g 22:39 Lv 19:18; Mt 19:19
^h 22:40 Mt 7:12; Rm 13:8-10; Gl 5:14
^i 22:41-46 Mk 12:35-37; Lk 20:41-44
^j 22:43 2Sm 23:2; Rv 1:10; 4:2
^k 22:44 Ps 110:1; Ac 2:34-35; 1Co 15:25; Heb 1:13; 10:13
^l 22:46 Mk 12:34; Lk 14:6; 20:40
^m 23:1-7 Mk 12:38-39; Lk 20:45-46
^n 23:1 Mt 10:42; 28:19; Lk 14:26; Jn 8:31; 13:35; 15:8; Ac 6:1
^o 23:2 Ezr 7:6,25; Neh 8:4
^p 23:3 Mt 5:20; 15:3-9; Rm 2:17-23

---

^A 22:24 Dt 25:5   ^B 22:28 Lit all had her   ^C 22:30 Other mss add God's   ^D 22:32 Ex 3:6,15-16   ^E 22:32 Other mss read God   ^F 22:37 Dt 6:5
^G 22:38 Lit and first   ^H 22:39 Lv 19:18   ^I 22:40 Or hang   ^J 22:43 Lit David in Spirit   ^K 22:44 Other mss read until I make your enemies your footstool'
^L 22:44 Ps 110:1   ^M 22:46 Lit answer him a word   ^N 23:4 Other mss omit that are hard to carry

---

wife after each one died, **whose wife** would she be **in the resurrection** (Matt 22:25-28)? **22:31-32** Though the patriarchs mentioned were physically dead even back in Moses's day, God was still their God. Spiritually speaking, they are very much alive.

22:37-38 Jesus wasted no time identifying **the greatest and most important command** by quoting from Deuteronomy 6:5: **Love the Lord your God with all your heart, with all your soul, and with all your mind** (Matt 22:37-38). God's entire law, in fact, can be reduced to this. At their core, the Ten Commandments are really a command to love God. While we frequently associate love with a *feeling*, it must be more than that because it's something that can be *commanded*.

God wants a relationship with you. He wants you to love him, to passionately and righteously pursue his glory. So what does loving God look like? It requires *all* of your heart, soul, and mind—in other words, your

entire being. Some of us Christians love God with *some* rather than with *all*, yet we want all of God. But you can't love God some and love the world some because these two are antithetical to one another (see 1 John 2:15). God will not share you with anyone. Your love for him must be comprehensive.

It's easy to say, "I love God," but words can be cheap. So remember, love for God is consistently expressed when you obey his commands (see John 14:15; 1 John 5:3). Align your decisions with his expectations.

22:39 Why does Jesus mention this particular command? Because you can't obey number one (22:37) without obeying number two. To love your neighbor is to make the decision to compassionately and righteously pursue his or her well-being. The two commands, then, are inseparable (see 1 John 4:20—5:2).

Do you want to draw closer to God? Help someone else draw closer to God. When you

love others, God will boomerang it back to you and provide you with a deeper experience of him.

22:40 All the Law and the Prophets depend on these two commands means all of God's commands are included in the first and second greatest commands. Fulfill these, through Christ, and you'll fulfill them all.

22:41-45 Inspired by the Spirit when he wrote Psalm 110:1 (Matt 22:43), David confessed that the Messiah would be more than **his son** (22:45). He would be divine. Though he would be fully human, a descendant of King David, he would also be fully God. The view of the Jewish leaders, though, was that the Messiah would be merely human—not divine. It was Jesus's claim of deity that would lead to his rejection and crucifixion (26:57-68).

23:4 The religious leaders were hypocrites. Instead of helping to relieve the burdens of others, they weighed them down with more burdens.

a 23:4 Lk 11:46; Ac 15:10; Gl 6:13
b 23:5 Ex 13:9; Dt 6:8; 11:18; Mt 6:1,5,16
c Mt 9:20; 14:36; Mk 6:56; Lk 8:44
d 23:6 Lk 11:43; 14:7; 20:46
e 23:7-8 Mk 9:5; 10:51; Jn 1:38,49; 11:8; Jms 3:1
f 23:9 Mal 1:6; Mt 6:9; 7:11
g 23:11 Mt 20:26-27; Mk 9:35; 3Jn 9
h 23:12 Pr 29:23; Ezk 21:26; Lk 14:11; 18:14; Jms 4:6,10; 1Pt 5:5-6
i 23:13 Mt 23:15,23,25; Lk 11:52
j 23:15 Ac 2:11; 6:5; 13:43
k 23:16 Mt 15:14; 23:24; Ac 1:16; Rm 2:19
l Lv 19:12; Nm 30:2; Dt 23:21; Mt 5:33; 14:7; 26:63,72

m 23:19 Ex 29:37; 30:29
n 23:21 1Kg 8:13; 2Ch 6:2; Ps 26:8; 132:14
o 23:22 Ex 17:16; Ps 11:4; Mt 5:34; Heb 8:1
p Ps 47:8; Mt 19:28; Rv 4:2
q 23:23 1Sm 15:22; Ps 33:5; Jr 5:1; Mc 6:8; Zch 7:9; Lk 11:42
r 23:24 Mt 15:14; 23:16
s 23:25 Mk 7:4; Lk 11:39
t 23:27 Lk 11:44; Ac 23:3

finger to move them.[a] [5] They do everything[A] to be seen by others: They enlarge their phylacteries[b] and lengthen their tassels.[B,C] [6] They love the place of honor at banquets, the front seats in the synagogues,[d] [7] greetings in the marketplaces, and to be called 'Rabbi' by people.

[8] "But you are not to be called 'Rabbi,' because you have one Teacher,[c] and you are all brothers and sisters.[e] [9] Do not call anyone on earth your father, because you have one Father, who is in heaven.[f] [10] You are not to be called instructors either, because you have one Instructor, the Messiah.[11] The greatest among you will be your servant.[g] [12] Whoever exalts himself will be humbled, and whoever humbles himself will be exalted.[h]

[13] "Woe to you, scribes and Pharisees, hypocrites! You shut the door of the kingdom of heaven in people's faces. For you don't go in, and you don't allow those entering to go in.[D,i]

[15] "Woe to you, scribes and Pharisees, hypocrites! You travel over land and sea to make one convert,[j] and when he becomes one, you make him twice as fit for hell[E] as you are!

[16] "Woe to you, blind guides,[k] who say, 'Whoever takes an oath by the temple, it means nothing. But whoever takes an oath[l] by the gold of the temple is bound by his oath.'[F] [17] Blind fools! For which is greater, the gold or the temple that sanctified the gold? [18] Also, 'Whoever takes an oath

by the altar, it means nothing; but whoever takes an oath by the gift that is on it is bound by his oath.' [19] Blind people![G] For which is greater, the gift or the altar that sanctifies the gift?[m] [20] Therefore, the one who takes an oath by the altar takes an oath by it and by everything on it. [21] The one who takes an oath by the temple takes an oath by it and by him who dwells[n] in it. [22] And the one who takes an oath by heaven takes an oath by God's throne[o] and by him who sits on it.[p]

[23] "Woe to you, scribes and Pharisees, hypocrites! You pay a tenth of[H] mint, dill, and cumin, and yet you have neglected the more important matters of the law — justice,[q] mercy, and faithfulness.[I] These things should have been done without neglecting the others. [24] Blind guides![r] You strain out a gnat, but gulp down a camel!

[25] "Woe to you, scribes and Pharisees, hypocrites! You clean the outside of the cup and dish, but inside they are full of greed[J] and self-indulgence.[s] [26] Blind Pharisee! First clean the inside of the cup,[k] so that the outside of it[L] may also become clean.

[27] "Woe to you, scribes and Pharisees, hypocrites! You are like whitewashed tombs,[t] which appear beautiful on the outside, but inside are full of the bones of the dead and every kind of impurity. [28] In the same way, on the outside you seem righteous to people, but inside you are full of hypocrisy and lawlessness.

[A] 23:5 Lit *do all their works*   [B] 23:5 Other mss add *on their robes*   [C] 23:8 Other mss add *the Christ*   [D] 23:13 Some mss include v. 14: *"Woe to you, scribes and Pharisees, hypocrites! You devour widows' houses and make long prayers just for show. This is why you will receive a harsher punishment.*   [E] 23:15 Lit *twice the son of gehenna*   [F] 23:16 Lit *is obligated*, also in v. 18   [G] 23:19 Other mss read *Fools and blind*   [H] 23:23 Or *You tithe*   [I] 23:23 Or *faith*   [J] 23:25 Or *full of violence*   [K] 23:26 Other mss add *and dish*   [L] 23:26 Other mss read *of them*

23:5 Phylacteries were small boxes containing copies of Scripture verses that were tied to the arm or the head and were worn as reminders to pray. **Tassels** were on the edges of prayer shawls. The Pharisees wore supersized versions of these items to impress people. They were like walking religious billboards, proclaiming to everyone, "Look how holy I am!" **23:6-7** It's not wrong to honor others. Paul said to give honor to whom honor is owed (Rom 13:7) and to "give recognition to those who labor among you . . . in the Lord" (1 Thess 5:12). But it's another thing altogether to love being honored and to seek it for yourself. The scribes and Pharisees thought too highly of themselves (see Rom 12:3). **23:8-10** We have different roles and job descriptions, but we're all equal in value before the Lord. No matter the position a brother in Christ holds, he's still your brother. **23:11-12** There is to be no elitism in the family of God, and the cure for elitism is servanthood (23:11). When was the last time you served someone—someone who couldn't

do anything for you in return? That's what Jesus did. The eternal Son of God became a servant to save those who couldn't save themselves (see Phil 2:5-8). As a result, God the Father exalted him (Phil 2:9-11). And that's what Jesus promises his disciples: **Whoever exalts himself will be humbled, and whoever humbles himself will be exalted** (Matt 23:12). **23:13** To say, **Woe to you, scribes and Pharisees** is to pronounce condemnation on them. These men had rejected **the kingdom of heaven** through Jesus Christ, and, as a result, they were preventing others from receiving him too. They were blocking the way of salvation. **23:15** By exhorting others to practice external religion without internal spirituality, they hindered them from true salvation and actually made them **fit for hell**. **23:16-22** Jesus explained how the Pharisees made false distinctions between different kinds of oaths. They considered some oaths binding and some not, but any oath made before God should be kept.

23:23-24 The **scribes and Pharisees** proudly paid **a tenth** of their possessions—even of tiny things like spices. However, while focusing on these minute details, they would neglect **the more important matters of the law—justice, mercy, and faithfulness** (23:23). They would major on the minors, and minor on the majors. Jesus's illustration is vivid: **You strain out a gnat, but gulp down a camel!** (23:24). **23:25** Be warned: when your chief concern is being seen and accepted by men, you'll concentrate on making a good outward impression while ignoring the corruption inside of you. **23:27-28 Whitewashed tombs** refers to the practice of painting tombs white so that they looked **beautiful**. On the inside, though, pretty tombs were still **full of . . . bones** (23:27). No matter how much you decorate the exterior of a grave, the interior still contains death. Similarly, the Pharisees seemed **righteous to people** on the outside, but on the inside they had wicked motives and desires (23:28).

²⁹ "Woe to you, scribes and Pharisees, hypocrites! You build the tombs of the prophets and decorate the graves of the righteous, ³⁰ and you say, 'If we had lived in the days of our ancestors, we wouldn't have taken part with them in shedding the prophets' blood.' ³¹ So you testify against yourselves that you are descendants of those who murdered the prophets. ³² Fill up, then, the measure of your ancestors' sins![a]

³³ "Snakes! Brood of vipers! How can you escape being condemned to hell?[A,b] ³⁴ This is why I am sending you prophets,[c] sages, and scribes. Some of them you will kill and crucify, and some of them you will flog in your synagogues[d] and pursue from town to town. ³⁵ So all the righteous blood shed on the earth will be charged to you,[B] from the blood of righteous Abel to the blood of Zechariah,[e] son of Berechiah, whom you murdered between the sanctuary and the altar.[f] ³⁶ Truly I tell you, all these things will come on this generation.[g]

JESUS'S LAMENTING OVER JERUSALEM

³⁷ "Jerusalem, Jerusalem,[h] who kills the prophets and stones those who are sent to her. How often I wanted to gather your children together, as a hen gathers her chicks[c] under her wings, but you were not willing![i] ³⁸ See, your house is left to you desolate.[j] ³⁹ For I tell you, you will not see me again until you say, 'Blessed is he who comes in the name of the Lord'!"[D,k]

DESTRUCTION OF THE TEMPLE PREDICTED

24 As Jesus left and was going out of the temple,[l] his disciples[m] came up and called his attention to its buildings. ² He replied to them, "Do you see all

these things? Truly I tell you, not one stone will be left here on another that will not be thrown down."

SIGNS OF THE END OF THE AGE

³ While he was sitting on the Mount of Olives, the disciples approached him privately and said, "Tell us, when will these things happen? And what is the sign of your coming and of the end of the age?"[n]

⁴ Jesus replied to them: "Watch out that no one deceives[o] you. ⁵ For many will come in my name, saying, 'I am the Messiah,' and they will deceive many.[p] ⁶ You are going to hear of wars and rumors of wars. See that you are not alarmed, because these things must take place, but the end is not yet. ⁷ For nation will rise up against nation, and kingdom against kingdom. There will be famines[E,q] and earthquakes in various places.[r] ⁸ All these events are the beginning of labor pains.[s]

PERSECUTIONS PREDICTED

⁹ "Then they will hand you over to be persecuted, and they will kill you. You will be hated by all nations because of my name.[t] ¹⁰ Then many will fall away, betray one another, and hate one another. ¹¹ Many false prophets[u] will rise up and deceive many. ¹² Because lawlessness[v] will multiply, the love of many will grow cold. ¹³ But the one who endures to the end will be saved. ¹⁴ This good news of the kingdom will be proclaimed in all the world[F] as a testimony to all nations,[w] and then the end will come.[x]

THE GREAT TRIBULATION

¹⁵ "So when you see **the abomination of desolation**,[G] spoken of by the prophet Daniel,[y] standing in the holy place"[z] (let the

---

Cross references (right margin):

[a] 23:31-32 Gn 15:16; Ac 7:51; 1Th 2:15-16
[b] 23:33 Mt 3:7; 5:22; 12:34
[c] 23:34 Ac 13:1; 1Co 12:28
[d] 2Ch 36:15-16; Mt 10:17; Ac 22:19
[e] 23:35 2Ch 24:21; Zch 1:1
[f] Gn 4:8; Heb 11:4; 1Jn 3:12; Rv 18:24
[g] 23:36 Mt 10:23; 16:28; 24:34
[h] 23:37-39 Lk 13:34-35
[i] 23:37 Dt 32:11-12; Ru 2:12; Mt 5:12
[j] 23:38 1Kg 9:7; Is 64:11; Jr 12:7; 22:5
[k] 23:39 Ps 118:26; Mt 21:9
[l] 24:1-51 Mk 13:1-37; Lk 21:5-36
[m] 24:1 Mt 9:10; Mk 10:10; Lk 6:1; Jn 6:3; 12:16

[n] 24:3 Mt 21:1; 24:27,37,39
[o] 24:4 Jr 29:8; Eph 5:6; Col 2:8; 2Th 2:3
[p] 24:5 Mt 1:17; Eph 5:2
[q] 24:7 Ac 11:28; Rv 6:8
[r] 2Ch 15:6; Is 19:2
[s] 24:8-20 Lk 21:12-24
[t] 24:9 Mt 10:17,22; Jn 16:2
[u] 24:11 Is 44:25; Mt 7:15; 24:24; Mk 13:22; Lk 6:26; Ac 13:6; 2Pt 2:1; 1Jn 4:1
[v] 24:12 Mt 13:41; 2Th 2:3
[w] 24:14 Mt 4:23; Rm 10:18; Col 1:6,23; 1Th 1:8
[x] Lk 2:1; 4:5; Ac 11:28; 17:6; Rv 3:10; 16:14
[y] 24:15 Dn 9:27; 11:31; 12:11; Mk 13:14; Lk 21:20
[z] Ac 6:13; 21:28

[A] 23:33 Lit *escape from the judgment of gehenna*   [B] 23:35 Lit *will come on you*   [C] 23:37 Or *as a mother bird gathers her young*   [D] 23:39 Ps 118:26
[E] 24:7 Other mss add *epidemics*   [F] 24:14 Or *in all the inhabited earth*   [G] 24:15 Dn 9:27

23:29-32 The **scribes and Pharisees** built **tombs of the prophets** and decorated **the graves of the righteous** (23:29), piously claiming that they wouldn't have joined with their forefathers who killed the Old Testament prophets (23:30). Yet, at the same time, they were rejecting the Messiah and planning to murder him! In truth, they were *just like* those who had gone before them (23:31).
23:35 Abel and **Zechariah** were martyred by unbelievers.
23:37 Jerusalem was the capital city of Israel and the home of God's temple. Though it ought to have been a holy city devoted to the Lord, those within the gates slew the servants of God **sent to her**. And unlike **chicks** that naturally run to a hen during times of danger, the religious leaders were not running to their Messiah.

23:39 Eventually the city and temple would be besieged and destroyed by the Romans. Nevertheless, Jesus will return to it one day to establish his millennial kingdom.
24:3 The disciples wanted to know the timing of the temple's destruction (see 24:1-2), which they connected to Jesus's return and **the end of the age**. While the Romans would overrun Jerusalem and decimate the temple in AD 70 under the Roman general Titus, the messianic age is yet future.
24:4-8 Here Jesus speaks of the first half of the seven-year tribulation period. The events of this time will be characterized by worldwide grief and agony (24:8). This will eventually lead to the birth of the messianic kingdom.
24:13 The one who endures to the end will be saved is not a reference to salvation but phys-

ical deliverance. Believers who endure to the end of the tribulation will be spared physical death and enter the millennium.
24:14 In spite of the horror on earth during the tribulation, the **good news of the kingdom will be proclaimed**. Many will be saved when they believe the good news of Jesus's coming kingdom rule.
24:15-20 A look at **Daniel** sheds light on this passage. (See the notes on Dan 9:24-27.) This **abomination** will be an image of the antichrist as he profanes the temple, sets himself up as God, and demands worship (Matt 24:15). Those who will not bow down to the antichrist will have to **flee**, leaving their property and possessions behind if they are to **escape** death (24:16-20; cf. Rev 13:15).

a 24:17 1Sm 9:25; Mt 10:27; Lk 5:19; 12:3; 17:31; Ac 10:9
b 24:21 Dn 12:1; Jl 2:2; Mt 24:29; Rv 7:14
c 24:22 Mt 22:14; 24:24,31; Mk 13:20,22,27; 1Tm 5:21; 2Tm 2:10; Rv 17:14
d 24:23 Lk 17:3; 21:28
e Mk 11:24; Jn 6:64
f 24:24 Dt 13:1-3; Mt 24:11; Ac 8:9; 2Th 2:9-11; Rv 13:13-14; 16:14; 19:20
g 24:27 Zch 9:14; Mt 8:20; 24:3,37,39; Lk 17:24
h 24:28 Jb 39:30; Lk 17:37
i 24:29 Is 13:10; 24:23; Ezk 32:7; Jl 2:10,31; 3:15; Zph 1:15; Rv 6:12-13
j 24:30 Dn 7:13; Zch 12:12; Mt 24:3; Rv 1:7
k 24:31 Is 27:13; 1Co 15:52; 1Th 4:16; Rv 8:2; 11:15
l Dn 7:2; Zch 2:6; Rv 7:1

m 24:32 Mt 13:3,34-36; 15:15; 21:33,45; 22:1
n 24:33 Jms 5:9; Rv 3:20
o 24:34 Mt 10:23; 16:28; 23:36
p 24:35 Ps 102:26; Is 51:6; Mt 5:18; Heb 12:27; 2Pt 3:10
q Ps 119:89; Is 40:8; Mk 13:31; Lk 21:33; 1Pt 1:23,25
r 24:36 Zch 14:7; Mt 25:13; Mk 13:32; Ac 1:7; 1Th 5:1-2
s 24:37-38 Gn 6:5; 7:6-23; Mt 22:30; Lk 17:26
t 24:41 Ex 11:5; Is 47:2; Lk 17:35
u 24:42 Mt 25:13; Lk 12:40; 21:36
v 24:43 Lk 12:39; 1Th 5:2; Rv 3:3
w 24:44 Mt 25:10; 1Th 5:6
x 24:45-51 Lk 12:42-46
y 24:45 Mt 7:24; 10:16; 25:2,21
z 24:46 Jn 13:17; Rv 16:15

reader understand), **16** "then those in Judea must flee to the mountains. **17** A man on the housetop[A] must not come down to get things out of his house,[a] **18** and a man in the field must not go back to get his coat. **19** Woe to pregnant women and nursing mothers in those days! **20** Pray that your escape may not be in winter or on a Sabbath. **21** For at that time there will be great distress,[B,b] the kind that hasn't taken place from the beginning of the world until now and never will again. **22** Unless those days were cut short, no one would[c] be saved. But those days will be cut short because of the elect.[c]

23 "If anyone tells you then, 'See, here is the Messiah!'[d] or, 'Over here!' do not believe it.[e] **24** For false messiahs and false prophets will arise and perform great signs and wonders to lead astray,[f] if possible, even the elect. **25** Take note: I have told you in advance. **26** So if they tell you, 'See, he's in the wilderness!' don't go out; or, 'See, he's in the storerooms!' do not believe it. **27** For as the lightning comes from the east and flashes as far as the west, so will be the coming of the Son of Man.[g] **28** Wherever the carcass is, there the vultures[D] will gather.[h]

THE COMING OF THE SON OF MAN

29 "Immediately after the distress[i] of those days, the sun will be darkened, and the moon will not shed its light; the stars will fall from the sky, and the powers of the heavens will be shaken. **30** Then the sign of the Son of Man will appear in the sky, and then all the peoples of the earth[E] will mourn;[F] and they will see the Son of Man coming on the clouds of heaven with power and great glory.[j] **31** He will send out his angels with a loud trumpet,[k] and they will gather his elect from the four winds,[l] from one end of the sky to the other.

THE PARABLE OF THE FIG TREE

32 "Learn this lesson[m] from the fig tree: As soon as its branch becomes tender and sprouts leaves, you know that summer is near. **33** In the same way, when you see all these things, recognize[G] that he[H] is near — at the door.[n] **34** Truly I tell you, this generation will certainly not pass away until all these things take place.[o] **35** Heaven and earth will pass away,[p] but my words will never pass away.[q]

NO ONE KNOWS THE DAY OR HOUR

36 "Now concerning that day and hour no one knows — neither the angels of heaven nor the Son[I] — except the Father alone.[r] **37** As the days of Noah were, so the coming of the Son of Man will be. **38** For in those days before the flood they were eating and drinking, marrying and giving in marriage, until the day Noah boarded the ark.[s] **39** They didn't know until the flood came and swept them all away. This is the way the coming of the Son of Man will be. **40** Then two men will be in the field; one will be taken and one left. **41** Two women will be grinding grain with a hand mill; one will be taken and one left.[t] **42** Therefore be alert, since you don't know what day[J] your Lord is coming.[u] **43** But know this: If the homeowner had known what time[K] the thief was coming, he would have stayed alert and not let his house be broken into.[v] **44** This is why you are also to be ready, because the Son of Man is coming at an hour you do not expect.[w]

FAITHFUL SERVICE TO CHRIST

45 "Who then is a faithful and wise servant,[x] whom his master has put in charge of his household, to give them food at the proper time?[y] **46** Blessed is that servant whom the master finds doing his job when he comes.[z] **47** Truly I tell you, he will put him

[A] 24:17 Or *roof* [B] 24:21 Or *tribulation,* also in v. 29 [C] 24:22 Lit *short, all flesh would not* [D] 24:28 Or *eagles* [E] 24:30 Or *all the tribes of the land* [F] 24:30 Lit *will beat*; that is, beat their chests [G] 24:33 Or *things, you know* [H] 24:33 Or *it*; that is, summer [I] 24:36 Other mss omit *nor the Son* [J] 24:42 Other mss read *hour*; = time [K] 24:43 Lit *watch*; a division of the night in ancient times

24:27 There will be no uncertainty when Christ returns. No one can miss a bolt of **lightning** when it **flashes**.
24:29 These spectacular signs are also predicted in the Old Testament (see Isa 13:10; 34:4; Joel 2:31).
24:30 The **peoples of the earth** who have not turned to Christ in repentance and faith **will mourn** when they **see the Son of Man coming** in **power and great glory.**
24:32-34 Following this revelation of the future to his disciples, Jesus applied the principles of the tribulation and his second coming. When a **fig tree . . . sprouts leaves,** any

Israelite knows that **summer** is on the horizon (24:32). It's an obvious sign that's not difficult to interpret. In the same way, when those living during the great tribulation witness the signs taking place (see 24:29-30), they can be certain that the Messiah is quickly returning (24:33). These are the people Jesus spoke of when he referred to **this generation** (24:34). They will see everything take place exactly as Jesus foretold.
24:42-44 **Be alert, since you don't know what day your Lord is coming** (24:42) is a reminder that Christians must always be watching— like a **homeowner** on alert for a **thief** to

break in—because the timing of the rapture is unknown (24:43-44). This is the event at which believers will be caught up in the air to be taken by Jesus to be with him (see the notes on 1 Thess 4:13-17). I believe Scripture teaches that the rapture will take place prior to the tribulation.
24:45-47 As believers waiting with anticipation for our Lord, we must be wise and trustworthy until he returns. When he does, Jesus will expect to find us busy serving him so he can reward us for faithfulness. Let us serve God with gladness and devotion, knowing his promises are certain.

in charge of all his possessions. **48** But if that wicked servant says in his heart, 'My master is delayed,' **49** and starts to beat his fellow servants, and eats and drinks with drunkards,[a] **50** that servant's master will come on a day he does not expect him and at an hour he does not know. **51** He will cut him to pieces and assign him a place with the hypocrites, where there will be weeping and gnashing of teeth.

THE PARABLE OF THE TEN VIRGINS

25 "At that time the kingdom of heaven will be like ten virgins[A] who took their lamps[B] and went out to meet the groom.[b] **2** Five of them were foolish and five were wise.[c] **3** When the foolish took their lamps, they didn't take oil with them; **4** but the wise ones took oil in their flasks with their lamps. **5** When the groom was delayed, they all became drowsy and fell asleep.

6 "In the middle of the night there was a shout: 'Here's the groom! Come out to meet him.'

7 "Then all the virgins got up and trimmed their lamps. **8** The foolish ones said to the wise ones, 'Give us some of your oil, because our lamps are going out.'

9 "The wise ones answered, 'No, there won't be enough for us and for you. Go instead to those who sell oil, and buy some for yourselves.'

10 "When they had gone to buy some, the groom arrived, and those who were ready went in with him to the wedding banquet,

and the door was shut.[d] **11** Later the rest of the virgins also came and said, 'Master, master, open up for us!'

12 "He replied, 'Truly I tell you, I don't know you!'

13 "Therefore be alert, because you don't know either the day or the hour.[c]

THE PARABLE OF THE TALENTS

14 "For it is just like a man about to go on a journey.[e] He called his own servants and entrusted his possessions to them. **15** To one he gave five talents,[D] to another two talents, and to another one talent, depending on each one's ability. Then he went on a journey.[f] Immediately **16** the man who had received five talents went, put them to work, and earned five more. **17** In the same way the man with two earned two more. **18** But the man who had received one talent went off, dug a hole in the ground, and hid his master's money.

19 "After a long time the master of those servants came and settled accounts with them. **20** The man who had received five talents approached, presented five more talents, and said, 'Master, you gave me five talents. See, I've earned five more talents.'

21 "His master said to him, 'Well done, good and faithful servant! You were faithful over a few things; I will put you in charge of many things. Share your master's joy.'[g]

22 "The man with two talents also approached. He said, 'Master, you gave me two talents. See, I've earned two more talents.'

[a] **24:49** Ac 2:15; 1Co 11:21; 1Th 5:7; Rv 17:6
[b] **25:1** Mt 13:24; Ac 20:8; Rv 4:5; 19:7; 21:2,9
[c] **25:2** Mt 7:24; 10:16; 24:45

[d] **25:10** Mt 22:2; Lk 13:25
[e] **25:14-30** Lk 19:12-27
[f] **25:15** Mt 18:24; Lk 19:13; Rm 12:6; 1Co 12:11; Eph 4:7
[g] **25:21** Mt 24:45,47; Lk 12:44; 22:28; Heb 12:2

[A] **25:1** Or *bridesmaids*   [B] **25:1** Or *torches*, also in vv. 3,4,7,8   [C] **25:13** Other mss add *in which the Son of Man is coming.*   [D] **25:15** A talent is worth about 6,000 denarii, or twenty years' wages for a laborer

---

25:1 As was the custom of the day for wedding ceremonies, **the groom** would go to the bride's home and take her to the marriage feast. A great procession would accompany them, and then all would enter into the feast. The **ten virgins** were bridesmaids waiting for the groom to arrive.

25:2-4 According to Jesus, **five of them were foolish and five were wise** (25:2). This was demonstrated by their preparation (or lack of it).

25:6-13 Jesus's parable is a description of Jewish believers during the great tribulation. The wise will be spiritually prepared so that when they see "the abomination of desolation" (24:15), they will be ready and sustained by the Lord until his kingdom reign begins. However, the foolish will make no such spiritual preparations. As a result, they won't enter into the blessedness of the kingdom and its rewards. Though the parable speaks of those alive during the tribulation, it serves as a warning to all. Don't wait until the last minute to be spiritually prepared, because then it will be too late.

25:14 This is a picture of what Jesus has done. Though he has gone away, he will return. In the meantime, he has given us **his possessions** to steward. Importantly, a steward is not an owner but one who manages the owner's possessions. The Bible makes clear that God owns "everything" (Pss 24:1; 50:10-12), and he expects us to protect and expand his possessions for the advancement of his kingdom in history.

If you're a Christian, God has given you three things to steward. First, until Jesus returns, you have *time*, the day-to-day context in which kingdom opportunities arise. Second, every believer has *talents* (abilities or skills) that are gifts from God to develop and use for his kingdom purposes. Third, you have *treasures* (financial resources). Your money isn't merely for your enjoyment but for kingdom advancement.

25:15-18 The Lord has distributed what we have to us based on his perfect will and knowledge of our capacities. The question is not what or how much you have. The ques-

tion is, what will you do with what you've been given?

25:19 After a long time the master . . . came and settled accounts with his servants. Similarly, one day all Christians will stand before God to give an account. Scripture calls this the "judgment seat of Christ" (2 Cor 5:10; cf. 1 Cor 3:12-15). Unbelievers will experience judgment too—the white throne judgment after the millennial kingdom (see Rev 20:11-15). But if you are a believer in Jesus Christ, your Lord is going to have a separate conversation with you about your stewardship of all that he put at your disposal. What will he say?

25:20-23 Notice that even though the one with five had more than the one with two, both received the same blessing: **Well done. . . . You were faithful over a few things; I will put you in charge of many things. Share your master's joy** (25:21, 23). The master gave to each according to his abilities; they were faithful with what they'd been given and were rewarded.

a 25:24 1Sm 25:3; 2Co 8:12
b 25:26 Pr 20:4; Mt 18:32;
　　Rm 12:11
c 25:29 Mt 13:12; Mk 4:25;
　　Lk 8:18; 19:26; Jn 15:2
d 25:30 Mt 8:12; 22:13;
　　Lk 13:28
e 25:31 Gn 16:7; Mt 5:34;
　　13:49; Lk 1:11; Ac 5:19;
　　Rv 14:6
f Mt 16:27; 19:28; 2Th 1:7;
　　Jd 14; Rv 1:7
g 25:32 Jl 3:12; Mt 24:14;
　　28:19; Rm 1:5; Gl 1:16
h Ezk 34:17,20; Mt 13:49
i 25:34 Mt 19:29; Lk 12:32;
　　1Co 15:50; Gl 5:21; Jms 2:5;
　　1Pt 3:9; Rv 21:7
j Mt 13:35; 20:23; 1Co 2:9;
　　Heb 4:3; 9:26; 11:16; Rv
　　13:8; 17:8

⇝ Questions & Answers ⇜

Q The third servant/steward in the parable of the talents explains his lack of investment on the misunderstanding that he served a "harsh" master (Matt 25:24–25). What are other misconceptions about God that can impact our ability to serve him well and steward our resources for his glory?

A One misconception about God is that he does not discipline us since we are saved by grace. But grace does not cancel out God's use of corrective measures with his people. We must not allow the biblical truths of God's love and grace to negate the biblical truth that Christians sometimes undergo divine chastisement. The author of Hebrews affirms this: "Endure suffering as discipline: God is dealing with you as sons. For what son is there that a father does not discipline?" (Heb 12:7).

Another misconception about God is that he is at our beck and call, that he is our divine Santa Claus, merely there to bless us. Yes, God does bless us. But many people want to be blessed without being a blessing to others. They want a one-sided relationship with God. But God does not exist simply to dole out goodies to us.

A final misconception that I'll mention is that religion is the same as relationship. Some assume that if they partake of religious activity, then they are in fellowship with God. However, what God wants is a personal relationship. Without a personal relationship, religion doesn't mean much to him.

FOR THE NEXT Q&A, SEE PAGE 1180.

23 "His master said to him, 'Well done, good and faithful servant! You were faithful over a few things; I will put you in charge of many things. Share your master's joy.'

24 "The man who had received one talent also approached and said, 'Master, I know you. You're a harsh man, reaping where you haven't sown and gathering where you haven't scattered seed.*a* **25** So I was afraid and went off and hid your talent in the ground. See, you have what is yours.'

26 "His master replied to him, 'You evil, lazy servant!*b* If you knew that I reap where I haven't sown and gather where I haven't scattered, **27** then^A you should have deposited my money with the bankers, and I would have received my money^B back with interest when I returned.

28 "'So take the talent from him and give it to the one who has ten talents. **29** For to everyone who has, more will be given, and he will have more than enough. But from the one who does not have, even what he has will be taken away from him.*c* **30** And throw this good-for-nothing servant into the outer darkness,*d* where there will be weeping and gnashing of teeth.'

THE SHEEP AND THE GOATS

31 "When the Son of Man comes in his glory, and all the angels^C,*e* with him, then he will sit on his glorious throne.*f* **32** All the nations^D,*g* will be gathered before him, and he will separate them one from another, just as a shepherd separates the sheep from the goats.*h* **33** He will put the sheep on his right and the goats on the left. **34** Then the King will say to those on his right, 'Come, you who are blessed by my Father; inherit the kingdom*i* prepared for you from the foundation of the world.*j*

35 "'For I was hungry and you gave me something to eat; I was thirsty and you gave me something to drink; I was a stranger and you took me in; **36** I was naked and you clothed me; I was sick and you

^A 25:26-27 Or *So you knew . . . scattered? Then* (as a question)　　^B 25:27 Lit *received what is mine*　　^C 25:31 Other mss read *holy angels*
^D 25:32 Or *the Gentiles*

25:24-27 While the first two servants were concerned with their master's affairs, this man was solely concerned with himself. He didn't want to be bothered with caring for his master's resources. Jesus is your King, and he expects you to live faithfully with a kingdom agenda. Live today with a future orientation, knowing that one day he will call you by name to settle accounts.
25:30 This text uses graphic language to speak not of eternal judgment (as some interpreters argue), but of the profound

regret that many believers will experience when they receive no rewards because of their unfaithfulness in stewarding God's resources. Those who were saved but whose earthly lives were useless to the King will lose out on full participation in and the benefits of Christ's millennial kingdom. Don't let this be you—making time for your personal priorities but giving no time for the kingdom.
25:31-40 This is a picture of Christ's second coming at the end of the great tribulation when he will judge the **nations** who will be

gathered before him. He will separate them— **the sheep from the goats** (25:32). The sheep will be **on his right**, the place of honor, and will be ushered into his millennial **kingdom** (25:34). The basis for their division from the goats will be the practical love and service they rendered during the tribulation to Jesus's **brothers and sisters**, the Jewish people, as an expression of their faith (25:35-40). Jesus will consider service rendered to his Jewish siblings as service rendered to him and as a demonstration of faith in him (25:40; see Joel 3:1-14).

took care of me; I was in prison and you visited me.'[a]

[37] "Then the righteous will answer him, 'Lord, when did we see you hungry and feed you, or thirsty and give you something to drink? [38] When did we see you a stranger and take you in, or without clothes and clothe you? [39] When did we see you sick, or in prison, and visit you?'

[40] "And the King will answer them, 'Truly I tell you, whatever you did for one of the least of these brothers and sisters of mine, you did for me.'[b]

[41] "Then he will also say to those on the left, 'Depart from me, you who are cursed, into the eternal fire prepared for the devil and his angels![c] [42] For I was hungry and you gave me nothing to eat; I was thirsty and you gave me nothing to drink; [43] I was a stranger and you didn't take me in; I was naked and you didn't clothe me, sick and in prison and you didn't take care of me.'

[44] "Then they too will answer, 'Lord, when did we see you hungry, or thirsty, or a stranger, or without clothes, or sick, or in prison, and not help you?'

[45] "Then he will answer them, 'Truly I tell you, whatever you did not do for one of the least of these, you did not do for me.'[d]

[46] "And they will go away into eternal punishment, but the righteous into eternal life."[e]

THE PLOT TO KILL JESUS

26 When Jesus had finished saying all these things,[f] he told his disciples, [2] "You know[A] that the Passover takes place after two days, and the Son of Man will be handed over to be crucified."[g]

[3] Then the chief priests[B] and the elders of the people assembled in the courtyard of the high priest, who was named Caiaphas,[h] [4] and they conspired to arrest Jesus in a treacherous way and kill him.[i] [5] "Not during the festival," they said, "so there won't be rioting among the people."

THE ANOINTING AT BETHANY

[6] While Jesus was in Bethany at the house of Simon[j] the leper,[c] [7] a woman approached him with an alabaster jar of very expensive perfume. She poured it on his head as he was reclining at the table. [8] When the disciples[k] saw it, they were indignant. "Why this waste?" they asked. [9] "This might have been sold for a great deal and given to the poor."

[10] Aware of this, Jesus said to them, "Why are you bothering this woman? She has done a noble thing for me. [11] You always have the poor with you, but you do not always have me.[l] [12] By pouring this perfume on my body, she has prepared me for burial. [13] Truly I tell you, wherever this gospel[m] is proclaimed in the whole world, what she has done will also be told in memory of her."

[14] Then[n] one of the Twelve, the man called Judas Iscariot, went to the chief priests[o] [15] and said, "What are you willing to give me if I hand him over to you?" So they weighed out thirty pieces of silver for him.[p] [16] And from that time he started looking for a good opportunity to betray him.

BETRAYAL AT THE PASSOVER

[17] On the first day of Unleavened Bread[q] the disciples came to Jesus and asked, "Where do you want us to make preparations for you to eat the Passover?"

[18] "Go into the city to a certain man," he said, "and tell him, 'The Teacher says: My time is near; I am celebrating the Passover at your place[D] with my disciples.'"[r] [19] So the disciples did as Jesus had directed them and prepared the Passover. [20] When evening came, he was reclining at the table with the Twelve. [21] While they were eating, he said, "Truly I tell you, one of you will betray me."[s]

[22] Deeply distressed, each one began to say to him, "Surely not I, Lord?"

[23] He replied, "The one who dipped his hand with me in the bowl — he will betray me. [24] The Son of Man will go just as

[a] 25:35-36 Jb 31:32; Is 58:7; Ezk 18:7; 2Tm 1:16; Heb 13:2; Jms 1:27; 2:15-16
[b] 25:40 Pr 19:17; Mt 10:42; 25:34; Heb 6:10
[c] 25:41 Mt 7:23; 13:40,42; Mk 9:48; 2Pt 2:4; Jd 6-7
[d] 25:45 Pr 14:31; 17:5; Ac 9:5
[e] 25:46 Dn 12:2; Jn 5:21; Ac 24:15; Rm 2:7
26:1-5 Mk 14:1-2; Lk 22:1-2; Jn 11:47-53
[g] 26:2 Jn 11:55; 13:1
[f] 26:3 Ps 2:2; Mt 26:57; Lk 3:2; Jn 11:47; 18:13,15; Ac 4:6
[i] 26:4 Mt 21:46; Jn 11:53

[j] 26:6-13 Mk 14:3-9; Jn 12:1-8
[k] 26:8 Mt 10:1; 26:56; Mk 3:7; 16:20; Lk 6:13; Jn 12:16
[l] 26:11 Dt 15:11; Jn 12:8
[m] 26:13 Mt 24:14; Mk 1:1; 13:10
[n] 26:14-16 Mk 14:10-11; Lk 22:3-6
[o] 26:14 Mt 10:4; Jn 6:71; 12:4; 13:30; Ac 1:16
[p] 26:15 Ex 21:32; Zch 11:12-13; Mt 27:3
[q] 26:17-19 Mk 14:12-16; Lk 22:7-13
[r] 26:18 Jn 7:6,8; 8:20; 13:1; 17:1
[s] 26:21-24 Mk 14:17-21; Lk 22:21-23; Jn 13:21-26

26:1-4 Jesus's enemies hatched their plot in secret, thinking they were in control. But clearly their actions were no surprise to Jesus. Everything was part of God the Father's plan to save sinners.
26:6 **Bethany** was less than two miles southeast of Jerusalem on the road to Jericho.
26:7 John 12:3 identifies this woman as "Mary," the sister of Lazarus.
26:8-9 John tells us in his Gospel that it was primarily Judas who was angry. Actually, he

cared nothing for **the poor** (26:9) but would steal from "the money-bag" (see John 12:4-6). 26:10-11 Jesus came to the woman's defense and called her actions **noble** (26:10). Though believers are called to minister to and care for **the poor**, our allegiance to and worship of Jesus Christ has primacy (26:11). 26:13 Since this story is in our Bibles, clearly his words have been fulfilled. 26:17 **Passover** commemorates God's deliverance of the Israelites from slavery in Egypt

(see Exod 12). The Lord's final plague on the Egyptians claimed the life of every Egyptian firstborn male, while the Israelites were spared by sacrificing a lamb and smearing its blood on their doorposts so that the Lord would pass over them. Jesus Christ is "our Passover lamb" (1 Cor 5:7). 26:18 Jesus said **My time is near**. In the days leading up to this, he had predicted that he would suffer and be killed in Jerusalem (16:21; 17:22-23; 20:17-19; 26:1-2).

a26:24 Dn 9:26; Mk 9:12; Lk 24:25-27; Ac 17:2-3; 26:22-23; 1Co 15:3; 1Pt 1:10
b26:25 Lk 22:70; Jn 1:38
c26:26-29 Mk 14:22-25; Lk 22:17-20; 1Co 11:23-25
d26:26 Mk 10:1; 26:56; Mk 3:7; 16:20; Lk 6:13; Jn 12:16
e Mt 14:19; 1Co 10:16
f26:28 Ex 24:8; Mt 20:28; Mk 1:4; Heb 9:20
g26:29 Mt 4:23; Mk 1:15; Ac 20:25
h26:30 Mt 21:1; Lk 22:39; Jn 18:1
i26:31 Zch 13:7; Mt 11:6; Jn 16:32
j26:32 Mt 28:7,10,16; Mk 16:7
k26:34 Mt 26:75; Lk 22:34; Jn 13:38
l26:36-46 Mk 14:32-42; Lk 22:40-46

m26:37 Mt 4:21; 17:1
n26:38 Ps 42:5-6; Mt 24:42; Jn 12:27
o26:39 Mt 20:22; Jn 5:30; 6:38; Php 2:8; Heb 5:7
p26:42 Mt 26:39; Mk 14:36; Lk 22:42; Jn 6:38
q26:45 Jn 12:27; 13:1
r26:47-56 Mk 14:43-50; Lk 22:47-53; Jn 18:3-11
s26:50 Mt 20:13; 22:12

it is written about him,[a] but woe to that man by whom the Son of Man is betrayed! It would have been better for him if he had not been born."

[25] Judas, his betrayer, replied, "Surely not I, Rabbi?"[b]

"You have said it," he told him.

THE FIRST LORD'S SUPPER

[26] As they were eating,[c] Jesus took bread, blessed and broke it, gave it to the disciples,[d] and said, "Take and eat it; this is my body."[e] [27] Then he took a cup, and after giving thanks, he gave it to them and said, "Drink from it, all of you. [28] For this is my blood of the covenant,[A] which is poured out for many for the forgiveness of sins.[f] [29] But I tell you, I will not drink from this fruit of the vine from now on until that day when I drink it new with you in my Father's kingdom."[g] [30] After singing a hymn, they went out to the Mount of Olives.[h]

PETER'S DENIAL PREDICTED

[31] Then Jesus said to them, "Tonight all of you will fall away because of me, for it is written:

**I will strike the shepherd,
and the sheep of the flock
will be scattered.**[B,i]

[32] But after I have risen, I will go ahead of you to Galilee."[j]

[33] Peter told him, "Even if everyone falls away because of you, I will never fall away."

[34] "Truly I tell you," Jesus said to him, "tonight, before the rooster crows, you will deny me three times."[k]

[35] "Even if I have to die with you," Peter told him, "I will never deny you," and all the disciples said the same thing.

THE PRAYER IN THE GARDEN

[36] Then Jesus came with them to a place called Gethsemane,[l] and he told the

disciples, "Sit here while I go over there and pray." [37] Taking along Peter and the two sons of Zebedee, he began to be sorrowful and troubled.[m] [38] He said to them, "I am deeply grieved[c] to the point of death. Remain here and stay awake with me."[n] [39] Going a little farther,[o] he fell facedown and prayed, "My Father, if it is possible, let this cup pass from me. Yet not as I will, but as you will."[o]

[40] Then he came to the disciples and found them sleeping. He asked Peter, "So, couldn't you stay awake with me one hour? [41] Stay awake and pray, so that you won't enter into temptation. The spirit is willing, but the flesh is weak."

[42] Again, a second time, he went away and prayed, "My Father, if this[E] cannot pass[F] unless I drink it, your will be done."[p] [43] And he came again and found them sleeping, because they could not keep their eyes open.

[44] After leaving them, he went away again and prayed a third time, saying the same thing once more. [45] Then he came to the disciples and said to them, "Are you still sleeping and resting? See, the time is near. The Son of Man is betrayed into the hands of sinners.[q] [46] Get up; let's go. See, my betrayer is near."

JUDAS'S BETRAYAL OF JESUS

[47] While he was still speaking, Judas, one of the Twelve, suddenly arrived.[r] A large mob with swords and clubs was with him from the chief priests and elders of the people. [48] His betrayer had given them a sign: "The one I kiss, he's the one; arrest him." [49] So immediately he went up to Jesus and said, "Greetings, Rabbi!" and kissed him.

[50] "Friend,"[s] Jesus asked him, "why have you come?"[G]

Then they came up, took hold of Jesus, and arrested him. [51] At that moment one of those with Jesus reached out his hand and

---

A26:28 Other mss read *new covenant*   B26:31 Zch 13:7   C26:38 Lit *"My soul is swallowed up in sorrow*   D26:39 Other mss read *Drawing nearer*
E26:42 Other mss add *cup*   F26:42 Other mss add *from me*   G26:50 Or *Jesus told him, "do what you have come for."*

26:25 **Judas** had already agreed to hand over Jesus to the religious leaders (see 26:14-16); nevertheless, he deceptively played along with the others who were saying in shock, "Surely not I" (26:22). Jesus not only knew he would be betrayed, but he knew his betrayer. 26:26-28 Jesus instituted what would become an ordinance of the church: Communion, or the Lord's Supper (see 1 Cor 11:23-26). The **bread** represents his **body** (Matt 26:26) and the **cup** represents his blood, which was about to be **poured out for many for the forgiveness of sins** (26:27-28). The church is to commemorate the work and spiritual presence of the true Passover

Lamb by remembering him and proclaiming him through Communion (see 1 Cor 5:7; 11:26). 26:33-35 Peter didn't believe such a thing could happen (26:33, 35), but he clearly didn't know himself very well. Jesus, in his omniscience, saw where the dangerous pride of Peter would lead (26:34). "Pride comes before destruction, and an arrogant spirit before a fall" (Prov 16:18). 26:36 **Gethsemane** is a garden at the foot of the Mount of Olives. Since the first Adam's fall occurred in a garden (see Gen 2–3), the last Adam entered into a garden to bring fallen man back into God's garden of fellowship through his substitutionary atonement. Since

the first Adam brought sin into the world by means of a tree, the last Adam would be crucified on a tree to bring salvation (see Rom 5:15-19; 1 Cor 15:21-22, 45). 26:38-39 Jesus was in anguish as he considered the wrath of God that would be poured out on him as he bore the sins of the world on the cross (26:38). Though in his humanity, he preferred that the **cup** of suffering might **pass**, he voluntarily submitted himself to his Father's **will** (26:39). "For the joy that lay before him" he was willing to endure the cross (Heb 12:2). 26:51-54 We learn in John 18:10 that it was Peter who jumped into action like a vigilante.

drew his sword. He struck the high priest's servant and cut off his ear.[a]

52 Then Jesus told him, "Put your sword back in its place because all who take up the sword will perish by the sword.[b] **53** Or do you think that I cannot call on my Father, and he will provide me here and now with more than twelve legions of angels?[c] **54** How, then, would the Scriptures be fulfilled[d] that say it must happen this way?"

55 At that time Jesus said to the crowds, "Have you come out with swords and clubs, as if I were a criminal,[A] to capture me? Every day I used to sit, teaching in the temple, and you didn't arrest me.[e] **56** But all this has happened so that the writings of the prophets[f] would be fulfilled." Then all the disciples[g] deserted him and ran away.

JESUS FACES THE SANHEDRIN

57 Those[h] who had arrested Jesus led him away to Caiaphas[i] the high priest, where the scribes and the elders had convened. **58** Peter was following him at a distance right to the high priest's courtyard. He went in and was sitting with the servants to see the outcome.[j]

59 The chief priests and the whole Sanhedrin were looking for false testimony against Jesus so that they could put him to death,[k] **60** but they could not find any, even though many false witnesses[l] came forward.[B] Finally, two[C] who came forward **61** stated, "This man said, 'I can destroy the temple of God[m] and rebuild it in three days.'"

62 The high priest stood up and said to him, "Don't you have an answer to what these men are testifying against you?" **63** But[n] Jesus kept silent.[o] The high priest said to him, "I charge you under oath[p] by the living God: Tell us if you are the Messiah, the Son of God."[q]

64 "You have said it," Jesus told him. "But I tell you, in the future[D] you will see **the Son of Man seated at the right hand** of Power and **coming on the clouds of heaven."**[E,r]

65 Then the high priest tore his robes and said, "He has blasphemed![s] Why do we still need witnesses? See, now you've heard the blasphemy.[t] **66** What is your decision?"

They answered, "He deserves death!"[u] **67** Then they spat in his face[v] and beat him; others slapped him **68** and said, "Prophesy to us, Messiah! Who was it that hit you?"[w]

PETER DENIES HIS LORD

69 Now Peter was sitting outside in the courtyard.[x] A servant girl approached him and said, "You were with Jesus the Galilean too."

70 But he denied it in front of everyone: "I don't know what you're talking about." **71** When he had gone out to the gateway, another woman saw him and told those who were there, "This man was with Jesus the Nazarene!"[y]

72 And again he denied it with an oath:[z] "I don't know the man!"

73 After a little while those standing there approached and said to Peter, "You really are one of them, since even your accent[F] gives you away."

74 Then he started to curse and to swear with an oath, "I don't know the man!" Immediately a rooster crowed, **75** and Peter remembered the words Jesus had spoken, "Before the rooster crows, you will deny me three times."[aa] And he went outside and wept bitterly.

JESUS HANDED OVER TO PILATE

27 When daybreak came, all the chief priests and the elders of the people plotted against Jesus to put him to death.[ab] **2** After tying him up, they led him away and handed him over to Pilate,[G] the governor.[ac]

JUDAS HANGS HIMSELF

3 Then Judas, his betrayer, seeing that Jesus had been condemned, was full of remorse

[a] 26:51 Lk 22:38; Jn 18:10
[b] 26:52 Gn 9:6; Rv 13:10
[c] 26:53 2Kg 6:17; Dn 7:10; Mt 4:11; Lk 8:30
[d] 26:54 Mt 1:22; 26:24
[e] 26:55 Mk 12:35; Lk 21:37; Jn 7:19; 8:2; 18:20
[f] 26:56 Mt 26:54; Rm 1:2; 2Pt 1:20
[g] Mt 10:1; 26:56; Mk 3:7; 16:20; Lk 6:13; Jn 12:16
[h] 26:57-68 Mk 14:53-65; Jn 18:12-13,19-24
[i] 26:57 Mt 26:3; Jn 11:49
[j] 26:58 Jn 7:32; 18:15
[k] 26:59 Mt 5:22; Ac 6:11
[l] 26:60 Dt 19:15; Ps 27:12; 35:11; Ac 6:13
[m] 26:61 Mt 27:40; Jn 2:19; Ac 6:14
[n] 26:63-66 Lk 22:67-71
[o] 26:63 Is 53:7; Mt 27:12,14; Jn 19:9
[p] Lv 19:12; Nm 30:2; Dt 23:21; Mt 5:33; 14:7; 23:16
[q] Lv 5:1; 1Sm 14:24,26; Mt 16:16

[r] 26:64 Ps 110:1; Dn 7:13; Mt 16:27; 24:30; Rv 1:7
[s] 26:65 Mk 3:29; Jn 10:33
[t] Nm 14:6; Mk 14:63; Ac 14:14
[u] 26:66 Lv 24:16; Jn 19:7
[v] 26:67 Mt 27:30; Mk 10:34; Lk 22:63-65; Jn 18:22
[w] 26:68 Mk 14:65; Lk 22:64
[x] 26:69-75 Mk 14:66-72; Lk 22:55-62; Jn 18:16-18,25-27
[y] 26:71 Mk 14:67; Ac 6:14
[z] 26:72 Lv 19:12; Nm 30:2; Dt 23:21; Mt 5:33; 14:7; 23:16
[aa] 26:75 Mt 26:34; Jn 13:38; Ac 3:13-14
[ab] 27:1 Mk 15:1; Lk 22:66; Jn 18:28
[ac] 27:2 Mt 20:19; Lk 13:1; Ac 3:13; 1Tm 6:13

[A] 26:55 Lit *as against a criminal* [B] 26:60 Other mss add *they found none* [C] 26:60 Other mss add *false witnesses* [D] 26:64 Lit *you, from now*
[E] 26:64 Ps 110:1; Dn 7:13 [F] 26:73 Or *speech* [G] 27:2 Other mss read *Pontius Pilate*

But Jesus corrected him for taking matters into his own hands. If it had been part of God's plan, Jesus could have summoned **twelve legions of angels** to deliver him (Matt 26:53). But these awful events had to happen (26:54).
26:64 The **Son of Man** on the **clouds of heaven** is a reference to the glorious heavenly King of Daniel 7:13-14, whose kingdom would have no end. Being **seated at the right hand of Power** was a reference to the Messiah taken from Psalm 110:1. Jesus had earlier used the passage to argue that the Messiah was a divine King (see Matt 22:41-46).

26:65 In Leviticus 21:10, **the high priest** is forbidden to tear **his robes**.
26:67-68 The Son of God submitted obediently to his Father's will for an important reason: he was winning your salvation. "Consider him who endured such hostility from sinners against himself, so that you won't grow weary and give up" (Heb 12:3).
26:69-75 Though Peter had boasted of his willingness to die for Jesus (see 26:35), God mercifully revealed to him the true condition of his heart. And Peter responded with tears of repentance.

27:2 Pontius **Pilate** was the Roman **governor** of Judea from AD 26–36. He was a brutal man with no love for the Jews. His residence was in Caesarea Maritima on the Mediterranean Sea. But given the Jewish crowds and potential for unrest, he was in Jerusalem during the Passover. Since Pilate had the power of execution, the Jewish leaders sought to convince him to put Jesus to death.
27:3-4 Though **Judas** felt the sting of guilt for his actions, he didn't turn to God in repentance like Peter had (see John 21:15-17). Repentance includes sorrow, but it's more than just sorrow.

*a*27:3 Mt 21:29; 26:14-15
*b*27:5 2Sm 17:23; Lk
1:19,21; Ac 1:18
*c*27:6 Mk 2:24; Jn 18:31
*d*27:9-10 Jr 32:6-9; Zch
11:12-13; Mt 1:22
*e*27:11-14 Mk 15:2-5; Lk
23:2-3; Jn 18:29-38
*f*27:11 Mt 2:2; 1Tm 6:13
*g*27:12 Mt 26:63; Jn 19:9
*h*27:14 Mk 15:5; Lk 23:9
*i*27:15-26 Mk 15:6-15; Lk
23:16-25; Jn 18:39-40;
19:16
*j*27:17 Mt 1:16; 27:22

*k*27:19 Gn 20:6; Nm
12:6; Jb 33:14-16; Mt 2:12;
Jn 19:13
*l*27:22 Mt 1:16; Ac 13:28
*m*27:23 Lk 23:41; Jn 8:46
*n*27:24 Dt 21:6-8; Ps 26:6;
Mt 26:5; 27:4,19
*o*27:25 Jos 2:19; Ac 5:28
*p*27:26 Is 53:5; Mk 15:15;
Lk 23:16; Jn 19:1
*q*27:27-31 Mk 15:16-20;
Jn 19:2-3
*r*27:27 Jn 18:28,33; 19:9;
Ac 10:1
*s*27:28 Lk 23:11; Jn 19:2
*t*27:30-31 Is 53:7; Mt 26:67

and returned the thirty pieces of silver to the chief priests and elders.*a* 4 "I have sinned by betraying innocent blood," he said.

"What's that to us?" they said. "See to it yourself!" 5 So he threw the silver into the temple*b* and departed. Then he went and hanged himself.

6 The chief priests took the silver and said, "It's not permitted*c* to put it into the temple treasury, since it is blood money." 7 They conferred together and bought the potter's field with it as a burial place for foreigners. 8 Therefore that field has been called "Blood Field" to this day. 9 Then what was spoken through the prophet Jeremiah was fulfilled: **They took**^A **the thirty pieces of silver, the price of him whose price was set by the Israelites, 10 and they gave**^B **them for the potter's field, as the Lord directed me.**^C,*d*

JESUS FACES THE GOVERNOR

11 Now Jesus stood before the governor.*e* "Are you the King of the Jews?" the governor asked him.

Jesus answered, "You say so."*f* 12 While he was being accused by the chief priests and elders, he didn't answer.*g*

13 Then Pilate said to him, "Don't you hear how much they are testifying against you?" 14 But he didn't answer him on even one charge, so that the governor was quite amazed.*h*

JESUS OR BARABBAS

15 At the festival*i* the governor's custom was to release to the crowd a prisoner they wanted. 16 At that time they had a notorious prisoner called Barabbas.^D 17 So when they had gathered together, Pilate said to them, "Who is it you want me to release for you — Barabbas, or Jesus who is called Christ?"*j* 18 For he knew it was because of envy that they had handed him over.

19 While he was sitting on the judge's bench, his wife sent word to him, "Have

nothing to do with that righteous man, for today I've suffered terribly in a dream because of him."*k*

20 The chief priests and the elders, however, persuaded the crowds to ask for Barabbas and to execute Jesus. 21 The governor asked them, "Which of the two do you want me to release for you?"

"Barabbas!" they answered.

22 Pilate asked them, "What should I do then with Jesus, who is called Christ?"

They all answered, "Crucify him!"*l*

23 Then he said, "Why? What has he done wrong?"

But they kept shouting all the more, "Crucify him!"*m*

24 When Pilate saw that he was getting nowhere, but that a riot was starting instead, he took some water, washed his hands in front of the crowd, and said, "I am innocent of this man's blood.^E See to it yourselves!"*n*

25 All the people answered, "His blood be on us*o* and on our children!" 26 Then he released Barabbas to them and, after having Jesus flogged, handed him over to be crucified.*p*

MOCKED BY THE MILITARY

27 Then*q* the governor's soldiers took Jesus into the governor's residence and gathered the whole company^F around him.*r* 28 They stripped him and dressed him in a scarlet robe.*s* 29 They twisted together a crown of thorns, put it on his head, and placed a staff in his right hand. And they knelt down before him and mocked him: "Hail, King of the Jews!" 30 Then they spat on him, took the staff, and kept hitting him on the head. 31 After they had mocked him, they stripped him of the robe, put his own clothes on him, and led him away to crucify him.*t*

CRUCIFIED BETWEEN TWO CRIMINALS

32 As they were going out, they found a Cyrenian man named Simon. They forced

---

^A27:9 Or *I took*   ^B27:10 Some mss read *I gave*   ^C27:9-10 Jr 32:6-9; Zch 11:12-13   ^D27:16 Other mss read *Jesus Barabbas*, also in v. 17
^E27:24 Other mss read *this righteous man's blood*   ^F27:27 Lit *cohort*

Repentance involves a change of mind— turning from sin and toward the God you have offended.

27:5 Guilt is a powerful motivator, and the only true remedy for your guilt before God is the cross of Christ.

27:16-17 Barabbas was a rebel and a murderer according to Luke 23:19.

27:24 Pilate **washed his hands in front of the crowd** to symbolize that he had nothing to do with Jesus's condemnation and was **innocent** of his **blood.** Some people today try to follow

a similar course. They attempt to withhold judgment about Jesus, thinking they can take a middle road. But Jesus said, "Anyone who is not with me is against me" (12:30). There is no neutral choice regarding the Messiah. There are only two eternal destinies, and each is based on acceptance or rejection of Jesus Christ.

27:26 Flogging involved the use of a whip of leather strips with bits of bone or metal tied to their ends. A cruel beating with this weapon would rip the skin from the victim's

back, exposing tissue and bones. Flogging alone could result in death.

27:27-31 Little did they know as they viciously beat and spit on him that every human being (including them!) will bow one day before this God-Man and confess, "Jesus Christ is Lord" (Phil 2:10-11). Through all of their brutality, the prophecy of Isaiah 50:6 was fulfilled.

27:32 The Romans typically made crucifixion victims carry their crosses to the execution site. But in this case, the soldiers forced a man **named Simon** to **carry** Jesus's **cross** (probably

him to carry his cross.[a] [33] When they came to a place called *Golgotha*[b] (which means Place of the Skull), [34] they gave him wine[A] mixed with gall to drink. But when he tasted it, he refused to drink it. [35] After crucifying him, they divided his clothes by casting lots.[B,C] [36] Then they sat down and were guarding him there. [37] Above his head they put up the charge against him in writing: THIS IS JESUS, THE KING OF THE JEWS.

[38] Then two criminals[c] were crucified with him, one on the right and one on the left.[d] [39] Those who passed by were yelling insults at[D] him, shaking their heads[e] [40] and saying, "You who would destroy the temple and rebuild it in three days, save yourself! If you are the Son of God, come down from the cross!"[f] [41] In the same way the chief priests, with the scribes and elders,[E] mocked him and said, [42] "He saved others, but he cannot save himself! He is the King of Israel![g] Let him[f] come down now from the cross, and we will believe in him. [43] He trusts in God; let God rescue him now — if he takes pleasure in him![G] For he said, 'I am the Son of God.'" [44] In the same way even the criminals who were crucified with him taunted him.[h]

THE DEATH OF JESUS

[45] From noon until three in the afternoon[H] darkness came over the whole land.[I,J] [46] About three in the afternoon Jesus cried out with a loud voice, "*Elí, Elí, lemá sabachtháni?*" that is, "**My God, my God, why have you abandoned me?**"[K,J]

[47] When some of those standing there heard this, they said, "He's calling for Elijah." [48] Immediately one of them ran and got a sponge, filled it with sour wine, put it on a stick, and offered him a drink.[k] [49] But the rest said, "Let's see if Elijah comes to save him."

[50] But Jesus cried out again with a loud voice and gave up his spirit.[l] [51] Suddenly, the curtain of the sanctuary[m] was torn in two from top to bottom, the earth quaked, and the rocks were split. [52] The tombs were also opened[n] and many bodies of the saints who had fallen asleep were raised. [53] And they came out of the tombs after his resurrection, entered the holy city, and appeared to many.

[54] When the centurion and those with him, who were keeping watch over Jesus, saw the earthquake and the things that had happened, they were terrified and said, "Truly this man was the Son of God!"[o]

[55] Many women who had followed Jesus from Galilee and looked after him were there, watching from a distance.[p] [56] Among them were Mary Magdalene, Mary the mother of James and Joseph, and the mother of Zebedee's sons.[q]

THE BURIAL OF JESUS

[57] When it was evening,[r] a rich man from Arimathea named Joseph came, who himself had also become a disciple[s] of Jesus. [58] He approached Pilate and asked for Jesus's body. Then Pilate ordered that it[L] be released. [59] So Joseph took the body, wrapped it in clean, fine linen, [60] and placed

[a] 27:32 Nm 15:35; Mk 15:21; Lk 23:26; Heb 13:12
[b] 27:33–44 Mk 15:22–32; Lk 23:33–43; Jn 19:17–24
[c] 27:34–35 Ps 22:17; 69:21
[d] 27:38 Is 53:12; Mt 20:21; Jn 18:40
[e] 27:39 Jb 16:4; Ps 22:7; 109:25; Lm 2:15; Mk 15:29
[f] 27:40 Mt 4:3,6; 26:61,63; Jn 2:19
[g] 27:42 Jn 1:49; 12:13
[h] 27:43–44 Ps 22:8; Lk 23:39–43
[i] 27:45–46 Mk 15:33–41; Lk 23:44–49; Jn 19:28–30
[j] 27:46 Ps 22:1; Heb 5:7

[k] 27:48 Ps 69:21; Mk 15:36; Lk 23:36; Jn 19:29
[l] 27:50 Mk 15:37; Lk 23:46; Jn 10:18; 19:30
[m] 27:51 Ex 26:31–33; 2Ch 3:14; Heb 9:3
[n] 27:52 Ezk 37:12
[o] 27:54 Jn 5:19; Heb 1:2
[p] 27:55 Ps 38:11; Lk 8:2-3; Jn 19:25
[q] 27:56 Mt 20:20; Mk 15:40; Jn 19:25
[r] 27:57–61 Mk 15:42–47; Lk 23:50–56; Jn 19:38–42
[s] 27:57 Mt 10:42; 28:19; Lk 14:26; Jn 8:31; 13:35; 15:8; Ac 6:1

[A] 27:34 Other mss read *sour wine* [B] 27:35 Other mss add *that what was spoken by the prophet might be fulfilled: "They divided my clothes among them, and for my clothing they cast lots."* [C] 27:38 Or *revolutionaries* [D] 27:39 Lit *passed by blasphemed*, or *were blaspheming* [E] 27:41 Other mss add *and Pharisees* [F] 27:42 Other mss read *If he ... Israel, let him* [G] 27:43 Or *if he wants him* [H] 27:45 Lit *From the sixth hour to the ninth hour* [I] 27:45 Or *whole earth* [J] 27:46 Some mss read *lama*; other mss read *lima* [K] 27:46 Ps 22:1 [L] 27:58 Other mss read *that the body*

its crossbeam), because he was so weakened by the flogging. Interestingly, as a **Cyrenian**, Simon was of African descent: Cyrene was in North Africa.

27:33 In Latin, this place is called Calvary.

27:34 This drink would help deaden the pain of crucifixion, but Jesus was resolved to endure the suffering.

27:35 Crucifixion was an extremely cruel form of execution. Victims were typically naked and either tied or nailed to their crosses. Their torture could last for days before death claimed them. While many criminals were crucified at the hands of the Romans, only Jesus was innocent and "pierced because of our rebellion" (Isa 53:5) so he might atone for the sins of the world.

27:37 On Christ's cross was a sign with this accusation: THIS IS JESUS, THE KING OF THE JEWS. In an ironic sense, this is the full revelation of the theme that Matthew has pursued

throughout his Gospel: on the cross Jesus was named King.

27:42-43 Because of his deity, Jesus could have done what the hecklers suggested (27:42), but his mission would have failed if he did. So while they ridiculed his trust in God and his claim that he was **the Son of God** (27:43), Jesus Christ steadfastly hung on that cross in obedience to his Father for our salvation.

27:46 Jesus's words here are both a quote and fulfillment of Psalm 22:1. Though he had previously known only unbroken divine fellowship from all eternity, Jesus experienced the horrible abandonment of his Father as God poured out his wrath on his Son as he bore the sins of the world.

27:51 This refers to the **curtain** separating the holy place from the most holy place (see Exod 26:33). Since the curtain was torn **from top to bottom**, clearly God did the tearing. In an

instant, full access to God's holy presence, through Jesus Christ, was granted. No further sacrifices were necessary. Truly, as Jesus declared, "It is finished" (John 19:30).

27:53 This was a small foretaste of the future resurrection that will take place when Christ resurrects the bodies of *all* deceased believers to live forevermore (see 1 Cor 15:20-23; 1 Thess 4:16).

27:54 Though the Jewish religious leaders had rejected him, these Gentiles believed Jesus was exactly who he'd claimed to be.

27:57-58 This **Joseph** was a prominent member of the Sanhedrin who had objected to their denunciation of Jesus (see Mark 15:43; Luke 23:50-51). Having **become a disciple**, he wanted to honor his Lord with a proper burial.

27:59-60 This wealthy man's actions fulfilled Isaiah 53:9.

a 27:60 Is 53:9; Mt 27:66;
    28:2; Mk 16:4
b 27:62 Mk 15:42; Lk 23:54;
    Jn 19:14,31,42
c 27:63 Mt 16:21; 17:22-23;
    20:19; Mk 8:31; 10:34; Lk
    9:22; 18:33
d 27:64 Mt 10:1; 26:56; Mk
    3:7; 16:20; Lk 6:13; Jn 12:16
e 27:66 Dn 6:17; Mt 28:2,11

f 28:1-8 Mk 16:1-8; Lk 24:1-
    10; Jn 20:1-8
g 28:2 Lk 24:4; Jn 20:12
h 28:3 Dn 7:9; 10:6; Mk
    9:3; Jn 20:12; Ac 1:10
i 28:5 Mt 14:27; 28:10;
    Rv 1:17
j 28:6 Mt 12:40; 16:21;
    27:63
k 28:7 Mt 10:1; 26:56; Mk
    3:7; 16:20; Lk 6:13; Jn 12:16
l Mt 26:32; Mk 16:7

⫸ KINGDOM LIVING ⫷
CHURCH
Accessing Heavenly Authority

The phrase "keys of the kingdom of heaven" (Matt 16:19) refers to our access to God's heavenly authority. We've been given the opportunity to act on God's behalf to accomplish his agenda. Similarly, the references to binding and loosing indicate that we as the church are called to take action when necessary. In other words, from his first mention of the word "church" (Matt 16:18), Jesus made it clear that we're expected to both reflect God's values and work to enact his kingdom agenda in the world.

So what does that look like? What are we supposed to actually do as an *ekklēsia* in our culture? Several passages of Scripture point us in the right direction, such as Micah 6:6-8; Romans 12:9-21; and James 1:26-27. Christians today need to understand this: The job of the church isn't to adopt the values of the culture in which it resides or merely to analyze or assess that culture. Instead, the job of the church is to set heaven in the context of the culture so that people can see God at work in the midst of their everyday lives.

It's also the job of the church to advance God's kingdom by making disciples. Take a moment to read the Great Commission found in Matthew 28:19-20. The church has operated for too long on the defensive side of the battle. We've been content to react to the movements of hell rather than actively advancing the values of heaven and the breadth of God's kingdom.

If we could ever see God's kingdom as he sees it and if we could ever see one another as he sees us—as individuals designed to come together in a unified goal under his overarching kingdom agenda—then the world would have to deal with the full strength of the church of Jesus Christ. We would truly be the salt and light he designed us to be.

FOR THE NEXT CHURCH
KINGDOM LIVING LESSON SEE PAGE 1259.

it in his new tomb, which he had cut into the rock. He left after rolling a great stone against the entrance of the tomb.*a* **61** Mary Magdalene and the other Mary were seated there, facing the tomb.

THE CLOSELY GUARDED TOMB

62 The next day, which followed the preparation day, the chief priests and the Pharisees gathered before Pilate*b* **63** and said, "Sir, we remember that while this deceiver was still alive he said, 'After three days I will rise again.'*c* **64** So give orders that the tomb be made secure until the third day. Otherwise, his disciples*d* may come, steal him, and tell the people, 'He has been raised from the dead,' and the last deception will be worse than the first."

65 "You have^ a guard of soldiers," Pilate told them. "Go and make it as secure as you know how." **66** They went and secured the tomb by setting a seal on the stone and placing the guard.*e*

RESURRECTION MORNING

28
After the Sabbath,*f* as the first day of the week was dawning, Mary Magdalene and the other Mary went to view the tomb. **2** There was a violent earthquake, because an angel of the Lord descended from heaven and approached the tomb. He rolled back the stone and was sitting on it.*g* **3** His appearance was like lightning, and his clothing was as white as snow.*h* **4** The guards were so shaken by fear of him that they became like dead men.

5 The angel told the women, "Don't be afraid, because I know you are looking for Jesus who was crucified.*i* **6** He is not here. For he has risen, just as he said. Come and see the place where he lay.*j* **7** Then go quickly and tell his disciples,*k* 'He has risen from the dead and indeed he is going ahead of you to Galilee; you will see him there.' Listen, I have told you."*l*

8 So, departing quickly from the tomb with fear and great joy, they ran to tell his

^27:65 Or *"Take*

27:62-66 The Jewish leaders were aware of Jesus's claims that he would **rise again** (27:63) and were fearful that Jesus's **disciples** would **steal** the body, announce that he was **raised from the dead**, and deceive the people (27:64). So Pilate granted **a guard of soldiers** and the sealing of the **tomb** (27:65-66).

28:1 Early on Sunday, **the first day of the week**, some of the women who followed Jesus went to **the tomb** so they could anoint his body with spices (see Mark 16:1).
28:2-4 This **angel** was no cute little cherub. He was so astonishing and fearsome that **the guards** who saw him were terrified and passed out (28:4).

28:6 Jesus had **risen** as promised! (See 12:40; 16:21; 17:9, 22-23; 20:19). That empty tomb was a glorious sight.

Who's In Charge?

STAR WARS IS ONE OF the most popular movie series ever made, and creator George Lucas is a rich man because of it. I read once that a Hollywood executive walked onto a set where they were shooting the movie, looking for Lucas. Not only had he never met the man, but he didn't even know what he looked like. After waiting on the set for two hours, looking for someone who appeared to be in charge, he approached a crew member to ask, "Which one is George?" She pointed to a skinny little guy in jeans and a plaid shirt who had a roll of cable on his shoulder and hadn't said one word the whole time. In fact, the Hollywood executive had assumed the "kid" was just one of the crew! He had been looking for a more dominant or charismatic person. And if he hadn't been told the truth, he would have continued to have no idea who was in charge.

You can find a similar story in the Bible. Jesus's disciples went to Galilee, and while standing on a mountain there, Jesus said, "All authority has been given to me in heaven and on earth" (MT 28:18). He had just risen from the dead, and was declaring to them that he is in charge. He rules over both everything and everyone. But while Jesus had all authority, *only his eleven disciples knew it*. Had anyone else approached him prior to this moment, they would have assumed that he was just another guy.

Jesus had a reason for only sharing this knowledge with the eleven disciples. He gave them a mission: "Go, therefore, and make disciples of all nations, baptizing them in the name of the Father and of the Son and of the Holy Spirit, teaching them to observe everything I have commanded you" (MT 28:19-20). He actually transferred authority to them so that they could go and make disciples. You only give that kind of responsibility to people who truly know who you are.

Do you know what Jesus looks like? Do you know the sound of his voice? Or are you just standing in the crowd, wondering who's in charge? Get to know the real Jesus, and experience his authority. Surrender your life to him, and commit to following where he leads.

[a] 28:9 Mk 16:9; Jn 20:14
[b] 28:10 Jn 20:17; Rm 8:29; Heb 2:11-12,17
[c] 28:14 Mt 27:2; Ac 12:20
[d] 28:15 Mt 9:31; 27:8; Mk 1:45

[e] 28:16 Mt 26:32; 28:7
[f] 28:18 Dn 7:13-14; Jn 17:2; Rm 14:9; Eph 1:20-22; Php 2:9-10; Col 2:10; 1Pt 3:22
[g] 28:19 Mt 10:42; 28:19; Lk 14:26; Jn 8:31; 13:35; 15:8; Ac 6:1
[h] Mk 16:15; Lk 24:47
[i] Ac 2:38; 8:16
[j] 28:20 Mt 13:39; 18:20; Ac 1:2; 2:42; 18:10

disciples the news. **9** Just then[A] Jesus met them and said, "Greetings!" They came up, took hold of his feet, and worshiped him.[a] **10** Then Jesus told them, "Do not be afraid. Go and tell my brothers to leave for Galilee, and they will see me there."[b]

THE SOLDIERS BRIBED TO LIE

11 As they were on their way, some of the guards came into the city and reported to the chief priests everything that had happened. **12** After the priests[B] had assembled with the elders and agreed on a plan, they gave the soldiers a large sum of money **13** and told them, "Say this, 'His disciples came during the night and stole him while we were sleeping.' **14** If this reaches the governor's ears, we will deal with[C] him and keep you out of trouble."[C] **15** They took the money and did as they were instructed, and this story has been spread among Jewish people to this day.[d]

THE GREAT COMMISSION

16 The eleven disciples traveled to Galilee, to the mountain where Jesus had directed them.[e] **17** When they saw him, they worshiped,[D] but some doubted. **18** Jesus came near and said to them, "All authority has been given to me in heaven and on earth.[f] **19** Go, therefore, and make disciples[g] of[E] all nations,[h] baptizing[i] them in the name of the Father and of the Son and of the Holy Spirit, **20** teaching them to observe everything I have commanded you. And remember,[F] I am with you always,[G] to the end of the age."[j]

APPLICATION QUESTIONS

READ MATTHEW 28:18-20

– What does it mean to make disciples in today's culture?
– How have you recently invested your time, money, or energy in making disciples?

[A] 28:9 Other mss add *as they were on their way to tell the news to his disciples*   [B] 28:12 Lit *After they*   [C] 28:14 Lit *will persuade*   [D] 28:17 Other mss add *him*   [E] 28:19 Or *and disciple*   [F] 28:20 Lit *see*   [G] 28:20 Lit *all the days*

28:12-13 Notice the fatal flaw in the story the soldiers were to spread. How could they know what had happened if they'd been sound asleep? And, even if they had been awake, how could a small band of civilians overpower armed and trained Roman soldiers? Here we see an attempt to deny a supernatural event by replacing it with a natural explanation. Jesus *really* rose from the dead! The resurrection is the greatest event of human history and is proof that Christianity is true. Without it, we have nothing. With it, we have hope in history and for eternity (see 1 Cor 15:12-19).
28:17 Even while they fell at the feet of the Son of God, they had lingering questions. Is this for real? Can I bank on this? The good news is that their doubts didn't keep them from him. God is not afraid of your questions either. But don't let them keep you away.

28:18-20 These final words of Jesus in Matthew's Gospel have become known as the Great Commission. In them we find the church's marching orders. **Authority** over the universe is in the hands of the Son of God, and it is he who commands his disciples to **make disciples** (28:18-19). A *disciple* is a learner who seeks to become like the one whom he is following. The goal of discipleship, then, is to help people become progressively like Christ in character and conduct, in attitudes and actions.

Discipleship is the key element of God's kingdom agenda, the visible manifestation of God's comprehensive rule over every area of life. The effectiveness of a church is therefore evaluated—not in the number of its members—but by its disciple making. It's the absence of discipleship that keeps a church

impotent and ineffective, because by not taking up Christ's mission of discipleship, its people cannot draw on Christ's authority. We accomplish disciple-making by *going* (evangelism), *baptizing* (public identification), and *teaching* (explaining the meaning and application of God's Word).

King Jesus closed the meeting with a powerful promise: **I am with you always, to the end of the age** (29:20). The second Person of the Trinity promises to uniquely engage and be involved with believers and churches that are making disciples. The church's mission in history, in fact, is possible because of Jesus's heavenly presence. The one who is called *Immanuel*—"God is with us" (1:23)—will be with us until the end. Therefore, we are to boldly live our lives as disciples and diligently equip others to do the same.

MARK

INTRODUCTION

Author

LIKE THE OTHER GOSPELS, THE Gospel of Mark is anonymous; it names no author. Nevertheless, the earliest existing copies (dating perhaps to the late first century BC) include the name "Mark" in the title. Moreover, the early church father Papias claimed that Mark wrote his Gospel based on Peter's preaching. Indeed, Peter mentions Mark as his companion (see 1 Pet 5:12-13), and this is the same "John Mark" from the book of Acts who also traveled with Paul on his missionary journeys (see Acts 12:12, 25; 13:5, 13; 15:36-39; Col 4:10; 2 Tim 4:11). This early evidence gives us good reason to believe that John Mark was the author of the Gospel bearing his name and that the apostle Peter provided him with eyewitness testimony of Jesus. Some interpreters have suggested that the unidentified young man who fled the night Jesus was betrayed (see Mark 14:50-52) was John Mark himself.

Historical Background

Many Bible scholars believe Mark's Gospel was written first, most likely during the AD 50s, and was used as a source by Matthew and Luke when they wrote their Gospels. It seems likely that Mark wrote primarily for a Gentile audience because he often explains Hebrew/Aramaic words and Jewish customs (e.g., 3:17; 5:41; 7:3-4, 11, 34; 15:34, 42). According to early church tradition, Mark wrote in Rome; therefore, his audience may have been Gentile churches in that city.

Message and Purpose

The book of Mark is written to disciples. It blends the two main topics of leadership and service. Mark unfolds what it means to serve as a kingdom leader and to lead as a servant, because both of these elements are included in what it means to be a follower of Jesus

Christ. Discipleship, in fact, is that process whereby we progressively learn what it means to bring every area of life under his lordship. The Gospel of Mark takes us on a pilgrimage as Jesus teaches his first disciples who he is, what he is about, and what it means to follow him.

The disciples had much to learn: they actually argued about which of them would be the greatest in the kingdom. Jesus had to turn their thinking upside down, so he showed them that leadership comes through service. He demonstrated this himself, for indeed he had come "to serve" (10:45). He is called both Son of God and Son of Man because Jesus is both divine and human. He serves the purposes of God, yet he does so by meeting the needs of people. Our challenge in studying Mark is to learn from Jesus's example how to lead and how to serve.

www.bhpublishinggroup.com/qr/te/41_00

Outline

THE MESSIAH'S HERALD

1 The beginning[a] of the gospel[b] of Jesus
Christ, the Son of God.[A,c] 2 As it is written in Isaiah[d] the prophet:[B,e]

See, I am sending my messenger[f]
ahead of you;
he will prepare your way.[C,D,g]
3 **A voice of one crying out**
in the wilderness:[h]
Prepare the way for the Lord;[i]
make his paths straight![E,j]

4 John came baptizing[F,k] in the wilderness[l]
and proclaiming a baptism of repentance[m]
for the forgiveness[n] of sins.[o] 5 The whole
Judean countryside and all the people of
Jerusalem[p] were going out to him, and
they were baptized by him in the Jordan[q]
River, confessing[r] their sins.[s] 6 John wore
a camel-hair garment with a leather belt
around his waist and ate locusts[t] and wild
honey.[u]
7 He proclaimed, "One who is more powerful[v] than I am is coming after me.[w] I am
not worthy[x] to stoop down and untie the
strap of his sandals.[y] 8 I baptize you with[G]
water,[z] but he will baptize you with the
Holy Spirit."[aa]

THE BAPTISM OF JESUS

9 In[ab] those days Jesus came from Nazareth[ac] in Galilee[ad] and was baptized in the
Jordan by John. 10 As soon as he came up
out of the water, he saw the heavens[ae] being torn open and the Spirit descending on
him like a dove. 11 And a voice[af] came from
heaven:[ag] "You are my beloved[ah] Son;[ai] with
you I am well-pleased."[aj]

THE TEMPTATION OF JESUS

12 Immediately[ak] the Spirit[al] drove[am] him
into the wilderness.[an] 13 He was in the wilderness forty days, being tempted[ao] by Satan.[ap] He was with the wild animals,[aq] and
the angels[ar] were serving him.

[a] 1:1 Jn 1:1; Php 4:15
[b] 1:1-8 Mt 3:1-12; Lk 3:1-18
[c] 1:1 Jn 5:19; Heb 1:2
[d] 1:2 Mt 3:3; 4:14; 12:17
[e] Lk 16:29
[f] Mt 13:49
[g] Mal 3:1
[h] 1:3 Jn 1:23
[i] Lk 10:1; 17:5
[j] Is 40:3
[k] 1:4 Lk 7:29; Ac 22:16
[l] Rv 12:6
[m] Lk 3:3; Ac 13:24; 19:4; 26:20
[n] Mt 9:2; Lk 24:47
[o] Jn 15:22; Ac 26:18
[p] 1:5 Mt 23:37; Jn 11:36
[q] Gn 13:10; Ps 114:3; Lk 3:3
[r] Ac 19:18
[s] Jn 15:22; Rm 6:23; 1Pt 4:1
[t] 1:6 Rv 9:3,7
[u] Rv 10:9-10
[v] 1:7 Rv 18:8
[w] Jn 1:15
[x] Mt 3:11
[y] Lk 3:16; Ac 13:23-25
[z] 1:8 Jn 1:26,31,33; Ac 1:5; 8:36; 11:16
[aa] Jn 1:33
[ab] 1:9-11 Mt 3:13-17; Lk 3:21-23
[ac] 1:9 Mt 2:23; 4:13; 21:11; Lk 1:26; 2:4,39,51; 4:16; Jn 1:45-46
[ad] Mt 17:22
[ae] 1:10 Mt 24:35; Lk 12:33; Ac 17:24; Eph 6:9; Rv 21:10
[af] 1:11 Jn 5:37
[ag] Rv 14:13
[ah] Lk 20:13; Eph 1:6; Phm 1
[ai] Ps 2:7
[aj] Is 42:1
[ak] 1:12-13 Mt 4:1-11; Lk 4:1-13
[al] 1:12 Jn 1:33
[am] 3Jn 10
[an] Mt 3:1; Rv 12:6
[ao] 1:13 Jms 1:13
[ap] Mt 4:1,10; Ac 13:10
[aq] Rv 6:8
[ar] Mt 13:49; Ac 5:19; Rv 14:6

KINGDOM LIVING
KINGDOM
Advancing God's Kingdom

If you are an American, it's likely because you were born here. But if you are a part of the kingdom of God, it is only because you have been born again into his kingdom. The reason why this is so important to know is that this foundational truth not only affects you greatly, but it is also the key to grasping the truths of the Bible.

The unifying, central themes running throughout the Bible are the glory of God and the advancement of his kingdom. The threads that run from Genesis to Revelation—from beginning to end—are focused on one thing: God's glory spreads through advancing God's kingdom.

When you do not focus on that, the Bible presents itself as disconnected stories that may be great for inspiration but seem to be unrelated in purpose and direction. The Bible exists to share God's movement in history toward the establishment and expansion of his kingdom. It highlights the connectivity of the kingdom. Understanding this principle increases the relevancy of this ancient manuscript to your everyday life because the kingdom is not only then, it is now.

In the same way that our culture and our country want us to be regularly reminded about our citizenship in this kingdom called America, there is another kingdom—a greater and more perfect one—of which we are a part. It is the kingdom of God.

FOR THE NEXT KINGDOM
KINGDOM LIVING LESSON SEE PAGE 1409.

[A] 1:1 Some mss omit *the Son of God* [B] 1:2 Other mss read *in the prophets* [C] 1:2 Other mss add *before you* [D] 1:2 Mal 3:1 [E] 1:3 Is 40:3 [F] 1:4 Or *John the Baptist came* [G] 1:8 Or *in*

1:1 **Jesus** is the Greek rendering of the Hebrew name *Joshua*, which means, "the Lord saves." **Christ** is the Greek word for the Hebrew "Messiah," which means, "Anointed One." This was the title of the promised King, the descendant of David who would rule the kingdom and deliver his people. The title **Son of God** tells us Jesus is more than a mere man. He's fully divine; he's the God-Man.

1:2 Typically, kings would send envoys ahead of them to prepare their way. Christ's ambassador was a man named John whose mission was foretold many years before by Isaiah (see Isa 40:3).

1:4-5 By **confessing their sins**, the people were agreeing with heaven's evaluation of their sins (1:5). By repenting they were adopting heaven's perspective on their sins, turning from them (1:4).

1:6-7 John's plain lifestyle was reflected in his clothing and his food (**locusts and wild honey**); (1:6). He was a simple, unworthy man pointing to someone **more powerful than** he (1:7).

1:8 That the coming one would **baptize** his followers **with the Holy Spirit** had been promised long ago (see Joel 2:28). In time, Jesus would deliver (see John 14:16-17; Acts 2:1-4).

1:9 Jesus **was baptized** to identify with sinners, whom he'd come to save (see the note on Matt 3:13-15), and so that he might be distinguished as the Messiah, the Son of God (see John 1:29-34).

1:10-11 We see the Trinity at work at this crucial kingdom moment: the ministry of God the **Son** begins with the loving affirmation of God the Father and the empowering presence of God the **Spirit** (1:10).

1:13 As Israel had spent forty years in the wilderness, so Jesus spent **forty days** identifying with God's people. And whereas Israel repeatedly failed to obey God during their time in the wilderness, Jesus would prove victorious.

MINISTRY IN GALILEE

14 After[a] John was arrested,[b] Jesus went to Galilee,[c] proclaiming[d] the good news[A,B,e] of God:[f] **15** "The time[g] is fulfilled, and the kingdom of God[h] has come[i] near.[j] Repent[k] and believe[l] the good news!"

APPLICATION QUESTIONS

READ MARK 1:15

– What ideas or images come to mind when you read the phrase "kingdom of God"?

THE FIRST DISCIPLES

16 As[m] he passed alongside the Sea of Galilee,[n] he saw Simon[o] and Andrew,[p] Simon's brother, casting a net into the sea[q] — for they were fishermen. **17** "Follow me,"[r] Jesus told them, "and I will make you fish for[C,s] people."[t] **18** Immediately they left their nets and followed[u] him.[v] **19** Going on a little farther, he saw James[w] the son of Zebedee[x] and his brother John[y] in a boat putting their nets in order. **20** Immediately he called them, and they left their father Zebedee in the boat with the hired men and followed him.[z]

DRIVING OUT AN UNCLEAN SPIRIT

21 They[aa] went into Capernaum,[ab] and right away he entered the synagogue[ac] on the Sabbath[ad] and began to teach.[ae] **22** They were astonished[af] at his teaching[ag] because he was teaching them as one who had authority, and not like the scribes.

23 Just then a man with an unclean[ah] spirit[ai] was in their synagogue.[aj] He cried out, **24** "What do you have to do with us,

Jesus of Nazareth?[ak] Have you come to destroy[al] us? I know who you are — the Holy[am] One of God!"[an]

25 Jesus rebuked[ao] him saying, "Be silent,[ap] and come out of him!" **26** And the unclean spirit threw him into convulsions,[aq] shouted with a loud voice, and came out of him.

27 They were all amazed,[ar] and so they began to ask[as] each other: "What is this? A new teaching[at] with authority![D,au] He commands even the unclean[av] spirits,[aw] and they obey him." **28** At once the news about him spread throughout the entire vicinity of Galilee.[ax]

HEALINGS AT CAPERNAUM

29 As[ay] soon as they left the synagogue,[az] they went into Simon[ba] and Andrew's[bb] house[bc] with James[bd] and John.[be] **30** Simon's mother-in-law was lying in bed with a fever, and they told him about her at once. **31** So he went to her, took her by the hand, and raised her up.[bf] The fever[bg] left her,[E] and she began to serve[bh] them.[bi]

32 When[bj] evening came, after the sun had set, they brought to him all those who were sick[bk] and demon-possessed.[bl] **33** The whole town was assembled at the door, **34** and he healed[bm] many who were sick with various diseases[bn] and drove out[bo] many demons.[bp] And he would not permit the demons to speak, because they knew him.[bq]

PREACHING IN GALILEE

35 Very[br] early in the morning, while it was still dark, he got up, went out, and made his way to a deserted place;[bs] and there he was praying.[bt] **36** Simon[bu] and his companions

[a] 1:14-15 Mt 4:17; Jn 4:45
[b] 1:14 Mt 3:12; Lk 3:20; 9:7-9; Jn 3:24
[c] Mt 17:22
[d] Mk 13:10
[e] Mk 1:1
[f] Rm 15:16; 1Th 2:2,8-9
[g] 1:15 Ps 37:39; Lk 20:10; Jn 7:8
[h] Mt 3:2; 6:33; 12:28; 19:24; 21:31,43; Mk 4:11; 9:1; 10:14; 12:34; 14:25; 15:43
[i] Mk 9:1
[j] Rm 13:11; 1Pt 4:7
[k] Ac 3:19; 26:20
[l] Mk 11:24; Jn 3:16; Ac 10:43; Rm 10:9; 1Pt 1:8-10
[m] 1:16-20 Mt 4:18-22; Lk 5:1-11
[n] 1:16 Mt 4:18; 15:29; Jn 6:1
[o] Mt 16:17
[p] Jn 6:8
[q] Mk 7:31
[r] 1:17 Mt 4:19
[s] Mt 4:18-19; Lk 5:2
[t] Mt 4:19
[u] 1:18 Lk 5:11; Jn 8:12
[v] Lk 18:28
[w] 1:19 Ac 12:2
[x] Jn 21:2
[y] Jn 21:7
[z] 1:20 Lk 18:28
[aa] 1:21-26 Lk 4:31-35
[ab] 1:21 Lk 10:15
[ac] Mk 3:1; Jms 2:2
[ad] Mk 2:23; Lk 13:10
[ae] Mt 28:20; Ac 4:2; 2Tm 4:11
[af] 1:22 Mk 6:2
[ag] Mt 7:28; 22:33; Mk 11:18; Lk 4:32; Ac 2:42; 17:19
[ah] 1:23 2Co 6:17
[ai] Lk 11:24
[aj] Jms 2:2
[ak] 1:24 Mk 14:67
[al] Jn 6:27
[am] 1Co 7:14
[an] Lk 4:34; Jn 6:69; Eph 4:30
[ao] 1:25 2Tm 4:2
[ap] Mt 22:12
[aq] 1:26 Mk 9:26; Lk 9:39
[ar] 1:27 Mk 10:24,32
[as] Mk 8:11
[at] Mk 11:18; Ac 2:42
[au] Jd 25
[av] 2Co 6:17
[aw] Lk 11:24
[ax] 1:28 Mt 17:22

[ay] 1:29-31 Mt 8:14-15; Lk 4:38-39 [az] 1:29 Jms 2:2 [ba] Mt 16:17 [bb] Jn 6:8 [bc] Mk 9:33 [bd] Ac 12:2 [be] Jn 21:7 [bf] 1:31 Mk 5:41 [bg] Lk 4:38 [bh] Phm 13 [bi] Rm 12:13 [bj] 1:32-34 Mt 8:16-17; Lk 4:40-41 [bk] 1:32 Lk 5:31 [bl] Mt 9:32 [bm] 1:34 Ac 8:7 [bn] Ac 19:12 [bo] 3Jn 10 [bp] Rv 9:20; 18:2 [bq] Mk 3:11-12;5:7 [br] 1:35-38 Mt 4:23-25; Lk 4:42-44 [bs] 1:35 Mt 14:13; Mk 6:31-32; Lk 4:42; 9:12; Rv 12:6 [bt] Mt 5:44; Ac 12:12 [bu] 1:36 Mt 16:17

[A] 1:14 Other mss add *of the kingdom*   [B] 1:14 Or *gospel*   [C] 1:17 Or *you to become fishers of*   [D] 1:27 Other mss read *"What is this? What is this new teaching? For with authority"*   [E] 1:31 Other mss add *at once*

1:14-15 The **kingdom of God** is the visible manifestation of the comprehensive rule of God over every area of life. How should people respond to this message? We should **repent** (change our minds about sin) **and believe** the saving message of Christ so the promise of the kingdom can come (1:15).
1:16-17 Jesus used the occupation of **Simon** (Peter) **and Andrew** to challenge them to follow him: **I will make you fish for people** (1:17). God will often do something similar when he calls us to become disciples; he'll link our backgrounds and experiences to his purposes for our lives.
1:21 Capernaum was a village on the north side of the Sea of Galilee.

1:22 The scribes who normally taught them were nothing like Jesus. He taught with **authority**, making God's Word powerfully clear.
1:23-24 An unclean spirit is a demon (1:23). What this one said about Jesus tells us that demons have the insight to know who Jesus is even as they're unwilling to worship him (1:24). As James says, it's possible to believe in God yet be unwilling to follow him (Jas 2:18-20).
1:25-28 Jesus had no intention of letting a follower of Satan be his spokesman to fuel the accusation that he was in league with the devil (see Matt 9:32-34).
1:31 It was equally important to Mark to point out that **she began to serve** Jesus as a result of what he did for her. The only appropriate

response to God's goodness in your life, in fact, is gratitude and service.
1:32 After the sun had set the Sabbath was over (see 1:21), so people had the freedom to carry burdens such as stretchers.
1:35 Jesus sought the fellowship of his heavenly Father—away from the distractions of the world. If the Son of God considered uninterrupted prayer such a priority, why do so many Christians consider it an afterthought?
1:36-38 The disciples' words in 1:37 suggest that they thought he wasn't capitalizing on the opportunities his popularity afforded him. Jesus, though, had not come merely to please the masses with miracles. He came to **preach** the good news and prepare people for God's kingdom (1:38).

*a*1:38 Mk 1:4
*b*1:39 Mt 17:22
c Mk 3:1
*d*1:40-44 Mt 8:2-4; Lk 5:12-14
*e*1:40 Mt 11:5
f Mt 17:14
*g*1Jn 1:7
*h*1:41 Lk 15:20
i Jn 20:17
*j*1:42 Lk 5:12
*k*1:43 Mt 9:30; Mk 14:5; Jn 11:33,38
*l*3Jn 10
*m*1:44 Mk 5:43; 7:36; 8:26,30; 9:9; 16:8; Lk 5:14
n Rv 1:1
o Ac 4:1
p Heb 5:1; 8:3
q Lv 13-14; Heb 1:3
r Mk 6:11; 1Tm 2:6
*s*1:45 Mk 1:4; Jn 18:32
t Mk 4:14
*u*2:1-12 Mt 9:1-8; Lk 5:17-26
*v*2:1 Lk 10:15
*w*2:2 Mk 4:14; Jn 18:32
*x*2:3 Mt 4:24; 8:6; 9:2,6; Mk 2:3-10

*y*2:5 Mt 8:10; Ac 3:16; Rm 1:8; 1Co 2:5; Gl 2:16; 1Tm 1:2; Heb 4:2
z Jn 15:22
aa Mt 9:2,5; Lk 5:20,23; 7:48
*ab*2:6 Mt 2:4
ac Mk 9:33
*ad*2:7 Ex 22:28; Mk 3:29; Rv 13:6
ae Ps 25:11; Mt 9:2
af Jn 15:22
ag Ex 34:6-7; Is 43:25; 44:2
*ah*2:8 Mk 10:52
ai Lk 5:22; 16:15; Jn 2:25
*aj*2:9 Lk 16:17; 18:25
ak Mk 2:3
al Mt 11:5

*am*2:10 Ps 8:4; Lk 5:24; Ac 7:56
an Mt 28:18; Mk 1:22
ao Jn 15:22
*ap*2:11 Mk 5:41
*aq*2:12 Ac 10:45
ar Jn 11:4; 17:1; 1Pt 2:12
as Lk 2:14
at Mt 9:33
*au*2:13-17 Mt 9:9-13; Lk 5:27-32
*av*2:13 Mt 28:20; Ac 4:2; 2Tm 4:11
*aw*2:14 Lk 5:27,29
ax Lk 5:27
ay Lk 5:27
az Lk 5:11; Jn 8:12
*ba*2:15 Lk 3:12; 18:13
bb Mt 9:10; 1Tm 1:15
*bc*2:16 Mt 2:4

searched for him, [37] and when they found him they said, "Everyone is looking for you."

[38] And he said to them, "Let's go on to the neighboring villages so that I may preach[a] there too. This is why I have come."

A MAN CLEANSED

[39] He went into all of Galilee,[b] preaching in their synagogues[c] and driving out demons. [40] Then[d] a man with leprosy[A,e] came to him and, on his knees,[B,f] begged him: "If you are willing, you can make me clean."[g] [41] Moved with compassion,[C,h] Jesus reached out his hand and touched[i] him. "I am willing," he told him. "Be made clean." [42] Immediately the leprosy[j] left him, and he was made clean. [43] Then he sternly warned[k] him and sent him away[l] at once, [44] telling him, "See that you say nothing to anyone;[m] but go and show[n] yourself to the priest,[o] and offer[p] what Moses commanded for your cleansing,[q] as a testimony[r] to them."[D] [45] Yet he went out and began to proclaim[s] it widely and to spread the news,[t] with the result that Jesus could no longer enter a town openly. But he was out in deserted places, and they came to him from everywhere.

THE SON OF MAN FORGIVES AND HEALS

2 When[u] he entered Capernaum[v] again after some days, it was reported that he was at home. [2] So many people gathered together that there was no more room, not even in the doorway, and he was speaking the word[w] to them. [3] They came to him bringing a paralytic,[x] carried by four of them. [4] Since they were not able to bring

him to[E] Jesus because of the crowd, they removed the roof above him, and after digging through it, they lowered the mat on which the paralytic was lying. [5] Seeing their faith,[y] Jesus told the paralytic, "Son, your sins[z] are forgiven."[aa]

[6] But some of the scribes[ab] were sitting there, questioning[ac] in their hearts: [7] "Why does he speak like this? He's blaspheming![ad] Who can forgive[ae] sins[af] but God alone?"[ag]

[8] Right away[ah] Jesus perceived in his spirit[ai] that they were thinking like this within themselves and said to them, "Why are you thinking these things in your hearts? [9] Which is easier:[aj] to say to the paralytic,[ak] 'Your sins are forgiven,' or to say, 'Get up, take your mat, and walk'?[al] [10] But so that you may know that the Son of Man[am] has authority[an] on earth to forgive sins"[ao] — he told the paralytic — [11] "I tell you: get up,[ap] take your mat, and go home."

[12] Immediately he got up, took the mat, and went out in front of everyone. As a result, they were all astounded[aq] and gave glory[ar] to God,[as] saying, "We have never seen anything like this!"[at]

THE CALL OF LEVI

[13] Jesus[au] went out again beside the sea. The whole crowd was coming to him, and he was teaching[av] them. [14] Then, passing by, he saw Levi[aw] the son of Alphaeus sitting at the toll booth,[ax] and he said to him, "Follow me,"[ay] and he got up and followed[az] him.

[15] While he was reclining at the table in Levi's house, many tax collectors[ba] and sinners[bb] were eating[F] with Jesus and his disciples, for there were many who were following him. [16] When the scribes[bc] who

A1:40 Gk *lepros*; a term for various skin diseases, also in v. 42; see Lv 13-14   **B**1:40 Other mss omit *on his knees*   **C**1:41 Other mss *Moved with indignation*   **D**1:44 Or *against them*   **E**2:4 Other mss read *able to get near*   **F**2:15 Lit *reclining together*

1:40-41 With this scene Mark wants his readers to know that Jesus's healing ministry wasn't perfunctory. When he heard and saw the man, he was **moved with compassion**. The sinless Son of God is able to sympathize with our weaknesses. Notice too the manner in which he healed him: **Jesus . . . touched him** (1:41). Understand: no one touched a leper. Doing so risked infection and made Jews unclean according to the Mosaic law. But the Son of God cannot be contaminated; he can only purify.
1:43-45 As a result of the man's disobedience, he hindered Jesus's ministry (1:45).
2:3-4 Some Christians will invite friends to church but not invite them to Jesus. They'll invite them to hear sermons, choir concerts, and to see special programs, but they won't tell them about the life-changing power of Jesus Christ. These four men knew that get-

ting their friend to a building wasn't the goal. Getting him to the Master was.
2:5 No matter how poor your physical condition, your spiritual condition must take priority. Unforgiven **sins** are more detrimental than unhealed limbs. Spiritual sickness is worse than broken circumstances. And spiritual healing can reverse sin's physical consequences.
2:7 While they were right that **God alone** could **forgive sins**, they had Jesus all wrong. He possessed divine authority because of his divine nature.
2:8 This is a reminder that there isn't a moment that goes by that Jesus doesn't know exactly what you're **thinking**.
2:9-11 Jesus's ability to accomplish a visible miracle would confirm his ability to accomplish an invisible spiritual one. Don't go to

Jesus for help with your physical circumstances unless you're willing for him to deal with your spiritual circumstances.
2:14 **Levi** is also known as Matthew (see Matt 9:9). Jews like him who served as tax collectors were considered unclean because they worked for Gentiles. Moreover, they typically charged extra taxes to keep for themselves (see Luke 19:1-10). Having a thieving tax collector as a disciple wouldn't improve Jesus's reputation among the religious elite.
2:16 These religious men couldn't understand why a holy man would hang out with such people. When was the last time you spent time with a sinner—not so you could share in sin but so you could point him to your Savior? If engaging with the lost is repulsive to you, you've lost sight of Jesus's mission and the calling on the church.

were Pharisees[A,a] saw that he was eating[b] with sinners[c] and tax collectors,[d] they asked his disciples, "Why does he eat[B] with tax collectors and sinners?"

17 When Jesus heard this, he told them, "It is not those who are well who need[e] a doctor,[f] but those who are sick.[g] I didn't come to call the righteous,[h] but sinners."[i]

A QUESTION ABOUT FASTING

18 Now[j] John's[k] disciples[l] and the Pharisees[c,m] were fasting.[n] People came and asked him, "Why do John's disciples and the Pharisees' disciples fast, but your disciples do not fast?"

19 Jesus said to them, "The wedding guests cannot fast while the groom[o] is with them, can they? As long as they have the groom with them, they cannot fast. **20** But the time[D] will come[p] when the groom will be taken away from them,[q] and then they will fast[r] on that day. **21** No one sews a patch of unshrunk cloth on an old garment. Otherwise, the new patch pulls away from the old cloth,[s] and a worse tear is made. **22** And no one puts new wine[t] into old wineskins. Otherwise, the wine will burst[u] the skins, and the wine is lost as well as the skins. No, new wine is put into fresh wineskins."

LORD OF THE SABBATH

23 On[v] the Sabbath he was going through the grainfields, and his disciples[w] began to make their way, picking some heads of grain. **24** The Pharisees[x] said to him, "Look, why are they doing what is not lawful[y] on the Sabbath?" **25** He said to them, "Have you never read what David[z] and those who were with him did when he was in need[aa] and hungry[ab] — **26** how he entered the house of God in the time of Abiathar[ac] the high priest[ad] and ate the bread of the Presence[ae] — which is not lawful for anyone to eat except the priests[af] — and also gave some to his companions?" **27** Then he told them, "The Sabbath was made for[E] man and not man for the Sabbath.[ag] **28** So then, the Son of Man[ah] is Lord[ai] even of the Sabbath."[aj]

3 Jesus[ak] entered the synagogue[al] again, and a man was there who had a shriveled[am] hand. **2** In order to accuse[an] him, they were watching him closely[ao] to see whether he would heal[ap] him on the Sabbath.[aq] **3** He told the man with the shriveled hand, "Stand before us." **4** Then he said to them, "Is it lawful[ar] to do good[as] on the Sabbath or to do evil,[at] to save life[au] or to kill?"[av] But they were silent.[aw] **5** After looking around at them with anger,[ax] he was grieved at the hardness[ay] of their hearts and told the man, "Stretch out your hand." So he stretched it out, and his hand was restored.[az] **6** Immediately the Pharisees[ba] went out and started plotting[bb] with the Herodians[bc] against him, how they might kill[bd] him.

MINISTERING TO THE MULTITUDE

7 Jesus[be] departed with his disciples to the sea, and a large crowd followed from Galilee,[bf] and a large crowd followed from Judea,[bg] **8** Jerusalem,[bh] Idumea, beyond the Jordan,[bi] and around Tyre[bj] and Sidon.[bk] The large crowd came to him because they heard about everything he was doing. **9** Then he told his disciples to have a small boat[bl] ready for him, so that the crowd wouldn't crush him. **10** Since he had healed[bm] many, all who had diseases were pressing toward him to touch[bn]

---

[a] 2:16 Mk 7:3
[b] Mt 11:18
[c] 1Tm 1:15
[d] Lk 3:12
[e] 2:17 Mt 6:8
[f] Col 4:14
[g] Lk 5:31
[h] Mt 13:17; Rm 1:17
[i] Lk 5:32
[j] 2:18-22 Mt 9:14-17; Lk 5:33-39
[k] 2:18 Mk 1:4
[l] Jn 3:25
[m] Mk 7:3
[n] Lk 18:12; Ac 13:2
[o] 2:19 Jn 2:9
[p] 2:20 Mk 13:24
[q] Lk 17:22; Jn 16:16-20
[r] Lk 18:12
[s] 2:21 Lk 19:36
[t] 2:22 Lk 5:37
[u] Jn 6:27
[v] 2:23-28 Mt 12:1-8; Lk 6:1-5
[w] 2:23 Mk 10:10
[x] 2:24 Mk 7:3
[y] Lk 6:2
[z] 2:25 Lk 1:27
[aa] Ac 2:45
[ab] Rv 7:16
[ac] 2:26 1Sm 21:1-6
[ad] Lv 16:32
[ae] Ex 25:30
[af] Ac 4:1
[ag] 2:27 Col 2:16
[an] 2:26 Mk 2:10
[af] Rm 7:25; 1Co 8:6; Col 3:22
[al] Lk 6:5
[ak] 3:1-6 Mt 12:9-14; Lk 6:6-11
[al] 3:1 Mk 1:21,39; Jms 2:2
[am] Mk 4:6; 5:29; 9:18; 11:20-21
[an] 3:2 Rv 12:10
[ao] Lk 6:7; 14:1; 20:20
[ap] Ac 8:7
[aq] Mk 2:23; Lk 13:10; 14:3
[ar] 3:4 Jn 18:31
[as] Ps 34:14; Lk 18:18
[at] Ps 34:12-16; 1Pt 3:17
[au] Php 2:12; Jms 5:20
[av] Lk 20:15
[aw] Lk 1:20; 19:40
[ax] 3:5 Jms 1:19
[ay] Ex 7:13; Rm 11:25
[az] Mk 8:25
[ba] 3:6 Mk 7:3
[bb] Mt 12:14; Mk 15:1

[bc] 3:6 Mt 22:16; Mk 12:13   [bd] Mk 11:18; Jn 5:18; 6:27   [be] 3:7-12 Mt 4:24-25; 12:15-16; Lk 6:17-19   [bf] 3:7 Mt 17:22   [bg] Lk 1:5   [bh] 3:8 Mt 23:37   [bi] Lk 3:3   [bj] Ac 21:7   [bk] Gn 49:13   [bm] 3:10 Ac 8:7   [bn] Jn 20:17

[A] 2:16 Other mss read *scribes and Pharisees*   [B] 2:16 Other mss add *and drink*   [C] 2:18 Other mss read *The disciples of John and of the Pharisees*
[D] 2:20 Or *the days*   [E] 2:27 Or *because of*

2:17 It's the bad who need good news (see 1:15). Jesus **didn't come to call the righteous** to enter into fellowship with God, nor the self-righteous (like the scribes and Pharisees) who didn't perceive a need for spiritual help. Rather, he came to call **sinners**, those who are spiritually bankrupt and know it.
2:18-20 The Old Testament certainly expected God's people to fast periodically, but the presence of the Messiah signaled a time for rejoicing and celebration. It would be no more appropriate for his followers to fast in his presence than for friends of a **groom** to **fast** at his **wedding** (2:19). Fasting would come later — when the groom was **taken away** (2:20). After Jesus's death, resurrection, and ascension, the legitimacy of fasting would resume.

2:23-24 The Jewish religious leaders accused Jesus of violating the Mosaic law. In their view, picking grain was tantamount to harvesting, harvesting was work, and work was forbidden **on the Sabbath** (2:24).
2:25-26 If **David**, the Lord's anointed, could eat the sacred bread when in need and be innocent, how much more could the Anointed One do the same?
2:27-28 **The Sabbath was made** to meet people's needs and benefit them. It was not to be a mere religious observance, absent of all compassion (2:27). As God, Jesus had established the day of rest; therefore, he knew its proper function (2:28).
3:4 The answer to Jesus's question was obvious. Failure **to do good** and **save life** would

actually be a violation of the law. The men opposed to Jesus were zealous for religious tradition but remained insensitive to the poor man's need.
3:5 Don't miss that here again Jesus healed by commanding a person to do what he was incapable of doing without divine help (see 2:10-12).
3:6 The **Herodians** were political supporters of Herod Antipas, the tetrarch of Galilee. Thus, religion and politics joined forces against the true King.
3:7-8 People from **Judea** and **Jerusalem** followed Jesus, but they also traveled from the outskirts: **Idumea** to the south, **beyond the Jordan** to the east, **and around Tyre and Sidon** in the northwest.

a 3:11 2Co 6:17
b Lk 11:24
c Lk 8:47
d Lk 4:34,41
e 3:12 2Tm 4:2
f Mk 1:34
g 3:13-19 Mt 10:2-4; Lk 6:12-16
h 3:13 Mt 4:8
i 3:14 Ac 1:2; Jd 17
j Mk 1:34
k 3:16 Mk 11:11; Jn 1:35-51
l Mt 16:17
m Ac 10:32
n 3:17 Ac 12:2
o Jn 21:2
p Jn 21:7
q Rv 6:1
r 3:18 Jn 6:8
s Jn 1:43-48; 6:5,7; 12:21-22; 14:8-9
t Ac 1:13
u Jn 11:16; 14:5; 20:24,26-28; 21:2
v 3:19 Mk 14:10,43; Ac 1:16,25
w 3:21 Jn 7:3
x Lk 2:48; Jn 2:3-4; 7:3-5
y 3:22 Mt 2:4
z Mt 10:25; 12:24,27; Lk 11:15-19
aa 3Jn 10
ab Rv 9:20; 18:2
ac Lk 12:58
ad Mt 9:34; 12:24; Lk 11:15
ae 3:23 Lk 18:16
af Mk 12:1
ag Mk 1:13; 4:15; 8:33
ah 3:23-27 Mt 12:25-29; Lk 11:17-22
ai 3:24 Lk 4:5
aj 3:27 Mk 15:1
ak 3:28-30 Mt 12:31-32; Lk 12:10
al 3:29 Ac 7:51
am Heb 6:4-6; 10:26-29; 1Jn 5:16
an Mk 14:64
ao 1Jn 5:16
ap 3:30 Lk 11:24
aq 3:31-35 Mt 12:46-50; Lk 8:19-21
ar 3:31 Mt 1:16
as Jn 2:12
at 3:32 Mk 6:3
au 3:34 Ac 9:30
av 3:35 Rm 8:27; Gl 1:4; Eph 1:9; 1Jn 2:17

him. **11** Whenever the unclean*a* spirits*b* saw him, they fell down*c* before him and cried out, "You are the Son of God!"*d* **12** And he would strongly warn*e* them not to make him known.*f*

THE TWELVE APOSTLES

13 Jesus*g* went up the mountain*h* and summoned those he wanted, and they came to him. **14** He appointed twelve, whom he also named apostles,*A,i* to be with him, to send them out to preach,*j* **15** and to have authority to*B* drive out demons. **16** He appointed the Twelve:*C,k* To Simon,*l* he gave the name Peter;*m* **17** and to James*n* the son of Zebedee,*o* and to his brother John,*p* he gave the name "Boanerges" (that is, "Sons of Thunder"*q*); **18** Andrew;*r* Philip*s* and Bartholomew; Matthew*t* and Thomas;*u* James the son of Alphaeus, and Thaddaeus; Simon the Zealot, **19** and Judas Iscariot,*v* who also betrayed him.

A HOUSE DIVIDED

20 Jesus entered a house, and the crowd gathered again so that they were not even able to eat.*D* **21** When his family*w* heard this, they set out to restrain him, because they said, "He's out of his mind."*x*

22 The scribes*y* who had come down from Jerusalem said, "He is possessed by Beelzebul,"*z* and, "He drives out*aa* demons*ab* by the ruler*ac* of the demons."*ad*

23 So he summoned*ae* them and spoke to them in parables:*af* "How can Satan*ag* drive out Satan?*ah* **24** If a kingdom*ai* is divided against itself, that kingdom cannot stand. **25** If a house is divided against itself, that

house cannot stand. **26** And if Satan opposes himself and is divided, he cannot stand but is finished. **27** But no one can enter a strong man's house and plunder his possessions unless he first ties up*aj* the strong man. Then he can plunder his house.

28 "Truly I tell you, people will be forgiven for all sins and whatever blasphemies*ak* they utter. **29** But whoever blasphemes*al* against the Holy Spirit never has forgiveness,*am* but is guilty*an* of an eternal sin"*E,ao* — **30** because they were saying, "He has an unclean spirit."*ap*

TRUE RELATIONSHIPS

31 His*aq* mother*ar* and his brothers*as* came, and standing outside, they sent word to him and called him. **32** A crowd was sitting around him and told him, "Look, your mother, your brothers,*at* and your sisters*F* are outside asking for you."

33 He replied to them, "Who are my mother and my brothers?" **34** Looking at those sitting in a circle around him, he said, "Here are my mother and my brothers!*au* **35** Whoever does the will of God*av* is my brother and sister and mother."

THE PARABLE OF THE SOWER

4 Again*aw* he began to teach*ax* by the sea, and a very large crowd gathered around him. So he got into a boat on the sea and sat down, while the whole crowd was by the sea on the shore. **2** He taught them many things in parables,*ay* and in his teaching*az* he said to them: **3** "Listen! Consider the sower who went out to sow.*ba*

aw 4:1-12 Mt 13:1-15; Lk 8:4-10   *ax* 4:1 Mt 28:20; Ac 4:2; 2Tm 4:11   *ay* 4:2 Mk 12:1   *az* Mk 11:18; Ac 2:42; 17:19   *ba* 4:3 Gl 6:7

A 3:14 Other mss omit *he also named them apostles*   *B* 3:15 Other mss add *heal diseases, and to*   *C* 3:16 Other mss omit *He appointed the Twelve*   *D* 3:20 Or *eat a meal*; lit *eat bread*   *E* 3:29 Other mss read *is subject to eternal judgment*   *F* 3:32 Other mss omit *and your sisters*

3:13-15 The role of the **apostles** was **to be with him** (to have a relationship to Jesus), to **preach** (to proclaim the message of Jesus; 3:14), and to **drive out demons** (to exercise the authority of Jesus; 3:15).

3:16-17 Peter functioned as something of a leader among the apostles (3:16). **James** and **John**, called the **Sons of Thunder** because of their intense personalities (3:17; see 10:35-45; Luke 9:51-56), were also fishermen. These three—Peter, James, and John—made up Jesus's inner circle and were often with him apart from the other apostles (see Mark 5:37; 9:2; 14:33).

3:19 Mark identifies **Judas Iscariot** as the apostle who **betrayed him** as a hint to the reader that the opposition to Jesus arose even among his companions. Judas was the only non-Galilean among the Twelve.

3:21 In light of everything he was doing, Jesus's biological family thought he'd gone crazy. His

brothers didn't believe in him during his ministry (see John 7:3-5), and even from an early age his parents misunderstood him (see Luke 2:41-50). After Jesus's resurrection, however, his mother and brothers would be counted among the first Christians in the early church (see Acts 1:14). His brothers James and Jude, in fact, would even write the Holy Spirit-inspired New Testament books now bearing their names.

3:22 In other words, they claimed the devil was the source of Christ's power.

3:25-26 Satan is the enemy of God, but he's not stupid (3:26). He's cunning like a serpent (see Gen 3:1) and prowls "like a roaring lion" (1 Pet 5:8). To attack his own kingdom would be to topple it without God's interference.

3:27 No one could render Satan (**the strong man** in view) helpless unless he was stronger—in this case, unless his power was divine.

3:28-30 To claim that the authority and power behind Jesus is actually the authority and power of the devil is to reject God's salvation in light of clear revelation. The one who rejects what the Holy Spirit makes clear, then, **is guilty of an eternal sin** (3:29). If you receive King Jesus as your Savior, he promises to forgive all. But if you spurn the King, call him the devil, and reject the Holy Spirit's testimony, you have no other option for salvation. As Jesus said, "I am the way, the truth, and the life. No one comes to the Father except through me." (John 14:6).

3:35 Jesus prioritized his relationship with those who submit themselves to God's **will**. If you want to experience more of Jesus and have a deeper relationship with him, respond to God's agenda for your life.

4:3-8 The parable of the sower shows what it looks like when different kinds of hearts encounter God's Word.

⁴ As he sowed, some seed fell along the path,[a] and the birds came and devoured[b] it. ⁵ Other seed fell on rocky ground where it didn't have much soil, and it grew up quickly,[c] since the soil wasn't deep. ⁶ When the sun came up, it was scorched, and since it had no root, it withered away.[d] ⁷ Other seed fell among thorns, and the thorns came up and choked it, and it didn't produce fruit. ⁸ Still other seed fell on good ground and it grew up, producing fruit that increased[e] thirty, sixty, and a hundred times."[f] ⁹ Then he said, "Let anyone who has ears to hear listen."[g]

WHY JESUS USED PARABLES

¹⁰ When he was alone, those around him with the Twelve,[h] asked him about the parables.[i] ¹¹ He answered them, "The secret[j] of the kingdom of God[k] has been given to you, but to those outside,[l] everything comes in parables ¹² so that

they may indeed look,
and yet not perceive;
they may indeed listen,
and yet not understand;[m]
otherwise, they might turn back
and be forgiven."[A,B,n]

THE PARABLE OF THE SOWER EXPLAINED

¹³ Then[o] he said to them: "Don't you understand this parable?[p] How then will you understand all of the parables? ¹⁴ The sower sows[q] the word.[r] ¹⁵ Some are like the word sown on the path.[s] When they hear, immediately Satan[t] comes and takes away the word[u] sown in them.[C] ¹⁶ And others are like seed sown on rocky ground. When they hear the word, immediately they receive it with joy.[v] ¹⁷ But they have no root; they are short-lived. When distress[w] or persecution comes because of the word, they immediately fall away.[x] ¹⁸ Others are like seed sown among thorns; these are the ones who hear the word, ¹⁹ but the worries[y] of this age,[z] the deceitfulness[D,aa] of wealth,[ab] and the desires[ac] for other things enter in and choke the word, and it becomes unfruitful.[ad] ²⁰ And those like seed sown on good ground hear the word,[ae] welcome it, and produce fruit[af] thirty, sixty, and a hundred times what was sown."

USING YOUR LIGHT

²¹ He[ag] also said to them, "Is a lamp brought in to be put under a basket or under a bed?[ah] Isn't it to be put on a lampstand?[ai] ²² For there is nothing hidden that will not be revealed,[aj] and nothing concealed that will not be brought to light. ²³ If anyone has ears to hear, let him listen."[ak] ²⁴ And he said to them, "Pay attention to what you hear. By the measure[al] you use,[am] it will be measured to you — and more will be added[an] to you. ²⁵ For whoever has, more will be given to him, and whoever does not have, even what he has will be taken away from him."[ao]

⌐ HOPE WORDS ⌐

I can't say it will never rain if you follow Jesus. But I can say that if you keep your eyes on him, he will cover you when the storms hit.

THE PARABLE OF THE GROWING SEED

²⁶ "The kingdom of God[ap] is like this," he said. "A man scatters seed on the ground. ²⁷ He sleeps[aq] and rises[ar] night[as] and day; the seed sprouts and grows, although he doesn't know how. ²⁸ The soil produces a crop[at] by itself — first the blade, then the head, and then the full grain[au] on the head.

a 4:4 Mk 8:27
b Gl 5:15
c 4:5 Mk 10:52
d 4:6 Mk 3:1
e 4:8 1Pt 2:2
f Jn 15:5; Col 1:6
g 4:9 Is 6:9; Jr 5:21; Ezk 12:2; Mk 8:18; Lk 14:35
h 4:10 Mk 11:11
i Mk 12:1
j 4:11 1Co 2:7
k Mk 1:15
l Rm 9:27
m 4:12 Mk 7:18
n Is 6:9-10
o 4:13-20 Mt 13:18-23; Lk 8:9-15
p 4:13 Mk 12:1
q 4:14 Gl 6:7
r Mk 16:20
s 4:15 Mk 8:27
t Mt 4:10
u Lk 6:47
v 4:16 Jn 5:43; 15:11
w 4:17 2Co 1:4
x Jn 16:1

y 4:19 1Pt 5:7
z Lk 16:8; Eph 1:21
aa Mt 13:22
ab Mt 13:22; Lk 8:14
ac 2Pt 1:4; 2:10
ad Rm 1:13; Ti 3:14; Jd 12
ae 4:20 Lk 6:47
af Col 1:10
ag 4:21-25 Lk 8:16-18
ah 4:21 Lk 5:18
ai Rv 1:12
aj 4:22 2Co 4:11
ak 4:23 Mk 4:9
al 4:24 2Co 10:13
am Mt 7:2; Lk 6:38
an Lk 17:5
ao 4:25 Mt 25:29; Lk 19:26
ap 4:26 Mk 1:15
aq 4:27 Mt 9:24
ar Mk 5:41
as Jn 9:4
at 4:28 Col 1:10
au Lk 16:7

A 4:12 Other mss read *and their sins be forgiven them*　B 4:12 Is 6:9-10　C 4:15 Other mss read *in their hearts*　D 4:19 Or *seduction*

4:10-12 That **the secret** or "mystery" of the **kingdom of God** had **been given to** them means that those things that had been hidden in the Old Testament about God's kingdom were being revealed to them through Christ. But for **those outside** who rejected Jesus's authority, the **parables** actually concealed truths (4:11). Unless they responded to the truth they had been given, they would not be given further insight to lead them to repentance (see also Matt 13:10-12).
4:15 The hardened **path** represents a hardened heart. People with such hearts refuse to believe; therefore, **Satan** easily removes the Word from them.

4:16-19 The seed that grows in **rocky ground** (4:16) and **among thorns** (4:18) represents believers who, either through spiritual immaturity or attachments to worldliness (such as **wealth**), fail to yield fruit (4:19). Spiritual growth cannot happen when God's kingdom is marginalized in a life.
4:20 The **good ground** represents hearts receptive to God's Word. They **welcome it**—that is, they believe and obey it. As a result, they **produce** abundant spiritual **fruit** because of the kingdom impact their lives have on others.
4:21-22 A lamp is put **on a lampstand** to light up a room and reveal its contents (4:21). In the same way, the light of God's Word is to shine

into people's hearts in order to bring **to light** that which is **hidden** (4:22).
4:24-25 To the degree that you welcome the Word in your life, you will bear fruit. The more believers accept God's kingdom agenda, the more fruitfulness God will entrust to them. But disobedience brings spiritual barrenness.
4:26-29 Similarly, the disciple of Jesus Christ who faithfully proclaims God's Word can have confidence that it will accomplish its work (see Isa 55:10-11). The Word has life within itself, so God will ensure growth and harvest as people respond to his Word when it is rightly explained.

Faith Is Always an Action

THE DIFFICULTIES OF BEING A Christian—one who is spiritually adopted into God's family—while living in the material world cannot be overstated. We worship a God we don't see with the naked eye, and we long to live in a kingdom we've never been to. It should come as no surprise, then, when we find ourselves more focused on our earthly problems than on heavenly solutions.

Such was the case for the disciples when a mighty storm rolled in and started knocking them about in their boat. And you can imagine their shock when they saw Jesus sleeping in the stern as though nothing was wrong. They cried, "Teacher! Don't you care that we're going to die?" (MK 4:38).

Jesus proceeded to supernaturally calm the storm. But what he said to the disciples should cut us all to the quick: "Why are you afraid? Do you still have no faith?" (MK 4:39-40). The disciples were afraid because they saw the storm instead of the God in the storm.

There is a bridge that God has constructed for everyone in the church today to move us from the natural to the supernatural. In order to move away from our storms and toward the one who calms the storm, we need to cross that bridge. It's called faith.

Faith is the only bridge that will allow you to travel beyond this world and all its problems. It's the only way for you to see things in the spiritual realm. Faith is acting like God is telling you the truth, even when what you see doesn't line up with what he's telling you. And when you start acting in faith, it's like crossing a bridge and starting to see things you've never seen.

Importantly, though, you must cross over the faith bridge if you ever hope to tap into the supernatural in your life. Faith requires action; it's not enough to merely say you believe something. It's not enough, for instance, to say we believe that God heals people and never pray for anybody to get well. Neither is it enough to believe that God has a job for you in the new year while you sit and wait for something to happen.

Crossing over the bridge—acting in faith—enables you to see what God is truly capable of. Remember, natural laws exist because God created them, and when he does something supernatural, he is actually superseding his own laws as he chooses to intervene in your life. Of course, crossing over the faith bridge can be scary. The disciples feared for their lives in that boat because believing in a supernatural solution in the middle of a storm is hard. What they lacked was an intimate knowledge of who Jesus is. The same is true for you and me; without a deeper understanding of Christ and his Word, we'll never experience his peace in the midst of our own trials. We'll never cross the bridge.

Lacking in faith is like being paralyzed. And not all paralysis is physical. You might be paralyzed by an addiction or depression. Maybe a bad relationship has you feeling stuck. Whatever your particular paralysis might be, it's time to make a faith journey and experience the supernatural power of God. The same Jesus who calmed the storm has the power to break your chains. The same Word that calmed the seas can set you free. Cross the bridge; it's time to start living out your faith.

29 As soon as the crop is ready, he sends for the sickle,[a] because the harvest[b] has come."

THE PARABLE OF THE MUSTARD SEED

30 And[c] he said, "With what can we compare the kingdom of God,[d] or what parable[e] can we use to describe it? **31** It's like a mustard seed[f] that, when sown upon the soil, is the smallest of all the seeds on the ground. **32** And when sown,[g] it comes up and grows taller than all the garden plants,[h] and produces large branches, so that the birds of the sky[i] can nest in its shade."

USING PARABLES

33 He was speaking the word[j] to them with many parables[k] like these, as they were able to understand.[l] **34** He did not speak to them without a parable. Privately, however, he explained everything to his own disciples.[m]

WIND AND WAVES OBEY JESUS

35 On[n] that day, when evening had come, he told them, "Let's cross over to the other side of the sea." **36** So they left the crowd and took him along since he was in the boat. And other boats were with him. **37** A great windstorm[o] arose, and the waves[p] were breaking over the boat, so that the boat was already being swamped. **38** He was in the stern, sleeping[q] on the cushion. So they woke him up[r] and said to him, "Teacher! Don't you care that we're going to die?"[s] **39** He got up, rebuked[t] the wind, and said to the sea, "Silence![u] Be still!" The wind ceased, and there was a great calm. **40** Then he said to them, "Why are you afraid?"[v] Do you still have no faith?"

41 And they were terrified[A,w] and asked one another, "Who then is this? Even the wind and the sea obey[x] him!"[y]

DEMONS DRIVEN OUT BY JESUS

5 They[z] came to the other side of the sea, to the region of the Gerasenes.[B] **2** As soon as he got out of the boat, a man with an unclean[aa] spirit[ab] came out of the tombs[ac] and met him. **3** He lived in the tombs,[ad] and no one was able to restrain him anymore — not even with a chain[ae] — **4** because he often had been bound with shackles and chains, but had torn the chains apart and smashed[af] the shackles. No one was strong enough to subdue[ag] him. **5** Night[ah] and day among the tombs[ai] and on the mountains,[aj] he was always crying out and cutting himself with stones.

6 When he saw Jesus from a distance, he ran and knelt down before him. **7** And he cried out with a loud voice, "What do you have to do with me, Jesus, Son[ak] of the Most High God?[al] I beg you before God, don't torment[am] me!" **8** For he had told him, "Come out of the man, you unclean[an] spirit!"[ao]

9 "What is your name?" he asked him.

"My name is Legion,"[ap] he answered him, "because we are many." **10** And he begged him earnestly not to send them out of the region.

11 A large herd of pigs[aq] was there, feeding[ar] on the hillside. **12** The demons[c] begged him, "Send us to the pigs, so that we may enter them." **13** So he gave them permission, and the unclean[as] spirits[at] came out and entered the pigs. The herd of about

---

a 4:29 Jl 3:13; Rv 14:14-19
b Rv 14:15
c 4:30-34 Mt 13:31-35; Lk 13:18-21
d 4:30 Mk 1:15
e Mk 12:1
f 4:31 Mt 17:20; Lk 17:6
g 4:32 Gl 6:7
h Lk 11:42
i Mt 24:35; Lk 12:33; Ac 17:24; Eph 6:9; Rv 21:10
j 4:33 Lk 6:47; Jn 18:32
k Mk 12:1
l Jn 16:12
m 4:34 Mt 9:10; Mk 10:10; Lk 6:1; Jn 6:3; Ac 6:1
n 4:35-41 Mt 8:23-27; Lk 8:22-25
o 4:37 Ps 107:25; Jnh 1:5-6
p Jd 13
q 4:38 Mk 9:24
r Mk 5:41
s Jn 6:27
t 4:39 2Tm 4:2
u Mt 22:12; Mk 3:4
v 4:40 Mt 8:26; Rv 21:8
w 4:41 Rv 11:11
x Mk 1:27
y Jnh 1:10,16; Mk 6:50-51
z 5:1-20 Mt 8:28-34; Lk 8:26-39
aa 5:2 2Co 6:17
ab Lk 11:24
ac Jn 5:28
ad 5:3 Lk 23:53
ae Mk 15:1
af 5:4 Rm 16:20; Rv 2:27
ag Jms 3:7-8
ah 5:5 Jn 9:4
ai Lk 23:53
aj Mt 4:8
ak 5:7 Jn 5:19; Heb 1:2
al Ps 78:35
am Rv 20:10
an 5:8 2Co 6:17
ao Lk 11:24
ap 5:9 Mt 26:53; Lk 8:30
aq 5:11 Mt 7:6; 8:30-32; Lk 8:32-33; 15:15-16
ar Jn 21:15
as 5:13 2Co 6:17
at Lk 11:24

A 4:41 Or *were filled with awe*   **B 5:1** Some mss read *Gadarenes*; other mss read *Gergesenes*   **C 5:12** Other mss read *All the demons*

4:30-32 In other words, though God's kingdom was starting small, with just a few disciples, it would grow tremendously in spite of its inauspicious beginning so that the operation of the kingdom in history would spread blessings everywhere.
4:35-37 Lying nearly seven hundred feet below sea level, **the Sea** of Galilee is surrounded by mountains and highlands. As a result of this geography, it is predisposed to violent windstorms, which is exactly what the disciples encountered. Though several of the apostles were hardened, lifelong fishermen, this storm filled them with terror.
4:38 When God lets us go through ordeals, it often feels like he doesn't **care**. The fear and pain lead to confusion ("Why would God let this happen?"). But in such moments, you must know your Bible and trust in the King of creation. There are no storms that come into your

life that do not first pass through his sovereign and loving fingers. If you know his character, you'll know that he does nothing that is not for your good and for his glory (see Rom 8:28).
4:40 The disciples had every reason to trust Jesus. They had *seen* his miraculous deeds; they *knew* God was with them. But it's easy to forget what Jesus did yesterday when we're going through a storm today. Importantly, before the storm arose, Jesus had told them, "Let's cross over to the other side" (4:35). He had let them know in advance that they would make it to their destination! But faith fails when we allow our circumstances to override God's Word.
4:41 Why does God put you in frightful circumstances? So that you'll learn to fear him more than your own circumstances. If you fear him above all else, you'll trust his Word above all else.

5:2-5 Mark has already told us about Jesus's encounters with demon-possessed people (see 1:23-26; 1:32-34; 3:11), but this account gets personal. Mark tells us what life was like for this particular man. First, **he lived in the tombs** (5:3). He was an utter social outcast. It's not that he had no human companions, but all of his human companions were dead! Second, he was out of control. Though people attempted to tie him up **with . . . chains**, he would simply break them. Because of his demonically inspired strength, **no one** could **subdue him** (5:4). Third, he endured self-inflicted agony. He was awake at all hours, **crying out and cutting himself** (5:5).
5:9 Since Jesus demanded to know the demon's **name**, we learn that the demon who had been talking was only a spokesman. His demonic aunts, uncles, cousins, and more had moved in with him.

two thousand rushed down the steep bank into the sea and drowned there.

14 The men who tended them[A] ran off[a] and reported it in the town and the countryside, and people went to see what had happened. **15** They came to Jesus and saw the man who had been demon-possessed,[b,c] sitting there, dressed and in his right mind;[d] and they were afraid.[e] **16** Those who had seen it described to them what had happened to the demon-possessed[f] man and told about the pigs. **17** Then they began to beg him to leave their region.

18 As he was getting into the boat, the man who had been demon-possessed begged him earnestly that he might remain with him. **19** Jesus did not let him but told him, "Go home to your own people, and report to them how much the Lord[g] has done[h] for you and how he has had mercy on you." **20** So he went out and began to proclaim[i] in the Decapolis[j] how much Jesus had done for him, and they were all amazed.[k]

A GIRL RESTORED AND A WOMAN HEALED

21 When[l] Jesus had crossed over again by boat[B] to the other side, a large crowd[m] gathered around him while he was by the sea. **22** One of the synagogue leaders, named Jairus,[n] came, and when he saw Jesus, he fell at his feet[o] **23** and begged him earnestly, "My little daughter is dying. Come and lay your hands on[p] her so that she can get well[C,q] and live." **24** So Jesus went with him, and a large crowd was following and pressing against him.

25 Now a woman suffering from bleeding[r] for twelve years **26** had endured[s] much under many doctors.[t] She had spent everything she had and was not helped at all. On the contrary, she became worse. **27** Having heard about Jesus, she came up behind him in the crowd and touched[u] his clothing.[v] **28** For she said, "If I just touch his clothes, I'll be made well."[w] **29** Instantly her flow of blood ceased, and she sensed in her body that she was healed[x] of her affliction. **30** At once Jesus realized in himself that power[y] had gone out from him. He turned around in the crowd[z] and said, "Who touched my clothes?"[aa]

31 His disciples said to him, "You see the crowd pressing against you, and yet you say, 'Who touched me?'"

32 But he was looking around to see who had done this. **33** The woman, with fear and trembling, knowing what had happened to her, came and fell down[ab] before him, and told him the whole truth.[ac] **34** "Daughter," he said to her, "your faith[ad] has saved you.[ae] Go in peace and be healed[af] from your affliction."[ag]

35 While he was still speaking, people came from the synagogue leader's house and said, "Your daughter is dead. Why bother the teacher[ah] anymore?"

36 When Jesus overheard[D] what was said, he told the synagogue leader, "Don't be afraid.[ai] Only believe." **37** He did not let anyone accompany him except Peter,[aj] James,[ak] and John,[al] James's brother. **38** They came to the leader's house, and he saw a commotion — people weeping and wailing loudly. **39** He went in and said to them, "Why are you making a commotion and weeping?[am]

5:14-17 Why **beg** Jesus **to leave their region?** Mark says they responded this way after learning **about the pigs** (5:16). "Two thousand" pigs to be exact (5:13). All that pork represented a lot of money. Were Jesus to continue doing similar things, he'd ruin the local economy. Notice that their livelihood was more important to them than a human being delivered from demonic oppression. They valued the material over the spiritual.

5:18 There has been a lot of begging in this chapter. The demons begged Jesus not to torment them or send them out of the region (see 5:7, 10). Then they begged to enter a herd of pigs (see 5:12). The locals begged Jesus to go away (see 5:17). But here we see some begging that's God-honoring. The man who had been demon possessed **begged** Jesus **that he might remain with him**.

5:19-20 Given the man's past, he was probably a fairly well known person. Those who knew him needed to hear his testimony to know what happens when the kingdom of God invades a

person's life. Christian, the people in your life need to hear what Jesus has done for you.

5:25-26 This **woman** had a severe *medical* problem. She had suffered from **bleeding for twelve years** (5:25). But she also had a severe *financial* problem. **She had spent everything she had** on **doctors** who were unable to help (5:26). Though Mark doesn't mention it, she also had a severe *religious* problem. Leviticus 15:25-27 indicates that the woman would have been ceremonially unclean during the course of her illness. Therefore, she was defiled, destitute, and desperate.

5:27 Imagine all the stories of this miracle-working teacher that could've been running through her mind. The lame were made to walk; the blind were made to see; the leprous were made clean; the demon-possessed were made free. She didn't want to stop him or call his name, but she needed to make contact with Jesus. He was her last and only hope.

5:30 Why did Jesus want to single this woman out in front of the crowd? In Psalm 50:15, God

says, "Call on me in a day of trouble; I will rescue you, and you will honor me." It would seem, then, that Jesus was determined to see that God was glorified publicly in this healing. When the Lord comes through in your life and no one knows about it but you, you need to declare his deeds and give him glory.

5:35 How heartbreaking to hear, **Your daughter is dead!** For a moment Jairus probably thought, "If only the crowd had let Jesus through; if only that woman hadn't stopped him." But though we often think that God has mismanaged our circumstances, his plan is perfect and brings him more glory than our plans would.

5:38-39 The **people weeping and wailing loudly** (5:38) probably included professional mourners, who were paid to attend funerals and express grief over the loss of a loved one. Jesus questioned their **weeping** (5:39) — not because mourning isn't appropriate in such cases, but because it signaled unbelief. The King, after all, had come to heal; Jesus's arrival was cause for hope.

The child[a] is not dead but asleep."[b] **40** They laughed at him, but he put them all outside. He took the child's father,[c] mother, and those who were with him, and entered the place where the child was. **41** Then he took the child[d] by the hand and said to her, "*Talitha koum*"[A] (which is translated, "Little girl, I say to you, get up"[e]). **42** Immediately the girl got up[f] and began to walk.[g] (She was twelve years old.) At this they were utterly astounded.[h] **43** Then he gave them strict orders that no one should know about this[i] and told them to give her something to eat.

REJECTION AT NAZARETH

6 He[j] left there and came to his hometown,[k] and his disciples[l] followed him. **2** When the Sabbath[m] came, he began to teach[n] in the synagogue,[o] and many who heard him were astonished. "Where did this man get these things?" they said. "What is this wisdom[p] that has been given to him, and how are these miracles[q] performed by his hands? **3** Isn't this the carpenter,[r] the son of Mary,[s] and the brother of James,[t] Joses, Judas,[u] and Simon? And aren't his sisters here with us?" So they were offended[v] by him. **4** Jesus said to them, "A prophet[w] is not without honor[x] except in his hometown, among his relatives, and in his household." **5** He was not able to do a miracle[y] there, except that he laid his hands on[z] a few sick[aa] people and healed[ab] them. **6** And he was amazed[ac] at their unbelief.[ad] He was going around the villages teaching.[ae]

COMMISSIONING THE TWELVE

7 He[af] summoned[ag] the Twelve[ah] and began to send[ai] them out in pairs and gave them authority over unclean[aj] spirits.[ak] **8** He instructed them to take nothing for the road except a staff — no bread, no traveling bag,[al] no money in their belts, **9** but to wear sandals and not put on an extra shirt.[am] **10** He said to them, "Whenever you enter a house, stay there until you leave that place. **11** If any place does not welcome[an] you or listen to you, when you leave there, shake the dust off your feet[ao] as a testimony[ap] against them."[B] **12** So they went out and preached[aq] that people should repent.[ar] **13** They drove out many demons,[as] anointed[at] many sick[au] people with oil[av] and healed them.[aw]

JOHN THE BAPTIST BEHEADED

14 King[ax] Herod[ay] heard about it, because Jesus's name[az] had become well known. Some[c] said, "John the Baptist[ba] has been raised from the dead,[bb] and that's why miraculous powers[bc] are at work[bd] in him." **15** But others said, "He's Elijah."[be] Still others said, "He's a prophet, like one of the prophets from long ago."[bf] **16** When Herod[bg] heard of it, he said, "John,[bh] the one I beheaded, has been raised!"[bi]

17 For[bj] Herod himself had given orders to arrest John and to chain[bk] him in prison on account of Herodias,[bl] his brother Philip's wife, because he had married her.[bm] **18** John had been telling Herod, "It is not lawful[bn] for you to have your brother's wife."[bo] **19** So Herodias held a grudge against him and wanted to kill[bp] him. But she could not, **20** because Herod feared[bq] John and protected him, knowing he was a righteous[br] and holy[bs] man. When Herod heard him he would be very perplexed,[D,bt] and yet he liked to listen to him.[bu]

[a] 5:39 Lk 1:7
[b] Mt 9:24
[c] 5:40 Col 3:21
[d] 5:41 Lk 1:7
[e] Mk 1:31; 2:11; 4:27,38; 9:27; 14:41-42
[f] 5:42 Mk 9:27
[g] Mt 11:5
[h] Mk 16:8; Ac 10:45
[i] 5:43 Mk 1:44; Lk 8:56
[j] 6:1-6 Mt 13:53-58
[k] 6:1 Mk 1:9
[l] Mt 9:10; Mk 10:10; Lk 6:1; Jn 6:3; Ac 6:1
[m] 6:2 Mk 2:23; Lk 13:10
[n] Mt 28:20; Ac 4:2; 2Tm 4:11
[o] Jms 2:2
[p] Pr 3:19; Ac 7:22; 1Co 1:21
[q] Ac 19:11
[r] 6:3 Mt 13:55
[s] Mt 1:16
[t] Jms 1:1; Jd 1
[u] Mt 13:55; Jd 1
[v] Jn 16:1
[w] 6:4 Mt 2:23
[x] Mt 13:57; 1Co 4:10; 12:23
[y] 6:5 Ac 19:11
[z] 1Tm 5:22
[aa] 1Co 11:30
[ab] Ac 8:7
[ac] 6:6 Rv 17:6
[ad] Heb 3:12,19
[ae] Mt 28:20; Ac 4:2; 2Tm 4:11
[af] 6:7-13 Mt 10:5-42; Lk 9:1-6
[ag] 6:7 Lk 18:16
[ah] Mk 11:11
[ai] Mk 3:14
[aj] 2Co 6:17
[ak] Lk 11:24
[al] 6:8 Lk 10:4
[am] 6:9 Jn 19:23
[an] 6:11 Lk 7:11
[ao] Mt 10:14; Lk 9:5; 10:11; Ac 13:51
[ap] 1Tm 2:6
[aq] 6:12 Mk 1:4
[ar] Ac 3:19; 26:20
[as] 6:13 Mk 3:15; Rv 9:20; 18:2
[at] Mk 16:1
[au] 1Co 11:30
[av] Jms 5:14
[aw] Ac 8:7
[ax] 6:14-16 Lk 9:7-9
[ay] 6:14 Mt 14:1
[az] Jn 10:25
[ba] Mk 1:4

[bb] 6:14 Mt 17:9; Jn 21:14   [bc] Mk 5:30   [bd] 1Co 12:6   [be] 6:15 Mk 8:28   [bf] Mt 2:23; Ac 7:52   [bg] 6:16 Mk 14:1   [bh] Mk 1:4   [bi] Mt 26:32   [bj] 6:17-29 Mt 14:6-12
[bk] 6:17 Mk 15:1   [bl] Mt 14:3,6; Lk 3:19   [bm] 1Tm 5:14   [bn] 6:18 Mk 2:24; Jn 18:31   [bo] Lv 18:16; 20:21   [bp] 6:19 Lk 20:15   [bq] 6:20 Ps 147:11; Pr 1:7;
Rv 14:7   [br] Mt 13:17   [bs] Ps 20:6; 1Co 7:14   [bt] Lk 24:4; Jn 13:22; Ac 25:20; 2Co 4:8; Gl 4:20   [bu] 2Co 11:19

[A] **5:41** An Aramaic expression   [B] **6:11** Other mss add *Truly I tell you, it will be more tolerable for Sodom or Gomorrah on judgment day than for that town.*   [C] **6:14** Other mss read *He*   [D] **6:20** Other mss read *When he heard him, he did many things*

5:41-42 Some parents have more difficulty waking their children in the morning for school than the Son of God had raising this little girl from the dead. That **she was twelve years old** (5:42) is particularly interesting given that the woman Jesus had just healed had been "bleeding for twelve years" (5:25).

6:4-5 They focused on his humanity and failed to recognize the supernatural nature of his words and works. Christ did not lack power; rather, an absence of faith caused God to withhold supernatural work. Don't hinder the work of God. His power is unlimited. But if you refuse to trust him, don't be surprised when eternity doesn't show up in your history.

6:7 Jesus gathered **the Twelve** together (see 3:14-19) and authorized these apostles to engage in an expansion of his ministry. As his ambassadors, they were to do what he'd been doing: preaching the kingdom, casting out demons, and healing the sick (see 6:12-13).

6:8-10 They were to take no extra provisions (6:8-9) because God would provide for them through the hospitality of those who'd submit to his kingdom agenda (6:10).

6:11 This is a reference to the Jewish practice of shaking **the dust off** one's feet upon returning to Israel from a Gentile region. If people would not receive the King's message, his ambassadors were to symbolically proclaim their coming judgment.

6:16 Herod Antipas was the son of Herod the Great, who'd tried to kill Jesus when he heard that a rival king had been born (see Matt 2:1-23). Superstitious man that he was, this Herod thought that Jesus was **John** the Baptist coming back to haunt him.

6:17-20 The mention of John's execution in 6:16 causes Mark to give his readers a flashback to explain what had happened to this man who hasn't been mentioned since he baptized Jesus in 1:9.

a 6:21 Jn 13:2
b Rv 6:15
c Ac 21:31
d Mt 17:22
e 6:22 Mt 11:17
f 6:23 Heb 6:16
g Mt 5:34
h Lk 4:5
i 6:24 Mk 1:4
j 6:25 Lk 7:20
k Mt 14:8
l 6:26 Mt 26:38; Mk 14:34
m Mt 5:33
n 1Th 4:8
o 6:29 Mk 10:10; Jn 3:25
p Jn 5:28
q 6:30–44 Mt 14:13–21; Lk 9:10–17; Jn 6:1–15
r 6:30 Ac 1:2; Jd 17
s 6:34 Lk 15:20
t Mt 7:15

u 6:35 Mk 10:10
v Jn 1:23; Rv 12:6
w 6:42 Mt 5:6
x 6:45–56 Mt 14:22–36; Jn 6:16–21
y 6:45 Jn 12:21
z 6:46 Mt 4:8
aa Mt 5:44; Ac 12:12

21 An opportune time came on his birthday, when Herod gave a banquet[a] for his nobles,[b] military commanders,[c] and the leading men of Galilee.[d] **22** When Herodias's own daughter[A] came in and danced,[e] she pleased Herod and his guests. The king said to the girl, "Ask me whatever you want, and I'll give it to you." **23** He promised her with an[f] oath:[g] "Whatever you ask me I will give you, up to half my kingdom."[h]

24 She went out and said to her mother, "What should I ask for?"

"John the Baptist's[i] head," she said.

25 At once she hurried to the king and said, "I want you to give me John the Baptist's[j] head on a platter[k] immediately." **26** Although the king was deeply distressed,[l] because of his oaths[m] and the guests[B] he did not want to refuse[n] her. **27** The king immediately sent for an executioner and commanded him to bring John's head. So he went and beheaded him in prison, **28** brought his head on a platter, and gave it to the girl. Then the girl gave it to her mother. **29** When John's disciples[o] heard about it, they came and removed his corpse and placed it in a tomb.[p]

FEEDING OF THE FIVE THOUSAND

30 The[q] apostles[r] gathered around Jesus and reported to him all that they had done and taught. **31** He said to them, "Come away by yourselves to a remote place and rest for a while." For many people were coming and going, and they did not even have time to eat.

32 So they went away in the boat by themselves to a remote place, **33** but many saw them leaving and recognized them, and they ran on foot from all the towns and arrived ahead of them.[c]

34 When he went ashore, he saw a large crowd and had compassion[s] on them, because they were like sheep[t] without a shepherd. Then he began to teach them many things.

35 When it grew late, his disciples[u] approached him and said, "This place is deserted,[v] and it is already late. **36** Send them away so that they can go into the surrounding countryside and villages to buy themselves something to eat."

37 "You give them something to eat," he responded.

They said to him, "Should we go and buy two hundred denarii[D] worth of bread and give them something to eat?"

38 He asked them, "How many loaves do you have? Go and see."

When they found out they said, "Five, and two fish." **39** Then he instructed them to have all the people sit down in groups on the green grass. **40** So they sat down in groups of hundreds and fifties. **41** He took the five loaves and the two fish, and looking up to heaven, he blessed and broke the loaves. He kept giving them to his disciples to set before the people. He also divided the two fish among them all. **42** Everyone ate and was satisfied.[w] **43** They picked up twelve baskets full of pieces of bread and fish. **44** Now those who had eaten the loaves were five thousand men.

WALKING ON THE WATER

45 Immediately[x] he made his disciples get into the boat and go ahead of him to the other side, to Bethsaida,[y] while he dismissed the crowd. **46** After he said good-bye to them, he went away to the mountain[z] to pray.[aa] **47** Well into the night, the boat was in

---

A 6:22 Other mss read *When his daughter Herodias* 　 B 6:26 Lit *and those reclining at the table* 　 C 6:33 Other mss add *and gathered around him* 　 D 6:37 A denarius = one day's wage

---

6:26-28 Herod didn't want to embarrass himself in front of everyone. He feared John, his wife, and his party guests—but he didn't fear God. 6:31 Sometimes, the most spiritual thing you can do is get some sleep. We need the reminder that we are created beings; we're not God. The fact that we need **rest** is a reminder that we are dependent on the One who "does not slumber or sleep" (Ps 121:4). 6:34 **Sheep** are dumb, defenseless, and directionless. They lack the knowledge to make the right choices, are vulnerable to attack from predators, and struggle with decision-making. But the Lord is "like a shepherd" who "gathers the lambs in his arms" (Isa 40:11).

6:35-36 From a purely human perspective, the disciples' concerns were justified. Mark tells us there were "five thousand men" present (6:44). Were women and children also counted, there could've been a total of fifteen to twenty thousand people. 6:37 These men had overlooked the fact that the kingdom power that had fed hundreds of thousands of Israelites in the wilderness for forty years (Exod 16:1-36) was the same kingdom power available to them through Jesus. 6:41 We are called to give God whatever we have—our time, our money, our abilities. If you have the compassionate Christ who has

access to the all-powerful Father, you have everything you need. 6:42-43 Miraculously, enough was provided for everyone. And it's not because everyone had a mere nibble or a few crumbs. **Everyone ate and was satisfied,** stuffed like a Thanksgiving turkey. And there were still leftovers! 6:45-46 As the disciples departed, Jesus went **to pray** (6:46). While they didn't know they were about to encounter a windstorm, Jesus did. And he was already interceding for them. Because of his resurrection from the dead, Jesus "always lives to intercede for" you too (Heb 7:25).

the middle of the sea, and he was alone on the land. [48] He saw them straining[a] at the oars,[A] because the wind was against them. Very early in the morning[B] he came toward them walking on the sea and wanted to pass by them. [49] When they saw him walking on the sea, they thought it was a ghost[b] and cried out, [50] because they all saw him and were terrified.[c] Immediately he spoke with them and said, "Have courage![d] It is I.[e] Don't be afraid."[f] [51] Then he got into the boat with them, and the wind ceased. They were completely astounded, [52] because they had not understood about the loaves. Instead, their hearts were hardened.[g]

MIRACULOUS HEALINGS

[53] When they had crossed over, they came to shore at Gennesaret[h] and anchored there.

[54] As they got out of the boat, people immediately recognized him. [55] They hurried throughout that region and began to carry the sick[i] on mats to wherever they heard he was. [56] Wherever he went, into villages, towns, or the country, they laid the sick in the marketplaces and begged him that they might touch just the end[j] of his robe.[k] And everyone who touched it was healed.

THE TRADITIONS OF THE ELDERS

7 The[l] Pharisees[m] and some of the scribes[n] who had come from Jerusalem[o] gathered around him. [2] They observed that some of his disciples were eating bread with unclean[p] — that is, unwashed — hands. [3] (For the Pharisees and all the Jews do not eat unless they give their hands a ceremonial washing, keeping the tradition of the elders. [4] When they come from the marketplace,[q] they do not eat unless they have washed.[r] And there are many other customs they have received and keep, like the washing of

cups, pitchers, kettles, and dining couches.[C,s]) [5] So the Pharisees[t] and the scribes[u] asked him, "Why don't your disciples live according to the tradition of the elders,[v] instead of eating bread with ceremonially unclean[b] hands?"

[6] He answered them, "Isaiah[w] prophesied[x] correctly about you hypocrites,[y] as it is written:[z]

This people honors[aa] me
    with their lips,
but their heart is far
    from me.
[7]   They worship me in vain,
    teaching[ab] as doctrines[ac]
    human commands. [E,ad]

[8] Abandoning the command of God, you hold on to human tradition."[F] [9] He also said to them, "You have a fine way of invalidating God's command in order to set up[G] your tradition! [10] For Moses[ae] said: Honor your father and your mother;[H,af] and Whoever speaks evil of father or mother must be put to death.[i,ag] [11] But you say, 'If anyone tells his father or mother: Whatever benefit[ah] you might have received from me is corban'" (that is, an offering[ai] devoted to God), [12] "you no longer let him do anything for his father or mother. [13] You nullify the word of God[aj] by your tradition that you have handed[ak] down. And you do many other similar things."

[14] Summoning[al] the crowd again, he told them, "Listen to me, all of you, and understand:[am] [15] Nothing that goes into a person from outside can defile him but the things that come out of a person are what defile him."[J]

[17] When he went into the house away from the crowd, his disciples asked him about the parable. [18] He said to them, "Are you also as lacking in understanding? Don't you realize that nothing going into a person from the outside can defile him?

[a] 6:48 Rv 20:10
[b] 6:49 Mt 14:26
[c] 6:50 Jn 5:7
[d] Jn 16:33
[e] Ex 3:14; Ps 45:8; Jn 8:24
[f] Jn 6:20
[g] 6:52 Mk 8:17; Heb 3:8
[h] 6:53 Mt 14:34; Lk 5:1
[i] 6:55 Lk 5:31
[j] 6:56 Mt 23:5
[k] Mt 9:20; 14:36; Lk 8:44; 19:36
[l] 7:1-23 Mt 15:1-20
[m] 7:1 Mk 7:3
[n] Mt 2:4
[o] Mt 23:37
[p] 7:2 Ac 10:28
[q] 7:4 Mk 6:56
[r] Heb 6:2; 9:10

[s] 7:4 Lk 5:18
[t] 7:5 Mk 7:3
[u] Mt 2:4
[v] 3Jn 1
[w] 7:6 Mt 3:3; 4:14; 12:17
[x] Jn 11:51
[y] Lk 6:42
[z] Ac 15:15
[aa] 1Tm 5:3
[ab] 7:7 Mt 28:20; Ac 4:2; 2Tm 4:11
[ac] Rm 15:4
[ad] Is 29:13; Col 2:22
[ae] 7:10 Ps 77:20; Mt 8:4; Heb 3:2
[af] Ex 20:12; Dt 5:16
[ag] Ex 21:17; Lv 20:9
[ah] 7:11 Mk 5:26
[ai] Heb 5:1; 9:9; 11:4
[aj] 7:13 Mk 4:14; Lk 8:21; Jn 18:32
[ak] Jd 3
[al] 7:14 Lk 18:16
[am] Mt 13:13

[A] 6:48 Or them being battered as they rowed   [B] 6:48 Lit Around the fourth watch of the night = 3 to 6 a.m.   [C] 7:4 Other mss omit and dining couches   [D] 7:5 Other mss read with unwashed   [E] 7:6-7 Is 29:13   [F] 7:8 Other mss add The washing of jugs, and cups, and many other similar things you practice.   [G] 7:9 Or to maintain   [H] 7:10 Ex 20:12; Dt 5:16   [I] 7:10 Ex 21:17; Lv 20:9   [J] 7:15 Some mss include v. 16: "If anyone has ears to hear, let him listen."

6:48 Don't miss that Jesus **saw them straining at the oars**. Though God may seem to be absent in your circumstances, rest assured that he sees you.

The CSB's **very early in the morning** is literally "around the fourth watch of the night." So this encounter occurred between three and six a.m.
6:51-52 The disciples were shocked by these events **because they had not understood about the loaves** (6:52). Something had happened the previous day (see 6:30-44) that should've affected how they reacted

this day. They didn't recognize Jesus because they weren't looking for him in the midst of their trial. And they weren't looking for him in this problem because they'd failed to see that Jesus was the answer to the previous problem.
7:9-12 The Pharisees and scribes were professionals at trumping God's Word with their own preferences (7:9). As an example of this, Jesus pointed to two Old Testament texts: the command to **honor** one's parents and the threat of **death** for those who curse their parents (7:10; see Exod 20:12; 21:17; Lev 20:9; Deut 5:16). God expects children, young and

old, to respect their parents. But, in order to avoid giving financial help to parents who were in need, these hypocrites would declare their money to be **corban**, which was **an offering devoted to God**, so that they could give it to the temple instead (Mark 7:11-12). In this way, they would appear to be generous supporters of God's work, when actually they were cheapskates avoiding family obligations (7:13). Paul makes it clear that "if anyone does not provide for his own family . . . he has denied the faith and is worse than an unbeliever" (1 Tim 5:8).

a 7:19 Php 3:19
b 1Jn 1:7
c 7:21 1Th 4:3
d Pr 1:16
e 7:22 Nm 5:11
f Eph 5:3
g Ps 10:7
h Rm 13:13; 2Co 12:21; Gl 5:19; Eph 4:19; 1Pt 4:3; 2Pt 2:2,7,18
i Jn 10:33; Rv 13:6
j Ps 17:10
k 2Co 11:1
l 7:24-30 Mt 15:21-28
m 7:24 Ac 21:7
n 7:25 Lk 11:24
o Lk 8:47
p 7:26 Ac 17:12
q Mk 3:15; Rv 9:20; 18:2
r 7:27 Ex 22:31
s 7:28 Lk 10:1
t 7:31 Ac 21:7
u Mt 4:18; 15:29; Mk 1:16; Jn 6:1

v 7:31 Mt 4:25; Mk 5:20
w 7:32 Lk 7:22
x Ex 4:11; Is 35:6; 56:10
y 1Tm 5:22
z 7:33 Jn 9:6
aa 7:34 Mt 24:35; Lk 12:33; Ac 17:24; Eph 6:9; Rv 21:10
ab 7:35 Phm 10
ac Lk 20:21
ad 7:36 Mk 1:44; Lk 8:56
ae Mk 1:4
af 7:37 Gn 1:31
ag Lk 7:22
ah Mk 9:17
ai 8:1-10 Mt 15:29-38
aj 8:1 Lk 18:16
ak Mt 9:10; Mk 10:10; Lk 6:1; Jn 6:3; Ac 6:1
al 8:2 Lk 15:20
am 8:3 Mk 8:27
an 8:4 Mt 5:6; 15:33
ao 8:6 Mk 14:22

19 For it doesn't go into his heart but into the stomach*a* and is eliminated" (thus he declared all foods clean*A,b*). **20** And he said, "What comes out of a person is what defiles him. **21** For from within, out of people's hearts, come evil thoughts, sexual immoralities,*c* thefts, murders,*d* **22** adulteries,*e* greed,*f* evil actions, deceit,*g* self-indulgence,*h* envy,*B* slander,*i* pride,*j* and foolishness.*k* **23** All these evil things come from within and defile a person."

A GENTILE MOTHER'S FAITH

24 He got up and departed from*l* there to the region of Tyre.*C,m* He entered a house and did not want anyone to know it, but he could not escape notice. **25** Instead, immediately after hearing about him, a woman whose little daughter had an unclean spirit*n* came and fell at his feet.*o* **26** The woman was a Gentile,*D,p* a Syrophoenician by birth, and she was asking him to cast the demon*q* out of her daughter. **27** He said to her, "Let the children be fed first, because it isn't right to take the children's bread and throw it to the dogs."*r*

28 But she replied to him, "Lord,*s* even the dogs under the table eat the children's crumbs."

29 Then he told her, "Because of this reply, you may go. The demon has left your daughter." **30** When she went back to her home, she found her child lying on the bed, and the demon was gone.

JESUS DOES EVERYTHING WELL

31 Again, leaving the region of Tyre,*t* he went by way of Sidon to the Sea of Galilee,*u*

through*E* the region of the Decapolis.*v* **32** They brought to him a deaf*w* man who had difficulty speaking*x* and begged Jesus to lay his hand on*y* him. **33** So he took him away from the crowd in private. After putting his fingers in the man's ears and spitting,*z* he touched his tongue. **34** Looking up to heaven,*aa* he sighed deeply and said to him, "*Ephphatha!*"*F* (that is, "Be opened!"). **35** Immediately his ears were opened,*ab* his tongue was loosened, and he began to speak clearly.*ac* **36** He ordered them to tell no one,*ad* but the more he ordered them, the more they proclaimed it.*ae*

37 They were extremely astonished and said, "He has done everything well.*af* He even makes the deaf*ag* hear and the mute speak."*ah*

FEEDING FOUR THOUSAND

8 In*ai* those days there was again a large crowd, and they had nothing to eat. He called*aj* the disciples*ak* and said to them, **2** "I have compassion*al* on the crowd, because they've already stayed with me three days and have nothing to eat. **3** If I send them home hungry, they will collapse on the way,*am* and some of them have come a long distance."

4 His disciples answered him, "Where can anyone get enough bread here in this desolate place to feed*an* these people?"

5 "How many loaves do you have?" he asked them.

"Seven," they said. **6** He commanded the crowd to sit down on the ground. Taking the seven loaves, he gave thanks, broke*ao* them, and gave them to his disciples to set before the people. So they served them

---

A 7:19 Other mss read *is eliminated, making all foods clean*   *B* 7:22 Or *evil eye*   *C* 7:24 Many early mss add *and Sidon*   *D* 7:26 Or *a Greek (speaker)*   *E* 7:31 Or *into*   *F* 7:34 An Aramaic expression

---

7:19-23 Bad food might make you sick, but it can't make you spiritually unclean. God had given Israel commands about unclean animals they couldn't eat to teach them about holiness and unholiness (see Lev 11). But, ultimately, we are not defiled by foods (Mark 7:14); we are defiled by **what comes out of** our **hearts** (7:21). Following customs and traditions can't fix your sinful heart any more than doing so could help the Pharisees. Only Jesus Christ, through his atoning work on the cross, can grant you forgiveness of sins and a transformed heart (see Heb 10:16-18) that is in sync with God.

7:24 Tyre was an area northwest of Galilee on the coast of the Mediterranean Sea. Previously, people from this region had come because they heard about his miraculous works (see 3:7-8).

7:27-28 Jesus was comparing the Jews to "children" and the Gentiles to "dogs"—the Greek word referred to house dogs or lapdogs. Matthew reports that Jesus told her he was sent to "the lost sheep of the house of Israel"

(Matt 15:24). Though his message of salvation would be for all people (Matt 28:19), his earthly ministry was primarily directed to the Jews. Nevertheless, this Gentile woman was humble and desperate. Picking up on Jesus's illustration, she told him that **even the dogs under the table eat the children's crumbs** (Mark 7:28). She didn't want to detract from his mission or prevent him from ministering to the people of Israel. All she wanted were some miracle leftovers to heal her daughter. The Jewish religious leaders were seeking to kill Jesus, but this poor Gentile woman had more faith than all of them put together.

7:31 The region of the Decapolis is where the man who had been possessed by the "legion" of demons went to proclaim how much Jesus had done for him (see 5:1-20).

7:33 Though Jesus could work the miraculous with mere words (e.g., 2:10-12; 3:5; 4:39; 7:29-30), frequently his miracles involved physical touch, demonstrating his compassion and

confirming that he was the author of the deed (e.g., 1:31, 41-42; 5:27-29, 41-42; 6:56).

7:34 He sighed deeply in sorrow over the man's broken condition. Similarly, Jesus wept before he raised Lazarus from the dead (John 11:35).

8:4 Unfortunately, none of the **disciples** thought to say, "Lord, remember that time when you fed thousands with only five loaves and two fish? Surely you can do that again!" Instead, they were perplexed, having no idea where the food would come from. When you forget God's past deeds in your life, you will forget the kingdom power available to you. You'll fail to believe that "all things are possible with God" (10:27).

8:5-10 As God fed the Israelite multitude in a wilderness with manna and quail, so Jesus fed the Israelite multitude in a "desolate place" (8:4) with **loaves** and **fish** (8:6-8). Like Father, like Son. Jesus's gratefulness in the midst of insufficiency is also a lesson to us (8:6). Giving thanks for what God has provided opens the door for him to respond with abundance.

to the crowd. [7] They also had a few small fish, and after he had blessed them, he said these were to be served as well. [8] They ate and were satisfied. Then they collected seven large baskets of leftover pieces. [9] About four thousand were there. He dismissed them. [10] And he immediately got into the boat with his disciples and went to the district of Dalmanutha.

THE LEAVEN OF THE PHARISEES AND HEROD

[11] The[a] Pharisees[b] came and began to argue with him, demanding of him a sign[c] from heaven[d] to test[e] him. [12] Sighing deeply in his spirit,[f] he said, "Why does this generation[g] demand a sign? Truly I tell you,[h] no sign will be given to this generation." [13] Then he left them, got back into the boat, and went to the other side.

[14] The disciples had forgotten to take bread and had only one loaf with them in the boat. [15] Then[i] he gave them strict orders: "Watch out! Beware of the leaven[A,j] of the Pharisees and the leaven of Herod."[k] [16] They were discussing among themselves that they did not have any bread. [17] Aware of this, he said to them, "Why are you discussing the fact you have no bread? Don't you understand or comprehend? Do you have hardened hearts?[l] [18] **Do you have eyes and not see; do you have ears and not hear?**[B,m] And do you not remember?[n] [19] When I broke the five loaves for the five thousand, how many baskets full of leftovers did you collect?"

"Twelve," they told him.

[20] "When I broke the seven loaves for the four thousand, how many baskets full of pieces did you collect?"

"Seven," they said.

[21] And he said to them, "Don't you understand yet?"[o]

HEALING A BLIND MAN

[22] They came to Bethsaida.[p] They brought a blind[q] man to him and begged him to touch him. [23] He took the blind man by the hand and brought him out of the village. Spitting[r] on his eyes and laying his hands on[s] him, he asked him, "Do you see anything?"

[24] He looked up and said, "I see people — they look like trees walking."[t]

[25] Again Jesus placed his hands on the man's eyes. The man looked intently and his sight was restored and he saw everything clearly. [26] Then he sent[u] him home, saying, "Don't even go into the village."[C,v]

PETER'S CONFESSION OF THE MESSIAH

[27] Jesus[w] went out with his disciples to the villages of Caesarea Philippi. And on the road he asked his disciples, "Who do people say that I am?"

[28] They answered him, "John the Baptist;[x] others, Elijah; still others, one of the prophets."[y]

[29] "But you," he asked them, "who do you say that I am?"

Peter[z] answered him, "You are the Messiah."[aa] [30] And he strictly warned[ab] them to tell no one about him.

HIS DEATH AND RESURRECTION PREDICTED

[31] Then[ac] he began to teach them that it was necessary for the Son of Man[ad] to suffer many things and be rejected[ae] by

---

a 8:11-12 Mt 16:1-4
b 8:11 Mk 7:3
c Mk 13:22; Jn 2:11; Heb 2:4
d Mt 24:35; Lk 12:33; Ac 17:24; Eph 6:9; Rv 21:10
e Jms 1:13
f 8:12 Ps 51:12
g Lk 11:29
h Rv 22:21
i 8:15-21 Mt 16:5-12
j 8:15 Lk 13:21; Gl 5:9
k Mt 14:1
l 8:17 Mk 6:52; Jn 12:40; Rm 11:7; 2Co 3:14
m 8:18 Jr 5:21; Ezk 12:2; Mk 4:9,40
n Rv 2:5

o 8:21 Mk 4:40
p 8:22 Jn 12:21
q Mt 15:14
r 8:23 Mk 7:33; 8:23; Jn 9:6
s 1Tm 5:22
t Mt 11:5
u 8:26 Mk 3:14
v Mk 1:44
w 8:27-30 Mt 16:13-20; Lk 9:18-20
x 8:28 Mk 1:4; Lk 7:20
y Mt 2:23; Ac 7:52
z 8:29 Lk 6:14
aa Mt 1:17; Eph 5:2
ab 8:30 2Tm 4:2
ac 8:31-9:1 Mt 16:21-28; Lk 9:21-27
ad 8:31 Mk 2:10
ae Mt 21:42; Mk 12:10; Lk 9:22; 17:25; 20:17; Heb 12:17; 1Pt 2:4,7

A 8:15 Or *yeast*   B 8:18 Jr 5:21; Ezk 12:2   C 8:26 Other mss add *or tell anyone in the village*

8:11-13 Jesus had already given more than sufficient proof of his messianic claims. He had performed a massive number of a variety of miracles before multiple witnesses. The Pharisees, then, had all the signs they needed. They'd just rejected them all.

8:15 It only takes a small amount of **leaven**, or yeast, to work through and affect an entire batch of dough. So, though they were few, the Pharisees and Herodians had a tremendous ability to influence the people with their human traditions and lead them away from God.

8:17-21 The disciples' worry about insufficient food demonstrated a lack of faith in Jesus. They failed to **remember** what he'd done (8:17-18)! Jesus had miraculously fed thousands on two different occasions using only a few loaves and fish (8:19-20; see 6:30-44; 8:1-10). His apostles' unbelief and inability to **understand** (8:21) was a result of forgetting

what Jesus had already done. Don't overlook how God worked in your life yesterday; you'll need that knowledge for the trials you'll face tomorrow.

8:22 Bethsaida was the hometown of Philip, Andrew, and Peter (see John 1:44).

8:23-25 After the first healing touch (8:23), the man was no longer blind; nevertheless, he still wasn't seeing clearly. After a second touch from Jesus, the man's **sight was restored** and he saw **clearly** (8:25). Likewise, Peter was about to demonstrate spiritual insight (see 8:29), but he did not yet see clearly enough. Though he believed that Jesus was the Messiah, Peter would also have to embrace everything that meant—including Jesus's suffering and death (see 8:31-33).

8:27 Caesarea Philippi was located about twenty-five miles north of the Sea of Galilee. The city had been rebuilt by Philip, the

son of Herod, and named after its builder and Caesar Augustus.

8:29-30 Indeed, Jesus is **the Messiah**, the Anointed One, the Son of David, the coming King (8:29). But he **warned them to tell no one** (8:30) because he didn't want people openly proclaiming him as the Messiah yet. There was still too much confusion about what the Messiah was to do, and that problem was about to be demonstrated by Peter himself.

8:31 For the first time, Jesus told his disciples what being the Messiah involved. Rejection and death certainly were not what the disciples were expecting for the Messiah. They were looking for victory, not defeat. Nevertheless, they had been with Jesus for a long time. They had heard his teaching; they'd seen his marvelous deeds. So if these difficult things were what Jesus said must happen, then they should've believed him.

the elders,[a] chief priests, and scribes,[b] be
killed, and rise[c] after three days.[d] 32 He
spoke openly about this. Peter took him
aside and began to rebuke him. 33 But turning around and looking at his disciples, he
rebuked Peter and said, "Get behind me,
Satan![e] You are not thinking about God's
concerns[A] but human concerns."

APPLICATION QUESTIONS

READ MARK 8:34

- Are you willing to follow God's divine calling for your life? Explain.
- How have you expressed your commitment to God?

HOPE WORDS

Jesus is not looking for fans.
He is looking for followers.

TAKE UP YOUR CROSS

34 Calling the crowd along with his disciples, he said to them, "If anyone wants
to follow after me, let him deny himself,[f]
take up his cross,[g] and follow me.[h] 35 For
whoever wants to save[i] his life will lose
it,[j] but whoever loses[k] his life[l] because of
me[m] and the gospel[n] will save it.[o] 36 For
what does it benefit[p] someone to gain[q]
the whole world[r] and yet lose[s] his life?[t]
37 What can anyone give in exchange for
his life?[u] 38 For whoever is ashamed[v] of me
and my words[w] in this adulterous and sinful[x] generation,[y] the Son of Man will also
be ashamed of him when he comes in the
glory[z] of his Father[aa] with the holy[ab] angels."[ac]

9 Then he said to them, "Truly I tell
you,[ad] there are some standing here
who will not taste death[ae] until they see
the kingdom of God come in power."[af]

THE TRANSFIGURATION

2 After[ag] six days[ah] Jesus took Peter, James,
and John[ai] and led them up a high mountain[aj] by themselves to be alone. He was
transfigured[ak] in front of them, 3 and his
clothes[al] became dazzling — extremely
white[am] as no launderer on earth could
whiten[an] them. 4 Elijah[ao] appeared to them
with Moses,[ap] and they were talking with
Jesus. 5 Peter said to Jesus, "Rabbi,[aq] it's
good[ar] for us to be here. Let us set up three
shelters:[as] one for you, one for Moses, and
one for Elijah" — 6 because he did not
know what to say,[at] since they were terrified.[au]
7 A cloud[av] appeared, overshadowing[aw] them, and a voice[ax] came from the
cloud:[ay] "This is my beloved[az] Son;[ba] listen
to him!"[bb]
8 Suddenly, looking around, they no longer saw anyone with them except Jesus.
9 As[bc] they were coming down the mountain,[bd] he ordered them to tell no one what
they had seen[be] until the Son of Man[bf] had
risen[bg] from the dead.[bh] 10 They kept this
word[bi] to themselves, questioning what
"rising from the dead" meant.
11 Then they asked him, "Why do the
scribes[bj] say that Elijah must come first?"[bk]
12 "Elijah does come first and restores[bl]
all things,"[bm] he replied. "Why then is it

[a] 8:31 3Jn 1 [b] Mt 2:4 [c] Mt 16:21; Lk 18:33; Ac 2:24 [d] Lk 9:22 [e] 8:33 Mt 4:1,10; Ac 13:10 [f] 8:34 Mk 10:45 [g] Lk 9:23 [h] Jn 8:12; 3Jn 9 [i] 8:35 Ac 16:30; Jms 5:20; Jd 23 [j] 1Jn 3:16 [k] Mt 16:26 [l] Mt 10:39 [m] Mk 10:29; Rm 8:36 [n] Mk 1:1; Php 1:5 [o] Mt 16:25; Lk 9:24 [p] 8:36 Mk 5:26 [q] Mt 16:26 [r] Mt 13:38 [s] 1Co 3:15; Php 3:7 [t] Rm 15:1 [u] 8:37 Mt 20:28 [v] 8:38 Rm 1:16 [w] Mk 4:14; Jn 18:32 [x] 1Tm 1:15 [y] Mt 12:39; Lk 11:29 [z] 8:38 Lk 9:32; Jn 17:24; 2Co 3:18; 2Pt 3:18 [aa] Mt 5:16; 11:27; Jn 8:42 [ab] 1Co 7:14 [ac] Mt 13:49; Ac 5:19; Jd 14; Rv 14:6 [ad] 9:1 Ps 72:19; Rv 22:21 [ae] Mk 13:28-32; 14:25; Jn 21:22-23; 2Pt 3:4 [af] Lk 6:19 [ag] 9:2-8 Mt 17:1-8; Lk 9:28-36 [ah] 9:2 Ex 24:15-18; Hs 6:2 [ai] Mt 10:2; Mk 5:37; 13:3; 14:33; Ac 1:13 [aj] Mt 4:8; 2Pt 1:18 [ak] Rm 12:2; 2Co 3:18 [al] 9:3 Lk 19:36 [am] Rv 3:4 [an] Rv 7:14 [ao] 9:4 Mk 8:28 [ap] Ps 77:20; Mt 8:4; Heb 3:2 [aq] 9:5 Jn 11:8 [ar] Gn 1:31 [as] Ex 25:9 [at] 9:6 Mk 14:40 [au] Heb 12:21 [av] 9:7 Ex 24:15; Mt 26:64 [aw] Lk 1:35

[ax] 9:7 Jn 5:37 [ay] 2Pt 1:16-18 [az] Eph 1:6; Phm 1 [ba] Lk 20:13; Jn 5:19 [bb] Dt 18:15 [bc] 9:9-13 Mt 17:9-13 [bd] 9:9 Mt 4:8 [be] Lk 8:56 [bf] Mk 2:10 [bg] Mt 16:21; Lk 18:33 [bh] Jn 20:9 [bi] 9:10 Mk 4:14 [bj] 9:11 Mt 2:4 [bk] Mal 4:5 [bl] 9:12 Mk 8:25 [bm] Lk 1:17

[A] 8:33 Or *about the things of God*

8:32-33 Peter had adopted Satan's way of thinking, which involved rejecting God's revealed truth for mere human logic. To oppose the true understanding of the Messiah is to oppose God.

8:34 If you want to be a disciple of Jesus—you must **deny** yourself, **take up** your **cross**, and **follow** him. It's easy to say you're a follower of Jesus—until the going gets hard. But Jesus expects you to identify with him, even if that means experiencing rejection and suffering.

8:35 In saying, **Whoever wants to save his life will lose it**, Jesus wasn't speaking to unbelievers. He was addressing those who had already decided to follow him. If you seek to preserve yourself from inconveniences and difficulties that come from identifying with Jesus, you will lose out on the abundant life Christ promises—that is, the experience of a relationship with him now and an eternal reward later.

On the other hand, **whoever loses his life because of [Jesus] and the gospel will save it.** So if you are willing to deny yourself (telling your desires no when they come in conflict with the kingdom), to pursue God's kingdom agenda in his Word, and to publicly identify with Jesus Christ, you will gain true life (that is, intimate experience with God) in history and even greater reward in eternity.

8:36-38 How **does it benefit** a believer to amass great wealth, notoriety, and power if he loses out on the abundant life God promises and his eternal rewards later? (8:36). We only get one chance to decide what kind of life we'll lead. As missionary C. T. Studd wrote, "Only one life, 'twill soon be past, / Only what's done for Christ will last." So don't let the pleasures this world has to offer replace the true meaning of life. Don't **be ashamed of** Christ and his words. Let his return be an experience of true joy, not of shame (8:38).

9:1 This statement refers to the fact that Peter, James, and John would **see** the Son of God's heavenly glory manifested before them (see 9:2-7). This would provide a preview of the glory of the coming kingdom.

9:4 **Moses** represented the Law, and **Elijah** represented the Prophets. The Old Testament ("the Law and the Prophets," Matt 5:17; 22:40) points to Jesus.

9:5-7 Have you ever known people who can't stop talking when they become nervous or afraid? That was Peter. He was **terrified** of what he saw and **did not know what to say** (9:6). So he suggested building **three shelters**, one for each of them (9:5), in fulfillment of Zechariah 14:16-19. However, by his affirmation of his **beloved Son**, God the Father made it clear that the disciples' focus was to be on Jesus alone (9:7).

written[a] that the Son of Man must suffer[b] many things and be treated with contempt?[c] 13 But I tell you that Elijah has come, and they did whatever they pleased to him, just as it is written[d] about him."

THE POWER OF FAITH OVER A DEMON

14 When[e] they came to the disciples, they saw a large crowd around them and scribes disputing[f] with them. 15 When the whole crowd saw him, they were amazed and ran to greet him. 16 He asked them, "What are you arguing with them about?"

17 Someone from the crowd answered him, "Teacher,[g] I brought my son to you. He has a spirit[h] that makes him unable to speak.[i] 18 Whenever it seizes him, it throws him down, and he foams at the mouth, grinds his teeth, and becomes rigid. I asked your disciples to drive it out, but they couldn't."

19 He replied to them, "You unbelieving[j] generation, how long will I be with you? How long must I put up with you? Bring him to me." 20 So they brought the boy to him. When the spirit saw him, it immediately threw the boy into convulsions. He fell to the ground and rolled around, foaming at the mouth. 21 "How long has this been happening to him?" Jesus asked his father.

"From childhood," he said. 22 "And many times it has thrown him into fire or water to destroy[k] him. But if you can do anything, have compassion[l] on us and help us."

23 Jesus said to him, "'If you can'?[A] Everything is possible[m] for the one who believes."[n]

24 Immediately the father of the boy cried out, "I do believe; help my unbelief!"

25 When Jesus saw that a crowd was quickly gathering, he rebuked[o] the unclean[p] spirit, saying to it, "You mute and deaf[q] spirit, I command you: Come out of him and never enter him again."

26 Then it came out, shrieking and throwing him[B] into terrible convulsions.[r] The boy became like a corpse, so that many said, "He's dead." 27 But Jesus, taking him by the hand, raised him,[s] and he stood up.

28 After he had gone into the house, his disciples asked him privately, "Why couldn't we drive it out?"

29 And he told them, "This kind can come out by nothing but prayer."[C,t]

THE SECOND PREDICTION OF HIS DEATH

30 Then[u] they left that place and made their way through Galilee, but he did not want anyone to know it.[v] 31 For he was teaching[w] his disciples and telling them, "The Son of Man[x] is going to be betrayed[D] into the hands of men. They will kill him, and after he is killed, he will rise[y] three days later."[z] 32 But they did not understand this statement, and they were afraid to ask him.[aa]

WHO IS THE GREATEST?

33 They[ab] came to Capernaum.[ac] When he was in the house,[ad] he asked them, "What were you arguing about on the way?"[ae] 34 But they were silent,[af] because on the way they had been arguing with one another about who was the greatest.[ag] 35 Sitting down, he called the Twelve[ah] and said to them, "If anyone wants to be first, he must be last and servant of all."[ai] 36 He took a child,[aj] had him stand among

a 9:12 Ac 15:15
b Mk 8:31
c Lk 23:11
d 9:13 Mk 1:2
e 9:14-29 Mt 17:14-20; Lk 9:37-42
f 9:14 Mk 8:11
g 9:17 Mk 4:38; Eph 4:11
h Lk 11:24; 1Tm 4:1; 1Jn 4:1
i Mk 7:37
j 9:19 Lk 12:46
k 9:22 Jn 6:27
l Lk 15:20

m 9:23 Mt 17:20; Jn 11:40
n Jn 3:16; Ac 10:43; Rm 10:9; 1Pt 1:8-10
o 9:25 2Tm 4:2
p 2Co 6:17
q Lk 7:22
r 9:26 Mk 1:26
s 9:27 Mk 1:31
t 9:29 Ac 12:5; 16:13; Phm 22
u 9:30-32 Mt 17:22-23; Lk 9:43-45
v 9:30 Mk 1:44
w 9:31 Mt 28:20; Ac 4:2; 2Tm 4:11
x Mk 2:10
y Mt 16:21; Lk 18:33; Ac 2:24
z Mk 8:31; Lk 9:22
aa 9:32 Mk 4:40; Lk 2:50
ab 9:33-50 Mt 18:1-10; Lk 9:46-50
ac 9:33 Lk 10:15
ad Mk 1:29
ae Mk 8:27
af 9:34 Mk 3:4
ag Lk 22:24-27; Ac 8:9
ah 9:35 Mk 11:11
ai Mt 20:16-27; 23:11; Mk 10:43-44; Lk 22:26
aj 9:36 Lk 1:7

A 9:23 Other mss add *believe*   B 9:26 Other mss omit *him*   C 9:29 Other mss add *and fasting*   D 9:31 Or *handed over*

9:13 In his account of this incident, Matthew makes it clear that Jesus was speaking about John the Baptist (Matt 17:13). On another occasion, Jesus said that John the Baptist "is the Elijah who is to come" (Matt 11:14). As Elijah is a messenger for God in the Old Testament, John is a messenger in the New. John came to "restore all things" (Mark 9:12) by calling Israel to repentance to prepare the way for the Messiah. But, the religious leaders **did whatever they pleased to him** by rejecting him (9:13; see Matt 3:7-10; Mark 11:29-31), and ultimately Herod had him executed (6:25-29).
9:14-18 The inability of the disciples to cast out the demon apparently led to a dispute with the **scribes**, who questioned their legitimacy (9:14).

9:22 The father was in such despair that he wondered **if** even Jesus could **do anything**. After all, his disciples had failed.
9:24 If you find yourself doubting God, let this man's cry be your prayer. Be honest with God about your doubts and proceed in faith. God will honor your faith and strengthen it.
9:28-29 A bit humiliated, the disciples asked Jesus privately why they'd failed (9:28). Some demons are worse and more powerful than others, he told them. Some require greater dependence on divine intervention that is only accessed through **prayer** (9:29). Past spiritual victory does not necessarily fuel today's spiritual battles. Today's battles require fresh dependency on and communication with God.

9:31-32 Again, Jesus told them that he would be **betrayed**, killed, and would **rise three days later** (9:31). However, they were just as confused about this second prediction (9:32) as they were about the first (see 8:31-33).
9:35 Greatness comes by being a **servant** to others—not by exalting yourself above others. You must believe that God will honor your servanthood in history and in eternity.
9:36-37 To show kindness to **a child**—who can offer nothing in return—is to serve God (9:37). Greatness is not achieved through marvelous actions that all see. It's often achieved through lowly and unseen acts of service toward those who cannot repay. But God sees, and God repays.

a 9:37 Jn 10:25
b Mt 15:24; Mk 12:6; '
Jn 3:16-17
c Mt 10:40
d 9:38 Jn 21:7
e Mk 4:38
f Mk 3:15; Rv 9:20
g Jn 10:25; 14:13
h Nm 11:26-30
i 9:39 Ac 19:11
j 9:40 Mt 12:30;
Lk 11:23
k 9:41 Mt 10:42; 25:35-42;
Rm 12:20
l Mt 1:17; Eph 5:2
m Rv 22:21
n Mt 10:42; 2Pt 2:13
o 9:42 Ex 23:33;
Jn 6:35
p Jdg 9:53; Mt 24:41;
Rv 18:22
q 9:43 Mt 5:29-30
r Mt 15:30-31
s Mt 3:12; 5:22; 25:41;
2Th 1:8
t 9:45 Jn 5:3

u 9:47 Mk 1:15
v 3Jn 10
w Jms 3:6
x 9:49 Lv 2:13;
Ezk 43:24
y 9:50 Mt 5:13; Lk 14:34
z Ex 30:35; 2Kg 2:19-23;
Col 4:6
aa Mt 5:9; Rm 12:18; 14:13;
2Co 13:11; 1Th 5:13;
Heb 12:14
ab 10:1-12 Mt 19:1-2
ac 10:1 Lk 1:5
ad Mt 4:15,25; Lk 3:3;
Jn 1:28; 3:26;
10:40
ae Mt 28:20; Ac 4:2;
2Tm 4:11
af 10:2 Mk 7:3
ag Jms 1:13
ah Jn 18:31
ai Lv 21:7　*ak* 10:3 Ps 77:20; Mt 8:4; Heb 3:2　*al* 10:4 Mt 5:31　*am* Dt 24:1,3　*an* 10:5 Mk 16:14　*ao* 10:6 Jn 1:1; Ac 26:4　*ap* Jn 1:3; Rv 3:14　*aq* Gn 1:27; 5:2
aj 1Pt 3:1　*ar* 10:7 Lk 15:4　*as* 10:7-8 Gn 2:24

them, and taking him in his arms, he said to them, 37 "Whoever welcomes[A] one little child such as this in my name[a] welcomes me. And whoever welcomes me does not welcome me, but him who sent[b] me."[c]

IN HIS NAME

38 John[d] said to him, "Teacher,[e] we saw someone[B] driving out demons[f] in your name,[g] and we tried to stop him because he wasn't following us."[h]

39 "Don't stop him," said Jesus, "because there is no one who will perform a miracle[i] in my name who can soon afterward speak evil of me. 40 For whoever is not against us is for us.[j] 41 And whoever gives you a cup of water to drink[k] in my name, because you belong to Christ[l] — truly I tell you,[m] he will never lose his reward.[n]

WARNINGS FROM JESUS

42 "But whoever causes one of these little ones who believe in me to fall away[o] — it would be better for him if a heavy millstone[p] were hung around his neck and he were thrown into the sea.

43 "And if your hand causes you to fall away, cut it off.[q] It is better for you to enter life maimed[r] than to have two hands and go to hell, the unquenchable fire.[C,S] 45 And if your foot causes you to fall away, cut it off. It is better for you to enter life lame[t]

than to have two feet and be thrown into hell.[D] 47 And if your eye causes you to fall away, gouge it out. It is better for you to enter the kingdom of God[u] with one eye than to have two eyes and be thrown[v] into hell,[w] 48 where their worm does not die, and the fire is not quenched.[E] 49 For everyone will be salted with fire.[F,G,x] 50 Salt is good, but if the salt should lose its flavor, how can you season it?[y] Have salt[z] among yourselves, and be at peace[aa] with one another."

THE QUESTION OF DIVORCE

10 He[ab] set out from there and went to the region of Judea[ac] and across the Jordan.[ad] Then crowds converged on him again, and as was his custom he taught[ae] them again.

2 Some Pharisees[af] came to test[ag] him, asking, "Is it lawful[ah] for a man to divorce[ai] his wife?"[aj]

3 He replied to them, "What did Moses[ak] command you?"

4 They said, "Moses permitted us to write divorce papers[al] and send her away."[am]

5 But Jesus told them, "He wrote this command for you because of the hardness of your hearts.[an] 6 But from the beginning[ao] of creation[ap] God[H] made them male and female.[I,aq] 7 For this reason a man will leave[ar] his father and mother[J] 8 and the two will become one flesh.[K,as] So they are no longer

A 9:37 Or "Whoever receives　B 9:38 Other mss add who didn't go along with us　C 9:43 Some mss include v. 44: Where their worm does not die, and the fire is not quenched.　D 9:45 Some mss include v. 46: Where their worm does not die, and the fire is not quenched.　E 9:48 Is 66:24　F 9:49 Other mss add and every sacrifice will be salted with salt　G 9:49 Lv 2:13; Ezk 43:24　H 10:6 Other mss omit God　I 10:6 Gn 1:27; 5:2　J 10:7 Some mss add and be joined to his wife　K 10:7-8 Gn 2:24

9:38-40 The disciples considered themselves part of an exclusive team (9:38). After all, they were the only ones who'd been deputized by Jesus to minister in his name. So who did that guy think he was? Jesus made it clear that someone cannot work for him and against him at the same time (9:39-40).

9:41 God sees and remembers all things done for his glory and for the good of others, especially those who **belong to Christ**, or "the household of faith" (Gal 6:10).

9:42 A **millstone** was used to grind grain, and it was so **heavy** that a donkey was typically used to move it. Thus, the consequences are grave for leading a follower of Christ astray through deception or false teaching. God's severe judgment will fall.

9:43-47 Jesus's point was that the **hand** (representing things you handle), the **foot** (representing the places you go), and the **eye** (symbolizing the things you look at) can open doors to sin; thus, people must take drastic

measures to remove sinful hindrances to faith.

9:48 There are several things we learn about **hell** from this brief statement. First, it's clear that Jesus considered it a real place. So though many today deny the existence of hell, their claims run contrary to Jesus's. Second, hell is a place of intense suffering, both external and internal. **The fire** represents the source of external suffering. The **worm** represents the source of internal suffering—the gnawing from within. Third, hell is eternal. Some today argue that unbelievers are "annihilated" after death, but Jesus says the worm doesn't die and the fire isn't quenched. The suffering of hell, then, is never-ending. The good news of Jesus Christ is so good because the bad news of hell is so bad.

9:49-50 Even believers (signified by the word **everyone**) have to deal with the salt of trial in their lives (9:49). As Old Testament sacrifices were offered with salt (Lev 2:13), so believers must live with sacrifice in mind. Salt had a

variety of helpful uses in New Testament times: it was a medicine, a seasoning, and a preservative. Similarly, believers are to be like **salt** in promoting peace among fellow believers (Mark 9:50). This demonstrates the preserving power of God.

10:2 There were two views about **divorce** held by first-century Jewish scholars. According to one, a man could divorce his wife if she committed sexual immorality. According to the other, a man could divorce his wife for any reason. The Pharisees wanted Jesus to take sides and, thus, alienate some of his listeners.

10:6 God's design for marriage is clear **from the beginning of creation**. It is to involve a **male and female**, which rules out a lot of what goes by the name of "marriage" in our culture.

10:7-9 Marriage was intended as a permanent bond. Therefore, **what God has joined together, let no one separate** (10:9). People, including civil judges, are not to overrule God.

two, but one flesh. **9** Therefore what God has joined together, let no one separate."[a]

10 When they were in the house again, the disciples questioned him about this matter. **11** He said to them, "Whoever divorces his wife[b] and marries[c] another commits adultery[d] against her. **12** Also, if she divorces her husband[e] and marries another, she commits adultery."

BLESSING THE CHILDREN

13 People[f] were bringing little children[g] to him in order that he might touch them, but the disciples rebuked[h] them. **14** When Jesus saw it, he was indignant[i] and said to them, "Let the little children come to me.[j] Don't stop[k] them, because the kingdom of God[l] belongs to such as these. **15** Truly I tell you,[m] whoever does not receive[A,n] the kingdom of God like a little child[o] will never enter it." **16** After taking them in his arms, he laid his hands on[p] them and blessed[q] them.

THE RICH YOUNG RULER

17 As[r] he was setting out on a journey,[s] a man ran up, knelt down[t] before him, and asked him, "Good[u] teacher,[v] what must I do to inherit[w] eternal life?"[x]

18 "Why do you call me good?" Jesus asked him. "No one is good except God alone.[y] **19** You know the commandments: **Do not murder;**[z] **do not commit adultery;**[aa] **do not steal;**[ab] **do not bear false witness;**[ac] **do not defraud;**[ad] **honor**[ae] **your father and mother."**[B,af]

20 He said to him, "Teacher,[ag] I have kept all these from my youth."

21 Looking at him, Jesus loved him[ah] and said to him, "You lack one thing: Go, sell all you have and give to the poor,[ai] and you will have treasure[aj] in heaven.[ak] Then come,[c] follow me."[al] **22** But he was dismayed by this demand, and he went away grieving,[am] because he had many possessions.[an]

POSSESSIONS AND THE KINGDOM

23 Jesus looked around and said to his disciples, "How hard it is for those who have wealth[ao] to enter the kingdom of God!"[ap] **24** The disciples were astonished at his words. Again Jesus said to them, "Children,[aq] how hard it is[D] to enter the kingdom of God! **25** It is easier for a camel to go through the eye of a needle than for a rich[ar] person to enter the kingdom of God." **26** They were even more astonished, saying to one another, "Then who can be saved?"[as] **27** Looking at them, Jesus said, "With man it is impossible,[at] but not with God, because all things are possible with God." **28** Peter[au] began to tell him, "Look, we have left everything and followed you." **29** "Truly I tell you,"[av] Jesus said, "there is no one who has left house or brothers or sisters or mother or father[E] or children or

a 10:9 1Co 7:10-15; Heb 7:26
b 10:11 1Pt 3:1
c 1Tm 5:14
d Mt 5:27-28
e 10:12 Mt 1:19
f 10:13-16 Mt 19:13-15; Lk 18:15-17
g 10:13 Lk 1:7
h 2Tm 4:2
i 10:14 Lk 13:14
j Lk 14:26
k 1Co 14:39
l Mk 1:15
m 10:15 Ps 72:19; Rv 22:21
n Ac 17:11
o Lk 1:7
p 10:16 1Tm 5:22
q Gn 48:15

t 10:17 Mt 17:14; 27:29; Mk 1:40　u Gn 1:31　v Mk 4:38; Eph 4:11　w Rv 21:7　x Lk 10:25-28; Jn 12:25; Ac 13:48　y 10:18 Ps 69:16　z 10:19 Mt 5:21 aa Mt 5:27-28　ab Eph 4:28

ac 10:19 Pr 6:19　ad 1Co 6:7-8; 7:5; 1Tm 6:5; Jms 5:4　ae 1Tm 5:3　af Ex 21:15　ag 10:20 Mk 4:38; Eph 4:11　ah 10:21 Lk 6:35; 2Th 2:13; Heb 12:6　ai 10:21 Lk 6:35; 2Th 2:13; Heb 12:6
ai Mk 14:7; Rm 15:26　aj 2Co 4:7　ak Mt 6:20; 13:44; Lk 12:33　al Jn 8:12　am 10:22 2Co 2:2　an Ac 2:45; 5:1　ao 10:23 Ac 4:37; 8:18,20; 24:26
ap Mk 1:15　aq 10:24 Lk 1:7　ar 10:25 Gn 24:35; Rv 2:9　as 10:26 Ac 16:30; Eph 2:8　at 10:27 Heb 6:4　au 10:28 Lk 6:14; Ac 10:32　av 10:29 Rv 22:21

10:31-37 Mt 19:16-30; Lk 18:18-30
s 10:17 Mk 8:27

A 10:15 Or *not welcome*　B 10:19 Ex 20:12-16; Dt 5:16-20　C 10:21 Other mss add *taking up the cross, and*　D 10:24 Other mss add *for those trusting in wealth*　E 10:29 Other mss add *or wife*

10:11-12 The one who illegitimately initiates divorce **and marries another** has entered an adulterous relationship because God has not canceled the first marriage (see the notes on Matt 19:4-9).

10:13-16 Jesus valued **children** so highly because they model what it takes for someone to come to God. They know what it is to have a low and dependent status. When they put their trust in someone, they do it wholeheartedly and with humility. We are not to be like the Pharisees, having pride in ourselves and in our own righteousness. We are to humble ourselves, acknowledging our sin, and put our whole trust and dependence on God.

10:17 Matthew adds that this individual was a "young man" (Matt 19:20). Luke says he was "a ruler" (Luke 18:18). All three Synoptic Gospels note that he was wealthy (see Mark 10:22; Matt 19:22; Luke 18:23). Thus, he is often described as the "rich young ruler."

His question suggests he not only wanted to know how to enter heaven but also how to gain inheritance rewards there.

10:18 All are sinners before a holy God. So, the only way Jesus could truly be called **good** is if he is the Son of **God**.

10:19-20 The **commandments** are divine standards of righteousness by which men can measure themselves (10:19). If someone could perfectly keep God's law, he or she would indeed be righteous before him. Yet we are all sinners. Our only hope of a righteous standing before God is to have a righteousness imputed or credited to us (Rom 4:22-25). Naively, the man claimed to have **kept all** of the commandments (Mark 10:20), but our sinful hearts have a habit of appraising us as better than we are.

10:21 In spite of the man's self-deception, **Jesus loved him**. The glorious good news is that Jesus loves sinners. He therefore sought to enlighten the man and expose his spiritual blindness. The clear problem in this man's life was that his love for money prevented him from loving his neighbor, proving that he was not as righteous as he perceived himself to be.

10:23 The problem is not **wealth** itself. Rather, an unhealthy dependence on worldly riches will obscure focus on kingdom values and eternal spiritual riches. Rich people can have a distorted picture of God's view of them, assuming that their wealth is proof of divine acceptance and blessing.

10:26 The disciples assumed that wealth was a sign of divine approval.

10:28 Peter's words are an indicator that if you intend to be the visible, vocal follower that Jesus calls you to be, it will cost you. You cannot grow as a disciple without paying a price.

10:29-30 Observe six things: *First*, Jesus's pronouncement is true for all who associate with him as kingdom disciples. There are no

a 10:29 Mk 1:1; Php 1:5
b 10:30 Lk 21:8
c Lk 20:10
d Mt 13:21
e Jn 12:25; Ac 13:48
f Mt 12:32; Lk 20:35; Eph 1:21; 2:7
g 10:31 Mk 9:35
h 10:32-34 Mt 20:17-19; Lk 18:31-34
i 10:32 Ps 79:1; Mt 23:37
j Ps 147:11; Pr 1:7; Rv 14:7
k Jn 6:61
l 10:33 Mk 2:10
m Mt 2:4
n 10:33-34 Mk 8:31; 9:31
o 10:34 Mt 16:21; Ac 2:24
p Lk 9:22
q 10:35-45 Mt 20:20-28; Ac 12:2
r 10:35 Jn 21:7
s Jn 21:2
t Mk 4:38; Eph 4:11
u 10:37 Mk 9:28; Lk 9:26
v 10:38 Jn 11:22
w 10:38 Ps 75:8
x Lk 12:50; Ac 22:16
y Lk 12:50; Rm 6:3; 2Co 4:10-11; Gl 2:20
z 10:39 Ac 12:2; Rv 1:9
aa 10:41 Jn 21:7
ab 10:42 Ac 19:16; 1Pt 5:3
ac 10:43 Mk 9:35; 10:45
ad 10:43-44 Lk 22:26
ae 10:44 Mt 10:24; Php 2:7; Rv 1:7
af 10:45 Mk 2:10
ag Jn 13:13-15; Php 2:7
ah Jn 6:51; 10:15; Gl 2:20
ai Lv 27:31; Ps 49:8; Mt 26:28; Eph 1:7
aj Is 52:13–53:12; Mt 20:28
ak 10:46-52 Mt 20:29-34; Lk 18:35-43
al 10:46 Nm 22:1
am Mt 15:14
an Jn 9:8
ao Mk 8:27
ap 10:47 Mk 14:67
aq 2Ch 1:1; Mt 1:1; Rm 1:3
ar 10:47 Mt 5:7; Mk 5:19; Lk 1:50
as Mt 15:22; 17:15; Mk 10:48; Lk 16:24
at 10:48 Mk 10:47

fields for my sake and for the sake of the gospel,*a* *30* who will not receive a hundred times*b* more, now at this time*c* — houses, brothers and sisters, mothers and children, and fields, with persecutions*d* — and eternal life*e* in the age to come.*f* *31* But many who are first will be last, and the last first."*g*

THE THIRD PREDICTION OF HIS DEATH

32 They*h* were on the road, going up to Jerusalem,*i* and Jesus was walking ahead of them. The disciples were astonished, but those who followed him were afraid.*j* Taking the Twelve aside again, he began to tell them the things that would happen to him.*k* *33* "See, we are going up to Jerusalem. The Son of Man*l* will be handed over to the chief priests and the scribes,*m* and they will condemn him to death. Then they will hand him over to the Gentiles,*n* *34* and they will mock him, spit on him, flog[A] him, and kill him, and he will rise*o* after three days."*p*

SUFFERING AND SERVICE

35 James*q* and John,*r* the sons of Zebedee,*s* approached him and said, "Teacher,*t* we want you to do whatever we ask you."

36 "What do you want me to do for you?" he asked them.

37 They answered him, "Allow us to sit at your right and at your left in your glory."*u*

38 Jesus said to them, "You don't know what you're asking.*v* Are you able to drink the cup*w* I drink or to be baptized with the baptism*x* I am baptized with?"*y*

39 "We are able," they told him.

Jesus said to them, "You will drink the cup I drink, and you will be baptized with the baptism I am baptized with.*z* *40* But to sit at my right or left is not mine to give; instead, it is for those for whom it has been prepared."

41 When the ten disciples heard this, they began to be indignant with James and John.*aa* *42* Jesus called them over and said to them, "You know that those who are regarded as rulers of the Gentiles lord it over*ab* them, and those in high positions act as tyrants over them. *43* But it is not so among you.*ac* On the contrary, whoever wants to become great among you will be your servant,*ad* *44* and whoever wants to be first among you will be a slave to all.*ae* *45* For even the Son of Man*af* did not come to be served, but to serve,*ag* and to give his life*ah* as a ransom*ai* for many."[B]*,aj*

A BLIND MAN HEALED

46 They*ak* came to Jericho.*al* And as he was leaving Jericho with his disciples and a large crowd, Bartimaeus (the son of Timaeus), a blind*am* beggar,*an* was sitting by the road.*ao* *47* When he heard that it was Jesus of Nazareth,*ap* he began to cry out, "Jesus, Son of David,*aq* have mercy*ar* on me!"*as* *48* Many warned him to keep quiet, but he was crying out all the more, "Have mercy on me,*at* Son of David!"

[A]10:34 Or *scourge*   [B]10:45 Or *in the place of many* ; Is 53:10-12

---

exceptions (**there is no one**, 10:29). *Second*, being a public disciple will cost you: maybe a location (**house**), relationships (**brothers or sisters or mother or father or children**), or even your business or means of employment (**fields**), (10:29). Jesus is not talking about abdicating one's responsibilities. A man does not become a Christian and stop providing for his children. But we are not to compromise our commitment to Christ for the sake of anything. *Third*, these prices are paid **for the sake of the gospel** (10:29)—that is, for the purpose of following Jesus and giving allegiance to his kingdom. *Fourth*, the very things that were left behind are what you receive. You don't truly lose anything; you make a trade. *Fifth*, you will also receive **persecutions** (10:30). The more committed you are to Christ, the more resistance there will be to the presence of Christ in your life. *Sixth*, a disciple's reward is divided between the ages: the present age and the age to come. Don't expect to receive all of your blessings now. Most of your reward is kept for you—and it's **a hundred times more** than anything you leave behind (10:30).

10:31 Believers whom God has blessed in the present life but who have been less than faithful with those blessings will find that God flips the script in the age to come. Let your motivation be for the reward that lies before you in the millennial kingdom and the new heaven and new earth.

10:33-34 Jesus knew what awaited him: mocking, spitting, flogging. But he also knew that victory was waiting. He would **rise** again (10:34).

10:37 Those sitting at a king's **right** and **left** held positions of significant honor and authority.

10:38-39 To **drink the cup** he would **drink** or **be baptized with** his **baptism** were metaphors for enduring suffering (10:38). We know from Scripture that because of their faith in Christ, James was executed (see Acts 12:1-2) and John was exiled (see Rev 1:9).

10:43-44 Jesus's use of the phrase **whoever wants to become great** indicates Jesus didn't quench his disciples' desire for greatness. Instead, he explained that you can't use the standards of the unrighteous to attain true greatness. To be great, you must be a **servant**

(10:43). According to Paul, believers are called to "serve one another through love" (Gal 5:13). God saves us by grace apart from good "works," but in Christ we are created "for good works" (Eph 2:8-10). So once we are saved, it's time to get to work! To practice servanthood among the people of God is to serve others with no strings attached for the glory of God. The church of Jesus Christ is a family, and we are called to serve each other (see 1 Pet 4:10).

10:45 Jesus didn't call his disciples to walk a path that he wouldn't walk. **To serve** was the reason he came into the world. When Paul exhorts the Philippians to reject "selfish ambition," live with "humility," and be concerned for "the interests of others" (Phil 2:3-4), in fact, he puts Christ forward as the perfect example of selfless, loving, God-honoring service. As John put it, "The one who says he remains in [Christ] should walk just as he walked" (1 John 2:6).

10:47 Son of David is a messianic title. Though he was physically blind, Bartimaeus could see better spiritually than the religious leaders could.

[49] Jesus stopped and said, "Call him."

So they called the blind man and said to him, "Have courage![a] Get up; he's calling for you." [50] He threw off his coat,[b] jumped up, and came to Jesus.

[51] Then Jesus answered him, "What do you want[c] me to do for you?"

"*Rabboni,*"[A,d] the blind man said to him, "I want to see."

[52] Jesus said to him, "Go, your faith has saved you."[e] Immediately he could see and began to follow Jesus on the road.

THE TRIUMPHAL ENTRY

11 When[f] they approached Jerusalem,[g] at Bethphage and Bethany[h] near the Mount of Olives, he sent two of his disciples [2] and told them, "Go into the village ahead of you. As soon as you enter it, you will find a colt tied there, on which no one has ever sat. Untie it and bring it. [3] If anyone says to you, 'Why are you doing this?' say, 'The Lord needs it and will send it back here right away.'"

[4] So they went and found a colt outside in the street, tied by a door. They untied it, [5] and some of those standing there said to them, "What are you doing, untying the colt?" [6] They answered them just as Jesus had said; so they let them go.

[7] They brought the colt to Jesus and threw their clothes on it, and he sat on it. [8] Many people spread their clothes on the road,[i] and others spread leafy branches cut from the fields.[B] [9] Those who went ahead and those who followed shouted:

Hosanna!
**Blessed is he who comes
in the name**[j] **of the Lord!**[C,k]
[10] Blessed is the
coming kingdom[l]
of our father David![m]
Hosanna[n] in the highest heaven!

[11] He went into Jerusalem[o] and into the temple.[p] After looking around at everything, since it was already late, he went out to Bethany[q] with the Twelve.

THE BARREN FIG TREE IS CURSED

[12] The[r] next day when they went out from Bethany, he was hungry. [13] Seeing in the distance a fig[s] tree with leaves, he went to find out if there was anything on it. When he came to it, he found nothing but leaves; for it was not the season for figs. [14] He said to it, "May no one ever eat fruit[t] from you again!"[u] And his disciples[v] heard it.

CLEANSING THE TEMPLE

[15] They came to Jerusalem,[w] and he went into the temple[x] and began to throw out those buying and selling. He overturned the tables of the money changers[y] and the chairs of those selling doves, [16] and would not permit anyone to carry goods through the temple. [17] He was teaching them: "Is it not written,[z] **My house**[aa] **will be called a house of prayer**[ab] **for all nations**?[D] But you have made it **a den of thieves**!"[E,ac]

[18] The chief priests and the scribes[ad] heard it and started looking for a way to kill him. For they were afraid[ae] of him, because the whole crowd was astonished by his teaching.

[19] Whenever evening came, they would go out of the city.

THE BARREN FIG TREE IS WITHERED

[20] Early[af] in the morning, as they were passing by, they saw the fig tree withered from the roots up. [21] Then Peter[ag] remembered and said to him, "Rabbi,[ah] look! The fig tree that you cursed[ai] has withered."

[22] Jesus replied to them, "Have faith in God.[aj] [23] Truly I tell you,[ak] if anyone says to

[a]10:49 Jn 16:33
[b]10:50 Lk 19:36
[c]10:51 Mk 1:40
[d]Jn 20:16
[e]10:52 Mk 9:22; Mk 6:56; Lk 5:20
[f]11:1-11 Mt 21:1-11; Lk 19:28-44; Jn 12:12-19
[g]11:1 Mt 23:37; Ac 8:1
[h]Mt 26:6; Lk 24:50; Jn 11:1,18; 12:1
[i]11:8 Mk 8:27
[j]11:9 Jn 10:25
[k]Lk 1:42; Heb 6:14
[l]11:10 Mk 1:15; 9:1
[m]Lk 1:27; Ac 2:29; 4:25
[n]Mk 11:9

[o]11:11 Mt 23:37
[p]Ac 21:26
[q]Mk 11:1
[r]11:12-19 Mt 21:12-19; Lk 19:45-48
[s]11:13 Lk 6:44; Jn 1:48
[t]11:14 Mt 3:8; 7:16-21
[u]Jr 8:13
[v]Mk 10:10
[w]11:15 Mt 23:37
[x]Ac 21:26
[y]Jn 2:15
[z]11:17 Mk 1:2; Ac 15:15
[aa]Lk 11:51; Jn 2:17
[ab]Ac 12:5; 16:13
[ac]Jr 7:11
[ad]11:18 Mt 2:4
[ae]Ps 147:11; Pr 1:7; Rv 14:7
[af]11:20-26 Mt 21:19-22
[ag]11:21 Lk 6:14; Ac 10:32
[ah]Jn 11:8
[ai]Jms 3:9
[aj]11:22 Mt 17:20
[ak]11:23 Ps 72:19; Rv 22:21

[A]10:51 Hb word for *my lord*   [B]11:8 Other mss read *others were cutting leafy branches from the trees and spreading them on the road*   [C]11:9 Ps 118:26   [D]11:17 Is 56:7   [E]11:17 Jr 7:11

11:2 That the **colt** was unused would make it naturally unwilling to receive a rider. Its submission would therefore demonstrate Jesus's authority over creation.
11:7-10 Matthew makes it clear that Jesus's actions in this scene were a fulfillment of messianic prophecy (see Matt 21:1-5; Zech 9:9). **Hosanna** is the Greek transliteration of a Hebrew phrase that means, "Please save!" (see Ps 118:25). **11:12-14** Ultimately, Jesus's actions in this instance were symbolic. Though the tree showed signs of life and productivity, in reality it was barren. The same was true of Israel—especially in the case of their religious leaders. They looked righteous and godly on the outside, but on the inside they were corrupt. Their lack of

faith meant that they were also barren—producing no fruit for God. Many people today are like that too. They attend church regularly, carry fancy Bibles, and shout "Amen!" But there's a lack of spiritual vitality inside them; thus, there's no kingdom fruit in their lives.
11:15-17 The business activities themselves were not necessarily a problem since pilgrims coming to worship needed to buy animals to make sacrifices. The problem was that these activities were taking place *in* the temple, hindering worship. Moreover, the businessmen themselves engaged in corrupt practices, cheating their customers.
11:22-23 Faith's authority allows the believer to speak directly to the obstacles of life (i.e.,

"mountains") and get them to move, and it's important to note that Jesus is not commending an extraordinary faith. After all, on one occasion he told his disciples something similar and said faith needed to be no larger than a tiny "mustard seed" (Matt 17:20). The most important aspect of faith, then, is the worthiness of its object. You can place tremendous faith in Santa Claus, but you'll be disappointed. If, however, you have true, vibrant faith in the God of the Bible, you have spiritual authority to access divine power. God has already blessed you "with every spiritual blessing in the heavens in Christ" (Eph 1:3). Through faith in Jesus, you have access to divine power. It's like having a contract with

a 11:23 Ac 10:20
b Jn 3:16; Ac 10:43; Rm 10:9; 1Pt 1:8-10
c Mk 9:23; Jn 11:22
d 11:24 Mt 5:44; Ac 12:12
e Jn 14:13; Jms 1:5 Mt 7:8
g 11:25 Lk 18:11
h Mt 6:12; 9:2
i Mt 5:16; Lk 11:13
j Mt 6:1; Lk 12:33
k Ps 25:11; Mt 9:2
l 11:27-33 Mt 21:23-27; Lk 20:1-8
m 11:27 Mt 23:37
n Ac 21:26
o Mt 2:4
p 3Jn 1
q 11:28 Mk 1:22
r 11:29 Mk 4:14
s 11:30 Lk 7:29; Ac 18:25; 19:3
t 11:31 1Jn 5:10
u 11:32 Mt 2:23; Ac 7:52

v 12:1-12 Mt 21:33-46; Lk 20:9-19
w 12:1 Gn 9:20
x 12:2 Mk 3:14
y Mt 10:24
z Mt 3:8; 7:16
aa 12:3 Lk 22:63
ab Col 2:8
ac 12:6 Eph 1:6; Phm 1
ad Heb 1:1-2
ae 12:9 Col 3:22
af 12:10 Mt 26:54; 2Pt 1:20
ag 12:10-11 Ps 118:22-23
ah 12:10 Ac 4:11; 1Pt 2:7
ai 12:11 Col 4:1; Jd 5

this mountain, 'Be lifted up and thrown into the sea,' and does not doubt*a* in his heart, but believes*b* that what he says will happen, it will be done for him.*c* 24 Therefore I tell you, everything you pray*d* and ask for*e* — believe that you have received[A,f] it and it will be yours. 25 And whenever you stand*g* praying, if you have anything against anyone, forgive*h* him, so that your Father*i* in heaven*j* will also forgive*k* you your wrongdoing."[B]

THE AUTHORITY OF JESUS CHALLENGED

27 They*l* came again to Jerusalem.*m* As he was walking in the temple,*n* the chief priests, the scribes,*o* and the elders*p* came 28 and asked him, "By what authority*q* are you doing these things? Who gave you this authority to do these things?" 29 Jesus said to them, "I will ask you one question;*r* then answer me, and I will tell you by what authority I do these things. 30 Was John's baptism*s* from heaven or of human origin? Answer me." 31 They discussed it among themselves: "If we say, 'From heaven,' he will say, 'Then why didn't you believe*t* him?' 32 But if we say, 'Of human origin'" — they were afraid of the crowd, because everyone thought that John was truly a prophet.*u* 33 So they answered Jesus, "We don't know."

And Jesus said to them, "Neither will I tell you by what authority I do these things."

THE PARABLE OF THE VINEYARD OWNER

12 He*v* began to speak to them in parables: "A man planted a vineyard,*w* put a fence around it, dug out a pit for a winepress, and built a watchtower. Then he leased it to tenant farmers and went away. 2 At harvest time he sent*x* a servant*y* to the farmers to collect some of the fruit*z* of the vineyard from them. 3 But they took him, beat*aa* him, and sent him away empty-handed.*ab* 4 Again he sent another servant to them, and they*c* hit him on the head and treated him shamefully.[D] 5 Then he sent another, and they killed that one. He also sent many others; some they beat, and others they killed. 6 He still had one to send, a beloved*ac* son. Finally*ad* he sent him to them, saying, 'They will respect my son.' 7 But those tenant farmers said to one another, 'This is the heir. Come, let's kill him, and the inheritance will be ours.' 8 So they seized him, killed him, and threw him out of the vineyard. 9 What then will the owner[E,ae] of the vineyard do? He will come and kill the farmers and give the vineyard to others. 10 Haven't you read this Scripture:*af*

The*ag* stone that
　the builders rejected
has become the cornerstone.*ah*
11　This came about from the Lord*ai*
　and is wonderful in our eyes?"[F]

12 They were looking for a way to arrest him but feared the crowd because they

---

A 11:24 Some mss read *you receive*; other mss read *you will receive*　B 11:25 Some mss include v. 26: *"But if you don't forgive, neither will your Father in heaven forgive your wrongdoing."*　C 12:4 Other mss add *threw stones and*　D 12:4 Other mss add *and sent him off*　E 12:9 Or *lord*　F 12:10-11 Ps 118:22-23

---

the electric company. Since you have a legal relationship with them, they provide you with electricity. Nevertheless, you must access that power by flipping the switch.

11:24-25 Spiritual authority comes through prayer and through repenting of sin—such as the sin of unforgiveness. Prayer enables us to access God's power in our lives, but unrepentant sin blocks God's power.

11:27-28 The religious leaders were furious with Jesus about the temple-cleansing incident (see 11:15-19).

11:30 In other words, he said, "You want to know if I'm legitimate, if I'm operating on God's authority? Tell me: Was John the Baptist legitimate? Did he minister on God's authority?"

11:31-32 The leaders had to huddle together to discuss their response options. If they admitted that John's authority was **from heaven**, then Jesus would ask them, **why didn't you believe him?** (11:31). After all, John testified that Jesus was the Messiah. But they were also reluctant to reject John

and his ministry because **they were afraid** of all the people who thought **John was truly a prophet** (11:32). If they denigrated John, the crowd might stone them!

11:33 These self-serving hypocrites demanded that Jesus answer their questions truthfully, but their refusal to answer his question meant they had no interest in the truth—only in advancing their own agenda.

12:1 As becomes clear, the vineyard owner represents God, the **vineyard** is Israel, and the **tenant farmers** are Israel's leaders. God was the source, provider, and protector of his people. He entrusted his vineyard to leaders who were to care for it on his behalf.

Those listening to Jesus would've been familiar with these details. Isaiah the prophet told a similar story about a vineyard that represented Israel (Isa 5:1-7, esp. 5:7). Instead of producing good grapes, it yielded worthless ones, so the Lord threatened to destroy it (Isa 5:2, 5-6). In Jesus's parable, he added an important character: the vineyard owner's son (see Mark 12:6). It's a reference to him.

12:2-5 This is a vivid description of how the leaders of Israel had abused God's prophets in the past. Though he sent them to warn his people to keep his covenant with them by pursuing righteousness, they refused. They owed God **fruit**—their obedience (12:2). But they scornfully mistreated and killed God's prophets, demonstrating their scorn for God himself.

12:6-8 Thus, Jesus revealed the intentions of the Jewish leaders to rule Israel without the Messiah.

12:9-11 Verse 9 speaks of God's coming judgment on the leaders and the temporary shifting of his kingdom program from Israel to the church. Jesus then quoted Psalm 118:22-23, identifying himself with the **rejected** stone that will ultimately be the preeminent **stone** in God's kingdom work—**the cornerstone** (Mark 12:10-11). Their rejection of God's agenda couldn't prevent him from accomplishing his plan.

knew he had spoken this parable against them. So they left him and went away.

GOD AND CAESAR

[13] Then[a] they sent some of the Pharisees[b] and the Herodians[c] to Jesus to trap him in his words.[d] [14] When they came, they said to him, "Teacher, we know you are truthful and don't care what anyone thinks, nor do you show partiality[e] but teach the way of God truthfully. Is it lawful to pay taxes[f] to Caesar or not? Should we pay or shouldn't we?"

APPLICATION QUESTIONS

READ MARK 12:14–17

– What are your initial reactions to this passage?

– What are some examples of services rendered by our government today?

– In what ways do we "give to Caesar the things that are Caesar's" (v. 17)?

---

[15] But knowing their hypocrisy,[g] he said to them, "Why are you testing[h] me? Bring me a denarius[A,i] to look at." [16] They brought a coin. "Whose image[j] and inscription[k] is this?" he asked them.

"Caesar's," they replied.

[17] Jesus told them, "Give to Caesar the things that are Caesar's, and to God the things that are God's."[l] And they were utterly amazed[m] at him.

THE SADDUCEES AND THE RESURRECTION

[18] Sadducees,[n] who say there is no resurrection,[o] came to him and questioned him: [19] "Teacher,[p] Moses[q] wrote for us that **if a man's brother dies**, leaving a wife behind but **no child,**[r] that man should take the wife[s] **and raise up offspring for his brother.**[B,t] [20] There were seven brothers. The first married a woman, and, dying, left no offspring. [21] The second also took her, and he died, leaving no offspring. And the third likewise. [22] None of the seven[c] left offspring. Last of all, the woman died too. [23] In the resurrection, when they rise,[D] whose wife will she be, since the seven had married her?"

[24] Jesus spoke to them, "Isn't this the reason why you're mistaken: you don't know the Scriptures[u] or the power[v] of God?" [25] For when they rise[x] from the dead,[y] they neither marry nor are given in marriage[z] but are like angels[aa] in heaven. [26] And as for the dead being raised — haven't you read in the book of Moses, in the passage about the burning bush, how God said to him: I[ab] **am the God of Abraham**[ac] **and the God of Isaac**[ad] **and the God of Jacob?**[E,ae] [27] He is not the God of the dead but of the living. You are badly mistaken."

THE PRIMARY COMMANDS

[28] One[af] of the scribes[ag] approached. When he heard them debating and saw that Jesus answered them well, he asked him, "Which command is the most important of all?"

[29] Jesus answered, "The most important[F] is **Listen, O Israel! The Lord**[ah] **our God, the Lord**[ai] **is one.**[G] [30] Love[aj] **the Lord your God**[ak] **with all your heart, with all your soul, with all your mind,**[al] **and with all your strength.**[H,I,am] [31] The second is, **Love your neighbor**[an] **as yourself.**[J,ao] There is no other command[ap] greater than these."

[32] Then the scribe said to him, "You are right, teacher. You have correctly said

[a] 12:13-17 Mt 22:15-22; Lk 20:20-26
[b] 12:13 Mk 7:3
[c] Mk 3:6
[d] Lk 11:54
[e] 12:14 Dt 1:17
[f] Mt 17:25
[g] 12:15 Mt 23:28; Lk 12:1; Gl 2:13; 1Tm 4:2; 1Pt 2:1
[h] Jms 1:13
[i] Mt 18:28
[j] 12:16 Rv 13:14
[k] Mk 15:26; Lk 23:38
[l] 12:17 Rm 13:7
[m] Rv 17:6
[n] 12:18-27 Mt 22:23-33; Lk 20:27-40
[o] 12:18 Ac 23:6
[p] 12:19 Mk 4:38; Eph 4:11
[q] Ps 77:20; Mt 8:4; Heb 3:2

[r] 12:19 Lk 1:7
[s] Mt 1:6
[t] Gn 38:8; Dt 25:5-10
[u] 12:24 Mt 26:54; 2Pt 1:20
[v] Lk 1:35; 6:19
[w] 2Co 13:4; Rv 11:17
[x] 12:25 Lk 18:33
[y] Jn 5:25; 20:9
[z] 1Tm 5:14
[aa] Mt 13:49; Ac 5:19; Rv 14:6
[ab] 12:26 Ex 3:6,15-16
[ac] Gl 3:6
[ad] Jms 2:21
[ae] Mt 1:2; Lk 1:33
[af] 12:28-34 Mt 22:34-40
[ag] 12:28 Mt 2:4
[ah] 12:29 Col 4:1; Jd 5
[ai] Dt 6:4
[aj] 12:30 Lk 6:35
[ak] Dt 6:5; Lk 10:27
[al] 1Jn 5:20
[am] Dt 6:4-5; Jos 22:5
[an] 12:31 Lk 10:29
[ao] Lv 19:18; 1Jn 4:21
[ap] Mk 7:8

[A] 12:15 A denarius = one day's wage   [B] 12:19 Gn 38:8; Dt 25:5   [C] 12:22 Other mss add *had taken her and*   [D] 12:23 Other mss omit *when they rise*
[E] 12:26 Ex 3:6,15-16   [F] 12:29 Other mss add *of all the commands*   [G] 12:29 Or *the Lord our God is Lord alone.*   [H] 12:30 Other mss add *This is the first commandment.*   [I] 12:30 Dt 6:4-5; Jos 22:5   [J] 12:31 Lv 19:18

12:14 The Pharisees and Herodians were no doubt gleeful over their question about **taxes**, assuming they had placed Jesus in a no-win situation. If he answered, yes, the crowd would be furious: they hated their Roman overlords. But if he said, no, the Pharisees and Herodians could announce that Jesus was promoting sedition, since the Jews were required to pay taxes to Rome.

12:17 It's appropriate to **give to Caesar**—that is, to the government—what belongs to him. As Paul told the Romans, "Let everyone submit to the governing authorities" (Rom 13:1). When government is functioning legitimately, it provides beneficial services to those living under its rule. So citizens rightly pay taxes to fund government services like police protection and adequate roads. Jesus

makes it clear, though, that our commitment to the state is not our only commitment. We also have a commitment to God, since we bear his image. And our commitment to God is greater because his authority is comprehensive.

12:18 The Jewish **Sadducees** had some faulty beliefs. For one, they said there was **no resurrection**, no physical life after death. Moreover, they only held the first five books of the Bible (the Pentateuch) as sacred Scripture.

12:19-23 The Sadducees assumed that their hypothetical situation proved **the resurrection** concept absurd (12:23). If it were true, they reasoned, it would result in mass confusion.

12:26-27 Jesus demonstrated that the Sadducees didn't "know the Scriptures" (12:24) as well as they thought by pointing to Exodus

3:6, which the Sadducees accepted as God's Word (see the note on Mark 12:18). God told Moses that he was (still) **the God of Abraham ... Isaac ... Jacob** (12:26), even though they had physically died. The point was that they were spiritually alive.

12:30 In other words, we are to **love** God with the totality of our being. It's one thing to claim that you love God. It's another thing to demonstrate it through everything you think, say, and do.

12:31 Jesus connected the vertical (love of God) with the horizontal (**love** of others). The two necessarily go together. To love God is to passionately pursue his glory with your total being. To love your neighbor is to decide to compassionately and righteously seek his or her well-being.

a 12:32 Rm 3:30
b Dt 4:35,39; 6:4; Is 37:20; 43:10; 44:6; 45:21
c 12:33 Lk 6:35
d 1Sm 15:22; Ps 51:16; Hs 6:6; Am 5:22; Mc 6:6-8
e 12:34 Mk 1:15
f Lk 20:40
g 12:35-37 Mt 22:41-46; Lk 20:41-44
h 12:35 Ac 21:26
i Mt 2:4
j Mt 1:17; Eph 5:2
k 2Ch 1:1; Mt 1:1; Rm 1:3
l 12:36 Lk 1:27
m Jn 1:33; Ac 19:21
n Lk 17:5
o Mt 20:21
p Ps 110:1
q 12:38-40 Mt 23:1-36; Lk 20:45-47
r 12:38 Rv 7:14
s Mk 6:56
t 12:39 Lk 11:43
u Jms 2:2
v Lk 14:7-8
w Jn 13:2
x 12:40 Gl 5:15
y Jms 1:27
z Mt 5:44; Ac 12:12
aa 12:41-44 Lk 21:1-4
ab 12:41 Jn 8:20
ac Gn 24:35; Rv 2:9
ad 12:42 Mk 14:7
ae 12:43 Mk 9:10; Mk 10:10; Lk 6:1; Jn 6:3; Ac 6:1
af Ps 72:19; Rv 22:21
ag Jn 8:20

an 12:44 1Co 15:58
ai Php 4:11
aj Lk 15:12
ak 1Jn 3:17
al 13:1-37 Mt 24:1-51; Lk 21:5-38
am 13:1 Ac 21:26
an Mk 4:38
ao 1Co 14:3
ap 13:2 Mk 14:58
aq 13:3 Mt 21:1
ar Ac 21:26
as Lk 6:14; Ac 10:32
at Ac 12:2
au Jn 21:7
av Jn 6:8
aw 13:6 Jn 10:25; 14:13
ax Ex 3:14; Ps 45:8; Jn 8:24
ay 1Jn 4:6
az 13:7 Jr 51:46; Dn 11:44
ba 2Th 2:2
bb Dn 2:28-29
bc 13:8 Is 19:2
bd Ac 26:4
be Gl 4:19
bf 13:9 Mt 10:17
bg Lk 22:63; Ac 5:40; 16:19-23,37
bh Jms 2:2
bi Ac 24:10-27; 25:1-12,23-27
bj Rm 8:36
bk Mk 6:11; 1Tm 2:6
bl Php 1:12
bm 13:10 Mk 1:1; Php 1:5

that he is one, and there is no one*a* else except him.*b* 33 And to love*c* him with all your heart, with all your understanding,^A and with all your strength, and to love your neighbor as yourself, is far more important than all the burnt offerings and sacrifices."*d*

34 When Jesus saw that he answered wisely, he said to him, "You are not far from the kingdom of God."*e* And no one dared*f* to question him any longer.

THE QUESTION ABOUT THE CHRIST

35 While*g* Jesus was teaching in the temple, he asked,*h* "How can the scribes*i* say that the Messiah*j* is the son of David?*k* 36 David*l* himself says by the Holy Spirit:*m*

> **The Lord*n* declared to my Lord,
> 'Sit at my right hand*o*
> until I put your enemies
> under your feet.'**^B,*p*

37 David himself calls him 'Lord.' How, then, can he be his son?" And the large crowd was listening to him with delight.

WARNING AGAINST THE SCRIBES

38 He*q* also said in his teaching, "Beware of the scribes, who want to go around in long robes*r* and who want greetings in the marketplaces,*s* 39 the best seats*t* in the synagogues,*u* and the places of honor*v* at banquets.*w* 40 They devour*x* widows' houses and say long prayers*z* just for show. These will receive harsher judgment."

THE WIDOW'S GIFT

41 Sitting*aa* across from the temple treasury,*ab* he watched how the crowd dropped money into the treasury. Many rich*ac* people were putting in large sums. 42 Then a poor*ad* widow came and dropped in two tiny coins worth very little. 43 Summoning his disciples,*ae* he said to them, "Truly I tell you,*af* this poor widow has put more into the treasury than all the others.*ag* 44 For

they all gave out of their surplus,*ah* but she out of her poverty*ai* has put in everything she had*aj* — all she had to live on."*ak*

DESTRUCTION OF THE TEMPLE PREDICTED

13 As*al* he was going out of the temple,*am* one of his disciples said to him, "Teacher,*an* look! What massive stones! What impressive buildings!"*ao*

2 Jesus said to him, "Do you see these great buildings?*ap* Not one stone will be left upon another — all will be thrown down."

SIGNS OF THE END OF THE AGE

3 While he was sitting on the Mount of Olives*aq* across from the temple,*ar* Peter,*as* James,*at* John,*au* and Andrew*av* asked him privately, 4 "Tell us, when will these things happen? And what will be the sign when all these things are about to be accomplished?"

5 Jesus told them, "Watch out that no one deceives you. 6 Many will come in my name,*aw* saying, 'I am he,'*ax* and they will deceive*ay* many. 7 When you hear of wars and rumors of wars,*az* don't be alarmed;*ba* these things must take place,*bb* but it is not yet the end. 8 For nation will rise up against nation, and kingdom against kingdom.*bc* There will be earthquakes in various places, and famines.^C These are the beginning*bd* of birth pains.*be*

PERSECUTIONS PREDICTED

9 "But you, be on your guard! They will hand you over to local courts,^D,*bf* and you will be flogged*bg* in the synagogues.*bh* You will stand before governors and kings*bi* because of me,*bj* as a witness*bk* to them.*bl* 10 And it is necessary that the gospel*bm* be preached to all nations. 11 So when they arrest you and hand you over, don't worry beforehand what you will say, but say whatever is given to you at that time, for it isn't you speaking, but the Holy Spirit.

---

^A 12:33 Other mss add *with all your soul*   ^B 12:36 Ps 110:1   ^C 13:8 Other mss add *and disturbances*   ^D 13:9 Or *sanhedrins*

12:33 Mere religious observance is worthless. Conforming to external religious regulations and practices—without **love**—will not get you close to God.

12:34 Jesus affirmed this particular scribe. His understanding of the law had brought him near to the Messiah and salvation—**not far from the kingdom of God.**

12:35-37 If David called his descendant **my Lord** (12:36), clearly he was more than merely David's **son** (12:37). Jesus was using the Scriptures to show that the Messiah would indeed be a human descendant of David, but he

would also be far more. He would be divine. The Son of David is also the Lord of David. Jesus is fully man and fully God.

12:38-40 The scribes were thought to be experts in and teachers of the law. They should've been examples of godliness and humility.

12:43-44 When God considers our Christian stewardship, he looks not merely at the amount of our gifts but at our motives.

13:1-2 Jesus's prediction became a reality in AD 70 when the Romans invaded Jerusalem under Titus, decimating the city.

13:3-4 The disciples connected the events Jesus mentioned in verse 2 with the end of

the age and the beginning of the messianic kingdom (see Matt 24:3), but they didn't understand that there would be an interval of time between the temple's destruction and Christ's millennial reign.

13:8 The prophets spoke of labor or **birth pains** as a symbol of God's outpouring of judgment (see Jer 30:5-7), so Jesus uses this symbol to refer to the beginning of the tribulation period prophesied by Daniel (see the notes on Dan 9:24-27). This time of sorrow will eventually lead to the end of the age, the return of Christ, and the "birth" of the messianic kingdom.

¹² "Brother will betray[a] brother to death,[b] and a father his child. Children will rise up against parents and have them put to death. ¹³ You will be hated by everyone because of my name,[c] but the one who endures to the end will be saved.[d]

THE GREAT TRIBULATION

¹⁴ "When you see **the abomination of desolation**[A,e] standing where it should not be" (let the reader understand), "then those in Judea[f] must flee to the mountains. ¹⁵ A man on the housetop must not come down or go in to get anything out of his house,[g] ¹⁶ and a man in the field must not go back to get his coat.[h] ¹⁷ Woe[i] to pregnant women and nursing mothers in those days!

¹⁸ "Pray[j] it[B] won't happen in winter. ¹⁹ For those will be days of tribulation,[k] the kind that hasn't been from the beginning[l] of creation[m] until now and never will be again. ²⁰ If the Lord[n] had not cut those days short,[o] no one would be saved. But he cut those days short for the sake of the elect,[p] whom he chose.[q]

²¹ "Then if anyone tells you, 'See, here is the Messiah!' See, there!' do not believe it. ²² For false messiahs and false prophets will arise and will perform signs and wonders[s] to lead astray, if possible, the elect. ²³ And you must watch! I have told you everything in advance.

THE COMING OF THE SON OF MAN

²⁴ "But in those days, after that tribulation:[t] The sun will be darkened, and the moon will not shed its light; ²⁵ the stars[u] will be falling from the sky, and the powers in the heavens will be shaken.[v] ²⁶ Then they will see the Son of Man[w] coming[x] in clouds[y] with great power[z] and glory.[aa] ²⁷ He will send out the angels[ab] and gather his elect[ac]

from the four winds, from the ends of the earth to the ends of heaven.[ad]

THE PARABLE OF THE FIG TREE

²⁸ "Learn[ae] this lesson[af] from the fig[ag] tree: As soon as its branch becomes tender and sprouts leaves, you know that summer is near.[ah] ²⁹ In the same way, when you see these things happening, recognize[c] that he[D] is near — at the door.

³⁰ "Truly I tell you,[ai] this generation will certainly not pass away until all these things take place. ³¹ Heaven and earth[aj] will pass away,[ak] but my words will never pass away.[al]

NO ONE KNOWS THE DAY OR HOUR

³² "Now concerning that day[am] or hour no one knows — neither the angels[an] in heaven nor the Son[ao] — but only the Father.[ap] ³³ "Watch! Be alert![E] For you don't know when the time[aq] is coming.[ar] ³⁴ "It is like[as] a man on a journey, who left his house, gave authority to his servants,[at] gave each one his work, and commanded the doorkeeper to be alert. ³⁵ Therefore be alert,[au] since you don't know when the master[av] of the house is coming — whether in the evening or at midnight or at the crowing of the rooster or early in the morning. ³⁶ Otherwise, when he comes suddenly he might find you sleeping.[aw] ³⁷ And what I say to you, I say to everyone: Be alert!"

THE PLOT TO KILL JESUS

14 It[ax] was two days before the Passover[ay] and the Festival[az] of Unleavened Bread.[ba] The chief priests and the scribes[bb] were looking for a cunning[bc] way to arrest Jesus and kill him.[bd] ² "Not during the festival," they said, "so that there won't be a riot among the people."

ᵃ 13:12 Jn 13:21
ᵇ Is 19:2; Mc 7:6
ᶜ 13:13 Mt 10:22; Lk 6:22; Jn 15:18-21
ᵈ 1Co 4:12; 2Th 1:4; 2Tm 2:12; Jms 1:12
ᵉ 13:14 Dn 9:27; 11:31; 12:11
ᶠ Lk 1:5
ᵍ 13:15 Mt 24:17; Lk 17:31
ʰ 13:16 Lk 19:36
ⁱ 13:17 Rv 9:12
ʲ 13:18 Mt 5:44; Ac 12:12
ᵏ 13:19 1Co 1:4
ˡ Ac 26:4
ᵐ Jn 1:3; Rv 3:14
ⁿ 13:20 Col 4:1; Jd 5
ᵒ Is 60:21-22
ᵖ Mt 24:22
ᵠ Eph 1:4
ʳ 13:21 Mt 1:17; Eph 5:2
ˢ 13:22 Ex 7:3; Dn 6:27; Jn 4:48; Ac 4:30; Rm 15:19; 2Th 2:9; Heb 2:4
ᵗ 13:24 2Co 1:4
ᵘ 13:25 Rv 1:16
ᵛ 13:24-25 Is 13:10; 34:4; Jl 2:10,31; 3:15
ʷ 13:26 Mk 2:10
ˣ Mk 8:38; 1Th 4:16
ʸ Dn 7:13-14
ᶻ Lk 6:19
ᵃᵃ Mk 10:37; Lk 9:32
ᵃᵇ 13:27 Mt 13:49; Ac 5:19; Rv 14:6
ᵃᶜ Mt 22:14,22
ᵃᵈ 13:27 Zch 2:6
ᵃᵉ 13:28 Jn 7:15
ᵃᶠ Mk 12:1
ᵃᵍ Jn 1:48
ᵃʰ Rv 1:1
ᵃⁱ 13:30 Ps 72:19; Rv 22:21
ᵃʲ 13:31 Lk 10:21
ᵃᵏ 2Pt 3:10
ᵃˡ Ps 102:25-27; Is 40:6-8; 51:6; Mt 5:18; Lk 16:17
ᵃᵐ 13:32 Mt 25:13
ᵃⁿ Mt 13:49
ᵃᵒ Jn 5:19; Heb 1:2
ᵃᵖ Mt 5:16; 11:27; Jn 8:42
ᵃᵠ 13:33 Lk 20:20
ᵃʳ Ac 1:7; 1Th 5:1-2; 1Pt 5:6
ᵃˢ 13:34 Lk 12:35-40
ᵃᵗ Mt 10:24
ᵃᵘ 13:35 Rv 16:15
ᵃᵛ Col 3:22
ᵃʷ 13:36 Pr 6:4
ᵃˣ 14:1-2 Mt 26:1-5; Lk 22:1-2
ᵃʸ 14:1 Ex 12:11
ᵃᶻ Jn 5:1
ᵇᵃ Ex 23:15
ᵇᵇ Mt 2:4
ᵇᶜ Ps 10:7
ᵇᵈ Jn 5:18

ᴬ 13:14 Dn 9:27   ᴮ 13:18 Other mss read *"Pray that your escape*   ᶜ 13:29 Or *you know*   ᴰ 13:29 Or *it*   ᴱ 13:33 Other mss add *and pray*

13:13 In this instance, **saved** does not refer to spiritual salvation but to preservation from physical death. In other words, believers who endure to the end of the tribulation will be spared physical death and enter the millennium. **13:14-16 The abomination of desolation** (13:14) is also prophesied by Daniel (see the note on Dan 9:24-27). The antichrist will arise during the seven-year tribulation period as a world ruler. At the midpoint of those seven years, he will break a covenant of peace made with Israel and set up an "abomination" in a rebuilt Jewish temple (see Dan 9:27). This will be an image in which he sets himself up as a god, revealing himself to be "the beast" who demands to be worshiped by all the people of earth (Rev 13:5-8). This abomination will coincide with an intense persecution of anyone

who refuses to worship the beast. Those who will not bow down will have to **flee**, leaving their property behind if they are to escape death (Mark 13:14-15). **13:21-23** Believers must be vigilant and discerning. Our theology has life-and-death consequences. **13:24-25** The prophets also foretold these amazing signs that will appear in the heavens (see Isa 13:10; 34:4; Joel 2:31). When they witness these celestial abnormalities, people will know that the Lord is coming soon. **13:26** This will happen in fulfillment of Daniel's prophecy (Dan 7:13-14). It will be an event visible to all. **13:32** In his humanity, the Son did not know because of his submission to the will of his Father.

13:35-37 After his resurrection, Jesus would ascend into heaven and give his church authority to minister in the world on his behalf. Christ's disciples, then, must not become spiritually lethargic but remain watchful and prepared for him to return at any time (13:35). The rapture of the church (see the notes on Matt 24:42-44; 1 Thess 4:13-17) will occur before the tribulation period begins. It has no preconditions and, therefore, could happen at any time. So believers must live constantly in light of Jesus's imminent return. **14:1-2** The Jewish leaders wanted things to proceed according to their timetable, but they were naïve. Jesus had predicted that he would be crucified and rise from the dead in Jerusalem (8:31; 9:30-31; 10:32-34). God is sovereign; everything proceeds according to his plan.

a 14:3-9 Mt 26:6-13; Jn 12:2-8
b 14:3 Mk 11:1
c Mt 11:5
d Lv 19:34
e Rm 12:13
f 14:5 Mt 18:28
g Rm 15:26
h 14:6 1Pt 2:12
i 14:7 Dt 15:11
j Lk 10:38-42
k 14:8 Lk 12:4
l Jn 19:40
m 14:9 Ps 72:19; Rv 22:21
n Mk 1:1; Php 1:5
o Mt 13:38; 1Jn 2:2
p 14:10-11 Mt 26:14-16; Lk 22:3-6
q 14:10 Mk 3:19
r Mk 11:11
s Mt 2:4
t Mk 9:31
u 14:11 Lk 19:15
v Jn 13:21
w 14:12-16 Mt 26:17-19; Lk 22:7-13
x 14:12 Ex 12:21
y Mt 9:10; Mk 10:10; Lk 6:1; Jn 6:3; Ac 6:1
z 14:14 Mk 4:38; Eph 4:11
aa 14:16 Mk 10:10
ab 14:17-21 Mt 26:20-25; Lk 22:21-23; Jn 13:21-30
ac 14:17 Mk 11:11
ad 14:21 Mk 2:10
ae Mk 1:2; Ac 15:15
af Dn 7:21,25; 9:26
ag Rv 9:12
ah 14:22-26 Mt 26:26-30; Lk 22:17-20; 1Co 11:23-25
ai 14:22 1Co 10:16
aj Mt 14:19; 15:36; Ac 2:46; 20:7,11; 27:35
ak Lk 24:30
al Lk 12:4; Jn 2:21; 6:51
am 14:23 Mk 8:6
an 14:24 Ex 24:8; Zch 9:11; Heb 9:18-20; 10:29; 13:20
ao Gn 4:11; Nm 35:33; Lm 4:13; Mt 23:35
ap Is 52:13–53:12
aq 14:25 Rv 22:21
ar Is 32:12; Hab 3:17; Jms 3:12
as Is 25:6; Lk 13:28-29; 14:15-24
at Mk 1:15
au 14:26 Mt 21:1
av 14:27-31 Mt 26:31-35; Lk 22:31-38; Jn 13:31-38
aw 14:27 Ac 15:15
ax Mt 7:15
ay Zch 13:7

THE ANOINTING AT BETHANY

3 While[a] he was in Bethany[b] at the house of Simon the leper,[A,c] as he was reclining at the table,[d] a woman came with an alabaster jar of very expensive perfume of pure nard. She broke the jar and poured it on his head.[e] **4** But some were expressing indignation to one another: "Why has this perfume been wasted? **5** For this perfume might have been sold for more than three hundred denarii[B,f] and given to the poor."[g] And they began to scold her.

6 Jesus replied, "Leave her alone. Why are you bothering her? She has done a noble thing[h] for me. **7** You always have the poor[i] with you, and you can do what is good for them whenever you want, but you do not always have me.[j] **8** She has done what she could; she has anointed my body[k] in advance for burial.[l] **9** Truly I tell you,[m] wherever the gospel[n] is proclaimed in the whole world,[o] what she has done will also be told in memory of her."

10 Then[p] Judas Iscariot,[q] one of the Twelve,[r] went to the chief priests[s] to betray Jesus[t] to them. **11** And when they heard this, they were glad and promised to give him money.[u] So he started looking for a good opportunity to betray[v] him.

PREPARATION FOR PASSOVER

12 On[w] the first day of Unleavened Bread, when they sacrifice the Passover lamb,[x] his disciples[y] asked him, "Where do you want us to go and prepare the Passover so that you may eat it?"

13 So he sent two of his disciples and told them, "Go into the city, and a man carrying a jar of water will meet you. Follow him. **14** Wherever he enters, tell the owner of the house, 'The Teacher[z] says, "Where is my guest room where I may eat the Passover with my disciples?"' **15** He will show

you a large room upstairs, furnished and ready. Make the preparations for us there." **16** So the disciples[aa] went out, entered the city, and found it just as he had told them, and they prepared the Passover.

BETRAYAL AT THE PASSOVER

17 When[ab] evening came, he arrived with the Twelve.[ac] **18** While they were reclining and eating, Jesus said, "Truly I tell you, one of you will betray me — one who is eating with me."

19 They began to be distressed and to say to him one by one, "Surely not I?"

20 He said to them, "It is one of the Twelve — the one who is dipping bread in the bowl with me. **21** For the Son of Man[ad] will go just as it is written[ae] about him,[af] but woe[ag] to that man by whom the Son of Man is betrayed! It would have been better for him if he had not been born."

THE FIRST LORD'S SUPPER

22 As[ah] they were eating, he took bread,[ai] blessed and broke[aj] it, gave it to them,[ak] and said, "Take it; this is my body."[al] **23** Then he took a cup, and after giving thanks,[am] he gave it to them, and they all drank from it. **24** He said to them, "This is my blood of the covenant,[C,an] which is poured out[ao] for many.[ap] **25** Truly I tell you,[aq] I will no longer drink of the fruit of the vine[ar] until that day when I drink it new[D,as] in the kingdom of God."[at]

26 After singing a hymn, they went out to the Mount of Olives.[au]

PETER'S DENIAL PREDICTED

27 Then[av] Jesus said to them, "All of you will fall away,[E] because it is written:[aw]

> **I will strike the shepherd,**
> **and the sheep[ax]**
> **will be scattered.**[F,ay]

A 14:3 Gk *lepros*; a term for various skin diseases; see Lv 13–14   **B** 14:5 A denarius = one day's wage   **C** 14:24 Other mss read *the new covenant*   **D** 14:25 Or *drink new wine*; lit *drink it new*   **E** 14:27 Other mss add *because of me this night*   **F** 14:27 Zch 13:7

14:3 The **woman** in this scene is Mary the sister of Lazarus (see John 12:3).

14:8-9 Mary sought to honor Jesus by sacrificially anointing him, and he wouldn't forget her actions. The Lord says, "Those who honor me I will honor" (1 Sam 2:30).

14:12 Passover commemorated the long-ago night in Egypt when God brought his judgment on that nation, killing every firstborn so that Pharaoh would set the Israelites free. God had instructed his people to slay unblemished lambs, wipe their blood on their doorposts, roast the lambs, and eat them. When he saw the blood on the doorposts of the Israelites, God would "pass over" them.

A reminder of God's deliverance from slavery, the Passover festival ultimately points to Jesus, "our Passover lamb" (1 Cor 5:7) who sets us free from sin (John 8:34-36).

14:18 To share a meal together is an act of friendship and trust, making Judas's betrayal especially despicable.

14:22-24 Jesus took the bread and wine, common elements during the Passover, and gave them new significance. He explained them in light of the new **covenant** (14:27). The **bread** represented his **body** (14:22), and the **cup** represented the **blood** that would be **poured out for many** (14:23-24). The sacrificial death of Jesus Christ on the cross would accomplish

what the old covenant had anticipated. It would atone for sins and make it possible for people to be forgiven and have a relationship with God. The church is to celebrate this Lord's Supper regularly. As often as we do, we "proclaim the Lord's death until he comes" (1 Cor 11:26). It's a visible proclamation of the gospel.

14:26 The **hymn** they sang was probably a psalm.

14:27-28 Though Jesus prophesied that **all** of them would **fall away** and abandon him (14:27), he also left them with hope. He spoke of their reunion after he had **risen** from the dead (14:28).

28 But after I have risen,[a] I will go ahead of you to Galilee."[b] **29** Peter[c] told him, "Even if everyone falls away, I will not." **30** "Truly I tell you," Jesus said to him, "today, this very night, before the rooster crows twice, you will deny me three times."[d] **31** But he kept insisting, "If I have to die with you, I will never deny you." And they all said the same thing.

THE PRAYER IN THE GARDEN

32 Then[e] they came to a place named Gethsemane, and he told his disciples,[f] "Sit here while I pray."[g] **33** He took Peter,[h] James,[i] and John[j] with him, and he began to be deeply distressed and troubled. **34** He said to them, "I am deeply grieved[A] to the point of death. Remain here and stay awake."[k] **35** He went a little farther, fell to the ground, and prayed that if it were possible, the hour[l] might pass from him. **36** And he said, "Abba,[B] Father![m] All things are possible[n] for you. Take this cup[o] away from me. Nevertheless, not what I will, but what you will." **37** Then he came and found them sleeping. He said to Peter, "Simon,[p] are you sleeping?[q] Couldn't you stay awake one hour? **38** Stay awake and pray[r] so that you won't enter into temptation.[C,s] The spirit[t] is willing, but the flesh[u] is weak." **39** Once again he went away and prayed, saying the same thing. **40** And again he came and found them sleeping, because they could not keep their eyes open. They did not know what to say to him.[v] **41** Then he came a third time and said to them, "Are you still sleeping and resting? Enough! The time has come. See, the Son of Man[w] is betrayed into the hands of sinners.[x] **42** Get up;[y] let's go. See, my betrayer is near."

JUDAS'S BETRAYAL OF JESUS

43 While[z] he was still speaking, Judas,[aa] one of the Twelve,[ab] suddenly arrived. With him was a mob, with swords and clubs, from the chief priests, the scribes,[ac] and the elders.[ad] **44** His betrayer had given them a signal. "The one I kiss," he said, "he's the one; arrest him and take him away under guard." **45** So when he came, immediately he went up to Jesus and said, "Rabbi!"[ae] and kissed him. **46** They took hold of him and arrested him. **47** One of those who stood by drew his sword, struck the high priest's servant, and cut off his ear. **48** Jesus said to them, "Have you come out with swords and clubs, as if I were a criminal,[D] to capture me? **49** Every day I was among you, teaching in the temple,[af] and you didn't arrest me. But the Scriptures[ag] must be fulfilled."[ah] **50** Then they all deserted him and ran away.[ai] **51** Now a certain young man, wearing nothing but a linen cloth, was following him. They caught hold of him, **52** but he left the linen cloth behind and ran away naked.[aj]

JESUS FACES THE SANHEDRIN

53 They[ak] led Jesus away to the high priest,[al] and all the chief priests, the elders, and the scribes[am] assembled.[an] **54** Peter[ao] followed him at a distance, right into the high priest's courtyard. He was sitting with the servants,[E,ap] warming himself by the fire. **55** The chief priests and the whole Sanhedrin[aq] were looking for testimony against Jesus to put him to death,[ar] but they could not find any. **56** For many were giving false testimony[as] against him, and the testimonies did not agree. **57** Some stood up and gave false testimony against him, stating, **58** "We heard him say, 'I will destroy this temple made with human hands,[at] and in three days I will build another not made by hands.'"[au] **59** Yet their testimony did not agree[au] even on this. **60** Then the high priest stood up before them all and questioned Jesus, "Don't you have an answer to what these men are testifying against you?" **61** But he kept silent

[a] 14:28 1Co 15:4
[b] Mt 17:22
[c] 14:29 Lk 6:14; Ac 10:32
[d] 14:30 Mk 14:72
[e] 14:32 Mt 26:36-46; Lk 22:39-46
[f] 14:32 Mk 1:10
[g] Mt 5:44; Ac 12:12
[h] 14:33 Lk 6:14
[i] Ac 12:2
[j] Jn 21:7
[k] 14:34 Rv 16:15
[l] 14:35 Jn 2:4
[m] 14:36 Rm 8:15; Gl 4:6
[n] Mt 19:26; Mk 9:23
[o] Ps 11:6; Is 51:17,22; Lm 4:21; Ezk 23:32-34; Mk 10:38-39; Jn 18:11
[p] 14:37 Mt 16:17
[q] Lk 6:14
[r] 14:38 Mt 5:44
[s] Mt 6:13; Lk 4:13
[t] Ps 51:12
[u] Php 3:3
[v] 14:40 Mk 4:40
[w] 14:41 Mk 2:10
[x] Mk 8:31; 9:31; 10:33-34
[y] 14:42 Mk 5:41
[z] 14:43-52 Mt 26:47-56; Lk 22:47-53; Jn 18:1-2
[aa] 14:43 Mk 3:19
[ab] Mk 11:11
[ac] 14:43 Mt 2:4
[ad] 3Jn 1
[ae] 14:45 Jn 11:8
[af] 14:49 Ac 21:26
[ag] 2Pt 1:20
[ah] Mt 1:22; Mk 9:12
[ai] 14:50 Mk 4:40; Jms 4:7
[aj] 14:52 Am 2:16
[ak] 14:53-65 Mt 26:57-68; Lk 22:54,63-65; Jn 18:24
[al] 14:53 Mt 26:3
[am] Mt 2:4
[an] Mk 8:31; 10:33
[ao] 14:54 Lk 6:14
[ap] Jn 18:18
[aq] 14:55 Mk 13:9
[ar] Mt 10:21
[as] 14:56 Pr 6:19; 1Jn 5:10
[at] 14:58 Col 2:11
[au] 14:59 Nm 35:30; Dt 17:6; 19:15; Php 2:6

[A] 14:34 Or *"My soul is swallowed up in sorrow*   [B] 14:36 Aramaic for *father*   [C] 14:38 Or *won't be put to the test*   [D] 14:48 Or *insurrectionist*
[E] 14:54 Or *temple police*, or *officers*, also in v. 65

14:29-31 Though his motives may've been good, Peter was not as spiritual as he thought he was. His pride and spiritual weakness would give Satan something to take advantage of. When we proudly exalt our abilities and fail to depend on God, we become bait for the evil one.
14:32-36 The true and full humanity of the Son of God is on display here. He asked that the **cup** of God's wrath might be taken away if it were **possible**; nevertheless, he was fully prepared to submit to his Father's **will** (14:36).

14:38 The spirit is willing, but the flesh is weak indicates that they had an inner desire to follow Jesus, but their physical exhaustion would make them susceptible to the devil. They needed to stay awake and seek the strengthening that only God could provide.
14:44-45 Judas's act of betrayal was vile. With a **kiss**—an act of kindness, friendship, intimacy—he handed over the Son of God to those who hated him.
14:47 We know from the other Gospels that it was Peter who **struck** the **servant** with vio-

lence and that Jesus rebuked him for it (see Matt 26:52-54; John 18:10-11).
14:51-52 Some interpreters believe this to be a veiled reference by the author (Mark) to himself.
14:61-62 When the high priest demanded that Jesus confess whether he was **the Messiah, the Son of the Blessed One** (14:61), Jesus responded, **I am** (14:62). But he didn't stop there. He attributed to himself the language of Psalm 110:1 and Daniel 7:13 (Mark 14:62), passages that prophesy of the glorious Messiah, human yet

a 14:61 Is 53:7; Mt 27:12,14; Mk 15:5; Lk 23:9; Jn 19:9
b Mt 1:17; Eph 5:2
c Jn 5:19; Heb 1:2
d Lk 1:68; Rm 1:25; 9:5; 2Co 1:3; 11:31; Eph 1:3; 1Pt 1:3
e 14:62 Ex 3:14; Ps 45:8; Jn 8:24
f Mk 2:10; Ac 7:56
g Mt 20:21
h Mt 26:64; Mk 13:26
i Ps 110:1; Dn 7:13
j 14:63 Mt 26:3
k Lv 10:6; 21:10; Nm 14:6; Jn 19:23
l Heb 12:1
m 14:64 Jn 10:33; Rv 13:6
n Mk 10:33
o 14:65 Jn 11:51
p Jn 18:18
q 14:66-72 Mt 26:69-75; Lk 22:54-62; Jn 18:15-18,25-27
r 14:66 Lk 6:14
s 14:67 Mk 1:24; 10:47; 16:6; Lk 4:34; 24:19
t 14:70 Jn 4:45
u 14:71 Mk 5:34
v 14:72 Mk 14:30
w 15:1-5 Mt 27:2,11-14; Lk 23:25; Jn 18:28-38
x 15:1 3Jn 1
y Mt 2:4
z 15:1 Mk 13:9
aa 1Tm 6:13
ab 15:2 Lk 19:38
ac Jn 19:21
ad 15:4 1Tm 6:13
ae 15:6-15 Mt 27:15-26; Lk 23:13-25; Jn 18:39-19:6
af 15:6 Mk 14:1
ag 1Tm 6:13
ah 15:7 Pr 1:16
ai Ac 23:7
aj 15:9 Lk 19:38
ak Jn 19:21
al 15:10 Ps 37:1
am 15:16-20 Mt 27:27-31
an 15:16 Jn 18:28,33; 19:9; Ac 23:35; Php 1:13
ao 15:17 Mk 15:20; Lk 16:19; Rv 18:12
ap Jn 19:2,5; Rv 12:1

and did not answer.[a] Again the high priest questioned him, "Are you the Messiah,[b] the Son[c] of the Blessed[d] One?"

62 "I am,"[e] said Jesus, "and you will see **the Son of Man**[f] **seated at the right hand**[g] of Power and **coming with the clouds**[h] **of heaven.**"[A,i]

63 Then the high priest[j] tore his robes[k] and said, "Why do we still need witnesses?[l] **64** You have heard the blasphemy.[m] What is your decision?" They all condemned him as deserving death.[n]

65 Then some began to spit on him, to blindfold him, and to beat him, saying, "Prophesy!"[o] The temple servants[p] also took him and slapped him.

PETER DENIES HIS LORD

66 While[q] Peter[r] was in the courtyard below, one of the high priest's maidservants came. **67** When she saw Peter warming himself, she looked at him and said, "You also were with Jesus, the man from Nazareth."[s]

68 But he denied it: "I don't know or understand what you're talking about." Then he went out to the entryway,[B] and a rooster crowed.[C]

69 When the maidservant saw him again, she began to tell those standing nearby, "This man is one of them."

70 But again he denied it. After a little while those standing there said to Peter again, "You certainly are one of them, since you're also a Galilean."[D,t]

71 Then he started to curse and swear,[u] "I don't know this man you're talking about!"

72 Immediately a rooster crowed a second time,[v] and Peter remembered when Jesus had spoken the word to him, "Before the rooster crows twice, you will deny me three times." And he broke down and wept.

JESUS FACES PILATE

15 As[w] soon as it was morning, having held a meeting with the elders,[x] scribes,[y] and the whole Sanhedrin, the chief priests[z] tied Jesus up, led him away, and handed him over to Pilate.[aa]

2 So Pilate asked him, "Are you the King[ab] of the Jews?"[ac]

He answered him, "You say so."

3 And the chief priests accused him of many things. **4** Pilate[ad] questioned him again, "Aren't you going to answer? Look how many things they are accusing you of!" **5** But Jesus still did not answer, and so Pilate was amazed.

JESUS OR BARABBAS

6 At[ae] the festival[af] Pilate[ag] used to release for the people a prisoner whom they requested. **7** There was one named Barabbas, who was in prison with rebels who had committed murder[ah] during the rebellion.[ai] **8** The crowd came up and began to ask Pilate to do for them as was his custom. **9** Pilate answered them, "Do you want me to release the King[aj] of the Jews[ak] for you?" **10** For he knew it was because of envy[al] that the chief priests had handed him over. **11** But the chief priests stirred up the crowd so that he would release Barabbas to them instead. **12** Pilate asked them again, "Then what do you want me to do with the one you call the King of the Jews?"

13 Again they shouted, "Crucify him!"

14 Pilate said to them, "Why? What has he done wrong?"

But they shouted all the more, "Crucify him!"

15 Wanting to satisfy the crowd, Pilate released Barabbas to them; and after having Jesus flogged, he handed him over to be crucified.

MOCKED BY THE MILITARY

16 The[am] soldiers led him away into the palace (that is, the governor's residence[an]) and called the whole company together. **17** They dressed him in a purple[ao] robe, twisted together a crown[ap] of thorns, and put it on

---

[A] 14:62 Ps 110:1; Dn 7:13　　[B] 14:68 Or *forecourt*　　[C] 14:68 Other mss omit *and a rooster crowed*　　[D] 14:70 Other mss add *and your speech shows it*

---

divine. Though the high priest was presiding over Jesus's "trial," one day all humanity will stand before Christ's judgment throne.

14:65 Don't skim over how the Son of God suffered for you.

14:66-72 Peter had brashly vowed to stand with Jesus, even if everyone else ran away. But he had placed his confidence in himself. Our flesh, no matter how sincere, cannot achieve righteousness apart from yielding to and depending on the Lord.

15:1 The **Sanhedrin**, the Jewish council over which the high priest presided, determined to hand Jesus over to Pontius **Pilate**, the Roman governor of Judea (from AD 26–36). Since the Jews were under Roman rule, they couldn't carry out the death penalty (see John 18:31); they would need the Roman governor's help. Pilate was a cruel man who was more than willing to execute enemies of Rome.

15:2 In order for Pilate to be willing to execute Jesus, he would need to be guilty of a crime against Rome—like sedition. Since he claimed to be the Messiah, a Jewish King, this was the charge the Sanhedrin brought against him. The Jews were to have no king

but Caesar. Jesus's answer, **You say so**, is an affirmation of the charge.

15:13-14 Pilate recognized that their demand made no sense. Incited by their religious leaders, the very ones who had been celebrating Jesus's teaching and miracles only a few days before were now calling for his death.

15:15 Flogging was a brutal means of punishment in which a whip, with pieces of bone or metal tied into its ends, was applied to the back of a person until his flesh was ripped to shreds.

15:16-20 Heed the words of the author of Hebrews, fellow Christian: "Consider him

him. **18** And they began to salute him, "Hail,[a] King[b] of the Jews!" **19** They were hitting him on the head with a stick and spitting on him. Getting down on their knees,[c] they were paying him homage. **20** After they had mocked[d] him, they stripped him of the purple robe and put his clothes on him.

CRUCIFIED BETWEEN TWO CRIMINALS

They led him out to crucify him. **21** They[e] forced a man coming in from the country, who was passing by, to carry Jesus's cross.[f] He was Simon of Cyrene,[g] the father of Alexander and Rufus.[h]

22 They[i] brought Jesus to the place called *Golgotha* (which means Place of the Skull[j]). **23** They tried to give him wine[k] mixed with myrrh,[l] but he did not take it.

24 Then they crucified him and divided his clothes, casting lots[m] for them to decide what each would get. **25** Now it was nine in the morning[A] when they crucified him. **26** The inscription of the charge written against him was: THE KING[n] OF THE JEWS.[o] **27** They[p] crucified two criminals[B,q] with him, one on his right and one on his left.[c]

29 Those[r] who passed by were yelling insults[s] at[D] him, shaking their heads,[t] and saying, "Ha! The one who would destroy the temple and rebuild it in three days,[u] **30** save yourself by coming down from the cross!"[v] **31** In the same way, the chief priests with the scribes[w] were mocking him among themselves and saying, "He saved others, but he cannot save himself! **32** Let the Messiah,[x] the King[y] of Israel,[z]

come down now from the cross,[aa] so that we may see and believe."[ab] Even those who were crucified with him taunted him.

THE DEATH OF JESUS

33 When[ac] it was noon,[E] darkness came over the whole land until three in the afternoon.[F,ad] **34** And at three Jesus cried out with a loud voice, *"Eloi, Eloi, lemá sabachtháni?"* which is translated, **"My God, my God, why have you abandoned me?"**[G,ae] **35** When some of those standing there heard this, they said, "See, he's calling for Elijah."

36 Someone ran and filled a sponge with sour wine, fixed it on a stick, offered him a drink,[af] and said, "Let's see if Elijah comes to take him down."

37 Jesus let out a loud cry and breathed his last. **38** Then the curtain[ag] of the temple was torn in two from top to bottom. **39** When the centurion, who was standing opposite him, saw the way he[H] breathed his last, he said, "Truly this man was the Son of God!"[i,ah]

40 There[ai] were also women watching from a distance. Among them were Mary Magdalene,[aj] Mary the mother of James the younger and of Joses, and Salome. **41** In Galilee[ak] these women followed him and took care of him. Many other women had come up with him to Jerusalem.[al]

THE BURIAL OF JESUS

42 When[am] it was already evening, because it was the day of preparation (that is, the day before the Sabbath), **43** Joseph of Arimathea, a prominent member of the Sanhedrin who

Video Devotional

"THE CROSS"

The cross provides the power, protection, authority, and provision of God to us.

www.bhpublishinggroup.com/qr/te/41-15

[a] 15:18 Mt 26:49; Lk 1:28; Jn 19:3
[b] Lk 19:38
[c] 15:19 Mk 5:6; Lk 22:41; Eph 3:14
[d] 15:20 Mk 10:34
[e] 15:21 Mt 27:32; Lk 23:26-31
[f] Lk 9:23
[g] Ac 6:9
[h] Rm 16:13
[i] 15:22-26 Mt 27:33-37; Lk 22:32-34; Jn 19:17-24
[j] 15:22 Jn 19:17
[k] 15:23 Gn 9:21; Dt 7:13; Ps 4:7; Pr 3:10; Lk 5:37
[l] Ps 69:21
[m] 15:24 Ps 22:18
[n] 15:26 Lk 19:38
[o] Jn 11:36
[p] 15:27-28 Mt 27:38,44; Lk 23:39-43
[q] 15:27 Mk 14:48
[r] 15:29-32 Mt 27:39-43; Lk 23:35-38
[s] 15:29 Ex 22:28; Mk 3:29; Rv 13:6
[t] Ps 22:7
[u] Jn 2:19
[v] 15:30 Lk 23:26
[w] 15:31 Mt 2:4
[x] 15:32 Mt 1:17; Eph 5:2
[y] Lk 19:38
[z] Jn 1:49

[aa] 15:32 Lk 23:26 [ab] Mk 8:11-12; 11:24; Jn 3:16; Ac 10:43; Rm 10:9; 1Pt 1:8-10 [ac] 15:33-39 Mt 27:45-54; Lk 23:44-48; Jn 19:28-30 [ad] 15:33 Am 8:9 [ae] 15:34 Ps 22:1 [af] 15:36 Ps 69:21 [ag] 15:38 Ex 26:31-33; 2Ch 3:14; Heb 6:19; 9:3; 10:20 [ah] 15:39 Is 19; Heb 1:2 [ai] 15:40-41 Mt 27:55-56; Lk 23:49; Jn 19:25-27 [aj] 15:40 Mt 28:1; Mk 16:1,9; Lk 8:2; 24:10; Jn 20:1-18 [ak] 15:41 Mt 17:22 [al] Mt 23:37 [am] 15:42-46 Mt 27:57-60; Lk 23:50-54; Jn 19:38-42

[A] 15:25 Lit *was the third hour*   [B] 15:27 Or *revolutionaries*   [C] 15:27 Some mss include v. 28: *So the Scripture was fulfilled that says: And he was counted among criminals.*   [D] 15:29 Or *passed by blasphemed*   [E] 15:33 Lit *the sixth hour*   [F] 15:33 Lit *the ninth hour*, also in v. 34   [G] 15:34 Ps 22:1
[H] 15:39 Other mss read *saw that he cried out like this and*   [i] 15:39 Or *a son of God*

---

who endured such hostility from sinners against himself, so that you won't grow weary and give up" (Heb 12:3).

15:21 Cyrene was the capital city of the Roman district of Cyrenaica in northern Africa.

15:22 The place of crucifixion was **called Golgotha**, an Aramaic name meaning **Place of the Skull**. Our English word *Calvary* is derived from the Latin translation, *Calvaria*. Scripture does not tell us why it had this name. Maybe people called it this because it was a customary place for executions, or perhaps it was because the place actually looked like a skull.

15:23 The drink would have helped dull the intense pain he was experiencing, but he refused it. He was determined not to lessen the suffering that he had voluntarily submitted to.

15:26 Ironically, the **charge** was true. Below it hung the divine King, atoning for the sins of the world.

15:31-32 They challenged him to **come down ...from the cross** if he was truly **the Messiah** (15:32). But remaining on the cross until death was exactly what the Messiah had to do.

15:33 The unnatural **darkness** signified God's judgment on sin.

15:34 Jesus's words were those of Psalm 22:1. Though the Trinitarian nature of God remained unbroken, yet the Son experienced a judicial separation from the Father as he suffered for the sins of the world.

15:38 This symbolized that he had achieved what he came to do—granting human beings access to God. Indeed, by atoning for sin,

Jesus made it possible for people to come into God's presence. We have no need for a mere human high priest to offer sacrifices repeatedly so that we can be right with God. Jesus Christ, the God-Man, is our great high priest who offered himself for sin once and for all (see Heb 4:14; 7:27; 10:10, 12).

15:40-41 Whereas the men had fled, these **women** stood faithfully by Jesus in his dying moments.

15:43 The Sanhedrin had condemned Jesus. **Joseph**, however, "had not agreed with their plan and action" (Luke 23:50-51). He identified with Jesus's kingdom message and wanted to honor him.

a 15:43 Jd 21
b Mk 1:15
c 1Tm 6:13
d Lk 12:4; Jn 2:21
e 15:46 Jn 5:28; 11:38; Ac 13:29
f Jn 20:1
g 15:47 Mt 27:61-66; Lk 23:55-56
h 16:1-4 Mt 28:1; Lk 24:1-2
i 16:1 Mk 15:40
j 16:2 Ac 20:7; 1Co 16:2
k Jn 5:28
l 16:5-8 Mt 28:5-8; Lk 24:3-8; Jn 20:1-2
m 16:5 Jn 5:28
n Lk 7:14
o Lk 12:27
p Rv 3:4
q 16:6 Mk 14:67
r 1Co 15:4
s 16:7 Lk 6:14
t Mt 17:22
u 16:8 Jn 5:28
v Mk 1:44; 4:40

w 16:9-11 Jn 20:11-18
x 16:9 Lk 24:1; Ac 20:7; 1Co 16:2
y Lk 18:33; Ac 2:24
z Mk 15:40
aa Mk 3:15; Lk 8:2
ab 16:11 Lk 24:5,11,23
ac 16:12 Jn 21:1; 2Co 4:11
ad Lk 24:13-35
ae 16:14 Lk 24:9
af Lk 24:38,41
ag 16:15-18 Mt 28:16-20
ah 16:15 Mt 13:38; 1Jn 2:2
ai Rm 8:22
aj 16:16 Mk 11:24; Jn 3:16; Ac 10:43; Rm 10:9; 1Pt 1:8-10
ak Ac 2:38; 22:16
al Mt 12:41; Jn 3:18,36; 5:11; 20:23
am 16:18 Lk 10:19; Ac 28:3-6
an Ac 28:5
ao Ac 9:12,17; 1Tm 5:22
ap 16:19 Lk 24:3
aq Lk 24:51; Ac 1:2,11,22; 1Tm 3:16
ar Lk 22:69; Heb 10:12

was himself looking forward[a] to the kingdom of God,[b] came and boldly went to Pilate[c] and asked for Jesus's body.[d] **44** Pilate was surprised that he was already dead. Summoning the centurion, he asked him whether he had already died. **45** When he found out from the centurion, he gave the corpse to Joseph. **46** After he bought some linen cloth, Joseph took him down and wrapped him in the linen. Then he laid him in a tomb[e] cut out of the rock and rolled a stone[f] against the entrance to the tomb. **47** Mary Magdalene[g] and Mary the mother of Joses were watching where he was laid.

RESURRECTION MORNING

16 When[h] the Sabbath was over, Mary Magdalene,[i] Mary the mother of James, and Salome bought spices, so that they could go and anoint him. **2** Very early in the morning, on the first day of the week,[j] they went to the tomb[k] at sunrise. **3** They were saying to one another, "Who will roll away the stone from the entrance to the tomb for us?" **4** Looking up, they noticed that the stone — which was very large — had been rolled away.

5 When[l] they entered the tomb,[m] they saw a young man[n] dressed[o] in a white[p] robe sitting on the right side; they were alarmed. **6** "Don't be alarmed," he told them. "You are looking for Jesus of Nazareth,[q] who was crucified. He has risen![r] He is not here. See the place where they put him. **7** But go, tell his disciples and Peter,[s] 'He is going ahead of you to Galilee;[t] you will see him there just as he told you.'" **8** They went out and ran from the tomb,[u] because trembling and astonishment overwhelmed them. And they said nothing to anyone,[v] since they were afraid.

[Some of the earliest mss conclude with 16:8.][A]

THE LONGER ENDING OF MARK: APPEARANCES OF THE RISEN LORD

[**9** Early[w] on the first day of the week,[x] after he had risen,[y] he appeared first to Mary Magdalene,[z] out of whom he had driven seven demons.[aa] **10** She went and reported to those who had been with him, as they were mourning and weeping. **11** Yet, when they heard that he was alive and had been seen by her, they did not believe it.[ab]

12 After this, he appeared[ac] in a different form to two of them walking on their way into the country.[ad] **13** And they went and reported it to the rest, who did not believe them either.

THE GREAT COMMISSION

14 Later he appeared to the Eleven[ae] themselves as they were reclining at the table. He rebuked their unbelief and hardness of heart, because they did not believe those who saw him after he had risen.[af] **15** Then[ag] he said to them, "Go into all the world[ah] and preach the gospel to all creation.[ai] **16** Whoever believes[aj] and is baptized will be saved,[ak] but whoever does not believe will be condemned.[al] **17** And these signs will accompany those who believe: In my name they will drive out demons; they will speak in new tongues;[B] **18** they will pick up snakes;[C,am] if they should drink anything deadly, it will not harm[an] them; they will lay hands on[ao] the sick, and they will get well."

THE ASCENSION

19 So the Lord Jesus, after speaking to them,[ap] was taken up into heaven[aq] and sat down at the right hand[ar] of God. **20** And they went out and preached everywhere, while the Lord worked with them and confirmed the word by the accompanying signs.]

A **16:8** Other mss include vv. 9-20 as a longer ending. The following shorter ending is found in some mss between v. 8 and v. 9 and in one ms after v. 8 (each of which omits vv. 9-20): *And all that had been commanded to them they quickly reported to those around Peter. After these things, Jesus himself sent out through them from east to west, the holy and imperishable proclamation of eternal salvation. Amen.* B **16:17** = languages
C **16:18** Other mss add *with their hands*

16:5 We know from Matthew's Gospel that the **man** was actually an angel (Matt 28:5). **16:7** **Peter**, the one who had denied Jesus, was perhaps singled out to reassure him of the Lord's forgiveness.

16:9-20 Some of the earliest existing ancient manuscripts of the Gospel of Mark do not contain this section. Therefore, many scholars believe that Mark originally concluded at 16:8 and that these verses were added later by someone other than the author. Most of what appears in these verses is reported in the other Gospels.

LUKE

INTRODUCTION

Author

ALL FOUR OF THE GOSPELS are anonymous, including the one attributed to Luke. However, we have good evidence for believing that Luke has been correctly identified as the author of the book bearing his name. First, the earliest manuscripts that exist include the name "Luke" in the title. Second, New Testament scholars agree that Luke and Acts are two works by the same author, and both are addressed to "Theophilus" (Luke 1:1-4; Acts 1:1-3). In Acts 16:10-17, during Paul's second missionary journey, the narrative changes from third person, "they," to first person, "we," (see also Acts 20:5-15; 21:1-18; 27:1-37; 28:1-16). Thus, the author of Acts—and of Luke—was one of Paul's traveling companions. Third, early Christian writers (e.g., Papias, Irenaeus, Justin Martyr, the Muratorian Canon, and Tertullian) unanimously affirm that Luke, the physician and companion of Paul (see Col 4:14; Phlm 24; 2 Tim 4:11), was the author. Granted, the writer could have been a different companion of Paul's. But since the early church didn't propose any other names, this is unlikely.

Identifying Luke as the author makes sense of features in the Gospel. For example, the author claims that he learned about the life and teaching of Jesus from "eyewitnesses" (Luke 1:2). Therefore, he was not himself an eyewitness to Jesus. In addition, Paul indicates that Luke was not "of the circumcised," that is, a Jew (Col 4:10-14). In other words, he was a Gentile. This would explain the emphasis on Gentiles in both Luke and Acts.

Historical Background

Many scholars believe Mark's Gospel was written first and that Matthew and Luke made use of it when they authored their Gospels. If this is the case, Luke would have been written after Mark, which probably dates to the AD 50s. But Luke would also have been written prior to Acts. Acts, which refers to the Gospel of Luke as "the first narrative" (Acts 1:1), was apparently written prior to Paul's release from prison in Rome (see Acts 28:16-31). After his release around AD 60, Paul continued his missionary work and was later imprisoned again and martyred about AD 66/67. So if Acts was completed around AD 60, then Luke would've been written in the late 50s.

Luke addressed his Gospel and Acts to "most honorable Theophilus" (Luke 1:3; see Acts 1:1). Since Luke addressed him in this way, he was apparently a person of high social status and perhaps wealthy too.

Many scholars believe Theophilus may have served as Luke's patron, funding the production of his work.

Message and Purpose

Luke wrote his Gospel to provide a well-documented account of the life of Jesus Christ. Luke shows Jesus—fully God and fully man—moving among the people in compassion to free them from the myriad of things oppressing them. The disregarded, the outcast, the forgotten, and the marginalized got to see and experience the love of Christ—even if Jesus had to confront the Jewish leaders to do it. Luke reveals to us that God is no respecter of persons; he opened his heart to the needy through the kingdom ministry of his Son. The Son of Man who heals the sick, raises the dead, and calls the prodigal back is also the transcendent God who calls all people to himself in salvation.

Luke also demonstrates through the genealogy and birth of Jesus that he has the right to claim the title of Son of David, the Messiah and King. Throughout the book, Jesus used the Word of God to open people's minds and hearts to who he is—just as he did on the road to Emmaus after his resurrection. The God of Luke is touchable and knowable!

VIDEO INTRO

www.bhpublishinggroup.com/qr/te/42_00

Outline

[a] 1:1 Rm 4:21; 14:5; Col 2:2; 4:12; 1Th 1:5; 2Tm 4:17; Heb 6:11; 10:22
[b] 1:2 Jn 15:27; Ac 1:21; 2Pt 1:16; 1Jn 1:1
[c] Ac 26:16; 1Co 4:1; Heb 2:3
[d] 1:3 Ac 23:26; 24:3; 26:25
[e] Ac 1:1
[f] 1:4 Ac 18:25; Rm 2:18; 1Co 14:19; Gl 6:6
[g] 1:5 Mt 2:1
[h] 1Ch 24:10
[i] 1:6 Gn 7:1; Ac 2:25; 8:21
[j] Php 2:15; 3:6; 1Th 3:13
[k] 1:7 Gn 4:1; 18:11; Jdg 13:2-3; 1Sm 1:2; 2:20; Ps 113:9; 127:3-5; Heb 11:11-12
[l] 1:8 1Ch 24:19; 2Ch 8:14; 31:2
[m] 1:9 Jos 18:6,8,10; 1Ch 24:31; 25:8; 26:13-14; Neh 10:34; 11:1; Ac 1:26
[n] Ex 30:7-8
[o] 1:11 Mt 2:13-14; 28:2; Lk 2:9; Ac 5:19; 8:26; 12:7
[p] Mk 16:5; Ac 2:33
[q] 1:12 Gn 21:17; Jdg 6:22-23; 2Kg 1:15; Mt 1:20; 28:5; Lk 2:10; Ac 10:3-4; 27:23-24
[r] 1:13 Gn 15:1; Mt 14:27; Lk 1:30
[s] Gn 25:21; 1Kg 8:45,49; 2Kg 20:5; Ps 6:9; Is 38:5
[t] Gn 16:11; 17:15,19; Is 8:3; Hs 1:4,9; Mt 1:20,23; Lk 1:60,63
[u] 1:13-15 Nm 6:3; Jdg 13:3-5; Mt 11:18; Lk 7:33
[v] 1:15 Ex 28:3; 31:3; 35:31; Dt 34:9; Mc 3:8; Lk 1:41,67; Ac 2:4; 4:8,31; 7:55; 9:17; 13:9; 13:52; Eph 5:18
[w] Is 44:2; Lk 1:41,44
[x] 1:16 Ps 22:27; Lm 3:40
[y] 1:16-17 Mal 4:5-6; Mt 11:14; 17:10-12
[z] 1:17 Is 40:3; Lk 1:76; 3:4
[aa] 1:19 Dn 8:16; 9:21; Lk 1:26
[ab] Mt 18:10
[ac] 1:22 Lk 1:62
[ad] 1:25 Gn 30:23; Is 4:1; 25:8
[ae] 1:26 Lk 1:19
[af] Mt 2:23
[ag] 1:27 Dt 21:23; Is 7:14; Mt 1:18,23

THE DEDICATION TO THEOPHILUS

1 Many have undertaken to compile a narrative about the events that have been fulfilled[A] among us,[a] [2] just as the original eyewitnesses[b] and servants of the word[c] handed them down to us. [3] It also seemed good to me, since I have carefully investigated everything from the very first, to write to you in an orderly sequence, most honorable[d] Theophilus,[e] [4] so that you may know the certainty of the things about which you have been instructed.[B,f]

GABRIEL PREDICTS JOHN'S BIRTH

[5] In the days of King Herod[g] of Judea, there was a priest of Abijah's division[h] named Zechariah. His wife was from the daughters of Aaron, and her name was Elizabeth. [6] Both were righteous in God's sight,[i] living without blame[j] according to all the commands and requirements of the Lord. [7] But they had no children because Elizabeth could not conceive, and both of them were well along in years.[k]

[8] When his division was on duty[l] and he was serving as priest before God, [9] it happened that he was chosen by lot,[m] according to the custom of the priesthood, to enter the sanctuary of the Lord and burn incense.[n] [10] At the hour of incense the whole assembly of the people was praying outside. [11] An angel of the Lord[o] appeared to him, standing to the right of the altar of incense.[p] [12] When Zechariah saw him, he was terrified and overcome with fear.[q] [13] But the angel said to him: "Do not be afraid,[r] Zechariah, because your prayer has been heard.[s] Your wife Elizabeth will bear you a son, and you will name him John.[t] [14] There will be joy and delight for you, and many will rejoice at his birth. [15] For he will be great in the sight of the Lord and will never drink wine or beer.[u] He will be filled with the Holy Spirit[v] while still in his mother's womb. [w] [16] He will turn many of the children of Israel to the Lord their God.[x] [17] And he will go before him in the spirit and power of Elijah, to turn the hearts of fathers to their children,[y] and the disobedient to the understanding of the righteous, to make ready for the Lord a prepared people."[z]

[18] "How can I know this?" Zechariah asked the angel. "For I am an old man, and my wife is well along in years."

[19] The angel answered him, "I am Gabriel,[aa] who stands in the presence of God,[ab] and I was sent to speak to you and tell you this good news. [20] Now listen. You will become silent and unable to speak until the day these things take place, because you did not believe my words, which will be fulfilled in their proper time."

[21] Meanwhile, the people were waiting for Zechariah, amazed that he stayed so long in the sanctuary. [22] When he did come out, he could not speak to them. Then they realized that he had seen a vision in the sanctuary. He was making signs to them[ac] and remained speechless. [23] When the days of his ministry were completed, he went back home.

[24] After these days his wife Elizabeth conceived and kept herself in seclusion for five months. She said, [25] "The Lord has done this for me. He has looked with favor in these days to take away my disgrace[ad] among the people."

GABRIEL PREDICTS JESUS'S BIRTH

[26] In the sixth month, the angel Gabriel[ae] was sent by God to a town in Galilee called Nazareth,[af] [27] to a virgin engaged[C,ag] to a man named Joseph, of the house of

---

[A] 1:1 Or *events that have been accomplished*, or *events most surely believed*   [B] 1:4 Or *informed*   [C] 1:27 Lit *betrothed*

1:3 Theophilus was apparently a man of high social standing who perhaps served as Luke's patron, funding the production of his Gospel and the book of Acts (see Acts 1:1). He may have been a new convert to Christianity.

1:5 Luke frequently emphasizes the historicity of his account by mentioning the rulers who were in power at the time (see 2:1-2; 3:1-2). Also known as Herod the Great, **King Herod** ruled over **Judea**, Samaria, Galilee, and portions of Perea and Syria from 37 to 4 BC. He was not a Jew but an Idumean whom the Roman emperor had put in power.

According to 1 Chronicles 24:7-18, the temple priests were divided into twenty-four divisions. Each **division** would serve for two weeks a year at the temple in Jerusalem.

1:6-7 Zechariah and Elizabeth were faithful followers of God, but Elizabeth had never been able to **conceive** (1:7). We must never assume that trials and difficulties only come our way because of our disobedience. God often brings or allows suffering in the lives of his people for his glorious purposes and for our sanctification.

1:8-9 Remember: "The lot is cast into the lap, but its every decision is from the Lord" (Prov 16:33). God is sovereign, working through even seemingly random processes (like the casting of the **lot**) to accomplish his will. There is no such thing as luck.

1:13-15 Given the couple's advanced age, John's birth would be miraculous. But God's purposes involved more than simply blessing an elderly couple with a child. This boy would

grow up to be John the Baptist, playing a special role in God's kingdom plans.

1:16-17 The angel's words show that John would be the fulfillment of Malachi 4:5-6, in which the Lord promised to send **Elijah**. John, then, would preach **in the spirit and power** of his Old Testament predecessor (Luke 1:17). Jesus later confirmed this when he told his disciples that John was "the Elijah . . . to come" (Matt 11:14; see also Matt 17:12).

1:19 Zechariah and other faithful Jews would've been familiar with Gabriel's name. He appears in the book of Daniel, where he explains the prophet's visions to him (see Dan 8:16; 9:21).

1:25 To be childless in that time and culture was considered a **disgrace**.

1:26-27 When Elizabeth was six months pregnant, **Gabriel** paid **Mary** a visit.

David.[a] The virgin's name was Mary. **28** And the angel came to her and said, "Greetings, favored woman! The Lord is with you."[A] **29** But she was deeply troubled[b] by this statement, wondering what kind of greeting this could be. **30** Then the angel told her: "Do not be afraid, Mary,[c] for you have found favor with God.[d] **31** Now listen: You will conceive and give birth to a son, and you will name him Jesus.[e] **32** He will be great and will be called the Son of the Most High,[f] and the Lord God will give him the throne of his father David.[g] **33** He will reign over the house of Jacob[h] forever, and his kingdom will have no end."[i]

34 Mary asked the angel, "How can this be, since I have not had sexual relations with a man?"[B]

35 The angel replied to her: "The Holy Spirit will come upon you,[j] and the power of the Most High will overshadow you. Therefore, the holy one to be born will be called the Son of God.[k] **36** And consider your relative Elizabeth — even she has conceived a son in her old age, and this is the sixth month for her who was called childless. **37** For nothing will be impossible with God."[l]

38 "I am the Lord's servant," said Mary. "May it be done to me according to your word." Then the angel left her.

MARY'S VISIT TO ELIZABETH

39 In those days Mary set out and hurried to a town in the hill country of Judah **40** where she entered Zechariah's house and greeted Elizabeth. **41** When Elizabeth heard Mary's greeting, the baby leaped inside her, and Elizabeth was filled with the Holy Spirit.[m] **42** Then she exclaimed with a loud cry: "Blessed are you among women, and your child will be blessed![c] **43** How could this happen to me, that the mother of my Lord should come to me? **44** For you see, when the sound of your greeting reached my ears, the baby leaped for joy inside me. **45** Blessed is she who has believed that the Lord would fulfill what he has spoken to her!"

MARY'S PRAISE

46 And Mary said:

My soul praises the greatness
of[D] the Lord,[n]
47 and my spirit rejoices[o] in God
my Savior,[p]
48 because he has looked with favor
on the humble condition
of his servant.
Surely, from now on
all generations
will call me blessed,[q]
49 because the Mighty One[r]
has done great things for me,[s]
and his name[t] is holy.
50 His mercy is from generation
to generation[u]
on those who fear him.
51 He has done a mighty deed
with his arm;[v]
he has scattered the proud
because of the thoughts
of their hearts;[w]
52 he has toppled the mighty
from their thrones
and exalted the lowly.[x]
53 He has satisfied the hungry
with good things[y]
and sent the rich away empty.
54 He has helped his servant Israel,
remembering his mercy
55 to Abraham and his
descendants[E] forever,[z]
just as he spoke to our ancestors.

56 And Mary stayed with her about three months; then she returned to her home.

THE BIRTH AND NAMING OF JOHN

57 Now the time had come for Elizabeth to give birth, and she had a son. **58** Then her neighbors and relatives heard that the

[a] 1:27 Mt 1:20; Lk 2:4
[b] 1:29 Lk 1:12
[c] 1:30 Mt 14:27; Lk 1:13
[d] Gn 6:8; Ex 33:12-17; Jr 31:2
[e] 1:31 Is 7:14; Mt 1:21,25; Lk 2:21
[f] 1:32 Lk 1:35,76; 3:38; 6:35; 8:28; 9:35; Jn 1:34,49; 11:27; Ac 7:48
[g] 2Sm 7:12-13; 1Kg 2:12; Ps 132:11; Is 9:7; Jr 33:17; Mk 11:10
[h] 1:33 Ex 19:3; Ps 114:1; Is 14:1; 29:22; 46:3
[i] Is 9:6 LXX; Dn 7:14
[j] 1:35 Mt 1:18
[k] Mt 14:33; Lk 4:3,9,41; 22:70
[l] 1:37 Gn 18:14; Lk 18:27
[m] 1:41 Lk 1:67; Ac 2:4; 4:8; 9:17; 13:9
[n] 1:46-53 1Sm 2:1-10
[o] 1:47 Ps 35:9; Hab 3:18
[p] 1Tm 1:1; 2:3; Ti 1:3; 2:10; 3:4; Jd 25
[q] 1:48 Lk 11:27
[r] 1:49 Ps 89:8; Zph 3:17
[s] Ps 71:19; 126:2-3
[t] Lv 20:3; 22:2,32; 1Ch 16:10,35; 29:16; Ps 30:4; 99:3; 103:1; 111:9; Is 57:15
[u] 1:50 Ps 100:5; 103:11,17
[v] 1:51 Ps 89:10; 98:1; 118:15
[w] Lk 2:35; 9:47
[x] 1:52 1Sm 2:7-8
[y] 1:53 Ps 34:10; 107:9; Lk 6:21,24-25
[z] 1:55 Gn 17:9,15; 21:12

[A] 1:28 Other mss add *Blessed are you among women.* [B] 1:34 Lit *since I do not know a man* [C] 1:42 Lit *and the fruit of your abdomen* (or *womb*) *is blessed* [D] 1:46 Or *soul magnifies* [E] 1:55 Or *offspring*; lit *seed*

1:31 Jesus is the Greek version of the Hebrew name Joshua, which means "the Lord saves." **1:32-33** Jesus would be **called the Son of the Most High**—he'd be a carbon copy of his Father, bearing the divine nature. He would also be the fulfillment of the Old Testament promises of the coming Son of **David**—the Messiah, who will rule forever (see 2 Sam 7:12-16). **1:35** Jesus would be both divine and human. Theologians describe this as the *hypostatic union*, the combining of a divine nature and

a human nature perfectly into one person. Indeed, he is God in the flesh. **1:38** Mary didn't understand all of the implications for her life that lay ahead, but she humbly submitted to the will of God. She's an example for us all. **1:41** That the **baby leaped inside** his mother at the sound of Mary's voice supports the fact that the unborn possess personhood. **1:43** Referring to her guest as **the mother of [her] Lord** confirmed what Mary had heard from the angel.

1:46-55 Mary's song is referred to as the *Magnificat*, which is the Latin translation of the Greek word rendered in English Bibles as **praises** or "magnifies" (1:46). Through his Messiah, God would extend **mercy** toward **those who fear him** (1:50). Those who recognize their need can expect good things from the Messiah. But he would also bring judgment, scattering **the proud** and toppling **the mighty** (1:51-52). God remembered his covenant and promises to his people, and he would fulfill them (1:54-55).

a 1:58 Gn 19:19
b 1:59 Gn 17:12; Lv 12:3; Lk 2:21; Php 3:5
c 1:60 Lk 1:13,63
d 1:62 Lk 1:22
e 1:64 Lk 1:20
f 1:66 Ac 11:21
g 1:67 Lk 1:41
h 1:68 Jl 2:28
i 1:68 Ps 41:13
j Lk 1:71; 2:38; Heb 9:12
k 1:69 1Sm 2:1,10; Ps 18:2; 89:17; 132:17; Ezk 29:21
l 2Sm 7:26; Ps 89:3,20; Ezk 34:23-24; 37:24-25
m 1:70 2Kg 21:10; Hs 12:10; Ac 3:21; Rm 1:2; Heb 1:1
n 1:72 Mc 7:20
o Ps 105:8-9,42; 106:45
p 1:73 Gn 22:16-17; Heb 6:13

q 1:76 Mt 11:9
r Lk 1:17; Is 40:3; Mal 3:1
s 1:77 Jr 31:34; Mk 1:4
t 1:78 Is 58:8; Jr 23:5; Zch 3:8; 6:12 LXX; Mal 4:2; Lk 24:49; Eph 4:8; 2Pt 1:19
u 1:79 Is 9:2; 60:2-3
v 1:80 Lk 2:40
w 2:1 Mt 22:17; Lk 3:1
x 2:2 Mt 4:24
y 2:4 Mt 2:23; 4:13; 21:11; Jn 1:45
z Gn 35:19; 48:7; Jos 19:15; Jdg 12:10; 17:7-9; Ru 1:1; 1Sm 16:1; Mc 5:2
aa Lk 1:27

Lord had shown her his great mercy,[a] and they rejoiced with her.

59 When they came to circumcise the child on the eighth day,[b] they were going to name him Zechariah, after his father. **60** But his mother responded, "No. He will be called John."[c]

61 Then they said to her, "None of your relatives has that name." **62** So they motioned to his father[d] to find out what he wanted him to be called. **63** He asked for a writing tablet and wrote: "His name is John." And they were all amazed. **64** Immediately his mouth was opened[e] and his tongue set free, and he began to speak, praising God. **65** Fear came on all those who lived around them, and all these things were being talked about throughout the hill country of Judea. **66** All who heard about him[f] took it to heart, saying, "What then will this child become?" For, indeed, the Lord's hand was with him.

ZECHARIAH'S PROPHECY

67 Then his father Zechariah was filled with the Holy Spirit[g] and prophesied:[h]

68 Blessed is the Lord, the God of Israel,[i]
because he has visited
and provided redemption
for his people.[j]
69 He has raised up a horn of salvation
for us[k]
in the house of his servant David,[l]
70 just as he spoke by the mouth
of his holy prophets in ancient times;[m]
71 salvation from our enemies
and from the hand of those
who hate us.
72 He has dealt mercifully
with our fathers[n]
and remembered
his holy covenant[o] —
73 the oath that he swore to our father
Abraham.[p]
He has given us the privilege,
74 since we have been rescued
from the hand of our enemies,
to serve him without fear

75 in holiness and righteousness
in his presence all our days.
76 And you, child, will be called
a prophet of the Most High,[q]
for you will go before the Lord
to prepare his ways,[r]
77 to give his people knowledge
of salvation
through the forgiveness
of their sins.[s]
78 Because of our God's merciful
compassion,
the dawn from on high[t]
will visit us
79 to shine on those who live
in darkness
and the shadow of death,[u]
to guide our feet into the way
of peace.

80 The child grew up and became spiritually strong,[v] and he was in the wilderness until the day of his public appearance to Israel.

THE BIRTH OF JESUS

2 In those days a decree went out from Caesar Augustus[w] that the whole empire[A] should be registered. **2** This first registration took place while[B] Quirinius was governing Syria.[x] **3** So everyone went to be registered, each to his own town.

4 Joseph also went up from the town of Nazareth[y] in Galilee, to Judea, to the city of David, which is called Bethlehem,[z] because he was of the house and family line of David,[aa] **5** to be registered along with Mary, who was engaged to him[c] and was pregnant. **6** While they were there, the time came for her to give birth. **7** Then she gave birth to her firstborn son, and she wrapped him tightly in cloth and laid him in a manger,[D] because there was no guest room available for them.

THE SHEPHERDS AND THE ANGELS

8 In the same region, shepherds were staying out in the fields and keeping watch at

---

[A] 2:1 Or *the whole inhabited world*   [B] 2:2 Or *This registration was the first while*, or *This registration was before*   [C] 2:5 Lit *betrothed*   [D] 2:7 Or *feeding trough*, also in vv. 12,16

1:67-79 Zechariah's prophecy of praise is called the *Benedictus*, which is the first word of the Latin rendering of **blessed is the Lord, the God of Israel** (1:68): *Benedictus Dominus Deus Israel.* He worshiped God for the **salvation** he was providing for his people through the Messiah, just as he had promised (1:68-75). As for Zechariah's son John, he would be **a prophet** who would **go before the Lord to prepare his ways** as the Old Testament prophets foretold

(1:76; see Isa 40:3; Mal 3:1). He would introduce Israel to the Messiah (see John 1:29-36).
2:1 Caesar Augustus ruled from 31 BC to AD 14.
2:4 Bethlehem was David's hometown (see 1 Sam 16:1). The distance between it and Nazareth was about ninety miles.
2:7 A manger was a feeding trough for animals. The King of creation, who deserved all honor and glory, was born into the humblest of circumstances.

2:8-11 God chose to announce his Son's birth—not to the political or religious leaders of the day—but to a group of humble **shepherds** (2:8). Why? He would be a Messiah **for all the people** (2:10) and offered as a sacrificial Lamb like those cared for by the shepherds. **The city of David** is another name for Bethlehem, King David's hometown (2:11).

night over their flock. **9** Then an angel of the Lord*a* stood before them,*b* and the glory of the Lord*c* shone around them, and they were terrified.^A **10** But the angel said to them, "Don't be afraid,*d* for look, I proclaim to you good news of great joy that will be for all the people:^B **11** Today in the city of David a Savior*e* was born for you, who is the Messiah,*f* the Lord.*g* **12** This will be the sign for you:*h* You will find a baby wrapped tightly in cloth and lying in a manger."

13 Suddenly there was a multitude of the heavenly host*c* with the angel, praising God and saying:

14　Glory to God in the highest heaven,*i*
　　and peace on earth*j* to people
　　　　he favors!^D,E,k

15 When the angels had left them and returned to heaven, the shepherds said to one another, "Let's go straight to Bethlehem and see what has happened, which the Lord has made known to us."

16 They hurried off and found both Mary and Joseph, and the baby who was lying in the manger. **17** After seeing them, they reported the message they were told about this child, **18** and all who heard it were amazed*l* at what the shepherds said to them. **19** But Mary was treasuring up all these things in her heart*m* and meditating on them. **20** The shepherds returned, glorifying and praising God*n* for all the things they had seen and heard, which were just as they had been told.

THE CIRCUMCISION AND PRESENTATION OF JESUS

21 When the eight days were completed for his circumcision,*o* he was named Jesus*p* — the name given by the angel before he was conceived. **22** And when the days of their purification according to the law of Moses were finished,*q* they brought him up to Jerusalem to present him to the Lord **23** (just as it is written in the law of the Lord, **Every firstborn male will be dedicated**^F **to the Lord**^G,*r*) **24** and to offer a sacrifice (according to what is stated in the law of the Lord, **a pair of turtledoves or two young pigeons**^H,*s*).

SIMEON'S PROPHETIC PRAISE

25 There was a man in Jerusalem whose name was Simeon. This man was righteous and devout,*t* looking forward to Israel's consolation,*u* and the Holy Spirit was on him. **26** It had been revealed to him by the Holy Spirit*v* that he would not see death before he saw the Lord's Messiah.*w* **27** Guided by the Spirit, he entered the temple. When the parents brought in the child Jesus to perform for him what was customary under the law, **28** Simeon took him up in his arms, praised God, and said,

29　Now, Master,
　　you can dismiss your servant
　　　in peace,
　　as you promised.
30　For my eyes have seen
　　　your salvation.*x*
31　You have prepared it
　　in the presence of all peoples —
32　a light for revelation
　　　to the Gentiles^I,*y*
　　and glory to your people Israel.*z*

33 His father and mother*j* were amazed at what was being said about him. **34** Then Simeon blessed them and told his mother Mary: "Indeed, this child is destined to cause the fall and rise of many in Israel*aa* and to be a sign that will be opposed*k* — **35** and a sword will pierce your own soul — that the thoughts*L* of many hearts may be revealed."

a 2:9 Mt 1:20; 2:13,19; 28:2; Lk 1:11; Ac 5:19; 8:26; 12:7; 12:23
b Lk 24:4; Ac 12:7
c Ex 24:16; 40:34-35; Lv 9:6,23; Nm 20:6; 1Kg 8:11; Is 35:2; 40:5; 60:1
d 2:10 Mt 14:27
e 2:11 Mt 1:21; Jn 4:42; Ac 5:31
f Mt 1:16; 16:16,20; Jn 11:27
g Lk 1:43; Ac 2:36; 10:36
h 2:12 1Sm 2:34; 2Kg 19:29; 20:8-9; Is 7:11,14
i 2:14 Mt 21:9; Lk 19:38
j Lk 12:51
k Lk 3:22; Eph 1:9; Php 2:13
l 2:18 Lk 1:63; 2:33; 4:22; 8:25; 9:43; 11:14,38; 20:26; 24:12,41
m 2:19 Lk 2:51
n 2:20 Mt 9:8
o 2:21 Lk 1:59
p Lk 1:31

q 2:22 Lv 12:6-8
r 2:23 Ex 11:5; 12:12,29; 13:2,12; 34:19; Dt 15:19
s 2:24 Lv 5:11; 12:8
t 2:25 Lk 1:6
u Ps 135:14; Is 40:1-2,11; 49:10,13; 51:3,12; 57:18; 61:2; 66:13; Jr 31:9; Mk 15:43; Lk 2:38; 23:51
v 2:26 Mt 2:12
w Ps 89:48; Jn 8:51; Heb 11:5
x 2:30 Ps 119:166,174; Is 52:10; Lk 3:6
y 2:32 Is 42:6; 49:6,9; Ac 13:47; 26:23
z Is 46:13 LXX
aa 2:34 Mt 21:44; 1Co 1:23; 2Co 2:16; 1Pt 2:8

^A 2:9 Lit *they feared a great fear*   ^B 2:10 Or *the whole nation*   ^C 2:13 Lit *heavenly army*   ^D 2:14 Other mss read *earth good will to people*   ^E 2:14 Or *earth to men of good will*   ^F 2:23 Lit *be called holy*   ^G 2:23 Ex 13:2,12   ^H 2:24 Lv 5:11; 12:8   ^I 2:32 Or *the nations*   ^J 2:33 Other mss read *But Joseph and his mother*   ^K 2:34 Or *spoken against*   ^L 2:35 Or *schemes*

2:12 The shepherds were responsible for making sure that newborn lambs had no defects since the sacrificial animals had to be without spot or wrinkle. So the shepherds would tightly wrap the lambs in cloth to keep them from becoming blemished and injuring themselves. This explains why Luke makes the point that Jesus was **wrapped tightly in cloth**, since at his birth he was the sinless Lamb of God whose substitutionary sacrifice would take away the sin of the entire world (see John 1:29; 2 Cor 5:21; 1 Pet 1:19-20; 1 John 2:2).
2:14 Peace on earth to people he favors is a reference to all those who would submit themselves to the Messiah. Importantly,

though, this angelic announcement of "peace on earth" that's repeated so often at Christmastime is not about quiet tranquility or merely the absence of animosity between people. It is a declaration of the coming end of hostilities between a holy God and sinful humanity through the atoning work of the Messiah. Only when "we have been declared righteous by faith," can "we have peace with God through our Lord Jesus Christ" (Rom 5:1). Peace among people is possible when humanity is living at peace with God and submitting to his kingdom rule.
2:21-24 Joseph and Mary fulfilled the law by circumcising their son "on the eighth day" (Lev

12:3). They further kept God's commands by presenting Jesus to the Lord in fulfillment of Exodus 13:2,12, and by offering a sacrifice in fulfillment of Leviticus 12:6-8. The kind of animals they offered indicates the couple was poor.
2:34 Indeed, some would **fall** by rejecting Jesus, and others would put their faith in him and **rise** to abundant and eternal life.
2:35 Simeon told Mary: **a sword will pierce your own soul**. Mary would misunderstand her son (2:41-50), think he was "out of his mind" (Mark 3:21), and experience the grief of his crucifixion (John 19:25-27). But later, after his resurrection, she would know joy (Acts 1:14).

a 2:36 Lk 2:38; Ac 21:9
b Jos 19:24
c 1Tm 5:9
d 2:37 Lk 5:33; Ac 13:3;
14:23; 1Tm 5:5
e 2:38 Is 52:9; Lk 1:68; 2:25
f 2:39 Mt 2:23; Lk 1:26;
2:51; 4:16
g 2:40 Lk 1:80; 2:52
h 2:41 Ex 12:11; 23:15; Dt
16:1-6
i 2:42 Dt 16:16-17
j 2:43 Ex 12:15

k 2:48 Mt 12:46
l Lk 2:49; 3:23; 4:22
m 2:50 Mk 9:32; Lk 9:45;
18:34
n 2:51 Lk 2:19
o 2:52 Lk 2:40
p 3:1 Mt 27:2; Lk 13:1; 23:1-
24,52; Ac 3:13; 4:27; 13:28;
1Tm 6:13
q Mt 14:1
r 3:2 Jn 18:13,24; Ac 4:6
s Mt 26:3
t 3:2-10 Mt 3:1-10; Mk
1:3-5
u 3:3 Mt 3:5
v Mk 1:4; Ac 2:38

ANNA'S TESTIMONY

36 There was also a prophetess,[a] Anna, a daughter of Phanuel, of the tribe of Asher.[b] She was well along in years, having lived with her husband seven years after her marriage,[A,c] **37** and was a widow for eighty-four years.[B] She did not leave the temple, serving God night and day with fasting and prayers.[d] **38** At that very moment,[c] she came up and began to thank God and to speak about him to all who were looking forward to the redemption of Jerusalem.[D,e]

THE FAMILY'S RETURN TO NAZARETH

39 When they had completed everything according to the law of the Lord, they returned to Galilee, to their own town of Nazareth.[f] **40** The boy grew up and became strong, filled with wisdom, and God's grace was on him.[g]

IN HIS FATHER'S HOUSE

41 Every year his parents traveled to Jerusalem for the Passover Festival.[h] **42** When he was twelve years old, they went up according to the custom of the festival.[i] **43** After those days were over,[j] as they were returning, the boy Jesus stayed behind in Jerusalem, but his parents[E] did not know it. **44** Assuming he was in the traveling party, they went a day's journey. Then they began looking for him among their relatives and friends. **45** When they did not find him, they returned to Jerusalem to search for him. **46** After three days, they found him in the temple sitting among the teachers, listening to them and asking them questions. **47** And all those who heard him were astounded at his understanding and his answers. **48** When his parents saw him, they were astonished, and his mother said to him,[k] "Son, why have you treated us like this? Your father and I have been anxiously searching for you."[l] **49** "Why were you searching for me?" he asked them. "Didn't you know that it was necessary for me to be in my Father's house?"[F] **50** But they did not understand what he said to them.[m]

IN FAVOR WITH GOD AND WITH PEOPLE

51 Then he went down with them and came to Nazareth and was obedient to them. His mother kept all these things in her heart.[n] **52** And Jesus increased in wisdom and stature, and in favor with God and with people.[o]

THE MESSIAH'S HERALD

3 In the fifteenth year of the reign of Tiberius Caesar, while Pontius Pilate was governor of Judea,[p] Herod was tetrarch[G] of Galilee,[q] his brother Philip tetrarch of the region of Iturea and Trachonitis, and Lysanias tetrarch of Abilene, **2** during the high priesthood of Annas[r] and Caiaphas,[s] God's word came to John the son of Zechariah in the wilderness.[t] **3** He went into all the vicinity of the Jordan,[u] proclaiming a baptism of repentance for the forgiveness of sins,[v] **4** as it is written in the book of the words of the prophet Isaiah:

A voice of one crying out
　in the wilderness:
Prepare the way for the Lord;
　make his paths straight!

A 2:36 Lit *years from her virginity*　B 2:37 Or *she was a widow until the age of eighty-four*　C 2:38 Lit *very hour*　D 2:38 Other mss read *in Jerusalem*　E 2:43 Other mss read *but Joseph and his mother*　F 2:49 Or *be involved in my Father's interests* (or *things*), or *be among my Father's people*　G 3:1 Or *ruler*

2:38 Anna thanked God and announced to everyone who was **looking forward to the redemption of Jerusalem** that the Messiah had come. Encountering Jesus is not something we should keep to ourselves.

2:40 In every way—physically, spiritually, and intellectually—Jesus matured in his humanity as God intended.

2:41 Jesus grew up in a godly Jewish home, demonstrated by the family's regular observance of things like **the Passover Festival** in **Jerusalem**. (See the note on 2:21-24.)

2:43-44 Since the family would've been in a caravan with many **relatives and friends** (2:44), it would have been easy to assume Jesus was among the larger group.

2:49-51 They **did not understand** that he had a unique kingdom mission from his heavenly Father (2:50). Nevertheless, he also had a responsibility to honor his earthly father and mother (see Exod 20:12). That's

why he went **with them** and **was obedient to them** (Luke 2:51).

2:52 Jesus wasn't simply God disguised as a man. He had both a perfect divine nature and a genuine human nature that matured as he grew.

3:1-2 By this point in the narrative, **Tiberius** had replaced Augustus as Roman emperor. When Herod the Great died in 4 BC, his territory was divided among his three sons: **Herod** Antipas, who ruled over **Galilee**; **Philip**, who ruled over areas in the northeastern part of Herod's kingdom beyond the Jordan; and Archelaus, who ruled over Judea. The latter was banished by Rome in AD 6 and replaced by a Roman governor. Thus, **Pontius Pilate** had been appointed the Roman **governor of Judea**.

Caiaphas was the actual Jewish high priest at the time. **Annas** was Caiaphas's father-in-law and the former high priest,

but he still retained the title. In their day, the Jewish people were oppressed by Gentile rulers and longed for deliverance, and **John** was going to prepare the way for their Deliverer. But Jesus wouldn't be the kind of Deliverer they were looking for. They wanted deliverance from Rome; Jesus would deliver them from sin and judgment, which is the prerequisite for social and political freedom.

3:3 John was calling Israel back to God, which begins with **repentance**: sorrow over sin and an inner resolve to turn from it. Water **baptism** would be a visible declaration of their repentance. A right attitude and disposition toward their sin was necessary to prepare them for the Messiah's arrival.

3:4-6 **The wilderness** in which John cried out reflected Israel's barren spiritual condition (3:4). True repentance would knock down **every mountain** of pride that kept the people

5 Every valley will be filled,
and every mountain and hill
will be made low;[A]
the crooked will become straight,
the rough ways smooth,
6 and everyone will see
the salvation of God.[B,a]

7 He then said to the crowds who came out to be baptized by him, "Brood of vipers![b] Who warned you to flee from the coming wrath?[c] 8 Therefore produce fruit[d] consistent with repentance. And don't start saying to yourselves, 'We have Abraham as our father,'[e] for I tell you that God is able to raise up children for Abraham from these stones. 9 The ax is already at the root of the trees. Therefore, every tree that doesn't produce good fruit will be cut down and thrown into the fire."[f]

10 "What then should we do?"[g] the crowds were asking him.

11 He replied to them, "The one who has two shirts must share with someone who has none, and the one who has food must do the same."[h]

12 Tax collectors[i] also came to be baptized, and they asked him, "Teacher, what should we do?"[j]

13 He told them, "Don't collect any more than what you have been authorized."

14 Some soldiers also questioned him, "What should we do?"

He said to them, "Don't take money from anyone by force or false accusation, and be satisfied with your wages."

15 Now the people were waiting expectantly, and all of them were questioning in their hearts whether John might be the Messiah.[k] 16 John answered them all,[l] "I baptize you with water, but one who is more powerful than I am is coming. I am not worthy to untie the strap of his sandals. He will baptize you with[c] the Holy Spirit and fire. 17 His winnowing shovel[m] is in his hand to clear his threshing floor and gather the wheat into his barn,[n] but the chaff he will burn with fire that never goes out."[o] 18 Then, along with many other exhortations, he proclaimed good news to the people. 19 But when John rebuked Herod the tetrarch[p] because of Herodias, his brother's wife, and all the evil things he had done,[q] 20 Herod added this to everything else — he locked up John in prison.[r]

THE BAPTISM OF JESUS

21 When all the people were baptized,[s] Jesus also was baptized. As he was praying,[t] heaven opened,[u] 22 and the Holy Spirit descended on him in a physical appearance like a dove. And a voice came from heaven: "You are my beloved Son; with you I am well-pleased."[v]

THE GENEALOGY OF JESUS CHRIST

23 As he began his ministry, Jesus was about thirty years old and was thought to be the
son of Joseph,[w] son of Heli,
24 son of Matthat, son of Levi,
son of Melchi, son of Jannai,
son of Joseph, 25 son of Mattathias,
son of Amos, son of Nahum,
son of Esli, son of Naggai,
26 son of Maath, son of Mattathias,
son of Semein, son of Josech,
son of Joda, 27 son of Joanan,
son of Rhesa, son of Zerubbabel,[x]
son of Shealtiel, son of Neri,
28 son of Melchi, son of Addi,
son of Cosam, son of Elmadam,
son of Er, 29 son of Joshua,
son of Eliezer, son of Jorim,
son of Matthat, son of Levi,

a 3:4-6 Is 40:3-5
b 3:7 Mt 12:34; 23:33
c Lk 3:7; Eph 5:6; Col 3:6; 1Th 1:10; Rv 6:17; 11:18
d 3:8 Lk 3:8; Jn 15:2,4,16
e Jn 8:33
f 3:9 Mt 3:10; 7:19; Lk 13:6-9
g 3:10 Ac 2:37-38
h 3:11 Is 58:7
i 3:12 Lk 5:29-30; 7:29,34; 15:1
j Mt 9:10-11; 21:31-32; Lk 5:29-30; 7:29; 15:1
k 3:15 Jn 1:19-20
l 3:16-17 Mt 3:11-12; Mk 1:7-8
m 3:17 Is 30:24
n Mt 13:29-30
o Mk 9:43,48
p 3:19 Mt 14:3; Mk 6:17
q Mt 14:1; Lk 3:1
s 3:21-22 Mt 3:13-17; Mk 1:9-11
t 3:21 Mt 14:23; Lk 5:16; 9:18,28-29
u Jn 1:51; Ac 7:55; 10:11; Rv 19:11
v 3:22 Ps 2:7; Is 42:1; Mt 3:17; 17:5; Mk 1:11; Lk 9:35; 2Pt 1:17
w 3:23 Mt 1:16
x 3:27 Hg 1:1,12,14; 2:4,21,23; Mt 1:12

A 3:5 Lit be humbled   B 3:4-6 Is 40:3-5   C 3:16 Or in

---

from God. John's proclamation and baptism would make a **straight** path for the Messiah to bring **salvation** and all of his kingdom promises to them (3:5-6).

3:8-9 John warned his hearers not to assume they were safe merely because they were descendants of **Abraham** (3:8). God had brought judgment on the people of Israel before because of their sins. That they were currently under foreign rule, in fact, was an indication that the nation had forsaken God in the past. The warning that **the ax is already at the root of the trees** (3:9) meant judgment was right around the corner—it's a reference to the destruction of Jerusalem by the Romans in AD 70.

3:10-11 Repentance is validated by how we relate to others. In the words of Paul, "the whole law is fulfilled in one statement: Love your neighbor as yourself" (Gal 5:14).

3:16 John's water baptism was inferior to the baptism of **the Holy Spirit and fire** that the Messiah would bring, a reference to the fact that Jesus would send the Holy Spirit at Pentecost (see Acts 2:1-4). Fire is used in the Bible as a metaphor of both purification and judgment.

3:18-19 John exhorted the people to repentance and proclaimed to them the **good news** of the coming kingdom of God (3:18). But John was no coward. He also spoke truth to power. Not only did he rebuke the masses, but he **rebuked** the rulers (3:19).

3:21 Jesus had not come for baptism to repent for his own sin but to identify with and represent the people he had come to save.

3:22 Scripture clearly teaches the Trinitarian nature of God. He is one (Deut 6:4), yet he exists in three coequal persons: Father, **Son**, and **Holy Spirit** (see Matt 28:19). Here Luke describes the actions of all three persons of the Godhead.

3:23-38 The genealogies of Luke and Matthew (Matt 1:1-16) demonstrate that Jesus was a legitimate heir to David's throne. The differences between the two lists have to do with the fact that Matthew provides Jesus's legal genealogy through Joseph, his adoptive father, and Luke provides Jesus's biological genealogy. Luke traces Jesus's genealogy back to **Adam** through Nathan (Luke 3:38) because Jesus is the promised "offspring" who would strike Satan's head in fulfillment of God's promise (Gen 3:15).

a 3:32-34 Mt 1:1-6
b 3:32 Ru 4:17,21-22
c 3:33 Gn 38:29; 46:12
d 3:34-36 Gn 11:26-30; 1Ch
   1:24-27
e 3:35 Gn 10:25; 11:16-19
f 3:36-38 Gn 5:3-32; 1Ch
   1:1-4
g 3:37 Gn 5:21-26
h 4:1-13 Mt 4:1-11; Mk
   1:12-13
i 4:1 Lk 3:3
j Lk 1:15,41,67; Ac 2:4;
   4:8,31; 9:17; 11:24; 13:9
k Gl 5:18
l 4:2 Ex 24:18; 34:28; Dt
   9:9,11,18,25; 10:10
m 4:4 Dt 8:3
n 4:5 Is 23:17; Jr 25:26
o 4:6 1Jn 5:19

✒ Questions & Answers ✒

Q Jesus came into the world to war against Satan's counter-kingdom. One of the significant battles in that war was Jesus's temptation in the wilderness (Matt 4:1-11; Luke 4:1-13). What can we learn from this confrontation about how to resist Satan?

A One of the first things we learn regarding Jesus's temptation in the wilderness is that God likes baseball: three strikes and you're out! Satan spoke three temptations; Jesus quoted three passages of Scripture. When the devil couldn't take it anymore, he left. That shows us the authority that the Word of God carries when used legitimately.

It also teaches us that we need to have a Bible study with the devil, not just with other Christians. Jesus actually opened up the Bible with the devil. When we are tempted, we need to use Scripture against the evil one and say, "Satan, what does the Lord say about what you are telling me right now?" What that does is remind you of what God says. It throws God's Word in the devil's face and reminds you that he can't handle spiritual weapons. If you keep pumping the Word of God in Satan's direction, sooner or later he has to yield to it.

Another thing we learn is that Jesus prepared for battle. He fasted forty days and forty nights before he went to war. To ready himself, he pushed the physical into the background so that the spiritual was in the foreground. We have to make sure that we are spiritually prepared if we are going to do spiritual warfare effectively.

FOR THE NEXT Q&A, SEE PAGE 1183.

30 son of Simeon, son of Judah,
   son of Joseph, son of Jonam,
   son of Eliakim, 31 son of Melea,
   son of Menna, son of Mattatha,
   son of Nathan, son of David,
32 son of Jesse,*a* son of Obed,*b*
   son of Boaz, son of Salmon,^A
   son of Nahshon,
33 son of Amminadab,
   son of Ram,^B son of Hezron,
   son of Perez,*c* son of Judah,
34 son of Jacob, son of Isaac,
   son of Abraham,*d* son of Terah,
   son of Nahor, 35 son of Serug,
   son of Reu, son of Peleg,*e*
   son of Eber, son of Shelah,
36 son of Cainan, son of Arphaxad,
   son of Shem, son of Noah,*f*
   son of Lamech, 37 son of Methuselah,
   son of Enoch,*g* son of Jared,
   son of Mahalalel, son of Cainan,
38 son of Enos, son of Seth,
   son of Adam, son of God.

THE TEMPTATION OF JESUS

4 Then Jesus*h* left the Jordan,*i* full of the Holy Spirit,*j* and was led by the Spirit*k* in the wilderness 2 for forty days*l* to be tempted by the devil. He ate nothing during those days, and when they were over, he was hungry. 3 The devil said to him, "If you are the Son of God, tell this stone to become bread."

4 But Jesus answered him, "It is written: **Man must not live on bread alone.**"^C,D,m

5 So he took him up^E and showed him all the kingdoms of the world*n* in a moment of time. 6 The devil said to him, "I will give you their splendor and all this authority, because it has been given over to me,*o* and I can give it to anyone I want. 7 If you, then, will worship me,^F all will be yours."

^A 3:32 Other mss read *Sala*   ^B 3:33 Other mss read *Amminadab, son of Aram, son of Joram*; other mss read *Amminadab, son of Admin, son of Arni*
   ^C 4:4 Other mss add *but on every word of God*   ^D 4:4 Dt 8:3   ^E 4:5 Other mss read *So the devil took him up on a high mountain*
                                                     ^F 4:7 Lit *will fall down before me*

4:1-2 Notice that the Spirit led Jesus **in the wilderness . . . to be tempted by the devil.** Evidently, then, being under the influence of the Spirit does not mean uninterrupted peace and tranquility. But why was Jesus in *the wilderness*? Jesus was the "second man" or "last Adam" (1 Cor 15:45, 47). The devil tempted the first Adam and succeeded in having him kicked out of the garden into the wilderness (Gen 3:1-24). The first Adam was on defense and lost, but the last Adam played offense. Empowered by the Holy Spirit, he went into the wilderness to face the devil so that he might bring humanity back to the garden.

4:3 Satan spoke three temptations to Jesus, but they were all driving at the same point. Would Jesus act independently of God? This is also the question that we face in each wilderness experience we encounter: Will I act independently of God? Satan had been watching Jesus, and he knew his human need: hunger (see 4:2). Therefore, Satan attacked at his point of crisis, at his point of need. He will do the same to you. You need to be aware of your weaknesses and vulnerabilities because you can be sure that Satan is. **4:4** Jesus quoted Deuteronomy 8:3, in which Moses reminded the Israelites—who were in a wilderness—that they hadn't survived merely because they ate manna. They sur-

vived because of the source of the manna. Jesus refused to act independently of his Father; he trusted in his provision.
4:5-7 How did Satan obtain the authority he claimed (4:5-6)? Adam was called to rule the world on God's behalf (Gen 1:26, 28). By rebelling against God, he abdicated his role and handed it over to Satan, who is now the "god of this age" (2 Cor 4:4).

Importantly, the Father had already promised his Son all of earth's kingdoms (see Ps 2:8). But obtaining that would require the fulfillment of a mission that included perfect obedience to the Father and a sacrificial atoning death for sinners.

8 And Jesus answered him,[A] "It is written: **Worship the Lord your God, and serve**[a] **him only.**"[B]

9 So he took him to Jerusalem, had him stand on the pinnacle of the temple, and said to him, "If you are the Son of God, throw yourself down from here. **10** For it is written:

> **He will give his angels orders concerning you,
> to protect you,**[C,b] **11** and
> **they will support you
>   with their hands,
> so that you will not strike
>   your foot against a stone.**"[D,c]

12 And Jesus answered him, "It is said: **Do not test the Lord your God.**"[E,d]
13 After the devil had finished every temptation, he departed from him for a time.

MINISTRY IN GALILEE

14 Then Jesus returned to Galilee in the power of the Spirit,[e] and news about him spread throughout the entire vicinity.[f] **15** He was teaching in their synagogues,[g] being praised[f] by everyone.

REJECTION AT NAZARETH

16 He came to Nazareth, where he had been brought up.[h] As usual, he entered the synagogue on the Sabbath day[i] and stood up to read.[j] **17** The scroll of the prophet Isaiah was given to him, and unrolling the scroll, he found the place where it was written:

> **18**   **The Spirit of the Lord is on me,
>   because he has anointed me
> to preach good news
>   to the poor.
> He has sent me**[G]
> **to proclaim release**[H]
>   **to the captives
> and recovery of sight
>   to the blind,
> to set free the oppressed,**
> **19**   **to proclaim the year
>   of the Lord's favor.**[i,k]

20 He then rolled up the scroll, gave it back to the attendant, and sat down.[i] And the eyes of everyone in the synagogue were fixed on him. **21** He began by saying to them, "Today as you listen, this Scripture has been fulfilled."[m]

22 They were all speaking well of him[J] and were amazed by the gracious words that came from his mouth; yet they said, "Isn't this Joseph's son?"[n]

23 Then he said to them, "No doubt you will quote this proverb[K] to me: 'Doctor, heal yourself. What we've heard that took place in Capernaum,[o] do here in your hometown also.'"

24 He also said, "Truly I tell you, no prophet is accepted in his hometown.[p] **25** But I say to you, there were certainly many widows in Israel in Elijah's days,[q] when the sky was shut up for three years and six months while a great famine came over all the land. **26** Yet Elijah was not sent to any of them except a widow at Zarephath in Sidon.[r] **27** And in the prophet Elisha's time, there were many in Israel who had leprosy,[L] and yet not one of them was cleansed except Naaman the Syrian."[s]

[a] 4:8 Dt 6:13
[b] 4:10 Ps 91:11
[c] 4:11 Ps 91:12
[d] 4:12 Dt 6:16
[e] 4:14 Mt 4:12
[f] Mt 4:24; 9:26,31; Mk 1:28,45; Lk 4:37; 5:15; 9:60
[g] 4:15 Mt 4:23; 9:35; Lk 4:44; 13:10; Ac 9:20; 13:5
[h] 4:16 Lk 2:39,51
[i] Mt 13:54; Mk 6:1-2
[j] Ac 13:14-16

[k] 4:18-19 Is 61:1-2; Mt 11:5; 12:18; Jn 3:34
[l] 4:20 Mt 26:55
[m] 4:21 Jn 13:18; 15:25; 17:12; 19:28,36; Ac 1:16; Jms 2:23
[n] 4:22 Mt 13:55; Mk 6:3; Jn 6:42
[o] 4:23 Mt 11:23; Mk 2:1-12; Jn 4:46-53
[p] 4:24 Mt 13:57; Mk 6:4; Jn 4:44
[q] 4:25 1Kg 17:1; 18:1; Jms 5:17
[r] 4:26 1Kg 17:8-24
[s] 4:27 2Kg 5:1-14

[A] 4:8 Other mss add *"Get behind me, Satan!* [B] 4:8 Dt 6:13 [C] 4:10 Ps 91:11 [D] 4:11 Ps 91:12 [E] 4:12 Dt 6:16 [F] 4:15 Or *glorified* [G] 4:18 Other mss add *to heal the brokenhearted,* [H] 4:18 Or *freedom,* or *forgiveness* [I] 4:18-19 Is 61:1-2 [J] 4:22 Or *They were testifying against him* [K] 4:23 Or *parable* [L] 4:27 Gk *lepros* ; a term for various skin diseases; see Lv 13–14

4:9-11 Following Satan's temptation would prove to be a spectacular, supernatural way to convince the Jews that Jesus was the Messiah. It would result in a safe landing. No suffering required. And no cross. To take the bait would be to leave us without hope.

4:12 Don't back God into a corner. We are not to intentionally create the need for a miracle. God will create miracle opportunities on his own.

4:13 Satan's departure demonstrates a very important principle for waging spiritual warfare. Satan is allergic to the proper use of Scripture. Three strikes, and he's out.

4:16 Notice what Luke identifies as Jesus's **usual** activity. Whereas Jesus's public ministry had just begun, his spiritual practice of engaging with God, God's Word, and God's people had always been a regular part of his life.

4:17-21 Indeed, Jesus had come to set **captives** free, open **blind** eyes, and **proclaim the year of the Lord's favor** (4:18-19). "The

year of the Lord's favor" is another name for the Year of Jubilee (every fifty years; see Lev 25:8-12) when Israel was instructed to set slaves free and release people from their debts, as well as allowing them to return to their family property. Jubilee is a symbol of the social and economic liberation of God's people. The key, however, to understanding the Year of Jubilee is that it was inaugurated by the Day of Atonement, when the issue of sin was addressed. Thus spiritual transformation is the foundation for the legitimate social, political, and economic restructuring of society.

Jesus's preaching, then, addresses both the content of the gospel (Jesus's coming death, burial, and resurrection for the forgiveness of sins) and the scope of the gospel (the impact this good news should make on issues of biblical justice—the equitable and impartial application of God's moral law in society). The

gospel of the kingdom that Jesus preaches saves us *from* hell, but it should also save us *for* making a kingdom impact on this world through our "good works" that bring glory to God and benefit to people (see Matt 5:16). Jesus, then, is offering his people and us a new Jubilee.

4:22 **Isn't this Joseph's son?** essentially meant, "Hey, this is the carpenter's kid. He's a local. Who does he think he is?"

4:25-27 Jesus knew that performing a miracle to *prove* he was the Messiah would not help those inclined to unbelief. After all, **Elijah** and **Elisha** were rejected by Israelites in spite of the miracles they performed. As a result, Gentiles received God's benefits instead, because they were willing to act in faith at the word of God given them through the prophets. Elijah provided for the **widow at Zarephath**, and Elisha healed **Naaman the Syrian** (see 1 Kgs 17:8-16; 2 Kgs 5:1-19).

a 4:29 Nm 15:35; Ac 7:58;
  Heb 13:12
b 4:30 Jn 10:39
c 4:31-37 Mk 1:21-28
d 4:32 Mt 7:28-29; Mk
  1:22; Jn 7:46
e 4:33-37 Mk 1:23-28
f 4:34 Mk 1:24; Jn 6:69
g 4:35 Mt 8:26; Mk 4:39;
  Lk 4:39,41; 8:24
h Mk 1:25; 9:25
i 4:38-41 Mt 8:14-17; Mk
  1:29-34
j 4:38 1Co 9:5
k 4:39 Mt 8:3; 14:31; 20:34;
  Mk 5:42; 10:52; Lk 1:64;
  5:13,25; Ac 9:34
l 4:40 Mt 4:23; Mk 5:23
m 4:41 Mt 4:3; 8:29;
  Mk 3:11
n Mt 8:16; Mk 1:34; 3:11-12
o 4:42-43 Mt 14:13; Mk
  1:35-38,45; 6:31-32;
  Lk 9:12

28 When they heard this, everyone in the synagogue was enraged. **29** They got up, drove him out of town,[a] and brought him to the edge of the hill that their town was built on, intending to hurl him over the cliff. **30** But he passed right through the crowd and went on his way.[b]

DRIVING OUT AN UNCLEAN SPIRIT

31 Then he went down to Capernaum,[c] a town in Galilee, and was teaching them on the Sabbath. **32** They were astonished at his teaching because his message had authority.[d] **33** In the synagogue there was a man with an unclean demonic spirit who cried out with a loud voice,[e] **34** "Leave us alone! What do you have to do with us, Jesus of Nazareth? Have you come to destroy us? I know who you are — the Holy One of God!"[f]

35 But Jesus rebuked him[g] and said, "Be silent and come out of him!"[h] And throwing him down before them, the demon came out of him without hurting him at all.

36 Amazement came over them all, and they were saying to one another, "What is this message? For he commands the unclean spirits with authority and power, and they come out!" **37** And news about him began to go out to every place in the vicinity.

HEALINGS AT CAPERNAUM

38 After he left the synagogue, he entered Simon's house.[i] Simon's mother-in-law was suffering from a high fever, and they asked him about her.[j] **39** So he stood over her and rebuked the fever, and it left her. She got up immediately[k] and began to serve them.

40 When the sun was setting, all those who had anyone sick with various diseases brought them to him. As he laid his hands on each one of them, he healed them.[l] **41** Also, demons were coming out of many, shouting and saying, "You are the Son of God!"[m] But he rebuked them and would not allow them to speak, because they knew he was the Christ.[n]

42 When it was day, he went out and made his way to a deserted place.[o] But the crowds were searching for him. They came to him and tried to keep him from leaving them. **43** But he said to them, "It is necessary for me to proclaim the good news about the kingdom of God to the other towns also, because I was sent for

---

☙ KINGDOM LIVING ❧
PERSONAL
Embracing the Unusual

Divine reversals are God's specialty. He loves turning around impossible circumstances. Joseph was taken from the prison to the palace, and Christ was taken from the grave to resurrected glory. Our God relishes the chance to make the impossible possible—like the time when Jesus climbed into Peter's boat, it was pushed out from land, and he began to teach the people before saying to Peter, "Put out into deep water and let down your nets for a catch" (Luke 5:1-4). What follows in Luke 5:5-6 demonstrates how unconventional our Lord can be. Peter had caught nothing all day, and while Jesus was a good Teacher, what did he really know about fishing? Nevertheless, when the disciples did as he instructed, they were surprised to find the catch of a lifetime in their nets.

So many of us want to experience a similar thrill: we want Jesus to fill our own empty nets with a mighty bounty. In order to receive Christ's blessing, though, we too have to embrace the unusual. God does things differently because he wants to show us who he is, who we are in him, what our purpose is, and (most importantly) how to follow him.

If we're willing to do things differently and follow him no matter what, we can experience real comebacks in our lives. But we also must remember that God blesses us so we can serve him more, not less. He doesn't desire to bless you so you will have less time to pray. He wants to bless you so you will have more time for him and truly know the power of prayer.

FOR THE NEXT PERSONAL
KINGDOM LIVING LESSON SEE PAGE 1197.

4:28 The people became **enraged** since Jesus was implying that God's grace would be withheld from them and given to the Gentiles (see the note on Luke 4:25-27).

4:29-30 Jesus's death would be at the appointed time and place.

4:32 Jesus wasn't merely conveying information. He was proclaiming the kingdom of God and the effect of God's kingdom agenda on every area of life. One couldn't be indifferent to Jesus's authoritative **message**. It had to be believed and obeyed—or rejected and defied.

4:33-35 Though the devil's forces understood Jesus's true identity, he wasn't going to let them handle his public relations campaign. Doing so would've fueled claims that his miracles were the work of Satan (see Matt 12:24).

4:38 The Simon in view here is better known as the apostle Peter.

4:39 This woman's actions are a reminder that when the Lord meets a need in your life, it should always motivate you to greater service.

4:40 They came to him **when the sun was setting** because that's when the Sabbath was over and they were free to travel.

4:41 Jesus didn't want acknowledgment from **demons**; he wants praise from people.

4:42-44 Jesus's miracles authenticated his message, but he didn't want to be known simply as a miracle worker. He had a message to announce.

this purpose." [44] And he was preaching in the synagogues of Judea.[A,a]

THE FIRST DISCIPLES

5 As the crowd was pressing in on Jesus to hear God's word,[b] he was standing by Lake Gennesaret.[c] [2] He saw two boats at the edge of the lake; the fishermen had left them and were washing their nets. [3] He got into one of the boats,[d] which belonged to Simon, and asked him to put out a little from the land. Then he sat down and was teaching the crowds from the boat.

[4] When he had finished speaking, he said to Simon, "Put out into deep water and let down your nets for a catch."[e]

[5] "Master,"[f] Simon replied, "we've worked hard all night long and caught nothing. But if you say so, I'll let down the nets."[B]

[6] When they did this, they caught a great number of fish, and their nets[B] began to tear. [7] So they signaled to their partners in the other boat to come and help them; they came and filled both boats so full that they began to sink.

[8] When Simon Peter saw this, he fell at Jesus's knees and said, "Go away from me, because I'm a sinful man, Lord!"[g] [9] For he and all those with him were amazed[h] at the catch of fish they had taken, [10] and so were James and John, Zebedee's sons, who were Simon's partners.

"Don't be afraid,"[i] Jesus told Simon. "From now on you will be catching people."[j] [11] Then they brought the boats to land, left everything, and followed him.[k]

A MAN CLEANSED

[12] While he was in one of the towns, a man was there who had leprosy[c] all over him.[l] He saw Jesus, fell facedown, and begged him: "Lord, if you are willing, you can make me clean."

[13] Reaching out his hand, Jesus touched him,[m] saying, "I am willing; be made clean," and immediately the leprosy left him.

❧ Questions & Answers ❧

Q What are some practical tips you can offer for becoming better at solitude and meditation in our busy and hyper-connected culture?

A Solitude allows us an opportunity to meditate on God's Word without distractions. Meditation is rolling something over and over again in your thinking. It's reflecting on who God is, what God can do, and what you need from him. If you are unaccustomed to it, yes, it's possible that your mind could wander and become distracted. So start by meditating for a few minutes a day. Over time, you can increase this to a few more minutes and then a few more. Soon you'll be shocked to find that you can spend a whole hour with God because you've increased the time little by little.

Read through the Psalms and let them speak to you. Let God's Word assist you by giving you something specific to meditate on. Also, place yourself in an environment that facilitates meditation. Perhaps play music, such as hymns, to lift your spirit. David played soothing songs with his harp. Such music can help facilitate the process of meditation. Furthermore, you can go for walks and allow nature to support your efforts as you spend time in God's creation. And yes, turn off your cell phone to minimize distractions.

FOR THE NEXT Q&A, SEE PAGE 1271.

---

[a] 4:44 Mt 4:23; Mk 1:39
[b] 5:1-11 Mt 4:18-22; Mk 1:16-20; Jn 1:40-42
[c] 5:1 Nm 34:11; Dt 3:17; Jos 12:3; 13:27; Mt 4:18
[d] 5:3 Mt 13:2; Mk 3:9-10; 4:1
[e] 5:4-6 Jn 21:3-6
[f] 5:5 Lk 8:24; 9:33,49; 17:13
[g] 5:8 Is 6:5; Lk 19:7
[h] 5:9 Lk 4:36; Ac 3:10
[i] 5:10 Mt 14:27
[j] 2Tm 2:26
[k] 5:11 Mt 4:20,22; 19:29; Mk 1:18,20; Lk 5:28; 18:43
[l] 5:12-14 Mt 8:2-4; Mk 1:40-44

[m] 5:13 Mt 8:15; 9:29; 17:7; 20:34; Lk 18:15; 22:51

[A] 4:44 Other mss read *Galilee*　[B] 5:5,6 Other mss read *net* (Gk sg)　[c] 5:12 Gk *lepros*; a term for various skin diseases, also in v. 13; see Lv 13–14

5:1 Lake Gennesaret is another name for the Sea of Galilee.
5:3 This move gave Jesus a platform from which to teach the people where he wouldn't run the risk of being smothered by them.
5:4 Peter had probably been fishing his whole life. Jesus was an itinerant preacher who had probably spent much of his life doing carpentry work like his dad (see Matt 13:55). Nevertheless, Jesus advised the professional fisherman how to do his job.
5:5 Through his Word, God calls you to action in your specific circumstances, but your instincts and experience may tell you that obeying won't work. We have to remember that our instincts and experience have been distorted by sin. We can't see things perfectly. We lack information.

Our understanding is flawed. We must depend on the almighty God who is all knowing and can accomplish the impossible.
5:6 This wasn't flimsy fishing gear; these were professional **nets** made to hold a lot of fish.
5:7 Jesus had blessed his followers with more than they could handle. If you will obey him in faith, then your vision of him, praise for him, trust in him, and experience of blessings from him will grow.
5:8 When humans are confronted with the holiness of God, their sinfulness is exposed. Isaiah was a godly man. But when he saw God on his throne in all his glory and the heavenly beings describing him as, "Holy, holy, holy," Isaiah said, "Woe is me for I am ruined because I am a man of unclean lips" (Isa 6:1-5). Peter

saw Jesus for who he really was, and thus saw himself for who he really was.
5:10 Previously Peter had caught fish for a living. From this point forward, he would fish for **people** as a kingdom ambassador so that they might become followers of Jesus. Jesus had blessed Peter, opening his eyes to his sinful condition and need for God so that Peter could extend that blessing to others. The same is true for you. Regardless of the blessings God brings into your life—physical, spiritual, financial, relational—they are not meant for your benefit and enjoyment alone. *Be* a blessing.
5:13 The Mosaic law required those with such skin conditions to separate from others. However, when **Jesus touched** the man, contamination didn't flow in; cleansing flowed out.

When God Doesn't Make Sense

JESUS HAD JUST FINISHED PREACHING from the wooden pulpit of a borrowed boat (SEE LK 5:1-11). Because the crowd was so large, he had taught them from a distance. Following the sermon, he narrowed his attention to the owner of the boat, Simon Peter. Thus, what started as a generic sermon to the multitude had become an instruction to someone in particular. What began as a message to the masses moved to personal directive for an individual. You've probably experienced that before—a time when the sermon had your name written all over it.

Jesus told Peter, "Put out into deep water and let down your nets for a catch" (LK 5:4).

In one short statement, Jesus told him where to go (into the deep), what to do (let down your nets), and what to expect (a great catch). But Peter complained: "Master, we've worked hard all night long and caught nothing" (LK 5:5). In other words, he said, "Sir, we have tried. There is no hope."

In those moments, Peter didn't know two clues that I am going to share with you. When we see these two clues in our lives, we should suspect that we are in the vicinity of receiving something very special from God. Clue number one is this: God is not allowing anything that you do to work. Perhaps you feel that you have done everything you can—you've gone job hunting, read the books, gone to counseling, but things still aren't working. When this happens, it's likely that you, like Peter, are exactly where God wants you to be. Clue number two is this: What God asks you to do doesn't make sense. Talk to any fisherman who has worked on the Sea of Galilee, and he will tell you that putting a net into the deep waters in the daytime is not the way to catch fish. What Jesus asked Peter to do contradicted his experience, knowledge, and training.

Thankfully for Peter, he eventually did the thing that Jesus asked him to do. And because he did, "They caught a great number of fish, and their nets began to tear" (LK 5:6). Do you know how many fish it takes to break a fisherman's net? If we were to ask Paul, he would probably tell us, "above and beyond all that we ask or think" (EPH 3:20). Indeed, God can do "above and beyond" for you as well when you are willing to follow his instructions, despite how far-reaching they may sound.

14 Then he ordered him to tell no one:[a] "But go and show yourself to the priest, and offer what Moses commanded for your cleansing as a testimony to them."

15 But the news[A] about him spread even more, and large crowds would come together to hear him and to be healed of their sicknesses. **16** Yet he often withdrew to deserted places and prayed.[b]

THE SON OF MAN FORGIVES AND HEALS

17 On one of those days while he was teaching, Pharisees and teachers of the law[c] were sitting there who had come from every village of Galilee and Judea, and also from Jerusalem. And the Lord's power to heal was in him.[d] **18** Just then some men came,[e] carrying on a stretcher a man who was paralyzed. They tried to bring him in and set him down before him. **19** Since they could not find a way to bring him in because of the crowd, they went up on the roof and lowered him on the stretcher through the roof tiles into the middle of the crowd before Jesus.

20 Seeing their faith he said, "Friend,[B] your sins are forgiven."

21 Then the scribes and the Pharisees[f] began to think to themselves: "Who is this man who speaks blasphemies? Who can forgive sins but God alone?"[g]

22 But perceiving their thoughts, Jesus replied to them, "Why are you thinking this in your hearts?[c] **23** Which is easier: to say, 'Your sins are forgiven,' or to say, 'Get up and walk'? **24** But so that you may know that the Son of Man has authority on earth to forgive sins" — he told the paralyzed man, "I tell you: Get up, take your stretcher, and go home."

25 Immediately he got up before them, picked up what he had been lying on, and went home glorifying God.[h] **26** Then everyone was astounded, and they were giving glory to God. And they were filled with awe[I] and said, "We have seen incredible things today."

THE CALL OF LEVI

27 After this, Jesus went out and saw a tax collector named Levi sitting at the tax office,[j] and he said to him, "Follow me." **28** So, leaving everything behind, he got up and began to follow him.

29 Then Levi hosted a grand banquet for him at his house. Now there was a large crowd of tax collectors and others who were guests[D] with them.[k] **30** But the Pharisees and their scribes[l] were complaining to his disciples, "Why do you eat and drink with tax collectors and sinners?"

31 Jesus replied to them, "It is not those who are healthy who need a doctor, but those who are sick. **32** I have not come to call the righteous, but sinners to repentance."

A QUESTION ABOUT FASTING

33 Then they said to him, "John's disciples fast often and say prayers, and those of the Pharisees do the same, but yours eat and drink."[E]

34 Jesus said to them, "You can't make the wedding guests fast while the groom is with them, can you? **35** But the time[F] will come[m] when the groom will be taken away from them — then they will fast in those days."

[a] 5:14 Mt 16:20; 17:9; Mk 1:44; 7:36; 8:30; Lk 8:56; 9:21
[b] 5:16 Mt 14:23; Mk 1:35; Lk 6:12
[c] 5:17 Ac 5:34; 1Tm 1:7
[d] Mk 5:30; Lk 6:19; 8:46
[e] 5:18-26 Mt 9:2-8; Mk 2:3-12
[f] 5:21 Mt 23:2; Lk 11:53; Jn 8:3
[g] Is 43:25

[h] 5:25 Lk 7:16; 13:13; 17:15; 18:43; 23:47
[i] 5:26 Lk 1:65; 7:16
[j] 5:27-39 Mt 9:9-17; Mk 2:14-22
[k] 5:29 Lk 15:1
[l] 5:30 Mk 2:16; Ac 23:9
[m] 5:35 1Sm 2:31; Ps 37:13; Ec 2:16; 12:1; Lk 17:22

[A] 5:15 Lit *the word*   [B] 5:20 Lit *"Man*   [C] 5:22 Or *minds*   [D] 5:29 Lit *were reclining*   [E] 5:33 Other mss read *"Why do John's . . . drink?"* (as a question)   [F] 5:35 Lit *days*

5:15-16 The greater the demand on him, the more Jesus in his humanity depended on God the Father.

5:20 Jesus saw **their faith**. How do you see faith? You see it by what it produces. Jesus saw their actions on behalf of their friend. But he also saw what no one else could. They saw a paralyzed man who needed healing. Jesus saw a sinner who needed forgiveness. The men had brought their **friend** for physical restoration, but Jesus knew he needed spiritual restoration. Getting right with God takes priority over getting your circumstances right.

5:21 They started with the (correct) assumption that **God alone** could **forgive sins**, and they arrived at the (correct) conclusion that Jesus was making himself equal to God. Coming from any other man, his claim would indeed be blasphemy. But not from the Son of God.

5:23-24 Jesus validated his divine **authority** to **forgive sins** in the spiritual realm by demonstrating his divine authority to heal lame legs in the physical realm. Since he could forgive sins, he should be acknowledged as the Son of Man, the Messiah.

5:27 **Levi** is also known as Matthew (see Matt 9:9). Jews who served as tax collectors for the Roman government were considered traitors by the Jewish people. Moreover, they often padded their own pockets by collecting more than necessary. But rather than avoid such a sinner, Jesus told him, **Follow me.**

5:29 When you truly encounter Jesus, it's not enough to follow him. You want others to know the joy of following him too. That's why Levi **hosted** this **grand banquet**.

5:30 They questioned the propriety of Jesus's association and fellowship with sinful people. But their concern confirmed that they didn't understand Jesus's mission—nor did they understand their own duty as supposed servants of God.

5:31-32 Jesus's mission was to invite the spiritually **sick** to repent and experience a restored relationship with God (5:31). He hadn't come simply to hang out with religious people.

5:33 The implication of these words was that Jesus was not encouraging his disciples to practice piety toward God.

5:34-35 Often fasting was a solemn occasion that involved sorrow over sins or an urgent request for divine intervention (see, e.g., 1 Sam 7:6; 2 Sam 12:16; Neh 1:4; Esth 4:15-16; Ps 35:13). But this wasn't a somber occasion; it was a time of celebration. Jesus compared it to a **wedding** and himself to **the groom** (Luke 5:34). When you attend a wedding, you don't fast because it's an event of merriment and rejoicing. The Messiah had finally come; it was party time! Later, though, when the **groom** was **taken away**—after his resurrection and ascension—his disciples would have opportunities for fasting (5:35).

a 6:1-5 Mt 12:1-8; Mk
2:23-28
b 6:2 Mt 19:3; Lk 14:3;
20:22
c 6:4 Ex 25:30; Lv 24:5-9
d 1Sm 21:6
e 6:6-11 Mt 12:9-14; Mk
3:1-6
f 6:7 Mk 3:2; Lk 14:1; 20:20
g Jn 8:6
h 6:8 Mt 9:4
i 6:9 Lk 14:3
j 6:10 Mk 3:5
k 1Kg 13:4

l 6:12 Mt 14:23; Lk 5:16;
9:18,28
m 6:13-16 Mt 10:2-4; Mk
3:16-19; Ac 1:13
n 6:13 Mk 6:30
o 6:15 Mt 9:9
p 6:17 Mt 11:21
q 6:19 Mt 9:21; 14:36;
Mk 3:10
r Lk 5:17
s 6:20-23 Mt 5:3-12

36 He also told them a parable: "No one tears a patch from a new garment and puts it on an old garment. Otherwise, not only will he tear the new, but also the piece from the new garment will not match the old. **37** And no one puts new wine into old wineskins. Otherwise, the new wine will burst the skins, it will spill, and the skins will be ruined. **38** No, new wine is put into fresh wineskins.[A] **39** And no one, after drinking old wine, wants new, because he says, 'The old is better.'"[B]

LORD OF THE SABBATH

6 On a Sabbath, he passed through the grainfields.[a] His disciples were picking heads of grain, rubbing them in their hands, and eating them. **2** But some of the Pharisees said, "Why are you doing what is not lawful on the Sabbath?"[b]

3 Jesus answered them, "Haven't you read what David and those who were with him did when he was hungry — **4** how he entered the house of God and took and ate the bread of the Presence, which is not lawful for any but the priests to eat?[c] He even gave some to those who were with him."[d] **5** Then he told them, "The Son of Man is Lord of the Sabbath."

6 On another Sabbath[e] he entered the synagogue and was teaching. A man was there whose right hand was shriveled. **7** The scribes and Pharisees were watching him closely,[f] to see if he would heal on the Sabbath, so that they could find a charge against him.[g] **8** But he knew their thoughts[h] and told the man with the shriveled hand, "Get up and stand here."[c] So he got up and stood there. **9** Then Jesus said to them, "I ask you: Is it lawful to do good on the Sabbath or to do evil, to save life or to destroy it?"[i] **10** After looking around at them all,[j] he told him, "Stretch out your hand."[k] He did,

and his hand was restored.[D] **11** They, however, were filled with rage and started discussing with one another what they might do to Jesus.

THE TWELVE APOSTLES

12 During those days he went out to the mountain to pray[l] and spent all night in prayer to God. **13** When daylight came, he summoned his disciples,[m] and he chose twelve of them, whom he also named apostles:[n] **14** Simon, whom he also named Peter, and Andrew his brother; James and John; Philip and Bartholomew; **15** Matthew and Thomas;[o] James the son of Alphaeus, and Simon called the Zealot; **16** Judas the son of James, and Judas Iscariot, who became a traitor.

TEACHING AND HEALING

17 After coming down with them, he stood on a level place with a large crowd of his disciples and a great number of people from all Judea and Jerusalem and from the seacoast of Tyre and Sidon.[p] **18** They came to hear him and to be healed of their diseases; and those tormented by unclean spirits were made well. **19** The whole crowd was trying to touch him,[q] because power was coming out from him and healing them all.[r]

THE BEATITUDES

20 Then looking up at his disciples, he said:[s]

Blessed are you who are poor,
  because the kingdom of God
    is yours.
21   Blessed are you who are now
    hungry,
  because you will be filled.
Blessed are you who weep now,
  because you will laugh.
22   Blessed are you when people
    hate you,

[A] **5:38** Other mss add *And so both are preserved.*   [B] **5:39** Other mss read *is good*   [C] **6:8** Lit *stand in the middle*   [D] **6:10** Other mss add *as sound as the other*

6:1-2 God had commanded Israel to remember **the Sabbath** as a time of rest, spiritual refreshment, and no labor (see Exod 20:8-11). But the Pharisees were extra-scrupulous. They added numerous laws to God's law about what kind of activities constituted labor. As far as they were concerned, Jesus and his disciples were harvesting and, thus, breaking the law.
6:3-5 As God's anointed one, **David** was authorized to eat **the bread of the Presence** because of his extreme need (6:3-4). If this was true in David's case, it was even more so in the case of God's true Anointed One (the Messiah). For Jesus was **Lord of the Sabbath** (6:5). By saying this, Jesus was making a

not-so-subtle affirmation of his deity. Since God had given the Sabbath command, Jesus would have to be equal to God to consider himself "Lord of the Sabbath."
6:6-8 The **Sabbath** was a frequent matter of contention between Jesus and the religious leaders (6:6-7). But Jesus wasn't one to back down from a fight (6:8).
6:9 His point was that if one chose not to do good to someone by alleviating that person's suffering, it was **evil**.
6:12 Given the mounting hostility to his ministry, Jesus sought time with his Father. This was how the Son of God approached critical moments. How do you approach them?

6:13-16 Luke names the **twelve** men whom Jesus designated as **apostles** (6:13). These handpicked individuals would travel with Jesus, learn from him, and be granted special authority to share in the responsibility of proclaiming his kingdom message.
6:20 Those **who are poor** are those who recognize their spiritual bankruptcy. They will see the authority of **the kingdom of God** overruling life's challenges.
6:21 Those **who are now hungry** with a passionate spiritual appetite for a relationship with God will receive satisfaction in their souls. Those **who weep** and mourn over their sin will have their sorrow replaced with joy.

when they exclude you,[a]
insult you,
and slander your name as evil[b]
because of the Son of Man.[c]
23 "Rejoice in that day and leap for joy. Take note — your reward is great in heaven, for this is the way their ancestors used to treat the prophets.[d]

WOE TO THE SELF-SATISFIED

24   But woe to you who are rich,
for you have received
your comfort.
25   Woe to you who are now full,
for you will be hungry.
Woe to you[A] who are now laughing,
for you will mourn and weep.
26   Woe to you[A]
when all people speak well
of you,
for this is the way
their ancestors
used to treat the false prophets.[e]

LOVE YOUR ENEMIES

27 "But I say to you who listen: Love your enemies, do what is good to those who hate you, **28** bless those who curse you, pray for those who mistreat you.[f] **29** If anyone hits you on the cheek,[g] offer the other also. And if anyone takes away your coat, don't hold back your shirt either. **30** Give to everyone who asks you, and from someone who takes your things, don't ask for them back. **31** Just as you want others to do for you, do the same for them.[h] **32** If you love those who love you, what credit is that to you? Even sinners love those who love them.[i] **33** If you do what is good to those who are good to you, what credit is that to you? Even sinners do that. **34** And if you lend to those from whom you expect to receive, what credit is that to you?[j] Even sinners lend to sinners to be repaid in full. **35** But love your enemies, do what

is good, and lend, expecting nothing in return. Then your reward will be great, and you will be children of the Most High.[k] For he is gracious to the ungrateful and evil. **36** Be merciful, just as your Father also is merciful.[l]

DO NOT JUDGE

37 "Do not judge, and you will not be judged.[m] Do not condemn, and you will not be condemned. Forgive, and you will be forgiven.[n] **38** Give, and it will be given to you; a good measure — pressed down, shaken together, and running over — will be poured into your lap.[o] For with the measure you use, it will be measured back to you."[p]

39 He also told them a parable: "Can the blind guide the blind? Won't they both fall into a pit?[q] **40** A disciple is not above his teacher, but everyone who is fully trained will be like his teacher.[r]

41 "Why do you look at the splinter in your brother's eye, but don't notice the beam of wood in your own eye? **42** Or how can you say to your brother, 'Brother, let me take out the splinter that is in your eye,' when you yourself don't see the beam of wood in your eye? Hypocrite! First take the beam of wood out of your eye, and then you will see clearly to take out the splinter in your brother's eye.

A TREE AND ITS FRUIT

43 "A good tree doesn't produce bad fruit; on the other hand, a bad tree doesn't produce good fruit.[B,s] **44** For each tree is known by its own fruit. Figs aren't gathered from thornbushes, or grapes picked from a bramble bush. **45** A good person produces good out of the good stored up in his heart. An evil person produces evil out of the evil stored up in his heart, for his mouth speaks from the overflow of the heart.

[a] 6:22 Jn 9:22; 16:2
[b] Heb 11:26; 1Pt 4:14
[c] Jn 15:21
[d] 6:23 Neh 9:26; Ezk 2:1-7; Ac 7:52
[e] 6:26 Jr 5:12-13; 6:13-15; Mc 2:11
[f] 6:28 Mt 5:44
[g] 6:29-30 Mt 5:39-42
[h] 6:31 Mt 7:12
[i] 6:32 Mt 5:46
[j] 6:34 Pr 19:17; Mt 5:42; Lk 14:12-14

[k] 6:35 Mt 5:45; Lk 1:32
[l] 6:36 Mt 5:7,48; Jms 5:11
[m] 6:37-42 Mt 7:1-5
[n] 6:37 Mt 6:14; 18:23-35; Lk 23:16; Ac 3:13
[o] 6:38 Ps 79:12; Is 65:6-7; Jr 32:18
[p] Mk 4:24
[q] 6:39 Mt 15:14
[r] 6:40 Mk 10:24; Jn 13:16; 15:20
[s] 6:43-44 Mt 7:16,18,20; 12:33-35

[A] 6:25,26 Other mss omit *to you*   [B] 6:43 Lit *on the other hand, again, a bad tree doesn't produce good fruit*

6:24 Those **who are rich** in the physical world but have no spiritual wealth toward God will ultimately lose their riches and find that they were meaningless.
6:25 Those who let this present age fill them will experience spiritual lack in the age to come.
6:26 Jesus's followers are not to regard complimentary words from the unrighteous as indicators of God's approval. The ungodly spoke well of **false prophets** during Old Testament times. God's people must remember that divine approval is more important than human praise.

6:27-31 Christ's followers have different values and are thus distinguishable from the rest of the world. All they do is done with a view toward bringing detractors to the knowledge of God's love in Jesus Christ.
6:37 Kingdom people won't **judge** and **condemn** others according to their own standards.
6:38 God's principle of reciprocity is activated when we minister to the needs of others with the result that he raises up people to minister in return to us in that same area of need (e.g., the widow of Zarephath, 1 Kgs 17:8-16).
6:39 What is true in the physical world is true spiritually too. Those who reject God's Mes-

siah and teach others to do so will lead them to destruction.
6:40 A disciple of Jesus is to **be like his teacher** in his attitudes and actions.
6:41-42 The splinter represents a minor fault, while **the beam of wood** represents a grievous sin (6:41). We must address the larger issues in our own hearts before we seek to address the small issues in the lives of our brothers and sisters in Christ (6:42).
6:43-45 Apple trees bear only apples. Orange trees bear only oranges. In the same way, you can identify people who follow God based on what they say and do—their **fruit** (6:43-44).

a 6:46 Mal 1:6; Mt 7:21
b 6:47-49 Mt 7:24-27
c 6:49 Ezk 13:10-16
d 7:1-10 Mt 8:5-13
e 7:5 Ac 10:22

f 7:7 Ps 107:20; Mt 8:16
g 7:12 Jdg 11:34; Lk 8:42;
   9:38; Heb 11:17
h 7:13 Mt 20:34
i 7:14 Mt 11:5; Mk 5:41;
Lk 7:22; 8:54; Jn 11:43;
   Ac 9:40
j 7:15 1Kg 17:23; 2Kg 4:36
k 7:16 Lk 5:26
l Mt 5:16; Lk 2:20; 13:13;
   23:47; Ac 4:21; 11:18
m Dt 18:15; Mt 21:11; Lk
   7:39; Jn 7:40
n Lk 1:68
o 7:18-35 Mt 11:2-19
p 7:19 Jn 4:25; 6:14; 11:27;
   Rm 5:14; Heb 10:37

HOPE WORDS

Don't forget that God is calling us to put into practice on Monday the truth that we said "amen" to on Sunday.

THE TWO FOUNDATIONS

46 "Why do you call me 'Lord, Lord,' and don't do the things I say?[a] 47 I will show you what someone is like who comes to me, hears my words, and acts on them:[b] 48 He is like a man building a house, who dug deep and laid the foundation on the rock. When the flood came, the river crashed against that house and couldn't shake it, because it was well built. 49 But the one who hears and does not act is like a man who built a house on the ground without a foundation. The river crashed against it, and immediately it collapsed. And the destruction of that house was great."[c]

A CENTURION'S FAITH

7 When he had concluded saying all this to the people who were listening, he entered Capernaum.[d] 2 A centurion's servant, who was highly valued by him, was sick and about to die. 3 When the centurion heard about Jesus, he sent some Jewish elders to him, requesting him to come and save the life of his servant. 4 When they reached Jesus, they pleaded with him earnestly, saying, "He is worthy for you to grant this, 5 because he loves our nation and has built us a synagogue."[e]

6 Jesus went with them, and when he was not far from the house, the centurion sent friends to tell him, "Lord, don't trouble yourself, since I am not worthy to have you come under my roof. 7 That is

why I didn't even consider myself worthy to come to you. But say the word, and my servant will be healed.[A,f] 8 For I too am a man placed under authority, having soldiers under my command. I say to this one, 'Go,' and he goes; and to another, 'Come,' and he comes; and to my servant, 'Do this,' and he does it."

9 Jesus heard this and was amazed at him, and turning to the crowd following him, he said, "I tell you, I have not found so great a faith even in Israel." 10 When those who had been sent returned to the house, they found the servant in good health.

A WIDOW'S SON RAISED TO LIFE

11 Afterward he was on his way to a town called Nain. His disciples and a large crowd were traveling with him. 12 Just as he neared the gate of the town, a dead man was being carried out. He was his mother's only son, and she was a widow.[g] A large crowd from the town was also with her. 13 When the Lord saw her, he had compassion on her[h] and said, "Don't weep." 14 Then he came up and touched the open coffin, and the pallbearers stopped. And he said, "Young man, I tell you, get up!"[i]

15 The dead man sat up and began to speak, and Jesus gave him to his mother.[j] 16 Then fear[B] came over everyone,[k] and they glorified God,[l] saying, "A great prophet has risen among us,"[m] and "God has visited[c] his people."[n] 17 This report about him went throughout Judea and all the vicinity.

IN PRAISE OF JOHN THE BAPTIST

18 Then John's disciples told him about all these things.[o] So John summoned two of his disciples 19 and sent them to the Lord, asking, "Are you the one[p] who is to come, or should we expect someone else?"

A 7:7 Other mss read *and let my servant be healed*   B 7:16 Or *awe*   C 7:16 Or *come to help*

6:46-49 The Bible isn't meant merely to be studied and memorized; it is meant to be believed and obeyed. We are to "be doers of the word and not hearers only" (Jas 1:22). When the storms of life come, it's what you do with what you hear that determines how much of Jesus you will experience. The foundation of God's Word operating in your life will determine the stability of your future—especially when serious trials come.
7:1-5 Many Gentiles, like this **centurion**, were drawn to the Jewish religion because of its monotheism (belief in one God) and moral teachings. They were known as *God fearers* and participated in much of the Jewish religious life (see, e.g., Acts 10:1-2). However,

they did not fully convert to Judaism—perhaps to avoid circumcision.
  This man believed that Jesus could heal his **servant**. But since he was uncertain whether Jesus would respond to a Gentile's request, he sent the message through some **Jewish elders** (7:2-3).
7:6-7 Clearly, the centurion's self-perception was quite different from that of the various Jewish religious leaders who had been critical of Jesus. This man had a high view of Jesus (**Lord**) and a humble view of himself (**I am not worthy;** 7:6).
7:8-9 The key to having truly **great . . . faith** is to be operating under legitimate spiritual authority.

7:12 With no husband or grown children to care for her, the **widow** would have no means of support, no hope.
7:14-16 Jesus had performed many miracles, but this is the first time (reported in Luke's Gospel) that he raised someone from the dead. It was a foretaste of the greater resurrection miracle to come (see 24:1-53).
7:18-20 John the Baptist had been locked up in prison by Herod Antipas (see 3:19-20). Receiving word about all that Jesus was doing, John was beginning to wonder if he had been wrong to herald Jesus as the Messiah. Though John was expecting the kingdom of God to come, it didn't appear to him that Jesus was planning to take the

20 When the men reached him, they said, "John the Baptist sent us to ask you, 'Are you the one who is to come, or should we expect someone else?'"

21 At that time Jesus healed many people of diseases,[a] afflictions, and evil spirits,[b] and he granted sight to many blind people.[c] **22** He replied to them, "Go and report to John what you have seen and heard: The blind receive their sight, the lame walk, those with leprosy[A] are cleansed, the deaf hear,[d] the dead are raised, and the poor are told the good news,[e] **23** and blessed is the one who isn't offended by me."

24 After John's messengers left, he began to speak to the crowds about John: "What did you go out into the wilderness to see? A reed swaying in the wind? **25** What then did you go out to see? A man dressed in soft clothes? See, those who are splendidly dressed and live in luxury are in royal palaces. **26** What then did you go out to see? A prophet?[f] Yes, I tell you, and more than a prophet. **27** This is the one about whom it is written:

> See, I am sending my messenger
> ahead of you;
> he will prepare your way
> before you.[B,g]

28 I tell you, among those born of women no one is greater than John,[c] but the least in the kingdom of God is greater than he."

29 (And when all the people, including the tax collectors, heard this, they acknowledged God's way of righteousness, because they had been baptized with John's baptism.[h] **30** But since the Pharisees and experts in the law[i] had not been baptized by him, they rejected the plan of God for themselves.[j])

AN UNRESPONSIVE GENERATION

31 "To what then should I compare the people of this generation, and what are they like? **32** They are like children sitting in the marketplace and calling to each other:

> We played the flute for you,
> but you didn't dance;
> we sang a lament,
> but you didn't weep!

33 For John the Baptist did not come eating bread or drinking wine,[k] and you say, 'He has a demon!' **34** The Son of Man has come eating and drinking, and you say, 'Look, a glutton and a drunkard, a friend of tax collectors and sinners!'[l] **35** Yet wisdom is vindicated by all her children."

MUCH FORGIVENESS, MUCH LOVE

36 Then one of the Pharisees invited him to eat with him. He entered the Pharisee's house and reclined at the table.[m] **37** And a woman in the town who was a sinner found out that Jesus was reclining at the table in the Pharisee's house.[n] She brought an alabaster jar of perfume **38** and stood behind him at his feet, weeping, and began to wash his feet with her tears. She wiped his feet with her hair, kissing them and anointing them with the perfume.[o]

39 When the Pharisee who had invited him saw this, he said to himself, "This man, if he were a prophet, would know who and what kind of woman this is who is touching him — she's a sinner!"[p]

40 Jesus replied to him, "Simon, I have something to say to you."

He said, "Say it, teacher."

41 "A creditor had two debtors. One owed five hundred denarii,[D,q] and the other fifty.

[a] 7:21 Mt 4:23
[b] Mk 1:34
[c] Mt 9:30; 12:22; Mk 8:25; Lk 18:42; Jn 9:7
[d] 7:22 Is 29:18; 35:5-6
[e] Is 61:1; Lk 4:18
[f] 7:26 Mt 14:5; Lk 1:76; 20:6
[g] 7:27 Mal 3:1; Mt 11:10; Mk 1:2; Lk 1:17
[h] 7:29 Mt 21:32; Lk 3:12; Ac 18:25; 19:3
[i] 7:30 Mt 22:35; Lk 10:25; 11:45-46,52; 14:3
[j] Mt 21:25,32; 23:13; Mk 7:9
[k] 7:33 Lk 1:15
[l] 7:34 Mt 9:10-11; Lk 15:2; 19:7
[m] 7:36 Lk 11:37; 14:1
[n] 7:37-39 Mt 26:6-13; Mk 14:3-9; Jn 12:1-8
[o] 7:38 Jn 11:2
[p] 7:39 Lk 7:16; Jn 4:19
[q] 7:41 Mt 18:28; Mk 6:37

throne. When experiencing suffering, even strong believers sometimes need reassurance and reaffirmation about Jesus and the gospel.

7:22 The miraculous works and message Jesus was performing were fulfilling Isaiah 61:1, which foretold of the Messiah's deeds.

7:28 The new covenant, which Jesus would bring about through his atoning death on the cross, was greater than the old covenant. Thus, the citizens in the kingdom operating under the new covenant will have a greater spiritual capacity than **John**, who had been operating under the old.

7:29-30 The people responded positively to Jesus's message about John. **They had been baptized** by him and received him as the forerunner of the Christ (7:29). In contrast, the religious leaders had rejected John,

rejected the One to whom John pointed, and thus **rejected the plan of God** (7:30). Such rejection would continue until Israel's leaders led the people in condemning their Messiah.

7:31-35 The point here is that the leaders were behaving like cranky **children** singing a silly song (7:32). They could not be pleased by the somberness of the kingdom, represented by John's ascetic lifestyle and call to repentance (7:33). Nor could they be pleased by the joy of the kingdom, represented by Jesus's gracious fellowship with sinners (7:34). The scribes and Pharisees saw John as demonic and Jesus as liberal. **Yet wisdom is vindicated by all her children** (7:35): those with spiritual insight validate it by their actions—their "children." The crowds who had received both John and Jesus demonstrated that they were wiser than

Israel's religious leaders.

7:37 All people are sinners. To call a particular woman **a sinner** was to say something about her lifestyle. She was probably either a loose woman or a prostitute.

7:38 This visitor was breaking all of the rules of decency—and she didn't care. She wanted to show love for Jesus and honor him for bringing the grace of God into her life.

7:40 Don't miss that Jesus **replied to** Simon. The Pharisee hadn't spoken. He had been thinking to himself (7:39); nevertheless, all humanity's deepest beliefs, feelings, and judgments are an open book before Jesus (see 5:21-22). You can't have a private reflection without Jesus knowing about it.

7:41 A denarius was the daily wage for the average laborer.

a 7:42 Mt 18:25
b 7:44 Gn 18:4; 19:2; 43:24;
Jdg 19:21; 1Tm 5:10
c 7:45 2Sm 15:5; 19:39;
20:9
d 7:46 2Sm 12:20; Ps 23:5;
Ec 9:8; Dn 10:3
e 7:48 Mt 9:2; Mk 2:5; Lk
5:20; Jms 5:15; 1Jn 2:12
f 7:49 Lk 5:21
g 7:50 Mt 9:22; Mk 10:52;
Lk 17:19; 18:42
h 1Sm 1:17; Mk 5:34;
Lk 8:48
i 8:1 Mk 6:6
j Mt 4:23; Lk 4:43
k 8:2 Mt 27:55; Mk 15:40-
41; Lk 23:49,55; Ac 1:14
l Mt 27:56,61; 28:1; Mk
16:9; Lk 24:10; Jn 19:25;
20:1,18

m 8:4-8 Mt 13:3-9; Mk
4:3-9
n 8:8 Gn 26:12
o Mt 11:15; Lk 13:34
p 8:9-10 Mt 13:10-11; Mk
4:10-11
q 8:10 Mt 19:11
r Is 6:9
s 8:11-15 Mt 13:18-23; Mk
4:13-20
t 8:11 Lk 8:21; 11:28; Ac
18:11; Jms 1:21; 1Pt 1:23
u 8:13 Ezk 33:31-32; Gl 1:9

[42] Since they could not pay it back,[a] he graciously forgave them both. So, which of them will love him more?"

[43] Simon answered, "I suppose the one he forgave more."

"You have judged correctly," he told him. [44] Turning to the woman, he said to Simon, "Do you see this woman? I entered your house; you gave me no water for my feet,[b] but she, with her tears, has washed my feet and wiped them with her hair. [45] You gave me no kiss,[c] but she hasn't stopped kissing my feet since I came in. [46] You didn't anoint my head with olive oil,[d] but she has anointed my feet with perfume. [47] Therefore I tell you, her many sins have been forgiven; that's why she loved much. But the one who is forgiven little, loves little." [48] Then he said to her, "Your sins are forgiven."[e]

[49] Those who were at the table with him began to say among themselves, "Who is this man who even forgives sins?"[f]

[50] And he said to the woman, "Your faith has saved you.[g] Go in peace."[h]

MANY WOMEN SUPPORT CHRIST'S WORK

8 Afterward he was traveling from one town and village to another,[i] preaching and telling the good news of the kingdom of God.[j] The Twelve were with him, [2] and also some women who had been healed of evil spirits and sicknesses:[k] Mary, called Magdalene (seven demons had come out[l] of her); [3] Joanna the wife of Chuza, Herod's steward; Susanna; and many others who were supporting them from their possessions.

THE PARABLE OF THE SOWER

[4] As a large crowd was gathering, and people were coming to Jesus from every town, he said in a parable:[m] [5] "A sower went out to sow his seed. As he sowed, some seed fell along the path; it was trampled on, and the birds of the sky devoured it. [6] Other seed fell on the rock; when it grew up, it withered away, since it lacked moisture. [7] Other seed fell among thorns; the thorns grew up with it and choked it. [8] Still other seed fell on good ground; when it grew up, it produced fruit: a hundred times what was sown."[n] As he said this, he called out, "Let anyone who has ears to hear listen."[o]

WHY JESUS USED PARABLES

[9] Then his disciples asked him, "What does this parable mean?"[p] [10] So he said, "The secrets of the kingdom of God have been given for you[q] to know, but to the rest it is in parables, so that

**Looking they may not see,
and hearing they may
not understand.[A,r]**

THE PARABLE OF THE SOWER EXPLAINED

[11] "This is the meaning of the parable:[s] The seed is the word of God.[t] [12] The seed along the path are those who have heard and then the devil comes and takes away the word from their hearts, so that they may not believe and be saved. [13] And the seed on the rock are those who, when they hear, receive the word with joy. Having no root, these believe for a while and fall away in a time of testing.[u] [14] As for the

^8:10 Is 6:9

7:42 Jesus's question implies that there should be a direct correlation between forgiveness and gratitude.

7:44-46 To provide a guest with **water** to wash his dusty sandaled **feet** was common hospitality in the first century (7:44). Moreover, greeting a guest with a **kiss** and **oil** for his **head** were signs of warmth and friendliness (7:45-46). Jesus took an uninvited, sinful woman to show hospitality to Jesus in this Pharisee's home.

7:47 Do you go to church for social connection? Do you read your Bible out of duty? Do you pray in boredom? Do you serve others for what you can get in return? If so, you have forgotten your sin before God and the cross of Christ that cancels all debt (see Col 2:14). Don't lose sight of how much you've **been forgiven**. Drink in the truth of the gospel, and it will drive you to a deep love for Jesus that spurs you to worship him with passion and serve others sacrificially.

7:48 If you are putting your faith in Christ as your substitutionary sacrifice, then he says these same words to you.

8:1-3 Many people followed Jesus, but there was a core group that went with him almost everywhere, which included women.

8:4 Jesus's parables were earthly stories with heavenly meanings. He taught his listeners valuable kingdom principles by using the familiar to explain the unfamiliar.

8:5-8 Jesus concluded this parable with, **Let anyone who has ears to hear listen** (8:8). Jesus told the people to "listen" because what he said was critically important. It would come up again.

8:10 The **secrets of the kingdom**—that is, things concealed in the Old Testament but revealed in the New Testament—were being made known to Jesus's followers. But to others his **parables** would make no sense because, though they had ears, they refused to "listen" (see 8:8).

8:11 **The seed** represented **the word of God**. The success of the seed, therefore, had nothing to do with the seed itself. If God's Word doesn't appear to be working in your life, you need to check the ground that it landed on.

The soil of your heart needs to be receptive to the seed in order for you to experience spiritual change and growth.

8:12 The word **saved** can have two meanings: "salvation" in eternity and "deliverance" in history. When an unbeliever hardens his heart against the gospel, Satan removes the Word that he's heard, lest he believe the good news about Christ and be saved—that is, become a Christian. When a believer hardens his heart against a specific truth of God's Word, he is susceptible to satanic deception. As a result of failing to embrace God's truth, a believer can fail to experience God's deliverance in his earthly struggles—that is, growing and overcoming persistent sin.

8:13 Believers who lack the discipline of spending time with God, living in obedience to his Word, and serving his people, are unable to stand up under the pressure when difficulties come their way. They become unproductive.

8:14 If the devil can't hinder you with difficulties, he'll choke you with distractions.

seed that fell among thorns, these are the ones who, when they have heard, go on their way and are choked with worries, riches, and pleasures of life,[a] and produce no mature fruit. **15** But the seed in the good ground — these are the ones who, having heard the word with an honest and good heart, hold on to it and by enduring,[b] produce fruit.

USING YOUR LIGHT

16 "No one, after lighting a lamp,[c] covers it with a basket or puts it under a bed, but puts it on a lampstand so that those who come in may see its light.[d] **17** For nothing is concealed that won't be revealed, and nothing hidden that won't be made known and brought to light.[e] **18** Therefore take care how you listen. For whoever has, more will be given to him;[f] and whoever does not have, even what he thinks he has will be taken away from him."

TRUE RELATIONSHIPS

19 Then his mother and brothers[g] came to him,[h] but they could not meet with him because of the crowd. **20** He was told, "Your mother and your brothers are standing outside, wanting to see you." **21** But he replied to them, "My mother and my brothers are those who hear and do the word of God."[i]

WIND AND WAVES OBEY JESUS

22 One day he and his disciples got into a boat,[j] and he told them, "Let's cross over to the other side of the lake."[k] So they set out, **23** and as they were sailing he fell asleep. Then a fierce windstorm came down on the lake; they were being swamped and were in danger. **24** They came and woke him up, saying, "Master, Master, we're going to die!"

Then he got up and rebuked the wind and the raging waves. So they ceased, and there was a calm.[l] **25** He said to them, "Where is your faith?"

They were fearful and amazed, asking one another, "Who then is this?[m] He commands even the winds and the waves, and they obey him!"

DEMONS DRIVEN OUT BY JESUS

26 Then they sailed to the region of the Gerasenes,[A,n] which is opposite Galilee. **27** When he got out on land, a demon-possessed man from the town met him. For a long time he had worn no clothes and did not stay in a house but in the tombs. **28** When he saw Jesus, he cried out,[o] fell down before him, and said in a loud voice, "What do you have to do with me,[p] Jesus, Son of the Most High God?[q] I beg you, don't torment me!" **29** For he had commanded the unclean spirit to come out of the man. Many times it had seized him, and though he was guarded, bound by chains and shackles, he would snap the restraints and be driven by the demon into deserted places.

30 "What is your name?" Jesus asked him.

"Legion,"[r] he said, because many demons had entered him. **31** And they begged him not to banish them to the abyss.[s]

32 A large herd of pigs was there, feeding on the hillside. The demons begged him to permit them to enter the pigs, and he gave them permission. **33** The demons came out of the man and entered the pigs, and the herd rushed down the steep bank into the lake and drowned.

34 When the men who tended them saw what had happened, they ran off and reported it in the town and in the countryside. **35** Then people went out to see what had happened. They came to Jesus and found the man the demons had departed from, sitting at Jesus's feet,[t] dressed and in his right mind. And they were afraid. **36** Meanwhile, the eyewitnesses reported to them how the demon-possessed man

[a] 8:14 Mt 6:25
[b] 8:15 Heb 10:36; Jms 5:7
[c] 8:16 Mt 5:15-16; Lk 11:33
[d] 8:16-18 Mk 4:21-25
[e] 8:17 Mt 10:26; Lk 12:2; 1Tm 5:25
[f] 8:18 Mt 13:12
[g] 8:19 Mt 13:55; Mk 6:3; Jn 2:12; 7:3,5,10; Ac 1:14; 1Co 9:5; Gl 1:19
[h] 8:19-21 Mt 12:46-50; Mk 3:31-35
[i] 8:21 Lk 11:28; Jms 1:22
[j] 8:22-25 Mk 8:23-27; Mk 4:36-41; Jn 6:16-21
[k] 8:22 Lk 5:1

[l] 8:24 Ps 65:7; 104:7; Mt 14:32; Mk 6:51; Lk 4:39
[m] 8:25 Mt 21:10; Lk 1:66; 5:21; 7:49; 9:9
[n] 8:26-39 Mt 8:28-34; Mk 5:1-20
[o] 8:28 Lk 4:33-34; Ac 8:7
[p] Jn 2:4
[q] Gn 14:18; Ps 57:2; Dn 3:26; Lk 1:32; Ac 16:17
[r] 8:30 Mt 26:53
[s] 8:31 Ps 140:10; Rm 10:7; Rv 9:1-2,11; 11:7; 17:8; 20:1,3
[t] 8:35 Lk 8:41; 10:39

---

^A **8:26** Other mss read *the Gadarenes*

8:15 The **good-ground** Christian consistently endures and bears **fruit** as his or her character and conduct are transformed as he or she lives in obedience to God's Word. To be one, you must come clean with God, confessing sin and seeking change.

8:16 If we understand the Word of God, our lifestyle should reflect that knowledge.

8:18 When we respond in faith to God's truth, more truth will be given. The one who refuses to respond to the truth will be lost.

8:19-21 Closeness with Christ is tied to obedience to **the word of God**. Importantly, we learn in the other Gospels that Jesus's biological family thought he was "out of his

mind" during his ministry and didn't believe in him (Mark 3:20-21; John 7:1-5). Those who not only **hear** but also **do** the Word will know true spiritual intimacy with Jesus (Luke 8:21).

8:22 Notice two things in this verse leading up to the account of the disciples' encounter with a stormy sea. First, they obeyed Jesus by getting in the boat and were thus in the middle of God's will. Sometimes he sends trials when we are in the center of his will because he has something bigger for us to experience. Second, as the following verses show, the disciples soon forgot Jesus's word. He told them, **Let's cross over to the other side of the lake**. Thus, whatever

happened along the way, they were going to reach the other side.

8:25 Fear of circumstances diminishes as righteous fear of Jesus increases.

8:28 Whatever power they possess over human beings, Satan's minions must bow to the authority of Jesus Christ.

8:34-37 It didn't matter to the people that a pitiful man had finally been set free from his suffering (8:35). The death of the pigs signaled a significant loss of revenue. Were Jesus to linger and cast out more demons, it would affect everyone—and the locals weren't interested in making such sacrifices. They **asked him to leave** (8:37).

When You Hit Rock Bottom

I HAVE BEEN ON THE SEA of Galilee. The guide told our group that the sea's location in the Jordan Rift causes tempests to flare up violently there with little or no notice. Getting caught in such a storm could be daunting, and the one that the disciples encountered came at night. In the dark, in the middle of the sea, the storm tested not only their boating expertise, but also their emotions.

When I read about what happened, I can feel their fear. I can see Peter drenched to the bone, along with the rest of the disciples in the boat. I'm not surprised that they woke Jesus up and asked him, "Teacher! Don't you care that we're going to die?" (MK 4:38). I probably would have done the same thing.

Sometimes it doesn't seem like God is in tune with our situations. Whatever our storms may be—whether health, finances, relationships, or employment—it can seem like God is asleep. Thus, when we find ourselves in stormy conditions we, like the disciples, may want to say, "Jesus, please wake up! We're in a mess, and we're afraid. Do something. We're not going to make it."

But it is precisely in those times when we feel weak and helpless that Jesus's authority is most visibly strong. God does some of his best work in those moments when we don't think he's working at all. Sometimes God lets you hit rock bottom so that you will discover he is the Rock at the bottom. Whatever the case, you can trust his work is motivated by a heart of love for your good (SEE RM 8:28).

Jesus got up from his slumber, faced the storm, and spoke to the sea: "Silence! Be still!" (MK 4:39). The Son of God gave two brief commands, and the storm obeyed. It stopped its noise; it hushed its fuss. Similar to a parent correcting an unruly toddler, Jesus told the sea to settle down. And, as simple and as immediately as that, there was a great calm.

Thunder and lightning might be chasing each other all around you. The wind could be blowing unexpected and unpleasant circumstances into your life. Nothing looks right. Nothing looks promising. All is night. But it is precisely in those times that Jesus's authority trumps the storm. With a simple word, he can calm the chaos.

So when you find yourself in a problem, don't forget the promises of God. Remember what Jesus has said. He is right there with you. Grab a pillow and trust him to calm the waves.

was delivered.[a] **37** Then all the people of the Gerasene region[A] asked him to leave them,[b] because they were gripped by great fear. So getting into the boat, he returned.

38 The man from whom the demons had departed begged him earnestly to be with him. But he sent him away and said, **39** "Go back to your home, and tell all that God has done for you." And off he went, proclaiming throughout the town how much Jesus had done for him.

A GIRL RESTORED AND A WOMAN HEALED

40 When Jesus returned, the crowd welcomed him,[c] for they were all expecting him.[d] **41** Just then, a man named Jairus came. He was a leader of the synagogue.[e] He fell down at Jesus's feet and pleaded with him to come to his house, **42** because he had an only daughter[f] about twelve years old, and she was dying.

While he was going, the crowds were nearly crushing him.[g] **43** A woman suffering from bleeding[h] for twelve years,[i] who had spent all she had on doctors[B] and yet could not be healed by any, **44** approached from behind and touched the end of his robe.[j] Instantly her bleeding stopped.

45 "Who touched me?" Jesus asked.

When they all denied it, Peter[c] said, "Master,[k] the crowds are hemming you in and pressing against you."[D]

46 "Someone did touch me," said Jesus. "I know that power has gone out from me."[l] **47** When the woman saw that she was discovered, she came trembling and fell down before him. In the presence of all the people, she declared the reason she had touched him and how she was instantly healed. **48** "Daughter," he said to her, "your faith has saved you.[E] Go in peace."[m]

49 While he was still speaking,[n] someone came from the synagogue leader's house and said, "Your daughter is dead. Don't bother[o] the teacher[p] anymore."

50 When Jesus heard it, he answered him, "Don't be afraid. Only believe, and she will be saved."[F] **51** After he came to the house, he let no one enter with him except Peter, John, James,[q] and the child's father and mother. **52** Everyone was crying[r] and mourning for her.[s] But he said, "Stop crying, because she is not dead but asleep."[t]

53 They laughed at him, because they knew she was dead. **54** So he[G] took her by the hand[u] and called out, "Child, get up!"[v] **55** Her spirit returned,[w] and she got up at once. Then he gave orders that she be given something to eat. **56** Her parents were astounded, but he instructed them to tell no one what had happened.[x]

COMMISSIONING THE TWELVE

9 Summoning the Twelve,[y] he gave them power and authority over all the demons and to heal diseases.[z] **2** Then he sent them to proclaim the kingdom of God and to heal the sick.[aa]

3 "Take nothing for the road,"[ab] he told them, "no staff,[ac] no traveling bag, no bread, no money; and don't take an extra shirt. **4** Whatever house you enter, stay there and leave from there. **5** If they do not welcome you, when you leave that town, shake off the dust from your feet as a testimony against them."[ad] **6** So they went out and traveled from village to village, proclaiming the good news and healing everywhere.

HEROD'S DESIRE TO SEE JESUS

7 Herod the tetrarch[ae] heard about everything that was going on.[af] He was perplexed, because some said that John had

[a] 8:36 Mt 4:24
[b] 8:37 1Kg 17:18; Lk 5:8; Ac 16:39
[c] 8:40 Lk 9:11
[d] 8:40-42 Mt 9:18-19; Mk 5:21-24
[e] 8:41 Lk 13:14; Ac 13:15; 18:8,17
[f] 8:42 Lk 7:12
[g] Mk 3:9
[h] 8:43 Lv 15:25
[i] 8:43-48 Mt 9:20-22; Mk 5:25-34
[j] 8:44 Nm 15:38-39; Dt 22:12; Mt 14:36; 23:5
[k] 8:45 Lk 5:5
[l] 8:46 Lk 5:17; 6:19; Ac 10:38
[m] 8:48 Lk 7:50
[n] 8:49-56 Mt 9:23-26; Mk 5:35-43
[o] 8:49 Lk 7:6
[p] Jn 11:28
[q] 8:51 Mk 3:17; 14:33; Lk 9:28
[r] 8:52 Lk 7:13
[s] Mt 11:17; Lk 23:27
[t] Jn 11:4,11; Ac 20:10
[u] 8:54 Mk 1:31
[v] Mt 11:5; Lk 7:14,22; Jn 11:43
[w] 8:55 Jdg 15:19; 1Sm 30:12
[x] 8:56 Mt 8:4
[y] 9:1 Lk 6:12-16
[z] Mt 10:1; Mk 3:13-15; 6:7
[aa] 9:2 Mt 10:5,7-8; Lk 4:43; 9:11,60; 10:1,9
[ab] 9:3-5 Mt 10:9-15; Mk 6:8-11; Lk 10:4-12; 22:35
[ac] 9:3 Mk 6:8
[ad] 9:5 Neh 5:13; Ac 13:51; 18:6
[ae] 9:7 Lk 3:1,19; 13:31; 23:7; Ac 13:1
[af] 9:7-9 Mt 14:1-2; Mk 6:14-16

[A] 8:37 Other mss read the Gadarenes   [B] 8:43 Other mss omit who had spent all she had on doctors   [C] 8:45 Other mss add and those with him   [D] 8:45 Other mss add and you say, 'Who touched me?'   [E] 8:48 Or has made you well   [F] 8:50 Or she will be made well   [G] 8:54 Other mss add having put them all outside

8:39 The man was to be a witness, spreading the good news of what God had done for him to the very people who wished Jesus to go away. We too must proclaim what he has done for us to those who have rejected him, in hope that they might believe.

8:41-42 Though many of the Jewish religious leaders were opposed to Jesus and his ministry, **Jairus** wasn't one of them.

8:43 Physical problems often lead to many other problems. This **woman** who had suffered **from bleeding for twelve years** was financially ruined, having spent every penny **on doctors** who couldn't help her. Moreover, her medical condition would've made her ceremonially unclean (see Lev 15:25-27), affecting her ability

to worship at the temple and to have contact with people.

8:45-46 Jesus was being accosted from every side. Everyone was touching him! But the Son of God knows when someone's persistent faith has accessed his spiritual authority (8:46).

8:56 Jesus told the astonished parents **to tell no one** of this because the formal acknowledgment of his messiahship awaited his entry into Jerusalem.

9:1-2 The Twelve refers to Jesus's small band of disciples whom he had named apostles (9:1; see 6:12-16). They had been with him everywhere, hearing him proclaim God's kingdom, watching him heal the sick, and observing as he rescued many from demonic oppression.

He gave **power and authority** to them so that they might go out in his name and do the same.

9:3-4 Jesus instructed them to take no provisions on their journey (9:3); rather, they were to accept hospitality from whoever would welcome them (9:4). Those who welcomed Jesus's kingdom message would welcome his ambassadors.

9:5 Those who rejected Jesus's disciples were spurning him and placing themselves in a position of judgment. To **shake off the dust** of a town **from [their] feet** was to separate themselves from those who separated themselves from God.

9:7 Jesus's reputation had reached every level of society, including those in political power.

a 9:8 Mt 11:14; 16:14; 17:3-
4,10–12; Lk 1:17; 4:26
b Mk 6:15
c 9:9 Lk 23:8
d 9:10–17 Mt 14:13–21; Mk
6:32–44; Jn 6:5–13
e 9:10 Mk 6:30
f Mt 11:21; Mk 8:22; Jn
1:44; 12:21
g 9:11 Lk 8:40
h 9:12 Lk 24:29
i Mt 15:23
j 9:13 Mt 16:9; Mk 8:19
k 9:16 Mk 7:34; Jn 11:41;
17:1
l Mt 26:26; Mk 8:7; 14:22;
Lk 24:30
m 9:18–20 Mt 16:13–16; Mk
8:27–29

n 9:19 Lk 9:7-8
o 9:20 Mt 1:17; Lk 23:35; Ac
3:18; Rv 12:10
p 9:21 Mt 12:16; 16:20;
Mk 7:36; 8:30; 9:9; Lk
5:14; 8:56
q 9:22–27 Mt 16:21–28; Mk
8:31–9:1
r 9:22 Lk 13:33; 18:31
s Mt 17:12,22–23; Lk 24:7
t Lk 17:25; 20:17; 1Pt 2:4
u Lk 20:1; 22:66
v Mt 27:63; Jn 2:19
w 9:23 2Tm 2:12–13
x Mt 10:38–39; Lk 14:27;
1Co 15:31
y 9:24 Lk 17:33; Jn 12:25
z 9:25 Lk 12:20
aa 9:26 Mt 10:33; Rm
1:16; 2Tm 1:8; Heb 11:16;
1Jn 2:28
ab Dn 7:10; Zch 14:5; Mt
24:30; Jn 1:51; Ac 1:11;
1Th 1:10
ac Lk 12:9; Rv 14:10
ad 9:27 Jn 8:52; Heb 2:9
ae Mt 10:23; 23:36; 24:34;
Mk 13:30; Lk 21:31–32
af 9:28–36 Mt 17:1–8; Mk
9:2–8
ag 9:28 Mk 14:33; Lk 8:51
ah Mt 14:23; Lk 3:21; 5:16;
6:12; 9:18

been raised from the dead, **8** some that Elijah had appeared,*a* and others that one of the ancient prophets had risen.*b* **9** "I beheaded John," Herod said, "but who is this I hear such things about?" And he wanted to see him.*c*

FEEDING OF THE FIVE THOUSAND

10 When the apostles returned,*d* they reported to Jesus all that they had done.*e* He took them along and withdrew privately to a^A town called Bethsaida.*f* **11** When the crowds found out, they followed him. He welcomed them,*g* spoke to them about the kingdom of God, and healed those who needed healing.

12 Late in the day,*h* the Twelve approached and said to him, "Send the crowd away,*i* so that they can go into the surrounding villages and countryside to find food and lodging, because we are in a deserted place here."

13 "You give them something to eat," he told them.

"We have no more than five loaves*j* and two fish," they said, "unless we go and buy food for all these people." **14** (For about five thousand men were there.)

Then he told his disciples, "Have them sit down^B in groups of about fifty each." **15** They did what he said, and had them all sit down. **16** Then he took the five loaves and the two fish, and looking up to heaven,*k* he blessed and broke them.*l* He kept giving them to the disciples to set before the crowd. **17** Everyone ate and was filled. They picked up twelve baskets of leftover pieces.

PETER'S CONFESSION OF THE MESSIAH

18 While he was praying in private*m* and his disciples were with him, he asked them, "Who do the crowds say that I am?"

19 They answered, "John the Baptist; others, Elijah; still others, that one of the ancient prophets has come back."^C,*n*

20 "But you," he asked them, "who do you say that I am?"

Peter answered, "God's Messiah."*o*

HIS DEATH AND RESURRECTION PREDICTED

21 But he strictly warned and instructed them to tell this to no one,*p* **22** saying,*q* "It is necessary that the Son of Man*r* suffer many things*s* and be rejected*t* by the elders, chief priests, and scribes,*u* be killed, and be raised the third day."*v*

⟶ HOPE WORDS ⟵

When you don't surrender to Christ, you surrender to chaos.

TAKE UP YOUR CROSS

23 Then he said to them all, "If anyone wants to follow after^D me, let him deny himself,*w* take up his cross daily,^E and follow me.*x* **24** For whoever wants to save his life will lose it, but whoever loses his life because of me will save it.*y* **25** For what does it benefit someone if he gains the whole world, and yet loses or forfeits himself?*z* **26** For whoever is ashamed of me and my words,*aa* the Son of Man will be ashamed of him when he comes in his glory*ab* and that of the Father and the holy angels.*ac* **27** Truly I tell you, there are some standing here who will not taste death*ad* until they see the kingdom of God."*ae*

THE TRANSFIGURATION

28 About eight days after this conversation,*af* he took along Peter, John, and James*ag* and went up on the mountain to pray.*ah*

---

^A 9:10 Other mss add *deserted place near a*   ^B 9:14 Lit *them recline*   ^C 9:19 Lit *has risen*   ^D 9:23 Lit *come after*   ^E 9:23 Other mss omit *daily*

Herod Antipas was **tetrarch** over Galilee. His father, Herod the Great, had been appointed by Rome to rule over Israel and had tried to kill the baby Jesus when he heard that a new king had been born (see Matt 2:16-18).
9:10-11 Notice that Jesus wasn't impatient with the masses that tracked him down. Rather, he **welcomed them**, taught them, and **healed** them.
9:13 By making them assess their situation, Jesus showed them that their resources were insufficient. Feeding the crowd was humanly impossible; it required divine assistance.
9:16-17 Jesus proved himself to be the source for the peoples' needs. He is a sufficient King who has an abundant supply.

9:20 Peter recognized Jesus as the Anointed One who is both King of the Jews and Savior of the world.
9:22 Notice that the correct appraisal of Christ's identity in **9:20** opened the door for Jesus to reveal further truth about himself.
9:23 To **deny** yourself is to place Jesus's glory ahead of your own. Taking up your **cross daily** is a clear allusion to crucifixion. As people condemned to it were required to carry their crosses to the place of execution, true disciples must daily submit to Christ's authority over their lives—even to the point of suffering and death. To **follow** King Jesus is to live according to God's comprehensive rule over every area of life.

9:24-25 In God's economy, true profit comes from giving away your life for God's purposes. Those who strive after this world's power, wealth, success, and values to the neglect of their spiritual lives will forfeit their experience of God's reality now and his kingdom reward at Christ's return (9:25).
9:27 Jesus was speaking of three of his disciples who, in a few days, would experience a foretaste of the glory of **the kingdom.**
9:28 **Peter, John, and James** were Jesus's inner circle of disciples, often accompanying him without the others (see 8:51; Mark 14:33).

29 As he was praying, the appearance of his face changed,[a] and his clothes became dazzling white.[b] **30** Suddenly, two men were talking with him — Moses and Elijah. **31** They appeared in glory and were speaking of his departure, which he was about to accomplish in Jerusalem.

32 Peter and those with him were in a deep sleep,[A,c] and when they became fully awake, they saw his glory and the two men who were standing with him. **33** As the two men were departing from him, Peter said to Jesus, "Master,[d] it's good for us to be here. Let us set up three shelters: one for you, one for Moses, and one for Elijah" — not knowing what he was saying.[e] **34** While he was saying this, a cloud appeared and overshadowed[f] them. They became afraid as they entered the cloud. **35** Then a voice came from the cloud,[g] saying: "This is my Son,[h] the Chosen One;[B,i] listen to him!"[j] **36** After the voice had spoken, Jesus was found alone. They kept silent, and at that time told no one what they had seen.

THE POWER OF JESUS OVER A DEMON

37 The next day,[k] when they came down from the mountain, a large crowd met him. **38** Just then a man from the crowd cried out, "Teacher, I beg you to look at my son, because he's my only child.[l] **39** A spirit seizes him; suddenly he shrieks, and it throws him into convulsions until he foams at the mouth; severely bruising him, it scarcely ever leaves him. **40** I begged your disciples to drive it out, but they couldn't."[m] **41** Jesus replied, "You unbelieving and perverse[c] generation,[n] how long will I be with you and put up with you?[o] Bring your son here."

42 As the boy was still approaching, the demon knocked him down and threw him into severe convulsions. But Jesus rebuked the unclean spirit, healed the boy,[p] and gave him back to his father.[q] **43** And they were all astonished at the greatness of God.[r]

THE SECOND PREDICTION OF HIS DEATH

While everyone was amazed at all the things he was doing,[s] he told his disciples, **44** "Let these words sink in:[D] The Son of Man is about to be betrayed into the hands of men."[t] **45** But they did not understand this statement;[u] it was concealed from them so that they could not grasp it,[v] and they were afraid to ask him about it.

WHO IS THE GREATEST?

46 An argument started among them about who was the greatest of them.[w] **47** But Jesus, knowing their inner thoughts,[E,x] took a little child and had him stand next to him. **48** He told them, "Whoever welcomes[F] this little child in my name welcomes me. And whoever welcomes me welcomes him who sent me.[y] For whoever is least among you — this one is great."[z]

IN HIS NAME

49 John responded,[aa] "Master, we saw someone driving out demons in your name,[ab] and we tried to stop him because he does not follow us."[ac] **50** "Don't stop him," Jesus told him, "because whoever is not against you is for you."[G,ad]

THE JOURNEY TO JERUSALEM

51 When the days were coming to a close for him to be taken up,[ae] he determined[H,af] to journey to Jerusalem.[ag] **52** He sent messengers ahead of himself,[ah] and on the way they entered a village of the Samaritans[ai]

a 9:29 Mk 16:12
b Ps 104:2; Dn 7:9; Mt 28:3
c 9:32 Gn 2:21; 15:12; 1Sm 26:12; Dn 8:18; 10:9; Mt 26:43
d 9:33 Lk 5:5; 9:49
e Mk 14:40
f 9:34 Lk 1:35; Ac 5:15
g 9:35 Ex 24:15-16; 2Pt 1:16-18
h Ex 4:23; Ps 2:7; Hs 11:1; Ac 13:33; Heb 1:5
i Ps 89:3; Is 42:1; Lk 23:35
j Ac 3:22
k 9:37-42 Mt 17:14-18; Mk 9:14-27
l 9:38 Lk 7:12
m 9:40 Lk 9:1; 10:17
n 9:41 Php 2:15
o Jn 14:9

p 9:42 Zch 3:2; Mt 8:26; Mk 1:25; Lk 4:35,39; Jd 9
q Lk 7:15
r 9:43 2Pt 1:16
s 9:43-45 Mt 17:22-23; Mk 9:30-32
t 9:44 Lk 9:22
u 9:45 Mk 6:52; Lk 2:50; 18:34; 24:25; Jn 10:6; 12:16; 16:17-19
v Lk 18:34; 24:16
w 9:46-48 Mt 18:1-5; Mk 9:33-37; Lk 22:24
x 9:47 Mt 9:4
y 9:48 Mt 10:40,42; Lk 10:16; Jn 13:20
z Lk 22:26
aa 9:49-50 Mk 9:38-40
ab 9:49 Mt 7:22; 12:27; Mk 16:17; Lk 10:17; Ac 19:13
ac Nm 11:28
ad 9:50 Mt 12:30; Lk 11:23
ae 9:51 Mk 16:19
af 2Kg 12:17; Is 50:7; Jr 42:15
ag Lk 13:22; 17:11; 18:31; 19:11,28
ah 9:52 Lk 10:1
ai Mt 10:5

A **9:32** Lit *were weighed down with sleep*   B **9:35** Other mss read *the Beloved*   C **9:41** Or *corrupt,* or *perverted,* or *twisted*; Dt 32:5   D **9:44** Lit "*Put these words in your ears*   E **9:47** Lit *the thoughts of their hearts*   F **9:48** Or *receives,* throughout the verse   G **9:50** Other mss read *against us is for us*   H **9:51** Lit *he stiffened his face to go*; Is 50:7

9:31 Moses and Elijah were talking about Jesus's death, resurrection, and ascension, which would open the door to salvation.
9:33 Peter suggested that they build **three shelters** in fulfillment of Zechariah 14:16-19, because he assumed it was time to inaugurate the kingdom.
9:36 Initially, **they told no one what they had seen** in obedience to Jesus's instructions (see Mark 9:9). After his resurrection, they could describe the glory that they had witnessed and heard (see 2 Pet 1:16-18).
9:45 What was it **they did not understand**? The disciples couldn't grasp how Jesus could

exercise extraordinary authority one moment and be killed the next.
9:46-47 The wisest thing to do with our concerns, emotions, thoughts, and desires is to come clean in prayer. Whether we speak about them or not, Jesus already knows about them the moment they enter our minds. Trying to hide them from him is pointless.
9:48 Kingdom greatness is not obtained in the way the world obtains greatness. It is achieved through service (see Mark 9:35-37), which includes caring for and valuing those with the lowest social standing who can do nothing for you in return. Children were a

prime example of this social tier in the first century.
9:49-50 The Twelve were not to think of themselves as an exclusive body of representatives; they were to rejoice that God's kingdom power was being manifested by others too. God's people ought to celebrate the ministries of fellow Christians when they are carried out in a spirit of love and faithfulness to God and his Word.
9:51 The time **for him to be taken up** is a reference to his death, resurrection, and ascension.
9:52-53 This passage reflects the racial and theological divide that existed between the Jews and the Samaritans (see, e.g., John 4:9, 20).

[a]9:53 Jn 4:9,20
[b]9:54 2Kg 1:9-16; Rv 13:13
[c]9:57-60 Mt 8:19-22
[d]9:60 Lk 8:1; 9:2; 16:16
[e]9:61 1Kg 19:20
[f]10:2 Mt 9:37-38; Jn 4:35
[g]Rv 14:15
[h]Mt 20:1
[i]2Th 3:1
[j]10:3 Mt 7:15; 10:16; Jn 10:12; Ac 20:29
[k]10:4 Lk 12:33; 22:35-36
[l]Mk 6:8; Lk 9:3; 22:35-36
[m]Mt 10:9-10

[n]10:5 Mt 11:26; Lk 10:21; 12:51
[o]10:6 Lk 7:50; 8:48; 24:36; Jn 20:19; Ac 15:33; 1Co 16:11; Jms 2:16
[p]10:7 Mt 10:10; 1Tm 5:18; 2Pt 2:13
[q]10:8 1Co 10:27
[r]10:9 Mt 10:8; 1Th 5:14
[s]Mt 12:28; Lk 11:20; 17:20
[t]Mt 10:7; Mk 1:15; 1Pt 4:7
[u]10:11 Mt 10:14; Mk 6:11; Lk 9:5; Ac 13:51; 18:6
[v]10:12 Mt 7:22; 13:1; Lk 17:31; 2Pt 3:10
[w]Rv 11:8
[x]Mt 10:15; 11:22,24; Lk 10:14
[y]10:13-15 Mt 11:20-24
[z]10:13 Ezk 16:23; Mt 23:13-16; Lk 6:24; Rv 9:12
[aa]Mt 11:21
[ab]Jn 12:21
[ac]Ex 3:20; Lk 19:37; Ac 2:22
[ad]Ezr 3:7; Jr 25:22; 47:4; Jl 3:4; Lk 6:17
[ae]Est 4:1,3; Dn 9:3; Jnh 3:6
[af]10:14 Ps 1:5; Mt 12:41
[ag]10:15 Mt 4:13; Lk 4:23,31; 7:1
[ah]Ac 2:33
[ai]Is 14:12-15; Ac 2:27
[aj]10:16 Mt 10:40; Jn 13:20
[ak]Mt 25:45; Lk 9:48; Jn 12:48
[al]Jn 5:23; 1Th 4:8
[am]10:17 Ezk 8:11
[an]10:17-20 Mk 16:17-18; Jn 12:31
[ao]10:17 Rv 9:20
[ap]Jn 10:25; 14:13

to make preparations for him. [53] But they did not welcome him, because he determined to journey to Jerusalem.[a] [54] When the disciples James and John saw this, they said, "Lord, do you want us to call down fire from heaven to consume them?"[A,b] [55] But he turned and rebuked them,[B] [56] and they went to another village.

FOLLOWING JESUS

[57] As they were traveling on the road someone said to him,[c] "I will follow you wherever you go." [58] Jesus told him, "Foxes have dens, and birds of the sky have nests, but the Son of Man has no place to lay his head." [59] Then he said to another, "Follow me."

"Lord," he said, "first let me go bury my father."

[60] But he told him, "Let the dead bury their own dead, but you go and spread the news of the kingdom of God."[d] [61] Another said, "I will follow you, Lord, but first let me go and say good-bye to those at my house."[e] [62] But Jesus said to him, "No one who puts his hand to the plow and looks back is fit for the kingdom of God."

SENDING OUT THE SEVENTY-TWO

10 After this, the Lord appointed seventy-two[c] others, and he sent them ahead of him in pairs to every town and place where he himself was about to go. [2] He told them,[f] "The harvest[g] is abundant, but the workers[h] are few. Therefore, pray to the Lord of the harvest to send out workers into his harvest.[i] [3] Now go; I'm sending you out like lambs among wolves.[j] [4] Don't carry a money-bag,[k] traveling bag,[l] or sandals;[m]

don't greet anyone along the road. [5] Whatever house you enter, first say, 'Peace[n] to this household.' [6] If a person of peace is there, your peace[o] will rest on him; but if not, it will return to you. [7] Remain in the same house, eating and drinking what they offer, for the worker is worthy of his wages.[p] Don't move from house to house. [8] When you enter any town, and they welcome you, eat the things set before you.[q] [9] Heal the sick[r] who are there, and tell them, 'The kingdom of God[s] has come near[t] you.' [10] When you enter any town, and they don't welcome you, go out into its streets and say, [11] 'We are wiping off even the dust of your town that clings to our feet as a witness against you.[u] Know this for certain: The kingdom of God has come near.' [12] I tell you, on that day[v] it will be more tolerable for Sodom[w] than for that town.[x]

UNREPENTANT TOWNS

[13] "Woe[y] to you,[z] Chorazin![aa] Woe to you, Bethsaida![ab] For if the miracles[ac] that were done in you had been done in Tyre and Sidon,[ad] they would have repented long ago, sitting in sackcloth and ashes.[ae] [14] But it will be more tolerable for Tyre and Sidon at the judgment[af] than for you. [15] And you, Capernaum,[ag] will you be exalted to heaven?[ah] No, you will go down to Hades.[ai] [16] Whoever listens to you listens to me.[aj] Whoever rejects you rejects me.[ak] And whoever rejects me rejects the one who sent me."[al]

THE RETURN OF THE SEVENTY-TWO

[17] The seventy-two[D,am] returned with joy, saying,[an] "Lord, even the demons[ao] submit to us in your name."[ap]

[A]9:54 Other mss add *as Elijah also did*   [B]9:55-56 Other mss add *and said, "You don't know what kind of spirit you belong to.* [56]*For the Son of Man did not come to destroy people's lives but to save them,"*   [C]10:1 Other mss read *seventy*   [D]10:17 Other mss read *The seventy*

9:54-55 The Son of God had not come to destroy but to save, to deliver, to heal (see John 3:17). Such should be the attitude of his followers as well.

9:57-58 Jesus's response in 9:58 means that following his call to become a disciple will become hard at times. There will be uncertainties. In fact, "All who want to live a godly life in Christ Jesus," Paul says, "will be persecuted" (2 Tim 3:12). Will you follow him no matter the cost?

9:59-60 Let me go bury my father (9:59) sounds like a reasonable request, but he wasn't asking to go to a funeral. He was referring to the *future* death of his father. He wanted to make sure he received his inheritance. Then, when his circumstances were secure, he'd be equipped to be a disciple.

Jesus challenged him: **Let the dead bury their own dead, but you go and spread the**

news of the kingdom of God (9:60). In other words, he said, let those who are *spiritually* dead worry about such things. Jesus calls you to be his follower right now, where you are, with whatever you have—not later, somewhere else, with a little bit more.

9:61-62 The man's mention of his family left the door open for them to persuade him to rethink his decision. To all who want to have it both ways—being the Lord's disciple *and* maintaining control of their own lives— Jesus insists, "You have to get off the fence to follow me."

10:5-8 The idea here is that those who accepted the kingdom message would support Jesus's workers by demonstrating hospitality.

10:12 The statement, **it will be more tolerable for Sodom than for that town**, is a reference to the wicked Old Testament city destroyed

by burning sulfur that rained from heaven (see Gen 19:24-25). Those who reject the clear revelation of God's kingdom message through his emissaries, then, will incur a more severe judgment than they. The rejection of greater light brings greater judgment.

10:13-15 The condemnation of these towns would be based on the revelation they'd received. **Capernaum** (10:15), in particular, had witnessed many of Jesus's miraculous works (see 4:31-41; 7:1-10), yet the majority of the city's inhabitants rejected him.

10:16 When Christ's disciples speak his Word, the listeners hear Christ; therefore, **whoever rejects [them] rejects** Jesus. And to reject Christ is to reject **the one who sent** him— God the Father. That chain reaction of rejection will lead to eternal damnation.

FOR THE NEXT PERSONAL
KINGDOM LIVING LESSON SEE PAGE 1219.

✎ KINGDOM LIVING ✎
PERSONAL
Do What You Know Now

God never tells you everything he is going to do or what he wants you to do all at once. He doesn't lay out the full plan step-by-step so that you know what to expect. If he did, there would be no need for faith. And "without faith it is impossible to please" him (Heb 11:6).

But God has told you something. Whatever he has instructed you to do in the circumstances you are in or in challenges you are facing, obey. However small, however insignificant it may seem—obey. However large, however daring it may seem—obey. Do what you know to do even if you don't know what end it is producing.

You can start with the simplest of all commandments to remember—though it's the most difficult to live out. I say it's simple to remember because it basically boils down to one word: love. I say it's difficult to live out because this one word contains the essence of all the other commandments we've ever been given (see Matt 22:37-40; Gal 5:14), "Love the Lord your God with all your heart, with all your soul, with all your strength, and with all your mind, and your neighbor as yourself" (Luke 10:27).

Start there, and you are on your way to living out your life as a kingdom disciple—despite the ups and downs you may be facing.

---

18 He said to them, "I watched Satan[a] fall from heaven like lightning.[b] **19** Look, I have given you the authority[c] to trample[d] on snakes[e] and scorpions[f] and over all the power of the enemy;[g] nothing at all will harm you.[h] **20** However, don't rejoice that[A] the spirits[i] submit to you,[j] but rejoice that your names are written[k] in heaven."

THE SON REVEALS THE FATHER

21 At that time[l] he[B] rejoiced in the Holy[C] Spirit[m] and said, "I praise[D] you, Father,[n] Lord of heaven and earth,[o] because you have hidden these things from the wise and intelligent[p] and revealed them to infants.[q] Yes, Father, because this was your good pleasure.[E,F] **22** All things have[F] been entrusted to me by my Father. No one knows who the Son is except the Father, and who the Father is except the Son, and anyone to whom the Son desires[G] to reveal him."[s] **23** Then turning to his disciples he said privately, "Blessed are the eyes that see the things you see! **24** For I tell you that many prophets and kings wanted to see the things you see but didn't see them; to hear the things you hear but didn't hear them."[t]

THE PARABLE OF THE GOOD SAMARITAN

25 Then[u] an expert in the law[v] stood up to test[w] him, saying, "Teacher,[x] what must I do to inherit eternal life?"[y] **26** "What is written in the law?" he asked him. "How do you read it?" **27** He answered, "**Love the Lord your God[z] with all your heart, with all your soul, with all your strength, and with all your mind,**"[aa] and "**your neighbor as yourself.**"[H,ab] **28** "You've answered correctly," he told him. "Do this and you will live."[ac]

29 But wanting to justify himself,[ad] he asked Jesus, "And who is my neighbor?"[ae] **30** Jesus took up the question and said: "A man was going down from Jerusalem to Jericho and fell into the hands of robbers. They stripped him, beat him up, and fled, leaving him half dead. **31** A priest happened

a 10:18 Mt 4:1,10; Ac 13:10; Rv 12:9
b Mt 28:3; Col 2:15
c 10:19 Mk 1:22
d Lk 21:24; Rv 11:2
e Gn 3:16; Mt 23:33; Rv 9:19
f Lk 11:12; Rv 9:3
g Mt 13:39; 1Co 15:25
h Ps 91:13; Mk 16:18; Ac 28:5
i 10:20 1Tm 4:1; 1Jn 4:1
j Mt 7:22-23
k Ex 32:32; Neh 9:38; Mal 3:16
l 10:21-24 Mt 11:25-27; 13:16-17
m 10:21 Lk 2:27; 4:1; 19:21; Ac 2:4
n Mt 7:21; Lk 23:34,46; Jn 8:42; 11:41; 12:27-28; 17:1-25
o Gn 14:19; Ac 17:24
p Is 44:25; Jr 8:9; Ac 13:7; 1Co 1:19-27; 3:19-20
q Ps 8:2; Mt 21:16
r Lk 2:14
s 10:22 Jn 1:18; 6:46; 7:29; 8:19; 10:15; 17:25-26
t 10:24 Jn 8:56; Heb 11:13; 1Pt 1:10-12
u 10:25-28 Mt 22:34-40; Mk 12:28-34
v 10:25 Lk 7:30
w Mt 16:1; 19:3
x Mt 8:19; Lk 3:12; Jn 1:38
y Mt 19:29; Lk 18:18; Jn 12:25; Rv 21:7
z 10:27 Lk 4:8
aa Dt 6:5
ab Lv 19:18
ac 10:28 Lv 18:5; Neh 9:29; Ezk 20:11; Rm 10:5; Gl 3:12
ad 10:29 Lk 16:15
ae Ex 20:16-17; Lv 6:2; 19:13-18; Pr 3:28-29; Mt 5:43; 19:19; Rm 13:9-10

A 10:20 Lit *don't rejoice in this, that*   B 10:21 Other mss read *Jesus*   C 10:21 Other mss omit *Holy*   D 10:21 Or *thank*, or *confess*   E 10:21 Lit *was well-pleasing in your sight*   F 10:22 Other mss read *And turning to the disciples, he said, "Everything has*   G 10:22 Or *wills*, or *chooses*   H 10:27 Lv 19:18; Dt 6:5

10:18 This is a reference to the judgment on **Satan** when he rebelled against God and was kicked out of **heaven** (see Isa 14:12-14). Not only does it affirm the preexistence of Jesus and that he was involved in Satan's judgment, but it gives insight into how the devil was sentenced to earth, setting the stage for the angelic conflict and the creation of humankind (see Eph 6:12; Heb 2:6-8).
10:20 To have a relationship with God—to be citizens of the kingdom and headed toward glory—is to be our supreme source of joy. Everything else is a bonus.
10:21 Infants here refers to those who trusted in Jesus's words and works through childlike faith.

10:24 Many Old Testament saints longed to **see** and **hear** the coming of the Messiah and his kingdom.
10:25 This concept of inheritance involves not merely entering the kingdom, which is by faith alone in Christ alone, but receiving the rewards and quality of life associated with following God.
10:27 Jesus identified these as the two greatest commands from the Old Testament (see Matt 22:34-40). To love **God** is to passionately pursue his glory; to love **your neighbor** is to compassionately, righteously, and responsibly seek his or her well-being. The two are inseparable.
10:29 The question implied that he had no objective way to determine whom he should

be loving. His assumption was that some people didn't qualify to be his neighbor and were therefore undeserving of his love.
10:31-32 Priests were responsible for interpreting the law and officiating in the temple. The Levites (the tribe from which the priests came) assisted them. Perhaps these men had fulfilled their religious obligations in Jerusalem and wanted to get home, or perhaps they were on their way to Jerusalem and didn't want to be late. Maybe they thought contact with the man would contaminate them or were afraid of being robbed too should they stop. Regardless, they didn't want to be bothered. Broken people need someone to show them compassion and give them life. Don't pass them by: take action.

a 10:33 Mt 10:5; Lk 9:52;
Ac 1:8
b Lk 7:13; 15:20
c 10:34 Is 1:6; Jms 5:14
d 10:37 Mt 23:23; Lk 1:72;
Jms 2:13
e 10:38 Jn 11:1,19-20; 12:2-3
f 10:39 Lk 8:35; Ac 22:3
g 10:40 Mk 4:38; 1Pt 5:7
h Rm 8:26

i 10:41 Lk 12:22; 1Co 7:32;
Php 4:6
j 10:42 Ps 16:5; 27:4;
Jn 6:27
k 11:1 Lk 3:21
l Lk 5:33
m 11:2-13 Mt 6:9-13
n 11:2 Jn 20:17; 1Pt 1:17
o Ps 9:10; Jn 10:25; 17:6
p Is 29:23; Lk 1:49; 1Pt 3:15
q Mk 9:1
r 11:3 Pr 30:8
s 11:4 Lk 6:12; 7:48; 24:47
t Mt 18:23-35
u Mt 26:41; Lk 4:13;
22:40,46; 1Co 10:13

to be going down that road. When he saw him, he passed by on the other side. **32** In the same way, a Levite, when he arrived at the place and saw him, passed by on the other side. **33** But a Samaritan*a* on his journey came up to him, and when he saw the man, he had compassion.*b* **34** He went over to him and bandaged his wounds, pouring on olive oil*c* and wine. Then he put him on his own animal, brought him to an inn, and took care of him. **35** The next day*A* he took out two denarii,*B* gave them to the innkeeper, and said, 'Take care of him. When I come back I'll reimburse you for whatever extra you spend.'

36 "Which of these three do you think proved to be a neighbor to the man who fell into the hands of the robbers?"

37 "The one who showed mercy*d* to him," he said.

Then Jesus told him, "Go and do the same."

MARTHA AND MARY

38 While they were traveling, he entered a village, and a woman named Martha*e* welcomed him into her home.*C* **39** She had a sister named Mary, who also sat at the Lord's*D* feet*F* and was listening to what he said.*E* **40** But Martha was distracted by her many tasks, and she came up and asked, "Lord, don't you care*g* that my sister has left me to serve alone? So tell her to give me a hand."*F,h*

41 The Lord*G* answered her, "Martha, Martha, you are worried and upset about many things,*I* **42** but one thing is necessary.*H,J* Mary has made the right choice,*I* and it will not be taken away from her."

> ⌁ **HOPE WORDS** ⌁
>
> *Forgiveness is not pretending like it didn't happen or didn't hurt. That's lying. Forgiveness is a decision to release a debt regardless of how you feel.*

THE LORD'S PRAYER

11 He was praying*k* in a certain place, and when he finished, one of his disciples said to him, "Lord, teach us to pray, just as John also taught his disciples."*l*

2 He said to them, "Whenever you pray, say,*m*

Father,*J,n*
your name*o* be honored as holy.*P*
Your kingdom come.*K,q*

3 Give us each day our daily bread.*L,r*

4 And forgive us our sins,*s*
for we ourselves also
forgive everyone
in debt to us.*M,t*
And do not bring us into temptation."*N,u*

A 10:35 Other mss add *as he was leaving*   *B* 10:35 A denarius = one day's wage.   *C* 10:38 Other mss omit *into her home*   *D* 10:39 Other mss read *at Jesus's*   *E* 10:39 Lit *to his word,* or *message*   *F* 10:40 Or *tell her to help me*   *G* 10:41 Other mss read *Jesus*   *H* 10:42 Some mss read *few things are necessary,* or *only one*   *I* 10:42 Lit *has chosen the good part,* or *has chosen the better portion* ; = the right meal   *J* 11:2 Other mss read *Our Father in heaven*   *K* 11:2 Other mss add *Your will be done on earth as it is in heaven*   *L* 11:3 Or *our bread for tomorrow*   *M* 11:4 Or *everyone who wrongs us*   *N* 11:4 Other mss add *But deliver us from the evil one*

10:33-35 The Jews' hatred of the Samaritans had historical roots (see 9:51-56; John 4:9, 20). When Assyria conquered the northern kingdom of Israel, many Israelites were exiled from the land, but some were left behind. Then the Assyrians brought many captives from other lands to Israel. As a result, many Jews intermarried with these peoples. The Samaritans of Jesus's day were descendants of those marriages, and the animosity between Jew and Samaritan was strong. Nevertheless, it was a Samaritan—not a Jewish religious leader—who **saw the man [and] had compassion** on him (Luke 10:33). Jesus chose to use a despised and rejected person to make his point.

Our neighbors, too, are found in any and every group. The church of Jesus Christ ought to be a place where wounded people of all backgrounds can come to receive love and life. **10:36-37** When you see a legitimate need with which you emotionally connect, and which is within your capacity to address, you are called in the name of Christ to demonstrate compassion. To experience the life, blessing, and reward that the kingdom has to offer, we are to reflect our vertical love for God through our horizontal love to others.

10:38-39 We see these sisters several times in the Gospels—the most well-known occasion being when Jesus raised their brother Lazarus from the dead (John 11:1-44). Interestingly, Scripture usually shows **Mary** at Jesus's **feet** (Luke 10:39). In John 11:32, she fell at Jesus's feet. In John 12:3, she anointed Jesus's feet. Here in Luke, she's listening at Jesus's feet. To sit at one's feet was the position of a learner in submission to a teacher.

10:40-42 Luke says **Martha was distracted by her many tasks** (10:40). It's easy for us to be distracted from God when we think we're ministering to him. So remember, when your work for the Lord damages your relationship with him, you need to reassess the amount of work and motivation for your service. God wants you to serve him—but not at the expense of spending quality time with him. If lately you are doing more for God but are colder toward God, if you are working harder but praying less, recall that it was **Mary [who] made the right choice** (10:42).

11:1 They had observed Jesus's commitment to and the results of his prayer, and they wanted to have the same experience.

11:2 Begin prayer by addressing God as **Father**. Regardless of what your earthly father is (or was) like, your heavenly Father is perfect. We are to honor his **name** (i.e., his character and reputation) **as holy**—that is, as separate from and transcendent over creation. Holiness, in fact, is God's chief characteristic. It's the attribute that ties all of his other attributes together. His love is holy; his justice is holy; his mercy is holy. He is "holy, holy, holy" (Isa 6:3).

11:3 We want to receive enough provision to last for years, but God will supply *today* everything that we need to accomplish his will *today*. This keeps us in **daily** dependence on him.

11:4 We are to pray that God would **forgive us our sins**. As the Holy Spirit reveals sin in our lives, we are to address it. After all, "If we confess our sins, he is faithful and righteous to forgive us our sins and to cleanse us from all unrighteousness" (1 John 1:9). Moreover, just as God in Christ forgave us, so we are called to **forgive** one another (see Eph 4:32).

ASK, SEARCH, KNOCK

5 He also said to them: "Suppose one of you[A] has a friend and goes to him at midnight and says to him, 'Friend, lend me three loaves of bread, **6** because a friend of mine on a journey has come to me, and I don't have anything to offer him.' **7** Then he will answer from inside and say, 'Don't bother me! The door is already locked, and my children and I have gone to bed. I can't get up to give you anything.' **8** I tell you, even though he won't get up and give him anything because he is his friend, yet because of his friend's shameless boldness,[B] he will get up and give him as much as he needs.[a]

9 "So[b] I say to you, ask,[c] and it will be given to you. Seek,[d] and you will find. Knock,[e] and the door will be opened to you. **10** For everyone who asks receives, and the one who seeks finds, and to the one who knocks, the door will be opened. **11** What father among you, if his son[c] asks for a fish, will give him a snake instead of a fish? **12** Or if he asks for an egg, will give him a scorpion? **13** If you then, who are evil,[f] know how to give good gifts to your children, how much more will the heavenly Father[g] give the Holy Spirit[h] to those who ask him?"

A HOUSE DIVIDED

14 Now[i] he was driving out a demon[j] that was mute.[k] When the demon came out, the man who had been mute spoke, and the crowds were amazed. **15** But some of them said, "He drives out demons by Beelzebul,[l] the ruler[m] of the demons."[n] **16** And others, as a test,[o] were demanding of him a sign[p] from heaven.

17 Knowing their thoughts,[q] he told them, "Every kingdom divided[r] against itself is headed for destruction, and a house divided against itself falls. **18** If Satan[s] also is divided against himself, how will his kingdom[t] stand? For you say I drive out demons by Beelzebul. **19** And if I drive out demons by Beelzebul, by whom do your sons[u] drive them out? For this reason they will be your judges. **20** If I drive out demons by the finger of God,[v] then the kingdom of God[w] has come upon you. **21** When a strong man, fully armed, guards his estate, his possessions are secure. **22** But when one stronger than he attacks and overpowers[x] him, he takes from him all his weapons[D,y] he trusted[z] in, and divides up his plunder.[aa] **23** Anyone who is not with me is against me,[ab] and anyone who does not gather with me scatters.

AN UNCLEAN SPIRIT'S RETURN

24 "When[ac] an unclean spirit[ad] comes out of a person, it roams through waterless places looking for rest,[ae] and not finding rest, it then[E] says, 'I'll go back to my house that I came from.' **25** Returning, it finds the house swept and put in order. **26** Then it goes and brings seven other spirits[af] more evil than itself, and they enter and settle down there. As a result, that person's last condition is worse than the first."[ag]

TRUE BLESSEDNESS

27 As he was saying these things, a woman from the crowd[ah] raised her voice and said to him, "Blessed is the womb that bore you and the one who nursed you!"[ai]

28 He said, "Rather, blessed are those who hear the word of God[aj] and keep it."[ak]

THE SIGN OF JONAH

29 As the crowds were increasing, he began saying: "This generation[al] is an evil generation.[am] It demands a sign,[an] but

---

a 11:8 Lk 18:1-6
b 11:9-13 Mt 7:7-11; Jn 14:13-14; 15:7; 16:24
c 11:9 Mt 18:19; 21:22; Mk 11:24; Jms 1:5-6,17; 1Jn 3:22; 5:14-15
d Dt 4:29; 1Ch 28:9; 2Ch 15:2; Pr 8:17; Is 55:6; Jr 29:13
e Lk 11:10; 12:36; 13:25; Ac 12:13,16; Rv 3:20
f 11:13 Rm 12:17; 1Th 5:22; 2Tm 3:13
g Mt 5:48
h Ps 51:11; Jn 1:33; Ac 2:4,38; Rm 8:9
i 11:14-23 Mt 9:32-34; 12:22-30; Mk 3:22-27; Jn 7:20; 8:48,52; 10:20
j 11:14 Mk 7:26
k Mt 7:37; 9:15-25; Lk 7:22
l 11:15 2Kg 1:2; Mt 10:25
m Lk 12:58
n Jn 12:31; 14:30; 16:11; Eph 2:2
o 11:16 Lk 10:25
p Jn 2:11; 8:6
q 11:17 Lk 5:22; Php 2:6
r Dn 5:28; 11:4; Lk 12:52-53

s 11:18 Mt 4:1,10; Ac 13:10
t Lk 4:5
u 11:19 Gl 3:7; 1Pt 5:13
v 11:20 Ex 8:19; 31:18; Dt 9:10; Ps 8:3
w Mt 19:24; 21:31,43; Lk 17:21
x 11:22 Jn 16:33; 1Jn 2:13
y Eph 6:11,13
z Ac 26:28
aa Is 49:24-26
ab 11:23 Mk 9:40; Lk 9:50
ac 11:24-26 Mt 12:43-45
ad 11:24 Mk 1:23-27; Lk 8:29; 9:42; Rv 18:2
ae Mt 11:29; Rv 4:8; 14:11
af 11:26 Lv 26:18-28; Dt 7:1; Pr 6:31; 26:25; Lk 8:2
ag Jn 5:14; 2Pt 2:20-22
ah 11:27 Lk 12:3
ai Lk 1:48; 23:29
aj 11:28 Lk 5:1; 8:21; Ac 13:7
ak Lv 22:31; Jn 13:17; Jms 1:22; Rv 1:3; 22:7
al 11:29 Lk 7:31; 17:25; 21:32
am 11:29-32 Mt 12:39-42; Mk 8:12
an 11:29 Lk 11:16

A 11:5 Lit *Who of you*   **B** 11:8 Or *persistence*   **C** 11:11 Other mss read *son asks for bread, would give him a stone? Or if he*   **D** 11:22 Gk *panoplia, the armor and weapons of a foot soldier; Eph 6:11,13*   **E** 11:24 Other mss omit *then*

11:5-8 Bold persistence in a relationship with God leads to needs being met.

11:9-10 We are not to sit back and wait for things to happen. Jesus calls us to **ask . . . seek . . . knock** in prayer (11:9).

11:13 The best heavenly gift that God gives to those who ask is **the Holy Spirit,** who in the new covenant delivers God's will to his children. The Spirit is available to operate on God's behalf through our prayers for our benefit and through us for the benefit of others.

11:16 The demand that Jesus give **a sign** to prove his authority suggested his many miracles weren't sign enough for them.

11:17-19 The devil will one day be defeated, but it won't be because he defeats himself (11:17-18). He'll be vanquished at the hands of King Jesus (see Rev 20:10). Furthermore, if

Jesus were driving out spirits by the hand of Satan, then by whose power were the followers of the religious leaders (their **sons**) driving **them out?** They couldn't condemn Jesus without condemning themselves (Luke 11:19).

11:20 If Jesus cast **out demons by the finger**—that is, the power—**of God,** then he must be the Messiah bringing his **kingdom.**

11:23 The refusal of Jesus's accusers to **gather** fellow Israelites to follow him as the Messiah made them complicit in the eventual destruction of the nation. There can be no neutrality when it comes to Jesus Christ. He is either the Messiah or he is Satan, but he cannot be a mere teacher or miracle worker.

11:24-26 It's not enough to be rid of demonic activity in one's life. The emptiness must be replaced by the Holy Spirit.

11:29-32 Jesus condemned those demanding **a sign** of him (11:29; see 11:16). Gentiles in **Nineveh** believed **Jonah,** though he performed no miracles (11:30). **The queen of the south** traveled from far away **to hear** Solomon's God-given **wisdom,** though he offered no heavenly signs (11:31). How much more should the crowds believe the Son of Man who is far **greater than** either Jonah or Solomon (11:32)? The only sign they would receive was **the sign of Jonah** (11:29), who had spent three days and nights in the belly of a huge fish, leading to the repentance of Gentiles. Similarly, Jesus would spend three days in the earth—dead and buried. Then he would rise again as proof of his identity as the Messiah, leading also to the repentance of the Gentiles (see Matt 12:40).

a 11:29 Jnh 1:1–4:9; Mt 16:4
b 11:30 Mk 2:10; Lk 5:24
c 11:31 1Kg 10:1; 2Ch 9:1
d Lk 10:14
e Heb 11:7
f 1Kg 4:34; Pr 1:1
g 11:33 Mt 5:15; Mk 4:21
h Lk 8:16
i 11:34–36 Mt 6:22-23
j 11:34 Jr 24:8; Mt 7:17
k 11:37 Lk 7:36
l 11:38 Heb 6:2
m Mt 15:2; Mk 7:2-5
n 11:39 Mt 23:25; Lk 12:20;
16:14; Heb 10:34
o Mk 7:22
p 11:40 Mt 23:17; Lk 12:20
q 11:41 Lk 12:33; Ac 24:17
r Ps 24:4; Ti 1:15

s 11:42 Lk 10:13
t Dt 14:22; Lk 18:12
u Mc 6:8; Zch 7:9; Mt
12:18,20; Jn 7:24; Ac 8:33
v Dt 6:5; Lk 10:27; Jn 5:42;
2Th 3:5
w 11:43 Mt 23:6; Mk 12:39;
Lk 20:46
x Jms 2:2
y 11:44 Mt 23:27
z 11:45 Lk 7:30
aa 11:46 Mt 23:4; Ac 27:10;
Gl 6:5
ab Mt 11:28-30; Ac 15:10
ac 11:47 Mt 2:23; Ac 7:52
ad Lk 20:15
ae 11:48 Mt 23:31
af Ac 22:20; Rm 1:32
ag 11:49 Pr 1:20–33; 8:1-36;
Mt 23:34
ah Lk 11:27; 13:1; 15:32;
21:9-10; Jn 13:16; Ac 1:2
ai 1Th 2:15; 2Tm 3:12
aj 11:50 Lk 11:29
ak Heb 9:26; Rv 18:24
al 11:51 Gn 4:9-10; Heb
12:24; 1Jn 3:12
am 24:20-22
an 11:52 1Co 14:6
ao 1Co 14:39
ap 11:53 Mk 6:19; Gl 5:1
aq 11:54 Ac 23:21
ar Is 29:21; Mt 22:15; Mk
3:2; 12:13; Lk 20:20; Jn 8:6

no sign will be given to it except the sign of Jonah.[A,a] 30 For just as Jonah became a sign to the people of Nineveh, so also the Son of Man[b] will be to this generation. 31 The queen of the south[c] will rise up at the judgment[d] with the men of this generation and condemn[e] them, because she came from the ends of the earth to hear the wisdom of Solomon,[f] and look — something greater than Solomon is here. 32 The men of Nineveh will stand up at the judgment with this generation and condemn it, because they repented at Jonah's preaching, and look — something greater than Jonah is here.

THE LAMP OF THE BODY

33 "No[g] one lights a lamp[h] and puts it in the cellar or under a basket,[B] but on a lampstand, so that those who come in may see its light. 34 Your eye is the lamp of the body.[i] When your eye is healthy, your whole body is also full of light. But when it is bad,[j] your body is also full of darkness. 35 Take care, then, that the light in you is not darkness. 36 If, therefore, your whole body is full of light, with no part of it in darkness, it will be entirely illuminated, as when a lamp shines its light on you."

RELIGIOUS HYPOCRISY DENOUNCED

37 As he was speaking, a Pharisee[k] asked him to dine with him. So he went in and reclined at the table. 38 When the Pharisee saw this, he was amazed that he did not first perform the ritual washing[C,l] before dinner.[m] 39 But the Lord said to him, "Now you Pharisees clean the outside of the cup and dish, but inside you are full of greed[n] and evil.[o] 40 Fools![D] Didn't he who made the outside make the inside too? 41 But give from what is within to the poor,[D,q] and then everything is clean[r] for you.

42 "But woe[s] to you Pharisees! You give a tenth[E,t] of mint, rue, and every kind of herb, and you bypass[F] justice[u] and love for God.[G,v] These things you should have done without neglecting the others.

43 "Woe to you Pharisees! You love the front seat[w] in the synagogues[x] and greetings in the marketplaces.

44 "Woe to you![H] You are like unmarked graves;[y] the people who walk over them don't know it."

45 One of the experts in the law[z] answered him, "Teacher, when you say these things you insult us too."

46 Then he said: "Woe also to you experts in the law! You load people with burdens[aa] that are hard to carry, and yet you yourselves don't touch these burdens with one of your fingers.[ab]

47 "Woe to you! You build tombs[i] for the prophets,[ac] and your fathers killed[ad] them. 48 Therefore, you are witnesses[ae] that you approve[J,af] the deeds of your fathers, for they killed them, and you build their monuments.[K] 49 Because of this, the wisdom of God[ag] said, 'I will send them prophets and apostles,[ah] and some of them they will kill and persecute,'[ai] 50 so that this generation[aj] may be held responsible for the blood of all the prophets shed since the foundation of the world[L,ak] — 51 from the blood of Abel[al] to the blood of Zechariah,[am] who perished between the altar and the sanctuary.

"Yes, I tell you, this generation will be held responsible.[M]

52 "Woe to you experts in the law! You have taken away the key to knowledge.[an] You didn't go in yourselves, and you hindered[ao] those who were trying to go in."

53 When he left there,[N] the scribes and the Pharisees began to oppose[ap] him fiercely and to cross-examine him about many things; 54 they were lying in wait[aq] for him to trap him in something he said.[O,ar]

A 11:29 Other mss add *the prophet*   B 11:33 Other mss omit *or under a basket*   C 11:38 Lit *he did not first wash*   D 11:41 Or *But donate from the heart as charity*   E 11:42 Or *a tithe*   F 11:42 Or *neglect*   G 11:42 Lit *the justice and the love of God*   H 11:44 Other mss add *scribes and Pharisees, hypocrites!*   I 11:47 Or *graves*   J 11:48 Lit *witnesses and approve*   K 11:48 Other mss omit *their monuments*   L 11:50 Lit *so that the blood of all . . . world may be required of this generation,*   M 11:51 Lit *you, it will be required of this generation*   N 11:53 Other mss read *And as he was saying these things to them*   O 11:54 Other mss add *so that they might bring charges against him*

11:39-41 Proof that one is clean on the inside is demonstrated through service to others, particularly charitable giving to those who can't pay you back (11:41). How you handle possessions reveals major truths about your inner life.
11:44 Instead of serving as safe spiritual guides for people, the Pharisees caused others to be contaminated by legalistic thinking—just as a Jew would become defiled by walking on an **unmarked** grave without knowing it (see Num 19:16).

11:46 He pronounced **woe** on these **experts in the [Mosaic] law** because their legal prescriptions went far beyond the Old Testament commandments so that they loaded people down with **burdens** too heavy to bear. They contributed to moving people further from God rather than closer to him.
11:47-52 While these men were happy to build **monuments** for dead **prophets**, it was the live ones they had a problem with (11:47-51). As their ancestors killed the Old Testament

prophets, so the Jewish religious leaders wanted to kill the Messiah. In reality, these **experts in the law** were anything but experts. They had **taken away the key to knowledge** (11:52). They lacked true knowledge of God, and they denied others access to the truth as well.
11:53-54 **The scribes and the Pharisees** considered Jesus their archenemy.

BEWARE OF RELIGIOUS HYPOCRISY

12 Meanwhile, a crowd of many thousands came together, so that they were trampling[a] on one another. He began to say to his disciples first,[b] "Be on your guard[c] against the leaven[A,d] of the Pharisees, which is hypocrisy.[e] **2** There is nothing covered that won't be uncovered,[f] nothing hidden that won't be made known.[g] **3** Therefore, whatever you have said in the dark will be heard in the light, and what you have whispered in an ear in private rooms[h] will be proclaimed on the housetops.[i]

FEAR GOD

4 "I say to you, my friends,[j] don't fear[k] those who kill the body, and after that can do nothing more. **5** But I will show you the one to fear: Fear[l] him who has authority to throw people into hell[m] after death. Yes, I say to you, this is the one to fear! **6** Aren't five sparrows sold for two pennies?[B] Yet not one of them is forgotten in God's sight.[n] **7** Indeed, the hairs of your head are all counted. Don't be afraid; you are worth more than many sparrows.

ACKNOWLEDGING CHRIST

8 "And I say to you, anyone who acknowledges[o] me before others, the Son of Man[p] will also acknowledge him before the angels of God,[q] **9** but whoever denies me before others will be denied before the angels of God.[r] **10** Anyone who speaks a word against the Son of Man will be forgiven,[s] but the one who blasphemes against the Holy Spirit[t] will not be forgiven. **11** Whenever[u] they bring you before synagogues and rulers and authorities,[v] don't worry[w] about how you should defend[x] yourselves or what you should say. **12** For the Holy Spirit will teach you at that very hour what must be said."[y]

THE PARABLE OF THE RICH FOOL

13 Someone from the crowd said to him, "Teacher,[z] tell my brother to divide the inheritance with me."

14 "Friend,"[c] he said to him, "who appointed me a judge or arbitrator over you?" **15** He then told them, "Watch out and be on guard[aa] against all greed,[ab] because one's life is not in the abundance of his possessions."[ac]

~ **HOPE WORDS** ~

Life isn't about what you accumulate this side of eternity. It's about what you accumulate for eternity.

---

16 Then he told them a parable:[ad] "A rich[ae] man's land was very productive. **17** He thought to himself, 'What should I do, since I don't have anywhere to store my crops? **18** I will do this,' he said. 'I'll tear down my barns and build bigger ones and store all my grain and my goods there. **19** Then I'll say to myself, "You have many goods stored up for many years. Take it easy;[af] eat, drink, and enjoy yourself." '[ag] **20** "But God said to him, 'You fool![ah] This very night your life is demanded of you. And the things you have prepared— whose will they be?'[ai] **21** "That's how it is with the one who stores up treasure[aj] for himself and is not rich toward God."[ak]

THE CURE FOR ANXIETY

22 Then he said to his disciples: "Therefore I tell you,[al] don't worry about your life, what you will eat; or about the body, what you will wear.[am] **23** For life is more than food and the body more than clothing. **24** Consider the ravens:[an] They don't sow or reap; they don't have a storeroom or a barn; yet God feeds them.[ao] Aren't you worth much

a 12:1 Lk 8:5
b Mt 16:5-6; Mk 8:14-15
c Jr 9:4; Lk 17:3; Ac 20:28
d Lk 13:21; Gl 5:9
e Mt 23:28; Mk 12:15; Gl 2:13; 1Pt 2:1
f 12:2-9 Mt 10:26-33; Mk 4:22; Lk 8:17
g 12:2 Lk 6:44
h 12:3 Mt 6:6; 24:26; Lk 12:24
i Ac 10:9
j 12:4 Ac 27:3
k Is 8:13; 51:12; Jr 1:8; Jn 6:20
l 12:5 Ps 147:11; Pr 1:7; Ac 10:2; Rv 14:7
m Mk 9:43; Jms 3:6
n 12:6 Ps 50:11
o 12:8 Mt 7:23; Jn 9:22
p Lk 5:24; 11:30
q Lk 15:10; Jn 1:51; Ac 10:3; Rm 10:9; Rv 3:5
r 12:9 Lk 9:26
s 12:10 Mt 12:31-32; Mk 3:28-30
t Lk 1:15,35; 2:25-26; 3:22
u 12:11-12 Mt 10:19-20; Mk 13:11; Lk 21:14-15
v 12:11 Lk 20:20; Eph 3:10; Col 2:15
w Php 4:6
x Ac 26:24
y 12:12 Pr 1:23; Jn 14:26

z 12:13 Lk 11:45
aa 12:15 1Tm 6:20; 2Tm 1:14; 4:15; 2Pt 3:17; 1Jn 5:21
ab Eph 5:3
ac Gn 12:5; Jb 20:20; 31:24; Ps 62:10
ad 12:16 Lk 5:36; 8:11
ae Lk 6:24; 16:19; 18:23; 19:2; 21:1
af 12:19 Mt 11:28; Mk 6:31; Rv 6:11; 14:13
ag Ec 2:24
ah 12:20 Jr 17:11; Lk 11:40
ai Ps 39:6; 49:10; Jr 17:11; Mt 16:26
aj 12:21 2Pt 3:7
ak Mt 6:19-20
al 12:22-32 Mt 6:25-34
am 12:22 Pr 31:25
an 12:24 1Kg 17:4,6; Jb 38:41; Ps 147:9; Pr 30:17
ao Rv 12:6

A 12:1 Or *yeast*   B 12:6 Lit *two assaria*; a small copper coin   C 12:14 Lit *Man*

12:1 Leaven, or yeast, slowly and imperceptibly permeates a batch of dough. Similarly, the undetected wicked influence of the Pharisees could spread to many—even the disciples—if not guarded against.
12:5 The one to truly **fear** is God, **who has authority to throw people into hell.**
12:10 Why is blasphemy of the Holy Spirit labeled the unforgiveable sin? Because it is deliberate, willful rejection of Christ whom the Holy Spirit reveals. To reject the Spirit's testimony of Christ is to reject the only means God has provided for salvation.

12:11-12 An example of the fulfillment of this promise (12:12) is seen in Peter's testimony in Acts 4:8-12.
12:13 This was an attempt to distract Jesus with temporal, earthly matters.
12:15 Greed appeals to people from all walks of life, regardless of income or social status. No one is immune to the attacks of covetousness. It is when the material takes priority over the spiritual. Remember, life does not consist of stuff. Don't let **possessions** take your eyes off Jesus.

12:16-21 The moral of this story is that God doesn't bless you just so you can build bigger storage spaces. He blesses you so that you can also bless others. The man's wealth is not the issue here; it's that he hoarded it for himself with no thought of God or the temporal nature of life. Though he was physically **rich,** he was spiritually poor. He had everything except **God**—which left him with nothing (12:21).
12:22-26 Worrying is foolish because it cannot bring about change to your situation. Think of it as a rocking chair: it will get you moving, but it can't take you anywhere.

Video Devotional

"FIRST"

When you put God's kingdom first, he will show up in your life in a way that will blow your mind.

more than the birds? [25] Can any of you add one moment to his life span[A] by worrying?[a] [26] If then you're not able to do even a little thing, why worry about the rest?

[27] "Consider how the wildflowers grow: They don't labor or spin thread. Yet I tell you, not even Solomon[b] in all his splendor was adorned like one of these. [28] If that's how God clothes the grass, which is in the field today and is thrown into the furnace tomorrow, how much more will he do for you — you of little faith?[c] [29] Don't strive for what you should eat and what you should drink, and don't be anxious. [30] For the Gentile world eagerly seeks[d] all these things, and your Father[e] knows that you need them.

[31] "But seek his kingdom,[f] and these things will be provided for you.[g] [32] Don't be afraid,[h] little flock,[i] because your Father delights[j] to give you the kingdom.[k] [33] Sell[l] your possessions and give to the poor.[m] Make money-bags[n] for yourselves that won't grow old, an inexhaustible treasure[o] in heaven, where no thief comes near and no moth destroys. [34] For where your treasure is, there your heart will be also.[p]

READY FOR THE MASTER'S RETURN

[35] "Be ready for service[B] and have your lamps lit.[q] [36] You are to be like people waiting for their master[r] to return from the wedding banquet[s] so that when he comes and knocks, they can open the door for him at once.[t] [37] Blessed will be those servants the master finds alert[u] when he comes. Truly I tell you, he will get ready,[c] have them recline at the table, then come and serve them.[v] [38] If he comes in the middle of the night, or even near dawn,[D] and

finds them alert, blessed are those servants. [39] But know this: If the homeowner had known at what hour the thief was coming,[w] he would not have let his house be broken into. [40] You also be ready,[x] because the Son of Man[y] is coming at an hour you do not expect."[z]

REWARDS AND PUNISHMENT

[41] "Lord," Peter asked, "are you telling this parable to us or to everyone?"

[42] The Lord said: "Who then is the faithful and sensible manager[aa] his master will put in charge of his household servants to give them their allotted food[ab] at the proper time? [43] Blessed is that servant whom the master finds doing his job when he comes. [44] Truly I tell you, he will put him in charge of all his possessions. [45] But if that servant says in his heart, 'My master is delaying his coming,'[ac] and starts to beat the male and female servants, and to eat and drink and get drunk, [46] that servant's master will come on a day he does not expect him and at an hour he does not know. He will cut him to pieces[E] and assign him a place with the unfaithful.[F] [47] And that servant who knew his master's will and didn't prepare himself or do it[G] will be severely beaten.[ad] [48] But the one who did not know and did what deserved[ae] punishment will receive a light beating. From everyone who has been given much, much will be required; and from the one who has been entrusted with much, even more will be expected.[H,af]

NOT PEACE BUT DIVISION

[49] "I came[ag] to bring fire on the earth, and how I wish it were already set ablaze!

---

[a] 12:25 Php 4:6
[b] 12:27 1Kg 10:4-7
[c] 12:28 Mt 8:26; 14:31; 16:8
[d] 12:30 Heb 11:14; 13:14
[e] Mt 5:16; 6:1; 11:27; Jn 8:42
[f] 12:31 Mt 5:6,20; Lk 11:2
[g] 1Kg 3:11-14; Mt 19:29; Mk 10:29-30
[h] 12:32 Lk 12:4,7
[i] Is 40:11; Ac 20:28; 1Pt 5:2-3
[j] Mt 11:26; Lk 10:21; Eph 1:5,9; Php 2:13
[k] Mt 13:19; 25:34; Lk 22:29
[l] 12:33-34 Mt 6:19-21
[m] 12:33 Ac 24:17
[n] Lk 10:4
[o] Mk 10:21; 2Co 4:7
[p] 12:34 1Pt 1:4
[q] 12:35-48 Mt 24:42-51; 25:1-13; Mk 13:33-37; Jn 13:4-5
[r] 12:36 2Pt 3:12
[s] Jn 2:1
[t] Rv 3:20
[u] 12:37 Rm 13:11
[v] Lk 17:8; 22:27
[w] 12:39 1Th 5:2
[x] 12:40 Lk 21:36
[y] Mk 2:10
[z] 1Th 5:2; 2Pt 3:10; Rv 3:3; 16:15
[aa] 12:42 Lk 16:1
[ab] 1Tm 6:8
[ac] 12:45 1Jn 2:28
[ad] 12:47 Dt 25:2; Jms 4:17   [ae] 12:48 Lv 5:17; Nm 15:29   [af] Lv 5:17; Mt 13:12; Rm 1:20; 2:14; 1Tm 1:13   [ag] 12:49-53 Mt 10:34-36; Mk 10:38

[A] 12:25 Or *add a cubit to his height*   [B] 12:35 Lit *"Let your loins be girded*; an idiom for tying up loose outer clothing in preparation for action; Ex 12:11
[C] 12:37 Lit *will gird himself*   [D] 12:38 Lit *even in the second or third watch*   [E] 12:46 Lit *him in two*   [F] 12:46 Or *unbelievers*   [G] 12:47 Lit *or do toward his will*,
[H] 12:48 Or *much*

12:29-32 It's one thing for unbelievers to worry, but believers who trust in the heavenly **Father** should not by filled with anxiety (12:29-30). Instead, Christ's disciples have access to the spiritual realm when they prioritize the **kingdom** of God (12:31), with its promises and provisions. As defenseless as his children are in the world, it would be the Father's joy to give them (the **little flock**) kingdom covering (12:32).
12:33-34 The disciples were to divest themselves of anything that would prohibit the pursuit of the kingdom and its priorities. They were to pursue spiritual treasures above physical ones. When we value heaven more than earth, we build and protect true wealth

that's unlike **treasure** accumulated here that is subject to decay and theft (12:33). The heart follows treasures and not vice versa. So wherever you want your **heart** to be, put your **treasure** there; your heart will follow it (12:34).
12:35-40 During the darkness of this present age, followers of Jesus are to **be ready** and active (12:35). Our witness must be visible and clear. We must live with a sense of expectancy as we wait for our master's appearing.
12:43-44 The faithful servant of Jesus is the one who is given a task, performs it, and is **blessed** by it (12:43). The reward that Jesus will give to the faithful steward will be far greater than the challenges encountered in this service (12:44).

12:47-48 Unfaithful believers will be weighed based on the level of their knowledge and responsibility, which means leaders will receive greater judgment than those who didn't have that level of responsibility (12:48).
12:49-53 Jesus would bring **division** and not **peace** (12:51) in that some would accept him, while others would reject him. In fulfillment of Scripture, in fact, he would bring division even within the same **household** (12:52; see Mic 7:6). His ministry would be **fire** that devours (Luke 12:49), but the goal of that blazing fire is national purification. This would involve Jesus's **baptism** (12:50)—which is not a reference to his baptism by John, but a metaphorical reference to his coming death

50 But I have a baptism to undergo,[a] and how it consumes[b] me until it is finished![c] **51** Do you think that I came here to bring peace on the earth?[d] No, I tell you, but rather division. **52** From now on, five in one household will be divided: three against two, and two against three.

53 They will be divided, father
        against son,
    son against father,
    mother against daughter,
    daughter against mother,
    mother-in-law against
        her daughter-in-law,
    and daughter-in-law
        against mother-in-law."[A,e]

INTERPRETING THE TIME

54 He also said to the crowds:[f] "When you see a cloud rising in the west, right away you say, 'A storm is coming,' and so it does.[g] **55** And when the south wind is blowing, you say, 'It's going to be hot,' and it is. **56** Hypocrites![h] You know how to interpret the appearance of the earth and the sky, but why don't you know how to interpret this present time?[i]

SETTLING ACCOUNTS

57 "Why don't you judge for yourselves what is right?[j] **58** As you are going with your adversary[k] to the ruler, make an effort to settle with him on the way. Then he won't drag you before the judge,[l] the judge hand you over to the bailiff, and the bailiff throw you into prison.[m] **59** I tell you, you will never get out of there until you have paid the last cent."[B,n]

REPENT OR PERISH

13 At that time,[o] some people came and reported to him about the Galileans[p] whose blood Pilate[q] had mixed with their sacrifices. **2** And he[c] responded to them, "Do you think that these Galileans were more sinful than all the other Galileans because they suffered these things?' **3** No, I tell you; but unless you repent, you will all perish as well. **4** Or those eighteen that the tower in Siloam[s] fell on and killed — do you think they were more sinful than all the other people who live in Jerusalem? **5** No, I tell you; but unless you repent, you will all perish as well."

THE PARABLE OF THE BARREN FIG TREE

6 And he told this parable:[t] "A man had a fig tree that was planted in his vineyard. He came looking for fruit on it and found none.[u] **7** He told the vineyard worker, 'Listen, for three years I have come looking for fruit on this fig tree and haven't found any. Cut it down![v] Why should it even waste the soil?'[w]

8 "But he replied to him, 'Sir,[D] leave it this year also, until I dig around it and fertilize it.[x] **9** Perhaps it will produce fruit next year, but if not, you can cut it down.'"

HEALING A DAUGHTER OF ABRAHAM

10 As he was teaching in one of the synagogues on the Sabbath,[y] **11** a woman was there who had been disabled by a spirit[E,z] for over eighteen years. She was bent over and could not straighten up at all.[F] **12** When Jesus saw her, he called out to her,[G] "Woman,

[a] 12:50 Ac 22:16; Rm 6:3; Eph 4:5
[b] 2Co 5:14
[c] Jn 19:28; 19:30
[d] 12:51 Lk 2:14
[e] 12:53 Mc 7:6
[f] 12:54-56 Mt 16:2-3
[g] 12:54 1Kg 18:43-44
[h] 12:56 Lk 6:42
[i] Lk 20:10; 21:8,30
[j] 12:57-59 Mt 5:25-26
[k] 12:58 1Pt 5:8
[l] 2Tm 4:8
[m] Pr 25:8
[n] 12:59 Lk 21:2

[o] 13:1 Mt 21:18-19; Mk 11:12-14
[p] Jn 4:45
[q] Mt 27:2
[r] 13:2 Jn 9:2
[s] 13:4 Jn 9:7
[t] 13:6 Lk 5:35; 12:16
[u] Mt 21:18-19; Mk 11:13

[v] 13:7 Mt 7:19; Lk 3:9; Jn 15:2; Rm 11:22   [w] Is 5:2   [x] 13:8 Lk 16:3   [y] 13:10 Lk 4:31; 6:6   [z] 13:11 Mt 8:17; Lk 4:33; 6:18; 7:21; 8:2,29; 9:39

[A] 12:53 Mc 7:6   [B] 12:59 Gk *lepton*, the smallest and least valuable copper coin in use   [C] 13:2 Other mss read *Jesus*   [D] 13:8 Or *Lord*   [E] 13:11 Lit *had a spirit of disability*   [F] 13:11 Or *straighten up completely*   [G] 13:12 Or *he summoned her*

and resurrection to bring about redemption for those who respond to him.

12:56 The problem was that they couldn't understand spiritual signs. Though many of them had seen the signs of his ministry, they refused to conclude that Jesus was the promised Messiah. They couldn't see what was right in front of their eyes.

12:57-59 Jesus compared the people's failure to discern the signs before them (see 12:54-56) with someone settling a legal dispute. Rather than waiting to address a matter in court, a person should seek to settle out of court to avoid prison time and to decrease the penalty that has to be paid (12:58-59). Likewise, those who continue to reject the Messiah while the day of opportunity to be reconciled to God is available, will in the end face a more severe judgment.

13:1-5 Even before **Pilate** confronts Jesus at the end of Luke's Gospel, readers learn of the Roman governor's violent nature. **Some people** told Jesus that he had killed some **Galileans** and **mixed** their **blood** with **their sacrifices** (13:1). Perhaps they wanted to hear Jesus condemn Pilate for that; instead, Jesus used the opportunity to urge his listeners to **repent** (13:3).

Repentance is the inner resolve and determination to turn from sin and toward the Lord. The goal of repentance is to reverse, avoid, limit, or cancel divine judgment and the consequences of sin. That **eighteen** people were **killed** when a **tower in Siloam fell on** them (13:4) is a sobering reminder that death can come when we least expect it—on the righteous and the unrighteous. Unless we as believers repent of sin, we are subject to

temporal judgment, including physical death. **Unless** the lost **repent**, they will **perish** eternally in hell (13:5).

13:6-9 A fig tree's well-being is dependent on its bearing **fruit** (13:9), and this parable follows Jesus's exhortation that people repent of sin (see 13:1-5). If good fruit is absent from a person's life, some kind of judgment is certain because inner repentance leads to an external demonstration of righteousness. Without visible fruit, professions of repentance are as genuine as a barren fig tree pretending to be healthy. **13:10-13** Though the woman had a physical ailment, Luke tells us twice that it was not the real source of her problem. She had been **disabled by a spirit** (13:11) and "bound" by "Satan" (13:16). Thus, she was under demonic attack. The evil spirit was the root, and her physical deformity was the fruit.

a 13:13 Mt 19:15; Mk 5:23;
6:2,5; 8:23; Lk 4:40
b Ac 15:16; Heb 12:12
c Jn 11:4
d 13:14 Mt 20:24; 21:15;
26:8; Mk 10:14,41; 14:4
e Ex 20:9; Ezk 46:1
f 13:15 Lk 6:42
g Lk 14:5,19; 1Co 9:9
h Lk 2:7,12,16
i Mt 12:11; Lk 14:5
j 13:16 Mt 4:1,10; Ac 13:10
k Mk 5:3; 15:1; 2Tm 2:9
l Gn 16:15; Jn 8:37; Heb
2:16
m 13:17 Lk 21:5; 1Co 16:9;
Php 1:28; 1Tm 5:14
n Ps 132:18; Is 45:16 LXX;
1Pt 3:16
o Is 12:5
p 13:18-19 Mt 13:31-32; Mk
4:30-32
q 13:20-21 Mt 13:33
r 13:21 Mt 16:6,11-12; Mk
8:15; Lk 12:1; 1Co 5:6-8;
Gl 5:9
s 13:22 Lk 9:51
t 13:23 Mt 22:14; Lk 18:26;
Ac 2:21; Rm 9:27; Eph 2:8;
1Pt 3:20; Rv 3:4

u 13:24 Mt 7:13-14
v 13:25 Mt 7:22-23; 10:33;
25:12
w 13:27 Ps 6:8; 2Tm 2:19;
Heb 3:12
x 13:28 Mt 13:42,50; 22:13;
24:51; 25:30
y 13:28-29 Mt 8:11-12
z 13:28 Mk 1:15; Lk 4:43
aa 13:30 Mt 19:30; 20:16;
Mk 10:31
ab 13:31 Mt 14:1
ac Mt 14:5; Mk 6:19; Jn
7:19-25; Ac 5:33
ad 13:32 Heb 2:10; 5:9; 7:28
ae 13:33 Ac 3:21; 17:3
af Mt 2:23; 21:11
ag Mk 8:31
ah 13:34-35 Mt 23:37-39;
Lk 19:41-44
ai 13:34 Heb 11:37
aj 2Ch 24:20-22; Mt 21:35;
Lk 20:15
ak Ps 147:2; Is 62:1,4

you are free of your disability." [13] Then he laid his hands on her,[a] and instantly she was restored[b] and began to glorify God.[c]

[14] But the leader of the synagogue, indignant[d] because Jesus had healed on the Sabbath, responded by telling the crowd, "There are six days when work should be done;[e] therefore come on those days and be healed and not on the Sabbath day."

[15] But the Lord answered him and said, "Hypocrites![f] Doesn't each one of you untie his ox[g] or donkey from the feeding trough[h] on the Sabbath and lead it to water?[i] [16] Satan[j] has bound[k] this woman, a daughter of Abraham,[l] for eighteen years — shouldn't she be untied from this bondage^A on the Sabbath day?"

[17] When he had said these things, all his adversaries[m] were humiliated,[n] but the whole crowd was rejoicing over all the glorious things he was doing.[o]

THE PARABLES OF THE MUSTARD SEED AND OF THE LEAVEN

[18] He said, therefore, "What is the kingdom of God like,[p] and what can I compare it to? [19] It's like a mustard seed that a man took and sowed in his garden. It grew and became a tree, and the birds of the sky nested in its branches."

[20] Again he said, "What can I compare the kingdom of God[q] to? [21] It's like leaven^B,[r] that a woman took and mixed into fifty pounds^C of flour until all of it was leavened."

THE NARROW WAY

[22] He went through one town and village after another, teaching and making his way to Jerusalem.[s] [23] "Lord," someone asked him, "are only a few people going to be saved?"[t]

He said to them, [24] "Make every effort to enter through the narrow door,[u] because I tell you, many will try to enter and won't be able [25] once the homeowner gets up and shuts the door.[v] Then you will stand outside and knock on the door, saying, 'Lord, open up for us!' He will answer you, 'I don't know you or where you're from.' [26] Then you will say, 'We ate and drank in your presence, and you taught in our streets.' [27] But he will say, 'I tell you, I don't know you or where you're from. Get away from me,[w] all you evildoers!' [28] There will be weeping and gnashing of teeth[x] in that place,[y] when you see Abraham, Isaac, Jacob, and all the prophets in the kingdom of God,[z] but yourselves thrown out. [29] They will come from east and west, from north and south, to share the banquet^D in the kingdom of God. [30] Note this: Some who are last will be first, and some who are first will be last."[aa]

JESUS AND HEROD ANTIPAS

[31] At that time some Pharisees came and told him, "Go, get out of here. Herod^ab wants to kill you."[ac]

[32] He said to them, "Go tell that fox, 'Look, I'm driving out demons and performing healings today and tomorrow, and on the third day I will complete my work.'^E,ad [33] Yet it is necessary that I[ae] travel today, tomorrow, and the next day, because it is not possible for a prophet^af to perish^ag outside of Jerusalem.

JESUS'S LAMENTATION OVER JERUSALEM

[34] "Jerusalem, Jerusalem,[ah] who kills the prophets and stones[ai] those who are sent to her.[aj] How often I wanted to gather your children[ak] together, as a hen gathers her

---

^A 13:16 Or isn't it necessary that she be untied from this bondage ^B 13:21 Or yeast ^C 13:21 Lit three sata; about forty liters ^D 13:29 Lit recline at the table ^E 13:32 Lit I will be finished

---

13:14-17 If **the leader of the synagogue** had known what fury Jesus was about to unleash with regard to his uncompassionate attitude (13:14), he perhaps would've kept his mouth shut. The exclamation **Hypocrites!** signaled that the synagogue leader and his companions didn't practice what they preached. Even **on the Sabbath**, they would **untie [their] ox or donkey** and **lead it to water** (13:15). Such care for an animal is expected and not the kind of work that God had prohibited by the Sabbath command. So, if an animal is worthy of such mercy, shouldn't **a daughter of Abraham**—a member of the covenant and its promises—be **untied from [her] bondage on the Sabbath day?** (13:16). Such stinging criticism from Jesus, rightly deserved, was humiliating (13:17).

13:18-19 While God's kingdom work began small and with seemingly insignificant people (fishermen and tax collectors), it would grow significantly and accommodate all of its citizens.
13:20-21 Over time, God's kingdom would continue to expand and work its way throughout the world.
13:24-27 Jesus made it clear that to enter the kingdom, one would have to accept him and his words. No other option was possible. He illustrated this by describing a **homeowner** shutting **the door** to his home, representing the kingdom (13:25). Once the entrance is closed, no one will be able to enter. Those who cry out for entry after it's too late will face the consequences. Meanwhile, the godly will be saved.

13:30 **Some who are last will be first, and some who are first will be last** implies a great reversal. For example, though many Jews would reject Jesus, Gentiles would receive him. Gentiles would be among the first to enter, while Jews would be the last.
13:31-33 Herod Antipas was the tetrarch over Galilee, appointed by the Romans. This warning was presumably a pretext to get Jesus out of their area (13:31). But even though it meant traveling through Herod's district, Jesus had to reach **Jerusalem**. That's where he would **complete [his] work** (13:32-33). He had a mission to fulfill and a schedule to meet, and nobody could thwart him.
13:34-35 At the thought of **Jerusalem**, the city that housed the temple, Jesus lamented over the centuries of rejecting God and his **proph-**

chicks under her wings,[a] but you were not willing![b] **35** See, your house is abandoned to you.[c] I tell you, you will not see me until the time comes when[A] you say, 'Blessed is he who comes in the name of the Lord'! "[B,d]

A SABBATH CONTROVERSY

14 One Sabbath, when he went in to eat[c] at the house of one of the leading Pharisees,[e] they were watching him closely.[f] **2** There in front of him was a man whose body was swollen with fluid. **3** In response, Jesus asked the law experts[g] and the Pharisees, "Is it lawful to heal on the Sabbath or not?"[h] **4** But they kept silent. He took the man, healed him, and sent him away. **5** And to them, he said, "Which of you whose son or ox falls into a well, will not immediately pull him out on the Sabbath day?"[i] **6** They could find no answer to these things.

TEACHINGS ON HUMILITY

7 He told a parable[j] to those who were invited, when he noticed how they would choose the best places[k] for themselves: **8** "When you are invited by someone to a wedding banquet, don't recline at the best place, because a more distinguished person[l] than you may have been invited by your host. **9** The one who invited both of you may come and say to you, 'Give your place to this man,' and then in humiliation, you will proceed to take the lowest place. **10** "But when you are invited, go and recline in the lowest place, so that when the one who invited you comes, he will say to you, 'Friend, move up higher.' You will then be honored[m] in the presence of all the other guests.[n] **11** For everyone who exalts himself will be humbled, and the one who humbles himself will be exalted."[o]

12 He also said to the one who had invited him, "When you give a lunch or a dinner, don't invite your friends, your brothers or sisters, your relatives, or your rich neighbors, because they might invite you back, and you would be repaid. **13** On the contrary, when you host a banquet,[p] invite those who are poor, maimed, lame, or blind.[q] **14** And you will be blessed, because they cannot repay you; for you will be repaid[r] at the resurrection of the righteous."[s]

THE PARABLE OF THE LARGE BANQUET

15 When[t] one of those who reclined at the table with him heard these things, he said to him, "Blessed is the one who will eat bread in the kingdom of God!"[u]

16 Then he told him: "A man was giving a large banquet and invited many. **17** At the time of the banquet, he sent his servant to tell those who were invited, 'Come, because everything is now ready.' **18** "But without exception[D] they all began to make excuses. The first one said to him, 'I have bought a field, and I must go out and see it. I ask you to excuse me.' **19** "Another said, 'I have bought five yoke of oxen, and I'm going to try them out. I ask you to excuse me.' **20** "And another said, 'I just got married,[v] and therefore I'm unable to come.' **21** "So the servant came back and reported these things to his master. Then in anger, the master of the house told his servant, 'Go out quickly into the streets and alleys of the city, and bring in here the poor, maimed, blind, and lame.'[w] **22** "'Master,' the servant said, 'what you ordered has been done, and there's still room.' **23** "Then the master told the servant, 'Go out into the highways and hedges and make them come in, so that my house may be filled. **24** For I tell you, not one of those people who were invited will enjoy my banquet.'"

THE COST OF FOLLOWING JESUS

25 Now[x] great crowds were traveling with him. So he turned and said to them: **26** "If

[a] **13:34** Dt 32:11; Ps 17:8; 36:7
[b] Jn 5:40
[c] **13:35** Is 64:11; Jr 12:7; 22:1-8
[d] Ps 118:26; Mt 21:9; Lk 19:38; Jn 12:13
[e] **14:1** Lk 7:36; 11:37
[f] Mk 3:2; Lk 6:7; 20:20
[g] **14:3** Lk 7:30; 14:30
[h] Mt 12:2; Mk 3:4; Lk 6:2,9; 13:14; Jn 5:10
[i] **14:5** Ex 21:33; Dt 22:4; Mt 12:11; Lk 13:15
[j] **14:7** Lk 5:36; 13:6
[k] Lk 11:43
[l] **14:8** Lk 7:2; Php 2:29; 1Pt 2:4
[m] **14:10** Jn 5:44; 7:18; Rm 2:7
[n] Pr 25:6-7; 29:23
[o] **14:11** Ezk 21:26; Mt 18:4; 23:12; Lk 1:51; 3:5; 18:14; Jms 4:10; 1Pt 5:5-6

[p] **14:13** Lk 5:29
[q] Lv 22:22; Lk 14:21
[r] **14:14** Rm 11:35; 12:19; 1Th 3:9; 2Th 1:6; Heb 10:30
[s] Ac 24:15
[t] **14:15-24** Mt 22:1-14
[u] **14:15** Lk 13:29; 22:16,30; Rv 9:9
[v] **14:20** Dt 24:5
[w] **14:21** Lk 14:13
[x] **14:25-33** Mt 10:37-38

---

ets. As a **hen** desires to protect her **chicks**, Jesus longed to do the same for Jerusalem (13:34). But since the holy city was rejecting the Messiah, he would have to reject the city. After Jesus's death and resurrection, Jerusalem would **not see** him again until his return to reign as King in his kingdom when believing Jews call out, **'Blessed is he who comes in the name of the Lord'!** (13:35).

14:2 The man was suffering from dropsy.

14:3-5 That they were unwilling to answer Jesus's question and remained **silent** showed that they were hypocrites (14:3-4). Any one of them would help a **son or [an] ox … on the Sabbath** if it fell

into a **well** (14:5). So why was it wrong in their eyes to do good to a man by healing him? They twisted God's law to suit themselves.

14:7-11 The Pharisees exalted themselves, assuming that they held important positions in the kingdom. But Jesus sought to teach them the relationship between humility and exaltation. We are to live with an eternal perspective in mind—not with a desire for notoriety. Followers of Christ are not to exalt themselves by presumptuously seeking positions of greatness; rather, they are to assume lower positions of service and allow God to exalt them. Humility is the true path to glory.

14:12-14 Inviting the outcasts of society would indicate that he had an eternal perspective, since repayment for such wouldn't come until **the resurrection** (14:14).

14:16-24 Jesus told a parable emphasizing that many who expected to be in the kingdom would be excluded. Since most of the Jews rejected Jesus, his kingdom message would be declared and received by others—by the Gentiles. There's no excuse for rejecting Jesus. The King and his kingdom must have priority.

14:26 Aren't children called to love and honor their parents (see Exod 20:12)? Aren't husbands

[a] 14:26 Mt 11:28; Mk 10:14; Lk 6:47; Jn 5:40
[b] Dt 21:15; 22:13; 24:3; Lk 16:13
[c] 14:27 Jn 19:17
[d] 14:28 Pr 24:27
[e] 14:33 Mt 19:21; Php 3:7; Heb 11:26
[f] 14:34-35 Mt 5:13; Mk 9:49-50
[g] 14:34 Jdg 9:45; Mk 9:50
[h] 14:35 Mt 11:15; 13:9; Mk 4:9
[i] 15:1-7 Mt 18:12-14
[j] 15:1 Mt 11:19; Lk 5:29
[k] 15:2 Lk 5:30; 7:39; Ac 11:3; Gl 2:12

[l] 15:3 Mk 12:1
[m] 15:4 Ps 119:176; Jr 50:6; Zch 11:16; Mt 10:6; 15:24
[n] 15:7 Jr 51:48; Rv 18:20
[o] 15:10 Lk 2:10
[p] 15:13 Lk 16:1
[q] Rm 6:2; 8:12; Gl 2:14; Col 3:7

anyone comes to me[a] and does not hate[b] his own father and mother, wife and children, brothers and sisters — yes, and even his own life — he cannot be my disciple. [27] Whoever does not bear his own cross[c] and come after me cannot be my disciple.

[28] "For which of you, wanting to build a tower, doesn't first sit down and calculate the cost[d] to see if he has enough to complete it? [29] Otherwise, after he has laid the foundation and cannot finish it, all the onlookers will begin to ridicule him, [30] saying, 'This man started to build and wasn't able to finish.'

[31] "Or what king, going to war against another king, will not first sit down and decide if he is able with ten thousand to oppose the one who comes against him with twenty thousand? [32] If not, while the other is still far off, he sends a delegation and asks for terms of peace. [33] In the same way, therefore, every one of you who does not renounce[A] all his possessions[e] cannot be my disciple.

[34] "Now,[f] salt[g] is good, but if salt should lose its taste, how will it be made salty? [35] It isn't fit for the soil or for the manure pile; they throw it out. Let anyone who has ears to hear listen."[h]

THE PARABLE OF THE LOST SHEEP

15 All[i] the tax collectors[j] and sinners were approaching to listen to him. [2] And the Pharisees and scribes were complaining, "This man welcomes sinners[k] and eats with them."

[3] So he told them this parable:[l] [4] "What man among you, who has a hundred sheep and loses one of them,[m] does not leave the ninety-nine in the open field[B] and go after the lost one until he finds it? [5] When he has found it, he joyfully puts it on his shoulders, [6] and coming home, he calls his friends and neighbors together, saying to them, 'Rejoice with me, because I have found my lost sheep!' [7] I tell you, in the same way, there will be more joy in heaven[n] over one sinner who repents than over ninety-nine righteous people who don't need repentance.

THE PARABLE OF THE LOST COIN

[8] "Or what woman who has ten silver coins,[C,D] if she loses one coin, does not light a lamp, sweep the house, and search carefully until she finds it? [9] When she finds it, she calls her friends and neighbors together, saying, 'Rejoice with me, because I have found the silver coin I lost!' [10] I tell you, in the same way, there is joy in the presence of God's angels[o] over one sinner who repents."

THE PARABLE OF THE LOST SON

[11] He also said: "A man had two sons. [12] The younger of them said to his father, 'Father, give me the share of the estate I have coming to me.' So he distributed the assets[E] to them. [13] Not many days later, the younger son gathered together all he had and traveled to a distant country, where he squandered[p] his estate in foolish living.[q]

[A] 14:33 Or *leave*   [B] 15:4 Or *the wilderness*   [C] 15:8 Gk *ten drachmas*   [D] 15:8 A Gk drachma was equivalent to a Roman denarius = one day's wage
[E] 15:12 Or *life*, or *livelihood*, also in v. 30

---

called to love their wives as Christ loved the church (see Eph 5:25)? What did Jesus mean? The parallel passage in Matthew helps explain. In Matthew 10:37, Jesus said, "The one who loves a father or mother more than me is not worthy of me; the one who loves a son or daughter more than me is not worthy of me." The point is that Jesus deserves priority over every other relationship. If you must choose between Jesus and **a** family member, then, Jesus wins.

14:27 A condemned person had to carry his cross to his crucifixion site, so Jesus's listeners knew what he was talking about. Many had seen it happen. Jesus was telling them that becoming his disciple would involve some form of suffering. Not every Christian disciple's suffering is the same, but every Christian disciple will suffer. This is because to **bear [your] cross** and follow Jesus means to identify with him. And as Jesus told his disciples, "If they persecuted me, they will also persecute you" (John 15:20).

14:33 You are a *steward* of all you have; you are not an *owner*. God has given you pos-

sessions to manage. You are to thank him for them, use them for his glory, and bless others with them. What you must *not* do is claim ownership.

14:34-35 If salt should lose its taste, how will it be made salty? The obvious answer is that it won't be (14:34). The saltiness of salt is what makes it salt! Likewise, unless a Christian is willing to endure the costly nature of being a disciple—which is an integral part of being one—he is useless to the kingdom of God (14:35).

15:1-2 As far as the religious leaders were concerned, **sinners** were to be avoided—not welcomed. They thought Jesus should be hanging out with religious people who were serious about keeping the law.

15:5-7 Jesus clearly considered joy and celebration to be the most natural response to finding a lost lamb. Hanging out with safe sheep when one is lost is as absurd as hanging out with only righteous people when you want to urge lost people to repent or to encourage erring believers to be restored to the Father. If you want to rescue the lost, you've got to go where

they are. Sinners who repent, and erring saints who return, experience restored fellowship with God, and **heaven** rejoices (15:7).

15:8-10 The principle here is the same as that of the previous parable. The Lord goes to great lengths to see salvation and restoration take place in a sinner's life. Do we?

15:11-13 This story is usually called the parable of the Prodigal Son. However, the prodigal son—the reckless and wasteful son who got himself lost—is not the focus of the story. He's an essential character, but ultimately the parable is about the older brother because Jesus was speaking to the Pharisees and scribes (see 15:1-3). Jesus wanted these self-righteous leaders who had no compassion on the lost to see themselves in that brother.

The younger of the **two sons** had become tired of the restrictions of living at home. He wanted to spread his wings; he wanted his freedom. In requesting his inheritance, it was tantamount to wishing his father were dead (15:11-12). The younger son was thus independent, unencumbered, and well funded.

14 After he had spent everything, a severe famine struck that country, and he had nothing.^A **15** Then he went to work for one of the citizens of that country, who sent him into his fields to feed pigs.^a **16** He longed to eat his fill from^B the pods that the pigs were eating, but no one would give him anything. **17** When he came to his senses,^c he said, 'How many of my father's hired workers have more than enough food, and here I am dying of hunger!^D **18** I'll get up, go to my father, and say to him, "Father, I have sinned^D against heaven^c and in your sight. **19** I'm no longer worthy^d to be called your son. Make me like one of your hired workers."' **20** So he got up and went to his father. But while the son was still a long way off, his father saw him and was filled with compassion.^e He ran, threw his arms around his neck, and kissed^f him. **21** The son said to him, 'Father, I have sinned against heaven and in your sight. I'm no longer worthy to be called your son.'

22 "But the father told his servants, 'Quick! Bring out the best robe^g and put it on him; put a ring^h on his finger and sandals^i on his feet. **23** Then bring the fattened calf^j and slaughter it, and let's celebrate with a feast, **24** because this son of mine was dead and is alive again;^k he was lost and is found!' So they began to celebrate.

25 "Now his older son was in the field; as he came near the house, he heard music and dancing. **26** So he summoned one of the servants, questioning what these things meant. **27** 'Your brother is here,' he told him, 'and your father has slaughtered the fattened calf because he has him back safe and sound.'^E

28 "Then he became angry and didn't want to go in. So his father came out and pleaded with him. **29** But he replied to his father, 'Look, I have been slaving many years for you, and I have never disobeyed your orders, yet you never gave me a goat so that I could celebrate with my friends. **30** But when this son of yours came, who has devoured your assets^f with prostitutes,^l you slaughtered the fattened calf for him.'

31 "'Son,'^G he said to him, 'you are always with me,^m and everything I have is yours. **32** But we had to celebrate and rejoice, because this brother of yours was dead and is alive again; he was lost and is found.'"

THE PARABLE OF THE DISHONEST MANAGER

16 Now he said to the disciples: "There was a rich^n man who received an accusation that his manager^o was squandering^p his possessions. **2** So he called the manager in and asked, 'What is this I hear about you? Give an account of your management,^q because you can no longer be my manager.'

3 "Then the manager said to himself, 'What will I do since my master is taking the management away from me? I'm not strong enough to dig; I'm ashamed to beg. **4** I know what I'll do so that when I'm removed from management, people will welcome me into their homes.'

^a 15:15 Lv 11:7; Dt 14:8
^b 15:18 Ex 10:16
^c Mt 21:25; Jn 3:27
^d 15:19 Lk 7:6-7
^e 15:20 Mt 9:36; Mk 1:41; Lk 7:13; 10:33
^f Gn 29:13; 33:4; 45:15; 2Sm 14:33
^g 15:22 Zch 3:3-5
^h Gn 41:42; Est 3:10; 8:2
^i Ezk 16:10
^j 15:23 1Sm 28:24
^k 15:24 Lk 15:32; Rm 11:15; 2Co 4:10; Col 2:13

^l 15:30 Pr 29:3
^m 15:31 Jn 8:35
^n 16:1 Lk 16:19
^o Lk 12:42
^p Lk 15:13
^q 16:2 1Tm 1:4

^A 15:14 Lit and he began to be in need   ^B 15:16 Other mss read to fill his stomach with   ^C 15:17 Lit to himself   ^D 15:17 Or dying in the famine; v. 14   ^E 15:27 Lit him back healthy   ^F 15:30 Or life, or livelihood   ^G 15:31 Lit Child

And it soon became clear why he wanted to leave: **He squandered his estate in foolish living** (15:13). A person's heart is revealed by his credit card statement. "Where your treasure is, there your heart will be also" (12:34). **15:15-17** The young man became so desperate that he accepted a job feeding **pigs** (15:15). Don't miss that. This is a Jewish man accepting a job to feed unclean animals. **The pods** were carob pods, the fruit of the carob tree, which were used to feed livestock. Since no one gave the prodigal anything to eat (15:16), the pigs were doing better than he. His newly acquired *freedom* had come at a high cost. Sometimes God lets us experience a tremendous fall because that's what it takes to open our eyes (15:17). **15:20-22** This is a beautiful picture of salvation and the restoration of erring saints. A destitute sinner comes to a holy God in repentance and faith with nothing to offer but desperate need. God the Father responds with love and **compassion** (15:20), granting the sinner all the privileges of sonship in the family and showering him with blessings—"every spiritual blessing in the heavens in Christ" (Eph 1:3).

15:25-30 Finally, Jesus introduced his listeners to the **older son**. Since he's telling this parable to the Pharisees and scribes (see 15:1-3), everything in the story leads us to the response of the older son. He was coming in from **the field**—which means he had been working—when **he heard music and dancing** (15:25). That meant there was a party going on. When he learned that the celebration was for his brother, **he became angry** and refused to go inside (15:26-28). The young fool had run off, wasted his inheritance, and wrecked his life. Then he came home to be treated like a king?

When his father tried to plead with him, the older son pointed to his years of service and obedience (15:28-29). In spite of all his hard work, he never even received **a goat** to **celebrate with [his] friends** (15:29). **But when this son of yours came** (notice that he didn't refer to him as *my brother* but as "this son of yours"), **you slaughtered the fattened calf for him** (15:30). In other words, "I slave for you all these years and get nothing. But he blows your money on decadence and gets a bash." **15:31-32** The Pharisees and scribes were angry with Jesus for welcoming tax collectors and sinners (see 15:1-2) because they failed to understand God's heart. He longs for the **lost** to be **found**. He's filled with joy when a single sinner repents and a relationship is restored (15:32).

16:3-4 The manager may have been dishonest, but he wasn't stupid. Immediately, the wheels of his mind started spinning: **What will I do? . . . I'm not strong enough to dig; I'm ashamed to beg** (16:3). He didn't have the physique to be a ditch digger, and he was too proud to stand on the street with a tin cup. He was a white-collar guy who didn't want to give up his lifestyle. He needed a plan so that when his job was gone, **people [would] welcome** him and provide for him (16:4).

a 16:8 Lk 18:6
b Mt 12:32; Lk 20:34
c Jn 12:46; Eph 5:8; 1Th 5:5
d 16:9 Lk 11:41
e Mt 6:24; 1Tm 6:10
f 16:10 Mt 25:21-23
g Lk 19:17
h 16:13 Mt 6:24

i 16:13 Lk 14:26
j 16:14 2Tm 3:2
k Lk 23:35
l 16:15 Lk 10:29; 18:9
m 1Sm 16:7; Ps 17:3; Pr 21:2;
Rm 8:27
n Dt 24:4
o 16:16-17 Mt 5:18; 11:12-
13; 24:35; Mk 13:31
p 16:16 Mt 7:12; 22:40; Ac
13:15; Rm 3:21
q Mt 4:23
r 16:17 Mt 5:18
s 16:18 Mt 5:32; 19:9; Mk
10:11-12
t Mt 1:19; 19:9
u Ex 20:14; Lv 20:10; Pr
6:32; 2Pt 2:14
v 16:19 Ex 28:6; 35:35; Est
8:15; Pr 31:22; Ezk 27:16;
Rv 18:16
w 16:20 Ac 3:2
x 16:21 Lk 15:16
y Mt 15:27
z 1Kg 21:19
aa 16:22 Jn 13:23

5 "So he summoned each one of his master's debtors. 'How much do you owe my master?' he asked the first one.

6 " 'A hundred measures of olive oil,' he said.

" 'Take your invoice,' he told him, 'sit down quickly, and write fifty.'

7 "Next he asked another, 'How much do you owe?'

" 'A hundred measures of wheat,' he said.

" 'Take your invoice,' he told him, 'and write eighty.'

APPLICATION QUESTIONS

READ LUKE 16:8-13

– What are some possessions that you value more than anyone else in the world values them?

– What are some possessions that are prized as highly valuable by our culture but not by you?

---

8 "The master praised the unrighteous manager*a* because he had acted shrewdly. For the children of this age*b* are more shrewd than the children of light*c* in dealing with their own people.*A* **9** And I tell you, make friends*d* for yourselves by means of worldly wealth*B,e* so that when it fails,*c* they may welcome you into eternal dwellings. **10** Whoever is faithful*f* in very little*g* is also faithful in much, and whoever is unrighteous in very little is also unrighteous in much. **11** So if you have not been faithful with worldly wealth, who will trust you with what is genuine? **12** And if you have not been faithful with what belongs to someone else, who will give you what is your own? **13** No*h* servant can serve

two masters, since either he will hate*i* one and love the other, or he will be devoted to one and despise the other. You cannot serve both God and money."

KINGDOM VALUES

14 The Pharisees, who were lovers of money,*j* were listening to all these things and scoffing*k* at him. **15** And he told them, "You are the ones who justify*l* yourselves in the sight of others, but God knows your hearts.*m* For what is highly admired by people is revolting*n* in God's sight.

16 "The*o* Law and the Prophets*p* were until John; since then, the good news of the kingdom of God*q* has been proclaimed, and everyone is urgently invited to enter it.*D* **17** But it is easier*r* for heaven and earth to pass away than for one stroke of a letter in the law to drop out.

18 "Everyone*s* who divorces*t* his wife and marries another woman commits adultery,*u* and everyone who marries a woman divorced from her husband commits adultery.

THE RICH MAN AND LAZARUS

19 "There was a rich man who would dress in purple and fine linen,*v* feasting lavishly every day. **20** But a poor man named Lazarus, covered with sores, was lying at his gate.*w* **21** He longed to be filled*x* with what fell from the rich man's table,*y* but instead the dogs*z* would come and lick his sores. **22** One day the poor man died and was carried away by the angels to Abraham's side.*E,aa* The rich man also died and was

---

A 16:8 Lit *own generation*   *B* 16:9 Lit *unrighteous money*, also in v. 11   *C* 16:9 Other mss read *when you fail*, or *pass away*   *D* 16:16 Or *everyone is forcing his way into it*   *E* 16:22 Or *to Abraham's bosom*; lit *to the fold of Abraham's robe*; Jn 13:23

16:5-7 Clearly he was being dishonest toward his employer, but he wasn't trying to get his job back. He was trying to ingratiate himself with his boss's debtors so that they might take him in or give him a job. **16:8-9** The **master** was impressed because even though the manager was out of a job, he had cleverly found a way to provide for his future. **The children of this age are more shrewd than the children of light** implies that unbelievers are often sharper than believers are (16:8). Though the manager had messed up his past, the man cunningly set things in motion to secure his future. So what should believers do? **Make friends . . . by means of worldly wealth so that when it fails, they may welcome you into eternal dwellings** (16:9).

Christians ought to use their earthly resources wisely and generously for kingdom purposes. In this way, lives will be changed and people saved by the gospel. "Shrewd" kingdom people will be greeted in eternity by a welcoming committee of friends whose

lives were forever transformed by their righteous use of worldly wealth.

16:10-12 If you aren't dependable in small things, you're not likely to be dependable in more significant ones. You must be trustworthy with what God has loaned you. The only way to properly use money and possessions is to use them in service to God.

16:13 Either your **money** will serve God, or you will ask **God** to serve your money. Use your resources with eternity in mind.

16:16 **The Law and the Prophets** is a shorthand way of referring to the Old Testament.

16:17 God's Word is more reliable than creation; it will last forever and will not fail.

16:18 Marriage was God's idea. In the beginning, he declared that a man and a woman come together as husband and wife "become one flesh" (Gen 2:24). Therefore, divorce and remarriage without a biblically authorized reason (see the notes on Matt 5:32; 19:4-9) ignores the authority of Scripture and results in adultery, since God has not canceled the original marriage.

16:19-21 The contrasts between the two men couldn't be starker. From a purely earthly perspective, the rich man (representing the Pharisees) was the clear winner. But Jesus was about to provide a heavenly perspective, highlighting that one's economic circumstances do not necessarily imply God's approval or disapproval.

16:22-24 **Abraham's side** (or bosom) is an idiom for heaven (16:22). In the Greek translation of the Old Testament, the Greek word *hades* was used to translate the Hebrew word *sheol*—the grave, the realm of the dead. In the New Testament, the unrighteous are tormented in **Hades** (16:23; see 10:15). Thus, it is synonymous with hell.

Many people argue that those who die simply cease to exist. But Scripture claims otherwise. The two men had different destinations: the poor man went up; the rich man went down. While some Christians prefer to believe that the unrighteous experience annihilation after death rather than conscious, eternal punishment, Jesus disagrees. The

buried. **23** And being in torment[a] in Hades,[b] he looked up and saw Abraham a long way off, with Lazarus at his side. **24** 'Father Abraham!'[c] he called out, 'Have mercy on me and send Lazarus to dip the tip of his finger in water and cool my tongue, because I am in agony[d] in this flame!'

25 "'Son,'[A] Abraham said, 'remember that during your life you received your good things,[e] just as Lazarus received bad things, but now he is comforted here,[f] while you are in agony. **26** Besides all this, a great chasm has been fixed between us and you, so that those who want to pass over from here to you cannot; neither can those from there cross over to us.'

27 "'Father,' he said, 'then I beg you to send him to my father's house — **28** because I have five brothers — to warn[g] them, so they won't also come to this place of torment.'

29 "But Abraham said, 'They have Moses and the prophets;[h] they should listen to them.'

30 "'No, father Abraham,' he said. 'But if someone from the dead goes to them, they will repent.'

31 "But he told him, 'If they don't listen to Moses and the prophets, they will not be persuaded if someone rises from the dead.'"[i]

WARNINGS FROM JESUS

17 He[j] said to his disciples, "Offenses will certainly come,[B] but woe[k] to the one through whom they come![l] **2** It would be better for him if a millstone were hung around his neck and he were thrown into the sea than for him to cause one of these little ones to stumble.[m] **3** Be[n] on your guard. If your brother sins,[c] rebuke[o] him, and if he repents, forgive[p] him. **4** And if he sins against you seven times in a day, and comes back to you seven times, saying, 'I repent,' you must forgive him."

FAITH AND DUTY

5 The[q] apostles[r] said to the Lord, "Increase our faith."[s]

6 "If you have faith the size of[D] a mustard seed," the Lord said, "you can say to this mulberry tree, 'Be uprooted and planted in the sea,' and it will obey you.

7 "Which one of you having a servant tending sheep or plowing will say to him when he comes in from the field, 'Come at once and sit down to eat'? **8** Instead, will he not tell him, 'Prepare something for me to eat, get ready, and serve me while I eat and drink; later you can eat and drink'?[u] **9** Does he thank that servant because he did what was commanded?[E] **10** In the same way, when you have done all that you were commanded, you should say, 'We are worthless[v] servants; we've only done our duty.'"

TEN MEN HEALED

11 While traveling to Jerusalem,[w] he passed between[F] Samaria and Galilee.[x] **12** As he entered a village, ten men with leprosy[G,y] met

---

[a] 16:23 Is 50:11
[b] Mt 11:23
[c] 16:24 Lk 3:8; 16:30; 19:9; Jn 8:33,39,53
[d] Is 66:24; Mt 25:41
[e] 16:25 Lk 6:24
[f] Mt 11:28
[g] 16:28 Ac 2:40; 8:25
[h] 16:29 Lk 24:27,44; Jn 1:45; Ac 26:22; 28:23
[i] 16:31 Mt 28:11-15; Jn 12:10-11
[j] 17:1-3 Mt 18:6-7; Mk 9:42; 1Co 11:19
[k] 17:1 Lk 22:22
[l] Mt 13:41

[m] 17:2 1Co 8:9
[n] 17:3-4 Mt 18:15,21-22
[o] 17:3 Lv 19:17
[p] Mt 6:14
[q] 17:5-6 Mt 17:19-20; Mk 9:28-29
[r] 17:5 Lk 6:13
[s] Mk 9:24
[t] 17:6 Mt 13:31; Mk 4:31; Lk 13:19
[u] 17:8 Lk 12:35-37
[v] 17:10 Jb 22:2-3; 35:7; Mt 25:30; Rm 11:35
[w] 17:11 Lk 9:51
[x] Jn 4:3-4
[y] 17:12 Lv 13:45-46

[A] 16:25 Lit *Child*   [B] 17:1 Lit "*It is impossible for offenses not to come*   [C] 17:3 Other mss add *against you*   [D] 17:6 Lit *faith like*   [E] 17:9 Other mss add *I don't think so*   [F] 17:11 Other mss read *through the middle of*   [G] 17:12 Gk *lepros*; a term for various skin diseases; see Lv 13-14

---

rich man was *not* annihilated. Not only did he undergo torment, but he could also see Lazarus in comfort **a long way off**, speak to Abraham of his **agony**, and cry out for **mercy** (16:23-24). His faculties were intact.

16:25 The rich man was receiving the just consequences of a life that had rejected God. He'd neither acknowledged God nor sought to care for his neighbor Lazarus with the wealth God had given him. His punishment was just.

16:26 Part of what makes the judgment of hell so awful is that it is forever. There's no escape.

16:27 His reference to Abraham as **Father** (cf. 16:24) shows that the rich man was Jewish, a descendant of Abraham, a member of the covenant people of Israel. Thus, he represents the Pharisees who thought they were right with God simply because of their ancestry.

16:29 In other words, he said, "Your brothers have God's Word. Let them heed it. If they believe God's promise of eternal life like their father Abraham did, they will be saved."

16:30 "Give them a tremendous miracle—a resurrection from the dead," he reasoned, "and then they'll believe and turn to God."

16:31 If one will not believe God's Word, a miracle will not convince him. Though Jesus had performed countless miracles, still the Pharisees refused to believe he was the Messiah. And while he would rise **from the dead**, even that miracle would not persuade them (see Acts 5:30-33). They were unwilling to believe.

17:2 Jesus warned against causing defenseless, vulnerable believers **to stumble**, to fall into sin. At the final judgment, the one who led them to sin will be better off to have a huge rock **hung around his neck** before being dropped in the ocean to drown. That's how severe God's retribution against such a person will be.

17:4 The number **seven** doesn't denote a limit to forgiveness. In the Bible, seven is the number of completion. Thus, our forgiveness of one another is to be complete. We are to always be ready to forgive our brothers and sisters when they repent.

17:5-6 The apostles wanted Jesus to give them a supersized faith (17:5), but Jesus said, "You only need a mustard-seed-sized faith." The *size* of the faith, then, isn't the issue. The *right kind* of faith is. That's because the right

kind of faith packs a powerful punch. A **mustard seed** is incredibly small (17:6). Don't be concerned with how big your faith is; be concerned with how big *the object of your faith* is. We don't require tremendous faith. All we need is genuine faith in our tremendous God.

17:7-10 The point here is that true faith, mustard-seed faith, submits to divine authority. The duty of **a servant** is to honor and obey his or her master (17:7). The reason why many Christians lack the faith to forgive (see 17:3-5) is that they're out of spiritual alignment. They make demands of God, and they're unwilling to submit to him. If you are out of alignment with your Master, you're not acting with mustard-seed faith. Trust God and obey him in the little things. Then you won't need him to "increase [your] faith" (17:5) because you'll have the right kind of faith to do what seems impossible.

17:12-13 These **ten men** all had the same tragic problem: **leprosy** (17:12). Upon learning that Jesus was visiting their town, they cried out, **Jesus, Master, have mercy on us!** (17:13). Indeed, they were in desperate need

Video Devotional

"WHY WE SHOULD PRAY ALWAYS"

Prayer is more than a few words thrown toward the ceiling. It is an ongoing fellowship with the living God.

---

him. They stood at a distance [13] and raised their voices, saying, "Jesus, Master,[a] have mercy on us!"

[14] When he saw them, he told them, "Go and show yourselves to the priests."[b] And while they were going, they were cleansed.

[15] But one of them, seeing that he was healed, returned and, with a loud voice, gave glory to God.[c] [16] He fell facedown[d] at his feet, thanking him. And he was a Samaritan.[e]

[17] Then Jesus said, "Were not ten cleansed? Where are the nine? [18] Didn't any return to give glory to God except this foreigner?" [19] And he told him, "Get up and go on your way. Your faith has saved you."[A,f]

THE COMING OF THE KINGDOM

[20] Being[g] asked by the Pharisees when the kingdom of God would come,[h] he answered them, "The kingdom of God is not coming with something observable; [21] no one will say,[B] 'See here!' or 'There!' For you see, the kingdom of God is in your midst."[C]

[22] Then he told the disciples: "The days are coming[i] when you will long to see one of the days of the Son of Man, but you won't see it.[j] [23] They will say to you,[k] 'See there!' or 'See here!' Don't follow or run after them.[l] [24] For as the lightning flashes from horizon to horizon and lights up the sky, so the Son of Man will be in his day.[m] [25] But first it is necessary that he suffer many things and be rejected by this generation.[n]

[26] "Just as it was in the days of Noah,[o] so it will be in the days of the Son of Man: [27] People went on eating, drinking, marrying and giving in marriage[p] until the day Noah boarded the ark,[q] and the flood came and destroyed them all. [28] It will be the same as it was in the days of Lot:[r] People went on eating, drinking, buying, selling, planting, building. [29] But on the day Lot left Sodom, fire and sulfur rained from heaven and destroyed[s] them all. [30] It[t] will be like that on the day the Son of Man is revealed. [31] On that day, a man on the housetop, whose belongings are in the house, must not come down to get them. Likewise the man who is in the field must not turn back. [32] Remember Lot's wife![v] [33] Whoever tries to make his life secure[D,E] will lose it, and whoever loses his life will preserve it.[w] [34] I tell you, on that night[x] two will be in one bed; one will be taken and the other will be left. [35] Two women will be grinding grain together; one will be taken and the other left."[F]

[37] "Where, Lord?"[y] they asked him.

He said to them, "Where the corpse is, there also the vultures[z] will be gathered."

THE PARABLE OF THE PERSISTENT WIDOW

18 Now he told them a parable on the need for them to pray[aa] always and not give up.[ab] [2] "There was a judge in a certain town who didn't fear God[ac] or respect

---

[a] **17:13** Lk 5:5
[b] **17:14** Lv 13:2–14:32; Mt 8:4; Lk 5:14
[c] **17:15** Mt 9:8; Mk 2:12; Lk 2:14; 5:26; Jn 9:24; Ac 4:21; 12:23; Rm 4:20
[d] **17:16** 1Sm 20:41; 2Sm 14:22; Mt 17:6; 1Co 14:25
[e] Mt 10:5; Jn 4:9
[f] **17:19** Mt 9:22; Mk 10:52; Lk 5:20; 18:42
[g] **17:20-21** Mt 24:23; Mk 13:21
[h] **17:20** Lk 19:11; Ac 1:6
[i] **17:22** Dt 32:35; Is 2:12; Jr 7:32; Am 4:2; Lk 5:35; 19:43; 21:6; 23:29
[j] Am 5:18
[k] **17:23-24** Mt 24:23,27; Mk 13:21
[l] **17:23** Lk 21:8
[m] **17:24** 1Co 1:8
[n] **17:25** Mt 16:21; Lk 9:22

[o] **17:26-27** Mt 24:37-38   [p] **17:27** Lk 20:34-35   [q] Gn 6:14   [r] **17:28** Gn 19:1-26   [s] **17:29** Gn 19:24-25   [t] **17:30-35** Mt 24:17,39-41; Mk 13:15
[u] **17:30** Mt 16:27; 24:44; 1Co 1:7; 2Th 1:7; 1Pt 1:7; 4:13   [v] **17:32** Gn 19:26   [w] **17:33** Mt 10:39; Jn 12:25   [x] **17:34** Lk 1:78-79   [y] **17:37** Lk 17:20
[z] Ezk 29:5; 32:4; 39:17-20   [aa] **18:1** Lk 11:5-13; 21:36; 1Th 5:17   [ab] 2Co 4:1   [ac] **18:2** Ps 147:11; Pr 1:7; Ac 10:2; Rv 14:7

[A] **17:19** Or *faith has made you well*   [B] **17:21** Lit *they will not say*   [C] **17:21** Or *within you*   [D] **17:33** Other mss read *to save his life*   [E] **17:33** Or *tries to retain his life*   [F] **17:35** Some mss include v. 36: *"Two will be in a field: One will be taken, and the other will be left."*

---

of heavenly intervention. Not only were they suffering from the dreaded physical skin condition, but lepers had to identify themselves by yelling, "Unclean! Unclean!" so that people would not get close enough to be contaminated by them. They had to live apart from others and could not participate in communal life (see Lev 13:45-46). Their condition was incurable from an earthly perspective.
17:14 According to Leviticus 13–14, **the priests** were responsible for examining those with skin diseases and pronouncing them either clean or unclean. Once the men were declared "clean," they could return to full participation in the covenant community under the blessing of God.
17:15-16 This guy didn't care what anyone thought: he was not ashamed to give God vocal praise and to pay physical homage for intervening in his life. Many people, even believers, only want physical blessings from the Lord and lose out on the true spiritual blessings that come through worship, praise,

and thanksgiving. (See the note on 10:33-35 on Samaritans.)
17:19 The word translated **saved** can also mean "deliver" or "make well," depending on the context.
17:20-21 The King was standing in front of them. He was the one who would usher in his **kingdom**, yet they didn't recognize him.
17:24 The coming of the Son of Man will be clear to all. It will not happen in secret.
17:25 The disciples still didn't understand that Jesus had come to suffer and die as an atoning sacrifice for sin. His return to rule on his throne in his millennial kingdom is still future.
17:26-29 Jesus compared the time of his future coming to **the days of Noah** (17:26). Back then there was both deliverance and destruction—deliverance for Noah and his family, and destruction for everyone else. **People went** about their daily lives, giving no attention to God, until **the flood came** and his judgment fell (17:27). Similarly, it will be like

the days of Lot (17:28). People were absorbed in the normal activities of life so that they failed to take God seriously. But when **Lot left Sodom**, God's retribution fell on the city (17:29). The rapture will introduce **the days of the Son of Man** (17:26).
17:34-37 A great separation of humanity will take place. No matter their location or the time of day, some **will be taken** in judgment, and some **will be left** to enter into the kingdom (17:34-35). People will be split apart based on their relationship to God. Where will this happen? Everywhere. Just as a dead body draws vultures, those who are spiritually dead will draw divine punishment (11:37).
18:2-3 From the outset, this doesn't look good for the **widow** (18:3). Since the **judge** cared nothing for **God** or **people** (18:2), what could persuade him to rule in her favor? Moreover, in those days, if a widow didn't remarry and had no family to care for her, she could easily end up destitute.

people. ³ And a widow[a] in that town kept coming to him, saying, 'Give me justice against my adversary.'

⁴ "For a while he was unwilling, but later he said to himself, 'Even though I don't fear God or respect people, ⁵ yet because this widow keeps[b] pestering me,[A] I will give her justice, so that she doesn't wear me out[B] by her persistent coming.' "

⁶ Then the Lord said, "Listen to what the unjust judge says. ⁷ Will not God grant justice[c] to his elect[d] who cry out to him day and night?[e] Will he delay[f] helping them?[C] ⁸ I tell you that he will swiftly grant them justice. Nevertheless, when the Son of Man comes,[g] will he find faith on earth?"

THE PARABLE OF THE PHARISEE AND THE TAX COLLECTOR

⁹ He[h] also told this parable to some who trusted in themselves[i] that they were righteous[j] and looked down[k] on everyone else: ¹⁰ "Two men went up to the temple to pray,[l] one a Pharisee and the other a tax collector. ¹¹ The Pharisee was standing[m] and praying like this about himself:[D] 'God, I thank you that I'm not like other people — greedy,[n] unrighteous,[o] adulterers,[p] or even like this tax collector. ¹² I fast[q] twice a week; I give a tenth[E,r] of everything I get.'

¹³ "But the tax collector, standing far off,[s] would not even raise his eyes to heaven[t] but kept striking his chest[u] and saying,

'God, have mercy on me,[F,v] a sinner!'[W] ¹⁴ I tell you, this one went down to his house justified[x] rather than the other; because everyone who exalts himself will be humbled, but the one who humbles himself will be exalted."[y]

BLESSING THE CHILDREN

¹⁵ People[z] were bringing infants to him so he might touch them, but when the disciples saw it, they rebuked them. ¹⁶ Jesus, however, invited them: "Let the little children come to me,[aa] and don't stop them, because the kingdom of God belongs to such as these. ¹⁷ Truly I tell you,[ab] whoever does not receive[ac] the kingdom of God like a little child[ad] will never enter it."

THE RICH YOUNG RULER

¹⁸ A[ae] ruler[af] asked him, "Good teacher, what must I do to inherit eternal life?"[ag] ¹⁹ "Why do you call me good?" Jesus asked him. "No one is good except God alone. ²⁰ You know the commandments: **Do not commit adultery; do not murder; do not steal; do not bear false witness; honor your father and mother.**"[G,ah] ²¹ "I have kept all these from my youth," he said. ²² When Jesus heard this, he told him, "You still lack one thing: Sell all you have and distribute it to the poor,[ai] and you will have treasure in heaven.[aj] Then come, follow me."[ak]

Cross references (right margin):

[a] 18:3 Lk 2:37; 4:26; 7:12; 21:2
[b] 18:5 Lk 11:8
[c] 18:7 Is 63:4; Rv 6:10
[d] Mt 24:22; Rm 8:33; 2Tm 2:10; Ti 1:1
[e] Ps 88:1
[f] 2Pt 3:9
[g] 18:8 Dn 7:13; Lk 9:26; 12:40
[h] 18:9-14 Mt 18:4; 23:12; Lk 14:11
[i] 18:9 Mt 5:20; 2Co 1:9
[j] Lk 16:15
[k] Lk 23:11; Ac 4:11; Rm 14:3,10
[l] 18:10 1Kg 10:5; 2Kg 20:5,8; Ac 3:1
[m] 18:11 Mt 6:5; Mk 11:25
[n] Mt 7:15; 1Co 5:10-11; 6:10
[o] Lk 16:10
[p] Ex 20:14; 1Co 6:9; Heb 13:4
[q] 18:12 Lk 5:33-35; Ac 13:2-3
[r] Lk 11:42
[s] 18:13 Lk 17:12
[t] Ezr 9:6
[u] Lk 23:48
[v] 18:13 Heb 2:17
[w] 1Tm 1:15
[x] 18:14 Lk 16:15; Php 3:8
[y] Is 2:11; Lk 1:52; 3:5; 14:11
[z] 18:15-17 Mt 18:3; 19:13-15; Mk 10:13-16
[aa] 18:16 Lk 14:26
[ab] 18:17 Ps 72:19; Rv 22:21
[ac] Lk 8:13
[ad] 1Co 14:20; 1Pt 2:2
[ae] 18:18-30 Mt 19:16-30; Mk 10:17-31; Lk 22:28-30
[af] 18:18 Lk 8:41; 12:58
[ag] Lk 10:25; Jn 3:15
[ah] 18:20 Ex 20:12-16; Dt 5:16-20
[ai] 18:22 Lk 12:33; 19:8; Ac 2:45; 4:34
[aj] Mt 6:19-20; Lk 5:11; 12:33
[ak] Lk 5:27

Footnotes:

[A] 18:5 Lit *widow causes me trouble*   [B] 18:5 Or *doesn't ruin my reputation*   [C] 18:7 Or *Will he put up with them?*   [D] 18:11 Or *by himself*
[E] 18:12 Or *give tithes*   [F] 18:13 Or *God, turn your wrath from me*   [G] 18:20 Ex 20:12-16; Dt 5:16-20

18:5 The Greek word translated **wear. . . out** can also mean to "ruin one's reputation." So, whether he was concerned with her nagging him to death or having his professionalism discredited, he finally ruled in her favor against her opponent. The key to the widow's persistence was her legal right to justice.
18:6-7 In other words, if an **unjust judge** (18:6) who doesn't fear God will rule justly in a poor woman's favor because of her persistence based on the law, won't a holy God **grant justice** (18:7) to his people who pray to him with perseverance based on his Word?
18:8 When the Son of Man comes, will he find faith on earth? In view here is our willingness to persevere by faith in prayer based on God's Word. Believers, then, have a legal right to answered prayer.
18:10 Most of Jesus's listeners would have immediately—and wrongly—assumed that they knew who the hero and the villain were in this story. The Pharisees were strict adherents to God's law. The common people considered them the epitome of orthodoxy and godliness. Meanwhile, the tax collectors were considered vile sinners. They were Jews who collected taxes from their own people on behalf of the

Roman Empire, and they often took extra to line their own pockets (see 19:1-10).
18:11-12 This guy used other people as his standard of righteousness. And since in his view he surpassed all of them, he celebrated his own virtue. Thinking himself better than everyone else, he assumed that God must be pleased with him.
18:13 Since **God** himself is the standard of righteousness, the **tax collector** knew that he fell far short. His only hope was God's grace.
18:14 Many of Jesus's parables feature surprising reversals or shocking endings (see 10:25-37; 12:13-21; 14:16-24; 15:11-32), and this one is no exception. Jesus said that the tax collector—not the Pharisee—went home **justified** (declared righteous) before God. He understood that he was a sinful man before a holy God, and he humbled himself in God's sight, pleading for mercy so that he might find salvation and restoration. The Pharisee, on the other hand, was self-righteous and self-sufficient. Grace will only be given to the humble, not to the proud (see Jas 4:6).
18:15-17 God's **kingdom** is only available to those who **receive [it] like a little child** (18:17). In a parent-child relationship, children bring

nothing to the table but their own weakness, need, and dependency. In the same way, we come to God through Jesus Christ, entirely dependent on him for both kingdom entry and kingdom blessing. These verses also support the importance of bringing children to Christ while they are young.
18:18 In Matthew, this fellow is described as a "young man" (Matt 19:20). Luke says here that he was **a ruler**. All three Synoptic Gospels tell us he was rich (Matt 19:22; Mark 10:22; Luke 18:23). Thus, he is typically referred to as the "rich young ruler."
18:19 The only way Jesus could be rightly called **good** is if he were, in fact, the Son of God.
18:20-23 When Jesus recited several of the Ten Commandments that address our relations with other people, the man assured him that he had **kept [them] all** since childhood (18:20-21). The man was either a bold liar or self-deceived. But rather than challenge this claim of perfect righteousness, Jesus appealed to the one thing that he knew the man lacked: love for his neighbor. So he told him to **sell** everything and give **to the poor**. Upon hearing this, the man **became extremely sad** (18:22-23). His love for his wealth superseded his love for people.

a 18:23 Mt 26:38; Mk
6:26; 14:34
b 18:26 Lk 18:42; Eph 2:8
c 18:27 Gn 18:14; Jb 42:2; Jr
32:17; Zch 8:6; Lk 1:37; Rm
4:21; 11:22
d 18:28 Lk 5:11; Jn 8:12
e 18:30 Jb 42:10; Mt 6:33;
Lk 21:8
f 18:31-34 Mt 20:17-19; Mk
10:32-34
g 18:31 Lk 9:51
h Ps 22; Is 52:13-53:12; Mt
1:22; 26:24
i Lk 22:37; Jn 19:28
j 18:32 Mt 27:2; Jn 18:30-
31; Ac 3:13
k Mt 27:26-31
l Mt 26:67; Mk 14:65; 15:19
m 18:33 Mt 16:21; Lk 9:22
n 18:34 Mk 9:32; Lk 2:50;
9:45
o Lk 1:29
p Lk 24:16
q 18:35-43 Mt 20:29-34;
Mk 10:46-52

r 18:37 Mt 2:23; Jn 18:5;
19:19; Ac 2:22
s 18:38 Lk 18:7
t Mt 1:1; 9:27; Lk 1:32;
Rm 1:3
u Lk 16:24
v 18:42 Lk 7:22; Jn 9:11;
Ac 9:12
w Mt 9:22; Lk 5:20; 7:50;
8:48; 17:19; 18:26
x 18:43 Lk 7:16; 13:13
y Lk 2:10
z 19:7 Lk 15:2
aa 19:8 Lk 18:22
ab Lk 3:14
ac Ex 22:1; 2Sm 12:6

23 After he heard this, he became extremely sad,*a* because he was very rich.

POSSESSIONS AND THE KINGDOM

24 Seeing that he became sad,*A* Jesus said, "How hard it is for those who have wealth to enter the kingdom of God! **25** For it is easier for a camel to go through the eye of a needle than for a rich person to enter the kingdom of God."

26 Those who heard this asked, "Then who can be saved?"*b*

27 He replied, "What is impossible with man is possible with God."*c*

28 Then Peter said, "Look, we have left what we had and followed*d* you."

29 So he said to them, "Truly I tell you, there is no one who has left a house, wife or brothers or sisters, parents or children because of the kingdom of God, **30** who will not receive many times more at this time,*e* and eternal life in the age to come."

THE THIRD PREDICTION OF HIS DEATH

31 Then*f* he took the Twelve aside and told them, "See, we are going up to Jerusalem.*g* Everything that is written*h* through the prophets about the Son of Man will be accomplished.*i* **32** For he will be handed over to the Gentiles,*j* and he will be mocked,*k* insulted, spit*l* on; **33** and after they flog him, they will kill him, and he will rise on the third day."*m*

34 They understood none of these things.*n* The meaning of the saying*B,o* was hidden*p* from them, and they did not grasp what was said.

A BLIND MAN RECEIVES HIS SIGHT

35 As*q* he approached Jericho, a blind man was sitting by the road begging. **36** Hearing a crowd passing by, he inquired what was happening. **37** "Jesus of Nazareth*r* is passing by," they told him.

38 So he called out,*s* "Jesus, Son of David,*t* have mercy*u* on me!" **39** Then those in front told him to keep quiet,*c* but he kept crying out all the more, "Son of David, have mercy on me!"

40 Jesus stopped and commanded that he be brought to him. When he came closer, he asked him, **41** "What do you want me to do for you?"

"Lord," he said, "I want to see."

42 "Receive your sight."*v* Jesus told him. "Your faith has saved you."*w* **43** Instantly he could see, and he began to follow him, glorifying God.*x* All the people,*y* when they saw it, gave praise to God.

JESUS VISITS ZACCHAEUS

19 He entered Jericho and was passing through. **2** There was a man named Zacchaeus who was a chief tax collector, and he was rich. **3** He was trying to see who Jesus was, but he was not able because of the crowd, since he was a short man. **4** So running ahead, he climbed up a sycamore tree to see Jesus, since he was about to pass that way. **5** When Jesus came to the place, he looked up and said to him, "Zacchaeus, hurry and come down because today it is necessary for me to stay at your house."

6 So he quickly came down and welcomed him joyfully. **7** All who saw it began to complain,*z* "He's gone to stay with a sinful man."

8 But Zacchaeus stood there and said to the Lord, "Look, I'll give half of my possessions to the poor,*aa* Lord. And if I have extorted*ab* anything from anyone, I'll pay back four times as much."*ac*

A **18:24** Other mss omit *he became sad*   *B* **18:34** Lit *This saying*   *C* **18:39** Or *those in front rebuked him*

18:25 The problem is that the **rich** tend to think that they are self-sufficient and that their wealth makes them acceptable before God.

18:26-27 Jesus's answer, **What is impossible with man is possible with God,** means that anyone can be saved—rich or poor. God can work in the hearts and minds of even the wealthy to humble them so that they look to him, rather than to their riches, as their source of eternal life.

18:29-30 No sacrifice made for God's kingdom agenda gets overlooked or forgotten. Faithful kingdom disciples will be repaid, sometimes in history but ultimately in eternity.

18:31-33 Jesus had predicted his approaching sacrificial death twice already (9:21-22; 9:43-45). **The prophets** is a reference to the Old Testament Scriptures (18:31). **The Gentiles** in this case is a reference to the Romans (18:32).

18:35-39 The beggar knew that if this man were the Messiah, he could transform his helpless situation. How desperate are you for Jesus to intervene in your circumstances?

18:40-43 This man's healing served as a spiritual lesson to the nation of Israel. If they would respond to the Messiah and acknowledge their spiritual blindness, God would grant them spiritual life and entrance into the kingdom that Jesus was offering. But would they humble themselves and receive him?

19:2 Since the Jews were subjugated by Rome, they paid taxes to the Roman Empire. Rome would employ Jews to collect taxes from their own kinspeople, and these men would often collect extra for themselves. They were thus considered traitors, and that's why in the New Testament you typically see tax collectors mentioned alongside prostitutes and sinners (e.g., Matt 11:19; 21:31; Luke 15:1). As **a chief tax collector, Zacchaeus** would have had a lot of money and few friends.

19:3-4 Zacchaeus's desperation caused him to do something a bit below his dignity, since he was short in stature. He was willing to endure some public scorn to see Jesus, the One everyone had been talking about.

19:7 Some people in the crowd were probably hoping to have Jesus as their own dinner guest. Why had he chosen to visit with that sinner instead? Because sinners were the reason he had come in the first place (19:10).

19:8 Repentance doesn't merely say, "I'm sorry," it makes amends for wrongdoing. Zacchaeus's outward actions were testimony of an inward transformation.

[a]19:9 Lk 1:77
[b]Lk 3:8; 13:16; Gl 3:7,29
[c]19:10 Ezk 34:16; Mt 9:13; 10:6; 15:24; 18:12; Lk 15:4
[d]19:11-27 Mt 25:14-30; Mk 13:34
[e]19:11 Lk 9:51
[f]Lk 17:20; Ac 1:6
[g]19:17 Lk 16:10; 1Co 4:2

[h]19:21 2Co 8:12
[i]19:26 Mt 13:12; Mk 4:25; Lk 8:18
[j]19:27 Lk 19:14
[k]19:28-44 Mt 21:1-11; Mk 11:1-11
[l]19:28 Lk 9:51

APPLICATION QUESTIONS

READ LUKE 19:11-27

– What ideas or images come to mind when you hear the word *stewardship*? Why?
– What does this passage teach about stewardship and our role as stewards in God's kingdom?
– What are some of the primary resources you're currently managing as a member of God's kingdom?
– In what ways are you currently using the resources you've been given to invest in God's kingdom agenda?

9 "Today salvation[a] has come to this house," Jesus told him, "because he too is a son of Abraham.[b] 10 For the Son of Man has come to seek and to save the lost."[c]

THE PARABLE OF THE TEN MINAS

11 As[d] they were listening to this, he went on to tell a parable because he was near Jerusalem,[e] and they thought the kingdom of God was going to appear right away.[f] 12 Therefore he said: "A nobleman traveled to a far country to receive for himself authority to be king[A] and then to return. 13 He called ten of his servants, gave them ten minas,[B] and told them, 'Engage in business until I come back.' 14 "But his subjects hated him and sent a delegation after him, saying, 'We don't want this man to rule over us.' 15 "At his return, having received the authority to be king, he summoned those servants he had given the money to, so that he could find out how much they had made in business. 16 The first came forward and said, 'Master, your mina has earned ten more minas.' 17 " 'Well done, good[c] servant!' he told him. 'Because you have been faithful[g] in

a very small matter, have authority over ten towns.' 18 "The second came and said, 'Master, your mina has made five minas.' 19 "So he said to him, 'You will be over five towns.' 20 "And another came and said, 'Master, here is your mina. I have kept it safe in a cloth 21 because I was afraid of you since you're a harsh man: you collect what you didn't deposit and reap what you didn't sow.'[h] 22 "He told him, 'I will condemn you by what you have said, you evil servant! If you knew I was a harsh man, collecting what I didn't deposit and reaping what I didn't sow, 23 why, then, didn't you put my money in the bank? And when I returned, I would have collected it with interest.' 24 So he said to those standing there, 'Take the mina away from him and give it to the one who has ten minas.' 25 "But they said to him, 'Master, he has ten minas.' 26 "I tell you, that to everyone who has, more will be given; and from the one who does not have, even what he does have will be taken away.[i] 27 But bring here these enemies of mine,[j] who did not want me to rule over them, and slaughter[D] them in my presence.'"

THE TRIUMPHAL ENTRY

28 When[k] he had said these things, he went on ahead, going up to Jerusalem.[l] 29 As he approached Bethphage and Bethany, at the

[A]19:12 Lit *to receive for himself a kingdom*, or *sovereignty*, also in v. 15   [B]19:13 = Gk coin worth a hundred drachmas or about a hundred days' wages   [C]19:17 Or *capable*   [D]19:27 Or *execute*

19:11-12 Jesus wanted his hearers to understand that his **kingdom** reign was not coming immediately (19:11). He would depart and **return** at a later time (19:12).
19:13 A mina was a coin worth about a hundred days' wages. The point here is that God would expect his followers (i.e., believers) to manage what he gave them until the King returned to be enthroned in Jerusalem. God's servants are called to follow him in obedience, even though the world rejects the King and his kingdom.
19:15-19 Everything we have is a gift from God. We must recognize that we are stewards of our resources, not owners. God will call us to give an account for how we have managed

our money, our possessions, our spiritual gifts, our relationships, and our time—and will reward or judge his people accordingly.
19:20-24 This lack of stewardship was fueled by a lack of relationship and the failure to take seriously the knowledge of his master's expectations and the fact that he would return. This servant (unfaithful believer) wanted nothing to do with the responsibilities of stewardship. Unfaithful believers will experience negative consequences at the judgment seat of Christ (see 1 Cor 3:15).
19:26-27 Faithfulness results in kingdom reward; unfaithfulness results in lack and loss of reward (19:26). But worst of all are the consequences that await those who make

themselves God's **enemies** (19:27; see 19:14). These will experience eternal judgment.
19:28-35 Three things are clear from these events. First, as Matthew informs his readers, these actions fulfilled the prophecy of Zechariah 9:9 (see Matt 21:4-5). Jesus was publicly presenting himself as the Messiah. Second, Jesus's knowledge of what would happen demonstrated his omniscience to his disciples. Third, a donkey that had never been ridden would not accept a rider easily. But Jesus showed himself to be the Master over creation. He came not on a horse as an emerging military king but as a humble servant of peace, which was represented by the donkey.

a **19:29** 2Sm 15:30; Zch
14:4; Lk 21:37; 22:39
b **19:32** Lk 22:13
c **19:35-38** Jn 12:12-15
d **19:35** Zch 9:9
e **19:36** 2Kg 9:13
f **19:38** Mt 2:2; 25:34
g Ps 118:26; Lk 13:35
h Lk 2:14
i Jb 16:19; Ps 148:1; Mt 21:9;
Mk 11:10; Lk 2:14
j **19:40** Hab 2:11
k **19:41** Lk 13:34-35; Jn
11:35; Heb 5:7
l **19:42** Lk 23:34
m Lk 8:9-10; 10:21
n **19:43** Lk 17:22
o Is 29:3; Jr 6:6; Ezk 4:2;
Lk 21:20
p **19:44** Mt 24:2; Mk 13:2
q Lk 21:6

r **19:44** Ex 3:16; Lk 1:68;
7:16; 1Pt 2:12
s **19:45-48** Mt 21:12-19;
Mk 11:12-19; Jn 2:13-17;
8:1-2; 11:45-53
t **19:46** Is 56:7
u Jr 7:11
v **19:47** Mt 26:55; Lk 20:1
w Lk 6:11; 11:53-54; 20:19
x **19:48** Lk 18:43; 20:6
y **20:1-8** Mt 21:23-27; Mk
11:27-33
z **20:1** Lk 19:47
aa Lk 4:18; 8:1
ab Lk 9:22; 22:66
ac **20:6** Lk 19:48
ad Mt 11:9; Lk 7:29-30
ae **20:9-19** Mt 21:33-46;
Mk 12:1-12
af **20:9** Is 5:1-7

place called the Mount of Olives,*a* he sent two of the disciples **30** and said, "Go into the village ahead of you. As you enter it, you will find a colt tied there, on which no one has ever sat. Untie it and bring it. **31** If anyone asks you, 'Why are you untying it?' say this: 'The Lord needs it.'"

32 So those who were sent left and found it just as he had told them.*b* **33** As they were untying the colt, its owners said to them, "Why are you untying the colt?"

34 "The Lord needs it," they said. **35** Then*c* they brought it to Jesus, and after throwing their clothes on the colt, they helped Jesus get on it.*d* **36** As he was going along, they were spreading their clothes on the road.*e* **37** Now he came near the path down the Mount of Olives, and the whole crowd of the disciples began to praise God joyfully with a loud voice for all the miracles they had seen:

38   Blessed is the King*f* who comes
        in the name of the Lord.*A,g*
        Peace in heaven
        and glory*h* in the highest heaven!*i*

39 Some of the Pharisees from the crowd told him, "Teacher, rebuke your disciples."

40 He answered, "I tell you, if they were to keep silent, the stones would cry out."*j*

JESUS'S LOVE FOR JERUSALEM

41 As he approached and saw the city, he wept*k* for it, **42** saying, "If you knew*l* this day what would bring peace — but now it is hidden*m* from your eyes. **43** For the days will come on you*n* when your enemies will build a barricade around you, surround you, and hem you in on every side.*o* **44** They will crush you and your children among you to the ground,*p* and they will not leave one stone on another*q* in your midst, because you did not recognize the time when God visited you."*r*

CLEANSING THE TEMPLE

45 He*s* went into the temple and began to throw out those who were selling,*B* **46** and he said, "It is written, **my house will be a house of prayer,**,*t* but you have made it **a den of thieves!**"*C,u*

47 Every day he was teaching*v* in the temple. The chief priests, the scribes, and the leaders of the people were looking for a way to kill*w* him, **48** but they could not find a way to do it, because all the people*x* were captivated by what they heard.

THE AUTHORITY OF JESUS CHALLENGED

20 One*y* day as he was teaching*z* the people in the temple and proclaiming the good news,*aa* the chief priests and the scribes, with the elders,*ab* came **2** and said to him: "Tell us, by what authority are you doing these things? Who is it who gave you this authority?"

3 He answered them, "I will also ask you a question. Tell me, **4** was the baptism of John from heaven or of human origin?"

5 They discussed it among themselves: "If we say, 'From heaven,' he will say, 'Why didn't you believe him?' **6** But if we say, 'Of human origin,' all the people*ac* will stone us, because they are convinced that John was a prophet."*ad* **7** So they answered that they did not know its origin.

8 And Jesus said to them, "Neither will I tell you by what authority I do these things."

THE PARABLE OF THE VINEYARD OWNER

9 Now*ae* he began to tell the people this parable: "A man planted a vineyard,*af* leased

---

A 19:38 Ps 118:26   **B** 19:45 Other mss add *and buying in it*   **C** 19:46 Is 56:7; Jr 7:11

19:37-39 They were quoting from Psalm 118. The people openly acknowledged Jesus as the Messiah, and he received their praise. But this was too much for **the Pharisees**. They demanded that Jesus **rebuke [his] disciples** (19:39). It was their way of saying, "Surely you don't believe this yourself, do you? Stop them!"

19:40 Jesus assured the Pharisees that if the crowd remained **silent, the stones would cry out**. God's long-awaited Messiah had finally come, and he deserved all honor and glory. If the Jewish leadership and the nation refused to accept him (see Matt 23:37), God would bring to life those who had died (indicated by the visible gravestones that surrounded the Mount of Olives) to bear testimony to Jesus (Luke 19:37-40).

19:41-44 When **the city** of Jerusalem finally came into view, Jesus **wept for it** (19:41). If the inhabitants would have accepted him nationally, they could have known **peace** (19:42). But they would soon reject him. As a result, God would hand the city over to judgment. Jerusalem's **enemies** would **surround** the city (19:43). This would be fulfilled in AD 70 when the Romans decimated the city.

19:45-46 Communicating with God had been replaced by religious activity for profit. The absence of the priority of prayer in the church is a significant indication that it has abandoned its primary calling.

19:47-48 Ultimately, Jesus's enemies would resort to using a traitor and the cover of darkness to accomplish their wicked plans (see 22:47-48, 52-53).

20:5-6 If they said that John's baptism was authorized by **heaven**, Jesus would ask, **Why didn't you believe him?** (20:5). After all, John had called all Israel to repent and be baptized—something the religious leaders didn't do. John had also pointed to Jesus as the Messiah (see John 1:29-34)—something the religious leaders refused to believe. On the other hand, if they said John's baptism was **of human origin**, they would probably be stoned to death by **the people**, since they believed **John was** a true **prophet** of God (Luke 20:6).

20:7-8 If you won't speak the truth, don't expect to receive the truth.

20:9 The vineyard owner represented God, and his **vineyard** was Israel. Isaiah the prophet had spoken of Israel as a vineyard too (Isa 5:1-7), so this would have sounded

it to tenant farmers, and went away for a long time. [10] At harvest time he sent a servant to the farmers so that they might give him some fruit from the vineyard. But the farmers beat him and sent him away empty-handed. [11] He sent yet another servant, but they beat that one too, treated him shamefully, and sent him away empty-handed. [12] And he sent yet a third, but they wounded this one too and threw him out.

[13] "Then the owner of the vineyard said, 'What should I do? I will send my beloved[a] son. Perhaps[A] they will respect him.'

[14] "But when the tenant farmers saw him, they discussed it among themselves and said, 'This is the heir. Let's kill him, so that the inheritance will be ours.'[b] [15] So they threw him out of the vineyard and killed him.

"What then will the owner of the vineyard do to them? [16] He will come and kill[c] those farmers and give the vineyard to others."

But when they heard this they said, "That must never happen!"[d]

[17] But he looked at them and said, "Then what is the meaning of this Scripture:[B,e]

The stone that
    the builders rejected
    has become the cornerstone?[C,f]

[18] Everyone who falls on that stone will be broken to pieces, but on whomever it falls, it will shatter him."[g]

[19] Then the scribes and the chief priests[h] looked for a way to get their hands on him[i] that very hour, because they knew he had told this parable against them, but they feared the people.[j]

GOD AND CAESAR

[20] They[k] watched closely[l] and sent spies[m] who pretended to be righteous,[D] so that they could catch him in what he said,[n] to hand him[o] over to the governor's[p] rule and authority. [21] They questioned him, "Teacher, we know that you speak and teach correctly,[q] and you don't show partiality[E,r] but teach truthfully the way of God.[s] [22] Is it lawful[t] for us to pay taxes[u] to Caesar[v] or not?"

[23] But detecting their craftiness, he said to them,[F] [24] "Show me a denarius.[G] Whose image and inscription does it have?"

"Caesar's," they said.

[25] "Well then," he told them, "give to Caesar[w] the things that are Caesar's, and to God the things that are God's."

[26] They were not able to catch him in what he said in public, and being amazed at his answer, they became silent.[x]

THE SADDUCEES AND THE RESURRECTION

[27] Some[y] of the Sadducees, who say there is no resurrection,[z] came up and questioned him: [28] "Teacher, Moses wrote for us that **if a man's brother** has a wife, and **dies childless, his brother should take the wife and produce offspring for his brother.**[H,aa] [29] Now there were seven brothers. The first took a wife and died without children. [30] Also the second[I] [31] and the third took her. In the same way, all seven died and left no children. [32] Finally, the woman died too. [33] In the resurrection, therefore, whose wife will the woman be? For all seven had married her."

[a] 20:13 Mt 17:5; Lk 3:22
[b] 20:14 Lk 16:16
[c] 20:16 Lk 19:27
[d] Rm 3:4; 1Co 6:15; Gl 2:17
[e] 20:17 Lk 4:17; 18:31; 21:22,37; 24:44
[f] Ps 118:22; Ac 4:11; Eph 2:20; 1Pt 2:4-7
[g] 20:18 Is 8:14-15; Dn 2:34-35,44-45; Rm 9:32-33; 1Pt 2:8
[h] 20:19 Mt 2:4; 20:18; 21:15; 22:2; 23:10
[i] Lk 19:47; 21:12
[j] Lk 22:2
[k] 20:20-26 Mt 20:15-22; Mk 12:13-17
[l] 20:20 Lk 6:7; 14:1
[m] Mt 22:15-16
[n] Lk 11:54
[o] Lk 24:20; Ac 3:13; Rm 8:32
[p] Mt 27:2; Lk 21:12
[q] 20:21 Jn 3:2
[r] Dt 1:17; 10:17; Mal 2:9; Mt 22:16
[s] Ac 13:10; 18:25-26
[t] 20:22 Lk 6:9; 14:3
[u] Mt 17:25; Lk 23:2; Rm 13:6-7
[v] Lk 2:1; 3:1; 20:24-25; 23:2
[w] 20:25 Mt 22:21
[x] 20:26 Lk 9:36; 14:4
[y] 20:27-40 Mt 22:23-33,46; Mk 12:18-27,34
[z] 20:27 Ac 23:6
[aa] 20:28 Dt 25:5

[A] 20:13 Other mss add *when they see him* [B] 20:17 Lit *"What then is this that is written* [C] 20:17 Ps 118:22 [D] 20:20 Or *upright* [E] 20:21 Lit *you don't receive a face* [F] 20:23 Other mss add *"Why are you testing me?* [G] 20:24 A denarius = one day's wage [H] 20:28 Dt 25:5 [I] 20:30 Other mss add *took her as wife, and he died without children*

familiar to Jesus's listeners. In Isaiah's song, the vineyard produced worthless grapes. In Jesus's parable, the vineyard doesn't fare much better.

20:10 Over the centuries, God had sent his servants the prophets to warn his people to bear fruit—to keep his covenant and to live righteously. But Israel repeatedly rejected God's Word spoken by his messengers, often mistreating them.

20:13-16 Jesus's declaration of judgment on Israel for their rebellion against God was too much for the religious leaders. They rejected his story and shouted, **That must never happen!** (20:16). They were unwilling to entertain the possibility that they had been unfaithful to God and were rejecting his Son.

20:17-18 Jesus made it clear to them that their rejection of him was a rejection of God and a fulfillment of **Scripture**. He quoted from

Psalm 118:22: **The stone that the builders rejected has become the cornerstone** (Luke 20:17). Though the religious leaders scorned Jesus as a worthless stone, he was the most important part of the building, the key element of the kingdom. One cannot reject him and go unharmed (20:18). Reject the cornerstone, and your building falls to ruin. Reject the Messiah, and your eternal condemnation is certain.

20:20-23 The **spies** approached Jesus under the guise of desiring a truthful answer from a God-honoring **teacher** on a complex, controversial subject (20:20-21). They asked, **Is it lawful for us to pay taxes to Caesar or not?** (20:22). If he answered, "Yes," the crowds (who hated the Romans) would be angry with him. But if he answered, "No," the religious leaders would have reason to accuse him of treason against Rome.

20:24-25 A **denarius** was the Roman coin used to pay taxes. Jesus pointed out that the coin with **Caesar's** image on it (20:24) belonged to Rome, so it was right to give Caesar what belonged to him for the services the empire provided. On the other hand, human beings bear **God's** "image" (Gen 1:26-27), so they are to give themselves in humble obedience to him (Luke 2:25).

20:27 The **Sadducees** had a lot of power since they were associated with aristocratic families and the high priests. They differed from the Pharisees on a number of theological issues. For example, they rejected belief in the **resurrection** and only believed in the first five books of the Bible (the Pentateuch) as Scripture.

20:28-33 The Sadducees believed that their hypothetical situation proved how ridiculous the idea of the resurrection was.

a 20:34 Lk 16:8
b Lk 17:27
c 20:35 Ac 5:41; 2Th 1:5
d Mk 10:30
e 20:36 1Co 15:54-55;
Rv 21:4
f Ps 82:6; Mt 5:45; Rm
8:14,19; Gl 3:26
g 20:37 Ex 3:6,15-16; 4:5;
Mt 1:2; Ac 3:13; 7:30-32
h 20:38 Rm 6:10-11; 14:7-8;
2Co 5:14-15; Gl 2:19-20;
1Th 4:14; 5:10
i 20:41-44 Mt 22:41-46;
Mk 12:34-37
j 20:41 Mt 1:1,17; Lk 1:27;
Rm 1:3; Eph 5:2
k 20:42 Lk 24:44; Ac 1:20
l 20:42-43 Ps 110:1; Ac
2:34-35; 1Co 15:25; Heb
1:13; 10:13
m 20:44 Rm 1:3-4
n 20:45-47 Mt 23:1-36; Mk
12:37-40
o 20:46 Mt 16:6
p Lk 11:43

q 21:1-4 Mk 12:41-44
r 21:2 2Kg 12:9; Mt 27:6;
Jn 8:20
s 21:2 Lk 12:59
t 21:3 2Co 8:2,12
u 21:5-38 Mt 24:1-51; Mk
13:1-37
v 21:6 Lk 17:22
w Lk 19:44
x 21:7 Ac 1:6-7
y 21:8 Jr 29:8; Eph 5:6;
2Th 2:3
z Jr 14:14; 1Jn 2:18
aa Jn 8:24
ab Lk 17:23
ac 21:10 2Ch 15:6; Is 19:2
ad 21:11 Is 29:6; Zch 14:5;
Rv 6:12
ae Rv 6:8
af Lk 11:16; 12:33
ag 21:12-17 Mt 10:19-22;
Mk 13:11-13
ah 21:12 Ps 119:84

34 Jesus told them, "The children of this age*a* marry and are given in marriage.*b* **35** But those who are counted worthy*c* to take part in that age*d* and in the resurrection from the dead neither marry nor are given in marriage. **36** For they can no longer die,*e* because they are like angels and are children of God,*f* since they are children of the resurrection. **37** Moses even indicated in the passage about the burning bush that the dead are raised, where he calls the Lord **the God of Abraham and the God of Isaac and the God of Jacob.**^A,g **38** He is not the God of the dead but of the living, because all are living to^B him."*h*

39 Some of the scribes answered, "Teacher, you have spoken well." **40** And they no longer dared to ask him anything.

THE QUESTION ABOUT THE CHRIST

41 Then*i* he said to them, "How can they say that the Christ is the son of David?*j* **42** For David himself says in the Book of Psalms:*k*

**The Lord declared to my Lord,
'Sit at my right hand**
**43 until I make your enemies
your footstool.'**^C,l

44 David calls him 'Lord'; how then can the Christ be his son?"*m*

WARNING AGAINST THE SCRIBES

45 While*n* all the people were listening, he said to his disciples, **46** "Beware*o* of the scribes, who want to go around in long robes and who love greetings in the marketplaces, the best seats in the synagogues, and the places of honor at banquets.*p* **47** They devour widows' houses and say long prayers just for show. These will receive harsher judgment."^D

THE WIDOW'S GIFT

21 He*q* looked up and saw the rich dropping their offerings into the temple treasury.*r* **2** He also saw a poor widow dropping in two tiny coins.^E,s **3** "Truly I tell you," he said, "this poor widow has put in more than all of them.*t* **4** For all these people have put in gifts out of their surplus, but she out of her poverty has put in all she had to live on."

DESTRUCTION OF THE TEMPLE PREDICTED

5 As*u* some were talking about the temple, how it was adorned with beautiful stones and gifts dedicated to God, he said, **6** "These things that you see — the days will come*v* when not one stone will be left on another that will not be thrown down."*w*

SIGNS OF THE END OF THE AGE

7 "Teacher," they asked him, "so when will these things happen? And what will be the sign when these things are about to take place?"*x*

8 Then he said, "Watch out that you are not deceived.*y* For many will come in my name,*z* saying, 'I am he,'*aa* and, 'The time is near.' Don't follow them.*ab* **9** When you hear of wars and rebellions,^F don't be alarmed. Indeed, it is necessary that these things take place first, but the end won't come right away."

10 Then he told them: "Nation will be raised up against nation, and kingdom against kingdom.*ac* **11** There will be violent earthquakes,*ad* and famines and plagues*ae* in various places, and there will be terrifying sights and great signs from heaven.*af* **12** But before all these things, they will lay their hands on you*ag* and persecute*ah*

---

^A 20:37 Ex 3:6,15   ^B 20:38 Or *with*   ^C 20:42-43 Ps 110:1   ^D 20:47 Or *judgment*   ^E 21:2 Lit *two lepta* ; the *lepton* was the smallest and least valuable Gk coin in use.   ^F 21:9 Or *insurrections*, or *revolutions*, or *chaos*

20:35-36 Though marriage is part of God's design for his creation, it will not be a feature of the new creation. So questions like, "Whose wife will the woman be?" (20:33) are irrelevant. Resurrected believers will **no longer die** (20:36). So there will be no need for procreation.

20:37-38 To say that he was still their God—after they had died—indicated that **the dead are raised** (20:37). Existence does not end with physical death.

20:39-40 Jesus had proven himself a formidable adversary. His understanding of the Scriptures and authority in teaching were vastly superior to those of the religious leaders.

20:41-44 That Christ would be the **son of David** was a universally accepted notion (20:41). Then Jesus quoted from Psalm 110:1, a

passage in which **David** (the author and highly revered king), speaking of the Messiah sitting at God's **right hand**, calls him **my Lord** (Luke 20:42-44). A father wouldn't call his descendant "Lord." Jesus wasn't denying the fact that the Christ would be descended from David. The Old Testament makes that clear. Rather, Jesus was emphasizing the fact that the Christ was *much more* than merely the son of David. Though he would be human, he wouldn't be merely human. He would also be God.

20:46-47 Just as there will be degrees of reward for believers, there will be degrees of punishment for unbelievers.

21:1-4 Jesus had just censured the scribes for devouring "widows' houses" (see 20:47). He further condemned their greed by contrasting it with one particular widow's virtue. To the

casual observer, it appeared that the widow had given next to nothing. But the percentage of what she gave, in relation to what she had, exceeded all the rest. The widow's willingness to give her livelihood demonstrated her great reliance on God as her source of provision.

21:5-6 **The temple**, which had been rebuilt and expanded by Herod the Great, was grand and **beautiful** (21:5). Nevertheless, Jesus's prediction would come true a few decades later in AD 70 when the Roman general (and later emperor) Titus conquered Jerusalem and leveled the temple (21:6).

21:7 The disciples believed the temple's destruction was linked to the start of the messianic kingdom (see Matt 24:3). They didn't yet realize that there would be a gap of time between these events.

you. They will hand you over to the synagogues[a] and prisons,[b] and you will be brought before kings and governors[c] because of my name. [13] This will give you an opportunity to bear witness.[d] [14] Therefore make up your minds[A] not to prepare your defense ahead of time,[e] [15] for I will give you such words[f] and a wisdom[g] that none of your adversaries will be able to resist or contradict.[h] [16] You will even be betrayed by parents, brothers, relatives, and friends.[i] They will kill some of you. [17] You will be hated by everyone because of my name,[j] [18] but not a hair of your head will be lost.[k] [19] By your endurance, gain[B] your lives.[l]

THE DESTRUCTION OF JERUSALEM

[20] "When you see Jerusalem surrounded by armies,[m] then recognize that its desolation[n] has come near. [21] Then those in Judea must flee[o] to the mountains.[p] Those inside the city must leave it, and those who are in the country must not enter it, [22] because these are days of vengeance[q] to fulfill all the things that are written. [23] Woe to pregnant women and nursing mothers in those days,[r] for there will be great distress in the land[C] and wrath against this people. [24] They will be killed by the sword[D,s] and be led captive into all the nations, and Jerusalem will be trampled by the Gentiles[E,t] until the times of the Gentiles[u] are fulfilled.

THE COMING OF THE SON OF MAN

[25] "Then there will be signs in the sun, moon, and stars;[v] and there will be anguish on the earth among nations bewildered by the roaring of the sea and the waves.[w]

[26] People will faint from fear and expectation of the things that are coming on the world, because the powers of the heavens will be shaken.[x] [27] Then they will see the Son of Man coming in a cloud[y] with power and great glory.[z] [28] But when these things begin to take place, stand up and lift up your heads, because your redemption is near."[aa]

THE PARABLE OF THE FIG TREE

[29] Then he told them a parable: "Look at the fig tree, and all the trees. [30] As soon as they put out leaves you can see for yourselves and recognize that summer is already near. [31] In the same way, when you see these things happening, recognize[F] that the kingdom of God is near. [32] Truly I tell you, this generation will certainly not pass away until all things take place.[ab] [33] Heaven and earth will pass away,[ac] but my words will never pass away.[ad]

THE NEED FOR WATCHFULNESS

[34] "Be on your guard,[ae] so that your minds are not dulled[G] from carousing,[H] drunkenness,[af] and worries of life,[ag] or that day will come on you unexpectedly[ah] [35] like a trap. For it will come on all who live on the face of the whole earth. [36] But be alert at all times,[ai] praying that you may have strength[I] to escape[aj] all these things that are going to take place and to stand before the Son of Man."

[37] During[ak] the day, he was teaching in the temple,[al] but in the evening he would go out and spend the night on what is called the Mount of Olives.[am] [38] Then all the people would come early in the morning to hear him in the temple.[an]

[a] 21:12 Ac 22:19; 26:11
[b] Ac 4:3; 5:18; 8:3; 12:4; 16:23
[c] Ac 17:6; 18:12; 24:1,27; 25:6; 27:24; 2Co 11:23
[d] 21:13 Php 1:12–19
[e] 21:14 Lk 12:11
[f] 21:15 Ex 4:12
[g] Ac 6:10
[h] Ac 4:14
[i] 21:16 Mt 10:35; Lk 12:53
[j] 21:17 Lk 6:22; Jn 15:18–19
[k] 21:18 1Sm 14:45; Mt 10:30; Lk 12:7; Jn 10:28
[l] 21:19 Mt 10:22; 24:13; Rm 2:7; 5:3; Heb 10:36; Jms 1:3
[m] 21:20 Lk 19:43
[n] Dn 9:27
[o] 21:21 Lk 17:31
[p] Mt 4:8
[q] 21:22 Is 34:8; 63:4; Dn 9:24–27; Hs 9:7; Lk 18:7–8
[r] 21:23 Lk 23:29
[s] 21:24 Heb 11:34
[t] Ps 79:1; Is 63:18; Dn 8:13; Rv 11:2
[u] Dn 12:7; Rm 11:25
[v] 21:25 Is 13:10; 24:23; Ezk 32:7; Jl 2:10; 3:15; Ac 2:20; Rv 6:12–13
[w] Ps 46:2–3; 65:7; Is 17:12; Jl 2:30–31

[x] 21:26 Is 34:4; Hg 2:6
[y] 21:27 Dn 7:13; Rv 1:7
[z] Mt 16:27; 26:64; Mk 9:1
[aa] 21:28 Lk 2:38; 24:21; Rm 8:23; 13:11
[ab] 21:32 Lk 9:27
[ac] 21:33 Ps 102:26; Is 51:6; 2Pt 3:10
[ad] Ps 119:89; Is 40:8; Mt 5:18; Lk 16:17; 1Pt 1:23,25
[ae] 21:34 Lk 17:3
[af] Rm 13:13
[ag] Mt 13:22; Mk 4:19; 1Th 5:6–7; 1Pt 4:7
[ah] Lk 12:40; 1Th 5:3
[ai] 21:36 Mt 25:13; 26:41; Mk 14:34–38; Lk 12:37; Ac 20:31; 1Co 16:13; Eph 6:18; 1Th 5:6; 1Pt 5:8
[aj] Rm 2:3; 1Th 5:3; Heb 2:3
[ak] 21:37–38 Jn 8:1–2
[al] 21:37 Mt 26:55
[am] Mt 21:1; Lk 22:39; Jn 8:1; 18:2
[an] 21:38 Jn 8:2

[A] 21:14 Lit *Therefore place* (determine) *in your hearts*   [B] 21:19 Other mss read *endurance, you will gain*   [C] 21:23 Or *the earth*   [D] 21:24 Lit *will fall by the edge of the sword*   [E] 21:24 Or *nations*   [F] 21:31 Or *you know*   [G] 21:34 Lit *your hearts are not weighed down*   [H] 21:34 Or *hangovers*   [I] 21:36 Other mss read *you may be counted worthy*

21:16-17 While many of Christ's followers throughout history have experienced persecution and death, Jesus spoke here primarily of the suffering of those who become believers during the tribulation.

21:20 When he mentioned **Jerusalem surrounded by armies,** Jesus returned to the disciples' question about the destruction of Jerusalem (see 21:7).

21:24 **The times of the Gentiles** referred to the period when Israel would no longer possess or live in peace in their homeland and the Messiah would not yet sit on the throne of David. Such could have been averted by the nation's repentance and acceptance of the Messiah.

Jesus had the destruction of Jerusalem in AD 70 in view here (21:20), but he also extends this to the future "abomination of

desolation" mentioned in Daniel 9:27, when the antichrist will set up his image in the Jerusalem temple and require everyone to worship that image (see Rev 13:4-8). Anyone who does not worship it will be persecuted (see Rev 13:15).

21:25-26 In other words, great upheaval will take place in the natural world as the end of evil nears.

21:31-32 When Jesus's followers see the signs described, they need to **recognize that the kingdom of God,** the earthly rule of Jesus's messianic reign in the millennium, **is near** (21:31). Such events will continue uninterrupted till the conclusion of Jesus's second coming.

21:33 Jesus claimed absolute sovereignty and authority over the fulfillment of his prophetic **words.**

21:34-36 The coming of the kingdom of God and the judgment that precedes it will have a universal affect. No one will escape. And those not prepared for God's judgment will not enter the peace and joy of Christ's millennial reign. Believers need to **be alert at all times, praying [for] strength** to be prepared for his second coming (21:36). What will be true for believers in that day is still true for his disciples today. We must be alert, ready, and living in anticipation of the coming rapture that will precede the period of the tribulation (see 1 Thess 4:13-18), when Christ will come in the clouds to summon believers to "always be with the Lord" (1 Thess 4:17).

21:37 Eventually, the religious leaders would find out where Jesus was staying each night—led there by a traitor (see 22:47-53).

Video Devotional

"WHAT GOD CALLS GREAT"

Greatness is not an external accomplishment as much as it is the character of one's spirit made manifest in actions, words, and thoughts.

THE PLOT TO KILL JESUS

22 The[a] Festival of Unleavened Bread,[b] which is called Passover,[c] was approaching. [2] The chief priests and the scribes were looking for a way to put him to death,[d] because they were afraid of the people.[e]

[3] Then[f] Satan entered Judas,[g] called Iscariot,[h] who was numbered among the Twelve. [4] He went away and discussed with the chief priests and temple police[i] how he could hand him over[j] to them. [5] They were glad and agreed to give him silver.[A] [6] So he accepted the offer and started looking for a good opportunity to betray him to them when the crowd was not present.

PREPARATION FOR PASSOVER

[7] Then[k] the Day of Unleavened Bread came when the Passover lamb had to be sacrificed.[l] [8] Jesus sent Peter and John,[m] saying, "Go and make preparations for us to eat the Passover."

[9] "Where do you want us to prepare it?" they asked him.

[10] "Listen," he said to them, "when you've entered the city, a man carrying a water jug will meet you. Follow him into the house he enters. [11] Tell the owner of the house, 'The Teacher asks you, "Where is the guest room where I can eat the Passover with my disciples?"' [12] Then he will show you a large, furnished room upstairs.[n] Make the preparations there."

[13] So they went and found it just as he had told them,[o] and they prepared the Passover.

THE FIRST LORD'S SUPPER

[14] When[p] the hour came, he reclined at the table, and the apostles with him. [15] Then he said to them, "I have fervently desired to eat this Passover with you before I suffer.

[16] For I tell you, I will not eat it again[B] until it is fulfilled in the kingdom of God."[q] [17] Then he took a cup,[r] and after giving thanks,[s] he said, "Take this and share it among yourselves. [18] For I tell you, from now on I will not drink of the fruit of the vine until the kingdom of God comes."

[19] And he took bread, gave thanks, broke it, gave it to them, and said, "This is my body,[t] which is given for you. Do this in remembrance[u] of me."

[20] In the same way he also took the cup after supper and said, "This cup is the new covenant[v] in my blood,[w] which is poured out for you.[C] [21] But[x] look, the hand of the one betraying me is at the table with me.[y] [22] For the Son of Man will go away as it has been determined,[z] but woe to that man by whom he is betrayed!"

[23] So they began to argue[aa] among themselves which of them it could be who was going to do it.

THE DISPUTE OVER GREATNESS

[24] Then a dispute also arose among them about who should be considered the greatest.[ab] [25] But he said to them,[ac] "The kings of the Gentiles lord it over them, and those who have authority over them have themselves called[D] 'Benefactors.' [26] It is not to be like that among you. On the contrary, whoever is greatest among you should become like the youngest,[ad] and whoever leads, like the one serving. [27] For who is greater, the one at the table or the one serving? Isn't it the one at the table? But I am among you as the one who serves.[ae] [28] You are those who stood by me in my trials.[af] [29] I bestow on you a kingdom,[ag] just as my Father bestowed one on me, [30] so that you may eat and drink at my table in my kingdom.[ah] And you will sit on thrones judging the twelve tribes of Israel.[ai]

[a] 22:1-2 Mt 26:1-5; Mk 14:1-2
[b] 22:1 Ex 23:15
[c] Ex 12:11; Jn 6:4; 11:55; 13:1
[d] 22:2 Mt 12:14; 21:46
[e] Lk 19:47-48; 20:19
[f] 22:3-6 Mt 26:14-16; Mk 14:10-11
[g] 22:3 Jn 13:2,27; Ac 5:3
[h] Lk 6:16
[i] 22:4 Lk 22:52; Ac 4:1; 5:24,26; 16:20,22,35-36,38
[j] Mk 9:31
[k] 22:7-13 Mt 26:17-19; Mk 14:12-16
[l] 22:7 Ex 12:21; 1Co 5:7
[m] 22:8 Ac 3:1; 8:14
[n] 22:12 Ac 1:13
[o] 22:13 Lk 19:32
[p] 22:14 Mt 26:20; Mk 14:17

[q] 22:16 Lk 14:15; Rv 19:9
[r] 22:17-20 Mt 26:26-29; Mk 14:22-25; 1Co 11:23-25
[s] 22:17 Mt 14:19; 15:36
[t] 22:19 Jn 6:51-53
[u] Heb 10:3
[v] 22:20 Ex 24:8; Jr 31:31; Zch 9:11; 1Co 11:25; 2Co 3:6; Heb 7:22; 8:8,13; 9:15; 12:24; 13:20
[w] 1Co 10:16

[x] 22:21-23 Mt 26:21-24; Mk 14:18-21; Jn 13:18-26

[y] 22:21 Ps 41:9   [z] 22:22 Ac 2:23; 10:42; 17:26,31   [aa] 22:23 Mt 21:25; Mk 9:10; Lk 24:15   [ab] 22:24 Mk 9:34; Lk 1:32   [ac] 22:25-27 Mt 20:25-28; Mk 10:42-45
[ad] 22:26 Lk 9:48; 1Pt 5:3   [ae] 22:27 Mt 20:28; Jn 13:1-17   [af] 22:28 Heb 2:18; 4:15   [ag] 22:29 Mt 5:34; 2Tm 2:12   [ah] 22:30 Lk 22:16   [ai] Mt 19:28

[A] 22:5 Or *money*   [B] 22:16 Other mss omit *again*   [C] 22:19-20 Other mss omit *which is given for you* (v. 19) through the end of v. 20   [D] 22:25 Or *them call themselves*

22:10 This guy would be easy to spot because such a task was typically carried out by women.
22:11-12 That the man would oblige and show them a **furnished room upstairs** that they could use suggests that he was a follower of Jesus (22:12).
22:19-20 Jesus instituted a meal that the church has partaken of together ever since: Communion, or the Lord's Supper. As the church consumes this meal together, we affirm our common faith in Christ's substitutionary atoning sacrifice, our new covenantal, unified relationship with him, and his ongoing spiritual presence in our lives. As the apostle Paul told the church in Corinth, "As often as you eat this bread and drink the cup, you proclaim the Lord's death until he comes" (1 Cor 11:26). We'll remember his death for us in the *past* and utilize its power and provisions for us in the *present*, until he returns for us in the *future*.
22:22 Christ's betrayal involved both divine sovereignty and human responsibility. **The Son of Man** would be killed **as ... determined**: it had been foretold long ago in Scripture.

God had predetermined to sacrifice his Son—the Suffering Servant—to atone for sin (see Isa 53:5-6). Nevertheless, **woe to that man by whom he is betrayed** is a reminder that Judas was accountable for his actions. He was no puppet being forced to do something against his will.
22:24-30 The disciples would attain high **kingdom** privilege—ruling with Christ and enjoying fellowship with him (22:29-30)—but not as a result of exalting themselves. Instead, such blessings would come as a result of serving God and others.

[a] 22:31 Mt 4:10
[b] Am 9:9
[c] 22:32 Jn 17:9–15; Rm 8:34
[d] Jn 21:15–17; 1Co 1:9; Php 1:6; 1Th 5:24; 2Tm 2:13
[e] 22:33–34 Mt 26:33–35; Mk 14:29–31; Jn 13:37–38
[f] 22:35 Mt 10:9–10; Mk 6:8; Lk 9:3; 10:4

[g] 22:37 Is 53:12
[h] Jn 17:4; 19:30
[i] 22:39 Mt 26:30; Mk 14:26; Lk 4:30; Jn 18:1
[j] Lk 21:37
[k] Mt 21:1

❧ KINGDOM LIVING ❧
PERSONAL
There Is Safety in Surrender

Surrender has never been a popular concept. This is particularly true in our social-media-saturated, me-crazed society. But you can't skip it if you want to pursue God fully as his kingdom disciple. God has a lot of benefits and blessings in store for the believer who is fully surrendered to him and aligned under his rule.

When your tires are out of alignment, you may feel your car pull to one side. Sometimes you can't detect the problem while driving, but you'll certainly know your car needs an alignment when the front tires begin to wear unevenly. Some Christians look at their lives and see the uneven wear. They may even feel themselves being pulled to one side or the other by the world, the flesh, and the devil. They may be experiencing more defeats than victories.

Understand that until you bring your thoughts and actions into proper alignment under God's authority, you are going to wear out as you face whatever circumstances life gives you. Living under God's kingdom rule means saying to God day by day, "Not my will, but your will be done. I submit my desires to your desires, my dreams to your dreams, my purposes and plans to your purposes and plans." That aligns you under his kingdom rule.

If you've been aligned with the world, taking your cues from the culture and from your flesh, you'll find it tough to get yourself back in line under the lordship of Jesus Christ. But doing so is a necessary first step to being in a right relationship with God and experiencing a victorious, abundant life.

FOR THE NEXT PERSONAL
KINGDOM LIVING LESSON SEE PAGE 1382.

PETER'S DENIAL PREDICTED

31 "Simon, Simon,[A] look out. Satan[a] has asked to sift you like wheat.[b] **32** But I have prayed[c] for you that your faith may not fail. And you, when you have turned back, strengthen[d] your brothers."

33 "Lord,"[e] he told him, "I'm ready to go with you both to prison and to death."

34 "I tell you, Peter," he said, "the rooster will not crow today until[B] you deny three times that you know me."

BE READY FOR TROUBLE

35 He also said to them, "When I sent you out[f] without money-bag, traveling bag, or sandals, did you lack anything?"

"Not a thing," they said.

36 Then he said to them, "But now, whoever has a money-bag should take it, and also a traveling bag. And whoever doesn't have a sword should sell his robe and buy one. **37** For I tell you, what is written must be fulfilled in me:[c] **And he was counted among the lawless.**[D,g] Yes, what is written about me is coming to its fulfillment."[h]

38 "Lord," they said, "look, here are two swords."

"That is enough!" he told them.

THE PRAYER IN THE GARDEN

39 He went out and made his way[i] as usual[j] to the Mount of Olives,[k] and the disciples

---

[A] 22:31 Other mss read *Then the Lord said, "Simon, Simon* [B] 22:34 Other mss read *before* [C] 22:37 Or *it is necessary that what is written be fulfilled in me* [D] 22:37 Is 53:12

22:31 The *you* in Greek is plural, so Satan wanted to wreak havoc on all of the disciples. Yet, Jesus addressed Simon Peter. That's because Peter served as the de facto leader of the group. His failure would be the worst and could lead to the defeat and defection of the rest of the disciples. But Jesus intended to use him to restore the others.

Notice that Satan needed permission. If you are a child of God, Satan has no power over you unless God grants it. The devil is powerful, but he's God's devil. He operates under the sovereign hand of God. Why would God grant a satanic request? Though Satan simply wants to harm and destroy, God uses Satan's activity for his own holy purposes. The Lord sometimes allows Satan to tempt us in

order to draw out the evil that's in us—evil of which we may not even be aware. By doing this, he reveals to us our sinful tendencies and weaknesses so that he might lead us to repent. **22:32** Notice that Jesus didn't tell Peter, "*If you* turn back," but *When* **you have turned back** (emphasis added). According to Matthew, Jesus foretold that "all" of the disciples would run away that night, and they did (Matt 26:31, 56). So Jesus exhorted Peter to encourage and help them afterwards. Jesus prophesied Peter's failure, his repentance, and his usefulness. This gives hope to believers who have fallen. Jesus offers a road to spiritual recovery and future ministry usefulness when they repent (see John 21:15–17). **22:33–34** In other words, he assured Jesus, "You can count on me to endure jail time

and execution alongside you. I'm your man!" But it would only take the accusations of a servant girl to cause him to fall to pieces (22:56–57; cf. Matt 26:69–70). In just a few hours, he would **deny three times** that he even knew who Jesus was (Luke 22:34). This is a clear illustration of Proverbs 16:18: "Pride comes before destruction, and an arrogant spirit before a fall." What happened to Peter can happen to you if you're long on pride and short on humility. "Whoever thinks he stands must be careful not to fall" (1 Cor 10:12). **22:38** Notice that when they told him they had **two swords** among them, he said that was **enough**. Jesus's goal was not a military overthrow. They were not to become a militia.

a **22:40-46** Mt 26:36-46;
Mk 14:32-42
b **22:40** Mt 6:13; Lk
4:13; 11:4
c **22:41** Lk 18:11
d **22:42** Jn 18:11
e **22:43** Mt 4:11; Heb 1:14
f **22:44** Heb 5:7
g **22:47-53** Mt 26:47-56;
Mk 14:43-50; Jn 18:3-12

h **22:53** Lk 2:46; Jn 18:20
i Jn 12:27; 16:4
j Ac 26:18; Eph 6:12;
Col 1:13
k **22:54** Mt 26:58; Mk
14:54; Jn 18:15
l **22:55-62** Mt 26:69-75;
Mk 14:66-72; Jn 18:16-
18,25-27
m **22:55** Mt 26:3
n **22:61** Mk 10:21
o Lk 22:31-34; Ac 3:13-14
p **22:63-65** Mt 26:67-68;
Mk 14:65; Jn 18:22-23
q **22:65** Mk 3:29

followed him. **40** When he reached the place,*a* he told them, "Pray that you may not fall into temptation."*b* **41** Then he withdrew from them about a stone's throw, knelt down, and began to pray,*c* **42** "Father, if you are willing, take this cup*d* away from me — nevertheless, not my will, but yours, be done."

APPLICATION QUESTIONS

READ LUKE 22:41-42

– What obstacles regularly prevent you from identifying God's will?
– What obstacles regularly hinder you from carrying out God's will?
– How can these obstacles be overcome?

---

43 Then an angel from heaven*e* appeared to him, strengthening him. **44** Being in anguish,*f* he prayed more fervently, and his sweat became like drops of blood falling to the ground.^ **45** When he got up from prayer and came to the disciples, he found them sleeping, exhausted from their grief. **46** "Why are you sleeping?" he asked them. "Get up and pray, so that you won't fall into temptation."

JUDAS'S BETRAYAL OF JESUS

47 While*g* he was still speaking, suddenly a mob came, and one of the Twelve named Judas was leading them. He came near Jesus to kiss him, **48** but Jesus said to him, "Judas, are you betraying the Son of Man with a kiss?"

49 When those around him saw what was going to happen, they asked, "Lord, should we strike with the sword?" **50** Then one of them struck the high priest's servant and cut off his right ear.

51 But Jesus responded, "No more of this!" And touching his ear, he healed him.

52 Then Jesus said to the chief priests, temple police, and the elders who had come for him, "Have you come out with swords and clubs as if I were a criminal?*B* **53** Every day while I was with you in the temple,*h* you never laid a hand on me. But this is your hour*i* — and the dominion of darkness."*j*

PETER DENIES HIS LORD

54 They seized him, led him away, and brought him into the high priest's house. Meanwhile Peter*k* was following at a distance. **55** They*l* lit a fire in the middle of the courtyard*m* and sat down together, and Peter sat among them. **56** When a servant saw him sitting in the light, and looked closely at him, she said, "This man was with him too."

57 But he denied it: "Woman, I don't know him."

58 After a little while, someone else saw him and said, "You're one of them too."

"Man, I am not!" Peter said.

59 About an hour later, another kept insisting, "This man was certainly with him, since he's also a Galilean."

60 But Peter said, "Man, I don't know what you're talking about!" Immediately, while he was still speaking, a rooster crowed. **61** Then the Lord turned and looked at Peter.*n* So Peter remembered the word of the Lord, how he had said to him, "Before the rooster crows today, you will deny me three times."*o* **62** And he went outside and wept bitterly.

JESUS MOCKED AND BEATEN

63 The men who were holding Jesus started mocking and beating him.*p* **64** After blindfolding him, they kept*c* asking, "Prophesy! Who was it that hit you?" **65** And they were saying many other blasphemous*q* things to him.

---

^ **22:43-44** Other mss omit vv. 43-44   *B* **22:52** Lit *as against a thief,* or *a bandit*   *C* **22:64** Other mss add *striking him on the face and*

22:41-42 If you are willing, take this cup away from me (22:41). These words tell us Jesus knew the suffering he was about to face. In his humanity, he wanted to avoid the intense physical and spiritual anguish if it were possible. Yet, he wanted even more to do the will of his Father: **Nevertheless, not my will, but yours, be done** (22:42).

22:45-46 Jesus rebuked them for seeking physical rest when what they needed more than anything was spiritual strength (22:46). Most of us are willing to prepare ourselves to meet physical threats. Few of us, however, are willing to engage in the deep spiritual preparation necessary to meet spiritual threats. Why? We do not recognize the danger.

22:47-48 Judas used an act of love, a kiss, as a weapon.

22:50-51 Peter cut off the **ear** of **the high priest's servant** (22:50; see John 18:10). But Jesus rebuked him. The Scripture had to be fulfilled. The divine plan had to be accomplished. Sin had to be atoned for. So he touched the servant's **ear [and] healed him** (Luke 22:51).

22:52-53 They arrested Jesus at night like **a criminal** (22:52) rather than publicly during the day **in the temple** so that the crowds could witness it. They didn't want anyone to see the injustice of their actions because they were cowards under demonic influence (22:53).

22:56-57 This was Peter's first opportunity to make good on his promise to his Lord: "I'm ready to go with you both to prison and to death" (22:33). Instead, he caved: **Woman, I don't know him** (22:57). Before long, in fact, he'd been granted three opportunities to boldly acknowledge his discipleship, and he made three vehement denials that he knew who they were talking about (22:56-60). Thus, he failed just as Jesus had predicted.

22:63-65 Luke recognized these words and actions as **blasphemous** (22:65). They treated the Son of God with disgrace and humiliation rather than with praise and worship.

JESUS FACES THE SANHEDRIN

66 When daylight came,[a] the elders[A] of the people, both the chief priests and the scribes,[b] convened and brought him before their Sanhedrin.[c] **67** They said,[d] "If you are the Messiah, tell us."

But he said to them, "If I do tell you, you will not believe. **68** And if I ask you, you will not answer. **69** But from now on, the Son of Man will be seated at the right hand of the power of God."[e]

70 They all asked, "Are you, then, the Son of God?"[f]

And he said to them, "You say that I am."[g]

71 "Why do we need any more testimony," they said, "since we've heard it ourselves from his mouth?"

JESUS FACES PILATE

23 Then[n] their whole assembly rose up and brought him before Pilate. **2** They began to accuse him, saying, "We found this man misleading our nation, opposing payment of taxes[i] to Caesar, and saying that he himself is the Messiah, a king."

3 So Pilate asked him,[j] "Are you the king of the Jews?"[k]

He answered him, "You say so."[B]

4 Pilate then told the chief priests and the crowds, "I find no grounds[l] for charging this man."

5 But they kept insisting, "He stirs up the people,[m] teaching throughout all Judea, from Galilee[n] where he started even to here."

JESUS FACES HEROD ANTIPAS

6 When Pilate[o] heard this,[c] he asked if the man was a Galilean. **7** Finding that he was under Herod's jurisdiction, he sent him to Herod,[p] who was also in Jerusalem during those days. **8** Herod was very glad to see Jesus; for a long time he had wanted to see him because he had heard about him and was hoping to see some miracle[D] performed by him. **9** So he kept asking him questions, but Jesus did not answer him.[q] **10** The chief priests and the scribes stood by, vehemently accusing him. **11** Then Herod, with his soldiers, treated him with contempt, mocked[r] him, dressed him in bright clothing,[s] and sent him back to Pilate. **12** That very day Herod and Pilate became friends.[E,t] Previously, they had been enemies.

JESUS OR BARABBAS

13 Pilate called together the chief priests, the leaders, and the people,[u] **14** and said to them, "You have brought me this man as one who misleads the people.[v] But in fact, after examining him in your presence, I have found no grounds[w] to charge this man with those things you accuse him of. **15** Neither has Herod, because he sent him back to us. Clearly, he has done nothing to deserve death. **16** Therefore, I will have him whipped[F,x] and then release him."[G]

18 Then[y] they all cried out together, "Take this man away![z] Release Barabbas to us!" **19** (He had been thrown into prison for a rebellion that had taken place in the city, and for murder.)

20 Wanting to release Jesus,[aa] Pilate addressed them again, **21** but they kept shouting, "Crucify! Crucify him!"

22 A third time he said to them, "Why? What has this man done wrong?[ab] I have found in him no grounds[ac] for the death penalty. Therefore, I will have him whipped and then release him."

23 But they kept up the pressure, demanding with loud voices that he be crucified, and

a **22:66** Mt 27:1; Mk 15:1; Jn 18:28
b **22:67** Lk 9:22; 20:1
c **22:67** Mk 13:9
d **22:67-71** Mt 26:63-66; Mk 14:61-64; Jn 18:19-21
e **22:69** Ps 110:1; Mk 16:19; Ac 7:56; Heb 1:3
f **22:70** Mt 4:3; Lk 1:32,35
g **22:70** Mt 26:64; 27:11; Lk 23:3
n **23:1-5** Mt 27:1,11-14; Mk 15:1-5; Jn 18:28-38
h **23:2** Lk 20:22-25
i **23:2** Mt 27:11; Mk 15:2
k **22:2** Lk 23:37-38; Jn 18:39; 19:3
l **23:4** Mt 27:24; Lk 23:14,22; Jn 19:4,6; 1Pt 2:22
m **23:5** Ac 17:5-8,13
n **23:5** Mt 4:12,23; Lk 4:14; Jn 1:43; 2:11
o **23:6** 1Tm 6:13
p **23:7** Lk 3:1; 9:7-9; 13:31

q **23:9** Is 53:7; Mt 27:12,14; Mk 15:4-5; Jn 19:9
r **23:11** Is 53:3; Mk 9:12; Lk 18:32; Ac 4:11
s **Mt 27:28; Mk 15:17
t **23:12** Ps 2:2; Ac 4:27
u **23:13** Lk 23:35; 24:20; Jn 7:26,48; 12:42
v **23:14** Lk 23:2
w Lk 23:4
x **23:16** Jn 19:1; Ac 5:40
y **23:18-23** Mt 27:15-23; Mk 15:6-14; Jn 18:40
z **23:18** Ac 21:36; 22:22
aa **23:20** Ac 3:13-14
ab **23:22** Jn 8:46
ac Lk 23:4

A **22:66** Or *council of elders*   B **23:3** Or *"That is true."*   C **23:6** Other mss read *heard "Galilee"*   D **23:8** Or *sign*   E **23:12** Lit *friends with one another*
F **23:16** Gk *paideuo*; to discipline or *"teach a lesson"*   G **23:16** Some mss include v. 17: *For according to the festival he had to release someone to them.*

22:66 The council of elders over which the high priest presided was a body of Jewish religious leaders known as the **Sanhedrin**.
22:69 Though the religious leaders thought they were about to be rid of him, Jesus knew that he would soon be seated in glory at **the right hand of** his Father.
23:1 Since the Jews were unable to execute anyone themselves, they needed the Roman governor's help.
23:2 They wanted to make Jesus appear to be an insurrectionist, someone who was a threat to Roman rule. If he was proclaiming himself to be a king and opposing Caesar, then Pilate would have to take action. Don't miss that they charged him with opposing paying **taxes to Caesar**. That was an outright lie (see 20:20-26).
23:7-8 **Herod** Antipas was the son of Herod the Great (who had sought to kill Jesus when he was a child; see Matt 2:16) and was the tetrarch who ruled over Galilee. It was this Herod who had put John the Baptist in prison and later beheaded him (Luke 3:18-20; 9:7-9). If he thought Jesus was going to do tricks for him, he was sorely disappointed.
23:11 Since Jesus wouldn't act like a performing seal, **Herod [and] his soldiers** made a mockery of him instead.
23:13-16 Pilate was not ultimately concerned with justice but with maintaining order.
23:18-19 Pilate would customarily perform an act of clemency during the Passover and set a Jewish prisoner free. Though he wanted to release Jesus, the leaders demanded **Barabbas** (23:18), a rebel and murderer, instead (23:19). This sheds light on how great their hatred of Jesus was. He had committed no sin. Yet he had won the adoration of the crowds, challenged the leaders' sacred traditions, and made them look like fools. Their jealousy and anger drove them to petition for the release of a murderer and to condemn a righteous man.
23:20-25 Pilate knew Jesus was innocent of the charges against him, but he preferred public order to justice—expediency to righteousness.

[a] 23:24-25 Mt 27:24-26; Mk 15:15; Jn 19:16
[b] 23:24 Php 4:6
[c] 23:25 Lk 24:20; Ac 4:24-28
[d] 23:26-32 Mt 27:31-32; Mk 15:20-21; Jn 19:17
[e] 23:26 Rm 16:3
[f] Lk 9:23; 14:27
[g] 23:27 Lk 8:52; Ac 8:2; Rv 1:7; 18:9
[h] 23:28 Sg 1:5; 2:7
[i] 23:29 Lk 17:22
[j] Mt 24:19; Mk 13:17; Lk 11:27; 21:23
[k] 23:30 Hs 10:8
[l] 23:31 Ezk 20:47; Lk 19:41
[m] 23:32 Is 53:12; Mt 27:38; Mk 15:27; Lk 22:37; Jn 19:18
[n] 23:33-34 Mt 27:33-38; Mk 15:22-27; Jn 19:17-24

[o] 23:34 Mt 5:16; 6:1; 11:27; Jn 8:42
[p] Mt 11:25; Lk 6:29,35; 22:42
[q] Ac 3:17; 1Co 2:6-8
[r] Ps 22:18
[s] 23:35-38 Mt 27:43,48; Mk 15:26,29-32; Jn 19:19,29
[t] 23:35 Ps 22:7,17; Lk 16:14; 23:13
[u] Is 42:1; Mt 1:17; 12:18; Lk 9:20,35; 1Pt 2:4
[v] 23:36 Ps 69:21
[w] 23:37 Lk 23:3
[x] 23:39-43 Mt 27:44; Mk 15:32
[y] 23:40 Ps 147:11; Pr 1:7; Ac
[z] 23:41 Lk 23:410:2; Rv 14:7
[aa] 23:42 Jdg 16:28; 1Sm 25:31; Neh 5:19; Jb 14:13; Ps 106:4
[ab] Mk 8:38; Ac 20:25
[ac] 23:43 2Co 12:4; Rv 2:7

their voices[A] won out. [24] So[a] Pilate decided to grant their demand[b] [25] and released the one they were asking for, who had been thrown into prison for rebellion and murder. But he handed Jesus over to their will.[c]

THE WAY TO THE CROSS

[26] As[d] they led him away, they seized Simon, a Cyrenian,[e] who was coming in from the country, and laid the cross[f] on him to carry behind Jesus. [27] A large crowd of people followed him, including women who were mourning and lamenting him.[g] [28] But turning to them, Jesus said, "Daughters of Jerusalem,[h] do not weep for me, but weep for yourselves and your children. [29] Look, the days are coming[i] when they will say, 'Blessed are the women without children, the wombs that never bore, and the breasts that never nursed!'[j] [30] Then they will begin **to say to the mountains, 'Fall on us!' and to the hills, 'Cover us!'**[B,k] [31] For if they do these things when the wood is green, what will happen when it is dry?"[l]

CRUCIFIED BETWEEN TWO CRIMINALS

[32] Two others — criminals[m] — were also led away to be executed with him. [33] When[n] they arrived at the place called The Skull, they crucified him there, along with the criminals, one on the right and one on the left. [34] Then Jesus said, "Father,[o] forgive[p] them, because they do not know what they are doing."[C,q] And they divided his clothes and cast lots.[r]

[35] The[s] people stood watching, and even the leaders were scoffing:[t] "He saved others; let him save himself if this is God's Messiah, the Chosen One!"[u] [36] The soldiers also mocked him. They came offering him sour wine[v] [37] and said, "If you are the King of the Jews,[w] save yourself!"

[38] An inscription was above him:[D] THIS IS THE KING OF THE JEWS.

[39] Then[x] one of the criminals hanging there began to yell insults at[E] him: "Aren't you the Messiah? Save yourself and us!"

[40] But the other answered, rebuking him: "Don't you even fear God,[y] since you are undergoing the same punishment? [41] We are punished justly, because we're getting back what we deserve for the things we did, but this man has done nothing wrong."[z] [42] Then he said, "Jesus, remember me[F,aa] when you come into your kingdom."[ab]

[43] And he said to him, "Truly I tell you, today you will be with me in paradise."[ac]

[A] 23:23 Other mss add *and those of the chief priests*　[B] 23:30 Hs 10:8　[C] 23:34 Other mss omit *Then Jesus said, "Father, forgive them, because they do not know what they are doing."*　[D] 23:38 Other mss add *written in Greek, Latin, and Hebrew letters*　[E] 23:39 Or *began to blaspheme*
[F] 23:42 Other mss add *Lord*

23:26 The other Gospels make it clear that Jesus had endured a brutal beating and scourging by this point (see Matt 27:26-31; Mark 15:15-20; John 19:1-3). So, even though a condemned man was typically forced to carry his cross to the place of crucifixion, Jesus was apparently too weakened to bear the burden. **Simon** was from Cyrene, a place on the coast of what is now Libya. He was African.

23:28 Jesus gave this warning in light of the judgment that was coming on the nation for rejecting the Messiah. Israel could not reject their Messiah without experiencing severe consequences.

23:31 **If they do these things when the wood is green** (that is, when the Messiah is with them), **what will happen when it is dry** (after he is gone)?

23:34 Even as he was being tortured to death, Jesus remembered the purpose for which he came—to open the door of divine forgiveness for all who would receive him. He prayed that the Father would **forgive** even his executioners, because they did not **know what they [were] doing**. Yet, even as he pleaded for mercy for them, they gambled for **his clothes**, fulfilling prophecy from Psalm 22:18 (see John 19:23-24). Behold our Savior: as sinners mocked him, he interceded for them so that they might repent and be saved.

23:35 Only by remaining on the cross and sacrificing his own life could Jesus provide salvation.

The religious leaders reveled in their "victory," but they had failed to grasp his mission. Even as he hung dying, the Son was winning the victory for which the Father had sent him.

23:36-38 The soldiers probably jeered at every criminal they were ordered to execute. But in this case, their ridicule reflected the **inscription** that Pilate had commanded to be placed on the cross: THIS IS THE KING OF THE JEWS (23:38; see John 19:19-22). Yet, ironically, the very thing they **mocked** was true (Luke 23:36). Before them hung the King of the Jews—and the King of all creation. One day, they will stand before him again. But on that day he will be seated on a throne pronouncing their judgment.

23:39-42 The two criminals crucified with Jesus reached different conclusions about who the man in the middle was. The rebellious criminal joined the crowd. He hurled **insults at** Jesus, ridiculing the idea that he was **the Messiah** (23:39). But the repentant one recognized that Jesus was both an innocent man who had **done nothing wrong** and a King about to enter his heavenly **kingdom** (23:41-42). Your eternal destiny is necessarily connected to your understanding of who Jesus is.

The men reached different conclusions regarding their own guilt. The first criminal failed to come to grips with his own sinfulness. There was no admission of blame, no **fear [of] God**. But his companion rebuked him. He rightly concluded that they were

being **punished justly** for their crimes (23:40-41). Without the comprehension that you are a sinner in rebellion against and separated from a holy God, you cannot be saved.

The two men reached different conclusions about what they needed to be delivered from. The unrepentant criminal simply wanted deliverance from his present earthly circumstances. **Save yourself and us**, he demanded of Jesus, meaning, "Keep us from dying!" (23:39). But the second criminal understood that there was something beyond their present trouble. One day, we all must face eternity and—unless we have a mediator—the wrath of God. With a repentant heart, this man recognized Jesus as the Mediator he needed: **Jesus, remember me when you come into your kingdom** (23:42). Hearing Jesus call his Father to forgive his executioners (see 23:34) was sufficient for this man to change his opinion about Jesus and place saving faith in him.

23:43 Salvation comes when we put our faith alone in Christ alone. The criminal didn't have an opportunity to follow the Lord in a life of obedience—though if he had lived he surely could have. Nevertheless, he did exactly what was required in order to be reconciled to God. And later that day, though his physical body died, his spirit and soul went to **paradise** with King Jesus, awaiting his future bodily resurrection. This affirms that believers go immediately into God's presence at death.

THE DEATH OF JESUS

44 It[a] was now about noon,[A] and darkness came over the whole land[B] until three,[C] **45** because the sun's light failed.[D] The curtain[b] of the sanctuary was split down the middle. **46** And Jesus called out with a loud voice, "Father, **into your hands I entrust my spirit.**"[E,c] Saying this, he breathed his last.

47 When the centurion saw what happened, he began to glorify[d] God, saying, "This man really was righteous!"[F] **48** All the crowds that had gathered for this spectacle, when they saw what had taken place, went home, striking their chests.[e] **49** But[f] all who knew him, including the women who had followed him from Galilee, stood at a distance,[g] watching these things.

THE BURIAL OF JESUS

50 There[h] was a good and righteous man named Joseph, a member of the Sanhedrin, **51** who had not agreed with their plan[i] and action. He was from Arimathea, a Judean town, and was looking forward to the kingdom of God.[j] **52** He approached Pilate and asked for Jesus's body. **53** Taking it down, he wrapped it in fine linen and placed it in a tomb cut into the rock, where no one had ever been placed.[G,k] **54** It was the preparation day, and the Sabbath was about to begin.[H] **55** The women[i] who had come with him from Galilee followed along and observed the tomb and how his body was placed. **56** Then they returned and prepared spices and perfumes.[m] And they rested on the Sabbath according to the commandment.[n]

RESURRECTION MORNING

24 On[o] the first day of the week,[p] very early in the morning, they[i] came to the tomb, bringing the spices they had prepared. **2** They found the stone rolled away from the tomb. **3** They went in but did not find the body[q] of the Lord Jesus.[r] **4** While they were perplexed about this, suddenly two men stood by them in dazzling[s] clothes. **5** So the women were terrified and bowed down to the ground.

"Why are you looking for the living among the dead?" asked the men. **6** "He is not here, but he has risen![t] Remember how he spoke to you when he was still in Galilee,[u] **7** saying, 'It is necessary that the Son of Man be betrayed[v] into the hands of sinful men, be crucified, and rise[w] on the third day'?" **8** And they remembered his words.

9 Returning from the tomb, they reported all these things to the Eleven[x] and to all the rest. **10** Mary Magdalene, Joanna, Mary the mother of James,[y] and the other women with them were telling the apostles[z] these things. **11** But these words seemed like nonsense to them, and they did not believe[aa] the women. **12** Peter,[ab] however, got up and ran to the tomb. When he stooped to look in, he saw only the linen cloths.[J,ac] So he went away, amazed[ad] at what had happened.

THE EMMAUS DISCIPLES

13 Now[ae] that same day two of them were on their way to a village called Emmaus, which was about seven miles[K,af] from Jerusalem.[ag] **14** Together they were discussing everything that had taken place. **15** And while they were discussing and arguing, Jesus himself came near and began to

[a] 23:44-49 Mt 27:45-56; Mk 15:33-41
[b] 23:45 Ex 26:31-33; Heb 6:19
[c] 23:46 Ps 31:5; Is 53:12; Jn 19:30; 1Co 15:55; 1Pt 4:19
[d] 23:47 Lk 13:13
[e] 23:48 Lk 18:13
[f] 23:49 Mt 27:55-56; Mk 15:40-41; Jn 19:25
[g] Ps 38:11; 88:8
[h] 23:50-56 Mt 27:57-61; Mk 15:42-47; Jn 19:38-42
[i] 23:51 Ac 2:23
[j] Lk 2:25,38
[k] 23:53 Is 53:9; Mk 11:2
[l] 23:55 Lk 1:42
[m] 23:56 Mk 16:1; Lk 24:1
[n] Ex 20:10; Dt 5:14

[o] 24:1-12 Mt 28:1-10; Mk 16:1-11; Jn 20:1-18
[p] 24:1 Ac 20:7; 1Co 16:2
[q] 24:3 Lk 12:4
[r] Lk 7:13; Ac 1:21
[s] 24:4 Lk 2:9; 17:24; Ac 12:7
[t] 24:6 Mt 26:32; Mk 5:41; 9:27; Jn 2:19; 1Co 15:4
[u] Mt 17:22-23; Mk 9:30-31; Lk 9:22,44
[v] 24:7 Lk 9:22,31,44; 18:32-33; 23:21
[w] Mt 17:9,23; Mk 8:31; 9:31; 10:34; Lk 18:33; 24:46
[x] 24:9 Ac 1:15-26; 2:14
[y] 24:10 Mk 15:40; 16:1; Lk 8:2-3
[z] Lk 6:13
[aa] 24:11 Mt 28:17; Lk 24:41; Jn 20:25,27
[ab] 24:12 Lk 6:14; Ac 10:32
[ac] Lk 23:53
[ad] Lk 1:21,63; 2:18,33; 4:22; Ac 2:7; 3:12
[ae] 24:13 Mk 16:12-13
[af] Rv 21:16
[ag] Mt 23:37; Ac 8:1

[A] 23:44 Lit *about the sixth hour*   [B] 23:44 Or *whole earth*   [C] 23:44 Lit *the ninth hour*   [D] 23:45 Other mss read *three, and the sun was darkened*
[E] 23:46 Ps 31:5   [F] 23:47 Or *innocent*   [G] 23:53 Or *interred*, or *laid*   [H] 23:54 Lit *was dawning*   [I] 24:1 Other mss add *and other women with them*
[J] 24:12 Other mss add *lying there*   [K] 24:13 Lit *about sixty stadia*; one *stadion* = 600 feet

---

23:44 It wasn't possible for the Son of God to be rejected and killed without it causing an ominous reaction from his creation.

23:45 The curtain symbolized the separation that existed between a holy God and sinful people. Only the high priest could enter the most holy place to make atonement for Israel's sins. But through the perfect atoning sacrifice of our "great high priest," Jesus Christ (see Heb 4:14; 7:27; 10:10, 12), human beings everywhere have access to God through him. The way to God is open. You no longer need the Old Testament sacrificial system; you only need Jesus and faith in his work.

23:46 When Jesus finally yielded up his life and **breathed his last**, he entrusted himself to his **Father**, quoting Psalm 31:5.

23:49 The women were anxious to know where he would be buried so that they could later anoint his body (see 23:55-56).

23:50-53 Though most of the Jewish religious leaders had opposed Jesus, there were notable exceptions. One of these was **a member of the Sanhedrin** who was named **Joseph**. He was **a . . . righteous man** who was **looking forward to the kingdom of God** (23:50-51). He boldly demonstrated his faith in Jesus by going publicly to **Pilate** and asking for **Jesus's body** so that he might bury him (23:52). Helped by Nicodemus, another Jewish leader who had opposed the Sanhedrin's plan (see John 3:1-2; 7:50-51; 19:39-40), Joseph **wrapped** and buried the body **in a tomb** that had never been used (Luke 23:53).

23:54 Jesus was crucified, died, and was buried on Friday. **The Sabbath** began at sundown on Friday.
24:1 The first day of the week is Sunday.
24:4 Though they appeared to be **men**, the two were actually angels (see 24:23; Matt 28:5).
24:10 Mary Magdalene, Joanna, [and] Mary the mother of James were among the women who played a prominent role in Jesus's ministry, supporting him from their own possessions (see 8:1-3). They were given the privilege of being the first to learn of the resurrection and to communicate it.
24:13-17 Two men were traveling to **Emmaus** (24:13). When Jesus—whom they didn't recognize—asked them what they were discussing, **they stopped walking and looked discouraged** (24:17). Their unbelief prevented them from recognizing him.

Video Devotional

"JESUS THROUGH THE BIBLE"

Jesus Christ is revealed in every book of the Bible.

a 24:16 Lk 9:45; 18:34; Jn 20:14-15; 21:4
b 24:18 Ac 26:26
c 24:19 Lk 4:34; 18:37; Ac 2:22
d Dt 18:15; Lk 4:24
e Lk 4:14; Ac 1:1; 2:22
f Lk 18:43
g 24:20 Lk 23:13
h Lk 9:44; 18:32; Ac 3:13; 13:27-28
i Lk 23:21,25; Ac 5:30
j 24:21 Lk 22:20; Ac 1:6
k Lk 9:22; 13:32; 18:33
l 24:24 Lk 24:12; Jn 20:2-10
m 24:25 Lk 16:31; 18:31; Ac 26:27; 2Pt 1:21
n 24:26 Lk 24:44-48; 1Co 15:3-5
o Lk 9:26,32; 21:27; 22:69; Ac 2:33; 7:55; 22:11
p 24:27 Gn 3:15; 12:3; 22:18; Nm 21:9; 24:17
q 2Sm 7:12-16; 5:7:14; 9:6; 52:13–53:12; Jr 23:5-6; Dn 7:13-14; Mc 5:2; Zch 9:9; 12:10
r Lk 16:16
s 24:28 Mk 6:48
t 24:30 Lk 9:16; 22:19
u 24:31 2Kg 6:17; Lk 24:16
v Jn 20:19,26
w 24:32 Ac 17:3; 1Co 15:3-8
x 24:33 Lk 24:9
y 24:34 Lk 22:32; 1Co 15:4-5
z 24:35 Ac 2:42
aa 24:36-44 Jn 20:19-20
ab 24:36 Lk 2:14; 7:50; 8:48; 10:5; 19:38; Ac 10:36
ac 24:37 Lk 24:5; Ac 10:4; 24:25

walk along with them. [16] But they[A] were prevented from recognizing him.[a] [17] Then he asked them, "What is this dispute that you're having[B] with each other as you are walking?" And they stopped walking and looked discouraged.

[18] The one named Cleopas answered him, "Are you the only visitor in Jerusalem who doesn't know the things that happened there in these days?"[b]

[19] "What things?" he asked them.

So they said to him, "The things concerning Jesus of Nazareth,[c] who was a prophet[d] powerful in action and speech[e] before God and all the people,[f] [20] and how our chief priests and leaders[g] handed him over to be sentenced to death,[h] and they crucified him.[i] [21] But we were hoping that he was the one who was about to redeem[j] Israel. Besides all this, it's the third day[k] since these things happened. [22] Moreover, some women from our group astounded us. They arrived early at the tomb, [23] and when they didn't find his body, they came and reported that they had seen a vision of angels who said he was alive. [24] Some of those who were with us went to the tomb and found it just as the women had said, but they didn't see him."[l]

[25] He said to them, "How foolish you are, and how slow[C] to believe all that the prophets have spoken![m] [26] Wasn't it necessary for the Messiah to suffer[n] these things and enter into his glory?"[o] [27] Then beginning with Moses[p] and all the Prophets,[q] he interpreted for them the things concerning himself in all the Scriptures.[r]

[28] They came near the village where they were going, and he gave the impression that he was going farther.[s] [29] But they urged him, "Stay with us, because it's almost evening, and now the day is almost over." So he went in to stay with them.

[30] It was as he reclined at the table with them that he took the bread, blessed and broke[t] it, and gave it to them. [31] Then their eyes were opened,[u] and they recognized him, but he disappeared from their sight.[v] [32] They said to each other, "Weren't our hearts burning within us while he was talking with us on the road and explaining the Scriptures[w] to us?" [33] That very hour they got up and returned to Jerusalem. They found the Eleven[x] and those with them gathered together, [34] who said, "The Lord has truly been raised and has appeared to Simon!"[y] [35] Then they began to describe what had happened on the road and how he was made known to them in the breaking of the bread.[z]

THE REALITY OF THE RISEN JESUS

[36] As[aa] they were saying these things, he himself stood in their midst. He said to them, "Peace[ab] to you!" [37] But they were startled and terrified[ac] and thought they were seeing a ghost.[ad] [38] "Why are you troubled?"[ae] he asked them. "And why do doubts arise in your hearts? [39] Look at my hands and my feet, that it is I myself![af] Touch me and see,[ag] because a ghost does not have flesh and bones as you can see I have." [40] Having said this, he showed them his hands and feet. [41] But while they still were amazed and in disbelief because of their joy, he asked them, "Do you have anything here to eat?" [42] So they gave him a piece of a broiled fish,[D] [43] and he took it and ate in their presence.

[44] He told them, "These are my words[ah] that I spoke to you while I was still with you — that everything written about me in the Law of Moses, the Prophets,[ai] and the Psalms[aj] must be fulfilled." [45] Then he opened their minds[ak] to understand[al] the Scriptures. [46] He also said to them, "This is

ad 24:37 Mt 14:26   ae 24:38 Jn 14:1,27   af 24:39 Jn 20:25,27   ag Mt 28:9; Ac 2:31; 17:18,31-32; 23:6-10; 24:15,21   ah 24:44 Lk 9:22,44; 17:25; 18:31-33; 22:37   ai Ac 13:15; 28:23   aj Ps 2:6-9; 16:10; 22:1-18; 34:20; 41:9; 69:1-9,20-21,26; 110:1-7; 118:22-26   ak 24:45 Lk 24:27,31   al Lk 9:45; 18:34

A 24:16 Lit *their eyes*   B 24:17 Lit *"What are these words that you are exchanging*   C 24:25 Lit *slow of heart*   D 24:42 Other mss add *and some honeycomb*

24:18-20 These guys proceeded to explain who **Jesus of Nazareth** was—to *Jesus* (24:19)! **24:21 We were hoping that he was the one who was about to redeem Israel.** This implies they had expected him to redeem them from Roman rule and set them free. They had put all of their eggs in the Jesus basket. But their dreams had been destroyed; their hearts were broken.

24:22-24 "We don't know where he is," was essentially the complaint these men made to the very man they were looking for! How wonderful that the one they couldn't find was walking alongside them.

24:25-27 Jesus is the Son of God, sitting now at the right hand of the Father, crowned with honor and glory. But he had to endure great suffering to get there (24:26). The disciples had missed what Scripture said about the Messiah. Likewise, many people today are excited about the promises and blessings of the Bible, but they avoid those passages that talk about trials and pain. However, you can't have one without the other. We must be willing to accept the total package.

Jesus **interpreted for them the things concerning himself in all the Scriptures**. It's a reminder that whether we're reading about Adam, Abraham, Moses, David, or Isaiah, we must always be looking for Jesus in the Old Testament Scriptures because they were written with him in mind.

24:29-30 Notice what happened. The guest became the host. They invited him in, and he fed them.

24:33 Once Jesus disappeared, the men hurried off to **Jerusalem**, making the same seven-mile journey they'd just traveled in reverse!

24:35 They recognized him during **the breaking of the bread** because they saw the nail prints in his hands.

24:41-43 He **ate** a **piece of a broiled fish** to give further proof that he was no apparition but had a resurrected body (24:42-43).

what is written:[A] The Messiah would suffer and rise from the dead the third day,[a] [47] and repentance for[B] forgiveness of sins[b] would be proclaimed in his name to all the nations,[c] beginning at Jerusalem.[d] [48] You are witnesses[e] of these things. [49] And look, I am sending you[c] what my Father promised.[f] As for you, stay in the city[D] until you are empowered[E,g] from on high."

THE ASCENSION OF JESUS

[50] Then he led them out to the vicinity of Bethany,[h] and lifting up his hands[i] he blessed them. [51] And while he was blessing them, he left them and was carried up into heaven.[j] [52] After worshiping him,[k] they returned to Jerusalem with great joy.[l] [53] And they were continually in the temple praising God.[F,m]

[a]24:46 Ps 16:10; Lk 9:22,44; 17:25; 18:32; Ac 8:26–40; 1Co 15:3–4
[b]24:47 Hs 14:2; Lk 3:3; Ac 2:38; 5:31; 8:22
[c]Gn 12:3; Ps 22:27; Is 2:2; 49:6; Hs 2:23; Mal 1:11; Mt 28:19–20; Mk 16:15
[d]24:47–49 Ac 1:4-8
[e]24:48 Ac 4:20,33
[f]24:49 Is 32:15; Jl 2:28-32; Jn 14:26; Ac 2:16–21; Eph 1:13
[g]Ac 4:33; Rm 15:13

[h]24:50 Lk 19:29; Ac 1:12   [i]Lv 9:22; 1Tm 2:8   [j]24:51 Mk 16:19; Jn 20:17; Ac 1:9–11   [k]24:52 Mt 28:17   [l]Lk 2:10   [m]24:53 Ac 2:46; 3:1; 5:42

[A]24:46 Other mss add *and thus it was necessary that*   [B]24:47 Many mss read *repentance and*   [C]24:49 Lit *upon you*   [D]24:49 Other mss add *of Jerusalem*   [E]24:49 Lit *clothed with power*   [F]24:53 Other mss read *praising and blessing God. Amen.*

24:49 The **Father** had **promised** the Holy Spirit.
24:50 **Bethany** was less than two miles from Jerusalem.
24:52-53 Worship, **joy**, praise—that's where our faith in the risen Lord Jesus Christ should lead us.

JOHN

INTRODUCTION

Author

THE TITLE OF THIS GOSPEL (also frequently called "the Fourth Gospel") indicates that its author was John. Early church fathers like Irenaeus and Clement of Alexandria attributed authorship to the apostle John, the son of Zebedee. Some modern critical scholars have attempted to argue that the Fourth Gospel was penned by a different John (or someone else entirely), but this is speculation lacking genuine proof.

In addition to the testimony of the early church, the internal evidence from the Gospel itself supports the idea that it was written by John the son of Zebedee. Not only was the author an eyewitness to Jesus (1:14; 19:35), but he also identifies himself in 21:20 as "the disciple Jesus loved" (see 13:23; 19:26; 20:2). This disciple was present at the Last Supper (13:23), a meal that Jesus shared with the Twelve (see Matt 26:20; Mark 14:17; Luke 22:14). Moreover, since this disciple is not named in the Fourth Gospel, he can't be any of the disciples who are named (Andrew, Nathanael, Peter, Philip, Thomas, Judas Iscariot, or Judas the son of James). We also see that this disciple whom Jesus loved was one of those present when the resurrected Jesus appeared to Peter, Thomas, Nathanael, Zebedee's sons (James and John), and two other disciples (see John 21:2; 21:20). That means he must be James, John, or one of the two unnamed disciples. James, however, died an early martyr's death in AD 42—a date too early for him to have written the Gospel. And there's no historical support for the Gospel being written by any of the remaining disciples. We thus have good reasons for believing that John the son of Zebedee authored the Fourth Gospel.

Historical Background

The author is aware of Peter's martyrdom (21:19), which happened in AD 65/66. The church historian Jerome claims that John died in about AD 98; thus, the Gospel was written sometime between these dates. Many evangelical scholars think a date in the 80s is most likely. Testimony from the church fathers indicates that the apostle John ministered in Ephesus during the latter years of his life. Therefore, he likely wrote it from there.

Message and Purpose

John was the beloved disciple of Jesus, with whom he had a close relationship. He wanted the readers of his Gospel to know Jesus Christ and become intimate with

him as well. To only know Jesus for heaven tomorrow is to miss the joy of heaven on earth in a growing, living relationship with Christ today.

John brings both of these concepts together in his book. He says Jesus is the divine Messiah—God dwelling in our midst—who has a kingdom that is not of this world. John records eight miracles to show that Jesus is no ordinary man. He is a man, to be sure, but he is the God-Man, the Word who became flesh (1:14). He wept at a grave one moment, and raised Lazarus from the dead the next.

John also records seven "I am" statements of Jesus, showing him to be the one who revealed himself to Moses at the burning bush. John conclusively demonstrates that Jesus is the Christ so that by believing in him you may have eternal life (20:31). But the Gospel of John is also about how to have abundant life (10:10), the fruitful, fulfilling, kingdom life that Jesus offers those who follow him.

www.bhpublishinggroup.com/qr/te/43_00

Outline

PROLOGUE

1 In the beginning[a] was the Word,[b] and the Word was with God, and the Word was God.[c] **2** He was with God in the beginning.[d] **3** All things were created[e] through him,[f] and apart from him not one thing was created that has been created. **4** In him was life,[A,g] and that life was the light[h] of men. **5** That light shines[i] in the darkness, and yet the darkness did not overcome[B] it.[j]

6 There was a man sent from God whose name was John.[k] **7** He came as a witness to testify about the light, so that all might believe through him.[C] **8** He was not the light, but he came to testify[l] about the light. **9** The true light[m] that gives light to everyone, was coming into the world.[D,n]

10 He was in the world, and the world was created[o] through him, and yet the world did not recognize him. **11** He came to his own, and his own people did not receive him. **12** But to all who did receive[p] him,[q] he gave them the right[r] to be[E] children[s] of God,[t] to those who believe[u] in his name,[v] **13** who were born,[w] not of natural descent,[F] or of the will[x] of the flesh,[y] or of the will of man,[G] but of God.[z]

14 The Word[aa] became flesh[ab] and dwelt[H] among us. We observed his glory,[ac] the glory as the one and only[ad] Son[i] from the Father, full of grace and truth. **15** (John testified concerning him and exclaimed, "This was the one of whom I said, 'The one coming after me[ae] ranks ahead of me,[af] because he existed before me.' ")[ag] **16** Indeed, we have all received grace[ah] upon[J] grace from his fullness, **17** for the law was given through Moses;[ai] grace and truth[aj] came through Jesus Christ. **18** No one has ever seen God. The one and only[ak] Son, who is himself God and is at the Father's[al] side[K] —he has revealed him.[am]

JOHN THE BAPTIST'S TESTIMONY

19 This was John's testimony when the Jews from Jerusalem[an] sent priests[ao] and Levites[ap] to ask him, "Who are you?"

[a]1:1 Gn 1:1; Col 1:18
[b]Jn 1:14; 1Jn 1:1; Rv 19:13
[c]Jn 20:28; Php 2:6
[d]1:2 Jn 8:38; 17:5; Ac 26:4
[e]1:3 Col 1:16; Heb 1:2
[f]Rm 11:36
[g]1:4 1Jn 2:5
[h]Ps 36:9; Jn 12:46
[i]1:5 1Jn 2:8
[j]Php 3:12
[k]1:6 Mk 1:4
[l]1:8 Jn 15:26
[m]1:9 Jn 12:46
[n]Jn 18:37; 1Jn 2:8
[o]1:10 Jn 1:3
[p]1:12 2Jn 10
[q]Jn 5:43
[r]Mk 1:22; Ac 9:14
[s]Lk 1:7

[t]1:12 Mt 5:9; Jn 11:52; Rm 8:16; 1Jn 3:1
[u]Jn 3:16
[v]Jn 10:25; 1Jn 3:23
[w]1:13 1Pt 1:3
[x]1Co 7:37; 16:12; Eph 2:3; 2Tm 2:26; 2Pt 1:21
[y]Php 3:3
[z]1Pt 1:3; 1Jn 2:29
[aa]1:14 Jn 1:1
[ab]Php 2:7; 1Jn 4:2; 5:20
[ac]Mk 10:37; Jn 17:24
[ad]Heb 11:17; 1Jn 4:9
[ae]1:15 Mt 3:11; Mk 1:7; Jn 1:27,30
[af]Col 1:19

[ag]Jn 3:13; 8:58; 10:30; 14:7-9,23; Php 2:6 [ah]1:16 Ac 15:11; 2Pt 3:18 [ai]1:17 Ps 77:20; Mt 8:4; Heb 3:2 [aj]Ps 119:142; Jn 14:6; 2Th 2:10
[ak]1:18 1Jn 4:9 [al]Mt 5:16; 11:27; Jn 8:42 [am]Mt 11:27; Lk 10:22; 1Jn 2:24 [an]1:19 Mt 23:37 [ao]1:15 Ac 4:1 [ap]Ex 6:19; Lk 10:32

[A]1:3-4 Other punctuation is possible: . . . *not one thing was created. What was created in him was life* [B]1:5 Or *grasp*, or *comprehend*, or *overtake*; Jn 12:35 [C]1:7 Or *it (the light)* [D]1:9 Or *The true light who comes into the world gives light to everyone*, or *The true light enlightens everyone coming into the world.* [E]1:12 Or *become* [F]1:13 Lit *blood* [G]1:13 Or *not of human lineage, or of human capacity, or of human volition* [H]1:14 Or *and dwelt in a tent*; lit *and tabernacled* [I]1:14 *Son* is implied from the reference to the Father and from Gk usage. [J]1:16 Or *in place of* [K]1:18 Other mss read *The one and only Son, who is at the Father's side*

1:1-3 When we read the Gospels of Matthew and Luke, the story begins in history with Jesus Christ conceived by the Holy Spirit and born to Joseph and Mary. But in the Fourth Gospel, John reaches back even further—into eternity. We are given access to the prequel, so to speak.

The Father **created** the world through **the divine Word**, his Son, who is the eternal expression of God (1:1, 3; see Col 1:16; Heb 1:2). The Word **was with God** (eternal intimate fellowship) and **was God** (sharing the same eternal divine nature) (1:1).

In light of the Spirit's involvement as well (see Gen 1:2), we see that each person of the triune God was unified in the work of creation. The Father, Son, and Spirit are co-equal members of the Trinity. Our one God (see Deut 6:4; 1 Cor 8:6) exists in three persons (see Matt 28:19).

1:5 Satan has blinded people's minds to keep them from seeing the glory of Christ (see 2 Cor 4:4), but Jesus has come to bring illumination **(light)** so that people can see things as they truly are. John's Gospel shows us how Jesus was continually rejected; nevertheless, the darkness **did not overcome** his light. Though his enemies crucified him, he was actually glorified in his death on the cross (see John 13:31-32) and victorious in his resurrection, resulting in the provision of salvation for all people (see 3:16; Rom 5:18; 1 Tim 2:6; Heb 2:9; 1 John 2:2).

1:6 Here John, the apostle and author of the Gospel, introduces **John** the Baptist.

1:7-8 Though he was the first to bear **witness** to Christ, John was not to be the last. All Christians have the responsibility **to testify about** him, to declare the truth of Jesus **so that all might believe** in him (1:7). That's the foundation of evangelism and missions.

1:10-11 Sin blinds people so that they don't know their Creator (1:10). Even **his own people**—the Jews, those who were waiting for the Messiah, those who should have recognized him—**did not receive him** (1:11). Of course, the first believers, including the apostles, were Jews. But by and large, the Jewish people rejected Jesus during his earthly ministry.

1:12-13 To **receive** Christ is not like passively receiving a letter in your mailbox. Instead, it means to welcome him (based on his substitutionary atonement), like one welcomes a guest into one's home. Those who do so are adopted into the family of God as his **children**. To **believe** in Jesus's **name** is to believe in his person (who he is) and work (what he has done) (1:12). When someone receives and believes in Jesus for the free gift of eternal life, he undergoes a supernatural birth, the impartation of spiritual life. He is **born . . . of God** (1:13)—what Jesus would call being "born again" (3:3).

1:14 The **Word became flesh and dwelt among us** testifies to the glory of the incarnation. Conceived by the Holy Spirit in the womb of Mary (see Matt 1:20), the divine Son of God became a man. Jesus is thus the God-Man—not half man and half God, but one person with a fully divine nature and a fully human nature. He is fully human so he cried as an infant, but he is fully divine and gave life to his mother! He is fully human so he had to sleep, but he is fully divine and can raise the dead. Our God experienced what it is to be human—yet without sinning (see Heb 4:15). Hunger, pain, temptation, grief, hardship, rejection: you face no category of human experience your Savior has not endured.

1:15 Though John was born before Jesus (see Luke 1:57-58; 2:1-7), he recognized that Jesus preceded him in eternity.

1:16-17 When we receive the substitutionary atoning death of Christ on the cross, our sins are forgiven and eternal life is imparted. That's amazing grace! The gospel, then, does what **the law** couldn't do (1:7). Through Jesus, we have access to the unmerited and unlimited favor of God. **Grace** is the inexhaustible supply of God's goodness that continuously brings his favor to his people (1:17), doing for us what we can't do for ourselves. God will provide believers with a never-ending supply of **grace upon grace** through Christ, as waves crashing on the seashore (1:16).

1:18 Even Moses saw only the backside of God's glory. No one can see God's face on this side of eternity and live (see Exod 33:18-23). Yet, since Jesus is fully God, to know Jesus is to know God. He has perfectly **revealed him**.

1:19-20 John had been preaching and baptizing, so they wondered if he thought he was **the Messiah**, the coming King foretold in Scripture (1:20).

*a*1:20 Mt 1:17; Eph 5:2
*b*1:21 Mal 4:5; Mt 11:14;
17:10-13; Mk 8:28; Lk 1:17
*c*Dt 18:15; Mt 2:23
*d*1:23 Is 40:3
*e*Mt 3:3; 4:14; 12:17
*f*1:24 Mk 7:3
*g*1:26 Mk 1:8
*h*1:27 Jn 1:15
*i*1:28 Mk 10:1; Lk 3:3
*j*1:29 Is 53:7; Ac 8:32; 1Pt
1:19; Rv 5:6
*k*Jn 15:22; 1Jn 3:5
*l*1:31 Jn 7:28
*m*2Co 4:11; 1Jn 1:2
*n*1:32 Ps 51:11; Jn 1:33; Ac
2:4; Rm 8:9; Gl 5:25; Ti
3:5; 1Jn 5:8; Rv 3:22
*o*Jms 4:5

*p*1:33 Mt 3:11; Mk 1:8; Lk
3:16; Ac 11:16
*q*1:34 Mt 3:17; 4:3; Jn 1:49;
5:19; Heb 1:2
*r*1:38 Jn 11:8
*s*1:40-42 Mt 4:18-22; Mk
1:16-20; Lk 5:2-11
*t*1:41 Mt 1:17
*u*Ex 29:29
*v*1:42 1Co 1:12; 3:22; 9:5;
15:5; Gl 1:18; 2:9,11,14
*w*1:43 Mk 3:18
*x*1:44 Jn 12:21
*y*1:45 Jn 1:46-49; 21:2
*z*Mt 2:23; Ac 7:52; Rm 3:21
*aa*Mt 1:16; Lk 1:27;
2:4,16,33; 3:23; Jn 6:42
*ab*Mk 1:9
*ac*1:46 Gn 1:31
*ad*1:47 2Co 11:22

20 He didn't deny it but confessed: "I am not the Messiah."[a]

21 "What then?" they asked him. "Are you Elijah?"[b]

"I am not," he said.

"Are you the Prophet?"[c]

"No," he answered.

22 "Who are you, then?" they asked. "We need to give an answer to those who sent us. What can you tell us about yourself?"

23 He said, "I am a **voice of one crying out in the wilderness: Make straight the way of the Lord**[A,d] — just as Isaiah[e] the prophet said."

24 Now they had been sent from the Pharisees.[f] **25** So they asked him, "Why then do you baptize if you aren't the Messiah, or Elijah, or the Prophet?"

26 "I baptize with[B] water,"[g] John answered them. "Someone stands among you, but you don't know him. **27** He is the one coming after me,[C,h] whose sandal strap I'm not worthy to untie." **28** All this happened in Bethany[D] across the Jordan,[i] where John was baptizing.

THE LAMB OF GOD

29 The next day John saw Jesus coming toward him and said, "Here is the Lamb of God,[j] who takes away the sin[k] of the world! **30** This is the one I told you about: 'After me comes a man who ranks ahead of me, because he existed before me.' **31** I didn't know him,[l] but I came baptizing with water so he might be revealed[m] to Israel." **32** And John testified, "I saw the Spirit[n] descending from heaven like a dove, and he rested on him.[o] **33** I didn't know him, but he who sent me to baptize with water told me, 'The one you see the Spirit descending and resting on — he is the one who baptizes with the Holy Spirit.'[p] **34** I have seen and testified that this is the Son of God."[E,q]

35 The next day, John was standing with two of his disciples. **36** When he saw Jesus passing by, he said, "Look, the Lamb of God!" **37** The two disciples heard him say this and followed Jesus. **38** When Jesus turned and noticed them following him, he asked them, "What are you looking for?"

They said to him, "Rabbi"[r] (which means "Teacher"), "where are you staying?"

39 "Come and you'll see," he replied. So they went and saw where he was staying, and they stayed with him that day. It was about four in the afternoon.[F]

40 Andrew,[s] Simon Peter's brother, was one of the two who heard John and followed him. **41** He first found his own brother Simon and told him, "We have found the Messiah"[G,t] (which is translated "the Christ"),[u] **42** and he brought Simon to Jesus.

When Jesus saw him, he said, "You are Simon, son of John.[H] You will be called Cephas"[v] (which is translated "Peter"[I]).

PHILIP AND NATHANAEL

43 The next day Jesus[J] decided to leave for Galilee. He found Philip[w] and told him, "Follow me."

44 Now Philip was from Bethsaida,[x] the hometown of Andrew and Peter. **45** Philip found Nathanael[y] and told him, "We have found the one Moses wrote about in the law (and so did the prophets[z]): Jesus son of Joseph,[aa] from Nazareth."[ab]

46 "Can anything good[ac] come out of Nazareth?" Nathanael asked him.

"Come and see," Philip answered.

47 Then Jesus saw Nathanael coming toward him and said about him, "Here truly is an Israelite[ad] in whom there is no deceit."

[A]**1:23** Is 40:3   [B]**1:26** Or *in*, also in vv. 31,33   [C]**1:27** Other mss add *who came before me*   [D]**1:28** Other mss read *in Bethabara*   [E]**1:34** Other mss read *is the Chosen One of God*   [F]**1:39** Lit *about the tenth hour*   [G]**1:41** Both Hb *Messiah* and Gk *Christos* mean "anointed one"   [H]**1:42** Other mss read *"Simon, son of Jonah"*   [I]**1:42** Both Aramaic *Cephas* and Gk *Petros* mean "rock"   [J]**1:43** Lit *he*

1:21 They were referring to the prophecy that **Elijah** would return (see Mal 4:5-6). **The Prophet** was a reference to Moses's prophecy that God would raise up a great prophet like him (see Deut 18:15-18).

1:23 The word **Lord** in this quotation refers to God, thus identifying the deity of Jesus.

1:27 Untying the sandals was the most menial job of a slave.

1:29 Behind John's statement is the Old Testament practice of animal sacrifice in general and the Passover offering of a lamb in particular. God had commanded Israel to sacrifice a lamb so that he might rescue them from Pharaoh before instituting the sacrificial system to atone for their sins. But ultimately the blood of animals couldn't "take away sins" (Heb 10:4). It

was a temporary measure (a layaway plan!) that pointed to a permanent means of salvation. Only the sacrifice of Jesus could truly address the sin "of the whole world" (1 John 2:2). For unbelievers, the problem is not that their sin hasn't been atoned for; the problem is that they are unwilling to *receive* the atonement that Jesus has already made (see John 1:12).

1:35-37 A Christian's testimony ought to accomplish what John the Baptist's testimony did: pointing people to Jesus so that they want to follow him.

1:40-42 Notice the domino effect in this passage. When you understand who Jesus is, you'll want others to know him.

1:43 An invitation to **follow** Jesus is an invitation to become his disciple.

1:46 Nazareth, a town in Galilee, had a poor reputation. Moreover, the Messiah was supposed to hail from Bethlehem (see Mic 5:2). Jesus had been born in Bethlehem, but he'd been raised in Nazareth (see Matt 2:1, 23).

1:47-51 Jesus displayed his omniscience, his supernatural knowledge of all things. Not only did he know about Nathanael's character and where he was when **Philip** found him (1:47-48), but he also knew what Nathanael had been thinking about. Notice that Jesus told Nathanael that he, along with the other disciples (the **you** is plural), would **see heaven opened and the angels of God ascending and descending on the Son of Man** (1:51). This statement is a reference to Jacob's experience of dreaming about a stairway reaching from earth to heaven with

48 "How do you know me?" Nathanael asked.

"Before Philip called you, when you were under the fig tree, I saw you," Jesus answered.

49 "Rabbi,"[a] Nathanael replied, "You are the Son[b] of God; you are the King of Israel! "[c]

50 Jesus responded to him, "Do you believe because I told you I saw you under the fig tree? You will see greater things than this." **51** Then he said, "Truly I tell you, you will see heaven opened and the angels of God[d] ascending and descending[e] on the Son of Man."[f]

THE FIRST SIGN: TURNING WATER INTO WINE

2 On the third day a wedding took place in Cana[g] of Galilee.[h] Jesus's mother[i] was there, and **2** Jesus and his disciples were invited to the wedding as well. **3** When the wine ran out, Jesus's mother told him, "They don't have any wine."

4 "What does that have to do with you and me,[A,j] woman? "[k] Jesus asked. "My hour has not yet come."

5 "Do whatever he tells you," his mother told the servants.

6 Now six stone water jars had been set there for Jewish purification.[l] Each contained twenty or thirty gallons.[B]

7 "Fill the jars with water," Jesus told them. So they filled them to the brim. **8** Then he said to them, "Now draw some out and take it to the headwaiter."[c] And they did.

9 When the headwaiter tasted the water (after it had become wine), he did not know where it came from — though the servants who had drawn the water knew.

He called the groom **10** and told him, "Everyone sets out the fine wine first, then, after people are drunk, the inferior. But you have kept the fine wine until now."

11 Jesus did this, the first of his signs, in Cana[m] of Galilee.[n] He revealed[o] his glory,[p] and his disciples believed in him.

12 After this, he went down to Capernaum,[q] together with his mother, his brothers,[r] and his disciples, and they stayed there only a few days.

CLEANSING THE TEMPLE

13 The Jewish Passover[s] was near, and so Jesus went up to Jerusalem.[t] **14** In the temple[u] he found people selling oxen, sheep, and doves, and he also found the money changers sitting there. **15** After making a whip out of cords,[v] he drove everyone out of the temple with their sheep[w] and oxen. He also poured out the money changers' coins and overturned the tables. **16** He told those who were selling doves, "Get these things out of here! Stop turning my Father's[x] house[y] into a marketplace! "[D,z]

17 And his disciples remembered that it is written: **Zeal**[aa] **for your house will consume**[ab] **me.** [E,ac]

18 So the Jews replied to him, "What sign will you show us for doing these things?"

19 Jesus answered, "Destroy this temple,[F,ad] and I will raise it up in three days."[ae]

20 Therefore the Jews said, "This temple took forty-six years to build,[G] and will you raise it up in three days?"[af]

21 But he was speaking about the temple of his body.[ag] **22** So when he was raised from the dead,[ah] his disciples remembered that he had said this,[ai] and they believed

---

[a] 1:49 Jn 11:8
[b] Jn 5:19
[c] Mt 27:42; Mk 15:32; Jn 12:13
[d] 1:51 Lk 12:8-9; 15:10; Ac 10:3
[e] Gn 28:12
[f] Mk 2:10
[g] 2:1 Jn 2:11; 4:46; 21:2
[h] Mt 17:22
[i] Mt 1:16
[j] 2:4 2Sm 16:10; 19:22
[k] Jn 19:26
[l] 2:6 Lv 13–14; Heb 1:3

[m] 2:11 Jn 2:1; 21:2
[n] Mt 17:22
[o] 2Co 4:11; 1Jn 1:2
[p] Mk 10:37; Jn 17:24
[q] 2:12 Lk 10:15
[r] Mt 12:46-50; Mk 3:31-35; 6:3; Lk 8:19-21; Ac 1:14
[s] 2:13 Ex 12:11
[t] Mt 23:37
[u] 2:14-17 Mt 21:12-13; Mk 11:15-17; Lk 19:45-46
[v] 2:15 Ac 27:32
[w] Mt 7:15
[x] 2:16 Mt 5:16; 11:27; Jn 8:42
[y] Lk 11:51; Jn 2:17
[z] Jr 7:11; Zch 14:21; Mal 3:1-3
[aa] 2:17 Nm 25:13
[ab] Gl 5:15
[ac] Ps 69:9
[ad] 2:19 Lk 1:21
[ae] Lk 9:22
[af] 2:20 Mk 15:29
[ag] 2:21 Mt 26:26; 27:52,58; Mk 14:22; 15:43; Lk 12:4; 22:19; 23:52,55; Jn 19:31,38,40; 20:12; 1Co 10:16; 11:23-26; Heb 10:5,10; 1Pt 2:24
[ah] 2:22 Mt 17:9; Rv 20:12
[ai] Jn 14:26

A 2:4 Or "*You and I see things differently*; lit "*What to me and to you*; Mt 8:29; Mk 1:24; 5:7; Lk 8:28   B 2:6 Lit *two or three measures*   C 2:8 Lit *ruler of the table*   D 2:16 Lit *a house of business*   E 2:17 Ps 69:9   F 2:19 Or *sanctuary*, also in vv. 20,21   G 2:20 Or *was built forty-six years ago*

---

angels "going up and down on it" (Gen 28:10-12). Not only did Jesus make explicit reference to this story, but he also told Nathanael that he was **an Israelite in whom there is no deceit** (John 1:47). Being a deceiver was exactly what Jacob was known for (see Gen 27:1-36). So by these two comments, Jesus was making Nathanael aware that he had read his thoughts.

We should not overlook that Jesus replaced the image of a stairway in Jacob's dream with "the Son of Man" (a reference to himself). Thus, Jesus Christ is the bridge between heaven and earth. He grants access to eternity. As he would tell his disciples later, "No one comes to the Father except through me" (John 14:6).

2:1-3 Though the Old Testament condemns drunkenness (e.g., Deut 21:20-21; Prov 20:1; 23:19-21; 31:4-5), **wine** is often spoken of in terms of celebration, blessing, and joy (John 2:3; e.g., Pss 4:7; 104:15; Prov 3:9-10; Song 1:2; Isa 25:6; 55:1).

2:4 Jesus's point was that it was not yet the time to publicly manifest his supernatural activity for all to see. In 2:7-8 he solved the dilemma without advertising his identity.

2:5 We too should **do whatever he** tells us. The Lord doesn't explain how he intends to deal with our problems. He simply calls us to obey his revealed Word. Once we do that, we will have the opportunity to experience him at a deeper level.

2:9-10 This miracle of transformation points to the drastic change in people's lives that takes place when they believe in Jesus and obey his Word.

2:11 John uses the term **signs** in reference to Jesus's miracles (see, e.g., 4:54; 6:2, 14).

2:14 Those who'd traveled from far away would need to purchase animals to offer as sacrifices, but sales were taking place in the outermost court of the temple—the court

of the Gentiles. Thus, non-Jews who came to worship the God of Israel were prevented from doing so. Moreover, the Synoptic Gospels make clear that the sellers were charging an exorbitant amount because Jesus said they had turned it into a "den of thieves." They were lining their pockets at the expense of the worshipers (cf. Matt 21:12-13).

2:19-22 He was speaking about the temple of his body (2:21). And though they couldn't understand him, he was right. The Jewish leaders would deliver Jesus over to be put to death. Then, in three days, he would rise from the grave. His resurrection would indeed demonstrate his authority for cleansing the temple. Interestingly, the **disciples** didn't comprehend everything he said either. It would require Jesus's resurrection for them to grow in their faith and understanding (2:22).

[a]**2:22** Mt 26:54; 2Pt 1:20
[b]**2:23** Mt 23:37
[c]Jn 5:1
[d]Jn 10:25; 1Jn 3:23
[e]**2:25** Jr 17:10
[f]**3:1** Mk 7:3
[g]Jn 3:4,9; 7:50; 19:39
[h]Lk 8:41; 12:58
[i]**3:2** Jn 11:8
[j]Mk 4:38; Eph 4:11
[k]Mk 1:45
[l]Ex 3:12; Jn 15:24; Ac 10:38; Rv 21:3
[m]**3:3** 1Pt 1:3; 1Jn 2:29
[n]Mk 1:15; 9:1
[o]**3:5** Mk 9:43
[p]Ezk 36:25-27; Ac 22:16; Ti 3:5
[q]**3:6** Php 3:3
[r]Jn 1:33
[s]**3:7** 1Pt 1:3
[t]**3:8** Jn 8:14
[u]1Co 2:13-16
[v]**3:11** Jn 1:51; Rv 22:21
[w]**3:13** Jn 20:17
[x]Dt 30:12; Jn 6:62; Ac 2:34; Rm 10:6; 1Co 15:47; Eph 4:8-10; Rv 11:12
[y]Jn 6:38; 8:23
[z]Mk 2:10
[aa]**3:14** Ps 77:20; Mt 8:4; Heb 3:2
[ab]Nm 21:4-9
[ac]**3:15** Mk 10:17; Jn 12:25; Ac 13:48
[ad]**3:16** Jn 12:43; 1Co 13:1; Gl 2:20; Col 1:13; 3:12; 1Th 1:4; 2Th 2:13,16; 1Jn 4:7-12; Jd 1
[ae]1Jn 4:9
[af]Jn 5:19; Heb 1:2
[ag]Jn 12:25; Rm 5:8; 1Jn 3:16; 4:9-10
[ah]**3:17** Jn 8:11
[ai]**3:18** Mt 12:41; Mk 16:16
[aj]Jn 10:25; 1Jn 3:23
[ak]Jn 5:19
[al]**3:19** Ps 36:9; Jn 12:46
[am]Jn 18:37; 1Jn 2:8

the Scripture[a] and the statement Jesus had
made.
23 While he was in Jerusalem[b] during
the Passover Festival,[c] many believed in
his name[d] when they saw the signs he was
doing. 24 Jesus, however, would not entrust
himself to them, since he knew them all
25 and because he did not need anyone to
testify about man; for he himself knew
what was in man.[e]

JESUS AND NICODEMUS

3 There was a man from the Pharisees[f]
named Nicodemus,[g] a ruler[h] of the
Jews. 2 This man came to him at night and
said, "Rabbi,[i] we know that you are a teacher[j] who has come from God,[k] for no one
could perform these signs you do unless
God were with him."[l]
3 Jesus replied, "Truly I tell you, unless
someone is born again,[A,m] he cannot see
the kingdom of God."[n]
4 "How can anyone be born when he is
old?" Nicodemus asked him. "Can he enter his mother's womb a second time and
be born?"
5 Jesus answered, "Truly I tell you, unless
someone is born[o] of water and the Spirit,[p] he cannot enter the kingdom of God.
6 Whatever is born of the flesh[q] is flesh,
and whatever is born of the Spirit[r] is spirit. 7 Do not be amazed that I told you that
you must be born[s] again. 8 The wind blows
where it pleases, and you hear its sound,
but you don't know where it comes from
or where it is going.[t] So it is with everyone
born of the Spirit."[u]
9 "How can these things be?" asked Nicodemus.
10 "Are you a teacher[B] of Israel and don't
know these things?" Jesus replied. 11 "Truly I tell you,[v] we speak what we know and
we testify to what we have seen, but you
do not accept our testimony. 12 If I have
told you about earthly things and you
don't believe, how will you believe if I tell
you about heavenly things? 13 No one has
ascended[w] into heaven[x] except the one
who descended from heaven[y] — the Son
of Man.[C,z]
14 "Just as Moses[aa] lifted up the snake
in the wilderness,[ab] so the Son of Man
must be lifted up, 15 so that everyone who
believes in him may[D] have eternal life.[ac]
16 For God loved[ad] the world in this way:[E]
He gave[F] his one and only[ae] Son,[af] so that
everyone who believes in him will not
perish but have eternal life.[ag] 17 For God
did not send his Son into the world to condemn[ah] the world, but to save the world
through him. 18 Anyone who believes in
him is not condemned, but anyone who
does not believe is already condemned,[ai]
because he has not believed in the name[aj]
of the one and only Son[ak] of God. 19 This is
the judgment: The light[al] has come into
the world,[am] and people loved darkness
rather than the light because their deeds

[A]**3:3** Or *from above*, also in v. 7 [B]**3:10** Or *the teacher* [C]**3:13** Other mss add *who is in heaven* [D]**3:15** Other mss add *not perish, but* [E]**3:16** Or *this much* [F]**3:16** Or *For in this way God loved the world, and so he gave*, or *For God so loved the world that he gave*

2:24 Jesus **would not entrust himself to them** because of their spiritual immaturity. They were not yet ready for full commitment to discipleship and public identification with him. Spiritual growth is important because it expands our capacity to experience more of God. Jesus does not relate to all believers the same way.

2:25 That Jesus **knew what was in man** is a reminder that he can see into our hearts.

3:1-2 **Nicodemus** went to Jesus under cover of darkness so that he could avoid the scorn of his fellow **Pharisees**.

3:3 The Greek word translated ***again*** can also mean "from above." Probably both ideas are intended. Indeed, we need to be born again (to have a spiritual birth in contrast to our physical birth), and that new birth comes only from heaven above. As the apostle Paul explains it, all people are dead in their sins, and only God can give us spiritual life (Eph 2:1-5). Nicodemus needed a spiritual rebirth; simply being a religious leader wouldn't cut it.

3:5-6 To enter God's kingdom, you must not only be **born** physically (of **water** and **flesh**) but also supernaturally (**of the Spirit**). Human birth and even an impressive physical ancestry are insufficient for obtaining eternal life.

3:8 God's **Spirit** invisibly does its work inside the human heart. We can't see it happening. All we see are the results.

3:9-13 The concept Nicodemus couldn't understand concerning the new kingdom age of the working of the Spirit was clearly taught in the Old Testament (3:9; see Isa 32:15; Ezek 36:25-27; Joel 2:28-29). As a teacher and leader, Nicodemus should have known of it. If he could not grasp **earthly things** that were plainly taught in the Scriptures, how could he grasp the **heavenly things** that only Jesus could reveal (John 3:12)—that is, that God in grace can give people a new heart (see 1 Sam 10:6; Jer 31:33)? Jesus could reveal deep heavenly truths since he had **descended from heaven** (John 3:13).

3:14-15 The mention of **Moses [lifting] up the snake** is a reference to an incident recorded in the book of Numbers (John 3:14; see Num 21:4-9). If anyone bitten trusted God and looked at the bronze snake, he would be healed. Similarly, **the Son of Man** would also be **lifted up** (on a cross; John 3:14), **so that everyone who believes in him may have eternal life** (John 3:15).

3:16 **God loved the world** of people, and his love was not merely sentimental. Rather, it prompted him to take action. God the Father **gave his one and only Son** as a substitute for sinful human beings. He would die in their place, bearing their sins. But salvation from sin through the Son requires faith: **Everyone who believes in him will not perish but have eternal life**. When you trust in Jesus alone as your personal sin-bearer, divine judgment is removed and eternal life is freely given.

3:18 Salvation from sin and judgment is free for the taking. But if you reject the miracle cure that the doctor offers you, don't blame him when you succumb to your fatal illness.

3:19-21 Those who love **darkness rather than the light**, so that they can try (in vain) to hide their sinful **deeds** (3:19-20), will experience eternal judgment for rejecting the free gift of God. Those who receive **the truth** and live in accordance with it come **to the light** (to Jesus) in order to show that their good **works** have been **accomplished by God** (3:21). Unbelievers are responsible for their evil deeds, but believers know that God gets the glory for their good ones.

were evil. **20** For everyone who does evil hates[a] the light and avoids it,[A] so that his deeds[b] may not be exposed. **21** But anyone who lives by[B] the truth comes to the light, so that his works[c] may be shown to be accomplished by God."

JESUS AND JOHN THE BAPTIST

22 After this, Jesus and his disciples went to the Judean countryside, where he spent time with them and baptized.

23 John[d] also was baptizing in Aenon near Salim, because there was plenty of water there. People were coming and being baptized, **24** since John had not yet been thrown into prison.[e]

25 Then a dispute arose between John's disciples[f] and a Jew[c] about purification.[g] **26** So they came to John and told him, "Rabbi,[h] the one you testified about, and who was with you across the Jordan,[i] is baptizing — and everyone is going to him."[j]

27 John responded, "No one can receive anything unless it has been given to him from heaven. **28** You yourselves can testify that I said, 'I am not the Messiah,[k] but I've been sent ahead of him.'[l] **29** He who has the bride[m] is the groom. But the groom's friend, who stands by and listens for him, rejoices greatly[D] at the groom's voice. So this joy[n] of mine is complete. **30** He must increase, but I must decrease."

THE ONE FROM HEAVEN

31 The one who comes from above[o] is above all. The one who is from the earth is earthly and speaks in earthly terms.[E] The one who comes from heaven is above all.[p] **32** He

testifies[q] to what he has seen and heard, and yet no one accepts his testimony. **33** The one who has accepted his testimony has affirmed that God is true.[r] **34** For the one whom God sent speaks God's words, since he[F] gives the Spirit[s] without measure. **35** The Father loves the Son[t] and has given all things into his hands.[u] **36** The one who believes in the Son has eternal life, but the one who rejects the Son[G] will not see life; instead, the wrath of God remains on him.[v]

JESUS AND THE SAMARITAN WOMAN

4 When Jesus[H] learned that the Pharisees[w] had heard he was making[x] and baptizing more disciples than John[y] **2** (though Jesus himself was not baptizing, but his disciples were), **3** he left Judea[z] and went again to Galilee.[aa] **4** He had to travel through Samaria;[ab] **5** so he came to a town of Samaria called Sychar near the property[ac] that Jacob[ac] had given his son Joseph.[ad] **6** Jacob's well[ae] was there, and Jesus, worn out from his journey, sat down at the well. It was about noon.[J]

7 A woman of Samaria came to draw water.[af]

"Give me a drink," Jesus said to her, **8** because his disciples had gone into town to buy food.

9 "How is it that you, a Jew,[ag] ask for a drink from me, a Samaritan[ah] woman?" she asked him. For Jews do not associate with[K] Samaritans.[L]

10 Jesus answered, "If you knew the gift of God,[ai] and who is saying to you, 'Give me a drink,' you would ask him, and he would give you living water."[aj]

[a]3:20 Lk 6:27; 19:14
[b]Mk 14:6; Gl 3:10; Jms 2:14-26
[c]3:21 Jn 5:36
[d]3:23 Mk 1:4
[e]3:24 Mk 1:14
[f]3:25 Mt 9:14; 11:2; 14:12; Mk 2:18; 6:29; Lk 5:33; 7:18-19; 11:1; Jn 1:35,37; 6:3
[g]Lv 13-14; Heb 1:3
[h]3:26 Jn 11:8
[i]Mk 10:1; Lk 3:3
[j]Mk 1:45
[k]3:28 Mt 1:17; Eph 5:2
[l]Lk 1:17
[m]3:29 Rv 21:2
[n]Jn 15:11
[o]3:31 Jms 1:17
[p]Jn 8:23; 1Jn 4:5-6

[q]3:32 Jn 15:26; Ac 26:5
[r]3:33 1Jn 5:20
[s]3:34 Jn 1:33
[t]3:35 Jn 5:20; 10:17; 1Co 13:1
[u]Jn 5:19
[v]3:36 Mk 16:16
[w]4:1 Mk 7:3
[x]Mt 28:19-20
[y]Mk 1:4
[z]4:3 Lk 1:5
[aa]Mt 17:22
[ab]4:4 Ac 1:8
[ac]4:5 Ps 22:23; Mt 1:2; Lk 1:33
[ad]Gn 30:24; 33:19; 48:22; 49:22
[ae]4:6 Jms 3:11
[af]4:7 Gn 24:11-17; 29:2-12
[ag]4:9 Jn 11:36; Ac 14:1; Rv 2:9
[ah]Lk 9:52; Ac 1:8
[ai]4:10 Ac 8:20
[aj]4:10 Gn 26:19; Ps 36:7-9; Is 49:10; 55:1; Jr 2:13; Zch 14:8; Jn 7:38; Rv 7:17; 21:6; 22:1,17

[A]3:20 Lit and does not come to the light   [B]3:21 Lit who does   [C]3:25 Other mss read and the Jews   [D]3:29 Lit with joy rejoices   [E]3:31 Or of earthly things   [F]3:34 Other mss read since God   [G]3:36 Or refuses to believe in the Son, or disobeys the Son   [H]4:1 Other mss read the Lord   [I]4:5 Lit piece of land   [J]4:6 Lit about the sixth hour   [K]4:9 Or do not share vessels with   [L]4:9 Other mss omit For Jews do not associate with Samaritans.

3:24 On John's imprisonment and execution, see the notes on Mark 6:16-28.

3:25-26 **John's disciples** had become concerned because **everyone [was] going to** Jesus. Thus, they essentially told their master, "This Jesus fella is moving in on your ministry. Now fewer people are coming to you."

3:28-30 John was simply the opening act, expected to warm up the crowd and then get off the stage. Jesus was the main event, the star attraction. John was content with and grateful for his role (3:30). Are you?

3:31-32 Jesus—**the one**—is the Son of God speaking from a heavenly perspective.

3:36 Jesus will one day rule the world as King. Thus, the matter is simple. Believe in **the Son** to receive **eternal life**. Reject him and experience divine **wrath**.

4:4-5 Don't miss that Jesus **had to travel through Samaria** (4:4). Typically, orthodox

Jews sought to avoid contact with Samaritans, so Jesus was taking a stance against that racist practice. The Jews disliked the Samaritans, considering them unclean. Originally, the name *Samaria* applied to the capital city of the northern kingdom of Israel (see 1 Kgs 16:23-24). But eventually the entire northern kingdom was referred to by this name. When the Assyrians conquered them, they deported many Israelites, but left others in the land. Then the Assyrians settled other conquered peoples there, who intermarried with the remaining Israelites. This mixture of peoples also involved the worship of various false gods (see 2 Kgs 17:24-41). The Samaritans of Jesus's day were their descendants, a people of mixed ancestry and syncretistic religious practices. Thus, the Jews despised them.

4:6 Notice that John emphasizes the full deity ("the Word was God," 1:1) and the full

humanity (he was **worn out**) of Jesus. In theological terminology, the uniting of two distinct natures (divine and human) in one person (Jesus Christ) is known as the *hypostatic* union.

Jacob's well represents common ground, since both Jews and Samaritans revered Jacob.

4:7 Typically people wouldn't **draw water** during the heat of the day. (Verse 6 says this encounter took place "about noon.") So, why would she arrive at a time when no one would be around? She was a woman of questionable character. Importantly, Jesus's willingness to engage her socially by drinking water from her cup opened the door for him to reach her spiritually. We too should seek to connect with different people as we share with them the good news of the gospel.

4:9 See the note on 4:4-5.

Cross-references (margin):

a 4:11 Lk 10:1
b 4:12 Mt 1:2; Lk 1:33
c 4:14 Jn 6:35; 7:37; 1Co 4:11; Rv 7:16; 21:6; 22:17
d Jms 3:11
e Jn 12:25; Ac 13:48; Rm 8:2; 1Jn 2:25
f 4:20 Dt 11:29–12:14; 27:3; Jos 24:1
g Mt 23:37
h 4:22 Gn 12:1-7; Is 2:3; Mal 1:11; Mt 15:24; Jn 11:36; Rm 3:1-2; 9:4-5; 15:8-9
i 4:23 Jn 5:25-29; 16:32
j 4:24 Jn 1:33; 2Th 2:10; Jd 20
k 2Th 2:10
l 4:25 Mt 1:17; Eph 5:2
m Ex 29:29; Jn 1:41
n 4:26 Ex 3:14; Ps 45:8; Jn 8:24
o 4:29 Mt 1:17
p 4:30 Mk 1:45
q 4:31 Jn 11:8
r 4:34 Eph 1:9; 1Jn 2:17
s Jn 5:30
t Jn 5:36
u 4:36 Mk 10:17; Jn 12:25; Ac 13:48
v 4:37 Lv 26:16; Dt 20:6; Jb 31:8; Mc 6:15; Mt 25:24; Lk 19:21

11 "Sir,"a said the woman, "you don't even have a bucket, and the well is deep. So where do you get this 'living water'? 12 You aren't greater than our father Jacob,b are you? He gave us the well and drank from it himself, as did his sons and livestock."

13 Jesus said, "Everyone who drinks from this water will get thirsty again. 14 But whoever drinks from the water that I will give him will never get thirsty again.c In fact, the water I will give him will become a wellA,d of water springing up in him for eternal life."e

15 "Sir," the woman said to him, "give me this water so that I won't get thirsty and come here to draw water."

16 "Go call your husband," he told her, "and come back here."

17 "I don't have a husband," she answered.

"You have correctly said, 'I don't have a husband,'" Jesus said. 18 "For you've had five husbands, and the man you now have is not your husband. What you have said is true."

19 "Sir," the woman replied, "I see that you are a prophet. 20 Our fathers worshiped on this mountain,f but you Jews say that the place to worship is in Jerusalem."g

21 Jesus told her, "Believe me, woman, an hour is coming when you will worship the Father neither on this mountain nor in Jerusalem. 22 You Samaritans worship what you do not know. We worship what we do know, because salvation is from the Jews.h 23 But an hour is coming, and is now here,i when the true worshipers will worship the Father in Spirit and in truth.B Yes, the Father wants such people to worship him. 24 God is spirit,j and those who worship him must worship in Spirit and in truth."k

25 The woman said to him, "I know that the Messiahl is coming" (who is called Christm).

HOPE WORDS

Knowing about Christ is no substitute for knowing Christ.

"When he comes, he will explain everything to us."

26 Jesus told her, "I, the one speaking to you, am he."n

THE RIPENED HARVEST

27 Just then his disciples arrived, and they were amazed that he was talking with a woman. Yet no one said, "What do you want?" or "Why are you talking with her?"

28 Then the woman left her water jar, went into town, and told the people, 29 "Come, see a man who told me everything I ever did. Could this be the Messiah?"o 30 They left the town and made their way to him.p

31 In the meantime the disciples kept urging him, "Rabbi,q eat something."

32 But he said, "I have food to eat that you don't know about."

33 The disciples said to one another, "Could someone have brought him something to eat?"

34 "My food is to do the will of himr who sent mes and to finish his work,"t Jesus told them. 35 "Don't you say, 'There are still four more months, and then comes the harvest'? Listen to what I'm telling you: OpenC your eyes and look at the fields, because they are readyD for harvest. 36 The reaper is already receiving pay and gathering fruit for eternal life,u so that the sower and reaper can rejoice together. 37 For in this case the saying is true: 'One sows and another reaps.'v 38 I sent you to reap what you didn't labor for; others have labored, and you have benefited fromE their labor."

A 4:14 Or spring   B 4:23 Or in spirit and truth, also in v. 24   C 4:35 Lit Raise   D 4:35 Lit white   E 4:38 Lit you have entered into

4:14 If you receive a drink from Jesus, you don't have to come back for another. His living water becomes its own everlasting well. Thirst no more.

4:16-18 Because Jesus was willing to drink from her cup (see the note on 4:7), he gained an opportunity to address her sin.

4:21 In John's Gospel, Jesus's **hour** is usually associated with his crucifixion and resurrection (see 2:4; 7:30; 8:20; 12:23, 27; 13:1; 16:32; 17:1). So through his death on the cross and triumph over the grave, Jesus would transform **worship** for God's people.

4:22 Salvation is from the Jews because the Messiah would be of Jewish lineage, descended from the tribe of Judah.

4:23-24 To **worship the Father in Spirit** (4:23) is to have a heart that is in pursuit of an intimate spiritual relationship with the **God** who **is spirit** (4:24). To worship God **in truth** is to worship him in a biblically accurate way—through the One who *is* the truth (see 14:6). God is on the hunt for those who will worship him spiritually through Jesus Christ based on the truth of his Word (4:23).

4:28-30 The woman hadn't attended seminary; she had no theological training. She had simply met Jesus. New believers should be encouraged to share their faith as soon as possible.

4:34 Jesus's greatest satisfaction and fulfillment was not in filling his belly but in obeying God. For us too, the spiritual must take precedence over the physical (see Matt 4:3-4; 6:31-33).

4:35 How often do we postpone sharing the gospel? How often do we put God's kingdom second, when Jesus commands us to seek it first (see Matt 6:33)? If we pay close attention, we will see God at work all around us and discover ministry opportunities right before us.

4:37 It may take several encounters with the gospel delivered through more than one messenger before a person believes it. One Christian explains the gospel to an unbeliever, and later another Christian eventually leads that unbeliever to Christ.

THE SAVIOR OF THE WORLD

39 Now many Samaritans[a] from that town believed in him because of what the woman said[A] when she testified,[b] "He told me everything I ever did." **40** So when the Samaritans came to him,[c] they asked him to stay with them, and he stayed there two days. **41** Many more believed because of what he said.[B] **42** And they told the woman, "We no longer believe because of what you said, since we have heard for ourselves and know that this really is the Savior[d] of the world."[c]

A GALILEAN WELCOME

43 After two days he left there for Galilee.[e] **44** (Jesus himself had testified[f] that a prophet has no honor in his own country.[g]) **45** When[h] they entered Galilee, the Galileans[i] welcomed him because they had seen everything he did in Jerusalem[j] during the festival.[k] For they also had gone to the festival.

THE SECOND SIGN: HEALING AN OFFICIAL'S SON

46 He went again to Cana[l] of Galilee, where he had turned the water into wine. There was a certain royal official whose son was ill at Capernaum.[m] **47** When this man heard that Jesus had come from Judea[n] into Galilee, he went to him and pleaded with him to come down and heal his son, since he was about to die. **48** Jesus told him, "Unless you people see signs and wonders,[o] you will not believe."[p] **49** "Sir,"[q] the official said to him, "come down before my boy dies." **50** "Go," Jesus told him, "your son will live." The man believed what[D] Jesus said to him and departed. **51** While he was still going down, his servants met him saying that his boy was alive. **52** He asked them at what time he got better. "Yesterday at one in the afternoon[E] the fever left him," they answered. **53** The father[r] realized this was the very hour at which Jesus had told him, "Your son will live." So he himself believed, along with his whole household.

54 Now this was also the second sign[s] Jesus performed after he came from Judea to Galilee.[t]

THE THIRD SIGN: HEALING THE SICK

5 After this, a Jewish festival took place, and Jesus went up to Jerusalem.[u] **2** By the Sheep Gate[v] in Jerusalem there is a pool, called Bethesda[F] in Aramaic, which has five colonnades. **3** Within these lay a large number of the disabled — blind, lame, and paralyzed.[G]

5 One man was there who had been disabled for thirty-eight years. **6** When Jesus saw him lying there and realized he had already been there a long time,[w] he said to him, "Do you want to get well?"

7 "Sir,"[x] the disabled man answered, "I have no one to put me into the pool when the water is stirred up, but while I'm coming, someone goes down ahead of me."

8 "Get up," Jesus told him, "pick up your mat and walk." **9** Instantly the man got well, picked up his mat, and started to walk.

Now that day was the Sabbath,[y] **10** and so the Jews[z] said to the man who had been healed, "This is the Sabbath.[aa] The law prohibits you from picking up your mat."

11 He replied, "The man who made me well[ab] told me, 'Pick up your mat and walk.'"

12 "Who is this man who told you, 'Pick up your mat and walk'?" they asked. **13** But the man who was healed did not know who it was,[ac] because Jesus had slipped away into the crowd that was there.[H]

---

[a] 4:39 Lk 9:52; Ac 1:8
[b] Jn 15:26; Ac 26:5
[c] 4:40 Mk 1:45
[d] 4:42 2Pt 3:18
[e] 4:43 Is 9:1-2; Mt 17:22
[f] 4:44 Jn 15:26; Ac 26:5
[g] Mt 13:57; Mk 6:4; Lk 4:24
[h] 4:45 Mt 4:17; Mk 1:14-15
[i] Mt 26:69; Mk 14:70; Lk 13:1-2; 22:59; 23:6; Ac 1:11; 2:7; 5:37
[j] Mt 23:37
[k] Jn 2:23; 5:1
[l] 4:46 Jn 2:1,11; 21:2
[m] Lk 10:15
[n] 4:47 Lk 1:5
[o] 4:48 Ex 7:3-4; Mk 13:22; Jn 2:23-25; 6:26
[p] Jn 3:16; 6:64; 20:25
[q] 4:49 Lk 10:1

[r] 4:53 Lk 11:11; Col 3:21
[s] 4:54 Jn 2:11
[t] Mt 17:22
[u] 5:1 Mt 23:37
[v] 5:2 Neh 3:1,32; 12:39
[w] 5:6 Is 46:10; Zch 14:7; Jn 5:6; 6:6; 8:14; 9:3; 11:11-15; 13:1-3,11
[x] 5:7 Lk 10:1
[y] 5:9 Mk 2:23
[z] 5:10 Jn 11:36
[aa] Lk 14:3
[ab] 5:11 Ti 2:8
[ac] 5:13 Jn 7:28

[A] 4:39 Lit *because of the woman's word*   [B] 4:41 Lit *because of his word*   [C] 4:42 Other mss add *, the Messiah*   [D] 4:50 Lit *the word*   [E] 4:52 Lit *at the seventh hour*   [F] 5:2 Some mss read *Bethzatha*; other mss read *Bethsaida*   [G] 5:3 Some mss include vv. 3b-4: — *waiting for the moving of the water,* [4] *because an angel would go down into the pool from time to time and stir up the water. Then the first one who got in after the water was stirred up recovered from whatever ailment he had.*   [H] 5:13 Lit *slipped away, there being a crowd in that place*

4:40 John indicated earlier that "Jews [did] not associate with Samaritans" (4:9; see the note on 4:4-5). Nevertheless, **the Samaritans ... asked [Jewish Jesus] to stay with them**. So he and his disciples hung out with them for **two days**. So, is racial reconciliation possible? If you're operating spiritually and united in Jesus, the answer is a resounding, yes! And it doesn't take long when people are right with Jesus.

4:53 That is, they all **believed** in Jesus as the Messiah and not just as a miracle worker.

5:6 Jesus's question suggests that some people have been stuck in their negative circumstances for so long that they have given up hope that things can ever change. God's work occurs in cooperation with our will. Keep hoping.

5:7 The healing was so near and yet so far away. The man's situation was hopeless, and he had no one to offer him aid.

5:8-9 Wherever your bed is, that's where your home is. Thanks to Jesus, this man would no longer be sleeping in a place of despair. It was time to roll up his **mat** and find a new home.

5:10 The Jewish religious leaders considered **picking up** a **mat** to be work (!) and, therefore, prohibited on **the Sabbath**. They had taken a divine command that provided physical rest for God's people and erroneously turned it into a human restriction on acts of mercy.

5:11 These words indicate that the healed man preferred to listen to the one with the miraculous power, not leaders who were just practicing religion! He had lain there for thirty-eight years, and the religious leaders had never aided in his healing.

a 5:14 Ac 21:26
b 5:15 Ti 2:8
c 5:16 Lk 6:28; 2Tm 3:12
d Lk 13:10
e 5:17 Mt 5:16; 11:27;
Jn 8:42
f 5:18 Mt 12:14; 26:4; 27:1;
Mk 3:6; 14:1; Lk 6:11; Jn
7:1,19; 10:33; 11:53
g 5:19 Jn 3:35; 6:38;
7:16,28; 8:26-42;
10:18,30,36-38; 12:49-50;
14:9,24,31; 15:9-10; 16:15;
17:9-10
h 5:20 Heb 3:9; Rv 15:3
i 5:21 Mk 9:27; Jn 2:19
j Jn 11:25-26
k 5:22 Mt 11:27
l 5:23 Jn 15:23
m Lk 10:16
n 5:24 Jn 6:53; 12:25; Ac
13:48; 1Jn 2:25

o 5:25 Jn 4:23
p Php 1:21
q 5:26 Jn 5:19; Col 1:19
r 5:27 2Th 1:5
s Mk 2:10; Heb 2:6; Rv
1:13; 14:14
t 5:30 Mt 12:41; 2Th 1:5
u Mt 6:33; Jn 8:16
v Mt 26:39; Jn 4:34; 6:38;
7:16-18; 8:28; 14:10; Rm
8:27; Eph 1:9
w 5:32 1Jn 5:20
x 5:33 Ps 119:142; Jn 14:6
y 5:35 Mk 1:4
z 2Sm 21:17; Mt 5:14-15; Lk
12:35; 2Pt 1:19; Rv 21:23
aa Ps 36:9; Jn 12:46
ab 5:36 Jn 15:24
ac Mk 9:37; Jn 1:6,33
ad 5:37 1Jn 5:9
ae Ex 33:11; 2Ki 4:12; Is 6:1;
Lk 3:22; Jn 1:18; 6:46-47;
14:9; 1Tm 1:17

14 After this, Jesus found him in the temple[a] and said to him, "See, you are well. Do not sin anymore, so that something worse doesn't happen to you." **15** The man went and reported to the Jews that it was Jesus who had made him well.[b] **16** Therefore, the Jews began persecuting[c] Jesus[A] because he was doing these things on the Sabbath.[d]

HONORING THE FATHER AND THE SON

17 Jesus responded to them, "My Father[e] is still working, and I am working also." **18** This is why the Jews began trying all the more to kill him:[f] Not only was he breaking the Sabbath, but he was even calling God his own Father, making himself equal to God.

19 Jesus replied, "Truly I tell you, the Son is not able to do anything on his own, but only what he sees the Father doing. For whatever the Father[B] does, the Son likewise does these things.[g] **20** For the Father loves the Son and shows him everything he is doing, and he will show him greater works[h] than these so that you will be amazed. **21** And just as the Father raises[i] the dead and gives them life, so the Son also gives life to whom he wants.[j] **22** The Father,[k] in fact, judges no one but has given all judgment to the Son, **23** so that all people may honor the Son just as they honor the Father.[l] Anyone who does not honor the Son does not honor the Father who sent him.[m]

LIFE AND JUDGMENT

24 "Truly I tell you, anyone who hears my word and believes him who sent me has eternal life[n] and will not come under judgment but has passed from death to life.

25 "Truly I tell you, an hour is coming, and is now here,[o] when the dead will hear the voice of the Son of God, and those who hear will live.[p] **26** For just as the Father has life in himself, so also he has granted to the Son[q] to have life in himself. **27** And he has granted him the right to pass judgment,[r] because he is the Son of Man.[s] **28** Do not be amazed at this, because a time is coming when all who are in the graves will hear his voice **29** and come out — those who have done good things, to the resurrection of life, but those who have done wicked things, to the resurrection of condemnation.

30 "I can do nothing on my own. I judge only as I hear, and my judgment[t] is just,[u] because I do not seek my own will, but the will of him who sent me.[v]

WITNESSES TO JESUS

31 "If I testify about myself, my testimony is not true. **32** There is another who testifies about me, and I know that the testimony he gives about me is true.[w] **33** You sent messengers to John, and he testified to the truth.[x] **34** I don't receive human testimony, but I say these things so that you may be saved. **35** John[C,y] was a burning and shining lamp,[z] and you were willing to rejoice for a while in his light.[aa]

36 "But I have a greater testimony than John's because of the works that the Father has given me to accomplish.[ab] These very works I am doing testify about me that the Father has sent[ac] me. **37** The Father who sent me has himself testified[ad] about me. You have not heard his voice at any time, and you haven't seen his form.[ae] **38** You don't have his word residing in you, because you don't believe the one he sent.

[A] 5:16 Other mss add *and trying to kill him* [B] 5:19 Lit *whatever that one* [C] 5:35 Lit *That man*

5:14 The man had been stuck because of **sin** in his life. Sin carries long-term consequences.
5:15-16 While Jesus was changing lives, the leaders were playing religion. No matter how much religious activity you are engaged in, if you're not in the life-changing business, then you're not in the business of Jesus.
5:17-18 No matter which day of the week it was, God the Father was engaged in kingdom work; therefore, his Son was too. As John himself has already said, "The Word was with God, and the Word was God" (1:1). But as far as the leaders were concerned, Jesus's claims were blasphemy.
5:19 The point here is that healing the man on the Sabbath was not blasphemy but an act of God.
5:20-21 **The Father loves the Son** is a subtle warning to the religious leaders. The one

whom they wanted to kill (5:18) was dearly loved by God the Father. And because of that, the Father would **show him greater works than these** so that they would be **amazed** (5:20); these works included raising **the dead** (5:21). So in a way, Jesus was telling them, "You think you're upset now because I healed a paralytic? Wait until you see what I do with Lazarus!" (see 11:1-44).
5:22 Jesus Christ has been made the final Judge of all humankind. Whether or not one accepts Jesus, then, has eternal consequences.
5:23 To reject Jesus is to reject God altogether. There's no true religion without Jesus Christ.
5:24 To believe in the Son is to pass **from death** (eternal separation from God) **to life** (eternal relationship with God). Faith in God's promise through Jesus Christ guarantees

eternal life to all who believe in him for it.
5:25-29 Whether people experience eternal life or condemnation after the resurrection will depend entirely on their response to Jesus in this life. If they believed in Jesus, they will **have done good things** because of the eternal life in them. If they did not believe in Jesus, they will **have done wicked things** because of the lack of life in them (5:29).
5:30 Everything Jesus did, he did at the initiative of his Father. He did **not seek [his] own will** but the Father's. That, in fact, is what a life looks like when it is completely yielded to God.
5:36 The miraculous signs Jesus performed were evidence that he was the Messiah **sent** from the Father. So in essence, Jesus told them, "My deeds are my validation." Everything had been done before their eyes.

39 You pore over the Scriptures[a] because you think you have eternal life in them, and yet they testify about me.[b] **40** But you are not willing[c] to come to me[d] so that you may have life.

41 "I do not accept glory[e] from people, **42** but I know you — that you have no love for God[f] within you. **43** I have come in my Father's name,[g] and yet you don't accept me.[h] If someone else comes in his own name, you will accept him. **44** How can you believe, since you accept glory from one another but don't seek the glory that comes from the only[i] God?[j] **45** Do not think that I will accuse you to the Father. Your accuser is Moses,[k] on whom you have set your hope. **46** For if you believed Moses, you would believe me, because he wrote about me. **47** But if you don't believe what he wrote,[l] how will you believe my words?"[m]

THE FOURTH SIGN: FEEDING OF THE FIVE THOUSAND

6 After[n] this, Jesus crossed the Sea of Galilee[o] (or Tiberias[p]). **2** A huge crowd was following him because they saw the signs that he was performing by healing the sick. **3** Jesus went up a mountain and sat down there with his disciples. **4** Now the Passover, a Jewish festival, was near. **5** So when Jesus looked up and noticed a huge crowd coming toward him,[q] he asked Philip,[r] "Where will we buy bread so that these people can eat?" **6** He asked this to test him,[s] for he himself knew what he was going to do.

7 Philip answered him, "Two hundred denarii[A,t] worth of bread wouldn't be enough for each of them to have a little." **8** One of his disciples, Andrew,[u] Simon Peter's[w] brother, said to him, **9** "There's a boy here who has five barley loaves and two fish — but what are they for so many?"

10 Jesus said, "Have the people sit down."

There was plenty of grass in that place; so they sat down. The men numbered about five thousand.[x] **11** Then Jesus took the loaves, and after giving thanks he distributed them to those who were seated — so also with the fish, as much as they wanted.[y]

12 When they were full, he told his disciples, "Collect the leftovers so that nothing is wasted."[z] **13** So they collected them and filled twelve baskets with the pieces from the five barley loaves that were left over by those who had eaten.

14 When the people saw the sign[B] he had done, they said, "This truly is the Prophet[aa] who is to come[ab] into the world."[ac]

15 Therefore, when Jesus realized that they were about to come and take him by force to make him king,[ad] he withdrew again to the mountain by himself.

THE FIFTH SIGN: WALKING ON WATER

16 When[ae] evening came, his disciples went down to the sea, **17** got into a boat, and started across the sea to Capernaum.[af] Darkness had already set in, but Jesus had not yet come to them. **18** A high wind arose, and the sea began to churn. **19** After they

[a] 5:39 Mt 26:54; 2Pt 1:20
[b] Lk 24:27,44; Ac 13:27
[c] 5:40 Lk 13:34
[d] Lk 14:26
[e] 5:41 Jn 17:24; Php 3:19; 1Pt 5:4
[f] 5:42 Lk 10:27; 11:42; 1Jn 4:20
[g] 5:43 Jn 10:25; 14:13; Ac 15:14; Rv 14:1
[h] Mk 4:16; Jn 1:12; 12:48; 13:20; 17:8
[i] 5:44 Dt 6:4; Jn 17:3; Rm 3:30; 16:27; 1Tm 1:17; 6:15-16; Jd 25; Rv 15:4
[j] 1Th 2:4
[k] 5:45 Ps 7:20; Mt 8:4; Heb 3:2
[l] 5:47 Mt 26:54; Rm 1:2
[m] Lk 16:29-31
[n] 6:1-15 Mt 14:13-21; Mk 6:30-44; Lk 9:10-17
[o] 6:1 Mk 1:16
[p] Jn 6:23; 21:1
[q] 6:5 Mk 1:45
[r] Mk 3:18
[s] 6:6 Ex 15:25

[t] 6:7 Mt 18:28
[u] 6:8 Mt 4:18; 10:2; Mk 1:16,29; 3:18; 13:3; Lk 6:14; Jn 1:40,44; 12:22; Ac 1:13
[v] Mt 16:17
[w] Lk 6:14; Ac 10:32
[x] 6:10 Mt 14:21
[y] 6:11 2Kg 4:42-44
[z] 6:12 Lk 15:4
[aa] 6:14 Dt 18:15
[ab] Mt 11:3; Lk 7:19-20; Rm 5:14; Heb 10:37
[ac] Jn 18:37
[ad] 6:15 Jn 19:21
[ae] 6:16-21 Mt 14:22-36; Mk 6:45-56
[af] 6:17 Lk 10:15

A **6:7** A denarius = one day's wage   B **6:14** Other mss read *signs*

5:39-40 A person can diligently study **the Scriptures** (the written Word) and still miss Jesus (the living Word). Knowing God's written Word is absolutely essential, but if your knowledge of it doesn't lead you to the living Word, then you have completely missed the point. This sad fact was illustrated when Jewish leaders told the wise men that Scripture foretold the Messiah's birth in Bethlehem, but they never bothered to make the trip to worship him (see Matt 2:1-6).

5:42-43 Jesus confronted the religious leaders with hard truth: **You have no love for God within you** (5:42). Why? Because Jesus had come in his **Father's name,** but they wouldn't **accept** him (5:43). They thought they loved God, claimed they loved God, boasted that they loved God. But they were unwilling to accept Jesus. Therefore, their professed love for God was a fraud. You simply can't have the Father without the Son. You can't have God without Jesus Christ.

5:44 Unconcerned with pleasing God, they sought to please each other.

5:45-47 Jesus told the religious leaders that **Moses,** the very person whose words they were reading in the Old Testament, would accuse them before God because they hadn't learned from him (5:45). Moses, Jesus told them, **wrote about me** (5:46). For example, Moses (who authored the books of Genesis–Deuteronomy) wrote about the Passover lamb (see Exod 12:1-28), and John the Baptist had identified Jesus as "the Lamb of God" (John 1:29, 36). Moses also wrote that God would "raise up . . . a prophet" like him from among God's people (Deut 18:15; see John 6:14; Acts 7:37). If they wouldn't believe Moses, they certainly weren't going to **believe** Jesus (John 5:47).

6:5-6 Teachers give students tests to allow them to apply what they've learned. When God tests us, he grants us opportunity to apply spiritual truth to the challenging circumstances we face. With thousands of hungry people gathering, Jesus gave Philip a pop quiz he'd never forget.

6:7 Two hundred denarii was over six months' wages. But in 6:5 Jesus wasn't asking about

the cost; he was asking where the food would come from.

6:10 Were women and children included in the count (see Matt 14:21), there could have been over fifteen **thousand** people present.

6:11 Jesus thanked God for what was not nearly enough! After that, **he distributed** the food and, miraculously, everyone ate **as much as they wanted.** Jesus took insufficiency, expressed gratitude for it, and provided more than enough. Don't let your lack of resources limit what God can do. Offer prayers of thanksgiving even in the midst of your insufficiency.

6:13 Twelve baskets equaled one big doggy bag per disciple. Each was a reminder of God's supernatural provision for each disciple.

6:14-15 As we'll see in 6:26-27, they only wanted the physical benefits Jesus offered. They wanted the blessings without the blesser.

6:19 They feared he was "a ghost" (see Matt 14:26).

a 6:20 Ex 3:14; Ps 45:8;
Jn 8:24
b 6:22 Jn 21:8
c 6:23 Jn 6:1; 21:1
d 6:25 Jn 11:8
e 6:27 Is 55:2
f Jn 12:25; Ac 13:48; 1Jn
2:25
g Dn 7:13; Mk 2:10; Jn
6:53,62
h 1Co 8:6; 15:24; Eph 5:20
i 6:29 Jn 5:36
j Mk 9:37; Jn 1:6

k 6:31 Ex 16:31
l Rv 12:6
m Ex 16:4,15; Ps 78:24
n 6:32 Ps 77:20; Mt 8:4;
Heb 3:2
o 6:35 Jn 8:24
p Lk 14:26
q Jn 4:14; Rv 7:16
r Mt 18:6; Mk 9:42; Jn
7:38; 11:25-26; 12:44,46;
14:12; 16:9
s Jn 7:37
t 6:37 Mt 24:22
u 6:38 Ex 3:8; Pr 30:4; Dn
4:13,23; Mt 28:2; Jn 1:51;
3:13; Eph 4:10; Rv 10:1;
18:1; 20:1
v Eph 1:9; 1Jn 2:17
w 6:39 Lk 18:33
x 6:40 Mt 11:27
y Jn 5:19
z Mt 16:21
aa 6:42 Jn 1:45

had rowed about three or four miles,[A] they saw Jesus walking on the sea. He was coming near the boat, and they were afraid. [20] But he said to them, "It is I.[B,*a*] Don't be afraid." [21] Then they were willing to take him on board, and at once the boat was at the shore where they were heading.

THE BREAD OF LIFE

[22] The next day, the crowd that had stayed on the other side of the sea saw there had been only one boat.[C,*b*] They also saw that Jesus had not boarded the boat with his disciples, but that his disciples had gone off alone. [23] Some boats from Tiberias[*c*] came near the place where they had eaten the bread after the Lord had given thanks. [24] When the crowd saw that neither Jesus nor his disciples were there, they got into the boats and went to Capernaum looking for Jesus. [25] When they found him on the other side of the sea, they said to him, "Rabbi,[*d*] when did you get here?"

[26] Jesus answered, "Truly I tell you, you are looking for me, not because you saw[D] the signs, but because you ate the loaves and were filled. [27] Don't work for the food that perishes[*e*] but for the food that lasts for eternal life,[*f*] which the Son of Man[*g*] will give you, because God the Father[*h*] has set his seal of approval on him."

[28] "What can we do to perform the works of God?" they asked.

[29] Jesus replied, "This is the work[*i*] of God — that you believe in the one he has sent."[*j*]

[30] "What sign, then, are you going to do so we may see and believe you?" they asked. "What are you going to perform? [31] Our ancestors ate the manna[*k*] in the wilderness,[*l*] just as it is written: **He gave them bread from heaven to eat.**"[E,*m*]

[32] Jesus said to them, "Truly I tell you, Moses[*n*] didn't give you the bread from heaven, but my Father gives you the true bread from heaven. [33] For the bread of God is the one who comes down from heaven and gives life to the world."

[34] Then they said, "Sir, give us this bread always."

[35] "I am[*o*] the bread of life," Jesus told them. "No one who comes to me[*p*] will ever be hungry,[*q*] and no one who believes in me[*r*] will ever be thirsty[*s*] again. [36] But as I told you, you've seen me,[F] and yet you do not believe. [37] Everyone the Father gives me will come to me, and the one who comes to me I will never cast out.[*t*] [38] For I have come down from heaven,[*u*] not to do my own will, but the will of him[*v*] who sent me. [39] This is the will of him who sent me: that I should lose none of those he has given me but should raise[*w*] them up on the last day. [40] For this is the will of my Father:[*x*] that everyone who sees the Son[*y*] and believes in him will have eternal life, and I will raise[*z*] him up on the last day."

[41] Therefore the Jews started complaining about him because he said, "I am the bread that came down from heaven." [42] They were saying, "Isn't this Jesus the son of Joseph,[*aa*] whose father and mother we know? How can he now say, 'I have come down from heaven'?"

[A] **6:19** Lit *twenty-five or thirty stadia* ; one *stadion* = 600 feet　[B] **6:20** Lit *"I am"*　[C] **6:22** Other mss add *into which his disciples had entered*
[D] **6:26** Or *perceived*　[E] **6:31** Ex 16:4; Ps 78:24　[F] **6:36** Other mss omit *me*

6:21 One moment they were in the middle of a stormy sea; the next moment they had miraculously reached their destination! Don't miss that once they **were willing to** receive Jesus into the boat, he dealt with their problem and delivered them where they needed to go. When believers recognize and respond to the presence of Jesus in the midst of their struggles, they invite the supernatural into their negative circumstances.
6:25 The crowd knew the disciples had departed in a boat (6:22) and knew Jesus hadn't left in one. Therefore, given his reputation, they suspected Jesus had arrived in some supernatural way.
6:26 They hadn't sought him for who he was. They sought him for what he could give them. They didn't want him, but his blessings. God isn't opposed to blessing people. He is opposed, however, to people who simply want to use him for his blessings—people who only want him for the stuff he can pro-

vide. He's looking for those who don't want his blessings without him.
　When the Israelites sinned against the Lord by constructing a golden calf, he told Moses that though he would give them the land of Canaan, he himself would not accompany them (see Exod 33:1-3). But Moses didn't want the promised land unless God would go with them (See Exod 33:15). When you want God more than you want his blessings, you will receive him—as well as whatever he graciously plans to give you. We are to pursue more *of* God, not just more *from* God.
6:27 They were striving for miraculous physical food (like the prioritization of the material over the spiritual in prosperity theology), when the Son was offering the free gift of spiritual food—that is, **eternal life**.
6:28-29 The only thing God demands of those wanting to receive the free gift of eternal life is belief in his Son, Jesus Christ.
6:32-33 Jesus's point was that God was their source, not Moses (6:32). And as sure as he'd

provided manna in the wilderness to address their ancestors' physical hunger, he was providing Jesus—**the true bread from heaven**—to meet their spiritual need (6:32).
　We must consider Jesus our source of life. If we "feed" on him (i.e., "believe in" him, 6:29) as **the bread of God** (6:33), we will never go hungry again (i.e., we "will never die," 11:26). This eternal life is permanent, secure, and irrevocable.
6:37 Just whom does the Father give to the Son? All those who believe in him. Whoever believes in the Son is a gift from the Father to the Son.
6:39 When you truly trust in Jesus Christ, you are eternally secure. If you come to him for salvation, you cannot be lost again.
6:40 As Jesus was raised from the dead (20:1-29), believers will also be raised **on the last day**.
6:42 They essentially said, "We know this guy. He's not **from heaven**; he's from Nazareth!"

43 Jesus answered them, "Stop complaining among yourselves. **44** No one can come to me unless the Father who sent me draws[A] him, and I will raise him up on the last day. **45** It is written in the Prophets:[a] **And they will all be taught by God.**[B,b] Everyone who has listened to and learned from the Father[c] comes to me — **46** not that anyone has seen the Father[d] except the one who is from God.[e] He has seen the Father.[f]

47 "Truly I tell you, anyone who believes[c] has eternal life. **48** I am the bread of life. **49** Your ancestors ate the manna[g] in the wilderness,[h] and they died. **50** This is the bread that comes down from heaven so that anyone may eat of it and not die.[i] **51** I am the living bread that came down from heaven. If anyone eats of this bread he will live[j] forever.[k] The bread that I will give for the life[l] of the world is my flesh."[m]

52 At that, the Jews argued[n] among themselves,[o] "How can this man give us his flesh to eat?"

53 So Jesus said to them, "Truly I tell you, unless you eat the flesh of the Son of Man[p] and drink his blood,[q] you do not have life in yourselves. **54** The one who eats my flesh and drinks my blood[r] has eternal life, and I will raise[s] him up on the last day, **55** because my flesh is true food and my blood is true drink. **56** The one who eats my flesh and drinks my blood remains in me, and I in him.[t] **57** Just as the living[u] Father sent me and I live because of the Father, so the one who feeds on me will live[v] because of me. **58** This is the bread that came down from heaven; it is not like the manna[D] your ancestors ate

— and they died. The one who eats this bread will live forever."[w]

59 He said these things while teaching in the synagogue[x] in Capernaum.[y]

MANY DISCIPLES DESERT JESUS

60 Therefore, when many of his disciples heard this, they said, "This teaching is hard. Who can accept[E] it?"

61 Jesus, knowing in himself[z] that his disciples were complaining about this, asked them, "Does this offend you? **62** Then what if you were to observe the Son of Man[aa] ascending[ab] to where he was before? **63** The Spirit[ac] is the one who gives life. The flesh doesn't help at all. The words that I have spoken to you are spirit and are life. **64** But there are some among you who don't believe." (For Jesus knew from the beginning[ad] those who did not[F] believe and the one who would betray[ae] him.) **65** He said, "This is why I told you that no one can come to me[af] unless it is granted to him by the Father."

66 From that moment[G] many of his disciples turned back and no longer accompanied him. **67** So Jesus said to the Twelve,[ag] "You don't want to go away too, do you?"

68 Simon Peter[ah] answered, "Lord, to whom will we go? You have the words of eternal life. **69** We have come to believe and know that you are the Holy One of God."[H,ai]

70 Jesus replied to them, "Didn't I choose you, the Twelve?[aj] Yet one of you is a devil."[ak] **71** He was referring to Judas,[al] Simon Iscariot's son,[l] one of the Twelve, because he was going to betray[am] him.

[a] 6:45 Mt 2:23; Ac 7:52
[b] Is 54:13
[c] 1Co 2:13; 1Th 4:9; 1Jn 2:20
[d] 6:46 Ex 33:20; Jn 5:47
[e] Jn 16:27
[f] Lk 10:22; Jn 8:38; 14:9
[g] 6:49 Ex 16:12-36
[h] Rv 12:6
[i] 6:50 Jn 11:26
[j] 6:51 Php 1:21
[k] Rv 4:9
[l] Jn 5:26; 6:53
[m] Php 3:3; Heb 10:10
[n] 6:52 2Tm 2:24
[o] Jn 9:16; 10:19
[p] 6:53 Mk 2:10
[q] Heb 9:12
[r] 6:54 Mt 26:26-29; Mk 14:22-25; Lk 22:15-20; 1Co 11:23-25
[s] Mt 16:21
[t] 6:56 Jn 15:4-5; 1Jn 3:24; 4:13-16
[u] 6:57 Mt 25:31-46; Heb 10:31
[v] Php 1:21; 1Pt 1:18
[w] 6:58 Rv 4:9
[x] 6:59 Jms 2:2
[y] Lk 10:15
[z] 6:61 Mk 10:32; Jn 1:47-48; 2:24-25; 4:17-18; 9:3; 11:4,11; 13:10-11,38
[aa] 6:62 Mk 2:10
[ab] Jn 3:13; 20:17; Ac 1:9
[ac] 6:63 Ps 51:11; Jn 1:33; Ac 2:4; Rm 8:9; Gl 5:25; Ti 3:5; Rv 3:22
[ad] 6:64 Jn 16:30; Ac 26:4
[ae] Mt 10:4; Jn 13:21
[af] 6:65 Lk 14:26
[ag] 6:67 Mk 11:11
[ah] 6:68 Lk 6:14
[ai] 6:69 Mk 1:24
[aj] 6:70 Jn 13:18
[ak] Mt 4:1,10; Jn 13:2,27; Ac 13:10
[al] 6:71 Mk 3:19
[am] Mt 10:4; Jn 13:21

[A] 6:44 Or *brings*, or *leads*   [B] 6:45 Is 54:13   [C] 6:47 Other mss add *in me*   [D] 6:58 Other mss omit *the manna*   [E] 6:60 Lit *hear*   [F] 6:64 Other mss omit *not*   [G] 6:66 Or *Because of this*   [H] 6:69 Other mss read *you are the Messiah, the Son of the Living God*   [I] 6:71 Or *Judas Iscariot, Simon's son*

6:44 This drawing is universal (see 12:32; 16:7-11) and can be rejected (see Acts 7:51).

6:48-51 Verse 48 is the first of Jesus's seven **I am** statements recorded in John's Gospel (see 8:12; 10:7, 11; 11:25; 14:6; 15:1). He would also say "I am" in an absolute sense to emphasize his divine identity (see 8:58).

The Jews wanted Jesus to give them physical bread like **the manna** God had given to their ancestors in the wilderness (see 6:30-31, 34), but Jesus reminded them that physical bread would only keep them alive for so long (6:49). Those who come to him—**the bread that comes down from heaven**—as their spiritual sustenance, however, will **not die** (6:50). In the same way that we eat bread to sustain our physical lives, we must eat **the living bread** (that is, believe in Jesus) to **live forever** (6:51).

In saying **the bread I will give for the life of the world is my flesh** (6:51), Jesus was speaking of the sacrifice of his body (his life) on the cross for the sins of the world (see 1:29; 19:18). Those who trust in Jesus as the atoning sacrifice for their sins will receive eternal life.

6:53-56 Jesus wasn't talking about cannibalism, though some listening may have misinterpreted it that way (see 6:60). He was using a rich metaphor to emphasize that believing in him is essential. Just as you will die without physical food, so also you can't have spiritual life apart from Jesus. You must **eat** him—that is, *receive* him, *trust* him, *believe* in him, *have faith* in him, *partake* of him.

It is by the believer's continuous act of faith through partaking spiritually of the body and blood of Christ in Communion that the benefits, power, and blessings of the new covenant are increasingly accessed (see 1 Cor 10:16-17; 11:23-26).

6:63 The Holy **Spirit** takes a person's belief in Jesus's words and activates Jesus's **life** in that person to give him spiritual life. Salvation cannot be attained through human effort.

6:64 The one who would betray him was Judas.

6:65 God only grants to Jesus those who are willing to respond to him. The Father cooperates with a person's decision to believe in his Son.

6:66-69 Only those who continue with Christ in the school of discipleship will receive more understanding from him. Those who drop out will not.

6:70-71 Nothing that happened throughout the course of his ministry, including Judas's betrayal, took Jesus by surprise. God's plan would be fulfilled even though it involved using Satan and his followers to accomplish it.

a 7:1 Mt 17:22
b Lk 1:5
c Jn 11:36
d Jn 5:18
e 7:2 Ex 23:16
f 7:3 Mk 3:21,31-35; 6:3; Lk 8:19
g Mk 6:28; Jn 5:36; Heb 3:9; Rv 15:3
h 7:6 Ps 37:39; Lk 20:10; Jn 7:8
i 7:7 Lk 6:27; 19:14
j 7:12 Gn 1:31
k Rv 20:10
l 7:14 Ac 21:26
m 7:15 Mt 26:54
n 7:16 Jn 5:19,30
o 7:17 Rm 8:27; Eph 1:9

p 7:18 Php 3:19
q Lk 9:32; Jn 17:24; 2Co 3:18; 1Pt 5:4; 2Pt 3:18
r Jn 8:14; 1Jn 5:20
s 1Jn 3:5
t 7:19 Ps 77:20; Mt 8:4; Heb 3:2
u Rm 2:12-29; 3:9-10,20-23,27-28
v 7:21 Jn 5:36; Heb 3:9; Rv 15:3
w 7:22 Ac 15:1; Gl 6:15
x Gn 17:9-14; Lv 12:3
y Mk 2:23
z 7:23 Lk 13:10
aa Lk 2:22
ab 7:24 Lk 6:37; Heb 9:27
ac 7:25 Mt 23:37
ad 7:26 Lk 8:41; 12:58
ae Mt 1:17; Eph 5:2
af 7:27 Mt 13:55; 21:11; Lk 4:22; Jn 6:42
ag 7:28 Ac 21:26
ah Jn 5:19
ai Jn 1:26-33; 5:13; 8:14,19,55; 9:29-30; 12:35; 13:7; 14:5; 15:15,21; 20:14; Gl 4:8; 1Th 4:5; 2Th 1:8; Ti 1:16
aj 7:29 Mk 9:37; Lk 10:22; Jn 1:6; 9:16
ak 7:31 Jn 15:24

THE UNBELIEF OF JESUS'S BROTHERS

7 After this, Jesus traveled in Galilee,*a* since he did not want to travel in Judea*b* because the Jews*c* were trying to kill him.*d* **2** The Jewish Festival of Shelters*A,e* was near. **3** So his brothers*f* said to him, "Leave here and go to Judea so your disciples can see your works*g* that you are doing. **4** For no one does anything in secret while he's seeking public recognition. If you do these things, show yourself to the world." **5** (For not even his brothers believed in him.)

6 Jesus told them, "My time*h* has not yet arrived, but your time is always at hand. **7** The world cannot hate*i* you, but it does hate me because I testify about it — that its works are evil. **8** Go up to the festival yourselves. I'm not going up to this festival,*B* because my time has not yet fully come." **9** After he had said these things, he stayed in Galilee.

JESUS AT THE FESTIVAL OF SHELTERS

10 After his brothers had gone up to the festival, then he also went up, not openly but secretly. **11** The Jews were looking for him at the festival and saying, "Where is he?" **12** And there was a lot of murmuring about him among the crowds. Some were saying, "He's a good*j* man." Others were saying, "No, on the contrary, he's deceiving*k* the people." **13** Still, nobody was talking publicly about him for fear of the Jews.

14 When the festival was already half over, Jesus went up into the temple*l* and began to teach. **15** Then the Jews were amazed and said, "How is this man so learned,*m* since he hasn't been trained?"

16 Jesus answered them, "My teaching isn't mine but is from the one who sent me.*n* **17** If anyone wants to do his will,*o* he will know whether the teaching is from God or whether I am speaking on my own. **18** The one who speaks on his own seeks his own glory;*p* but he who seeks the glory*q* of the one who sent him is true,*r* and there is no unrighteousness in him.*s* **19** Didn't Moses*t* give you the law? Yet none of you keeps the law.*u* Why are you trying to kill me?"

20 "You have a demon!" the crowd responded. "Who is trying to kill you?"

21 "I performed one work,*v* and you are all amazed," Jesus answered. **22** "This is why Moses has given you circumcision*w* — not that it comes from Moses but from the fathers*x* — and you circumcise a man on the Sabbath.*y* **23** If a man receives circumcision on the Sabbath*z* so that the law of Moses*aa* won't be broken, are you angry at me because I made a man entirely well on the Sabbath? **24** Stop judging*ab* according to outward appearances; rather judge according to righteous judgment."

THE IDENTITY OF THE MESSIAH

25 Some of the people of Jerusalem*ac* were saying, "Isn't this the man they are trying to kill? **26** Yet, look, he's speaking publicly and they're saying nothing to him. Can it be true that the authorities*ad* know he is the Messiah?*ae* **27** But we know where this man is from.*af* When the Messiah comes, nobody will know where he is from."

28 As he was teaching in the temple,*ag* Jesus cried out, "You know me and you know where I am from. Yet I have not come on my own, but the one who sent me*ah* is true. You don't know him;*ai* **29** I know him because I am from him, and he sent me."*aj*

30 Then they tried to seize him. Yet no one laid a hand on him because his hour had not yet come. **31** However, many from the crowd believed in him and said, "When the Messiah comes, he won't perform more signs than this man has done,*ak* will he?"

7:2-5 Matthew 13:55 identifies Jesus's **brothers** as "James, Joseph, Simon, and Judas." James believed in Jesus after his resurrection, became a leader in the early church, and authored the New Testament letter that bears his name (see, e.g., Acts 15:13; 21:18; 1 Cor 15:7; Gal 1:19; Jas 1:1). Judas (better known as Jude) is the author of the New Testament letter that bears his (see Jude 1).

7:6 My time has not yet arrived means it was not the moment for his public presentation as the Messiah (see 12:12-19). Jesus knew his death would follow soon after that open acknowledgment.

7:8-10 Jesus does things according to his Father's ways and timetable, not ours. And

God's ways and timing are perfect (see Gal 4:4-5).

7:13 Interestingly, when a man eventually did speak favorably of Jesus in public, the religious leaders banned him from the synagogue (see 9:13-34).

7:15 The people were puzzled that Jesus was so **learned** because he hadn't been **trained** by the religious leaders.

7:16 Jesus accurately represented the Father in everything he said.

7:22-23 Many of the Jews had become **angry** with Jesus because he healed a lame man **on the Sabbath** (7:23; see 5:1-13). Yet the Jews obeyed the law of **Moses** by performing **cir- cumcision** on "the Sabbath" (7:22). So if the act

of circumcision didn't break the law, how could making **a man entirely well** break it? (7:23).

7:24 They were to use God's standards for judgments and not their personal preferences.

7:27 They *thought* they knew all about Jesus. But though they assumed he was merely a preacher from Nazareth, he was much more. He was the Son of God from heaven.

7:30 An angry mob wanted **to seize** Jesus. He stood before them, alone and defenseless. But nothing happened, because their plans weren't in God's sovereign schedule. Similarly, no matter how bad your circumstances appear, nothing can harm you outside of God's will and timing.

32 The Pharisees[a] heard the crowd murmuring these things about him, and so the chief priests[b] and the Pharisees sent servants[A] to arrest him. **33** Then Jesus said, "I am only with you for a short time.[c] Then I'm going to the one who sent me.[d] **34** You will look for me, but you will not find me; and where I am, you cannot come."[e]

35 Then the Jews[f] said to one another, "Where does he intend to go so we won't find him? He doesn't intend to go to the Jewish people dispersed[B,g] among the Greeks[h] and teach the Greeks, does he? **36** What is this remark he made: 'You will look for me, and you will not find me; and where I am, you cannot come'?"

THE PROMISE OF THE SPIRIT

37 On the last and most important day of the festival,[i] Jesus stood up and cried out, "If anyone is thirsty, let him come to me[c,k] and drink.[l] **38** The one who believes in me,[m] as the Scripture[n] has said, will have streams of living water[o] flow[p] from deep within him." **39** He said this about the Spirit.[q] Those who believed in Jesus were going to receive the Spirit,[r] for the Spirit[D] had not yet been given[E] because Jesus had not yet been glorified.

THE PEOPLE ARE DIVIDED OVER JESUS

40 When some from the crowd heard these words, they said, "This truly is the Prophet."[s] **41** Others said, "This is the Messiah." But some said, "Surely the Messiah doesn't come from Galilee, does he? **42** Doesn't the Scripture[t] say that the Messiah comes from David's[u] offspring[F] and from the town of Bethlehem,[v] where David lived?" **43** So the crowd was divided[w] because of

him. **44** Some of them wanted to seize him,[x] but no one laid hands on him.

DEBATE OVER JESUS'S CLAIMS

45 Then the servants[y] came to the chief priests[z] and Pharisees, who asked them, "Why didn't you bring him?" **46** The servants answered, "No man ever spoke like this!"[G,aa] **47** Then the Pharisees responded to them: "Are you fooled[ab] too? **48** Have any of the rulers[ac] or Pharisees believed in him? **49** But this crowd, which doesn't know the law, is accursed."

50 Nicodemus[ad] — the one who came to him previously and who was one of them — said to them, **51** "Our law doesn't judge a man before it hears from him and knows what he's doing, does it?"[ae] **52** "You aren't from Galilee[af] too, are you?" they replied. "Investigate and you will see that no prophet arises from Galilee."[ag]

[The earliest mss do not include 7:53–8:11.][H]

8 [**53** Then each one went to his house. **1** But Jesus went to the Mount of Olives.[ah]

AN ADULTERESS FORGIVEN

2 At dawn he went to the temple[ai] again, and all the people were coming to him.[aj] He sat down[ak] and began to teach them. **3** Then the scribes and the Pharisees[al] brought a woman caught in adultery,[am] making her stand in the center. **4** "Teacher," they said to him, "this woman was caught in the act of committing adultery.[an] **5** In the law Moses[ao] commanded us to stone such women.[ap] So what do you say?" **6** They

[a] 7:32 Mk 7:3
[b] Mt 2:4
[c] 7:33 Jn 12:35; 14:19; 16:5,16
[d] Jn 14:12; 16:5,10,17,28
[e] 7:34 Jn 8:21; 13:33
[f] 7:35 Jn 11:36
[g] Jms 1:1; 1Pt 1:1
[h] Gl 2:3
[i] 7:36 Jn 8:21
[j] 7:37 Lv 23:34-36; Nm 29:35; Dt 16:13-14; Neh 8:18; Jn 5:1
[k] Lk 14:26
[l] Is 55:1; Rv 22:17
[m] 7:38 Jn 6:35
[n] Mt 26:54
[o] Jn 4:10-14
[p] Ex 17:1-6; Ps 78:15-16; 105:40-41; Pr 18:4; Is 12:3; Ezk 47:1-11; Zch 14:8; Rv 22:1-2
[q] 7:39 Ps 51:11; Jn 1:33; Ac 2:4; 8:15; Rm 8:9; Gl 5:25; Ti 3:5; Rv 3:22
[r] Ac 2:33
[s] 7:40 Jn 6:14
[t] 7:42 2Pt 1:20
[u] Lk 1:27
[v] Gn 35:19
[w] 7:43 Jn 9:16; 1Co 1:10
[x] 7:44 Jn 10:39
[y] 7:45 Jn 18:18
[z] Mt 2:4
[aa] 7:46 Mt 7:28-29
[ab] 7:47 Rv 20:10
[ac] 7:48 Lk 8:41
[ad] 7:50 Jn 3:1; 19:39
[ae] 7:51 Dt 1:16; 17:6; 19:15
[af] 7:52 Mt 17:22
[ag] 2Kg 14:25
[ah] 8:1 Mt 21:1
[ai] 8:2 Ac 21:26
[aj] Mk 1:45
[ak] Mk 9:35
[al] 8:3 Mk 7:3
[am] Nm 5:11
[an] 8:4 Mt 5:27-28
[ao] 8:5 Ps 77:20; Mt 8:4; Heb 3:2
[ap] Lv 20:10; Dt 22:22-24; Ezk 16:38-41

[A] 7:32 Or *temple police*, or *officers*, also in vv. 45,46   [B] 7:35 Gk *diaspora*; Jewish people scattered throughout Gentile lands   [C] 7:37 Other mss omit *to me*   [D] 7:39 Other mss read *Holy Spirit*   [E] 7:39 Lit *the Spirit was not yet*   [F] 7:42 Lit *seed*   [G] 7:46 Other mss read *like this man*   [H] 7:53–8:11 Other mss include all or some of the passage after Jn 7:36,44,52; 21:25; or Lk 21:38.

7:33-36 Approaching God's Word at the purely physical level as these Jews did will inevitably result in confusion. We need our antennae tuned to God's heavenly broadcast.

7:37 There is only one oasis for those who are in a spiritual desert. If you're spiritually parched, go to Jesus.

7:39 In this case, **glorified** refers to Jesus's crucifixion and resurrection.

7:42 They didn't realize that Jesus actually *was* born from the line of **David** (see Matt 1:1-17) in **Bethlehem** as Scripture had foretold (see Mic 5:2; Matt 2:1; Luke 2:1-7), but he grew up and ministered in Galilee—which Scripture had also foretold (see Isa 9:1-2; Matt 2:19-23; 4:14-15).

7:46 In other words, they said, "We intended to arrest him like you told us to,

but then we heard him talk and changed our minds!" Jesus's sermon was so mesmerizing that it prevented them from obeying wicked men.

7:47-51 Actually, there was a Pharisee named Nicodemus who had been captivated by Jesus's teaching. But he had kept his interest under wraps by only visiting Jesus at night (see 3:1-13). Interestingly, though, when he heard these words, **Nicodemus** spoke up: **Our law doesn't judge a man before it hears from him . . . does it?** (7:51). Thus, he wisely sought to calm everyone and to urge them against condemning someone without proper investigation.

7:52 Not only were they wrong about Jesus's birthplace (see 7:41-42), but they also were

wrong about no prophets coming **from Galilee**. Jonah's hometown of Gath-hepher was located there (see 2 Kgs 14:25).

8:3-5 This scene should make us ask, Where was the man who was involved with the woman? The law required that both parties be judged (see Lev 20:10; Deut 22:22). This, therefore, smells like a setup.

Importantly, if Jesus opposed stoning the adulteress, he would be opposing **the law Moses commanded** (John 8:5; see Deut 22:22). But if he advocated her death, he would be in trouble with the Romans because the Jews (under Roman rule) weren't permitted to execute anyone (see 18:31).

8:6 Just as the Ten Commandments had been "inscribed by the finger of God" (Exod 31:18),

[a] 8:6 Lk 11:54
[b] 8:7 Rm 3:23;6:23
[c] Rm 2:1,22
[d] Dt 17:7
[e] 8:11 Jn 3:17
[f] 8:12 Ex 3:14; Jn 8:24,58
[g] Ps 36:9; Jn 12:46; 1Jn 2:8
[h] Ex 13:21-22; 14:19-25; Is
42:6; 49:6; 60:19-22; Zch
14:5-8; Jn 9:5; 12:46
[i] 8:14 Jn 3:8; 7:28; 9:29;
12:35; 13:3,36; 14:5;
16:5,28; 1Jn 2:11
[j] 8:15 Lk 6:37; Rv 19:11
[k] Php 3:3
[l] Jn 3:17; 12:47
[m] 8:16 Mt 12:41; Jn 16:32;
2Th 1:5
[n] 8:17 Nm 35:30; Jn 8:14
[o] 8:18 1Jn 5:7,9

[p] 8:19 Jn 7:28; 1Jn 2:23
[q] Lk 10:22; Jn 17:3; 1Jn 4:8
[r] 8:20 Mk 12:41,43; Lk 21:1
[s] 8:21 Jn 14:2; 16:5
[t] Dt 24:16; Ezk 3:18; 33:8; Jn
15:22; Rm 3:23; 6:23
[u] Jn 7:34,36; 8:22; 13:33
[v] 8:22 Jn 8:21
[w] 8:23 Jn 3:13,31; 18:36;
Col 3:1-2
[x] 1Jn 4:5
[y] Jn 15:19; 17:14-16; 18:36
[z] 8:26 Jn 5:19
[aa] Jn 3:32; 15:15
[ab] 8:28 Mk 2:10
[ac] Jn 8:24
[ad] Mk 6:5; Jn 9:33; 15:5
[ae] 8:29 Jn 16:32; Ac 10:38

asked this to trap him,[a] in order that they might have evidence to accuse him.

Jesus stooped down and started writing on the ground with his finger. [7] When they persisted in questioning him, he stood up and said to them, "The one without sin[b] among you[c] should be the first to throw a stone at her."[d] [8] Then he stooped down again and continued writing on the ground. [9] When they heard this, they left one by one, starting with the older men. Only he was left, with the woman in the center. [10] When Jesus stood up, he said to her, "Woman, where are they? Has no one condemned you?"

[11] "No one, Lord,"[A] she answered.

"Neither do I condemn you,"[e] said Jesus. "Go, and from now on do not sin anymore."]

THE LIGHT OF THE WORLD

[12] Jesus spoke to them again: "I am[f] the light[g] of the world. Anyone who follows me will never walk in the darkness but will have the light of life."[h]

[13] So the Pharisees said to him, "You are testifying about yourself. Your testimony is not valid."

[14] "Even if I testify about myself," Jesus replied, "My testimony is true, because I know where I came from and where I'm going. But you don't know where I come from or where I'm going.[i] [15] You judge[j] by human standards.[j,k] I judge no one.[l] [16] And if I do judge, my judgment is true, because it is not I alone who judge, but I and the Father who sent me.[m] [17] Even in your law it is written that the testimony of two witnesses is true.[n] [18] I am the one who testifies[o] about myself, and the Father who sent me testifies about me."

[19] Then they asked him, "Where is your Father?"

"You know neither me nor my Father,"[p] Jesus answered. "If you knew me, you would also know my Father."[q] [20] He spoke these words by the treasury,[r] while teaching in the temple. But no one seized him, because his hour had not yet come.

JESUS PREDICTS HIS DEPARTURE

[21] Then he said to them again, "I'm going away;[s] you will look for me, and you will die in your sin.[t] Where I'm going, you cannot come."[u]

[22] So the Jews said again, "He won't kill himself, will he, since he says, 'Where I'm going, you cannot come'[v]?"

[23] "You are from below," he told them, "I am from above.[w] You are of this world;[x] I am not of this world.[y] [24] Therefore I told you that you will die in your sins. For if you do not believe that I am he, you will die in your sins."

[25] "Who are you?" they questioned.

"Exactly what I've been telling you from the very beginning," Jesus told them. [26] "I have many things to say and to judge about you, but the one who sent me[z] is true, and what I have heard from him — these things I tell the world."[aa]

[27] They did not know he was speaking to them about the Father. [28] So Jesus said to them, "When you lift up the Son of Man,[ab] then you will know that I am[ac] he, and that I do nothing on my own.[ad] But just as the Father taught me, I say these things. [29] The one who sent me is with me. He has not left me alone,[ae] because I always do what pleases him."

[A] 8:11 Or *Sir*; Jn 4:15,49; 5:7; 6:34; 9:36   [B] 8:15 Lit *You judge according to the flesh*

---

whatever Jesus was **writing** was a subtle way of communicating to them that he himself was the divine author of the law. Writing on the dirt was also an allusion to the fact that the law had been given to humankind who had been created out of dust and were therefore vulnerable to weakness and sin.
8:7 The point of Jesus's words was that not one of them was qualified to judge her. Their hypocrisy was revealed because they only brought the woman. The law commanded that both the man and the woman were guilty (Lev 20:10; Deut 22:22).
8:11 Notice that Jesus demonstrated grace and mercy to the woman (removing her condemnation) *before* he told her to start living right. A true understanding of grace and mercy does not endorse or promote **sin**; rather, it's designed to produce gratitude and holiness (see Rom 6:1-7).

We do not obey God in order to earn forgiveness. Rather, grace and mercy are to motivate our obedience. When we truly understand God's amazing grace, we do not go out and merely sin *less*—we go out and seek to sin *no more*.
8:14 Jesus **came from** and was **going** to heaven. The divine Son of God isn't capable of giving false **testimony**.
8:17-18 Jesus pointed to the **law** of Moses, which declared **the testimony of two witnesses** to be **true** (8:17). Jesus's words passed this requirement because he testified about himself through his messianic claims, **and the Father** also testified about him through his miraculous deeds (8:18; see the note on 5:36).
8:19 Anyone who rejects Jesus cannot know God because the former provides access to the latter (see the note on 14:4-7).

8:20 See the notes on 7:30 and 7:46.
8:23-24 Jesus and his interlocutors approached their debates from two different realms, the physical and the spiritual. Unless the Jewish leaders could see Jesus from a heavenly perspective, they would experience eternal judgment. Unless they believed that Jesus was the Messiah and received his payment for their sins, they would **die in [their] sins** (8:24).
8:28-30 Though the Father had **sent** the Son into the world, he had **not left [him] alone**. Jesus affirmed that the Father was **with** him because **he always [does] what pleases him** (8:29). In response to these words, **many believed in him** (8:30). Those who likewise place their faith in Jesus can have confidence that God will receive them—not because of their perfect faith but because of Jesus's perfect obedience.

TRUTH AND FREEDOM

30 As he was saying these things, many believed in him.

31 Then Jesus said to the Jews who had believed him, "If you continue in my word,[A,a] you really are my disciples. **32** You will know the truth,[b] and the truth will set you free."

33 "We are descendants[B] of Abraham,"[c] they answered him, "and we have never been enslaved to anyone. How can you say, 'You will become free'?"

34 Jesus responded, "Truly I tell you, everyone who commits sin is a slave of sin.[d] **35** A slave does not remain in the household forever,[e] but a son does remain forever.[f] **36** So if the Son sets you free, you really will be free. **37** I know you are descendants of Abraham,[g] but you are trying to kill me because my word has no place among you. **38** I speak what I have seen[h] in the presence of the Father;[c,i] so then, you do what you have heard from your father."

39 "Our father is Abraham," they replied.

"If you were Abraham's children," Jesus told them, "you would do what Abraham did.[j] **40** But now you are trying to kill me, a man who has told you the truth[k] that I heard from God. Abraham did not do this. **41** You're doing what your father does."[l]

"We weren't born[m] of sexual immorality,"[n] they said. "We have one Father — God."[o]

42 Jesus said to them, "If God were your Father, you would love me,[p] because I came from God[q] and I am here. For I didn't come on my own, but he sent me. **43** Why don't you understand what I say? Because you cannot listen to[D] my word.[r] **44** You are of your father the devil,[s] and you want to carry out your father's

desires. He was a murderer[t] from the beginning[u] and does not stand in the truth,[v] because there is no truth in him. When he tells a lie, he speaks from his own nature,[E] because he is a liar and the father of lies. **45** Yet because I tell the truth, you do not believe me. **46** Who among you can convict me of sin?[w] If I am telling the truth, why don't you believe me? **47** The one who is from God listens to God's words. This is why you don't listen, because you are not from God."

JESUS AND ABRAHAM

48 The Jews responded to him, "Aren't we right in saying that you're a Samaritan[x] and have a demon?"[y]

49 "I do not have a demon," Jesus answered. "On the contrary, I honor my Father and you dishonor me. **50** I do not seek my own glory;[z] there is one who seeks it and judges. **51** Truly I tell you, if anyone keeps my word,[aa] he will never see death."

52 Then the Jews said, "Now we know you have a demon. Abraham died and so did the prophets. You say, 'If anyone keeps my word, he will never taste death.' **53** Are you greater than our father Abraham who died? And the prophets died. Who do you claim to be?"

54 "If I glorify myself," Jesus answered, "my glory is nothing. My Father — about whom you say, 'He is our God' — he is the one who glorifies me. **55** You do not know him, but I know him. If I were to say I don't know him,[ab] I would be a liar like you. But I do know him,[ac] and I keep his word. **56** Your father Abraham rejoiced to see my day; he saw it[ad] and was glad."

57 The Jews replied, "You aren't fifty years old yet, and you've seen Abraham?"[F]

[a]8:31 Jn 2:22; 18:32
[b]8:32 Ps 119:142; Jn 14:6; 2Th 2:10
[c]8:33 Gn 16:15; Jn 8:37; Heb 2:16
[d]8:34 Rm 6:17-20; 2Pt 2:19
[e]8:35 1Jn 2:17
[f]Gn 21:10; Lk 15:31; Gl 4:30
[g]8:37 Lk 19:9; Jn 8:31-47; Ac 13:26; Rm 4:11,16; Gl 3:7
[h]8:38 Jn 3:32; 5:19; 6:46
[i]Mt 5:16; 11:27; Lk 11:13; Jn 8:42
[j]8:39 Gl 3:7,9
[k]8:40 Ps 119:142; Jn 14:6
[l]8:41 2Jn 9
[m]1Jn 2:29
[n]Hs 2:4; 1Th 4:3
[o]Dt 32:6
[p]8:42 Dt 6:5; Lk 10:27; 1Jn 5:1
[q]Jn 13:3; 16:27; 1Jn 5:20
[r]8:43 Lk 6:47; Jn 18:32
[s]8:44 Mt 4:1; Jn 13:2,27; Eph 2:1-3
[t]8:44 1Jn 3:15
[u]Gn 3:1-4; 4:8-9; Ac 26:4; 2Co 11:3; 1Jn 3:8-15; Rv 12:9
[v]Jn 14:6; Rm 3:7
[w]8:46 Jn 15:22; 1Jn 3:5
[x]8:48 Lk 9:52; Ac 1:8
[y]Jn 7:20; 10:20; Rv 9:20; 18:2
[z]8:50 Jn 17:24; Php 3:19; 1Pt 5:4
[aa]8:51 Jn 8:52,55; 14:23-24; 15:20; 17:6; 18:32; 1Jn 2:5; Rv 1:3; 3:8,10; 22:7,9
[ab]8:55 Jn 7:28
[ac]Mt 11:27
[ad]8:56 Lk 10:24; Heb 11:13-19

[A]8:31 Or *my teaching*, or *my message*, also in v. 37   [B]8:33 Or *offspring* ; lit *seed*, also in v. 37; Jn 7:42   [C]8:38 Other mss read *of my Father*   [D]8:43 Or *cannot hear*   [E]8:44 Lit *from his own things*   [F]8:57 Other mss read *and Abraham has seen you?*

8:31 Notice that you can believe in Jesus but not **continue in [his] word** and, thus, not function as a true disciple. Justification does not automatically result in continuous discipleship.

8:32 Truth is the absolute standard by which reality is measured. We live in a relativistic society that denies absolute truth, claiming, "What's true for you may not be true for me." But truth is not based on feelings, experiences, or desires. Truth is God's viewpoint on every matter, and it is not subject to redefinition. Pilate would ask, "What is truth?" (18:38), and the answer to that question is "Jesus" (see 14:6).

8:33 The Jews were basing their spiritual status on their physical link to Abraham.

8:36 The *living* Word (Jesus) provides us with legal freedom from sin through his atoning death on the cross; thus, we no longer stand condemned before God. But we must continue in his *written* Word (Scripture) in order to enjoy freedom from the sin to which we can be enslaved in our daily lives.

8:41 In other words, **they said**, "We know all about your illegitimate birth, Jesus! Your mother was pregnant before she was married" (see Matt 1:18).

8:42 In saying, **If God were your Father, you would love me, because I came from God**, Jesus denied their accusation (see the note on 8:41); his birth wasn't immoral but supernatural.

8:44-47 These Jews had lied about Jesus's mama (8:41), but in 8:44 he was telling the truth about their daddy! Their opposition to Jesus was Satanic in origin. They wanted to do whatever their father did, which explained all of their actions. Their religion was a fiction, and their allegiance was to the wrong kingdom. They were **not from God** (8:47).

8:48 See the note on 4:4-5.

8:51 Every person who believes in Jesus Christ as his or her Savior will escape **death** because when a Christian dies, he or she is immediately ushered into the presence of the Lord. Have no fear. Physical death is merely a transition into eternity.

a 8:58 Ex 3:14; Ps 45:8; Jn
1:15; 8:24; 17:5; Col 1:17
b 8:59 Jn 10:33
c Ex 17:4; Lv 24:16; 1Sm
30:6; 1Kg 21:10–13; Jn
10:31; 11:8
d Lk 4:30; Jn 12:36
e Ac 21:26
f 9:2 Jn 11:8
g Ezk 18:20
h Ex 20:5; Jb 21:19
i 9:3 Jn 5:36; 6:28–29; Rm
14:20; Heb 3:9; Rv 15:3
j 9:4 Jn 5:17; 2Jn 8
k Jn 11:9; 12:35; Rm 13:12
l 9:5 Mt 5:14; Jn 8:12; 12:46
m 9:6 Gn 2:7
n 9:7 Lk 13:4; Jn 9:11
o Is 35:5
p 9:11 Jn 9:7
q Ac 9:12
r 9:13 Mk 7:3

s 9:14 Mk 2:23
t 9:16 Jn 7:29
u Mt 26:45; Lk 24:7; Jn
9:24; Rm 5:19
v Jn 7:43; 10:19; 1Co 1:10
w 9:17 Jn 6:14
x 9:22 Mt 1:17; Eph 5:2
y 9:24 Jn 17:24
z Jos 7:19; 1Sm 6:5; Is
42:12; Jr 13:16; Lk 2:14;
Rm 4:20

58 Jesus said to them, "Truly I tell you, before Abraham was, I am."[a]

59 So they picked up stones[b] to throw at him.[c] But Jesus was hidden[A,d] and went out of the temple.[B,e]

THE SIXTH SIGN: HEALING A MAN BORN BLIND

9 As he was passing by, he saw a man blind from birth. **2** His disciples asked him: "Rabbi,[f] who sinned, this man[g] or his parents,[h] that he was born blind?"

3 "Neither this man nor his parents sinned," Jesus answered. "This came about so that God's works[i] might be displayed in him. **4** We[c] must do the works[j] of him who sent me[b] while it is day.[k] Night is coming when no one can work. **5** As long as I am in the world, I am the light of the world."[l]

6 After he said these things he spit on the ground, made some mud[m] from the saliva, and spread the mud on his eyes. **7** "Go," he told him, "wash in the pool of Siloam"[n] (which means "Sent"). So he left, washed, and came back seeing.[o]

8 His neighbors and those who had seen him before as a beggar said, "Isn't this the one who used to sit begging?" **9** Some said, "He's the one." Others were saying, "No, but he looks like him."

He kept saying, "I'm the one."

10 So they asked him, "Then how were your eyes opened?"

11 He answered, "The man called Jesus made mud, spread it on my eyes, and told me, 'Go to Siloam[p] and wash.' So when I went and washed I received my sight."[q]

12 "Where is he?" they asked.

"I don't know," he said.

THE HEALED MAN'S TESTIMONY

13 They brought the man who used to be blind to the Pharisees.[r] **14** The day that Jesus

made the mud and opened his eyes was a Sabbath.[s] **15** Then the Pharisees asked him again how he received his sight.

"He put mud on my eyes," he told them. "I washed and I can see."

16 Some of the Pharisees said, "This man is not from God,[t] because he doesn't keep the Sabbath." But others were saying, "How can a sinful man[u] perform such signs?" And there was a division[v] among them.

17 Again they asked the blind man, "What do you say about him, since he opened your eyes?"

"He's a prophet,"[w] he said.

18 The Jews did not believe this about him — that he was blind and received sight — until they summoned the parents of the one who had received his sight. **19** They asked them, "Is this your son, the one you say was born blind? How then does he now see?"

20 "We know this is our son and that he was born blind," his parents answered. **21** "But we don't know how he now sees, and we don't know who opened his eyes. Ask him; he's of age. He will speak for himself." **22** His parents said these things because they were afraid of the Jews, since the Jews had already agreed that if anyone confessed him as the Messiah,[x] he would be banned from the synagogue. **23** This is why his parents said, "He's of age; ask him."

24 So a second time they summoned the man who had been blind and told him, "Give glory[y] to God.[z] We know that this man is a sinner."

25 He answered, "Whether or not he's a sinner, I don't know. One thing I do know: I was blind, and now I can see!"

26 Then they asked him, "What did he do to you? How did he open your eyes?"

27 "I already told you," he said, "and you didn't listen. Why do you want to hear it

---

A 8:59 Or *Jesus hid himself*   B 8:59 Other mss add *and having gone through their midst, he passed by*   C 9:4 Other mss read *I*   D 9:4 Other mss read *us*

8:58 This is one of Jesus's most profound claims to deity in the Gospels. He didn't say, "Before Abraham was, I *was*," but "**I am.**" The former wording could be ambiguous and misunderstood, but not the latter. Not only was he claiming to have existed in Abraham's day, but he was also claiming divine identity.

When Moses asked God his name so that he could tell the Israelites who had sent him to them, God responded, "I AM WHO I AM. This is what you are to say to the Israelites: I AM has sent me to you" (Exod 3:14). Thus, Jesus identified himself as the God who had spoken to Moses.

8:59 Wrongly assuming Jesus was speaking blasphemy, **they picked up stones to** stone him.

9:1-5 Many in ancient times believed serious birth defects were the product of personal sin—thus the disciples' question in verse 2. But sickness, disease, and defect are not necessarily the result of personal sin (consider Job). Sometimes God allows negative conditions and circumstances in our lives in order to accomplish positive goals: our good, his glory, and bringing benefit to others (see Gen 50:19-20; Rom 8:28).

9:6 In this instance, the word of God (i.e., **saliva** from Jesus's mouth) was mixed with

humanity (i.e., dirt from which man was created) to provide the basis for a miracle.

9:12 He could hardly be expected to lead them to Jesus's current location. After all, he had never seen him!

9:18-23 These **parents** were interested in self-preservation (9:22). If you publicly confess Christ, you will likely experience some form of ridicule or ostracism. Believing in a generic "God" is safe; confessing Christ will earn you mockery.

9:26-27 When they asked him to give another account of his healing, it was clear that they hadn't believed him the first time. That may explain the bold tone of his reply.

Tearing Down Partitions

WHAT IS A PARTITION? In a number of classrooms, a high wall can be placed down the middle so that one room is made into two. These separators can decrease the possibility of noise from one side passing to the other. So if a group is meeting in one part of the room and another group is in the other, a partition will ensure that they do not disturb each other. It is designed to decrease disturbance and minimize the leaking of information from one space into another.

Satan creates a stronghold by creating a partition in your mind. He wants to block the free flow of the knowledge of God from entering into the thinking of the saint. Every day, we wrestle with emotionally-charged situations that have the potential to cripple us spiritually: the death of a loved one, the loss of a job, divorce, addictions, and unresolved anger. These are large matters, but smaller ones happen too: an unkind word, a disrespectful boss, something you see or read that carries negativity or causes envy. All are catalysts for creating partitions in our minds. And when they do, God's spiritual truth gets blocked, and we become paralyzed in our circumstances.

Of course, it doesn't have to be this way. But first, you must acknowledge a hard truth: living under the burden of emotional strongholds reflects a poor understanding of your identity in Christ. It's sin. Worry, fear, doubt, hate—such things are sins because they prevent us from trusting in and recognizing the truth of God.

Take a look in the mirror. That person you see was co-crucified, co-buried, and co-resurrected with Christ. Even though you may only have received Christ a short time ago, God took what happened to Jesus so many years ago and made it a part of your spiritual reality. That means every victory Jesus secured over sin and death already belongs to you.

Yes, Satan is a master at planting thoughts in your mind and making you think they are your own: "I can't overcome worry; I can't be free from this emotional bondage; I can't resist this old habit of falling into depression." But though you may say things like this to yourself, you must stop believing the lies so that you can overcome. All those statements may have been true when the old you was alive, but that person died on the cross along with Christ. You are a completely new creation.

To be fair, it's one thing to articulate this simple truth in writing; it's another thing entirely to apply it to the heat of one's own personal battles. Some strongholds, after all, may have been with you for a long time, and tearing them down might seem impossible. But God's Word doesn't lie, and Jesus *has* given you the power to shake free from the chains of sin. Meditate on, memorize, and apply the truths of his Word: you will see partitions begin to fall.

a **9:28** Ps 77:20; Mt 8:4; Heb 3:2
b **9:29** Jn 7:27-28; 8:14
c **9:31** Jb 27:9; Ps 66:18; Pr 28:9; Is 1:15; 1Jn 3:21
d Eph 1:9
e Ps 34:15,16; 145:19; Pr 15:20; Jms 5:16-18; 1Jn 5:14-15
f **9:32** Jn 15:24
g **9:33** Jn 8:28
h **9:34** Ps 51:5
i Is 66:5
j **9:35** Mk 2:10
k **9:36** Lk 10:1
l **9:39** Jn 18:37
m Mk 12:40; Jn 5:22-30
n Lk 4:18; Jn 3:19; 12:47-50
o **9:41** Jn 15:22,24; 1Jn 1:8; 3:5

p **10:1** Jr 7:11; Hs 6:9; 1Th 5:2,4; 2Pt 3:10; Rv 3:3; 16:15
q **10:2** Gn 4:2; Ps 23:1
r Mt 7:15
s **10:6** Mk 9:32; Lk 2:50; 9:45; 18:34; Jn 2:24; 12:16
t **10:7** Ex 3:14; Ps 45:8; Jn 8:24
u Mt 7:15
v **10:10** Eph 4:28
w Jn 6:27
x **10:11** Ps 23; Is 40:11; Ezk 34:12,23; 37:24; Zch 13:7; Jn 21:15-17; Heb 13:20; 1Pt 2:25; 5:4; Rv 7:17
y Mt 20:28; Mk 10:45; 2Co 5:21; Gl 3:13; 1Jn 3:16
z **10:12** Lk 10:3
aa **10:15** Mt 11:27; Lk 10:22
ab Mt 20:28
ac **10:16** Is 56:8; Ezk 34:11-13; Mt 8:11,12; Jn 12:32; Ac 10:34-35; 1Pt 2:25

again? You don't want to become his disciples too, do you?"

28 They ridiculed him: "You're that man's disciple, but we're Moses's*a* disciples. **29** We know that God has spoken to Moses. But this man—we don't know where he's from."*b*

30 "This is an amazing thing!" the man told them. "You don't know where he is from, and yet he opened my eyes. **31** We know that God doesn't listen to sinners,*c* but if anyone is God-fearing and does his will,*d* he listens to him.*e* **32** Throughout history*A* no one has ever heard of someone opening the eyes of a person born blind.*f* **33** If this man were not from God, he wouldn't be able to do anything."*g*

34 "You were born entirely in sin,"*h* they replied, "and are you trying to teach us?" Then they threw him out.*i*

SPIRITUAL BLINDNESS

35 Jesus heard that they had thrown the man out, and when he found him, he asked, "Do you believe in the Son of Man?"*B,j*

36 "Who is he, Sir,*k* that I may believe in him?" he asked.

37 Jesus answered, "You have seen him; in fact, he is the one speaking with you."

38 "I believe, Lord!" he said, and he worshiped him.

39 Jesus said, "I came into this world*l* for judgment,*m* in order that those who do not see will see and those who do see will become blind."*n*

40 Some of the Pharisees who were with him heard these things and asked him, "We aren't blind too, are we?"

41 "If you were blind," Jesus told them, "you wouldn't have sin.*o* But now that you say, 'We see,' your sin remains.

THE GOOD SHEPHERD

10 "Truly I tell you, anyone who doesn't enter the sheep pen by the gate but climbs in some other way is a thief and a robber.*p* **2** The one who enters by the gate is the shepherd*q* of the sheep.*r* **3** The gatekeeper opens it for him, and the sheep hear his voice. He calls his own sheep by name and leads them out. **4** When he has brought all his own outside, he goes ahead of them. The sheep follow him because they know his voice. **5** They will never follow a stranger; instead they will run away from him, because they don't know the voice of strangers." **6** Jesus gave them this figure of speech, but they did not understand*s* what he was telling them.

7 Jesus said again, "Truly I tell you, I am*t* the gate for the sheep.*u* **8** All who came before me*C* are thieves and robbers, but the sheep didn't listen to them. **9** I am the gate. If anyone enters by me, he will be saved and will come in and go out and find pasture. **10** A thief comes only to steal*v* and kill and destroy.*w* I have come so that they may have life and have it in abundance.

11 "I am the good shepherd.*x* The good shepherd lays down his life for the sheep.*y* **12** The hired hand, since he is not the shepherd and doesn't own the sheep, leaves them*D* and runs away when he sees a wolf*z* coming. The wolf then snatches and scatters them. **13** This happens because he is a hired hand and doesn't care about the sheep.

14 "I am the good shepherd. I know my own, and my own know me, **15** just as the Father knows me, and I know the Father.*aa* I lay down my life*ab* for the sheep. **16** But I have other sheep*ac* that are not from this

---

A **9:32** Lit *From the age* *B* **9:35** Other mss read *the Son of God* *C* **10:8** Other mss omit *before me* *D* **10:12** Lit *leaves the sheep*

9:30-34 In going toe-to-toe with the Jewish religious leaders, the healed man soundly bested them. Humiliated, they kicked him out of the synagogue to limit his influence on others.

9:35 Whatever negative consequences you experience for confessing Christ are not the last word.

9:38 Were Jesus not divine, accepting worship would be an endorsement of idolatry.

9:39 Jesus used the man's physical blindness to teach spiritual truth. Jesus had come into the world to give spiritual sight to those who desperately acknowledge their spiritual blindness. But to those who claimed to be spiritual know-it-alls, Jesus promised the **judgment** of becoming even more spiritually blind.

9:41 If they had been willing to admit their blindness—their lostness, their sinfulness—Jesus would have shown them grace. But since they claimed to **see**, their **sin** remained. When you think that nothing is wrong with you (see 1 John 1:8), everything is wrong.

10:2-4 Jesus was using this imagery to describe himself and to emphasize the importance of his followers (his **sheep**) having a personal knowledge of and relationship with him (their **shepherd**).

10:9 Jesus is "the way" to safety and life (14:6). We must go through him to **be saved**.

10:10 Jesus doesn't want you *merely* to posses eternal life but also to possess the full experience of **life**. Following the shepherd leads to blessing and joy and a growing experience of eternal life. It allows him to rebuke and reverse the enemy's attempts at blocking the blessings, purpose, and spiritual fulfillment God has for your life (see Joel 2:25; Mal 3:11).

10:15 In saying, **I lay down my life for the sheep,** Jesus was speaking of his substitutionary atonement when he would sacrifice his life on the cross for the sins of the world—though that would not have been clear to his audience. As he would tell his disciples later, "No one has greater love than this: to lay down his life for his friends" (15:13).

10:16 God the Father gave his one and only Son because he loved *the world*—all humankind, without exception (see 3:16; 1 Tim 2:6; Heb 2:9; 1 John 2:2). The **other sheep** that Jesus would save are Gentiles who would believe in him so that the church would con-

sheep pen; I must bring them also, and they will listen to my voice. Then there will be one flock, one shepherd.[a] **17** This is why the Father loves me,[b] because I lay down my life[c] so that I may take it up again. **18** No one takes it from me, but I lay it down on my own. I have the right to lay it down, and I have the right to take it up again. I have received this command from my Father."[d]

19 Again the Jews were divided[e] because of these words. **20** Many of them were saying, "He has a demon[f] and he's crazy. Why do you listen to him?" **21** Others were saying, "These aren't the words of someone who is demon-possessed. Can a demon open the eyes of the blind?"[g]

~ **HOPE WORDS** ~

If you are living outside of God's purpose, you are living outside of God's power.

JESUS AT THE FESTIVAL OF DEDICATION

22 Then the Festival of Dedication took place in Jerusalem, and it was winter. **23** Jesus was walking in the temple in Solomon's Colonnade.[h] **24** The Jews surrounded him and asked, "How long are you going to keep us in suspense?[A] If you are the Messiah,[i] tell us plainly."[B,j] **25** "I did tell you and you don't believe," Jesus answered them. "The works[k] that I do in my Father's name testify about me. **26** But you don't believe because you are not of my sheep.[C,l] **27** My sheep hear my voice, I know them, and they follow me. **28** I give them eternal life,[m] and they will

never perish.[n] No one will snatch[o] them out of my hand. **29** My Father,[p] who has given them to me, is greater than all. No one is able to snatch them out of the Father's hand. **30** I and the Father are one."[q]

RENEWED EFFORTS TO STONE JESUS

31 Again the Jews picked up rocks to stone him.[r]

32 Jesus replied, "I have shown you many good works[s] from the Father. For which of these works are you stoning me?"

33 "We aren't stoning[t] you for a good work," the Jews answered, "but for blasphemy, because you — being a man — make yourself God."

34 Jesus answered them, "Isn't it written in your law,[D] **I said, you are gods**?[E,u] **35** If he called those whom the word[v] of God came to 'gods' — and the Scripture[w] cannot be broken — **36** do you say, 'You are blaspheming' to the one the Father set apart and sent into the world, because I said: I am the Son of God?[x] **37** If I am not doing my Father's works,[y] don't believe me. **38** But if I am doing them and you don't believe me, believe the works. This way you will know and understand[F] that the Father is in me and I in the Father."[z] **39** Then they were trying again to seize him,[aa] but he eluded their grasp.[ab]

MANY BEYOND THE JORDAN BELIEVE IN JESUS

40 So he departed again across the Jordan[ac] to the place where John[ad] had been baptizing earlier, and he remained there. **41** Many came to him[ae] and said, "John never did a sign, but everything John said about this man was true." **42** And many believed in him there.

---

[a] **10:16** Ezk 34:23; 37:24; Jn 11:52; 17:11,20-22; Eph 2:11-19
[b] **10:17** Jn 3:35; 5:20
[c] **10:18** Jn 5:19
[d] **10:18** Jn 5:19
[e] **10:19** Jn 7:43; 9:16
[f] **10:20** Jn 7:20; 8:48; Rv 9:20; 18:2
[g] **10:21** Ex 4:11; Ps 146:8; Jn 9:32-33
[h] **10:23** Ac 3:11; 5:12
[i] **10:24** Mt 1:17; Eph 5:2
[j] **10:24** Mt 26:63; Lk 22:67; 2Co 3:12
[k] **10:25** Jn 5:36; 6:28-29; Rm 14:20; Heb 3:9; 2Jn 8; Rv 15:3
[l] **10:26** Jn 6:37; 8:47
[m] **10:28** Jn 12:25; Ac 13:48; 1Jn 2:25
[n] **10:28** Mt 10:42; Mk 9:41; Lk 21:18; Jn 3:16; 6:27,39; 17:12; 18:9; 2Co 4:9; 2Jn 8
[o] **10:29** Mt 11:27
[p] **10:30** Jn 1:15; 14:10; 17:11; 1Jn 2:24
[q] **10:31** Jn 11:8
[r] **10:32** Jn 5:36; 15:24
[s] **10:33** Lv 24:16; Mt 9:3; 26:62-66; Jn 5:18; 8:59
[t] **10:34** Ps 82:6
[u] **10:35** Lk 8:21; Jn 2:22; 18:32
[v] **10:36** Jn 5:19; Heb 1:2
[w] **10:36** Mt 26:54
[x] **10:37** Jn 5:36; 15:24; Heb 3:9; Rv 15:3
[y] **10:38** Jn 14:10; 1Jn 5:20
[z] **10:39** Jn 7:44
[aa] **10:39** Lk 4:30
[ab] **10:40** Mk 10:1; Lk 3:3
[ac] **10:41** Mk 1:4
[ad] **10:41** Mk 1:45

[A] **10:24** Lit *"How long are you taking away our life?"*　[B] **10:24** Or *openly*, or *publicly*　[C] **10:26** Other mss add *just as I told you*　[D] **10:34** Other mss read *in the scripture*　[E] **10:34** Ps 82:6　[F] **10:38** Other mss read *know and believe*

---

sist of both Jewish and Gentile believers (see Eph 2:11-22). **There will be one flock.**

10:17-18 Jesus was under no obligation to sacrifice himself for sinners. And though the Jews would hunt him over and the Romans would crucify him, this was only possible because he let them (see 19:10-11). No one *takes* the life of the Son of God. He lays it down voluntarily because he is willing to give his life in obedience to the Father's **command** and in love for sinners (10:18).

10:19-21 Notice the polarization here. No one was on the fence about Jesus. Indeed, each of us will believe either the truth about him or will embrace a lie instead.

10:22 Today **the Festival of Dedication** is commonly known as Hanukkah, which celebrates the rededication of the temple in

165 BC after its desecration by Antiochus IV Epiphanes in 168 BC.

10:28-29 Believers are not eternally secure because of their grip on God but because of his grip on them. If you come to Jesus by faith, he's got you. When you're too weak and your hands go limp, he'll still be hanging on.

10:30 I and the Father are one—in essence and in purpose. You don't get a clearer claim to deity than that. Remember, our Creator is one God in three persons: Father, Son, and Holy Spirit. And Jesus Christ is one person with two natures (divine and human).

10:34-36 Jesus pointed to Psalm 82:6: **I said, you are gods** (John 10:34). There God referred to human rulers, who were made in God's image and responsible to imitate God's char-

acter, as "gods." So if sinful men in honored positions could be called "gods," what about a perfect man?

10:39 You'd think that by this point they would realize that seizing Jesus is a dead-end street (see 7:30-32, 44-46; 8:20). No one could take his life from him (see 10:17-18), but soon he would lay it down. Jesus was sovereign over his own death.

10:40-42 Given the hostility directed against him in Jerusalem, Jesus **departed . . . across the Jordan** (10:40). But that didn't put a damper on his ministry or the success of his message (10:41-42).

a 11:1 Mk 11:1
b Lk 10:38-42
c 11:2 Lk 7:38; Jn 12:3
d 11:4 Lk 9:32; Jn 9:3;
10:38; 11:40; 17:24; 2Co
3:18; 2Pt 3:18
e Jn 5:19; Heb 1:2
f 11:7 Lk 1:5
g 11:8 Mt 23:7-8; 26:25,49;
Mk 9:5; 11:21; 14:45; Jn
1:38,49; 3:2,26; 4:31;
6:25; 9:2
h Jn 10:31
i 11:9 Mt 5:14; Jn 8:12
j 11:10 Jn 9:4
k 11:11 Ac 13:36; 1Co 11:30

l 11:16 Mk 3:18
m 11:17 Jn 5:28
n 11:18 Mt 23:37
o 11:23 Mk 9:27
p 11:24 Jn 2:4; 6:39; 1Pt 1:5;
3:3; 2Pt 3:3; Jd 18
q 11:25 Ex 3:14; Jn 8:24,58
r Jn 6:35
s Php 1:21
t 11:26 Jn 6:50; 8:51
u 11:27 Mt 1:17; Eph 5:2
v Jn 5:19
w Jn 18:37

LAZARUS DIES AT BETHANY

11 Now a man was sick, Lazarus from Bethany,*a* the village of Mary and her sister Martha.*b* **2** Mary was the one who anointed the Lord with perfume and wiped his feet with her hair,*c* and it was her brother Lazarus who was sick. **3** So the sisters sent a message to him: "Lord, the one you love is sick."

4 When Jesus heard it, he said, "This sickness will not end in death but is for the glory of God,*d* so that the Son of God*e* may be glorified through it." **5** Now Jesus loved Martha, her sister, and Lazarus. **6** So when he heard that he was sick, he stayed two more days in the place where he was. **7** Then after that, he said to the disciples, "Let's go to Judea*f* again."

8 "Rabbi,"*g* the disciples told him, "just now the Jews tried to stone you,*h* and you're going there again?"

9 "Aren't there twelve hours in a day?" Jesus answered. "If anyone walks during the day, he doesn't stumble, because he sees the light of this world.*i* **10** But if anyone walks during the night,*j* he does stumble, because the light is not in him."

11 He said this, and then he told them, "Our friend Lazarus has fallen asleep,*k* but I'm on my way to wake him up."

12 Then the disciples said to him, "Lord, if he has fallen asleep, he will get well." **13** Jesus, however, was speaking about his death, but they thought he was speaking about natural sleep. **14** So Jesus then told them plainly, "Lazarus has died. **15** I'm glad for you that I wasn't there so that you may believe. But let's go to him."

16 Then Thomas*l* (called "Twin"*A*) said to his fellow disciples, "Let's go too so that we may die with him."

THE RESURRECTION AND THE LIFE

17 When Jesus arrived, he found that Lazarus had already been in the tomb*m* four days. **18** Bethany was near Jerusalem*n* (less than two miles*B* away). **19** Many of the Jews had come to Martha and Mary to comfort them about their brother.

20 As soon as Martha heard that Jesus was coming, she went to meet him, but Mary remained seated in the house. **21** Then Martha said to Jesus, "Lord, if you had been here, my brother wouldn't have died. **22** Yet even now I know that whatever you ask from God, God will give you."

23 "Your brother will rise*o* again," Jesus told her.

24 Martha said to him, "I know that he will rise again in the resurrection at the last day."*p*

25 Jesus said to her, "I am*q* the resurrection and the life. The one who believes in me,*r* even if he dies, will live.*s* **26** Everyone who lives and believes in me will never die.*t* Do you believe this?"

27 "Yes, Lord," she told him, "I believe you are the Messiah,*u* the Son*v* of God, who comes into the world."*w*

A 11:16 Gk *Didymus*   *B* 11:18 Lit *fifteen stadia*; one *stadion* = 600 feet

---

11:1-2 Lazarus and his two sisters, **Mary** and **Martha**, appear several times in the Gospels (see 12:1-8; Luke 10:38-42).

11:4 If someone says that a Christian walking with the Lord can't become ill or contract a disease, that person is simply wrong. Lazarus's **sickness** was not a means of punishment, not a sign of rebellion. Rather, it had a spiritual purpose.

11:5-6 Jesus loved Martha, her sister, and Lazarus (11:5), and they knew of his love for them (see 11:3). They shared an intimate relationship with him. But, in spite of this, Jesus **stayed two more days in the place where he was** (11:6). His delay appeared to contradict his promise of healing. However, it was *because* he loved them that he delayed his arrival.

This passage demonstrates an important theological truth regarding prayer. In our times of struggle, we want God to respond immediately. When he doesn't, we're tempted to assume he doesn't care. But the reality is that we don't understand his timing or his purposes because his ways are not our ways (see Isa 55:8-9). There's a method to his (apparent) contradictions. He responds as he does because he loves us and because he's seeking his glory. Trust him in his delays.

11:9-10 The day—the time of his public, earthly ministry—was the opportunity for action. While Jesus, **the light of this world**, was with them, they could walk and not **stumble** (11:9). Later, they would have the light of the Holy Spirit's presence. But to function apart from Jesus is like walking around at **night** (11:10). Operating without his illumination will cause you to trip and wind up on your face. **11:11** For those who trust in the Lord, the Bible describes death as sleep (i.e., a new level of spiritual consciousness), from which we will one day be physically raised (see 1 Thess 4:13). **11:15** Jesus was not **glad** concerning Lazarus's death but glad concerning what he was about to do.

11:16 Later, **Thomas** would express doubt over Jesus's resurrection (see 20:24-29). But for now, he was ready to **die with [Jesus]**. Those who are spiritually confident today may find themselves in the depths of uncertainty tomorrow.

11:21-22 Translation: "This is all your fault, Jesus! I called you, but you didn't come. If you had listened to me, none of this would have happened." Though Martha was filled with frustration that Jesus hadn't done things her way, she hadn't lost all hope. **Even now I know that whatever you ask from God, God will give you (11:22)**. Thus, Martha was filled with both faith and doubt. So here she is like the man who cried out to Jesus in desperation, "I do believe; help my unbelief! (Mark 9:24).

Take your doubts to God in prayer (he's omniscient and knows about them anyway). Believe that he can deal with your disappointment and help you in your spiritual struggle. **11:24-26** Resurrection isn't just an event; the **resurrection** is a person (11:24-25). The Son of God has "life in himself" (5:26) and can give life so that a person may "live forever" (6:51). Jesus himself is the basis of eternal life. That's how he can say that the one who **believes in [him] will never die**—that is, he will pass from physical life immediately into eternal life (11:26; see Phil 1:23). The present tense (**lives and believes in me**) also shows that Jesus is a right-now deliverer, not just a future one (John 11:26).

11:27 Though she still didn't comprehend everything or know what exactly was going to happen, Martha trusted Jesus and confessed him as **the Messiah, the Son of God**. Choose to hang on to that conviction when your own world is rocked by grief.

It's Time for a Resurrection

WHEN YOU GO TO A restaurant, someone will give you a written description of what they have to offer. You can read the menu for yourself. Sometimes you may salivate just scanning the menu because it looks so good. But you won't be satisfied to leave the restaurant after merely reading the menu because you don't go to a restaurant just to read.

When a waiter comes to your table, he will likely proclaim parts of the menu to you. He will walk through and exegete it for you. The waiter will tell you what different terms mean and how stuff is made. He may even give you his personal opinion about what he likes to eat. But you will not be satisfied by his words because no one goes to a restaurant to hear somebody else preach about it.

You go to a restaurant to taste and experience what it has in store for you. Therefore, you will not be satisfied until you have partaken of all it has to offer you, until you have tasted it fully.

God longs for us to taste what he offers. He wants us to experience that he is the great "I AM" (EX 3:14). Reading about him is good. Hearing about him is good. But if you leave this life without having deeply experienced God, then you may have known a nice truth from a distance, but you will never have known all that he can do for you. You will never know the power of hearing God say (like he did in John 11:43 when he called Lazarus from the grave), "Career, come forth. Marriage, come forth. Health, come forth. Relationship, come forth. Hope, come forth. Future, come forth. Family, come forth. Finances, come forth. Joy, come forth. Peace, come forth. Significance, come forth."

Whatever is dying in your life can be called forth. Jesus can call even dead things to life. And when he does, you won't need somebody else to tell you how good God is because you will have experienced him for yourself. You won't need somebody else to tell you how great God can be because you will have seen him for yourself.

God longs to be more than just theology on a shelf. He wants to be real to you right now. To accomplish this, sometimes he allows us to get, or even puts us, between a rock and a hard place. He lets something die for the express purpose of letting us experience a resurrection. Because God knows that when we see him for who he really is, we will never see life the same way again.

JESUS SHARES THE SORROW OF DEATH

28 Having said this, she went back and called her sister Mary, saying in private, "The Teacher is here and is calling for you."

29 As soon as Mary heard this, she got up quickly and went to him.[a] 30 Jesus had not yet come into the village but was still in the place where Martha had met him. 31 The Jews who were with her in the house consoling her saw that Mary got up quickly and went out. They followed her, supposing that she was going to the tomb[b] to cry there.

32 As soon as Mary came to where Jesus was and saw him, she fell at his feet[c] and told him, "Lord, if you had been here, my brother would not have died!"

33 When Jesus saw her crying, and the Jews who had come with her crying, he was deeply moved[A] in his spirit[d] and troubled. 34 "Where have you put him?" he asked.

"Lord," they told him, "come and see."

35 Jesus wept.[e]

36 So the Jews said, "See how he loved[f] him!" 37 But some of them said, "Couldn't he who opened the blind man's eyes[g] also have kept this man from dying?"

THE SEVENTH SIGN: RAISING LAZARUS FROM THE DEAD

38 Then Jesus, deeply moved again, came to the tomb. It was a cave, and a stone was lying against it.[h] 39 "Remove the stone," Jesus said.

Martha, the dead man's sister, told him, "Lord, there is already a stench because he has been dead four days."

40 Jesus said to her, "Didn't I tell you that if you believed you would see the glory[i] of God?"[j]

41 So they removed the stone. Then Jesus raised his eyes and said, "Father, I thank[k] you that you heard me.[l] 42 I know that you always hear me, but because of the crowd standing here I said this, so that they may believe you sent[m] me." 43 After he said this, he shouted with a loud voice, "Lazarus, come out!" 44 The dead man came out bound hand and foot with linen strips and with his face wrapped in a cloth. Jesus said to them, "Unwrap him and let him go."

THE PLOT TO KILL JESUS

45 Therefore, many of the Jews who came to Mary and saw what he did believed in him.[n] 46 But some of them went to the Pharisees[o] and told them what Jesus had done.

47 So the chief priests and the Pharisees convened the Sanhedrin[p] and were saying, "What are we going to do since this man is doing many signs? 48 If we let him go on like this, everyone will believe in him, and the Romans[q] will come and take away both our place and our nation."

49 One of them, Caiaphas,[r] who was high priest[s] that year, said to them, "You know nothing at all! 50 You're not considering that it is to your[B] advantage that one man should die for the people rather than the whole nation perish."[t] 51 He did not say this on his own, but being high priest that year he prophesied that Jesus was going to die[u] for the nation, 52 and not for the nation only, but also to unite the scattered children[v] of God. 53 So from that day on they plotted to kill him.[w]

54 Jesus therefore no longer walked openly[x] among the Jews but departed from there to the countryside near the wilderness,[y] to a town called Ephraim, and he stayed there with the disciples.

[a] 11:29 Mk 1:45
[b] 11:31 Jn 5:28
[c] 11:32 Rv 19:10
[d] 11:33 Ps 51:12
[e] 11:35 Lk 19:41
[f] 11:36 Mk 14:44; Jn 5:20
[g] 11:37 Jn 9:6-7
[h] 11:38 Mt 27:60; Mk 15:46; Lk 24:2; Jn 20:1
[i] 11:40 Jn 17:24
[j] Mk 9:23; 1Jn 3:2
[k] 11:41 Mk 8:6; Rm 1:8
[l] Jn 9:31
[m] 11:42 Mk 9:37; Jn 1:6
[n] 11:45 Jn 2:23; 12:11
[o] 11:46 Mk 7:3
[p] 11:47 Mk 13:9
[q] 11:48 Ac 16:21
[r] 11:49 Mt 26:3,57; Lk 3:2; Jn 18:13-14,24,28; Ac 4:6
[s] Lv 16:32
[t] 11:50 Is 53:8; Jn 18:14
[u] 11:51 2Co 4:10
[v] 11:52 Lk 1:7
[w] 11:53 Jn 5:18
[x] 11:54 Jn 7:1
[y] Mt 3:1; Rv 12:6

[A] 11:33 Or *angry*, also in v. 38 [B] 11:50 Other mss read *to our*

11:35 Even though Jesus knew he was about to call Lazarus back to life, he grieved with personal pain and sorrow over the death-dealing effects of sin on those he loves. "We do not have a high priest who is unable to sympathize" (Heb 4:15).

11:37 If they thought keeping a **man from dying** would be spectacular, they were in for the shock of their lives.

11:39-40 Jesus called **Martha** to demonstrate her faith in him by her action—allowing **the stone** to be **remov[ed]** (11:39). Faith must precede sight if we want to see God's supernatural intervention in our circumstances. We'll never know what God plans to do until we obey what he has clearly revealed.

11:41-42 He could've showed up on time and conducted a private miracle to heal Lazarus. Instead, he arrived late to put on a public, supernatural display, validating his messianic identity and sparking faith in a mass gathering of people. The latter, though it resulted in temporary grief, would produce tremendous spiritual impact and bring God greater glory.

Jesus's prayer for his Father's supernatural intervention illustrates his current intercessory work of deliverance for believers when we respond in faith and obedience (see Heb 7:25). This is why we pray to the Father in the name of Jesus.

11:43-44 This scene is a foretaste of what is to come. And though Lazarus would physically die again, those who believe in Jesus will take part in the everlasting resurrection and live forever.

11:47-48 Notice that they didn't deny Jesus's miraculous **signs** (11:47). Rather, they lamented them. Instead of cheering his raising of the dead, they worried that Jesus's winning of followers would cause **the Romans** to think there was an insurrection, thus bringing the Roman hammer down on their **nation** (11:48).

11:49-53 This wicked **high priest** was merely thinking on the physical level, but his words providentially foretold a spiritual reality. Indeed, the **one man** would **die for** the sins of the many. **Jesus was going to die for the nation** (11:49-51). And not only for Israel, but also for Gentiles (11:52). Even as the religious leaders **plotted** evil, though, God planned to use it for good (11:53; see Gen 50:20).

55 Now the Jewish Passover[a] was near, and many went up to Jerusalem[b] from the country to purify themselves before the Passover. **56** They were looking for Jesus and asking one another as they stood in the temple:[c] "What do you think? He won't come to the festival,[d] will he?" **57** The chief priests[e] and the Pharisees had given orders that if anyone knew where he was, he should report it so that they could arrest him.

THE ANOINTING AT BETHANY

12 Six days before the Passover, Jesus came to Bethany[f] where Lazarus[A] was, the one Jesus had raised from the dead.[g] **2** So[h] they gave a dinner for him there; Martha[i] was serving them, and Lazarus was one of those reclining at the table with him. **3** Then Mary took a pound of perfume, pure and expensive nard, anointed Jesus's feet, and wiped his feet with her hair.[j] So the house was filled with the fragrance of the perfume.

4 Then one of his disciples, Judas Iscariot[k] (who was about to betray him), said, **5** "Why wasn't this perfume sold for three hundred denarii[B,l] and given to the poor?" **6** He didn't say this because he cared about the poor but because he was a thief.[m] He was in charge of the money-bag and would steal part of what was put in it.

7 Jesus answered, "Leave her alone; she has kept it for the day of my burial.[n] **8** For you always have the poor with you,[o] but you do not always have me."

THE DECISION TO KILL LAZARUS

9 Then a large crowd of the Jews learned he was there. They came not only because of Jesus but also to see Lazarus, the one he had raised from the dead.[p] **10** But the chief priests had decided to kill Lazarus also, **11** because he was the reason many of the Jews were deserting them[c] and believing in Jesus.

THE TRIUMPHAL ENTRY

12 The[q] next day, when the large crowd that had come to the festival heard that Jesus was coming to Jerusalem, **13** they took palm branches[r] and went out to meet him. They kept shouting:

> "*Hosanna!*[s]
> **Blessed is he who comes in**
>   **the name of the Lord**[D,t] — the
>   King of Israel!"[u]

14 Jesus found a young donkey[v] and sat on it, just as it is written:

> **15** **Do not be afraid,**[w]
> **Daughter Zion. Look, your King**
>   **is coming,**
> **sitting on a donkey's colt.**[E,x]

16 His disciples did not understand these things at first. However, when Jesus was glorified, then they remembered that these things had been written about him[y] and that they had done these things to him.

17 Meanwhile, the crowd, which had been with him when he called Lazarus out of the tomb[z] and raised him from the dead, continued to testify.[F] **18** This is also why the crowd met him, because they heard he had done this sign. **19** Then the Pharisees said to one another, "You see? You've accomplished nothing. Look, the world has gone after him!"[aa]

JESUS PREDICTS HIS CRUCIFIXION

20 Now some Greeks were among those who went up to worship at the festival.

Cross-references (right margin):

[a] 11:55 Ex 12:11
[b] Mt 23:37
[c] 11:56 Ac 21:26
[d] Jn 2:23
[e] 11:57 Mt 2:4
[f] 12:1 Mk 11:1
[g] Jn 11:43-44
[h] 12:2-8 Mt 26:6-13; Mk 14:3-9
[i] 12:2 Jn 11:1
[j] 12:3 Mk 14:3; Jn 11:2
[k] 12:4 Mt 26:14; Mk 3:19
[l] 12:5 Mt 18:28
[m] 12:6 Jn 10:1
[n] 12:7 Jn 19:40
[o] 12:8 Dt 15:11
[p] 12:9 Jn 21:14
[q] 12:12-19 Mt 21:1-11; Mk 11:1-11; Lk 19:28-44
[r] 12:13 Lv 23:40; Rv 7:9
[s] Lk 1:42
[t] Ps 118:25-26
[u] Jn 1:49
[v] 12:14 Lk 13:15
[w] 12:15 Jn 6:20
[x] Zch 9:9
[y] 12:16 Jn 2:22; 14:26
[z] 12:17 Jn 5:28
[aa] 12:19 Mk 15:6-15; Lk 19:39-44; Jn 11:47-48; 12:36-43; 19:15

[A] 12:1 Other mss read *Lazarus who died*   [B] 12:5 A denarius = one day's wage   [C] 12:11 Lit *going away*   [D] 12:13 Ps 118:25-26   [E] 12:15 Zch 9:9   [F] 12:17 Other mss read *Meanwhile, the crowd, which had been with him, continued to testify that he had called Lazarus out of the tomb and raised him from the dead.*

11:55 Jerusalem began filling with people because it was time for **the Passover**, celebrating God's deliverance of Israel from Egyptian slavery (see Exod 12:1-28). Soon God would provide a new and ultimate means of deliverance from slavery to sin.

12:4-6 Three hundred denarii was about a year's wages (12:5). Adding such a sum to the piggy bank would've meant more cash in Judas's pocket.

12:7 Jesus's **burial** was only a few days away.

12:8 Providing for **the poor** is a biblical mandate for God's people (see Lev 19:9-10; Prov 19:17; 2 Cor 9:7; Eph 4:28). (Of course, the Bible is talking about those who are legitimately poor, not those who are poor through their own laziness; see 2 Thess 3:10.) But dealing with poverty is an unending reality in this sinful, fallen world. And this reality was not to prevent Jesus's followers from honoring their long-awaited Lord and Messiah who would only be with them a short while longer.

12:9-11 When they learned that Jesus had **raised** Lazarus **from the dead**, crowds of people wanted to get a glimpse of the ex-corpse (12:9). Because of Jesus's miraculous deed, **many of the Jews were deserting** the Jewish religious leaders **and believing in Jesus** (12:11). How did **the chief priests** respond to this? They **decided to kill Lazarus** too (12:10)! Their wickedness knew no bounds.

12:13 Hosanna is Hebrew for "save us"—it's a cry of deliverance. By applying Psalm 118:25-26 to Jesus and identifying him as their King, they were hailing Jesus as the Messiah who would deliver them from Roman domination.

12:14-16 Jesus fulfilled Scripture and entered Jerusalem in exactly the manner foretold in Zechariah 9:9. Fulfilled prophecies like this one testify to the divine inspiration and inerrancy of Scripture. The many Old Testament prophecies about the Messiah were written hundreds of years before his birth, yet they were fulfilled in his life accurately and in detail. This should encourage all believers to trust that the Bible is indeed the authoritative Word of God.

12:19 The Gospels make clear that the religious leaders in Jerusalem were motivated in their hatred of Jesus by jealousy (see Matt 27:18; Mark 15:10).

12:20-21 These **Greeks** were Gentile proselytes who worshiped the God of Israel (12:20). Earlier Jesus had said, "I have other

²¹ So they came to Philip,ᵃ who was from Bethsaidaᵇ in Galilee,ᶜ and requested of him, "Sir,ᵈ we want to see Jesus." ²² Philip went and told Andrew;ᵉ then Andrew and Philip went and told Jesus.

²³ Jesus replied to them, "The hour has come for the Son of Manᶠ to be glorified. ²⁴ Truly I tell you, unless a grain of wheatᵍ falls to the ground and dies, it remains by itself. But if it dies, it produces much fruit.ʰ ²⁵ The one who loves his life will lose it,ⁱ and the one who hatesʲ his lifeᵏ in this world will keep it for eternal life. ²⁶ If anyone serves me, he must follow me. Where I am, there my servantˡ also will be.ᵐ If anyone serves me, the Father will honorⁿ him.

²⁷ "Now my soul is troubled. What should I say — Father, save meᵒ from this hour? But that is why I came to this hour. ²⁸ Father, glorify your name."ᴬ,ᵖ

Then a voice�q came from heaven:ʳ "I have glorified it, and I will glorify it again."ˢ

²⁹ The crowd standing there heard it and said it was thunder. Others said, "An angel has spoken to him."

³⁰ Jesus responded, "This voice came, not for me, but for you.ᵗ ³¹ Now is the judgment of this world.ᵘ Now the ruler of this worldᵛ will be cast out.ʷ ³² As for me, if I am lifted upᴮ from the earth I will draw all people to myself."ˣ ³³ He said this to indicate what kind of death he was about to die.ʸ

³⁴ Then the crowd replied to him, "We have heard from the law that the Messiah will remain forever.ᶻ So how can you say,

'The Son of Manᵃᵃ must be lifted up'? Who is this Son of Man?"

³⁵ Jesus answered, "The light will be with you only a little longer.ᵃᵇ Walk while you have the lightᵃᶜ so that darkness doesn't overtake you.ᵃᵈ The one who walks in darkness doesn't know where he's going.ᵃᵉ ³⁶ While you have the light,ᵃᶠ believe in the light so that you may become children of light." Jesus said this, then went away and hid from them.ᵃᵍ

ISAIAH'S PROPHECIES FULFILLED

³⁷ Even though he had performed so many signs in their presence, they did not believe in him. ³⁸ This was to fulfillᵃʰ the word of Isaiahᵃⁱ the prophet, who said:ᶜ

Lord, who has believed
  our message?
And to whom has the armᵃʲ
  of the Lord been revealed?ᴰ,ᵃᵏ

³⁹ This is why they were unable to believe, because Isaiah also said:

⁴⁰ He has blindedᵃˡ their eyes
  and hardened their hearts,ᵃᵐ
so that they would not see
  with their eyes
or understand with their hearts,
  and turn,ᵃⁿ
  and I would heal them.ᴱ,ᵃᵒ

⁴¹ Isaiah said these things becauseᶠ he saw his gloryᵃᵖ and spoke about him.

⁴² Nevertheless, many did believe in him even among the rulers,ᵃ�q but because of

ᵃ 12:21 Mk 3:18
ᵇ Mt 11:21; Mk 6:45; 8:22; Lk 9:10; 10:13; Jn 1:44
ᶜ 12:22 Jn 6:8
ᵈ Col 3:22
ᵉ 12:23 Mk 2:10
ᶠ 12:24 Lk 16:7
ᵍ 1Co 15:36
ʰ 12:25 Jn 10:28
ⁱ Lk 6:27; 19:14
ʲ Mt 10:39
ᵏ 12:26 1Co 3:5
ˡ Jn 14:3; 17:24; 2Co 5:8; Php 1:23; 1Th 4:17
ᵐ 1Tm 5:3
ⁿ 12:27 Ps 3:7
ᵒ 12:28 Jn 10:25; Ac 15:14; Rv 14:1
ᵖ Jn 5:37
�q Rv 14:13
ʳ 12:30 Jn 11:42
ˢ Jn 11:4; 17:1; 1Pt 2:12
ᵗ 12:31 Lk 4:6
ᵘ Jn 3:16; 14:30; 16:11
ᵛ Col 2:15; 1Jn 3:8
ʷ 12:32 Jn 11:51
ˣ 12:33 Jn 18:32
ʸ 12:34 Ps 89:36; Jn 15:4; 1Jn 2:17

ᵃᵃ 12:34 Mk 2:10   ᵃᵇ 12:35 Ps 118:27; Jn 7:33; 9:4   ᵃᶜ Ps 36:9; Jn 12:46; 1Jn 2:8   ᵃᵈ Php 3:12   ᵃᵉ Jn 7:28; 8:14; 1Jn 2:11   ᵃᶠ 12:36 Jn 7:33; 1Th 5:5   ᵃᵍ Lk 4:30   ᵃʰ 12:38 Mt 1:22   ᵃⁱ Mt 3:3; 4:14; 12:17   ᵃʲ Ex 15:16   ᵃᵏ Is 53:1   ᵃˡ 12:40 Jn 8:59   ᵃᵐ Heb 3:8   ᵃⁿ Is 56:3,6; Mt 18:3; 23:15; Ac 15:3; 28:27; Rm 16:5; 1Tm 3:6   ᵃᵒ Is 6:10; 1Pt 2:24   ᵃᵖ 12:41 Mk 10:37; Jn 17:24   ᵃ�q 12:42 Lk 8:41

ᴬ 12:28 Other mss read *your Son*   ᴮ 12:32 Or *exalted*, also in v. 34   ᶜ 12:38 Lit *which he said*   ᴰ 12:38 Is 53:1   ᴱ 12:40 Is 6:10   ᶠ 12:41 Other mss read *when*

---

sheep that are not from this sheep pen; I must bring them also" (10:16). By "other sheep" he meant Gentiles. Jesus came to be the Savior of the world (see 3:16). And now the world was starting to come to him, saying, **We want . . . Jesus** (12:21).

12:23 We've seen repeatedly in John's Gospel that it was not Jesus's time or that his hour had not yet come (see 2:4; 7:6, 8, 30; 8:20). Jesus operated on a divine clock. But when his disciples told him that these Greeks wanted to see him, Jesus finally said, "It's time"—**the hour has come for the Son of Man to be glorified.** The Son's glorification involves his death, resurrection, and ascension back to the Father.

12:24 In the same way that a single **grain** produces much **wheat**, Jesus's death would yield much spiritual **fruit**—salvation and eternal life for all who trust in him.

12:25 To hate your **life in this world** means *not* living in a self-centered way but being a servant of others. The one who lives a life of

service in the name of the Lord Jesus will be rewarded in this life and in the life to come. **12:27** Jesus's **soul** was **troubled** because he knew the suffering that would be required. He would die for the sins of the world, enduring separation from his Father. Nevertheless, his grief didn't cause him to flee from his task. To suffer and die for sinners is **why [Jesus] came**.

12:28 Throughout the Son's ministry, the Father had been **glorified** through the miraculous signs. But the ultimate glorification was coming in the cross and resurrection.

12:30 The Father validated the Son so that they might believe.

12:31 Adam and Eve were given the responsibility to rule the world on God's behalf. Instead, they chose to sin against God and thereby granted rule to Satan (see 2 Cor 4:4; Eph 2:2; 1 John 5:19). So the Son of God became a man to defeat the devil. The cross guarantees the enemy's defeat because Satan achieves vic-

tory through accusing sinners. But through the cross, Jesus Christ would deal with sin once and for all (see Heb 7:26-27; 9:12; 10:10).

12:32-33 When Jesus spoke of being **lifted up** (12:32), he was speaking about the **kind of death he was about to die**—crucifixion (12:33). The message of the cross draws **people** to the Savior. That's why we are to share the gospel with everyone in the world.

12:35 Jesus himself is **the light** (see 1:9; 8:12). If you reject him, your life will consist of **darkness**. This, in fact, is why we live in such a dark and sin-scarred world.

12:36 To **believe in the light** is to trust in Jesus Christ. Do this and God will grant you understanding so that you may walk in his ways.

12:40 When Pharaoh repeatedly and willfully hardened his heart against God, the Lord eventually cooperated with Pharaoh and **hardened** his heart further (see Exod 8:32; 9:12). If a person persists in pursuing darkness, eventually God will confirm his desire.

the Pharisees they did not confess him, so that they would not be banned from the synagogue. **43** For they loved human praise[a] more than praise from God.[b]

A SUMMARY OF JESUS'S MISSION

44 Jesus cried out, "The one who believes in me[c] believes not in me, but in him who sent me. **45** And the one who sees me sees him[d] who sent me. **46** I have come as light into the world, so that everyone who believes in me would not remain in darkness. **47** If anyone hears my words and doesn't keep[e] them, I do not judge him; for I did not come to judge the world[f] but to save the world.[g] **48** The one who rejects me[h] and doesn't receive my sayings has this as his judge:[A] The word I have spoken will judge him on the last day.[i] **49** For I have not spoken on my own, but the Father[j] himself who sent me has given me a command to say everything I have said. **50** I know that his command is eternal life.[k] So the things that I speak, I speak just as the Father has told me."[l]

JESUS WASHES HIS DISCIPLES' FEET

13 Before the Passover Festival, Jesus knew that his hour had come to depart from this world to the Father.[m] Having loved his own who were in the world,[n] he loved them to the end.

2 Now when it was time for supper, the devil[o] had already put it into the heart of Judas,[p] Simon Iscariot's son,[B] to betray[q] him. **3** Jesus knew that the Father had given everything into his hands,[r] that he had come from God,[s] and that he was going back to God.[t] **4** So he got up from supper, laid aside his outer clothing,[u] took a towel, and tied it around himself.[v] **5** Next, he poured water into a basin and began to wash his disciples' feet and to dry them with the towel tied around him.

6 He came to Simon Peter,[w] who asked him, "Lord, are you going to wash my feet?" **7** Jesus answered him, "What I'm doing you don't realize now, but afterward you will understand."[x]

8 "You will never wash my feet," Peter said.

Jesus replied, "If I don't wash you, you have no part with me."

9 Simon Peter said to him, "Lord, not only my feet, but also my hands and my head." **10** "One who has bathed," Jesus told him, "doesn't need to wash anything except his feet, but he is completely clean. You are clean, but not all of you." **11** For he knew who would betray him. This is why he said, "Not all of you are clean."

THE MEANING OF FOOT WASHING

12 When Jesus had washed their feet and put on his outer clothing, he reclined again and said to them, "Do you know what I have done for you? **13** You call me Teacher and Lord — and you are speaking rightly, since that is what I am. **14** So if I, your Lord and Teacher, have washed your feet, you also ought to wash one another's feet.[y] **15** For I have given you an example,[z] that you also should do just as I have done for you.

> ### ⟶ HOPE WORDS ⟶
> *God is looking for servants, not celebrities.*

16 "Truly I tell you, a servant is not greater than his master,[c,aa] and a messenger is not greater than the one who sent him. **17** If you know these things, you are blessed if you do them.[ab]

18 "I'm not speaking about all of you; I know those I have chosen.[ac] But the

[a] **12:43** Php 3:19
[b] Lk 9:32; 2Co 3:18; 1Th 2:4; 2Pt 3:18
[c] **12:44** Jn 6:35
[d] **12:45** Jn 14:9
[e] **12:47** Lk 11:28; 2Tm 1:14; 2Pt 3:17
[f] Lk 6:37; Jn 3:18; 8:15; Rv 6:10
[g] Jn 3:17; Ac 16:30; Eph 2:8
[h] **12:48** Lk 10:16
[i] Jn 2:4; 6:39; 1Pt 1:5; 3:3; 2Pt 3:3; Jd 18
[j] **12:49** Mt 11:27
[k] **12:50** Jn 5:26; 12:25; Ac 13:48; 1Jn 2:25
[l] Jn 5:19; 14:24
[m] **13:1** Jn 10:18; 12:23; 16:28
[n] Jn 1:11; 6:37
[o] **13:2** Mt 4:1,10; Jn 8:44; Ac 13:10
[p] Mk 3:19
[q] Mt 10:4; Jn 12:4; 13:21
[r] **13:3** Mt 11:27; 28:18; Jn 17:2
[s] Jn 8:42; 16:27; 17:8
[t] Jn 8:14; 14:12; 16:28; 17:11
[u] **13:4** Lk 19:36
[v] Lk 12:37
[w] **13:6** Mt 16:17
[x] **13:7** Jn 3:11; 7:28; 12:16
[y] **13:14** 1Tm 5:10; 1Pt 5:5
[z] **13:15** 1Pt 2:21
[aa] **13:16** Jn 15:20
[ab] **13:17** Mt 7:24-25; Lk 6:47; 11:28; Jms 1:22-25
[ac] **13:18** Jn 6:70; Eph 1:4

[A] **12:48** Lit *has the one judging him*   [B] **13:2** Or *Judas Iscariot, Simon's son*   [C] **13:16** Or *lord*

12:43 May that never be said of us.

12:44-45 To reject Jesus Christ, the Son of God, is to reject the Father who sent him. And the opposite is also true: **The one who believes in [him] believes** in the one **who sent [him]** (12:44). Salvation is a package deal. You cannot say you believe in God while simultaneously rejecting Jesus. We only truly come to God through the Son.

12:47 Jesus powerfully summarizes why he came into the world. He **did not come to judge the world but to save** it.

13:1 John tells us that Jesus **loved his own**, a reference to his disciples. He had spent three years with the Twelve—teaching them, leading them, and praying for them.

13:2 In intending **to betray** Jesus, **Judas** had opened the door for **the devil** to put a specific idea **into [his] heart**.

13:3-5 Jesus took the humble role of a servant, washing the dirty feet of those who should have been washing his. Why? Because he came to serve (see Mark 10:45). To this servanthood mind-set, the Lord calls each one of us.

13:10 In other words, if you're already saved, you don't need to be saved again. You just need to address the dirty areas in your life so that you can stay **clean**. To maintain fellowship with the Lord, we must regularly come to him in confession and repentance. "If we confess our sins, he is faithful and righteous

to forgive us our sins and to cleanse us from all unrighteousness" (1 John 1:9).

13:14-15 How does Jesus's foot-washing command apply in our modern context? We are to serve people in the family of God—especially by helping them when things get dirty. Our service is most needed in the messiness of life where people are hurting and suffering.

13:18 Importantly, **those** he had **chosen** is a reference to those chosen for service, not for salvation.

The Scripture Jesus quoted is from Psalm 41:9. Just as David was betrayed, so also the Messiah—the Son of David—would be betrayed.

[a] Mt 26:54
[b] 13:18 Mt 1:22
[c] Ps 41:9
[d] 13:19 Jn 13:19
[e] Mk 11:24; Jn 3:16; Ac 10:43; Rm 10:9; 1Pt 1:8-10
[f] Ex 3:14; Jn 8:24,58
[g] 13:20 Jn 5:43; 2Jn 10
[h] 13:21-30 Mt 26:20-25; Mk 14:17-21; Lk 22:21-23
[i] 13:21 Ps 51:12
[j] Jn 15:26; Ac 26:5
[k] 13:23 Jn 19:26; 20:2; 21:7,20
[l] 13:26 Ps 41:9
[m] Mk 14:20
[n] 13:27 Mt 4:1,10; Jn 8:44; Ac 13:10
[o] 13:29 Mk 3:19
[p] Jn 2:23
[q] 13:30 Jn 9:4

[r] 13:31-38 Mt 26:31-35; Mk 14:27-31; Lk 22:31-34
[s] 13:31 Mk 2:10
[t] Jn 11:4; 17:1; 1Pt 2:12
[u] 2Th 1:12; 1Jn 2:5
[v] 13:33 Jn 7:33
[w] Jn 8:21-22; 14:2; 16:5
[x] 13:35 1Co 13:1
[y] 13:36 Jn 14:2; 16:5
[z] 13:37 1Jn 3:16
[aa] Mk 14:31
[ab] 14:1 Jn 14:27
[ac] Ac 16:34; 27:25; Rm 4:3,17,24; Gl 3:6; Ti 3:8; Jms 2:23; 1Jn 5:10
[ad] 14:2 Jn 8:21-22; 13:33,36; 16:7
[ae] 14:3 Mk 8:38
[af] Jn 12:26
[ag] 14:4 Jn 7:28; 8:14; 16:5; 1Jn 2:11

Scripture[a] must be fulfilled:[b] **The one who eats my bread**[A] **has raised his heel against me.**[B,C] [19] I am telling you now before it happens,[d] so that when it does happen you will believe[e] that I am he.[f] [20] Truly I tell you, whoever receives anyone I send receives me, and the one who receives[g] me receives him who sent me."

JUDAS'S BETRAYAL PREDICTED

[21] When[h] Jesus had said this, he was troubled in his spirit[i] and testified,[j] "Truly I tell you, one of you will betray me."

[22] The disciples started looking at one another — uncertain which one he was speaking about. [23] One of his disciples, the one Jesus loved,[k] was reclining close beside Jesus.[C] [24] Simon Peter motioned to him to find out who it was he was talking about. [25] So he leaned back against Jesus and asked him, "Lord, who is it?"

[26] Jesus replied, "He's the one I give the piece of bread to after I have dipped it."[l] When he had dipped the bread,[m] he gave it to Judas, Simon Iscariot's son.[D] [27] After Judas ate the piece of bread, Satan[n] entered him. So Jesus told him, "What you're doing, do quickly."

[28] None of those reclining at the table knew why he said this to him. [29] Since Judas[o] kept the money-bag, some thought that Jesus was telling him, "Buy what we need for the festival,"[p] or that he should give something to the poor. [30] After receiving the piece of bread, he immediately left. And it was night.[q]

THE NEW COMMAND

[31] When[r] he had left, Jesus said, "Now the Son of Man[s] is glorified, and God is glorified[t] in him.[u] [32] If God is glorified in him,[E] God will also glorify him in himself and will glorify him at once. [33] Children, I am with you a little while longer.[v] You will look for me, and just as I told the Jews, so now I tell you: 'Where I am going, you cannot come.'[w]

[34] "I give you a new command: Love one another. Just as I have loved you, you are also to love one another. [35] By this everyone will know that you are my disciples, if you love[x] one another."

PETER'S DENIALS PREDICTED

[36] "Lord," Simon Peter said to him, "where are you going?"

Jesus answered, "Where I am going[y] you cannot follow me now, but you will follow later."

[37] "Lord," Peter asked, "why can't I follow you now? I will lay down my life[z] for you."[aa]

[38] Jesus replied, "Will you lay down your life for me? Truly I tell you, a rooster will not crow until you have denied me three times.

THE WAY TO THE FATHER

14 "Don't let your heart be troubled.[ab] Believe[F] in God;[ac] believe also in me. [2] In my Father's house are many rooms; if not, I would have told you. I am going away[ad] to prepare a place for you. [3] If I go away and prepare a place for you, I will come again[ae] and take you to myself, so that where I am you may be also.[af] [4] You know the way to where I am going."[G,ag]

[A] 13:18 Other mss read *eats bread with me*   [B] 13:18 Ps 41:9   [C] 13:23 Lit *reclining at Jesus's breast*; that is, on his right; Jn 1:18   [D] 13:26 Or *Judas Iscariot, Simon's son*   [E] 13:32 Other mss omit *If God is glorified in him*   [F] 14:1 Or *You believe*   [G] 14:4 Other mss read this verse: *And you know where I am going, and you know the way*

13:20 When we go into the world in the name of Jesus and proclaim his gospel and his teachings, we go as his and the Father's authorized representatives.

13:26 To offer food was a sign of friendship; therefore, Jesus was extending a final offer of grace and mercy to the one who was about to betray him. Judas took **the bread**, but he rejected the more important offer.

13:27 Satan only **entered him** because Judas had invited him by rejecting Jesus and intending to betray him (see the note on 13:2).

13:31-32 The Son would glorify the Father, and the Father would **glorify** the Son (13:32); they would mutually advertise one another's glory. Highlighting the greatness of God, in fact, is what Christians are called to as well. Everything we do—in thought, word, and deed—is to be done for the glory of God (see 1 Cor 10:31).

13:33 In **a little while**, Jesus would ascend to God the Father (see Acts 1:9).

13:34 Biblical **love** is the decision to compassionately, responsibly, and righteously pursue the well-being of another person. Love is a decision to seek another's best, regardless of your feelings.

13:35 Notice that he didn't say everyone would recognize his **disciples** by how much of the Bible they knew. Knowing the Bible is essential, but knowledge means nothing without **love** (see 1 Cor 13:1-3). A loveless Christian actually undermines the gospel. Why? Because, as John says elsewhere, "God is love" (1 John 4:8). How can people come to know the God who perfectly expresses love—both within the Trinity and to humanity—if his representatives don't demonstrate love?

13:38 Jesus poured cold water on this fiery disciple because he wanted Peter to put his pride to death. He was talking a good game, but he wouldn't be able to back it up with action (see 18:15-18, 25-27).

Too often we're exactly like Peter. In our minds we envision ourselves as better disciples than we actually are. Pride will cause us to think too highly of ourselves and then fall flat on our faces.

14:2 In Jewish wedding custom, the father would add rooms onto his house for his newly married son. Jesus wasn't abandoning them but heading out to get their eternal home ready. When your time comes, have no fear. Heaven has been prepared **for you** too.

14:3 This return of which Jesus prophesied is what we call the *rapture*, the time when he will return to receive his saints and take them to heaven (see 1 Thess 4:16-17). Though we can't know the precise timing of this event, it will happen prior to his return to earth to establish his millennial kingdom.

14:4-7 Thomas had misunderstood (14:5). **The way** mentioned in verse 4 isn't a path; it's a person: Jesus said, **I am the way, the truth, and the life. No one comes to the Father except through me** (14:6). Christ is the universal

He Is for You

I COULD TELL YOU THAT IF you come to Jesus, it won't rain. Or that you will no longer have to experience difficulties, trials, delays, or disappointments. And if I did tell you that, you just might shout, clap, and smile. But I can't tell you that—because it's not true.

Yet what I *can* tell you ought to put a smile on your face, and it will change the way you view life's storms when you fully grasp it. God never allows anything in your life that he does not promise to use for good if you are one of his children and living according to his purposes (SEE RM 8:28). If you will make Jesus your focus, he will make his love both your comfort and your strength. Place your eyes on him because he is *for* you.

Paul reminds us of the comfort we have as children of God when he writes, "Blessed be the God and Father of our Lord Jesus Christ, the Father of mercies and the God of all comfort. He comforts us in all our affliction" (2 CO 1:3-4). Jesus assures us that he has asked his Father to send us the comfort we need: "I will ask the Father, and he will give you another Counselor [or *comforter*, see CSB note] to be with you forever" (JOHN 14:16).

I can't say that if you come to Jesus—or focus on Jesus—that it will never storm. But I can tell you that if you will keep your eyes on him and the promises in his Word, he will be your covering when it does. He will be your umbrella. He will be the shelter that guards your emotions, dreams, and even the deepest part of who you are. He will protect and nurture that tender part of you, which we often refer to as the core, or spirit. It is that place within you that embodies the truest and most authentic parts of who you are.

Yet not only will Jesus cover you, but he will also use the trials and troubles of this life to guide you into your brighter tomorrow. I know that life can and does hurt. And I know that many have experienced pain at a level that even I cannot fully identify with. But rather than allow that hurt to lead you onto a path of bitterness, you can receive the comfort Jesus offers. Take him at his Word. He is with you. You are not alone. You may feel alone, but you are not. Focus your gaze on the one who promises to cover you. And in his covering, you will discover his comfort.

a 14:5 Mk 3:18
b 14:6 Ex 3:14; Jn 8:24,58
c Heb 10:20
d 14:7 Mt 11:27; 1Jn 2:23
e Jn 17:3; 1Jn 4:8
f 14:8 Mk 3:18
g 14:9 Jn 5:19,37; 12:45
h 14:10 Jn 10:30; 14:11,20;
1Jn 2:24; 4:17
i Jn 5:30
j Jn 5:36; 6:28; Heb 3:9;
Rv 15:3
k 14:11 Jn 10:38
l 14:12 Jn 6:35
m Jn 5:20
n Jn 7:33; 13:1,3;
16:5,10,17,28; 17:11,13; 20:17
o 14:13 Jn 11:4; 17:1; 1Pt 2:12
p Jn 5:19
q 14:14 Jn 10:25
r 11:22; 15:7,16; 16:23-24
s 14:15 1Jn 5:3
t 14:16 Lk 24:49; Jn 14:26;
15:26; 16:7; 1Jn 2:1; Ac 2:33
u 14:17 Jn 1:33
v Ps 119:142; 2Th 2:10;
1Jn 4:6
w 1Jn 4:4
x 14:19 Jn 7:33
y Jn 16:16
z Php 1:21
aa 14:20 Jn 14:10
ab 14:21 Jn 8:31; 1Jn 2:5
ac Dt 7:12-13; Jn 16:27
ad 14:22 Lk 6:16; Ac 1:13
ae Ac 10:40-41
af 14:23 Jn 14:2; 1Jn 2:24
ag 14:24 Jn 5:19; 7:16; 8:28;
12:49-50
ah 14:26 Ps 51:11; Jn 1:33;
Ac 2:4; Rm 8:9; Gl 5:25; Ti
3:5; Rv 3:22
ai Lk 24:49; Jn 14:16; 15:26;
16:7; Ac 2:33
aj Jn 16:13; 1Co 2:10;
1Jn 2:27
ak Jn 2:22; 2Pt 1:21

5 "Lord," Thomas[a] said, "we don't know where you're going. How can we know the way?"

6 Jesus told him, "I am[b] the way,[c] the truth, and the life. No one comes to the Father except through me. **7** If you know me, you will also know[A] my Father.[d] From now on you do know him[e] and have seen him."

JESUS REVEALS THE FATHER

8 "Lord," said Philip,[f] "show us the Father, and that's enough for us."

9 Jesus said to him, "Have I been among you all this time and you do not know me, Philip? The one who has seen me has seen the Father.[g] How can you say, 'Show us the Father'? **10** Don't you believe that I am in the Father and the Father is in me?[h] The words I speak to you I do not speak on my own.[i] The Father who lives in me does his works.[j] **11** Believe me that I am in the Father and the Father is in me. Otherwise, believe[B] because of the works themselves.[k]

PRAYING IN JESUS'S NAME

12 "Truly I tell you, the one who believes in me[l] will also do the works that I do. And he will do even greater works than these,[m] because I am going to the Father.[n] **13** Whatever you ask in my name, I will do it so that the Father may be glorified[o] in the Son.[p] **14** If you ask me[c] anything in my name,[q] I will do it.[D,r]

ANOTHER COUNSELOR PROMISED

15 "If you love me, you will keep[E] my commands.[s] **16** And I will ask the Father, and he will give you another Counselor[F,t] to

be with you forever. **17** He is the Spirit[u] of truth.[v] The world is unable to receive him because it doesn't see him or know him. But you do know him, because he remains with you and will be[G] in you.[w]

THE FATHER, THE SON, AND THE HOLY SPIRIT

18 "I will not leave you as orphans; I am coming to you. **19** In a little while the world will no longer see me,[x] but you will see me.[y] Because I live, you will live[z] too. **20** On that day you will know that I am in my Father,[aa] you are in me, and I am in you. **21** The one who has my commands and keeps them is the one who loves me.[ab] And the one who loves me will be loved by my Father.[ac] I also will love him and will reveal myself to him."

22 Judas[ad] (not Iscariot) said to him, "Lord, how is it you're going to reveal yourself to us and not to the world?"[ae]

23 Jesus answered, "If anyone loves me, he will keep my word. My Father will love him, and we will come to him and make our home with him.[af] **24** The one who doesn't love me will not keep my words. The word that you hear is not mine but is from the Father who sent me.[ag]

25 "I have spoken these things to you while I remain with you. **26** But the Counselor, the Holy Spirit,[ah] whom the Father will send[ai] in my name, will teach you all things[aj] and remind you of everything I have told you.[ak]

JESUS'S GIFT OF PEACE

27 "Peace I leave with you. My peace I give to you. I do not give to you as the world gives.

A 14:7 Other mss read *If you had known me, you would have known*   **B** 14:11 Other mss read *believe me*   **C** 14:14 Other mss omit *me*   **D** 14:14 Other mss omit all of v. 14   **E** 14:15 Other mss read *"If you love me, keep* (as a command)   **F** 14:16 Or *advocate*, or *comforter*, also in v. 26   **G** 14:17 Other mss read *and is*

point of access to God. If you want to know the Father, you must come to him through his Son. Jesus assured Thomas that if he knew the Son, he knew the **Father** (14:7).

14:8-9 Philip wanted to be like Moses, who got to catch a glimpse of God (14:8; see Exod 33:12–34:9). But he didn't understand that fully revealing God the Father was exactly what Jesus had come to do. Whereas Moses only saw a hint of the glory of the invisible God, Jesus said, **The one who has seen me has seen the Father** (John 14:9). Jesus Christ is God incarnate, the God-Man.

14:12 Jesus was talking about scope of impact. His travels were limited, as were the number of people who heard his voice. But in the years since, the church has carried his message to billions all over the world.

14:15 According to Jesus, obedience is the proof of love. Our relationship with him, not a fear of disappointing him, drives our desire to please him.

14:16 In Greek there are two words that could be used to mean *another*. One means "another of a different kind"; the other means "another of the same kind." The latter is used here. The Holy Spirit is **another Counselor**, but one who shares in the divine nature. Therefore, God would still be with them in the person of God the Holy Spirit. The same sovereign love and power they enjoyed in Jesus, then, would be present in their lives. Importantly, when you trust in Christ to take away your sins and give you eternal life, the Holy Spirit also comes to dwell within you, ministering the presence of God to you.

14:17 The only way to know and receive **the Spirit of** God is through knowing and receiving the Son of God, Jesus Christ.

14:18 Not only would he send the Holy Spirit to be with them, but one day the Son will also return to take his followers to the place prepared for them (see 14:2-4).

14:19 Because I live, you will live too. Jesus shares his resurrection life with his followers through the Holy Spirit.

14:21 When you are connected to the love of the Father and Son in obedience, Jesus promises to **reveal** more of himself to you. If you listen to a radio station in your car, you know that the further you get from the broadcast station, the worse your reception of the signal gets. Many people have difficulty connecting with God because they've wandered too far away to pick up his signal. But if you come back home in obedience, relating to God through Christ in love, he will disclose more of himself to you.

14:26 This applies to the first disciples because **the Holy Spirit** helped them to recall Jesus's words, sharing them with others and recording them in the pages of Scripture (see 2 Pet 1:21). But the Spirit also helps believers today, enabling us to recall Scripture at the appropriate time and helping us to understand its meaning and its application to our

Don't let your heart be troubled or fearful.[a] [28] You have heard me tell you, 'I am going away[b] and I am coming to you.' If you loved me, you would rejoice that I am going to the Father,[c] because the Father is greater than I.[d] [29] I have told you now before it happens[e] so that when it does happen you may believe. [30] I will not talk with you much longer, because the ruler of the world[f] is coming. He has no power over me.[A,g] [31] On the contrary, so that the world may know that I love the Father, I do as the Father commanded me.

"Get up; let's leave this place."

⤳ HOPE WORDS ⤳

Spiritual intimacy with God expands spiritual capacity.

THE VINE AND THE BRANCHES

15 "I am[h] the true vine, and my Father is the gardener. [2] Every branch in me that does not produce fruit he removes,[i] and he prunes every branch that produces fruit so that it will produce more fruit. [3] You are already clean[j] because of the word I have spoken to you. [4] Remain in me, and I in you. Just as a branch is unable to produce fruit by itself unless it remains on the vine, neither can you unless you remain in me.[k] [5] I am the vine;[l] you are the branches. The one who remains in me and I in him produces much fruit,[m] because you can do nothing without me. [6] If anyone does not remain in me, he is thrown aside[n] like a branch and he withers. They gather them, throw them into the fire,[o] and they are burned.[p] [7] If you remain in me and my words remain in you, ask whatever you want and it will be done for you.[q] [8] My Father is glorified[r] by this: that you produce much fruit and prove to be[B] my disciples.

CHRISTLIKE LOVE

[9] "As the Father has loved me, I have also loved you. Remain in my love.[s] [10] If you keep my commands you will remain in my love, just as I have kept my Father's commands and remain in his love.[t]

[11] "I have told you these things so that my joy may be in you and your joy may be complete.[u] [12] This is my command: Love one another as I have loved[v] you. [13] No one has

a 14:27 2Tm 1:7
b 14:28 Jn 16:5
c Jn 16:10
d Jn 10:29; 1Jn 3:20; 4:4
e 14:29 Jn 13:19; 16:4
f 14:30 Mt 4:1; Jn 12:31
g Lk 4:6
h 15:1 Ex 3:14; Jn 8:24,58
i 15:2 Mt 3:10; 7:19; 15:13; Lk 3:9; 13:6-9; Jn 15:6; Rm 11:17,22
j 15:3 Ps 24:4; Ti 1:15

k 15:4 Jn 6:56; 8:28; 1Jn 2:5
l 15:5 Jms 3:12
m Mk 4:8
n 15:6 Jn 15:2
o 2Th 1:8
p 1Th 1:8; 2Pt 3:7
q 15:7 Jn 14:14
r 15:8 Jn 11:4; 17:1; 1Pt 2:12
s 15:9 Col 1:13; 1Jn 5:20; Jd 21
t 15:10 Jn 5:19
u 15:11 1Jn 1:4; 2Jn 12
v 15:12 Jn 3:16

A 14:30 Lit *He has nothing in me*   B 15:8 Or *and become*

---

lives, as he activates "the mind of Christ" in us (1 Cor 2:10-16).
14:27 In saying, **My peace I give to you,** Jesus is *not* promising the absence of storms. He's talking about peace in the midst of tribulation—at a time when you shouldn't have any peace. This is the peace *of God,* "which surpasses all understanding, [and guards] your hearts and minds in Christ Jesus" (Phil 4:7).

In the coming hours, the disciples would have good reason to be **troubled.** Likewise, you will have experiences that prompt you to fear. But with a sovereign God ruling the world and "the peace of Christ" ruling in your heart (see Col 3:15), you can overcome.
14:28 Jesus's imminent departure to be with **the Father** meant that his mission—the reason for which he'd come into the world—was almost complete.
14:30 When Adam and Eve sinned, they gave up their role of ruling creation on God's behalf, and turned it over to Satan. Therefore, the devil is appropriately called **the ruler of the world,** "the god of this age" (2 Cor 4:4), and "the ruler of the power of the air" (Eph 2:2). He holds "the power of death" and keeps people in slavery by "the fear of death" (see Heb 2:14-15). But Satan has **no power over** Jesus because Jesus is without sin. The Son of God became a man so that he might defeat the devil as a man and restore God's kingdom rule.
15:1 The prophet Isaiah had spoken of Israel as the Lord's vineyard. God expected his vineyard to bear fruit, but it produced nothing but worthless grapes (see Isa 5:1-7). In contrast,

the Son of God came as the authentic **vine,** perfectly obeying the Father and revealing his will to the people.
15:2 The Greek verb translated **removes** in this verse can also be rendered "takes away" or "lifts up." The branches in a vineyard could become heavy and drag on the ground easily. So God the gardener "takes them away" from the ground by lifting them up. God will, therefore, seek to make you fruitful by lifting you up, encouraging you, and motivating you—for example, through his Word and through the people of God.

God's goal for every Christian is an increase in fruit bearing. Fruitfulness is a life of spiritual usefulness and productivity for the good of others and the glory of God. Those who are fruitful God also **prunes** so that they bear **more fruit.** So know that sometimes God will bring challenges and trials into our lives to enable us to grow in our faith and cast off anything hindering full productivity.
15:3 The disciples were **clean** through the washing of Christ's **word** (see Eph 5:26). This is how we stay clean too.
15:5 The idea of remaining (or abiding) in Christ has to do with intimacy of relationship. Jesus Christ is our source, the only One who can provide the spiritual sustenance and vitality we need to be useful believers. Thus, we need to hang out with him. You can't avoid Jesus all week and then show up on Sunday morning expecting growth.
15:6 If you disconnect from the vine for too long, don't be surprised to find yourself experiencing divine discipline, getting

burned (this is not a description of hell but of spiritual discipline), and seeing your spiritual life withering. Such a believer is useless to himself, God, and others. So, if you find such things happening to you, repent! "Draw near to God, and he will draw near to you" (Jas 4:8).
15:7 To have Jesus's **words remain in you** requires more than merely reading or listening to them. You must internalize them. Another way to describe this is *meditating* on God's Word, rolling it around in your mind to grasp what it means and how to apply it to your specific circumstances. We must chew and swallow Scripture, so to speak, so that it becomes part of us. Doing so will align our wills with his.
15:8 The more useful you become to the kingdom, the more glory God will receive.
15:9-10 Obedience produces a deeper relationship with Jesus. The Son wants us to enjoy the intimate kind of loving relationship with him that he enjoys with the **Father.**
15:11 *Joy* is internal stability in spite of external circumstances because of the knowledge that God is in control. It is a settled assurance and quiet confidence in God's sovereignty that results in the decision to praise him.
15:12-13 Biblical **love** is the decision to compassionately, righteously, responsibly, and sacrificially seek the well-being of another (15:12). You can love people whom you may not necessarily like because love is not dependent on your feelings. That's why Jesus can command you to "love your enemies" (Matt 5:44). It's true that love may include feelings of affection, and such feelings may develop over time. But it's

You Can Overcome

MANY CHRISTIANS ARE PRISONERS OF addictive behavior. And it's easy to feel overwhelmed and hopeless when you just can't seem to beat a habit. In fact, letting go of your addictive behavior may feel like letting go of the very thing that helps you cope, gets you through each day, and sustains you. But it isn't truly sustaining you. It's pulling you under.

Drugs, extramarital sex, pornography, alcoholism, unhealthy relationships, negative self-talk, overwork, gluttony, gambling, overspending—these things can become the go-to coping mechanisms for life's pain, disappointments, and boredom. But they can leave you feeling trapped. A counselor and an accountability partner can be great assets to help you overcome addictive behavior. But the cure ultimately lies with you and God. Of course, there are things like chemical addictions that must be dealt with appropriately—that's another discussion. But dealing with behavioral addictions takes shifting your thinking to a new place.

To be set free from addictive behavior, you need to "be transformed by the renewing of your mind" (RM 12:2). You need a new way of looking at yourself, God, others, and the things you do. Satan's strategy to keep you in addictive behavior is to mess with your mind. He wants to plant thoughts in your head so they'll take root and bear deadly, destructive fruit in your actions. Remember that whoever or whatever controls your mind, also controls you.

God doesn't want you to be focused on negative thoughts and controlled by them. Rather, God wants you to focus on him, to allow his Word and Spirit to control you and bear good and lasting fruit in your life. Jesus said, "If you remain in me and my words remain in you, ask whatever you want and it will be done for you" (JOHN 15:7). The key to your victory is in that verse, so let Christ's words (thoughts) remain in you. When Christ's thoughts begin to dominate your soul, you'll experience the new and abundant life he died to give you.

Christian, let me encourage you with this truth: God is at work in you. You are his workmanship, and you are a masterpiece (SEE EPH 2:10). Things may not be perfect in your life right now, but life is a process. Don't look at tomorrow—for "tomorrow will worry about itself" (MT 6:34). Just focus on living this day, this moment—trusting that God will get you through. That's all the faith you need. By faith, you will overcome your addictive behavior with moment-by-moment victories that will add up to days, weeks, months, and years. God loves you so much that he's not giving up on you. He'll continue to chisel and carve away what doesn't need to be there, and when he reveals who you truly are in him, you'll be amazed!

When things appear to take a turn for the worse in your life, remind yourself that God may be setting things up for a comeback. You just might not be able to see it. In 2 Kings we read an account of an attack on the prophet Elisha. He was a man of God, so closely tied to God that he could discern things beyond the natural realm. But in this particular instance, Elisha called on God to help the person he was with to see as well. Elisha prayed that God would "open his eyes and let him see." When the Lord answered, that servant "saw that the mountain was covered with horses and chariots of fire" (2 KGS 6:17).

When Elisha prayed, God opened the eyes of the servant to see the Lord's protection and provision. So when things get difficult for you, take a moment to pray that God would reveal to you what he is doing as well. Then, have faith that he will come through. Remember, believing *is* seeing.

greater love than this: to lay down his life[a] for his friends. **14** You are my friends if you do what I command you. **15** I do not call you servants anymore, because a servant doesn't know what his master[A,b] is doing. I have called you friends, because I have made known to you everything I have heard from my Father. **16** You did not choose me, but I chose you.[c] I appointed you to go and produce fruit and that your fruit should remain, so that whatever you ask[d] the Father in my name,[e] he will give you.[f]

17 "This is what I command you: Love one another.

PERSECUTIONS PREDICTED

18 "If the world hates[g] you, understand that it hated me before it hated you. **19** If you were of the world, the world would love you as its own. However, because you are not of the world, but I have chosen[h] you out of it, the world hates you. **20** Remember the word I spoke to you: 'A servant is not greater than his master.'[i] If they persecuted me, they will also persecute you. If they kept my word,[j] they will also keep yours. **21** But they will do all these things to you on account of my name,[k] because they don't know[l] the one who sent me. **22** If I had not come and spoken to them, they would not be guilty of sin.[m] Now they have no excuse for their sin. **23** The one who hates me also hates my Father.[n] **24** If I had not done the works[o] among them that no one else has done,[p] they would not be guilty of sin.[q] Now they have seen and hated both me and my Father. **25** But this happened so that the statement written in their law might be fulfilled:[r] **They hated me for no reason.**[B,s]

THE COUNSELOR'S MINISTRY

26 "When the Counselor[t] comes, the one I will send to you from the Father[u] — the Spirit of truth[v] who proceeds from the Father — he will testify about me. **27** You also will testify,[w] because you have been with me from the beginning.

16 "I have told you these things to keep you from stumbling. **2** They will ban you from the synagogues.[x] In fact, a time is coming when anyone who kills you will think he is offering service[y] to God. **3** They will do these things because they haven't known[z] the Father or me. **4** But I have told you these things so that when their time[c] comes you will remember[aa] I told them to you. I didn't tell you these things from the beginning, because I was with you. **5** But now I am going away[ab] to him who sent me, and not one of you asks me, 'Where are you going?'[ac] **6** Yet, because I have spoken these things to you, sorrow has filled your heart. **7** Nevertheless, I am telling you the truth.[ad] It is for your benefit that I go away, because if I don't go away the Counselor will not come to you. If I go, I will send him to you.[ae] **8** When he comes, he will convict the world about sin, righteousness, and judgment: **9** About sin, because they do not believe in me; **10** about righteousness, because I am going to the Father[af] and you will no longer see me; **11** and about judgment,[ag] because the ruler of this world[ah] has been judged.[ai]

12 "I still have many things to tell you, but you can't bear them now.[aj] **13** When the Spirit of truth[ak] comes, he will guide you into all the truth.[al] For he will not speak on his own, but he will speak whatever he hears. He will also declare to you what is to come. **14** He will glorify me, because he will

[a] 15:13 Rm 5:8; 1Jn 3:16
[b] 15:15 Col 3:22
[c] 15:16 Mt 24:22
[d] Jn 10:25
[e] Jn 14:13
[f] Jn 11:22; 16:23
[g] 15:18 Lk 6:27; 19:14
[h] 15:19 Eph 1:4
[i] 15:20 Jn 13:16
[j] Jn 8:51
[k] 15:21 Mk 13:13; Jn 10:25
[l] Jn 3:11; 7:28; 20:9
[m] 15:22 Ezk 2:5; 3:7; Jn 9:41; Rm 1:20; 2:1; 6:23
[n] 15:23 Jn 5:23
[o] 15:24 Jn 5:36; Heb 3:9; Rv 15:3
[p] Jn 3:2; 7:31; 9:32; 10:32,37
[q] Jn 9:41
[r] 15:25 Jn 12:38; 13:18; 17:12; 18:9,32; 19:24,36
[s] Ps 69:4

[t] 15:26 Jn 14:16
[u] Jn 14:26
[v] Ps 119:142; Jn 1:33; 14:17; 16:13; Rm 3:7; 1Jn 4:6
[w] 15:27 Ac 4:20
[x] 16:2 Jn 9:22; 12:42
[y] Ex 12:25
[z] 16:3 Jn 7:28
[aa] 16:4 Jn 14:29; Rv 2:5
[ab] 16:5 Jn 7:33; 8:14,21-22; 13:3,33,36; 14:4-5,28; 16:10,17
[ac] Jn 8:14
[ad] 16:7 Ps 119:142
[ae] Jn 14:26
[af] 16:10 Jn 14:12,28; 16:17
[ag] 16:11 Mt 12:41; Jn 5:22; 2Th 1:5; Rv 19:11
[ah] Mt 4:1; Jn 12:31
[ai] Col 2:15; Heb 2:14
[aj] 16:12 Mk 4:33
[ak] 16:13 Rm 3:7; 1Jn 4:6
[al] Jn 1:17; 14:6; 2Th 2:10

[A] 15:15 Or *lord*   [B] 15:25 Ps 69:4   [C] 16:4 Other mss read *when the time*

---

not driven by them. Love is driven by sacrifice for the welfare of others. And the greatest expression of love is to **lay down** one's **life for … friends** (John 15:13). That's the kind of love Jesus modeled for us.

15:15 A **master** doesn't reveal things to a servant, but a friend would reveal things to his **friends**.

15:16 When the Bible refers to God's choice (or election) of people, it's a choosing for service, not salvation. Jesus **chose** his disciples so that they would **produce fruit** that would be useful to his kingdom and reflect God's character. He didn't simply save them for heaven only; he **appointed** them to a mission on earth that would involve winning people to Christ and growing them in the faith.

15:18-21 When you faithfully represent Jesus, the world (which is under the influence of Satan) will relate to you as it did to him.

15:25 Those in Jesus's day **fulfilled** the Scripture spoken by David in Psalm 69:4: **They hated me for no reason**. As the wicked showed their disdain for King David, so they showed disdain for the Son of David.

15:26-27 Since the role of the Holy **Spirit** is to **testify about** the Son of God, the Spirit has a Christocentric ministry. He does not merely draw attention to himself; he draws attention to Jesus (15:26). Therefore, we should be wary of those who claim the Spirit's involvement in a ministry that ignores Jesus. If the Spirit makes much of Jesus, then his disciples should too (15:27).

16:2-4 We shouldn't be shocked when we experience rejection or censure for our Christian beliefs and standards. This could come from family, friends, employers, customers, coworkers, the government—and the list

goes on. As Paul told Timothy, "All who want to live a godly life in Christ Jesus will be persecuted" (2 Tim 3:12).

16:7 The coming of the Holy Spirit would **benefit** the disciples because his presence would not be physically limited (as Jesus's was). He would dwell within each of them (see 14:17) and go with them wherever they traveled (see Eph 1:22-23). If you have trusted Jesus Christ, you are never alone.

16:8 To **convict** in this sense is to convince concerning the truth.

16:13 Indeed, **the Spirit** would **declare to** them things that were yet **to come** (such as the prophecies in Revelation). He would ensure that the apostles' writings were true, guaranteeing that they wrote Scripture, the very words of God.

^a16:15 Mt 11:27
^bJn 17:10
^cJn 5:19
^d16:16 Jn 7:33
^eMk 2:20; 14:19
^f16:17 Jn 14:12; 16:10
^g16:20 Mt 11:17; Lk 7:32; 23:27
^hJn 16:6; 2Co 2:2
ⁱ16:21 Gl 4:19
^jLk 1:7
^k16:22 Jn 20:20
^lJn 15:11
^m16:23 Jn 11:22; 14:13–14; 15:16
ⁿ16:24 Jn 10:25
^oMt 7:8
^p1Jn 1:4; 2Jn 12

^q16:26 Jn 14:16
^rJn 10:25
^s16:27 Jn 14:21
^tJn 6:46; 8:42; 13:3; 16:30
^u16:28 Jn 14:12
^v16:30 Mk 2:8; Jn 1:48; 2:24–25; 6:64; 21:17
^wJn 16:27
^x16:32 Jn 4:23
^yJn 8:16,29

take from what is mine and declare it to you. [15] Everything the Father[a] has is mine.[b] This is why I told you that he takes from what is mine and will declare it to you.[c]

SORROW TURNED TO JOY

[16] "A little while[d] and you will no longer see me;[e] again a little while and you will see me."[A]

[17] Then some of his disciples said to one another, "What is this he's telling us: 'A little while and you will not see me; again a little while and you will see me,' and, 'Because I am going to the Father'[f]?" [18] They said, "What is this he is saying,[B] 'A little while'? We don't know what he's talking about."

[19] Jesus knew they wanted to ask him, and so he said to them, "Are you asking one another about what I said, 'A little while and you will not see me; again a little while and you will see me'? [20] Truly I tell you, you will weep and mourn,[g] but the world will rejoice. You will become sorrowful,[h] but your sorrow will turn to joy. [21] When a woman is in labor, she has pain[i] because her time has come. But when she has given birth to a child,[j] she no longer remembers the suffering because of the joy that a person has been born into the world. [22] So you also have sorrow[c] now. But I will see you again. Your hearts will rejoice,[k] and no one will take away your joy from you.[l]

[23] "In that day you will not ask me anything. Truly I tell you, anything you ask the Father in my name, he will give you.[m] [24] Until now you have asked for nothing in my name.[n] Ask and you will receive,[o] so that your joy may be complete.[p]

JESUS THE VICTOR

[25] "I have spoken these things to you in figures of speech. A time is coming when I will no longer speak to you in figures, but I will tell you plainly about the Father. [26] On that day you will ask[q] in my name, and[r] I am not telling you that I will ask the Father on your behalf. [27] For the Father himself loves you, because you have loved[s] me and have believed that I came from God.[D,t] [28] I came from the Father and have come into the world. Again, I am leaving the world and going to the Father."[u]

[29] His disciples said, "Look, now you're speaking plainly and not using any figurative language. [30] Now we know that you know everything[v] and don't need anyone to question you. By this we believe that you came from God."[w]

[31] Jesus responded to them, "Do you now believe? [32] Indeed, an hour is coming, and has come,[x] when each of you will be scattered to his own home, and you will leave me alone. Yet I am not alone, because the Father is with me.[y] [33] I have told you these things so that in me you may have peace. You will have suffering in this world. Be courageous! I have conquered the world."

⌒ **HOPE WORDS** ⌒

Trials are unavoidable, but that doesn't mean that they have to be unprofitable.

---

^A16:16 Other mss add *because I am going to the Father*　^B16:18 Other mss omit *he is saying*　^C16:22 Other mss read *will have sorrow*　^D16:27 Other mss read *from the Father*

16:16 In **a little while**, the disciples would **no longer see** him because he would be dead and buried. But in another **little while**, they would see him **again** when he rose from the grave.

16:17-18 Don't be upset when you don't understand what Jesus is doing in your life. After all, Jesus's first disciples were confused, and they had Jesus right there with them! Choose to pursue him in the midst of your confusion.

16:20 Their grief would **turn to joy** at his resurrection.

16:22 Joy is rooted in the presence and work of Christ on the inside—not on the ever-changing circumstances of life.

16:24 God is still in the prayer-answering business when we love and seek to honor the Son, and there's nothing like the **joy** that comes when the Creator of the universe answers your personal prayer.

16:25 There is a principle at work here for believers in Christ: God only explains what you are ready and able to handle. You may not understand the circumstances that you're experiencing, but God loves you and is taking you through a growth process. He calls for your trust and obedience now. Further understanding will come later, when you're prepared to receive it.

16:26-27 Notice that **the Father** himself **loves** due to a disciple's relationship to his Son.

16:31-32 Jesus said, **Do you now believe? Indeed, an hour is coming, and has come, when each of you will be scattered . . . and you will leave me alone.** Translation: "You don't believe as strongly as you think you do. Now, while all is quiet and safe, this is easy for you to say. But very soon you're going to forget your fragile faith and run."

Have you ever made a vow to God only to back away from it later—perhaps as quickly as when you left the church parking lot? It's easy to boast about our faith as the disciples did in 16:30; it's harder to live it, as Peter would soon discover (see 18:15-18, 25-27). This is one of the reasons why God causes us to experience challenges. Through them, we come to see how brittle our faith is and how mighty our Savior is; thus, our faith is made a little stronger.

16:33 Regardless of how the world beats you down, you have reason to live with bold faith because Jesus is the sovereign King over the world. He has defeated sin, Satan, and death. If you're a believer, your eternity is secure. And Jesus has the power to overrule your earthly circumstances. Knowing this truth and maintaining an intimate relationship with the Lord will radically change your perspective as you face whatever obstacles come your way.

a 17:1 Jn 5:19; Heb 1:2
b Jn 12:28
c 17:2 Php 3:3
d Jn 12:25; Ac 13:48;
1Jn 2:25
e Mt 24:22
f 17:3 Jn 5:44; Rm 16:27
g Jn 4:23; 1Jn 5:20
h Mk 9:37; Jn 1:6
i Jn 5:38; 6:29
j 17:5 Mt 11:27

k 17:5 Mk 10:37; Jn 17:24;
1Pt 5:1
l Pr 8:23; Jn 1:1-2; 8:58
m 17:6 Jn 10:25; Ac 15:14;
Rv 14:1
n Mt 24:22; Jn 6:37
o Jn 8:23; 13:1; 15:19; 17:14-
16; 18:36; 1Co 5:10; 1Jn
2:16; 4:5
p Jn 18:9
q Jn 8:51
r 17:8 Jn 14:24
s Jn 5:43; 13:3
t 17:9 Rm 9:11
u 17:10 Jn 16:15
v 17:11 Jn 13:3; 14:12
w Ps 20:6; 1Co 7:14
x Pr 18:10
y Jn 11:52
z Jn 10:16,30; 17:22; Gl 3:28

⚜ KINGDOM LIVING ⚜
CHURCH
The Power of Unity

Jesus's high priestly prayer found in John 17 shows how much is at stake with regard to the church's unity. God's name, his glory, and his love are tied to the unity in which his people are to live. You see, our bond as believers in Christ is much more than something to keep us from fussing and fighting among ourselves. It is a testimony to the world that the Lord and the faith we preach are real.

God will respond to us on the basis of our unity, or lack thereof. Whether it includes unity across denominations, economic statuses, ethnicities, or genders, unity is critical to the movement of God's kingdom agenda by the church.

Let me state this principle another way. If we are functioning in conflict and disunity, God will limit his work in our lives. If we have time to be blessed but not to be blessings, if we are selfish saints who want things from God but don't want to mess with

being functioning members of a local church, or if we are causing disruption in the church by our attitudes or tongues, then we are wasting our time when we ask God to do something for us.

In fact, Scripture goes so far as to tell us that if we are people like that, then others in the church need to steer clear of us: "Watch out for those who create divisions and obstacles contrary to the teaching that you learned. Avoid them" (Rom 16:17). Elsewhere Paul said concerning the church, "If anyone destroys God's temple, God will destroy him" (1 Cor 3:17). And among those things God hates is "one who stirs up trouble among brothers" (Prov 6:19). This is not a small issue because God responds to his people's unity or lack thereof.

FOR THE NEXT CHURCH
KINGDOM LIVING LESSON SEE PAGE 1326.

JESUS PRAYS FOR HIMSELF

17 Jesus spoke these things, looked up to heaven, and said: "Father, the hour has come. Glorify your Son so that the Son*a* may glorify you,*b* **2** since you gave him authority over all flesh,^A,c so that he may give eternal life*d* to everyone you have given him.*e*

⚜ HOPE WORDS ⚜
The essence of heaven is the uninterrupted knowledge of God.

3 This is eternal life: that they may know you, the only*f* true*g* God, and the one you have sent*h* — Jesus Christ.*i* **4** I have glorified you on the earth by completing the work you gave me to do. **5** Now, Father,*j* glorify me in your presence with that

glory*k* I had with you before the world existed.*l*

JESUS PRAYS FOR HIS DISCIPLES

6 "I have revealed your name*m* to the people you gave me*n* from the world.*o* They were yours, you gave them to me,*p* and they have kept your word.*q* **7** Now they know that everything you have given me is from you, **8** because I have given them the words you gave me.*r* They have received them and have known for certain that I came from you.*s* They have believed that you sent me.

9 "I pray^B for them. I am not praying for the world but for those you have given me,*t* because they are yours. **10** Everything I have is yours, and everything you have is mine,*u* and I am glorified in them. **11** I am no longer in the world, but they are in the world, and I am coming to you.*v* Holy*w* Father, protect^C them by your name*x* that you have given me, so that they may be one*y* as we are*z* one.

---

^A 17:2 Or *people*   ^B 17:9 Lit *ask* (throughout this passage)   ^C 17:11 Lit *keep* (throughout this passage)

17:3 Eternal life does not merely refer to an existence that lasts forever. After all, everyone will live eternally, either in heaven or in hell. To receive eternal life, then, is to enter into the divine realm with the goal of experiencing an intimate relationship with God through Jesus, a relationship that will grow throughout eternity. It is the uninterrupted, deepening knowledge and experience of

God. This is the purpose for which we were created.
17:4 We bring glory to God in the same way—by pursuing his will for our lives. Do you consider **completing the work** he intends you to do to be as desirous and life-sustaining as eating?
17:5 Before the incarnation, before Jesus was conceived by the Holy Spirit in the womb of

Mary, **before** the creation week even began, God the Son eternally existed in the glorious presence of God the Father. And to this glory he would soon return.
17:11 In Scripture, names do not merely identify people but speak of their character. Therefore, Jesus was asking that God would protect them by keeping them connected to their holy and righteous Father.

I Pledge Allegiance to the King

FOURTH-CENTURY THEOLOGIAN SAINT AMBROSE MADE a name for himself by stamping out heresy in the early days of the church. Another of Ambrose's claims to fame is his penning of the now-famous phrase, "When in Rome, do as the Romans do." Today we use the phrase to encourage people to embrace someone else's customs when engaging those of a different culture. Ambrose's original intent for the phrase was to express his belief in flexibility in a church service when it comes to worship.

In those days (much like today), churches had different ways of doing things. Some churches observed fasting on Saturday; some did not. Some preferred one type of songbook over another. Ambrose believed that when visiting a local church, it was good to observe their way of doing things. There were limits, of course. All churches needed to follow the orthodox teaching of Scripture. Think of it like a boundary separating right from wrong. Christians are free to worship God in different ways in accordance with their local cultures and languages—as long as they stay inside the boundary.

We are born and live our lives inside earthly nations; we learn to speak earthly languages; and we engage those who are living in earthly cultures. We all have citizenship in an earthly nation, and we submit to the governing authorities of that nation. But our true citizenship lies upward. As Christians, our first allegiance is to the kingdom of heaven and its Sovereign, the triune God. Heaven follows a standard called holiness. One day, we will spend eternity living out that standard in perfect fellowship with God and with each other.

But today, we are aliens; we are not of the world, just as Christ is not of the world (SEE JOHN 17:16). From an eternal perspective, then, we must remember that even though we serve a kingdom agenda, we are not absolved from actively engaging the culture into which we've been sent. God doesn't just rule in heaven; he rules both heaven *and* earth. The agenda of his kingdom is the visible manifestation of that comprehensive rule over every area of life. Our allegiance to God means that how we live on earth matters. We are not mere observers of a fallen culture; we are meant to serve as transformational agents within it.

We believers are called to be agents of change in this world, seeking to bring the good news of Christ to all people. We are to show others what it means to worship God through our own diversity, respecting the differences between us as we live our lives. But we must never lose sight of the big picture: eternity awaits, and the seeds we plant here on earth today will come to bear when we dwell with God in heaven later.

Therefore, I encourage you to embrace the culture in which you live without straying beyond the boundaries and into sin. Put your true citizenship on display without disrespecting the ways of those who live around you. Above all, keep your eyes on eternity, never forgetting that how we worship God and how we live matter, both in the nasty here-and-now and in the sweet by-and-by.

HOPE WORDS

God calls us to go against the grain when the grain is going against God. Be in the world, not of the world.

12 While I was with them, I was protecting them by your name that you have given me. I guarded[a] them and not one of them is lost, except the son of destruction,[A] so that the Scripture[b] may be fulfilled.[c] **13** Now I am coming to you, and I speak these things in the world so that they may have my joy completed in them. **14** I have given them your word. The world hated[d] them because they are not of the world,[e] just as I am not of the world.[f] **15** I am not praying that you take them out of the world but that you protect them from the evil one.[g] **16** They are not of the world, just as I am not of the world.[h] **17** Sanctify[i] them by the truth;[j] your word is truth. **18** As you sent me into the world,[k] I also have sent them into the world. **19** I sanctify myself for them, so that they also may be sanctified by the truth.

APPLICATION QUESTIONS

READ JOHN 17:17

– In what areas of life are you trusting your feelings and experiences more than the truth of God's Word?

JESUS PRAYS FOR ALL BELIEVERS

20 "I pray not only for these, but also for those who believe in me through their word. **21** May they all be one,[l] as you, Father, are in me and I am in you.[m] May they

APPLICATION QUESTIONS

READ JOHN 17:20-23

– How would you summarize Jesus's intercession on behalf of his followers?
– How does Jesus's prayer contribute to your understanding of unity in the church?
– What barriers are currently preventing you from experiencing a greater level of unity with other members of the church?

also be[B] in us, so that the world may believe you sent me. **22** I have given them the glory[n] you have given me, so that they may be one as we are one. **23** I am in them and you are in me,[o] so that they may be made completely one, that the world may know you have sent me and have loved[p] them as you have loved me.[q]

24 "Father, I want those you have given me to be with me where I am,[r] so that they will see my glory, which you have given me because you loved me before the world's foundation. **25** Righteous Father, the world has not known you. However, I have known you,[s] and they have known that you sent me. **26** I made your name[t] known to them and will continue to make it known, so that the love you have loved me with may be in them and I may be in them."[u]

[a]17:12 2Tm 1:14
[b]Mt 26:54
[c]Ps 41:9; Jn 13:18; 15:25; 19:24,36
[d]17:14 Lk 6:22,27; 19:14
[e]Jn 15:19
[f]Jn 8:23; 18:36
[g]17:15 2Th 3:3
[h]17:16 Jn 18:36; 1Jn 4:17
[i]17:17 Lk 11:2
[j]Ps 119:142; 2Th 2:10; 1Jn 5:20
[k]17:18 1Jn 4:17

[l]17:21 Jn 11:52; 17:11
[m]1Jn 2:24; 5:20
[n]17:22 Mk 10:37; Jn 17:24; 1Pt 5:1,4
[o]17:23 1Jn 4:4
[p]Jn 3:16; 12:43; 1Co 13:1; 2Th 2:13
[q]Jn 15:9
[r]17:24 Jn 12:26
[s]17:25 Mt 11:27; Lk 10:22
[t]17:26 Jn 10:25
[u]1Jn 4:4

[A]17:12 The one destined for destruction, loss, or perdition   [B]17:21 Other mss add *one*

17:12 The son of destruction is a reference to Judas. God knew far in advance that Judas would betray the Messiah. Understand, then, that even wickedness falls under the sovereignty of God—not because God prescribes it, but because he uses it. How much better would it be for you to fulfill God's purposes through your obedience than through your rebellion? **17:13-14** To experience peace in the midst of suffering is for Jesus to share his **joy** with you, and this comes by means of confidence in his **word** (17:14). **17:15-16** Christians must function in this **world**— in our families, neighborhoods, schools, workplaces, marketplaces, and civic arenas (17:15). Yet, we are not to adopt the world's perspective or let it dictate our values. We must operate on earth from a heavenly perspective, God's perspective. God's Word is to shape our understanding of right and wrong. Though we are *in* the world, we must not be *of* it. **17:17** To be *sanctified* is to be set apart for God's purposes. This process happens through internalizing the eternal **truth** of God's **word.** Think of the Word like food. You can chew it all day, but unless you swallow it, you receive no health benefits from it. You internalize God's Word not by merely hearing or reading it, but by trusting and obeying it. Then its work of spiritual transformation is activated in your life (see 2 Cor 3:17-18). **17:18** Jesus was sending his disciples **into the world**—that is, sending them on a mission. They would not be cloistered in a monastery but making their God-glorifying presence known in the culture. **17:20** The disciples/apostles with him that night would proclaim the gospel through their preaching and through their Holy Spirit-inspired writings, which would become the New Testament. Therefore, **those who believe in [him] through their word** includes all those who have trusted in Christ down through the ages. Jesus, then, was praying for you and me. **17:21** A football team consists of different players filling different positions with different roles. But the entire team has one purpose: reaching the goal line. Their unity (oneness) consists of pursuing that goal according to the rules of the game. The church of Jesus Christ is composed of people from every walk of life. But we have the common purpose of proclaiming the gospel and pursuing God's kingdom agenda. Our effectiveness is determined by our unity. That's why Satan works so hard at causing division among Christians and within churches. Being **one** in adherence to truth is critical to experiencing the presence and power of God (see Acts 2:1-2, 43-44; 4:24-31). Illegitimate disunity disconnects us from God and causes us to be ineffective in our lives and in our prayers (see 1 Pet 3:7). **17:23** Our involvement in the church is not trivial. We are caught up in something much bigger than us. We are called to serve the Lord in unity so that the love and glory of our Trinitarian God is visibly and powerfully manifested to a watching **world.**

a 18:1-12 Mt 26:47-56; Mk 14:43-52; Lk 22:47-53
b 18:2 Mk 3:19
c Mt 10:4; Mk 9:31; Jn 13:21
d 18:3 Mk 7:3
e 18:4 Jn 16:30
f 18:5 Ex 3:14; Jn 8:24,58
g 18:9 Mt 1:22
h Jn 17:6,12
i 18:10 Mt 16:17
j Lk 6:14; Ac 10:32
k Mk 14:47; Heb 4:12
l Lv 16:32
m 18:11 Is 51:22; Jr 49:12; Mt 20:22; 26:39,42; Mk 14:36; Lk 22:42

n 18:13 Lk 3:2; Jn 18:24; Ac 4:6
o Mt 26:3; Jn 11:49
p 18:14 Jn 11:50
q 18:15 Lk 6:14
r 18:19 Mt 26:3
s 18:20 Jms 2:2
t Ac 21:26

JESUS BETRAYED

18 After*a* Jesus had said these things, he went out with his disciples across the Kidron Valley, where there was a garden, and he and his disciples went into it. 2 Judas,*b* who betrayed*c* him, also knew the place, because Jesus often met there with his disciples. 3 So Judas took a company of soldiers and some officials*A* from the chief priests and the Pharisees*d* and came there with lanterns, torches, and weapons.

4 Then Jesus, knowing everything that was about to happen to him,*e* went out and said to them, "Who is it that you're seeking?"

5 "Jesus of Nazareth," they answered.

"I am he,"*f* Jesus told them.

Judas, who betrayed him, was also standing with them. 6 When Jesus told them, "I am he," they stepped back and fell to the ground.

7 Then he asked them again, "Who is it that you're seeking?"

"Jesus of Nazareth," they said.

8 "I told you I am he," Jesus replied. "So if you're looking for me, let these men go." 9 This was to fulfill*g* the words he had said: "I have not lost one of those you have given me."*h*

10 Then Simon*i* Peter,*j* who had a sword,*k* drew it, struck the high priest's*l* servant, and cut off his right ear. (The servant's name was Malchus.)

11 At that, Jesus said to Peter, "Put your sword away! Am I not to drink the cup*m* the Father has given me?"

JESUS ARRESTED AND TAKEN TO ANNAS

12 Then the company of soldiers, the commander, and the Jewish officials arrested Jesus and tied him up. 13 First they led him to Annas,*n* since he was the father-in-law of Caiaphas,*o* who was high priest that year. 14 Caiaphas was the one who had advised the Jews that it would be better for one man to die for the people.*p*

PETER DENIES JESUS

15 Simon Peter*q* was following Jesus, as was another disciple. That disciple was an acquaintance of the high priest; so he went with Jesus into the high priest's courtyard. 16 But Peter remained standing outside by the door. So the other disciple, the one known to the high priest, went out and spoke to the girl who was the doorkeeper and brought Peter in.

17 Then the servant girl who was the doorkeeper said to Peter, "You aren't one of this man's disciples too, are you?"

"I am not." he said. 18 Now the servants and the officials had made a charcoal fire, because it was cold. They were standing there warming themselves, and Peter was standing with them, warming himself.

JESUS BEFORE ANNAS

19 The high priest*r* questioned Jesus about his disciples and about his teaching.

20 "I have spoken openly to the world," Jesus answered him. "I have always taught in the synagogue*s* and in the temple,*t* where all the Jews congregate, and I haven't spoken anything in secret. 21 Why do you question me? Question those who heard what I told them. Look, they know what I said."

22 When he had said these things, one of the officials standing by slapped Jesus, saying, "Is this the way you answer the high priest?"

A 18:3 Or *temple police*, or *officers*, also in vv. 12,18,22

18:1 The Kidron Valley lay between Jerusalem and the Mount of Olives.

18:2 Notice that Jesus wasn't hiding from his enemies. He went to a location where he knew **Judas** could find him. Jesus was ready to complete his mission in obedience to the Father.

18:5-6 The Greek words behind the translation **I am he** can simply be rendered as "I am"—the divine name, the self-designation that God revealed to Moses (see the note on 8:58). Jesus is no mere man. He's the Word who was with God, was God, and became flesh (see 1:1, 14). Jesus spoke the divine name using the same voice that had spoken the world into existence. And it knocked the betrayer and his accomplices off their feet.

18:8-9 When Jesus intervenes to protect you, his intervention is always effective.

18:10 Though John doesn't tell us anything further about the servant's injury, we learn in Luke's Gospel that Jesus healed his **ear** before they led him away (see Luke 22:50-51).

18:11 Jesus rebuked Peter for stepping between him and God's will: **Am I not to drink the cup the Father has given me?**

18:12 Since the **soldiers** and **Jewish officials** had been knocked over by Jesus's mere words and then watched him reattach a severed ear, you might assume that they would be rethinking their plans to arrest him. But apparently they were so determined to do evil that nothing else mattered.

18:13 Though **Caiaphas** was the **high priest**, **Annas** was the former high priest and thus retained the title.

18:15-16 This unnamed **disciple** was John, the author of this Gospel. John never identifies himself by name but typically calls himself "the disciple Jesus loved" (see 13:23; 19:26; 20:2; also see the introduction).

18:18 The Greek word translated **charcoal fire** appears only one other time in John's Gospel. When it shows up in 21:9, it will be significant.

18:19-20 Annas wanted Jesus to tell him what he had been doing to get everyone so riled up (18:19). But Jesus wasn't about to recount everything he'd done and said. After all, he had **spoken openly** both **in the synagogue and in the temple**. He had done nothing **in secret**, nor did he lead any secret organization (18:20).

18:21-23 If this trial were to be legitimate, they would have to bring forward witnesses to testify about what he had done wrong. Jesus requested that the high priest do so (18:21). Instead, someone simply **hit** him! They had no interest in justice. They wanted blood (18:22-23).

a 18:23 Gn 1:31
b 18:24-27 Mt 26:57-75; Mk 14:53-72; Lk 22:54,62-65
c 18:24 Jn 18:13
d 18:27 Jn 13:38
e 18:28-38 Mt 27:2,11-14; Mk 15:1-5; Lk 23:25
f 18:28 Mk 15:16
g 18:29 1Tm 6:13
h 1Tm 5:19; Ti 1:6
i 18:32 Jn 12:32-33

j 18:33 Jn 19:21
k 18:36 Mk 1:15; Ac 20:25
l Jn 17:6
m Lk 1:2; Jn 18:18; Ac 26:16; 1Co 4:1
n Jn 8:23; 17:14,16
o 18:37 Jn 1:9; 3:19; 6:14; 9:39; 11:27; 12:46; 16:28; 1Tm 1:15
p Jn 15:26; Ac 26:5
q Ps 119:142; 2Th 2:10
r 18:38 Mt 27:37; Mk 15:26; 25:18; 28:18
s 18:39—19:6 Mt 27:15-26; Mk 15:6-15; Lk 23:13-25
t 18:40 Mk 15:7
u Mk 14:48
v 19:2 Mk 15:17

23 "If I have spoken wrongly," Jesus answered him, "give evidence^A about the wrong; but if rightly,^a why do you hit me?" **24** Then^b Annas^c sent him bound to Caiaphas the high priest.

PETER DENIES JESUS TWICE MORE

25 Now Simon Peter was standing and warming himself. They said to him, "You aren't one of his disciples too, are you?"

He denied it and said, "I am not."

26 One of the high priest's servants, a relative of the man whose ear Peter had cut off, said, "Didn't I see you with him in the garden?" **27** Peter denied it again. Immediately a rooster crowed.^d

JESUS BEFORE PILATE

28 Then^e they led Jesus from Caiaphas to the governor's headquarters.^f It was early morning. They did not enter the headquarters themselves; otherwise they would be defiled and unable to eat the Passover.

29 So Pilate^g came out to them and said, "What charge^h do you bring against this man?"

30 They answered him, "If this man weren't a criminal,^B we wouldn't have handed him over to you."

31 Pilate told them, "You take him and judge him according to your law."

"It's not legal for us to put anyone to death," the Jews declared. **32** They said this so that Jesus's words might be fulfilled indicating what kind of death he was going to die.^i

33 Then Pilate went back into the headquarters, summoned Jesus, and said to him, "Are you the King of the Jews?"^j

34 Jesus answered, "Are you asking this on your own, or have others told you about me?"

35 "I'm not a Jew, am I?" Pilate replied. "Your own nation and the chief priests handed you over to me. What have you done?"

36 "My kingdom^k is not of this world," said Jesus. "If my kingdom were of this world,^l my servants^m would fight, so that I wouldn't be handed over to the Jews. But as it is,^c my kingdom is not from here."^n

37 "You are a king then?" Pilate asked.

"You say that I'm a king," Jesus replied. "I was born for this, and I have come into the world^o for this: to testify^p to the truth.^q Everyone who is of the truth listens to my voice."

38 "What is truth?" said Pilate.

JESUS OR BARABBAS

After he had said this, he went out to the Jews again and told them, "I find no grounds^r for charging him. **39** You^s have a custom that I release one prisoner to you at the Passover. So, do you want me to release to you the King of the Jews?"

40 They shouted back, "Not this man, but Barabbas!"^t Now Barabbas was a revolutionary.^D,u

JESUS FLOGGED AND MOCKED

19 Then Pilate took Jesus and had him flogged. **2** The soldiers also twisted together a crown^v of thorns, put it on his

---

^A **18:23** Or *him, "testify*   ^B **18:30** Lit *an evil doer*   ^C **18:36** Or *But now*   ^D **18:40** Or *robber*; see Jn 10:1,8 for the same Gk word used here

---

18:25-27 By this point, Peter had already denied a direct question about whether he was a disciple of Jesus (see 18:17). Here he denies twice more having any relationship with Jesus. One of those who accused him of being with Jesus was **a relative of the man whose ear Peter had cut off** (18:26; see 18:10). Surrounded by the stares of an inquisitive crowd, Peter was asked in essence, "Aren't you the one who drew my kin's blood?" In spite of his former boasting that he would die for Jesus, Peter wasn't ready to put his life on the line. And **immediately** after his third denial, **a rooster crowed** (18:27)—just as Jesus had predicted (see 13:38).

18:28 The Jewish officials had rejected God's Messiah and were seeking to put to death an innocent man, but they were worried about being made ceremonially unclean by entering the Gentile **governor's headquarters**! They couldn't see that their wicked actions had already made them filthy.

18:29 Pontius **Pilate** was the Roman governor over Judea. Typically, he governed in Caesarea Maritima on the Mediterranean Sea.

But during the Passover, when large crowds were present in Jerusalem, Pilate was on the scene to squelch any Jewish disturbances. He was a ruthless man with no affection for the Jews, and they had no fondness for him either. But since the Romans alone had the power of execution, the Jewish leaders needed Pilate to condemn Jesus.

18:32 Clearly, Jesus was not a victim of fate; he is the sovereign Lord who proceeded toward his death according to plan.

18:36-37 In saying, **My kingdom is not of this world** (18:36), Jesus essentially answered, "Yes, I'm a King. But not from here." So, was he the King of the Jews? Of course. He was also King of the Romans. In fact, he is King of the entire world. But the *source* of his kingship and authority is in heaven.

18:38 Pilate's question is repeated by our postmodern world today. Many in our culture reject the notion of absolute truth. "Truth" to them is relative—that is, what's true for one person isn't necessarily true for another. But this is preposterous. *Truth* is the absolute standard by which reality is measured. It's

not something that changes based on feelings or perspective. A person can deny that gravity is true, but if he decides to jump off a building to prove it, he's going to find that truth doesn't care about his feelings or perspective. Truth exists whether you embrace it or not.

18:40 **Barabbas** was an insurrectionist who had created havoc for Rome because he wanted the Jews out from under Roman rule. Don't miss that the leaders preferred a criminal who had fought for physical deliverance from Rome because that's all they cared about. They wanted political deliverance from Gentile rule, when what they needed was spiritual deliverance from sin.

19:1 Flogging involved the use of a whip of leather strips with bits of bone or metal tied to the ends. It would rip the skin from the victim's back.

19:2-3 Though **the soldiers** no doubt thought they were merely exercising the might of Rome over a simple Jew, they were actually fulfilling biblical prophecy about the Messiah in detail (see Isa 50:6; 53:5).

a 19:3 Mk 1:45
b 19:4 Jn 18:38
c 19:5 Lk 19:36
d Zch 6:12
e 19:7 Lv 24:16; Jn 10:33,36
f Jn 5:18; 19:12; Heb 1:2
g 19:9 Mk 15:16
h Mk 14:61

i 19:11 Jn 15:22; 18:13-14,19-24,28
j 19:17-24 Mt 27:33-37; Mk 15:22-26; Lk 23:32-34
k 19:17 Lk 9:23; 23:26

head, and clothed him in a purple robe. **3** And they kept coming up to him*a* and saying, "Hail, King of the Jews!" and were slapping his face.

4 Pilate went outside again and said to them, "Look, I'm bringing him out to you to let you know I find no grounds*b* for charging him." **5** Then Jesus came out wearing the crown of thorns and the purple robe.*c* Pilate said to them, "Here is the man!"*d*

PILATE SENTENCES JESUS TO DEATH

6 When the chief priests and the temple servants*A* saw him, they shouted, "Crucify! Crucify!"

Pilate responded, "Take him and crucify him yourselves, since I find no grounds for charging him."

7 "We have a law," the Jews replied to him, "and according to that law he ought to die,*e* because he made himself the Son of God."*f*

8 When Pilate heard this statement, he was more afraid than ever. **9** He went back into the headquarters*g* and asked Jesus, "Where are you from?" But Jesus did not give him an answer.*h* **10** So Pilate said to him, "Do you refuse to speak to me? Don't you know that I have the authority to release you and the authority to crucify you?"

11 "You would have no authority over me at all," Jesus answered him, "if it hadn't been given you from above. This is why the one who handed me over to you has the greater sin."*i*

12 From that moment Pilate kept trying*B* to release him. But the Jews shouted, "If you release this man, you are not Caesar's friend. Anyone who makes himself a king opposes Caesar!"

13 When Pilate heard these words, he brought Jesus outside. He sat down on the judge's seat in a place called the Stone Pavement (but in Aramaic,*c* *Gabbatha*). **14** It was the preparation day for the Passover, and it was about noon.*D* Then he told the Jews, "Here is your king!"

15 They shouted, "Take him away! Take him away! Crucify him!"

Pilate said to them, "Should I crucify your king?"

"We have no king but Caesar!" the chief priests answered.

16 Then he handed him over to be crucified.

THE CRUCIFIXION

Then they took Jesus away.*E* **17** Carrying*J* the cross by himself,*k* he went out to what is called Place of the Skull, which in Aramaic is called *Golgotha*. **18** There they crucified him and two others with him, one on either side, with Jesus in the middle. **19** Pilate also had a sign made and put on the cross. It said: JESUS OF NAZARETH, THE KING OF THE

---

*A*19:6 Or *temple police*, or *officers*   *B*19:12 Lit *Pilate was trying*   *C*19:13 Or *Hebrew*, also in vv. 17,20   *D*19:14 Lit *about the sixth hour*   *E*19:16 Other mss add *and led him out*

19:5-6 Given the fact that he judged Jesus innocent, Pilate surely thought the Jewish crowd would be satisfied with the brutality and humiliation that Jesus had experienced (19:5). But only one thing would satisfy them. They wanted Jesus crucified (19:6).
19:7 Jesus had made claims that only God could make. The Jews therefore accused him of blasphemy, saying, "You—being a man—make yourself God" (10:33).
19:8 What would make Pilate fearful? Jesus had told Pilate that he ruled a kingdom that was "not of this world" (see 18:36). Now the Jews were telling him that Jesus claimed to be the Son of God. In Matthew 27:19 we learn that Pilate's wife told him she had dreamed about this "righteous man" and that he should have nothing to do with him. Pilate was likely a superstitious pagan who feared the gods. He was perhaps thinking, "Who *is* this guy?"
19:9 Given Pilate's rising fear, he was essentially saying, "Where are you from, *really*?"
19:10 When someone insists on shouting, "**Don't you know** that I'm in charge here?," it usually means he's uncertain himself.
19:11 If a person exercises any **authority** on earth, ultimately that authority has been granted by God (from **above**). Whether or not an individual chooses to wield that authority

for kingdom purposes has serious consequences because we all will one day be called to give an account for our use of authority—whether in government, at work, in the community, or even at home. Remember, God is the ultimate authority. While the human in charge may be *a* boss, he or she isn't *the* boss.
  God would hold Pilate accountable for his gross violation of justice. The **sin** of the Jewish high priest was much worse though since he had the Scriptures available to him and was aware of Jesus's teachings and miracles, yet closed his eyes to the truth.
19:12 The Jewish leaders won the battle of whether or not Jesus should be released because they pitted Pilate against the emperor. What would Caesar think if he heard one of his governors was setting free some would-be revolutionary who claimed to be a rival king in the Roman Empire? Caesar didn't mind religion—as long as it didn't compete with his absolute authority.
19:13 Mention of **the judge's seat** here is a subtle reminder that one day every Christian will stand before the judgment seat of Christ so that he may render a verdict, not regarding salvation, but regarding service and faithfulness to him.
19:14 That these events coincided with **Passover** was no accident. When the Israelites

were slaves in Egypt, God had commanded them to slaughter a lamb and place its blood on the doorposts of their homes. Then, when he struck down the firstborn of Egypt, he "passed over" the homes with a blood covering. By means of this, God rescued his people from slavery (see Exod 12:1-28). Jesus, "the Lamb of God, who takes away the sin of the world" (John 1:29) was about to shed his blood so that all those who believe in him would be saved from slavery to sin.
19:15 Notice that **the chief priests** didn't say, "We have no king but God." Their hatred of Jesus was so great that they were willing to disregard their divine ruler and align themselves with a pagan king. Placing human government above God never ends well.
19:17 The Latin translation of **Golgotha** is *Calvaria*, from which we get the English rendering *Calvary*.
19:19-22 Pilate had made the sign read as a title, a fact. The Jewish leaders wanted it to clearly indicate that this was merely Jesus's *claim* (19:21). But Pilate rebuffed them, saying, **What I have written, I have written** (19:22). He meant for the sign to sting the Jews. But, in his sovereignty, God meant it to declare to the world the truth about his Son.

JEWS. **20** Many of the Jews read this sign, because the place where Jesus was crucified was near the city,[a] and it was written in Aramaic, Latin, and Greek. **21** So the chief priests of the Jews said to Pilate, "Don't write, 'The King of the Jews,'[b] but that he said, 'I am the King of the Jews.'"

22 Pilate replied, "What I have written, I have written."

23 When the soldiers crucified Jesus, they took his clothes and divided them into four parts, a part for each soldier. They also took the tunic, which was seamless, woven in one piece from the top. **24** So they said to one another, "Let's not tear it, but cast lots for it, to see who gets it." This happened that the Scripture[c] might be fulfilled[d] that says: **They divided my clothes among themselves, and they cast lots for my clothing.**[A,e] This is what the soldiers did.

JESUS'S PROVISION FOR HIS MOTHER

25 Standing[f] by the cross[g] of Jesus were his mother,[h] his mother's sister, Mary the wife of Clopas, and Mary Magdalene.[i] **26** When Jesus saw his mother and the disciple he loved[j] standing there, he said to his mother, "Woman, here is your son." **27** Then he said to the disciple, "Here is your mother." And from that hour the disciple took her into his home.

THE FINISHED WORK OF JESUS

28 After[k] this, when Jesus knew that everything was now finished[l] that the Scripture might be fulfilled, he said, "I'm thirsty."[m] **29** A jar full of sour wine was sitting there; so they fixed a sponge full of sour wine on a hyssop branch[n] and held it up to his mouth. **30** When Jesus had received the sour wine, he said, "It is finished."[o] Then bowing his head, he gave up his spirit.[p]

JESUS'S SIDE PIERCED

31 Since it was the preparation day,[q] the Jews did not want the bodies[r] to remain on the cross[s] on the Sabbath[t] (for that Sabbath was a special[B] day). They requested that Pilate have the men's legs broken and that their bodies be taken away.[u] **32** So the soldiers came and broke the legs of the first man and of the other one who had been crucified with him. **33** When they came to Jesus, they did not break his legs since they saw that he was already dead.[v] **34** But one of the soldiers pierced[w] his side[x] with a spear, and at once blood and water[y] came out. **35** He who saw this has testified[z] so that you also may believe. His testimony is true, and he knows he is telling the truth.[aa] **36** For these things happened so that the Scripture would be fulfilled:[ab] **Not one of his bones will be broken.**[C,ac] **37** Also, another Scripture says: **They will look at the one they pierced.**[D,ad]

JESUS'S BURIAL

38 After[ae] this, Joseph of Arimathea, who was a disciple of Jesus — but secretly because of his fear of the Jews — asked Pilate that he might remove Jesus's body.[af] Pilate gave him permission; so he came and took his body away. **39** Nicodemus[ag] (who had previously come to him at night) also came, bringing a mixture of about seventy-five pounds[E] of myrrh and aloes. **40** They took Jesus's body[ah] and wrapped it in linen cloths[ai] with the fragrant spices, according to the burial[aj] custom of the Jews. **41** There was a garden in the place where he was crucified. A new tomb was in the garden; no one had yet been placed in it. **42** They placed Jesus there because of the Jewish day of preparation and since the tomb was nearby.

THE EMPTY TOMB

20 On[ak] the first day of the week[al] Mary Magdalene[am] came to the tomb[an] early, while it was still dark. She saw that the stone[ao] had been removed

[a] 19:20 Heb 13:12
[b] 19:21 Mt 2:2; 27:11,29,37; Mk 15:2,9,12,18,26; Lk 23:3,37-38; Jn 18:33,39; 19:3,19
[c] 19:24 Mt 26:54
[d] Mt 1:22
[e] Ps 22:18
[f] 19:25-27 Mt 27:55-56; Mk 15:40-41; Lk 23:49
[g] 19:25 Lk 23:26
[h] Mt 1:16
[i] Mk 15:40
[j] 19:26 Jn 13:23; 21:7
[k] 19:28-30 Mt 27:45-54; Mk 15:33-39; Lk 23:44-48
[l] 19:28 Lk 12:50; 18:31; 22:37; Jn 19:30; Ac 13:29; Heb 10:14; 11:40
[m] Ps 22:15; 69:21
[n] 19:29 Ex 12:22
[o] 19:30 Lk 12:50; Jn 4:34; 17:4; 19:28
[p] 1Jn 5:8
[q] 19:31 Jn 19:14
[r] Lk 12:4

[s] 19:31 Lk 23:26
[t] Mk 2:23
[u] Dt 21:22-23; Jos 8:29; 10:26-27
[v] 19:33 Ex 12:46; Nm 9:12; Ps 34:20
[w] 19:34 Zch 12:10; Rv 1:7
[x] Jn 20:20
[y] 1Jn 5:6-9
[z] 19:35 Jn 1:14-15,34
[aa] Jn 21:24
[ab] 19:36 Jn 13:18; 17:12; 19:24
[ac] Ex 12:46; Nm 9:12; Ps 34:20
[ad] 19:37 Zch 12:10
[ae] 19:38-42 Mt 27:57-60; Mk 15:42-46; Lk 23:50-54
[af] 19:38 Lk 12:4; Jn 2:21
[ag] 19:39 Jn 3:1-9; 7:50
[ah] 19:40 Jn 2:21; 19:40
[ai] Jn 20:5
[aj] Mk 14:8
[ak] 20:1-2 Mt 28:5-8; Mk 16:5-8; Lk 24:3-8
[al] 20:1 Lk 24:1; Ac 20:7; 1Co 16:2
[am] Mk 15:40
[an] Jn 5:28
[ao] Mt 27:60,66; Mk 15:46

[A] 19:24 Ps 22:18   [B] 19:31 Lit great   [C] 19:36 Ex 12:46; Nm 9:12; Ps 34:20   [D] 19:37 Zch 12:10   [E] 19:39 Lit a hundred litrai; a Roman litrai = 12 ounces

19:26-27 Even while dying, Jesus fulfilled his obligation to care for his widowed **mother**, entrusting her to the care of John, his **disciple** and the author of this Gospel. Jesus entrusted the well-being of his mother to John rather than to one of her biological sons because they had not yet believed in him (see 7:5). Spiritual relationships are to take precedence over biological and physical relationships (see Matt 12:46-50).
19:29 Hyssop was the plant used to brush lamb's blood on the doorposts during the Passover (see Exod 12:21-23). As the apostle Paul says, "Christ our Passover lamb has been sacrificed" (1 Cor 5:7).

19:30 Jesus's declaration, **It is finished**, meant the debt for sin had been paid in full.
19:31 Victims hanging on a cross had to put weight on their **legs** in order to lift themselves to breathe.
19:33-34 That **blood and water** flowed out (19:34) indicated that Jesus's heart was no longer beating. In the early years of the church, a heresy arose claiming that Jesus was totally divine and only pretended to be human (see 1 John 4:1-2). But John wants his readers to know that such talk is a complete lie. As sure as Jesus was fully God, he was fully human: he bled and died.

19:36-37 Down to the slightest detail, our sovereign God was fulfilling his Word.
19:38-40 The other Gospels inform us that **Joseph of Arimathea** was wealthy and a prominent member of the Jewish Sanhedrin (19:38; see Matt 27:57; Mark 15:43). Joining Joseph was **Nicodemus**, another secret disciple **who had previously** spoken with Jesus **at night** (John 19:39; see 3:1-13).
19:41 That **no one had yet been placed** in the tomb is a significant detail because later, when Jesus's body was gone, no one was able to point to any bones there as being Jesus's remains.
20:1 The first day of the week was Sunday.

*20:2 Lk 6:14; Jn 21:7;
Ac 10:32
*Jn 5:28
*20:5 Lk 24:12; Jn 19:40;
20:5-7
*20:7 Lk 19:20; Jn 11:44;
Ac 19:12
*Jn 20:5
*20:9 Mt 26:54
*Lk 18:33; Ac 2:24
*Mk 9:9-10; 12:25; Lk
16:31; 24:46; Ac 10:41;
13:34; 17:3,31
*20:11-18 Mk 16:9-11
*20:11 Jn 5:28
*20:12 Gn 16:7; Mt 13:49;
Ac 5:19; Rv 14:6
*Lk 12:4; Jn 2:21
*20:13 Lk 10:1; 1Co 8:6

*20:14 Jn 21:4
*20:16 Mk 4:38; Eph 4:11
*20:17 Lk 24:51; Jn 3:13;
6:62; Ac 1:9-11; 2:33-34;
Rm 10:6; Eph 1:20-21; 4:8;
1Pt 3:22
*Mt 5:16; 11:27; Jn 8:42
*Ac 9:30
*Jn 14:12
*Mt 27:46
*20:18 Mk 16:10
*20:19 Lk 24:1; Ac 20:7;
1Co 16:2
*Jn 14:27; 16:33
*20:20 Lk 24:39-40; Jn
19:34; 20:25-29
*20:21 Jn 3:17; 17:18;
Heb 3:1
*Jn 13:20; Ac 1:2
*20:22 Gn 2:7; Ezk 37:9
*Ps 51:11; Jn 1:33; 14:17;
16:7; Ac 2:4; 8:15; Rm 8:9;
Gl 5:25; Ti 3:5; Rv 3:22
*20:23 Mt 16:19; 18:18;
Jn 9:41

from the tomb. [2] So she went running to Simon Peter[a] and to the other disciple, the one Jesus loved, and said to them, "They've taken the Lord out of the tomb,[b] and we don't know where they've put him!"

[3] At that, Peter and the other disciple went out, heading for the tomb. [4] The two were running together, but the other disciple outran Peter and got to the tomb first. [5] Stooping down, he saw the linen cloths[c] lying there, but he did not go in. [6] Then, following him, Simon Peter also came. He entered the tomb and saw the linen cloths lying there. [7] The wrapping[d] that had been on his head was not lying with the linen cloths[e] but was folded up in a separate place by itself. [8] The other disciple, who had reached the tomb first, then also went in, saw, and believed. [9] For they did not yet understand the Scripture[f] that he must rise[g] from the dead.[h] [10] Then the disciples returned to the place where they were staying.

MARY MAGDALENE SEES THE RISEN LORD

[11] But[i] Mary stood outside the tomb,[j] crying. As she was crying, she stooped to look into the tomb. [12] She saw two angels[k] in white sitting where Jesus's body[l] had been lying, one at the head and the other at the feet. [13] They said to her, "Woman, why are you crying?"

"Because they've taken away my Lord,"[m] she told them, "and I don't know where they've put him."

[14] Having said this, she turned around and saw Jesus standing there, but she did not know it was Jesus.[n] [15] "Woman," Jesus said to her, "why are you crying? Who is it that you're seeking?"

Supposing he was the gardener, she replied, "Sir, if you've carried him away, tell me where you've put him, and I will take him away."

[16] Jesus said to her, "Mary."

Turning around, she said to him in Aramaic,[A] "Rabboni!"—which means "Teacher."[o]

[17] "Don't cling to me," Jesus told her, "since I have not yet ascended[p] to the Father.[q] But go to my brothers[r] and tell them that I am ascending to my Father[s] and your Father, to my God[t] and your God."

[18] Mary Magdalene went and announced to the disciples, "I have seen the Lord!"[u] And she told them what[B] he had said to her.

THE DISCIPLES COMMISSIONED

[19] When it was evening of that first day of the week,[v] the disciples were gathered together with the doors locked because they feared the Jews. Jesus came, stood among them, and said to them, "Peace be with you."[w]

[20] Having said this, he showed them his hands and his side.[x] So the disciples rejoiced when they saw the Lord.

[21] Jesus said to them again, "Peace be with you. As the Father has sent me,[y] I also send you."[z] [22] After saying this, he breathed on them[aa] and said,[c] "Receive the Holy Spirit.[ab] [23] If you forgive the sins of any, they are forgiven them; if you retain the sins of any, they are retained."[ac]

^20:16 Or Hebrew   ^20:18 Lit these things   ^20:22 Lit he breathed and said to them

20:7 One of the many theories concocted to explain away the resurrection is that Jesus was merely resuscitated. This theory proposes that after enduring the intense brutality of being beaten and crucified, Jesus was revived by the cool interior of the tomb. But this doesn't explain why a half-dead man would remove **his head** cloth, neatly fold it, and place it **separate** from his intact **linen** wrappings! Nor does it explain how he could have had the strength to move the heavy stone blocking the entrance. Like other attempts to deny the resurrection, this one fails to adequately explain the evidence. One thing is clear: when the disciples saw Jesus later (see 20:19-23), he didn't look like a man who had been merely resuscitated from a near death experience!

20:8 Previously John (the man in view here) had believed in Jesus's identity. Now he **believed** in the resurrection that Jesus had predicted (see Luke 9:21-22; 18:31-34).

20:13 Mary couldn't grasp what had happened. The only thing she could conclude was that someone had **taken away** Jesus's body, and it broke her heart. Apparently resurrection was not an option she considered.

20:15 Perhaps she supposed **he was the gardener** since the tomb was in a garden (see 19:41).

20:17-18 Don't overlook that the resurrection of Jesus Christ was first announced by a woman. In first-century Judaism, a woman's testimony wasn't considered credible. So if the disciples were going to invent a resurrection story, they wouldn't choose women to be the first to see and declare it. The fact that the first witnesses were women (see Matt 28:1-10) provides evidence for the historicity of the resurrection. It also affirms the communication gifting of women as long as the gift is exercised under the legitimately authorized spiritual authority and covering of the home and the church (see 1 Cor 11:5, 10).

20:19 Clearly, Jesus had a physical body. Mary touched him (see 20:17); Thomas would touch him (see 20:27); later he would eat with his disciples (see 21:12-13). He was no mere phantom (see Luke 24:39). He had risen bodily from the grave. But his resurrected body no longer had material limitations. Apparently, he could

pass through **locked** doors if he wanted. And later he would ascend on a cloud into heaven (see Acts 1:9). The apostles tell us that our resurrection bodies will be like his (see 1 Cor 15:45-57; Phil 3:21; 1 John 3:2).

20:20 Jesus's scars will serve as eternal reminders of the cost of our redemption, and they will forever give us reason to praise him.

20:21 The Father had **sent** the Son on a kingdom mission to atone for the sins of the world so that all who believe would receive eternal life. Now the Son was sending his disciples on a kingdom mission to proclaim that message and make other disciples throughout the world (see Matt 28:16-20).

20:22 Most interpreters recognize this as an anticipatory act. **The Holy Spirit** would come to dwell within the apostles on the day of Pentecost (see Acts 2:1-21), enabling them to accomplish the mission on which Jesus was sending them. Jesus was visibly and physically preparing them for what was spiritually to come.

20:23 The Holy Spirit would enable them to authoritatively declare that God had indeed forgiven **the sins of any** who believe in Jesus.

THOMAS SEES AND BELIEVES

24 But Thomas[a] (called "Twin"[A]), one of the Twelve, was not with them when Jesus came. **25** So the other disciples were telling him, "We've seen the Lord!"

But he said to them, "If I don't see the mark of the nails in his hands, put my finger into the mark of the nails,[b] and put my hand into his side,[c] I will never believe."[d]

26 A week later his disciples were indoors again, and Thomas was with them. Even though the doors were locked, Jesus came and stood among them and said, "Peace be with you."

27 Then he said to Thomas, "Put your finger here and look at my hands. Reach out your hand and put it into my side. Don't be faithless, but believe."[e]

28 Thomas responded to him, "My Lord and my God!"

29 Jesus said, "Because you have seen me, you have believed.[8] Blessed are those who have not seen and yet believe."[f]

THE PURPOSE OF THIS GOSPEL

30 Jesus performed many other signs[g] in the presence of his disciples that are not written[h] in this book.[i] **31** But these are written so that you may believe that Jesus is the Messiah,[j] the Son[k] of God,[c,l] and that by believing you may have life in his name.[m]

JESUS'S THIRD APPEARANCE TO THE DISCIPLES

21 After this, Jesus revealed[n] himself again to his disciples by the Sea of Tiberias.[o] He revealed himself in this way: **2** Simon Peter,[p] Thomas[q] (called "Twin"[A]), Nathanael[r] from Cana of Galilee,[s] Zebedee's[t] sons, and two others of his disciples were together. **3** "I'm going fishing," Simon Peter said to them.

"We're coming with you," they told him. They went out and got into the boat, but that night they caught nothing.[u]

4 When daybreak came, Jesus stood on the shore, but the disciples did not know it was Jesus.[v] **5** "Friends,"[D] Jesus called to them, "you don't have any fish, do you?"

"No," they answered.

6 "Cast the net on the right side of the boat," he told them, "and you'll find some." So they did,[E] and they were unable to haul it in because of the large number of fish. **7** The disciple, the one Jesus loved, said to Peter, "It is the Lord!"[w]

When Simon Peter heard that it was the Lord, he tied his outer clothing around him (for he had taken it off) and plunged into the sea. **8** Since they were not far from land (about a hundred yards[F,x] away), the other disciples came in the boat,[y] dragging the net full of fish.

9 When they got out on land, they saw a charcoal fire there, with fish lying on it, and bread. **10** "Bring some of the fish you've just caught," Jesus told them. **11** So Simon Peter climbed up and hauled the net ashore, full of large fish — 153 of them. Even though there were so many, the net was not torn.[z]

12 "Come and have breakfast," Jesus told them. None of the disciples dared ask him, "Who are you?" because they knew it was the Lord. **13** Jesus came, took the bread, and gave it to them. He did the same with the fish. **14** This was now the third time[aa] Jesus appeared[G,ab] to the disciples after he was raised from the dead.

JESUS'S THREEFOLD RESTORATION OF PETER

15 When they had eaten breakfast, Jesus asked Simon Peter, "Simon, son of John,[H] do you love me more than these?"

[a] 20:24 Mk 3:18; Jn 11:16
[b] 20:25 Ps 22:16
[c] Jn 20:20
[d] Dt 9:23; Mk 16:11; Lk 22:67; Jn 4:48; 6:64; Ac 13:41
[e] 20:27 Nm 12:7
[f] 20:29 2Co 5:7; 1Pt 1:8
[g] 20:30 Jn 2:11; 21:25
[h] 1Jn 1:4
[i] 2Tm 4:13
[j] 20:31 Mt 1:17; Ac 18:5; 1Jn 2:22; 5:1
[k] Jn 5:19
[l] Heb 1:2
[m] Jn 10:27; 1Jn 3:23
[n] 21:1 Mk 16:12; Jn 21:14; 2Co 4:11; 5:10; 1Tm 3:16; Heb 9:26; 1Pt 1:10; 1Jn 1:2; 3:5,8
[o] Jn 6:1,23
[p] 21:2 Lk 6:14; Ac 10:32
[q] Mk 3:18
[r] Jn 1:45-49
[s] Mt 17:22
[t] Mt 4:21; 10:2; 20:20; 26:37; 27:56; Mk 1:19-20; 3:17; 10:35; Lk 5:10; Jn 21:7; Ac 12:2

[u] 21:3 Lk 5:5
[v] 21:4 Jn 20:14,19,26
[w] 21:7 Lk 10:1; 1Co 8:6
[x] 21:8 Lk 12:25
[y] Mk 3:9; Jn 6:22-24
[z] 21:11 Lk 5:4-10
[aa] 21:14 Jn 20:19,26
[ab] Jn 21:1; 2Co 4:11; 1Jn 1:2

[A] 20:24; 21:2 Gk *Didymus* [B] 20:29 Or *have you believed?* [C] 20:31 Or *that the Messiah, the Son of God, is Jesus* [D] 21:5 Lit *"Children"* [E] 21:6 Lit *they cast* [F] 21:8 Lit *about two hundred cubits* [G] 21:14 Lit *was revealed* (v. 1) [H] 21:15-17 Other mss read *"Simon, son of Jonah"*; Mt 16:17; Jn 1:42

20:24-25 In church history, **Thomas** earned the nickname "Doubting Thomas." But this isn't a fair appraisal of his character. Previously, Thomas was prepared to go into hostile territory and die with Jesus (see 11:7-8, 16). A believer can be spiritually strong one moment and spiritually deflated the next.

20:27 Jesus responded to Thomas's unbelief with grace. He gave the struggling disciple the opportunity to do exactly what he had wanted: to touch the wounds of his risen Savior.

20:31 Here John gives us the evangelistic purpose for his book. He wrote it **so that** readers might **believe that Jesus is the Messiah**—the God-Man—who died as a substitutionary

atonement for sins and that, **by believing**, they will receive eternal life—that is, an eternal relationship with God and an ever-expanding experience of this reality in our lives (see 17:3). That's what salvation is all about.

21:1 **The Sea of Tiberias** is another name for the Sea of Galilee.

21:4 They didn't recognize **Jesus** because it was only **daybreak**, and they were still some distance away.

21:9 The Greek word for **charcoal fire** appears two times in John's Gospel: here and at 18:18, when Peter was warming himself by another such blaze. On that occasion, Peter had denied three times that he knew Jesus. Thus, the Lord was using scents and sights

to remind Peter of his recent past. We can be certain of this because of the conversation that follows in 21:15-19. Peter never forgot this meal Jesus provided; he even mentioned it in his preaching (see Acts 10:41).

21:14 The resurrection of Jesus Christ was neither a fairy tale nor a hallucination. He "presented himself alive to [his disciples] by many convincing proofs . . . over a period of forty days" (Acts 1:3).

21:15 When Jesus asked Peter if he loved him, the Greek verb used is *agapaō*, often used to describe self-sacrificial love. But when Peter affirmed his **love** for Jesus, the Greek verb is *phileō*, a brotherly kind of love and affection—a love between good

[a] 21:15 Mt 8:30,33; Mk 5:11,14; Lk 8:32,34; 15:15; Jn 21:17
[b] Rv 5:6
[c] 21:16 Lk 6:35; Rv 12:11
[d] Lk 10:27
[e] 1Pt 5:2
[f] Mt 7:15; Jn 10:11
[g] 21:17 Mk 14:44; Jn 5:20
[h] 2Co 2:2
[i] Jn 16:30
[j] Jn 21:15
[k] 21:18 Jn 1:51; Rv 22:21
[l] 21:19 2Pt 1:14

[m] 21:19 Jn 11:4; 17:1; 1Pt 2:12
[n] Jn 1:43; 8:12; 10:27
[o] 21:20 Jn 21:7
[p] Jn 13:21,23-25
[q] 21:22 Mk 8:38
[r] 21:23 Ac 9:30
[s] Mk 9:1
[t] 21:25 Jn 20:30

"Yes, Lord," he said to him, "you know that I love you."

"Feed[a] my lambs,"[b] he told him. [16] A second time he asked him, "Simon, son of John, do you love[c] me?"[d]

"Yes, Lord," he said to him, "you know that I love you."

"Shepherd[e] my sheep,"[f] he told him.

[17] He asked him the third time, "Simon, son of John, do you love[g] me?"

Peter was grieved[h] that he asked him the third time, "Do you love me?" He said, "Lord, you know everything;[i] you know that I love you."

⤳ HOPE WORDS ⤳

Your future doesn't have to be determined by your failures.

"Feed[j] my sheep," Jesus said. [18] "Truly I tell you,[k] when you were younger, you would tie your belt and walk wherever you wanted. But when you grow old, you will stretch out your hands and someone else will tie you and carry you where you don't want to go." [19] He said this to indicate by what kind of death[l] Peter would glorify

God.[m] After saying this, he told him, "Follow me."[n]

CORRECTING A FALSE REPORT

[20] So Peter turned around and saw the disciple Jesus loved[o] following them, the one who had leaned back against Jesus at the supper and asked, "Lord, who is the one that's going to betray you?"[p] [21] When Peter saw him, he said to Jesus, "Lord, what about him?"

[22] "If I want him to remain until I come,"[q] Jesus answered, "what is that to you? As for you, follow me."

[23] So this rumor[A] spread to the brothers and sisters[r] that this disciple would not die.[s] Yet Jesus did not tell him that he would not die, but, "If I want him to remain until I come, what is that to you?"

EPILOGUE

[24] This is the disciple who testifies to these things and who wrote them down. We know that his testimony is true.

[25] And there are also many other things that Jesus did, which, if every one of them were written down, I suppose not even the world itself could contain the books[B] that would be written.[t]

[A] 21:23 Lit *this word*   [B] 21:25 Lit *scroll*

---

friends. Previously, Peter had claimed that his love for and commitment to Jesus was superior to that of the others (the **these** to whom Jesus referred). But after his failure and denial, he wasn't willing to arrogantly say that he loved Jesus with a sacrificial love. In light of this humble response, Jesus told him, **Feed my lambs**. In other words, "Since you're not thinking so highly of yourself anymore, I can use you to lead and care for my people."

21:17 Peter could later write to other church leaders, "Shepherd God's flock among you . . . not lording it over those entrusted to you, but being examples to the flock" (1 Pet 5:2-3). Why? Because Peter had taken to heart Jesus's command, **Feed my sheep**.

21:18-19 According to tradition passed down in the early church, Peter was martyred in Rome under Emperor Nero for his faith in Jesus Christ: he was crucified upside down.

21:20-22 God has a *general will* for all of his people. This is expressed in his biblical commands for all of his followers. But he also has a *specific will* for each individual Christian. Jesus graciously revealed to Peter his will for him. But he wasn't about to tell Peter his specific will for John.

Christians are called to follow Jesus *corporately* as the church and *personally* as individuals. Each of us is to discern how he wants us to serve and glorify him. You are not to use God's specific will for you to measure anyone else, nor are you to take his specific will

for another and use it to measure your own circumstances. We are not to sit as judges regarding how God chooses to use other believers.

21:22-23 Jesus wasn't saying that John would **remain** alive until his second coming. He was simply saying, "Whatever my specific will is for John, it doesn't concern you" (21:22). Read and interpret the Bible carefully. Poor interpretation leads to erroneous conclusions!

21:25 John has only given us a highlight reel of Jesus's ministry! But God providentially determined that what we have in Scripture is enough. You don't need to know *everything* Jesus did and said. But, John says, you *do* need to "believe that Jesus is the Messiah . . . by believing you . . . have life in his name" (20:31).

ACTS

INTRODUCTION

Author

IF LUKE WAS THE AUTHOR of the Gospel that bears his name (and we have good reason for believing that; see the introduction to Luke), then he was also the author of the book of Acts. First, the two books are clearly connected and written to the same man, Theophilus (see Luke 1:1-4; Acts 1:1-3). Second, the author was one of Paul's traveling companions, because during Paul's second missionary journey, the narrative changes from third person, "they," to first person, "we" (16:10-17; see also 20:5-15; 21:1-18; 27:1-37; 28:1-16), indicating that the author had joined Paul. And we know from Paul's Letters that Luke the physician was one of Paul's companions (see Col 4:14; 2 Tim 4:11; Phlm 24). Third, beginning in the second century, early Christian writers affirm that Luke was the author of Acts.

Historical Background

Acts is the second volume of Luke's two-volume work. He refers to his Gospel as "the first narrative" that described "all that Jesus began to do and teach until the day he was taken up" (Acts 1:1-2). In Acts the narrative continues with the Holy Spirit coming to empower the disciples in proclaiming Jesus to both Jews and Gentiles.

Theophilus, to whom Luke wrote, was most likely his patron—that is, a wealthy person who funded Luke's research and writing of his two books (notice that he calls him "most honorable Theophilus" in Luke 1:3).

Acts appears to have been written before Paul was released from prison in Rome (see Acts 28:16-31). The Gospel of Luke was probably written in the late AD 50s, and Paul was released from his first Roman imprisonment about AD 60. Since the Gospel was written first (see 1:1), Acts would have been completed around that time.

Message and Purpose

Acts is unique because it links the Gospels with the Epistles by recording the birth and early history of the church, the expression of God's kingdom for this age. When the disciples asked Jesus if the kingdom was

coming at that moment, he told them it was not for them to know, but that they would see a manifestation of the kingdom's power in the work of the church through the power of the Holy Spirit (1:6-8).

The rest of Acts records what happened when the Holy Spirit's power infused the church. That makes the book critical because it is the blueprint for the church today. It reveals how the church functions when not filled with the Spirit and what happens when the Spirit fills the church so that it explodes with power and kingdom authority. We see what we are supposed to be and do today as the church of the Lord Jesus.

Acts is a kingdom book: Jesus spoke about the kingdom of God at the beginning (1:3), and Paul proclaimed the kingdom of God at the end (28:30-31). That's crucial because the whole Bible wraps around this theme of the kingdom agenda, the visible manifestation of the comprehensive rule of God over every area of life. And that rule is to be reflected in and through the church.

VIDEO   INTRO

www.bhpublishinggroup.com/qr/te/44_00

Outline

I. The Holy Spirit's Empowerment of the Church for Kingdom Witness (1:1–2:47)

II. Kingdom Witness in Jerusalem (3:1–7:60)

III. Kingdom Witness beyond Jerusalem (8:1–20:38)
- A. Kingdom Witness in Judea and Samaria and the Conversion of Paul (8:1–9:43)
- B. Peter's Kingdom Witness to the Gentiles and Escape from Prison (10:1–12:25)
- C. Paul's First Missionary Journey (13:1–14:28)
- D. The Jerusalem Council (15:1-35)
- E. Paul's Second Missionary Journey (15:36–18:21)
- F. F. Paul's Third Missionary Journey (18:22–20:38)

IV. Paul's Arrest, Trial, and Kingdom Witness in Rome (21:1–28:31)

[a] 1:1 Lk 1:3; 24:19
[b] 1:2 Mt 28:19-20; Lk 24:47; Jn 20:21
[c] 1:3 Mt 28:17; Mk 16:14; Lk 24:34,36; Jn 20:19; 1Co 15:5-7
[d] 1:4 Lk 24:49; Ac 2:33
[e] 1:5 Jl 3:18; Mt 3:11; Ac 11:16
[f] 1:7 Mt 24:36; Mk 13:32; 1Th 5:1
[g] 1:8 Lk 24:48; Ac 2:1,4; 4:33; 8:1,14; 13:47

[h] 1:10 Mt 28:13; Mk 16:5; Lk 24:4; Jn 20:12
[i] 1:11 Mt 16:27; Ac 2:7; 1Th 1:10; 2Th 1:10
[j] 1:13 Ac 9:37,39; 20:8
[k] 1:14 Mt 10:2-4; Mk 3:16-19; Lk 6:14-16
[l] 1:14 Ac 2:46; 4:24; 5:12; 15:25; Rm 15:6
[m] Mt 12:46; Lk 23:49,55; Rm 12:12; Col 4:2
[n] 1:16 Lk 22:37,47; 24:44; Jn 13:18; 18:3
[o] 1:17 Jn 6:71; Ac 20:24; 21:19
[p] 1:18 Mt 26:14-15; 27:5,7-8

PROLOGUE

1 I wrote the first narrative, Theophilus, about all that Jesus began to do and teach[a] [2] until the day he was taken up, after he had given instructions through the Holy Spirit to the apostles he had chosen.[b] [3] After he had suffered, he also presented himself alive to them by many convincing proofs, appearing to them over a period of forty days and speaking about the kingdom of God.[c]

THE HOLY SPIRIT PROMISED

[4] While he was[A] with them, he commanded them not to leave Jerusalem, but to wait for the Father's promise.[d] "Which," he said, "you have heard me speak about; [5] for John baptized with water, but you will be baptized with the Holy Spirit in a few days."[e]

[6] So when they had come together, they asked him, "Lord, are you restoring the kingdom to Israel at this time?"

[7] He said to them, "It is not for you to know times or periods that the Father has set by his own authority.[f] [8] But you will receive power when the Holy Spirit has come on you, and you will be my witnesses in Jerusalem, in all Judea and Samaria, and to the end of the earth."[g]

⟍ HOPE WORDS ⟋

The quickest way for God to get you where he wants you is for him to be able to use you where he has you.

THE ASCENSION

[9] After he had said this, he was taken up as they were watching, and a cloud took him out of their sight. [10] While he was going, they were gazing into heaven, and suddenly two men in white clothes stood by them.[h] [11] They said, "Men of Galilee, why do you stand looking up into heaven? This same Jesus, who has been taken from you into heaven, will come in the same way that you have seen him going into heaven."[i]

UNITED IN PRAYER

[12] Then they returned to Jerusalem from the Mount of Olives, which is near Jerusalem — a Sabbath day's journey away. [13] When they arrived, they went to the room[j] upstairs where they were staying: Peter, John, James, Andrew, Philip, Thomas, Bartholomew, Matthew, James the son of Alphaeus, Simon the Zealot, and Judas the son of James.[k] [14] They all were continually united[l] in prayer,[B] along with the women, including Mary the mother of Jesus, and his brothers.[m]

MATTHIAS CHOSEN

[15] In those days Peter stood up among the brothers and sisters[c] — the number of people who were together was about a hundred and twenty — and said: [16] "Brothers and sisters, it was necessary that the Scripture be fulfilled that the Holy Spirit through the mouth of David foretold about Judas, who became a guide to those who arrested Jesus.[n] [17] For he was one of our number and shared in this ministry."[o] [18] Now this man acquired a field with his unrighteous wages. He fell headfirst, his body burst open and his intestines spilled out.[p] [19] This became known to all the residents of Jerusalem, so that in their own language that field is called *Hakeldama* (that is, Field of

---

[A] 1:4 Or *he was eating*, or *he was lodging*   [B] 1:14 Other mss add *and petition*   [C] 1:15 Other mss read *disciples*

1:1 The first narrative is the Gospel of Luke. **Theophilus** was probably the patron who funded Luke's work.
1:3 The disciples didn't have a corporate delusion. Nor did they see a ghost. Jesus showed them **by many convincing proofs** that he was the same flesh-and-blood man they'd seen crucified and buried—though he'd since gained a glorified body (see Luke 24:36-43).
   What did Jesus talk to his disciples about for **forty days** between his resurrection and his ascension? **The kingdom of God**. God's kingdom agenda is the unifying theme of Scripture. We may take it as the visible manifestation of the comprehensive rule of God in every area of life. Thus, the church exists to serve King Jesus and his kingdom.

1:5 Just as new Christians are immersed in the waters of baptism, Jesus's disciples are also immersed in **the Holy Spirit** so that they have power to obey their King and proclaim his kingdom.
1:6-8 The disciples wanted to know whether it was finally time for **Israel** to be delivered from the yoke of Rome. Though it was not yet time for Christ's millennial kingdom, in which he will rule over the entire earth from Jerusalem on David's throne (1:7), it *was* nearly time for the power of the kingdom to arrive in **the Holy Spirit**. Empowered by the Spirit, the disciples would go as Jesus's **witnesses** to proclaim him and make kingdom disciples **in Jerusalem**. From there the gospel would expand to **all Judea and Samaria** and then **to the end of the earth** (1:8). This is what we see

in the book of Acts, and this kingdom work continues today, as the church proclaims King Jesus in the power of the Holy Spirit.
1:14 Prayer is our link to heaven. The Holy Spirit uses it to deliver our requests to heaven and to bring heaven's deliverance to earth. The disciples' unity in prayer was critical for experiencing God's divine intervention.
1:16-19 Matthew's Gospel sheds further light on Judas's end. Realizing that he had sinned by betraying Jesus—but unwilling to repent—Judas threw the money he'd received from the chief priests into the temple and hanged himself. But refusing to take back the blood money, the chief priests used it to buy the field in which Judas committed suicide (see Matt 27:3-10). There, Judas's decaying body eventually **fell** and **burst open**

Questions & Answers

Q What are some ways you have seen God move in response to collective prayer—prayer offered in community with other brothers and sisters in Christ?

A I can think of a number of examples of how God provided for us through collective prayer. Once we thought our church would have to leave the school building where we were meeting, so our congregation started to pray. When the time came for the people making the decision to vote, some of those who wanted to vote against our church were delayed in traffic. As a result, they missed the opportunity to vote, and we were allowed to stay.

On a later occasion, we did have to leave the school and had nowhere to go. Once again, we prayed. Then God supernaturally brought a person—whom I had never met and whom I had not asked for help—to provide the resources for our first church building.

Later, we were able to acquire twenty acres of land for the Tony Evans Training Center because through a series of events—and through our prayers asking God to show us what our next step would be to provide biblical, kingdom-based training—God made financial provision.

I know what it is like when God's people pray and he answers.

FOR THE NEXT Q&A, SEE PAGE 1273.

Blood). **20** "For it is written in the Book of Psalms:

> Let his dwelling become
>   desolate;
> let no one live in it;ᴬ and
> Let someone else take
>   his position.ᴮ,ᵃ

21 "Therefore, from among the men who have accompanied us during the whole time the Lord Jesus went in and out among us — **22** beginning from the baptism of John until the day he was taken up from us — from among these, it is necessary that one become a witness with us of his resurrection."ᵇ

23 So they proposed two: Joseph, called Barsabbas, who was also known as Justus, and Matthias.ᶜ **24** Then they prayed,ᵈ "You, Lord, know everyone's hearts;ᵉ show which of these two you have chosenᵉ **25** to take the placeᶜ in this apostolic ministryᶠ that Judas left to go where he belongs." **26** Then they cast lotsᵍ for them, and the lot fell to Matthias and he was added to the eleven apostles.

PENTECOST

2 When the day of Pentecost had arrived, they were all together in one place.ʰ **2** Suddenly a sound like that of a violent rushing windⁱ came from heaven, and it filled the whole house where they were staying.ʲ **3** They saw tongues like flames of fire that separated and rested on each one of them. **4** Then they were all filledᵏ with the Holy Spirit and began to speak in different tongues,ᴰ as the Spirit enabled them.ˡ

5 Now there were Jews staying in Jerusalem, devout people from every nationᵐ under heaven. **6** When this sound occurred, a crowd came together and was confused because each one heard them speaking in his own language. **7** They were astounded and amazed, saying,ᴱ "Look, aren't all these who are speaking Galileans?ⁿ **8** How is it that each of us can hear them in our own native language? **9** Parthians, Medes, Elamites; those who live in Mesopotamia, in Judea and Cappadocia, Pontus and Asia,ᵒ **10** Phrygia and Pamphylia, Egypt and the parts of Libya near Cyrene; visitors from Rome (both Jews and converts),ᵖ **11** Cretans and Arabs — we hear them declaring the magnificent acts of God in our own tongues." **12** They were all astounded and

(Acts 1:18). Therefore, they named the place **Field of Blood** (1:19; see Matt 27:8).
1:20 If those who betrayed King David, the psalmist behind the quoted passages, should have been judged and replaced, how much more should the one who betrayed the Son of David experience judgment and be replaced?
1:24-26 Casting lots is a practice analogous to throwing dice. According to Proverbs,

"The lot is cast into the lap, but its every decision is from the Lord" (Prov 16:33). Interestingly, though, after the coming of the Holy Spirit in Acts 2, the apostles never again made a decision by this method. Instead, they depended on the Holy Spirit through prayer.
2:1 The day of Pentecost marks the time of the wheat harvest and commemorates the giving of the law on Mount Sinai. Many Jews

would travel to Jerusalem for Pentecost or else stay there after Passover to await it.
2:4-6 The **tongues** (2:4) in which the apostles were miraculously enabled to speak were the various native languages (2:6, 8) of the visitors to Jerusalem (not some unintelligible heavenly language). This was the fulfillment of Jesus's promise that they would receive power from the Holy Spirit to be his witnesses to the world (1:8).

a 2:13 Ac 17:32; 1Co 14:23
b 2:17 Is 44:3; Jn 7:38; Ac 10:45; 21:9
c 2:18 Ac 21:10; 1Co 12:10
d 2:20 Mt 24:29; 1Th 5:2
e Is 58:13; Ezk 13:5; Am 5:18; Ob 15; Zph 1:14; Zch 14:1; Mal 4:5
f 2:17-21 Jl 2:28-32; Ac 16:31; Rm 10:13
g 2:22 Jn 3:2; 4:48; Ac 10:38; Heb 2:4
h 2:23 Mt 26:24; Lk 22:22; 24:20; Ac 3:18; 4:28; 5:30
i 2:24 Rm 8:11; 1Co 6:14; 2Co 4:14; Eph 1:20; Col 2:12; 1Th 1:10; Heb 13:20
j 2:27 Mt 11:23; Lk 2:26; Ac 13:35; Heb 7:26
k 2:25-28 Ps 16:8-11
k 2:29 1Kg 2:10; Neh 3:16; Ac 7:8-9; 13:36
m 2:30 2Sm 23:2; Ps 132:11; Mt 22:43; Lk 1:32; Ac 1:8; Heb 11:32
n 2:31 Ps 16:10; Ac 2:27
o 2:32 Lk 18:33; Ac 2:24
p 2:33 Php 2:9; Heb 10:12
q Jn 7:39; 14:26; 16:7,13
r Ac 2:17; 10:45
s 2:34-35 Ps 110:1; Mt 5:35; 22:44; Mk 12:36; Lk 20:42-43; Jn 3:13; 1Co 15:25; Heb 1:13

perplexed, saying to one another, "What does this mean?" [13] But some sneered and said, "They're drunk on new wine."[a]

PETER'S SERMON

[14] Peter stood up with the Eleven, raised his voice, and proclaimed to them: "Fellow Jews and all you residents of Jerusalem, let me explain this to you and pay attention to my words. [15] For these people are not drunk, as you suppose, since it's only nine in the morning.[A] [16] On the contrary, this is what was spoken through the prophet Joel:

[17] And it will be in the last days,
    says God,
that I will pour out my Spirit
    on all people;
then your sons and your daughters
    will prophesy,
your young men will see visions,
and your old men will
    dream dreams.[b]
[18] I will even pour out my Spirit
    on my servants in those days, both
        men and women
    and they will prophesy.[c]
[19] I will display wonders
    in the heaven above
    and signs on the earth below:
    blood and fire and a cloud of smoke.
[20] The sun will be turned to darkness
    and the moon to blood[d]
    before the great and glorious day
        of the Lord[e] comes.
[21] Then everyone who calls
    on the name of the Lord
    will be saved.[B,f]

[22] "Fellow Israelites, listen to these words: This Jesus of Nazareth was a man attested to you by God with miracles, wonders, and signs that God did among you through him, just as you yourselves know.[g] [23] Though he was delivered up according to God's determined plan and foreknowledge, you used[c] lawless people to nail him to a cross and kill him." [24] God raised him up, ending the pains of death,[i] because it was not possible for him to be held by death. [25] For David says of him:

I saw the Lord ever before me;
because he is at my right hand,
I will not be shaken.
[26]   Therefore my heart is glad
    and my tongue rejoices.
    Moreover, my flesh will rest
        in hope,
[27]   because you will not abandon me
        in Hades
    or allow your holy one
        to see decay.[j]
[28]   You have revealed the paths of life
        to me;
    you will fill me with gladness
        in your presence.[D,k]

[29] "Brothers and sisters, I can confidently speak to you about the patriarch David: He is both dead and buried, and his tomb is with us to this day.[l] [30] Since he was a prophet, he knew that God had sworn an oath to him to seat one of his descendants[E] on his throne.[m] [31] Seeing what was to come, he spoke concerning the resurrection of the Messiah: **He**[F] **was not abandoned in Hades, and** his flesh **did not experience decay.**[G,n] [32] "God has raised[o] this Jesus; we are all witnesses of this. [33] Therefore, since he has been exalted to the right hand of God[p] and has received from the Father the promised Holy Spirit,[q] he has poured out[r] what you both see and hear. [34] For it was not David who ascended into the heavens, but he himself says:

The Lord declared to my Lord,
'Sit at my right hand
[35]   until I make your enemies
        your footstool.'[H,s]

[A] 2:15 Lit *it's the third hour of the day*   [B] 2:17-21 Jl 2:28-32   [C] 2:23 Other mss read *you have taken*   [D] 2:25-28 Ps 16:8-11   [E] 2:30 Other mss add *according to the flesh to raise up the Messiah*   [F] 2:31 Other mss read *His soul*   [G] 2:31 Ps 16:10   [H] 2:34-35 Ps 110:1

2:16-18 What the people were witnessing was actually the fulfillment of Old Testament prophecy. Peter quoted **the prophet Joel** (2:16), who foretold the day when God would **pour out [his] Spirit on [his] servants** without distinction when repentance occurred (2:17-18; see Joel 2:28-32).
2:22-23 Jesus was not unknown to the Jews listening to Peter. They had witnessed his **miracles** (2:22) yet **used lawless people to . . . kill him** (2:23). Though God had a sovereign plan to sacrifice his Son for sinners, that did not absolve these free moral agents of their actions. Some of those listening to Peter had

joined with the mob on that day, crying out, "Crucify him!" (see Luke 23:13-25).
2:24-31 Death could not hold Jesus (2:24). To explain, Peter quoted **David** from Psalm 16:8-11; he spoke of **the Lord** not abandoning him to the grave or allowing his **holy one to see decay** (Acts 2:25, 27). David, though, wasn't speaking about himself. He was speaking about Jesus (2:25). Peter could say **confidently** that **David** was **dead and buried** (2:29). David, then, had been talking about someone else— one of his own **descendants** whom **God had sworn . . . to seat** on David's **throne** (2:30; see Ps 110:1). That descendant was none other

than **the Messiah**, who was raised so that **his flesh did not experience decay** (Acts 2:31).
2:32 Peter said, **We are all witnesses of this**. The frightened disciples (see John 20:19) had been transformed by the Holy Spirit to risk their lives by boldly and publicly proclaiming the resurrection. What explains their transformation and willingness to face persecution and death? The only sane answer is that they were truly witnesses to the resurrected Jesus.
2:34-35 Many years prior, David overheard God the Father telling the Messiah, **Sit at my right hand until I make your enemies your footstool.** (See the note on Ps 110:1.)

[a] 2:36 Mt 28:18; Lk 2:11; Rm 14:9; 2Co 4:5

[b] 2:37 Lk 3:10; Ac 16:30
[c] 2:38 Lk 24:47; Ac 3:19; 26:20
[d] Ac 8:12; 22:16
[e] Ac 3:16; 15:14
[f] 2:39 Is 44:3; Ac 3:25; Eph 2:13
[g] 2:40 Dt 32:5; Mt 17:17; Php 2:15
[h] 2:42 Ac 5:28; 13:12; 17:19; 1Co 14:6
[i] Ac 1:14; Heb 10:25
[j] 2:43 Mk 16:17,20; Ac 5:12
[k] 2:44 Mt 19:21; Ac 4:32
[l] 2:46 Lk 24:53; Ac 5:42; 20:7
[m] 2:47 Ac 5:14; 11:24; 16:5; Rm 14:18
[n] 3:1 Ps 55:17; Mt 27:46; Ac 10:3,30

Questions & Answers

Q The growth and discipleship of the early church presented in Acts 2:42-47 is framed by the four vital experiences of worship, fellowship, education, and outreach. How do these experiences shape your approach to kingdom growth and discipleship in your own life and ministry?

A I do believe that Acts 2 shows us the four critical experiences of the first New Testament church, experiences that should be integral to every church if it wants to have a well-rounded ministry in the personal development of its members. The first vital experience of the church was worship, the recognition of God for who he is, what he has done, and what we are trusting him to do. God inhabits the worship of his people. Second, the church experienced fellowship, which describes believers' connection with one another, their mutual sharing of the life of Christ with each other. Next, there was education. These early Christians grew in the knowledge of the Word and the apostles' doctrine. You can't grow beyond what you know. Finally, the church engaged in outreach. They were meeting peoples' needs, and God was adding to the church daily. When those four components are engrafted into the life of the church and, therefore, engrafted into the individual lives of its members, their spiritual development will be well balanced, and growth will occur.

FOR THE NEXT Q&A, SEE PAGE 1281.

36 "Therefore let all the house of Israel know with certainty that God has made this Jesus, whom you crucified, both Lord and Messiah."[a]

CALL TO REPENTANCE

37 When they heard this, they were pierced to the heart and said to Peter and the rest of the apostles: "Brothers, what should we do?"[b]

38 Peter replied, "Repent[c] and be baptized,[d] each of you, in the name[e] of Jesus Christ for the forgiveness of your sins, and you will receive the gift of the Holy Spirit. **39** For the promise is for you and for your children, and for all who are far off,[f] as many as the Lord our God will call." **40** With many other words he testified and strongly urged them, saying, "Be saved from this corrupt[A] generation!"[g] **41** So those who accepted his message were baptized, and that day about three thousand people were added to them.

A GENEROUS AND GROWING CHURCH

42 They devoted themselves to the apostles' teaching,[h] to the fellowship, to the breaking of bread, and to prayer.[i] **43** Everyone was filled with awe, and many wonders and signs were being performed through the apostles.[j] **44** Now all the believers were together and held all things in common.[k] **45** They sold their possessions and property and distributed the proceeds to all, as any had need. **46** Every day they devoted themselves to meeting together in the temple, and broke bread from house to house. They ate their food with joyful and sincere hearts,[l] **47** praising God and enjoying the favor of all the people. Every day the Lord added to their number[B] those who were being saved.[m]

HEALING OF A LAME MAN

3 Now Peter and John were going up to the temple for the time of prayer[n] at three in the afternoon.[c] **2** A man who was lame from birth was being carried there.

[A] 2:40 Or *crooked*, or *twisted*   [B] 2:47 Other mss read *to the church*   [C] 3:1 Lit *at the ninth hour*

2:38 The New Testament is clear that we are saved by grace through faith in Jesus Christ apart from works (see Eph 2:8-9; Rom 4:4-5). But repentance and baptism are to accompany faith. To repent is to turn from sin to God. To be baptized in the name of Jesus is to obediently go public with a profession of faith in him.

Since the goal of repentance is to reduce or remove the consequences of sin, Peter was calling on the Jews who had witnessed and endorsed the crucifixion of Jesus (in identification with their Jewish leaders), to publicly renounce their actions via baptism.

2:41 With **three thousand** conversions to faith in Christ, the church was off to an amazing start.

2:42-47 The early church was known for four activities that should be foundational to every kingdom-minded local church. First, they had devotion to **the apostles' teaching**. Thus, believers learned God's perspective (based on his inerrant Word) on every matter so that they could obey him, experience spiritual growth, and make kingdom impact. Second, they devoted themselves to **fellowship**—mutually sharing the life of Christ within the family of God. A disconnected Christian is a disobedient and unfruitful Christian. Third, the church regularly prioritized worship, reflected in **the breaking of bread** (i.e., the Lord's Supper) and **prayer** (2:42). Fourth, they were engaged in evan-

gelistic outreach because **every day the Lord added to their number those who were being saved** (2:47). Everyone was involved in evangelism; they weren't merely letting the apostles take care of it.

3:2-7 The forty-year-old **lame** man (see 4:22) was hopeless, helpless, and dependent. He could not stand on his own two feet. He asked for what he *wanted* (**money**; 3:3); he was about to receive what he *needed* (healing; 3:6-7). Notice that after pronouncing the man's healing, Peter took the initiative and **raised him up** (3:7). The church must *both* speak hope into a broken life *and* extend practical help.

When God meets your needs, he may not give you what you asked for, but what he

*a*3:2 Lk 16:20; Jn 9:8; Ac 14:8
*b*3:6 Ac 4:10; 2Co 6:10
*c*3:8 Is 35:4-6; Ac 14:10
*d*3:10 Jn 9:8; Ac 3:2
*e*3:11 Lk 22:8; Jn 10:23; Ac 5:12
*f*3:13 Ac 5:30; 7:32; 22:14
*g*Mt 27:2; Lk 23:4; Jn 19:15; Ac 13:28
*h*3:14 Mk 1:24; Ac 4:27; 7:52
*i*Mk 15:11; Lk 23:18,25

*j*3:15 Ac 2:24; 5:31
*k*3:17 Lk 23:34; Ac 13:27
*l*3:18 Lk 24:27; Ac 2:23; 17:3; 26:23
*m*3:19 Ac 2:38; 8:22; 17:30; 26:20
*n*Ps 51:1,9; Is 43:25; 44:22; Col 2:14
*o*3:20 Ac 22:14; 26:16
*p*3:21 Mt 17:10; Lk 1:70; Ac 1:11
*q*3:22-23 Dt 18:15-19; Ac 7:37
*r*3:25 Gn 22:18; Ac 2:39; Rm 9:4
*s*3:26 Ac 2:24; 13:46; Rm 1:16

He was placed each day at the temple gate called Beautiful, so that he could beg from those entering the temple.*a* **3** When he saw Peter and John about to enter the temple, he asked for money. **4** Peter, along with John, looked straight at him and said, "Look at us." **5** So he turned to them, expecting to get something from them. **6** But Peter said, "I don't have silver or gold, but what I do have, I give you: In the name of Jesus Christ of Nazareth, get up and walk!"*b* **7** Then, taking him by the right hand he raised him up, and at once his feet and ankles became strong. **8** So he jumped up and started to walk, and he entered the temple with them — walking, leaping, and praising God.*c* **9** All the people saw him walking and praising God, **10** and they recognized that he was the one who used to sit and beg at the Beautiful Gate of the temple. So they were filled with awe and astonishment at what had happened to him.*d*

PREACHING IN SOLOMON'S COLONNADE

11 While he*A* was holding on to Peter and John, all the people, utterly astonished, ran toward them in what is called Solomon's Colonnade.*e* **12** When Peter saw this, he addressed the people: "Fellow Israelites, why are you amazed at this? Why do you stare at us, as though we had made him walk by our own power or godliness? **13** The God of Abraham, Isaac, and Jacob, the God of our ancestors,*f* has glorified his servant Jesus, whom you handed over and denied before Pilate,*g* though he had decided to release him. **14** You denied the Holy and Righteous One*h* and asked to have a murderer released to you.*i* **15** You killed the source*B* of life, whom God raised from the dead;

we are witnesses of this.*j* **16** By faith in his name, his name has made this man strong, whom you see and know. So the faith that comes through Jesus has given him this perfect health in front of all of you.

17 "And now, brothers and sisters, I know that you acted in ignorance, just as your leaders also did.*k* **18** In this way God fulfilled what he had predicted through all the prophets — that his Messiah would suffer.*l* **19** Therefore repent*m* and turn back, so that your sins may be wiped out,*n* **20** that seasons of refreshing may come from the presence of the Lord, and that he may send Jesus, who has been appointed*o* for you as the Messiah. **21** Heaven must receive him until the time of the restoration of all things, which God spoke about through his holy prophets from the beginning.*p* **22** Moses said:*c* **The Lord your God will raise up for you a prophet like me from among your brothers and sisters. You must listen to everything he tells you. 23 And everyone who does not listen to that prophet will be completely cut off from the people.**D,q*

24 "In addition, all the prophets who have spoken, from Samuel and those after him, have also foretold these days. **25** You are the sons*E* of the prophets and of the covenant that God made with your ancestors, saying to Abraham, **And all the families of the earth will be blessed through your offspring.***F,r* **26** God raised up his servant*G* and sent him first to you to bless you by turning each of you from your evil ways."*s*

PETER AND JOHN ARRESTED

4 While they were speaking to the people, the priests, the captain of the temple police, and the Sadducees confronted

*A*3:11 Other mss read *the lame man who was healed*   *B*3:15 Or *the Prince*, or *the Ruler*   *C*3:22 Other mss add *to the fathers*   *D*3:22-23 Dt 18:15-19
*E*3:25 = heirs   *F*3:25 Gn 12:3; 18:18; 22:18; 26:4   *G*3:26 Other mss add *Jesus*

provides will always be greater than what you want. Peter and John invited him to look deeper than his mere external circumstances. His expectations were too small. It would be the spiritual focus that would transform his circumstances. This story shows why we need spiritual people in our lives who help get us to God. It was in accepting spiritual help that his external need was addressed. Also note that regularly hanging out in the vicinity of the temple gate never changed the man. Only an encounter with the authority (i.e., **name**; 3:6) of the risen Christ would do that. This is also true for us today.
3:9-10 Your response to God's work in your life should be visible and vocal. And it should lead you to greater public praise and worship. The man went from limping to leaping. His

transformation ultimately led to the salvation of many souls (see 4:4). When God does something amazing in an individual's life, he usually has a greater purpose in mind than that individual's benefit. He wants to do something even more amazing *through* that individual.
3:16 It was through **faith in [the] name** of the resurrected Lord Jesus that this lame man had been made well. Peter exercised faith when he told the man to walk, and the lame man exercised faith when he responded to the spiritual help that enabled him to get up.
3:17-18 Though they were still accountable for their sin, they hadn't truly realized that they had been dealing with the **Messiah** whom **the prophets** had **predicted . . . would suffer** (3:18).

3:20 That God would **send Jesus** is a reference to the coming millennial reign of **the Messiah**.
3:21 **The time of the restoration of all things** refers to the time when Israel will repent and receive the Messiah as predicted by the **prophets** (see Rom 11:25-27). The coming of the earthly messianic kingdom is directly connected to the repentance of the Jewish nation (see Zech 12:10; Matt 23:39).
4:1-4 Jesus told his disciples, "If they persecuted me, they will also persecute you" (John 15:20). That persecution was about to begin. They seized Peter and John and threw them in jail **until the next day since** the Jewish council, the Sanhedrin, didn't meet at night (Acts 4:3). Nevertheless, beginning with the healing of one lame man (3:1-10), God brought **about five thousand** men to Christ

them,[a] [2] because they were annoyed that they were teaching the people and proclaiming in Jesus the resurrection of the dead.[b] [3] So they seized them and took them into custody until the next day since it was already evening. [4] But many of those who heard the message believed, and the number of the men[A] came to about five thousand.

PETER AND JOHN FACE THE JEWISH LEADERSHIP

[5] The next day, their rulers, elders, and scribes assembled in Jerusalem [6] with Annas the high priest, Caiaphas, John, Alexander, and all the members of the high-priestly family.[c] [7] After they had Peter and John stand before them, they began to question them: "By what power or in what name have you done this?"

[8] Then Peter was filled with the Holy Spirit and said to them, "Rulers of the people and elders:[B,d] [9] If we are being examined today about a good deed done to a disabled man, by what means he was healed, [10] let it be known to all of you and to all the people of Israel, that by the name of Jesus Christ of Nazareth, whom you crucified and whom God raised from the dead — by him this man is standing here before you healthy.[e] [11] This Jesus is

> the stone rejected by you
>   builders,
> which has become
>   the cornerstone.[c,f]

[12] There is salvation in no one else, for there is no other name under heaven given to people by which we must be saved."[g]

THE BOLDNESS OF THE DISCIPLES

[13] When they observed the boldness of Peter and John and realized that they were uneducated and untrained men, they were amazed and recognized that they had been with Jesus.[h] [14] And since they saw the man who had been healed standing with them, they had nothing to say in opposition. [15] After they ordered them to leave the Sanhedrin, they conferred among themselves, [16] saying, "What should we do with these men? For an obvious sign has been done through them, clear to everyone living in Jerusalem, and we cannot deny it.[i] [17] But so that this does not spread any further among the people, let's threaten them against speaking to anyone in this name again." [18] So they called for them and ordered them not to speak or teach at all in the name of Jesus.

[19] Peter and John answered them, "Whether it's right in the sight of God for us to listen to you rather than to God, you decide;[j] [20] for we are unable to stop speaking about what we have seen and heard."[k]

[21] After threatening them further, they released them. They found no way to punish them because the people were all giving glory to God over what had been done.[l] [22] For this sign of healing had been performed on a man over forty years old.

PRAYER FOR BOLDNESS

[23] After they were released, they went to their own people and reported everything the chief priests and the elders had said to them. [24] When they heard this, they raised their voices together to God and said, "Master, you are the one who made the heaven, the earth, and the sea, and everything in them.[m] [25] You said through the Holy Spirit, by the mouth of our father David your servant:[D]

> Why do the Gentiles rage
>   and the peoples plot futile things?
> [26]   The kings of the earth
>   take their stand

[a] 4:1 Mt 3:7; Lk 22:4; Ac 5:24
[b] 4:2 Ac 3:15; 17:18
[c] 4:6 Mt 26:3; Lk 3:2; Jn 18:13
[d] 4:8 Lk 23:13; Ac 4:5
[e] 4:10 Ac 2:24; 3:6
[f] 4:11 1Pt 2:7
[g] 4:12 Mt 1:21; Ac 10:43; 1Tm 2:5
[h] 4:13 Mt 11:25; Lk 22:8; Jn 7:15
4:16 Jn 11:47; Ac 3:9-10
[i] 4:19 Ac 4:13; 5:28
[k] 4:20 Ac 22:15; 1Co 9:16; 1Jn 1:1,3
[l] 4:21 Mt 9:8; 21:26; Lk 20:6,19; 22:2; Ac 5:26
[m] 4:24 Ex 20:11; 2Ch 2:12; Neh 9:6; Ps 102:25; 124:8; 134:3; 146:6; Is 37:16

[A] 4:4 Or *people*   [B] 4:8 Other mss add *of Israel*   [C] 4:11 Ps 118:22   [D] 4:25 Other mss read *through the mouth of David your servant*

(4:4). There's no stopping the kingdom of God manifested through the power of the Holy Spirit when Jesus is being glorified.

4:7-8 In essence they demanded of **Peter and John**, "Who authorized you to say and do these things?" But unless they truly wanted to hear the answer, they shouldn't have asked the question. When previously asked about Jesus, **Peter** said, "I don't know him" (Luke 22:57). Giving himself over to the influence of the Spirit's power, however, would enable him (as it does for us) to confidently bear witness to Christ.

4:10-11 Jesus is the fulfillment of Psalm 118:22; he is **the stone** that the Jewish leaders had **rejected**, which became **the cornerstone**, the stone upon which the rest of the build-

ing depends (Acts 4:11). The only way to avoid the implications of what they had done was to repent and turn to the risen Lord Jesus, the one whom they had **crucified** (4:10).

4:12 The **name** *Jesus* is the Greek version of the Hebrew name *Joshua*, which means, "The Lord saves." Jesus's name, then, speaks to who he is, what he has done, and what he can do. **Salvation** from sin, death, and hell is found in him alone.

4:13 That **they were uneducated** means that they had received no formal rabbinical training, the ancient equivalent of seminary. But they **had been with Jesus**. *That's* where they got their training. Over the course of three years, the Son of God had taught the former fishermen everything they knew.

You can receive extensive, formal, theological education and have degrees after your name. But if you've never "been with Jesus" in a spiritual relationship and enrolled in his school of discipleship, you'll make no lasting spiritual impact on others.

4:15-18 The Jewish religious leaders didn't care about truth; they cared only about preserving their own religious authority.

4:19-20 Christians are to "submit to the governing authorities" (Rom 13:1) and "to every human authority" (1 Pet 2:13). We are to be model citizens. But when the commands of the government conflict with the clearly revealed commands of God, our allegiance must be to the King of creation.

[a]4:25-26 Ps 2:1-2; Dn 9:24-25; Lk 4:18; Ac 1:16; 10:38; Heb 1:9
[b]4:27 Mt 14:1; 27:2; Lk 23:1,12
[c]4:29 Ac 9:27; 13:46; 14:3; 19:8; Php 1:14
[d]4:30 Jn 4:48; Ac 3:6
[e]4:31 Ac 2:2,4; 16:26; Php 1:14
[f]4:32 Ac 2:44; Php 1:27
[g]4:33 Lk 24:48; Ac 1:8,22

[h]4:34 Mt 19:21; Ac 2:45
[i]4:35 Ac 2:45; 4:37; 5:2; 6:1
[j]4:36 Ac 9:27; 1Co 9:6
[k]4:37 Ac 4:35; 5:2
[l]5:2 Ac 4:37; 5:3
[m]5:3 Mt 4:10; Lk 22:3; Jn 13:2,27
[n]5:5 Ezk 11:13; Ac 5:10-11
[o]5:6 Ezk 29:5; Jn 19:40; Ac 8:2
[p]5:9 Ac 5:3-4; 15:10; 1Co 10:9

and the rulers assemble together against the Lord and against his Messiah.[A,a]

[27] "For, in fact, in this city both Herod and Pontius Pilate, with the Gentiles and the people of Israel, assembled together against your holy servant Jesus, whom you anointed,[b] [28] to do whatever your hand and your will had predestined to take place. [29] And now, Lord, consider their threats, and grant that your servants may speak your word with all boldness,[c] [30] while you stretch out your hand for healing, and signs and wonders[d] are performed through the name of your holy servant Jesus." [31] When they had prayed, the place where they were assembled was shaken, and they were all filled with the Holy Spirit and began to speak the word of God boldly.[e]

APPLICATION QUESTIONS

READ ACTS 4:24-31

– What were the results when the entire congregation joined together in prayer?

ALL THINGS IN COMMON

[32] Now the entire group of those who believed were of one heart and mind, and no one claimed that any of his possessions was his own, but instead they held everything in common.[f] [33] With great power the apostles were giving testimony to the resurrection of the Lord Jesus, and great grace was on all of them.[g] [34] For there was not a needy person among them because all those who owned lands or houses sold them, brought the proceeds of what was

sold,[h] [35] and laid them at the apostles' feet. This was then distributed to each person as any had need.[i]

[36] Joseph, a Levite from Cyprus by birth, the one the apostles called Barnabas (which is translated Son of Encouragement),[j] [37] sold a field he owned, brought the money, and laid it at the apostles' feet.[k]

LYING TO THE HOLY SPIRIT

5 But a man named Ananias, with his wife Sapphira, sold a piece of property. [2] However, he kept back part of the proceeds with his wife's knowledge, and brought a portion of it and laid it at the apostles' feet.[l]

[3] "Ananias," Peter asked, "why has Satan filled your heart[m] to lie to the Holy Spirit and keep back part of the proceeds of the land? [4] Wasn't it yours while you possessed it? And after it was sold, wasn't it at your disposal? Why is it that you planned this thing in your heart? You have not lied to people but to God." [5] When he heard these words, Ananias dropped dead, and a great fear came on all who heard.[n] [6] The young men got up, wrapped his body, carried him out, and buried him.[o]

[7] About three hours later, his wife came in, not knowing what had happened. [8] "Tell me," Peter asked her, "did you sell the land for this price?"

"Yes," she said, "for that price."

[9] Then Peter said to her, "Why did you agree to test the Spirit of the Lord? Look, the feet of those who have buried your husband are at the door, and they will carry you out."[p]

[10] Instantly she dropped dead at his feet. When the young men came in, they found

---

[A]4:25-26 Ps 2:1-2

4:27-28 Wicked rulers did exactly what they wanted to do. Nevertheless, God used their actions to accomplish his holy purposes. God can take humanity's worst and accomplish his best. Through the killing of Jesus at the hands of sinners, God was providing a way to save sinners.

4:29 The disciples didn't want threats to shut them up; rather, they wanted even more confidence to speak about Jesus. Persecution—whatever form it takes—should move us similarly.

4:31 They had already received the Holy Spirit (2:1-4), but a Christian who is indwelt by the Spirit can be powerfully **filled with** (i.e., under the control of) the Spirit for bold proclamation. This is the kind of boldness the church needs, and it's the kind of boldness that God makes available to you.

4:32 They **were of one heart and mind**. Unity among the people of God is critical

for the revealing of the visible manifestation of his glory (see 2 Chr 5:1-14). It's what Jesus prayed for (see John 17:20-23), and it's what these first believers demonstrated. When there is disunity, the Spirit does not work.

No one claimed that any of his possessions was his own means they were generous and met one another's needs voluntarily.

4:36-37 Barnabas demonstrated the appropriateness of his name—which means **Son of Encouragement**—by selling **a field he owned** and giving **the money** to the apostles. His generosity makes the selfishness of the couple described in chapter 5 all the more glaring.

5:1-2 When Ananias **laid** the money from his property's sale **at the apostles' feet**, he gave the impression that he was giving it all (5:2).

5:3 Peter's words tell us that believers can allow **Satan** to manipulate them.

5:4 Ananias owned the land, and he hadn't been forced to sell it. Even when he did, he wasn't required to give the church the money. His sin was that he made a *commitment* to give all of the proceeds to meet the needs of others (like Barnabas did) and then deceptively kept back some for himself—to the detriment of those in need. Thus, he **lied . . . to God** by not providing for his brothers and sisters as he'd claimed he would. A lie that damages the family of God incurs greater judgment (see 1 Cor 3:17).

5:7-10 Sapphira condemned herself by following her husband into sin and telling the same lie (5:7-8). Though a husband is to love his wife sacrificially and a wife is to submit to the leadership of her husband, neither is to follow the other into sin. Our relationship with and commitment to God must always be primary.

her dead, carried her out, and buried her beside her husband. **11** Then great fear came on the whole church and on all who heard these things.

APOSTOLIC SIGNS AND WONDERS

12 Many signs and wonders were being done among the people through the hands of the apostles.[a] They were all together in Solomon's Colonnade.[b] **13** No one else dared to join them, but the people spoke well of them.[c] **14** Believers were added to the Lord in increasing numbers — multitudes of both men and women. **15** As a result, they would carry the sick out into the streets and lay them on cots and mats so that when Peter came by, at least his shadow[d] might fall on some of them. **16** In addition, a multitude came together from the towns surrounding Jerusalem, bringing the sick and those who were tormented by unclean spirits, and they were all healed.

IN AND OUT OF PRISON

17 Then the high priest rose up. He and all who were with him, who belonged to the party of the Sadducees, were filled with jealousy.[e] **18** So they arrested the apostles and put them in the public jail.[f] **19** But an angel of the Lord opened the doors of the jail during the night, brought them out, and said,[g] **20** "Go and stand in the temple, and tell the people all about this life."[h] **21** Hearing this, they entered the temple at daybreak and began to teach.

THE APOSTLES ON TRIAL AGAIN

When the high priest and those who were with him arrived, they convened the Sanhedrin — the full council of the Israelites — and sent orders to the jail to have them brought.[i] **22** But when the servants[A] got there, they did not find them in the jail, so they returned and reported, **23** "We found the jail securely locked, with the guards standing in front of the doors, but when we opened them, we found no one inside." **24** As[B] the captain of the temple police and the chief priests heard these things, they were baffled about them, wondering what would come of this.

25 Someone came and reported to them, "Look! The men you put in jail are standing in the temple and teaching the people." **26** Then the commander went with the servants and brought them in without force, because they were afraid the people might stone them.[j] **27** After they brought them in, they had them stand before the Sanhedrin, and the high priest asked, **28** "Didn't we strictly order you not to teach in this name?[k] Look, you have filled Jerusalem with your teaching and are determined to make us guilty of this man's blood."[l] **29** Peter and the apostles replied, "We must obey God rather than people. **30** The God of our ancestors raised up Jesus,[m] whom you had murdered by hanging him on a tree.[n] **31** God exalted this man to his right hand as ruler and Savior, to give repentance to Israel and forgiveness of sins.[o] **32** We are witnesses of these things, and so is the Holy Spirit[p] whom God has given to those who obey him."

GAMALIEL'S ADVICE

33 When they heard this, they were enraged and wanted to kill them.[q] **34** But a Pharisee named Gamaliel, a teacher of the law who was respected by all the people, stood up in the Sanhedrin and ordered the men[c] to be taken outside for a little while.[r] **35** He said to them, "Men of Israel, be careful about what you're about to do to these men. **36** Some time ago Theudas rose up, claiming to be somebody, and a group of about four hundred men rallied to him. He was killed, and all his followers were dispersed and came to nothing.[s] **37** After this man, Judas the Galilean rose up in the days of the census and attracted a following. He also perished, and all his followers were scattered. **38** So in the present case, I tell you, stay away from these men and leave them alone. For if this plan or this work is of human origin, it will fail;[t] **39** but

[a] 5:12 Ac 2:43; 14:3; 19:11; Rm 15:19; 2Co 12:12; Heb 2:4
[b] Jn 10:23; Ac 4:21,32
[c] 5:13 Ac 2:47; 3:11
[d] 5:15 Mt 14:36; Ac 19:12
[e] 5:17 Ac 4:1; 15:5
[f] 5:18 Lk 21:12; Ac 4:3
[g] 5:19 Mt 1:20; Lk 1:11; Ac 8:26; 12:7; 16:26; 27:23
[h] 5:20 Jn 6:63,68; Php 2:16
[i] 5:21 Mt 5:22; Ac 4:6; 5:27,34,41
[j] 5:26 Ac 4:21; 5:13
[k] 5:28 Jn 14:13; Ac 3:16; 1Jn 3:23
[l] Mt 27:25; Ac 2:23,36; 3:15; 4:10; 7:52
[m] 5:30 Ac 2:24; 3:13
[n] Ac 10:39; 13:29; Gl 3:13; 1Pt 2:24
[o] 5:31 Ac 2:33; 3:15
[p] 5:32 Lk 24:48; Jn 15:26; Ac 15:28; Heb 2:4
[q] 5:33 Ac 2:37; 7:54
[r] 5:34 Lk 2:46; 5:17; Ac 22:3
[s] 5:36 Ac 8:9; Gl 2:6; 6:3
[t] 5:38 Mt 15:17; Mk 11:30

[A] **5:22** Or *temple police*, or *officers*, also in v. 26   [B] **5:24** Other mss add *the high priest and*   [C] **5:34** Other mss read *apostles*

5:11 It was obvious to everyone that the supernatural work of God was operating in the apostles' ministry; therefore, people who hadn't been taking God seriously before were definitely taking him seriously after that. Church discipline is designed to enhance the believer's reverence for God and proper treatment of God's people.

5:15-16 Jesus had promised his disciples that they would do miraculous works like he had done (see John 14:12), and they were doing so with gusto.

5:17 Were the Jewish leaders concerned that the apostles were teaching bad theology? No. They **were filled with jealousy.** They cared nothing for God's glory, only for their own.

5:19 A locked cell is hardly capable of stopping the supernatural.

5:25 In other words, they were doing the very thing they had been locked up for in the first place!

5:28 Notice that they weren't even willing to say Jesus's name nor act under his authority: **Didn't we strictly order you not to teach in this name?** **5:29** Our chief authority is not merely *a* king. He is *the* King. When a human command contradicts a divine one, our obligation to God is supreme.

[a]5:39 Pr 21:30; Ac 7:51; 11:17
[b]5:40 Mt 10:17; Mk 13:9; Ac 4:18
[c]5:41 Mt 5:12; Jn 15:21; 1Pt 4:13
[d]6:1 Mt 9:10; Mk 10:10; Lk 6:1; Jn 6:3; Ac 9:1,10,19,25-26; 21:4,16
[e]Ac 2:41; 4:4,35; 5:14; 9:29,39; 11:20
[f]6:3 Dt 1:13; 1Tm 3:7
[g]Lk 4:1; Ac 7:55; 11:19,24
[h]6:5 Ac 6:8-9; 11:19; 22:20
[i]Mt 23:15; Ac 8:5,26; 21:8
[j]6:6 Ac 1:24; 8:17; 13:3; 2Tm 1:6
[k]Nm 8:10; Ac 9:17; 1Tm 4:14
[l]6:7 Ac 12:24; 19:20; Col 1:6

[m]6:11 1Kg 21:10,13; Mt 26:59-60
[n]6:13 Mt 24:15; Ac 7:58; 21:28; 25:8
[o]6:14 Dn 9:26; Ac 15:1; 21:21; 26:3; 28:17
[p]7:2 Gn 11:31; 15:7; Ps 29:3; Ac 22:1; 1Co 2:8
[q]7:3 Gn 12:1
[r]7:4 Gn 11:31; 12:4-5

if it is of God, you will not be able to overthrow them. You may even be found fighting against God." They were persuaded by him.[a] [40] After they called in the apostles and had them flogged, they ordered them not to speak in the name of Jesus and released them.[b] [41] Then they went out from the presence of the Sanhedrin, rejoicing that they were counted worthy to be treated shamefully on behalf of the Name.[A,c] [42] Every day in the temple, and in various homes, they continued teaching and proclaiming the good news that Jesus is the Messiah.

SEVEN CHOSEN TO SERVE

6 In those days, as the disciples[d] were increasing in number, there arose a complaint by the Hellenistic Jews against the Hebraic Jews that their widows were being overlooked in the daily distribution.[e] [2] The Twelve summoned the whole company of the disciples and said, "It would not be right for us to give up preaching the word of God to wait on tables. [3] Brothers and sisters, select from among you seven men of good reputation,[f] full of the Spirit[g] and wisdom, whom we can appoint to this duty. [4] But we will devote ourselves to prayer and to the ministry of the word." [5] This proposal pleased the whole company. So they chose Stephen,[h] a man full of faith and the Holy Spirit, and Philip, Prochorus, Nicanor, Timon, Parmenas, and Nicolaus, a convert from Antioch.[i] [6] They had them stand before the apostles, who prayed[j] and laid their hands on[k] them.

[7] So the word of God spread, the disciples in Jerusalem increased[l] greatly in number, and a large group of priests became obedient to the faith.

STEPHEN ACCUSED OF BLASPHEMY

[8] Now Stephen, full of grace and power, was performing great wonders and signs among the people. [9] Opposition arose, however, from some members of the Freedmen's Synagogue, composed of both Cyrenians and Alexandrians, and some from Cilicia and Asia, and they began to argue with Stephen. [10] But they were unable to stand up against his wisdom and the Spirit by whom he was speaking.

[11] Then they secretly persuaded some men to say, "We heard him speaking blasphemous words against Moses and God."[m] [12] They stirred up the people, the elders, and the scribes; so they came, seized him, and took him to the Sanhedrin. [13] They also presented false witnesses who said, "This man never stops speaking against this holy place and the law.[n] [14] For we heard him say that this Jesus of Nazareth will destroy this place and change the customs that Moses handed down to us."[o] [15] And all who were sitting in the Sanhedrin looked intently at him and saw that his face was like the face of an angel.

STEPHEN'S SERMON

7 "Are these things true?" the high priest asked.

[2] "Brothers and fathers," he replied, "listen: The God of glory appeared to our father Abraham when he was in Mesopotamia, before he settled in Haran,[p] [3] and said to him: **Leave your country and relatives, and come to the land that I will show you.**[B,q] [4] "Then he left the land of the Chaldeans and settled in Haran. From there, after his father died, God had him move to this land in which you are now living.[r] [5] He

---

[A]5:41 Other mss add *of Jesus,* or *of Christ*　[B]7:3 Gn 12:1

5:41 Consider this response. Having just been beaten, the disciples didn't depart in fear or grief. Instead, they rejoiced that they were deemed **worthy** to suffer for the name of Jesus. As Peter would later write to Christians experiencing persecution, "Rejoice as you share in the sufferings of Christ" (1 Pet 4:13; see also 2:18-21; 3:17). Suffering for Jesus is far better than living at ease without him. He won't forget what you do for his name.

6:1 A kingdom disciple is a believer in Christ who takes part in the spiritual development process of progressively learning to live all of life in submission to the lordship of Jesus Christ. The goal of the church is not merely for people to become Christians, but for them to develop into fully committed disciples.

Hellenistic Jews spoke Greek. **Hebraic Jews** spoke Aramaic. While they were racially the same, they were culturally different.

6:2-3 Many interpreters understand this passage to describe the selection of the first deacons, who would serve the physical needs of God's people, while the apostles (and, eventually, the elders/overseers) addressed the spiritual needs.

6:5 All of the selected men had Greek names. These men, then, could relate to the Hellenistic Jews so that they could address their specific needs and concerns.

6:8-10 **Stephen**, one of the men selected in 6:5, was "full of faith and the Holy Spirit" (6:5), was **full of grace and power**, and was **performing great wonders** (6:8). That's quite a résumé. When **opposition arose** from various unbelieving Jews, they were no match for

his wisdom or for **the Spirit** who empowered his **speaking** (6:9-10).

6:11-14 Since they couldn't best Stephen in legitimate argument, they sought to destroy him by deception. The gist of the accusations is that Stephen was a threat to Judaism.

6:15 The man whom they wanted to kill had the appearance of one who had been in the holy presence of God.

7:2-5 The Jewish leaders of Stephen's day had become so focused on their religion—encapsulated in the law, the land, and the temple—that they had forgotten the fact that God wanted relationship. While the land was a benefit received by Abraham's descendants, the main idea here is that Abraham's relationship with God was key.

didn't give him an inheritance in it — not even a foot of ground — but he promised to give it to him as a possession, and to his descendants after him,[a] even though he was childless. **6** God spoke in this way: His **descendants** would **be strangers in a foreign country, and they** would **enslave and oppress them for four hundred years.** **7** **I will judge the nation that they will serve as slaves,** God said. **After this, they will come out and worship me in this place.**[A,b] **8** And so he gave Abraham the covenant of circumcision. After this, he fathered Isaac and circumcised[c] him on the eighth day. Isaac became the father of Jacob, and Jacob became the father of the twelve patriarchs.[d]

THE PATRIARCHS IN EGYPT

9 "The patriarchs became jealous of Joseph and sold him into Egypt, but God was with him[e] **10** and rescued him out of all his troubles. He gave him favor and wisdom in the sight of Pharaoh, king of Egypt, who appointed him ruler over Egypt and over his whole household.[f] **11** Now a famine and great suffering came over all of Egypt and Canaan,[g] and our ancestors could find no food. **12** When Jacob heard there was grain in Egypt, he sent our ancestors there the first time. **13** The second time, Joseph revealed himself to his brothers, and Joseph's family became known to Pharaoh. **14** Joseph invited his father Jacob and all his relatives, seventy-five people in all,[h] **15** and Jacob went down to Egypt. He and our ancestors died there,[i] **16** were carried back to Shechem, and were placed in the tomb that Abraham had bought for a sum of silver from the sons of Hamor in Shechem.[j]

MOSES, A REJECTED SAVIOR

17 "As the time was approaching to fulfill the promise that God had made to Abraham, the people flourished and multiplied in Egypt[k] **18** until a different king who did not know Joseph ruled over Egypt.[B] **19** He dealt deceitfully with our race and oppressed our ancestors by making them abandon their infants outside so that they wouldn't survive.[l] **20** At this time Moses was born, and he was beautiful in God's sight. He was cared for in his father's home for three months. **21** When he was put outside, Pharaoh's daughter adopted and raised him as her own son.[m] **22** So Moses was educated in all the wisdom of the Egyptians and was powerful in his speech and actions.[n]

23 "When he was forty years old, he decided to visit his own people, the Israelites. **24** When he saw one of them being mistreated, he came to his rescue and avenged the oppressed man by striking down the Egyptian. **25** He assumed his people would understand that God would give them deliverance through him, but they did not understand. **26** The next day he showed up while they were fighting and tried to reconcile them peacefully, saying, 'Men, you are brothers. Why are you mistreating each other?'[o] **27** "But the one who was mistreating his neighbor pushed Moses aside, saying: **Who appointed you a ruler and a judge over us? 28 Do you want to kill me, the same way you killed the Egyptian yesterday?**[C,p] **29** "When he heard this, Moses fled and became an exile in the land of Midian, where he became the father of two sons.[q] **30** After forty years had passed, an angel[D] appeared to him in the wilderness of Mount Sinai, in the flame of a burning bush. **31** When Moses saw it, he was amazed at the sight. As he was approaching to look at it, the voice of the Lord came: **32 I am the God of your ancestors — the God of Abraham, of Isaac, and of Jacob.**[E,r] Moses began to tremble and did not dare to look.

33 "The Lord said to him: **Take off the sandals from your feet, because the place where you are standing is holy ground. 34 I have certainly seen the oppression of my people in Egypt; I have heard their groaning and have come

[a]7:5 Gn 12:7; 13:15; 15:18; 17:8; Gl 3:16; Heb 8:8–9
[b]7:6–7 Gn 15:13–14; Ex 3:12; 12:40
[c]7:8 Gn 17:9–11; 21:2–4
[d]Gn 25:26; 29:31; 30:5; 35:23
[e]7:9 Gn 37:11,28; 39:2,21; 45:4; Ps 105:17
[f]7:10 Gn 41:37–43; 42:6; Ps 105:21
[g]7:11 Gn 41:54; 42:5
[h]7:13–14 Gn 45:1–4,9–10,16,27; 46:26–27; Ex 1:5; Dt 10:22
[i]7:15 Gn 46:5; 49:33; Ex 1:6
[j]7:16 Gn 23:16; 33:19; 50:13; Ex 13:19; Jos 24:32
[k]7:17 Gn 15:13; Ex 1:7; Ps 105:24
[l]7:18–19 Ex 1:8–10,22; Ps 105:25
[m]7:20–21 Ex 2:2–10; Heb 11:23
[n]7:22 1Kg 4:30; Is 19:11; Lk 24:19
[o]7:23–26 Ex 2:11–14; Heb 11:24–26
[p]7:27–28 Ex 2:14; Lk 12:14; Ac 7:35
[q]7:29 Ex 2:15,22; 18:3–4
[r]7:32 Ex 3:6; Mt 22:32; Mk 12:26; Lk 20:37

[A]7:6–7 Gn 15:13–14   [B]7:18 Other mss omit *over Egypt*   [C]7:27–28 Ex 2:14   [D]7:30 Other mss add *of the Lord*   [E]7:32 Ex 3:6,15

7:7 This place refers to the land of Israel. It was to be the geographical context for knowing and worshiping God. Being God's people, however, was about more than living in the land.

7:9-16 This section highlights another theme from Stephen's sermon. Unbelieving Israelites often rejected those whom God chose. God exalted Joseph and used him, even though his brothers (**the patriarchs**) rejected and persecuted him (7:9). In a similar way, the Jewish leaders rejected and persecuted Jesus.

7:17-28 In fulfillment of what God told Abraham (see 7:6-7), the people **multiplied** and eventually a new Pharaoh enslaved them (7:17-19). Though the Egyptians sought to kill the infant sons of the Israelites, **Moses** was preserved and raised by **Pharaoh's** own **daughter** so that he became wise and **powerful** (7:19-22). Later, when Moses tried to help his fellow **Israelites**, his attempts at leadership were rejected (7:23-28).

7:30-33 Moses encountered God **in the wilderness of Mount Sinai** (7:30-32). Again, the Lord initiated a relationship outside the promised land. Moreover, the land where God appeared to Moses was **holy ground** because of God's presence (7:33). Land is only holy if God is present; a church is only holy if Jesus is in its midst.

a 7:33-34 Ex 3:5,7-8,10
b 7:35 Ex 14:19; Nm 20:16
c 7:36 Ex 12:41; 33:1; Heb 8:9
d Ex 14:21; 16:35; Nm 14:33; Ps 95:10; Ac 13:18
e 7:37 Dt 18:15; Ac 3:22
f 7:38 Ex 19:17; Is 63:9; Ac 7:53
g Dt 5:27; 32:47; Jn 1:17; Rm 3:2; Heb 4:12; 5:12; 1Pt 4:11
h 7:39 Ex 16:3; Nm 11:4; 14:3-4; Ezk 20:8,24
i 7:40 Ex 32:1,23
j 7:41 Dt 9:16; Ps 106:19-20; Rv 9:20
k 7:42 Jos 24:20; Is 63:10
l Dt 4:19; 2Kg 21:3; Jr 19:13; Zph 1:5
m 7:42-43 1Kg 11:7; Am 5:25-27; Ac 7:36

n 7:44 Ex 25:8-9,40; 38:21; Heb 8:5
o 7:45 Jos 3:14; 18:1; 23:9; 24:18; Ps 44:2
p 7:46 2Sm 7:1,8; 1Ch 22:7; Ps 89:19; 132:5
q 7:47 1Kg 6:1-2; 8:17-20; 2Ch 3:1
r 7:48 1Kg 8:27; 2Ch 2:6
s 7:49-50 Is 66:1-2; Mt 5:34-35
t 7:51 Ex 32:9; Dt 10:16; Heb 3:13
u Lv 26:41; Jr 4:4; 6:10; 9:26
v 7:52 2Ch 36:16; Mt 5:12; 21:35; 23:31,37; 1Th 2:15
w Ac 3:14; 5:28
x 7:53 Ac 7:38; Gl 3:19; Heb 2:2
y 7:55 Jn 12:41; Ac 6:5

down to set them free. And now, come, I will send you to Egypt.[A,a]

35 "This Moses, whom they rejected when they said, **Who appointed you a ruler and a judge?**[B] — this one God sent as a ruler and a deliverer through the angel who appeared to him in the bush.[b] **36** This man led them out and performed wonders and signs in the land of Egypt,[c] at the Red Sea, and in the wilderness for forty years.[d]

ISRAEL'S REBELLION AGAINST GOD

37 "This is the Moses who said to the Israelites: God[c] **will raise up for you a prophet like me from among your brothers and sisters.**[D,e] **38** He is the one who was in the assembly in the wilderness, with the angel who spoke to him on Mount Sinai, and with our ancestors.[f] He received living oracles to give to us.[g] **39** Our ancestors were unwilling to obey him. Instead, they pushed him aside, and in their hearts turned back to Egypt.[h] **40** They told Aaron: **Make us gods who will go before us. As for this Moses who brought us out of the land of Egypt, we don't know what's happened to him.**[E,i] **41** They even made a calf in those days, offered sacrifice to the idol, and were celebrating what their hands had made.[j] **42** God turned away[k] and gave them up to worship[l] the stars of heaven, as it is written in the book of the prophets:

> House of Israel, did you bring me
>   offerings and sacrifices
>   for forty years in the wilderness?
> **43** You took up the tent of Moloch
>   and the star of your god Rephan,
>   the images that you made
>   to worship.
> So I will send you into exile
>   beyond Babylon.[F,m]

GOD'S REAL TABERNACLE

44 "Our ancestors had the tabernacle of the testimony in the wilderness, just as he who spoke to Moses commanded him to make it according to the pattern he had seen.[n] **45** Our ancestors in turn received it and with Joshua brought it in when they dispossessed the nations that God drove out before them,[o] until the days of David. **46** He found favor in God's sight and asked that he might provide a dwelling place for the God[G] of Jacob.[p] **47** It was Solomon, rather, who built him a house,[q] **48** but the Most High does not dwell in sanctuaries made with hands, as the prophet says:[r]

> **49** Heaven is my throne,
>   and the earth my footstool.
>   What sort of house will you build
>   for me?
>   says the Lord,
>   or what will be my resting place?
> **50** Did not my hand make all
>   these things?[H,s]

RESISTING THE HOLY SPIRIT

51 "You stiff-necked[t] people with uncircumcised hearts and ears![u] You are always resisting the Holy Spirit. As your ancestors did, you do also. **52** Which of the prophets did your ancestors not persecute?[v] They even killed those who foretold the coming of the Righteous One, whose betrayers and murderers[w] you have now become. **53** You received the law under the direction of angels[x] and yet have not kept it."

THE FIRST CHRISTIAN MARTYR

54 When they heard these things, they were enraged[I] and gnashed their teeth at him. **55** Stephen, full of the Holy Spirit, gazed into heaven. He saw the glory of God, and Jesus standing at the right hand of God.[y] **56** He said, "Look, I see the heavens opened

A 7:33-34 Ex 3:5,7-8,10   B 7:35 Ex 2:14   C 7:37 Other mss read The Lord your God   D 7:37 Dt 18:15   E 7:40 Ex 32:1,23   F 7:42-43 Am 5:25-27
G 7:46 Other mss read house   H 7:49-50 Is 66:1-2   I 7:54 Or were cut to the quick

7:35-36 Moses, the man whom the Israelites had **rejected**, was God's chosen **deliverer** (7:35). Thus, when the Jewish leaders rejected Jesus whom God had sent, they were following in the footsteps of their ancestors.

7:37 Moses's prophecy was fulfilled in Jesus (see Deut 18:15-18; John 6:14).

7:44-50 Their **ancestors had the tabernacle** that God **commanded** Moses to make (7:44). Later, **Solomon** constructed God's temple in Jerusalem (7:47). But, ultimately, God doesn't **dwell** in a man-made structure because **heaven is [his] throne, and the earth [his] footstool** (7:48-49). The Jewish leaders were devoted to the temple (see 6:13-14), but

they had lost sight of the God to whom the temple pointed.

7:51 Don't miss that **the Holy Spirit** can be resisted. Though the Spirit brings the truth to bear on a heart and mind, a person can be stubborn and unwilling to respond. Don't be obstinate to what God says through his Word and by his Spirit. The consequences can be disastrous.

7:52-53 The **ancestors** of those to whom Stephen was speaking had persecuted **the prophets**, even killing **those who foretold the coming of** the Messiah. And Stephen's listeners had followed in their footsteps, betraying and murdering Jesus Christ when he came (7:52)! Though they professed to

treasure God's **law** as law keepers, they demonstrated by their actions that their hearts were lawless (7:53).

7:54 When the listeners **were enraged** at this man who was full of the Holy Spirit, they were really mad at God himself and the truth that was spoken about them.

7:56 Stephen's Lord and Savior, about whom he had faithfully testified, was ready to receive him into glory with a standing ovation! This is the way our Lord wants to receive all of his faithful servants. He received a glimpse of heaven before he died, one of the glorious privileges God gives to faithful believers as they transition from earth to heaven.

and the Son of Man standing at the right hand of God!"[a]

57 They yelled at the top of their voices, covered their ears, and together rushed against him. **58** They dragged him out of the city and began to stone[b] him. And the witnesses laid their garments at the feet of a young man named Saul.[c] **59** While they were stoning Stephen, he called out: "Lord Jesus, receive my spirit!"[d] **60** He knelt down and cried out with a loud voice,[e] "Lord, do not hold this sin against them!" And after saying this, he died.[A,f]

SAUL THE PERSECUTOR

8 Saul agreed with putting him to death. On that day a severe persecution broke out against the church in Jerusalem, and all except the apostles were scattered throughout the land of Judea and Samaria.[g] **2** Devout men buried Stephen and mourned deeply over him. **3** Saul,[h] however, was ravaging the church. He would enter house after house, drag off men and women, and put them in prison.[i]

PHILIP IN SAMARIA

4 So those who were scattered went on their way preaching the word. **5** Philip went down to a[B] city in Samaria and proclaimed the Messiah to them.[j] **6** The crowds were all paying attention to what Philip said, as they listened and saw the signs he was performing. **7** For unclean spirits, crying out with a loud voice, came out of many who were possessed, and many who were paralyzed and lame were healed.[k] **8** So there was great joy in that city.

THE RESPONSE OF SIMON

9 A man named Simon had previously practiced sorcery in that city and amazed the Samaritan people, while claiming to be somebody great.[l] **10** They all paid attention to him, from the least of them to the greatest, and they said, "This man is called the Great Power of God."[C,m] **11** They were attentive to him because he had amazed them with his sorceries for a long time. **12** But when they believed Philip, as he proclaimed the good news about the kingdom of God and the name of Jesus Christ, both men and women were baptized.[n] **13** Even Simon himself believed. And after he was baptized, he followed Philip everywhere and was amazed as he observed the signs and great miracles[o] that were being performed.

[a] 7:56 Mt 3:16; Jn 1:51
[b] 7:58 Lv 24:14-16; Dt 13:9; Heb 13:12
[c] Ac 8:1; 22:20
[d] 7:59 Ps 31:5; Lk 23:46; Ac 9:14
[e] 7:60 Mt 5:44; Lk 22:41; 23:34; Ac 9:40
[f] Jn 11:11; 1Co 11:30; 1Th 4:13-15
[g] 8:1 Ac 9:31; 11:19
[h] 8:3 Ac 7:58; 22:20
[i] Ac 22:4,19; 26:10; 1Co 15:9; Gl 1:13; Php 3:6; 1Tm 1:13
[j] 8:4-5 Ac 6:5; 15:35
[k] 8:7 Mt 4:24; Mk 16:17
[l] 8:9 Ac 5:36; 13:6
[m] 8:10 Ac 14:11; 28:6
[n] 8:12 Ac 1:3; 2:38
[o] 8:13 Ac 8:6; 19:11

❧ Questions & Answers ❧

Q What would you say are some of the strengths and weaknesses of the charismatic movement?

A A strength of the charismatic movement is that it has called attention to the primacy of the Holy Spirit in our lives. Far too often, the Holy Spirit has been forgotten, neglected, or minimized. So charismatics have called a full frontal assault on the rejection of him in a practical way for people's lives, not just as a point of theology. But like any doctrine, the emphasis on the Holy Spirit can be carried to an extreme and become an unbiblical fanaticism. When the gifting of the Holy Spirit is made an end in itself, and not tied to the exaltation of Jesus Christ, you have moved beyond the realm in which he is working.

FOR THE NEXT Q&A, SEE PAGE 1289.

[A] 7:60 Lit *he fell asleep*   [B] 8:5 Other mss read *the*   [C] 8:10 Or *"This is the power of God called Great*

7:58 Luke introduces us to the man who would become one of the most significant persons in the book of Acts and who would write more New Testament Letters than any other: **Saul** (eventually known as Paul the apostle).

7:59-60 Stephen followed in Jesus's footsteps, commending his **spirit** to the **Lord** and praying that God would forgive his attackers (see Luke 23:34, 46).

8:1 Jesus had promised his disciples that they would be his witnesses in Jerusalem and "in all Judea and Samaria" (1:8). God was using this persecution to send his people out to spread the gospel and grow the church. Remember this when hardship comes into your own life because of your faith in Christ. Your circumstances are not outside of God's sovereign control and care. He can use your adversity to glorify himself, accomplish his purposes, bring others to Christ, and strengthen your faith.

8:2 The loss of a beloved Christian friend or family member can bring great pain and sorrow, but the apostle Paul reminds us that, though we grieve, we don't do so like unbelievers "who have no hope" (1 Thess 4:13). At the moment of his death, Stephen was with his Lord in heaven.

8:3 Don't ever tell yourself that an unbeliever you know could never become a Christian. **Saul** was as opposed to Christ as a person can be. But when God converted him (see 9:1-22), he became the greatest missionary the world has ever known.

8:4 The persecutors certainly didn't intend this consequence, but God used their wicked actions to fulfill his purposes.

8:5-7 The miracles served to give visible validity to the gospel message **Philip** proclaimed.

8:14-17 Today, when a person trusts in Christ, he or she receives the Holy Spirit at that moment (see 1 Cor 12:13). But this Holy Spirit activity in the book of Acts represented a unique moment in the early church. That each new group (Samaritans, Gentiles, et al.) received the Holy Spirit when the apostles were present demonstrated the unity of the believers and that all were embracing the same faith (see Acts 10:44-46; 19:1-7).

8:18-20 **The Holy Spirit** cannot be bought but is sovereignly and freely given.

a 8:14 Lk 22:8; Ac 8:1
b 8:16 Mt 28:19; Ac 2:38;
10:48; 19:2
c 8:20 2Kg 5:16; Is 55:1; Dn
5:17; Mt 10:8; Ac 2:38
d 8:21 2Kg 10:15; Ps 78:37
e 8:22-23 Is 55:6-7; Dn
4:27; 2Tm 2:25; Heb 12:15
f 8:24 Gn 20:7; Ex 8:8; Nm
21:7; Jms 5:16
g 8:26 Ac 5:19; 8:29

h 8:27 Ps 68:31; 87:4; Is
56:3; Zph 3:10
i 1Kg 8:41; Jn 12:20
j 8:29 Ac 10:19; 11:12; 13:2;
20:23; 21:11
k 8:32-33 Is 53:7-8; Php 2:8
l 8:35 Lk 24:27; Ac 17:2;
18:28
m 8:39 1Kg 18:12; 2Kg 2:16;
Ezk 3:12,14; 8:3; 11:1,24;
43:5

SIMON'S SIN

14 When the apostles who were at Jerusalem heard that Samaria had received the word of God, they sent Peter and John to them.*a* **15** After they went down there, they prayed for them so the Samaritans might receive the Holy Spirit because he had not yet come down on any of them. **16** (They had only been baptized in the name of the Lord Jesus.*b*) **17** Then Peter and John laid their hands on them, and they received the Holy Spirit.

18 When Simon saw that the Spirit*A* was given through the laying on of the apostles' hands, he offered them money, **19** saying, "Give me this power also so that anyone I lay hands on may receive the Holy Spirit."

20 But Peter told him, "May your silver be destroyed with you, because you thought you could obtain the gift of God with money!*c* **21** You have no part or share in this matter, because your heart is not right before God.*d* **22** Therefore repent of this wickedness of yours, and pray to the Lord that, if possible, your heart's intent may be forgiven. **23** For I see you are poisoned by bitterness and bound by wickedness."*e*

24 "Pray to the Lord for me," Simon replied, "so that nothing you have said may happen to me."*f*

25 So, after they had testified and spoken the word of the Lord, they traveled back to Jerusalem, preaching the gospel in many villages of the Samaritans.

THE CONVERSION
OF THE ETHIOPIAN OFFICIAL

26 An angel of the Lord spoke to Philip: "Get up and go south to the road that goes down from Jerusalem to Gaza." (This is the desert road.*B,g*) **27** So he got up and went.

There was an Ethiopian man, a eunuch*h* and high official of Candace, queen of the Ethiopians, who was in charge of her entire treasury. He had come to worship in Jerusalem*i* **28** and was sitting in his chariot on his way home, reading the prophet Isaiah aloud.

29 The Spirit told Philip, "Go and join that chariot."*j*

30 When Philip ran up to it, he heard him reading the prophet Isaiah, and said, "Do you understand what you're reading?"

31 "How can I," he said, "unless someone guides me?" So he invited Philip to come up and sit with him. **32** Now the Scripture passage he was reading was this:

He was led like a sheep
    to the slaughter,
and as a lamb is silent
    before its shearer,
so he does not open his mouth.
33   In his humiliation justice
    was denied him.
Who will describe his generation?
For his life is taken
    from the earth.*c,k*

34 The eunuch said to Philip, "I ask you, who is the prophet saying this about — himself or someone else?" **35** Philip proceeded to tell him the good news about Jesus, beginning with that Scripture.*l*

36 As they were traveling down the road, they came to some water. The eunuch said, "Look, there's water. What would keep me from being baptized?"*D* **38** So he ordered the chariot to stop, and both Philip and the eunuch went down into the water, and he baptized him. **39** When they came up out of the water, the Spirit of the Lord*m* carried Philip away, and the eunuch did not see him any longer but went on his way

---

A 8:18 Other mss add *Holy*   *B* 8:26 Or *is a desert place*   *C* 8:32-33 Is 53:7-8   *D* 8:36 Some mss include v. 37: *Philip said, "If you believe with all your heart you may." And he replied, "I believe that Jesus Christ is the Son of God."*

8:21-24 It is clear that Simon was a believer (see 8:13)—though one in extreme error. Years of practicing magic and claiming to have divine power (see 8:9-11) had resulted in **bitterness** and **wickedness** in his heart (8:23). Repentance and prayer were needed (8:22) to root out the evil ways and desires that had so long been part of his life. God is not a slot machine to be used to fulfill our carnal desires.

8:25 The good news of Jesus Christ and the kingdom of God was being preached across racial lines, and barriers were falling.

8:27-28 In ancient times, a **eunuch** was a castrated man—usually a slave who was used to watch over a harem or a treasury. However, the practice of a eunuch serving as a treasurer

became so common that frequently the title "eunuch" was used even for treasurers who were not physical eunuchs. So it may be that the term simply denotes his high position in the queen's administration. Regardless, he had obviously come to believe in the God of Israel because he was returning home after worshiping **in Jerusalem**.

8:29-35 Pray regularly for God to bring people across your path with whom you can share the love of God in Jesus Christ. There are individuals out there whom the Spirit has prepared. Like the Ethiopian man, they're asking themselves, **How can I** understand **unless someone guides me?** (8:31). Believers are to know the Scriptures so that they are prepared to help unbelievers properly under-

stand and respond to the gospel, as well as to help fellow believers grow in their faith (see 1 Pet 3:15).

8:36-39 The account of the Ethiopian official is significant. First, it acknowledges the existence of a royal kingdom of dark-skinned people in the first century AD. Second, it records the continuation of Christianity in Africa after having been initiated through the first African Jewish proselytes who were converts at Pentecost (see 2:10). Third, it verifies God's promise in Zephaniah 3:9-10 about followers of God coming from Cush (that is, Ethiopia). God calls to himself peoples from the African continent to serve him in fellowship with all humanity.

rejoicing. **40** Philip appeared in[A] Azotus,[B] and he was traveling and preaching the gospel in all the towns until he came to Caesarea.[a]

THE DAMASCUS ROAD

9 Now Saul was still breathing threats and murder against the disciples[b] of the Lord. He went to the high priest[c] **2** and requested letters[d] from him to the synagogues in Damascus, so that if he found any men or women who belonged to the Way,[e] he might bring them as prisoners to Jerusalem. **3** As[f] he traveled and was nearing Damascus, a light from heaven suddenly flashed around him. **4** Falling to the ground, he heard a voice saying to him, "Saul, Saul, why are you persecuting me?"

5 "Who are you, Lord?" Saul said.

"I am Jesus, the one you are persecuting," he replied. **6** "But get up and go into the city, and you will be told what you must do."

7 The men who were traveling with him stood speechless, hearing the sound but seeing no one.[g] **8** Saul got up from the ground, and though his eyes were open, he could see nothing. So they took him by the hand and led him into Damascus. **9** He was unable to see for three days and did not eat or drink.

SAUL'S BAPTISM

10 There was a disciple in Damascus named Ananias, and the Lord said to him in a vision, "Ananias."

"Here I am, Lord," he replied.[h]

11 "Get up and go to the street called Straight," the Lord said to him, "to the house of Judas, and ask for a man from Tarsus[i] named Saul, since he is praying there. **12** In a vision[c] he has seen a man named Ananias coming in and placing his hands on him so that he may regain his sight."[j]

13 "Lord," Ananias answered, "I have heard from many people about this man, how much harm he has done to your saints in Jerusalem.[k] **14** And he has authority here from the chief priests to arrest all who call on your name."[l]

15 But the Lord said to him, "Go, for this man is my chosen instrument[m] to take my name to Gentiles,[n] kings, and Israelites.[o] **16** I will show him how much he must suffer for my name."[p]

17 Ananias went and entered the house. He placed his hands on him and said, "Brother Saul, the Lord Jesus, who appeared to you on the road you were traveling, has sent me so that you may regain your sight and be filled with the Holy Spirit."[q]

18 At once something like scales fell from his eyes, and he regained his sight. Then he got up and was baptized. **19** And after taking some food, he regained his strength.[r]

SAUL PROCLAIMING THE MESSIAH

Saul was with the disciples in Damascus for some time. **20** Immediately he began proclaiming Jesus in the synagogues: "He is the Son of God."[s]

21 All who heard him were astounded and said, "Isn't this the man in Jerusalem who was causing havoc for those who called on this name and came here for the purpose of taking them as prisoners to the chief priests?"[t]

22 But Saul grew stronger and kept confounding the Jews who lived in Damascus by proving that Jesus is the Messiah.

23 After many days had passed, the Jews conspired to kill him, **24** but Saul learned of their plot. So they were watching the gates day and night intending to kill him,[u] **25** but his disciples took him by night and lowered him in a large basket through an opening in the wall.[v]

---

[a] 8:40 Ac 10:1,24; 12:19; 21:8,16; 23:23,33; 25:1,4,6,13
[b] 9:1 Mt 9:10; Mk 10:10; Lk 6:1; Jn 6:3; Ac 6:1
[c] Ac 8:3; 9:13,21
[d] 9:2 Ac 15:30; 22:5; 23:25,33
[e] Ac 19:9,23; 22:4; 24:14,22
[f] 9:3–8 Ac 22:6–11; 26:12–18; 1Co 15:8
[g] 9:7 Dn 10:7; Jn 12:29; Ac 22:9
[h] 9:10 Ac 10:3,17,19; 22:12; 21:39; 22:3
[i] 9:11 Ac 9:30; 11:25; 21:39; 22:3
[j] 9:12 Mk 5:23; Ac 9:17

[k] 9:13 Ac 8:3; 9:32; Rm 1:7; 15:25–26,31; 16:2,15
[l] 9:14 Ac 7:59; 1Co 1:2; 2Tm 2:22
[m] 9:15 Ac 13:2; Rm 1:1; Gl 1:15
[n] Mt 28:19; Rm 1:5; Gl 1:16
[o] Ac 25:22; 26:1
[p] 9:16 Ac 20:23; 21:4,11; 2Co 6:4–5; 11:23–27; 1Th 3:3
[q] 9:17 Ac 6:6; 22:13
[r] 9:19 Ac 11:26; 26:20
[s] 9:20 Mt 4:3; Ac 13:5,14
[t] 9:21 Ac 8:3; 9:13–14; Gl 1:13,23
[u] 9:24 Ac 20:3,19; 23:12,30; 25:3; 2Co 11:26
[v] 9:25 Jos 2:15; 1Sm 19:12; 2Co 11:33

[A] 8:40 Or Philip was found at, or Philip found himself in [B] 8:40 Or Ashdod [C] 9:12 Other mss omit In a vision

---

9:1-2 Damascus was a city located about one hundred and fifty miles north of Jerusalem in Syria. **The Way** was an early name referring to Christianity because Jesus was "the way" (see John 14:6). "The Way" also represented the new life of believers as they followed the pattern of their Messiah (Acts 9:2). The gospel was expanding outside of Judea (see 1:8), and **Saul** had become a religious bounty hunter to put a stop to it (9:1).
9:4 Jesus so identifies with his people that to persecute them is to persecute him. The church is "the body of Christ" (1 Cor 12:27). So anyone who attacks God's people is attacking the One who loved them, died for them, and united them to himself.

9:8 The encounter left Saul blind, a reflection of his spiritual blindness.
9:13-14 Ananias was probably thinking, "You want me to go talk to the man who's in town to arrest believers—like me?" But even when it looks like obedience could result in trouble, God calls us to trust and obey. He is usually up to something much bigger than we realize.
God used a faithful (though frightened!) disciple to launch Saul in a sudden new direction in life. A menace was about to become a missionary. If you know someone whom you think could never be converted, don't forget what the grace and mercy of God accomplished in the life of a wicked man named Saul.
9:20 What did Saul do after a supernatural encounter with Jesus? **Immediately he began**

proclaiming Jesus in the synagogues. He was filled with the Spirit and became a vocal and formidable witness. Anyone who walks around bragging about being filled with the Spirit, but who does not bear testimony to Jesus Christ, is a walking contradiction.
9:22 Saul was a Pharisee (see Phil 3:5), and he knew the Old Testament well. His encounter with Jesus made the Scriptures come together for him. Everything made sense.
9:23 The Jews conspired to kill him because their star persecutor of Christians had switched his allegiance. Saul had become a liability to them.
9:25 Those whom he had previously come to imprison were saving his life.

a 9:26 Ac 22:17; 26:20;
   GI 1:17
b 9:27 Ac 13:46; 14:3; 18:26;
   19:8; 26:26; Eph 6:20;
   1Th 2:2
c Ac 4:36; 9:3-6,20,22
d 9:29 Ac 6:1; 2Co 11:26
e 9:30 Ac 8:40; GI 1:21
f 9:31 Mt 16:18; 1Co 14:4;
   Rv 1:4
g 9:32 Rm 1:7; Eph 5:3; 6:18
h 1Ch 8:12; Ezr 2:23; Neh
   7:37; 11:35
i 9:34 Ac 3:6,16; 4:10
j 9:35 1Ch 5:16; 27:29; Sg
   2:1; Is 33:9; 35:2; 65:10
k 9:36 Jos 19:46; 2Ch 2:16;
   Ezr 3:7; Jnh 1:3; Ac 10:5

l 9:36 1Tm 2:10; Ti 3:8
m 9:40 Mt 9:25; Mk 5:41;
   Lk 22:41; Jn 11:43; Ac 7:60
n 9:43 Ac 10:6,17,32
o 10:1 Mt 27:27; Mk 15:16;
   Jn 18:3,12; Ac 8:40
p 10:2 Ac 10:22,35; 13:16,26
q 10:3 Ac 3:1; 5:19; 9:10;
   10:17,19
r 10:4 Ac 9:43; 11:14

SAUL IN JERUSALEM

26 When he arrived in Jerusalem,*a* he tried to join the disciples, but they were all afraid of him, since they did not believe he was a disciple. **27** Barnabas, however, took him and brought him to the apostles and explained to them how Saul had seen the Lord on the road and that the Lord had talked to him, and how in Damascus he had spoken boldly*b* in the name of Jesus.*c* **28** Saul was coming and going with them in Jerusalem, speaking boldly in the name of the Lord. **29** He conversed and debated with the Hellenistic Jews, but they tried to kill him.*d* **30** When the brothers found out, they took him down to Caesarea and sent him off to Tarsus.*e*

THE CHURCH'S GROWTH

31 So the church*f* throughout all Judea, Galilee, and Samaria had peace and was strengthened. Living in the fear of the Lord and encouraged by the Holy Spirit, it increased in numbers.

THE HEALING OF AENEAS

32 As Peter was traveling from place to place, he also came down to the saints*g* who lived in Lydda.*h* **33** There he found a man named Aeneas, who was paralyzed and had been bedridden for eight years. **34** Peter said to him, "Aeneas, Jesus Christ heals you. Get up and make your bed,"*A* and immediately he got up.*i* **35** So all who lived in Lydda and Sharon*j* saw him and turned to the Lord.

DORCAS RESTORED TO LIFE

36 In Joppa*k* there was a disciple named Tabitha (which is translated Dorcas). She

was always doing good works*l* and acts of charity. **37** About that time she became sick and died. After washing her, they placed her in a room upstairs. **38** Since Lydda was near Joppa, the disciples heard that Peter was there and sent two men to him who urged him, "Don't delay in coming with us." **39** Peter got up and went with them. When he arrived, they led him to the room upstairs. And all the widows approached him, weeping and showing him the robes and clothes that Dorcas had made while she was with them. **40** Peter sent them all out of the room. He knelt down, prayed, and turning toward the body said, "Tabitha, get up." She opened her eyes, saw Peter, and sat up.*m* **41** He gave her his hand and helped her stand up. He called the saints and widows and presented her alive. **42** This became known throughout Joppa, and many believed in the Lord. **43** Peter stayed for some time in Joppa with Simon,*n* a leather tanner.

CORNELIUS'S VISION

10 There was a man in Caesarea named Cornelius, a centurion of what was called the Italian Regiment.*o* **2** He was a devout man and feared God along with his whole household. He did many charitable deeds for the Jewish people and always prayed to God.*p* **3** About three in the afternoon*B* he distinctly saw in a vision an angel of God who came in and said to him, "Cornelius."*q*

4 Staring at him in awe, he said, "What is it, Lord?"

The angel told him, "Your prayers and your acts of charity have ascended as a memorial offering before God.*r* **5** Now send

---

A 9:34 Or *and get ready to eat*   *B* 10:3 Lit *About the ninth hour*

9:26-27 Though everyone else was **afraid** of Saul, **Barnabas** was willing to embrace the work of grace that God was doing in his life. **9:30 Tarsus** was Saul's hometown (see 9:11). It was located in the Roman province of Cilicia (in modern-day south-central Turkey). **9:31** What about the "severe persecution" (8:1) that had broken out against the church? How could things be going so well for Christ's followers when their external circumstances were so bad? In God's sovereignty, the period of persecution actually caused the church to increase and grow stronger. True Christianity, in fact, prospers in spite of outward pressure when believers depend on God's peace that "surpasses all understanding" (Phil 4:7), receive comfort that only the Holy Spirit can provide, and take God and his Word seriously.

In many places in the world today, Christians are persecuted and even killed for their faith. Though believers in many places may not face such severity, they can still undergo persecution in other forms like rejection, mocking, ostracism, and discrimination. "All who want to live a godly life in Christ Jesus will be persecuted" (2 Tim 3:12). So if a believer experiences no form of persecution, it may mean that he or she doesn't have a faith worth persecuting. Don't be a secret agent Christian: go public with your trust in Christ. **9:32-35** The miracles the apostles were performing were not merely for shock and awe. Their purpose was to draw people to Christ (9:35). **9:40** This was the first time that one of the apostles, raised the dead like Jesus had (see Luke 7:11-15; 8:50-56; John 11:1-44). But it wouldn't be the last (see Acts 20:7-12). God brought Tabitha's good works back to her (see 9:36). She had sacrificially served oth-

ers, and thus God showed mercy to her. Our God is a God of reciprocity (see Luke 6:38). **10:1-2 Cornelius** was a Gentile God fearer—that is, he believed in the God of Israel. But he was not a Jewish proselyte—that is, he was not circumcised as a full-fledged convert to Judaism. He engaged in **charitable deeds for the Jewish people and always prayed to God.** **10:14** Peter had been faithful to the dietary restrictions God had given Israel under the old covenant (see Lev 11:1-47). But during his ministry Jesus had "declared all foods clean" (Mark 7:19). The previous standards Peter had learned, then, were irrelevant in light of what God had done and was doing. The Lord was getting ready to teach Peter about more than mere changes to his diet. He was about to break down racial divides and signal the dawning of a new day.

men to Joppa and call for Simon, who is also named Peter. [6] He is lodging with Simon, a tanner, whose house is by the sea."[a]

[7] When the angel who spoke to him had gone, he called two of his household servants and a devout soldier, who was one of those who attended him. [8] After explaining everything to them, he sent them to Joppa.

PETER'S VISION

[9] The[b] next day, as they were traveling and nearing the city, Peter went up to pray on the roof[c] about noon.[A] [10] He became hungry and wanted to eat, but while they were preparing something, he fell into a trance. [11] He saw heaven opened[d] and an object that resembled a large sheet coming down, being lowered by its four corners to the earth. [12] In it were all the four-footed animals and reptiles of the earth, and the birds of the sky. [13] A voice said to him, "Get up, Peter; kill and eat."

[14] "No, Lord!" Peter said. "For I have never eaten anything impure and ritually unclean."[e]

[15] Again, a second time, the voice said to him, "What God has made clean, do not call impure."[f] [16] This happened three times, and suddenly the object was taken up into heaven.

PETER VISITS CORNELIUS

[17] While Peter was deeply perplexed about what the vision he had seen might mean, right away the men who had been sent by Cornelius, having asked directions to Simon's house, stood at the gate. [18] They called out, asking if Simon, who was also named Peter, was lodging there.

[19] While Peter was thinking about the vision, the Spirit told him, "Three men are here looking for you.[g] [20] Get up, go downstairs, and go with them with no doubts at all, because I have sent them."[h]

[21] Then Peter went down to the men and said, "Here I am, the one you're looking for. What is the reason you're here?"

[22] They said, "Cornelius, a centurion, an upright and God-fearing man, who has a good reputation with the whole Jewish nation, was divinely directed by a holy angel to call you to his house and to hear a message from you."[i] [23] Peter then invited them in and gave them lodging.

The next day he got up and set out with them, and some of the brothers from Joppa went with him.[j] [24] The following day he entered Caesarea. Now Cornelius was expecting them and had called together his relatives and close friends. [25] When Peter entered, Cornelius met him, fell at his feet, and worshiped him.

[26] But Peter lifted him up and said, "Stand up. I myself am also a man."[k] [27] While talking with him, he went in and found a large gathering of people. [28] Peter said to them, "You know it's forbidden for a Jewish man to associate with or visit a foreigner,[l] but God has shown me that I must not call any person impure or unclean.[m] [29] That's why I came without any objection when I was sent for. So may I ask why you sent for me?"

[30] Cornelius replied, "Four days ago at this hour, at three in the afternoon,[B] I was[c] praying in my house. Just then a man in dazzling clothing stood before me[n] [31] and said, 'Cornelius, your prayer has been heard, and your acts of charity have been remembered in God's sight. [32] Therefore send someone to Joppa and invite Simon here, who is also named Peter. He is lodging in Simon the tanner's house by the sea.'[D] [33] So I immediately sent for you, and it was good of you to come. So now we are all in the presence of God to hear everything you have been commanded by the Lord."

GOOD NEWS FOR GENTILES

[34] Peter began to speak: "Now I truly understand that God doesn't show favoritism,[o] [35] but in every nation the person who fears him and does what is right is acceptable to him. [36] He sent the message to the Israelites, proclaiming the good news of peace through Jesus Christ — he is Lord of all.[p] [37] You know the events that took place

[a]10:6 Lk 16:13; Rm 14:4; 1Pt 2:18
[b]10:9-32 Ac 11:5-14
[c]10:9 Ps 55:17; Jr 19:13; 32:29; Zph 1:5; Mt 24:17
[d]10:10-11 Jn 1:51; Ac 22:17
[e]10:14 Lv 11:4; 20:25; Dt 4:4-20; Ezk 4:14; Dn 1:8; Ac 9:5
[f]10:15 Mt 15:11; Mk 7:19; Rm 14:14; 1Co 10:25; 1Tm 4:4; Ti 1:15
[g]10:19 Ac 8:29; 10:3
[h]10:20 Ac 15:7-9

[i]10:22 Mk 8:38; Ac 10:2; 11:14
[j]10:23 Ac 10:45; 11:12
[k]10:26 Ac 14:15; Rv 19:10; 22:8
[l]10:28 Jn 4:9; 18:28; Ac 11:3
[m]Ac 10:14-15,35; 15:8-9
[n]10:30 Ac 1:10; 3:1
[o]10:34 Dt 10:17; 2Ch 19:7; Rm 2:11; Gl 2:6; Eph 6:9; Col 3:25; 1Pt 1:17
[p]10:36 Mt 28:18; Ac 2:36; 13:32; Rm 10:12; Eph 2:17; Rv 17:14

[A]10:9 Lit about the sixth hour [B]10:30 Lit at the ninth hour [C]10:30 Other mss add fasting and [D]10:32 Other mss add When he arrives, he will speak to you.

10:16 Notice that Peter received two reruns of the message (two or three witnesses are God's method of divine confirmation; see, e.g., Deut 17:6; Matt 18:16; 2 Cor 13:1; 1 Tim 5:19).
10:28-29 Jews didn't associate with those who lived on the other side of the tracks, so to speak. But at a clear word from God, Peter had changed his convictions on that matter and obeyed at once. Given the Bible's clear teach-

ing on racial equality, since all people come from one source (see 17:26), it doesn't require years of training and seminars to embrace the truth. It simply requires a willingness to take God at his Word.
10:30-33 Don't miss that God had sovereignly orchestrated events so that Peter had been invited to his own evangelistic crusade with a crowd ready and willing to listen (10:33).

10:34-35 Peter had come to understand what Paul would later write: "Is God the God of Jews only? Is he not the God of Gentiles too? Yes, of Gentiles too" (Rom 3:29). No ethnic or racial group is superior to another or gets preferential treatment from God. He accepts all who come to him on his terms (Acts 10:35).

*a*10:38 Mt 4:23; Lk 4:18; Jn
3:2; Ac 4:26
*b*10:39 Lk 24:48; Ac
2:32; 5:30
*c*10:41 Lk 24:43; Jn 14:17,22
*d*10:42 Jn 5:22; Ac 17:31;
Rm 14:9; 2Co 5:10; 2Tm
4:1; 1Pt 4:5
*e*10:43 Is 53:11; Jr 31:34
*f*1Jn 2:12; 3:23
*g*Lk 24:47; Ac 15:9; Rm
10:11; Gl 3:22
*h*10:44 Ac 11:15; 15:8
*i*10:45 Ac 2:33,38; 10:23;
11:18
*j*10:47 Ac 2:4; 8:36;
11:17; 15:8
*k*10:48 Ac 2:38; 8:16; 1Co
1:14-17

*l*11:2 Ac 10:45; Col 4:11;
1Tm 1:10
*m*11:3 Ac 10:28; Gl 2:12
*n*11:5-14 Ac 10:9-32
*o*11:12 Ac 8:29; 10:23; 15:9
*p*11:14 Jn 4:53; Ac 10:2;
16:15,31-34; 18:8; 1Co 1:16
*q*11:15 Ac 2:4; 10:44
*r*11:16 Mt 3:11; Mk 1:8; Lk
3:16; Jn 1:33; Ac 1:5
*s*11:17 Ac 5:39; 10:45,47
*t*11:18 Rm 10:12-13;
2Co 7:10

throughout all Judea, beginning from Galilee after the baptism that John preached: **38** how God anointed Jesus of Nazareth with the Holy Spirit and with power, and how he went about doing good and healing all who were under the tyranny of the devil, because God was with him.*a* **39** We ourselves are witnesses of everything he did in both the Judean country and in Jerusalem, and yet they killed him by hanging him on a tree.*b* **40** God raised up this man on the third day and caused him to be seen, **41** not by all the people, but by us whom God appointed as witnesses, who ate and drank with him after he rose from the dead.*c* **42** He commanded us to preach to the people and to testify that he is the one appointed by God to be the judge of the living and the dead.*d* **43** All the prophets testify*e* about him that through his name*f* everyone who believes in him receives forgiveness of sins."*g*

GENTILE CONVERSION AND BAPTISM

44 While Peter was still speaking these words, the Holy Spirit came down*h* on all those who heard the message. **45** The circumcised believers who had come with Peter were amazed because the gift of the Holy Spirit had been poured out even on the Gentiles.*i* **46** For they heard them speaking in other tongues*A* and declaring the greatness of God.

Then Peter responded, **47** "Can anyone withhold water and prevent these people from being baptized, who have received the Holy Spirit just as we have?"*j* **48** He commanded them to be baptized in the name of Jesus Christ.*k* Then they asked him to stay for a few days.

GENTILE SALVATION DEFENDED

11 The apostles and the brothers and sisters who were throughout Judea heard that the Gentiles had also received the word of God. **2** When Peter went up to Jerusalem, the circumcision party criticized him,*l* **3** saying, "You went to uncircumcised men and ate with them."*m*

4 Peter began to explain to them step by step: **5** "I*n* was in the town of Joppa praying, and I saw, in a trance, an object that resembled a large sheet coming down, being lowered by its four corners from heaven, and it came to me. **6** When I looked closely and considered it, I saw the four-footed animals of the earth, the wild beasts, the reptiles, and the birds of the sky. **7** I also heard a voice telling me, 'Get up, Peter; kill and eat.'

8 " 'No, Lord!' I said. 'For nothing impure or ritually unclean has ever entered my mouth.' **9** But a voice answered from heaven a second time, 'What God has made clean, you must not call impure.'

10 "Now this happened three times, and everything was drawn up again into heaven. **11** At that very moment, three men who had been sent to me from Caesarea arrived at the house where we were. **12** The Spirit told me to accompany them with no doubts at all. These six brothers also accompanied me, and we went into the man's house.*o* **13** He reported to us how he had seen the angel standing in his house and saying, 'Send*B* to Joppa, and call for Simon, who is also named Peter. **14** He will speak a message to you by which you and all your household*p* will be saved.'

15 "As I began to speak, the Holy Spirit came down on them, just as on us at the beginning.*q* **16** I remembered the word of the Lord, how he said, 'John baptized with water, but you will be baptized with the Holy Spirit.'*r* **17** If, then, God gave them the same gift that he also gave to us when we believed in the Lord Jesus Christ, how could I possibly hinder God?"*s*

18 When they heard this they became silent. And they glorified God, saying, "So then, God has given repentance resulting in life even to the Gentiles."*t*

10:44-46 This was a Gentile Pentecost mirroring what happened in 2:1-11. It was an event bringing Jews and Gentiles together into the family of God.

When an Olympic athlete wins a gold medal, no one asks the athlete what song he or she would like to hear played at the award ceremony. They play the anthem of the country that the athlete represents. No matter how diverse the athletes are from a given country, they compete under the same flag. Similarly, believers in Jesus Christ come from every tribe, tongue, nation, race, and gender. These different aspects of humanity are part of God's creation and, therefore, are not obliterated by the gospel. But they are not the most important things about us. We do not primarily represent our race; we represent God's kingdom. We live, work, and worship together under *his* banner, not our own.

11:1-3 Those who were members of **the circumcision party criticized** Peter for eating with Gentiles without having required their circumcision first (11:2-3). They were more concerned with law keeping than they were excited about the news that **Gentiles had also received the word of God** (11:1).

11:17-18 In other words, Peter was saying, illegitimate racial divisions stand in God's way and oppose the truth of the gospel (see Gal 2:11-14). To oppose something that so clearly had a divine stamp of approval on it would be to oppose God. Peter's explanation caused the other Jewish believers to give glory to God for granting **repentance resulting in life even to the Gentiles** (Acts 11:18).

THE CHURCH IN ANTIOCH

[19] Now those who had been scattered as a result of the persecution that started because of Stephen made their way as far as Phoenicia, Cyprus, and Antioch,[a] speaking the word to no one except Jews. [20] But there were some of them, men from Cyprus and Cyrene, who came to Antioch and began speaking to the Greeks[A] also, proclaiming the good news about the Lord Jesus.[b] [21] The Lord's hand was with them, and a large number who believed turned to the Lord.[c] [22] News about them reached[B] the church in Jerusalem, and they sent out Barnabas to travel[c] as far as Antioch. [23] When he arrived and saw the grace of God, he was glad and encouraged all of them to remain true to the Lord with devoted hearts,[d] [24] for he was a good man, full of the Holy Spirit[e] and of faith. And large numbers of people were added[f] to the Lord.

[25] Then he[o] went to Tarsus to search for Saul, [26] and when he found him he brought him to Antioch. For a whole year they met with the church and taught large numbers. The disciples[g] were first called Christians at Antioch.[h]

FAMINE RELIEF

[27] In those days some prophets came down from Jerusalem to Antioch.[i] [28] One of them, named Agabus, stood up and predicted by the Spirit that there would be a severe famine throughout the Roman world.[E] This took place during the reign of Claudius.[j] [29] Each of the disciples, according to his ability, determined to send relief to the brothers and sisters who lived in Judea.[k] [30] They did this, sending it to the elders[l] by means of Barnabas and Saul.

JAMES MARTYRED AND PETER JAILED

12 About that time King Herod violently attacked some who belonged to the church, [2] and he executed James,[m] John's brother, with the sword. [3] When he saw that it pleased the Jews, he proceeded to arrest Peter too, during the Festival of Unleavened Bread.[n] [4] After the arrest, he put him in prison and assigned four squads of four soldiers each to guard him, intending to bring him out to the people after the Passover. [5] So Peter was kept in prison, but the church was praying fervently to God for him.

PETER RESCUED

[6] When Herod was about to bring him out for trial, that very night Peter, bound with two chains, was sleeping between two soldiers, while the sentries in front of the door guarded the prison. [7] Suddenly an angel of the Lord[o] appeared, and a light shone in the cell. Striking Peter on the side, he woke him up and said, "Quick, get up!" And the chains fell off his wrists.[p] [8] "Get dressed," the angel told him, "and put on your sandals." And he did. "Wrap your cloak around you," he told him, "and follow me." [9] So he went out and followed, and he did not know that what the angel did was really happening, but he thought he was seeing a vision.[q] [10] After they passed the first and second guards, they came to the iron gate that leads into the city, which opened to them by itself. They went outside and passed one street, and suddenly the angel left him.[r]

[11] When Peter came to himself, he said, "Now I know for certain that the Lord has sent his angel and rescued me from Herod's grasp and from all that the Jewish

[a]11:19 Ac 6:5; 13:1; 14:26; 15:22-23,30,35; 18:22; Gl 2:11
[b]11:20 Mt 27:32; Ac 4:36
[c]11:21 Lk 1:66; Ac 2:47; 9:35
[d]11:23 Ac 13:43; 14:26; 15:40; 20:24,32
[e]11:24 Lk 4:1; Ac 6:5; 7:55
[f]Ac 2:41,47; 5:14
[g]11:26 Ac 6:1; 9:1; 13:52; 14:20; 15:10; 16:1; 19:1
[h]Ac 26:28; 1Pt 4:16
[i]11:27 Ac 13:1; 15:32; 1Co 12:28; Eph 4:11
[j]11:28 Ac 24:14; Ac 18:2; 21:10; Gl 2:2
[k]11:29 Rm 15:26; 2Co 9:1-2; Gl 2:10
[l]11:30 Ac 14:23; 15:2; 16:4; 20:17; 21:18; 1Tm 5:17,19; Jms 5:14; 2Jn 1

[m]12:2 Mt 4:21; 20:23
[n]12:3 Ex 12:15; 23:15; Ac 12:5; 20:6; 24:27; 25:9; 2Co 1:11; Eph 6:18
[o]12:7 Lk 1:11; Col 4:1; Jd 5
[p]Lk 2:9; 5:19; 16:26; 24:4
[q]12:9 Ps 126:1; Ac 9:10
[r]12:10 Ac 5:19; 16:26

11:19 The persecution that started because of Stephen caused believers to be **scattered . . . as far as Phoenicia** (on the Mediterranean Coast in Syria), **Cyprus** (an island south of Asia Minor), **and Antioch** (in southeast Turkey). Antioch would become a dominant church, sending missionaries (including Paul) throughout the Roman Empire.
11:25-26 For a second time Barnabas served as a bridge to help Saul get connected to other believers (see 9:26-30). Do you make opportunities to facilitate and encourage the ministries of others?
It was in **Antioch** that **disciples** of Jesus Christ **were first called Christians** (11:26); they were named for the One whom they worshiped and obeyed. If we are going to bear Christ's name in the world, then we

must likewise bear his attitudes and actions, his character and conduct.
11:27-30 Recognizing that they were all part of the same family of God, Gentile believers in Antioch provided loving support to Jewish believers in need. Regardless of past divisions between their people groups, these individuals saw other Christians as their brothers and sisters and acted accordingly. Do you?
12:1 This man was **Herod** Agrippa I (grandson of Herod the Great; see Matt 2:1-23). He ruled over Judea from AD 41 to 44.
12:2 Why wasn't James, one of the Twelve, delivered from such a violent fate? The Bible does not enable us to answer such questions, but Scripture does assure us that all suffering falls under the sovereign purposes of God

(see, e.g., Rom 8:28-39). We can be certain that whatever he does or allows is ultimately for our good and his glory. God's purposes are not the same for each Christian—after all, Peter would be delivered from Herod's plans (see Acts 12:3-7). Therefore, we must never compare our circumstances to those of others (see John 21:21-23). Rather, we ought to ask ourselves, "Am I, to the best of my ability, following the Word of God and the leading of the Holy Spirit in determining God's will for my life?" James and Peter were both operating in the will of God, but God had different plans for how each would bring him glory.
12:5 Prayer is the divinely authorized method for accessing heavenly authority for earthly intervention.

a 12:11 Ps 33:18-19; 34:7;
Dn 3:28; 6:22; Lk 15:17;
2Co 1:10
b 12:12 Ac 12:25; 15:37,39;
Col 4:10; 2Tm 4:11; Phm
24; 1Pt 5:13
c 12:13-15 Mt 18:10; Lk
24:21
d 12:17 Ac 13:16; 19:33;
21:40
e Ac 15:13; 21:18; Gl 1:19;
2:9,12
f 12:19 Ac 8:40; 16:27;
27:42
g 12:20 1Kg 5:11; Ezr 3:7;
Ezk 27:17; Mt 11:21

h 12:23 Lk 1:11; Col 4:1; Jd 5
i 1Sm 25:38; 2Sm 24:16-17;
Ps 115:1
j 12:24 Ac 6:7; 19:20
k 12:25 Ac 4:36; 11:30; 12:12
l 13:1 Mt 14:1; Ac 4:36;
11:19,22,27; 1Co 12:28
m 13:2 Ac 8:29; 9:15; Rm
1:1; Gl 1:15
n 13:3 Ac 6:6; 14:26
o 13:5 Ac 9:20; 12:12
p 13:6 Mt 7:15; Ac 8:9

people expected."*a* **12** As soon as he realized this, he went to the house of Mary, the mother of John Mark,*^,b* where many had assembled and were praying. **13** He knocked at the door of the outer gate, and a servant named Rhoda came to answer. **14** She recognized Peter's voice, and because of her joy, she did not open the gate but ran in and announced that Peter was standing at the outer gate.

15 "You're out of your mind!" they told her. But she kept insisting that it was true, and they said, "It's his angel."*c* **16** Peter, however, kept on knocking, and when they opened the door and saw him, they were amazed.

17 Motioning to them with his hand*d* to be silent, he described to them how the Lord had brought him out of the prison. "Tell these things to James*e* and the brothers," he said, and he left and went to another place.

18 At daylight, there was a great commotion among the soldiers as to what had become of Peter. **19** After Herod had searched and did not find him, he interrogated the guards and ordered their execution. Then Herod went down from Judea to Caesarea and stayed there.*f*

HEROD'S DEATH

20 Herod had been very angry with the people of Tyre and Sidon. Together they presented themselves before him. After winning over Blastus, who was in charge of the king's bedroom, they asked for peace, because their country was supplied with food from the king's country.*g* **21** On

an appointed day, dressed in royal robes and seated on the throne, Herod delivered a speech to them. **22** The assembled people began to shout, "It's the voice of a god and not of a man!" **23** At once an angel of the Lord*h* struck him because he did not give the glory to God, and he was eaten by worms and died.*i*

24 But the word of God flourished and multiplied.*j* **25** After they had completed their relief mission, Barnabas and Saul returned to*B* Jerusalem, taking along John who was called Mark.*k*

PREPARING FOR THE MISSION FIELD

13 Now in the church at Antioch there were prophets and teachers: Barnabas, Simeon who was called Niger, Lucius of Cyrene, Manaen, a close friend of Herod the tetrarch,*l* and Saul.

2 As they were worshiping*c* the Lord and fasting, the Holy Spirit said, "Set apart for me Barnabas and Saul for the work to which I have called them."*m* **3** Then after they had fasted, prayed, and laid hands on them, they sent them off.*n*

THE MISSION TO CYPRUS

4 So being sent out by the Holy Spirit, they went down to Seleucia, and from there they sailed to Cyprus. **5** Arriving in Salamis, they proclaimed the word of God in the Jewish synagogues. They also had John as their assistant.*o* **6** When they had traveled the whole island as far as Paphos, they came across a sorcerer, a Jewish false prophet named Bar-Jesus.*p* **7** He was with the proconsul, Sergius Paulus,

A **12:12** Lit *John who was called Mark*   *B* **12:25** Other mss read *from*   *C* **13:2** Or *were ministering to*

12:15 The church had been "praying fervently to God" for Peter (12:5). But when God miraculously answered, they couldn't believe it and told Rhoda, **You're out of your mind!** Do you ever pray because you know you're supposed to, but you don't actually expect God to answer? Don't put God in a box. Believe that he "is able to do above and beyond all that we ask or think according to the power that works in us" (Eph 3:20).
12:17 This **James** was the brother of Jesus (see 15:13; 1 Cor 15:7; Gal 1:19).
12:19 After his search for Peter turned up empty, **Herod** had **the guards** executed and then left town for a change of scenery at his palace in **Caesarea**. Yet, this despot would soon give an account to God for his arrogance.
12:20 **Tyre and Sidon** were Phoenician cities north of Caesarea on the Mediterranean Coast that Herod **supplied with food**.
12:22-23 When Herod received blasphemous praise and failed to **give the glory to God**, he **died** (12:23). Years prior, when King Nebu-

chadnezzar arrogantly claimed credit for the glory of Babylon, God made him insane and caused him to live with animals, until the king was willing to humbly praise and honor the Lord who alone deserves glory (see Dan 4:28-37). God declared through Isaiah, "I will not give my glory to another" (Isa 42:8). Pride is an ugly sin and will come under the Lord's just condemnation—perhaps in this life, but definitely in eternity. When you are tempted to think more highly of yourself than you ought, remember that you have nothing which has not been given to you by God.
12:24 Contrast the downfall of Herod with the flourishing of **the word of God**. The narcissistic king had attempted to stop the spread of the gospel by murdering and imprisoning the church's leaders (see 12:1-4) and had ended up as worm food (12:23). Meanwhile, the church was growing.
13:1 We know of at least two black leaders **in the church at Antioch**. Their names were **Simeon who was called Niger** (meaning

"black" or "dark") and **Lucius of Cyrene** (a city in North Africa). Already then, the church of Jesus Christ was becoming the racially mixed group that it was intended and destined to be (see Rev 7:9).
13:2 Note that the Holy Spirit spoke in the context of corporate worship and fasting.
13:3 The laying on of **hands** gave official recognition of the Spirit's ministry call and endorsement.
13:4 The island of **Cyprus** was Barnabas's home territory (see 4:36).
13:6-8 **Bar-Jesus** was also known as **Elymas** (13:6, 8). He was **a sorcerer** and **a Jewish false prophet**, having mixed Jewish religion with pagan practices (13:6). Elymas was hanging out with the island's intelligent **proconsul** (a governor of the province under Roman authority), **Sergius Paulus**. He was trying to keep him from listening to **the word of God** spoken by Barnabas and Saul (13:7-8).

FOR THE NEXT Q&A, SEE PAGE 1295.

Questions & Answers

Q What are some key resources for spiritual growth that you urge Christians to make a regular part of their lives?

A God has given us key resources to use for our spiritual development. We start with the Bible because the Bible is food for the soul: "Desire the pure milk of the word, so that you may grow up into your salvation" (1 Pet 2:2). If you leave out the Bible, it doesn't matter what else you do.

But of crucial importance alongside reading the Bible is prayer. Prayer is essential because it involves inviting heaven into history to change earth. Prayer invokes the role of the Holy Spirit. Why is that critical? Because the Holy Spirit's job is to take the truth of the Word and apply it to our own personal decision-making.

Then there are other Christians, the environment of the church. The church is one of God's primary confirming mechanisms: "Every matter must be established by the testimony of two or three witnesses" (2 Cor 13:1). One of these witnesses is the Holy Spirit, as in Acts 13:1-3 when the Spirit spoke to the church about what God wanted Paul and Barnabas to do. So God allows other people in our spiritual circles to be voices confirming what God said in his Word about a decision we need to make.

Ancillary to all of this are the many Christian devotionals and books that address spiritual development. None of those resources can replace the Word of God, prayer, or the church, but they can be support mechanisms to further spiritual growth.

---

an intelligent man. This man summoned Barnabas and Saul and wanted to hear the word of God.[a] **8** But Elymas the sorcerer (that is the meaning of his name) opposed[b] them and tried to turn the proconsul away from the faith.[c]

9 But Saul — also called Paul — filled with the Holy Spirit, stared straight at Elymas **10** and said, "You are full of all kinds of deceit and trickery, you son of the devil[d] and enemy of all that is right. Won't you ever stop perverting the straight paths[e] of the Lord? **11** Now, look, the Lord's hand is against you.[f] You are going to be blind, and will not see the sun for a time." Immediately a mist and darkness fell on him, and he went around seeking someone to lead him by the hand.

12 Then, when he saw what happened, the proconsul believed, because he was astonished at the teaching of the Lord.[g]

PAUL'S SERMON IN ANTIOCH OF PISIDIA

13 Paul and his companions set sail from Paphos and came to Perga in Pamphylia, but John left them and went back to Jerusalem.[h] **14** They continued their journey from Perga and reached Pisidian Antioch. On the Sabbath day they went into the synagogue and sat down.[i] **15** After the reading of the Law and the Prophets, the leaders of the synagogue sent word to them, saying, "Brothers, if you have any word of encouragement for the people, you can speak."[j]

16 Paul stood up and motioned with his hand and said: "Fellow Israelites, and you who fear God, listen![k] **17** The God of this people Israel chose our ancestors, made the people prosper during their stay in the land of Egypt, and led them out of it with a mighty[A] arm.[l] **18** And for about forty years he put up with them[B] in the wilderness;[m] **19** and after destroying seven nations in the land of Canaan,[n] he gave them their land as an inheritance. **20** This all took about 450 years. After this, he gave them judges until

[a]13:7 Ac 18:12; 19:38
[b]13:8 Ex 7:11; 2Tm 3:8
[c]Ac 6:7; 8:9
[d]13:10 Mt 13:38; Jn 8:44
[e]Hs 14:9; 2Pt 2:15
[f]13:11 Ex 9:3; 1Sm 5:6-7; Ps 32:4; Heb 10:31
[g]13:12 Ac 13:49; 15:35-36
[h]13:13 Ac 12:12; 13:6; 15:38
[i]13:14 Ac 9:20; 14:19,21; 16:3; 17:2; 18:4
[j]13:15 Mk 5:22; Ac 15:21
[k]13:16 Ac 10:2; 12:17
[l]13:17 Ex 1:6; 6:6; Dt 7:6-8; Ac 7:17
[m]13:18 Dt 1:31; Ac 7:36
[n]13:19 Dt 7:1; Jos 14:1; 19:51; Ps 78:55; Ac 7:45

[A]13:17 Lit *with an uplifted*   [B]13:18 Other mss read *he cared for them*

13:9 Saul was a Hebrew name, and **Paul** was a Roman name. From this point forward in Acts (and in all of his letters), the man who would become known as the "apostle to the Gentiles" (Rom 11:13) is called Paul.
13:11 Since he had embraced *spiritual* blindness, Elymas would now be *physically* **blind**.
13:12 Although Elymas had tried to prevent Sergius Paulus from becoming a Christian, God used **what happened** to Elymas to bring the proconsul to faith. Whether God

accomplishes his will through your obedience resulting in your blessing, or in spite of your rebellion resulting in your shame is your choice.
13:13 Apparently, the intense mission work had proven to be too much for **John** (that is, John Mark, author of the Gospel of Mark). In the future, Paul and Barnabas would go their separate ways because Barnabas wanted to give him a second chance and Paul did not (see 15:36-41). Eventually, though, Paul would

be reconciled to John Mark and find his ministry helpful (see 2 Tim 4:11).
13:14 Pisidian Antioch is not to be confused with Syrian Antioch where their sending church was located (see 13:1).
13:15-22 Paul wasn't about to pass up an invitation to proclaim the gospel. He started with the Old Testament, with which his audience was familiar, to work his way to Jesus. Along the way, he emphasized the sovereign hand of God in Israel's history.

a 13:20 Jdg 2:16; 1Sm 3:20; Ac 3:24
b 13:21 1Sm 8:5; 9:1; 10:1
c 13:22 1Sm 15:23,26; 16:13
d 1Sm 13:14; Ps 89:20
e 13:23 Ps 132:1; Mt 1:1; Lk 2:11; Ac 13:32
f 13:24 Mt 3:1; Mk 1:4; Lk 3:3; Ac 1:22; 19:4
g 13:25 Mt 3:11; Mk 1:7; Lk 3:16; Jn 1:20,27; Ac 20:24
h 13:26 Ac 4:12; 5:20
i 13:27 Lk 24:27; Ac 3:17
j 13:28 Mt 27:22-23; Ac 3:14
k 13:29 Mt 27:59; Lk 23:53; Ac 5:30
l 13:30 Mt 28:6; Ac 2:24
m 13:31 Mt 28:16; Lk 24:48; Ac 1:3
n 13:32 Ac 5:42; 26:6; Rm 4:13; 9:4
o 13:33 Ps 2:7; Heb 1:5; 5:5

p 13:34 Is 55:3; Ac 13:30,37
q 13:35 Ps 16:10; Ac 2:27
r 13:36 Ac 7:60; 1Co 11:30; 15:6,18,20,51; 1Th 4:13-15
s 1Kg 2:10; Ac 2:29; 13:22; 20:27
t 13:38 Lk 24:47; Ac 2:38
u 13:39 Rm 3:28; 10:4
v 13:41 Is 29:14; Hab 1:5
w 13:43 Ac 11:23; 14:22
x 13:45 Ac 18:6; 1Th 2:16; 1Pt 4:4; Jd 10

Samuel the prophet.[a] [21] Then they asked for a king, and God gave them Saul the son of Kish, a man of the tribe of Benjamin, for forty years.[b] [22] After removing him,[c] he raised up David as their king and testified about him: 'I have found David the son of Jesse to be **a man after my own heart**,[A,d] who will carry out all my will.'

[23] "From this man's descendants, as he promised, God brought to Israel[e] the Savior, Jesus.[B] [24] Before his coming to public attention, John had previously proclaimed a baptism of repentance to all the people of Israel.[f] [25] Now as John was completing his mission, he said, 'Who do you think I am? I am not the one. But one is coming after me, and I am not worthy to untie the sandals on his feet.'[g]

[26] "Brothers and sisters, children of Abraham's race, and those among you who fear God, it is to us that the word of this salvation has been sent.[h] [27] Since the residents of Jerusalem and their rulers did not recognize him or the sayings of the prophets that are read every Sabbath, they have fulfilled their words by condemning him.[i] [28] Though they found no grounds for the death sentence, they asked Pilate to have him killed.[j] [29] When they had carried out all that had been written about him, they took him down from the tree and put him in a tomb.[k] [30] But God raised him from the dead,[l] [31] and he appeared for many days to those who came up with him from Galilee to Jerusalem, who are now his witnesses to the people.[m] [32] And we ourselves proclaim to you the good news of the promise that was made to our ancestors.[n] [33] God has fulfilled this for us, their children, by raising up Jesus, as it is written in the second Psalm:

You are my Son;
today I have become
your Father.[C,D,o]

[34] As to his raising him from the dead, never to return to decay, he has spoken in this way, **I will give you the holy and sure promises of David.**[E,p] [35] Therefore he also says in another passage, **You will not let your Holy One see decay.**[F,q] [36] For David, after serving God's purpose in his own generation, fell asleep,[r] was buried with his fathers, and decayed,[s] [37] but the one God raised up did not decay. [38] Therefore, let it be known to you, brothers and sisters, that through this man forgiveness of sins is being proclaimed to you.[t] [39] Everyone who believes is justified[G] through him from everything that you could not be justified from through the law of Moses.[u] [40] So beware that what is said in the prophets does not happen to you:

[41]   Look, you scoffers,
        marvel and vanish away,
        because I am doing a work
            in your days,
        a work that you will never believe,
        even if someone were to explain it
            to you."[H,V]

PAUL AND BARNABAS IN ANTIOCH

[42] As they were leaving, the people[I] urged them to speak about these matters the following Sabbath. [43] After the synagogue had been dismissed, many of the Jews and devout converts to Judaism followed Paul and Barnabas, who were speaking with them and urging them to continue in the grace of God.[w]

[44] The following Sabbath almost the whole town assembled to hear the word of the Lord.[J] [45] But when the Jews saw the crowds, they were filled with jealousy and began to contradict what Paul was saying, insulting him.[x]

[46] Paul and Barnabas boldly replied, "It was necessary that the word of God be spoken to you first. Since you reject it and

A 13:22 1Sm 13:14; Ps 89:20   B 13:23 Other mss read *brought salvation*   C 13:33 Or *I have begotten you*   D 13:33 Ps 2:7   E 13:34 Is 55:3
F 13:35 Ps 16:10   G 13:39 Or *freed*, also later in this verse   H 13:41 Hab 1:5   I 13:42 Other mss read *they were leaving the synagogue of the Jews, the Gentiles*   J 13:44 Other mss read *of God*

13:23 From the **descendants** of King David, **God brought to Israel the Savior, Jesus**, just **as he promised** David (see 2 Sam 7:11-16). Jesus is the fulfillment of God's Old Testament promises to send a Messiah.

13:34-37 The Lord had prophesied through David of the resurrection. However, **David** had not been speaking about himself rising from the dead but about his descendant, the Messiah, God's **Holy One** (13:34-35; see the note on 2:24-31). David **decayed** in his tomb; Jesus walked out of his (13:35-37).

God expects each of his servants to fulfill his or her kingdom purpose during his or her lifetime. And that purpose will always involve influencing the lives of people for both time and eternity.

13:38-39 If we believe in Jesus as the One who died for our sins, we are **justified through him from everything that [we] could not be justified from through the law of Moses** (13:39). The law was unable to set people free. All it could do was show them the problem of sin in their hearts. Only the gospel of Jesus Christ can justify us—make us right before God.

13:44-45 Paul's message had earned him quite an audience (13:44). But just as the Jewish leaders had been jealous of Jesus (see Mark 15:10), these Jews were jealous when they observed Paul drawing larger crowds than they ever had (Acts 13:45).

13:46-47 Paul delivered the gospel message to the Jews **first** because God had made a covenant with them, given them his Word, and brought the Messiah into the world through Israel. But since they rejected God's offer, Paul determined to take the gospel straight **to the Gentiles** (13:46). It had always been

judge yourselves unworthy of eternal life, we are turning to the Gentiles.[a] [47] For this is what the Lord has commanded us:

> I have made you
> a light for the Gentiles
> to bring salvation
> to the end of the earth."[A,b]

[48] When the Gentiles heard this, they rejoiced and honored the word of the Lord, and all who had been appointed to eternal life believed. [49] The word of the Lord spread through the whole region. [50] But the Jews incited the prominent God-fearing women and the leading men of the city. They stirred up persecution against Paul and Barnabas and expelled them from their district.[c] [51] But Paul and Barnabas shook the dust off their feet[d] against them[e] and went to Iconium. [52] And the disciples were filled with joy and the Holy Spirit.[f]

GROWTH AND PERSECUTION IN ICONIUM

14 In Iconium they entered the Jewish synagogue, as usual, and spoke in such a way that a great number of both Jews and Greeks believed.[g] [2] But the unbelieving Jews stirred up the Gentiles and poisoned their minds against the brothers.[h] [3] So they stayed there a long time and spoke boldly for the Lord, who testified to the message of his grace by enabling them to do signs and wonders.[i] [4] But the people of the city were divided, some siding with the Jews and others with the apostles.[j] [5] When an attempt was made by both the Gentiles and Jews, with their rulers, to mistreat and stone them, [6] they found out about it and fled to the Lycaonian towns of Lystra and Derbe and to the surrounding countryside.[k] [7] There they continued preaching the gospel.[l]

MISTAKEN FOR GODS IN LYSTRA

[8] In Lystra a man was sitting who was without strength in his feet, had never walked, and had been lame from birth. [9] He listened as Paul spoke. After looking directly at him and seeing that he had faith to be healed, [10] Paul said in a loud voice, "Stand up on your feet!" And he jumped up and began to walk around.[m]

[11] When the crowds saw what Paul had done, they shouted, saying in the Lycaonian language, "The gods have come down to us in human form!"[n] [12] Barnabas they called Zeus, and Paul, Hermes, because he was the chief speaker. [13] The priest of Zeus, whose temple was just outside the town, brought bulls and wreaths to the gates because he intended, with the crowds, to offer sacrifice.

[14] The apostles Barnabas and Paul tore their robes when they heard this and rushed into the crowd, shouting:[o] [15] "People! Why are you doing these things? We are people also, just like you, and we are proclaiming good news to you, that you turn from these worthless things[p] to the living God, **who made the heaven, the earth, the sea, and everything in them.**[B,q] [16] In past generations he allowed all the nations[r] to go their own way, [17] although he did not leave himself without a witness,[s] since he did what is good by giving you rain from heaven and fruitful seasons[t] and filling you with food and your[c] hearts with joy." [18] Even though they said these things, they barely stopped the crowds from sacrificing to them.

[19] Some Jews came from Antioch and Iconium, and when they won over the crowds, they stoned Paul and dragged him out of the city, thinking he was dead.[u] [20] After the disciples gathered around him, he

[a] 13:46 Mt 21:43; Ac 3:26; 18:6; 22:21; 28:28
[b] 13:47 Is 42:6; 49:6; Lk 2:32
[c] 13:50 Ac 14:2,19; 2Tm 3:11
[d] 13:51 Mt 10:14; Mk 6:11; Lk 9:5; Ac 18:6
[e] Ac 14:1,19,21; 16:2; 2Tm 3:11
[f] 13:52 Mt 5:12; Jn 16:22; Ac 2:4
[g] 14:1 Ac 13:5,51; 14:19
[h] 14:2 Jn 3:36; Ac 13:50
[i] 14:3 Mk 16:20; Jn 4:48; Ac 4:29; 20:32; Heb 2:4
[j] 14:4 Ac 17:4-5; 19:9; 28:24
[k] 14:6 Mt 10:23; 2Tm 3:11
[l] 14:7 Ac 14:15,21; 16:10

[m] 14:8-10 Mk 6:56; Php 2:12
[n] 14:11 Ac 8:10; 28:6
[o] 14:14 Mt 26:65; Mk 14:63
[p] 14:15 1Sm 12:21; 1Co 8:4; 1Th 1:9
[q] Gn 1:1; Ex 20:11; Ps 146:6; Jr 14:22; Rv 14:7
[r] 14:16 Ps 81:2; Mc 4:5; Ac 17:30; 1Pt 4:3
[s] 14:17 Ac 17:26-27; Rm 1:19-20
[t] Lv 26:4; Dt 11:14; 28:12; Jb 5:10; Ps 65:10; 147:8; Ezk 34:26; Jl 2:23
[u] 14:19 Ac 13:45,51; 2Co 11:25; 2Tm 3:11

[A] 13:47 Is 49:6   [B] 14:15 Ex 20:11; Ps 146:6   [c] 14:17 Other mss read *our*

God's plan **to bring [his] salvation** to all people (13:47; see Isa 49:6).

13:49-50 Don't miss that the gospel prevails in spite of opposition. No matter how much unbelievers seek to silence Jesus's followers, God's Word can't be stopped.

13:51 Shaking **the dust off their feet** was a sign of the coming judgment against these unbelievers because of their rebellion.

13:52 When **the Holy Spirit** is doing his work within you, you can experience internal peace and **joy** regardless of your external circumstances.

14:5-7 Knowing when to stay in spite of persecution (see 14:2-3) and when to leave to escape it requires wisdom. There's no one-size-fits-all answer. We need to follow the Spirit's leading.

14:12-13 The people assumed **Barnabas** was **Zeus** (the king of the gods) and **Paul** was **Hermes** (the messenger of the gods), **because he was the chief speaker** (14:12). They intended **to offer sacrifice** to them (14:13) because their superstitious, pagan worldview left them with no alternative way to interpret and respond to the miracle witnessed.

14:14-16 Unlike Herod, who foolishly embraced being treated like a god (and paid the price for it; see 12:20-23), Paul and Barnabas were horrified at being mistaken for gods. They deflected the glory to the only true God. They told the people to **turn from these worthless things** (their polytheistic worship) and turn **to the living God** who created all things (14:15).

14:17 As David explains in Psalm 19:1, God testifies to his own existence through the world he made: "The heavens declare the glory of God." As Paul says, **He did not leave himself without a witness.**

14:19 Notice the fickleness of sinful human hearts. Human devotion can quickly turn to animosity when it's not tethered to truth. The crowds that hailed Jesus as the Messiah (see Matt 21:8-11) were shouting for his crucifixion a few days later (see Matt 27:20-23).

14:20 **The disciples** thought the missionary had died from the stoning, but **he got up and** continued his mission elsewhere. Paul had been a vile persecutor of the church, but when the Lord poured out his mercy on him, there wasn't anything he wouldn't endure for the sake of the gospel. What about you?

*a*14:20 Ac 11:26; 14:22,28
*b*14:21 Mt 28:19; Ac 13:51
*c*14:22 Ac 11:23; 13:43
*d*Lk 22:48; Jn 15:20; 16:33;
Ac 9:16; Rm 8:17; 1Th 3:3;
2Tim 3:12
*e*14:23 Ac 11:30; 13:3;
20:32; Ti 1:5
*f*14:26 Ac 11:19; 13:3
*g*14:27 Ac 15:12; 21:19
*h*1Co 16:9; 2Co 2:12; Col
4:3; Rv 3:8
*i*15:1 Ac 15:24; Gl 2:12
*j*Ac 15:5; 16:3; 21:21; 1Co
7:18; Gl 5:2
*k*Lv 12:3; Ac 6:14
*l*15:2 Ac 11:30; 16:4;
Gl 2:1-2
*m*15:3 Ac 11:18; 21:5; Rm
15:24; 1Co 16:6,11; 2Co
1:16; Ti 3:13; 3Jn 6

*n*15:4 Ac 14:27; 15:12
*o*15:8 Ac 1:24; 10:44,47
*p*15:9 Ac 10:28,34; 11:12
*q*Ac 10:43; 1Pt 1:22
*r*15:10 Mt 23:4; Gl 5:1
*s*15:11 Rm 3:24; Eph 2:5-8;
Ti 2:11
*t*15:12 Jn 4:48; Ac 14:27;
15:4
*u*15:13-14 Ac 12:17; 15:7

got up and went into the town. The next day he left with Barnabas for Derbe.*a*

CHURCH PLANTING

21 After they had preached the gospel in that town and made many disciples, they returned to Lystra, to Iconium, and to Antioch,*b* **22** strengthening the*A* disciples by encouraging them to continue in the faith*c* and by telling them, "It is necessary to go through many hardships*d* to enter the kingdom of God." **23** When they had appointed elders*e* for them in every church and prayed with fasting, they committed them to the Lord in whom they had believed.

24 They passed through Pisidia and came to Pamphylia. **25** After they had spoken the word in Perga, they went down to Attalia. **26** From there they sailed back to Antioch where they had been commended to the grace of God for the work they had now completed.*f* **27** After they arrived and gathered the church together, they reported everything God had done with them*g* and that he had opened the door*h* of faith to the Gentiles. **28** And they spent a considerable time with the disciples.

DISPUTE IN ANTIOCH

15 Some men*i* came down from Judea and began to teach the brothers: "Unless you are circumcised*j* according to the custom prescribed by Moses,*k* you cannot be saved." **2** After Paul and Barnabas had engaged them in serious argument and debate, Paul and Barnabas and some others were appointed to go up to the apostles and elders in Jerusalem about this issue.*l* **3** When they had been sent on their way by the church,*m* they passed through both Phoenicia and Samaria, describing in detail the conversion of the Gentiles, and they brought great joy to all the brothers and sisters.

4 When they arrived at Jerusalem, they were welcomed by the church, the apostles, and the elders, and they reported all that God had done with them.*n* **5** But some of the believers who belonged to the party of the Pharisees stood up and said, "It is necessary to circumcise them and to command them to keep the law of Moses."

THE JERUSALEM COUNCIL

6 The apostles and the elders gathered to consider this matter. **7** After there had been much debate, Peter stood up and said to them: "Brothers and sisters, you are aware that in the early days God made a choice among you,*o* that by my mouth the Gentiles would hear the gospel message and believe. **8** And God, who knows the heart, bore witness to them by giving them the Holy Spirit, just as he also did to us.*o* **9** He made no distinction between us and them,*p* cleansing their hearts by faith.*q* **10** Now then, why are you testing God by putting a yoke on the disciples' necks*r* that neither our ancestors nor we have been able to bear? **11** On the contrary, we believe that we are saved through the grace*s* of the Lord Jesus in the same way they are." **12** The whole assembly became silent and listened to Barnabas and Paul describe all the signs and wonders God had done through them among the Gentiles.*t* **13** After they stopped speaking, James responded: "Brothers and sisters, listen to me. **14** Simeon*c* has reported how God first intervened to take from the Gentiles a people for his name.*u* **15** And the words of the prophets agree with this, as it is written:

16   **After these things I will return
    and rebuild David's fallen tent.
    I will rebuild its ruins**

---

*A*14:22 Lit *the souls of the*   *B*15:7 Other mss read *us*   *C*15:14 Simon (Peter)

14:22 Walking as a kingdom disciple of Jesus is challenging because it involves **many hardships.** Although not all believers will experience the same kinds of problems or the same level of persecution, "all who want to live a godly life in Christ Jesus will be persecuted" (2 Tim 3:12). We need the encouragement of a church community to help strengthen and sustain us.
14:23 Jesus's church polity calls for a plurality of **elders** (governing body of male spiritual leaders; see 1 Tim 3:1) in each local **church.**
14:27 Just as God had promised, he was bringing his blessing to all peoples of the earth through the ultimate offspring of Abraham, Jesus Christ (see Gen 12:3; Gal 3:16).
15:1-3 This controversy would be the basis of Paul's writing his letter to the Galatians.

When theological controversies arise, godly church leaders need to come together in submission to Scripture and with openness to the Holy Spirit's direction. Many times throughout history, church councils have assembled to address difficult theological issues. The first of these met **in Jerusalem** (15:2).
15:5 We are not saved by trusting in Christ *and* keeping **the law.** The message of the gospel calls people to believe in Christ and his substitutionary atonement alone to be saved.
15:9 **Us** here refers to the Jews. **Them** refers to the Gentiles. Ethnic distinctions should not matter within the body of Christ (see Gal 3:28; Eph 2:11-22).
15:10 The Jews had been unable to keep the law. What made them think the Gentiles could?

15:11 We are **saved [by] grace** through faith in Christ—not through law keeping.
15:13 This **James** was the half brother of the Lord Jesus. He became a believer after the resurrection, rose to leadership in the Jerusalem church, and wrote the New Testament letter that bears his name (see Matt 13:55; Acts 12:17; 21:18; 1 Cor 15:7; Gal 1:19; Jas 1:1).
15:15-16 James quoted from Amos 9:11-12 to show that Scripture testified to God's comprehensive plan of redemption for all people. James sets a good example for us all. Many of our questions would be answered if we would look to the Bible more than we look to human opinions.

and set it up again,
17 so the rest of humanity
may seek the Lord —
even all the Gentiles
who are called by my name —
declares the Lord
who makes these things 18 known
from long ago.A,B,a

19 Therefore, in my judgment, we should not cause difficulties for those among the Gentiles who turn to God, 20 but instead we should write to them to abstain from things polluted by idols, from sexual immorality,b from eating anything that has been strangled, and from blood. 21 For since ancient times, Moses has had those who proclaim him in every city, and every Sabbath day he is read aloud in the synagogues."c

THE LETTER TO THE GENTILE BELIEVERS

22 Then the apostles and the elders, with the whole church, decided to select men who were among them and to send them to Antioch with Paul and Barnabas: Judas, called Barsabbas, and Silas,d both leading men among the brothers. 23 They wrote:
"From the apostles and the elders, your brothers,
To the brothers and sisters among the Gentiles in Antioch, Syria, and Cilicia:e
Greetings.
24 Since we have heard that some without our authorization went out from usf and troubled you with their words and unsettled your hearts,c,g 25 we have unanimouslyh decided to select men and send them to you along with our dearly loved Barnabas and Paul, 26 who have risked their livesi for the name of our Lord Jesus Christ. 27 Therefore we have sent Judas and Silas, who will personally report the same things by word of mouth. 28 For it was the Holy Spirit's decision — and ours — not to

place further burdens on you beyond these requirements:j 29 that you abstain from food offered to idols, from blood, from eating anything that has been strangled, and from sexual immorality.k You will do well if you keep yourselves from these things. Farewell."

THE OUTCOME OF THE JERUSALEM LETTER

30 So they were sent off and went down to Antioch, and after gathering the assembly, they delivered the letter. 31 When they read it, they rejoiced because of its encouragement. 32 Both Judas and Silas, who were also prophets themselves, encouraged the brothers and sisters and strengthened them with a long message.l 33 After spending some time there, they were sent back in peacem by the brothers and sisters to those who had sent them.D,E 35 But Paul and Barnabas, along with many others, remained in Antioch, teaching and proclaiming the word of the Lord.n

PAUL AND BARNABAS PART COMPANY

36 After some time had passed, Paul said to Barnabas, "Let's go back and visit the brothers and sisters in every towno where we have preached the word of the Lord and see how they're doing." 37 Barnabas wanted to take along John Mark.F 38 But Paul insisted that they should not take along this man who had deserted them in Pamphylia and had not gone on with them to the work. 39 They had such a sharp disagreement that they parted company, and Barnabas took Markp with him and sailed off to Cyprus. 40 But Paul chose Silas and departed, after being commended by the brothers and sisters to the grace of the Lord.q 41 He traveled through Syriar and Cilicia, strengthening the churches.

a 15:16-18 Is 45:21; Jr 14:9; Dn 9:19; Am 9:11-12
b 15:20 1Co 8:7,13; 10:7-8,14-28; Rv 2:14,20
c 15:21 Ac 13:15; 2Co 3:14
d 15:22 Ac 1:23; 15:2; 1Pt 5:12
e 15:23 Ac 15:1; 23:26; Jms 1:1
f 15:24 Gl 2:4; 5:12; Ti 1:10
g Gl 1:7; 5:10
h 15:25 Ac 1:14; 2:46; 4:24; 5:12; 7:57; 8:6; 12:20; 18:12; 19:29
i 15:26 Ac 9:23-25; 14:19
j 15:28 Ac 5:32; 15:8
k 15:29 Ac 15:20; 21:25; Rv 2:14,20
l 15:32 Ac 14:22; 15:1
m 15:33 Mk 5:34; Ac 16:36; 1Co 16:11; Heb 11:31
n 15:35 Ac 8:4; 13:1
o 15:36 Ac 13:4,13-14,51; 14:6,24
p 15:37-39 Ac 12:12; 13:13; Col 4:10
q 15:40 Ac 11:23; 14:26; 15:22
r 15:41 Ac 6:9; 15:23; 16:5

A 15:17-18 Other mss read says the Lord who does all these things. Known to God from long ago are all his works.   B 15:16-18 Am 9:11-12; Is 45:21   C 15:24 Other mss add by saying, 'Be circumcised and keep the law,'   D 15:33 Other mss read the brothers to the apostles   E 15:33 Other mss add v. 34: But Silas decided to stay there.   F 15:37 Lit John who was called Mark

15:20 Associating with things polluted by idols and eating things strangled or containing blood were forbidden to Jews in the law of Moses and were linked to Gentile idolatry (see 1 Cor 10:19-20). Abstaining from such would not save the Gentile Christians or cause them to break fellowship with God (see 1 Cor 10:28-32), but it would prevent them from unnecessarily offending Jewish Christians and would facilitate fellowship with them.

15:30-35 What had started as controversy (15:1) ended in unity, edification, and joy. This is what happens when godly leaders address problems in obedience to God's Word, recognizing how God's Spirit has been at work, and encouraging God's people to seek one another's well-being. 15:37-38 The prior work had apparently been too much for John Mark, and he had thrown in the towel (see 13:13). Ministry is hard business because it necessarily involves people and their problems. For the missionary serving

in a foreign culture and away from family and friends, the difficulties are compounded. 15:39-41 Both men had a point and neither was wrong, yet they couldn't convince one another. Therefore, they split into two missionary teams. Thus, God took their disagreement and used it to expand their gospel reach. Though Paul and Barnabas would part ways, in God's providence their gospel impact would be doubled. God knows how to take a mess and make a miracle.

a 16:1 Ac 17:14-15; 18:5;
19:22; 20:4; Rm 16:21; 1Co
4:17; Php 2:19; 1Th 3:2,6
b 2Tm 1:5; 3:15
c 16:2 Ac 13:51; 16:40
d 16:3 Gl 2:3
e 16:4 Ac 11:30; 15:2,28
f 16:5 Ac 2:47; 9:31; 15:41
g 16:6 Ac 2:9; 18:23; Gl
1:2; 3:1
h 16:7 Ac 8:29; Rm 8:9; Gl
4:6; Php 1:19; 1Pt 1:11
i 16:8 Ac 16:11; 20:5-6; 2Co
2:12; 2Tm 4:13
j 16:9 Ac 9:10; 20:1,3
k 16:10-17 Ac 20:5-15;
21:1-18; 27:1-28:16
l 16:12 Ac 20:6; Php 1:1;
1Th 2:2

m 16:14 Lk 24:45; Ac 18:7;
Rv 1:11
n 16:15 Gn 19:3; Lk 24:29;
Ac 11:14
o 16:16 Lv 19:31; Dt 18:11;
1Sm 28:3,7
p 16:17-18 Mk 5:7; 16:17
q 16:19 Mt 10:18; Ac 8:3;
15:22; 17:6-8; 19:25-26;
21:30; Jms 2:6
r 16:21 Est 3:8; Ac 16:12

PAUL SELECTS TIMOTHY

16 Paul went on to Derbe and Lystra, where there was a disciple named Timothy,*a* the son of a believing Jewish woman,*b* but his father was a Greek. **2** The brothers and sisters at Lystra and Iconium spoke highly of him.*c* **3** Paul wanted Timothy to go with him; so he took him and circumcised*d* him because of the Jews who were in those places, since they all knew that his father was a Greek. **4** As they traveled through the towns, they delivered the decisions reached by the apostles and elders at Jerusalem for the people to observe.*e* **5** So the churches were strengthened in the faith and grew daily in numbers.*f*

EVANGELIZATION OF EUROPE

6 They went through the region of Phrygia and Galatia; they had been forbidden by the Holy Spirit to speak the word in Asia.*g* **7** When they came to Mysia, they tried to go into Bithynia, but the Spirit of Jesus*h* did not allow them. **8** Passing by Mysia they went down to Troas.*i* **9** During the night Paul had a vision in which a Macedonian man was standing and pleading with him, "Cross over to Macedonia and help us!"*j* **10** After*k* he had seen the vision, we immediately made efforts to set out for Macedonia, concluding that God had called us to preach the gospel to them.

LYDIA'S CONVERSION

11 From Troas we put out to sea and sailed straight for Samothrace, the next day to Neapolis, **12** and from there to Philippi,*l* a Roman colony and a leading city of the district of Macedonia. We stayed in that city for several days. **13** On the Sabbath day we went outside the city gate by the river, where we expected to find a place of prayer. We sat down and spoke to the women gathered there. **14** A God-fearing woman named Lydia, a dealer in purple cloth from the city of Thyatira, was listening. The Lord opened her heart to respond to what Paul was saying.*m* **15** After she and her household were baptized, she urged us, "If you consider me a believer in the Lord, come and stay at my house."*n* And she persuaded us.

PAUL AND SILAS IN PRISON

16 Once, as we were on our way to prayer, a slave girl met us who had a spirit by which she predicted the future.*o* She made a large profit for her owners by fortune-telling. **17** As she followed Paul and us she cried out, "These men, who are proclaiming to you^ the way of salvation, are the servants of the Most High God." **18** She did this for many days.

Paul was greatly annoyed. Turning to the spirit, he said, "I command you in the name of Jesus Christ to come out of her!" And it came out right away.*p*

19 When her owners realized that their hope of profit was gone, they seized Paul and Silas*q* and dragged them into the marketplace to the authorities. **20** Bringing them before the chief magistrates, they said, "These men are seriously disturbing our city. They are Jews **21** and are promoting customs that are not legal for us as Romans to adopt or practice."*r* **22** The crowd joined in the attack against them, and the chief magistrates stripped off their clothes

^16:17 Other mss read *us*

16:1 Timothy's mother was a **Jewish** Christian, and **his father was a Greek**. Thus, Timothy was the son of what might be called an interracial marriage. Paul would come to call Timothy his "true son in the faith" (1 Tim 1:2) and his "dearly loved son" (2 Tim 1:2); therefore, it's likely that Timothy had been converted during Paul's first visit to Lystra (see Acts 14:8-20; also 1 Cor 4:17). In time, Paul would assign Timothy to lead the church in Ephesus (see 1 Tim 1:3-4; 4:11-16).

16:3 The Jerusalem Council (see 15:1-35), including Paul, had just concluded that Gentiles did not need to be circumcised and keep the law of Moses in order to be saved. So why would Paul have Timothy **circumcised**?

Paul didn't do this so that Timothy could be saved but so that he could effectively minister among Jews. Having an uncircumcised man as part of his team would have distracted Jews from the gospel; therefore, Paul was willing to be flexible on non-essential issues for the sake of his gospel ministry: "I have become all things to all people, so that I may by every possible means save some" (1 Cor 9:22). We should adopt Paul's attitude and flexibility.

16:6-7 **The Spirit** provides guidance by stirring up inner convictions about decisions we need to make. He will never lead us to do anything contrary to Scripture. But within the framework of God's moral will, he can place within us a burden that doesn't go away. If this happens, slow down, get quiet with God, and ask him to help you understand how he's trying to guide you. One primary way the Holy Spirit provides guidance is through the confirmation of two or three witnesses (see Deut 19:15; 2 Cor 13:1). Notice Paul was twice forbidden to more forward.

16:10 This is the first instance in which the author of the book uses the pronoun **we**. Thus, Luke had obviously joined Paul in his mission work at this point (see the authorship discussion in the introduction to Acts).

16:11-12 The church in **Philippi** (16:12) would be the first one Paul would start in Europe, and he would pen his letter to the Philippians about a decade later.

16:14-15 **Lydia** was a God-fearer; she was a Gentile believer in the God of Israel who had not become a proselyte—that is, a convert to Judaism. It appears she was a businesswoman of some means. Her dealings **in purple cloth** (16:14) provided her with a home large enough to house all of the missionaries in Paul's group (16:15).

16:16-18 Understandably, Paul didn't want a demonic, fortune-telling spirit shouting about his work and marketing the gospel in such a manner. He thus commanded the spirit **to come out of her** (16:18).

16:19-24 Paul would later write that they "were treated outrageously in Philippi" (1 Thess 2:2).

and ordered them to be beaten with rods.[a]
23 After they had severely flogged them, they threw them in jail, ordering the jailer to guard them carefully. **24** Receiving such an order, he put them into the inner prison and secured their feet in the stocks.[b]

A MIDNIGHT DELIVERANCE

25 About midnight Paul and Silas were praying and singing hymns to God, and the prisoners were listening to them. **26** Suddenly there was such a violent earthquake that the foundations of the jail were shaken, and immediately all the doors were opened, and everyone's chains came loose.[c] **27** When the jailer woke up and saw the doors of the prison standing open, he drew his sword and was going to kill himself, since he thought the prisoners had escaped. **28** But Paul called out in a loud voice, "Don't harm yourself, because we're all here!"

⟶ HOPE WORDS ⟵

Brokenness is often the road to breakthrough.

29 The jailer called for lights, rushed in, and fell down trembling before Paul and Silas. **30** He escorted them out and said, "Sirs, what must I do to be saved?"[d] **31** They said, "Believe in the Lord Jesus, and you will be saved — you and your household."[e] **32** And they spoke the word of the Lord to him along with everyone in his house. **33** He took them the same hour of the night and washed their wounds. Right away he and all his family were baptized. **34** He brought them into his house, set a meal before them, and rejoiced because he had come to believe in God with his entire household.[f]

AN OFFICIAL APOLOGY

35 When daylight came, the chief magistrates sent the police to say, "Release those men."

36 The jailer reported these words to Paul: "The magistrates have sent orders for you to be released. So come out now and go in peace."[g]

⟶ Questions & Answers ⟵

Q You have discussed how life-changing your dad's coming to Christ was for your family. Could you describe your dad's salvation experience and its impact on you, as well as how you came to faith?

A My dad was led to Christ by two men when he visited a church with my mother. Those men witnessed to him after the service. He didn't accept Christ right away, but he went home and thought about it. Then, in the basement of our home, he got on his knees and trusted Jesus. My mother wasn't a believer at that time, so he led her to Christ. Afterwards, the two of them gathered the four of us kids (I'm the oldest of four) and shared the gospel with us, and we accepted Christ.

I was about twelve years old then, and our home completely changed. We had devotions and Bible studies, and my dad led us to a Bible teaching church. He took us out on the street corner to witness to others. All of this was part of my Christian experience growing up. Our home that had been in disarray was suddenly brand new and coming together. We kids experienced the harmony of having a father and mother who had been fighting but now were loving each other. We were taught biblical principles that affected my life and ultimately my direction. I fell in love with the Word, which led me to fall in love with Christian ministry. The transformed life of my dad transformed my life, my future, and my family. I will always be grateful for the example he set for me.

FOR THE NEXT Q&A, SEE PAGE 1298.

[a] 16:22 2Co 6:5; 11:25; 1Th 2:2
[b] 16:24 Jb 13:27; 33:11; Jr 20:2-3; 29:26
[c] 16:26 Ac 4:31; 5:19; 12:7,10
[d] 16:30 Ac 2:37; 22:10
[e] 16:31 Mk 16:16; Ac 11:14
[f] 16:34 Ac 11:14; 16:15

[g] 16:36 Ac 15:33; 16:27

16:25 Paul and Silas weren't weeping or complaining or feeling sorry for themselves. In the middle of their pain and difficulty, they were praising! Their external circumstances did not dictate their internal disposition. They were demonstrating to those around them that King Jesus wasn't just ruling their message; he was also ruling their lives. As you encounter troubling times, pray for God to help you bring him glory as you praise

him in the midst of your pain. The world is watching.
16:27 If prisoners escaped in that era, the one guarding them was subject to capital punishment. Remember the fate of the soldiers who had been guarding Peter when Herod locked him up (see 12:6-10, 18-19).
16:31-33 Typically, when the leader of the household believed, the family would follow. That's what happened here, as the jailer and

his whole **family** became disciples of Jesus Christ and **were baptized** (16:33).
16:37 Paul demanded that the magistrates **come . . . and escort [them] out** of the jail to demonstrate their innocence. Having just established a new church in Philippi, he didn't want the citizens to think that its founders were disreputable men. This illustrates the legitimacy of righteous social protest; Paul essentially conducted a sit-in against injustice.

a 16:37 Ac 22:25-29
b 16:39-40 Mt 8:34; Ac 16:14
c 17:1 Ac 20:4; Php 4:16; 1Th 1:1; 2Tm 4:10
d 17:2 Ac 8:35; 9:20; 13:13-14
e 17:3 Lk 24:26; Jn 20:9; Ac 3:18; 9:22; 18:28
f 17:4 Jn 7:35; Ac 14:4; 15:22
g 17:5 Ac 17:13; Rm 16:21; 1Th 2:14-16

h 17:7 Lk 2:1; Rm 1:32; Eph 2:15
i Lk 23:2; Jn 19:12
j 17:10 Ac 17:13-14; 20:4
k 17:11 Is 34:16; Lk 16:29; Jn 5:39
l 17:14 Mt 10:23; Ac 15:22; 16:1
m 17:15 Ac 18:1,5; 1Th 3:1
n 17:16-17 Ac 9:20; 2Pt 2:8

37 But Paul said to them, "They beat us in public without a trial, although we are Roman citizens, and threw us in jail. And now are they going to send us away secretly? Certainly not! On the contrary, let them come themselves and escort us out."[a] **38** The police reported these words to the magistrates. They were afraid when they heard that Paul and Silas were Roman citizens. **39** So they came to appease them, and escorting them from prison, they urged them to leave town. **40** After leaving the jail, they came to Lydia's house, where they saw and encouraged the brothers and sisters, and departed.[b]

A SHORT MINISTRY IN THESSALONICA

17 After they passed through Amphipolis and Apollonia, they came to Thessalonica,[c] where there was a Jewish synagogue. **2** As usual, Paul went into the synagogue, and on three Sabbath days reasoned with them from the Scriptures,[d] **3** explaining and proving that it was necessary for the Messiah to suffer and rise from the dead: "This Jesus I am proclaiming to you is the Messiah."[e] **4** Some of them were persuaded and joined Paul and Silas, including a large number of God-fearing Greeks, as well as a number of the leading women.[f]

RIOT IN THE CITY

5 But the Jews became jealous, and they brought together some wicked men from the marketplace, formed a mob, and started a riot in the city. Attacking Jason's house, they searched for them to bring them out to the public assembly.[g] **6** When they did not find them, they dragged Jason and some of the brothers before the city officials, shouting, "These men who have turned the world upside down have come

here too, **7** and Jason has welcomed them. They are all acting contrary to Caesar's decrees,[h] saying that there is another king — Jesus."[i] **8** The crowd and city officials who heard these things were upset. **9** After taking a security bond from Jason and the others, they released them.

THE BEREANS SEARCH THE SCRIPTURES

10 As soon as it was night, the brothers and sisters sent Paul and Silas away to Berea.[j] Upon arrival, they went into the synagogue of the Jews. **11** The people here were of more noble character than those in Thessalonica, since they received the word with eagerness and examined the Scriptures[k] daily to see if these things were so. **12** Consequently, many of them believed, including a number of the prominent Greek women as well as men. **13** But when the Jews from Thessalonica found out that the word of God had been proclaimed by Paul at Berea, they came there too, agitating and upsetting[A] the crowds. **14** Then the brothers and sisters immediately sent Paul away to go to the coast, but Silas and Timothy[l] stayed on there. **15** Those who escorted Paul brought him as far as Athens, and after receiving instructions for Silas and Timothy to come to him as quickly as possible, they departed.[m]

PAUL IN ATHENS

16 While Paul was waiting for them in Athens, he was deeply distressed when he saw that the city was full of idols. **17** So he reasoned in the synagogue with the Jews and with those who worshiped God, as well as in the marketplace every day with those who happened to be there.[n] **18** Some of the Epicurean and Stoic philosophers also debated with him. Some said, "What is this ignorant show-off[B] trying to say?"

A 17:13 Other mss omit and upsetting   *B 17:18 Lit this seed picker*

17:1 Thessalonica was the capital of Macedonia. Since the Jews believed in the Old Testament, he could start at their **synagogue** to show them how Jesus fulfilled the Scriptures.

17:5-9 Like the antagonists in Philippi (see 16:19-21), the **jealous** Jews tried to make the Christians political opponents of Rome by claiming that they were **acting contrary to Caesar's decrees** and following **another king—Jesus**—who was proclaiming another kingdom (17:5, 7). They wanted to discredit Christianity by politicizing it.

    Similar attempts to discredit the Christian faith happen today—not on religious grounds but for political expediency. Traditional Christianity is deemed unacceptable

because its adherents' moral views prevent them from affirming, for example, abortion and homosexual marriage. Thus, followers of Christ can find themselves running afoul of the law for standing true to their Christian convictions. Here we must follow the apostle Peter's counsel by regarding Christ as holy and giving a defense for our faith "with gentleness and respect. . . . For it is better to suffer for doing good, if that should be God's will, than for doing evil" (1 Pet 3:15-17).

17:10-11 How a person receives the Word of God will determine the effect that the Word has on him. God will not hide the truth from the one who honestly seeks it (see Jer 29:12-13). All believers, then, should seek to be like

the Bereans, welcoming God's Word with anticipation and regularly mining it in order to be transformed by it through obedience.

17:12 As a result of this attitude toward Scripture, many were saved, including **prominent** men and women.

17:13 The opponents from **Thessalonica** couldn't leave well enough alone. They came and stirred up the Berean **crowds** too!

17:18 Epicureanism and Stoicism were two popular schools of philosophical thought in ancient Greece. The former was founded by Epicurus, who did not believe in the afterlife and emphasized the pursuit of pleasure and freedom from pain. Founded by Zeno, Stoicism was pantheistic and emphasized the pursuit of virtue.

Others replied, "He seems to be a preacher of foreign deities" — because he was telling the good news about Jesus and the resurrection.[a]

19 They took him and brought him to the Areopagus,[A] and said, "May we learn about this new teaching you are presenting?[b] **20** Because what you say sounds strange to us, and we want to know what these things mean." **21** Now all the Athenians and the foreigners residing there spent their time on nothing else but telling or hearing something new.

THE AREOPAGUS ADDRESS

22 Paul stood in the middle of the Areopagus and said: "People of Athens! I see that you are extremely religious in every respect. **23** For as I was passing through and observing the objects of your worship, I even found an altar on which was inscribed: 'To an Unknown God.' Therefore, what you worship in ignorance, this I proclaim to you. **24** The God who made the world and everything in it[c] — he is Lord of heaven and earth[d] — does not live in shrines made by hands.[e] **25** Neither is he served by human hands, as though he needed anything,[f] since he himself gives everyone life and breath and all things.[g] **26** From one man[B] he has made every nationality to live over the whole earth and has determined their appointed times and the boundaries of where they live.[h] **27** He

did this so that they might seek God, and perhaps they might reach out and find him, though he is not far from each one of us.[i] **28** For in him we live and move and have our being, as even some of your own poets have said, 'For we are also his offspring.'[j] **29** Since we are God's offspring then, we shouldn't think that the divine nature is like gold or silver or stone, an image fashioned by human art and imagination.[k]

30 "Therefore, having overlooked[l] the times of ignorance, God now commands all people everywhere to repent, **31** because he has set a day when he is going to judge the world in righteousness by the man he has appointed. He has provided proof of this to everyone by raising him from the dead."[m]

32 When they heard about the resurrection of the dead, some began to ridicule him, but others said, "We'd like to hear from you again about this." **33** So Paul left their presence. **34** However, some people joined him and believed, including Dionysius the Areopagite, a woman named Damaris, and others with them.

FOUNDING THE CORINTHIAN CHURCH

18 After this, he[c] left Athens and went to Corinth,[n] **2** where he found a Jew named Aquila,[o] a native of Pontus, who had recently come from Italy with his wife Priscilla because Claudius had ordered all the Jews to leave Rome. Paul came to

[a] 17:18 Ac 4:2; 17:31-32
[b] 17:19 Mk 1:27; Ac 17:22
[c] 17:24 Is 42:5; Ac 14:15
[d] Dt 10:14; Ps 115:16; Mt 11:25
[e] Ac 7:48
[f] 17:25 Jb 22:2; Ps 50:10-12
[g] Gn 2:7; Jb 27:3; 33:4; Zch 12:1
[h] 17:26 Dt 32:8; Jb 12:23; Mal 2:10

[i] 17:27 Dt 4:7; Jr 23:23-24; Ac 14:17
[j] 17:28 Jb 12:10; Dn 5:23; Ti 1:12
[k] 17:29 Is 40:18-19; Rm 1:23
[l] 17:30 Lk 24:47; Ac 14:16; Rm 3:25; Ti 2:11-12; 1Pt 1:14; 4:3
[m] 17:31 Ps 9:8; 98:9; Mt 10:15; Ac 2:24; Rm 2:16
[n] 18:1 Ac 17:15; 19:1; 1Co 1:2; 2Co 1:1,23; 2Tm 4:20
[o] 18:2 Ac 18:18,26; Rm 16:3-5; 1Co 16:19; 2Tm 4:19

[A] 17:19 Or *Mars Hill*   [B] 17:26 Other mss read *blood*   [C] 18:1 Other mss read *Paul*

17:19-21 The **Areopagus**, meaning "Mars Hill," was a place where philosophical and religious beliefs were debated and discussed. There will always be people who love to debate theology and spirituality but who are never willing to commit. They like to know about new ideas. But God wants us to know *him* (see John 17:3). **17:23** The people of Athens would be called *spiritual* today. Religion was so important to them that they even had an **altar** honoring **an Unknown God**, just to make sure they had all of their bases covered! That which was unknown to them, Paul would be happy to explain.

When evangelizing Jews, Paul sought to show them from Scripture that Jesus is the Messiah. When evangelizing Gentiles who didn't know the Bible, Paul started with their general interest in religion, moved to the living and true God who created the world, explained human sin and accountability before God, and then made his way to Christ. His approach serves as a good model for our own evangelism efforts. We must tailor our methods to meet our listeners where they are and take them to what they need—the gospel, the free gift of eternal life through faith alone in Christ alone.

17:24-27 God is the source, ruler, and sustainer of the universe and all it contains, including human **life**. He neither dwells in temples nor depends on humans to serve him because he is transcendent—above, beyond, and independent of the physical universe that he made. God needs nothing (17:25). God determines where everyone fits in history and geography. All of his sovereign plans are designed to prompt people to **seek** him (17:27). **From one man he has made every nationality** (17:26). This affirms that the human race exists because of a personal Creator, not some random, impersonal evolutionary process. It also affirms the historicity of Adam and the essential unity and dignity of the human race, leaving no basis for racial superiority. **17:28** The statement, **In him we live and move and have our being** gets at the idea that God is not only transcendent, but he is immanent—he is present within and interacts with the world he has made. He exists outside of time and space yet is closer to you than your own breath. Since God is the sum total of all of life, it is in getting to know him intimately that you truly come to know who you are and what you were created to be.

17:29 Idols are any nouns (person, place, thing, or thought) that you look to as your source. They misrepresent and diminish the glory of the living and true God. **17:32-34** Paul received varied responses to his preaching: some **believed**, some mocked him with **ridicule**, and some wanted **to hear** more (17:32, 34). As we share the gospel, then, we can expect the same kinds of reactions. Whenever and wherever you have opportunity, be faithful to make Jesus known and invite people to place their faith in him for the gift of eternal life. Then leave the rest in God's hands as the Holy Spirit works in their hearts. **18:1 Corinth** was a significant city located along important trade routes with close access to port cities. It also had multiple pagan temples and was known for its immorality. Paul obviously saw the city as strategic for his ministry since he remained there for "a year and a half" (18:11). **18:2** Roman emperor **Claudius had ordered all the Jews to leave Rome** in AD 49. According to Roman historical sources, the expulsion was because of riots over someone named *Chrestus*, probably a garbled reference to *Christos*, the Greek rendering of *Christ*.

a 18:3 Ac 20:34; 1Co 4:12; 9:15; 2Co 11:7; 12:13; 1Th 2:9; 2Th 3:8
b 18:4 Ac 9:20; 13:14; 14:1; 18:19

c 18:5 Jb 32:18; Ac 15:22; 16:1,9; 17:3,14–15; 18:28; 1Th 3:6
d 18:6 Ac 13:45; Rm 3:8; 1Co 4:13; Ti 3:2
e Neh 5:13; Mt 10:14; Ac 13:51
f 2Sm 1:16; Ezk 18:13; 33:4; Mt 27:25
g Ezk 3:18; Ac 13:46
h 18:8 Mk 5:22; Ac 11:14; 1Co 1:14
i 18:9–10 Mt 28:20; Ac 23:11
j 18:12 Ac 13:7; 18:27
k 18:15 Ac 23:29; 25:11,19
l 18:17 1Co 1:1

❧ Questions & Answers ❧

Q Can there be a difference between your job and your calling?

A Our jobs can be our kingdom calling, or they can simply be a support for our kingdom calling. In professional ministry, you get paid for the ministry that you do, whether as a pastor, a missionary, a Bible school teacher, or someone serving in a parachurch ministry. But, for others, a job can serve as a support mechanism for ministry. The apostle Paul was a tentmaker; that's how he earned a living. Tentmaking was the support mechanism for his ministry to the Gentiles to whom God had called him.

If you have not been called to professional ministry and you work in the marketplace of the world, you ought to do whatever ministry God will allow you to do in that sphere. My physician, Dr. Kenneth Cooper, who has had a worldwide impact as the "father of aerobics," will readily tell you that his job as a physician is also his calling in ministry as a person under the kingdom umbrella of God. He uses the physical needs of people to introduce them to their spiritual need, and the two go together. Whenever you can unite these two, then what is viewed as a secular occupation can certainly also be the ministry to which God has called you.

FOR THE NEXT Q&A, SEE PAGE 1302.

them, ³ and since they were of the same occupation, tentmakers by trade,*a* he stayed with them and worked. ⁴ He reasoned in the synagogue every Sabbath and tried to persuade both Jews and Greeks.*b*

⁵ When Silas and Timothy arrived from Macedonia, Paul devoted himself to preaching the word[A] and testified to the Jews that Jesus is the Messiah.*c* ⁶ When they resisted and blasphemed,*d* he shook out his clothes*e* and told them, "Your blood is on your own heads!*f* I am innocent.*g* From now on I will go to the Gentiles."*g* ⁷ So he left there and went to the house of a man named Titius Justus, a worshiper of God, whose house was next door to the synagogue. ⁸ Crispus, the leader of the synagogue, believed in the Lord, along with his whole household.*h* Many of the Corinthians, when they heard, believed and were baptized.

⁹ The Lord said to Paul in a night vision, "Don't be afraid, but keep on speaking and don't be silent. ¹⁰ For I am with you, and no one will lay a hand on you to hurt you, because I have many people in this city."*i* ¹¹ He stayed there a year and a half, teaching the word of God among them.

¹² While Gallio was proconsul of Achaia, the Jews made a united attack against Paul and brought him to the tribunal.*j* ¹³ "This man," they said, " is persuading people to worship God in ways contrary to the law."

¹⁴ As Paul was about to open his mouth, Gallio said to the Jews, "If it were a matter of wrongdoing or of a serious crime, it would be reasonable for me to put up with you Jews. ¹⁵ But if these are questions about words, names, and your own law, see to it yourselves. I refuse to be a judge of such things."*k* ¹⁶ So he drove them from the tribunal. ¹⁷ And they all[C] seized Sosthenes,*l* the leader of the synagogue, and beat him in front of the tribunal, but none of these things mattered to Gallio.

THE RETURN TRIP TO ANTIOCH

¹⁸ After staying for some time, Paul said farewell to the brothers and sisters and sailed away to Syria, accompanied by

[A] 18:5 Other mss read *was urged by the Spirit*   [B] 18:6 Lit *clean*   [C] 18:17 Other mss read *Then all the Greeks*

18:3-4 Paul made tents to pay the bills so that he could engage in his primary work: trying **to persuade both Jews and Greeks** to believe in and follow Christ (18:4).
18:5 Previously, Paul had left **Silas and Timothy** in Berea (see 17:14-15).
18:6 Shaking **out his clothes** was a symbolic gesture like brushing the dust from his garment (cf. 13:51). By it Paul was communicating that he was **innocent** of responsibility for the judgment the Jews would incur for scorning God's Messiah.
18:7-8 Though the Jews as a whole rejected Paul's message, the Lord saw to it that Paul's base of operations moved right

next to their gathering place and the local synagogue leader became a Christ-follower.
18:9-10 We sometimes think of Paul as a missionary superman, but he was as human as the rest of us. If the Lord had to tell him not to be fearful, apparently Paul struggled with fear. When you similarly find your emotions getting the better of you, heed God's Word and go to him in prayer, accessing his heavenly resources for your earthly circumstances so that "the peace of God, which surpasses all understanding, [can] guard your hearts and minds in Christ Jesus" (Phil 4:6-7).
18:12 Archaeological evidence verifies that **Gallio** became **proconsul** in AD 51. **Tribunal**

translates the Greek word *bēma*. It refers to the seat on which an authority figure sat to render judicial judgments (see, e.g., Matt 27:19; John 19:13). Archaeological excavations have unearthed the Corinthian *bēma* in the marketplace; this is probably the site at which Paul's encounter with Gallio took place. Regardless, Paul would later tell the Corinthians that all believers will "appear before the judgment seat [*bēma*] of Christ, so that he may judge our work on earth to determine our rewards (see 2 Cor 5:10).
18:18 That Paul **shaved his head . . . because of a vow** is probably a reference to a Nazirite vow (see Num 6:1-21).

Priscilla and Aquila. He shaved his head at Cenchreae because of a vow he had taken.[a] **19** When they reached Ephesus[b] he left them there, but he himself entered the synagogue and debated with the Jews. **20** When they asked him to stay for a longer time, he declined, **21** but he said farewell and added,[A] "I'll come back to you again, if God wills."[c] Then he set sail from Ephesus.

22 On landing at Caesarea, he went up to Jerusalem and greeted the church, then went down to Antioch.[d]

23 After spending some time there, he set out, traveling through one place after another in the region of Galatia and Phrygia, strengthening all the disciples.[e]

THE ELOQUENT APOLLOS

24 Now a Jew named Apollos,[f] a native Alexandrian, an eloquent man who was competent in the use of the Scriptures, arrived in Ephesus. **25** He had been instructed in the way of the Lord; and being fervent in spirit,[B] he was speaking and teaching accurately about Jesus, although he knew only John's baptism.[g] **26** He began to speak boldly in the synagogue. After Priscilla and Aquila heard him, they took him aside[c] and explained the way of God to him more accurately.[h] **27** When he wanted to cross over to Achaia, the brothers and sisters wrote to the disciples to welcome him. After he arrived, he was a great help to those who by grace had believed.[i] **28** For he vigorously refuted the Jews in public, demonstrating through the Scriptures that Jesus is the Messiah.[j]

TWELVE DISCIPLES OF JOHN THE BAPTIST

19 While Apollos was in Corinth, Paul traveled through the interior regions and came to Ephesus. He found some disciples[k] **2** and asked them, "Did you receive the Holy Spirit when you believed?"[l]

"No," they told him, "we haven't even heard that there is a Holy Spirit."[m]

3 "Into what then were you baptized?" he asked them.

"Into John's baptism," they replied.[n]

4 Paul said, "John baptized with a baptism of repentance,[o] telling the people that they should believe in the one who would come after him, that is, in Jesus."[p]

5 When they heard this, they were baptized into the name of the Lord Jesus. **6** And when Paul had laid his hands on[q] them, the Holy Spirit came on them, and they began to speak in other tongues[D] and to prophesy.[r] **7** Now there were about twelve men in all.

IN THE LECTURE HALL OF TYRANNUS

8 Paul entered the synagogue and spoke boldly over a period of three months, arguing and persuading them about the kingdom of God.[s] **9** But when some became hardened and would not believe, slandering the Way in front of the crowd, he withdrew from them, taking the disciples, and conducted discussions every day in the lecture hall of Tyrannus.[t] **10** This went on for two years, so that all the residents of Asia, both Jews and Greeks,[u] heard the word of the Lord.[v]

[a] 18:18 Nm 6:2,5,9,18; Ac 21:24; Rm 16:1
[b] 18:19 Ac 19:1; 20:16; 1Co 15:32; 1Tm 1:3; 2Tm 1:18
[c] 18:21 Rm 1:10; 1Co 4:19; 16:7; Heb 6:3; Jms 4:15; 1Pt 3:17
[d] 18:22 Ac 8:40; 11:19
[e] 18:23 Ac 14:22; 16:6
[f] 18:24 Ac 19:1; 1Co 1:12; 3:5; 4:6; 16:12; Ti 3:13
[g] 18:25 Lk 7:29; Ac 9:2; 19:3; Rm 12:11
[h] 18:26 Mt 2:8; Lk 1:3; Ac 18:25; 23:15,20; 24:22; Eph 5:15; 1Th 5:2
[i] 18:27 Ac 18:12,18; 1Co 3:6
[j] 18:28 Ac 9:22; 17:2-3; 18:5

[k] 19:1 Ac 18:1,24; 1Co 1:12; 3:5-6
[l] 19:2 Ac 8:15-17; 10:44-45
[m] Jn 7:39; Ac 8:16; 11:16
[n] 19:3 Ac 18:25
[o] 19:4 Lk 3:3; Ac 13:24
[p] Mt 3:11; Jn 1:7,27; Ac 13:24-25
[q] 19:6 Ac 6:6; 8:17
[r] Mk 16:17; Ac 2:4; 10:46
[s] 19:8 Ac 1:3; 9:20; 28:23
[t] 19:9 Ac 9:2; 11:26; 14:4; 19:23,30
[u] 19:10 Ac 14:1; 18:4; 19:17; 20:21; 1Co 1:24
[v] Ac 19:8,22,26-27; 20:31

[A] **18:21** Other mss add *"By all means it is necessary to keep the coming festival in Jerusalem. But*   [B] **18:25** Or *in the Spirit*   [C] **18:26** Lit *they received him*
[D] **19:6** languages

18:20-21 Notice Paul's phrase, **if God wills** (18:21). It was no mere pious sentiment but Paul's humble acknowledgment that his life and plans were in God's hands. Similarly, James warns his readers not to boast arrogantly about their intentions, schedules, and efforts. Instead, he urges them to say, "If the Lord wills, we will live and do this or that" (see Jas 4:13-17). It wasn't to be merely a religious saying Christians were to quote, but a heart philosophy they were to adopt. We must allow for divine flexibility, welcoming God to disturb our plans when he has other purposes for us.
18:23 Paul was not the kind to stay at home when churches needed **strengthening** and the lost needed the gospel. So, after **some time**, he began his third missionary journey.
18:26 Priscilla's involvement in this passage affirms that men and women in the body of Christ can discuss and explain Scripture to

one other person. This is distinct from the restriction on women serving in the office of elder/pastor (see the note on 1 Tim 2:11-12). Notice also that she and Aquila didn't embarrass Apollos by correcting him publicly; they addressed him privately: **they took him aside**.
18:28 Believers today should likewise seek to be equipped to explain the Scriptures. How sad it is to see Christians who are unable to use their Bibles to explain the gospel to an unbeliever! All of us who claim the name of Christ should have a growing knowledge of God's Word and an ability to defend what we say we believe (see 1 Pet 3:15).
19:1-7 Paul had expected all Christians to receive the Spirit (notice he said, **when you believed** in 19:2). But, we must remember that the book of Acts chronicles a unique transition stage after the death and resurrection of Jesus (see the note on 8:14-17). As different groups came to believe the gospel, their reception

of the Spirit came later when an apostle was present: this showed the unity of their faith.
19:8 The kingdom was the constant focus of Jesus's teaching, from the start of his ministry (Mark 1:14-15) to after his resurrection (Acts 1:3). Therefore, we shouldn't be surprised that it was the focus of Paul's preaching throughout the book of Acts (see 28:30-31). The goal of redemption is that believers in Jesus Christ would live their entire lives under God's sovereign rule as kingdom disciples.
19:9-10 The Way was an early title for Christianity (see, e.g., 9:2; 19:23; 24:14, 22). Believers in Christ were to follow a new way of life because Jesus is "the way" (see John 14:6; Rom 6:1-7).
Notice that the opposition to the gospel drove Paul to a different setting that resulted in more spiritual fruit than the original location. God knows how to take the actions of wicked men and use them to accomplish his good purposes.

a 19:11–12 Ac 5:15; 8:13
b 19:13 Mt 12:27; Mk 9:38;
Lk 11:19
c 19:17 Ac 8:16; 19:5,13;
21:13; 1Co 6:11; Col 3:17
d Ac 5:5,11; 18:19
e 19:19 Is 3:3; Ezk 13:18–20
f 19:20 Ac 6:6–7; 12:24
g 19:21 Ac 16:9; 18:12;
20:16,22; Rm 15:24–25,28
h 19:22 Rm 16:23; 2Tm 4:20
i Ac 13:5; 16:1,23; 19:10;
2Tm 4:20

j 19:23 Ac 9:2; 2Co 1:8
k 19:26 Dt 4:28; Ps 115:4; Is
44:10–20; Jr 10:3; Ac 17:29;
1Co 8:4; Rv 9:20
l 19:29 Rm 16:23; 1Co 1:14
m Ac 20:4; 27:2; Col 4:10;
Phm 24
n 19:32 Ac 21:34
o 19:32–33 Ac 12:17; 21:34

DEMONISM DEFEATED AT EPHESUS

11 God was performing extraordinary miracles by Paul's hands, **12** so that even facecloths or aprons[A] that had touched his skin were brought to the sick, and the diseases left them, and the evil spirits came out of them.[a]

13 Now some of the itinerant Jewish exorcists also attempted to pronounce the name of the Lord Jesus over those who had evil spirits, saying, "I command you by the Jesus that Paul preaches!"[b] **14** Seven sons of Sceva, a Jewish high priest, were doing this. **15** The evil spirit answered them, "I know Jesus, and I recognize Paul — but who are you?" **16** Then the man who had the evil spirit jumped on them, overpowered them all, and prevailed against them, so that they ran out of that house naked and wounded. **17** When this became known to everyone who lived in Ephesus, both Jews and Greeks, they became afraid, and the name of the Lord Jesus[c] was held in high esteem.[d]

18 And many who had become believers came confessing and disclosing their practices, **19** while many of those who had practiced magic[e] collected their books and burned them in front of everyone. So they calculated their value and found it to be fifty thousand pieces of silver. **20** In this way the word of the Lord flourished and prevailed.[f]

THE RIOT IN EPHESUS

21 After these events, Paul resolved by the Spirit[B] to pass through Macedonia and Achaia and go to Jerusalem. "After I've been there," he said, "It is necessary for me to see Rome as well."[g] **22** After sending to Macedonia two of those who assisted him, Timothy and Erastus,[h] he himself stayed in Asia for a while.[i]

23 About that time there was a major disturbance about the Way.[j] **24** For a person named Demetrius, a silversmith who made silver shrines of Artemis, provided a great deal of business for the craftsmen. **25** When he had assembled them, as well as the workers engaged in this type of business, he said: "Men, you know that our prosperity is derived from this business. **26** You see and hear that not only in Ephesus, but in almost all of Asia, this man Paul has persuaded and misled a considerable number of people by saying that gods made by hand are not gods.[k] **27** Not only do we run a risk that our business may be discredited, but also that the temple of the great goddess Artemis may be despised and her magnificence come to the verge of ruin — the very one all of Asia and the world worship."

28 When they had heard this, they were filled with rage and began to cry out, "Great is Artemis of the Ephesians!" **29** So the city was filled with confusion, and they rushed all together into the amphitheater, dragging along Gaius[l] and Aristarchus,[m] Macedonians who were Paul's traveling companions. **30** Although Paul wanted to go in before the people, the disciples did not let him. **31** Even some of the provincial officials of Asia, who were his friends, sent word to him, pleading with him not to venture[c] into the amphitheater. **32** Some were shouting one thing and some another,[n] because the assembly was in confusion, and most of them did not know why they had come together. **33** Some Jews in the crowd gave instructions to Alexander[D] after they pushed him to the front. Motioning with his hand, Alexander wanted to make his defense to the people.[o] **34** But when they recognized that he was a Jew, they all shouted

---

19:11–12 People took the **aprons** Paul used in his tent-making trade to heal others of **diseases** (19:12). Paul was so devoted to the Lord that after a hard day's work, he had sanctified sweat.

19:13–14 Some **itinerant Jewish exorcists** had seen the amazing power Paul displayed, and they wanted in on it. They decided to imitate him, using Jesus's **name** like a magical formula to wield power against **evil spirits** (19:13). They didn't believe Jesus was the Messiah, but they didn't mind using his name for their benefit. But understand this: Jesus won't be used for our selfish ends.

19:18–20 They **burned** their sorcery **books** (19:18–19) because they no longer wanted to be associated with false and deceptive

spirituality. And when they rid their lives of these things, **the word of [God] flourished and prevailed** even more (19:20).

Christian, are you dabbling with horoscopes? Tarot cards? Palm reading? God doesn't work through superstitious practices. The only way for the power of God to be present in your life is for you to leave them behind. "Guard yourselves from idols" (1 John 5:21).

19:23 A major disturbance occurred **about the Way** (on "the Way," see the note on 19:9–10). Wherever Paul preached, two things regularly happened: people got saved, and people got mad. That pattern was about to repeat itself.

19:24–27 Artemis was a Greek goddess (known among the Romans as *Diana*), and Ephesus was home to the great temple of Artemis—one

of the Seven Wonders of the Ancient World (19:24, 27). It was the major Ephesian tourist attraction; people from all over Asia visited it to worship. But as a result of Paul preaching that **gods made by hand are not gods**, many people had stopped buying the idolatrous trinkets produced by Demetrius and his comrades (19:25–26). Instead, they were coming to Christ and tossing their Artemis statues in the trash. Thus, these craftsmen were watching their religion suffer and their **business** flatline (19:27).

19:29 This **amphitheater** seated approximately twenty-four thousand.

19:34 These people didn't want to hear about this Jewish Messiah who was a rival to their goddess. Instead, they shouted on and on about Artemis's supposed greatness.

in unison for about two hours: "Great is Artemis of the Ephesians!"

35 When the city clerk had calmed the crowd down, he said, "People of Ephesus! What person is there who doesn't know that the city of the Ephesians is the temple guardian of the great[A] Artemis, and of the image that fell from heaven? **36** Therefore, since these things are undeniable, you must keep calm and not do anything rash. **37** For you have brought these men here who are not temple robbers or blasphemers of our[B] goddess. **38** So if Demetrius and the craftsmen who are with him have a case against anyone, the courts are in session, and there are proconsuls. Let them bring charges against one another.[a] **39** But if you seek anything further, it must be decided in a legal assembly. **40** In fact, we run a risk of being charged with rioting[b] for what happened today, since there is no justification that we can give as a reason for this disturbance." **41** After saying this, he dismissed the assembly.

PAUL IN MACEDONIA

20 After the uproar was over, Paul sent for the disciples, encouraged them, and after saying farewell, departed to go to Macedonia.[c] **2** And when he had passed through those areas and offered them many words of encouragement, he came to Greece **3** and stayed three months. The Jews plotted against him when he was about to set sail for Syria, and so he decided to go back through Macedonia.[d] **4** He was accompanied[c] by Sopater son of Pyrrhus[D] from Berea, Aristarchus and Secundus from Thessalonica, Gaius from Derbe, Timothy,[e] and Tychicus[f] and Trophimus[g] from the province of Asia. **5** These men went on ahead and waited for us in Troas,[h] **6** but we sailed away from Philippi after the Festival of Unleavened Bread.[i] In five days we reached them at Troas, where we spent seven days.

EUTYCHUS REVIVED AT TROAS

7 On the first day of the week, we[E] assembled to break bread.[j] Paul spoke to them, and since he was about to depart the next day, he kept on talking until midnight. **8** There were many lamps in the room upstairs where we were assembled, **9** and a young man named Eutychus was sitting on a window sill and sank into a deep sleep as Paul kept on talking. When he was overcome by sleep, he fell down from the third story and was picked up dead. **10** But Paul went down, bent over him, embraced him, and said, "Don't be alarmed, because he's alive."[k] **11** After going upstairs, breaking the bread, and eating, Paul talked a long time until dawn. Then he left. **12** They brought the boy home alive and were greatly comforted.

FROM TROAS TO MILETUS

13 We went on ahead to the ship and sailed for Assos, where we were going to take Paul on board, because these were his instructions, since he himself was going by land. **14** When he met us at Assos, we took him on board and went on to Mitylene. **15** Sailing from there, the next day we arrived off Chios. The following day we crossed over to Samos, and[F] the day after, we came to Miletus.[l] **16** For Paul had decided to sail past Ephesus to avoid spending time in the province of Asia, because he was hurrying to be in Jerusalem, if possible, for the day of Pentecost.[m]

FAREWELL ADDRESS
TO THE EPHESIAN ELDERS

17 Now from Miletus, he sent to Ephesus and summoned the elders of the church. **18** When they came to him, he said to them: "You know, from the first day I set foot in Asia, how I was with you the whole time,[n] **19** serving the Lord with all humility, with tears, and during the trials that came to me through the plots of the Jews.[o] **20** You know that I did not avoid proclaiming to you anything that was profitable or from

[a] 19:37-38 Ac 13:7; Rm 2:22
[b] 19:40 Mt 26:5; 27:24; Ac 17:5
[c] 20:1 Ac 11:26; 16:9; 19:21; 2Co 2:12-13
[d] 20:3 Ac 9:23; 20:19; 23:12; 25:3; 2Co 11:26
[e] 20:4 Ac 14:6; 16:1; 17:1; 19:29
[f] Eph 6:21; Col 4:7; 2Tm 4:12; Ti 3:12
[g] Ac 21:29; 2Tm 4:20
[h] 20:5 Ac 16:8,10; 20:6-8,13-15
[i] 20:6 Ex 12:14-15; 23:15

[j] 20:7 Ac 2:42; 1Co 10:16
[k] 20:10 1Kg 17:21; 2Kg 4:34; Mt 9:23-24; Mk 5:39
[l] 20:15 Ac 20:17; 2Tm 4:20
[m] 20:16 Ac 2:1; 18:19; 19:21; 1Co 16:8
[n] 20:18 Ac 18:19; 19:1,10
[o] 20:19-20 Ac 20:3,27

[A]**19:35** Other mss add *goddess*   [B]**19:37** Other mss read *your*   [C]**20:4** Other mss add *to Asia*   [D]**20:4** Other mss omit *son of Pyrrhus*
[E]**20:7** Other mss read *the disciples*   [F]**20:15** Other mss add *after staying at Trogyllium*

19:41 The word translated *assembly* here is the Greek word *ekklēsia*. When it refers to the assembly of believers, it's translated "church." So when Jesus and the apostles started speaking of the *church*, they were not coining a new term. It was a common word used to speak of a gathering of people to address an issue, especially one legal in nature. The church of Jesus Christ is God's legally authorized assembly on earth to call on the power of heaven

to execute the will of God in history (see the notes on Matt 16:18-19).
20:6 Notice the appearance of the first-person plural **we**. It tells us that Luke, the author of Acts, had once again joined Paul (see the note on 16:10).
20:9-10 Just as Jesus had done before them, both Peter and Paul raised the dead through the power of the Holy Spirit (see 9:36-43).

20:18-20 It was an emotional time. Paul was on his way to Jerusalem, opposition awaited, and he realized he might never see the Ephesians again. Therefore, he wanted to give them a final exhortation so that they might continue the work to which God had called them, teaching and leading his people.

a 20:21 Mk 1:15; Ac 2:38;
18:5
b Ac 24:24; 26:18; Eph 1:15;
Col 2:5; Phm 5
c 20:22 Ac 17:16; 20:16
d 20:23 Ac 9:16; 21:4,11;
1Th 3:3
e 20:24 Ac 1:17; 21:13; 2Co
4:1; 2Tm 4:7
f Gl 1:1; Ti 1:3
g 20:25-26 Ac 18:6; 20:38;
28:31
h 20:27 Lk 7:30; Ac 20:20;
Eph 1:11
i 20:28 Lk 12:32; Jn 10:16;
1Co 9:7; 1Pt 5:2-3
j Php 1:1; 1Tm 3:2; Ti 1:7;
1Pt 2:25
k Eph 1:7,14; Heb 9:12; 1Pt
1:19; Rv 5:9
l 20:30 Ac 11:26; 1Tm 1:20;
1Jn 2:19
m 20:31 Ac 19:10; 20:19
n 20:32 Ac 14:23; Heb 13:9
o Ac 26:18; Eph 1:14; Col
1:12; 3:24; Heb 9:15; 1Pt 1:4
p 20:33 1Sm 12:3; 1Co 9:12;
2Co 7:2; 11:9; 12:17

➤ Questions & Answers ➤

Q In Acts 20:17-38, Paul delivers his final message to the leaders of the Ephesian church, summarizing the themes that were important to him and the message he wanted to hand off to the leaders. If you had to give a final message to the next generation of leaders at your church, what would be your key points and highlights?

A My last message to our church and our leadership would be similar to Paul's. I would want to encourage them to protect the church from error, from evil people, and from division. Also, I would urge them to maintain the vision that the church exists to advance the kingdom of God—not merely to have church programming.

When the church becomes ingrown and only exists for itself, it is no longer fulfilling the purpose for which it was created. We are called to advance God's kingdom—which is the visual manifestation of the comprehensive rule of God over every area of life. And we are to do so through the individual, the family, and the members of the church, moving outward to the community. If church leaders keep that vision and philosophy in sight and hold tenaciously to the authority of God's Word, the church will always remain strong, relevant, and effective.

FOR THE NEXT Q&A, SEE PAGE 1325.

teaching you publicly and from house to house. [21] I testified to both Jews and Greeks about repentance toward God*a* and faith in our Lord Jesus.*b* [22] "And now I am on my way to Jerusalem, compelled by the Spirit,[A] not knowing what I will encounter there,*c* [23] except that in every town the Holy Spirit warns me that chains and afflictions are waiting for me.*d* [24] But I consider my life of no value to myself; my purpose is to finish my course[B] and the ministry*e* I received from the Lord Jesus,*f* to testify to the gospel of God's grace. [25] "And now I know that none of you, among whom I went about preaching the kingdom, will ever see me again. [26] Therefore I declare to you this day that I am innocent[C] of the blood of all of you,*g* [27] because I did not avoid declaring to you the whole plan of God.*h* [28] Be on guard for yourselves and for all the flock*i* of which the Holy Spirit has appointed you as overseers,*j* to shepherd the church of God,[D] which he purchased with his own blood.*k* [29] I know that after my departure savage wolves will come in among you, not sparing the flock. [30] Men will rise up even from your own number and distort the truth to lure the disciples into following them.*l* [31] Therefore be on the alert, remembering that night and day for three years I never stopped warning each one of you with tears.*m* [32] "And now[E] I commit you to God and to the word of his grace,*n* which is able to build you up and to give you an inheritance*o* among all who are sanctified. [33] I have not coveted anyone's silver or gold or clothing.*p* [34] You yourselves know that

[A] 20:22 Or *in my spirit*   [B] 20:24 Other mss add *with joy*   [C] 20:26 Lit *clean*   [D] 20:28 Some mss read *church of the Lord*; other mss read *church of the Lord and God*   [E] 20:32 Other mss add *brothers and sisters*

20:21 **Repentance** is an internal decision and determination to turn from sin. To have **faith** in Jesus is to trust in Christ alone for the gift of eternal life.

20:22 Being **compelled by the Spirit** is that feeling of God having a vice grip on your soul, confirming his purpose for you and urging you in a particular direction.

20:24 Despite his trials and uncertainties, Paul had an eternal perspective: **I consider my life of no value to myself**. Instead, what he valued above all things was the opportunity to **testify to the gospel of God's grace**. Therefore, Paul wanted to faithfully **finish [his] course**, to reach the finish line.

Are you prepared to live the rest of your life the same way? Don't let your days pass you by. Pursue God and his plans for you. Whatever the future held, Paul wanted to complete his life, saying in essence, "I have done what

God put me on earth to do" (see 2 Tim 4:6-8).

20:25-27 Paul was confident that he had faithfully proclaimed **the kingdom**—the rule of God—among the Ephesians (20:25). Therefore, he was **innocent of [their] blood** (20:26), like the "watchman" the prophet Ezekiel spoke of (see Ezek 3:16-27). If someone needed to hear truth from God's Word, he avoided nothing and exhorted everyone (20:27). No one could blame Paul for failing to talk about Jesus. Could the same be said of you?

20:28 It is a pastoral duty to guide the people of God in biblical truth and protect them from error—to provide spiritual direction and warn against dangerous spiritual influences. To fail at this is to fail as a spiritual shepherd.

20:29-30 Protecting **the flock** sometimes means confronting **wolves**, people who don't have the best interests of others

in mind but only care to satisfy their own desires. The church needs pastors who know God's Word, can discern negative influences, and will step in to guard the flock that God has entrusted to them. These leaders should also be motivated by a deep love for God's people.

20:32 Pastors, don't neglect the ministry of **the word**. No matter how eloquent a preacher, dynamic a leader, or competent an administrator you are, never forget that you are nothing without the Word of God. The church is founded on and edified through the Bible. Let it be at the center of your ministry.

20:33-34 Beware of those who seek to use the church merely to line their pockets. A faithful pastor/elder is "worthy of his wages" (1 Tim 5:17-18), but that's quite different from someone who is fleecing the flock for personal gain.

I worked with my own hands to support myself and those who are with me.[a] 35 In every way I've shown you that it is necessary to help the weak by laboring like this and to remember the words of the Lord Jesus, because he said, 'It is more blessed to give than to receive.'"

36 After he said this, he knelt down and prayed with all of them.[b] 37 There were many tears shed by everyone. They embraced Paul and kissed him, 38 grieving most of all over his statement that they would never see his face again. And they accompanied him to the ship.[c]

WARNINGS ON THE JOURNEY TO JERUSALEM

21 After[d] we tore ourselves away from them, we set sail straight for Cos, the next day to Rhodes, and from there to Patara. 2 Finding a ship crossing over to Phoenicia, we boarded and set sail. 3 After we sighted Cyprus, passing to the south of it,[A] we sailed on to Syria and arrived at Tyre, since the ship was to unload its cargo there. 4 We sought out the disciples and stayed there seven days. Through the Spirit they told Paul not to go to Jerusalem.[e] 5 When our time had come to an end, we left to continue our journey, while all of them, with their wives and children, accompanied us out of the city. After kneeling down on the beach to pray, 6 we said farewell to one another and boarded the ship, and they returned home.

7 When we completed our voyage[B] from Tyre, we reached Ptolemais, where we greeted the brothers and sisters and stayed with them for a day.[f] 8 The next day we left and came to Caesarea, where we entered the house of Philip[g] the evangelist,[h] who was one of the Seven, and stayed with him. 9 This man had four virgin daughters who prophesied.[i]

10 After we had been there for several days, a prophet named Agabus came down from Judea. 11 He came to us, took Paul's belt, tied his own feet and hands, and said, "This is what the Holy Spirit says: 'In this way the Jews in Jerusalem will bind the man who owns this belt and deliver him over to the Gentiles.'"[j] 12 When we heard this, both we and the local people pleaded with him not to go up to Jerusalem.

13 Then Paul replied, "What are you doing, weeping and breaking my heart? For I am ready not only to be bound but also to die in Jerusalem for the name of the Lord Jesus."[k]

14 Since he would not be persuaded, we said no more except, "The Lord's will be done."[l]

CONFLICT OVER THE GENTILE MISSION

15 After this we got ready and went up to Jerusalem. 16 Some of the disciples from Caesarea also went with us and brought us to Mnason of Cyprus, an early disciple, with whom we were to stay.[m]

17 When we reached Jerusalem, the brothers and sisters welcomed us warmly.[n] 18 The following day Paul went in with us to James, and all the elders were present.[o] 19 After greeting them, he reported in detail what God had done among the Gentiles through his ministry.[p]

20 When they heard it, they glorified God and said, "You see, brother, how many thousands of Jews there are who have believed, and they are all zealous[q] for the law. 21 But they have been informed about you — that you are teaching all the Jews who are among the Gentiles to abandon Moses, telling them not to circumcise their children or to live according to our customs.[r] 22 So what is to be done?[c] They

a 20:34 Ac 18:3; 19:22
b 20:36 Lk 22:41; Ac 7:60; 21:5
c 20:37-38 Ac 15:3; 20:25
d 21:1 Ac 16:10-11
e 21:4 Ac 11:26; 20:23; 21:11
f 21:7 Jn 21:23; Ac 12:20
g 21:8 Ac 6:5; 8:5
h Eph 4:11; 2Tm 4:5
i 21:9 Lk 2:36; Ac 2:7; 13:1; 1Co 11:5
j 21:11 1Kg 22:11; Jr 13:1-11; Mt 20:19; Ac 20:23; 21:33
k 21:13 Ac 5:41; 9:16; 20:24
l 21:14 Mt 6:10; Lk 22:42
m 21:16 Ac 8:40; 21:3-4
n 21:17 Ac 15:4; 21:7
o 21:18 Ac 11:30; 12:17; 15:13
p 21:19 Ac 1:17; 14:27; Rm 15:18-19
q 21:20 Ac 22:3; Rm 10:12; Gl 1:14
r 21:21 Ac 6:14; 15:19-20; 21:28; 1Co 7:18

A 21:3 Lit leaving it on the left   B 21:7 Or As we continued our voyage   C 21:22 Other mss add A multitude has to come together, since

---

20:35 **It is more blessed to give than to receive** because in God's economy you will be more blessed if you're a spiritual conduit rather than a spiritual cul-de-sac. God wants to work through you so that you will be a blessing to others. If you have the capacity to address a need (with your money, your time, or your encouragement), be used by God to give to and meet that need. God will return the favor (see Luke 6:38).
20:37-38 Paul had the heart of a shepherd; that truth was reflected in the response to his departure.
21:8 **Philip** was **one of the Seven**—that is, one of the first seven deacons appointed by the

church (see 6:1-6)—and he shared the gospel with the Ethiopian eunuch (see 8:26-40).
21:9 Notice that the gift of prophecy was bestowed by the Spirit without gender distinction. Though women were restricted from the office of elder/overseer/pastor (see 1 Tim 2:11-13), the Spirit makes no gender distinction in the distribution of spiritual gifts.
21:13 When the excitement of spending eternity with **Jesus** is real in your heart, whether you live or die doesn't make a difference as long as the Lord is glorified. As Paul told the Philippians, "For me, to live is Christ and to die is gain" (Phil 1:21).

21:14 We will frequently be unable to understand the reason God allows certain circumstances in our lives. Nevertheless, like Paul and the Lord Jesus himself (see Luke 22:42), we must have hearts that submit to our King's **will** for our lives.
21:21 Though Paul clearly told all people (Jews and Gentiles) that salvation came through faith in Christ alone, he didn't argue that Jewish customs couldn't be practiced. After all, Paul had Timothy circumcised to make it easier for the two of them to conduct ministry among the Jews (see 16:1-3). Circumcision is not a problem as long as one doesn't rely on it for salvation or sanctification (see Gal 5:1-6).

*21:24 Jn 11:55; Ac 18:18;
21:26; 24:18
*21:26 Nm 6:13; Ac 24:18
*21:27 Ac 24:18; 26:21
*21:28 Mt 24:15; Ac 24:6
*21:29 Ac 18:19; 20:4
*21:30 2Kg 11:15; Ac 16:19;
26:21

*21:33 Ac 12:6; 20:23;
21:11; Eph 6:20; 2Tm
1:16; 2:9
*21:34 Ac 19:32; 23:10
*21:36 Lk 23:18; Jn 19:15;
Ac 22:22
*21:38 Mt 24:26; Ac 5:36
*21:39 Ac 9:11; 22:3
*21:40 Jn 5:2; Ac 12:17
*22:1-2 Ac 7:2; 21:40
*22:3-16 Ac 9:1-22;
26:9-18
*22:3 Dt 33:3; Ac 5:34;
9:11; 21:39; 2Co 11:22;
Php 3:5
*Ac 26:5; Rm 10:2; Php 3:6
*22:4 Ac 9:2; 24:14,22
*Ac 8:3; 22:19-20; 26:10
*22:5 Lk 22:66; Ac 13:26;
1Tm 4:14

will certainly hear that you've come. [23] Therefore do what we tell you: We have four men who have made a vow. [24] Take these men, purify yourself along with them, and pay for them to get their heads shaved. Then everyone will know that what they were told about you amounts to nothing, but that you yourself are also careful about observing the law.[a] [25] With regard to the Gentiles who have believed, we have written a letter containing our decision that[A] they should keep themselves from food sacrificed to idols, from blood, from what is strangled, and from sexual immorality."

THE RIOT IN THE TEMPLE

[26] So the next day, Paul took the men, having purified himself along with them, and entered the temple, announcing the completion of the purification days when the offering would be made for each of them.[b] [27] When the seven days were nearly over, some Jews from the province of Asia saw him in the temple, stirred up the whole crowd, and seized him,[c] [28] shouting, "Fellow Israelites, help! This is the man who teaches everyone everywhere against our people, our law, and this place. What's more, he also brought Greeks into the temple and has defiled this holy place."[d] [29] For they had previously seen Trophimus the Ephesian in the city with him, and they supposed that Paul had brought him into the temple.[e]

[30] The whole city was stirred up, and the people rushed together. They seized Paul, dragged him out of the temple, and at once the gates were shut.[f]

[31] As they were trying to kill him, word went up to the commander of the regiment that all Jerusalem was in chaos. [32] Taking along soldiers and centurions, he immediately ran down to them. Seeing the commander and the soldiers, they stopped beating Paul. [33] Then the commander approached, took him into custody, and

ordered him to be bound with two chains.[g] He asked who he was and what he had done. [34] Some in the crowd were shouting one thing and some another. Since he was not able to get reliable information because of the uproar, he ordered him to be taken into the barracks.[h] [35] When Paul got to the steps, he had to be carried by the soldiers because of the violence of the crowd, [36] for the mass of people followed, yelling, "Get rid of him!"[i]

PAUL'S DEFENSE
BEFORE THE JERUSALEM MOB

[37] As he was about to be brought into the barracks, Paul said to the commander, "Am I allowed to say something to you?"

He replied, "You know how to speak Greek? [38] Aren't you the Egyptian who started a revolt some time ago and led four thousand men of the Assassins into the wilderness?"[j]

[39] Paul said, "I am a Jewish man from Tarsus of Cilicia,[k] a citizen of an important city. Now I ask you, let me speak to the people."

[40] After he had given permission, Paul stood on the steps and motioned with his hand to the people. When there was a great hush, he addressed them in Aramaic:[B,l]

22
[1] "Brothers and fathers, listen now to my defense before you." [2] When they heard that he was addressing them in Aramaic,[B] they became even quieter.[m] [3] He[n] continued, "I am a Jew, born in Tarsus of Cilicia but brought up in this city, educated at the feet of Gamaliel[o] according to the law of our ancestors. I was zealous for God, just as all of you are today.[p] [4] I persecuted this Way[q] to the death, arresting and putting both men and women in jail,[r] [5] as both the high priest and the whole council of elders can testify about me. After I received letters from them to the brothers, I traveled to Damascus to arrest those who were there and bring them to Jerusalem to be punished.[s]

21:23-24 This was probably a reference to the Nazirite **vow** (see Num 6:1-21), something Paul had done himself (see Acts 18:18). Once the other Jews saw Paul do as he was told here, they would realize that the rumors they had heard about him rejecting Jewish customs amounted **to nothing** (21:24).
21:25 The **letter** to the **Gentiles** that had been written was a result of the Jerusalem Council (see 15:22-29).
21:28-29 Because they had seen Paul walking around the city with a Gentile man from

Ephesus, they assumed he **had brought him [inside] the temple**.
21:35 The commander had his **soldiers** carry Paul because **the crowd** wouldn't stop attacking him. When we read Paul's letters, we might be tempted to think that he was just a heady theologian. But actually Paul wrote from an incredible Christian experience that included genuine love for people, intense emotional and physical suffering, and active pursuit of his King's agenda.

22:1-5 Paul began to address the crowd that only moments before had been beating him to a pulp. They had become angry with him based on false pretenses, so Paul wanted to clarify who he was and what he had been doing. He began by explaining how much they had in common.
   The Way was an early title given to Christianity (22:4; see 9:2; 19:9, 23; 24:14, 22).

PAUL'S TESTIMONY

6 "As[a] I was traveling and approaching Damascus, about noon an intense light from heaven suddenly flashed around me. **7** I fell to the ground and heard a voice saying to me, 'Saul, Saul, why are you persecuting me?'

8 "I answered, 'Who are you, Lord?'

"He said to me, 'I am Jesus of Nazareth, the one you are persecuting.' **9** Now those who were with me saw the light,[A] but they did not hear the voice of the one who was speaking to me.[b]

10 "I said, 'What should I do, Lord?'

"The Lord told me, 'Get up and go into Damascus, and there you will be told everything that you have been assigned to do.'

11 "Since I couldn't see because of the brightness of the light,[B] I was led by the hand by those who were with me, and went into Damascus.[c] **12** Someone named Ananias, a devout man according to the law, who had a good reputation with all the Jews living there,[d] **13** came and stood by me and said, 'Brother Saul, regain your sight.' And in that very hour I looked up and saw him. **14** And he said, 'The God of our ancestors has appointed[e] you to know his will, to see[f] the Righteous One,[g] and to hear the words from his mouth, **15** since you will be a witness for him to all people of what you have seen and heard.[h] **16** And now, why are you delaying? Get up and be baptized, and wash away your sins,[i] calling on his name.'[j]

17 "After I returned to Jerusalem and was praying in the temple, I fell into a trance[k] **18** and saw him telling me, 'Hurry and get out of Jerusalem quickly, because they will not accept your testimony about me.'

19 "But I said, 'Lord, they know that in synagogue after synagogue I had those who believed in you imprisoned and beaten.[l] **20** And when the blood of your witness Stephen was being shed, I stood there giving approval[c] and guarding the clothes of those who killed him.'[m]

21 "He said to me, 'Go, because I will send you far away to the Gentiles.' "[n]

PAUL'S ROMAN PROTECTION

22 They listened to him up to this point. Then they raised their voices, shouting, "Wipe this man off the face of the earth! He should not be allowed to live!"[o]

23 As they were yelling and flinging aside their garments and throwing dust into the air,[p] **24** the commander ordered him to be brought into the barracks, directing that he be interrogated with the scourge to discover the reason they were shouting against him like this. **25** As they stretched him out for the lash, Paul said to the centurion standing by, "Is it legal for you to scourge a man who is a Roman citizen and is uncondemned?"[q]

26 When the centurion heard this, he went and reported to the commander, saying, "What are you going to do? For this man is a Roman citizen."

27 The commander came and said to him, "Tell me, are you a Roman citizen?"

"Yes," he said.

28 The commander replied, "I bought this citizenship for a large amount of money."

"But I was born a citizen," Paul said.

29 So those who were about to examine him withdrew from him immediately. The commander too was alarmed when he realized Paul was a Roman citizen and he had bound him.[r]

PAUL BEFORE THE SANHEDRIN

30 The next day, since he wanted to find out exactly why Paul was being accused by the Jews, he released him[D] and instructed the chief priests and all the Sanhedrin to convene.[s] He brought Paul down and placed him before them. **23** **1** Paul looked straight at the Sanhedrin and said, "Brothers, I have lived my life

[a]22:6-11 Ac 9:3-8; 26:12-18
[b]22:9 Dn 10:7; Ac 9:7; 26:13
[c]22:10-11 Ac 9:8; 16:30
[d]22:12 Ac 9:10,17; 10:22
[e]22:14 Ac 3:13; 9:15; 26:16
[f]1Co 9:1; 15:8
[g]Ac 3:14; 7:52
[h]22:15 Ac 23:11; 26:16
[i]22:16 Ac 2:38; 1Co 6:11; Heb 10:22
[j]Ac 9:14; Rm 10:13
[k]22:17 Ac 9:26; 10:10
[l]22:19 Mt 10:17; Ac 8:3; 22:4

[m]22:20 Ac 7:58; 8:1; Rm 1:32
[n]22:21 Ac 9:15; 13:46
[o]22:22 Ac 21:36; 25:24
[p]22:23 2Sm 16:13; Ac 7:58
[q]22:24-25 Ac 16:37; 21:34; 22:29
[r]22:29 Ac 16:38; 21:33
[s]22:30 Mt 5:22; Ac 23:3-8

[A]22:9 Other mss add *and were afraid*   [B]22:11 Lit *the glory of that light*   [C]22:20 Other mss add *of his murder*   [D]22:30 Other mss add *from his chains*

22:10 The Lord didn't inform Paul about his purpose until he went to **Damascus** as commanded. Many Christians want to know God's purposes for their lives, but they're unwilling to obey the clear commands that he's already given. But God hits a moving target. Follow God in faith; do what you already know you're supposed to do. By doing so, you'll show him that you're serious about pursuing him so that he can begin guiding, directing, and ordering your steps.
22:14-15 Paul was saved for a purpose, and the same is true of all believers. Christians are

God's "workmanship, created in Christ Jesus for good works, which God prepared ahead of time for us to do" (Eph 2:10).
22:21 God sent Paul to **the Gentiles**. And what Paul said about the Ephesian church was also once true of most of us: "At one time you were Gentiles . . . without Christ, excluded from the citizenship of Israel, and foreigners to the covenants of promise, without hope and without God in the world" (Eph 2:11-12). Praise God for his grace to Gentiles and for Paul's faithfulness to his Gentile mission.

22:24 The Roman **commander** ordered Paul to be taken to the barracks—not to protect him—but to whip him **with the scourge to discover** why everyone was so angry with him. Clearly, then, he wasn't concerned with justice.
22:25-29 Paul shrewdly used his citizenship to his advantage. He wasn't afraid to be beaten for Christ. But he also wasn't afraid to exercise his legal rights to escape illegitimate punishment and to take his case and message to a higher governmental authority—ultimately to Caesar (see 25:11-12).

[a] 23:1 Ac 24:16; 1Co 4:4; 1Tm 3:9; 2Tm 1:5; Heb 13:18; 1Pt 3:16
[b] 23:2 1Kg 22:24; Jn 18:22; Ac 24:1
[c] 23:3 Lv 19:15; Dt 25:1-2; Mt 23:27; Jn 7:51
[d] 23:5 Ex 22:28; Ac 24:17
[e] 23:6 Ac 26:5; Php 3:5
[f] Ac 24:15,21; 26:6-8; 28:20
[g] 23:8 Mt 22:23; Mk 12:18; Lk 20:27
[h] 23:9 Mk 2:16; Lk 5:30
[i] Ac 23:29; 25:25; 26:31
[j] Jn 12:29; Ac 22:7,17-18
[k] 23:10 Ac 21:34; 23:16,32
[l] 23:11 Ac 18:9; 19:21; 27:23

[m] 23:12 Ac 23:14,21,30; 25:3
[n] 23:15 Ac 22:30; 23:1
[o] 23:21 Lk 11:54; Ac 23:12,14

before God in all good conscience[a] to this day." [2] The high priest Ananias ordered those who were standing next to him to strike him on the mouth.[b] [3] Then Paul said to him, "God is going to strike you, you whitewashed wall! You are sitting there judging me according to the law, and yet in violation of the law are you ordering me to be struck?"[c]

[4] Those standing nearby said, "Do you dare revile God's high priest?"

[5] "I did not know, brothers, that he was the high priest," replied Paul. "For it is written, **You must not speak evil of a ruler of your people.**"[A,d] [6] When Paul realized that one part of them were Sadducees and the other part were Pharisees, he cried out in the Sanhedrin, "Brothers, I am a Pharisee, a son of Pharisees.[e] I am being judged because of the hope of the resurrection of the dead!"[f] [7] When he said this, a dispute broke out between the Pharisees and the Sadducees, and the assembly was divided. [8] For the Sadducees say there is no resurrection,[g] and neither angel nor spirit, but the Pharisees affirm them all.

[9] The shouting grew loud, and some of the scribes of the Pharisees'[h] party got up and argued vehemently: "We find nothing evil in this man.[i] What if a spirit or an angel has spoken to him?"[B,j]

[10] When the dispute became violent, the commander feared that Paul might be torn apart by them and ordered the troops to go down, take him away from them, and bring him into the barracks.[k] [11] The following night, the Lord stood by him and said, "Have courage! For as you have testified about me in Jerusalem, so it is necessary for you to testify in Rome."[l]

THE PLOT AGAINST PAUL

[12] When it was morning, the Jews formed a conspiracy and bound themselves under a curse not to eat or drink until they had killed Paul.[m] [13] There were more than forty who had formed this plot. [14] These men went to the chief priests and elders and said, "We have bound ourselves under a solemn curse that we won't eat anything until we have killed Paul. [15] So now you, along with the Sanhedrin, make a request to the commander that he bring him down to you[c] as if you were going to investigate his case more thoroughly. But, before he gets near, we are ready to kill him."[n]

[16] But the son of Paul's sister, hearing about their ambush, came and entered the barracks and reported it to Paul. [17] Paul called one of the centurions and said, "Take this young man to the commander, because he has something to report to him."

[18] So he took him, brought him to the commander, and said, "The prisoner Paul called me and asked me to bring this young man to you, because he has something to tell you."

[19] The commander took him by the hand, led him aside, and inquired privately, "What is it you have to report to me?"

[20] "The Jews," he said, "have agreed to ask you to bring Paul down to the Sanhedrin tomorrow, as though they are going to hold a somewhat more careful inquiry about him. [21] Don't let them persuade you, because there are more than forty of them lying in ambush — men who have bound themselves under a curse not to eat or drink until they have killed him. Now they are ready, waiting for your consent."[o]

[22] So the commander dismissed the young man and instructed him, "Don't tell anyone that you have informed me about this."

TO CAESAREA BY NIGHT

[23] He summoned two of his centurions and said, "Get two hundred soldiers ready with seventy cavalry and two hundred spearmen

[A] 23:5 Ex 22:28 [B] 23:9 Other mss add *Let us not fight God.* [C] 23:15 Other mss add *tomorrow*

23:3 The phrase **whitewashed wall** refers to a thing made to look clean on the outside though it is actually dirty on the inside.
23:4-5 Some interpreters think Paul truly didn't know to whom he was speaking in verse 3. Others think Paul's eyesight was bad. But more likely, Paul considered Ananias an illegitimate high priest because of his unjust actions in conducting the trial (see Lev 19:15). In any case, by quoting Exodus 22:28, Paul was acknowledging respect for the leader's office but saying, "This is a fake leader."
23:6-9 It was clear to Paul that he wasn't going to get a fair hearing. So when he **realized** that some of those gathered **were**

Sadducees (a group that denied the resurrection of the dead) and some were **Pharisees** (a group that believed in the resurrection of the dead), he told them he was **a Pharisee** on trial **because of the hope of the resurrection** (23:6, 8). That was a shrewd move because technically, he was right. His message was the proclamation that Jesus was the Messiah who had risen from the dead. But he used that truth to highlight the theological conflict that existed between the two groups, winning sympathy for himself from the Pharisees (23:9).
23:11 God would ultimately take Paul to the heart of the Roman Empire, but it wouldn't be

a smooth ride. Sometimes, in his providence, God will take you on a long and difficult road to get you where he wants you. Trust God, maintain your kingdom perspective, and (as the Lord told Paul) **have courage.**
23:12-22 If the Lord knows how to have a nephew at the right place at the right time to foil the plans of a band of killers (23:16-22), then he knows how to take care of you no matter what you're up against.
23:23-24 The commander was under obligation to look after this Roman citizen in his charge. Therefore, he gathered **two hundred soldiers . . . with seventy cavalry and two hundred spearmen** (470 armed Romans

to go to Caesarea at nine tonight.^A,a^ 24 Also provide mounts for Paul to ride and bring him safely to Felix the governor."

25 He wrote the following letter:^B^ 26 Claudius Lysias,

To the most excellent governor Felix: Greetings.^b^

27 When this man had been seized by the Jews and was about to be killed by them, I arrived with my troops and rescued him because I learned that he is a Roman citizen.^c^ 28 Wanting to know the charge they were accusing him of, I brought him down before their Sanhedrin. 29 I found out that the accusations were concerning questions of their law,^d^ and that there was no charge that merited death or imprisonment.^e^ 30 When I was informed that there was a plot against the man,^c,f^ I sent him to you right away. I also ordered his accusers^g^ to state their case against him in your presence.^D^

31 So the soldiers took Paul during the night and brought him to Antipatris as they were ordered. 32 The next day, they returned to the barracks, allowing the cavalry to go on with him. 33 When these men entered Caesarea and delivered the letter to the governor, they also presented Paul to him.^h^ 34 After he^E^ read it, he asked what province he was from. When he learned he was from Cilicia,^i^ 35 he said, "I will give you a hearing whenever your accusers also get here." He ordered that he be kept under guard in Herod's palace.^F,j^

THE ACCUSATION AGAINST PAUL

24 Five days later Ananias^k^ the high priest came down with some elders and a lawyer named Tertullus. These men presented their case against Paul to the governor.^l^ 2 When Paul was called in,

Tertullus began to accuse him and said: "We enjoy great peace because of you, and reforms are taking place for the benefit of this nation because of your foresight. 3 We acknowledge this in every way and everywhere, most excellent^m^ Felix, with utmost gratitude. 4 But, so that I will not burden you any further, I request that you would be kind enough to give us a brief hearing. 5 For we have found this man to be a plague,^n^ an agitator^o^ among all the Jews throughout the Roman world, and a ringleader of the sect of the Nazarenes.^p^ 6 He even tried to desecrate the temple, and so we apprehended him.^G^ By examining him yourself you will be able to discern the truth about these charges we are bringing against him." 9 The Jews also joined in the attack, alleging that these things were true.

PAUL'S DEFENSE BEFORE FELIX

10 When the governor motioned for him to speak, Paul replied: "Because I know you have been a judge of this nation for many years, I am glad to offer my defense in what concerns me.^q^ 11 You can verify for yourself that it is no more than twelve days since I went up to worship in Jerusalem.^r^ 12 They didn't find me arguing with anyone or causing a disturbance among the crowd, either in the temple or in the synagogues or anywhere in the city.^s^ 13 Neither can they prove the charges they are now making against me. 14 But I admit this to you: I worship the God of my ancestors according to the Way,^t^ which they call a sect, believing everything that is in accordance with the law and written in the prophets.^u^ 15 I have a hope in God, which these men themselves also accept, that there will be a resurrection,^H,v^ both of the righteous and the unrighteous.^w^ 16 I always strive to have a clear conscience^x^ toward God and men.

^a^23:23 Ac 8:40; 23:33
^b^23:26 Lk 1:3; Ac 15:23; 24:3; 26:25
^c^23:27 Ac 21:32-33; 22:25-29
^d^23:29 Ac 18:15; 25:19
^e^23:29 Ac 25:25; 26:31
^f^23:30 Ac 9:24; 23:12,20
^g^Ac 24:19; 25:16
^h^23:33 Ac 8:40; 23:23-24,26
^i^23:34 Ac 6:9; 21:39; 25:1
^j^23:35 Mt 27:27; Ac 24:27; 25:16
^k^24:1 Ac 23:2
^l^Ac 21:27; 23:2,24,30

^m^24:3 Lk 1:3; Ac 23:26; 26:25
^n^24:5 Ac 16:20; 17:6
^o^Ac 21:28; 26:5; 28:22
^p^Mt 2:23; 26:71; Mk 1:24; 10:47; 16:6; Lk 18:37; 24:19; Jn 19:19; Ac 2:22; 3:6; 4:10; 6:14; 22:8
^q^24:9-10 Ac 23:24; 1Th 2:16
^r^24:11 Ac 21:27; 24:1
^s^24:12 Ac 25:8; 28:17
^t^24:14 Ac 9:2; 22:4; 24:22
^u^Ac 3:13; 26:22; 28:23
^v^24:15 Ac 23:6; 28:20
^w^Dn 12:2; Jn 5:28-29
^x^24:16 Ac 23:1; 1Co 4:4; 1Tm 3:9; 2Tm 1:5; Heb 13:18; 1Pt 3:16

^A^23:23 Lit *at the third hour tonight* ^B^23:25 Or *He wrote a letter to this effect:* ^C^23:30 Other mss add *by the Jews* ^D^23:30 Other mss add *Farewell* ^E^23:34 Other mss read *the governor* ^F^23:35 Or *headquarters* ^G^24:6 Some mss include vv. 6b-8a: *and wanted to judge him according to our law.* ^7^*But Lysias the commander came and took him from our hands with great force,* ^8^*commanding his accusers to come to you.* ^H^24:15 Other mss add *of the dead*

against 40 fasting Jews sounds like pretty good odds!) to transport Paul by night **to ... the governor.** So not only was Paul being delivered safely from the hands of those who wanted to kill him, he was getting a massive armed escort.

23:26 Marcus Antonius **Felix** was the Roman **governor** (or procurator) of Judea from AD 52 to 58. According to historical sources, Felix was a lousy and brutal ruler.

23:34 Paul **was from Cilicia**, a Roman **province** on the coast of modern-day Turkey. His

hometown, Tarsus, was located there (see 9:11; 21:39; 22:3).

23:35 Though Paul was **kept under guard**, Luke makes it clear throughout the narrative that Paul is ultimately in God's hands—not in the hands of Rome.

24:5 The sect of the Nazarenes is a reference to the fact that Jesus grew up in Nazareth.

24:6 The accusation that Paul had tried **to desecrate the temple** was plainly untrue, but they knew they had to make Paul guilty of something that would concern a Roman ruler.

If Paul were disturbing the peace and causing riots, Rome would need to do something.

24:10-14 When given opportunity, Paul did not hesitate to speak the truth and seek to address his illegitimate incarceration through the legal means available to him. The only thing to which Paul would **admit** was being a worshiper of God **according to the Way**—that is, Christianity, which his Jewish accusers rejected as **a sect** but which was nonetheless a fulfillment of Scripture (24:14).

*a*24:17 Ac 11:29; Rm 15:25-28; 1Co 16:1-3; 2Co 8:1-4; Gl 2:10
*b*24:18 Ac 21:26-27; 26:21
*c*24:22 Ac 9:2; 22:4; 24:14
*d*24:23 Ac 23:35; 27:3; 28:16
*e*24:25 Gl 5:23; Ti 2:12; 2Pt 1:6
*f*24:27 Ac 25:1,4,9; 26:24
*g*Ac 12:3; 25:9
*h*Ac 23:35; 25:14

*i*25:1 Ac 8:40; 23:34
*j*25:2 Ac 24:1; 25:15
*k*25:3-4 Ac 9:24; 24:23
*l*25:6 Mt 27:19; Ac 25:10,17
*m*25:7 Mk 15:3; Lk 23:2,10; Ac 24:5,13
*n*25:8 Ac 6:13; 24:12; 28:17
*o*25:9 Ac 24:27; 25:20
*p*25:11 Ac 25:21,25; 26:32; 28:19

17 After many years, I came to bring charitable gifts and offerings to my people.*a* **18** While I was doing this, some Jews from Asia found me ritually purified in the temple, without a crowd and without any uproar.*b* **19** It is they who ought to be here before you to bring charges, if they have anything against me. **20** Or let these men here state what wrongdoing they found in me when I stood before the Sanhedrin, **21** other than this one statement I shouted while standing among them, 'Today I am on trial before you concerning the resurrection of the dead.'"

THE VERDICT POSTPONED

22 Since Felix was well informed about the Way,*c* he adjourned the hearing, saying, "When Lysias the commander comes down, I will decide your case." **23** He ordered that the centurion keep Paul under guard, though he could have some freedom, and that he should not prevent any of his friends from meeting*A* his needs.*d*

24 Several days later, when Felix came with his wife Drusilla, who was Jewish, he sent for Paul and listened to him on the subject of faith in Christ Jesus. **25** Now as he spoke about righteousness, self-control, and the judgment to come,*e* Felix became afraid and replied, "Leave for now, but when I have an opportunity I'll call for you." **26** At the same time he was also hoping that Paul would offer him money.*B* So he sent for him quite often and conversed with him.

27 After two years had passed, Porcius Festus*f* succeeded Felix, and because Felix wanted to do the Jews a favor,*g* he left Paul in prison.*h*

APPEAL TO CAESAR

25 Three days after Festus arrived in the province, he went up to Jerusalem from Caesarea.*i* **2** The chief priests and the leaders of the Jews presented their case against Paul to him; and they appealed,*j* asking for a favor against Paul, that Festus summon him to Jerusalem. They were, in fact, preparing an ambush along the road to kill him. **4** Festus, however, answered that Paul should be kept at Caesarea, and that he himself was about to go there shortly.*k* **5** "Therefore," he said, "let those of you who have authority go down with me and accuse him, if he has done anything wrong."

6 When he had spent not more than eight or ten days among them, he went down to Caesarea. The next day, seated at the tribunal, he commanded Paul to be brought in.*l* **7** When he arrived, the Jews who had come down from Jerusalem stood around him and brought many serious charges that they were not able to prove.*m* **8** Then Paul made his defense: "Neither against the Jewish law,*n* nor against the temple, nor against Caesar have I sinned in any way."

9 But Festus, wanting to do the Jews a favor,*o* replied to Paul, "Are you willing to go up to Jerusalem to be tried before me there on these charges?"

10 Paul replied: "I am standing at Caesar's tribunal, where I ought to be tried. I have done no wrong to the Jews, as even you yourself know very well. **11** If then I did anything wrong and am deserving of death, I am not trying to escape death; but if there is nothing to what these men accuse me of, no one can give me up to them. I appeal to Caesar!"*p*

*A*24:23 Other mss add *or visiting*　　*B*24:26 Other mss add *so that he might release him*

24:17 Delivering **charitable gifts** to his fellow Jews was hardly something Paul would do if he despised them.

24:18-21 Those men who had seized Paul in the temple and accused him of wrongdoing hadn't even shown up for his trial (24:19)! Moreover, the men who *were* there couldn't explain what Paul had done wrong when he had **stood before the Sanhedrin**, except that he affirmed **the resurrection of the dead** (24:20-21)—something which the Pharisees in the Sanhedrin agreed with (see 23:6-9).

24:22 **Lysias the commander** was the one who had sent Paul to Felix (see 23:23-30).

24:24-25 When Paul **spoke about** the subjects of **righteousness, self-control, and the judgment to come**, Felix became afraid (24:25). Why? Because someone who is unrighteous and lacking self-control doesn't want to hear how divine judgment will be poured out. Felix

was apparently interested in religious matters (see 24:22). But when the conversation turned to his own sins and his accountability before God, Felix squirmed.

24:27 Felix knew that Paul was innocent of all charges, but he was unwilling to upset the Jews by setting him free. Nevertheless, God providentially used this injustice to move him toward the goal of proclaiming the gospel in Rome, the center of earthly power in Paul's day.

25:2-3 They had devised a similar plot two years ago, and it had resulted in Paul being transferred to Caesarea in the first place (see 23:12-30).

25:4 Once again, God was working behind the scenes to protect Paul from the murderous plans of the Jewish leaders. He was at work to take Paul far from their grasp—to stand before Caesar. No matter how grim your circumstances appear, do not forget the glori-

ous truth that God is in control. Trust him to accomplish his will for your life as he sovereignly directs your path.

25:6-9 Like his predecessor, Festus could find no reason to condemn Paul. Nevertheless, he had a province to run, and he wanted his constituents to be peaceable citizens. So as **a favor** to **the Jews**, he asked Paul if he'd be willing to stand trial in **Jerusalem** (25:9).

25:10-11 Paul had not wronged **the Jews**, so he argued that he shouldn't be given over to them. As a Roman citizen, Paul had the full right of appeal, so he declared, **I appeal to Caesar!** Paul had been exercising every legal right available to him. He wanted to make it clear to all that neither he nor Christianity was guilty of subverting the empire. Moreover, he wanted to go to Rome, the highest level of earthly authority, with a message from the supreme authority: believe in the Lord Jesus.

12 Then after Festus conferred with his council, he replied, "You have appealed to Caesar; to Caesar you will go."

KING AGRIPPA AND BERNICE VISIT FESTUS

13 Several days later, King Agrippa and Bernice arrived in Caesarea and paid a courtesy call on Festus. **14** Since they were staying there several days, Festus presented Paul's case to the king, saying, "There's a man who was left as a prisoner by Felix. **15** When I was in Jerusalem, the chief priests and the elders of the Jews presented their case and asked that he be condemned.*a* **16** I answered them that it is not the Roman custom to give someone up^A before the accused faces the accusers and has an opportunity for a defense against the charges.*b* **17** So when they had assembled here, I did not delay. The next day I took my seat at the tribunal and ordered the man to be brought in. **18** The accusers stood up but brought no charge against him of the evils I was expecting. **19** Instead they had some disagreements*c* with him about their own religion and about a certain Jesus, a dead man Paul claimed to be alive. **20** Since I was at a loss in a dispute over such things, I asked him if he wanted to go to Jerusalem and be tried there regarding these matters. **21** But when Paul appealed to be held for trial by the Emperor,^B I ordered him to be kept in custody until I could send him to Caesar."

22 Agrippa said to Festus, "I would like to hear the man myself."

"Tomorrow you will hear him," he replied.*d*

PAUL BEFORE AGRIPPA

23 So the next day, Agrippa and Bernice*e* came with great pomp and entered the auditorium with the military commanders and prominent men of the city. When Festus gave the command, Paul was brought in. **24** Then Festus said: "King Agrippa and all men present with us, you see this man. The whole Jewish community has appealed to me concerning him, both in Jerusalem and here, shouting that he should not live any longer.*f* **25** I found that he had not done anything deserving of death, but when he himself appealed to the Emperor, I decided to send him.*g* **26** I have nothing definite to write to my lord about him. Therefore, I have brought him before all of you, and especially before you, King Agrippa, so that after this examination is over, I may have something to write. **27** For it seems unreasonable to me to send a prisoner without indicating the charges against him."

PAUL'S DEFENSE BEFORE AGRIPPA

26 Agrippa said to Paul, "You have permission to speak for yourself."

Then Paul stretched out his hand and began his defense: **2** "I consider myself fortunate, that it is before you, King Agrippa, I am to make my defense today against all the accusations of the Jews, **3** especially since you are very knowledgeable about all the Jewish customs and controversies. Therefore I beg you to listen to me patiently.

4 "All the Jews know my way of life from my youth, which was spent from the beginning among my own people and in Jerusalem.*h* **5** They have known me for a long time, if they are willing to testify, that according to the strictest sect of our religion I lived as a Pharisee.*i* **6** And now I stand on trial because of the hope*j* in what God promised^k to our ancestors, **7** the promise our twelve tribes hope to reach as they earnestly serve him night and day. King Agrippa, I am being accused by the Jews because of this hope.*l* **8** Why do any of you consider it incredible that God raises the dead? **9** In fact, I myself was convinced that it was necessary to do many things in opposition to the

a 25:14-15 Ac 24:27; 25:2
b 25:16 Ac 23:30; 24:4-5
c 25:19 Ac 18:15; 23:29
d 25:20-22 Ac 9:15; 25:9,11
e 25:23 Ac 25:13; 26:30

f 25:24 Ac 22:22; 25:2,7
g 25:25 Ac 23:29; 25:11-12
h 26:3-4 Ac 6:14; 25:19; Gl 1:13
i 26:5 Ac 22:3; 23:6; Php 3:5
j 26:6 Ac 24:15; 28:20
k Ac 13:32; Rm 15:8
l 26:7 Php 3:11; 1Th 3:10; 1Tm 5:5; Jms 1:1

---

^A 25:16 Other mss add *to destruction* ^B 25:21 Lit *his majesty,* also in v. 25

25:13 King Agrippa was Herod Agrippa II, the son of Herod Agrippa I (see 12:1-5, 20-23) and the last member of the Herodian Dynasty to rule. The Romans had put him in charge of a few territories that did not include Judea.
25:22 Because Agrippa said, **I would like to hear the man myself,** Paul was about to have an opportunity to talk to a human king about King Jesus.
25:23 Bernice was Agrippa's sister.
25:24-27 Festus was understandably embarrassed **to send a prisoner** to Caesar without

indicating the charges against him (25:27). Doing so was no small matter. So in essence Festus was saying, "Help me out, Agrippa. Don't let me look like a fool in front of the emperor!"
26:1 Stretching **out his hand** was a show of respect.
26:2-3 Paul knew that a government office is to be respected—even if the person holding the office isn't worthy of respect—because such governmental authorities were established by the Lord. In his letter to the church in Rome, Paul writes, "Let everyone submit

to the governing authorities, since there is no authority except from God, and the authorities that exist are instituted by God" (Rom 13:1).
26:6-7 Indeed, the reason Paul was on trial boiled down to his belief in something that had been **promised** to the Jewish people in the Old Testament Scriptures: the **hope** of the resurrection of the dead.
26:9-11 Paul wanted Agrippa to know that if anything could transform him from being the chief persecutor of Christianity to its chief advocate, it would have to be miraculous.

a 26:9 Jn 16:2; 1Tm 1:13
b 26:10 Ac 8:3; 9:13-14,21;
22:5,20
c 26:11 Ac 25:21,25; 26:32;
28:19
d 26:12-18 Ac 9:3-8;
22:6-11
e 26:14 Ac 9:7; 21:40
f 26:16 Ezk 2:1; Dn 10:11;
Ac 22:14-15
g 26:17 1Ch 16:35; Jr 1:8,19;
Ac 9:15
h 26:18 Is 35:5; 42:7
i Ac 20:32; Eph 5:8; Col
1:13; 1Pt 2:9
j 26:20 Mt 3:8; Lk 3:8; Ac
9:19-20,22,26-29; 13:46;
22:17-20

k 26:22 Lk 24:27; Ac 10:43;
24:14
l 26:23 Lk 24:26; 1Co
15:20,23; Col 1:18; Rv 1:5
m 26:24 2Kg 9:11; Jn 10:20;
1Co 1:23; 2:14; 4:10
n 26:25 Ac 23:26; 24:3
o 26:28-29 Ac 11:26; 21:33;
1Co 7:7
p 26:30-31 Ac 23:9,29;
25:23
q 26:32 Ac 25:11; 28:18

name of Jesus of Nazareth.*a* **10** I actually did this in Jerusalem, and I locked up many of the saints in prison, since I had received authority for that from the chief priests. When they were put to death, I was in agreement against them.*b* **11** In all the synagogues I often punished them and tried to make them blaspheme.*c* Since I was terribly enraged at them, I pursued them even to foreign cities.

PAUL'S ACCOUNT OF HIS
CONVERSION AND COMMISSION

12 "I was traveling to Damascus under*d* these circumstances with authority and a commission from the chief priests. **13** King Agrippa, while on the road at midday, I saw a light from heaven brighter than the sun, shining around me and those traveling with me. **14** We all fell to the ground, and I heard a voice speaking to me in Aramaic,*A* 'Saul, Saul, why are you persecuting me? It is hard for you to kick against the goads.'*e*

15 "I asked, 'Who are you, Lord?'

"And the Lord replied: 'I am Jesus, the one you are persecuting. **16** But get up and stand on your feet. For I have appeared to you for this purpose, to appoint you as a servant and a witness of what you have seen and will see of me.*f* **17** I will rescue you from your people and from the Gentiles. I am sending you to them*g* **18** to open their eyes*h* so that they may turn*B* from darkness to light and from the power of Satan to God, that they may receive forgiveness of sins and a share among those who are sanctified by faith in me.'*i*

19 "So then, King Agrippa, I was not disobedient to the heavenly vision. **20** Instead, I preached to those in Damascus first, and to those in Jerusalem and in all the region of Judea, and to the Gentiles, that they should repent and turn to God, and do works worthy of repentance.*j* **21** For this reason the Jews seized me in the temple

and were trying to kill me. **22** To this very day, I have had help from God, and I stand and testify to both small and great, saying nothing other than what the prophets and Moses said would take place*k* — **23** that the Messiah would suffer, and that, as the first to rise from the dead, he would proclaim light to our people and to the Gentiles."*l*

AGRIPPA NOT QUITE PERSUADED

24 As he was saying these things in his defense, Festus exclaimed in a loud voice, "You're out of your mind,*m* Paul! Too much study is driving you mad."

25 But Paul replied, "I'm not out of my mind, most excellent Festus. On the contrary, I'm speaking words of truth and good judgment.*n* **26** For the king knows about these matters, and I can speak boldly to him. For I am convinced that none of these things has escaped his notice, since this was not done in a corner. **27** King Agrippa, do you believe the prophets? I know you believe.

28 Agrippa said to Paul, "Are you going to persuade me to become a Christian so easily?"*c*

29 "I wish before God," replied Paul, "that whether easily or with difficulty,*D* not only you but all who listen to me today might become as I am — except for these chains."*o*

30 The king, the governor, Bernice, and those sitting with them got up, **31** and when they had left they talked with each other and said, "This man is not doing anything to deserve death or imprisonment."*p*

32 Agrippa said to Festus, "This man could have been released if he had not appealed to Caesar."*q*

SAILING FOR ROME

27 When it was decided that we were to sail to Italy, they handed over Paul and some other prisoners to a

---

A 26:14 Or *Hebrew*   *B* 26:18 Or *to turn them*   *C* 26:28 Or *so quickly*   *D* 26:29 Or *whether a short time or long*

26:19-23 Whereas formerly Paul was an aggressive opponent of Christ, he'd become an aggressive soldier for Christ. Instead of keeping people *from* the kingdom, Paul's energies were redirected toward bringing them *into* the kingdom.

Though some Jews were outraged by his message of salvation for the Gentiles (26:21), Paul hadn't invented it or pulled it out of thin air. Everything he had preached was consistent with and in fulfillment of **what the prophets and Moses said would take place** (26:22; see Ps 16:10; Isa 52:13–53:12).

26:24-25 Divine visions? A voice from heaven? A dead man raised to life? This was

too much for **Festus**, who thought **Paul** had gone crazy: **Too much study is driving you mad** (26:24). But Paul was unfazed by Festus's insult. Far from being **out of [his] mind**, Paul was **speaking words of truth and good judgment** (26:25). He would have been crazy *not* to submit to King Jesus.

26:27 Putting the Jewish king on the spot, Paul asked, **Do you believe the prophets? I know you believe.** Although Paul was the one on trial, he turned the tables on Agrippa and played the prosecutor.

26:28-29 Paul was willing to talk to anyone about Jesus, regardless of their social status:

government officials (13:7, 12), the lame (14:8-10), women (16:13-15), a jailer (16:25-34), and intellectuals (17:16-34). What about you? Are you willing to step outside of your comfort zone to share the good news with those whom others might avoid?

26:32 More than his freedom, Paul wanted to testify about Jesus to the Roman emperor. And God was going to give him that opportunity.

27:1-2 The use of the first-person plural (**we**) once again indicates that the author, Luke, and a believer from **Thessalonica** named **Aristarchus** were with Paul (see 16:8-10; 20:1-6).

centurion named Julius, of the Imperial Regiment.[A,a] [2] When we had boarded a ship of Adramyttium, we put to sea, intending to sail to ports along the coast of Asia. Aristarchus, a Macedonian of Thessalonica, was with us.[b] [3] The next day we put in at Sidon, and Julius treated Paul kindly and allowed him to go to his friends to receive their care.[c] [4] When we had put out to sea from there, we sailed along the northern coast[B] of Cyprus because the winds were against us. [5] After sailing through the open sea off Cilicia and Pamphylia, we reached Myra in Lycia.[d] [6] There the centurion found an Alexandrian ship sailing for Italy and put us on board. [7] Sailing slowly for many days, with difficulty we arrived off Cnidus. Since the wind did not allow us to approach it, we sailed along the south side of Crete off Salmone. [8] With still more difficulty we sailed along the coast and came to a place called Fair Havens near the city of Lasea.

PAUL'S ADVICE IGNORED

[9] By now much time had passed, and the voyage was already dangerous. Since the Day of Atonement[C,e] was already over, Paul gave his advice [10] and told them, "Men, I can see that this voyage is headed toward disaster and heavy loss, not only of the cargo and the ship but also of our lives." [11] But the centurion paid attention to the captain and the owner of the ship rather than to what Paul said.[f] [12] Since the harbor was unsuitable to winter in, the majority decided to set sail from there, hoping somehow to reach Phoenix, a harbor on Crete[g] facing the southwest and northwest, and to winter there.

STORM-TOSSED SHIP

[13] When a gentle south wind sprang up, they thought they had achieved their purpose. They weighed anchor and sailed along the shore of Crete. [14] But before long, a fierce wind called the "northeaster" rushed down from the island. [15] Since the ship was caught and unable to head into the wind, we gave way to it and were driven along. [16] After running under the shelter of a little island called Cauda,[D] we were barely able to get control of the skiff. [17] After hoisting it up, they used ropes and tackle and girded the ship. Fearing they would run aground on the Syrtis, they lowered the drift-anchor, and in this way they were driven along. [18] Because we were being severely battered by the storm, they began to jettison the cargo the next day.[h] [19] On the third day, they threw the ship's tackle overboard with their own hands. [20] For many days neither sun nor stars appeared, and the severe storm kept raging. Finally all hope was fading that we would be saved.

[21] Since they had been without food for a long time, Paul then stood up among them and said, "You men should have followed my advice not to sail from Crete and sustain this damage and loss. [22] Now I urge you to take courage, because there will be no loss of any of your lives, but only of the ship. [23] For last night an angel of the God I belong to and serve stood by me[i] [24] and said, 'Don't be afraid, Paul. It is necessary for you to appear before Caesar. And indeed, God has graciously given you all those who are sailing with you.' [25] So take courage, men, because I believe God that it will be just the way it was told to me.[j] [26] But we have to run aground on some island."[k]

[27] When the fourteenth night came, we were drifting in the Adriatic Sea, and about midnight the sailors thought they were approaching land. [28] They took soundings and found it to be a hundred and twenty feet[E] deep; when they had sailed a little farther and sounded again, they found it to be ninety feet[F] deep. [29] Then, fearing we might run aground on the rocks, they dropped four anchors from the stern and prayed for daylight to come. [30] Some sailors tried to escape from the ship; they had let down the skiff into the sea, pretending that they were going to put out anchors from the bow. [31] Paul said to the centurion and the soldiers, "Unless these men stay

---

[a] 27:1 Ac 10:1; 16:10; 25:12,25
[b] 27:2 Ac 17:1; 19:29; 20:4; Col 4:10; Phm 24
[c] 27:3 Ac 24:23; 27:43; 28:16
[d] 27:5 Ac 6:9; 13:13
[e] 27:9 Lv 16:29-31; 23:27-29; Nm 29:7
[f] 27:10-11 Ac 27:21; Rv 18:17
[g] 27:12 Ac 2:11; Ti 1:5

[h] 27:18 Jnh 1:5; Ac 27:38
[i] 27:23 Dn 6:16; Ac 18:9; 23:11; Rm 1:9; 2Tm 4:17
[j] 27:25 Ac 27:22,36; Rm 4:20-21
[k] 27:26 Ac 27:17,29; 28:1

[A] 27:1 Or *Augustan Cohort* [B] 27:4 Lit *sailed under the lee,* also in v. 7 [C] 27:9 Lit *the Fast* [D] 27:16 Or *Clauda* [E] 27:28 Lit *twenty fathoms*
[F] 27:28 Lit *fifteen fathoms*

27:9 That **the Day of Atonement was already over** means it was late in the year.
27:11 Listening to the "professional" rather than the man with a connection to God (see 27:9-10) would prove costly. But as you read about the upcoming storm those on the ship would face, remember that Paul was not outside God's will. He had been obedient to the Lord, seeking to take his case to Rome, which was exactly where God wanted him to go (see 23:11). Sometimes, then, being in a storm does not mean you're out of God's will. It may be exactly where he wants you to be so that he can accomplish his purposes in you and through you (see Mark 4:35-41; 6:45-52).

27:19 **The ship's tackle** was its rigging and other essential equipment.
27:23-24 God had a mission for Paul, and he wouldn't die before that mission was accomplished.
27:25 We too can have **courage** in life's storms because **God** is faithful to keep his promises.

a 27:34 1Kg 1:52; Mt 10:30; Lk 21:18
b 27:35 Mt 14:19; 15:36
c 27:37 Ac 2:41; 7:14; Rm 13:1; 1Pt 3:20
d 27:38-39 Ac 27:18; 28:1
e 27:41-44 Ac 12:19; 27:3,22; 2Co 11:25
f 28:1 Ac 16:10; 27:1
g Ac 27:26,39
h 28:2 Rm 1:14; 1Co 14:11; Col 3:11

i 28:4 Lk 13:2,4; Jn 9:2
j 28:5 Mk 16:18; Lk 10:19
k 28:6 Ac 8:10; 14:11
l 28:8 Ac 9:40; Jms 5:14-15
m 28:14 Jn 21:23; Ac 1:16
n 28:16 Ac 24:23; 27:3

in the ship, you cannot be saved." **32** Then the soldiers cut the ropes holding the skiff and let it drop away.

33 When it was about daylight, Paul urged them all to take food, saying, "Today is the fourteenth day that you have been waiting and going without food, having eaten nothing. **34** So I urge you to take some food. For this is for your survival, since none of you will lose a hair from your head."*a* **35** After he said these things and had taken some bread, he gave thanks to God in the presence of all of them, and after he broke it, he began to eat.*b* **36** They all were encouraged and took food themselves. **37** In all there were 276 of us on the ship.*c* **38** When they had eaten enough, they began to lighten the ship by throwing the grain overboard into the sea.

SHIPWRECK

39 When daylight came, they did not recognize the land but sighted a bay with a beach. They planned to run the ship ashore if they could.*d* **40** After cutting loose the anchors, they left them in the sea, at the same time loosening the ropes that held the rudders. Then they hoisted the foresail to the wind and headed for the beach. **41** But they struck a sandbar and ran the ship aground. The bow jammed fast and remained immovable, while the stern began to break up by the pounding of the waves. **42** The soldiers' plan was to kill the prisoners so that no one could swim away and escape. **43** But the centurion kept them from carrying out their plan because he wanted to save Paul, and so he ordered those who could swim to jump overboard first and get to land. **44** The rest were to follow, some on planks and some on debris from the ship. In this way, everyone safely reached the shore.*e*

MALTA'S HOSPITALITY

28 Once safely ashore, we*f* then learned that the island was called Malta.*g* **2** The local people*h* showed us extraordinary kindness. They lit a fire and took us all in, since it was raining and cold.

3 As Paul gathered a bundle of brushwood and put it on the fire, a viper came out because of the heat and fastened itself on his hand. **4** When the local people saw the snake hanging from his hand, they said to one another, "This man, no doubt, is a murderer. Even though he has escaped the sea, Justice has not allowed him to live."*i* **5** But he shook the snake off into the fire and suffered no harm.*j* **6** They expected that he would begin to swell up or suddenly drop dead. After they waited a long time and saw nothing unusual happen to him, they changed their minds and said he was a god.*k*

MINISTRY IN MALTA

7 Now in the area around that place was an estate belonging to the leading man of the island, named Publius, who welcomed us and entertained us hospitably for three days. **8** Publius's father was in bed suffering from fever and dysentery. Paul went to him, and praying and laying his hands on him, he healed him.*l* **9** After this, the rest of those on the island who had diseases also came and were healed. **10** So they heaped many honors on us, and when we sailed, they gave us what we needed.

ROME AT LAST

11 After three months we set sail in an Alexandrian ship that had wintered at the island, with the Twin Gods*A* as its figurehead. **12** Putting in at Syracuse, we stayed three days. **13** From there, after making a circuit along the coast,*B* we reached Rhegium. After one day a south wind sprang up, and the second day we came to Puteoli. **14** There we found brothers and sisters*m* and were invited to stay a week with them. And so we came to Rome. **15** Now the brothers and sisters from there had heard the news about us and had come to meet us as far as the Forum of Appius and the Three Taverns. When Paul saw them, he thanked God and took courage. **16** When we entered Rome,*C* Paul was allowed to live by himself with the soldier who guarded him.*n*

A 28:11 Gk *Dioscuri*, twin sons of Zeus, Castor and Pollux   *B* 28:13 Other mss read *From there, casting off,*   *C* 28:16 Other mss add *the centurion turned the prisoners over to the military commander; but*

27:35-36 When times are hard and you don't know what God is up to, do you continue to thank him for his provision in your life (see Phil 4:6-7)? Not only will you remind yourself of the goodness of God, but you may also be a witness to those around you that God is worthy of our trust in difficult times.

27:42 A soldier or guard who allowed a prisoner to get away would forfeit his own life (see 12:6-10, 18-19; 16:26-27).
28:4 **Justice** was a Greek goddess.
28:10 God provided for all of the men's needs through the island's inhabitants. But don't overlook the fact that the islanders' admira-

tion for Paul began when he was bitten by a snake (see 28:3-6). God's providence sometimes requires that we pass through painful experiences so that he can give us—and even others—his blessing.

PAUL'S FIRST INTERVIEW WITH ROMAN JEWS

17 After three days he called together the leaders of the Jews. When they had gathered he said to them: "Brothers, although I have done nothing against our people or the customs of our ancestors, I was delivered as a prisoner from Jerusalem into the hands of the Romans.[a] **18** After they examined me, they wanted to release me, since there was no reason for the death penalty in my case.[b] **19** Because the Jews objected, I was compelled to appeal to Caesar;[c] even though I had no charge to bring against my people. **20** For this reason I've asked to see you and speak to you. In fact, it is for the hope of Israel that I'm wearing this chain."[d]

21 Then they said to him, "We haven't received any letters about you from Judea. None of the brothers has come and reported or spoken anything evil about you. **22** But we want to hear what your views are, since we know that people everywhere are speaking against this sect."[e]

THE RESPONSE TO PAUL'S MESSAGE

23 After arranging a day with him, many came to him at his lodging. From dawn to dusk he expounded and testified about the kingdom of God. He tried to persuade them about Jesus from both the Law of Moses and the Prophets.[f] **24** Some were persuaded by what he said, but others did not believe.[g]

25 Disagreeing among themselves, they began to leave after Paul made one statement:[A] "The Holy Spirit was right in saying to your[B] ancestors through the prophet Isaiah **26** when he said,

Go to these people and say:
You will always be listening,
but never understanding;
and you will always be looking,
but never perceiving.
27 For the hearts of these people
have grown callous,
their ears are hard of hearing,
and they have shut their eyes;
otherwise they might see
with their eyes
and hear with their ears,
understand with their heart
and turn,
and I would heal them.[C,h]

28 Therefore, let it be known to you that this salvation of God has been sent to the Gentiles; they will listen."[D]

PAUL'S MINISTRY UNHINDERED

30 Paul stayed two whole years in his own rented house. And he welcomed all who visited him, **31** proclaiming the kingdom of God[i] and teaching about the Lord Jesus Christ with all boldness[j] and without hindrance.

a 28:17 Ac 6:14; 25:8
b 28:18 Ac 22:24; 23:29; 26:31
c 28:19 Ac 25:11; 26:32
d 28:20 Ac 21:33; 26:6-7,29; Eph 6:20; 2Tm 1:16
e 28:22 Lk 2:34; Ac 24:5; 1Pt 2:12; 4:14
f 28:23 Ac 8:35; 17:3; 19:8; 26:22; Phm 22
g 28:24 Ac 14:4; 19:9
h 28:26-27 Ps 119:70; Is 6:9-10; Mt 13:14-15; Mk 4:12; Lk 8:10; Jn 12:40; Rm 11:8
i 28:31 Mt 4:23; Ac 20:25; 28:23
j Ac 4:29,31; 2Tm 2:9

28:17-20 Paul gathered the local Jewish **leaders** and explained all of the events surrounding the circumstances of his case. He wanted them to know that he bore no animosity against his fellow **Jews** in Jerusalem but instead wanted to talk to the Jews in Rome about why he was in chains (28:17). He had been imprisoned because of his belief in **the hope of Israel**, the resurrection of the dead (28:20; see 23:6; 24:15; 26:23).
28:23 The Old Testament anticipates Jesus and points to him. Rightly interpreted, it leads people to the King who came to establish God's kingdom.

28:25-27 Those who refused to believe departed in anger when they heard Paul say that **the Holy Spirit was right** about their **ancestors** when he chastised them **through the prophet Isaiah** for failing to believe the Word of God (28:25; see Isa 6:9-10). Their response is ironic given that Paul was essentially telling them, "Don't be like your foolish forefathers. Believe the Scriptures—all of which point to Jesus as the Messiah."
28:28 God's gift of grace will not go unappreciated. If some reject it, there are others who will gladly accept it.

28:30-31 The book of Acts ends where it began—with an emphasis and focus on the kingdom of God (see 1:3). Paul engaged in **proclaiming** (preaching) **the kingdom of God and teaching** people **about . . . Christ**. Biblical *preaching* focuses on persuading people with kingdom truth in order to bring about an obedient response. Biblical *teaching* focuses on delivering a clear understanding of the King. This dual emphasis of the kingdom and its King should dominate every pulpit.

ROMANS

INTRODUCTION

Author

THE APOSTLE PAUL CLAIMS TO be the author of this letter (1:1), and no serious objections have been made to suggest otherwise. According to 16:22, Paul used Tertius as his amanuensis, or secretary, to write it—a common first-century practice.

Historical Background

Paul addressed his letter to Christians living in Rome (1:7), the capital of the vast Roman Empire. The people living there in the first century represented the empire's various cultures and religions and included many Jews. The Christian churches in Rome were not founded by Paul, though he was anxious to visit them (1:13-15). The first Christians there were probably those "visitors from Rome (both Jews and converts)" who came to Jerusalem at Pentecost (Acts 2:10), were converted under the gospel preaching of Peter (see Acts 2:14-41), and later returned to the capital city to begin churches.

According to Acts, Aquila and Priscilla were two Jewish Christians from Rome whom Paul met during his ministry in Corinth. This husband and wife had to leave their home because the Roman emperor "Claudius, had ordered all the Jews to leave Rome" (Acts 18:2)—which happened in AD 49. A first-century Roman historian named Suetonius reported that Claudius did this because of Jewish unrest over "Chrestus"—which is most likely a reference to Christ. Given all of the quarreling in Rome between Jews who had embraced Jesus as the Messiah and Jews who had not, the Roman emperor simply kicked out all of the Jews. This exit of Jewish Christians would have left local church leadership in the hands of Gentile Christians. When Claudius's decree expired at his death, many Jewish Christians returned to Rome. The cultural diversity between Jewish and Gentile Christians would have caused tensions between the groups—a fact evident in Paul's letter to the Romans (e.g., Rom 2; 11; 14–15).

Paul most likely wrote the letter in AD 57 during his third missionary journey while in Corinth (in Greece). He was on his way to Jerusalem to deliver a contribution from Gentile churches to the poor Jewish Christians in Jerusalem. After this, he planned to visit Rome (Acts 19:21; 20:3, 16; Rom 15:25-29).

Message and Purpose

Romans is the constitution of the church. Its major theme is the righteousness of God. Paul wanted the Romans to understand this great truth both theologically and practically—what it means and how it is to be lived out. He began by teaching that all human beings have failed to meet God's standards of righteousness. They have been turned over to the passive wrath of God—yet, instead of destroying them instantly, God made provision for redemption.

The apostle continues by teaching that God, recognizing we had a problem we could not fix, freely provided a way we could be made righteous. Faith in the sacrifice of Jesus Christ on the cross and his resurrection results in his righteousness being applied to our accounts in payment for our sins. But this great transaction was only the beginning, because now we can have a relationship with Jesus Christ because we have a new identity. That doesn't mean we sin no longer. Even though Christians are saved, we still struggle with our flesh, as Paul related very honestly about himself.

Romans also tells us what God is going to do about his people Israel. Though they rejected him, God still has a plan for them. The book ends with a celebration of the faith we have in Christ and the power it gives us for victorious living as his kingdom representatives, individually and in community.

VIDEO · INTRO

www.bhpublishinggroup.com/qr/te/45_00

Outline

THE GOSPEL OF GOD FOR ROME

1 Paul, a servant of Christ Jesus, called as an apostle[A,a] and set apart[b] for the gospel of God[c] — 2 which he promised beforehand[d] through his prophets[e] in the Holy Scriptures — 3 concerning his Son, Jesus Christ our Lord, who was a descendant of David[B,f] according to the flesh[g] 4 and was appointed to be the powerful[h] Son of God[i] according to the Spirit of holiness[c] by the resurrection of the dead. 5 Through him we have received grace and apostleship[j] to bring about[b] the obedience[k] of faith for the sake of his name among all the Gentiles,[E,l] 6 including you who are also called by Jesus Christ.[m]

7 To all who are in Rome, loved by God,[n] called[o] as saints.[p]

Grace to you and peace from God our Father and the Lord Jesus Christ.

PAUL'S DESIRE TO VISIT ROME

8 First, I thank my God through Jesus Christ for all of you because the news of your faith[f] is being reported in all the world.[q] 9 God is my witness,[r] whom I serve with my spirit[s] in telling the good news about his Son — that I constantly mention you,[t] 10 always asking in my prayers that if it is somehow in God's will, I may now at last succeed in coming to you.[u] 11 For I want very much to see you,[v] so that I may impart to you some spiritual gift to strengthen you, 12 that is, to be mutually encouraged by each other's faith, both yours and mine.

13 Now I don't want you to be unaware,[w] brothers and sisters, that I often planned to come to you (but was prevented until now[x]) in order that I might have a fruitful ministry[G] among you,[y] just as I have had among the rest of the Gentiles. 14 I am obligated both to Greeks and barbarians,[H,z] both to the wise and the foolish. 15 So I am eager to preach the gospel[aa] to you also who are in Rome.

THE RIGHTEOUS WILL LIVE BY FAITH

16 For I am not ashamed of the gospel,[I,ab] because it is the power of God for salvation[ac] to everyone who believes, first to the Jew,[ad] and also to the Greek.[ae] 17 For in it the righteousness of God is revealed from faith to faith,[J,af] just as it is written: **The righteous will live by faith.**[K,L,ag]

THE GUILT OF THE GENTILE WORLD

18 For God's wrath[ah] is revealed from heaven against all godlessness and unrighteousness of people who by their unrighteousness suppress the truth,[ai] 19 since

a1:1 1Co 1:1; 9:1; 2Co 1:1
b Ac 9:15; 13:2; Gl 1:15
c Mk 1:14
d1:2 Ti 1:2
e Lk 1:70; Rm 3:21; 16:26
f1:3 Mt 1:1
g Jn 1:14; Rm 4:1; 9:3,5;
1Co 10:18
h1:4 Ac 10:38; 13:33; 17:31;
26:23
i Mt 4:3
j1:5 Ac 1:25; Gl 1:16
k Ac 6:7; Rm 16:26
l Ac 9:15
m1:6 Jd 1; Rv 17:14
n1:7 Rm 5:5; 8:39; 1Th 1:4
o Rm 8:28; 1Co 1:24
p 1Co 1:2–4
q1:8 Rm 16:19
r1:9 Rm 9:1; 2Co 1:23;
11:31; Php 1:8; 1Th 2:5,10
s 2Tm 1:3
t Eph 1:16; Php 1:3–5; 1Th
1:2; 2Tm 1:3; Phm 4

u1:10 Ac 18:21; Rm 15:32
v1:11 Ac 19:21; Rm 15:23
w1:13 1Co 10:1; 11:3
x Ac 19:21
y Jn 4:36; Rm 15:16; Php
1:22; Col 1:6
z1:14 Ac 28:2
aa1:15 Rm 15:20; 1Co 9:16
ab1:16 2Tm 1:8,12,16
ac 1Co 1:18,24
ad Ac 3:26; Rm 2:9
ae Jn 7:35
af1:17 Rm 3:21; 9:30; Php 3:9
ag Hab 2:4; Gl 3:11; Heb
10:38
ah1:18 Rm 5:9; Eph 5:6;
Col 3:6
ai 2Th 2:6-10

A1:1 Or *Jesus, a called apostle*   B1:3 Lit *was of the seed of David*   C1:4 Or *the spirit of holiness,* or *the Holy Spirit*   D1:5 Or *him for;* lit *him into*
E1:5 Or *nations,* also in v. 13   F1:8 Or *because your faith*   G1:13 Lit *have some fruit*   H1:14 Or *non-Greeks*   I1:16 Other mss add *of Christ*   J1:17 Or
revealed out of faith into faith   K1:17 Or *The one who is righteous by faith will live*   L1:17 Hab 2:4

1:1 The word *gospel* means "good news." Throughout Romans it refers to the entirety of salvation: justification (salvation past), sanctification (salvation present), and glorification (salvation future).
1:2-4 The Jews had expected a Messiah who would reign on David's throne; they had not anticipated him to also be divine (see Matt 22:41-46; 26:63-65; John 5:18). **The resurrection** served as a demonstration and validation of Jesus's divinity (Rom 1:4).
1:7 Paul greets the Roman Christians in his characteristic way: **Grace to you and peace from God our Father and the Lord Jesus Christ**. The grace of God our Father *leads* to peace with Jesus Christ. We can't have one without the other.
1:8 These were not secret agent Christians; these people went public with their allegiance to God's kingdom agenda. They were open in their testimony, just as all churches and believers should be.
1:10-11 Why was Paul so insistent on seeing the Roman believers? He wanted to **impart to [them] some spiritual gift to strengthen** them (1:11). He wanted to have a spiritual impact on them and bring them spiritual benefit so that their ministry would grow even stronger.
1:12 Consider the idea of being **mutually encouraged by each other's faith**. The Chris-

tian life is one of giving in every direction, always seeking to encourage and enrich others. Ideally, we encourage the one who ministers to us *while* he ministers to and encourages us.
1:14 Paul felt **obligated** to preach the gospel. Why? Because the cost of *not* sharing the gospel is too high. If you see your neighbor's house on fire, do you shrug and say, "Glad that's not my home"? No! You feel an obligation to act, because something valuable is at stake, and doing nothing is too costly.
1:16 If we're **ashamed** to share the **gospel**, it's because we do not understand the power embedded in it. If we really believe it has **power** not only to save sinners but also to give victory to saints, we'll share it.
1:17 One reason Paul had confidence in the gospel was that **in it the righteousness of God is revealed**. The word *righteousness* means "to be right." Not "better than others" or "good enough," but *right*, as in, *right with God*. Our problem is that we mentally dumb down God, reducing him to our level so that our sin doesn't seem so bad. The gospel, though, makes God's righteousness the standard. So it doesn't matter how nice of a sinner you are, you are still a sinner.
The gospel also gives us a provision: **The righteous will live by faith**. If we appeal to

our relative goodness, we'll always fall short. But if we appeal to God by faith, then the gospel has already saved us. Think of it this way. If I can't afford a house, but a generous oil baron puts up his bankroll for me, my finances are irrelevant. He bought the house *for me*. I am dependent on his resources, and he can afford it. That's what the gospel is like: God has resources available for every believer who lives by faith. The act of faith in the finished work of Christ justifies us, and it is the lifestyle of faith that sanctifies and transforms us.
1:18 **God's wrath** is his righteous and just retribution against sin. The focus here has to do with God's wrath in history not in eternity. He does not apologize for it. Sinful human beings, conversely, would rather **suppress the truth**. *Suppress* means "to hold down." A beach ball held underwater resists and wants to pop back up; so if you want to keep the ball under, you have to force it down. Humans tend to do the same thing to the truth about God's righteousness because we don't want to deal with it.
1:19-20 Whether a man lives in Timbuktu or Dallas, he knows something about God because God's **invisible attributes** are **clearly seen** (1:20). Consider the wind: even though we cannot see it, we know it's there because

a 1:19 Ac 14:17; 17:24-27
b 1:20 Mk 10:6
c Jb 12:7-9; Ps 19:1-6; Jr 5:21-22
d 1:21 2Kg 17:15; Jr 2:5; Eph 4:17-20
e 1:22 Jr 10:14; 1Co 1:20
f 1:23 Ps 106:20; Jr 2:11; Ac 17:29
g 1:24 Eph 2:3; 4:19
h 1:25 Is 44:20; Jr 10:14; 13:25; 16:19
i Rm 9:5; 2Co 11:31
j 1:26 1Th 4:5
k 1:27 Lv 18:22; 20:13; 1Co 6:9

l 1:29 2Co 12:20
m 1:30 Ps 5:5
n 2Tm 3:2
o 1:31 2Tm 3:3
p 1:32 Rm 6:21
q Lk 11:48; Ac 8:1; 22:20
r 2:1 Lk 12:14; Rm 9:20
s Rm 1:20
t 2Sm 12:5-7; Mt 7:1; Rm 14:22
u 2:4 Rm 11:22
v Rm 3:25
w Ex 34:6; Rm 9:22; 1Tm 1:16; 1Pt 3:20; 2Pt 3:15
x 2Pt 3:9
y 2:5 Dt 32:34; Pr 1:18
z Ps 110:5; 2Co 5:10; 2Th 1:5; Jd 6
aa 2:6 Ps 62:12; Pr 24:12; Mt 16:27
ab 2:7 1Co 15:42,50,53
ac Lk 8:15; Heb 10:36
ad Heb 2:7; 1Pt 1:7
ae Mt 25:46
af 2:8 2Co 12:20; Gl 5:20; Php 2:3; Jms 3:14,16
ag 2Th 2:12
ah 2:9 Rm 8:35
ai Ac 3:26; Rm 1:16; 1Pt 4:17
aj 2:11 Dt 10:17; Ac 10:34

what can be known[A] about God is evident among them,[a] because God has shown it to them. [20] For his invisible attributes, that is, his eternal power and divine nature, have been clearly seen since the creation of the world,[b] being understood through what he has made.[c] As a result, people are without excuse. [21] For though they knew God, they did not glorify him as God or show gratitude. Instead, their thinking became worthless, and their senseless hearts were darkened.[d] [22] Claiming to be wise, they became fools[e] [23] and exchanged the glory of the immortal God for images resembling mortal man, birds, four-footed animals, and reptiles.[f]

[24] Therefore God delivered them over in the desires of their hearts[g] to sexual impurity, so that their bodies were degraded among themselves. [25] They exchanged the truth of God for a lie,[h] and worshiped and served what has been created instead of the Creator, who is praised forever.[i] Amen.

FROM IDOLATRY TO DEPRAVITY

[26] For this reason God delivered them over to disgraceful passions.[j] Their women[B] exchanged natural sexual relations[C] for unnatural ones. [27] The men[D] in the same way also left natural relations with women and were inflamed in their lust for one another. Men committed shameless acts with men[k] and received in their own persons[E] the appropriate penalty of their error.

[28] And because they did not think it worthwhile to acknowledge God, God delivered them over to a corrupt mind so that they do what is not right. [29] They are filled with all unrighteousness,[F] evil, greed, and wickedness. They are full of envy, murder, quarrels, deceit, and malice. They are

gossips,[l] [30] slanderers, God-haters, arrogant, proud, boastful,[m] inventors of evil, disobedient to parents,[n] [31] senseless, untrustworthy, unloving,[G,o] and unmerciful. [32] Although they know God's just sentence —that those who practice such things deserve to die[H,p] —they not only do them, but even applaud[i,q] others who practice them.

GOD'S RIGHTEOUS JUDGMENT

2 Therefore, every one of you[J,r] who judges is without excuse.[s] For when you judge another,[t] you condemn yourself, since you, the judge, do the same things. [2] We know that God's judgment on those who do such things is based on the truth. [3] Do you really think —anyone of you who judges those who do such things yet do the same —that you will escape God's judgment? [4] Or do you despise the riches of his kindness,[u] restraint,[v] and patience,[w] not recognizing[k] that God's kindness[x] is intended to lead you to repentance? [5] Because of your hardened and unrepentant heart you are storing up wrath[y] for yourself in the day of wrath,[z] when God's righteous judgment is revealed. [6] **He will repay each one according to his works:**[L,aa] [7] eternal life[ab] to those who by persistence in doing good[ac] seek glory, honor,[ad] and immortality;[ae] [8] but wrath and anger to those who are self-seeking[af] and disobey the truth[ag] while obeying unrighteousness. [9] There will be affliction and distress[ah] for every human being who does evil, first to the Jew, and also to the Greek;[ai] [10] but glory, honor, and peace for everyone who does what is good, first to the Jew, and also to the Greek. [11] For there is no favoritism with God.[aj]

[A] **1:19** Or *what is known* [B] **1:26** Lit *females*, also in v. 27 [C] **1:26** Lit *natural use*, also in v. 27 [D] **1:27** Lit *males*, also later in v. [E] **1:27** Or *in themselves* [F] **1:29** Other mss add *sexual immorality* [G] **1:31** Other mss add *unforgiving* [H] **1:32** Lit *things are worthy of death* [i] **1:32** Lit *even take pleasure in* [J] **2:1** Lit *Therefore, O man, every one* [K] **2:4** Or *patience, because you do not recognize* [L] **2:6** Ps 62:12; Pr 24:12

---

its effects are obvious. Creation testifies to the existence, greatness, power, and glory of God (see Ps 19:1-6).

1:24 This verse shows God taking his hand of restraint off, essentially saying, "You want to do life without me? You've got it." But understand: this is the passive wrath of God at work in history. He lets people experience the built-in negative consequences of living independent of him.

1:26-27 When sex becomes a god, lust reigns. And so we find men and women exchanging **natural sexual relations for unnatural ones** (1:26)—that is homosexuality and lesbianism. God allows us to pursue all kinds of sexual lusts, but the result is a mess. Broken homes, broken hearts, sexually transmitted diseases,

unplanned and unwanted pregnancies—all are the fallout of letting lust rule.

1:32 You know a person or culture has descended into ultimate corruption when people give public and legal approval to sin.

2:1-2 At this point in Paul's argument, his Jewish listeners would be nodding their heads in agreement: "Get those pagans, Paul!" But Paul turns the tables, showing the impartiality of God when it comes to judgment. The moralistic Jews were practicing the same things for which they judged others. Paul's response? **When you judge another, you condemn yourself** (2:1). God's judgment is not based on our self-evaluation of our morals, but **is based on the truth** as measured by his divine standard (2:2).

2:4 People often assume that if God has not judged them yet, he will not judge at all. But Paul says that **God's kindness is intended to lead . . . to repentance**. He waits to pour out his wrath—not because his wrath is a myth, but because he knows that once it begins, there is no reprieve.

2:5 We should never envy the wicked. They are accumulating a greater degree of divine **judgment**.

2:6-8 Paul's point here is not that we can be saved by **works** (2:6, the rest of Romans makes that obvious), but that God is an impartial Judge.

2:11 *All* have sinned and *all* are justified only by God's grace (see 3:23-24).

12 All who sin without the law[a] will also perish without the law, and all who sin under[A] the law will be judged by the law. **13** For the hearers of the law[b] are not righteous before God, but the doers of the law will be justified.[B] **14** So, when Gentiles, who do not by nature have the law,[c] do[c] what the law demands, they are a law to themselves even though they do not have the law. **15** They show that the work of the law[D] is written on their hearts.[d] Their consciences confirm this. Their competing thoughts either accuse or even excuse them[E] **16** on the day when God judges[e] what people have kept secret, according to my gospel through Christ Jesus.[f]

JEWISH VIOLATION OF THE LAW

17 Now if[F] you call yourself a Jew, and rely on the law,[g] and boast in God, **18** and know his will, and approve the things that are superior,[h] being instructed from the law, **19** and if you are convinced that you are a guide for the blind, a light to those in darkness, **20** an instructor of the ignorant, a teacher of the immature, having the embodiment of knowledge and truth[i] in the law — **21** you then, who teach another,[j] don't you teach yourself? You who preach, "You must not steal" — do you steal? **22** You who say, "You must not commit adultery" — do you commit adultery? You who detest idols, do you rob their temples?[k] **23** You who boast in the law,[l] do you dishonor God by breaking the law? **24** For, as it is written: **The name of God is blasphemed among the Gentiles because of you.**[G,m]

CIRCUMCISION OF THE HEART

25 Circumcision benefits you if you observe the law, but if you are a lawbreaker, your circumcision has become uncircumcision.[n] **26** So if an uncircumcised[o] man keeps the law's requirements,[p] will not his uncircumcision be counted as circumcision? **27** A man who is physically uncircumcised, but who keeps the law, will judge you[q] who are a lawbreaker in spite of having the letter of the law and circumcision. **28** For a person is not a Jew who is one outwardly,[r] and true circumcision is not something visible in the flesh. **29** On the contrary, a person is a Jew who is one inwardly,[s] and circumcision is of the heart — by the Spirit, not the letter.[H,t] That person's praise is not from people but from God.[u]

PAUL ANSWERS AN OBJECTION

3 So what advantage does the Jew have? Or what is the benefit of circumcision? **2** Considerable in every way. First, they were entrusted[v] with the very words of God.[w] **3** What then? If some were unfaithful,[x] will their unfaithfulness nullify God's faithfulness? **4** Absolutely not![y] Let God be true, even though everyone is a liar,[z] as it is written:

> **That you may be justified**
> **in your words**
> **and triumph when you judge.**[I,aa]

5 But if our unrighteousness highlights[J] God's righteousness,[ab] what are we to say?[ac] I am using a human argument:[K,ad] Is God unrighteous to inflict wrath? **6** Absolutely not! Otherwise, how will God judge the world?[ae] **7** But if by my lie God's truth abounds to his glory, why am I also still being judged as a sinner?[af] **8** And why not say, just as some people slanderously claim we say, "Let us do what is evil so that good may come"?[ag] Their condemnation is deserved!

THE WHOLE WORLD GUILTY BEFORE GOD

9 What then? Are we any better off?[L] Not at all! For we have already charged that both

---

[a]2:12 1Co 9:21
[b]2:13 Mt 7:21,24; Jn 13:17; Jms 1:22
[c]2:14 Ac 10:35; Rm 1:19
[d]2:15 Rm 2:27
[e]2:16 Ac 10:42; 17:31; Rm 3:6; 14:10
[f]Rm 16:25; 1Co 15:1; Gl 1:11; 1Tm 1:11; 2Tm 2:8
[g]2:17 Mc 3:11; Jn 5:45; Rm 9:4
[h]2:18 Php 1:10
[i]2:20 Is 2:1-4; 42:6-7; 49:6
[j]2:21 Mt 23:3-7
[k]2:22 Ac 19:37
[l]2:23 Mc 3:11; Jn 5:45; Rm 9:4
[m]2:24 Is 52:5; Ezk 36:20-23; 2Pt 2:2
[n]2:25 Jr 4:4; 9:25
[o]2:26 Rm 3:30; 1Co 7:19; Eph 2:11
[p]Rm 8:4

[q]2:27 Mt 12:41
[r]2:28 Jn 8:39; Rm 9:6; Gl 6:15
[s]2:29 Php 3:3; Col 2:11
[t]Rm 7:6; 2Co 3:6
[u]Jn 5:44; 12:43; 1Co 4:5; 2Co 10:18
[v]3:2 Dt 4:8; Ps 147:19; Rm 9:4
[w]Ac 7:38
[x]3:3 Rm 10:16; Heb 4:2
[y]3:4 Lk 20:16; Rm 3:31
[z]Ps 116:11
[aa]Ps 51:4
[ab]3:5 Rm 5:8; 2Co 6:4; Gl 2:18
[ac]Rm 4:1; 7:7; 8:31; 9:14,30
[ad]Rm 6:19; 1Co 9:8; 15:32; Gl 3:15
[ae]3:6 Rm 2:16
[af]3:7 Rm 9:19
[ag]3:8 Rm 6:1

[A]2:12 Lit in [B]2:13 Or acquitted [C]2:14 Or who do not have the law, instinctively do [D]2:15 The code of conduct required by the law [E]2:15 Internal debate, either in a person or among the pagan moralists [F]2:17 Other mss read Look— [G]2:24 Is 52:5 [H]2:29 Or heart— spiritually, not literally [I]3:4 Ps 51:4 [J]3:5 Or shows, or demonstrates [K]3:5 Lit I speak as a man [L]3:9 Are we Jews any better than the Gentiles?

2:12-15 God will judge people according to the light they have (2:12). Although **the Gentiles** may not have had the Jewish **law**, they had their consciences, which were sufficient to **either accuse or even excuse them** (2:14-15). Knowledge and understanding affects the level of judgment.
2:17-23 The Jews felt that because they had **the law**, they were **superior** (2:17-18). But having the law only made them more self-righteous and hypocritical (2:19-22). External religion without internal conversion has absolutely no value to God. He never intended for his people to simply memorize

his law. He intends for us to keep it, and we can only do that when we are changed from the inside out.
2:24 Perhaps the most tragic result of the Jews dishonoring God was their terrible witness to the world. May the hypocrisy of the saved never keep the gospel from getting to the lost!
2:28-29 Those who were authentic Jews were not those who had merely performed external rituals like **circumcision**, but those who followed God in obedient relationship. When religion trumps relationship, God is not present.

3:3-4 God's **faithfulness** is not overcome by our faithlessness, however great it may be (3:3). As Paul puts it, **Let God be true, even though everyone is a liar** (3:4). Our very unrighteousness demonstrates God's righteousness.
3:5-8 The questions asked here reflect an attitude common to proud humanity: when God turns our evil toward his good plan, we ask to be let off for our evil. But just because God uses our unrighteousness to reveal his righteousness does not negate the fact that we broke the law.
3:9 The **Jews** may have sinned by ignoring the law, but the **Gentiles** sinned by ignoring

a 3:9 Rm 2:1-29
b Rm 1:18-32
c Rm 3:19,23; 11:32; Gl 3:22
d 3:10–12 Ps 14:1-3; 53:1-3;
Ec 7:20
e 3:13 Ps 5:9
f Ps 140:3
g 3:14 Ps 10:7
h 3:15–17 Is 59:7-8
i 3:18 Ps 36:1
j 3:19 Jn 10:34
k Rm 2:12
l Rm 2:9
m 3:20 Ps 143:2; Ac 13:39;
Gl 2:16
n Rm 4:15; 5:13,20; 7:7
o 3:21 Rm 1:17; 9:30
p Ac 10:43; Rm 1:2

q 3:22 Rm 4:5
r Ac 3:16; Gl 2:16,20; 3:22;
Eph 3:12
s Rm 4:11,16; 10:4
t Rm 10:12; Gl 3:28; Col 3:11
u 3:23 Rm 3:9
v 3:24 Rm 4:4,16; Eph 2:8
w 1Co 1:30; Eph 1:7; Col
1:14; Heb 9:15
x 3:25 1Jn 2:2; 4:10
y 1Co 5:7; Heb 9:14,28; 1Pt
1:19; Rv 1:5
z Rm 2:4
aa Ac 17:30; 14:16
ab 3:27 Rm 2:17,23; 4:2; 1Co
1:29-31
ac Rm 9:31
ad 3:28 Ac 13:39; Rm 9:31;
Eph 2:9; Jms 2:20,24,26
ae 3:29 Ac 10:34; Rm 9:24;
10:12; 15:9; Gl 3:28
af 3:30 Rm 10:12
ag Rm 4:11,16; Gl 3:8
ah 3:31 Lk 20:16; Rm 3:4
ai Mt 5:17; Rm 4:3; 8:4
aj 4:1 Rm 1:3
ak 4:2 1Co 1:31

Jews*a* and Gentiles*A,b* are all under sin,*B,c* **10** as it is written:

> There is no one righteous,
>   not even one.
> **11** There is no one who understands;
>   there is no one who seeks God.
> **12** All have turned away;
>   all alike have become worthless.
> There is no one who does
>   what is good,
>   not even one.*c,d*
> **13** Their throat is an open grave;
> they deceive with their tongues.*D,e*
> Vipers' venom is
>   under their lips.*E,f*
> **14** Their mouth is full of cursing
>   and bitterness.*F,g*
> **15** Their feet are swift to shed blood;
> **16** ruin and wretchedness are
>   in their paths,
> **17** and the path of peace
>   they have not known.*G,h*
> **18** There is no fear of God
>   before their eyes.*H,i*

19 Now we know that whatever the law says,*j* it speaks to those who are subject to the law,*i,k* so that every mouth may be shut and the whole world may become subject to God's judgment.*j,l* **20** For no one will be justified*k* in his sight by the works of the law,*m* because the knowledge of sin comes through the law.*n*

THE RIGHTEOUSNESS OF GOD THROUGH FAITH

21 But now, apart from the law, the righteousness of God has been revealed,*o* attested by the Law and the Prophets.*L,p*

22 The righteousness of God is through faith*q* in Jesus Christ*M,r* to all who believe,*s* since there is no distinction.*t* **23** For all have sinned*u* and fall short of the*N* glory of God. **24** They are justified freely by his grace*v* through the redemption that is in Christ Jesus.*w* **25** God presented him as an atoning sacrifice*O,x* in his blood,*y* received through faith, to demonstrate his righteousness, because in his restraint God*z* passed over the sins previously committed.*aa* **26** God presented him to demonstrate his righteousness at the present time, so that he would be righteous and declare righteous*p* the one who has faith in Jesus.

BOASTING EXCLUDED

27 Where, then, is boasting?*ab* It is excluded. By what kind of law?*Q,ac* By one of works? No, on the contrary, by a law*R* of faith. **28** For we conclude that a person is justified by faith apart from the works of the law.*ad* **29** Or is God the God of Jews only?*ae* Is he not the God of Gentiles too? Yes, of Gentiles too, **30** since there is one God*af* who will justify the circumcised by faith*ag* and the uncircumcised through faith. **31** Do we then nullify the law through faith? Absolutely not!*ah* On the contrary, we uphold the law.*ai*

ABRAHAM JUSTIFIED BY FAITH

4 What then will we say that Abraham, our forefather*aj* according to the flesh, has found?*S* **2** If Abraham was justified*T* by works,*ak* he has something to boast about — but not before God. **3** For what does the Scripture say? **Abraham**

A 3:9 Lit *Greeks*   *B* 3:9 Under sin's power or dominion   *C* 3:10–12 Ps 14:1-3; 53:1-3; Ec 7:20   *D* 3:13 Ps 5:9   *E* 3:13 Ps 140:3   *F* 3:14 Ps 10:7
G 3:15–17 Is 59:7-8   *H* 3:18 Ps 36:1   *I* 3:19 Lit *those in the law*   *J* 3:19 Or *become guilty before God,* or *may be accountable to God*   *K* 3:20 Or *will be declared righteous,* or *will be acquitted*   *L* 3:21 When capitalized, *the Law and the Prophets* = OT   *M* 3:22 Or *through the faithfulness of Jesus Christ*   *N* 3:23 Or *and lack the*   *O* 3:25 Or *a propitiation,* or *a place of atonement*   *P* 3:26 Or *and justify,* or *and acquit*   *Q* 3:27 Or *what principle?*   *R* 3:27 Or *a principle*   *S* 4:1 Or *What then shall we say? Have we found Abraham to be our forefather according to the flesh?* or *What, then, shall we say that Abraham our forefather found according to the flesh?*   *T* 4:2 Or *was declared righteous,* or *was acquitted*

their consciences. We started on different paths, but we ended up in the same hopeless place.

3:12-18 People use every part of their bodies to rebel against the Word and will of God (3:13-18). **All** of us stand under condemnation; **all** of us need salvation (3:12).

3:20 Think of **the law** as a mirror that shows you who you really are. While a mirror reveals your messed-up hair, you don't pull it off the wall and brush your hair with it! Mirrors don't fix anything; they show us what needs fixing. The law was not designed to fix you, but to reveal what needs fixing.

3:23 If two men are running to catch a plane, and one man is an hour late, while the other is one minute late, both men miss the flight!

It doesn't matter if you are "better" than your neighbor. Your neighbor is not the standard. **God** is the standard, and we all **fall short**.

3:24 Justification is a legal concept meaning that in God's courtroom, he pronounced believers innocent of all charges. He does this through what theologians call "imputation"—taking Jesus's perfect record and crediting it to our accounts.

3:25 Forgiveness *always* comes at a cost. A man once owned a Rolls-Royce that started to give him trouble. At his call, the company sent an expert to repair the car. Over time, the man noticed that he never got billed. And when he called Rolls-Royce to check on the matter, they said, "Sir, there is no recorded problem with any Rolls-Royce." So what hap-

pened to the repair bill? Rolls-Royce absorbed it. Likewise, God sent Jesus to repair our sin problem, but he didn't leave a bill behind because he absorbed the cost himself.

3:31 Do we . . . nullify the law through faith? No. When you understand grace, you find that you do the right thing, not because you're driven to (as under the law), but because you're grateful. If you really understand grace, you can't help but worship God, give to him, and love other people. Grace isn't license to sin; it's God's inexhaustible supply of goodness.

4:2 Works can't save us because they give us something to brag about. As long as we're boasting, we aren't clinging to God's grace.

4:3 It doesn't matter how sincere or passionate your faith is if its object is wrong. Back in

believed God, and it was credited to him for righteousness.[A,a] [4] Now to the one who works,[b] pay is not credited as a gift, but as something owed. [5] But to the one who does not work, but believes on him who declares the ungodly to be righteous,[c] his faith is credited for righteousness.

DAVID CELEBRATING THE SAME TRUTH

[6] Just as David also speaks of the blessing of the person to whom God credits righteousness apart from works:

[7] Blessed are those whose lawless acts are forgiven
    and whose sins are covered.

[8] Blessed is the person
    the Lord will never charge
    with sin.[B,d]

ABRAHAM JUSTIFIED BEFORE CIRCUMCISION

[9] Is this blessing only for the circumcised,[e] then? Or is it also for the uncircumcised? For we say, **Faith was credited to Abraham for righteousness.**[A,f] [10] In what way then was it credited — while he was circumcised, or uncircumcised? It was not while he was circumcised, but uncircumcised. [11] And he received the sign of circumcision[g] as a seal of the righteousness that he had by faith[c,h] while still uncircumcised. This was to make him the father[i] of all who believe[j] but are not circumcised, so that righteousness may be credited to them also. [12] And he became the father of the circumcised, who are not only circumcised but who also follow in the footsteps of the faith our father Abraham had while he was still uncircumcised.

THE PROMISE GRANTED THROUGH FAITH

[13] For the promise to Abraham[k] or to his descendants that he would inherit the world[l] was not through the law, but through the righteousness that comes by faith. [14] If those who are of the law are heirs,[m] faith is made empty and the promise nullified, [15] because the law produces wrath.[n] And where there is no law,[o] there is no transgression.

[16] This is why the promise is by faith, so that it may be according to grace,[p] to guarantee it to all the descendants[q] — not only to those who are of the law[D] but also to those who are of Abraham's faith. He is the father of us all. [17] As it is written: **I have made you the father of many nations.**[E,r] He is our father in God's sight, in whom Abraham believed — the God who gives life to the dead[s] and calls[t] things into existence that do not exist.[u] [18] He believed, hoping against hope, so that he became **the father of many nations**[E,v] according to what had been spoken: **So will your descendants be.**[F,w] [19] He did not weaken in faith when he considered[G] his own body to be already dead[x] (since he was about a hundred years old)[y] and also the deadness of Sarah's womb.[z] [20] He did not waver in unbelief at God's promise but was strengthened in his faith and gave glory to God,[aa] [21] because he was fully convinced[ab] that what God had promised, he was also able to do.[ac] [22] Therefore, **it was credited to him for righteousness.**[A,ad] [23] Now **it was credited to him**[A] was not written for Abraham alone,[ae] [24] but also for us. It will be credited to us who believe in him[af] who raised Jesus our Lord from the dead.[ag] [25] He was delivered up for[H] our trespasses[ah] and raised for our justification.[ai]

[a] 4:3 Gn 15:6; Gl 3:6; Jms 2:23
[b] 4:4 Rm 11:6
[c] 4:5 Jn 3:33; Rm 3:22
[d] 4:7-8 Ps 32:1-2; 2Co 5:19
[e] 4:9 Rm 3:30
[f] Gn 15:6
[g] 4:11 Gn 17:10-11
[h] Jn 3:33
[i] Lk 19:9
[j] Rm 3:22

[k] 4:13 Rm 9:8; Gl 3:16; Heb 6:15,17; 7:6; 11:9,17
[l] Gn 17:4-6; 21:17-18
[m] 4:14 Gl 3:18
[n] 4:15 Rm 7:7,10-25; 1Co 15:56; Gl 3:10
[o] Rm 3:20
[p] 4:16 Rm 3:24
[q] Rm 9:8; 15:8
[r] 4:17 Gn 17:5
[s] Jn 5:21
[t] Is 48:13; 51:2
[u] 1Co 1:28
[v] 4:18 Gn 17:5
[w] Gn 15:5
[x] 4:19 Heb 11:12
[y] Gn 17:17
[z] Gn 18:11
[aa] 4:20 Mt 9:8
[ab] 4:21 Rm 14:5
[ac] Gn 18:14; Heb 11:19
[ad] 4:22 Gn 15:6; Rm 4:3
[ae] 4:23 Rm 15:4; 1Co 9:9; 10:11; 2Tm 3:16
[af] 4:24 Rm 10:9; 1Pt 1:21
[ag] Ac 2:24
[ah] 4:25 Rm 5:6,8; 8:32; Gl 2:20; Eph 5:2
[ai] Rm 5:18; 1Co 15:17; 2Co 5:15

[A] 4:3,9,22,23 Gn 15:6   [B] 4:7-8 Ps 32:1-2   [C] 4:11 Lit *righteousness of faith*, also in v. 13   [D] 4:16 Or *not to those who are of the law only*   [E] 4:17,18 Gn 17:5   [F] 4:18 Gn 15:5   [G] 4:19 Other mss read *He did not consider*   [H] 4:25 Or *because of*

---

the 1980s, there was a tragic case in Chicago where some Tylenol had become laced with cyanide. Those involved believed they were just getting pain medicine, but their belief was insufficient: the contents of the bottles couldn't be trusted. It is the *object* of our faith, and not our faith itself, that matters.
4:4-5 Salvation is a gift, plain and simple. If you just reach out your hand and take it, then it's yours. But if you work for it, you dismiss the gift and treat it as a wage that is earned.
    Many people will stand before God and list their credentials: I went to church every Sunday; I helped the needy; I read my Bible. But God will not grant salvation **as something owed** (4:4; see Eph 2:8-9).

4:6-8 The point here is that even King **David** recognized that sins are not overcome by hard work, and lawless acts are not outweighed by good deeds (4:6-7). **The Lord** does the forgiving; he does the covering; we simply believe it and receive it (4:8).
4:9-12 The timing of Abraham's circumcision was not a historical accident, but an intentional orchestration of God. Since Abraham believed before circumcision (circumcision was the physical confirmation of faith), he could become **the father of all who believe**— Gentile as well as Jew (4:11). All come to God on the same basis: faith.
4:18-19 Abraham's great act of faith actually didn't have anything to do with circumcision

or the law at all. It had to do with God's promise to give Abraham and Sarah a son. Given their advanced age, this required a supernatural level of **hope** (4:18).
4:21 Can God pull off what God said? To doubt him is to question whether he tells the truth. It is to challenge God's integrity.
4:22-25 What Abraham only saw in shadows and hints, we see fully. We know that the object of our faith is **Jesus our Lord**, who was raised **from the dead** (4:24). Abraham trusted the power of God to bring life from a seemingly dead situation (barrenness). We have seen the power of God bring life from the literal death of the Son.

Against All Hope

YEARS AGO, THIRTY-THREE MINERS IN Chile became trapped more than two thousand feet underground. For weeks, they found themselves in a deep, dark pit and were unable to do anything to get out of their situation. No one even knew exactly where they were. Trapped beneath the surface, they were helpless, hopeless, and desperate. If they were ever going to be saved, help would have to come from above.

After several weeks, the miners' location was pinpointed and rescue workers were able to lower essential items down to them through a small tube. Things like toothpaste, food, and other survival items were sent to the miners, not just to help them in the midst of their dark and desperate situation, but also to give them hope. Indeed, this tube provided hope to the miners that someone was up above them, doing everything in their power to reach them and deliver them from their pit. The tube itself did not deliver them, but it gave them hope that deliverance was on the way.

It could be that today you find yourself in a similar circumstance. Life has caved in on you—perhaps spiritually, financially, relationally, or emotionally. Regardless, you see no way out. At the moment, you aren't even sure that anyone above knows where you are.

After fifty-nine days, every miner was successfully brought to the surface. All survived. One miner, Mario Sepúlveda, said, "We always knew that we would be rescued; we never lost faith." Another miner said that there were not thirty-three people down in that pit: there were thirty-four. God was with them the entire time.

God's Word does not automatically and immediately undo all of life's negative realities. Christians still face the same troubles as anyone else (SEE JOHN 16:33). But what God does provide is a sustaining hope. God is aware of your plight and is working on your behalf for good. No matter how dark your situation is, keep the faith because ultimately it will keep you. If you are still stuck deep in a pit, look for the lifeline—the tube—that God uses to send you what you need to sustain you as you wait on your breakthrough. He is Jehovah Jireh, our God who shall supply all our needs. And when the day comes for your victory, praise him. Praise the Lord because he saw you through what seemed like a hopeless situation.

Scripture tells us that Abraham was in a hopeless situation. He and his wife were past the age of bearing children. But God had promised him an heir. So we read that Abraham "believed, hoping against hope" (ROM 4:18). As a result, Abraham saw the fruit of his belief in his son.

You, too, will see the fruit of your belief—either in this world or in the next. It is a promise from God who says, "Those who put their hope in me will not be put to shame" (ISA 49:23). So put your hope in God today. He sees you. He knows you. He loves you. He is with you. And he will deliver you when you trust him.

The great news is that you can get it back. You don't have to live a life of defeat, or a life in which you simply get by without maximizing all you were created to be. You can reclaim your spiritual authority. It is never too late. Start now.

FAITH TRIUMPHS

5 Therefore, since we have been declared righteous by faith,[a] we have peace[A] with God through our Lord Jesus Christ.[b] **2** We have also obtained access through him[c] by faith[B] into this grace in which we stand,[d] and we rejoice[c] in the hope of the glory of God. **3** And not only that,[e] but we also rejoice in our afflictions,[f] because we know that affliction produces endurance,[g] **4** endurance produces proven character,[h] and proven character produces hope. **5** This hope will not disappoint us,[i] because God's love has been poured out in our hearts[j] through the Holy Spirit who was given to us.

THOSE DECLARED RIGHTEOUS ARE RECONCILED

6 For while we were still helpless, at the right time,[k] Christ died for the ungodly. **7** For rarely will someone die for a just person — though for a good person perhaps someone might even dare to die. **8** But God proves[l] his own love for us[m] in that while we were still sinners, Christ died for us. **9** How much more then, since we have now been declared righteous by his blood,[n] will we be saved through him from wrath.[o] **10** For if, while we were enemies,[p] we were reconciled to God through the death of his Son, then how much more, having been reconciled, will we be saved by his life.[q] **11** And not only that, but we also rejoice in God through our Lord Jesus Christ, through whom we have now received this reconciliation.[r]

DEATH THROUGH ADAM AND LIFE THROUGH CHRIST

12 Therefore, just as sin entered the world through one man,[s] and death through sin,[t] in this way death spread to all people,[u] because all sinned.[D] **13** In fact, sin was in the world before the law, but sin is not charged to a person's account when there is no law.[v] **14** Nevertheless, death reigned from Adam to Moses, even over those who did not sin in the likeness of Adam's transgression.[w] He is a type of the Coming One.[x] **15** But the gift is not like the trespass. For if by the one man's trespass the many died, how much more have the grace of God and the gift which comes through the grace of the one man[y] Jesus Christ overflowed to the many. **16** And the gift is not like the one man's sin, because from one sin came the judgment,[z] resulting in condemnation, but from many trespasses came the gift, resulting in justification.[E] **17** Since by the one man's trespass, death reigned through that one man, how much more will those who receive the overflow of grace and the gift of righteousness reign in life[aa] through the one man, Jesus Christ. **18** So then, as through one trespass there is condemnation for everyone, so also through one righteous act there is justification leading to life[ab] for everyone. **19** For just as through one man's disobedience the many were made sinners,[ac] so also through the one man's obedience[ad] the many will be made righteous. **20** The law came along to multiply the trespass.[ae] But where sin multiplied, grace multiplied

[a] 5:1 Rm 3:28
[b] Rm 5:11
[c] 5:2 Eph 2:18; 3:12; Heb 10:19-20; 1Pt 3:18
[d] 1Co 15:1
[e] 5:3 Rm 5:11; 8:23; 9:10; 2Co 8:19
[f] Mt 5:12; Jms 1:2-3
[g] Lk 21:19
[h] 5:4 Php 2:22; Jms 1:12
[i] 5:5 Ps 119:116; Rm 9:33; Heb 6:18-20
[j] Ac 2:33; 10:45; Gl 4:6; Ti 3:6
[k] 5:6 Gl 4:4
[l] 5:8 Rm 3:5
[m] Jn 3:16; 15:13; Rm 8:39
[n] 5:9 Rm 3:25
[o] Rm 1:18; 1Th 1:10
[p] 5:10 Rm 11:28; 2Co 5:18-20; Eph 2:3; Col 1:21
[q] Rm 8:34; Heb 7:25
[r] 5:11 Rm 11:15; 2Co 5:18-20

[s] 5:12 Gn 2:17; 3:6,19; 1Co 15:21
[t] Rm 6:23; 1Co 15:56; Jms 1:15
[u] Rm 5:19,21; 1Co 15:22
[v] 5:13 Rm 4:15
[w] 5:14 Hs 6:7
[x] 1Co 15:45
[y] 5:15 Ac 15:11
[z] 5:16 1Co 11:32
[aa] 5:17 2Tm 2:12; Rv 22:5
[ab] 5:18 Rm 4:25
[ac] 5:19 Rm 11:32
[ad] Php 2:8
[ae] 5:20 Rm 3:20; 7:7; Gl 3:19

[A] 5:1 Other mss read *faith, let us have peace,* which can also be translated *faith, let us grasp the fact that we have peace*   [B] 5:2 Other mss omit *by faith*   [C] 5:2 Lit *boast,* also in vv. 3,11   [D] 5:12 Or *have sinned*   [E] 5:16 Or *acquittal*

5:1-2 Previously, we were God's enemies. We were at war with him. Through **Jesus**, however, he has drawn us close and made us his friends (5:1). Although the grace that saves and grows us can't be earned (see 11:6), it can be accessed by faith.

5:3-4 If we are in Christ, then we can **rejoice in our afflictions** (5:3) because God is working in those afflictions for our good.

5:6-8 On occasions like Memorial Day, we honor the sacrifices of people who died so others might live. Remembering those heroes brings to my mind what Paul says here, that **for a just person . . . perhaps someone might even dare to die** (5:7). It's rare for someone to lay his life down for others. It's tremendously loving and worthy of honor. But God's love is even more worthy of recognition than this. Jesus died, but not for friends; God proved **his own love for us** by dying for us while we were his enemies (5:8)! It's as if he says to unbelievers, "I know

you're rebelling against me. But I still love you so much that I'll go to the cross for you" (5:6).

5:9-11 Though the death of Christ addressed the penalty of sin, it is the resurrected life of Christ that saves or delivers his people in history from the power of sin and its consequences through his intercessory work on our behalf (see Heb 7:25).

5:14 Adam **is a type of the Coming One** in that he foreshadowed Jesus. We got our physical life from Adam, and we get our spiritual life from the last Adam, Christ. But just as Adam gave us sin through imputation, depositing sin into our accounts so that we were born with it, Christ imputes righteousness and life into us. He is our representative, and in his righteousness we find ours.

5:15 Unlike Adam, who gave us life and death, Jesus gives only life. And while we *earned* Adam's penalty of death—after all, every time we sin we show that we wouldn't have

chosen any better than he did—we *receive* **the grace of God** as a **gift**.

5:17 You can group the human race under two people—Adam or Christ. Every person you meet is either in Adam or in Christ, and that's a difference with eternal consequences.

5:18 Even though we are all born sinners, having inherited original sin from Adam, Christ's blood covers us until we reach an age of accountability, that time when a person is capable of choosing to transgress and reject his revelation. So while **there is condemnation for everyone**, there is divine covering through Christ for those who have not yet chosen to rebel against God's law. This explains how babies or people with mental handicaps are saved by Christ's death, since original sin is no longer the issue in those cases.

5:19 We are saved by works—just not our own. We are saved by the works of Christ.

5:20-21 It is essential for all believers to grow in their understanding and appreciation of

[a] 5:20 Rm 6:1; 1Tm 1:14
[b] 5:21 Rm 5:12,14
[c] Jn 1:17; Rm 6:23
[d] 6:1 Rm 3:5
[e] Rm 3:8; 6:15
[f] 6:2 Lk 20:16
[g] Rm 7:4,6; Gl 2:19; Col 2:20; 3:3; 1Pt 2:24
[h] 6:3 Mt 28:19; 1Co 1:13-17; 12:13; Gl 3:27
[i] Ac 2:38; 8:16; 19:5
[j] 6:4 Col 2:12
[k] Ac 2:24
[l] Jn 11:40; 2Co 13:4
[m] Rm 7:6; 2Co 5:17; Gl 6:15; Eph 4:23-24; Col 3:10
[n] 6:5 2Co 4:10; Php 3:10; Col 2:12; 3:1
[o] 6:6 Eph 4:22; Col 3:9
[p] Gl 2:20; 5:24; 6:14
[q] Rm 7:24
[r] 6:7 1Pt 4:1
[s] 6:8 2Co 4:10; 2Tm 2:11
[t] 6:9 Ac 2:24
[u] Rv 1:18

[v] 6:11 Rm 7:4,6; Gl 2:19; Col 2:20; 3:3; 1Pt 2:24
[w] 6:13 Rm 7:5; Col 3:5
[x] Rm 12:1; 2Co 5:14; 1Pt 2:24
[y] 6:14 Rm 5:18; 7:4,6; Gl 4:21
[z] Rm 5:17,21
[aa] 6:15 Rm 6:1
[ab] Lk 20:16
[ac] 6:16 Rm 11:2; 1Co 3:16; 5:6; 6:2-3,9,15-16,19; 9:13,24
[ad] Jn 8:34; 2Pt 2:19
[ae] Rm 6:23
[af] 6:17 Rm 1:8; 2Co 2:14
[ag] 2Tm 1:3
[ah] 6:18 Jn 8:32; Rm 8:2
[ai] 6:19 Rm 3:5

even more[a] [21] so that, just as sin reigned in death,[b] so also grace will reign[c] through righteousness, resulting in eternal life through Jesus Christ our Lord.

THE NEW LIFE IN CHRIST

6 What should we say then?[d] Should we continue in sin so that grace may multiply?[e] [2] Absolutely not![f] How can we who died to sin[g] still live in it? [3] Or are you unaware that all of us who were baptized[h] into Christ Jesus were baptized into his death?[i] [4] Therefore we were buried with him by baptism into death,[j] in order that, just as Christ was raised from the dead[k] by the glory of the Father,[l] so we too may walk in newness[A] of life.[m] [5] For if we have been united with him in the likeness of his death,[n] we will certainly also be[B] in the likeness of his resurrection. [6] For we know that our old self[C,o] was crucified with him[p] so that the body ruled by sin[D] might be rendered powerless[q] so that we may no longer be enslaved to sin, [7] since a person who has died[r] is freed[E] from sin. [8] Now if we died with Christ,[s] we believe that we will also live with him, [9] because we know that Christ, having been raised from the dead,[t] will not die again. Death no longer rules over him.[u] [10] For the death he died, he died to sin once for all time; but the life he lives, he lives to God. [11] So, you too consider yourselves dead to sin[v] and alive to God in Christ Jesus.[F]

[12] Therefore do not let sin reign in your mortal body, so that you obey[G] its desires. [13] And do not offer any parts[H] of it to sin[W] as weapons for unrighteousness. But as those who are alive from the dead, offer yourselves to God,[X] and all the parts of yourselves to God as weapons for righteousness. [14] For sin will not rule over you, because you are not under the law[Y] but under grace.[Z]

FROM SLAVES OF SIN TO SLAVES OF GOD

[15] What then? Should we sin because we are not under the law but under grace?[aa] Absolutely not![ab] [16] Don't you know that if you offer yourselves to someone[I] as obedient slaves,[ac] you are slaves of that one you obey[ad] — either of sin leading to death[ae] or of obedience leading to righteousness? [17] But thank God that, although you used to be slaves of sin,[af] you obeyed from the heart that pattern of teaching to which you were handed[J] over,[ag] [18] and having been set free from sin,[ah] you became enslaved to righteousness. [19] I am using a human analogy[ai] because of the weakness of your flesh.[K] For just as you offered the parts of yourselves as slaves to impurity, and to

---

[A] 6:4 Or *a new way*   [B] 6:5 Be joined with him   [C] 6:6 Lit *man*   [D] 6:6 Lit *that the body of sin*   [E] 6:7 Or *justified* ; lit *acquitted*   [F] 6:11 Other mss add *our Lord*   [G] 6:12 Other mss add *sin* (lit *it*) *in*   [H] 6:13 Or *members*, also in v. 19   [I] 6:16 Lit *that to whom you offer yourselves*   [J] 6:17 Or *entrusted*   [K] 6:19 Or *your human nature*

---

the magnificent grace of God (see Titus 2:11-14; 2 Pet 3:18).

6:1 People often make the mistake of seeing **grace** as license to do whatever they want: If more sin means more grace, why not just sin on purpose? Remember: no judge shows mercy to a criminal so that he can go out and commit more crimes.

6:2 Anyone who says that salvation makes him free to sin has totally misunderstood his or her new identity in Christ. As believers, we are dead to what once controlled us.

6:3-4 When Jesus died two thousand years ago, we died too. When he was buried, **we were buried with him** (6:4). Paul uses baptism to illustrate how this works. In Greek, the word translated **baptism** was used for dyeing clothes. You would dip a cloth in purple dye, let it soak (or be "baptized"), and it would absorb the color. The properties of the dye became part of the cloth, so that its visible identity was transformed. That's what happens to Christians: we are dipped in the blood of Jesus, so that the properties of Jesus become a part of us (see Gal 2:20).

6:6-7 If the Christian has the resurrection power of Jesus to overcome sin, why is it so hard to do? If **our old self was crucified with him** (6:6), why does that "old self" still have such power?

A mortician I know says that sometimes the muscles within cadavers twitch. He even saw a twitch that actually catapulted a cadaver off the table! But after sharing that insight, he told me, "That stuff doesn't bother me, because I know that *dead* is *dead*, even when it acts alive." Indeed, it's the same with our body of sin. Yes, it's moving around like it's still in charge. Yes, we'll still sin. But previously we *had* to, because we were sin's slaves. Now we **no longer** need to **be enslaved** (6:6). If we continue to sin, it's because we've forgotten our true identity.

6:11 During the Civil War, it was legal for men who wanted to avoid the draft to pay for personal replacements. In one particular instance, a man paid for another to go into battle for him, and that individual was killed. A few months later, the man who paid for the replacement received a second draft notice. But he took the legal agreement to the draft board, saying, "The second draft is invalid. Someone already went to war and died in my place." This is a picture of the Christian's situation. When Satan wants to re-draft us into sin, we must oppose him by pointing to Jesus's victory: "Satan, you can't force me to that old life anymore. The payment has already been paid. Jesus died in my place."

6:15 If you are living **under grace**, you will actually keep **the law**. And if you don't, it only proves you're not operating under the grace of God. Christians obey the standard, but the motivation isn't the standard. The motivation is God's grace.

6:16-18 In 1863, President Lincoln issued his famous Emancipation Proclamation, freeing all slaves throughout the Confederacy. But even years later, there were certain places where that announcement had been kept secret. Thus, even after being declared free, African Americans were still acting like slaves. No one had told them the truth of their situation! How foolish is it for those of us who *know* we're free in Christ to keep saying yes to sin?

6:19-22 If you become a slave of sin, you get some short-term pleasure, but that pleasure leads to death. What kind of a trade-off is that? If, however, you become a slave of God, you get sanctification and righteousness—both of which lead to life (6:22).

The New Way

"OUT WITH THE OLD AND in with the new" is a cliché most of us are familiar with. It's a phrase meant to communicate the importance of moving forward with the times and leaving behind what has become outdated.

This may surprise you, but I have a flip phone. In this age of tablets and smartphones, I know my ancient piece of technology probably seems useless to most. But though my staff wants to communicate with me through text messages and emails, the truth is I'd rather just stick to paper memos and handwritten notes.

The reason I have not embraced the newer technology is simply because I am too comfortable with the old way of doing things. When someone gives me directions, I pull out a pen and paper. While everyone else on a plane pulls out their laptops, I pull out my yellow legal pad. I have been taking care of business in one way for so long that changing to an entirely new method has no appeal.

That is how many Christians respond to the new way that God has made available to them—that is, the grace of God. You see, we live in a world that teaches the value of hard work, which yields a reward. And while I am a firm believer in hard work, that is not how grace works. What separates Christianity from all other religions is that we operate in God's kingdom under his grace. It's not about what we can do for God, but about what he has already done for us. That requires a major adjustment for most Christians. Rather than working to earn God's favor, we are to trust that it is given freely to us, even though we don't deserve it (SEE ROM 3:23; 6:23).

We want to make it right. We want to fill the tank with good deeds to make up for the bad deeds, but we can never repay the debt and don't need to. You see, grace is about getting what we *don't* deserve. The grace for God is best shown in the greatest gift ever given. Jesus Christ paid the price for all our sin with his death on a cross, and we no longer need to try to earn God's favor. He offers it to us freely.

The old way of doing things was hardly as effective. In the Old Testament, God gave the Jews a system of offerings and sacrifices accomplished through a priest. This old covenant way was complicated, messy, and time-consuming. But even more than that, it was temporary. God meant for the sacrifices to point to the ultimate sacrifice of his Son. The animal sacrifices and burnt offerings had to keep going on since they only covered the sins of the people for a season. Thanks be to God for a new covenant through Jesus!

The new way releases us from having to try to earn God's favor. Grace is about unconditionally accepting his favor as a free gift. Our sins have been forgiven; our eternal future is secured. God eagerly desires to fill our lives with his blessings and protection from spiritual wickedness. I encourage you to let go of the old way of doing things and embrace God's grace in your life.

[a] 6:20 Mt 6:24
[b] 6:21 Jr 12:13; Ezk 16:63; Rm 7:5
[c] Rm 1:32; 5:12; 8:6,13; Gl 6:8
[d] 6:22 1Co 7:22; 1Pt 2:16
[e] Rm 7:4
[f] 1Pt 1:9
[g] 6:23 Mt 25:46; Rm 5:21; 8:39
[h] 7:1 Rm 1:13
[i] 7:2 1Co 7:39
[j] 7:4 Rm 6:2
[k] Rm 8:2; Gl 2:19; 5:18
[l] Col 1:22
[m] 7:5 Rm 8:8-10; 2Co 10:3
[n] Rm 6:13,21,23
[o] 7:6 Rm 2:29

[p] 7:7 Rm 3:5
[q] Lk 20:16
[r] Rm 4:15; 5:20
[s] Ex 20:17
[t] 7:8 Rm 3:20
[u] 1Co 15:56
[v] 7:10 Lv 18:5; Lk 10:28; Rm 10:5; Gl 3:12
[w] 7:11 Gn 3:13
[x] 7:12 1Tm 1:8
[y] 7:13 Lk 20:16
[z] 7:14 1Co 3:1
[aa] 1Kg 21:20,25; 2Kg 17:17; Rm 6:6; Gl 4:3
[ab] Rm 3:9
[ac] 7:15 Jn 15:15
[ad] Gl 5:17
[ae] 7:18 Jn 3:6; Rm 8:3

greater and greater lawlessness, so now offer them as slaves to righteousness, which results in sanctification. [20] For when you were slaves of sin, you were free with regard to righteousness.[A,a] [21] So what fruit was produced[B] then from the things you are now ashamed of?[b] The outcome of those things is death.[c] [22] But now, since you have been set free from sin and have become enslaved to God,[d] you have your fruit, which results in sanctification[e] — and the outcome is eternal life![f] [23] For the wages of sin is death, but the gift of God is eternal life in Christ Jesus our Lord.[g]

AN ILLUSTRATION FROM MARRIAGE

7 Since I am speaking to those who know the law, brothers and sisters,[h] don't you know that the law rules over someone as long as he lives? [2] For example, a married woman is legally bound to her husband while he lives.[i] But if her husband dies, she is released from the law regarding the husband. [3] So then, if she is married to another man while her husband is living, she will be called an adulteress. But if her husband dies, she is free from that law. Then, if she is married to another man, she is not an adulteress.

[4] Therefore, my brothers and sisters, you also were put to death[j] in relation to the law[k] through the body of Christ[l] so that you may belong to another. You belong to him who was raised from the dead in order that we may bear fruit for God. [5] For when we were in the flesh,[m] the sinful passions aroused through the law were working in us[C,n] to bear fruit for death. [6] But now we have been released from the law, since we have died to what held us, so that we may serve in the newness of the Spirit[o] and not in the old letter of the law.

SIN'S USE OF THE LAW

[7] What should we say then?[p] Is the law sin? Absolutely not![q] On the contrary, I would not have known sin if it were not for the law.[r] For example, I would not have known what it is to covet if the law had not said, **Do not covet.**[D,s] [8] And sin, seizing an opportunity through the commandment,[t] produced in me coveting of every kind. For apart from the law sin is dead.[u] [9] Once I was alive apart from the law, but when the commandment came, sin sprang to life again [10] and I died. The commandment that was meant for life[v] resulted in death for me. [11] For sin, seizing an opportunity through the commandment, deceived me,[w] and through it killed me. [12] So then, the law is holy,[x] and the commandment is holy and just and good. [13] Therefore, did what is good become death to me? Absolutely not![y] On the contrary, sin, in order to be recognized as sin, was producing death in me through what is good, so that through the commandment, sin might become sinful beyond measure.

THE PROBLEM OF SIN IN US

[14] For we know that the law is spiritual,[z] but I am of the flesh,[E] sold[aa] as a slave to sin.[F,ab] [15] For I do not understand what I am doing,[ac] because I do not practice what I want to do,[ad] but I do what I hate. [16] Now if I do what I do not want to do, I agree with the law that it is good. [17] So now I am no longer the one doing it, but it is sin living in me. [18] For I know that nothing good lives in me, that is, in my flesh.[ae] For the desire to do what is good is with me, but there is no ability to do it. [19] For I do not do the good that I want to do, but I practice the evil that I do not want to do. [20] Now if I do what I do not want, I am no longer the one that does it, but it is the sin that lives in me.

[A] 6:20 Lit free to righteousness   [B] 6:21 Lit what fruit do you have   [C] 7:5 Lit in our members   [D] 7:7 Ex 20:17   [E] 7:14 Or unspiritual   [F] 7:14 Lit under sin

6:23 Paul is writing to Christians here. The point is that believers can still choose **sin**, but when they do, they collect their rightful **wages**: weakness, sickness, meaninglessness, and the loss of spiritual fellowship with God (see 1 John 1:5–9). Unbelievers, on the other hand, live in a perpetual state of spiritual death (i.e., separation from God).
7:5 **The law** is designed to reveal sin, but knowing what is forbidden also has a way of arousing **sinful passions.**
7:7 Just because the law instigated our sinful passions doesn't mean something is wrong with the law. It is like a mirror; it shows us what's wrong, but it's not designed to fix it.

Without it, we **would not have known,** for instance, **what it is to covet.** The law, then, is also like a speed limit sign that reads, "Speed Limit 55," which may or may not slow us down. Nevertheless, that sign validates the police officer who pulls us over when we're driving 80! Because that sign is posted, our **sin** is revealed, and we're without excuse.
7:11 Have you ever seen a "Don't Touch" sign? The sign itself makes you want to reach out your hand! Likewise, **sin** conjures up the desire to do the opposite of what the law says.
7:12 **The law** came from God and represents his holy character.

7:15 It's encouraging to know that Paul suffered the same struggles we do. Haven't we all asked, "What's wrong with me? I know better than to do this!" Indeed, there is a spiritual war within us.
7:18 Our sin nature was like a factory that produced unrighteousness, evil, and sin. When we came to Christ, God shut that factory down. That solved the problem of future production from our old sin nature, but it didn't address what was already produced. Existing sin from that factory lingers in our **flesh.**
7:20 Paul is not excusing our sin. He is reminding us that our true identity is no longer found in our actions, even if we keep sinning.

❧ Questions & Answers ❧

Q How should Paul's description of the Spirit's work in Romans 8 be of comfort to us in our own battles with sin?

A Romans 8, full of references to the work and ministry of the Spirit, comes right after Paul's description of the intense battle with the flesh in Romans 7:14-24. Paul's expression of the victory he achieved in Romans 8 over the struggle he was experiencing in Romans 7 should lead us to one conclusion: you can't fix the flesh with the flesh. Paul tried, but he failed. Only when he learned to walk in the Spirit—that is, to live life under the Spirit's power—was he lifted above the debilitating, gravitational pull of sin. So as we yield to God's truth and depend on the Spirit to make that truth operative in our lives, it is like putting helium in a balloon. It lifts us up to a higher level of victory than we can experience on our own. Living under God's control, based on his Word, gives us power to have victory over what our flesh cannot do by itself.

FOR THE NEXT Q&A, SEE PAGE 1344.

21 So I discover this law:[A,a] When I want to do what is good,[B] evil is present with me. **22** For in my inner self[c] I delight in God's law,[b] **23** but I see a different law in the parts of my body,[D,c] waging war against the law of my mind and taking me prisoner to the law of sin in the parts of my body. **24** What a wretched man I am! Who will rescue me from this body of death?[d] **25** Thanks be to God through Jesus Christ our Lord![e] So then, with my mind I myself am serving the law of God, but with my flesh, the law of sin.

THE LIFE-GIVING SPIRIT

8 Therefore, there is now no condemnation[f] for those in[g] Christ Jesus, [E,n] **2** because the law of the Spirit of life[i] in Christ Jesus has set you[F] free from the law of sin and death.[j] **3** What the law could not do[k] since it was weakened by the flesh,[l] God did. He condemned sin in the flesh by sending his own Son in the likeness of sinful flesh[m] as a sin offering,[G,n] **4** in order that the law's requirement would be fulfilled[o] in us who do not walk according to the flesh[p] but according to the Spirit. **5** For those who live according to the flesh have their minds set on the things of the flesh,[q] but those who live according to the Spirit have their minds set on the things of the Spirit. **6** Now the mind-set of the flesh[r] is death,[s] but the mind-set of the Spirit is life and peace. **7** The mind-set of the flesh is hostile[t] to God because it does not submit to God's law. Indeed, it is unable to do so. **8** Those who are in the flesh[u] cannot please God. **9** You, however, are not in the flesh, but in the Spirit, if indeed the Spirit of God lives in you.[v] If anyone does not have the Spirit of Christ,[w] he does not belong to him. **10** Now if Christ is in you,[x] the body is dead because of sin, but the Spirit[H] gives life[i] because of righteousness. **11** And if the Spirit of him who raised Jesus from the dead[y] lives in you, then he who raised

[a] 7:21 Rm 8:2
[b] 7:22 2Co 4:16; Eph 3:16; 1Pt 3:4
[c] 7:23 Rm 6:19; Gl 5:17; Jms 4:1; 1Pt 2:11
[d] 7:24 Rm 6:6; 8:2; Col 2:11
[e] 7:25 1Co 15:57
[f] 8:1 Rm 5:16; 8:34
[g] Rm 8:9-10
[h] Rm 8:11,39; 16:3
[i] 8:2 1Co 15:45
[j] Jn 8:32,36; Rm 6:14,18; 7:4
[k] 8:3 Ac 13:39; Heb 10:1-2
[l] Rm 7:18; Heb 7:18
[m] Php 2:7; Heb 2:14,17; 4:15
[n] Lv 5:6-7,11; 14:31; Is 53:10
[o] 8:4 Lk 1:6; Rm 2:26
[p] Gl 5:16
[q] 8:5 Gl 5:19-25
[r] 8:6 Gl 6:8
[s] Rm 6:21
[t] 8:7 Jms 4:4
[u] 8:8 Rm 7:5
[v] 8:9 Jn 14:23; 1Co 3:16; 6:19; 2Co 6:16; 2Tm 1:14
[w] Jn 14:17; Gl 4:6; Php 1:19; 1Jn 4:13
[x] 8:10 Jn 17:23; Gl 2:20; Eph 3:17; Col 1:27
[y] 8:11 Ac 2:24; Rm 6:4

[A] 7:21 Or *principle*   [B] 7:21 Or *I find with respect to the law that when I want to do good*   [C] 7:22 Lit *inner man*   [D] 7:23 Lit *my members*   [E] 8:1 Other mss add *who do not walk according to the flesh but according to the Spirit*   [F] 8:2 Other mss read *me*   [G] 8:3 Or *for sin*   [H] 8:10 Or *spirit*   [I] 8:10 Or *your spirit is alive*

7:21 Note the word **with** here. Evil is *with* me; it doesn't define me. When sin wants me to define myself by what I've done wrong, I remember that God defines me by who I am in Christ.

7:24-25 All throughout this chapter, Paul has been struggling to pull himself out of his inner war, but as if battling quicksand, he found that the more he struggled, the deeper he sank. The power of positive thinking did nothing for him. Until he finally lifted his eyes to the only One who could rescue him, his situation was hopeless. Then, like a bolt of lightning, he finally shouts, **Thanks be to God through Jesus Christ our Lord!** (7:25). *Jesus* lifted Paul out of the muck and mire.

8:1 If you are a believer in **Jesus**, it does not matter what your heart tells you; God says you stand before him with zero **condemnation**.

8:2-3 Which law you operate by determines whether you live in victory or defeat. **The law of sin and death** is like gravity. It inherently pulls you down, no matter how high you jump. But **the law of the Spirit** overrides gravity (8:2). It's like climbing aboard an airplane, where the laws of aerodynamics apply. You cannot get rid of the law of gravity, but you can transcend it. The Spirit's law transcends the law of sin so that sin no longer controls the agenda (8:3).

8:4 The word **walk** refers to our entire way of life, and it has three concepts imbedded in it. First, it implies a destination: you must point your life toward the will and glory of God. Second, it implies dependence: when you walk, you place one foot in front of another, putting all your weight on that foot for that step. You must rest all of the weight of your soul on God's power, not your own. Third, walking implies dedication: you must continually take steps, perpetually calling on God to do in you what you could never do alone.

8:5-7 If our **minds** are set on the wrong things, our feet will automatically go the wrong way (8:5). Setting your mind is like choosing a television station. You can watch channel 5 or channel 8, but you can't watch both simultaneously. Nor can you simultaneously listen to AM and FM frequencies on the same device. You have two different channels—one that leads to **death** and one that leads to **life and peace** (8:6).

8:11 The Spirit is like an engine in a car that can take us where God wants us to go. Too many of us are trying to push the car of life around, when God wants us to let the engine do the work.

[a] 8:13 Col 3:5
[b] 8:14 Gl 5:18
[c] Hs 1:10; Mt 5:9; Jn 1:12; Rm 9:8,26; 2Co 6:18; Gl 3:26; 1Jn 3:1; Rv 21:7
[d] 8:15 2Tm 1:7; Heb 2:15
[e] Gl 4:5
[f] Mk 14:36; Gl 4:6
[g] 8:16 Ac 5:32

[h] 8:17 Ac 20:32; Gl 3:29; 4:7; Eph 3:6; Ti 3:7; Heb 1:14; Rv 21:7
[i] 2Co 1:5,7; Php 3:10; Col 1:24; 2Tm 2:12
[j] 8:18 2Co 4:17; 1Pt 4:13
[k] Rm 1:5; Col 3:4; Ti 2:13; 1Pt 5:1
[l] 8:19 Php 1:20
[m] 1Co 1:7; Col 3:4; 1Pt 1:7,13; 1Jn 3:2
[n] 8:20 Gn 3:17-19
[o] Ps 39:5; Ec 1:2
[p] Gn 3:17; 5:29
[q] 8:21 Ac 3:21; 2Pt 3:13; Rv 21:1
[r] 8:22 Jr 12:4,11

❧ KINGDOM LIVING ❧
CHURCH
The Church's Mission

Entire books have been written on the church's mission, but perhaps the most comprehensive summary of our calling is the text commonly called the Great Commission (Matt 28:19-20). These are the last words spoken by Jesus Christ before his ascension to heaven, which makes them crucial. They are also very important words because they contain Christ's final instructions to his church, which is to "make disciples of all nations" (28:19).

There's more to discipleship than the personal dimension of a believer's growth in grace. *Discipleship* is the developmental process of the local church by which Christians are brought from spiritual infancy to spiritual maturity so that they can reproduce the process with others, which the Bible calls being "conformed to the image of [God's] Son" (Rom 8:29). This verse goes on to explain the goal of our becoming like Jesus: "so that he would be the firstborn among many brothers and sisters."

The process of discipleship that leads to believers becoming Christlike is designed to be repeated until Jesus has many siblings who look like him. You and I can't grow in this way if we are living as isolated Christians. Someone has said that Christianity was never meant to be "Jesus and me, under a tree." Rather, God placed us in a body of people called the church so that together we can accomplish the mission. The church is God's place to produce disciples who think, talk, and act so much like Jesus that the world can look at us and say, "This must be what Jesus is like." After all, Jesus said, "It is enough for a disciple to become like his teacher" (Matt 10:25). The primary role of the local church is to provide an environment in which authentic discipleship can occur.

FOR THE NEXT CHURCH KINGDOM LIVING LESSON SEE PAGE 1353.

Christ from the dead will also bring your mortal bodies to life through[A] his Spirit who lives in you.

THE HOLY SPIRIT'S MINISTRIES

12 So then, brothers and sisters, we are not obligated to the flesh to live according to the flesh, **13** because if you live according to the flesh, you are going to die. But if by the Spirit you put to death the deeds of the body,[a] you will live. **14** For all those led by God's Spirit[b] are God's sons.[c] **15** For you did not receive a spirit of slavery to fall back into fear.[d] Instead, you received the Spirit of adoption,[e] by whom we cry out, "*Abba*,[B] Father!"[f] **16** The Spirit himself testifies together with our spirit[g] that we are God's children, **17** and if children, also

heirs[h] — heirs of God and coheirs with Christ — if indeed we suffer with him[i] so that we may also be glorified with him.

FROM GROANS TO GLORY

18 For I consider that the sufferings of this present time are not worth comparing[j] with the glory[k] that is going to be revealed to us. **19** For the creation eagerly waits with anticipation[l] for God's sons[m] to be revealed. **20** For the creation was subjected[n] to futility[o] — not willingly, but because of him who subjected it[p] — in the hope **21** that the creation itself[q] will also be set free from the bondage to decay into the glorious freedom of God's children. **22** For we know that the whole creation has been groaning together with labor pains[r] until

[A] 8:11 Other mss read *because of*　　[B] 8:15 Aramaic for *father*

8:14-15 If we walk according to the Spirit as God desires, we prove ourselves to be **God's sons** (8:14). Not only are we sons (and daughters), but we are *adopted* children. If a person was adopted in Paul's time, that individual immediately received all of the rights of an adult heir. The chief right that Paul mentions here is intimacy with God. We therefore can pray, ***Abba*, Father** (8:15). *Abba* is a term of intimacy meaning "Papa" or "Daddy." We can say it with complete assurance that God is listening.

8:16-17 Being adopted as **God's children** (8:16) may come with extreme benefits, but it also carries with it intense responsibility. Yes, we are already **heirs of God**, but we can only become **coheirs with Christ** if we **suffer with him** (8:17). If we do suffer, we will be **glorified with him** (8:17). If we shrink back in the day of trial, we'll lose something valuable. We cannot lose our salvation, but we can certainly lose some of the reward God intends to give. **8:18** For believers, **the glory** ahead is not only greater than our **present** suffering. It is *so much*

greater that should we look back on our earthly existence from the joys of eternity, our only response will be, "Suffering? *What* suffering?" **8:19-21** Human sin corrupted **creation** and dragged it down into the messes we see today. It brought about things like earthquakes, volcanoes, and disease. But our righteousness, bought and perfected by Christ, will act as the agent of change in creation. When the children of God are ruling, the earth will once again have order, perfection, and untarnished beauty.

APPLICATION QUESTIONS

READ ROMANS 8:28
- What emotions do you experience when you read this verse? Why?
- When has God caused difficult circumstances to work together for good in your life?
- What situations seem out of control in your life right now?

now. **23** Not only that,[a] but we ourselves who have the Spirit as the firstfruits[b] — we also groan within ourselves,[c] eagerly waiting for adoption,[d] the redemption of our bodies.[e] **24** Now in this hope[f] we were saved, but hope[g] that is seen is not hope, because who hopes for what he sees? **25** Now if we hope for what we do not see,[h] we eagerly wait for it with patience.

26 In the same way the Spirit also helps us in our weakness, because we do not know what to pray for as we should,[i] but the Spirit himself intercedes for us[A,j] with unspoken groanings. **27** And he who searches our hearts[k] knows the mind of the Spirit, because he intercedes for the saints according to the will of God.

28 We know that all things work together[B] for the good[c] of those who love God, who are called according to his purpose.[l] **29** For those he foreknew he also predestined[m] to be conformed to the image of his Son,[n] so that he would be the firstborn among many brothers and sisters.[o] **30** And those he predestined, he also called; and those he called, he also justified;[p] and those he justified, he also glorified.[q]

THE BELIEVER'S TRIUMPH

31 What then are we to say about these things?[r] If God is for us, who is against us?[s] **32** He did not even spare his own Son[t] but offered him up for us all.[u] How will he not also with him grant us everything?

⤳ HOPE WORDS ⤳

Sometimes God rescues us from things. Sometimes he rescues us out of things. And sometimes he changes us in things. Let him choose. He knows best.

33 Who can bring an accusation against God's elect?[v] God is the one who justifies.[w] **34** Who is the one who condemns?[x] Christ Jesus is the one who died,[y] but even more, has been raised;[z] he also is at the right hand of God[aa] and intercedes for us.[ab] **35** Who can separate us from the love of Christ? Can affliction[ac] or distress or persecution[ad] or famine or nakedness or danger or sword? **36** As it is written:

**Because of you
we are being put to death
all day long;[ae]
we are counted as sheep
to be slaughtered.[D,af]**

37 No, in all these things we are more than conquerors[ag] through him who loved us.[ah] **38** For I am persuaded that neither death nor life,[ai] nor angels nor rulers,[aj] nor things present nor things to come,[ak] nor powers, **39** nor height nor depth, nor any other created thing will be able to separate us from the love of God[al] that is in Christ Jesus our Lord.[am]

⤳ HOPE WORDS ⤳

You may run out of a lot of things in life, but you will never run out of God's love.

[a] 8:23 Rm 5:3
[b] Nm 15:17-21; 1Co 16:15; 2Co 1:22
[c] 2Co 5:2,4
[d] Gl 5:5
[e] Rm 7:24
[f] 8:24 1Th 5:8; Ti 3:7
[g] Rm 4:18; 2Co 5:7; Heb 11:1
[h] 8:25 1Th 1:3
[i] 8:26 Mt 20:22; 2Co 12:8
[j] Jn 14:16; Rm 8:15-16; Eph 6:18
[k] 8:27 Ps 139:1-5; Lk 16:15; Ac 1:24; Rv 2:23
[l] 8:28 Rm 9:24; 11:29; 1Co 1:9; Gl 1:6,15; 5:8; Eph 1:11; 3:11; 2Th 2:14; Heb 9:15; 1Pt 2:9; 3:9
[m] 8:29 Rm 9:23; 1Co 2:7; Eph 1:5,11
[n] 1Co 15:49; Php 3:21; Col 3:10; 1Jn 3:2
[o] Col 1:18; Heb 1:6
[p] 8:30 1Co 6:11
[q] Jn 17:22; Rm 9:23; 1Co 2:7; 6:9; 11:23
[r] 8:31 Rm 3:5; 4:1
[s] Ps 118:6; Mt 1:23
[t] 8:32 Jn 3:16; Rm 5:8
[u] Rm 4:25

[v] 8:33 Lk 18:7
[w] Is 50:8-9
[x] 8:34 Rm 8:1
[y] Rm 5:6-8
[z] Ac 2:24
[aa] Mk 16:19
[ab] Heb 7:25; 9:24; 1Jn 2:1
[ac] 8:35 Rm 2:9; 2Co 4:8
[ad] 1Co 4:11; 2Co 11:26-27
[ae] 8:36 Ac 20:24; 1Co 4:9; 15:30-31; 2Co 1:9; Is 53:7; Zch 11:4,7
[af] 8:37 Jn 16:33; 1Co 15:57
[ah] Gl 2:20; Eph 5:2; Rv 1:5
[ai] 8:38 1Co 3:22
[aj] 1Co 15:24; Eph 1:21; 1Pt 3:22
[ak] 1Co 3:22
[al] 8:39 Rm 5:8
[am] Rm 8:1

[A] 8:26 Some mss omit *for us*   [B] 8:28 Other mss read *that God works together in all things*   [C] 8:28 The ultimate good   [D] 8:36 Ps 44:22

8:23 It may be difficult, but our groaning *now* is leading to life *then*. And just as a mother forgets the pain of childbirth once her baby is born, we too will forget our pains in the world to come.
8:24 Hope is a joyful expectation about the future, a trust that our tomorrows will be greater than our yesterdays. Real hope combines radical trust in God with the candid admission that we don't know the details about our futures. What we *do* know, however, outweighs what we do *not*.

8:26 We don't know the language of prayer like God does. We're like foreigners, wandering around a country completely helpless. But in this unknown territory, **the Spirit** of God translates for us.
8:27 The Greek word for **intercedes** that Paul uses means "to appeal." In our weakness, we may simply be groaning, but the Spirit translates that into an appeal that is **according to the will of God.** If we pray from the heart— even if our prayers are only groans—they are exactly as they should be by the time they reach God.

8:28-29 The promise of 8:28 is a conditional one. If believers are not loving God and progressively being **conformed to the image of** Christ, they will not see things working together for good.
8:30 God always finishes what he starts. Note that all who are **called** reach glorification, which guarantees the eternal security of all believers.
8:33 If God says you're not guilty because you've placed faith in Christ (and he does), then charges against you are irrelevant.
8:37 With God's love, we don't just get by. We overwhelmingly conquer.

a 9:1 Rm 1:9; 2Co 11:10; Gl 1:20; 1Tm 2:7
b 9:3 Ex 32:32
c 1Co 12:3; 16:22; Gl 1:8,9
d 9:4 Rm 8:6
e Ex 4:22; Rm 8:15
f Ex 40:34; 1Kg 8:11; Ezk 1:28; Heb 9:5
g Gn 17:2; Dt 29:14; Lk 1:72; Ac 3:25; Eph 2:12
h Dt 4:13-14; Ps 147:19
i Dt 7:6; 14:1; Heb 9:1,6
j Ac 2:39; 13:32; Eph 2:12
k 9:5 Ac 3:13; Rm 11:28
l Mt 1:1-16; Rm 1:3
m Jn 1:1; Col 2:9
n Col 1:16-19
o Rm 1:25
p 9:6 Nm 23:19
q Jn 1:47; Rm 2:28-29; Gl 6:16
r 9:7 Jn 8:33,39; Gl 4:23
s Gn 21:12; Heb 11:18
t 9:8 Rm 8:14
u Rm 4:13,16; Gl 3:29; 4:28; Heb 11:11
v 9:9 Gn 18:10,14
w 9:10 Rm 5:3
x Gn 25:21

y 9:11 Rm 4:17; 8:28
z 9:12 Gn 25:23
aa 9:13 Mal 1:2-3
ab 9:14 Rm 3:5
ac 2Ch 19:7; Rm 2:11
ad Lk 20:16
ae 9:15 Ex 33:19
af 9:16 Gl 2:2
ag Eph 2:8
ah 9:17 Ex 9:16
ai 9:18 Ex 4:21; 7:3; 9:12; 10:20,27; 11:10; 14:4,7; Dt 2:30; Jos 11:20; Jn 12:40; Rm 11:7,25
aj 9:19 Rm 11:19; 1Co 15:25; Jms 2:18
ak Rm 3:7
al 2Ch 20:6; Jb 9:12; Dn 4:35
am 9:20 Jb 33:13
an Is 29:16; 45:9; 64:8; Jr 18:6; 2Tm 2:20
ao 9:21 Is 64:8; Jr 18:6
ap 9:22 Rm 2:4

ISRAEL'S REJECTION OF CHRIST

9 I speak the truth in Christ[a] — I am not lying; my conscience testifies to me through the Holy Spirit[A] — **2** that I have great sorrow and unceasing anguish in my heart. **3** For I could wish[b] that I myself were cursed[c] and cut off[B] from Christ for the benefit of my brothers and sisters, my own flesh and blood. **4** They are Israelites,[d] and to them belong the adoption,[e] the glory,[f] the covenants,[g] the giving of the law,[h] the temple service,[i] and the promises.[j] **5** The ancestors are theirs,[k] and from them, by physical descent,[c] came the Christ,[l] who is God[m] over all,[n] praised forever.[D,o] Amen.

GOD'S GRACIOUS ELECTION OF ISRAEL

6 Now it is not as though the word of God has failed,[p] because not all who are descended from Israel are Israel.[q] **7** Neither are all of Abraham's children his descendants.[E,r] On the contrary, **your offspring will be traced**[F] **through Isaac.**[G,s] **8** That is, it is not the children by physical descent[H] who are God's children,[t] but the children of the promise[u] are considered to be the offspring. **9** For this is the statement of the promise: **At this time I will come, and Sarah will have a son.**[I,v] **10** And not only that,[w] but Rebekah conceived children[x] through one man, our father Isaac. **11** For though her sons had not been born yet or done anything good or bad, so that

God's purpose according to election might stand[y] — **12** not from works but from the one who calls — she was told, **The older will serve the younger.**[J,z] **13** As it is written: **I have loved Jacob, but I have hated Esau.**[K,aa]

GOD'S SELECTION IS JUST

14 What should we say then?[ab] Is there injustice with God?[ac] Absolutely not![ad] **15** For he tells Moses, **I will show mercy to whom I will show mercy, and I will have compassion on whom I will have compassion.**[L,ae] **16** So then, it does not depend on human will or effort[af] but on God who shows mercy.[ag] **17** For the Scripture tells Pharaoh, **I raised you up for this reason so that I may display my power in you and that my name may be proclaimed in the whole earth.**[M,ah] **18** So then, he has mercy on whom he wants to have mercy and he hardens whom he wants to harden.[ai]

19 You will say to me,[aj] therefore, "Why then does he still find fault?[ak] For who can resist his will?"[al] **20** But who are you, a mere man, to talk back to God?[am] Will what is formed say to the one who formed it, "Why did you make me like this?"[an] **21** Or has the potter no right over the clay,[ao] to make from the same lump one piece of pottery for honor and another for dishonor? **22** And what if God, wanting to display his wrath and to make his power known, endured with much patience[ap] objects of

[A] 9:1 Or *testifying with me by the Holy Spirit*   [B] 9:3 Lit *to be anathema*   [C] 9:5 Lit *them, according to the flesh*   [D] 9:5 Or *the Messiah, the one who is over all, the God who is blessed forever,* or *Messiah. God, who is over all, be blessed forever*   [E] 9:7 Lit *seed*   [F] 9:7 Lit *called*   [G] 9:7 Gn 21:12   [H] 9:8 Lit *children of the flesh*   [I] 9:9 Gn 18:10,14   [J] 9:12 Gn 25:23   [K] 9:13 Mal 1:2-3   [L] 9:15 Ex 33:19   [M] 9:17 Ex 9:16

9:1-3 Like the Lord whom he followed, Paul was willing to experience divine judgment so others might be saved (9:3). Do you have the same intense **anguish** (9:2) for those who don't know Jesus?

9:4-7 The nation of Israel received special privileges, including **the covenants, the giving of the law,** the unique opportunity to worship God in **the temple service,** and the **promises** of the Savior (9:4). Israel had been favored by God in a way no other nation had. They were not diminished in the least by God drawing Gentiles into his family.

9:6-7 It seemed as if **the word of God** to Israel had **failed** because while the Jews were supposed to welcome their Messiah, many (in fact, most) of them rejected Jesus. Thus, Paul reminds us of an Old Testament idea known as "the remnant" (e.g., Isa 10:21). He says that not **all who are descended from Israel are Israel** (Rom 9:6). There had *always* been a true people of God within the nation, a spiritual Israel within the physical Israel. So it is today. Only those who accept Christ are truly **Abraham's children** and **descendants** (9:7).

9:8 Israel assumed that **children by physical descent** were **God's children.** Don't we similarly assume that our kids, because they grow up in church, are all right—even if everything in their lives says otherwise? God has a lot of *children,* but he doesn't have any *grandchildren.* Each one of our kids must accept Christ personally, because only **the children of the promise are considered . . . offspring.**

9:10-13 Election is about service, not individual eternal salvation (9:11). Jacob—not Esau—was chosen to be the Messiah's ancestor even though both were Abraham's descendants.

In saying, **I have loved Jacob, but I have hated Esau** (9:13), Paul switches from individual to national election by quoting Malachi 1:2-3, where the two sons represent nations (see Gen 25:23) as Esau's descendants (the Edomites) served Jacob (Israel). The concepts of *love* and *hate* refer to God's decision to bestow inheritance, blessings, and kingdom responsibility on Jacob's descendants rather than on Esau's. Although Esau never served Jacob personally, Jacob called himself Esau's

servant (see Gen 33:3, 5, 8, 14). God was pointing to his favor of Israel (Jacob's descendants) over the Edomites (Esau's descendants). God has the sovereign right to choose whom he will use to accomplish his kingdom purposes.

9:15-16 Mercy is given for the purpose of receiving blessing to accomplish and advance God's kingdom program, not for individual salvation.

9:17-18 Hardening is not predestination to damnation; it's an expression of God's prerogative to choose whom he will use to serve his purposes and how he will use them (see Jer 18:1-12). God punishes the wicked by using their wickedness to accomplish his purposes. God uses obedience and disobedience to accomplish his kingdom agenda while holding people responsible for their own decisions.

9:19-24 The Creator has rights over his creation, plain and simple. Whether God is acting in **wrath** or in **mercy** (9:22-23), he is accomplishing his plan. The big difference is in how *we* experience that plan—as willing sons and daughters, or as unwilling slaves.

wrath prepared for destruction?[a] **23** And what if he did this to make known the riches of his glory[b] on objects of mercy[c] that he prepared beforehand for glory[d] — **24** on us, the ones he also called,[e] not only from the Jews but also from the Gentiles?[f] **25** As it[A] also says in Hosea,

> I will call Not My People, My People,
> and she who is Unloved,
> Beloved.[B,g]

26 And it will be in the place where they were told,
> you are not my people,
> there they will be called sons of the living God.[C,h]

27 But Isaiah cries out concerning Israel,
> Though the number
> of Israelites
> is like the sand of the sea,[i]
> only the remnant will be saved;[j]

28 since the Lord will execute
> his sentence
> completely and decisively
> on the earth.[D,E,K]

29 And just as Isaiah predicted:
> If the Lord of Hosts[F] had not left
> us offspring,[l]
> we would have become
> like Sodom,
> and we would have been made
> like Gomorrah.[G,m]

ISRAEL'S PRESENT STATE

30 What should we say then?[n] Gentiles, who did not pursue righteousness, have obtained righteousness — namely the righteousness that comes from faith.[o]

31 But Israel, pursuing the law of righteousness,[p] has not achieved the righteousness of the law.[H,q] **32** Why is that? Because they did not pursue it by faith, but as if it were by works.[i] They stumbled over the stumbling stone.[r] **33** As it is written,

> Look, I am putting a stone in Zion
> to stumble over
> and a rock to trip over,
> and the one who believes
> on him[s]
> will not be put to shame.[J,t]

RIGHTEOUSNESS BY FAITH ALONE

10 Brothers and sisters, my heart's desire and prayer to God concerning them[k] is for their salvation. **2** I can testify about them that they have zeal for God,[u] but not according to knowledge. **3** Since they are ignorant of the righteousness of God[v] and attempted to establish their own righteousness, they have not submitted to God's righteousness. **4** For Christ is the end[L] of the law for righteousness[w] to everyone who believes,[x] **5** since Moses writes about the righteousness that is from the law: **The one who does these things will live by them.**[M,y] **6** But the righteousness that comes from faith[z] speaks like this: **Do not say in your heart, "Who will go up to heaven?"**[N,aa] that is, to bring Christ down **7** or, **"Who will go down into the abyss?"**[O,ab] that is, to bring Christ up from the dead.[ac] **8** On the contrary, what does it say? **The message is near you, in your mouth and in your heart.**[P,ad] This is the message of faith that we proclaim:

[a] 9:22 Pr 16:4; 1Pt 2:8
[b] 9:23 Rm 2:4; Eph 3:16
[c] Ac 9:15
[d] Rm 8:29
[e] 9:24 Rm 8:28
[f] Rm 3:29
[g] 9:25 Hs 2:23; 1Pt 2:10
[h] 9:26 Hs 1:10; Mt 16:16
[i] 9:27 Gn 22:17
[j] Rm 11:5
[k] 9:27-28 Is 10:22-23; 28:22
[l] 9:29 Jms 5:4
[m] Dt 29:23; Is 1:9; 13:19; Jr 49:18; 50:40; Am 4:11
[n] 9:30 Rm 9:14
[o] Rm 1:17; 3:21; 10:6; Gl 2:16; 3:24; Php 3:9; Heb 11:7

[p] 9:31 Is 51:1; Rm 10:2,20; 11:7
[q] Gl 5:4
[r] 9:32 1Pt 2:6,8
[s] 9:33 Rm 10:11
[t] Is 8:14; 28:16; Rm 5:5
[u] 10:2 Ac 21:20
[v] 10:3 Rm 1:17
[w] 10:4 Rm 7:1-4; Gl 3:24; 4:5
[x] Rm 3:22
[y] 10:5 Lv 18:5; Neh 9:29; Ezk 20:11,13,21; Rm 7:10
[z] 10:6 Rm 9:30
[aa] Dt 9:4; 30:12
[ab] 10:7 Dt 30:13; Lk 8:31
[ac] Heb 13:20
[ad] 10:8 Dt 30:14

[A] 9:25 Or he   [B] 9:25 Hs 2:23   [C] 9:26 Hs 1:10   [D] 9:28 Or land   [E] 9:27-28 Is 10:22-23; 28:22; Hs 1:10   [F] 9:29 Gk Sabaoth; or the Lord of Armies   [G] 9:29 Is 1:9   [H] 9:31 Other mss read the law for righteousness   [I] 9:32 Other mss add of the law   [J] 9:33 Is 8:14; 28:16   [K] 10:1 Other mss read God for Israel   [L] 10:4 Or goal   [M] 10:5 Lv 18:5   [N] 10:6 Dt 9:4; 30:12   [O] 10:7 Dt 30:13   [P] 10:8 Dt 30:14

9:25-26 Between wrath and mercy, God leans toward mercy, as the example of Hosea reminds us. Even though Israel was subjected to God's wrath in history, their remnant will return as God's **Beloved** and **People** (9:25).

9:30-33 From one perspective, it was God's sovereign will to extend grace to the Gentiles. From another perspective, though, the Gentiles **have obtained righteousness** because they pursued it the right way, by faith (9:30). Israel, by contrast, failed to achieve **the law of righteousness** (9:31) because **they did not pursue it by faith** (9:32). As long as anyone pursues salvation by works, as Israel did, the grace of Jesus will act like a **stumbling stone** (9:32). Jesus is either the stone we trip over in our self-righteousness, or he's the rock we build our lives upon.

10:1-2 The problem with Israel, Paul points out, is not a lack of passion. He testifies that **they have zeal for God**. They believe in God and think they are pleasing to him. But their

zeal is **not according to knowledge** (10:2). So, although they're running a race, it's the race of religion—the Jewish equivalent of going to church and trying to be a good person. Paul knew this race well, because he too had been running it for years.

10:3 There are two approaches to getting to heaven: God's approach and man's. They lead to very different outcomes. Though society may tell us there are dozens of ways to get to heaven, in the end there's only one.

Consider a game of basketball. Two guys take shots to win the game: the first guy misses the rim completely, an air ball; the second guy puts up a shot that rattles around, *nearly* goes in, but still misses. Which shot is of greater value? Neither. There's a set standard for scoring (the ball must go through the hoop), and both guys missed it. The worst thing in the world is

thinking that just because your ball went around the rim, spiritually speaking, it went in.

10:4 The point of **the law** wasn't the law; the point of the law was to point us to Jesus.

10:5 If you want **the law** to judge you, fine. Have it your way. God will judge you by the law. But it won't be pretty. God demands absolute perfection, so if you're hoping to be justified by the law, you had better live a life without sin. And history tells us there's only been one such life.

10:6-8 The **righteousness that comes from faith** (10:6) is not difficult or complicated. The righteousness of the law is hard, always making us wonder whether we've done enough. It makes us ask, **Who will go up to heaven?** (10:6) or **Who will go down into the abyss?** (10:7), because we want to have some assurance from beyond the grave. But somebody has already come from heaven and gotten

[a] 10:9 Mt 10:32; Lk 12:8; Rm 14:9; 1Co 12:3; Php 2:11
[b] Ac 16:31; Rm 4:24
[c] Ac 2:24
[d] 10:11 Is 28:16
[e] 10:12 Rm 3:22,29
[f] Ac 10:36
[g] Rm 3:29
[h] 10:13 Jl 2:32; Ac 2:21; 7:59
[i] 10:14 Eph 2:17; 4:21
[j] Ac 8:31; Ti 1:3
[k] 10:15 Is 52:7; Nah 1:15; Rm 1:15; 15:20
[l] 10:16 Rm 3:3
[m] Is 53:1; Jn 12:38
[n] 10:17 Gl 3:2,5
[o] Col 3:16
[p] 10:18 Ps 19:4; Rm 1:8; Col 1:16,23; 1Th 1:8
[q] 10:19 Rm 11:11,14

[r] 10:19 Dt 32:21
[s] 10:20 Is 65:1; Rm 9:30
[t] 10:21 Is 65:2
[u] 11:1 1Sm 12:22; Jr 33:24-26
[v] Lk 20:16
[w] 11:2 2Co 11:22; Php 3:5
[x] 11:2 1Sm 12:22; Ps 94:14; Rm 8:29; 1Pt 1:2
[y] Rm 6:16
[z] 11:3 1Kg 19:10,14; 1Th 2:14
[aa] 11:4 1Kg 19:18
[ab] 11:5 2Kg 19:4; Rm 9:27
[ac] 11:6 Rm 4:4
[ad] 11:7 Rm 9:31
[ae] Mk 6:52; Rm 9:18; 11:25; 2Co 2:14

[9] If you confess with your mouth, "Jesus is Lord,"[a] and believe in your heart[b] that God raised him from the dead,[c] you will be saved. [10] One believes with the heart, resulting in righteousness, and one confesses with the mouth, resulting in salvation. [11] For the Scripture says, **Everyone who believes on him will not be put to shame.**[A,d] [12] since there is no distinction between Jew and Greek,[e] because the same Lord[f] of all[g] richly blesses all who call on him. [13] For **everyone who calls on the name of the Lord will be saved.**[B,h]

ISRAEL'S REJECTION OF THE MESSAGE

[14] How, then, can they call on him they have not believed in? And how can they believe without hearing about him?[i] And how can they hear without a preacher?[j] [15] And how can they preach unless they are sent? As it is written: **How beautiful**[c] **are the feet of those who bring good news.**[D,k] [16] But not all obeyed the gospel.[l] For Isaiah says, **Lord, who has believed our message?**[E,m] [17] So faith comes from what is heard,[n] and what is heard comes through the message about Christ.[F,o] [18] But I ask, "Did they not hear?" Yes, they did:

Their voice has gone out to
the whole earth,
and their words to the ends
of the world.[G,p]

[19] But I ask, "Did Israel not understand?" First, Moses said,

I will make you jealous
of those who are not a nation;[q]

I will make you angry by a nation
that lacks understanding.[H,r]
[20] And Isaiah says boldly,

I was found
by those who were not looking
for me;
I revealed myself
to those who were not asking
for me.[I,s]

[21] But to Israel he says, **All day long I have held out my hands to a disobedient and defiant people.**[J,t]

ISRAEL'S REJECTION NOT TOTAL

11 I ask, then, has God rejected his people?[u] Absolutely not![v] For I too am an Israelite, a descendant of Abraham,[w] from the tribe of Benjamin. [2] God has not rejected his people whom he foreknew.[x] Or don't you know[y] what the Scripture says in the passage about Elijah — how he pleads with God against Israel? [3] **Lord, they have killed your prophets and torn down your altars. I am the only one left, and they are trying to take my life![K,z]** [4] But what was God's answer to him? **I have left seven thousand for myself who have not bowed down to Baal.**[L,aa] [5] In the same way, then, there is also at the present time a remnant chosen by grace.[ab] [6] Now if by grace,[ac] then it is not by works; otherwise grace ceases to be grace.[M]

[7] What then? Israel did not find what it was looking for,[ad] but the elect did find it. The rest were hardened,[ae] [8] as it is written,

**God gave them a spirit of stupor,
eyes that cannot see**

[A] 10:11 Is 28:16 [B] 10:13 Jl 2:32 [C] 10:15 Or *welcome*, or *timely* [D] 10:15 Is 52:7; Nah 1:15 [E] 10:16 Is 53:1 [F] 10:17 Other mss read *God* [G] 10:18 Ps 19:4 [H] 10:19 Dt 32:21 [I] 10:20 Is 65:1 [J] 10:21 Is 65:2 [K] 11:3 1Kg 19:10,14 [L] 11:4 1Kg 19:18 [M] 11:6 Other mss add *But if of works it is no longer grace; otherwise work is no longer work.*

up from the grave. In Jesus you have a gospel message that is **in your heart** (10:8).

10:9-10 When a person believes, he receives justification. But in order to receive deliverance from temporal wrath in history (see 1:18-32; 5:9-10), a believer must also publicly acknowledge the lordship of Jesus Christ and call on him for divine assistance. This, in fact, is why **confess** and **believe** are flipped here (10:10). When a person believes, he receives God's righteousness (i.e., he is born again). But when he publicly acknowledges identification with Christ, he receives temporal divine intervention. Failure to do so results in the loss of that intervention (i.e., deliverance; see Matt 10:32-33).

10:11 We often think of coming to Jesus as a chance for our sins to be wiped away. And Jesus certainly does that. But he also removes our **shame**, delivering us in our everyday circumstances.

10:16 From Isaiah's time down to Paul's, the normal response to the Word of the Lord was rejection. The faithful will always be in the minority. **10:18** The word of God has gone out to every individual, whether he or she knows Jesus's name or not. *General revelation* is the idea that in the beauty and majesty of nature, people are confronted with the reality and power of God. The problem, as Paul brought up in the first chapter of Romans, is that they reject and suppress this knowledge of God. Thus, *special revelation* is necessary for people to be reconciled to him.

10:19-20 By extending grace to the Gentiles, **who were not looking for** or **asking for** him (10:20), God's goal was to **make** Israel **jealous of those who are not a nation** (10:19).

10:21 Nobody is more heartbroken by your disobedience than God. And nobody but God will show you more patience. If you're living in defiance on some issue, return to him.

11:1 God's grace toward Paul illustrates the kind of compassion God desires to show Israel as a whole.

11:2-5 In verse 5 we again see the idea of the **remnant**, which Paul introduced in 9:6 (though without the specific word). The nation of Israel was always a mixed group, a combination of faithful and faithless people. And while those who remained faithful, like Elijah, often felt completely alone, God reminds the remnant that they are not (see 1 Kgs 19:14-18). For **Elijah**, God preserved **seven thousand** (Rom 11:2-4); for Paul, **there is also . . . a remnant chosen by grace** (11:5); and for us, too, God keeps a remnant of faithful believers to remind us that we are never alone.

11:7-10 Just as Pharaoh's heart was hardened because he rejected God's command (see the note on 9:17-18; see Exod 10:1, 20), Israel's heart was hardened because they rejected

and ears that cannot hear,
to this day.[A,a]

9 And David says,

Let their table become a snare
and a trap,
a pitfall and a retribution to them.

10 Let their eyes be darkened
so that they cannot see,
and their backs be bent
continually.[B,b]

ISRAEL'S REJECTION NOT FINAL

11 I ask, then, have they stumbled so as to fall? Absolutely not! On the contrary, by their transgression, salvation has come to the Gentiles[c] to make Israel jealous. **12** Now if their transgression brings riches for the world, and their failure riches for the Gentiles, how much more will their fullness bring![d]

13 Now I am speaking to you Gentiles. Insofar as I am an apostle to the Gentiles,[e] I magnify my ministry, **14** if I might somehow make my own people[C,f] jealous and save some of them.[g] **15** For if their rejection brings reconciliation[h] to the world, what will their acceptance mean but life from the dead?[i] **16** Now if the firstfruits are holy,[j] so is the whole batch. And if the root is holy, so are the branches.

17 Now if some of the branches were broken off,[k] and you, though a wild olive branch, were grafted in among them[l] and have come to share in the rich root[D] of the cultivated olive tree, **18** do not boast that you are better than those branches. But if you do boast — you do not sustain the root, but the root sustains you.[m] **19** Then you will say,[n] "Branches were broken off so that I might be grafted in." **20** True enough; they were broken off because of unbelief, but you stand by faith.[o] Do not be arrogant, but beware,[E,p] **21** because if God did not spare the natural branches, he will not spare you either. **22** Therefore, consider God's kindness and severity: severity toward those who have fallen but God's kindness[q] toward you — if you remain in his kindness.[r] Otherwise you too will be cut off.[s] **23** And even they, if they do not remain in unbelief,[t] will be grafted in, because God has the power to graft them in again. **24** For if you were cut off from your native wild olive tree and against nature were grafted into a cultivated olive tree, how much more will these — the natural branches — be grafted into their own olive tree?

25 I don't want you to be ignorant[u] of this mystery,[v] brothers and sisters, so that you will not be conceited:[w] A partial hardening has come upon Israel[x] until the fullness of the Gentiles has come in.[y] **26** And in this way all[F] Israel will be saved, as it is written,

The Deliverer will come
from Zion;
he will turn godlessness away
from Jacob.

27 And this will be my covenant
with them[G,z]
when I take away their sins.[H,aa]

28 Regarding the gospel, they are enemies for your advantage,[ab] but regarding election, they are loved because of the patriarchs,[ac] **29** since God's gracious gifts and calling[ad] are irrevocable.[I,ae] **30** As you once disobeyed God but now have received mercy through their disobedience, **31** so they too have now disobeyed, resulting in mercy to you, so that they also may now[J] receive mercy. **32** For God has imprisoned all in disobedience[af] so that he may have mercy on all.

[a] 11:8 Dt 29:4; Is 29:10; Mt 13:13-14
[b] 11:9-10 Ps 69:22-23
[c] 11:11 Ac 28:28
[d] 11:12 Rm 11:25
[e] 11:13 Ac 9:15
[f] 11:14 Gn 29:14; 2Sm 19:12-13; Rm 9:3
[g] 1Co 1:21; 7:16; 9:22; 1Tm 1:15; 2:4; 2Tm 1:9; Ti 3:5
[h] 11:15 Rm 5:11
[i] Lk 15:24,32
[j] 11:16 Nm 15:17-21; Neh 10:37; Ezk 44:30
[k] 11:17 Jr 11:16; Jn 15:2
[l] Eph 2:12-13
[m] 11:18 Jn 4:22
[n] 11:19 Rm 9:19
[o] 11:20 Rm 5:2; 1Co 10:12; 2Co 1:24

[p] 11:20 Rm 12:16; 1Tm 6:17; 1Pt 1:17
[q] 11:22 Rm 2:4
[r] 1Co 15:2; Heb 3:6,14
[s] Jn 15:2
[t] 11:23 2Co 3:16
[u] 11:25 Rm 1:13
[v] Mt 13:11; Rm 16:25; 1Co 2:7-10; Eph 3:3-5,9
[w] Rm 12:16
[x] Rm 11:7
[y] Lk 21:24; Jn 10:16
[z] 11:26-27 Is 59:20-21
[aa] 11:27 Jr 31:31-34; Heb 8:10,12
[ab] 11:28 Rm 5:10
[ac] Dt 7:8; 10:15; Rm 9:5
[ad] 11:29 Rm 8:28; 1Co 1:26; Eph 1:18; 4:1,4; Php 3:14; 2Th 1:11; 2Tm 1:9; Heb 3:1; 2Pt 1:10
[ae] Heb 7:21
[af] 11:32 Rm 3:9; Gl 3:22-23

[A] 11:8 Dt 29:4; Is 29:10   [B] 11:9-10 Ps 69:22-23   [C] 11:14 Lit *flesh*   [D] 11:17 Other mss read *the root and the richness*   [E] 11:20 Lit *fear*   [F] 11:26 Or *And then all*   [G] 11:26-27 Is 59:20-21   [H] 11:27 Jr 31:31-34   [I] 11:29 Or *are not taken back*   [J] 11:31 Other mss omit *now*

God's Son. Thus, **God gave them ... eyes that cannot see and ears that cannot hear** (Rom 11:8) so that they would **not find what [they] were looking for** (11:7)—namely, salvation, because they sought it by works.

11:11 Israel may have **stumbled**, but not so badly **as to fall** away from God forever. In fact, God planned on their rejection as the vehicle for delivering salvation **to the Gentiles.**

11:12-15 When Christ returns, the **failure** of Israel will be reversed by **their fullness** because they will believe on Jesus as their Messiah. Not only will this reversal lead to the salvation of Israel, but it will lead to **riches for the world** (11:12) and **life from the dead** (11:15).

11:16 If the **firstfruits** of a particular crop are healthy and sweet, that's a guarantee that the rest of the crop will follow suit. God's promises to Abraham form **the root**, and that root produces the fruit: the remnant of Israel. Through this remnant, God will be able to fulfill his promises to Abraham and restore Israel as a nation.

11:17-21 Paul warns Gentile readers to avoid having a haughty attitude about the grace God has shown them: **Do not be arrogant** (11:20) and **do not boast that you are better than those branches** (11:18)—that is, the nation of Israel. After all, Israel was cut off **because of unbelief** (11:20), and God may just as readily cut off Gentile branches as Israelite ones (11:21). All who remain grafted into God's tree of salvation **stand by faith** (11:20), and faith cannot coexist with arrogant pride.

11:22 God is severe toward our sin, but kind enough to cover it in Christ. His kindness saves us from his severity.

11:25-27 God will fulfill his promises to Israel. Even though **a partial hardening has come upon** them (11:25), they will experience future salvation. Once **the fullness of the Gentiles has come** (11:25), God will pick up his program with Israel again. All of this will happen during the tumultuous end times, when Jesus returns as **the Deliverer** to eliminate all **godlessness**. In that day, **all Israel** that survives the great tribulation **will be saved** (11:26).

11:28 *Election* is the selection of a people through whom God would fulfill his kingdom purpose and program. It is not an election to individual, eternal salvation.

a 11:33 Rm 2:4; Eph 3:8
b Col 2:3; Eph 3:10
c Jb 5:9; 11:7; 15:8
d 11:34 Is 40:13-14; 1Co 2:16
e 11:34-35 Jb 35:7; 41:11; Is 40:13; Jr 23:18
f 11:36 1Co 8:6; 11:12; Col 1:16; Heb 2:10
g 12:1 1Co 1:10; 2Co 10:2; Eph 4:1; 1Pt 2:11
h Rm 6:13,16,19; 1Co 6:20; Heb 13:15; 1Pt 2:5
i 12:2 1Pt 1:14
j Mt 13:22; Gl 1:4; 1Jn 2:15
k Eph 4:23; Ti 3:5
l Eph 5:10,17; Col 1:9
m 12:3 Rm 1:5; 15:15; 1Co 3:10; 15:10; Gl 2:9; Eph 3:7-8
n Rm 11:20
o 1Co 7:17; 2Co 10:13; Eph 4:7; 1Pt 4:11
p 12:4 1Co 12:12-14; Eph 4:4,16
q 12:5 1Co 10:17,23
r 1Co 12:20,27; Eph 4:12,25
s 12:6 1Co 7:7; 12:4; 1Pt 4:10-11
t Ac 13:1; 1Co 12:10
u 12:7 Ac 6:1; 1Co 12:28
v Ac 13:1; 1Co 14:26
w 12:8 Ac 4:36; 11:23; 13:15
x 2Co 8:2; 9:11,13
y 1Co 12:28; 1Tm 5:17
z 2Co 9:7
aa 12:9 2Co 6:6; 1Tm 1:5
ab 1Th 5:21-22

APPLICATION QUESTIONS

READ ROMANS 11:33-36

– What's your initial reaction to these verses? Why?

– What do these verses teach you about God?

A HYMN OF PRAISE

33 Oh, the depth of the riches[a]
both of the wisdom
and of the knowledge of God![b]
How unsearchable
his judgments[c]
and untraceable his ways!

34 **For who has known the mind
of the Lord?[d]
Or who has been
his counselor?**

35 **And who has ever given to God,
that he should be repaid?[A,e]**

36 For from him and through him
and to him are all things.[f]
To him be the glory forever. Amen.

∽ HOPE WORDS ∽

*In order to transform
what you do, you must first
transform how you think.*

A LIVING SACRIFICE

12 Therefore, brothers and sisters, in view of the mercies of God, I urge you[g] to present your bodies as a living sacrifice,[h] holy and pleasing to God; this is your true worship.[B] **2** Do not be conformed[i] to this age,[j] but be transformed by the renewing of your mind,[k] so that you may discern what is the good, pleasing, and perfect will[l] of God.

MANY GIFTS BUT ONE BODY

3 For by the grace[m] given to me, I tell everyone among you not to think of himself more highly than he should think.[n] Instead, think sensibly, as God has distributed a measure of faith[o] to each one. **4** Now as we have many parts in one body,[p] and all the parts do not have the same function, **5** in the same way we who are many[q] are one body in Christ[r] and individually members of one another. **6** According to the grace given to us, we have different gifts:[s] If prophecy,[t] use it according to the proportion of one's[c] faith; **7** if service,[u] use it in service; if teaching,[v] in teaching; **8** if exhorting,[w] in exhortation; giving, with generosity;[x] leading,[y] with diligence; showing mercy, with cheerfulness.[z]

CHRISTIAN ETHICS

9 Let love be without hypocrisy.[aa] Detest evil;[ab] cling to what is good. **10** Love one

---

A 11:34-35 Jb 41:11; Is 40:13; Jr 23:18   B 12:1 Or *your reasonable service*   C 12:6 Or *the,* also in v. 19

11:33-36 The word **glory** comes from a word meaning "weighty" or "heavy" (11:36). Those who grew up in the 1960s may remember that back then we would say, "That dude is heavy." The expression meant that a person was deep; there was a lot to him. God is the weightiest, heaviest, deepest being in the universe. His glory is unmatched: no one can even outline his actions (11:33); no one can get inside his head to know what he's thinking (11:34); no one can offer something to God that puts him in their debt (11:35). All of life, history, and creation exist for the supreme purpose of recognizing the greatness of the glory of God (11:36).

12:1 To **present** our **bodies as a living sacrifice, holy and pleasing to God** means complete and total surrender. It's the difference between what a chicken and a pig bring to a bacon-and-egg breakfast. The chicken makes a contribution; the pig gives everything. What we often try to do with God is give an egg here and an egg there, but God wants sacrifice—the ham and bacon. Only total surrender can be called **true worship**.

12:2 Notice that we aren't conforming or transforming our minds. Someone else is. When God has all of us, and when the

world has none of us, God does the work of **renewing** our confused minds. He brings our thoughts in line with his own so that we think God's thoughts after him (see 1 Cor 2:16).

God has a goal in this. Renewal allows him to merge his thoughts with ours so that he can bring his plans into our lives. He calls it **the good, pleasing, and perfect will of God**. God has a purpose and a plan for each of our lives—one that finds us when we are fully surrendered.

12:3 Nobody should **think of himself more highly than he** ought because everything we have is a gift. You don't brag about a birthday present as if you made it and paid for it. Don't brag about the God-given gifts you have, either. On the flip side, though, don't disparage yourself as if God has given you nothing. **God has distributed a measure . . . to each one,** including you.

12:4-5 Paul compares the local church to a human **body,** in which every part functions for the good of the whole. If you're not a functioning, serving member of a local church, you are living outside the will of God. Because you're a part of the body, you matter. But because you're only one part, it's not all about you.

12:6 We serve one another because of **the grace given to us.** The more you understand grace, the easier it is to serve others. Imagine a boy leaving his mother a note, saying, "For mowing the lawn, a dollar. For washing the dishes, a dollar. For making the bed, a dollar. You owe me, Mother, three dollars." That's works-based service in a nutshell. Now, imagine a mother leaving her own note: "For being in labor with you for sixteen hours, no charge. For staying up with you all night when you were sick, no charge. For buying you clothing and food, no charge." That's grace-based service.

12:9 Paul says our **love** for one another must **be without hypocrisy**. The Greek word for *hypocrite* was used of an actor who wore a mask. Some of the best actors and actresses I know come to church with their masks on. They fake it when people ask them, "How you doing?" They fake it because they're worried that people won't love them unless they wear a mask. So to all of us Paul says, be the kind of community where it's safe for people to take their masks off.

12:10 We can **love one another deeply** once we recognize that we don't have to like someone to love them well. Love is often associated with emotion, but it starts with a decision to compassionately and righteously

another deeply as brothers and sisters.[a] Outdo one another in showing honor.[b] [11] Do not lack diligence in zeal; be fervent in the Spirit;[A,c] serve the Lord.[d] [12] Rejoice in hope;[e] be patient in affliction;[f] be persistent in prayer.[g] [13] Share with the saints in their needs;[h] pursue hospitality.[i] [14] Bless those who persecute you;[j] bless and do not curse. [15] Rejoice with those who rejoice;[k] weep with those who weep. [16] Live in harmony with one another.[l] Do not be proud;[m] instead, associate with the humble. Do not be wise in your own estimation.[n] [17] Do not repay anyone evil for evil.[o] Give careful thought to do what is honorable[p] in everyone's eyes. [18] If possible, as far as it depends on you, live at peace with everyone.[q] [19] Friends, do not avenge yourselves; instead, leave room for God's wrath, because it is written, **Vengeance belongs to me; I will repay,**[B,r] says the Lord. [20] But

> **If your enemy is hungry,**
>   **feed him.**[s]
> **If he is thirsty, give him something**
>   **to drink.**
> **For in so doing**
>   **you will be heaping fiery coals**
>   **on his head.**[C,t]

[21] Do not be conquered by evil, but conquer evil with good.

Video Devotional
"THE MERCIES OF GOD"

The mercies of God as outlined in Paul's letter to the Romans.

www.bhpublishinggroup.com/qr/te/45-12

⚜ KINGDOM LIVING ⚜
COMMUNITY
God's Rule in Culture

Since God is just (Deut 32:4) and the ultimate lawgiver (Jas 4:12), his laws and judgments are just and righteous (Pss 19:7-9; 111:7-8). They are to be applied without partiality (Lev 19:15; Num 15:16; Deut 1:17) because justice is the moral standard by which God measures human conduct (Is 26:7). A government's role, then, is to be his instrument of divine justice by impartially establishing, reflecting, and applying his divine standards of justice in society (Deut 4:7-8; 2 Sam 8:15; Ps 72:1-2, 4).

Biblical justice is the equitable and impartial application of the rule of God's moral law in society. Whether exercising itself through economic, political, social, or criminal justice, the one constant within all four realms is the understanding and application of God's moral law within the social realm.

The Bible expressly states that the reason there is social disintegration in the form of all kinds of immorality and domestic and international chaos is that humanity wrongfully segregates the spiritual from the social (2 Chr 15:3-6). When God created man, he gave him the responsibility to rule the earth under divine authority while simultaneously spreading God's image throughout the world (Gen 1:26-28).

It was man's refusal to submit to divine authority that led to social disintegration. When man disobeyed God, the result was family breakdown, economic struggle, emotional instability, and physical death (Gen 3:1-19). The closer God's rule is followed in society, the more ordered society will be. The further God's rule is removed from culture, the more chaotic culture becomes.

FOR THE NEXT COMMUNITY
KINGDOM LIVING LESSON SEE PAGE 1500.

[a] 12:10 Jn 13:34; 1Th 4:9; Heb 13:1; 2Pt 1:7
[b] Rm 13:7; Php 2:3; 1Pt 2:17
[c] 12:11 Ac 18:25
[d] Ac 20:19
[e] 12:12 Rm 5:2
[f] Heb 10:32,36
[g] Ac 1:14
[h] 12:13 Rm 15:25; 1Co 16:15; 2Co 9:1; Heb 6:10
[i] Mt 25:35; 1Tm 3:2
[j] 12:14 Mt 5:44; Lk 6:22; 1Co 4:12
[k] 12:15 Jb 30:25; Heb 13:3
[l] 12:16 Rm 15:5; 2Co 13:11; Php 2:2; 4:2; 1Pt 3:8
[m] Rm 11:20
[n] Rm 11:25; Pr 3:7
[o] 12:17 Pr 20:22; 24:29
[p] 2Co 8:21

[q] 12:18 Mk 9:50; Rm 14:19
[r] 12:19 Dt 32:35; Ps 94:1; 1Th 4:6; Heb 10:30
[s] 12:20 Mt 5:44; Lk 6:27
[t] 2Kg 6:22; Pr 25:21-22

[A] 12:11 Or *in spirit*   [B] 12:19 Dt 32:35   [C] 12:20 Pr 25:21-22

---

seek the well-being of others. Just like the small gauge on a boiler indicates how full the vessel is, our love for one another indicates how full our hearts are with the love of Jesus. **12:11** *Behind the Greek word translated* **fervent** is the idea of boiling water. If you're **fervent in the Spirit**, you're boiling for the kingdom of God; you're fired up to **serve the Lord**. Have you ever noticed how kids, who otherwise might seem tired, get a sudden burst of energy if you offer to play some game they love? They boil over with enthusiasm because they love it. **12:13** God gave you a job, which brings you money, which pays for your house. If all of the doors in your life stay closed, you don't understand **hospitality**—or grace. **12:14** If Jesus forgave you when you were his enemy (after all, your sins put him on the cross), shouldn't that change the way you view your enemies? **12:16** If you want to keep from thinking too highly of yourself, make it a regular part of your agenda to connect **with the humble**, people who have nothing to give back. Look for people in the church who are without designer clothes, high school degrees, or even steady jobs. They may be nobodies in the world's eyes, but in the church they ought to feel like somebodies. **12:17** When reading Paul's reminder to the Romans not to **repay anyone evil for evil**, remember that he's still talking to the church! Don't attack the hurting parts of your body; they're part of you. If you repay people for the wrong they do you, you'll end up hurting yourself. **12:18** Many misinterpret this verse to say, in essence, "Be patient for as long as you can, but once your patience runs out, get ready to throw down." This verse is actually saying, **as far as it depends on you,** that is, on your side of the relationship, **live at peace.** Do everything you can to get along with people, and if they should still harbor a grudge, that's on them. **12:19-20** It could be that one of the reasons God hasn't dealt with your enemy yet is that you are still in the way! **12:21** As Dr. Martin Luther King Jr. once said, "Darkness cannot drive out darkness; only light can do that. Hate cannot drive out hate; only love can do that."

a 13:1 Ti 3:1; 1Pt 2:13
b Dn 2:21; 4:17; Jn 19:1
c 13:3 1Pt 2:14
d 13:4 1Th 4:6
e 13:5 1Pt 2:13,19
f 13:7 Mt 22:21
g Lk 20:22; 23:2
h Mt 17:25

i 13:8 Mt 7:12; 22:39; Jn 13:34; Rm 12:10; Gl 5:14; Jms 2:8
j 13:9 Ex 20:13-17; Dt 5:17-21
k Lv 19:18; Mt 19:19
l 13:11 1Co 7:29; 10:11; Jms 5:8; 1Pt 4:7; 2Pt 3:9,11; 1Jn 2:18; Rv 1:3; 22:10
m Mk 13:37; 1Co 15:34; Eph 5:14; 1Th 5:6
n Ac 19:2; 1Co 3:5; 15:2
o 13:12 Heb 10:25; 1Jn 2:8; Rv 1:3; 22:10
p Eph 5:11
q 2Co 6:7; 10:4; Eph 6:11,13; 1Th 5:8
r 13:13 1Th 4:12
s Lk 21:34; Gl 5:21; Eph 5:18; 1Pt 4:3
t 13:14 Jb 29:14; Gl 3:27; Eph 4:24; Col 3:10,12
u Gl 5:16; 1Pt 2:11
v 14:1 Ac 28:2; Rm 11:15; 12:3; 15:7
w Rm 15:1; 1Co 8:9-11; 9:22
x 14:2 Rm 14:14
y 14:3 Lk 18:9

APPLICATION QUESTIONS

READ ROMANS 13:1-7

– What do these verses teach about our rights and responsibilities in regard to human governments?

A CHRISTIAN'S DUTIES TO THE STATE

13 Let everyone submit to the governing authorities,*a* since there is no authority except from God,*b* and the authorities that exist are instituted by God. **2** So then, the one who resists the authority is opposing God's command, and those who oppose it will bring judgment on themselves. **3** For rulers are not a terror*c* to good conduct, but to bad. Do you want to be unafraid of the authority? Do what is good, and you will have its approval. **4** For it is God's servant for your good. But if you do wrong, be afraid, because it does not carry the sword for no reason. For it is God's servant, an avenger*d* that brings wrath on the one who does wrong. **5** Therefore, you must submit, not only because of wrath but also because of your conscience.*e* **6** And for this reason you pay taxes, since the authorities are God's servants, continually attending to these tasks.*A* **7** Pay your obligations*f* to everyone: taxes to those you owe taxes,*g* tolls to those you owe tolls, respect to those you owe respect,*h* and honor to those you owe honor.

LOVE, OUR PRIMARY DUTY

8 Do not owe anyone anything, except to love one another, for the one who loves another has fulfilled the law.*i* **9** The commandments, **Do not commit adultery; do not murder; do not steal;**B **do not covet,**CJ and any other commandment, are summed up by this commandment: **Love your neighbor as yourself.**D,K **10** Love does no wrong to a neighbor. Love, therefore, is the fulfillment of the law.

PUT ON CHRIST

11 Besides this, since you know the time, it is already the hour*l* for you*E* to wake up from sleep,*m* because now our salvation is nearer than when we first believed.*n* **12** The night is nearly over, and the day is near;*o* so let us discard the deeds of darkness*p* and put on the armor of light.*q* **13** Let us walk with decency,*r* as in the daytime: not in carousing and drunkenness;*s* not in sexual impurity and promiscuity; not in quarreling and jealousy. **14** But put on the Lord Jesus Christ,*t* and don't make plans to gratify the desires of the flesh.*u*

THE LAW OF LIBERTY

14 Accept*v* anyone who is weak in faith,*w* but don't argue about disputed matters. **2** One person believes he may eat anything,*x* while one who is weak eats only vegetables. **3** One who eats must not look down on one who does not eat,*y*

A 13:6 Lit *to this very thing*   B 13:9 Other mss add *do not bear false witness*   C 13:9 Ex 20:13-17; Dt 5:17-21   D 13:9 Lv 19:18   E 13:11 Other mss read *for us*

13:1 Since God has placed governmental rulers over us, we should **submit to the governing authorities**, recognizing them as God's agents. While there is an institutional separation between church and state, there must never be a separation between God and government. The closer God is to a government and its citizens, the more ordered the society will be. The further God is from a government and its citizens, the more chaotic the society will become (see 2 Chr 15:3-6).

13:2 The one who resists the authority of God—whether that's a person rebelling against the government or the government rebelling against God—**is opposing God's command** and **will** reap **judgment**.

13:3 Much of the time, what the government promotes as good aligns with the Bible. But when it doesn't, we must **do what is good** before God and trust him with the political results. God and his Word give us the definitive standard of what should be viewed as right and wrong. The biblical responsibility of civil government is to maintain a safe, just, righteous, and compassionately responsible environment in which freedom can flourish.

13:4-5 Twice in this passage Paul calls the governing authorities **God's servant**, which

reinforces their role (13:4). In a democratic republic like ours, we citizens can be servants to our leaders, pointing them to his truth. If we don't, then "one nation under God" will become "one nation under chaos."

13:6-7 Paul's words here intentionally echo those of Jesus. Jesus said, "Give . . . to Caesar the things that are Caesar's, and to God the things that are God's" (Matt 22:21). We owe government leaders our taxes. We owe them earthly honor. But both Paul and Jesus remind us that we must never give them our hearts. They cannot have our ultimate allegiance, since we are created in the image of God. He is above all.

13:8-9 Biblical **love** is the decision to compassionately and righteously seek the benefit and well-being of another (13:8). We owe that to others without end, because that kind of love is the underlying factor in all of God's horizontal commandments: **Do not commit adultery; do not murder; do not steal; do not covet** (13:9).

13:10 Jesus said, "All the Law and the Prophets depend" on two commands: (1) Love God with all of your heart, soul, and mind; (2) love your neighbor as yourself (Matt 22:37-40).

13:11 The phrase **wake up from sleep** references the spiritual lethargy that plagues so

many people in our churches. God didn't save us just for heaven after we die, but also to experience his salvation in history and spare us the consequences of our sin.

13:14 We put on the armor of light in two ways. First, we **put on the Lord Jesus Christ**, living by faith in him, studying his Word, and seeking to reflect him in our actions. Second, we **don't make plans to gratify the desires of the flesh**, which would counteract being clothed in Christ. Imagine you just put on your best suit or dress for church. As you're walking to service, you notice a shortcut—but it's through a back alley and involves climbing through two dumpsters. Do you take that route? No! That dirty environment would foul your pristine clothes. Put on the purity of Christ and don't climb through the dumpsters of sin.

14:1 Many man-made rules address things that aren't clearly spelled out in Scripture. When we talk about human rules as if they're God's ideas, we harm those who are **weak in faith**.

14:2-3 Paul addresses man-made rules regarding diet that were tripping up these particular believers. Some thought eating meat was sinful, so they would eat **only vegetables**. Others thought it was okay to **eat anything** (14:2). The first group didn't become vegetarian for

and one who does not eat must not judge one who does,[a] because God has accepted him.[b] **4** Who are you to judge[c] another's household servant? Before his own Lord he stands or falls. And he will stand, because the Lord is able[A] to make him stand.

5 One person judges one day to be more important than another day.[d] Someone else judges every day to be the same. Let each one be fully convinced in his own mind.[e] **6** Whoever observes the day, observes it for the honor of the Lord.[B] Whoever eats, eats for the Lord, since he gives thanks to God;[f] and whoever does not eat, it is for the Lord that he does not eat it, and he gives thanks to God. **7** For none of us lives for himself, and no one dies for himself.[g] **8** If we live, we live for the Lord; and if we die, we die for the Lord. Therefore, whether we live or die, we belong to the Lord.[h] **9** Christ died and returned to life[i] for this: that he might be Lord over both the dead and the living.[j] **10** But you, why do you judge your brother or sister? Or you, why do you despise your brother or sister? For we will all stand before the judgment seat of God.[C,k] **11** For it is written,

As I live, says the Lord,
every knee will bow to me,[l]
and every tongue will give praise to God.[D,m]

12 So then, each of us will give an account of himself to God.[n]

THE LAW OF LOVE

13 Therefore, let us no longer judge one another.[o] Instead decide never to put a stumbling block or pitfall in the way of your brother or sister.[p] **14** I know and am persuaded in the Lord Jesus that nothing is unclean in itself.[q] Still, to someone who considers a thing to be unclean, to that one it is unclean.[r] **15** For if your brother or sister is hurt by what you eat, you are no longer walking according to love.[s] Do not destroy, by what you eat, someone for whom Christ died.[t] **16** Therefore, do not let your good be slandered,[u] **17** for the kingdom of God is not eating and drinking,[v] but righteousness, peace, and joy[w] in the Holy Spirit. **18** Whoever serves Christ[x] in this way is acceptable to God and receives human approval.[y]

19 So then, let us pursue what promotes peace[z] and what builds up one another.[aa] **20** Do not tear down God's work because of food. Everything is clean, but it is wrong to make someone fall by what he eats.[ab] **21** It is a good thing not to eat meat, or drink wine, or do anything that makes your brother or sister stumble.[E] **22** Whatever you believe about these things, keep between yourself and God. Blessed is the one who does not condemn himself by what he approves.[ac] **23** But whoever doubts stands condemned if he eats,[ad] because his eating is not from faith,[F] and everything that is not from faith is sin.

PLEASING OTHERS, NOT OURSELVES

15 Now we who are strong have an obligation to bear the weaknesses of those without strength,[ae] and not to please ourselves. **2** Each one of us is to please his neighbor for his good, to build him up.[af]

[a] 14:3 Col 2:16
[b] Ac 28:2; Rm 11:15; 15:7
[c] 14:4 Rm 9:20; Jms 4:12
[d] 14:5 Gl 4:10
[e] Lk 1:1; Rm 4:21
[f] 14:6 Mt 14:19; 1Co 10:30; 1Tm 4:3-4
[g] 14:7 Rm 8:38; 2Co 5:15; Gl 2:20; Php 1:20
[h] 14:8 Lk 20:38; Php 1:20; 1Th 5:10; Rv 14:13
[i] 14:9 Rv 1:18; 2:8
[j] Mt 28:18; Jn 12:24; Php 2:11; 1Th 5:10
[k] 14:10 Rm 2:16; 2Co 5:10
[l] 14:11 Php 2:10-11
[m] Is 45:23; 49:18
[n] 14:12 Mt 12:36; 16:27; 1Pt 4:5
[o] 14:13 Mt 7:1; Rm 14:3

[p] 14:13 1Co 8:13
[q] 14:14 Ac 10:15; Rm 14:2,20
[r] 1Co 8:7
[s] 14:15 Eph 5:2
[t] 1Co 8:11
[u] 14:16 1Co 10:30; Ti 2:5
[v] 14:17 1Co 8:8
[w] Rm 15:13; Gl 5:22
[x] 14:18 Rm 16:18
[y] 2Co 8:21; Php 4:8; 1Pt 2:12
[z] 14:19 Ps 34:14; Rm 12:18; 1Co 7:15; 2Tm 2:22; Heb 12:14
[aa] Rm 15:2; 1Co 10:23; 14:3,26; 2Co 12:19; Eph 4:12,29
[ab] 14:20 1Co 8:9-13
[ac] 14:22 1Jn 3:21
[ad] 14:23 Rm 14:5
[ae] 15:1 Rm 14:1; Gl 6:2; 1Th 5:14
[af] 15:2 1Co 9:22; 10:24,33; 2Co 13:9

[A] **14:4** Other mss read *For God has the power*　[B] **14:6** Other mss add *but whoever does not observe the day, it is to the Lord that he does not observe it*　[C] **14:10** Other mss read *of Christ*　[D] **14:11** Is 45:23; 49:18　[E] **14:21** Other mss add *or offended or weakened*　[F] **14:23** Or *conviction*

dietary reasons, but convictional ones. The meat in Rome had been offered to idols; therefore, many people felt it was tainted with the demonic. The second group, however, thought, "Well, what's an idol, anyway? It's not a real god, so whatever happens to the meat before it arrives on my table is fine."

The problem was that these two hard stances kept the believers from fully accepting each other (14:3). And while we don't usually argue over meat in the church today, we do sometimes say things like, "If you were really saved, you wouldn't go to the movies." Understand that it's fine to have personal convictions, but if the Bible hasn't condemned a thing, we should give space to believers whose convictions differ on matters that Scripture does not address plainly.

14:5 This discussion resonates with me because my father-in-law didn't celebrate Christmas: he thought our culture had taken it over with commercialism. My wife, my kids, and I, however, do. The Bible says that I would be wrong to condemn him for what he was doing, just as he would've been wrong to condemn us. If **each one** is **fully convinced in his own mind** that he's honoring God regarding a matter on which Scripture isn't crystal clear, we need to let our brothers and sisters exercise liberty.

14:10-12 Jesus said it's foolishness to point out a speck of sawdust in your brother's eye if you have a two-by-four in your own (see Matt 7:3). Paul is getting at the same idea here: **Why do you judge your brother or sister** (Rom 14:10), when you know that **each of us will give an account of himself to God** (14:12)? God won't be asking you about the opinions and preferences of your brother. He'll be looking into your account. So get out of your neighbor's business and tend to your own.

14:13 Rather than asking, what faults can I find in my neighbors' lives? we should ask, how will my actions affect them?

14:19-21 The goal of the kingdom is not to keep other people in line with our preferences, but to **pursue what promotes peace** (14:19). We can use our freedom in two ways: either we **tear down God's work** (14:20) in people's lives by flaunting our liberty, or we build **up one another** (14:19) by being sensitive to our weaker brothers and sisters. The irony is that while we may have the freedom to do something, if we continue to do it knowing it will make our brother stumble, that action suddenly becomes evil. On the contrary, **it is a good thing not to ... do anything that makes** someone **stumble**, which means to trip them up spiritually (14:21).

14:23 Your conscience is like a metal detector: it beeps when you approach something God hasn't freed you to do. You may watch a dozen people walk through that metaphorical gate without the beep going off. Don't bother about them. If your conscience beeps, don't follow.

15:1-3 Patience for others should flow from our understanding of how patient Jesus has been toward us.

a 15:3 2Co 8:9
b Ps 69:9
c 15:4 Rm 4:23; 2Tm 3:16
d 15:5 2Co 1:3
e Rm 12:16
f 15:6 Rv 1:6
g 15:7 Rm 14:1
h 15:8 Mt 15:24; Ac 3:26
i Rm 4:16; 2Co 1:20
j 15:9 Rm 3:29; 11:30
k Mt 5:49
l 2Sm 22:50; Ps 18:49
m 15:10 Dt 32:43
n 15:11 Ps 117:1
o 15:12 Rv 5:5; 22:16
p Is 11:10; Mt 12:21
q 15:13 Rm 14:17
r 1Co 2:4; 1Th 1:5

s 15:14 Eph 5:9; 2Th 1:11
t 1Co 1:5; 8:1,7,10; 12:8; 13:2
u 15:15 Rm 12:3
v 15:16 Ac 9:15; Rm 11:13
w Rm 1:1
x Rm 12:1; Eph 5:2; Php 2:17
y 15:17 Php 3:3
z Heb 2:17; 5:1
aa 15:18 Ac 15:12; 21:19; Rm 1:5; 2Co 3:5
ab 15:19 Jn 4:48
ac Ac 22:17-21
ad Ac 20:1
ae 15:20 Rm 1:15; 10:15
af 1Co 3:10; 2Co 10:15-16
ag 15:21 Is 52:15
ah 15:22 Rm 1:13; 1Th 2:18
ai 15:23 Ac 19:21; Rm 1:10
aj 15:24 Ac 15:3

3 For even Christ did not please himself.[a] On the contrary, as it is written, **The insults of those who insult you have fallen on me.**[A,b] **4** For whatever was written in the past was written for our instruction,[c] so that we may have hope through endurance and through the encouragement from the Scriptures. **5** Now may the God who gives[B] endurance and encouragement[d] grant you to live in harmony with one another,[e] according to Christ Jesus, **6** so that you may glorify the God and Father of our Lord Jesus Christ[f] with one mind and one voice.

GLORIFYING GOD TOGETHER

7 Therefore accept one another,[g] just as Christ also accepted you, to the glory of God. **8** For I say that Christ became a servant of the circumcised[C] on behalf of God's truth,[h] to confirm the promises to the fathers,[i] **9** and so that Gentiles[j] may glorify God for his mercy.[k] As it is written,

Therefore I will praise you
among the Gentiles,
and I will sing praise
to your name.[D,l]

10 Again it says, **Rejoice, you Gentiles, with his people!**[E,m] **11** And again,

Praise the Lord, all you Gentiles;
let all the peoples praise him![F,n]

12 And again, Isaiah says,

The root of Jesse[o] will appear,
the one who rises to rule
the Gentiles;
the Gentiles will hope in him.[G,p]

13 Now may the God of hope fill you with all joy and peace as you believe[q] so that you may overflow with hope by the power of the Holy Spirit.[r]

FROM JERUSALEM TO ILLYRICUM

14 My brothers and sisters, I myself am convinced about you that you also are full of goodness,[s] filled with all knowledge,[t] and able to instruct one another. **15** Nevertheless, I have written to remind you more boldly on some points[u] because of the grace given me by God[u] **16** to be a minister of Christ Jesus to the Gentiles,[v] serving as a priest of the gospel of God.[w] My purpose is that the Gentiles may be an acceptable offering,[x] sanctified by the Holy Spirit. **17** Therefore I have reason to boast in Christ Jesus[y] regarding what pertains to God.[z] **18** For I would not dare say anything except what Christ has accomplished through me[aa] by word and deed for the obedience of the Gentiles, **19** by the power of miraculous signs and wonders,[ab] and by the power of God's Spirit. As a result, I have fully proclaimed the gospel of Christ from Jerusalem[ac] all the way around to Illyricum.[I,ad] **20** My aim is to preach the gospel where Christ has not been named,[ae] so that I will not build on someone else's foundation,[af] **21** but, as it is written,

Those who were not told
about him will see,
and those who have not heard
will understand.[J,ag]

PAUL'S TRAVEL PLANS

22 That is why I have been prevented many times from coming to you.[ah] **23** But now I no longer have any work to do in these regions,[k] and I have strongly desired for many years to come to you[ai] **24** whenever I travel to Spain.[L] For I hope to see you when I pass through and to be assisted by you for my journey there,[aj] once I have

A 15:3 Ps 69:9 **B** 15:5 Lit *God of* **C** 15:8 The Jews **D** 15:9 2Sm 22:50; Ps 18:49 **E** 15:10 Dt 32:43 **F** 15:11 Ps 117:1 **G** 15:12 Is 11:10 **H** 15:15 Other mss add *brothers* **I** 15:19 A Roman province northwest of Greece on the eastern shore of the Adriatic Sea **J** 15:21 Is 52:15 **K** 15:23 Lit *now, having no longer a place in these parts* **L** 15:24 Other mss add *I will come to you.*

15:5 God wants us to be united around our common Savior and toward a common kingdom agenda. Just as in an orchestra each instrument makes a unique sound but plays the same song, so also each believer possesses unique traits but moves in a common direction.

15:6 Paul chooses the word **one** intentionally. Note that he doesn't say we have the *same* mind and the *same* voice. Unity is not a matter of sameness, but of oneness. Like a quilt with various colors and patterns blended into a beautiful whole, the body of Christ blends different people together into a beautiful array of redeemed lives. Unity doesn't wash out our differences; it combines them to form something greater.

15:7 As wide as we imagine the gap to be between ourselves and our most disliked enemies, Paul reminds us that there was never a gap wider than the one between us and God. If **Christ . . . accepted you** when you were weak and ungodly, certainly you can accept others when they differ from you in much less significant ways.

15:9-12 To remind his audience that God had multi-ethnic unity in mind all along, Paul quotes from a number of Old Testament prophets who all preach the same message: God has always desired for **all the peoples** to **praise him** together (15:11).

15:14 The Greek word Paul uses when he tells us **to instruct one another** means "to admonish" or "to counsel." Every mature believer has a responsibility to be a counselor to his or her brother and sister. To do this, we need two things. First, we must be **full of goodness**. If

you aren't seeking to please the Lord, don't try leading others folks to please him. You can only lead someone where you're traveling yourself. Second, we must be **filled with all knowledge**. This refers to the knowledge of God that comes from the Scriptures. Biblical counseling comes from the overflow of the Word of God in you—not from your own opinions.

15:20 At a moment's notice, Paul was able to offer up his mission statement in a single line. Do you have the same confidence about God's call on your life? Ask God to ignite his fire in you and to direct you to your mission for him.

15:24 Even the strongest saints need each other, to enjoy the **company** of other believers **for a while**.

first enjoyed your company[a] for a while. [b] Right now I am traveling to Jerusalem[b] to serve the saints,[c] [26] because Macedonia[d] and Achaia[e] were pleased to make a contribution for the poor among the saints in Jerusalem. [27] Yes, they were pleased, and indeed are indebted to them. For if the Gentiles have shared in their spiritual benefits,[f] then they are obligated to minister to them in material needs. [28] So when I have finished this and safely delivered the funds[A] to them,[B,g] I will visit you on the way to Spain. [29] I know that when I come to you, I will come in the fullness of the blessing[c] of Christ.

[30] Now I appeal to you, brothers and sisters, through our Lord Jesus Christ and through the love of the Spirit,[h] to strive together with me in fervent prayers to God on my behalf.[i] [31] Pray that I may be rescued from the unbelievers in Judea,[j] that my ministry to[D] Jerusalem[k] may be acceptable to the saints,[l] [32] and that, by God's will,[m] I may come to you with joy[n] and be refreshed together with you.

[33] May the God of peace be with all of you.[o] Amen.

PAUL'S COMMENDATION OF PHOEBE

16 I commend to you[p] our sister Phoebe, who is a servant[E] of the church in Cenchreae.[q] [2] So you should welcome her in the Lord[r] in a manner worthy of the saints and assist her in whatever matter she may require your help. For indeed she has been a benefactor of many — and of me also.

GREETING TO ROMAN CHRISTIANS

[3] Give my greetings to Prisca[F] and Aquila,[s] my coworkers in[t] Christ Jesus,[u] [4] who risked their own necks for my life. Not only do I thank them, but so do all the Gentile churches. [5] Greet also the church that

meets in their home.[v] Greet my dear friend Epaenetus, who is the first convert[G,w] to Christ from Asia.[H,x] [6] Greet Mary,[i] who has worked very hard for you.[j] [7] Greet Andronicus and Junia, my fellow Jews[K,y] and fellow prisoners.[z] They are noteworthy in the eyes of the apostles,[L] and they were also in Christ before me. [8] Greet Ampliatus, my dear friend in the Lord. [9] Greet Urbanus, our coworker in Christ, and my dear friend Stachys. [10] Greet Apelles, who is approved in Christ. Greet those who belong to the household of Aristobulus.[aa] [11] Greet Herodion, my fellow Jew.[M] Greet those who belong to the household of Narcissus who are in the Lord. [12] Greet Tryphaena and Tryphosa, who have worked hard in the Lord. Greet my dear friend Persis, who has worked very hard in the Lord. [13] Greet Rufus,[ab] chosen in the Lord; also his mother — and mine. [14] Greet Asyncritus, Phlegon, Hermes, Patrobas, Hermas, and the brothers and sisters who are with them. [15] Greet Philologus and Julia, Nereus and his sister, and Olympas, and all the saints who are with them.[ac] [16] Greet one another with a holy kiss.[ad] All the churches of Christ send you greetings.

WARNING AGAINST DIVISIVE PEOPLE

[17] Now I urge you, brothers and sisters, to watch out for those who create divisions and obstacles contrary to the teaching that you learned.[ae] Avoid them,[af] [18] because such people do not serve our Lord Christ[ag] but their own appetites.[N,ah] They deceive the hearts of the unsuspecting with smooth talk and flattering words.[ai]

PAUL'S GRACIOUS CONCLUSION

[19] The report of your obedience has reached everyone.[aj] Therefore I rejoice over you, but I want you to be wise about what is good, and yet innocent about what

[a] 15:24 Rm 1:12
[b] 15:25 Ac 19:21
[c] Ac 24:17
[d] 15:26 Ac 16:9; 1Co 16:5; 2Co 1:16; 2:13; 7:5; 8:1; 9:2,4; 11:9; Php 4:15; 1Th 1:7; 4:10; 1Tm 1:3
[e] Ac 18:12; 19:21
[f] 15:27 1Co 9:11
[g] 15:28 Jn 3:33
[h] 15:30 Gl 5:22; Col 1:8
[i] 2Co 1:11; Col 4:12
[j] 15:31 2Co 1:10; 2Th 3:2; 2Tm 3:11; 4:17
[k] 2Co 8:4; 9:1
[l] Ac 9:13; Rm 15:15
[m] 15:32 Ac 18:21; Rm 1:10
[n] Rm 15:23
[o] 15:33 Rm 16:20; 2Co 13:11; Php 4:9; 1Th 5:23; 2Th 3:16; Heb 13:20
[p] 16:1 2Co 3:1
[q] Ac 18:18
[r] 16:2 Php 2:29
[s] 16:3 Ac 18:2
[t] Rm 8:11; 2Co 5:17; 12:2; Gl 1:22
[u] Rm 8:1

[v] 16:5 1Co 16:19; Col 4:15; Phm 2
[w] 1Co 16:15
[x] Ac 16:6
[y] 16:7 Rm 9:3; 16:21
[z] Col 4:10; Phm 23
[aa] 16:10 1Co 1:11
[ab] 16:13 Mk 15:21
[ac] 16:15 Rm 16:2
[ad] 16:16 1Co 16:20; 2Co 13:12; 1Th 5:26; 1Pt 5:14
[ae] 16:17 1Tm 1:3; 6:3
[af] Mt 7:15; Gl 1:8-9; 2Th 3:6,14; Ti 3:10; 2Jn 10
[ag] 16:18 Rm 14:18
[ah] Php 3:19
[ai] Col 2:4; 2Pt 2:3
[aj] 16:19 Rm 1:8

[A] 15:28 Lit *delivered this fruit*   [B] 15:28 Or *and placed my seal of approval on this fruit for them*   [C] 15:29 Other mss add *of the gospel*   [D] 15:31 Lit *that my service for*   [E] 16:1 Others interpret this term in a technical sense: *deacon*, or *deaconess*, or *minister*, or *courier*   [F] 16:3 Traditionally, *Priscilla*, as in Ac 18:2,18,26   [G] 16:5 Lit *the firstfruits*   [H] 16:5 Other mss read *Achaia*   [I] 16:6 Or *Maria*   [J] 16:6 Other mss read *us*   [K] 16:7 Or *family members*   [L] 16:7 Or *They are noteworthy among the apostles*   [M] 16:11 Or *family member*   [N] 16:18 Lit *belly*

15:25-26 In addition to evangelizing the unsaved, churches always have been, and always should be, the primary organization for alleviating poverty in communities, especially among Christians (see Gal 6:10). When we assume that someone else should take care of the poor, not only do we harm those in poverty, but we also send out a terrible false message about our Lord, who "though he was rich, for [our] sake he became poor" (2 Cor 8:9). **15:30-33** Paul knows that he will fail if not sustained by prayer. We have the same need Paul did. Do we have the same conviction?

16:1-2 The word Paul uses for **servant** is the same root word that is translated "deacon" in other parts of Scripture. Therefore, **Phoebe** had an official capacity as a deaconess in the Roman church, showing that women have critical roles to play in church leadership under male authority. The legitimate leadership ministry of women in the church should be publicly recognized and supported. **16:3-16** What we see here is an example of unity within diversity. There is ethnic diversity: **Prisca and Aquila** (16:3), **Andronicus and Junia** (16:7), and **Herodion** (16:11) are all Jewish

believers; they are included right alongside the many Gentile believers. There is diversity of gender, as several prominent women are named, including **Junia** (16:7), **Tryphaena and Tryphosa** (16:12), and **Julia** (16:15). There is even a diversity of class: **Aristobulus** (16:10) and **Narcissus** (16:11) are called heads of "households," indicating a high position in society; they appear alongside others who probably owned nothing at all. These people co-labored with Paul in the ministry of the gospel. They **worked very hard in the Lord** (16:12).

a 16:19 Jr 4:22; Mt 10:16;
1Co 14:20
b 16:20 Rm 15:33
c Mt 4:10
d 1Co 16:23; 2Co 13:13; Gl
6:18; Php 4:23; 1Th 5:28;
2Th 3:18; Rv 22:21
e 16:21 Ac 16:1
f Ac 13:1
g Ac 17:5
h Ac 20:4
i 16:22 1Co 16:21; Gl
6:11; Col 4:18; 2Th 3:17;
Phm 19
j 16:23 Ac 20:4; 1Co 1:14
k Ac 19:22

is evil.*ª* **20** The God of peace*ᵇ* will soon crush Satan*ᶜ* under your feet. The grace of our Lord Jesus be with you.*ᵈ*

21 Timothy,*ᵉ* my coworker, and Lucius,*ᶠ* Jason,*ᵍ* and Sosipater,*ʰ* my fellow countrymen, greet you.

22 I Tertius, who wrote this letter,*ⁱ* greet you in the Lord.*ᴬ*

23 Gaius,*ʲ* who is host to me and to the whole church, greets you. Erastus,*ᵏ* the city treasurer, and our brother Quartus greet you.*ᴮ*

GLORY TO GOD

25 Now to him who is able to strengthen you*ˡ* according to my gospel and the proclamation about Jesus Christ,*ᵐ* according to the revelation of the mystery kept silent*ⁿ* for long ages*ᵒ* **26** but now revealed and made known through the prophetic Scriptures,*ᵖ* according to the command of the eternal God to advance the obedience of faith*ۊ* among all the Gentiles — **27** to the only wise God, through Jesus Christ — to him be the glory forever!*ᶜʳ* Amen.

l 16:25 Eph 3:20; Jd 24   *m* Rm 2:16   *n* Mt 13:35; Rm 11:25; 1Co 2:1,7; 4:1; Eph 1:9; 3:3,9; 6:19; Col 1:26; 2:2; 4:3; 1Tm 3:16   *o* 2Tm 1:9; Ti 1:2
p 16:26 Rm 1:2   *q* Rm 1:5   *r* 16:27 Rm 11:36

ᴬ 16:22 Or *letter in the Lord, greet you*   ᴮ 16:23 Some mss include v. 24: *The grace of our Lord Jesus Christ be with you all.*   ᶜ 16:25-27 Other mss have these vv. at the end of chap. 14 or 15.

1 CORINTHIANS

INTRODUCTION

Author

THIS LETTER IDENTIFIES THE APOSTLE Paul as its author (1:1; 16:21). Though critical scholars often question the authenticity of several other Pauline letters, most biblical scholars are unanimous in affirming that Paul wrote 1 Corinthians.

Historical Background

Paul visited Corinth in the Roman province of Achaia in about AD 50 during his second missionary journey and ministered there for a year and a half (see Acts 18:1-18). While there, he met a Jewish couple named Aquila and Priscilla. Since he shared their tent-making trade, he stayed with them (Acts 18:2-3). He also preached in the Jewish synagogue in Corinth, but when the Jews resisted him, he began teaching in a house next door to the synagogue and saw many Corinthians place faith in Christ (Acts 18:4-8).

Paul probably wrote 1 Corinthians around AD 54 while he ministered in Ephesus for about three years during his third missionary journey (1 Cor 16:8; see Acts 19:1–20:1, 31). This was actually the second letter that Paul wrote to the Corinthians, the first having been lost to history (see 1 Cor 5:9). A number of problems had arisen in the church that Paul felt the need to address. He learned of these issues from "members of Chloe's people" (1:11; cf. 5:1; 11:18) and from a letter the Corinthians had sent him (see 7:1; cf. 7:25; 8:1; 12:1; 16:1).

Message and Purpose

The apostle Paul wrote this letter to deal with the worldliness that had entered the church in Corinth. It was full of divisions, as well as gross immorality that was tolerated and even approved of by the church.

Paul addressed a variety of topics in his letter. He explained the importance and purpose of marriage. He wanted the Corinthians to understand the principle of spiritual freedom because some of them were holding fellow believers hostage to rules that no longer apply

in the church age. Paul addressed the Lord's Supper, which the church was abusing. He was also concerned about the people's excitement over spiritual gifts alongside their lack of love for one another and their misunderstanding of the resurrection.

Paul had first visited the Corinthians several years prior; therefore, they should have been more spiritually mature than reports suggested. Sadly, the people were carnal, at times living like unbelievers rather than as servants of Jesus Christ. They needed to allow the Holy Spirit to bring them to maturity so that they could have a godly influence on their world and advance God's kingdom agenda.

www.bhpublishinggroup.com/qr/te/46_00

Outline

I. Introduction (1:1-9)
II. Response to Reports from within the Church (1:10–6:20)
   A. Divisions in the Church (1:10–4:21)
   B. Immorality and Settling Disputes in the Church (5:1–6:20)
III. Response to the Corinthians' Letter (7:1–16:4)
   A. Sex and Marriage (7:1-40)
   B. Food Sacrificed to Idols (8:1–11:1)
   C. Proper Order, Love, and Spiritual Gifts in the Church (11:2–14:40)
   D. The Resurrection (15:1-58)
   E. Collection for the Church in Jerusalem (16:1-4)
IV. Conclusion (16:5-24)

a 1:1 Ac 13:9
b Rm 1:1
c 2Co 1:1; Eph 1:1; Col 1:1; 2Tm 1:1
d Ac 18:17
e 1:2 Ac 18:1; 19:1; 2Co 1:1,23; 2Tm 4:20
f Ac 20:32; 26:18; 1Co 6:11; Heb 10:10
g Rm 1:6-7
h Gn 4:26; Ps 79:6; Jn 10:25; Ac 9:14; 15:14; Rv 14:1
i 1:3 Rm 1:7; 2Co 1:2; Gl 1:3; Eph 1:2; Php 1:2; 2Th 1:2; Ti 1:4
j 1:4 Rm 1:8; Php 1:3; Col 1:3; 1Th 1:2; 2Th 1:3; 2Tm 1:3; Phm 4
k 1:5 2Co 8:9; 9:11
l Rm 15:14; 1Co 12:8; 2Co 8:7; 1Jn 2:20
m 1:6 2Th 1:10; 1Tm 2:6; 2Tm 1:8; Rv 1:2
n 1:7 Lk 17:30; Rm 8:19; Php 3:20; Heb 9:28; 2Pt 3:12
o 1Pt 4:13
p 1:8 Php 1:6; 1Th 3:13
q Lk 17:24; 1Co 5:5; 2Co 1:14; Php 2:16; Col 1:22
r 1:9 Dt 7:9; Is 49:7; 1Co 10:13; 2Co 1:18
s Rm 8:28
t Jn 5:19; Heb 1:2; 1Jn 1:3
u 1:11 Ti 3:9

v 1:12 Ti 3:13
w Jn 1:42
x Mt 23:9-10
y 1:13 1Co 12:5; 2Co 11:4; Eph 4:5
z 1:14 Ac 18:8
aa Rm 16:23
ab 1:16 Rm 16:5
ac 1Co 16:15,17
ad 1:17 Lk 23:26; Php 3:18
ae 1:18 Ac 19:11; Rm 1:16; 2Co 13:4
af 1:19 Is 29:14
ag 1:20 Lk 16:8
ah 1:22 Mt 12:38
ai 1:23 Lk 23:26; 1Co 2:2; Gl 3:1; 5:11
aj 1:24 Rm 1:6

GREETING

1 Paul,*a* called as an apostle*b* of Christ Jesus by God's will,*c* and Sosthenes our brother:*d*

2 To the church of God at Corinth,*e* to those sanctified*f* in Christ Jesus, called*g* as saints, with all those in every place who call on the name*h* of Jesus Christ our Lord — both their Lord and ours. 3 Grace to you and peace from God our Father*i* and the Lord Jesus Christ.

THANKSGIVING

4 I always thank*j* my God for you because of the grace of God given to you in Christ Jesus, 5 that you were enriched in him*k* in every way, in all speech and all knowledge.*l* 6 In this way, the testimony about Christ was confirmed among you,*m* 7 so that you do not lack any spiritual gift as you eagerly wait*n* for the revelation*o* of our Lord Jesus Christ. 8 He will also strengthen you to the end,*p* so that you will be blameless in the day of our Lord Jesus Christ.*q* 9 God is faithful;*r* you were called by him*s* into fellowship with his Son,*t* Jesus Christ our Lord.

DIVISIONS AT CORINTH

10 Now I urge you, brothers and sisters, in the name of our Lord Jesus Christ, that all of you agree in what you say, that there be no divisions among you, and that you be united with the same understanding and the same conviction. 11 For it has been reported to me about you, my brothers and sisters, by members of Chloe's people, that there is rivalry*u* among you. 12 What I am saying is this: One of you says, "I belong to Paul," or "I belong to Apollos,"*v* or "I belong to Cephas,"*w* or "I belong to Christ."*x* 13 Is Christ divided?*y* Was Paul crucified for you? Or were you baptized in Paul's name? 14 I thank God*A,B* that I baptized none of you except Crispus*z* and Gaius,*aa* 15 so that no one can say you were baptized in my name. 16 I did, in fact, baptize the household*ab* of Stephanas;*ac* beyond that, I don't recall if I baptized anyone else. 17 For Christ did not send me to baptize, but to preach the gospel — not with eloquent wisdom, so that the cross*ad* of Christ will not be emptied of its effect.

CHRIST THE POWER AND WISDOM OF GOD

18 For the word of the cross is foolishness to those who are perishing, but it is the power of God to us who are being saved.*ae* 19 For it is written,

I will destroy the wisdom
of the wise,
and I will set aside the intelligence
of the intelligent.*C,af*

20 Where is the one who is wise? Where is the teacher of the law?*D* Where is the debater of this age?*ag* Hasn't God made the world's wisdom foolish? 21 For since, in God's wisdom, the world did not know God through wisdom, God was pleased to save those who believe through the foolishness of what is preached. 22 For the Jews ask for signs*ah* and the Greeks seek wisdom, 23 but we preach Christ crucified,*ai* a stumbling block to the Jews and foolishness to the Gentiles.*E* 24 Yet to those who are called,*aj* both Jews and

---

A 1:14 Other mss omit *God*   *B* 1:14 Or *I am thankful*   *C* 1:19 Is 29:14   *D* 1:20 Or *scholar*   *E* 1:23 Other mss read *Greeks*

1:1 The letter expresses the thoughts of **Paul** himself (see the repeated uses of "I" throughout), so it's possible that **Sosthenes** served as Paul's *amanuensis*—that is, his secretary who wrote down his words (as Tertius did in Paul's letter to the Romans; see Rom 16:22).

1:2 Although the church **at Corinth** had become quite carnal (see 3:1-3), as reflected in their actions, Paul knew they were saved and had been **sanctified** through their faith **in Christ**. Thus, it is possible (though detrimental) to be an immature Christian whose life reflects more worldly thinking and living than heavenly. We need to be transformed "by the renewing of" our minds (Rom 12:2) so that we experience the realities and benefits of our salvation.

To **call on the name of [the] Lord** is a privilege uniquely available to Christians for requesting divine intervention in their lives (see Acts 7:59; Rom 10:9-14; 2 Tim 2:21-22).

1:9 God is faithful to keep his promises to save us through our faith in Christ. As a result

of our salvation, we have access to **fellowship with** Christ. But we are called to live out our fellowship with our Savior through fellowship with his saints. Sadly, the prevalent sins in the church were hindering their intimate fellowship with the Savior. This is why Paul needed to write to them.

1:10 Illegitimate divisions among believers block God's work in their lives and in the church. A football team is unified—not because everyone plays the same position—but because everyone is straining for the same goal line. An orchestra is unified—not because everyone performs on the same instrument—but because everyone harmoniously plays the same song under the direction of one conductor. Likewise, the church is to be **united**—not because every Christian is exactly alike—but because we all pledge allegiance to the same Lord.

1:11-12 Reports had reached Paul that rivalries existed among the church members based on allegiance to a favorite ministry leader (1:11).

Some preferred **Paul** (probably those who'd been around since the church's founding) or **Apollos** (likely those who preferred a more eloquent and sophisticated speaker; see Acts 18:24-28) or **Cephas**/Peter (probably Jewish believers who lamented the loss of their traditions)—or even **Christ** (likely the super spiritual ones) (1 Cor 1:12).

1:13 These rhetorical questions are intended to shame the Corinthian believers over their divisive factions. The answer to all of them is a resounding no! Christ alone is the One to whom we owe our loyalty.

1:18 Having been delivered from hell, believers in Jesus are now **being saved**—delivered from the power and effects of sin in history.

1:20-21 How is **the world's wisdom foolish** (1:20)? It lacks the divine point of view and considers life from a merely human perspective. **God's wisdom**, by contrast, enables us to see things from a divine perspective, make wise choices, and open ourselves to his intervention in our circumstances (1:21). Human

Greeks, Christ is the power of God and the wisdom of God, **25** because God's foolishness is wiser than human wisdom, and God's weakness is stronger than human strength.

BOASTING ONLY IN THE LORD

26 Brothers and sisters, consider your calling: Not many were wise from a human perspective,[A] not many powerful,[a] not many of noble birth. **27** Instead, God has chosen[b] what is foolish in the world to shame the wise, and God has chosen what is weak in the world to shame the strong. **28** God has chosen what is insignificant and despised in the world[c] — what is viewed as nothing — to bring to nothing what is viewed as something, **29** so that no one[B] may boast in his presence.[d] **30** It is from him that you are in Christ Jesus, who became wisdom from God for us — our righteousness,[e] sanctification,[f] and redemption,[g] **31** in order that, as it is written:[h] **Let the one who boasts, boast in the Lord.**[C,i]

PAUL'S PROCLAMATION

2 When I came to you, brothers and sisters, announcing the mystery[D] of God to you, I did not come with brilliance[j] of speech[k] or wisdom. **2** I decided to know nothing among you except Jesus Christ and him crucified.[l] **3** I came to you in weakness,[m] in fear,[n] and in much trembling.[o] **4** My speech[p] and my preaching were not with persuasive[q] words of wisdom[E] but with a demonstration of the Spirit's power, **5** so that your faith might not be based on human wisdom but on God's power.[r]

SPIRITUAL WISDOM

6 We do, however, speak a wisdom among the mature,[s] but not a wisdom of this age, or of the rulers[t] of this age, who are coming to nothing.[u] **7** On the contrary, we speak God's hidden wisdom in a mystery, a wisdom God predestined[v] before the ages for our glory.[w] **8** None of the rulers of this age knew this wisdom, because if they had known it, they would not have crucified the Lord of glory.[x] **9** But as it is written,

**What no eye has seen, no ear
　has heard,
and no human heart
　has conceived —
God has prepared these things
　for those who love him.**[F,y]

10 Now God has revealed these things to us by the Spirit, since the Spirit searches everything,[z] even the depths of God. [aa] **11** For who knows a person's thoughts[G] except his spirit[ab] within him? In the same way, no one knows[ac] the thoughts of God except the Spirit of God. **12** Now we have not received the spirit of the world, but the Spirit who comes from God, so that we may understand what has been freely given to us by God. **13** We also speak these things, not in words[ad] taught by human wisdom, but in those taught by the Spirit, explaining spiritual things to spiritual people.[H] **14** But the person without the Spirit[I] does not receive what comes from God's Spirit, because it is foolishness to him; he is not able to understand it since it is evaluated[J] spiritually. **15** The spiritual person, however, can evaluate[K] everything, and yet he himself cannot be evaluated by anyone. **16** For

[a]1:26 Ac 25:5
[b]1:27 Mt 24:22; Eph 1:4
[c]1:28 Lk 18:9
[d]1:29 Ac 7:46
[e]1:30 Mt 6:33; Rm 1:17; 2Pt 1:1
[f]1Th 4:3
[g]Eph 1:7
[h]1:31 Mk 1:2
[i]Jr 9:23-24
[j]2:1 1Tm 2:2
[k]Col 4:6
[l]2:2 1Co 1:23-24; Gl 6:14
[m]2:3 2Co 11:30
[n]Rv 11:11
[o]Php 2:12
[p]2:4 Mt 12:37
[q]Php 1:25
[r]2:5 Mk 5:30; Lk 1:35; 6:19; Ac 19:11; 2Co 13:4; 2Tm 1:7; Rv 11:17

[s]2:6 Mt 5:48
[t]Lk 12:58
[u]Heb 2:14
[v]2:7 Eph 1:5
[w]Lk 24:26; 1Pt 5:1,4
[x]2:8 Ps 24:7
[y]2:9 Is 52:15; 64:4; Lk 10:27; 1Jn 4:20
[z]2:10 Ps 17:3; Jn 14:26
[aa]Rm 8:39; 11:33; Eph 3:18
[ab]2:11 Rm 1:9
[ac]1Jn 4:8
[ad]2:13 Mt 12:37

[A]1:26 Lit *wise according to the flesh*　[B]1:29 Lit *that not all flesh*　[C]1:31 Jr 9:24　[D]2:1 Other mss read *testimony*　[E]2:4 Other mss read *human wisdom*　[F]2:9 Is 52:15; 64:4　[G]2:11 Or *things*　[H]2:13 Or *things with spiritual words*　[I]2:14 Lit *natural person*　[J]2:14 Or *judged, or discerned,* also in v. 15　[K]2:15 Or *judge, or discern*

---

wisdom considers the word of the cross to be **foolishness**, but God uses this so-called foolishness to save people (1:21).

1:26-29 If you have low self-esteem, come from humble beginnings, have experienced significant struggles, or are despised by the in crowd, then you're a choice candidate to be used by God for his kingdom program. If you are a child of God through Jesus Christ, it's not because of who you are but in spite of it.

2:1-5 Where do you place your confidence when you share Christ with others? Is it in your own rhetorical and persuasive abilities? Or does your confidence rest solely in the **power** of God to bring salvation and life transformation (2:4-5)? We cannot achieve what only divine sovereignty can accomplish.

2:6 Believers whose life perspectives have been nurtured by the Spirit of God are

mature; on the other hand, **the rulers of this age** do not use divine truth as the reference point for their lives.

2:8 The rulers of this age didn't comprehend God's wisdom; otherwise, **they would not have crucified** Jesus Christ. In their attempt to destroy this Jewish rabbi, they were actually furthering God's plan of redemption. In his glorious sovereignty and providence, the Lord is able to use unbelievers to achieve his purposes.

2:9-10 The point here is that God can help believers understand things that they cannot learn through natural means. Though God has revealed to us his inspired, written Word, believers need the Spirit's illumination to help us supernaturally learn, grasp, and apply the things of God. Illumination does not involve new revelation; rather, it involves God giving a believer understanding of the

meaning and application of Scripture in the midst of his own experiences.

2:11 We are dependent on **the Spirit** to enable us to make a spiritual connection with **God**. When this happens, God illuminates his Word so that it becomes relevant to specific circumstances.

2:14-15 The person without the Spirit (literally, the "natural person") refers to an unbeliever (2:14). Worldly thinking doesn't have access to the things of God. Using it to discern them is like trying to connect your television to a signal when you don't have the right equipment. All you get is static. The **spiritual** believer evaluates everything from a divine perspective, but he or she **cannot be** correctly **evaluated** by the world (2:15).

2:16 The mind of Christ is the capacity to think Christ's thoughts after him so that we

[a] 2:16 Is 40:13
[b] Col 2:2
[c] 3:1 1Co 14:20; Heb 5:13; 1Pt 2:2
[d] 3:3 Jms 3:14,16
[e] Ti 3:9
[f] 3:4 Ti 3:13
[g] 3:6 Ac 18:4-11; 1Co 4:15; 9:1; 15:1
[h] 3:9 1Pt 2:5
[i] 3:11 Is 28:16; Rm 15:20; 2Co 10:16; 11:4; Gl 1:6-9

[j] 3:12 Jms 5:3
[k] Rv 17:4
[l] 3:13 2Th 1:8; 1Pt 1:7
[m] Ps 62:12; Pr 24:12; Mt 16:27; 2Co 5:10; 1Pt 1:17
[n] 3:15 Mt 9:22; Ac 16:30; Eph 2:8
[o] Jd 23
[p] 3:16 Lk 1:21
[q] Lv 26:11; Jms 4:5
[r] 3:17 Heb 6:8
[s] Ps 20:6; 1Co 7:14
[t] 3:18 2Co 11:3
[u] Lk 16:8
[v] Mt 5:22
[w] Is 5:21; Jr 8:8-9; Gl 6:3
[x] 3:19 1Co 1:18
[y] Ac 15:15; Gl 4:22
[z] Jb 5:13; Lk 20:23
[aa] 3:20 Mt 15:19; 1Tm 2:8
[ab] Ps 94:11
[ac] 3:21 Rm 8:32
[ad] 3:22 Jn 1:42
[ae] 1Jn 5:12
[af] Mt 10:21; Jn 8:51; Php 3:10
[ag] Rm 8:38

who has known the Lord's mind, that he may instruct him?[A,a] But we have the mind of Christ.[b]

THE PROBLEM OF IMMATURITY

3 For my part, brothers and sisters, I was not able to speak to you as spiritual people but as people of the flesh, as babies in Christ.[c] **2** I gave you milk to drink, not solid food, since you were not yet ready for it. In fact, you are still not ready, **3** because you are still worldly. For since there is envy[d] and strife[B,e] among you, are you not worldly and behaving like mere humans? **4** For whenever someone says, "I belong to Paul," and another, "I belong to Apollos,"[f] are you not acting like mere humans?

THE ROLE OF GOD'S SERVANTS

5 What then is Apollos? What is Paul? They are servants through whom you believed, and each has the role the Lord has given. **6** I planted,[g] Apollos watered, but God gave the growth. **7** So then neither the one who plants nor the one who waters is anything, but only God who gives the growth. **8** Now he who plants and he who waters are one,[C] and each will receive his own reward according to his own labor. **9** For we are God's coworkers.[D] You are God's field, God's building.[h]

10 According to God's grace that was given to me, I have laid a foundation as a skilled master builder,[E] and another builds on it. But each one is to be careful how he builds on it. **11** For no one can lay any other foundation[I] than what has been laid down. That foundation is Jesus Christ. **12** If anyone builds on the foundation with gold, silver,[j] costly stones,[k] wood, hay, or straw, **13** each one's work will become obvious. For the day will disclose it, because it will be revealed by fire;[l] the fire will test the quality of each one's work.[m] **14** If anyone's work that he has built survives, he will receive a reward. **15** If anyone's work is burned up, he will experience[F] loss, but he himself will be saved[n] — but only as through fire.[o]

16 Don't you yourselves know that you are God's temple[p] and that the Spirit of God lives in you?[q] **17** If anyone destroys God's temple, God will destroy him;[r] for God's temple is holy,[s] and that is what you are.

THE FOLLY OF HUMAN WISDOM

18 Let no one deceive[t] himself. If anyone among you thinks he is wise in this age,[u] let him become a fool[v] so that he can become wise.[w] **19** For the wisdom of this world is foolishness[x] with God, since it is written,[y] **He catches the wise in their craftiness;**[G,z] **20** and again, **The Lord knows that the reasonings**[aa] **of the wise are futile.**[H,ab] **21** So let no one boast in human leaders, for everything is yours[ac] — **22** whether Paul or Apollos or Cephas[ad] or the world or life[ae] or death[af] or things present or things to come[ag] — everything

[A] 2:16 Is 40:13   [B] 3:8 Other mss add and divisions   [C] 3:8 Or of equal status, or united in purpose   [D] 3:9 Or are coworkers belonging to God   [E] 3:10 Or wise master builder   [F] 3:15 Or suffer   [G] 3:19 Jb 5:13   [H] 3:20 Ps 94:11

APPLICATION QUESTIONS

READ 1 CORINTHIANS 3:10-15

– What do these verses teach about our role as stewards?
– What steps can you take to raise your investment in God's kingdom?

---

will live as we ought. A spiritual person seeks to think about a matter as Christ would—he or she is biblically informed and spiritually illumined—and then applies that perspective to life decisions.

3:1-4 Milk refers to the gospel message and the doctrinal ABCs of the faith. **Solid food** refers to spiritual discernment in the use of God's Word (3:2; see Heb 5:11-14). These Corinthians were saved, but not living in light of the spiritual realm into which they had been adopted. Without spiritual growth, believers will continue to live as they did before coming to Christ. They will operate from a worldly and earthly perspective and behave **like mere humans** (i.e., unbelievers), rather than spiritual people. How did Paul know that the Corinthians were **acting** this way? Because they were dividing themselves into factions behind various leaders, causing nothing but **envy and strife** among

themselves (1 Cor 3:3-4; see 1:10-13). This is worldliness at its worst!

3:5-9 If believers are to align themselves with anyone, it should be with the Lord—not with his **servants** (3:5). He's our source of spiritual life and growth.

3:10-11 Spiritually speaking, the only **foundation** you want to build on is **Jesus** (3:11) because he paid top dollar, so to speak, to save you from your sins so that you might have eternal life and fellowship with God.

3:12-13 To obey God's Word and be faithful with what he has given is to build wisely using precious metals and **stones** (3:12). But to disregard his Word and live for yourself is to build foolishly using worthless materials. Such work just won't last. **The day** is a reference to that time when Christians will stand before the judgment seat of Christ (3:13; see 2 Cor 5:10). Under the revealing gaze of the Lord Jesus, the

quality of our **work** will be tested **by fire** to determine our level of loss or rewards (1 Cor 3:13).

3:15 This verse affirms the eternal security of unfaithful believers who enter heaven with little or nothing to show in terms of service to God and his kingdom.

3:17 It is no small thing in God's eyes to bring destruction upon his church (his **temple**) (see Acts 5:1-11).

3:19-20 You can call it **wisdom**, if you like, but if a worldview disagrees with God's view of things, it's nothing but folly.

4:2 Whether or not you serve in fulltime Christian ministry, if you have believed in Jesus as the atoning sacrifice for your sins, you are a manager over a sphere of influence. Therefore, you must live as a full-time servant of Christ and not just as a part-time Christian. You are called to operate under his authority, to be **faithful** to your King's agenda.

is yours, 23 and you belong to Christ,[a] and
Christ belongs to God.

THE FAITHFUL MANAGER

4 A person should think of us in this
way: as servants[b] of Christ and managers[c] of the mysteries of God.[d] 2 In this
regard, it is required that managers be
found faithful.[e] 3 It is of little[f] importance
to me that I should be judged[g] by you or
by any human court.[A] In fact, I don't even
judge myself. 4 For I am not conscious of
anything against myself, but I am not justified[h] by this. It is the Lord who judges me.
5 So don't judge[i] anything prematurely, before the Lord comes,[j] who will both bring
to light what is hidden in darkness and reveal the intentions of the hearts. And then
praise will come to each one from God.[k]

HOPE WORDS

The more you become a slave to Jesus, the freer you become as a person.

THE APOSTLES' EXAMPLE OF HUMILITY

6 Now, brothers and sisters,[l] I have applied
these things to myself and Apollos[m] for
your benefit, so that you may learn from
us the meaning of the saying: "Nothing beyond what is written." The purpose is that
none of you will be arrogant, favoring one
person over another. 7 For who makes you
so superior? What do you have that you
didn't receive? If, in fact, you did receive it,
why do you boast as if you hadn't received
it? 8 You are already full! You are already
rich! You have begun to reign as kings
without us — and I wish you did reign, so
that we could also reign with you! 9 For I
think God has displayed us, the apostles,
in last place, like men condemned to die:
We have become a spectacle to the world,
both to angels and to people. 10 We are fools
for Christ, but you are wise in Christ![n] We
are weak, but you are strong! You are distinguished, but we are dishonored! 11 Up
to the present hour we are both hungry
and thirsty; we are poorly clothed, roughly treated, homeless; 12 we labor, working[o]
with our own hands.[p] When we are reviled,
we bless; when we are persecuted, we endure it; 13 when we are slandered, we respond graciously. Even now, we are like the
scum of the earth, like everyone's garbage.[q]

PAUL'S FATHERLY CARE

14 I'm not writing this to shame you, but to
warn you as my dear children.[r] 15 For you
may have countless instructors in Christ,
but you don't have many fathers. For I became your father[s] in Christ Jesus through
the gospel. 16 Therefore I urge you to imitate me. 17 This is why I have sent[t] Timothy
to you. He is my dearly loved and faithful[u]
child in the Lord. He will remind you about
my ways in Christ Jesus, just as I teach everywhere in every church.

18 Now some are arrogant, as though
I were not coming to you. 19 But I will
come to you soon,[v] if the Lord wills, and
I will find out not the talk, but the power of those who are arrogant. 20 For the

[a] 3:23 Nm 3:12
[b] 4:1 Jn 18:36
[c] Lk 16:1
[d] 1Co 2:7
[e] 4:2 Nm 12:7
[f] 4:3 Mt 5:19
[g] 1Co 2:14
[h] 4:4 Ac 13:39
[i] 4:5 Lk 6:37
[j] Mk 8:38; 1Pt 5:6
[k] 2Co 10:18
[l] 4:6 Ac 9:30
[m] Ti 3:13
[n] 4:10 1Pt 5:14
[o] 4:12 2Jn 8
[p] Ac 18:3
[q] 4:13 Is 64:6; Lm 3:45
[r] 4:14 1Th 2:11; Phm 1
[s] 4:15 Gl 4:19; Phm 10
[t] 4:17 2Co 9:3; Eph 6:21-22; Col 4:7-8; Phm 12
[u] Nm 12:7
[v] 4:19 Ac 19:21; 1Co 16:5; 2Co 1:15-16

[A] 4:3 Lit *a human day*

4:4-5 Sin-scarred human beings can't perfectly assess the motives of others (or even their own). Only God knows all of the facts and can render a perfect and righteous judgment.

4:6 Everything Christ's "servants" (see 4:1) think, say, and do is to be rooted in and derived from God's authoritative, inerrant Word. Scripture is sufficient; worldly opinions are not.

4:7 God's stewards must never think or act like owners. Kingdom stewards faithfully manage the time, talents, and treasures that God has given them to oversee on his behalf.

4:8 The Corinthians wanted **to reign as kings** who needed nothing, but those who live in pride and self-sufficiency do not submit to the divine King who requires that we live in dependence on him to experience his blessing.

4:9-13 Paul and his coworkers were treated **like the scum of the earth** by the world (4:13). Yet the Corinthians expected nothing but the best for themselves. Is your assessment of what it means to live as a disciple of Christ based on the Bible? Or is it based on worldly assumptions and viewpoints? Are you willing to be **dishonored** for Christ? Or do you expect to be **distinguished** and admired (4:10)? If you are **reviled** or **slandered** for your Christian faith, do you **respond graciously** (4:12-13), or do you repay evil with evil?

4:14-15 Paul wasn't merely pretending to be a father figure. He had actually served as their spiritual **father**, bringing the Corinthians to faith through his ministry (4:15; see Acts 18:1-11). He warned them because he had their best interests and their spiritual development at heart.

4:16 Do you place faithfulness to God above your personal satisfaction so that in essence you can say to others (perhaps to your children), "Follow me and, inasmuch as I follow Christ, do what I do"?

4:20-21 **The kingdom of God** is accompanied with visible **power** and authority not merely verbal declarations (4:20; see Matt 16:19). Paul desired that they would be convinced by the truth of his words and the conviction of the Holy Spirit so that he didn't have to resort to extreme disciplinary measures.

5:1 Paul doesn't say the **father's wife** was the man's mother, so the implication is that she was his stepmother. We know that she was unsaved and not a part of the church because Paul only concerns himself with the actions of the man.

That something was **not even tolerated among the Gentiles** means that unbelievers wouldn't allow it. As depraved as the city of Corinth often was, the non-Christians there would at least draw the line at the kind of immorality taking place in the church!

a 4:21 2Co 1:23; 2:1,3;
12:20-21; 13:2,10
b Jms 3:13
c 5:1 1Th 4:3
d Gl 1:16
e Lv 18:8; Dt 22:30; 27:20
f 5:2 Lk 6:25
g 5:3 Col 2:5; 1Th 2:17

h 5:5 1Jn 5:16
i Mt 25:13; Ac 2:20; Php 1:6
j 5:6 Lk 13:21; Gl 5:9
k 5:6-8 Lk 13:21
l 5:7 Ex 12

☙ Questions & Answers ☙

Q Who were some of your mentors/influencers who shaped your emphasis on a kingdom worldview? How did they impact your ministry?

A There were some great people in my life. I'll start with my father. I saw him hold God's Word up high even though he was living during a more difficult time in terms of race relations. I saw that his commitment to Scripture trumped his circumstances, even in spite of the poverty that our family often had to deal with when he didn't have work. He showed me what a man—a kingdom man—looks like.

Then there was evangelist B. Sam Hart, who held a crusade in which I participated. He saw my enthusiasm and extended a formal invitation for me to serve in his ministry. When I attended college in Atlanta to learn the Word of God further, a professor named Doug

Macintosh encouraged me to attend Dallas Theological Seminary (DTS). I hadn't considered attending DTS, but he paid the application fee, and I enrolled as a student.

I was also greatly influenced by a preacher named Tom Skinner. He was ahead of his time. He kept emphasizing, "the kingdom, the kingdom, the kingdom," specifically as it relates to the race issue. So this bell was continually ringing in my ear. Then there were Gene Getz and Reuben Conner, who both challenged me to start a church to model the kingdom principles that I was beginning to talk about.

All of these voices helped shape my thinking, which led to the development of the kingdom agenda worldview.

FOR THE NEXT Q&A, SEE PAGE 1347.

kingdom of God is not a matter of talk but of power. **²¹** What do you want? Should I come to you with a rod,*a* or in love and a spirit of gentleness?*b*

IMMORAL CHURCH MEMBERS

5 It is actually reported that there is sexual immorality*c* among you, and the kind of sexual immorality that is not even tolerated^A among the Gentiles*d* — a man is sleeping with his father's wife.*e* **²** And you are arrogant! Shouldn't you be filled with grief*f* and remove from your congregation the one who did this? **³** Even though I am absent in the body, I am present in spirit.*g* As one who is present with you in this way,

I have already pronounced judgment on the one who has been doing such a thing. **⁴** When you are assembled in the name of our Lord Jesus, and I am with you in spirit, with the power of our Lord Jesus, **⁵** hand that one over to Satan for the destruction of the flesh,*h* so that his spirit may be saved in the day of the Lord.*i*

⁶ Your boasting is not good. Don't you know that a little leaven*B j* leavens the whole batch of dough?*k* **⁷** Clean out the old leaven so that you may be a new unleavened batch, as indeed you are. For Christ our Passover lamb*l* has been sacrificed.*C* **⁸** Therefore, let us observe the feast, not with old leaven or with the leaven of

^A 5:1 Other mss read *named*   ^B 5:6 Or *yeast*, also in vv. 7,8   ^C 5:7 Other mss add *for us*

5:2 One of the marks of a true and spiritually healthy church is how it deals with sin—particularly, an ongoing pattern of rebellious behavior against God. When you hear about a fellow Christian entrapped in a web of sin, does it break your heart and cause you to seek to rescue them (see Jas 5:19-20)? Or does it prompt you to pick up your phone and gossip?

5:3 Of Paul's pronouncement of **judgment**, some people might say, "What a person does is his or her own business." No, what a professing believer does is God's business because it's his church. And it's the church's business because we are a family. If a member of your family is physically sick or injured, you wouldn't simply say, "That's his business." Rather, the problem is a family matter.

5:5 By excommunicating the man from the church, believers could help him see that God's covenant protection was removed from his life. The goal of this was to drive the man to repentance so that he could be delivered from this sin before facing Christ's judgment.
5:6 Left unchecked, sin (often represented by **leaven** in the Bible) will harm an entire congregation. Consider the account of Israel at the battle of Ai (see Josh 7:1-26). The sin of one man (Achan), who lived among God's people, cost other men their lives and resulted in the temporary loss of victory for the congregation.
5:7-8 Prior to Israel's exodus experience, the Israelites were commanded to sacrifice a lamb and put its blood on their doorframes so that the angel of death would pass over them when

the Lord brought judgment on Egypt's firstborn. In addition, the Israelites were to remove leaven from their homes and eat unleavened bread for seven days to serve as a reminder of their hurried departure from Egypt (see Exod 12:1-28).

Paul tells the Corinthians that **Christ** is the fulfillment of the **Passover lamb**. He was **sacrificed** to protect them from judgment. Furthermore, leaven is symbolic of sin. So just as the Israelites were to rid their homes of all leaven, so the Corinthians must **clean out the old leaven so that** they might **be a new unleavened batch** (1 Cor 5:7). In other words, sin—the old way of life—must be left behind so that the church can live as the new people we are in Christ. One person's sin (leaven) can hinder or stop God's blessing for everyone (5:8).

malice and evil,[a] but with the unleavened bread of sincerity and truth.

CHURCH DISCIPLINE

[9] I wrote to you in a letter not to associate[b] with sexually immoral people.[c] [10] I did not mean the immoral people of this world or the greedy[d] and swindlers[e] or idolaters; otherwise you would have to leave the world.[f] [11] But actually, I wrote[A] you not to associate with anyone who claims to be a brother or sister[g] and is sexually immoral or greedy, an idolater or verbally abusive, a drunkard[h] or a swindler. Do not even eat with such a person. [12] For what business is it of mine to judge[i] outsiders? Don't you judge those who are inside? [13] God judges outsiders. **Remove the evil person from among you.**[B,j]

LAWSUITS AMONG BELIEVERS

6 If any of you has a dispute against another, how dare you take it to court[k] before the unrighteous,[c] and not before the saints? [2] Or don't you know that the saints will judge the world? And if the world is judged by you, are you unworthy to judge the trivial cases? [3] Don't you know that we will judge angels — how much more matters of this life? [4] So if you have such matters, do you appoint as your judges those who have no standing[l] in the church? [5] I say this to your shame![m] Can it be that there is not one wise person among you who is able to arbitrate between fellow believers?[n] [6] Instead, brother goes to court against brother, and that before unbelievers![o]

[7] As it is, to have legal disputes against one another is already a defeat for you.[p] Why not rather be wronged?[q] Why not rather be cheated?[r] [8] Instead, you yourselves do wrong and cheat — and you do this to brothers and sisters! [9] Don't you know that the unrighteous[s] will not inherit God's kingdom?[t] Do not be deceived: No sexually immoral people, idolaters,[u] adulterers,[v] or males who have sex with males,[D,W] [10] no thieves,[x] greedy[y] people, drunkards, verbally abusive people,[z] or swindlers[aa] will inherit God's kingdom. [11] And some of you used to be like this.[ab] But you were washed, you were sanctified,[ac] you were justified in the name of the Lord Jesus Christ and by the Spirit of our God.

GLORIFYING GOD IN BODY AND SPIRIT

[12] "Everything is permissible[ad] for me," but not everything is beneficial. "Everything is permissible for me," but I will not be mastered by anything. [13] "Food[ae] is for the stomach and the stomach for food,"

---

[a] 5:8 Mk 7:22; Rm 1:29
[b] 5:9 2Th 3:14
[c] 1Co 6:9; Eph 5:5; 1Tm 1:10; Heb 12:16; 13:4; Rv 21:8; 22:15
[d] 5:10 Eph 5:5
[e] Lk 18:11
[f] Jn 17:6
[g] 5:11 2Th 3:6
[h] 1Co 6:10
[i] 5:12 Lk 6:37
[j] 5:13 Dt 17:7
[k] 6:1 Mt 18:15-17
[l] 6:4 Lk 18:9

[m] 6:5 1Co 4:14
[n] Ac 9:30
[o] 6:6 Lk 12:46
[p] 6:7 Rm 11:12
[q] Rv 2:11
[r] Mk 10:19
[s] 6:9 Lk 16:10
[t] Mk 1:15; Ac 20:25
[u] Eph 5:5
[v] Lk 18:11
[w] Gn 19:5
[x] 6:10 Jn 10:1
[y] Eph 5:5
[z] 1Co 5:11
[aa] Lk 18:11
[ab] 6:11 Eph 2:2-3; 4:22; 5:8; Ti 3:3
[ac] Lk 11:2
[ad] 6:12 Jn 18:31
[ae] 6:13 1Tm 6:8

[A] 5:11 Or *But now I am writing*   [B] 5:13 Dt 17:7   [C] 6:1 Unbelievers; v. 6   [D] 6:9 Both passive and active participants in homosexual acts

---

5:9 The Corinthians should have known better than to ignore this church member's sexual immorality. For Paul had sent a previous **letter** telling them **not to associate with sexually immoral people**—that is, with professing believers who indulged in sexual sin (see 5:11). Clear patterns of sin are not acceptable and must be confronted. To call oneself a child of God and live like a child of the devil is a contradiction.

5:12-13 It is not the church's business **to judge outsiders**—unbelievers (5:12). **God** will deal with them (5:13). But the church is called to judge its own, to **judge those who are inside** (5:12; see 1 Pet 4:17), for the good of the sinning member, the purity of the church, and the glory of God. Churches that refuse to lovingly and clearly address unrepentant sin are not functioning as biblically centered, New Testament churches. Therefore, they are limiting or negating God's powerful presence in their midst.

The local church is to be a hospital for the sick, a place where sinners can come to be healed. Indeed, we must welcome the sick and never keep them away. But what the church must *not* do is allow the sick to be content with being sick. When we do that, we cease to be a hospital and devolve into a hospice that simply makes people comfortable in their sin.

6:2-3 If when they reign with Christ (see Rev 20:4-6), Christians will participate in worldwide judgment—including judging fallen **angels** (6:3)—then surely they can handle **trivial cases** among themselves (1 Cor 6:2). **6:5-6** Every local church should have a church court of sorts. **Wise**, spiritual church leaders should **arbitrate between fellow believers** (6:5). This enables a body of believers to bring God's point of view to bear on specific situations in order to settle disputes between members and provide resolution. To call on **unbelievers** to arbitrate disputes between Christians—those who have been reconciled to God and to one another—hinders the proclamation of the gospel and reputation of the church before the world (6:6).

6:7-8 Their actions did not bring God glory in the eyes of unbelievers but brought division to the church.

6:9-11 Inheritance has to do with the kingdom rewards and blessings to be received or lost by believers at the judgment seat of Christ based on our obedience, faithfulness, and righteous living (6:9-10; see 2 Tim 2:12; Heb 12:16-17). By the grace of God, believers have been **washed** (cleansed of guilt by the blood of Jesus), **sanctified** (spiritually set apart to God), and **justified** (declared righteous before

God) (1 Cor 6:11). Thus, we are called to live in a way reflecting the reality of what God has done for us.

6:12 Everything is permissible for me was a slogan spoken by the Corinthians that they used to justify and rationalize their immorality. Paul counters it by telling them that "permissible" things aren't necessarily **beneficial**. Christian freedom should never be used to sin or harm fellow believers. Liberty becomes detrimental when it negates the law of love—whether to another person or to yourself by bringing you into bondage.

6:13 Food is for the stomach and the stomach for food was a Corinthian slogan conveying the idea, "I've got a bodily appetite, so I need to satisfy it." But the Corinthians extended this argument beyond just eating. Some were arguing that *sexual* cravings also needed to be satisfied—even by visiting pagan temple prostitutes (see 6:15)!

However, Paul would have none of that kind of thinking: **The body is not for sexual immorality**. God created sex for procreation and intimacy between a husband and wife within the covenant bond of marriage. Our bodies are not our own to do with as we please but are **for the Lord**. What we do with them is not irrelevant and is to be determined by the Lord.

[a] 6:13 1Th 4:3
[b] 6:14 Mk 5:30; Lk 1:35; 6:19; Ac 19:11; 2Co 13:4; Rv 11:17
[c] 6:15 Rm 12:5; 1Co 12:27; Eph 5:30
[d] 6:16 Gn 2:24
[e] 6:17 Jn 11:52
[f] Ps 51:12
[g] 6:18 Jms 4:7
[h] 1Co 10:8
[i] 6:19 Lk 1:21
[j] Rm 8:9,23; 1Co 7:40; 2Co 4:13; Jd 19
[k] Jms 4:5; 1Jn 4:4
[l] 6:20 2Pt 2:1
[m] 7:2 1Th 4:3
[n] Mt 1:6; 1Pt 3:1
[o] 7:3 Rm 13:7

[p] 7:5 Mk 10:19
[q] 7:7 2Co 1:11
[r] 7:8 Jms 1:27
[s] 7:9 1Co 9:25
[t] 1Tm 5:14
[u] 7:10 1Tm 5:14
[v] 7:11 Dt 22:19
[w] 7:12 Ac 9:30
[x] 7:14 Lk 11:2

and God will do away with both of them. However, the body is not for sexual immorality[a] but for the Lord, and the Lord for the body. [14] God raised up the Lord and will also raise us up by his power.[b] [15] Don't you know that your bodies are a part of Christ's body?[c] So should I take a part of Christ's body and make it part of a prostitute? Absolutely not! [16] Don't you know that anyone joined to a prostitute is one body with her? For Scripture says, **The two will become one flesh.**[A,d] [17] But anyone joined[e] to the Lord is one spirit[f] with him.

[18] Flee[g] sexual immorality! Every other sin[B] a person commits is outside the body, but the person who is sexually immoral[h] sins against his own body. [19] Don't you know that your body is a temple[i] of the Holy Spirit[j] who is in you,[k] whom you have from God? You are not your own, [20] for you were bought[l] at a price. So glorify God with your body.[c]

PRINCIPLES OF MARRIAGE

7 Now in response to the matters you wrote[D] about: "It is good for a man not to use[E] a woman for sex." [2] But because sexual immorality is so common,[F,m] each man should have sexual relations with his own wife,[n] and each woman should have sexual relations with her own husband. [3] A husband should fulfill his marital duty[o] to his wife, and likewise a wife to her husband. [4] A wife does not have the right

over her own body, but her husband does. In the same way, a husband does not have the right over his own body, but his wife does. [5] Do not deprive[p] one another — except when you agree for a time, to devote yourselves to[G] prayer. Then come together again; otherwise, Satan may tempt you because of your lack of self-control. [6] I say this as a concession, not as a command. [7] I wish that all people were as I am. But each has his own gift[q] from God, one person has this gift, another has that.

A WORD TO THE UNMARRIED

[8] I say to the unmarried[H] and to widows:[r] It is good for them if they remain as I am. [9] But if they do not have self-control,[s] they should marry, since it is better to marry[t] than to burn with desire.

ABOUT MARRIED PEOPLE

[10] To the married I give this command[u] — not I, but the Lord — a wife is not to leave[I] her husband. [11] But if she does leave, she must remain unmarried or be reconciled to her husband — and a husband is not to divorce his wife.[v] [12] But I (not the Lord) say to the rest: If any brother[w] has an unbelieving wife and she is willing to live with him, he must not divorce her. [13] Also, if any woman has an unbelieving husband and he is willing to live with her, she must not divorce her husband. [14] For the unbelieving husband is made holy[x]

[A] 6:16 Gn 2:24   [B] 6:18 Lit *Every sin*   [C] 6:20 Other mss add *and in your spirit, which belong to God.*   [D] 7:1 Other mss add *to me*   [E] 7:1 Lit *"It is good for a man not to touch a woman"*   [F] 7:2 Lit *because of immoralities*   [G] 7:5 Other mss add *fasting and to*   [H] 7:8 Or *widowers*   [I] 7:10 Or *separate from, or divorce*

6:15-17 To sexually unite with a prostitute is to be illegitimately **one body with her**. According to Genesis 2:24, when a man and woman are joined sexually in marriage, they legitimately **become one flesh** (1 Cor 6:16). Thus, to engage in prostitution or any other sexually immoral relationship is to make Christ and his **body** (the church) part of an illegitimate union (6:15). And that's exactly what happens when a person is both **joined to a prostitute** *and* **joined to the Lord** (6:16-17). We should never make our Savior part of such an unrighteous union!

6:18 Sexual sin is unique because by joining to someone other than one's spouse, a person enters into an illegitimate one-flesh union (see 6:16) and **sins against his own body.** This, in fact, is why people experience emotional, psychological, and spiritual scars as a result of sexual sin.

6:19-20 A Christian's **body** is a house of worship; therefore, sexual immorality brings such sin directly into God's presence! When you have sex, you are going to church. The Lord is present when a husband and wife experience physical intimacy too, but sexual pleasure within marriage brings God glory because it

honors his design for sex. Sexual immorality, in whatever form it takes (adultery, fornication, homosexuality, pornography, etc.), makes a mockery of God's design. God will call everyone to account for how they manage their sexuality.

7:1 A literal rendering of the Greek text into English is, "It is good for a man not to touch a woman." *Touching a woman* is a euphemism for engaging in sexual activity with her. Thus, for those who are single, abstinence is God's good plan until marriage. God created sex and knows best how it is to be expressed. Pursuing it outside of the covenant bond of marriage is sin and will not bring the fulfillment that God intends.

7:2 Sexual expression within marriage is *not* immoral.

7:3-4 By encouraging husbands and wives to fulfill their **marital** responsibilities to one another, Paul isn't suggesting that having sex is a mere **duty** (7:3). Rather, he's emphasizing that husbands and wives should not be selfish and should focus on the needs of their spouses.

7:5 *To fast* is to temporarily give up satisfying a craving of the body in order to focus and give extra attention to a spiritual need. If a

husband and wife need God to intervene in a situation, a sexual fast for the purpose of **prayer** is in order.

7:7-9 Paul was single. But unless God has granted the gift of celibacy, marriage is a wise and legitimate pursuit.

7:10-11 When two people marry, there will always be struggles and challenges. But, even when there are difficult problems, Paul urges the pursuit of reconciliation—not **divorce** (7:11).

7:12 By saying that his instructions are from himself and **not the Lord**, Paul means that Jesus never spoke directly on this subject during his earthly ministry. Nevertheless, as an inspired apostle, Paul provides guidance from the Holy Spirit.

7:13-14 Not only can the believing spouse share the gospel with the **unbelieving** spouse and their children, but he or she also brings a covering of God's blessing to the marriage and family. Consider Rahab's situation (see Josh 2:8-14). When she confessed faith in the Lord and sheltered his people, she *and her unbelieving family* were delivered from the destruction that God brought upon Jericho.

a 7:17 Col 3:15
b 7:22 Rm 1:1; 2Tm 2:24
c 7:23 2Pt 2:1
d 7:25 Mt 5:7; Mk 5:19; Lk 1:50
e Nm 12:7
f 7:28 1Tm 5:14
g 7:29 Rm 13:11

Questions & Answers

Q Fasting as a spiritual discipline to accompany prayer is unfamiliar to many people. How important is fasting?

A Fasting is important because it prioritizes the spiritual over the physical. Fasting involves giving up something that appeals to the five senses. Typically it involves food, but the Bible also speaks of sexual fasting in marriage (see 1 Cor 7:5). The point of fasting is to deny a desire in the physical realm because you need something greater in the spiritual realm. Such actions notify God of how seriously you take a particular need. Although God already knows about your need, fasting practically demonstrates to him that the spiritual matters deeply to you.

Too often, we neglect prayer in favor of television, friends, entertainment, or food. Such prioritization pushes the physical to the front. But kingdom prayer gives priority to the spiritual. It must come first. Jesus said, "My kingdom is not of this world" (John 18:36). His kingdom is spiritual. Therefore, when you fast, you bump the spiritual to first place. It's like placing a Bunsen burner under your prayer request.

FOR THE NEXT Q&A, SEE PAGE 1355.

by the wife, and the unbelieving wife is made holy by the husband.[A] Otherwise your children would be unclean, but as it is they are holy. **15** But if the unbeliever leaves, let him leave. A brother or a sister is not bound in such cases. God has called you[B] to live in peace. **16** Wife, for all you know, you might save your husband.

Husband, for all you know, you might save your wife.[C]

VARIOUS SITUATIONS OF LIFE

17 Let each one live his life in the situation the Lord assigned when God called[a] him.[D] This is what I command in all the churches. **18** Was anyone already circumcised when he was called? He should not undo his circumcision. Was anyone called while uncircumcised? He should not get circumcised. **19** Circumcision does not matter and uncircumcision does not matter. Keeping God's commands is what matters. **20** Let each of you remain in the situation[E] in which he was called. **21** Were you called while a slave? Don't let it concern you. But if you can become free, by all means take the opportunity.[F] **22** For he who is called by the Lord as a slave[b] is the Lord's freedman. Likewise he who is called as a free man is Christ's slave. **23** You were bought[c] at a price; do not become slaves of people. **24** Brothers and sisters, each person is to remain with God in the situation in which he was called.

ABOUT THE UNMARRIED AND WIDOWS

25 Now about virgins:[G] I have no command from the Lord, but I do give an opinion as one who by the Lord's mercy[d] is faithful.[e] **26** Because of the present distress, I think that it is good for a man to remain as he is. **27** Are you bound to a wife? Do not seek to be released. Are you released from a wife? Do not seek a wife. **28** However, if you do get married,[f] you have not sinned, and if a virgin[H] marries, she has not sinned. But such people will have trouble in this life,[I] and I am trying to spare you.

29 This is what I mean, brothers and sisters: The time is limited,[g] so from now on those who have wives should be as though they had none, **30** those who weep

---

[A] 7:14 Lit *the brother*   [B] 7:15 Other mss read *us that you will save your wife?*   [C] 7:16 Or *Wife, how do you know that you will save your husband? Husband, how do you know*   [D] 7:17 Lit *called each*   [E] 7:20 Lit *in the calling*   [F] 7:21 Or *But even though you can become free, make the most of your position as a slave*   [G] 7:25 Or *betrothed*, or *those not yet married*   [H] 7:28 Or *betrothed woman*   [I] 7:28 Lit *in the flesh*

7:15 If a Christian spouse has done everything possible to preserve the marriage but the **unbeliever** still **leaves** the home or their divinely ordained role, Scripture considers such a situation legitimate grounds for divorce (and, thus, the believing spouse would be free to remarry). Importantly, though, accusations of abandonment must be validated by the church.
7:16 Daily exposure to the verbal and visual message of the gospel is a powerful testimony that God might use to bring someone to faith in Christ.

7:22-23 Christian, no matter your vocation, you are called first and foremost to render faithful service to the Lord who saved you.
7:25 Paul refers to single believers as **virgins** because according to a biblical worldview unmarried believers are not to be sexually active. A *kingdom single* is an unmarried Christian who is committed to fully and freely maximizing his or her life under the rule of God and the lordship of Jesus Christ.
7:26-27 Paul's instructions here follow the same principle he just outlined in 7:17, 20, and

24: believers ought to remain in the situation in which they were called to Christ.
7:28 Marriage, even Christian marriage, has unique challenges because it's the uniting of two imperfect people. So no one should go running about in a flippant search for a spouse.
7:29-31 We must not live with a temporal mindset as if **this world** is all there is (7:31). Make decisions based on an eternal perspective and not based on earthly pressures.

a 7:30 Php 1:18
b 7:31 Mk 13:7; 1Jn 2:8
c 7:32 1Th 4:1
d 7:34 1Tm 5:5
e 7:37 Jn 1:13

f 8:1 Ac 15:29; 21:25; 1Co 10:19; Rv 2:14,20
g 1Co 4:6
h 1Co 13:1-13
i 8:2 1Co 3:18; 13:8-12; 1Tm 3:7
j 8:3 Dt 6:5; Lk 10:27
k Pr 2:6
l 8:4 Dt 6:4
m 8:5 2Th 2:4
n 8:6 Mt 5:16; 11:27; Lk 11:13; Jn 8:42; Eph 5:20
o Ps 104:24; Col 1:16; Rv 3:14
p Jn 1:3
q 8:8 Rm 14:17
r 8:9 Ex 23:33; Rm 14:20
s 8:11 Jn 11:51; Rm 5:6,8; 8:34; 14:9,15; 1Co 15:3; Gl 2:21; Eph 5:2; 1Th 5:10
t Heb 6:8
u Mt 25:45
v 8:13 Dt 12:15

as though they did not weep, those who rejoice[a] as though they did not rejoice, those who buy as though they didn't own anything, 31 and those who use the world as though they did not make full use of it. For this world in its current form is passing away.[b]

32 I want you to be without concerns. The unmarried man is concerned about the things of the Lord — how he may please[c] the Lord. 33 But the married man is concerned about the things of the world — how he may please his wife — 34 and his interests are divided. The unmarried woman or virgin is concerned about the things of the Lord,[d] so that she may be holy both in body and in spirit. But the married woman is concerned about the things of the world — how she may please her husband. 35 I am saying this for your own benefit, not to put a restraint on you, but to promote what is proper and so that you may be devoted to the Lord without distraction.

36 If any man thinks he is acting improperly toward the virgin he is engaged to, if she is getting beyond the usual age for marriage, and he feels he should marry — he can do what he wants. He is not sinning; they can get married. 37 But he who stands firm in his heart (who is under no compulsion, but has control over his own will[e]) and has decided in his heart to keep her as his fiancée, will do well. 38 So then he who marries his fiancée does well, but he who does not marry will do better.[A]

39 A wife is bound[B] as long as her husband is living. But if her husband dies, she is free to be married to anyone she wants — only in the Lord. 40 But she is happier if she remains as she is, in my opinion. And I think that I also have the Spirit of God.

FOOD OFFERED TO IDOLS

8 Now about food sacrificed to idols:[f] We know that "we all have knowledge." Knowledge puffs up,[g] but love[h] builds up. 2 If anyone thinks he knows anything, he does not yet know it as he ought to know it.[i] 3 But if anyone loves God,[j] he is known[k] by him.

4 About eating food sacrificed to idols, then, we know that "an idol is nothing in the world,"[c] and that "there is no God but one."[l] 5 For even if there are so-called gods,[m] whether in heaven or on earth — as there are many "gods" and many "lords" — 6 yet for us there is one God, the Father.[n] All things are from him,[o] and we exist for him. And there is one Lord, Jesus Christ. All things are through him, and we exist through him.[p]

7 However, not everyone has this knowledge. Some have been so used to idolatry up until now that when they eat food sacrificed to an idol, their conscience, being weak, is defiled. 8 Food will not bring us close to God.[D] We are not worse off if we don't eat, and we are not better if we do eat.[q] 9 But be careful that this right of yours in no way becomes a stumbling block[r] to the weak. 10 For if someone sees you, the one who has knowledge, dining in an idol's temple, won't his weak conscience be encouraged[E] to eat food offered to idols? 11 So the weak person, the brother or sister for whom Christ died,[s] is ruined[F,t] by your knowledge.[u] 12 Now when you sin like this against brothers and sisters and wound their weak conscience, you are sinning against Christ. 13 Therefore, if food causes my brother or sister to fall, I will never again eat meat,[v] so that I won't cause my brother or sister to fall.

A 7:36-38 Or 36*If any man thinks he is acting improperly toward his virgin daughter, if she is getting beyond the usual age for marriage, and he feels she should marry — he can do what he wants. He is not sinning; she can get married.* 37*But he who stands firm in his heart (who is under no compulsion, but has control over his own will) and has decided in his heart to keep his own virgin daughter will do well.* 38*So then he who gives his own virgin daughter in marriage does well, but he who does not give his own virgin daughter in marriage will do better.* B 7:39 Other mss add *by law* C 8:4 Or *an idol has no real existence* D 8:8 Or *bring us before* (the judgment seat of) *God* E 8:10 Or *built up* F 8:11 Or *destroyed*

7:32-35 Adam was consumed with his calling until God gave him Eve. Likewise, every Christian single should maximize the freedom of his or her single status until God brings a mate. It is okay to have the desire for a mate; it is not okay to allow the desire to become a spiritual distraction.

7:39 The phrase **only in the Lord** means a believer must marry a fellow believer. Many people talk about finding a *soul*-mate, but the Lord wants us to find a *spirit*-mate. Within that context, there is freedom of choice. As Paul writes to the Corinthians later, "Don't become partners with those who do not believe. . . . What fellowship does light have with darkness?" (2 Cor 6:14).

8:5-6 No matter how many so-called **gods** and **lords** the Greeks and Romans revered, for Christians there is **one God, the Father,** the source of all things. **And there is one Lord, Jesus Christ,** the agent of creation.

8:9-11 We don't want to do something that causes a fellow Christian to fail to move forward in his or her faith (8:9). Some of the Corinthians rightly recognized that idols are nothing and, so, had no problem eating food sacrificed to idols. But, if their liberty **encouraged** a believer with a **weak conscience** to

also **eat** the **food,** the latter would experience spiritual harm. We must not ruin the faith of another (8:10-11). Let's act in love toward other believers so that their faith is strengthened and not undermined.

8:12 To insist on exercising our liberty at the expense of weaker Christians is not only to sin against them but also to sin **against Christ.** As Paul himself learned, Jesus takes sins against his church (his body) seriously (see Acts 9:3-5).

8:13 Paul would go out of his way to avoid hindering the spiritual development of another Christian. Would you? Don't trip up others

PAUL'S EXAMPLE AS AN APOSTLE

9 Am I not free? Am I not an apostle? Have I not seen Jesus our Lord? Are you not my work in the Lord? [2] If I am not an apostle to others, at least I am to you, because you are the seal[a] of my apostleship in the Lord.

[3] My defense to those who examine me is this: [4] Don't we have the right to eat and drink?[b] [5] Don't we have the right to be accompanied by a believing wife[A] like the other apostles,[c] the Lord's brothers, and Cephas?[d] [6] Or do only Barnabas[e] and I have no right to refrain from working? [7] Who serves as a soldier at his own expense?[f] Who plants a vineyard and does not eat its fruit? Or who shepherds a flock and does not drink the milk from the flock?

[8] Am I saying this from a human perspective? Doesn't the law also say the same thing? [9] For it is written in the law of Moses, **Do not muzzle an ox[g] while it treads out grain.**[B,h] Is God really concerned about oxen? [10] Isn't he really saying it for our sake? Yes, this is written for our sake,[i] because he who plows ought to plow in hope,[j] and he who threshes should thresh in hope of sharing the crop.[k] [11] If we have sown spiritual things for you, is it too much if we reap material benefits from you? [12] If others have this right to receive benefits from you, don't we even more? Nevertheless, we have not made use of this right; instead, we endure everything[l] so that we will not hinder the gospel of Christ.

[13] Don't you know that those who perform the temple services eat the food from the temple, and those who serve at the altar[m] share in the offerings of the altar? [14] In the same way, the Lord has commanded that those who preach the gospel should earn their living by the gospel.[n]

[15] For my part I have used none of these rights, nor have I written these things that they may be applied in my case. For it would be better for me to die than for anyone to deprive me of my boast! [16] For if I preach the gospel, I have no reason to boast, because I am compelled to preach[c] — and woe to me if I do not preach the gospel! [17] For if I do this willingly, I have a reward, but if unwillingly, I am entrusted[o] with a commission. [18] What then is my reward? To preach the gospel and offer it free of charge and not make full use of my rights in the gospel.[p]

[19] Although I am free from all and not anyone's slave, I have made myself a slave to everyone, in order to win[q] more people. [20] To the Jews I became like a Jew, to win Jews; to those under the law, like one under the law — though I myself am not under the law[D] — to win those under the law.[r] [21] To those who are without the law,[s] like one without the law — though I am not without God's law but under the law of Christ — to win those without the law. [22] To the weak I became weak, in order to win the weak. I have become all things to all people, so that I may by every possible means save some.[t] [23] Now I do all this because of the gospel, so that I may share in the blessings.

[24] Don't you know that the runners in a stadium all race,[u] but only one receives the prize? Run in such a way to win the prize.[v] [25] Now everyone who competes exercises

---

[a] 9:2 Rv 5:1
[b] 9:4 2Th 3:8-9
[c] 9:5 Jd 17
[d] Jn 1:42
[e] 9:6 Ac 4:36
[f] 9:7 Lk 3:14
[g] 9:9 Lk 13:15
[h] Dt 25:4
[i] 9:10 Rm 4:24
[j] Ac 23:6; 1Th 1:3
[k] 2Tm 2:6
[l] 9:12 Ac 20:33-35; 2Co 6:3-10; 11:7-12
[m] 9:13 Lv 6:16,26; 7:6,31-32; Nm 5:9-10; 18:8-20,31; Dt 18:1
[n] 9:14 Mt 10:8-10; Lk 10:7
[o] 9:17 Lk 16:11
[p] 9:18 2Co 11:7; 12:13
[q] 9:19 1Pt 3:1
[r] 9:20 Ac 16:3; 21:23-26
[s] 9:21 Rm 2:12,14; Gl 2:3; 3:2
[t] 9:22 Rm 11:14; 1Co 7:16
[u] 9:24 Jd 3
[v] Col 2:18

[A] 9:5 Lit *a sister as a wife*   [B] 9:9 Dt 25:4   [C] 9:16 Lit *because necessity is laid upon me*   [D] 9:20 Other mss omit *though I myself am not under the law*

---

in their spiritual progress; rather, help them on their journey.

9:3-6 Of those who wonder if he practices what he preaches, Paul asks questions to show that he has rights as an apostle. These rights included eating and drinking whatever he chose, taking a spouse, and ceasing his tent-making vocation to support himself.

9:7 Similarly, an apostle of Jesus Christ is certainly entitled to receive remuneration for his work.

9:9-10 The point is that those who engage in Christian ministry have the right to receive compensation for their work.

9:12 Paul didn't want to risk staining the credibility of the gospel or be the cause of anyone rejecting the message of **Christ**, so he had relinquished his **right** to financial support while among the Corinthians.

9:13-14 The priests who served in the **temple** had the right to receive the sacrificial

offerings as their **food** (9:13; see, e.g., Num 18:8-32). **In the same way, the Lord** Jesus had **commanded that those who preach the gospel should earn their living by the gospel** (1 Cor 9:14; see Matt 10:8-10; Luke 10:7).

9:17-18 Paul had been **entrusted with a commission** from the Lord Jesus to serve as his ambassador, proclaiming the gospel to the world (9:17; see Acts 26:12-18). Paul's **reward** was seeing lives transformed by God (1 Cor 9:18); therefore, he preferred to secure his own financial support rather than lose out on that joy.

9:19-22 In non-essential matters, Paul was willing to adopt the ways of either **Jews** or Gentiles so that he might gain a hearing among them for the sake of the gospel (9:20-22). When we truly grasp God's great love for us, we come to see that serving him and winning others to him should be our passion. After all, "God proves his own love for us in

that while we were still sinners, Christ died for us" (Rom 5:8). Let that be your motivation, and resolve to let nothing prevent you from exalting your Savior and making the good news known to others.

9:24 In the race of the Christian life, Paul wasn't content to receive a participation ribbon. He wanted to obtain the gold medal. As sure as true athletes compete to win, followers of Christ should **run** the Christian **race** for the **prize**. You should long to hear Jesus say to you, "Well done, good and faithful servant!" (Matt 25:23).

9:25 In ancient times, athletes competed to **receive a perishable crown**. They labored long and hard to obtain something that lacked long-term value. Paul tips his hat to such devotion but nevertheless says, in effect, "That's not our plan. We aim higher. Christians strive from an eternal perspective." We seek **an imperishable crown**. God's

a 9:25 Gl 5:23
b 1Pt 1:18; 5:4
c 9:27 Heb 6:8
d 10:1 Ps 44:1; Ac 7:11
e Ex 13:21
f Ex 14:29
g 10:2 Ac 22:16
h Ps 77:20; Mt 8:4; Heb 3:2
i 10:3 Ex 16:31
j 10:4 Ex 17:6; Nm 20:7-13
k Jn 4:14; 6:30-35
l 10:5 Jd 5
m 10:6 Mt 27:23; Jms 4:2
n Nm 11:4,33-34; Ps 78:18; 106:14
o 10:7 Eph 5:5
p Ex 32:6
q 10:8 1Co 6:18; Rv 2:14,20; 17:2; 18:3,9
r Nm 25:1-18; Ps 106:29
s 10:9 Nm 21:6
t 10:10 Jn 6:41; Jd 16
u Nm 16:41-50
v Ex 12:23; 2Sm 24:16; 1Ch 21:15; Ps 78:49
w 10:11 Ps 102:18
x Mk 13:7
y Mk 10:30
z 10:12 Pr 24:16; Heb 6:8

aa 10:13 Nm 12:7
ab 2Pt 2:9
ac 10:16 Mt 26:27; Mk 14:23; Lk 22:17,20; 1Co 11:25-26
ad Mk 6:41; Gl 3:14
ae Mt 26:26; Mk 14:22; Lk 22:19; Ac 2:42,46; 20:7
af 10:17 Jn 11:52; Eph 4:4
ag 10:18 Gn 8:20; Lv 1:5; Nm 3:26; Dt 12:27; 1Sm 2:28; 1Ch 6:49; Ps 26:6; Ezk 8:15; Heb 7:13
ah 10:22 Ec 6:10

self-control*a* in everything. They do it to receive a perishable crown,*b* but we an imperishable crown. **26** So I do not run like one who runs aimlessly or box like one beating the air. **27** Instead, I discipline my body and bring it under strict control, so that after preaching to others, I myself will not be disqualified.*c*

WARNINGS FROM ISRAEL'S PAST

10 Now I do not want you to be unaware, brothers and sisters, that our ancestors*d* were all under the cloud,*e* all passed through the sea,*f* **2** and all were baptized*g* into Moses*h* in the cloud and in the sea. **3** They all ate the same spiritual food,*i* **4** and all drank the same spiritual drink. For they drank from the spiritual rock*j* that followed them, and that rock was Christ.*k* **5** Nevertheless God was not pleased with most of them, since they were struck down in the wilderness.*l*

6 Now these things took place as examples for us, so that we will not desire*m* evil things as they did.*A,n* **7** Don't become idolaters*o* as some of them were; as it is written, **The people sat down to eat and drink, and got up to party.***B,C,p* **8** Let us not commit sexual immorality*q* as some of them did,*p* and in a single day twenty-three thousand people died.*r* **9** Let us not test Christ as some of them did*E* and were destroyed by snakes.*s* **10** And don't complain*t* as some of them did,*F,u* and were killed by the destroyer.*G,v* **11** These things happened to them as examples, and they were written for our instruction,*w* on whom the ends of the ages*H,x* have come.*y* **12** So, whoever thinks he stands must be careful not to fall.*z* **13** No temptation has come upon

you except what is common to humanity. But God is faithful;*aa* he will not allow you to be tempted beyond what you are able, but with the temptation he will also provide a way out*ab* so that you may be able to bear it.

⌐ **HOPE WORDS** ⌐
God is greater than your struggle.

WARNING AGAINST IDOLATRY

14 So then, my dear friends, flee from idolatry. **15** I am speaking as to sensible people. Judge for yourselves what I am saying. **16** The cup*ac* of blessing*ad* that we bless, is it not a sharing in the blood of Christ? The bread*ae* that we break, is it not a sharing in the body of Christ? **17** Because there is one bread, we who are many are one*af* body, since all of us share the one bread. **18** Consider the people of Israel.*I* Do not those who eat the sacrifices participate in the altar?*ag* **19** What am I saying then? That food sacrificed to idols is anything, or that an idol is anything? **20** No, but I do say that what they*J* sacrifice, they sacrifice to demons and not to God. I do not want you to be participants with demons! **21** You cannot drink the cup of the Lord and the cup of demons. You cannot share in the Lord's table and the table of demons. **22** Or are we provoking the Lord to jealousy? Are we stronger than he?*ah*

CHRISTIAN LIBERTY

23 "Everything is permissible,"*K* but not everything is beneficial. "Everything is

---

A 10:6 Lit *they desired*   B 10:7 Or *to dance*   C 10:7 Ex 32:6   D 10:8 Lit *them committed sexual immorality*   E 10:9 Lit *them tested*   F 10:10 Lit *them complained*   G 10:10 Or *the destroying angel*   H 10:11 Or *goals of the ages*, or *culmination of the ages*   I 10:18 Lit *Look at Israel according to the flesh*   J 10:20 Other mss read *Gentiles*   K 10:23 Other mss add *for me*

---

rewards do not fade, rust, or perish. So, maintain a kingdom perspective and strive for the imperishable reward.

9:27 Only one passion in your life is worth your total commitment and pursuit: loving Christ and serving him. Don't disqualify yourself for the prize by quitting the race, running in the wrong direction, or breaking the rules. Run to win.

10:1-5 Every Israelite (**all**) had access to these spiritual benefits (10:1-4). Likewise, every Christian believer has equal access to the spiritual benefits that God offers his people. The point here is that being recipients of God's kindness is no guarantee of avoiding his disciplining hand for ongoing rebellion. The **rock** mentioned is verse 4 is another indicator that the Son of God was active in Old Testament times before his incarnation.

10:7-10 Idolatry, **sexual immorality**, and complaining: these sins led to the downfall of the Israelites (see, e.g., Exod 32:1-6; Num 16:41-50; 25:1-15), and they can lead to ours.

10:11 Christians are those **on whom the ends of the ages have come**. The consequences are high for any believers in the church age who choose to follow the sinful example of Israel's wilderness generation. Remember God's warning to the Galatians: "God is not mocked. For whatever a person sows he will also reap" (Gal 6:7).

10:13 Take heart. No **temptation** will prove overpowering because Christians are no longer slaves to sin; we have the freedom to choose what is good. God will **provide a way out**; he will grant you the strength so that you may say no to sinful enticements.

Through the power of the Holy Spirit, we have the ability to withstand the temptation and pass the test.

10:19-22 Some of the Corinthians were apparently attempting to **share in the Lord's table and the table of demons** (10:21) by partaking of Communion and also eating with unbelievers who were sacrificing to idols in pagan temples. Though **idols** are not truly gods, Paul contends that **demons** stand behind them (10:19-20). A sacrifice offered to a false god, then, has actually been offered to a demon. You **cannot** draw closer in intimacy with Christ and experience his kingdom blessings, while at the same time drawing closer to demonic activity (10:21).

10:23-24 Paul gives the proper balance and understanding of Christian liberty by saying

permissible,"[A] but not everything builds up. [24] No one is to seek his own good, but the good of the other person.[a]

[25] Eat everything that is sold in the meat market, without raising questions for the sake of conscience, [26] since **the earth is the Lord's,**[b] and all that is in it. [B,C] [27] If any of the unbelievers invites you over and you want to go, eat everything that is set before you, without raising questions for the sake of conscience. [28] But if someone says to you, "This is food from a sacrifice," do not eat it,[d] out of consideration for the one who told you, and for the sake of conscience.[c] [29] I do not mean your own conscience, but the other person's. For why is my freedom judged[e] by another person's conscience? [30] If I partake with thanksgiving,[f] why am I criticized because of something for which I give thanks?

[31] So, whether you eat or drink, or whatever you do, do everything for the glory of God.[g] [32] Give no offense[h] to Jews or Greeks or the church of God, [33] just as I also try to please everyone in everything, not seeking my own benefit, but the benefit of many,[i] so that they may be saved. [1] Imitate me, as I also imitate Christ.[j]

INSTRUCTIONS ABOUT HEAD COVERINGS

[2] Now I praise you[D] because you remember me in everything and hold fast to the traditions[k] just as I delivered[l] them to you. [3] But I want you to know that Christ is the head[m] of every man, and the man is the head of the woman,[E,n] and God is the head of Christ.[o] [4] Every man who prays or prophesies with something on his head dishonors[p] his head. [5] Every woman who prays or prophesies with her head uncovered dishonors her head, since that is one and the same as having her head shaved.[q] [6] For if a woman doesn't cover her head, she should have her hair cut off. But if it is disgraceful for a woman to have her hair cut off or her head shaved, let her head be covered.

[7] A man should not cover his head, because he is the image[r] and glory of God.[s] So too, woman is the glory of man. [8] For man did not come from woman, but woman came from man.[t] [9] Neither was man created for the sake of woman, but woman for the sake of man. [10] This is why a woman should have a symbol of authority on

[a] 10:24 Mk 10:45; Php 2:4
[b] 10:26 Mk 13:19
[c] Ps 24:1
[d] 10:28 Lk 10:8
[e] 10:29 Lk 6:37
[f] 10:31 Mk 8:6; Rm 1:8
[g] 10:31 Mk 10:37; Lk 9:32; Jn 17:24; 2Co 3:18; 2Pt 3:18
[h] 10:32 Ac 24:16; Php 1:10

[i] 10:33 Mk 10:45
[j] 11:1 Php 2:5; 1Pt 2:21
[k] 11:2 2Th 2:15; 3:6
[l] Jd 3
[m] 11:3 Eph 1:22; 4:15; Col 1:18; 2:10,19
[n] Gn 3:16; Eph 5:23
[o] 1Co 3:23
[p] 11:4 1Pt 3:16
[q] 11:5 Dt 21:11-12
[r] 11:7 Gn 1:27
[s] Mk 10:37; Lk 9:32; Jn 17:24; 2Co 3:18; 2Pt 3:18
[t] 11:8 Gn 2:21-23; 1Tm 2:13

[A] 10:23 Other mss add *for me*   [B] 10:26 Ps 24:1   [C] 10:28 Other mss add *"For the earth is the Lord's and all that is in it."*   [D] 11:2 Other mss add brothers,   [E] 11:3 Or *the husband is the head of the wife*

---

that the exercise of freedom must be tempered and regulated by the principle of love. We are called to seek **the good of** others, not our own (10:24).

10:25 The point is that Corinthian believers didn't need to research whether or not a piece of **meat** had been part of a pagan sacrifice prior to being delivered to the **market**.

10:28-29 If a believer knowingly eats food sacrificed to idols, someone might interpret it as a compromise of their faith and a participation in idolatry. This could hinder some from coming to Christ, and it could injure a weak believer's **conscience**.

10:32–11:1 Paul exhorts the Corinthians to **imitate** his example as he imitates **Christ**, giving no unnecessary **offense to Jews or Greeks or the church** (10:32; 11:1). Why? Because God's reputation is more important than our personal preferences! The gospel is at stake. Eternity hangs in the balance! Let us not seek our **own benefit** but seek to compassionately, righteously, and responsibly pursue the well-being of others **so that they may be saved** (10:33).

11:3 When the apostle says, **the man is the head of the woman,** he's not saying that every man is the head of every woman. Rather, here he is speaking of the headship of the husband over the wife (see Eph 5:22-33; Col 3:18-19). Paul is also not saying that the husband is superior to the wife. As the Father and Son are equal in essence while different in function, so the husband and wife are equal as human beings and in their spiritual standing before God (see Gal 3:28-29) but different in their roles in marriage. The wife is called to submit to her husband's spiritual leadership—though, of course, she is never to follow her husband into sin or to submit to abuse, since her commitment to Christ is to transcend her commitment to her husband (see the notes on Eph 5:22-33; 1 Pet 3:1-7).

Importantly, the man is not autonomous either. He is also called to submit: **Christ is the head of every man.** He is not free to lead his wife and children as he deems fit; instead, he is to lead in full submission to the lordship of Christ. When God's people operate within this divine order, there is covering and protection. But, like a car, we're in danger of crashing when we get out of alignment.

11:5-6 Paul argues that if either the wife or husband (see 11:4) rejected the common cultural distinctions between men and women, it would signal a rejection of God's design. But apparently, women in the Corinthian church were expressing their own version of women's liberation, rebelling against any sense of submission to their husbands' spiritual authority by refusing to wear a head covering during worship. Paul said if a woman disregarded this male-female role distinction by uncovering her head, she might as well go all the way and shave **her head**—and thus look like a man! To reject submission to authority is to reject God's prescribed order.

11:7-9 Paul is not talking about a distinction in essence between men and women but a distinction in function. The husband glorifies God through his kingdom role as head, and the wife glorifies God by fulfilling her kingdom role to help her husband (see the notes on Gen 2:18-25).

11:10 Because of the angels is Paul's way of saying that if a woman operates out of alignment with God's will (uncovered), either in the home or in the church (see 14:34-35; 1 Tim 2:11-14), she will lose angelic assistance. Angels serve as God's heavenly messengers, helping to bring about his will in our lives. But when a wife rebels against his revealed will, she will lose divine support. The same is true for the husband (see 1 Pet 3:7).

*a*11:12 Ps 104:24; Rv 3:14
*b*11:13 Jn 5:22-30
*c*11:14 Mt 28:20; Ac 4:2;
2Tm 4:11
*d*2Co 6:8
*e*11:15 Php 3:19
*f*11:19 2Pt 2:1
*g*11:20 Mt 26:26-29; Mk
14:22-25; Lk 22:14-20; 1Co
10:14-22

*h*11:23 Jd 3
*i*11:24 Lk 22:19
*j*11:25 Lk 22:20
*k*Jn 6:54
*l*11:26 Php 2:8; 3:10
*m*Mk 8:38
*n*11:29 Mk 12:40; 1Jn 5:16

her head, because of the angels. **11** In the Lord, however, woman is not independent of man, and man is not independent of woman. **12** For just as woman came from man, so man comes through woman, and all things come from God.*a*

13 Judge*b* for yourselves: Is it proper for a woman to pray to God with her head uncovered? **14** Does not even nature itself teach*c* you that if a man has long hair it is a disgrace*d* to him, **15** but that if a woman has long hair, it is her glory?*e* For her hair is given to her*A* as a covering. **16** If anyone wants to argue about this, we have no other*B* custom, nor do the churches of God.

THE LORD'S SUPPER

17 Now in giving this instruction I do not praise you, since you come together not for the better but for the worse. **18** For to begin with, I hear that when you come together as a church there are divisions among you, and in part I believe it. **19** Indeed, it is necessary that there be factions*f* among you, so that those who are approved may be recognized among you. **20** When you come together, then, it is not to eat the Lord's Supper.*g* **21** For at the meal, each one eats his own supper.*c* So one person is hungry while another gets drunk! **22** Don't

you have homes in which to eat and drink? Or do you despise the church of God and humiliate those who have nothing? What should I say to you? Should I praise you? I do not praise you in this matter!

23 For I received from the Lord what I also passed on to you:*h* On the night when he was betrayed, the Lord Jesus took bread, **24** and when he had given thanks, broke it, and said,*D* "This is my body, which is*E* for you. Do this in remembrance of me."*i*

25 In the same way also he took the cup, after supper, and said, "This cup is the new covenant*j* in my blood.*k* Do this, as often as you drink it, in remembrance of me." **26** For as often as you eat this bread and drink the cup, you proclaim the Lord's death*l* until he comes.*m*

SELF-EXAMINATION

27 So then, whoever eats the bread or drinks the cup of the Lord in an unworthy manner will be guilty of sin against the body*F* and blood of the Lord. **28** Let a person examine himself; in this way let him eat the bread and drink from the cup. **29** For whoever eats and drinks without recognizing the body,*G* eats and drinks judgment*n* on himself. **30** This is why many are sick and ill among you, and many have

*A*11:15 Other mss omit *to her*   *B*11:16 Or *no such*   *C*11:21 Or *eats his own supper ahead of others*   *D*11:24 Other mss add *"Take, eat.*   *E*11:24 Other mss add *broken*   *F*11:27 Lit *be guilty of the body*   *G*11:29 Other mss read *drinks unworthily, not discerning the Lord's body*

11:11-12 Men and women should view themselves as mutually dependent. God has demonstrated through his creation design that neither can do without the other, and neither is superior.

11:13-16 **Even nature itself**, Paul argues, confirms the distinction between men and women. In his day, women wore **long hair**, and men wore short hair. To do otherwise was disgraceful (11:14-15) because men ought to be distinguished from women. We should not do anything to blur the lines between the two. God designed and created men and women equal, yet different. And as he concludes this topic, Paul maintains that this is not merely his own opinion. All of **the churches of God** submit to the teaching that gender distinctions are to be evidenced visibly (11:16). Our humble submission to divine design and the theological, covenantal kingdom principle of headship frees God to accomplish his work in our lives.

11:17-22 In other words, what was supposed to be an intimate time of worship and remembrance had turned into a circus. There was nothing about the warped way the Corinthians celebrated the sacrificial death of Christ that Paul could **praise** (11:22).

11:23-25 The Lord's Supper offers a uniquely powerful time of spiritual intimacy with the Lord in the same way that physical intimacy

in marriage serves as a special time of intimacy between a couple. It is a special sharing with Christ beyond the normal relationship, enabling access to heaven at a deeper level. Communion is also designed to demonstrate the unity of the church at a common meal with the Savior.

11:26 When the church of Christ gathers to partake of the Lord's Supper, we evangelistically **proclaim** his sacrifice to the world to invite them to trust in Christ for forgiveness and eternal life. We triumphantly proclaim it to the devil and the demonic realm (see Col 2:15; 1 Pet 3:18-19) to remind them of their defeat and their coming judgment. And we gloriously proclaim it to one another to recognize anew the victory over sin and the spiritual authority that Christ won for us on the cross.

11:27 Paul isn't referring to personal worthiness. We are all sinful; no person is worthy of salvation. That's why we need God's grace. Rather, Paul is talking about the illegitimate **manner** in which they participated in Communion. They were treating something sacred as common. This special moment of remembrance and intimacy with the Lord and his people had lost its solemn significance because of the self-centered way they engaged in it. We are not required to come to the Lord's Supper without any sin in our lives.

If we had to be perfect, we'd never be able to partake. But we must take it seriously, recognizing its spiritual and physical significance, as well as the principle of the unity of his body (the church), which this ordinance is designed to encourage.

11:28-29 How we relate to Christ's **body** affects how God relates to us. To treat it with anything other than respect is to eat and drink **judgment on** oneself (11:29), which brings to mind the case of Ananias and Sapphira (see Acts 5:1-11). Unless you recognize that the Lord's Supper represents Christ's victory on the cross and unless you are also in fellowship with his spiritual family, the Communion moment that's intended to bless you could actually hurt you.

11:30-32 Paul explains that the Corinthian believers had been experiencing such divine judgment. Their selfish actions around the Lord's Table had resulted in **many** of them becoming **ill** or falling **asleep** (11:30; i.e., dying). Since they had not **judged** their own actions **properly**, God had severely **disciplined** them (11:31-32).

The Bible is clear that suffering and poor health are not necessarily a result of personal sin. Job, for instance, was a righteous man who suffered much. A man whom Jesus healed was not born blind because of anyone's sin but "so that God's works might be

a 11:30 Jn 11:11; Ac 7:60; 1Th 4:13-15
b 11:32 Jn 5:22-30
c Mt 12:41; Jn 5:22
d 11:34 1Co 4:19

e 12:2 Ac 8:32; 1Co 14:10; 2Pt 2:16
f 1Co 8:4
g 12:4 Rm 12:6; 1Co 14:1; Eph 4:8; Heb 2:4; 1Pt 4:10
h 12:7 Jms 4:5
i 12:8-10 Rm 12:7-8; Eph 4:11; 1Pt 4:11
j 12:8 1Co 2:6-7
k 12:9 Lk 13:32; Ac 4:22,30; 10:38

⚜ KINGDOM LIVING ⚜
CHURCH
The Body of Christ

As followers of Jesus Christ our Lord, our spiritual well-being depends on our connection with Christ through his body, the church. In 1 Corinthians 12, the word *body* appears eighteen times as an illustration of how believers are to act in concert with each other as the expression of Christ on earth. Paul's conclusion in this chapter is that we must be connected to each other in order to be what God wants us to be and to live with the kingdom authority we have been delegated to carry out.

In the New Testament, the human body became the primary picture representing the church. At the end of 1 Corinthians 12:12, Paul writes, "So also is Christ." What the human body is, so also is Christ's body, the church. There are many different parts doing many different things within a body, but those parts comprise one unit. The reason your physical body is one is that all the parts are connected. If you cut off a finger,

the finger dies. If you want a severed appendage to function, you must get it reconnected quickly. Connection is absolutely necessary for life. Likewise, any time a part of the body decides to go off and do its own thing, that is a clue that the body is not well.

Christ's body, the church, is not merely an organization, but an organism. We can create a robot and have organization. The parts connect to each other so that it works. But the problem with the robot is that it has no life. A human body, by contrast, has organization that makes it function, but it also is a living, breathing organism. Connection with the body of believers is essential if we are to exist as the divine legislative authority on earth that the church has been created to be.

FOR THE NEXT CHURCH
KINGDOM LIVING LESSON SEE PAGE 1392.

---

fallen asleep.*a* **31** If we were properly judging ourselves, we would not be judged, **32** but when we are judged*b* by the Lord, we are disciplined, so that we may not be condemned*c* with the world.

33 Therefore, my brothers and sisters, when you come together to eat, welcome one another.^A **34** If anyone is hungry, he should eat at home, so that when you gather together you will not come under judgment. I will give instructions about the other matters whenever I come.*d*

DIVERSITY OF SPIRITUAL GIFTS

12 Now concerning spiritual gifts:^B brothers and sisters, I do not want you to be unaware. **2** You know that when you

were pagans, you used to be enticed and led astray by mute*e* idols.*f* **3** Therefore I want you to know that no one speaking by the Spirit of God says, "Jesus is cursed," and no one can say, "Jesus is Lord," except by the Holy Spirit.

4 Now there are different gifts,*g* but the same Spirit. **5** There are different ministries, but the same Lord. **6** And there are different activities, but the same God produces each gift in each person. **7** A manifestation of the Spirit is given to each person*h* for the common good: **8** to one*i* is given a message of wisdom*j* through the Spirit, to another, a message of knowledge by the same Spirit, **9** to another, faith by the same Spirit, to another, gifts of healing*k* by the one Spirit, **10** to another, the performing

---

^A 11:33 Or *wait for one another*   ^B 12:1 Or *spiritual things,* or *spiritual people*

---

displayed in him" (John 9:3). Nevertheless, sin *can* result in suffering, sickness, and even death. That's what had happened to many of the Christians in Corinth. So examine yourself before you partake of the Lord's Supper. Ask, Do I recognize that it points to the judgment of God, the forgiveness of sin, the defeat of Satan, the victory of grace, and the unity of the church? Do I expect God's blessings to flow to me through Communion, while I ignore known sin and disunity in my life?

11:33-34 Approach the Lord's Table with reverence—not only for him but also for his spiritual family—and receive his blessing, which can include physical healing (Isa 53:5; Jas 5:15).

12:2-3 The essential feature of all those who have trusted in Jesus Christ is that they are indwelt by the Holy Spirit. Before coming to faith in Christ, the Corinthian believers were **pagans . . . enticed and led astray by mute idols** (12:2). But by the power of the Spirit, they were enabled to turn to God and say, **Jesus is Lord** (12:3).

12:4-7 Just as the church of Jesus Christ is made up of a variety of people of both genders and of different ethnicities, nationalities, languages, and ages, it is made up of individuals who receive from God a variety of spiritual **gifts** (12:4). A *spiritual gift* is a God-given and empowered ability to serve him in ways that benefit others. Our variety is to be

unified in submission to our King's agenda for the good of all. We must not use our spiritual gifts for selfish ends, promoting division among God's people.

12:8-11 Notice that **one** Christian is given this gift, and **another** Christian is given that gift (12:8-10); thus, no one obtains a spiritual monopoly. Rather, within the church, we are dependent on one another for the exercise of all these different gifts. Furthermore, **one and the same Spirit** distributes **to each person as he wills** (12:11). You don't choose the spiritual gift of your preference. The Spirit gives as he sees fit. He knows what you and his kingdom need better than you do, so trust him to supply you with the spiritual

Video Devotional

"UNITING THE BODY OF CHRIST"

Unity in the church invites God's presence into our assembly and grants the authority Christ died to provide.

*a*12:10 Ac 19:11
*b*1Co 13:2
*c*1Jn 4:1-3
*d*12:12 Jn 11:52
*e*Eph 4:4
*f*12:13 Gl 3:28; Eph 2:13-18;
Col 3:11

*g*12:18 Ps 143:10; Pr 16:9;
Jn 5:30; Gl 1:4; Eph 1:9;
1Jn 2:17
*h*12:23 Mk 6:4; 1Pt 2:7
*i*12:25 1Co 1:10
*j*12:27 Eph 1:23; Col 1:18
*k*12:28 Mt 16:18; 1Co 14:4;
Rv 1:4
*l*Eph 4:11; Jms 3:1

of miracles,*a* to another, prophecy,*b* to another, distinguishing between spirits,*c* to another, different kinds of tongues,*A* to another, interpretation of tongues. **11** One and the same Spirit is active in all these, distributing to each person as he wills.

APPLICATION QUESTIONS

READ 1 CORINTHIANS 12:1-12

– What gifts have you been given that can be used in the church?

UNITY YET DIVERSITY IN THE BODY

12 For just as the body is one*d* and has many parts, and all the parts of that body, though many, are one body — so also is Christ.*e* **13** For we were all baptized by*B* one Spirit into one body — whether Jews or Greeks, whether slaves or free — and we were all given one Spirit to drink.*f* **14** Indeed, the body is not one part but many. **15** If the foot should say, "Because I'm not a hand, I don't belong to the body," it is not for that reason any less a part of the body. **16** And if the ear should say, "Because I'm not an eye, I don't belong to the body," it is not for that reason any less a part of the body. **17** If the whole body were an eye, where would the hearing be? If the whole body were an ear, where would the sense of smell be? **18** But as it is, God has arranged each one of the parts

in the body just as he wanted.*g* **19** And if they were all the same part, where would the body be? **20** As it is, there are many parts, but one body. **21** The eye cannot say to the hand, "I don't need you!" Or again, the head can't say to the feet, "I don't need you!" **22** On the contrary, those parts of the body that are weaker are indispensable. **23** And those parts of the body that we consider less honorable,*h* we clothe these with greater honor, and our unrespectable parts are treated with greater respect, **24** which our respectable parts do not need.

Instead, God has put the body together, giving greater honor to the less honorable, **25** so that there would be no division*i* in the body, but that the members would have the same concern for each other. **26** So if one member suffers, all the members suffer with it; if one member is honored, all the members rejoice with it.

27 Now you are the body of Christ,*j* and individual members of it. **28** And God has appointed these in the church:*k* first apostles, second prophets, third teachers,*l* next miracles,*m* then gifts of healing,*n* helping, administrating, various kinds of tongues.*C* **29** Are all apostles? Are all prophets? Are all teachers? Do all do miracles? **30** Do all have gifts of healing? Do all speak in other tongues? Do all interpret?*o* **31** But desire*p* the greater gifts. And I will show you an even better way.

*m*12:28 Mk 13:22   *n*1Co 12:9   *o*12:30 Lk 24:27   *p*12:31 Nm 25:13; Jms 4:2

^A^12:10 languages   ^B^12:13 Or *with*, or *in*   ^C^12:28 languages, also in v. 30

---

ability with which you can best serve him and bless others.
12:12-14 A human **body** best illustrates what the church is: **many parts** that are **one** (12:12). Not only does the body consist of a variety of external parts but also many complex internal systems, including the circulatory, respiratory, nervous, skeletal, and digestive systems. Nevertheless (when working properly) all of the parts and systems function together for the good of the whole. **Indeed, the body** of Christ, the church, **is not one part but many** (12:14).

Though the Corinthians consisted of **Jews or Greeks . . . slaves or free,** they were all made a part of the same entity. Paul elaborates, noting that believers are **baptized by one Spirit into one body** (12:13). The Greek verb *baptizō* means "to immerse." It could be used to describe the action of immersing a cloth into a dye to change its color. The baptism of the cloth in such a case brings about a transformation that changes its visible identity. In the same way, the Spirit transforms all believers for a new way of life that is to be done together. They are baptized "into one body"—the body of Christ, the family of God (12:13).

12:15-16 What happens when Christians operate on their own, when they disconnect from the church and do not benefit others? Paul describes the absurdity of this by again using the human body analogy. If **a hand** or an **ear** says, **I don't belong to the body,** breakdown results. Because of the loss of use of the hand or ear, the body is left incomplete. Moreover, the severed hand or ear does not benefit from the rest of the body.

12:17-20 No single person in the church is more valuable than any other. In the same way that God designed the human body with each part functioning exactly as he intended, so also **God has arranged each** part of **the body** of Christ **just as he wanted** (12:18). The one who created you gave you the spiritual gift that he wanted you to have. To insist that you want to serve the church in a different capacity than what God intended is like an ear insisting on being an eye. Not only is such a stance futile, but it is also a prideful rejection of your King's wise and perfect plan for you.

12:21-22 Often we place too much emphasis on members and ministries that are visible. But this wrongly equates visibility with value. Not every member has the same gift, the same role, or the same level of responsibil-

ity. But every member matters. Those whose ministries go on behind the scenes are vital to the health of the church.

12:23-24 Though private parts are not displayed for the world to see, they perform indispensable functions. So it is in the body of Christ.

12:26 A little toe may seem fairly insignificant. But if you stub yours, it will shut you down! The pain affects the whole body. Indeed, **if one member** of the body **suffers, all the members suffer with it.** Therefore, don't be concerned only for your own needs within Christ's body. As Paul says elsewhere, "Rejoice with those who rejoice; weep with those who weep" (Rom 12:15). This is simply an application of the second greatest commandment: "Love your neighbor as yourself" (Matt 22:39).

12:27-31 Paul mentions several offices within the church for which individuals are spiritually equipped. Their ranking (**first . . . second . . . third**) has to do with the level of the office (12:28). The **apostles** were those who had seen the risen Jesus and were appointed by him as foundational leaders to teach doctrine to the church. The **prophets** communicate God's revelation to God's people. **Teachers** explain the meaning of God's truth (12:28).

❧ Questions & Answers ❧

Q Why do you think the church is crucial to the spiritual growth of a Christian, and why, in particular, should we commit to membership in a local church?

A Whenever people got saved in the New Testament era, they were connected to a local body of believers. Connectivity to a local church is critical and commanded (see Heb 10:24-25) because of the illustration that Paul gives of the church in 1 Corinthians 12:12-31. He defines the church as a body in which all members are to be attached. Attachment of the members brings life to the body, and the body brings life to the members. If you were to cut off a hand, the hand couldn't function as intended because it will have lost the blood flow that gives life. Membership is formal attachment. Our body parts aren't casually attached; they are formally attached.

But notice this: Parts are formally attached for functional purposes. The hand doesn't simply hang there; it grabs stuff. The feet aren't merely attached; they move the body. The members

of the body are to serve and improve the life of the body. Members of a local church are to serve God by serving the church and improving the lives of others. In turn, their own lives are improved as well.

Sociologists of religion in the US have noted the rise of the religious "nones," those who claim no identification with a religion or no formal affiliation with a church or denomination. At the same time, these people speak of their love for Jesus and appreciation for spirituality. Yet people who claim to be spiritual and love Christ—yet are unattached to a local church, his body—are not obeying God's command for attachment. Now, part of this is the church's fault, because sometimes local churches have not been what they ought to be. As a result, people are hindered from joining. But that simply means you need to find the real deal—a faithful, Bible-teaching church—and not merely exempt yourself from this essential entity that God has established.

FOR THE NEXT Q&A, SEE PAGE 1360.

FOR THE NEXT Q&A, SEE PAGE 1360.

Video Devotional
"HORIZONTAL JESUS"

www.bhpublishinggroup.com/qr/te/46-13

Loving others horizontally is a reflection of Christ's hands and feet to humanity.

a 13:1 Jn 13:35; 1Jn 4:7-12
b Mt 10:9
c 13:2 1Co 14:1,3-6,22-39; Eph 4:11; 1Th 5:20
d Mt 17:20

e 13:4 1Th 5:14
f Nm 25:13; Gl 4:17
g 1Co 4:6
h 13:5 Mk 10:45; Php 2:4
i Ac 17:16
j 13:6 Ps 119:142; Jn 8:14; 14:6
k 13:7 Jms 1:12
l 13:8 Mt 7:25,27; Lk 6:49; 11:17; 13:4; 16:17; Ac 15:16; Heb 11:30; Rv 11:13; 16:19

LOVE: THE SUPERIOR WAY

13 If I speak human or angelic tongues[A] but do not have love,[a] I am a noisy gong[b] or a clanging cymbal. ² If I have the gift of prophecy[c] and understand all mysteries and all knowledge, and if I have all faith so that I can move mountains[d] but do not have love, I am nothing. ³ And if I give away all my possessions, and if I give over my body in order to boast[B] but do not have love, I gain nothing.

⁴ Love is patient,[e] love is kind. Love does not envy,[f] is not boastful, is not arrogant,[g] ⁵ is not rude, is not self-seeking,[h] is not irritable,[i] and does not keep a record of wrongs. ⁶ Love finds no joy in unrighteousness but rejoices in the truth.[j] ⁷ It bears all things, believes all things, hopes all things, endures[k] all things.

⁸ Love never ends.[l] But as for prophecies, they will come to an end; as for tongues, they will cease; as for knowledge, it will

---

[A] 13:1 languages, also in v. 8   [B] 13:3 Other mss read *body to be burned*

Notice that **various kinds of tongues** are mentioned last on the list (12:28). And since it comes last in the list, it should not be given such supreme importance as some have assigned it. Moreover, observe that Paul asks, **Do all speak in other tongues?** (12:30). This question implies that not all Christians have been given this gift; therefore, it is not a super-Christian status indicator or the only sign that someone has been baptized by the Holy Spirit. Paul's instruction regarding tongues is written to a carnal, divided church (see 3:1-3). Thus, the exercise of the gift of tongues is not necessarily a sign of spiritual maturity.

Paul's questions in 12:29-30 indicate that no one receives every gift. But each

receives the gift that God intends each person to receive. Nevertheless, Paul says it is not wrong to **desire the greater gifts** to be manifested in the church (12:31)—that is, the higher-ranking gifts (if God chooses to grant them)—in order to provide the broadest edification to the church.

13:1 Angels only spoke human languages in Scripture.

13:2-3 No matter how visible and effective my **gift** or ministry may be, if I **do not have love** for my fellow Christians, **I am nothing** and **I gain nothing** because spiritual gifts are for the benefit of others. The gift does not matter when love is missing.

13:4-5 Biblical **love** is the decision (not merely a feeling) to compassionately (out of concern

for someone else), righteously (based on God's standards), and sacrificially (giving to meet a need) seek the well-being of another. Notice each of the characteristics of love: it is **patient . . . kind . . . not [envious] . . . not arrogant . . . not irritable**. These things are only possible when we put others before ourselves.

13:6 Love does not affirm someone in their sin or their false beliefs because **love finds no joy in unrighteousness but rejoices in the truth**.

13:7 Love does not quit; it endures through thick and thin.

13:8-10 As we mature spiritually (i.e., **when the perfect comes**), we are less dependent on the gift of prophecy and tongues. Ultimately, when we experience the joyous intimacy of

a13:12 1Jn 3:2
bPr 2:6; Jn 17:3; 1Jn 4:8
c1Co 8:3; Gl 4:9
d13:13 1Th 1:3
e14:2 1Co 12:10
f14:6 1Pt 4:13
g14:7 Rv 5:8; 14:2; 15:2

h14:8 Nm 10:9; Is 58:1; Jr 4:19; Ezk 33:3-6; Jl 2:1
i14:12 Nm 25:13; Gl 1:14
jPs 51:11; Lk 11:34; Jn 1:33; Ac 2:4; Rm 8:9; Gl 5:25; Ti 3:5; 1Jn 4:1; Rv 3:22
k14:14 Ps 51:12
lGl 5:22; Ti 3:14
m14:16 Ps 72:19; Rv 22:21
n14:18 Rm 1:8
o14:19 Mt 12:37
p14:20 Ps 131:2; Is 28:9; Mt 18:3; Rm 16:19; Eph 4:14; Heb 5:12-13

come to an end. [9] For we know in part, and we prophesy in part, [10] but when the perfect comes, the partial will come to an end. [11] When I was a child, I spoke like a child, I thought like a child, I reasoned like a child. When I became a man, I put aside childish things. [12] For now we see only a reflection[A] as in a mirror, but then face to face.[a] Now I know in part, but then I will know fully,[b] as I am fully known.[c] [13] Now these three remain: faith, hope,[d] and love — but the greatest of these is love.

PROPHECY: A SUPERIOR GIFT

14 Pursue love and desire spiritual gifts, and especially that you may prophesy. [2] For the person who speaks in another tongue[B,e] is not speaking to people but to God, since no one understands him; he speaks mysteries in the Spirit.[c] [3] On the other hand, the person who prophesies speaks to people for their strengthening,[D] encouragement, and consolation. [4] The person who speaks in another tongue builds himself up, but the one who prophesies builds up the church. [5] I wish all of you spoke in other tongues,[E] but even more that you prophesied. The person who prophesies is greater than the person who speaks in tongues, unless he interprets so that the church may be built up.

[6] So now, brothers and sisters, if I come to you speaking in other tongues, how will I benefit you unless I speak to you with a revelation[f] or knowledge or prophecy or teaching? [7] Even lifeless instruments that produce sounds — whether flute or harp[g] — if they don't make a distinction in the notes, how will what is played on the flute

or harp be recognized? [8] In fact, if the bugle makes an unclear sound, who will prepare for battle?[h] [9] In the same way, unless you use your tongue for intelligible speech, how will what is spoken be known? For you will be speaking into the air. [10] There are doubtless many different kinds of languages in the world, none is without meaning. [11] Therefore, if I do not know the meaning of the language, I will be a foreigner[F] to the speaker, and the speaker will be a foreigner to me. [12] So also you — since you are zealous[i] for spiritual gifts, [G,j] seek to excel in building up the church.

[13] Therefore the person who speaks in another tongue should pray that he can interpret. [14] For if I pray in another tongue, my spirit[k] prays, but my understanding is unfruitful.[l] [15] What then? I will pray with the spirit, and I will also pray with my understanding. I will sing praise with the spirit, and I will also sing praise with my understanding. [16] Otherwise, if you praise with the spirit,[H] how will the outsider[I] say "Amen"[m] at your giving of thanks, since he does not know what you are saying? [17] For you may very well be giving thanks, but the other person is not being built up. [18] I thank[n] God that I speak in other tongues more than all of you; [19] yet in the church I would rather speak five words[o] with my understanding, in order to teach others also, than ten thousand words in another tongue.

[20] Brothers and sisters, don't be childish in your thinking, but be infants in regard to evil and adult in your thinking.[p] [21] It is written in the law,

**I will speak to this people
by people of other tongues**

A13:12 Lit *we see indirectly*　B14:2 language, also in vv. 4,13,14,19,26,27　C14:2 Or *in spirit*, or *in his spirit*　D14:3 Lit *building up*　E14:5 languages, also in vv. 6,18,21,22,23,39　F14:11 Gk *barbaros*, or *barbarian*　G14:12 Lit *zealous of spirits*　H14:16 Or *praise by the Spirit*　I14:16 Lit *the one filling the place of the uninformed*

God's presence, spiritual gifts will come to an end because we will no longer need them. But not love. **Love never ends** (13:8).

13:12 Even **as I am fully known** to God now, one day **I will know fully** reality as God meant me to know it. All will be made clear.

13:13 In eternity, you will no longer need **faith** because you will have sight. You will no longer need **hope** because your expectations and anticipations will all have been met and exceeded. But the **love** that will characterize our eternal relationship with God will continue since "God is love" (1 John 4:8).

14:1 **Love** is superior to **spiritual gifts** and enables one to understand and utilize spiritual gifts rightly.

14:2-5 It's important to understand what Paul means regarding the gift of speaking **in another tongue** (14:2). Though some inter-

pret this to mean "a heavenly language," the New Testament evidence favors the meaning "human language." Note the key passage in Acts 2:4-11. The apostles were "filled with the Holy Spirit and began to speak in different tongues" (2:4). The context makes clear that these "tongues" (2:4, 11) were actually various native languages (2:6, 8) spoken by those who came to Jerusalem for Pentecost.

14:6-12 Shared understanding is necessary for communication to be meaningful. Thus, Paul wants their zeal **for spiritual gifts** to be matched by an equal zeal for **building up the church** (14:12) so that the Spirit could do his work among them.

How do you view the spiritual gift that you have received from the Holy Spirit? Is it a tool for winning attention, admiration, and praise from others? Or do you consider your gift to

be an opportunity to glorify God and lovingly build up your brothers and sisters in Christ? Also, unintelligible and uninterpreted praying and singing are for private, not public, use.

14:18-19 Though Paul himself spoke **in other tongues more than all** the Corinthians, he didn't consider it a badge of honor to be flaunted (14:18). He preferred to utter **five** comprehensible **words** that edified others, **than ten thousand** incoherent **words** that benefited no one (14:19). May God grant that our convictions be the same as Paul's.

14:20 Excitement about exercising exotic spiritual gifts that no one can understand is immature. A more mature stance is to exercise gifts for the good of others.

14:21-22 Paul quotes from Isaiah 28:11-12, which recounts the defeat of the rebellious and unbelieving Israelites at the hands of

God Is Real

ICAN'T TELL YOU THE NUMBER of times that people have come up to me to ask, "Is God real?" Even in church, it seems that some men and women have spent years reading and singing about him, but aren't really sure if God even exists. Others have become weary of the burdens of daily living and have thrown in the towel as far as their commitment to God is concerned. They think, "He might exist, but he doesn't seem that interested in me or my troubles."

For many of us, reality is rooted in our personal experiences. Therefore, we assume that what we can see, hear, taste, touch, and smell is more trustworthy than anything else. And since we can't see God with our eyes or hear him with our ears, how can we be sure he's even real?

God wants you to *know* that there is a reality beyond what you perceive through your five senses. In 1 Corinthians 13:12, Paul writes, "For now we see only a reflection as in a mirror, but then face to face. Now I know in part, but then I will know fully, as I am fully known." In other words, our experiences today pale in comparison to the experiences that await us when we spend eternity with God.

That isn't to say we can't experience God in a personal way each day before then. God reveals himself to all of creation, and he greatly desires to have a personal relationship with you. The benefits of experiencing him are immeasurable. God gives us spiritual wisdom to prevent us from making wrong turns on life's roads. He gives us spiritual deliverance from life's crises. He gives formidable power to all those who feel worn out and want to give up so that they don't have to be owned by their problems.

If you are struggling, I pray that God will strengthen you, fill you with his wisdom, and deliver you from crisis. This is how we can experience God's fullness every day. To those who submit themselves to obeying him and dedicate themselves to hearing his voice through the reading of his Word comes a greater degree of closeness to him.

a 14:21 Is 28:11-12
b 14:25 Is 45:14; Zch 8:23
c 14:26 1Co 12:10
d 14:29 1Jn 4:1

e 14:31 Lk 16:25
f 14:33 Eph 6:18
g 14:34 1Tm 2:11-12; 1Pt 3:1
h 14:35 Mt 1:19; 1Pt 3:1
i 14:39 Nm 25:13; Gl 4:17
j 14:40 Rm 13:13
k 15:1 Pr 24:16
l 15:2 Gl 4:11; Heb 6:8
m 15:3 Jd 3
n 1Co 8:11
o Mt 26:54; 1Pt 1:20
p 15:4 Mt 27:59-60;
Mk 15:46; Lk 23:53; Jn
19:41-42
q 15:4 1Th 4:14
r Ps 16:10; Is 53:10; Hs 6:2;
Mt 12:40; Jn 2:22; Ac 2:25-
32; 13:33-35; 26:22-23

and by the lips of foreigners,
and even then, they will not listen
to me,[A,a]

says the Lord. [22] Speaking in other tongues, then, is intended as a sign, not for believers but for unbelievers, while prophecy is not for unbelievers but for believers. [23] If, therefore, the whole church assembles together and all are speaking in other tongues and people who are outsiders or unbelievers come in, will they not say that you are out of your minds? [24] But if all are prophesying and some unbeliever or outsider comes in, he is convicted by all and is called to account by all. [25] The secrets of his heart will be revealed, and as a result he will fall facedown and worship God, proclaiming, "God is really among you."[b]

ORDER IN CHURCH MEETINGS

[26] What then, brothers and sisters? Whenever you come together, each one[B] has a hymn, a teaching, a revelation, another tongue, or an interpretation.[c] Everything is to be done for building up. [27] If anyone speaks in another tongue, there are to be only two, or at the most three, each in turn, and let someone interpret. [28] But if there is no interpreter, that person is to keep silent in the church and speak to himself and God. [29] Two or three prophets should speak, and the others should evaluate.[d] [30] But if something has been revealed to another person sitting there, the first prophet should be silent. [31] For you can all prophesy one by one, so that

everyone may learn and everyone may be encouraged.[e] [32] And the prophets' spirits are subject to the prophets, [33] since God is not a God of disorder but of peace.

As in all the churches of the saints,[f] [34] the women[c] should be silent in the churches,[g] for they are not permitted to speak, but are to submit themselves, as the law also says. [35] If they want to learn something, let them ask their own husbands[h] at home, since it is disgraceful for a woman to speak in the church. [36] Or did the word of God originate from you, or did it come to you only?

[37] If anyone thinks he is a prophet or spiritual, he should recognize that what I write to you is the Lord's command. [38] If anyone ignores this, he will be ignored.[D] [39] So then, my brothers and sisters, be eager[f] to prophesy, and do not forbid speaking in other tongues. [40] But everything is to be done decently[j] and in order.

RESURRECTION ESSENTIAL TO THE GOSPEL

15 Now I want to make clear for you, brothers and sisters, the gospel I preached to you, which you received, on which you have taken your stand[k] [2] and by which you are being saved, if you hold to the message I preached to you — unless you believed in vain.[l] [3] For I passed on to you[m] as most important what I also received: that Christ died[n] for our sins according to the Scriptures,[o] [4] that he was buried,[p] that he was raised on the third day[q] according to the Scriptures,[r] [5] and

---

A 14:21 Is 28:11-12   B 14:26 Other mss add *of you*   C 14:34 Other mss read *your women*   D 14:38 Other mss read *he should be ignored*

---

the Assyrian army that spoke a language the people couldn't understand. Based on this, he says, **Speaking in other tongues . . . is intended as a sign . . . for unbelievers**—that is, a sign of judgment—while **prophecy** is **for believers**.

14:26-28 Still concerned that the church be edified, Paul next moves to the issue of orderliness in the gathered church. His point is that a coherent process should be followed.

14:32-33 That **the prophets' spirits are subject to the prophets** means they must exercise self-control in giving prophecy because **God is not a God of disorder but of peace** (14:33). These last words are important for both individual believers and the church as a whole to apply. Since "God is not a God of disorder" (since he is unified in his triune nature), then he expects his people to do everything in a proper and orderly way (see 14:40). Such behavior promotes understanding, edification, and harmony.

14:34-35 Paul is not forbidding a woman from praying and prophesying when the church gathers. After all, he has already made clear

that a woman can do so if she submits to the spiritual authority of her husband and the church's leadership (see 11:5). Apparently, though, some of the women in Corinth were being disruptive during the church service.

14:36-38 For those who might become disgruntled and oppose Paul's instructions on the matters regarding church orderliness, comes this reminder: **the word of God** did not **originate from** them (14:36). Rather, Paul had proclaimed it. And to reject his teaching is to reject the Lord. Those who do that will **be ignored** by the Lord (14:38).

14:40 Indeed, "God is not a God of disorder but of peace" (see 14:33). Righteous unity is critical for the church to experience God's presence in its midst.

15:2 *Being saved* here refers to present tense salvation for deliverance from the power of sin. Believers must continually abide (i.e., **hold** fast) in the knowledge and application of God's Word.

15:3-4 Why did Paul consider Christ's death **according to the Scriptures** to be **most important**? (15:3). Because of who Christ

is and what his death accomplished. Jesus Christ is the Word of God who became flesh (see John 1:14). He is the Son of God, the Second Person of the Godhead, who became a man without giving up his deity (see Phil 2:5-8). He is the one and only person with both a divine nature and a human nature, unmixed forever. Therefore, he could serve as a perfect substitutionary sacrifice for sinners because as God he is without sin, and as a man he could die in our place. By bearing our sins on the cross, he suffered the wrath of God that we deserved so that we might be forgiven, receive eternal life, and be saved (see, e.g., 2 Cor 5:21; 1 Pet 2:24).

Also topping Paul's priority list was the truth that Christ **was buried** (1 Cor 15:4). Jesus didn't merely swoon on the cross; he died. The Old Testament predicted that the Messiah would give his life as a sacrificial offering (see Isa 53:4-12), and the New Testament record assures us that this was indeed true of Jesus (see John 19:33-42; Phil 2:8).

Third, Paul emphasized that Jesus **was raised on the third day**. He suffered and

that he appeared to Cephas,[a] then to the Twelve.[b] [6] Then he appeared to over five hundred brothers and sisters at one time;[c] most of them are still alive, but some have fallen asleep. [7] Then he appeared to James,[d] then to all the apostles.[e] [8] Last of all, as to one born at the wrong time,[A,f] he also appeared to me.[g]

[9] For I am the least of the apostles,[h] not worthy to be called an apostle, because I persecuted[i] the church of God. [10] But by the grace of God I am what I am, and his grace toward me was not in vain. On the contrary, I worked harder than any of them, yet not I, but the grace of God that was with me.[j] [11] Whether, then, it is I or they, so we proclaim and so you have believed.

RESURRECTION ESSENTIAL TO THE FAITH

[12] Now if Christ is proclaimed as raised from the dead,[k] how can some of you say, "There is no resurrection of the dead"?[l] [13] If there is no resurrection of the dead, then not even Christ has been raised; [14] and if Christ has not been raised, then our proclamation is in vain, and so is your faith.[B] [15] Moreover, we are found to be false witnesses[m] about God, because we have testified[n] wrongly about God that he raised up Christ — whom he did not raise up, if in fact the dead are not raised. [16] For if the dead are not raised, not even Christ has been raised. [17] And if Christ has not been raised, your faith is worthless; you are still in your sins. [18] Those, then, who have fallen asleep in Christ[o] have also perished. [19] If we have put our hope in Christ for this life only, we should be pitied more than anyone.

CHRIST'S RESURRECTION GUARANTEES OURS

[20] But as it is, Christ has been raised from the dead, the firstfruits[p] of those who have fallen asleep. [21] For since death[q] came through a man,[r] the resurrection of the dead also comes through a man.[s] [22] For just as in Adam all die, so also in Christ all will be made alive.[t]

[23] But each in his own order:[u] Christ, the firstfruits; afterward, at his coming, those who belong to Christ. [24] Then comes the end,[v] when he hands over the kingdom to God the Father,[w] when he abolishes all rule and all authority and power.[x] [25] For he must reign[y] until he puts all his enemies under his feet.[z] [26] The last enemy to be abolished is death.[aa] [27] For **God has put everything under his feet.**[c,ab] Now when it says "everything" is put under him, it is obvious that he who puts everything under him is the exception. [28] When everything is subject to Christ, then the Son[ac] himself will also be subject to the one who subjected everything to him, so that God may be all in all.[ad]

[a] 15:5 Lk 24:34
[b] Mk 16:14; Lk 24:36; Jn 20:19,26; Ac 10:41
[c] 15:6 Mt 28:10-20
[d] 15:7 Jms 1:1
[e] Ac 1:3-11
[f] 15:8 1Tm 1:13-16
[g] Ac 9:1-8
[h] 15:9 Eph 3:8; 1Tm 1:16-17
[i] Php 3:6
[j] 15:10 2Co 3:5; Php 2:13; Col 1:29
[k] 15:12 Mt 17:9
[l] Mt 22:23; Mk 12:18; Lk 20:27; Ac 23:8; 2Tm 2:18
[m] 15:15 Mt 26:60
[n] Jn 15:26
[o] 15:18 1Th 4:16; 1Pt 5:14
[p] 15:20 Ex 23:19; Lv 2:12; Rm 8:23; Col 1:18
[q] 15:21 Mt 10:21; Jn 8:51; Php 3:10
[r] Gn 3:1-7; Rm 5:12-14
[s] Mt 28:5-6; Mk 16:6; Lk 24:5-8,34; Jn 11:25; 20:9,15-18
[t] 15:22 Rm 14:9
[u] 15:23 1Th 4:17
[v] 15:24 Mt 24:6; Mk 13:7
[w] Mt 5:16; 11:27; Lk 11:13; Jn 8:42; Eph 5:20
[x] Ac 8:10; Eph 1:21; 1Pt 3:22
[y] 15:25 Lk 1:33; Rv 11:15
[z] Ps 110:1; Mt 22:44; Eph 1:22
[aa] 15:26 2Co 5:4
[ab] 15:27 Ps 8:6
[ac] 15:28 Jn 5:19; Heb 1:2
[ad] Ps 104:24; Eph 1:23

[A] 15:8 Or *one whose birth was unusual* [B] 15:14 Or *proclamation is useless, and your faith also is useless*, or *proclamation is empty, and your faith also is empty* [C] 15:27 Ps 8:6

---

died on our behalf; he made payment for our sins. Was this payment accepted? We can be certain that it was because God raised him from the dead. This is the clear and consistent testimony of the early church (see, e.g., Acts 2:24-32; 3:15; 5:30; 10:39-41; 13:29-37; 17:31). The resurrection is your receipt that God accepted Christ's payment for your sins and mine.

15:6 The resurrected Jesus **appeared to over five hundred brothers and sisters at one time; most** of whom were **still alive** and could verify this claim. This was no conspiracy concocted by a small band of people, then. *Hundreds* saw him!

15:7 One of the qualifications of being an apostle was to have seen the risen Christ (see Acts 1:21-22). **James** was the Lord's own half-brother. Though he didn't believe in Jesus during his earthly ministry (see John 7:3-5), when he witnessed the resurrection, James believed, became a leader in the early church (see Acts 12:17; 15:13; 21:18), and wrote the New Testament letter bearing his name.

15:8 This persecutor of the church had been called by the risen Lord Jesus himself to be an apostle (see Acts 9:1-22).

15:9 Paul never forgot the horrific actions he had taken against God's people when he was an unbeliever.

15:10 Paul's understanding of and appreciation for God's **grace** through Christ inspired his labor and love. This appreciation for grace is what should empower and motivate Christians for service.

15:12-14 Our salvation depends on the truth that Jesus Christ is the sinless Son of God whose death paid for our sins and whom God vindicated by raising him from the grave. Without this, we have no sinless Savior, no high priest who always lives to intercede for us (see Heb 7:25), no forgiveness, no hope of being raised from the dead ourselves.

15:19 Indeed, if our belief in the resurrection is something that does not extend beyond the grave — that is, if it's not true — then we have no hope of eternal life after death, are living a lie, and ought to **be pitied** by the world.

15:20 The use of **firstfruits** here calls to mind Leviticus 23:10-14. In that passage, the Israelites were to bring the first portion of their harvests to the priest as an offering to the Lord. This was done in anticipation of the full harvest that was to come, as they trusted in God to provide. Thus, Christ's resurrection

is the promise that believers will one day be raised.

15:21-22 Adam disobeyed God and brought both spiritual and physical **death** to the human race. But through his own **resurrection, Christ** — the last Adam (see 15:45-47) — has made eternal life available to all.

15:23-28 God has a plan and an order to his resurrection process. **Christ, the firstfruits**, was the first to rise. **At his** next **coming**, all those who belong to Christ will receive resurrection bodies (15:23; see 1 Thess 4:13-18). At the end, after his millennial reign, he will hand **over the kingdom to God the Father**, and abolish all his enemies — including **death** — putting **everything under his feet** (1 Cor 15:24-27; see Ps 110:1). With everything else **subjected** to him, **the Son** will in turn **be subject** to the Father (1 Cor 15:28).

The Son will have succeeded where Adam failed and fulfilled the created kingdom destiny of man to rule (see Ps 8:4-6). He will have established a kingdom to defeat Satan's kingdom, ruling on behalf of humanity for God. When he hands over the kingdom to the Father at the end of his millennial reign, his earthly mission in history will be complete, ushering in eternity. And **God** will be **all in all** (1 Cor 15:28).

*a*15:31 Rm 8:36
*b*15:32 Eph 1:1
*c*1Th 2:19
*d*15:34 Ti 2:12
*e*Is 22:13
*f*1Co 4:14
*g*15:36 Jn 12:24
*h*15:38 Ps 143:10; Pr 16:9;
Jn 5:30; Gl 1:4; Eph 1:9;
1Jn 2:17
*i*15:39 Php 3:3
*j*15:40 Lk 9:31-32; Ac 22:11
*k*15:42 Rm 2:7; Eph 6:24;
2Tm 1:10
*l*15:43 2Co 6:8
*m*1Pt 5:4
*n*Mk 5:30; Lk 1:35; 6:19; Ac
19:11; 2Co 13:4; Rv 11:17
*o*15:45 Gn 2:7
*p*Rm 8:2
*q*15:47 Gn 2:7; 3:19;
Ps 90:3

⇝ Questions & Answers ⇝

Q You have stated that knowing the stories of the first Adam and the last Adam are key to understanding history. Can you explain how the relationship between them sums up the history and future of our world?

A It's really intriguing to see that the world boils down to the actions of two people: the first Adam and the last Adam. The first Adam plunged the world into sin (see Rom 5:12). Paul says, "in Adam all die" (1 Cor 15:22). But then he goes on to say that Christ, "the last Adam," made all alive (Rom 5:17; 1 Cor 15:22, 45). So the first Adam brought defeat and death; the last Adam brings about victory and life. The first Adam turned the world over to Satan. But the last Adam, Jesus Christ, hands the world back over to God. The first Adam set in motion the ruin of history and society. The last Adam is going to renew history and society. And he will rule the earth so that we see what it looks like when humans are leading the world as God intended when he first created them. The difference between these two Adams is the difference between two worldviews, two world orders, two world perspectives. So you need to be attached to the right Adam.

FOR THE NEXT Q&A, SEE PAGE 1371.

RESURRECTION SUPPORTED BY CHRISTIAN EXPERIENCE

29 Otherwise what will they do who are being baptized for the dead?[A] If the dead are not raised at all, then why are people baptized for them?[B] **30** Why are we in danger every hour? **31** I face death every day,[a] as surely as I may boast about you, brothers and sisters, in Christ Jesus our Lord. **32** If I fought wild beasts in Ephesus[b] as a mere man, what good did that do me?[c] If the dead are not raised, **Let us eat and drink, for tomorrow we die.**[c,d] **33** Do not be deceived: "Bad company corrupts good morals." **34** Come to your senses[D,e] and stop sinning; for some people are ignorant about God. I say this to your shame.[f]

THE NATURE OF THE RESURRECTION BODY

35 But someone will ask, "How are the dead raised? What kind of body will they have when they come?" **36** You fool! What you sow does not come to life[g] unless it dies. **37** And as for what you sow — you are not sowing the body that will be, but only a seed, perhaps of wheat or another grain. **38** But God gives it a body as he wants,[h] and to each of the seeds its own body. **39** Not all flesh[i] is the same flesh; there is one flesh for humans, another for animals, another for birds, and another for fish. **40** There are heavenly bodies and earthly bodies, but the splendor[j] of the heavenly bodies is different from that of the earthly ones. **41** There is a splendor of the sun, another of the moon, and another of the stars; in fact, one star differs from another star in splendor. **42** So it is with the resurrection of the dead: Sown in corruption, raised in incorruption;[k] **43** sown in dishonor,[l] raised in glory;[m] sown in weakness, raised in power;[n] **44** sown a natural body, raised a spiritual body. If there is a natural body, there is also a spiritual body. **45** So it is written, **The first man Adam became a living being;**[E,o] the last Adam[p] became a life-giving spirit. **46** However, the spiritual is not first, but the natural, then the spiritual. **47** The first man was from the earth, a man of dust;[q] the second man is[F] from

---

A15:29 Or *baptized on account of the dead*   B15:29 Other mss read *for the dead*   C15:32 Is 22:13   D15:34 Lit *Sober up*   E15:45 Gn 2:7
F15:47 Other mss add *the Lord*

15:29 It appears that some were being **baptized** by proxy on behalf of those who had died before they could be baptized. Paul isn't advocating this practice; rather, he's pointing out its absurdity if there's no resurrection.
15:32 If there's no resurrection, Paul says, quoting the self-indulgent attitude of the Israelites in Isaiah 22:13, **Let us eat and drink, for tomorrow we die.**
15:33 The Corinthian believers needed to stop hanging out with those who were promoting false doctrine, denying the resurrection, and living unrighteously. You cannot make unbelievers your constant, intimate companions

and think you will escape unscathed. Cozying up to heretical teachings and lifestyles is dangerous.
15:35-44 Just as seeds are transformed when planted, so our bodies will be transformed at Christ's return. A dead **natural body** will be raised as an eternal **spiritual body** (15:44).
15:45-49 Paul compares Adam to Christ; he discusses the first Adam and the last Adam. *Adam* is Hebrew for "man." **The first man**, made of **dust**, **became a living being** through the power of God. But **the second man**, who has come **from heaven**, **became a life-giving spirit** (15:45, 47). **The natural** man could only

die; **the spiritual** man can give life (15:46). **We have** all **borne the image of the man of dust**. What we need is to **bear the image of the man of heaven** (15:49). From birth, all human beings are "in Adam," but through faith in the gospel we are "in Christ" and granted the hope of resurrection to life (see 15:22).
15:52-55 Pain, sickness, disease, disability, and suffering of every kind will be gone **in the twinkling of an eye** at Jesus's return (15:52). Our resurrection bodies will be indestructible and incorruptible. For all those who are in Christ Jesus, then, there is no **sting** to **death**, for **death** will be **swallowed up in victory** (15:54-55).

heaven. **48** Like the man of dust, so are those who are of the dust; like the man of heaven, so are those who are of heaven.[a] **49** And just as we have borne the image[b] of the man of dust, we will also bear the image of the man of heaven.[c]

VICTORIOUS RESURRECTION

50 What I am saying, brothers and sisters, is this: Flesh[d] and blood[e] cannot inherit the kingdom of God, nor can corruption inherit incorruption. **51** Listen, I am telling you a mystery: We will not all fall asleep, but we will all be changed, **52** in a moment, in the twinkling of an eye, at the last trumpet.[f] For the trumpet will sound, and the dead will be raised incorruptible, and we will be changed. **53** For this corruptible body must be clothed[g] with incorruptibility,[h] and this mortal body must be clothed with immortality. **54** When this corruptible body is clothed with incorruptibility, and this mortal body is clothed with immortality, then the saying that is written will take place:

> Death has been swallowed up[i] in
> victory.[A,j]
55 Where, death, is your victory?
> Where, death, is your sting?[B,k]

56 The sting of death is sin, and the power of sin[l] is the law.[m] **57** But thanks be to God, who gives us the victory[n] through our Lord Jesus Christ! **58** Therefore, my dear brothers and sisters, be steadfast, immovable, always excelling in the Lord's work,[o] because you know that your labor in the Lord is not in vain.

COLLECTION FOR THE JERUSALEM CHURCH

16 Now about the collection[p] for the saints: Do the same as I instructed the Galatian[q] churches. **2** On the first day of the week,[r] each of you is to set something

aside and save in keeping with how he is prospering, so that no collections will need to be made when I come.[s] **3** When I arrive, I will send with letters[t] those you recommend to carry your gift to Jerusalem.[u] **4** If it is suitable for me to go as well, they will travel with me.

APPLICATION QUESTIONS

READ 1 CORINTHIANS 16:1-2

– How satisfied are you with your current level of financial giving? Explain.

PAUL'S TRAVEL PLANS

5 I will come to you after I pass through Macedonia[v] — for I will be traveling through Macedonia — **6** and perhaps I will remain with you or even spend the winter, so that you may send me on my way wherever I go. **7** I don't want to see you now just in passing, since I hope to spend some time with you, if the Lord allows.[w] **8** But I will stay in Ephesus[x] until Pentecost,[y] **9** because a wide door[z] for effective ministry has opened for me[c] — yet many oppose me. **10** If Timothy comes, see that he has nothing to fear while with you, because he is doing the Lord's work,[aa] just as I am. **11** So let no one look down[ab] on him. Send him on his way in peace so that he can come to me, because I am expecting him with the brothers.

12 Now about our brother Apollos:[ac] I strongly urged him to come to you with the brothers, but he was not at all willing to come now. However, he will come when he has an opportunity.

FINAL EXHORTATION

13 Be alert, stand firm in the faith,[ad] be courageous,[D] be strong. **14** Do everything in love.[ae]

Cross references (right column):

a 15:48 Php 3:20-21
b 15:49 Gn 1:27
c 1Jn 3:2
d 15:50 Php 3:3
e Mt 16:17
f 15:52 Mt 24:31; 1Pt 1:5
g 15:53 Pr 31:25
h 1Pt 1:18
i 15:54 Mt 23:24
j Is 25:8
k 15:55 Hs 13:14
l 15:56 Rm 4:15
m Gl 5:4
n 15:57 1Jn 5:5
o 15:58 Mk 14:6; Gl 3:10; Jms 2:14-26
p 16:1 Ac 11:30; 2Co 8:4
q Gl 1:2
r 16:2 Mt 28:1; Mk 16:9; Lk 24:1; Jn 20:1,19; Ac 20:7
s 16:2 2Co 9:1-5
t 16:3 2Co 8:16-22
u 16:5 Ac 16:9
v 16:5 Ac 16:9
w 16:7 Ps 143:10; Pr 16:9; Jn 5:30; Gl 1:4; Eph 1:9; 1Jn 2:17
x 16:8 Eph 1:1
y Ex 34:22
z 16:9 Col 4:3
aa 16:10 Jn 5:17; 2Jn 8
ab 16:11 Lk 18:9
ac 16:12 Ti 3:13
ad 16:13 Jd 3
ae 16:14 1Co 13:1

Footnotes:

A 15:54 Is 25:8　B 15:55 Hs 13:14　C 16:9 Lit *door has opened to me, great and effective*　D 16:13 Lit *act like men*

15:58 In light of our victory over sin and death due to our faith in King Jesus believers are encouraged to labor for their Lord. Therefore, make God's kingdom agenda your own. Don't become weary or give up because your labor **is not in vain**. It won't be wasted. You're not spinning your wheels when you engage in faithful kingdom service. God sees your work for him, and he has a reward in store for you that will exceed your wildest expectations. **16:1** Though Paul doesn't say explicitly whom the **collection** is for, references elsewhere make it clear that he's talking about a relief gift for the impoverished believers in Jerusalem (see Acts 24:17; Rom 15:25-26; 2 Cor 8:1–9:15).

16:2 The first day of the week is Sunday; therefore, giving is a part of the day of worship. Setting **aside** the offerings in advance would prevent Paul from having to chide or browbeat them when he visited, avoiding embarrassment for everyone. **16:3-4** Paul greatly desired that the Gentile believers might bless Jewish believers in their time of distress. As he told the Christians in Rome, "If the Gentiles have shared in [the Jewish believers'] spiritual benefits, then they are obligated to minister to them in material needs" (Rom 15:27). His plan was to send the **gift to Jerusalem** through trusted representatives whom the Corinthians selected (1 Cor 16:3).

16:8-9 Notice how Paul describes the situation presented to him in Ephesus. He sees it as **a wide door for effective ministry** (16:9). And since God had provided a significant opening for the gospel, Paul was willing to trust him and be faithful no matter the opposition he faced from unbelievers. **16:10-12** This is the same **Timothy** to whom the books of 1 and 2 Timothy are addressed (16:10-11). For more on **Apollos (16:12)**, see Acts 18:24-28. **16:13-14** The church was beset with self-centeredness, arrogance, and division; therefore, Paul wants to move them to a godly, love-centered mentality (see 13:1-13).

^{a}16:15 Lv 2:12
^{b}Ac 18:12
^{c}16:18 Ps 51:12
^{d}1Th 5:12

^{e}16:19 Ac 6:9
^{f}16:19-20 Rm 16:3-23; 2Co 13:12; Php 4:21-22; Col 4:10-15; 1Th 5:26; Phm 23-24
^{g}16:19 Ac 18:2
^{h}Rm 16:5
^{i}16:20 2Co 13:12
^{j}16:21 2Th 3:17
^{k}16:23-24 2Co 13:13; Gl 6:18; Eph 6:23-24; Php 4:23; Col 4:18; 1Th 5:28; 2Th 3:18

15 Brothers and sisters, you know the household of Stephanas: They are the firstfruits^a of Achaia^b and have devoted themselves to serving the saints. I urge you **16** also to submit to such people, and to everyone who works and labors with them. **17** I am delighted to have Stephanas, Fortunatus, and Achaicus present, because these men have made up for your absence. **18** For they have refreshed my spirit^c and yours. Therefore recognize^d such people.

CONCLUSION

19 The churches of Asia^e send you greetings.^{f} Aquila and Priscilla^g send you greetings warmly in the Lord, along with the church that meets in their home.^{h} **20** All the brothers and sisters send you greetings. Greet one another with a holy kiss.^{i}

21 This greeting is in my own hand^j — Paul. **22** If anyone does not love the Lord, a curse be on him. Our Lord, come!^{A} **23** The grace of the Lord Jesus be with you.^{k} **24** My love be with all of you in Christ Jesus.

^{A}16:22 Aramaic *Marana tha*

16:15 Describing **the household of Stephanas** as **the firstfruits of Achaia** (the Roman province in which Corinth was located) means that they were among the first Christian converts in Corinth.

16:17-18 Stephanas and others had personally ministered to Paul on the Corinthians' behalf. Just as "bad company corrupts good morals" (15:33), hanging out with godly people will encourage you to follow their example of faith, love, and service.

16:19 Paul had first met **Aquila and Priscilla** in Corinth, and the Corinthians knew well (see Acts 18:1–19:1).

16:21 Paul probably dictated the letter to a secretary (see Rom 16:22) and then added a personal greeting, as was his custom (see 2 Thess 3:17).

16:22 Paul announces divine chastisement on professing believers who do **not love the Lord**, which is demonstrated by promoting dissension and division in the church. Lack of affection for God's people is proof of a lack of affection for God, which results in being outside of his divine covering (see 1 John 4:11, 20-21).

2 CORINTHIANS

INTRODUCTION

Author

VIRTUALLY NO BIBLICAL SCHOLAR QUESTIONS the authenticity of 2 Corinthians as a Pauline letter. It contains more personal information about him than any of his other letters.

Historical Background

On Paul's initial ministry among the Corinthians, see the historical background in the introduction to 1 Corinthians. It appears that Paul wrote at least four letters to the church in Corinth: (1) a letter which has been lost (see 1 Cor 5:9), (2) 1 Corinthians, (3) a tearful letter (see 2 Cor 2:3-4, 9; 7:8, 12), and (4) 2 Corinthians.

Between the penning of 1 and 2 Corinthians, Paul made a visit to Corinth that proved to be "painful" (2 Cor 2:1; see 13:2). Perhaps this was because Timothy, who had visited the church (see 1 Cor 16:10-11), had reported to him that they didn't respond well to 1 Corinthians. Later Paul sent his tearful letter (2 Cor 2:3-4, 9; 7:8, 12), probably by means of Titus, who returned and reported that the majority had corrected someone in the church who had sinned against Paul (2:6; 7:6-16). At some point, some "super-apostles"—better known as "false apostles"—had infiltrated the church in Corinth, seeking to undermine Paul (11:5, 12-15, 20-23). In 2 Corinthians, Paul defends his ministry and encourages the Corinthians to complete their collection for the relief of the believers in Jerusalem.

Message and Purpose

This is Paul's most intimate letter to a church; it expresses his heart and his passion. False teachers had entered the church in Corinth, and they were receiving a hearing even though they were undermining Paul's message. They also questioned his kingdom calling and responsibility as an apostle of Jesus Christ. So Paul offered a defense of his ministry because the gospel was being undermined by Jewish teachers who were trying to put Christians back under the law of Moses.

Paul also called the Corinthians to show concern for the poor. He wanted the Jewish and Gentile Christians to understand that they are one people in Christ. What better way to show this than for Gentile believers to help Jewish believers in need?

The apostle appealed to the Corinthians' hearts and minds, showing them that truth without love is damaging, while love without truth is deceptive. Paul even spoke of his personal experience of a heavenly vision. If Paul could humble himself after receiving such a privilege, surely the Corinthians could see that he was not operating with pride but with a servant's heart.

www.bhpublishinggroup.com/qr/te/47_00

Outline

a 1:1 1Co 1:1; Eph 1:1; Col 1:1; 2Tm 1:1
b 1Th 3:2; 1Tm 1:2
c 1Co 1:2
d Ac 18:12; Php 1:1
e 1:2 Lk 12:51; Rm 1:7; 2Tm 1:2; 3Jn 14
f Mt 5:16; 11:27; Lk 11:13; Jn 8:42; Eph 5:20
g 1:3 Mk 14:61
h Heb 10:28
i Lk 2:25
j 1:5 Gl 5:24; Php 3:10
k Rm 8:17; 2Co 4:10; Gl 6:17; Php 3:10; Col 1:24
l Php 1:29
m 1:6 Heb 11:37
n Php 1:29
o 1:7 1Th 1:3
p Phm 17
q 1:8 Ac 6:9
r Ac 8:10; 1Co 15:24; Eph 1:21; 1Pt 3:22
s 2Co 4:8
t 1:9 Ps 25:2; 26:1; Jr 17:5-7; Lk 18:9
u Mk 9:27; Jn 2:19
v 1:10 Mt 27:43
w Mt 10:21; Jn 8:51; Php 3:10

x 1:12 1Tm 2:6
y Heb 13:18
z Pr 3:19; 1Co 1:21
aa Ac 23:1; 2Co 4:2; 5:12; 1Th 2:10
ab 1:14 Rm 2:17; Gl 6:4
ac 2Co 9:3; Php 2:16; 4:1; 1Th 2:19-20
ad Php 1:6
ae 1:15 Ac 18:1-18; 1Co 4:19
af 1:16 Ac 16:9
ag Ac 20:38
ah Ac 19:21; 1Co 16:5-7
ai Lk 1:5
aj 1:17 Php 3:3; Col 3:2
ak 1:18 Nm 23:19
al 1:19 Jn 5:19; Heb 1:2
am 1Th 1:1
an Heb 13:8
ao 1:20 Gn 12:7
ap Ps 72:19; Rv 22:21
aq Mk 10:37; Lk 9:32; Jn 17:24; 2Co 3:18; 2Pt 3:18
ar 1:21 Lk 4:18; 1Jn 2:20

GREETING

1 Paul, an apostle of Christ Jesus by God's will,*a* and Timothy*b* our*A* brother:

To the church of God at Corinth,*c* with all the saints who are throughout Achaia.*d* ² Grace to you and peace*e* from God our Father*f* and the Lord Jesus Christ.

THE GOD OF COMFORT

³ Blessed be*g* the God and Father of our Lord Jesus Christ, the Father of mercies*h* and the God of all comfort.*i* ⁴ He comforts us in all our affliction,*B* so that we may be able to comfort those who are in any kind of affliction, through the comfort we ourselves receive from God. ⁵ For just as the sufferings*j* of Christ*k* overflow to us, so also through Christ our comfort overflows.*l* ⁶ If we are afflicted,*m* it is for your comfort and salvation. If we are comforted, it is for your comfort, which produces in you patient endurance of the same sufferings that we suffer.*n* ⁷ And our hope*o* for you is firm, because we know that as you share*p* in the sufferings, so you will also share in the comfort.

APPLICATION QUESTIONS

READ 2 CORINTHIANS 1:3-7

– What are some painful areas in your life right now—physical or otherwise? What's causing you discomfort or agony?

– How do you typically respond to pain and difficult circumstances?

⁸ We don't want you to be unaware, brothers and sisters, of our affliction that took place in Asia.*q* We were completely overwhelmed — beyond our strength*r* — so that we even despaired*s* of life itself. ⁹ Indeed, we felt that we had received the sentence of death, so that we would not trust in ourselves but in God*t* who raises*u* the dead. ¹⁰ He has delivered*v* us from such a terrible death,*w* and he will deliver us. We have put our hope in him that he will deliver us again ¹¹ while you join in helping us by your prayers. Then many will give thanks on our*c* behalf for the gift that came to us through the prayers of many.

A CLEAR CONSCIENCE

¹² Indeed, this is our boast: The testimony*x* of our conscience*y* is that we have conducted ourselves in the world, and especially toward you, with godly sincerity and purity, not by human wisdom*z* but by God's grace.*aa* ¹³ For we are writing nothing to you other than what you can read and also understand. I hope you will understand completely — ¹⁴ just as you have partially understood us — that we are your reason for pride,*ab* just as you also are ours*ac* in the day of our*D* Lord Jesus.*ad*

A VISIT POSTPONED

¹⁵ Because of this confidence, I planned to come to you first,*ae* so that you could have a second benefit,*E* ¹⁶ and to visit you on my way to Macedonia,*af* and then come to you again from Macedonia and be helped by you*ag* on my journey*ah* to Judea.*ai* ¹⁷ Now when I planned this, was I of two minds? Or what I plan, do I plan in a purely human*F,aj* way so that I say "Yes, yes" and "No, no" at the same time? ¹⁸ As God is faithful,*ak* our message to you is not "Yes and no." ¹⁹ For the Son of God,*al* Jesus Christ, whom we proclaimed among you — Silvanus,*G,am* Timothy, and I — did not become "Yes and no." On the contrary, in him it is always "Yes."*an* ²⁰ For every one of God's promises*ao* is "Yes" in him. Therefore, through him we also say "Amen"*ap* to the glory of God.*aq* ²¹ Now it is God who strengthens us together with you in Christ, and who has anointed*ar* us. ²² He has also put his seal on us and given us

---

A 1:1 Lit *the*   *B* 1:4 Or *trouble,* or *tribulation,* or *trials,* or *oppression*   *C* 1:11 Other mss read *your*   *D* 1:14 Other mss omit *our*   *E* 1:15 Other mss read *a second joy*   *F* 1:17 Or *a worldly,* or *a fleshly,* or *a selfish*   *G* 1:19 Or *Silas*; Ac 15:22-32; 16:19-40; 17:1-16

1:1 The city of **Corinth** was located in the Roman province of **Achaia**, in modern-day Greece.

1:3-4 God often lets us experience difficult circumstances so that he can use us to experientially minister to others and empathize with their pain. When you offer **comfort** to a fellow believer, you serve as a conduit for the comfort of God, and you open yourself

up to experience a deeper level of his reality at work in your life.

1:6 Paul was a visible and verbal follower of Christ who stood head and shoulders above other Christians in terms of faithfulness. And he suffered greatly—not in spite of his faith but because of his faith in and obedience to Christ. Paul's suffering and ours is directly related to God's purpose of using us to min-

ister to others. So if you're suffering, read on.

1:9-10 When you encounter a seemingly hopeless situation, it opens your eyes to the reality that you cannot depend on and deliver yourself. Allow personal brokenness that strips you of your self-sufficiency to move you to a deeper level of trust in and dependence on our all-sufficient God. The One who is able to raise **the dead** can surely

More than You Can Bear

THERE IS A MYTH AMONG Christians that I often hear people say: "God will not put more on me than I can bear." Maybe you've heard it. Maybe you've even said it. Some people even think it's in the Bible. But let me debunk that myth right now with a look at the life of Paul. In 2 Corinthians, Paul wrote, "We don't want you to be unaware, brothers and sisters, of our affliction.... We were completely overwhelmed—beyond our strength—so that we were even despaired of life itself" (2 COR 1:8).

If ever there was a hopeless situation, Paul was in one. He hadn't done anything to cause it. In fact, he had followed God's leading straight into a place of despair. If you share similar feelings today, you are in good company. The apostle Paul was a man who served God, knew God, and pursued his calling at all costs. That should demonstrate to us that a life of service to our King doesn't guarantee a life without difficulties, sorrows, or sacrifices. In fact, the opposite is typically true.

God sometimes allows situations in your life to appear hopeless because he is trying to direct your focus onto him. You may feel like giving up because you can't seem to fix the situation you are in, and no one you know can fix it either. All of your human resources have been depleted. But Paul reveals a key principle in his next statement: "We felt that we had received the sentence of death, so that we would not trust in ourselves but in God who raises the dead. . . . We have put our hope in him" (2 COR 1:9-10).

In order to take Paul deeper in faith, God put him in a situation that his résumé, abilities, and connections could not change. Why? So that Paul would learn to trust God even more than he had done so far.

Is God being mean in such situations? No. I understand that it may feel like it sometimes when you're going through it, but what he's really doing is trying to take you deeper. Because it is in these times—these hopeless scenarios in which you see no way up, over, or out (and yet God somehow ultimately "raises the dead" for you)—that God becomes real to you in a new way. So seek him when life's situations have you struggling. Don't be ashamed of the pain or despair you may feel. Paul himself felt it. Never deny your emotions. Simply turn them Godward and look to the one who knows how to raise the dead.

a 1:22 Jms 4:5
b Eph 1:14
c 1:23 Rm 1:9; Php 1:8; Heb 12:1
d 1Co 4:21; 2Co 13:2,10
e 1:24 Pr 24:16
f 2:3 Php 1:25
g 2:5 2Th 3:8
h 2:7 Mt 6:12
i 2:9 Rm 5:4
j Php 2:8

k 2:11 2Co 12:17
l 2:12 Ac 16:8
m Col 4:3
n 2:13 2Th 1:7
o Ti 1:4
p Ac 16:9
q 2:14 1Co 15:57
r Jn 17:3; 1Jn 4:8
s 2:15 Eph 5:2; Php 4:18
t Mt 9:22; Ac 16:30; Eph 2:8
u Jn 6:27
v 2:16 Mt 10:21; Jn 8:51; Php 3:10
w 1Jn 5:12

x 2:17 Mt 12:36; Mk 4:14; Lk 6:47; 8:21; Jn 1:1; 2:22; 18:32; Ac 17:11; 2Tm 2:15; Heb 4:12
y 3:2 1Co 9:2
z 3:3 Phm 13
aa Dt 5:26

the Spirit in our hearts[a] as a down payment.[b]

23 I call on God as a witness,[c] on my life, that it was to spare you that I did not come to Corinth.[d] 24 I do not mean that we lord it over your faith, but we are workers with you for your joy, because you stand firm in your[e] faith. 2 1 In fact, I made up my mind about this: I would not come to you on another painful visit.[A] 2 For if I cause you pain, then who will cheer me other than the one being hurt by me?[B] 3 I wrote this very thing so that when I came I wouldn't have pain from those who ought to give me joy, because I am confident[f] about all of you that my joy will also be yours. 4 For I wrote to you with many tears out of an extremely troubled and anguished heart — not to cause you pain, but that you should know the abundant love I have for you.

A SINNER FORGIVEN

5 If anyone has caused pain, he has caused pain not so much to me but to some degree — not to exaggerate[g] — to all of you. 6 This punishment by the majority is sufficient for that person. 7 As a result, you should instead forgive[h] and comfort him. Otherwise, he may be overwhelmed by excessive grief. 8 Therefore I urge you to reaffirm your love to him. 9 I wrote for this purpose: to test your character[i] to see if you are obedient[j] in everything. 10 Anyone you forgive, I do too. For what I have forgiven — if I have forgiven anything — it is for your benefit in the presence of Christ,

11 so that we may not be taken advantage[k] of by Satan. For we are not ignorant of his schemes.

A TRIP TO MACEDONIA

12 When I came to Troas[l] to preach the gospel of Christ, even though the Lord opened a door[m] for me, 13 I had no rest[n] in my spirit because I did not find my brother Titus.[o] Instead, I said good-bye to them and left for Macedonia.[p]

A MINISTRY OF LIFE OR DEATH

14 But thanks be to God,[q] who always leads us in Christ's triumphal procession and through us spreads the aroma of the knowledge of him in every place.[r] 15 For to God we are the fragrance[s] of Christ among those who are being saved[t] and among those who are perishing.[u] 16 To some we are an aroma of death[v] leading to death, but to others, an aroma of life[w] leading to life. Who is adequate for these things? 17 For we do not market the word of God[x] for profit like so many.[C] On the contrary, we speak with sincerity in Christ, as from God and before God.

LIVING LETTERS

3 Are we beginning to commend ourselves again? Or do we need, like some, letters of recommendation to you or from you? 2 You yourselves are our letter, written on our hearts, known and read by everyone.[y] 3 You show that you are Christ's letter,[z] delivered[D] by us, not written with ink but with the Spirit of the living God[aa]

[A] 2:1 Lit *not again in sorrow to come to you*   [B] 2:2 Lit *the one pained*   [C] 2:17 Other mss read *like the rest*   [D] 3:3 Lit *ministered to*

---

breathe life into your seemingly impossible circumstances (1:9).

2:1-4 Someone in the Corinthian church had publicly opposed and sinned against Paul (see 2:5-10), so he wanted to avoid a **painful visit** like his previous one (2:1). Therefore, Paul had written a tearful letter to them from an **anguished heart** so that they could deal with the sin, have their **joy** restored, and know of Paul's **abundant love** for them (2:3-4).

2:5 A troublemaker within a congregation causes harm not just to an individual but to the whole church.

2:6-8 Biblical instructions on church discipline are crucial for dealing with sin in the church (see the notes on Matt 18:15-17; 1 Cor 5:3). But it's also crucial that the church **forgive** a sinning believer who repents (2 Cor 2:7) and then to lead them to a place of spiritual restoration (see Gal 6:1; Jas 5:19-20).

2:10-11 Satan's goal is to incite disunity in the church, and this was a perfect opportunity for him to take advantage of them. Don't be **ignorant of his schemes** (2:11). He'll tempt

you both to ignore sin and to refuse to **forgive** (2:10).

2:12-13 The problems in the Corinthian church had unnecessarily prevented Paul's ministry from moving forward. They'd become a distraction.

2:14 After a victorious battle, a Roman general would engage in a parade that included those whom he had conquered. In addition, incense was burned along the parade route, providing a sweet aroma of victory. Here Paul compares Jesus Christ to a conquering general who **leads** the apostle and other believers in **triumphal procession** and in spreading **the aroma of the knowledge of** Christ everywhere they go. The imagery also reminds us of Old Testament sacrifices that offered pleasing aromas to God (see, e.g., Lev 1:13).

2:15-16 This is a reminder that a person's response to the gospel has eternal consequences. When you share the good news of Jesus Christ with someone, eternity hangs in the balance. It's for this reason that Paul was

engaged with a high degree of integrity in authentic ministry. This is no game; heaven and hell are on the line.

2:17 Paul knew he spoke a message **from God** and ministered **before God** for the well-being of the church and for God's glory. That should be the motivation of every Christian.

3:1-3 Paul's ministry had received divine validation. The Corinthians themselves—won to the gospel from pagan idolatry—were Paul's **letter** of recommendation. This evidence was available for **everyone** to read (3:2). Just as the new covenant was greater than the old covenant (with God's law written on **human hearts** rather than on **tablets of stone**; see Heb 8:8-10), so Paul's commendation is greater than any false teacher's because of the visible effect **the Spirit of the living God** had on the lives of the Corinthians through Paul's ministry (2 Cor 3:3).

If no one's life is being changed at a local church, then the ministry taking place there lacks validation. A church's goal is not the installation of nice carpets and comfortable

— not on tablets of stone[a] but on tablets of human hearts.[A,b]

PAUL'S COMPETENCE

[4] Such is the confidence we have through Christ before God. [5] It is not that we are competent in[b] ourselves to claim anything as coming from ourselves, but our adequacy is from God.[c] [6] He has made us competent to be ministers of a new covenant,[d] not of the letter,[e] but of the Spirit. For the letter kills, but the Spirit gives life.

NEW COVENANT MINISTRY

[7] Now if the ministry that brought death, chiseled in letters on stones, came with glory,[f] so that the Israelites were not able to gaze steadily at Moses's face because of its glory, which was set aside, [8] how will the ministry of the Spirit not be more glorious? [9] For if the ministry that brought condemnation had glory, the ministry that brings righteousness overflows with even more glory. [10] In fact, what had been glorious is not glorious now by comparison because of the glory that surpasses it. [11] For if what was set aside[g] was glorious, what endures will be even more glorious.

[12] Since, then, we have such a hope,[h] we act with great boldness. [13] We are not like Moses, who used to put a veil over his face[i] to prevent the Israelites from gazing steadily until the end[c] of the glory of what was being set aside, [14] but their minds were hardened.[j] For to this day, at the reading of the old covenant,[k] the same veil remains; it is not lifted, because it is set aside only in Christ.[l] [15] Yet still today, whenever Moses is read, a veil lies over their hearts, [16] but whenever a person turns[m] to the Lord, the veil is removed.[n] [17] Now the Lord is the Spirit, and where the Spirit of the Lord is, there is freedom. [18] We all, with unveiled faces, are looking as in a mirror at[D,o] the glory of the Lord[p] and are being transformed[q] into the same image[r] from glory to glory; this is from the Lord who is the Spirit.[E]

> ⇨ **HOPE WORDS** ⇦
>
> *Transformation is the demonstration that the information has taken root.*

THE LIGHT OF THE GOSPEL

[4] Therefore, since we have this ministry because we were shown mercy,[s] we do not give up.[t] [2] Instead, we have renounced secret and shameful things, not acting[u] deceitfully or distorting the word of God,[v] but commending ourselves before God to everyone's conscience by an open display of the truth.[w] [3] But if our gospel is

[a] 3:3 Ex 24:12
[b] Pr 3:3; 7:3; Jr 17:1; 31:33; Ezk 11:19; 36:26; Heb 8:10
[c] 3:5 1Co 15:10
[d] 3:6 Lk 22:20; Heb 7:22
[e] Rm 7:6
[f] 3:7 Ex 34:29–35; Mk 10:37; Lk 9:32; Jn 17:24; 2Co 3:18; 2Pt 3:18
[g] 3:11 Heb 2:14
[h] 3:12 1Th 1:3
[i] 3:13 Ex 34:33
[j] 3:14 Mk 8:17; Heb 3:13
[k] Ac 13:15; 15:21; Heb 7:22
[l] Rm 16:7; 1Pt 5:14
[m] 3:16 1Pt 2:25
[n] Ex 34:34
[o] 3:18 1Co 13:12
[p] Jn 17:24; 2Co 1:20; 4:4–6; 1Tm 1:11,17
[q] Mk 9:2
[r] Gn 1:27; 1Jn 3:2
[s] 4:1 Mt 5:7; Mk 5:19; Lk 1:50
[t] 2Th 3:13
[u] 4:2 Jn 6
[v] 2Co 2:17; 2Tm 2:15; Heb 4:12
[w] 2Co 5:11–12; 6:7; 7:14

[A] 3:3 Lit *fleshly hearts* [B] 3:5 Lit *from* [C] 3:13 Or *at the outcome* [D] 3:18 Or *are reflecting* [E] 3:18 Or *from the Spirit of the Lord*, or *from the Lord, the Spirit*

---

pews, but the life-transforming work of producing kingdom disciples.

3:4-5 Replace your self-confidence with God-confidence. Regardless of your personal abilities and competencies, you are incapable of producing spiritual results via earthly means. Humbly depend on the power of the Holy Spirit so that he can accomplish his kingdom agenda through you.

3:7-11 The old covenant **ministry . . . brought death** because the sinful hearts of the people were unable to keep the law. Nevertheless, **glory** accompanied the old covenant when God's glory rubbed off on **Moses's face** as he spent time in his presence (3:7; see Exod 34:29-35). So if a **ministry** that ultimately brought **condemnation** was glorious, how much **more glorious** must new covenant ministry be since it brings **righteousness** (2 Cor 3:8-9)? In fact, the glorious ministry of Jesus Christ so far **surpasses** the old covenant that the latter is not even **glorious** by **comparison** (3:10). Thus, any attempt to return to the law and the old covenant for righteousness and transformation is a spiritually backward step. By contrast, the new covenant transforms sinners into saints and **endures** forever (3:11).

3:14-15 In Paul's day, many who were still looking to the old covenant of law were coming to God's Word with a veil **over their hearts** (3:15)—that is, they were not pursuing an intimate relationship like Moses did. We must approach God's Word with unveiled hearts as we obediently welcome his truth into our lives (see Jas 1:19-25) and give the Holy Spirit permission to do his transforming work.

3:17-18 The transforming work that God accomplished through Christ is intended for *all* believers—not merely for a small subset of super saints—so that we live in spiritual victory and freedom (3:18; see John 8:31-32, 36).

Transformation is *not* the mere accumulation of information. You can attend church and acquire a tremendous amount of Bible knowledge—both of which are important things. But these actions in and of themselves won't change you. Moreover, transformation is not simply behavior modification. If parents tell their child to take out the trash and he or she refuses, they can threaten punishment to get him or her to conform to their instructions. But this won't necessarily produce internal transformation and a change of character. In fact, as the child takes out the trash, he or she may be boiling with rebellion on the inside.

Spiritual transformation is an internal change that reflects the character of Christ and brings about a corresponding external change. And though it requires your involvement, you don't actually transform yourself. Notice that Paul says we are **being transformed**. God accomplishes it as the Holy Spirit uses our exposure, openness, and obedience to the Word of God (i.e., the **mirror**; 2 Cor 3:18; see Jas 1:21-25) to grow us from one level of spiritual development to the next (i.e., "from glory to glory"; see below).

Believers are to be transformed into **the same image from glory to glory** (2 Cor 3:18). With this phrase Paul is speaking about being made to resemble and reflect Jesus who is "the image of the invisible God" (Col 1:15). God doesn't intend that we look like Jesus physically, of course, but that we look like him in our attitudes and actions, in our character and conduct.

4:2 Paul and his companions were men of integrity. As a result, no one had a shred of evidence to substantiate an accusation against them. Let the same be true of you.

a 4:4 Lk 16:8
b Mk 10:37
c Gn 1:27
d 4:5 Php 2:11
e 4:6 Gn 1:3; Mt 6:23
f Php 3:8; 1Jn 4:8
g Mk 10:37; Lk 9:32; Jn 17:24; 2Co 3:18; 2Pt 3:18
h 4:7 Mk 5:30; Lk 1:35; 6:19; Ac 19:11; 2Co 13:4; Rv 11:17
i 4:10 Lk 9:23; Rm 5:6-8; 6:5-8; 8:34-36; Gl 6:17
j 4:11 Mt 10:21; Jn 8:51; Php 3:10
k 4:13 Ps 116:10 LXX
l 4:14 1Th 4:14

m 4:15 2Co 9:11
n 4:16 2Th 3:13
o Rm 7:22
p 4:17 Gl 6:2
q Lk 24:26; 1Pt 5:1,4
r 4:18 Rm 8:24
s 5:1 2Pt 1:13
t Eph 6:9; Php 2:10
u Col 2:11
v 5:2 1Pt 2:2

veiled, it is veiled to those who are perishing. **4** In their case, the god of this age[a] has blinded the minds of the unbelievers to keep them from seeing the light of the gospel of the glory of Christ,[A,b] who is the image of God.[c] **5** For we are not proclaiming ourselves but Jesus Christ as Lord,[d] and ourselves as your servants for Jesus's sake. **6** For God who said, "Let light shine out of darkness,"[e] has shone in our hearts to give the light of the knowledge[f] of God's glory[g] in the face of Jesus Christ.

TREASURE IN CLAY JARS

7 Now we have this treasure in clay jars, so that this extraordinary power[h] may be from God and not from us. **8** We are afflicted in every way but not crushed; we are perplexed but not in despair; **9** we are persecuted but not abandoned; we are struck down but not destroyed. **10** We always carry the death of Jesus[i] in our body, so that the life of Jesus may also be displayed in our body. **11** For we who live are always being given over to death[j] for Jesus's sake, so that Jesus's life may also be displayed in our mortal flesh. **12** So then, death is at work in us, but life in you. **13** And since we have the same spirit of faith in keeping with what is written, **I believed, therefore I spoke,**[B,k] we also believe, and therefore speak. **14** For we know that the one who raised the Lord Jesus will also raise us with Jesus[l] and present us with you. **15** Indeed, everything is for your benefit so that,

~ **HOPE WORDS** ~

God never said that the kingdom life would be easy. He just said that it would be worth it.

as grace extends through more and more people, it may cause thanksgiving[m] to increase to the glory of God.

16 Therefore we do not give up.[n] Even though our outer person is being destroyed, our inner person[o] is being renewed day by day. **17** For our momentary light affliction[p] is producing for us an absolutely incomparable eternal weight of glory.[q] **18** So we do not focus on what is seen,[r] but on what is unseen. For what is seen is temporary, but what is unseen is eternal.

~ **HOPE WORDS** ~

If all you see is what you see, you will never see all there is to be seen.

OUR FUTURE AFTER DEATH

5 For we know that if our earthly tent we live in[s] is destroyed, we have a building from God, an eternal dwelling in the heavens,[t] not made with hands.[u] **2** Indeed, we groan in this tent, desiring[v] to put on

---

A 4:4 Or *the gospel of the glorious Christ*, or *the glorious gospel of Christ*   B 4:13 Ps 116:10 LXX

4:4 Satan is **the god of this age**. His mention here is a reminder that we who share the gospel do not struggle "against flesh and blood" but "against evil, spiritual forces in the heavens" (Eph 6:12).
4:6 Just as he created visible **light** at the dawn of creation, so also God shines spiritual **light** into darkened **hearts**.
4:7 The **treasure** Paul is talking about is the knowledge of God experienced through Christ that he just mentioned in 4:6. Paul speaks of our bodies as **clay jars**, fragile containers made from earth (see Gen 2:7). On our best days, then, we're just dignified dirt. The weakness of such humble vessels is set in sharp contrast to their valuable and supernatural contents.
4:8-9 How will you know when you're truly connecting with Christ and allowing him to work in and through you? As Paul says, you'll be **afflicted** but **not crushed**—that is, in the midst of life's turmoil, you won't sink into despair.
4:11 God lets us experience problems so that the divine **life** of Jesus is manifested **in our mortal flesh**. It couldn't be more clear, then:

Those who claim that faithfully following Jesus brings only blessings and never complications are dead wrong. God will allow hard circumstances into your life to force you to rely on Jesus.
4:13 What do you do when you're experiencing hardship? Paul says, **I believed, therefore I spoke.** So, speak God's Word into your situation.
4:16 If you have not yet experienced signs of aging, you will! But though our bodies grow older and decay, we believers are becoming strengthened in **our inner person**, which is where our treasure is (4:7). Believers should be growing spiritually younger (i.e., healthier) as they grow physically older. We are being made fit for our future heavenly home, and this happens through a process that comes **day by day**. As when the Israelites received the manna in the wilderness, the Lord provides you with the grace you need for today. Next week's grace must wait until next week.
4:17 Paul calls his troubles **momentary light affliction**. How can he refer to such intense, prolonged suffering this way? Well, he understands that negative circumstances have a

positive effect when we trust and obey God through them. In fact, they are **producing for us an absolutely incomparable eternal weight of glory**. The pain and suffering of this life can be truly awful. But when the input of affliction is compared to the output of glory that Christ is accomplishing on your behalf, Paul insists that the difference between them is like night and day.
4:18 If your tribulations seem long and heavy, you're looking at the wrong thing. To put it another way, if all you see is what you see, then you do not see all there is to be seen! Paul is not saying we must close our eyes to the reality of our suffering; he's saying we need to open our eyes by faith to **unseen** realities that will last forever. An eternal perspective gives the believer the ability to handle the struggles of this life.
5:1 When Paul speaks of **our earthly tent**, he's talking about our physical bodies. When this life on earth is over, and our bodies return to dust, life has only just begun. Eternity awaits! And for those who trust in Christ, God has **an eternal dwelling** prepared for our incorruptible resurrection bodies—something Paul

Treasures in Darkness

A ROCK COLLECTOR NAMED ROB CUTSHAW once found a rock he described as "purdy and big." He tried to sell it, and when that failed, he kept the rock under his bed in the dark. Rob guessed the blue chunk of rock could bring as much as $500, but he would have taken less for it if an urgent bill needed paying. That's how close he came to selling for a few hundred dollars what turned out to be the largest, most valuable sapphire ever found. The blue rock that Rob had once abandoned to the darkness—now known as the "Star of David" sapphire—weighs nearly a pound and could easily sell for several million dollars.

Cutshaw's story makes me wonder how many of us have a treasure hidden in the darkness of our lives and are unaware of its immense value? God wants nothing more than for us to have full access to all his blessings and to the reward that he has already laid aside for us. The problem is that far too many of us are unaware of this treasure he has for us. We live in desperation, wondering when we're going to get a break, wondering when God's finally going to come through for us.

So, how can we discover this fantastic treasure for ourselves and let God use it to take care of our needs? Sometimes, in order for God to meet a need, we must first plant a seed. Many years ago, our church ministry was about to be kicked out of a school where we had been meeting for Sunday services. While we had no idea what would happen, we continued to teach the Word and take care of each other like brothers and sisters in Christ should. I was still at Dallas Seminary at the time, and one day as I walked by a staff member there, he casually said to me, "Oh, by the way, did you know that that small church on Camp Wisdom Road is getting ready to move, and they're looking to sell?" Before the year was done, we moved to our permanent church home. Because we had stayed diligent in fulfilling our calling as a ministry, teaching the Word and caring for each other, God revealed a wonderful treasure that was mere blocks from the school we had been occupying.

God has called you to a mighty work as well. I know that the hardships you face can be distracting, even paralyzing sometimes. But God wants to know if your focus is on him or your circumstances. If you stay diligent with what he has given you, he will fill you to overflowing with blessings down the road.

If you went to the right store looking for a particular amount of rice, the person behind the counter would pour that rice into a measuring pot or scale of some kind. But he would not fill it to the precise measure straight away; he would only go three quarters of the way up and then shake the pot and press on the rice. The reason for such shaking is to both level out the rice and fill in any gaps that formed underneath. Such shaking and pressing allows you to go home with more rice.

That's what God can do in the midst of your trouble; he lets life press down on you so he can fill in the gaps. Paul writes in 2 Corinthians 4:8, "We are afflicted in every way but not crushed; we are perplexed but not in despair." After all, it is in the darkness of life that God prepares us for his best.

a 5:3 Mt 25:36; Lk 10:30
b 5:4 Rm 7:24; 8:23; 1Co 15:26
c 5:7 Mt 8:10; Ac 3:16; Rm 1:8; 1Co 2:5; Gl 2:16; 1Tm 1:2; Heb 4:2
d Lk 3:22
e 5:8 Php 1:23
f 5:9 Heb 13:21
g 5:10 Jn 5:22-30
h Mt 25:31-46; Php 1:6; Heb 10:31
i Mt 16:27
j 5:11 Ps 147:11; Pr 1:7; 1Pt 1:17; Rv 14:7

k 5:13 Ac 10:45
1 1Pt 4:7
m 5:14 Jn 11:51; 2Co 4:10
n 5:15 Lk 20:38; Heb 2:9
o Rm 14:7
p Lk 20:38
q 5:17 Jn 1:3; Rv 3:14
r Rm 8:24
s Is 43:19; 65:17; Rm 6:4; Eph 4:24; Rv 21:5
t 5:18 Rm 5:11
u 5:19 2Pt 2:20
v Ti 2:11

our heavenly dwelling, **3** since, when we have taken it off,[A] we will not be found naked.[a] **4** Indeed, we groan while we are in this tent, burdened as we are, because we do not want to be unclothed but clothed, so that mortality[b] may be swallowed up by life. **5** Now the one who prepared us for this very purpose is God, who gave us the Spirit as a down payment.

6 So we are always confident and know that while we are at home in the body we are away from the Lord. **7** For we walk by faith,[c] not by sight.[d] **8** In fact, we are confident, and we would prefer to be away from the body and at home with the Lord.[e] **9** Therefore, whether we are at home or away, we make it our aim to be pleasing[f] to him. **10** For we must all appear before the judgment seat[g] of Christ,[h] so that each may be repaid[i] for what he has done in the body, whether good or evil.

11 Therefore, since we know the fear of the Lord,[j] we try to persuade people. What we are is plain to God, and I hope it is also plain to your consciences. **12** We are not commending ourselves to you again, but giving you an opportunity to be proud of us, so that you may have a reply for those who take pride in outward appearance rather than in the heart. **13** For if we are out of our mind,[k] it is for God; if we are in our right mind,[l] it is for you. **14** For the love of Christ compels us, since we have reached this conclusion: If one died for all,[m] then all died. **15** And he died for all[n] so that those who live should no longer live for themselves,[o] but for the one[p] who died for them and was raised.

THE MINISTRY OF RECONCILIATION

16 From now on, then, we do not know anyone from a worldly perspective.[B] Even if we have known Christ from a worldly perspective,[c] yet now we no longer know him in this way. **17** Therefore, if anyone is in Christ, he is a new creation;[q] the old has passed away, and see,[r] the new has[D] come![s] **18** Everything is from God, who has reconciled us to himself through Christ and has given us the ministry of reconciliation.[t] **19** That is, in Christ, God was reconciling the world[u] to himself,[v] not counting

[A] 5:3 Other mss read *when we have put on*   [B] 5:16 Lit *anyone according to the flesh*   [C] 5:16 Lit *Christ according to the flesh*   [D] 5:17 Other mss read *look, all new things have*

had previously explained to the Corinthians (see 1 Cor 15:35-57).

5:4-5 According to Ecclesiastes 3:11, God has "put eternity in [our] hearts." Though we operate in time, we ache for what is everlasting because God created us to last forever. He made us **for this very purpose** (2 Cor 5:5)! **We do not want to be unclothed but clothed** is Paul's way of saying we don't want life to end but desire our **mortality [to] be swallowed up by life** (5:4).

How do we know God will follow through on his promise to grant believers eternal life? Because he has given us the Holy **Spirit as a down payment** guaranteeing what is to come (2 Cor 5:5).

5:7 We must live based on what God's Word teaches us to believe instead of on what we can see. We walk by faith, trusting that God is telling the truth. Though we can't see the eternal realities that he has promised, we act—living heavenly in a hellish world—because we are confident in him.

5:9-10 The Greek word translated **judgment seat** is *bēma* (5:10). In the ancient world, it was on a *bēma* that a ruler or person with authority would sit to render judicial deci-

sions. Paul, for example, stood before the judgment seat (or "tribunal") of Gallio when the Jews made charges against him (see Acts 18:12-13).

One day every Christian will have to stand before Christ's *bēma* to have his or her faithfulness (or lack thereof) evaluated. Believers will be granted or denied rewards based on whether or not they have lived for Christ. Therefore, knowing that everything **good or evil** will be repaid (2 Cor 5:10), how do you want to spend the few days allotted to you?

5:11 In light of his fear of God (i.e., taking God seriously), Paul sought **to persuade people** to believe in King Jesus and submit their lives to his kingdom agenda. Do you?

5:15 The Son of God suffered the wrath of God to purchase our eternal destiny in glory. What greater privilege is there than serving him, living for him during our brief pilgrimages on earth as our loving response to his overwhelming love for us?

5:16 In other words, Christians are not to evaluate people based on mere physical appearances like age, gender, or ethnicity but based on their eternal destinies. Similarly, we don't evaluate **Christ from a worldly perspective**. He is no

mere crucified first-century Jewish man; rather, he is the risen Savior and King who is seated at the right hand of the Father. We must see and evaluate things according to their heavenly, spiritual realities—not their mere earthly, physical, racial, and temporal appearances.

5:17 If you are a Christian, you have been born again of imperishable seed and share in the divine nature (see John 3:3; 1 Pet 1:23; 2 Pet 1:4). God has brought about a spiritual transformation inside of you, and your identity is tied to your **new** birth. You are no longer who you once were: **The old has passed away.** Therefore, you are called to live in accordance with your new identity.

5:20 An *ambassador* is an officially designated representative authorized to speak in a foreign land on behalf of the country by which he was sent. Therefore, we must speak faithfully for the one who sent us. Scripture declares that God wants "everyone to be saved and to come to the knowledge of the truth" (1 Tim 2:4). He desires that all people would hear and understand the gospel so that they may have the opportunity to believe for eternal life. Remarkably, he makes **his appeal through us.**

their trespasses against them, and he has committed the message of reconciliation to us. **20** Therefore, we are ambassadors[a] for Christ, since God is making his appeal through us. We plead on Christ's behalf:[b] "Be reconciled to God." **21** He made the one who did not know sin[c] to be sin[A] for us,[d] so that in him we might become the righteousness of God.

6 Working together with him, we also appeal to you, "Don't receive the grace of God in vain." **2** For he says:

> At an acceptable time I listened to you,
> and in the day of salvation I helped you.[B,e]

See, now is the acceptable time; now is the day of salvation![f]

THE CHARACTER OF PAUL'S MINISTRY

3 We are not giving anyone an occasion for offense, so that the ministry will not be blamed. **4** Instead, as God's ministers, we commend ourselves in everything: by great endurance, by afflictions, by hardships, by difficulties, **5** by beatings, by imprisonments,[g] by riots, by labors, by sleepless nights, by times of hunger, **6** by purity,[h] by knowledge,[i] by patience,[j] by kindness,[k] by the Holy Spirit, by sincere love,[l] **7** by the word of truth,[C,m] by the power of God;[n] through weapons of righteousness for the right hand and the left, **8** through glory[o] and dishonor, through slander and good report; regarded as deceivers, yet true; **9** as unknown, yet recognized; as dying, yet see — we live; as being disciplined, yet not killed; **10** as grieving, yet always rejoicing;[p] as poor, yet enriching many; as having nothing, yet possessing everything. **11** We have spoken openly to you, Corinthians; our heart has been opened wide. **12** We are not withholding our affection from you, but you are

withholding yours from us. **13** I speak as to my children; as a proper response, open your heart to us.

⊰ Questions & Answers ⊱

Q There are a number of different metaphors for the saving work that Christ accomplished through his atoning work on the cross. But you believe that the penal substitutionary approach is the central and most important biblical understanding of the atonement. Could you describe what this is, and why it is important to our understanding of salvation?

A The *penal substitutionary* death of Christ is central to our salvation. It is consistent with the nature of God and his just wrath against sin. You see, God must respond to sin. He can't act like it didn't happen; his holy and righteous nature cannot allow that. Sin must be punished. In order for me to escape God's just judgment for my sin, one who shares my humanity but who never sinned must be punished (penal) in my place (as a substitute). By taking on humanity and living a sinless life, Jesus could die in my place. God *imputed* or credited my sins to Jesus on the cross—he put them on Jesus as if they were his. Then Jesus suffered and died for my sins as a *propitiation*—that is, as an atoning sacrifice that satisfied the demands of God's holy wrath and turned away his anger. Penal substitution is the key to my salvation. When I accept Jesus's sacrificial death on my behalf, God is satisfied with me and credits the righteousness of Christ to me (see 2 Cor 5:21).

FOR THE NEXT Q&A, SEE PAGE 1383.

---

[a]5:20 Eph 6:20
[b]2Co 12:10; Php 1:29
[c]5:21 1Jn 3:5
[d]Rm 8:3; Gl 3:13; 1Pt 2:24
[e]6:2 Is 49:8
[f]Is 49:8; 55:6; Lk 4:19; Heb 3:13
[g]6:5 Jdg 16:21
[h]6:6 2Co 11:3
[i]Php 3:8; 1Jn 4:8
[j]Ex 34:6; 2Tm 3:10
[k]Rm 2:4; 3:12; 11:22; Gl 5:22; Eph 2:7; Col 3:12; Ti 3:4
[l]1Co 13:1
[m]6:7 2Th 2:10
[n]Mk 5:30; Lk 1:35; 6:19; Ac 19:11; 2Co 13:4; Rv 11:17
[o]6:8 1Pt 5:4
[p]6:10 Mt 5:4; Jn 16:22; 2Co 7:4; Php 1:4,25; 2:17-18; 3:1; 4:1,4; Col 1:24; 1Th 1:6; 1Pt 1:6-8

[A]5:21 Or *be a sin offering* [B]6:2 Is 49:8 [C]6:7 Or *by truthful speech*

5:21 In exchange for our sins, Jesus offers to give us his perfect righteousness—that is, when we place our faith in him, he credits our spiritual bank accounts with his own perfection. The theological term for this transaction is *imputation*. When you believe in Jesus as your substitutionary atonement, your **sin** is imputed (or credited) to Christ, and his **righteousness** is imputed to you. This is the glorious exchange that the gospel offers to everyone who will receive it. And this is the good news of which we Christians are ambassadors.

6:1-2 Since Paul urges the Corinthians not to **receive the grace of God in vain** (6:1), it may be that false teachers were telling them to focus on keeping the law by their own self-effort, rather than relying on God's gracious provision to live the Christian life (see Gal 3:1-5). Paul quotes from Isaiah 49:8 to emphasize that **the day of salvation** has arrived (2 Cor 6:2). Today, we must operate in light of God's grace if we are to maximize the salvation we have received.

6:4-5 Paul lists a series of **hardships** that he had endured on behalf of his ministry,

demonstrating that he was willing to suffer many intense **afflictions** to honor Christ and see lives transformed for his kingdom.

6:6-10 Through his personal character, the divine affirmation of his work, and his spiritual successes in spite of adversity, Paul's apostleship was validated.

6:11-13 Like Paul, those who serve in positions of leadership ought to have a deep love for those under their spiritual care. Likewise, the congregation should have warm affection and respect for their leaders who will one day "give an account" to God for the souls of those whom

Video Devotional

"ALIGNMENT"

A kingdom marriage is a marriage that is properly aligned under the rule of God over every area of life.

SEPARATION TO GOD

14 Don't become partners with those who do not believe. For what partnership is there between righteousness and lawlessness?[a] Or what fellowship does light[b] have with darkness?[c] **15** What agreement does Christ have with Belial?[A] Or what does a believer have in common with an unbeliever? **16** And what agreement does the temple of God have with idols?[d] For we[B] are the temple of the living God, as God said:

> I will dwell[e]
> and walk among them,
> and I will be their God,[f]
> and they will be my people.[C,g]

17 Therefore, **come out**
> **from among them**
> and **be separate, says the Lord;**
> **do not touch any unclean thing,**
> and I will welcome you.[D,h]

18 And **I will be a Father**[i] to you,
> **and** you will be **sons**[j] and daughters to me,
> says the Lord Almighty.[E,k]

7 So then, dear friends, since we have these promises,[l] let us cleanse ourselves from every impurity of the flesh and spirit,[m] bringing holiness to completion[F] in the fear of God.[n]

JOY AND REPENTANCE

2 Make room for us in your hearts. We have wronged no one, corrupted[o] no one, taken advantage of no one. **3** I don't say this to condemn you, since I have already said that you are in our hearts, to die together and to live together. **4** I am very frank with you; I have great pride in you. I am filled with encouragement; I am overflowing with joy in all our afflictions.

5 In fact, when we came into Macedonia,[p] we[G] had no rest. Instead, we were troubled in every way: conflicts[q] on the outside, fears[r] within. **6** But God, who comforts the downcast,[s] comforted us by the arrival of Titus, **7** and not only by his arrival but also by the comfort he received from you. He told us about your deep longing, your sorrow, and your zeal[t] for me, so that I rejoiced even more. **8** For even if I grieved you with my letter,[u] I don't regret it. And if I regretted it — since I saw that the letter grieved you, yet only for a while — **9** I now rejoice, not because you were grieved, but because your grief led to repentance. For you were grieved as God willed, so that you didn't experience any loss from us. **10** For godly grief produces a repentance that leads to salvation without regret, but worldly grief produces death.[v] **11** For consider how much diligence this very thing — this grieving as God wills — has produced in you: what a desire to clear yourselves, what indignation, what fear, what deep longing, what zeal, what justice! In every way you showed yourselves to be pure[w] in this matter. **12** So even though I wrote to you, it was not because of the one who did wrong, or because of the one who was wronged, but in order that your devotion to us might be made plain to you in the sight of God. **13** For this reason we have been comforted.

In addition to our own comfort, we rejoiced even more over the joy Titus[x] had, because his spirit was refreshed by all of you. **14** For if I have made any boast to him about you, I have not been disappointed; but as I have spoken everything to you in truth,[y] so our boasting to Titus has also turned out to be the truth. **15** And his affection toward you is even greater as he remembers the obedience of all of you, and how you received him with fear and trembling. **16** I rejoice that I have complete confidence in you.

---

[a] 6:14 Mt 13:41
[b] Jn 12:46
[c] Mt 6:23
[d] 6:16 Gn 31:19; 1Co 8:4
[e] Jms 4:5
[f] Heb 3:6
[g] Lv 26:12
[h] 6:17 Is 52:11
[i] 6:18 Mt 5:16; 11:27; Lk 11:13; Jn 8:42; Eph 5:20
[j] Mt 5:9
[k] 2Sm 7:14; Rv 1:8
[l] 7:1 Gn 12:7
[m] Ps 51:12
[n] Ps 147:11; Pr 1:7; Rv 14:7
[o] 7:2 1Co 3:17; 15:33; 2Co 11:3; Eph 4:22; 2Pt 2:12; Jd 10; Rv 19:2
[p] 7:5 Ac 16:9
[q] 7:5 Jms 4:1; Ti 3:9
[r] Jn 7:13; Ac 27:29
[s] 7:6 Mt 11:29
[t] 7:7 Nm 25:13
[u] 7:8 2Co 2:2,4
[v] 7:10 Mt 10:21; Jn 8:51; Php 3:10
[w] 7:11 Php 4:8
[x] 7:13 Ti 1:4
[y] 7:14 Ps 119:142; Jn 8:14; 14:6; 2Co 11:10; 1Jn 5:20; 3Jn 3

[A] 6:15 Or *Beliar*   [B] 6:16 Other mss read *you*   [C] 6:16 Lv 26:12; Jr 31:33; 32:38; Ezk 37:26   [D] 6:17 Is 52:11   [E] 6:18 2Sm 7:14; Is 43:6; 49:22; 60:4; Hs 1:10   [F] 7:1 Or *spirit, perfecting holiness*   [G] 7:5 Lit *our flesh*

---

they serve (Heb 13:17). Without this two-way openness, it's difficult for those within a church to care for and protect one another spiritually.
6:14 To **become partners with** someone can also be translated "be unequally yoked." The idea comes from Deuteronomy 22:10, in which the Israelites were commanded not to have "an ox and a donkey" plowing together. Whether it's a romantic relationship, intimate friendship, or a business partnership, such compromise negatively affects your intimacy with God. When you align yourself with those whose beliefs and lives are far from God, you'll find God distancing himself from you too.

7:2-4 Regarding any accusations or rumors that the false apostles had made against him, Paul reiterates that he has not **wronged** or **taken advantage of** anyone and pleads with the Corinthians to open their **hearts** to him (7:2). He quickly explains that he and his coworkers are not attempting to **condemn** the Corinthians. Their **hearts** are filled with affection, **pride**, and **joy** over them in spite of the **afflictions** suffered (7:3-4). The false apostles were to blame for the unrest they had caused.
7:5-7 God often **comforts** his children through their fellow believers (see 1:3-7). In his providence, he will bring people alongside those experiencing conflict who can offer a sympathetic ear and speak words of truth and encouragement. So when you see a brother or sister in Christ suffering, don't pass up the opportunity to be used by God.
7:10 Worldly grief is what Judas experienced after he betrayed Jesus. He knew he had sinned and was filled with remorse, but he was unwilling to repent to God (see Matt 27:3-5). In contrast, Peter experienced **godly grief** after denying Christ. This led to his **repentance** and recommitment to the Lord, resulting in his spiritual restoration (see Matt 26:75; John 21:15-19).

APPEAL TO COMPLETE
THE COLLECTION

8 We want you to know, brothers and sisters, about the grace of God that was given to the churches[a] of Macedonia:[b] 2 During a severe trial brought about by affliction, their abundant joy and their extreme poverty overflowed in a wealth of generosity on their part.[c] 3 I can testify that, according to their ability and even beyond their ability, of their own accord, 4 they begged us earnestly for the privilege of sharing[d] in the ministry to the saints, 5 and not just as we had hoped. Instead, they gave themselves first to the Lord and then to us by God's will.[e] 6 So we urged Titus that just as he had begun, so he should also complete among you this act of grace.

7 Now as you excel in everything — in faith, speech, knowledge,[f] and in all diligence, and in your love for us[A] — excel also in this act of grace. 8 I am not saying this as a command. Rather, by means of the diligence of others, I am testing the genuineness of your love. 9 For you know the grace of our Lord Jesus Christ: Though he was rich,[g] for your sake he became poor,[h] so that by his poverty you might become rich. 10 And in this matter I am giving advice because it is profitable for you, who began last year not only to do something but also to want to do it.[i] 11 Now also finish the task, so that just as there was an eager desire, there may also be a completion, according to what you have. 12 For if the eagerness is there, the gift is acceptable according to what a person has, not according to what he does not have.[j] 13 It is not that there should be relief for others

and hardship for you, but it is a question of equality.[B] 14 At the present time your surplus is available for their need, so that their abundance may in turn meet your need, in order that there may be equality. 15 As it is written: **The person who had much did not have too much, and the person who had little did not have too little.**[C,k]

ADMINISTRATION
OF THE COLLECTION

16 Thanks be to God, who put the same concern for you into the heart of Titus. 17 For he welcomed our appeal and, being very diligent, went out to you by his own choice. 18 We have sent with him the brother[l] who is praised among all the churches for his gospel ministry.[D] 19 And not only that, but he was also appointed by the churches to accompany us with this gracious gift that we are administering for the glory of the Lord himself and to show our eagerness to help. 20 We are taking this precaution so that no one will criticize us about this large sum that we are administering. 21 Indeed, we are giving careful thought[m] to do what is right,[n] not only before the Lord but also before people. 22 We have also sent with them our brother. We have often tested him in many circumstances and found him to be diligent — and now even more diligent because of his great confidence in you. 23 As for Titus, he is my partner[o] and coworker[p] for you; as for our brothers, they are the messengers[q] of the churches, the glory of Christ.[r] 24 Therefore, show them proof before the churches of your love and of our boasting[s] about you.

a 8:1 Mt 16:18; 1Co 14:4; Rv 1:4
b Ac 16:9
c 8:2 Php 4:10
d 8:4 Ac 24:17; Rm 15:26,31; 2Co 8:19-20; 9:1,12-13
e 8:5 Ps 143:10; Pr 16:9; Jn 5:30; Gl 1:4; Eph 1:9; 1Jn 2:17
f 8:7 Php 3:8; 1Jn 4:8
g 8:9 Mt 20:28; 2Co 6:10; Php 2:6-7
h Php 2:7
i 8:10 1Co 16:1-4; 2Co 9:1-2
j 8:12 Lk 21:3
k 8:15 Ex 16:18
l 8:18 2Co 12:18
m 8:21 1Tm 5:8
n 1Pt 2:12
o 8:23 Phm 17
p 1Co 3:9
q Jn 13:16
r Mk 10:37
s 8:24 2Co 12:5; Jms 4:16

A 8:7 Other mss read *in our love for you*   B 8:13 Lit *but from equality*   C 8:15 Ex 16:18   D 8:18 Lit *churches, in the gospel*

8:1-5 From Paul's other letters, we know that he had taken up a collection among the Gentile churches on behalf of the poor believers in Jerusalem (see Rom 15:25-28; Gal 2:9-10). He had previously urged the Corinthians to take up an offering of their own that he could deliver when he traveled to Jerusalem (see 1 Cor 16:1-4). In this chapter, he makes an appeal for them to complete their collection.

Paul begins by highlighting **the churches of Macedonia** (this would have included the churches in Philippi, Thessalonica, and Berea; see Acts 16:6–17:15) as an example of generosity to motivate the Corinthians' own giving (2 Cor 8:1). Although the Macedonian believers had experienced **a severe trial**, this did not prevent them from expressing **generosity** (8:2).

Why do you give to gospel ministry? Is it because you feel guilty? Is it because you're

trying to cut a deal with God? Or is it because you know and have experienced the unmerited goodness of God in your life? When you are characterized by spiritual satisfaction and a true understanding and appreciation of grace, giving to the Lord's work will be something you are excited to do.

8:7 The apostle longs to see them **excel in** giving to the poor Jewish Christians, just as they have excelled in other ways. When we respond to God's **grace** in our lives with a willingness to give to others, his grace to us and through us is magnified all the more. It makes God look good.

8:8-9 The eternal Son of God had enjoyed heavenly glory and fellowship with the Father from all eternity. But "he emptied himself" and took "on the likeness of humanity" (Phil 2:7). Then he gave "his life as a ransom for many" (Mark 10:45). Christ exemplified the

spirit and attitude that Paul longs to see from the Corinthian church. It wasn't asking too much to prompt them to honor what Christ did for them by meeting the needs of fellow saints.

8:12 God looks at the heart of the giver, not at the size of the gift.

8:15 God provided a sufficient supply of manna to the Israelites in the wilderness so that everyone had enough. In the same way, he wanted the church in Corinth (and churches today) to help other saints when it was in their capacity to do so. The church of Jesus Christ is the means by which God meets needs.

8:20-21 Local churches should similarly ensure that financial matters are handled in a manner that is above reproach. Our Christian testimony is at stake, as well as the Lord's reputation.

[a] 9:2 Ac 16:9
[b] Ac 18:12
[c] Nm 25:13
[d] 2Co 8:18; 12:18
[e] 9:5 Ac 11:30
[f] Eph 5:3
[g] 9:7 Lk 6:35; Jn 3:16;
12:43; 2Th 2:13; Rv 12:11
[h] 9:8 Eph 3:20
[i] 9:9 Jn 16:32
[j] Ps 112:9; 1Jn 2:17

[k] 9:10 Is 55:10-11; Hs 10:12
[l] 9:11 1Co 1:5; 2Co 6:10
[m] 9:12 Heb 8:6
[n] 9:13 Php 4:10
[o] 10:2 Php 3:3
[p] 10:4 1Tm 1:18
[q] Ac 25:5

MOTIVATIONS FOR GIVING

9 Now concerning the ministry to the saints, it is unnecessary for me to write to you. [2] For I know your eagerness, and I boast about you to the Macedonians:[a] "Achaia[b] has been ready since last year," and your zeal[c] has stirred up most of them.[d] [3] But I am sending the brothers so that our boasting about you in this matter would not prove empty, and so that you would be ready just as I said. [4] Otherwise, if any Macedonians come with me and find you unprepared, we, not to mention you, would be put to shame in that situation.[A] [5] Therefore I considered it necessary to urge the brothers to go on ahead to you and arrange in advance the generous gift[e] you promised, so that it will be ready as a gift and not as an extortion.[f]

[6] The point is this:[g] The person who sows sparingly will also reap sparingly, and the person who sows generously will also reap generously. [7] Each person should do as he has decided in his heart — not reluctantly or out of compulsion, since God loves[g] a cheerful giver. [8] And God is able[h] to make every grace overflow to you, so that in every way, always having everything you need, you may excel in every good work. [9] As it is written:

He distributed freely;[i]
he gave to the poor;
his righteousness
endures forever.[CJ]

[10] Now the one who provides seed for the sower and bread for food will also provide and multiply your seed and increase the harvest of your righteousness.[k] [11] You will be enriched[l] in every way for all generosity, which produces thanksgiving to God through us. [12] For the ministry of this service[m] is not only supplying the needs of the saints but is also overflowing in many expressions of thanks to God. [13] Because of the proof provided by this ministry, they will glorify God for your obedient confession of the gospel of Christ, and for your generosity[n] in sharing with them and with everyone. [14] And as they pray on your behalf, they will have deep affection for you because of the surpassing grace of God in you. [15] Thanks be to God for his indescribable gift!

PAUL'S APOSTOLIC AUTHORITY

10 Now I Paul, myself, appeal to you by the meekness and gentleness of Christ — I who am humble among you in person but bold toward you when absent. [2] I beg you that when I am present I will not need to be bold with the confidence by which I plan to challenge certain people who think we are behaving according to the flesh.[o] [3] For although we live in the flesh, we do not wage war according to the flesh, [4] since the weapons of our warfare[p] are not of the flesh, but are powerful[q] through God for the demolition of

[A] 9:4 Or *in this confidence*   [B] 9:6 Lit *And this*   [C] 9:9 Ps 112:9

9:6 The seed deposited in the ground is an investment made in faithful expectation of reaping something much more significant. The same is true of the investments we make in the Lord's work.

In spite of what some health-and-wealth gospel advocates may say, Paul is not promising that giving **generously** to gospel ministry will result in earthly material prosperity and the elimination of all your problems. Anyone who says that is claiming biblical support for false teaching.

Nevertheless, if you give generously to a legitimate need from sincere gospel motives when it is in your capacity to do so, God will give you his blessing. A *blessing* is the God-given capacity to experience, enjoy, and extend the goodness and favor of God in your life. Regardless of what God provides to you, he will bless you with his presence and the ability to use what he provides.

9:7 We are to be **cheerful** in our giving because of an understanding that God is our source. One way you know you are growing in your faith is when you give with a glad heart in response to the goodness of God. Giving should be a joy not a job.

9:8 This statement applies to all cheerful givers: **God is able to make every grace overflow to you**. God's superabundant grace includes all that he can do for you that you are unable to do for yourself. He can guide you when you're lost and provide for you when you're in need. He can heal a relationship that's broken and grant peace where there's conflict. When God's kingdom is given priority in your life, you open yourself to waves of grace that are bigger than your gift. History and eternity have more grace available than we could ever access (see Eph 2:7).

9:10 The emphasis here is that God is both the source of what is planted and also the source of what is harvested.

9:12 God's goal is that both giver and receiver obtain his blessing as he himself is exalted.

9:13-14 Cheerful and willing contributions to legitimate needs result in an overabundance of grace and blessing, leading to increased prayer and praise to God, which lead to more giving and grace. Those who refuse to give, or who give from mere compulsion, short-circuit this chain of blessing before it can even begin.

9:15 The "surpassing grace of God" (9:14) so overwhelms Paul that he doesn't have a vocabulary capable of describing it.

10:1-2 Some Corinthians were being influenced by false teachers who had infiltrated the church. Thus, Paul pleads with the believers in a spirit of **meekness and gentleness** (10:1) to listen to him to avoid his having to boldly confront those who were **behaving according to the flesh** (10:2) and had accused Paul of being self-serving.

10:3-5 By **strongholds** (10:4), Paul isn't talking about physical fortresses but about destructive patterns of thought that lead people astray and hold them hostage to sinful, harmful, and addictive behavior. This is accomplished through blocking **the knowledge of God** (10:5) from penetrating the mind and life of the believer. If addictive behavior is present in a person's life, that behavior is not the stronghold but merely its fruit. Strongholds can only be demolished by the knowledge of God — that is, by truth. As Jesus told his disciples, "The truth will set you free" (John 8:32). When your relationship to the living Word connects to the written Word, "you really will be free" (John 8:36). If you're not taking **every thought captive to obey Christ** (2 Cor 10:5) and are instead succumbing to a stronghold, it's because you either don't know the truth or aren't making use of the truth you know

strongholds. We demolish arguments [5] and every proud thing that is raised up against the knowledge[a] of God, and we take every thought captive to obey Christ. [6] And we are ready to punish any disobedience, once your obedience is complete.

[7] Look at what is obvious.[A] If anyone is confident that he belongs to Christ,[b] let him remind himself of this: Just as he belongs to Christ, so do we. [8] For if I boast a little too much about our authority, which the Lord gave for building you up[c] and not for tearing you down, I will not be put to shame. [9] I don't want to seem as though I am trying to terrify you with my letters. [10] For it is said, "His letters are weighty and powerful, but his physical presence is weak and his public speaking amounts to nothing." [11] Let such a person consider this: What we are in our letters, when we are absent, we will also be in our actions when we are present.

[12] For we don't dare classify or compare ourselves with some who commend[d] themselves. But in measuring themselves by themselves and comparing themselves to themselves,[e] they lack understanding.[f] [13] We, however, will not boast beyond measure but according to the measure of the area of ministry that God has assigned[g] to us, which reaches even to you. [14] For we are not overextending ourselves, as if we had not reached you, since we have come to you with the gospel of Christ. [15] We are not boasting beyond measure about other people's labors. On the contrary, we have the hope[h] that as your faith increases, our

area of ministry will be greatly enlarged, [16] so that we may preach the gospel to the regions beyond you[i] without boasting about what has already been done in someone else's area of ministry.[j] [17] So **let the one who boasts, boast in the Lord.**[B,k] [18] For it is not the one commending himself who is approved, but the one the Lord commends.[l]

PAUL AND THE FALSE APOSTLES

11 I wish you would put up with a little foolishness[m] from me. Yes, do put up with me![c] [2] For I am jealous[n] for you with a godly jealousy,[o] because I have promised you in marriage to one husband — to present a pure[D] virgin to Christ. [3] But I fear that, as the serpent[q] deceived[r] Eve[s] by his cunning, your minds may be seduced from a sincere and pure[D] devotion to Christ.[t] [4] For if a person comes and preaches another Jesus,[u] whom we did not preach, or you receive a different spirit,[v] which you had not received, or a different gospel,[w] which you had not accepted, you put up with it splendidly!

[5] Now I consider myself in no way inferior to those "super-apostles."[x] [6] Even if I am untrained in public speaking,[y] I am certainly not untrained in knowledge.[z] Indeed, we have in every way made that clear to you in everything. [7] Or did I commit a sin by humbling[aa] myself so that you might be exalted,[ab] because I preached the gospel of God to you free of charge?[ac] [8] I robbed other churches by taking pay from them to minister to you. [9] When I

[a] 10:5 Jn 17:3; 1Jn 4:8
[b] 10:7 1Co 3:23; Gl 5:24
[c] 10:8 1Co 14:3
[d] 10:12 Gl 2:18
[e] Pr 26:12; 27:2
[f] Mt 13:13
[g] 10:13 Rm 12:3; 1Co 7:17; Heb 7:2
[h] 10:15 1Th 1:3
[i] 10:16 Ac 19:21
[j] Rm 15:20
[k] 10:17 Jr 9:24
[l] 10:18 1Th 2:4
[m] 11:1 Mk 7:22; 2Co 11:17,21
[n] 11:2 Jms 3:16
[o] Nm 25:13; Gl 4:17
[p] Php 4:8
[q] 11:3 Gn 3:1; Lk 10:19
[r] Rm 7:11; 16:18; 1Co 3:18; 2Th 2:3; 1Tm 2:14
[s] Gn 3:20
[t] 1Th 3:5
[u] 11:4 1Co 3:11
[v] 1Jn 4:1
[w] Gl 1:6
[x] 11:5 Jd 17
[y] 11:6 1Co 1:17
[z] Php 3:8; 1Jn 4:8
[aa] 11:7 Lk 14:11
[ab] Lk 1:52
[ac] Ac 18:3

[A] **10:7** Or *You are looking at things outwardly*   [B] **10:17** Jr 9:24   [C] **11:1** Or *Yes, you are putting up with me*   [D] **11:3** Other mss omit *and pure*

10:6 In order for Paul to deal effectively with the **disobedience** of the false apostles, the Corinthians would need to be unified in their commitment to the Lord and to Paul by complete—not partial—obedience. If a minority of the Corinthians still allowed themselves to be influenced by heretical teachers, it would affect the entire church.

10:8 Paul used his authority **for building** the church in Corinth **up**, not for **tearing [them] down** as the false apostles had. How do you use your own influence within the body of Christ?

10:12-16 The false teachers to whom some of the Corinthians were listening had a faulty view of themselves. They were **measuring themselves by themselves and comparing themselves to themselves** (10:12). In other words, they served as their own standard. This is the epitome of human wisdom and pride. Paul, however, refused to **boast beyond measure** (10:13; cf. 10:15)—that is, to boast and operate outside of the God-designed boundaries in which he'd been placed. He knew what Christ had

equipped and called him to do, unlike these false apostles who exalted themselves and criticized Paul.

We too must realize that we can't serve as our own standard because sin has contaminated us. Our only legitimate standard is Scripture. Furthermore, we must be content with the boundaries in which God has placed us. To live within God-given boundaries is freedom; it maximizes your uniqueness and abilities. To try to function outside of those boundaries will produce frustration and will often lead to sin.

10:17-18 How do you know you're operating in the right spot and for the right reasons? Because you find that you're consciously doing what you do for the glory of God—that is, you're making God look good by how you live. Boasting in yourself, your abilities, and your accomplishments is a dead-end street because it's a lie (**the Lord** is your source, not you) and it ultimately won't satisfy.

11:1 In order to respond to his opponents and try to win back those among the Corinthians who had embraced them, Paul feels

compelled to engage in the very thing that he hates: the **foolishness** of boasting.

11:5 The false teachers had promoted themselves as being superior to Paul, but he knew he was not **inferior** to these so-called **super-apostles**.

11:6 Paul knew that his **knowledge** of the true gospel and the content of his message were far more important that oratorical skill. You may be a dynamic and persuasive public speaker. Nevertheless, if you're not proclaiming, "Jesus Christ and him crucified" (1 Cor 2:2), your message is insufficient and will be devoid of the spiritual power that comes only from the Word of God.

11:8 Paul means that other Christians paid for his ministry among them when he could rightly have expected the Corinthians to support him themselves.

11:9-11 Paul hadn't wanted to **burden** them and hinder the work of the gospel among them (11:9). This kind of **boasting** Paul was willing to engage in—that is, boasting about how he had sacrificed for them and about his great **love** for them (11:10-11).

a 11:9 Ac 16:9
b Php 4:10
c 11:10 Ac 18:12
d 11:13 Rv 2:2
e 11:15 Gl 3:10
f 11:19 Pr 3:7
g 11:20 Gl 5:15
h Mt 5:39
i 11:22 Php 3:5
j Gn 16:15; Gl 3:29

k 11:24 Dt 25:3
l 11:25 Ac 16:22
m Ac 14:19
n Ac 27:1-44; 1Tm 1:19
o 11:26 Mk 14:48
p Ac 9:23; 13:50; 14:5;
17:5; 18:12; 20:3,19; 21:27;
23:10-12; 25:3
q 11:27 Rm 8:35
r 11:29 Jn 16:1
s 11:31 Mt 5:16; 11:27; Lk
11:13; Jn 8:42; Eph 5:20
t 11:32 2Sm 8:5
u 11:33 Ac 9:19-25
v 12:1 Lk 1:22
w 1Pt 4:13
x 12:2 1Th 4:17
y 12:4 Lk 23:43

was present with you and in need, I did not burden anyone, since the brothers who came from Macedonia[a] supplied my needs.[b] I have kept myself, and will keep myself, from burdening you in any way. [10] As the truth of Christ is in me, this boasting of mine will not be stopped[A] in the regions of Achaia.[c] [11] Why? Because I don't love you? God knows I do!

[12] But I will continue to do what I am doing, in order to deny[B] an opportunity to those who want to be regarded as our equals in what they boast about. [13] For such people are false apostles,[d] deceitful workers, disguising themselves as apostles of Christ. [14] And no wonder! For Satan disguises himself as an angel of light. [15] So it is no great surprise if his servants also disguise themselves as servants of righteousness. Their end will be according to their works.[e]

PAUL'S SUFFERINGS FOR CHRIST

[16] I repeat: Let no one consider me a fool. But if you do, at least accept me as a fool so that I can also boast a little. [17] What I am saying in this matter[c] of boasting, I don't speak as the Lord would, but as it were, foolishly. [18] Since many boast according to the flesh, I will also boast. [19] For you, being so wise, gladly put up with fools![f] [20] In fact, you put up with it if someone enslaves you, if someone exploits[g] you, if someone takes advantage of you, if someone is arrogant toward you, if someone slaps[h] you in the face. [21] I say this to our shame: We have been too weak for that!

But in whatever anyone dares to boast — I am talking foolishly — I also dare: [22] Are they Hebrews?[i] So am I. Are they Israelites? So am I. Are they the descendants of Abraham?[j] So am I. [23] Are they servants of Christ? I'm talking like a madman — I'm a better one: with far more labors, many

more imprisonments, far worse beatings, many times near death. [24] Five times I received the forty lashes minus one from the Jews.[k] [25] Three times I was beaten with rods.[l] Once I received a stoning.[m] Three times I was shipwrecked.[n] I have spent a night and a day in the open sea. [26] On frequent journeys, I faced dangers from rivers, dangers from robbers,[o] dangers from my own people,[p] dangers from Gentiles, dangers in the city, dangers in the wilderness, dangers at sea, and dangers among false brothers; [27] toil and hardship, many sleepless nights, hunger and thirst, often without food, cold, and without clothing.[q] [28] Not to mention[D] other things, there is the daily pressure on me: my concern for all the churches. [29] Who is weak, and I am not weak? Who is made to stumble,[r] and I do not burn with indignation?

[30] If boasting is necessary, I will boast about my weaknesses. [31] The God and Father[s] of the Lord Jesus, who is blessed forever, knows I am not lying. [32] In Damascus,[t] a ruler[E] under King Aretas guarded the city of Damascus in order to arrest me. [33] So I was let down in a basket through a window in the wall and escaped from his hands.[u]

SUFFICIENT GRACE

12 Boasting is necessary. It is not profitable, but I will move on to visions[v] and revelations[w] of the Lord. [2] I know a man in Christ who was caught up[x] to the third heaven fourteen years ago. Whether he was in the body or out of the body, I don't know; God knows. [3] I know that this man — whether in the body or out of the body I don't know; God knows — [4] was caught up into paradise[y] and heard inexpressible words, which a human being is not allowed to speak. [5] I will boast about

[A] 11:10 Or *silenced*   [B] 11:12 Lit *cut off*   [C] 11:17 Or *business*, or *confidence*   [D] 11:28 Lit *Apart from*   [E] 11:32 Gk *ethnarches*; a leader of an ethnic community

11:12 The false apostles wouldn't boast in these kinds of humble attitudes and actions; thus, they were clearly not Paul's **equals.**
11:13 Paul calls these opponents exactly what they were: **false apostles** and **deceitful workers.** They weren't Christians but devilish impostors.
11:14-15 Don't assume that Satan's temptations and tactics will always be obvious. He's a liar and deceiver, and he's been plying his trade for millennia. The enemy knows how to make succumbing to his temptations appear like good and right things to do. "Put on the full armor of God so that you can stand

against the schemes of the devil" (Eph 6:11), and "resist him, [being] firm in the faith" (1 Pet 5:9).
11:22-29 Paul's point in recounting all his hardships is this: suffering was not an indicator of his failure as an apostle; it was a sign of his superiority. His superior suffering on behalf of his Savior (who suffered!) demonstrated his superior service and commitment.
11:32-33 On one occasion **in Damascus**, he had been lowered down **in a basket through a window in the wall** of the city to escape those who wanted to kill him. The point is he was

willing to be weak and helpless for the sake of proclaiming the gospel.
12:2 The first heaven refers to the earth's atmosphere, and the second heaven is the area that includes the sun, moon, planets, stars, and galaxies. The **third heaven** is the dwelling place of God.

Paul experienced a personal tour of heaven and came back to talk about it! Nevertheless, he speaks of his experience humbly in the third person (**a man, he**) because ultimately he prefers to boast in his weakness (see 12:6-10) since this is where true strength lies and how God is most glorified.

this person, but not about myself, except of my weaknesses.

6 For if I want to boast, I wouldn't be a fool, because I would be telling the truth.[a] But I will spare you, so that no one can credit me with something beyond what he sees in me or hears from me, **7** especially because of the extraordinary revelations. Therefore, so that I would not exalt myself, a thorn in the flesh[b] was given to me, a messenger of Satan[c] to torment me so that I would not exalt myself. **8** Concerning this, I pleaded with the Lord three times that it would leave me. **9** But he said to me, "My grace is sufficient for you, for my power[d] is perfected in weakness."[e]

⟶ HOPE WORDS ⟶

God knows how to teach us to pray. He puts us in situations where prayer is our only option.

Therefore, I will most gladly boast all the more about my weaknesses, so that Christ's power may reside in me. **10** So I take pleasure in weaknesses, insults, hardships, persecutions, and in difficulties, for the sake of Christ.[f] For when I am weak, then I am strong.[g]

SIGNS OF AN APOSTLE

11 I have been a fool; you forced it on me. You ought to have commended me, since I am not in any way inferior to those "super-apostles," even though I am nothing.[h] **12** The signs[i] of an apostle[j] were performed with unfailing endurance among you, including signs and wonders[k] and miracles.[l] **13** So in what way are you worse off than the other churches, except that I personally did not burden you? Forgive me for this wrong!

PAUL'S CONCERN FOR THE CORINTHIANS

14 Look, I am ready to come to you this third time.[m] I will not burden you, since I am not seeking what is yours, but you. For children ought not save up for their parents, but parents for their children. **15** I will most gladly spend and be spent for you.[A,n] If I love you more, am I to be loved less? **16** Now granted, I did not burden[o] you; yet sly as I am, I took you in by deceit![p] **17** Did I take advantage of you by any of those I sent you? **18** I urged Titus[q] to go, and I sent the brother with him. Titus didn't take advantage of you, did he? Didn't we walk in the same spirit[r] and in the same footsteps?

19 Have you been thinking all along that we were defending ourselves to you? No, in the sight of God we are speaking in Christ, and everything, dear friends, is for building you up.[s] **20** For I fear that

[a] 12:6 Ps 119:142; Jn 8:14; 14:6; 2Co 11:10; 1Jn 5:20; 3Jn 3
[b] 12:7 Nm 33:55; Ezk 28:24; Php 3:3
[c] Mt 4:1,10; Ac 13:10
[d] 12:9 Mk 5:30; Lk 1:35; 6:19; Ac 19:11; 2Co 13:4; Rv 11:17
[e] Is 40:29-31; 1Co 2:5; Php 4:13
[f] 12:10 Mt 5:11-12; Rm 5:3; 2Co 13:4
[g] Eph 6:10

[h] 12:11 Gl 6:3
[i] 12:12 Heb 2:4
[j] Ac 1:2; Jd 17
[k] Mk 13:22
[l] Ac 19:11
[m] 12:14 Ac 18; 2Co 2:1; 13:1
[n] 12:15 2Co 1:6; Php 2:17; Col 1:24; 1Th 2:8; 2Tm 2:10
[o] 12:16 1Th 2:7
[p] Ps 10:7
[q] 12:18 Ti 1:4
[r] Ps 51:12
[s] 12:19 1Co 14:3-4

[A] 12:15 Lit *for your souls*, or *for your lives*

12:7 In this context, a **thorn** is something or someone that painfully nags or irritates one's humanity on a continuous basis. Many interpreters have speculated about what Paul's particular thorn might be. That we're left to guess at exactly what it was gives us the freedom to apply any of our "thorns" to this passage, but Paul tells us several things about his. First, it was clearly painful. It brought him **torment**. Second, though God was the ultimate source of the thorn (see 12:8-9), **Satan** served as the delivery system. As in Job's experience, God allowed Satan to bring suffering into Paul's life, but (unlike Satan) God had good purposes in mind. Third, God's intention was that Paul **not exalt** himself as a result of his astonishing experiences. The Lord wanted to keep Paul humble because removing his self-sufficiency would eliminate any stubborn pride, make him more useful, cause him to bear more fruit in ministry, and bring more glory to God.

If God gives you a "thorn in the flesh," you can be certain that it's for your good and because he loves you. Such a thing is intended to unveil anything in your life (an

actual or potential sin) that is not in sync with God's kingdom agenda. Your self-sufficient attitude stands in his way; he wants you to see him as your all-sufficient God. Thus, sometimes God acts like a recycling plant in our lives: he breaks us down so that he can reuse us and increase our anointing.

12:9 When I have a really bad headache, I take extra-strength pain reliever because it has the power to address my problem. My **weakness** drives me to a pill so that its power may be demonstrated in my life. If not for the weaknesses that God allows us to endure, we would lack opportunities to seek his sufficient **grace** and experience his perfect **power**. **12:10** The Lord has grace and power to accomplish in your life only what is possible in the midst of your profound weakness. So by God's grace, **take pleasure in [your] weaknesses** so that his power can be revealed. Then you will be able to say along with the apostle Paul, **When I am weak, then I am strong**.

12:11-12 The Corinthians had compelled Paul to act like **a fool** with his boasting. Rather than putting him in a situation in which he had to defend his ministry, they should

have **commended** him (12:11). Unlike the deceivers, Paul had his ministry validated by supernatural **signs and wonders and miracles** (12:12).

12:13 Some of the Corinthians, no doubt instigated by the false apostles, accused Paul of making them inferior to **other churches**. But given the divine affirmation that accompanied his ministry (see 12:12), the only thing they'd suffered was not being burdened by Paul (see 11:7-9). For this, Paul sarcastically begs, **Forgive me for this wrong!**

12:14-15 Paul had refused funds from the Corinthian church because he was concerned for their spiritual condition, not their money. Like a father, he felt responsible to care for his spiritual **children**—not to have them take care of him (12:14). Nevertheless, because of his **love** for them, he longed that they would love him in return (12:15).

12:20-21 Paul is worried that when he comes he will find the church full of strife and sin (12:20). He laments the fact that he might discover a lack of repentance among those who had **sinned** previously, insisting that this would bring him nothing but grief (12:21).

a 12:20 Ti 3:9
b Jms 3:14
c Rm 2:8
d 1Pt 2:1
e 1Co 14:33,40
f 12:21 Ac 3:19
g 1Th 4:3
h Mk 7:21-22
i 13:1 2Co 12:14
j Dt 17:6; 19:15
k 13:2 Gl 5:21; 1Th 3:4
l 13:3 Mt 10:20; 1Co 5:4
m 13:4 Mt 27:22; Php 2:7-8
n Rm 14:9; Php 1:21;
1Pt 3:18
o 2Co 12:10
p Rm 6:4,8
q 13:5 Jms 1:13

r 13:7 1Pt 2:12
s 13:8 2Th 2:10
t 13:9 Ac 25:5
u 13:10 1Co 14:3
v 2Co 10:4,8
w 13:11 Rm 12:16; Php 1:7
x Mk 9:50; Rm 16:20;
2Tm 1:2
y 1Jn 4:16
z 13:12 Rm 16:16; 1Co
16:20; 1Th 5:26; 1Pt 5:14
aa 13:13 1Co 13:1; 1Jn 4:16
ab 2Th 3:16

perhaps when I come I will not find you to be what I want, and you may not find me to be what you want. Perhaps there will be quarreling,[a] jealousy,[b] angry outbursts, selfish ambitions,[c] slander,[d] gossip, arrogance, and disorder.[e] 21 I fear that when I come my God will again[A] humiliate me in your presence, and I will grieve for many who sinned before and have not repented[f] of the moral impurity, sexual immorality,[g] and sensuality[h] they practiced.

FINAL WARNINGS AND EXHORTATIONS

13 This is the third time I am coming to you.[i] **Every matter must be established by the testimony of two or three witnesses.[B]** [j] 2 I gave a warning when I was present the second time, and now I give a warning[k] while I am absent to those who sinned before and to all the rest: If I come again, I will not be lenient, 3 since you seek proof of Christ speaking in me.[l] He is not weak in dealing with you, but powerful among you. 4 For he was crucified[m] in weakness, but he lives[n] by the power of God. For we also are weak in him,[o] but in dealing with you we will live[p] with him by God's power.

5 Test[q] yourselves to see if you are in the faith. Examine yourselves. Or do you yourselves not recognize that Jesus Christ is in you? — unless you fail the test.[c] 6 And

I hope you will recognize that we ourselves do not fail the test. 7 But we pray to God that you do nothing wrong — not that we may appear to pass the test, but that you may do what is right,[r] even though we may appear to fail. 8 For we can't do anything against the truth,[s] but only for the truth. 9 We rejoice when we are weak and you are strong.[t] We also pray that you become fully mature.[D] 10 This is why I am writing these things while absent, so that when I am there I may not have to deal harshly with you, in keeping with the authority the Lord gave me for building up[u] and not for tearing down.[v]

11 Finally, brothers and sisters, rejoice.[E] Become mature, be encouraged,[F] be of the same mind,[w] be at peace,[x] and the God of love[y] and peace will be with you. 12 Greet one another with a holy kiss.[z] All the saints send you greetings.

13 The grace of the Lord Jesus Christ, and the love[aa] of God, and the fellowship of the Holy Spirit be with you all.[G,ab]

[A] 12:21 Or *come again my God will*   [B] 13:1 Dt 17:6; 19:15   [C] 13:5 Or *you are disqualified*, or *you are counterfeit*   [D] 13:9 Or *become complete*, or *be restored*   [E] 13:11 Or *farewell*   [F] 13:11 Or *listen to my appeal*   [G] 13:12-13 Some translations divide these two vv. into three vv. so that v. 13 begins with *All the saints . . .* and v. 14 begins with *The grace of . . .*

13:1-4 Though Paul himself was **weak**, the risen Christ was operating in him; thus, **God's power** would be displayed among the Corinthians unless the sin was addressed (13:3-4). 13:5 This testing was not for the purpose of determining whether they were saved. Paul was confident that they had experienced God's saving grace in Christ (see, e.g., 1 Cor 1:4-9). Instead, he wants them to **examine** whether Christ's abiding presence was operating through them. They needed to **test** whether they were operating in sync with the true faith or with the heretical teachings of the false apostles. Were they progressing in the faith as disciples? Or were they regressing due to sin and error?
13:7-10 The driving force behind Paul's ministry was fidelity to the truth and the building up of the saints, not personal popularity and acceptance. He would do whatever it took, including disciplining them, in order for God's truth to be preserved.
13:11-13 These exhortations apply to all believers: **rejoice, become mature, be encouraged, be of the same mind, be at peace.** We are capable of all these actions because of the work of God in our lives. If the Corinthians followed through, **the God of love and peace** would be with them and grant them his power (13:11).

GALATIANS

INTRODUCTION

Author

THE WRITER OF THIS BOOK identifies himself as the apostle Paul (1:1), and even most critical New Testament scholars agree that he was the author. Interpreters believe Galatians may be the earliest of his letters.

Historical Background

Paul wrote this letter "to the churches of *Galatia*" (1:2, emphasis added). In his day, the term Galatia could be used to refer to an ethnic group or a province. If Paul was using the term ethnically, then Galatians was written to the people who lived in north central Asia Minor (modern-day Turkey). Alternatively, Paul could have been using the term to speak of the Roman province of Galatia in southern Asia Minor. New Testament scholars describe these two options as the North Galatian theory and the South Galatian theory.

Though certainty is impossible, the South Galatian theory seems most likely for at least two reasons. First, we know Paul ministered extensively in southern Asia Minor during his missionary journeys as described in the book of Acts. However, no clear evidence exists that Paul visited northern Asia Minor. The second reason has to do with when Paul wrote the letter. Those who argue for the South Galatian theory believe he wrote it after his first missionary journey to that region. Those who argue for the North Galatian theory believe Paul wrote later, giving him time to visit that region at some point.

As a result of these two perspectives, interpreters disagree over how to identify Paul's visit to Jerusalem mentioned in Galatians 2:1-10. North Galatian interpreters believe the visit is identical with the Jerusalem Council visit of Acts 15:1-29. But, if so, it's strange that Paul didn't tell the Galatians about the letter that the leaders of the Jerusalem church wrote to Gentile believers after the council (Acts 15:22-29). Doing so would've made sense. After all, the Jerusalem Council dealt with the same problem that Paul seems to address in Galatians: Judaizers were telling Gentile Christians that they had to become circumcised to be saved (see Acts 15:1; Gal 5:1-6; 6:12-13). Thus, it seems more likely that Paul's visit to Jerusalem in Galatians 2:10 is the famine relief visit of Acts 11:27-30.

If "Galatians" refers to the churches Paul visited on his first missionary journey in AD 47–48 (the South Galatian theory), then Paul likely wrote it in AD 48 or 49, prior to the Jerusalem Council in AD 49. That would make Galatians Paul's earliest New Testament letter.

Message and Purpose

The Galatians were bewitched by false teachers known as Judaizers; these people were teaching a gospel that was no gospel at all. Paul wrote to the confused believers in Galatia to help them see that what they were being taught was a false gospel that depended on human efforts to make a person acceptable to God, which was completely contrary to the true gospel of salvation and sanctification by grace through the power of the Holy Spirit.

Throughout Galatians, the contrast between the flesh and the Spirit—between living by human perspective and living by God's perspective—is highlighted. Paul says it's impossible to live by both because they are diametrically opposed to one another. The flesh and the Spirit are at war. That's why Galatians teaches us that the only way to obtain victory over the flesh is to walk by the Spirit. God knows we need this truth because we will continue to battle with the flesh as long as we are in these imperfect bodies. If we are to experience the liberty, freedom, and victory that the true gospel offers, we must adopt a spiritual, kingdom-based mindset so that we live in the power of the Spirit and not in the defeat of the flesh.

VIDEO | INTRO

www.bhpublishinggroup.com/qr/te/48_00

Outline

a 1:1 Ac 13:9
b Mt 5:16; 6:1; 11:27; Jn 8:42
c Ac 9:6; 20:24; 22:10-21; 26:16
d 1:2 Ac 16:6; 18:23; 1Co 16:1; 2Tm 4:10; 1Pt 1:1
e 1:4 Rm 6:23; Ti 2:14
f Mt 20:28; Rm 4:25; 1Co 15:3; Gl 2:20
g Php 4:20; 1Th 1:3; 3:11,13; Heb 10:7; 1Pt 3:17; Rv 10:7
h 1:6 Col 3:15; 1Pt 1:15
i 1:7 Ac 4:12; 1Co 3:11
j Jd 4
k 1:8 Gn 16:7; Mt 13:49; Lk 1:11; Ac 5:19; Rv 14:6
l Rm 15:20
m 1:9 Jd 3
n 1:10 1Th 2:4

o 1:12 1Pt 4:13
p 1Co 11:23; 15:3
q 1:13 2Pt 3:11
r Ac 8:1–9:2; 26:4; Php 3:5-6
s Php 3:6; 2Tm 3:12
t 1:14 Mk 7:3
u 1:15 Mt 24:22; Col 3:15
v 1:16 Jn 5:19; Heb 1:2
w 1:17 Mt 23:37; Ac 8:1
x Jd 17
y Is 21:13; Jr 25:24; Ezk 27:21; Gl 4:25
z 2Sm 8:5
aa 1:18 Ac 9:26
ab Jn 1:42
ac 1:19 Jd 1
ad 1:21 Nm 23:7; Lk 2:2
ae Ac 9:30; 11:25-26
af 1:23 Ac 8:1-3
ag Jd 3
ah 2:1 Ac 15:2-30
ai Ac 4:36
aj Ti 1:4

GREETING

1 Paul,*a* an apostle — not from men or by man, but by Jesus Christ and God the Father*b* who raised him from the dead*c* — **2** and all the brothers who are with me: To the churches of Galatia.*d*

3 Grace to you and peace from God the Father and our Lord^A Jesus Christ, **4** who gave himself for our sins*e* to rescue us from this present evil age,*f* according to the will of our God and Father.*g* **5** To him be the glory forever and ever. Amen.

NO OTHER GOSPEL

6 I am amazed that you are so quickly turning away from him who called*h* you by the grace of Christ and are turning to a different gospel — **7** not that there is another gospel,*i* but there are some*j* who are troubling you and want to distort the gospel of Christ. **8** But even if we or an angel*k* from heaven should preach to you a gospel contrary to what we have preached to you,*l* a curse be on him!^B **9** As we have said before, I now say again: If anyone is preaching to you a gospel contrary to what you received,*m* a curse be on him!

10 For am I now trying to persuade people,*c* or God?*n* Or am I striving to please people? If I were still trying to please people, I would not be a servant of Christ.

PAUL DEFENDS HIS APOSTLESHIP

11 For I want you to know, brothers and sisters, that the gospel preached by me is not of human origin. **12** For I did not receive it from a human source and I was not taught it, but it came by a revelation*o* of Jesus Christ.*p*

13 For you have heard about my former way of life*q* in Judaism:*r* I intensely persecuted*s* God's church and tried to destroy it. **14** I advanced in Judaism beyond many contemporaries among my people, because I was extremely zealous for the traditions of my ancestors.*t* **15** But when God, who from my mother's womb set me apart and called*u* me by his grace, was pleased **16** to reveal his Son*v* in me, so that I could preach him among the Gentiles, I did not immediately consult with anyone.^D **17** I did not go up to Jerusalem*w* to those who had become apostles*x* before me; instead I went to Arabia*y* and came back to Damascus.*z*

18 Then after three years I did go up to Jerusalem*aa* to get to know Cephas,^E,ab and I stayed with him fifteen days. **19** But I didn't see any of the other apostles except James,*ac* the Lord's brother. **20** I declare in the sight of God: I am not lying in what I write to you.

21 Afterward, I went to the regions of Syria*ad* and Cilicia.*ae* **22** I remained personally unknown to the Judean churches that are in Christ. **23** They simply kept hearing: "He who formerly persecuted*af* us now preaches the faith*ag* he once tried to destroy." **24** And they glorified God because of me.^F

PAUL DEFENDS HIS GOSPEL AT JERUSALEM

2 Then after fourteen years I went up again*ah* to Jerusalem with Barnabas,*ai* taking Titus*aj* along also. **2** I went up

---

^A 1:3 Other mss read *God our Father and the Lord*   ^B 1:8 Or *you, let him be condemned*, or *you, let him be condemned to hell*; Gk *anathema*   ^C 1:10 Or *win the approval of people*   ^D 1:16 Lit *flesh and blood*   ^E 1:18 Other mss read *Peter*   ^F 1:24 Or *in me*

1:1-2 Paul wrote his letter to counter a false gospel that was being preached to **the churches of Galatia**. He was God's messenger carrying God's message. They couldn't reject what he had to say without serious consequences.

1:3-4 Holy God cannot overlook humanity's sin and rebellion. He must punish it. But because of God's great love, he sent his Son—fully God and fully man—to suffer and die in our place, bearing the wrath of God against sin. Everyone who trusts in the free gift of Christ's sin-bearing sacrifice on his or her behalf will be saved. This rescue not only justifies sinners for heaven but also gives saints the ability to be delivered from the power of sin on earth in **this present evil age** (1:4).

1:6 The Galatians had been visited by false teachers. These appear to be the same as the "Judaizers" mentioned in Acts who were telling Gentile Christians, "Unless you are circumcised according to the custom pre-

scribed by Moses, you cannot be saved" (Acts 15:1). The good news of justification—being granted a righteous legal standing before God through faith in Jesus Christ—was being undermined by these Judaizers with the result that the Galatian believers would either question the authenticity of their salvation or return to the law as a means for sanctification.

1:7 What was being urged upon the Galatians was an attempt to **distort the gospel of Christ** and to leave grace for the law, which equaled a loss in Christian liberty.

1:10 We must not soft-pedal the good news of salvation through faith in Jesus Christ. Let us, like Paul, desire the approval of God more than people. Obey God and love the lost enough to share the gospel with them.

1:11-12 Christ (1:12) revealed **the gospel** message directly to Paul (1:11) and called him to be his apostle to the Gentiles (see Acts 9:1-19; 26:12-23).

1:13-14 Paul (Saul) had wanted nothing more than to **destroy** the church (1:13), which he

believed was corrupting his Jewish religion. Furthermore, Paul was a rising star in Judaism. He was surpassing his peers in his zeal for **the traditions of** his Jewish **ancestors** (1:14). When it came to Pharisaical law keepers, Paul was the cream of the crop (see Phil 3:4-6).

1:15 Paul's talk of God setting him apart for service when he was in his **mother's womb** uses the same kind of language used to describe Jeremiah's ministry calling from God (see Jer 1:4-5).

1:18-19 Paul wanted the Galatians to know that his apostleship was not derivative from the other apostles. He had not been "ordained" by them. Paul didn't get his gospel authority via **Cephas** (Peter); he got it directly from Christ (1:18).

1:23 Paul's story is a reminder that no one is beyond the grace of God. The vilest sinner can repent and believe. The heart that hates Christ can be softened and filled with love.

2:1 Barnabas and **Titus** were two of Paul's ministry partners.

according to a revelation[a] and presented to them the gospel I preach among the Gentiles, but privately to those recognized as leaders. I wanted to be sure I was not running, and had not been running, in vain. [3] But not even Titus, who was with me, was compelled to be circumcised, even though he was a Greek. [4] This matter arose because some false brothers[b] had infiltrated our ranks to spy on the freedom we have in Christ Jesus in order to enslave us. [5] But we did not give up and submit to these people for even a moment, so that the truth[c] of the gospel would be preserved for you.

[6] Now from those recognized as important (what they[A] once were makes no difference to me; God does not show favoritism[B,d]) — they added nothing to me. [7] On the contrary, they saw that I had been entrusted with the gospel for the uncircumcised,[e] just as Peter[f] was for the circumcised, [8] since the one at work in Peter for an apostleship to the circumcised was also at work in me for the Gentiles. [9] When James,[g] Cephas,[c,h] and John[i] — those recognized as pillars[j] — acknowledged the grace that had been given to me, they gave the right hand of fellowship to me and Barnabas, agreeing that we should go to the Gentiles and they to the circumcised. [10] They asked only that we would remember the poor,[k] which I had made every effort to do.

FREEDOM FROM THE LAW

[11] But when Cephas[c] came to Antioch, I opposed him to his face because he stood condemned.[D] [12] For he regularly ate with the Gentiles before certain men came from James. However, when they came, he withdrew and separated himself, because he feared those from the circumcision party. [13] Then the rest of the Jews[l] joined his hypocrisy,[m] so that even Barnabas was led astray by their hypocrisy. [14] But when I saw that they were deviating from the truth of the gospel, I told Cephas[c] in front of everyone, "If you, who are a Jew, live like a Gentile[n] and not like a Jew,[o] how can you compel Gentiles to live[p] like Jews?"[E]

[15] We are Jews by birth and not "Gentile sinners," [16] and yet because we know that a person is not justified by the works of the law[q] but by faith in Jesus Christ,[F] even we ourselves have believed in Christ Jesus.

a2:2 1Pt 4:13
b2:4 2Pt 2:1
c2:5 2Th 2:10
d2:6 Dt 16:19
e2:7 Col 3:11
fLk 6:14; Ac 10:32

g2:9 Jd 1
h Jn 1:42
i Jn 21:7
j 1Tm 3:15; Rv 3:12; 10:1
k2:10 Mk 14:7; Rm 15:26
l2:13 Rm 2:28-29
m Mk 12:15
n2:14 Rm 1:13
o Rm 14:2
p Rm 6:2
q2:16 Rm 3:20; Gl 3:2,5,10

A2:6 Lit *the recognized ones*   B2:6 Or *God is not a respecter of persons*; lit *God does not receive the face of man*   C2:9,11,14 Other mss read *Peter*
D2:11 Or *he was in the wrong*   E2:14 Some translations continue the quotation through v. 16 or v. 21.   F2:16 Or *by the faithfulness of Jesus Christ*

2:3 **Titus** knew submitting to circumcision could add nothing to the standing Christ had obtained for him before God. Thus, Titus serves as an object lesson of Gentile salvation and ministry involvement apart from the law.
2:4 The **false brothers** only pretended to be followers of **Christ**. They sought **to enslave** the church to legalism—the attempt to earn salvation and sanctification by keeping the law.
2:5 The **truth of the gospel** is that salvation and sanctification come through faith and not through law keeping.
2:6 **Those** who were **recognized as important**, including the other apostles, didn't intimidate Paul. He did not need their validation. God had revealed the message of the gospel directly to Paul through Christ. He needed no human endorsement or permission to preach it.
2:7-8 The church leaders in Jerusalem recognized Paul's apostolic authority. Though Peter and Paul were ministering primarily to different audiences (Jews and Gentiles), their gospel was the same: circumcision is not a requirement for salvation. Salvation is by grace apart from works (see Titus 3:5).

2:10 In the Old Testament, God regularly showed concern for the impoverished and oppressed. He commanded Israel to show compassion and care to the marginalized, including widows and orphans (see Exod 22:22; 23:6; Lev 19:10), and he commands the church to do the same (see 1 John 3:17). His agenda should be our agenda. We should **remember the poor**.
2:11 When Peter (**Cephas**) was in the wrong, Paul loved God, Peter, and others enough to confront his fellow apostle and try to reverse his direction.
2:12-13 Both **Gentiles** (2:12) and their food were considered unclean. To fellowship with Gentiles over a meal, then, would make **Jews** (2:13) spiritually unclean before God.
Previously, when God showed Peter a vision of various unclean animals and commanded him to eat (see Acts 10:9-13), God wasn't merely teaching Peter that he could eat any kind of food. He was assuring him that he could eat with any kind of person. All are equal before God. That's why Peter **regularly ate with Gentiles** (Gal 2:12). The gospel had broken down the racial barrier.

But then **certain men** said to Peter that they clearly found his behavior inappropriate. Perhaps they said, "Of course we 'accept' the Gentile Christians, Peter. But we need to maintain our Jewish identity. Sure we're all equal. But we need to be 'separate but equal.'" And at that moment, because **he feared** these Jews (2:12), Peter failed. He separated himself from his Gentile brothers in Christ. He and those who followed his example thus became hypocrites, preaching about the unifying nature of the gospel message but living contrary to it (2:13).
2:14 **The gospel** had been undermined by Peter's behavior. Gentiles watching Peter (**Cephas**) would have thought, "In order to fellowship with Jewish Christians, I guess we need to adopt Jewish practices like the food laws and circumcision." Such thinking would have convinced them that the gospel hadn't really worked and that racial unity and right standing before God would only result from keeping the law. Legalism and hypocrisy go hand in hand, disrupting the gospel's power to produce racial harmony

*a*2:17 Rm 6:23; 1Tm 1:15
*b*1Co 3:5
*c*Lk 20:16
*d*2:18 Ac 20:32
*e*Rm 2:25,27; Jms 2:9,11
*f*2:19 Rm 7:4; 1Pt 2:24

*g*2:19 Php 1:21
*h*2:20 Mk 10:38; 2Co 13:5
*i*Jn 5:19; Heb 1:2
*j*Jn 3:16
*k*2Th 2:13
*l*Ti 2:14
*m*Lk 20:38; Rm 14:8
*n*2:21 Rm 7:5; 9:31; Gl 5:4;
Php 3:6
*o*1Co 8:11; Php 3:10
*p*3:1 Rm 1:14
*q*Mt 27:22

✥ KINGDOM LIVING ✥
PERSONAL
The Great Prescription

When you are sick, you go to the doctor, and if she finds an infection, she writes you a prescription. Guess what the doctor expects you to do in your pain while you are waiting to get better? Take the medicine she gave you. She doesn't expect you to read about the medicine. She doesn't expect you to talk about the medicine. She doesn't even expect you to understand what the medicine is and how it works. She wants you to take the medicine and allow it to do its job. When you do what the doctor tells you to do, the positive outcome will present itself in time.

Far too many Christians like to talk to other people about what God's Word says we are to do in our lives. We like to think about his Word. Consider it. Mull it around. Research it. Dissect it. But far too few of us actually act on it—putting it into practice.

And yet in his Word, God, the Great Physician, has prescribed what we need in order to live the victorious kingdom life. Whether or not we follow what he has revealed—embracing things like love, forgiveness, trust, faith, humility, self-control, and gentleness—will determine how long it takes for us to see improvement. These are the things being developed within us as God walks with us through the journey of life. These are the characteristics of Christ and the fruit of his Spirit.

When you align your thoughts with his and allow those thoughts to manifest themselves in your choices, you are living out Galatians 2:20 to its fullest: "I have been crucified with Christ, and I no longer live, but Christ lives in me. The life I now live in the body, I live by faith in the Son of God, who loved me and gave himself for me." You are aligned under his kingdom rule.

FOR THE NEXT PERSONAL
KINGDOM LIVING LESSON SEE PAGE 1401.

This was so that we might be justified by faith in Christ[A] and not by the works of the law, because by the works of the law no human being will[B] be justified. **17** But if we ourselves are also found to be "sinners" while seeking to be justified by Christ,[a] is Christ then a promoter[c,b] of sin? Absolutely not![c] **18** If I rebuild[d] those things that I tore down, I show myself to be a lawbreaker.[e] **19** For through the law I died to the law,[f] so that I might live for God.[g] **20** I have been crucified with Christ, and I no longer live, but Christ lives in me.[h] The life I now live in the body,[b] I live by faith in the Son of God,[i] who loved[j] me[k] and gave himself[l] for me.[m] **21** I do not set aside the grace of God, for if righteousness comes through the law,[n] then Christ died[o] for nothing.

JUSTIFICATION THROUGH FAITH

3 You foolish[p] Galatians! Who has cast a spell on you,[E] before whose eyes Jesus Christ was publicly portrayed[F] as crucified?[q] **2** I only want to learn this from you: Did you receive the Spirit by the works of the law or by believing what you heard?[G] **3** Are you so foolish? After beginning by

✥ HOPE WORDS ✥

While other people may walk on you, Jesus will walk with you.

[A]2:16 Or *by the faithfulness of Christ*   [B]2:16 Lit *law all flesh will not*   [C]2:17 Or *servant*   [D]2:20 Lit *flesh*   [E]3:1 Other mss add *not to obey the truth*   [F]3:1 Other mss add *among you*   [G]3:2 Lit *hearing with faith*, also in v. 5

2:18 Paul's point is that the real sin was turning back to the law after one had believed in Christ alone for justification—building up what had been torn down.
2:20 I no longer live, but Christ lives in me. Indeed, my identity in Christ is the most important thing about me. Everything else is secondary. When I place racial or ethnic identity above my identity in Christ (as Peter did), I forget God's amazing grace. I forget **the Son of God . . . gave himself for me** so that I might be reconciled to God and reconciled to others. The cross is not merely a historical event; it affects contemporary life, as well as social and racial relationships.

2:21 By his actions, Peter unwittingly negated God's **grace**. If the Galatians listened to the Judaizers and became law keepers, they would too. And that would be declaring the gospel irrelevant and cancelling the power of grace to work in their lives and ours. Spirituality, then, does not come from performing an external list of rules (this is at the heart of legalism); rather, it comes from the internal flow of grace in and through the life of the believer. In order to live under grace, we must die to the law (see Rom 7:1-4).
3:1 In the Bible, a *fool* isn't someone who lacks intelligence, formal education, or rational capacity. It's someone who lacks spiritual

sense. To believe the false teachers who were encouraging the Galatians to embrace circumcision was, in essence, to make Christ's death unnecessary (see 2:21). It showed a lack of spiritual sense.
3:2 In other words, did you get saved and **receive the Spirit** by keeping the Ten Commandments? Clearly, the Galatians were saved and received the Holy Spirit when they put their faith in Christ alone.
3:3 In other words, were you justified (**beginning**) by the Spirit's application of the death of Christ to your life, but being sanctified (**finishing**) by your flesh—by your human effort apart from the work of the Spirit? Remember,

the Spirit, are you now finishing by the flesh? **4** Did you experience[A,a] so much for nothing — if in fact it was for nothing? **5** So then, does God give you the Spirit and work miracles[b] among you by your doing the works of the law? Or is it by believing what you heard — **6** just like Abraham who **believed God,**[c] **and it was credited to him for righteousness?**[B,d]

7 You know, then, that those who have faith, these are Abraham's sons.[e] **8** Now the Scripture saw in advance that God would justify the Gentiles by faith and proclaimed the gospel ahead of time to Abraham,[f] saying, **All the nations**[c] **will be blessed through you.**[D,g] **9** Consequently those who have faith are blessed with Abraham,[h] who had faith.[E]

LAW AND PROMISE

10 For all who rely on the works of the law are under a curse,[i] because it is written, **Everyone who does not do everything written in the book of the law is cursed.**[F,k] **11** Now it is clear that no one is justified before God by the law, because **the righteous will live**[l] **by faith.**[G,m] **12** But the law is not based on faith; instead, **the one who does these things will live by them.**[H,n] **13** Christ redeemed us from the curse of the law by becoming a curse for us,[o] because it is written, **Cursed is everyone who is hung on a tree.**[I,p] **14** The purpose was that the blessing of Abraham would come to the Gentiles by Christ Jesus, so that we could receive the promised Spirit through faith.[q]

15 Brothers and sisters, I'm using a human illustration. No one sets aside or makes additions to a validated human

[a]3:4 Php 1:29
[b]3:5 Mk 13:22
[c]3:6 Jn 14:1
[d]Gn 15:6
[e]3:7 Jn 8:37,39

[f]3:8 Gn 16:15; Jn 8:37; Heb 2:16
[g]Gn 12:3; 18:18
[h]3:9 Jn 8:39
[i]3:10 Jms 3:10
[j]Ac 15:15
[k]Dt 27:26; Rm 4:15
[l]3:11 Php 1:21
[m]Hab 2:4
[n]3:12 Lv 18:5
[o]3:13 1Pt 2:24
[p]Dt 21:23; Ac 5:30
[q]3:14 Rm 4:16

[A]3:4 Or *suffer* [B]3:6 Gn 15:6 [C]3:8 Or *Gentiles* [D]3:8 Gn 12:3; 18:18 [E]3:9 Or *with believing Abraham* [F]3:10 Dt 27:26 [G]3:11 Hab 2:4 [H]3:12 Lv 18:5 [I]3:13 Dt 21:23

---

sanctification comes through the empowerment of the Spirit in our lives (see 2 Cor 3:17-18)—not from our own will power, effort, or rule keeping.

3:5 Miracles by definition involve the invasion of the supernatural world into the natural world. No matter how hard you work, you can't pull off the miraculous. This can only happen through faith in the power of the Holy **Spirit.**

3:6 When God promised **Abraham** numerous descendants, Abraham didn't try to earn that promise from God; he simply **believed** what **God** said. If, therefore, the great patriarch Abraham was declared righteous on account of his faith (and not because he was circumcised), why did the Galatians need to become circumcised?

3:7-9 Abraham's sons—his spiritual children, both Jews and Gentiles—are **those who have** faith in God, not those who seek to keep the law (3:7). The Judaizers were just plain wrong. **The gospel** was announced **ahead of time to Abraham** when God promised that **all the nations** would be **blessed** through him (3:8; see Gen 12:3). They would be blessed through "the Seed" of Abraham, Jesus Christ (Gal 3:16, 19). God's blessings come to **those who have faith** like **Abraham** (3:9), who exercised faith before the giving of the law. Trying to keep the law to earn acceptance from God is a dead-end street.

3:10 The point here is that unless you obey *everything* in God's **law**, you're under his judgment. His righteous nature demands it. As James says, "Whoever keeps the entire law, and yet stumbles at one point, is guilty of breaking it all" (Jas 2:10).

3:11 Paul continues to point to the Old Testament to underscore the idea that justification comes through faith, not through the law.

Even according to Habakkuk the prophet, **the righteous will live by faith** (see Hab 2:4).

3:13 On the cross, God took the sins of the whole world and credited them to Christ's account. Thus, he was cursed for us so that he might serve as a perfect substitute for us, and so that he might fulfill Scripture: **Cursed is everyone who is hung on a tree** (see also Deut 21:23).

3:14 Remember: God promised to bless "all the nations" (Jews and Gentiles, 3:8) through **Abraham** (3:14; see Gen 12:3). This **blessing**—justification by faith—comes to the world through the Seed, the descendant of Abraham: Jesus Christ (Gal 3:16, 19). As a result of Christ's work, all people who have **faith** in him can **receive the promised** Holy **Spirit.** It is the Spirit's role to activate the perfect righteousness of Christ, who has already fulfilled the law, in the life of the believer who lives by faith.

[a]3:16 Gn 12:7; 13:15;
  17:8; 24:7
[b]3:17 Gn 15:13; Ex 12:40;
  Ac 7:6
[c]3:19 Rm 4:15; 5:20
[d]Gn 16:7; Mt 13:49; Lk 1:11;
  Ac 5:19; Rv 14:6
[e]Heb 8:6
[f]3:20 Dt 6:4

[g]3:22 Rm 6:23
[h]Rm 3:22
[i]Mk 11:24; Jn 3:16; Ac
  10:43; Rm 10:9; 1Pt 1:8-10
[j]3:23 Jd 3
[k]Lk 10:21
[l]3:24 Mt 5:17; Col 2:17;
  Heb 9:10
[m]3:25 Jd 3
[n]3:27 Pr 31:25
[o]3:28 Jn 8:33
[p]Rm 10:12; 1Co 12:13;
  Gl 5:6
[q]Jn 17:11
[r]3:29 Rm 4:14; 8:17
[s]Rm 4:13
[t]4:1 Nm 26:52-62
[u]Col 3:22

will.[A] **16** Now the promises were spoken to Abraham and to his seed. He does not say "and to seeds," as though referring to many, but referring to one, **and to your seed,**[B,a] who is Christ. **17** My point is this: The law, which came 430 years later,[b] does not invalidate a covenant previously established by God[c] and thus cancel the promise. **18** For if the inheritance is based on the law, it is no longer based on the promise; but God has graciously given it to Abraham through the promise.

THE PURPOSE OF THE LAW

19 Why then was the law given?[c] It was added for the sake of transgressions[D] until the Seed to whom the promise was made would come. The law was put into effect through angels[d] by means of a mediator.[e] **20** Now a mediator is not just for one person alone, but God is one.[f] **21** Is the law therefore contrary to God's promises? Absolutely not! For if the law had been granted with the ability to give life, then righteousness would certainly be on the basis of the law. **22** But the Scripture imprisoned everything under sin's

power,[E,g] so that the promise might be given on the basis of faith[h] in Jesus Christ to those who believe.[i] **23** Before this faith[j] came, we were confined under the law, imprisoned until the coming faith was revealed.[k] **24** The law, then, was our guardian until Christ,[l] so that we could be justified by faith. **25** But since that faith[m] has come, we are no longer under a guardian, **26** for through faith you are all sons of God in Christ Jesus.

SONS AND HEIRS

27 For those of you who were baptized into Christ have been clothed with Christ.[n] **28** There is no Jew or Greek, slave or free,[o] male and female;[p] since you are all one[q] in Christ Jesus. **29** And if you belong to Christ, then you are Abraham's seed, heirs[r] according to the promise.[s]

4 **1** Now I say that as long as the heir[t] is a child, he differs in no way from a slave, though he is the owner[u] of everything. **2** Instead, he is under guardians and trustees until the time set by his father. **3** In the same way we also, when we were children, were in slavery under the

[A]3:15 Or *a human covenant that has been ratified*   [B]3:16 Gn 12:7; 13:15; 17:8; 24:7   [C]3:17 Other mss add *in Christ*   [D]3:19 Or *because of transgressions*   [E]3:22 Lit *under sin*

3:16-17 Just as a human will cannot be supplanted (see 3:15), so the Abrahamic covenant could not be supplanted by the Mosaic law. God's covenant with Abraham existed long before he gave Israel the law. And it was ratified unilaterally since it was solely dependent on God (see Gen 15:1-21).

3:18 By pushing **the law** as the basis for salvation, the Judaizers were essentially saying that God's law had eradicated God's promises **to Abraham**.

3:19-20 Why . . . was the law given? Paul gives three answers. First, God gave the law because of Israel's **transgressions** (3:19). Their sin produced the need for the law, which served as a means of restraint. The law identified the actions that were contrary to God's will that would result in his wrath.

Second, the law was set in place as a temporary measure. It was given **until the Seed to whom the promise was made would come** (3:19). Paul has already said that this Seed is Christ (see 3:16). God's promise to bless all the nations through Abraham has been fulfilled through Christ (see 3:8, 14). Through faith in him, we receive the blessing of justification, a righteous standing before God, and the power for sanctification through the work of the Holy Spirit. The coming of Christ issued in a new administration of grace, cancelling the old administration of the law (Eph 1:9-12).

Third, the law was second class. God used both divine intermediaries (**angels**, Gal 3:19; see Acts 7:53; Heb 2:2) and a human intermediary (Moses; see Exod 32:15-16) to establish the law (Gal 3:19). But when it came to God's covenant with Abraham, God spoke his promises *directly* to the patriarch. **A mediator** is used when two parties are involved. Such was the case with the law. God established the law, and Israel was obligated to keep it. In the case of the Abrahamic covenant, though, only **one** party was obligated: **God** (3:20). God alone would fulfill his promises.

3:21-23 God doesn't work against himself. One simply has to understand what **the law** *can do* and what it *cannot*. People couldn't become righteous **on the basis of the law** because people are sinners, incapable of keeping it. The law can't empower sinners to obey; it can't **give life** (3:21). Instead, the law served the promises by helping prepare the way. It revealed God's righteous standards and **imprisoned** everyone **under sin's power** so that people were positioned to receive **the promise** through **faith in Jesus** (3:22).

The law is like a mirror. When you look in a mirror, it shows you that you need to brush your hair, wash your face, and straighten your clothes. But it can't do any of those things for you. The mirror shows your faults, but it can't fix them. That's what the law does for sinful people. It reveals our problem, our disobedience. But it can't enable us to obey.

3:24 In ancient Greco-Roman society, the *paidagōgos* (translated here as **guardian**) was a household slave who was responsible for looking after younger children, providing them with moral instruction and discipline.

3:27 Here Paul speaks of spiritual baptism, the baptism of the Holy Spirit, which is shared by all believers (see 1 Cor 12:13). Everyone who puts faith in Christ is **baptized** into his body and **clothed** with his righteousness. Spiritual growth is the ongoing process of the Holy Spirit making our condition equal to our position.

3:28 Paul is not saying that these distinctions cease to exist. He is saying that in spite of our human differences we are all unified because we are **one in Christ**. No one is superior to anyone else before God. We all share equally in our relationship with him through Jesus. Thus, the Galatians didn't have to keep the law and undergo circumcision as the Judaizers insisted. They didn't have to become Jews.

3:29 Since **Christ** is the true Seed of Abraham (3:16, 19), then those united with him by faith are **heirs** with Christ and, by extension, **Abraham's seed** spiritually (since God still has a plan for the physical seed of Abraham, Rom 11:1).

4:1-3 The point here is that Jews and Gentiles, **when we were children** (before coming to faith in Christ), **were in slavery under the elements of the world** (4:3). Jews were slaves under the law and Gentiles were slaves under false religion. Both systems were based on a philosophy that you have to perform to get God to accept you and to bless you. This perspective is the essence of legalism and has the effect of putting God in our debt—which, of course, he cannot be.

Q Jesus told his disciples to pray to God as "Father," emphasizing the relational side of prayer. What would you say to a person who struggles with relating to God as Father?

A A broken relationship or lack of relationship with an earthly father can affect a person's understanding of the heavenly Father. I urge those who've had such experiences not to let a poor earthly father define the heavenly Father. Instead, they should look for other examples. There are good, godly men out there—men to be emulated, respected, and followed. We should look to those men, and if possible, be mentored by them, not only to see an ongoing illustration of what the heavenly Father is like, but to multiply that example by a billion through our own actions!

What you stare at will determine how you feel. You deal with real feelings because of experiences that truly happened to you. So you need to shift your eyes. Identify a spiritual person who can help you make a clearer connection with your heavenly Father. Then, as you try to increase your intimacy with God, speak to God in his own words. Pray God's Word back to him and assume that what he says is true, even though you may not feel it right now because of your experiences. Again, emulate the right people and assume God is telling the truth. The Holy Spirit's job is to make God's reality real in your life.

FOR THE NEXT Q&A, SEE PAGE 1391.

elements^A^ of the world.^?^ ^4^ When the time came to completion, God sent his Son,^b^ born of a woman,^c^ born under the law,

^5^ to redeem those under the law, so that we might receive adoption as sons.^d^ ^6^ And because you are sons, God sent the Spirit of his Son^e^ into our^B^ hearts, crying, "*Abba,*^c^ Father!"^f^ ^7^ So you are no longer a slave^g^ but a son,^h^ and if a son, then God has made you an heir.^i^

PAUL'S CONCERN FOR THE GALATIANS

^8^ But in the past, since you didn't know God,^j^ you were enslaved to things^D^ that by nature are not gods. ^9^ But now, since you know God,^k^ or rather have become known by God, how can you turn back again to the weak and worthless^l^ elements?^m^ Do you want to be enslaved to them all over again? ^10^ You are observing special days, months, seasons, and years.^n^ ^11^ I am fearful for you, that perhaps my labor for you has been wasted.

^12^ I beg you, brothers and sisters: Become like me, for I also became like you. You have not wronged me; ^13^ you know^E^ that previously I preached the gospel to you because of a weakness of the flesh. ^14^ You did not despise or reject me though my physical condition was a trial for you.^F^ On the contrary, you received me as an angel of God, as Christ Jesus himself.

^15^ Where, then, is your blessing? For I testify to you that, if possible, you would have torn out your eyes and given them to me. ^16^ So then, have I become your enemy because I told you the truth?^o^ ^17^ They court you eagerly, but not for good. They want to exclude you from me, so that you would pursue them. ^18^ But it is always good to be pursued^G^ in a good manner — and not just when I am with you. ^19^ My children,^p^ I am again suffering labor pains^q^ for you until Christ is formed in you. ^20^ I would like to be with you right now and change my tone of voice, because I don't know what to do about you.

^a^4:3 Rm 7:6; 2Pt 2:20
^b^4:4 Jn 5:19; Heb 1:2
^c^Gn 3:15; Lk 2:7; Php 2:7
^d^4:5 Dt 14:1; Mt 5:9
^e^4:6 Ac 16:7; Rm 5:5,20; 8:9,16; 2Co 3:17
^f^Mk 14:36; Rm 8:15
^g^4:7 Mt 10:24; Rv 1:1
^h^Dt 14:1; Mt 5:9
^i^Nm 26:52-62; Rm 4:14; 8:17
^j^4:8 Jn 7:28; Php 3:8
^k^4:9 Pr 2:6; Php 3:8
^l^Mk 14:17; Rm 15:26
^m^Col 2:8
^n^4:10 Rm 14:5; Col 2:16
^o^4:16 Eph 4:15
^p^4:19 1Th 2:11
^q^1Co 4:15; Jms 1:18

^A^4:3 Or *spirits*, or *principles* ^B^4:6 Other mss read *your* ^C^4:6 Aramaic for *father* ^D^4:8 Or *beings* ^E^4:12-13 Or ^12^ *Become like I am, because I — inasmuch as you are brothers and sisters — am not requesting anything of you. You wronged me.* ^13^ *You know* ^F^4:14 Other mss read *me* ^G^4:18 Lit *zealously courted*

4:4-5 Jesus was **born of a woman, born under the law** because the Son of God had to become incarnate as a Jew, a member of the Mosaic covenant, so that he could perfectly obey and fulfill the law (4:4; see Matt 5:17-18). Only then could he **redeem those under** it (Gal 4:5; see 3:13). Those who place faith in him are adopted into God's family.
4:6-7 One implication here is that our former father, Satan (see Eph 2:3), has lost all rights over us, and we have no obligation to obey

him or the flesh (see Rom 8:12). We have a brand-new family under the stewardship of a new teacher and guide.
4:8-9 Indeed, why return to something that binds you when Christ came to set you free?
4:10, 12 The Judaizers had sought to convince the Galatians to observe the Jewish religious calendar as part of their law-keeping efforts to obtain acceptance from God (4:10). Paul therefore urges the Galatians to **become like** him because he had become **like** them

(4:12)—that is, he was like a Gentile who was under no obligation to keep the law. They, on the other hand, were placing themselves back under the law.
4:19 Paul compares himself to a mother in **labor** because he was **suffering** on their behalf, wanting to deliver them from false doctrine and see them transformed into the image of **Christ**. His confusion, pain, and sorrow for them demonstrate the great love he had for those he brought to Christ.

a 4:22 Gn 16:15; Jn 8:37;
Heb 2:16
b Rm 8:15,21; Heb 2:15
c 4:24 Ex 16:1
d Gn 16:1
e 4:25 Is 21:13; Jr 25:24; Ezk
27:21; Gl 1:17
f Mt 23:37; Ac 8:1
g 4:26 Heb 12:22; Rv 3:12;
21:2,10
h 4:27 Ac 15:15
i Gn 11:30; Lk 1:7
j Is 54:1
k 4:28 Ps 105:9; Jms 2:21
l Gn 12:7; Rm 9:8; Gl 3:29
m 4:29 Ps 51:11; Jn 1:33; Ac
2:4; Rm 8:9; Gl 5:25; Ti
3:5; Rv 3:22
n Gn 21:9

o 4:30 Gn 21:10
p 4:31 1Pt 3:6
q 5:1 Rm 14:4; Php 1:27
r 4:21—5:1 Gl 4:22
s 5:4 2Pt 3:18
t 5:5 Jd 21
u Rm 8:23-25; 1Th 1:3
v 5:6 1Th 1:3
w 1Co 13:1; Jms 2:18-22
x 5:7 Jn 8:14; 1Jn 5:20
y 5:8 Col 3:15; 1Pt 1:15

SARAH AND HAGAR: TWO COVENANTS

21 Tell me, you who want to be under the law, don't you hear the law? **22** For it is written that Abraham[a] had two sons, one by a slave[b] and the other by a free woman. **23** But the one by the slave was born as a result of the flesh, while the one by the free woman was born through promise. **24** These things are being taken figuratively, for the women represent two covenants. One is from Mount Sinai[c] and bears children into slavery — this is Hagar.[d] **25** Now Hagar represents Mount Sinai in Arabia[e] and corresponds to the present Jerusalem,[f] for she is in slavery with her children. **26** But the Jerusalem above[g] is free, and she is our mother. **27** For it is written,[h]

Rejoice, childless woman,[i]
unable to give birth.
Burst into song and shout,
you who are not in labor,
for the children of the desolate
woman will be many,
more numerous than those
of the woman who has
a husband.[A,j]

28 Now you too, brothers and sisters, like Isaac,[k] are children of promise.[l] **29** But just as then the child born as a result of the flesh persecuted the one born as a result of the Spirit,[m] so also now.[n] **30** But what does the Scripture say? "Drive out the slave and her son, for the son of the slave

~ HOPE WORDS ~

Freedom means being released from illegitimate restrictions.

will never be a coheir with the son of the free woman."[B,o] **31** Therefore, brothers and sisters, we are not children of a slave but of the free woman.[p]

FREEDOM OF THE CHRISTIAN

5 For freedom, Christ set us free. Stand firm[q] then and don't submit again to a yoke of slavery.[r] **2** Take note! I, Paul, am telling you that if you get yourselves circumcised, Christ will not benefit you at all. **3** Again I testify to every man who gets himself circumcised that he is obligated to do the entire law. **4** You who are trying to be justified by the law are alienated from Christ; you have fallen from grace.[s] **5** For we eagerly await[t] through the Spirit, by faith, the hope[u] of righteousness. **6** For in Christ Jesus neither circumcision nor uncircumcision accomplishes anything; what matters is faith[v] working through love.[w]

7 You were running well. Who prevented you from being persuaded regarding the truth?[C,x] **8** This persuasion does not come from the one who calls you.[y] **9** A little leaven[D] leavens the whole batch of dough. **10** I myself am persuaded in the Lord you will

A 4:27 Is 54:1   B 4:30 Gn 21:10   C 5:7 Or *obeying the truth*   D 5:9 Or *yeast*

4:21-23 It was clear to Paul that many of the Galatians had been deceived and desired **to be under the law** (4:21). So he wanted to make sure that they understood what the law was all about. Paul uses two of Abraham's **sons** and their mothers to make his appeal. Ishmael was born to Hagar, **a slave**. Isaac was born to Sarah, **a free woman** (4:22). Though Ishmael was born by natural means, Isaac was born through supernatural intervention to a woman past her child-bearing years—as a result of God's **promise** (4:23).

4:24-26 Paul is treating the women **figuratively** in order to contrast law and grace. This contrast is reflected in **two covenants** (4:24). **Hagar represents** the Mosaic covenant given at **Mount Sinai.** The Jews who remain under this covenant are, like Hagar, slaves—slaves to the law (4:25). Such was the earthly Jerusalem. **But the Jerusalem above is free** (4:26)—that is, "the new Jerusalem," which will come "down out of heaven from God" one day (Rev 21:2). This city corresponds to Sarah, who represents God's covenant of promise with Abraham, which was fulfilled in Christ and his new covenant sacrifice. The children of this covenant are free children of grace.

4:29-30 Just as Ishmael **persecuted** Isaac (4:29; see Gen 21:9), so the Judaizers who promoted law keeping in order to be made right or remain right with God were persecuting believers with their false teaching (Gal 4:29). In the same way that Sarah cast out the slave woman and her son for mocking Isaac (see Gen 21:10), so too the Galatians should cast out the Judaizers for their legalism (Gal 4:30). Law and grace cannot coexist in the same house (or in the same church).

5:1 Spiritual **freedom** is living a "thank you" life and a "want to" life (relationship), rather than a "have to" life (law). We are to seek to please God and gain approval for our obedience because of our acceptance—not to earn it.

5:2-3 Paul explains that you can't pick and choose which laws you want to obey. If they, for example, insisted on getting **circumcised** (5:2), they would be obligating themselves **to do the entire law** (5:3; see 3:10). Such would keep them from experiencing the power of the substitutionary life of Christ in their lives.

5:4 For believers to be **alienated from Christ** and to **have fallen from grace** is not a reference to losing salvation. The phrase refers to ceasing to operate from a grace standard and adopting a works-based mentality

rather than a relationship-driven one. Doing so leads to nothing but a life of slavery and spiritual defeat—a life lacking joy, love, true obedience, spiritual intimacy, and the power that only grace can provide.

5:5 The hope of righteousness refers to that time when righteousness will flow throughout the earth during the millennial reign of Christ. The life to which God calls us is **by faith** from beginning to end (see Rom 1:17).

5:6 God is not looking for obedience through law keeping; he's looking for obedience motivated by **love** that naturally comes from **faith**.

5:8 The negative influence on them had not come from God (**the one who calls you**) but from Satan working through the false teachers.

5:9 A little leaven leavens the whole batch of dough implies that small things can have a huge impact. The believers in the Galatian churches may have outnumbered the Judaizing teachers, but it only took a few people pushing false doctrine to produce destructive results among the flock.

5:10 Paul was optimistic, believing the truth would prevail: the Galatians would adopt God's view of justification and sanctification by grace, and the false teachers would **pay the penalty**—that is, they'd be judged.

not accept any other view. But whoever it is that is confusing you will pay the penalty.[a] **11** Now brothers and sisters, if I still preach circumcision, why am I still persecuted? In that case the offense of the cross[b] has been abolished. **12** I wish those who are disturbing you might also let themselves be mutilated!

13 For you were called[c] to be free, brothers and sisters; only don't use this freedom as an opportunity[A] for the flesh, but serve one another through love. **14** For the whole law is fulfilled[d] in one statement: **Love your neighbor as yourself.**[B,e] **15** But if you bite and devour[f] one another, watch out, or you will be consumed by one another.

⟋ HOPE WORDS ⟋
You were saved to serve.

THE SPIRIT VERSUS THE FLESH

16 I say then, walk by the Spirit[g] and you will certainly not carry out the desire of the flesh. **17** For the flesh desires[h] what is against the Spirit, and the Spirit desires what is against the flesh; these are opposed to each other, so that you don't do what you want.[i] **18** But if you are led by the Spirit, you are not under the law.

19 Now the works of the flesh are obvious:[c] sexual immorality,[j] moral impurity,[k] promiscuity,[l] **20** idolatry,[m] sorcery,[n] hatreds,[o] strife,[p] jealousy,[q] outbursts of anger,[r] selfish ambitions,[s] dissensions,[t] factions,[u] **21** envy,[D,v] drunkenness, carousing,[w] and anything similar. I am warning you about these things — as I warned you before — that those who practice such things will not inherit the kingdom of God.[x]

22 But the fruit of the Spirit[y] is love,[z] joy,[aa] peace, patience,[ab] kindness,[ac] goodness, faithfulness, **23** gentleness,[ad] and self-control.[ae] The law is not against such things.[E] **24** Now those who belong to Christ Jesus[af] have crucified the flesh[ag] with its passions and desires.[ah] **25** If we live[ai] by the Spirit, let us also keep in step

[a] 5:10 Mt 12:40
[b] 5:11 Lk 9:23
[c] 5:13 Col 3:15
[d] 5:14 Mt 1:22
[e] Lv 19:18; Mt 7:12; 19:19; 22:37-40; Jn 13:34
[f] 5:15 Gl 5:20; Php 3:2,20
[g] 5:16 Rm 8:4; 1Tm 3:16; 2Pt 1:4; 2:10

[h] 5:17 1Pt 2:11
[i] Rm 7:15,23; Php 2:13
[j] 5:19 Mk 7:21; 1Th 4:3
[k] 1Th 4:7
[l] Mk 7:22
[m] 5:20 Col 3:5; 1Pt 4:3
[n] Rv 18:23
[o] Rm 8:7
[p] Ti 3:9
[q] Jms 3:4
[r] Rv 14:19
[s] Rm 2:8
[t] Rm 16:17
[u] 2Pt 2:1
[v] 5:21 Rm 1:29
[w] Rm 13:13; 1Pt 4:3
[x] 1Co 6:10; 15:50
[y] 5:22 Mt 7:16-20; Rm 6:21; 7:4; 8:5; Eph 5:9
[z] 1Co 13:1; Phm 5
[aa] Jn 15:11; 2Co 6:10
[ab] Ex 34:6; 2Tm 3:10
[ac] Ps 25:6; 2Co 6:6
[ad] 5:23 Jms 3:13
[ae] 2Pt 1:6
[af] 5:24 Nm 3:12
[ag] Rm 8:12
[ah] 2Pt 1:4; 2:10
[ai] 5:25 Php 1:21; 3:16

[A] 5:13 Lit *a pretext*; a military term for abuse of position　[B] 5:14 Lv 19:18　[C] 5:19 Other mss add *adultery,*　[D] 5:21 Other mss add *murders,*　[E] 5:23 Or *Against such things there is no law*

5:11 Paul was being **persecuted** by Jews because he didn't preach the need to keep the law, illustrated through **circumcision**. The fact of his persecution demonstrated that he was truly preaching the cross. The message **of the cross**—that we are justified by faith alone in Christ's substitutionary sacrifice alone—is an **offense** or stumbling block to those who proudly insist on pleasing God through their own efforts.

5:12 As sure as emasculation would make a man unable to reproduce physically, Paul wanted the Judaizers to be unable to reproduce spiritually.

5:13 Spiritual **freedom** is not the absence of boundaries. Suppose a football player catches the ball and wants to play the game without restrictions. He proceeds to run out of bounds and into the stands to avoid being tackled. Eventually, he re-enters the stadium and crosses into the end zone from the opposite direction. He's no longer playing football but creating chaos. Football can only be football when played within the boundaries of sidelines.

So what does Christian freedom look like? Serving **one another through love**. Remember: biblical love is the decision to compassionately, righteously, and sacrificially seek the well-being of another. Since the Son of God served *us* through love, why would his disciples expect to do anything less?

5:14-15 When crabs are cooked, they're placed in a pot of water. As the water temperature within the pot starts to rise, the crabs attempt to climb out, only to discover that their fellow crabs pull them back in as they likewise attempt to escape. When church members

assume an every-man-for himself mind-set rather than a serve-through-**love** mind-set, they will claw and grab one another until all are roasted in the pot.

5:16 When Scripture talks about our "walk," it's talking about the conduct of our lives. To **carry out the desire of the flesh** is to live life based on a sinful human viewpoint. To **walk by the Spirit** is to *discover* God's view on a matter, *decide* to act on that divine perspective, and *depend* on the Holy Spirit to empower your obedience. Notice that walking by the Spirit doesn't mean resting while the Spirit does all the work. We are called to *walk* while trusting in the Spirit's empowerment. It's much like walking on a moving sidewalk at the airport. You are walking in dependence on a power at work underneath you.

Note too that you focus on walking by the Spirit first, and he overrides—not necessarily cancels—the desires of the flesh. To flip that order is either to lose the battle or to settle for flesh management rather than true spiritual transformation.

5:17 There's a civil war happening in every Christian, a battle between **the flesh** and **the Spirit.** Thus, in our decision-making, we face the pull of living from two very different perspectives with different goals. Choices will lead to different outcomes. The life of faith is the life of walking by the Spirit.

5:18 Since in the Greek text there is no article before law, Paul is not only speaking of the **law**, of Moses but the "law principle," which is seeking to use our own strength (the flesh) to have victory or to motivate God to do something. The difference between living

under law versus living under grace is the difference between utilizing a battery that you must keep recharging versus being continually plugged-in to an electrical outlet.

5:19-21 No one has to guess at what **the works of the flesh** might be (5:19). They don't reside only in the mind but demonstrate themselves in human deeds. They include sexual sins (summarized by **sexual immorality**), superstitious sins (like **sorcery**), and social sins (like **hatreds . . . jealousy . . . selfish ambitions** (5:19-20). They also include **anything similar** (5:21). Such things are the natural result of living according to the flesh and are evidence we are not walking in the Spirit.

5:22-23 While the works of the flesh destroy (see 5:19-21), **the fruit of the Spirit** provides life and refreshment. It benefits others. To *love* is to seek another person's good—especially when that person can do nothing for you in return. *Joy* is the settled celebration of the soul within us, even when circumstances don't make us happy. *Peace* results when strife gives way to harmony. To exercise *patience* is to be long-suffering instead of short-tempered. We demonstrate *kindness* when we help rather than hurt. *Goodness* summarizes the virtuous acts and attitudes that advance the kingdom of God and benefit others. *Faithfulness* means constancy, perseverance, and dependability. *Gentleness* is seen in the one who practices tenderness in submission to God. When we say no to sin and yes to God in the midst of temptation, we exhibit *self-control*. The fruit of the Spirit is primarily manifested in our relationships.

5:25 The verb for **"keep in step"** is different from the word for "walk" in 5:16. It means

a 5:26 Php 2:3
b 6:1 Jms 3:13
c Ps 51:12
d Jms 1:13
e 6:2 1Co 9:21
f 6:3 1Co 3:18; 2Co 12:11; Gl 2:6
g 6:4 Mk 14:6; Gl 3:10; Jms 2:14-26
h 6:6 Rm 15:27; 1Pt 5:2

i 6:8 Ps 51:11; Jn 1:33; Ac 2:4; Rm 8:9; Gl 5:25; Ti 3:5; Rv 3:22
j Jn 12:25; Ac 13:48
k 6:9 2Th 3:13
l Lk 18:18; Jms 4:17
m 6:10 2Jn 8
n Gn 1:31; 3Jn 11
o 1Tm 5:8
p Jd 3
q 6:12 Php 3:3
r Ac 15:1
s 2Tm 3:12
t Php 3:18
u 6:13 Lk 11:28

with the Spirit. [26] Let us not become conceited, provoking one another, envying one another.[a]

CARRY ONE ANOTHER'S BURDENS

6 Brothers and sisters, if someone is overtaken in any wrongdoing, you who are spiritual, restore such a person with a gentle[b] spirit,[A,c] watching out for yourselves so that you also won't be tempted.[d] [2] Carry one another's burdens; in this way you will fulfill the law of Christ.[e] [3] For if anyone considers himself to be something when he is nothing,[f] he deceives himself. [4] Let each person examine his own work,[g] and then he can take pride in himself alone, and not compare himself with someone else. [5] For each person will have to carry his own load.

[6] Let the one who is taught the word share[h] all his good things with the teacher. [7] Don't be deceived: God is not mocked. For whatever a person sows he will also reap, [8] because the one who sows to his flesh will reap destruction from the flesh, but the one who sows to the Spirit[i] will reap eternal life[j] from the Spirit. [9] Let us not get tired[k] of doing good,[l] for we will reap at the proper time if we don't give up. [10] Therefore, as we have opportunity, let us work[m] for the good[n] of all, especially for those who belong to the household[o] of faith.[p]

CONCLUDING EXHORTATION

[11] Look at what large letters I use as I write to you in my own handwriting. [12] Those who want to make a good impression in the flesh[q] are the ones who would compel you to be circumcised[r] — but only to avoid being persecuted[s] for the cross[t] of Christ. [13] For even the circumcised don't keep[u] the law themselves, and yet they want you to be circumcised in order to boast about your flesh. [14] But as for me, I will never boast about anything except the cross of our Lord Jesus Christ. The world has been crucified to me through

[A] 6:1 Or *with the Spirit of gentleness*

---

to march in step with your commander so that he can lead you, step-by-step. Therefore, the Holy Spirit must be included in every move we make if we truly want him to lead us. Live based on the divine perspective of God's Word and pray for the Spirit's empowerment. The result will be victory over the flesh, the production of spiritual fruit (see 5:22-23), and service through love (see 5:13).

5:26 To **become conceited** regarding spiritual fruit in your life is to forget its source, and it will serve as a quick way to end the Spirit's fruit production in you. The same is true of **envying** the fruit bearing of another. To "love your neighbor as yourself" (5:14) is to celebrate the goodness in the lives of our spiritual brothers and sisters, just as we would desire them to do for us.

6:1 When you help a fellow Christian in trouble due to a sin from which they can't free themselves, you must do so **with a gentle spirit.** Gentleness doesn't mean soft-pedaling the diagnosis or the prescription. We're not to compromise the truth. Instead, we are to treat the person as we'd want to be treated—with patience, care, and kindness, restoring him or her with the least amount of pain possible. But be careful. Watch out that you aren't **tempted** as well. The tempter who wreaked havoc in your brother's life has his eye on you too.

6:2 Burdens don't necessarily imply sin. The burdens of life can include all sorts of weighty problems: physical, relational, financial, and emotional. Believers are to serve one another like spotters serving those who are lifting weights. When the strain of a burden becomes more than an individual can bear, a

spotter helps lift the weight off of his chest. Carrying the burden of another can take an unlimited number of forms, including prayer, making time for a person, providing practical assistance, giving financial assistance, and providing a listening ear. Such burden bearing **will fulfill the law of Christ,** the law of love (see 5:13-14; see John 13:34).

6:3 No one is too good to serve and carry burdens. After all, the Lord Jesus served his disciples by washing their feet (see John 13:2-15). If the Master didn't consider himself above service, how can we?

6:4 The only one to whom you should **compare** yourself is Jesus. Do that, and you'll never think more of yourself than you ought.

6:5 Helping with burdens doesn't mean carrying someone's full **load** for them so that they are alleviated of all responsibility. Each must be willing **to carry** his own backpack.

6:6 It's right and good to invest materially in that which brings you spiritual life and growth. Reciprocity in ministry keeps believers from becoming selfish and self-centered.

6:7 God has established certain laws that govern the universe he has made. This is true in the physical world (e.g., the law of gravity). But it's true of the spiritual world as well. Paul articulates an important spiritual law or principle when he says, **Whatever a person sows he will also reap.** A farmer harvests exactly what he plants. If he sows potatoes, he won't be looking to harvest green beans. Decide what you want to harvest spiritually, and let that control what you decide to sow.

This law is universal (it applies to all people everywhere) and inviolable (it proves true

without fail). Don't kid yourself into believing that you can rebel against God without consequence.

6:9 Remember that there's an appropriate seasonal time gap for the purpose of development between sowing and reaping.

6:10 We are to sow in the Spirit by busily doing **good** works that benefit others in Jesus's name. And while we are called to show love to all people, we are to have a special love for the people of God.

6:11 It's possible that Paul may have used an amanuensis, a secretary, to write his letter (see Rom 16:22), before taking up the pen himself to write these final words. Regardless, Paul calls attention to the **large letters** he uses here to add emphasis to his argument. We sometimes use bold type, italics, or all capital letters for similar purposes.

6:12-13 Not only was the message of the Judaizers corrupt, but their motives also were corrupt. They pushed circumcision **to avoid being persecuted for the cross of Christ** (6:12). Since they knew it would lead to persecution from fellow Jews, they adopted and pushed a false gospel instead. The Judaizers were also motivated by a desire **to boast about** the Galatians—that is, to boast in the fact that they had convinced them to become **circumcised** (6:13). Thus returning them to life under the law and removing them from life under grace.

6:14 Our lives should identify more with our Savior than with **the world** that is opposed to him. When being covered by Christ's blood shed on **the cross** becomes our claim to fame, we will find ourselves fulfilling the law by the Spirit and not attempting to do so by the works of the flesh.

the cross, and I to the world. **15** For[A] both circumcision and uncircumcision[a] mean nothing; what matters instead is a new creation.[b] **16** May peace come to all those who follow this standard, and mercy even to the Israel[c] of God![B]

17 From now on, let no one cause me trouble, because I bear on my body the marks of Jesus.[d] **18** Brothers and sisters, the grace of our Lord Jesus Christ be with your spirit.[e] Amen.

6:15 Col 3:11
6:16 Jn 1:3; Rv 3:14
6:16 Lk 3:8

6:17 Php 3:10
6:18 Ps 51:12

[A] **6:15** Other mss add *in Christ Jesus*   [B] **6:16** Or *And for those who follow this standard, may peace and mercy be upon them, even upon the Israel of God,* or *And as many who will follow this standard, peace be upon them and mercy even upon the Israel of God.*

6:15 Christianity is not about a set of rules but about a growing dynamic relationship with the living God. As Paul said earlier, "There is no Jew or Greek" (3:28)—not that these distinctions don't exist but that they don't matter before God. Being made **a new creation** is what matters (6:15). "If anyone is in Christ, he is a new creation" (2 Cor 5:17). Your relationship with Christ is the most important thing about you.

6:17 These **marks of Jesus** are probably visible wounds and scars that Paul carried with him as a result of his gospel ministry (see Acts 14:19; 16:22-23; 2 Cor 6:4-5; 11:23-25).

EPHESIANS

INTRODUCTION

Author

THE AUTHOR OF EPHESIANS TWICE identifies himself as Paul (1:1; 3:1), and the early church accepted the book as being written by the apostle. Some scholars think the writing style, vocabulary, and even some teachings of the letter are not typical of Paul, but the objections are exaggerated. Furthermore, the evidence we have from the early church indicates that early Christians rejected letters known to be pseudonymous (falsely written under someone else's name). So there is no good reason to dispute that Paul authored Ephesians.

Historical Background

Paul stayed at Ephesus, the capital city of the province of Asia, for almost three years (see Acts 20:31)—probably from AD 51 to 54 or 52 to 55. He subsequently penned this letter while in prison (Eph 3:1; 4:1; 6:20). Disagreement exists concerning whether Paul wrote Ephesians while imprisoned in Caesarea (Acts 23:23, 33-35; 24:22-23, 27) around AD 57–59 or while held in Rome (Acts 28:30) in about AD 60–62, but Christian tradition suggests that Paul wrote Ephesians from Rome around AD 60–61. Paul was under house arrest in guarded rental quarters (Acts 28:30). He most likely wrote Colossians, Philemon, and Philippians during the same imprisonment.

Little is known about the Christian recipients of the letter. It was carried to its destination by Tychicus, who in Ephesians 6:21 and Colossians 4:7 is identified as Paul's emissary. The Ephesian and Colossian letters probably were delivered at the same time since the apostle noted in both that Tychicus would inform the churches concerning Paul's situation.

Message and Purpose

Central to the message of Ephesians is the re-creation of the human family according to God's original kingdom intention for humankind. Jews and Gentiles are brought together in Christ as one people. For those who trust in Jesus, the distinction between Jew and Gentile is abolished by his sacrificial death. No more hindrance remains to reuniting all humanity as the people of God with Christ as the head (Eph 1:22-23). The new body, the church, has been endowed by the power of the Holy Spirit to enable those comprising it to serve together in unity (1:3–2:10), and to live new lives of faith and maturity for the fulfillment of God's kingdom program (4:1–6:9).

www.bhpublishinggroup.com/qr/te/49_00

Outline

EXPOSITION OF EPHESIANS

www.bhpublishinggroup.com/qr/te/49-07

GREETING

1 Paul,[a] an apostle of Christ Jesus by God's will:[b]

To the faithful saints[c] in Christ Jesus[A] at Ephesus.[B,d]

2 Grace to you and peace from God our Father and the Lord Jesus Christ.

GOD'S RICH BLESSINGS

3 Blessed is the God and Father of our Lord Jesus Christ, who has blessed us with every spiritual blessing in the heavens in Christ.[e] **4** For he chose us in him, before the foundation of the world, to be holy and blameless in love before him.[c,f] **5** He predestined us to be adopted as sons through Jesus Christ for himself, according to the good pleasure of his will, **6** to the praise of his glorious grace[g] that he lavished on us in the Beloved One.[h]

7 In him we have redemption[i] through his blood, the forgiveness[j] of our trespasses, according to the riches of his grace **8** that he richly poured out on us with all wisdom and understanding.[D] **9** He made known to us the mystery of his will,[k] according to his good pleasure that he purposed in Christ[l] **10** as a plan for the right time[E] — to bring everything together in Christ,[m] both things in heaven and things on earth[n] in him.[o]

11 In him we have also received an inheritance,[f] because we were predestined[p] according to the plan of the one who works out everything in agreement with the

purpose of his will, **12** so that we who had already put our hope[q] in Christ might bring praise to his glory.[r]

13 In him you also were sealed with the promised Holy Spirit[s] when you heard the word of truth,[t] the gospel of your salvation, and when you believed. **14** The Holy Spirit is the down payment[u] of our

⮞ Questions & Answers ⮜

Q In Ephesians 1:10 Paul states that God's plan is "to bring everything together in Christ." Why is this the goal of the outworking of God's plan for this world, and why should it be good news for us?

A Ephesians 1:10 is Paul's philosophy of history. God intends for all things to culminate in the rule of Jesus Christ. Why is that important? It means God is going to fulfill his kingdom purpose for man to rule the world under him (see Ps 8:3-8). The first Adam failed, submitting to the devil's agenda instead of God's. But the last Adam, Jesus Christ, won't fail. He will fulfill all of God's purposes. Regardless of what you see happening in the world, God's program is still in place. Jesus has won the victory, and he will rule.

———————————————
FOR THE NEXT Q&A, SEE PAGE 1394.

[a] 1:1 Ac 13:9
[b] Eph 1:9
[c] Eph 5:2
[d] Ac 18:19-21; 19:9-10; 20:3,17; 1Co 15:32; Rv 2:1
[e] 1:3 Eph 1:20; 2:6; 3:10; 6:12
[f] 1:4 Jd 24
[g] 1:6 Jn 1:14; Rm 5:2; 2Co 4:15
[h] Mt 3:17; Jn 3:35; 10:17; Col 1:13
[i] 1:7 Heb 9:12
[j] Ps 25:11; Mt 9:2; Mk 2:5; Lk 24:47
[k] 1:9 Rm 11:25; 16:25; Eph 3:3; Col 1:27
[l] Rm 9:11
[m] 1:10 Mt 1:17; Eph 5:2
[n] Php 2:10
[o] Col 1:16
[p] 1:11 Pr 19:21

[q] 1:12 1Th 1:3
[r] Mk 10:37
[s] 1:13 Ps 51:11; Jn 1:33; Ac 2:4; Rm 8:9; Gl 5:25; Ti 3:5; Rv 3:22
[t] Col 1:5; 2Th 2:10
[u] 1:14 Gn 38:17-18,20; 2Co 1:22; 5:5

[A] 1:1 Or *to the saints, the believers in Christ Jesus* [B] 1:1 Other mss omit *at Ephesus* [C] 1:4 Or *in his sight. In love* [D] 1:8 Or *on us. With all wisdom and understanding,* [E] 1:10 Or *the fulfillment of times* [F] 1:11 Or *In him we are also an inheritance,*

1:2 This is Paul's trademark salutation: **Grace to you**.

1:3 To bless the name of God is to speak well of him, to praise him. *Worship* is the celebration of who God is, what he has done, and what we are trusting him to do. God is not interested in spectators. He invites us to praise him.

Paul says, **in Christ**, God **has [already] blessed [believers] with every spiritual blessing in the heavens**—or we could translate it "heavenly places" (see 1:20-21; 2:6; 3:10; 6:12). This is a reference to the spiritual *realm where God and Satan battle* for our allegiance. We live in the physical realm with our problems, needs, struggles, and sins. But whatever happens in the physical realm originates in the spiritual realm. Although conflict is visible fruit, its root is spiritual in nature.

Paul says God has already done everything he is ever going to do for believers. He's blessed them with "every spiritual blessing" in the heavenly places. And, as Paul will soon say, believers are "seated" there with Jesus (2:6). Think of this like a video teleconference in which you're in two places at once—seated physically in one

place but operating in another. Believers are present in two places at the same time: We're physically located on earth but operate from heavenly places. God wants our position there to dictate our activity on earth.

1:4 God created us for himself, for *his* happiness. He's chosen us **to be holy and blameless** so that the church will bring *him* pleasure.

1:5-6 The focus of the book of Ephesians is on the corporate church, not on individual Christian salvation (see 1:22-23; 2:14, 16, 22; 3:10, 21; 4:16; 5:32). Therefore, the choosing and election to which Paul refers is not for individuals to eternal life but regards God's choice to establish a people (the body of Christ) **in the Beloved One** (1:6) whose purpose is to reflect his holy character in a sinful world. God predetermined to bring a group of people into his family, drafting them into his Son so they'd receive spiritual benefits and manifest his heavenly rule in their lives. Election is for service and spiritual benefit, not for individual, personal salvation.

1:7-8 In the ancient world, slaves could be redeemed; a price could be paid for their free-

dom. **Redemption** from sin comes through the price paid by Jesus Christ **through his blood** (1:7). Why blood? Because the judgment for sin is death (Rom 6:23), and shedding blood means taking life (see Deut 12:23). The sinless Son of God had to die to pay for our sins so we might have **forgiveness** (Eph 1:7)— God's grace **richly poured out on us** (1:8).

1:9-10 In Christ, **things in heaven and things on earth** are unified (1:10) so that we might be aligned under God's kingdom reign, living transformed lives for his pleasure. God's philosophy of history is to bring all things under the rule of his Son.

1:13 Official documents were **sealed** in antiquity, implying protection and ownership. When you believe in Christ as your Savior, God puts you inside an envelope called Jesus. You are "in Christ." But God also guarantees delivery. He registers the letter and seals it with the **Holy Spirit**—indicating that he is its owner and the only one qualified to open it.

1:14 Like an engagement ring, the Holy Spirit is a **down payment** on an eternal commitment. The Spirit is a heavenly first

a 1:17 Ps 51:12
b 1Pt 4:13
c 1:18 1Th 1:3

d 1:18 Col 3:15
e 1:19 Ac 4:33
f 1:20 Php 2:9
g Jn 20:17; Eph 1:3; 2:6;
3:10; 6:12; Php 2:10;
1Pt 3:22
h 1:21 2Tm 2:19
i Mk 10:30

⋙ KINGDOM LIVING ⋘
CHURCH
We Are the House of God

The church is a microcosm of the kingdom, which is the larger expression of God's rule. In fact, it is the church's chief responsibility to introduce Jesus Christ and his kingdom to society at large. Our job as members of the church is to live in a way that shows the world a clear picture of the kingdom and that all things are to fall underneath the Lord Jesus Christ (see Eph 1:22-23). The church should present to the broader culture a working illustration of God's solutions to the problems the culture faces so that the culture can replicate the solutions in society at large. People who want to see heaven at work on earth should be able to discover it in the church.

Paul says in Ephesians 2:21 that the church is a building "being put together [and growing] into a holy temple in the Lord." What does a temple do? It houses God. That's what the temple did in the Old Testament; that's where the presence and the glory of God resided. In the same way,

the glory of God in this age resides within the church—within us.

Therefore, we should be seeing society impacted because of the church's presence. A faulty eschatology and ecclesiology, however, lead to a church in history having little impact on the culture. Where the glory of God is, transformation is close by.

When the powerful reality of God's kingdom is brought to bear in society, that society should be in the process of being transformed because God's kingdom institution—the church—is present in its midst, mediating the blessings of comprehensive rule to the broader society. The church is to be the visible manifestation of the kingdom in history.

FOR THE NEXT CHURCH
KINGDOM LIVING LESSON SEE PAGE 1394.

---

inheritance, until the redemption of the possession, to the praise of his glory.

PRAYER FOR SPIRITUAL INSIGHT

15 This is why, since I heard about your faith in the Lord Jesus and your love for all the saints, **16** I never stop giving thanks for you as I remember you in my prayers. **17** I pray that the God of our Lord Jesus Christ, the glorious Father,[A] would give you the Spirit[B,a] of wisdom and revelation[b] in the knowledge of him. **18** I pray that the eyes of your heart may be enlightened so that you may know what is the hope[c] of his

calling,[d] what is the wealth of his glorious inheritance in the saints, **19** and what is the immeasurable greatness of his power[e] toward us who believe, according to the mighty working of his strength.

GOD'S POWER IN CHRIST

20 He exercised this power in Christ by raising him from the dead and seating him at his right hand[f] in the heavens[g] — **21** far above every ruler and authority, power and dominion, and every title given,[C,h] not only in this age but also in the one to come.[i] **22** And **he subjected everything**

A 1:17 Or *the Father of glory*   *B* 1:17 Or *a spirit*   *C* 1:21 Lit *every name named*

---

installment given in anticipation of eternal life, a life that is eternally secure. He's a foretaste of what's ahead.

1:17 Paul prays God would give them **wisdom**. *Wisdom* is effectively applying divine truth to the twists, turns, and dangers of everyday life. But Paul correlates the ability to be wise with the **knowledge of** God. They are tied together. Trying to be wise without knowing God *is like flying a plane without having a control tower to help you navigate*. We all need the help of someone who can see what we can't.

1:18 Paul prays that **the eyes of [their] heart[s] may be enlightened**. Since I'm a platinum flyer for an airline, I was given a booklet explaining the privileges of membership. But

for a long time, I never read it. When I finally did, I found that I had privileges available to me that could make my life and travel much more convenient. A lack of awareness about what's available to those in the family of God similarly causes people to miss out, so Paul wants the Ephesians to be aware of their family privileges. Knowing who their Daddy is has *staggering* implications.

Many Christians are living spiritually poor lives, while sitting on a pile of spiritual **wealth**. While God holds most of your spiritual **inheritance** for eternity, he will give you what you need now to fulfill his purpose for you.

1:19 God can flip, turn, and twist things around. If you're a believer in Jesus, you're

a candidate to see the working of God's immeasurably great **power** in your life.

1:20 If your circumstances are bad, remember that God's immeasurably great **power** raised Jesus **from the dead**. And that same resurrection power is available to help you in whatever you face. God can invade the circumstances of your life and demonstrate his sufficiency.

1:22-23 God the Father has **appointed** his Son **as head over everything for the church, which is his body**. Therefore, the church, operating under Christ's kingdom authority (i.e., headship), can give the world a picture of what life under God's kingdom authority looks like.

under his feet[A,a] and appointed him[B] as head[b] over everything for the church, **23** which is his body,[c] the fullness[d] of the one who fills all things[e] in every way.

APPLICATION QUESTIONS

READ EPHESIANS 1:20-23

– What do you like best about your local church? Why?

– Do you view your church as a place where you can meet with and experience God? Explain.

FROM DEATH TO LIFE

2 And you were dead[f] in your trespasses and sins **2** in which you previously lived according to the ways of this world,[g] according to the ruler of the power of the air,[h] the spirit[i] now working in the disobedient.[c] **3** We too all previously lived among them in our fleshly[j] desires, carrying out the inclinations[k] of our flesh and thoughts, and we were by nature children under wrath[l] as the others were also. **4** But God, who is rich in mercy,[m] because of his great love[n] that he had for us,[D] **5** made us alive[o] with Christ even though we were dead[p] in trespasses. You are saved by grace! **6** He also raised us up with him and seated us with him in the heavens in Christ Jesus,[q] **7** so that in the coming ages[r] he might display the immeasurable

Video Devotional

"PUSH PLAY AND BELIEVE"

www.bhpublishinggroup.com/qr/te/49-02

Salvation comes by faith alone in Christ alone.

∽ HOPE WORDS ∾

Where you stand must be determined by where you're seated.

---

riches[s] of his grace through his kindness[t] to us in Christ Jesus. **8** For you are saved by grace[u] through faith, and this is not from yourselves; it is God's gift — **9** not from works, so that no one can boast. **10** For we are his workmanship, created[v] in Christ Jesus for good works, which God prepared ahead of time[w] for us to do.

∽ HOPE WORDS ∾

Grace is all that God has done and will do because of what Jesus Christ did.

UNITY IN CHRIST

11 So then, remember that at one time you were Gentiles in the flesh — called "the uncircumcised" by those called "the circumcised,"[x] which is done in the flesh by human hands.[y] **12** At that time you were without Christ, excluded from the citizenship of Israel, and foreigners to the covenants of promise,[z] without hope[aa] and without God in the world. **13** But now in Christ Jesus, you who were far away have been brought near by the blood[ab] of Christ. **14** For he is our peace, who made both groups one[ac] and tore down the dividing wall of hostility. In his flesh, **15** he made of no effect the law consisting of commands and expressed in regulations, so that he might create[ad] in himself one[ae] new man from the two, resulting in peace. **16** He did this so that he might reconcile both to God

---

[a] 1:22 Ps 8:6; Rm 13:1; 1Co 15:27; 1Pt 3:22
[b] Col 2:10
[c] 1:23 Eph 4:4
[d] Jn 1:16
[e] Col 3:11
[f] 2:1 Jn 5:25
[g] 2:2 2Pt 2:20
[h] 2Pt 2:10; Jd 8
[i] 1Co 2:12; 1Tm 4:1
[j] 2:3 Php 3:3
[k] Mt 21:31; Lk 12:47; 23:25; Jn 1:13; 1Co 7:37; 2Pt 1:21
[l] Rm 2:5; Rv 6:16
[m] 2:4 Lk 1:50
[n] 1Co 13:1; 1Jn 4:16
[o] 2:5 Col 2:13; 1Tm 5:6
[p] Jn 5:25
[q] 2:6 Eph 1:3,20; 3:10; 6:12; Php 2:10; 1Pt 3:22
[r] 2:7 Mk 10:30
[s] 2:7 Lk 8:14; 2Co 8:9
[t] Ps 25:6
[u] 2:8 Rm 3:24; 6:14; 11:6; Gl 2:21; 2Tm 1:9
[v] 2:10 Jn 1:3; Rv 3:14
[w] Rm 9:23
[x] 2:11 Gl 6:15
[y] Php 3:3
[z] 2:12 Gn 12:7
[aa] 1Th 1:3; 4:13
[ab] 2:13 Heb 9:12
[ac] 2:14 Rm 10:12; Gl 3:28
[ad] 2:15 Rv 3:14
[ae] Jn 11:52

[A] 1:22 Ps 8:6   [B] 1:22 Lit *gave him*   [C] 2:2 Lit *sons of disobedience*   [D] 2:4 Lit *love with which he loved us*

2:1-3 When displaying diamonds, a jeweler places them against a black cloth because diamonds shine more brilliantly against a dark backdrop. Before he describes God's grace, Paul wants the Ephesians to know how dark things were without it. Paul places the diamond of grace against the backdrop of sin so that grace will glitter even more.

Being in Satan's kingdom is like being the living **dead** (2:1). In it, we had mobility, but no life—that is, no spiritual life. Indeed, those who are spiritually dead are unable to respond to spiritual stimuli. There is no capacity to relate to the spiritual realm. So while outside of Christ, you may have been pretty, educated, and rich, you were alienated from the life of God. No clever arrangement of bad eggs can result in a good omelet.

2:4 The words **but God** remind us that salvation came at God's initiative.

2:5 **Grace** is the unmerited favor of God. It is the inexhaustible supply of God's goodness, based on the work of Christ, whereby he does for us what we do not deserve, could never earn, and would never be able to repay.

2:6 Paul said previously that Jesus was seated in the heavenly places with resurrection power and dominion (1:20-21). Now he says God relocated us there too **in Christ Jesus**. Believers are linked with Christ, in union with him. This is how you have access to your spiritual privileges—to "every spiritual blessing" (1:3)—that God has placed in your account.

2:7 To put this another way, you haven't seen anything yet! Eternity with God will be a nonstop, never-ending, blow-your-mind experience.

2:8-9 Grace **is God's gift** (2:8)—received, not earned (see Rom 4:4-5; 11:6). It doesn't come by means of **works** (Eph 2:9). Therefore, there will be no strutting like peacocks in heaven.

You will only be able to brag about the magnificent grace of God.

2:10 A *good work* is a divinely prescribed action that benefits others in such a way that God is glorified (see Matt 5:16). Many Christians are unfulfilled and miserable because they've never gotten around to doing the **works** God has for them.

2:11 The Gentiles were **called "the uncircumcised"** by Jews—**those called "the circumcised."** The cross of Christ not only deals with our separation from God, but also deals with our separation from one another. We are saved by grace "for good works" (2:10). And those works are to be lived out in the Christian dynamic called the church—heaven's kingdom community.

2:15-16 This new group—this **one new man** (2:15)—that incorporates Jews and Gentiles is called the church. Heaven's new community is a new race, reconciled **to God in one body through the cross** (2:16).

a 2:16 Eph 4:4
b 2:17 Lk 4:18; 1Pt 1:12

c 2:17 Is 57:19
d 2:18 Jn 10:7-9; Rm 5:2;
Eph 3:12

➢ Questions & Answers ❧

Q Paul tells us in Ephesians 2:8-9 that works cannot save us. But in Ephesians 2:10 he says that we have been created to do good works. So what is the proper role of good works in the life of the believer?

A To do good works is to express appreciation to God for his free gift of salvation. At the same time, though, good works allow God to use us to advance his cause in the world. To accept a free gift and then to neglect or abuse the gift is to insult the giver. When we respond to God's salvation by being unwilling to give our time, talents, or resources for his purposes, we demonstrate a lack of gratitude and ascribe little value to his salvation. He not only saved you for glory,

but he also saved you for your usefulness on your way there.

There is another dimension of good works: God will reward you for the work you have done. At the judgment seat of Christ, God will reward believers based on their faithful service to him. Imagine the shame of standing before him on that day and having little to show for your time on earth. The Bible says some will be saved, but they will experience the loss of rewards because of the poor quality of their works (see 1 Cor 3:13-15). You do not want the grief of standing before the Lord who saved you with no good works to show for the advancement of his glory.

FOR THE NEXT Q&A, SEE PAGE 1395.

in one body*a* through the cross by which he put the hostility to death.[A] **17** He came and proclaimed the good news*b* of peace to you who were far away and peace to those who were near.*c* **18** For through him we both have access*d* in one Spirit to the

➢ KINGDOM LIVING ❧
CHURCH
Upon This Rock

After Peter's declaration that Jesus is the Messiah in Matthew 16:16, Jesus responded by blessing Peter and giving him a new name. Jesus called him *petros*, the Greek word for a single stone of a size that can be thrown or carried. But when Jesus said, "On this rock I will build my church" (Matt 16:18), he used the Greek word *petra*, which refers to a cliff or a large collection of rocks. In other words, Jesus didn't say he'd build his church on Peter, an individual stone (*petros*). He said he'd build his church on a huge mass (*petra*) of stones like Peter—men and women who recognize Jesus as the Messiah—by joining those stones together into a single entity. Peter himself expressed this idea in a letter to the early church in 1 Peter 2:5.

The apostle Paul also used this imagery when he taught in Ephesians 2:19-22 what it means to be part of the church. Thus, the church is

a living collection of individual stones joined together to serve as the foundation of God's kingdom work in this world. Notice that the church doesn't exist solely in terms of stones that are living and breathing now. Rather, we who live as Christians today are "fellow citizens with the saints" (Eph 2:19). The church is the unified collection of *all* Christians throughout history.

Also notice that we aren't isolated from God in our attempts to be the church. Instead, we are "of God's household" (Eph 2:19). Jesus himself is the cornerstone of the church; we are constructed around him. And we're being made "for God's dwelling in the Spirit" (Eph 2:22). In other words, the church is supported by all three members of the Trinity.

FOR THE NEXT CHURCH
KINGDOM LIVING LESSON SEE PAGE 1484.

[A] 2:16 Or *death in himself*

2:17 The reason we have racial, ethnic, gender, and class divisions in the church is that we have not fully and properly understood the cross. Christians divided along such lines don't see themselves as part of the "one new man" (2:15). All barriers based on factors such as race and gender are obliterated by the cross. This doesn't mean these distinctions don't exist; instead, these distinctions are absorbed into something bigger. In

terms of spiritual relationship and development, a white person has no advantage over a black person. A man has no spiritual advantage over a woman. We can embrace our differences with a common commitment to Christ because we are at peace with one another through our peace with God. We live with **the good news of peace**.

If you don't see yourself belonging to this new race, to this "one new man," you will fol-

low the world's agenda. You will say things like, "Races don't mix, just like oil and water don't mix." But, you see, there is an exception. When you add an emulsifier, it allows two liquids to mix that normally don't. The atoning death of Jesus is God's emulsifier to bring into harmony those who wouldn't otherwise mix.

2:18-19 The church is a family.

Father.[a] **19** So then you are no longer foreigners and strangers, but fellow citizens with the saints, and members of God's household, **20** built on the foundation of the apostles and prophets,[b] with Christ Jesus himself as the cornerstone. **21** In him the whole building, being put together,[c]

➤ Questions & Answers ❧

Q What does Paul mean when he describes the church as "God's household, built on the foundation of the apostles and prophets, with Christ Jesus himself as the cornerstone" (Eph 2:19-20)?

A When Jesus built the church, he used his human leaders to establish it. Remember, the church began at Pentecost after Jesus ascended to heaven. So he wasn't physically present to build it. However, he was spiritually present in the person of the Holy Spirit through his leaders. He took the disciples, trained them for three years, and made them apostles. As a result, they became the foundation for the establishment of the church, the development of doctrine, and the expansion of God's kingdom program. Because of the apostles and prophets, we have the witness of the Word of God to tell us what the church is, what it believes, how it functions, and how we ought to relate to it.

FOR THE NEXT Q&A, SEE PAGE 1396.

grows into a holy temple in the Lord.[d] **22** In him you are also being built together[e] for God's dwelling[f] in the Spirit.

～ HOPE WORDS ～

If Jesus is your foundation, you'll be able to withstand the storm.

PAUL'S MINISTRY TO THE GENTILES

3 For this reason, I, Paul, the prisoner[g] of Christ Jesus on behalf of you Gentiles — **2** you have heard, haven't you, about the administration of God's grace that he gave to me for you? **3** The mystery was made known to me by revelation,[h] as I have briefly written above. **4** By reading this you are able to understand my insight into the mystery of Christ.[i] **5** This was not made known to people[A] in other generations as it is now revealed to his holy apostles and prophets[j] by the Spirit: **6** The Gentiles are coheirs, members of the same body, and partners in the promise[k] in Christ Jesus through the gospel. **7** I was made a servant of this gospel by the gift of God's grace that was given to me by the working of his power.[l]

8 This grace was given to me — the least of all the saints — to proclaim to the Gentiles the incalculable riches[m] of Christ, **9** and to shed light for all about the administration of the mystery hidden for ages in God who created[n] all things. **10** This is so that God's multi-faceted wisdom[o] may now be made known through the church to the rulers and authorities in the heavens.[p] **11** This is according to his eternal purpose[q] accomplished in Christ Jesus our Lord. **12** In him we have boldness and confident access[r] through faith in him.[B] **13** So then I ask you not to be discouraged[s]

[a] 2:18 Jn 4:23; 1Co 12:13; Eph 4:4; Col 1:12
[b] 2:20 1Co 12:28; Eph 3:5
[c] 2:21 Eph 4:16
[d] 2:21 1Pt 2:5
[e] 2:22 Rm 11:18
[f] 1Pt 2:5
[g] 3:1 2Tm 1:8
[h] 3:3 1Pt 4:13
[i] 3:4 Col 4:3
[j] 3:5 1Co 12:28-29; Eph 2:20
[k] 3:6 Gn 12:7
[l] 3:7 Mk 5:30; Lk 1:35; 6:19; Ac 19:11; 2Co 13:4; Rv 11:17
[m] 3:8 Rm 1:15; 10:12; 11:12; 1Pt 1:12
[n] 3:9 Mk 13:19
[o] 3:10 Pr 3:19; Rm 11:33; 1Co 1:21,24; Rv 7:12
[p] Eph 1:3,20; 2:6; 6:12; Php 2:10
[q] 3:11 Pr 19:21
[r] 3:12 Rm 5:2
[s] 3:13 2Th 3:13

[A] 3:5 Lit *to the sons of men*   [B] 3:12 Or *through his faithfulness*

2:20-22 When a building is constructed, its stones must be placed in alignment with the **cornerstone**. So, as God's building, we Christians must be in alignment with Christ (2:20). After all, **in him the whole building . . . grows into a holy temple in the Lord** (2:21). In the Old Testament, the glory of God was manifested in the temple. It was where God hung out. Today he's in the new temple, the church. Together we believers are the temple of God, **God's dwelling** (2:22), meant to display God's glory. But that glory isn't on display when we are not aligned with Christ.

3:1 Paul calls himself a **prisoner of Christ Jesus**. Though he is writing from jail, Paul knows he is no prisoner of man. When you're in the will of God, the negative circumstances

of your life happen with God's purposes in mind. God's purpose was that Paul would proclaim the truth of the gospel.

3:6 You and I are **coheirs . . . and partners**, too. As Christians, we are fellow partakers of grace, on equal footing before God. If you've been brought into God's family through the blood of Christ, the color of your skin doesn't matter. You get the same spiritual DNA that is given to every other believer—planted within you by the Spirit as soon as you are born into the family of God. You come as an equal. There are no insignificant people in God's army.

3:8 Paul referred to himself as **the least of all the saints**. When Mr. Big Stuff met Jesus, he shrunk in his own estimation.

3:10 The church is like a prism displaying the rich colors of God's manifold **wisdom**. Through it God is teaching the angelic realm—both good angels and demons, as well as their human representatives—his wisdom as he brings together sinners from every tribe, tongue, and nation into one heavenly community. And no doubt the righteous angels stare at this in wonder (see 1 Pet 1:12). God checks with the church before he deals with the principalities and powers that affect history (see Matt 16:18-19).

3:12 You can't stroll into the office of the president of the United States, but through Jesus Christ, all believers can boldly and confidently come into the presence of God the Father—the Creator and Sustainer of the universe.

a 3:13 Jn 5:44; 7:18; Rm 2:7; 1Pt 5:4
b 3:14 Php 2:10

c 3:16 Lk 8:14; 2Co 8:9
d Lk 9:32; Jn 17:24; 2Co 3:18; 2Pt 3:18
e 2Tm 1:7
f Rm 7:22; Php 4:13
g 3:18 Jb 11:7–9; Ps 103:11–14
h 3:20 Rm 16:25; 2Co 9:8; Jd 24
i Mk 14:36
j Rm 15:13; 16:25; 2Tm 1:7; Jd 24
k 3:21 Php 4:20
4:1 2Tm 1:8
m 4:2 Col 3:12
n Ex 34:6; 2Tm 3:10
o Heb 13:22
p 1Co 13:1
q 4:3 Eph 4:13
r Ps 51:11; Jn 1:33; Ac 2:4; Rm 8:9; Gl 5:25; Ti 3:5; Rv 3:22
s 4:4 Rm 12:4–5; 1Co 10:17; 12:9,12–13; Eph 2:16,18; Col 3:15

✎ Questions & Answers ✎

Q Why does Paul emphasize that God's mystery of reconciling Jew and Gentile is being demonstrated through the church "to the rulers and authorities in the heavens" (Eph 3:10)?

A The church is a revelation "to the rulers and authorities in the heavens" because what God does in history, he does through the church. The church is his vehicle; it is his embassy to carry out his program. There are both good and evil spiritual beings in the heavens, angels and demons, and they respond to God's spiritual agency—the church. When angels see our unity, they can act on God's behalf in our midst to advance God's program. But when the demonic realm sees our disunity, it can carry out its program of wickedness unabated. This principle also flows over to what happens in the culture, since angels influence believers and demons influence unbelievers and rebellious believers. Victory over the powers in the culture comes when the church supports the agenda of God and not the regime of the devil.

FOR THE NEXT Q&A, SEE PAGE 1397.

over my afflictions on your behalf, for they are your glory.*a*

PRAYER FOR SPIRITUAL POWER

14 For this reason I kneel*b* before the Father*A* **15** from whom every family in heaven

and on earth is named. **16** I pray that he may grant you, according to the riches*c* of his glory,*d* to be strengthened with power*e* in your inner being*f* through his Spirit, **17** and that Christ may dwell in your hearts through faith. I pray that you, being rooted and firmly established in love, **18** may be able to comprehend with all the saints what is the length and width, height and depth of God's love,*g* **19** and to know Christ's love that surpasses knowledge, so that you may be filled with all the fullness of God.

20 Now to him who is able*h* to do above and beyond all that we ask or think*i* according to the power*j* that works in us — **21** to him be glory in the church and in Christ Jesus to all generations, forever and ever. Amen.*k*

⇌ HOPE WORDS ⇌

*Stop focusing on what you can't do.
Start focusing on what God can do.*

UNITY AND DIVERSITY IN THE BODY OF CHRIST

4 Therefore I, the prisoner in the Lord,*l* urge you to live worthy of the calling you have received, **2** with all humility*m* and gentleness, with patience,*n* bearing*o* with one another in love,*p* **3** making every effort to keep the unity*q* of the Spirit*r* through the bond of peace. **4** There is one body and one Spirit*s* — just as you were called to

A 3:14 Other mss add *of our Lord Jesus Christ*

3:16 When my cell phone is out of power, no external alterations will make a difference. The problem is an uncharged battery. We need the internal strength that only the **Spirit** can provide. **3:17** The Greek word for *dwell* means to make yourself at home. That's what we tell people to do when they come to visit. Nevertheless, we don't mean that we want them roaming the entire house and rummaging through our closets. But if you want spiritual power, Jesus must be free to be fully at home in your heart. He must have access to every room. He wants to clean and straighten out the messy closets that you're hiding. If you want to realize all that God has for you, Christ must be Lord of your heart. **3:18-19** Paul wants them to know something that is beyond their capacity to grasp: **The length and width, height and depth of God's love** (3:18)! Even when you've been in God's presence for one hundred quadrillion years, you will have just been introduced to him. Because the God of the Bible is inexhaustible. There's no end to knowing God and the "great love that he [has] for us" (2:4).

3:20-21 What does Scripture say God **is able to do**? He is able to rescue from a fiery furnace (see Dan 3:17). He is able to deliver from lions' mouths (see Dan 6:20-22). He is able to give sight to the blind (see Matt 9:28-30). He is able to keep you from stumbling (see Jude 24). "He is able to save completely" (see Heb 7:25). He is able "to make . . . grace overflow" (2 Cor 9:8). He is able to do **above and beyond** even these things (Eph 3:20).

A fire hydrant is small, but it can gush water in volume and force that is out of proportion to its size. That's because the water isn't in the hydrant. The hydrant is connected to a reservoir that is always full. When the church is in sync with Jesus Christ, it has a connection to a reservoir that is always overflowing. When God's people's internal connection to him is tight, they will gush out the power of God in and through their lives individually and collectively. **4:1-2** Paul begins the second half of his letter with the word **therefore**. In light of the gracious riches the Ephesian believers have

in Christ and the glorious reality of this new community called the church, there are now accompanying responsibilities.

He urges them **to live worthy of [their] calling** (4:1). They must conduct themselves in a way that reflects their new status (4:2). **4:3** Notice Paul commands them to *keep* this **unity**, not to *establish* it. The church didn't create the unity. God calls us to preserve what he's already created (see 2:11-22). This unity is tied to our Christian character (see 4:2) and is based on the work of the Holy Spirit. If your point of reference isn't the Spirit of God, you'll be operating from a merely human point of view. But when you relate to people based on God's point of view, the Spirit can override human differences and hold us together **through the bond of peace**. *Peace*—harmony where once there was conflict—will act like a belt to hold us together. **4:4-6** Cancer is a dreaded disease in which cells no longer unify with the body as a whole. Cancerous cells have their own independent vision

[a] 4:4 Ac 26:6-7; 28:20; Rm 5:2; 8:23-25; Eph 1:18; Col 1:5; 1Th 1:3
[b] 4:5 1Co 1:13; 8:6
[c] Jd 3
[d] 4:6 Dt 6:4
[e] Mt 5:16; 11:27; Lk 11:13; Jn 8:42
[f] Ps 104:24
[g] 4:7 1Co 12:7-11
[h] 4:8 Jn 20:17
[i] Ps 68:18
[j] 4:9 Jn 3:13; 6:62; Rm 10:6-7; Php 2:6-11
[k] 4:10 Jn 3:13; 6:38
[l] Eph 1:23; Heb 4:14; 7:26; 9:24

[m] 4:12 Rm 7:4; 1Co 10:16; 12:27; Col 2:17
[n] 4:13 Jn 5:19; Heb 1:2
[o] Lk 2:52
[p] 4:14 Rm 15:4; Heb 13:9
[q] 4:15 Col 2:10

Questions & Answers

Q How has a biblical vision for building up believers in the church shaped your own approach to ministry?

A Paul says Christ "gave some to be apostles, some prophets, some evangelists, some pastors and teachers, equipping the saints for the work of ministry, to build up the body of Christ" (Eph 4:11-12). "Equipping the saints" refers to giving them the spiritual, biblical, and practical tools needed to fulfill the service and ministry they have been called to do. The church is a place of preparation and training. Whatever ministry believers embark on, the role of the church is to enable them to know what to do, know how to do it, and have the resources with which to do it.

This has affected our own church's ministry. When people come through our pre-membership program, we give them a list of over 130 ministry opportunities they can choose from, based on their time, talents, and interests. We ask every member to do one thing. If everybody does one thing, everything gets done, and nobody gets burned out. So we have thousands of people serving because they understand they are not just doing a job, they are serving the kingdom of God.

Coupled with this idea of equipping the saints is helping them grow in their faith. We do not want people merely doing jobs; we want people growing in their relationship to Christ. We want to draw them to Christ and help them grow and develop in him. So when they go through our pre-membership program, the first thing they do is go through a spiritual growth class because we want to lay the groundwork for their spiritual development. We want their service to be infused with God and not merely with activity.

FOR THE NEXT Q&A, SEE PAGE 1399.

one hope[A][a] at your calling — **5** one Lord,[b] one faith,[c] one baptism, **6** one God[d] and Father[e] of all, who is above all and through all and in all.[f]

7 Now grace was given to each one of us[g] according to the measure of Christ's gift. **8** For it says:

> When he ascended[h] on high,
> he took the captives captive;
> he gave gifts to people.[B][j]

9 But what does "he ascended" mean except that he[c] also descended to the lower parts of the earth?[D][j] **10** The one who descended is also the one who ascended far above all the heavens,[k] to fill all things.[l]

11 And he himself gave some to be apostles, some prophets, some evangelists, some pastors and teachers, **12** equipping the saints for the work of ministry, to build up the body of Christ,[m] **13** until we all reach unity in the faith and in the knowledge of God's Son,[n] growing into maturity with a stature[o] measured by Christ's fullness. **14** Then we will no longer be little children, tossed by the waves and blown around by every wind of teaching,[p] by human cunning with cleverness in the techniques of deceit. **15** But speaking the truth in love, let us grow in every way into him who is the head[q] — Christ. **16** From him the

---

[A] 4:4 Lit *called in one hope*   [B] 4:8 Ps 68:18   [C] 4:9 Other mss add *first*   [D] 4:9 Or *the lower parts, namely, the earth*

---

and program. They want to stay in your body, but they want to do their own thing—and multiply. Their goal is to shut you down. Similarly, Satan wants to shut down God's people. And he knows nothing will shut us down like disunity, since God is a God of order (see 1 Cor 14:33).
4:7-8 To equip the church for unity and service, God graciously gives every believer a spiritual **gift** (4:7)—a spiritual ability to be used in service to God's people for the expansion of his kingdom.
4:9 After defeating Satan on the cross, Jesus's spirit **descended** and declared victory to the demons (see 1 Pet 3:19).
4:11-12 Some people attend church only for personal benefit. But that's called being a leech. God saved and equipped *you* for the

work of ministry, the work of service. Why? We are **to build up the body of Christ** (4:12). The church will only grow and mature when all the parts operate in harmony, in unity. If you have a Lone Ranger personality, you will be a feeble saint—and the body will suffer for it. Our relationship to the corporate body is crucial to our own spiritual development and the development of the church.
4:13-14 **Children** are unstable in their thinking, easily tossed to and fro. Christians need the right theological and spiritual foundation to keep from being **blown around by every wind of teaching, by human cunning (4:14).** We need to be stabilized by **maturity**, and maturity only comes when we're connected to each other (4:13).

4:15 **Truth** is what God says about a matter. And it shouldn't be used like a destructive hammer. Rather, it must be spoken with **love**, which involves compassionately, righteously, and responsibly seeking the well-being of its recipient.
4:16 California redwood trees grow to be massive in size and ancient in age. The secret to their stability and longevity is that their roots intertwine. Underground, they're all interconnected. You can't mess with one without messing with the whole grove. When fierce winds blow, their connectedness allows them to borrow from one another and stand strong. So it is, Paul says, with the **body** of Christ, the church.

a 4:16 Col 2:2
b Col 2:19
c 4:19 1Th 4:17
d 4:21 2Th 2:10
e 4:22 Rm 13:12
f 2Pt 3:11
g Rm 6:6; 7:6; 1Co 5:7-8; 2Co 3:14; Col 3:9
h 4:23 Ps 51:12
i 4:24 Rm 13:12
j Mk 13:19; Jn 1:13; Rv 3:14
k Col 3:10; 2Pt 1:4
l 4:25 Pr 31:25
m Zch 8:16
n 4:26 Ps 4:4; 37:8; Mt 18:21; Jms 1:19-20
o 4:28 1Th 2:8; 1Tm 6:18
p 4:30 Ps 51:11; Jn 1:33; Ac 2:4; Rm 8:9; Gl 5:25; Ti 3:5; Rv 3:22
q Php 1:6
r 4:32 Mt 11:30; Lk 5:39; 6:35; Rm 2:4; 1Co 15:33; 1Pt 2:3
s 1Pt 3:8
t Ps 25:11; Mt 9:2; Mk 2:5; Lk 24:47; Col 3:12-13
u 5:2 2Th 2:13; Ti 2:14
v 5:3 1Th 4:3
w 1Th 4:7
x Lk 12:15; Rm 1:29; Eph 4:19; Col 3:5; 1Th 2:5; 2Pt 2:3,14

APPLICATION QUESTIONS

READ EPHESIANS 4:11-12

- How do these verses contribute to your understanding of the church?
- Why do you go to church? What do you hope to encounter or experience?
- When do you feel most connected with other Christians around the world?

whole body, fitted and knit together*a* by every supporting ligament, promotes the growth*b* of the body for building up itself in love by the proper working of each individual part.

LIVING THE NEW LIFE

17 Therefore, I say this and testify in the Lord: You should no longer live as the Gentiles live, in the futility of their thoughts. **18** They are darkened in their understanding, excluded from the life of God, because of the ignorance that is in them and because*A* of the hardness of their hearts. **19** They became callous and gave themselves over to promiscuity for the practice of every kind of impurity*c* with a desire for more and more.*B*

20 But that is not how you came to know Christ, **21** assuming you heard about him and were taught by him, as the truth*d* is in Jesus, **22** to take off*C,e* your former way of life,*f* the old self*g* that is corrupted by deceitful desires, **23** to be renewed*D* in the spirit*h* of your minds, **24** and to put on*E,i* the new self, the one created*j* according to God's likeness*k* in righteousness and purity of the truth.

25 Therefore, putting away*l* lying, **speak the truth, each one to his neighbor,**F,m because we are members of one another. **26** Be angry and do not sin.*G,n* Don't let the sun go down on your anger, **27** and don't give the devil an opportunity. **28** Let the thief no longer steal. Instead, he is to do honest work with his own hands, so that he has something to share*o* with anyone in need. **29** No foul language should come from your mouth, but only what is good for building up someone in need,*H* so that it gives grace to those who hear. **30** And don't grieve God's Holy Spirit.*p* You were sealed by him*i* for the day of redemption.*q* **31** Let all bitterness, anger and wrath, shouting and slander be removed from you, along with all malice. **32** And be kind*r* and compassionate*s* to one another, forgiving*t* one another, just as God also forgave you*j* in Christ.

5 Therefore, be imitators of God, as dearly loved children, **2** and walk in love, as Christ also loved us and gave himself for us,*u* a sacrificial and fragrant offering to God. **3** But sexual immorality*v* and any impurity*w* or greed*x* should not even be heard of*k* among you, as is proper for saints. **4** Obscene and foolish talking or crude joking are not suitable, but rather

---

A 4:18 Or *in them because*   *B* 4:19 Lit *with greediness*   *C* 4:21-22 Or *Jesus. This means: take off* (as a command)   *D* 4:22-23 Or *desires; renew* (as a command)   *E* 4:23-24 Or *minds; and put on* (as a command)   *F* 4:25 Zch 8:16   *G* 4:26 Ps 4:4   *H* 4:29 Lit *for the building up of the need*   *I* 4:30 Or *Spirit, by whom you were sealed*   *J* 4:32 Other mss read *us*   *K* 5:3 Or *be named*

4:17 Describing unbelievers, Paul speaks of **the futility of their thoughts**. Their thinking has no aim or purpose. Although you can go to an airport to buy gum or a newspaper, doing so is ancillary to the main purpose for going to an airport: to catch a plane and reach a new destination.

4:19 In other words, their consciences are dead. They have committed sins for so long that their consciences no longer feel. Things that might have shocked them once don't shock anymore.

4:21 Jesus *is* **the truth** (John 14:6), and everyone who is of the truth "listens to" him (John 18:37).

4:22-24 When you were saved, you received a new wardrobe. But you've got **to take off** the old clothes and **put on** the new (4:22, 24). When God makes your inside clean, you want your outside to match.

How do we make this happen? Speaking of unbelievers, Paul uses words like "thoughts," "understanding," and "ignorance" (4:17-18). The common denominator is their thinking. Your lifestyle too is controlled by your brain.

So the key to taking off the old and putting on the new is **to be renewed in the spirit of [our] minds** (4:23). Christians must not go back to the worldview they had before Christ. To "put on the new self" requires a new way of thinking grounded in biblical truth (4:24).

4:25 Satan is "the father of lies" (John 8:44), so children of God must **speak the truth**. We can't be in community unless we honestly address and admit our faults, failures, and weaknesses.

4:26-27 Paul says control your anger, deal with it daily, and **don't give the devil an opportunity** to inflame it into something bigger. Anger is sinful when it attacks people and seeks revenge rather than addressing the problem.

4:28 Christians are not to rip each other off but are to be productive and serve one another. That includes putting in a full day's work and serving in ministry that blesses others for the advancement of God's kingdom.

4:29-31 The Spirit's joy, presence, and power will not be yours if you make him sad when you open your mouth.

4:32 If your credit card company said they were canceling your debt but continued sending you a bill every month, it would mean they hadn't really canceled what you owed. So really forgive, as you have been forgiven.

5:1 As a child often mimics the characteristics and behavior of a parent, so God's **children** are to copy their heavenly Father. The Son put the Father on display (see John 1:18). So if you don't know how to pattern yourself after the Father, just take a close look at Jesus.

5:2 Christians are to reflect the nature of God's **love** by serving others rather than themselves. Christ's sacrifice on the cross is the supreme illustration of what it means to love. It was **a fragrant offering**—it was acceptable **to God**. Similarly, when we love others by seeking what is best for their lives, it smells good to God.

5:3-5 The culture of Ephesus embraced all forms of **immorality**. But Paul told the church there not to let the culture set the standard for them. As **saints** or "holy ones," they were to be set apart for God (5:3). God wants us to see sin the way he sees it.

LIGHT VERSUS DARKNESS

6 Let no one deceive you with empty arguments, for God's wrath[e] is coming on the disobedient[A] because of these things. **7** Therefore, do not become their partners. **8** For you were once darkness, but now you are light[f] in the Lord. Live as children of light[g] — **9** for the fruit of the light[B] consists of all goodness, righteousness, and truth[h] — **10** testing[i] what is pleasing[j] to the Lord. **11** Don't participate in the fruitless[k] works of darkness, but instead expose them. **12** For it is shameful even to mention what is done by them in secret. **13** Everything exposed by the light is made visible,[l] **14** for what makes everything visible is light. Therefore it is said:

Get up, sleeper,[m] and rise up
    from the dead,[n]
and Christ will shine on you.[o]

CONSISTENCY IN THE CHRISTIAN LIFE

15 Pay careful attention, then, to how you live — not as unwise people but as wise — **16** making the most of the time,[C,p] because the days are evil. **17** So don't be foolish, but understand[q] what the Lord's will[r] is. **18** And don't get drunk[s] with wine,[t] which leads to reckless living, but be filled by the Spirit:[u] **19** speaking to one another in psalms, hymns, and spiritual songs, singing and making music with your heart to the Lord, **20** giving thanks always for everything to God the Father in the name of our Lord Jesus Christ, **21** submitting to one another in the fear of Christ.[v]

WIVES AND HUSBANDS

22 Wives,[w] submit[D,x] to your husbands[y] as to the Lord, **23** because the husband is the head of the wife[z] as Christ is the head[aa] of the church. He is the Savior of

giving thanks. **5** For know and recognize this: Every sexually immoral[a] or impure[b] or greedy[c] person, who is an idolater, does not have an inheritance in the kingdom[d] of Christ and of God.

[a] 5:5 1Co 5:9
[b] 2Co 6:17
[c] 1Co 5:10-11; 6:10
[d] Mk 1:15

[e] 5:6 Rm 2:5; Rv 6:16
[f] 5:8 Ps 36:9; Jn 12:46
[g] Is 2:5; Lk 16:8; Jn 12:35-36
[h] 5:9 Eph 5:17
[i] 5:10 Rm 12:2
[j] Lk 18:18
[k] 5:11 Gl 5:22; Ti 3:14
[l] 5:13 1Jn 1:2
[m] 5:14 Pr 6:4
[n] Jn 5:25
[o] Is 26:19; 51:17; 52:1; 60:1; Mal 4:2; Lk 1:78-79; Rm 13:11
[p] 5:16 Col 4:5
[q] 5:17 Jr 31:31-34; Ezk 36:26-27; Rm 12:2; Php 1:9-10; 1Th 5:21
[r] Ps 143:10; Pr 16:9; Gl 1:4; Eph 1:9
[s] 5:18 Lk 12:45; Jn 2:10; 1Th 5:7; Rv 17:2
[t] Gn 9:21; Dt 7:13; Ps 4:7; Pr 3:10; Lk 5:37
[u] Lk 1:15; Ac 13:52
[v] 5:18-21 Col 3:16-17; 1Pt 1:17
[w] 5:22 1Pt 3:1
[x] Gn 3:16; 1Co 11:3,7-9,11-12; Col 3:18; Ti 2:4-5; 1Pt 3:1-6
[y] 1Pt 3:1
[z] 5:23 1Co 11:3
[aa] Col 2:10

[A] 5:6 Lit *sons of disobedience*   [B] 5:9 Other mss read *fruit of the Spirit*   [C] 5:16 Lit *buying back the time*   [D] 5:22 Other mss omit *submit*

5:8 Jesus is "the light of the world" (John 8:12). His followers must reflect him the way the moon reflects the sun—not as crescent-moon Christians but as full-moon Christians. And we can't *reflect* his **light** unless we're *in* the light. So, if you want to reflect Christ, you have to be absorbing Christ through cultivating an intimate walk and relationship with him (see John 15:1-16).

5:13-14 **Everything exposed by the light is made visible** (5:13). So, does that mean we go around telling on people? No. **What makes everything visible is light** (5:14). If cockroaches are in a room, all you have to do is turn on the light, and they scatter. Similarly, if you live as children of light, shameful deeds will

be exposed by your lifestyle and words that reflect God's standard. You know how Jesus got in trouble with the religious leaders? By being Jesus. He just showed up, speaking truth and living righteousness. So if you're spiritually sleeping, get up and **Christ will shine** (5:14).

5:16 Don't waste your life. What opportunity is God giving you to maximize your potential?

5:18 When you come to Christ, you are indwelt by the Spirit, and he will never leave you. But being **filled by the Spirit** is different (emphasis added). A person filled by the Spirit is under the Spirit's influence. Since the Greek verb "filled" is plural, Paul is emphasizing that the church must collectively operate as a Spirit-controlled environment.

5:19-21 This is a reminder that we need spiritual input. We also need to speak God's perspective to one another so that we all become full of spiritual things. We need to worship and give thanks to God regularly, being subject to one another. But not just on Sundays. After all, the moment your car leaves the filling station, you begin burning fuel. So let worship become a lifestyle and regularly fill the tanks of others with God's perspective. That way we will be filled by the Spirit—and not some cheap substitute.

5:22 **Wives** are called to **submit to**—to voluntarily place themselves under the legitimate authority of—their husbands. Importantly, though, a wife is equal to her husband in her

Video Devotional
"RINGS"

A prayer for your marriage with the truth of God's Word and principles.

APPLICATION QUESTIONS

READ EPHESIANS 5:22-33

- How would you summarize what it means to be a good husband?
- How would you summarize what it means to be a good wife?
- What ideas or images come to mind when you hear the word *submit*?
- What emotions do you typically experience when you submit to someone or something? Why?

the body.ᵃ **24** Now as the church submits to Christ, so also wives are to submit to their husbands in everything. **25** Husbands, love your wives,ᵇ just as Christ loved ᶜ the church and gave himself ᵈ for her **26** to make her holy, cleansingᴬ her

with the washing of water by the word. **27** He did this to present the church to himself in splendor, without spot or wrinkle or anything like that, but holy and blameless.ᵉ **28** In the same way, husbands are to love their wives as their own bodies. He who loves his wife loves himself. **29** For no one ever hates his own flesh but provides and cares for it, just as Christ does for the church, **30** since we are members of his body.ᴮ **31 For this reason a man will leave his father and mother and be joined to his wife,ᶠ and the two will become one flesh.**ᶜᵍ **32** This mysteryʰ is profound, but I am talking about Christ and the church. **33** To sum up, each one of you is to love his wife as himself, and the wife is to respect her husband.

ᵃ5:23 Col 3:18–4:1
ᵇ5:25 Col 3:19; 1Pt 3:7
ᶜJn 3:16; 1Co 13:1; 2Th 2:13
ᵈTi 2:14

ᵉ5:27 Jd 24
ᶠ5:31 1Pt 3:1
ᵍGn 2:24
ʰ5:32 1Co 2:7

☞ KINGDOM LIVING ☜
FAMILY
The Sacrifice of Love

God commands husbands to love their wives (see Eph 5:25). However, he never instructs a wife to love her husband. Instead, wives are commanded to respect them (see Eph 5:33). This may seem like an odd way to address the subject of love, but God isn't saying that women should dismiss the commandment to love. Rather, God is love (1 John 4:8), and his love lives within all of us. Therefore, we are all commanded to love one another with the love of Christ. From God's perspective, a woman's love is a response to her husband's salvation and the love he gives to her.

If husbands are going to be biblical lovers, they also must become biblical saviors. Jesus Christ died for us, not because we were lovable but in order to make us lovable. The Bible says Jacob loved Rachel so much that he worked fourteen years to gain her hand (Gen 29:20,

30). That's a high price to pay, but it's a reasonable price tag for love. Too many men want to run away from their wives when there's a problem. But if there were no problems, if your wife were perfect, she wouldn't need a Savior. Christ looked at us in our mess and said, "You have a Savior. Here I am." Kingdom man, if there is no sacrifice, there is no love.

A husband who truly loves his wife says, "If you want out of this marriage, you're going to have to leave me because I'm not going anywhere. No matter how you treat me or what happens, I want you to know you have a savior." Only a man who has abandoned himself to a kingdom agenda rather than a personal one can make this level of commitment.

FOR THE NEXT **FAMILY**
KINGDOM LIVING LESSON SEE PAGE 1482.

ᴬ5:26 Or *having cleansed*   ᴮ5:30 Other mss add *and of his flesh and of his bones*   ᶜ5:31 Gn 2:24

---

being—both are made in God's "image" (Gen 1:27). And a wife's submission to her husband is not absolute. It is **as to the Lord**. The husband cannot ask his wife to do anything outside of God's will.

But what if the wife is the better leader in the home or has greater intelligence or more ability than her spouse? Think of it this way. A merging tractor-trailer may be bigger, longer, and carry more cargo than a tiny car coming down the road. Nevertheless, the tractor-trailer doesn't have the right of way but must yield as instructed to avoid catastrophe.

God as Creator has placed a husband on the highway and given his wife the yield sign within the will of God.

5:24 This doesn't mean a wife can't disagree with her spouse, but it means God has placed husbands in a position that is to be honored. A kingdom wife "is to respect her husband" (5:33), even when expressing disagreement.

5:25-27 Far too many men think headship means playing dictator and telling everyone what to do. But *biblical* headship means being a responsible governing authority. The husband is responsible for leading his family in

the advancement of God's kingdom in the context of love (5:25). Biblical love compassionately, righteously, and sacrificially pursues the well-being of another.

Husbands are to love according to Christ's standard. How did Christ love the church? To death! Therefore, a husband is to sacrifice for his wife and be her deliverer—protecting her and paying the price for her well-being. A kingdom husband is also to be his wife's sanctifier—taking her (and all her history) from where she is and helping her to where she ought to be, just as Christ sanctifies the

[a]6:1 Pr 1:8; 6:20; 23:22; Col 3:20
[b]6:2-3 Ex 20:12
[c]6:4 Rm 10:19
[d]Heb 12:5
[e]6:5 Col 3:22; 1Pt 2:18
[f]Php 2:12
[g]2Co 9:11
[h]6:6 Ps 143:10; Pr 16:9; Gl 1:4; Eph 1:9
[i]6:7 Col 3:23
[j]6:9 Ac 4:29; 9:1
[k]Col 3:25
[l]Col 4:1

APPLICATION QUESTIONS

READ EPHESIANS 6:4

- What are your initial reactions to this verse? Why?
- In what ways do you nurture and nourish your children?
- How do you personally invest your time and resources in the spiritual nourishment of your children?

CHILDREN AND PARENTS

6 Children, obey[a] your parents in the Lord, because this is right. ² **Honor your father and mother**, which is the first commandment with a promise, ³ **so that it may go well with you and that you may have a long life in the land.**[A,B,b] ⁴ Fathers, don't stir up anger[c] in your children, but bring them up in the training[d] and instruction of the Lord.

SLAVES AND MASTERS

⁵ Slaves, obey your human[c] masters[e] with fear and trembling,[f] in the sincerity[g] of your heart, as you would Christ. ⁶ Don't work only while being watched, as people-pleasers, but as slaves of Christ, do God's will[h] from your heart. ⁷ Serve with a good attitude, as to the Lord and not to people,[i] ⁸ knowing that whatever good each one does, slave or free, he will receive this back from the Lord. ⁹ And masters, treat your slaves the same way, without threatening[j] them, because you know that both their Master and yours is in heaven, and there is no favoritism[k] with him.[l]

⤳ **KINGDOM LIVING** ⤶

PERSONAL

Waging Victorious Warfare

When Paul established the church at Ephesus, he wanted the believers to know they had the power to withstand the attacks of the enemy, Satan. He wanted them to realize that they could stand firm in their faith and refuse to yield to sin and thoughts of defeat. They had been given spiritual weapons more powerful and effective than the enemy's.

Paul lists those weapons in Ephesians 6, but sums up their usage in verses 10-11 where he writes, "Be strengthened by the Lord and by his vast strength. Put on the full armor of God so that you can stand against the schemes of the devil." In order to stand and fight valiantly, they needed to understand they were not strong enough on their own to resist Satan's temptations and tactics. It was *God's* power and strength that empowered them to overcome the wiles of the devil.

Paul explained to the Ephesians that they needed to use weapons of spiritual warfare on a daily basis. God protected them, and he protects us. But one way he does this is through believers putting on the full armor of God each day.

Always keep this truth in mind: You are not fighting for victory; you are fighting from a position of victory. Christ has secured the victory for you, and he offers it through the armor of God. The victory is yours when you are well-dressed for warfare.

FOR THE NEXT FAMILY
KINGDOM LIVING LESSON SEE PAGE 1411.

---

^6:3 Or *life on the earth*   ^B6:2-3 Ex 20:12   ^C6:5 Lit *according to the flesh*

---

church (5:26-27). A kingdom husband outserves his wife.

5:33 God has created husbands to lead and wives to respond. And when a woman sees her man initiating, owning responsibility, treating her as special, and sacrificing for her well-being, she is apt to respond to him with heartfelt respect and submission.

When a car is out of alignment, its tires are going to wear unevenly, and getting new tires won't fix the problem. Many married people think that if they could just find a new mate, their problems would go away. But that's not the answer. If kingdom husbands and wives expect to draw on their heavenly blessings, they must align their roles in the family according to God's good design through love and respect.

6:1-2 When adult **children** leave the home and are no longer dependent on their parents for provision and protection, they are not obligated to **obey** them. Nevertheless, no one

outgrows the requirement to **honor** mother and father.

6:4 Paul says, **Fathers, don't stir up anger in your children**. In other words, don't correct your kids in such a way that they become embittered. Be an encourager, not a discourager. Praise them and make sure they know you are proud to be their dad. Furthermore, **bring them up in the training and instruction of the Lord**. To bring up children is to nurture and care for them. "The training and instruction" has to do with teaching and discipline. Thus, fathers who have been given the primary biblical role for childrearing (see Gen 18:19) should teach kids God's divine guidelines on their own level and break it down in such a way that they can grasp it. We must give them age-appropriate discipline—not in anger, but in love. Discipline isn't the same thing as venting. God disciplines us in love in order to correct our behavior (Heb 12:5-6). We owe our children the same.

6:5-9 Most of what we know of slavery (especially American antebellum slavery) is condemned in the Bible: human beings were not to be kidnapped and sold (Exod 21:16); slaves were not to be abused (Exod 21:26-27); fugitive slaves were not to be returned to their masters (Deut 23:15-16).

In a Roman culture infused with an unrighteous institution of slavery, Paul writes to tell a church how to live with a heavenly perspective. We can apply Paul's principles here to our own workplaces. God wants to be an integral part of your daily nine-to-five. For Christian employees and employers to access their heavenly blessings, they must bring a heavenly perspective to bear on the job.

To serve Christ in your job, obey your employer as long as he doesn't ask you to disobey Christ. Whether or not the boss is around, God is always watching. And even if your boss doesn't appreciate your efforts or

*a*6:10 Ac 4:33
*b*6:11 Pr 31:25
*c*Eph 6:11-17
*d*6:12 Php 3:3
*e*1Pt 3:22
*f*Mt 6:13; Jn 17:15
*g*Eph 1:3,20; 2:6; 3:10;
Php 2:10
*h*6:13 1Th 5:8

*i*6:13 2Tm 4:15; 1Pt 5:9
*j*6:14 Pr 24:16; Php 1:27
*k*Jn 14:6; 1Jn 5:20
*l*Mt 6:33; Rm 1:17; 2Pt 1:1
*m*1Th 5:8
*n*6:16 Gn 15:1
*o*Mt 8:10; Ac 3:16; Rm 1:8;
1Co 2:5; Gl 2:16; 1Tm 1:2;
Heb 4:2
*p*2Th 3:3
*q*6:17 1Th 5:8
*r*Mk 14:47
*s*Ps 51:11; Jn 1:33; Ac 2:4;
Rm 8:9; Gl 5:25; Ti 3:5;
Rv 3:22
*t*6:18 Mt 5:44; Ac 12:12
*u*Jd 20
*v*Pr 6:4
*w*6:19 2Co 3:12
*x*6:20 2Co 5:20
*y*6:21 Ti 3:12
*z*6:22 Lk 16:25
*aa*Col 4:8
*ab*6:23 Mt 5:16; 11:27; Lk
11:13; Jn 8:42

⚭ HOPE WORDS ⚭

Standing firm in the armor of God doesn't stop the spiritual warfare from raging. It stops it from defeating you.

CHRISTIAN WARFARE

10 Finally, be strengthened by the Lord and by his vast strength.*a* **11** Put on*b* the full armor*c* of God so that you can stand against the schemes of the devil. **12** For our struggle is not against flesh*d* and blood, but against the rulers, against the authorities,*e* against the cosmic powers of this darkness, against evil,*f* spiritual forces in the heavens.*g* **13** For this reason take up the full armor*h* of God, so that you may be able to

⚭ HOPE WORDS ⚭

We don't wrestle against flesh and blood. The people are real. The problems are real. They are just not the root problem.

resist*i* in the evil day, and having prepared everything, to take your stand. **14** Stand,*j* therefore, with truth*k* like a belt around your waist, righteousness*l* like armor on your chest,*m* **15** and your feet sandaled with readiness for the gospel of peace. **16** In every situation take up the shield*n* of faith*o* with which you can extinguish all the flaming arrows of the evil one.*p* **17** Take the helmet*q* of salvation and the sword*r* of the Spirit*s* — which is the word of God. **18** Pray*t* at all times in the Spirit*u* with every prayer and request, and stay alert*v* with all perseverance and intercession for all the saints. **19** Pray also for me, that the message may be given to me when I open my mouth to make known with boldness*w* the mystery of the gospel. **20** For this I am an ambassador*x* in chains. Pray that I might be bold enough to speak about it as I should.

PAUL'S FAREWELL

21 Tychicus,*y* our dearly loved brother and faithful servant^A in the Lord, will tell you all the news about me so that you may be informed. **22** I am sending him to you for this very reason, to let you know how we are and to encourage*z* your hearts.*aa*

23 Peace to the brothers and sisters, and love with faith, from God the Father*ab* and the Lord Jesus Christ. **24** Grace be with all who have undying love for our Lord Jesus Christ.^B,C

^A 6:21 Or *deacon*   ^B 6:24 Other mss add *Amen.*   ^C 6:24 Lit *all who love our Lord Jesus Christ in incorruption*

---

is unfair, your work will never go unnoticed or be in vain. You work for an unseen employer who sees all and will reward you.

If you're the boss, you're under divine authority too. Employees may be under you in position, but they are equal to you in value. They bear the image of God, so honor their dignity. And treat all your employees with equity, consistently applying righteous standards to them.

6:10-13 What we call *spiritual warfare* is the conflict in the spiritual realm that affects the physical realm. The daily problems we face here are rooted there. But, importantly, the resources you need to fight the battle are there too.

The battle Christians face every day is rooted in **the schemes of the devil** (6:11), in his efforts to deceive us. He is happy for you to picture him as a cartoon character wearing a red jumpsuit with horns and carrying a pitchfork so that you won't take him seriously. Meanwhile, like an opposing football team, his demonic realm watches your game film. They know your history, your weak spots, and your sin patterns. Their goal is to keep you from experiencing God's will for your life. You're not their first assignment. They're good at what they do.

You, then, have to fight the spiritual with the spiritual. Your human strength won't work. Your only hope is to **be strengthened by the Lord** and to **put on the full armor of God** (6:10-11). Through the cross and resurrection of Christ, victory is already won. The devil has lost. The only power he has is the power you give him. We are to stand firm in Christ's victory.

6:14 To wear **truth like a belt** is to live in authenticity before God. Since Satan is a liar, he can't function in an environment of integrity.

Our **righteousness** is not our own. God *imputed* Christ's perfect righteousness to us (see 2 Cor 5:21). When Satan accuses you, then, protect your heart with the truth of your righteous standing in Christ that is to be reflected by righteous living based on the truth. Unrighteousness acts like an open invitation to Satan and his demonic forces to invade our hearts and lives in order to defeat us spiritually.

6:15 Having **your feet sandaled with readiness for the gospel of peace** refers to the peace of God that confirms we are moving in the right direction.

6:16 What is **faith**? It's acting like God's telling the truth—being obedient to God's

view on a matter. Whatever temptations the devil fires at you, you can overcome him by believing God's Word and acting on it. Acting in faith is like activating a divine fire extinguisher.

6:17 To wear **the helmet of salvation** means to make decisions with a biblical mindset. We are to think God's thoughts and not operate in human wisdom.

The sword of the Spirit—which is the word of God—is the only offensive weapon in the spiritual armor ensemble. The term Paul uses does not describe a long sword but something more like a dagger intended for hand-to-hand combat. He's talking about the Word of God spoken, made effective by the Spirit, to cut through the devil's lies. When Jesus was tempted, he declared, "It is written" (Matt 4:1-11), defeating the devil by using the Word. And just as Jesus did when tempted in the wilderness, Christians must learn to use Bible study against the devil. He is allergic to the Word of God when it is consistently used against him.

6:18 Prayer is the divine means of putting on our spiritual armor, which is a reflection of the person and work of Jesus Christ on our behalf.

6:21-22 Tychicus probably delivered the letter (6:21).

The Real Enemy

THE WORLD IS AT WAR—A conflict is wreaking havoc on civilians, injuring and killing many, even innocent children. Countless lives have been lost in battle after battle, and many people are uncertain there will ever be decisive victory. I'm not talking about a war of physical combat. I'm grateful, as all Americans should be, for the sacrifice and valor of our men and women serving in the armed services. But I speak of a war with consequences that will reverberate throughout eternity.

Spiritual warfare is an epic battle between good and evil that began when Satan was cast out of heaven. Confrontation escalated in the garden of Eden, where the first man, Adam, received a near fatal blow that has affected the history of God's people. Then Jesus came to earth and faced battle daily. The devil tempted him in the wilderness, and the battle raged. Jesus was sent to the cross to die, and the battle raged. He rose victoriously on the third day, but the enemy still hasn't surrendered.

The destiny of the entire world's population lies in the outcome of this great spiritual war. The situation is clearly described by Paul, the apostle: "Our struggle is not against flesh and blood, but against the rulers, against the authorities, against the cosmic powers of this darkness, against evil, spiritual forces in the heavens" (EPH 6:12).

Surrounding us is a spiritual conflict: angels versus demons, good versus evil, light versus darkness. But amazingly, most believers live as if this conflict is not even happening, as if the battle of the ages is just a fantasy or sci-fi story. What's worse is that most people think the only battle is what they can see—as if the real enemy is the person with whom they're arguing, their job, their health, the economy, or any number of other things.

What would you say if I told you that every problem in your life is a direct result of the spiritual war I've been describing? Indeed, discouragement, divorce, addiction, uncontrolled anger, debt—all are a direct result of the duel for the hearts and souls of individuals. Not one of us is immune to the consequences of spiritual warfare. And although the players fight in an invisible realm, we all face the effects of their conflict every day of our lives: it shows up as pain, struggle, defeat, and heartache.

PHILIPPIANS

INTRODUCTION

Author

THE APOSTLE PAUL IDENTIFIES HIMSELF as the author of this letter, and even the most critical scholars agree that he is. Though the greeting mentions "Paul and Timothy" (1:1), Paul is simply noting Timothy's physical presence with him. The first person "I" used throughout the letter makes it clear that this is not a case of joint authorship.

Historical Background

Paul indicates that he was imprisoned at the time he wrote Philippians (1:7, 13). We cannot be certain which imprisonment this was. Bible scholars debate about the three most likely locations: Rome, Caesarea, or Ephesus. Paul experienced frequent troubles in Ephesus (see Acts 19:21-41; 1 Cor 15:32; 16:8-9), but though he indicates that he had been imprisoned many times (2 Cor 11:23), we don't have conclusive evidence of an Ephesian imprisonment. We know he was jailed in Caesarea from AD 57 to 59 (see Acts 24:22-27). But it's more likely that Philippians was written from Rome around AD 62. This would make sense of Paul's reference to the saints of "Caesar's household" sending greetings (Phil 4:22).

During his second missionary journey in AD 51, Paul received a vision of "a Macedonian man" (Acts 16:9-10). As a result, he traveled to Philippi and founded a church in that leading city in Macedonia (see Acts 16:11-15). He also experienced persecution and imprisonment there (see Acts 16:16-40). The congregation at Philippi was the first church in Europe.

Message and Purpose

Philippians is the book of joy. Paul wants God's saints to live in the joy of the Lord and his kingdom instead of just reacting to their circumstances. Joy consists of internal stability in spite of external circumstances. And Paul was particularly qualified to teach on the subject because he wrote this book from a prison cell.

Philippians is in part a thank-you letter to the saints at Philippi for sending Epaphroditus to comfort Paul and deliver him a financial gift when they heard of his arrest and dire straits. But Paul also used the occasion to send some correction to the Philippians. He wrote the famous passage in chapter 2 to instruct the church to bring the mindset of Christ into the church rather than conforming to the world's mindset. Since two prominent women were fighting within the church, Paul knew he had to challenge the prevailing mentality.

He went on to explain that the church affects the angelic realm when it is operating properly. But that requires unity, which is why Paul prays in chapter 3 that the church might be unified. His conclusion is an exhortation to victory, to prayer instead of worry, and to choosing the mind of Christ that brings peace and joy.

www.bhpublishinggroup.com/qr/te/50_00

Outline

I. Greeting and Prayer (1:1-11)
II. The Progress of the Gospel (1:12-30)
III. Christian Humility (2:1-11)
IV. Christ-like Character (2:12-30)
V. Knowing Christ (3:1-11)
VI. Reaching Forward to God's Goal (3:12-21)
VII. Practical Counsel (4:1-9)
VIII. Appreciation of Support (4:10-23)

GREETING

1 Paul[a] and Timothy,[b] servants of Christ Jesus:

To all the saints in Christ Jesus who are in Philippi,[c] including the overseers[d] and deacons.[e]

2 Grace to you and peace from God our Father and the Lord Jesus Christ.

THANKSGIVING AND PRAYER

3 I give thanks to my God for every remembrance of you,[A] **4** always praying with joy for all of you in my every prayer, **5** because of your partnership in the gospel from the first day[f] until now.[g] **6** I am sure of this, that he who started a good work[h] in you[B] will carry it on to completion[i] until the day of Christ Jesus. **7** Indeed, it is right[j] for me to think this way about all of you, because I have you in my heart,[c] and you are all partners with me in grace, both in my imprisonment[k] and in the defense[l] and confirmation of the gospel. **8** For God is my witness,[m] how deeply I miss all of you[n] with the affection of Christ Jesus. **9** And I pray this: that your love[o] will keep on growing[p] in knowledge and every kind of discernment,[q] **10** so that you may approve the things that are superior[r] and may be pure[s] and blameless[t] in the day of Christ,[u] **11** filled with the fruit[v] of righteousness[w] that comes through Jesus Christ to the glory[x] and praise of God.

> #### ~ HOPE WORDS ~
>
> *If God is powerful enough to get you to heaven, then he is powerful enough to sustain you on earth.*

ADVANCE OF THE GOSPEL

12 Now I want you to know, brothers and sisters, that what has happened to me has actually advanced the gospel,[y] **13** so that it has become known throughout the whole imperial guard, and to everyone else, that my imprisonment is because I am in Christ. **14** Most of the brothers have gained confidence in the Lord from my imprisonment and dare even more to speak the word[D,z] fearlessly. **15** To be sure, some preach Christ out of envy and rivalry,[aa] but others out of good will. **16** These preach out of love,[ab] knowing that I am appointed for the defense of the gospel; **17** the others proclaim Christ out of selfish ambition,[ac] not sincerely, thinking that they will cause me trouble in my imprisonment. **18** What does it matter? Only that in every way, whether from false motives[ad] or true, Christ is proclaimed, and in this I rejoice. Yes, and I will continue to rejoice **19** because I know this will lead to my salvation[E,ae] through your prayers and help from the Spirit[af] of Jesus Christ.[ag] **20** My eager expectation and hope[ah] is that I will not be ashamed about anything, but that now as always, with all courage, Christ will be highly honored in my body, whether by life[ai] or by death.[aj]

LIVING IS CHRIST

21 For me, to live is Christ[ak] and to die is gain.[al] **22** Now if I live on in the flesh, this means fruitful[am] work[an] for me; and I don't know which one I should choose. **23** I am torn between the two. I long to depart and be with Christ[ao] — which is far better[ap] — **24** but to remain in the flesh is more necessary for your sake. **25** Since I am persuaded of this, I know that I will remain and continue with all of you for your progress and joy in the faith,[aq] **26** so that, because of my

[a] 1:1 Ac 13:9
[b] Ac 16:1; 1Tm 1:2
[c] Ac 16:12-40; 20:3-6; 1Th 2:2
[d] Ac 20:28; Ti 1:7
[e] 1Co 3:5
[f] 1:5 Ac 16:12-40
[g] 1Co 9:15-18; 2Co 11:7-9; Php 4:10,16,18
[h] 1:6 2Co 9:8; Gl 3:10
[i] 2Co 7:1
[j] 1:7 Rm 1:17
[k] Php 1:13-14,17-20,25,30; 2:17,24; 4:22
[l] Ac 22:1
[m] 1:8 Rm 1:9
[n] 1Th 3:6
[o] 1:9 1Co 13:1
[p] 1Co 15:58
[q] Eph 5:17
[r] 1:9-10 Rm 12:2
[s] 1:10 2Pt 3:1
[t] Ac 24:16; 1Co 10:32
[u] Php 1:6,15
[v] 1:11 Mt 3:8; Gl 5:22
[w] Rm 1:17
[x] Lk 9:32; Jn 17:24; 2Co 3:18; 2Pt 3:18

[y] 1:12 Mk 13:9; Ac 21–26
[z] 1:14 Lk 8:21; Jn 18:32; Ac 17:11; Heb 4:12
[aa] 1:15 Rm 1:29; Ti 3:9
[ab] 1:16 1Co 13:1
[ac] 1:17 Rm 2:8
[ad] 1:18 1Th 2:5
[ae] 1:19 Jb 13:16-18
[af] Gl 5:25
[ag] Ac 16:7; Rm 8:9; 1Pt 1:11
[ah] 1:20 Ac 23:6; 1Th 1:3
[ai] 1Jn 5:12
[aj] Jn 8:51
[ak] 1:21 Rm 14:7-9; Gl 2:19-20; Php 1:11,15; Col 2:6–3:11
[al] Rm 8:38-39; Php 3:7; Gl 5:22
[am] 1:22 Mt 3:8; Rm 1:13; Gl 5:22
[an] Mk 14:6; Gl 3:10; Jms 2:14-26
[ao] 1:23 Rm 6:8; 2Co 4:14; 13:4-5; 1Th 4:14; 5:9-10
[ap] Jn 12:26
[aq] 1:25 Mt 8:10; Ac 3:16; Rm 1:8; 1Co 2:5; Gl 2:16; 1Tm 1:2; Heb 4:2; Jd 3

[A] 1:3 Or *for your every remembrance of me*   [B] 1:6 Or *work among you*   [C] 1:7 Or *because you have me in your heart*   [D] 1:14 Other mss add *of God*
[E] 1:19 Or *vindication*

1:1 Paul includes **Timothy**, his son in the faith, in his greeting since Timothy had ministered with Paul in the Philippi region (see Acts 16:1-15). Though the letter was written to the whole congregation, Paul makes special mention of **the overseers and deacons** because they were responsible to lead the church in love and obedience.
1:2 This greeting could be called a summary of the gospel.
1:3-4 All believers in Jesus Christ should follow Paul's lead. Remembering fellow Christians provides opportunity to praise God for their faith and to seek God for their good.
1:6 People often start projects with great enthusiasm. However, when their zeal fades,

the work fizzles out. But God is not like us. He never undertakes anything that he doesn't finish. When he begins **a good work** in a believer's heart, it's as good as done.
1:7 Just how did the Philippians partner with the apostle in ministry? They supported him in his **imprisonment and in the defense and confirmation of the gospel**. They were not, then, fair-weather Christians. When the gospel was spreading powerfully, they supported him. And when the name of Jesus landed Paul in a jail cell, the Philippian believers still remained true to him.
1:9-10 **Love** must be more than sentimental emotion; it must conform with the truth of the Word of God.

1:12-14 **The gospel** is not hindered by struggle and persecution when they are tied to our faith and witness.
1:15-18 It takes a radical kind of God-centeredness to **rejoice** in insincere gospel proclamation—even when the preachers intend your harm (1:17-18). But as long as Jesus was exalted and people were believing in him, Paul was content.
1:21-26 Ministry requires self-sacrifice, and Paul was pleased to contribute to the spiritual growth of others so that their **boasting in Christ Jesus [could] abound** (1:26). By willingly laying down his life for the Philippians, Paul was simply following in the footsteps of his Master, Jesus Christ.

[a] 1:26 1Co 15:58
[b] Rm 16:7; Eph 2:6; 1Pt 5:14
[c] 1:27 Ac 23:1
[d] 1Co 16:13; Gl 5:1; Eph
6:13-17; Php 4:1; 2Th 2:15
[e] Jn 11:52
[f] 1Tm 3:9; 4:1,6; 5:8;
6:10,21
[g] 1:28 1Co 16:9
[h] Mt 7:13; Rm 9:22
[i] Ac 4:12; 2Co 7:10; Heb 5:9
[j] 1:29 Mk 11:24; Jn 3:16; Ac
10:43; Rm 10:9; 1Pt 1:8-10
[k] 2:1 Rm 5:8; 15:30; 2Th
2:16; 1Jn 3:16; 4:9-10,16
[l] 1Co 12:13; 2Co 13:13;
Eph 4:3
[m] Col 3:12
[n] 2:2 Rm 12:16; 15:5; 2Co
13:11; Php 4:2
[o] 2Th 1:3; 1Jn 3:16
[p] Jn 11:52
[q] 2:3 Rm 2:8
[r] Gl 5:26
[s] Col 3:12
[t] Rm 13:1; Php 3:8; 4:7;
1Pt 2:13
[u] 2:4 Rm 15:1
[v] Lv 19:18; Mk 10:45; 12:31;
1Co 10:24; 13:5; Php 2:21

[w] 2:6 Is 9:6; Jn 1:1,14;
20:28; Rm 9:5; Col 1:15-16;
Ti 2:13; Heb 1:2-13; 2Pt 1:1;
1Jn 4:14-15
[x] 2:7 Mk 9:12; 2Co 8:9; 13:4
[y] Is 42:1; 53:12; Mt 20:28;
Mk 10:45
[z] Jn 1:14; Rm 8:3; Gl 4:4;
1Tm 2:5; Heb 2:17
[aa] 2:8 Lk 23:26; Php 3:10
[ab] 2:9 Is 52:13; 53:12; Dn
7:14; Ac 2:32-33; 5:30-31;
Eph 1:20-21; Heb 2:9
[ac] 2:10 Is 45:23
[ad] 2Co 5:1; Eph 1:20; 2:6;
3:10; 6:12; Heb 3:1; 12:22
[ae] Mt 28:18; Eph 1:10;
Rv 5:13
[af] 2:11 Is 45:23; Rm 10:9; 14:11; 1Co 12:3
[ag] Lk 9:32; Jn 17:24; 2Co 3:18; 2Pt 3:18

coming to you again, your boasting[a] in Christ Jesus[b] may abound.

27 Just one thing: As citizens of heaven, live your life[c] worthy of the gospel of Christ. Then, whether I come and see you or am absent, I will hear about you that you are standing firm[d] in one[e] spirit, in one accord,[A] contending together for the faith[f] of the gospel, **28** not being frightened in any way by your opponents.[g] This is a sign of destruction for them,[h] but of your salvation[i] — and this is from God. **29** For it has been granted to you on Christ's behalf not only to believe[j] in him, but also to suffer for him, **30** since you are engaged in the same struggle that you saw I had and now hear that I have.

CHRISTIAN HUMILITY

2 If then there is any encouragement in Christ, if any consolation of love,[k] if any fellowship with the Spirit,[l] if any affection and mercy,[m] **2** make my joy complete by thinking the same way,[n] having the same love,[o] united in spirit, intent on one[p] purpose. **3** Do nothing out of selfish ambition[q] or conceit,[r] but in humility[s] consider others as more important[t] than yourselves. **4** Everyone should look out not only for his own interests,[u] but also for the interests of others.[v]

CHRIST'S HUMILITY AND EXALTATION

5 Adopt the same attitude as that of Christ Jesus,

~ **HOPE WORDS** ~

*Unity does not mean uniformity.
It means oneness of purpose.*

6 who, existing in the form of God,
did not consider equality
with God[w]
as something to be exploited.[B]
7 Instead he emptied himself[x]
by assuming the form of a servant,[y]
taking on the likeness
of humanity.[z]
And when he had come
as a man,
8 he humbled himself
by becoming obedient
to the point of death —
even to death on a cross.[aa]
9 For this reason God
highly exalted him[ab]
and gave him the name
that is above every name,
10 so that at the name of Jesus
every knee will bow[ac] —
in heaven[ad] and on earth
and under the earth[ae] —
11 and every tongue[af] will confess
that Jesus Christ is Lord,
to the glory[ag] of God the Father.

[A] 1:27 Lit *soul*   [B] 2:6 Or *to be grasped*, or *to be held on to*

1:27 Paul summarizes the believer's calling as living in a manner **worthy of the gospel of Christ**. Do you live in such a way? Paul's hope is to hear of them **standing firm in one spirit, in one accord, contending together for the faith of the gospel**.

1:28 Courage is crucial to our gospel witness. **God**, the sovereign King, can embolden failing hearts and eradicate stumbling blocks. Don't be **frightened** by **opponents** of the good news.

1:29 Suffering may appear to be a strange gift, but it's not. Suffering for the sake of Christ is *purposeful*, not purposeless. He allows it for our good and for his glory—and that makes all the difference.

1:30 Believers are called to take a stand for the gospel in love and truth regardless of repercussions, knowing that some people will support us and others will oppose us. Our goal, whether it leads to life or death, is to make Christ look good and glorify his name. He takes note of everything and will not forget it.

Like the Philippians who endured **the same struggle** as Paul, we are called to live for Christ despite opposition. Far from being a miserable existence, though, this is the only way to find true life and purpose.

2:2 Notice the dual use of the word *same*. It has to do with harmony and unity in the body of Christ. Where there is disunity, the spirit of God backs up. Conversely, where there is unity, the Spirit of God is at home. A football team is unified, not because every player plays the same position—that would be *uniformity*. A football team is unified because they are operating in harmony to reach the same goal line. Each player is playing his position with the objective of either helping his team score or stopping the opposing team from scoring. Everyone is moving in the same direction.

2:3 By definition servants serve others, not themselves. The word *nothing* doesn't allow for exceptions. It would be a lot easier if Paul had said, Don't do *most* things **out of selfish ambition or conceit**. That would allow us an escape clause. But "nothing" requires ongoing commitment to humility.

2:5-7 What does it mean that Jesus **emptied himself by assuming the form of a servant** (2:7)? He didn't empty himself of deity; he didn't stop being God. Rather, he poured the fullness of deity into his humanity. He took on human flesh and became a servant. He didn't let his deity stop him from expressing humanity. The incarnation resulted in Jesus being fully God and fully man. In theology, this is known as the *hypostatic union*—two natures in one person, unmixed forever.

Serving was never a threat to Jesus because he never lost sight of who he was. He knew his position with the Father. Similarly, when you know who you are—a son or daughter of God—rendering service won't be a problem. It's when you don't know who you are that serving becomes a problem. When you are unsure of your identity, you'll fear that serving is beneath you, that you'll somehow be taken advantage of if you serve.

2:8-9 People will pump you up, but they will also stick a pin in your balloon. Jesus was after something more than the praises of people; he lived for divine recognition.

2:10-11 All people are to recognize and bow down to the comprehensive kingdom rule of **Jesus Christ** (2:11). This can now be done voluntarily, but one day all will do it mandatorily.

a 2:12 Phm 1
b Mk 1:27; Ac 16:14,32–33; Rm 6:12
c 2:14 Jn 7:12; Ac 6:1; 1Pt 4:9
d 1Tm 2:8
e 2:15 Lk 1:6
f Mt 10:16; Rm 16:19
g Jd 24
h Lk 3:5; Ac 2:40; 1Pt 2:18
i Mt 17:17
j Dt 32:5
k 2:16 Lk 8:21; Jn 18:32; Ac 17:11; Heb 4:12
l Rm 2:17; Gl 6:4; Php 1:26
m Php 1:6,15
n 2:17 Php 1:7
o Ex 25:29; Nm 28:7
p 2:19 Lk 24:3
q Ac 16:1; 1Tm 1:2

r 2:21 Rm 15:1; 2Tm 3:2
s 1Co 10:24; Php 1:15
t 2:24 Php 1:7
u 2:25 Php 4:18
v Mt 6:8

❧ Questions & Answers ❧

Q The early church faced resistance to proclaiming Jesus as Lord because they were entering a cultural and political world in which Caesar, the Roman ruler, mandated that he himself be proclaimed as Lord. In our own day and time, what do you think are the most pressing challenges to confessing Jesus's lordship over every aspect of life?

A Today, many things are pulling at us so that they might rule over us. Race, for instance, is a challenging issue because sometimes we tend to worship our race or our culture. Rather than letting our commitment to Christ lead us, we let our race dictate our actions and reactions, causing even more division within the family of God. Politics can also become a lord when you are more Democrat than Christian,

or more Republican than Christian. Materialism and success can become American idols, if you will, should we let the value systems of society determine what we hold to be valuable in order to please people or to keep up with the Joneses. Another significant challenge is the idol of technology, which has become a "lord" for many. Technological advancement tempts us to believe that we need God less because we have more tools to make our lives easier. But of course, in spite of all the advancements, money, and power, our lives are often still a mess. So it should be clear that we desperately need Jesus to be Lord over all these things in our lives.

FOR THE NEXT Q&A, SEE PAGE 1417.

LIGHTS IN THE WORLD

12 Therefore, my dear friends,*a* just as you have always obeyed,*b* so now, not only in my presence but even more in my absence, work out your own salvation with fear and trembling. **13** For it is God who is working in you both to will and to work according to his good purpose. **14** Do everything without grumbling*c* and arguing,*d* **15** so that you may be blameless*e* and pure,*f* children of God who are faultless*g* in a crooked*h* and perverted*i* generation,*j* among whom you shine like stars in the world, **16** by holding firm to the word*k* of life. Then I can boast*l* in the day of Christ*m* that I didn't run or labor for nothing. **17** But even if I am poured out*n* as a drink offering*o* on the sacrificial service of your faith, I am glad and rejoice with all of you. **18** In the same way you should also be glad and rejoice with me.

TIMOTHY AND EPAPHRODITUS

19 Now I hope in the Lord Jesus*p* to send Timothy*q* to you soon so that I too may be encouraged by news about you. **20** For

I have no one else like-minded who will genuinely care about your interests; **21** all seek their own interests,*r* not those of Jesus Christ.*s* **22** But you know his proven character, because he has served with me in the gospel ministry like a son with a father. **23** Therefore, I hope to send him as soon as I see how things go with me. **24** I am confident in the Lord that I myself will also come soon.*t*

25 But I considered it necessary to send you Epaphroditus*u* — my brother, coworker, and fellow soldier, as well as your messenger and minister to my need*v* — **26** since he has been longing for all of you and was distressed because you heard that he was sick. **27** Indeed, he was so sick that he nearly died. However, God had mercy on him, and not only on him but also on me, so that I would not have sorrow upon sorrow. **28** For this reason, I am very eager to send him so that you may rejoice again when you see him and I may be less anxious. **29** Therefore, welcome him in the Lord with great joy and hold people like

---

2:12 We are not to work *for* our salvation but to **work out** our **salvation**. Salvation is by grace through faith in Jesus Christ.

Paul encourages the church in Philippi to develop the salvation that has been deposited within them. They were to do this **with fear and trembling**. To *fear God* is to take God seriously. We're to honor God in our decisions, regardless of the cost, so that he might be glorified. God brings circumstances into our lives, in fact, that will require us to "work out" our salvation, to gain an increasingly high reverence for God and to choose his will over

our own. This allows us to have an ever-increasing experience of his saving work and kingdom purpose in and through us.

2:13 Obedience is not based on our willpower, but on God's power **working in** us.

2:14 *Grumbling* refers to any negative emotional response to something you don't like. We all know what **arguing** is. Both hinder obedience. If we want to see God at work, we shouldn't waste our time fussing about his will.

2:15-16 We reflect God's perspective to a watching **world** when we hold tight to his **word** through trust and obedience.

2:19 **Timothy**, Paul's protégé and "son in the faith" (1 Tim 1:2), could act as an extension of Paul himself. Timothy shared the same love for the Lord and love for the church that Paul did. He serves as a wonderful example of humble servanthood.

2:27 The phrase **sorrow upon sorrow** refers to emotional sorrow over losing a friend and also ministry sorrow because the church would have lost Epaphroditus's gospel commitment to ministry.

2:29 The church ought to **hold people like** Epaphroditus **in honor**. His great service is an

[a] 2:30 Mk 14:6; 2Co 9:8; Gl 3:10; Jms 2:14-26
[b] 3:1 Rm 12:12; 2Co 6:10; Php 1:18
[c] 3:2 2Co 13:7
[d] 3:3 Gl 6:15
[e] Rm 8:4; Gl 5:25; 1Tm 3:16
[f] Rm 16:7; Eph 2:6; Php 1:1,15; 1Pt 5:14
[g] 3:5 Gn 17:12,25; 21:4; Lv 12:3; Lk 1:59; 2:21
[h] Rm 9:6
[i] Ps 68:27
[j] Ac 5:34; 22:3; Gl 1:14; 5:4
[k] 3:6 Rm 10:2
[l] Ac 22:2-5; 26:9-11; 1Co 15:9; Gl 1:13; 1Tm 1:13; 2Tm 3:12
[m] Rm 3:21; 9:31; 10:4-5; Gl 2:21; 3:21
[n] Lk 1:6; Rm 7:9-10
[o] 3:8 Php 2:3
[p] Jn 17:3; 2Co 4:6; Gl 4:8-9; Php 1:15; Col 2:2; 1Jn 4:8

[q] 3:8 1Pt 3:1
[r] 3:9 Rm 10:5
[s] Rm 3:22; 10:4; Gl 2:21; Heb 11:7
[t] 3:10 Rm 8:17; 2Co 1:5-7; Col 1:24; 1Pt 4:13; 5:1,9
[u] Rm 6:5; 8:36; 2Co 4:7-12; 12:9-10; Gl 6:17
[v] 3:12 Jn 1:5; 12:35; Rm 9:30; 1Co 9:24; Eph 3:18
[w] 3:13 Lk 9:62; 17:31
[x] 3:14 Rm 16:7; Eph 2:6; Php 1:1,15; 1Pt 5:14

him in honor, [30] because he came close to death for the work[a] of Christ, risking his life to make up what was lacking in your ministry to me.

KNOWING CHRIST

3 In addition, my brothers and sisters, rejoice[b] in the Lord. To write to you again about this is no trouble for me and is a safeguard for you.

[2] Watch out for the dogs, watch out for the evil[c] workers, watch out for those who mutilate the flesh. [3] For we are the circumcision,[d] the ones who worship by the Spirit[e] of God, boast in Christ Jesus,[f] and do not put confidence in the flesh — [4] although I have reasons for confidence in the flesh. If anyone else thinks he has grounds for confidence in the flesh, I have more: [5] circumcised the eighth day;[g] of the nation of Israel,[h] of the tribe of Benjamin,[i] a Hebrew born of Hebrews; regarding the law,[j] a Pharisee; [6] regarding zeal,[k] persecuting[l] the church; regarding the righteousness that is in the law,[m] blameless.[n]

[7] But everything that was a gain to me, I have considered to be a loss because of Christ. [8] More than that, I also consider everything to be a loss in view of the surpassing value[o] of knowing Christ[p] Jesus my Lord. Because of him I have suffered the loss of all things and consider them as dung, so that I may gain Christ[q] [9] and be found in him, not having a righteousness of my own from the law,[r] but one that is through faith in Christ[A] — the righteousness from God based on faith.[s] [10] My goal is to know him and the power of his resurrection and the fellowship of his sufferings,[t] being conformed to his death,[u] [11] assuming that I will somehow reach the resurrection from among the dead.

REACHING FORWARD TO GOD'S GOAL

[12] Not that I have already reached the goal or am already perfect, but I make every effort to take hold[v] of it because I also have been taken hold of by Christ Jesus. [13] Brothers and sisters, I do not[B] consider myself to have taken hold of it. But one thing I do: Forgetting what is behind[w] and reaching forward to what is ahead, [14] I pursue as my goal the prize promised by God's heavenly[c] call in Christ Jesus.[x] [15] Therefore, let all of us who are mature think this way. And if you think differently about anything,

[A] 3:9 Or *through the faithfulness of Christ*   [B] 3:13 Other mss read *not yet*   [C] 3:14 Or *upward*

---

example of the kind of commitment believers are to have to Christ and also to each other.
3:1 We can't be reminded too often to **rejoice in** Jesus. We can find joy in the Lord even when our circumstances are bad.
3:2 In biblical times, **dogs** were considered unclean animals; thus, Paul is saying to beware of false, *unclean* teachers. Paul had a perpetual problem with a group called the Judaizers. These Jews said one must keep the Old Testament law to be saved and sanctified. They tried to combine faith and works as a way of getting right and staying right with God. In spreading that message, they were undermining the ministry of Paul and the truth of the gospel—a message of grace, not law keeping.

We must beware of any system of theology that says we must earn our standing with God. All the spiritual calisthenics we might do, including good things like going to church, reading our Bibles, praying, and giving will not help us earn right standing with him. Religion, in fact, only weighs us down. It never tells us when we've done enough because it allows no such end. The Judaizers highlighted circumcision, but that ritual—and all things similar—was made obsolete by the death and resurrection of Christ. God gives us right standing with him

only through the righteousness of his Son, Jesus Christ.
3:3 Confidence in the flesh refers to the conviction that I can do on my own what's necessary for me to become what I'm supposed to be as a Christian. But when you put confidence in yourself about your relationship with God, you nullify his work in your life.
3:4-6 If we place our **confidence in** our accomplishments, or in anything other than Christ, we will find it impossible to rejoice in the Lord when things don't go well (3:4). When we struggle in our marriages or in our careers, we'll be miserable if we've placed our confidence in things. To be steady and joyful in all circumstances, we must place our confidence in Jesus.
3:7-8 Paul counts his past accomplishments and anything in the present or future as **loss** compared to knowing Jesus. Indeed, things are worthless when compared to Christ. But the only way a person can view life from this perspective is to see how valuable Christ truly is.
3:10 When you are going through a rough time, remember that Jesus Christ invites you to get **to know him** better through it. He will hurt with you, and you will get to understand him better in the process. Suffering is a call to intimacy with Jesus.

3:11 Paul is not talking about rising from **the dead** when Jesus comes back, though that will happen. He's talking about experiencing Jesus's **resurrection** power in this life to joyously overcome every challenge. Paul desired an outside-the-box experience of the living Christ operating in and through his life. Do you?
3:12-13 Paul has a holy discontent that keeps him pressing on. Therefore, he forgets **what is behind** and reaches for **what is ahead** (3:13).

To become an excellent Christian and fulfill your kingdom purpose, you too must have a short memory and a clear direction. So, what aspects of yesterday must you forget? All of them—the good, the bad, and the ugly. You've got to let go of your successes, your failures, and the ways others have hurt you. It's not that you don't remember the past; it's that you don't allow the past to be a controlling factor in your life. Don't spend too much time looking in the rearview mirror. A much bigger piece of glass called the windshield should have your focus because where you're going is a lot bigger than where you've been.
3:14 The way to get over yesterday is to have a forward focus, to press on. Look to the future, not the past.

^a 3:15 Lk 10:21
^b 3:18 Lk 23:26; 1Co 1:17; Gl 6:12
^c 3:19 Lk 14:10; Jn 5:41,44; 8:50,54; 12:43; Rm 9:4; 1Co 11:15; 2Co 6:8; 1Th 2:6
^d 3:21 1Pt 5:4
^e 1Co 6:13; 1Jn 3:2

^f 4:1 Rv 12:1
^g Rm 14:4; 1Co 16:13; Php 1:27; 2:2

☙ KINGDOM LIVING ❧
KINGDOM
Citizens of God's Kingdom

The message of God's kingdom agenda is sorely lacking today, even in the church. That's not to say that we don't speak about God's kingdom in the church. We do. But too much of what we say ends up being esoteric, theological code words that are unrelated to the realities of life in the here and now.

The absence of a comprehensive agenda for life has led to deterioration of cosmic proportions. Few followers of Christ have developed a true kingdom worldview, and the result has been chaos and confusion in all areas of life. We live segmented, compartmentalized lives as individuals because we lack an overarching blueprint to give us direction. Families disintegrate because they exist for their own fulfillment. Churches have a limited impact on society because they fail to understand that the goal of the church is to advance God's kingdom. Society at large has nowhere to turn for solid solutions to the perplexing challenges that confront us today, including a myriad of social ills.

It's time for Christians to recognize our place as citizens of God's kingdom. We need a comprehensive worldview based on the way our Creator intended life to be lived. We need an agenda big enough to include both individuals and societal structures, clear enough to be understood and appropriated by the average person on the street, and flexible enough to allow for considerable differences among peoples and societies. In other words, we need to embrace God's kingdom agenda.

FOR THE NEXT KINGDOM
KINGDOM LIVING LESSON SEE PAGE 1414.

God will reveal^a this also to you. **16** In any case, we should live up to whatever truth we have attained. **17** Join in imitating me, brothers and sisters, and pay careful attention to those who live according to the example you have in us. **18** For I have often told you, and now say again with tears, that many live as enemies of the cross^b of Christ. **19** Their end is destruction; their god is their stomach; their glory^c is in their shame. They are focused on earthly things, **20** but our citizenship is in heaven, and we eagerly wait for a Savior from there, the Lord Jesus Christ. **21** He will transform the body of our humble condition into the likeness of his glorious^d body,^e by the power that enables him to subject everything to himself.

4 So then, my dearly loved and longed for brothers and sisters, my joy and crown,^f in this manner stand firm^g in the Lord, dear friends.

PRACTICAL COUNSEL

2 I urge Euodia and I urge Syntyche to agree in the Lord. **3** Yes, I also ask you, true partner,^A to help these women who have contended for the gospel at my side, along with Clement and the rest of my co-workers whose names are in the book of life. **4** Rejoice in the Lord always. I will say it again: Rejoice! **5** Let your graciousness^B

^A 4:3 Or *true Syzygus*, possibly a person's name   ^B 4:5 Or *gentleness*

3:16 In other words, we should practice what we know to do.
3:17 We will never ascend to an excellent life if we're constantly hanging out with get-by people who are thinking in a mediocre way. We can't be excellent if we follow the world's ways. Excellent people—spiritually minded people who want to excel in their walk with God—hang around excellent people. They spend time with others sharing that same goal.
3:18 To **live as enemies of the cross** is to engage in lives of physical gratification and self-centeredness.
3:20 Don't let your earthly experience crowd out the reality of your heavenly **citizenship**. We are to focus on the returning King and his kingdom, not on this world and its lesser kingdoms.

4:2-3 Paul urges **Euodia and . . . Syntyche to agree in the Lord** (4:2). And he calls the church **to help these women** get along; they **have contended for the gospel at [his] side** (4:3). These faithful women had lost sight of the big picture. Evidently, the dispute between them had spread throughout the church, so Paul tells them to set aside their differences for the sake of the gospel.
4:4 The church faces opposition within and without, yet here is Paul, writing a letter about joy and telling the Philippians to rejoice. From a human perspective, it doesn't make sense. And yet the path to joy is to actually choose to rejoice, so Paul tells them to **rejoice in the Lord always**.

Worldly happiness is not the same as godly happiness. Godly happiness is called joy. In the Bible, the word *joy* is a celebration term. Thus, Paul is calling for celebration. The difference between joy and secular happiness is that the latter depends on what happens; it is circumstantially driven. So, if things are going in an upward direction in life, you feel up, but if things are going down, you feel down. This keeps you on an emotional roller coaster Biblical joy, by contrast, has to do with stability and celebration on the inside regardless of circumstances on the outside. We must choose to rejoice in order to experience the joy God promises us.
4:5 In other words, don't spread unhappiness to others. Being gracious means we don't use our ministries to be vindictive or hateful when things aren't going well. Rather, we embrace a good attitude because we know

Keep Your Eyes on the Prize

HAVE YOU EVER WATCHED "The Price is Right"? There is a particular game on that show called Plinko. Contestants drop giant chips down a slanted board covered in wooden spikes. At its bottom are nine slots, each labeled with a different cash prize amount, ranging in value. The goal is to get one of your chips to land in the $10,000 slot in the middle. But as a chip slides down the board, it will hit many of the spikes as it falls, causing it to move erratically downward. Therefore, though a contestant will start out aiming his or her chip for the middle slot, the chip often veers way off course in its travels. It might land in the big money slot, or it might land in the end slot, earning the player a whole dollar. The point for us is that even when we aim straight for the big prize, our journeys to it seldom go as we plan.

Think about how God often works in our lives. He tells us to aim for the big prize (his will for our lives), but along the way, he takes us on detours. As a young man, I felt that God was calling me to become a full-time evangelist. I was living in Baltimore, and it would have been easy to conclude that God wanted me to evangelize from there. But God took me on many detours, including my time attending school in Atlanta and then attending seminary in Dallas. Years went by before I eventually became a pastor, and not an evangelist after all. But in pastoring, I was able to help start a national ministry through which we began broadcasting the teaching of God's Word all across America and around the world. And I take advantage of this platform to present the gospel regularly.

Indeed, then, God made me an evangelist—but not according to the path I had expected. If I had chosen to look at all those detours as departures or setbacks, the church where I pastor and the national ministry from which I broadcast might never have existed. I would have missed out on my own destiny.

It was the same for Joseph. If he had taken his eyes off of the prize, his story might have turned out quite differently, too. His brothers sold him into slavery. He was falsely accused of sleeping with Potiphar's wife and unjustly imprisoned. But every step of the way, Joseph kept looking to bring God into otherwise bad situations. Eventually, the Lord used the evil that had been done to him to elevate him to one of the highest positions in the land. And when the chance came to seek retribution against his brothers, Joseph told them, "You planned evil against me; God planned it for good to bring about the present result—the survival of many people" (GEN 50:20).

Don't miss that. The very actions Joseph's brothers meant for evil God meant for good. Put another way, when evil is present, and God is brought into the situation, good will always come out of it. It's like playing a game of Plinko in which a positive outcome is certain. No matter what happens along the way, if we include God in it, the end result will always be rewarding beyond measure.

Seek God in every aspect of your life. And know that as he leads you toward his perfect will, he will probably take you in a direction that seems off course as he zigzags you toward your destiny. When that happens, don't be discouraged. Keep your eyes on the prize.

[a] 4:5 1Co 16:22; Php 1:6; Heb 10:24-25; Jms 5:8; Rv 1:7; 3:11; 22:20
[b] 4:7 Php 2:3
[c] Rm 16:7; Eph 2:6; Php 1:1,15; 1Pt 5:14
[d] 4:8 Jn 8:14
[e] 1Tm 3:8,11; Ti 2:2
[f] Rm 1:17
[g] 2Co 7:11; 11:2; 1Tm 5:22; Ti 2:5; Jms 3:17; 1Pt 3:2; 1Jn 3:3
[h] 1Pt 2:9; 2Pt 1:3,5
[i] 4:9 Jd 3

[j] 4:10 Php 1:5
[k] 2Co 8:1-2; 11:9

✦ KINGDOM LIVING ✦
PERSONAL
The Key to a Kingdom Mind

A kingdom mind is ultimately responsible for how you live out your life as a kingdom citizen. As you think, so you are. One of the most important things that you can do as a follower of Jesus Christ is to think on the things that are true. Far too often, Satan tries to place subtle lies within our thoughts. They aren't enough to attract our attention, but they are enough to get our line of thinking off of the truth. In order to remain focused on the truth, it is essential to commit the Word of God to memory.

Scripture tells us to think on the things that are lovely, pure, sensible, and true. We read in Paul's letter to the church at Philippi, "Brothers and sisters, whatever is true, whatever is honorable, whatever is just, whatever is pure, whatever is lovely, whatever is commendable—if there is any moral excellence and if there is anything praiseworthy—dwell on these things" (Phil 4:8).

The reverse of that holds true as well. Whatever is untrue, dishonorable, unjust, impure, unlovely, and not commendable—we are to guard our minds against. Our minds are integral to how we live our lives: they steer what decisions we make, what words we choose to use, and even the level of faith we exhibit toward God. One of the most helpful things you can do is commit Philippians 4:8 to memory and make it your guiding force throughout your day. Do this and watch what God does both in and through you.

be known to everyone. The Lord is near.[a] [6] Don't worry about anything, but in everything, through prayer and petition with thanksgiving, present your requests to God. [7] And the peace of God, which surpasses[b] all understanding, will guard your hearts and minds in Christ Jesus.[c]

[8] Finally[A] brothers and sisters, whatever is true,[d] whatever is honorable,[e] whatever is just,[f] whatever is pure,[g] whatever is lovely, whatever is commendable — if there is any moral excellence[h] and if there is anything praiseworthy — dwell on these things. [9] Do what you have learned and received[i] and heard from me, and seen in me, and the God of peace will be with you.

❤ HOPE WORDS ❤
You cannot dwell on both the things of God and the lies of Satan.

APPRECIATION OF SUPPORT

[10] I rejoiced in the Lord greatly because once again[j] you renewed your care for me.[k] You were, in fact, concerned about me but lacked the opportunity to show

---

[A] 4:8 Or *In addition*

---

the Lord is near. If we refuse to rejoice and instead complain, we can make the very near God feel very far off indeed.

4:6 Every time we begin to **worry**, we should see that as a call from God telling us that it's time to pray. *Prayer* is relational communication with God. It seeks to draw resources from the invisible spiritual realm into visible, physical reality. The sobering truth is that the more you worry, the less you pray. But the more you pray, the less you worry.

When you make a **petition**, be specific. A moment in which you are plagued by worry is not the time for one of those general prayers for God to bless the world. To deal with anxiety, make sure your petitions are precise. Get real with God.

Prayer can often feel frustrating—like when you go to a soda machine, put in your money, punch the button, and nothing comes out. But thinking of it in those terms causes us to miss how prayer works. God wants us to make

requests **with thanksgiving**. Give thanks, not for the problem itself, but for the God you are inviting into your specific problem. Offering thanks is a demonstration of faith in God's goodness and provision despite what you see.

4:7 When you pray as instructed in 4:6, **the peace of God, which surpasses all understanding, will guard [you] in Christ Jesus**. In other words, you'll experience calm in the midst of chaos. You will know God heard your prayer, not necessarily because the problem is solved, but because of the peace that God gives you. It's as if God puts soldiers and sentries around your feelings and thoughts.

4:8 We don't want to lose the peace God grants us in the next hour or the next day. So to prevent that, Paul says we're to dwell on **whatever is true**, **honorable**, **just**, **pure**, **lovely**, and **commendable**, and **if there is any moral excellence and . . . anything praiseworthy**, we're to focus our attention there. One of the reasons we don't keep our peace

is that we tend to dwell on the things that are set in opposition to the peace we're asking for. If we continue to entertain messages that work against our peace, anxiety will soon return. We must, therefore, ask ourselves if we are able to praise God for the things that we are dwelling on. If we can't, then we'll soon lose the peace God has given us.

4:9 The Philippians were to handle things the way they had seen Paul handle things. He was in prison, but he was praising God instead of worrying. One of the purposes of the church is to connect believers with other kingdom-minded people. We need support, and we need good examples. When we're rejoicing and praying and dwelling on the right things and watching the right people, we don't just have the peace of God, we have **the God of peace**. We get his peace, and we get his presence.

4:10-12 *Contentment* means being satisfied and at rest about where God has you, despite

it. [11] I don't say this out of need, for I have learned to be content in whatever circumstances I find myself. [12] I know both how to make do with little, and I know how to make do with a lot.[a] In any and all circumstances I have learned the secret of being content — whether well fed or hungry, whether in abundance or in need. [13] I am able to do all things through him[A] who strengthens me.[b] [14] Still, you did well by partnering with me in my hardship.

[15] And you Philippians[c] know that in the early days of the gospel,[d] when I left Macedonia,[e] no church shared with me in the matter of giving and receiving except you alone. [16] For even in Thessalonica[f] you sent gifts for my need[g] several times. [17] Not that I seek the gift, but I seek the profit[B,h] that

is increasing to your account. [18] But I have received everything in full,[i] and I have an abundance. I am fully supplied,[c] having received from Epaphroditus[j] what you provided — a fragrant offering, an acceptable sacrifice, pleasing[k] to God. [19] And my God[l] will supply all your needs according to his riches in glory in Christ Jesus. [20] Now to our God and Father[m] be glory forever and ever.[n] Amen.[o]

FINAL GREETINGS

[21] Greet every saint in Christ Jesus. The brothers who are with me send you greetings. [22] All the saints send you greetings, especially those who belong to Caesar's[p] household.[q] [23] The grace of the Lord Jesus Christ be with your spirit.[D,r]

---

[a] 4:12 1Co 15:58   [b] 4:13 2Co 12:9; Eph 3:16; Col 1:11; 1Tm 1:12; 2Tm 4:17   [c] 4:15 Php 1:1   [d] Ac 16:6-40; Php 1:5   [e] Ac 16:9   [f] 4:16 Ac 17:1   [g] Mt 6:8   [h] 4:17 Mt 3:8; Rm 1:13; Gl 5:22

[i] 4:18 Php 1:5   [j] Php 2:25   [k] Heb 13:21   [l] 4:19 Mt 27:46; Rm 1:8; Php 1:8   [m] 4:20 Gl 1:4; 1Th 1:3; 3:11,13   [n] Gl 1:5; 1Tm 1:17; 2Tm 4:18; Heb 13:21   [o] Rm 11:36; Rv 22:21   [p] 4:22 Mt 22:17; Lk 20:22   [q] Php 1:7   [r] 4:23 Rm 1:9

[A] 4:13 Other mss read *Christ*   [B] 4:17 Lit *fruit*   [C] 4:18 Or *Here, then, is my receipt for everything, I have an abundance, for I am fully supplied*
[D] 4:23 Other mss add *Amen.*

---

what's happening around you. It's not natural or automatic; it must be learned. God teaches us contentment through the ups and downs of changing circumstances. He wants us to learn to depend on him and his divine enabling no matter what.

4:13 Many times, it seems that God doesn't come through for us until we can't take one

more step. Then he provides at just the right time, strengthening us. The lesson of contentment is most effectively learned during times of suffering or need.

4:17 That Paul desires to increase the Philippians **account** means he wants to increase their heavenly reward.

4:18 **A fragrant offering, an acceptable sacrifice**: these are Old Testament images that describe the Philippians faithful service to Paul.

4:23 Indeed, all Christians need God's **grace** to continue to joyfully stand firm in the Lord.

COLOSSIANS

INTRODUCTION

Author

THE AUTHOR OF THIS LETTER claims to be the apostle Paul (1:1). Many modern critical scholars, though, deny Pauline authorship. They believe Colossians differs in style and theology from Paul's undisputed letters and conclude that some later imitator of Paul wrote it in his name. But no theological truths in the letter contradict what Paul says elsewhere. Moreover, there are many stylistic and theological similarities between Colossians and Paul's other letters. Importantly, the early church—including church fathers Irenaeus, Tertullian, Clement of Alexandria, and Justin—believed that Paul was the author. Therefore, we are justified in believing the same.

Historical Background

Colossae was a city located in the Lycus River Valley in Phrygia—a part of modern-day Turkey. The church in Colossae was not established by Paul but by his co-worker Epaphras (1:7; 4:12-13). It is clear that Paul was imprisoned while writing Colossians (4:3, 18). Many scholars agree that Paul most likely wrote Ephesians, Philippians, Colossians, and Philemon (the Prison Epistles) while he was imprisoned in Rome in AD 60–62 (see Acts 28:30). There are a number of links between these letters. Tychicus delivered both Colossians and Ephesians to their recipients (Eph 6:21-22; Col 4:7-8). Both the letter to the Colossians and the one to Philemon mention Onesimus, Archippus, and Epaphras (Col 4:9, 17; Phlm 1-2, 9-10, 23). It appears, then, that Philemon was a member of the Colossian church.

Message and Purpose

Paul wrote Colossians from jail to deal with some heresies that were circulating among the churches—particularly one false teaching about the uniqueness and deity of Jesus Christ. Such teachings involved a blending of Jewish and Greek ideas with a smattering of Christian perspective that resulted in a dumbing down of the truth about Christ. Paul counters this with a striking argument for the deity of Jesus—"he is the image of the invisible God" (Col 1:15) who was responsible for creation and is the head of the church. He is King over all of his kingdom.

Paul calls for rejection of any so-called knowledge, religious or secular, that diminishes the uniqueness of Christ. But he didn't want believers' stance on the topic to be merely theoretical. He therefore calls the Colossian believers to reflect Christ's character in every area of their lives, to put the truth into practice. The key to doing this is to submit to Jesus as Lord, both because he is God and because he is the final word of authority in the life of every believer. In the book of Colossians, Paul exalts Christ and calls the church to display his glory and truth by the way we live for his kingdom.

www.bhpublishinggroup.com/qr/te/51_00

Outline

*a*1:1 1Co 1:1; 2Co 1:1; Eph
1:1; 2Tm 1:1
*b*Ac 16:1; 1Tm 1:2
*c*1:5 Ps 119:142; Jn 14:6;
2Co 11:10; Eph 1:13; 2Tm
2:15; 3Jn 3
*d*1:6 Mk 4:8
*e*Mt 13:38; 24:14; Rm 3:6;
2Pt 2:20
*f*2Th 2:10
*g*2Pt 3:18
*h*1:7 Col 4:12; Phm 23
*i*Mt 1:17; Eph 5:2
*j*1:8 Ps 51:11; Jn 1:33; Ac
2:4; Rm 8:9; Ti 3:5; Rv
1:10; 3:22
*k*1:9 Jn 14:13; Jms 1:5
Pr 2:6; Col 3:10
*m*Eph 1:9
*n*1:10 2Co 9:8; Gl 3:10
*o*Pr 2:6; Jn 17:3; 2Pt 1:2;
1Jn 4:8
*p*1:11 Php 4:13
*q*Ac 4:33; 2Co 13:4
*r*Lk 9:32; Jn 17:24; 2Co
3:18; 2Pt 3:18

*s*1:12 Ps 36:9; Jn 12:46
*t*1:13 Mt 27:43
*u*Mt 3:2; Mk 1:15; Ac 20:25

GREETING

1 Paul, an apostle of Christ Jesus by God's will,*a* and Timothy*b* our brother:

2 To the saints in Christ at Colossae, who are faithful brothers and sisters.

Grace to you and peace from God our Father.^A

THANKSGIVING

3 We always thank God, the Father of our Lord Jesus Christ, when we pray for you, **4** for we have heard of your faith in Christ Jesus and of the love you have for all the saints **5** because of the hope reserved for you in heaven. You have already heard about this hope in the word of truth,*c* the gospel **6** that has come to you. It is bearing fruit*d* and growing all over the world,*e* just as it has among you since the day you heard it and came to truly appreciate*f* God's grace.*B,g* **7** You learned this from Epaphras,*h* our dearly loved fellow servant. He is a faithful minister of Christ*i* on your*c* behalf, **8** and he has told us about your love in the Spirit.*j*

⌁ HOPE WORDS ⌁

God longs to be more than just theology on a shelf. He wants to be real to you right now.

PRAYER FOR SPIRITUAL GROWTH

9 For this reason also, since the day we heard this, we haven't stopped praying for you. We are asking*k* that you may be filled with the knowledge*l* of his will*m* in all wisdom and spiritual understanding,^D **10** so that you may walk worthy of the Lord, fully pleasing to him: bearing fruit in every good work*n* and growing in the knowledge of God,*o* **11** being strengthened*p* with all power,*q* according to his glorious*r* might, so that you may have great endurance and patience, joyfully **12** giving thanks to

---

⌁ KINGDOM LIVING ⌁

KINGDOM

God's Comprehensive Rule

The kingdom of God is his rule, plan, and program. It is all-embracing, covering everything in the universe. We can define *the kingdom* as God's comprehensive rule over all creation. If God's kingdom is comprehensive, so is his kingdom agenda. *The kingdom agenda* may be defined as the visible manifestation of the comprehensive rule of God over every area of life.

The Greek word that Scripture uses for "kingdom" is *basileia*. It means "a rule" or "authority." It includes the concept of power. So when we talk about a kingdom, we're talking first about a king or a ruler. And if there is a ruler, there also have to be "rulees," or kingdom subjects (see Col 1:13). In addition, a kingdom includes a realm; that is, a domain over which the king rules. Moreover, a kingdom has regulations or guidelines that govern the relationship between the ruler and the subjects. These are necessary so that the subjects will know whether they are doing what the ruler wants done.

God's kingdom includes all of these elements. He is the absolute ruler of his domain, which encompasses all of creation. Likewise, his authority is total. Everything God rules, he runs. And he's made his guidelines known in his Word.

Yes, living in God's kingdom brings blessings, but you don't get to enjoy the blessings of the King if you're not willing to live under his sovereign authority. In other words, until you become a kingdom person who makes decisions based on God's kingdom agenda, you'll miss out on the abundant life he has in store for you.

FOR THE NEXT KINGDOM
KINGDOM LIVING LESSON SEE PAGE 1438.

---

the Father, who has enabled you^E to share in the saints' inheritance in the light.*s* **13** He has rescued*t* us from the domain of darkness and transferred us into the kingdom*u*

---

^A1:2 Other mss add *and the Lord Jesus Christ*   ^B1:6 Or *and truly recognized God's grace*   ^C1:7 Other mss read *our*   ^D1:9 Or *all spiritual wisdom and understanding*   ^E1:12 Other mss read *us*

1:1 Paul considered **Timothy** his "son in the faith" (1 Tim 1:2).
1:4-5 These believers had a vertical-horizontal connection: their **faith in Christ** (vertical) could intersect with their **love** for **the saints** (horizontal) because both (1:4) came from the same **hope** that was waiting for them. The **gospel** not only offers the hope of eternal life but also rewards us in this life (1:5).

1:7 Epaphras was evidently the founder and teacher of the church at Colossae.
1:9-10 Most of us want to bear good **fruit** (1:10)—i.e., have a spiritually productive life. The problem is that though many Christians hear about God and carry his book around, they're not really getting to know him, not really experiencing him. Don't just visit God for two hours on Sunday. Talk to him all the

time. And while you're walking or while you're driving, "whether you eat or drink, or whatever you do" (1 Cor 10:31), stay plugged in. You don't need a *microwave* experience with God; you need a *crockpot* experience with him. Simmer in his presence, and leave an impact on the lives of others with the impact the Lord has had on you.
1:13-14 We were under the rule of the devil, but Jesus Christ provided **redemption**.

of the Son[a] he loves.[b] **14** In him we have redemption,[A] the forgiveness of sins.

THE CENTRALITY OF CHRIST

15 He is the image of the invisible God,[c]
the firstborn over all creation.[d]
16 For everything was created by him,[e]
in heaven and on earth,
the visible and the invisible,
whether thrones or dominions
or rulers or authorities —
all things have been created
through him and for him.[f]
17 He is before all things,[g]
and by him all things[h] hold together.

APPLICATION QUESTIONS

READ COLOSSIANS 1:17

– How do you need Jesus to hold things together for you right now?

---

18 He is also the head of the body,
the church;
he is the beginning,[i]
the firstborn from the dead,[j]
so that he might come to have
first place in everything.
19 For God was pleased to have
all his fullness[k] dwell in him,[l]
20 and through him to reconcile
everything to himself,
whether things on earth or things
in heaven,
by making peace[m]

through his blood,[n] shed
on the cross.[B,o]

21 Once you were alienated and hostile in your minds expressed in your evil actions. **22** But now he has reconciled you by his physical body through his death,[p] to present you holy, faultless,[q] and blameless before him[r] — **23** if indeed you remain grounded and steadfast in the faith[s] and are not shifted away from the hope[t] of the gospel that you heard. This gospel has been proclaimed in all creation[u] under heaven,[v] and I, Paul,[w] have become a servant of it.

PAUL'S MINISTRY

24 Now I rejoice in my sufferings[x] for you, and I am completing in my flesh what is lacking in Christ's afflictions for his body,[y] that is, the church. **25** I have become its servant, according to God's commission that was given to me for you, to make the word of God fully known, **26** the mystery hidden for ages and generations but now revealed to his saints. **27** God wanted to make known among the Gentiles the glorious wealth of this mystery, which is Christ[z] in you, the hope[aa] of glory. **28** We proclaim him, warning and teaching everyone with all wisdom, so that we may present everyone mature in Christ. **29** I labor for this, striving[ab] with his strength that works powerfully in me.[ac]

2 For I want you to know how greatly I am struggling[ad] for you, for those in Laodicea,[ae] and for all who have not seen

Video Devotional
"POPCORN"

The secret to maturity as a kingdom disciple is Christ in you.

www.bhpublishinggroup.com/qr/te/51-01

[a] 1:13 Jn 5:19; Heb 1:2
[b] Mt 3:17; Jn 3:16; 15:10; 17:26; 1Jn 4:16
[c] 1:15 Php 2:6
[d] Jn 1:3; Rv 3:14
[e] 1:16 Gn 1:1; Mk 13:19
[f] Jn 1:3; Rm 11:36; 1Co 8:6; Eph 1:10,21
[g] 1:17 Jn 1:1-2; 8:58; Heb 1:2-3
[h] Ps 104:24
[i] 1:18 Gn 1:1; Mk 1:1; Jn 1:1; Ac 26:4
[j] Ac 26:23; 1Co 15:20,23; Rv 1:5
[k] 1:19 Ps 72:19; Is 6:3; Jr 23:24; Ezk 43:5; 44:4; Jn 1:14,16; Eph 3:19; Php 2:6; Col 2:9
[l] Dt 12:5
[m] 1:20 Ac 7:26; Eph 2:14

[n] 1:20 Heb 9:12
[o] Lk 9:23; 23:26
[p] 1:22 Php 2:8
[q] Jd 24
[r] 2Co 4:14
[s] 1:23 Gl 2:16; Jd 3

[t] 1:23 1Th 1:3   [u] Rv 3:14   [v] Rm 10:18; Eph 6:9   [w] Ac 13:9   [x] 1:24 2Co 1:4; Php 1:29; 3:10   [y] Eph 4:4   [z] 1:27 Col 2:2   [aa] 1Th 1:3   [ab] 1:29 Jd 3   [ac] 1Co 15:10
[ad] 2:1 2Tm 4:7   [ae] Col 4:13-16; Rv 1:11; 3:14   [s] 1:23 Gl 2:16; Jd 3

[A] **1:14** Other mss add *through his blood*   [B] **1:20** Other mss add *through him*

A slave could be redeemed in the ancient world if a price was paid for his freedom. We were slaves to sin and Satan, but through his atoning death Christ purchased us off the slave block, granting us **forgiveness of sins** and transferring us into his glorious kingdom (1:14).

1:15 The word *image* means perfect replica. That Christ is **the firstborn over all creation** has nothing to do with time but with rank. It's like the term *first lady*. The president's wife is not the first woman ever to live in the White House. She holds the rank of first lady because of her connection to the one in charge. By his divine connection to God the Father, Christ inherits creation and the right to rule: "God has appointed him heir of all things" (Heb 1:2). He is the rightful King of creation.

1:16 Genesis 1:1 says, "God created the heavens and the earth." Yet Jesus is the uncreated Creator of all things (see John 1:1-4), and there is only one uncreated, eternal being. Thus, Jesus is God. What, then, should we make of

the claim in Isaiah 9:6 that "A child will be born for us, a son will be given"? Well, the child (that is, Jesus) had to be *born* because the incarnation was a new thing, but the Son was *given* because he already existed.

1:17 The planets stay in their orbits because Jesus holds them there. If he can do that, you can be confident that he can hold you together too.

1:18 Jesus is the down payment on our resurrection. You can be raised **from the dead** because Jesus was raised from the dead.

1:19 The Second Person of the Trinity took on human flesh; he is fully God and fully man. Every attribute of God is manifested in the Son; Jesus is God in bodily form (see 2:9). That's why we see in Scripture that one minute Jesus is thirsty because he's a man, and the next minute he calms the sea because he's the Son of God.

1:20 Jesus reconciles sinners to God **through his blood, shed on the cross**. If you've placed faith in Christ, your bank statement of righteousness is reconciled by him; you have

perfect righteousness because you receive a credit from him.

1:24 Paul wanted believers to be filled with what was necessary for their spiritual development, and that includes suffering. Paul's ministry and stewardship was to prepare the church for the judgment seat of Christ.

1:26-27 The mystery refers to the exciting fact that Christ indwells every believer so that they increasingly reflect his character, conduct, attitude, and actions as they use God's Word to deal with life and become more mature (see Heb 5:11-14). Christ's indwelling presence functions within us like a new motor in an old car.

1:28-29 People are at various stages in their spiritual experience. Every minister should strive with God's **strength** (1:29) for the spiritual development of his entire congregation.

2:1-3 Paul's labor of love not only went to the Colossians, but it extended to people he'd never met (2:1). He wanted them to understand the fullness of the gospel. In Christ is found the secret to truth and to **knowledge**

*a*2:2 Lk 16:25; Col 4:8
*b*Php 3:8
*c*Col 1:27
*d*2:3 Pr 3:19; Is 11:2; 45:3; Jr 23:5; Ac 7:22; 1Co 1:21
*e*1Co 14:6
*f*2:5 Ps 51:12; 1Th 2:17
*g*2:6 Jd 3
*h*Eph 3:11
*i*2:7 Eph 2:20
*j*Eph 4:21; Heb 13:9
*k*2:8 Mk 7:3

*l*2:8 1Tm 6:20
*m*2:9 Php 2:6; Col 1:19
*n*2:10 1Co 11:3; Eph 1:22; 4:15; 5:23
*o*2:11 Col 1:22; 3:9
*p*Mt 1:17; Eph 5:2
*q*2:12 Rm 6:4
*r*Eph 2:6; Col 3:1
*s*Mt 17:9; Jn 5:25; 20:9; 21:14; Ac 2:24
*t*2:14 Lk 9:23; 23:26
*u*2:15 Lk 10:18; Jn 12:31; 16:11; Eph 6:12; Heb 2:14
*v*2:16 Lk 6:37
*w*Jn 6:55; Rm 14:3,17; 1Co 8:4; Heb 9:10
*x*Ps 81:3
*y*2:17 Heb 8:5; 10:1
*z*Rm 8:38
*aa*Gl 3:24; 5:2
*ab*2:18 1Co 9:24; Php 3:14
*ac*Col 3:12
*ad*1Co 4:6
*ae*2:19 1Co 6:13; Eph 4:4

me in person. ² I want their hearts to be encouraged*a* and joined together in love, so that they may have all the riches of complete understanding and have the knowledge of God's mystery*b* — Christ.*A,C* ³ In him are hidden all the treasures of wisdom*d* and knowledge.*e*

CHRIST VERSUS THE COLOSSIAN HERESY

⁴ I am saying this so that no one will deceive you with arguments that sound reasonable. ⁵ For I may be absent in body, but I am with you in spirit,*f* rejoicing to see how well ordered you are and the strength of your faith in Christ.

⁶ So then, just as you have received*g* Christ Jesus as Lord,*h* continue to live in him, ⁷ being rooted and built up in him*i* and established in the faith, just as you were taught,*j* and overflowing with gratitude.

⬥ HOPE WORDS ⬥

You are exactly who God intended you to be.

⁸ Be careful that no one takes you captive through philosophy and empty deceit based on human tradition,*k* based on the elements of the world, rather than

Christ.*l* ⁹ For the entire fullness*m* of God's nature dwells bodily*B* in Christ, ¹⁰ and you have been filled by him, who is the head*n* over every ruler and authority. ¹¹ You were also circumcised in him with a circumcision not done with hands, by putting off the body of flesh,*o* in the circumcision of Christ,*p* ¹² when you were buried with him*q* in baptism, in which you were also raised with him*r* through faith in the working of God, who raised him from the dead.*s* ¹³ And when you were dead in trespasses and in the uncircumcision of your flesh, he made you alive with him and forgave us all our trespasses. ¹⁴ He erased the certificate of debt, with its obligations, that was against us and opposed to us, and has taken it away by nailing it to the cross.*t* ¹⁵ He disarmed the rulers and authorities and disgraced them publicly; he triumphed over them in him.*C,u*

¹⁶ Therefore, don't let anyone judge*v* you in regard to food and drink*w* or in the matter of a festival or a new moon*x* or a Sabbath day.*D* ¹⁷ These are a shadow*y* of what was to come;*z* the substance is*E* Christ.*aa* ¹⁸ Let no one condemn*F* you*ab* by delighting in ascetic practices*ac* and the worship of angels, claiming access to a visionary realm. Such people are inflated*ad* by empty notions of their unspiritual*G* mind. ¹⁹ He doesn't hold on to the head, from whom the whole body,*ae*

---

*A*2:2 Other mss read *mystery of God, both of the Father and of Christ*; other ms variations exist on this v.   *B*2:9 Or *nature lives in a human body*
*C*2:15 Or *them through it*   *D*2:16 Or *or sabbaths*   *E*2:17 Or *substance belongs to*   *F*2:18 Or *disqualify*   *G*2:18 Lit *fleshly*

---

and to life; apprehending that truth leads to **wisdom** (2:2-3). *Knowledge* is the comprehension of truth; *wisdom* is the application of that truth to life.

2:4 Paul's concern was that the Colossians would go to false teachers offering supposed insider, secret spiritual understanding that was inconsistent with reality. Lies can **sound reasonable**, but they're still lies. Remember, the Bible is our standard for discerning truth from error. Only the full understanding of Christ can keep believers from being deceived by persuasive arguments.

2:5 Paul was delighted in how these particular believers were standing fast in the truth even in his absence.

2:6-7 Like mighty trees, believers are to remain **rooted in Jesus**, both in knowledge and in practice. That way, growth will occur and protection from false teachers will be provided.

2:9-10 In Genesis 3:1-19, Adam abdicated his role as manager of creation, turning rule over to Satan—"the god of this age" (2 Cor 4:4). But the "last Adam" (1 Cor 15:45), Jesus Christ, succeeded where the first Adam failed. He came to solve the problem. As the Second Person of the Trinity, he possesses **the entire**

fullness of God's nature (Col 2:9). But he also became a man, because God the Father intended that that man would rule over his kingdom on earth and defeat Satan. Through his sinless life, atoning death, and resurrection, Jesus defeated Satan's legal authority and reclaimed the earthly kingdom.

2:11-13 Note the recurring theme: "by him" (2:10), **in him** (2:11), **with him** (2:12[x2]; 2:13). Paul is expressing the great theological truth of our union with Christ. By faith, we are united inseparably with him, like cream stirred into coffee.

If you watch a replay of yesterday's football game—and you already know the final score is in your team's favor—you won't get upset if your team falls behind. Knowing how the game ends will have a stabilizing effect. Scripture tells us how everything is going to turn out. If you are trusting in Christ, you can have confidence whatever your struggles because you know how the story ends. Jesus is already victorious, and you are in union with him.

2:14 When a person was executed under Roman law, the sentence was attached to the accused's cross (see John 19:19). But Jesus took *our* sentence away, effectively

nailing our certificates of debt to *his* **cross**. He paid our penalty; he died for our guilt. God "made the one who did not know sin to be sin for us, so that in him we might become the righteousness of God" (2 Cor 5:21).

2:15 A fallen angel is no match for the Son of God, who took away Satan's rulership. *Satan* is actually the transliteration of a Hebrew word meaning "adversary" or "accuser." He is "the accuser of our brothers and sisters," whom he "accuses . . . before our God day and night" (Rev 12:10). But in light of the atoning sacrifice of Christ, Satan's accusations are empty.

If somebody has a gun pointed at you, whether or not it's loaded is a huge deal. The devil doesn't want you to know that his gun has been emptied by the cross. Now, if you don't know that, you're still going to cower and run, living in fear and shame. But you don't have to listen to him. Though he is right about your sin, your debt has been paid by Christ. You are free to live for God. Satan still has power, but he no longer possesses final authority in history.

2:18-19 Don't let a puffed-up false prophet tell you that you are in trouble unless you

nourished and held together by its ligaments and tendons, grows with growth from God.

20 If you died with Christ[a] to the elements of this world, why do you live as if you still belonged to the world? Why do you submit to regulations: **21** "Don't handle, don't taste, don't touch"? **22** All these regulations refer to what is destined to perish by being used up; they are human commands and doctrines. **23** Although these have a reputation for wisdom[b] by promoting self-made religion, false humility, and severe treatment of the body, they are not of any value in curbing self-indulgence.[A,c]

THE LIFE OF THE NEW MAN

3 So if you have been raised with Christ, seek the things above, where Christ is, seated at the right hand of God.[d] **2** Set your minds on things above, not on earthly things.[e] **3** For you died,[f] and your life is hidden with Christ in God. **4** When Christ, who is your[g] life, appears,[g] then you also will appear with him in glory.[h]

5 Therefore, put to death what belongs to your earthly nature: sexual immorality, impurity,[i] lust,[j] evil desire, and greed,[k] which is idolatry.[l] **6** Because of these, God's wrath[m] is coming upon the disobedient,[c] **7** and you once walked in these things when you were living[n] in them. **8** But now, put away[o] all the following: anger,[p] wrath,[q] malice,[r] slander,[s] and filthy language from your mouth.[t] **9** Do not lie[u] to one another, since you have put off[v] the old self[w] with its practices **10** and have put on[x] the new self. You are being renewed in knowledge according to the image of your[D] Creator.[y] **11** In Christ there is not Greek and Jew, circumcision

and uncircumcision, barbarian, Scythian, slave and free; but Christ is all and in all.[z]

THE CHRISTIAN LIFE

12 Therefore, as God's chosen ones, holy and dearly loved,[aa] put on compassion,

---

> ❧ **Questions & Answers** ❧

Q What are some Scripture passages that address the issue of shaping and transforming the mind?

A A key Scripture that addresses the shaping of our minds is Colossians 3:2: "Set your minds on things above, not on earthly things." This earth is temporary, so develop an eternal perspective. Another relevant passage is Jesus's rebuke of Peter in Matthew 16:23. Peter thought he was doing something good. But his mind was being shaped by the devil, and he didn't know it! Spiritual discernment is critical. You need to be able to discern the sources that are influencing your thinking. In addition, it's helpful to talk to spiritual people who are further along in the faith than you are, people who can help shape your mind.

Paul had the opportunity to influence the mindset of numerous people, such as Timothy, Titus, and the Ephesian elders (see Acts 20:17-38). All of these examples demonstrate the importance of having spiritual influencers in your life to keep you focused on an eternal perspective rooted in Scripture.

FOR THE NEXT Q&A, SEE PAGE 1421.

---

[a] 2:20 Rm 6:8; 1Pt 2:24
[b] 2:23 Ac 7:22
[c] 1Tm 4:8
[d] 3:1 Heb 10:12
[e] 3:2 Php 3:19
[f] 3:3 Rm 6:8
[g] 3:4 2Co 4:11; 1Jn 1:2; 2:28
[h] Lk 9:32; Jn 17:24; 2Co 3:18; 2Pt 3:18
[i] 3:5 1Th 4:3,7
[j] Rm 1:26; 1Th 4:5
[k] Eph 5:3
[l] 1Co 10:14; Gl 5:20; 1Pt 4:3
[m] 3:6 Jms 1:19; Rv 6:16
[n] 3:7 Lk 15:13; Rm 6:2
[o] 3:8 Rm 13:12
[p] Jms 1:19
[q] Rv 14:19
[r] 1Co 14:20
[s] Jn 10:33; Rv 13:6
[t] Eph 4:22-31
[u] 3:9 Lv 19:11; 1Tm 2:7
[v] Col 2:15
[w] Eph 4:22
[x] 3:10 Pr 31:25
[y] Mk 13:19; Jn 1:3; Rv 3:14

[z] 3:11 Eph 1:23
[aa] 3:12 Jn 3:16; 2Th 2:13; Rv 12:11

[A] 2:23 Lit *value against indulgence of the flesh*   [B] 3:4 Other mss read *our*   [C] 3:6 Other mss omit *upon the disobedient*   [D] 3:10 Lit *his*

---

know some secret information to which only he has access (2:18). What you need is to be part of **the body**, the church, which is connected to **the head**, Jesus Christ. This is the *only* way to receive ongoing spiritual **growth from God** (2:19). Any unchurched Christian will be a spiritually malnourished one.

2:21-23 Adding to God's commands might sound wise and religious, but such **human commands** (2:22) carry no authority. Add-on rules function like extra carry-on bags: they'll rob you of the freedom to fly. The world's decrees and precepts don't help a person to be spiritual. They are of no value in the eternal kingdom of God.

3:1-2 Believers must be tuned in to the Heavenly Broadcasting Network to receive the data needed for daily living. Take a good look at heaven's perspective on every issue so you will know how to live on earth.

3:3-4 To help the Colossians develop a new mentality, Paul reminds them of their new identity. First, he says, **you died.** Your old life has no more power over you. Second, **your life is hidden with Christ in God (3:3).** In fact, Christ is not merely to be in your life; he is to *be* the total sum of **your life** (3:4).

3:5 Paul calls Christians to **put to death what belongs to [the] earthly nature** (cf. Rom 8:12-13)—to kick out that earthly perspective.

Don't give it a chance to breathe or rear its ugly head.

3:8-10 Put away even **anger** and **filthy language.** They don't belong in your life. When you have taken a shower, you naturally put on clean clothes. They complement what the shower was designed to do. Jesus Christ cleansed you by his blood. Therefore, you must ask yourself concerning your actions, "Will those clothes match what Jesus did in my life? Or will they dirty up what Jesus made clean?" Because Christ has set you free, your mouth no longer rules you.

3:11 God does not have favorites. All who place faith in Christ are part of his family.

Video Devotional

"FORGIVE-NESS"

Forgive, not only because the other person needs it, but because you need to be set free.

kindness,[a] humility,[b] gentleness,[c] and patience,[d] 13 bearing with one another and forgiving one another if anyone has a grievance against another. Just as the Lord has forgiven you, so you are also to forgive.[e] 14 Above all, put on love, which is the perfect bond of unity. 15 And let the peace of Christ, to which you were also called[f] in one body, rule your hearts. And be thankful. 16 Let the word of Christ dwell richly among you, in all wisdom teaching and admonishing one another through psalms, hymns, and spiritual songs,[A] singing to God with gratitude in your hearts. 17 And whatever you do, in word or in deed, do everything in the name[g] of the Lord Jesus, giving thanks to God the Father through him.

CHRIST IN YOUR HOME

18 Wives, submit yourselves to your husbands, as is fitting in the Lord.[h] 19 Husbands,[i] love your wives[j] and don't be bitter[k] toward them. 20 Children,[l] obey your parents in everything, for this pleases the Lord. 21 Fathers,[m] do not exasperate[n] your children, so that they won't become discouraged. 22 Slaves, obey your human[o] masters in everything. Don't work only while being watched, as people-pleasers, but work wholeheartedly, fearing

a 3:12 2Co 6:6
b Ac 20:19; Eph 4:2; Php 2:3; Col 2:18,23; 1Pt 5:5
c Jms 3:13
d 2Tm 3:10
e 3:13 2Co 2:7,10; 12:13; Eph 4:32
f 3:15 Jn 14:27; 1Co 7:15; Php 4:7
g 3:17 Jn 14:13; Php 2:10
h 3:18–4:1 Eph 5:22–6:9
i 3:19 1Pt 3:1
j Eph 5:25; 1Pt 3:1
k Rv 8:11; 10:9-10
l 3:20 Gn 3:16; Lv 10:14; Dt 31:12; Ps 37:25; Pr 20:7; Lk 1:7; Ac 2:39; Heb 2:13
m 3:21 Ps 103:13; Eph 6:4; Heb 11:23
n 2Co 9:2
o 3:22 Rm 1:3; 4:1; 8:4-5,12-13; 9:3,5; 1Co 1:26; 10:18; 2Co 1:17; 5:16; 10:2-3; 11:18; Gl 4:23,29; Eph 6:5
p 3:22 Pr 1:7; Rv 14:7
q 3:23 Eph 6:7
r 3:25 Rv 2:11
s 4:1 Col 3:22
t 4:2 Rm 12:12

the Lord.[p] 23 Whatever you do, do it from the heart, as something done for the Lord and not for people,[q] 24 knowing that you will receive the reward of an inheritance from the Lord. You serve the Lord Christ. 25 For the wrongdoer[r] will be paid back for whatever wrong he has done, and there is no favoritism.

4 Masters,[s] deal with your slaves justly and fairly, since you know that you too have a Master in heaven.

SPEAKING TO GOD AND OTHERS

2 Devote yourselves[t] to prayer; stay alert in it with thanksgiving. 3 At the same time,

A 3:16 Or *and songs prompted by the Spirit*

3:13 Forgiveness does *not* mean approving a sin or excusing evil. Rather, forgiveness means releasing people from obligations incurred by their wrongs against you. This may come in the form of unilateral forgiveness—that is, forgiving someone who has not asked for forgiveness. Or it may come in the form of transactional forgiveness, which involves the confession of the offender, his repentance, and reconciliation.

What makes forgiveness possible is recognizing that **the Lord has forgiven you**. If you refuse to forgive, you have blocked God's operation in your life (see Matt 18:21-35). But when you forgive, you no longer "grieve" the Holy Spirit (Eph 4:30), and you imitate the one who shows you mercy.

3:15 When you are committed to setting your mind "on things above" (3:2), God will give you **the peace of Christ**—inner calm despite trying circumstances to help confirm your decisions and the directions for your life. If you don't have that, something is out of alignment.

3:16 When I visit with members of my church, they say, "Make yourself at home, pastor." But they don't want me going into every room and doing whatever I want! God's Word, by contrast, must **dwell** in us. It must have

access to every inch of the house of your heart—every bedroom, closet, and attic. You may have junk and dirt in places that you don't want God to see. But rest assured: He already knows about it. And if you'll let him, he can clean it up.

3:17 Jesus's **name** signed at the bottom of your day means his power is behind your life. You are to do all things with his reputation in mind.

3:18 Wives are to align themselves under the legitimate leadership of their **husbands**. This doesn't mean that wives have no input. A wise kingdom husband, in fact, will always value the input of the kingdom wife God has given him! But the point here is that the husband has the ultimate responsibility for making decisions under God that affect the well-being of the family.

Importantly, wives' submission is limited to what is **fitting in the Lord**—that is, to what falls within the boundaries of God's will. If a husband asks his wife to sin, she does not owe him her submission.

3:19 A kingdom man is not a dictator, ruling his home with a heavy hand and expecting his family to wait on him. Instead, he is a benevolent leader under the authority of God, acting with **love** and seeking the well-being of his wife and children. The husband's model is

Christ, who sacrificially loved his bride—the church—to the point of death (see Eph 5:25).

3:20 Dads and moms need to teach their sons and daughters the spiritual motivation for their obedience: it **pleases the Lord**. This fact should be emphasized from an early age.

3:21 When you correct your children, you want to break their will—their stubbornness—without breaking their spirit. The goal is to lead them to willing obedience and righteousness. Our children need to know that they are significant and important and that we as their parents will love them and not place demands on them that they can never satisfy. Remember, rules without relationship lead to rebellion.

3:22 We can apply this principle to our own vocations. Ultimately, regardless of our occupations, we all serve God and are accountable to him for the quality of our work (see 1 Cor 10:31; Eph 6:5-6).

3:23 Since you work for God, you are to produce excellence. Since you produce excellence, you should satisfy your earthly employer and your customers.

4:1 As with 3:22, this principle has wider application. Employers ought to treat their employees with dignity, justness, and fairness. God will deal with your business and

pray also for us that God may open a door[a] to us for the word, to speak the mystery of Christ,[b] for which I am in chains,[c] [4] so that I may make it known as I should. [5] Act wisely toward outsiders, making the most of the time.[d] [6] Let your speech always be gracious, seasoned with salt,[e] so that you may know how you should answer each person.[f]

FINAL GREETINGS

[7] Tychicus,[g] our dearly loved brother, faithful[h] minister, and fellow servant in the Lord, will tell you all the news about me. [8] I have sent him to you for this very purpose, so that you may know how we are[A] and so that he may encourage[i] your hearts.[j] [9] He is coming with Onesimus,[k] a faithful and dearly loved brother, who is one of you. They will tell you about everything here.

[10] Aristarchus, my fellow prisoner, sends you greetings, as does Mark,[l] Barnabas's[m] cousin (concerning whom you have received instructions: if he comes to you, welcome him), [11] and so does Jesus who is called Justus. These alone of the circumcised are my coworkers for the kingdom of God, and they have been a comfort to me. [12] Epaphras,[n] who is one of you, a servant of Christ Jesus, sends you greetings. He is always wrestling[o] for you in his prayers, so that you can stand mature and fully assured[B] in everything God wills.[p] [13] For I testify about him that he works hard[C,q] for you, for those in Laodicea,[r] and for those in Hierapolis. [14] Luke, the dearly loved physician, and Demas[s] send you greetings. [15] Give my greetings to the brothers and sisters in Laodicea, and to Nympha and the church in her home.[t] [16] After this letter has been read at your gathering, have it read also in the church of the Laodiceans; and see that you also read the letter from Laodicea. [17] And tell Archippus,[u] "Pay attention to the ministry you have received in the Lord, so that you can accomplish it."[v]

[18] I, Paul, am writing this greeting with my own hand. Remember my chains.[w] Grace be with you.[D,x]

---

[a] 4:3 Ac 14:27; 1Co 16:9; 2Co 2:12
[b] 1Co 2:7; Eph 3:4; 5:2
[c] Ac 27:2; 28:16,30; Eph 6:18-20
[d] 4:5 Eph 5:15-17
[e] 4:6 Mk 9:50; Lk 14:34
[f] 1Pt 3:15
[g] 4:7 Ac 20:4; Ti 3:12
[h] Nm 23:19
[i] 4:8 Lk 16:25
[j] Eph 6:21-22; Col 2:2
[k] 4:9 Phm 10,16
[l] 4:10 Phm 24
[m] Ac 4:36

[n] 4:12 Col 1:7; Phm 23
[o] Jd 3
[p] Gl 1:4; Eph 1:9
[q] 4:13 Jd 3
[r] Col 2:1
[s] 4:14 2Tm 4:10
[t] 4:15 Ac 12:12; Rm 16:5
[u] 4:17 Phm 2
[v] 2Tm 4:5
[w] 4:18 Php 1:7
[x] 1Tm 6:21; 2Tm 4:22; Ti 3:15

[A] 4:8 Other mss read *that he may know how you are*   [B] 4:12 Other mss read *and complete*   [C] 4:13 Other mss read *he has a great zeal*   [D] 4:18 Other mss add *Amen.*

---

your life in accordance with how you deal with those who work for you. Your employment practices are to reflect the character of the God you serve.

4:2 A believer who is outfitted with "the full armor of God" (Eph 6:10-17) but refuses to "pray" (Eph 6:18) is like a front-line soldier outfitted with the best weapons technology and protective gear but who has no communication with his command authority. He won't last long.

4:5-6 Don't waste opportunities to share the gospel. Combine tact with spice. Our witness should be crafted for **each person** in his or her unique situation (4:6) so that the gospel message is applied rightly to those who need to know about the Christian faith.

4:15-16 Laodicea was located about ten miles from Colossae (4:15). Though we do not have a copy of Paul's letter to the Laodiceans, we do have the risen Lord Jesus's letter to the church in Laodicea that the apostle John recorded in the book of Revelation (Rev 3:14-22).

Don't miss that Paul wanted these churches to pass around the letters he had written. It shows how Paul's letters were first circulated (Col 4:16).

4:18 Paul provided a handwritten **greeting** as a stamp of authenticity that the letter was indeed from him.

1 THESSALONIANS

INTRODUCTION

Author

PAUL IDENTIFIES HIMSELF AS THE author of 1 and 2 Thessalonians (1 Thess 1:1; 2 Thess 1:1). No serious objections have been made about his authorship of the former, but some critical scholars have questioned his authorship of the latter. Some argue that the two letters are too different from one another to have been penned by the same author. Alleged differences, however, are overblown. We are fully justified in believing that the apostle Paul wrote both. And though he mentions Silvanus and Timothy in his initial greetings (1 Thess 1:1; 2 Thess 1:1), clearly Paul is the primary author.

Historical Background

Paul visited Thessalonica (the modern-day Greek city of Thessaloniki) during his second missionary journey. It was an important port city on the Aegean Sea, the capital of the Roman province of Macedonia, and was located at the crossroads of two major trade routes. Thus, it was significant culturally and economically.

Though a large number of Greeks in Thessalonica initially believed Paul's preaching, the Jews there stirred up persecution against him so that he had to flee to Berea (see Acts 17:1-10). Paul probably wrote 1 and 2 Thessalonians in AD 50–51 during his lengthy ministry in Corinth (see Acts 18:1-17).

Message and Purpose

Paul wrote to the believers in Thessalonica because false teachers had infiltrated and were threatening damage to the church. He also wanted to challenge the moral laxity that had penetrated the church and to correct confusion that had arisen concerning Christ's second coming. Some believers in Thessalonica were suffering for their commitment to Christ, so Paul also wrote to encourage them to remain faithful given that Christ could return at any moment. If these believers would live in light of Christ's imminent return, they would have lifestyles pleasing to the Lord.

The apostle balanced encouragement, correction, and challenge to call this church to remain faithful to Christ even though things were not going their way. He wanted them to operate with a kingdom mentality so that they would live out the values of God's kingdom in their daily lives.

www.bhpublishinggroup.com/qr/te/52_00

Outline

I. An Authentic Message for an Authentic Community (1:1-10)
II. Paul's Authentic Ministry (2:1-12)
III. The Authentic Testimony (2:13-20)
IV. The Authentic Touch (3:1-13)
V. The Authentic Walk (4:1-12)
VI. The Authentic Hope (4:13–5:11)
VII. An Authentic Farewell (5:12-28)

GREETING

1 Paul, Silvanus,[A,a] and Timothy:[b] To the church of the Thessalonians[c] in God the Father and the Lord Jesus Christ.
Grace to you and peace.[B]

THANKSGIVING

2 We always thank God for all of you, making mention of you constantly in our prayers. **3** We recall, in the presence of our God and Father,[d] your work produced by faith,[e] your labor motivated by love, and your endurance inspired by hope in our Lord Jesus Christ.[f] **4** For we know, brothers and sisters loved[g] by God,[h] that he has chosen you,[i] **5** because our gospel did not come to you in word only, but also in power, in the Holy Spirit,[j] and with full assurance. You know how we lived among you[k] for your benefit, **6** and you yourselves became imitators of us and of the Lord when, in spite of severe persecution, you welcomed the message[l] with joy from the Holy Spirit. **7** As a result, you became an example to all the believers in Macedonia[m] and Achaia.[n] **8** For the word of the Lord rang out from you, not only in Macedonia and Achaia, but in every place that your faith[c,o] in God has gone out. Therefore, we don't need to say anything, **9** for they themselves report[D] what kind of reception[p] we had from you: how you turned[q] to God from idols[r] to serve the living[s] and true[t] God **10** and to wait[u] for his Son[v] from heaven, whom he raised from the dead[w] — Jesus, who rescues us[x] from the coming wrath.[y]

⤜ Questions & Answers ⤛

Q What role should hope or trust in God's future promises play in prayer?

A Hope is joyful and confident expectation about the future. It's not merely wishful thinking. Through hope we know that where we are going is different than where we are right now. When you approach God in prayer, you are to approach him expectantly. You are looking for him to answer, not simply because you are asking him, but because you are claiming a promise that he has made in his Word. If you do that and are willing to adjust to his will, then you can have hope that he will answer. You'll start to see where and how he is working around you.

There are things that I'm praying for right now. The answers are outside of my control, but I am expecting answers from him. Why? Because I know my God is big enough to help. He may not answer exactly as I would like, but I trust him to do what's right. You put those ingredients together, and you keep hope alive.

FOR THE NEXT Q&A, SEE PAGE 1425.

PAUL'S CONDUCT

2 For you yourselves know, brothers and sisters, that our visit[z] with you was not without result. **2** On the contrary, after we had previously suffered[aa] and

[a] 1:1 Ac 15:22; 2Co 1:19; 2Th 1:1; 1Pt 5:12
[b] Ac 16:1; 1Tm 1:2
[c] Ac 17:1
[d] 1:3 Php 4:20
[e] Rm 3:28; 9:32; Gl 2:16; 5:6; 2Th 1:11; Heb 6:1; Jms 2:14-26; Rv 2:19
[f] Ac 15:26
[g] 1:4 Jn 3:16; Rv 12:11
[h] Dt 33:12; 2Th 2:13
[i] Mt 24:22; Eph 1:4
[j] 1:5 Jn 1:33; Ac 2:4; Rm 8:9; 1Co 2:4; Gl 5:25; Ti 3:5; Rv 3:22
[k] Ac 20:18; 1Th 2:10
[l] 1:6 Heb 4:12
[m] 1:7 Ac 16:9
[n] Ac 18:12
[o] 1:8 Gl 2:16
[p] 1:9 Ac 17:1-9
[q] 1Pt 2:25
[r] Gn 31:19; 1Co 8:4
[s] Dt 5:26
[t] Jn 4:23; 1Jn 5:20
[u] 1:10 Jd 21
[v] Heb 1:2
[w] Mt 17:9; Jn 5:25
[x] Mt 27:43
[y] Rm 2:5; 1Th 5:9; Rv 6:16

[z] 2:1 Ac 17:1-9
[aa] 2:2 Ac 16:19-24

[A] 1:1 Or *Silas*; Ac 15:22-32; 16:19-40; 17:1-16   [B] 1:1 Other mss add *from God our Father and the Lord Jesus Christ*   [C] 1:8 Or *in every place news of your faith*   [D] 1:9 Lit *report about us*

1:1 The word translated *church, ekklēsia*, means a "called-out group." In the first century, anytime people gathered for a common purpose, especially to address legal matters (as in a town hall meeting; see Acts 19:39-41), it was called an *ekklēsia*. Scripture takes this everyday word and gives it new meaning: *we* as believers are the "called-out ones"—called out from the agenda of hell to a kingdom agenda that executes the rule of heaven on earth.
1:2-3 When people truly receive Jesus, **faith, hope,** and **love** start radiating outward from them. You, then, have a *working* faith, a *laboring* love, and an *enduring* hope. What will distinguish you in a cold, indifferent world is not how many Bible verses you quote, or how intense your emotions are, but how you tangibly serve others.
1:4 The point is you are saved to serve God by choice, not by chance. God found you before

you found him. And that choice was for fulfilling a divinely ordained purpose on earth.
1:5 Don't miss Paul's statement, **You know how we lived among you.** His life was an open book. Just as our words tell people the good news about Jesus, our lives need to *show* them the good news too.
1:6 Even in tribulation, an authentic Christian community has **joy from the Holy Spirit.** In spite of rejection, in spite of difficulties, in spite of hard times, you have internal stability that external troubles can't touch because you have the Spirit.
1:7-8 If you want to show off a new clothing line, you put samples on a beautiful model. The model's role is to make the clothes look good. Similarly, the Thessalonians wore kingdom clothes—godly attitudes and actions—well. When they reacted to tragedy, they made Jesus look good. The language they used made Jesus look good. The way

they conducted themselves at home made Jesus look good. Could the same be said of you?
1:9 An idol is anyone or anything, other than God, that holds your confidence, trust, and allegiance. It is anything that you look to as your source. While many American households lack idols of stone, many of us drive idols of steel. And though we don't have idols of wood, we stash idols of paper in our bank accounts. Further, even though we don't have idols of gold, we put all our hope into particular people in our lives. Everybody has a god. Everybody has a master. The only question is this: what (or who) is yours?
1:10 An authentic Christian community becomes an expectant community. And if we are truly waiting for Jesus's return, we'll be about his kingdom work.
2:2 Paul was beaten and wrongly imprisoned **in Philippi.**

a 2:2 Php 1:1
b 2:3 1Th 4:7
c Ps 10:7
d 2:4 Lk 16:11
e Ac 15:7; Gl 2:7; 1Tm 1:11
f Jn 5:44; 12:43; 1Co 4:5;
2Co 10:18; Gl 1:10; Php
3:19; 1Th 2:15; 1Pt 3:4
g Ps 17:3; Pr 21:2; Rm 8:27
h 2:5 Eph 5:3
i Mk 12:40; Lk 20:47; Jn
15:22; Ac 27:30; Php 1:18
j Rm 1:9
k 2:6 Php 3:19
l 2:7 Ac 1:2; Jd 17
m 2:9 2Jn 8
n 2:10 Rm 1:9
o Ti 2:12
p 1Th 5:23
q 2:11 1Co 4:14; Gl 4:19;
1Tm 1:2; Phm 10
r 2:12 3Jn 6
s Mk 1:15; Ac 20:25
t Lk 9:32; 24:26; Jn 17:24;
2Co 3:18; 1Pt 5:1; 2Pt 3:18
u 2:13 2Th 3:1
v Lk 8:21

w 2:14 Lk 1:5
x Php 1:29
y Ac 17:5
z 2:15 Lk 24:20
aa Rm 11:3
ab 2:16 Mt 23:30-32
ac 2:17 Col 2:5
ad 1Th 3:10
ae 2:18 Mt 4:1,10; Ac 13:10
af 2:19 Jn 15:11; 2Co 6:10
ag Rv 12:1
ah 2Co 12:5; Jms 4:16
ai Rv 11:8
aj 1Th 1:10; 1Jn 2:28
ak 1Co 15:31; 2Co 1:14; Php
4:1; 2Th 1:4
al 2:20 Jn 12:43; Php 3:19
am 3:1 Ac 17:15
an 3:2 Ac 16:1; 1Tm 1:2
ao Php 1:27

were treated outrageously in Philippi,*a* as you know, we were emboldened by our God to speak the gospel of God to you in spite of great opposition. **3** For our exhortation didn't come from error or impurity*b* or an intent to deceive.*c* **4** Instead, just as we have been approved by God to be entrusted*d* with the gospel,*e* so we speak, not to please people, but rather God,*f* who examines our hearts.*g* **5** For we never used flattering speech, as you know, or had greedy*h* motives*i* — God is our witness*j* — **6** and we didn't seek glory*k* from people, either from you or from others. **7** Although we could have been a burden as Christ's apostles,*l* instead we were gentle^A among you, as a nurse^B nurtures her own children. **8** We cared so much for you that we were pleased to share with you not only the gospel of God but also our own lives, because you had become dear to us. **9** For you remember our labor and hardship, brothers and sisters. Working*m* night and day so that we would not burden any of you, we preached God's gospel to you. **10** You are witnesses,*n* and so is God, of how devoutly, righteously,*o* and blamelessly*p* we conducted ourselves with you believers. **11** As you know, like a father with his own children,*q* **12** we encouraged, comforted, and implored each one of you to live worthy of God,*r* who calls you into his own kingdom*s* and glory.*t*

RECEPTION AND OPPOSITION TO THE MESSAGE

13 This is why we constantly thank God, because when you received the word of God that you heard from us, you welcomed it not as a human message, but as it truly is,*u* the word of God,*v* which also works effectively in you who believe. **14** For you, brothers and sisters, became imitators of God's churches in Christ Jesus that are in Judea,*w* since you have also suffered*x* the same things from people of your own country,*y* just as they did from the Jews **15** who killed the Lord Jesus*z* and the prophets and persecuted us.*aa* They displease God and are hostile to everyone, **16** by keeping us from speaking to the Gentiles so that they may be saved. As a result, they are constantly filling up their sins to the limit,*ab* and wrath has overtaken them at last.^C

PAUL'S DESIRE TO SEE THEM

17 But as for us, brothers and sisters, after we were forced to leave you^D for a short time (in person, not in heart*ac*), we greatly desired and made every effort to return*ad* and see you face to face. **18** So we wanted to come to you — even I, Paul, time and again — but Satan*ae* hindered us. **19** For who is our hope or joy*af* or crown*ag* of boasting*ah* in the presence of our Lord*ai* Jesus at his coming?*aj* Is it not you?*ak* **20** Indeed you are our glory*al* and joy!

ANXIETY IN ATHENS

3 Therefore, when we could no longer stand it, we thought it was better to be left alone in Athens.*am* **2** And we sent Timothy,*an* our brother and God's coworker^E in the gospel of Christ,*ao* to strengthen and encourage you concerning your faith, **3** so that no one will be shaken by these afflictions. For you yourselves know that we are appointed to this. **4** In fact, when we were with you, we told you in advance that we were going to experience affliction, and as you know, it happened. **5** For this reason, when I could no longer stand it, I also sent

---

^A **2:7** Many mss read *infants*   ^B **2:7** Or *nursing mother*   ^C **2:16** Or *to the end*   ^D **2:17** Lit *orphaned from you*   ^E **3:2** Other mss read *servant*

2:4 Paul was interested in one audience only—**God.**

2:5 God is our witness. Now, that's a powerful thought. If you walk with God, God himself will testify on your behalf. No slanderous accusation of greed or self-interest or flattery will stick when God takes the witness stand for you.

2:7-12 Caring relationships—not merely sermons—were the key to Paul's ministry. And that principle applies to everyone in the church, not just to the pastor. Lives touching lives is what makes a church. Individuals can't care for hundreds or thousands of people, but they can care for each other.

2:13 The Greek word translated **welcomed** means more than just hearing the Word and appreciating it. It means they respected, reverenced, embraced, and inculcated it. Like

people enjoying a good meal, they not only tasted and chewed the Word but digested it. It does us no good merely to read a few Bible passages. We have to swallow and digest them by acting on what they say.

2:19 Paul's **crown** is the Thessalonians themselves. In light of Jesus's return, Paul's greatest joy was leading people to Jesus. He had a kingdom perspective, an *eternal* perspective. When I get to heaven, I want to see a welcoming committee there because of what I've done on earth. I want to look around and say, "I invested in her"; "I led him to Christ"; "I discipled and built them up." There is a deep, unshakable joy in saying, "Lord Jesus, let me deliver to you these other saints."

3:2 We live in a high tech world, but even the best technology is no replacement for relationship. We can be high tech, but we

need high *touch* to grow spiritually. We in the church need real intimacy, and that only comes through authentic touch.

The Greek verb Paul uses for **encourage** is *parakaleō*. It shares a root with the noun (*paraklētos*) that describes the Holy Spirit in John 14:26 ("Counselor") and 1 John 2:1 ("advocate"). When God wants to encourage a believer, he uses his Holy Spirit to do it, but he often does that *through* another believer.

3:3 Believers **are appointed to** trouble. We are elected, chosen, destined *for trouble.* It knows our address, and it will arrive (see John 16:33). But the good news is that God intends to use it for our good.

3:5 When Paul thought of the devil, he didn't have in mind some ridiculous caricature. He knew that the devil is an evil spirit who hates God and seeks to tempt God's children and

God's Kingdom Agenda

ONE DAY A MAN WENT to visit his friend who lived on a farm. As he was driving down the long, winding road that led to his friend's house, he saw a barn with over twenty different targets painted on its side. Intrigued, he pulled his truck off the edge of the road and went closer to take a better look. As he did, he was amazed. Every target had one solitary hole in it, and every hole was in the center of the bull's eye. Getting back into his truck, the man continued down the road to his friend's house. The first question out of his mouth after greeting his friend was, "Who is the sharp-shooter that can hit a bull's eye with every shot?"

His friend smiled and replied, "Oh, that's me. I make every shot."

"Where in the world did you learn to shoot like that?"

"It was easy," he said. "I shoot first, and then I draw a target around the bullet hole."

This story illustrates our society's approach to life. We do everything we can to fool ourselves, and others, into thinking that we are on target when in reality all we have done is learn how to paint well. We attempt to camouflage our emptiness and failures with materialism, success, and other pursuits. What's more unfortunate is that we even try to fill our emptiness through religious activities. We learn to look, act, and talk like Christians while oftentimes we are simply attempting to obscure the fact that we are a culture and a people tragically off target.

God, on the other hand, can hit a bull's eye with a crooked stick. Every time. And he has set forth a plan by which we can do the same—if we submit to his way. I like to call this plan God's "kingdom agenda," which is the visible manifestation of the comprehensive rule of God over every area of life.

The absence of submission to the kingdom agenda in our personal and family lives, churches, and communities has led to deterioration of immense proportions. People live segmented, compartmentalized lives because they lack God's kingdom worldview. Families disintegrate because they exist for their own satisfaction rather than for the kingdom. Churches are limited in the scope of their impact because they fail to comprehend that the goal of the church is not the church itself, but the kingdom. Communities have nowhere to turn to find real solutions for real people who have real problems because the church has become divided, ingrown, and unable to transform the cultural landscape in any relevant way.

The kingdom agenda offers us a way to view and live life with a solid hope by optimizing the solutions of heaven. When God is no longer the final and authoritative standard under which all else falls, hope leaves. But the reverse of that is true as well: as long as you have God, you have hope. He's the only one whom you or I can truly bank on. If God is still in the picture, and as long as his agenda is still on the table, it's not over.

Even if relationships collapse, God will sustain you. Even if finances dwindle, God will keep you. Even if dreams die, God will revive you. As long as God is still present in your life, family, church, and community, there is hope.

a 3:6 Ac 18:5
b 1Co 11:2; Php 1:8
c 3:8 Rm 14:4; 1Co 16:13; Php 1:27
d 3:9 Jn 15:11; 2Co 6:10; Php 1:18
e 3:10 1Th 2:17
f Col 1:24
g 3:11 Jn 8:42; Php 4:20
h Ac 20:21
i 3:12 Lk 7:42
j Rm 13:8
k 3:13 Lk 1:6
l Rm 1:4; 1Co 7:14; 2Co 7:1
m 1Th 1:10; 1Jn 2:28
n Rv 11:8

o 4:3 1Th 5:18
p Rm 6:19,22; 1Co 1:30; 2Th 2:13; 1Tm 2:15; Heb 12:14; 1Pt 1:2
q 1Tm 4:3
r 4:5 2Pt 1:4; 2:10
s 4:6 2Co 12:17
t 4:7 Mt 23:27; 2Co 12:21; Gl 5:19; Eph 4:19; 5:3; Col 3:5; 1Th 2:3
u 4:8 Ps 51:11; Jn 1:33; Ac 2:4; Rm 8:9; Gl 5:25; Ti 3:5; 1Jn 5:8; Rv 3:22
v 4:9 Jn 6:45
w 1Jn 3:11
x 4:10 Ac 16:9
y 4:11 Lk 14:4; 23:56; Ac 11:18; 21:14
z 2Th 3:12; 2Jn 8
aa 4:12 Rm 13:13; 1Co 14:40

him to find out about your faith, fearing that the tempter had tempted you and that our labor might be for nothing.

ENCOURAGED BY TIMOTHY

6 But now Timothy has come to us[a] from you and brought us good news about your faith and love. He reported that you always have good memories of us and that you long to see us, as we also long to see you.[b] **7** Therefore, brothers and sisters, in all our distress and affliction, we were encouraged about you through your faith. **8** For now we live, if you stand firm[c] in the Lord. **9** How can we thank God for you in return for all the joy[d] we experience before our God because of you, **10** as we pray very earnestly night and day to see you face to face[e] and to complete what is lacking in your faith?[f]

PRAYER FOR THE CHURCH

11 Now may our God and Father[g] himself, and our Lord Jesus,[h] direct our way to you. **12** And may the Lord cause you to increase and overflow with love[i] for one another[j] and for everyone, just as we do for you. **13** May he make your hearts blameless[k] in holiness[l] before our God and Father at the coming[m] of our Lord[n] Jesus with all his saints. Amen.[A]

THE CALL TO SANCTIFICATION

4 Additionally then, brothers and sisters, we ask and encourage you in the Lord Jesus, that as you have received instruction from us on how you should live and please God — as you are doing[B] — do this even more. **2** For you know what commands we gave you through the Lord Jesus.

3 For this is God's will,[o] your sanctification:[p] that you keep away[q] from sexual immorality, **4** that each of you knows how to control his own body[c] in holiness and honor, **5** not with lustful passions,[r] like the Gentiles, who don't know God. **6** This means one must not transgress against and take advantage[s] of a brother or sister in this manner, because the Lord is an avenger of all these offenses, as we also previously told and warned you. **7** For God has not called us to impurity[t] but to live in holiness. **8** Consequently, anyone who rejects this does not reject man, but God, who gives you his Holy Spirit.[u]

LOVING AND WORKING

9 About brotherly love: You don't need me to write you because you yourselves are taught by God[v] to love one another.[w] **10** In fact, you are doing this toward all the brothers and sisters in the entire region of Macedonia.[x] But we encourage you, brothers and sisters, to do this even more, **11** to seek to lead a quiet life,[y] to mind your own business,[D] and to work[z] with your own hands, as we commanded you, **12** so that you may behave properly[aa]

A 3:13 Other mss omit *Amen.*   B 4:1 Lit *walking*   C 4:4 Or *to acquire his own wife*; lit *to possess his own vessel*   D 4:11 Lit *to practice one's own things*

---

destroy their faith. Paul was concerned that **the tempter** might have **tempted** the Thessalonians and that his own **labor might be for nothing.** Satan is real, and he is after you and me.

3:7 Everybody loses faith. Everybody falls down. We need somebody to pick us up again. Paul had the Thessalonians. Whom do you have? Connectivity with a solid, biblically centered local church is indispensable for properly progressing in the Christian life.

3:8 This is staggering! Paul, the greatest missionary ever, says to the Thessalonians, How **you stand** will determine how **we live**. In other words, he says, "I can't make it without you." Even apostles and pastors need encouragement in this vicious and divided world.

3:10 Faith needs community. I need you, and you need me. On our own, our faith **is lacking.** If we believe all by ourselves, we will not believe for long. Any unchurched, uninvolved Christian is living outside the will of God.

3:12-13 Paul wants the Thessalonians **to . . . overflow with love for one another** (3:12). Love is a choice to serve someone for his or her good. It is a decision of the will, which is why we can—and should—love people even if we do not *like* them. We choose to love, and then we ask God to help our emotions catch up. He also wants the Thessalonians to have love **for everyone** (3:12). If the only people we love are just like us, there's room for improvement. Paul further asks that God would make their **hearts blameless in holiness** because Jesus is coming back (3:13). Indeed, living in light of Jesus's second coming means living in holiness. If Jesus came back today—in the next hour—would he find you doing kingdom work? Would he say to you, "Well done, good and faithful servant" (Matt 25:23)?

4:2 Details are slim here because the Thessalonians already knew **what commands** they'd received **through the Lord.** Most believers know God's commands—at least in part—but they are not obedient to what they already know. To that Paul would say, "Remember what Jesus said? Don't ask me for the next lesson unless you're obeying *that*."

4:3 Paul knows that believers need to be sanctified in a lot of areas, but he starts with the topic of sex on purpose. He knows that if Jesus can help us to win in this matter, we can win in any other. Indeed, if Jesus helps us to walk away from pornography or to stop sleeping around, then he's really the Master of our lives.

4:5 When we believers succumb to sexual strongholds, we are worshiping the wrong thing. We are proving that we are **like the** unsaved **Gentiles, who don't know God.** Sexual immorality is a fruit of an idolatrous root—of the worship of pleasure over God, something that should not be true of believers who possess the Spirit.

4:6 One of the most attractive lies about sexual immorality is that we can get away with the thrill and not experience negative consequences. But **the Lord is an avenger of all these offenses.** He sees what we are doing, even if no one else does.

4:7 Though we do not stay pure to earn God's love, we are to stay pure *because* God loves us.

4:9-10 Unlike most churches, the Thessalonian church seemed to have mastered the art of loving each other.

4:11 Evidently, some of the Thessalonians had gotten so excited about Jesus's return that they had quit their jobs. But Paul reminds them **to work with [their] own hands,** because their laziness had become a liability to their friends and neighbors. Waiting

THE COMFORT OF CHRIST'S COMING

[13] We do not want you to be uninformed, brothers and sisters, concerning those who are asleep, so that you will not grieve like the rest, who have no hope.[b] [14] For if we believe that Jesus died and rose[c] again,[d] in the same way, through Jesus,[e] God will bring with him those who have fallen asleep. [15] For we say this to you by a word from the Lord:[f] We who are still alive at the Lord's coming[g] will certainly not precede those who have fallen asleep.[h] [16] For the Lord himself will descend from heaven with a shout,[B,i] with the archangel's[j] voice, and with the trumpet of God, and the dead in Christ[k] will rise first. [17] Then[l] we who are still alive, who are left, will be caught up together with them in the clouds[m] to meet the Lord in the air, and so we will always be with the Lord. [18] Therefore encourage[c] one another with these words.

THE DAY OF THE LORD

5 About the times and the seasons:[n] Brothers and sisters, you do not need anything to be written to you. [2] For you yourselves know very well that the day of the Lord[o] will come just like a thief[p] in the night. [3] When they say, "Peace and security," then sudden destruction[q] will come upon them, like labor pains on a pregnant woman, and they will not escape. [4] But you, brothers and sisters, are not in the dark, for this day to surprise you like a thief.[r] [5] For you are all children of light and children of the day. We do not belong to the night or the darkness.[s] [6] So then, let us not sleep, like the rest, but

[a] 4:12 Eph 4:28

[b] 4:13 Jr 14:19; Eph 2:12; 1Th 1:3
[c] 4:14 Lk 18:33
[d] Rm 4:9,15; 1Co 8:11; 15:3-4; 2Co 5:15
[e] Jn 14:19; Rm 8:11; 1Co 6:14; 15:18-20; 2Co 4:14; Php 1:23
[f] 4:15 2Pt 1:21; Rv 11:8
[g] 1Jn 2:28
[h] 1Co 15:51
[i] 4:16 Jn 5:25
[j] Jd 9
[k] Rm 16:7; 1Co 15:18; 1Pt 5:14; Rv 14:13; 20:5
[l] 4:17 1Co 15:23,51-52
[m] Mt 26:64
[n] 5:1 Dn 2:21; Ac 1:7
[o] 5:2 Jl 2:1; Mt 25:13; Ac 2:20; Php 1:6
[p] Jn 10:1
[q] 5:3 2Th 1:9
[r] 5:4 Jb 24:13-17
[s] 5:5 Col 1:13

in the presence of outsiders and not be dependent on anyone.[A,a]

[A] 4:12 Or *not need anything*, or *not be in need* [B] 4:16 Or *command* [C] 4:18 Or *comfort*

expectantly for Jesus's return does not mean that we stop working and sit around doing nothing, wasting time until the rapture. It means we work *differently*, looking to Jesus (and not our work) for our hope.
4:13 What kind of ignorance is Paul concerned with? Here he mentions **those who are asleep**, referring to people in the Thessalonian congregation who have died. Their living loved ones were afraid that they had missed the rapture. But Christians need not **grieve like** those **who have no hope** because they are uncertain about what happens after death. For the Christian, death is not the end. It is the beginning of a brand new life.
4:14-15 If we believe in Jesus, what we call "death" is no more permanent or harmful than sleep. We need not fear it anymore than we'd fear a nap. Christian loved ones who pass away remain alive in heaven with Jesus (see 2 Cor 5:8; Phil 1:22-23). At the rapture, they'll return with Christ to reclaim their resurrected, glorified bodies.

4:16 What will Jesus be shouting when he returns? There's another instance in Scripture when Jesus shouted—when he called the dead man Lazarus by name, and Lazarus walked out of the grave (see John 11:43-44). When Jesus comes back, he will do that again, many times over. I'm going to hear, "Evans, come out!" And my old body, decayed in the grave, is going to jump back to life again and be united with my spirit and soul.
4:17 The Latin word for *caught up* is *rapturo*. At the rapture, those of us who **are still alive** will join other brothers and sisters in Christ, and we will meet **them in the clouds**. And importantly, our bodies will not have the same limitations that they do today. Not only will our busted bodies be put back together, but you and I also will literally be able to walk on cloud nine since we will have resurrected bodies like Christ's (see 1 John 3:2).
5:1 To want to hear **about the times and the seasons** is to desire a timeline for Jesus's return. Jesus's second coming is imminent—

that is, we should expect him to return at any time. But God does not provide us with a specific date to circle on our calendars. One thing is certain: it will be a surprise for people who do not expect it.
5:2 The day of the Lord is the future time of judgment and blessing after the rapture through the conclusion of the millennial kingdom (see Isa 13:9-11; Joel 2:28-32; Zeph 1:14-18; 3:14-15). A **thief** doesn't send you a note in advance, saying, "Tomorrow night, around 11:00 p.m., I plan to break your back door with a sledgehammer and take your television." So, if you are not prepared for a thief to arrive at any hour, you are not prepared at all.
5:3 When a baby decides to come, Mom isn't going anywhere. In one moment, everything changes for her. The day of the Lord is that time after the rapture when God directly intervenes in world affairs for judgment during the tribulation and for blessings in Messiah's millennial reign.

a 5:8 1Pt 5:8
b Eph 6:14; Rv 9:9,17
c 1Sm 17:5,38; Ps 60:7;
108:8; Is 59:17; Eph 6:17
d 5:9 Rv 11:8
e Ac 15:26
f 5:10 Jn 11:51; Rm 14:9;
1Co 8:11; Gl 1:4
g 1Th 5:6
h Lk 20:38; Php 1:23
i 5:12 1Co 16:18; Php 2:29
j 5:13 Mk 9:50
k 5:14 2Th 3:15

l 5:14 Mt 18:26,29; Lk 18:7;
1Co 13:4; Heb 6:15; Jms
5:7-8; 2Pt 3:9
m 5:15 Mt 5:44; Rm 12:17;
1Pt 3:9
n Lk 7:47
o Rm 12:9; Gl 6:10; 1Th 5:21
p 5:16 2Co 6:10; Php 1:18
q 5:18 Eph 6:6; 1Th 4:3; 1Pt
2:15; 4:2; 1Jn 2:17
r 5:21 Eph 5:17
s 5:22 1Tm 4:3
t 5:23 Rm 15:33
u Ps 51:12
v 1Th 1:10
w Rv 11:8
x 1Jn 2:28
y 5:24 Col 3:15
z 1Pt 1:15
aa 5:27 Col 4:16

let us stay awake and be self-controlled. **7** For those who sleep, sleep at night, and those who get drunk, get drunk at night. **8** But since we belong to the day, let us be self-controlled[a] and put on the armor[b] of faith and love, and a helmet[c] of the hope of salvation. **9** For God did not appoint us to wrath, but to obtain salvation through our Lord[d] Jesus Christ,[e] **10** who died for us,[f] so that whether we are awake or asleep,[g] we may live together with him.[h] **11** Therefore encourage one another and build each other up as you are already doing.

EXHORTATIONS AND BLESSINGS

12 Now we ask you, brothers and sisters, to give recognition[i] to those who labor among you and lead you[A] in the Lord and admonish you, **13** and to regard them very highly in love because of their work. Be at peace[j] among yourselves. **14** And we exhort you, brothers and sisters:[k] warn those who are idle,[B] comfort the discouraged, help the weak, be patient[l] with everyone. **15** See to it that no one repays evil for evil[m] to anyone,[n] but always pursue what is good for one another and for all.[o] **16** Rejoice[p] always, **17** pray constantly, **18** give thanks in everything; for this is God's will[q] for you in Christ Jesus. **19** Don't stifle the Spirit. **20** Don't despise prophecies, **21** but test all things.[r] Hold on to what is good. **22** Stay away[s] from every kind of evil.

23 Now may the God of peace[t] himself sanctify you completely. And may your whole spirit,[u] soul, and body be kept sound and blameless at the coming[v] of our Lord[w] Jesus Christ.[x] **24** He who calls[y] you[z] is faithful; he will do it. **25** Brothers and sisters, pray for us also. **26** Greet all the brothers and sisters with a holy kiss. **27** I charge you by the Lord that this letter be read to all the brothers and sisters.[aa] **28** The grace of our Lord Jesus Christ be with you.

[A] 5:12 Or *care for you*   [B] 5:14 Or *who are disorderly*, or *who are undisciplined*

5:8-9 We must put these on: **the armor of faith and love** and the **helmet of the hope of salvation** (5:8). Without these, we have no protection in this world. With them, however, we can be confident in our deliverance since God has not destined us for **wrath** (5:9).

5:11 These theological truths are not for personal education alone but for our corporate edification. We stand or we fall—together.

5:14 It takes great wisdom to shepherd God's people well. Part of that wisdom lies in being aware of the different seasons in which people live. For **those who are idle**, Paul says we should **warn** them. There comes a time we must, out of love for fellow believers, confront them when they are not walking with Jesus.

To those who are **discouraged**, Paul says we should offer **comfort**. Not every problem a person experiences in life is a result of their sin. When a fellow believer is lacking in courage, he or she needs you to believe for them and be a comfort.

To those who are **weak**, we should offer **help**. After all, as the old song says, we all need somebody to lean on. Today I may help you in your weakness, but tomorrow I will need you to help me in mine. That's how the body of Christ works.

Finally—and this is the most difficult part—we should **be patient with everyone**. We must be patient with people who are sinning and with people who are suffering, with people who want to change and with people who do not. Patience aims for every target.

We must demonstrate compassion without compromise.

5:16-22 These commands are simple, but following them certainly isn't! The only way we can constantly **give thanks** and **rejoice** is by knowing that God is working something out in our lives.

5:23-24 God has never started a project he did not finish. And if he has started on you, you can be sure that he *will* **sanctify you completely** as you allow him to transform you from the inside out (**spirit, soul, and body**) (5:23).

5:28 Paul began the letter with the mention of **grace** (see 1:1) and ends it the same way. From first to last, and every step along the way, the Christian life is lived by grace.

2 THESSALONIANS

INTRODUCTION

Author

See discussion in 1 Thessalonians.

Historical Background

See discussion in 1 Thessalonians.

Message and Purpose

Paul wrote this letter to correct doctrinal error because many of the Thessalonian Christians were confused. Their misunderstanding about the day of the Lord, the time of God's judgment preceded by the rapture (see 1 Thess 4:13-18), had caused some of the believers to live slothfully. They reasoned that since Christ's coming could happen any day, there was no point in working every day and dealing with daily burdens. Many were quitting their jobs and using prophecy as an excuse to be irresponsible, surviving off of the generosity of others.

Paul sought to correct the church's thinking and to explain how they should live responsibly in light of the truth about the day of the Lord. Paul was concerned that the Thessalonians understand right doctrine, but he also wanted them to engage in right living in light of it as part of God's kingdom people.

VIDEO INTRO

www.bhpublishinggroup.com/qr/te/53_00

Outline

I. Standing Firm in Suffering (1:1-12)
II. Standing Firm in Doctrine (2:1-12)
III. Standing Firm in Faithfulness (2:13-17)
IV. Standing Firm in Obedience (3:1-18)

[a] 1:1 Ac 15:22; 2Co 1:19;
1Th 1:1; 1Pt 5:12
[b] Ac 16:1; 1Tm 1:2
[c] Ac 17:1
[d] 1:3 1Co 13:1; 1Jn 4:16
[e] Php 2:2
[f] 1Th 4:10
[g] 1:4 2Co 12:5
[h] 1:5 1Jn 1:9
[i] Mt 12:41; Jn 5:22,27,30;
8:16; 16:11; Heb 9:27;
Jms 2:13; 2Pt 3:7; Rv 14:7;
16:7; 19:2
[j] Php 1:29
[k] 1:8 1Co 3:13; Heb 10:27;
12:29; 2Pt 3:7; Rv 14:10
[l] Ps 79:6; Is 66:15; Jr 10:25
[m] 1Pt 4:17
[n] 1:9 1Tm 6:9
[o] Gn 4:14
[p] Is 2:10,19,21
[q] 1:10 Mk 8:38

[r] 1:10 Jn 17:10; Rm 8:17
[s] Eph 5:3; 6:18
[t] 1:11 Eph 4:1; Col 3:15
[u] Gl 2:16; 1Th 1:3
[v] 1:12 Jn 14:13; Ac 3:16;
15:14; Php 2:10
[w] Is 24:15; 49:3; 66:5; Mal
1:11; 2Co 8:23
[x] Jn 13:31
[y] 2:1 1Th 1:10; 1Jn 2:28
[z] Rv 11:8
[aa] 2:2 1Jn 4:1
[ab] Mt 25:13; Ac 2:20;
Php 1:6
[ac] 2Tm 2:18; 1Jn 2:28
[ad] 2:4 1Co 8:5
[ae] Is 14:12-15; Ezk 28:2;
Ac 17:23

GREETING

1 Paul, Silvanus,[A,a] and Timothy:[b] To the church of the Thessalonians[c] in God our Father and the Lord Jesus Christ. ² Grace to you and peace from God our Father and the Lord Jesus Christ.

GOD'S JUDGMENT AND GLORY

³ We ought to thank God always for you, brothers and sisters, and rightly so, since your faith is flourishing and the love[d] each one of you has for one another[e] is increasing.[f] ⁴ Therefore, we ourselves boast[g] about you among God's churches — about your perseverance and faith in all the persecutions and afflictions that you are enduring. ⁵ It is clear evidence of God's righteous[h] judgment[i] that you will be counted worthy of God's kingdom, for which you also are suffering,[j] ⁶ since it is just for God to repay with affliction those who afflict you ⁷ and to give relief to you who are afflicted, along with us. This will take place at the revelation of the Lord Jesus from heaven with his powerful angels, ⁸ when he takes vengeance with flaming fire[k] on those who don't know God[l] and on those who don't obey the gospel of our Lord Jesus.[m] ⁹ They will pay the penalty of eternal destruction[n] from the Lord's presence[o] and from his glorious strength[p] ¹⁰ on that day when he comes[q] to be glorified[r] by his saints[s] and to be marveled at by all those who have believed, because our testimony among you was believed. ¹¹ In view of this, we always pray for you that our God will make you worthy of his calling,[t] and by his power fulfill your every desire to do good[B] and your work produced by faith,[u] ¹² so that the name[v] of our Lord Jesus will be glorified[w] by you, and you by him,[x] according to the grace of our God and the Lord Jesus Christ.

THE MAN OF LAWLESSNESS

2 Now concerning the coming[y] of our Lord[z] Jesus Christ and our being gathered to him: We ask you, brothers and sisters, ² not to be easily upset or troubled, either by a prophecy[C,aa] or by a message or by a letter supposedly from us, alleging that the day of the Lord[D,ab] has come.[ac] ³ Don't let anyone deceive you in any way. For that day will not come unless the apostasy[E] comes first and the man of lawlessness[F] is revealed, the man doomed to destruction. ⁴ He opposes and exalts himself above every so-called god[ad] or object of worship,[ae] so that he sits[G] in God's temple, proclaiming that he himself is God.

⁵ Don't you remember that when I was still with you I used to tell you about this? ⁶ And you know what currently restrains him, so

[A] 1:1 Or *Silas*; Ac 15:22-32; 16:19-40; 17:1-16   [B] 1:11 Or *power bring to fruition your desire to do good*   [C] 2:2 Or *spiritual utterance*   [D] 2:2 Other mss read *Christ*   [E] 2:3 Or *rebellion*   [F] 2:3 Other mss read *man of sin*   [G] 2:4 Other mss add *as God*

1:3 Though the Thessalonians were experiencing difficult times, their **faith** was strong. Trials expand faith, just like exercise develops muscle. After all, how will you know God is bigger than your problems unless God gives you some you can't handle on your own— some "faith weights"?

1:4-5 Other **churches** were being encouraged by the Thessalonians' spiritual commitment, patience, and love for one another, in spite of the persecution they were enduring. Remember, you go to church not just for yourself, but also to impact the lives of others through meaningful service. Don't disconnect. When believers suffer for the faith, they are gaining greater kingdom rewards and authority (see Rom 8:17).

1:9-10 What's the most frightening doctrine in the Bible? The doctrine of hell. If you don't know Christ, pay attention: a day of reckoning is coming! Eternal destruction means never-ending pain and regret. Those who like to hang out with Satan in life will be away **from the Lord's presence** after death (1:9). There will be no answered prayers in hell. There will be no light and no peace, because God is light, and God is peace. Those who choose God, on the other hand, will experience glory unspeakable when they pass from this life (1:10).

1:11-12 Paul knew that if the Thessalonian church was recharged by prayer, it would have an even more powerful witness: **The name of our Lord Jesus will be glorified by you** (1:12).

If you go through a particularly difficult season and choose to lean on the Lord in prayer, somebody may look at you and ask, "How can you smile at a time like this? How are you standing when you ought to be stooping?" The answer will be that "those who trust in the LORD will renew their strength . . . they will run and not become weary" (Isa 40:31).

2:1-2 The Thessalonians were being told that they had missed the rapture and were thus living in the tribulation (2:1)! First, they were deceived by a **prophecy**—a spiritual or religious utterance (2:2). Paul had told them previously, "Don't despise prophecies" (1 Thess 5:20), but the devil tries to talk in the name of God. That's why John said we must "test the spirits" (1 John 4:1). Beware anyone who says, "God told me such-and-such," if it doesn't agree with God's Word.

Second, they were deceived by a **message**—hearsay (2:2). You might still be doing things merely because "Mama said." But the only legitimate messages we are to follow are those that agree with the message that really comes from God.

Third, they were deceived by **a letter**—by

things written down (2:2). Some of us need to change the books we're reading. Rat poison is 90% food. But it's that last 10% that's designed to kill.

2:3 Even new believers need to seek to understand prophecy because knowledge of the future will control decisions in the present. You don't need to study every religion in the world; you just need to know Christianity well. After all, federal agents learn to identify counterfeit dollars by studying the real thing. **2:4** Satan convinced Adam and Eve to rebel, to operate independently of God. That's what couples who do illegitimately give up on their marriages; that's what children do who disrespect their parents. Eventually, the human preference for lies through Satanic deception will lead to the appearance of "the man of lawlessness" (2:3). He will be empowered to bring the rebellion against God to ultimate fruition. The lawless one will exalt himself as the supreme object of worship and proclaim himself to be God (see Rev 13:5-8).

2:6-8 The only reason the world is not as wicked as it could be is *that* something **currently restrains** the lawless one (2:6). **The mystery of lawlessness** is Satan's program of sin, and **the one now restraining** is the Holy

that he will be revealed in his time.[a] [7] For the mystery of lawlessness[b] is already at work, but the one now restraining will do so until he is out of the way, [8] and then the lawless one will be revealed. The Lord Jesus will destroy him with the breath of his mouth[c] and will bring him to nothing at the appearance of his coming. [9] The coming of the lawless one is based on Satan's working, with all kinds of false miracles, signs, and wonders,[d] [10] and with every wicked deception among those who are perishing. They perish because they did not accept the love of the truth and so be saved.[e] [11] For this reason God sends them a strong delusion so that they will believe the lie, [12] so that all will be condemned[f] — those who did not believe[g] the truth but delighted in unrighteousness.

STAND FIRM

[13] But we ought to thank God always for you, brothers and sisters loved by the Lord, because from the beginning[A] God has chosen[h] you for salvation through sanctification[i] by the Spirit and through belief in the truth. [14] He called you to this through our gospel, so that you might obtain the glory[j] of our Lord Jesus Christ. [15] So then, brothers and sisters, stand firm[k] and hold to the traditions you were taught,[l] whether by what we said or what we wrote.

[16] May our Lord Jesus Christ himself and God our Father, who has loved[m] us and given us eternal encouragement and good hope by grace, [17] encourage your hearts and strengthen you in every good work and word.

PRAY FOR US

3 In addition, brothers and sisters, pray for us that the word of the Lord may spread rapidly and be honored, just as it was with you,[n] [2] and that we may be delivered[o] from wicked and evil people, for not all have faith.[B] [3] But the Lord is faithful; he will strengthen and guard you from the evil one.[p] [4] We have confidence in the Lord about you, that you are doing and will continue to do what we command. [5] May the Lord direct your hearts to God's love and Christ's endurance.[q]

➤ HOPE WORDS ➤

It is not information about Jesus that will deliver you. It is Jesus who will deliver you.

WARNING AGAINST IRRESPONSIBLE BEHAVIOR

[6] Now we command you, brothers and sisters, in the name[r] of our Lord Jesus Christ, to keep away from every brother or sister[s] who is idle and does not live according to the tradition[t] received[u] from us. [7] For you yourselves know how you should

[a] 2:6 Lk 21:8
[b] 2:7 Mt 13:41
[c] 2:8 Is 11:4; 30:28
[d] 2:9 Mt 24:24; Mk 13:22; Rv 13:13
[e] 2:10 Ac 16:30; Eph 2:8
[f] 2:12 Jn 5:22-30
[g] Jn 6:64
[h] 2:13 Rm 9:11; 11:5; Eph 1:4; 1Th 1:4
[i] Rm 6:19; 1Co 1:30; 1Th 4:3; 1Tm 2:15; Heb 12:14; 1Pt 1:2
[j] 2:14 Lk 9:32; Jn 17:24; 2Co 3:18; 1Pt 5:1,4; 2Pt 3:18
[k] 2:15 Rm 14:4; 1Co 16:13; Php 1:27
[l] Mk 7:3; 1Tm 4:11; Jd 3
[m] 2:16 Jn 3:16; Rv 12:11

[n] 3:1 1Th 2:13
[o] 3:2 Mt 27:43; Rm 15:31
[p] 3:3 Mt 5:37; 6:13; 13:19,38; Jn 17:15; Eph 6:16; 1Jn 2:13-14; 3:12; 5:18-19
[q] 3:5 Rm 15:5; Rv 13:10
[r] 3:6 Jn 14:13; Ac 3:16; 15:14; Php 2:10
[s] 1Th 18:17; 1Co 5:11; 2Tm 3:5; 2Jn 10
[t] Mk 7:3
[u] Jd 3

[A] 2:13 Other mss read *because as a firstfruit*   [B] 3:2 Or *for the faith is not in everyone*

Spirit working through the church (2:7). The Spirit sets himself up like a dam to hold back the full expression of evil until God removes his church out of the world at the rapture. The relationship of the church (and individual Christians) to the Holy Spirit affects the expansion or limitation of sin in our lives, our families, and the broader society.

2:9 Satan is no ninety-pound weakling. He is a powerful spiritual being, and he can mimic supernatural wonders.

2:10 When you reject **truth**, you invite lies into your life. The Word of God is truth; therefore, we should measure everything by Scripture.

2:11-12 The only way to heaven is through God's channel, Jesus Christ. Those who allow themselves to believe anything else **will be condemned** (2:12). They will be judged for their decision to reject the truth. Delusion and deception will be greatly amplified during the tribulation (see Rev 13:11-18).

2:13 The surrounding context makes it clear that this choosing does not refer to personal salvation but to deliverance from the tribulation through the rapture (see 2:1-4, 11-12; cf. 1 Thess 5:1-9).

2:14 Remarkably, God wants Christians to be partners with his Son, to **obtain the glory of our Lord Jesus**. God will eventually turn the whole universe over to Christ. That's why Jesus refused Satan's temptation to worship him in exchange for all the kingdoms of the world (see Matt 4:8-10). Jesus knew that he would one day rule the world anyway—through faithfulness to the Father. Some of us seek the things of this world through unrighteousness, but God already intends to give the world to his people, if we stand firm.

2:15 **Stand firm.** You are to be like a member of the Queen's Guard in England—no matter what happens around you and while everybody else is waffling and buying into different worldviews, you hold onto the truth of Scripture. If you only follow Christ when he gives you good things, and not when you struggle, then you're not following Christ at all.

The **traditions** in view here are those **taught** by apostolic authority, by the Word of God. Importantly, personal preference and cultural practice are not equal to Scripture. Don't let human traditions enslave you; your Master is Christ (see Col 2:8).

2:16-17 God has given us **eternal encouragement and good hope** (2:16). He has already put on deposit in eternity all the comfort you need to deal with any situation you face. Think of it as having a well-supplied account at the bank; all you have to do is write a withdrawal slip. And prayer is the slip.

When teams row together in the Olympics, eight men in the boat have their backs to the finish line, but they're looking at the coxswain. He's looking at the line and talking to them: "Row harder! The finish line is coming; don't give up!" Jesus is your coxswain. He knows where the end point is. You just watch him and row. Keep your eyes on "the source and perfecter of our faith" (Heb 12:2), and stand firm.

3:2 Many people talk as if they're saved, but they're not. And their hypocrisy can rub off on us if we're not careful.

3:6 Just because people are members of your church doesn't mean they're spiritual. A church serves like a hospital: sick people go there to get better. Not every professing Christian, then, is somebody to follow—a person may be spiritually immature and still "sick," or just plain lazy and not concerned with growing in the Lord. As the psalmist says, don't "walk in the advice of the wicked" (Ps 1:1).

[a] 3:7 3Jn 11
[b] 3:8 1Co 10:25
[c] 1Th 2:7
[d] Rv 14:13
[e] 2Co 11:27; 1Th 2:9
[f] Ac 18:3; Eph 4:28; 2Jn 8
[g] 2Co 2:5; 1Th 2:9
[h] 3:9 Mk 1:22; Ac 9:14; Rm 13:1; 1Co 9:4-14
[i] Heb 8:5
[j] 3:10 1Th 4:11
[k] 3:11 1Tm 5:13

[l] 3:13 Lk 18:1; 2Co 4:1,16; Gl 6:9; Eph 3:13
[m] 3:16 1Th 5:23
[n] Nm 6:26; Eph 6:23
[o] Rm 15:33; 1Co 16:24; 2Co 13:13; Ti 3:15; Heb 13:25
[p] 3:17 1Co 16:21

imitate[a] us: We were not idle among you; [8] we did not eat[b] anyone's food free of charge;[c] instead, we labored[d] and toiled,[e] working[f] night and day, so that we would not be a burden[g] to any of you. [9] It is not that we don't have the right[h] to support, but we did it to make ourselves an example to you so that you would imitate[i] us. [10] In fact, when we were with you, this is what we commanded you: "If anyone isn't willing to work, he should not eat."[j] [11] For we hear that there are some among you who are idle. They are not busy but busybodies.[k] [12] Now we command and exhort such people by the Lord Jesus Christ to work quietly and provide for themselves.[A]

[13] But as for you, brothers and sisters, do not grow weary[l] in doing good.

[14] If anyone does not obey our instruction in this letter, take note of that person; don't associate with him, so that he may be ashamed. [15] Yet don't consider him as an enemy, but warn him as a brother.

FINAL GREETINGS

[16] May the Lord of peace[m] himself give you peace always in every way.[n] The Lord be with all of you.[o] [17] I, Paul, am writing this greeting with my own hand,[p] which is an authenticating mark in every letter; this is how I write. [18] The grace of our Lord Jesus Christ be with you all.

[A] 3:12 Lit *they may eat their own bread*

3:7-9 Paul took responsibility for his well-being. If your theology makes you irresponsible, you're reading the Bible wrongly.

3:10 There are four tiers of responsibility. First is *personal* responsibility: you shouldn't expect anybody else to do for you what you ought and are able to do for yourself (see 3:6-8, 10). The second tier is *family* responsibility. Relatives are to care for each other: "If anyone does not provide for his own family . . . [he] is worse than an unbeliever" (1 Tim 5:8; see also 1 Tim 5:4). If the family can't help, then there's *church* responsibility (see 1 Tim 5:9-10, 16); after all, it's God's extended family. *State* responsibility is to be the very last tier. Unfortunately, for many, the state is tier number one in addressing human need. It is the primary role of civil government to maintain a safe, just, righteous, and compassionately responsible environment for freedom and personal responsibility to flourish (see Rom 13:1-7).

3:11-13 If you don't occupy your time with the right thing, you're going to occupy it with the wrong thing. If you're minding everyone's business but your own, there's a spiritual problem.

3:14-15 We often assume we're not supposed to make people feel guilty or **ashamed**. But understand that Christians who won't take personal responsibility and obey the Word of God need to experience legitimate guilt.

We must **warn** them and, if necessary due to a refusal to repent, break our fellowship with them (3:15). Sometimes a brother needs a lesson.

3:16 You know you're where God wants you to be when you are objectively in his Word and he subjectively confirms it with his **peace**. *Peace* is harmony on the inside **always in every way**—that is, regardless of your circumstances.

3:18 *Grace* is God doing for you what you don't deserve and can't earn (see Rom 11:6). It is his unmerited favor. You have an account in heaven, and God gives you the grace needed for today—but only for today. Nevertheless, it's more than you'll ever need.

1 TIMOTHY

INTRODUCTION

Author

THE LETTERS OF 1–2 TIMOTHY and Titus are often referred to as the Pastoral Epistles. Each indicates that Paul was the author (1 Tim 1:1; 2 Tim 1:1; Titus 1:1). Nine of Paul's thirteen letters were written to churches. Four were written to individuals. The three Pastoral Epistles were written to two of Paul's coworkers and sons in the ministry—Timothy and Titus—who were serving in pastoral roles within churches. Early church fathers such as Irenaeus identified Paul as the author as well.

It was not until critical scholars began to question Pauline authorship in the nineteenth century that these assertions were disputed. Many critical scholars today deny Pauline authorship because they claim that the Pastoral Epistles differ in style, vocabulary, and theology from Paul's other letters. However, some differences in style and vocabulary hardly demand different authors. One has to keep in mind the different audiences of Paul's letters: some were penned to individuals and others to whole churches. It's not unreasonable, then, to believe that Paul might express himself differently in style and vocabulary when writing to an entire church versus when writing to a colleague in ministry. Importantly, regarding the supposed differences in theology, none of the examples raised are actual contradictions. Rather, they involve different theological emphases or topics. There are no serious objections, then, to believing that the letters were authored by the apostle Paul.

Historical Background

Timothy hailed from Lystra in Asia Minor (modern-day Turkey), a place Paul visited on his first missionary journey (see Acts 14:5-23). Timothy was the son of a believing Jewish woman and a Greek father (Acts 16:1), and he was likely converted under Paul's ministry (1 Cor 4:17; 1 Tim 1:2). During Paul's second missionary journey, he visited Lystra again and took Timothy with him as a coworker (see Acts 16:2-3). Over time, the man served as a trusted companion and ministry ally of unquestionable commitment and character (see, e.g., Acts 17:14-15; 19:22; 20:4; Rom 16:21; 1 Cor 4:17; 16:10; 2 Cor 1:19; Phil 2:19-22; 1 Thess 3:2, 6). Titus was also a Gentile convert and coworker of Paul. He accompanied Paul in his missionary work and was often sent on ministry missions (see, e.g., 2 Cor 7:6-7; 8:16-18, 23; 12:18; Gal 2:1, 3).

Paul probably wrote these letters after the time period covered in the book of Acts. Released from Roman imprisonment, Paul continued his missionary work. During this time, he left Timothy to minister in Ephesus (1 Tim 1:3-4). Paul also visited Crete and left Titus to minister there (Titus 1:5). Later Paul wrote 2 Timothy when he was again imprisoned in Rome (2 Tim 1:8, 16; 4:16)—that imprisonment would lead to his martyrdom (2 Tim 4:6-8).

Message and Purpose

This is the first of the Pastoral Epistles that instruct church leaders and members how to do church God's way. Having left Timothy behind in Ephesus to grow what Paul had himself established, Paul explained to him how the church should work. The key verse of the book is 1 Timothy 3:15, in which Paul says, "I have written so that you will know how people ought to conduct themselves in God's household, which is the church of the living God."

Paul spends a lot of time explaining how to grow and develop church leadership, how leaders are to function, and what their responsibilities entail. Timothy was to study, learn, and grow himself from God's Word, and then preach what he was learning. The letter also points out that the quality of leaders affects the quality of the members. This, in fact, is why Paul was so concerned that Timothy develop the right kind of leaders. First Timothy can help pastors and church members maximize their potential in making their church all that God designed it to be in the ministry of his kingdom.

www.bhpublishinggroup.com/qr/te/54_00

Outline

I. False Teaching and the True Gospel (1:1-20)
II. The Priority of Prayer and the Reality of Gender Roles (2:1-15)
III. Qualifications for Leaders in God's Household (3:1-16)
IV. The Hard but Essential Work of Ministry (4:1–6:2)
V. The Gain of Godliness and the Deception of Greed (6:3-21)

[a] 1:1 Ac 13:9
[b] Rm 16:26; Ti 1:3
[c] 1Tm 2:3; Ti 1:3; 2:10; 3:4; Jd 25
[d] 1Co 15:19; Col 1:27; 1Th 1:3; 1Pt 3:13,13
[e] 1:2 Ac 16:1; 20:4; 1Co 4:17; 16:10
[f] 1:3 Ac 16:9
[g] Eph 1:1
[h] Jd 4
[i] 1:4 1Tm 4:7; 2Tm 4:4; Ti 1:14; 2Pt 1:16
[j] Eph 1:10; 3:2,9; Col 1:25
[k] 1:5 Rm 13:10
[l] Ps 24:4; 2Tm 2:22; 1Pt 1:22
[m] Ac 23:1; 24:16; Rm 9:1; 2Co 1:12; 1Tm 1:19; 3:9; Heb 10:22; 1Pt 3:21
[n] 2Tm 1:5
[o] 1:8 Rm 7:12,16
[p] 1:9 Ti 1:6,10; Heb 2:8
[q] 1:10 1Co 5:9
[r] Gn 19:5; Rm 1:27; 1Co 6:9
[s] Jn 8:44
[t] 1Tm 6:3; 2Tm 1:13; Ti 1:9; 2:1
[u] 1:11 2Co 4:4
[v] 1Tm 6:15
[w] Lv 6:4; Lk 12:48; 1Co 9:17; Gl 2:7; 1Th 2:4; 1Tm 1:11; 6:20; 2Tm 1:12,14; Ti 1:3
[x] 1:12 Ac 9:22; Php 4:13

[y] 1:13 Ac 6:11; 2Tm 3:2; 2Pt 2:11
[z] Php 3:6
[aa] 1Co 15:8
[ab] 1:15 1Tm 3:1; 4:9; 2Tm 2:11; Ti 3:8
[ac] Jn 3:17; 12:46; 18:37; 1Jn 4:9
[ad] Mk 2:17; Lk 19:10; Rm 11:4
[ae] 1Co 15:9
[af] 1:16 Lk 1:50
[ag] Ex 34:6; Rm 2:4
[ah] Jn 12:25; Ac 13:48
[ai] 1:17 Ps 47:7
[aj] Ps 90:2
[ak] 1Co 9:25
[al] Jn 5:44; 1Co 8:6; Eph 4:6; 1Tm 2:5; 6:15; Jd 25
[am] 2Pt 1:17; Rv 5:12
[an] Mk 10:37
[ao] Php 4:20; 1Tm 6:16; Rv 22:21
[ap] 1:18 1Co 13:2; 1Tm 4:14; 2Tm 1:6

GREETING

1 Paul,[a] an apostle of Christ Jesus by the command[b] of God our Savior[c] and of Christ Jesus our hope:[d] [2] To Timothy,[e] my true son in the faith. Grace, mercy, and peace from God the[A] Father and Christ Jesus our Lord.

FALSE DOCTRINE AND MISUSE OF THE LAW

[3] As I urged you when I went to Macedonia,[f] remain in Ephesus[g] so that you may instruct certain people[h] not to teach false doctrine [4] or to pay attention to myths[i] and endless genealogies. These promote empty speculations rather than God's plan,[j] which operates by faith. [5] Now the goal of our instruction is love[k] that comes from a pure heart,[l] a good conscience,[m] and a sincere faith.[n] [6] Some have departed from these and turned aside to fruitless discussion. [7] They want to be teachers of the law, although they don't understand what they are saying or what they are insisting on. [8] But we know that the law is good,[o] provided one uses it legitimately. [9] We know that the law is not meant for a righteous person, but for the lawless and rebellious,[p] for the ungodly and sinful, for the unholy and irreverent, for those who kill their fathers and mothers, for murderers, [10] for the sexually immoral[q] and homosexuals,[r] for slave traders, liars,[s] perjurers, and for whatever else is contrary to the sound teaching[t] [11] that conforms to the gospel[u] concerning the glory of the blessed God,[v] which was entrusted to me.[w]

PAUL'S TESTIMONY

[12] I give thanks to Christ Jesus our Lord who has strengthened[x] me, because he considered me faithful, appointing me to the ministry — [13] even though I was formerly a blasphemer,[y] a persecutor,[z] and an arrogant man.[aa] But I received mercy because I acted out of ignorance in unbelief, [14] and the grace of our Lord overflowed, along with the faith and love that are in Christ Jesus. [15] This saying is trustworthy[ab] and deserving of full acceptance: "Christ Jesus came into the world[ac] to save sinners"[ad] — and I am the worst of them.[ae] [16] But I received mercy[af] for this reason, so that in me, the worst of them, Christ Jesus might demonstrate his extraordinary patience[ag] as an example to those who would believe in him for eternal life.[ah] [17] Now to the King[ai] eternal,[aj] immortal,[ak] invisible, the only[B] God,[al] be honor[am] and glory[an] forever and ever. Amen.[ao]

ENGAGE IN BATTLE

[18] Timothy, my son, I am giving you this instruction in keeping with the prophecies[ap] previously made about you, so that by recalling them you may fight the good fight, [19] having faith[aq] and a good conscience.[ar] Some[as] have rejected these and have shipwrecked their faith. [20] Among them are Hymenaeus[at] and Alexander,[au] whom I have delivered to Satan,[av] so that they may be taught not to blaspheme.

INSTRUCTIONS ON PRAYER

2 First of all, then, I urge that petitions, prayers, intercessions, and thanksgivings be made for everyone, [2] for kings and all those who are in authority,[aw] so that we may lead a tranquil and quiet life

[aq] 1:19 Eph 3:12; 6:16; Col 1:23; 2:5; 1Th 5:8; 1Tm 3:13; 6:12; 2Tm 4:7; 1Jn 5:4
[ar] Heb 10:22
[as] 2Tm 2:18; Jd 4
[at] 1:20 2Tm 2:17
[au] 2Tm 4:14
[av] 1Co 5:5
[aw] 2:2 Ezr 6:10; Rm 13:1; 1Co 2:1

A 1:2 Other mss read our   B 1:17 Other mss add wise

1:2 Paul served as a spiritual mentor to Timothy, who was perhaps converted under his ministry. **1:5 The goal of** biblical **instruction is love**— love for God (to love God is to passionately pursue his glory and submit to his will) and love for neighbor (to love people is the decision to compassionately, righteously, and responsibly seek the well-being of others). The absence of love means that teaching (no matter how accurate) has not fully accomplished its goal. **1:7** When you act like an expert about spiritual and biblical subjects that you know little about, you're going to confuse and harm those who trust your supposed expertise. **1:8-11** Paul emphasizes that he is not disparaging the law but those who misunderstand it and use it legalistically. **The law is good**, but it must be understood **legitimately** (1:8). The law shows us how sinful we are (see Rom

7:7-13), how incapable we are of keeping it. The law was intended to point us to our need for a Savior (see Gal 3:21-26). It can't make us righteous. Believers satisfy the demands of the law as they walk in the Spirit (see Rom 8:1-13; Gal 5:16-18). The law is for those who have not yet become convinced of their sin. **1:12-14** Timothy had no doubt heard Paul's testimony before, but Paul apparently never tired of telling the story of the power of God's grace in his life. No matter where you came from or what you did, if you trust in Jesus as your substitutionary sacrifice, you too have a testimony of grace to proclaim. **1:15-16** This statement includes both doctrine (the mission of Christ) and experience (the personal application of the gospel to Paul). The apostle was grateful to serve as a testimony of hope and encouragement so that

others might be motivated to believe the gospel. Are you? **1:17** Jesus Christ *is* **God**. He is sovereign above all earthly and spiritual power. He deserves our worship and service because of who he is and what he has done. **1:20** In his second letter to Timothy, Paul explains that **Hymenaeus** was teaching that the resurrection had already happened (2 Tim 2:17-18). In excommunicating false teachers from the church (turning them over **to Satan**), Paul hoped they would see the error of their deeds and be led to repentance. **2:1-2** God expects us to submit to his rule regardless of the political environments in which we live, but in a culture of religious freedom, believers are able to have a more public witness and can share their faith in ways that they could not under an oppressive regime. An

in all godliness[a] and dignity.[b] **3** This is good, and it pleases God our Savior,[c] **4** who wants everyone[d] to be saved[e] and to come to the knowledge of the truth.[f]

5 For there is one God[g] and one mediator[h] between God and humanity, the man[i] Christ Jesus, **6** who gave himself as a ransom for all,[j] a testimony at the proper time.

7 For this I was appointed a herald, an apostle[k] (I am telling the truth;[A] I am not lying), and a teacher of the Gentiles[l] in faith and truth.

INSTRUCTIONS TO MEN AND WOMEN

8 Therefore, I want the men in every place to pray, lifting up holy hands without anger or argument.[m] **9** Also, the women are to dress themselves in modest clothing,[n] with decency and good sense, not with elaborate hairstyles, gold,[o] pearls, or expensive apparel, **10** but with good works,[p] as is proper for women who profess to worship God. **11** A woman is to learn quietly with full submission.[q] **12** I do not allow a woman to teach or to have authority over a man; instead, she is to remain quiet. **13** For Adam was formed first, then Eve.[r] **14** And Adam was not deceived, but the woman was deceived and transgressed.[s] **15** But she will be saved through childbearing, if they continue in faith, love, and holiness,[t] with good sense.

QUALIFICATIONS FOR OVERSEERS AND DEACONS

3 This saying is trustworthy:[u] "If anyone aspires to be an overseer,[B,v] he desires a noble work." **2** An overseer,[w] therefore, must be above reproach, the husband of

[a] 2:2 2Pt 1:3
[b] 1Tm 3:4; Ti 2:7
[c] 2:3 1Tm 1:1
[d] 2:4 Ti 2:11
[e] Ezk 18:23,32; Jn 3:17; 1Tm 4:10; Ti 2:11; 2Pt 3:9
[f] Jn 14:6,17
[g] 2:5 Dt 6:4; Gl 3:20
[h] Heb 8:6
[i] Jn 1:14; Php 2:7; 3:3; 1Jn 4:2; 5:20
[j] 2:6 Mt 20:28; Gl 1:4
[k] 2:7 Eph 3:7-8; 1Tm 1:11; 2Tm 1:11
[l] Ac 9:15
[m] 2:8 Mk 7:21; Lk 9:46-47; 24:38; Rm 14:1; Php 2:14
[n] 2:9 1Pt 3:3
[o] 2:9 Rv 3:18
[p] 2:10 2Co 9:8; Gl 3:10
[q] 2:11 1Co 14:34; Ti 2:5
[r] 2:13 Gn 2:7,22; 3:16; 1Co 11:8-12
[s] 2:14 Gn 3:6,13; 2Co 11:3
[t] 2:15 1Th 3:12-4:10
[u] 3:1 1Tm 1:15; 4:9
[v] 3:2-4 Ti 1:7
[w] Ac 20:28; Php 1:1; Ti 1:6-8

A2:7 Other mss add *in Christ*   **B3:1** Or *bishop, pastor*

---

orderly, free society is a positive environment for the proliferation of the gospel.

2:3-4 When natural disasters strike, rescue units mobilize and enter the devastation so that they might help those who will surely perish without them. God has a mobilized rescue unit: it's called the church. And the church's job is to enter this sin-scarred world and rescue the dying with the King's message of life. Notice that God's desire is universal: he wants **everyone to be saved**. This is God's emotional basis and motivation for unlimited atonement (see John 3:16; Heb 2:9). The gospel is not restricted to any race, gender, ethnicity, class, or individual. So don't let anything prevent you from going to the lost: you have the message with the power to rescue them.

2:5-6 A *mediator* is someone who brings two estranged parties together (2:5). Sinful humanity stands condemned under the righteous wrath of a holy God. And only Jesus Christ, the God-Man, can reconcile us. Because of his divine nature, he is sinless. Because of his human nature, he can serve as a substitutionary sacrifice for sinful humans. Knowing this, he **gave himself as a ransom for all** (2:6)—that is, he paid the price for everyone (theologians call this *unlimited atonement*).

The judgment of God against rebellious humanity has been completely satisfied through Christ's sin-bearing work (see 1 John 2:2). But to receive the benefits of this sacrifice, you must personally receive Christ's payment by faith.

2:7 Whatever lies the false teachers were spreading (see 1:3-4), Paul was devoted to **telling the truth**, to proclaiming the standard of reality. Are you?

2:8 Men are to take the lead in calling heaven down to earth. Men are to be leaders in their homes and in their churches. And there's no more important way to lead among the people of God than by praying for divine intervention. Jesus is looking for men who are willing to get in the game and get dirty on the field. Leading in prayer is frontline ministry.

Lifting up holy hands refers to a common prayer stance (e.g., Exod 9:29; 1 Kgs 8:22; Ps 28:2) that is to be done in the context of purity and unity.

2:9-10 Godly character is to be reflected outwardly in godly apparel. Worldly standards are often unacceptable—and this is sometimes true when it comes to clothing choices. Do not dress in a way that draws inappropriate attention by either underdressing or overdressing. Walk in godliness, dress with godliness, and be worthy of respect.

2:11-12 Paul allows women to speak in the church when it is under the proper covering of legitimate male authority (see 1 Cor 11:2-10). What he's talking about here is the exercise of a role, an office. He's talking about *teaching* and *having authority*. An overseer/elder/pastor (these terms are interchangeable in the New Testament) is expected both to teach and to govern and lead the church (see 1 Tim 3:2, 5; 5:17; Titus 1:9; cf. 1 Thess 5:12; Heb 13:17). Women are restricted from serving in this role of final authority in the church, where teaching and exercising authority are combined (senior pastor, elder, bishop).

2:13 In other words, the limitation on women serving in a role of final authority in the church is based on a creation principle. There was an order to God's creation of humanity. He created the man first *not* because the man was superior to the woman, but because he was to be the positional leader. This established a pattern for the home and the church.

The married couple was to function as an inseparable team, exercising dominion together over God's creation, with the man exhibiting godly servant leadership. The man's role as "head" (i.e., governing authority) over the woman (Eph 5:22-23) does not make him superior to her any more than God the Father's role as "head" makes him superior in essence to God the Son (see 1 Cor 11:3). They are coequal members of the Trinity, though they have different functions.

Likewise, the husband is to submit to Christ's headship over him and the wife is to submit to her husband's headship (Eph 5:24; Col 3:18; 1 Pet 3:1); nonetheless, they are unified in Christ (Gal 3:28) and "coheirs of the grace of life" (1 Pet 3:7). When this clearly defined covenantal order is breached, the door is opened for Satan to sow discord (see Gen 3:1-6).

2:14 Though Eve **was deceived**, Scripture lays responsibility for humankind's fall into sin at the feet of Adam (see Rom 5:12; 1 Cor 15:21). As the "head," he should have defended both his wife and God's garden against the lying intruder (see Eph 5:22-23). Similarly, God-called men are to serve as spiritual guardians and overseers in the church, leading God's people, teaching the truth, and equipping the church to guard against Satanic intrusion.

2:15 Every time a believing woman has a baby and raises her child **in faith, love, and holiness**, she's preparing another offspring to help put hell on the run. Only Jesus's work on the cross ultimately defeats the devil. But, as his body, we the church are promised that the devil will also be crushed under our feet (see Rom 16:20). Women are to influence their children to be agents of God's kingdom, battling the enemy through the power of the Holy Spirit. Such a faithful kingdom woman will **be saved**—that is, delivered—and experience spiritual victory. Single women and those unable to bear children can share in this victory by teaching and discipling the next generation of kingdom warriors.

3:1 The term **overseer** is interchangeable in the New Testament with the term *elder* (see Acts 20:28; Titus 1:5-7). It is also interchangeable with the office of *pastor*, because overseers and elders are charged with the pastoral duty of "shepherding" (see Acts 20:28; 1 Pet 5:1-2) and serving as the final human authority in the church.

3:2 That an overseer should be **the husband of one wife** was a necessary stipulation in a culture in which men often took more than one.

[a] 3:2 Ti 2:2,5
[b] Lv 19:34; 1Pt 4:9; 2Jn 10
[c] 3:3 1Tm 6:10
[d] 3:6 1Tm 5:12; 2Pt 2:3; Rv 20:1-15
[e] 3:7 Ac 13:10
[f] 3:8 Php 1:1
[g] 3:9 Php 1:27; 1Tm 1:2,19; Jd 3
[h] Heb 13:18
[i] 3:11 1Pt 3:1-6
[j] Ti 2:2
[k] 3:14 1Tm 4:13

[l] 3:15 1Co 3:16; 2Co 6:16; Eph 2:21-22; 1Pt 2:5; 4:17
[m] Mt 16:16; 1Tm 4:10
[n] Ps 119:142; 2Co 11:10; 2Th 2:10
[o] 3:16 2Pt 1:3
[p] Jn 1:14; Php 2:7; 1Jn 4:2; 5:20
[q] Rm 1:3-4; 2:28-29; 7:5-6; 8:4; 1Co 5:5; 6:16-17; Gl 3:3; 4:29; 5:16-24; 6:8; Php 3:3; Col 2:5; Rv 1:10
[n] Mt 11:24; Jn 3:16; Ac 10:43; Rm 10:9; 1Pt 1:8-10
[s] Mk 16:19; Jn 20:17; 1Pt 3:22
[t] 4:1 Jn 14:17; 16:13; Ac 20:23; 21:11; 1Co 2:10-11
[u] 2Th 2:3-9; 2Tm 3:1; 2Pt 3:3; Jd 18
[v] Php 1:27; 1Tm 1:2; Jd 3
[w] Mt 7:15; 1Jn 4:6
[x] Jms 3:15
[y] 4:2 Mk 12:15
[z] Heb 13:18
[aa] 4:3 1Tm 5:14; Heb 13:4
[ab] Rm 14:6; Col 2:16,23; 1Th 4:3; 5:22; 1Pt 2:11
[ac] Gn 1:29; 9:3
[ad] 4:4 Gn 1:31
[ae] Ac 10:15
[af] 4:5 Lk 8:21; 1Tm 2:1; Heb 4:12
[ag] 4:6 Php 1:27; 1Tm 1:2; Jd 3

one wife, self-controlled, sensible,[a] respectable, hospitable,[b] able to teach, [3] not an excessive drinker, not a bully but gentle, not quarrelsome, not greedy.[c] [4] He must manage his own household competently and have his children under control with all dignity. [5] (If anyone does not know how to manage his own household, how will he take care of God's church?) [6] He must not be a new convert, or he might become conceited and incur the same condemnation as the devil.[d] [7] Furthermore, he must have a good reputation among outsiders, so that he does not fall into disgrace and the devil's[e] trap.

[8] Deacons,[f] likewise, should be worthy of respect, not hypocritical, not drinking a lot of wine, not greedy for money, [9] holding the mystery of the faith[g] with a clear conscience.[n] [10] They must also be tested first; if they prove blameless, then they can serve as deacons. [11] Wives,[A,j] too, must be worthy of respect, not slanderers, self-controlled,[j] faithful in everything. [12] Deacons are to be husbands of one wife, managing their children and their own households competently. [13] For those who have served well as deacons acquire a good standing for themselves and great boldness in the faith that is in Christ Jesus.

THE MYSTERY OF GODLINESS

[14] I write these things to you, hoping to come[k] to you soon. [15] But if I should be delayed, I have written so that you will know how people ought to conduct themselves in God's household,[l] which is the church of the living God,[m] the pillar and foundation of the truth.[n] [16] And most certainly, the mystery of godliness[o] is great:

He[B] was manifested in the flesh,[p]
vindicated in the Spirit,[q]
seen by angels,
preached among the nations,
believed[r] on in the world,
taken up in glory.[s]

DEMONIC INFLUENCE

4 Now the Spirit[t] explicitly says that in later times[u] some will depart from the faith,[v] paying attention to deceitful spirits[w] and the teachings of demons,[x] [2] through the hypocrisy[y] of liars whose consciences[z] are seared. [3] They forbid marriage[aa] and demand abstinence[ab] from foods that God created[ac] to be received with gratitude by those who believe and know the truth. [4] For everything created by God is good,[ad] and nothing is to be rejected if it is received with thanksgiving,[ae] [5] since it is sanctified by the word of God[af] and by prayer.

A GOOD SERVANT OF JESUS CHRIST

[6] If you point these things out to the brothers and sisters, you will be a good servant of Christ Jesus, nourished by the words of the faith[ag] and the good

[A] 3:11 Or *The women*   [B] 3:16 Other mss read *God*

3:4-5 To competently **manage** one's home or congregation does not mean that no problems arise. Rather, it means that when they do, a man takes responsibility for addressing them biblically.

3:6-7 Though outsiders may not believe what the church teaches, they should be able to respect the overseer for his character and integrity (3:7).

3:8-10 The Greek word for **deacons** is *diakonos*, which means "servant." The deacon is to execute the ministry for the well-being of the people by serving them under the leadership of the overseers/elders. The qualifications for deacons are similar to those of overseers, demanding high-quality character (3:8-9). Deacons, though, are not required to be able to teach or to manage the church (see 3:2, 4-5).

3:11 The Greek word rendered **wives** in the CSB could also be rendered "women." Thus, it could be referring to the wives of deacons or to female deacons (deaconesses). Most likely, Paul speaks here of the latter (see Rom 16:1-2). First, the fact that he returns to deacon qualifications in 1 Timothy 3:12 indicates that he is speaking throughout 3:11-13 of the requirements for male and female deacons.

Second, it would be odd for Paul to provide qualifications for deacons' wives but say nothing about overseers' wives in 3:1-7.

3:16 Here we see the distinctive *message* or confession of the church—**the mystery of godliness**, something that was formerly unknown but which has now been revealed. What follows this phrase was a hymn sung by the church in Paul's day, affirming the good news about Jesus Christ. It sets forth the core beliefs about Christ that need to operate in a believer's life to promote godliness.

Manifested in the flesh is a reference to the incarnation of the Son of God. **Vindicated in the Spirit** means Jesus was declared by the Father as his beloved Son, empowered by the Spirit to perform supernatural works, and raised from the dead. **Seen by angels** reminds us that heavenly beings attended Jesus at his birth, temptation, resurrection, and ascension, signifying divine approval. **Preached among the nations** refers to the proclamation of the gospel to the world. **Believed on in the world** refers to faith in Christ for forgiveness of sins and eternal life. **Taken up in glory** references Christ's ascension into heaven.

4:2 The conscience, rightly trained, helps us to know right from wrong. But these

false teachers (**liars**) had burned theirs to the point that they were numb; they could no longer discern goodness from wickedness.

4:3 What did the heretics' demonic teachings look like? Were they commanding animal sacrifices? Were they instructing people to commit murder and mayhem? No. They were forbidding divinely ordained institutions and provisions like **marriage** and certain **foods**—things that **God** had **created to be received with gratitude**. Lack of gratitude and demonic, idolatrous influence go hand in hand (see Rom 1:21-23).

4:4 There is nothing from which you receive godly enjoyment and benefit that cannot be traced back to God. Therefore, we are to give thanks to God "always" and "in everything" (Eph 5:20; 1 Thess 5:18). This should be one of the chief characteristics of a Christian.

4:6 Shepherds of God's people are called to feed his Word to the flock. If they don't, the church will end up malnourished and useless. Moreover, if pastors and teachers do not sustain their own spiritual development by feeding on Scripture, it will be impossible for them to provide spiritual sustenance to others.

[a] 4:6 2Tm 3:10-15
[b] 4:7 1Tm 1:4; 2Tm 4:4; Ti 1:14; 2Pt 1:16
[c] 2Pt 1:3
[d] 4:8 Col 2:23
[e] Ps 37:9,11; Pr 19:23; 22:4; Mt 6:33; Mk 10:30; Jn 12:25; Ac 13:48; 1Pt 3:9
[f] 4:9 1Tm 1:15; 3:1; 2Tm 2:11
[g] 4:10 Dt 5:26; Jos 3:10; 1Sm 17:26; Ps 42:2; Jr 10:10; Dn 6:20; Ac 14:15; 1Tm 3:15
[h] 1Tm 1:1
[i] 1Tm 2:4; Ti 2:11

[j] 4:12 Pr 12:6
[k] 2Pt 3:11
[l] 1Co 13:1
[m] 1Tm 5:2
[n] 4:13 1Tm 3:14
[o] 4:14 1Co 13:2; 1Tm 1:18; 2Tm 1:6
[p] 1Tm 5:22
[q] 4:16 Eph 2:8; Jd 23
[r] Ezk 33:9; Ac 20:28; Rm 11:14

Questions & Answers

Q What early experiences in your ministry shaped your understanding of the need for a kingdom worldview?

A I observed a sharp conflict between what was happening around me in the world and what I was being taught. I was receiving great biblical teaching and theology, but it often seemed irrelevant to the realities of what people were dealing with. Take the civil rights movement, for example. Many were preaching about God's love, but churches were still segregated. There were places I couldn't go as an African American, even though they were being led and staffed by evangelical Christians. Missionaries couldn't be accepted for various mission agencies because they were black. In fact, if I had applied a few years earlier to the seminary I attended, I wouldn't have been able to enter because it held to segregation.

What I saw was a significant disconnect between theology and practice, between what people believed and how they were operating. I believed the Bible, but I also observed many inconsistencies among Christians. This confronted me with questions: How does the Bible answer questions relevant to life? What is the ethical value of the Bible—not merely the informational value of the Bible? I was also hearing those on the other side—those emphasizing liberation theology. But they too were doing damage to what the Bible clearly taught. And so I was struggling with these polar opposites. When I discovered the Bible's emphasis on God's kingdom, I discovered the unifying force I was looking for.

FOR THE NEXT Q&A, SEE PAGE 1441.

teaching that you have followed.[a] **7** But have nothing to do with pointless and silly myths.[b] Rather, train yourself in godliness.[c] **8** For the training of the body has limited benefit,[d] but godliness is beneficial in every way, since it holds promise for the present life and also for the life to come.[e] **9** This saying is trustworthy and deserves full acceptance.[f] **10** For this reason we labor and strive,[A] because we have put our hope in the living God,[g] who is the Savior[h] of all people,[i] especially of those who believe.

INSTRUCTIONS FOR MINISTRY

11 Command and teach these things. **12** Don't let anyone despise your youth, but set an example for the believers in speech,[j] in conduct,[k] in love,[B][l] in faith, and in purity.[m] **13** Until I come,[n] give your attention to public reading, exhortation, and teaching. **14** Don't neglect the gift that is in you; it was given to you through prophecy,[o] with the laying on of hands[p] by the council of elders. **15** Practice these things; be committed to them, so that your progress may be evident to all. **16** Pay close attention to your life and your teaching; persevere in these things, for in doing this you will save[q] both yourself and your hearers.[r]

[A] 4:10 Other mss read *and suffer reproach*   [B] 4:12 Other mss add *in spirit,*

4:7 Godliness—becoming more like God in actions, attitudes, character, and conduct—should be the Christian's goal. Listening to silly **myths** (popular, speculative fables and unbiblical stories promoted by false teachers) produces nothing of value in a person's life, but the Word of God produces godliness when obeyed.

4:8 Our passion for and pursuit of spiritual growth should be greater than our drive to be physically fit. Our souls need a regular workout program. You don't become godly by chance.

4:10 Given the value of the reward, Paul urges Timothy to **labor and strive** in the pursuit of godliness—both for himself and for those he serves.

The cross made all humankind savable. But he is the Savior **especially of those who**

believe—those who have received the gift of eternal life through placing faith alone in Christ alone.

4:11 Pastors are to instruct the people of God in the truths of God, admonishing them to believe and obey so that they may properly respond.

4:12 It's hard to disregard people for their **youth** when their character and conduct are impeccable. Teaching the truth is not enough; church leaders must model the truth they proclaim.

4:13 To what was Timothy to **give** his **attention**? To the **public reading** of Scripture, to **exhortation** to apply the truth to life, and to **teaching** others how to understand and follow the Word. Passivity in ministry is sin.

4:14 You must not **neglect** the development and use of your spiritual gifts either.

God gives gifts to be used for the benefit of others, not to be buried for safekeeping. You will be called to give an account of how you used the blessings God entrusted to you.

4:15-16 Timothy was to devote himself fully to his ministry so that his spiritual **progress** would be **evident to all** (4:15). Gospel ministry should produce growth in the gospel minister, not only in those to whom he ministers. He does not serve others well, in fact, if he doesn't **pay close attention** to his own **life** and **teaching**. By persevering in spiritual development, both personally and professionally, he **will save**—in the sense of "deliver"—**both** himself and those under his care (4:16). Timothy had already experienced personal salvation through faith in Christ, but through the delivering and

a 5:3 Ex 22:22; Jms 1:27
b 5:5 1Co 7:34
c 5:6 Lk 15:24; Eph 2:1,5;
5:14; Rv 3:1
d 5:8 Rm 12:17; 2Co 8:21
e Mt 10:33; Php 1:27; 1Tm
1:2; 2Pt 2:1; Jd 4; Rv 2:13
f 5:10 Mk 14:6; 2Co 9:8; Gl
3:10; Jms 2:14-26
g 2Jn 10
h Lk 7:44; Jn 13:5-14
i Heb 11:37
j 2Co 9:8
k 5:11 1Tm 5:14
l 5:12 Mk 12:40
m 5:13 Pr 17:9; 3Jn 10
n 5:14 Gn 2:18-25; 1Co
7:9-10; 1Tm 4:3; 5:11

o 5:14 Ti 2:4-5
p 5:15 Heb 12:13
q 5:17 1Th 5:12
r 5:18 Dt 25:4; 1Co 9:9
s Lv 19:13; Dt 24:14-15; Mt
10:10; Lk 10:7; 1Co 9:4-14;
2Pt 2:13
t 5:19 Dt 19:15
u 5:21 Lk 11:28
v 5:22 Ex 29:10; Lv 4:15;
Lk 4:40; Ac 6:6; 28:8; 1Tm
4:14; Heb 6:2
w Php 4:8
x 5:24 Mt 12:41; Jn 5:22-30;
Heb 9:27
y 6:1 Jn 10:25; Ac 15:14;
Rv 14:1

5 Don't rebuke an older man, but exhort him as a father, younger men as brothers, [2] older women as mothers, and the younger women as sisters with all purity.

THE SUPPORT OF WIDOWS

[3] Support[A] widows[a] who are genuinely in need. [4] But if any widow has children or grandchildren, let them learn to practice godliness toward their own family first and to repay their parents, for this pleases God. [5] The widow who is truly in need and left all alone has put her hope in God[b] and continues night and day in her petitions and prayers; [6] however, she who is self-indulgent is dead even while she lives.[c] [7] Command this also, so that they will be above reproach. [8] But if anyone does not provide[d] for his own family, especially for his own household, he has denied the faith[e] and is worse than an unbeliever.

[9] No widow is to be enrolled on the list for support unless she is at least sixty years old, has been the wife of one husband, [10] and is well known for good works[f] — that is, if she has brought up children, shown hospitality,[g] washed the saints' feet,[h] helped the afflicted,[i] and devoted herself to every good work.[j] [11] But refuse to enroll younger widows, for when they are drawn away from Christ by desire, they want to marry[k] [12] and will therefore receive condemnation[l] because they have renounced their original pledge. [13] At the same time, they also learn to be idle, going from house to house; they are not only idle, but are also gossips[m] and busybodies, saying things they shouldn't say. [14] Therefore, I want younger women to marry,[n] have children, manage their households,

and give the adversary no opportunity to accuse us.[o] [15] For some have already turned away[p] to follow Satan. [16] If any[B] believing woman has widows in her family, let her help them. Let the church not be burdened, so that it can help widows in genuine need.

HONORING THE ELDERS

[17] The elders who are good leaders are to be considered worthy of double honor,[c] especially those who work hard[q] at preaching and teaching. [18] For the Scripture says: **Do not muzzle an ox while it is treading out the grain,**[D,r] and, "The worker is worthy of his wages."[s]

[19] Don't accept an accusation against an elder unless it is supported by two or three witnesses.[t] [20] Publicly rebuke those who sin, so that the rest will be afraid. [21] I solemnly charge you before God and Christ Jesus and the elect angels to observe[u] these things without prejudice, doing nothing out of favoritism. [22] Don't be too quick to appoint[E,v] anyone as an elder, and don't share in the sins of others. Keep yourself pure.[w] [23] Don't continue drinking only water, but use a little wine because of your stomach and your frequent illnesses. [24] Some people's sins are obvious, preceding them to judgment,[x] but the sins of others surface[F] later. [25] Likewise, good works are obvious, and those that are not obvious cannot remain hidden.

HONORING MASTERS

6 All who are under the yoke as slaves should regard their own masters[G] as worthy of all respect, so that God's name[y] and his teaching will not be blasphemed. [2] Let those who have believing masters not

---

A 5:3 Lit *Honor*   **B** 5:16 Other mss add *believing man or*   **C** 5:17 Or *of respect and remuneration*   **D** 5:18 Dt 25:4   **E** 5:22 Lit *to lay hands on*   **F** 5:24 Lit *follow*   **G** 6:1 Or *owners*

---

transforming power of God's Word, he and the church could experience daily victory over the power of sin.
5:1-2 Through Jesus Christ we have been adopted as sons and daughters of God, so the church is the family of God. This family mind-set transforms how we think about and respond to fellow believers.
5:4 Children have an obligation to **practice godliness** toward **their parents** for the investment they made in their lives. No widow should be in want who has believing children.
5:8 God calls parents, and especially husbands, to **provide for** their families. Men are to reflect the fatherhood of God. A man who will not take care of his wife and children lies about what God is like. Believing men (and women) should also care for widows in their

extended families because God is "a champion of widows" (Ps 68:5).
5:9-10 An elderly **widow** who has demonstrated faithful service *to* the church deserves the faithful support *of* the church.
5:14-15 Notice that Paul does not give cultural reasons for the directive in verse 14. Rather, he provides a theological and spiritual reason. By devoting her primary focus to her home, a kingdom woman protects herself and her family from **Satan** (5:15).
5:18 If **an ox** is provided with food for his work (see Deut 25:4), how much more is a hard-working minister of the gospel **worthy of his wages**?
5:19-21 It should not be easy for a disgruntled church member to falsely accuse **an elder**. Therefore, all accusations must be confirmed **by two or three witnesses** (5:19). If an elder

is found guilty of unrepentantly continuing in **sin**, he must be rebuked **publicly, so that the rest** of the elders (and the congregation) will fear the consequences of sin (5:20). God's people see that their leaders are held to the same standards as they are—and to an even higher level.
5:22 We do not want to fail to take the appropriate time to observe a man's life and spiritual condition, as outlined in 3:1-7.
5:23 In a day before modern medicine, a moderate amount of **wine** provided medicinal benefits to those who needed them.
5:24-25 What we do—whether good or bad—will come to light.
6:1-2 On slavery in the Bible, see the note on Ephesians 6:5-9. These principles still apply to employer-employee relationships today.

be disrespectful to them because they are brothers, but serve them even better, since those who benefit from their service are believers and dearly loved.[A,a]

FALSE DOCTRINE AND HUMAN GREED

Teach and encourage these things. **3** If anyone teaches false doctrine and does not agree with the sound teaching of our Lord[b] Jesus Christ and with the teaching that promotes godliness,[c] **4** he is conceited and understands nothing, but has an unhealthy interest in disputes and arguments over words.[d] From these come envy,[e] quarreling,[f] slander,[g] evil suspicions, **5** and constant disagreement among people whose minds are depraved and deprived of the truth, who imagine that godliness is a way to material gain.[B,n] **6** But godliness with contentment is great gain.[i] **7** For we brought nothing into the world, and[c] we can take nothing out.[j] **8** If we have food and clothing,[D] we will be content with these. **9** But those who want to be rich fall into temptation, a trap, and many foolish and harmful desires, which plunge people into ruin and destruction. **10** For the love of money is a root[E] of all kinds of evil, and by craving it, some have wandered away from the faith[k] and pierced themselves with many griefs.

FIGHT THE GOOD FIGHT

11 But you, man of God, flee from these things, and pursue righteousness, godliness, faith, love,[l] endurance,[m] and gentleness. **12** Fight the good fight[n] of the faith. Take hold of eternal life[o] to which you were called and about which you have made a good confession in the presence of many witnesses. **13** In the presence of God, who gives life to all,[p] and of Christ Jesus, who gave a good confession before Pontius Pilate,[q] I charge you **14** to keep this command without fault or failure until the appearing[r] of our Lord[s] Jesus Christ. **15** God will bring this about in his own time.[t] He is the blessed and only[u] Sovereign, the King of kings,[v] and the Lord of lords,[w] **16** who alone is immortal and who lives in unapproachable light,[x] whom no one has seen or can see,[y] to him be honor and eternal power.[z] Amen.[aa]

INSTRUCTIONS TO THE RICH

17 Instruct those who are rich in the present age not to be arrogant[ab] or to set their

[a] 6:2 2Th 2:12; 1Jn 4:16
[b] 6:3 Rv 11:8
[c] 2Pt 1:3
[d] 6:4 2Tm 2:14,23; Ti 3:9
[e] Ps 37:1
[f] Ti 3:9
[g] Rv 13:6
[h] 6:5 Eph 4:22; 2Tm 3:8; Ti 1:11,15
[i] 6:6 Ps 37:16; Pr 15:16; 16:8; Php 4:11; Heb 13:5
[j] 6:7 Jb 1:21; Ps 49:17; Ec 5:15
[k] 6:10 Php 1:27; 1Tm 1:2; Jd 3

[l] 6:11 1Co 13:1
[m] Rv 13:10
[n] 6:12 1Tm 4:7; Jd 3
[o] 1Jn 5:12
[p] 6:13 Mk 13:19; Rm 1:25
[q] Mt 27:11-14
[r] 6:14 Ti 2:13; 1Jn 2:28
[s] Rv 11:8
[t] 6:15 Lk 21:8
[u] Rm 16:27
[v] Rv 17:14
[w] Dt 10:17; Ps 136:2-3; Rv 17:14; 19:16
[x] 6:16 Ps 36:9; 104:2; Jn 12:46
[y] Ex 33:20; Jn 1:18
[z] Jd 25
[aa] 1Tm 1:17; Rv 22:21
[ab] 6:17 1Sm 2:3; Ec 7:8; Rm 11:20; 12:16

APPLICATION QUESTIONS

READ 1 TIMOTHY 6:15

– What ideas or images come to mind when you hear the word *sovereignty*? Why?

[A] **6:2** Or *because, as believers who are dearly loved, they are devoted to others' welfare*   [B] **6:5** Other mss add *From such people withdraw yourself.*
[C] **6:7** Other mss add *it is clear that*   [D] **6:8** Or *food and shelter*   [E] **6:10** Or *is the root*

6:3-5 Anyone who **teaches false doctrine and does not agree with . . . sound teaching** has disqualified himself for godliness. **Godliness** is a lifestyle that consistently pursues and reflects the character of God (6:3). It is a way of life. It's the way Christians should roll.

The reason Paul had left Timothy behind in Ephesus was so that he might deal with false teachers who were causing problems (see 1:3-4; see also 1:18-20). These men may have promoted themselves as superior instructors of deep doctrine. But Paul had a different appraisal of them. They were spreading "the teachings of demons" (4:1), were **conceited**, and understood **nothing**. They were known for their godlessness. They saw godliness as **a way of material gain** (6:4-5), meaning that their motivation for ministry was money.

6:6 Contentment is being at ease (inner sufficiency) where you are and being thankful for what you have. Contentment doesn't mean complacency; rather, it's learning to be satisfied until God gives you more (see Prov 30:8-9; Phil 4:11-13). Complaining is empirical proof of discontentment. Content people know that God is acting on their behalf.

6:8 Godliness with a full stomach, clothes on your back, and a roof over your head is enough for you to be content. Everything else is a bonus.

6:10 Paul didn't say that *money* leads to evil—rather, *the love of* money leads to evil. When we make time to grow our material lives, while allowing our spiritual lives to decline (cutting back on church participation, prayer, Bible study, and fellowship), then we are demonstrating that we love money.

King Solomon was once the wealthiest man in the world, and he said, "The one who loves silver is never satisfied with silver, and whoever loves wealth is never satisfied with income" (Eccl 5:10). One can be filled to overflowing with wealth and material possessions. But without an eternal perspective, such earthly focus will only result in **craving** for more.

6:11 Of course it's important to flee what harms, but we must also pursue what gives life. As the writer of Hebrews says, "Lay aside every hindrance and . . . run with endurance" (Heb 12:1). Leave sin behind and pursue spiritual development.

6:12 Timothy must **take hold of eternal life**. Since Timothy was already a believer, this is a reference to aggressively pursuing a deeper experience in the knowledge of God (see John 17:3).

6:15-16 When trials and tribulations strike, remember that God is **Sovereign** (6:15). When you think more highly of yourself than you ought, remember that God is sovereign.

When your life hits rock bottom, remember that God is sovereign. The worst nightmare of the wicked is that God is sovereign. The overruling hope of the saint is that God is sovereign.

6:17 To be **rich** means to have an abundance beyond your needs (think food, clothes, and shelter). In gauging whether or not you are wealthy, then, don't confuse wants with needs.

Paul highlights two threats or side effects of wealth without godliness. First, when you prioritize the material over the spiritual, you quickly become **arrogant** and conceited—thinking more highly of yourself than others simply because you have more money than they. Thus, a dangerous potential side effect of wealth is pride.

A second threat or side effect is that you misplace your hope. If your hope is in the riches you possess **in the present age**, you have forgotten that money can't deliver. **The uncertainty of wealth** means it cannot be depended upon, either in this age or the one to come. Instead, we must set our hope **on God**. We must not expect money to do what only God can. God **richly provides us with all things**.

It is not a sin to be rich, but we must not let wealth blind us to the "great gain" of "godliness with contentment" (6:6). Riches

a 6:17 Ac 17:25
b 6:18 Mk 14:6; Gl 3:10;
Jms 2:14-26; 1Pt 2:12
c Rm 12:8,13; Eph 4:28
d 6:19 Mt 6:20

e 6:20 1Tm 1:11; 2Tm
1:12,14; Ti 1:3
f Heb 12:13
g Col 2:8; 2Tm 2:16; 4:4;
Ti 1:14
h 6:21 2Tm 2:18
i Php 1:27; 1Tm 1:2

☙ KINGDOM LIVING ❧
KINGDOM
Operating Under the Rule of the King

Do you know what it means to be part of a kingdom? In America, we have a president, but that office is part of our larger governing body. In addition to the executive branch of government, we have legislative and judicial branches. It's a system of checks and balances designed to ensure that one person or even a group of people doesn't gain too much power.

In a true kingdom, by contrast, all facets of life operate under the direct rule and authority of a king or queen. The monarch is in charge. The monarch makes decisions and creates laws that steer the course and fortune of the entire nation—for better or for worse. Therefore, the boundaries of a kingdom extend as far as the influence and control of the ruler. Wherever a king's direct authority is acknowledged and obeyed, that place is part of the king's realm—part of his kingdom.

It's important for us as Christians to understand these principles because the Bible tells us

repeatedly that we're part of the kingdom of God. We're subjects in God's kingdom, which means we're under the direct authority and rule of God as our King—that is, we're supposed to be.

Too often, however, we drift into rebellion and actively or passively seek to dethrone the one we're supposed to serve. We seek to treat God as if he runs a democracy in which we have the right to vote on whether or not we want to accept something as truth. There are two answers to every question in a kingdom, though—the king's and everyone else's. And when everyone else disagrees with the king, they are wrong. God is our rightful King, the author of all truth and the ruler over all. Our lives, families, culture, and churches will experience his covering, protection, and favor when we abide by and embrace this reality.

FOR THE NEXT KINGDOM
KINGDOM LIVING LESSON SEE PAGE 1532.

hope on the uncertainty of wealth, but on God,[A] who richly provides us with all things[a] to enjoy. **18** Instruct them to do what is good, to be rich in good works,[b] to be generous and willing to share,[c] **19** storing up treasure for themselves as a good foundation for the coming age,[d] so that they may take hold of what is truly life.

GUARD THE HERITAGE

20 Timothy, guard what has been entrusted to you,[e] avoiding[f] irreverent and empty speech and contradictions from what is falsely called knowledge.[g] **21** By professing it, some[h] people have departed from the faith.[i]

Grace be with you all.

[A] 6:17 Other mss read *on the living God*

were not meant to replace or compete with our trust in God and our pursuit of godliness. We must never lose sight of the fact that God is the only source of all that we **enjoy**.
6:18 How does a Christian to whom God has given wealth position himself or herself so that he or she is not taken captive by

arrogance? Paul tells Timothy the antidote: **Instruct them to do what is good** (that is, to prioritize the pursuit of godliness), **to be rich in good works** (to let exceptional net worth be matched by exceptional service to benefit others), **to be generous and willing to share** (to acknowledge God as source and be characterized by generosity).

6:19 **What is truly life** is the spiritual fulfillment and purpose that God gives in this life—and future rewards in the life to come.
6:20 By **avoiding** things that are a waste of time—whatever has no basis in Scripture and no spiritual benefit—Timothy would keep himself and those he shepherded on the road to godliness.

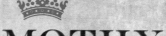

2 TIMOTHY

INTRODUCTION

Author and Historical Background

SEE THE INTRODUCTION TO 1 TIMOTHY for a discussion of the author and historical background of the Pastoral Epistles (1 Timothy, 2 Timothy, and Titus).

Message and Purpose

Second Timothy is the apostle Paul's final letter, written to his beloved son in the faith. Paul gives clear indications in the book that he knows his departure is soon at hand, and therefore he wanted to encourage Timothy in his ministry. The aging apostle knew that Timothy was struggling. He had been having health problems, and it was easy for some people to write him off. This highly personal letter was meant to encourage him to step up to the plate, to take his ministry seriously, and to see it as a long-term commitment.

It was important for Timothy to gain right perspective in the face of the stresses and strains, demands and disappointments of ministry. Paul wanted to encourage him by his own testimony of having fought the good fight and finished his own race (4:7). Paul didn't throw in the towel when things got tough; he chose the right

battles to fight and he won them. He desired that Timothy did the same.

Paul also wanted Timothy to pass this message along to those coming behind him in ministry. And the apostle gave Timothy—and all of us—the best reason of all for being faithful: to receive the crown of righteousness from the Lord himself, which is available to all believers who faithfully serve the King and his kingdom.

www.bhpublishinggroup.com/qr/te/55_00

Outline

I. Persuaded by God's Power (1:1-18)
II. Persevering in Ministry (2:1-26)
III. Prepared for Perilous Times (3:1-17)
IV. Preaching the Word (4:1-22)

a 1:1 Ac 13:9
b 1Co 1:1; Eph 1:1; Col 1:1
c 1Jn 2:25; 5:12
d 1:2 1Tm 1:2; 2Jn 3
e 1:3 Ac 23:1; 24:16; Rm 9:1;
2Co 1:12; 1Tm 1:19; 3:9;
Heb 10:22; 1Pt 3:21
f Eph 1:6
g 1:5 1Tm 1:5
h Ac 16:1
i 1:6 1Tm 4:14; 5:22
j 1:7 Jn 7:13; 14:27; Rm 8:15
k Lk 1:35; 4:14; 24:49; Ac
1:8; 4:33; Rm 15:13,19; 1Co
2:4; Eph 3:16,20; 1Th 1:5
l 1Co 13:1
m 1:8 Mk 8:38; Rm 1:16;
2Tm 1:12,16
n Ac 4:33; 1Co 1:6; Rv 1:2,9;
12:17; 19:10; 20:4
o Eph 3:1; 4:1; Phm 1,9
p Lk 1:35; 2Co 13:4
q 1:9 Rm 8:28; 11:14,29;
Heb 3:1
r Eph 2:9
s Pr 19:21; Is 42:6; 46:10; Ac
2:23; 4:28; 26:16; Rm 8:28;
9:11; Eph 1:11; Php 2:13
t 1:10 Lk 21:8; 2Tm 4:1;
1Jn 2:28
u Jn 8:51; Php 3:10
v 1:10 1Jn 5:12
w 1:11 1Tm 2:7
x 1:12 Php 1:29; 2Tm 2:9
y 1Tm 1:11; 6:20; Ti 1:3
z Php 1:6; 2Tm 4:8
aa 1:13 1Tm 1:10; 6:3; Ti
1:9; 2:1
ab 2Tm 2:2; 3:14
ac 1:15 Ac 6:9; 16:6
ad 2Tm 4:10-16
ae 1:16 Lk 1:50
af 2Tm 4:19
ag Phm 7,20
ah Ac 16:26; 20:23; 21:33;
23:29; 26:29; Eph 6:20;
Phm 10
ai 1:17 Rm 1:7
aj 1:18 Lk 1:50
ak Eph 1:1
al 2:1 Gl 1:6; 2Pt 3:18
am 2:2 2Tm 1:13
an Nm 12:7
ao 2:3 1Tm 1:18

GREETING

1 Paul,[a] an apostle of Christ Jesus by God's will,[b] for the sake of the promise of life[c] in Christ Jesus:

[2] To Timothy, my dearly loved son.

Grace, mercy, and peace[d] from God the Father and Christ Jesus our Lord.

THANKSGIVING

[3] I thank God, whom I serve with a clear conscience[e] as my ancestors did, when I constantly remember you in my prayers night and day.[f] [4] Remembering your tears, I long to see you so that I may be filled with joy. [5] I recall your sincere faith[g] that first lived in your grandmother Lois and in your mother Eunice[h] and now, I am convinced, is in you also.

[6] Therefore, I remind you to rekindle the gift of God that is in you through the laying on of my hands.[i] [7] For God has not given us a spirit of fear,[j] but one of power,[A,k] love,[l] and sound judgment.

NOT ASHAMED OF THE GOSPEL

[8] So don't be ashamed[m] of the testimony about our Lord,[n] or of me his prisoner.[o] Instead, share in suffering for the gospel, relying on the power[p] of God. [9] He has saved us and called us with a holy calling,[q] not according to our works,[r] but according to his own purpose[s] and grace, which was given to us in Christ Jesus before time began. [10] This has now been made evident through the appearing[t] of our Savior Christ Jesus, who has abolished death[u] and has brought life[v] and immortality to light through the gospel. [11] For this gospel I was appointed[w] a herald, apostle, and teacher,[B] [12] and that is why I suffer[x] these things. But I am not ashamed, because I know whom I have believed and am persuaded that he is able to guard what has been entrusted to me[C,y] until that day.[z]

BE LOYAL TO THE FAITH

[13] Hold on to the pattern of sound teaching[aa] that you have heard from me,[ab] in the faith and love that are in Christ Jesus. [14] Guard the good deposit through the Holy Spirit who lives in us. [15] You know that all those in the province of Asia[ac] have deserted me,[ad] including Phygelus and Hermogenes. [16] May the Lord grant mercy[ae] to the household of Onesiphorus,[af] because he often refreshed me[ag] and was not ashamed of my chains.[ah] [17] On the contrary, when he was in Rome,[ai] he diligently searched for me and found me. [18] May the Lord grant that he obtain mercy[aj] from him on that day. You know very well how much he ministered at Ephesus.[ak]

BE STRONG IN GRACE

2 You, therefore, my son, be strong in the grace[al] that is in Christ Jesus. [2] What you have heard from me[am] in the presence of many witnesses, commit to faithful[an] men[D] who will be able to teach others also.

[3] Share in suffering as a good soldier of Christ Jesus.[ao] [4] No one serving as a soldier gets entangled in the concerns of civilian

---

A 1:7 Or *For the Spirit God gave us does not make us fearful, but gives us power*   B 1:11 Other mss add *of the Gentiles*   C 1:12 Or *guard what I have entrusted to him,* or *guard my deposit*   D 2:2 Or *faithful people*

1:2 This is Paul's second letter **to Timothy**, his son in the ministry. It's also the last New Testament letter he wrote.

1:3-4 Paul had a deep affection for this young man who had served with him so faithfully in ministry. He remembers Timothy's **tears**, perhaps shed during their last parting, and longs to see him so that sorrow can be replaced by **joy** (1:4).

1:5 This passage shows the powerful influence women can have on the life of a young man should his father be either absent or spiritually inactive. It is critical that parents and grandparents pass on their **faith**, in word and deed, to the next generation (see Judg 2:10).

1:6 Timothy could not be passive about his spiritual **gift** and neither can we. God intends that we develop—keep fresh and vibrant—the gifts he provides for the benefit of others. We will be held accountable for failure to do so.

1:7 Like many believers, Timothy struggled with **a spirit of fear**. His timidity probably resulted from a variety of factors. Regardless, God's Holy Spirit provides **power, love, and sound judgment**—the necessary spiritual resources for fulfilling ministry and employing spiritual gifts. Such divine resources are available to all—that is, power for the use of our gifts, love for those who benefit from them, and good discernment in the application of our gifts.

1:9-10 Even the possibility of death should not nullify an effective ministry since it is no longer an issue for the believer.

1:11 A herald proclaims the good news. An **apostle** serves as God's authoritative leader and messenger. A **teacher** instructs others in the Word of God.

1:12 Because of his faithfulness to the message, Paul had been persecuted. Nevertheless, in spite of the pain and sorrow, suffering brought him no shame or regret. For the apostle was **persuaded that** God had the power to care for him and deliver him through any obstacles and trials **until that day** when he would call him home. He wanted Timothy

(and all believers) to have that same confidence in God.

1:14 We must recognize the gospel's value and not treat it casually. With the empowerment of **the Holy Spirit who lives in us**, we must **guard** the gospel, proclaiming it faithfully and defending it against error and ministering its truth to others for their spiritual development.

1:16 A believer named **Onesiphorus** is unknown to us apart from this mention; nevertheless, he is immortalized in the pages of Scripture because of his love and care for the aging apostle. We too must pray for God's favor on those who support the ministry and its ministers.

2:1 Timothy was Paul's **son** in the faith.

2:2 Timothy couldn't bear the ministry burden alone; he needed to pass the spiritual baton to faithful men and women who could transfer God's truth to others.

2:3-6 Paul uses three illustrations to encourage Timothy in the work he was called to perform. *First*, he was to **share in suffering as a**

⇝ Questions & Answers ⇜

Q In your teaching, you emphasize how crucial a commitment to read and study the Bible is to spiritual growth. Can you give some practical suggestions to help us grow through God's Word?

A When it comes to getting into God's Word, you must simply read it! No, you won't understand all of it at once, and you may find some of it boring. But since it is the Word of God, it still does its work even when you are not connecting with it like you feel you should be. If you are seriously reading it, it will do its work.

Second, you must learn it! Learning Scripture can be facilitated in a number of ways: through your church's ministries, through your pastor's preaching from the pulpit, and through your Sunday school class and small group studies. Through all of these avenues, you can grow in your understanding of the Bible.

Third, you must use it! You must apply what Scripture says to your life. "The word of God is living and effective" (Heb 4:12) whether you believe and obey it or not. But when you apply it, it becomes alive in you and for you. Many people read and study the Word, but they aren't changed by the Word because they don't use the Word. If you want to benefit from the Bible, don't stop with merely studying it. "But be doers of the word and not hearers only, deceiving yourselves" (Jas 1:22).

FOR THE NEXT Q&A, SEE PAGE 1447.

life; he seeks to please the commanding officer. **5** Also, if anyone competes as an athlete, he is not crowned unless he competes according to the rules. **6** The hardworking farmer ought to be the first to get a share of the crops.*a* **7** Consider what I say, for the Lord will give you understanding in everything.

8 Remember Jesus Christ, risen from the dead*b* and descended from David, according to my gospel, **9** for which I suffer to the point of being bound like a criminal. But the word of God is not bound. **10** This is why I endure*c* all things for the elect:*d* so that they also may obtain salvation, which is in Christ Jesus, with eternal glory.*e* **11** This saying is trustworthy:*f*

For if we died with him,*g*
we will also live with him;
12 if we endure, we will also reign*h*
with him;
if we deny him, he will also deny us;
13 if we are faithless,
he remains faithful,
for he cannot deny himself.

AN APPROVED WORKER

14 Remind them of these things, and charge them before God^A not to fight about words.*i* This is useless and leads to the ruin of those who listen. **15** Be diligent to present yourself to God as one approved, a worker who doesn't need to be ashamed, correctly teaching the word of truth.*j*

^A **2:14** Other mss read *before the Lord*

good soldier of Christ Jesus (2:3). Paul thus presents the Christian life as warfare against Satan in a hostile world (see Eph 6:10-18). To be victorious in battle, no **soldier gets entangled** in **civilian** affairs but **seeks to please** his or her **commanding officer** (2 Tim 2:4). Military service places restrictions on personal liberty—so does Christian ministry. The *second* illustration involves an **athlete**. All of his or her efforts are wasted unless **he competes according to the rules**—that is, operates within biblical guidelines and does not yield to worldly pleasures. He cannot be **crowned** a victor otherwise (2:5). You cannot disobey God's Word in the pursuit of spiritual victory. To disregard God's boundaries is to disqualify yourself from receiving reward. *Third*, Paul compares Timothy's work to that of a **farmer** (2:6). Farmers must work long

hours in all conditions. Laziness will fail to produce a harvest.
2:11-13 This series of four couplets was perhaps a common **saying** among first-century Christians. **If we died with him, we will also live with him** (2:11) refers to our union with Christ. Through trusting in him as Savior, we have died with Christ (see Gal 2:19-20) and are also raised with him (see Eph 2:6). Your eternal future is secure through your connection to and identification with Jesus. **If we endure, we will also reign with him** means that if we live a consistent Christian life, we will be rewarded with reigning with Christ in his millennial kingdom (2 Tim 2:12; see Rev 20:4). **If we deny him, he will also deny us** (2 Tim 2:12) means that if our Christian lives are more covert than public (see the notes on Matt 10:32-33), if we seek

to please ourselves more than to please our Lord, we will lose the opportunity to partake in his millennial reign. This does not involve loss of salvation but loss of rewards and privileges. The final couplet repeats the idea of the first in a different way: **if we are faithless, he remains faithful** (2 Tim 2:13). When our faith grows weak or even fails, God remains true to his promise to save us through Christ. To fail to keep his promise would be for him to **deny himself**, and that **he cannot** do (2:13).
2:14-15 In the same way that federal agents identify counterfeit currency through their intimate knowledge of the real thing, it is believers' knowledge of the truth that will enable them to identify error. Local churches need pastors who know the Word and help God's people know and apply it.

a 2:16 Jd 18
b 2:17 1Tm 1:20
c 2:18 Ac 17:32; 1Co 15:12-17;
2Th 2:1-2
d 1Tm 1:19; 6:21
e 2:19 Jos 23:7; Est 9:4; Is
26:13; Rm 15:20; Eph 1:21
f Nm 16:5; Pr 2:6; Jn
10:14,27; 1Co 8:3
g Ac 15:14
h Lv 24:11,16; Nm 16:26-27;
Jos 23:7; Ps 6:9; 33:15; Pr
3:7; Is 26:13; 52:11; Jr 20:9
i 2:20 Rm 9:21
j Rm 9:21
k 2:21 1Co 9:8; Gl 3:10;
1Tm 5:10
l 2:22 1Tm 4:12; 6:11; Jms 4:7
m Lk 12:51; 2Tm 1:2; Heb
12:14; 3Jn 14
n Gn 13:4
o 2:24 Rv 11:8
p Jn 6:52; Pr 7:26; Jms 4:2
q 2:25 Jms 3:13
r Ac 26:20; Rm 2:4; 2Co
7:9-10
s 2:26 1Tm 3:7
t Jn 1:13

u 3:1 Jn 6:39; Php 1:6; 1Pt
1:5; 2Pt 3:3; Jd 18
v 3:2 Php 2:21; 1Tm 6:4
w Lk 16:14; 1Tm 3:3; 6:10
x Pr 16:18; Lk 1:51; Rm 1:30
y 1Tm 1:9
z 3:3 Jn 14:6
aa Ti 1:8
ab 3:4 Lk 6:16; Ac 7:52
ac Ac 19:36
ad 1Tm 3:6; 6:4
ae Php 3:19
af 3:5 1Co 4:20; 2Co 13:4;
Ti 1:16
ag Mt 7:15; 2Th 3:6
ah 3:6 2Pt 1:4; 2:10
ai 3:7 2Co 11:10; 1Tm 2:4;
2Tm 2:25; Ti 1:1
aj 3:8 Ex 7:11-12; 8:18; 9:11
ak Ps 77:20; Mt 8:4; Heb 3:2
al 1Co 14:14; Php 4:7
am 2Co 13:5-7
an 3:10 Pr 19:21; Ac 11:23
ao 1Co 13:1; 1Jn 4:16
ap 3:11 Gl 5:24; Php 3:10
aq Ac 13:14; 14:19,21
ar Ac 13:51; 16:2
as Ac 14:6,8; 27:5
at 3:12 Jn 15:20; Ac 14:22;
2Co 4:9-10

16 Avoid irreverent and empty speech, since those who engage in it will produce even more godlessness,*a* **17** and their teaching will spread like gangrene. Hymenaeus*b* and Philetus are among them. **18** They have departed from the truth, saying that the resurrection has already taken place,*c* and are ruining the faith of some.*d* **19** Nevertheless, God's solid foundation stands firm, bearing this inscription:*e* **The Lord knows those who are his,**[A],*f* and let everyone who calls on the name*g* of[B] the Lord turn away from wickedness.*h*

20 Now in a large house there are not only gold and silver vessels,*i* but also those of wood and clay; some for honorable[C] use and some for dishonorable.[D],*j* **21** So if anyone purifies himself from anything dishonorable,[E] he will be a special[F] instrument, set apart, useful to the Master, prepared for every good work.*k*

22 Flee*l* from youthful passions, and pursue righteousness, faith, love, and peace,*m* along with those who call on the Lord*n* from a pure heart. **23** But reject foolish and ignorant disputes, because you know that they breed quarrels. **24** The Lord's*o* servant must not quarrel,*p* but must be gentle to everyone, able to teach,[G] and patient, **25** instructing his opponents with gentleness.*q* Perhaps God will grant them repentance*r* leading them to the knowledge of the truth. **26** Then they may come to their senses and escape the trap of the devil,*s* who has taken them captive to do his will.*t*

DIFFICULT TIMES AHEAD

3 But know this: Hard times will come in the last days.*u* **2** For people will be lovers of self,*v* lovers of money,*w* boastful, proud,*x* demeaning, disobedient to parents, ungrateful, unholy,*y* **3** unloving, irreconcilable, slanderers,*z* without self-control, brutal, without love for what is good,*aa* **4** traitors,*ab* reckless,*ac* conceited,*ad* lovers of pleasure*ae* rather than lovers of God, **5** holding to the form of godliness but denying its power.*af* Avoid these people.*ag*

6 For among them are those who worm their way into households and deceive gullible women overwhelmed by sins and led astray by a variety of passions,*ah* **7** always learning and never able to come to a knowledge of the truth.*ai* **8** Just as Jannes and Jambres*aj* resisted Moses,*ak* so these also resist the truth. They are men who are corrupt in mind*al* and worthless*am* in regard to the faith. **9** But they will not make further progress, for their foolishness will be clear to all, as was the foolishness of Jannes and Jambres.

STRUGGLES IN THE CHRISTIAN LIFE

10 But you have followed my teaching, conduct, purpose,*an* faith, patience, love,*ao* and endurance, **11** along with the persecutions and sufferings*ap* that came to me in Antioch,*aq* Iconium,*ar* and Lystra.*as* What persecutions I endured — and yet the Lord rescued me from them all. **12** In fact, all who want to live a godly life in Christ Jesus will be persecuted.*at* **13** Evil people

---

[A] 2:19 Nm 16:5 [B] 2:19 Lit *everyone who names the name of* [C] 2:20 Or *special* [D] 2:20 Or *ordinary* [E] 2:21 Lit *from these* [F] 2:21 Or *an honorable* [G] 2:24 Or *everyone, skillful in teaching*

2:16 Not only do believers need to avoid unbiblical teaching, but they must also **avoid irreverent and empty speech** (cf. Eph 4:29).

2:19 God is intimately acquainted with his children. Therefore, anyone who **calls on** God's **name** should pursue him and **turn away from wickedness**. Calling on God's name is the special privilege given to believers to invoke his supernatural intervention into the circumstances of life for his divine deliverance (see Rom 10:9, 13; 1 Cor 1:2).

2:20-21 Common household vessels (containers) would be made of **wood and clay**. These would be used for practically anything. **Gold and silver** vessels were special and used only for **honorable** purposes (2:20). Believers are to be vessels of honor, cleansing themselves from false teaching so that they will be **useful to** God's kingdom and prepared **for every good work** (2:21).

2:22 Believers must understand that it's not enough to run away from sin; we must go after holiness. If we remove our filthy rags, we must put on clean clothes.

2:23-26 As **the Lord's servant**, a believer is to be about *his* business (2:24). We should not be known for our quarreling but for our gentleness and patience. When someone errs through sin or unbiblical teaching, correct him gently, not harshly.

3:1 **The last days** refers to the period of time between Christ's resurrection and the rapture, the period in which we live (see Heb 1:2; 2 Pet 3:3).

3:5 To hold to **the form of godliness** while **denying its power** is to project a religious appearance absent of true spiritual reality. Religion without the presence and power of God is like wax fruit—it looks real but possesses no nutritional value. True **godliness** moves people from sin to righteousness.

3:8-9 **Jannes and Jambres** were Pharaoh's magicians who had opposed **Moses** and **the truth** (see Exod 7:8-12). The **men** who opposed God in Paul and Timothy's day were similarly **corrupt** and **worthless** (2 Tim 3:8). But as sure as God overruled the Egyptian magicians, he would also overrule the false teachers and make their folly evident **to all** (3:9).

3:10-11 The point here is that Timothy was not alone in his struggles. Paul had been through worse, and he could testify to the sustaining grace of God.

3:12 Notice the universal nature of this statement: **all who want to live a godly life in Christ Jesus will be persecuted**. Not everyone will suffer in the same way because persecution takes many forms, but if you seek to be a visible and verbal follower of Christ and give allegiance to his kingdom agenda in every area of your life, you will face significant opposition from the devil and the world. As Jesus told his disciples, "If they persecuted me, they will also persecute you" (John 15:20). The good news is that whatever persecution

[a] 3:13 Rv 20:10
[b] 3:14 2Tm 1:13
[c] 3:15 Mt 26:54; 2Pt 1:20-21
[d] Ac 4:12; 2Co 7:10; Heb 5:9
[e] 3:16 2Pt 1:20-21
[f] 3:17 2Co 9:8; Gl 3:10; 1Tm 5:10; 2Tm 2:21

[g] 4:1 Jn 5:22-30; Rm 5:18; 1Pt 4:5
[h] Jn 5:25; Rm 14:9; 1Pt 4:5; Rv 18:8; 19:11
[i] Mk 1:15; Ac 20:25
[j] 4:3 Rm 15:4
[k] 4:4 1Tm 1:4; 4:7; Ti 1:14; 2Pt 1:16
[l] 4:5 Ac 21:8; Eph 4:11
[m] 4:6 Gn 35:14; Php 2:17

～ HOPE WORDS ～

The job of parenting is to extend the kingdom of God into the next generation.

～ HOPE WORDS ～

We are not called to adapt the Bible to our lives, but to adapt our lives to the Bible.

and impostors will become worse, deceiving[a] and being deceived. **14** But as for you, continue in what you have learned and firmly believed. You know those who taught you,[b] **15** and you know that from infancy you have known the sacred Scriptures,[c] which are able to give you wisdom for salvation[d] through faith in Christ Jesus. **16** All Scripture is inspired by God[A,e] and is profitable for teaching, for rebuking, for correcting, for training in righteousness, **17** so that the man of God may be complete, equipped for every good work.[f]

APPLICATION QUESTIONS

READ 2 TIMOTHY 3:16-17

- How do you intentionally expose yourself to preaching and teaching that are based on the authority of God's Word?
- What steps do you take to apply what you learn?

FULFILL YOUR MINISTRY

4 I solemnly charge you before God and Christ Jesus, who is going to judge[g] the living and the dead,[h] and because of his appearing and his kingdom:[i] **2** Preach the word; be ready in season and out of season; rebuke, correct, and encourage with great patience and teaching. **3** For the time will come when people will not tolerate sound doctrine,[j] but according to their own desires, will multiply teachers for themselves because they have an itch to hear what they want to hear. **4** They will turn away from hearing the truth and will turn aside to myths.[k] **5** But as for you, exercise self-control in everything, endure hardship, do the work of an evangelist,[l] fulfill your ministry.

6 For I am already being poured out as a drink offering,[m] and the time for my departure is close. **7** I have fought the good fight, I have finished the race, I have kept the faith. **8** There is reserved for me the

---

[A] 3:16 Lit *breathed out by God*

---

you face, God can deliver you from it or through it.

3:14-15 Timothy's mother and grandmother taught him the sacred Scriptures from an early age (see 1:5).

3:16 The doctrine of inspiration refers to the process by which God oversaw the composition of Scripture, guiding the authors to write exactly what he wanted them to write without error. The Greek word translated **inspired** is literally "breathed out by God." Our God communicates, and he has worked supernaturally through the Holy Spirit to communicate perfectly to us (see 1 Cor 2:9-16; 2 Pet 1:19-21). When we read the Bible, we are reading the very words of the living God.

All Scripture is **profitable for teaching** (instructing you in the truths that you need to know), **for rebuking** (reproving you for what you've done wrong), **for correcting** (showing you what it right), and **for training in righteousness** (guiding you to approach life as God intended) (2 Tim 3:16). Everything a believer needs to become all that God has redeemed him to be has been deposited in the Scriptures.

4:1 Notice the solemn **charge**. The God who called Timothy into ministry was delivering a sacred command to him through his authoritative messenger Paul. And he directs that

same sacred command to every man who takes up the mantle of pastor in a local church.

4:2 What should believers expect to be the standard of authority at their churches? Feelings? Intellect? Tradition? Paul says there is only one standard by which a church is to properly function: God's **word**. The Bible—and only the Bible—is the final authority for Christian individuals, families, churches, and even the broader culture.

What does it mean to **preach**? The action calls to mind the role of a herald who was responsible for receiving the message of a king and delivering it the king's subjects. *To preach* is to declare what God has to say to his people and to exhort them to act on that by believing and obeying it. Biblical preaching confronts us with God, through the Word, inspired by the Holy Spirit, through the personality of a preacher, so that we will understand and respond to God. Preaching includes reading the Word, explaining the Word, and applying it.

In a world that claims everything is relative, people ought to be able to hear the absolute truth of the Word of God (John 17:17) preached in "the church of the living God, the pillar and foundation of the truth" (1 Tim 3:15). Each person might have his or her own view. But

when we come to church, we need to hear *God's* view.

4:3-4 Sinful people don't naturally run toward what is holy and righteous. They prefer what makes them feel good. That's why they need to hear the Word faithfully preached.

4:5 Timothy couldn't control the response to his sermons. But he could commit himself to faithfully fulfilling God's calling on his life. He could **exercise self-control** (letting the gospel transform his life), **endure hardship** (suffering for the gospel), and **do the work of an evangelist** (proclaiming the gospel).

4:6 Paul uses Old Testament imagery to describe his impending death. Just as drink offerings were poured out to God on the altar, the apostle recognized that his life was being poured out, and **the time for [his] departure** was **close**. He was sitting in a Roman prison, awaiting execution.

4:7 It's not enough to *start* the Christian **race**. It's not enough to *run* the race. You must *finish* the race. Your goal in life must be to finish well. Paul didn't reach the end of his days to contemplate the things he hadn't done. In fact, he had no sense of incompleteness. Christ can get you to the finish line, but you must focus your attention on him. Even if you have fallen, get up, and keep running. "Let us run with endurance the race that lies before

a 4:8 Jn 15:17; Rv 12:1
b Lk 18:2,6; Jn 5:22–30; Ac 10:42; Heb 12:23
c Ti 2:13; 1Jn 2:28
d 4:9 Ti 3:12
e 4:10 Col 4:14; Phm 24
f 2Tm 1:15
g Ac 17:1
h Gl 1:2
i Ti 1:4
j 4:11 Col 4:14; Phm 24
k Ac 15:37–39
l 4:12 Ac 20:4; Ti 3:12
m 4:13 Ac 16:8
n 4:14 1Tm 1:20
o 4:15 2Tm 1:14; 2Pt 3:17
p 4:16 2Tm 1:15
q 4:18 Mk 1:15; Ac 20:25
r 4:19 Ac 18:2
s 2Tm 1:16
t 4:20 Ac 19:22; Rm 16:23
u Ac 20:4; 21:29
v Ac 20:15,17

crown*a* of righteousness, which the Lord, the righteous Judge,*b* will give me on that day, and not only to me, but to all those who have loved his appearing.^,*c*

FINAL INSTRUCTIONS

9 Make every effort to come to me soon,*d* **10** because Demas*e* has deserted me,*f* since he loved this present world, and has gone to Thessalonica.*g* Crescens has gone to Galatia,*h* Titus*i* to Dalmatia. **11** Only Luke*j* is with me. Bring Mark*k* with you, for he is useful to me in the ministry. **12** I have sent Tychicus*l* to Ephesus. **13** When you come, bring the cloak I left in Troas*m* with Carpus, as well as the scrolls, especially the parchments. **14** Alexander*n* the coppersmith did great harm to me. The Lord will repay him according to his works. **15** Watch out*o* for him yourself because he strongly opposed our words.

16 At my first defense, no one stood by me, but everyone deserted me.*p* May it not be counted against them. **17** But the Lord stood with me and strengthened me, so that I might fully preach the word and all the Gentiles might hear it. So I was rescued from the lion's mouth. **18** The Lord will rescue me from every evil work and will bring me safely into his heavenly kingdom.*q* To him be the glory forever and ever! Amen.

BENEDICTION

19 Greet Prisca and Aquila,*r* and the household of Onesiphorus.*s* **20** Erastus*t* has remained at Corinth; I left Trophimus*u* sick at Miletus.*v* **21** Make every effort to come before winter. Eubulus greets you, as do Pudens, Linus, Claudia, and all the brothers and sisters.

22 The Lord be with your spirit. Grace be with you all.

^ 4:8 Or *have longed for his appearing*

---

us, keeping our eyes on Jesus, the source and perfecter of our faith" (Heb 12:1-2).

4:8 According to ancient tradition, Paul was beheaded. But that frightening fate made no difference to Paul. Not only would the Lord restore his head to his body, but he would also place a **crown** on it. And **not only** on *his* head, but on the heads of **all those who have loved** Christ's **appearing** through faithful living.

A football team can perform poorly during the first quarter—or even during the first half of the game. But what's most important is how they finish. Don't, then, look backward on the mess in your past. The grace of God can cover it. Instead, look forward. There's still time. Fight the good fight, finish the race, and keep the faith (see 4:7). Your reward is waiting.

4:11 This **Luke** was the same "dearly loved physician" (Col 4:14) who penned the Gospel bearing his name.

It's interesting that Paul asks Timothy to **bring Mark with** him. Mark (also called "John" or "John Mark") had traveled with Paul before (see Acts 13:5). But after Mark left Paul in the middle of his first missionary journey (Acts 13:13), Paul was unwilling to take him the next time. Paul and Barnabas had such a sharp disagreement over Mark that they parted ways (Acts 15:36-40). By this point, the relationship had been mended.

4:13 Most likely, **the scrolls** were copies of Scripture. If so, Paul was a diligent student of the Word until the end.

4:14-15 It's likely that this is the same **Alexander** of Ephesus who was a false teacher that Paul "delivered to Satan" (1 Tim 1:19-20) because Paul warns Timothy, who was ministering in Ephesus, to **watch out for him** and his opposition to sound teaching (2 Tim

4:15). Regardless, Paul knew that ultimately **the Lord** would **repay** Alexander for his deeds (4:14). "Don't be deceived: God is not mocked. For whatever a person sows he will also reap" (Gal 6:7).

4:16-17 Paul didn't put his hope in people. After all, during his trial, at his **first defense**, he was **deserted** by everyone. Yet, he followed in the footsteps of the Lord Jesus and the first Christian martyr (Stephen) by asking the Lord to forgive them (4:16; see Luke 23:34; Acts 7:59-60). Regardless of who had abandoned Paul, **the Lord** consistently **stood with** him (4:17).

The lion's mouth (4:17) may either refer metaphorically to evil people like Emperor Nero (see Ps 22:13, 19-21) or literally to the wild animals that killed Christians in the Roman coliseum (see Dan 6:22).

TITUS

INTRODUCTION

Author and Historical Background

SEE THE INTRODUCTION TO 1 TIMOTHY for a discussion of the author and historical background of the Pastoral Epistles (1 Timothy, 2 Timothy, and Titus).

Message and Purpose

Titus was one of the apostle Paul's sons in the ministry. Paul sent him to lead the churches on the island of Crete, and then he wrote this brief letter to equip Titus to effectively lead them in serving the body of Christ. Paul explained to Titus the importance of leadership, noting that part of Titus's responsibility as a pastor and spiritual leader was to develop leaders who would help the church fulfill its role. This included encouraging the older men to disciple the younger men and the older women to disciple the younger women so that the members of the body of Christ could help one another grow.

Titus contains solid teaching on the importance of good works—those ministries that benefit the members of the church and others as well. It also includes instructions on the absolute necessity of teaching sound

doctrine through the proclamation of God's Word with both love and clarity. Two words summarize Paul's message here: proclamation and coordination. Titus was to preach the Word and coordinate the ministry so that lives would be changed and God's kingdom expanded.

www.bhpublishinggroup.com/qr/te/56_00

Outline

I.   Greetings (1:1-4)
II. Instructions for Leadership (1:5-16)
III. Virtues and Ethics for God's People (2:1-15)
IV. Christian Behavior and Good Works toward Others (3:1-11)
V.   Final Words (3:12-15)

a 1:1 Ac 13:9
b Ac 16:17; Rm 1:1; Eph 6:6; Jms 1:1; 1Pt 2:16; Rv 1:1
c Mt 22:14; 24:22; Lk 18:7; Rm 8:33; Col 3:12; 1Co 1:27-28; 1Th 1:4; Jms 2:5
d 1Tm 2:4; 2Tm 3:7
e 1Tm 6:3
f 1:2 1Co 15:19; Ti 3:7; Heb 9:15
g Nm 23:19; Heb 6:18
h Rm 1:2; 2Tm 1:9
i 1:3 Jn 21:1; 2Co 4:11; 1Pt 5:4; 1Jn 1:2
j Jn 1:1; 2:22; 2Tm 2:15; Heb 4:12
k 1Tm 1:11; 6:20; 2Tm 1:12,14
l 1Tm 1:1
m 1Tm 1:1; 2:3; Ti 2:10; 3:4; Jd 25
n 1:4 2Co 2:13; 7:6,13-14; 8:6,16,23; 12:18; Gl 2:1,3; 2Tm 4:10
o 1Tm 1:2
p Rm 1:7; 1Co 1:3
q 1:5 Ac 27:7,12-13
r 1Tm 3:1-7; 5:17
s 1:6-8 1Tm 3:2-4
t 1:6 Col 1:22
u 1:7 Ac 20:28; Php 1:1; 1Pt 2:25
v 1:9 Ac 2:42
w 1Tm 1:10; 6:3; 2Tm 1:13; Ti 2:1
x 1:13 Jn 8:14
y 2Co 13:10
z 1:14 1Tm 1:4; 4:7; 2Tm 4:4; 2Pt 1:16
aa 2Tm 4:4
ab 1:15 Heb 13:18
ac 1:16 Jn 7:28
ad Mk 14:6; 2Co 9:8; Gl 3:10; Jms 2:14-26
ae 2Co 9:8
af 2:1 Ti 1:9
ag 2:2 1Tm 5:1
ah 1Co 13:1; 1Jn 4:16
ai 2:3 1Tm 5:2
aj 2:5 Lk 10:17; Eph 5:22
ak Lk 8:21; 2Tm 2:15; Heb 4:12

GREETING

1 Paul,[a] a servant of God[b] and an apostle of Jesus Christ, for[A] the faith of God's elect[c] and their knowledge of the truth[d] that leads[e] to godliness,[e] 2 in the hope of eternal life[f] that God, who cannot lie,[g] promised before time began.[h] 3 In his own time he has revealed[i] his word[j] in the preaching with which I was entrusted[k] by the command[l] of God our Savior:[m]

4 To Titus,[n] my true son[o] in our common faith.

Grace and peace from God the Father and Christ Jesus our Savior.[p]

TITUS'S MINISTRY IN CRETE

5 The reason I left you in Crete[q] was to set right what was left undone and, as I directed you, to appoint elders[r] in every town. 6 An elder[s] must be blameless:[t] the husband of one wife, with faithful[c] children who are not accused of wildness or rebellion. 7 As an overseer[u] of God's household, he must be blameless: not arrogant, not hot-tempered, not an excessive drinker, not a bully, not greedy for money, 8 but hospitable, loving what is good, sensible, righteous, holy, self-controlled, 9 holding to the faithful message as taught,[v] so that he will be able both to encourage with sound teaching[w] and to refute those who contradict it.

10 For there are many rebellious people, full of empty talk and deception, especially those from the circumcision party. 11 It is necessary to silence them; they are ruining entire households by teaching what they shouldn't in order to get money dishonestly. 12 One of their very own prophets said, "Cretans are always liars, evil beasts, lazy gluttons." 13 This testimony is true.[x] For this reason, rebuke them sharply,[y] so that they may be sound in the faith 14 and may not pay attention to Jewish myths[z] and the commands of people who reject the truth.[aa]

15 To the pure, everything is pure, but to those who are defiled and unbelieving nothing is pure; in fact, both their mind and conscience[ab] are defiled. 16 They claim to know God,[ac] but they deny him by their works.[ad] They are detestable, disobedient, and unfit for any good work.[ae]

SOUND TEACHING AND CHRISTIAN LIVING

2 But you are to proclaim things consistent with sound teaching.[af] 2 Older men[ag] are to be self-controlled, worthy of respect, sensible, and sound in faith, love,[ah] and endurance. 3 In the same way, older women[ai] are to be reverent in behavior, not slanderers, not slaves to excessive drinking. They are to teach what is good, 4 so that they may encourage the young women to love their husbands and to love their children, 5 to be self-controlled, pure, workers at home, kind, and in submission[aj] to their husbands, so that God's word[ak] will not be slandered.

A 1:1 Or according to   B 1:1 Or corresponds   c 1:6 Or believing

1:1-2 Paul speaks of Christians as **God's elect**. Election is to godliness (see Eph 1:4) and to service (see 2 Pet 1:8-11)

1:3 The timing for Jesus's entry into the world was perfect—and so is the timing for everything God does in your life.

1:4 **Titus** was Paul's pastoral delegate on Crete. He either led Titus to Christ or nurtured him in the faith since he calls him his **true son** in their **common faith**.

1:5 These **elders** would serve Titus's need to **set right** things that were broken in the church so that the ministry would be healthy and operate effectively based on sound doctrine. Qualified spiritual leadership is critical for a church to function properly.

1:6-9 Notice that the criteria for serving as an **elder** are quite stout! What we see here are not descriptions of *performance* but of *character*. Paul wanted a certain kind of man to serve as an elder. An "elder," also called **an overseer** (1:6-7), is not necessarily an old man, but a mature one who knows and walks with God.

Elders are to **encourage with sound teaching** or **refute those who contradict it** (1:9).

This is a weighty responsibility. It takes men of integrity to submit faithfully to their King's agenda, to teach others to do likewise, and to correct those who oppose it. That's why Paul gave Titus such high expectations for elder candidates. Character is everything.

1:10-11 Because many false teachers are outside the church, elders must equip Christians with sound, biblical teaching to help them discern truth from lies. But should false teachers try to operate inside the church, elders must **silence them** (1:11).

1:12-14 Paul quotes a Cretan poet from the sixth century BC: **Cretans are always liars, evil beasts, lazy gluttons** (1:12). It's never good when someone describes his own fellow citizens like that. But unfortunately, Paul found the saying to be **true** of at least some of the Cretans. He thus urged Titus to **rebuke them sharply** (1:13). Of course, for Paul rebuke is never the end but only the means to an end. He wanted church members in Crete to **be sound in the faith** and to ignore those **who reject the truth** (1:13-14). Only by conforming your thinking to God's truth can you live a life that is pleasing to God.

1:16 Similarly, lips that claim to praise God mean nothing when they are combined with a lifestyle that denies him.

2:2 If **older men** are **self-controlled, worthy of respect, sensible, and sound in faith, love, and endurance** they can serve as authentic models and spiritual mentors for young Christian men who are confronted by a very different kind of "manhood" on exhibit in the surrounding culture. Gender-based discipleship should be a major part of every local church's ministry.

2:3-5 Where can a young Christian wife find holy women to disciple her to live faithfully and build up her family? According to Paul, she ought to find such kingdom women in the church. By aligning their lives with God's principles for a kingdom wife (2:4-5; see Eph 5:22-24, 33), young women will not only experience God's blessing but also prevent **God's word** from being **slandered** (Titus 2:5). When wives and mothers abandon the priority of the home, they bring shame and dishonor to the authority, truthfulness, and power of God's Word. They also call into question the seriousness of their spiritual

❧ Questions & Answers ❧

Q How has the apostle Paul's ministry shaped your own approach to ministry?

A Paul's ministry has affected me from the standpoint of biblical exposition. Paul was a tactician. He threaded the needle in detail. That's why teachers and believers spend so much time in his letters. (I'm thankful God let him write so many of them!) Paul's writing—his use of words, his use of the Old Testament, and his arguments to address practical problems—forces me to go deep in my study and in my preaching. I've been helped, in particular, by *biblical theology*. Systematic theology looks at what all of Scripture teaches on different topics. But biblical theology looks at what a particular author has to say to his audience on a subject. Since Paul wrote more letters than any other New Testament author (thirteen), he has a lot to say on a variety of topics that are critical for church ministry, spiritual growth, and meeting life's challenges. Paul has forced me to dig in the context for the content, which takes me deeper in my exposition of Scripture.

FOR THE NEXT Q&A, SEE PAGE 1456.

⁶ In the same way, encourage the young men[a] to be self-controlled ⁷ in everything. Make yourself an example of good works with integrity and dignity[A] in your teaching. ⁸ Your message is to be sound beyond reproach,[b] so that any opponent will be ashamed, because he doesn't have anything bad to say about us.

⁹ Slaves are to submit to their masters[c] in everything, and to be well-pleasing,[d] not talking back ¹⁰ or stealing, but demonstrating utter faithfulness, so that they may adorn the teaching of God our Savior[e] in everything.

¹¹ For the grace of God has appeared, bringing salvation[B] for all people,[f] ¹² instructing us to deny godlessness[g] and worldly lusts[h] and to live in a sensible, righteous,[i] and godly[j] way in the present age, ¹³ while we wait for the blessed hope,[k] the appearing of the glory[l] of our great God and Savior, Jesus Christ. ¹⁴ He gave himself for us[m] to redeem us from all lawlessness and to cleanse for himself a people for his own possession,[n] eager to do good works.

¹⁵ Proclaim these things; encourage and rebuke with all authority. Let no one disregard[c] you.

CHRISTIAN LIVING AMONG OUTSIDERS

3 Remind them to submit[o] to rulers and authorities, to obey, to be ready for every good work, ² to slander no one, to avoid fighting, and to be kind, always showing gentleness[p] to all people. ³ For we too were once foolish, disobedient, deceived, enslaved by various passions[q] and pleasures,[r] living in malice and envy, hateful, detesting one another.

[a] 2:6 1Tm 5:1; 1Pt 5:5; 1Jn 2:13-14
[b] 2:8 1Tm 2:2
[c] 2:9 Eph 6:5-9; Col 3:22; 1Tm 6:1; 1Pt 2:18; Jd 4
[d] Heb 13:21
[e] 2:10 1Tm 1:1; 2:3; Ti 1:3; 3:4; Jd 25
[f] 2:11 Ac 1:8; Rm 10:14; 2Co 5:18-21; 1Tm 2:4; 4:10; 2Pt 3:9
[g] 2:12 Jd 18
[h] 2Tm 4:10; 2Pt 1:4; 2:10
[i] Lk 23:41; 1Co 15:34; 1Th 2:10; 1Pt 2:24
[j] 2Tm 3:12
[k] 2:13 Ac 23:6; 1Th 1:3
[l] Lk 9:32; Jn 17:1,24; 2Co 3:18; 2Pt 3:18
[m] 2:14 Mt 20:28; Mk 10:45; Rm 8:32; Gl 1:4; 2:20; Eph 5:2,25; 1Tm 2:6
[n] Ex 19:5; Lk 1:68
[o] 3:1 Rm 13:1-7; 1Pt 2:13-14
[p] 3:2 Jms 3:13
[q] 3:3 2Pt 1:4; 2:10
[r] Jms 4:1

[A] 2:7 Other mss add *and incorruptibility*   [B] 2:11 Or *appeared with saving power*   [C] 2:15 Or *despise*

---

commitment.

2:6-7 Be self-controlled in everything. If young men today need any advice, surely that is it. In a culture that encourages men to indulge their every desire, self-control is a radical message.

2:9-10 Scripture condemns most of what we know of slavery (especially American antebellum slavery). For example, humans are not to be kidnapped and sold (Exod 21:16); slaves are not to be abused (Exod 21:26-27); and fugitive slaves are not to be returned to their masters (Deut 23:15-16). But given the unrighteous institution of slavery as it existed in the Roman Empire, Paul tells Christian slaves how to live with a heavenly perspective.

Paul's principles for slaves ought to be applied by believers in their workplaces. When employers think of their Christian employees, they ought to consider them **to be well-pleasing, not** given to **talking back**

(2:9) **or stealing, but demonstrating utter faithfulness** (2:10). Does that describe your approach to your daily nine-to-five?

2:11-13 All people are within the hopeful reach of God's **salvation** (2:11). No one is beyond God's rescue, no matter who he or she is or what's been done. In fact, the "worst" people in society are exactly those whom God seeks for his rescue project. The **grace of God has appeared** (2:11)—that is, it has emerged out of the shadows of the law (see John 1:15-17). Grace is not just a doctrine; it's a person. And grace has a name: Jesus Christ, **our great God and Savior**, who says to all, "Come to me" (Titus 2:13). Grace grows us in godliness and increases our victory over sin.

2:14 Jesus paid the price to free us from slavery to sin. So, how should redeemed people live? Only by adopting a godly perspective, living in obedience to his commands, and being **eager to do good works** can believers see the power of heaven at work in their

earthly lives. *Good works* are the divinely approved acts that benefit people and bring glory to God.

2:15 Paul gave Titus some serious marching orders. The work of ministry is not for the faint of heart. It is to be exercised with loving but firm kingdom authority.

3:1 This is a hard bit of instruction, but government officials, employers, and any other persons of authority should be the recipients of our **every good work**. In the end, Christians are serving God in all they do, and he is always watching our motives and actions. When we cheat the time clock at work, we are really cheating God himself—and giving the world a poor reflection of our Master.

3:2-3 Paul wants us to remember where we came from. We are to show **gentleness to all people** (3:2) because God showed the same to us when we were **foolish, disobedient, deceived** (3:3). Believers are often tempted to look down their noses at unbelievers—for-

a 3:4 1Tm 1:1; 2:3; Ti 1:3;
2:10; Jd 25
b 3:5 Rm 11:14; 2Tm 1:9
c Eph 2:9
d Eph 2:4; 1Pt 1:3
e Jn 3:5; Eph 5:26; 1Pt 3:21
f Rm 12:2
g 3:6 Jl 2:28; Ac 2:33; 10:45;
Rm 5:5
h 3:7 Ac 13:43; 15:11; 1Co
8:1; Gl 1:6; 1Pt 4:10
i Ti 1:2
j 3:8 1Tm 1:15; 3:1; 4:9;
2Tm 2:11
k 3:9 1Tm 6:4
l 1Tm 1:4
m Rm 1:29; 13:13; 1Co 1:11;
3:3; 2Co 12:20; Gl 5:20;
Php 1:15; 1Tm 6:4

n 3:10 1Tm 1:9
o Mt 18:15; 2Th 3:15
p 3:12 Ac 20:4; Eph 6:21;
Col 4:7; 2Tm 4:12
q Lk 14:26; 2Tm 4:9
r 3:13 Ac 18:24; 19:1; 1Co
1:12; 3:4–6,22; 4:6; 16:12
s Jms 2:15

4 But when the kindness of God our Savior and his love for mankind appeared,[a] **5** he saved us[b] —not by works of righteousness that we had done,[c] but according to his mercy[d] — through the washing of regeneration[e] and renewal by the Holy Spirit.[f] **6** He poured out his Spirit on us abundantly[g] through Jesus Christ our Savior **7** so that, having been justified by his grace,[h] we may become heirs with the hope of eternal life.[i] **8** This saying is trustworthy.[j] I want you to insist on these things, so that those who have believed God might be careful to devote themselves to good works. These are good and profitable for everyone. **9** But avoid foolish debates,[k] genealogies,[l] quarrels,[m] and disputes about the law, because they are unprofitable and worthless. **10** Reject a divisive[n] person after a first and second warning.[o] **11** For you know that such a person has gone astray and is sinning; he is self-condemned.

FINAL INSTRUCTIONS AND CLOSING

12 When I send Artemas or Tychicus to you,[p] make every effort to come to me[q] in Nicopolis, because I have decided to spend the winter there. **13** Diligently help Zenas the lawyer and Apollos[r] on their journey, so that they will lack[s] nothing.

14 Let our people learn to devote themselves to good works for pressing needs, so that they will not be unfruitful.[t] **15** All those who are with me send you greetings. Greet those who love us in the faith. Grace be with all of you.[u]

t 3:14 Mt 13:22; Mk 4:19; 1Co 14:14; Gl 5:22; Eph 5:11; 2Pt 1:8; Jd 12   *u* 3:15 Col 4:18; 2Th 3:16

---

getting that they too were once lost.

3:7 We are now **heirs**, sons and daughters of the King, **with the hope of eternal life**. So live like a royal heir and make his kingdom vision your own.

3:8 Good works are divinely prescribed actions that benefit others and glorify God (see Matt 5:16). They bless those in the church, and they bless those outside it by giving them an accurate picture of the love and grace of God and his offer of the free gift of salvation (see Eph 2:8-9).

3:9-11 Few things drive away seekers like church infighting. So Satan loves to encourage selfish strife and division among church members. What should churches do with **a** divisive person (3:10) who quarrels about unprofitable and worthless matters (3:9)? Warn him twice and then **reject** him (3:10-11).

3:14 Trusting in Christ the King as your sin-bearer will get you from earth to heaven. But adopting his kingdom agenda will bring heaven's help to your earthly life.

PHILEMON

INTRODUCTION

Author

PAUL WROTE HIS LETTER TO Philemon while in prison (vv. 1, 9-10, 13). He most likely wrote Ephesians, Philippians, Colossians, and Philemon during the same imprisonment in Rome. In AD 60–62, he was under house arrest in guarded rental quarters (see Acts 28:30).

Historical Background

Paul addressed his letter to Apphia, Archippus, and the church that met in Philemon's home; nevertheless, his main addressee is Philemon who lived in Colossae (see the reference to Onesimus in Col 4:9). Apparently he was a wealthy man, since he owned slaves and a house large enough to accommodate church meetings. In any case, it appears Philemon had become a convert through the ministry of Paul himself (Phlm 19). Importantly, though this letter is a personal appeal to Philemon, it was not private. The rest of the church would have heard it read aloud and witnessed Philemon's response to Paul.

Message and Purpose

This is an intimate letter from the apostle Paul to his friend Philemon. This man had a slave named Onesimus, who stole from him, ran away to Rome, and through a series of circumstances encountered Paul. Not only did Paul lead Onesimus to Christ but discipled him to such an extent that Onesimus ministered back to Paul. Nevertheless, when the apostle learned about the circumstances that had brought Onesimus to Rome, Paul sent Onesimus back to Philemon to make things right. The theme of Paul's letter to Philemon is thus forgiveness and reconciliation. Philemon was in a position to forgive Onesimus and restore their relationship, showing Onesimus the same forgiveness that Philemon himself had received from God, since the two men had become brothers in Christ.

Here we see a very tender side of Paul as he pleads with his friend Philemon to forgive and reconcile with Onesimus. His words are a reminder that forgiveness is prerequisite to reconciliation, and reconciliation is prerequisite to restoration. The message of Philemon is desperately needed in our day of division and strife. As believers, we need to be kingdom agents of forgiveness and reconciliation in each other's lives and in the world.

VIDEO | INTRO

www.bhpublishinggroup.com/qr/te/57_00

Outline

I. Address and Greeting (1-3)
II. Thanksgiving for Philemon (4-7)
III. Paul's Appeal for Onesimus (8-20)
IV. Closing (21-25)

a 1 Ac 13:9
b 2Tm 1:8; Heb 13:3
c Rm 1:1
d Ac 16:1; 1Tm 1:2
e 2 Col 4:17
f Php 2:25
g Ac 12:12; Rm 16:5
h 5 Dt 6:5; Mt 22:37; Gl 5:6,22; Eph 6:23; 1Th 1:3; 3:6; 5:8; 1Tm 1:14; 1Jn 4:20
i 6 Gl 5:6
j Gn 1:31; 18:18; 3Jn 11
k 7 Lk 12:19; 2Tm 1:16
l 9 2Tm 1:8; Heb 13:3
m 10 1Th 2:11
n Col 4:9
o 1Co 4:15

p 16 Php 3:3
q 1Co 16:19; Rv 11:8
r 17 Rm 14:1
s 18 Rm 5:13
t 19 1Co 16:21
u 23 Col 1:7; 4:12
v 24 Ac 12:12,25; 15:37,39; Col 4:10; 2Tm 4:11; 1Pt 5:13
w Ac 19:29
x Col 4:14; 2Tm 4:10-11
y 25 2Th 3:18; Rv 11:8
z Ps 51:12

GREETING

Paul,*a* a prisoner*b* of Christ Jesus,*c* and Timothy*d* our brother:

To Philemon our dear friend and co-worker, **2** to Apphia our sister,*A* to Archippus*e* our fellow soldier,*f* and to the church that meets in your home.*g*

3 Grace to you and peace from God our Father and the Lord Jesus Christ.

PHILEMON'S LOVE AND FAITH

4 I always thank my God when I mention you in my prayers, **5** because I hear of your love*h* for all the saints and the faith that you have in the Lord Jesus. **6** I pray that your participation in the faith may become effective*i* through knowing every good thing*j* that is in us*B* for the glory of Christ. **7** For I have great joy and encouragement from your love, because the hearts of the saints have been refreshed*k* through you, brother.

AN APPEAL FOR ONESIMUS

8 For this reason, although I have great boldness in Christ to command you to do what is right, **9** I appeal to you, instead, on the basis of love. I, Paul, as an elderly man*c* and now also as a prisoner*l* of Christ Jesus, **10** appeal to you for my son,*m* Onesimus.*D,n* I became his father*o* while I was in chains. **11** Once he was useless to you, but now he is useful both to you and to me. **12** I am sending him back to you — I am sending my very own heart.*E,F* **13** I wanted to keep him with me, so that in my imprisonment for the gospel he might serve me in your place. **14** But I didn't want to do anything without your consent, so that your good deed might not be out of obligation, but of your own free will. **15** For perhaps this is why he was separated from you for a brief time, so that you might get him back permanently, **16** no longer as a slave, but more than a slave — as a dearly loved brother. He is especially so to me, but how much more to you, both in the flesh*p* and in the Lord.*q*

17 So if you consider me a partner, welcome*r* him as you would me. **18** And if he has wronged you in any way, or owes you anything, charge that to my account.*s* **19** I, Paul, write this with my own hand:*t* I will repay it — not to mention to you that you owe me even your very self. **20** Yes, brother, may I benefit from you in the Lord; refresh my heart in Christ. **21** Since I am confident of your obedience, I am writing to you, knowing that you will do even more than I say. **22** Meanwhile, also prepare a guest room for me, since I hope that through your prayers I will be restored to you.

FINAL GREETINGS

23 Epaphras,*u* my fellow prisoner in Christ Jesus, sends you greetings, and so do **24** Mark,*v* Aristarchus,*w* Demas, and Luke,*x* my coworkers.

25 The grace of the Lord*G,y* Jesus Christ be with your spirit.*z*

A 2 Other mss read *our beloved*   *B* 6 Other mss read *in you*   *C* 9 Or *an ambassador*   *D* 10 In Gk, *Onesimus* means "useful"   *E* 12 Other mss read *him back. Receive him, my own heart.*   *F* 12 Lit *you—that is, my own heart*   *G* 25 Other mss read *our Lord*

1-2 Apphia was probably Philemon's wife; **Archippus** was perhaps their son (v. 2). Paul, though, is writing primarily to **Philemon** (v. 1). In the Greek language in which Paul wrote, the instances of "you" and "your" in the body of the letter (vv. 2, 4-21, 23) are singular, not plural. Nonetheless, since it was also addressed to **the church** that met in Philemon's house (v. 2), the principles of forgiveness and reconciliation raised in this personal letter are applicable to the whole church.

4-5 It's a contradiction to say you love God if you fail to **love** your fellow Christians (v. 5; see 1 John 4:7-12, 20-21). Encourage and minister to them.

9-10 Previously, Philemon had a slave named **Onesimus** who wronged him by perhaps stealing from him (v. 10; see v. 18) and then running away. Somehow Onesimus came into contact with Paul in Rome and believed the gospel (v. 10). The question addressed in this passage is this: How do you relate to a person who has wronged you based on his or her new status with Jesus Christ?

11 Since the name *Onesimus* actually means "useful," Paul makes a play on words: the man who was formerly **useless to you** is now **useful both to you and to me**. Paul has seen that Onesimus's new status in Christ matches his name.

12-16 Given his **imprisonment for the gospel**, Paul would like Onesimus to stay and **serve** him on Philemon's behalf (v. 13). Philemon's runaway slave could become his representative to support God's premier missionary. But Paul doesn't want to obligate his friend without his **consent** (v. 14), so he is **sending [Onesimus] back** (v. 12). Why? Because Onesimus needs to face up to what he's done. He has to make things right. But, also, Paul is helping Philemon grow in love and forgiveness.

Philemon has the opportunity to receive Onesimus back **as a dearly loved brother** (v. 16). These men have a chance to show the church what reconciliation looks like.

17 The body of Christ is one: we're family.

18 We need mediators in the church like Paul, who mirrored his Savior. After all, Jesus Christ took every sinful debt that we owed God and said, **Charge [it] to my account**.

19-21 Paul reminds Philemon that he owes his own conversion to him (v. 19). Though this letter is short, it demonstrates the great power of the gospel when it comes to interpersonal relationships. Whether we have done wrong like Onesimus, been wronged like Philemon, or need to mediate between two brothers like Paul did, following Jesus Christ means submitting to his kingdom agenda for reconciliation. Forgiveness is a divine condition for experiencing and exercising kingdom authority in prayer (see Mark 11:22-26).

HEBREWS

INTRODUCTION

Author

THE LETTER TO THE HEBREWS does not identify an author; therefore, there has been much speculation as to his identity. Some argue for Paul, Luke, Barnabas, Apollos, Timothy, Silvanus, or others. But in the end, we cannot be certain. Regardless, the writer has an in-depth understanding of the Old Testament and the conventions of the religious life of Israel, including the priesthood (see 5:1-10; 7:1-28), the tabernacle/tent of meeting (see 9:1-14), and the sacrificial system (see 10:1-25). He also demonstrates a command of the Greek language. His range of vocabulary and the style in which he presented his arguments, in fact, resulted in what many have agreed is some of the most sophisticated writing in the New Testament.

Historically, many opted for either Paul or a missionary associate of his as the author of Hebrews because the writer was familiar with Paul's companion Timothy (see 13:23). But while Paul was identified as the author by the early Christian writer Clement (ca. AD 150–215), and he was followed by other prominent church fathers like Eusebius and Augustine, no definitive case can be made. The best position might be that of Origen who wrote, "Who wrote the epistle, in truth God knows." This uncertainty should not, however, trouble us. The early church received the letter as inspired and authoritative Scripture. It has unquestioned value for the Christian life.

Historical Background

The author presumably knew the Christian recipients of his letter well because he referred to them as "brothers and sisters" (3:12; 10:19; 13:22). Like him, they had heard about the gospel through the earliest followers of Jesus (2:3). They were Jewish Christians, having familiarity with the old covenant sacrificial system. Moreover, they were a group enduring various forms of persecution (10:32-34) under Emperor Nero prior to the destruction of the temple in AD 70. As a result, some among them had grown unwilling to grow spiritually and risked forfeiting—not their salvation—but the blessings and rewards God had in store for them. Thus, the author urges them to "go on to maturity" (6:1) and to hold fast to their commitment to Christ.

Message and Purpose

Hebrews is often considered one of the most difficult books in the New Testament to interpret, second only to Revelation. That's because Hebrews is very dependent on the Old Testament for much of what the author has to say to Jewish Christians who have come upon hard times and are considering bailing out on their Christian commitment to return to Judaism.

This letter's recipients were wondering whether following Christ was worth the persecution. In effect, the author of Hebrews urged them, "Yes it is! Keep going. Don't turn back. Jesus is worth the trouble." That's also the same message Hebrews offers to anyone today who is encountering opposition in the Christian faith and thinking of throwing in the towel. Some things are worth the struggle, and some things aren't. But Jesus definitely is!

The author has a lot to say about how Jesus is superior to the Old Testament sacrificial system. Hebrews will rev up your faith in Christ and his unshakeable kingdom. Following him is worth it.

www.bhpublishinggroup.com/qr/te/58_00

Outline

Video Devotional
"JESUS CHRIST"

Jesus Christ lived on earth to display the image of God in history. His life, death, and resurrection provide our hope and salvation.

THE NATURE OF THE SON

1 Long ago God spoke[a] to the fathers by the prophets[b] at different times and in different ways.[c] **2** In these last days,[d] he has spoken to us by his Son. God has appointed him heir of all things[e] and made the universe[A,f] through him. **3** The Son is the radiance[B] of God's glory and the exact expression[c] of his nature,[g] sustaining all things by his powerful word.[h] After making purification for sins,[D] he sat down at the right hand of the Majesty on high.[E,i] **4** So he became superior to the angels, just as the name he inherited is more excellent than theirs.[j]

THE SON SUPERIOR TO ANGELS

5 For to which of the angels did he ever say,

You are my Son;
today I have become your Father,[F,G]

or again,

I will be his Father,
and he will be my Son?[H,k]

6 Again, when he[i] brings his firstborn into the world,[i] he says,

And let all God's angels worship him.[J,m]

7 And about the angels he says:

He makes his angels winds,[K]
and his servants[L] a fiery flame,[M,n]

8 but to[N] the Son:

Your throne, O God,
is forever and ever,
and the scepter of your kingdom
is a scepter of justice.[o]
9 You have loved righteousness
and hated lawlessness;
this is why God, your God,
has anointed you
with the oil of joy[p]
beyond your companions.[O,P]

10 And:

In the beginning, Lord,
you established the earth,
and the heavens are the works
of your hands;[q]
11 they will perish, but you remain.
They will all wear out like clothing;[r]
12 you will roll them up like a cloak,[Q]
and they will be changed
like clothing.
But you are the same,
and your years will never end.[R,S]

13 Now to which of the angels has he ever said:

Sit at my right hand
until I make your enemies
your footstool?[S,t]

14 Are they not all ministering spirits sent out to serve those who are going to inherit salvation?[u]

---

a 1:1 Jn 9:29; Heb 2:2-3 *b* 2Kg 17:13; 21:10; 24:2; Jr 7:25; 26:5; 29:19; 35:15; 44:4; Ezk 38:17; Dn 9:6; Hs 12:10; Zch 1:6; 8:9; Mt 2:23; Lk 1:70; 24:44; Ac 2:30; 3:21,24 *c* Nm 12:6,8; Jl 2:28 *d* 1:2 Ac 2:17; Gl 4:4; 2Tm 3:1; 2Pt 3:3; Jd 18 *e* Jr 3:19; 10:16; Zch 8:12 *f* Ps 2:8; Jn 1:3; Col 1:16; Rv 4:11 *g* 1:3 2Co 4:4 *h* Ps 33:6 *i* Mt 22:44; Mk 16:19; Col 1:17

j 1:4 Eph 1:21; Php 2:9 *k* 1:5 2Sm 7:14; Ps 2:7; Ac 13:33 *l* 1:6 Col 1:15,18; Rv 1:5 *m* Dt 32:43; Ps 97:7 *n* 1:7 Ps 104:4 *o* 1:8 Ps 45:6-7 *p* 1:9 Is 61:1,3; Php 2:9 *q* 1:10 Ps 102:25 *r* 1:11 Is 50:9; 51:6 *s* 1:12 Ps 102:26-27; Heb 13:8 *t* 1:13 Jos 10:24; Ps 110:1; Mt 22:44; Mk 12:36; Ac 2:34-35; Heb 10:13 *u* 1:14 Ps 103:20; Mt 18:10; Heb 5:9

A 1:2 Lit *ages*   B 1:3 Or *reflection*   C 1:3 Or *representation*, or *copy*, or *reproduction*   D 1:3 Other mss read *for our sins by himself*   E 1:3 Or *he sat down on high at the right hand of the Majesty*   F 1:5 Or *have begotten you*   G 1:5 Ps 2:7; 2Sm 7:14; 1Ch 17:13   H 1:6 Or *When he again*   J 1:6 Dt 32:43 LXX; Ps 97:7   K 1:7 Or *spirits*   L 1:7 Or *ministers*   M 1:7 Ps 104:4   N 1:8 Or *about*   O 1:9 Or *associates*   P 1:8-9 Ps 45:6-7   Q 1:12 Other mss omit *like a cloak*   R 1:10-12 Ps 102:25-27   S 1:13 Ps 110:1

1:1 The recipients of Hebrews were Jewish Christians struggling to persevere in their commitment to Christ in the face of temptation and persecution.

The Bible is God's revelation to us. But in times past, he communicated to his people **in different ways:** by **prophets,** angels (e.g., Josh 5:13-15), and even a donkey (Num 22:22-41). **1:2** When the author mentions **these last days,** he's talking about the New Testament days—everything that falls between the time of Christ's birth and his return. Jesus is God's final Word on every subject. Furthermore, God has bequeathed all of creation to his Son, the **heir of all things.**
1:3 **The Son is the radiance of God's glory and the exact expression of his nature.** Jesus Christ possesses *all* of the divine attributes. After Christ completed his work of redemption, **making purification for sins, he sat down at the right hand of the Majesty on high.** By contrast, when the high priest entered the most holy place in the tabernacle/temple to offer sacrifice for the sins of

the people, there was no chair. He couldn't sit because his work was never done.

The sacrificial system was God's temporary solution, pointing forward to something better. But when Jesus died on the cross for sin, he declared, "It is finished" (John 19:30)—that is, "The sin debt is paid in full." With his resurrection, his work was complete, and he sat down in the seat of authority and power to rule from heaven through his people on earth (Heb 7:25; see Matt 28:19-20; Eph 1:22-23).
1:4-9 Jesus **became superior to the angels, just as the name he inherited is more excellent than theirs** (1:4). He demonstrated by his perfect life, substitutionary death, and bodily resurrection his legitimate right to rule.

Many first-century Jewish Christians revered **angels** because they were a means of divine revelation. But God never said to an angel, **You are my Son** (1:5). Nor does an angel have the right to receive worship, which is for God alone (see Exod 20:3-5). Rather, **all God's angels worship** the Son (Heb 1:6). Not only that, but God calls the Son **God** (1:8-9)!

Angels are merely "ministering spirits" who "serve those who are going to inherit salvation" (1:14).

The psalm quoted by the author in verse 9 speaks of Christ's **companions**. The eternal bond between believers and Christ shows up several times in Hebrews (e.g., 3:1, 14). What does it mean? Well, believers have the opportunity to be Christ's companions, his partners, who will rule with him as part of his inner circle. This honor is distinct from justification. Those who accept him as their sin-bearer gain entrance by grace into the kingdom of God as heirs. But your participation as Christ's *companion* determines the level of your inheritance in the kingdom. Faithfulness to the King is the criterion for becoming part of Christ's administrative cabinet when he establishes his earthly millennial kingdom on his return (3:14; see Rom 8:17; 2 Tim 2:12; Rev 2:16-17).
1:14 God has assigned **ministering** angels to oversee, serve, and cover believers.

WARNING AGAINST NEGLECT

2 For this reason, we must pay attention all the more to what we have heard, so that we will not drift away.[a] **2** For if the message spoken through angels was legally binding[A,b] and every transgression and disobedience received a just punishment,[c] **3** how will we escape if we neglect such a great salvation?[d] This salvation had its beginning when it was spoken of by the Lord, and it was confirmed to us by those who heard him.[e] **4** At the same time, God also testified by signs and wonders, various miracles, and distributions of gifts from the Holy Spirit according to his will.[f]

JESUS AND HUMANITY

5 For he has not subjected to angels the world to come that we are talking about. **6** But someone somewhere has testified:

What is man
  that you remember him,
or the son of man that you care
  for him?
7 You made him lower
  than the angels
for a short time;
you crowned him with glory
  and honor.[B]
8 and subjected everything
  under his feet.[c]

For in **subjecting everything** to him, he left nothing that is not subject to him. As it is, we do not yet see **everything subjected**

to him.[g] **9** But we do see Jesus — **made lower than the angels for a short time** so that by God's grace he might taste death[h] for everyone — **crowned with glory and honor**[i] because he suffered death.[j]

10 For in bringing many sons and daughters to glory, it was entirely appropriate that God — for whom and through whom all things exist — should make the source[D] of their salvation perfect through sufferings.[k] **11** For the one who sanctifies and those who are sanctified all have one Father.[E] That is why Jesus is not ashamed to call them brothers and sisters,[l] **12** saying:

I will proclaim your name
  to my brothers and sisters;
I will sing hymns to you
  in the congregation.[F,m]

13 Again, **I will trust in him.**[G] And again, **Here I am with the children God gave me.**[H,n]

14 Now since the children have flesh and blood in common, Jesus also shared in these, so that through his death he might destroy the one holding the power of death — that is, the devil[o] — **15** and free those who were held in slavery all their lives by the fear of death.[p] **16** For it is clear that he does not reach out to help angels, but to help Abraham's offspring.[q] **17** Therefore, he had to be like his brothers and sisters in every way, so that he could become a merciful and faithful high priest in matters[i] pertaining to God, to make

[a]2:1 Jos 24:27; Mc 5:13; 1Co 9:27; 10:6; 11:34; Ti 3:14
[b]2:2 Dt 33:2; Ac 7:53; Heb 1:1
[c]Nm 15:30; Heb 10:28
[d]2:3 Is 45:17
[e]Lk 1:2; Heb 1:2; 10:29
[f]2:4 Jn 4:48; Ac 2:22,43; 5:12; 8:13; 14:3; 15:12; Rm 12:3–8; 15:19; 1Co 12:4; 2Co 12:12; Eph 1:5; 4:8
[g]2:6-8 Ps 7:17; Ps 8:4-6; Mt 22:44; Ac 2:35; 1Co 15:25–27; Eph 1:22; Heb 10:13
[h]2:9 Jn 8:52; 1Co 15:54–56; Php 2:8; Col 1:22; Heb 9:15; 1Pt 3:18
[i]Ac 2:33; 3:13
[j]Jn 3:16; 2Co 5:15; Php 2:9
[k]2:10 Lk 13:32; 24:26; Rm 11:36; Heb 7:28
[l]2:11 Mt 28:10; Jn 20:17; Ac 17:28; Heb 10:10
[m]2:12 Ps 22:22; Heb 12:23
[n]2:13 Ps 18:2; Is 8:17-18; 12:2; Jn 10:29; 17:6
[o]2:14 Jn 1:14; 1Co 15:54–56; Col 2:15; 2Tm 1:10; 1Jn 3:8
[p]2:15 Rm 8:15; 2Tm 1:7
[q]2:16 Lk 19:9; Jn 8:39; Rm 4:16; Gl 3:7–9,29

[A]2:2 Or valid, or reliable   [B]2:7 Other mss add and set him over the works of your hands   [C]2:6-8 Ps 8:5-7 LXX   [D]2:10 Or pioneer, or leader
[E]2:11 Or father, or origin; lit all are of one   [F]2:12 Ps 22:22   [G]2:13 2Sm 22:3 LXX; Is 8:17 LXX; 12:2 LXX   [H]2:13 Is 8:18 LXX   [I]2:17 Lit things

2:1 If you're bobbing along on the ocean and do nothing, you're going to drift. Similarly, if you're neglecting your spiritual life, you're going to drift from God and you will inevitably find trouble.

2:5-9 After Satan rebelled and took a host of fallen angels with him, God created humans—constitutionally inferior beings—and **subjected** the **world** to them instead of **angels** (2:5). Why? So God could show what he can do with less when less is dependent on him than he can do with more when more is in rebellion against him. According to Psalm 8 as quoted here, God made Adam **lower than the angels** but **crowned him with glory and honor and subjected everything under his feet** (Heb 2:7-8).

The problem is this: the first Adam failed and handed over ruling authority to Satan. That's why **we do not yet see everything subjected to [humanity]** (2:8). What did God do in response? He committed himself to bringing about his kingdom rule on earth through a man. He even accomplished it himself through the person of his Son, Jesus Christ. The Son temporarily became **lower**

than the angels to realign heaven and earth. He came down to **taste death for everyone** and was **crowned with glory and honor** (2:9). The Son became a man and won the victory over Satan and sin through his obedience, sacrificial death, and resurrection.

Even in Christ's victory, though, we do not yet "see" the full results with our eyes (2:8). It's like when a person wins the presidential election but whose presidency has yet to be experienced. We still await Christ's returning to judge and rule on the earth. But make no mistake: Jesus is already in the victor's chair (2:9).

2:10 Jesus was perfect in his deity, but he had to learn obedience as a man (5:8-9) so that he might accomplish God's kingdom purposes. To do that, he had to suffer. He received glory and honor on Sunday, in fact, because of his obedient suffering and death on Friday.

2:11-12 When you became a Christian, you entered into the family of God. He adopted you, and you became a brother or sister to Jesus. Now, he's working to sanctify you so that he's **not ashamed to call** you his brother or sister.

2:14-15 Jesus conquered death to free people from **the fear of death** (2:15). Yet because Satan is "the father of lies" (John 8:44), he'll try to trick you. Remember, then, that the devil no longer has **the power of death** (Heb 2:14). The gun he's been intimidating you with has no bullets. Jesus Christ emptied its chamber into himself. Thus, all Satan can do is deceive you into thinking the gun still has ammunition. But the fear of death should no longer make you a slave (see 1 Cor 15:51-57).

2:16 The fallen **angels** that rebelled against God had no opportunity for redemption. Yet, remarkably, God offers help to us—Abraham's children through faith.

2:17-18 Academically speaking, a male doctor knows the pain a laboring mom is going through. But a female doctor who has actually experienced childbirth herself can truly empathize. As a mother, she's felt that pain. As a doctor, she can help others through it. Jesus is **a merciful and faithful high priest** (2:17). He has truly felt your pain, and he can empathize with you. Moreover, he can deliver you from sin and enable you to overcome your circumstances (see John 16:33).

Well-Dressed for Warfare

EVERY YEAR, MY WIFE LOIS and I take a trip to New York City. I grew up not too far from the Big Apple, and returning there always brings back great memories. On our most recent trip to New York, however, we weren't able to get out in the city as much as usual. A hurricane named Irene had also come to town with winds strong enough to knock a man over. Few people took to the streets of New York during Irene's visit. Those who did venture outside didn't bother to carry an umbrella to protect them from the rain because an umbrella isn't enough to stop you from getting soaked by a hurricane. Those who didn't want to be affected by the storm—like Lois and me—chose to stay inside.

That choice didn't stop the wind or the rain. It simply stopped the wind and the rain from stopping us. It didn't still the storm. It changed how the storm affected us. Likewise, standing firm in the armor of God doesn't stop the spiritual warfare from raging all around you. Instead, it stops the warfare from defeating you. That is why one scheme of the devil is to get you to step out from under the protective covering God has given you (SEE EPH 6:10-18). Once you step outside and away from God's protection, you expose yourself to whatever Satan wants to bring your way.

Most people would question the wisdom of walking around outside when a hurricane is in full force. But believers who walk into a world full of spiritual warfare without the armor of God are even more foolish. The key to victory in spiritual warfare comes in recognizing the truth that Jesus Christ has already secured the victory you seek. There is no safer place you or I can be than fully armed with our identity in Christ.

Everything that happens in the visible, physical world has its root in the invisible, spiritual world. Therefore, in order to overcome a visible, physical stronghold in your life, you must battle it with the invisible, spiritual weaponry of the armor of God. The book of Hebrews tells us that through Christ's death, he rendered Satan powerless: "Since the children have flesh and blood in common, Jesus also shared in these, so that through his death he might destroy the one holding the power of death—that is, the devil—and free those who were held in slavery all their lives by the fear of death" (HEB 2:14-15).

In Jesus Christ, you have been set free and no longer have to cower under fear of life's hurricanes. Your victory is rooted in the reality that every-thing is underneath the one who has made us complete in him: "He subjected everything under his feet and appointed him as head over everything for the church, which is his body, the fullness of the one who fills all things in every way" (EPH 1:22-23).

If Satan defeats you, he must do so with permission that has been given to him. This is a truth that Satan does not want you to know, or own, because once you walk in this truth, you will treat him differently, look at him differently, and respond to him differently. You will know that in Christ you are safe and secure, even in the midst of life's hurricanes.

atonement[A,a] for the sins of the people.[b] **18** For since he himself has suffered when he was tempted, he is able to help those who are tempted.

OUR APOSTLE AND HIGH PRIEST

3 Therefore, holy brothers and sisters, who share in a heavenly calling, consider Jesus, the apostle and high priest of our confession.[c] **2** He was faithful to the one who appointed him, just as Moses was in all God's household. **3** For Jesus is considered worthy of more glory than Moses, just as the builder has more honor than the house. **4** Now every house is built by someone, but the one who built everything is God.[d] **5** Moses was faithful as a servant[e] in all God's household, as a testimony to what would be said in the future. **6** But Christ was faithful as a Son over his household. And we are that household if we hold on to our confidence and the hope in which we boast.[B,f]

WARNING AGAINST UNBELIEF

7 Therefore, as the Holy Spirit says:

Today, if you hear his voice,
8   do not harden your hearts
    as in the rebellion,
  on the day of testing
    in the wilderness,
9   where your fathers tested me,
    tried me,
  and saw my works **10** for forty years.

Therefore I was provoked to anger
  with that generation
  and said, "They always go astray
    in their hearts,
  and they have not known
    my ways."
11   So I swore in my anger,
    "They will not enter my rest."[C,g]

12 Watch out, brothers and sisters, so that there won't be in any of you an evil, unbelieving heart that turns away[h] from the living God. **13** But encourage each other daily,[i] while it is still called **today**, so that none of you is hardened[j] by sin's deception.[k] **14** For we have become participants in Christ if we hold firmly until the end the reality[D] that we had at the start.[l] **15** As it is said:

Today, if you hear his voice,
  do not harden your hearts
    as in the rebellion.[E,m]

16 For who heard and rebelled? Wasn't it all who came out of Egypt under Moses?[n] **17** With whom was God angry for forty years? Wasn't it with those who sinned, whose bodies fell in the wilderness?[o] **18** And to whom did he swear that they would not enter his rest, if not to those who disobeyed? **19** So we see that they were unable to enter because of unbelief.

THE PROMISED REST

4 Therefore, since the promise to enter his rest remains, let us beware[F] that none of you be found to have fallen

[a]2:17 2Co 5:21
[b]Lk 18:13; Rm 3:25; Php 2:7; Heb 4:15; 5:1-2; 7:26-28; 1Jn 2:2; 4:10
[c]3:1 Rm 15:8; Php 3:14; Heb 2:11,17; 4:14-15
[d]3:4 Eph 2:10; 3:9
[e]3:5 Ex 14:31; Nm 12:7-8; Dt 18:19; 34:5; Jos 1:2,7,13,15; 11:12,15; 12:6; 1Kg 8:53,56; Mal 4:4
[f]3:6 Mt 10:22; Rm 5:2; 11:22; 1Co 3:16; Heb 1:2

[g]3:7-11 Ps 95:7-11; Ac 7:36; Heb 4:3,5
[h]3:12 Lk 8:13; Ac 15:38; 1Tm 4:1
[i]3:13 1Th 2:12; 2Th 3:12; Heb 10:25
[j]Ac 19:9; Rm 9:18; Heb 3:8,15; 4:7
[k]Eph 4:22; Heb 10:24
[l]3:14 1Co 15:2; Heb 3:6; 10:23; 11:1
[m]3:15 Ps 95:7-8
[n]3:16 Nm 14:2; Dt 1:35-38
[o]3:17 Nm 14:29; Ps 106:26

[A]2:17 Or *propitiation*   [B]3:6 Other mss add *firm to the end*   [C]3:7-11 Ps 95:7-11   [D]3:14 Or *confidence*   [E]3:15 Ps 95:7-8   [F]4:1 Lit *fear*

3:1 The author reminds Christians that God didn't save us just so we could go to heaven. He saved us to partner with him in his kingdom agenda on earth, to **share in a heavenly calling**—to be his companions in the messianic kingdom that is to come (see 11:16). **3:2-6** Moses faithfully served God, delivered his word to Israel, and oversaw the establishment of the tabernacle and sacrificial system. These Jewish Christian readers revered Moses. But Jesus is **worthy of more glory than Moses, just as the builder has more honor than the house** (3:3). Thus, the two cannot be fairly compared. Though **Moses was faithful as a servant in all God's household** (3:5), **Christ was faithful as a Son over [God's] household** (3:6). The Son over the house has more say-so than a faithful servant. **3:7-11** Psalm 95, quoted here, speaks of Israel's period of forty years in the wilderness after departing Egypt. Numbers 13-14 recount how the Israelites refused to listen to God and enter the promised land of Canaan because they feared the inhabitants. As a result of that rebellion, God made them wander in the wilderness where they continued to rebel. God was angry because

his chosen people did not know his **ways** (Heb 3:10).

The Bible teaches that God's ways with his people include three stages: deliverance, development, and destiny. First, Israel experienced *deliverance* when God set them free from Egyptian bondage. Similarly, when he saved you—caused you to be born again in Christ—he delivered you. But his involvement in your life doesn't end there. Second, the next stage is *development*, in which he brings you into a deeper relationship with him. This includes the trials and tests of life; there's no development without these experiences. Most of the Israelites in the wilderness failed in the development stage because they wouldn't trust God to provide for them.

Third, the developmental process leads to *destiny*. This is where God wants you to wind up. But you can't go from deliverance to destiny and skip development. God swore that the people would not **enter [his] rest** (3:11). The "rest" in view is a way of referring to their inheritance. Because of their continual rebellion, they forfeited living in the land of Canaan. **3:12** If there is no development in their lives, they could miss out on their own inheri-

tance—the spiritual blessings God has for them in history and in eternity. You can be saved but refuse to develop. In other words, you can end up in the bleachers rather than on the playing field. In terms of your spiritual progress and kingdom rewards, then, don't have **an evil, unbelieving heart** that allows sin to disconnect you from fellowship with God. **3:13-14** One of the primary purposes of the local church is to create an environment in which believers can help each other persevere. This is why the New Testament emphasizes (and why churches should emphasize) the "one anothers"—the exhortations to care for and encourage each other (e.g., John 15:12; Gal 6:2; Eph 4:32; 1 Thess 5:11). If we want to be Christ's companions, those who partner with him in his kingdom agenda, we must **hold firmly until the end** (Heb 3:14). To do that, we must help one another avoid sin's deception. **3:15** If we don't want to **harden [our] hearts**, we need regular exposure to God's Word and the spiritual encouragement of God's people (see 10:24-25). It's the only thing with the power to keep a heart soft (see 4:12-13). **4:1** Don't run the risk of falling short of your inheritance. If you're seriously living the

a 4:1-2 1Th 2:13; Heb 12:15
b 4:3 Ps 95:11; Heb 3:11
c 4:4 Gn 2:2; Ex 20:11
d 4:5-6 Ps 95:11; Heb 3:19

e 4:7 Ps 95:7-8; Heb 3:7
f 4:8 Jos 22:4
g 4:10 Heb 4:4; Rv 14:13

❧ Questions & Answers ❧

Q Philippians 2:7 notes that in Christ's incarnation "he emptied himself by assuming the form of a servant, taking on the likeness of humanity." Why is understanding Christ's self-emptying, his *kenosis*, important to understanding what he came to accomplish for us?

A Jesus's *kenosis*, or self-emptying, is critical for understanding his person, purpose, and work. At the incarnation, Jesus did not stop being God. He poured deity into his humanity.

Thus, he "emptied himself" by humbling himself to become human. As a result, he is able to fully express deity and humanity. So it can truly be said that Jesus is God with us (see Matt 1:23) because of his incarnation.

On account of that union of deity and humanity, Jesus can reach out one hand to touch the Father and reach out the other hand to touch people. Hebrews 4:15 says, "For we do not have a high priest who is unable to sympathize with our weaknesses, but one who has been tempted in every way as we are, yet without sin." The high priest presented God to men and men to God. Jesus can do both because he can relate to both. He has both a divine nature and a human nature. This connecting point allows him to serve as the only perfect sacrifice for our sin. Since Jesus is eternally the God-Man, he will forever be the connecting point between humanity and the Father.

FOR THE NEXT Q&A, SEE PAGE 1457.

short.^A ^2 For we also have received the good news just as they did. But the message they heard did not benefit them, since they were not united with those who heard it in faith.^B,a ^3 For we who have believed enter the rest, in keeping with what^c he has said,

So I swore in my anger,
"They will not enter my rest,"^D,b

even though his works have been finished since the foundation of the world. ^4 For somewhere he has spoken about the seventh day in this way: **And on the seventh day God rested from all his works.**^E,c ^5 Again, in that passage he says, **They will never enter my rest.**^D ^6 Therefore, since it remains for some to enter it, and those who formerly received the good news did not enter because of disobedience,^d ^7 he again specifies a certain day — **today.** He specified this speaking through David after such a long time:

Today, if you hear his voice,
do not harden your hearts.^F,e

^8 For if Joshua^f had given them rest, God would not have spoken later about another day. ^9 Therefore, a Sabbath rest remains for God's people. ^10 For the person who has entered his rest has rested from his own works, just as God did from his.^g ^11 Let us then make every effort to enter that rest, so that no one will fall into the same pattern of disobedience.

❧ HOPE WORDS ❧

Speak God's Word into your circumstances rather than speaking your circumstances into God's Word.

^A 4:1 Or *that any of you might seem to have missed it*   ^B 4:2 Other mss read *since it was not united by faith in those who heard*   ^C 4:3 Or *rest, just as*
^D 4:3,5 Ps 95:11   ^E 4:4 Gn 2:2   ^F 4:7 Ps 95:7-8

Christian life, you will run into challenges and trials. The temptation is to acquiesce to your environment to ease the pressure. But if you follow the route of least resistance, you will fail to be Christ's *companion,* or *partner* (1:9; 3:1, 14). And while you won't lose your salvation, you will lose the opportunity to experience his plans for you in his kingdom. Don't squander your inheritance (i.e., your rest).
4:2 Who were **those who heard** the **good news** about Canaan **in faith**? Well, when God brought Israel to the edge of the promised land, twelve spies entered on a reconnais-

sance mission. Afterward, ten of them said, "We can't take Canaan. The job's too big for us." Only two—Joshua and Caleb—believed God and said, "Yes, we can do it with God's help." Unfortunately, the people of Israel believed the majority report. As a result, God refused to let anyone of that generation enter the land except Joshua and Caleb. Unbelief for the believer is the refusal to act like God is telling the truth.
4:3-6 God's rest **on the seventh day** of creation week (4:4) doesn't mean he took a nap. It means he enjoyed his work, for he saw that

it "was very good" (Gen 1:31). But the people of Israel failed to enter God's rest (i.e., the place of promised blessing) and find enjoyment **because of disobedience** (Heb 4:5-6).
4:7 To **harden your hearts** means to tell God no. Expose yourself to godly people and principles that help chip away at whatever keeps the truth from getting through.
4:9-11 The principle of **Sabbath rest** still operates today (4:9). Believers are called to enter the **rest** God has prepared for them rather than following Israel's example **of disobedience** (4:10-11).

OUR GREAT HIGH PRIEST

14 Therefore, since we have a great high priest who has passed through the heavens — Jesus the Son of God — let us hold fast to our confession.[e] **15** For we do not have a high priest who is unable to sympathize with our weaknesses, but one who has been tempted in every way as we are,[f] yet without sin.[g] **16** Therefore, let us approach the throne of grace with boldness, so that we may receive mercy and find grace to help us in time of need.

CHRIST, A HIGH PRIEST

5 For every high priest taken from among men is appointed in matters pertaining to God for the people, to offer both gifts and sacrifices for sins. **2** He is able to deal gently with those who are ignorant and are going astray, since he is also clothed with weakness.[h] **3** Because of this, he must make an offering for his own sins as well as for the people.[i] **4** No one takes this honor on himself; instead, a person is called by God, just as Aaron was.[j] **5** In the same way, Christ did not exalt himself to become a high priest, but God who said to him,

> **You are my Son;
> today I have become
>   your Father,**[A,B,K]

6 also says in another place,

> **You are a priest forever
> according to the order
>   of Melchizedek.**[C,l]

7 During his earthly life,[D] he offered prayers and appeals[m] with loud cries and tears[n] to the one who was able to save him from death, and he was heard because of his reverence. **8** Although he was the Son, he learned obedience from what he suffered.[o] **9** After he was perfected, he became the source of eternal salvation for all who

[a] 4:12 Jr 23:29; 1Pt 1:23
[b] Is 49:2; Eph 6:17; Rv 1:16; 2:12
[c] 1Co 14:24-25
[d] 4:13 2Ch 16:9; Jb 26:6; 34:21; Ps 33:13-15
[e] 4:14 Heb 3:1; 6:20; 10:23
[f] 4:15 Is 53:3; Heb 2:18
[g] 2Co 5:21; 1Pt 2:22
[h] 5:2 Heb 2:18; 4:15; 7:28
[i] 5:3 Lv 4:3; 9:7; Heb 9:7
[j] 5:4 Ex 28:1; 1Ch 23:18
[k] 5:5 Ps 2:7; Jn 8:54; Heb 1:1
[l] 5:6 Ps 110:4; Heb 7:17
[m] 5:7 Mt 26:39; Mk 14:36
[n] Ps 22:1; Mt 27:46,50; Mk 15:34,37; Lk 23:46
[o] 5:8 Php 2:7-8; Heb 1:2

12 For the word of God is living and effective[a] and sharper than any double-edged sword,[b] penetrating as far as the separation of soul and spirit, joints and marrow. It is able to judge the thoughts and intentions of the heart.[c] **13** No creature is hidden from him, but all things are naked and exposed to the eyes of him to whom[d] we must give an account.

[A] 5:5 Lit *I have begotten you*   [B] 5:5 Ps 2:7   [C] 5:6 Gn 14:18-20; Ps 110:4   [D] 5:7 Lit *In the days of his flesh*

4:12-13 Have you ever had an experience with God's Word that made you feel exposed? Have you ever heard it preached and felt like it was directed right at you? Have you ever felt your soul sliced open by the Word? Remember, we have no private lives. We don't even get to have private thoughts. Everything is laid bare before the One **to whom we must give an account** (4:13).

4:15 In one sense, Jesus is like all of us—he has endured incredible temptation, suffering, and hardship. Yet, in another, he's like none of us—he has never sinned. Therefore, he is the perfect **high priest**. He can **sympathize** with you in your weakness and suffer-

ing. Yet, since he resisted completely, he can also help you.

4:16 Prayer is the believer's passport into the spiritual realm. So, when you're tempted to give up, that *temptation* is actually an *invitation* to draw near to the King's throne so you **may receive mercy and find grace**. *Mercy* is not getting what you deserve; *grace* is getting what you don't deserve.

5:1-3 Israel's **high priest** stood between God and the people. He entered the tabernacle/temple to offer **sacrifices** on their behalf to make atonement **for sins** (5:1). He was a mediator. But, given that the high priest was also **clothed with weakness**, he could **deal gently**

with those who were **going astray** (5:2). Since he was himself a sinner, the sin **offering** he made was **for his own sins as well as** theirs (5:3).

5:4 One didn't just jump into the office of high priest. Rather, a person had to be **called by God, just as** Moses's brother **Aaron was**.

5:6 Jesus Christ wasn't appointed to the priesthood of Aaron but to the priesthood of Melchizedek. The author will return to discussing Melchizedek in chapter 7.

5:8 **Although he was the Son, he learned obedience**—in his human nature, not in his divine nature (see Luke 2:52).

5:9 The Greek verb and noun that we translate "saved" and "salvation" don't always

a 5:12 1Co 3:2; Heb 6:1;
1Pt 2:21
b 5:14 Is 7:15; 1Co 2:6
c 6:1 Php 3:13; Heb 5:12;
9:14
d 6:2 Jn 3:25; Ac 6:6; 17:31-
32; 19:4-6

e 6:4 Gl 3:3; Eph 2:8; Heb
10:32
f 6:6 Heb 10:29; 2Pt 2:21;
1Jn 5:16
g 6:7-8 Gn 3:17-18; Ps
65:10; Is 5:6
h 6:10 Pr 19:17; Mt 10:42;
25:40; 2Co 8:4; 1Th 1:3;
2Tm 1:18

obey him, **10** and he was declared by God a high priest according to the order of Melchizedek.

THE PROBLEM OF IMMATURITY

11 We have a great deal to say about this, and it is difficult to explain, since you have become too lazy to understand. **12** Although by this time you ought to be teachers, you need someone to teach you the basic principles of God's revelation again. You need milk, not solid food.*a* **13** Now everyone who lives on milk is inexperienced with the message about righteousness, because he is an infant. **14** But solid food is for the mature — for those whose senses have been trained to distinguish between good and evil.*b*

WARNING AGAINST FALLING AWAY

6 Therefore, let us leave the elementary teaching about Christ and go on to maturity, not laying again a foundation of repentance from dead works, faith in God,*c* **2** teaching about ritual washings,*A* laying on of hands, the resurrection of the dead, and eternal judgment.*d* **3** And we will do this if God permits.
4 For it is impossible to renew to repentance those who were once enlightened,

who tasted the heavenly gift, who shared in the Holy Spirit,*e* **5** who tasted God's good word and the powers of the coming age, **6** and who have fallen away. This is because,*B* to their own harm, they are recrucifying the Son of God and holding him up to contempt.*f* **7** For the ground that drinks the rain that often falls on it and that produces vegetation useful to those for whom it is cultivated receives a blessing from God. **8** But if it produces thorns and thistles, it is worthless and about to be cursed, and at the end will be burned.*g*
9 Even though we are speaking this way, dearly loved friends, in your case we are confident of things that are better and that pertain to salvation. **10** For God is not unjust; he will not forget your work and the love*c* you demonstrated for his name by serving the saints — and by continuing to serve them.*h* **11** Now we desire each of you to demonstrate the same diligence for the

A 6:2 Or *about baptisms*   *B* 6:6 Or *while*   *C* 6:10 Other mss read *labor of love*

refer to salvation from the penalty of sin and eternal judgment. Depending on the context, the words can also be rendered "delivered" or "deliverance"—implying rescue from challenges or dangers in life, and from divine wrath in history (see, e.g., Matt 14:30; Acts 27:20; Rom 5:9-10). This is the meaning of the use of the word **salvation** here, since the author's readers are already believers (Heb 3:1, 12; 10:19; 13:22). Having become our great high priest who endured suffering and remained faithful to God, Jesus Christ is the source of deliverance for all believers who obey him.
5:11 The Greek word translated *lazy* can mean "dull" or "stubborn." So, in other words, they had become mule-headed and refused to grow spiritually.
5:12 Something is wrong if a thirty-year-old is still eating baby food. Knowing the ABCs and 123s of the Bible is crucial, but there comes a time to build on this foundation with further understanding and growth. Any believer who fails to move on from **milk** to **solid food**— "milk" being the content of God's Word, while "solid food" is the spiritual application and use of God's Word in life—has some developmental issues and becomes stagnant in spiritual development.
5:14 If you chew your **food** but don't swallow, you will starve. You have to internalize and put God's Word into practice (see Jas 1:21-

25). Only then will you be equipped to make Word-driven decisions rather than circumstance-driven decisions.
6:4-6 Some feel that the description, **those who were once enlightened, who tasted the heavenly gift, who shared in the Holy Spirit, who tasted God's good word** (6:4-5), isn't a reference to believers. Some say that the people described here merely *tasted* the heavenly gift and didn't go all the way and ingest it. But Hebrews also says that Jesus *tasted* death for everyone (2:9). You can be certain that he didn't just nibble death! He died. The people described in 6:4-5 are Christians.
So, what's going on here? The author says if such people **have fallen away** (6:6), it's **impossible to renew [them] to repentance** (6:4). Some interpreters think this means Christians can lose their salvation, but the rest of the Bible clearly teaches our eternal security in Christ (see, e.g., John 6:37-40; 10:26-29; Rom 8:28-39; Eph 1:13-14; 1 John 5:13). And if this text teaches that believers can lose their salvation, it also teaches that it's impossible for them to return to Christ. But no one claims that those who deny Jesus (like Peter; see Matt 26:69-75) can't repent and return to him.
Remember that the author has just urged the readers to "go on to maturity" (Heb 6:1). The problem is that they are in danger of having hardened, rebellious hearts because

they refuse to press on in spiritual growth. To persist in this state is to forget what God has done for you, acting like those who crucified **the Son of God** and held **him up to contempt** (6:6). To stubbornly refuse to follow Christ in obedience is to mock him.
It's impossible to renew such unfaithful believers to repentance. But we should ask, impossible for whom? After all, Jesus said, "With God all things are possible" (Matt 19:26). The issue, then, is not God's inability to bring someone back to repentance; it's man's inability to do so. God has to directly intervene.
6:7-8 The author is not describing eternal judgment here. The Bible speaks of fire in hell, but fire is also used to describe God's discipline of believers (see 1 Cor 3:11-15). At the judgment seat of Christ, then, a believer's faithless works will **be burned** up (Heb 6:8). "He himself will be saved—but only as through fire" (1 Cor 3:15). So don't give up. Persevere! If you're falling down, get back in the game. Press on to maturity.
6:10-12 God's purpose in saving you was not merely so you will go to heaven when you die; he wants to use you here until you die and then reward you with your kingdom inheritance when he returns (see Luke 19:11-19). Your usefulness increases as you grow in spiritual maturity during your pilgrimage from earth to glory.

full assurance of your hope until the end, [12] so that you won't become lazy but will be imitators of those who inherit the promises through faith and perseverance.[a]

INHERITING THE PROMISE

[13] For when God made a promise to Abraham, since he had no one greater to swear by, he swore by himself: [14] **I will indeed bless you, and I will greatly multiply you.**[A,b] [15] And so, after waiting patiently, Abraham obtained the promise. [16] For people swear by something greater than themselves, and for them a confirming oath ends every dispute. [17] Because God wanted to show his unchangeable purpose even more clearly to the heirs of the promise, he guaranteed it with an oath,[c] [18] so that through two unchangeable things, in which it is impossible for God to lie, we who have fled for refuge might have strong encouragement to seize the hope set before us.[d] [19] We have this hope as an anchor for the soul, firm and secure. It enters the inner sanctuary behind the curtain.[e] [20] Jesus has entered there on our behalf as a forerunner,[f] because he has become a high priest forever according to the order of Melchizedek.[g]

THE GREATNESS OF MELCHIZEDEK

7 For this Melchizedek, king of Salem, priest of God Most High, met Abraham and blessed him as he returned from defeating the kings, [2] and Abraham gave him a tenth of everything. First, his name means king of righteousness, then also, king of Salem, meaning king of peace. [3] Without father, mother, or genealogy, having neither beginning of days nor end of life, but resembling the Son of God,[h] he remains a priest forever.

[4] Now consider how great this man was: even Abraham the patriarch[i] gave a tenth of the plunder to him. [5] The sons of Levi who receive the priestly office have a command according to the law to collect a tenth from the people[j] — that is, from their brothers and sisters — though they have also descended from Abraham. [6] But one without this[g] lineage collected a tenth from Abraham and blessed the one who had the promises.[k] [7] Without a doubt, the inferior is blessed by the superior. [8] In the one case, men who will die receive a tenth, but in the other case, Scripture testifies that he lives.[l] [9] And in a sense Levi himself, who receives a tenth, has paid a tenth through Abraham, [10] for he was still within his ancestor[c] when Melchizedek met him.

A SUPERIOR PRIESTHOOD

[11] Now if perfection came through the Levitical priesthood (for on the basis of it the people received the law[m]), what further need was there for another priest to appear, said to be according to the order of Melchizedek and not according to the

[a] 6:12 Heb 10:36; 13:7
[b] 6:13-15 Gn 21:5; 22:16-17; Lk 1:73
[c] 6:16-17 Ex 22:11; Heb 11:9
[d] 6:18 Ti 1:2; Heb 12:1
[e] 6:19 Lv 16:2,15; Heb 9:7
[f] 6:20 Heb 4:14; 8:1; 9:24
[g] Heb 5:6,10; 7:17

[h] 7:1-3 Gn 14:18-20; Mt 4:3; Mk 5:7; Heb 7:6
[i] 7:4 Gn 14:20; Ac 2:29; 7:8-9
[j] 7:5 Nm 18:21,26; 2Ch 31:4-5
[k] 7:6 Gn 14:19; Rm 4:13
[l] 7:8 Heb 5:6; 6:20
[m] 7:11 Gl 2:21; Heb 7:18-19; 8:7

A 6:14 Gn 22:17   B 7:6 Lit *their*   C 7:10 Lit *still in his father's loins*

6:13-15 Twenty-five years passed between God's promise of a son and the birth of Isaac. Then many more years passed before that fateful day when Abraham faithfully offered Isaac on the altar and God **swore by himself** (6:13) that he would **bless** and **multiply** Abraham (6:14).

6:17 God's *promise* is his declaration of what he will do, and his *oath* is his announcement that he is ready to do it. God made a promise to Abraham in Genesis 12:1-3, but many years passed before he swore the oath in Genesis 22:16-17. In between, there was a long gap. During such gaps, God prepares the promise for the person and prepares the person for the promise. This is why persevering in faith is so important.

7:1-3 Melchizedek appears in Genesis 14:17-24. Then he's mentioned briefly in Psalm 110:4. But here in Hebrews, he suddenly becomes a key figure in the Bible. The author tells us that Melchizedek's **name means king of righteousness** (based on the Hebrew) and **king of peace** (*Salem* means "peace"; 7:2). Who comes to mind when you consider those titles?

Moreover, the Old Testament doesn't mention this man's **beginning** or **end**. Of course, the author of Hebrews isn't saying that he literally had no parents and never died. He's saying that there is no record of his birth or death. Thus, **he remains a priest forever** (7:3).

The point is that Melchizedek is a prototype of Jesus, the true King of righteousness and peace. As the divine Son of God, he had no beginning of days. And as the resurrected Lord, he has no end. Like Melchizedek, Jesus is both a priest and a King. Such a dual role was unheard of in Israel, where the offices of priest and king were intentionally distinct.

7:4-10 Not only is Jesus different from the Levitical priests (since he's both priest and King), but he's also superior to them. How? Because he's a priest like Melchizedek. The author draws attention to the fact that Abraham paid a tithe to Melchizedek (7:4). The Levites also collected tithes. They received them from **the people** of Israel—Abraham's descendants (7:5). But **the inferior is blessed by the superior** (7:7). In other words, as great as Abraham was as the father of Israel, he was inferior to Melchizedek because Melchizedek blessed him.

Abraham acknowledged his submission to Melchizedek and expressed his gratitude by giving him a tithe. And notice this: he didn't tithe to get a blessing; he tithed out of thankfulness for the blessing he received. In a sense, though, **Levi** *also* paid tithes to Melchizedek because **he was still within his ancestor** Abraham at the time (7:9-10). So Melchizedek's priesthood is superior because he blessed Abraham (and his descendants) and received tithes from them. Furthermore, his priesthood is superior because, though the Levitical priests died, **Scripture testifies that [Melchizedek] lives** (7:8).

It is because of Jesus's continuity with the Melchizedekian priesthood that it is legitimate for the church to receive tithes today. They are, in fact, a tangible indication of submission to our great high priest who has already "blessed us with every spiritual blessing in the heavens" (Eph 1:3). Jesus mediates the experience of these blessings to his people around Communion (1 Cor 10:16; 11:23-26). **7:11-12** These Jewish Christians were tempted to return to Judaism, but they couldn't go back. When a new coach comes to a team, he brings his own playbook. If you look back to the old coach and old playbook, you'll run the wrong plays and frustrate your new coach.

a 7:11 Heb 7:17; 10:1
b 7:14 Is 11:1; Mc 5:2; Mt 1:3; Lk 3:33; Rv 5:5
c 7:17 Ps 110:4; Heb 5:6; 6:20; 7:21
d 7:18 Rm 8:3; Gl 4:9
e 7:19 Ac 13:39; Rm 3:20; Heb 9:9
f Heb 4:16; 6:18
g 7:21 1Sm 15:29; Ps 110:4
h 7:22 Heb 8:6-10; 9:15; 12:24; 13:20
i 7:25 Rm 8:34; Heb 9:24

j 7:26 2Co 5:21; Heb 4:15
k 7:27 Eph 5:2; Heb 5:1,3; 9:12,28
l 7:28 Heb 1:2; 2:10; 5:2,9
m Php 3:12; Heb 10:14; 11:40
n 8:1 Col 3:1; Heb 2:17
o 8:2 Ex 33:7; Heb 9:11,24
p 8:3 Eph 5:2; Heb 5:1; 9:14
q 8:5 Col 2:17; Heb 9:23; 10:1
r Ex 25:40; Heb 11:7; 12:25
s 8:6 Jb 33:23; Is 29:1; Gl 3:19-20; 1Tm 2:5; Heb 9:15; 12:24
t Heb 7:22; 9:15; 12:24; 13:20
u Lk 22:20; 2Co 3:6,8

order of Aaron?*ᵃ* **12** For when there is a change of the priesthood, there must be a change of law as well. **13** For the one these things are spoken about belonged to a different tribe. No one from it has served at the altar. **14** Now it is evident that our Lord came from Judah,*ᵇ* and Moses said nothing about that tribe concerning priests.

15 And this becomes clearer if another priest like Melchizedek appears, **16** who did not become a priest based on a legal regulation about physical^A descent but based on the power of an indestructible life. **17** For it has been testified:

> **You are a priest forever**
> **according to the order**
> **of Melchizedek.** ^B,C

18 So the previous command is annulled because it was weak and unprofitable*ᵈ* **19** (for the law perfected*ᵉ* nothing), but a better hope is introduced, through which we draw near to God.*ᶠ* **20** None of this happened without an oath. For others became priests without an oath, **21** but he became a priest with an oath made by the one who said to him:

> **The Lord has sworn**
> **and will not change his mind,**
> **"You are a priest forever."** ^B,g

22 Because of this oath, Jesus has also become the guarantee of a better covenant.*ʰ* **23** Now many have become Levitical priests, since they are prevented by death from remaining in office. **24** But because he remains forever, he holds his priesthood permanently. **25** Therefore, he is able to save completely those who come to God through him, since he always lives to intercede*ⁱ* for them. **26** For this is the kind of high priest we need: holy, innocent, undefiled, separated

from sinners, and exalted above the heavens.*ʲ* **27** He doesn't need to offer sacrifices every day, as high priests do — first for their own sins, then for those of the people. He did this once for all time when he offered himself.*ᵏ* **28** For the law appoints as high priests men who are weak, but the promise of the oath, which came after the law, appoints a Son,*ˡ* who has been perfected*ᵐ* forever.

A HEAVENLY PRIESTHOOD

8 Now the main point of what is being said is this: We have this kind of high priest, who sat down at the right hand of the throne of the Majesty in the heavens,*ⁿ* **2** a minister of the sanctuary and the true tabernacle that was set up by the Lord and not man.*ᵒ* **3** For every high priest is appointed to offer gifts*ᵖ* and sacrifices; therefore, it was necessary for this priest also to have something to offer. **4** Now if he were on earth, he wouldn't be a priest, since there are those*ᶜ* offering the gifts prescribed by the law. **5** These serve as a copy and shadow*ᵍ* of the heavenly things, as Moses was warned when he was about to complete the tabernacle. For God said, **Be careful that you make everything according to the pattern that was shown to you on the mountain.** ^D,f **6** But Jesus has now obtained a superior ministry, and to that degree he is the mediator*ˢ* of a better covenant,*ᵗ* which has been established on better promises.*ᵘ*

A SUPERIOR COVENANT

7 For if that first covenant had been faultless, there would have been no occasion for a second one. **8** But finding fault with his people,*ᴱ* he says:*ᶠ*

^A 7:16 Or *fleshly*   ^B 7:17,21 Ps 110:4   ^C 8:4 Other mss read *priests*   ^D 8:5 Ex 25:40   ^E 8:8 Lit *with them*   ^F 8:8 Other mss read *finding fault, he says to them*

7:13-17 You can't mix Jesus with the Old Testament system. The Levites have been superseded. Jesus descended from the line of Judah, so the priesthood to whom believers owe allegiance has changed. His priesthood, though, isn't dependent on his lineage (no priests ever came from Judah); it's **based on the power of an indestructible life** (7:16). By virtue of his resurrection from the dead, Jesus is a **priest forever** (7:17).
7:25 As in 5:9, the author is not talking about being *saved* in terms of forgiveness of sin and eternal life here. He's talking about being *delivered* from and through trials and circumstances in this life. Jesus's full-time job is to intercede for believers and to rescue them from the power of sin, Satan, and

adverse circumstances as they draw near to him (see 4:16).
8:2-6 The system that **Moses** established was good and was done in obedience to God, but it was all preparatory. It was **a copy and shadow of the heavenly things** (8:5). It pointed forward to Jesus who **obtained a superior ministry**, mediating **a better covenant**, which is **established on better promises** (8:6).
   Readers couldn't go back to Judaism because everything behind them was inferior to Jesus. Their only option was pursuing Christ.
8:7 A *covenant* is a special agreement that God makes with his people. It is a divinely created, relational bond through which God

reveals himself and administers his kingdom program. The old covenant made with the people of Israel was good, but it was also temporary and weak because God had something better in store.
8:10 God promised that under the new covenant he would **put [his] laws into their minds and write them on their hearts**. Therefore, you as a follower of Jesus now have the capacity to experience God and obey him. But while every Christian has this ability, not every Christian has developed it (5:11-14; see 1 Cor 3:1-3).
8:12 If you really understand the greatness of this grace, you will be motivated to live to please the One who saved you. You will transfer from a "have to" life to a "thank you" life.

See, the days are coming,
  says the Lord,
when I will make a new covenant
  with the house of Israel
  and with the house of Judah —
9 not like the covenant
  that I made with their ancestors
  on the day I took them
    by the hand
  to lead them out of the land
    of Egypt.
  I showed no concern for them,
    says the Lord,
  because they did not continue
    in my covenant.
10 For this is the covenant
  that I will make with the house
    of Israel
  after those days, says the Lord:
  I will put my laws
    into their minds
  and write them on their hearts.
  I will be their God,
  and they will be my people.[a]
11 And each person will not teach
    his fellow citizen,[A]
  and each his brother or sister,
    saying, "Know the Lord,"
  because they will all know me,
  from the least to the greatest
    of them.[b]
12 For I will forgive
    their wrongdoing,
  and I will never again remember
    their sins.[B,C,C]
13 By saying a new covenant, he has declared that the first is obsolete. And what
is obsolete and growing old is about to
pass away.[d]

OLD COVENANT MINISTRY

9 Now the first covenant also had regulations for ministry and an earthly sanctuary. 2 For a tabernacle was set
up, and in the first room, which is called
the holy place, were the lampstand, the
table, and the presentation loaves.[e]
3 Behind the second curtain was a tent
called the most holy place.[f] 4 It had the
gold altar of incense and the ark of
the covenant, covered with gold on all
sides, in which was a gold jar containing
the manna, Aaron's staff that budded,
and the tablets of the covenant.[g] 5 The
cherubim of glory were above the ark
overshadowing the mercy seat. It is not
possible to speak about these things in
detail right now.[h]
6 With these things prepared like this,
the priests enter the first room repeatedly,
performing their ministry.[i] 7 But the high
priest alone enters the second room, and
he does that only once a year, and never
without blood, which he offers for himself
and for the sins the people had committed
in ignorance.[j] 8 The Holy Spirit was making it clear that the way into the most holy
place had not yet been disclosed while the
first tabernacle was still standing.[k] 9 This
is a symbol for the present time, during
which gifts and sacrifices are offered
that cannot perfect the worshiper's conscience.[l] 10 They are physical regulations
and only deal with food, drink, and various washings imposed until the time of
the new order.[m]

NEW COVENANT MINISTRY

11 But Christ has appeared as a high priest
of the good things that have come.[D] In the
greater and more perfect tabernacle not
made with hands (that is, not of this creation[n]), 12 he entered the most holy place
once for all time, not by the blood of goats
and calves, but by his own blood, having
obtained eternal redemption.[o] 13 For if the
blood of goats and bulls and the ashes of a
young cow, sprinkling those who are defiled, sanctify for the purification of the
flesh,[p] 14 how much more will the blood
of Christ, who through the eternal Spirit[q]
offered himself without blemish to God,

[a] 8:10 Zch 8:8; 2Co 3:3; Heb 10:16
[b] 8:11 Is 54:13; Jn 6:45; 1Jn 2:27
[c] 8:12 Jr 31:31-34; Rm 11:27; Heb 10:17
[d] 8:13 2Co 5:17

[e] 9:2 Ex 25:8-9,23-39; 26:1; Lv 24:5-8
[f] 9:3 Ex 26:31-33; 40:3
[g] 9:4 Ex 16:33; 25:10,16; 30:1-5; Nm 17:10; Dt 10:2
[h] 9:5 Ex 25:18-19; Lv 16:2
[i] 9:6 Nm 28:3
[j] 9:7 Ex 30:10; Lv 16:15,34; Heb 5:3
[k] 9:8 Jn 14:6; Heb 10:19-20
[l] 9:9 Heb 5:1; 7:19
[m] 9:10 Lv 11:2-3; Col 2:16
[n] 9:11 Heb 2:17; 8:2; 10:1
[o] 9:12 Dn 9:24; Heb 7:27; 10:4
[p] 9:13 Lv 16:14-15; Nm 19:2,9,17-18
[q] 9:14 1Pt 3:18; 1Jn 1:7

[A] 8:11 Other mss read neighbor   [B] 8:12 Other mss add and their lawless deeds   [C] 8:8-12 Jr 31:31-34   [D] 9:11 Other mss read that are to come

9:1-3 Originally, Israel's **sanctuary** (9:1) was
a **tabernacle** (9:2). Later, under God's direction, they built a permanent structure—a
temple—the interior of which was laid out
in a similar way. The main sections of both
structures were separated by a curtain
between **the holy place** and **the most holy
place** (9:2-3).
9:4-7 Once a year **the high priest alone**
passed through the curtain and entered the
most holy place (9:7). Why? This was where
God manifested his holy presence above
the **ark of the covenant** (9:4). On the Day of

Atonement, the high priest would enter with
the **blood** of a sacrifice offered **for himself
and for the sins the people had committed
in ignorance** (9:7).
9:9 The **sacrifices** couldn't **perfect the
worshiper's conscience**—that is, the old
covenant couldn't change people. God had
prescribed external acts to deal temporarily
with sin because of his holy nature. But following them couldn't bring about an internal
change.
9:12 What the Old Testament high priest did
every year with **the blood of** animals, Christ

did once and for all with **his own blood**. The
Old Testament sacrifices only had a one-year
warranty. But Christ's sacrifice was eternal
and, therefore, obtained lasting redemption.
9:13-14 Whereas the Old Testament sacrifices could cleanse the outside, **the blood
of Christ** can **cleanse our consciences from
dead works so that we can serve the living
God** (9:14). And if you're clean on the inside,
it can work its way out so that dead works
that formerly sought to earn God's favor
become good works that are the result of
our response to God's favor.

a 9:14 Ti 2:14; Heb 6:1;
10:2,22
b 9:15 1Tm 2:5; Heb 8:6;
12:24
c Jr 31:31-34; 1Co 11:25;
2Co 3:6; Heb 7:22; 8:8;
13:20
d Gn 12:7; Rm 8:28; Gl 3:19;
Heb 4:1
e Rm 3:25; 5:6
f 9:19 Ex 24:6-8; Lv 14:4-6
g 9:20 Ex 24:8; Mt 26:28
h 9:21 Ex 29:12; Lv 8:15
i 9:22 Lv 17:11
j 9:23 Heb 8:5
k 9:24 Rm 8:34; Heb
7:25; 8:2
l 9:25 Heb 9:7; 10:19
m 9:26 Mt 24:3; 28:20;
1Co 10:11
n Heb 4:3; 7:27

o 9:27 Gn 3:19; 2Co 5:10
p 9:28 Is 53:12; 1Pt 2:24
q Mk 8:38; 1Th 4:16
r Mt 26:28; 1Co 1:7; Ti 2:13
s 10:1 Col 2:17; Heb
8:5; 9:11
t 10:5-7 Ps 40:6-8; Jr 36:2;
Heb 1:6
u 10:8 Mk 12:33; Heb
10:5-6
v 10:10 Jn 17:19; Heb
7:27; 9:12

cleanse our[A] consciences from dead works so that we can serve the living God?[a]

15 Therefore, he is the mediator[b] of a new covenant,[B,c] so that those who are called might receive the promise[d] of the eternal inheritance, because a death has taken place for redemption from the transgressions committed under the first covenant.[e] **16** Where a will exists, the death of the one who made it must be established. **17** For a will is valid only when people die, since it is never in effect while the one who made it is living. **18** That is why even the first covenant was inaugurated with blood. **19** For when every command had been proclaimed by Moses to all the people according to the law, he took the blood of calves and goats,[c] along with water, scarlet wool, and hyssop, and sprinkled the scroll itself and all the people,[f] **20** saying, **This is the blood of the covenant that God has ordained for you.**[D,g] **21** In the same way, he sprinkled the tabernacle and all the articles of worship with blood.[h] **22** According to the law almost everything is purified with blood, and without the shedding of blood there is no forgiveness.[i]

23 Therefore, it was necessary for the copies of the things in the heavens to be purified with these sacrifices, but the heavenly things themselves to be purified with better sacrifices than these.[j] **24** For Christ did not enter a sanctuary made with hands (only a model[E] of the true one) but into heaven itself, so that he might now appear in the presence of God for us.[k] **25** He did not do this to offer himself many times, as the high priest enters the sanctuary yearly with the blood of another.[l] **26** Otherwise, he would have had to suffer many times since the foundation of the world. But now he has appeared one time, at the end of the ages,[m] for the removal of sin by the sacrifice of himself.[n] **27** And just as it is appointed for people to die once — and

after this, judgment[o] — **28** so also Christ, having been offered once to bear the sins of many,[p] will appear a second time,[q] not to bear sin, but[F] to bring salvation to those who are waiting for him.[r]

THE PERFECT SACRIFICE

10 Since the law has only a shadow of the good things[s] to come, and not the reality itself of those things, it can never perfect the worshipers by the same sacrifices they continually offer year after year. **2** Otherwise, wouldn't they have stopped being offered, since the worshipers, purified once and for all, would no longer have any consciousness of sins? **3** But in the sacrifices there is a reminder of sins year after year. **4** For it is impossible for the blood of bulls and goats to take away sins.

5 Therefore, as he was coming into the world, he said:

> **You did not desire sacrifice**
> **and offering,**
> **but you prepared a body for me.**
> **6** **You did not delight**
> **in whole burnt offerings**
> **and sin offerings.**
> **7** **Then I said, "See —**
> **it is written about me**
> **in the scroll —**
> **I have come to do your will,**
> **O God."**[G,t]

8 After he says above, **You did not desire or delight in sacrifices and offerings, whole burnt offerings and sin offerings** (which are offered according to the law[u]), **9** he then says, **See, I have come to do your will.**[H] He takes away the first to establish the second. **10** By this will, we have been sanctified through the offering of the body of Jesus Christ once for all time.[v]

11 Every priest stands day after day ministering and offering the same sacrifices time after time, which can never

A 9:14 Other mss read *your*　　**B** 9:15 The Gk word used here can be translated covenant, will, or testament, also in vv. 16,17,18.　　**C** 9:19 Some mss omit *and goats*　　**D** 9:20 Ex 24:8　　**E** 9:24 Or *antitype*, or *figure*　　**F** 9:28 Lit *time, apart from sin*,　　**G** 10:5-7 Ps 40:6-8　　**H** 10:9 Other mss add *God*

9:24-26 In other words, Jesus didn't enter a man-made tabernacle that was "a copy and shadow of" God's dwelling (8:5) to offer an animal sacrifice that could only provide temporary external purification (see 9:13). This had been done — over and over (9:25). Instead, Christ offered **the sacrifice of himself** (9:26) to remove sin — internal and external — once and for all so that he might appear in God's presence for you in **heaven** (9:24). Jesus isn't the copy; he's the real thing. His sacrifice doesn't have limited application; it endures forever. **9:27** The phrase, **It is appointed for people to die once—and after this, judgment,**

reminds us that death isn't the end. Human beings, however, typically live as if death is the last word. Therefore, people want to fulfill all their desires before they reach the end. Remember that death is a transition — not a conclusion. Judgment is coming. **9:28** Jesus came the first time **to bear the sins of many**. He's coming **a second time** to grab us. We're now living in the interim between Christ's death and return. **10:1** We need to understand the purpose of **the law**. It reveals our sinfulness and weakness. The law's job was to prove that you and I are sinners based on the holy standard of God.

10:2-4 The sacrifices offered in accordance with the law couldn't purify a person's conscience (10:2), and they certainly couldn't take sin away permanently. Instead, the annual sacrifices served as a **reminder of sins** (10:3). The Old Testament sacrificial system prepared for and pointed the way to something better. **10:10** By trusting in the saving power of Christ's death and resurrection, you **have been sanctified** — that is, you've been set apart for God's purposes and glory. You've been set apart to be Christ's kingdom companion and to live your life in submission to his lordship and kingdom agenda.

APPLICATION QUESTIONS

READ HEBREWS 10:19-25

– How do you typically draw near to God?
– How has your church helped you draw near to God?

take away sins.[a] [12] But this man, after offering one sacrifice for sins forever, sat down at the right hand of God.[A,b] [13] He is now waiting until his enemies are made his footstool.[c] [14] For by one offering he has perfected forever those who are sanctified. [15] The Holy Spirit also testifies to us about this. For after he says:

[16]　　**This is the covenant I will make
　　　　with them
　　after those days,**
the Lord says,
　　**I will put my laws on their hearts
　　and write them on their minds,**
[17]　　and **I will never again remember
　　their sins** and their lawless acts.[B,d]
[18] Now where there is forgiveness of these, there is no longer an offering for sin.

EXHORTATIONS TO GODLINESS

[19] Therefore, brothers and sisters, since we have boldness to enter the sanctuary through the blood of Jesus[e] — [20] he has inaugurated[c] for us a new and living way through the curtain (that is, through his flesh[f]) — [21] and since we have a great high priest over the house of God,[g] [22] let us draw near with a true heart in full assurance of faith, with our hearts sprinkled clean from an evil conscience and our bodies washed in pure water.[h] [23] Let us hold on to the confession of our hope without wavering, since he who promised is faithful.[i] [24] And let us watch out for one another to provoke love and good works, [25] not neglecting to gather together, as some are in the habit of doing, but encouraging each other,[j] and all the more as you see the day approaching.

WARNING AGAINST DELIBERATE SIN

[26] For if we deliberately go on sinning after receiving the knowledge of the truth, there no longer remains a sacrifice for sins,[k] [27] but a terrifying expectation of judgment and the fury of a fire about to consume the adversaries.[l] [28] Anyone who disregarded the law of Moses died without mercy, based on the testimony of two or three witnesses.[m] [29] How much worse punishment do you think one will deserve

[a] 10:11 Nm 28:3; Heb 5:1
[b] 10:12 Rm 8:34; Eph 1:20; Col 3:1; Heb 1:3; 8:1; 12:2; 1Pt 3:22
[c] 10:13 Ps 110:1; Mt 22:44; Mk 12:36; Lk 20:43; Ac 2:34-35; 1Co 15:25; Heb 1:13
[d] 10:16-17 Jr 31:33-34; Heb 8:10,12
[e] 10:19 Eph 2:18; Heb 9:25
[f] 10:20 Jn 10:9; Heb 9:3,8
[g] 10:21 Heb 2:17; 4:14
[h] 10:22 Ezk 36:25; Heb 9:14
[i] 10:23 1Co 1:9; Heb 3:6
[j] 10:25 Ac 2:42; Rm 13:11; Heb 3:13
[k] 10:26 Nm 15:30; Dt 17:12; Heb 6:4; 2Pt 2:20-21; 1Jn 5:16
[l] 10:27 Is 26:11; Zph 1:18; 2Th 1:8
[m] 10:28 Dt 17:6; Heb 2:2

[A] 10:12 Or *offering one sacrifice for sins, sat down forever at the right hand of God*　[B] 10:16-17 Jr 31:33-34　[C] 10:20 Or *opened*

10:11-12 The Levitical priests were fighting a losing battle. They offered **the same sacrifices time after time**, which could not **take away sins** (10:11). This, however, was all part of God's plan so that, at the right time, he could send **this man**—"the last Adam" (1 Cor 15:45)—to offer **one sacrifice for sins forever** and then sit down **at the right hand of God** (Heb 10:12). Jesus finished the job. And when he sat, it was in the seat of authority to exercise his kingdom rule.

10:13 At Christ's return, everyone—those who submit to him now and those who don't (**his enemies**)—will be placed under his authority, and he will rule in his millennial kingdom.

10:16 Through the new covenant work of Christ, God puts his **laws** on your heart. That means God's standard is within you. That's why you experience conviction when you sin by breaking his law. As you grow in your Christian faith, you become more aware of the fact that you fall short of God's standard but increase in your desire to obey him.

10:17-18 At the heart of the new covenant is this beautiful promise: **I will never again remember their sins** (10:17). Your sin debt is paid. There is complete **forgiveness** (10:18). Thus, you are freed to walk with the Lord without guilt or shame and to pursue his purpose for your life with joy.

10:19-21 In light of who Jesus is and what he has done (7:1–10:18), **we have boldness to enter the sanctuary through the blood of Jesus** (10:19). The author is again using the imagery of the tabernacle. You couldn't just go waltzing into God's presence in the most holy place. Only the high priest could enter and only once a year. But through the blood of Jesus our **great high priest**, the **curtain** between God and humanity has been removed (10:20-21). Access has been granted. You can now confidently enter into the presence of God—and you don't have to be ashamed.

10:22 Draw near with a true heart in full assurance of faith. After all, Jesus has already dealt with the things you're ashamed to discuss. God knows our issues, and he's dealt with our problems. You never have to beat around the bush in prayer. Be real with the Father. Boldness in drawing near to God is critical for avoiding divine discipline associated with the willful sin the author addresses later in the chapter.

10:24-25 Connecting to a vibrant, biblically based, loving church is a critical tool that can steer us away from disobedience so that we can avert sin's consequences and avoid divine discipline. Believers who are not a functioning part of a local church are living outside of the will of God and limiting God's work in their lives.

Tragically, some of this letter's readers had started **neglecting to gather together**. They were avoiding the means God had provided to help them. Remember, when your get-up-and-go has gotten up and gone, you need someone who can lift you up. It can be hard to be a Christian. We need to be **encouraging each other** (10:25).

10:26-27 In view here is willful sin against God, sin committed because a believer develops a defiant spirit. Think of a teenager who, when corrected for disobedience, becomes stubborn and says to his parents, "I don't care what you say."

This is rebellion. And it has to be dealt with because unaddressed rebellion only gets worse and can spread. What we see in this passage is not a description of a struggling believer who sins. That's why the author uses the word **deliberately** (10:26). This is a determined mindset to have one's own way.

When a believer continues in this kind of unrepentant rebellion, there are consequences: **judgment** and **fire** (10:27). This is not, however, a reference to hell. Scripture sometimes uses fire to describe God's discipline for believers (see 1 Cor 3:11-15). We've seen throughout Hebrews that the author is speaking to Christians (e.g., "brothers and sisters"; Heb 10:19) whose salvation is secure (e.g., 10:14), so the consequences he's describing refer to the stern discipline of God.

10:28-31 The most severe form of discipline for spiritual disobedience is physical death (see 1 John 5:16). This was the case in Israel for those **who disregarded** the Mosaic law

[a] 10:29 Mt 12:31-32; Eph 4:30; Heb 6:6
[b] 10:30 Dt 32:35-36; Ps 135:14; Rm 12:19
[c] 10:31 Mt 16:16; Lk 12:5
[d] 10:32 Php 1:29-30; Heb 6:4
[e] 10:33 1Co 4:9; Php 4:14; 1Th 2:14
[f] 10:34 Mt 5:12; 1Pt 1:4-5
[g] 10:35 Heb 2:2; 11:26
[h] 10:36 Lk 21:19; Heb 12:1

[i] 10:37-38 Hab 2:3-4; Lk 18:8; Rm 1:17; Gl 3:11; Rv 22:20
[j] 11:1 Rm 8:24; 2Co 4:18
[k] 11:3 Gn 1:1; Jn 1:3; 2Pt 3:5
[l] 11:4 Gn 4:4; 1Jn 3:12
[m] 11:5 Gn 5:21-24; 2Kg 2:11

who has trampled on the Son of God, who has regarded as profane[A] the blood of the covenant by which he was sanctified, and who has insulted the Spirit of grace?[a] 30 For we know the one who has said,

Vengeance belongs to me;
I will repay,[B,C]

and again,

The Lord will judge his people.[D,b] 31 It is a terrifying thing to fall into the hands of the living God.[c]

32 Remember the earlier days when, after you had been enlightened, you endured a hard struggle with sufferings.[d] 33 Sometimes you were publicly exposed to taunts and afflictions, and at other times you were companions of those who were treated that way.[e] 34 For you sympathized with the prisoners[E] and accepted with joy the confiscation of your possessions, because you know that you yourselves have a better and enduring possession.[F,f] 35 So don't throw away your confidence, which has a great reward.[g] 36 For you need endurance, so that after you have done God's will, you may receive what was promised.[h]

37 For yet in a very little while,
the Coming One will come
and not delay.

38 But my righteous one[G] will live
by faith;
and if he draws back,
I have no pleasure[H] in him.[i,j]

39 But we are not those who draw back and are destroyed, but those who have faith and are saved.

LIVING BY FAITH

11 Now faith is the reality[j] of what is hoped for, the proof[k] of what is not seen.[j] 2 For by it our ancestors won God's approval.

3 By faith we understand that the universe was[L] created by the word of God,[k] so that what is seen was made from things that are not visible.[M]

4 By faith Abel offered to God a better sacrifice than Cain did. By faith he was approved as a righteous man, because God approved his gifts, and even though he is dead, he still speaks through his faith.[l]

5 By faith Enoch was taken away, and so he did not experience death. He was not to be found because God took him away.[N] For before he was taken away, he was approved as one who pleased God.[m] 6 Now without faith it is impossible to please God, since the one who draws near to him

[A] 10:29 Or ordinary [B] 10:30 Other mss add says the Lord [C] 10:30 Dt 32:35 [D] 10:30 Dt 32:36 [E] 10:34 Other mss read sympathized with my imprisonment [F] 10:34 Other mss add in heaven [G] 10:38 Other mss read the righteous one [H] 10:38 Lit my soul has no pleasure [I] 10:37-38 Is 26:20 LXX; Hab 2:3-4 [J] 11:1 Or assurance [K] 11:1 Or conviction [L] 11:3 Or the worlds were, or the ages were [M] 11:3 Or so that what is seen was made out of what was not visible [N] 11:5 Gn 5:21-24

(Heb 10:28). Their fellow Jews stoned them. The author says that for the Christian who defies God, there will be a **worse punishment** even than this (10:29). And while we don't see it happen very often, the very idea demonstrates how serious God is about his holiness. In Corinth, some believers became sick and even died because of their disobedience regarding the Lord's Supper (see 1 Cor 11:27-32).

If you persist willfully in the very sin for which Christ died to set you free, you've **trampled on the Son of God** and **insulted the Spirit of grace** (Heb 10:29). Such is the willful rebellion of believers who treat with contempt the high sacrificial price paid by God's Son to bring us our great salvation. God will not ignore this. The sacrifice that saves you from the eternal consequences of sin will not necessarily deliver you from the consequences of sin in history. The Lord vows to **judge his people** (10:30). This is not the side of God you want to see, because **it is a terrifying thing** (10:31; see Rom 11:22).

10:32-34 To **remember the earlier days** is a call to remember what it was like after they were first saved. Their passion for Christ and for the gospel was so strong that they **endured** intense **sufferings (10:32)**, mistreatment, and the **confiscation** of their property.

They didn't quit but **sympathized** with others who were similarly mistreated (10:34). "Persevere as you did before," the author tells them in essence. "Don't give up now!"

10:36 God always keeps his promises. But notice what the writer says: you **receive** what was promised **after** you have done the Lord's **will**. The promise, the reward, the inheritance—some of which is granted in history and the rest in eternity—is attached to performing the will of God.

The longer obedience takes, the longer it takes for the promise to be fulfilled.

Israel should have possessed the promised land in minimal time. However, it took them forty years to enter—not because the promise changed but because they refused to do God's will.

10:37 Make no mistake: Jesus **will come and not delay**. He will move on our behalf in history as we trust and obey him (Jas 5:7-8).

10:38 The writer's talking to believers, describing the difference between those who do and do not experience God's deliverance from or through circumstances. If you want to experience Christ's **pleasure** now and when he comes, then keep moving forward, press on to maturity, and **live by faith**. You became a Christian by faith, and you can only live the Christian life by faith.

11:1-2 To exercise **faith** is to have confidence about an expectation without visible proof that it will happen. What makes this confidence possible? The trustworthiness of the object of faith. The question we must answer is this: Is God trustworthy? And as I like to say, faith is acting like God is telling the truth. Notice that each of the heroes of the faith mentioned in this chapter acted on what they believed.

11:3 God created everything, in all its vastness and complexity. That should encourage us that God may be doing extraordinary things in our lives for our good even when we can't see what he's doing.

11:4 **By faith Abel** worshiped God based on God's standards and expectations: he offered shed blood as a sacrifice rather than just giving him something his own hands had produced. He offered God his best and **was approved**. In fact, **even though he is dead**—murdered by his brother—Abel's faith **still speaks**. It teaches us that access to God's presence is through the blood. That's the kind of legacy you want to leave. You want your life of faith to be a testimony to others, to point them to the truth.

11:5 **Enoch** is one of only two people who **did not experience death** (Elijah is the other; see 2 Kgs 2:1-12). Why? Hebrews says it's because

God Has a Plan for You

GOD LONGS TO BE MORE than just theology on a shelf. He wants to be real to you right now. To accomplish this, sometimes he allows you to get in, or even puts you in, what seems like a hopeless scenario. Similar to what he did with Martha and Mary when their brother Lazarus died, God lets something die for the express purpose of letting you experience a resurrection. He does this because he knows that when you see him for who he really is, you will never view life the same way again.

God wants you to take this new sight and view all of life differently, even the ordinary experiences that you face. He wants you to view them through spiritual eyes rather than through the eyes of a physical world that defines your existence day by day. The reason why so many people are not experiencing more resurrections in their hopeless situations is because they are too earthbound. They are so tied to the physical definitions and expectations of life that they wind up missing out on the spiritual.

No matter what you are facing today, I want to remind you of one very important truth: there is still hope. God has stated in his Word that he has a plan for you and that his plan for you includes both "a future and a hope" (JER 29:11). What stops many people from fully living out God's plan in their lives is losing hope and not trusting in God. God says that "without faith it is impossible to please" him (HEB 11:6). He also says that he will reward your faith if you place it in him.

Friend, before you give up, look up. Fix your eyes on Jesus and set your heart on the truth that what he has said about you will come to pass if you will but believe in him and his Word.

a 11:7 Gn 6:13-22; 1Pt 3:20
b 11:8 Gn 12:1-4,7; Ac 7:2-4
c 11:9 Gn 12:8; 18:1; Ac 7:5;
Heb 6:17
d 11:10 Heb 12:22; 13:14; Rv
21:2,10,14
e 11:11 Gn 17:19; 18:11-14;
21:2
f 11:12 Gn 22:17; Rm 4:19

g 11:13 Mt 13:17; Jn 8:56;
Heb 11:39
h Gn 23:4; 1Ch 29:15; Ps
39:12; 1Pt 1:17
i 11:16 Ex 3:6,15; Mk 8:38;
2Tm 4:18; Heb 13:14
j 11:17 Gn 22:1-10; Jms 2:21
k 11:18 Gn 21:12; Rm 9:7
l 11:19 Rm 4:17
m 11:20 Gn 25:25;
27:26-40
n 11:21 Gn 47:31;
48:1,5,16,20
o 11:22 Gn 50:24-25;
Ex 13:19
p 11:23 Ex 1:16,22; 2:2

must believe that he exists and that he rewards those who seek him. [7] By faith Noah, after he was warned about what was not yet seen and motivated by godly fear, built an ark to deliver his family. By faith he condemned the world and became an heir of the righteousness that comes by faith.[a]

[8] By faith Abraham, when he was called, obeyed and set out for a place that he was going to receive as an inheritance. He went out, even though he did not know where he was going.[b] [9] By faith he stayed as a foreigner in the land of promise, living in tents as did Isaac and Jacob, coheirs of the same promise.[c] [10] For he was looking forward to the city that has foundations, whose architect and builder is God.[d]

➤ HOPE WORDS ➤

The opposite of faith is not doubt;
the opposite of faith is disobedience.

[11] By faith even Sarah herself, when she was unable to have children, received power to conceive offspring, even though she was past the age, since she[A] considered that the one who had promised was faithful.[e] [12] Therefore, from one man — in fact, from one as good as dead — came offspring as numerous as the stars of the sky and as innumerable as the grains of sand along the seashore.[f]

[13] These all died in faith, although they had not received the things that were promised. But they saw them from a distance,[g] greeted them, and confessed that they were foreigners and temporary residents on the earth.[h] [14] Now those who say such things make it clear that they are seeking a homeland. [15] If they were thinking about where they came from, they would have had an opportunity to return. [16] But they now desire a better place — a heavenly one. Therefore, God is not ashamed to be called their God, for he has prepared a city for them.[i]

[17] By faith Abraham, when he was tested, offered up Isaac.[j] He received the promises and yet he was offering his one and only son, [18] the one to whom it had been said, **Your offspring**[B] **will be traced through Isaac.**[c,k] [19] He considered God to be able even to raise someone from the dead;[l] therefore, he received him back, figuratively speaking.[D]

[20] By faith Isaac blessed Jacob and Esau[m] concerning things to come. [21] By faith Jacob, when he was dying, blessed each of the sons of Joseph, and **he worshiped, leaning on the top of his staff.**[E,n] [22] By faith Joseph, as he was nearing the end of his life, mentioned[F] the exodus of the Israelites and gave instructions concerning his bones.[o]

[23] By faith Moses, after he was born, was hidden by his parents for three months, because they saw that the child was beautiful, and they didn't fear the king's edict.[p] [24] By faith Moses, when he had grown up, refused to be called the son of Pharaoh's daughter [25] and chose to suffer with the people of God rather than to enjoy the

---

A 11:11 Or *By faith Abraham, even though he was past age — and Sarah herself was barren — received the ability to procreate since he* B 11:18 Lit seed C 11:18 Gn 21:12 D 11:19 Or *back, as a foreshadowing,* or *as a type* E 11:21 Gn 47:31 F 11:22 Or *remembered*

---

he **pleased God**. That doesn't mean, of course, that if you're pleasing God you won't die! But it does mean that his departure from the world was a direct result of how he lived. **11:6** Do you want to live in a way that pleases God? Then you must operate by **faith**, even if you must do so alone and go against the accepted norms of the day. You must believe with expectation that God responds when you seek to please him.

11:7 Noah took God seriously and acted on what he said. But just consider the obstacles he faced! There was a 120-year gap between God's command to build the ark and the flood, and Noah was instructed to build a tremendously huge boat on dry land. Nevertheless, Noah believed God and obeyed—even though what he'd been asked to do didn't make sense since it had never rained a drop at that point in history (see Gen 2:5).
11:8-10 Often in life, you won't know where God is taking you either. And if you overlook

the spiritual, you will become discouraged. God is the **architect** of the eternal **city**, and he's the architect of the opportunities in your life (11:10).
11:11 When God promised her a child, the aged Sarah laughed (Gen 18:11-12). She thought it was a joke. Eventually, though, she had faith that **the one who had promised was faithful**. It took twenty-five years to get from promise to baby. Oftentimes God doesn't complete what he wants to do in your life until you're spiritually prepared.
11:13-16 Though they could have turned around and given up (11:15), each of the people mentioned in Hebrews 11 was **seeking a homeland** (11:14); they desired **a better place—a heavenly one** (11:16). Their approach to life, then, was based on an eternal perspective, a kingdom perspective. When you know the One who's preparing a better city for you, you can survive any wait.

11:17-19 God told **Abraham** to sacrifice **Isaac**—the very son through whom Abraham was to become the father of a nation (11:17-18). Make no mistake. In one way or another, God will test how much you love him. Do you love the gift or the Giver more?

So, how did Abraham cope when it seemed like God's command contradicted his promise? He considered that God was able to **raise** the **dead** (11:19). And why would he think that? Because Sarah was barren (11:11), and Abraham was "as good as dead" (11:12); nevertheless, it is God who gives life, and he had promises to keep. The receiving back of Isaac is an illustration of the same type of divine intervention that God's people can expect today if they live by faith.
11:20-21 If you're a parent, you're going to pass on many things to your kids. Make sure that you pass them the baton of faith in God above all else.

fleeting pleasure of sin.[a] **26** For he considered reproach for the sake of Christ to be greater wealth than the treasures of Egypt, since he was looking ahead to the reward.[b] **27** By faith he left Egypt behind, not being afraid of the king's anger, for Moses persevered as one who sees him who is invisible.[c] **28** By faith he instituted the Passover and the sprinkling of the blood, so that the destroyer of the firstborn might not touch the Israelites. **29** By faith they crossed the Red Sea as though they were on dry land. When the Egyptians attempted to do this, they were drowned.[d]

30 By faith the walls of Jericho fell down after being marched around by the Israelites for seven days. **31** By faith Rahab the prostitute welcomed the spies in peace and didn't perish with those who disobeyed.[e]

32 And what more can I say? Time is too short for me to tell about Gideon, Barak, Samson, Jephthah,[f] David, Samuel, and the prophets,[g] **33** who by faith conquered kingdoms,[h] administered justice, obtained promises, shut the mouths of lions,[i] **34** quenched the raging of fire, escaped the edge of the sword, gained strength in weakness, became mighty in battle, and put foreign armies to flight.[j] **35** Women received their dead, raised to life again. Other people were tortured, not accepting release, so that they might gain a better resurrection. **36** Others experienced mockings and scourgings, as well as bonds and imprisonment.[k] **37** They were stoned,[A,l] they were sawed in two, they died by the sword, they wandered about in sheepskins, in goatskins,[m] destitute, afflicted, and mistreated. **38** The world was not worthy of them. They wandered in deserts and on mountains, hiding in caves and holes in the ground.

39 All these were approved through their faith, but they did not receive what was promised, **40** since God had provided something better for us, so that they would not be made perfect without us.[n]

THE CALL TO ENDURANCE

12 Therefore, since we also have such a large cloud of witnesses[o] surrounding us, let us lay aside every hindrance and the sin that so easily ensnares us. Let us run with endurance[p] the race that lies before us, **2** keeping our eyes on Jesus,[B] the source and perfecter[c] of our faith. For the joy that lay before him,[D] he endured the cross, despising the shame,[q] and sat down at the right hand of the throne of God.

⟿ HOPE WORDS ⟿

No matter the situation, your Savior is bigger and stronger. Keep your eyes on him.

FATHERLY DISCIPLINE

3 For consider him who endured such hostility from sinners against himself, so that you won't grow weary and give up.[r] **4** In struggling against sin, you have not yet resisted to the point of shedding your blood. **5** And you have forgotten the exhortation that addresses you as sons:

> My son, do not take the Lord's
>   discipline lightly
> or lose heart when you are
>   reproved by him,
> **6**   for the Lord disciplines the one
>   he loves
> and punishes every son
>   he receives.[E,s]

7 Endure suffering as discipline: God is dealing with you as sons. For what son is there that a father does not discipline?

[a] 11:24-25 Ex 2:10-11; Ps 84:10
[b] 11:26 Heb 10:35; 13:13
[c] 11:27 Rm 1:20; Col 1:15-16; 1Tm 1:17
[d] 11:29 Ex 14:22-30
[e] 11:31 Jos 2:1; 6:23
[f] 11:32 Jdg 4:6; 11:1; 13:24
[g] 1Sm 1:20; 16:1,13
[h] 11:33 2Sm 7:11; 8:1-3
[i] Jdg 14:5-6; 1Sm 17:34-37; Dn 6:22
[j] 11:34 Jdg 15:8; 2Kg 20:7; Dn 3:25
[k] 11:36 Gn 39:20; Jr 20:2
[l] 11:37 1Kg 21:13; 2Ch 24:20-21
[m] 1Kg 19:10; 2Kg 1:8

[n] 11:40 Heb 11:16; Rv 6:11
[o] 12:1 Heb 11:2,4-5,39
[p] 1Co 9:24; Heb 10:36
[q] 12:2 Lk 24:26; Php 2:8-9; Heb 13:13
[r] 12:3 Mt 10:24; Gl 6:9
[s] 12:5-6 Jb 5:17; Ps 94:12; Pr 3:11-12; Rv 3:16

A 11:37 Other mss add *they were tempted,*   **B** 12:2 Or *us, looking to Jesus*   **C** 12:2 Or *the founder and completer,* or *pioneer and perfecter*   **D** 12:2 Or *who instead of the joy lying before him*   **E** 12:6 Pr 3:11-12

11:30-31 The walls of Jericho fell as a result of the most bizarre military strategy enacted in history (11:30). And as a result of her willingness to align with God's people in it, **Rahab the prostitute** got recognized alongside Abraham and Moses as a hero in the Hall of Faith (11:31). How can this be? Simple. God tells us, "Your ways are not my ways" (Isa 55:8).

11:37-38 The world neither approved of nor deserved them, but God applauded them. Whose approval are you seeking? You can't please both the world and God.

11:39 The believer is to seek divine approval above the approval of man.

12:1 An Olympic sprinter strips off his warm-up gear to eliminate extra weight and wind resistance. Similarly, we need to jettison unbelief and anything in our lives that might trip us up spiritually and prevent us from running **the race** well all the way to the finish line.

12:2-3 Have you ever been running and felt like you wanted to quit? If someone draws alongside you and encourages you to keep going, it enables you to go farther than you could have managed by yourself. It shifts the focus from your pain to the person helping you, and you get a second wind. Similarly, if you keep your attention on him, **Jesus** will enable you to persevere.

How did Jesus himself reach the finish line? **For the joy that lay before him, he endured the cross.** The Son of God made it through Friday by keeping his eyes on Sunday when he'd go back to the Father in heaven and sit **down at the right hand of the throne of God** (12:2). Regardless of the suffering and trials you're facing, know that resurrection day is coming. Don't **grow weary and give up** (12:3).

12:5-7 Discipline includes both positive and negative repercussions, both instruction and correction. Parents are to instruct their children and train them to live with wisdom (see Prov 1:7-9). But when a child is disobedient, a loving father also disciplines him or her. If a

[a] 12:7-8 Dt 8:5; 1Pt 5:9
[b] 12:9 Nm 16:22; Is 38:16
[c] 12:10 Lv 11:44; 2Pt 1:4
[d] 12:11 Is 32:17; Jms 3:17-18
[e] 1Pt 1:6
[f] 12:12 Jb 4:3-4; Is 35:3
[g] 12:13 Pr 4:26; Gl 6:1
[h] 12:14 Rm 6:22; 14:19
[i] Mt 5:8; 2Co 7:1
[j] 12:15 2Co 6:1; Gl 5:4; Heb 3:12; 10:39
[k] 12:16 1Tm 1:9; 4:7; 6:20; 2Tm 2:16
[l] Gn 25:33
[m] 12:17 Gn 27:34-38

[n] 12:18-20 Ex 19:12-13,18; 20:18-21; Dt 4:11; 5:5,25
[o] 12:21 Dt 9:19
[p] 12:22 Gl 4:26; Heb 11:10
[q] 12:23 Ps 94:2; Lk 10:20; Php 3:12
[r] 12:24 1Tm 2:5; Heb 7:22; 8:6; 9:15
[s] 1Co 11:25; 2Co 3:6; Heb 13:20
[t] Gn 4:10; Heb 11:4
[u] 12:25 Heb 2:2-4; 8:5; 11:7
[v] 12:26 Ex 19:18; Hg 2:6
[w] 12:27 1Co 7:31; 2Pt 3:10
[x] 12:28 Dn 2:44; Heb 13:15
[y] 12:29 Dt 4:24; 2Th 1:8
[z] 13:1 Rm 12:10; 1Pt 1:22

[8] But if you are without discipline — which all receive[A] — then you are illegitimate children and not sons.[a] [9] Furthermore, we had human fathers discipline us, and we respected them. Shouldn't we submit even more to the Father of spirits and live?[b] [10] For they disciplined us for a short time based on what seemed good to them, but he does it for our benefit, so that we can share his holiness.[c] [11] No discipline seems enjoyable at the time, but painful. Later on, however, it yields the peaceful fruit[d] of righteousness to those who have been trained by it.[e]

[12] Therefore, strengthen your tired hands and weakened knees,[f] [13] and make straight paths for your feet, so that what is lame may not be dislocated[B] but healed instead.[g]

WARNING AGAINST REJECTING GOD'S GRACE

[14] Pursue peace with everyone, and holiness[h] — without it no one will see the Lord.[i] [15] Make sure that no one falls short of the grace of God and that no root of bitterness springs up, causing trouble and defiling many.[j] [16] And make sure that there isn't any immoral[c] or irreverent[k] person like Esau, who sold his birthright in exchange for a single meal.[l] [17] For you know that later, when he wanted to inherit the blessing, he was rejected, even though he sought it with tears, because he didn't find any opportunity for repentance.[m]

[18] For you have not come to what could be touched, to a blazing fire, to darkness, gloom, and storm, [19] to the blast of a trumpet, and the sound of words. Those who heard it begged that not another word be spoken to them, [20] for they could not bear what was commanded: **If even an animal touches the mountain, it must be stoned.**[D,n] [21] The appearance was so terrifying that Moses said, **I am trembling with fear.**[E,O] [22] Instead, you have come to Mount Zion, to the city of the living God (the heavenly Jerusalem), to myriads of angels, a festive gathering,[p] [23] to the assembly of the firstborn whose names have been written[r] in heaven, to a Judge, who is God of all, to the spirits of righteous people made perfect,[q] [24] and to Jesus, the mediator[r] of a new covenant,[s] and to the sprinkled blood, which says better things than the blood of Abel.[t]

[25] See to it that you do not reject the one who speaks. For if they did not escape when they rejected him who warned them on earth, even less will we if we turn away from him who warns us from heaven.[u] [26] His voice shook the earth at that time, but now he has promised, **Yet once more I will shake not only the earth but also the heavens.**[G,v] [27] This expression, "Yet once more," indicates the removal of what can be shaken[w] — that is, created things — so that what is not shaken might remain. [28] Therefore, since we are receiving a kingdom that cannot be shaken, let us be thankful. By it, we may serve God acceptably, with reverence and awe,[x] [29] for our God is a consuming fire.[y]

FINAL EXHORTATIONS

13 Let brotherly love[z] continue. [2] Don't neglect to show hospitality, for by doing this some have welcomed angels

[A] 12:8 Lit *discipline, of which all have become participants*   [B] 12:13 Or *so that the lame will not be turned aside*   [C] 12:16 Or *sexually immoral*   [D] 12:20 Ex 19:12   [E] 12:21 Dt 9:19   [F] 12:23 Or *registered*   [G] 12:26 Hg 2:6

good parent takes this matter seriously, how much more does God?

12:8 Illegitimate children in ancient Rome had no rights and could not be beneficiaries of an inheritance. The phrase, **which all receive,** could be translated "of which all are partakers." The Greek term for "partaker" is the same word we saw earlier meaning "companion" or "partner" (1:9; 3:1, 14). Thus, the author is reminding them that if they want to be Christ's special companions/partners/ partakers and receive the inheritance—his kingdom blessings in history and eternity— they must be willing to submit to his fatherly discipline.

12:11 As with any kind of training, regular submission to godly discipline leads to increased strength and righteousness.

12:15 When you're experiencing troublesome circumstances, you're in danger of resenting what God is doing in your life. But **bitterness** will only serve to compound the problems.

12:16-17 The point here is that God has blessings in store for you, an inheritance. Don't be like Esau and foolishly throw away your reward for fleeting, temporal gratification.

12:18-24 Here the author contrasts Mount Sinai with Mount Zion. When the Lord appeared to Israel on Mount Sinai to deliver the law, the people were filled with terror (12:18-21). You won't find comfort in the Ten Commandments either. The law can only identify your weaknesses and indict you. So don't climb Sinai. That's not your mountain. **Instead, you have come to Mount Zion** (12:22). Zion represents the **new covenant** in Jesus Christ (12:24). Only through him are **the spirits of righteous people made perfect** (12:23). Only Jesus can make you everything God wants you to be.

12:25-28 God disrupts the natural order of things in the physical earthly realm in order to reveal his spiritual, eternal kingdom that can't be shaken.

12:29 Tomorrow you may press a hot iron to your wrinkled clothes. But your intent won't be to ruin them. Your goal will be to remove the wrinkles to make your garment fit to wear. Guess what? God wants to wear you and look good in you. So he will apply **a consuming fire** to you. Even though there will be steam and heat, you're going to look good when he's through.

13:2 The Greek word translated **angels** can also mean "messengers." Angels can be divine or human messengers. So whether the messenger God sends you is supernatural or not, remember that **hospitality** opens the door to those who are on a divine mission for your good.

as guests without knowing it.[a] **3** Remember those in prison, as though you were in prison with them, and the mistreated,[A] as though you yourselves were suffering bodily.[b] **4** Marriage is to be honored by all and the marriage bed kept undefiled, because God will judge the sexually immoral and adulterers.[b] **5** Keep your life free from the love of money. Be satisfied with what you have, for he himself has said, **I will never leave you or abandon you.**[c,c] **6** Therefore, we may boldly say,

> **The Lord is my helper;**
> **I will not be afraid.**
> **What can man do to me?**[D,d]

7 Remember your leaders who have spoken God's word to you. As you carefully observe the outcome of their lives, imitate their faith.[e] **8** Jesus Christ is the same yesterday, today, and forever.[f] **9** Don't be led astray by various kinds of strange teachings; for it is good for the heart to be established by grace and not by food regulations, since those who observe them have not benefited.[g] **10** We have an altar from which those who worship at the tabernacle do not have a right to eat.[h] **11** For the bodies of those animals whose blood is brought into the most holy place by the high priest[i] as a sin offering are burned outside the camp.[j] **12** Therefore, Jesus also suffered outside the gate,[k] so that he might sanctify[E] the people by his own blood. **13** Let us then go to him outside the camp, bearing his disgrace.[l] **14** For we do not have an enduring city here; instead, we seek the one to come.[m] **15** Therefore, through him let us continually offer up to God a sacrifice of praise, that is, the fruit of

⌐ **HOPE WORDS** ⌐

Always remember that in
our changing seasons of life,
we have a changeless God.

lips that confess his name.[n] **16** Don't neglect to do what is good and to share, for God is pleased with such sacrifices.[o] **17** Obey your leaders[F] and submit to them, since they keep watch[p] over your souls as those who will give an account, so that they can do this with joy and not with grief, for that would be unprofitable for you. **18** Pray for us, for we are convinced that we have a clear conscience, wanting to conduct ourselves honorably in everything.[q] **19** And I urge you all the more to pray[G] that I may be restored to you very soon.

BENEDICTION AND FAREWELL

20 Now may the God of peace, who brought up from the dead our Lord Jesus — the great Shepherd of the sheep[r] — through the blood of the everlasting covenant,[s] **21** equip[H] you with everything good to do his will, working in us what is pleasing in his sight, through Jesus Christ, to whom be glory forever and ever.[i,f] Amen.

22 Brothers and sisters, I urge you to receive this message of exhortation, for I have written to you briefly. **23** Be aware that our brother Timothy has been released. If he comes soon enough, he will be with me when I see you. **24** Greet all your leaders and all the saints. Those who are from Italy send you greetings. **25** Grace be with you all.[u]

[a] 13:2 Gn 18:3; Mt 25:35
[b] 13:3–4 Mt 25:36; 1Co 6:9
[c] 13:5 Dt 31:6,8; Jos 1:5; Php 4:11
[d] 13:6 Ps 27:1; 56:4,11; 118:6
[e] 13:7 Heb 6:12; 13:17,24
[f] 13:8 Jn 8:58; Heb 1:12
[g] 13:9 Eph 4:14; Col 2:16
[h] 13:10 1Co 9:13; 10:18
[i] 13:11 1Co 9:13; 10:18
[j] Ex 29:14; Lv 16:27
[k] 13:12 Jn 19:17; Ac 7:58
[l] 13:13 Heb 11:26; 1Pt 4:14
[m] 13:14 Mc 3:10; Heb 12:22

[n] 13:15 Lv 7:12; Hs 14:2; Eph 5:20
[o] 13:16 Rm 12:13; Php 4:18
[p] 13:17 Is 62:6; Ezk 3:17; Ac 20:28
[q] 13:18 Ac 23:1; 1Th 5:25
[r] 13:20 Jn 10:11; Ac 2:24; Rm 15:33
[s] Zch 9:11; Heb 7:22; 8:6–10; 9:15; 12:24
[t] 13:21 Rm 11:36; Php 2:13; 1Pt 5:10
[u] 13:22–25 Ac 16:1; Col 4:18; 1Th 3:2; Heb 13:7,17; 1Pt 5:12

[A] 13:3 Or *tortured*   [B] 13:3 Or *mistreated, since you are also in a body*   [C] 13:5 Dt 31:6   [D] 13:6 Ps 118:6   [E] 13:12 Or *set apart*, or *consecrate*   [F] 13:17 Or *rulers*   [G] 13:19 Lit *to do this*   [H] 13:21 Or *perfect*   [I] 13:21 Other mss omit *and ever*

13:3 We are called to care for fellow believers who are being persecuted and incarcerated. Don't focus so much on your problems that you overlook those who are worse off than you. Most of our problems in the western world pale in comparison to the persecution our brothers and sisters are facing around the globe.

13:4 Christians are to respect and celebrate the institution of marriage between one man and one woman because it is God's creation order (see Matt 19:4-6). One way this is accomplished is through honoring **the marriage bed**—that is, through maintaining godly sexual morality and fidelity in marriage.
13:5 Money itself is not bad. Rather, **the love of money** (see 1 Tim 6:10) leads to character corruptions like greed, covetousness, and discontentment.

13:6 A Christian who fears the Lord and not people is free and unstoppable.
13:7-8 Don't forget those who influenced you spiritually and keep their legacy alive. Even though human spiritual leadership may change, **Jesus** remains **the same**, so keep following him (13:8).
13:10-13 The priests in **the tabernacle** served at an altar. Yet, we have a better **altar**—Jesus Christ, who nourishes us with grace (13:10). After the priests sacrificed the **blood** of the **animals**, the animal **bodies** were **burned outside the camp** (13:11). Similarly, **Jesus also suffered**. But he did so **outside the gate** of Jerusalem (13:12). His blood was shed *outside*, not inside the tabernacle or temple.
   There's no refuge in the old covenant sacrificial system. Jesus isn't there. Thus, we also need to go **outside** (i.e., away from dead

religious activity) with him, identifying with him, and **bearing his disgrace** (13:13). Being a serious Christian will mean enduring ridicule and reproach at some level, even by the religious establishment. But take heart. You're in good company.
13:14 This fallen world is not our home; it's a temporary residence. Do you **seek the [city] to come** by living life with an eternal perspective as an unapologetically visible and verbal follower of Jesus Christ?
13:17 Indeed, you should always **obey your** church **leaders** (when they're following Scripture) and pray for them, as well as bring them **joy**.
13:20 The resurrection verifies the truth of Christianity and sets it apart from all other religions. The grave is empty; our Savior and King is alive and reigning.

JAMES

INTRODUCTION

Author

THE AUTHOR IDENTIFIES HIMSELF AS James, but that's a name shared by several New Testament personalities. The first candidate is James the son of Zebedee, brother of John. But he died in AD 44 (see Acts 12:1-2), a date which is too early for him to have written this letter. A second possibility is James the son of Alphaeus (see Mark 3:18). But no early Christian tradition acknowledges him as the author. Most likely, the writer is James the brother of Jesus (Mark 6:3; Acts 1:14; 12:17; 15:13; 21:18; 1 Cor 15:7; Gal 2:9).

Though not a follower of his brother during his earthly ministry (see John 7:3-5), James came to believe in Jesus after his resurrection (Acts 1:14; 1 Cor 15:7). He was a leader in the Jerusalem church and exerted significant influence.

Historical Background

Since James died in AD 62 or 66, his letter was written before this time. There are some similarities between themes in James's letter and the writings of Paul. If time is allowed for the events of Acts 15 and 21 to have occurred (these chapters recount events in which Paul and James were together), then a date between AD 48 and 52 seems the most likely time for the writing of the letter.

The reference "to the twelve tribes dispersed abroad" in James 1:1 suggests that James was writing to Jewish Christians living in or around Palestine. The reference to a synagogue in 2:2 strengthens this view. Since James led the Jerusalem church, it's likely the audience lived in and around there.

Message and Purpose

James is the in-your-face, no-holds-barred apostle. He says in essence, "If you are going to be a Christian, be a real one." This book thus explains what practical Christianity looks like. It's about living out your faith in everyday situations with everyday people, and doing it victoriously.

James opens by talking about trials that affect every area of life. He then exhorts his readers to stop whining and keep going because there's a crown waiting for each of us, not only in heaven but here on earth. Then James tackles discrimination in the church and tells God's people to stop honoring the wrong folks. Some, for instance, had rewarded the rich and ignored the poor even as the ones they were honoring were awaiting their day of reckoning and the ones they were ignoring were God's kingdom priority. James also warns believers to watch their tongues and to quit living by earthly wisdom. He urges God's people to quit fighting and fussing with each other, to submit themselves to God. James says that if God's people will get right with God, they will have his power at their disposal. But if we aren't using our faith, it is dead (useless).

www.bhpublishinggroup.com/qr/te/59_00

Outline

GREETING

1 James,[a] a servant of God[b] and of the Lord Jesus Christ:
To the twelve tribes[c] dispersed abroad.[A,d] Greetings.[e]

TRIALS AND MATURITY

[2] Consider it a great joy, my brothers and sisters, whenever you experience various trials,[f] [3] because you know that the testing of your faith produces endurance. [4] And let endurance have its full effect, so that you may be mature and complete, lacking nothing.

➤ HOPE WORDS ➤

Your greatest lessons in faith are often learned in the dark.

[5] Now if any of you lacks wisdom, he should ask God — who gives to all generously and ungrudgingly — and it will be given to him.[g] [6] But let him ask in faith without doubting.[B] For the doubter is like the surging sea, driven and tossed by the wind. [7] That person should not expect to receive anything from the Lord, [8] being double-minded and unstable in all his ways.[C,h]

APPLICATION QUESTIONS

READ JAMES 1:5-8

– Where do you typically turn when you need to make a decision?

– What does your answer to the previous question reveal about your priorities in life?

➤ HOPE WORDS ➤

Behind every physical disturbance, setback, ailment, or issue that we face lies a spiritual root.

---

[9] Let the brother of humble circumstances boast in his exaltation, [10] but let the rich boast in his humiliation because he will pass away like a flower of the field.[i] [11] For the sun rises and, together with the scorching wind, dries up the grass; its flower falls off, and its beautiful appearance perishes. In the same way, the rich person will wither away while pursuing his activities.[j]

[12] Blessed is the one who endures trials, because when he has stood the test he will receive the crown[k] of life that God[D] has promised to those who love him.[l]

[13] No one undergoing a trial should say, "I am being tempted by God," since God is not tempted by evil, and he himself doesn't tempt anyone. [14] But each person is tempted when he is drawn away and enticed by his own evil desire.[m] [15] Then after desire has conceived, it gives birth to sin, and when sin is fully grown, it gives birth to death.[n]

[16] Don't be deceived, my dear brothers and sisters.[o] [17] Every good and perfect gift is from above, coming down from the Father of lights, who does not change like shifting shadows.[p] [18] By his own choice, he gave us birth by the word of truth so that we would be a kind of firstfruits of his creatures.[q]

---

[a]1:1 Mt 13:55; Mk 6:3; Ac 12:17; 15:13; 21:18; Gl 1:19; 2:9,12; Jd 1
[b]Ac 16:17; Rm 1:1; Eph 6:6; Jms 1:1; 1Pt 2:16; Rv 1:1
[c]Gn 49:28; Ex 24:4; Ezk 47:13; Mt 19:28; Ac 26:7; Rv 21:12
[d]Jn 7:35; 1Pt 1:1
[e]Ti 1:1
[f]1:2 Mt 5:12; 1Pt 1:6
[g]1:5 1Kg 3:9; Pr 2:3–6; Mt 7:7
[h]1:8 Jms 4:8; 2Pt 2:14

[i]1:10 1Co 7:31; 1Pt 1:24
[j]1:11 Ps 102:4,11; Is 40:7
[k]1:12 1Co 9:25; 2Tm 4:8; 1Pt 5:4; Rv 2:10; 3:11
[l]Mt 10:22; Jms 2:5
[m]1:14 Pr 7:6-23
[n]1:15 Jb 15:35; Ps 7:14; Is 59:4; Rm 6:23
[o]1:16 1Co 6:9; Jms 1:19
[p]1:17 Nm 23:19; Mal 3:6; Jn 3:27; 1Jn 1:5
[q]1:18 Jn 1:13; Eph 1:12

[A]1:1 Gk *diaspora*; Jewish people scattered throughout Gentile lands   [B]1:6 Or *without divided loyalties*   [C]1:8 Or *in all his conduct*   [D]1:12 Other mss read *that the Lord*

1:2 In God's providence, you have bad days on purpose. God uses **trials** to develop us spiritually. A *trial* is a divinely-ordained difficulty that God causes or permits so that he may grow us and conform us into the image of his Son (see Rom 8:28-29).

1:3-4 God is working to produce **endurance** in you (1:3), so don't try to short-circuit a trial by illegitimately seeking to exit it. God is trying to make you spiritually **mature and complete** (1:4). Conflicts you experience in the physical world are a means he uses to draw your attention to something in the spiritual world.

1:5 Wisdom is the ability to apply spiritual truth to life's circumstances. How does **God** communicate this **wisdom**? Primarily through prayer and his Word and secondarily through godly counsel.

1:6-8 The **double-minded** person **should not expect to receive** wisdom from God because

he's **unstable**, mixing divine answers with conflicting human answers (1:7-8).

1:9 **The brother of humble circumstances** is a fellow who doesn't have much. James tells this person to **boast in his exaltation**—that is, to glory in the fact that God is conforming him to Christ through his struggle.

1:12 **The crown of life** is kingdom victory in history as a result of passing a test. Everyone is looking for a blessing. Unfortunately, what they often mean by blessing is a car, a house, a mate, a job, or a raise. A true *blessing*, however, is a God-given capacity to experience, enjoy, and extend his goodness in life. Regardless of whether God's blessings include external components, they are intended to bring about *internal* change so that our lives display his kingdom relationship and rule.

1:14-15 Like an expert football coach, the devil studies your game films. He knows

your distinctive weaknesses and tendencies. He knows how to appeal to your **evil desire** so that you'll be **drawn away** to sin (1:14). And **sin** leads to **death**—separation from God (1:15). When believers sin, we break fellowship with God.

1:17 God never changes and always shines. Why does a portion of the earth become dark even though the sun always shines? Because earth keeps turning. God is consistently shining forth his goodness, truth, and grace. So turn *to* him, not *away* from him.

1:18 The Israelites gave God the **firstfruits** of their crops, flocks, and herds. They demonstrated how they valued him by giving him the first and best of what they owned. As God's "firstfruits," you are of highest value to him. You are a son or daughter of the living God. Don't succumb to temptation and lower your dignity.

a 1:19 Pr 10:19; 17:27;
Ec 5:1-2
b 1:21 Eph 1:13; 4:22;
Col 3:8
c 1:22-25 Mt 7:24-27; Rm
2:13; Jms 2:14-20
d 1:25 Jn 13:17; Jms 2:12
e 1:26 Ps 34:13; 39:1; 141:3;
Jms 3:2-3; 1Pt 3:10
f 1:27 Jb 31:17; Is 1:17,23;
Mt 25:36
g Rm 12:2; 1Jn 5:18
h 2:1 Lv 19:15; Dt 1:17; Ac
10:34; Rm 2:11; Eph 6:9;
Col 3:25

HEARING AND DOING THE WORD

19 My dear brothers and sisters, understand this: Everyone should be quick to listen, slow to speak, and slow to anger,*a* **20** for human anger does not accomplish God's righteousness. **21** Therefore, ridding yourselves of all moral filth and the evil that is so prevalent,^A humbly receive the implanted word, which is able to save your souls.*b*

22 But*c* be doers of the word and not hearers only, deceiving yourselves. **23** Because if anyone is a hearer of the word and not a doer, he is like someone looking at his own face^B in a mirror. **24** For he looks at himself, goes away, and immediately forgets what kind of person he was. **25** But the one who looks intently into the perfect law of freedom and perseveres in it, and is not a forgetful hearer but a doer who works — this person will be blessed in what he does.*d*

26 If anyone*c* thinks he is religious without controlling his tongue,*e* his religion is useless and he deceives himself. **27** Pure and undefiled religion before God the Father is this: to look after orphans and widows*f* in their distress and to keep oneself unstained from the world.*g*

THE SIN OF FAVORITISM

2 My brothers and sisters, do not show favoritism as you hold on to the faith in our glorious Lord Jesus Christ.*h* **2** For if someone comes into your meeting wearing a gold ring and dressed in fine clothes, and a poor person dressed in filthy clothes also comes in, **3** if you look with favor on the one wearing the fine clothes and say, "Sit here in a good place," and yet you say to the poor person, "Stand over there," or "Sit here on the floor by my footstool," **4** haven't you made distinctions among yourselves and become judges with evil thoughts?

❧ Questions & Answers ❧

Q In Ephesians 2:11-22, Paul describes the church as a site where God is reconciling Jews and Gentiles into one body. In a world that is still experiencing racial and ethnic strife, what role do you think the church has to play?

A The church should be the model of racial unity. The Bible condemns illegitimate discrimination—that is, discrimination that's not related to sin. James 2:1-4 condemns class discrimination between the rich and the poor. Galatians 2:11-14 condemns racial discrimination between Jews and Gentiles. We thwart the Spirit's work when we deny people the rights and privileges of full participation in the body of Christ based on illegitimate criteria. One of the things that is hindering the church in our culture is our refusal to welcome people based solely on their commitment to Christ, using secular unbiblical criteria as a means of judgment. The church is called to be made up of people from all nations, races, and ethnic groups (see Matt 28:19; Acts 10:34-35; 13:1; Rev 5:9; 7:9), unified and confessing "one faith, one baptism," and "one Lord" (Eph 4:1-6).

FOR THE NEXT Q&A, SEE PAGE 1476.

^A **1:21** Or *the abundance of evil*   ^B **1:23** Or *at his natural face*   ^C **1:26** Other mss add *among you*

1:19-20 Be quick to listen to God's thoughts on a matter, **slow to speak** your own point of view, and **slow to anger** (1:19) should you not like what God has to say in contrast to your own human perspective. God's Word will confront you, but getting angry with him will **not** achieve his righteous plan for your life (1:20). **1:21** Confess and repent of your sin and **humbly receive the implanted word**. Through it, after all, God has implanted in you a new nature. You have everything you need for spiritual growth. But you have to receive it, humbly placing yourself under its authority so that it can **save** you—that is, deliver and transform you. **1:22-25** Without application there can be no spiritual transformation. The Bible calls us to true **freedom**, which is submission to God's perfect Word. To live this way requires going to the Word intentionally—not casually—in

prayer and meditation. The one who submits to transformation by the Word and is **a doer** will be **blessed** (1:25). **1:26-27 If anyone thinks he [or she] is religious**, his or her Christianity must be seen in his or her conversation, compassion, and conduct. First, then, your *conversation* ought to demonstrate mastery of your **tongue** (1:26). Talk less and bless more. Second, if your religion is to be **pure**, it must express itself in *compassion*. **Look after orphans and widows.** Provide for those who can do nothing for you in return because that's what your heavenly Father did for you. Third, practice an in-the-world-but-not-of-the-world religion (see John 17:15-16)—that is, in your *conduct*, keep yourself **unstained** (Jas 1:27). Don't let the world rub off on you. Instead, let your faith rub off on the world.

2:1 One of the ways we become stained by the world (see 1:27) is by practicing discrimination. To illegitimately discriminate against people (we *are* to discriminate against evil) is to make a value judgment based on unbiblical criteria (such as race, class, or culture) and act inappropriately toward them. **2:2-4** If a GQ-looking rich guy **in fine clothes** receives preferential treatment in your church because of his status and wealth, while a **poor person** is disregarded because he seemingly has nothing to offer (2:2-3), you have **made distinctions . . . with evil thoughts** (2:4). Regardless of the motivation for the favoritism—whether race, class, education, gender, or culture—we cannot blame society or our upbringing for this tendency that James calls "evil."

[5] Listen, my dear brothers and sisters: Didn't God choose the poor in this world[a] to be rich in faith[b] and heirs[c] of the kingdom that he has promised to those who love him? [6] Yet you have dishonored the poor.[d] Don't the rich oppress you and drag[e] you into court? [7] Don't they blaspheme the good name that was invoked over you?[f]

[8] Indeed, if you fulfill the royal law prescribed in the Scripture, **Love your neighbor as yourself,**[A,g] you are doing well. [9] If, however, you show favoritism,[h] you commit sin and are convicted by the law as transgressors. [10] For whoever keeps the entire law, and yet stumbles at one point, is guilty of breaking it all.[i] [11] For he who said, **Do not commit adultery,**[B] also said, **Do not murder.**[C,j] So if you do not commit adultery, but you murder, you are a lawbreaker.

[12] Speak and act as those who are to be judged by the law of freedom.[k] [13] For judgment is without mercy to the one who has not shown mercy.[l] Mercy triumphs over judgment.

FAITH AND WORKS

[14] What good is it, my brothers and sisters, if someone claims to have faith but does not have works? Can such faith save him?

[15] If a brother or sister is without clothes and lacks daily food [16] and one of you says to them, "Go in peace, stay warm, and be well fed," but you don't give them what the body needs, what good is it?[m] [17] In the same way faith, if it doesn't have works, is dead by itself.

[18] But someone will say, "You have faith, and I have works."[D] Show me your faith without works, and I will show you faith by my works.[n] [19] You believe that God is one. Good! Even the demons believe — and they shudder.[o]

---

[20] Senseless person! Are you willing to learn that faith without works is useless? [21] Wasn't Abraham our father justified by works in offering Isaac his son on the altar? [22] You see that faith was active together with his works, and by works, faith was made complete,[p] [23] and the Scripture was fulfilled that says, **Abraham believed God, and it was credited to him as righteousness,**[E,q] and he was called God's friend.[r] [24] You see that a person is justified by works and not by faith alone. [25] In the same way, wasn't Rahab the prostitute also justified by works in receiving the messengers and sending them out by a different route?[s] [26] For just as the body without the spirit is dead, so also faith without works is dead.

---

[a] 2:5 Jb 34:19; 1Co 1:27
[b] Lk 12:21; Rv 2:9
[c] Rm 4:13-14; 8:17; Gl 3:29; 4:7; Ti 3:7; Heb 1:2; 11:7
[d] 2:6 1Co 11:22
[e] Ac 8:3; 17:6; 18:12
[f] 2:7 Is 63:19; 65:1; Am 9:12; Ac 15:17
[g] 2:8 Lv 19:18; Mt 22:39
[h] 2:9 Lv 19:15; Dt 1:17; Ac 10:34; Rm 2:11; Eph 6:9; Col 3:25
[i] 2:10 Mt 5:10; Gl 3:10
[j] 2:11 Ex 20:13-14; Dt 5:17-18
[k] 2:12 Mt 7:12,24-29; 19:17-21; 22:36-40; 28:20
[l] 2:13 Jb 22:6; Pr 21:13; Mt 5:7; 18:32-35
[m] 2:14-16 Mt 25:35-36; Lk 3:11; 1Jn 3:16-18
[n] 2:18 Rm 3:28; Heb 11:33; Jms 3:13
[o] 2:19 Dt 6:4; Mt 8:29; Lk 4:34
[p] 2:21-22 Gn 22:9; 1Th 1:3; Heb 11:17
[q] 2:23 Gn 15:6; Rm 4:3; Gl 3:6
[r] 2Ch 20:7; Is 41:8
[s] 2:25 Jos 2:4,6,15; Heb 11:31

[A] 2:8 Lv 19:18   [B] 2:11 Ex 20:14; Dt 5:18   [C] 2:11 Ex 20:13; Dt 5:17   [D] 2:18 The quotation may end here or after v. 18b or v. 19.   [E] 2:23 Gn 15:6

2:5-7 Those who are destitute often recognize their need for a Savior while those living proudly in wealth and comfort frequently miss their need for God.

2:8 When asked about the greatest commandment, Jesus said the law has two sides to it: love God and love your neighbor (see Matt 22:34-40).

2:9 You can't claim to love God while you hate your brother or sister (1 John 4:20). If **you show favoritism**, you don't merely do something socially unacceptable—**you commit sin**.

2:10-11 James's point here is that if you practice discrimination against those made in the image of God, you're **guilty** of sin no matter how many rules you follow.

2:12 In other words, **speak and act** with the knowledge that you will stand before the judgment seat of Christ one day.

2:14 James wants us to know that it's possible for a believer to have a useless **faith**—one that's devoid of good **works**. Some people think that James is contradicting Paul, who said, "A person is justified by faith apart from the works of the law" (Rom 3:28). But Paul is talking about how a sinner becomes a saint, whereas James

is talking about how a saint brings heaven to earth. You cannot merit salvation; it is received by grace through faith in Christ alone (see Eph 2:8-9). Our sanctification, however, requires that our faith express itself in works.

In Greek, the word for **save** can have different meanings based on context. It can refer to being delivered or rescued from challenges or dangers in life (see, e.g., Matt 14:30; Acts 27:20). Here James is discussing a faith that can "save" or "deliver" from the power of sin's consequences in history (cf. Jas 1:21).

2:15-16 James isn't deriding the spiritual; he's simply insisting that it's not enough. If a brother is hungry, he doesn't need a sermon. He needs a ham sandwich! Put your faith in action by helping those in need.

2:17 It's possible to have a useless **faith** that's not accomplishing anything in life. If you say you trust God, it should affect your feet. Once you become a Christian by faith alone, your faith has to get married to works. Then, what you believe about eternity will become alive and real in your history.

2:18 In the Hall of Faith of Hebrews 11, the author repeatedly describes what various Old

Testament figures *accomplished* "by faith." Belief was demonstrated by what they did.

2:21-24 Offering Isaac . . . on the altar (2:21) didn't save **Abraham**; after all, he had already believed God and had his faith credited **as righteousness** (2:23) in Genesis 15:6. It's in Genesis 22 that God called him to sacrifice his son. When Abraham obeyed, God confirmed his intent to bless him and make a great nation of him (Gen 22:15-18). **By works, [his] faith was made complete** or matured (Jas 2:22).

Faith must be demonstrated, not just discussed, to be beneficial in history. A person is *justified by faith* alone apart from works for heaven, but he is *justified by works* for usefulness on earth (2:24).

2:25 Rahab (see Josh 2:15-18) was **justified by works** that others could see—she helped Israel's spies, evidencing the trust she'd already placed in God. This justification by works brought her deliverance and victory in history (see Josh 2:8-19; 6:22-23).

2:26 The **faith** of a believer can atrophy. We can become orthodox corpses unless our faith is put to work.

[a] 3:1 Mt 23:8; Rm 2:20-21;
1Tm 1:7
[b] 3:2 1Kg 8:46; Pr 20:9;
Jms 2:10
[c] Mt 12:37; Jms 1:26;
1Pt 3:10
[d] 3:3 Ps 32:9; 39:1
[e] 3:5 Ps 12:3-4; 73:8-9
[f] 3:6 Ps 120:2-3; Pr 16:27;
Mt 15:11,18
[g] 3:8 Ps 140:3; Ec 10:11;
Rm 3:13
[h] 3:9 Gn 1:26; 1Co 11:7

[i] 3:13 Jms 1:21; 2:18
[j] 3:14 Rm 2:8; 13:13; 2Co
12:20
[k] 3:15 2Th 2:9; 1Tm 4:1;
Jms 1:17; Rv 2:24
[l] 3:17 Lk 6:36; Rm 12:9; 1Co
2:6; Heb 12:11; Jms 2:4
[m] 3:18 Pr 11:18; Is 32:17;
Hs 10:12; Am 6:12; Gl 6:8;
Php 1:11
[n] 4:1 Rm 7:23; Ti 3:9
[o] 4:3 Ps 18:41; 1Jn 3:22; 5:14
[p] 4:4 Jn 15:19; Jms 1:27;
1Jn 2:15

CONTROLLING THE TONGUE

3 Not many should become teachers, my brothers,[A] because you know that we will receive a stricter judgment.[a] [2] For we all stumble in many ways.[b] If anyone does not stumble in what he says, he is mature, able also to control the whole body.[c] [3] Now if we put bits into the mouths of horses so that they obey us,[d] we direct their whole bodies. [4] And consider ships: Though very large and driven by fierce winds, they are guided by a very small rudder wherever the will of the pilot directs. [5] So too, though the tongue is a small part of the body, it boasts great things.[e] Consider how a small fire sets ablaze a large forest. [6] And the tongue is a fire. The tongue, a world of unrighteousness, is placed[B] among our members. It stains the whole body,[f] sets the course of life on fire, and is itself set on fire by hell. [7] Every kind of animal, bird, reptile, and fish is tamed and has been tamed by humankind, [8] but no one can tame the tongue. It is a restless evil, full of deadly poison.[g] [9] With the tongue we bless our Lord and Father, and with it we curse people who are made in God's likeness.[h] [10] Blessing and cursing come out of the same mouth. My brothers and sisters, these things should not be this way. [11] Does a spring pour out sweet and bitter water from the same opening? [12] Can a fig tree produce olives, my brothers and sisters, or a grapevine produce figs? Neither can a saltwater spring yield fresh water.

THE WISDOM FROM ABOVE

[13] Who among you is wise and understanding? By his good conduct he should show that his works are done in the gentleness that comes from wisdom.[i] [14] But if you have bitter envy and selfish ambition in your heart, don't boast and deny the truth.[j] [15] Such wisdom does not come down from above but is earthly, unspiritual, demonic.[k] [16] For where there is envy and selfish ambition, there is disorder and every evil practice. [17] But the wisdom from above is first pure, then peace-loving, gentle, compliant, full of mercy and good fruits, unwavering, without pretense.[l] [18] And the fruit of righteousness[m] is sown in peace by those who cultivate peace.

PROUD OR HUMBLE

4 What is the source of wars and fights among you? Don't they come from your passions[n] that wage war within you?[C] [2] You desire and do not have. You murder and covet and cannot obtain. You fight and wage war.[D] You do not have because you do not ask. [3] You ask and don't receive because you ask with wrong motives, so that you may spend it on your pleasures.[o]

[4] You adulterous people![E] Don't you know that friendship with the world is hostility toward God? So whoever wants to be the friend of the world becomes the enemy of God.[p] [5] Or do you think it's without reason that the Scripture says:

[A] 3:1 Or *brothers and sisters*　　[B] 3:6 Or *places itself*, or *appoints itself*　　[C] 4:1 Or *war in your members*　　[D] 4:2 Or *You desire and do not have, so you murder. You covet and cannot obtain, so you fight and wage war.*　　[E] 4:4 Lit *Adulteresses*

3:1 Why shouldn't **many ... become teachers**? Teachers influence the thinking of others and have the power to lead them astray.

3:3-6 A mouth can set the whole **course of life on fire** (3:6). It can destroy self-esteem, devastate relationships, ruin careers, and kill ministries As sure as a tiny match can set a forest ablaze, the mouth causes harm that is out of proportion to its size. If you want to change the course of your life, you need to ask God to help steer that little rudder called your tongue.

3:7-8 We have seals that clap, dolphins that talk, birds that flip, and dogs that jump through hoops. But the only successful tongue-tamer is God. You need to be filled with Scripture and the Holy Spirit.

3:9-12 James isn't writing to the world. He's exhorting Christians, reminding them that their mouths are polluted. After singing hallelujahs, some families start tearing each other down before they've even departed the church parking lot. If criticizing, gossiping, and swearing come out of your mouth, the content of your heart needs to be addressed.

3:13 James doesn't say that it's the one who has read widely, attained advanced degrees, and can wax eloquently about any subject that **is wise and [has] understanding**. Rather, the wise person shows **that his works are done in the gentleness that comes from wisdom**. In other words, wise deeds are the proof of a wise individual.

3:14-15 **Bitter envy and selfish ambition** may help people to rise on the world stage (3:14). But remember, mere human **wisdom** is an expression of Satan's agenda (3:15). To convey heavenly wisdom, you must communicate with heaven.

4:1 Ask people why they're fighting, and they're likely to point their fingers at others. But James insists that wars **come from ... within you**.

4:2-3 The human heart manufactures desires, frequently selfish ones. These can range from the mundane ("I want a little peace and quiet") to the weighty ("I want power and significance"). When someone prevents you from satisfying a **desire**, you are tempted to view that person as an enemy to be defeated. Therefore, the natural tendency is to **murder and covet** (4:2). It's not necessarily that you intend to slay anyone physically. Jesus, after all, reminds us that murder begins in the heart with hatred (see Matt 5:21-26).

Many people **don't receive** what they want from God either because they **do not ask** or they **ask with wrong motives** (Jas 4:2-3). The kingdom of God and the needs of others don't factor into the equation. A helpful question to pose when we pray about something for ourselves is this: How will God's program be advanced through the granting of my request?

4:4 When we want the satisfaction of our own desires above all else, we commit idolatry and worship something other than God. Worldliness and godliness cannot coexist.

4:5-6 The **Lord is a jealous God** (see Exod 34:14) who won't share his bride (the church) with false gods. So, what does a holy, jealous God do when his people foolishly pursue the

The spirit he made to dwell in us envies intensely?[A,a]

6 But he gives greater grace. Therefore he says:

> God resists the proud,
> but gives grace to the humble.[B,b]

7 Therefore, submit to God. Resist the devil, and he will flee from you.[c] **8** Draw near to God, and he will draw near to you. Cleanse your hands, sinners, and purify your hearts, you double-minded.[d] **9** Be miserable and mourn and weep. Let your laughter be turned to mourning and your joy to gloom.[e] **10** Humble yourselves before the Lord, and he will exalt you.

11 Don't criticize one another, brothers and sisters. Anyone who defames or judges a fellow believer[c] defames and judges the law. If you judge the law, you are not a doer of the law but a judge.[f] **12** There is one lawgiver and judge[D] who is able to save

and to destroy. But who are you to judge your neighbor?[g]

OUR WILL AND GOD'S WILL

13 Come now, you who say, "Today or tomorrow we will travel to such and such a city and spend a year there and do business and make a profit."[h] **14** Yet you do not know what tomorrow will bring — what your life will be! For you are like vapor that appears for a little while, then vanishes.[i] **15** Instead, you should say, "If the Lord wills, we will live and do this or that." **16** But as it is, you boast in your arrogance. All such boasting is evil.[j] **17** So it is sin to know the good and yet not do it.[k]

WARNING TO THE RICH

5 Come now, you rich[l] people, weep and wail over the miseries that are coming on you. **2** Your wealth has rotted and your clothes are moth-eaten.[m] **3** Your gold and silver are corroded, and their corrosion will be a witness against you and will eat your flesh like fire. You have stored up treasure in the last days.[n] **4** Look! The pay that you withheld from the workers[o] who mowed your fields cries out, and the outcry of the harvesters has reached the ears of the Lord of Hosts.[E,p] **5** You have lived luxuriously on the earth and have indulged yourselves. You have fattened your hearts[q] in a day of slaughter.[r] **6** You have

a 4:5 1Co 6:19; 2Co 6:16
b 4:6 Ps 138:6; Pr 3:34; Mt 23:12
c 4:7 Eph 4:27; 6:11; 1Pt 5:8-9
d 4:8 2Ch 15:2; Is 1:16; Jms 1:8
e 4:9 Mt 5:4; Lk 6:25
f 4:11 Mt 7:1; Jms 1:22; 1Pt 2:1
g 4:12 Mt 10:28; Rm 14:4
h 4:13 Pr 27:1; Lk 12:18-20
i 4:14 Jb 7:7; Ps 102:3
j 4:15-16 Ac 18:21; 1Co 5:6
k 4:17 Lk 12:47-48; Jn 9:41; 2Pt 2:21
l 5:1 Pr 11:28; Lk 6:24
m 5:2 Jb 13:28; Is 50:9; Mt 6:19-20
n 5:3 Rm 2:5; Jms 5:8
o 5:4 Lv 19:13; Jb 24:10-11; Jr 22:13; Mal 3:5
p Dt 24:15; Rm 9:29
q 5:5 Jb 21:13; Am 6:1
r Jr 12:3; 25:34

A 4:5 Or Scripture says: He jealously yearns for the spirit he made to live in us?, or Scripture says: The Spirit he made to dwell in us longs jealously?
B 4:6 Pr 3:34   C 4:11 Or his brother or sister   D 4:12 Other mss omit and judge   E 5:4 Gk Sabaoth ; or the Lord of Armies

world and treat him like an enemy? Well, **God resists the proud** (Jas 4:6).

If you place yourself in opposition to God through your attachment to the world, he'll oppose you because such pride imitates the king of pride, Satan, who exalted himself above God (see Isa 14:12-14). The only solution is to **humble** yourself before him in order to experience the outpouring of his **grace** (Jas 4:6). Pride is like a beard. It grows without our cultivation, and we have to daily, humbly shave it off.

4:7 To **submit to God** is to recognize your weakness, to stop fighting, and to surrender to him as your ultimate and final authority (see Rom 12:1-2).

Satan is stronger than you, smarter than you, and has been practicing his craft for millennia. There's only one way to **resist** him: the same way the King of kings resisted him—by wielding Scripture (see Matt 4:1-11). When the devil whispers his lies to your conscience, proclaim the truth of the Word of God, and **he will flee from you** as he fled from Christ (see Matt 4:11). **4:8** To **draw near to God** is to come into his presence with prayer, praise, and obedience.

However, if you reserve this for Sundays only, you won't draw near enough.

To **cleanse your hands** requires taking personal responsibility for sin and refusing to downplay it. Some people don't receive the help they need from God because they "don't sin." Rather, they "make mistakes." But Jesus didn't die for mistakes; he died for sins. To call sin anything else is a symptom of pride. **4:11-12** Jesus said the great commandments are love God and love **your neighbor** as yourself (4:12; see Mark 12:28-31). So if you judge **a fellow believer**, you're judging **the law** that commands us to love others (Jas 4:11). Remember, that brother or sister you criticize could have been you. As God has shown you grace and mercy, practice grace and mercy. **4:14** Life has too many variables for you to guarantee your tomorrow. By contrast, God's kingdom agenda is assured because he's an omniscient (all-knowing) and omnipotent (all-powerful) eternal King. Your agenda is uncertain at best. You're like **vapor** that **vanishes**. Here for a moment and then gone. **4:15** You should acknowledge that your plans fall within a larger, controlling reality: the will

of God. Make your plans (see Prov 16:9), but then submit them to the Lord for approval. To do something **if the Lord wills** is not a pious phrase but a philosophy of life. Jesus's "food" was doing the will of his Father (John 4:34), so put it on your menu.
5:1 Some of God's servants were wealthy (e.g., Abraham, Job), and money was not their problem. What is condemned here is a mindset that turns gold into a god. The key is to recall Jesus's teaching, "Don't store up for yourselves treasures on earth. . . . But store up for yourselves treasures in heaven. . . . For where your treasure is, there your heart will be also" (Matt 6:19-21).
5:4 God greatly condemns economic injustice in the workplace.
5:5 Remember the rich young ruler of Matthew 19:16-22? Remember Jesus's story of the rich man and Lazarus in Luke 16:19-31? Materialism (when the physical and financial take precedence over the spiritual and the eternal) has a high price tag.
5:6 That they had **murdered the righteous** probably means they hated (murdered in their hearts; see 4:2) those less fortunate than they.

[a] 5:6 Heb 10:38; Jms 4:2
[b] 5:7 Dt 11:14; Jr 5:24;
Hs 6:3
[c] 5:8 Rm 13:11; Php 4:5;
1Pt 4:7
[d] 5:9 Mt 24:33; 1Co 4:5;
Jms 4:12; 1Pt 4:5
[e] 5:11 Jb 1:21-22; 2:10;
42:10-12
[f] Ex 34:6; Nm 14:18;
Mt 5:10

[g] 5:12 Mt 5:33-37; 23:16-
22; Mk 7:9-13
[h] 5:13 Ps 50:15; Col 3:16
[i] 5:14 Mk 6:13; 16:18
[j] 5:15 Is 33:24; Mt 9:2; Mk
2:5; Lk 24:47
[k] 5:16 Nm 11:2; Mt 3:6; Jn
9:31; 1Pt 2:24

❧ Questions & Answers ❧

Q Since prayer is an important part of accessing God's power, what are some tips you can give to those seeking to deepen their prayer lives?

A First, we have to understand what prayer is. Prayer is our communication vehicle, given to us by God to connect us with him. God wants to be involved in history, but he has determined that he will do this through humanity. To pray is to invite the involvement of eternity into time. So the idea behind prayer is to go to God, recognizing who he is through praise and worship, and communicating what you need. When you make specific requests in prayer, you must make sure that you are in alignment with God's expectations. For example, Peter tells husbands that if they are at odds with their wives and don't live with them "in an understanding way," their prayers will "be hindered" (1 Pet 3:7). Division between husband and wife blocks the prayer from getting through. Therefore, you have to make sure you deal with any unaddressed issues so that you are in alignment. Then you make your request known to God, giving him permission "to do above and beyond all that we ask or think" (Eph 3:20). Make your request specific, but then submit to his will. After all, God's will is always better than your request.

FOR THE NEXT Q&A, SEE PAGE 1497.

condemned, you have murdered the righteous, who does not resist you.[a]

WAITING FOR THE LORD

7 Therefore, brothers and sisters, be patient until the Lord's coming. See how the farmer waits for the precious fruit of the earth and is patient with it until it receives the early and the late rains.[b] **8** You also must be patient. Strengthen your hearts, because the Lord's coming is near.[c]

9 Brothers and sisters, do not complain about one another, so that you will not be judged. Look, the judge stands at the door![d]

10 Brothers and sisters, take the prophets who spoke in the Lord's name as an example of suffering and patience. **11** See, we count as blessed those who have endured.[A] You have heard of Job's endurance[e] and have seen the outcome that the Lord brought about — the Lord is compassionate and merciful.[f]

TRUTHFUL SPEECH

12 Above all, my brothers and sisters, do not swear, either by heaven or by earth or with any other oath.[g] But let your "yes" mean "yes," and your "no" mean "no," so that you won't fall under judgment.[B]

EFFECTIVE PRAYER

13 Is anyone among you suffering? He should pray. Is anyone cheerful? He should sing praises.[h] **14** Is anyone among you sick? He should call for the elders of the church, and they are to pray over him, anointing him with oil in the name of the Lord.[i] **15** The prayer of faith will save the sick person, and the Lord will raise him up; if he has committed sins, he will be forgiven.[j] **16** Therefore, confess your sins to one another and pray for one another, so that you may be healed. The prayer of a righteous person is very powerful in its effect.[k] **17** Elijah was a human being as we are, and he prayed earnestly that it would not rain, and for three years and six months it did

[A] 5:11 Or *persevered*   [B] 5:12 Other mss read *fall into hypocrisy*

5:7-8 The Lord's coming is a reference to God's divine intervention into our historical circumstances. Many people equate patience with twiddling their thumbs. But that's not biblical patience. James illustrates the concept using the **farmer**. He doesn't sit on his porch in a rocker. The farmer must fulfill his responsibilities on earth. Similarly, Christians must act responsibly and faithfully in history.
5:12 Give a simple **yes** or **no** because if you have to swear to convince someone that you're sincere, you have a reliability problem.

5:13 These responses acknowledge that affliction and blessing both come from the Lord, who works through them to accomplish his purposes.
5:14 In these verses, James addresses any person who is **sick**. The Greek word from which this is translated can mean "weak." Thus, it can refer to any kind of weakness, physical or otherwise. Those beaten down and struggling to pray, then, can seek help from **the elders**—the male spiritual leadership of the church.
5:15 This cannot be saying that *every* physical sickness will be healed. That would suggest

we would never die. The application is wider. The **prayer** offered in **faith** will provide divine encouragement in the midst of problems.
5:16 Suffering and sickness do not necessarily result from sin. Job, for instance, was afflicted even though he didn't sin (Job 1). Moreover, Jesus made it clear that a person can be stricken with an illness or condition that has no connection to wrongdoing (John 9:1-3). On the other hand, a sinful lifestyle *can* result in weakness and suffering. Therefore, if needed, **confess your sins to** a trusted, spiritually mature believer. If you will deal with your sin, you will see God work in your life.

not rain on the land.*ª* **¹⁸** Then he prayed again, and the sky gave rain and the land produced its fruit.*ᵇ*

¹⁹ My brothers and sisters, if any among you strays from the truth,*ᶜ* and someone turns him back,*ᵈ* **²⁰** let that person know that whoever turns a sinner from the error of his way will save his soul from death and cover a multitude of sins.*ᵉ*

ª 5:17 1Kg 17:1; 18:1; Lk 4:25; Ac 14:15
ᵇ 5:18 1Kg 18:41–45; Jms 3:17–18
ᶜ 5:19 Mt 18:15; Gl 6:1; Jms 3:14

5:19 *ᵈ* Ps 51:13; Dn 12:3; Mal 2:6; Lk 1:16   *ᵉ* 5:20 Pr 10:12; Rm 11:14; 1Pt 4:8

5:19-20 One who **strays from the truth** is a backslider (5:19). He or she is not progressing in the faith but regressing. The most famous example of this is Peter, who denied his Lord (see Matt 26:69-75).

These verses are not so much about the backslider as they are about those around him or her. Though many believers fail to comprehend their responsibility to the family of faith, your Christianity is real when you see a brother or sister in Christ backsliding

and act in love. You cannot be a passive believer.

The one who **turns a sinner from the error of his way will save his soul from death** (Jas 5:20). James is referring to a Christian, so he's not talking about losing salvation. "Death" here may mean untimely physical death. The New Testament describes instances in which Christians died early. Sometimes God takes a straying and unrepentant believer home (see 1 Cor 11:30). It also can refer metaphorically

to deterioration in circumstances because the intimate presence of God is no longer operating in a rebellious person's life.

God says you and I have the power to intercept straying Christians on the road to spiritual misery. By doing so, we **cover a multitude of sins** (Jas 5:20). James alludes here to Proverbs 10:12, which says, "Love covers all offenses." Believers can be used of God to provide a covering for past sins and lead an erring brother or sister to restoration. May we do so.

1 PETER

INTRODUCTION

Author

THE AUTHOR CLAIMS TO BE "Peter, an apostle of Jesus Christ" (1:1). He maintains he is an "elder and witness" to Christ's sufferings (5:1). Moreover, his exhortation to "shepherd God's flock" (5:2) is reminiscent of the charge Jesus gave to Peter in John 21:15-17. Several themes in 1 Peter appear in Peter's sermons in Acts, such as the God "who judges impartially" (1 Pet 1:17; cf. Acts 10:34); the idea that God "raised [Jesus] from the dead and gave him glory" (1 Pet 1:21; cf. Acts 2:32-36); and truth about "the stone that the builders rejected" being the cornerstone (1 Pet 2:7-8; cf. Acts 4:10-11).

Some critical scholars have disputed this claim of authorship, arguing that someone else wrote the letter in Peter's name. But their theories are inconclusive and cannot be proven. Several early church leaders—Irenaeus, Tertullian, and Clement of Alexandria—accepted 1 Peter as authentic. Furthermore, there are examples of the early church rejecting the practice of writing under an apostolic pseudonym as forgery. They likely would have dismissed the letter if they had believed it to be falsely attributed to Peter. In light of this, the book should be accepted as the apostle Peter's work.

Historical Background

Peter wrote to Christians in various regions of Asia Minor, the area we know today as Turkey. The recipients of the letter were primarily Jewish believers (but included some Gentile believers) since Peter refers to them as sojourners of the *dispersion* ("dispersed abroad," 1:1). The Greek word *diaspora*, which is behind that phrase, referred to Jews who were separated from their homeland. Though they had earlier been involved in idolatry (4:3) and were ignorant (1:14) and empty (1:18) before coming to Christ, they had since been accepted as "God's people" (2:9-10). They were experiencing some form of persecution for their faith (1:6; 2:19; 3:16; 4:12-19).

The cryptic statement in 5:13 suggests that Peter probably wrote the letter from Rome. "Babylon" was used cryptically for the capital of the Roman Empire. Peter doesn't mention Paul's presence at the end of the letter, and Paul doesn't mention Peter's presence in the letters he wrote while under house arrest in Rome (AD 60–62). Therefore, Peter likely wrote 1 Peter in Rome

after Paul was released and before 2 Peter was written—between AD 62 and 64.

Message and Purpose

Peter loved to lead, but he had to go through a lot of brokenness to learn how. He thus wrote this book to churches to encourage them to persevere in spite of their own suffering, trials, and persecution. Peter wanted believers to know that new birth in Christ gives hope that will aid perseverance in spite of what we go through. Peter blends doctrinal truth about our salvation with practical truth about how it is to be lived out in our various life situations—including in the relationships between husbands and wives.

Peter knew about suffering because he had experienced it as a disciple of Christ. But he also learned how to endure it with joy and victory rather than with sadness and defeat. This is a lesson we need today as our own culture grows increasingly hostile against the Christian faith. If we are going to be real kingdom citizens, our salvation has to become a visible reality that affects all we do. Peter tells us we need a Christianity that can be seen, even in a world that opposes and rejects us.

www.bhpublishinggroup.com/qr/te/60_00

Outline

GREETING

1 Peter,[a] an apostle of Jesus Christ:
To those chosen, living as exiles[b] dispersed[c] abroad[A] in Pontus, Galatia, Cappadocia, Asia, and Bithynia,[d] chosen[e] **2** according to the foreknowledge[f] of God the Father, through the sanctifying work of the Spirit,[g] to be obedient[h] and to be sprinkled with the blood[i] of Jesus Christ.
May grace and peace be multiplied to you.

A LIVING HOPE

3 Blessed be the God and Father of our Lord Jesus Christ.[j] Because of his great mercy[k] he has given us new birth[l] into a living hope[m] through the resurrection of Jesus Christ from the dead[n] **4** and into an inheritance that is imperishable,[o] undefiled, and unfading, kept in heaven[p] for you. **5** You are being guarded by God's power[q] through faith for a salvation that is ready to be revealed in the last time.[r] **6** You rejoice in this,[B] even though now for a short time, if necessary, you suffer grief in various trials[s] **7** so that the proven character of your faith[t] — more valuable than gold which, though perishable, is refined by fire[u] — may result[v] in praise, glory, and honor[w] at the revelation of Jesus Christ.[x] **8** Though you have not

---

∽ HOPE WORDS ∽

The purpose of trials is to see if you believe what you say you believe.

---

seen[y] him, you love him;[z] though not seeing him now, you believe in him, and you rejoice[aa] with inexpressible and glorious joy, **9** because you are receiving the goal of your faith, the salvation of your souls.

10 Concerning this salvation, the prophets,[ab] who prophesied about the grace that would come to you, searched and carefully investigated. **11** They inquired into what time or what circumstances the Spirit of Christ[ac] within them was indicating when he testified in advance[ad] to the sufferings of Christ[ae] and the glories[af] that would follow.[c] **12** It was revealed to them that they were not serving themselves but you. These things have now been announced to you through those who preached the gospel to you[ag] by the Holy Spirit sent from heaven[ah] — angels long to catch a glimpse of these things.

A CALL TO HOLY LIVING

13 Therefore, with your minds ready for action,[ai] be sober-minded[aj] and set your hope[ak] completely on the grace to be brought to you at the revelation[al] of Jesus Christ. **14** As obedient children,[am] do not be conformed to the desires of your former ignorance. **15** But as the one who called you[an] is holy,[ao] you also are to be holy in all your conduct; **16** for it is written, **Be holy, because I am holy.**[D,ap] **17** If you appeal to the Father who judges impartially[aq] according to each one's work,[ar] you are to conduct yourselves in reverence[as] during your time living as strangers. **18** For you know that

---

Cross references:
[a]1:1 Lk 6:14; Ac 10:32
[b]Gn 23:4; Ps 39:12; Heb 11:9,13; 1Pt 2:11
[c]Jn 7:35; Jms 1:1
[d]Ac 2:9; 6:9; 16:6-7; Gl 1:2
[e]Mt 22:14; 24:22; Ti 1:1
[f]1:2 Rm 8:29; 1Pt 1:20
[g]2Th 2:13
[h]1Pt 1:14,22
[i]Heb 9:12; 10:22; 12:24
[j]1:3 2Co 1:3; Eph 1:3
[k]Gl 6:16; Ti 3:5
[l]Jn 1:13; 3:3,7; Jms 1:18; 1Pt 1:23
[m]Ac 23:6; 1Th 1:3
[n]1Co 15:20; 1Pt 3:21
[o]1:4 Ac 20:32; Rm 8:17; Col 3:24
[p]2Tm 4:8
[q]1:5 Jn 10:28; Php 4:7
[r]Rm 8:18; 2Co 4:17; Heb 12:11; 1Pt 4:13; 5:1,10; Rv 15:1; 21:9
[s]1:6 Jms 1:2; 1Pt 4:12
[t]1:7 Jms 1:3
[u]Is 48:10; Zch 13:9; Mal 3:3; 1Co 3:13
[v]2Co 5:3; Php 3:9; Rv 14:5
[w]Rm 2:7,10,29; 1Co 4:5
[x]Lk 17:30
[y]1:8 Ex 33:20; Rm 8:24
[z]1Jn 4:20
[aa]1:10 Lk 1:70; 10:24; 16:16,29; 18:31; 24:25,27,44
[ac]1:11 Rm 8:9
[ad]Mt 26:24
[ae]Mk 8:31; Lk 24:26; Php 3:10
[af]Lk 24:26
[ag]1:12 Mk 16:15; 1Co 9:14; 2Co 10:16
[ah]Jn 14:26; 15:26; Ac 1:8; 2:2-4; 13:4
[ai]1:13 Ex 12:11
[aj]1Pt 5:8
[ak]Mt 12:21; Rm 8:24; 1Th 1:3
[al]1Pt 4:13; 5:4
[am]1:14 Heb 2:13
[ao]Lk 1:49; 1Co 7:14
[ap]1:16 Lv 11:44-45; 19:2; 20:7
[aq]1:17 Ac 10:34; Rm 2:11; Gl 2:6; Eph 6:9
[ar]1Co 3:12
[as]1:15 Ac 9:31; Rm 3:18; 2Co 5:11; 7:1; Eph 5:21; Php 2:12
[an]1:15 Gl 1:6; 5:8; 1Th 2:12; 5:24; 1Pt 5:10

[A]1:1 Gk *diaspora*; Jewish people scattered throughout Gentile lands　　[B]1:6 Or *In this fact rejoice*　　[C]1:11 Or *the glories after that*　　[D]1:16 Lv 11:44-45; 19:2; 20:7

1:1-2 Peter was writing to Jewish (and some Gentile) Christians who were **dispersed** among Gentile nations. His greeting highlights the saving work of each member of the Trinity. The Christian recipients were **chosen according to the foreknowledge of God the Father, through the sanctifying work of the Spirit, to be obedient and to be sprinkled with the blood of Jesus Christ.**

1:3 Salvation is a **new birth into a living hope**, which is a positive expectation about the future. When you were born the first time, it was into a dead hope. You were born to die. But, **through the resurrection of Jesus**, there's a better future on the horizon. His resurrection guarantees your own (see 1 Cor 15:30-32).

1:4 Inheritance includes our rewards for faithfulness and fidelity to the King and his kingdom. Ever made a hotel reservation only to discover that the hotel had no record of it when you showed up? That won't happen with this reservation because it is **kept in**

heaven. No one can take it, lose it, or hack it out of God's heavenly computer.

1:5 If you are truly born again, you're not going anywhere—not because of your power to hold on to God, but because God has an omnipotent grip on you (see John 10:27-29).

1:6-7 All **trials** are designed to do three things: prove your faith, develop your faith, and glorify your Savior. You never know what you believe until you face a test. The heavenly goldsmith wants to refine your character.

1:8-9 You **love** Christ by seeking his glory, so determine how you can bring him the most glory in a given circumstance and do it. You **believe** Christ—or trust him—by obeying him. Trusting Christ isn't a feeling; it's a decision to obey (1:8). *Rejoicing* in Christ means thanking and praising him **because you are receiving the goal of your faith . . . salvation** (1:9). This is not a reference to eternal salvation; the first readers already had it (see 1:4). It's about the future rewards that await us.

1:14-16 God is **holy**, which means, "separate" or "set apart" (1:15-16).He's distinct from his creation, unstained by sin, and is the standard of righteousness. Holiness is central to who God is. He is never described in the Bible as "love, love, love" or "sovereign, sovereign, sovereign." But the angelic beings emphasize that he is "holy, holy, holy" (Isa 6:3; Rev 4:8). This perfect holiness is at the heart of his other attributes. Everything about him is in a class by itself. And he calls his people to pursue holiness by seeking to please him in every dimension of their lives.

1:17 Those who come to God through Jesus address him as **Father** and are to **conduct** themselves **in reverence** for God by taking him seriously. Since he is holy, we are to be holy. Non-Christians should be viewing you as a little strange because you're seeking to conform to God's standards and not the world's.

1:18-19 To *redeem* is to pay a price to set someone free. What did it cost to free you from slavery to sin? Not **silver or gold** but

a 1:18 2Pt 3:11
b Is 52:3; 1Co 6:20; Ti 2:14; Heb 9:12
c 1:19 Jn 6:53; Ac 20:28; 1Co 10:16; Eph 2:13; Heb 10:19
d Ex 12:5; Lv 4:32; Is 53:7; Jn 1:29
e 1:20 Ac 2:23; Eph 1:4; 1Pt 1:2; Rv 13:8
f 2Pt 3:3; Jd 18
g 1:21 Ac 10:45; Rm 4:24; 10:9; Eph 1:1; 1Tm 4:12; 6:2
h Ac 2:24; Rm 10:9
i Jn 17:5,24; 1Tm 3:16; Heb 2:9
j 1:22 Zch 7:9; Jn 13:34; 12:10; 1Th 4:9; 1Jn 4:7
k 1Tm 1:5
l 1:23 1Pt 1:3
m 1Jn 3:9
n Lk 8:21; Heb 4:12
o 1:24 1Pt 5:4
p 1:24-25 Is 40:6-8; Lk 21:33; Jms 1:10-11; 1Jn 2:17
q 2:1 Rm 13:12
r 2Co 12:20
s 2:2 1Co 3:2; 9:7; Heb 5:12-13

t 2:3 Heb 6:4-5
u Ps 34:8; Ti 3:4
v 2:5 Rm 12:1; Heb 13:15
w 2:6 Ps 9:11; Heb 12:22
x Eph 2:20
y Is 28:16; Rm 9:33; 10:11
z 2:7 Ps 118:22; Mt 21:42; Lk 20:17; Ac 4:11
aa 2:8 Is 8:14; Rm 9:33; 14:20
ab Ac 2:23; 4:27-28; Rm 9:22; 11:7; Jd 4
ac 2:9 Dt 7:6; 10:15; Is 43:20
ad Is 61:6; Rv 1:6; 5:10; 20:6
ae Ex 19:6
af Ex 34:9; Dt 7:6; Ps 33:12; Is 43:21; Ti 2:14
ag Is 42:12; 43:21
ah Is 9:2; Ac 26:18; Eph 5:8; Col 1:12-13
ai 2:10 Mt 5:7; Mk 5:19; Lk 1:50

you were redeemed from your empty way of life*a* inherited from your fathers, not with perishable things like silver or gold,*b* 19 but with the precious blood of Christ,*c* like that of an unblemished and spotless lamb.*d* 20 He was foreknown*e* before the foundation of the world but was revealed in these last times*f* for you. 21 Through him you believe in God,*g* who raised him from the dead*h* and gave him glory,*i* so that your faith and hope are in God.

22 Since you have purified yourselves by your obedience to the truth,*A* so that you show sincere brotherly love for each other,*j* from a pure*B* heart love one another constantly,*C,k* 23 because you have been born again*l* — not of perishable seed*m* but of imperishable — through the living and enduring word of God.*n* 24 For

> All flesh is like grass,
>   and all its glory*o* like a flower
>   of the grass.
> The grass withers,
>   and the flower falls,
> 25 but the word of the Lord
>   endures forever.*D,p*

And this word is the gospel that was proclaimed to you.

THE LIVING STONE AND A HOLY PEOPLE

2 Therefore, rid yourselves of*q* all malice, all deceit, hypocrisy, envy, and all slander.*r* 2 Like newborn infants, desire the pure milk of the word,*E,s* so that you may grow up into your salvation,*F* 3 if you have tasted*t* that the Lord is good.*G,u* 4 As you come to him, a living stone — rejected by people but chosen and honored by*H* God — 5 you yourselves, as living stones, a spiritual house, are being built to be a holy priesthood*I* to offer spiritual sacrifices acceptable to God*v* through Jesus Christ. 6 For it stands in Scripture:

> See, I lay a stone in Zion,*w*
> a chosen
>   and honored*J* cornerstone,*x*
> and the one who believes in him
>   will never be put to shame.*K,y*

7 So honor will come to you who believe; but for the unbelieving,

> The stone that the builders
>   rejected —
> this one has become
>   the cornerstone,*L,z*

8 and

> A stone to stumble over,
>   and a rock to trip over.*M,aa*

They stumble because they disobey the word; they were destined*ab* for this.

9 But you are a chosen race,*N,O,ac* a royal priesthood,*P,ad* a holy nation,*Q,ae* a people for his possession,*R,af* so that you may proclaim the praises*S,T,ag* of the one who called you out of darkness into his marvelous light.*ah* 10 Once you were not a people, but now you are God's people; you had not received mercy,*ai* but now you have received mercy.

A 1:22 Other mss add *through the Spirit*   *B* 1:22 Other mss omit *pure*   *C* 1:22 Or *fervently*   *D* 1:24-25 Is 40:6-8   *E* 2:2 Or *desire pure spiritual milk*   *F* 2:2 Other mss omit *for your salvation*   *G* 2:3 Ps 34:8   *H* 2:4 Or *precious to*   *I* 2:5 Or *you yourselves, as living stones, are being built into a spiritual house for a holy priesthood*   *J* 2:6 Or *precious*   *K* 2:6 Is 28:16 LXX   *L* 2:7 Ps 118:22   *M* 2:8 Is 8:14   *N* 2:9 Or *generation,* or *nation*   *O* 2:9 Dt 7:6; 10:15; Is 43:20 LXX   *P* 2:9 Ex 19:6; 23:22 LXX; Is 61:6   *Q* 2:9 Ex 19:6; 23:22 LXX   *R* 2:9 Ex 19:5; 23:22 LXX; Dt 4:20; 7:6; Is 43:21 LXX   *S* 2:9 Or *the mighty deeds*   *T* 2:9 Is 42:12; 43:21

something much more valuable: **the precious blood of Christ**. Why? Well, if you and I are both stuck in a ditch, we can't help each other. We need someone who's not in the ditch. Sinners can't redeem sinners. Under Israel's sacrificial system, to atone for sin you had to offer **an unblemished and spotless lamb** (1:19). But that was not a once-and-for-all offering. Jesus Christ, however, is the perfect Lamb of God (see John 1:29). He was without sin (see 1 Pet 2:22), so he could serve as a perfect Savior. Our holy God demanded a price for sin, and he met his own demands through the sacrificial death of his Son.

1:23 If you have believed in Jesus Christ, you received a **seed** (i.e., the divine nature; see 2 Pet 1:4) that is **imperishable** (which implies believers cannot lose their salvation). God sparked life in you where once there was death, and he did it **through the living and enduring word**.

2:1 These actions belong to the former life of sin, but they lead to death (i.e., separation from fellowship with God).

2:2 The word that caused us to be born again is the same Word that causes growth. But, unfortunately, many Christians choose malnourishment.

You don't have to command babies to eat; they know when they're hungry. Christians must be reminded that they are spiritually hungry and must be fed. You also won't find infants consuming big meals on Sunday in order to last them the whole week. Babies eat regularly for day-to-day nourishment; Christians need the same. Some believers are consuming spiritual junk food that can't nourish and won't produce growth. They need a steady diet and application of God's Word instead of man's opinion.

2:4-5 Peter is not just talking about each individual's coming to Jesus but to our corporate coming to him (2:4). God is taking **living stones**—that have life because of *the* living stone—and building **a spiritual house** (2:5). He's not building *houses* but a *house*. And he wants all of us stones to fit snugly into that building. We were dug out of the quarry of sin to be cemented together by the grace of God.

2:6-8 You have only two choices with Jesus: accept him or reject him. Those who accept him know he is the Lord's **honored cornerstone**—the stone on which God's household aligns. We are to live our lives with reference to him, and we **will never be put to shame** (2:6). But for those who reject him, he is a **stone to stumble over**; thus, they will **trip over** him right into judgment (2:7-8).

2:9-10 Believers are **a chosen race** (2:9). As the last Adam (see Rom 5:12-21; 1 Cor 15:45-49), Jesus is the head of a new race of people. The first Adam brought sin and death on the whole human race, but the last Adam brought spiritual life to believers from every ethnic group. All physical or cultural distinctions are

A CALL TO GOOD WORKS

11 Dear friends, I urge you as strangers and exiles[a] to abstain[b] from sinful[c] desires that wage war against the soul.[d] **12** Conduct[e] yourselves honorably among the Gentiles,[A] so that when they slander you as evildoers, they will observe your good works and will glorify God on the day he visits.[f]

13 Submit[g] to every human authority because of the Lord, whether to the emperor[B] as the supreme authority[h] **14** or to governors as those sent out by him to punish those who do what is evil and to praise those who do what is good. **15** For it is God's will[i] that you silence the ignorance[j] of foolish people by doing good. **16** Submit as free people, not using your freedom as a cover-up for evil,[k] but as God's slaves.[l] **17** Honor everyone. Love[m] the brothers and sisters.[n] Fear God.[o] Honor the emperor.

⮞ HOPE WORDS ⮜

Freedom does not mean getting to do whatever you want to do. Freedom means getting to do what you ought to do.

SUBMISSION OF SLAVES TO MASTERS

18 Household slaves, submit to your masters[p] with all reverence[q] not only to the good and gentle ones but also to the cruel.[r] **19** For it brings favor if, because of a consciousness of God, someone endures grief from suffering unjustly. **20** For what credit is there if when you do wrong and are beaten, you endure it? But when you do what is good and suffer,[s] if you endure it, this brings favor with God.

21 For you were called to this, because Christ also suffered[t] for you, leaving you an example,[u] that you should follow[v] in his steps. **22** He did not commit sin,[w] **and no deceit[x] was found in his mouth**;[C,y] **23** when he was insulted, he did not insult in return; when he suffered, he did not threaten but entrusted himself to the one who judges[z] justly. **24** He himself bore our sins[aa] in his body[ab] on the tree;[ac] so that, having died to sins,[ad] we might live for righteousness.[ae] **By his wounds**[D,af] **you have been healed**. **25** For you **were like sheep going astray**,[E,ag] but you have now returned to the Shepherd[ah] and Overseer[F] of your souls.

WIVES AND HUSBANDS

3 In the same way, wives,[ai] submit yourselves to your own husbands so that, even if some disobey the word,[aj]

Cross references (right margin):

a 2:11 1Pt 1:1
b 1Tm 4:3
c Rm 7:23; Php 3:3
d Gl 5:17; Jms 4:1
e 2:12 2Pt 3:11
f Is 10:3; Jr 6:15; 8:12; 10:15; Lk 1:68; 7:16; 19:44
g 2:13-14 Rm 13:1-7; Ti 3:1
h 2:13 Rm 13:1
i 2:15 Gl 1:4; Eph 1:9
j 1Pt 3:16
k 2:16 1Co 14:20
l Rm 1:1; Ti 1:1; Rv 2:20
m 2:17 Rm 12:11
n Heb 13:1; 1Pt 5:9
o Pr 1:7; 24:21; Ac 10:2; Rv 14:7

p 2:18 Eph 6:5; Col 3:22; Ti 2:9; Jd 4
q Rm 13:3,7
r Php 2:15
s 2:20 1Pt 4:14
t 2:21 Mk 8:31; 1Pt 3:18;
u Jn 3:16
v Jn 13:15
w Jn 8:12
x 2:22 1Pt 4:1; 1Jn 3:5
y 2Pt 2:1
z Is 53:9
aa 2:23 Rv 18:8; 19:11
ab 2:24 Heb 7:27-28; 9:27-28
ac Is 53:4-5,12; Jn 2:21
ad Ac 5:30; 10:39; 13:29; Gl 3:13
ae Rm 6:2,8-11; 7:6; Gl 2:19; Col 2:20; 3:3
af Rm 6:2,11; Ti 2:12
ag Is 53:5; Mt 13:15; Jn 12:40; Ac 28:27
ah 2:25 Ps 119:176; Is 53:6
ai Gn 48:15; 49:24; Ps 23:1; Jr 31:10
aj 3:1 Eph 5:22-33; Col 3:18-19; 1Tm 3:11
ak 1Co 7:16; 1Pt 1:24-25

A 2:12 Or *among the nations*, or *among the pagans*　　B 2:13 Or *king*　　C 2:22 Is 53:9　　D 2:24 Is 53:5　　E 2:25 Is 53:6　　F 2:25 Or *Guardian*

---

subservient to this greater category: we are children of God.

The people of God are **a holy nation**—not a perfect people, but a people set apart with a passion to live corporately to please God. We are **a people for his possession**—we're not special because of who we are, but because of the One to whom we belong (2:9).

Along with this new identity, God's people are to live a new lifestyle. You are to **proclaim the praises of the one who called you out of darkness into his marvelous light** (2:9). You are to serve as an advertising agency tasked with sharing the message of his love.

2:11-12 Christ's followers are actually **strangers and exiles**. This fallen world, then, is not your home. It's roughly a seventy- or eighty-year pit stop on the way to your eternal destination. The Christian's job in this interim period is to make a difference for God in the world. You are to **abstain from sinful desires** (2:11)—that is, don't do what everyone else is doing. You are to **conduct yourselves honorably among the Gentiles**, those who don't know God (2:12).

Jesus told his disciples to let their light shine before unbelievers so that they would see their good works and glorify God (Matt 5:14-16). So go public with your faith, and

influence neighbors and communities for God.

2:13-14 Christians have a responsibility to civil government.

2:16-17 In a fallen world, governments can be unjust and act in ways that are contrary to God's rule. When that happens, we have a legitimate basis to protest (see, e.g., Acts 4:19-20; 5:29). But we are not to use our **freedom** as God's people **as a cover-up for evil** (1 Pet 2:16). The world should find Christians to be exemplary citizens who **honor** all people, **love** others, **fear God**, and respect ruling authorities (2:17).

2:18 Paul does not condone slavery. Rather, he takes the reality of an unrighteous institution in the Roman world and tells believers how to honor God within it

2:19-20 Consider Joseph's story. Though he acted with integrity toward his master, he was treated **unjustly** (2:19; see Gen 39:1-20). Nevertheless, he entrusted himself to the Lord who "extended kindness to him" and "granted him favor" (Gen 39:21). This principle does not, however, negate using just means to address unrighteous treatment.

2:21-23 Jesus is the perfect example of someone enduring unjust suffering, since he alone is sinless (2:22). Rather than return-

ing evil for evil, he **entrusted himself to the one who judges justly** (2:23). Joseph son of Jacob serves as a type of Jesus the Suffering Servant.

2:24 What was the purpose of Christ's righteousness? **So that, having died to sins, we might live for righteousness**. Righteousness is the standard that God requires. If you're saved, Jesus gave you the ability to turn sin off and turn righteousness on. We can say no to sin and yes to righteousness—no to Satan's agenda and yes to God's.

By his wounds you have been healed is not a promise that followers of Jesus never get sick (though some teach that false theology). There are various kinds of healing that we need. Yes, sometimes God grants physical healing, but we also need emotional healing and relational healing. And all healing is connected to Jesus's wounds, and Jesus's wounds are connected to his death for sin. So if you want healing in a relationship, you have to be willing to address the sins that brought about the relational problems. Jesus can bring such healing only if the root sins are dealt with (see Jas 5:14-16).

3:1 **Wives** are to **submit** by choice, not by coercion. Moreover, submission has nothing to do with intrinsic value. Men and women

a 3:1 1Co 9:19-22; Php 3:8
b 2Pt 3:11
c 3:2 Ti 2:5
d 3:3 Is 3:18-24; 1Tm 2:9
e 3:4 Rm 2:29; 7:22
f Mt 5:5
g 1Tm 2:2
h 3:5 Ps 20:6; 1Co 7:14
i 1Tm 5:5; 1Pt 1:3
j 3:6 Gn 17:15-21; 18:6-15;
Heb 11:11
k Pr 3:25
l 3:7 Mt 1:19; 1Co 14:35;
Eph 5:22-28; Col 3:18-19;
Ti 2:4-5
m 1Th 4:4
n 3:8 Heb 13:1
o Eph 4:32
p 3:9 Rm 12:17
q Lk 6:28; Rm 12:14;
1Co 4:12

APPLICATION QUESTIONS

READ 1 PETER 3:1-7

— How do these verses contribute to your understanding of biblical submission?
— According to Peter, what are the benefits of biblical submission?
— What makes you feel honored and cherished by your spouse?
— What steps have you recently taken to honor and cherish your spouse?
— What steps can you take to improve your prayer life with your spouse?

they may be won over[a] without a word by the way their wives live[b] [2] when they observe your pure, reverent lives.[c] [3] Don't let your beauty consist of outward things like elaborate hairstyles and wearing gold jewelry or fine clothes,[d] [4] but rather what is inside the heart[A,e] — the imperishable quality of a gentle[f] and quiet[g] spirit, which is of great worth in God's sight. [5] For in the past, the holy[h] women who put their hope[i] in God also adorned themselves in this way, submitting to their own husbands, [6] just as Sarah[j] obeyed Abraham, calling him lord. You have become her children when you do what is good and do not fear any intimidation.[k]

[7] Husbands,[l] in the same way, live with your wives in an understanding way, as with a weaker partner,[m] showing them honor as coheirs of the grace of life, so that your prayers will not be hindered.

DO NO EVIL

[8] Finally, all of you be like-minded and sympathetic, love one another,[n] and be compassionate[o] and humble,[B] [9] not paying back evil for evil[p] or insult for insult but, on the contrary, giving a blessing,[q] since you were called for this, so that you may inherit a blessing.

> ⚜
> ⇝ KINGDOM LIVING ⇜
> FAMILY
> ## A Wife's Trust Is in The Lord
>
> The motivation that led the women in biblical times to reverence their husbands is that they "put their hope in God" (1 Pet 3:5). Hoping in God means focusing your trust on the Lord. It implies that a woman recognizes there is something bigger going on behind her respect for her husband. In fact, the Bible tells wives to submit to their husbands "as to the Lord" (Eph 5:22). You see, God overrules a wife's husband in terms of authority.
>
> Here is the answer to those who think the biblical framework makes a man the absolute ruler in his kingdom, with his wife and children functioning as his indentured servants. The man does not have ultimate rule; God does. Thus, a wife's trust is to be in the Lord.
>
> It's one thing to trust when things are fine and a husband is fulfilling his roles as leader and lover. But it's another story altogether for a wife to trust God when the husband isn't doing his part. That's why a woman's eyes need to be on the Lord, not on her husband. Her perspective can make all the difference. With her faith in God, a wife can see things that others can't. The definition of a spiritual man or a spiritual woman is not someone who does spiritual things like reading the Bible, praying, or going to church. The definition of a spiritual individual is someone who sees things spiritually and responds in faith.
>
> A wife may look at her husband and say, "Surrendering to him doesn't make sense." But when she sees things through the eyes of faith, life becomes clearer. She may not see in her husband what she wants to see, but she'll never be ultimately disappointed if her eyes are fixed on Jesus.

[A] **3:4** Or *rather, the hidden person of the heart*   [B] **3:8** Other mss read *courteous*

are equal before God; both are created in his image. Neither is more significant. And submission is not passivity. A wife is not to give up who she is and become a doormat. This matter is all about being in alignment under God and recognizing the God-given roles he assigned to husbands and wives. A kingdom husband is to lead his family with love. A kingdom wife is to support that leadership with her gifts and abilities.

3:3-4 Don't be captivated by store-bought beauty. Outward attractiveness can give a false impression about what someone is like on the inside. God wants internal beauty—

what is inside the heart—to take precedence (3:4). Someone can be gorgeous outside and ugly inside.

3:5-6 Sarah used her words to build up **Abraham** rather than tear him down—even though he was often a poor leader (3:6). As a result, she received the miracle of God opening her womb at the age of ninety. Peter expects Christian women to take their cues from Sarah (not their contemporary culture) in the way they honor their husbands. This way they too can see God's divine intervention in their lives. **3:7** The Bible says in effect that if you're going to be God's kingdom man, you've got to

spend time with your wife, listen to her, know what her needs are, and grow in **understanding** of her. You can't lead someone whom you don't understand. Wives may be physically **weaker**, but they are their husbands' **coheirs of the grace of life**. So **honor** your wife as an equal partner in the relationship. A husband who refuses to align himself under God's agenda and value, appreciate, and utilize the contributions of his wife cannot expect God to answer his **prayers**.

3:8-12 Too many church congregations are characterized by attitudes and actions that are shameful. But Jesus told his followers the

---

www.bhpublishinggroup.com/qr/te/6o-03

⟋ HOPE WORDS ⟍

As you become a blessing to others,
you set yourself up to be blessed.

---

10 For the[a] one who wants to love life
   and to see good days,
   let him keep his tongue from evil[b]
   and his lips from speaking deceit,[c]
11 and let him turn away[d] from evil
   and do what is good.
   Let him seek peace[e] and pursue it,
12 because the eyes of the Lord are
   on the righteous
   and his ears are open
   to their prayer.
   But the face of the Lord is against
   those who do what is evil.[A]

UNDESERVED SUFFERING

13 Who then will harm you if you are devoted to what is good? 14 But even if you should suffer for righteousness,[f] you are blessed. **Do not fear what they fear**[B,g] **or be intimidated,**[C,h] 15 but in your hearts regard[D] Christ[E] the Lord as holy, ready at any time to give a defense to anyone who asks you for a reason for the hope that is in you.[i] 16 Yet do this with gentleness and respect, keeping a clear conscience,[j] so that when you are accused,[F] those who disparage your good conduct in Christ will be put to shame. 17 For it is better to suffer[k] for doing good, if that should be God's will, than for doing evil.

18 For Christ also suffered[l] for sins once for all,[m] the righteous for the unrighteous, that he might bring you to God.[n] He was put to death in the flesh[G,o] but made alive by the Spirit,[H] 19 in which[i] he also went and made proclamation to the spirits[p] in

prison 20 who in the past were disobedient, when God patiently waited in the days of Noah[q] while the ark was being prepared. In it a few — that is, eight people[J,r] — were saved through water. 21 Baptism, which corresponds to this, now saves you (not as the removal of dirt from the body,[s] but the pledge[K] of a good conscience toward God) through the resurrection of Jesus Christ,[t] 22 who has gone into heaven[u] and is at the right hand of God[v] with angels, authorities, and powers subject to him.[w]

FOLLOWING CHRIST

4 Therefore, since Christ suffered[L] in the flesh, arm yourselves also with the same understanding[M] — because the one who suffers in the flesh is finished[x] with sin[N] — 2 in order to live the remaining time in the flesh no longer for human desires, but for God's will.[y] 3 For there has already been enough time spent in doing what the Gentiles choose to do: carrying on in unrestrained behavior, evil desires,[z] drunkenness, orgies,[aa] carousing, and lawless idolatry. 4 They are surprised that you don't join them in the same flood of wild living — and they slander[o] you. 5 They will give an account to the one who stands ready to judge the living and the dead.[ab] 6 For this reason the gospel was also preached to those who are now dead,[P,ac] so that, although they might be judged in the flesh according to human standards,[ad] they might live[ae] in the spirit according to God's standards.

END-TIME ETHICS

7 The end of all things is near;[af] therefore, be alert and sober-minded[ag] for prayer. 8 Above all, maintain constant love[ah] for one another, since **love covers a multitude of sins.**[Q,ai] 9 Be hospitable[aj] to one

---

Video Devotional

"KINGDOM MEN NEEDED"

A kingdom man is a man who rightly aligns himself underneath the lordship of Jesus Christ.

---

[a] 3:10-12 Ps 34:12-16
[b] 3:10 Jms 1:26
[c] Rm 3:13; Jms 3:5-8
[d] 3:11 Ps 37:27
[e] Lk 12:51; 2Tm 1:2; Heb 12:14; 3Jn 14
[f] 3:14 Mt 6:33; Rm 1:17; 2Pt 1:1
[g] Jn 6:20; 7:13
[h] 3:14-15 Is 8:12-13
[i] 3:15 1Jn 4:4
[j] 3:16 Ac 23:1; 24:16; Rm 9:1; 2Co 1:12; 1Tm 1:5,19; 3:9; Heb 10:22; 1Pt 3:21
[k] 3:17 Php 1:29; 1Pt 2:19
[l] 3:18 Mk 8:31; Rm 5:8
[m] Rm 9:28; Heb 9:28; 10:10; 1Pt 2:21; 4:1
[n] Rm 5:2
[o] Eph 2:14
[p] 3:19 1Jn 4:1

[q] 3:20 Gn 5:29
[r] Gn 5:32; 6:18; 7:7,13; 8:16,18
[s] 3:21 Heb 9:14; 10:22
[t] 1Pt 1:3
[u] 3:22 Ac 1:10,12; 1Tm 3:16; Heb 4:14; 6:20
[v] Ps 110:1; Mk 16:19; Ac 2:33-34; Rm 8:34; 1Pt 3:10-12
[w] Eph 1:20-22

---

[x] 4:1 Rm 6:10; Heb 4:15; 7:26; 9:28 [y] 4:2 Mk 3:35; Rm 6:11; 12:2 [z] 4:3 Mk 7:22 [aa] Rm 13:13; Gl 5:21 [ab] 4:5 Ac 10:42; Rm 14:9; 2Tm 4:1 [ac] 4:6 Jn 5:25 [ad] 1Pt 3:18 [ae] Php 1:21 [af] 4:7 Rm 13:11-12; Heb 9:26; Jms 5:8; 1Jn 2:18; Rv 1:3 [ag] 1Pt 5:8 [ah] 4:8 1Pt 1:22 [ai] Pr 10:12; Jms 5:20 [aj] 4:9 1Tm 3:2; Ti 1:8

[A] 3:10-12 Ps 34:12-16 [B] 3:14 Or *Do not fear them* [C] 3:14 Is 8:12 [D] 3:15 Or *sanctify,* or *set apart* [E] 3:15 Other mss read *set God* [F] 3:16 Other mss read *when they speak against you as evildoers* [G] 3:18 Or *by the flesh,* or *in the fleshly realm* [H] 3:18 Or *in the spirit,* or *in the Spirit,* or *in the spiritual realm* [I] 3:19 Or *by whom,* or *in whom,* or *at that time* [J] 3:20 Or *souls* [K] 3:21 Or *the appeal* [L] 4:1 Other mss read *suffered for us* [M] 4:1 Or *perspective,* or *attitude* [N] 4:1 Or *The one who suffered in the flesh has finished with sin* [O] 4:4 Or *blaspheme* [P] 4:6 Or *those who are dead* [Q] 4:8 Pr 10:12

---

world would know they are his disciples if they **love one another** (3:8; see John 13:35). The church is like an embassy in a foreign land. It's where the rules and ethics of eternity operate within history.

3:15-16 God is not looking for spectators but players who live for their King with righteousness and then give testimony about him **with gentleness and respect** (3:16).

3:20-21 Deliverance does not come through water **baptism** (3:21) but by testifying of entering **the ark** of safety (3:20; i.e., Jesus

Christ), which is the basis of spiritual baptism (see Rom 6:1-7).

4:4-5 We should ask ourselves, Which is worse? Being slandered by the ungodly or judged by God?

4:6 Between Christ's crucifixion and resurrection, he **preached** to people who had died, proclaiming his salvation to Old Testament believers in preparation for his leading them to paradise (see Eph 4:8-10). It was also the victorious proclamation of the victory of the cross over sin and Satan's authority (see Col 2:14-15).

4:7 You and I are on death row; we're fuses burning out. So, how should we live? From God's viewpoint, time is the boundary of opportunity. Peter explains how to make the most of the opportunity you've been given. At the top of the list is **prayer**. It replaces self-focus with a God-focus.

4:8 Biblical **love** is not defined by our feelings but by sacrificing for the good of others.

4:9 Biblical hospitality is an authentic welcoming and serving, especially toward those who can do nothing in return. Jesus reminds

a 4:10 1Co 12:7
b 4:11 Rm 12:6-8; 1Co 15:58
   c 4:12 1Pt 1:6-7
d 4:13 Gl 5:24; Php 3:10
e 1Co 1:7; Eph 1:17; 2Th 1:7;
   1Pt 1:7,13
f 4:14 Ps 89:50-51; Ac 5:41;
   1Pt 2:20
g Ac 4:33; Rv 3:22
h 4:17 Mk 12:40; Jn 5:22;
   Heb 10:27; 13:4
i Gl 6:10; Eph 2:19; 1Tm
   3:15; Heb 3:2
j 4:18 Pr 11:31
k 4:19 Ps 10:14; 2Co 1:9

   l 5:1 Ac 4:20
m Rm 8:18; Col 3:4
n 5:2 Jr 3:15; 23:1; Jn 21:16;
   Ac 20:28

HOPE WORDS

Greatness is maximizing your potential for the glory of God and the good of others.

another without complaining. **10** Just as each one has received a gift, use it to serve others,*a* as good stewards of the varied grace of God. **11** If anyone speaks, let it be as one who speaks God's words; if anyone serves, let it be from the strength God provides,*b* so that God may be glorified through Jesus Christ in everything. To him be the glory and the power forever and ever. Amen.

CHRISTIAN SUFFERING

12 Dear friends, don't be surprised when the fiery ordeal comes among you to test you as if something unusual were happening to you.*c* **13** Instead, rejoice as you share in the sufferings of Christ,*d* so that you may also rejoice with great joy when his glory is revealed.*e* **14** If you are ridiculed for the name of Christ,*f* you are blessed, because the Spirit*g* of glory and of God*A* rests on you. **15** Let none of you suffer as a murderer, a thief, an evildoer, or a meddler.*B* **16** But if anyone suffers as a Christian, let him not be ashamed but let him glorify God in having that name.*c* **17** For the time has come for judgment*h* to begin with God's household,*i* and if it begins with us, what will the outcome be for those who disobey the gospel of God?

18   And **if a righteous person is saved with difficulty, what will become of the ungodly and the sinner?**[D,j]

19 So then, let those who suffer according to God's will entrust themselves*k* to a faithful Creator while doing what is good.

KINGDOM LIVING
CHURCH
The Household of God

The church isn't a gathering of strangers, like fans at a sporting event who just happen to be sitting next to each other. Rather, the church is a community of individuals spiritually linked together with the purpose of reflecting and spreading the values of the kingdom of God. It is therefore critical to the process of growing mature disciples who imitate Jesus Christ. Jesus, after all, is relational. He even stated that the key characteristic that would identify his disciples was their love for one another (see John 13:35).

God's people are so vitally connected that we're like members of the same physical body. The parts of your body are in a relationship together. Just smash your thumb or stub your toe, and you'll have a good biblical reminder of the interrelationship of your bodily members! And should you disconnect a body part, you'll see that you've cut off its ability to function because it is separated from the source of its life.

Factors like these are why Peter and Paul both call the church "God's household" (Eph 2:19; 1 Pet 4:17). Your home is supposed to be the place where you give and receive love unconditionally. It takes more than the paid professional staff in a church to produce this kind of love. It comes from each one of us being in dynamic relationships so that we can encourage and edify one another.

FOR THE NEXT CHURCH
KINGDOM LIVING LESSON SEE PAGE 1531.

ABOUT THE ELDERS

5 I exhort the elders among you as a fellow elder and witness*l* to the sufferings of Christ, as well as one who shares in the glory about to be revealed:*m* **2** Shepherd God's flock among you,*n* not overseeing*E*

us that what we do for "the least of these" we do for him (Matt 25:40).

4:10 We are to **serve others** based on the spiritual **gift** we have **received.** Full-service gas stations are hard to find today. Most are self-service. Unfortunately, many attend church like a self-service station. They fill up on preaching and go home until they need more fuel. But God intends his church to

be full service with each member providing for the well-being of others. Since you are a receptor of grace, you ought to be a conduit for grace. So whatever your spiritual gift, it's all about God—not you.

4:12-14 No one looks forward to suffering. We want to reign with Christ, not suffer with him. But to reign with Christ in glory, we must suffer with him now. If you suffer because of

your decision to follow Jesus, **you are blessed** (4:14).

4:17-18 If God's fatherly discipline is painful, how much worse will his **judgment** be on **the ungodly**?

5:1-4 Elders are to **shepherd God's flock** (5:1-2). The church is a flock the Lord "purchased with his own blood" (Acts 20:28). And a shepherd's job is to preserve and protect the sheep.

out of compulsion but willingly, as God would have you;[A] not out of greed for money but eagerly; [3] not lording it over those entrusted to you, but being examples to the flock. [4] And when the chief Shepherd[a] appears, you will receive the unfading crown[b] of glory. [5] In the same way, you who are younger, be subject to the elders. All of you clothe yourselves with[B] humility toward one another, because

> God resists the proud
> but gives grace to the humble.[C,c]

CONCLUSION

[6] Humble[d] yourselves, therefore, under the mighty hand[e] of God, so that he may exalt you at the proper time, [7] casting all your cares on him, because he cares about you.[f] [8] Be sober-minded,[g] be alert.[h] Your adversary the devil[i] is prowling around like a roaring lion, looking for anyone he can devour. [9] Resist him,[j] firm in the faith, knowing that the same kind of sufferings are being experienced by your fellow believers throughout the world.

[10] The God of all grace, who called you to his eternal glory[k] in Christ,[D] will himself restore, establish, strengthen, and support you after you have suffered a little while.[E] [11] To him be dominion[F] forever.[G] Amen.

[12] Through Silvanus,[H,l] a faithful brother (as I consider him), I have written to you briefly in order to encourage you and to testify that this is the true grace of God. Stand firm in it! [13] She who is in Babylon,[m] chosen together with you, sends you greetings, as does Mark, my son. [14] Greet one another with a kiss of love.[n] Peace[o] to all of you who are in Christ.[l]

[a] 5:4 Jn 10:11,14; 21:15-17; Heb 13:20; 1Pt 2:25
[b] 1Co 9:25; Rv 12:1
[c] 5:5 Pr 3:34; Jms 4:6
[d] 5:6 Lk 14:11
[e] 1Kg 8:42; 2Ch 6:32; Dn 9:15
[f] 5:7 Ps 55:22
[g] 5:8 1Th 5:6,8; 2Tm 4:5; 1Pt 1:13; 4:7
[h] Rv 16:15
[i] Mt 4:1,10; Ac 13:10
[j] 5:9 Eph 6:13-14; Jms 4:7
[k] 5:10 1Pt 5:1,4; 2Pt 3:18
[l] 5:12 Ac 15:22; 1Th 1:1; 2Th 1:1
[m] 5:13 Rv 14:8; 16:19; 17:5,18; 18:2,10,21
[n] 5:14 Rm 16:16; 1Co 16:20; 2Co 13:12; 1Th 5:26
[o] Eph 6:23

[A] 5:2 Other mss omit *as God would have you* [B] 5:5 Or *you tie around yourselves* [C] 5:5 Pr 3:34 LXX [D] 5:10 Other mss read *in Christ Jesus*
[E] 5:10 Or *to a small extent* [F] 5:11 Some mss read *dominion and glory*; other mss read *glory and dominion* [G] 5:11 Other mss read *forever and ever*
[H] 5:12 Or *Silas*; Ac 15:22-32; 16:19-40; 17:1-16 [I] 5:14 Other mss read *Christ Jesus. Amen.*

I once saw a magazine advertisement for a mail-in ordination certificate. You could become a reverend by mail without even answering questions about doctrine, conduct, or character. The problem is that doctrine, conduct, and character are everything! It is only when pastors and elders serve as **examples to the flock** that they will be rewarded by the **chief Shepherd**, Jesus Christ (1 Pet 5:3-4; see John 10:7-11; Heb 13:20).

5:8-9 When you transferred out of Satan's realm and into Christ's kingdom, you became a target. **The devil** prowls **like a roaring lion** looking for food. He wants to keep you from advancing God's kingdom on earth, and don't think you can fly under his radar (5:8). He wants to destroy you. So be **firm in the faith** (5:9). Remember that you can conquer Satan, but only through your faith in and obedience to Jesus Christ.

2 PETER

INTRODUCTION

Author

THE AUTHOR OF THIS LETTER identifies himself as "Simeon Peter, a servant and an apostle of Jesus" (1:1). Though Simeon is not the name typically used for Peter, it is a Semitic spelling of his name and does occur at Acts 15:14. The letter writer includes a reference to being personally present at the transfiguration of Jesus (2 Pet 1:16-18)—an event the Gospels say happened when Peter, James, and John were with him (see Matt 17:1-13; Mark 9:2-8; Luke 9:28-36). Moreover, the author is personally familiar with the apostle Paul, a truth we know from Acts 15 and Paul's own letter to the Galatians (Gal 2:9-14). Based on the letter itself, then, we have every reason to believe that it comes from the hand of Peter.

Many modern critical scholars, though, deny Peter's authorship. They believe the letter is pseudonymous—that is, written by someone else under Peter's name. They also argue that the style of writing is different from 1 Peter, and that 2 Peter copied from the letter of Jude—with which it shares common themes and language. But none of these arguments should prevent us from accepting Peter as the author. First, we know from testimony in the early church that the practice of people writing falsely under the name of an apostle was soundly rejected. Such writings were not accepted as Scripture. Second, two letters from the same author are not required to be exactly alike in style to be authentic. Furthermore, it may be that Peter used Silvanus as an amanuensis (secretary) to write 1 Peter (see 1 Pet 5:12). If so, this could easily account for stylistic differences. Finally, the fact that Peter may have borrowed from Jude, Jude may have borrowed from Peter, or both may have borrowed from another source is no stumbling block to authenticity. Therefore, we are justified in believing that the apostle Peter penned the letter.

Historical Background

Peter claims in 3:1 that this is "the second letter" he has written to his readers. But 2 Peter doesn't list any recipients, like 1 Peter does (1 Pet 1:1). So we cannot know for sure if he is writing to the same Christians, or if the statement in 2 Peter 3:1 refers to another letter that has been lost to history.

According to early church tradition, Peter was martyred during the rule of the Roman emperor Nero around AD 67. Since he acknowledges that his death is approaching ("I will soon lay aside my tent," 1:14), it is likely that he wrote near the end of his life and, thus, probably from Rome.

The Christians to whom he wrote were obviously confronted by false teachers (see chapter 2). So Peter warns them to reject false doctrine, urges them to be faithful to grow spiritually, and reminds them that certain judgment is coming on such teachers.

Message and Purpose

Shortly before his death, Peter desired to build up the faith of these believers so that they could recognize what was counterfeit by knowing what is true. He knew that if they increased in their understanding and application of Scripture, they would grow in their relationship with Jesus Christ. Believers have a new nature from God, but it needs to be fed and nurtured as they participate with Christ in their growth in grace.

Before concluding, Peter warns the believers under his charge against the influence of false teachers infiltrating the churches, denying the Scriptures and the Lord in an attempt to destroy the faith. Peter urges believers to hold tightly to their faith, to continue growing in grace, to keep alert for false teaching, to know the Word, and to be ready and watching for Christ's return when they will receive their kingdom reward. Patient waiting for Christ is not wasted faith.

VIDEO · INTRO

www.bhpublishinggroup.com/qr/te/61_00

Outline

I. Greeting (1:1-2)
II. Growing in the Faith (1:3-15)
III. The Trustworthy Prophetic Word (1:16-21)
IV. False Teachers (2:1-22)
V. The Day of the Lord (3:1-13)
VI. Final Words (3:14-18)

GREETING

1 Simeon[A] Peter,[a] a servant and an apostle[b] of Jesus Christ:

To those who have received a faith equal to ours through the righteousness[c] of our God and Savior[d] Jesus Christ.

2 May grace and peace be multiplied to you through the knowledge of God[e] and of Jesus our Lord.

GROWTH IN THE FAITH

3 His[B] divine power[f] has given us everything required for life and godliness through the knowledge[g] of him who called[h] us by[c] his own glory and goodness. **4** By these he has given us very great and precious promises,[i] so that through them you may share in the divine nature,[j] escaping the corruption that is in the world because of evil desire. **5** For this very reason, make every effort to supplement your faith with goodness, goodness with knowledge, **6** knowledge with self-control,[k] self-control with endurance, endurance with godliness, **7** godliness with brotherly affection,[l] and brotherly affection with love. **8** For if you possess these qualities in increasing measure, they will keep you from being useless[m] or unfruitful[n] in the knowledge of our Lord Jesus Christ. **9** The person who lacks these things is blind and shortsighted and has forgotten the cleansing from his past sins. **10** Therefore, brothers and sisters, make every effort to confirm your calling and election,[o] because if you do these things you will never stumble. **11** For in this way, entry into the eternal kingdom[p] of our Lord and Savior Jesus Christ will be richly provided for you.

12 Therefore I will always remind you about these things, even though you know them and are established in the truth[q] you now have. **13** I think it is right, as long as I am in this bodily tent,[r] to wake you up with a reminder, **14** since I know that I will soon lay aside my tent, as our Lord Jesus Christ has indeed made clear to me.[s] **15** And I will also make every effort so that you are able to recall these things at any time after my departure.[D]

THE TRUSTWORTHY PROPHETIC WORD

16 For we did not follow cleverly contrived myths when we made known to you the power and coming of our Lord Jesus Christ;[t] instead, we were eyewitnesses of his majesty.[u] **17** For he received honor and glory from God the Father when the voice came to him from the Majestic Glory, saying "This is my beloved Son,[E] with whom I am well-pleased!"[v] **18** We ourselves heard this voice when it came from heaven while we were with him on the holy mountain.[w] **19** We also have the prophetic word strongly confirmed, and you will do well to pay attention to it, as to a lamp shining in a dark place,[x] until the day dawns[y] and the morning star[z] rises in your hearts. **20** Above all, you know this: No prophecy of Scripture comes from the prophet's

[a] 1:1 Mt 16:17; Lk 6:14; Ac 10:32; 15:14
[b] Rm 1:1; Ti 1:1
[c] Rm 5:17,21; Php 1:11
[d] Ti 2:13
[e] 1:2 Jn 17:3; Php 3:8; 2Pt 1:3,8; 2:20; 3:18
[f] 1:3 1Pt 1:5
[g] Jn 17:3; Php 3:8; 2Pt 1:2,8; 2:20; 3:18
[h] 1Th 2:12; 2Th 2:14; 1Pt 5:10
[i] 1:4 Jos 21:45; 1Kg 8:56; Is 38:16; Jr 33:14; Rm 9:4; 15:8; 2Co 7:1
[j] Eph 4:24; Heb 12:10; 1Jn 3:2
[k] 1:6 Ac 24:25; Gl 5:23
[l] 1:7 Rm 12:10; Heb 13:1; 1Pt 1:22
[m] 1:8 Jms 2:20
[n] Mt 7:16-21; Gl 5:22; Ti 3:14
[o] 1:10 Mt 22:14; Rm 11:29; 2Pt 1:3

[p] 1:11 Col 1:13; 2Tm 4:18
[q] 1:12 2Co 11:10; Col 1:5-6; 2Jn 2; 3Jn 3-4
[r] 1:13 2Co 5:1-4
[s] 1:14 Jn 21:18-23
[t] 1:16 Mk 13:26; 14:62; 1Th 2:19
[u] Mt 17:1-6
[v] 1:17 Is 42:1; Mt 3:17; 17:5; Mk 1:11; 9:7; Lk 3:22
[w] 1:18 Ps 2:6; Mt 17:1; Mk 9:2; Lk 9:28
[x] 1:19 Ps 119:105
[y] Mal 4:2; Rm 13:12; 2Pt 3:18
[z] Nm 24:17; Rv 22:16

[A] 1:1 Other mss read *Simon* [B] 1:3 Lit *As his* [C] 1:3 Or *to* [D] 1:15 Or *death* [E] 1:17 Other mss read *my Son, my beloved*

1:1 The author identifies himself as **Simeon Peter**, which has led some to conclude incorrectly that someone other than Peter wrote the letter. A better explanation for the alternate spelling is that "Simeon" was a Semitic rendering of Simon, used especially in first-century Palestinian settings (cf. Acts 15:14).

1:3 The spiritual blessings we need are already available to us (see Eph 1:3), but it's up to us to access them. These comprehensive blessings are appropriated **through the knowledge of** God—that is, through the specific knowledge of God's will for and blessings to believers. This knowledge is the difference between merely meeting the president of the United States and having a personal relationship with him.

1:4 The **divine nature** is implanted into believers in seed form (cf. 1 Pet 1:23) and doesn't immediately translate into mature, godly living. Rather, it gives every Christian potential to escape **the corruption that is in the world**, much like a seed gives the person who possesses it the potential to grow a plant. When the seed is tended and grows,

the life of the Spirit expands in a believer's soul, and the expansion is manifested in the body through righteous living.

1:5-7 These qualities act like vitamin supplements, enabling believers to adopt God's kingdom perspective and live in accordance with it. God instructs believers to add these qualities to their saving faith in order to actualize the potential for maturity and godly living.

1:8 When you're growing in Christ, you don't have to strain to bear fruit. It will emerge as naturally as apples develop on a healthy apple tree.

1:10 The admonition to **make every effort to confirm your calling and election** is not about making sure you're saved. It's about making sure you are spiritually productive, since the purpose of election is service not individual salvation.

1:12-14 Peter's urgency to issue the reminder stemmed not from any failure on the part of Christians but from the impending reality of his own death, about which Jesus **made a clear** prophecy (1:14; see John 21:18-19).

1:16 Peter and his fellow apostles (cf. 1:1) could speak authoritatively about spiritual matters because they **were eyewitnesses of** Christ's **majesty**.

1:17-18 This is a reference to the events that unfolded on the Mount of Transfiguration (cf. Mark 9:2-8).

1:19 God's revelation of Christ's glory to Peter **confirmed** the authority and truthfulness of the **prophetic word** Peter presented. Hence, believers **do well to pay attention to it**. God's Word functions like **a lamp shining in a dark place**, sustaining believers in their spiritual walks. Indeed, the entire Bible causes Christ (**the morning star**; see Rev 22:16) to come alive **in [our] hearts**.

1:20-21 The Bible is uncontaminated and completely without error in the same way that the Holy Spirit protected Jesus from sin in his conception and birth, even though it included human involvement. Thus, we can confidently say that Scripture's true author is God.

Winning at Scrabble™

WHEN MY MOTHER WAS ALIVE, she loved to play Scrabble™. For her birthday one year, we bought her an actual Scrabble™ table for the sole purpose of playing the game. She played for countless hours, and understandably, was very good at it. She could take the twenty-six letters of the alphabet and make words I never even knew existed. It's fair to say that none of us ever won a game of Scrabble™ against her.

In the English language, there are approximately 225,000 words, and all you need are twenty-six letters to get to all of them. Anything you want to accomplish with words can be achieved by using those twenty-six characters. This remarkable truth reminds me of a greater one: with God's divine power at work in us, we have been provided with everything we need to live a life of godliness.

As a Christian, you move a little closer to glory every day. You are on a journey toward heaven, and once you arrive, nothing you experienced prior to that will compare to the unending joy that awaits you. And so, you wait eagerly for that day to arrive. But waiting for heaven is not the same as waiting for a bus. God does not intend for you to wait passively for something to happen as if nothing you do on earth matters.

The road to glory is paved with purpose, and that purpose lives within you. You don't need to go find it; God has planted a seed within every believer. It's a measure of his righteous character, and he desires to see that character flourish within you. Like any seed, though, it requires nurturing; it's meant to grow. But it's not going to grow just because you desire it to do so. The apostle Peter says that we need to "make every effort" when it comes to moral excellence (2 PET 1:5). That means living a godly life requires more than a Sunday-only effort; it's an all-the-time activity.

At any rate, the means for godly living lie within you, so I recommend a workout program. But I'm not talking about a physical workout. Any time you spend in a gym might benefit your body, but in order for the spiritual seed inside you to grow, it requires spiritual exercise. Philippians 2:12 says, "Just as you have always obeyed, so now, . . . work out your own salvation with fear and trembling." You might be thinking, "But I already have salvation!" But assuming that is the case, you now need to work out that salvation—that is, you need to start the practice of living like a child of God.

This is how God intends for us to move toward glory—actively participating in the building of godly character within us. It includes obedience to him, and it also means showing the love and compassion of Jesus Christ to others.

own interpretation, **21** because no prophecy ever came by the will of man;[a] instead, men spoke from God as they were carried along by the Holy Spirit.[b]

THE JUDGMENT OF FALSE TEACHERS

2 There were indeed false prophets[c] among the people, just as there will be false teachers[d] among you. They will bring in destructive heresies, even denying the Master who bought[e] them, and will bring swift destruction on themselves. **2** Many will follow their depraved ways, and the way of truth will be maligned because of them.[f] **3** They will exploit[g] you in their greed[h] with made-up stories. Their condemnation,[i] pronounced long ago, is not idle, and their destruction does not sleep.

4 For if God didn't spare[j] the angels who sinned but cast them into hell[A,k] and delivered them in chains[B] of utter darkness to be kept for judgment;[l] **5** and if he didn't spare the ancient world, but protected Noah,[m] a preacher of righteousness, and seven others,[C,n] when he brought the flood on the world of the ungodly; **6** and if he reduced the cities of Sodom and Gomorrah[o] to ashes and condemned them to extinction,[D] making them an example of what is coming to the ungodly;[E,p] **7** and if he rescued righteous Lot,[q] distressed by the depraved behavior of the immoral **8** (for as that righteous man lived among them day by day, his righteous soul was tormented by the lawless deeds he saw and heard) — **9** then the Lord knows how to rescue[s]

the godly from trials and to keep the unrighteous under punishment for the day of judgment,[t] **10** especially those who follow the polluting desires of the flesh and despise authority.[u]

Bold, arrogant people! They are not afraid to slander the glorious ones; **11** however, angels, who are greater in might and power, do not bring a slanderous charge against them before the Lord.[f] **12** But these people, like irrational animals — creatures of instinct born to be caught and destroyed — slander what they do not understand, and in their destruction they too will be destroyed. **13** They will be paid back with harm for the harm they have done. They consider it a pleasure to carouse in broad daylight. They are spots and blemishes, delighting in their deceptions[G] while they feast with you. **14** They have eyes full of adultery[v] that never stop looking for sin. They seduce unstable people and have hearts trained in greed. Children under a curse![w] **15** They have gone astray by abandoning the straight path[x] and have followed the path of Balaam,[y] the son of Bosor,[H] who loved the wages of wickedness[z] **16** but received a rebuke for his lawlessness: A speechless donkey spoke with a human voice and restrained the prophet's madness.[aa]

17 These people are springs without water, mists driven by a storm. The gloom of darkness has been reserved for them.[ab] **18** For by uttering boastful, empty words,[ac] they seduce, with fleshly desires

a 1:21 Jr 23:26; 2Tm 3:16
b 2Sm 23:2; Lk 1:70; Ac 1:16; 3:18; 1Pt 1:11
c 2:1 Dt 13:1-5; Mt 7:15
d Ac 20:29; 2Co 11:13-15; Gl 2:4; 1Tm 4:1; 2Tm 4:3
e 1Co 6:20; 7:23
f 2:2 Rm 2:24
g 2:3 Jms 4:13
h Eph 5:3
i Mt 12:41; 23:33; Rm 3:8
j 2:4 Rm 8:32; Jd 6
k Rv 20:2-3,10
l Mt 25:41
m 2:5 Gn 5:29
n 1Pt 3:20
o 2:6 Gn 19:24; Jd 7
p Is 1:9; Jd 15
q 2:7 Gn 19:16
r 2:8 Ps 119:136,158; Ezk 9:4
s 2:9 1Co 10:13

t 2:9 Mt 10:15; Jd 6
u 2:10-13 Jd 8-12
v 2:14 Mt 5:27-28
w Jr 23:14; Hs 4:2; Eph 2:3; Heb 2:13
x 2:15 Ac 13:10
y Nm 22:5-7; Dt 23:4; Neh 13:2; Jd 11; Rv 2:14
z Hs 9:1; Mc 1:7; Ac 1:18
aa 2:16 Nm 22:22-35
ab 2:17 Jd 13
ac 2:18 Jd 16

A 2:4 Gk *Tartarus*　B 2:4 Other mss read *in pits*　C 2:5 Lit *Noah, the eighth, a preacher of righteousness*　D 2:6 Other mss omit *to extinction*　E 2:6 Other mss read *an example of what is going to happen to the ungodly*　F 2:11 Other mss read *them from the Lord*　G 2:13 Other mss read *delighting in the love feasts*　H 2:15 Other mss read *Beor*

2:1 The assertion that some people deny **the Master who bought them** affirms an unlimited and universal *atonement*. But this doesn't imply a universal *salvation*. Christ's atoning work is available to all, but effective only for those who will receive it.

2:3 The false teachers referenced here do not veer unknowingly into error but intentionally perpetuate lies. Therefore, they will receive **condemnation** and eternal **destruction**.

2:4-6 Peter gives three examples to demonstrate that God judges evil and that punishment, therefore, awaits false teachers. First, God judged **the angels who sinned** and **cast them into hell** (2:4). This is a reference to the prehistoric rebellion of Satan and the angels who sided with him (see Isa 14:12-15). Second, God **didn't spare the ancient world... when he brought the flood on the world of the ungodly** (2 Pet 2:5; see Gen 6-8). This example highlights the fact that God preserves the godly even as he judges the wicked, a theme picked up again in 2:7-10. In the flood, the

godly person spared was **Noah**, along with **seven** of his family members (2:5). Third, God **reduced the cities of Sodom and Gomorrah to ashes ... making them an example of what is coming to the ungodly** (2:6; see Gen 19:23-29). This example highlights the Lord's judgment of those who lead ungodly lifestyles and are unrepentant.

2:7-8 Even today, feeling **tormented** by wickedness is one indication of a person's desire for righteousness (2:8).

2:9 Ultimate deliverance for believers will come at the rapture of the church (cf. 1 Thess 4:13-18), yet God also brings deliverance in history at times. For the wicked, there is no hope apart from repentance and faith in Christ, only the fearful expectation of eternal destruction in hell.

2:10 Though false teachers identify with Christ's church publicly (see 2:1), they refuse to live under his lordship. They are **bold** and **arrogant**, even mocking the spiritual power of Satan and demons—referenced here as

glorious ones (2:10) to denote their status as celestial beings, but not any moral goodness within them.

2:13-14 False teachers are not only evil at night when their deeds can be hidden. They are flagrant with their unrighteousness, feasting at the Lord's Table and fellowshiping with the church while using their Christian veneers to hide evil intentions.

2:15-16 Peter sheds light on the narrative of Balaam in Numbers 22–24, clarifying that he attempted to curse Israel in hopes of financial gain. However, a **rebuke** from a **speechless donkey** illustrated that an animal had more spiritual insight than Balaam (2 Pet 2:16; see Num 22:28-30). So too with the false teachers.

2:17 Like **springs without water** and clouds without rain, the false teachers arrive with a pretense of offering refreshment but in reality offer nothing to sustain spiritual life.

2:18 Contrary to the way of spiritual growth, false teachers use their communication

The Greatest Truth

SKEPTICS AREN'T THE ONLY ONES who raise questions about the Bible. Even Christians might ask, "How can believers claim that the Bible is true compared with any other religious book? What makes Scripture stand out from other pieces of writing that claim to be from God?"

So, how do we authenticate the Bible? Consider its historical authenticity. The Bible has been substantiated both historically and archaeologically as being more accurate than any other book handed down through time. Research and analysis by historians, linguists, sociologists, and archaeologists have demonstrated the soundness of the Scriptures through forensic science, the discovery and study of other ancient literature, and much more.

The Bible is also set apart from all other books in another way: its prophetic accuracy. A large portion of its prophecy has already been fulfilled with unblemished precision. A classic example is the foretelling of Jesus's birth in Bethlehem. In Micah 5:2, the prophet told of our Savior's birth over seven hundred years before it happened. Matthew recorded the fulfillment of this for us in Matthew 2:1-6. What makes this prophecy stand out is the obscurity of Bethlehem. Had Micah mentioned a major metropolis in Israel, one could argue that Micah had merely guessed well. Yet Micah recorded the mind of God by pinpointing this remote region as the site of Christ's birth. Prophetic Scripture is accurate in all its details because God himself moved the writers to record it.

Of course, Micah's prophecy is just one of several hundred that have already been fulfilled. Each is a reminder that God is not bound by time, space, or matter. He knows the beginning from the end, and prophecy involves the recording of his thoughts before an event historically happens. The apostle Peter wrote, "No prophecy of Scripture comes from the prophet's own interpretation, because no prophecy ever came by the will of man; instead, men spoke from God as they were carried along by the Holy Spirit" (2 PET 1:20-21).

Imagine one hundred prophecies being accurately fulfilled (without any errors). The odds against this happening are astronomical. It would be impossible. Yet the Bible contains hundreds of prophecies, written by a number of inspired writers over a period of centuries that already have come true. That's because these prophecies are not based on chance, but on the eternal knowledge of God.

Isaiah 53, for instance, contains a number of prophecies, including one about Jesus's piercing, his scourging, and even his silence in the face of oppression and accusation. The passage speaks of his grave and his purity; it also mentions that our own iniquities would be placed on Jesus, our sinless Savior. "He himself bore our sicknesses, and he carried our pains" (ISA 53:4). Grief and sorrow tell a tale much more painful than scourging itself. Jesus came not only to bear our sins, but also our burdens.

In your pain, know this truth: you are not alone. Jesus sees. He knows. He cares. He's been there. And because he has suffered, he offers a comfort not merely rooted in intellectual assent but in compassionate understanding.

and debauchery, people who have barely escaped[A] from those who live in error. [19] They promise them freedom, but they themselves are slaves of corruption, since people are enslaved to whatever defeats them.[a] [20] For if, having escaped the world's impurity through the knowledge of the Lord[B] and Savior Jesus Christ,[b] they are again entangled in these things and defeated, the last state is worse for them than the first.[c] [21] For it would have been better for them not to have known the way of righteousness[d] than, after knowing it, to turn back from the holy command[e] delivered[f] to them.[g] [22] It has happened to them according to the true proverb: **A dog returns to its own vomit,**[c,h] and, "A washed sow returns to wallowing in the mud."

THE DAY OF THE LORD

3 Dear friends, this is now the second letter[i] I have written to you; in both letters, I want to stir up your sincere[j] understanding by way of reminder, [2] so that you recall the words previously spoken by the holy prophets and the command of our Lord and Savior given through your apostles. [3] Above all, be aware of this: Scoffers will come in the last days[k] scoffing and following their own evil desires, [4] saying, "Where is his 'coming' that he promised?[l] Ever since our ancestors fell asleep,[m] all things continue as they have been since the beginning of creation." [5] They deliberately overlook this: By the word of God[n] the heavens came into being long ago and the earth was brought about from water and through water.[o] [6] Through these the world of that time perished when it was flooded.[p] [7] By the same word,[q] the present heavens and earth are stored up for fire, being kept for the day of judgment[r] and destruction of the ungodly.

[8] Dear friends, don't overlook this one fact: With the Lord one day is like a thousand years, and a thousand years like one day.[s] [9] The Lord does not delay his promise,[t] as some understand delay, but is patient with you, not wanting any[u] to perish[v] but all to come to repentance.[w]

[10] But the day of the Lord[x] will come like a thief;[D,y] on that day the heavens will pass away[z] with a loud noise, the elements will burn and be dissolved,[aa] and the earth and the works on it will be disclosed.[E,F] [11] Since all these things are to be dissolved in this way, it is clear what sort of people you should be in holy conduct and godliness [12] as you wait for the day of God and hasten its coming.[G,ab] Because of that day, the heavens will be dissolved with fire and the elements will melt with heat. [13] But based on his promise, we wait for new heavens and a new earth,[ac] where righteousness dwells.[ad]

> ⌘ **HOPE WORDS** ⌘
>
> *God's timing is always perfect. Trust his delays.*

---

[a] 2:19 Jn 8:34; Rm 6:16; 7:5
[b] 2:20 2Pt 1:2
[c] Mt 12:45; Lk 11:26
[d] 2:21 Pr 8:20; 12:28; 16:31; 21:21; Mt 21:32
[e] Rm 7:12; 1Tm 6:14
[f] Jd 3
[g] Ezk 18:1-32; Heb 6:4-6; 10:26-27
[h] 2:22 Pr 26:11
[i] 3:1 1Pt 1:1
[j] Php 1:10
[k] 3:3 2Tm 3:1; Heb 1:2; Jms 5:3; 1Pt 1:20
[l] 3:4 1Th 2:19; 2Pt 3:12
[m] Ac 7:60
[n] 3:5 Gn 1:3-30; Ps 148:5; Jn 1:1-3; Heb 4:12; 11:3

[o] 3:5 Ps 24:1-2; 33:6-7; 136:5-6; Pr 8:24-29
[p] 3:6 2Pt 2:5
[q] 3:7 Is 66:15-16; Ezk 38:22; Am 7:4; Zph 1:18; Mal 4:1
[r] Php 1:6; 2Th 1:5; 1Jn 4:17
[s] 3:8 Ps 90:4
[t] 3:9 Hab 2:3
[u] Ti 2:11
[v] Ezk 18:23,32; 33:11; 1Tm 2:4
[w] Jl 2:12-13; Jnh 3:10; 4:2; Ac 17:31; Rm 2:4
[x] 3:10 Php 1:6
[y] Mt 24:43; Lk 12:39; 1Th 5:2
[z] Mt 5:18; 24:35; Rv 21:1
[aa] Is 24:19; Mc 1:4
[ab] 3:12 Lk 12:36; 1Co 1:7; 1Th 1:10; Ti 2:13; Jd 21
[ac] 3:13 Is 65:17; 66:22; Mt 19:28; Rm 8:21; Rv 21:1
[ad] Is 32:16; Rm 14:17

---

abilities to arouse the **fleshly desires** of recent converts to Christianity—referenced here as **people who have barely escaped**—and drag them backward into their old lifestyles rather than forward in righteousness.

2:20-21 When Christians are tricked by false teachers into returning to their previous, unrighteous lifestyle that the **knowledge** of Christ had delivered them from, they will find themselves in a worse state since they now know better (2:20).

2:22 In the end, those believers who follow false teachers become like them in their lifestyles. They seek ultimately to satisfy their sinful desires above all else. That situation is depicted by appropriate proverbs, portraying such lifestyles as behaving like disgusting animals.

3:1 The other letter referenced could be either 1 Peter or a letter that has been lost.

3:4 The incorrect implication of their observation—which itself is inaccurate, as Peter will demonstrate—is that world affairs will always continue as they are, and God will not intervene in human history.

3:5-6 Those with a scoffing mentality **deliberately overlook** the fact that God has intervened in human history numerous times. For one, he intervened **long ago** by bringing **the heavens . . . into being** and bringing forth **the earth** (3:5; see Gen 1). This happened **by the word of God** (2 Pet 3:5)—that is, when God spoke at creation, things happened. Likewise today, when God speaks his authoritative Word over an individual's life, things happen. The scoffers also ignore Genesis 6–8, where **the world of that time perished when it was flooded** (3:6).

3:7 By the same word that created the world and brought the flood, God will intervene in human history again by destroying **the present heavens and earth** with **fire** and bringing a **day of judgment and destruction of the ungodly**.

3:8-9 Christians should remember that God can do in **one day** what it would take humans **a thousand years** to do (3:8). God's apparent slowness to intervene on some occasions provides an opportunity for humans to fulfill their responsibilities. The supreme example of this principle is that God delays final judgment because he does not want **any to perish but all to come to repentance** and believe the gospel (3:9). Many are waiting on God, when God is actually waiting on them.

3:10 Here the phrase **day of the Lord** refers specifically to the coming great tribulation period when God will govern the affairs of man in a more direct and open way than he does at present.

3:12 In using the phrase **hasten its coming**, Peter is not saying humans can change God's sovereign timetable. Rather, when a believer focuses every moment of life on pleasing God and doing his will, time seems to fly by as it does on a busy workday in which we hasten from one task to another.

3:13 The **new heavens and a new earth** refer to a promise God made to his people long ago (see Isa 65:17; 66:22).

a 3:14 Php 2:15; 1Th 5:23;
   11m 6:14; Jms 1:27
b 3:15 Ac 9:17; 15:25;
   2Pt 3:2

c 3:16 Heb 5:11; 2Pt 2:14
d 3:17 Lk 12:15; 2Tm
   1:14; 4:15
e 3:18 2Pt 1:2
f Rm 11:36; 2Tm 4:18; Rv 1:6

CONCLUSION

14 Therefore, dear friends, while you wait for these things, make every effort to be found without spot or blemish in his sight, at peace.*a* **15** Also, regard the patience of our Lord as salvation, just as our dear brother Paul has written to you according to the wisdom given to him.*b* **16** He speaks about these things in all his letters. There are some matters that are hard to understand. The untaught and unstable will twist them to their own destruction,*c* as they also do with the rest of the Scriptures.

17 Therefore, dear friends, since you know this in advance, be on your guard,*d* so that you are not led away by the error of lawless people and fall from your own stable position. **18** But grow in the grace and knowledge*e* of our Lord and Savior Jesus Christ. To him be the glory both now and to the day of eternity.*A,f*

A 3:18 Other mss add *Amen.*

3:14 As sacrificial animals in the Old Testament were to be **without spot or blemish in [God's] sight,** new covenant believers are to be without moral defect before the Lord, repenting when they do sin.
3:15 The Lord's delay in coming is designed to give men and women time to repent of sin and come to **salvation.**

3:16 The distortions did not reflect any fault in Paul's writings. Rather, the fault was with **the untaught and unstable** false teachers who **[twisted] them to their own destruction.**

A passing comment acknowledges that Paul's letters already were regarded by the church as among **the Scriptures**.

3:17 Indeed, don't be **led away by the error of** men who talk like Christians but live rebellious, ungodly lives. Maintaining a **stable position** spiritually is the key to godly living.
3:18 The theme of spiritual growth bookends the letter, recurring here after its introduction in 1:1–15.

1 JOHN

INTRODUCTION

Author

ANCIENT MANUSCRIPTS UNANIMOUSLY NAME the author of this letter as John, the son of Zebedee who also authored the Fourth Gospel. The style and vocabulary of 1–3 John and the Fourth Gospel are so similar that it seems they must have come from the same hand. Some scholars, however, believe a different John (that is, someone other than the apostle) is responsible for these New Testament books. Others claim they are a product of a "Johannine school"—the work of early followers of John. Nevertheless, the view with the best support is that John, the disciple of Jesus, is the author.

Historical Background

Second-century Christian sources report that John eventually relocated to Ephesus and ministered to churches there. He continued his pastoral work in that region until nearly AD 100. Thus, Ephesus is the likely location from which John penned 1–3 John. These letters could have been written at any time in the last quarter of the first century.

Message and Purpose

John is the apostle of intimacy. He's very concerned with our fellowship—that is, our closeness with the Lord. His epistles form a trilogy of intimacy. John wrote to Christians, whom he addressed in 1 John as "little children" (2:1, 28; 4:4; 5:21). He speaks of obedience, walking with God in righteousness, submission to the truth, and functioning together in love as being key elements of intimacy with God.

In 2 John 1, the apostle addresses the church as "the elect lady and her children," since the church is the bride of Christ. He writes about truth and love. *Truth* is the absolute standard by which reality is measured, and *love* is the expression of that truth in our care for others. John says that when the church operates in truth and love, we experience true intimacy with God

In 3 John, he addresses Gaius, a hospitable leader who loved to bring in outside teachers who presented the truth. But the church had a problem in the person of Diotrephes, who tried to reject these sound teachers. So John warned about this power-seeking man and the evil behind any attempt to stop true teachers of the Word.

All three epistles seek to promote intimacy with the King as well as with fellow citizens of the kingdom.

www.bhpublishinggroup.com/qr/te/62_00

Outline

I. Fellowship with God by Walking in the Light (1:1-10)
II. Obey, Remain, and Love (2:1-11)
III. Spiritual Maturity and the Enemies of Fellowship (2:12-29)
IV. Being a Child of God and Loving the Children of God (3:1-24)
V. The Spirit of Truth and the Love of God (4:1-19)
VI. Intimacy with God and Praying with Confidence (4:20—5:21)

Video Devotional

"FROM EARTH TO HEAVEN"

Our pathway to heaven is found through complete and total trust in the salvation of Jesus Christ as our substitutionary sacrifice.

PROLOGUE: OUR DECLARATION

1 What was from the beginning,[a] what we have heard, what we have seen with our eyes, what we have observed and have touched with our hands, concerning the word[b] of life — [2] that life was revealed,[c] and we have seen it and we testify and declare to you the eternal life that was with the Father and was revealed to us[d] — [3] what we have seen and heard we also declare to you, so that you may also have fellowship[e] with us; and indeed our fellowship is with the Father[f] and with his Son Jesus Christ. [4] We are writing these things[A] so that our[B] joy[g] may be complete.

FELLOWSHIP WITH GOD

[5] This is the message we have heard from him and declare to you: God is light,[h] and there is absolutely no darkness in him.[i] [6] If we say, "We have fellowship[j] with him," and yet we walk in darkness,[k] we are lying and are not practicing the truth.[l] [7] If we walk in the light[m] as he himself is in the light, we have fellowship with one another, and the blood of Jesus[n] his Son cleanses us from all sin. [8] If we say, "We have no sin,"[o] we are deceiving ourselves, and the truth is not

in us. [9] If we confess our sins, he is faithful and righteous to forgive[p] us our sins and to cleanse us from all unrighteousness. [10] If we say, "We have not sinned," we make him a liar, and his word[q] is not in us.[r]

2 My little children, I am writing you these things so that you may not sin. But if anyone does sin, we have an advocate[s] with the Father — Jesus Christ the righteous one. [2] He himself is the atoning sacrifice[c,t] for our sins, and not only for ours, but also for those of the whole world.[u]

GOD'S COMMANDS

[3] This is how we know[v] that we know him: if we keep his commands.[w] [4] The one who says, "I have come to know him," and yet doesn't keep his commands, is a liar, and the truth is not in him. [5] But whoever keeps his word,[x] truly in him the love of God is made complete. This is how we know we are in him:[y] [6] The one who says he remains in him[z] should walk just as he walked.

[7] Dear friends, I am not writing you a new command[aa] but an old command that you have had from the beginning. The old command is the word[ab] you have heard. [8] Yet I am writing you a new command,

[a] 1:1 Jn 1:1; 1Jn 2:13-14
[b] Ps 119:25; Jn 1:1,4; 5:24; Php 2:16
[c] 1:2 Jn 1:31; 21:1,14; Col 3:4; 1Pt 5:4; 1Jn 2:28; 3:5,8
[d] 1Jn 5:20
[e] 1:3 Php 3:10
[f] Mt 11:27
[g] 1:4 2Co 2:3; Php 1:4,25; 2:18
[h] 1:5 Ps 27:1; 36:9; Jn 12:46; 1Tm 6:16

[i] 1Jn 2:5 [j] 1:6 2Co 8:4 [k] Pr 2:13; Is 9:2; 50:10; Jn 8:12; 12:35; 1Jn 2:11 [l] Jn 14:6; 2Co 11:10; 3Jn 3 [m] 1:7 Eph 5:8-14; Php 2:15; Col 1:12-14; 1Th 5:5 [n] Heb 10:19; 12:24; 1Pt 1:2,19; Rv 1:5 [o] 1:8 Pr 20:9; Jr 2:35; Rm 3:9-23; Jms 3:2

[p] 1:9 Ps 103:3; Jr 31:34; Mt 9:6; 26:28; Col 1:14; Jms 5:15 [q] 1:10 Lk 8:21; Heb 4:12 [r] Jn 8:37 [s] 2:1 Jn 14:26 [t] 2:2 Rm 3:25; 2Co 5:21; Heb 2:17; 1Jn 4:10 [u] Mt 26:13; 28:19-20; Mk 14:9; Rm 1:8 [v] 2:3 Jn 13:35; 1Jn 2:5; 3:19,24; 4:2,6,13; 5:2 [w] Jn 14:15; 15:10 [x] 2:5 Jn 14:23 [y] Jn 6:56; 14:20; 15:1-7; Rm 8:1; 2Co 5:17; Eph 2:10; Php 1:1 [z] 2:6 Jn 15:4-7; 1Jn 2:24,27-28; 3:6,24; 4:13,15-16 [aa] 2:7 Mk 7:8; Jn 13:34; 2Jn 5 [ab] Lk 6:47; Jn 1:1

[A] 1:4 Other mss add *to you*   [B] 1:4 Other mss read *your*   [C] 2:2 Or *the propitiation*

1:1-2 When John talks about Jesus, he's not delivering second-hand information. He's communicating about what he saw and **observed** and **touched**.

1:3 How can you, in the twenty-first century, hang out with the apostles so you can have the same level of intimate **fellowship** (Greek, *koinonia*) with God that they enjoyed? Through studying the New Testament in general and 1 John in particular. This goes beyond the legal relationship of justification to intimate communion with the Savior that is available to all believers. The truth of the Bible, when applied to the life of the believer, enhances their fellowship and spiritual intimacy with God.

1:4 True joy transcends external circumstances. It is stability on the inside in spite of what is occurring on the outside.

1:5 When John describes **God** as **light**, he calls to mind Jesus's words as recorded in his Gospel: "The light has come into the world, and people loved darkness rather than the light because their deeds were evil" (John 3:19). The function of light is to reveal things as they truly are, to expose. If you shine a light down a city alley at night, you'll see cockroaches scatter because they want to do their dirty work in secret. If you want God's personal presence and activity in your life, you must be

willing to allow his light to expose your sinful thoughts, attitudes, speech, and actions that are inconsistent with his character.

1:6-7 Fellowship with God is determined by our walk not by our talk. Only as we live fully exposed to the truth of God is the ongoing cleansing work of **the blood of Jesus** activated to reveal, cleanse, and empower us to address the sin that has been exposed (1:7). Then fellowship with God is maintained and expanded. Failure to do this keeps God's work dormant in the life of the believer (see 2 Cor 3:17-18).

1:8-10 When we **confess our sins** to God, we are agreeing with what God's Word reveals about us (1:9). We are admitting that what the light exposes is not just a mistake, a bad habit, or a mere product of our upbringing. It's sin. This allows forgiveness and cleansing power to flow. To deny your sin is to call God **a liar** and forfeit the hope of his **word** doing its transforming work in your life (1:10).

2:1 Consider the advocacy of **Jesus**. If you are a believer, Jesus represents you before the bar of God's judgment. You were a bankrupt sinner who couldn't afford a lawyer, but the Father appointed his own Son in your defense. This advocate doesn't share your sin problem; he's the only **righteous one**. He paid

your debt on the cross, and his shed blood continues to cleanse you today.

2:2 Jesus has appeased God's just wrath against sin by his sacrificial death for the whole human race (i.e., unlimited atonement). He satisfied (i.e., propitiation) God's righteous demands so that the Creator is favorably disposed toward those who place faith in him for eternal life. Let this sink in: God himself paid the price for a legal relationship and intimate fellowship with you.

2:3-4 Obedience rooted in love is the requirement for ongoing, deepening fellowship with God. To **know him** is a reference to intimate fellowship not justification, since John's readers are already believers (2:4; see 2:1, 28; 4:4; 5:21).

2:5-6 Some people dip their teabags in and out of hot water to steep their tea. Many Christians approach their relationship with Jesus like this—dipping in and out of church on Sunday mornings, with little change resulting. Other tea drinkers place their teabags in the water and let them remain. In time, the tea seeps into the water and transforms it. For Christ to influence and transform your life, you must remain (or abide) **in him** (2:6).

2:7-8 John's thinking of the **command** to love one another. It summarizes the others. It's **old** because it's found in Leviticus 19:18, but

which is true in him and in you, because the darkness is passing away[a] and the true light[b] is already shining.[c] **9** The one who says he is in the light but hates his brother or sister[d] is in the darkness until now. **10** The one who loves his brother or sister[e] remains in the light, and there is no cause for stumbling in him.[A] **11** But the one who hates his brother or sister[f] is in the darkness, walks in the darkness,[g] and doesn't know where he's going,[h] because the darkness has blinded his eyes.

REASONS FOR WRITING

12   I am writing to you, little children, since your sins have been forgiven on account of his name.[i]

13   I am writing to you, fathers, because you have come to know the one who is from the beginning.[j]
       I am writing to you, young men, because you have conquered the evil one.[k]

14   I have written to you, children, because you have come to know the Father.
       I have written to you, fathers, because you have come to know the one who is from the beginning.
       I have written to you, young men, because you are strong, God's word[l] remains in you, and you have conquered the evil one.

A WARNING ABOUT THE WORLD

15 Do not love the world[m] or the things in the world. If anyone loves the world, the

love of the Father is not in him. **16** For everything in the world — the lust of the flesh,[n] the lust of the eyes,[o] and the pride[p] in one's possessions — is not from the Father, but is from the world. **17** And the world with its lust is passing away,[q] but the one who does the will of God[r] remains forever.[s]

THE LAST HOUR

18 Children, it is the last hour.[t] And as you have heard that antichrist[u] is coming, even now many antichrists have come. By this we know that it is the last hour. **19** They went out from us, but they did not belong to us; for if they had belonged to us, they would have remained with us. However, they went out so that it might be made clear that none of them belongs to us.

20 But you have an anointing[v] from the Holy One,[w] and all of you know the truth.[B] **21** I have not written to you because you don't know the truth, but because you do know it, and because no lie comes from the truth. **22** Who is the liar, if not the one who denies that Jesus is the Christ?[x] This one is the antichrist: the one who denies

[a] **2:8** Rm 13:12; 1Co 7:31; 1Jn 2:17
[b] Jn 1:9; 3:19-21; 8:12; 12:46
[c] Jn 1:5; 12:35-36; Rv 22:5
[d] **2:9** 1Jn 2:11; 3:15; 4:20
[e] **2:10** Rm 12:10; 1Th 4:9; Heb 13:1; 1Pt 1:22; 1Jn 3:10,14-17; 4:20-21
[f] **2:11** Lv 19:17; 1Jn 3:15; 4:20
[g] 1Jn 1:6
[h] Jn 14:6
[i] **2:12** Ps 25:11; Lk 24:47; Ac 2:38; 10:43
[j] **2:13** 1Jn 1:1
[k] Jn 16:33; 17:15; Eph 6:10; 1Jn 2:14; 4:4; 5:4-5; Rv 2:7
[l] **2:14** 1Jn 1:10
[m] **2:15** Jn 15:19; 17:16; Rm 12:2; Jms 1:27; 4:4

[n] **2:16** Rm 13:14; Eph 2:3; 1Pt 4:2; 2Pt 2:18
[o] Gn 3:6; Pr 27:20
[p] Jms 4:16
[q] **2:17** 1Jn 2:8
[r] Mk 3:35; Eph 6:6; 1Th 4:3; 1Pt 2:15
[s] Jn 8:35; 12:34; 2Co 9:9; 1Pt 1:25
[t] **2:18** Jn 2:4; 1Pt 4:7
[u] Mt 24:5,24; 1Jn 2:22; 4:3; 2Jn 7
[v] **2:20** 2Co 1:21
[w] Ps 89:18; Mk 1:24; Ac 10:38
[x] **2:22** Jn 20:31; Ac 18:5; Eph 5:2; 1Jn 5:1

it's also **new** because it's the governing commandment for the Christian life.

2:9-11 When you love your **brother or sister**, you seek to comprehensively and righteously meet his or her need in a way that brings glory to God (2:9). It is no mere expression of feelings but an expression of something higher, something eternal. "God is love" (4:8).

2:12-14 All Christians enjoy God's judicial forgiveness and have been adopted as his children. **Fathers . . . young men . . . children** are terms corresponding to different stages of spiritual development. Their goal is maturity.

2:15 When the moon shines, it's actually reflecting the light of the sun. Sometimes the earth gets in the way, though, so that the moon's light is diminished. Similarly, we have an enemy that prevents us from reflecting the *Son's* light on us. That enemy is called the world.

When John talks about not loving the world, he's not talking about planet earth. He's talking about an organized system

headed by Satan that draws us away from God's love and will. You **love the world** when it owns your affections and governs your choices by getting you to exclude God.

2:16-17 What does the world offer you? First, it promises to satisfy legitimate desires in illegitimate ways (**the lust of the flesh**). Eating is legitimate; gluttony is worldly. Sex is legitimate; immorality is worldly. Second, the world tempts your mind through what your eyes see (**the lust of the eyes**). The biblical word for this is *covetousness*, which is desiring and pursuing that which is not legitimate for you to have. Third, there is **the pride in one's possessions**—that is, living to impress others (2:16). What those in love with the world forget, however, is that **the world with its lust is passing away**. Worldliness makes the "now" more important than eternity. But you are passing through, and the world is passing by. It's transient. Only **the one who does the will of God remains forever** (2:17). The price

tag for loving the world is the loss of personal intimacy with God.

2:18 **The last hour** refers to the period of history that falls between the coming of Christ and his return. Though the antichrist will appear during the tribulation when the church is raptured (see Dan 9:26-27; 1 Thess 4:13-18; 2 Thess 2:3; Rev 11:2; 13:1-8), *little* **antichrists** are active already. An antichrist *opposes* and *replaces* Christ with the goal of distracting and derailing Christians from pursuing Jesus.

2:20-23 What power and protection do believers have against spiritual liars? **An anointing** and **the truth** (2:20-21). "An anointing" is not some special gift shared by only elite clergy. John is addressing spiritual "children" (2:18). Every Christian has the anointing: the internal teaching ministry of the Holy Spirit who illuminates the believer's mind to understand and apply God's truth, as well as to detect deception.

[a] 2:23 Jn 5:23
[b] Jn 8:19; 16:3; 17:3; 1Jn 4:15; 5:1; 2Jn 9
[c] 2:24 Jn 15:4-7; 1Jn 2:6,27-28; 3:6,24; 4:13,15-16
[d] Jn 10:38; Col 3:3; 1Th 1:1; 1Jn 4:15-16
[e] 2:25 Jn 4:14; 1Tm 4:8; 2Tm 1:1; Ti 1:2
[f] 2:27 Jn 14:26
[g] Jn 15:4-7; 1Jn 2:6; 3:6,24; 4:13,15-16
[h] 2:28 Lk 17:30; Col 3:4; 1Jn 3:2
[i] 1Th 2:19
[j] 2:29 Gn 18:19; Dt 6:18; 1Jn 3:7,10
[k] Jn 1:12-13; 3:3-7; 8:41; 1Jn 3:9; 4:7; 5:1,4,18

[l] 3:2 2Co 4:11; 1Pt 5:4; 1Jn 2:28
[m] Rm 8:29; 1Co 15:49; 2Co 3:18; Php 3:21; 2Pt 1:4
[n] 1Co 13:12; Heb 12:14; Rv 22:4
[o] 3:3 Ac 23:6; 1Th 1:3
[p] Php 4:8
[q] 3:5 Jn 1:29; 1Co 15:3; Heb 10:4; 1Pt 2:24
[r] 2Co 5:21; Heb 4:15; 7:26; 1Pt 2:21-22; 3:18; 1Jn 2:29
[s] 3:6 Jn 15:4-7; 1Jn 2:6,24,27-28; 3:24; 4:13,15-16
[t] Rm 6:11-12; 1Jn 2:29; 5:18
[u] 3:8 Mk 1:11
[v] Jn 21:1; 2Co 4:11; 1Pt 5:4; 1Jn 5:20
[w] 3:9 1Jn 2:29
[x] 1Pt 1:23
[y] 3:10 1Jn 2:10; 3:14-17; 4:20-21
[z] 3:12 Gn 4:1; Jd 11
[aa] 2Th 3:3

the Father and the Son. [23] No one who denies the Son has the Father;[a] he who confesses the Son has the Father as well.[b]

REMAINING WITH GOD

[24] What you have heard from the beginning is to remain in you. If what you have heard from the beginning remains in you, then you will remain in the Son[c] and in the Father.[d] [25] And this is the promise that he himself made to us: eternal life.[e]

[26] I have written these things to you concerning those who are trying to deceive you. [27] As for you, the anointing you received from him remains in you, and you don't need anyone to teach you. Instead, his anointing teaches you about all things[f] and is true and is not a lie; just as it has taught you,[A] remain in him.[g]

GOD'S CHILDREN

[28] So now, little children, remain in him so that when he appears[h] we may have confidence and not be ashamed before him at his coming.[i] [29] If you know that he is righteous, you know this as well: Everyone who does what is right[j] has been born of him.[k] 3 [1] See what great love[B] the Father has given us that we should be called God's children — and we are! The reason the world does not know us is that it didn't know him. [2] Dear friends, we are God's children now, and what we will be

has not yet been revealed.[l] We know that when he appears,[c] we will be like him[m] because we will see him as he is.[n] [3] And everyone who has this hope[o] in him purifies himself just as he is pure.[p]

[4] Everyone who commits sin practices lawlessness; and sin is lawlessness. [5] You know that he was revealed so that he might take away sins,[D,q] and there is no sin in him.[r] [6] Everyone who remains in him[s] does not sin;[E,f] everyone who sins[F] has not seen him or known him.

[7] Children, let no one deceive you. The one who does what is right is righteous, just as he is righteous. [8] The one who commits[G] sin is of the devil, for the devil has sinned from the beginning. The Son of God[u] was revealed[v] for this purpose: to destroy the devil's works. [9] Everyone who has been born of God[w] does not sin,[H] because his seed[x] remains in him; he is not able to sin,[I] because he has been born of God. [10] This is how God's children and the devil's children become obvious. Whoever does not do what is right is not of God, especially the one who does not love his brother or sister.[y]

LOVE IN ACTION

[11] For this is the message you have heard from the beginning: We should love one another, [12] unlike Cain,[z] who was of the evil one[aa] and murdered his brother. And why

[A] 2:27 Or as he has taught you   [B] 3:1 Or what sort of love   [C] 3:2 Or when it appears   [D] 3:5 Other mss read our sins   [E] 3:6 Or not keep on sinning   [F] 3:6 Or who keeps on sinning   [G] 3:8 Or practices   [H] 3:9 Or not practice sin   [I] 3:9 Or to keep on sinning

---

2:24 John's point here is that the Holy Spirit's ministry always remains available to teach Christians, but the truth (**what you have heard from the beginning**) *must* remain in us. Think of it like satellite TV. The satellite communicates, but your satellite dish must receive the signal. The power of the Holy Spirit is available to every believer, but many believers do not operate in a position of dependence on the Spirit because their satellite dishes only function on Sunday mornings.
2:28 A Christian can be accepted but not acceptable. A child who plays in the mud, for instance, is accepted by his or her parents; he or she is not, however, in an acceptable condition. Live everyday on high alert, looking for Jesus to return, and it will influence how you live.
3:1 This **Father** business isn't mere religious talk or an attempt to tap into the power of positive thinking. If you are a Christian, you have a perfect heavenly Father who loves you and who doesn't share any of the failures of your earthly father. What's more, he's the King of creation. You are royalty. Nevertheless, do not be surprised when the world rejects you; it rejected God's Son because **it didn't know him** either. You're in good company.

3:2 At Christ's return, you will be miraculously changed, and it will be manifest to all. At his appearing, the graves will be robbed, and we will be transformed with resurrected bodies.
3:4 When you sin, you're a lawbreaker; you're acting in rebellion against God.
3:6-10 John said "there is no sin in" Christ (3:5). Therefore, whoever remains in him **does not sin** either (3:6). Since believers are called to remain in him (see 2:6; John 15:5-7), we sin only because we're not remaining in Christ. John says, **Everyone who has been born of God does not sin**. The reason is that God's **seed remains in him** (1 John 3:9). When you placed your faith in Jesus Christ, God gave you new life—which John describes as God's "seed." Every Christian is born again. This new spiritual life or seed is from God, so it is pure and sinless.
Why, then, do we still sin in thought, word, and deed even though we'd prefer not to? Because the old part of us is still contaminated by sin. Paul calls our unredeemed humanity "the flesh," and he wrestles with this in Romans 7:13-25. The new life of Christ is planted in us in seed form, but we still bear the damage of sin in our souls. When Christ returns, the flesh will be completely eradicated, and we will be

without sin. Until then, we must continually repent of sin, submit to God's Word, and walk with the Spirit so that the seed of the new divine nature may grow.
Don't be deceived. **The one who does what is right is righteous** (1 John 3:7). **The one who commits sin is of the devil** (3:8). How, then, can a believer do what is right *and* commit sin in the space of a few seconds? Consider Peter. He boldly confessed that Jesus is the Christ, and Jesus blessed him because God had revealed it to him (see Matt 16:13-17). However, in no time, Jesus told Peter, "Get behind me, Satan," when he denied that Christ must suffer (Matt 16:21-23).
Throughout each day, your actions will either be influenced by God or the devil. Satan can't make you sin, but he can entice you. So, to whom will you listen? Will you be **of the devil** so that he gets credit for your deeds (1 John 3:8)? Or will you live by the truth, come to the light, and do works for which God gets the credit (see John 3:21)? Do **what is right** and love fellow believers in submission to the Holy Spirit (1 John 3:10).
3:11 How important is it to love your brothers and sisters in Christ? Imagine a patient claims to have the flu but has no symptoms.

❧ Questions & Answers ❧

Q C.S. Lewis, in his classic work *The Screw-tape Letters*, once noted, "There are two equal and opposite errors into which our race can fall about the devils. One is to disbelieve in their existence. The other is to believe, and to feel an excessive and unhealthy interest in them. They themselves are equally pleased by both errors and hail a materialist or a magician with the same delight." What would you say is a healthy, balanced, biblical response to the reality of the demonic realm?

A A healthy biblical response to the demonic realm is to believe in its existence and take that belief seriously. Scripture tells us that "our struggle is not against flesh and blood, but . . . against the cosmic powers of this darkness, against evil, spiritual forces in the heavens"

(Eph 6:12). Urging the Corinthians to flee from idolatry, Paul warns them to avoid "the cup of demons" and "the table of demons" (1 Cor 10:21). They *are* around us, and they are working against us, so they cannot be ignored.

Nevertheless, "the one who is in you is greater than the one who is in the world" (1 John 4:4). So you must not be so obsessed with them that you cower in fear and feel that they are controlling you. God's work in you through his Holy Spirit (and his work governing the angelic world on your behalf) is superior to the demonic forces coming against you. Take the evil one seriously, but don't give him the final word because he doesn't have the final word.

FOR THE NEXT Q&A, SEE PAGE 1498.

did he murder him? Because his deeds were evil, and his brother's were righteous. **13** Do not be surprised, brothers and sisters, if the world hates[a] you. **14** We know that we have passed from death to life because we love our brothers and sisters. The one who does not love remains in death.[b] **15** Everyone who hates his brother or sister[c] is a murderer,[d] and you know that no murderer has eternal life residing in him. **16** This is how we have come to know love: He laid down his life[e] for us.[f] We should also lay down our lives for our brothers and sisters.[g] **17** If anyone has this world's goods[h] and sees a fellow believer[A] in need[i] but withholds compassion[j] from him — how does God's love reside in him?[k] **18** Little children, let us not love in word or speech, but in action and in truth.[l] **19** This is how we will know that we belong to the truth[m] and will reassure our hearts before him **20** whenever our hearts

condemn us; for God is greater than our hearts, and he knows all things.[n] **21** Dear friends, if our hearts don't condemn us, we have confidence before God **22** and receive whatever we ask from him because we keep his commands[o] and do what is pleasing in his sight. **23** Now this is his command: that we believe in the name[p] of his Son Jesus Christ, and love one another as he commanded us. **24** The one who keeps his commands remains in him,[q] and he in him. And the way we know that he remains in us[r] is from the Spirit[s] he has given us.

THE SPIRIT OF TRUTH AND THE SPIRIT OF ERROR

4 Dear friends, do not believe every spirit, but test the spirits[t] to see if they are from God, because many false prophets have gone out into the world. **2** This is how you know the Spirit of God: Every spirit that confesses that Jesus

[a] 3:13 Jn 17:14
[b] 3:14 Jn 8:51
[c] 3:15 1Jn 2:9,11; 4:20
[d] Mt 5:21-22; Jn 8:44
[e] 3:16 Jn 10:11,14,17-18; 13:37-38; 15:13
[f] Is 53:10; Mk 10:45
[g] Mk 8:34-35; 1Co 11:1; Php 2:5-8
[h] 3:17 Mk 12:44; Lk 15:12; 1Jn 2:16
[i] Ac 2:45
[j] 2Co 7:15
[k] Jms 2:15-16; 1Jn 2:5
[l] 3:18 Mt 7:21; Jn 13:34-35; 15:12-17; Jms 1:22-25; 2:14-17
[m] 3:19 Jn 14:6; 2Co 11:10; 3Jn 3
[n] 3:20 Ps 139:6; Pr 2:6; Jn 14:28
[o] 3:22 Mk 7:8; Jn 14:15; 1Jn 2:3; 5:2
[p] 3:23 Ps 33:21; Is 50:10; Jn 1:12; 3:18; 1Jn 5:13
[q] 3:24 Jn 11:13; Jn 15:4-7; Ac 5:32; 15:8
[r] Jn 6:56
[s] Rm 8:9-16
[t] 4:1 1Th 5:21

[A] 3:17 Lit *sees his brother or sister*

A doctor would say, "You don't have the flu." Similarly, the ultimate "symptom" or proof of your vertical intimacy with God is your horizontal love for his children. *Love* is the decision to compassionately, righteously, and responsibly seek the well-being of another.
3:15 To hate is to murder in your heart, and **no murderer has eternal life residing in him**. This is not referring to salvation but to enjoyment of the Christian life and intimacy with God.
3:17 Meeting the needs of **fellow** Christians — whether physical, emotional, or financial — is

the most practical demonstration of **love** and the most telling symptom of fellowship with God.
3:18 Beware of merely declaring your love with your mouth. What your lips proclaim, your life must support.
3:19-20 The idea here is that when you serve other believers in love, God will calm your heart when you are in turmoil.
3:21-22 Lack of **confidence** is a tremendous stumbling block to prayer. But when you love others and act as an answer to their prayers, you can be confident that your Father will

put things in motion to answer your prayer according to his will.
4:1 Some deceivers may even come in the name of Jesus. So if you watch Christian television, listen to Christian radio, or read Christian books, be discerning. "Satan disguises himself as an angel of light" (2 Cor 11:14).
4:2-3 According to early Christian tradition, a heresy circulated in John's day that distinguished between Jesus (a man) and Christ (a supernatural being). Proponents taught that Christ descended on Jesus at his baptism and departed at the crucifixion.

[a]4:2 Jn 1:14; Php 2:7; 3:3
[b]1Co 12:3
[c]4:3 1Jn 2:18,22; 2Jn 7
[d]4:4 Rm 8:31; Col 1:27;
1Jn 3:20
[e]Jn 12:31
[f]4:5 Jn 17:6; 2Pt 2:20
[g]4:6 Jn 8:47
[h]Mk 13:5-6; 1Co 2:12;
1Tm 4:1
[i]4:7 1Jn 2:29
[j]4:9 Mk 9:37
[k]Jn 1:14,18; 3:16,18
[l]Jn 10:28
[m]4:10 Jn 3:16
[n]2Co 5:21; 1Jn 2:2
[o]4:11 Jn 13:14; 15:12; Rm
13:8; 1Th 4:9; 1Pt 1:22
[p]4:12 Ex 33:20
[q]4:13 Jn 15:4-7; 1Jn
2:6,24,27-28; 3:6,24;
4:15-16
[r]Rv 3:22
[s]4:14 Rm 1:3
[t]4:15 Jn 9:22; Php 2:6

[u]4:17 Mt 10:15; 11:22,24;
12:36; 2Pt 2:9; 3:7; Jd 6
[v]Jn 14:10-11; 15:9-10;
17:11,15,18
[w]4:18 Rm 8:15

Christ has come in the flesh[a] is from God,[b] [3] but every spirit that does not confess Jesus[A] is not from God. This is the spirit of the antichrist,[c] which you have heard is coming; even now it is already in the world.

[4] You are from God, little children, and you have conquered them, because the one who is in you[d] is greater than the one who is in the world.[e] [5] They are from the world.[f] Therefore what they say is from the world, and the world listens to them. [6] We are from God. Anyone who knows God listens to us;[g] anyone who is not from God does not listen to us. This is how we know the Spirit of truth and the spirit of deception.[h]

KNOWING GOD THROUGH LOVE

[7] Dear friends, let us love one another, because love is from God, and everyone who loves has been born of God[i] and knows God. [8] The one who does not love does not know God, because God is love. [9] God's love was revealed among us[B] in this way: God sent[j] his one and only Son[k] into the world so that we might live[l] through him. [10] Love consists in this: not that we loved God, but that he loved us[m] and sent his Son to be the atoning sacrifice[C,n] for our sins. [11] Dear friends, if God loved us in this way, we also must love one another.[o] [12] No one has ever seen God.[p] If we love one another, God remains in[D] us and his love is made complete in us. [13] This is how we know that we remain in him[q] and he in us: He has given us of his Spirit.[r] [14] And we have seen and we testify that the Father has sent his Son[s] as the world's Savior. [15] Whoever confesses[t] that Jesus is the Son of God — God remains in him and he in God. [16] And we have come to know and to believe the love that God has for us.

God is love, and the one who remains in love remains in God, and God remains in him. [17] In this, love is made complete with us so that we may have confidence in the day of judgment,[u] because as he is, so also are we in this world.[v] [18] There is no fear in love; instead, perfect love drives out fear,[w]

[A]4:3 Other mss read *confess that Jesus has come in the flesh*   [B]4:9 Or *in us*   [C]4:10 Or *the propitiation*   [D]4:12 Or *remains among*

To this lie John says, "No." Jesus *is* the Christ (see 2:22), and Jesus Christ came **in the flesh** (4:2). He is the unique, eternal Son of God who offers salvation from sin only by grace through faith in him. He is the God-Man. His mother gave birth to him because he was man, but he created her because he is God. He went to sleep because he was a man, but he commanded the wind and waves to go to sleep because he's God. The truth about the uniqueness of Jesus must be your spiritual foundation.
4:4 The tremendous pressure in the ocean's depths can crush a diver. But if you descend inside a pressurized diving bell, it exerts pres-

sure *outward* to protect you from destruction. When Christians go into the world, they will experience extreme pressure—especially as they go deeper. But have no fear. The pressure inside of you is **greater than** the pressure on you.
4:6 Anyone who knows God listens to us. The apostles were Jesus's chosen representatives. They witnessed his resurrection, and they composed the New Testament under the inspiration of the Holy Spirit. Read and know what they wrote.
4:7-8 As sure as the magnetic pull of the earth causes a compass to point north, the magnetic pull of God's **love** at work in your heart

will always point you to other brothers and sisters who need love.
4:10-11 We hated God. We were fools, rebelling against the King of the universe. Nevertheless, he set his **love** on us (4:10). You're going to love people who won't respond in kind. But they need your love nonetheless.
4:12 People can't see God, but they should see the **love** of **God** operating through you.
4:15 Living in the atmosphere of love means you are living in the atmosphere of God.
4:17-18 Every believer will stand before the **judgment** seat of Christ (4:17). Don't think of it as a trial to determine your salvation but as the Judge's opportunity to evaluate the

Be Strong in the Lord

OING BATTLE AGAINST SATAN REQUIRES more than a New Year's resolution and a dose of will power. Spiritual warfare requires spiritual weaponry. The strength you need to successfully do such battle is supplied by God. That may seem obvious. But, judging from the way we treat this truth, it bears repeating.

Many of us tend to swing toward one of two extremes when it comes to the devil. Some overestimate him. They become fearful and timid, lest Satan leap upon them. Remember: "The one who is in you is greater than the one who is in the world" (1 JOHN 4:4).

Others underestimate the devil. Yes, Satan is a defeated foe. But even though he is nothing more than a condemned death row inmate awaiting execution, it is not wise to sleep in his cell. When the apostle Paul spoke about spiritual warfare, he made a very critical point. Paul reminded us that our strength is not in ourselves, but in God. He said, "Be strengthened by the Lord and by his vast strength" (EPH 6:10).

In our humanity, we do not have the power to overcome the evil spirits at work in this world. You cannot beat the devil on your own. Only God is capable of putting the devil in his place, and that is exactly what he will do someday (SEE REV 20). In the meantime, however, God limits Satan's reach and empowers us to achieve victory in our day-to-day encounters with darkness when we put on "the full armor of God" (EPH 6:13).

I can envision Paul in his prison cell, dictating this letter to the Ephesian church. Perhaps he paused, searching for a perfect illustration to help him communicate this vital truth. Suddenly, his gaze fell on the Roman centurion to whom he was chained. Noticing the various components of the guard's uniform, Paul set about to describe six vital pieces of armor necessary for victory in spiritual warfare: the belt of truth, breastplate of righteousness, shoes of peace, shield of faith, helmet of salvation, and the sword of the spirit. It is only when you put on and use the full armor of God that you will experience the victory that is yours for the taking.

A young boy once went to the zoo with his dad. As they passed the lions' den, one of the lions let out a ferocious roar. Startled, the boy grabbed onto his father, covered his face, and began to cry. His father asked, "What's wrong?"

The little boy replied, "Don't you see the lion?"

"Yes," his father answered, "but I also see the cage."

Satan is a defeated foe, a caged lion. But your victory in spiritual warfare must rest on the reality that God has given you everything you need to live in light of this truth in order to experience and become all that he has created you to be. God will not dress you. You are going to have to put on the armor of God every day in order to experience the victory that is yours.

Until you recognize that your struggle is not with man but with spiritual forces of wickedness in the heavenly places, you will never live in victory. The first key in winning the battles of spiritual warfare comes in identifying the true enemy you and I face. The enemy is not that which we can see. Satan lies beneath the surface, seeking to create havoc in God's people.

a 4:18 Eph 4:11-16
b 4:19 2Th 2:13
c 4:20 1Jn 2:9,11; 3:15
d 1Jn 1:10
e 1Jn 2:10; 3:10,14-17
f 5:1 1Jn 2:29

g 5:3 Dt 30:11; Mt 11:30;
　　23:4,23
h 5:5 1Co 15:57; 2Pt 2:20
i Jn 5:19; 14:1; Heb 1:2
j 5:6 Mk 1:11; Jn 1:34
k Jn 17:1; 1Jn 1:7; 4:10
l Jn 15:26; Ac 26:5

☙ KINGDOM LIVING ❧
COMMUNITY
Good Works and God's Glory

Jesus's earthly ministry consistently modeled the integration of justice through the spiritual and the social in that he dwelt among the oppressed, ate with them (Luke 5:27-32), comforted them (Luke 12:22-34), fed them (Luke 9:10-17), restored them (Luke 5:12-16), and ministered to them (Luke 7:18-23) in fulfillment of his Father's will. All of Jesus's good works were clearly connected to the spiritual purposes of God (Matt 4:23-24).

Christ's followers are to influence society for God through the good works they do for others in the name of God, too. Good works are not good words, nor are they simply good things. After all, you don't have to be a Christian to do good things or to say something kind. The unsaved can build orphanages and houses, give money, and visit the sick. But the unsaved cannot glorify God through good works. What we do for others must always be tied to God's glory.

The apostle John stressed the connection between love for God and love for others: "If anyone says, 'I love God,' and yet hates his brother or sister, he is a liar. For the person who does not love his brother or sister whom he has seen cannot love God whom he has not seen" (1 John 4:20). John reminded us that this love is to be expressed through actions and not just words as it is carried out "in action and in truth" (1 John 3:18). A just society is comprised of people who truly understand what biblical justice entails and daily seek to promote it in the lives of all.

Biblical justice isn't simply a ministry to be relegated to a special event. Biblical justice is a foundational part of fulfilling the purpose of the church as intimated by the heart of God. It results from God's people being what he has called us to be and participating in what he has called us to do.

because fear involves punishment.[A] So the one who fears is not complete in love.[a] **19** We love[B] because he first loved us.[b] **20** If anyone says, "I love God," and yet hates his brother or sister,[c] he is a liar.[d] For the person who does not love his brother or sister[e] whom he has seen cannot love God whom he has not seen.[c] **21** And we have this command from him: The one who loves God must also love his brother and sister.

5 Everyone who believes that Jesus is the Christ has been born of God,[f] and everyone who loves the Father[D] also loves the one born of him. **2** This is how we know that we love God's children: when we love God and obey[E] his commands. **3** For this

is what love for God is: to keep his commands. And his commands are not a burden,[g] **4** because everyone who has been born of God conquers the world. This is the victory that has conquered the world: our faith.

THE CERTAINTY OF GOD'S TESTIMONY

5 Who is the one who conquers the world[h] but the one who believes that Jesus is the Son of God?[i] **6** Jesus Christ — he is the one who came by water and blood, not by water only, but by water[j] and by blood.[k] And the Spirit is the one who testifies,[l] because the Spirit is the truth. **7** For there are three

---

[A] 4:18 Or *fear has its own punishment* or *torment*　[B] 4:19 Other mss add *him*　[C] 4:20 Other mss read *has seen, how is he able to love . . . seen?* (as a question)　[D] 5:1 Or *loves the one who has given birth*　[E] 5:2 Other mss read *keep*

Christian life you lived (see 2 Cor 5:10). In spite of your sins and failures, if you actively sought to minister in love to members of God's family, you will be able to stand with confidence on that day because "love covers a multitude of" offenses (1 Pet 4:8). You will have no reason to **fear** (1 John 4:18).
4:20-21 Many Christians began their spiritual lives with excitement about Jesus only to become discouraged at some point. According to John, victory over this problem is achieved when faith in Christ leads to love of God's children. Your love for God is not measured by what you say (**I love God**) but

what you do. You cannot claim to **love** the invisible **God** if you refuse to actively **love** the Christian **brother or sister** standing in front of you (4:20). God has intertwined loving him and loving his children (4:21).
5:2 You are not an only child in the family of God. To ignore your brother in Christ is to cut yourself off from intimacy with God.
5:3 If your Christian life is weighing you down, you're not living the real Christian life. God's **commands are not a burden**. When obedience is driven by love, it loses its burden. Ask any mother of a newborn. She doesn't feed, change, clean, and comfort her baby because

of a command—but because of love. Does she become tired and dirty? Of course. But the work isn't a burden per se because it's her baby she's attending.
5:5 The faith that saved you, that gave you positional, spiritual victory at conversion, will continue to give you victory through what you do. Why? Because the faith that acts—that loves one's neighbor—is placed in the same victorious **Jesus**.
5:6-8 These **three** witnesses **testify** together: **the Spirit, the water, and the blood** (5:7-8). The *water* refers to Christ's baptism when the Father praised his Son and the Holy

that testify:[A,a] [8] the Spirit,[b] the water, and the blood[c] — and these three are in agreement. [9] If we accept human testimony, God's testimony[d] is greater, because it is God's testimony that he has given about his Son. [10] The one who believes in the Son of God has this testimony within himself. The one who does not believe God has made him a liar,[e] because he has not believed in the testimony God has given about his Son. [11] And this is the testimony: God has given us eternal life, and this life is in his Son. [12] The one who has the Son has life.[f] The one who does not have the Son of God does not have life. [13] I have written these things to you who believe in the name[g] of the Son of God so that you may know that you have eternal life.

EFFECTIVE PRAYER

[14] This is the confidence we have before him: If we ask[h] anything according to his will, he hears us.[i] [15] And if we know that he hears whatever we ask,[j] we know that we have what we have asked of him.[k]

[16] If anyone sees a fellow believer[B] committing a sin that doesn't lead to death, he should ask, and God will give life to him — to those who commit sin that doesn't lead to death. There is sin[c] that leads to death. I am not saying he should pray about that. [17] All unrighteousness is sin, and there is sin that doesn't lead to death.

CONCLUSION

[18] We know that everyone who has been born of God does not sin, but the one who is born of God keeps him,[D,l] and the evil one does not touch him. [19] We know that we are of God, and the whole world is under the sway of the evil one. [20] And we know that the Son of God has come[m] and has given us understanding so that we may know the true one.[E] We are in the true one — that is, in his Son Jesus Christ.[n] He is the true God and eternal life.

[21] Little children, guard yourselves from idols.

---

[a] 5:7 Dt 19:15; Mt 18:16; Jn 8:17-18
[b] 5:8 Jn 1:32; 19:30; 20:22
[c] Jn 19:34
[d] 5:9 Jn 5:36-37; 8:18
[e] 5:10 Gn 3:4
[f] 5:12 Jn 3:15,36; 5:24; 6:40,47
[g] 5:13 1Jn 3:23
[h] 5:14 Mt 7:7; Jn 14:13; 1Jn 3:22
[i] Mt 7:8; Jn 9:31; 11:22
[j] 5:15 Jms 1:5
[k] Jn 11:22; 16:24

[l] 5:18 Jn 17:12; 1Pt 1:5; Jd 24; Rv 3:10
[m] 5:20 Jn 1:14; 8:42; 1Jn 1:2; 3:5,8
[n] Jn 10:38; 15:9; 17:21; 1Th 1:1; 1Jn 2:23-24

A 5:7-8 A few late Gk mss and some late Vg mss add *testify in heaven: the Father, the Word, and the Holy Spirit, and these three are one.* [8] *And there are three who bear witness on earth:*   B 5:16 Lit *sees his brother or sister*   C 5:16 Or *is a sin*   D 5:18 Other mss read *himself*   E 5:20 Other mss read *the true God*

Spirit descended on him (see Matt 3:16-17). The *blood* refers to Christ's sacrificial death when darkness covered the land, the earth quaked, and the temple veil split in two (see Matt 27:45, 51). In these events, God gave testimony to the truthfulness of his Son and his mission. The third witness is the *Spirit*, who validates on the inside what God does on the outside.

5:9-10 A basic principle of God's Word is that a "matter must be established by the testimony of two or three witnesses" (2 Cor 13:1; see Deut 19:15). The tragic truth is that in spite of the threefold **testimony** God has provided (see the note on 1 John 5:6-8), too many believe man rather than God. That's equivalent to calling God **a liar** (5:10).

5:11 What does God want you to believe? **God has given us eternal life.** In John's Gospel, Jesus defined eternal life this way: "that they may know you, the only true God, and the one you have sent—Jesus Christ" (John 17:3). *Eternal life* is the knowledge of God. You receive this at the moment of salvation, but that's only the beginning. You must grow in your knowledge and understanding, as sure as an infant must progress toward childhood. God wants us to grow in our knowledge of

him—he wants us to deepen in our experience of eternal life. To do that, you must have intimacy with his Son, because **this life is in his Son.**

5:13 God wants you to **know that you have eternal life**—not based on your fluctuating faith—but based on the object of your faith, Jesus.

5:14 How do we know that we're on the same wavelength with God and praying **according to his will**? We begin with the Word of God. Pray the Bible with all of its promises and commands. Let it be in your heart and on your tongue. God wants his Word to be done, so pray for it to be done in your life and in the lives of others. Prayer is a toll-free number; the tab is picked up at the other end.

5:16 If you see a brother or sister **committing a sin**, that person needs a believer who is intimate with God to intercede for him or her. As a result of his own intimacy with God, Moses intervened on behalf of Israel (see Exod 32:7-14). When the four men who carried the paralytic took him to Jesus, he forgave and healed when he saw *their* faith (see Mark 2:5). When we reach out in love to a brother or sister who is being defeated, God can allow that believer to piggyback on our faith to receive deliverance. That's what the family of God is about.

There is a more serious kind of sin, though—a **sin that leads to death**. This is sin that results in the physical death of a believer. We see examples of this in Scripture when God takes unrepentant believers home before their time (see 1 Cor 3:16-17; 11:30). These are typically gross sins against the body of Christ. In view here is not a believer struggling with sin (after all, the church is a hospital for sinners) but a hard-headed fool who adopts a harsh, unloving attitude toward God's people. When someone wreaks havoc in the family of God, he or she may experience severe discipline from the Lord.

5:18-19 See the note on 3:6-10. Your victory over sin is determined by the degree to which you "walk by the Spirit" (Gal 5:16). When you live by the Spirit (not by willful determination, or through the "power of positive thinking"), Satan cannot touch you (1 John 5:18)—even though **the whole world is under the sway of the evil one** (5:19; see Eph 2:3; 2 Cor 4:4).

5:20-21 Idols are false gods, cheap imitations (5:21). John urges you to pursue the real deal. Accept no imitations. Jesus **is the true God** (5:20).

2 JOHN

INTRODUCTION

Author

See discussion in 1 John.

Historical Background

See discussion in 1 John.

Message and Purpose

See discussion in 1 John.

Outline

I. Greetings (1-2)
II. Walking in Truth and Love (3-6)
III. Warning to Remain in Christ's Teaching (7-11)
IV. Farewell (12-13)

VIDEO   INTRO

www.bhpublishinggroup.com/qr/te/62_oo

GREETING

The elder:

To the elect[a] lady and her children, whom I love in the truth — and not only I, but also all who know the truth[b] — [2] because of the truth that remains in us[c] and will be with us forever.

[3] Grace, mercy, and peace[d] will be with us from God the Father and from Jesus Christ, the Son[e] of the Father, in truth and love.[f]

TRUTH AND DECEPTION

[4] I was very glad to find some of your children walking in truth,[g] in keeping with a command we have received from the Father. [5] So now I ask you, dear lady — not as if I were writing you a new command, but one we have had from the beginning — that we love one another.[h] [6] This is love:[i] that we walk according to his commands.[j] This is the command as you have heard it from the beginning: that you walk in love.[A]

[7] Many deceivers have gone out into the world; they do not confess the coming of Jesus Christ in the flesh.[k] This is the deceiver and the antichrist.[l] [8] Watch

yourselves so you don't lose what we[B] have worked for, but that you may receive a full reward.[m] [9] Anyone who does not remain in Christ's teaching[n] but goes beyond it does not have God.[o] The one who remains[p] in that teaching, this one has both the Father[q] and the Son.[r] [10] If anyone comes to you and does not bring this teaching, do not receive[s] him into your home, and don't greet him; [11] for the one who greets him shares[t] in his evil works.[u]

FAREWELL

[12] Though I have many things to write to you,[v] I don't want to use paper and ink. Instead, I hope to come to you and talk face to face so that our joy[w] may be complete.

[13] The children of your elect sister send you greetings.

[a] 1 Rm 16:13; 1Pt 5:13; 2Jn 13
[b] Jn 8:32; 14:6; 1Tm 2:4
[c] 2 1Jn 1:8
[d] 3 1Tm 1:2; 2Tm 1:2
[e] Heb 1:2
[f] 1Jn 4:12
[g] 4 3Jn 3–4
[h] 5 1Jn 3:11
[i] 6 1Jn 2:5; 5:3
[j] Ps 103:18; Mk 7:8; Jn 14:15,21,23; 15:10
[k] 7 Php 3:3
[l] 1Jn 2:18,22; 4:3

[m] 8 2Pt 2:13
[n] 9 Jn 8:31–32; 1Jn 2:21–23,27
[o] Jn 5:12; 8:41; 1Jn 2:23
[p] Jn 15:4–16
[q] Mt 11:27
[r] Heb 1:2; 1Jn 2:23
[s] 10 Jn 1:12; 6:21; 13:20
[t] 11 1Tm 5:22
[u] Eph 5:11; 1Tm 5:22; Jd 23
[v] 12 3Jn 13
[w] Jn 15:11

[A] 6 Or *in it*   [B] 8 Other mss read *you*

---

1 John is using the term **lady** metaphorically. New Testament writers speak of the church using female terminology because the church is "the bride" of Christ (Rev 22:17; see also Eph 5:22-33). Thus, John is writing to a congregation and its members, **her children.**

2 One plus one still equals two. **Truth** is that which corresponds to reality, and it finds its roots in God. He is the absolute standard against which a claim is to be measured. The revealed Word of God speaks truth about life and death, heaven and hell, money and parenting, marriage and sex, and every other topic relevant to life's big questions. Therefore, we don't have to wallow in a sea of relativity. On the contrary, we must adopt and stand for truth.

4 We walk **in truth**—that is, live in accordance with God's Word—by keeping the Father's commands.

6 The test of a true church is not whether or not it has problems, but whether or not

it addresses those problems with God's standard of truth. Yet, we can't be "walking in truth" (v. 4) if we don't **walk in love**. We love others when we compassionately, righteously, and responsibly seek their wellbeing—that which God desires for them.

7 It doesn't matter how eloquently a person speaks or what social causes he or she advocates. If that person suggests Jesus is anything less than the eternal Son of God who became a sinless man, died to atone for sins, and rose from the dead, he or she is **the deceiver and the antichrist**. *The* antichrist is coming and will appear during the great tribulation (see Dan 9:26-27; 1 Thess 4:13-18; 2 Thess 2:3; Rev 11:2; 13:1-8), but *little* antichrists are active now (see 1 John 2:18). The category of *antichrist* applies to those who oppose and replace Christ.

8 God has rewards in store for his followers. Most of those are reserved for our heavenly

eternity. But if you are unfaithful and allow yourself to be tricked regarding the truth, you can **lose** some of what God has in store.

9 **Remain** can also be translated "stay" or "abide"; the idea is to "be in close proximity." You can't be close to Christ without being close to his **teaching**. Intimacy with God requires remaining in his Word.

10-11 In the early church, believers didn't have church buildings but often met in each other's homes (see Acts 2:46; 5:42; 20:20; Rom 16:5; 1 Cor 16:19; Col 4:15). Thus, John warns the church to give no hearing or exposure to deceivers who do not hold to the truth of Christ. This doesn't mean you can't talk to unbelievers and try to evangelize them. Rather, it means the church must not give audience to those who deny who Christ is.

12 The most effective form of ministry—the kind that brings the most **joy**—is that done **face to face**.

3 JOHN

INTRODUCTION

Author

See discussion in 1 John.

Historical Background

See discussion in 1 John.

Message and Purpose

See discussion in 1 John.

Outline

I. Greetings (1-4)
II. Being Coworkers with the Truth (5-8)
III. Good and Evil Leaders (9-12)
IV. Farewell (13-15)

www.bhpublishinggroup.com/qr/te/62_00

GREETING

The elder:[a]
To my dear friend Gaius, whom I love in the truth.[b]

2 Dear friend, I pray that you are prospering in every way and are in good health,[c] just as your whole life is going well.[A] **3** For I was very glad when fellow believers came and testified[d] to your fidelity to the truth — how you are walking in truth.[e] **4** I have no greater joy[f] than this: to hear that my children[g] are walking in truth.

GAIUS COMMENDED

5 Dear friend, you are acting faithfully in whatever you do for the brothers and sisters, especially when they are strangers. **6** They have testified to your love before the church.[h] You will do well to send them on their journey[i] in a manner worthy of God,[j] **7** since they set out for the sake of the Name,[k] accepting nothing from pagans.[B,l] **8** Therefore, we ought to support such people so that we can be coworkers with the truth.

DIOTREPHES AND DEMETRIUS

9 I wrote something to the church, but Diotrephes, who loves to have first place among them,[m] does not receive our authority.[n] **10** This is why, if I come, I will remind him of the works he is doing, slandering[o] us with malicious words. And he is not satisfied with that! He not only refuses to welcome fellow believers, but he even stops those who want to do so and expels them from the church.

11 Dear friend, do not imitate what is evil,[p] but what is good. The one who does good is of God;[q] the one who does evil has not seen God.[r] **12** Everyone speaks well of Demetrius — even the truth itself. And we also speak well of him, and you know[s] that our testimony is true.[t]

FAREWELL

13 I have many things to write you, but I don't want to write to you with pen and ink. **14** I hope to see you soon, and we will talk face to face.

15 Peace to you. The friends send you greetings. Greet the friends by name.

A 2 Or *as your soul prospers*   B 7 Or *Gentiles*

[a] 1 2Jn 1
[b] Jn 14:6; 1Jn 5:20
[c] 2 1Tm 1:10
[d] 3 Jn 15:26; Ac 26:5
[e] 2Jn 4
[f] 4 Jn 15:11
[g] 1Co 4:14; Gl 4:19; Php 2:22
[h] 6 Mt 16:18; 1Co 14:4; Rv 1:4
[i] Ac 15:3; 20:38; 21:5; Rm 15:24; 1Co 16:6; 2Co 1:16; Ti 3:13
[j] 1Co 10:31; 1Th 2:12
[k] 7 Jn 10:25; Ac 15:14; Rv 14:1
[l] 1Co 9:15-18

[m] 9 Mt 20:25-28; 23:5-12; Col 1:18; 1Pt 5:2-3; 2Jn 9
[n] Ac 18:27; Rm 16:1-2; 2Co 3:1
[o] 10 1Tm 5:13
[p] 11 1Pt 3:17
[q] 1Jn 4:4
[r] Ex 33:20
[s] 12 1Jn 2:20-21
[t] Jn 21:24

1 **Gaius** was probably a church leader.
2 Some have wrongly tried to advocate a "prosperity gospel" using this verse. There's nothing inherently evil in having money or being physically fit. Getting a raise and improving your fitness are fine. But without a prospering soul—that is, without spiritual development—your motivations will be misplaced, and health and wealth will leave you hollow.
3 The measuring rod for your spiritual well-being, for the success of your Christian life, is whether or not **you are walking in truth**—whether you're living by the standard of God's Word.
7-8 We should **support** those who **set out for the sake of the Name** of Jesus—those who

are doing the work of God as evangelists, teachers, church planters, and missionaries. By providing them with financial support, hospitality, encouragement, and prayer, **we can be coworkers with the truth.** God thus credits to our accounts the blessings that he gives to them because we are their helpers.
9 That Diotrephes refused to receive John's **authority** is a big deal. Understand that John had been chosen by the Son of God himself to serve as one of his apostles and to write Scripture.
10 Whereas Gaius supported traveling believers who were doing the work of Christ (see vv. 5-8), Diotrephes slammed the door in their faces and excommunicated church members for helping them. A leader

submits to the truth and exercises godly authority for the good of those under him or her. A despot refuses to submit to the truth and rules over others for his or her own gain. The apostle John was not afraid to call him out.
11-12 Demetrius's life showed consistency: the way he lived matched the truth of Scripture. When you see this kind of pattern in a leader, you know you can follow him.
13-14 John's words here are a reminder that writing can be useful, but it can't replace talking **face to face** (v. 14). Whether someone needs warning or encouragement, emails and text messages don't compare to looking a brother or sister in the eye and "speaking the truth in love" (Eph 4:15).

JUDE

INTRODUCTION

Author

THIS AUTHOR IDENTIFIES HIMSELF AS Jude, "brother of James" (v. 1). It's unlikely he would be referring to James the son of Zebedee, who was martyred at an early date (see Acts 12:1-2). Likely, he is referencing the well-known leader of the Jerusalem church (Acts 15:13-21; Gal 2:9) and brother of Jesus (Mark 6:3). Yet though Jude was also Jesus's brother, he humbly calls himself a "servant of Jesus Christ" instead (Jude 1).

Historical Background

The first readers of Jude's letter were probably Jewish Christians because of his several references to Jewish history. He identifies them as "those who are called, loved by God the Father and kept for Jesus Christ" (v. 1), which could be a general designation referring to believers anywhere. But in verse 3 he also calls them "dear friends" and goes on to address a specific situation; thus, he likely has a specific group in mind—perhaps several churches. Aside from this, we do not know who Jude's recipients were.

It's hard to determine the date of the letter. All we know is that it was written within Jude's lifetime, and the false teaching he addresses had time to develop. A reasonable date for it, then, would be between AD 65 and 80. Nothing in the letter points to a date beyond this period.

Message and Purpose

Jude had intended to write about the great salvation that believers share, but he had to adjust his message because false teachers had infiltrated the church. He wanted these troublemakers to be identified by their false teaching and false living because the former inevitably leads to the latter. It's imperative that believers learn to distinguish truth from error.

In a series of contrasts, Jude shows the difference between doctrinal error that manifests itself in corrupt living and the truth of God that leads to righteous living. Jude also warned about rebelling against God's ordained authorities; to do so is to rebel against God. Jude wanted believers to stand and fight for the truth—combining holy kingdom truth with holy kingdom living.

www.bhpublishinggroup.com/qr/te/65_oo

Outline

I. Introduction and Purpose (1-4)
II. Illustrations of Past Rebels (5-11)
III. False Teachers and their Judgment (12-19)
IV. Exhortations for Believers (20-23)
V. Benediction (24-25)

GREETING

Jude,[a] a servant of Jesus Christ and a brother of James:

To those who are the called,[b] loved[A,c] by God the Father and kept for Jesus Christ.[d]

2 May mercy, peace, and love be multiplied to you.[e]

JUDE'S PURPOSE IN WRITING

3 Dear friends, although I was eager to write you about the salvation we share,[f] I found it necessary to write, appealing to you to contend for the faith[g] that was delivered[h] to the saints once for all. **4** For some people, who were designated for this judgment long ago,[B,i] have come in by stealth;[j] they are ungodly,[k] turning the grace of our God into sensuality and denying[l] Jesus Christ, our only Master and Lord.

APOSTATES: PAST AND PRESENT

5 Now I want to remind you, although you came to know all these things once and for all, that Jesus[c] saved a people out of Egypt and later destroyed those who did not believe;[m] **6** and the angels[n] who did not keep their own position but abandoned their proper dwelling, he has kept in eternal chains in deep darkness for the judgment on the great day. **7** Likewise, Sodom and Gomorrah[o] and the surrounding towns committed sexual immorality and perversions,[D] and serve as an example by undergoing the punishment of eternal fire.[p] **8** In the same way these people — relying on their dreams — defile their flesh, reject authority, and slander glorious ones.[q] **9** Yet when Michael[r] the archangel[s] was disputing with the devil[t] in an argument about Moses's[u] body, he did not dare utter a slanderous condemnation against

him but said, "The Lord rebuke you!"[10] **10** But these people blaspheme anything they do not understand. And what they do understand — by instinct — like irrational animals — by these things they are destroyed. **11** Woe to them! For they have gone the way of Cain,[v] have plunged into Balaam's error[w] for profit, and have perished in Korah's rebellion.[x]

THE APOSTATES' DOOM

12 These people are dangerous reefs[E] at your love feasts[y] as they eat with you without reverence. They are shepherds who only look after themselves. They are waterless clouds carried along by winds;[z] trees in late autumn — fruitless, twice dead and uprooted. **13** They are wild waves of the sea, foaming up their shameful deeds; wandering stars[aa] for whom the blackness of darkness[ab] is reserved forever.[ac]

14 It was about these that Enoch,[ad] in the seventh generation from Adam, prophesied: "Look! The Lord comes with tens of thousands of his holy ones[ae] **15** to execute judgment on all and to convict all the ungodly[af] concerning all the ungodly acts that they have done in an ungodly way, and concerning all the harsh things ungodly sinners have said against him." **16** These people are discontented grumblers, living according to their desires;[ag] their mouths utter arrogant words, flattering[ah] people for their own advantage.

17 But you, dear friends, remember what was predicted by the apostles of our Lord Jesus Christ. **18** They told you, "In the end time[ai] there will be scoffers[aj] living according to their own ungodly desires." **19** These people create divisions and are worldly,[ak] not having the Spirit.

[a]1 Mt 13:55; Mk 6:3
[b]Rm 1:7; 1Co 1:24
[c]1Th 1:4; 2Th 2:13
[d]Jn 17:11, 15; 1Th 5:23; 1Pt 1:5
[e]2 1Pt 1:2; 2Pt 1:2
[f]3 Ti 1:4
[g]1Tm 6:12; 2Tm 4:7
[h]2Pt 2:21
[i]4 1Pt 2:8
[j]Gl 2:4; 2Tm 3:6
[k]Mk 7:22; Rm 5:6
[l]Ti 1:16; 2Pt 2:1; 1Jn 2:22
[m]5 1Co 10:1-11
[n]6 Gn 6:1-4; 2Pt 2:4
[o]7 2Pt 2:6
[p]2Th 1:8
[q]8 2Pt 2:10
[r]9 Dn 10:13,21; 12:1; Rv 12:7
[s]Lk 1:19; 1Th 4:16
[t]Mt 4:1,10; Ac 13:10
[u]Ps 77:20; Mt 8:4; Heb 3:2
[v]11 Gn 4:1-17,24-25; Heb 11:4; 1Jn 3:12
[w]Nm 22:5; 2Pt 2:15
[x]Nm 16:1
[y]12 1Co 11:17-22; 2Pt 2:13
[z]Pr 25:14
[aa]13 Is 14:12-15; Rv 1:16; 8:10; 9:1
[ab]Mt 6:23; Jd 6
[ac]2Pt 2:17
[ad]14 Gn 5:18
[ae]Dt 33:2; Dn 7:10; Mk 8:38; 1Th 3:13; 2Th 1:7; Heb 12:22
[af]15 2Pt 2:5-6
[ag]16 2Pt 2:10
[ah]Lv 19:15; Dt 10:17; 2Ch 19:7; Pr 28:21
[ai]18 1Tm 4:1; 2Tm 3:1; 1Pt 1:5,20
[aj]2Pt 3:3
[ak]19 Rm 8:9; Php 3:3

[A]1 Other mss read *sanctified*   [B]4 Or *whose judgment was written about long ago*   [C]5 Other mss read *the Lord*, or *God*   [D]7 Or *and went after other flesh*   [E]12 Other mss read *are like blemishes*

---

1 Jude was a half-brother of Jesus (see Mark 6:3), but he saw himself as **a servant of Jesus Christ** and radically submitted to his lordship. **3 To contend for the faith** is to wage battle on behalf of the true faith as deposited in God's inerrant Word (see 2 Tim 3:14-17). **4** The New Testament emphasizes that grace teaches us to live at a higher moral standard than those in the world do (see Titus 2:11-12). Yet, tragically, these false teachers turned **grace** into something it was never meant to be—an excuse for sin (see Rom 6:1-7). **6** This is an insight into the angelic rebellion in which Lucifer led a *coup d'état* and was followed by **angels who . . . abandoned their proper dwelling**.

7 God's judgment on these cities is **an example** of the **eternal fire** that will fall on those who legitimize evil (see Gen 19:1-29). **11** Interestingly, Jude compares the blaspheming false teachers to **Cain** (who gave a bloodless offering), Balaam (who only ministered for money), and Korah (who rejected the authority of God's word). For rebelling against spiritual authority, all of them were judged. **12** Indeed, heretics are like **dangerous reefs**, which are hidden dangers to ships. They are **waterless clouds**, putting on a big show as if they will relieve the spiritually parched even though there's no substance behind what they say. They are like **fruitless** trees that produce nothing of spiritual value.

14 Enoch walked with God in the midst of moral decay in the days of Noah and spoke of the coming judgment (see Gen 5:21-24). **15-16** Notice how many times Jude uses the word **ungodly** to describe them (v. 15). They used their positions and their mouths to exploit others and to satisfy their own lusts. Thus, believers have to be on guard. Scripture warns us to "test the spirits" (1 John 4:1) to discern what is legitimate and what is not. If you are led by a blind teacher on spiritual matters, you'll wind up falling into a ditch with him. **18 Scoffers** make a joke of the faith. **19 Divisions** provide the devil with the opportunities he wants. All Satan needs is a crack

There Is Still Time

CHANCES ARE YOU'VE DONE SOMETHING over the course of your life that you're not proud of. In fact, you might have even done a few "some-things" and feel they are taking their toll. You told one too many lies. You kept one too many secrets. You hurt one too many people. Indeed, after a lifetime of bad behavior, you might feel like it's too late to do anything about righting your wrongs. Too late to make a difference. Too late to be used by God for anything worthwhile. And though you know that God has forgiven your sin through your faith in Jesus so that you will enter heaven when you die, you can't shake the feeling that the chance to do something good on earth has come and gone.

If you feel this way, let me be straight with you. We serve a big God who is capable of overcoming the impossible and restoring the unrestorable. In fact, God is in the business of taking the worst of us and using us in mighty ways for the glory of his name and kingdom.

Consider Moses. He was a prince of Egypt, but one mistake cost him the respect of Pharaoh and the trust of his own people. He murdered an Egyptian and tried to cover up his crime. Then he spent years as an outcast, convinced that his wickedness rendered him ineligible for good works. God's response was to show up in a burning bush with a message for Moses that no matter what he had done, the plan was for him to lead God's people out of Egypt and into the promised land. He would be given authority over the people and power from God to bring judgment on Egypt.

Think about Rahab. She was a prostitute living in the pagan city of Jericho. She lived on the furthest outskirts of the city, on the wall, which was a place for the lowest in society. Shortly before her nation's downfall, she knew enough of the Lord and of God's chosen people to know what was coming. It would have been easy for her to conclude that her fate was sealed and that God would kill her along with everyone else in Jericho. But faith compelled her to help Joshua's spies, to align herself with Israel's God. Thus, God used her to grant victory to the Israelites, and he saved her by protecting her from Jericho's fall.

The Bible is full of stories about sinners whom God ended up redeeming and using to bring about his perfect plan of deliverance and restoration. So, if God could use murderers and prostitutes to become great heroes of the faith, why do you assume he wouldn't do the same for you?

Tapping into the future God wants for you starts with a living, active faith that God is who he says he is and that he will do what he promises to do. He is "able to protect you from stumbling and to make you stand in the presence of his glory, without blemish and with great joy" (JUDE 24). By choosing to believe that God will keep his promise regardless of what you have done, you open the door to being used by God for greatness in his kingdom.

Don't give up. Defeat is not permanent. Our victory has already been won through Jesus Christ. All you have to do is draw near to God and start experiencing all he has in store for you on earth.

EXHORTATION AND BENEDICTION

20 But you, dear friends, as you build yourselves up in your most holy faith, praying in the Holy Spirit,[a] **21** keep yourselves in the love of God,[b] waiting expectantly for the mercy of our Lord Jesus Christ for eternal life. **22** Have mercy on those who waver; **23** save others by snatching them from the fire;[c] have mercy on others but with fear,[d] hating[e] even the garment[f] defiled by the flesh.

24 Now to him[g] who is able to protect you from stumbling[h] and to make you stand in the presence of his glory, without blemish[i] and with great joy, **25** to the only[j] God our Savior, through Jesus Christ our Lord,[A] be glory, majesty, power, and authority before all time,[B] now and forever. Amen.

[a] 20 Rm 8:15–16,26–27; Eph 6:18
[b] 21 Jn 15:9–10; 1Jn 4:16
[c] 23 1Co 3:15; 2Th 1:8
[d] Rv 11:11

[e] 23 Pr 6:16–19
[f] Zch 3:3–4
[g] 24 Rm 16:25; Eph 3:20
[h] Jn 17:12
[i] Eph 1:4; 5:27; Php 2:15; Col 1:22
[j] 25 Lk 5:44; Rm 16:27

[A] 25 Other mss omit *through Jesus Christ our Lord*   [B] 25 Other mss omit *before all time*

---

to slither through so he can amplify problems and hinder God's work.

20 Build yourselves up in your most holy faith means don't be a static Christian: grow. If your son finished sixth grade and said, "I'm done with school," you'd probably point out that no matter what he has learned so far, it's insufficient to carry him through to the end of life successfully.

To pray **in the Holy Spirit** is to pray with a spiritual mind-set, in concert with God's desires and God's design based on God's Word.

22-23 Some Christians struggle in their faith and need compassion. Others need to be aggressively snatched **from the fire**, that is, redirected from a behavior or relationship that will burn them. But as sure as clothing contaminated by a leper's skin could infect you, helping others overcome their sinful tendencies could drag you down with them (v. 23). Reject the sin; help the sinner.

24 God is able to keep you from being duped by the deceptions of false teachers. He can keep you from being tripped up so that you stand before him **without blemish and with great joy.** No one is sinless. To be *blameless* means that whatever your failures, they are sufficiently covered. When you stand before God, based on your commitment to the truth, he's going to declare that you look just right.

25 This closing is a reminder that God has the attributes, the position, and the legitimate right to get you through whatever challenges confront you and the moral decay in the world around you.

REVELATION

INTRODUCTION

Author

THE TRADITIONAL VIEW IS THAT the apostle John, the son of Zebedee, wrote the book of Revelation. This position has been challenged by critical scholars; nevertheless, it is still the most defensible view. The writer identifies himself as "John" (1:1, 4, 9; 22:8)—presumably a well-known John among first-century Christians. The many allusions to the Old Testament found in the book, as well as the style of writing, suggest the author was a Jewish Christian from Palestine. According to early church tradition, the apostle John ministered from about AD 70 to 100 in Asia Minor—the location of the "seven churches in Asia" (1:4, 11; 2:1–3:22). Thus, these believers would have been well acquainted with him. Furthermore, all of the earliest Christian writers attributed the book to John the apostle.

Historical Background

John addressed Revelation to seven churches in Asia Minor (modern-day Turkey): in Ephesus, in Smyrna, in Pergamum, in Thyatira, in Sardis, in Philadelphia, and in Laodicea (1:4, 11). Conservative evangelical scholars have suggested various dates for this writing. Some believe that the persecution experienced by these churches reflects the reign of Nero in the late AD 60s. But the majority favor a date in the mid-90s, during the reign of the Roman emperor Domitian who ruled from AD 81 to 96. Early church tradition attests that local persecution of Christians took place under Domitian and that John was exiled to the island of Patmos (1:9) during his reign. These early Christian writers support a mid-90s date for the writing of Revelation. Thus, the aged apostle wrote what Jesus Christ revealed to him while he endured exile for his faithful preaching ministry.

Message and Purpose

The book of Revelation is specifically designed to explain what happens before, during, and after the return of Jesus Christ. It can be summarized in one phrase: "Things to come." It explains what God's prophetic kingdom program is and how it works, and it offers the most comprehensive detail in all of Scripture.

This book has two goals: to encourage Christians to live righteous and holy lives in light of the prophetic timetable that is to come and to challenge unbelievers about the judgment ahead if they reject Christ.

The apostle John begins by telling the church how it ought to live. He tells each church the special reward believers will receive for living holy lives that are pleasing to the Lord. Then he enters into an extensive description of the tribulation that fulfills many Old Testament prophecies, as well as Jesus's Olivet discourse. This section also describes God's dealings with Israel after the church has been raptured and the times of the Gentiles have ended. This leads to Christ's millennial kingdom on earth, followed by the judgment of unbelievers and the transition into the new heaven and new earth—the eternal state in which believers will be with the Lord forever.

VIDEO   INTRO

www.bhpublishinggroup.com/qr/te/66_00

Outline

PROLOGUE

1 The revelation of^A Jesus Christ that God gave him to show his servants^a what must soon take place.^b He made it known by sending his angel^c to his servant John,^d ^2 who testified to the word of God and to the testimony^B of Jesus Christ,^e whatever he saw.^c ^3 Blessed is the one who reads aloud the words of this prophecy,^f and blessed are those who hear the words of this prophecy and keep^D what is written in it, because the time is near.

^4 John: To the seven churches in Asia. Grace and peace^g to you from^E the one who is, who was, and who is to come,^h and from the seven spirits^F,i before his throne, ^5 and from Jesus Christ, the faithful witness,^j the firstborn from the dead^k and the ruler of the kings of the earth.^l

To him who loves us and has set us free^G from our sins by his blood,^m ^6 and made us a kingdom,^H priests^i,n to his God and Father — to him be glory and dominion forever and ever. Amen.^o

^7   Look, he is coming
         with the clouds,^p
     and every eye will see him,
     even those who pierced him.
     And all the tribes^j of the earth^K,q
     will mourn over him.^L,M,r
     So it is to be. Amen.

^8 "I am the Alpha and the Omega,"^s says the Lord God, "the one who is, who was, and who is to come, the Almighty."

JOHN'S VISION OF THE RISEN LORD

^9 I, John, your brother and partner in the affliction,^t kingdom,^u and endurance^v that are in Jesus, was on the island called Patmos because of the word of God and the testimony of Jesus.^w ^10 I was in the Spirit^N,x on the Lord's day, and I heard a loud voice behind me like a trumpet^y ^11 saying, "Write^z on a scroll^o what you see and send it to the seven churches: Ephesus, Smyrna, Pergamum, Thyatira, Sardis, Philadelphia, and Laodicea."

^12 Then I turned to see whose voice^aa it was that spoke to me. When I turned I saw seven golden lampstands,^ab ^13 and among the lampstands was one like the Son of Man,^P,ac dressed in a robe^ad and with a golden sash wrapped around his chest.^ae ^14 The hair of his head was white as wool — white as snow^af — and his eyes like a fiery flame.^ag ^15 His feet were like fine bronze as it is fired in a furnace,^ah and his voice like the sound of cascading^Q waters.^ai ^16 He had seven stars in his right hand; a sharp double-edged sword came from his mouth,^aj and his face was shining like the sun at full strength.^ak

^17 When I saw him, I fell at his feet like a dead man.^al He laid his right hand on me and said, "Don't be afraid. I am the First and the Last,^am ^18 and the Living One.^an I was dead, but look — I am alive forever and ever,^ao and I hold the keys^ap of death and Hades. ^19 Therefore write what you have seen,^aq what is, and what will take place after this. ^20 The mystery^ar of the seven

^a 1:1 Ac 2:18; Rm 6:19; 1Pt 2:16; Rv 22:6
^b Dn 2:28–29,45; Rv 22:6
^c Gn 24:7; Mt 1:24; Ac 12:11
^d Jn 21:7; Rv 22:8
^e 1:2 1Co 1:6; Rv 12:17; 19:10; 20:4
^f 1:3 Rv 14:13; 16:15; 19:9; 20:6; 22:7,14
^g 1:4 Ti 1:4
^h Rv 1:8,17; 4:8; 16:5
^i 1:5 Rv 3:1; 4:5; 5:6
^j 1:5 Rv 19:37; Jn 18:37; Rv 2:13; 3:14
^k Ps 89:27; Ac 26:23; Rm 8:29; 1Co 15:20–23; Col 1:18
^l Ps 89:27; Rv 17:14; 19:16
^m Dt 7:8; Rm 8:2
^n 1:6 Ex 19:6; 1Pt 2:9; Rv 5:10; 20:6
^o Rm 11:36; 1Pt 4:11; Jd 25; Rv 7:12
^p 1:7 Is 19:1; Zch 12:10; Jn 19:34-37
^q Gn 12:3; 28:14; Zch 14:17
^r Dn 7:13; Zch 12:10
^s 1:8 Is 44:6; Rv 21:6; 22:13

^t 1:9 Jn 16:33; Ac 14:22; Rm 5:3; 2Tm 2:12; Rv 2:9
^u Mt 25:34; Jms 2:5
^v Rm 5:3–4; 8:25; 15:4; Col 1:11; 2Th 1:4; Heb 10:36; 12:1; Jms 1:3–4; Rv 2:3; 3:10; 13:10; 14:12
^w Rv 1:2; 6:9; 12:17; 19:10; 20:4
^x 1:10 1Kg 18:12; Ezk 3:12; 2Co 12:2; Rv 4:2; 17:3; 21:10
^y Ex 19:16,19; 20:18; Ps 47:5
^z 1:11 Ex 34:27; Dt 31:19; Is 8:1; 30:8; Jr 30:2; 36:2,28; Hab 2:2; Rv 2:1,8,12,18; 3:1,7,14; 14:3; 19:9; 21:5
^aa 1:12 Ex 20:18
^ab 1:13 Ex 25:37; 37:23; 2Ch 4:20; Zch 4:2
^ac 1:13 Dn 7:13; 10:16; Rv 14:14
^ad Dn 10:5
^ae Rv 15:6

^af 1:14 Is 1:18; Dn 7:9   ^ag Dn 10:6; Rv 2:18; 19:12   ^ah 1:15 Ezk 1:7; Dn 10:6; Rv 2:18   ^ai Ezk 1:24; 43:2; Rv 14:2; 19:6   ^aj 1:16 Is 49:2; Heb 4:12; Rv 2:12,16; 19:15   ^ak Mt 17:2; Rv 10:1   ^al 1:17 Gn 17:3; Jdg 6:22-23; 13:20; Jb 42:5-6; Is 6:5; Ezk 1:28; Dn 8:17; Mt 17:6; Lk 1:12; 5:8   ^am Is 41:4; 44:6; 48:12; Rv 2:8; 22:13   ^an 1:18 Mt 16:16; 26:63; Jn 6:57; Rv 4:10; 10:6   ^ao Rm 6:9; 14:9; Rv 2:8; 10:6   ^ap Mt 16:19   ^aq 1:19 Ex 17:14; 34:27; Dt 31:19; Jr 30:2; Hab 2:2   ^ar 1:20 Mt 13:35; Rm 16:25

^A 1:1 Or Revelation of, or A revelation of   ^B 1:2 Or witness   ^C 1:2 Or as many as he saw   ^D 1:3 Or follow, or obey   ^E 1:4 Other mss add God   ^F 1:4 Or the sevenfold Spirit   ^G 1:5 Other mss read has washed us   ^H 1:6 Other mss read kings and   ^I 1:6 Or made us into (or to be) a kingdom of priests; Ex 19:6   ^J 1:7 Or peoples   ^K 1:7 Gn 12:3; 28:14; Zch 14:17   ^L 1:7 Or will wail because of him   ^M 1:7 Dn 7:13; Zch 12:10   ^N 1:10 Or in spirit; lit I became in the Spirit   ^O 1:11 Or book   ^P 1:13 Or like a son of man   ^Q 1:15 Lit many

1:1 The revelation of Jesus Christ refers to Christ's unveiling or disclosure of matters related to his second coming to earth.
1:3 That **the time is near** means the return of Christ is imminent. It could happen at any time.
1:4 Speaking of **the seven churches in Asia** is a way of speaking of all churches because the number seven represents completion or fullness. These churches are representative of all Christian churches throughout history.
1:5 Jesus is **the firstborn from the dead**, the first of a whole company of people who will one day rise from the grave because they are **set . . . free from [their] sins by his blood.** Though his personal earthly kingdom rule is not yet visible in history, it will become so at his second coming.
1:6 As **priests** of God's kingdom, believers are to represent people to God and God to people.

1:7 Every eye will see him as he rotates around the sun at his return.
1:8 Alpha and **Omega** are the first and last letters of the Greek alphabet, signifying that God is the beginning and the end. He's the Creator of all things, and he'll bring history to its conclusion. He is **the one who is, who was, and who is to come.** God is yesterday, today, and tomorrow because he exists eternally. But later in the letter, it's Jesus who calls himself "the Alpha and the Omega" (22:13), and clearly he is the coming One (22:7, 12, 20). This is not surprising, though, because Jesus is the Second Person of the Trinity and coequal with the Father (see John 1:1; Col 1:15).
1:10 To be **in the Spirit** is to be thinking and functioning spiritually, to be engulfed in a spiritual framework. **The Lord's day** is Sunday, the first day of the week.
1:11 See the note on 1:4.
1:12 The seven churches are represented

by **seven golden lampstands** to signify the expression of divine life that should radiate through all churches. Indeed, churches are to illuminate their communities.
1:13 Jesus is situated **among the lampstands** to signify his visible rulership of the church as Judge and King, even before his second coming to personally and directly rule the entire world (see 1:20). The church, then, cannot view Jesus merely as a gentle figure with long hair and a loving gaze. Christians must view him as a Ruler, for there is a judgment side of Jesus along with the blessing side we love to talk about.
1:14-16 This image assures us that when Christ returns, the rulership he has always possessed by virtue of his position as God's Son will be realized in practice.
1:18 These **keys** represent access to **death and Hades**, and by extension, access to heaven.
1:20 The Greek word translated **angels** in the CSB, angelos, means "messenger," and that's

a 1:20 Mt 5:14-15
b 2:1 Ac 21:11; Rv 1:16,20
c 2:2 Rv 2:19; 3:1,8,15
d 2Co 11:13
e 1Jn 4:1
f 2:3 Mt 24:9
g 2:4 Jr 2:2
h 2:5 Heb 10:32
i 2:7 1Jn 5:4-5
j Gn 2:8-9; Lk 23:43; 2Co 12:4; Rv 22:2,14,19
k 2:8 Rv 1:17

l 2:9 Rv 3:9-10
m 2:10 Mt 4:1; Eph 4:27; 6:11; 1Tm 3:6; Jms 4:7; 1Pt 5:8; Rv 12:9,12; 20:2
n Dn 1:12,14
o Mt 10:22; 24:13; Rv 12:11
p 1Co 9:25; Jms 1:12; Rv 3:11
q 2:11 Rv 20:6,14; 21:8

stars you saw in my right hand and of the seven golden lampstands is this: The seven stars are the angels[A] of the seven churches, and the seven lampstands[B] are the seven churches.[a]

THE LETTERS TO THE SEVEN CHURCHES

THE LETTER TO EPHESUS

2 "Write to the angel[c] of the church in Ephesus: Thus says the one who holds the seven stars in his right hand and who walks among the seven golden lampstands:[b] **2** I know your works, your labor, and your endurance,[c] and that you cannot tolerate evil people. You have tested those who call themselves apostles and are not,[d] and you have found them to be liars.[e] **3** I know that you have persevered and endured hardships for the sake of my name,[f] and have not grown weary. **4** But I have this against you: You have abandoned the love you had at first.[g] **5** Remember then how far you have fallen; repent, and do the works you did at first.[h] Otherwise, I will come to you[D] and remove your lampstand from its place, unless you repent. **6** Yet you do have this: You hate the practices of the Nicolaitans, which I also hate.

7 "Let anyone who has ears to hear listen to what the Spirit says to the churches. To the one who conquers, I will give[i] the right to eat from the tree of life, which is in[E] the paradise of God.[j]

THE LETTER TO SMYRNA

8 "Write to the angel of the church in Smyrna: Thus says the First and the Last,[k] the one who was dead and came to life: **9** I know your[F] affliction and poverty, but

you are rich. I know the slander of those who say they are Jews and are not, but are a synagogue of Satan.[l] **10** Don't be afraid of what you are about to suffer. Look, the devil[m] is about to throw some of you into prison to test you, and you will experience affliction for ten days.[n] Be faithful to the point of death,[o] and I will give you the crown[G] of life.[p]

11 "Let anyone who has ears to hear listen to what the Spirit says to the churches. The one who conquers will never be harmed by the second death.[q]

[A] 1:20 Or *messengers* [B] 1:20 Other mss add *that you saw* [C] 2:1 Or *messenger*, also in vv. 8,12,18 [D] 2:5 Other mss add *quickly* [E] 2:7 Other mss read *in the midst of* [F] 2:9 Other mss add *works and* [G] 2:10 Or *wreath*

the intended sense here. The pastors who declare God's Word, then, are God's messengers to the churches.

2:2-4 Many positive things were happening in this church. They tested everything by the Scriptures and rightly found that some so-called apostles did not teach pure doctrine. But Jesus shifts from patting them on the back to rebuke: **You have abandoned the love you had at first** (2:4). They had correct doctrine, but not a correct heart. The key word here is *first*. As with romantic love between a man and a woman, first love always involves passion. Yet there was not passionate pursuit of an intimate relationship with Christ in the church. They were merely following a program. Duty had replaced devotion.

2:5-6 If a church's activity is about us rather than about Jesus, he'll **remove** his presence from it. They needed to remember the primacy of relationship over performance, to repent of their spiritual departure, and to resume prioritizing intimate fellowship with God (see Luke 10:38-42).

2:7 The Greek verb translated **conquers** is *nikaō*, and it means to be victorious in the midst of, over, in, or through whatever circumstances are holding a believer hostage. In 1 John 5:5 we read, "Who is the one who conquers the world but the one who believes that Jesus is the Son of God?" If by believing in Jesus we are conquerors, then why in these letters to the churches are we still exhorted to conquer? John is addressing the contrast

between our legal status (our declared position in Christ) and our experiential reality. We must work out this position of being a conqueror in the experiences of our everyday lives in order to have special intimacy with Christ in the kingdom (i.e., **the right to eat from the tree of life . . . in the paradise of God**).

2:9 Some who claimed to be **Jews** were actually **a synagogue of Satan** because they were doing the devil's work, slandering believers.

2:11 To **never be harmed by the second death** refers to enjoying a sense of full gain when Christ separates believers from unbelievers at the end of history. At the final judgment, some Christians will experience a sense of loss, despite their eternal salvation, when

THE LETTER TO PERGAMUM

12 "Write to the angel of the church in Pergamum: Thus says the one who has the sharp, double-edged sword:[a] **13** I know[A] where you live — where Satan's throne is. Yet you are holding on to my name and did not deny your faith in me,[B,b] even in the days of Antipas, my faithful witness[c] who was put to death among you, where Satan lives. **14** But I have a few things against you. You have some there who hold to the teaching of Balaam,[d] who taught Balak to place a stumbling block[c] in front of the Israelites: to eat meat sacrificed to idols[e] and to commit sexual immorality.[f] **15** In the same way, you also have those who hold to the teaching of the Nicolaitans.[D] **16** So repent! Otherwise, I will come to you quickly[g] and fight against them with the sword of my mouth.[h]

17 "Let anyone who has ears to hear listen to what the Spirit says to the churches. To the one who conquers, I will give some of the hidden manna.[E,i] I will also give him a white stone, and on the stone a new name[j] is inscribed that no one knows except the one who receives it.

THE LETTER TO THYATIRA

18 "Write to the angel of the church in Thyatira: Thus says the Son of God,[k] the one whose eyes are like a fiery flame and whose feet are like fine bronze:[l] **19** I know your works — your love, faithfulness,[F] service, and endurance.[m] I know that your last works are greater than the first. **20** But I have this against you: You tolerate the woman Jezebel,[n] who calls herself a prophetess and teaches and deceives my servants to commit sexual immorality and to eat meat sacrificed to idols.[o] **21** I gave her time to repent,[p] but she does not want to repent of her sexual immorality.[q] **22** Look, I will throw her into a sickbed[r] and those who commit adultery with her[s] into great affliction.[t] Unless they repent of her[G] works, **23** I will strike her children dead. Then all the churches will know that I am the one who examines minds and hearts,[v] and I will give to each of you according to your works.[w] **24** I say to the rest of you in Thyatira, who do not hold this teaching, who haven't known "the so-called secrets[I,x] of Satan"[y] — as they say — I am not putting any other burden on you.[z] **25** Only hold on to what you have until I come.[aa] **26** The one who conquers and who keeps my works to the end: I will give him authority over the nations —

27   **and he will rule[J,ab] them**
        with an iron scepter;
        he will shatter them
              like pottery[K,ac] —

28 just as I have received this from my Father. I will also give him the morning star.[ad] **29** "Let anyone who has ears to hear listen to what the Spirit says to the churches.

THE LETTER TO SARDIS

3 "Write to the angel[L] of the church in Sardis: Thus says the one who has the seven spirits of God[ae] and the seven stars:[af] I know your works;[ag] you have a reputation[M] for being alive, but you are dead.[ah] **2** Be alert[ai] and strengthen[N] what remains, which is about to die,[o] for I have not found

[a] 2:12 Is 49:2; Heb 4:12; Rv 1:16; 2:16; 19:15
[b] 2:13 1Tm 5:8
[c] Ac 22:20
[d] 2:14 2Pt 2:15
[e] Ac 15:29; 1Co 8:10; 10:19
[f] Nm 25:1; 31:16; 1Co 10:8
[g] 2:16 Rv 22:7
[h] 2Th 2:8
[i] 2:17 Ex 16:32-34
[j] Is 55:13; 56:5; 62:2
[k] 2:18 Ps 2:7-9
[l] Rv 1:14-15
[m] 2:19 1Tm 1:3; Rv 2:2
[n] 2:20 1Kg 16:30-33; 21:25; 2Kg 9:7,30-37

[o] 2:20 2Kg 9:22; Ac 15:29; 1Co 10:20
[p] 2:21 Rm 2:4; 2Pt 3:9
[q] Rv 9:20-21; 16:9,11
[r] 2:22 2Kg 9:22
[s] Rv 17:2; 18:9
[t] Mt 24:21; Ac 7:11
[u] 2:23 Ezk 33:27
[v] Ps 7:9; 26:2; 139:1; Jr 11:20; 17:10; Mt 16:27; Lk 16:15; Ac 1:24; Rm 8:27
[w] Rm 2:6; 2Co 11:15; 2Tm 4:14; Rv 18:6; 20:12-13
[x] 2:24 2Co 2:10
[y] Rv 2:9
[z] Mt 11:30; Ac 15:28; 24:4; 1Jn 5:3
[aa] 2:25 Rv 3:11
[ab] 2:27 Rv 19:15
[ac] Ps 2:9
[ad] 2:28 Is 14:12; 2Pt 1:19; Rv 22:1
[ae] 3:1 Rv 1:4; 4:5; 5:6
[af] Rv 1:16,20; 2:1
[ag] Rv 2:2,19; 3:8,15
[ah] Rm 6:11
[ai] 3:2 Mt 25:13; 26:40-41; Ac 20:31; 1Co 16:13; 1Pt 5:8; 2Pt 3:10

[A] 2:13 Other mss add *your works and*   [B] 2:13 Or *deny my faith*   [C] 2:14 Or *to place a trap*   [D] 2:15 Other mss add *which I hate to eat*   [F] 2:19 Or *faith*   [G] 2:22 Other mss read *their*   [H] 2:23 Or *with a plague*   [I] 2:24 Or *the secret things*   [J] 2:27 Or *shepherd*   [K] 2:27 Ps 2:9   [L] 3:1 Or *messenger*, also in vv. 7,14   [M] 3:1 Or *have a name*   [N] 3:2 Other mss read *guard*   [O] 3:2 Or *strengthen who remain, who are about to die*

Jesus rebukes their unfaithfulness (see Matt 25:28-30; 1 Cor 3:15).

2:12 **The one who has the sharp, double-edged sword** is Jesus speaking the Word of God.

2:14 **Balaam** claimed God's name (see Num 22–24) while also enticing his people to compromise (Num 25:1; 31:16). It's a big deal to God when we cause other people to stumble, especially when we do it knowingly and for profit.

2:17 **Manna** was the supernatural food God sent from heaven to sustain Israel in the wilderness (see Deut 8:16). This manna is **hidden** in that it is not available to all. It represents exclusive sustenance and kingdom fellowship with God for Christians who reject the way "of Balaam" (see the note on Rev 2:14).

In the Roman world, **a white stone** was used as an admission ticket. A white stone

with someone's **name** on it was a personalized, all-access pass. This image, then, reinforces the idea of exclusive, personal fellowship with God as the conquering Christian's reward. For the one who rises above being a nominal Christian, Jesus has special benefits. You get invited to the private reception.

2:20 Though perhaps this was her real name, **Jezebel** also brings to mind the wife of Israel's King Ahab (see 1 Kgs 16:31; 2 Kgs 9) and represents an entire category of immoral and idolatrous women.

2:22-23 The **affliction** described here illustrates that one purpose of repentance is to limit or remove sin's consequences (2:22). Repentance allows Christians to regain fellowship with the Lord. Those not following the way of Jezebel did not have to worry about the burdens listed.

2:26-27 The reward for obeying Christ is **authority over the nations** (2:26), a reference to the thousand-year reign of Jesus following his second coming. During that time, believers who exhibit purity in this life will help the Lord rule the world. That millennial reign, though, is merely a down payment on eternity.

2:28 Jesus himself is **the morning star** (see 22:16). Thus, the reward for a pure life is a greater experience of Jesus during his millennial reign and for eternity. Naturally, a coruler of the universe will have greater access to the King than a common citizen.

3:1-2 This church had a **reputation for being alive** (3:1). It was the kind of place about which people today might say, "They have great music and great preaching." Yet because Jesus knew their **works**, he saw there was no true spiritual life there (3:2). They were merely playing church.

[a]3:3 Mt 24:42-44; Mk 13:32-37; Lk 12:35-40; 1Th 5:1-11; Rv 16:15
[b]3:4 Zch 3:3-4; 2Co 7:1; Rv 14:4
[c]3:5 1Jn 2:13-14; 4:4; 5:4-5; Rv 2:7,11,17,26; 3:12,21
[d]Mt 17:2; Rv 3:18; 4:4
[e]Dt 32:32-33; Ps 69:28; Dn 12:1; Rv 13:8; 17:8; 20:12,15; 21:27
[f]Mt 10:32; Lk 12:8
[g]3:6 Mt 11:15; 13:9,43; Lk 8:8; 14:35
[h]Ac 8:29; 10:19; 11:12; 13:2; 21:11; 28:25; 1Tm 4:1; Heb 3:7; 10:15; Rv 14:13; 22:17
[i]3:7 1Jn 5:20; Rv 6:10; 19:11
[j]Is 22:22; Mt 16:19
[k]3:8 Ac 14:27; 1Co 16:9; 2Co 2:12; Col 4:3
[l]3:9 Is 45:14; 49:23; 60:14; 1Co 14:25
[m]Is 43:4
[n]3:10 Lk 8:13; Heb 3:8; 1Pt 4:12
[o]Rv 6:10; 8:13; 11:10; 13:8,14; 17:8
[p]3:11 Rv 22:7,12,20
[q]Rv 2:25
[r]1Co 9:25; 1Th 2:19; 2Tm 4:8; Jms 1:12; 1Pt 5:4
[s]3:12 1Kg 7:21; 2Ch 3:17; Jr 1:18; Gl 2:9

[t]3:12 Ezk 48:35; Gl 4:26; Heb 12:22; Rv 21:2
[u]Rv 2:17; 7:3; 14:1; 22:4
[v]3:14 2Co 1:20
[w]Mk 10:6; 13:19; Jn 1:1-5; Col 1:18; 2Pt 3:4
[x]3:17 Hs 12:8; Zch 11:5; 1Co 4:8
[y]3:18 Zch 13:9; 1Pt 1:7
[z]Gn 2:25; Is 20:4; Ezk 23:29; Rv 16:15
[aa]3:19 Heb 12:26
[ab]3:20 Lk 24:29-30
[ac]3:21 Mt 19:28; 2Tm 2:12; Rv 20:4
[ad]4:1 Ex 19:19; 20:18; Rv 47:5; Zch 9:14; Rv 1:10
[ae]Rv 11:12
[af]Gn 12:1; Zch 1:9; Rv 17:1; 21:9

your works complete before my God. [3] Remember, then, what you have received and heard; keep it, and repent. If you are not alert, I will come[A] like a thief, and you have no idea at what hour I will come upon you.[a] [4] But you have a few people[B] in Sardis who have not defiled[c] their clothes,[b] and they will walk with me in white, because they are worthy.

[5] "In the same way, the one who conquers[c] will be dressed in white clothes,[d] and I will never erase his name from the book of life[e] but will acknowledge his name before my Father and before his angels.[f]

[6] "Let anyone who has ears to hear listen[g] to what the Spirit says[h] to the churches.

THE LETTER TO PHILADELPHIA

[7] "Write to the angel of the church in Philadelphia: Thus says the Holy One, the true one,[i] the one who has the key of David, who opens and no one will close, and who closes and no one opens:[j] [8] I know your works. Look, I have placed before you an open door that no one can close because you have but little power; yet you have kept my word and have not denied my name.[k] [9] Note this: I will make those from the synagogue of Satan, who claim to be Jews and are not, but are lying — I will make them come and bow down at your feet,[l] and they will know that I have loved you.[m] [10] Because you have kept my command to endure, I will also keep you from the hour of testing[n] that is going to come on the whole world to test those who live on the earth.[o] [11] I am coming soon.[p] Hold on to what you have,[q] so that no one takes your crown.[r]

[12] "The one who conquers I will make a pillar[s] in the temple of my God, and he will never go out again. I will write on him the name of my God and the name of the city of my God — the new Jerusalem,[t] which comes down out of heaven from my God — and my new name.[u]

[13] "Let anyone who has ears to hear listen to what the Spirit says to the churches.

THE LETTER TO LAODICEA

[14] "Write to the angel of the church in Laodicea: Thus says the Amen,[v] the faithful and true witness, the originator[D,w] of God's creation: [15] I know your works, that you are neither cold nor hot. I wish that you were cold or hot. [16] So, because you are lukewarm, and neither hot nor cold, I am going to vomit[E] you out of my mouth. [17] For you say, 'I'm rich; I have become wealthy and need nothing,'[x] and you don't realize that you are wretched, pitiful, poor, blind, and naked. [18] I advise you to buy from me gold refined in the fire so that you may be rich,[y] white clothes so that you may be dressed and your shameful nakedness not be exposed,[z] and ointment to spread on your eyes so that you may see. [19] As many as I love, I rebuke and discipline.[aa] So be zealous and repent. [20] See! I stand at the door and knock. If anyone hears my voice and opens the door, I will come in to him and eat with him, and he with me.[ab]

[21] "To the one who conquers I will give the right to sit with me on my throne,[ac] just as I also conquered and sat down with my Father on his throne.

[22] "Let anyone who has ears to hear listen to what the Spirit says to the churches."

THE THRONE ROOM OF HEAVEN

4 After this I looked, and there in heaven was an open door. The first voice that I had heard speaking to me like a trumpet[ad] said, "Come up here,[ae] and I will show you what must take place after this."[af]

[A]3:3 Other mss add upon you   [B]3:4 Lit few names   [C]3:4 Or soiled   [D]3:14 Or beginning of God's creation, or ruler of God's creation   [E]3:16 Or spit

---

3:4 **A few** believers in this church were committed spiritually and not acquiescing to spiritual apathy.
3:5 **White clothes** for **the one who conquers** represent the garments required for a special event, like a gown or tuxedo of today. They are qualified for a special invitation to kingdom events, as well as for public recognition.
3:10 This verse suggests a pre-tribulational rapture because it says, **I will also keep you from the hour of testing that is going to come on the whole world**. Jesus will not merely keep believers from the test but from the period of the test—that is, the tribulation period.

3:12 In the end, everyone will know the spiritually serious person (i.e., **pillar**) is special to God because Jesus will publicly identify that person.
3:15-16 The Everyday English Tony Evans Translation puts it this way: "Y'all make me want to throw up!" Nobody orders a lukewarm drink. They want iced tea or hot coffee. In the spiritual realm, God finds tepidness unappealing as well.
3:17 The Laodiceans said, **I have become wealthy and need nothing**. But the external appearance of prosperity was not indicative of the condition of their hearts or their level of fellowship with God. They were spiritually

uncommitted, carnal, and compromising. As Jesus put it, they were spiritually **wretched, pitiful, poor, blind, and naked**.
3:18 The Laodicean Christians needed to acquire from Jesus true wealth—those character traits, behaviors, and beliefs that have eternal value. Then they truly would **be rich**.
3:20 Jesus will not force himself into a church. But if any member of a congregation will open **the door** by submitting to his will, he will **come in . . . and eat**—that is, he will have intimate fellowship with believers who respond to his invitation.
4:1 The second use of the phrase after this marks a transition to the next section of Rev-

[2] Immediately I was in the Spirit,[a] and there was a throne in heaven[b] and someone was seated on it. [3] The one seated[A] there had the appearance of jasper and carnelian stone.[c] A rainbow that had the appearance of an emerald surrounded the throne.[d]

[4] Around the throne were twenty-four thrones, and on the thrones sat twenty-four elders[e] dressed in white clothes,[f] with golden crowns on their heads.[g]

[5] Flashes of lightning and rumblings and peals of thunder came from the throne.[h] Seven fiery torches were burning before the throne, which are the seven spirits of God.[i] [6] Something like a sea of glass, similar to crystal, was also before the throne.[j]

Four living creatures covered with eyes in front and in back were around the throne on each side. [7] The first living creature was like a lion; the second living creature was like an ox; the third living creature had a face like a man; and the fourth living creature was like a flying eagle.[k] [8] Each of the four living creatures had six wings;[l] they were covered with eyes around and inside. Day and night[m] they never stop,[B] saying,

Holy, holy, holy,
Lord God, the Almighty,

who was, who is,
and who is to come.[n]

[9] Whenever the living creatures give glory, honor, and thanks to the one seated on the throne, the one who lives forever and ever,[o] [10] the twenty-four elders fall down before the one seated on the throne[p] and worship the one who lives forever and ever. They cast their crowns before the throne and say,

[11]   Our Lord and God,[c]
       you are worthy[q] to receive
       glory and honor and power,[r]
       because you have created all things,[s]
       and by your will
       they exist and were created.

THE LAMB TAKES THE SCROLL

5 Then I saw in the right hand of the one seated on the throne a scroll with writing on both sides, sealed with seven seals.[t] [2] I also saw a mighty angel[u] proclaiming with a loud voice, "Who is worthy to open the scroll and break its seals?" [3] But no one in heaven or on earth or under the earth was able to open the scroll or even to look in it. [4] I wept and wept because no one was found worthy to open[D] the scroll or even to look in it. [5] Then one of the elders said to me, "Do not weep. Look, the Lion from the tribe of Judah,[v] the Root of David,[w] has conquered[x] so that he is able to open the scroll and[E] its seven seals."

[6] Then I saw one like a slaughtered lamb[y] standing in the midst of the throne and the four living creatures and among the elders. He had seven horns and seven eyes, which are the seven spirits of God[z] sent into all the earth. [7] He went and took

[a] 4:2 Ac 19:21; Rm 8:9; 14:17; Eph 2:18,22; 3:5; 6:18; Rv 1:10; 17:3; 21:10
[b] 1Kg 22:19; Ps 11:4; 103:19; Is 66:1; Mt 5:34; 23:22; Dn 7:9
[c] 4:3 Ex 28:17,20; 39:10,13; Ezk 28:13; Rv 21:11,18-20
[d] Gn 9:13-17; Ezk 1:28; Rv 10:1
[e] 4:4 Mt 19:28; Rv 11:16; 5:8; 19:4; 20:4
[f] Rv 3:4,18
[g] Zch 6:11; Rv 9:7
[h] 4:5 Ex 19:16; 20:18; Ps 77:18; Rv 8:5; 11:19; 16:18
[i] Rv 1:4; 3:1; 5:6
[j] 4:6 Rv 15:2; 21:18,21
[k] 4:7 Ezk 1:5-28; 10:9-14
[l] 4:8 Is 6:2
[m] Rv 7:15

[n] 4:8 Is 6:3
[o] 4:9 Rv 10:6; 15:7
[p] 4:10 2Ch 20:18; Mk 5:33; Rv 5:8
[q] 4:11 2Sm 22:4; Ps 18:3; Heb 3:3; Rv 5:2,9,12
[r] Rv 5:12; 7:12
[s] Gn 1:1; Ac 14:15; Rv 10:6; 14:7
[t] 5:1 Is 29:11; Ezk 2:9-10; Dn 12:4
[u] 5:2 Rv 10:1
[v] 5:5 Gn 49:9
[w] Is 11:1,10; Rm 15:12; Rv 22:16
[x] Jn 16:33
[y] 5:6 Rv 5:12; 13:8
[z] Rv 1:4

[A] 4:3 Other mss omit *The one seated*   [B] 4:8 Or *rest*   [C] 4:11 Some mss add *the Holy One* ; other mss read *Lord*   [D] 5:4 Other mss add *and read*
[E] 5:5 Other mss add *loose*

---

elation. This refers to the church age—that is, the period of history between Christ's ascension and his rapture of believers. All events described in Revelation from this point forward will occur following the rapture. But not only has John shifted in the time period he is describing, the venue has shifted from earth to heaven.
4:3 The **rainbow** hearkens back to Genesis 9:12-17, where God designated the rainbow as a sign of his covenant with Noah never to destroy the whole earth with a flood again. Each time one appears in Scripture, it's a reminder of God's faithfulness.
4:4 Twenty-four has special significance in Scripture, pointing to people who stand out as spiritual leaders like the twenty-four priestly divisions among Aaron's descendants (see 1 Chr 24). These **elders** are believers who have overcome during the church age and are ruling with Christ.

4:7 The appearances of the four living creatures may symbolize the portraits of Jesus in the four Gospels. In Matthew, Jesus is King of the Jews, represented by a regal **lion**. In Mark, he is a servant, represented by **an ox**—a beast of burden. In Luke, he is the Son of Man, represented by the face of a **man**. And in John, he is the Son of God who gives eternal life, represented by a majestic **eagle**.
4:8 In Isaiah 6:2-3, each creature covered its face with two **wings**, its feet with two wings, and flew with two. They called to one another, "Holy, holy, holy is the Lord of Armies; his glory fills the whole earth."
4:11 The worship of God as Creator sets the stage for subsequent chapters in which God is depicted as moving into creation and setting it right from the effects of sin.
5:1 The **scroll** is like a title deed to the earth. It depicts God's ownership of all creation and

right to hold accountable those who misuse it and thus dishonor him. Through judgment administered by Jesus, God once again will lay claim to his creation, which was plunged into sin in Genesis 3.
5:5 This scene reflects the fact that sinful people, even when they are redeemed as John was, fall short of the qualifications necessary for one who could judge the earth. But Christ—**the Lion from the tribe of Judah** and **the Root of David**—by virtue of his full divinity, sinless humanity, and atoning death, is qualified. Jesus died to redeem humanity at his first coming. He will judge in order to redeem the entire creation at his second.
5:6 As sure as Jesus is regal like a lion, he was slain like a sacrificial **lamb** to atone for the sins of the whole world (cf. Isa 53:7; 1 John 2:2).

a 5:8 Ps 33:2; 71:22; 150:3;
       Dn 3:5
     b Rv 15:7
c Ps 141:2; Lk 1:10; Rv 8:3-4
d 5:9 Ps 40:3; 96:1; 98:1;
       144:9; 149:1; Is 42:10;
       Rv 14:3
e Ex 19:5; Rv 7:9; 11:9; 14:6
f 5:10 Ex 19:6; Rv 1:5-6

g 5:11 Dn 7:10; Heb 12:22
h 5:13 Php 2:10
i Ps 69:34; 96:11; 145:21;
       Rv 12:12

❧ Questions & Answers ❧

Q God's work through Christ was in part for the reconciliation of Jews and Gentiles (see Eph 2:11-22). What can we do to better embrace God's vision and seek unity and reconciliation in the church?

A First, we must understand why division exists in the church. Though there are many underlying reasons for the lack of unity, the top reason is that the devil foments divisiveness. You see, he knows something that many Christians don't. The devil knows that God recoils from illegitimate disunity. He won't fellowship with it; it will keep prayers from being answered. When you are divided, the Spirit of God *cannot* work because he *will not* work.

Because of this, we must fight for the unity of the church—just like the early church had to fight for the unity of Jews and Gentiles coming together through the gospel. Such unity wasn't natural to them. To overcome cultural racial biases, we must fight for the unity of all nationalities, races, and

ethnicities. To put it another way, you must place your history, background, culture, and personality under the rule of Christ.

From a human perspective, we often have division in the church because we make Christ subject to our unique identities. If we do this, division will inevitably take place because we are all different! But if we acknowledge our differences and place them under divine authority, we are able to be unified in our purpose and mission. Players on a football team have different positions and tasks, but they are united with one team goal. In the same way, the body of Christ is diverse, made up of people from "every tribe and language and people and nation" (Rev 5:9). We have one goal: the advancement of the kingdom. When we come together, in spite of our differences, and unify around Jesus Christ and his kingdom, the power of God is manifested to the world.

FOR THE NEXT Q&A, SEE PAGE 1536.

the scroll out of the right hand of the one seated on the throne.

THE LAMB IS WORTHY

8 When he took the scroll, the four living creatures and the twenty-four elders fell down before the Lamb. Each one had a harp[a] and golden bowls[b] filled with incense,[c] which are the prayers of the saints. **9** And they sang a new song:[d]

You are worthy to take the scroll
   and to open its seals,
because you were slaughtered,
   and you purchased[A] people[B]
   for God by your blood
from every tribe and language
   and people and nation.[e]
10   You made them a kingdom[c]
   and priests to our God,[f]
   and they will reign on the earth.

11 Then I looked and heard the voice of many angels around the throne, and also of the living creatures and of the elders.

Their number was countless thousands, plus thousands of thousands.[g] **12** They said with a loud voice,

Worthy is the Lamb who was
   slaughtered
to receive power and riches
   and wisdom and strength
   and honor and glory
   and blessing!
13 I heard every creature in heaven, on earth, under the earth,[h] on the sea, and everything in them say,[i]

Blessing and honor and glory
   and power
be to the one seated on the throne,
   and to the Lamb, forever
   and ever!
14 The four living creatures said, "Amen," and the elders fell down and worshiped.

THE FIRST SEAL ON THE SCROLL

6 Then I saw the Lamb open one of the seven[D] seals, and I heard one of the four living creatures say with a

---

A 5:9 Or *redeemed*   B 5:9 Other mss read *us*   C 5:10 Other mss read *them kings*   D 6:1 Other mss omit *seven*

5:9 The mention of redeemed people in heaven being **from every tribe and language and people and nation** portrays the ethnic, linguistic, and national diversity that will be present in eternity. Difference and diversity are not problems to be solved; they were

part of God's plan from the beginning. God delights in the variety and beauty of his creation.
5:12 The song repeats the word **worthy** for the fifth time since 4:11, over which span it first was applied to God the Father and then

twice to the Son, emphasizing their coequality and divinity. The first two persons of the Trinity are worshiped together in 5:13.
6:1 With the opening of the first seal, the tribulation period begins on earth—a seven-year span following the rapture of the church in

voice like thunder,[a] "Come!" [2] I looked, and there was a white horse.[b] Its rider held a bow;[c] a crown[d] was given to him, and he went out as a conqueror in order to conquer.[A]

THE SECOND SEAL

[3] When he opened the second seal, I heard the second living creature say, "Come!" [4] Then another horse went out, a fiery red one,[e] and its rider was allowed to take peace from the earth, so that people would slaughter one another. And a large sword was given to him.[f]

THE THIRD SEAL

[5] When he opened the third seal, I heard the third living creature say, "Come!" And I looked, and there was a black horse.[g] Its rider held a set of scales in his hand.[h] [6] Then I heard something like a voice among the four living creatures say, "A quart of wheat for a denarius,[B] and three quarts of barley for a denarius,[i] but do not harm the oil and the wine."[j]

THE FOURTH SEAL

[7] When he opened the fourth seal, I heard the voice of the fourth living creature say, "Come!" [8] And I looked, and there was a pale green[c] horse. Its rider was named Death, and Hades was following after him.[k] They were[D] given authority[l] over a fourth of the earth, to kill by the sword, by famine, by plague, and by the wild animals of the earth.[m]

THE FIFTH SEAL

[9] When he opened the fifth seal, I saw under the altar the souls of those who had been slaughtered because of the word of God and the testimony they had given.[E,n] [10] They cried out with a loud voice: "Lord,[F] the one who is holy and true,[o] how long until you judge those who live on the earth and avenge our blood?[p] " [11] So they were each given a white robe, and they were told to rest a little while longer until the number would be completed of their fellow servants and their brothers and sisters, who were going to be killed just as they had been.

THE SIXTH SEAL

[12] Then I saw him open[G] the sixth seal. A violent earthquake occurred;[q] the sun turned black like sackcloth[r] made of hair; the entire moon[H] became like blood;[s] [13] the stars[i] of heaven fell to the earth as a fig tree drops its unripe figs when shaken by a high wind; [14] the sky was split apart like a scroll being rolled up;[t] and every mountain and island was moved from its place.[u]

[15] Then the kings of the earth, the nobles, the generals, the rich, the powerful, and every slave and free person hid in the caves and among the rocks of the mountains.[v] [16] And they said to the mountains and to the rocks, "Fall on us and hide us[w] from the face of the one seated on the throne and from the wrath of the Lamb, [17] because the great day of their[j] wrath has come! And who is able to stand?"[x]

[a] 6:1 Rv 14:2; 19:6
[b] 6:2 Zch 6:1-3; Rv 19:11
[c] Zch 9:13-14
[d] Rv 14:14
[e] 6:4 Zch 1:8; 6:2
[f] Mt 10:34
[g] 6:5 Zch 6:2,6
[h] 1Sm 2:3; Jb 6:2; 31:6; Ps 62:9; Pr 16:2
[i] 6:6 2Kg 6:25; 7:1
[j] Rv 7:3; 9:4
[k] 6:8 Hs 13:14; Rv 1:18; 20:13
[l] Mt 10:1; 28:18; Rv 9:3
[m] Jr 14:12; 15:2-3; 24:10; 29:17-18; Ezk 5:12,17; 14:21; 29:5

[n] 6:9 Rv 1:2,9; 12:17; 19:10; 20:4
[o] 6:10 Rv 3:7
[p] Dt 32:43; Ps 79:10; 119:84; Rv 19:2
[q] 6:12 Rv 11:13; 16:18
[r] Is 13:10; 50:3; Jl 2:10; 3:15; Mt 24:29
[s] Jl 2:31; Ac 2:20
[t] 6:14 Is 34:4
[u] Ezk 38:20; Nah 1:5; Rv 16:20
[v] 6:15 Jdg 6:2; 1Sm 13:6; Is 2:10,19,21; Heb 11:38
[w] 6:16 Hs 10:8; Lk 23:30
[x] 6:17 1Sm 6:20; Ezr 9:15; Ps 1:5; 24:3; 76:7; 130:3; Jl 2:11; Mal 3:2

[A] 6:2 Or *went out conquering and in order to conquer*   [B] 6:6 A denarius = one day's wage   [C] 6:8 Or *a greenish gray*   [D] 6:8 Other mss read *He was*
[E] 6:9 Other mss add *about the Lamb*   [F] 6:10 Or *"Master*   [G] 6:12 Or *I saw when he opened*   [H] 6:12 Or *the full moon*   [I] 6:13 Perhaps meteors
[J] 6:17 Other mss read *his*

---

which God brings judgment to earth in order to reclaim it.

6:2 The **rider** on **a white horse** is referenced elsewhere as the antichrist (see 1 John 2:18; 4:3) who will rise to power following the rapture and bring order out of chaos. This person will claim victory—represented by his white mount and **crown**—and gain world power. Notably, there is no mention of an arrow with his **bow**, indicating the bloodless nature of his coup. The ensuing sense of peace throughout the world, however, will prove false.

6:4 The **fiery red** horse represents chaos. Like Adolf Hitler before him, the antichrist is going to transition from pretending to be peaceful to wielding **a large sword**, representative of his capacity to slay people. The parallel to Hitler is instructive because the German chancellor rose to power amid the turbulence of the Great Depression by

building consensus and support before his administration devolved into violence and dictatorship.

6:5-6 The opening of **the third seal** heightens the world chaos, bringing economic instability to the tribulation period, a reality depicted by **a black horse** whose rider holds **a set of scales** (6:5). Inflation will be so severe that **a quart of wheat** will cost a day's wage, which was **a denarius** in Roman currency (6:6). The antichrist will take over the world's economic order.

6:8 If this occurred today, the fourth seal would bring the demise of approximately two billion people!

6:9-10 These people were **slaughtered** for their faith during the tribulation by the antichrist (6:9). Obviously, then, people will come to faith in Jesus following the rapture because all believers of the church age will have been removed from earth.

6:12-14 It will appear that God is undoing the created elements he formed in Genesis 1.

6:15-16 While it would be logical for individuals who know they are under judgment to call for mercy, these people's hearts have become so hardened that they prefer death to salvation! Notice that they know God's identity precisely: he is God the Father **on [heaven's] throne** and God the Son, **the Lamb** (6:16). Nevertheless, they want nothing to do with him.

6:17 The great day of . . . wrath marks a transition point in the tribulation.

Approximately three and a half years through the seven-year period, earth will experience what Jesus called "great distress" (Matt 24:21, or the "great tribulation" [KJV, NASB]). Though the CSB renders it as merely a description, it can also be taken as a proper name.

[a] 7:1 Rv 9:14
[b] Is 11:12; Jr 49:36; Ezk 7:2; Dn 7:2; Zch 6:5; Mt 24:31; Rv 20:7-8
[c] 7:2 Is 41:2
[d] Rv 7:3; 9:4
[e] 7:3 Rv 3:12; 6:6; 9:4
[f] Ezk 9:4,6; Rv 13:16; 14:1,9; 20:4; 22:4
[g] 7:4 Gn 35:23-26
[h] 7:9 Rv 5:9; 11:9; 13:7; 14:6
[i] Gn 15:5; 32:12
[j] 7:10 Ex 15:2; 2Ch 20:17; Ps 3:8; 67:2; Is 12:2; 49:6; 51:6,8; 52:10; Jnh 2:9; Ac 4:12; Rm 1:6; 1Pt 1:5; Rv 12:10; 19:1

[l] 7:12 Rv 4:11
[m] 7:14 Dn 12:1; Mk 13:19; Rv 3:10; 6:11
[n] Ps 51:7; Is 1:18; 43:25; 44:22; Heb 9:24; 1Jn 1:7
[o] 7:15 Rv 4:8
[p] Rv 3:12; 11:1,2,19; 14:15,17; 15:5-6,8; 16:1,17; 21:22
[q] Ps 27:5; 31:20; 61:4; Is 25:4; Rv 21:3
[r] 7:16 Dt 28:22; Is 49:10; Jn 6:35
[s] 7:17 Ps 23:1; Ezk 34:23
[t] Ps 23:2; Is 49:10; Jr 2:13
[u] Is 25:8; Rv 21:4
[v] 8:1 Hab 2:20; Zph 1:7; Zch 2:13

THE SEALED OF ISRAEL

7 After this I saw four angels[a] standing at the four corners of the earth, restraining the four winds of the earth[b] so that no wind could blow on the earth or on the sea or on any tree. [2] Then I saw another angel rising up from the east,[c] who had the seal of the living God.[d] He cried out in a loud voice to the four angels who were allowed to harm the earth and the sea: [3] "Don't harm the earth or the sea or the trees[e] until we seal the servants of our God on their foreheads."[f] [4] And I heard the number of the sealed:

144,000 sealed from every tribe
   of the Israelites:[g]
[5] 12,000 sealed from the tribe of Judah,
12,000[A] from the tribe of Reuben,
12,000 from the tribe of Gad,
[6] 12,000 from the tribe of Asher,
12,000 from the tribe of Naphtali,
12,000 from the tribe of Manasseh,
[7] 12,000 from the tribe of Simeon,
12,000 from the tribe of Levi,
12,000 from the tribe of Issachar,
[8] 12,000 from the tribe of Zebulun,
12,000 from the tribe of Joseph,
12,000 sealed from the tribe
   of Benjamin.

A MULTITUDE FROM THE GREAT TRIBULATION

[9] After this I looked, and there was a vast multitude from every nation, tribe, people, and language,[h] which no one could number,[i] standing before the throne and before the Lamb. They were clothed in white robes with palm branches in their hands.[j] [10] And they cried out in a loud voice:

Salvation belongs to our God,[k]
who is seated on the throne,
and to the Lamb!

[11] All the angels stood around the throne, and along with the elders and the four living creatures they fell facedown before the throne and worshiped God, [12] saying,

Amen! Blessing and glory
   and wisdom
and thanksgiving and honor
and power and strength
be to our God forever and ever.[l]
   Amen.

[13] Then one of the elders asked me, "Who are these people in white robes, and where did they come from?"

[14] I said to him, "Sir,[B] you know."

Then he told me: These are the ones coming out of the great tribulation.[m] They washed their robes and made them white[n] in the blood of the Lamb.

[15] For this reason they are
   before the throne of God,
and they serve him day and night[o]
   in his temple.[p]
The one seated on the throne
   will shelter[c] them:[q]
[16] They will no longer hunger;
they will no longer thirst;
the sun will no longer strike them,
nor will any scorching heat.[r]
[17] For the Lamb who is at the center
   of the throne
will shepherd them;[s]
he will guide them to springs of the
   waters of life,[t]
and God will wipe away every tear
   from their eyes.[u]

THE SEVENTH SEAL

8 When he opened the seventh seal, there was silence[v] in heaven for about half an hour. [2] Then I saw the seven angels

---

[A] 7:5-8 Other mss add *sealed* after each number   [B] 7:14 Or *"My lord*   [C] 7:15 Or *will spread his tent over*

7:1 Up to this point, John's depictions of judgment have focused on events. In describing this interlude before the breaking of the seventh seal in chapter 8, he focuses on the followers of Jesus who will be alive on earth during the tribulation, including 144,000 Jews (7:4) and "a vast multitude" (7:9) of Jews and Gentiles. **Four angels** hold back the wind during this time so it cannot serve as a force of destruction and judgment until the servants of God are sealed. **The four corners** represent north, south, east, and west.

7:3 To **seal the servants of our God** is to designate them as subject to his ownership and protection.

7:4 These **144,000** individuals are Jewish evangelists who will be God's witnesses during the tribulation. A reliance on the witness of Jewish evangelists is in keeping

with Isaiah 49:6, in which Isaiah prophesied the Jews would become "a light for the nations" so that people "to the ends of the earth" might be saved. That promise remains largely unfulfilled during the church age because most Jews have rejected Jesus's claim to be the Messiah and have failed to become the light of the world (cf. Rom 9–11).

7:5-8 The 144,000 Jewish evangelists who proclaim the gospel during the tribulation will be divided evenly among the twelve tribes of Israel: **Judah, Reuben, Gad, Asher, Naphtali, Manasseh, Simeon, Levi, Issachar, Zebulun, Joseph,** and **Benjamin**.

7:9 The presence of those **from every nation, tribe, people, and language** confirms the truthfulness of 5:9, where the Lamb is praised for redeeming such a diverse multitude. This

indicates that racial distinctions and uniquenesses are retained in eternity.

7:13-14 The elder's answer suggests the 144,000 Jewish evangelists (see the note on 7:4) will lead a large number of Jews and Gentiles to embrace Christ as their Lord and Savior (7:14). God wants everyone to know that even amid judgment, he offers abundant mercy and opportunity for pardon as well as abundant opportunity for turning from evil. Of course, that opportunity will close at Christ's second coming.

7:15 The phrase **for this reason** refers to the salvation described in 7:14.

8:1 The pause allows for repentance before God unleashes the next round of judgment. This provision underscores God's mercy, but its brevity highlights the need to repent quickly as opportunity remains.

who stand in the presence of God;[a] seven trumpets were given to them.[b] 3 Another angel, with a golden incense burner, came and stood at the altar. He was given a large amount of incense to offer with the prayers of all the saints on the golden altar in front of the throne.[c] 4 The smoke of the incense, with the prayers of the saints, went up in the presence of God from the angel's hand. 5 The angel took the incense burner, filled it with fire from the altar,[d] and hurled it to the earth; there were peals of thunder, rumblings, flashes of lightning, and an earthquake.[e]

THE SEVEN TRUMPETS

6 And the seven angels who had the seven trumpets prepared to blow them.

THE FIRST TRUMPET

7 The first angel blew his trumpet, and hail and fire, mixed with blood, were hurled to the earth.[f] So a third of the earth was burned up, a third of the trees were burned up, and all the green grass was burned up.[g]

THE SECOND TRUMPET

8 The second angel blew his trumpet, and something like a great mountain ablaze with fire was hurled into the sea.[h] So a third of the sea became blood,[i] 9 a third of the living creatures in the sea died, and a third of the ships were destroyed.

THE THIRD TRUMPET

10 The third angel blew his trumpet, and a great star, blazing like a torch, fell from heaven.[j] It fell on a third of the rivers and springs of water. 11 The name of the star is Wormwood,[k] and a third of the waters became wormwood. So, many of the people died from the waters, because they had been made bitter.

THE FOURTH TRUMPET

12 The fourth angel blew his trumpet, and a third of the sun was struck, a third of the moon, and a third of the stars, so that a third of them were darkened. A third of the day was without light and also a third of the night.[l]

13 I looked and heard an eagle[A] flying high overhead, crying out in a loud voice, "Woe![m] Woe! Woe to those who live on the earth, because of the remaining trumpet blasts that the three angels are about to sound!"

THE FIFTH TRUMPET

9 The fifth angel blew his trumpet, and I saw a star that had fallen from heaven to earth.[n] The key for the shaft to the abyss[o] was given to him. 2 He opened the shaft to the abyss, and smoke came up out of the shaft like smoke from a great[B] furnace[p] so that the sun and the air were darkened by the smoke from the shaft.[q] 3 Then locusts came out of the smoke on to the earth,[r] and power[c] was given to them[s] like the power that scorpions have on the earth.[t] 4 They were told not to harm the grass of the earth, or any green plant, or any tree,[u] but only those people who do not have God's seal on their foreheads.[v] 5 They were not permitted to kill them but were to torment them for five months;

[a]8:2 Lk 1:19; Rv 15:1,6-8; 16:1; 17:1; 21:9
[b]Jos 6:6; Zph 1:14-16
[c]8:3 Rv 5:8
[d]8:5 Lv 6:12-13; Nm 16:46
[e]Rv 4:5
[f]8:7 Ex 9:13-35; Jl 2:30-31
[g]Ezk 5:12; 38:22; Zch 13:8-9; Lk 21:25-26; Rv 9:15,18; 12:4
[h]8:8 Jr 51:25; Mk 11:23
[i]Ex 7:20-21
[j]8:10 Is 14:12; Rv 9:1
[k]8:11 Pr 5:3-4; Jr 9:15; Lm 3:19
[l]8:12 Ex 10:21-23; Is 13:10; Jl 2:2; Am 5:18; 8:9; Mk 13:24
[m]8:13 Rv 9:12; 11:14; 12:12
[n]9:1 Is 14:12; Lk 10:18; Rv 8:10
[o]Lk 8:31; Rm 10:7; Rv 9:11; 11:7; 17:8; 20:1-3
[p]9:2 Gn 19:28; Ex 19:18
[q]Jl 2:2,10
[r]9:3 Ex 10:1-20; Dt 28:42; 1Kg 8:37; Ps 78:46
[s]Mt 10:1; 28:18; Rv 6:8
[t]Dt 8:15; Ezk 2:6; Lk 10:19
[u]9:4 Rv 6:6; 7:3
[v]Rv 7:3

[A]8:13 Other mss read *angel*　[B]9:2 Other mss omit *great*　[c]9:3 Or *authority*, also in v. 10

8:3 These **prayers** are the petitions of martyrs from the tribulation who cried out previously for divine vengeance and justice and were told to wait (cf. 6:10-11). That they rise with sweet smelling **incense** suggests it is a pleasant experience for God to receive the prayers of his people.

8:6 Within the seventh seal are **seven trumpets**, which depict a whole new round of judgments.

8:7 **Hail and fire, mixed with blood** depicts a firestorm that dwarfs even the most gigantic contemporary wildfires. While wildfires in the western United States, for example, burn tens of thousands of acres, this firestorm will affect **a third of** the planet.

8:8-9 This may be part of the same firestorm triggered by the sounding of the first trumpet.

8:10-11 The **great star** (8:10) appears to be a meteor or asteroid. Science fiction works commonly have depicted the damage such a celestial body could cause were it to collide with earth, but in this instance the damage will be real. **Wormwood** (8:11) means bitter, referencing the effect this thing will have on the fresh water supply.

8:12 Normal cycles of daylight and darkness will be thrown off, perhaps somewhat resembling an Alaskan winter, whose lingering darkness has physical, emotional, and psychological effects.

8:13 The eagle's warning suggests the remaining judgments will be harsh. That is because they are intended to purify and reclaim the earth. It also underscores the graciousness of God in offering an opportunity for humanity to repent before judgment falls.

9:1 The **star** is not an inanimate object but has a personal identity, for John says a key was given **to him**. Specifically, the star represents Satan. In Isaiah 14:12, the prophet says the "shining morning star" had "fallen from the heavens." The subsequent description of that star in Isaiah 14:12-14 has led many Bible interpreters to conclude that the passage is describing Satan, in addition to its reference to King Nebuchadnezzar of Babylon. In other words, Isaiah spoke of Satan's original fall into rebellion and applied it to Babylon's prideful king.

Just as a key grants access to a jail, this **key** grants Satan access to **the shaft to the abyss**. The *abyss* is the abode of demons. During the tribulation, Satan will be granted authority to unlock it. A principle illustrated in this verse is that Satan only has as much authority as God grants him. Nowhere in Scripture is that principle more prominently displayed than in Job 1:12 and 2:6, in which Satan cannot harm Job without God's permission. But what the devil intends for evil, God intends for good.

9:4 This marks a departure from the activity of normal locusts, which eat **grass**, plants, and trees. But as indicated by their origin in the abode of demons, these "locusts" are demonic (9:2-3). The **seal** represents God's divine protection of believers. These demons will have to leave followers of Jesus alone.

a 9:6 Jb 3:20-22; Rv 6:16
b 9:7 Jl 2:4-5
c 9:8 Jl 1:6
d 9:11 Jb 26:6; 28:22; 31:12;
Ps 88:11; Pr 15:11; 27:20
e 9:12 Rv 8:13; 11:14
f 9:13 Ex 39:38; 40:5
g 9:14 Rv 7:1-2
h Rv 16:12
i 9:15 Gn 7:11; 2Kg 25:1; Jr
39:2; 52:4,12,31
j Rv 8:7-12

k 9:17 Gn 19:24; Dt 29:23;
Jb 18:15; Ps 11:6; Is 34:9;
Lk 17:29; Rv 14:10; 19:20;
20:10; 21:8
l 9:20 1Kg 13:33; 2Ch
34:25; Ps 7:12; Jr 1:16; Rv
16:9,11
m 1Co 10:20
n Dt 29:17; Dn 2:32,35,45;
Hab 2:19; Ac 17:29
o Dt 4:28; Ps 115:4-7;
135:15-17; Dn 5:23
p 10:1 Rv 5:2; 18:21
q Rv 4:3
r Rv 3:12
s 10:4 Dn 8:26; 12:4,9
t 10:6 Dn 12:7

their torment is like the torment caused by a scorpion when it stings someone. **6** In those days people will seek death and will not find it; they will long to die, but death will flee from them.*a*

7 The appearance of the locusts was like horses prepared for battle.*b* Something like golden crowns was on their heads; their faces were like human faces; **8** they had hair like women's hair; their teeth were like lions' teeth;*c* **9** they had chests like iron breastplates; the sound of their wings was like the sound of many chariots with horses rushing into battle; **10** and they had tails with stingers like scorpions, so that with their tails they had the power to harm people for five months. **11** They had as their king*A* the angel of the abyss; his name in Hebrew is Abaddon,*B,d* and in Greek he has the name Apollyon.*c*

12 The first woe has passed. There are still two more woes to come after this.*e*

THE SIXTH TRUMPET

13 The sixth angel blew his trumpet. From the four*D* horns of the golden altar*f* that is before God, I heard a voice **14** say to the sixth angel who had the trumpet, "Release the four angels*g* bound at the great river Euphrates."*h* **15** So the four angels who were prepared for the hour, day, month, and year*i* were released to kill a third*j* of the human race. **16** The number of mounted troops was two hundred million;*E* I heard their number. **17** This is how I saw the horses and their riders in the vision: They had breastplates that were fiery red, hyacinth blue, and sulfur yellow. The heads of the

horses were like the heads of lions, and from their mouths came fire, smoke, and sulfur.*k* **18** A third of the human race was killed by these three plagues — by the fire, the smoke, and the sulfur that came from their mouths. **19** For the power of the horses is in their mouths and in their tails, because their tails, which resemble snakes, have heads that inflict injury.

20 The rest of the people, who were not killed by these plagues, did not repent of the works of their hands*l* to stop worshiping demons*m* and idols of gold, silver, bronze, stone, and wood,*n* which cannot see, hear, or walk.*o* **21** And they did not repent of their murders, their sorceries, their sexual immorality, or their thefts.

THE MIGHTY ANGEL
AND THE SMALL SCROLL

10 Then I saw another mighty angel*p* coming down from heaven, wrapped in a cloud, with a rainbow*q* over his head.*F* His face was like the sun, his legs*G* were like pillars of fire,*r* **2** and he held a little scroll opened in his hand. He put his right foot on the sea, his left on the land, **3** and he called out with a loud voice like a roaring lion. When he cried out, the seven thunders raised their voices. **4** And when the seven thunders spoke, I was about to write, but I heard a voice from heaven, saying, "Seal up what the seven thunders said,*s* and do not write it down!" **5** Then the angel that I had seen standing on the sea and on the land raised his right hand to heaven. **6** He swore by the one who lives forever and ever,*t* who created

---

A 9:11 Or *as king over them*   *B* 9:11 Or *Destruction*   *C* 9:11 Or *Destroyer*   *D* 9:13 Other mss omit *four*   *E* 9:16 Other mss read *a hundred million*
F 10:1 Or *a halo on his head*   *G* 10:1 Or *feet*

9:6 Unbelievers will be forced to live through a period of prolonged demonic suffering intended for those who do not know Jesus as their Savior.

9:7-8 This description emphasizes the ferociousness of the locusts and their intimidating looks. In the Old Testament, locusts were instruments of judgment, as in the eighth plague God brought upon the Egyptians (see Exod 10:1-20). The placement of **something like golden crowns...on their heads** signifies authority—in this case, authority from hell (Rev 9:7).

9:9 Because the locusts have **chests like iron**, they will be protected from harm as they torment others.

9:11 The **angel of the abyss**, the **Hebrew** name **Abaddon**, and the **Greek** name **Apollyon** are references to Satan. He is directing the entire locust attack.

9:15 The deaths noted here, combined with the fourth of the earth killed in 6:8, bring the

death total during the first three and a half years of the tribulation to more than half of the world's population.

9:18 The mode of death is specified for the third of humankind mentioned in 9:15.

9:19 Likely, the agents of judgment associated with the sixth trumpet are the same as those of the fifth.

9:20-21 This is a picture of utterly hardened hearts. Already, technology could allow every human on the planet to witness these catastrophic judgments; and as 6:16-17 explained, all will know that God is the source of them. Yet most men and women won't **repent**.

The anti-God movement in America today is a harbinger of this tragic reality. As Romans 1:21-25 explains, when people possess ample evidence of God's activity but fail to honor or give thanks to him, he gives them over to the just consequences of their actions. Those

consequences come in the form of passive wrath during the church age, in which God's hand of restraint and protection are removed. But during the tribulation period, his wrath will be active.

10:2 The presentation of this **scroll**, which likely contains more prophecy of events to transpire during the tribulation, is accompanied by a roaring in nature signified by the angel's **right foot on the sea** and **his left on the land**.

10:4 For all the information Revelation tells about Christ's second coming, there are still some things God has opted not to disclose.

10:6 What has been **delay[ed]** to this point is the full and final outpouring of God's wrath. As Peter put it, "The Lord does not delay his promise, as some understand delay, but is patient with you, not wanting any to perish but all to come to repentance" (2 Pet 3:9).

heaven and what is in it, the earth and what is in it, and the sea and what is in it: "There will no longer be a delay, [7] but in the days when the seventh angel[a] will blow his trumpet, then the mystery of God[b] will be completed, as he announced to his servants the prophets."[c]

[8] Then the voice that I heard from heaven spoke to me again and said, "Go, take the scroll that lies open in the hand of the angel who is standing on the sea and on the land."

[9] So I went to the angel and asked him to give me the little scroll. He said to me, "Take and eat it; it will be bitter in your stomach, but it will be as sweet as honey in your mouth."[d]

[10] Then I took the little scroll from the angel's hand and ate it. It was as sweet as honey in my mouth, but when I ate it, my stomach became bitter.[e] [11] And they said to me, "You must prophesy again about[A] many peoples, nations, languages, and kings."[f]

THE TWO WITNESSES

11 Then I was given a measuring reed[g] like a rod,[B] with these words: "Go[c] and measure the temple of God and the altar, and count those who worship there.

[2] But exclude the courtyard outside the temple.[h] Don't measure it, because it is given to the nations,[D,i] and they will trample the holy city[j] for forty-two months.[k] [3] I will grant[E] my two witnesses authority to prophesy for 1,260 days, dressed in sackcloth."[l] [4] These are the two olive trees and the two lampstands that stand before the Lord[F] of the earth.[m] [5] If anyone wants to harm them, fire comes from their mouths and consumes their enemies;[n] if anyone wants to harm them, he must be killed in this way. [6] They have authority to close up the sky so that it does not rain during the days of their prophecy.[o] They also have power over the waters to turn them into blood[p] and to strike the earth with every plague whenever they want.[q]

THE WITNESSES MARTYRED

[7] When they finish their testimony, the beast[r] that comes up out of the abyss[s] will make war on them, conquer them, and kill them. [8] Their dead bodies[G,t] will lie in the main street[H] of the great city,[u] which figuratively[I] is called Sodom[v] and Egypt,[w] where also their Lord was crucified. [9] And some of[J] the peoples, tribes, languages, and nations[x] will view their bodies for three and a half days and not permit their

[a] 10:7 Rv 11:15; 16:17
[b] Rv 1:20; 17:5,7
[c] 2Kg 9:7; 17:23; Ezk 38:17; Am 3:7; Zch 1:6; 1Pt 2:10-12
[d] 10:9 Ps 119:103; Jr 15:16; Ezk 2:8–3:3
[e] 10:10 Nm 5:24; Ezk 3:1-3
[f] 10:11 Dn 3:4,7; 4:1; 5:19; 7:14; Rv 5:9; 7:9; 11:9
[g] 11:1 Ezk 40:3,5; 42:15-19; Rv 21:15

[h] 11:2 Ezk 40:17,20; 42:14
[i] Lk 21:24
[j] Rv 21:1
[k] Dn 7:25; 12:7,11; Rv 12:6,14; 13:5
[l] 11:3 Gn 37:34; 2Sm 3:31; 1Kg 20:31-32; 21:25-29; 2Kg 19:1-2; 1Ch 21:16; Is 3:24; 20:2; Jr 6:26
[m] 11:4 Zch 4:3,11-14
[n] 11:5 2Kg 1:10-12; Jr 5:14; Rv 9:17
[o] 11:6 Gn 8:2; Dt 11:17; 1Kg 8:35; 17:1; 2Ch 6:26; 7:13; Lk 4:25
[p] Ex 4:9; 7:17-21; Rv 16:4
[q] Ex 5:3; 9:15; Jr 21:6; Ezk 28:23; Zch 14:12,15
[r] 11:7 Dn 7:11; Rv 13:1-18; 17:8
[s] Ps 140:10; Lk 8:31; Rm 10:7; Rv 9:1,11; 17:8; 20:1-3
[t] 11:8 Is 66:24
[u] Rv 16:19; 17:18; 18:10,16-21,24
[v] Is 1:9,10; 3:9; Jr 23:14; Ezk 16:46,49
[w] Ezk 23:3,8,19,27
[x] 11:9 Rv 5:9; 7:9; 10:11

[A] 10:11 Or *prophesy again against*   [B] 11:1 Other mss add *and the angel stood up*   [C] 11:1 Lit *"Arise*   [D] 11:2 Or *Gentiles*   [E] 11:3 Or *I will give to*
[F] 11:4 Other mss read *God*   [G] 11:8 Or *Their corpse*   [H] 11:8 Or *lie on the broad street*   [I] 11:8 Or *spiritually*   [J] 11:9 Lit *And from*

10:7 When the seventh angel will blow his trumpet in 11:15, it will mark a shift to the end of the tribulation, when the seven bowls of God's wrath will be poured out (16:1-21). At that point, the narrative truly will begin rushing toward the return of Jesus to set up his throne on earth. It might seem puzzling that John would announce a rush to the second coming when there are still twelve chapters remaining in Revelation. However, some of those chapters will rehash from a different perspective events already described. Thus far, God has revealed events to come. Beginning in chapter 11, he will focus on the personalities involved in those events.

10:10 In Ezekiel 2:8–3:15, the prophet had a similar experience. When he obeyed, he reported the scroll to be "as sweet as honey in [his] mouth" (Ezek 3:3). Yet after learning the people of Israel would not listen to God, the prophet reported feeling "bitterness" and "an angry spirit" and that "the Lord's hand was on [him] powerfully" (Ezek 3:14). The hard word of prophecy is pleasant to receive because it is, after all, the very word of God. Processing the prophecy internally, however, is a different matter that can prove difficult and even unpleasant.

10:11 Equipped with a harsh word from God, John is instructed to **prophesy**. Even when the word of God is difficult, then, the man of God must continue to proclaim it.

11:1 To **measure** a structure or piece of property in Scripture is a means of laying claim to it. In this case, then, God is laying claim to the Jewish **temple** in Jerusalem that will be rebuilt during the tribulation. Today a Muslim mosque known as the Dome of the Rock sits on the temple site. Orthodox Jews, however, pray daily for the return of the temple at the Western Wall—the one remaining structure from the ancient Jewish temple complex.

11:2 Nations is a translation of the Greek word that refers to Gentiles in this context. The outer court of the temple will be the only place in the complex that Gentiles are allowed to enter. **Forty-two months** correspond with three and a half years, indicating that the events described in this chapter will occur during the latter half of the seven-year tribulation.

11:3 This equals a period of three and a half years on the Jewish calendar of thirty-day months. One reason to be confident in the Bible's truth is its specificity in passages like this. It not only prophesies events, but precise details about their occurrence.

11:4 The two witnesses are pictured metaphorically as **two olive trees** and **two lampstands**. Olive trees stand for God's people in the Old and New Testaments (see Ps 52:8; Jer 11:16; Rom 11:24). Lampstands signify

that God will provide spiritual illumination through these witnesses.

11:5 These witnesses are two extraordinary individuals. Yet that should not come as a surprise because the tribulation is not an ordinary period of history. To underscore the divine anointing on them, as well as the seriousness of coming against them, the death penalty is pronounced even upon **anyone who just wants to harm them.**

11:6 In the Old Testament, Elijah prophesied a drought (see 1 Kgs 17:1-7). Moses pronounced a series of plagues on Egypt, including the water being turned **into blood** (see Exod 7–12). Perhaps, then, the two witnesses are Elijah and Moses—who have returned to earth at least once before at the Mount of Transfiguration (see Matt 17:1-13). What's more, Elijah did not die (see 2 Kgs 2:1-14) and Moses's body was hidden by God (Deut 34:6), possibly hinting at the Lord's intention to use both of the men on earth again.

11:7 The beast that comes up out of the abyss is also known as the antichrist.

11:8 The wickedness of the city during the tribulation is highlighted by the reference to it as **Sodom and Egypt.**

11:9 Just as some individuals from every "nation, tribe, people, and language" will be saved (7:9), some from every ethnic group

[a] 11:9 Lv 26:30; 2Sm 4:12;
Is 66:24
[b] 11:10 Ps 25:2; 94:3; Pr
24:17; Ob 12-13
[c] 11:11 Gn 2:7; 6:17; 7:15,22;
Ezk 37:5
[d] 11:12 2Kg 2:1; Mk 16:19;
Lk 24:51; Ac 1:9-10
[e] 11:13 Is 29:6; Ezk 38:19
[f] 11:14 Rv 8:13; 9:12
[g] 11:15 Is 27:13
[h] 2Sm 7:16; Is 37:16; Dn
7:14,18; Lk 1:32-33
[i] 11:17 Rv 1:4,8; 4:8; 16:5

[j] 11:17 Lk 1:33; 1Co 15:25;
Rv 19:6
[k] 11:18 Ps 2:1
[l] Rv 10:7
[m] 2Kg 23:2; Ps 115:13;
Rv 19:5
[n] 11:19 Rv 4:5; 8:5
[o] 12:1 Mt 24:30
[p] Gn 37:9-10
[q] 12:2 Ps 48:6; Is 13:8;
Jr 22:23
[r] 12:3 Rv 13:2,4,11; 20:2
[s] Dn 7:7,20,24; Rv 13:1;
17:3-18
[t] 12:4 Dn 8:10; Rv 8:7,12

bodies to be put into a tomb.[a] **10** Those who live on the earth will gloat[b] over them and celebrate and send gifts to one another because these two prophets had tormented those who live on the earth.

THE WITNESSES RESURRECTED

11 But after three and a half days, the breath[A] of life[c] from God entered them, and they stood on their feet. Great fear fell on those who saw them. **12** Then they heard[B] a loud voice from heaven saying to them, "Come up here." They went up to heaven in a cloud, while their enemies watched them.[d] **13** At that moment a violent earthquake took place,[e] a tenth of the city fell, and seven thousand people were killed in the earthquake. The survivors were terrified and gave glory to the God of heaven.

14 The second woe[f] has passed. Take note: The third woe is coming soon!

THE SEVENTH TRUMPET

15 The seventh angel blew his trumpet,[g] and there were loud voices in heaven saying,

The kingdom of the world
has become the kingdom
of our Lord and of his Christ,
and he will reign forever and ever.[h]

16 The twenty-four elders, who were seated before God on their thrones, fell facedown and worshiped God, **17** saying,

We give you thanks, Lord God,
the Almighty,
who is and who was,[c,i]

because you have taken
your great power
and have begun to reign.[j]
18 The nations were angry,[k]
but your wrath has come.
The time has come
for the dead to be judged
and to give the reward
to your servants the prophets,[l]
to the saints, and to those who fear
your name,
both small and great,[m]
and the time has come to destroy
those who destroy the earth.

19 Then the temple of God in heaven was opened, and the ark of his covenant[D] appeared in his temple. There were flashes of lightning, rumblings and peals of thunder,[n] an earthquake,[E] and severe hail.

THE WOMAN, THE CHILD, AND THE DRAGON

12 A great sign[F] appeared in heaven:[o] a woman clothed with the sun, with the moon under her feet and a crown of twelve stars on her head.[p] **2** She was pregnant and cried out in labor and agony as she was about to give birth.[q] **3** Then another sign[G] appeared in heaven: There was a great fiery red dragon[r] having seven heads and ten horns,[s] and on its heads were seven crowns.[H] **4** Its tail swept away a third of the stars in heaven and hurled them to the earth.[t] And the dragon stood in front of the woman who was about to give birth, so that when she did give birth it might

[A] 11:11 Or *spirit*   [B] 11:12 Other mss read *Then I heard*   [C] 11:17 Other mss add *and who is to come*   [D] 11:19 Other mss read *ark of the covenant of the Lord*   [E] 11:19 Other mss omit *an earthquake*   [F] 12:1 Or *great symbolic display*; see Rv 12:3   [G] 12:3 Or *another symbolic display*   [H] 12:3 Or *diadems*

also will harden their hearts against God and his messengers.

11:10 Imagine a celebration that will involve **gifts**, like those given at a Christmas party, because wicked men and women will delight in the death of two figures who **tormented** them with supernatural judgments and preaching about righteousness!

11:11-12 After three and a half days of gloating over the slain witnesses, the party will end for the beast and his followers. **The breath of life** will enter the two witnesses, bringing about a resurrection (11:11).

11:13 As God often does, in this instance he will allow negative events to occur because those events will bring him greater **glory**.

11:15 The **seventh . . . trumpet** announces the imminent arrival of Christ's reign. This sequence depicts events strikingly close to the end of the tribulation and the coming of God's kingdom. Take note that the rapture is not synonymous with the second coming. The rapture is when Christ will come in the

air to receive believers into heaven. He will not come all the way down to earth in the rapture. He will only do that at the second coming, when he will be accompanied by the saints.

11:16-18 The twenty-four elders (11:16) speak of another resurrection, which is not the resurrection of New Testament believers because that occurs at the rapture. This is the resurrection of Old Testament **saints—** God's **servants the prophets**, who will be given **the reward** they are due along with **those who fear [his] name** (11:18). The Old Testament has a unique connection to the tribulation because it prophesies this seven-year period (cf. Jer 30:3-7; Dan 9:24-27). Therefore, Old Testament saints will receive their resurrection bodies following the tribulation.

12:1-2 The twelve stars represent the twelve tribes of Israel, and the **woman** is Israel (12:1). Her pregnancy symbolizes the fact that Jesus the Messiah came through Israel. At his first

coming, Jesus was born of a Jewish woman. His second coming must again originate with that people. The purpose of the tribulation is for Israel to give birth, so to speak, to the Messiah once again. In other words, Jesus cannot return until Israel receives him. Most of the Jewish people currently reject him. Yet through the **labor** (12:2) of the tribulation, overwhelming numbers of Jews will receive Christ.

12:3-4 John states in 12:9 that this **dragon** is the devil. The sweeping **away [of] a third of the stars** (12:4) depicts Satan's control over a third of the angels, who rebelled against God and help carry out Satan's evil schemes.

During the tribulation, Satan will seek to destroy Israel and **devour her child** (12:4). That is, he wants to preclude the possibility that Christ will return to the world through Israel. He employed a similar strategy at Jesus's first coming, with King Herod's attempt to kill the Christ child (see Matt 2:1-18).

devour her child.[a] [5] She gave birth to a Son, a male who is going to rule[A] all nations with an iron rod.[b] Her child was caught up to God and to his throne. [6] The woman fled into the wilderness, where she had a place prepared by God,[c] to be nourished there[B] for 1,260 days.[d]

THE DRAGON THROWN OUT OF HEAVEN

[7] Then war broke out in heaven: Michael[e] and his angels fought against the dragon. The dragon and his angels also fought, [8] but he could not prevail,[f] and there was no place for them in heaven any longer.[g] [9] So the great dragon was thrown out — the ancient serpent,[h] who is called the devil and Satan,[i] the one who deceives the whole world.[j] He was thrown to earth, and his angels with him.[k] [10] Then I heard a loud voice in heaven say,

The salvation and the power
and the kingdom of our God
and the authority of his Christ
have now come,[l]
because the accuser[m]
    of our brothers and sisters,
who accuses them
before our God day and night,
has been thrown down.
[11]   They conquered him
by the blood of the Lamb[n]
and by the word
    of their testimony;[o]
for they did not love their lives
to the point of death.[p]
[12]   Therefore rejoice, you heavens,
and you who dwell in them![q]
Woe to the earth and the sea,

because the devil has come down
    to you
with great fury,
because he knows his time is short.

THE WOMAN PERSECUTED

[13] When the dragon saw that he had been thrown down to the earth, he persecuted[c] the woman who had given birth to the male child. [14] The woman was given two wings of a great eagle,[r] so that she could fly from the serpent's presence to her place in the wilderness, where she was nourished for a time, times, and half a time.[s] [15] From his mouth the serpent spewed water like a river flowing after the woman, to sweep her away with a flood. [16] But the earth helped the woman. The earth opened its mouth and swallowed up the river that the dragon had spewed from his mouth. [17] So the dragon was furious with the woman and went off to wage war[t] against the rest of her offspring[D,u] — those who keep the commands of God[v] and hold firmly to the testimony about Jesus.[w]

THE BEAST FROM THE SEA

[18] The dragon[E] stood on the sand of the sea.[F]

13 And I saw a beast coming up out of the sea.[x] It had ten horns and seven heads. On its horns were ten crowns,[G,y] and

[a] 12:4 Mt 2:16
[b] 12:5 Ps 2:7-9; Rv 2:27; 19:15
[c] 12:6 Ex 16:4; 1Kg 19:3-8; Hs 2:14
[d] Dt 1:31; 2:7; Dn 12:11; Rv 11:2-3; 12:14; 13:5
[e] 12:7 Dn 10:13,21; 12:1; Jd 9
[f] 12:8 1Sm 2:9; Ps 21:11; Jr 20:11
[g] Jb 2:1
[h] 12:9 Gn 3:1
[i] Lk 10:18; Rm 16:20; Rv 2:9; 3:9; 20:2,7
[j] Rv 13:14; 20:3,8,10
[k] Mt 25:41; Lk 10:18; Jn 12:31
[l] 12:10 Rv 11:17; 19:1
[m] Jb 1:6-12; 2:1-5; Zch 3:1; Rm 8:33-34
[n] 12:11 1Pt 1:19; Rv 5:9; 7:14
[o] Rv 6:9
[p] Lk 14:26; Jn 12:25; Heb 11:32-37; Rv 2:10
[q] 12:12 Ps 96:11; Is 49:13

[r] 12:14 Ex 19:4; Dt 32:10-11; Is 40:31
[s] Dn 7:25; 12:7; Rv 11:2; 13:5
[t] 12:17 Rv 11:7; 13:7
[u] Gn 3:15
[v] 1Co 7:19
[w] Rv 1:2,9; 19:10; 20:4
[x] 13:1 Dn 7:3
[y] Rv 12:3

[A] **12:5** Or *shepherd*   [B] **12:6** Or *God, that they might feed her there*   [C] **12:13** Or *pursued*   [D] **12:17** Or *seed*   [E] **12:18** Or *he*; other mss read *I*
[F] **12:18** Some translations put Rv 12:18 either in Rv 12:17 or Rv 13:1.   [G] **13:1** Or *diadems*

12:5 The **birth [of] a Son** is a reference to Jesus's advent as a baby in Bethlehem. His **rule [of] all nations** refers to the millennial kingdom, in which he will reign over the earth with his people for a thousand years. The child's being **caught up to God** pictures Jesus's ascension (see Acts 1:6-11).
12:6 This depicts God's protection of Israel during the second half of the tribulation. During that time, the Jewish people will receive Jesus as Messiah en masse and hasten his second coming.
12:7-8 As **Michael** fought on Daniel's behalf against demons in the Old Testament era (12:7; see Dan 10:13), angels fight for believers today and will fight for Israel in the tribulation to come.
12:9 Satan's expulsion from heaven is the same episode referenced in Isaiah 14:12-15 and Revelation 9:1, which occurred sometime

before the fall of humankind (see Gen 3). We allow Satan to achieve victories in our lives when we act on his deception rather than rejecting it.
12:10 A major strategy of Satan is to be an accuser of believers (see Zech 3:1-7) in order to rob them of their joy, power, and fellowship with God.
12:11 Every Christian is saved from eternal condemnation by Christ's **blood**. Those who defeat Satan's schemes in this life and receive the reward of eternal authority do so by a godly public **testimony**.
12:12-13 The **devil** knows (see 20:1-3) that he will be locked up for a thousand years following Christ's return. This reality will prompt him to take full advantage of his final forty-two months of freedom to wreak havoc (12:12). His goal will be to destroy Israel and thus render God's Word false. As John puts

it, **when the dragon saw that he had been thrown down . . . , he persecuted the woman [Israel] who had given birth to the male child [Jesus]** (12:13).
12:14 A time, times, and half a time refers to the three and a half years during which Satan will come against Israel with wild fury. God will protect Israel supernaturally.
12:15-16 This prophecy illustrates a broader principle: We discover God most powerfully in the context of being overwhelmed. When believers are flooded with opposition, often they are able to watch God supernaturally suck up the **flood** of despair and avert Satan's plan for destruction.
13:1 The sea represents the Gentiles. So depicting the antichrist as a **beast coming up out of the sea** signifies that he will be a Gentile. The antichrist's **ten horns** represent a ten-nation confederacy that he will rule

b 13:2 Dn 7:4-6
c 13:3 Rv 17:8
d 13:4 Rv 12:3
e Ex 15:11; Is 46:5
f 13:5 Dn 7:8,11,20
g Rv 11:2
h 13:7 Rv 12:17
i Jr 27:6; Dn 7:6,14; Lk 4:6;
    Jn 19:11
j Rv 5:9; 7:9; 11:9; 14:6
k 13:8 Ex 32:32-33; Ps
    69:28; Php 4:3; Rv 3:5;
    17:8; 20:12,15; 21:27
l 1Pt 1:19-20; Rv 5:6,12; 7:14
m 13:9 Mt 11:15; Rv
    2:7,11,17,19; 3:6,13,22

n 13:10 Jr 15:2; 43:11
o Rv 14:12
p 13:11 Dn 8:3
q 13:13 Dt 13:1-3; Mk 13:22;
    2Th 2:9-11
r 1Kg 18:38; 2Kg 1:10;
    Lk 9:54
s 13:14 Rv 12:9
t 2Th 2:9-12; Rv 19:20
u 13:15 Dn 3:5-6; Rv 20:4
v 13:16 Rv 14:1,9,11; 16:2;
    19:20; 20:4

on its heads were blasphemous names.[A,a] [2] The beast I saw was like a leopard, its feet were like a bear's, and its mouth was like a lion's mouth.[b] The dragon gave the beast his power, his throne, and great authority. [3] One of its heads appeared to be fatally wounded, but its fatal wound was healed.

The whole earth was amazed and followed the beast.[c] [4] They worshiped the dragon[d] because he gave authority to the beast. And they worshiped the beast, saying, "Who is like the beast?[e] Who is able to wage war against it?"

[5] The beast was given a mouth to utter boasts and blasphemies.[f] It was allowed to exercise authority[B,c] for forty-two months.[g] [6] It began to speak[D] blasphemies against God: to blaspheme his name and his dwelling — those who dwell in heaven. [7] And it was permitted to wage war against the saints and to conquer them.[h] It was also given authority[i] over every tribe, people, language, and nation.[j] [8] All those who live on the earth will worship it, everyone whose name was not written from the foundation of the world in the book[E] of life[k] of the Lamb who was slaughtered.[F,l]

[9] If anyone has ears to hear, let him listen.[m]

[10]   If anyone is to be taken captive,
       into captivity he goes.

    If anyone is to be killed[G]
       with a sword,
       with a sword he will be killed.[n]
This calls for endurance[H] and faithfulness from the saints.[o]

THE BEAST FROM THE EARTH

[11] Then I saw another beast coming up out of the earth; it had two horns like a lamb,[i,p] but it spoke like a dragon. [12] It exercises all the authority of the first beast on its behalf and compels the earth and those who live on it to worship the first beast, whose fatal wound was healed. [13] It also performs great signs,[q] even causing fire to come down from heaven to earth in front of people.[r] [14] It deceives those who live on the earth[s] because of the signs that it is permitted to perform in the presence of the beast,[t] telling those who live on the earth to make an image[j] of the beast who was wounded by the sword and yet lived. [15] It was permitted to give breath[k] to the image of the beast, so that the image of the beast could both speak and cause whoever would not worship the image of the beast to be killed.[u] [16] And it makes everyone — small and great, rich and poor, free and slave — to receive a mark on his right hand or on his forehead,[v] [17] so that no one

in   [A] 13:1 Other mss read *heads was a blasphemous name*   [B] 13:5 Other mss read *to wage war*   [C] 13:5 Or *to rule*   [D] 13:6 Or *He opened his mouth*
    anyone kills   [H] 13:10 Or *Here is the perseverance*   [I] 13:11 Or *ram*   [J] 13:14 Or *a statue*, or *a likeness*   [K] 13:15 Or *a spirit*, or *life*
    [E] 13:8 Or *scroll*   [F] 13:8 Or *written in the book of life of the Lamb who was slaughtered from the foundation of the world*   [G] 13:10 Other mss read

(see Dan 7:7-8). The setting of this chapter is the second half of the tribulation, during which time the antichrist will oppose Israel after appearing to be its ally. This figure will blaspheme the name of God, signified by the **names** on **its heads**.

13:2 The antichrist will be a human monster. That's why he's described as a predator **like a leopard [with] feet . . . like a bear's** and a mouth **like a lion's**. The reason we classify people like Hitler, Stalin, Lenin, and Mao this way is that they sought to exterminate people en masse. This is precisely what the antichrist will seek to do with Israel. This man's **great authority** will come directly from Satan.

13:3-4 At some point, the antichrist will appear **to be fatally wounded**, but the **wound [will be] healed**. This will lead **the whole earth** to be **amazed** and to follow him (13:3). As they do, he will direct worship toward the devil **(the dragon)**. Mass worship of the devil may seem unthinkable to us, but it is not so absurd in a culture that has dismissed God (13:4).

13:5-7 If the thought of a world ruler with such sweeping authority seems farfetched, think of Hitler. If not for a series of providential interventions, he might have achieved the goal of world domination. For example, a snowstorm kept the Germans from conquering Russia, and America's entrance into

World War II pushed them back on the western front. Hitler wasn't *the* antichrist, but he was *an* antichrist. And his near conquest of the world makes an actual conquest by this future leader seem less implausible.

13:8 Only believers will refuse to worship the antichrist. All others will bow—**everyone whose name was not written from the foundation of the world in the book of life**. This verse implies that God the Father reckoned the death of Jesus to humans as righteousness before "the foundation of the world." Christ's death occurred at a specific point in history some two thousand years ago, but for God all moments are the present. Thus, even before creating the universe, he counted Christ's death as atoning for the sin each person inherits from Adam (cf. Rom 5:18).

Importantly, no one is condemned for original, inherited sin. The only cause for anyone's consignment to hell is his or her own personal sin, including rejection of Jesus as Savior. That's why children who die in infancy and people born with severe mental disabilities go to heaven. They have no conscience, personal sin, or spiritual rejection of the Savior for which to be condemned. Yet when a person knowingly sins and rejects the revelation of God in creation, his or her name is erased from the book of life and only reinserted

should he or she place faith in Jesus as Savior. **13:10** The tribulation will be a rough period for followers of Jesus. The heightened cost of discipleship will make it much less desirable to be saved then than it is now.

13:11 The earth is a reference to the promised land. Thus, the **beast coming up out of the earth** will be Jewish. He will have a gentle side **like a lamb** but will speak the very words of Satan **like a dragon**.

13:12 This second beast, the false prophet, completes the unholy trinity, which imitates the work of the Holy Trinity. Within the Godhead, the Father seeks worship; the Son gives glory to the Father; and the Holy Spirit gives glory to the Son. Here, Satan seeks worship for himself; the first beast glorifies Satan; and the second beast glorifies the first. Specifically, this second beast **compels the earth . . . to worship the first beast**. Additionally, he will heal the antichrist's fatal wound, imitating the Holy Spirit's work of raising Christ from the dead (see Rom 8:11).

13:13-15 Even if someone can call down flames and raise the dead, he is an instrument of Satan if he does not also point people to Jesus.

13:16-18 Such a **mark** may take the form of a chip embedded under the skin. The mark will contain **the number** of the antichrist, which

can buy or sell unless he has the mark: the beast's name or the number of its name.

18 This calls for wisdom:[A],[a] Let the one who has understanding calculate[B] the number of the beast, because it is the number of a person. Its number is 666.[c]

THE LAMB AND THE 144,000

14 Then I looked, and there was the Lamb, standing on Mount Zion,[b] and with him were 144,000 who had his name and his Father's name written on their foreheads.[c] **2** I heard a sound[D] from heaven like the sound of cascading waters[d] and like the rumbling of loud thunder. The sound I heard was like harpists playing on their harps.[e] **3** They sang[E] a new song[f] before the throne and before the four living creatures and the elders,[g] but no one could learn the song except the 144,000 who had been redeemed from the earth. **4** These are the ones who have not defiled themselves with women, since they remained virgins.[h] These are the ones who follow the Lamb wherever he goes. They were redeemed[F] from humanity as the firstfruits[i] for God and the Lamb. **5** No lie was found in their mouths; they are blameless.[j]

THE PROCLAMATION OF THREE ANGELS

6 Then I saw another angel[k] flying high overhead,[l] with the eternal gospel to announce to the inhabitants of the earth — to every nation, tribe, language, and people.[m] **7** He spoke with a loud voice:[n] "Fear God[o] and give him glory,[p] because the hour of his judgment has come.[q]

Worship the one who made heaven and earth,[r] the sea and the springs of water."

8 And another, a second angel, followed, saying, "It has fallen, Babylon the Great[s] has fallen.[G] She made all the nations drink the wine of her sexual immorality,[H] which brings wrath."[t]

9 And another, a third angel, followed them and spoke with a loud voice: "If anyone worships the beast and its image and receives a mark on his forehead or on his hand, **10** he will also drink the wine of God's wrath, which is poured full strength into the cup of his anger.[u] He will be tormented with fire and sulfur[v] in the sight of the holy angels and in the sight of the Lamb, **11** and the smoke of their torment will go up forever and ever.[w] There is no rest[I],[X] day or night for those who worship the beast and its image, or anyone who receives the mark[y] of its name. **12** This calls for endurance from the saints,[z] who keep God's commands and their faith in Jesus."[J]

13 Then I heard a voice from heaven saying, "Write: Blessed are the dead who die in the Lord from now on."[aa]

"Yes," says the Spirit, "so they will rest from their labors, since their works follow them."

REAPING THE EARTH'S HARVEST

14 Then I looked, and there was a white cloud, and one like the Son of Man[K],[ab] was seated on the cloud, with a golden crown on his head and a sharp sickle in his hand. **15** Another angel came out of the temple, crying out in a loud voice to the one who was seated on the cloud, "Use your sickle and reap, for the time to reap has come,

[a] 13:18 Rv 17:9
[b] 14:1 Is 18:7; 24:23; Mc 4:7
[c] Dt 6:8; Ezk 9:4; Rv 3:12; 7:3; 9:4; 13:16; 22:4
[d] 14:2 Ezk 1:24; 43:2; Rv 1:15; 19:6
[e] Rv 5:8
[f] 14:3 Rv 5:9
[g] Rv 4:4,6
[h] 14:4 1Sm 21:4-5
[i] Dt 21:17; Jr 2:3; Jms 1:18
[j] 14:5 Zph 3:13; Jn 1:47
[k] 14:6 Rv 7:2; 8:3; 14:15,17-18; 18:1
[l] Rv 8:13
[m] Rv 5:9; 7:9; 11:9; 13:7
[n] 14:7 Rv 1:10; 8:13; 10:3
[o] Gn 22:12; 42:18; Ps 66:16; Ec 5:7; 12:13; Ac 13:16,26; 1Pt 2:17
[p] Jos 7:19; 1Sm 6:5; Jr 13:16; Lk 17:18; Rv 4:9; 16:9; 19:7
[q] Rv 18:10

[r] 14:7 Ps 115:15; 121:2; 124:8; 134:3; 146:6
[s] 14:8 Dn 4:30; Rv 16:19; 17:5; 18:2
[t] Is 21:9; Jr 51:7-8,49; Rv 17:2,4; 18:2-3
[u] 14:10 Ps 75:8; Is 51:17; Jr 25:15-17; Rv 17:2,4; 18:2-3
[v] Lk 17:29; Rv 20:10; 21:8
[w] 14:11 Is 1:31; 34:10; 66:24; Rv 19:3
[x] Ps 22:2; Is 23:12; 62:6; Jr 45:3; Lm 2:18
[y] Rv 4:15; Ex 12:13; Ezk 9:4,6; Rv 13:16; 16:2; 19:20
[z] 14:12 Rv 13:10
[aa] 14:13 Rv 1:3; 16:15; 19:9; 20:6; 22:7,14
[ab] 14:14 Dn 7:13; Lk 21:27; Rv 1:13

[A] 13:18 Or *Here is wisdom* [B] 13:18 Or *count*, or *figure out* [C] 13:18 Other Gk mss read 616 [D] 14:2 Or *voice* [E] 14:3 Other mss add *as it were* [F] 14:4 Other mss add *by Jesus* [G] 14:8 Other mss omit the second *has fallen* [H] 14:8 Or *wine of her passionate immorality* [I] 14:11 Or *They have no rest* [J] 14:12 Or *and the faith of Jesus*, or *and faithfulness to Jesus* [K] 14:14 Or *like a son of man*

is 666. Six is the number of man; it contrasts with seven, which is the number of God. The numeral six is repeated three times, once each for Satan, the antichrist, and the false prophet. Note that the centralized, governmental control of trade is the economics of the antichrist (13:17).

14:1 These **144,000** are Jewish evangelists, whose job is to announce the gospel worldwide during the tribulation to lead many more to faith in Christ. They will prepare the way for the return of Jesus. The name **on their foreheads** contrasts with the mark placed on nonbelievers by the false prophet (cf. 13:16).

14:4 As Jesus is the "firstfruits" of the resurrection (see 1 Cor 15:23), the 144,000 Jewish evangelists are the **firstfruits** of those to be saved during the tribulation. There will be a multitude saved at that time, but these are presented to God the Father and God the

Son as the initial harvest **redeemed from humanity**.

14:6 Even while judgment and persecution are being poured out on the earth, widespread evangelism will be occurring.

14:7 Worship of God as Maker of **heaven and earth** marks a contrast with the false worship of Satan and the antichrist.

14:8 **Babylon the Great** is a metaphorical expression depicting the system of false religion and rebellion against God established by the devil and the two beasts (cf. 17:1-18). Unlike worship of God, which will endure, this false religion will prove temporary.

14:9-10 Receiving the **mark** of 666 (14:9; see 13:18) may appear to be a harmless formality to enable commerce, but it designates its recipients for judgment at **full strength** in hell—a place where the wicked are **tormented with fire** (14:10).

14:11 Hell is separation from God, and God is the one who gives **rest** (see Matt 11:28). So picture the unpleasantness of battling insomnia for a week. Then extend that into eternity. Then contrast that potential future with heaven, which is depicted in Scripture as a place of eternal rest (Heb 3:7–4:11). Consignment to hell is a free choice, a penalty people bring on themselves, as when they elect to receive **the mark of** the beast.

14:13 **The dead who die in the Lord from now on** is a reference to those who are persecuted for their faith in Christ during the tribulation. They will find **rest**, a fate that is the opposite of that experienced by those who receive the mark of the beast (see the note on 14:11).

14:14-16 The **sickle** here is an instrument to inflict judgment and death on those who reject God. It is mentioned six times in five verses (14:14-18) to underscore the impending

a 14:15 Jl 3:13
b 14:19 Rv 16:19; 19:15
c 14:20 Is 63:1-6
d 15:1 Mt 16:1; 24:30; Lk 21:11; Ac 2:19; Rv 12:1,3; 13:13
e Jn 19:30; Rv 10:7; 16:17; 17:17
f 15:2 Rv 4:6
g Rv 5:8; 14:2
h 15:3 Ex 15:1; Dt 31:22

i 15:3 Rv 16:7; 19:2
j Dn 2:37; Lk 22:25; 1Tm 6:15; Rv 17:14; 19:16
k 15:4 Is 8:13
l Ps 86:9; 113:4; Is 52:10; 61:11; Jr 3:17; 33:9
m 15:5 Ex 38:21; Nm 17:7; 18:2
n Rv 11:19
o 15:7 Ex 15:18; Ps 10:16; 45:6; 48:14; Gl 1:5; Eph 3:21; Php 4:20; 1Tm 1:17; 2Tm 4:18; Heb 1:8; 13:21; 1Pt 4:11; Rv 1:6,18; 4:9-10; 5:13; 7:12; 10:6; 11:15
p 15:8 Ex 19:18; 20:18; Is 4:5; 6:4
q 16:1 Rv 8:2,6; 15:1,6-8
r Rv 17:1; 21:9
s 16:2 Ex 9:9-11; Dt 28:27,35; Jb 2:7; Is 1:6; Jr 30:12-17

since the harvest of the earth is ripe."[a] [16] So the one seated on the cloud swung his sickle over the earth, and the earth was harvested.

[17] Then another angel who also had a sharp sickle came out of the temple in heaven. [18] Yet another angel, who had authority over fire, came from the altar, and he called with a loud voice to the one who had the sharp sickle, "Use your sharp sickle and gather the clusters of grapes from the vineyard of the earth, because its grapes have ripened." [19] So the angel swung his sickle at the earth and gathered the grapes from the vineyard of the earth, and he threw them into the great winepress of God's wrath.[b] [20] Then the press was trampled outside the city, and blood flowed out of the press up to the horses' bridles for about 180 miles.[A,c]

PREPARATION FOR THE BOWL JUDGMENTS

15 Then I saw another great and awe-inspiring sign[B] in heaven:[d] seven angels with the seven last plagues; for with them God's wrath will be completed.[e] [2] I also saw something like a sea of glass[f] mixed with fire, and those who had won the victory over the beast, its image,[c] and the number of its name, were standing on the sea of glass with harps from God.[g] [3] They sang the song of God's servant Moses[h] and the song of the Lamb:

Great and awe-inspiring are
your works,

Lord God, the Almighty;
just and true[i] are your ways,
King of the nations.[D,j]
[4] Lord, who will not fear
and glorify your name?
For you alone are holy.[k]
All the nations will come
and worship before you[l]
because your righteous acts
have been revealed.

[5] After this I looked, and the heavenly temple — the tabernacle of testimony[m] — was opened.[n] [6] Out of the temple came the seven angels with the seven plagues, dressed in pure, bright linen, with golden sashes wrapped around their chests. [7] One of the four living creatures gave the seven angels seven golden bowls filled with the wrath of God who lives forever and ever.[o] [8] Then the temple was filled with smoke from the glory of God and from his power,[p] and no one could enter the temple until the seven plagues of the seven angels were completed.

THE FIRST BOWL

16 Then I heard a loud voice from the temple saying to the seven angels,[q] "Go and pour out the seven[E] bowls[r] of God's wrath on the earth." [2] The first went and poured out his bowl on the earth, and severely painful sores[s] broke out on the people who had the mark of the beast and who worshiped its image.

[A] 14:20 Lit *1,600 stadia*   [B] 15:1 Or *and awesome symbolic display*   [C] 15:2 Other mss add *his mark*   [D] 15:3 Other mss read *ages*   [E] 16:1 Other mss omit *seven*

---

doom for those who reject him during the tribulation. In general, a *sickle* is a tool used to harvest crops.

14:18-19 The angel's declaration that the harvest has **ripened** is a reminder that God does not pour out his wrath on people at the first hint of their sinful rebellion, though that would be entirely justified. Instead, he provides extended opportunity for repentance and strikes with the sickle of judgment when rebellion has matured into an unmistakable pattern (14:18).

14:20 When God brings final judgment against the nations who attack him at Armageddon (cf. 16:14-16), the bloodletting will be so severe that **blood** will splatter up to the level of a horse's bridle for approximately **180 miles**.

15:1 In view here is the cessation of the temporal judgments of the tribulation. Final judgment will remain, in which the wicked and the righteous are consigned to their eternal destinies.

15:2 In all likelihood, this is a body of water that is utterly smooth. The calmness, however, does not indicate serenity, for the **sea** is **mixed with fire**, an indication that the calm is merely a dramatic pause before a display of God's burning wrath. **Standing on the sea** are believers who presumably have been martyred because they are in heaven rather than on earth.

15:3 As **Moses** sang in triumph after Israel's Egyptian enemies had been swallowed by the Red Sea (see Exod 15:1-18), followers of Christ from the tribulation will sing at the prospect of Satan, the antichrist, and the false prophet being overwhelmed with judgment. This **song** will be even more glorious than that of Moses, though, because the judgment will be carried out by the Lamb of God. Jesus was active in Moses's day, following Israel through the wilderness (see 1 Cor 10:1-4). But he was not yet openly identified as the incarnate Messiah and Redeemer, as he is here. The worship song celebrates God's **awe-inspiring . . . works**, which are never capricious or unfair, but **just**.

15:4 The two specific reasons for which God is worshiped are his character and his works.

15:5-6 The procession of **the seven angels** (15:6) out of **the heavenly temple** (15:5) indicates the judgments they are to bear come directly from God's presence, for in the Old Testament, the temple was where God's presence dwelt.

15:8 The temple's filling **with smoke** hearkens back to two Old Testament scenes. The first occurred in 1 Kings 8:10-11, in which Solomon dedicated the temple and God's presence was manifested as a cloud that filled the building. The second scene occurred in Isaiah 6:4. In both instances, the cloud/smoke signified God's manifest presence. That's the point of the smoke in Revelation as well. God wants all to recognize him as the source of the fierce judgments to ensue.

16:1 **The seven bowls** represent God's final judgments during the latter three and a half years of the tribulation. Foreshadowed by the "song of . . . Moses" (15:3), some of these judgments parallel the plagues God brought upon Egypt through Moses (Exod 7-12).

THE SECOND BOWL

3 The second[A] poured out his bowl into the sea. It turned to blood like that of a dead person, and all life in the sea died.[a]

THE THIRD BOWL

4 The third[A] poured out his bowl into the rivers and the springs of water, and they became blood.[b] **5** I heard the angel of the waters say,

You are just,
the Holy One,[c] who is and who was,[d]
because you have passed judgment
on these things.
6 Because they poured out
the blood of the saints
and the prophets,[e]
you have given them blood
to drink;
they deserve it![f]

7 I heard the altar say,

Yes, Lord God, the Almighty,
true and just are your judgments.[g]

THE FOURTH BOWL

8 The fourth[A] poured out his bowl on the sun. It was allowed to scorch people with fire, **9** and people were scorched by the intense heat. So they blasphemed the name of God,[h] who has the power[B] over these plagues, and they did not repent and give him glory.[i]

THE FIFTH BOWL

10 The fifth[A] poured out his bowl on the throne of the beast,[j] and its kingdom was plunged into darkness.[k] People[C] gnawed their tongues because of their pain **11** and blasphemed the God of heaven[l] because of their pains and their sores, but they did not repent of their works.

THE SIXTH BOWL

12 The sixth[A] poured out his bowl on the great river Euphrates,[m] and its water was dried up[n] to prepare the way for the kings from the east. **13** Then I saw three unclean spirits like frogs[o] coming from the dragon's mouth,[p] from the beast's mouth,[q] and from the mouth of the false prophet.[r] **14** For they are demonic spirits performing signs,[s] who travel to the kings of the whole world to assemble them[t] for the battle on the great day of God, the Almighty.[u] **15** "Look, I am coming like a thief. Blessed[v] is the one who is alert and remains clothed[D,w] so that he may not go around naked and people see his shame."[x] **16** So they assembled the kings at the place called in Hebrew, Armageddon.[E,y]

THE SEVENTH BOWL

17 Then the seventh[A] poured out his bowl into the air,[F] and a loud voice came out of the temple[G,z] from the throne, saying, "It is done!"[18] There were flashes of lightning, rumblings, and peals of thunder. And a severe earthquake occurred like no other since people have been on the earth, so great was the quake.[aa] **19** The great city[ab] split into three parts, and the cities of the nations[H] fell. Babylon the Great was remembered in God's presence; he gave her the cup filled with the wine of his fierce anger.[ac] **20** Every island fled, and the mountains disappeared.[ad] **21** Enormous hailstones, each weighing about a hundred

[a]16:3 Rv 8:8-9
[b]16:4 Ex 7:17-21
[c]16:5 Is 5:19; 41:20; 45:11
[d]Rv 11:17
[e]16:6 2Kg 9:7; Mt 23:30; Lk 11:50; Rv 17:6; 18:24
[f]Is 49:26
[g]16:7 Ps 19:9; Rv 19:2
[h]16:9 Lv 24:11; Is 52:5; Rm 2:24; 1Tm 6:1; Rv 13:6
[i]Rv 9:20-21
[j]16:10 Rv 2:13; 13:2
[k]Ex 10:21
[l]16:11 Rv 13:6

[m]16:12 Gn 2:14; 15:18; Dt 11:24; 1Kg 4:21; Rv 9:14
[n]Ex 14:21-22,29; 15:19; Jos 2:10; 4:23; 5:1; 2Kg 2:8; Neh 9:11; Is 51:10
[o]16:13 Ex 8:2-14; Lv 11:9-12,41-47
[p]Rv 12:9
[q]Rv 13:1
[r]Rv 13:11-17
[s]16:14 2Th 2:9-10
[t]1Kg 22:20-23; Mt 24:24; 2Th 2:10
[u]Ezk 38-39; Jl 2:11; 3:2; Zch 14:2; Rv 19:11-21
[v]16:15 Rv 1:3; 14:13; 19:9; 20:6; 22:7,14
[w]Lk 12:35-40; 1Th 5:2,6-8
[x]Rv 3:18
[y]16:16 Jdg 5:19; 2Kg 9:27; Ezk 38:8
[z]16:17 Is 66:6
[aa]16:18 Ex 19:16-19; Rv 4:5; 8:5; 11:19
[ab]16:19 Rv 18:10,16,18-19,21
[ac]Rv 14:19; 19:15
[ad]16:20 Ezk 38:20; Rv 6:14

[A]16:3,4,8,10,12,17 Other mss add *angel* [B]16:9 Or *authority* [C]16:10 Lit *They* [D]16:15 Or *and guards his clothes* [E]16:16 Some mss read *Armagedon*; other mss read *Harmegedon*; other mss read *Mageddon*; other mss read *Mageddon* [F]16:17 Or *bowl on the air* [G]16:17 Other mss add *of heaven* [H]16:19 Or *the Gentile cities*

16:5 Because God is **just**, his judgment is always an expression of his righteous standard. Since God is eternal—the one **who is and who was**—he never lowers that standard. We must either meet his standard or have a substitute, Jesus Christ, meet it in our place. When a person accepts Jesus as his Savior, God imputes his righteous life to the saved person's account; thus, that person is counted as having met the standard.
16:6 Those who will not receive Jesus get what they **deserve** for their actions.
16:10-11 As in 16:9, the scene is reminiscent of a child cursing his or her parent while he or she is being spanked. Such a reaction to punishment inevitably triggers more punishment.
16:12 As God carries out the **sixth** bowl judgment, he is providentially guiding history toward the battle of Armageddon. **The great**

river Euphrates dries up and opens a travel route for armies of the Orient(i.e., **kings from the east**) to converge on the Middle East with the forces of the antichrist and other world armies.
16:13-14 The convergence of armies for history's final war will not be merely a geopolitical event. Rather, it will be a supernatural event because **demonic spirits performing signs [will]** travel to the **kings of the whole world to assemble them for . . . battle** (16:14). John pictures these demonic spirits **like frogs coming from [Satan's] mouth, from the [antichrist's] mouth, and from the mouth of the false prophet** (16:13). These three evil figures will employ miraculous signs to rally the nations behind their cause.
16:15 During the lead-up to war, Jesus injects a personal warning that his return will be sud-

den and unexpected. The only way to avoid **shame** on that day is to be spiritually **alert and . . . clothed** with a righteous life.
16:16 Armageddon is a Greek transliteration of the Hebrew phrase **Har Megiddo**, meaning "Mount of Megiddo." It is the name of an ancient hilltop settlement in northern Israel near Haifa. Near it is a huge plain that has been the site of several historic battles, though the greatest battle on this site has yet to occur.
16:17-18 Though the armies have gathered, the direct and mighty acts of God are what draw John's attention as the Lord begins to convulse nature in opposition to his enemies.
16:19 The great city referenced at the beginning of the verse is synonymous with **Babylon the Great** in the next sentence. Identified by the name of the wicked Old

a 16:21 Rv 16:9,11
b Jos 10:11; Ezk 38:22
c 17:1 Rv 15:7; 16:1; 21:9
d Rv 19:2
e Jr 51:13; Rv 17:15
f 17:2 Ps 2:2; 76:12; Is 24:21; Ezk 27:33; Rv 1:5; 6:15; 18:9; 19:19; 21:24
g Is 23:16-17; Nah 3:4; Rv 14:8; 18:3
h 17:3 Ezk 8:3; 11:24; Lk 4:1,14; Rv 1:10; 4:2; 21:10
i Rv 12:3,6; 13:1
j 17:4 Ezk 28:13; Rv 18:16
k Mt 24:15; Mk 13:14; Lk 16:15; Rv 21:27
l 17:5 Rv 14:1
m 17:6 Dt 32:42; Is 49:26; 63:6; Ezk 39:19

n 17:8 Ps 140:10; Lk 8:31; Rm 10:7; Rv 9:1,11; 11:7; 20:1-3
o Mt 7:13; Jn 17:12; Rm 9:22; Php 3:19; 2Th 2:3; 2Pt 3:7; Rv 1:18; 2:8
p Ps 69:28; Is 4:3; Mt 25:34; Eph 1:4; Php 4:3; 1Pt 1:20; Rv 3:5; 13:8; 20:12,15; 21:27
q Ps 48:5; Rv 13:3,12,14
r 17:9 Rv 13:18
s 17:12 Dn 7:24; Rv 13:1
t Rv 18:10,17,19
u 17:14 Dt 10:17; Ps 136:2-3; Dn 2:47; 1Tm 6:15; Rv 1:5; 19:11-21
v Rv 12:11; 13:8
w 17:15 Jr 51:13
x Is 17:12; Jr 51:58; Dn 5:19; Hab 2:8; Rv 5:9; 7:9; 10:11; 11:9; 13:7; 14:6
y 17:16 2Sm 13:15-20; Ezk 23:22-35
z Lv 20:14; 21:9

pounds,[A] fell from the sky on people, and they blasphemed God[a] for the plague of hail because that plague was extremely severe.[b]

THE WOMAN AND THE SCARLET BEAST

17 Then one of the seven angels who had the seven bowls[c] came and spoke with me: "Come, I will show you the judgment of the notorious prostitute[B,d] who is seated on many[c] waters.[e] **2** The kings of the earth[f] committed sexual immorality with her, and those who live on the earth became drunk on the wine of her sexual immorality."[g] **3** Then he carried me away in the Spirit[D,h] to a wilderness.

I saw a woman sitting on a scarlet beast that was covered[E] with blasphemous names and had seven heads and ten horns.[i] **4** The woman was dressed in purple and scarlet, adorned with gold, jewels, and pearls.[j] She had a golden cup in her hand filled with everything detestable[k] and with the impurities of her[F] prostitution. **5** On her forehead was written a name, a mystery:[l] BABYLON THE GREAT, THE MOTHER OF PROSTITUTES AND OF THE DETESTABLE THINGS OF THE EARTH. **6** Then I saw that the woman was drunk with the blood of the saints and with the blood of the witnesses to Jesus.[m] When I saw her, I was greatly astonished.

THE MEANING OF THE WOMAN AND OF THE BEAST

7 Then the angel said to me, "Why are you astonished? I will explain to you the mystery of the woman and of the beast, with the seven heads and the ten horns, that carries her. **8** The beast that you saw was, and is not, and is about to come up from the abyss[n] and go to destruction.[o] Those who live on the earth whose names have not been written in the book of life from the foundation of the world[p] will be astonished when they see the beast that was, and is not, and is to come.[q] **9** This calls for a mind that has wisdom.[G,r]

"The seven heads are seven mountains on which the woman is seated. They are also seven kings: **10** Five have fallen, one is, the other has not yet come, and when he comes, he must remain for only a little while. **11** The beast that was and is not, is itself an eighth king, but it belongs to the seven and is going to destruction. **12** The ten horns you saw are ten kings[s] who have not yet received a kingdom, but they will receive authority as kings with the beast for one hour.[t] **13** These have one purpose, and they give their power and authority to the beast. **14** These will make war against the Lamb, but the Lamb will conquer them because he is Lord of lords and King of kings.[u] Those with him are called, chosen, and faithful."[v]

15 He also said to me, "The waters you saw,[w] where the prostitute was seated, are peoples, multitudes, nations, and languages.[x] **16** The ten horns you saw, and the beast, will hate the prostitute.[y] They will make her desolate and naked, devour her flesh, and burn her up with fire.[z] **17** For

---

[A] 16:21 Lit *about a talent*; talents varied in weight upwards from 75 pounds   [B] 17:1 Traditionally translated *the great whore*   [C] 17:1 Or *by many*   [D] 17:3 Or *in spirit*   [E] 17:3 Or *was filled*   [F] 17:4 Other mss read *earth's*   [G] 17:9 Or *Here is the mind of wisdom*

Testament kingdom that conquered Israel, *Babylon* represents secular, worldly institutions opposed to God.
16:21 As in 6:16-17, people know the source of their judgment, yet they refuse to repent or honor God. Instead, they blaspheme him, enraged at the severity of the **plague**. Their response is as irrational as it is immoral.
17:1-5 Prostitute is used as a metaphor for people who are unfaithful to God (17:1). What John calls **the MOTHER**, or origin, of such unfaithfulness is the city of **Babylon** (17:5), introduced in Genesis 11:1-9. Led by a man named Nimrod, the people of Babylon rejected God's rule and put humankind at the center of their civilization. God dispersed that city in judgment by confusing its languages (Gen 10:8-12). Throughout subsequent history, though, it spawned other civilizations in which man attempted to elevate himself to the role of deity—such as in the later kingdom of Babylon led by Nebuchadnezzar. After that, the Roman Empire embodied the values of ancient Babylon. Eventually, the

term *Babylon* came to be used for any worldly system that attempted to replace God. Today, secularism and worldliness are children of this great mother of prostitutes.
The image of this prostitute **seated on many waters** (Rev 17:1) depicts worldliness and secularism dispersed among the many people groups and nations of the world (cf. 17:15) who **became drunk**, so to speak, on immorality (17:2). The prostitute is riding on **a scarlet beast** (17:3), which is the antichrist, because he will carry godlessness across his dominion. The materialism associated with worldly systems is depicted as the woman's clothing as well as her adornment. Perversion is depicted as the **detestable** content of a **golden cup** (17:4).
17:9-11 Key to understanding this scene is John's description of the beast's **seven heads [as] seven mountains on which the woman is seated** (17:9). Historically, the Roman Empire has been described as a nation built on seven hills or seven mountains. Accordingly, John seems to be saying the antichrist will lead

a renewed Roman Empire. Worldliness and rebellion against God will spread across it, personified by the unfaithful woman seated on it.
The seven heads also represent **seven kings** (17:9) or world leaders. The presence of **five [kings who] have fallen** (17:10) indicates the antichrist will depose some world leaders in order to increase his power. Nevertheless, he will leave some leaders in power and allow still others to rise. The antichrist will govern alongside his political contemporaries, although eventually, as John repeats, he **is going to destruction** (17:11).
17:12-14 There will be **ten** nations in the renewed Roman Empire that form an alliance under the antichrist and **make war against the Lamb** at the battle of Armageddon. **But the Lamb will conquer them because he is ... King of kings** (17:12, 14).
17:16-17 The image of **ten** nations devouring **the prostitute** and burning **her up with fire** (17:16) serves as a reminder that the worldly system, which promises pleasure, will soon

God has put it into their hearts to carry out his plan by having one purpose[a] and to give their kingdom[A] to the beast until the words of God are fulfilled.[b] **18** And the woman you saw is the great city that has royal power over the kings of the earth."

THE FALL OF BABYLON THE GREAT

18 After this I saw another angel with great authority coming down from heaven,[c] and the earth was illuminated by his splendor. **²** He called out in a mighty voice:

It has fallen,[B]
Babylon the Great has fallen![d]
She has become a home for demons,
a haunt for every unclean spirit,
a haunt for every unclean bird,
and a haunt[c] for every unclean
    and despicable beast.[D,e]
3 For all the nations have drunk[E]
the wine of her sexual immorality,
which brings wrath.[f]
The kings of the earth
have committed sexual immorality
    with her,
and the merchants of the earth
have grown wealthy
    from her sensuality and excess.[g]
4 Then I heard another voice from heaven:
Come out of her, my people,
so that you will not share
    in her sins[h]
or receive any of her plagues.
5 For her sins are piled up[F] to heaven,[i]
and God has remembered
    her crimes.[j]
6 Pay her back the way she also paid,[k]
and double it
    according to her works.[l]
In the cup in which she mixed,[m]

mix a double portion for her.
7 As much as she glorified herself
and indulged her sensual and
    excessive ways,
give her that much torment
    and grief.
For she says in her heart,
"I sit as a queen;
I am not a widow,
and I will never see grief."[n]
8 For this reason her plagues
    will come in just one day —
death and grief and famine.[o]
She will be burned up with fire,[p]
because the Lord God
    who judges[q] her is mighty.[r]

THE WORLD MOURNS BABYLON'S FALL

9 The kings of the earth who have committed sexual immorality and shared her sensual and excessive ways will weep and mourn over her when they see the smoke from her burning. **10** They will stand far off in fear of her torment,[s] saying,

Woe, woe, the great city,[t]
Babylon, the mighty city!
For in a single hour
your judgment has come.

11 The merchants of the earth will weep and mourn over her, because no one buys their cargo any longer — **12** cargo of gold, silver, jewels, and pearls; fine linen, purple, silk, and scarlet; all kinds of fragrant wood products; objects of ivory; objects of expensive wood, brass,[G] iron, and marble; **13** cinnamon, spice,[H] incense, myrrh,[I] and frankincense; wine, olive oil, fine flour, and grain; cattle and sheep; horses and carriages; and slaves — human lives.[u]

[a]17:17 Gn 50:20
[b]Jr 51:12; Rv 10:7
[c]18:1 Dn 4:13,23; Rv 10:1; 20:1
[d]18:2 Is 21:9; Dn 4:30; Rv 14:8; 16:19; 17:5
[e]Is 13:20-22; Mal 1:3
[f]18:3 Rv 14:8; 17:2
[g]Ezk 16:29
[h]18:4 Is 52:11; Jr 50:8; 51:6,9,45; 2Co 6:17
[i]18:5 Jr 51:9
[j]2Sm 19:19; Neh 6:14; Ps 74:22; Is 64:9; Jr 14:10; 31:34; Hs 8:13
[k]18:6 Jr 50:29
[l]Ex 22:4,7,9; Is 40:2; Jr 16:18; 17:18
[m]Rv 14:8

[n]18:7 Is 47:7-8; Ezk 28:2-8; Zph 2:15
[o]18:8 Is 47:9
[p]Ps 21:9; 97:3; Is 33:12; 47:14; Jr 16:8; 17:16
[q]Ps 7:8; 58:11; 96:10
[r]Dt 10:17; Jos 4:24; Ps 24:8; Is 1:24
[s]18:10 Ezk 26:16-18
[t]Rv 11:8; 16:19; 17:18
[u]18:13 Gn 36:6; Nm 31:32-35; 1Ch 5:21; Ezk 27:12-22

[A]17:17 Or *sovereignty*   [B]18:2 Other mss omit *It has fallen*   [C]18:2 Or *prison*   [D]18:2 Other mss omit the words *and a haunt for every unclean beast.* The words *and despicable* then refer to the *bird* of the previous line.   [E]18:3 Some mss read *collapsed*; other mss read *fallen*   [F]18:5 Or *sins have reached up*   [G]18:12 Or *bronze,* or *copper*   [H]18:13 Other mss omit *spice*   [I]18:13 Or *perfume*

---

pass away. Those who embrace that system seek self-glorification and thrills. But in the end, their long-sought gratification will amount to nothing, and they will be given **to the beast** as his pawns (17:17).
18:1 Angels are present and active in the church age as well, and indeed some followers of Christ "have welcomed angels as guests without knowing it" (Heb 13:2). But after the church is removed from the earth, angels will assume a more visible role to fill the spiritual void.
18:2-3 The angel proclaims that human-centered society **has fallen** (18:2) because **all the nations** became unfaithful to God, which is depicted metaphorically as society's drinking **the wine of [Babylon's] sexual immorality**. As

a result of this wicked activity, **the merchants of the earth** are said to **have grown wealthy** (18:3). This passage, then, illustrates that all wealth does not come as a blessing from God. Satan can give wealth too, as is evident from his promise to give Jesus worldly kingdoms in exchange for worship (see Matt 4:8-9). It would be a mistake to assume that the presence of wealth in a particular life indicates God's blessing and approval.
18:4-5 God's **people** are called to withdraw from worldly living in order to avoid the judgment to come upon godless society.
18:7-8 Babylon says, **I sit as a queen; I am not a widow, and I will never see grief** (18:7). God hates brazen rejection of his ways and an accompanying view of oneself as indestruc-

tible. Therefore, he will send **death and grief and famine** (18:8).
18:10 Judgment of the antichrist's realm will be swift.
18:11-14 God's judgment will involve economic disruption. Divine destruction of wealth in this instance should not be taken to indicate divine condemnation of wealth per se. There are many wealthy people in the Bible who walked with God—Abraham, Joseph, and Solomon to name a few. In Solomon's case, Scripture says explicitly that great wealth was a gift and reward from God (see 2 Chr 1:12). What the Lord condemns is a person being controlled by wealth. In the case of Babylon, wealth led to self-centeredness and denial of God.

a 18:16 Rv 17:4
b 18:18 Ex 15:11; Dt 33:29; 2Sm 7:23; Ezk 27:32; Rv 13:4
c 18:19 Ezk 27:30
d Rv 18:10,16
e 18:20 Rv 12:12
f Ps 48:11; 97:8
g 18:21 Rv 5:2; 10:1
h Jr 51:59-64
i Rv 16:20; 18:11,14,22-23
j 18:22 Is 24:8

k 18:23 Jr 25:10
l 18:24 Rv 16:6
m Rv 6:10; 16:6
n 19:1 Rv 7:9
o Ps 104:35; 106:1,48; 146:10; 148:14; 150:1
p Jb 12:13; Dn 9:9; Rv 7:10
q 19:2 Jn 8:16; 19:35; Rv 15:3; 16:7
r Rv 17:1
s Dt 32:43; 2Kg 9:7; Rv 6:10; 16:6; 17:6; 18:24
t 19:3 Is 34:8-10; Rv 14:11
u 19:4 Rv 4:8-10; 5:6-14; 7:11; 11:16
v Ps 106:48
w 19:5 Dt 1:17; 2Ch 18:30; 34:30; Jb 3:19; Ps 115:13; Rv 11:18

¹⁴ The fruit you craved has left you.
All your splendid
  and glamorous things are gone;
they will never find them again.

¹⁵ The merchants of these things, who became rich from her, will stand far off in fear of her torment, weeping and mourning, ¹⁶ saying,

Woe, woe, the great city,
dressed in fine linen, purple,
  and scarlet,
adorned with gold, jewels,
  and pearls;*a*
¹⁷ for in a single hour
  such fabulous wealth
  was destroyed!

And every shipmaster, seafarer, the sailors, and all who do business by sea, stood far off ¹⁸ as they watched the smoke from her burning and kept crying out: "Who was like the great city?"*b* ¹⁹ They threw dust on their heads and kept crying out, weeping, and mourning,*c*

Woe, woe, the great city,*d*
where all those who have ships
  on the sea
became rich from her wealth;
for in a single hour
  she was destroyed.
²⁰ Rejoice over her, heaven,
and you saints, apostles,
  and prophets,*e*
because God has pronounced on her
  the judgment*f* she passed on you!

THE FINALITY OF BABYLON'S FALL

²¹ Then a mighty angel*g* picked up a stone like a large millstone and threw it into the sea, saying,

In this way, Babylon the great city
will be thrown down violently*h*
and never be found again.*i*
²² The sound of harpists, musicians,
flutists, and trumpeters
will never be heard in you again;*j*
no craftsman of any trade

will ever be found in you again;
the sound of a mill
will never be heard in you again;
²³ the light of a lamp
will never shine in you again;
and the voice of a groom and bride
will never be heard in you again.*k*
All this will happen
because your merchants
were the nobility of the earth,
because all the nations
  were deceived
by your sorcery.
²⁴ In her was found the blood
  of prophets and saints,*l*
and of all those slaughtered
  on the earth.*m*

CELEBRATION IN HEAVEN

19 After this I heard something like the loud voice of a vast multitude*n* in heaven, saying,

Hallelujah!*o*
Salvation, glory, and power belong
  to our God,*p*
² because his judgments are true^A
  and righteous,*q*
because he has judged
  the notorious prostitute*r*
who corrupted the earth
  with her sexual immorality;
and he has avenged the blood
  of his servants
that was on her hands.*s*
³ A second time they said,
Hallelujah!
Her smoke ascends forever
  and ever!*t*

⁴ Then the twenty-four elders and the four living creatures fell down and worshiped God,*u* who is seated on the throne, saying,

Amen! Hallelujah!*v*
⁵ A voice came from the throne, saying,
Praise our God,
all his servants, and the ones
  who fear him,
both small and great!*w*

^A 19:2 Valid; Jn 8:16; 19:35

18:15-17 That wealth controlled the inhabitants of the antichrist's kingdom is evident from the **mourning** of **the merchants** upon the destruction of their material goods (18:15). They lament not the loss of life or swift removal of other people's livelihood, but that **in a single hour such fabulous wealth was destroyed** (18:17).
18:21 Not only will the destruction of godless secular society be severe, but it will also be final.

18:24 Not surprisingly, worship of the wrong object (wealth) is accompanied by wrath misdirected at an improper target (Christians). In the antichrist's kingdom, as with other godless societies throughout history, **the blood of prophets and saints** testifies to the slaughter of those who stand for God's values in opposition to the religion of materialism.
19:1 The scene shifts from earth to heaven as **a vast multitude** praises God with cries of **Hallelujah!** This Greek word is the transliteration

of a Hebrew compound: *hallal* (praise) and *Yah* (an abbreviated form of Yahweh). Thus, the word means "praise Yahweh." *Praise* is the declaration of the glory, greatness, power, and majesty of God.
19:2 The reasons for praising God are manifold, but here the praise comes specifically **because his judgments are true and righteous**. At Christ's second coming, he will judge those who are unfaithful to their Creator, and doing so will be entirely appropriate.

a 19:6 Ezk 1:24; 43:2; Rv 1:15; 14:2
b Ex 15:18; Ps 93:1; 96:10; 97:1; 99:1; 146:10; Is 24:23; Lk 1:33; 1Co 15:25; Rv 11:15,17
c 19:7 Mt 5:12; Rm 1:21; 4:20
d Is 54:5-7; Hs 2:19; Mt 22:2-14; Eph 5:27,32; Rv 21:2
e 19:8 Gn 41:42; Ezk 16:10,13; Mt 27:59; Lk 16:19; Rv 15:6; 19:14
f Eph 2:10
g 19:9 Rv 17:1; 22:8-9
h Is 25:6-8; Lk 13:29
i Rv 21:5; 22:6

j 19:10 Ac 10:25; Rv 22:9
k Rv 1:2,9; 12:17; 20:4
l 19:11 Jn 1:51; Rv 4:1; 11:19; 15:5
m Is 3:14
n Ps 9:8; 96:13; Rv 16:7; 19:2
o 19:12 Rv 1:14; 2:18
p Rv 12:3; 13:1
q Rv 2:17; 3:12
r 19:13 Is 63:1-6; Rv 14:14-20
s Jn 1:1-5; Heb 4:12
t 19:15 Is 49:2; Heb 4:12; Rv 1:16; 2:12,16
u Is 11:4; 2Th 2:8; Rv 1:16; 2:12
v 19:15 Ps 2:9; Rv 12:5

⚜ KINGDOM LIVING ⚜
CHURCH
Christ's Millennial Reign

After Jesus gathers his church to himself, we will celebrate with a magnificent feast: the marriage supper of the Lamb. The bride (the church) and bridegroom (Christ) will celebrate their union and will begin an eternity together.

A bride spends a lot of time getting ready, making herself look perfect for her groom. In the same way, the church of Christ will be purified, glorious, and perfect in every detail because all the sinfulness of earth will be burned away and the righteousness of Christ will shine forth. This will truly be a celebration, a party like none we have ever seen. The wedding reception will last a millennium—one thousand years.

Before this wedding feast takes place, Jesus will inaugurate his millennial rule by dealing with all his enemies. He will come back to earth with his army to set up his kingdom rule. God will judge the earth through the great tribulation, and the sheep will be separated from the goats (believers from the unbelievers). Those who come through the tribulation as believers in Jesus Christ will participate in the wedding feast along with the other believers, his church.

We will have this wedding feast because man will finally realize the destiny he was created for, all due to the person and work of the perfect man, Jesus Christ. The purpose of the millennial reign is for humanity to fulfill its God-ordained destiny to rule the earth and to fellowship with the Creator.

⁶ Then I heard something like the voice of a vast multitude, like the sound of cascading waters,*a* and like the rumbling of loud thunder, saying,

Hallelujah, because our Lord God,
    the Almighty,
    reigns!*b*
⁷ Let us be glad, rejoice,
    and give him glory,*c*
because the marriage of the Lamb
    has come,
and his bride
    has prepared herself.*d*
⁸ She was given fine linen to wear,
    bright and pure.*e*
For the fine linen represents the righteous acts of the saints.*f*

⁹ Then he*A* said to me,*g* "Write: Blessed are those invited to the marriage feast*h* of the Lamb!" He also said to me, "These words of God are true."*i* ¹⁰ Then I fell at his feet to worship him, but he said to me, "Don't do that!*j* I am a fellow servant with you and your brothers and sisters who hold firmly to the testimony of Jesus.*k* Worship God, because the testimony of Jesus is the spirit*B* of prophecy."

THE RIDER ON A WHITE HORSE

¹¹ Then I saw heaven opened,*l* and there was a white horse. Its rider is called Faithful and True,*m* and he judges and makes war with justice.*n* ¹² His eyes were like a fiery flame,*o* and many crowns*C* were on his head.*p* He had a name written that no one knows except himself.*q* ¹³ He wore a robe dipped in blood,*r* and his name is called the Word of God.*s* ¹⁴ The armies that were in heaven followed him on white horses, wearing pure white linen. ¹⁵ A sharp*D* sword*t* came from his mouth, so that he might strike the nations with it.*u* He will rule*E* them with an iron rod.*v* He will also trample the winepress of the fierce anger

A 19:9 Probably an angel; Rv 17:1; 22:8-9   *B* 19:10 Or *the Spirit*   *C* 19:12 Or *diadems*   *D* 19:15 Other mss add *double-edged*   *E* 19:15 Or *shepherd*

19:7-9 In the church's spiritual **marriage** to Christ, the betrothal period is the church age, when Christians are pledged to him. The wedding will occur when Jesus returns to take his bride to his heavenly Father's house. The celebration will occur during the millennium, after the church **has prepared herself** (19:7) through **righteous acts** (19:8).

The marriage feast of the Lamb destroys the common caricature of heaven as a place where each believer simply sits on a cloud playing a harp. During this thousand-year-long party, believers' rewards and responsibilities will be determined by their levels of faithfulness to Christ on earth. Jesus will ensure the complete absence of disorder and discord.

19:11 This verse takes the reader back in time to the second coming of Jesus, which will occur before the millennium. The public nature of the coming is depicted by heaven's visible opening. Jesus rides **a white horse**, the Roman symbol of victory. Christ's main task upon returning to earth is making **war** against the enemies of God.

19:13 The meekness and mildness of Jesus at his first coming contrast with his disposition at his second coming. On that day, he will establish his reign on earth by force. Thus, he is pictured wearing **a robe dipped in blood**.

19:14 These armies are followers of Jesus from the church age and the tribulation who will rule on earth with him during the millennial kingdom.

19:15 This **sword** is the Word of God. From Genesis to Revelation, Jesus is pictured as possessing and wielding the authoritative Word. As followers of Jesus, then, we must not simply know God's Word or study it, but also verbally quote it. It carries intrinsic

a 19:15 Jr 25:15; Rv
14:8,10,19–20; 16:19; 18:3
b 19:16 Dt 10:17; Dn 2:47;
1Tm 6:15; Rv 17:14
c 19:18 Ezk 32:4; 39:17-20
d 19:19 Rv 16:13-14; 17:2;
18:3,9
e Nm 27:3; Jdg 6:33; Is 13:4;
Hs 1:11

f 19:20 Rv 13:13-17
g Mt 5:22; Mk 9:43; Rv
20:10,14; 21:8
h 20:1 Ps 140:10; Lk
8:31; Rm 10:7; Rv 9:1,11;
11:7; 17:8
i Ps 107:10; 149:8; Jr 39:7;
Ezk 7:23
j 20:2 Rv 12:9
k Is 24:22
l 20:3 Dn 6:17; Mt 27:66
m Rv 12:9

♚

❧ KINGDOM LIVING ❧
KINGDOM
The Golden Era of Jesus Christ

What will Christ's millennial rule look like? According to Revelation 20:1-10, this golden era will be ushered in by the captivity of Satan. Scripture tells us that Satan will be bound for one thousand years and then thrown into the lake of fire. There will be theocratic rule during this time, meaning Jesus will have total dominion and power over the earth.

The Word of God will be a sword in the mouth of Christ according to Revelation 19:15, so Jesus need only say the word to crush any rebellion. Righteousness and faithfulness will be his belt, and the wolf will dwell with the lamb. There will be harmony. With Christ ruling at the helm, this will definitely be a golden age on planet earth.

God and his Word will dominate then. Everyone will function in harmony with the knowledge of God because everyone will have that knowledge. According to Isaiah 30:23-24, men will be prosperous, with a yield from the ground that is "rich and plentiful." We believers will rule with Christ and serve in his government.

After the wedding supper and the millennial rule, we'll go home with our bridegroom to the new Jerusalem. Jesus has been preparing this place for us, where "He will wipe away every tear from their eyes. Death will be no more; grief, crying, and pain will be no more, because the previous things have passed away" (Rev 21:4). Jesus will take us home to the Father, and we will live as citizens in the kingdom of God.

of God,*a* the Almighty. **16** And he has a name written on his robe and on his thigh: KING OF KINGS AND LORD OF LORDS.*b*

THE BEAST AND ITS ARMIES DEFEATED

17 Then I saw an angel standing in the sun, and he called out in a loud voice, saying to all the birds flying high overhead, "Come, gather together for the great supper of God, **18** so that you may eat the flesh of kings, the flesh of military commanders, the flesh of the mighty, the flesh of horses and of their riders, and the flesh of everyone, both free and slave, small and great."*c*

19 Then I saw the beast, the kings of the earth, and their armies*d* gathered together to wage war*e* against the rider on the horse and against his army. **20** But the beast was taken prisoner, and along with it the false prophet, who had performed the

signs in its presence. He deceived those who accepted the mark of the beast and those who worshiped its image with these signs.*f* Both of them were thrown alive into the lake of fire that burns with sulfur.*g* **21** The rest were killed with the sword that came from the mouth of the rider on the horse, and all the birds ate their fill of their flesh.

SATAN BOUND

20 Then I saw an angel coming down from heaven holding the key to the abyss*h* and a great chain*i* in his hand. **2** He seized the dragon, that ancient serpent who is the devil and Satan,*A,j* and bound*k* him for a thousand years. **3** He threw him into the abyss, closed it, and put a seal on it*l* so that he would no longer deceive the nations*m* until the thousand years were completed. After that, he must be released for a short time.

A 20:2 Other mss add *who deceives the whole world*

authority to accomplish God's purposes. In some cases, it draws a person to salvation. In others, it causes a hardened sinner to be without excuse for his or her conduct. In no situation, however, will a child of God verbally quote and obey the Word of God and have that Word return empty (see Isa 55:11).
19:17-18 The context of this summons is that Satan, the antichrist, and their allies will seek to destroy Jesus when he returns at the battle of Armageddon (16:12-16). Nevertheless,

Jesus will utterly defeat them and leave their bodies to be eaten by **birds** of prey (19:17), a reality mentioned in Matthew 24:27-28 as well.
19:19 Jesus will not return to bring capricious judgment against unsuspecting innocent parties. He will strike down the wicked who are **gathered . . . to wage war against** him.
19:20 This **lake** makes it clear that there is no annihilation in store for those who reject Christ, just ongoing eternal separation from God (see 21:8).

20:2 We derive the word *millennium* from the Latin words for "thousand years." Theologians use this term to reference various interpretations of the **thousand years** in Revelation 20. *Premillennialism*, which is the position adopted in these notes, teaches that Christ will return before his thousand-year reign on earth.
20:3 The sinfulness of humanity will not be removed during this period, but the devil's ability to exacerbate it through deception will be.

THE SAINTS REIGN WITH CHRIST

4 Then I saw thrones, and people seated on them who were given authority to judge.[a] I also saw the souls of those[b] who had been beheaded because of their testimony about Jesus[c] and because of the word of God, who had not worshiped the beast or his image, and who had not accepted the mark on their foreheads or their hands.[d] They came to life[e] and reigned with Christ for a thousand years.[f] **5** The rest of the dead did not come to life until the thousand years were completed.

This is the first resurrection. **6** Blessed[g] and holy is the one who shares in the first resurrection! The second death[h] has no power[A] over them, but they will be priests of God and of Christ, and they will reign with him for a thousand years.[i]

SATANIC REBELLION CRUSHED

7 When the thousand years are completed, Satan will be released from his prison **8** and will go out to deceive the nations[j] at the four corners of the earth,[k] Gog and Magog, to gather them for battle.[l] Their number is like the sand of the sea.[m] **9** They came up across the breadth of the earth and surrounded the encampment of the saints, the beloved city.[n] Then fire came down from heaven[B] and consumed them.[o] **10** The devil who deceived them was thrown into the lake of fire and sulfur where the beast and the false prophet are,[p] and they will be tormented day and night forever and ever.[q]

⟶ HOPE WORDS ⟵
When the devil reminds you of your past, remind him of his future.

THE GREAT WHITE THRONE JUDGMENT

11 Then I saw a great white throne and one seated on it. Earth and heaven fled from his presence, and no place was found for them.[r] **12** I also saw the dead, the great and the small, standing before the throne, and books were opened.[s] Another book was opened, which is the book of life,[t] and the dead were judged according to their works[u] by what was written in the books. **13** Then the sea gave up the dead that were in it, and death and Hades[v] gave up the dead that were in them; each one was judged according to their works. **14** Death and Hades were thrown into the lake of fire.[w] This is the second death, the lake of fire.[c] **15** And anyone whose name was not found written in the book of life was thrown into the lake of fire.

THE NEW CREATION

21 Then I saw a new heaven and a new earth;[x] for the first heaven and the first earth had passed away,[y] and the sea was no more.[z] **2** I also saw the holy city,[aa] the new Jerusalem, coming down out of

[a] 20:4 Dn 7:22; Mt 19:28; 1Co 6:2-3; Rv 3:21; 6:9
[b] Rv 6:9
[c] Rv 1:2,9; 12:11,17; 19:10
[d] Rv 7:3; 9:4; 13:12-16; 14:1; 22:4
[e] Is 25:6-8; Mt 9:18; 26:29; Lk 13:29; Rv 2:8; 13:14
[f] 2Tm 2:12
[g] 20:6 Rv 1:3; 14:13; 16:15; 19:9; 22:7,14
[h] Rv 2:11; 20:14; 21:8
[i] Rv 1:6; 5:10
[j] 20:8 Gn 3:13; 2Co 11:3; 1Tm 2:14; 2Jn 7; Rv 12:9; 18:23; 19:20
[k] Is 11:12; Ezk 7:2; Rv 7:1
[l] Ezk 38–39
[m] Gn 32:12; Is 10:22; Jr 33:22; Hs 1:10
[n] 20:9 Ezk 38:16; Jl 3:2,11-12; Zch 14:2
[o] 2Kg 1:10,12; Ezk 38:22; 39:6; Lk 9:54
[p] 20:10 Rv 19:20
[q] Mt 25:41

[r] 20:11 Is 51:6; Mt 24:35; 2Pt 3:10; Rv 18:21
[s] 20:12 Dn 7:10
[t] Is 4:3; 34:16; Dn 12:1; Rv 3:5; 13:8; 17:8; 20:15; 21:27
[u] Ps 62:12; Jr 17:10; Rm 2:6; 1Pt 1:17
[v] 20:13 Rv 1:18; 6:8
[w] 20:14 Is 25:7-8; 1Co 15:26
[x] 21:1 Is 65:17; 66:22; 2Pt 3:13
[y] Lk 21:33; 1Co 7:31; 2Pt 3:10
[z] Is 57:20; Rv 13:1,6-7
[aa] 21:2 Neh 11:1; Is 48:2; 52:1; Dn 9:24; Mt 4:5; 27:53; Rv 11:2; 22:19

20:5-6 Nonbelievers from all periods of history other than the tribulation will not be raised for judgment **until the thousand years [are] completed**. That postmillennial resurrection will be **the first resurrection** of that group (20:5). Importantly, in verse 6, the phrase **the first resurrection** is used with a different referent: the resurrection of believers at the beginning of the millennium to reign with Jesus. Over such people, **the second death** (i.e., eternal judgment) **has no power**. **20:7-8** Even following a **thousand years** of utopia on earth under the reign of Christ, there will be people who rebel against him and fall for Satan's deception. Such people follow Jesus outwardly but have experienced no heart transformation. When Satan is **released from** captivity (20:7), he will not force anyone to rebel against Christ. He will simply take advantage of what's already inside them.

The people Satan deceives are referred to as **Gog and Magog**, which are the names of an evil man in Ezekiel 38–39 and the land over which he ruled, respectively. Here the phrase is symbolic of the enemies of God in general (Rev 20:8).

20:9 These allies of Satan will come **up across the breadth of the earth** and surround Jerusalem. But unlike the protracted battle God wages against his enemies during the tribulation, divine victory in this situation will come quickly. **20:11-12** The **great white throne** (20:11) is the site at which unbelievers from all ages of history will be judged by God. This will involve the consultation of two heavenly records: the **books** and **the book of life**. The former are records of people's deeds, by which their levels of judgment will be determined, since their names will be shown not to be in the book of life. Each nonbeliever's level of punishment will be **according to their works** (20:12)—that is, in proportion to their sins and good things committed while in the body. The book of life lists those who have trusted Christ as Savior and been credited with his imputed righteousness. No one will receive salvation based on what's written in a book of deeds because everyone has sinned and fallen short of God's perfect standard (see Rom 3:23; 6:23).

20:13 At death, the soul is separated from the body, with the soul going immediately into the presence of God (see Luke 23:43) or to a state of judgment (see Luke 16:22-24). At the rapture, believers' souls will be united with glorified bodies appropriate to their eternal existence in paradise. Here, nonbelievers' souls are united with bodies suited for their eternal location. **20:14-15 The second death** (20:14) is another way of speaking of eternal judgment. The first death is the physical death of the body. The second is eternal separation from the love, blessings, and benefits of God. **21:1** The eternal state must be completely free from sin's consequences. But that doesn't mean the end for planet earth. Every molecule, atom, proton, and neutron in existence today will disintegrate only to be replaced by a glorious new creation. And while three-quarters of the planet on which we live is currently under water that vast expanse will be made habitable for God's people. **21:2-4** Right now, Christ dwells in a heavenly city with the souls of all believers who have died (see John 14:2-3). During the millennium,

a 21:2 Gl 4:26; Php 3:20;
Heb 11:10; 12:22; 13:14;
Rv 3:12
b Is 61:10; Rv 19:7
c 21:3 Dt 5:22; Ezk 9:1; Mt
27:46,50; Jn 11:43; Rv 1:10;
-11:12; 16:1
d Mt 19:28
e Lv 26:11-12; Jr 7:23; 30:22;
31:33; Ezk 37:27; Hs 2:23;
Zch 8:8
f 21:4 Is 25:8; 30:19; 35:10;
51:11; 65:19; Rv 7:16-17
g Hs 13:14; 1Co 15:54
h Is 60:20
i Is 42:9; 2Co 5:17
j 21:5 Rv 3:14; 19:11; 22:6
k 21:6 Rv 16:17
l Rv 1:8; 22:13
m Is 44:6; 48:12
n Ps 42:1-2; Is 41:17; 44:3;
55:1; Jn 4:14; 7:37
o Ps 36:9; Jr 2:13; Jn 4:14
p 21:7 Rv 2:7
q 2Sm 7:14
r 21:8 Rm 1:28-32; 1Co
6:9-10; Rv 22:15
s Rv 19:20
t Rv 20:6
u 21:9 Rv 16:1
v 21:10 Rv 1:10; 4:2; 17:3
w Ezk 40:2
x 21:11 Is 60:1-2

y 21:13 Ezk 48:30-34
z 21:15 Rv 11:1
aa Ezk 40:3
ab 21:19 Ex 28:15-21;
Is 54:11
ac 21:23 Is 24:23; 30:26;
60:19-20; Zch 14:6-7;
Rv 22:5
ad 21:24 Is 42:6; 49:6;
60:3,5
ae Is 49:7,23; 60:10
af 21:25 Neh 7:3

heaven from God,*a* prepared like a bride adorned for her husband.*b*

³ Then I heard a loud voice*c* from the throne:*A,d* Look, God's dwelling*B* is with humanity, and he will live with them. They will be his peoples,*C,e* and God himself will be with them and will be their God.*D* ⁴ He will wipe away every tear from their eyes.*f* Death will be no more;*g* grief, crying, and pain will be no more,*h* because the previous things*E* have passed away.*i*

⁵ Then the one seated on the throne said, "Look, I am making everything new." He also said, "Write, because these words*F* are faithful and true."*j* ⁶ Then he said to me, "It is done!*k* I am the Alpha and the Omega,*l* the beginning and the end.*m* I will freely give to the thirsty*n* from the spring of the water of life.*o* ⁷ The one who conquers*p* will inherit these things, and I will be his God, and he will be my son.*q* ⁸ But the cowards, faithless,*G* detestable, murderers, sexually immoral, sorcerers, idolaters, and all liars*r* — their share will be in the lake that burns with fire and sulfur,*s* which is the second death."*t*

THE NEW JERUSALEM

⁹ Then one of the seven angels, who had held the seven bowls filled with the seven last plagues,*u* came and spoke with me: "Come, I will show you the bride, the wife of the Lamb." ¹⁰ He then carried me away in the Spirit*H,v* to a great, high mountain*w* and showed me the holy city, Jerusalem, coming down out of heaven from God, ¹¹ arrayed with God's glory.*x* Her radiance was like a precious jewel, like a jasper stone, clear as crystal. ¹² The city had a massive high wall, with twelve gates. Twelve angels were at the gates;

the names of the twelve tribes of Israel's sons were inscribed on the gates. ¹³ There were three gates on the east, three gates on the north, three gates on the south, and three gates on the west.*y* ¹⁴ The city wall had twelve foundations, and the twelve names of the twelve apostles of the Lamb were on the foundations.

¹⁵ The one who spoke with me had a golden measuring rod*z* to measure the city, its gates, and its wall.*aa* ¹⁶ The city is laid out in a square; its length and width are the same. He measured the city with the rod at 12,000 *stadia*.*I* Its length, width, and height are equal. ¹⁷ Then he measured its wall, 144 cubits according to human measurement, which the angel used. ¹⁸ The building material of its wall was jasper, and the city was pure gold clear as glass. ¹⁹ The foundations of the city wall were adorned with every kind of jewel:*ab* the first foundation is jasper, the second sapphire, the third chalcedony, the fourth emerald, ²⁰ the fifth sardonyx, the sixth carnelian, the seventh chrysolite, the eighth beryl, the ninth topaz, the tenth chrysoprase, the eleventh jacinth, the twelfth amethyst. ²¹ The twelve gates are twelve pearls; each individual gate was made of a single pearl. The main street*J* of the city was pure gold, transparent as glass.

²² I did not see a temple in it, because the Lord God the Almighty and the Lamb are its temple. ²³ The city does not need the sun or the moon to shine on it, because the glory of God illuminates it, and its lamp is the Lamb.*ac* ²⁴ The nations*K* will walk by its light,*ad* and the kings of the earth will bring their glory into it.*L,ae* ²⁵ Its gates will never close by day because it will never be night there.*af* ²⁶ They will bring the glory

---

A 21:3 Other mss read *from heaven*   *B* 21:3 Or *tent*, or *tabernacle*   *C* 21:3 Other mss read *people*   *D* 21:3 Other mss omit *and will be their God*
E 21:4 Or *the first things*   *F* 21:5 Other mss add *of God*   *G* 21:8 Other mss add *the sinful,*   *H* 21:10 Or *in spirit*   *I* 21:16 A *stadion* (sg) = about 600
feet; 12,000 *stadia* = 1,400 miles.   *J* 21:21 Or *The public square*   *K* 21:24 Other mss add *of those who are saved*   *L* 21:24 Other mss read *will bring
to him the nations' glory and honor*

God's people will live and work on the earth we know now, with their capital in Jerusalem. But after God destroys and makes the earth new, he's going to send that heavenly city **down out of heaven** to the new earth. That city will become the capital of the new creation and be known as **the new Jerusalem** (Rev 21:2). And there God will dwell in the midst of his new creation and **live with** his people (21:3). All sadness, hurt, and disappointment will be no more as we live alongside our Creator (21:4).
21:8 Unbelievers, with their unglorified bodies and unredeemed souls, will enter a place where every problem from this life will be amplified without any hope of improvement.

They will become locked at varying levels in the consequences of their sinfulness.
21:9-11 Although believers will dwell across the entire new creation, the angel focuses John's attention on the new earth's capital, **Jerusalem** (21:10).
21:12, 14 The two sets of **names** signify that old- and new-covenant followers of the Lord will dwell together in the new creation.
21:15-16 A *stadia* is approximately six hundred feet, which means each dimension of **the city** is approximately fourteen hundred miles—about half the distance from New York to Los Angeles. The most mind-blowing aspect of these dimensions is the height (21:16). It's a multistory city that extends up—and this is just the capital of God's new creation!

21:22 There will be a temple in Jerusalem during the tribulation and during the millennium. But there will be no **temple** in the new Jerusalem because a representation of God's presence will no longer be necessary. We will have his direct presence.
21:24, 26 There will be **nations** and **kings** (21:24) functioning in a national context and bringing their **glory and honor** into the city (21:26). Everyone will come to the new Jerusalem as a highlight of their lives on the new earth. And why not, given its splendor?
21:25 That **it will never be night there** suggests believers' glorified bodies will never get tired and need to sleep.

and honor of the nations into it.^A,a ^27 Nothing unclean will ever enter it,^b nor anyone who does what is detestable or false, but only those written in the Lamb's book of life.^c

---

~ **HOPE WORDS** ~

When God writes your name in the book of life, he does so in ink—not pencil.

THE SOURCE OF LIFE

22 Then he showed me the river^8 of the water of life,^d clear as crystal,^e flowing from the throne of God and of the Lamb^f ^2 down the middle of the city's main street. The tree of life was on each side of the river, bearing twelve kinds of fruit, producing its fruit every month.^g The leaves of the tree are for healing the nations,^h ^3 and there will no longer be any curse.^i The throne of God and of the Lamb will be in the city, and his servants will worship him. ^4 They will see his face,^j and his name will be on their foreheads.^k ^5 Night will be no more;^l people will not need the light of a lamp or the light of the sun, because the Lord God will give them light,^m and they will reign forever and ever.

THE TIME IS NEAR

^6 Then he said to me, "These words are faithful^c and true.^n The Lord, the God of the spirits of the prophets,^D has sent his angel to show his servants what must soon take place."^o

^7 "Look, I am coming soon!^p Blessed is the one who keeps the words of the prophecy of this book."^q

^8 I, John, am the one who heard and saw these things. When I heard and saw them, I fell down to worship at the feet of the angel who had shown them to me. ^9 But he said to me, "Don't do that! I am a fellow servant with you, your brothers the prophets, and those who keep the words of this book. Worship God!"^r

^10 Then he said to me, "Don't seal up the words of the prophecy of this book, because the time is near.^s ^11 Let the unrighteous go on in unrighteousness; let the filthy still be filthy; let the righteous go on in righteousness; let the holy still be holy."^t

^12 "Look, I am coming soon, and my reward is with me^u to repay each person according to his work.^v ^13 I am the Alpha and the Omega,^w the first and the last,^x the beginning and the end.^y

^14 "Blessed^z are those who wash their robes,^E so that they may have the right to the tree of life and may enter the city by the gates. ^15 Outside are the dogs,^aa the sorcerers, the sexually immoral, the murderers, the idolaters, and everyone who loves and practices falsehood.^ab

^16 "I, Jesus, have sent my angel to attest these things to you for the churches. I am the Root^ac and descendant of David,^ad the bright morning star."^ae

^17 Both the Spirit and the bride say, "Come!" Let anyone who hears, say, "Come!" Let the one who is thirsty come. Let the one who desires take the water of life freely.^af

^a 21:26 Is 60:11
^b 21:27 Is 35:8; 52:1
^c Rv 3:5; 13:8; 17:8; 20:12,15
^d 22:1 Jr 2:13; 17:13; Jn 4:10
^e Rv 4:6
^f Ps 46:4; Ezk 47:1-2; Jl 3:18; Zch 14:8
^g 22:2 Gn 2:9; 3:22,24; Pr 13:12
^h Is 19:22; 57:19; 61:1; Jr 51:8-9; Zch 8:22-23; Mal 4:2; Mt 4:24; Jn 4:47; Ac 28:8
^i 22:3 Gn 3:14-19; Zch 14:11
^j 22:4 Ex 33:20,23; Ps 17:15; Mt 5:8; 1Jn 3:2
^k Rv 7:3; 9:4; 13:16; 14:1,9; 17:5; 20:4
^l 22:5 Zch 14:7; Rv 21:25
^m Ps 56:13; 118:27; Is 60:19; 1Jn 1:5
^n 22:6 Rv 3:14; 19:11; 21:5
^o Dn 2:28-29,45; Rv 1:1

^p 22:7 Rv 3:11
^q Rv 1:3; 14:13; 19:9; 20:6; 22:14
^r 22:9 Rv 19:10
^s 22:10 Is 8:16; Dn 8:26; 9:24; 12:4; Rv 1:3; 10:4
^t 22:11 Ezk 3:27; Dn 12:10
^u 22:12 Is 40:10; 62:11
^v Ps 62:12; Is 59:18; Jr 17:10; 25:14; Rm 2:6
^w 22:13 Rv 1:8
^x Rv 1:17
^y Rv 21:6
^z 22:14 Rv 1:3; 14:13; 16:15; 19:9; 20:6; 22:7
^aa 22:15 Ps 22:16,20; Mt 15:26-27; Php 3:2
^ab Rm 1:28-32; 1Co 6:9-10; Rv 21:8
^ac 22:16 Rv 5:5
^ad Is 11:1,10; Rm 1:3
^ae Nm 24:17; Rv 2:28
^af 22:17 Is 55:1; Jn 4:10

---

^A 21:26 Other mss add *in order that they might go in* ^B 22:1 Other mss read *pure river* ^C 22:6 Or *trustworthy* ^D 22:6 Other mss read *God of the holy prophets* ^E 22:14 Other mss read *who keep his commands*

21:27 While the invitation to dwell in this city is universal, the requirements to enter are specific: **only those** who have received Jesus as their Savior by faith can.
22:1 The throne of God and of the Lamb indicates that a single throne is shared by God the Father and God the Son.
22:2 The tree of life first appeared in the garden of Eden (Gen 2:9). Humans were barred from eating from it after Adam and Eve sinned (Gen 3:22-24). **The leaves of the tree are for healing the nations.** Why would healing be necessary in the new heaven and new earth? Because there is a group of people who have access to the heavenly Jerusalem but who do not live there (see Rev 21:24-26). There is only one group of people left on earth to go into eternity in their physical bodies—those who were true to Jesus Christ and served him during his millennial reign. They go into eternity after the millennium with physically

glorified bodies not spiritually glorified bodies (see 1 Cor 15:38-41)—that is, like Adam and Eve in the garden. These will make up the nations who do not live in the new Jerusalem but who will have access to the city. They will need the leaves of the tree for their continued health and well-being.
22:3-5 In the new heaven and new earth, **there will no longer be any curse**. Everything will be just as God intended it, and **his servants will worship him** (22:3). Use of the term "servants" implies that believers will be happily serving and working in the new creation, overseeing the planet to varying degrees corresponding to their rewards. In this environment, God's people **will see his face** (22:4), and his radiant presence will provide all necessary illumination (22:5).
22:10-11 The words of Revelation will lead people to one of two responses. Some will not heed the admonitions and continue

on a path of rebellion against God. As John puts it, **the filthy [will] still be filthy**. Others, however, will heed the warnings and move in the direction God wants them to go, namely, toward **righteousness** (22:11).
22:16 The bright morning star is one name for the sun. In the daytime, it is the one star sufficiently luminous and powerful to light the entire earth. Spiritually speaking, Jesus is "the bright morning star" because he is the most powerful source of spiritual illumination and is the sole source of eternal life.
22:17 *Anyone* who is spiritually **thirsty** may have his or her thirst quenched by Jesus. Best of all, this spiritual satisfaction is free. **The water of life** is a gift. All that is required to possess eternal life in the paradise that has been described is to receive the free gift of salvation by placing your faith in Jesus Christ alone and his substitutionary death.

a **22:19** Dt 4:2; 12:32
b **22:20** Rv 1:2
c 1Co 16:22

❧ *Questions & Answers* ❧

Q You have been a life-long reader, and spiritual resources can play a critical role in shaping a kingdom mind. Who are some of your favorite authors who have shaped the way you think biblically and theologically?

A Theologically, my thinking has been affected by Joseph Dillow's great book *Final Destiny*, a comprehensive soteriology and eschatology. It provides a proper theological framework and solves a lot of confusion that exists today. I have tried to vary my devotional readings among different authors, including A. W. Tozer, John MacArthur, David Jeremiah, and Chuck Swindoll. Another significant author in my life was Charles Ryrie. When the Ryrie Study Bible was first released, I dove into his study notes because they were succinct and authentic.

18 I testify to everyone who hears the words of the prophecy of this book: If anyone adds to them, God will add to him the plagues that are written in this book. **19** And if anyone takes away from the words of the book of this prophecy, God will take away his share of the tree of life and the holy city, which are written about in this book.*a*

20 He who testifies about these things*b* says, "Yes, I am coming soon."

Amen! Come, Lord Jesus!*c*

21 The grace of the Lord Jesus^A be with everyone.^B Amen.^C

---

^A **22:21** Other mss add *Christ*   ^B **22:21** Other mss read *with all the saints*   ^C **22:21** Other mss omit *Amen.*

22:18-19 Don't mess with the Word. That's John's admonition in these verses, and it applies specifically to the book of Revelation. It has two components. First, do not add to **the prophecy of this book**. The penalty for doing so will be **the plagues that are written in** it (22:18). Second, do not take **away from the words of the book**. Those who do so will have their heavenly rewards taken away,

namely, their **share of the tree of life and the holy city** (21:19).

22:20 Jesus is **coming soon**. You can understand this even if details of the rapture, the tribulation, the second coming of Jesus, the millennium, and the eternal state remain unclear.

Moreover, the glorious future in store for followers of Jesus should inspire worship.

John's response to all that was revealed to him was, **Amen! Come, Lord Jesus!** If reading Revelation makes you a better worshiper, it has achieved its goal.

22:21 The wrath to come on all who do not acknowledge Jesus as Savior contrasts with **the grace of the Lord Jesus** available to **everyone** during the church era.

DEFINITIONS OF KEY TERMS AND DOCTRINES
OF THE CHRISTIAN FAITH

Knowing key terms and sound doctrine matters as we come to know God in all of his of triune fullness as Father, Son, and Holy Spirit, as far as we can with our finite minds. God wants us to know him. Paul prayed "that the God of our Lord Jesus Christ, the glorious Father, would give you the Spirit of wisdom and revelation in the knowledge of him" (Eph 1:17). Knowing God is the foundation of the wisdom we need to live victorious and abundant Christian lives (Prov 9:10). Below are explanations of key terms and a selection of doctrinal topics from God's Word, as well as relevant Scripture for each.

Baptism: *The ordinance of water baptism is an outward testimony of an inward reality—the salvation of a soul by the blood of Christ and the baptism of that person into the body of Christ by the Holy Spirit, formally initiating the life of discipleship.*

Because water baptism is symbolic of this inner, spiritual work, it was never intended to have saving power in itself. The primary meaning of baptism for the believer is public identification with Christ in his death, burial, and resurrection, pictured by the immersion of the believer in the waters of baptism. Baptism inaugurates the formal beginning of the believer's life of discipleship (Matt 28:19; Rom 6:1-4; 1 Cor 12:13; Col 2:12; 1 Pet 3:21).

Biblical Justice: *The equitable and impartial application of the rule of God's moral law in society.*

Biblical justice provides society with a divine frame of reference from which to operate. The word *justice* in Scripture means to prescribe the right way. Biblical justice is not a man-made, socially imposed, top-down system ultimately leading to the negation of freedom. Biblical justice promotes freedom by emphasizing accountability, equality, and responsibility in providing a spiritual underpinning in the personal and social realms. Biblical justice must always be coupled with righteousness (Gen 18:19; Pss 7:6; 9:16; 11:7; 33:5; 89:14; Matt 12:18-20).

Blessing: *The capacity to experience, enjoy, and extend the goodness and favor of God in your life.*

A blessing is not merely what God does for you or to you. A blessing is also what God is able to do through you in order to similarly bring a blessing to others. Christians who want God to bless them must be willing for God to bless others through them. We must align ourselves under the fundamentals of God's covenant to be in a position to receive the blessings he has promised. Living in God's kingdom brings blessings, but these blessings are often contingent upon living for his kingdom and underneath

his authority (Gen 1:28; Luke 6:38; Acts 20:35; Gal 3:14; Eph 1:3; 1 Pet 3:9).

Calling: *The customized life purpose God has ordained and equipped you to accomplish in order to bring him the greatest glory and achieve the maximum expansion of his kingdom.*

As followers of Jesus and subjects in God's kingdom, believers have been placed on earth to carry out God's will according to their personal gifts and his plan for each life. Your calling is unique to you and will often involve an intersection of your past experiences, passions, gifts, skills, position, and personality when God ushers you into its fulfillment (Acts 13:36; Gal 2:20; Eph 2:10; Phil 2:12-13).

Church: *The spiritually redeemed body of believers that is to legislate the heavenly values of the kingdom of God on earth.*

The church is built and God's kingdom is advanced by faithful believers who serve Christ to the best of their ability. God designed the church to be the epicenter of culture, and the church's strength or weakness is a major determining factor in the success or failure of human civilization, since the church alone possesses the keys of the kingdom and its authority. A church also provides a community in which spiritual gifts are to be used for the benefit of others, and a place where believers partake in worship, study, fellowship, and outreach (Matt 16:18-19; Acts 2:42-47; Eph 1:22; 2:11-22; 3:10; Col 1:18-24).

Confession: *To acknowledge to God and others, as appropriate, that what God calls a sin we also call a sin in our own lives, thoughts, and actions.*

Every misery we encounter is related to sin to some extent—whether it is our own sin, someone else's sin, or just the evil, sinful world in which we live. But God's mercy and grace extend beyond our sin through the blood of Christ. When God sees our pain, he feels and experiences it with us. But grace must precede mercy because God can't help us with our pain until he first deals with our sin. That's why we are told to confess our sins. Confession of your sin enables God to extend his mercy to you (Prov 28:13; Eph 2:1-5; Jas 5:16; 1 John 1:9).

Covenant: *A divinely created relational bond through which God reveals himself and administers his kingdom program that's designed to bring his greatest blessing to human beings who operate under its guidelines.*

A biblical covenant involves far more than a contract. In a biblical covenant, you enter into an

intimate relationship with another person or persons. Jesus's blood has established the new covenant under which you are to align your life in order to receive its full covenantal blessings, covering, and protection. There must be covenantal alignment under the lordship of Jesus Christ in order to experience his kingdom presence, power, authority, provision, and covering (Deut 29:9; 1 Cor 10:16; Heb 8:6; 9:15; 12:24).

Dispensations: *Divisions of time that can be defined as progressive stages in God's revelation, each consisting of a distinct stewardship or rule of life.*

Since each dispensation is distinct and identifiable—such as Innocence, Law, Grace, and Kingdom—there are different characteristics, administrations, jurisdictions and judgments in each period. Dispensationalism recognizes the movement of God in redemption history and identifies how he related to people in the time in which they lived with the divine revelation that he had communicated to them (Matt 5:21-22; John 1:17; Acts 17:31-32; 1 Cor 9:17; Eph 1:10; 3:2; Col 1:25).

Election: *The sovereign prerogative of God to choose individuals, families, groups, and nations to serve his kingdom purposes as he so wills.*

Election is specifically related to service, usefulness, and blessings—not individual salvation. Jesus died for all human beings without exception and desires for all to be saved (Rom 9:10-13; 1 Tim 2:4; 4:10; Heb 2:9; 2 Pet 3:8-11; 1 John 2:2).

Eternal Life: *The never-ending reality of growing in our experiential knowledge of God while abiding in his unabated presence forever.*

It's important to see that Jesus did not define eternal life solely in terms of its length. Eternal life certainly means that we are going to live forever. But there's much more to it than that. Even the lost will exist forever. The eternal life that God gives is a quality of life that Jesus defined as knowing God the Father and God the Son. This is personal, intimate knowledge, and it begins the moment we trust Christ (John 4:13-14; 10:27-30; 17:2-3; 2 Pet 1:2-3).

Eternal Security: *The clear teaching of Scripture that those who come to know Christ as their Savior enter into an eternal relationship with God that guarantees their eternal security.*

God's power is able to keep believers from falling because it is up to him, not to us, to make good on the Bible's guarantee of eternal life for true believers in Christ. Simply put, the doctrine of eternal security means that our redemption in Christ Jesus is permanent (John 10:27-30; Rom 8:31-39; Eph 1:13-14; 1 Tim 2:10-13; 1 John 5:11-13).

Evangelism: *Sharing the good news of Christ's substitutionary death and resurrection and his free offer of forgiveness of sin and eternal life to all who come to him by faith to receive it.*

Every believer is called to share the gospel with every lost person possible, both at home and abroad. The act of sharing your faith is not reserved for ministers or evangelists. Jesus has given believers the task of telling others about him and the gospel of saving grace as we go about our daily lives. It can be as simple as doing a kind act for someone in need and then asking to pray with them afterwards while sharing the gospel, or it could be more elaborate (Mark 16:15; Acts 1:8; 21:8; 2 Cor 5:18-21; Eph 4:11; 2 Tim 4:5).

Faith: *Acting like God is telling the truth; acting like it is so even when it is not so in order that it might be so simply because God said so.*

Faith is the opposite of sight, acting and judging things based solely on what we can see and perceive with our human senses. Faith always involves your feet. It is an action of your life, not merely words from your lips. A person can feel like they lack faith but still be full of faith if they choose to obey what God has revealed to do or say. Faith is not merely a feeling; it is an action in response to God's revealed will (Rom 4:17; 2 Cor 5:7; Eph 2:8-9; Heb 11:1-3, 6).

Fellowship: *Intimate communion with God and his people as they share the life and love of Christ with one another.*

Biblical fellowship is not just coffee and donuts in Sunday school, or a meal in the fellowship hall. Fellowship is the sharing of our lives and sharing the life and love of Christ with other believers. The Bible teaches that Christians are bonded together in a relationship of unity as members of one another. In fact, those who withdraw from the community of believers will find their relationship with God limited by their failure to participate in the fellowship of the saints. (Acts 2:42; Rom 12:5; 1 Cor 11:29; Heb 10:25; 1 John 1:5-9).

Forgiveness: *The decision to no longer credit an offense against an offender with a view to executing personal vengeance.*

There are two basic categories of forgiveness: (1) *Unilateral forgiveness* is the decision to release someone from an offense who is either unable or unwilling to repent in order that the offended person is set free. Give to the Lord that situation in which someone misunderstood you, misread your motives, hurt you, or sinned against you. Forgive the people involved if that's needed, and rest your case with God, realizing that he knows your heart. (2) *Transactional forgiveness* is the decision to release someone from an offense who repents of his or her sin, thus opening up the opportunity for reconciliation (Matt 6:12, 14-15; 18:21-35; 2 Cor 2:10; Eph 4:32; Col 3:12-13).

Freedom: *The release from illegitimate bondage so that you can choose to exercise responsibility in maximizing all that you were created to be.*

The freedom that is actualized through a kingdom perspective, that of embracing God's sovereignty, generates a faith more powerful than any human weapon or system of philosophy could ever produce. It accesses God's grace in such a way so as to grant a freedom that is not dependent upon externals. Authentic biblical freedom releases people from sin and illegitimate bondage to righteousness so that they can serve God and others as they fulfill his will for their lives (John 8:32-36; 2 Cor 3:17; Gal 5:1-4).

God: *The eternally perfect uncreated Creator, Sustainer, and Ruler of all things who is one in essence but exists in three coequal persons: Father, Son, and Holy Spirit (the Trinity).*

God exists before time and will exist beyond time. He sits outside of the confines of our finite humanity. He is the great "I AM," dependent upon no one. Within him lies all wisdom, knowledge, and understanding. His multiplicity of attributes comprise a sovereign and supreme being exhibiting an array of emotion, power, authority, and gentleness unlike any other. The many declarations in Scripture that God exists as a triune being have made the doctrine of the Trinity a central tenet of true, biblical faith (Gen 1:26; Matt 3:16-17; 28:19; 2 Cor 13:14).

Grace: *The inexhaustible goodness of God which he freely bestows upon human beings, which is undeserved, unearned, and unable to be repaid.*

Grace is God's unmerited favor. It is by grace that we are saved, and it is grace that is to serve as a believer's motivation for righteous living and good works. Our gratitude for God's grace provides the impetus for obedience, worship, and fellowship with the Lord. Personal power and strength become perfected as we experience a greater level of God's grace. We are to grow in our understanding of grace and are also called to extend grace to one another as a reflection of God's grace in our own lives (John 1:16; Rom 3:24; 5:15; 2 Cor 12:9; Eph 1:7-8; 2:8-9, 1 Pet 4:10; 2 Pet 3:18).

Grace over Law: *The grace of God saves us totally apart from any merit of our own, overcoming the power of the law to condemn.*

As Christians we often tend to get our Bible doctrines confused and start mixing truths that were never meant to be mixed. The Christians in Galatia got sidetracked because a group of people called the Judaizers had confused them about the relationship between the gospel of grace and the works of the law. Their message was that people needed to add law-keeping to grace to truly be saved and sanctified. But Paul wrote that salvation and sanctification is by grace through faith from first to last. The demands of the law are met as believers grow in grace (Rom 1:17; 3:20; 8:1-4; 11:6; Gal 2:21; 5:1-4; Eph 2:8-9; Titus 2:11, 12).

Hierarchy: *A covenantally authorized functional order that operates within a particular alignment and chain of command.*

The triune God perfectly illustrates this concept. Although the Father, Son, and Holy Spirit are equally God, the Son obeys and glorifies the Father, and the Spirit only speaks what the Father and Son tell him to say. Likewise, the Spirit's calling is not to glorify himself but rather to glorify the Son. Based on the activity in the Trinity, God has established a hierarchy in human relationship as well. Hierarchy does not delineate value or equality; rather, it establishes an order for effective kingdom function (John 5:19; 16:14; 17:4; 1 Cor 11:3; Heb 13:17).

Hope: *Confident expectation about the future based on the character and promises of God.*

Local churches are to be centers of hope in every community where they minister. The church is supposed to be a little bit of heaven a long way from home. It is to be that place where the values of eternity operate in history—a place where weary people can go to find truth, acceptance, equality, freedom, safety, forgiveness, justice, and hope. Jesus is working to bring glory to himself and hope to mankind in fulfillment of his kingdom purposes and provisions (Jer 29:11-14; Matt 5:13-14; Rom 5:3-5; Heb 10:23; 1 Pet 3:15).

Hypostatic Union: *Two natures (divine and human) in one person (Jesus Christ) unmixed forever.*

This is the term theologians use to describe the perfect union of Christ's divine and human natures, both in their fullness without any confusion. Christ's undiminished deity and perfect humanity are united forever in one person. Jesus was no less God when he became a perfect man. He was fully human but without sin. Jesus is the God-man, united forever in heaven. He is unique—God in the flesh (John 1:1, 14; Luke 2:52; Phil 2:5-8; Heb 2:14).

Inheritance: *The temporal and eternal blessings and privileges afforded to faithful Christians for the enjoyment of all the rights and benefits of the King and his kingdom.*

Believers are heirs of the kingdom promises to Abraham, having already been blessed by the King with all spiritual blessings (Eph 1:3). We only receive a portion of the rights and benefits of our inheritance in the present age. But when Jesus comes, we will receive our full inheritance based on our obedience, faithfulness, and fulfillment of God's will for our lives (Rom 4:13-16; 8:17; Eph 1:3, 14, 18; Col 1:12; 3:24; Heb 9:15; 1 Pet 1:4).

Joy: *The feeling and expression of the inner celebration and satisfaction of the soul that transcends circumstances.*

Joy is the overflow of life, the stability inside despite chaos on the outside. The influence of the first-century church was so powerful in society that it brought

great joy to the entire city of Samaria when Philip took the gospel there (Acts 8:8). The Holy Spirit's task is to make real in the lives of true believers the comfort and confidence of their security in Christ (Neh 8:10; Luke 2:10-11; John 15:11; Rom 14:17; Phil 1:25; 1 Pet 1:8-9).

Justification: *Justification is a legal term that means to acquit, to find the defendant not guilty.*

In the New Testament, it means to declare the former defendant righteous. A basic definition of biblical justification is a judicial act by which God declares righteous those who believe in Jesus Christ. The picture is a courtroom in which we stand condemned by our sin. But justification is a pardon from a death penalty. On the cross, Jesus announced that the price for sin had been paid in full. Justification comes from God alone. The opposite of justification is condemnation (John 19:30; Rom 3:19-24; 5:1, 8-9; 8:33).

Kingdom: *The sovereign and comprehensive rule of God over all of his creation.*

The Bible declares that God's kingdom is the entire universe, which includes the earth and all of its inhabitants (Ps 24:1). The job of the Holy Spirit is to bring people to recognize God's right to rule as King and to submit to his authority. Jesus told the apostles that God will indeed establish his earthly kingdom someday, but in his own time. In the meantime, God has decided to set up his own kingdom communities. This community is called the church, brought into being by the Holy Spirit in order to exercise God's kingdom authority in history (1 Chr 29:11; Ps 115:3; Dan 4:34-35; Matt 6:33; 16:18-19; 1 Thess 2:12; Heb 12:28).

Kingdom Agenda: *The visible manifestation of the comprehensive rule of God over every area of life.*

We are called to align our lives underneath God's over-arching rule. His kingdom rule needs to remain at the forefront of our thinking in order to fully penetrate our choices and decisions thus bringing about the full realization of his covenantal blessings and authority. It transcends the politics of men and offers the solutions of heaven, removing the division humanity often erects between the sacred and the secular. This agenda is manifested through the four covenantal spheres of the individual, family, church, and community—which includes civil government (Ps 128:1-6; Matt 6:10, 33; John 18:36; Rom 13:1-7; Col 1:13; 4:11).

Kingdom Authority: *The sovereign and comprehensive rule of God over all of his creation.*

Kingdom authority is the divinely authorized right and responsibility delegated to disciples to act on God's behalf in spiritually ruling over his creation under the lordship of Jesus Christ. Believers are given authority to rule in God's kingdom under his direction and in accordance with his will and purposes. We gain access to this authority through living under the comprehensive rule of God in our lives. While authority is offered through Christ, it is not always accessed. There is a process to entering into the complete realization and execution of the divine mission for our individual lives, families, church, nation, and world (Gen 1:26-28; Deut 4:28-37, Dan 4:34-37; Matt 25:14-30; 28:18-20; Phil 3:14-20).

Kingdom Citizen: *A visible, verbal follower of Jesus Christ who consistently applies the principles of heaven to the concerns of the culture.*

Kingdom citizens have an obligation to fully utilize and fulfill their assigned tasks through the use of God-given resources and abilities for the benefit of society. Spiritual ministry and social responsibility work hand-in-hand. When the two are properly connected and integrated, people become productive citizens of society while also becoming prepared for life in eternity (Jer 29:7; Matt 5:13-16; Rom 13:1-7; Gal 6:10; 1 Tim 2:1-3; 1 Pet 2:17).

Kingdom Disciple: *A believer who takes part in the spiritual developmental process of progressively learning to live all of life under the lordship of Jesus Christ.*

This process of growth from spiritual infancy to spiritual maturity enables the believer to become increasingly more like Christ. Kingdom discipleship is designed to be replicated again and again until Jesus has many brothers and sisters who look, act, and think like him (Matt 28:18-20; Rom 8:29, 2 Cor 3:17-18; 2 Tim 1:13; 2:2).

Kingdom Man: *A male who is consistently living under the rule of God and lordship of Jesus Christ over every area of his life.*

A kingdom man accepts his responsibilities under God and faithfully carries them out. When this man is faithful, God will move even pagan powers and other forces and circumstances on earth to support his kingdom man doing his kingdom business. Jesus is the perfect example of a kingdom man in his earthly ministry (Gen 18:19; Exod 34:23-24; John 17:4; 19:30; 1 Cor 11:3; Phil 3:7-14).

Kingdom Marriage: *A covenantal union between a man and a woman who commit themselves to function in unison under divine authority in order to replicate God's image and expand his rule in the world through both their individual and joint callings.*

God established marriage and created the first family. A man and a woman together were to reflect God's image, which is unity in diversity—God the Father, the Son, and the Holy Spirit. The marriage union most fully expresses who God truly is, and it is the most comprehensive manifestation of his image on earth as well as the foundation for a stable society. Paul uses the sacred covenant of marriage to illustrate both the bond and function between Christ and his church (Gen 1:26-28; 2:22-25; Mal 2:10-17; Matt 19:3-10, Eph 5:22-23).

Kingdom Parenting: *The responsibility to intentionally oversee the generational transfer of a comprehensive Christian worldview so that children learn to consistently live all of life under God's divine authority.*

Parents are to train children in the biblical principles of a kingdom worldview. Through consistent time in imparting truths from God's Word to their children, parents disciple their children in spiritual growth. Kingdom parents leave a legacy and inheritance not only for their children but also for their children's children. Children are to be "like young olive plants around your table"—indicating a regular pattern of purposeful development. Parents are also to encourage their children and lovingly correct them when they disobey (Deut 6:4-9; Psalm 128:3; Prov 13:22; 22:6; Eph 6:1-4; Col 3:20-21).

Kingdom Prayer: *The divinely authorized methodology to access heavenly authority for earthly intervention.*

Prayer links us to a heavenly realm we are unfamiliar navigating. Prayer is the God given communication link between heaven and earth, time and eternity, the finite and the infinite. Simply put, it is relational communication with God (Luke 18:1; Phil 4:4-7; 1 Thess 5:17; 1 Tim 2:1-2).

Kingdom Single: *An unmarried Christian who has committed to fully and freely maximizing his or her completeness under the rule of God and the Lordship of Jesus Christ.*

According to the apostle Paul, being single is a very good thing (1 Cor 7:26). In fact, a kingdom single is in the best possible spiritual position. Singlehood is a unique platform and position provided to you for great enjoyment, accomplishment, discovery, exploration, freedom, meaning and spiritual fellowship as well as eternal impact (1 Cor 6:17-20; 7:20, 25-40; Phil 4:11-13).

Kingdom Steward: *A believer who faithfully oversees, protects, and expands the assets God has given him or her to manage on his behalf.*

A kingdom steward carries out the divinely ordained responsibility of faithfully managing God's assigned resources (time, talent, and treasures) in such a way that they bring him glory and expand his kingdom rule in the world. Stewardship is the responsibility to protect and expand the possessions of another, which for believers means recognizing that everything we have is a gift from God for which we are accountable as his stewards or managers (Matt 25:14-30; Luke 16:9-13; 19:11-27; 1 Cor 4:2; 16:2; Titus 1:7; 1 Pet 4:10).

Kingdom Woman: *A female who is consistently living under the rule of God and lordship of Jesus Christ over every area of her life.*

A kingdom woman has been uniquely tasked with the purpose of not only living out her own calling but also providing a strong help (*ezer kenegdo*) in the home and to her husband. In addition, she is to utilize her spiritual gifts and exercise her delegated positions of leadership for the benefit of the church and society. She models strength, diligence, charity, compassion, entrepreneurism, and dedication to those placed within her sphere of influence (Prov 31:10-31; Luke 8:2-3; Rom 16:1-2; 1 Cor 11:1-10; Eph 5:22-24, 33; 2 Tim 3:10-11; 1 Pet 3:1-6).

Local Church/Membership: *A local church is called an* ekklesia, *meaning a body of "called out ones" taken from the world and joined to Jesus Christ in a living union, a body of which he is the head.*

Many of the references to the church in the New Testament refer to a specific local church, or a group of local assemblies, whether in Rome, Corinth, Ephesus, etc. Every Christian becomes a member of the universal church at salvation, but is also exhorted to become a functioning, faithful member of a biblically sound local church. The role of the local church is to exercise the authority of the kingdom in history (Matt 16:18-19; 1 Cor 1:2; 2 Cor 1:1; 1 Thess 1:1; 2 Thess 1:1; Heb 10:25).

The Lord's Supper: *Also known as communion, the Lord's Supper is one of the two ordinances (along with baptism) given by Jesus Christ to his church through which believers publicly proclaim their association with and surrender to him through his death, burial, and resurrection.*

The Lord's Supper was instituted by Jesus on the night before his crucifixion, as he observed the Jewish Passover with his disciples. Jesus transformed the elements by teaching that the bread represented his body which would soon be broken to atone for sin and that the cup represented the "new covenant" in his blood—the promise of the Passover lamb being fulfilled in the salvation he provided. In communion, the believer can experience the unique spiritual presence of Christ as well as accesses his authority in a unique way over the spiritual realms of darkness (Luke 22:14-23; 1 Cor 10:16; 11:23-29).

Lordship: *The recognition of and submission to the rule of Christ over the life of a believer.*

Believers in Jesus Christ are called to bring every area of life under Christ's rule and lordship. Only as a believer acknowledges and submits to the lordship of Christ can the power and authority of God's kingdom be made visible in history. God explicitly states that it is his determined purpose to bring all of history under the rule of Jesus Christ. There must be covenantal alignment under the lordship of Jesus Christ in order to experience his kingdom power, authority, provision, and covering (Rom 14:6-9; 1 Cor 8:5-6; Eph 1:9-10; Phil 2:9-11; Col 1:13).

Love: *The decision to compassionately, righteously, and sacrificially seek the well-being of another.*

Love is not first and foremost an emotion. Love is a decision. We are to choose love even when we do not feel like loving because we are called to love others as God has loved us. Our relationship with Christ is first and foremost one of love. Out of our intimate abiding with him, we are to extend love to those around us. It is by the mark of love that people are to recognize us as followers of Christ (John 3:16; 13:35; Rom 5:5; 1 Cor 13:1-8; 1 John 3:1; 4:10-11, 19-20).

Mercy: *The expression of God's steadfast love that relieves misery and does not give all that the sinner deserves.*

Believers can praise God that even though they were once destined for death as members of Satan's kingdom, God saved them by his mercy. Biblical justice also comes tempered with the potential for mercy toward the offender. The cross of Jesus Christ is the greatest example of this appeal for mercy. While on the cross, Jesus asked his Father to forgive those who were killing him. Through the parable of the two slaves who owed money, Jesus teaches that this principle of mercy that he offers us should govern how we treat others (Lam 3:22; Matt 5:7; 18:21-34; Eph 2:4-5; Heb 4:16).

Offices of Christ: *The three major offices or categories of leaders for God's people, Israel, in the Old Testament were prophet, priest, and king.*

Each office was a separate calling and duty. Each of these offices was a type and a foretaste of the coming Messiah, Jesus Christ, who now fulfills all three offices. Christ is the prophet we need to instruct us in the things of God. He is also our great high priest who redeemed us by offering his own body as the final and full sacrifice for sin. Christ is also our glorious, coming King, ruling over all things now from heaven as he awaits his triumphant return to earth (Deut 18:15; Luke 4:24; Acts 3:22; Heb 4:14-16; Rev 19:16).

Original Sin: *The entrance of sin into the human race through Adam's sin in the garden of Eden.*

When Adam fell by disobeying God and eating from the tree of the knowledge of good and evil, his spirit died and his soul became contaminated by sin. His nature was changed and became corrupted, separated from God and in need of forgiveness and redemption. Since Adam is the father of the human race, every child of Adam is born in sin with what theologians call the Adamic nature (Gen 2:15-17; 3:6-7; Ps 51:5; Rom 5:12-14; Eph 2:1-3).

Peace: *Well-being, contentment, and wholeness produced through an abiding faith in and relationship with God.*

Peace does not mean that you will have no troubles. Peace means that God's provision of his presence will lighten the stress those troubles produce. Peace is the umbrella in the storm, calming nerves and covering you from the results of worry. Peace comes through prayer and also through keeping your mind fixed on the truth of God's Word. Peace is the order and calm the Holy Spirit brings into the life of a believer despite external circumstances (John 14:27; Rom 14:17; Eph 2:14-17; Phil 4:4-6).

Rapture: *The split-second moment when Christ will return in the air to take his people, the church, home to be with him forever.*

This is one of the themes of prophecy in the Bible. The Christians at Thessalonica were shaken because they feared they would never see their dead loved ones again. Paul wrote to assure them with the truth of the church's rapture when the church is taken out of the world. The world will not realize the restraining and sanctifying influence of the church until God raptures his church and all of hell breaks loose on the earth in the tribulation (1 Thess 4:13-18; 2 Thess 2:7; Titus 2:13).

Reconciliation: *The restoration of a previously broken relationship based on repentance and forgiveness.*

Reconciliation involves removing the hostility between parties and restoring peace and harmony in a relationship. It means that the wall separating the hostility has been broken down; the breach has been healed. Jesus accomplished our reconciliation with God when He died on the cross for our sins. This should encourage believers to be reconciled with one another (Matt 5:24; Luke 12:58; Rom 5:10; 2 Cor 5:18-19; Eph 2:11-22; 2:14-16).

Redemption: *To deliver through the payment of a price.*

Christ's death was the price God demanded to redeem us from slavery to sin. God never skips sin. Someone has to pay the price—either you or an acceptable substitute. On the cross Jesus said, "It is finished" (John 19:30), meaning, "paid in full." All the requirements necessary to pay for our redemption were put up by Jesus Christ on the cross (Mark 10:45; 1 Cor 6:20; Gal 1:4; Eph 1:7-11 Titus 2:14; 1 Pet 1:18-19).

Repentance: *The inner resolve and determination to turn away from a sin that is manifested by an external change in behavior coupled with appropriate restitution.*

When a person bows to Jesus in repentance and submission, He becomes Lord of that person's life. Christ's death removed the barrier keeping sinners from being reconciled to a holy God, thus freeing God to save any and everyone who believes. We are still responsible to come to Christ in faith to be saved and in repentance to be in fellowship with him, but Christ's death makes that avenue open and available to all (Mark 1:15; Luke 13:1-5; 19:1-10; Rom 2:4; 2 Cor 7:10).

Resurrection: *To become alive again from the dead.*

Six distinct resurrections are mentioned in Scripture. In the order of their occurrence they are

the resurrection of Jesus Christ; the resurrection of an unnamed number of believers in Jerusalem who were resurrected when Christ arose from the grave; the resurrection of the church at the rapture; the resurrection of Old Testament saints at Christ's second coming; the resurrection of tribulation believers; and the resurrection of the wicked for judgment (Matt 27:52-53; John 20:1-10; 1 Thess 4:13-18; Rev 20:5; 20:11-15).

Righteousness: *The divine standard God has established for mankind's actions and attitudes to be acceptable to him.*

The vast difference between God and mankind is that he is righteous in his character and we are not. Since perfect righteousness on our part is required to enter God's presence, Jesus Christ lived a perfectly sinless, righteous life and died on the cross for the payment of our sins. As a result, God could bestow on those who trust in Christ through faith his own righteousness as a gift of grace. We are then to live out God's righteous standards in our daily lives (Rom 1:18-21; 3:10-22; 9:30; 2 Cor 5:21; Phil 1:9-11; 1 Tim 6:11; Heb 12:14).

Sanctification: *The process of the believer's growth in Christ.*

Positional sanctification was accomplished for every believer at the moment of salvation by receiving Christ's righteousness (the same root word as "sanctify"). *Progressive* sanctification is the growth process by which believers seek to become more like Christ in their decisions and lifestyle. *Entire* or *ultimate* sanctification will only be achieved when we stand perfect before Christ in glory (1 Cor 1:2; 1 Thess 4:3; 5:22-23; 2 Thess 2:13).

Sanctions: *The negative and positive consequences of obedience and disobedience.*

The progress or regression of our lives, families, churches, and society is directly tied to divine sanctions operating in history. Sanctions, both positive and negative, are one of the distinctions of a spiritual covenant. This is the cause and effect relationship that is built into history. Sin brings destruction, and righteousness brings blessing (Deut 30:15-20; 2 Chr 15:3-6; Mal 2:13-16; 1 Cor 11:23-32).

Sin: *The failure of man to measure up to God's perfect standard of righteousness, whether in thought, word, or deed.*

Human beings are sinners by nature—their sin inherited from the first Adam—as well as sinners by personal choice. The human heart has been thoroughly corrupted by sin, leaving people without Christ in a state of total depravity—a doctrine that means we have nothing within ourselves to commend us to God. To sin is to "miss the mark," to fall short of God's standard of righteousness and perfection. The result, or punishment, for sin is death,

which is removed only by the saving grace of Jesus Christ (Jer 17:9; Rom 3:10-12, 23; 5:19; 6:23; 11:32).

Sovereignty/Providence: *The sovereignty of God means that he exercises his prerogative to do whatever he pleases with his creation. His providence is the outworking of God's eternal plan for mankind and all of his creation.*

Providence is the invisible and mysterious hand of God at work in the details of history to bring to pass his sovereign will. God's providence includes every part of creation, from the inanimate world to individuals and entire nations. In his righteous, wise, and loving providence, God is bringing to pass his eternal purposes for his glory and our eternal good (Pss 22:28; 24:1; 66:7; 103:19; Rom 8:28).

Spiritual Warfare: *The cosmic conflict waged in the invisible spiritual realm but simultaneously fleshed out in the visible physical realm, which our enemy the devil uses when he seeks to defeat us.*

Satan seeks to discourage and distract us from the real battle and convince us that we have to fight him physically rather than spiritually. Yet while Satan may have power, he does not have authority. The victory in spiritual warfare rests in the authority of Christ made available to believers through the weapons of warfare. When it comes to spiritual warfare and the issue of our victory, the matter has already been settled. Jesus Christ defeated the devil and all of his forces on the cross, and nothing can cancel out that victory. We are not fighting for victory, but from a position of victory. Satan is a defeated foe (1 Cor 2:11; 2 Cor 10:3-5; Eph 6:10-18; Col 2:15; 1 Pet 5:8-9; Rev 12:10-11).

Stronghold: *A sin or circumstance that illegitimately holds a person in spiritual bondage; a negative, destructive pattern of thinking or actions used by Satan to promote a recurrence of sin in our lives.*

God says these strongholds have to be destroyed, which means he didn't build them. Once a stronghold is built, it gives our enemy Satan a place from which to launch further attacks against our minds and a fortification from which to repel our attempts to dislodge him. But the Word of God gives us the weapons to tear down these satanic fortresses (Rom 12:2; 2 Cor 10:3-5; 6:7; Eph 6:10-18).

Substitutionary Atonement: *Christ's death was a blood atonement as a sacrificial substitution, in our place, to satisfy the demands of the law in order to appease a holy God for the payment of sin.*

God has always required the shedding of blood to atone for sin. This requirement of blood goes all the way back to Eden, when God killed an animal to cover Adam and Eve after they sinned. The animal's death temporally satisfied God's requirement and substituted for their deaths. Jesus didn't die just to leave us a good example or to show us how to bear

up under suffering. Our guilt was transferred to him; therefore, he took the death stroke that should have fallen on us for all eternity (Gen 3:21; 2 Cor 5:21; Heb 9:12-14; 1 Pet 2:24).

Total Depravity: *Every facet of human nature has been polluted, defiled, and contaminated by sin.*

This is the inborn corruption we inherited as children of Adam, which means there is nothing within us to commend us to a holy God. We are sold into sin—unable to save ourselves, and totally dependent on God's grace in Christ, which he offers to all mankind (Jer 17:9; Rom 1:29 3:23; Phil 2:15; 2 Tim 3:8; 2 Pet 2:19).

Truth: *The absolute standard by which reality is measured. It is God's view on every subject.*

Absolute truth cannot be perceived by human beings apart from the revelation of God. The Bible is the sole repository and determiner of absolute truth, and God guarantees the truth of every word he has given in Scripture. The believer is dependent on the ministry of the Holy Spirit as the illuminator of Scripture in order to understand and obey what God has revealed to us (Num 23:19; Ps 19:1-10; John 17:17, 2 Tim 3:7).

Universal Church: *The church is revealed in the New Testament as the body and bride of Christ through whom God is accomplishing his purposes in this present age.*

The church is that company of redeemed people called out from the world and joined together in one living union by the baptism and indwelling of the Holy Spirit. As such, the universal church refers to every believer from the church's birthday on the day of Pentecost to the future rapture, when Christ will come for his church and take his people out of the world (Matt 16:18; Acts 2:1-4; Eph 1:22-23; 3:10; Col 1:18).

Unlimited Atonement: *This refers to the universal extent of Christ's atoning death.*

The Bible teaches that Christ's sacrifice is sufficient for all mankind, even though not every person is saved. Sin has to be atoned for, because God is too holy to ignore sin, and too loving to let us plunge headlong into hell. Atonement is paying what must be paid—the penalty of death—to settle God's righteous claim against us. And the only death that satisfied this demand was that of Christ on the cross for all sin for all mankind without exception (John 3:16, 36; Rom 5:15-17; 2 Cor 5:15; 1 Tim 2:6; Heb 2:9; 1 John 2:2).

Worship: *The recognition of God for who he is, what he has done, and what we are trusting him to do.*

The job of believers as worshipers is to praise and exalt the glory of our great God and his Son, the Lord Jesus Christ. God fills all of the universe and eternity. There is no lack in him that requires us to magnify him so that He becomes bigger. Rather, worship recognizes and extolls how big he truly is. Magnifying God is when we focus our praise and worship on him. We see him for the great and awesome God that he is; he is bigger than our problems and circumstances. That's the power worship has. It changes us by changing our perspective of God. Worship is to be the lifestyle of the believer (Pss 29:2; 66:4; Matt 4:10; John 4:23; Rom 12:1; Phil 2:9-11).

TOPICAL INDEX OF THE KINGDOM

KINGDOM
Exodus 19:6
Numbers 24:7
2 Samuel 3:10
2 Samuel 7:12
2 Samuel 7:13
2 Samuel 7:16
1 Kings 9:5
1 Chronicles 17:14
1 Chronicles 22:10
1 Chronicles 28:7
2 Chronicles 1:1
2 Chronicles 13:8
Psalm 22:28
Psalm 45:6
Psalm 145:11
Psalm 145:12
Psalm 145:13
Isaiah 9:7
Isaiah 13:4
Isaiah 37:16
Ezekiel 37:24
Daniel 2:44
Daniel 4:3
Daniel 4:34
Daniel 4:36
Daniel 6:26
Daniel 7:14
Daniel 7:18
Daniel 7:27
Obadiah 1:21
Micah 4:8
Matthew 4:23
Matthew 6:10
Matthew 6:13
Matthew 6:33
Matthew 8:12
Matthew 9:35
Matthew 12:26
Matthew 13:19
Matthew 13:38
Matthew 13:41
Matthew 13:43
Matthew 16:28
Matthew 20:1

Matthew 20:21
Matthew 24:7
Matthew 24:14
Matthew 25:34
Matthew 26:29
Luke 1:33
Luke 4:5
Luke 11:2
Luke 11:18
Luke 12:31
Luke 12:32
Luke 22:29
Luke 22:30
Luke 23:42
John 18:36
Acts 1:6
Acts 20:25
1 Corinthians 15:24
Ephesians 5:5
Colossians 1:13
1 Thessalonians 2:12
2 Timothy 4:1
2 Timothy 4:18
Hebrews 1:8
Hebrews 12:28
James 2:5
2 Peter 1:11
Revelation 1:6
Revelation 1:9
Revelation 5:10
Revelation 11:15
Revelation 12:10

KINGDOM OF GOD
Matthew 12:28
Matthew 19:24
Matthew 21:31
Matthew 21:43
Mark 1:15
Mark 4:11
Mark 4:26
Mark 4:30
Mark 9:1
Mark 9:47
Mark 10:14

Mark 10:15
Mark 10:23
Mark 10:24
Mark 10:25
Mark 11:10
Mark 12:34
Mark 14:25
Mark 15:43
Luke 4:43
Luke 6:20
Luke 7:28
Luke 8:1
Luke 8:10
Luke 9:2
Luke 9:11
Luke 9:27
Luke 9:60
Luke 9:62
Luke 10:9
Luke 10:11
Luke 11:20
Luke 13:18
Luke 13:20
Luke 13:28
Luke 13:29
Luke 14:15
Luke 16:16
Luke 17:20
Luke 17:21
Luke 18:16
Luke 18:17
Luke 18:24
Luke 18:25
Luke 18:29
Luke 19:11
Luke 21:31
Luke 22:16
Luke 22:18
Luke 23:51
John 3:3
John 3:5
Acts 1:3
Acts 8:12
Acts 14:22
Acts 19:8

Acts 28:23
Acts 28:31
Romans 14:17
1 Corinthians 4:20
1 Corinthians 6:9
1 Corinthians 6:10
1 Corinthians 15:50
Galatians 5:21
Colossians 4:11
2 Thessalonians 1:5

KINGDOM OF HEAVEN
Matthew 3:2
Matthew 4:17
Matthew 5:3
Matthew 5:10
Matthew 5:19
Matthew 5:20
Matthew 7:21
Matthew 8:11
Matthew 10:7
Matthew 11:11
Matthew 11:12
Matthew 13:11
Matthew 13:24
Matthew 13:31
Matthew 13:33
Matthew 13:44
Matthew 13:45
Matthew 13:47
Matthew 13:52
Matthew 16:19
Matthew 18:1
Matthew 18:3
Matthew 18:4
Matthew 18:23
Matthew 19:12
Matthew 19:14
Matthew 19:23
Matthew 22:2
Matthew 23:13
Matthew 22:2
Matthew 23:13
Matthew 25:1

ALIGNMENT

Our understanding must align with God's order
  - Prov 3:5
We must align our lives with that of Jesus Christ
  - 1 Cor 11:1
Being in alignment with God makes our paths
  straight - Prov 3:5-6
God has a prescribed hierarchical order - 1 Cor 11:3
God has a unique plan for you - Phil 1:6
Prayer must be in alignment with God's will
  - 1 John 5:14

ANGELS

Archangels - Dan 10:13
Theophany/Angel of the Lord - Gen 16:7; Exod 3:2;
  Josh 5:14; Judg 13:15-16
Fall of the angels - Isa 14:12-14; Luke 10:18; Jude 1:6;
  Rev 12:1-17
Guardian angels - Ps 91:11; Heb 1:14
Angels are curious - 1 Pet 1:12
Angels rejoice at the salvation of people - Luke 15:10
Angels do not marry - Matt 22:30
Angels minister to people - Heb 1:14
Angels are messengers - Luke 1:1-38; Hebrews 13:1
Sacrifice to demons - Deut 2:17; 1 Cor 10:20-21; Rev 9:20

ATONEMENT

The Passover lamb - Exod 12:1-13
The day of Atonement - Lev 16:1-34
Substitutionary atonement - Isa 53:1-12; 1 Pet 2:24
Requirement of blood - Heb 9:22

BAPTISM

Purpose of baptism - Rom 6:1-7
Commanded by Christ - Matt 28:19
Demonstrated by Christ - Matt 3:13-17
Ordinance of the church - Matt 28:19
One baptism - Eph 4:5
Baptism of the Spirit - Mark 1:8; Acts 1:5
Water baptism - Acts 10:47
Not a requirement for salvation - 1 Cor 1:17
Baptism of repentance - Mark 1:4
Baptism for the dead - 1 Cor 15:29

BIBLE

Authority - John 10:35
Uniqueness - Matt 21:42; 2 Pet 1:21
Power - Heb 4:12-13
Sufficiency - Ps 19:7-11; Prov 30:5-6
Inerrancy - 2 Tim 3:16
Source of truth - John 17:17
Inspiration - 2 Tim 3:16-17
Life-giving - John 6:68-69
Symbolized as food - 1 Pet 2:2
Power of the Word - Heb 4:12

CHRISTIAN LIFE

Discipline - 1 Tim 4:7
Confession - Jas 5:16; 1 John 1:9
Submission - Eph 5:20
Community - Heb 10:25
Growing/Maturing - Heb 5:11-14; 2 Pet 3:18;
  1 John 2:12-14
Use of spiritual gifts - Eph 4:7-16; 1 Pet 4:10-11
Accountability - 1 Cor 12:14-31; Heb 13:17
Loving one another - John 13:34-35; Rom 12:10;
  1 John 4:11

CHURCH

Authority of the church - Matt 16:18-19; 18:18
Church discipline - Matthew 18:15-20
Church leadership - Acts 14:23; 1 Thess 5:12
Unity of the church - John 17:20-23; 1 Cor 1:10; Eph 4:3
Power of the church - Eph 3:14-21
Rapture of the church - 1 Thess 4:13-18

CONFESSION

Confessing sins to others - Jas 5:16
Confessing sins to God - Ps 32:5
Confession as an affirmation of identity - Luke 12:8;
  1 John 2:23
Confession leads to forgiveness - 1 John 1:9-10
Confession leads to healing - Jas 5:16
Confession of Christ - Matt 10:32-33
Confession of lordship - Rom 10:9

CREATION

God created everything - Gen 1:1
Jesus is the agent of creation - Col 1:16
The Holy Spirit oversees creation - Gen 1:2
Creation reveals God - Rom 1:20
Creation is fallen - Rom 8:20-21
Creation longs to be redeemed - Rom 8:22
Creation will be restored - Rev 21:1-5

DEATH

The great enemy - Rev 20:14
A result of the Fall - Gen 2:15-17
Mortality of humanity - Heb 9:27; Jas 4:14
Defeated at the cross - 1 Cor 15:55-57
Death of Jesus - 1 Pet 3:18
Physical vs spiritual death - Gen 2:17; John 14:6;
  Rom 6:23
Grief and mourning - John 11:32-38

DOUBT

Faith when facing doubt - Ps 73
Doubt hinders prayer - Jas 1:6-8
Combatting doubt when facing difficult
  circumstances - Ps 69:1-3
Combatting doubt with God's Word - Acts 17:11-12

END TIMES

The antichrist - Rev 13:1-18
The abomination of desolation - Dan 12:1-13; Matt 24:15;
Rapture - 1 Thess 4:13-17
Return of Christ - Acts 1:11
New heaven and new earth - Rev 21:1
Resurrection of the dead - 1 Cor 15:1-58
Judgement seat of Christ - 2 Cor 5:10
The great tribulation - Matt 24:1-54
The millennium - Rev 20:1-15
The fate of the devil - Rev 20:10
The fate of death - Rev 20:14
The end of sin - Rev 21:4
Timing - Matt 24:36; 2 Thess 2:3-12

ETERNAL LIFE

Eternal life begins at conversion - John 4:13-14
God is the God of the living - Mark 12:24-27
Eternal life is a free gift - Rom 6:23
Eternal life is found through faith in Jesus - John 3:16
Eternal life is spent with Christ - Luke 23:43;
    2 Cor 5:6-8
Eternal life is the knowledge of God - John 17:3

EVANGELISM

Commanded by Jesus - Matt 28:19-20; Acts 1:8
Evangelism spreads the gospel beyond
    all barriers - Acts 1:8
Gift of evangelism - Eph 4:11
Who should evangelize? - 1 Pet 3:15
Cross-cultural ministry - Acts 17:22-34
Responsibility of all believers - 2 Cor 5:18-20

FAILURE

Failure and the anger of the Lord - Ps 106:7-43
Peter's denial of Christ - Matt 26:69-75
Failure as a result of pride - Gen 11:3-8
Failure as a result of disobedience - Num 14:40-45
God helps us through failure - Ps 37:23-24
Encouragement through failures - John 21:12-17
Jesus will finish working in you - Phil 1:6

FAITH

Faith defined - Heb 11:1
Faith leads to salvation - Eph 2:8-9
Faith means trusting God's ways - Isa 55:8-9
God's faithfulness - 1 Cor 1:9
Faith and works - Rom 4:1-5; Jas 2:14-26
Examples of faith - Heb 11:1-40
Rewards of faith - Heb 11:32-40
Faith should be childlike - Matt 18:3
Focus of faith - Heb 12:1-2
The power of faith - Matt 21:21-22; 1 Pet 1:5
Walking by faith - 2 Cor 5:7

FALL

The occurrence of the fall - Gen 3:1-7
The curse of the fall - Gen 3:8-24
The reversal of the fall - Rev 22:1-5
The fall led to death - 1 Cor 15:22

The fall separated mankind from God - Eph 4:18
The fall planted evil in the hearts of
    all people - Eph 2:1-3
The condemnation of the fall - Rom 5:18-19

FAMILY

Family roles - Col 3:18-21
Raising children - Prov 22:6
Honor parents - Exod 20:12
Family as a picture of the church - Eph 2:19; 5:22-33
Fighting for the family - Neh 4:14
Providing for the family - 1 Tim 5:4, 8

FEAR

Source of fear - Gen 3:10
Fear of God - Ps 111:10
Commands not to be afraid - Phil 4:6
God is our refuge - Ps 46:1-2
We do not have a spirit of fear - 2 Tim 1:7
Fear is the opposite of love - 1 John 4:8
Bring your fears to God - Ps 34:4-5; 56:3-4

FORGIVENESS

God forgives us - Ps 103:12
Forgiving others - Matt 18:21-35
Confession leads to forgiveness - 1 John 1:9
Forgiveness brings fellowship with God - Ps 85:2
Jesus has the authority to forgive sins - Matt 9:1-8
Christians should forgive others - Eph 4:32
Petition for forgiveness - Ps 51:1-19
Blessedness of forgiveness - Ps 32:1-7

GOD

Glory - Ps 8:1
Immutability - 1 Sam 15:29
Omnipresence - Ps 139:7-12
Omniscience - Matt 10:30; 1 John 3:20
Omnipotence - Matt 19:26
Wisdom of God - Rom 11:33
Goodness - Ps 34:8
Graciousness - Titus 2:11
Mercy - Eph 2:4-5
Wrath - Rom 12:19
Love - 1 John 4:8

GOD'S WILL

Discerning God's will - John 7:17
God's timing is perfect - Ps 37:34
God's will is beyond our understanding - Isa 55:9
Growing in holiness demonstrates the
    will of God - Rom 12:2
Submitting to God's will - Jas 4:13-17

GOVERNMENT

Leaders are placed by God - Rom 13:1-7
Governments wield power to enforce law - Rom 13:4
Governments will overextend their authority
    - 1 Sam 8:10-18
Governments are subject to God - Rom 13:1-7
Pray for those in leadership - 1 Tim 2:1-2

Earthly governments are temporary - Isa 9:6-7;
  Rev 19:15-16
God is sovereign over government - Isa 40:23;
  Prov 21:1
Submitting to government - 1 Pet 2:13-15

GRACE

God's grace is sufficient - 2 Cor 12:9
Grace is the means of salvation - Eph 2:8-9
Grace is the perfection of the law - John 1:17
Grace is a gift - Rom 11:6
Grace is essential to the health of a church
  - Acts 13:43
Grace and peace - 1 Cor 1:3; Gal 1:3; Eph 1:2; Phil 3
Grace is essential to the gospel - Titus 2:11-14
Grace is the foundation of spiritual growth - 2 Pet 3:18

HEAVEN

The dwelling place of God - Matt 6:9
Where the stars reside - Gen 1:1; Ps 19:1-4
Third heaven - 2 Cor 12:2-4
Heavenly citizenship - Phil 3:20
Free of the curse - Rev 21:4
Worship of God - Rev 22:1-5
Prepared by Jesus - John 14:1-3

HELL

Eternal separation from God - Matt 25:46
Characterized by fire - Mark 9:43
Second death - Rev 2:11
Outer darkness - Matt 13:41-42
For fallen angels - Matt 25:41; 2 Pet 2:4
The final dwelling of death and the devil - Rev 19:20;
  20:13-14
The second death - Rev 20:14-15

HOLY SPIRIT

Member of the Trinity - Matt 28:19
The Spirit proceeds from the Father and the Son -
  John 15:26; Gal 4:6
Role in salvation - Acts 2:38; Gal 5:16-26
Baptism of the Holy Spirit - Acts 1:4-5
Filling of the Holy Spirit - Eph 5:18
Illumination of the Holy Spirit - 1 Cor 2:10-16
Seals the believer - Eph 4:30
Fruit of the Spirit - Gal 5:22-23
Source of life - Rom 8:11
The Holy Spirit was active in creation - Gen 1:2
The Holy Spirit intercedes on our behalf - Rom 8:26
The Holy Spirit can be resisted - Acts 7:51

INDIVIDUAL

God deals with individuals - Eph 4:7
God loves individuals - Luke 15:4-7
God has a plan for your life - Phil 1:9-11
Salvation is provided to individuals - John 3:16
Each person will give an individual account before
  God - 1 Cor 3:10-15
The resurrection is promised to individual
  people - John 5:25-30

ISRAEL

Given the law - Exod 19
God's chosen people - Deut 7:6
Settled in the promised land - Josh 1:4
As a national identity - Exod 19:5-6
Jacob was renamed Israel - Gen 32:28
The civil war - 2 Sam 2:12-32
Jerusalem the capital - 2 Chr 6:5-6
The Babylonian exile - 2 Kgs 25:21
The Assyrian exile - 2 Kgs 18:11
Coronation of Saul, the first king - 1 Sam 10
Building of Solomon's temple - 1 Kgs 6
Destruction of the first temple - Ezra 5:12
Rebuilding of the temple - Ezra 3:8-13
Restoration of the nation - Isa 43:4-6; Ezek 39:25-29

JESUS CHRIST

Jesus is divine - John 1:1; Titus 2:13
Jesus is human - Rom 1:3-4; Gal 4:4
Jesus has power - Mark 4:35-41
Jesus has all authority - Matt 28:18
Jesus's death, burial and resurrection - John 19-21;
  1 Cor 15:12-20
Spoke in parables - Matt 13:10-17
Sermon on the Mount - Matt 5-7
Second Coming - Acts 1:11; Rev 19:11-19
The union of Jesus's two natures - Phil 2:5-11
He is the eternal God - Col 1:17; 2:9; Heb 1:3
Our great high priest - Heb 7:25; Heb 4:14-16

JUSTICE

God is just - Deut 32:4
God's laws are just - Pss 19:7-9; 111:7-8
God's laws are to be applied impartially - Num 15:16;
  Deut 1:17; Rom 2:11
Justice is to be applied in society - Ps 72:1-2, 4;
  Amos 5:21-24
God requires men to do justice - Mic 6:8; Zech 7:9-10
Justice is to be connected to righteousness - Ps 89:14;
  Amos 5:24
Justice for the orphan, widow, and alien - Deut 10:17-19

KINGDOM

God's kingdom agenda - Ps 128:1-6
Jesus proclaimed the kingdom - Mark 1:14-15
The kingdom must be prioritized - Matt 6:33-34
The kingdom is not of this world - John 18:36
The kingdom has a King - John 18:37
The kingdom brings order to chaos - Gen 1:1-3;
  Isa 32:1-4
The kingdom glorifies its King - Rom 11:36
The kingdom has subjects - Matt 25:34-40
The kingdom is unshakeable - Heb 12:28
The kingdom operates by covenants - Exod 19:5-6
The mysteries of the kingdom - Matt 13:24-50
Paul proclaimed the kingdom - Acts 28:23, 30-31
The disciples proclaimed the kingdom - Luke 9:1-2
The church possesses the keys to the
  kingdom - Matt 16:18-19
The kingdom covenant of dominion - Gen 1:26-28; Ps 8:3-6

LOVE
God is love - 1 John 4:8
We are to love one another - John 13:34
We are to love God - Deut 6:5
God loves the world - John 3:16
Love exists between the persons of the
    Trinity - John 17:24; 1 John 4:7-14
Love described - 1 Cor 13:1-13
Love your enemies - Matt 5:44
Time to love - Eccl 3:8
Love casts out fear - 1 John 4:18

MEN
A man provides for his family - 1 Tim 5:8
A man loves his wife - Eph 5:25
A man disciplines his children in love - Eph 6:4
A man should be strong and firm in the
    faith - 1 Cor 16:13
Men of exceeding moral character should lead the
    church well - 1 Tim 3:1-10
A man is under divine authority - Exod 34:23-24;
    1 Cor 11:3
Men are to be the foundation of the family
    - Exod 18:19
Men are to lead in prayer - 1 Tim 2:8

MARRIAGE
Marriage should reflect Christ and the
    church - Eph 5:22-33
Marriage was created before the fall - Gen 2:24
Marriage is permanent until death - Matt 19:3-9;
    Rom 7:1-3; 1 Cor 7:39
Marriage does not exist in heaven - Luke 20:34-38
God hates divorce - Mal 2:16
Sexual activity should only happen within
    marriage - Prov 5:15-20
Marriage is between a man and a woman - Gen 2:24
Husbands and wives have unique roles in
    marriage - Eph 5:22-33
Husbands and wives are to be unified in
    prayer - 1 Cor 7:5; 1 Pet 3:7

MERCY
God has mercy on people - Ps 86:15
Mercy is a spiritual virtue - Matt 5:7; Luke 6:36
Jesus's throne dispenses mercy - Heb 4:14
Mercy given can be received - Matt 5:7; Jas 2:13
Mercy should be given to others - Jude 22-23

MONEY
The love of money - Eccl 5:10; 1 Tim 6:10
The worship of money - Matt 6:24
Treasure in heaven - Matt 6:19-21
Money and contentment - 1 Tim 6:6-8
Money and temptation - 1 Tim 6:9
Money and pride - 1 Tim 6:17-19
Danger of greed - Luke 12:13-21
Money and stewardship - Matt 25:14-30; Luke 19:11-27
The power to make wealth - Deut 8:17-18; Isa 48:17
Making friends with money - Luke 16:1-13

Financial sowing and reaping - Luke 6:38; 2 Cor 9:6-10
Slavery of debt - Prov 22:7
Priority of giving - Ps 50:14-15, 23; Prov 3:9-10;
    Luke 6:38; 1 Cor 16:2

PATIENCE
God is patient with us - 2 Pet 3:9
We are to be patient with others - Gal 5:22-23
We are to be patient in times of tribulation
    - Rom 12:12; Jas 5:7-8
Patience is developed through trials - Jas 1:3-4
Joy should accompany patience - Col 1:9-12
God is the source of patience - Rom 15:5
Patience is a fruit of the spirit - Gal 5:22
Patience in ministry - 2 Cor 6:6; 2 Tim 4:2

PEACE
A unique kind of peace comes from God - Phil 4:7
God's kingdom will usher in permanent peace
    between people - Isa 2:4
Peace should exist among Christians - 2 Cor 13:11
Christ is our peace - Eph 2:14
Jesus gives us inner peace - Mat 11:28-30
Peace in the midst of tribulation - John 16:33
The peace of God - Phil 4:6-7
Peace with God - Rom 5:1

PRAYER
Prayer brings the peace of God - Phil 4:6-7
God listens to our prayers - Ps 34:17-18
God answers prayer - Pss 50:15; 91:15; Jer 33:3; Matt 7:7
People should pray together - Acts 2:42
People can pray alone - Dan 6:10
Prayer can be brief and wordless - Neh 2:4-5
Jesus's instructions on prayer - Matt 6:5-15
A person's attitude and relationships affect the
    efficacy of prayer - Jas 4:1-3; 1 Pet 3:7
Power of prayer - Eph 3:14-20; Jas 5:16-18
The seasons for unanswered prayer - Jas 1:5-7; 4:1-5
Praying in faith - Jas 1:5-7; 5:13-15

REPENTANCE
Humility accompanies repentance - 2 Chr 7:14
Repentance and the kingdom - Matt 3:2
Unrepentance brings the wrath of God - Rom 2:4-5
National repentance - Joel 1:14
Baptism of repentance - Mark 1:4
Repentance from dead works - Heb 6:1
All should repent - Acts 17:30

RECONCILIATION
People should be reconciled to God - Rom 5:10;
    2 Cor 5:20
People should be reconciled to each other
    - Matt 5:24
Racial reconciliation - Zeph 3:9; Eph 2:11-22;
    Gal 2:11-20
Global reconciliation - Rev 7:9
Believers have the ministry of reconciliation
    - 2 Cor 5:18-19

RESURRECTION

Resurrection of the body - 1 Cor 15:42-45
Resurrection of Christ - 1 Cor 15:3-4
OT references to the resurrection - Dan 12:2
God is the God of the living - Mark 12:24-27
Jesus will raise the dead - John 5:25-29
Resurrection at the rapture - 1 Thess 4:16
Resurrection at the white throne judgement -
     Rev 20:11-15

SALVATION

Need for salvation - Rom 6:23; Eph 2:1-3
Cure for sin - Rom 7:24-25; 8:1-3
Justification - Rom 3:21-31
Sanctification - Rom 5:9-10; Jas 1:19-21
Glorification - Col 3:4
Regeneration - Titus 3:5
Free gift - Rom 3:24; 6:23
Security - John 10:27-29; Rom 8:31-39
Salvation belongs to the Lord - Ps 3:8
Helmet of salvation - Eph 6:17

SATAN

Satan fell from heaven - Isa 14:12-17; Luke 10:18;
Satan deceived Eve - Gen 3:1-7
The ruler of this world - John 12:31
The deceiver - Rev 12:9
The accuser - Zech 3:1; Rev 12:10
Frustrates the work of God's Word - Mark 4:15
Father of lies - John 8:44
Tempts Jesus - Matt 4:1-11
Hell prepared for - Matt 25:41

SIN

Original sin - Ps 51:5
Separates man from God - Isa 59:2
Harms interpersonal relationships - 1 Cor 6:9-11
Leads to death - Rom 5:12; 6:23
Entered the world at the fall - Rom 5:12
God forgives sin - Eph 4:32
Jesus became sin for us - 2 Cor 5:21
Sin is universal - Ecc 7:20; Rom 3:10-12; 6:23
Confession is the remedy for sin - 1 John 1:9
Christ died for us in our sin - Rom 5:8
Christ died for our sins - 1 Cor 15:3

SPIRITUAL GIFTS

The variety of gifts - Rom 12:4-8; 1 Cor 12:4-11
The sovereign distribution of gifts - 1 Cor 12:11, 18
The servanthood of spiritual gifts - 1 Pet 4:10-11
The purpose of spiritual gifts - Rom 1:11; Eph 4: 8-16
The importance of each spiritual gift - 1 Cor 12:14-31
The unity of spiritual gifts - 1 Cor 12:25-26
The abuse of spiritual gifts - 1 Cor 14:1-40
The motivation behind spiritual gifts - 1 Cor 13:1-13

SPIRITUAL GROWTH

Bearing good fruit - Matt 3:8-10
Seek first the kingdom of God - Matt 6:33
God will complete the work he started in you - Phil 1:6

Fruit of the Spirit - Gal 5:22-23
A theology of spiritual growth - 2 Pet 1:2-11
The role of the Word of God - 2 Tim 2:15
Help others grow in their faith - 2 Tim 4:11-15
God is the source of spiritual growth - 1 Cor 3:7
Grow in grace - 2 Pet 3:18
Grow in the Word - 1 Pet 2:2

SPIRITUAL WARFARE

The armor of God - Eph 6:10-16
God is our protection - Ps 91:1-16
The enemy seeks to destroy us - 1 Pet 5:8
God's Word is powerful - Heb 4:12
God provides a way to escape temptation of the devil
     - 1 Cor 10:13
Jesus has overcome the world - John 16:33
Jesus was tempted and came through victorious -
     Matt 4:1-11
Overcoming the devil - Rev 12:11
The cross defeated the demonic realm - Col 2:15

TRIALS

The purpose of trials - Jas 1:2-4
Trials test our faith - 1 Pet 1:7
The expectation of trials - 1 Pet 4:12
The ministry of trials - 2 Cor 1:3-11
The victory over trials - John 16:33
Entering the kingdom through tribulation - Acts 14:22

TRINITY

God has a triune name - Matt 28:19
Jesus spoke of the other two persons of the Trinity as
     distinct - John 14:26
The Spirit proceeds from the Father and the Son -
     John 15:26; Rom 8:9
All three members of the Godhead were active in
     creating the world - Gen 1:1-2; Col 1:16
God speaks in the first person plural - Gen 1:26; Isa 6:8
Trinitarian formats are used throughout the
     New Testament - 2 Cor 13:13
All three members were involved in Jesus
     baptism - Luke 3:22
Trinitarian construction can be found in the Old
     Testament - Isa 42:1

UNITY

The blessing of unity - Ps 133:1-3
The preservation of unity - Eph 4:3
The condemnation of disunity - 1 Cor 1:10-13
The condemnation of racial disunity - Num 12:1-10;
     Gal 2:11-20
The unity of the body - 1 Cor 12:7-26
The power of unity - Acts 4:24-31
The mindset of unity - Rom 15:5-6; Phil 1:27
The goal of unity - Eph 4:11-16
The prayer for unity - John 17:20-23

WOMEN

First at the resurrection - John 20:11-18
Role in the church - Rom 16:1-2; 1 Tim 3:11; 1 Cor 11:5

Role in marriage - Eph 5:22-33

Jesus ministered to women - Luke 10:38-42;
   John 4:1-38

Importance to the ministry of Jesus - Luke 8:1-3

Provided political and military leadership - Judg 4-5

WORSHIP

Worship is reserved only for God - Luke 4:8

Continuous worship in heaven - Rev 4:1-11

Worship should be continuous on earth - Phil 4:4

Worship glorifies God - Ps 86:9

Creation sings praises to God - Isa 55:12

Worship includes singing - Isa 12:5

Worship includes music and instruments - Ps 150

Our lives should be an act of worship - Rom 12:1

Worship is a community event - Ps 95:1-6; Eph 5:19

Worship is a private event - Eph 5:19

Worship is to be in spirit and truth - John 4:24

The word *doctrine* means "teaching" or "instruction." Applied to the study of the Scriptures, another word for doctrine is "truth," the gathering together in a systematic way of all that God's infallible, inerrant Word says about a given subject.

While the Bible contains all the truth God wants us to know about himself, these teachings are not arranged in an alphabetic, systematic way because the Bible is not a textbook. The challenge is to organize the truths of God's Word in a way that clearly communicates what the Bible teaches on any subject it addresses. This process is called *systematic theology* and is needed because we cannot turn to any one portion of Scripture to find the full biblical revelation on any subject. So it's important to bring together the Bible's teachings on any doctrine so that they can be studied in an orderly way.

This is the purpose of this section, which summarizes the major doctrines of systematic theology. I have dealt with this at length in my Understanding God series (Moody Publishers) and in detail in my book, *Theology You Can Count On* (Moody, 2008).

THEOLOGY PROPER

Virtually all studies on theology begin with this subject, which is so-called because it focuses on God the Father. These truths will help you grasp the greatness of our God. (See the Doctrinal Outlines for more detail.)

1. God is an eternal, transcendent being. God has no beginning or end (Ps 90:1-2). He told Moses, "I AM WHO I AM" (Exod 3:14). God exists prior to, above, and distinct from his creation (Isa 40:18-25). God is distinct in his person (Ps 50:21) and in his thoughts (Isa 55:8-9).

2. God is a spirit being. God in his essence is pure spirit (John 4:23-24a). He is immaterial in that he does not have a body; therefore, God is invisible (John 1:18).

3. God is an immutable being. Immutability means not having the ability to change. God cannot, does not, and will not change (Num 23:19; Mal 3:6), either in his person or in his purposes, although he can and does change in his methods. Therefore, we can trust his promises and eternal love for us (Jer 31:3; Jas 1:17).

4. God is a triune being. The Bible makes it inextricably clear that there is only one true God, and he is one (Deut 6:4; Isa 45:5; 1 Cor 8:4). However, this one God exists in three co-eternal and co-equal—yet distinct—persons: Father, Son, and Holy Spirit. They are unified in their essence, yet each has a different function in the Godhead.

We use the words *Trinity* or *Triune* to speak of the unity of this three-in-one God, although these words themselves do not appear in Scripture. But the truth of the divine Trinity appears throughout the Bible. In Matt 28:18-20, Jesus used the singular "name" of the Father, Son, and Holy Spirit, a strong proof of both the unity and the "threeness" of God.

The Trinitarian nature of God is also demonstrated in that the Father (Gal 1:1, 3; Eph 1:2-3), the Son (John 20:28), and the Holy Spirit (Acts 5:3-4) are each called God.

CHRISTOLOGY

Christology consists of what the Bible teaches about Jesus Christ in his person and work. (See further under "Christology" in the Doctrinal Outlines.) Jesus is unique, the only "one-of-a-kind" Son of God (John 3:16) who is both fully God and man, perfect in both natures without any mixture, division, or confusion.

Jesus made a clear claim to his pre-existence and divine nature as God (John 10:30), a statement his hearers understood so well that they tried to stone him for making himself equal with God (10:33). The prophecy of his birth also included a claim to his eternal existence (Mic 5:2). Isaiah called Jesus Christ "Eternal Father" or "Father of eternity" (Isa 9:6).

Fully divine, Jesus also became a man in his birth, or incarnation. He was born as no other person has been born, because he was born of a virgin (Isa 7:14; 9:6; Matt 1:22-23). The apostle Paul tied these prophecies together in Gal 4:4. Jesus is also unique in his death and resurrection.

PNEUMATOLOGY

The formal name for study of the person and ministry of the Holy Spirit is derived from the Greek word *pneuma*, which means "breath" or "spirit." He is the Third Person of the Trinity, co-equal and co-eternal with the Father and Son. (See the Doctrinal Outlines for more detail.)

The Holy Spirit's unique role is to make the truth of God's Word and the reality of his presence a living experience in the lives of Christians. The Spirit is active on every page of Scripture, from his work in creation (Gen 1:2) to his invitation to salvation and eternity with Jesus in heaven (Rev 22:17).

Two of the Holy Spirit's most important ministries have already been accomplished. He was the

life-giving force in Jesus's virgin birth (Luke 1:35), protecting the Savior from the contamination of human sin inherited through one's father. The Spirit inspired the writers of God's Word so that what was written is infallible, inerrant, and wholly trustworthy, protected from human contamination (1 Pet 1:20-21).

The Holy Spirit's primary roles today include glorifying Christ (John 16:14), indwelling believers for the power to do what God has called us to do (Acts 1:8), and convicting unbelievers of their sin and coming judgment (John 16:7-11).

SOTERIOLOGY

Salvation is the miracle by which a lost person is granted forgiveness and given eternal life through the death and resurrection of Christ. The term *soteriology* comes from the Greek word *sōtēr*, which means "savior."

1. Sin: the need for salvation. The Bible declares that all of us are under the curse and penalty of sin (Rom 3:23; 6:23) because we have failed to measure up to God's demands of perfection. We inherited a sin nature from Adam (Rom 5:12). Our sin debt is so great, we cannot pay it ourselves, which is why the sinless Son of God had to die for our sins on the cross.

2. Justification: the verdict of salvation. The Greek word translated "justify" means to announce a favorable verdict in a courtroom, or to declare righteous. Justification is a judicial act by which God declares righteous those who believe in Jesus Christ. The Bible is clear that justification comes from God alone, for "God is the one who justifies" (Rom 8:33). Every person ever born is lost in sin and needs to be justified through Christ's redemptive sacrifice (Rom 3:23-24). Justification is a gift of God's grace. We have nothing to offer God to make us acceptable to him.

3. Regeneration: the miracle of salvation. Regeneration is the process by which God implants new spiritual life, his very life, in the heart of a sinner who believes on Jesus Christ for salvation. The Bible describes regeneration as a new birth (John 3:1-8), a spiritual resurrection (Rom 6:4-5), and a new creation (2 Cor 5:17). Salvation not only brings such a complete change that we are born again spiritually and raised from the dead, but we are also completely remade people.

4. Security: the assurance of salvation. Our assurance of salvation is bound up in the promise of the gospel and the finished work of Christ (John 5:24; 10:27-30). John built a powerful case for our security (1 John 5:11-13), concluding with this assuring statement: "I have written these things to you who believe in the name of the Son of God so that you may know that you have eternal life" (5:13).

There is certainty in our salvation. Jesus never brought anyone from spiritual death to eternal life only to let that person fall back under God's judgment.

BIBLIOLOGY

This doctrine involves the study of God's Word. The Bible is unique among all other books and so-called sacred writings, because it alone is the very Word of God (Isa 55:10-11).

1. The Bible is truth. God's Word is pure, unadulterated truth (Ps 12:6). God declares that when he speaks, everything he says is true (Isa 45:19). Jesus also affirmed the absolute truth of Scripture (John 17:17).

2. The Bible is authoritative. Christ said that the Bible carries the imprint of his divine authority (Matt 24:35). The authority of God's Word is a settled issue in heaven (Ps 119:89).

3. The Bible is Holy Spirit-inspired: The Spirit inspired the writing of Scripture to protect it from contamination by human ideas or opinions (2 Pet 1:20-21). So it is accurate to say that God himself is the author of the Bible, and the result is pure truth from him.

ECCLESIOLOGY

The doctrine of the church comes from the Greek word *ekklēsia*, which means "assembly" or "called out ones." From this term we can formulate a definition of the church as a special called-out assembly of people, chosen by God to become part of what Paul called both the body and the bride of Christ (1 Cor 12:12-31; Eph 5:22-27, 32). The Bible also makes it clear that the church is God's family (Rom 1:13; 16:1; Heb 2:11). Thus, the church consists of people; it is not merely an organization or a building.

The church is the most important entity on earth in terms of God's program for this age. God has commissioned the church alone to be his representative agency. And the church alone has been granted the authority to bring the realities of God's kingdom program to bear on history since it has been given the keys of the kingdom (i.e., heavenly authority to be utilized on earth, Matt 16:18-19).

Jesus prophesied the coming of the church during a critically important time of teaching with the apostles (Matt 16:13-19). This passage is unmistakably clear that the church is built on Christ, not Peter or any other apostle. Jesus said it is "my church." Both Paul and Peter agreed that Christ alone is the church's "cornerstone" (Eph 2:20; 1 Pet 2:6).

The universal church is made up of all believers from the church's birthday at Pentecost (Acts 2) to the future day when Christ will rapture his church

(1 Thess 4:13-18) from the world. But the universal church is visibly expressed and functions through the many local churches where believers assemble to carry out the mandates Christ gave to his people and live out the principles of the Christian life.

The church is the apex of God's eternal plan for mankind (Eph 3:1-21). It is the means by which God will demonstrate to the angelic realm—including both holy angels and Satan and his demons—his infinite wisdom in choosing weak, lesser creatures like us to manifest his glory and carry out his kingdom program.

ANGELOLOGY

This doctrine deals with angelic beings, both the holy (elect) angels and the evil ones (Satan and his demonic realm). Angels are not eternal but were created by God as part of his original creation (Col 1:16). This verse also teaches the important truth that angels were not created for themselves, but for Christ and for God's divine purposes. Angels were created to give God endless worship around his throne (Ps 148:2). This is important because a heresy that arose in the early church was the worship of angels (Col 2:18). Although angels are far more glorious and powerful than human beings, they were also created to be "ministering spirits" (Heb 1:14) to serve God and his people.

Angels are spirit beings, although they can take on a human appearance in order to accomplish a specific, God-given mission on earth. An example of this is when the angels visited Abraham and destroyed Sodom (Genesis 18–19; see also Heb 13:2). The word *angel* means "messenger," which provides a basic understanding of their ministry. As God's creation, angels also possess intellect, emotion, and will—the fundamental attributes of personhood.

Since angels do not reproduce (Mark 12:25) and do not die, the number of angels God created is the same number of those who exist now. We aren't told their numbers, but they are said to exist in unimaginable numbers (Deut 33:2; Rev 5:11).

The first category of angels are those called holy who stayed true to God and did not follow Satan in his rebellion. Satan, formerly known as Lucifer (Isa 14:12, KJV) or "morning star," heads the second category, the evil angels known as demons. This includes one-third of the angels who followed Lucifer when he tried to usurp God's throne because he wanted to be worshiped as God (Rev 12:4) and build his own demonic kingdom to rival the righteous kingdom of God (Isa 14:13-14; Col 1:13).

Satan's evil character was formed the moment his pride led him to rebel against God and seek to establish his own kingdom (Isa 14:12-15). He was transformed from the most beautiful of all God's creatures into the prince of darkness, kicked out of heaven to earth, falling with the speed of lightning (Luke 10:18).

Lucifer was also given some new names. SATAN means "adversary, opposer." DEVIL means "*accuser*" or "*slanderer.*" He was defeated the moment he challenged God, was defeated again at the cross (Col 2:15), will one day be confined during Christ's millennial reign, and then judged and sent forever to hell (Matt 25:41, Rev 20: 7-10).

In the meantime, Satan and his demons have access to earth to deceive the world and carry out spiritual warfare against believers (Eph 6:10-12). Satan has also been granted temporary access to heaven, to accuse believers before God (Job 1:6; 2:1-2). But Jesus is our defense attorney to counter those accusations with his blood (1 John 2:2).

ESCHATOLOGY

The study of Bible prophecy is so-named because it is derived from a compound of two Greek words meaning "last things." It's astounding to realize that God has chosen to reveal his plan for the future ahead of time—not to satisfy our curiosity or so we can guess at dates for Christ's return, but as a stimulus to holy living (2 Pet 3:1-15). The Scriptures set forth several major events that are yet to come on God's prophetic timetable:

1. *The rapture of the church.* The rapture will be instantaneous and could occur at any moment. It will end the church age as Christ comes in the clouds to take his church home to be with him (1 Thess 4:13-18). This is the "blessed hope" we look forward to as God's people (Titus 2:13). After the rapture, believers will appear before the judgment seat of Christ to receive or lose rewards based on their faithfulness or lack thereof (2 Cor 5:10).

2. *The tribulation.* The joy of the rapture for believers will usher in a time of unprecedented judgment, terror, and suffering on the unbelieving world left behind, as the antichrist and his false prophet take center stage.

Jesus great prophesied the tribulation (Matt 24:4-28), and the book of Revelation (particularly chapters 4–18) chronicles its unfolding. Although this seven-year period will begin peacefully as the antichrist makes a peace treaty with Israel, at the midpoint he will break this treaty and reveal himself in all of his evil. The second half of the tribulation will be a literal "hell on earth" for those who have to endure it.

3. *Christ's second coming and millennial kingdom.* At his triumphant return, Christ will defeat Satan, the antichrist, and all the forces of evil (Rev 19:11-21). He will then bind Satan and establish his glorious one-thousand-year reign on the throne in Jerusalem as Israel's Messiah (Rev 20:1-2).

4. *The great white throne judgment and the eternal state.* The great white throne judgment (Rev 20:11-15)

is the last event before God brings in the eternal state. This is a judgment for those who have rejected Christ. Their eternal doom is announced and carried out. But for believers, our judgment for sin is past and the bliss of our eternal life in heaven is described in Revelation 21–22. We will forever be with the Lord.

Scan this code with your mobile device or follow this link for videos *of Tony Evans providing an overview of theology.*

www.bhpublishinggroup.com/qr/te/67-10

God possesses a number of attributes or essential qualities that are inherent in his essential being. These attributes are eternally held by the Triune God and are true of each member of the Trinity—God the Father, God the Son, and God the Holy Spirit.

Because human beings are uniquely created in God's image (Gen 1:26), we share some of his attributes such as love and anger. These are called God's *communicable* attributes. But God also possesses divine attributes that belong to him alone, known as his *incommunicable* attributes. These include perfections such as his eternality and absolute holiness.

The study below reviews these attributes of God as Father, Son, and Holy Spirit. Because each person of the Trinity displays these attributes, the study below includes verses that speak to all three Persons, rather than separating each member of the Trinity into a separate list.

1. The Transcendence of God: God is before, above, and totally distinct or transcendent from his creation. God is unique, one of a kind. No comparison can be made between God and any portion of his creation because there is nothing or no one to compare him to (Is 6:1; 40:18; 55:8-9).

2. The Infinity of God: God is eternal with no limitations except those imposed by his own nature. He is not bound by the succession of events. Jesus claimed eternality in his dealings with the Jews. The Bible also calls the Holy Spirit "eternal" (Ps 90:2; John 8:56-58; Heb 9:14).

3. The Self–Existence of God: God does not depend on anyone or anything outside of himself for his life. He has the ground of existence in himself. God is independent in his Being and in everything else—his virtues, decrees, and works. He also causes everything in creation to depend on him (Ps 50:12; Jer 10:10-13).

4. The Self-Sufficiency of God: God is totally and absolutely complete within himself. Jesus claimed his self-sufficiency in predicting his death, making it clear that he retained complete control over his life (Ps 23:1-6; John 10:17-18; Acts 17:24-25).

5. The Holiness of God: God's intrinsic and transcendent purity is the standard of righteousness to which the whole universe must conform. God's holiness is the key to understanding everything else about Him; this attribute infiltrates all the other attributes. Jesus is called holy, and the Holy Sprit's very name reveals his divine character (Isa 6:1-3; Luke 1:35; Acts 1:8; 4:27-30; 1 Pet 1:13-19; Rev 4:8).

6. The Sovereignty of God: God rules and controls all of his creation, including human affairs. God sits on the universe's throne as Lord. Everything that happens comes about because he either directly causes it or permits it to occur. Nothing enters into history or could ever exist outside of history that does not come under God's absolute control (Job 23:13; 42:2; Pss 115:3; 135:6; Dan 4:28-37).

7. The Glory of God: God's glory is the visible manifestation of his attributes. The word translated "glory" in the Old Testament means "to be weighted, to be heavy." When we discuss God's glory, we mean someone with an awesome reputation because he has awesome splendor (Exod 33:12-23; Ps 29:3; Luke 2:9; 1 Tim 6:15-16; Rev 21:23).

8. The Omniscience of God: God has intuitive knowledge of all things both actual and potential. This word is a compound of two words: *omni*, which means "all," and *science*, which has to do with knowledge. There is absolutely nothing God doesn't know (Ps 139:1-6; 147:5; Isa 40:13-14; Heb 4:13).

9. The Omnipresence of God: God's complete essence is fully present in all places at all time. There is no place in creation where God does not exist in all his divine fullness. God's presence is in the sphere of immensity and infinitude. *Infinitude* (or infinity) means that which is without limit. *Immensity* refers to that which cannot be contained (1 Kgs 8:26-27; Ps 139:7-12).

10. The Omnipotence of God: God is all-powerful. But his omnipotence involves more than just raw power. Rather, it involves the exercise of his prerogative to use his unlimited power to reflect his divine glory and accomplish his sovereign will. The unlimited power of deity is also ascribed to Jesus and to the Holy Spirit (Pss 62:11; 147:5; Matt 19:26; Rom 1:4; 1 Cor 2:4; Eph 3:8-21).

11. The Wisdom of God: God has the unique ability to so interrelate his attributes that he accomplishes his predetermined purposes by the best means possible. God's ability to use his attributes in perfect wisdom is unique because no one else can accomplish this (Exod 31:1-5; Dan 2:19-20; Rom 11:33; 16:27; Jas 3:13-18).

12. The Goodness of God: This attribute describes the collective perfections of God's nature and benevolence of his acts. God is good by nature and good in what he does. The goodness of God is the standard by which anything called good must be judged. Jesus was also called "good teacher" (Pss 107:1-15; 119:68; Mark 10:17-18; Jas 1:17).

13. The Wrath of God: God's wrath is his necessary, righteous retribution against sin. God's wrath is not an easy subject to consider, but it is as integral to his nature as any of his other perfections. The Bible has more to say about God's wrath than about his love. God's wrath against sin arises by necessity because of the justice of his law and the righteousness of his character. God must judge sin, although he takes no pleasure in punishing the unrighteous (Exod 34:7; Deut 32:41; Ezek 33:11; Rom 5:8-9; 11:22).

14. The Love of God: God's love is his joyful self-determination to reflect the goodness of his will and glory by meeting the needs of mankind. God did not become love after he made the world and mankind. God's love is eternal. In and of himself, God is love. God's love is also inextricably tied to his own glory (John 3:16; Rom 5:8; Eph 1:4-6; 1 John 4:7-21).

15. The Grace of God: Grace is God's inexhaustible supply of goodness that does for mankind what they could never do for themselves. God has supplied every true believer with a magnificent provision of grace. We can't earn it and we don't deserve it, but he has made it abundantly available to all mankind in general (common grace) and to believers in particular. God's endless supply of grace also means that it is sufficient for our every need (2 Cor 9:8; 12:9; Eph 2:1-10; 1 Tim 4:10; Heb 4:16).

16. The Veracity of God: God is always reliable and completely truthful. He cannot lie. The first challenge Satan made against God was to question his truthfulness to Eve (Gen 3:1-5). Jesus Christ and the Holy Spirit are also called true and "the truth" (Num 23:19; Heb 6:16-18; 1 John 4:6; 5:20).

17. The Immutability of God: The immutability of God means he never alters his purposes or changes his nature. Immutability means not having the ability to change. As the eternal Son of God, Jesus also does not change (Mal 3:6; Heb 12:17; 13:8; Jas 1:17).

THE UNIQUENESS OF SCRIPTURE

There is no other book in history that can be compared with the Bible. It is not merely human words about God; it is the very Word of God to humanity. It is in fact the voice of God in print, and as such Scripture is of divine origin and in a class by itself.

The Bible is composed of sixty-six books, divided into two testaments. There are thirty-nine books in the Old Testament and twenty-seven books in the New Testament. The Bible was written over a period of 1,500 years by almost forty different authors who were unified in the central purpose of perfectly communicating the truth of God to humanity so that he could be glorified and his Kingdom advanced. The ultimate uniqueness of Scripture is that it is *alive* and is able to pierce into the deepest depths of a person's life, emotions, and thoughts (Heb 4:12-13) and to transform the lives of those who respond to its message.

THE AUTHORITY OF SCRIPTURE

Many Christians live their lives according to their own set of laws because they do not respect God or acknowledge his rule over every area of their lives. Just as a driver should fear the authority of a police officer (i.e., take the officer seriously) whether they see him or not, Christians show true reverence for God by how they acknowledge his authority. As it turns out, God has infused his authority into the truth of Scripture.

Scripture is authoritative because it is truth (John 17:17). Truth is the absolute standard by which reality is measured. It's God's view on every subject. In Scripture, God has made truth knowable (John 8:32). Since God cannot lie (Heb 6:18) and since his Word is eternally settled in heaven (Ps 119:89), then his Word can be completely trusted (Pss 12:6; 18:30).

Christian doctrine has developed over the centuries but not out of thin air or out of the imaginations of men gone by. These doctrines we hold dear were articulated from Scripture itself. For those of us who take Scripture seriously, we affirm the divine authority of the Bible: *Sola Scriptura*—that is, by Scripture alone.

Since God's nature is perfectly true (1 John 5:20) then his Word is inerrant. Inerrancy means that the original autographs of Scripture are completely true concerning everything about which they speak and were completely recorded without error down to the most minute detail (Matt 5:17-18). Therefore, Scripture is binding on every aspect of our lives (John 10:35).

What can we say, then, about Scripture? It is divine in its authority. It is the absolute final authority for all matters of our lives. We can live under God's perfect rule, trusting that he has given us the governance we need through the pages of Scripture.

THE REVELATION OF SCRIPTURE

Imagine going to a play, sitting while the curtain is closed waiting for the performance, and then watching the curtain open to reveal the scene. If you go to a play, you receive a program in which you can read about that play, but you're waiting for the curtain to open because you want to see it on display. That's revelation.

In theology, revelation refers to the initiative of God to disclose or reveal himself to humanity (Heb 1:1-3) so that we could know what otherwise we would not know or understand. Since he is totally unique and distinct from his creation (Isa 55:10-11), revelation is needed for finite people to understand and properly relate to an infinite God. God has revealed his eternal attributes in general revelation (i.e., nature/creation, Rom 1:19-20), and he has also revealed himself in special revelation through the living Word, Jesus Christ (John 1:1, 14), and the written Word of Scripture.

It is in this special revelation that we find God revealing to humanity his true nature, done primarily through the pages of the Bible (Ps 19:1-6; Rom 1:18-20; 2:14-16; John 1:14-18; Acts 17:24-34). All creation can plainly see *that* he exists, but those who have been illuminated by the Holy Spirit can begin to see *who* he really is.

THE INSPIRATION OF SCRIPTURE

Inspiration refers to the process by which God oversaw the composition of Scripture so that its message was perfectly recorded (2 Tim 3:16) without error through the instrumentality and personalities of human authors. Human authors were perfectly guided by the Holy Spirit in the writing of every word of Scripture (2 Pet 1:19-21). In the same way that the Holy Spirit used humanity's instrumentality in the birth of the living Word (the incarnation) keeping the sin nature of Mary from being

transferred to Jesus, he likewise kept sin and error from being transferred from the human authors in the writing of Scripture.

Hebrews 4:12 tells us that Scripture is the "living and effective" Word from God, one that is able to pierce the very soul and spirit and to discern our thoughts and intentions. In other words, the Bible is no empty collection of stories about people who lived long ago. Rather, in its pages, we encounter the living God, and its words are enlivened by the Spirit of God. When we open the Bible, we are not just opening a book, we are opening ourselves up to the discerning, piercing voice of God that calls forth an active response from us.

By studying inspiration we seek to understand the origin of Scripture, the process of faithfully recording God's revelation about himself, and how these inspired ("living and effective") Scriptures are uniquely authoritative in the life of the believer.

Word of God, ultimately the Lord is the originator, or encoder, of his message, and we are the decoder, the person tasked with understanding the message that is being communicated.

Interpretation refers to meaning—what is the text actually saying. It seeks to understand what the author was saying to the audience to whom he was speaking, and then, relate that meaning to us today. Interpretation is a *science* since words have meaning and language follows certain rules of grammar and composition that can be observed and cataloged.

Interpretation is also an *art* as we seek to understand and match the meaning of words from one language, culture, and context to another. Thus, God wants us to be diligent in our study of his Word so that we will understand what the biblical authors were communicating in their day and how his eternal truth relates to us today (Ezra 7:10; 2 Tim 2:15; 3:16-17).

THE CANONICITY OF SCRIPTURE

We might think that the Holy Scriptures always existed in the perfectly convenient form that we find today, yet the process was more complex than that. The journey through time and culture to compile our Bible has always been a *divine process* in which the Holy Spirit supervised both its writing and development.

Canonicity refers to the principles and processes of recognizing which writings were the inspired books to be included in the Bible. Jesus stated that the whole Old Testament was Scripture (Luke 24:27). He also prophesied that the Holy Spirit would disclose to the apostles the truths that would become New Testament Scripture (John 16:13-15).

While it may seem uncomfortable at first to dissect the manner in which all sixty-six books came to be recognized as God's Word, you will find that the hand of God was present at every turn, guiding this process through the church. The same God who inspired holy men to record every word exactly as he wanted it also oversaw the process by which the books were assembled into the complete and authoritative collection of Scripture.

THE ILLUMINATION OF SCRIPTURE

Illumination refers to the Holy Spirit's work of personally enlightening the human mind to the understanding and application of biblical truth (1 Cor 2:9-16) for the purpose of bringing spiritual conviction to unbelievers (John 16:7-11) and transforming believers into the image of Christ (2 Cor 3:17-18). Through the *process* of illumination, you and I are able not only to grasp the truths of God but to internalize and live out his precepts.

There is a danger in speaking of illumination as a lightbulb moment, such that spiritual insight into the Scriptures may seem like something that is instantaneous. Thomas Edison, the inventor of the lightbulb, famously stated that the genius behind his inventions was "one percent inspiration and ninety-nine percent perspiration." Similarly, there is a process at work that brings the experience of the illumination of God's Word to the heart and mind of the Christian. This process of illumination finds its origin in the Holy Spirit, yet it also involves the responsiveness of the believer. We must be careful, though, not to think that spiritual illumination will come through our study alone. Spiritual insight is also founded on the Holy Spirit working within us.

THE INTERPRETATION OF SCRIPTURE

Perhaps you have heard the popular phrase, "Something got lost in translation." When people use that phrase, what they mean is that what someone says isn't always understood by the one who receives the message. If this is true with people who speak the same language in the same society, then you can only imagine the complexities in communication that can occur when we study a more complex subject matter such as the Holy Scriptures. With the

THE SUFFICIENCY OF SCRIPTURE

Sufficiency refers to the comprehensive nature of Scripture in its ability to address every area of life. It is therefore the standard by which all of life is understood and evaluated. Scripture also possesses the power to address what it proclaims (Isa 55:11) both in creation (Ps 33:6) and in every aspect of our daily lives (Ps 19:7-14).

Paul writes in 2 Tim 3:16-17, "All Scripture is inspired by God and is profitable for teaching, for rebuking, for correcting, for training in righteousness, so that the man of God may be complete, equipped for every good work." That means we do not need to rely on extra knowledge, wisdom, or insight to do what God wants us to do. We have been fully equipped for living abundantly in his kingdom based on the truth he has provided in the pages of the Bible.

NAMES OF GOD

Elohim-God (Gen 1:1)
– The strong creator
Jehovah-LORD (Gen 2:4)
– The self-existing One
Adonai-LORD /Master (Gen 15:2)
– The Headship Name

THE COMPOUND NAMES OF THE LORD GOD
"Jehovah El and Jehovah Elohim"
Jehovah El Elohim (Josh 22:22)
– The LORD God of Gods
Jehovah Elohim (Gen 2:4; 3:9-13, 21)
– The LORD God
Jehovah Elohe Abothekem (Josh 18:3)
– The LORD God of Your Fathers
Jehovah El Elyon (Gen 14:22)
– The LORD, the Most High God
Jehovah El Emeth (Ps 31:5)
– LORD God of Truth
Jehovah El Gemuwal (Jer 51:56)
– The LORD God of Recompenses
Jehovah Elohim Tsebaoth (Ps 59:5; Isa 28:22)
– LORD God of Hosts
Jehovah Elohe Yeshuathi (Ps 88:1)
– LORD God of My Salvation
Jehovah Elohe Yisrael (Ps 41:13)
– The LORD God of Israel

THE COMPOUND NAMES OF GOD
"El, Elohim, and Elohe"
Elohim (Gen 1:1)
– God
Elohim Bashamayim (Josh 2:11)
– God in Heaven
El Bethel (Gen 35:7)
– God of the House of God
Elohe Chaseddi (Ps 59:10)
– The God of My Mercy
Elohe Yisrael (Gen 33:20)
– God, the God of Israel
El Elyon (Gen 14:18; Ps 78:56; Dan 3:26)
– The Most High God
El Emunah (Deut 7:9)
– The Faithful God
El Gibbor (Isa 9:6)
– Mighty God
El Hakabodh (Ps 29:3)
– The God of Glory
El Hay (Josh 3:10; Jer 23:36; Dan 3:26)
– The Living God
El Hayyay (Ps 42:8)
– God of My Life
Elohim Kedoshim (Josh 24:19)
– Holy God

El Kanna (Exod 20:5)
– Jealous God
El Kanno (Josh 24:19)
– Jealous God
Elohe Mauzi (Ps 43:2)
– God of My Strength
Elohim Machase Lanu (Ps 62:8)
– God Our Refuge
Eli Maelekhi (Ps 68:24)
– God My King
El Marom (Mic 6:6)
– God Most High
El Nekamoth (Ps 18:47)
– God that Avengeth
El Nose (Ps 99:8)
– God that Forgave
Elohenu Olam (Ps 48:14)
– Our Everlasting God
Elohim Ozer Li (Ps 54:4)
– God My Helper
El Rai (Gen 16:13)
– God Seest Me
Elsali (Ps 42:9)
– God, My Rock
El Shaddai (Gen 17:1,2; Ezek 10:5)
– Almighty God
Elohim Shophtim Ba-arets (Ps 58:11)
– God that Judgeth in the Earth
El Simchath Gili (Ps 43:4)
– God My Exceeding Joy
Elohim Tsebaoth (Ps 80:7; Jer 35:17; 38:17)
– God of Hosts
Elohe Tishuathi (Ps 18:46; 51:14)
– God of My Salvation
Elohe Tsadeki (Ps 4:1)
– God of My Righteousness
Elohe Yakob (Ps 20:1)
– God of Israel
Elohe Yisrael (Ps 59:5)
– God of Israel

THE COMPOUND NAMES OF JEHOVAH
Jehovah (Exod 6:2,3)
– The LORD
Adonai Jehovah (Gen 15:2)
– Lord God
Jehovah Adon Kol Ha-arets (Josh 3:11)
– The LORD, the Lord of All the Earth
Jehovah Bore (Isa 40:28)
– The LORD Creator
Jehovah Chereb (Deut 33:29)
– The LORD . . . the Sword
Jehovah Eli (Ps 18:2)
– The LORD My God
Jehovah Elyon (Gen 14:18-20)

– The Lord Most High
Jehovah Gibbor Milchamah (Ps 24:8)
– The Lord Mighty In Battle
Jehovah Maginnenu (Ps 89:18)
– The Lord Our Defense
Jehovah Goelekh (Isa 49:26; 60:16)
– The Lord Thy Redeemer
Jehovah Hashopet (Judg 11:27)
– The Lord the Judge
Jehovah Hoshiah (Ps 20:9)
– O Lord Save
Jehovah Immeka (Judg 6:12)
– The Lord Is with You
Jehovah Izuz Wegibbor (Ps 24:8)
– The Lord Strong and Mighty
Jehovah-jireth (Gen 22:14)
– The Lord Shall Provide
Jehovah Kabodhi (Ps 3:3)
– The Lord My God
Jehovah Kanna Shemo (Exod 34:14)
– The Lord Whose Name Is Jealous
Jehovah Keren-Yishi (Ps 18:2)
– The Lord the Horn of My Salvation
Jehovah Machsi (Ps 91:9)
– The Lord My Refuge
Jehovah Magen (Deut 33:29)
– The Lord the Shield
Jehovah Makkeh (Ezek 7:9)
– The Lord that Smiteth
Jehovah Mauzzam (Ps 37:39)
– The Lord Their Strength
Jehovah Mauzzi (Jer 16:19)
– The Lord My Fortress
Ha-Melech Jehovah (Ps 98:6)
– The Lord the King
Jehovah Melech Olam (Ps 10:16)
– The Lord King Forever
Jehovah Mephalti (Ps 18:2)
– The Lord My Deliverer
Jehovah Mekaddishkem (Exod 31:13)
– The Lord that Sanctifies You
Jehovah Metsudhathi (Ps 18:2)
– The Lord My High Tower
Jehovah-Moshiekh (Isa 49:26; 60:16)
– The Lord Your Savior
Jehovah Nissi (Exod 17:15)
– The Lord My Banner
Jehovah Ori (Ps 27:1)
– The Lord My Light
Jehovah Uzzi (Ps 28:7)
– The Lord My Strength
Jehovah Rophe (Exod 15:26)
– The Lord (our) Healer
Jehovah Roi (Ps 23:1)
– The Lord My Shepherd
Jehovah Sabaoth (Tsebaoth) (1 Sam 1:3)
– The Lord of Hosts
Jehovah Sali (Ps 18:2)
– The Lord My Rock
Jehovah Shalom (Judg 6:24)

– The Lord (our) Peace
Jehovah Shammah (Ezek 48:35)
– The Lord Is There
Jehovah Tsidkenu (Jer 23:6)
– The Lord Our Righteousness
Jehovah Tsuri (Ps 19:14)
– O Lord My Strength

NAMES OF JESUS

Alpha and Omega (Rev 22:13)
Advocate (1 John 2:1)
Anointed One (Luke 4:18)
Apostle and High Priest (Heb 3:1)
Author and Finisher of Our Faith (Heb 12:2)
Authority (Matt 28:18)
Bread of Life (John 6:35)
Beloved (Matt 3:17)
Bridegroom (Matt 9:15)
Chief Cornerstone (Ps 118:22)
Christ (John 11:27)
Christ the Lord (Luke 2:11)
Chosen One (Luke 9:35)
Deliverer (1 Thess 1:10)
Door (John 10:9)
Everlasting Father (Isa 9:6)
Faithful and True (Rev 19:11)
Freedom Maker (John 8:36)
Good Shepherd (John 10:11)
Great High Priest (Heb 4:14)
Head of the Church Body (Eph 1:22)
Helper (John 14:16)
Hope (1 Tim 1:1)
Servant (Acts 4:29-30)
I Am (John 8:58)
Immanuel (Isa 7:14)
Gift from God (2 Cor 9:15)
Jesus of Nazareth (Acts 10:38)
Judge (Acts 10:42)
King of the Jews (Matt 27:37)
King of Kings (Rev 17:14)
Last Adam (1 Cor 15:45)
Lamb of God (John 1:29)
Light of the World (John 8:12)
Lion of the Tribe of Judah (Rev 5:5)
Lord of All (Phil 2:9-11)
Master (Luke 5:5)
Mediator (1 Tim 2:5)
Messiah (John 1:41)
Mighty God (Isa 9:6)
Mighty One (Isa 60:16)
Morning Star (Rev 22:16)
Prince of Peace (Isa 9:6)
Peace (Eph 2:14)
Prophet (Mark 6:4)
Rabbi (John 3:26)
Redeemer (Job 19:25)
Resurrection and the Life (John 11:25)
Risen Lord (1 Cor 15:3-4)
Rock (1 Cor 10:4)
Sacrifice for Our Sins (1 John 4:10)

Savior (John 4:42)
Son of David (Matt 9:27)
Son of God (Matt 14:33)
Son of Man (Mark 9:31)
Son of the Most High (Luke 1:32)
Supreme Creator (1 Cor 1:16-17)
The Almighty (Rev 1:8)
Way (John 14:6)
Word of Life (John 1:1)
Word of God (Rev 19:13)
True Vine (John 15:1)
Truth (John 8:32)
Victorious One (Rev 3:21)
Wonderful Counselor (Isa 9:6)

NAMES OF THE HOLY SPIRIT

Ruah qadesow – Holy Spirit (Is 63:10)
Ruah qadse a – Holy Spirit (Ps 51:11)
Ruah Elohim – Spirit of God (Gen 1:2)
Nismat Ruah hayyim – The Breath of the Spirit of Life (Gen 7:22)
Ruah YHWH – Spirit of YHWH (Isa 11:2)
Ruach hakmah ubinah – Spirit of Wisdom (Isa 11:2)
Ruah esah ugeburah – Spirit of Counsel and Might (Isa 11:2)
Ruah daat weyirat YHWH – Spirit of Understanding and Fear of YHWH (Isa 11:2)
Pneumatos Hagiou – Holy Spirit (Matt 1:18)
Pneumati Theou – Spirit of God (Matt 12:28)
Ho Paraclētos – The Intercessor (John 16:7)
Pneuma tēs Alētheias – Spirit of Truth (John 16:13)
Pneuma – Spirit (John 3:8)
Pneumatos – Spirit (John 3:8)
Breath of the Almighty (Job 33:4)

Comforter (John 14:16)
Eternal Spirit (Heb 9:14)
Free Spirit (Ps 51:12)
God (Acts 5:3)
Good Spirit (Neh 9:20)
His Spirit (Eph 2:22)
Lord (2 Thess 3:5)
My Spirit (Gen 6:3)
Power of the Highest (Luke 1:35)
Spirit (Matt 4:1)
Spirit of the Lord God (Isa 61:1)
Spirit of the Lord (Isa 11:2)
Spirit of God (1 Cor 2:11)
Spirit of the Father (Matt 10:20)
Spirit of Christ (Rom 8:9)
Spirit of the Son (Gal 4:6)
Spirit of life (Rom 8:2)
Spirit of grace (Zech 12:10)
Spirit of prophecy (Rev 19:10)
Spirit of adoption (Rom 8:15)
Spirit of wisdom (Isa 11:2)
Spirit of counsel (Isa 11:2)
Spirit of might (Isa 11:2)
Spirit of understanding (Isa 11:2)
Spirit of knowledge (Isa 11:2)
Spirit of the fear of the Lord (Isa 11:2)
Spirit of truth (John 14:17)
Spirit of holiness (Rom 1:4)
Spirit of revelation (Eph 1:17)
Spirit of judgment (Isa 28:6)
Spirit of burning (Isa 4:4)
Spirit of glory (1 Pet 4:14)
Seven Spirits of God (Rev 1:4)

DOCTRINAL OUTLINES OF GOD, JESUS, AND THE HOLY SPIRIT

The most important study one can embark on is the study of God. The Lord says through the prophet Jeremiah, "The wise person should not boast in his wisdom; the strong should not boast in his strength; the wealthy should not boast in his wealth. But the one who boasts should boast in this: that he understands and knows me—that I am the Lord, showing faithful love, justice, and righteousness on the earth, for I delight in these things" (Jer 9:23-24). To grow in experiential knowledge of God should be the primary pursuit of every believer since this knowledge affects all of life in time and for eternity.

I. THE KNOWLEDGE OF GOD

A. **The Concept of Knowing God**
   I. It involves the acquisition of accurate facts about God (John 17:17; 2 Tim 3:16-17)
   II. It involves a saving encounter with God (John 3:3; 1 John 5:20)
   III. It involves an ongoing intimacy with God (2 Pet 1:5-8; 3:18)
   IV. It involves personal experiences with God (Jas 1:2-5; 1 Pet 1:6-7; 5:10)

B. **The Possibility of Knowing God**
   I. God commands us to know Him (Jer. 9:23-24)
   II. God desires to be known intimately (Exod 33:11; Ps 25:14)
   III. God has prescribed a way to know him (Acts 2:40-47)
   – Worship
   – Fellowship
   – Education
   – Outreach
   IV. God has limitations on what can be known about him (Isa 40:12-14; 45:15; Deut 29:29)
   V. God has given believers the Holy Spirit to reveal the things of God (John 16:13-15; 1 Cor 2:10)

C. **The Importance of Knowing God**
   I. It is the only way a person can escape judgment and enter into eternal life (John 17:3)
   II. It is the only way a person can truly know themselves (Isa 6:5)
   III. It is the best way of having an accurate knowledge of the world (Rom 1:20; Col 1:15-17)
   IV. It is essential for personal holiness (Jer 9:23-24)
   V. It enables people to be strong as they face the challenges of life (Dan 11:32)
   VI. It generates the true worship of God (Rom 11:33-36)

II. THE REVELATION OF GOD

A. **Naturalistic Arguments for God's Existence**
   I. Argument of Cause-Effect (Cosmological): For every effect there must be a cause. Thus, there must be a powerful cause for the existence of the universe. This argument does not prove that the cause is the Christian's God, but it does prove that the cause is powerful.
   II. Argument of Purpose (Teleological): There is definite order and design in the universe (seasons, earth rotating on axis, planets revolving around the sun, etc.). Thus, the first cause must be intelligent (just as a watch proves there must exist a watchmaker).
   III. Argument from the nature of man (Anthropological): Man's conscience, moral nature (sense of right and wrong), intelligence, and mental capacities have to be accounted for. His Creator must thus bear these same qualities of personhood. Personal existence must have a personal source.
   IV. Argument from the idea of God (Ontological): Man has the idea of a most perfect being (where did that idea come from given the imperfections of man and the universe). Since a most perfect being who does not exist is not as perfect as one who does exist, there must be a God.

B. **Biblical Arguments for God's Existence**
   I. General revelation (that which is universally available in creation to all mankind)
   – Creation reveals God's glory and power (Ps 19:1)
   – Creation reveals God's supremacy and divine nature (Rom 1:20)
   – Creation reveals God's providential control of nature (Acts 14:17)

– Creation reveals God's
goodness (Matt 5:45)
– Creation reveals God's
intelligence (Acts 17:24-29)
– Creation reveals God's
existence (Acts 17:24-28)
– Man's conscience universally affirms
the existence of God (Rom 1:19)

II. Special revelation (that which is
limited to Jesus Christ and the Bible)
– Jesus Christ is the supreme and final
revelation of God to man (Heb 1:1-2)
– Jesus Christ "exegetes" (explains)
the person of God (John 1:18)
– Jesus Christ reveals the
glory of God (John 1:14)
– Jesus Christ reveals the power
and wisdom of God (1 Cor 1:24)
– Jesus Christ reveals the
grace of God (Titus 2:11)
– Jesus Christ reveals the
love of God (Rom 5:8)
– The Bible assumes and does not
seek to prove the existence of
God (Gen 1:1; Ps 14:1; Heb 11:6)
– The Bible is the inerrant revelation
of God (2 Tim 3:16-17)

III. THE TRIUNITY OF GOD

A. **The Definition of the Trinity**: Trinity is a
theological term (not a biblical one) used to
describe the biblical teaching of the nature
of God. There is one God who exists in three
co-equal persons who are one in essence yet
distinct in personality. Thus, God is three in one.

B. **The Delineation of the Trinity**
I. There is only one true God (Deut
6:4; Isa 44:6; John 17:3; 1 Cor 8:4)

II. There is plurality in God (Gen
1:26-27; Isa 48:16; 63:7-10)
– The Father is recognized as
God (John 6:27; 1 Pet 1:2)
– Jesus Christ is recognized as God
(John 1:1, 14, 18; Titus 2:13; Heb 1:8)
– The Holy Spirit is recognized as
God (Acts 5:3-4; 1 Cor 3:16)

III. These three are distinct persons.
– The Father and the Son are distinct
persons (John 5:20, 32, 37; 17:5)
– The Father and the Son are distinct
from the Spirit (John 14:16; 15:26)

IV. These three are unified (Matt
28:19; 3:12-16; 2 Cor 13:13)

C. **The Work of the Trinity**
I. The Trinity works together to
provide salvation (John 6:63;
1 Cor 6:19-21; Eph 1:7-9)
II. The Trinity works together in the revelation
of God's truth (John 1:17-18; 16:13)
III. The Trinity works together in prayer
(John 14:14; Eph. 1:6; 2:18; 6:18)
IV. The Trinity works together in
creation (Gen 1:1-3,26; Col 1:16)
V. The Trinity works together in
confirmation (Matt 3:16-17)

D. **The Praise of the Trinity**
I. The Father glorifies the Son
(John 6:37-40; Eph 1:4)
II. The Son honors the Father
(John 5:19, 30-31; 12, 28)
III. The Spirit honors the Son
(John 15:26; 16:8-10,14)

E. **The Essence of the Trinity**: All three
members of the trinity possess the attributes or perfection of deity.

Jesus Christ is unique in history; he is fully God and fully man. His deity is from all eternity because he is the Son of God. But he also chose to leave heaven and come to earth as a man to save us and establish God's promised kingdom on earth. Jesus partook of human nature in his earthly ministry as the "Son of Man." This was Jesus's favorite title for himself during his ministry. At his birth, his incarnation, Jesus became flesh and blood, fully identifying with humanity, without relinquishing his divine attributes.

I. THE PERSON OF JESUS CHRIST

A. Christ's Pre-Existence as the Eternal Son of God

I. Jesus is the Second Person of the Trinity, co-eternal and co-equal with God the Father and the Holy Spirit (John 1:1-2; 8:58; Heb 1:2-4)

II. Jesus clearly claimed to be God when he declared, "I and the Father are one" (John 10:30 see also John 5:17-18)

III. Jesus is also the co-Creator with God the Father (John 1:3, Col 1:16-17)

IV. Jesus made pre-incarnate appearances in the Old Testament (Gen 18:1-3; Josh 5:13-15; Judg 13:3, 9-8)

V. The prophet Micah declared that Jesus has no beginning; his existence reaches into eternity past (Mic 5:2)

VI. Jesus is also designated "Eternal Father" (Isa 9:6) or "Father of eternity"

B. Christ's Incarnation as the Unique God/Man

I. Jesus was born in Bethlehem to the virgin Mary, fulfilling biblical prophecy (Isa 7:14; Matt 1:22-23; Luke 1:26-35)

II. Jesus's was born without sin because he was conceived by the Holy Spirit, avoiding the contamination of sin through a human father (Luke 1:35; 3:23; Rom 5:12)

III. Jesus took on human flesh with its frailties and limitations, except for sin (John 1:14)

IV. Jesus experienced the range of human emotions, further proof that his incarnation was not merely a mirage; he did not simply appear to be a man. He became tired and thirsty (John 4:6-7); he wept at the grave of Lazarus; he felt compassion for people (Matt 9:36); he experienced exultant joy (Luke 10:21)

II. THE WORK OF JESUS CHRIST

A. His Ministry on Earth

I. Jesus preached the gospel and called people to repentance (Matt 4:17; Luke 4:18, 43-44; 13:1-6)

II. Jesus called the twelve apostles to himself, then trained and commissioned them for ministry (Matt 10:1-4; Luke 5:1-11; John 1:35-51)

III. Jesus died on the cross as the atonement for our sins (John 19:17-30; Rom 5:6-8; 1 Cor 15:3)

IV. Jesus was buried in Joseph's tomb, and his body was guarded by Roman soldiers, proving that he died (Matt 27:57-66; 1 Cor 15:4)

V. Jesus rose bodily on the third day, triumphing over the devil, sin, and the grave (John 20:1-9; 1 Cor 15:4, 55-57; Col 2:15; Heb 2:14; 1 John 3:8)

VI. The risen Christ appeared to hundreds of people (Matt 28:16-20; Luke 24:13-43; John 20:10-18; 1 Cor 15:5-8)

VII. Christ ascended back to the Father's right hand in heaven (John 20:17; Acts 1:11; Eph 4:8-10)

B. His Present Ministry in Heaven and Future Return

I. Christ is in heaven today fulfilling his ministry as our great high priest, interceding with God for believers (Heb 4:14-16; 7:25; 1 John 2:2)

II. Christ will come in the clouds *for* his saints at the rapture, and return to the earth in power and glory *with* his saints to judge the earth and assume his millennial kingdom throne (1 Thess 4:13-18; Rev 19:11—20:4).

C. The Importance of Knowing Christ

I. The knowledge of Christ begins with the acquisition of accurate facts about him (Matt 16:13-17; John 17:3, 6-8)

II. It continues as the Holy Spirit convicts of sin and the need for salvation (John 3:3, 7; 16:8-11)

III. It brings the sinner to a saving encounter with Christ by faith (Acts 9:1-19; 16:30-31)

IV. It grows as the believer becomes conformed to the image of Christ through a life of holiness, fellowship with Christ, and obedience to Christ (John 14:15, 23; 1 Cor 1:9; 2 Cor 3:17-18; 1 Pet 1:15-16; 2 Pet 1:5-8; 3:18; 1 John 1:3b)

v. It will continue at the rapture of the church when believers see Christ face-to-face (1 Thess 4:13-18: 1 John 3:2)

vi. It will culminate in Jesus's kingdom rule with his saints (Rom 8:17; Rev 19:11-6)

PNEUMATOLOGY

The Holy Spirit is not merely an addendum to the Christian faith. He is at the heart and core of it. He is not merely a force or an influence but rather the third Person of the Trinity to whom we must personally relate. Therefore, if we are going to live the victorious Christian life, it is critical that we understand the person and ministry of the Holy Spirit.

I. THE PERSON OF THE HOLY SPIRIT

A. **The Holy Spirit's eternality as the Third Person of the Triune God**
   I. The Holy Spirit is co-eternal and co-equal with God the Father and Jesus Christ (Matt 28:19; Acts 5:1-9; 2 Cor 13:14)
   II. The Holy Spirit is thus a person, not merely a force or influence. He displays intellect, emotion, and will—the fundamental attributes of personhood (Rom 8:27; 1 Cor 2:10-13; 12:11; Eph 4:30)

B. **The Bible's Proof of the Holy Spirit's Deity and Personhood**
   I. Jesus used personal pronouns for the Holy Spirit (John 15:26; 16:13)
   II. The Spirit refers to himself in the first person and can speak his thoughts to others, which only a person can do (Acts 13:2)
   III. The Holy Spirit expresses emotions (Eph 4:30)

II. THE WORK OF THE HOLY SPIRIT

A. **His Ministry in the Old Testament (before the Incarnation of Christ)**
   I. The Holy Spirit was the active agent in creation (Gen 1:2)

II. The Spirit came upon believers at specific (limited) times for specific tasks, but did not permanently indwell them (Exod 31:1-11; 35:30-31; Num 11:16-17, 25-26; Judg 3:10; 6:34; 11:29; 13:25; 14:6, 19; 15:14)

III. The Spirit inspired the authors of the Old Testament to record God's Word without error (2 Pet 1:19-21)

B. **His Ministry in the New Testament**
   I. The Holy Spirit was the active agent in Christ's virgin birth, his incarnation (Matt 1:18; Luke 1:26-35)
   II. The Spirit came in answer to Jesus's promise to give birth to the church on the day of Pentecost (John 14:16-17; 15:26; Acts 1:8; 2:1-4)
   III. The Spirit is the active Agent in the salvation of every believer (John 3:5-8)
   IV. Beginning at Pentecost, the Spirit baptizes every believer into the church, the body of Christ (1 Cor 12:13)
   V. The Spirit permanently indwells every believer in the church age (John 14:16-17; Rom 8:9-11)
   VI. The Spirit is the divine teacher of God's Word as the Spirit of truth (John 14:26; 16:12-13, 15; 1 Cor 2:10-13)
   VII. The Spirit empowers Christians for service, equips them with his sovereignly given gifts, and sends them out in ministry (Acts 13:1-2; Rom 15:13; 1 Cor 12:1-11; 2 Cor 3:6)
   VIII. The Spirit is sent to glorify Christ (John 16:14)
   IX. The Spirit convicts the world of sin, righteousness, and judgment (John 16:7-11)
   X. The Spirit inspired the authors of the New Testament to record God's Word without error (2 Pet 1:19-21)

Spiritual growth is offered to every true believer, resulting in an ever-increasing experience of the abundant life Christ died to supply (John 10:10). Yet while it is offered, it is not automatic. Spiritual growth requires your participation for it to take place.

Spiritual growth may be defined as that transformational process by which we allow the indwelling Christ to increasingly express himself in and through us. This, then, enables us to bring God greater glory as we also experience more of his power and presence in our own lives. As you mature spiritually, you gain access to the kingdom benefits that result from living as a fully committed kingdom disciple.

The process of spiritual growth occurs through feeding the seed you were supplied by the Holy Spirit at the moment of your conversion so that you may, as Peter wrote, "grow up into your salvation" (Eph 4:15; 1 Pet 2:2; 2 Pet 1:2-11; 3:18). In so doing, you progressively learn to let Christ live his life through you, as you abide with him in an intimate relationship (John 15:5; Gal 2:20.)

Information about the Christian faith is critical, because our faith has specific content. But it is also critical that this information gets connected to the living reality of Jesus Christ if you are going to experience spiritual growth. God will transform you as you make him your focus, thus reflecting his glory and becoming more like him (Rom 8:29; 2 Cor 3:17-18).

THE ESSENTIALS OF SPIRITUAL GROWTH

1. Conversion: The Foundation of Spiritual Growth. Conversion, or salvation, is the process whereby God deposits within every believer a new nature that is from him and is, therefore, perfect. When you receive Christ, everything becomes new at the core of your being, giving you the disposition and the capacity to know and serve God rather than serving sin and self.

God's will for a believer is spiritual growth, to the end that what is on the inside becomes visible on the outside. God often applies the heat and the pressure to bring about this release. That's why our greatest times of spiritual growth are almost always our times of greatest trial. Lasting spiritual growth comes about through internal transformation, not just external reformation. Paul wrote, "I say then, walk by the Spirit and you will certainly not carry out the desire of the flesh" (Gal 5:16).

We think that if we can just stop fulfilling the lust of the flesh, then we can begin walking in the Spirit. But it's just the opposite. The Holy Spirit working on the inside produces spiritual victory on the outside. All that we need to walk in victory and grow in Christ is already present within us (2 Pet 1:3).

2. Identity: The Key to Spiritual Growth. The moment you placed your faith in Christ alone for salvation, God implanted a new nature deep within your being. This new nature, also called the new birth, is the reference point for your identity. But when God gave you this new nature, through which you are now alive spiritually, he also put to death your old nature. This death occurred on the cross of Jesus Christ, when he died for the sins of the world. This is why your identity as a Christian begins at the cross.

The truth of this is expressed so clearly in Gal 2:20, which contains all we need to know about our identity as believers in one power-packed capsule. If you can absorb and apply the truth of this verse, you are well on your way to growing spiritually, because your identity is the key to your spiritual development.

Our old self is dead and gone, crucified with Christ on the cross and buried with him when he was buried in the tomb (Rom 6:4). Since that's true, we had better be looking for our identity somewhere else. A key step in spiritual growth and our identity with Christ is coming to grips with the fact of our death to sin and the old life.

3. Sin: The Hindrance to Spiritual Growth. Sin's impact on our lives is not by accident, since we have three formidable enemies arrayed against us. These include the world (an evil system, 1 John 5:19), the flesh (our evil desires, Rom 7:14-15), and the devil (an evil spiritual being, Rev 12:9). They join forces in a well-planned campaign to use sin to block our spiritual development.

But we are not alone, because Jesus has overcome the world (John 16:33; 1 John 4:4), God has given us victory over our evil desires (Rom 7:25), and he has stripped the devil of his power through Jesus's death on the cross (Heb 2:14). That's why it's so important that you grow in Christ. The more you grow spiritually, the more the Spirit dominates the flesh rather than the flesh defeating us and thwarting the Spirit's work in your life. When we confess our sins to God, we have the tremendous promise of his forgiveness and cleansing (1 John 1:9).

4. Grace: The Environment of Spiritual Growth. A failure to understand and grow in grace (i.e., God's unmerited favor) inevitably results in faulty

development and stunted spiritual growth. Christians who do not learn to function under grace are underdeveloped saints. This failure is the single greatest cause of spiritual regression.

Read Eph 2:4-5 and notice especially the last sentence: "You are saved by grace!" This is the key. Do you understand that if you know Christ as your Savior, you are saved not because of your decision or anything else you did, but because God took the initiative to reach down and save you by grace? Salvation is God's work from beginning to end. Similarly, it is by grace that you need to live the Christian life after you are saved (2 Pet 3:18). God's promise of abundant grace is found in 2 Cor 9:8, a verse you ought to memorize if you haven't already done so.

5. Faith: The Action of Spiritual Growth. Faith is so important to our spiritual growth because it is the mechanism God has given us whereby we can tap into the spiritual realm that is above and beyond the world of our five senses. Living by faith is so crucial that spiritual growth is impossible without it, because the absence of faith means we are displeasing rather than pleasing to God (Heb 11:6).

In other words, faith and spiritual growth are inextricably woven together. A life of faithfulness to God demands that we live by faith, just as we were saved by faith. Biblical faith is a settled confidence in the person and the promises of God as revealed in his Word. Faith trusts in the integrity of God because it believes that God has told the truth about unseen realities. Faith also transports us to a supernatural realm that transcends our senses—a truth Paul prayed we would grasp (Eph 3:14-21). Practically speaking, faith is acting like God is telling the truth.

6. The Holy Spirit: The Enabler for Spiritual Growth. Only as we are empowered by the indwelling Holy Spirit will we produce what our lives are supposed to produce. The Holy Spirit is God's supernatural gift to make experiential, alive, and real the new beings we have become. The Spirit is the heart and soul of a growing, flourishing Christian life, and if we don't get plugged in to him, we will continue to stagnate and remain stunted in our spiritual development. The Spirit is the most active member of the Godhead when it comes to the matter of spiritual growth.

The issue for believers is not how much of the Spirit we have, but how much he has of us. Ephesians 5:14-17 tell us that it is possible to be a Christian, and yet be asleep spiritually as well as unwise and foolish. This is why Paul issued the familiar command of Scripture: "Don't get drunk with wine, which leads to reckless living, but be filled by the Spirit" (Eph 5:18). We are to live our lives from a spiritual perspective (Rom 8:1-13; Gal 5:16-18).

7. Scripture: The Food of Spiritual Growth. In refuting the devil's temptation, Christ explicitly stated the connection between spiritual health and the Word of God (Matt 4:4). Given the essential part the Word plays in our spiritual growth, it is unfortunate today that the Bible has been reduced to a menu to be studied rather than a nourishing meal to be enjoyed and consumed.

When learning the Scriptures becomes merely an academic exercise, we can actually increase in biblical knowledge while regressing in spiritual understanding. Jesus told the people of his day that while they were diligent to search the Scriptures, their study didn't do them any good because it did not lead them to believe in him (John 5:39-40).

We need to be absolutely clear that the Bible is the inspired, inerrant revelation of God (Isa 55:8-9; Matt 5:17-18; 2 Tim 3:16). But its purpose is not just to give us information for our heads, but food for the new nature to feed upon so that spiritual growth can be maximized (1 Pet 2:2). What milk is to a baby's body, the Word of God is to the soul. It is the food that fuels healthy spiritual growth.

8. Prayer: The Access of Spiritual Growth. Prayer is that which causes all the parts of the Christian life to relate properly to one another, because prayer is the primary means by which we relate to and communicate with God (Matt 6:5-7).

God has made us in such a way that the power of the Holy Spirit flows along the wires of prayer, which makes prayer absolutely vital to our spiritual growth. Prayer is so important that the Bible tells us, "Pray constantly" (1 Thess 5:17). The Holy Spirit understands prayers that we can't express adequately, and makes sense of thoughts that we don't even understand ourselves, because he knows the language of prayer and can interpret it for us (Rom 8:26).

We need to pray constantly because prayer is the link between the physical and the spiritual worlds. And since the spiritual world controls the physical world, getting connected to and accessing the authority of the spiritual world affects your functioning in the physical world.

9. The Church: The Context of Spiritual Growth. The church is the most exciting entity that God has placed on this earth, because it is the life-support system for individual Christians. God never meant for us to grow spiritually in isolation from other believers. Spiritual growth is a group project, which should be good news to you because it means you don't have to do it all yourself.

The Bible uses a number of terms to illustrate this community, corporate aspect of the church. One of these terms is the family. One of Paul's synonyms for salvation is adoption, the act by which God places all believers into his family (Gal 4:5; Eph 1:5).

The great thing about God's adoption program is that no believer is left out. The church is not just a classroom for spiritual instruction, but a living and growing organism to enhance our spiritual development. The book of Ephesians especially teaches the importance of the church to the spiritual development of its members (Eph 2:19-22; 4:11-16; see also Heb 10:23-25).

10. Giving: The Generosity of Spiritual Growth. Everything we have, including the breath in our lungs, is a gift from God (Jas 1:17).

Our giving is part of what the Bible calls our stewardship—the fact that we are merely managers of God's possessions and called to handle them wisely (2 Cor 4:4). But before we can understand this responsibility, we need to be reminded that we have *been given* everything, including the money God entrusted to us. So anything we give back to God is just returning to him a small part of what he has given to us.

A steward is a manager who oversees the property of another. God owns everything (Ps 24:1), yet he has given each of us time, talents, and treasures to manage for him until he returns (Matt 25:14-30). A key text on the stewardship of giving is (2 Cor 9:6-7). It teaches that the person who gives little will receive little, and the person who gives generously will receive much. Tithing, as well as using resources to carry out good works, gives tangible evidence that we recognize God as our source and that we take him seriously (Deut 14:23). It also testifies that we recognize and are submitted to the priesthood of Jesus Christ (Heb 7:1-25).

11. Trials: The Test of Spiritual Growth. A lot of people don't want to hear that trials are necessary for Christians, but it's true. Scripturally, a trial comes as an adverse set of circumstances in your life, either permitted or created by God, to develop you spiritually.

Each part of this definition is important, because we don't want to gloss over or deny that a trial is an adversity. Trials are not easy to handle. But God is behind our trials, which means we are not the victims of random fate. And because God is in control, our trials have a good purpose, which is to grow and mature us spiritually.

Christians can even rejoice in the middle of a trial (Jas 1:2) because we know trials are opportunities for us to grow into spiritual maturity. Spiritual maturity is the process of our becoming more like Jesus Christ (Gal 4:19). God assures that he will successfully guide us through our trials when we look to him in the midst of them (1 Cor 10:13).

12. Temptation: The Battle of Spiritual Growth. We need to be clear that the temptation to sin we face in the Christian life is not from God (Jas 1:13-14). God won't cause you to sin, and the devil can't make you sin. Satan can offer you a temptation and make it look inviting, but he cannot force you to sin. You have to cooperate.

The devil's power is influence and deception, not coercion. Jesus experienced all of our temptations without sinning (Heb 4:15). So don't let the devil put you on a guilt trip for being tempted. Your response determines whether a temptation becomes sin. The problem with sin is that the devil uses false advertising. Sin almost never comes with a sticker that says, "Warning: Will Cause Death." Sin looks attractive, and its price seems reasonable. But it always costs more than the advertised price. Satan's goal is to use sin to break our fellowship with God.

13. Calling: The Ministry of Spiritual Growth. Your calling is the customized life purpose that God has shaped, fashioned, and equipped for you, in order to expand his kingdom and bring himself greater glory (Jer 29:11).

Ephesians 2:10 also deals with our calling, which is to produce "good works" that bless and help others and glorify God (Matt 5:16). So your calling is not just what you do for a living, but your divinely preplanned service for God that is your response to the great grace he has shown you in salvation (Rom 12:1-8). God has a calling that is tailor-made for you (Acts 13:36).

14. Obedience: The Response of Spiritual Growth. The connection between the new nature that God put within us at salvation and our obedience to him is so vital that I want to establish it first.

God announced in Jeremiah 31:31-34 that someday he would relate to human beings in a new way called the new covenant. This covenant is not based on law and animal sacrifice, but on the once-and-for-all sacrifice of Jesus Christ. The main feature of the new covenant is this: "I will put my teaching within them and write it on their hearts" (v. 33). The fact that these desires are built-in, or internal, is crucial, because it revolutionizes our understanding of obedience.

Not only has God given us his law, but when he made us new creations in Christ, he also gave us the internal desire to obey his law by walking in his ways (Phil 2:12-13). Jesus called our obedience his "yoke," which he also said is the source of rest for those who are weary (Matt 11:28-30). Obedience activates the word and work of God in our lives (Jas 1:19-25).

15. Maturity: The Goal of Spiritual Growth. Paul challenged the often infantile Corinthians to grow up (1 Cor 14:20). Spiritual maturity is the ability to consistently view and live life from the perspective of the Spirit rather than the flesh, with the result that we maximize our God-given capacity to bring him glory.

In other words, mature Christians consistently see things that human eyes can't see. They hear things that the most acute hearing on earth cannot detect. And they have thoughts that they did not originate on their own because the Holy Spirit is helping them think God's thoughts. The Holy Spirit is free to send his message clearly and directly to the spiritually mature (see Heb 5:11-14).

The promise to a person who is listening to the Spirit is that he or she will "understand what has been freely given to us by God" (1 Cor 2:12). This puts you in another world from the mass of people (1 Cor 2:14). A mature believer is worlds removed from the understanding of the unsaved person. Mature believers have transformed lives that reflect and transfer the values of the kingdom of God (2 Cor 3:17-18).

www.bhpublishinggroup.com/qr/te/67-08

Scan this code with your mobile device or follow this link for videos of Tony Evans as he disciples you to grow in spiritual maturity.

In Ephesians 6:10-18, Paul illuminates the reality that life is a battle. In this powerful passage on spiritual warfare, Paul instructs us that the battles we face are not physical battles but, rather, spiritual ones. Satan is our fierce enemy, and he uses every opportunity to try to get us to depart from God's path and to destroy our trust in God. The devil is a skilled fighter, and he doesn't fight fair. So we must take him seriously and be prepared to resist his devious schemes.

The good news is that we are not in this fight alone. God has equipped us to stand against all the devil's schemes. He has provided the tools we need for victory, which Paul refers to as "the full armor of God" (6:11). Paul modelled this armor after what a typical Roman soldier would have worn in the culture of his day. Understanding the unique nature of each piece of the armor, along with when and how to use it, will enable you to wage victorious spiritual warfare in the evil day of intense satanic attack.

The belt of truth: A belt was an essential piece of equipment for a Roman warrior because it provided a place to tuck in his sword so that it would always be within reach. It was also key for keeping the rest of his equipment in place. Similarly, truth for the spiritual warrior is the foundation for everything. Since Satan is a liar by nature, he can't handle the truth. Without the foundation of a commitment to truthfulness and integrity based on God's truth, one should not dare to venture into battle. But with God's truth as our standard and basis of authority, we can be assured of the victory.

The breastplate of righteousness: The breastplate was a piece of armor that was worn over the chest to protect the heart of the warrior. The fastest way to stop an opposing soldier was to strike him in the heart, so this was the place that required the sturdiest protection. The strongest protection for our heart is the righteousness that comes from being right before God. Since Jesus has forgiven our sins, our heart is protected by his righteousness but we must also practice righteousness in our lifestyle.

Feet sandaled with the gospel of peace: A soldier can't stand firmly in place if he doesn't have solid and dependable footwear. Roman soldiers, therefore, wore sturdy leather sandals with hobnails driven through the sole to give them traction, so they wouldn't be slipping and sliding in the heat of conflict. The good news of what Jesus has done *for us* and *in us* gives us peace and confidence even in the fiercest combat against the enemy of our soul. It is the peace of God that gives us firm footing for any battle we face and confirms that we are moving in the right direction.

The shield of faith: Every Roman soldier needed a large shield to protect him against arrows fired by enemies. These shields were usually covered with tough animal hides to make them impregnable and were often as large as two and a half feet wide and four feet tall. They were an essential defensive component of their gear. For the Christian, faith (acting like God is telling the truth) is our shield. Our trust in Christ is what protects us from all the fiery projectiles that the enemy aims at us. But we must always remember a shield is of little use unless you put it between yourself and the danger you face!

The helmet of salvation: Even today, soldiers, police officers, and first responders going into a dangerous situation wear a helmet. A helmet protects them by absorbing the force that is targeted at their head. Since we need to use our brains in spiritual battle, we need to keep them safe. If our mind is focused on the divine, spiritual resources of our salvation and not upon our own human resources, then we will have the protection we need to keep up the fight.

The sword of the Spirit: All the other pieces of armor that we have discussed are primarily defensive in nature. They protect us from harm by minimizing our vulnerabilities and covering our potentially weak areas. But no Roman soldier would ever have wanted to go into battle with only protective gear. They would have had a sword at their side which could be used against any combatant coming against them. We too have an offensive weapon for our warfare against the enemy of our souls: the Word of God, the Bible. When Jesus was tempted by the devil, he gave us an example of how to deal with such an attack. He quoted Scripture to confirm God's way and reject the falsehoods that Satan was trying to implant in His mind. We will never find real victory in spiritual warfare if we do not take up the sword of the Spirit. And just as a Roman soldier needed to become familiar with his sword before he could use it effectively, so we must become ever more familiar with the Word of God so that we can be prepared to use the power of specific passages when the decisive moment arises. Believers need to learn how to have a Bible study with the devil when he attacks.

Each piece of armor is essential for those who wish to defeat the enemy and live a life of victory. It is no coincidence that immediately after providing this inventory of the believer's spiritual armor that Paul turns to the topic of prayer, urging that we pray "at all times in the Spirit with every prayer and request" (6:18). Prayer is the divine means of putting on the six pieces of armor. As you pray, it is critical that you not only pray for yourself but also for others. Prayer connects us intimately with God in a spirit of trust and dependence. We cannot and dare not face such a

ferocious battle alone. Prayer is a reminder that God fights for us and at our side. Prayer polishes up every essential piece of our armor and gets us fully ready for the fight. As believers live life well-dressed for warfare, they experience the victory that is theirs in Christ Jesus. Always remember, you are not fighting *for* victory. You are fighting *from* victory. The battle has already been won.

HARMONY OF THE GOSPELS

		MATTHEW	MARK	LUKE	JOHN
PART I. INTRODUCTORY STATEMENTS					
1.	Luke's Historical Introduction			1:1-4	
2.	John's Theological Introduction				1:1-18
3.	Matthew's and Luke's Genealogical Introductions	1:1-17		3:23-38	
PART II. THE BIRTH AND YOUTH OF JOHN THE BAPTIST AND JESUS					
4.	Gabriel's Announcement to Zechariah				
	Place: Jerusalem			1:5-25	
5.	Gabriel's Announcement to Mary				
	Place: Nazareth			1:26-38	
6.	Songs of Elizabeth and Mary				
	Place: Judea			1:39-56	
7.	Birth and Youth of John the Baptist				
	Place: Judea			1:57-80	
8.	The Angel's Announcement to Joseph				
	Place: Nazareth	1:18-25			
9.	The Birth of Jesus				
	Place: Bethlehem			2:1-7	
10.	The Shepherds and the Angels				
	Place: Near Bethlehem			2:8-20	
11.	Circumcision and Naming of Jesus				
	Place: Bethlehem			2:21	
12.	The Presentation in the Temple				
	Place: Jerusalem			2:22-38	
13.	The Visit of the Wise Men				
	Places: Jerusalem, Bethlehem	2:1-12			
14.	Flight to Egypt and Return to Nazareth				
	Places: Nazareth, Egypt	2:13-23		2:39	
15.	His Youth in Nazareth and Visit to Jerusalem				
	Places: Nazareth, Jerusalem			2:40-52	
PART III. JOHN THE BAPTIST'S MINISTRY					
16.	The Coming of the Word				
	Place: Wilderness		1:1	3:1-2	
17.	Response of John in the Wilderness				
	Place: Wilderness	3:1-6	1:2-6	3:3-6	
18.	The Boldness of His Preaching				
	Place: Wilderness	3:7-10		3:7-14	
19.	John's Idea of the Messiah	3:11-12	1:7-8	3:15-18	
PART IV. EARLY MINISTRY OF JESUS					
20.	The Baptism in the Jordan				
	Place: Jordan	3:13-17	1:9-11	3: 21-23	

		MATTHEW	MARK	LUKE	JOHN
21.	The Temptation of Jesus by Satan				
	Place: Judean Wilderness	4:1-11	1:12-13	4:1-13	
22.	Testimony of John and Disciples				
	Place: Bethany				1:19-51
23.	The First Miracle				
	Place: Cana				2:1-11
24.	The First Stay in Capernaum				
	Place: Capernaum				2:12
25.	First Passover and Cleansing Temple				
	Place: Jerusalem				2:13–3:21
26.	Closing Ministry and Arrest of John				
	Place: Aenon			3:19-20	3:22-36; 4:1-3
27.	Jesus and the Samaritan Woman				
	Place: Samaria				4:4-42
28.	Jesus Returns to Galilee				
	Place: Galilee	4:12	1:14	4:14	4:43-45
PART V. THE MINISTRY IN GALILEE					
29.	The Message of Jesus—Repentance				
	Place: Galilee	4:17	1:14-15	4:14-15	
30.	Healing the Centurion's Son				
	Place: Capernaum				4:46-54
31.	Jesus Rejected by the People				
	Place: Nazareth	4:13-16		4:16-30	
32.	Calling the Fishermen				
	Place: Capernaum	4:18-22	1:16-20	5:1-11	
33.	A Busy Sabbath in Capernaum				
	Place: Capernaum	8:14-17	1:21-34	4:31-41	
34.	The First Tour of Galilee				
	Place: Galilee	4:23-25	1:35-39	4:42-44	
35.	The Healing of a Man with Leprosy				
	Place: Galilee	8:2-4	1:40-45	5:12-16	
36.	Healing the Paralyzed Man in Peter's Home				
	Place: Capernaum	9:1-8	2:1-12	5:17-26	
37.	The Call of Matthew (Levi)				
	Place: Sea of Galilee	9:9-13	2:13-17	5:27-32	
38.	Three Parables About Fasting				
	Place: The Seaside	9:14-17	2:18-22	5:33-39	
39.	First Sabbath Controversy in Jerusalem				
	Place: Jerusalem				5:1-47
40.	Further Controversies in Galilee				
	Place: Galilee	12:1-14	2:23–3:6	6:1-11	
41.	Choosing the Twelve				
	Place: Near Capernaum	5:1–8:1	3:14-19	6:12-49	

		MATTHEW	MARK	LUKE	JOHN
42.	Healing the Centurion's Servant				
	Place: Capernaum	8:5-13		7:1-10	
43.	Raising the Son of a Widow				
	Place: Nain			7:11-17	
44.	Doubt of John and Praise of Jesus				
	Place: Nain	11:2-19		7:18-35	
45.	The Cities of Opportunity				
	Place: Capernaum	11:20-30			
46.	The Sinful Woman in House of Simon				
	Place: Capernaum			7:36-50	
47.	Jesus and Disciples Go to Galilee			8:1-3	
48.	Jesus Accused of Blasphemy				
	Place: Galilee	12:15-45	3:20-30		
49.	The Mother of Jesus Calls Him	12:46-50	3:31-35	8:19-21	
50.	The First Extended Group of Parables				
	Place: Sea of Galilee	13:1-53	4:1-34	8:4-18	
51.	Jesus Stills the Storm and Casts Out Demons				
	Places: Sea of Galilee; Gadara	8:23-34	4:35—5:20	8:22-39	
52.	Healing Jairus's Daughter and Woman with Issue of Blood				
	Place: Capernaum	9:18-26	5:21-43	8:40-56	
53.	Two Blind Men and Demon-Possessed Man Healed				
	Place: Capernaum	9:27-34			
54.	Last Rejection at Nazareth				
	Place: Nazareth	13:54-58	6:1-6		
55.	The Disciples Given Power to Heal				
	Place: Capernaum	10:1-42	6:6-13	9:1-6	
56.	Herod Fears John and Jesus	14:1-12	6:14-29	9:7-9	

PART VI. THE WITHDRAWAL FROM GALILEE

		MATTHEW	MARK	LUKE	JOHN
57.	Feeding of the Five Thousand	14:13-21	6:30-44	9:10-17	6:1-13
58.	The Return to Gennesaret				
	Place: Lake of Gennesaret	14:22-36	6:45-56		6:14-21
59.	Rejection of Christ in the Synagogue				
	Place: Capernaum				6:22-71
60.	Criticism of the Pharisees Concerning Unwashed Hands				
	Place: Capernaum	15:1-20	7:1-23		7:1
61.	Healing Daughter of Syrophoenician				
	Place: Phoenicia	15:21-28	7:24-30		
62.	Jesus Departs to Sea of Galilee	15:29-38	7:31—8:9		
63.	Pharisees and Sadducees Attack Jesus, Again Asking a Sign				
	Place: Magdala	15:39—16:4	8:10-12		

		MATTHEW	MARK	LUKE	JOHN
64.	Jesus Again Withdraws to Bethsaida-Julias				
	Place: Bethsaida	16:5-12	8:13-26		
65.	The Great Confession of Peter				
	Place: Caesarea-Philippi	16:13-20	8:27-30	9:18-21	
66.	Jesus Predicts His Death and Resurrection				
	Place: Galilee	16:21-28	8:31-38	9:22-27	
67.	The Transfiguration of Jesus				
	Place: Mt. Tabor	17:1-13	9:2-13	9:28-36	
68.	Disciples Unable to Cast Out Evil Spirit	17:14-21	9:14-29	9:37-42	
69.	Further Reference to His Death and Resurrection				
	Place: Galilee	17:22-23	9:30-32	9:43b-45	
70.	Jesus Pays Tax by Miracle				
	Place: Capernaum	17:24-27			
71.	Disciples Contending Who Is Greatest				
	Place: Capernaum	18:1-5	9:33-37	9:46-48	
72.	Jesus Rebukes the Narrowness of John				
	Place: Capernaum	18:6-14	9:38-50	9:49-50	
73.	On Forgiving a Brother				
	Place: Capernaum	18:15-35			
74.	Christ Requires Full Consecration				
	Place: Capernaum	8:19-22		9:57-62	
75.	His Unbelieving Brothers Rebuked				
	Place: Capernaum				7:2-10
76.	James and John Rebuked for Anger				
	Place: Samaria			9:51-56	

PART VII. THE MINISTRY IN JUDEA

		MATTHEW	MARK	LUKE	JOHN
77.	At the Festival of Shelters				
	Place: Jerusalem				7:11–8:11
78.	Jesus the Light of the World				
	Place: Jerusalem				8:12-59
79.	Healing a Man Born Blind				
	Place: Jerusalem				9:1-41
80.	Parable of the Good Shepherd				
	Place: Jerusalem				10:1-21
81.	The Seventy Sent Out			10:1-24	
82.	Parable of the Good Samaritan				
	Place: Jerusalem			10:25-37	
83.	Jesus Received by Martha and Mary				
	Place: Bethany			10:38-42	
84.	The Disciples Taught How to Pray	6:9-13		11:1-13	
85.	Accused of Healing Through Beelzebub			11:14-36	
86.	The Criticism of Pharisee and Lawyer			11:37-54	

		MATTHEW	MARK	LUKE	JOHN
87.	Warning the Disciples Against the Leaven of the Pharisees			12:1-12	
88.	Covetousness and the Parable of the Rich Fool			12:13-21	
89.	The Ravens and Lilies			12:22-34	
90.	The Second Coming Referred to by Jesus			12:35-48	
91.	Christ's Eagerness for His Baptism of Death on the Cross			12:49-59	
92.	Repentance and Parable of Fig Tree			13:1-9	
93.	The Infirm Woman Healed on Sabbath			13:10-21	
94.	Jesus at the Festival of Dedication				
	Place: Jerusalem				10:22-39

PART VIII. THE MINISTRY IN PEREA

		MATTHEW	MARK	LUKE	JOHN
95.	Many Believe on Jesus				
	Place: Bethany				10:40-42
96.	Asked Concerning Number of the Saved				
	Place: Perea			13:22-35	
97.	Jesus Teaches Humility and Service				
	Place: Near Jerusalem			14:1-24	
98.	To Be Christ's Disciple Requires Forsaking All				
	Place: Jerusalem			14:25-35	
99.	Christ Justifies Himself in Receiving Sinners			15:1-32	
100.	Parables Concerning Stewardship			16:1–17:10	
101.	The Raising of Lazarus				
	Place: Bethany				11:1-54
102.	Jesus Goes to Jerusalem for the Passover				
	Places: Samaria, Galilee			17:11-37	
103.	Parables on Prayer on Way to Jerusalem			18:1-14	
104.	Pharisees Tempt Jesus Concerning Divorce	19:1-12	10:1-12		
105.	Christ Welcoming Little Children				
	Place: Perea	19:13-15	10:13-16	18:15-17	
106.	Parable of the Rich Young Ruler	19:16-29	10:17-30	18:18-30	
107.	Parable of the Laborers in Vineyard	20:1-16	10:31		
108.	Jesus Again Refers to Death and Resurrection	20:17-19	10:32-34	18:31-34	
109.	Selfishness of James and John	20:20-28	10:35-45		
110.	Bartimaeus Receives His Sight	20:29-34	10:46-52	18:35-43	
111.	Zacchaeus and Parable of the Pounds				
	Place: Jericho			19:1-28	

PART IX. THE LAST JERUSALEM MINISTRY

		MATTHEW	MARK	LUKE	JOHN
112.	The Interest in Jesus and Lazarus				
	Place: Bethany				11:55-57; 12:1, 9-11

	MATTHEW	MARK	LUKE	JOHN
113. The Challenge to the Sanhedrin				
Place: Jerusalem	21:1-17	11:1-11	19:29-44	12:12-19
114. Cursing the Fig Tree—Cleansing the Temple				
Place: Jerusalem	21:12-13,18-19	11:12-18	19:45-48	
115. The Greeks Seek Jesus While He Is in Agony of Soul				
Place: Jerusalem				12:20-50
116. The Withered Fig Tree, and the Power of Faith				
Place: Jerusalem	21:19-22	11:19-26	21:37-38	
117. Sanhedrin Questions the Authority of Jesus				
Place: Jerusalem	21:23-46; 22:1-14	11:27—12:12	20:1-19	
118. An Attempt to Trap Jesus Concerning Tribute to Caesar				
Place: Jerusalem	22:15-22	12:13-17	20:20-26	
119. A Further Attempt to Puzzle Jesus				
Place: Jerusalem	22:23-33	12:18-27	20:27-40	
120. The Legal Problem of a Lawyer				
Place: Jerusalem	22:34-40	12:28-34		
121. Jesus Silences Enemies by Appeal to David				
Place: Jerusalem	22:41-46	12:35-37	20:41-44	
122. A Denunciation of Scribes and Pharisees				
Place: Jerusalem	23:1-39	12:38-40	20:45-47	
123. The Widow's Two Tiny Coins				
Place: Jerusalem		12:41-44	21:1-4	

PART X. JESUS COUNSELS HIS DISCIPLES LEADING UP TO HIS SACRIFICE

	MATTHEW	MARK	LUKE	JOHN
124. Jesus's Olivet Discourse				
Place: Jerusalem	24:1—25:46	13:1-37	21:5-36	
125. Jesus Predicts His Arrest				
Place: Jerusalem	26:1-5	14:1-2	22:1-2	
126. Jesus Anointed by Mary				
Place: Bethany	26:6-13	14:3-9		12:2-8
127. The Act of Judas Iscariot				
Place: Jerusalem	26:14-16	14:10-11	22:3-6	
128. Preparation for Passover and Jealousy of the Disciples				
Place: Jerusalem	26:17-20	14:12-17	22:7-16,24-30	
129. Jesus Washes the Disciples' Feet				
Place: Jerusalem				13:1-20
130. Judas Named as the Betrayer				
Place: Jerusalem	26:21-25	14:18-21	22:21-23	13:21-30
131. Steadfastness of the Disciples Questioned				
Place: Jerusalem	26:31-35	14:27-31	22:31-38	13:34-38
132. The Memorial Supper Instituted (See 1Co 11:23-26)				
Place: Jerusalem	26:26-29	14:22-25	22:17-20	

		MATTHEW	MARK	LUKE	JOHN
133.	Jesus Opens His Heart to the Disciples Concerning His Departure				
	Place: Upper Room and on Way to Gethsemane				14:1–16:33
134.	The Intercessory Prayer				
	Place: Near Gethsemane				17:1-26
135.	The Agony in Gethsemane	26:36-46	14:32-42	22:39-46	18:1
PART XI. THE CONDEMNATION AND THE CROSS					
136.	The Betrayal, Arrest, and Desertion by the Disciples				
	Place: Gethsemane	26:47-56	14:43-52	22:47-53	18:2-12
137.	The Examination by Annas				
	Place: Jerusalem				18:13-14, 19-23
138.	Condemned on Perjured Testimony				
	Place: Jerusalem	26:57-68	14:53-65	22:54,63-65	18:24
139.	Peter's Three Denials				
	Place: Jerusalem	26:58,69-75	14:54,66-72	22:54-62	18:15-18,25-27
140.	An Attempt to Make the Trial Legal				
	Place: Jerusalem	27:1	15:1	22:66-71	
141.	Judas Realizes His Sin (see Acts 1:18-19)				
	Place: Jerusalem	27:3-10			
142.	Jesus Before Pilate				
	Place: Jerusalem	27:2,11-14	15:2-5	23:1-5	18:28-38
143.	Jesus Is Sent to Herod				
	Place: Jerusalem			23:6-12	
144.	Herod Returns Jesus to Pilate				
	Place: Jerusalem	27:15-26	15:6-15	23:13-25	18:39–19:16
145.	Jesus Is Mocked by Soldiers				
	Place: Jerusalem	27:27-30	15:16-19		
146.	Simon Bears the Cross				
	Place: On Way to Calvary	27:31-34	15:20-23	23:26-33	19:16-17
147.	Jesus Is Crucified				
	Place: Calvary	27:35-50	15:24-37	23:33-46	19:18-30
148.	Events that Accompanied Jesus's Death				
	Place: Jerusalem	27:51-56	15:38-41	23:45-49	
149.	Burial in Joseph's Tomb				
	Place: Gethsemane	27:57-60	15:42-46	23:50-54	19:31-42
150.	The Women by the Tomb	27:61-66	15:47	23:55-56	
PART XII. THE RESURRECTION AND ASCENSION					
151.	At the Tomb on the Sabbath				
	Place: Gethsemane	28:1			
152.	Anointing with Spices		16:1		

	MATTHEW	MARK	LUKE	JOHN
153. The Tomb Is Opened	28:2-4			
154. Women Find the Empty Tomb and Angels	28:5-8	16:2-8	24:1-8	20:1
155. The Women Report to the Apostles				
Place: Jerusalem			24:9-12	20:2-10
156. Jesus Appears to Mary Magdalene				
Place: Jerusalem		16:9-11		20:11-18
157. Then Other Women See Him	28:9-10			
158. The Watchmen Bribed to Claim the Body Taken by the Disciples	28:11-15			
159. Jesus Appears on Way to Emmaus		16:12-13	24:13-32	
160. Simon Peter Sees Jesus (see also 1Co 15:5)			24:33-35	
161. Entire Group, Except Thomas, See Him, and He Eats Before Them		16:14	24:36-43	20:19-25
162. Entire Group Sees Him, Thomas Now Believes				20:25-31
163. Jesus Appears by Sea of Galilee				21:1-25
164. The Apostles Commissioned to Preach				
Place: Galilee	28:16-20	16:15-18		
165. James the Brother of Jesus Sees Him (see also 1Co 15:7)				
166. Jesus and Disciples Counsel for the Last Time and Jesus Ascends (see also Acts 1:3-12)				
Place: Olivet		16:19-20	24:44-53	

THE TEN COMMANDMENTS

COMMANDMENT	PASSAGE	RELATED OLD TESTAMENT PASSAGES	RELATED NEW TESTAMENT PASSAGES	JESUS'S TEACHING
You shall have no other gods before me.	Ex 20:3; Dt 5:7	Ex 34:14; Dt 6:4,13-14; 2Kg 17:35; Ps 81:9; Jr 25:6; 35:15	Ac 5:29	Mt 4:10; 6:33; 22:37-40
You shall not make for yourself an idol.	Ex 20:4-6; Dt 5:8-10	Ex 20:23; 32:8; 34:17; Lv 19:4; 26:1; Dt 4:15-20; 7:25; 32:21; Ps 115:4-7; Is 55:12-20	Ac 17:29; 1Co 8:4-6,10-14; 1Jn 5:21	Mt 6:24; Lk 16:13
You shall not misuse the name of the Lord.	Ex 20:7; Dt 5:11	Ex 22:28; Lv 18:21; 19:12; 22:2; 24:16; Ezk 39:7	Rm 2:23-24; Jms 5:12	Mt 5:33-37; 6:9; 23:16-22
Remember the Sabbath day by keeping it holy.	Ex 20:8-11; Dt 5:12-15	Gn 2:3; Ex 16:23-30; 31:13-16; 35:2-3; Lv 19:30; Is 56:2; Jr 17:21-27	Ac 20:7; Heb 10:25	Mt 12:1-13; Mk 2:23-27; 3:1-6; Lk 6:1-11; Jn 5:1-18
Honor your father and your mother.	Ex 20:12; Dt 5:16	Ex 21:17; Lv 19:3; Dt 21:18-21; 27:16; Pr 6:20	Eph 6:1-3; Col 3:20	Mt 15:4-6; 19:19; Mk 7:9-13; Lk 2:51; 18:20; Jn 19:26-27
You shall not murder.	Ex 20:13; Dt 5:17	Gn 9:6; Lv 24:17; Nm 35:33	Rm 13:9-10; 1Pt 4:15	Mt 5:21-24; 19:18; 26:52; Mk 10:19; Lk 18:20
You shall not commit adultery.	Ex 20:14; Dt 5:18	Lv 18:20; 20:10; Dt 22:22; Nm 5:12-31; Pr 6:29,32	Rm 13:9-10; 1Co 6:9; Heb 13:4; Jms 2:11	Mt 5:27-30; 19:18; Mk 10:19; Lk 18:20; Jn 8:1-11
You shall not steal.	Ex 20:15; Dt 5:19	Lv 19:11,13; Ezk 18:7	Rm 13:9-10; Eph 4:28; Jms 5:4	Mt 19:18; Mk 10:19; 12:40; Lk 18:20
You shall not give false testimony.	Ex 20:16; Dt 5:20	Ex 23:1,7; Lv 19:11; Pss 15:2; 101:5; Pr 10:18; Jr 9:3-5; Zch 8:16	Eph 4:25,31; Col 3:9; Ti 3:2	Mt 5:37; 19:18; Mk 10:19; Lk 18:20
You shall not covet.	Ex 20:17; Dt 5:21	Dt 7:25; Jb 31:24-28; Ps 62:10	Rm 7:7; 13:9; Eph 5:3-5; Heb 13:5; Jms 4:1-2	Lk 12:15-34

DOCTRINES RELATED TO THE PARABLES OF OUR LORD

PARABLE	TEXT	RELATED DOCTRINES
Lamp Under Bowl	Mt 5:14-15; Mk 4:21-22; Lk 8:16; 11:33	Discipleship
Builders	Mt 7:24-27; Lk 6:47-49	Discipleship
New Cloth on Old Coat	Mt 9:16; Mk 2:21; Lk 5:36	Jesus Christ
New Wine in Old Skins	Mt 9:17; Mk 2:22; Lk 5:37-38	Jesus Christ
Sower and Soils	Mt 13:3-8,18-23; Mk 4:3-8,14-20; Lk 8:5-8,11-15	Evil and Suffering, Evangelism, Christian Ethics, Election, Revelation, Missions
Weeds and Wheat	Mt 13:24-30,36-43	The Church, Evil and Suffering, Sin, Christian Ethics, Jesus Christ, Election, Revelation
Mustard Seed	Mt 13:31-32; Mk 4:30-32; Lk 13:18-19	The Church, Election
Yeast	Mt 13:33; Lk 13:20-21	The Church, Holy Scripture, Election
Hidden Treasure	Mt 13:44	The Church, Salvation, Revelation
Valuable Pearl	Mt 13:45-46	The Church, Revelation
Net	Mt 13:47-50	The Church
Owner of a House	Mt 13:52	The Church, Education
Lost Sheep	Mt 18:12-14; Lk 15:4-7	Evangelism, God
Unmerciful Servant	Mt 18:23-24	The Church, Salvation, Christian Ethics
Vineyard Workers	Mt 20:1-16	The Church, Humanity, God
Two Sons	Mt 21:28-32	The Church, Salvation
Tenants	Mt 21:33-44; Mk 12:1-11	Jesus Christ, Holy Scripture, Election
Wedding Banquet	Mt 22:2-14	The Church, Jesus Christ, Election
Fig Tree	Mt 24:32-35; Mk 13:28-29; Lk 21:29-31	Jesus Christ, Election, Creation, Last Things
Faithful and Wise Servant	Mt 24:45-51; Lk 12:42-48	Last Things
Ten Virgins	Mt 25:1-13	The Church, Salvation, Humanity
Talents	Mt 25:14-30; Lk 19:12-27	Stewardship, Humanity, Jesus Christ, Last Things
Sheep and Goats	Mt 25:31-46	Stewardship, Evil and Suffering, Salvation, Christian Ethics, Jesus Christ, Last Things, Creation, Discipleship
Growing Seed	Mk 4:26-29	The Church, Evangelism
Watchful Servants	Mk 13:35-37; Lk 12:35-40	Jesus Christ, Last Things History
Moneylender	Lk 7:41-43	Stewardship, Salvation, Revelation
Good Samaritan	Lk 10:30-37	Christian Ethics, Discipleship
Friend in Need	Lk 11:5-8	Humanity, Prayer
Rich Fool	Lk 12:16-21	Stewardship, Humanity, Christian Ethics, Election
Unfruitful Fig Tree	Lk 13:6-9	Discipleship

PARABLE	TEXT	RELATED DOCTRINES
Low Seat at Feast	Lk 14:7-14	Christian Ethics, Election, Discipleship
Great Banquet	Lk 14:16-24	Election
Cost of Discipleship	Lk 14:28-33	Discipleship
Lost Coin	Lk 15:8-10	Salvation
Prodigal Son	Lk 15:11-32	Sin, Salvation, Humanity, Christian Ethics, Revelation
Shrewd Manager	Lk 16:1-8	Christian Ethics
Rich Man and Lazarus	Lk 16:19-31	Evil and Suffering, Salvation, Evangelism, Holy Scripture, Last Things, Prayer
Master and Servant	Lk 17:7-10	Discipleship
Persistent Widow	Lk 18:2-8	Evil and Suffering, Jesus Christ, Election, Prayer
Pharisee and Tax Collector	Lk 18:10-14	Stewardship, Salvation, Christian Ethics, Prayer

DOCTRINAL EMPHASES IN THE MIRACLES OF OUR LORD

MIRACLE	BIBLICAL PASSAGE	
Water Turned to Wine		
Healings	Matthew 4:23-24	Mark 1:32-34
Healing of a Leper	Matthew 8:1-4	Mark 1:40-42
Healing of a Roman Centurion's Servant	Matthew 8:5-13	
Healing of Peter's Mother-in-Law	Matthew 8:14-15	Mark 1:29-31
Calming of the Storm at Sea	Matthew 8:23-27	Mark 4:35-41
Healing of the Wild Men of Gadara	Matthew 8:28-34	Mark 5:1-15
Healing of a Paralytic	Matthew 9:1-7	Mark 2:1-12
Healing of a Woman with a Hemorrhage	Matthew 9:20-22	Mark 5:25-29
Raising of Jairus's Daughter	Matthew 9:23-25	Mark 5:22-42
Healing of Two Blind Men	Matthew 9:27-31	
Healing of a Demon-Possessed Man	Matthew 8:32-33	
Healing of a Man with a Shriveled Hand	Matthew 12:10-13	Mark 3:1-5
Feeding of 5,000 People	Matthew 14:15-21	Mark 6:35-44
Walking on the Sea	Matthew 14:22-25	Mark 6:47-51
Healing of the Syrophoenician's Daughter	Matthew 15:21-28	Mark 7:24-30
Feeding of 4,000 People	Matthew 15:32-38	Mark 8:1-9
Healing of a Boy with Seizures	Matthew 17:14-18	Mark 9:14-29
Healing of Two Blind Men at Jericho	Matthew 20:30-34	
Healing of a Man with an Unclean Spirit		Mark 1:23-26
Healing of a Deaf, Speechless Man		Mark 7:31-37
Healing of a Blind Man at Bethsaida		Mark 8:22-26
Healing of Blind Bartimaeus		Mark 10:46-52
A Miraculous Catch of Fish		
Raising a Widow's Son		
Healing of an Infirm Woman		
Healing of a Man with the Dropsy		
Healing of Ten Lepers		
Healing of Malchus's Ear		
Healing of Official's Son		
Healing of a Lame Man at Bethesda		
Healing of a Blind Man		
Raising of Lazarus		

BIBLICAL PASSAGE		DOCTRINAL EMPHASIS
	John 2:1-11	Vocabulary in defining miracles
		Christ as the agent of miracles
Luke 5:12-13		Christ as the agent of miracles
Luke 7:1-10		Faith as the context of miracles
Luke 4:38-39		Christ as the agent of miracles
Luke 8:22-25		Nature as the context of miracles
Luke 8:26-35		Christ as the agent of miracles
Luke 5:18-25		Christ as the agent of miracles
Luke 8:43-48		Faith as the context of miracles
Luke 8:41-56		Faith as the context of miracles
		Faith as the context of miracles
		Revelation as the purpose of miracles
Luke 6:6-10		Redemption as the purpose of miracles
Luke 9:12-17	John 6:1-13	Christ as the agent of miracles
	John 6:16-21	Christ as the agent of miracles
		Faith as the context of miracles
		Christ as the agent of miracles
Luke 9:37-43		Faith as the context of miracles
		Faith as the context of miracles
Luke 4:33-35		Christ as the agent of miracles
		Methods in defining miracles
		Christ as the agent of miracles
Luke 18:35-43		Faith as the context of miracles
Luke 5:4-11	John 21:1-11	Nature as the context of miracles
Luke 7:11-15		Christ as the agent of miracles
Luke 13:11-13		Praise as the purpose of miracles
Luke 14:1-4		Christ as the agent of miracles
Luke 17:11-19		Faith as the context of miracles
Luke 22:50-51	John 18:3-11	Christ as the agent of miracles
	John 4:46-54	Faith as the context of miracles
	John 5:1-9	John 5:1-9
	John 9:1-12	Faith as the context of miracles
	John 11:38-44	Christ as the agent of miracles

BIBLE READING PLANS

The *CSB Tony Evans Study Bible* offers two plans for reading through the Bible. The first plan developed by Heather Collins-Grattan Floyd is structured to take a person through the Bible in three years. This plan may appeal to busy persons who have a limited amount of time each day to read the Scriptures. Reading a smaller portion each day may enable the person to spend more time reading, studying, and meditating on the passage for the day.

The second plan was developed by the late Robert Murray M'Cheyne. This plan takes the reader to four portions of Scripture each day from various parts of the Bible. Following this plan, a person will read through the Old Testament once and the New Testament twice within a year.

APPROACHING THE BIBLE

In reading and studying the Bible, we draw on the same knowledge, skills, and competencies we use in reading other documents. However, with the Bible there is an added dimension. The Bible was written by human beings but the ultimate Author who worked through a variety of human authors is God himself. In what may have been his last written words to Timothy, Paul reminded his protégé that all Scripture is inspired by God. For this reason, John Wesley said that Scripture can only be understood with the help of the Spirit who inspired these sixty-six books. Therefore, as believers come to read and study Scripture, they need to remember the Author of Scripture and ask for the Spirit's help in understanding what they read.

As you read the Scriptures daily, you will find help in the article, "How to Study the Bible" on pages XV-XVII of the *CSB Tony Evans Study Bible*.

- Come to the Bible expecting to grow. It is like both milk (1Pt 2:2) and solid food (Heb 5:14) providing nourishment for both the young and those more mature.
- Come to the Bible for understanding and direction. It is like a counselor (Ps 119:24) and provides light for your journey (Pss 119:105,130).
- Come to the Bible for correction and purification. It is like:
  - a mirror in which the believer sees himself and the changes that God requires,
  - fire and a hammer (Jer 23:29),
  - a scalpel by which God performs spiritual surgery on the heart (Heb 4:12),
  - water that washes and purifies (Eph 5:26)
- Come to the Bible for pleasure. God's Word is like honey (Pss 19:10; 119:103).

Come daily to the Bible with these attitudes and expectations, and you will be changed. This is God's multifaceted instrument for conforming you to the image of his Son.

THREE-YEAR BIBLE READING PLAN

Edited by Heather Collins-Grattan Floyd

YEAR ONE

JANUARY

Genesis 1:1-26	1st
Genesis 1:27–2:25	2nd
Genesis 3:1-24	3rd
Genesis 4:1-26	4th
Genesis 5:1-32	5th
Genesis 6:1–7:10	6th
Genesis 7:11–8:22	7th
Genesis 9:1-29	8th
Genesis 10:1-32	9th
Genesis 11:1–12:9	10th
Genesis 12:10–13:18	11th
Genesis 14:1-24	12th
Genesis 15:1–16:16	13th
Genesis 17:1-27	14th
Genesis 18:1-15	15th
Genesis 18:16-33	16th
Genesis 19:1-29	17th
Genesis 19:30–20:18	18th
Genesis 21:1-34	19th
Genesis 22:1-24	20th
Genesis 23:1–24:14	21st
Genesis 24:15-44	22nd
Genesis 24:45-67	23rd
Genesis 25:1-18	24th
Genesis 25:19-34	25th
Genesis 26:1-25	26th
Genesis 26:26–27:20	27th
Genesis 27:21-46	28th
Genesis 28:1–29:12	29th
Genesis 29:13–30:11	30th
Genesis 30:12-43	31st

FEBRUARY

Genesis 31:1-35	1st
Genesis 31:36-55	2nd
Genesis 32:1-32	3rd
Genesis 33:1-20	4th
Genesis 34:1-31	5th
Genesis 35:1–36:8	6th
Genesis 36:9-43	7th
Genesis 37:1-36	8th
Genesis 38:1-30	9th
Genesis 39:1-23	10th
Genesis 40:1–41:14	11th
Genesis 41:15-49	12th
Genesis 41:50–42:26	13th
Genesis 42:27–43:14	14th
Genesis 43:15-34	15th

Genesis 44:1-34	16th
Genesis 45:1-28	17th
Genesis 46:1-34	18th
Genesis 47:1-31	19th
Genesis 48:1-22	20th
Genesis 49:1-28	21st
Genesis 49:29–50:26	22nd
Exodus 1:1-22	23rd
Exodus 2:1-25	24th
Exodus 3:1-22	25th
Exodus 4:1-31	26th
Exodus 5:1–6:13	27th
Exodus 6:14–7:13	28th

MARCH

Exodus 7:14–8:19	1st
Exodus 8:20–9:12	2nd
Exodus 9:13-35	3rd
Exodus 10:1-20	4th
Exodus 10:21–11:10	5th
Exodus 12:1-28	6th
Exodus 12:29–13:16	7th
Exodus 13:17–14:31	8th
Exodus 15:1-27	9th
Exodus 16:1-36	10th
Exodus 17:1-16	11th
Exodus 18:1-27	12th
Exodus 19:1-25	13th
Exodus 20:1-26	14th
Exodus 21:1-36	15th
Exodus 22:1-31	16th
Exodus 23:1-33	17th
Exodus 24:1–25:9	18th
Exodus 25:10-40	19th
Exodus 26:1-37	20th
Exodus 27:1–28:14	21st
Exodus 28:15-43	22nd
Exodus 29:1-34	23rd
Exodus 29:35–30:21	24th
Exodus 30:22–31:18	25th
Exodus 32:1-35	26th
Exodus 33:1–34:9	27th
Exodus 34:10-35	28th
Exodus 35:1–36:1	29th
Exodus 36:2-38	30th
Exodus 37:1-24	31st

APRIL

Exodus 37:25–38:20	1st
Exodus 38:21–39:7	2nd
Exodus 39:8-43	3rd

Exodus 40:1-38	4th
Leviticus 1:1–2:16	5th
Leviticus 3:1–4:12	6th
Leviticus 4:13-35	7th
Leviticus 5:1–6:7	8th
Leviticus 6:8–7:10	9th
Leviticus 7:11-38	10th
Leviticus 8:1-36	11th
Leviticus 9:1-24	12th
Leviticus 10:1–11:8	13th
Leviticus 11:9-40	14th
Leviticus 11:41–13:8	15th
Leviticus 13:9-39	16th
Leviticus 13:40-59	17th
Leviticus 14:1-32	18th
Leviticus 14:33-57	19th
Leviticus 15:1-33	20th
Leviticus 16:1-34	21st
Leviticus 17:1-16	22nd
Leviticus 18:1-30	23rd
Leviticus 19:1-37	24th
Leviticus 20:1-27	25th
Leviticus 21:1–22:16	26th
Leviticus 22:17–23:8	27th
Leviticus 23:9-32	28th
Leviticus 23:33–24:23	29th
Leviticus 25:1-17	30th

MAY

Leviticus 25:18-46	1st
Leviticus 25:47–26:13	2nd
Leviticus 26:14-46	3rd
Leviticus 27:1-34	4th
Numbers 1:1-31	5th
Numbers 1:32-54	6th
Numbers 2:1-34	7th
Numbers 3:1-39	8th
Numbers 3:40–4:20	9th
Numbers 4:21-49	10th
Numbers 5:1-31	11th
Numbers 6:1-27	12th
Numbers 7:1-35	13th
Numbers 7:36-65	14th
Numbers 7:66–8:4	15th
Numbers 8:5-26	16th
Numbers 9:1-23	17th
Numbers 10:1-36	18th
Numbers 11:1-30	19th
Numbers 11:31–13:16	20th
Numbers 13:17–14:10	21st
Numbers 14:11-38	22nd

Numbers 14:39–15:21	23rd
Numbers 15:22-41	24th
Numbers 16:1-24	25th
Numbers 16:25-50	26th
Numbers 17:1–18:7	27th
Numbers 18:8-32	28th
Numbers 19:1-22	29th
Numbers 20:1-29	30th
Numbers 21:1-20	31st

JUNE

Numbers 21:21-35	1st
Numbers 22:1-21	2nd
Numbers 22:22–23:12	3rd
Numbers 23:13–24:14	4th
Numbers 24:15–25:18	5th
Numbers 26:1-37	6th
Numbers 26:38-65	7th
Numbers 27:1–28:8	8th
Numbers 28:9–29:6	9th
Numbers 29:7-40	10th
Numbers 30:1–31:24	11th
Numbers 31:25-54	12th
Numbers 32:1-42	13th
Numbers 33:1-49	14th
Numbers 33:50–34:29	15th
Numbers 35:1-34	16th
Numbers 36:1-13	17th
Deuteronomy 1:1-25	18th
Deuteronomy 1:26-46	19th
Deuteronomy 2:1-23	20th
Deuteronomy 2:24–3:20	21st
Deuteronomy 3:21–4:14	22nd
Deuteronomy 4:15-49	23rd
Deuteronomy 5:1-33	24th
Deuteronomy 6:1-25	25th
Deuteronomy 7:1-26	26th
Deuteronomy 8:1–9:6	27th
Deuteronomy 9:7–10:11	28th
Deuteronomy 10:12–11:7	29th
Deuteronomy 11:8-32	30th

JULY

Deuteronomy 12:1-32	1st
Deuteronomy 13:1–14:21	2nd
Deuteronomy 14:22–15:23	3rd
Deuteronomy 16:1–17:7	4th
Deuteronomy 17:8–18:22	5th
Deuteronomy 19:1-21	6th
Deuteronomy 20:1–21:14	7th
Deuteronomy 21:15–22:21	8th
Deuteronomy 22:22–23:25	9th
Deuteronomy 24:1–25:4	10th
Deuteronomy 25:5–26:15	11th
Deuteronomy 26:16–27:26	12th
Deuteronomy 28:1-35	13th
Deuteronomy 28:36-68	14th
Deuteronomy 29:1-29	15th
Deuteronomy 30:1–31:8	16th

Deuteronomy 31:9-29	17th
Deuteronomy 31:30–32:25	18th
Deuteronomy 32:26-52	19th
Deuteronomy 33:1-19	20th
Deuteronomy 33:20–34:12	21st
Joshua 1:1-18	22nd
Joshua 2:1-24	23rd
Joshua 3:1-17	24th
Joshua 4:1-5:9	25th
Joshua 5:10–6:21	26th
Joshua 6:22–7:15	27th
Joshua 7:16–8:23	28th
Joshua 8:24–9:15	29th
Joshua 9:16–10:15	30th
Joshua 10:16-43	31st

AUGUST

Joshua 11:1-23	1st
Joshua 12:1–13:7	2nd
Joshua 13:8–14:5	3rd
Joshua 14:6–15:19	4th
Joshua 15:20–16:4	5th
Joshua 16:5–17:18	6th
Joshua 18:1-28	7th
Joshua 19:1-39	8th
Joshua 19:40–21:8	9th
Joshua 21:9-42	10th
Joshua 21:43–22:20	11th
Joshua 22:21–23:16	12th
Joshua 24:1-33	13th
Judges 1:1-36	14th
Judges 2:1-23	15th
Judges 3:1-31	16th
Judges 4:1–5:5	17th
Judges 5:6-31	18th
Judges 6:1-24	19th
Judges 6:25-40	20th
Judges 7:1-25	21st
Judges 8:1-35	22nd
Judges 9:1-21	23rd
Judges 9:22-57	24th
Judges 10:1–11:11	25th
Judges 11:12-40	26th
Judges 12:1-15	27th
Judges 13:1-25	28th
Judges 14:1-20	29th
Judges 15:1-20	30th
Judges 16:1-22	31st

SEPTEMBER

Judges 16:23–17:13	1st
Judges 18:1-31	2nd
Judges 19:1-30	3rd
Judges 20:1-18	4th
Judges 20:19-48	5th
Judges 21:1-25	6th
Ruth 1:1-22	7th
Ruth 2:1-23	8th
Ruth 3:1-18	9th

Ruth 4:1-22	10th
1 Samuel 1:1-28	11th
1 Samuel 2:1-26	12th
1 Samuel 2:27–3:18	13th
1 Samuel 3:19–5:5	14th
1 Samuel 5:6–6:18	15th
1 Samuel 6:19–8:9	16th
1 Samuel 8:10–9:17	17th
1 Samuel 9:18–10:16	18th
1 Samuel 10:17–11:15	19th
1 Samuel 12:1-25	20th
1 Samuel 13:1-22	21st
1 Samuel 13:23–14:30	22nd
1 Samuel 14:31-52	23rd
1 Samuel 15:1-35	24th
1 Samuel 16:1-23	25th
1 Samuel 17:1-37	26th
1 Samuel 17:38-58	27th
1 Samuel 18:1-30	28th
1 Samuel 19:1-24	29th
1 Samuel 20:1-34	30th

OCTOBER

1 Samuel 20:35–22:5	1st
1 Samuel 22:6–23:6	2nd
1 Samuel 23:7-29	3rd
1 Samuel 24:1–25:13	4th
1 Samuel 25:14-44	5th
1 Samuel 26:1–27:4	6th
1 Samuel 27:5–28:25	7th
1 Samuel 29:1–30:20	8th
1 Samuel 30:21–31:13	9th
2 Samuel 1:1-27	10th
2 Samuel 2:1–3:5	11th
2 Samuel 3:6-39	12th
2 Samuel 4:1–5:16	13th
2 Samuel 5:17–6:23	14th
2 Samuel 7:1-29	15th
2 Samuel 8:1–9:13	16th
2 Samuel 10:1-19	17th
2 Samuel 11:1-27	18th
2 Samuel 12:1-31	19th
2 Samuel 13:1-27	20th
2 Samuel 13:28–14:17	21st
2 Samuel 14:18–15:12	22nd
2 Samuel 15:13–16:4	23rd
2 Samuel 16:5-22	24th
2 Samuel 16:23–17:29	25th
2 Samuel 18:1-27	26th
2 Samuel 18:28–19:23	27th
2 Samuel 19:24–20:10	28th
2 Samuel 20:11–21:14	29th
2 Samuel 21:15–22:24	30th
2 Samuel 22:25–23:7	31st

NOVEMBER

2 Samuel 23:8-39	1st
2 Samuel 24:1-25	2nd
1 Kings 1:1-31	3rd

1 Kings 1:32–2:12	4th	1 Chronicles 2:10-41	31st	2 Chronicles 30:1–31:1	20th
1 Kings 2:13-38	5th			2 Chronicles 31:2-21	21st
1 Kings 2:39–3:28	6th			2 Chronicles 32:1-31	22nd
1 Kings 4:1-34	7th	**YEAR TWO**		2 Chronicles 32:32–33:25	23rd
1 Kings 5:1-18	8th			2 Chronicles 34:1-28	24th
1 Kings 6:1-38	9th			2 Chronicles 34:29–35:19	25th
1 Kings 7:1-26	10th	**JANUARY**		2 Chronicles 35:20–36:8	26th
1 Kings 7:27-51	11th	1 Chronicles 2:42–3:16	1st	2 Chronicles 36:9-23	27th
1 Kings 8:1-26	12th	1 Chronicles 3:17–4:23	2nd	Ezra 1:1-2:42	28th
1 Kings 8:27-43	13th	1 Chronicles 4:24–5:10	3rd		
1 Kings 8:44-66	14th	1 Chronicles 5:11–6:15	4th	**MARCH**	
1 Kings 9:1-28	15th	1 Chronicles 6:16-53	5th	Ezra 2:43–3:7	1st
1 Kings 10:1-29	16th	1 Chronicles 6:54-81	6th	Ezra 3:8–4:16	2nd
1 Kings 11:1-25	17th	1 Chronicles 7:1-29	7th	Ezra 4:17–5:17	3rd
1 Kings 11:26–12:11	18th	1 Chronicles 7:30–8:40	8th	Ezra 6:1-22	4th
1 Kings 12:12-33	19th	1 Chronicles 9:1-34	9th	Ezra 7:1-28	5th
1 Kings 13:1-34	20th	1 Chronicles 9:35–11:9	10th	Ezra 8:1-30	6th
1 Kings 14:1-31	21st	1 Chronicles 11:10-47	11th	Ezra 8:31–9:15	7th
1 Kings 15:1-32	22nd	1 Chronicles 12:1-37	12th	Ezra 10:1-17	8th
1 Kings 15:33–16:28	23rd	1 Chronicles 12:38–14:17	13th	Ezra 10:18-44	9th
1 Kings 16:29–17:24	24th	1 Chronicles 15:1–16:6	14th	Nehemiah 1:1–2:10	10th
1 Kings 18:1-35	25th	1 Chronicles 16:7-43	15th	Nehemiah 2:11–3:19	11th
1 Kings 18:36–19:18	26th	1 Chronicles 17:1-27	16th	Nehemiah 3:20–4:14	12th
1 Kings 19:19–20:28	27th	1 Chronicles 18:1-17	17th	Nehemiah 4:15–5:19	13th
1 Kings 20:29–21:10	28th	1 Chronicles 19:1–20:8	18th	Nehemiah 6:1-7:3	14th
1 Kings 21:11-29	29th	1 Chronicles 21:1–22:1	19th	Nehemiah 7:4-60	15th
1 Kings 22:1-28	30th	1 Chronicles 22:2–23:14	20th	Nehemiah 7:61–8:12	16th
		1 Chronicles 23:15–24:19	21st	Nehemiah 8:13–9:18	17th
DECEMBER		1 Chronicles 24:20–25:31	22nd	Nehemiah 9:19-37	18th
1 Kings 22:29-53	1st	1 Chronicles 26:1-32	23rd	Nehemiah 9:38–10:39	19th
2 Kings 1:1-18	2nd	1 Chronicles 27:1-34	24th	Nehemiah 11:1-36	20th
2 Kings 2:1-25	3rd	1 Chronicles 28:1-21	25th	Nehemiah 12:1-26	21st
2 Kings 3:1–4:7	4th	1 Chronicles 29:1-30	26th	Nehemiah 12:27–13:5	22nd
2 Kings 4:8-44	5th	2 Chronicles 1:1–2:10	27th	Nehemiah 13:6-31	23rd
2 Kings 5:1-27	6th	2 Chronicles 2:11–3:17	28th	Esther 1:1-22	24th
2 Kings 6:1-33	7th	2 Chronicles 4:1–5:1	29th	Esther 2:1-23	25th
2 Kings 7:1-20	8th	2 Chronicles 5:2–6:11	30th	Esther 3:1–4:17	26th
2 Kings 8:1-29	9th	2 Chronicles 6:12-31	31st	Esther 5:1–6:14	27th
2 Kings 9:1-29	10th			Esther 7:1–8:17	28th
2 Kings 9:30–10:17	11th	**FEBRUARY**		Esther 9:1-17	29th
2 Kings 10:18-36	12th	2 Chronicles 6:32–7:11	1st	Esther 9:18–10:3	30th
2 Kings 11:1-20	13th	2 Chronicles 7:12–8:18	2nd	Job 1:1–2:10	31st
2 Kings 11:21–12:21	14th	2 Chronicles 9:1-31	3rd		
2 Kings 13:1-25	15th	2 Chronicles 10:1–11:4	4th	**APRIL**	
2 Kings 14:1-29	16th	2 Chronicles 11:5–12:16	5th	Job 2:11–4:11	1st
2 Kings 15:1-31	17th	2 Chronicles 13:1–14:1	6th	Job 4:12–5:27	2nd
2 Kings 15:32–17:6	18th	2 Chronicles 14:2–15:19	7th	Job 6:1-30	3rd
2 Kings 17:7-33	19th	2 Chronicles 16:1–17:19	8th	Job 7:1-21	4th
2 Kings 17:34-18:18	20th	2 Chronicles 18:1-27	9th	Job 8:1-22	5th
2 Kings 18:19-37	21st	2 Chronicles 18:28–19:11	10th	Job 9:1-35	6th
2 Kings 19:1-28	22nd	2 Chronicles 20:1-30	11th	Job 10:1-22	7th
2 Kings 19:29–20:21	23rd	2 Chronicles 20:31–21:20	12th	Job 11:1-20	8th
2 Kings 21:1-26	24th	2 Chronicles 22:1–23:15	13th	Job 12:1–13:19	9th
2 Kings 22:1–23:3	25th	2 Chronicles 23:16–24:22	14th	Job 13:20–14:22	10th
2 Kings 23:4-27	26th	2 Chronicles 24:23–25:16	15th	Job 15:1-35	11th
2 Kings 23:28–24:20	27th	2 Chronicles 25:17–26:10	16th	Job 16:1–17:16	12th
2 Kings 25:1-30	28th	2 Chronicles 26:11–28:8	17th	Job 18:1–19:20	13th
1 Chronicles 1:1-31	29th	2 Chronicles 28:9–29:11	18th	Job 19:21–20:29	14th
1 Chronicles 1:32–2:9	30th	2 Chronicles 29:12-36	19th	Job 21:1-34	15th

Job 22:1-30	16th	Psalm 68:1-27	10th	Proverbs 9:1-18	4th
Job 23:1-17	17th	Psalms 68:28–69:21	11th	Proverbs 10:1-32	5th
Job 24:1–25:6	18th	Psalms 69:22–71:16	12th	Proverbs 11:1-31	6th
Job 26:1–27:23	19th	Psalms 71:17–72:20	13th	Proverbs 12:1-28	7th
Job 28:1-28	20th	Psalm 73:1-28	14th	Proverbs 13:1-25	8th
Job 29:1-25	21st	Psalms 74:1–75:10	15th	Proverbs 14:1-35	9th
Job 30:1-31	22nd	Psalms 76:1–77:20	16th	Proverbs 15:1-33	10th
Job 31:1-40	23rd	Psalm 78:1-39	17th	Proverbs 16:1-33	11th
Job 32:1-22	24th	Psalm 78:40-72	18th	Proverbs 17:1-28	12th
Job 33:1-33	25th	Psalms 79:1–80:19	19th	Proverbs 18:1-24	13th
Job 34:1-37	26th	Psalms 81:1–82:8	20th	Proverbs 19:1-29	14th
Job 35:1-16	27th	Psalms 83:1–84:12	21st	Proverbs 20:1-30	15th
Job 36:1-33	28th	Psalms 85:1–86:17	22nd	Proverbs 21:1-31	16th
Job 37:1-24	29th	Psalms 87:1–88:18	23rd	Proverbs 22:1-29	17th
Job 38:1-41	30th	Psalm 89:1-18	24th	Proverbs 23:1-35	18th
		Psalm 89:19-52	25th	Proverbs 24:1-34	19th
MAY		Psalms 90:1–91:16	26th	Proverbs 25:1-28	20th
Job 39:1-30	1st	Psalms 92:1–94:23	27th	Proverbs 26:1-28	21st
Job 40:1-24	2nd	Psalms 95:1–97:12	28th	Proverbs 27:1-27	22nd
Job 41:1-34	3rd	Psalms 98:1–99:9	29th	Proverbs 28:1-28	23rd
Job 42:1-17	4th	Psalms 100:1–102:17	30th	Proverbs 29:1-27	24th
Psalms 1:1–3:8	5th			Proverbs 30:1-33	25th
Psalms 4:1–6:10	6th	**JULY**		Proverbs 31:1-31	26th
Psalms 7:1–8:9	7th	Psalms 102:18–103:22	1st	Ecclesiastes 1:1-18	27th
Psalm 9:1-20	8th	Psalm 104:1-35	2nd	Ecclesiastes 2:1-26	28th
Psalm 10:1-18	9th	Psalm 105:1-45	3rd	Ecclesiastes 3:1-22	29th
Psalms 11:1–13:6	10th	Psalm 106:1-39	4th	Ecclesiastes 4:1-16	30th
Psalms 14:1–16:11	11th	Psalms 106:40–107:22	5th	Ecclesiastes 5:1–6:12	31st
Psalms 17:1–18:15	12th	Psalms 107:23–108:13	6th		
Psalm 18:16-50	13th	Psalm 109:1-31	7th	**SEPTEMBER**	
Psalms 19:1–21:7	14th	Psalms 110:1–112:10	8th	Ecclesiastes 7:1-29	1st
Psalms 21:8–22:26	15th	Psalms 113:1–115:18	9th	Ecclesiastes 8:1–9:10	2nd
Psalms 22:27–24:10	16th	Psalms 116:1–117:2	10th	Ecclesiastes 9:11–10:20	3rd
Psalm 25:1-22	17th	Psalm 118:1-29	11th	Ecclesiastes 11:1–12:14	4th
Psalms 26:1–27:14	18th	Psalm 119:1-48	12th	Song of Songs 1:1–2:7	5th
Psalms 28:1–30:12	19th	Psalm 119:49-88	13th	Song of Songs 2:8–3:11	6th
Psalm 31:1-24	20th	Psalm 119:89-136	14th	Song of Songs 4:1–5:2	7th
Psalms 32:1–33:22	21st	Psalms 119:137–120:7	15th	Song of Songs 5:3–6:13	8th
Psalm 34:1-22	22nd	Psalms 121:1–124:8	16th	Song of Songs 7:1–8:14	9th
Psalm 35:1-28	23rd	Psalms 125:1–129:8	17th	Isaiah 1:1-20	10th
Psalms 36:1–37:20	24th	Psalms 130:1–134:3	18th	Isaiah 1:21–2:11	11th
Psalms 37:21–38:12	25th	Psalms 135:1–136:26	19th	Isaiah 2:12–3:15	12th
Psalms 38:13–40:10	26th	Psalms 137:1–138:8	20th	Isaiah 3:16–5:7	13th
Psalms 40:11–42:4	27th	Psalm 139:1-24	21st	Isaiah 5:8-30	14th
Psalms 42:5–44:16	28th	Psalms 140:1–141:10	22nd	Isaiah 6:1–7:9	15th
Psalms 44:17–46:3	29th	Psalms 142:1–143:12	23rd	Isaiah 7:10–8:10	16th
Psalms 46:4–48:14	30th	Psalm 144:1-15	24th	Isaiah 8:11–9:7	17th
Psalm 49:1-20	31st	Psalm 145:1-21	25th	Isaiah 9:8–10:4	18th
		Psalms 146:1–147:20	26th	Isaiah 10:5-26	19th
JUNE		Psalms 148:1–150:6	27th	Isaiah 10:27–11:16	20th
Psalm 50:1-23	1st	Proverbs 1:1-33	28th	Isaiah 12:1–13:22	21st
Psalm 51:1-19	2nd	Proverbs 2:1-22	29th	Isaiah 14:1-27	22nd
Psalms 52:1–54:7	3rd	Proverbs 3:1-35	30th	Isaiah 14:28–15:9	23rd
Psalms 55:1–56:13	4th	Proverbs 4:1-27	31st	Isaiah 16:1-14	24th
Psalms 57:1–58:11	5th			Isaiah 17:1–18:7	25th
Psalms 59:1–60:12	6th	**AUGUST**		Isaiah 19:1–20:6	26th
Psalms 61:1–63:11	7th	Proverbs 5:1–6:19	1st	Isaiah 21:1-17	27th
Psalms 64:1–65:13	8th	Proverbs 6:20–7:27	2nd	Isaiah 22:1-25	28th
Psalms 66:1–67:7	9th	Proverbs 8:1-36	3rd	Isaiah 23:1-18	29th

Isaiah 24:1-23	30th	Jeremiah 13:1-27	24th	Ezekiel 4:1–5:17	14th
		Jeremiah 14:1-22	25th	Ezekiel 6:1–7:9	15th
OCTOBER		Jeremiah 15:1-21	26th	Ezekiel 7:10-27	16th
Isaiah 25:1-12	1st	Jeremiah 16:1-21	27th	Ezekiel 8:1–9:11	17th
Isaiah 26:1-21	2nd	Jeremiah 17:1-27	28th	Ezekiel 10:1–11:15	18th
Isaiah 27:1-13	3rd	Jeremiah 18:1-23	29th	Ezekiel 11:16–12:28	19th
Isaiah 28:1-22	4th	Jeremiah 19:1–20:6	30th	Ezekiel 13:1–14:11	20th
Isaiah 28:23–29:12	5th			Ezekiel 14:12–16:14	21st
Isaiah 29:13-30:7	6th	**DECEMBER**		Ezekiel 16:15-43	22nd
Isaiah 30:8-33	7th	Jeremiah 20:7–21:14	1st	Ezekiel 16:44-63	23rd
Isaiah 31:1–32:20	8th	Jeremiah 22:1-23	2nd	Ezekiel 17:1-24	24th
Isaiah 33:1-24	9th	Jeremiah 22:24–23:17	3rd	Ezekiel 18:1-32	25th
Isaiah 34:1–35:3	10th	Jeremiah 23:18–24:10	4th	Ezekiel 19:1-14	26th
Isaiah 35:4–36:22	11th	Jeremiah 25:1-31	5th	Ezekiel 20:1-31	27th
Isaiah 37:1-20	12th	Jeremiah 25:32–26:24	6th	Ezekiel 20:32–21:13	28th
Isaiah 37:21-38	13th	Jeremiah 27:1-22	7th	Ezekiel 21:14-32	29th
Isaiah 38:1–39:8	14th	Jeremiah 28:1-17	8th	Ezekiel 22:1-31	30th
Isaiah 40:1-26	15th	Jeremiah 29:1-32	9th	Ezekiel 23:1-34	31st
Isaiah 40:27–41:16	16th	Jeremiah 30:1-24	10th		
Isaiah 41:17–42:9	17th	Jeremiah 31:1-22	11th	**FEBRUARY**	
Isaiah 42:10–43:7	18th	Jeremiah 31:23-40	12th	Ezekiel 23:35–24:14	1st
Isaiah 43:8–44:5	19th	Jeremiah 32:1-25	13th	Ezekiel 24:15–25:17	2nd
Isaiah 44:6-23	20th	Jeremiah 32:26–33:9	14th	Ezekiel 26:1-21	3rd
Isaiah 44:24–45:17	21st	Jeremiah 33:10–34:7	15th	Ezekiel 27:1-27	4th
Isaiah 45:18–46:13	22nd	Jeremiah 34:8–35:19	16th	Ezekiel 27:28–28:10	5th
Isaiah 47:1-15	23rd	Jeremiah 36:1-32	17th	Ezekiel 28:11-26	6th
Isaiah 48:1-22	24th	Jeremiah 37:1–38:13	18th	Ezekiel 29:1-21	7th
Isaiah 49:1-21	25th	Jeremiah 38:14–39:18	19th	Ezekiel 30:1-26	8th
Isaiah 49:22–51:3	26th	Jeremiah 40:1–41:10	20th	Ezekiel 31:1–32:6	9th
Isaiah 51:4-23	27th	Jeremiah 41:11–42:22	21st	Ezekiel 32:7-28	10th
Isaiah 52:1-15	28th	Jeremiah 43:1–44:6	22nd	Ezekiel 32:29–33:20	11th
Isaiah 53:1-12	29th	Jeremiah 44:7-30	23rd	Ezekiel 33:21–34:19	12th
Isaiah 54:1–55:5	30th	Jeremiah 45:1–46:19	24th	Ezekiel 34:20–35:15	13th
Isaiah 55:6–56:12	31st	Jeremiah 46:20–47:7	25th	Ezekiel 36:1-32	14th
		Jeremiah 48:1-25	26th	Ezekiel 36:33–37:28	15th
NOVEMBER		Jeremiah 48:26-47	27th	Ezekiel 38:1-23	16th
Isaiah 57:1-21	1st	Jeremiah 49:1-22	28th	Ezekiel 39:1–40:4	17th
Isaiah 58:1-14	2nd	Jeremiah 49:23-39	29th	Ezekiel 40:5-37	18th
Isaiah 59:1-21	3rd	Jeremiah 50:1-16	30th	Ezekiel 40:38–41:12	19th
Isaiah 60:1-22	4th	Jeremiah 50:17-32	31st	Ezekiel 41:13–42:20	20th
Isaiah 61:1–62:12	5th			Ezekiel 43:1-27	21st
Isaiah 63:1-19	6th			Ezekiel 44:1-31	22nd
Isaiah 64:1–65:7	7th			Ezekiel 45:1-25	23rd
Isaiah 65:8–66:4	8th	**YEAR THREE**		Ezekiel 46:1-24	24th
Isaiah 66:5-24	9th			Ezekiel 47:1-23	25th
Jeremiah 1:1–2:3	10th			Ezekiel 48:1-35	26th
Jeremiah 2:4-25	11th	**JANUARY**		Daniel 1:1–2:16	27th
Jeremiah 2:26–3:13	12th	Jeremiah 50:33–51:10	1st	Daniel 2:17-49	28th
Jeremiah 3:14-4:4	13th	Jeremiah 51:11-32	2nd		
Jeremiah 4:5-31	14th	Jeremiah 51:33-48	3rd	**MARCH**	
Jeremiah 5:1-19	15th	Jeremiah 51:49-64	4th	Daniel 3:1-30	1st
Jeremiah 5:20–6:12	16th	Jeremiah 52:1-34	5th	Daniel 4:1-27	2nd
Jeremiah 6:13-30	17th	Lamentations 1:1-15	6th	Daniel 4:28–5:16	3rd
Jeremiah 7:1-34	18th	Lamentations 1:16–2:9	7th	Daniel 5:17–6:18	4th
Jeremiah 8:1-22	19th	Lamentations 2:10–3:9	8th	Daniel 6:19–7:14	5th
Jeremiah 9:1-22	20th	Lamentations 3:10-57	9th	Daniel 7:15–8:22	6th
Jeremiah 9:23–10:18	21st	Lamentations 3:58–4:15	10th	Daniel 8:23–9:19	7th
Jeremiah 10:19–11:23	22nd	Lamentations 4:16–5:22	11th	Daniel 9:20–11:4	8th
Jeremiah 12:1-17	23rd	Ezekiel 1:1-28	12th	Daniel 11:5-35	9th
		Ezekiel 2:1–3:27	13th		

Daniel 11:36–12:13	10th	Matthew 9:35–10:31	4th	Luke 11:29-54	30th
Hosea 1:1–2:13	11th	Matthew 10:32–11:30	5th		
Hosea 2:14–4:11	12th	Matthew 12:1-37	6th	**JULY**	
Hosea 4:12–5:15	13th	Matthew 12:38–13:23	7th	Luke 12:1-34	1st
Hosea 6:1–7:16	14th	Matthew 13:24-58	8th	Luke 12:35-59	2nd
Hosea 8:1–9:9	15th	Matthew 14:1-36	9th	Luke 13:1-30	3rd
Hosea 9:10–10:15	16th	Matthew 15:1-39	10th	Luke 13:31–14:24	4th
Hosea 11:1–12:14	17th	Matthew 16:1–17:13	11th	Luke 14:25–15:32	5th
Hosea 13:1–14:9	18th	Matthew 17:14–18:20	12th	Luke 16:1-31	6th
Joel 1:1-20	19th	Matthew 18:21–19:15	13th	Luke 17:1-37	7th
Joel 2:1-17	20th	Matthew 19:16–20:19	14th	Luke 18:1-34	8th
Joel 2:18-32	21st	Matthew 20:20–21:22	15th	Luke 18:35–19:27	9th
Joel 3:1-21	22nd	Matthew 21:23-46	16th	Luke 19:28-48	10th
Amos 1:1–2:5	23rd	Matthew 22:1-46	17th	Luke 20:1-26	11th
Amos 2:6–3:15	24th	Matthew 23:1-39	18th	Luke 20:27–21:4	12th
Amos 4:1-13	25th	Matthew 24:1-35	19th	Luke 21:5-38	13th
Amos 5:1-27	26th	Matthew 24:36–25:30	20th	Luke 22:1-38	14th
Amos 6:1-7:9	27th	Matthew 25:31–26:25	21st	Luke 22:39-65	15th
Amos 7:10–8:14	28th	Matthew 26:26-68	22nd	Luke 22:66–23:25	16th
Amos 9:1-15	29th	Matthew 26:69–27:26	23rd	Luke 23:26–24:12	17th
Obadiah	30th	Matthew 27:27-56	24th	Luke 24:13-53	18th
Jonah 1:1–2:10	31st	Matthew 27:57–28:20	25th	John 1:1-34	19th
		Mark 1:1-39	26th	John 1:35–2:12	20th
APRIL		Mark 1:40–2:22	27th	John 2:13–3:21	21st
Jonah 3:1–4:11	1st	Mark 2:23–3:35	28th	John 3:22–4:26	22nd
Micah 1:1–2:5	2nd	Mark 4:1-41	29th	John 4:27-54	23rd
Micah 2:6–4:2	3rd	Mark 5:1-43	30th	John 5:1-30	24th
Micah 4:3–5:9	4th	Mark 6:1-29	31st	John 5:31–6:24	25th
Micah 5:10–6:16	5th			John 6:25-71	26th
Micah 7:1-20	6th	**JUNE**		John 7:1-44	27th
Nahum 1:1–2:10	7th	Mark 6:30-56	1st	John 7:45–8:29	28th
Micah 2:11–3:19	8th	Mark 7:1-37	2nd	John 8:30-59	29th
Habakkuk 1:1-17	9th	Mark 8:1–9:1	3rd	John 9:1-41	30th
Habakkuk 2:1-20	10th	Mark 9:2-37	4th	John 10:1-42	31st
Habakkuk 3:1-19	11th	Mark 9:38–10:22	5th		
Zephaniah 1:1-18	12th	Mark 10:23–11:11	6th	**AUGUST**	
Zephaniah 2:1-15	13th	Mark 11:12–12:17	7th	John 11:1-44	1st
Zephaniah 3:1-20	14th	Mark 12:18-44	8th	John 11:45–12:19	2nd
Haggai 1:1-15	15th	Mark 13:1-37	9th	John 12:20-50	3rd
Haggai 2:1-23	16th	Mark 14:1-31	10th	John 13:1-38	4th
Zechariah 1:1–2:13	17th	Mark 14:32-72	11th	John 14:1-31	5th
Zechariah 3:1–5:11	18th	Mark 15:1-41	12th	John 15:1–16:4	6th
Zechariah 6:1–7:14	19th	Mark 15:42–16:20	13th	John 16:5-33	7th
Zechariah 8:1–9:8	20th	Luke 1:1-38	14th	John 17:1-26	8th
Zechariah 9:9–10:12	21st	Luke 1:39-80	15th	John 18:1-24	9th
Zechariah 11:1–12:14	22nd	Luke 2:1-40	16th	John 18:25-40	10th
Zechariah 13:1–14:21	23rd	Luke 2:41–3:20	17th	John 19:1-27	11th
Malachi 1:1-14	24th	Luke 3:21–4:13	18th	John 19:28–20:18	12th
Malachi 2:1–3:6	25th	Luke 4:14-44	19th	John 20:19–21:14	13th
Malachi 3:7–4:6	26th	Luke 5:1-39	20th	John 21:15-25	14th
Matthew 1:1–2:6	27th	Luke 6:1-36	21st	Acts 1:1–2:13	15th
Matthew 2:7–3:17	28th	Luke 6:37–7:17	22nd	Acts 2:14-40	16th
Matthew 4:1–5:12	29th	Luke 7:18-50	23rd	Acts 2:41–3:26	17th
Matthew 5:13–6:4	30th	Luke 8:1-25	24th	Acts 4:1-31	18th
		Luke 8:26-56	25th	Acts 4:32–5:16	19th
MAY		Luke 9:1-36	26th	Acts 5:17–6:7	20th
Matthew 6:5–7:12	1st	Luke 9:37-62	27th	Acts 6:8–7:22	21st
Matthew 7:13–8:27	2nd	Luke 10:1-37	28th	Acts 7:23-53	22nd
Matthew 8:28–9:34	3rd	Luke 10:38–11:28	29th	Acts 7:54–8:25	23rd

Acts 8:26—9:9	24th	1 Corinthians 6:1-20	5th	2 Timothy 3:10—4:22	18th
Acts 9:10-43	25th	1 Corinthians 7:1-40	6th	Titus 1:1—2:15	19th
Acts 10:1-43	26th	1 Corinthians 8:1—9:27	7th	Titus 3:1-15	20th
Acts 10:44—11:30	27th	1 Corinthians 10:1—11:1	8th	Philemon	21st
Acts 12:1—13:3	28th	1 Corinthians 11:2-34	9th	Hebrews 1:1—2:4	22nd
Acts 13:4-41	29th	1 Corinthians 12:1—13:13	10th	Hebrews 2:5—3:19	23rd
Acts 13:42—14:7	30th	1 Corinthians 14:1-40	11th	Hebrews 4:1—5:10	24th
Acts 14:8-28	31st	1 Corinthians 15:1-34	12th	Hebrews 5:11—7:10	25th
		1 Corinthians 15:35-58	13th	Hebrews 7:11—8:13	26th
SEPTEMBER		1 Corinthians 16:1-24	14th	Hebrews 9:1-28	27th
Acts 15:1-35	1st	2 Corinthians 1:1-2:4	15th	Hebrews 10:1-39	28th
Acts 15:36—16:15	2nd	2 Corinthians 2:5—3:18	16th	Hebrews 11:1-40	29th
Acts 16:16-40	3rd	2 Corinthians 4:1—5:15	17th	Hebrews 12:1-29	30th
Acts 17:1-34	4th	2 Corinthians 5:16—7:1	18th		
Acts 18:1—19:7	5th	2 Corinthians 7:2—8:15	19th	**DECEMBER**	
Acts 19:8-41	6th	2 Corinthians 8:16—9:15	20th	Hebrews 13:1-25	1st
Acts 20:1-38	7th	2 Corinthians 10:1—11:15	21st	James 1:1—2:13	2nd
Acts 21:1-36	8th	2 Corinthians 11:16—12:10	22nd	James 2:14—3:18	3rd
Acts 21:37—22:21	9th	2 Corinthians 12:11—13:13	23rd	James 4:1—5:20	4th
Acts 22:22—23:10	10th	Galatians 1:1—2:10	24th	1 Peter 1:1-25	5th
Acts 23:11-35	11th	Galatians 2:11—3:26	25th	1 Peter 2:1—3:7	6th
Acts 24:1-27	12th	Galatians 3:27—4:31	26th	1 Peter 3:8—4:11	7th
Acts 25:1-27	13th	Galatians 5:1—6:18	27th	1 Peter 4:12—5:14	8th
Acts 26:1-32	14th	Ephesians 1:1—2:10	28th	2 Peter 1:1-21	9th
Acts 27:1-26	15th	Ephesians 2:11—3:21	29th	2 Peter 2:1-22	10th
Acts 27:27—28:10	16th	Ephesians 4:1—5:14	30th	2 Peter 3:1-18	11th
Acts 28:11-31	17th	Ephesians 5:15—6:24	31st	1 John 1:1—2:17	12th
Romans 1:1-32	18th			1 John 2:18—3:24	13th
Romans 2:1-29	19th	**NOVEMBER**		1 John 4:1—5:21	14th
Romans 3:1-31	20th	Philippians 1:1—2:11	1st	2 John—3 John	15th
Romans 4:1-25	21st	Philippians 2:12—3:11	2nd	Jude	16th
Romans 5:1—6:14	22nd	Philippians 3:12—4:23	3rd	Revelation 1:1-2:7	17th
Romans 6:15—7:25	23rd	Colossians 1:1—2:3	4th	Revelation 2:8—3:6	18th
Romans 8:1-39	24th	Colossians 2:4—3:17	5th	Revelation 3:7—4:11	19th
Romans 9:1-33	25th	Colossians 3:18—4:18	6th	Revelation 5:1—6:11	20th
Romans 10:1—11:10	26th	1 Thessalonians 1:1—2:16	7th	Revelation 6:12—8:6	21st
Romans 11:11-36	27th	1 Thessalonians 2:17—4:12	8th	Revelation 8:7—9:21	22nd
Romans 12:1—13:14	28th	1 Thessalonians 4:13—5:28	9th	Revelation 10:1—11:19	23rd
Romans 14:1—15:13	29th	2 Thessalonians 1:1—2:12	10th	Revelation 12:1—13:10	24th
Romans 15:14-33	30th	2 Thessalonians 2:13—3:18	11th	Revelation 13:11—14:20	25th
		1 Timothy 1:1—2:15	12th	Revelation 15:1—16:16	26th
OCTOBER		1 Timothy 3:1—5:2	13th	Revelation 16:17—17:18	27th
Romans 16:1-27	1st	1 Timothy 5:3-25	14th	Revelation 18:1-24	28th
1 Corinthians 1:1—2:5	2nd	1 Timothy 6:1-21	15th	Revelation 19:1—20:6	29th
1 Corinthians 2:6—3:23	3rd	2 Timothy 1:1—2:13	16th	Revelation 20:7—21:27	30th
1 Corinthians 4:1—5:13	4th	2 Timothy 2:14—3:9	17th	Revelation 22:1-21	31st

DAILY BREAD: THE WORD OF GOD IN A YEAR

Edited by Heather Collins-Grattan Floyd

JANUARY

This is my beloved Son, with whom I am well-pleased. Listen to him (Mt 17:5)!

Genesis 1	Matthew 1	1st	Ezra 1	Acts 1
Genesis 2	Matthew 2	2nd	Ezra 2	Acts 2
Genesis 3	Matthew 3	3rd	Ezra 3	Acts 3
Genesis 4	Matthew 4	4th	Ezra 4	Acts 4
Genesis 5	Matthew 5	5th	Ezra 5	Acts 5
Genesis 6	Matthew 6	6th	Ezra 6	Acts 6
Genesis 7	Matthew 7	7th	Ezra 7	Acts 7
Genesis 8	Matthew 8	8th	Ezra 8	Acts 8
Genesis 9–10	Matthew 9	9th	Ezra 9	Acts 9
Genesis 11	Matthew 10	10th	Ezra 10	Acts 10
Genesis 12	Matthew 11	11th	Nehemiah 1	Acts 11
Genesis 13	Matthew 12	12th	Nehemiah 2	Acts 12
Genesis 14	Matthew 13	13th	Nehemiah 3	Acts 13
Genesis 15	Matthew 14	14th	Nehemiah 4	Acts 14
Genesis 16	Matthew 15	15th	Nehemiah 5	Acts 15
Genesis 17	Matthew 16	16th	Nehemiah 6	Acts 16
Genesis 18	Matthew 17	17th	Nehemiah 7	Acts 17
Genesis 19	Matthew 18	18th	Nehemiah 8	Acts 18
Genesis 20	Matthew 19	19th	Nehemiah 9	Acts 19
Genesis 21	Matthew 20	20th	Nehemiah 10	Acts 20
Genesis 22	Matthew 21	21st	Nehemiah 11	Acts 21
Genesis 23	Matthew 22	22nd	Nehemiah 12	Acts 22
Genesis 24	Matthew 23	23rd	Nehemiah 13	Acts 23
Genesis 25	Matthew 24	24th	Esther 1	Acts 24
Genesis 26	Matthew 25	25th	Esther 2	Acts 25
Genesis 27	Matthew 26	26th	Esther 3	Acts 26
Genesis 28	Matthew 27	27th	Esther 4	Acts 27
Genesis 29	Matthew 28	28th	Esther 5	Acts 28
Genesis 30	Mark 1	29th	Esther 6	Romans 1
Genesis 31	Mark 2	30th	Esther 7	Romans 2
Genesis 32	Mark 3	31st	Esther 8	Romans 3

FEBRUARY

I have treasured the words from his mouth more than my daily food (Jb 23:12).

Genesis 33	Mark 4	1st	Esther 9–10	Romans 4
Genesis 34	Mark 5	2nd	Job 1	Romans 5
Genesis 35–36	Mark 6	3rd	Job 2	Romans 6
Genesis 37	Mark 7	4th	Job 3	Romans 7
Genesis 38	Mark 8	5th	Job 4	Romans 8
Genesis 39	Mark 9	6th	Job 5	Romans 9
Genesis 40	Mark 10	7th	Job 6	Romans 10
Genesis 41	Mark 11	8th	Job 7	Romans 11
Genesis 42	Mark 12	9th	Job 8	Romans 12
Genesis 43	Mark 13	10th	Job 9	Romans 13
Genesis 44	Mark 14	11th	Job 10	Romans 14
Genesis 45	Mark 15	12th	Job 11	Romans 15
Genesis 46	Mark 16	13th	Job 12	Romans 16
Genesis 47	Luke 1:1-38	14th	Job 13	1 Corinthians 1
Genesis 48	Luke 1:39-80	15th	Job 14	1 Corinthians 2
Genesis 49	Luke 2	16th	Job 15	1 Corinthians 3

Genesis 50	Luke 3	17th	Job 16−17	1 Corinthians 4
Exodus 1	Luke 4	18th	Job 18	1 Corinthians 5
Exodus 2	Luke 5	19th	Job 19	1 Corinthians 6
Exodus 3	Luke 6	20th	Job 20	1 Corinthians 7
Exodus 4	Luke 7	21st	Job 21	1 Corinthians 8
Exodus 5	Luke 8	22nd	Job 22	1 Corinthians 9
Exodus 6	Luke 9	23rd	Job 23	1 Corinthians 10
Exodus 7	Luke 10	24th	Job 24	1 Corinthians 11
Exodus 8	Luke 11	25th	Job 25−26	1 Corinthians 12
Exodus 9	Luke 12	26th	Job 27	1 Corinthians 13
Exodus 10	Luke 13	27th	Job 28	1 Corinthians 14
Exodus 11−12:21	Luke 14	28th	Job 29	1 Corinthians 15

MARCH
But Mary was treasuring up all these things in her heart and meditating on them (Lk 2:19).

Exodus 12:22ff.	Luke 15	1st	Job 30	1 Corinthians 16
Exodus 13	Luke 16	2nd	Job 31	2 Corinthians 1
Exodus 14	Luke 17	3rd	Job 32	2 Corinthians 2
Exodus 15	Luke 18	4th	Job 33	2 Corinthians 3
Exodus 16	Luke 19	5th	Job 34	2 Corinthians 4
Exodus 17	Luke 20	6th	Job 35	2 Corinthians 5
Exodus 18	Luke 21	7th	Job 36	2 Corinthians 6
Exodus 19	Luke 22	8th	Job 37	2 Corinthians 7
Exodus 20	Luke 23	9th	Job 38	2 Corinthians 8
Exodus 21	Luke 24	10th	Job 39	2 Corinthians 9
Exodus 22	John 1	11th	Job 40	2 Corinthians 10
Exodus 23	John 2	12th	Job 41	2 Corinthians 11
Exodus 24	John 3	13th	Job 42	2 Corinthians 12
Exodus 25	John 4	14th	Proverbs 1	2 Corinthians 13
Exodus 26	John 5	15th	Proverbs 2	Galatians 1
Exodus 27	John 6	16th	Proverbs 3	Galatians 2
Exodus 28	John 7	17th	Proverbs 4	Galatians 3
Exodus 29	John 8	18th	Proverbs 5	Galatians 4
Exodus 30	John 9	19th	Proverbs 6	Galatians 5
Exodus 31	John 10	20th	Proverbs 7	Galatians 6
Exodus 32	John 11	21st	Proverbs 8	Ephesians 1
Exodus 33	John 12	22nd	Proverbs 9	Ephesians 2
Exodus 34	John 13	23rd	Proverbs 10	Ephesians 3
Exodus 35	John 14	24th	Proverbs 11	Ephesians 4
Exodus 36	John 15	25th	Proverbs 12	Ephesians 5
Exodus 37	John 16	26th	Proverbs 13	Ephesians 6
Exodus 38	John 17	27th	Proverbs 14	Philippians 1
Exodus 39	John 18	28th	Proverbs 15	Philippians 2
Exodus 40	John 19	29th	Proverbs 16	Philippians 3
Leviticus 1	John 20	30th	Proverbs 17	Philippians 4
Leviticus 2−3	John 21	31st	Proverbs 18	Colossians 1

APRIL
Send your light and your truth; let them lead me (Ps 43:3).

Leviticus 4	Psalms 1−2	1st	Proverbs 19	Colossians 2
Leviticus 5	Psalms 3−4	2nd	Proverbs 20	Colossians 3
Leviticus 6	Psalms 5−6	3rd	Proverbs 21	Colossians 4
Leviticus 7	Psalms 7−8	4th	Proverbs 22	1 Thessalonians 1
Leviticus 8	Psalm 9	5th	Proverbs 23	1 Thessalonians 2
Leviticus 9	Psalm 10	6th	Proverbs 24	1 Thessalonians 3
Leviticus 10	Psalms 11−12	7th	Proverbs 25	1 Thessalonians 4
Leviticus 11−12	Psalms 13−14	8th	Proverbs 26	1 Thessalonians 5
Leviticus 13	Psalms 15−16	9th	Proverbs 27	2 Thessalonians 1
Leviticus 14	Psalm 17	10th	Proverbs 28	2 Thessalonians 2
Leviticus 15	Psalm 18	11th	Proverbs 29	2 Thessalonians 3

Leviticus 16	Psalm 19	12th	Proverbs 30	1 Timothy 1
Leviticus 17	Psalms 20–21	13th	Proverbs 31	1 Timothy 2
Leviticus 18	Psalm 22	14th	Ecclesiastes 1	1 Timothy 3
Leviticus 19	Psalms 23–24	15th	Ecclesiastes 2	1 Timothy 4
Leviticus 20	Psalm 25	16th	Ecclesiastes 3	1 Timothy 5
Leviticus 21	Psalms 26–27	17th	Ecclesiastes 4	1 Timothy 6
Leviticus 22	Psalms 28–29	18th	Ecclesiastes 5	2 Timothy 1
Leviticus 23	Psalm 30	19th	Ecclesiastes 6	2 Timothy 2
Leviticus 24	Psalm 31	20th	Ecclesiastes 7	2 Timothy 3
Leviticus 25	Psalm 32	21st	Ecclesiastes 8	2 Timothy 4
Leviticus 26	Psalm 33	22nd	Ecclesiastes 9	Titus 1
Leviticus 27	Psalm 4	23rd	Ecclesiastes 10	Titus 2
Numbers 1	Psalm 35	24th	Ecclesiastes 11	Titus 3
Numbers 2	Psalm 36	25th	Ecclesiastes 12	Philemon
Numbers 3	Psalm 37	26th	Song of Songs 1	Hebrews 1
Numbers 4	Psalm 38	27th	Song of Songs 2	Hebrews 2
Numbers 5	Psalm 39	28th	Song of Songs 3	Hebrews 3
Numbers 6	Psalms 40–41	29th	Song of Songs 4	Hebrews 4
Numbers 7	Psalms 42–43	30th	Song of Songs 5	Hebrews 5

MAY

From infancy you have known the sacred Scriptures (2Tm 3:15).

Numbers 8	Psalm 44	1st	Song of Songs 6	Hebrews 6
Numbers 9	Psalm 45	2nd	Song of Songs 7	Hebrews 7
Numbers 10	Psalms 46–47	3rd	Song of Songs 8	Hebrews 8
Numbers 11	Psalm 48	4th	Isaiah 1	Hebrews 9
Numbers 12-13	Psalm 49	5th	Isaiah 2	Hebrews 10
Numbers 14	Psalm 50	6th	Isaiah 3–4	Hebrews 11
Numbers 15	Psalm 51	7th	Isaiah 5	Hebrews 12
Numbers 16	Psalms 52–54	8th	Isaiah 6	Hebrews 13
Numbers 17–18	Psalm 55	9th	Isaiah 7	James 1
Numbers 19	Psalms 56–57	10th	Isaiah 8–9:7	James 2
Numbers 20	Psalms 58–59	11th	Isaiah 9:8–10:4	James 3
Numbers 21	Psalms 60–61	12th	Isaiah 10:5ff.	James 4
Numbers 22	Psalms 62–63	13th	Isaiah 11–12	James 5
Numbers 23	Psalms 64–65	14th	Isaiah 13	1 Peter 1
Numbers 24	Psalms 66–67	15th	Isaiah 14	1 Peter 2
Numbers 25	Psalm 68	16th	Isaiah 15	1 Peter 3
Numbers 26	Psalm 69	17th	Isaiah 16	1 Peter 4
Numbers 27	Psalms 70–71	18th	Isaiah 17–18	1 Peter 5
Numbers 28	Psalm 72	19th	Isaiah 19–20	2 Peter 1
Numbers 29	Psalm 73	20th	Isaiah 21	2 Peter 2
Numbers 30	Psalm 74	21st	Isaiah 22	2 Peter 3
Numbers 31	Psalms 75–76	22nd	Isaiah 23	1 John 1
Numbers 32	Psalm 77	23rd	Isaiah 24	1 John 2
Numbers 33	Psalm 78:1-37	24th	Isaiah 25	1 John 3
Numbers 34	Psalm 78:38ff.	25th	Isaiah 26	1 John 4
Numbers 35	Psalm 79	26th	Isaiah 27	1 John 5
Numbers 36	Psalm 80	27th	Isaiah 28	2 John
Deuteronomy 1	Psalms 81–82	28th	Isaiah 29	3 John
Deuteronomy 2	Psalms 83–84	29th	Isaiah 30	Jude
Deuteronomy 3	Psalm 85	30th	Isaiah 31	Revelation 1
Deuteronomy 4	Psalms 86–87	31st	Isaiah 32	Revelation 2

JUNE

Blessed is the one who reads aloud the words of this prophecy, and blessed are those who hear the words of this prophecy and keep what is written in it (Rv 1:3).

Deuteronomy 5	Psalm 88	1st	Isaiah 33	Revelation 3
Deuteronomy 6	Psalm 89	2nd	Isaiah 34	Revelation 4
Deuteronomy 7	Psalm 90	3rd	Isaiah 35	Revelation 5

Deuteronomy 8	Psalm 91	4th	Isaiah 36	Revelation 6
Deuteronomy 9	Psalms 92–93	5th	Isaiah 37	Revelation 7
Deuteronomy 10	Psalm 94	6th	Isaiah 38	Revelation 8
Deuteronomy 11	Psalms 95–96	7th	Isaiah 39	Revelation 9
Deuteronomy 12	Psalms 97–98	8th	Isaiah 40	Revelation 10
Deuteronomy 13–14	Psalms 99–101	9th	Isaiah 41	Revelation 11
Deuteronomy 15	Psalm 102	10th	Isaiah 42	Revelation 12
Deuteronomy 16	Psalm 103	11th	Isaiah 43	Revelation 13
Deuteronomy 17	Psalm 104	12th	Isaiah 44	Revelation 14
Deuteronomy 18	Psalm 105	13th	Isaiah 45	Revelation 15
Deuteronomy 19	Psalm 106	14th	Isaiah 46	Revelation 16
Deuteronomy 20	Psalm 107	15th	Isaiah 47	Revelation 17
Deuteronomy 21	Psalms 108–109	16th	Isaiah 48	Revelation 18
Deuteronomy 22	Psalms 110–111	17th	Isaiah 49	Revelation 19
Deuteronomy 23	Psalms 112–113	18th	Isaiah 50	Revelation 20
Deuteronomy 24	Psalms 114–115	19th	Isaiah 51	Revelation 21
Deuteronomy 25	Psalm 116	20th	Isaiah 52	Revelation 22
Deuteronomy 26	Psalms 117–118	21st	Isaiah 53	Matthew 1
Deuteronomy 27–28:19	Psalm 119:1-24	22nd	Isaiah 54	Matthew 2
Deuteronomy 28:2off.	Psalm 119:25-48	23rd	Isaiah 55	Matthew 3
Deuteronomy 29	Psalm 119:49-72	24th	Isaiah 56	Matthew 4
Deuteronomy 30	Psalm 119:73-96	25th	Isaiah 57	Matthew 5
Deuteronomy 31	Psalm 119:97-120	26th	Isaiah 58	Matthew 6
Deuteronomy 32	Psalm 119:121-144	27th	Isaiah 59	Matthew 7
Deuteronomy 33–34	Psalm 119:145-176	28th	Isaiah 60	Matthew 8
Joshua 1	Psalms 120–122	29th	Isaiah 61	Matthew 9
Joshua 2	Psalms 123–125	30th	Isaiah 62	Matthew 10

JULY

They received the word with eagerness and examined the Scriptures daily to see if these things were so (Ac 17:11).

Joshua 3	Psalms 126–128	1st	Isaiah 63	Matthew 11
Joshua 4	Psalms 129–131	2nd	Isaiah 64	Matthew 12
Joshua 5–6:5	Psalms 132–134	3rd	Isaiah 65	Matthew 13
Joshua 6:6ff.	Psalms 135–136	4th	Isaiah 66	Matthew 14
Joshua 7	Psalms 137–138	5th	Jeremiah 1	Matthew 15
Joshua 8	Psalm 139	6th	Jeremiah 2	Matthew 16
Joshua 9	Psalms 140–141	7th	Jeremiah 3	Matthew 17
Joshua 10	Psalms 142–143	8th	Jeremiah 4	Matthew 18
Joshua 11	Psalm 144	9th	Jeremiah 5	Matthew 19
Joshua 12–13	Psalm 145	10th	Jeremiah 6	Matthew 20
Joshua 14–15	Psalms 146–147	11th	Jeremiah 7	Matthew 21
Joshua 16–17	Psalm 148	12th	Jeremiah 8	Matthew 22
Joshua 18–19	Psalms 149–150	13th	Jeremiah 9	Matthew 23
Joshua 20–21	Acts 1	14th	Jeremiah 10	Matthew 24
Joshua 22	Acts 2	15th	Jeremiah 11	Matthew 25
Joshua 23	Acts 3	16th	Jeremiah 12	Matthew 26
Joshua 24	Acts 4	17th	Jeremiah 13	Matthew 27
Judges 1	Acts 5	18th	Jeremiah 14	Matthew 28
Judges 2	Acts 6	19th	Jeremiah 15	Mark 1
Judges 3	Acts 7	20th	Jeremiah 16	Mark 2
Judges 4	Acts 8	21st	Jeremiah 17	Mark 3
Judges 5	Acts 9	22nd	Jeremiah 18	Mark 4
Judges 6	Acts 10	23rd	Jeremiah 19	Mark 5
Judges 7	Acts 11	24th	Jeremiah 20	Mark 6
Judges 8	Acts 12	25th	Jeremiah 21	Mark 7
Judges 9	Acts 13	26th	Jeremiah 22	Mark 8
Judges 10–11:11	Acts 14	27th	Jeremiah 23	Mark 9
Judges 11:12ff.	Acts 15	28th	Jeremiah 24	Mark 10
Judges 12	Acts 16	29th	Jeremiah 25	Mark 11
Judges 13	Acts 17	30th	Jeremiah 26	Mark 12

Judges 14	Acts 18	31st	Jeremiah 27	Mark 13

AUGUST
"Speak, for your servant is listening" (1Sm 3:10).

Judges 15	Acts 19	1st	Jeremiah 28	Mark 14
Judges 16	Acts 20	2nd	Jeremiah 29	Mark 15
Judges 17	Acts 21	3rd	Jeremiah 30–31	Mark 16
Judges 18	Acts 22	4th	Jeremiah 32	Psalms 1–2
Judges 19	Acts 23	5th	Jeremiah 33	Psalms 3–4
Judges 20	Acts 24	6th	Jeremiah 34	Psalms 5–6
Judges 21	Acts 25	7th	Jeremiah 35	Psalms 7–8
Ruth 1	Acts 26	8th	Jeremiah 36	Psalm 9
Ruth 2	Acts 27	9th	Jeremiah 37	Psalm 10
Ruth 3–4	Acts 28	10th	Jeremiah 38	Psalms 11–12
1 Samuel 1	Romans 1	11th	Jeremiah 39	Psalms 13–14
1 Samuel 2	Romans 2	12th	Jeremiah 40	Psalms 15–16
1 Samuel 3	Romans 3	13th	Jeremiah 41	Psalm 17
1 Samuel 4	Romans 4	14th	Jeremiah 42	Psalm 18
1 Samuel 5–6	Romans 5	15th	Jeremiah 43	Psalm 19
1 Samuel 7–8	Romans 6	16th	Jeremiah 44	Psalms 20–21
1 Samuel 9	Romans 7	17th	Jeremiah 46	Psalm 22
1 Samuel 10	Romans 8	18th	Jeremiah 47	Psalms 23–24
1 Samuel 11	Romans 9	19th	Jeremiah 48	Psalm 25
1 Samuel 12	Romans 10	20th	Jeremiah 49	Psalms 26–27
1 Samuel 13	Romans 11	21st	Jeremiah 50	Psalms 28–29
1 Samuel 14	Romans 12	22nd	Jeremiah 51	Psalm 30
1 Samuel 15	Romans 13	23rd	Jeremiah 52	Psalm 31
1 Samuel 16	Romans 14	24th	Lamentations 1	Psalm 32
1 Samuel 17	Romans 15	25th	Lamentations 2	Psalm 33
1 Samuel 18	Romans 16	26th	Lamentations 3	Psalm 34
1 Samuel 19	1 Corinthians 1	27th	Lamentations 4	Psalm 35
1 Samuel 20	1 Corinthians 2	28th	Lamentations 5	Psalm 36
1 Samuel 21–22	1 Corinthians 3	29th	Ezekiel 1	Psalm 37
1 Samuel 23	1 Corinthians 4	30th	Ezekiel 2	Psalm 38
1 Samuel 24	1 Corinthians 5	31st	Ezekiel 3	Psalm 39

SEPTEMBER
The instruction of the Lord is perfect, renewing one's life (Ps 19:7).

1 Samuel 25	1 Corinthians 6	1st	Ezekiel 4	Psalms 40–41
1 Samuel 26	1 Corinthians 7	2nd	Ezekiel 5	Psalms 42–43
1 Samuel 27	1 Corinthians 8	3rd	Ezekiel 6	Psalm 44
1 Samuel 28	1 Corinthians 9	4th	Ezekiel 7	Psalm 45
1 Samuel 29–30	1 Corinthians 10	5th	Ezekiel 8	Psalms 46–47
1 Samuel 31	1 Corinthians 11	6th	Ezekiel 9	Psalm 48
2 Samuel 1	1 Corinthians 12	7th	Ezekiel 10	Psalm 49
2 Samuel 2	1 Corinthians 13	8th	Ezekiel 11	Psalm 50
2 Samuel 3	1 Corinthians 14	9th	Ezekiel 12	Psalm 51
2 Samuel 4–5	1 Corinthians 15	10th	Ezekiel 13	Psalms 52–54
2 Samuel 6	1 Corinthians 16	11th	Ezekiel 14	Psalm 55
2 Samuel 7	2 Corinthians 1	12th	Ezekiel 15	Psalms 56–57
2 Samuel 8–9	2 Corinthians 2	13th	Ezekiel 16	Psalms 58–59
2 Samuel 10	2 Corinthians 3	14th	Ezekiel 17	Psalms 60–61
2 Samuel 11	2 Corinthians 4	15th	Ezekiel 18	Psalms 62–63
2 Samuel 12	2 Corinthians 5	16th	Ezekiel 19	Psalms 64–65
2 Samuel 13	2 Corinthians 6	17th	Ezekiel 20	Psalms 66–67
2 Samuel 14	2 Corinthians 7	18th	Ezekiel 21	Psalm 68
2 Samuel 15	2 Corinthians 8	19th	Ezekiel 22	Psalm 69
2 Samuel 16	2 Corinthians 9	20th	Ezekiel 23	Psalms 70–71
2 Samuel 17	2 Corinthians 10	21st	Ezekiel 24	Psalm 72
2 Samuel 18	2 Corinthians 11	22nd	Ezekiel 25	Psalm 73

2 Samuel 19	2 Corinthians 12	23rd	Ezekiel 26	Psalm 74
2 Samuel 20	2 Corinthians 13	24th	Ezekiel 27	Psalms 75–76
2 Samuel 21	Galatians 1	25th	Ezekiel 28	Psalm 77
2 Samuel 22	Galatians 2	26th	Ezekiel 29	Psalm 78:1-37
2 Samuel 23	Galatians 3	27th	Ezekiel 30	Psalm 78:38ff.
2 Samuel 24	Galatians 4	28th	Ezekiel 31	Psalm 79
1 Kings 1	Galatians 5	29th	Ezekiel 32	Psalm 80
1 Kings 2	Galatians 6	30th	Ezekiel 33	Psalms 81–82

OCTOBER

How I love your instruction! It is my meditation all day long (Ps 119:97).

1 Kings 3	Ephesians 1	1st	Ezekiel 34	Psalms 83–84
1 Kings 4–5	Ephesians 2	2nd	Ezekiel 35	Psalm 85
1 Kings 6	Ephesians 3	3rd	Ezekiel 36	Psalm 86
1 Kings 7	Ephesians 4	4th	Ezekiel 37	Psalms 87–88
1 Kings 8	Ephesians 5	5th	Ezekiel 38	Psalm 89
1 Kings 9	Ephesians 6	6th	Ezekiel 39	Psalm 90
1 Kings 10	Philippians 1	7th	Ezekiel 40	Psalm 91
1 Kings 11	Philippians 2	8th	Ezekiel 41	Psalms 92–93
1 Kings 12	Philippians 3	9th	Ezekiel 42	Psalm 94
1 Kings 13	Philippians 4	10th	Ezekiel 43	Psalms 95–96
1 Kings 14	Colossians 1	11th	Ezekiel 44	Psalms 97–98
1 Kings 15	Colossians 2	12th	Ezekiel 45	Psalms 99–101
1 Kings 16	Colossians 3	13th	Ezekiel 46	Psalm 102
1 Kings 17	Colossians 4	14th	Ezekiel 47	Psalm 103
1 Kings 18	1 Thessalonians 1	15th	Ezekiel 48	Psalm 104
1 Kings 19	1 Thessalonians 2	16th	Daniel 1	Psalm 105
1 Kings 20	1 Thessalonians 3	17th	Daniel 2	Psalm 106
1 Kings 21	1 Thessalonians 4	18th	Daniel 3	Psalm 107
1 Kings 22	1 Thessalonians 5	19th	Daniel 4	Psalms 108–109
2 Kings 1	2 Thessalonians 1	20th	Daniel 5	Psalms 110–111
2 Kings 2	2 Thessalonians 2	21st	Daniel 6	Psalms 112–113
2 Kings 3	2 Thessalonians 3	22nd	Daniel 7	Psalms 114–115
2 Kings 4	1 Timothy 1	23rd	Daniel 8	Psalm 116
2 Kings 5	1 Timothy 2	24th	Daniel 9	Psalms 117–118
2 Kings 6	1 Timothy 3	25th	Daniel 10	Psalm 119:1-24
2 Kings 7	1 Timothy 4	26th	Daniel 11	Psalm 119:25-48
2 Kings 8	1 Timothy 5	27th	Daniel 12	Psalm 119:49-72
2 Kings 9	1 Timothy 6	28th	Hosea 1	Psalm 119:73-96
2 Kings 10	2 Timothy 1	29th	Hosea 2	Psalm 119:97-120
2 Kings 11–12	2 Timothy 2	30th	Hosea 3–4	Psalm 119:121-144
2 Kings 13	2 Timothy 3	31st	Hosea 5–6	Psalm 119:145-176

NOVEMBER

Like newborn infants, desire the pure milk of the word, so that you may grow up into your salvation (1Pt 2:2).

2 Kings 14	2 Timothy 4	1st	Hosea 7	Psalms 120–122
2 Kings 15	Titus 1	2nd	Hosea 8	Psalms 123–125
2 Kings 16	Titus 2	3rd	Hosea 9	Psalms 126–128
2 Kings 17	Titus 3	4th	Hosea 10	Psalms 129–131
2 Kings 18	Philemon 1	5th	Hosea 11	Psalms 132–134
2 Kings 19	Hebrews 1	6th	Hosea 12	Psalms 135–136
2 Kings 20	Hebrews 2	7th	Hosea 13	Psalms 137–138
2 Kings 21	Hebrews 3	8th	Hosea 14	Psalm 139
2 Kings 22	Hebrews 4	9th	Joel 1	Psalms 140–141
2 Kings 23	Hebrews 5	10th	Joel 2	Psalm 142
2 Kings 24	Hebrews 6	11th	Joel 3	Psalm 143
2 Kings 25	Hebrews 7	12th	Amos 1	Psalm 144
1 Chronicles 1–2	Hebrews 8	13th	Amos 2	Psalm 145
1 Chronicles 3–4	Hebrews 9	14th	Amos 3	Psalms 146–147
1 Chronicles 5–6	Hebrews 10	15th	Amos 4	Psalms 148–150

1 Chronicles 7–8	Hebrews 11	16th	Amos 5	Luke 1:1-38
1 Chronicles 9–10	Hebrews 12	17th	Amos 6	Luke 1:39ff.
1 Chronicles 11–12	Hebrews 13	18th	Amos 7	Luke 2
1 Chronicles 13–14	James 1	19th	Amos 8	Luke 3
1 Chronicles 15	James 2	20th	Amos 9	Luke 4
1 Chronicles 16	James 3	21st	Obadiah	Luke 5
1 Chronicles 17	James 4	22nd	Jonah 1	Luke 6
1 Chronicles 18	James 5	23rd	Jonah 2	Luke 7
1 Chronicles 19–20	1 Peter 1	24th	Jonah 3	Luke 8
1 Chronicles 21	1 Peter 2	25th	Jonah 4	Luke 9
1 Chronicles 22	1 Peter 3	26th	Micah 1	Luke 10
1 Chronicles 23	1 Peter 4	27th	Micah 2	Luke 11
1 Chronicles 24–25	1 Peter 5	28th	Micah 3	Luke 12
1 Chronicles 26–27	2 Peter 1	29th	Micah 4	Luke 13
1 Chronicles 28	2 Peter 2	30th	Micah 5	Luke 14

DECEMBER

The instruction of his God is in his heart; his steps do not falter (Ps 37:31).

1 Chronicles 29	2 Peter 3	1st	Micah 6	Luke 15
2 Chronicles 1	1 John 1	2nd	Micah 7	Luke 16
2 Chronicles 2	1 John 2	3rd	Nahum 1	Luke 17
2 Chronicles 3–4	1 John 3	4th	Nahum 2	Luke 18
2 Chronicles 5–6:11	1 John 4	5th	Nahum 3	Luke 19
2 Chronicles 6:12ff.	1 John 5	6th	Habakkuk 1	Luke 20
2 Chronicles 7	2 John	7th	Habakkuk 2	Luke 21
2 Chronicles 8	3 John	8th	Habakkuk 3	Luke 22
2 Chronicles 9	Jude	9th	Zephaniah 1	Luke 23
2 Chronicles 10	Revelation 1	10th	Zephaniah 2	Luke 24
2 Chronicles 11–12	Revelation 2	11th	Zephaniah 3	John 1
2 Chronicles 13	Revelation 3	12th	Haggai 1	John 2
2 Chronicles 14–15	Revelation 4	13th	Haggai 2	John 3
2 Chronicles 16	Revelation 5	14th	Zechariah 1	John 4
2 Chronicles 17	Revelation 6	15th	Zechariah 2	John 5
2 Chronicles 18	Revelation 7	16th	Zechariah 3	John 6
2 Chronicles 19–20	Revelation 8	17th	Zechariah 4	John 7
2 Chronicles 21	Revelation 9	18th	Zechariah 5	John 8
2 Chronicles 22–23	Revelation 10	19th	Zechariah 6	John 9
2 Chronicles 24	Revelation 11	20th	Zechariah 7	John 10
2 Chronicles 25	Revelation 12	21st	Zechariah 8	John 11
2 Chronicles 26	Revelation 13	22nd	Zechariah 9	John 12
2 Chronicles 27–28	Revelation 14	23rd	Zechariah 10	John 13
2 Chronicles 29	Revelation 15	24th	Zechariah 11	John 14
2 Chronicles 30	Revelation 16	25th	Zechariah 12–13:1	John 15
2 Chronicles 31	Revelation 17	26th	Zechariah 13:2ff.	John 16
2 Chronicles 32	Revelation 18	27th	Zechariah 14	John 17
2 Chronicles 33	Revelation 19	28th	Malachi 1	John 18
2 Chronicles 34	Revelation 20	29th	Malachi 2	John 19
2 Chronicles 35	Revelation 21	30th	Malachi 3	John 20
2 Chronicles 36	Revelation 22	31st	Malachi 4	John 21

TABLE OF WEIGHTS AND MEASURES

WEIGHTS

Gerah	Hebrew	1/20 shekel	1/50 ounce	.6 gram	gerah; oboli
Bekah	Hebrew	1/2 shekel or 10 gerahs	1/5 ounce	5.7 grams	bekah; half a shekel; quarter ounce; fifty cents
Pim	Hebrew	2/3 shekel	1/3 ounce	7.6 grams	2/3 of a shekel; quarter
Shekel	Hebrew	2 bekahs	2/5 ounce	11.5 grams	shekel; piece; dollar; fifty dollars
Litra (pound)	Greco-Roman	30 shekels	12 ounces	.4 kilogram	pound; pounds
Mina	Hebrew/Greek	50 shekels	1¼ pounds	.6 kilogram	mina; pound
Talent	Hebrew/Greek	3,000 shekels or 60 minas	75 pounds/88 pounds	34 kilograms/40 kilograms	talent/talents; 100 pounds

LENGTH

Handbreadth	Hebrew	1/6 cubit or 1/3 span	3 inches	8 centimeters	handbreadth; three inches; four inches
Span	Hebrew	1/2 cubit or 3 handbreadths	9 inches	23 centimeters	span
Cubit/Pechys	Hebrew/Greek	2 spans	18 inches	.5 meter	cubit/cubits; yard; half a yard; foot
Fathom	Greco-Roman	4 cubits	2 yards	2 meters	fathom; six feet
Kalamos	Greco-Roman	6 cubits	3 yards	3 meters	rod; reed; measuring rod
Stadion	Greco-Roman	1/8 milion or 400 cubits	1/8 mile	185 meters	miles; furlongs; race
Milion	Greco-Roman	8 stadia	1,620 yards	1.5 kilometers	mile

DRY MEASURE

Xestes	Greco-Roman	1/2 cab	1 1/6 pints	.5 liter	pots; pitchers; kettles; copper pots; copper bowls; vessels of bronze
Cab	Hebrew	1/18 ephah	1 quart	1 liter	cab; kab
Choinix	Greco-Roman	1/18 ephah	1 quart	1 liter	measure; quart
Omer	Hebrew	1/10 ephah	2 quarts	2 liters	omer; tenth of a deal; tenth of an ephah; six pints
Seah/Saton	Hebrew/Greek	1/3 ephah	7 quarts	7.3 liters	measures; pecks; large amounts
Modios	Greco-Roman	4 omers	1 peck or 1/4 bushel	9 liters	bushel; bowl; peck
Ephah [Bath]	Hebrew	10 omers	3/5 bushel	22 liters	bushel; peck; deal; part; measure; six pints; seven pints
Lethek	Hebrew	5 ephahs	3 bushels	110 liters	half homer; half sack
Kor [Homer]/Koros	Hebrew/Greek	10 ephahs	6 bushels or 200 quarts	220 liters/525 liters	cor; homer; sack; measures; bushels

LIQUID MEASURE

Log	Hebrew	1/72 bath	1/3 quart	.3 liter	log; pint; cotulus
Xestes	Greco-Roman	1/8 hin	1 1/6 pints	.5 liter	pots; pitchers; kettles; copper bowls; vessels of bronze
Hin	Hebrew	1/6 bath	1 gallon or 4 quarts	4 liters	hin; pints
Bath/Batos	Hebrew/Greek	1 ephah	6 gallons	22 liters	gallon(s); barrels; liquid measures
Metretes	Greco-Roman	10 hins	10 gallons	39 liters	firkins; gallons

CONCORDANCE

A

AARON

Levite, brother of Moses (Ex 4:14; 6:16-20). Spokesman for Moses (4:14-16; 7:1-2). Consecrated (Ex 29) and ordained (Lv 8) as priest (Ex 28:1; 1Ch 6:49; Heb 5:1-4; 7). Made golden calf (Ex 32). Died outside the promised land (Nm 20:1-12,22-29; 33:38-39).

ABADDON

your faithfulness in A? .... Ps 88:11
Sheol and A lie open
   before the LORD .... Pr 15:11
his name in Hebrew is A, ... Rv 9:11

ABANDON

I will a them and hide my face. Dt 31:17
I will not leave you or a you..... Jos 1:5
certainly not a the LORD ...... Jos 24:16
the LORD has a-ed us........... Jdg 6:13
LORD will not a his people,...... 1Sm 12:22
but if you a him, he will a you.. 2Ch 15:2
For you will not a me to Sheol;.. Ps 16:10
my God, why have you
   a-ed me?..................... Ps 22:1
or a his heritage,............... Ps 94:14
Don't a wisdom,................. Pr 4:6
My God, why have
   you a-ed me? .... Mt 27:46
will never leave you or a you.. Heb 13:5
a-ed the love you had at first..... Rv 2:4

ABBA

He said, "A, Father!........... Mk 14:36
we cry out, "A, Father!" .... Rm 8:15
crying, "A, Father!"............. Gl 4:6

ABEL

Shepherd, second son of Adam; brought acceptable sacrifice; was murdered (Gn 4:2-8; Mt 23:35; Heb 11:4).

ABIGAIL

Intelligent wife of the fool Nabal; pled for his life; married David after Nabal died (1Sm 25).

ABIJAH

1. Tragic son of King Jeroboam of Israel (1Kg 14:1,13).
2. Son of Rehoboam, King of Judah (2Ch 13). Also known as Abijam (1Kg 15:1-8).

ABILITY

depending on each one's a.... Mt 25:15
according to their a............ 2Co 8:3

ABIMELECH

1. King of Gerar at the time of Abraham (Gn 20:1-18; 21:22-32).
2. King of Gerar at the time of Isaac (Gn 26:1-31).
3. Son of Gideon, tried to become king of Shechem (Jdg 9).

ABLE

count the stars, if you are a.... Gn 15:5
Moses chose a men........... Ex 18:25
God is a to raise up
   children .... Mt 3:9
Are you a to drink the cup....Mt 20:22
the Lord is a to make
   him stand.................... Rm 14:4
tempted beyond what
   you are a,................... 1Co 10:13
Now to him who is a to do ....Eph 3:20
to him who is a to protect you....Jd 24
a to open the scroll .... Rv 5:3

ABNER

Saul's cousin and commander of his army (1Sm 14:50). At first supported Saul's son Ish-bosheth (2Sm 2:8-9) but defected to David (3:6-21). Killed by Joab and mourned by David (3:22-39).

ABOMINATION

and set up the a of
   desolation...................Dn 11:31
see the a of desolation, ... Mt 24:15

ABOVE

the LORD is God in heaven a ....Dt 4:39
the name that is a
   every name, ... Php 2:9
Set your minds on things a,..... Col 3:2

ABRAHAM

Born Abram son of Terah in Ur, Mesopotamia; married Sarai, then lived in Haran (Gn 11:31; Ac 7:2-4). Called to Canaan and given a promise of progeny and prosperity (Gn 12:1-3). Lied to Pharaoh in Egypt about Sarai (12:10-20). Separated from his nephew Lot (Gn 13). Rescued Lot (14:1-16) and was blessed by Melchizedek (14:17-20; Heb 7:1-10). God declared him righteous because of his faith (Gn 15:6; Rm 4:3,20-22; Gl 3:6; Jms 2:23).

Fathered Ishmael by Hagar (Gn 16). Name changed (17:5); circumcised (17:9-27; Rm 4:9-12). Visited by angels (Gn 18); promised a son with Sarah (18:9-14; cp. 17:15-19). Lied to Abimelech in Gerar about Sarah (Gn 20). Fathered Isaac (21:1-7). Sent Hagar away at Sarah's request (21:8-14). Tested by God concerning Isaac (Gn 22; Heb 11:17-19; Jms 2:21-24). Buried Sarah at Machpelah (Gn 23). Sent servant to find wife for Isaac (24:1-9). Died and was buried with Sarah (25:7-11).

God promised a covenant with Abraham, then made it and confirmed it (Gn 12:1-3; 13:14-17; 15; 17; 22:15-18). It was the basis of future blessings for many people (Ex 2:24; Lv 26:42; 2Kg 13:23; Ps 105:6-11; Ac 3:25).

ABSALOM

Son of David by Maacah (2Sm 3:3). Known for his looks and hair (14:25-26). Killed Amnon for raping Tamar and was banished by David (2Sm 13). Reinstated by David at Joab's insistence (2Sm 14). Rebelled, ousted David (2Sm 15–17). Killed by Joab (18:9-15) despite David's warning (18:5). Greatly mourned by David (18:33–19:4).

ABSENT

a in the body, I am present
   in spirit, ... 1Co 5:3
I may be a in body, but .... Col 2:5

ABSTAIN

he is to a from wine and beer. . Nm 6:3
a from food offered to idols,.. Ac 15:29
a from sinful desires........... 1Pt 2:11

ABUNDANCE

Seven years of great a .... Gn 41:29
bearing spices, gold in great a,.. 1Kg 10:2
have life and have it in a. ...... Jn 10:10

ABUNDANTLY

He poured out his Spirit on us a.. Ti 3:6

ABUSED

a her all night ....Jdg 19:25

ABYSS

not to banish them to the a. ....Lk 8:31
Who will go down into the a?.. Rm 10:7

ACCEPT

Should we a only good from
   God ....Jb 2:10
the LORD a-ed Job's prayer......Jb 42:9
My son, if you a my words....... Pr 2:1
A my instruction............... Pr 8:10
Not everyone can a this
   saying,.......................Mt 19:11
a one another,................. Rm 15:7

ACCEPTABLE

the meditation of my heart
   be a ....Ps 19:14
See, now is the a time; 2Co 6:2
spiritual sacrifices a to God......1Pt 2:5

ACCEPTANCE

what will their a mean........ Rm 11:15
and deserving of full a: 1Tm 1:15

ACCESS

a through him by faith
   into ... grace.................Rm 5:2
we both have a in one spirit......Eph 2:18

ACCOMPANY

signs will a those who
   believe: ....Mk 16:17

ACCOMPLISH

it will a what I please ....Is 55:11
I watch over my word to a it."......Jr 1:12

ACCORDING

be done for you a to your faith!.. Mt 9:29
be done to me a to your word...Lk 1:38

who do not walk a to the flesh.. Rm 8:4
ask anything a to his will,...... 1Jn 5:14
were judged a to their works .. Rv 20:12

ACCOUNT

a for every careless word..... Mt 12:36

ACCUSATION

Who can bring an a.......... Rm 8:33
an a against an elder.......... 1Tm 5:19

ACCUSE

He will not always a us ....Ps 103:9
standing at his right side to a...Zch 3:1
in order to a him...... Mt 12:10; Mk 3:2
They began to a him,........... Lk 23:2
Your a-r is Moses,...............Jn 5:45
so that when you are a-d,...... 1Pt 3:16

ACHAIA

he wanted to cross over to A,.. Ac 18:27

ACHAN

Sinned at Jericho; stoned (Jos 7; 1Ch
   2:7).

ACHISH

King of Gath before whom David
feigned madness (1Sm 21:10-15). Later,
he favored David (1Sm 27–29).

ACKNOWLEDGE

Then I a-d my sin to you ....Ps 32:5
I will also a him before my
   Father in heaven .... Mt 10:32

ACQUIT

I know you will not a me........Jb 9:28

ACT (N)

an outstretched arm and
   great a-s ....Ex 6:6
deeds and mighty a-s like
   yours? ....Dt 3:24
this woman was caught in the a.. Jn 8:4

ACT (V)

trust in him, and he will a,......Ps 37:5
I a-ed for the sake of my
   name,...................... Ezk 20:9
these words of mine and a-s... Mt 7:24

a-ed out of ignorance in
   unbelief................... 1Tm 1:13

ACTION

a-s are weighed by him. 1Sm 2:3
with your minds ready for a, ...1Pt 1:13
word or speech, but in a. 1Jn 3:18

ACTIVE

You see that faith was a.......Jms 2:22

ADAM

First man. Created by God (Gn 1:26-27;
2:7). Named animals (2:18-20). Given
Eve (2:21-25). Failed to obey and was
evicted (1:15-17; 3:6-24; Rm 5:14; 1Co
15:22). Died at 930 years (Gn 5:3-5).

ADD

no a-ing to it or taking from it.. Ec 3:14
Can any of you a one moment.. Mt 6:27
three thousand people
   were a-ed.....................Ac 2:41

ADMINISTER

gifts of healing, helping,
   a-ing, ... 1Co 12:28

ADMINISTRATION

the a of the mystery ....Eph 3:9

ADMONISHING

teaching and a one another ...Col 3:16

ADONIJAH

Son of David (2Sm 3:4). Conspired for
the throne and was executed by Solomon (1Kg 1–2).

ADOPTION

you received the Spirit of a,......Rm 8:15
to them belong the a, ...Rm 9:4
that we might receive a as sons.. Gl 4:5

ADORN

A yourself with majesty ....Jb 40:10
as a bride a-s herself...........Is 61:10
it was a-ed with beautiful
   stones ....Lk 21:5
a the teaching of God our
   Savior....................... Ti 2:10

also **a-ed** themselves in this
way,...........................1Pt 3:5
a-ed with gold, jewels, and
pearls.........................Rv 17:4
a bride **a-ed** for her husband ...Rv 21:2

ADORNMENT

life for you and **a** for your
neck..........................Pr 3:22

ADULTERER

both the **a** and the adulteress.. Lv 20:10
a-'s eye watches for twilight, .. Jb 24:15
you associate with **a-s**.........Ps 50:18
the land is full of **a-s**;..........Jr 23:10
idolaters, **a-s**, male who have...1Co 6:9
judge sexually immoral and
a-s,..........................Heb 13:4

ADULTERESS

both the adulterer and the **a**...Lv 20:10
This is the way of an **a**: she
eats ....Pr 30:20
they are **a-es** ....Ezk 23:45

ADULTEROUS

You **a** wife, ...Ezk 16:32
An evil and **a**
generation.............Mt 12:39; 16:4
this **a** and sinful generation,.. Mk 8:38
You **a** people! Don't you know. Jms 4:4

ADULTERY

Do not commit **a**. ..... Ex 20:14; Dt 5:18
If a man commits **a** ....Lv 20:10
already committed **a**
with her ....Mt 5:28
marries another, commits **a**. .. Mt 19:9
do not commit **a**; do not
steal;........................Mt 19:18
brought a woman caught in **a**,...Jn 8:3
who said, Do not commit **a**,
also ....Jms 2:11

ADVANCE (N)

Scripture saw in **a** that God......Gl 3:8

ADVANCE (V)

has actually **a-d** the gospel,....Php 1:12

ADVANTAGE

the **a** of wisdom...............Ec 10:10
So what **a** does the Jew have?... Rm 3:1

ADVERSARY

I will take vengeance on
my **a-ies** ....Dt 32:41
You exalt me above my **a-ies**; .. Ps 18:48
give the **a** no opportunity.....1Tm 5:14
Your **a** the devil is prowling 1Pt 5:8

ADVERSITY

life and prosperity, death
and **a**........................Dt 30:15
only good from God and not **a**?..Jb 2:10
both **a** and good come from ...Lm 3:38

ADVICE

rejected the elders' **a**......... 2Ch 10:13
walk in the **a** of the wicked ....Ps 1:1
should have followed my **a** ....Ac 27:21

ADVISERS

with many **a** they succeed. ....Pr 15:22

ADVOCATE

we have an **a** with the Father ... 1Jn 2:1

AFFECTION

not withholding our **a**
from you 2Co 6:12
with the **a** of Christ Jesus. ..... Php 1:8

AFFLICT

the Almighty has **a-ed** me?......Ru 1:20
He was oppressed and **a-ed**,......Is 53:7
you who are **a-ed**, along
with us.......................2Th 1:7
destitute, **a-ed**, and
mistreated.................Heb 11:37

AFFLICTION

fruitful in the land of my **a**......Gn 41:52
Lord saw that the **a** of Israel .. 2Kg 14:26
Consider my **a** and trouble,....Ps 25:18
He does not enjoy bringing **a** .. Lm 3:33
she was healed of her **a**. ...... Mk 5:29
a-s are waiting for me.........Ac 20:23
a produces endurance, ...Rm 5:3
momentary light **a** is
producing 2Co 4:17

AFRAID

I was **a** because I was naked, .. Gn 3:10
not be **a**, Abram. I am your
shield........................Gn 15:1
he was **a** to look at God..........Ex 3:6

Do not be **a**, alarmed,
or terrified ....Dt 20:3
Do not be **a** or discouraged,......Jos 1:9
I will not be **a** of the thousands.. Ps 3:6
of whom should I be **a**? .... Ps 27:1
When I am **a**, I will trust in
you............................Ps 56:3
She is not **a** for her
household..................Pr 31:21
I will trust him and not be **a**,.....Is 12:2
Do not be **a** of anyone, for I
will be ....Jr 1:8
don't be **a** to take Mary .... Mt 1:20
Jesus told them, "Do not be **a**.. Mt 28:10
Don't be **a**. Only believe....... Mk 5:36
they were **a** of him, ... Mk 11:18
they were **a** of the
crowd.................Mk 11:32; 12:12
Do not be **a**, Mary,..............Lk 1:30
they were **a** of the people. ..... Lk 22:2
It is I. Don't be **a**! ....Jn 6:20
they were **a** of the Jews, ...Jn 9:22
I will not be **a**. What can
man do ....Heb 13:6

AGABUS

Early church prophet (Ac 11:28; 21:10).

AGAG

Amalekite king spared by Saul, executed by Samuel (1Sm 15).

AGAINST

who is not with me is **a** me,... Mt 12:30
whoever is not **a** us is for us. . Mk 9:40
If God is for us, who is **a** us? ...Rm 8:31

AGE

already existed in the **a-s**
before .... Ec 1:10
the worries of this **a**... Mt 13:22; Mk 4:19

AGONY

a like a woman in labor. ....Jr 22:23
I am in **a** in this flame! ....Lk 16:24

AGREE

If two of you on earth **a** .... Mt 18:19
the testimonies did not **a**......Mk 14:56
Why did you **a** to test the Spirit. Ac 5:9
Saul **a-d** with putting him
to death.......................Ac 8:1
I **a** with the law that it is good...Rm 7:16
does not **a** with the sound
teaching 1Tm 6:3

AGREEMENT

making a binding **a** in
    writing ....Neh 9:38
we have an **a** with Sheol;....... Is 28:15
a does Christ have
    with Belial?.................. 2Co 6:15
these three are in a.............1Jn 5:8

AGRIPPA

Herodian king who heard Paul's testimony (Ac 25–26).

AHAB

Son of Omri, king of Israel (1Kg 16:28–22:40). Married Jezebel and promoted Baalism (16:31-33). Killed Naboth (21:1-14). Condemned by Elijah (18:18; 21:17-24) and other prophets (20:35-43; 22:19-28). Died in disguise in battle (22:29-40).

AHASUERUS

King of Persia, son of Darius and grandson of Cyrus. Greek name is Xerxes. Dismissed Vashti and married Esther (Est 1–2). Signed Haman's decree (Est 3) then was convinced by Esther to reverse it and hang Haman (Est 4–7) and allow the Jews to defend themselves (Est 8–9).

AHAZ

Idolatrous king of Judah (2Kg 16:2-4). Son of Jotham. Attacked by Aram and Israel (16:5-6; 2Ch 28:5-7). Refused Isaiah's advice and turned to Assyria for help (Is 7). Not buried among the kings (2Ch 28:27).

AHAZIAH

1. Son of Ahab; king of Israel (1Kg 22:40). Injured in a fall; condemned by Elijah for seeking Baal (2Kg 1:2-17).
2. Son of Jehoram; king of Judah (2Kg 8:25-27). Mortally wounded by Jehu while visiting King Joram of Israel (9:27).

AHEAD

Each creature went
    straight a..............Ezk 1:9; 10:22
sending my messenger **a**
    of you; ....Mt 11:10
I will go a of you to Galilee. ...Mt 26:32
which God prepared a of time.. Eph 2:10
reaching forward to what is a,.. Php 3:13

AHIJAH

1. Priest at the time of Saul (1Sm 14:3-4,18).
2. Prophet from Shiloh to Jeroboam (1Kg 4:3; 11:29-39).

AI

Bethel on the west and **A**
    on the........................ Gn 12:8
they fled from the men of **A**. ... Jos 7:4
Joshua burned A...............Jos 8:28

AIJALON

moon, over the Valley of A.... Jos 10:12
A with its pasturelands, ...Jos 21:24

AIMLESSLY

do not run like one who
    runs a......................1Co 9:26

AIR

box like one beating the a..... 1Co 9:26
meet the Lord in the **a** 1Th 4:17
poured out his bowl into the a,.. Rv 16:17

ALABASTER

an **a** jar................ Mt 26:7; Mk 14:3

ALARM

sound the **a** on my holy
    mountain!.....................Jl 2:1

ALARMED

and rumors of wars,
    don't be a; ....Mk 13:7

ALERT

be **a**, since you don't know....Mt 24:42
Be **a**, stand firm in the faith, ..1Co 16:13
stay **a** with all perseverance.. Eph 6:18
prayer; stay **a** in it...............Col 4:2
Be sober-minded! Be a! 1Pt 5:8

ALEXANDER

Hymenaeus and A 1Tm 1:20
A the coppersmith............2Tm 4:14

ALIEN

Your offspring will be
    resident a................... Gn 15:13
"I have been a resident a"...... Ex 2:22
the land they lived in as a-s...... Ex 6:4

and resident **a-s** in Canaan,...Ps 105:12
no longer oppress the
    resident a, ...Jr 7:6

ALIENATED

are **a** from Christ; ....Gl 5:4
Once you were **a** and hostile... Col 1:21

ALIVE

to keep them **a** with you. ...... Gn 6:19
when they heard that he
    was a .... Mk 16:11
he also presented himself a......Ac 1:3
dead to sin and a to God .... Rm 6:11
in Christ all will be made a... 1Co 15:22
made us **a** with Christ .... Eph 2:5
he made you a with him.......Col 2:13
We who are still a.............1Th 4:17
made **a** by the Spirit, ... 1Pt 3:18
but look—I am a forever .... Rv 1:18

ALL

with **a** your heart, with **a** your soul,
    and with **a** your strength......Dt 6:5
search for me with **a** your
    heart.........................Jr 29:13
love the Lord ... with **a** your
    heart.........................Lk 10:27
a have sinned and fall short .. Rm 3:23
He died to sin once for **a** ....Rm 6:10
We will not **a** fall asleep, but we will **a**
    be changed,.................1Co 15:51
the one who fills **a** things..... Eph 1:23
I am able to do **a** things .... Php 4:13
A Scripture is inspired by
    God 2Tm 3:16
but **a** to come to repentance. ...2Pt 3:9

ALLEGIANCE

every tongue will swear a......Is 45:23

ALLIANCE

Solomon made an **a** with
    Pharaoh 1Kg 3:1
they will form an a, ...Dn 11:6

ALLOTMENT

Israel according to their tribal
    a-s:........................... Jos 12:7

ALLOW

will not **a** your faithful one to
    see ....Ps 16:10
A it for now, ... Mt 3:15

a your holy one to see decay. . . Ac 2:27
will not a you to be tempted . .1Co 10:13

ALMIGHTY

I am God A. . . . . Gn 17:1
Isaac, and Jacob as God A, ...Ex 6:3
discover the limits of the A? . . . . . .Jb 11:7
dwells in the shadow of the A. . . Ps 91:1
was, and who is coming, the A. . . Rv 1:8
Holy, holy, holy, Lord God, the A, . .Rv 4:8
God, the A, reigns! . . . . .Rv 19:6

ALMOND

the a tree blossoms, ...Ec 12:5

ALONE

not good for the man to be a. . . Gn 2:18
man does not live on bread a . . . .Dt 8:3
I a am left, .1Kg 19:10
Against you—you a— . . . . Ps 51:4
the LORD a will be exalted . . . . Is 2:11
Man must not live on bread a . . Mt 4:4
to a remote place to be a. . . . . . Mt 14:13
Who can forgive sins but
    God a? . . . . Mk 2:7
by works and not by faith a. . .Jms 2:24

ALPHA

the A and the Omega, . . .Rv 1:8; 21:6; 22:13

ALREADY

Whatever is, has a been, and
    whatever will be, a is. . . . . Ec 3:15
has a committed adultery . . . . . .Mt 5:28
how I wish it were a set
    ablaze! . . . . .Lk 12:49
does not believe is a judged, ...Jn 3:18
You are a clean. . . . . .Jn 15:3
You are a full! You are a rich! . . .1Co 4:8
Not that I have a reached . . . . . Php 3:12
it is a in the world now. 1Jn 4:3

ALTAR

Noah built an a to the LORD. . . . . Gn 8:20
Isaac and placed him on the a . .Gn 22:9
construct the a of acacia wood. . Ex 27:1
an a for the burning of
    incense; . . . . .Ex 30:1
tear down their a-s, ...Ex 34:13
take hold of the horns of the a. .1Kg 1:50
I will come to the a of God, ... Ps 43:4
leave your gift . . . in front of
    the a. . . . . Mt 5:24
takes an oath by the a, ... Mt 23:18
We have an a from which . . . . . .Heb 13:10

in offering Isaac . . . on the a? . . Jms 2:21
I saw under the a the souls . . . . . .Rv 6:9

ALTOGETHER

reliable and a righteous. . . . . Ps 19:9
righteous and a trustworthy. . Ps 119:138

ALWAYS

my sin is a before me. . . . . Ps 51:3
You a have the poor with you, . .Mt 26:11
I am with you a, ...Mt 28:20
Rejoice in the Lord a. . . . . Php 4:4
A be ready to give a defense. 1Pt 3:15

AM SEE I AM

AMASA

David's nephew; commander of Absalom's army (2Sm 17:25). Reinstated by
David (19:13). Killed by Joab (20:10).

AMAZED

a and asked, "What kind of
    man. . . . . Mt 8:27
the crowds were a, ... Mt 9:33
he was a at their unbelief. . . . . . .Mk 6:6
they were astounded and a, ...Ac 2:7

AMAZIAH

Son of Joash; king of Judah. Defeated
Edom but adopted their gods (2Ch 25:11-
14). Rejected God's rebuke, challenged
King Jehoash of Israel, and was defeated
(26:15-24). Killed by a conspiracy (25:27).

AMBASSADOR

we are a-s for Christ, ...2Co 5:20
For this I am an a in chains.. . .Eph 6:20

AMBITION

bitter envy and selfish a . . . . . . Jms 3:14

AMBUSH

Set an a behind the city. . . . . Jos 8:2
set up an a around Gibeah. . . Jdg 20:29
Let's set an a and kill someone. . .Pr 1:11
forty of them lying in a, ... Ac 23:21

AMEN

all the people will reply, 'A!'. . . . Dt 27:15
be the LORD forever. A and a. . Ps 89:52

will the outsider say "A" 1Co 14:16
through him we also say "A" . . 2Co 1:20
The A, the faithful and true . . . . . .Rv 3:14
A! Come, Lord Jesus! . . . . .Rv 22:20

AMNON

Oldest son of David (2Sm 3:2). Raped his
sister Tamar; killed by Absalom (2Sm 13).

AMON

Son of Manasseh; king of Judah; killed
by his servants (2Kg 21:18-26).

AMOS

Prophet against moral decay in Israel
under Jeroboam II (Am 5:24).

ANANIAS

1. Lied about gift to the church at Jerusalem and died (Ac 5:1-6).
2. Disciple in Damascus who visited Paul
   (Ac 9:10-19).
3. High priest at Paul's arrest (Ac 23:1-5;
   24:1).

ANCESTOR

from the day their a-s came
    out. 2Kg 21:15
a clear conscience as
    my a-s did, ...2Tm 1:3

ANCHOR

this hope as an a for our lives, . . Heb 6:19

ANCIENT

Will you continue on the a
    path. . . . . .Jb 22:15
Rise up, a doors! . . . . Ps 24:7,9
Ask about the a paths, ... Jr 6:16
the A of Days took his seat. . . . . . Dn 7:9
since a times, Moses . . . . .Ac 15:21
if he didn't spare the a world, . . 2Pt 2:5
seized the dragon, that a serpent. .Rv 20:2

ANDREW

Apostle; fisherman; Peter's brother (Mt
4:18; 10:2; Mk 1:16,29; 3:18; 13:3; Lk 6:14; Jn
1:35-44; 6:8-9; 12:12; Ac 1:13).

ANGEL

two a-s entered Sodom . . . . .Gn 19:1
a of the LORD called to him. . . . . Gn 22:11

he will send his **a** before you,.. Gn 24:7
a-s were going up and down.. Gn 28:12
going to send an **a** before you ..Ex 23:20
a of the LORD took his stand . Nm 22:22
God sent an **a** to Jerusalem ...1Ch 21:15
A of the LORD encamps around ..Ps 34:7
he will give his **a-s** orders ...... Ps 91:11
Bless the LORD, all his **a-s**......Ps 103:20
the **a** of the LORD ... struck
  down .... Is 37:36
He sent his **a** and rescued ...... Dn 3:28
My God sent his **a** and shut..... Dn 6:22
Jacob struggled with the **a**......Hs 12:4
a of the Lord appeared .... Mt 2:13
he will give his **a-s** orders...... Mt 4:6
is going to come with his **a-s**.. Mt 16:27
their **a-s** continually view..... Mt 18:10
are like **a-s** in heaven.........Mt 22:30
for the devil and his **a-s!** ...... Mt 25:41
the **a-s** were serving him....... Mk 1:13
the **a** Gabriel was sent ....Lk 1:26
a said to them, "Don't be afraid..Lk 2:10
the **a-s** of God ascending .... Jn 1:51
face was like the face of an **a**....Ac 6:15
we will judge **a-s**................1Co 6:3
If I speak human or **a-ic**
  tongues.....................1Co 13:1
disguises himself as an **a**
  of light. 2Co 11:14
even if we or an **a** from heaven.. Gl 1:8
the worship of **a-s**,.............Col 2:18
some have welcomed **a-s** as
  guests .... Heb 13:2
A-s long to catch a glimpse......1Pt 1:12
if God didn't spare the **a-s** 2Pt 2:4
Write to the **a** of the church in ..Rv 2–3

ANGER

until your brother's **a**
  subsides ....Gn 27:44
alone, so that my **a** can burn.. Ex 32:10
gracious God, slow to **a**........ Ex 34:6
LORD's **a** burned against Israel ..Jdg 2:14
his **a** may ignite at any moment. . Ps 2:12
do not rebuke me in your **a**; ..... Ps 6:1
For his **a** lasts only a moment, .. Ps 30:5
I swore in my **a**, "They will not.. Ps 95:11
A gentle answer turns away **a**, .. Pr 15:1
A fool gives full vent to his **a**, .. Pr 29:11
compassionate, slow to **a**, ...Jl 2:13
slow to **a**,........................ Jnh 4:2
jealousy, outbursts of **a**,.........Gl 5:20
sun go down on your **a**,.......Eph 4:26
All bitterness, **a** and wrath, ... Eph 4:31
a, wrath, malice, slander, ...Col 3:8
So I swore in my **a**, ...Heb 3:11
slow to speak, and slow to **a**, .. Jms 1:19
the cup of his **a**.................Rv 14:10
winepress of the fierce **a** of
  God,..........................Rv 19:15

ANGRY

the Son or he will be **a** ....Ps 2:12
Be **a** and do not sin; ....Ps 4:4
An **a** person stirs up conflict, ..Pr 29:22
Is it right for you to be **a**? ...... Jnh 4:4
who is **a** with his brother...... Mt 5:22
Be **a** and do not sin. ....Eph 4:26

ANGUISH

After his **a**, he will see light,..... Is 53:11
in **a**, he prayed more
  fervently, ... Lk 22:44
I wrote to you with ...
  a-ed heart 2Co 2:4

ANIMAL

LORD God formed ... every
  wild **a**...................... Gn 2:19
with an **a** must be put to
  death......................... Ex 22:19
may eat all these ... land **a-s**..... Lv 11:2
every **a** of the forest is mine,...Ps 50:10
cares about his **a-'s** health, ... Pr 12:10
and the fate of **a-s** is the same... Ec 3:19
four-footed **a-s** and reptiles ...Ac 10:12

ANNIHILATE

a all the Jewish people......... Est 3:13

ANNOUNCE

I **a** them to you before they
  occur .... Is 42:9

ANOINT

A Aaron and his sons .... Ex 30:30
LORD sent me to **a** you as king ..1Sm 15:1
The LORD **a-ed** you king...... 1Sm 15:17
You **a** my head with oil; ....Ps 23:5
a-ed me to bring good news..... Is 61:1
a-ed my body in advance ......Mk 14:8
a-ed me to preach good news ..Lk 4:18
You didn't **a** my head with ...
  oil, ...Lk 7:46
a-ed Jesus's feet, ...Jn 12:3
against ... Jesus, whom you
  a-ed, ... Ac 4:27
pray over him, **a-ing** him ..... Jms 5:14

ANOINTED (ADJ)

If the **a** priest sins, ...Lv 4:3
he will walk before my **a** one ..1Sm 2:35
Do not touch my **a** ones...... 1Ch 16:22
against the LORD and his **A** One: ..Ps 2:2
Do not touch my **a** ones, ...Ps 105:15
an **a** guardian cherub, ... Ezk 28:14

until the **A** One, the ruler ...... Dn 9:25
These are the two **a** ones,......Zch 4:14

ANOINTED (N)

lift my hand against ...
  LORD's **a**....................1Sm 24:6

ANOINTING (N)

an **a** from the Holy One,........1Jn 2:20
his **a** teaches you 1Jn 2:27

ANOINTING (ADJ)

spices for the **a** oil .... Ex 25:6

ANOTHER

Let **a** praise you, and not your .. Pr 27:2
I will not give my glory to **a**...... Is 48:11
he will give you **a** Counselor... Jn 14:16
not that there is **a** gospel, ...Gl 1:7

ANSWER (N)

A gentle **a** turns away anger, ... Pr 15:1
a of the tongue is from the
  LORD........................... Pr 16:1
who gives an **a** before he
  listens .... Pr 18:13
money is the **a** for
  everything....................Ec 10:19
were astounded at ... his **a-s**....Lk 2:47

ANSWER (V)

he **a-ed** him with fire 1Ch 21:26
but you do not **a** me; .... Jb 30:20
a me, for I am poor and needy .. Ps 86:1
Don't **a** a fool according to......Pr 26:4
A a fool according to ....Pr 26:5
But Jesus still did not **a** ....Mk 15:5

ANT

Go to the **a**, you slacker! ....Pr 6:6
a-s are not a strong people,......Pr 30:25

ANTICHRIST

heard that **a** is coming, even now
  many **a-s** have come.........1Jn 2:18
is the **a**: the one who denies ...1Jn 2:22
spirit of the **a**; which you have.. 1Jn 4:3
This is the deceiver and the **a**...... 2Jn 7

ANTIOCH

first called Christians at **A**...... Ac 11:26
reached Pisidian **A**.............Ac 13:14

ANTIQUITY

origin is from a, from eternity. . Mc 5:2

ANXIETY

A in a person's heart weighs . . Pr 12:25

ANXIOUS

don't be a. . . . . Lk 12:29

ANYTHING

Is a impossible for the LORD? . . Gn 18:14
Is a too difficult for me? . . . . Jr 32:27
A you ask the Father . . . . Jn 16:23

APART

Set a for me Barnabas and
    Saul . . . . Ac 13:2
a from the law, the
    righteousness . . . . Rm 3:21
my mother's womb set me a and
    called . . . . Gl 1:15

APOLLOS

Alexandrian Jew, became a Christian
apologist after being instructed in doctrine by Priscilla and Aquila in Ephesus
(Ac 18:24-28). Was popular like Paul and
Peter (1Co 1:12) but not a rival (3:5-6,22;
4:6; 16:12; Ti 3:13).

APOSTASY

a-ies will reprimand you . . . . Jr 2:19
save them from all their
    a-ies . . . . Ezk 37:23
I will heal their a; . . . . Hs 14:4
unless the a comes first. 2Th 2:3

APOSTLE

the names of the twelve a-s: . . . Mt 10:2
twelve, whom he also named
    a-s, ... Mk 3:14
he was added to the eleven a-s. . Ac 1:26
laid it at the a-s' feet. . . . . Ac 5:2
called as an a and set apart . . . . . Rm 1:1
I am an a to the Gentiles, ... Rm 11:13
first a-s, second prophets, ... 1Co 12:28
not worthy to be called an a, . . . 1Co 15:9
such people are false a-s, ... 2Co 11:13
signs of an a. 2Co 12:12
on the foundation of the a-s . . Eph 2:20
some to be a-s, some
    prophets, ... Eph 4:11
Jesus, the a and high priest . . . . . Heb 3:1
twelve names of twelve a-s . . . . . . Rv 21:14

APOSTLESHIP

We have received grace and a . . Rm 1:5
you are the seal of my a. 1Co 9:2
Peter for an a to the circumcised. . Gl 2:8

APPEAL (N)

God is making his a through
    us. 2Co 5:20

APPEAL (V)

I a to Caesar! . . . . Ac 25:11
I a, . . . on the basis of love. . . . . . . Phm 9

APPEAR

the LORD a-ed to Abram . . . . Gn 12:7
sign of the Son of Man will a. . Mt 24:30
and a-ed to many. . . . . Mt 27:53
the third time Jesus a-ed . . . . . . Jn 21:14
he a-ed to over five hundred . . 1Co 15:6
all a before the judgment seat. . 2Co 5:10
until the a-ing of our Lord. . . . 1Tm 6:14
those who have loved his
    a-ing. 2Tm 4:8
blessed hope, the a-ing of
    the glory. . . . . Ti 2:13
will a a second time, ... Heb 9:28

APPEARANCE

Do not look at his a 1Sm 16:7
no a that we should desire him. . Is 53:2
judging according to
    outward a-s; . . . . Jn 7:24

APPETITE

A worker's a works for him . . . . . . Pr 16:26
if you have a big a; . . . . Pr 23:2
yet the a is never satisfied. . . . . . . Ec 6:7
He enlarges his a like Sheol, . . . Hab 2:5
Lord Christ but their own
    a-s. . . . . Rm 16:18

APPLES

is like gold a in silver settings. . Pr 25:11

APPLY

A yourself to discipline . . . . Pr 23:12
I a-ied my mind to seek . . . . Ec 1:13

APPOINT

These are the LORD's
    a-ed times, ... Lv 23:4
a a king to judge us 1Sm 8:5
A a king for them. 1Sm 8:22

I will a peace as your
    government . . . . Is 60:17
A harvest is also a-ed for you, . . Hs 6:11
the LORD a-ed a great fish . . . . . Jnh 1:17
God a-ed a worm . . . . Jnh 4:7
vision is yet for the a-ed time; Hab 2:3
He a-ed twelve, ... Mk 3:14
been a-ed for you as the
    Messiah. . . . . Ac 3:20
God did not a us to wrath, ... 1Th 5:9
For this I was a-ed a herald, . . . 1Tm 2:7
Don't be too quick to a
    anyone 1Tm 5:22
a elders in every town: . . . . Ti 1:5
God has a-ed him heir of
    all things . . . . Heb 1:2
it is a-ed for people to die
    once . . . . Heb 9:27

APPROACH

let us a the throne of grace . . . Heb 4:16

APPROPRIATE

Luxury is not a for a fool. . . . . . . Pr 19:10
made everything a in its time. . . Ec 3:11

APPROVAL

I stood there giving a . . . . Ac 22:20
and receives human a. . . . . Rm 14:18
by it our ancestors won
    God's a. . . . . Heb 11:2

APPROVE

just as we have been a-d by
    God 1Th 2:4
to present yourself . . . as one
    a-d, ... 2Tm 2:15

AQUILA

Husband of Priscilla; tentmaker; Jewish Christian; teacher; coworker with
Paul (Ac 18:2,18,26; Rm 16:3; 1Co 16:19;
2Tm 4:19).

ARAB

Geshem the A. . . . . Neh 2:19; 6:1
Cretans and A-s. . . . . Ac 2:11

ARABAH

in the A opposite Suph, ... Dt 1:1
the Sea of the A—the Dead
    Sea— . . . . Jos 3:16
along the route to the A, ... 2Kg 25:4
and goes down to the A. . . . . . . Ezk 47:8

ARAM

Son of Shem (Gn 10:22). The nation named for him, perennial enemy of Israel (Jdg 3:8; 2Sm 8:6; 1Kg 11:25; 20; 22; 2Kg 6:8-24; 8:12-13; 13:3,22; 16:7).

ARAMAIC

speak to your servants in A, . .2Kg 18:26
The letter was written in A . . . . . . Ezr 4:7
spoke to the king (A begins
     here): . . . . Dn 2:4

ARAMEAN

My father was a wandering A. . Dt 26:5

ARARAT

on the mountains of A. . . . . Gn 8:4

ARAUNAH

Man whose threshing floor David bought (2Sm 24:15-25); also called Or-nan (1Ch 21:15-28); threshing floor be-came site of the temple (1Ch 22:1; 2Ch 3:1).

ARCHANGEL

a shout, with the a-'s voice, ...1Th 4:16
Michael the a, .Jd 9

ARCHER

the a-s found him and
     severely 1Sm 31:3
The a-s shot King Josiah, ...2Ch 35:23
like an a who wounds
     everyone . . . . .Pr 26:10

ARCHITECT

whose a and builder is God. . .Heb 11:10

AREOPAGUS

stood in the middle of the A . . .Ac 17:22

ARGUE

Let him who a-s with God give. . Jb 40:2
Pharisees . . . began to a with
     him, ... Mk 8:11
What were you a-ing about . . Mk 9:33
don't a about disputed
     matters. . . . . Rm 14:1
without grumbling and
     a-ing, ... Php 2:14

ARGUMENT

Hear now my a, ... Jb 13:6
An a started among them . . . . . Lk 9:46
We demolish a-s 2Co 10:4
deceive you with empty a-s, . . . Eph 5:6
deceive you with
     persuasive a-s. . . . . .Col 2:4
holy hands without anger or a. .1Tm 2:8

ARISE

God a-s. His enemies scatter, . . .Ps 68:1
A, my darling. Come away, ...Sg 2:10
A, shine, for your light has come . .Is 60:1
false prophets will a . . . . .Mt 24:24

ARK

Make . . . an a of gopher wood. . .Gn 6:14
make an a of acacia wood, ... Ex 25:10
Put the tablets . . . into the a. . . . . .Ex 25:16
The a of God was captured, ...1Sm 4:11
Nothing was in the a except 1Kg 8:9
a place there for the a, ...1Kg 8:21
the day Noah boarded the a. . . .Mt 24:38
built an a to deliver his family. . .Heb 11:7
while the a was being
     prepared. 1Pt 3:20
the a of his covenant appeared . .Rv 11:19

ARM

with an outstretched a . . . . .Ex 6:6
a strong hand and an
     outstretched a, ...Dt 4:34
underneath are the
     everlasting a-s. . . . . .Dt 33:27
Do you have an a like God's?. . . .Jb 40:9
a-s can bend a bow of bronze. .Ps 18:34
holy a have won him victory. . . . Ps 98:1
as a seal on your a. . . . . .Sg 8:6
taking them in my a-s, ... Hs 11:3
taking them in his a-s, ... Mk 10:16
to whom has the a of the Lord been
     revealed? . . . . .Jn 12:38

ARMAGEDDON

place called in Hebrew, A. . . . . . .Rv 16:16

ARMOR

Saul . . . had him put on a. 1Sm 17:38
one who puts on his a boast . .1Kg 20:11
through the joints of his a. . .1Kg 22:34
penetrate his double
     layer of a? . . . . Jb 41:13
put on the a of light. . . . . .Rm 13:12
Put on the full a of God . . . . . . .Eph 6:11
put on the a of faith and love, . . .1Th 5:8

ARMY

chariots and his a into the sea; .Ex 15:4
commander of the LORD's a. . . . Jos 5:14
defied the a-ies of the living
     God 1Sm 17:36
a great a, like an a of God. . . . 1Ch 12:22
Though an a deploys against
     me, ...Ps 27:3
king is not saved by a large a; . .Ps 33:16
Jerusalem surrounded by
     a-ies, ... Lk 21:20
The a-ies that were in heaven . .Rv 19:14
on the horse and agains this a. .Rv 19:19

ARREST

Herod had a-ed John, ... Mt 14:3
looking for a way to a him, . . . Mt 21:46
hold of Jesus, and a-ed him. . .Mt 26:50
they a-ed the apostles . . . . .Ac 5:18
he proceeded to a Peter too, ...Ac 12:3

ARROGANCE

your a have reached
     my ears, ... 2Kg 19:28
A leads to nothing but strife, . . Pr 13:10
gossip, a, and disorder. 2Co 12:20
you boast in your a. . . . . Jms 4:16

ARROGANT

For I envied the a; . . . . .Ps 73:3
a people have attacked me; . . . . .Ps 86:14
I hate a pride, evil conduct, ... Pr 8:13
an a spirit before a fall. . . . . Pr 16:18
Do not be a, but beware. . . . . . .Rm 11:20

ARROW

I will shoot three a-s
     beside it 1Sm 20:20
Elisha said, "Take the a-s!" . . . 2Kg 13:18
a-s of the Almighty have pierced. Jb 6:4
the a that flies by day, ...Ps 91:5
a-s in the hand of a warrior . . .Ps 127:4
He made me like a sharpened a; . . Is 49:2
Their tongues are deadly a-s— . . .Jr 9:8
extinguish all the flaming a-s. .Eph 6:16

ARTAXERXES

King of Persia who allowed Ezra to rebuild the temple (Ezr 6:14; 7:1-26) and Nehemiah to rebuild the wall of Jeru-salem (Neh 2:1-6).

ARTEMIS

Greek goddess (Ac 19:24-35).

ASA

Son of Abijam; king of Judah (1Kg 15:8). Instituted reforms (15:13). Rebuked for relying on Aram for military help and on doctors for healing rather than on the Lord (2Ch 16:1-12).

ASCEND

Who may a the mountain ......Ps 24:3
I will a to the heavens; ....Is 14:13
No one has a-ed into heaven ...Jn 3:13
observe the Son of Man a-ing ..Jn 6:62
not yet a-ed to the Father. ......Jn 20:17
is also the one who a-ed ......Eph 4:10

ASCENTS

song of a..................Pss 120–134

ASCRIBE

a to the Lord glory and 1Ch 16:28;
Ps 96:7
A power to God................. Ps 68:34

ASENATH

Wife of Joseph (Gn 41:45,50; 46:20).

ASHAMED

All my enemies will be a........Ps 6:10
Jacob will no longer be a ......Is 29:22
is a of me and of my words......Mk 8:38
I am not a of the gospel, ...Rm 1:16
don't be a of the testimony.....2Tm 1:8
who doesn't need to be a,.....2Tm 2:15
not a to call them brothers,....Heb 2:11
is not a to be called their God,..Heb 11:16
Christian, let him not be a 1Pt 4:16

ASHER

Jacob's eighth son, born of Zilpah (Gn 30:13; 35:26). The tribe's territory was in the northwest on the Phoenician coast (Jos 19:24-31). Also, a town (17:7).

ASHERAH

cut down the A pole beside it. . Jdg 6:25
and the 400 prophets of A....1Kg 18:19
an obscene image of A....... 2Ch 15:16

ASHES

even though I am dust and a .. Gn 18:27
is to gather up the cow's a .....Nm 19:9
Tamar put a on her head.....2Sm 13:19
the a poured from the altar, ...1Kg 13:5

put on sackcloth and a, ... Est 4:1
he sat among the a.............. Jb 2:8
I am dust and a................. Jb 42:6
a crown of beauty instead of a,..Is 61:3
put on sackcloth, and sat in a.. Jnh 3:6
in sackcloth and a long ago!...Mt 11:21
the a of a young cow.......... Heb 9:13

ASIA

forbidden ... to speak the
word in A....................Ac 16:6
first convert to Christ from A..Rm 16:5
To the seven churches in A......Rv 1:4

ASIDE

Do not turn a to the right or ...Dt 28:14
took the twelve disciples a ... Mt 20:17
set something a and save......1Co 16:2
let us lay a every hindrance ..Heb 12:1

ASK

When your children a you, ... Ex 12:26
When your son a-s you ....Dt 6:20
A of me, and I will make ....Ps 2:8
Two things I a of you; ....Pr 30:7
sought by those who did not a; ..Is 65:1
Give to the one who a-s you,... Mt 5:42
you need before you a him...... Mt 6:8
A, and it will be given.........Mt 7:7
you pray and a for—believe.. Mk 11:24
Holy Spirit to those who a ..... Lk 11:13
Whatever you a in my name, .. Jn 14:13
a whatever you want ....Jn 15:7
A and you will receive,.........Jn 16:24
the Jews a for signs 1Co 1:22
lacks wisdom, he should a God,..Jms 1:5
You a and don't receive because
you a with wrong motives,.. Jms 4:3
a anything according to
his will, ...1Jn 5:14

ASLEEP

The child is not dead but a. ... Mk 5:39
as they were sailing he fell a... Lk 8:23
Lazarus has fallen a, ...Jn 11:11
We will not all fall a, ...1Co 15:51
concerning those who are a, ..1Th 4:13

ASSEMBLE

a the whole community ....Lv 8:3
A on the mountains of Samaria..Am 3:9
to gather nations, to a
kingdoms, ...Zph 3:8
a-d together against your
holy servant Jesus, ... Ac 4:27
to a them for the battle ....Rv 16:14

ASSEMBLY

sacred a on the first day and another
sacred a on the seventh day. .Ex 12:16
the a in front of the rock, ... Nm 20:10
his praise in the a of the
faithful...................... Ps 149:1
the a was divided.............. Ac 23:7
the a of the firstborn.........Heb 12:23

ASSOCIATE

you a with adulterers. ....Ps 50:18
Don't a with those who drink. . Pr 23:20
don't a with rebels, ...Pr 24:21
a with the humble.............Rm 12:16
not to a with anyone who claims
to be a believer 1Co 5:11
don't a with him,.............. 2Th 3:14

ASSURANCE

Holy Spirit, and with full a. 1Th 1:5
true heart in full a of faith,......Heb 10:22

ASSURED

stand mature and fully a.......Col 4:12

ASSYRIA

From that land he went to A...Gn 10:11
The king of A deported the Israelites
to A.........................2Kg 18:11
Woe to A, the rod of my anger...Is 10:5

ASTONISHED

crowds were a at his teaching,..Mt 7:28
were a and said, "Where
did this .... Mt 13:54
they were a at his teaching....Mt 22:33
were a. "Where did this
man get....................... Mk 6:2
disciples were a at his words.. Mk 10:24
parents saw him, they were a,..Lk 2:48
all a at the greatness of God....Lk 9:43

ASTOUNDED

were a at his understanding......Lk 2:47

ASTRAY

led a to bow down ... to other
gods ....Dt 30:17
who rejects correction
goes a. .... Pr 10:17
We all went a like sheep;....... Is 53:6
their shepherds led them a,......Jr 50:6
and one of them goes a, ... Mt 18:12
lead a, if possible, the elect....Mk 13:22

always go a in their hearts, ... Heb 3:10
you were like sheep going a, .. 1Pt 2:25

ATHALIAH

Wife of Jehoram and mother of Ahaziah, kings of Judah; descendant of Omri (2 Kg 8:26). Encouraged Baal worship (8:27). Killed heirs and ruled after her son's death (2Kg 11:1-3). Jehoiada the priest executed her and crowned Josiah, the only surviving heir (11:4-20).

ATHENS

City in Greece (Ac 17; 1Th 3:1).

ATHLETE

if anyone competes as an a, ... 2Tm 2:5

ATONE

only you can a for our
    rebellions....................Ps 65:3
Rescue us and a for our sins, ...Ps 79:9

ATONEMENT

blood of the sin offering
    for a..........................Ex 30:10
priest will make a on their
    behalf, ...Lv 4:20
make a before the LORD........Lv 14:31
is the Day of A.................Lv 23:27
he ... made a for the
    Israelites...................Nm 25:13
to make a for the sins of the .. Heb 2:17

ATONING SACRIFICE

him as an a through faith..... Rm 3:25
himself is the a for our sins, ...1Jn 2:2
Son to be the a for our sins.....1Jn 4:10

ATTACK

he may come and a me,........ Gn 32:11
I will a him while he is weary..2Sm 17:2
a worm that a-ed the plant,.....Jnh 4:7

ATTEMPTED

a to establish their ...
    righteousness,..............Rm 10:3
When the Egyptians a to
    do this,.....................Heb 11:29

ATTENDANT

gave it back to the a, and sat... Lk 4:20

ATTENTION

to pay a is better than the fat ..1Sm 15:22
Pay a to the sound of my cry,......Ps 5:2
The God of Jacob doesn't pay a.. Ps 94:7
My son, pay a to my words;......Pr 4:20
pay a to the words of the wise,..Pr 22:17
pay a to myths and endless.... 1Tm 1:4
give your a to public reading,.. 1Tm 4:13
not pay a to Jewish myths ....Ti 1:14
pay a all the more to what we have
    heard ....Heb 2:1

ATTIRE

attendants' service and
    their a,......................1Kg 10:5

ATTITUDE

Serve with a good a, as to the
    Lord ....Eph 6:7
Adopt the same a as that of
    Christ......................Php 2:5

ATTRIBUTES

For his invisible a, ...Rm 1:20

AUTHORITY

Confer some of your a on
    him ....Nm 27:20
like one who had a, ...Mt 7:29
Son of Man has a on earth...... Mt 9:6
gave them a over unclean
    spirits.........................Mt 10:1
All a has been given to me.... Mt 28:18
you gave him a over all flesh;... Jn 17:2
You would have no a over me... Jn 19:11
submit to the governing a-ies,..Rm 13:1
there is no a except from God,..Rm 13:1
a symbol of a on her head,....1Co 11:10
far above every ruler and a, ..Eph 1:21
rulers, against the a-ies, ...Eph 6:12
disarmed the rulers and a-ies..Col 2:15
teach or to have a over a man;..1Tm 2:12
submit to rulers and a-ies,........Ti 3:1
Submit to every human a......1Pt 2:13
a-ies, and powers subject to
    him...........................1Pt 3:22
glory, majesty, power, and a .....Jd 25
I will give him a over the
    nations ....Rv 2:26
who were given a to judge..... Rv 20:4

AVENGE

He will a the blood............ Dt 32:43
Should I not a myself .... Jr 5:9
do not a yourselves;..........Rm 12:19
how long until you ... a.........Rv 6:10

AVENGER

cities as a refuge from
    the a,......................Nm 35:12
hand him over to the a of
    blood ....Dt 19:12
to silence the enemy and the a...Ps 8:2
Lord is an a of all these
    offenses,.....................1Th 4:6

AVOID

a irreverent and empty
    speech......................2Tm 2:16
But a foolish debates,
    genealogies, ...Ti 3:9

AWAKE

A! A, Deborah! ....Jdg 5:12
when I a, I will be satisfied..... Ps 17:15
or a-n love until..........Sg 2:7; 3:5; 8:4
I a-ned you under the apricot
    tree.........................Sg 8:5
He a-ns me each morning;
    he a-ns my ear to listen ...... Is 50:4
in the dust of the earth will a, ..Dn 12:2
Couldn't you stay a one
    hour?.......................Mk 14:37
let us stay a and be
    self-controlled................1Th 5:6
whether we are a or asleep, ...1Th 5:10

AWAY

All have turned a;..............Ps 53:3

AWE

of the world stand in a of him...Ps 33:8
I tremble in a of you;........Ps 119:120
so that people will be in a of
    him...........................Ec 3:14
stand in a of the God of Israel.. Is 29:23
I stand in a of your deeds........Hab 3:2

AWE-INSPIRING

the great, mighty, and a God, .. Dt 10:17
glorious and a name—the
    Lord,.......................Dt 28:58
looked like the a Angel of
    God..........................Jdg 13:6
the great and a God who keeps ..Neh 1:5
great, mighty, and a God......Neh 9:32
right hand show your a acts. ...Ps 45:4
the LORD, the Most High is a, ...Ps 47:2
You answer us ... with a works,.. Ps 65:5
his acts for humanity are a...... Ps 66:5
you are a in your sanctuaries.. Ps 68:35
LORD—the great and a God ......Dn 9:4
Great and a are your works,......Rv 15:3

AWESOME

What an **a** place this is! .... Gn 28:17

AX

iron **a** head fell into the water, .. 2Kg 6:5
Does an **a** exalt itself .... Is 10:15
the **a** is already at the root
   of .... Mt 3:10; Lk 3:9

AZARIAH

1. Prophet (2Ch 15:1-8).
2. King of Judah, also called Uzziah
   (2Kg 15:1-7).

B

BAAL

Israel aligned itself with **B**
   of Peor, ... Nm 25:3
the 450 prophets of **B** 1Kg 18:19
knee that has not bowed to **B** .. 1Kg 19:18
no longer call me, "My **B**." ...... Hs 2:16
who have not bowed
   down to **B**. .... Rm 11:4

BAASHA

King of Israel (1Kg 15:16–16:7). Exterminated Jeroboam's family (15:29).

BABY

Give the living **b** to the first. 1Kg 3:27
the **b** leaped inside her, ... Lk 1:41
You will find a **b** wrapped ...... Lk 2:12
and the **b** who was lying in ...... Lk 2:16

BABYLON

Mesopotamian city; place of captivity
(2Kg 24; Dn 1:1-6); symbol of wickedness
(Rv 17:5).
Therefore it is called **B**, ... Gn 11:9
from a distant country,
   from **B**. 2Kg 20:14
went up from **B** to Jerusalem. . . Ezr 1:11
By the rivers of **B**—........... Ps 137:1
B has fallen, has fallen. .... Is 21:9
the king of **B** for seventy years. . Jr 25:11
She who is in **B**, chosen 1Pt 5:13
It has fallen, **B** the Great .... Rv 14:8

BACK (N)

gave my **b** to those who beat
   me, ... Is 50:6

BACK (ADV)

looked **b** and became a pillar . . Gn 19:26
ahead ten steps or go **b** ten
   steps? 2Kg 20:9
plow and looks **b** is fit for. ..... Lk 9:62

BAD

but a **b** tree produces **b** fruit. . . . Mt 7:17
B company corrupts good . . . 1Co 15:33

BAG

in each man's sack was his
   b of .... Gn 42:35
different weights in your **b**, . . . Dt 25:13
David put his hand in the **b**, . . 1Sm 17:49
weeping, carrying the **b**
   of seed, ... Ps 126:6
or **b-s** of deceptive weights? . . . Mc 6:11
wages into a **b** with a hole in it . . Hg 1:6

BAKE

b-d unleavened bread for
   them, ... Gn 19:3
b-d the dough they had
   brought. .... Ex 12:39
B what you want to **b**, ... Ex 16:23
a grain offering **b-d** in an oven, . . Lv 2:4

BAKER

king of Egypt's cupbearer
   and **b** .... Gn 40:1

BALAAM

Prophet hired by King Balak of Moab
to curse Israel (Nm 22). His donkey
talked (22:21-30; 2Pt 2:16). He blessed
Israel (Nm 23–24; Jos 24:10; Neh 13:2).
Executed for practicing divination
(Nm 31:8; Jos 13:22; 2Pt 2:15; Jd 11; Rv
2:14).

BALAK

King of Moab who hired Balaam to
curse Israel (Nm 22–24).

BALANCE

You are to have honest **b-s**, ... Lv 19:36
b-s and scales are the LORD's; . . . Pr 16:11
weighed the mountains
   on a **b** .... Is 40:12

BALDY

chanting, "Go up, **b**! 2Kg 2:23

BALM

Is there no **b** in Gilead? .... Jr 8:22

BAN

will **b** you from the
   synagogues. .... Jn 16:2

BANDAGE

For he wounds but also **b-s**; . . . . Jb 5:18
and **b-s** their wounds. .... Ps 147:3
cleansed, **b-d**, or soothed
   with oil. .... Is 1:6
LORD **b-s** his people's
   injuries .... Is 30:26
Look, it has not been **b-d**. ..... Ezk 30:21
healed the sick, **b-d** the
   injured .... Ezk 34:4
and **b-d** his wounds, ... Lk 10:34

BANDIT

your need, like a **b**. .... Pr 6:11; 24:34

BANISH

plans so that the one **b-ed** from him
   does not remain **b-ed**. 2Sm 14:14
not **b** me from your presence . . Ps 51:11
nations where I will **b** them. . . . Ezk 4:13

BANK

put my money in the **b**? .... Lk 19:23

BANNER

The LORD Is My **B**. .... Ex 17:15
lift the **b** in the name of our
   God. .... Ps 20:5
as an army with **b-s** .... Sg 6:4,10

BANQUET

the king held a week-long **b** .... Est 1:5
He brought me to the **b** hall, ... Sg 2:4
love the place of honor at **b-s**, . . Mt 23:6
a **b**, invite those who are poor, . . Lk 14:13

BAPTISM

Sadducees coming to his **b**, ... Mt 3:7
proclaiming a **b** of repentance . . Mk 1:4
with the **b** I am baptized
   with? .... Mk 10:38
baptized with John's **b**. .... Lk 7:29
I have a **b** to undergo, ... Lk 12:50
he knew only John's **b**. .... Ac 18:25
we were buried with him by **b** . . Rm 6:4
one Lord, one faith, one **b**, ... Eph 4:5

BAPTIST

buried with him in **b**, ... Col 2:12
B ... now saves you 1Pt 3:21

BAPTIST

In those days John the **B** came, ..Mt 3:1
Give me John the **B**-'s head .... Mt 14:8
Some say John the **B**; .... Mt 16:14
John the **B** sent us to ask you, ...Lk 7:20

BAPTIZE

I **b** you with water for. .... Mt 3:11
b-ing them in the name of. ... Mt 28:19
to be **b**-d with the baptism I ..Mk 10:38
and is **b**-d will be saved, ... Mk 16:16
Tax collectors also came to
  be **b**-d, ... Lk 3:12
Jesus also was **b**-d. .... Lk 3:21
b-ing more disciples than
  John .... Jn 4:1
will be **b**-d with the Holy Spirit .. Ac 1:5
Repent and be **b**-d, ... Ac 2:38
there's water. What would keep
  me from being **b**-d? .... Ac 8:36
who were **b**-d into Christ Jesus were
  b-d into his death? .... Rm 6:3
Christ did not send me to **b**,
  but. 1Co 1:17
all were **b**-d into Moses. 1Co 10:2
we were all **b**-d by one
  Spirit. 1Co 12:13
are being **b**-d for the dead? .. 1Co 15:29

BARABBAS

Insurrectionist released by Pilate instead of Jesus (Mt 27:16-26; Mk 15:7-15; Lk 23:18; Jn 18:40).

BARAK

Reluctantly joined Deborah to fight Canaanites (Jdg 4–5; 1Sm 12:11; Heb 11:32).

BARBARIAN

obligated both to Greeks and
  b-s, ... Rm 1:14
b, Scythian, slave and free; .... Col 3:11

BAREFOOT

he did that, going stripped
  and **b** .... Is 20:2

BARK

peeled the **b**, exposing
  white .... Gn 30:37

BARLEY

a loaf of **b** bread came
  tumbling .... Jdg 7:13
five **b** loaves and two fish. ...... Jn 6:9

BARN

sow or reap or gather into **b**-s, ..Mt 6:26
but collect the wheat in my **b**. ..Mt 13:30
I'll tear down my **b**-s and build..Lk 12:18

BARNABAS

Levite from Cyprus, named Joseph (Ac 4:36). Introduced Paul to Jerusalem church (9:26-27). Worked with Paul, initially as leader in Antioch (11:19-30), then on a journey (Ac 13–14), then in Jerusalem (15:1-21). Separated from Paul over whether to bring John Mark with them again (15:36-41).

BARTHOLOMEW

Apostle (Mt 10:3; Mk 3:18; Lk 6:14; Ac 1:13), possibly also called Nathanael (Jn 1:43-51).

BARUCH

Jeremiah's scribe (Jr 36).

BASED

not be **b** on human wisdom 1Co 2:5
the law is not **b** on faith; .... Gl 3:12
righteousness from God **b**
  on faith. .... Php 3:9
b on the testimony of two ...Heb 10:28
b on what seemed good to
  them .... Heb 12:10

BASHAN

the rest of Gilead and all **B**, ...Dt 3:13
strong ones of **B** encircle me...Ps 22:12
against all the oaks of **B**, ... Is 2:13
you cows of **B** .... Am 4:1

BASIN

Make a bronze **b** for washing.. Ex 30:18
he made ten bronze **b**-s........1Kg 7:38
poured water into a **b** and
  began to .... Jn 13:5

BASKET

Three **b**-s ... were on my
  head. .... Gn 40:16
she got a papyrus **b** for him ..... Ex 2:3

LORD showed me two **b**-s of figs..Jr 24:1
A **b** of summer fruit. .... Am 8:1
a woman sitting inside the **b**. ...Zch 5:7
a lamp and puts it under a **b**, .. Mt 5:15
they picked up twelve **b**-s full ..Mt 14:20
lowered him in a large **b** .... Ac 9:25

BATCH

holy, so is the whole **b**. .... Rm 11:16
a little leaven leavens the
  whole **b** 1Co 5:6

BATHE

he saw a woman **b**-ing 2Sm 11:2
One who has **b**-d, ... Jn 13:10

BATHSHEBA

Wife of Uriah the Hethite. David committed adultery with her, then married her (2Sm 11). Solomon's mother (2Sm 12; 1Kg 1–2).

BATTLE

the **b** is the LORD's. 1Sm 17:47
the **b** is not yours, but God's. . 2Ch 20:15
He smells the **b** from a
  distance .... Jb 39:25
clothed me with strength
  for **b**; .... Ps 18:39
the LORD, mighty in **b**. .... Ps 24:8
A horse is prepared for ...**b**, .. Pr 21:31
or the **b** to the strong, ... Ec 9:11
nations against Jerusalem
  for **b**. .... Zch 14:2
like horses prepared for **b**. ...... Rv 9:7
the **b** on the great day of God, .. Rv 16:14
Magog, to gather them for **b**. ... Rv 20:8

BEAM

b of wood in your own eye? .... Mt 7:3

BEAR (N)

Whenever a lion or a **b** came ..1Sm 17:34
two female **b**-s came out 2Kg 2:24
to meet a **b** robbed of her cubs ..Pr 17:12
The cow and the **b** will graze, ...Is 11:7
He is a **b** waiting in ambush, ...Lm 3:10
second one, that looked like a **b**..Dn 7:5

BEAR (V)

b children with painful effort.. Gn 3:16
punishment is too great to **b**!.. Gn 4:13
wife Sarah will **b** you a son, ...Gn 17:19
that **b**-s its fruit in season .... Ps 1:3

a burden too heavy for me to **b**. .Ps 38:4
he **b-s** our burdens; ....Ps 68:19
They will still **b** fruit in old
　age, ...Ps 92:14
he himself **bore** our sicknesses,. .Is 53:4
yet he **bore** the sin of many ... Is 53:12
"Blessed is the womb that **bore**
　you ....Lk 11:27
does not **b** his own cross ......Lk 14:27
but you can't **b** them now. .....Jn 16:12
that we may **b** fruit for God.......Rm 7:4
b the weaknesses of those..... Rm 15:1
so that you may be able to
　b it. 1Co 10:13
b-s all things, believes all 1Co 13:7
b-ing with one another... Eph 4:2; Col
　3:13
offered once to **b** the sins of . .Heb 9:28
He himself **bore** our sins 1Pt 2:24
tree of life ... **b-ing** twelve
　kinds .... Rv 22:2

BEARD

shaved off half their **b-s**,......2Sm 10:4
on the **b**, running down
　Aaron's **b**,....................Ps 133:2

BEAST

Four huge **b-s** came up .... Dn 7:3
b that comes up out of the
　abyss ....Rv 11:7
a **b** coming up out of the sea....Rv 13:1
calculate the number of the **b**,. .Rv 13:18
who had the mark of the **b** ......Rv 16:2
who accepted the mark of
　the **b** ....Rv 19:20

BEAT

gave my back to those who **b**
　me,............................. Is 50:6
will **b** their swords into plows, ..Mc 4:3
they spat in his face and
　b him;......................Mt 26:67
to **b** him, saying, "Prophesy!" ..Mk 14:65
they stopped **b-ing** Paul........ Ac 21:32
or box like one **b-ing** the air... 1Co 9:26
Three times I was **b-en** 2Co 11:25

BEATING (N)

by **b-s**, by imprisonments,
　by riots,......................2Co 6:5

BEAUTIFUL

daughters of mankind were **b**,. .Gn 6:2
know what a **b** woman you
　are. ....Gn 12:11

Now the girl was very **b**,...... Gn 24:16
Rebekah, for she is a **b**
　woman........................ Gn 26:7
but Rachel was shapely and **b**. .Gn 29:17
when she saw that he was **b**, ...Ex 2:2
woman was intelligent and **b**,. .1Sm 25:3
Let a search be made for **b**
　young........................ Est 2:2
praise from the upright is **b**.....Ps 33:1
How **b** you are, my darling.. .Sg 1:15; 4:1
How **b** on the mountains are ... Is 52:7
which appear **b** on the
　outside,.......................Mt 23:27
used to sit and beg at the
　B Gate.........................Ac 3:10

BEAUTY

gazing on the **b** of the LORD.....Ps 27:4
Zion, the perfection of **b**,........Ps 50:2
Don't lust in your heart for
　her **b**.......................Pr 6:25
is deceptive and **b** is fleeting, . .Pr 31:30
a crown of **b** instead of ashes, . ..Is 61:3
you declared: I am perfect in **b**. .Ezk 27:3
b consist of outward things......1Pt 3:3

BED

on my **b**, I meditate on you ......Ps 63:6
if I make my **b** in Sheol, ...Ps 139:8
prepare evil plans on their **b-s**!. .Mc 2:1
under a basket or under a **b**? . .Mk 4:21
I have gone to **b**. I can't get up . . Lk 11:7
be in one **b**: one will be taken. .Lk 17:34
the marriage **b** kept
　undefiled, ... Heb 13:4

BEE

b-s with honey in the carcass. . Jdg 14:8

BEELZEBUL

if I drive out demons by **B**, ... Mt 12:27

BEER

he is to abstain from wine
　and **b**........................ Nm 6:3
eat food or drink wine or **b** .....Dt 29:6
Wine is a mocker, **b** is a brawler,. .Pr 20:1
or for rulers to desire **b**. ....Pr 31:4
Give **b** to one who is dying......Pr 31:6
in the morning in pursuit of **b**, . .Is 5:11
who are champions at
　pouring **b**, ...Is 5:22
they stagger, but not with **b**.....Is 29:9
preach to you about wine
　and **b**,........................ Mc 2:11
will never drink wine or **b**. ..... Lk 1:15

BEER-SHEBA

place was called **B** because ... Gn 21:31
Abraham settled in **B**..........Gn 22:19
All the Israelites from Dan to **B**. .Jdg 20:1
throne of David ... from Dan
　to **B**...........................2Sm 3:10

BEFORE

B a word is on my tongue, ...Ps 139:4
No god was formed **b** me,...... Is 43:10
Even **b** they call, I will answer;. .Is 65:24
messenger ... clear the way
　b me..........................Mal 3:1
Father knows ... **b** you ask him. . Mt 6:8
B the rooster crows twice,....Mk 14:72
B Philip called you, ...Jn 1:48
B Abraham was, I am..........Jn 8:58
For the joy that lay **b** him ..... Heb 12:2

BEG

At that time I **b-ged** the LORD: . .Dt 3:23
or his children **b-ging** for
　bread.........................Ps 37:25
b-ging him, 'Be patient with
　me .... Mt 18:29
I'm ashamed to **b**................Lk 16:3
the one who used to sit **b-ging**?. .Jn 9:8

BEGGAR

a blind **b**, was sitting by.......Mk 10:46
who had seen him before as a **b** . .Jn 9:8

BEGINNING

In the **b** God created the heavens. . Gn 1:1
of the LORD is the **b** of
　wisdom; ....Ps 111:10
of the LORD is the **b** of
　knowledge;.....................Pr 1:7
The LORD acquired me at the **b**. . Pr 8:22
of the LORD is the **b** of wisdom, . .Pr 9:10
of a matter is better than its **b**;. . .Ec 7:8
I declare the end from the **b**,... Is 46:10
The **b** of the gospel of Jesus..... Mk 1:1
In the **b** was the Word,............Jn 1:1
What was from the **b**,............1Jn 1:1
as you have heard it from the **b**:. . 2Jn 6
Omega, the **b** and the end. ......Rv 21:6

BEHEADED

had John **b** in the prison. ...... Mt 14:10
"I **b** John," Herod said, ...Lk 9:9
b because of their testimony . . Rv 20:4

BEHEMOTH

Look at **B**, which I made ....Jb 40:15

BEHIND

told Peter, "Get **b** me, Satan!... Mt 16:23
Forgetting what is **b** .... Php 3:13

BEING

the man became a living **b**. ..... Gn 2:7
Adam became a living **b**;..... 1Co 15:45

BELIEVE

Abram **b-d** the LORD,.......... Gn 15:6
they did not **b** God or rely on...Ps 78:22
inexperienced one **b-s**
　anything, ... Pr 14:15
one who **b-s** will be
　unshakable. .... Is 28:16
Who has **b-d** what we have
　heard?.......................... Is 53:1
Do you **b** that I can do this? .... Mt 9:28
of these little ones who **b**
　in me .... Mt 18:6
if you **b**, you will receive...... Mt 21:22
or, 'Over here!' do not **b** it! ....Mt 24:23
Repent and **b** the good news!.. Mk 1:15
I do **b**; help my unbelief!" ..... Mk 9:24
not doubt in his heart, but **b-s**..Mk 11:23
Don't be afraid. Only **b**, ... Lk 8:50
slow you are to **b** in your
　hearts........................ Lk 24:25
so that all might **b** through him.. Jn 1:7
so that everyone who **b-s** in
　him .... Jn 3:16
if you **b-d** Moses, you would **b**..Jn 5:46
you **b** in the one he has sent..... Jn 6:29
b-s in me will ever be thirsty ...Jn 6:35
who sees the Son and **b-s** in
　him .... Jn 6:40
Anyone who **b-s** has eternal
　life........................... Jn 6:47
who **b-s** in me, as the Scripture.. Jn 7:38
you don't **b** me, **b** the works....Jn 10:38
b-s in me will never die........ Jn 11:26
Lord, who has **b-d** our
　message?.................... Jn 12:38
B in God; **b** also in me. .... Jn 14:1
B me that I am in the Father ... Jn 14:11
By this we **b** that you came ....Jn 16:30
world may **b** you sent me. ...... Jn 17:21
went in, saw, and **b-d**........... Jn 20:8
seen me, you have **b-d**. Blessed are
　those who have not seen
　and yet **b**. .... Jn 20:29
written so that you may **b** .....Jn 20:31
by **b-ing** you may have life ....Jn 20:31
appointed to eternal life **b-d**. . Ac 13:48
B in the Lord Jesus, ...Ac 16:31
but others did not **b**. .... Ac 28:24
salvation to everyone who **b-s**,.. Rm 1:16
in Jesus Christ, to all who **b**, ... Rm 3:22
Abraham **b-d** God, and it was ..Rm 4:3

the father of all who **b** .... Rm 4:11
b in your heart that God
　raised........................ Rm 10:9
b-s with the heart,
　resulting in .... Rm 10:10
call on him they have not **b-d** in? And
　how can they **b** without....Rm 10:14
who has **b-d** our message? ...Rm 10:16
b-s all things, hopes
　all things, ... 1Co 13:7
unless you **b-d** for no purpose. .1Co 15:2
I **b-d**, therefore I spoke, ... 2Co 4:13
just like Abraham who **b-d** God,..Gl 3:6
if we **b** that Jesus died and.....1Th 4:14
b-d on in the world, taken up ..1Tm 3:16
especially of those who **b**. 1Tm 4:10
must **b** that he exists........... Heb 11:6
You **b** that God is one, ...Even the
　demons **b** .... Jms 2:19
Abraham **b-d** God, and it was ..Jms 2:23
not seeing him now, you **b**.......1Pt 1:8
do not **b** every spirit, but test ... 1Jn 4:1
Everyone who **b-s** that Jesus is the
　Christ has been born of God, ..1Jn 5:1

BELIEVER

intended as a sign, not for **b-s**..1Co 14:22
what does a **b** have in
　common.................... 2Co 6:15
an example to all the **b-s**........ 1Th 1:7

BELLY

move on your **b** and eat dust .. Gn 3:14
For as Jonah was in the **b** of .. Mt 12:40

BELONG

that **b-s** to your neighbor....... Ex 20:17
hidden things **b** to the LORD our God,
　but the revealed things **b**... Dt 29:29
under heaven **b-s** to me......... Jb 41:11
Salvation **b-s** to the LORD;........ Ps 3:8
kingship **b-s** to the LORD; ..... Ps 22:28
the leaders of the earth **b** to
　God;.......................... Ps 47:9
for all the nations **b** to you. ..... Ps 82:8
Look, every life **b-s** to me...... Ezk 18:4
forgiveness **b** to the Lord our
　God .... Dn 9:9
you may **b** to another........... Rm 7:4
to them **b** the adoption,
　the glory..................... Rm 9:4
we live or die, we **b** to the Lord...Rm 14:8
you **b** to Christ, and Christ
　b-s to 1Co 3:23
I don't **b** to the body, ...1Co 12:15
if they had **b-ed** to us, they would
　have remained with us. 1Jn 2:19
Salvation **b-s** to our God,........ Rv 7:10

BELOVED

The LORD's **b** rests securely ....Dt 33:12
This is my **b** Son, with whom
　I am........................... Mt 3:17
my **b** in whom my I delight;... Mt 12:18
I will send my **b** son........... Lk 20:13
This is my **b** Son, with whom ...2Pt 1:17

BELSHAZZAR

King of Babylon (Dn 5; 7:1; 8:1).

BELT

his sword, his bow, and his **b**.. 1Sm 18:4
a leather **b** around his waist. ...2Kg 1:8
with a leather **b** around his
　waist, ... Mt 3:4
took Paul's **b**, tied his own feet ..Ac 21:11
with truth like a **b** around
　your .... Eph 6:14

BELTESHAZZAR

Daniel's Babylonian name (Dn 1:7).

BENAIAH

Heroic warrior in charge of David's body-
guard (2Sm 8:18; 20:23; 23:20-23). Loyal to
Solomon (1Kg 1; 4:4); executed Adonijah,
Joab, and Shimei (2:25-46).

BENEFICIAL

but godliness is **b** in every way,..1Tm 4:8

BENEFIT

and do not forget all his **b-s**....Ps 103:2
What will it **b** a someone if
　he gains .... Mt 16:26
you have **b-ed** from their labor. .Jn 4:38
It is for your **b** that I go away, ...Jn 16:7
what is the **b** of circumcision?.. Rm 3:1
Christ will not **b** you at all........ Gl 5:2

BEN-HADAD

1. King of Aram in Asa's time (1Kg 15:18-
20; 2Ch 16:2-4).
2. King of Aram from Ahab's time (1Kg
20; 2Kg 6:24; 8:7-13).
3. King of Aram in Jehoash's time (2Kg
13:24-25).

BENJAMIN

Second son of Rachel, twelfth son of
Jacob (Gn 35:17-18,24). Tribe with the
smallest territory; Jerusalem may have

originally been in it (Jos 18:16; Jdg 1:21).
Nearly wiped out (Jdg 20–21). Saul and
Paul were Benjaminites (1Sm 9:1; Rm
11:1; Php 3:5).

BERNICE

Wife of Agrippa (Ac 25:13,23; 26:30).

BEREA

sent Paul and Silas away to B... Ac 17:10

BESIDES

not have other gods b
    me..................... Ex 20:3; Dt 5:7
no Savior exists b me...........Hs 13:4

BEST

He chose the b part for
    himself,......................Dt 33:21
spared . . . the b of the sheep,. . 1Sm 15:9
don't recline at the b place, ...Lk 14:8

BETHANY

to B, and spent the night
    there. ....Mt 21:17
He led them to the vicinity
    of B,........................ Lk 24:50
in B . . . where John was
    baptizing......................Jn 1:28
Lazarus from B,.................Jn 11:1
came to B where Lazarus was,.. Jn 12:1

BETHEL

east of B and pitched his tent,.. Gn 12:8
and named the place B,....... Gn 28:19
He set up one in B, ... 1Kg 12:29

BETHLEHEM

B Ephrathah, you are small..... Mc 5:2
After Jesus was born in B........Mt 2:1
city of David, which is called B,..Lk 2:4
Let's go straight to B and see ...Lk 2:15

BETRAY

have finished b-ing, they will
    b you..........................Is 33:1
Brother will b brother to
    death,...................... Mt 10:21
a good opportunity to b him. . Mt 26:16
One of you will b me. .... Mt 26:21
that man by whom he is b-ed! ..Lk 22:22
b-ing the Son of Man with a
    kiss? .... Lk 22:48

He knew who would b him. .... Jn 13:11
the night when he was b-ed, ..1Co 11:23

BETTER

to obey is b than sacrifice, ...1Sm 15:22
Your faithful love is b than life. . Ps 63:3
B a little with the fear of .... Pr 15:16
B a meal of vegetables where.. Pr 15:17
B a dry crust with peace ....Pr 17:1
B a poor person . . . with
    integrity .... Pr 19:1
B to live on the corner of a roof.. Pr 21:9
B to live in a wilderness .... Pr 21:19
B an open reprimand ....Pr 27:5
b a neighbor nearby ....Pr 27:10
nothing b for a person than to
    eat,..........................Ec 2:24
B one handful with rest.........Ec 4:6
Two are b than one ....Ec 4:9
B that you do not vow ....Ec 5:5
good name is b than fine
    perfume .... Ec 7:1
The end of a matter is b than .... Ec 7:8
a live dog is b than a dead lion...Ec 9:4
Your caresses are much b
    than wine, ...Sg 4:10
it is b that you lose one of
    the parts.....................Mt 5:29
b for him if a heavy millstone.. Mt 18:6
Are we any b off? Not at all! ....Rm 3:9
it is b to marry than to burn 1Co 7:9
we are not b if we do eat. 1Co 8:8
I will show you an even b
    way..........................1Co 12:31
be with Christ—which is
    far b .... Php 1:23
confident of things that are b ..Heb 6:9
the guarantee of a b
    covenant...................... Heb 7:22
to be purified with b
    sacrifices ....Heb 9:23
it is b to suffer for doing good,..1Pt 3:17

BETWEEN

hostility b you and the woman,
    and b your offspring and her
    offspring.................... Gn 3:15
torch . . . b the divided
    animals. ....Gn 15:17
the LORD judge b me and you... Gn 16:5
and to discern b good and evil. .1Kg 3:9
passed b the pieces of the calf ..Jr 34:19
lifted me up b earth and
    heaven...................... Ezk 8:3
you murdered b the
    sanctuary...................Mt 23:35
distinction b Jew and Greek,.. Rm 10:12
one mediator b God and
    humanity,...................1Tm 2:5

BEWARE

b of the leaven of the Pharisees..Mt 16:6
B of the scribes . . . in long
    robes .... Lk 20:46

BEYOND

not too difficult or b your
    reach......................... Dt 30:11
b these, my son, be warned: ...Ec 12:12
Nothing b what is written.......1Co 4:6
tempted b what you are able,..1Co 10:13
able to do above and b all ......Eph 3:20
in Christ's teaching, but goes b it,.. 2Jn 9

BILHAH

Rachel's slave, mother of Dan and
Naphtali (Gn 30:1-7).

BIND

He bound his son Isaac........ Gn 22:9
her vows are b-ing, ... Nm 30:7
B them as a sign on your hand .. Dt 6:8
b them as a sign on your
    hands, ... Dt 11:18
Always b them to your heart;... Pr 6:21
B up the testimony. ....Is 8:16
and he will b up our wounds.....Hs 6:1
Whatever you b on earth is already
    bound in heaven,......Mt 16:19; 18:18
I am ready not only to be
    bound ....Ac 21:13
A wife is bound as long as......1Co 7:39
but the word God is not bound. .. 2Tm
    2:9
and bound him for a
    thousand years. .... Rv 20:2

BIRD

You may eat every clean b,..... Dt 14:11
b-s of the sky, and the fish of
    the sea........................Ps 8:8
in its branches the b-s of the sky ...Dn
    4:21
Consider the b-s of the sky:.... Mt 6:26
b-s of the sky have nests, but .. Mt 8:20
the b-s came and devoured
    them. .... Mt 13:4
worth much more than the
    b-s? ....Lk 12:24

BIRTH

the Rock who gave you b;.....Dt 32:18
a time to give b and a time to
    die;...........................Ec 3:2
to a stone, "You gave b to me." .. Jr 2:27
b of Jesus Christ came about ...Mt 1:18

she gave **b** to her firstborn Son,.. Lk 2:7
new **b** into a living hope 1Pt 1:3

BIRTHDAY

Herod's **b** celebration came,.... Mt 14:6

BIRTHRIGHT

First sell me your **b**............ Gn 25:31
b in exchange for a single
    meal...................... Heb 12:16

BIT

put **b-s** into the mouths of
    horses .... Jms 3:3

BITE

anyone who is **bitten** looks
    at it,.......................Nm 21:8
In the end it **b-s** like a snake .. Pr 23:32
If the snake **b-s** before it is..... Ec 10:11
if you **b** and devour one
    another, ...Gl 5:15

BITTER

and made their lives **b** .... Ex 1:14
unleavened bread and **b** herbs...Ex 12:8
water at Marah because it
    was **b** .... Ex 15:23
in the end she's as **b** as
    wormwood................... Pr 5:4
wine to one whose life is **b**...... Pr 31:6
who substitute **b** for sweet ..... Is 5:20
pour out sweet and **b** water ...Jms 3:11

BITTERNESS

The heart knows its own **b**,......Pr 14:10
All **b**, anger and wrath, ... Eph 4:31
that no root of **b** springs up,.. Heb 12:15

BLACK

the second chariot **b** horses,... Zch 6:2
make a single hair white or **b**.. Mt 5:36
I looked, and there was a **b**
    horse.........................Rv 6:5
the sun turned **b** like sackcloth..Rv 6:12

BLAMELESS

b you prove yourself **b**, ... 2Sm 22:26
happy are those whose way
    is **b**, ... Ps 119:1
b in the day of our Lord Jesus ..1Co 1:8
to be holy and **b** in love
    before him.................. Eph 1:4

so that you may be **b** and
    pure, ... Php 2:15
in the law, **b**..................... Php 3:6
May he make your hearts **b** ...1Th 3:13
body be kept sound and **b**......1Th 5:23
b: the husband of one wife,.......Ti 1:6

BLASPHEME

my name is continually **b-d**.... Is 52:5
He has **b-d**!.....................Mt 26:65
He's **b-ing**! Who can forgive
    sins .... Mk 2:7
b-s against the Holy Spirit .... Mk 3:29
tried to make them **b** ....Ac 26:11
God is **b-d** among the Gentiles..Rm 2:24
they may be taught not to **b**....1Tm 1:20

BLASPHEMER

I was formerly a **b**,............ 1Tm 1:13

BLASPHEMOUS

We heard him speaking **b**
    words.........................Ac 6:11
and on its heads were **b** names...Rv 13:1

BLASPHEMY

b against the Spirit will not... Mt 12:31
you've heard the **b**. ....Mt 26:65
stoning you ... for **b**,...........Jn 10:33
to utter boasts and **b-ies**.......Rv 13:5

BLAZE

fire from the Lord **b-d** among..Nm 11:1
mountain was **b-ing** with fire...Dt 5:23
in the morning it **b-s** like ....Hs 7:6

BLAZING (ADJ)

into the furnace of **b** fire.......Dn 3:20

BLEMISH

he is to present one without **b**... Lv 3:1
offered himself without **b** to
    God,......................... Heb 9:14
b in his sight, at peace..........2Pt 3:14
b and with great joy, ...Jd 24

BLESS

God **b-ed** them: "Be fruitful,......Gn 1:22
God **b-ed** the seventh day....... Gn 2:3
I will **b** you,..................... Gn 12:2
I will **b** her; indeed, ...Gn 17:16
b you and make your
    offspring .... Gn 22:17

B me too, my father! ....Gn 27:34
let you go unless you **b** me. ...Gn 32:26
Lord **b-ed** the Sabbath day..... Ex 20:11
Lord **b** you and protect you;.. Nm 6:24
since he has **b-ed**, I cannot ..Nm 23:20
they curse, you will **b**......... Ps 109:28
A generous person will be
    b-ed,...........................Pr 22:9
b-es his neighbor with a loud.. Pr 27:14
the nations will be **b-ed** by him ..Jr 4:2
from this day on I will **b** you... Hg 2:19
took bread, **b-ed** and
    broke it,..................... Mt 26:26
he **b-ed** and broke the loaves. . Mk 6:41
hands on them and **b-ed**
    them........................Mk 10:16
b those who curse you, ... Lk 6:28
families of the earth will be
    b-ed .... Ac 3:25
B those who persecute you; **b** ..Rm 12:14
When we are reviled, we **b**; 1Co 4:12
nations will be **b-ed**
    through you. .... Gl 3:8
has **b-ed** us with every
    spiritual .... Eph 1:3
inferior is **b-ed** by the superior. .Heb 7:7

BLESSED (ADJ)

You will be **b** in the city and **b** in the
    country...................... Dt 28:3
May you be **b** by the Lord,.... Ps 115:15
He who comes in the name of the
    Lord is **b**. .... Ps 118:26
Let your fountain be **b**, ... Pr 5:18
children rise up and call her **b**. .Pr 31:28
who trusts in the Lord... is **b**. .....Jr 17:7
B are the poor in spirit, ... Mt 5:3
B is he who comes in the
    name of...................... Mt 21:9
B are you among women, ...Lk 1:42
B are those who have not
    seen and.................... Jn 20:29
more **b** to give than to
    receive. .... Ac 20:35
while we wait for the **b** hope .. Ti 2:13
B is the one who endures
    trials, ...Jms 1:12
for righteousness, you are **b**... 1Pt 3:14
B is the one who reads aloud the
    words of this prophecy, and
    b are those .... Rv 1:3
B is the one who keeps the words of
    the prophecy of this book. ...Rv 22:7

BLESSING (N)

you will be a **b**.................. Gn 12:2
deceitfully and took your **b**. ..Gn 27:35
set before you a **b** and a curse:..Dt 11:26
He turned the curse into a **b** ....Dt 23:5

these **b-s** will come and
  overtake......................Dt 28:2
God turned the curse into a **b**. .Neh 13:2
May the LORD's **b** be on you....Ps 129:8
B-s are on the head of the
  righteous, ...Pr 10:6
send down . . . showers of **b**. .Ezk 34:26
pour out a **b** for you ....Mal 3:10
cup of **b** that we bless, ...1Co 10:16
b of Abraham . . . to the Gentiles. .Gl 3:14
blessed us with every
  spiritual **b** ....Eph 1:3
so that you may inherit a **b**......1Pt 3:9
and honor and glory and **b**! ....Rv 5:12

BLIND (ADJ)

mute or deaf, seeing or **b**? ......Ex 4:11
When you present a **b** animal . .Mal 1:8
Woe to you, **b** guides, ...Mt 23:16
a **b** beggar, was sitting ....Mk 10:46
I was **b**, and now I can see!......Jn 9:25
are wretched, pitiful, poor, **b**,...Rv 3:17

BLIND (N)

block in front of the **b**, ...Lv 19:14
I was eyes to the **b** ....Jb 29:15
LORD opens the eyes of the **b**...Ps 146:8
the eyes of the **b** will be opened, . .Is 35:5
the **b** receive their sight,
  the lame ....Mt 11:5
Can the **b** guide the **b**? ....Lk 6:39
you are a guide for the **b**, ...Rm 2:19

BLIND (V)

a bribe **b-s** the clear-sighted... Ex 23:8
king of Babylon **b-ed**
  Zedekiah,.....................2Kg 25:7
deafen their ears and **b** their
  eyes;...........................Is 6:10
He has **b-ed** their eyes ....Jn 12:40
the god of this age has **b-ed** ... 2Co 4:4
the darkness has **b-ed** his eyes. . 1Jn 2:11

BLOCK

I will bow down to a **b** of
  wood? .... Is 44:19
became a sinful stumbling **b** . . Ezk 44:12
Christ crucified, a stumbling **b**. .1Co 1:23

BLOOD

Your brother's **b** cries out to
  me .... Gn 4:10
Whoever sheds human **b**, by humans
  his **b** will be shed, ... Gn 9:6
You are a bridegroom of **b**..... Ex 4:25
Nile . . . will turn to **b**............ Ex 7:17

see the **b**, I will pass over you. . Ex 12:13
This is the **b** of the covenant... Ex 24:8
must not eat any fat or any **b**.... Lv 3:17
life of a creature is in the **b**, ...Lv 17:11
a man of war and have shed **b**. 1Ch 28:3
or drink the **b** of goats?........Ps 50:13
land became polluted with **b**. .Ps 106:38
I have no desire for the **b** of bulls,. .Is 1:11
hold you responsible for his **b**. . . Ezk 3:18
moon to **b** before the great ......Jl 2:31
flesh and **b** did not reveal this . .Mt 16:17
this is my **b** . . . the covenant;. .Mt 26:28
field has been called "**B** Field" . .Mt 27:8
sweat became like drops of **b**. .Lk 22:44
who were born, not of **b**, ... Jn 1:13
and drinks my **b** has eternal
  life,...........................Jn 6:54
Hakeldama (that is, Field of **B**).. . Ac 1:19
and the moon to **b** before the
  great...........................Ac 2:20
been strangled, and from **b**. . . Ac 15:20
through faith in his **b**, ... Rm 3:25
declared righteous by his **b**,......Rm 5:9
is it not a sharing in the **b** 1Co 10:16
covenant in my **b**.............1Co 11:25
Flesh and **b** cannot inherit . . 1Co 15:50
redemption through his **b**,......Eph 1:7
brought near by the **b** .... Eph 2:13
struggle is not against flesh
  and **b**,....................... Eph 6:12
by making peace through
  the **b**.........................Col 1:20
not by the **b** of goats and
  calves, but by his own **b**,.... Heb 9:12
without . . . **b** there is no
  forgiveness.................Heb 9:22
with the precious **b** of us 1Jn 1:7
one who came by water and **b**, . 1Jn 5:6
set us free from our sins by
  his **b**,.........................Rv 1:5
purchased people . . . by your **b**. . Rv 5:9
the entire moon became like **b**;. .Rv 6:12
made them white in the **b** ......Rv 7:14
a third of the sea became **b**,......Rv 8:8
conquered . . . by the **b** of the
  Lamb .... Rv 12:11
He wore a robe dipped in **b**, . . .Rv 19:13

BLOODSHED

no one is guilty of **b**. .... Ex 22:2
b defiles the land,............ Nm 35:33
responsibility for **b** will be
  wiped........................Dt 21:8
Save me from the guilt of **b**,......Ps 51:14

BLOSSOM (N)

cups shaped like almond **b-s**,.. Ex 25:33
has budded, if the **b** has
  opened,......................Sg 7:12

their **b-s** will blow away like
  dust, ... Is 5:24

BLOSSOM (V)

sprouted, formed buds, **b-ed**,. .Nm 17:8
the almond tree **b-s**, ...Ec 12:5
Jacob will take root. Israel will **b**. .Is 27:6

BLOT

I will destroy them and **b** out ...Dt 9:14
b out all my guilt. ....Ps 51:9

BLOW

B the horn in Zion; sound the.....Jl 2:1
blew and pounded that house. . Mt 7:25
The wind **b-s** where it pleases, . .Jn 3:8
b-n around by every wind......Eph 4:14
seven trumpets prepared to
  b them.........................Rv 8:6

BOAST

who puts on his armor **b** like . .1Kg 20:11
I will **b** in the LORD; ....Ps 34:2
We **b** in God all day long;.......Ps 44:8
The one who **b-s** about a gift . .Pr 25:14
Don't **b** about tomorrow, ... Pr 27:1
the wise man should not **b** in his
  wisdom;........................Jr 9:23
the one who **b-s** should **b**
  in this:.......................... Jr 9:24
You who **b** in the law, ... Rm 2:23
one who **b-s**, **b** in the Lord...... 1Co 1:31
give over my body in order
  to **b** 1Co 13:3
gladly **b** . . . about my
  weaknesses,................. 2Co 12:9
b about anything except
  the cross...................... Gl 6:14
so that no one can **b**........... Eph 2:9
it **b-s** great things............... Jms 3:5

BOASTFUL

b cannot stand in your sight;......Ps 5:5
Love does not envy, is not **b**, ...1Co 13:4

BOAT

they left the **b** and their
  father....................... Mt 4:22
the **b** was being swamped..... Mt 8:24
climbing out of the **b**, Peter... Mt 14:29

BOAZ

Husband of Ruth (Ru 4:13), kinsman
redeemer (Ru 2:20; 3:1; 4:3-10,16-17).

Ancestor of David (Ru 4:21-22; 1Ch 2:11-12) and Jesus (Mt 1:5; Lk 3:32).

BODY

one who comes from your
　own **b** .... Gn 15:4
He must not go near a dead **b**.. Nm 6:6
The eye is the lamp of the **b**. ... Mt 6:22
Don't fear those who kill
　the **b** .... Mt 10:28
Take and eat it; this is my **b**....Mt 26:26
the temple of his **b**. ....Jn 2:21
let sin reign in your mortal **b**, .. Rm 6:12
rescue me from this **b** of
　death? ....Rm 7:24
present your **b-ies** as a living.. Rm 12:1
absent in the **b**, I am present ...1Co 5:3
b-ies are a part of Christ's **b**? ..1Co 6:15
know that your **b** is a temple ..1Co 6:19
This is my **b**, which is for you ..1Co 11:24
the **b** is one and has many
　parts, ...1Co 12:12
sown a natural **b**, raised a
　spiritual **b**.................. 1Co 15:44
away from the **b** and at home
　with 2Co 5:8
I bear on my **b** the marks of
　Jesus. .... Gl 6:17
There is one **b** and one
　Spirit— .... Eph 4:4
to build up the **b** of Christ, ... Eph 4:12
their wives as their own
　b-ies. ....Eph 5:28
since we are members of
　his **b**........................Eph 5:30
control his own **b** in holiness...1Th 4:4
spirit, soul, and **b** be kept
　sound........................ 1Th 5:23
bore our sins in his **b** on 1Pt 2:24

BODILY

God's nature dwells **b** in Christ, ..Col 2:9

BOIL (N)

festering **b-s** on people and
　animals......................Ex 9:9
infected Job with terrible **b-s**......Jb 2:7

BOIL (V)

not **b** a ... goat in ...
　milk................Ex 23:19; Dt 14:21

BOLD

but **b** toward you when
　absent................2Co 10:1
Pray that I might be **b** enough.. Eph 6:20

BOLDLY

to speak the word of God **b**...... Ac 4:31

BOLDNESS

In him we have **b**............. Eph 3:12
make known with **b** .... Eph 6:19
approach the throne ...
　with **b**, ... Heb 4:16

BOND

the perfect **b** of unity...........Col 3:14

BONE

This one, at last, is **b** of my **b** ... Gn 2:23
not break any of its **b-s**........ Ex 12:46
Joseph's **b-s**, ... were buried ..Jos 24:32
all my **b-s** are disjointed; ......Ps 22:14
b-s; not one of them is broken..Ps 34:20
jealousy is rottenness to the
　b-s........................Pr 14:30
a gentle tongue can break a **b**. . Pr 25:15
shut up in my **b-s**...............Jr 20:9
valley; it was full of **b-s**........Ezk 37:1
the **b-s** came together, **b** to **b**..Ezk 37:7
are full of **b-s** of the dead......Mt 23:27
Not one of his **b-s** will be ......Jn 19:36

BOOK

erase me from the **b** you
　have .... Ex 32:32
this **b** of the law and place it...Dt 31:26
b of instruction must not
　depart .... Jos 1:8
I have found the **b** of the law .. 2Kg 22:8
Ezra read out of the **b** of the law of
　God every day,..............Neh 8:18
be erased from the **b** of life......Ps 69:28
no end to the making of many
　b-s,...........................Ec 12:12
seal the **b** until the time of..... Dn 12:4
that are not written in this **b**.. Jn 20:30
could contain the **b-s** that .....Jn 21:25
whose names are in the
　b of life......................Php 4:3
written in the Lamb's **b** of life. .Rv 21:27

BORN

cursed the day he was **b**.......... Jb 3:1
I was guilty when I was **b**;......Ps 51:5
I was **b** when there were no......Pr 8:24
a child will be **b** for us,..........Is 9:6
LORD called me before I was **b**. .Is 49:1
I set you apart before you
　were **b**...........................Jr 1:5
who has been **b** King of the
　Jews .... Mt 2:2

was **b** for you, who is the
　Messiah, ...Lk 2:11
you must be **b** again..............Jn 3:7
as to one **b** at the wrong time,..1Co 15:8
b of a woman, **b** under the law, ..Gl 4:4
was **b** as a result of the flesh, ...Gl 4:23
because you have been **b** again..1Pt 1:23
who loves has been **b** of God ..1Jn 4:7

BORROW

When a man **b-s** an animal...... Ex 22:14
You will lend to many nations, but you
　will not **b**.....................Dt 28:12
wicked person **b-s** and does
　not repay ....Ps 37:21
the **b-er** is a slave to the lender...Pr 22:7
one who wants to **b** from you.. Mt 5:42

BOUNDARY

move your neighbor's **b**
　marker, ... Dt 19:14
he set the **b-ies** of the peoples ..Dt 32:8
when I determined its **b-ies** ...Jb 38:10
set all the **b-ies** of the earth;......Ps 74:17
You set a **b** they cannot cross;..Ps 104:9
set the sand as the **b** of the sea,..Jr 5:22

BOW (N)

placed my **b** in the clouds, ... Gn 9:13
arms can bend a **b** of
　bronze...................... 2Sm 22:35
I do not trust in my **b**, ...Ps 44:6
bent their tongues like their **b-s**; Jr 9:3

BOW (V)

May ... nations **b** in worship
　to you. .... Gn 27:29
and **b-ed** down to my sheaf......Gn 37:7
knee that has not **b-ed** to Baal. .1Kg 19:18
Come, let us worship and **b**
　down;........................Ps 95:6
Every knee will **b** to me, ...Is 45:23
coast and islands ... will **b** ...Zph 2:11
every knee will **b** to me, ... Rm 14:11
name of Jesus every knee
　will **b** .... Php 2:10

BOWL

the gold **b** is broken, ...Ec 12:6
one who dipped his hand
　with me in the **b** ....Mt 26:23
the seven **b-s** of God's wrath......Rv 16:1

BOX

or **b** like one beating the air... 1Co 9:26

BOY

some small **b-s** came out 2Kg 2:23
b here who has five barley
    loaves........................... Jn 6:9

BOZRAH

Edomite city (Gn 36:33; 1Ch 1:44; Is 34:6;
63:1; Jr 49:13,22; Am 1:12).

BRANCH

B of the Lord will be beautiful...... Is 4:2
a **b** from his roots will bear fruit... Is 11:1
raise up a Righteous **B** for
    David............................ Jr 23:5
about to bring my servant,
    the **B**. .... Zch 3:8
a man whose name is **B**; ...... Zch 6:12
I am the vine; you are the **b-es**.. Jn 15:5
root is holy, so are the **b-es**.... Rm 11:16
a wild olive **b**, were grafted in.. Rm 11:17

BRAWLER

Wine is a mocker, beer is a **b**, ... Pr 20:1

BREAD

eat **b** by the sweat of your
    brow........................... Gn 3:19
Festival of Unleavened **B** ...... Ex 12:17
B of the Presence on the table.. Ex 25:30
man does not live on **b** alone...... Dt 8:3
You provided **b** from heaven.. Neh 9:15
I trusted, one who ate my **b**,..... Ps 41:9
b eaten secretly is tasty! .... Pr 9:17
b on the surface of the waters, ..Ec 11:1
tell these stones to become **b**... Mt 4:3
Man must not live on **b** alone..... Mt 4:4
Give us today our daily **b**........ Mt 6:11
if his son asks him for **b**,........ Mt 7:9
took **b**, blessed and broke it, ..Mt 26:26
one who is dipping **b** with
    me ....Mk 14:20
I am the **b** of life, ... Jn 6:35
breaking of **b**, and to prayers... Ac 2:42
the Lord Jesus took **b**,......... 1Co 11:23

BREAK *SEE ALSO* BROKEN (ADJ)

I will **b** down your strong
    pride........................... Lv 26:19
I will never **b** my covenant ...... Jdg 2:1
will **b** them with an iron scepter;.. Ps 2:9
a gentle tongue can **b** a bone... Pr 25:15
three strands is not easily
    broken........................ Ec 4:12
He will not **b** a bruised reed,...... Is 42:3
long ago I **broke** your yoke;...... Jr 2:20

where thieves don't **b** in and .. Mt 6:19
He will not **b** a bruise dreed,.. Mt 12:20
bread, blessed and **broke** it, ..Mt 26:26
She **broke** the jar and
    poured it..................... Mk 14:3
Not only was he **b-ing** the
    Sabbath...................... Jn 5:18
the Scripture cannot be
    broken .... Jn 10:35
they did not **b** his legs .... Jn 19:33
of his bones will be **broken**.... Jn 19:36
broke bread from house to
    house .... Ac 2:46
Branches were **broken** off
    so that .... Rm 11:19
given thanks, **broke** it,........ 1Co 11:24
is guilty of **b-ing** it all. .... Jms 2:10
to open the scroll and **b** its
    seals?........................ Rv 5:2
war **broke** out in heaven:....... Rv 12:7

BREAKERS

b and your billows swept
    over me..................... Jnh 2:3

BREAST

let her **b-s** always satisfy you; .. Pr 5:19
Your **b-s** are like two fawns, ..Sg 4:5; 7:3

BREATH

breathed the **b** of life into....... Gn 2:7
Remember that my life is but a **b**.. Jb 7:7
the **b** entered them,.......... Ezk 37:10
gives everyone life and **b** ......Ac 17:25
b of life from God entered
    them, ... Rv 11:11

BREATHE

b-d the breath of life into .... Gn 2:7
Let everything that **b-s** praise.. Ps 150:6
b into these slain so that they .. Ezk 37:9
a loud cry and **b-d** his last..... Mk 15:37
He **b-d** on them and said, ... Jn 20:22

BRIBE

not take a **b**, for a **b** blinds ..... Ex 23:8
no partiality and taking no **b**. . Dt 10:17
Do not accept a **b**, for it blinds.. Dt 16:19
the one who hates **b-s** will live. .Pr 15:27
a **b** corrupts the mind........... Ec 7:7
love graft and chase after **b-s**.... Is 1:23

BRICK

They used **b** for stone........... Gn 11:3
require the same quota of **b-s** ...Ex 5:8

BRIDE

rejoices over his **b**, so your
    God........................... Is 62:5
I will remove ... the voices of the
    groom and the **b**, ... Jr 7:34
the **b** her honeymoon chamber. . Jl 2:16
He who has the **b** is the groom.. Jn 3:29
the **b**, the wife of the Lamb......Rv 21:9

BRIDEGROOM *SEE ALSO* GROOM

You are a **b** of blood to me! ......Ex 4:25

BRIGHT

B eyes cheer the heart;......... Pr 15:30
suddenly a **b** cloud covered......Mt 17:5
dressed in pure, **b** linen, ...Rv 15:6
the **b** morning star. .... Rv 22:16

BRIGHTER

shining **b** and **b** until midday.... Pr 4:18

BRILLIANCE

I did not come with **b** of
    speech....................... 1Co 2:1

BRING

brought each to the man
    to see .... Gn 2:19
b into the ark two of all........ Gn 6:19
Lord who **brought** you
    from Ur.......................Gn 15:7
I **brought** you out of Egypt ..... Jdg 2:1
Lord **b-s** death and gives life;.. 1Sm 2:6
b an offering and enter......... Ps 96:8
don't know what a day might **b**. . Pr 27:1
I **brought** you from the ends of ..Is 41:9
B my sons from far away, ... Is 43:6
I have spoken; so I will also **b** it.. Is 46:11
anointed me to **b** good news...... Is 61:1
about to **b** a sword against you,.. Ezk 6:3
will **b** you into your own
    land....................... Ezk 36:24
B the full tenth into the
    storehouse .... Mal 3:10
I did not come to **b** peace, but.. Mt 10:34
brought to him all who
    were sick.................... Mt 14:35
I came to **b** fire on the earth,...Lk 12:49
b in here the poor, maimed, ...Lk 14:21
feet of those who **b** good
    news........................Rm 10:15
more will their fullness **b**! .... Rm 11:12
b them up in the training and.. Eph 6:4
brought nothing into the
    world, ... 1Tm 6:7

BROAD

b that leads to destruction, ...Mt 7:13

BROKEN (ADJ) *SEE ALSO*
BREAK

sacrifice pleasing to God is a b spirit.
  You will not despise a b and
  humbled heart, God. .... Ps 51:17

BROKENHEARTED

The LORD is near the b;........Ps 34:18
He heals the b and bandages ..Ps 147:3
He has sent me to heal the b, ...Is 61:1

BRONZE

So Moses made a b snake.....Nm 21:9
The sky above you will be b, .. Dt 28:23
my arms can bend a bow
  of b........................2Sm 22:35
a third kingdom, of b,..........Dn 2:39

BROOD

B of vipers! Who warned you... Mt 3:7

BROTHER

Am I my b-'s guardian? .... Gn 4:9
His b-s were jealous of him, ...Gn 37:11
When b-s ... and one of them dies
  without a son,................ Dt 25:5
pleasant it is when b-s live
  together .... Ps 133:1
a b is born for a difficult time.. Pr 17:17
offended b is harder to
  reach .... Pr 18:19
friend who stays closer than
  a b..........................Pr 18:24
be reconciled with your b,..... Mt 5:24
B will betray b to death,....... Mt 10:21
If your b sins against you, ...Mt 18:15
Whoever does the will of God is my b
  and sister and mother...... Mk 3:35
no one who has left house
  or b-s ....Mk 10:29
b of yours was dead and is
  alive ....Lk 15:32
my b-s ... my own flesh and
  blood........................Rm 9:3
b goes to court against b,.......1Co 6:6
if food causes my b to fall,.... 1Co 8:13
but warn him as a b........... 2Th 3:15
not ashamed to call them
  b-s,..........................Heb 2:11
the one who hates his b is in the
  darkness, ...1Jn 2:11
lay down our lives for
  our b-s. 1Jn 3:16

BROTHER-IN-LAW

Perform your duty as her b..... Gn 38:8
Her b is to take her as his wife,..Dt 25:5

BROTHERLY

show sincere b love for each ,..1Pt 1:22

BRUISED

He will not break a
  b reed, ... Is 42:3; Mt 12:20

BUD

let's see if the vine has b-ded, .. Sg 7:12
Though the fig tree does not b ..Hab 3:17

BUILD

let us b ourselves a city ....Gn 11:4
cities that you did not b, ...Dt 6:10
So he built it in seven years... 1Kg 6:38
who will b a house for me,....1Ch 17:12
began to b the LORD's temple ...2Ch 3:1
appointed me to b him a house..Ezr 1:2
Unless the LORD b-s a house,... Ps 127:1
Wisdom has built her house;.... Pr 9:1
wise woman b-s her house, ... Pr 14:1
to tear down and a time to b;....Ec 3:3
B houses and live in them.......Jr 29:5
who built his house on the
  rock.......................... Mt 7:24
on this rock I will b my
  church, ... Mt 16:18
which is able to b you up .....Ac 20:32
for his good, to b him up.......Rm 15:2
be careful how he b-s on it.....1Co 3:10
puffs up, but love b-s up.........1Co 8:1
but not everything b-s up.... 1Co 10:23
Lord gave for b-ing you up ... 2Co 10:8
built on the foundation of the
  apostles and prophets, ...Eph 2:20
to b up the body of Christ,......Eph 4:12
rooted and built up in him......Col 2:7
and b each other up 1Th 5:11

BUILDING (N)

Do you see these great b-s?..... Mk 13:2
You are God's field, God's b......1Co 3:9
we have a b from God,..........2Co 5:1
the whole b, being put
  together,.................... Eph 2:21

BUILDER

The stone that the b-s
  rejected....................Ps 118:22
The stone that the b-s
  rejected....................Mt 21:42

whose architect and b is God.. Heb 11:10
The stone that the b-s rejected .. 1Pt 2:7

BULL

their hands on the b-'s head. .. Ex 29:10
unblemished b as a sin offering..Lv 4:3
Many b-s surround me;........Ps 22:12
I will not take a b from..........Ps 50:9
Do I eat the flesh of b-s ....Ps 50:13
no desire for the blood of b-s, ... Is 1:11
impossible for the blood of
  b-s ....Heb 10:4

BULLY

not a b but gentle,..............1Tm 3:3
not a b, not greedy for money,.... Ti 1:7

BURDEN (N)

bear the b of the people, ... Nm 11:17
Cast your b on the LORD,...... Ps 55:22
Day after day he bears our b-s;..Ps 68:19
They have become a b to me;.......Is 1:14
no longer refer to the b of the
  LORD, ...Jr 23:36
yoke is easy and my b is light...Mt 11:30
You load people with b-s ....Lk 11:46
Carry one another's b-s;.........Gl 6:2

BURDEN (V)

have b-ed me with your sins;.. Is 43:24
you who are weary and b-ed,..Mt 11:28
I will not b you, ...2Co 12:14
Let the church not be b-ed, ...1Tm 5:16

BURIAL

Give me b property among
  you .... Gn 23:4
does not even have a proper b, ..Ec 6:3
she has prepared me for b...... Mt 26:12

BURN

Why isn't the bush b-ing up? ....Ex 3:3
b for b, bruise for bruise, ... Ex 21:25
b-ing on the altar continually;.. Lv 6:13
Israel did not b any of the
  cities........................Jos 11:13
to b their sons and daughters ...Jr 7:31
king not to b the scroll, ...Jr 36:25
the chaff he will b with fire..... Mt 3:12
into the fire, and they are b-ed...Jn 15:6
If anyone's work is b-ed up, ...1Co 3:15
better to marry than to b 1Co 7:9
a third of the earth was b-ed up,.. Rv 8:7
lake of fire that b-s with
  sulfur........................ Rv 19:20

BURNING (ADJ)

turned from his **b** anger........Jos 7:26
my insides are full of **b** pain,....Ps 38:7
in my **b** zeal I speak against... Ezk 36:5

BURNT

If his offering is a **b** offering..... Lv 1:3

BURST

vast watery depths **b** open,......Gn 7:11
about to **b** like new wineskins.. Jb 32:19
the new wine will **b** the skins, ..Lk 5:37
He fell headfirst, his body **b**
    open..........................Ac 1:18

BURY

be **b-ied** at a ripe old age..... Gn 15:15
so that I can **b** my dead.........Gn 23:4
Joseph's bones, ...
    were **b-ied**.................Jos 24:32
first let me go **b** my father...... Mt 8:21
let the dead **b** their own dead.. Mt 8:22
were **b-ied** with him by
    baptism.....................Rm 6:4
was **b-ied**, that he was raised..1Co 15:4
b-ied with him in baptism, ...Col 2:12

BUSH

the **b** was on fire but was not...... Ex 3:2
passage about the burning **b**, ..Mk 12:26
in the flame of a burning **b**......Ac 7:30

BUSINESS

to mind your own **b**, ...1Th 4:11
and do **b** and make a profit. ... Jms 4:13

BUSYBODIES

are also gossips and **b**,........1Tm 5:13

BUTTER

churning of milk produces **b**, ..Pr 30:33

BUY

B—and do not sell—truth,......Pr 23:23
She evaluates a field and **b-s** it;..Pr 31:16
b wine and milk without silver ..Is 55:1
threw out all those **b-ing** and ..Mt 21:12
for you were **bought** at a
    price. 1Co 6:20
denying the Master who
    bought 2Pt 2:1
b from me gold refined.........Rv 3:18
no one can **b** or sell unless .....Rv 13:17

BUYER

it's worthless!" the **b** says, ...Pr 20:14

C

CAESAREA

came to the region of **C**
    Philippi, ... Mt 16:13
a man in **C** named Cornelius, ...Ac 10:1
Paul should be kept at **C**,....... Ac 25:4

CAIAPHAS

High priest, along with his father-in-law Annas, who sentenced Jesus (Mt 23:6; Lk 3:2; Jn 18:13). Spoke prophetically (Jn 11:49-52). Threatened Peter and John (Ac 4:6).

CAIN

Firstborn of Adam and Eve; crop farmer; murdered his brother; God marked and banished him (Gn 4:1-25; Heb 11:4; 1Jn 3:12; Jd 11).

CALAMITY

will laugh at your **c**.............Pr 1:26
your brother in the day of his **c**; ..Ob 12

CALCULATE

first sit down and **c** the cost...... Lk 14:28
c the number of the beast,......Rv 13:18

CALEB

Judahite who scouted Canaan and, along with Joshua, recommended invasion (Nm 13:30–14:38). Entered the promised land (Dt 1:36); received Hebron (Jos 14:13).

CALF

made it into an image of a **c**.... Ex 32:4
Then he made two golden
    c-ves, ...1Kg 12:28
bring the fattened **c** and
    slaughter ....Lk 15:23
not by the blood of goats and
    c-ves.......................Heb 9:12

CALL

people began to **c** on the
    name ....Gn 4:26

I **c** heaven and earth as
    witnesses....................Dt 4:26
Then the LORD **c-ed** Samuel, ... 1Sm 3:4
I **c-ed** to the LORD in my
    distress; 2Sm 22:7
c on the name of your god, and I will
    c on the name of LORD..... 1Kg 18:24
C on me in a day of trouble;....Ps 50:15
I **c** to you from the ends of the
    earth.......................Ps 61:2
is near all who **c** out to him, ..Ps 145:18
Doesn't wisdom **c** out?........... Pr 8:1
Her children rise up and **c** her
    blessed......................Pr 31:28
Woe to those who **c** evil good... Is 5:20
c to him while he is near. .... Is 55:6
Even before they **c**, I will
    answer;......................Is 65:24
everyone who **c-s** on the
    name of ....Jl 2:32
I didn't come to **c** the
    righteous, ...Mt 9:13
Why do you **c** me 'Lord,
    Lord,' ....Lk 6:46
He **c-s** his own sheep by name.. Jn 10:3
You **c** me Teacher and Lord......Jn 13:13
I do not **c** you servants
    anymore, ...Jn 15:15
those he **c-ed**, he also
    justified;....................Rm 8:30
everyone who **c-s** on the
    name of......................Rm 10:13
God's heavenly **c** in Christ
    Jesus. ....Php 3:14
God has not **c-ed** us to
    impurity.....................1Th 4:7

CALLING (N)

God's ... and **c** are
    irrevocable..................Rm 11:29
Brothers and sisters, consider
    your **c**: 1Co 1:26
live worthy of the **c** you have .. Eph 4:1
confirm your **c** and election, .. 2Pt 1:10

CALM (N)

And there was a great **c**........ Mt 8:26

CALM (V)

I have **c-ed** and quieted myself.. Ps 131:2
one slow to anger **c-s** strife. ... Pr 15:18

CAMEL

she got down from her **c**......Gn 24:64
easier for a **c** to go through the
    eye..........................Mt 19:24
gnat, but gulp down a **c**! ......Mt 23:24

CAMP (N)

Jacob said, "This is God's c." ... Gn 32:2
outside the c and slaughtered .. Nm 19:3
go to him outside the c, ... Heb 13:13

CAMP (V)

c around the tent of meeting .. Nm 2:2

CANA

a wedding took place in C of
    Galilee. .... Jn 2:1

CANAAN

Son of Ham, his descendants, and the
land they populated (Gn 9:18-27; 10:15-
19). God promised the land to Abraham (12:4-7; 17:8; Ex 6:4; 1Ch 16:15-18).

CANAANITE

"Do not marry a C woman." ... Gn 28:6
drive out the C-s, Amorites, ... Ex 33:2
so the C-s have lived among
    them. .... Jdg 1:30
a C woman from that region
    came. .... Mt 15:22

CANAL

among the exiles by the
    Chebar C, ... Ezk 1:1
I was beside the Ulai C. .... Dn 8:2

CANCEL

seven years you must c debts. .. Dt 15:1

CANOPY

made darkness a c around
    him, ... 2Sm 22:12
spreading out the sky like a c, .. Ps 104:2

CAPERNAUM

went to live in C by the sea, ... Mt 4:13
teaching in the synagogue in C. .. Jn 6:59

CAPITALS

made two c of cast bronze 1Kg 7:16
Strike the c of the pillars. .... Am 9:1

CAPTIVE

the king of Babylon took
    him c 2Kg 24:12
took many c-s to Damascus ... 2Ch 28:5

to the heights, taking
    away c-s; .... Ps 68:18
to proclaim liberty to the c-s .... Is 61:1
to proclaim freedom to the c-s .. Lk 4:18
take every thought c 2Co 10:5
took the captives c; he gave
    gifts. .... Eph 4:8
Be careful that no one takes
    you c. .... Col 2:8
taken c, into captivity he
    goes. .... Rv 13:10

CAPTIVITY

returned to Jerusalem from
    the c, ... Ezr 3:8
those destined for c, to c. .... Jr 15:2
taken captive, into c he goes. .. Rv 13:10

CARCASS

who touches its c will be
    unclean. .... Lv 11:39
honey from the lion's c. .... Jdg 14:9

CARE (N)

the sheep under his c. .... Ps 95:7
I was sick and you took c
    of me; .... Mt 25:36
to an inn, and took c of him... Lk 10:34
casting all your c-s on him, ... 1Pt 5:7

CARE (V)

what is a human that you c for
    him, ... Ps 144:3
son of man that you c for
    him? .... Heb 2:6
because he c-s about you. 1Pt 5:7

CAREFUL

be c not to forget the LORD. ...... Dt 6:12
Be c to obey all these things ... Dt 12:28
c not to practice your
    righteousness .... Mt 6:1
each one is to be c how he
    builds. 1Co 3:10
But be c that this right of yours. .. 1Co 8:9
c attention, then, to how you
    live. .... Eph 5:15

CARELESS

to account for every c word .. Mt 12:36

CARMEL

gathered the prophets at
    Mount C 1Kg 18:20

CARMI

Son of Reuben (Gn 46:9; Nm 26:6).

CAROUSING

not in c and drunkenness; .... Rm 13:13

CARPENTER

Isn't this the c-'s son? .... Mt 13:55
Isn't this the c, the son of Mary, .. Mk 6:3

CARRY

I c-ied you on eagles' wings ..... Ex 19:4
God c-ied you as a man c-ies
    his son. .... Dt 1:31
No one but the Levites may c .. 1Ch 15:2
shepherd them, and c them
    forever. .... Ps 28:9
lambs in his arms and c-ies
    them. .... Is 40:11
and he c-ied our pains; .... Is 53:4
not c-ing a load ... on the
    Sabbath day .... Jr 17:22
He himself ... c-ied our
    diseases. .... Mt 8:17
Don't c a money-bag, traveling
    bag, ... Lk 10:4
not c out the desire of the flesh. .. Gl 5:16
C one another's burdens; .... Gl 6:2

CASE

argue my c before God. .... Jb 13:3
The first to state his c seems
    right .... Pr 18:17
Let's argue the c together. ...... Is 43:26
the LORD has a c against his
    people, ... Mc 6:2

CAST (ADJ)

Do not make c images of gods .. Ex 34:17
his c images are a lie; ...... Jr 10:14; 51:17

CAST (V)

c spells, consult a medium or .. Dt 18:11
Joshua c lots for them at
    Shiloh. .... Jos 18:10
He c the Pur—that is, the
    lot— .... Est 9:24
they c lots for my clothing. ..... Ps 22:18
C your burden on the LORD, .. Ps 55:22
The lot is c into the lap, ... Pr 16:33
who comes to me I will never
    c out. .... Jn 6:37
they c lots for my clothing. ..... Jn 19:24
Who has c a spell on you, ... Gl 3:1
c-ing all your care on him, ... 1Pt 5:7

c their crowns before the
throne . . . . Rv 4:10

CATCH

your sin will c up with you . . . Nm 32:23
C the foxes for us—the little
foxes . . . . Sg 2:15
now on you will be c-ing
people! . . . . Lk 5:10
brought a woman caught in
adultery, ... Jn 8:3
caught up to the third heaven . . 2Co 12:2
be caught up together with
them 1Th 4:17
her child was caught up to God . . Rv 12:5

CATTLE

is mine, the c on a thousand
hills. . . . . Ps 50:10

CAUSE (N)

For you have upheld my just c; . . Ps 9:4
have persecuted me
without c, ... Ps 119:161
upholds the just c of the poor, . . Ps 140:12
Don't accuse anyone without c, . . Pr 3:30
he will champion their c
against you. . . . . Pr 23:11

CAUSE (V)

and c-s grass to grow on the
hills. . . . . Ps 147:8
Even if he c-s suffering, ... Lm 3:32
c you to follow my statutes . . Ezk 36:27
whoever c-s . . . to fall away— . . Mt 18:6
c one of these little ones to
stumble . . . . Lk 17:2

CAVE

give me the c of Machpelah . . . Gn 23:9
took refuge in the c of
Adullam. 1Sm 22:1
Then Saul left the c and
went on 1Sm 24:7
hid them, fifty men to a c, ... 1Kg 18:4
hid in the c-s and among the
rocks . . . . Rv 6:15

CEASE

and day and night will not c. . . . Gn 8:22
there will never c to be poor
people . . . . Dt 15:11
sin . . . by c-ing to pray for
you 1Sm 12:23
He makes wars c . . . . Ps 46:9

got into the boat, the wind
c-d. . . . . Mt 14:32
otherwise grace c-s to be
grace. . . . . Rm 11:6
as for tongues, they will c; 1Co 13:8

CEDAR

I am living in a c
house while 2Sm 7:2
command that c-s from
Lebanon be 1Kg 5:6
and grow like a c tree in
Lebanon. . . . . Ps 92:12

CELEBRATE

c it as a festival to the
Lord . . . . Lv 23:41

CENSUS

Take a c of the entire . . . . . . Nm 1:2; 26:2
he had taken a c of the
troops 2Sm 24:10

CENTURION

a c came to him, pleading with
him . . . . Mt 8:5
When the c saw what
happened, ... Lk 23:47
in Caesarea named
Cornelius, a c . . . . Ac 10:1

CEPHAS

Aramaic for "Rock"; Peter (Jn 1:42; 1Co
1:12; 3:22; 9:5; 15:5; Gl 1:18; 2:9,11,14).

CERTIFICATE

he may write her a
divorce c, ... Dt 24:1
He erased the c of debt, ... Col 2:14

CHAFF

were shattered and became
like c . . . . Dn 2:35
But the c he will burn up with
fire . . . . Mt 3:12

CHAIN

and broke their c-s apart . . . . . . Ps 107:14
the c-s fell off his wrists . . . . Ac 12:7
I am an ambassador in
c-s. . . . . Eph 6:20
in c-s of utter darkness 2Pt 2:4
a great c in his hand. . . . . Rv 20:1

CHALDEA

Another name for the Babylonian Empire (Jr 51:24; Ezk 12:13; 23:15).

CHALDEAN

Inhabitants of Chaldea (Gn 11:28).
Known as sages or magicians (Dn 2:2;
4:7). Took Judah into exile (2Kg 25; 2Ch
36:17-19; Ezr 5:12; Jr 32).

CHAMBER

the king would bring me to his
c-s. . . . . Sg 1:4

CHAMPION

a c named Goliath, from Gath, . . 1Sm 17:4

CHANCE

time and c happen to all of
them. . . . . Ec 9:11

CHANGE

c-d my wages ten times. . . . . Gn 31:7
or a son of man, that he
might c his mind . . . . Nm 23:19
does not lie or c his mind, ... 1Sm 15:29
You will c them like a
garment, ... Ps 102:26
Can the Cushite c his skin, ... Jr 13:23
Because I, the Lord, have
not c-d, ... Mal 3:6
but we will all be c-d, ... 1Co 15:51
and they will be c-d like
clothing. Heb 1:12
and will not c his mind, ... Heb 7:21

CHANGERS

overturned the tables of the
money c . . . . Mt 21:12

CHANNEL

Who cuts a c for the flooding
rain . . . . Jb 38:25

CHARACTER

you are a woman of noble c . . . . . Ru 3:11
c, and proven c produces hope. . Rm 5:4
so that the proven c of your
faith 1Pt 1:7

CHARGE (N)

Joseph was in c of the country; . . . Gn 42:6

CHARGE

Above his head they put up
the c .... Mt 27:37
that they could find a c against
him............................ Lk 6:7
the gospel and offer it free of c ..1Co 9:18

CHARGE (V)

Do not c your brother
interest .... Dt 23:19
man the Lord will never c
with sin! .... Rm 4:8
I solemnly c you before
God 1Tm 5:21
c them before God not to
fight 2Tm 2:14
c that to my account........... Phm 18

CHARIOT

came back and covered
the c-s .... Ex 14:28
even though they have
iron c-s .... Jos 17:18
because those people had
iron c-s.................... Jdg 1:19
nine hundred iron c-s,.......... Jdg 4:3
Solomon accumulated
1,400 c-s 1Kg 10:26
a c of fire with horses of fire ..2Kg 2:11
covered with horses and
c-s of fire 2Kg 6:17
Some take pride in c-s,.......... Ps 20:7
God's c-s are tens of
thousands,.................. Ps 68:17
making the clouds his c,...... Ps 104:3
saw four c-s coming .... Zch 6:1
I will cut off the c from
Ephraim.................... Zch 9:10

CHARITY

doing good works and acts
of c.......................... Ac 9:36
your acts of c have
ascended .... Ac 10:4

CHARM

C is deceptive and beauty is ...Pr 31:30

CHARMED

If the snake bites before it
is c, ... Ec 10:11

CHASE

whoever c-s fantasies
lacks sense.................. Pr 12:11

CHEAT

c-ed me and changed my
wages....................... Gn 31:7
Why not rather be c-ed? 1Co 6:7

CHEEK

My c-s to those who tore out
my .... Is 50:6
Let him offer his c to the one ..Lm 3:30
if anyone slaps you on your
right c,...................... Mt 5:39

CHEERFUL

God loves a c giver............. 2Co 9:7

CHEMOSH

Moab's god (Jdg 11:24; 1Kg 11:7,33).

CHERUB

Make one c at one end and ... Ex 25:19
He rode on a c and flew, ...2Sm 22:11
The first c-'s height was 15
feet 1Kg 6:26
one was the face of a c, ...Ezk 10:14

CHERUBIM

stationed the c and the
flaming, ... Gn 3:24
he made two c 15 feet high ... 1Kg 6:23
You who sit enthroned
between the c,............... Ps 80:1
four wheels beside the c, ...Ezk 10:9

CHEST

righteousness like armor on
your c, ... Eph 6:14

CHICKS

as a hen gathers
her c .... Mt 23:37; Lk 13:34

CHIEF

the c-s of David's warriors.... 1Ch 11:10
rejected by the elders, the
c priests,..................... Mk 8:31
when the c Shepherd appears, ..1Pt 5:4

CHILD

quieted my soul like a
weaned c .... Ps 131:2
For a c will be born for us, ...Is 9:6
and a c will lead them........... Is 11:6

Can a woman forget her
nursing c,.................... Is 49:15
When Israel was a c, I loved
him,......................... Hs 11:1
He called a c and had him ..... Mt 18:2
When I was a c, I spoke like
a c,......................... 1Co 13:11
give birth it might devour
her c......................... Rv 12:4

CHILDBEARING

But she will be saved
through c, ... 1Tm 2:15

CHILDISH

a man, I put aside c things.. .... 1Co 13:11

CHILDLESS

I am c and the heir of my
house is...................... Gn 15:2
No woman will miscarry
or be c .... Ex 23:26
who is c gives birth to seven, .. 1Sm 2:5
Rejoice, c one,.................... Is 54:1
Rejoice, c woman,............... Gl 4:27

CHILDREN

you will bear c with painful
effort......................... Gn 3:16
When your c ask you,........ Ex 12:26
punishing the c for the
fathers' iniquity,............. Ex 20:5
Teach them to your c,.......... Dt 11:19
Fathers are not to be put to death for
their c, and c ... for their
fathers; .... Dt 24:16
In the future, when your c ask
you,........................ Jos 4:6
Rachel weeping for her c, refusing to
be comforted for her c
because...................... Jr 31:15
and the c-'s teeth are set on
edge........................ Jr 31:29
and the c-'s teeth are set on
edge .... Ezk 18:2
c for Abraham from these
stones....................... Mt 3:9
how to give good gifts to y
our c, ... Mt 7:11
you turn and become like c, ... Mt 18:3
Let the little c come to me..... Mk 10:14
C will rise up against parents.. Mk 13:12
women without c, ... are
fortunate!.................... Lk 23:29
gave them the right to be c of
God,......................... Jn 1:12
testifies ... that we are God's c,..Rm 8:16

C, obey your parents in the
   Lord,........................ Eph 6:1
C, obey your parents in
   everything, ... Col 3:20
Fathers, do not exasperate
   your c,......................Col 3:21
managing their c and their
   own.........................1Tm 3:12
that we should be called
   God's c—.................... 1Jn 3:1

CHINNERETH

Another name for the Sea of Galilee
(Nm 34:11; Jos 13:27) and a city there
(Jos 19:35).

CHOICE

I am offering you three c-s...2Sm 24:12

CHOOSE SEE ALSO CHOSEN (ADJ)

Lot **chose** the entire plain of the
   Jordan.......................Gn 13:11
He will let the one he **c-s**
   come........................Nm 16:5
He **chose** their descendants .... Dt 4:37
LORD ... **chose** you, not because..Dt 7:7
the place the LORD your God
   c-s.........................Dt 12:5
C life so that you ....Dt 30:19
c for yourselves today:........Jos 24:15
who **chose** me over your
   father......................2Sm 6:21
the LORD has **chosen** Zion;....Ps 132:13
A good name is to be
   chosen over .... Pr 22:1
servant, Jacob, whom I have
   chosen,.......................Is 41:8
I **chose** you before I formed you..Jr 1:5
are invited, but few are
   chosen..................... Mt 22:14
and he **chose** twelve of them...Lk 6:13
You did not c me, but I
   chose you.................... Jn 15:16
a remnant **chosen** by grace.... Rm 11:5
he **chose** us in him, before the..Eph 1:4
loved by God, that he has
   chosen you.................1Th 1:4

CHOSEN (ADJ)

this is my c one; I delight
   in him........................Is 42:1
This is my Son, the C One;...... Lk 9:35
God's c ones, holy and dearly ..Col 3:12
a c and honored cornerstone, .. 1Pt 2:6
you are a c race, a royal
   priesthood,................... 1Pt 2:9

CHRIST SEE ALSO MESSIAH

The birth of Jesus C came
   about.......................Mt 1:18
Messiah is coming" (... called C)...Jn 4:25
Scriptures that Jesus is the C.....Ac 18:28
through faith in Jesus C, to all..Rm 3:22
we were still sinners, C died for
   us...........................Rm 5:8
if we died with C, we believe
   that.........................Rm 6:8
heirs of God and coheirs
   with C .... Rm 8:17
can separate us from the
   love of C? .... Rm 8:35
For C is the end of the law .....Rm 10:4
who are many are one body
   in C ....Rm 12:5
But put on the Lord Jesus C, ..Rm 13:14
but we preach C crucified,.....1Co 1:23
and that rock was C...........1Co 10:4
Imitate me, as I also imitate C.. 1Co 11:1
C is the head of every man,......1Co 11:3
you are the body of C,........1Co 12:27
C died for our sins
   according to.................1Co 15:3
also in C all will be made
   alive....................... 1Co 15:22
Jesus C as Lord, and ourselves
   as 2Co 4:5
is in C, he is a new creation; ...2Co 5:17
I no longer live, but C lives
   in me........................Gl 2:20
except the cross of ...Jesus C... Gl 6:14
into him who is the head—C..Eph 4:15
just as C loved the church ....Eph 5:25
to live is C and to die is gain....Php 1:21
considered ... a loss because
   of C........................... Php 3:7
C is all and in all................ Col 3:11
the dead in C will rise first.....1Th 4:16
the coming of our Lord Jesus C..2Th 2:1
C ... came into the world to
   save......................... 1Tm 1:15
salvation, which is in C Jesus,..2Tm 2:10
C also suffered for sins once
   for all,....................... 1Pt 3:18
ridiculed for the name of C, ... 1Pt 4:14
who denies that Jesus is the C?..1Jn 2:22
with C for a thousand years ... Rv 20:4

CHRISTIAN

were first called C-s at
   Antioch. ....Ac 11:26
if anyone suffers as a C,........ 1Pt 4:16

CHURCH

on this rock I will build my c, ..Mt 16:18
pay attention to them,
   tell the c......................Mt 18:17

as overseers, to shepherd
   the c ....Ac 20:28
the c that meets in their home.. Rm 16:5
one who prophesies builds
   up the c. 1Co 14:4
for a woman to speak in the c..1Co 14:35
wife as Christ is the head of
   the c..........................Eph 5:23
regarding zeal, persecuting
   the c;......................... Php 3:6
the head of the body, the c;......Col 1:18
are the angels of the seven
   c-es,...........................Rv 1:20
to the angel of the c in Ephesus ..Rv 2:1

CIRCUMCISE

your males must be **c-d**. ....Gn 17:10
Abraham **c-d** him, ... Gn 21:4
Therefore, **c** your hearts.......Dt 10:16
God will **c** your heart ....Dt 30:6
C yourselves to the LORD; .... Jr 4:4
they came to **c** the child ....Lk 1:59
you **c** a man on the Sabbath.....Jn 7:22
Unless you are **c-d** according to..Ac 15:1
if ... **c-d**, Christ will not
   benefit you .... Gl 5:2
c-d the eighth day; .... Php 3:5

CIRCUMCISION

and c is of the heart........... Rm 2:29
c and uncircumcision mean
   nothing; .... Gl 6:15
we are the c, the ones who
   worship .... Php 3:3
with a c not done with hands,.. Col 2:11

CIRCUMSTANCES

learned to be content in
   whatever c .... Php 4:11

CISTERN

may drink water from his
   own c 2Kg 18:31
Drink water from your own c,.. Pr 5:15
dug c-s for themselves,
   cracked c-s .... Jr 2:13
Jeremiah had been put into
   the c......................... Jr 38:7

CITIZEN

realized Paul was a Roman c.. Ac 22:29

CITIZENSHIP

I bought this c for a large
   amount .... Ac 22:28

CITY

but our **c** is in
heaven, ...Php 3:20

CITY

Lot lived in the **c**-ies on the
plain......................... Gn 13:12
give **c**-ies . . . for the Levites . . . Nm 35:2
will include six **c**-ies of
refuge, ... Nm 35:6
Select your **c**-ies of refuge,.....Jos 20:2
gave the Levites these **c**-ies ....Jos 21:3
and **c**-ies you did not build, . . .Jos 24:13
which he named the **c** of
David........................2Sm 5:9
unless the Lord watches over
a **c**,........................... Ps 127:1
her works praise her at the
c gates........................ Pr 31:31
Say to the **c**-ies of Judah, "Here is your
God!" .... Is 40:9
c situated on a hill cannot be
hidden. .... Mt 5:14
I have many people in this **c**....Ac 18:10
he was looking forward to
the **c** ....Heb 11:10
we do not have an enduring **c** .....Heb
13:14
saw the holy **c**, the new
Jerusalem, ...Rv 21:2

CLAIM

rose up, **c**-ing to be
somebody, ... Ac 5:36
while **c**-ing to be somebody
great. ....Ac 8:9
C-ing to be wise, . . . became
fools ....Rm 1:22

CLAN

small among the **c**-s of Judah; . . Mc 5:2

CLANGING

a noisy gong or a **c** cymbal........1Co 13:1

CLAP

C your hands, all you peoples;.. Ps 47:1
Let the rivers **c** their hands;......Ps 98:8
trees of the field will **c** their . . . Is 55:12

CLAY

strength is dried up like
baked **c**;.....................Ps 22:15
out of the muddy **c**, and set my
feet ....Ps 40:2
Does **c** say to the one forming it, . . Is 45:9

we are the **c**, and you are our
potter; .... Is 64:8
Just like **c** in the potter's hand, . . Jr 18:6
partly iron and partly fired **c**... Dn 2:33
has the potter no right over
the **c**,.......................Rm 9:21
Now we have this treasure
in **c** jars,..................... 2Co 4:7

CLEAN

of all the **c** animals, and two.... Gn 7:2
The one who has **c** hands
and a.........................Ps 24:4
with hyssop, and I will be **c**; .... Ps 51:7
create a **c** heart for me and .... Ps 51:10
You can make me **c**.............. Mt 8:2
You **c** the outside of the cup
and ....Mt 23:25
he declared all foods **c**)........Mk 7:19
You are **c**, but not all of you. ... Jn 13:10
You are already **c** because
of the ....Jn 15:3
God has made **c**, do not call.......Ac 10:15

CLEANSE

my guilt and **c** me from my sin.. Ps 51:2
holy, **c**-ing her with the
washing ....Eph 5:26
to **c** for himself a people........ Ti 2:14
C your hands, sinners, and .... Jms 4:8
Jesus his Son **c**-s us from all sin. .1Jn 1:7
to **c** us from all
unrighteousness.............. 1Jn 1:9

CLEAR

and he will **c** the way before
me ....Mal 3:1
and he will **c** his threshing ..... Mt 3:12
strive to have a **c** conscience .. Ac 24:16
the faith with a **c** conscience...1Tm 3:9
keeping a **c** conscience,........ 1Pt 3:16

CLIFF

your nest is set in the **c**-s..... Nm 24:21

CLIMB

I will **c** the palm tree and take ... Sg 7:8
he **c**-ed up a sycamore tree to
see............................Lk 19:4
by the door but **c**-s in some
other.......................... Jn 10:1

CLING

"Don't **c** to me," Jesus told her.. Jn 20:17
Detest evil; **c** to what is good...Rm 12:9

CLOAK

Put your hand inside your **c**......Ex 4:6
neighbor's **c** as collateral,..... Ex 22:26
Wrap your **c** around you, ...Ac 12:8
bring the **c** I left in Troas with ..2Tm 4:13
You will roll them up like a **c**, .Heb 1:12

CLOSE (ADV)

who stays **c-r** than a brother...Pr 18:24

CLOSE (V)

what he opens, no one can **c**; .. Is 22:22
who opens and no one will **c**,....Rv 3:7

CLOTH

of unshrunk **c** on an old
garment ....Mk 2:21
him tightly in **c** and laid him.....Lk 2:7
he saw the linen **c**-s lying there,. .Jn 20:5

CLOTHE

and **c-d** me with gladness ......Ps 30:11
If that's how God **c**-s the
grass of ....Mt 6:30
I was naked and you **c-d** me;..Mt 25:36
mortal . . . is **c-d** with
immortality, ...1Co 15:54
not want to be unclothed but
c-d,........................... 2Co 5:4
All of you **c** yourselves with
humility 1Pt 5:5
a woman **c-d** with the sun,
with the ....Rv 12:1

CLOTHES

your **c** . . . did not wear out; .....Dt 29:5
anointed himself, changed
his **c**,...................... 2Sm 12:20
fire and his **c** not be burned? . . .Pr 6:27
Tear your hearts, not just your **c**,..Jl 2:13
And why do you worry
about **c**? ....Mt 6:28
get in here without
wedding **c**? .... Mt 22:12
in fine **c**, and a poor man dressed in
filthy **c** also comes in. .... Jms 2:2

CLOTHING

Your **c** did not wear out, and.....Dt 8:4
and they cast lots for my **c**. ....Ps 22:18
Strength and honor are her **c**,.. Pr 31:25
and the body more than **c**?......Mt 6:25
come to you in sheep's **c**........Mt 7:15
they cast lots for my **c**..........Jn 19:24
If we have food and **c**,..........1Tm 6:8

CLOUD

I have placed my bow in the
    c-s,............................. Gn 9:13
a pillar of c to lead them........Ex 13:21
the mountain, the c covered it.. Ex 24:15
the c filled the LORD's temple, ...1Kg 8:10
a c as small as a man's hand ..1Kg 18:44
your faithfulness reaches
    the c-s............................Ps 57:10
making the c-s his chariot, ...Ps 104:3
temple was filled with the c,...Ezk 10:4
coming with the c-s of heaven.. Dn 7:13
a bright c covered them, and a voice
    from the c said:..............Mt 17:5
coming on the c-s of heaven
    with ....Mt 24:30
coming in c-s with great
    power ....Mk 13:26
of Man coming in a c with
    power ....Lk 21:27
a c took him out of their sight....Ac 1:9
ancestors were all under the c,..1Co 10:1
in the c-s to meet the Lord in
    the..........................1Th 4:17
have such a large c of
    witnesses...................Heb 12:1
he is coming with the c-s,........ Rv 1:7

CLOUDLESS

the sun rises on a c morning,..2Sm 23:4

COAL

rain burning c-s and sulfur..... Ps 11:6
will heap burning c-s on his
    head,....................... Pr 25:22
a glowing c that he had taken ....Is 6:6
be heaping fiery c-s on his
    head....................... Rm 12:20

COAT

let him have your c as well..... Mt 5:40

COFFIN

and placed him in a c in
    Egypt.......................Gn 50:26

COHEIRS *SEE ALSO* HEIRS

heirs of God and c with Christ...Rm 8:17
The Gentiles are c, members of..Eph 3:6
them honor as c of the grace of... 1Pt 3:7

COIN

open its mouth you'll find a c .. Mt 17:27
Show me the c used for
    the tax...................... Mt 22:19

if she loses one c, ...Lk 15:8
widow dropping in two
    tiny c-s.......................Lk 21:2

COLD

is like c water to a parched
    throat....................... Pr 25:25
even a cup of c water to one .. Mt 10:42
the love of many will grow c.. Mt 24:12
that you are neither c nor hot...Rv 3:15

COLLAPSED

a great shout, and the wall c. ..Jos 6:20
pounded that house, and it c... Mt 7:27

COLLECTION

Now about the c for the saints:..1Co 16:1

COLLECTOR

even the tax c-s do the same?.. Mt 5:46
Thomas and Matthew the
    tax c;........................ Mt 10:3
a friend of tax c-s and sinners!..Mt 11:19
let him be like ... a tax c to
    you..........................Mt 18:17
Tax c-s and prostitutes are
    entering .... Mt 21:31
Tax c-s also came to be
    baptized,....................Lk 3:12
a Pharisee and the other a
    tax c........................Lk 18:10
chief tax c, and he was rich. ....Lk 19:2

COLORS

made a robe of many c for him.. Gn 37:3

COLT

on a donkey, on a c, the foal of .. Zch 9:9
a donkey and on a c, the foal .. Mt 21:5
sitting on a donkey's c. .... Jn 12:15

COME

Spirit ... c powerfully on
    him,.......................Jdg 14:6,19
Spirit ... c powerfully on
    David 1Sm 16:13
who c-s in the name of the
    LORD ....Ps 118:26
Your kingdom c. Your will be .. Mt 6:10
to another, 'C!' and he c-s .... Mt 8:9
Are you the one who is to c,..... Mt 11:3
who c-s in the name of the
    Lord .... Mt 21:9
Father gives me will c to me,....Jn 6:37

No one c-s to the Father except..Jn 14:6
who is, who was, and who
    is c-ing;......................Rv 1:4
Spirit and the bride say, "C! ....Rv 22:17
Let the one who is thirsty c. ...Rv 22:17
Amen! C, Lord Jesus!.........Rv 22:20

COMFORT (N)

This is my c in my affliction:..Ps 119:50
it is for your c and salvation; ...2Co 1:6

COMFORT (V)

rod and your staff—they c me.. Ps 23:4
LORD, have helped and
    c-ed me. ....Ps 86:17
they have no one to c them. ..... Ec 4:1
"C, c my people," says your God. .Is 40:1
For the LORD has c-ed his
    people,...................... Is 49:13
I—I am the one who c-s you....Is 51:12
refusing to be c-ed for her......Jr 31:15
mourn, for they will be c-ed. ... Mt 5:4
able to c those who are in any kind of
    affliction, through the c we ..2Co 1:4

COMFORTERS

You are all miserable c. .... Jb 16:2

COMING

can endure the day of his c? ... Mal 3:2
what is the sign of your c
    and of the................... Mt 24:3
still alive at the Lord's c........1Th 4:15
Now concerning the c of our
    Lord 2Th 2:1
be patient until the Lord's c.... Jms 5:7
"Where is his 'c' that he
    promised?...................2Pt 3:4

COMMAND (N)

who love him and keep his c-s... Dt 7:9
the c of the LORD is radiant,..... Ps 19:8
I love your c-s more than
    gold, ...Ps 119:127
but let your heart keep my c-s; .. Pr 3:1
who respects a c will be
    rewarded. .... Pr 13:13
least of these c-s and teaches.. Mt 5:19
teaching as doctrines
    human c-s................... Mt 15:9
the greatest and most
    important c.................Mt 22:38
Abandoning the c of God, ...Mk 7:8
I give you a new c:.............Jn 13:34
love me, you will keep
    my c-s....................... Jn 14:15

If you keep my **c-s** you will
  remain........................Jn 15:10
This is my **c**: Love one another..Jn 15:12
I write to you is the Lord's **c**...1Co 14:37
I am not writing you a new **c** ... 1Jn 2:7
Now this is his **c**: that we 1Jn 3:23
love for God is: to keep his **c-s**. And
  his **c-s** are not a burden,......1Jn 5:3
saints, who keep God's **c-s**.....Rv 14:12

COMMAND (V)

the tree about which I **c-ed**
  you,...........................Gn 3:17
everything that God had **c-ed**
  him............................Gn 6:22
You must say whatever I **c** you;..Ex 7:2
not add anything to what I **c** you..Dt 4:2
so that you may **c** your
  children .... Dt 32:46
you have **c-ed** us we will do, ... Jos 1:16
he **c-ed**, and it came into
  existence ....Ps 33:9
for he **c-ed**, and they were
  created.......................Ps 148:5
everything I have **c-ed** you....Mt 28:20
I do as the Father **c-ed** me......Jn 14:31
God ... **c-s** all people
  everywhere ....Ac 17:30
love one another as he **c-ed** us. .1Jn 3:23

COMMANDER

I have ... come as **c** of the
  LORD's .... Jos 5:14

COMMANDMENT

He wrote the Ten **C-s**, ... Ex 34:28
follow the Ten **C-s**, which he
  wrote ....Dt 4:13
the **c** is holy and just and good.. Rm 7:12
is the first **c** with a promise ... Eph 6:2

COMMISSION

and **c** him in their sight. ..... Nm 27:19
The LORD **c-ed** Joshua son
  of Nun,.......................Dt 31:23

COMMIT

Do not **c** adultery...... Ex 20:14; Dt 5:18
C your way to the LORD;........Ps 37:5
one who **c-s** adultery lacks
  sense;..........................Pr 6:32
C your activities to the LORD.... Pr 16:3
c-ted adultery with her in
  his heart. ....Mt 5:28
Everyone who **c-s** sin is a
  slave of ....Jn 8:34

he has **c-ted** the
  message ... to us............. 2Co 5:19
c to faithful men who will be ..2Tm 2:2
He did not **c** sin, and no deceit ..1Pt 2:22

COMMON

between the holy and the **c**, ...Lv 10:10
and the poor have this in **c**:.....Pr 22:2
the oppressor have this in **c**:...Pr 29:13
between the holy and the **c**, .. Ezk 22:26
and held all things in **c**......... Ac 2:44
except what is **c** to
  humanity....................1Co 10:13
believer have in **c** with an 2Co 6:15

COMPANION

but a **c** of fools will suffer
  harm.........................Pr 13:20
a **c** of gluttons humiliates his
  father........................Pr 28:7
falls, his **c** can lift him up;.......Ec 4:10

COMPANY

Bad **c** corrupts good morals. . 1Co 15:33

COMPARE

none can **c** with you............Ps 40:5
To what should I **c** this
  generation?..................Mt 11:16
What can I **c** it to?............. Lk 13:20
are not worth **c-ing** with the
  glory.........................Rm 8:18
c-ing themselves to
  themselves,................. 2Co 10:12

COMPASSION

will have **c** on whom I will
  have **c**...................... Ex 33:19
and have **c** on his servants..... Dt 32:36
because of your great **c**. ...... Neh 9:19
according to your abundant **c**, .. Ps 51:1
As a father has **c** on his
  children,.....................Ps 103:13
my **c** is stirred! .... Hs 11:8
crowds, he felt **c** for them..... Mt 9:36
will have **c** on whom I will
  have **c**........................Rm 9:15
put on **c**, kindness, humility,...Col 3:12

COMPASSIONATE

the LORD your God is a **c** God....Dt 4:31
gracious and **c**, slow to anger.. Neh 9:17
The LORD is **c** and gracious, ...Ps 103:8
you are a gracious and **c**
  God,.......................... Jnh 4:2

And be kind and **c** to one
  another.....................Eph 4:32
Lord is **c** and merciful.........Jms 5:11

COMPELS

love of Christ **c** us, since we... 2Co 5:14

COMPETE

Their **c-ing** thoughts either....Rm 2:15
Now everyone who **c-s**
  exercises 1Co 9:25
if anyone **c-s** as an athlete,......2Tm 2:5

COMPETENT

not that we are **c** in ourselves.. 2Co 3:5
He has made us **c** to be
  ministers 2Co 3:6

COMPLAIN

So the people **c-ed** to Moses,....Ex 17:2
All the Israelites **c-ed** about
  Moses ....Nm 14:2
And don't **c** as some of them
  did, ...1Co 10:10
do not **c** about one another, ... Jms 5:9
to one another without **c-ing**... 1Pt 4:9

COMPLAINT

He has heard your **c-s** about
  him...........................Ex 16:7
the Israelites' **c-s** that they
  make .... Nm 14:27
I will give vent to my **c** .... Jb 10:1
I pour out my **c** before him;....Ps 142:2
anyone has a **c** against
  another.......................Col 3:13

COMPLETE (ADJ)

seventy years for Babylon
  are **c**,.......................... Jr 29:10
So this joy of mine is **c**...........Jn 3:29
in you and your joy may be **c**...Jn 15:11
that your joy may be **c**.........Jn 16:24
that the man of God may be **c**,..2Tm 3:17
that you may be mature and **c**, .. Jms 1:4
so that our joy may be **c**......... 1Jn 1:4

COMPLETE (V)

God had **c-d** his work that he
  had done ....Gn 2:2
When the seventy years are
  c-d,........................... Jr 25:12
When the thousand years are
  c-d,........................... Rv 20:7

COMPLETION

carry it on to c until the day ... Php 1:6

COMPREHEND

may be able to c with all the .. Eph 3:18

CONCEAL

I did not c your constant
    love..........................Ps 40:10
the glory of God to c a matter...Pr 25:2
an open reprimand than c-ed
    love..........................Pr 27:5
who c-s his sins will not
    prosper,......................Pr 28:13
For nothing is c-ed that
    won't be ....Lk 8:17
it was c-ed from them so
    that they....................Lk 9:45

CONCEIT

So that you will not be c-ed, .. Rm 11:25
Let us not become c-ed,
    provoking....................Gl 5:26
nothing from selfish ambition
    or c,.........................Php 2:3
or he might become c-ed and
    incur........................1Tm 3:6
he is c-ed and understands
    nothing, ...1Tm 6:4

CONCEIVE

Sarai was unable to c;......... Gn 11:30
Rachel was unable to c........ Gn 29:31
Did I c all these people?....... Nm 11:12
Manoah; his wife was unable
    to c.........................Jdg 13:2
was sinful when my mother
    c-d me......................Ps 51:5
the virgin will c, have a son......Is 7:14
what has been c-d in her is
    by the......................Mt 1:20
You will c and give birth to a.... Lk 1:31
desire has c-d, it gives birth ...Jms 1:15

CONCERN (N)

Then I had c for my holy
    name,...................... Ezk 36:21
have the same c for each
    other........................ 1Co 12:25

CONCERN (V)

master does not c himself
    with ....Gn 39:8
married man is c-ed about......1Co 7:33

CONCUBINES

and three hundred c, ...1Kg 11:3

CONDEMN

my own mouth would c me;....Jb 9:20
GOD will help me; who will
    c me? .... Is 50:9
by your words you will be
    c-ed.........................Mt 12:37
can you escape being c-ed
    to hell?......................Mt 23:33
They all c-ed him as
    deserving...................Mk 14:64
does not believe will be c-ed. . Mk 16:16
Do not c, and you will not be
    c-ed........................Lk 6:37
"Neither do I c you," said Jesus .. Jn 8:11
He c-ed sin in the flesh by
    sending......................Rm 8:3
Who is the one who c-s?...... Rm 8:34
doubts stands c-ed if he eats, ..Rm 14:23
Let no one c you by delighting..Col 2:18
whenever our hearts c us;......1Jn 3:20

CONDEMNATION

Their c is deserved! ....Rm 3:8
there is now no c for those in... Rm 8:1
the same c as the devil. 1Tm 3:6

CONDUCT (N)

shameful c is pleasure for a
    fool,.........................Pr 10:23
are to be holy in all your c;......1Pt 1:15

CONDUCT (V)

knows how to c himself before.. Ec 6:8
you are to c yourselves in.......1Pt 1:17
C yourselves honorably among
    the 1Pt 2:12

CONFESS

the live goat and c over it all ...Lv 16:21
But if they will c their
    iniquity..................... Lv 26:40
person is to c the sin he has..... Nm 5:7
I will c my transgressions to......Ps 32:5
If you c with your mouth,
    "Jesus.......................Rm 10:9
tongue will c that Jesus........Php 2:11
c your sins to one another
    and .... Jms 5:16
If we c our sins, he is faithful......1Jn 1:9
he who c-es the Son has the
    Father 1Jn 2:23
Every spirit that c-es that Jesus..1Jn 4:2

CONFESSION

good c in the presence of
    many 1Tm 6:12
let us hold fast to the c. .... Heb 4:14

CONFIDENCE

Lord GOD, my c from my youth.. Ps 71:5
will be your c and will keep..... Pr 3:26
and do not put c in the flesh... Php 3:3
So don't throw away your c,..Heb 10:35

CONFIRM

to c the promises to the
    fathers......................Rm 15:8
every effort to c your calling .. 2Pt 1:10
the prophetic word
    strongly c-ed,............... 2Pt 1:19

CONFLICT

A hot-tempered person stirs
    up c, ... Pr 15:18

CONFORMED

predestined to be c to the
    image...................... Rm 8:29
Do not be c to this age,
    but be......................Rm 12:2
being c to his death,........... Php 3:10
do not be c to the desires of..... 1Pt 1:14

CONFUSE

down there and c their
    language ....Gn 11:7

CONFUSION

So the city was filled with c, .. Ac 19:29

CONGREGATION

sing hymns to you in the c......Heb 2:12

CONQUER

I have c-ed the world..........Jn 16:33
Do not be c-ed by evil, but c
    evil..........................Rm 12:21
victory that has c-ed the world: ..1Jn 5:4
as a conqueror in order to c......Rv 6:2

CONQUEROR

are more than a c through
    him ....Rm 8:37
I will give the c the right to ......Rv 2:7

CONSCIENCE

a clear c toward God and men...Ac 24:16
Their c-s confirm this..........Rm 2:15
but also because of your c. ....Rm 13:5
their c, being weak, is defiled. 1Co 8:7
of liars whose c-s are seared...1Tm 4:2
cleanse our c-s from dead
    works to..................... Heb 9:14
sprinkled clean from an
    evil c.......................Heb 10:22
keeping a clear c, so that.......1Pt 3:16

CONSECRATE

C every firstborn male to me,...Ex 13:2
c them to serve me as priests. ..Ex 29:1
c it along with all its
    furnishings..................Ex 40:9
C yourselves and be holy, for I..Lv 20:7
Joshua told the people,
    "C yourselves ....Jos 3:5
I have c-d this temple you have..1Kg 9:3

CONSECRATED (ADJ)

However, there is c bread, but..1Sm 21:4

CONSIDER

Have you c-ed my servant Job?.. Jb 1:8
LORD; c my sighing. ....Ps 5:1
Even a fool is c-ed wise
    when he ....Pr 17:28
C how the wildflowers grow:..Lk 12:27
you too c yourselves dead to
    sin .... Rm 6:11
Brothers and sisters, c your
    calling:....................1Co 1:26
but in humility c others as
    more........................Php 2:3
I also c everything to be a loss ..Php 3:8
she c-ed that the one who
    had ....Heb 11:11
C it a great joy, my brothers......Jms 1:2

CONSISTENT

produce fruit c with repentance..Mt 3:8

CONSOLATION

Christ, if any c of love, if any...... Php 2:1

CONSOLE

refused to be c-d, because they..Mt 2:18

CONSPIRE

all of you have c-d against
    me! 1Sm 22:8

and the rulers c together ....Ps 2:2
they c-d to arrest Jesus .... Mt 26:4

CONSTANTLY

Pray c........................1Th 5:17

CONSULT

Saul said, "C a spirit for me....1Sm 28:8
Rehoboam c-ed with the
    elders......................1Kg 12:6
even c-ed a medium for
    guidance 1Ch 10:13
shouldn't a people c their God?. .Is 8:19
not immediately c with anyone. . Gl 1:16

CONSUME

bush was on fire but was not
    c-d.........................Ex 3:2
so I may c them instantly......Nm 16:21
the LORD your God is a c-ing
    fire,..........................Dt 4:24
fire fell and c-d the burnt
    offering. 1Kg 18:38
zeal for your house has c-d me,..Ps 69:9
For we are c-d by your anger; ..Ps 90:7
Zeal for your house will c me. ... Jn 2:17
for our God is a c-ing fire. ....Heb 12:29

CONTAIN

heaven, cannot c you,
    much less...................1Kg 8:27
highest heaven cannot c him? ..2Ch 2:6
itself could c the books that ...Jn 21:25

CONTEMPT

some to disgrace and
    eternal c. ....Dn 12:2
things and be treated with c?..Mk 9:12
treated him with c, mocked
    him ....Lk 23:11
of God and holding him up
    to c........................Heb 6:6

CONTEND

Let Baal c with him ....Jdg 6:32
Will the one who c-s with the ..Jb 40:2
c with the one who c-s with
    you ....Is 49:25
appealing to you to c for the faith..Jd 3

CONTENT

have learned to be c in
    whatever ....Php 4:11
we will be c with these.........1Tm 6:8

CONTENTMENT

godliness with c is a great gain ..1Tm 6:6

CONTINUE

If you c in my word,..............Jn 8:31
urging them to c in the grace..Ac 13:43
Should we c in sin so that grace ..Rm 6:1
c in what you have learned ...2Tm 3:14

CONTRARY

a gospel c to what you received,..Gl 1:9
law therefore c to God's
    promises? .... Gl 3:21
whatever else is c to the
    sound.......................1Tm 1:10

CONTRIVED

we did not follow cleverly
    c myths 2Pt 1:16

CONTROL (N)

have his children under c.......1Tm 3:4

CONTROL (V)

the one who c-s his lips is
    prudent. ....Pr 10:19
person who does not c his
    temper is .... Pr 25:28
able also to c the whole body ..Jms 3:2

CONVERT

land and sea to make one c...Mt 23:15
from Rome (both Jews and c-s)..Ac 2:10
must not be a new c, or he
    might.......................1Tm 3:6

CONVICT

Who among you can c me
    of sin? ....Jn 8:46
He will c the world about sin,...Jn 16:8
he is c-ed by all and is judged
    by...........................1Co 14:24
c all the ungodly ....Jd 15

CONVICTION

same understanding and the
    same c.....................1Co 1:10

CONVINCED

fully c that what he had
    promised ....Rm 4:21
be fully c in his own mind...... Rm 14:5

CONVINCING

alive to them by many c proofs,..Ac 1:3

COPING

from foundation to c and from..1Kg 7:9

COPPER

whose hills you will mine c......Dt 8:9
and c is smelted from ore.......Jb 28:2
All of them are c, tin, iron....Ezk 22:18
gathers silver, c, iron, lead...Ezk 22:20
it becomes hot and its c glows..Ezk 24:11
gold, silver, or c for your.......Mt 10:9

COPPERSMITH

blacksmiths and c-s to repair
the.........................2Ch 24:12
Alexander the c did great
harm......................2Tm 4:14

COPY

These serve as a c and shadow
of...............................Heb 8:5
c-ies of the things in the
heavens......................Heb 9:23

CORBAN

have received from me is c......Mk 7:11

CORD

A c of three strands is not.....Ec 4:12
before the silver c is snapped,......Ec 12:6
them with human c-s, with
ropes.........................Hs 11:4

CORINTH

left Athens and went to C,......Ac 18:1

CORNELIUS

Centurion; Christian (Ac 10).

CORNER

cut off the c of Saul's robe.....1Sm 24:4
on the street c-s to be seen
by people.......................Mt 6:5
since this was not done in a c..Ac 26:26
at the four c-s of the earth,...Rv 7:1; 20:8

CORNERSTONE

rejected has become the c....Ps 118:22
a precious c, a sure foundation;..Is 28:16

The c will come from
Judah........................Zch 10:4
builders rejected has become
the c........................Mt 21:42
This Jesus...has become the c..Ac 4:11
Christ Jesus himself as the c..Eph 2:20
in Zion, a chosen and
honored c,....................1Pt 2:6

CORPSE

The boy became like a c,......Mk 9:26
he gave the c to Joseph.......Mk 15:45
Where the c is, there also.....Lk 17:37

CORRECT

The one who c-s a
mocker will....................Pr 9:7
if you really c your ways.........Jr 7:5
rebuking, for c-ing, for
training.....................2Tm 3:16
rebuke, c, and encourage.....2Tm 4:2

CORRECTION

but one who hates c is stupid...Pr 12:1

CORRESPONDS

Hagar...c to the present
Jerusalem,....................Gl 4:25
Baptism, which c to this, now
saves.........................1Pt 3:21

CORRUPT (N)

the earth was c in God's
sight,...........................Gn 6:11
all alike have become c.........Ps 14:3
Be saved from this c
generation!...................Ac 2:40

CORRUPT (V)

splendor you c-ed your
wisdom....................Ezk 28:17
Bad company c-s good
morals.....................1Co 15:33
prostitute who c-ed the
earth with...................Rv 19:2

CORRUPTIBLE

For this c body must be
clothed...................1Co 15:53

CORRUPTION

Sown in c, raised in..........1Co 15:42
escaping the c that is in the.....2Pt 1:4

COST

offerings that c me nothing...2Sm 24:24
without silver and without c!......Is 55:1
calculate the c to see if he has..Lk 14:28

COUNCIL

praise him in the c of the
elders........................Ps 107:32
on of hands by the c of elders..1Tm 4:14

COUNSEL

c and understanding are his...Jb 12:13
with my eye on you, I will
give c.........................Ps 32:8
whoever listens to c is wise....Pr 12:15
Plans fail when there is no c,...Pr 15:22
and no c will prevail against..Pr 21:30
Has c perished from the
prudent?.....................Jr 49:7

COUNSELOR

He leads c-s away barefoot and..Jb 12:17
but with many c-s there is......Pr 11:14
victory comes with many c-s...Pr 24:6
He will be named Wonderful C,..Is 9:6
you another C to be with you..Jn 14:16
But the C, the Holy Spirit,....Jn 14:26
When the C comes, the one I...Jn 15:26
go away the C will not come to..Jn 16:7
Or who has been his c?.......Rm 11:34

COUNT

c the stars, if you are able
to c them......................Gn 15:5
incited David to c the people..1Ch 21:1
of your head have all been
c-ed..........................Mt 10:30
we are c-ed as sheep to be.....Rm 8:36
not c-ing their trespasses
against......................2Co 5:19
May it not be c-ed against
them.........................2Tm 4:16

COUNTRY

has no honor in his own c.......Jn 4:44

COURAGE

Have c, son, your sins...........Mt 9:2
Have c! It is I. Don't be afraid..Mt 14:27
stood by him and said, "
Have c!........................Ac 23:11

COURAGEOUS

Be strong and c; don't be........Dt 31:6

Be strong and c, for you will.... Jos 1:6
be strong and let your heart
   be c............................Ps 27:14
Be c! I have conquered the
   world. ....Jn 16:33

COURSE

to finish my c and the.........Ac 20:24

COURT

If one wanted to take him to c, ..Jb 9:3
a day in your c-s than a
   thousand ....Ps 84:10
an offering and enter his c-s....Ps 96:8
and his c-s with praise.........Ps 100:4
Don't take a matter to c hastily..Pr 25:8
The c was convened, and the
   books ....Dn 7:10
you and drag you into c? ......Jms 2:6

COURTYARD

make the c for the tabernacle...Ex 27:9
Peter was sitting outside in
   the c.........................Mt 26:69
Jesus into the high priest's c. ..Jn 18:15

COVENANT

I will establish my c with you,...Gn 6:18
I am establishing my c with
   you ....Gn 9:9
the LORD made a c with
   Abram, ...Gn 15:18
listen to me and keep my c, ...Ex 19:5
will remember my c with
   Jacob. ....Lv 26:42
will never break my c with you. .Jdg 2:1
book of the c that had been
   found 2Kg 23:2
Let us ... make a c before our
   God ....Ezr 10:3
I have made a c with my eyes. ...Jb 31:1
who keep his c, who
   remember ....Ps 103:18
have made a c with death......Is 28:15
I will make a new c with.......Jr 31:31
I will establish a
   permanent c...............Ezk 16:60
Messenger of the c you desire..Mal 3:1
This cup is the new c..........Lk 22:20
the adoption, the glory, the c-s,..Rm 9:4
this will be my c with them...Rm 11:27
This cup is the new c.........1Co 11:25
to be ministers of a new c, ...2Co 3:6
the women represent two c-s...Gl 4:24
the guarantee of a better c....Heb 7:22
he is the mediator of a
   new c,......................Heb 9:15

COVER (N)

He spread a cloud as a c-ing ..Ps 105:39
hair is given to her as a c-ing..1Co 11:15

COVER (V)

the rock and c you with my
   hand.......................Ex 33:22
is forgiven, whose sin is c-ed! ..Ps 32:1
You c-ed all their sin. ....Ps 85:2
He will c you with his feathers;..Ps 91:4
but love c-s all offenses. ....Pr 10:12
with two they c-ed their faces, ...Is 6:2
as the water c-s the sea........Hab 2:14
and to the hills, 'C us!'.........Lk 23:30
forgiven and whose sins are
   c-ed!.........................Rm 4:7
if a woman doesn't c her
   head,.........................1Co 11:6
man should not c his head.....1Co 11:7
and c a multitude of sins......Jms 5:20
since love c-s a multitude of
   sins 1Pt 4:8

COVER-UP (N)

using your freedom as a c for
   evil............................1Pt 2:16

COVET

Do not c your
   neighbor's............Ex 20:17; Dt 5:21
quarter, I c-ed them and
   took them....................Jos 7:21
I have not c-ed anyone's
   silver........................Ac 20:33
what it is to c if the law had not..Rm 7:7
do not steal; do not c;.........Rm 13:9
You murder and c and cannot..Jms 4:2

COW

seven other c-s, sickly and thin ..Gn 41:3
you c-s of Bashan who are
   on the.........................Am 4:1

COWARDS

But the c, faithless, detestable,..Rv 21:8

CRAFTINESS

He traps the wise in their c .....Jb 5:13
He catches the wise in
   their c 1Co 3:19

CRAFTSMAN

I was a skilled c beside him...... Pr 8:30
business for the c-men........Ac 19:24

CRAVE

by c-ing it, some have
   wandered 1Tm 6:10

CRAZY

the man is c," Achish said.... 1Sm 21:14
He has a demon and he's c. ....Jn 10:20

CREATE

In the beginning God c-d the
   heavens.......................Gn 1:1
God c-d man in his own image; Gn 1:27
c a clean heart for me..........Ps 51:10
You who c-d my inward
   parts; ....Ps 139:13
commanded, and they
   were c-d......................Ps 148:5
who c-d the heavens and
   stretched ....Is 42:5
All things were c-d through him, ..Jn 1:3
served what has been c-d
   instead ....Rm 1:25
man was not c-d for the sake of
   woman,.......................1Co 11:9
c-d in Christ Jesus for good
   works........................ Eph 2:10
c in himself one new man
   from ....Eph 2:15
everything was c-d by him,......Col 1:16
everything c-d by God is good,..1Tm 4:4
you have c-d all things, and by your
   will they ... were c-d.......... Rv 4:11

CREATION

he rested from all his work of c.. Gn 2:3
the beginning of c God made
   them..........................Mk 10:6
preach the gospel to all c......Mk 16:15
have been clearly seen since
   the c ....Rm 1:20
For the c eagerly waits with ...Rm 8:19
is in Christ, he is a new c; 2Co 5:17
the firstborn over all c. ....Col 1:15
been since the beginning of c...2Pt 3:4

CREATOR

God Most High, C of heaven
   and ....Gn 14:22
So remember your C in the days..Ec 12:1
created instead of the C,.......Rm 1:25
entrust themselves to a
   faithful C.....................1Pt 4:19

CREATURE

and every living c that moves ..Gn 1:21
No c is hidden from him, ...Heb 4:13

Four living **c-s** covered
  with eyes . . . . .Rv 4:6

CRETE

Island in the Mediterranean Sea. Paul
assigned Titus as supervisor there (Ti
1:5) and moored there on his way to
Rome (Ac 27).

My eyes are worn out from
c-ing. . . . . .Ps 88:9
A voice of one c-ing out:. . . . . . . Is 40:3
the stones will c out from
the wall, ...Hab 2:11
A voice of one c-ing out in the. . Mt 3:3
silent, the stones would c out!. . Lk 19:40
grief, c-ing, and pain will be no . .Rv 21:4

CRYSTAL

gleamed like awe-inspiring c, . .Ezk 1:22
a sea of glass, similar to c, ...Rv 4:6

CUP

head with oil; my c overflows. . . . . . .Ps 23:5
even a c of cold water to . . . . . .Mt 10:42
to drink the c that I am about Mt 20:22
Then he took a c, and after . . .Mt 26:27
let this c pass from me. . . . . . . .Mt 26:39
This c is the new covenant. . . . Lk 22:20
This c is the new covenant. 1Co 11:25
full strength into the c of
his anger. . . . . .Rv 14:10

CUPBEARER

The king of Egypt's c and baker. .Gn 40:1
I was the king's c. . . . . .Neh 1:11

CURE

But he cannot c you or heal
your . . . . .Hs 5:13

CURSE (N)

come and put a c on these
people . . . . Nm 22:6
before you a blessing and a c:. . .Dt 11:26
hung on a tree is under
God's c. .Dt 21:23
all these c-s will come . . . . .Dt 28:15
an undeserved c goes nowhere. Pr 26:2
preached to you, a c be on him! . . .Gl 1:8
redeemed us from the c of the
law by becoming a c for us, . . Gl 3:13
Blessing and c-ing come
out of . . . . Jms 3:10

CURSE (V)

will never again c the ground. . .Gn 8:21
I will c anyone who treats you . .Gn 12:3
Those who c you will be c-d,. . .Gn 27:29
C God and die! . . . . .Jb 2:9
and c-d the day he was born. . . . . Jb 3:1
Whoever c-s his father or
mother . . . . Pr 20:20
he started to c and to swear . .Mt 26:74

fig tree that you c-d has
withered. . . . . Mk 11:21
bless those who c you, pray for. .Lk 6:28
persecute you; bless and do
not c. . . . . .Rm 12:14
with it we c people who are . . . Jms 3:9

CURSED (ADJ)

The ground is c because of you. .Gn 3:17
I could wish that I myself
were c . . . . .Rm 9:3
C is everyone who is hung
on a tree. Gl 3:13

CURTAIN

the c of the sanctuary
was torn . . . . Mt 27:51
inaugurated . . . through
the c . . . . .Heb 10:20

CUSTOM

and are promoting c-s that are
not. . . . . .Ac 16:21
or the c-s of our ancestors, ...Ac 28:17

CUT

right hand causes you to
sin, c it off . . . . .Mt 5:30
servant, and c off his right ear. . .Jn 18:10
you too will be c off. . . . . .Rm 11:22

CYMBAL

Praise him with resounding
c-s;. . . . . .Ps 150:5
noisy gong or a clanging c. 1Co 13:1

CYRUS

King of Persia; used by God (Is 44:28;
45:1); permitted the exiles to return
and rebuild the temple (2Ch 36:22–Ezr
1:8; 3:7; 4:3-5; 5:13–6:14).

D

DAGON

Philistine god (Jdg 16:23; 1Sm 5:2-7; 1Ch
10:10).

DAILY

Give us today our d bread. . . . . . .Mt 6:11
up his cross d, and follow me. . Lk 9:23

DAMASCUS

he traveled and was nearing D, . .Ac 9:3

DAN

Son of Jacob and Bilhah (Gn 30:4-6;
35:25). Tribe; unable to conquer allotted land west of Jerusalem and up
the coast to Joppa; took land in the far
north (Jos 19:40-48; Jdg 18). City (Jdg
18:29).

DANCE (N)

You turned my lament into
d-ing;. . . . . .Ps 30:11
Praise him with tambourine
and d;. . . . . .Ps 150:4

DANCE (V)

David was d-ing with all his
might. 2Sm 6:14
time to mourn and a time to d; . .Ec 3:4
flute for you, but you didn't d;. .Mt 11:17
Herodias's daughter d-d. . . . . . . Mt 14:6

DANGER

I fear no d, for you are with. . . . . .Ps 23:4
or nakedness or d or sword? . .Rm 8:35
d-s in the city, d-s in the. 2Co 11:26

DANIEL

1. Son of David (1Ch 3:1).
2. Prophet during the exile in Babylon.
Called Belteshazzar (Dn 1:7); refused to
eat the king's food (1:8-20); interpreted the king's dreams (Dn 3; 4) and the
writing on the wall (Dn 5); thrown in
the lion's den (Dn 6). Received visions
(Dn 7–12).

DARE

someone might even d to die. . .Rm 5:7

DARIUS

1. The Mede, who conquered Babylon
(Dn 5:31).
2. Darius I of Persia allowed the rebuilding of the temple (Ezr 4:5; 5–6; Hg 1:1;
Zch 1:1).
3. Darius II of Persia (Neh 12:22).

DARK

the darkness is not d to you. . .Ps 139:12
have said in the d will be heard. .Lk 12:3

DARKEST

when I go through the **d**
　valley,.........................Ps 23:4

DARKNESS

walking in **d** have seen a great ...Is 9:2
I form light and create **d**, ... Is 45:7
if the light within you is **d**, how deep
　is that **d**! ....Mt 6:23
shines in the **d**, and yet the **d**
　did not........................Jn 1:5
and people loved **d** rather than..Jn 3:19
fellowship does light have
　with **d**? 2Co 6:14
you were once **d**, but now......Eph 5:8
called you out of **d** into his 1Pt 2:9
is absolutely no **d** in him. 1Jn 1:5
but hates his brother or sister
　is in the **d**.......................1Jn 2:9

DAUGHTER

the sons of God came to the
　d-s of ....Gn 6:4
sons and your **d-s** will
　prophesy,.......................Jl 2:28
Rejoice greatly, D Zion!........ Zch 9:9
mother against **d, d** against
　mother ....Lk 12:53

DAVID

Youngest son of Jesse, anointed king by
Samuel (Ru 4:17-22; 1Sm 16:1-13). Sought
God's heart (1Sm 13:14; Ac 13:22). Killed
Goliath (1Sm 17). Covenant of friendship
with Jonathan (18:1-4; 19–20; 23:16-18).
Spared Saul's life (1Sm 24; 26). Anointed king of Judah (2Sm 2:1-11) and Israel
(5:1-4).
　Conquered Jerusalem (5:6-9) and
brought the ark there (2Sm 6). Was
promised by God that he would keep
his descendant on the throne (2Sm 7).
Prepared for building the temple (1Ch
22–29). Psalmist, musician (Ps 23:1), and
prophet (Mt 22:43; Ac 1:16; 4:25).
　Committed adultery with Bathsheba
and murdered Uriah, then was confronted by Nathan (2Sm 11–12). Family
and political troubles followed: Amnon, Tamar, and Absalom (2Sm 13–18);
Sheba (2Sm 20); punished for military
census (2Sm 24; 1Ch 21); Adonijah and
Solomon (1Kg 1–2).
　Named Solomon as successor (1Kg
1:29-30). Died (2Sm 23:1-7; 1Kg 2:10-12).
Ancestor of Jesus (Mt 1:1,6); Jesus is heir
to his throne forever (Mt 12:23; 21:9; Mk
11:10; Lk 1:32; Rv 22:16).

DAWN (N)

righteousness shine like the **d**,..Ps 37:6
appearance is as sure as the **d**. ..Hs 6:3

DAWN (V)

a light has **d-ed** on those
　living in........................Is 9:2
of death, light has **d-ed**........ Mt 4:16

DAY

God called the light "**d**,"..........Gn 1:5
he meditates on it **d** and night... Ps 1:2
pursue me all the **d-s** of my life,..Ps 23:6
Teach us to number our **d-s** ..Ps 90:12
This is the **d** the LORD has
　made ....Ps 118:24
Creator in the **d-s** of your youth:..Ec 12:1
can endure the **d** of his
　coming? ....Mal 3:2
that **d** and hour no one ....Mt 24:36
Give us each **d** our daily bread.. Lk 11:3
will raise him up on the last **d**...Jn 6:40
now is the **d** of salvation. 2Co 6:2
time, because the **d-s** are evil...Eph 5:16
well that the **d** of the Lord will..1Th 5:2
entrusted to me until that **d**... 2Tm 1:12
one **d** is like a thousand years,..2Pt 3:8

DEACONS

D, likewise, should be..........1Tm 3:8

DEAD

and let the **d** bury their own **d**. Mt 8:22
He is not the God of the **d**,......Mt 22:32
'He has been raised from the **d**.. Mt 28:7
looking for the living among
　the **d**?........................ Lk 24:5
consider yourselves **d** to sin... Rm 6:11
you were **d** in your trespasses ..Eph 2:1
the firstborn from the **d**,....... Col 1:18
and the **d** in Christ will rise....1Th 4:16
also faith without works is **d**.. Jms 2:26

DEAD SEA

The end of the Jordan River, forming
the southeastern border of Canaan
(Nm 34:3; Jos 15:5); also called the Sea
of the Arabah (Dt 3:17; Jos 3:16; 12:3; 2Kg
14:25) and the Eastern Sea (Ezk 47:18;
Zch 14:8).

DEAF

makes him mute or **d**, seeing or..Ex 4:11
On that day the **d** will hear the ..Is 29:18
the **d** hear, the dead are raised,.. Mt 11:5

DEATH

You put me into the dust of **d**. .Ps 22:15
The **d** of his faithful ones is... Ps 116:15
Rescue those being taken off
　to **d**,.........................Pr 24:11
he will destroy **d** forever........ Is 25:8
D, where are your barbs?......Hs 13:14
will not taste **d** until
　they see.....................Mt 16:28
but has passed from **d** to life....Jn 5:24
he will never see **d**. ....Jn 8:51
d reigned from Adam to
　Moses, ...Rm 5:14
For the wages of sin is **d**,...... Rm 6:23
rescue me from this
　body of **d**? ....Rm 7:24
neither **d** nor life, nor angels
　nor rulers, ... Rm 8:38
Where, **d**, is your victory?..... 1Co 15:55
passed from **d** to life because.. 1Jn 3:14
I hold the keys of **d** and
　Hades. ....Rv 1:18
D and Hades were thrown into
　the.............................Rv 20:14
D will be no more; ....Rv 21:4

DEBATE

Where is the **d-r** of this age?...1Co 1:20
But avoid foolish **d-s**,
　genealogies..................... Ti 3:9

DEBORAH

Prophet and judge (Jdg 4–5).

DEBT

forgive us our **d-s**, as we also......Mt 6:12
forgive everyone in **d** to us...... Lk 11:4
He erased the certificate of **d**,.. Col 2:14

DEBTORS

as we also have forgiven our **d**.. Mt 6:12

DECAY

allow your faithful one to
　see **d**. ....Ps 16:10
allow your holy one to see **d**. .. Ac 2:27
not allow your holy one to
　see **d**. ....Ac 13:35

DECEIT

and in whose spirit is no **d**!..... Ps 32:2
Israelite in whom there is no **d**.. Jn 1:47
quarrels, **d**, and malice........Rm 1:29
and no **d** was found in his
　mouth;......................1Pt 2:22

DECEITFUL

heart is more **d** than anything...Jr 17:9

DECEIVE

I am he,' and they will **d** many..Mk 13:6
Let no one **d** himself............1Co 3:18
Don't be **d-d**: God is not mocked..Gl 6:7
Let no one **d** you with empty......Eph 5:6
worse, **d-ing** and being **d-d**...2Tm 3:13
have no sin," we are **d-ing**
ourselves....................1Jn 1:8

DECENCY

clothing, with **d** and good
sense,.......................1Tm 2:9

DECEPTIVE

Charm is **d** and beauty is......Pr 31:30

DECISION

but its every **d** is from the
LORD.......................Pr 16:33
multitudes in the valley of **d**!......Jl 3:14

DECLARE

The heavens **d** the glory of God,..Ps 19:1

DECREE

In those days a **d** went out from..Lk 2:1

DEDICATE

the Israelites **d-d** the LORD'S..1Kg 8:63
for anyone to **d** something
rashly......................Pr 20:25

DEED

whatever you do, in word or
in **d**,..........................Col 3:17

DEEP

D calls to **d** in the roar of........Ps 42:7

DEER

As a **d** longs for streams of......Ps 42:1
like those of a **d** and enables
me..........................Hab 3:19

DEFECT

No man who has any **d** is to
come......................Lv 21:18

DEFENSE

At my first **d**, no one stood by
me,..........................2Tm 4:16
ready... to give a **d** to anyone
who.........................1Pt 3:15

DEFILE

that Shechem had **d-d** his
daughter....................Gn 34:5
out of the mouth—this **d-s**
a man.......................Mt 15:11
These are the things that **d**
a person,....................Mt 15:20
conscience, being weak,
is **d-d**.........................1Co 8:7

DELIGHT (N)

his **d** is in the LORD'S............Ps 1:2
Take **d** in the LORD, and he
will.........................Ps 37:4
your instruction is my **d**..Pss 119:77,174

DELIGHT (V)

rescued me because he **d-ed**
in me.......................Ps 18:19
disciplines the son in whom
he **d-s**......................Pr 3:12
my beloved in whom I **d**;......Mt 12:18

DELILAH

Philistine woman who betrayed Samson (Jdg 16:4-22).

DELIVER

but **d** us from the evil one......Mt 6:13
He was **d-ed** up for our
trespasses...................Rm 4:25
has **d-ed** us from such a
terrible.....................2Co 1:10
faith that was **d-ed** to the
saints once..................Jd 3

DELIVERANCE

d will come to the Jewish people from
another place,...............Est 4:14
me with joyful shouts of **d**......Ps 32:7

DELIVERER

the LORD raised up...a **d** to
save........................Jdg 3:9
my fortress, and
my **d**,..............2Sm 22:2; Ps 18:2
You are my help and
my **d**;..................Ps 40:17; 70:5

DELUSION

them a strong **d** so that they...2Th 2:11

DEMOLISH

We **d** arguments..............2Co 10:4

DEMOLITION

for the **d** of strongholds.......2Co 10:4

DEMON

sacrificed to **d-s**, not God,......Dt 32:17
drive out **d-s** in your name.....Mt 7:22
and they say, 'He has a **d**!'......Mt 11:18
spirits and the teachings
of **d-s**,......................1Tm 4:1
Even the **d-s** believe—and
they.........................Jms 2:19
stop worshiping **d-s** and
idols of.....................Rv 9:20

DEMON-POSSESSED

brought...the **d**, the
epileptics,..................Mt 4:24
two **d** men met him as
they came..................Mt 8:28

DEMONSTRATE

to **d** his righteousness.....Rm 3:25,26

DEN

threw him into the lions' **d**......Dn 6:16
are making it a **d** of thieves!..Mt 21:13

DENY

But whoever **d-ies** me before others, I
will also **d** him before my..Mt 10:33
let him **d** himself, take up.....Mt 16:24
you will **d** me three times!......Mt 26:34
he has **d-ied** the faith and
is worse.....................1Tm 5:8
if we **d** him, he will also **d** us;..2Tm 2:12
of godliness but **d-ing** its
power.......................2Tm 3:5
but they **d** him by their works...Ti 1:16
d-ing the Master who bought
them,........................2Pt 2:1
who **d-ies**...Jesus is the
Christ?......................1Jn 2:22

DEPART

scepter will not **d** from
Judah......................Gn 49:10
is old he will not **d** from it......Pr 22:6

on the left, 'D from me, you
who............................ Mt 25:41
I long to d and be with........ Php 1:23

DEPRIVE

Do not d one another— 1Co 7:5

DEPTH

height nor d, nor any other... Rm 8:39
the d of the riches both
  of the ....Rm 11:33
everything, even the d-s of
  God............................1Co 2:10

DESCEND

the Spirit d-ing from heaven
  like............................Jn 1:32
ascending and d-ing on the
  Son of........................ Jn 1:51
the one who d-ed from heaven..Jn 3:13
The one who d-ed is also the
  one .... Eph 4:10
himself will d from heaven
  with 1Th 4:16

DESCENDANT

So will your d-s be..............Rm 4:18

DESERT (N)

highway for our God in the d. .. Is 40:3
rivers in the d, to give drink.......Is 43:20

DESERT (V)

disciples d-ed him and ran
  away.......................Mt 26:56

DESERVE

has not dealt with us as our
  sins d ....Ps 103:10
He has done nothing to d
  death........................Lk 23:15

DESIRE (N)

Your d will be for your
  husband .... Gn 3:16
will give you your heart's d-s...Ps 37:4
my heart's d and prayer to
  God .... Rm 10:1
plans to gratify the d-s of the
  flesh........................Rm 13:14
to marry than to burn with d. ..1Co 7:9
carry out the d of the flesh...... Gl 5:16
and enticed by his own evil d...Jms 1:14

DESIRE (V)

or d your neighbor's house,...... Dt 5:21
nothing you d can equal her. ... Pr 3:15
that we should d him............ Is 53:2
For I d loyalty and not ....Hs 6:6
I d mercy and not sacrifice..Mt 9:13; 12:7
I have fervently d-d to eat this ..Lk 22:15
But d the greater gifts.........1Co 12:31
d-ing to put on our heavenly
  dwelling 2Co 5:2

DESOLATE

your house is left to you d......Mt 23:38
the children of the d woman,... Gl 4:27

•

DESOLATION

set up the abomination of d....Dn 11:31
the abomination of d,........ Mt 24:15
abomination of d standing
  where it .... Mk 13:14
that its d has come near....... Lk 21:20

DESPAIR (N)

myself over to d concerning all. .Ec 2:20
we are perplexed but not in d; ..2Co 4:8

DESPAIR (V)

so that we even d-ed of life..... 2Co 1:8

DESPISE

So Esau d-d his birthright.....Gn 25:34
and she d-d him in her heart. . 2Sm 6:16
fools d wisdom and discipline. ...Pr 1:7
He was d-d and rejected by
  men, ... Is 53:3
devoted to one and d the other. .Mt 6:24
Don't let anyone d your
  youth,.......................1Tm 4:12
endured a cross, d-ing the
  shame .... Heb 12:2

DESTINED

this child is d to cause the fall .. Lk 2:34

DESTITUTE

in goatskins, d, afflicted ..... Heb 11:37

DESTROY

who is able to d both soul and. .Mt 10:28
Have you come to d us?........Mk 1:24
to steal and kill and d.........Jn 10:10
we are struck down but not
  d-ed........................ 2Co 4:9

our outer person is being
  d-ed,........................ 2Co 4:16
if our earthly tent ... is d-ed,....2Co 5:1
who is able to save and to d... Jms 4:12

DESTRUCTION

set apart to the LORD for d......Jos 6:17
Pride comes before d,.......... Pr 16:18
road broad that leads to d,.....Mt 7:13
objects of wrath prepared
  for d? .... Rm 9:22
Their end is d; their god is.......Php 3:19
the penalty of eternal d........2Th 1:9
twist them to their own d, ... 2Pt 3:16

DETERMINE

Since a person's days are
  d-d and .... Jb 14:5
I have d-d that my mouth
  will not .... Ps 17:3
but the LORD d-s his steps....... Pr 16:9
person's steps are d-d by
  the LORD, ... Pr 20:24

DETEST

D evil; cling to what is good....Rm 12:9

DETESTABLE

committed all these d acts,......Lv 18:27
imitating the d practices 2Kg 16:3

DEVIL

to be tempted by the d. ....Mt 4:1
enemy who sowed them is
  the d......................... Mt 13:39
for the d and his angels! ...... Mt 25:41
Yet one of you is the d!..........Jn 6:70
don't give the d an
  opportunity .... Eph 4:27
against the schemes of the d..Eph 6:11
Resist the d, and he will........ Jms 4:7
adversary the d is prowling......1Pt 5:8
who is called the d and
  Satan,........................Rv 12:9

DEVOTED

be d to one and despise the
  other. .... Mt 6:24

DEVOUR

Must the sword d forever? .. 2Sm 2:26
if you bite and d one
  another, ... Gl 5:15
looking for anyone he can d. ... 1Pt 5:8

DEVOUT

This man was righteous and **d**, . .Lk 2:25

DEW

If **d** is only on the fleece, ...Jdg 6:37

DICTATION

At Jeremiah's **d**, Baruch
  wrote on. .Jr 36:4

DIE

from it, you will certainly **d**. . . . .Gn 2:17
Where you **d**, I will **d**, and
  there I . . . . .Ru 1:17
but fools **d** for lack of sense. . . . Pr 10:21
him with a rod, he will not **d**. . .Pr 23:13
a time to give birth and a time
  to **d**; . . . . .Ec 3:2
and drink, for tomorrow we
  d! . . . . Is 22:13
Even if I have to **d** with you, . .Mt 26:35
believes in me will never **d**. . . . . Jn 11:26
wheat falls to the ground and
  d-s, ...Jn 12:24
time, Christ **d-d** for the ungodly. . . . Rm
  5:6
How can we who **d-d** to sin
  still . . . . .Rm 6:2
and if we **d**, we **d** for the Lord. .Rm 14:8
that Christ **d-d** for our sins. 1Co 15:3
the law I **d-d** to the law, ... Gl 2:19
to live is Christ and to **d** is
  gain. . . . . .Php 1:21
for people to **d** once . . . . Heb 9:27
The dead who **d** in the Lord . . . . . .Rv 14:13

DIG

cisterns that you did not **d**, ... Dt 6:11
fence around it, **dug** a
  winepress . . . . Mt 21:33

DINAH

Daughter of Jacob and Leah (Gn 30:21).
Raped by Shechem; avenged by Simeon and Levi (Gn 34).

DIP

the one who is **d-ping** bread. .Mk 14:20

DIRECT

He **d-s** it wherever he
  chooses. . . . . .Pr 21:1
May the Lord **d** your
  hearts to. 2Th 3:5

DISAPPOINT

hope will not **d** us, because
  God's . . . . .Rm 5:5

DISARM

He **d-ed** the rulers and
  authorities . . . . .Col 2:15

DISASTER

the wicked for the day of **d**. . . . . . Pr 16:4
I make success and create **d**; . . . . .Is 45:7
If a **d** occurs in a city, hasn't . . . .Am 3:6
No **d** will overtake us. . . . . Mc 3:11

DISCERN

so that you may **d** what is the. .Rm 12:2

DISCIPLE

Summoning his twelve **d-s**,
  he gave .Mt 10:1
A **d** is not above his teacher, . . Mt 10:24
and make **d-s** of all nations, . . Mt 28:19
come after me cannot be
  my **d**. . . . . .Lk 14:27
and his **d-s** believed in him. . . . . . Jn 2:11
my word, you really are my
  d-s. . . . . .Jn 8:31
and the **d** he loved . . . . .Jn 19:26
d-s were first called Christians
  at . . . . .Ac 11:26

DISCIPLINE (N)

Apply yourself to **d** and
  listen to. . . . . .Pr 23:12
Don't withhold **d** from a
  youth; . . . . .Pr 23:13
No **d** seems enjoyable at the
  time. . . . . .Heb 12:11

DISCIPLINE (V)

your anger or **d** me in your
  wrath . . . . .Ps 38:1
for the LORD **d-s** the one he
  loves, ...Pr 3:12
D your son while there is
  hope; . . . . .Pr 19:18
judged . . . we are **d-d**, so that
  we 1Co 11:32
for the Lord **d-s** the one he
  loves . . . . Heb 12:6

DISCOURAGED

Do not be afraid or **d**, ... Jos 1:9
stopped walking and looked **d**. . Lk 18:1

DISCUSS

And they were **d-ing** among
  themselves, ...Mt 16:7

DISEASE

all the terrible **d-s** of Egypt that. .Dt 7:15
he heals all your **d-s**. . . . . .Ps 103:3
and healing every **d** and
  sickness . . . . Mt 4:23
weaknesses and carried our
  d-s. . . . . .Mt 8:17
demons and to heal **d-s**. . . . . Lk 9:1

DISFIGURED

was so **d** that he did not. . . . . Is 52:14

DISGRACE

When arrogance comes,
  d follows, ... Pr 11:2
but sin is a **d** to any people. . . . . Pr 14:34
has long hair it is a **d** to him, ...1Co 11:14

DISGRACEFUL

But if it is **d** for a woman to. 1Co 11:6
for it is **d** for a woman to
  speak 1Co 14:35

DISGUISE

king of Israel **d-d** himself. . . . 1Kg 22:30
Satan **d-s** himself as an angel. .2Co 11:14

DISHONEST

D scales are detestable to the. . . .Pr 11:1
one who hates **d** profit prolongs. .Pr 28:16

DISHONOR (N)

for honor and another for **d**?. .Rm 9:21
sown in **d**, raised in glory; . . . 1Co 15:43

DISHONOR (V)

her head uncovered **d-s** her
  head, ...1Co 11:5

DISMISS

You can **d** your servant in
  peace, ... Lk 2:29

DISOBEDIENCE

through one man's **d** the many. .Rm 5:19
received mercy through
  their **d**, ... Rm 11:30

DISOBEDIENT

out my hands to a **d** and
defiant......................Rm 10:21
spirit now working in the **d**.... Eph 2:2

DISORDER

is not a God of **d** but of peace. .1Co 14:33

DISPERSE

Jewish people **d-d** among the ..Jn 7:35

DISPLAY

I will **d** my glory among the ..Ezk 39:21
I think God has **d-ed** us,.........1Co 4:9
ages he might **d** the
immeasurable..............Eph 2:7

DISPUTE

was **d-ing** with the devil...........Jd 9

DISQUALIFY

others, I myself will not be
d-ied.......................1Co 9:27

DISSENSIONS

selfish ambitions, **d**, factions,...Gl 5:20

DISTINCTION

They make no **d** between the
holy......................Ezk 22:26
believe, since there is no **d**.... Rm 3:22
for there is no **d** between Jew ..Rm 10:12

DISTINGUISH

You must **d** between the holy
and ....Lv 10:10
to another, **d-ing** between
spirits......................1Co 12:10

DISTRACTED

But Martha was **d** by her
many ....Lk 10:40

DISTRESS

to be sorrowful and deeply
d-ed.......................Mt 26:37
will be great **d** in the land......Lk 21:23

DISTRIBUTE

d the land as an inheritance......Jos 13:6

This was then **d-d** to each
person......................Ac 4:35
d-ing to each person as he
wills.......................1Co 12:11

DIVIDE

your hand over the sea, and
d it..........................Ex 14:16
They **d-d** my garments
among......................Ps 22:18
Every kingdom **d-d** against
itself......................Mt 12:25
him, they **d-d** his clothes......Mt 27:35
my brother to **d** the
inheritance..................Lk 12:13
Is Christ **d-d**? Was it Paul who.. 1Co 1:13

DIVINATION

not to practice **d** or sorcery....Lv 19:26
rebellion is like the sin of **d**, ..1Sm 15:23

DIVINE

his eternal power and **d**
nature,......................Rm 1:20
His **d** power has given us
everything...................2Pt 1:3
you may share in the **d** nature, ..2Pt 1:4

DIVISION

No, I tell you, but rather **d**!.....Lk 12:51
that there be no **d-s** among
you,..........................1Co 1:10
church there are **d-s** among
you,..........................1Co 11:18
would be no **d** in the body,......1Co 12:25

DIVORCE

he cannot **d** her as long as he ..Dt 22:19
may write her a **d** certificate,...Dt 24:1
given her a certificate of **d**.......Jr 3:8
If he hates and **d-s** his wife,... Mal 2:16
decided to **d** her secretly.......Mt 1:19
must give her a written
notice of **d**. ....Mt 5:31
permitted you to **d** your
wives ....Mt 19:8

DIVORCED (ADJ)

marries a **d** woman commits.. Mt 5:32

DOCTOR

who are well who need a **d**,.... Mt 9:12
proverb to me: 'D, heal
yourself ....Lk 4:23

DOCTRINE

teaching as **d-s** human
commands..................Mt 15:9
people not to teach false **d**.....1Tm 1:3
they will not tolerate sound **d**,..2Tm 4:3

DOER

But be **d-s** of the word and not..Jms 1:22

DOG

'The **d-s** will eat Jezebel in the ..1Kg 21:23
As a **d** returns to its vomit,..... Pr 26:11
since a live **d** is better than a ..... Ec 9:4
bread and throw it to the **d-s**...Mk 7:27
A **d** returns to its own vomit, ..2Pt 2:22

DOMAIN

us from the **d** of darkness ..... Col 1:13

DOMINION

His **d** is an everlasting **d** ......Dn 4:34; 7:14
power and **d**, and every title...Eph 1:21
to him be glory and **d** forever......Rv 1:6

DONKEY

the LORD opened the **d-**'s
mouth,......................Nm 22:28
riding on a **d**, on a colt, the foal
of .... Zch 9:9
mounted on a **d** and on a colt.. Mt 21:5
A speechless **d** spoke with a
human......................2Pt 2:16

DOOR

Rise up, ancient **d-s**! Then
the King ....Ps 24:7
keep watch at the **d** of my lips. . Ps 141:3
and the **d** will be opened to you ..Mt 7:7
to enter through the
narrow **d**,...................Lk 13:24
the Lord opened a **d** for me......2Co 2:12
that God may open a **d** to us for..Col 4:3
you an open **d** that no one can...Rv 3:8
I stand at the **d** and knock...... Rv 3:20

DOORPOST

blood and put it on the two **d-s** ..Ex 12:7
Write them on the **d-s** of your
house........................Dt 6:9

DOUBLE-EDGED

and as sharp as a **d** sword........Pr 5:4
and sharper than any **d** sword, ..Heb 4:12

DOUBT

sharp **d** sword came from
his mouth,................... Rv 1:16

DOUBT

of little faith, why did
you **d**? .... Mt 14:31
If you have faith and do not **d**, ..Mt 21:21
they worshiped, but some
d-ed. .... Mt 28:17
whoever **d**-s stands
condemned. ....Rm 14:23
let him ask in faith without
d-ing..........................Jms 1:6

DOUGH

took their **d** before it was
leavened, ... Ex 12:34
leavens the whole batch of **d**? ..1Co 5:6
leavens the whole batch of **d**. .... Gl 5:9

DOVE

he sent out a **d** to see whether.. Gn 8:8
Spirit of God descending
like a **d**...................... Mt 3:16
serpents and as innocent as
d-s.......................... Mt 10:16

DOWNFALL

Before his **d** a person's heart
is proud, ... Pr 18:12

DRAGON

And the **d** stood in front of the..Rv 12:4
He seized the **d**, that ancient
serpent .... Rv 20:2

DRAW

the Father who sent me **d**-s
him,...........................Jn 6:44
earth I will **d** all people to......Jn 12:32
let us **d** near with a true
heart.......................Heb 10:22
D near to God, and he will **d**
near .... Jms 4:8

DREAM (N)

Joseph had a **d**................. Gn 37:5
Daniel also understood ... **d**-s ..Dn 1:17
Daniel had a **d** with visions in ...Dn 7:1
your old men will have **d**-s, and. .Jl 2:28
appeared to Joseph in a **d**, ... Mt 2:13
terribly in a **d** because of him. . Mt 27:19
and your old men will
dream **d**-s................... Ac 2:17

DREAM (V)

he **d**-ed: A stairway was set
on........................... Gn 28:12

DRESS

the women are to **d** themselves
in 1Tm 2:9

DRINK

D water from your own cistern,. .Pr 5:15
eat and **d**, for tomorrow
we die! .... Is 22:13
and you gave me something
to **d**; ....Mt 25:35
and they all **drank** from it. ...Mk 14:23
Do this, as often as you **d** it, ...1Co 11:25
we were all given one Spirit
to **d**. 1Co 12:13

DRIVE

did not **d** them out completely.. .Jos 17:13
He **drove** everyone out of
the temple..................... Jn 2:15
perfect love **d**-s out fear, ...1Jn 4:18

DRUNK (ADJ)

And don't get **d** with wine,.... Eph 5:18

DRUNKARD

a glutton and a **d**, a friend of...Mt 11:19
abusive, a **d** or a swindler. 1Co 5:11

DRUNKENNESS

not in carousing and **d**; ....Rm 13:13
envy, **d**, carousing, and
anything...................... Gl 5:21
evil desires, **d**, orgies 1Pt 4:3

DRY

and let the **d** land appear..........Gn 1:9
go through the sea on **d**
ground.......................Ex 14:16
D bones, hear the word of......Ezk 37:4

DULL

Make the minds of these
people **d**; .... Is 6:10

DUST

man out of the **d** from the
ground .... Gn 2:7
belly and eat **d** all the days..... Gn 3:14

offspring like the **d** of the
earth, ... Gn 13:16
I am **d** and ashes.................Jb 42:6
remembering that we are **d**...Ps 103:14
all come from **d**, and all
return to **d**. .... Ec 3:20
shake the **d** off your feet
when .... Mt 10:14
The first man was ... a man
of **d**;.........................1Co 15:47

DUTY

we've only done our **d**.........Lk 17:10

DWELL

LORD, who can **d** in your tent?.. Ps 15:1
and I will **d** in the house of
the............................Ps 23:6
became flesh and **dwelt**
among us.................... Jn 1:14
that Christ may **d** in your
hearts....................... Eph 3:17
praiseworthy—**d** on these
things....................... Php 4:8
all his fullness **d** in him, ... Col 1:19
God's nature **d**-s bodily in
Christ, ... Col 2:9

DWELLING

a place for your **d** forever. 1Kg 8:13
being built together for
God's **d**. .... Eph 2:22

E

EAGLE

I carried you on **e**-s' wings
and ....Ex 19:4
youth is renewed like the **e**.......Ps 103:5
they will soar on wings like
e-s; .... Is 40:31
the left, and the face of an **e**....Ezk 1:10
creature was like a flying **e**.......Rv 4:7

EAR

One who shaped the **e** not
hear, ...Ps 94:9
otherwise they ... hear with
their **e**-s, ...Is 6:10
Let anyone who has **e**-s listen!. .Mt 11:15
servant, and cut off his right **e**. . Jn 18:10
no eye has seen, no **e** has heard, 1Co 2:9
And if the **e** should say 1Co 12:16
who has **e**-s to hear listen to.......Rv 2:7

EARTH

God created the heavens and
    the e............................Gn 1:1
may know the e belongs to
    LORD........................ Ex 9:29
The e and everything in it,...... Ps 24:1
whole e sing to the LORD........ Ps 96:1
he is coming to judge the e.....Ps 96:13
his glory fills the whole e........Is 6:3
they will inherit the e........... Mt 5:5
Heaven and e will pass away,.. Mt 24:35
and peace on e to people he......Lk 2:14
we wait for ... a new e, ...2Pt 3:13

EARTHLY

if our e tent we live in...........2Co 5:1
They are focused on e things,..Php 3:19
not ... above but is e,
    unspiritual,................. Jms 3:15

EARTHQUAKE

but the LORD was not in the e...1Kg 19:11
be famines and e-s in various .. Mt 24:7
There was a violent e,............ Mt 28:2
was such a violent e that the ..Ac 16:26
A violent e occurred; ....Rv 6:12

EASIER

For which is e: to say, 'Your ..... Mt 9:5
it is e for a camel to go........ Mt 19:24
But it is e for heaven and earth..Lk 16:17

EAST

As far as the e is from the
    west,.......................Ps 103:12
wise men from the e arrived......Mt 2:1

EASY

For my yoke is e and my
    burden..................... Mt 11:30

EAT

You are free to e from any tree ..Gn 2:16
took some of its fruit and ate it;..Gn 3:6
words were found, and I
    ate them.....................Jr 15:16
E this scroll, then go and speak..Ezk 3:1
of Man came e-ing and
    drinking, ...Mt 11:19
Everyone ate and was
    satisfied.................... Mt 14:20
They all ate and were
    satisfied.................... Mt 15:37
and said, "Take and e it;.......Mt 26:26
sinners and e-s with them!......Lk 15:2

who e-s my flesh and drinks ...Jn 6:54
Get up, Peter; kill and e!........Ac 10:13
believes he may e anything, ...Rm 14:2
whether you e or drink, or......1Co 10:31
work, he should not e......... 2Th 3:10
He said to me, "Take and e it; ...Rv 10:9

EDEN

LORD God planted a garden in E,..Gn 2:8
You were in E, the garden of
    God .... Ezk 28:13

EDOM

is why he was also named E. .Gn 25:30
land of Seir, the territory of E. . Gn 32:3

EFFECTIVE

is living and e and sharper
    than .... Heb 4:12

EFFORT

not depend on human will
    or e .... Rm 9:16
then make every e to enter
    that .... Heb 4:11
make every e to supplement
    your 2Pt 1:5

EGYPT

Abram went down to E to stay..Gn 12:10
sold Joseph in E to Potiphar,.. Gn 37:36
his offspring with him came
    to E.......................... Gn 46:6
lived in E was 430 years....... Ex 12:40
out of E I called my son.......... Hs 11:1
Out of E I called my Son........ Mt 2:15

EHUD

Benjaminite judge (Jdg 3:12-30).

ELAH

1. Valley where David fought Goliath
    (1Sm 17:2,19; 21:9).
2. Son of Baasha; king of Israel (1Kg
    16:6-14).

ELDER

break the tradition of the e-s?.. Mt 15:2
appointed e-s ... in every
    church..................... Ac 14:23
The e-s who are good leaders..1Tm 5:17
accusation against an e
    unless 1Tm 5:19

call for the e-s of the church,..Jms 5:14
thrones sat twenty-four e-s...... Rv 4:4

ELEAZAR

Son of Aaron; high priest (Ex 6:23; Nm
20:25-28). Helped Joshua distribute
land (Jos 14:1).

ELECT

if possible, even the e. ....Mt 24:24
justice to his e who cry out to ..Lk 18:7
but the e did find it............. Rm 11:7

ELECTION

purpose according to
    e might stand................ Rm 9:11
to confirm your calling and e,..2Pt 1:10

ELEMENTS

based on the e of the world, ...Col 2:8

ELEVEN

appeared to the E
    themselves as .... Mk 16:14

ELI

High priest at Samuel's birth (1Sm 1–4).
Blessed Hannah (1:17; 2:20). Failed to
discipline his sons (2:12-17,22-36). Died
when the ark was captured (4:11-18).

ELÍ

E, E, lemá sabachtháni? .... Mt 27:46

ELIAKIM

1. Son of Hilkiah; Hezekiah's administrator (2Kg 18:18; Is 22:20; 36:3).
2. Son of Josiah; king of Judah. Called
    Jehoiakim (2Kg 23:34; 2Ch 36:4).

ELIEZER

1. Abraham's servant (Gn 15:2).
2. Son of Moses (Ex 18:4; 1Ch 23:15).
3. Ancestor of Jesus (Lk 3:29).

ELIJAH

Prophet against Ahab and Ahaziah.
Predicted famine (1Kg 17:1; Jms 5:17).
Fed by ravens (1Kg 17:2-7); fed by widow (17:8-16; Lk 4:26); raised widow's
son (1Kg 17:17-24). Defeated prophets

of Baal (18:19-40). Fled Jezebel (19:1-3). Chose Elisha to succeed him (19:16,19-21); taken up into heaven (2Kg 2:1-12).

Forerunner to the Messiah, embodied in John the Baptist (Mal 4:5; Mt 11:14; 17:10-13; Lk 1:17). Appeared with Jesus (Mt 17:3-4).

ELISHA

Prophet; successor to Elijah (1Kg 19:16-21; 2Kg 2:1-18). Made bad water good (2Kg 2:19-22); called bears to punish boys (2:23-24); provided water for army (3:13-22). Provided miraculous supply of oil for widow (4:1-7); granted son to barren woman and restored him to life (4:8-37). Healed Naaman and punished Gehazi (5:1-27). Made iron ax float (6:5-7). Blinded Aramean army (6:8–7:20). A man was revived by touching his dead bones (13:20-21).

Made Hazael king of Aram (2Kg 8:7-15) and Jehu king of Israel (9:1-13).

ELIZABETH

Mother of John the Baptist; Mary's relative (Lk 1).

ELKANAH

Father of Samuel; husband of Hannah (1Sm 1:1).

ELOI

voice, "*E, E, lemá*
     sabachtháni . . . . Mk 15:34

EMBRACE

Can a man e fire and his
     clothes. Pr 6:27

EMMAUS

on their way to a village
     called E, ... Lk 24:13

EMPTY (ADJ)

mouth will not return to me e, . . Is 55:11
deceive you with e
     arguments, ... Eph 5:6

EMPTY (V)

cross of Christ will not be
     e-ied 1Co 1:17
he e-ied himself by assuming . . Php 2:7

EMPTY-HANDED

No one is to appear before
     me e. . . . . Ex 23:15

ENCAMPS

of the LORD e around those
     who . . . . Ps 34:7

ENCOURAGE

Therefore e one another and . . 1Th 4:18

ENCOURAGEMENT

(which is translated Son of E), . . Ac 4:36
through the e from the
     Scriptures . . . . Rm 15:4
then there is any e in Christ, . . . Php 2:1

END (N)

to put an e to every creature, . . Gn 6:13
and the e-s of the earth your . . . . . . Ps 2:8
make me aware of my e . . . . Ps 39:4
but its e is the way to death . . . . Pr 14:12
The e of a matter is better than . . Ec 7:8
endures to the e will be saved . . Mt 10:22
endures to the e will be saved . . Mt 24:13
and his kingdom will have no e . . Lk 1:33
He loved them to the e. . . . . Jn 13:1
and to the e-s of the earth . . . . Ac 1:8
Christ is the e of the law for . . . Rm 10:4
who keeps my works to the e: . . Rv 2:26
last, the beginning and the e . . Rv 22:13

END (V)

Love never e-s. But as for 1Co 13:8

ENDURANCE

that affliction produces e, ... Rm 5:3
faith, love, e, and gentleness. . 1Tm 6:11
Let us run with e the race that. . Heb 12:1
the testing of your faith
     produces e. . . . . Jms 1:3

ENDURE

of the LORD is pure, e-ing forever;. . Ps 19:9
May they fear you while the sun
     e-s . . . . Ps 72:5
But who can e the day of his . . . Mal 3:2
the one who e-s to the end
     will . . . . Mt 10:22
e-d with much patience objects
     of . . . . Rm 9:22
hopes all things, e-s all things. . 1Co 13:7
if we e, we will also reign
     with 2Tm 2:12

a better and e-ing
     possession. . . . . Heb 10:34
that lay before him, he e-d the
     cross. . . . . Heb 12:2
the word of the Lord e-s
     forever. 1Pt 1:25

ENEMY

an e to your e-ies and a foe to . . Ex 23:22
me in the presence of my e-ies; . . Ps 23:5
do not let my e-ies gloat
     over me. Ps 25:2
I make your e-ies your
     footstool. . . . . Ps 110:1
If your e is hungry, give him . . . Pr 25:21
a man's e-ies are the men of
     his own . . . . Mc 7:6
love your e-ies and pray for
     those . . . . Mt 5:44
a man's e-ies will be the
     members . . . . Mt 10:36
e who sowed them is the
     devil. . . . . Mt 13:39
I put your e-ies under your
     feet . . . . Mt 22:44
if, while we were e-ies, we
     were . . . . Rm 5:10
But If your e is hungry, feed
     him. . . . . Rm 12:20
The last e he abolishes is
     death 1Co 15:26
the world becomes the e of
     God. . . . . Jms 4:4

ENGAGED

to a virgin e to a man named . . . Lk 1:27

ENJOY

to eat, drink, and e his work. . . . Ec 2:24
provides us with all things
     to e. 1Tm 6:17

ENLIGHTENED

eyes of your heart may be e . . . Eph 1:18
those who were once e, ... Heb 6:4

ENOCH

Father of Methuselah (Gn 5:18-21); prophet (Jd 14); walked with God, and God took him (Gn 5:22-24; Heb 11:5).

ENSLAVE

we may no longer be e-d to sin, . . Rm 6:6
put up with it if someone e-s
     you, ... 2Co 11:20

want to be **e-d** to them all over

again? ....Gl 4:9

ENSNARE

the sin that so easily **e-s** us.....Heb 12:1

ENTANGLE

The ropes of Sheol **e-d** me;... 2Sm 22:6
soldier gets **e-d** in the
concerns 2Tm 2:4
they are again **e-d** in these
things......................2Pt 2:20

ENTER

anger, "They will not **e** my
rest."..........................Ps 95:11
E his gates with thanksgiving..Ps 100:4
you will never **e** the
kingdom of..................Mt 5:20
E through the narrow gate......Mt 7:13
like a little child will never
e it..........................Mk 10:15
he cannot **e** the kingdom of God...Jn 3:5
just as sin **e-ed** the world
through.....................Rm 5:12
anger, "They will not **e** my
rest."........................Heb 3:11

ENTHRONED

e between the cherubim,......2Kg 19:15
But the LORD sits **e** forever; ......Ps 9:7
e on the praises of Israel.......Ps 22:3

ENTICE

son, if sinners **e** you, don't be......Pr 1:10
drawn away and **e-d** by his
own..........................Jms 1:14

ENTRUST

Into your hand I **e** my spirit;......Ps 31:5
into your hands I **e** my spirit..Lk 23:46
what has been **e-ed** to me
until 2Tm 1:12

ENVY (N)

They are full of **e**, murder......Rm 1:29
For where there is **e** and
selfish ....Jms 3:16

ENVY (V)

Don't let your heart **e** sinners;..Pr 23:17
Don't **e** the evil or desire to be..Pr 24:1
Love does not **e**, is not boastful, ...1Co 13:4

EPHESUS

City in Asia Minor visited by Paul (Ac 18:19; 19:1; 1Co 16:8; Eph 1:1; Rv 2:1).

EPHOD

are to make the **e** of finely
spun .... Ex 28:6

EPHRAIM

Son of Joseph (Gn 41:52); tribe with territory north and west of Bethel (Gn 48; Jos 14:4; 16:4-5); designation for Israel (Is 11:13; Jr 7:15; Ezk 37:16; Hs 5:13).

EPHRATHAH

Bethlehem **E**, you are small
among........................Mc 5:2

EQUAL

making himself **e** to God........Jn 5:18

EQUALITY

did not consider **e** with God as..Php 2:6

EQUIP

be complete, **e-ped** for
every good 2Tm 3:17
e you with everything good
to .... Heb 13:21

ERASE

Let them be **e-d** from the book
of .... Ps 69:28
and I will never **e** his name from..Rv 3:5

ERROR

appropriate penalty of their **e**.. Rm 1:27
from the **e** of his way will.....Jms 5:20

ESAU

Son of Isaac; elder twin of Jacob (Gn 25:24-26); rejected by God (Mal 1:2-3; Rm 9:13); sold birthright (Gn 25:30-34; Heb 12:16); tricked out of blessing (Gn 27:1-30; Heb 11:20); reconciled with Jacob (12:16). Progenitor of Edomites in Seir (Dt 2:4-29).

ESCAPE (V)

can I go to **e** your spirit? ....Ps 139:7
that you will **e** God's judgment?..Rm 2:3

how will we **e** if we neglect

such ....Heb 2:3

ESTABLISH

But I will **e** my covenant with.. Gn 6:18
and I will **e** his kingdom. 2Sm 7:12
up in him and **e-ed** in the faith,.. Col 2:7

ESTHER

Persian name of Hadassah, Mordecai's cousin (Est 2:7). Chosen queen of Persia (2:16-18); interceded at great risk to foil a plot to exterminate the Jews (Est 3–9).

ESTIMATION

Do not be wise in your
own **e**. ....Rm 12:16

ETERNAL

for he is good. His faithful
love **e** ....Ps 136:1
must I do to have **e** life?....... Mt 19:16
will go away into **e** punishment, but
the righteous into **e** life.....Mt 25:46
not perish but have **e** life........ Jn 3:16
that he may give **e** life to
everyone .... Jn 17:2
gift of God is **e** life in Christ... Rm 6:23
incomparable **e** weight of
glory..........................2Co 4:17
pay the penalty of **e**
destruction, ...2Th 1:9
Now to the King **e**, immortal...1Tm 1:17
may know that you have **e** life. 1Jn 5:13

ETERNITY

from **e** to **e**, you are God........Ps 90:2
has also put **e** in their hearts ... Ec 3:11

ETHIOPIAN

There was an **E** man, a eunuch.. Ac 8:27

EUNUCH

For there are **e-s** who were
born .... Mt 19:12
The **e** said to Philip, "I ask...... Ac 8:34

EUPHRATES

And the fourth river is the **E**. .. Gn 2:14

EVALUATE

it since it is **e-d** spiritually......1Co 2:14

EVANGELIST

prophets, some e-s, some
   pastors ....Eph 4:11
the work of an e, fulfill your......2Tm 4:5

EVE

First woman; wife of Adam (Gn 3:20;
4:1-2,25). Gave in to temptation (3:1; 2Co
11:3; 1Tm 2:13-14).

EVERLASTING

and underneath are the e
   arms. ....Dt 33:27
The LORD is the e God, ...Is 40:28
have loved you with an e love;.. Jr 31:3

EVERYTHING

you do, do e for the glory of
   God..........................1Co 10:31
has given us e required for life.. 2Pt 1:3

EVIL

of the knowledge of good and e.. Gn 2:9
To fear the LORD is to hate e.......Pr 8:13
who call e good and good e,......Is 5:20
but deliver us from the e one... Mt 6:13
then, who are e, know how to .. Mt 7:11
an e man produces e things
   from ....Mt 12:35
protect them from the e one... Jn 17:15
Do not repay anyone e for e......Rm 12:17
Stay away from every kind
   of e.........................1Th 5:22
is a root of all kinds of e,......1Tm 6:10
since God is not tempted by e,..Jms 1:13

EVILDOER

I tell you, don't resist an e. ......Mt 5:39

EWE

one small e lamb that he had. .2Sm 12:3

EXACT

the e expression of his nature,..Heb 1:3

EXALT

the rock of my salvation, is
   e-ed. 2Sm 22:47
let us e his name together.......Ps 34:3
be e-ed above the heavens;......Ps 57:5,11
You are e-ed above all the gods. Ps 97:9
Righteousness e-s a
   nation, but..................Pr 14:34

humbles himself will be
   e-ed..........................Mt 23:12
God highly e-ed him and gave ..Php 2:9
the Lord, and he will e you.... Jms 4:10

EXAMINE

and e-d the Scriptures daily
   to see ....Ac 17:11
Let a person e himself;........1Co 11:28

EXAMPLE

given you an e, that you also .. Jn 13:15
things took place as e-s for
   us,...........................1Co 10:6
to the e you have in us. .... Php 3:17
set an e for the believers......1Tm 4:12
you, but being e-s to the flock... 1Pt 5:3

EXASPERATE

Fathers, do not e your children..Col 3:21

EXCHANGE

anyone give in e for his life?.. Mt 16:26

EXCHANGED

They e their glory for the
   image......................Ps 106:20
and the glory of the
   immortal ....Rm 1:23

EXCUSE

they have no e for their sin......Jn 15:22
As a result, people are
   without e. ....Rm 1:20

EXHORT

older man, but e him as a
   father......................1Tm 5:1

EXHORTATION

with many other e-s, he
   proclaimed ....Lk 3:18

EXILE

went into e from its land...... 2Kg 25:21
the returned e-s were building. . Ezr 4:1
I urge you as strangers and e-s. .1Pt 2:11

EXILED

So Israel has been e-d to
   Assyria 2Kg 17:23

EXIST

who, e-ing in the form of God,..Php 2:6
and through whom all
   things e ....Heb 2:10
believe that he e-s and that he ..Heb 11:6
your will they e and were ....Rv 4:11

EXPECT

coming at an hour you do
   not e........................Mt 24:44
and lend, e-ing nothing in
   return........................Lk 6:35

EXPECTANTLY

the LORD and wait e for him; ... Ps 37:7

EXPECTATION

e of the wicked comes will
   perish......................Pr 10:28
but a terrifying e of
   judgment ....Heb 10:27

EXPLAIN

He will e everything to us.......Jn 4:25

EXPOSE

so that his deeds may not
   be e-d.......................Jn 3:20
darkness, but instead e them. .Eph 5:11
Everything e-d by the light is..Eph 5:13

EXPRESSION

the exact e of his nature,....... Heb 1:3

EXTEND

would bless me, e my border,..1Ch 4:10

EXTINGUISH

you can e all the flaming
   arrows......................Eph 6:16

EYE

e for e, tooth for
   tooth..............Ex 21:24; Lv 24:20
For the e-s of the LORD roam ..2Ch 16:9
have made a covenant with
   my e-s.......................Jb 31:1
Protect me as the pupil of
   your e;.......................Ps 17:8
I lift my e-s toward the.........Ps 121:1
they might see with their
   e-s and.......................Is 6:10

Your **e-s** are too pure to
 look on .... Hab 1:13
If your right **e** causes you to ... Mt 5:29
An **e** for an **e** and a tooth for... Mt 5:38
The **e** is the lamp of the body... Mt 6:22
the splinter in your brother's
 e but .... Mt 7:3
And their **e-s** were opened...... Mt 9:30
see with their **e-s** and hear
 with .... Mt 13:15
and it is wonderful in our **e-s**?..Mt 21:42
Then their **e-s** were opened,
 and ....Lk 24:31
keeping our **e-s** on Jesus, ... Heb 12:2
what we have seen with our **e-s**,..1Jn 1:1
clouds, and every **e** will see him .. Rv 1:7
away every tear from their
 e-s. .... Rv 7:17; 21:4

EYEWITNESSES

the original **e** ... handed them
 down .... Lk 1:2
we were **e** of his majesty....... 2Pt 1:16

EZEKIEL

Hebrew prophet at the time of the
exile, writing from Babylon (Ezk 1:1;
2Kg 24:14-16). Wrote about the fall of
Jerusalem (Ezk 33:21) and the ultimate
restoration of the city and temple (Ezk
40–48).

EZRA

Priest and teacher of the law; leader of
the returning exiles, sent by King Artaxerxes of Persia to reestablish worship
in the temple (Ezr 7–8). Nehemiah's
colleague (Neh 8:2,6; 12:31-37). Made
priests stop intermarriage with foreigners (Ezr 9–10).

F

FACE

I have seen God **f** to **f**, ...Gn 32:30
LORD would speak ... **f** to **f**, ...Ex 33:11
Moses, the skin of his **f** shone!..Ex 34:30
LORD make his **f** shine on you..Nm 6:25
LORD, I will seek your **f**..........Ps 27:8
I have set my **f** like flint, ...Is 50:7
oil on your head and wash
 your **f**, ...Mt 6:17
and his **f** shone like the sun......Mt 17:2
spat in his **f** and beat him;.....Mt 26:67
appearance of his **f** changed,.. Lk 9:29

a mirror, but then **f** to **f**........1Co 13:12
with unveiled **f-s** are looking .. 2Co 3:18
But the **f** of the Lord is against..1Pt 3:12
and his **f** was shining like the
 sun............................ Rv 1:16

FACTIONS

it is necessary that there be **f**..1Co 11:19
ambitions, dissensions, **f**,......Gl 5:20

FADE

the flowers **f**, but the word of... Is 40:8
a crown that will never **f**
 away. 1Co 9:25

FAIL

you that your faith may not **f**.. Lk 22:32
as though the word of God
 has **f-ed**......................Rm 9:6

FAILURE

and their **f** riches for the...... Rm 11:12

FAINT

my body **f-s** for you in a land
 that ....Ps 63:1
they will walk and not **f**........ Is 40:31

FAIR

The Lord's way isn't **f**......Ezk 18:25,29;
 33:17,20

FAIRLY

He judges the peoples **f**. ....Ps 96:10
with your slaves justly and **f**, ... Col 4:1

FAITH

righteous one will live by his **f**.. Hab 2:4
Your **f** has saved you. .... Mt 9:22
If you have **f** the size of a
 mustard .... Mt 17:20
woman, "Your **f** has saved you.. Lk 7:50
to the Lord, "Increase our **f**......Lk 17:5
will he find **f** on earth?.........Lk 18:8
that he had **f** to be healed, ... Ac 14:9
is justified by **f** apart from..... Rm 3:28
been declared righteous by **f**,... Rm 5:1
So **f** comes from what is
 heard,.......................Rm 10:17
that is not from **f** is sin.......Rm 14:23
if I have all **f** so that I can 1Co 13:2
three remain: **f**, hope, and
 love.........................1Co 13:13

stand firm in the **f**, be
 courageous, ...1Co 16:13
For we walk by **f**, not by sight ..2Co 5:7
I live by **f** in the Son of God,.....Gl 2:20
the righteous will live by **f**...... Gl 3:11
patience, kindness, goodness, **f**,..Gl 5:22
you are saved by grace
 through **f**,................... Eph 2:8
one Lord, one **f**, one baptism,.. Eph 4:5
situation take up the shield
 of **f**, ... Eph 6:16
righteousness from God based
 on **f**........................... Php 3:9
the armor of **f** and love,.........1Th 5:8
some will depart from the **f**,... 1Tm 4:1
Fight the good fight of the **f**;.. 1Tm 6:12
finished the race, I have kept
 the **f**.......................2Tm 4:7
righteous one will live by **f**;.. Heb 10:38
Now **f** is the reality of what is ..Heb 11:1
By **f** we understand that the ...Heb 11:3
By **f** Abel offered to God a......Heb 11:4
Now without **f** it is impossible..Heb 11:6
source and perfecter of our **f**, ..Heb 12:2
f, if it doesn't have works, is
 dead .... Jms 2:17
supplement your **f** with
 goodness,..................... 2Pt 1:5

FAITHFUL *SEE ALSO* FAITHFUL LOVE

he is **f** in all my household. .....Nm 12:7
the **f** God who keeps his
 gracious .... Dt 7:9
With the **f** you prove
 yourself **f**; 2Sm 22:26
Love the LORD, all his **f** ones....Ps 31:23
Who then is a **f** and wise
 servant,......................Mt 24:45
Well done, good and **f**
 servant!..................... Mt 25:21
God is **f**; you were called by him.. 1Co 1:9
God is **f**, he will not allow you ..1Co 10:13
He who calls you is **f**; he will.. 1Th 5:24
commit to **f** men who will be
 able 2Tm 2:2
he remains **f**, for he cannot
 deny 2Tm 2:13
since he who promise dis **f**.. Heb 10:23
entrust themselves to a **f**
 Creator....................... 1Pt 4:19
he is **f** and righteous to forgive.. 1Jn 1:9
Its rider is called F and True,... Rv 19:11

FAITHFUL LOVE

goodness and **f** will pursue......Ps 23:6
because your **f** is better.........Ps 63:3
will sing about the LORD's **f**
 forever;.......................Ps 89:1

FAITHFULNESS

to declare your f in the
   morning.......................Ps 92:2
so great is his f toward those. . Ps 103:11
For I desire f and not sacrifice. . . Hs 6:6
slow to anger, abounding in f, . . Jnh 4:2
because he delights in f. . . . . Mc 7:18

FAITHFULNESS

to heaven, your f to the clouds. . Ps 36:5
Your f reaches the clouds. . . . . . Ps 57:10
proclaim your f to all generations. .Ps 89:1
his f, through all generations. .Ps 100:5
great is your f! . . . . .Lm 3:23
unfaithfulness nullify God's f?. . Rm 3:3

FAITHLESS

if we are f, he remains
   faithful,. 2Tm 2:13

FALL

How the mighty have f-en! . . . 2Sm 1:19
Though he f-s, he will not be . . Ps 37:24
Though a thousand f at your
   side . . . . Ps 91:7
an arrogant spirit before a f. . . Pr 16:18
a righteous person f-s seven
   times, ...Pr 24:16
you have f-en from the heavens. . . . . Is
   14:12
Babylon has f-en, has f-en. . . . . . .Is 21:9
some seed fell along the path, . . Mt 13:4
to cause the f and rise of many. . Lk 2:34
I watched Satan f from heaven. . Lk 10:18
grain of wheat f-s to the
   ground . . . . .Jn 12:24
have sinned and f short of the. . Rm 3:23
must be careful not to f. 1Co 10:12
you have f-en from grace. . . . . Gl 5:4
and who have f-en away, ... Heb 6:6
thing to f into the hands . . . . . Heb 10:31
a great star . . . fell from
   heaven. .Rv 8:10
f-en, Babylon the Great has
   f-en, ...Rv 14:8

FALSE

Do not give f testimony
   against . . . . Ex 20:16
Beware of f prophets who
   come. . . . . .Mt 7:15
do not bear f witness; . . . . Mt 19:18
Many f prophets will rise up
   and . . . . .Mt 24:11
F messiahs and f prophets
   will . . . . .Mt 24:24
whether from f motives or
   true, ...Php 1:18

there will be f teachers
   among you. 2Pt 2:1
the mouth of the f prophet. . . . . Rv 16:13

FALSEHOOD

I hate and abhor f, but I love . . Ps 119:163
Keep f and deceitful words far. . Pr 30:8

FALSELY

f say every kind of evil against
   you . . . . Mt 5:11
what is f called knowledge. 1Tm 6:20

FAMILY

As for me and my f, we will. . . . . . .Jos 24:15
All the f-ies of the nations will . .Ps 22:27
makes their f-ies multiply
   like. . . . . .Ps 107:41
All the f-ies of the earth will be . .Ac 3:25
he and all his f were baptized. . .Ac 16:33
from whom every f in heaven
   and . . . . Eph 3:15

FAMINE

There was a f in the land, ... Gn 12:10
seven years of f will take
   place. . . . . .Gn 41:30
by sword, f, and plague. . . . . . . .Jr 14:12
not a f of bread or a thirst for. . Am 8:11
There will be f-s and
   earthquakes. . . . . Mt 24:7
or persecution or f or
   nakedness . . . . Rm 8:35

FAR

As f as the east is from the. . . .Ps 103:12
yet their hearts are f from me, . . Is 29:13
but their heart is f from me. . . . Mt 15:8
You are not f from the
   kingdom. . . . . .Mk 12:34
you who were f away have
   been. . . . . Eph 2:13

FAST (N)

Will the f I choose be like this: . . Is 58:5
Announce a sacred f; . . . . Jl 1:14; 2:15

FAST (V)

baby was alive, you f-ed 2Sm 12:21
After he had f-ed forty
   days and forty . . . . Mt 4:2
Whenever you f, don't be
   gloomy . . . . Mt 6:16
but your disciples do not f?. . . . Mt 9:14

guests cannot f while the
   groom .Mk 2:19
I f twice a week; I give a tenth. . . .Lk 18:12
after they had f-ed, prayed, and . .Ac 13:3

FASTING

so that their f is obvious to
   people . . . . Mt 6:16

FAT

is better than the f of rams. . . 1Sm 15:22

FATAL

but its f wound was healed. . . . .Rv 13:3

FATE

there is one f for everyone. . . . . . Ec 9:3
and who considered his f?. . . . . . Is 53:8

FATHER

a man leaves his f and mother. .Gn 2:24
become the f of many nations . .Gn 17:4
Honor your f and your
   mother so . . . . Ex 20:12
Honor your f and your mother. .Dt 5:16
F-s are not to be put to death
   for . . . . .Dt 24:16
Isn't he your F and Creator?. . . . . Dt 32:6
I will his f, and he 2Sm 7:14
today I have become your F. . . . . . Ps 2:7
You are my F, my God, the
   rock. . . . . Ps 89:26
Listen, my son, to your f-'s
   instruction . . . . Pr 1:8
A wise son brings joy to his f, . . . Pr 10:1
Eternal F, Prince of Peace. . . . . . . Is 9:6
not die for his f-'s iniquity. . . . . Ezk 18:17
Our F in heaven, your name be . . . Mt 6:9
who loves a f or mother more . .Mt 10:37
Honor your f and your mother; . .Mt 15:4
will leave his f and mother and . .Mt 19:5
you have one F, who is in
   heaven. Mt 23:9
Abba, F! All things are
   possible. . . . . .Mk 14:36
for me to be in my F-'s house?. .Lk 2:49
What f among you, if his son
   asks. . . . . .Lk 11:11
Jesus said, "F, forgive them . . . Lk 23:34
Stop turning my F-'s house into. . Jn 2:16
was even calling God his own F, . .Jn 5:18
You are of your f the devil, ...Jn 8:44
snatch them out of the F-'s
   hand. .Jn 10:29
I and the F are one. . . . . .Jn 10:30
the F is in me and I in the F. . . . .Jn 10:38

In my F-'s house are many
   rooms ....Jn 14:2
comes to the F except through.. Jn 14:6
show us the F, and that's
   enough ....Jn 14:8
who has seen me has seen
   the F..........................Jn 14:9
you ask the F in my name, ... Jn 15:16
by whom we cry out,
   "Abba, F!" ....Rm 8:15
I will be a F to you, and you... 2Co 6:18
one God and F of all, who is ... Eph 4:6
Honor your f and mother,
   which........................Eph 6:2
F-s, don't stir up anger in ...... Eph 6:4
F-s, do not exasperate your.... Col 3:21
I will be his F, and he will be... Heb 1:5
what son is there that a f does
   not...........................Heb 12:7
down from the F of lights,......Jms 1:17

FATHERLESS

He executes justice for the
   f and.........................Dt 10:18
You are a helper of the f........ Ps 10:14
a father of the f and a
   champion ....Ps 68:5
and helps the f and the widow,.. Ps 146:9
don't encroach on the fields
   of the f......................Pr 23:10

FATTENED

Then bring the f calf and ......Lk 15:23
You have f your hearts......... Jms 5:5

FAULT

Cleanse me from my hidden
   f-s...........................Ps 19:12
Why then does he still find f?.. Rm 9:19
without f or failure until...... 1Tm 6:14

FAULTLESS

who are f in a crooked........ Php 2:15

FAVOR (N)

Noah ... found f with the LORD.. Gn 6:8
moment, but his f, a lifetime. ...Ps 30:5
and obtains f from the LORD,...... Pr 8:35
for you have found f with God. Lk 1:30
and in f with God and with..... Lk 2:52
God and enjoying the f of all ... Ac 2:47
trying to win the f of people, ...Gl 1:10

FAVOR (V)

peace on earth to people he f-s!.. Lk 2:14

FAVORITISM

that God doesn't show f,...... Ac 10:34
There is no f with God.......... Rm 2:11
and there is no f with him...... Eph 6:9
doing nothing out of f......... 1Tm 5:21
do not show f as you
   hold on to....................Jms 2:1

FEAR (N)

The f of the LORD is pure, ... Ps 19:9
and rescued me from all my f-s. .Ps 34:4
f of the LORD is the beginning.. Ps 111:10
The f of the LORD is the
   beginning ....Pr 1:7
delight will be in the f of the
   LORD. ....Is 11:3
of slavery to fall back into f, .. Rm 8:15
salvation with f and
   trembling. ....Php 2:12
There is no f in love; instead,
   perfect love drives out f, ... 1Jn 4:18

FEAR (V)

For now I know that you f
   God,..........................Gn 22:12
F the LORD your God ... worship
   him...........................Dt 6:13
f-ed the LORD, but they also.. 2Kg 17:33
He is f-ed above all gods........1Ch 16:25
f-s God and turns away from.. Jb 1:8; 2:3
darkest valley, I f no danger, for ..Ps 23:4
my salvation—whom should
   I f?...........................Ps 27:1
To f the LORD is to hate evil...... Pr 8:13
but a woman who f-s the LORD
   will ....Pr 31:30
f God and keep his commands,.. Ec 12:13
Do not f, for I am with you; .....Is 41:10
f him who is able to destroy
   both ....Mt 10:28
town who didn't f God or
   respect ....Lk 18:2
So the one who f-s is not
   complete 1Jn 4:18

FEARFULNESS

has not given us a spirit of f,... 2Tm 1:7

FEAST

I hate, I despise your f-s!.......Am 5:21
us observe the f, not with old...1Co 5:8
to the marriage f of the Lamb!.. Rv 19:9

FEASTING (N)

than a house full of f with strife.. Pr 17:1
than to go to a house of f,........Ec 7:2

FEATHERS

He will cover you with his f;.... Ps 91:4

FEED

He fed you in the wilderness
   with ....Dt 8:16
shepherds f themselves
   rather than .... Ezk 34:8
your heavenly Father f-s
   them.........................Mt 6:26
so the one who f-s on me will
   live...........................Jn 6:57
"F my lambs," He told him...... Jn 21:15
If your enemy is hungry,
   f him........................ Rm 12:20

FEEDING

no oxen, the f trough i sempty, .. Pr 14:4

FELLOWSHIP

this is the law of the f sacrifice.. Lv 7:11
We used to have close f;........Ps 55:14
teaching, to the f, to the
   breaking..................... Ac 2:42
Or what f does light have
   with 2Co 6:14
and the f of the Holy Spirit be ..2Co 13:13
we say, "We have f with him" ... 1Jn 1:6

FEMALE

he created them male and f.....Gn 1:27
new ... a f will shelter a man... Jr 31:22
beginning made them male
   and f, ...Mt 19:4
slave or free, male or f; ....Gl 3:28

FERVENT

and being f in spirit, he was .. Ac 18:25
be f in the Spirit; serve the
   Lord......................... Rm 12:11

FESTIVAL

Celebrate a f in my honor
   three........................ Ex 23:14
"Not during the f," they said ...Mk 14:2
the matter of a f or a new
   moon ....Col 2:16

FESTIVE

leading the f procession to the.. Ps 42:4

FEVER

was lying in bed with a f, ...Mk 1:30

FEW

were f in number, very f
indeed . . . . Ps 105:12
Let his days be f; let another . . . Ps 109:8
but the workers are f . . . . Mt 9:37
are invited, but f are chosen . . Mt 22:14
a f people going to be saved? . . Lk 13:23

FEWEST

you were the f of all peoples . . . . Dt 7:7

FIELD

Let the f-s and everything in
them . . . . Ps 96:12
blooms like a flower of the f; . . Ps 103:15
I went by the f of a slacker
and . . . . Pr 24:30
how the wildflowers of the f
grow: . . . . Mt 6:28
f is the world; and the good
seed. . . . . Mt 13:38
out in the f-s and keeping watch. . Lk 2:8
your eyes and look at the f-s, . . . Jn 4:35
You are God's f, God's building . . 1Co 3:9

FIERY

surprised when the f ordeal
comes 1Pt 4:12

FIG

so they sewed f leaves together. . Gn 3:7
Though the f tree does not bud. . Hab 3:17
At once the f tree withered. . . . Mt 21:19
F-s aren't gathered from
thornbushes. . . . . Lk 6:44
Can a f tree produce olives, . . . Jms 3:12

FIGHT (N)

Fight the good f of the faith; . . 1Tm 6:12
I have fought the good f, I have. . 2Tm 4:7

FIGHT (V)

The LORD will f for you; . . . . Ex 14:14
LORD; f those who f me. . . . . Ps 35:1
F the good fight of the faith; . . 1Tm 6:12
God not to f about words; 2Tm 2:14
I have fought the good fight,
I have 2Tm 4:7

FILL

Be fruitful, multiply, f the
earth, ... Gn 1:28
glory of the LORD f-ed the
temple. 1Kg 8:11

whole earth is f-ed with his
glory, ... Ps 72:19
His glory f-s the whole earth. . . . . . Is 6:3
Do I not f the heavens and the. . Jr 23:24
and I will f this house with
glory, ... Hg 2:7
He will be f-ed with the Holy . . . Lk 1:15
"F the jars with water," Jesus . . . . Jn 2:7
you ate the loaves and were
f-ed. . . . . Jn 6:26
they were all f-ed with the Holy . . Ac 2:4
Then Peter was f-ed with the
Holy . . . . Ac 4:8
sight and be f-ed with the Holy. . Ac 9:17
called Paul—f-ed with the
Holy . . . . Ac 13:9
the God of hope f you with all. . Rm 15:13
who f-s all things in every
way. . . . . Eph 1:23
heavens, to f all things. . . . . Eph 4:10
but be f-ed by the Spirit: . . . . . . Eph 5:18
f-ed with the fruit of. . . . . Php 1:11

FILTH

of all moral f and the evil, ... Jms 1:21
removal of the f of the flesh, . . . 1Pt 3:21

FILTHY

was dressed with f clothes
as he . . . . Zch 3:3
and f language from your
mouth. . . . . Col 3:8
Let the f still be f; . . . . Rv 22:11

FIND

If I f fifty righteous people . . . . Gn 18:26
you will f him when you seek . . Dt 4:29
those who search for me f me. . Pr 8:17
For the one who f-s me f-s life. . Pr 8:35
who f-s a wife f-s a good thing. . Pr 18:22
Who can f a wife of noble. . . . . . Pr 31:10
the LORD while He may be
found; . . . . Is 55:6
will seek me and f me when
you . . . . Jr 29:13
Seek, and you will f. . . . . Mt 7:7
and you will f rest for . . . . Mt 11:29
life because of me will f it. . . . . Mt 16:25
whom master f-s doing his
job . . . . Mt 24:46
I have found my lost sheep! . . . . Lk 15:6
he was lost and is found! . . . . . Lk 15:24
whose name was not found
written . . . . Rv 20:15

FINISH

He said, "It is f-ed!" . . . . Jn 19:30

to f my course and the
ministry . . . . Ac 20:24
I have f-ed the race, I have
kept. 2Tm 4:7

FIRE

and the pillar of f by night . . . . . Ex 13:22
a chariot of f with horses of f. . 2Kg 2:11
their f will never go out, ... Is 66:24
he will be like a refiner's f . . . . . Mal 3:2
you with the Holy Spirit and f. . Mt 3:11
burn with f that never goes
out. . . . . Mt 3:12
into the eternal f prepared for. . Mt 25:41
and the f is not quenched. . . . . Mk 9:44
I came to bring f on the earth, . Lk 12:49
like flames of f that separated. . Ac 2:3
the f will test the quality of . . . 1Co 3:13
for our God is a consuming f. . Heb 12:29
And the tongue is a f. . . . . Jms 3:6
second death, the lake of f. . . . Rv 20:14

FIRM

Stand f and see the LORD's. . . . . Ex 14:13
If you do not stand f in your faith, . Is 7:9
Be alert, stand f in the faith . . 1Co 16:13
stand f and hold to the. 2Th 2:15

FIRMLY

The world is f
established; . . . . Ps 93:1; 96:10
are like f embedded nails. . . . . . Ec 12:11
being rooted and f
established . . . . Eph 3:17
if we hold f until the end. . . . . . Heb 3:14

FIRST

The f to state his case seems. . . Pr 18:17
I and the LORD, the f and with
the . . . . Is 41:4
I am the f and I am the last. . . . . . Is 44:6
But seek f the kingdom of God . Mt 6:33
F take the beam . . . out of
your eye, ... Mt 7:5
f will be last, and the last f. . . . Mt 19:30
wants to be f among you
must be. Mt 20:27
F clean the inside of the cup, . . Mt 23:26
this, the f of his signs, in Cana . . Jn 2:11
were f called Christians at
Antioch. Ac 11:26
who does evil, f to the Jew, and. . Rm 2:9
The f man Adam became a
living 1Co 15:45
the dead in Christ will rise f. . . 1Th 4:16
We love because he f loved us. . 1Jn 4:19
I am the F and the Last, ... Rv 1:17

abandoned the love you
had at f.............................Rv 2:4
for the f heaven and the f
earth had ....Rv 21:1

FIRSTBORN

LORD struck every f male in .. Ex 12:29
Consecrate every f male
to me,............................Ex 13:2
He struck all the f in Egypt,......Ps 78:51
she gave birth to her f Son, ...Lk 2:7
the f from the dead and the......Rv 1:5

FIRSTFRUITS

the f of those who have
fallen 1Co 15:20

FISH (N)

will rule the f of the sea, ... Gn 1:26
Jonah was in . . . the f three
days ....Jnh 1:17
he asks for a f, will give him..... Mt 7:10
have five loaves and two f
here,............................Mt 14:17
the seven loaves and the f,......Mt 15:36
full of large f—153 of them.......Jn 21:11

FISH (V)

I will make you f for people.... Mt 4:19

FISHERMEN

Then the f will mourn.............Is 19:8
the sea—for they were f.......Mk 1:16

FIT

looks back is f for the
kingdom..................... Lk 9:62

FITTING

husbands, as is f in the Lord. . .Col 3:18

FIVE

hand and chose f smooth
stones 1Sm 17:40
For you've had f husbands, ...Jn 4:18

FIVE HUNDRED

to over f brothers 1Co 15:6

FIVE THOUSAND

who ate were about f men, ... Mt 14:21

FIX

great chasm has been f-ed
between ....Lk 16:26

FIXED (ADJ)

it is firmly f in heaven.........Ps 119:89
If this f order departs from
before ....Jr 31:36

FLAME

to him in a f of fire within ....Ex 3:2
Love's f-s are fiery f-s............Sg 8:6
a fire, and its Holy One, a f....Is 10:17

FLAMING

cherubim and the f, whirling
sword............................Gn 3:24
can extinguish all the f arrows
of .... Eph 6:16

FLASH

the lightning f-es from
horizon to ....Lk 17:24

FLATTER

they f with their tongues.........Ps 5:9
A person who f-s his
neighbor spreads ....Pr 29:5
f-ing people for their own
advantage ....Jd 16

FLATTERING (ADJ)

and a f mouth causes ruin....... Pr 26:28

FLEE

But Moses **fled** from Pharaoh
and ....Ex 2:15
Where can I f from your
presence?......................Ps 139:7
The wicked f when no one is ... Pr 28:1
dear friends, f from
idolatry..........................1Co 10:14
F from youthful passions,
and 2Tm 2:22
devil, and he will f from you. . . Jms 4:7

FLEECE

If dew is only on the f, ...Jdg 6:37

FLEETING

is deceptive and beauty is f, ...Pr 31:30
all the days of your f life,.........Ec 9:9

FLESH

bone of my bone, and f of
my f; ....Gn 2:23
wife, and they become one f. . . Gn 2:24
yet I will see God in my f.......Jb 19:26
and give them a heart of f,.... Ezk 11:19
and give you a heart of f. ....Ezk 36:26
f and blood did not reveal
this ....Mt 16:17
and the two will become
one f?.........................Mt 19:5
is willing, but the f is weak.... Mt 26:41
Whatever is born of the f is f,....Jn 3:6
one who eats my f and drinks
my ....Jn 6:56
are not in the f, but in the
Spirit,..........................Rm 8:9
sisters, my own f and blood......Rm 9:3
a thorn in the f was given to
me,............................2Co 12:7
the works of the f are obvious:.. Gl 5:19
is not against f and blood,......Eph 6:12

FLOCK

protects his f like a shepherd; . .Is 40:11
You have scattered my f,........ Jr 23:2
but you do not tend the f...... Ezk 34:3
sheep of the f will be
scattered.................... Mt 26:31
watch at night over their f.......Lk 2:8
will be one f, one shepherd. ... Jn 10:16

FLOGGED

having Jesus f, handed
him over................... Mt 27:26

FLOOD

I am bringing a f ....Gn 6:17
LORD sits enthroned over
the f;..........................Ps 29:10
They didn't know until the
f came ....Mt 24:39
When the f came, the river.......Lk 6:48

FLOODGATES

the f of the sky were opened,...Gn 7:11
will not open the f of heaven.. Mal 3:10

FLOODWATERS

f on the earth to destroy every.. Gn 6:17
Don't let the f sweep over
me or ....Ps 69:15

FLOW

streams of living water f from. . Jn 7:38

FLOWER

blooms like a f of the field;...... Ps 103:15
withers, the f-s fade, but the
   word...................... Is 40:8
withers, and the f falls, ... 1Pt 1:24

FLUTE

We played the f for you,
   but you .... Mt 11:17

FLY (N)

send swarms of f-ies against
   you,.......................Ex 8:21
will whistle to the f-ies at the....Is 7:18

FLY (V)

the arrow that f-ies by day,..... Ps 91:5

FOAL

on a colt, the f of a donkey...... Zch 9:9
the f of a donkey............... Mt 21:5

FOCUS

So we do not f on what is
   seen, ... 2Co 4:18
They are f-ed on earthly
   things, ... Php 3:19

FOLD (V)

little f-ing of the arms to
   rest,.................... Pr 6:10; 24:33
but was f-ed up in a separate
   place .... Jn 20:7

FOLLOW

Do not f other gods, the gods of .. Dt 6:14
If the Lord is God, f him.......1Kg 18:21
F me, ... and I will make you..... Mt 4:19
take up his cross, and f me.... Mt 16:24
Anyone who f-s me will
   never walk .... Jn 8:12
The sheep f him because they .. Jn 10:4
These are the ones who f the
   Lamb .... Rv 14:4

FOLLY

F is a rowdy woman;........... Pr 9:13

FOOD

every green plant for f. .... Gn 1:30
Every creature... will be f .... Gn 9:3
He gives f to every creature. . Ps 136:25

feed me with the f I need........Pr 30:8
Isn't life more than f .... Mt 6:25
(thus he declared all f-s clean).. Mk 7:19
My f is to do the will of him......Jn 4:34
Don't work for the f that
   perishes .... Jn 6:27
Now about f sacrificed to
   idols:........................1Co 8:1

FOOL

The f says in his heart,
   "... no God." .... Pss 14:1; 53:1
f-s despise wisdom and
   discipline......................Pr 1:7
A f despises his father's
   discipline, ... Pr 15:5
Don't answer a f according to .. Pr 26:4
Whoever says, 'You f!' will be .. Mt 5:22
to be wise, they became f-s......Rm 1:22
We are f-s for Christ, but
   you are 1Co 4:10

FOOLISH

A f son is grief to his father.... Pr 17:25
like a f man who built his
   house on..................... Mt 7:26
of them were f and five were.. Mt 25:2
God made the world's
   wisdom f? 1Co 1:20
f Galatians! Who has cast a
   spell on .... Gl 3:1

FOOLISHNESS

but the f of fools produces f....Pr 14:24
a fool according to his f....... Pr 26:4,5
the word of the cross is f 1Co 1:18
of this world is f with God,..... 1Co 3:19

FOOT

Remove the sandals from your
   feet,..........................Ex 3:5
You put everything under his
   feet:.........................Ps 8:6
strike your f against a stone. .. Ps 91:12
is a lamp for my feet and a
   light .... Ps 119:105
on the mountains are the
   feet of .... Is 52:7
strike your f against a stone.......Mt 4:6
f causes you to fall away,
   cut it off .... Mt 18:8
to wash his feet with her tears.. Lk 7:38
showed them his hands and
   feet........................... Lk 24:40
began to wash his disciples'
   feet .... Jn 13:5
beautiful are the feet of those ..Rm 10:15

soon crush Satan under your
   feet..................... Rm 16:20
If the f should say, "Because ..1Co 12:15
all his enemies under his
   feet...................... 1Co 15:25
and your feet sandaled with .. Eph 6:15

FOOTSTOOL

I make your enemies your f.... Ps 110:1
and earth is my f. ....Is 66:1
is my throne, and earth my f... Ac 7:49
His enemies are made his f. . Heb 10:13

FORBID

f-den by the Holy Spirit to
   speak ....Ac 16:6
do not f speaking in other ... 1Co 14:39

FORBIDDEN (ADJ)

the lips of the f woman drip ..... Pr 5:3

FORCE (N)

violent have been seizing it
   by f...........................Mt 11:12
take him by f to make him king,..Jn 6:15
the elemental f-s of the world. .. Gl 4:3
against evil, spiritual f-s in
   the.......................... Eph 6:12

FORCE (V)

And if anyone f-s you to go one..Mt 5:41
They f-d him to carry his....... Mt 27:32

FORCED (ADJ)

the Canaanites serve as f labor ..Jdg 1:28

FORDS

captured the f of the Jordan ...Jdg 12:5

FOREHEAD

and as a reminder on your f,......Ex 13:9
hit the Philistine on his f. 1Sm 17:49
a mark on the f-s of the men
   who.......................... Ezk 9:4
servants of our God on their f-s.. Rv 7:3
not have God's seal on their f-s. .Rv 9:4
on his right hand or on his f, ..Rv 13:16
mark on their f-s or their
   hands. .... Rv 20:4

FOREIGN

get rid of the f gods that are......Jos 24:23

must not bow down to a f god. . Ps 81:9
sing the Lord's song on f soil? . . Ps 137:4

FOREIGNER

the land where you live as a f, . . Gn 28:4
the Passover: no f may eat it. . Ex 12:43
by the lips of f-s, and even
   then, ...1Co 14:21
are no longer f-s and
   strangers, ... Eph 2:19
that they were f-s and
   temporary . . . . .Heb 11:13

FOREKNEW

For those he f he also . . . . Rm 8:29
rejected his people whom he f. . Rm 11:2

FORERUNNER

entered there on our behalf
   as a f, ...Heb 6:20

FORESKIN

circumcise the flesh of your f. . Gn 17:11

FOREVER

will not remain with
   mankind f, ... Gn 6:3
your throne will be
   established f. 2Sm 7:16
But the Lord sits enthroned f; . . . Ps 9:7
"You are a priest f . . . . Ps 110:4
for wealth is not f; . . . . .Pr 27:24
of this bread he will live f. . . . . . . Jn 6:51
You are a priest f according to . .Heb 5:6
same yesterday, today, and f . . . . .Heb 13:8
the word of the Lord endures f. .1Pt 1:25
and they will reign f and ever. . Rv 22:5

FORFEITS

whole world, and yet loses or
   f himself? . . . . Lk 9:25

FORGET

be careful not to f the Lord
   who . . . . .Dt 6:12
you f-got the God who gave
   birth . . . . .Dt 32:18
and do not f all his benefits. . . .Ps 103:2
If I f you, Jerusalem, may my
   right hand f its skill . . . . .Ps 137:5
My son, don't f my teaching, but Pr 3:1
Can a woman f her nursing
   child . . . . Is 49:15
F-ting what is behind. . . . . Php 3:13

you have f-gotten the
   exhortation. . . . . Heb 12:5
and immediately f-s what
   kind of . . . . Jms 1:24

FORGIVE

if you would only f their sin... Ex 32:32
f their sin, and heal their land. . 2Ch 7:14
one whose transgression is f-n, . .Ps 32:1
For I will f their iniquity and . . Jr 31:34
And f us our debts, as we also
   have f-n our debtors. . . . . Mt 6:12
Who can f sins but God alone? . .Mk 2:7
But the one who is f-n little, ...Lk 7:47
and if he repents, f him. . . . . Lk 17:3
Father, f them, because . . . . Lk 23:34
f-ing one another, just as God also
   f-gave you in Christ. . . . . .Eph 4:32
and f-gave us all our
   trespasses. . . . . .Col 2:13
committed sins, he will be f-n. .Jms 5:15
and righteous to f us our sins . . 1Jn 1:9

FORGIVENESS

you there is f, so that you may. .Ps 130:4
poured out for many for the f
   of sins. .Mt 26:28
through his blood, the f of our. . Eph 1:7
have redemption, the f of sins... Col 1:14
shedding of blood there is
   no f . . . . .Heb 9:22

FORM (N)

He didn't have . . . f or majesty . . Is 53:2
and you haven't seen his f. . . . . .Jn 5:37
existing in the f of God, did not. .Php 2:6
holding to the f of godliness
   but 2Tm 3:5

FORM (V)

Then the Lord God f-ed the
   man out . . . . Gn 2:7
when I was f-ed in the depths
   of . . . . .Ps 139:15
Will what is f-ed say to the one
   who f-ed it, ... Rm 9:20
you until Christ is f-ed in you. . . Gl 4:19

FORMLESS

Now the earth was f and empty, . .Gn 1:2

FORTRESS

The Lord is my rock, my f, . . . 2Sm 22:2
refuge and my f, my God in
   whom . . . . Ps 91:2

FORTUNES

Lord restores the f of his
   people, ... Ps 14:7

FORTY

Rain fell . . . f days and f nights. . . . . . Gn 7:12
on the mountain f days and f . . Ex 24:18
in the wilderness for f years . .Nm 14:33
f days to be tempted by the
   devil. . . . . .Lk 4:2
appearing to them during f days . .Ac 1:3

FORWARD

and reaching f to what is
   ahead . . . . Php 3:13
he was looking f to the city . . .Heb 11:10

FOUND

The Lord f-ed the earth by
   wisdom. . . . . Pr 3:19

FOUNDATION

established the earth on
   its f-s; . . . . .Ps 104:5
precious cornerstone, a sure f; . .Is 28:16
because its f was on the rock. . . . .Mt 7:25
builds on the f with gold, ...1Co 3:12
built on the f of the apostles . .Eph 2:20
God's solid f stands firm, ... 2Tm 2:19
looking . . . to the city that has
   f-s, ...Heb 11:10

FOUNTAIN

for with you is life's f . . . . .Ps 36:9
abandoned me, the f of living
   water, ... Jr 2:13

FOUR HUNDRED

will be . . . oppressed f years. . . . . . .Gn 15:13
enslave and oppress them f
   years. . . . . .Ac 7:6

FOX

F-es have dens, and birds of
   the . . . . Mt 8:20
Go tell that f, 'Look! . . . . .Lk 13:32

FRAGRANCE

we are the f of Christ among . . 2Co 2:15

FRAGRANT

sacrificial and f offering to God. . Eph 5:2

FRANKINCENSE

carry gold and f and proclaim.. Is 60:6
gold, f, and myrrh.............Mt 2:11

FREE (ADJ)

and the truth will set you f.....Jn 8:32
Jesus has set you f from
  the law...............Rm 8:2
slave or f, male or female; ......Gl 3:28
For freedom, Christ has set us f.. Gl 5:1
and has set us f from our sins ...Rv 1:5

FREE (V)

The LORD f-s prisoners........Ps 146:7
who has died is f-d from sin. ...Rm 6:7

FREEDOM

to proclaim ... f to the
  prisoners; ....Is 61:1
Spirit of the Lord is, there is f.. 2Co 3:17
For freedom, Christ has set us f....Gl 5:1
don't use this f as an
  opportunity .... Gl 5:13
not using your f as a cover-up......1Pt 2:16

FREELY

our God, for he will f forgive.... Is 55:7
are justified f by his grace.... Rm 3:24

FRESH

put new wine into f wineskins, ..Mt 9:17
saltwater spring yield f water. . Jms 3:12

FRIEND

as a man speaks with his f, ...Ex 33:11
Now when Job's three
  f-s—Eliphaz.................Jb 2:11
A f loves at all times,.......... Pr 17:17
but there is a f who stays
  closer.....................Pr 18:24
wounds of a f are
  trustworthy .... Pr 27:6
a f of tax collectors and........Mt 11:19
lay down his life for his f-s.....Jn 15:13
and he was called God's f......Jms 2:23
be the f the world becomes
  the...........................Jms 4:4

FRIENDSHIP

f with the world is hostility......Jms 4:4

FRONT

the f seats in the synagogues,...Mt 23:6

FRUIT

that bears its f in season......... Ps 1:3
The f of the righteous is a tree.. Pr 11:30
produce f consistent with ...... Mt 3:8
recognize them by their f. ......Mt 7:16
not drink from this f of the
  vine........................Mt 26:29
that does not produce f he
  removes,...................Jn 15:2
But the f of the Spirit is love,
  joy,..........................Gl 5:22
bearing f in every good work.. Col 1:10
tree of life ... bearing twelve
  kinds of f,...................Rv 22:2

FRUITFUL

blessed them: "Be f, multiply, .. Gn 1:22
But the Israelites were f,......... Ex 1:7

FULFILL

May the LORD f all your
  requests...................Ps 20:5
F what you vow..................Ec 5:4
not come to abolish but to f....Mt 5:17
this Scripture has been f-ed.......Lk 4:21
and the Psalms must be f-ed.. Lk 24:44
loves another has f-ed the
  law.........................Rm 13:8
husband should f his marital...1Co 7:3
whole law is f-ed in one
  statement....................Gl 5:14
way you will f the law of
  Christ ....Gl 6:2

FULFILLMENT

therefore, is the f of the law...Rm 13:10

FULL

land will be as f of the
  knowledge ....Is 11:9
whole body will be f of light. .. Mt 6:22
from the Father, f of grace and ..Jn 1:14
Stephen, f of the Holy..........Ac 7:55
You are already f!...............1Co 4:8

FULLNESS

grace upon grace from his f, ... Jn 1:16
until the f of the Gentiles......Rm 11:25
the f of the one who fills all... Eph 1:23
filled with all the f of God...... Eph 3:19
have all his f dwell in him,..... Col 1:19
entire f of God's nature dwells ..Col 2:9

FULLY

I will know f, as I am f known...1Co 13:12

FURNACE

tested you in the f of affliction. . Is 48:10
thrown into a f of blazing fire... Dn 3:6
throw them into the blazing f . Mt 13:42

FURY

who have drunk the cup of
  his f............................Is 51:17
and the f of a fire about to ... Heb 10:27

FUTILE

Everything is f...................Ec 1:2

FUTILITY

"Absolute f," says the Teacher. ... Ec 1:2
For he comes in f and he goes in..Ec 6:4
creation was subjected to f.......Rm 8:20
in the f of their thoughts...... Eph 4:17

FUTURE

person of peace will have a f...Ps 37:37
For the evil have no f;........ Pr 24:20
to give you a f and a hope. ......Jr 29:11

G

GABRIEL

Angel who explained Daniel's visions (Dn 8:16; 9:21) and announced John's and Jesus's births (Lk 1:19,26).

GAD

1. Son of Jacob by Zilpah (Gn 30:9-11). Tribe with Transjordan territory north of the Dead Sea (Nm 32; Dt 3:16-17; Jos 18:7).
2. Seer at time of David (1Sm 22:5; 2Sm 24:11-19; 1Ch 21:9-19; 29:29; 2Ch 29:25).

GAIN (N)

Ill-gotten g-s do not profit......Pr 10:2
to live is Christ and to die is g. .Php 1:21
with contentment is a great g.. 1Tm 6:6

GAIN (V)

someone if he g-s the whole
  world........................Mt 16:26
someone to g the whole
  world .... Mk 8:36
dung, so that I may g
  Christ.........................Php 3:8

GALILEAN

You were with Jesus the G
  too. . . . . Mt 26:69

GALILEE

1. Region in northern Palestine (Jos
20:7; 21:32; 1Kg 9:11); where Jesus
lived (Mt 2:22; 3:13; 21:11) and ministered (Is 9:1; Mt 4:12,15,23); where he
appeared after the resurrection (Mt
26:32; Ac 1:11).
2. Sea along the Jordan (Mt 4:18; 15:29).

GALL

they gave me g for my food, ... Ps 69:21
him wine mixed with g to
  drink. . . . . Mt 27:34

GALLOWS

he had the g constructed. . . . . . . Est 5:14

GAMALIEL

Pharisee (Ac 5:34); Paul's teacher (22:3).

GANG

a g of evildoers has closed in . . Ps 22:16

GANGRENE

their teaching will spread
  like g; 2Tm 2:17

GAP

and stand in the g before me
  on. . . . . Ezk 22:30

GARDEN

LORD God planted a g in Eden, . . Gn 2:8
A new tomb was in the g; . . . . . . Jn 19:41

GARDENER

and my Father is the g. . . . . Jn 15:1
Supposing he was the g, she . . . Jn 20:15

GARMENT

But leaving his g in her hand, . . Gn 39:12
They divided my g-s among . . . Ps 22:18
You will change them like
  a g, ... Ps 102:26
clothed me with the g-s of
  salvation. Is 61:10
patches an old g with

unshrunk. . . . . Mt 9:16

GATE

Lift up your heads, you g-s! . . . . . . Ps 24:7
Enter his g-s with
  thanksgiving . . . . Ps 100:4
Enter through the narrow g. . . . . . Mt 7:13
and the g-s of Hades will
  not. . . . . Mt 16:18
I am the g. If anyone enters by. . Jn 10:9
also suffered outside the g, . . Heb 13:12
Its g-s will never
  close by day . . . . Rv 21:25

GATHER

and g enough for that day. . . . . . . Ex 16:4
G my faithful ones to me, ... Ps 50:5
and a time to g stones; . . . . Ec 3:5
he g-s the lambs in his arms
  and . . . . Is 40:11
who does not g with me
  scatters . . . . Mt 12:30
or three are g-ed together
  in my . . . . Mt 18:20
I wanted to g your children together,
  as a hen g-s her chicks . . . . . . Mt 23:37

GAZE (N)

fix your g straight ahead. . . . . Pr 4:25

GAZE (V)

So I g on you in the sanctuary . . Ps 63:2
they were g-ing into heaven . . . Ac 1:10

GEHAZI

Elisha's attendant (2Kg 4:11-37; 5:20-27;
8:4-5).

GENEALOGY

Israel was registered in the
  g-ies 1Ch 9:1
to myths and endless g-ies. 1Tm 1:4
Without father, mother, or g, . . Heb 7:3

GENERATION

to the third and fourth g. . . . . Ex 34:7
been our refuge in every g. . . . . . Ps 90:1
There is a g that . . . . Pr 30:11
To what should I compare
  this g? . . . . Mt 11:16
adulterous g demands a
  sign, ... Mt 12:39
This g will certainly not pass. . . Mt 24:34
from now on all g-s will call me. . Lk 1:48

GENEROSITY

giving, with g; . . . . Rm 12:8

GENEROUS

A g person will be blessed, ... Pr 22:9
to be g and willing to share, . . 1Tm 6:18

GENEROUSLY

who sows g will also reap g. . . . 2Co 9:6

GENTILE

Don't even the G-s do the
  same? . . . . Mt 5:47
They will hand him over to the
  G-s . . . . Mt 20:19
a light for revelation to the
  G-s . . . . Lk 2:32
trampled by the G-s until the
  times of the G-s are fulfilled. . Lk 21:24
Why do the G-s rage . . . . Ac 4:25
poured out even on the G-s. . . Ac 10:45
Is he not also the God of G-s . . Rm 3:29
fullness of the G-s has come. . Rm 11:25
he regularly ate with the G-s
  before . . . . Gl 2:12

GENTLE

A g answer turns away anger, . . Pr 15:1
a g tongue can break a bone. . . Pr 25:15
is coming to you, g, and
  mounted. Mt 21:5
peace-loving, g, compliant,
  full. . . . . Jms 3:17
quality of a g and quiet spirit, . . 1Pt 3:4

GENTLENESS

or in love and a spirit of g? 1Co 4:21
appeal to you by the . . . g of
  Christ. 2Co 10:1
goodness, faithfulness, g, s
  elf-control. . . . . Gl 5:23
humility and g, with patience. . Eph 4:2
faith, love, endurance, and g. . 1Tm 6:11
do this with g and respect, ... 1Pt 3:16

GENUINELY

widows who are g in need. 1Tm 5:3

GENUINENESS

am testing the g of your love. . . 2Co 8:8

GERASENE

sailed to the region of the G-s, . . Lk 8:26

GET

G wisdom .... Pr 16:16

GETHSEMANE

with them to a place called G, ..Mt 26:36

GHOST

they thought it was a **g** and
  cried .... Mk 6:49
because a **g** does not have
  flesh .... Lk 24:39

GIBEON

inhabitants of G heard what.... Jos 9:3
Sun, stand still over G, ... Jos 10:12

GIDEON

Judge (Jdg 6–8; Heb 11:32). The fleece
(Jdg 6:36-40). God reduced his army
(7:2-8).

GIFT

person's **g** opens doors for
  him .... Pr 18:16
leave your **g** there in front of .. Mt 5:24
to give good **g-s** to your
  children, ... Mt 7:11
will receive the **g** of the Holy .. Ac 2:38
but the **g** of God is eternal life ..Rm 6:23
we have different **g-s**: .... Rm 12:6
each has his own **g** from God, .. 1Co 7:7
Now there are different **g-s**, ...1Co 12:4
to God for his indescribable **g**! ..2Co 9:15
good and perfect **g** is from
  above, ... Jms 1:17

GILEAD

Region east of the Jordan and north
of Moab, allotted to Reuben, Gad, and
half of Manasseh (Nm 32:40; Dt 3:12-13;
Jos 13:8-31; 17:1-6).

GIRL

by the hand, and the **g** got up . Mt 9:25
"Little **g**, I say to you, get up" ...Mk 5:41

GIVE

I will **g** this land to your
  offspring. .... Gn 12:7
The LORD **g-s**, and the LORD
  takes. .... Jb 1:21
G thanks to the God of gods....Ps 136:2
if he is thirsty, **g** him water ....Pr 25:21

leech has two daughters:
  "G, G!" .... Pr 30:15
be born for us, a son will be
  g-n to us, ... Is 9:6
I will not **g** my glory to another.. Is 42:8
I will **g** you a new heart and ..Ezk 36:26
G us today our daily bread ...... Mt 6:11
Ask, and it will be **g-n**. .... Mt 7:7
hungry and you **gave** me....Mt 25:35
G, and it will be **g-n** to you; ..... Lk 6:38
is my body, which is **g-n** for
  you. .... Lk 22:19
He **gave** them the right to be ...... Jn 1:12
He **gave** his one and only Son, .. Jn 3:16
I **g** them eternal life, ... Jn 10:28
not **g** to you as the world **g-s**... Jn 14:27
since he himself **g-s** everyone
  life .... Ac 17:25
blessed to **g** than to receive. .. Ac 20:35
he himself **gave** some to be.... Eph 4:11
gave himself as a ransom for
  all, ... 1Tm 2:6
ready . . . to **g** a defense to...... 1Pt 3:15

GIVER

since God loves a cheerful **g**. .. 2Co 9:7

GLAD

Let the heavens be **g** and 1Ch 16:31
let us rejoice and be **g** in it...... Ps 118:24
Be **g** and rejoice, because your.. Mt 5:12

GLADNESS

Let me hear joy and **g**; .... Ps 51:8
Serve the LORD with **g**; .... Ps 100:2

GLASS

Something like a sea of **g**, ... Rv 4:6
city was pure gold clear as **g**... Rv 21:18

GLEAN

do not **g** what is left. .... Dt 24:21
saw what she had **g-ed**.......... Ru 2:18

GLOAT

not let my enemies **g** over me.. Ps 25:2

GLOOM

a day of darkness and **g**, ... Jl 2:2
to darkness, **g**, and storm, ... Heb 12:18

GLOOMY

don't be **g** like the hypocrites.. Mt 6:16

GLORIFY

I have **g-ied** it, and I will **g** it
  again! .... Jn 12:28
the Son of Man is **g-ied**, and God is
  g-ied in him.................. Jn 13:31
G your Son so that the Son
  may **g** .... Jn 17:1
those he justified, he also
  g-ied. .... Rm 8:30
So **g** God in your body. 1Co 6:20

GLORIOUS

Who is like you, **g** in holiness.. Ex 15:11
G things are said about you, ...Ps 87:3

GLORY

Please, let me see your **g**. ..... Ex 33:18
The **g** has departed from
  Israel, ... 1Sm 4:21
Declare his **g** among the
  nations 1Ch 16:24
crowned him with **g** and honor. ..Ps 8:5
Then the King of **g** will come in.. Ps 24:7
ascribe to the LORD **g** and
  strength...................... Ps 29:1
the whole earth is filled with
  his **g**...................... Ps 72:19
ascribe to the LORD **g** and
  strength...................... Ps 96:7
His **g** fills the whole earth........Is 6:3
And the **g** of the LORD will
  appear, ... Is 40:5
the **g** of the LORD filled...Ezk 43:5; 44:4
the Son of Man comes in
  his **g**, ... Mt 25:31
and the **g** of the Lord shone .....Lk 2:9
G to God in the highest heaven, ..Lk 2:14
We observed his **g**, the **g** as the one
  and only Son.................. Jn 1:14
exchanged the **g** of the
  immortal .... Rm 1:23
and fall short of the **g** of God.. Rm 3:23
not worth comparing with
  the **g** .... Rm 8:18
adoption, the **g**, the covenants.. Rm 9:4
do everything for the **g** of
  God........................1Co 10:31
incomparable eternal
  weight of **g**.................. 2Co 4:17
Christ in you, the hope of **g**. ... Col 1:27
crowned him with **g** and
  honor....................... Heb 2:7
worthy to receive **g** and honor.. Rv 4:11

GLUTTON

and the **g** will become poor....Pr 23:21
they say, 'Look, a **g** and a
  drunkard .... Mt 11:19

GNASH

they **g-ed** their teeth at me.....Ps 35:16
will be weeping and **g-ing** of
   teeth. ....Mt 8:12; 13:12; 25:30
and **g-ed** their teeth at him.....Ac 7:54

GNAT

strain out a **g**, yet gulp down..Mt 23:24

GO

Let my people **g**, ...Ex 5:1
For wherever you **g**, I will **g**, ...Ru 1:16
Where can I **g** to escape your..Ps 139:7
We all **went** astray like sheep;..Is 53:6
I say to this one, 'G!' and he **g-es**;..Mt 8:9
G, therefore, and make
   disciples ....Mt 28:19
G into all the world and
   preach.....................Mk 16:15
I am **g-ing** away to prepare a
   place..........................Jn 14:2

GOAL

I pursue as my **g** the prize......Php 3:14
receiving the **g** of your faith,.....1Pt 1:9

GOAT

put them on the **g-'s** head and
   send ....Lv 16:21
bulls or drink the blood of **g-s**?..Ps 50:13
separates the sheep from
   the **g-s**......................Mt 25:32
For if the blood of **g-s** and
   bulls ....Heb 9:13

GOD

In the beginning G created the ..Gn 1:1
you will be like G, knowing
   good ....Gn 3:5
the sons of G saw that the ......Gn 6:2
he was a priest to G Most
   High........................Gn 14:18
saying, "I am G Almighty.......Gn 17:1
LORD, the Everlasting G. ......Gn 21:33
G planned it for good to bring ..Gn 50:20
I am the G of your father, the G of
   Abraham, the G of Isaac, and the G
   of Jacob.......................Ex 3:6
LORD, the G of your fathers......Ex 3:15
LORD, the G of the Hebrews,.....Ex 3:18
This is my G, and I will praise
   him,..........................Ex 15:2
Do not have other **g-s** besides
   me............................Ex 20:3
I, LORD your G, am a jealous G, ..Ex 20:5
G is not a man, that he might lie,..Nm 23:19

G is a consuming fire, a
   jealous G......................Dt 4:24
the voice of the living G
   speaking......................Dt 5:26
LORD your G is G, the faithful G..Dt 7:9
the LORD your G is the G of **g-s**..Dt 10:17
The G of old is your dwelling ..Dt 33:27
and your G will be my G.........Ru 1:16
there is no rock like our G.....1Sm 2:2
will know that Israel has
   a G,.......................1Sm 17:46
LORD G of Armies was with
   him........................2Sm 5:10
But will G indeed live on earth..1Kg 8:27
G who answers with fire,
   he is G 1Kg 18:24
Their **g-s** are **g-s** of the hill...1Kg 20:23
they had worshiped other **g-s**..2Kg 17:7
And G granted his request......1Ch 4:10
Save us, G of our salvation; ..1Ch 16:35
our G is greater than any of
   the **g-s**.......................2Ch 2:5
says in his heart, "There's
   no G." ....Pss 14:1; 53:1
My G, my G, why have you......Ps 22:1
the nation whose G is the
   LORD— ....Ps 33:12
G is our refuge and strength, ...Ps 46:1
Our G is a G of salvation,......Ps 68:20
What **g** is great like G? ....Ps 77:13
For he is our G, and we are the ..Ps 95:7
Acknowledge that the LORD
   is G...........................Ps 100:3
Give thanks to the G of **g-s**. ....Ps 136:2
fear G and keep his
   commands,..................Ec 12:13
Wonderful Counselor, Mighty G, ..Is 9:6
of Judah, "Here is your G!" ......Is 40:9
The LORD is the everlasting G,..Is 40:28
There is no G but me. ....Is 44:6
I will be their G, and they will ..Jr 31:33
I am the LORD, the G of every ..Jr 32:27
people, and I will be your G. ..Ezk 36:28
Didn't one G create us? ....Mal 2:10
is translated "G is with us.".....Mt 1:23
heart, for they will see G. ....Mt 5:8
Therefore, what G has joined ..Mt 19:6
and to G the things that are
   G-'s ....Mt 22:21
that is, "My G, My G, why have..Mt 27:46
Who can forgive sins but
   G alone? ....Mk 2:7
was with G, and the Word was G...Jn 1:1
For G loved the world in this
   way: ....Jn 3:16
G is spirit, and those who
   worship ....Jn 4:24
I said, you are **g-s**? ....Jn 10:34
to him, "My Lord and my G!"..Jn 20:28
We must obey G rather than
   people ....Ac 5:29

The **g-s** have come down to
   us in ....Ac 14:11
g-s made by hand are not **g-s**!..Ac 19:26
Let G be true, even though
   everyone ....Rm 3:4
If G is for us, who is against......Rm 8:31
G is the one who justifies.......Rm 8:33
Be reconciled to G.............2Co 5:20
I will be their G, and they
   will be 2Co 6:16
that by nature are not **g-s**........Gl 4:8
one G and Father of all, who is..Eph 4:6
who, existing in the form of G,..Php 2:6
one G and one mediator
   between G....................1Tm 2:5
our great G and Savior, Jesus......Ti 2:13
for our G is a consuming
   fire.........................Heb 12:29
G is light, and there is..........1Jn 1:5
does not know G, because
   G is love......................1Jn 4:8
holy, holy, Lord G, the Almighty, ..Rv 4:8
G-'s dwelling is with humanity,..Rv 21:3

GODDESS

Ashtoreth, the **g** of the
   Sidonians, ...1Kg 11:5
temple of the great **g** Artemis..Ac 19:27

GOD-FEARING

centurion, an upright and
   G man,......................Ac 10:22

GODLESS

the hope of the **g** will perish. ....Jb 8:13

GODLESSNESS

heaven against all **g** and.......Rm 1:18
he will turn **g** away from
   Jacob........................Rm 11:26

GODLINESS

life in all **g** and dignity..........1Tm 2:2
but **g** is beneficial in every way..1Tm 4:8
But **g** with contentment is.....1Tm 6:6
holding to the form of **g** but ...2Tm 3:5
required for life and **g** 2Pt 1:3
endurance, endurance with **g**,.. 2Pt 1:6

GODLY

is the one seeking? G
   offspring....................Mal 2:15
For **g** grief produces a 2Co 7:10
want to live a **g** life in Christ ..2Tm 3:12
and **g** way in the present age,... Ti 2:12

GOG

the day when G comes
   against .... Ezk 38:18
G and Magog, to gather them.. Rv 20:8

GOLD

G cannot be exchanged for it, .. Jb 28:15
They are more desirable
   than g........................ Ps 19:10
more than g, even the
   purest g, ... Ps 119:127
is better than silver and g....... Pr 22:1
is like g apples in silver
   settings. .... Pr 25:11
street of the city was pure g,.. Rv 21:21

GOLGOTHA

they came to a place called G .Mt 27:33

GOLIATH

Philistine giant from Gath killed by
David (1Sm 17).

GOMER

Hosea's wife (Hs 1:3,8).

GOOD

And God saw that it was g....... Gn 1:10
God planned it for g to bring
   about .... Gn 50:20
There is no one who
   does g.................... Ps 14:1; 53:1
Taste and see that the LORD is g. .Ps 34:8
withhold the g from those
   who........................... Ps 84:11
How g and pleasant it is when..Ps 133:1
A joyful heart is g medicine,... Pr 17:22
who brings news of g things,... Is 52:7
to do what is g on the Sabbath. .Mt 12:12
Well done, g and faithful
   slave! .... Mt 25:21
Why do you call me g? ... No
   one is g except God.........Mk 10:18
I am the g shepherd............. Jn 10:11
together for the g of those
   who.......................... Rm 8:28
by evil, but conquer evil
   with g....................... Rm 12:21
in Christ Jesus for g works, ... Eph 2:10

GOODNESS

cause all my g to pass in front ..Ex 33:19
Only g and faithful love will..... Ps 23:6
patience, kindness, g,
   faithfulness,................... Gl 5:22

GOODS

You have many g stored
   up for........................ Lk 12:19
has this world's g and sees 1Jn 3:17

GOSHEN

Region of Egypt where Israel settled
(Gn 45:10; 46:28-34); the best part of the
land (47:6,27); excluded from plagues
(Ex 8:22; 9:26).

GOSPEL

and preach the g to all
   creation.................... Mk 16:15
For I am not ashamed of
   the g,....................... Rm 1:16
But if our g is veiled, ... 2Co 4:3
and are turning to a different g... Gl 1:6
with the eternal g to
   announce.................... Rv 14:6

GOSSIP

A g goes around revealing a....Pr 11:13
but are also g-s and
   busybodies,................ 1Tm 5:13

GOVERNMENT

and the g will be on his
   shoulders...................... Is 9:6

GRACE

g flows from your lips........... Ps 45:2
g and truth came through Jesus. Jn 1:17
sin so that g may multiply? ..... Rm 6:1
My g is sufficient for you, ... 2Co 12:9
you have fallen from g........... Gl 5:4
you are saved by g through
   faith .... Eph 2:8
For the g of God has appeared .. Ti 2:11
having been justified by his g,....Ti 3:7
But he gives greater g........... Jms 4:6

GRACIOUS

I will be g to whom I will be g, ..Ex 33:19
Be g to me, God, according to... Ps 51:1
are a compassionate and g
   God,........................ Ps 86:15
Let your speech always be g, ...Col 4:6

GRAFT

wild olive branch, were
   g-ed in...................... Rm 11:17
God has the power to g
   them in .... Rm 11:23

GRANDCHILDREN

G are the crown of the elderly,.. Pr 17:6

GRAPE

not drink any g juice or eat .... Nm 6:3
with a single cluster of g-s, .. Nm 13:23
The fathers have eaten sour
   g-s,.......................... Jr 31:29
because its g-s have ripened...Rv 14:18

GRASP

so that they could not g it, ... Lk 9:45
him, but he eluded their g......Jn 10:39

GRASS

As for man, his days are like g ..Ps 103:15
All humanity is g, and all its .... Is 40:6
The g withers, the flowers fade.. Is 40:7
God clothes the g of the field,.. Mt 6:30
All flesh is like g, and all its 1Pt 1:24
The g withers, and the flower .. 1Pt 1:24

GRASSHOPPER

To ourselves we seemed like
   g-s,......................... Nm 13:33

GRATITUDE

to God with g in your hearts. ...Col 3:16

GRAVE

their throat is an open g; .... Ps 5:9
He was assigned a g with the
   wicked....................... Is 53:9
You are like unmarked g-s; ....Lk 11:44
Their throat is an open g; ...... Rm 3:13

GRAY

G hair is a glorious crown;..... Pr 16:31

GREAT

God made the two g lights...... Gn 1:16
will make you into a g
   nation,....................... Gn 12:2
LORD is a g God, a g King
   above all..................... Ps 95:3
g is your faithfulness! ....Lm 3:23
wants to become g among
   you ....Mt 20:26
because of his g love that he .. Eph 2:4
with contentment is g gain. 1Tm 6:6
we neglect such a g salvation?.. Heb 2:3
Then I saw a g white
   throne and .... Rv 20:11

GREATER

something g than the temple.. Mt 12:6
You will see g things than this. . Jn 1:50
No one has g love than this, ... Jn 15:13
But desire the g gifts. 1Co 12:31
the one who is in you is g
    than the 1Jn 4:4

GREATEST

Who is g in the kingdom........Mt 18:1
g among you will be your
    servant....................Mt 23:11
But the g of these is love. 1Co 13:13

GREED

be on guard against all g, ...Lk 12:15

GREEDY

A g person stirs up conflict, .. Pr 28:25
thieves, g people, drunkards ..1Co 6:10

GREEK

to the Jew, and also to the G.... Rm 1:16
signs and the G-s seek
    wisdom, ...1Co 1:22
is no Jew or G, slave or free, ...Gl 3:28

GREEN

lets me lie down in g pastures;.. Ps 23:2

GRIEF

and joy may end in g. ....Pr 14:13
because your g led to
    repentance.................2Co 7:9
this with joy and not with g, ..Heb 13:17

GRIEVE

rebelled and g-d his Holy
    Spirit.........................Is 63:10
Peter was g-d that he asked
    him ....Jn 21:17
And don't g God's Holy Spirit. .Eph 4:30
you will not g like the rest,......1Th 4:13

GROAN

we also g within ourselves,...... Rm 8:23

GROANING

God heard their g; ....Ex 2:24
the whole creation has been g ..Rm 8:22
intercedes for us with
    unspoken g-s. .... Rm 8:26

GROOM SEE ALSO
BRIDEGROOM

as a g rejoices over his bride, ... Is 62:5
I will eliminate... the voice of
    the g and the bride,.......... Jr 7:34
Let the g leave his bedroom,.....Jl 2:16
sad while the g is with them?.. Mt 9:15
When the g was delayed,
    they.........................Mt 25:5
He who has the bride is the g. ..Jn 3:29

GROUND

The g is cursed because of
    you...........................Gn 3:17
you are standing is holy g.......Ex 3:5
Others fell on rocky g, ... Mt 13:5

GROW

He grew up before him like a
    young.......................Is 53:2
the wildflowers of the field g: . Mt 6:28
boy grew up and became
    strong,......................Lk 2:40
let us g in every way into
    him ....Eph 4:15
But g in the grace and
    knowledge 2Pt 3:18

GROWTH

but only God who gives the g. ..1Co 3:7

GUARD (N)

The g-s were so shaken by fear. .Mt 28:4

GUARD (V)

G your heart above all else,......Pr 4:23
will g your hearts and minds.. Php 4:7
g what has been entrusted
    to you, ...1Tm 6:20

GUARDIAN

Am I my brother's g?........... Gn 4:9
law, then, was our g until
    Christ, ...Gl 3:24
Shepherd and G of your souls. 1Pt 2:25

GUIDE

And if the blind g the blind,... Mt 15:14
He will g you into all the truth ..Jn 16:13

GUILT

You forgave the g of my sin.......Ps 32:5
my sins and blot out all my g.... Ps 51:9

GUILTY

I will not justify the g...........Ex 23:7
I was g when I was born; ....Ps 51:5
Acquitting the g and
    condemning................ Pr 17:15
but is g of an eternal sin" ..... Mk 3:29

H

HABAKKUK

Prophet in Judah before the exile (Hab 1:1).

HADES SEE ALSO SHEOL

You will go down to H......... Mt 11:23
and the gates of H will not......Mt 16:18
You will not abandon me in H.. Ac 2:27
I hold the keys of death and H. . Rv 1:18

HAGAR

Sarah's slave; mother of Ishmael (Gn 16; Gl 4:21-31). Sent away by Sarah (Gn 16:5-9; 21:9-21).

HAGGAI

Prophet after the exile, who encouraged rebuilding the temple (Ezr 5:1; 6:14; Hg 1–2).

HAIL

I will rain down the worst
    h that ....Ex 9:18
and mocked him: "H, King
    of the ....Mt 27:29

HAILSTONES

LORD threw large h on
    them from..................Jos 10:11
Enormous h, each weighing
    about ....Rv 16:21

HAIR

is to let the h of his head grow.. Nm 6:5
But his h began to grow back. .Jdg 16:22
are more than the h-s of my
    head,........................Ps 40:12
make a single h white or
    black........................Mt 5:36
But even the h-s of your head
    have ....Mt 10:30
and wiped his feet with her h,.. Jn 11:2
she should have her h cut off. . 1Co 11:6

HAIRSTYLES

with elaborate **h**, gold, pearls,..1Tm 2:9
elaborate **h** and wearing gold .. 1Pt 3:3

HAIRY

A **h** man with a leather belt......2Kg 1:8

HALF

give you, up to **h** my kingdom. . Mk 6:23

HALLELUJAH

H! My soul, praise the LORD.......Ps 146:1
multitude in heaven,
   saying, **H**!......................Rv 19:1

HAM

Son of Noah (Gn 5:32; 9:18-27). Ancestor of Cushites, Egyptians, and Canaanites (Gn 9:18-27; 10:6; Pss 78:51; 105:23,27; 106:22).

HAMAN

Nobleman of Persia at the time of Esther (Est 3:1-2); enemy of Jews (3:3-15). Hanged on his own gallows (7:9-10).

HANANIAH

1. False prophet; opposed Jeremiah (Jr 28).
2. Shadrach's original name (Dn 1:6).

HAND (N)

rock and cover you with my **h**..Ex 33:22
lay their **h-s** on the bull's head....Lv 4:15
they pierced my **h-s** and my
   feet...........................Ps 22:16
Sit at my right **h** until I make .. Ps 110:1
even there your **h** will lead
   me;..........................Ps 139:10
Whatever your **h-s** find to do, ..Ec 9:10
of the field will clap their **h-s**. . Is 55:12
man's **h** appeared and began
   writing .... Dn 5:5
if your right **h** causes you to...Mt 5:30
let your left **h** know what
   your right .... Mt 6:3
Sit at my right **h** until I put....Mt 22:44
into your **h-s** I entrust my
   spirit........................ Lk 23:46
he showed them his **h-s** and
   feet.......................... Lk 24:40
will snatch them out of my **h**.. Jn 10:28
Because I'm not a **h**, I don't ...1Co 12:15
dwelling...not made with **h-s**...2Co 5:1

lifting up holy **h-s** without
   anger 1Tm 2:8
to fall into the **h-s** of the
   living .... Heb 10:31

HAND (V)

h-ed him over to be crucified.. Mt 27:26
when he **h-s** over the
   kingdom to 1Co 15:24

HANDLE

Don't **h**, don't taste, don't
   touch"? ....Col 2:21

HANG

anyone **hung** on a tree is
   under ....Dt 21:23
Then he went and **h-ed**
   himself...................... Mt 27:5
everyone who is **hung** on a tree ..Gl 3:13

HANNAH

Wife of Elkanah; mother of Samuel (1Sm 1–2).

HAPPY

How **h** is the one who does not...Ps 1:1
H is the nation whose God is ..Ps 33:12
H is the man who has filled his ..Ps 127:5
H is a man who finds wisdom
   and .... Pr 3:13

HARD

It will be **h** for a rich person .. Mt 19:23
This teaching is **h**! Who can
   accept ....Jn 6:60
that are **h** to understand.......2Pt 3:16

HARDEN

But I will **h** his heart so that..... Ex 4:21
Do not **h** your hearts as at
   Meribah,.....................Ps 95:8
and he **h-s** whom he wants
   to **h**......................Rm 9:18
elect did find it. The rest were
   h-ed .... Rm 11:7
A partial **h-ing** has come upon
   Israel ....Rm 11:25
do not **h** your hearts as in the.. Heb 3:8

HAREM

beautiful young women to
   the **h**...................... Est 2:3

HARM (N)

Don't plan any **h** against your ..Pr 3:29

HARM (V)

But they were planning to
   h me..........................Neh 6:2

HARP

praise him with **h** and lyre. ......Ps 150:3
Each one had a **h** and golden
   bowls ....Rv 5:8

HARSH

but a **h** word stirs up wrath......Pr 15:1

HARVEST

earth endures, seedtime
   and **h**,......................... Gn 8:22
observe the Festival of **H** with .. Ex 23:16
sleeps during **h** is disgraceful... Pr 10:5
The **h** is abundant, but the
   workers .... Mt 9:37
because they are ready for **h**....Jn 4:35
since the **h** of the earth is ripe..Rv 14:15

HASTY

Do not be **h** to speak, ...Ec 5:2

HATE

You who love the LORD, **h** evil! ..Ps 97:10
To fear the LORD is to **h** evil...... Pr 8:13
will not use the rod **h-s** his
   son, ...Pr 13:24
a time to love and a time to **h**; ...Ec 3:8
H evil and love good;...........Am 5:15
I loved Jacob, but I **h-d** Esau.... Mal 1:3
If he **h-s** and divorces......... Mal 2:16
your neighbor and **h** your
   enemy........................Mt 5:43
do what is good to those who
   h you ....Lk 6:27
me and does not **h** his own
   father........................Lk 14:26
want to do, but I do what I **h**. ..Rm 7:15
loved Jacob, but I have **h-d**
   Esau.........................Rm 9:13

HATRED

not harbor **h** against your
   brother.......................Lv 19:17

HAY

stones, wood, **h**, or straw,......1Co 3:12

HEAD

will strike your **h**, and you will . . Gn 3:15
lay their hands on the bull's **h** . . Lv 4:15
You anoint my **h** with oil; . . . . Ps 23:5
will heap burning coals on
    his **h**, ... Pr 25:22
Man has no place to lay his **h** . . Mt 8:20
His **h** was brought on a platter . . Mt 14:11
Christ is the **h** of every man, and the
    man is the **h** of the woman, . . 1Co 11:3
her **h** uncovered dishonors
    her **h**, ... 1Co 11:5
husband is the **h** of the
    wife as . . . . Eph 5:23

HEAL

For I am the LORD who
    h-s you. . . . . Ex 15:26
their sin, and **h** their land. 2Ch 7:14
He **h-s** the brokenhearted . . . . . Ps 147:3
a time to kill and a time to **h**; . . . . Ec 3:3
and we are **h-ed** by his wounds. . Is 53:5
H the sick, raise the dead . . . . . . Mt 10:8
it lawful to **h** on the Sabbath? . . Mt 12:10
Doctor, **h** yourself. . . . . Lk 4:23
turn, and I would **h** them. . . . . . . Jn 12:40
so that you may be **h-ed**. . . . . . . Jms 5:16
By his wounds you have been
    h-ed. 1Pt 2:24

HEALING

will rise with **h** in its wings, . . . Mal 4:2
gifts of **h** by the one Spirit, ... 1Co 12:9
the tree are for **h** the nations, . . Rv 22:2

HEALTHY

The **h** don't need a doctor, ... Lk 5:31

HEAR

may you **h** in heaven and
    forgive. 1Kg 8:34
One who shaped the ear not **h**, . . Ps 94:9
with their eyes and **h** with
    their ears, ... Is 6:10
Have you not **h-d**? Has it not
    been . . . . Is 40:21
Dry bones, **h** the word of the
    LORD . . . . Ezk 37:4
You have **h-d** that it was said . . Mt 5:21
longed . . . to **h** the things
    you **h** . . . . Mt 13:17
Anyone who **h-s** my word and . Jn 5:24
My sheep **h** my voice, ... Jn 10:27
And how can they **h**
    without a . . . . Rm 10:14
So faith comes from
    what is **h-d**, ... Rm 10:17

no eye has seen, no ear has **h-d**, . . 1Co 2:9
according to his will, he **h-s** us. . . 1Jn 5:14
If anyone **h-s** my voice and
    opens . . . . Rv 3:20

HEARERS

For the **h** of the law are not . . . . Rm 2:13
of the word and not **h** only, . . . Jms 1:22

HEARING (N)

works of the law or by
    h with faith? . . . . Gl 3:2

HEART

I will harden his **h** so that he . . . . . . Ex 4:21
when you seek him with all
    your **h** . . . . Dt 4:29
LORD your God with all your **h**, . . Dt 6:5
found a man after his own **h** . . 1Sm 13:14
but the LORD sees the **h** 1Sm 16:7
meditation of my **h** be
    acceptable . . . . Ps 19:14
create a clean **h** for me and . . . . Ps 51:10
Your word in my **h** so that
    I may. . . . . Ps 119:11
Search me, God, and know
    my **h**; . . . . Ps 139:23
Trust in the LORD with all your **h**, . . Pr 3:5
The **h** is more deceitful than . . . . . . Jr 17:9
them and write it on their **h-s**. . Jr 31:33
I will give you a new **h** . . . . . . Ezk 36:26
Blessed are the pure in **h**, ... Mt 5:8
there your **h** will be also. . . . . . . Mt 6:21
the law is written on their
    h-s. . . . . Rm 2:15
and circumcision is of the **h** . . Rm 2:29
believe in your **h** that God
    raised. Rm 10:9
you do, do it from the **h**, as
    done . . . . Col 3:23

HEAVEN

God created the **h-s** and the
    earth. . . . . Gn 1:1
Most High, Creator of **h** and
    earth, ... Gn 14:19
h, the highest **h**, cannot
    contain 1Kg 8:27
When I observe your **h-s**, the
    work. . . . . Ps 8:3
The **h-s** declare the glory of
    God, ... Ps 19:1
Your faithful love reaches
    to **h**, ... Ps 36:5
Who do I have in **h** but you? . . Ps 73:25
Let the **h-s** be glad and the
    earth. Ps 96:11

For as high as the **h-s** are
    above . . . . Ps 103:11
time for every activity under **h**: . . Ec 3:1
create a new **h** and a new
    earth; . . . . Is 65:17
coming with the clouds of **h**. . . . Dn 7:13
the kingdom of **h** has come
    near! . . . . Mt 3:2
The **h-s** suddenly opened for
    him, ... Mt 3:16
for yourselves treasures in **h**, . . Mt 6:20
H and earth will pass away, . . . Mt 24:35
Who will go up to **h**? . . . . Rm 10:6
to the third **h** fourteen
    years ago. 2Co 12:2
but our citizenship is in **h**, ... Php 3:20
Christ did not enter a sanctuary . . .
    but into **h** itself, ... Heb 9:24
that day the **h-s** will pass
    away. 2Pt 3:10
I saw a new **h** and a new
    earth. . . . . Rv 21:1

HEAVENLY

and your **h** Father knows
    that you. . . . . Mt 6:32
a multitude of the **h** host with . . Lk 2:13
There are **h** bodies and
    earthly. 1Co 15:40
by God's **h** call in Christ. . . . . . . Php 3:14
who share in a **h** calling, ... Heb 3:1

HEBREW

came and told Abram the H, . . Gn 14:13
This is one of the H boys. . . . . Ex 2:6
LORD, the God of the H-s, ... Ex 3:18
He answered them, "I'm a H . . . . Jnh 1:9
of Benjamin, a H born of H-s; . . Php 3:5

HEEL

and you will strike his **h**. . . . . . . Gn 3:15
Esau's **h** with his hand. . . . . Gn 25:26
has raised his **h** against me. . . . . Ps 41:9
has raised his **h** against me. . . . Jn 13:18

HEIGHT

h nor depth, nor any other. . . . . Rm 8:39
length and width, **h** and
    depth . . . . Eph 3:18

HEIR SEE ALSO COHEIRS

born in my house will be my **h**. . Gn 15:3
if children, also **h-s**—**h-s** of
    God . . . . Rm 8:17
h-s according to the promise. . . Gl 3:29
then God has made you an **h**. . . . Gl 4:7

HELL *SEE ALSO* HADES, SHEOL

to have two hands and
   go to **h** .... Mk 9:43
authority to throw people
   into **h** ....Lk 12:5

HELMET

and a **h** of salvation on his
   head; ....Is 59:17
Take the **h** of salvation .... Eph 6:17

HELP (N)

He is our **h** and shield. .... Ps 33:20
Where will my **h** come from? .. Ps 121:1
gifts of healing, **h-ing**,
   administrating, ... 1Co 12:28

HELP (V)

LORD has **h-ed** us to this
   point. 1Sm 7:12
I do believe; **h** my unbelief! ... Mk 9:24
He is able to **h** those who are .. Heb 2:18

HELPER

I will make a **h** corresponding
   to him. .... Gn 2:18
You are a **h** of the fatherless.... Ps 10:14
a **h** who is always found in
   times .... Ps 46:1
Lord is my **h**; I will not be
   afraid. .... Heb 13:6

HELPLESS

For while we were still **h**, ...Rm 5:6

HEN

as a **h** gathers her chicks
   under .... Mt 23:37

HERALD

are the feet of the **h**, who
   proclaims .... Is 52:7

HERB

unleavened bread and
   bitter **h-s**. .... Ex 12:8

HERE

"**H** I am," he answered. .... Ex 3:4
ran to Eli and said, "**H** I am; 1Sm 3:5
I said: **H** I am. Send me. .... Is 6:8

HERITAGE

Sons are indeed a **h** from the
   LORD, ... Ps 127:3

HEROD

1. The Great; king in Judea at the time of
   Jesus's birth; executed male babies (Mt 2).
2. Archelaus; son of 1. (Mt 2:22).
3. Philip; son of 1. (Mk 6:17).
4. Antipas; son of 1.; tetrarch of Galilee;
   arrested and executed John the Baptist (Mt 14:1-12).
5. Agrippa I; grandson of 1.; persecuted
   the church; died when he didn't give
   glory to God (Ac 12).
6. Agrippa II; son of 5. (Ac 25:13). Heard
   Paul's defense (25:22–26:32).

HERODIAS

Wife of Herod Antipas, formerly of
Herod Philip; requested head of John the
Baptist (Mt 14:3-11; Mk 6:17-28; Lk 3:19).

HETHITES

Ancient people of the promised land
(Gn 10:15-18; 15:20; Jos 1:4); Abraham
lived among them (Gn 23); Esau married them (26:34; 27:46; 36:2). Formerly
lived in the hill country (Nm 13:29; Jos
9:1; 11:3; 12:8); dispossessed by Israel
(Ex 23:23; Dt 7:1; 20:17; Jos 3:10); some
remained (Jdg 3:5; 1Kg 9:20-21); fought
alongside Israel (1Sm 26:6).
H-s, Perizzites, Rephaim ...... Gn 15:20
and spoke to the H-s: .... Gn 23:20
daughter of Beeri the H. ...... Gn 26:34
wife of Uriah the H? 2Sm 11:3
and your mother a H. .... Ezk 16:3

HEZEKIAH

Son of Ahaz; king of Judah (2Kg 18–20;
2Ch 29–32; Is 36–39). Reformer (2Kg
18:4; 2Ch 29–31). Healed of fatal illness
(2Kg 20:1-11); showed treasuries to Babylonians (20:12-19).

HIDDEN (ADJ)

The **h** things belong to the
   LORD .... Dt 29:29
Cleanse me from my **h** faults... Ps 19:12
and nothing **h** that won't be
   made .... Mt 10:26

HIDE

they **hid** from the LORD .... Gn 3:8

she **hid** him for three months.... Ex 2:2
because she **hid** the messengers. Jos 6:17
h me in the shadow of your
   wings .... Ps 17:8
hid me in the shadow of his
   hand. .... Is 49:2
situated on a hill cannot be
   h-den. .... Mt 5:14
and went off and **hid** your
   talent .... Mt 25:25
your life is **h-den** with Christ... Col 3:3
Fall on us and **h** us from the ......Rv 6:16

HIDING (ADJ)

You are my **h** place; .... Ps 32:7

HIGH *SEE ALSO* HIGH PLACE, HIGH PRIEST, MOST HIGH

For as **h** as the heavens are ... Ps 103:11
took him to a very **h** mountain .. Mt 4:8

HIGH PLACE

people were sacrificing on the
   h-s, ... 1Kg 3:2
LORD at the **h** in Gibeon 1Ch 16:39
They enraged him with
   their **h-s** .... Ps 78:58

HIGH PRIEST

led him away to Caiaphas
   the **h**, ... Mt 26:57
become a merciful and
   faithful **h** .... Heb 2:17
this is the kind of **h** we need:.. Heb 7:26

HIGHER

so my ways are **h** than your
   ways, ... Is 55:9

HIGHLY

the LORD is great and is **h**
   praised; .... Ps 145:3
of himself more **h** than he
   should .... Rm 12:3

HIGHWAY

make a straight **h** for our
   God in .... Is 40:3
Go out into the **h-s** and
   hedges and .... Lk 14:23

HILL

the cattle on a thousand **h-s**. .. Ps 50:10

mountain and **h** will be leveled;. .Is 40:4
situated on a **h** cannot be
   hidden........................ Mt 5:14
mountain and **h** will be made
   low ....Lk 3:5
and to the **h-s**, 'Cover us!'......Lk 23:30

HINDER

your prayers will not be **h-ed**... 1Pt 3:7

HIP

He struck Jacob's **h** socket......Gn 32:25

HIRAM

1. King of Tyre; helped David build his palace and Solomon build the temple (2Sm 5:11; 2Kg 5). Manned Solomon's fleet (1Kg 9:27).
2. Craftsman; helped build the temple and its furnishings (1Kg 7:13-14); also called Huram (2Ch 4:11) or Huram-abi (2:13; 4:16).

HIRE

the morning to **h** workers for
   his .... Mt 20:1

HIRED (ADJ)

of my father's **h** workers have
   more.......................... Lk 15:17
he is a **h** hand and doesn't care..Jn 10:13

HIT

Who was it that **h** you? .... Lk 22:64

HITTITE

Ancient people from Asia Minor (modern Turkey) in contrast to the Hethites, who were Canaanites.
all the land of the **H-s** .... Jos 1:4
to all the kings of the **H-s** 1Kg 10:29
Solomon loved ... **H** women... 1Kg 11:1

HOLD

Your right hand **h-s** on to me....Ps 63:8
You **h** my right hand. ....Ps 73:23
Your heart must **h** on to my
   words............................Pr 4:4
I will **h** on to you with my ......Is 41:10
h-ing firm to the word of life.. Php 2:16
by him all things **h** together.... Col 1:17
test all things. **H** on to what is..1Th 5:21
take **h** of eternal life 1Tm 6:12

Let us **h** on to the
   confession of..............Heb 10:23

HOLIDAY

It is a **h** when they send gifts .. Est 9:19

HOLINESS

Who is like you, glorious in **h**,.. Ex 15:11
in the splendor of his **h** .. Pss 29:2; 96:9
so that we can share his **h**.... Heb 12:10

HOLY *SEE ALSO* HOLY PLACE, HOLY SPIRIT

you are standing is **h** ground. ...Ex 3:5
and be **h** because I am **h**........Lv 11:44
is no one **h** like the LORD. 1Sm 2:2
H, h, h is the LORD of............Is 6:3
who is my equal?" asks the
   H One. ....Is 40:25
So then, the law is **h**, and the .. Rm 7:12
and called us with a **h** calling,..2Tm 1:9
is written, Be **h**, because I am **h**. .1Pt 1:16
regard Christ the Lord as **h**......1Pt 3:15
H, h, h, Lord God, the ....Rv 4:8
I also saw the **h** city, new ......Rv 21:2

HOLY PLACE

between the **h** and the
   most **h**. ....Ex 26:33
enter the most **h** in this way: ...Lv 16:3
Then he made the most **h**;. 2Ch 3:8
Who may stand in his **h**? ....Ps 24:3
standing in the **h**" (let the
   reader ....Mt 24:15
entered the most **h** once for
   all...........................Heb 9:12

HOLY SPIRIT

Third person of the Trinity, through whom God acts, reveals his will, empowers individuals, and discloses his personal presence.
or take your **H** from me........ Ps 51:11
and grieved his **H**. ....: Is 63:10
baptize you with the **H** and fire.. Mt 3:11
speaks against the **H**, it will
   not......................... Mt 12:32
Father and of the Son and of
   the **H**, ... Mt 28:19
The **H** will come upon you......Lk 1:35
and the **H** descended on....... Lk 3:22
Father give the **H** to those who
   ask........................... Lk 11:13
the Counselor, the **H**,..........Jn 14:26
they were all filled with the **H** ..Ac 4:31
H had been poured out even on..Ac 10:45

forbidden by the **H** to speak......Ac 16:6
Did you receive the **H** when
   you ....Ac 19:2
your body is a temple of the **H**. .1Co 6:19
sealed with the promised **H**....Eph 1:13
don't grieve God's **H**,.........Eph 4:30
carried along by the **H**. 2Pt 1:21

HOME

God provides **h-s** for those who
   are............................Ps 68:6
sparrow finds a **h**, and a
   swallow ....Ps 84:3
Go back to your **h**, and tell all.. Lk 8:39
to him and make our **h** with
   him...........................Jn 14:23
is hungry, he should eat at **h**,..1Co 11:34
from the body and at **h** with
   the Lord..................... 2Co 5:8

HOMEOWNER

If the **h** had known what time
   the..........................Mt 24:43

HOMETOWN

not without honor except in
   his **h** .... Mt 13:57

HOMOSEXUAL

for the sexually immoral and
   h-s, ... 1Tm 1:10

HONEST

How painful **h** words can be!...Jb 6:25
word with an **h** and good heart,..Lk 8:15

HONEY

land flowing with milk and **h** ...Ex 3:8
What is sweeter than **h**?......Jdg 14:18
sweeter than **h** dripping
   from a .... Ps 19:10
It is not good to eat too
   much **h**......................Pr 25:27
his food was locusts and wild **h**. .Mt 3:4

HONOR (N)

crowned him with glory and **h**. . Ps 8:5
is not without **h** except in his.. Mt 13:57

HONOR (V)

H your father and your
   mother .... Ex 20:12
H the LORD with your possessions..Pr 3:9

your name be **h-ed** as holy. ...... Mt 6:9
H your father and your
mother; .... Mt 15:4
This people **h** me with their ... Mt 15:8
if one member is **h-ed**, all
the 1Co 12:26

HONORABLE

whatever is **h**, whatever is
just .... Php 4:8

HONORABLY

ourselves **h** in everything. ... Heb 13:18

HOPE (N)

where then is my **h**? Who
can see. .... Jb 17:15
Put your **h** in God, for I will ..... Ps 42:5
This **h** will not disappoint ...... Rm 5:5
Rejoice in **h**; be patient in ..... Rm 12:12
three remain: faith, **h**, and
love. 1Co 13:13
what is the **h** of his calling, ... Eph 1:18
Christ in you, the **h** of glory. ... Col 1:27
like the rest, who have no **h**. ... 1Th 4:13
a helmet of the **h** of salvation. ... 1Th 5:8
birth into a living **h** through 1Pt 1:3
reason for the **h** that is in you .. 1Pt 3:15
who has this **h** in him purifies. .. 1Jn 3:3

HOPE (V)

He kills me, I will **h** in him. ..... Jb 13:15
all things, **h-s** all things 1Co 13:7
the reality of what is **h-d** for, .. Heb 11:1

HORN

caught in the thicket by its
h-s. .... Gn 22:13
My shield, the **h** of my
salvation. 2Sm 22:3
and it had ten **h-s**. .... Dn 7:7
has raised up a **h** of salvation. ... Lk 1:69

HORSE

has thrown the **h** and its
rider into. .... Ex 15:1
chariots, and others in **h-s**, but
we .... Ps 20:7
The **h** is a false hope for safety .. Ps 33:17
and there was a white **h**. .... Rv 6:2
and there was a white **h**. .... Rv 19:11

HOSANNA

H in the highest heaven! .... Mt 21:9

HOSEA

Prophet in Israel near the end of the
kingdom; his marriage modeled God's
love and Israel's unfaithfulness (Hs
1–3).

HOSHEA

Son of Elah; last king of Israel (2Kg
15:30; 17:1-6).

HOSPITABLE

respectable, **h**, able to teach, ... 1Tm 3:2
Be **h** to one another without. 1Pt 4:9

HOSPITALITY

in their needs; pursue **h**. ...... Rm 12:13
neglect to show **h**, for by
doing .... Heb 13:2

HOST

of the heavenly **h** with the
angel. .... Lk 2:13

HOSTILE

mind-set of the flesh is **h** to
God .... Rm 8:7

HOSTILITY

I will put **h** between you and
the .... Gn 3:15
down the dividing wall of **h**. ... Eph 2:14
who endured such **h** from
sinners .... Heb 12:3
with the world is **h** toward
God? .... Jms 4:4

HOT

you are neither cold nor **h**. ...... Rv 3:15

HOT-TEMPERED

not **h**, not an excessive drinker, .. Ti 1:7

HOUR

that day and **h** no one knows .. Mt 24:36
But an **h** is coming, and is now .. Jn 4:23
The **h** has come for the Son of .. Jn 12:23
Father, the **h** has come. .... Jn 17:1
keep you from the **h** of testing .. Rv 3:10

HOUSE

dwell in the **h** of the LORD as. ... Ps 23:6

zeal for your **h** has consumed
me, ... Ps 69:9
Unless the LORD builds a **h**, ... Ps 127:1
Wisdom has built her **h**; .... Pr 9:1
for my **h** will be called a **h** of
prayer .... Is 56:7
who built his **h** on the rock. ... Mt 7:24
And everyone who has left
h-s, ... Mt 19:29
My **h** will be called a **h** of
prayer. .... Mt 21:13
he was of the **h** and family line .. Lk 2:4
my Father's **h** into a
marketplace. .... Jn 2:16
In my Father's **h** are many ...... Jn 14:2
builder has more honor
than the **h**. .... Heb 3:3
a spiritual **h**, are being built ... 1Pt 2:5

HOUSEHOLD

will be the members of his **h**. .. Mt 10:36
believed, along with his
whole **h**. .... Jn 4:53
believe God with his entire **h**. .. Ac 16:34
manages his own **h** competently .. 1Tm 3:4

HULDAH

Wife of Shallum; prophetess in Josiah's time (2Kg 22:14).

HUMAN

heaven on the **h** race to see if. .. Ps 14:2
Even **h** wrath will praise you; .. Ps 76:10
I led them with **h** cords, with ... Hs 11:4
is he served by **h** hands, ... Ac 17:25
not depend on **h** will or effort. Rm 9:16
is wiser than **h** wisdom, ... 1Co 1:25
is one flesh for **h-s**, another
for 1Co 15:39

HUMANITY

and all **h** together will see it. ..... Is 40:5
pour out my Spirit on all **h**; ..... Jl 2:28
you except what is common
to **h**. 1Co 10:13
between God and **h**, Jesus
Christ, ... 1Tm 2:5

HUMBLE (ADJ)

Moses was a very **h** man, ... Nm 12:3
He leads the **h** in what is right .. Ps 25:9
but gives grace to the **h**. ...... Pr 3:34
h and riding on a donkey, ... Zch 9:9
Blessed are the **h**, for they
I am lowly and **h** in heart, ... Mt 11:29
but gives grace to the **h**. .... Jms 4:6

HUMBLE (V)

that he might **h** you and test
  you . . . . Dt 8:2
despise a broken and **h-d**
  heart. . . . . Ps 51:17
whoever **h-s** himself like this
  child . . . . Mt 18:4
who exalts himself will be **h-d**, . . Lk 14:11
he **h-d** himself by becoming. . . Php 2:8
H yourselves before the Lord, . . Jms 4:10
H yourselves, therefore, under
  the 1Pt 5:6

HUMBLY

and to walk **h** with your God. . . . Mc 6:8

HUMILIATION

In his **h** justice was denied
  him. . . . . Ac 8:33

HUMILITY

and **h** comes before honor. . . . . . Pr 15:33
but in **h** consider others as
  more. . . . . Php 2:3
clothe yourselves with **h**
  toward one 1Pt 5:5

HUNGER

Those who **h** . . . for
  righteousness . . . . Mt 5:6
They will no longer **h**; . . . . Rv 7:16

HUNGRY

If I were **h**, I would not tell. . . . . Ps 50:12
and giving food to the **h**. . . . . . . Ps 146:7
your enemy is **h**, give him food. . Pr 25:21
days and forty nights, he was **h**. . . . Mt 4:2
For I was **h** and you gave me . . . Mt 25:35
Blessed are you who are now **h**, . . Lk 6:21
who comes to me will ever
  be **h**, ... Jn 6:35
If your enemy is **h**, feed him. . . Rm 12:20

HURAM *SEE* HIRAM

HURAM-ABI *SEE* HIRAM

HURRY

You are to eat it in a **h**; . . . . Ex 12:11

HURT

sister is **h** by what you eat. . . . . . Rm 14:15

HUSBAND

Your desire will be for your **h**, . . Gn 3:16
"Go call your **h**," he told her, ... Jn 4:16
you've had five **h-s**, and the man you
  now have is not your **h**. . . . . . . Jn 4:18
A **h** should fulfill his marital . . . 1Co 7:3
for the **h** is the head of the
  wife. . . . . Eph 5:23
H-s, love your wives, just as . . Eph 5:25
the **h** of one wife, ... 1Tm 3:2
encourage... women to love
  their **h-s** . . . . Ti 2:4
H-s, in the same way, live with. . 1Pt 3:7

HUSHAI

David's friend and spy in Absalom's
court (2Sm 15:32–17:15).

HYMN

praying and singing **h-s** to
  God, ... Ac 16:25
in psalms, **h-s**, and spiritual . . Eph 5:19
psalms, **h-s**, and spiritual
  songs . . . . Col 3:16

HYPOCRISY

are full of **h** and
  lawlessness. . . . . Mt 23:28
Let love be without **h**. . . . . Rm 12:9

HYPOCRITE

you must not be like the **h-s**, ... Mt 6:5
H! First take the beam of wood . . Mt 7:5
scribes and Pharisees, **h-s**! . . . . . . Mt 23:13

HYSSOP

Purify me with **h**, and I will be. . Ps 51:7

I

I AM

I WHO I. . . . . Ex 3:14
I the first and I the last. There is
  no. . . . . Is 44:6
"I," said Jesus, ... Mk 14:62
"I . . . am he" . . . . Jn 4:26
Before Abraham was, I. . . . . Jn 8:58
"I he," Jesus told them . . . . Jn 18:6

IDLE

warn those who are **i**,
  comfort. 1Th 5:14

IDOL

Do not make an **i** for yourself, . . Ex 20:4
Their **i-s** are silver and gold, . . . Ps 115:4
incense, another praises
  an **i**— . . . . Is 66:3
abstain from food offered to
  i-s, ... Ac 15:29
about food sacrificed to **i-s**: 1Co 8:1
we know that "an **i** is nothing . . 1Co 8:4

IDOLATRY

my dear friends, flee from **i**. . 1Co 10:14
i, sorcery, hatreds, strife, ... Gl 5:20
desire, and greed, which is **i**. . . . Col 3:5

IGNORANCE

overlooked the times of **i**, ... Ac 17:30
silence the **i** of foolish people . . 1Pt 2:15

IGNORANT

reject foolish and **i** disputes, . . 2Tm 2:23
those who are **i** and are going . . Heb 5:2

ILLEGITIMATE

then you are **i** children
  and not . . . . Heb 12:8

ILLNESSES

stomach and your frequent **i**. . 1Tm 5:23

ILLUMINATE

my God **i-s** my darkness. . . . . Ps 18:28

IMAGE

Let us make man in our **i**, ... Gn 1:26
Whose **i** and inscription
  is this? . . . . Mt 22:20
he is the **i** and glory of God, ... 1Co 11:7
He is the **i** of the invisible God, . . Col 1:15
an **i** of the beast . . . . Rv 13:14

IMITATE

I urge you to **i** of me. 1Co 4:16
I me, as I also **i** Christ. 1Co 11:1
of their lives, **i** their faith. . . . . . Heb 13:7
do not **i** what is evil,
  but what is. 3Jn 11

IMITATORS

Therefore, be **i** of God, as . . . . . . Eph 5:1
but will be **i** of those
  who inherit. . . . . Heb 6:12

IMMANUEL

have a son, and name him I......Is 7:14
they will name him I,
   which is ....Mt 1:23

IMMORAL

associate with sexually i
   people 1Co 5:9
No sexually i people, idolaters,..1Co 6:9
Every sexually i or impure or..Eph 5:5
there isn't any i or
   irreverent ....Heb 12:16
murderers, sexually i,
   sorcerers ....Rv 21:8

IMMORALITY

except in a case of sexual i,.....Mt 5:32
except for sexual i, and
   marries.....................Mt 19:9
We weren't born of sexual i,......Jn 8:41
abstain...from sexual i,.....Ac 15:20
The body is not for sexual i
   but for 1Co 6:13
Flee sexual i! Every other sin..1Co 6:18
Let us not commit sexual i as
   some.......................1Co 10:8
But sexual i and any impurity
   or ....Eph 5:3
that you keep away from
   sexual i,......................1Th 4:3

IMMORTAL

glory of the i God for images..Rm 1:23
the King eternal, i, invisible......1Tm 1:17

IMMORTALITY

body must be clothed with i...1Co 15:53
the only One who has i,
   dwelling 1Tm 6:16
brought life and i to light.....2Tm 1:10

IMPERISHABLE

into an inheritance that is i,......1Pt 1:4

IMPLANTED

humbly receive the i word, ...Jms 1:21

IMPORTANT

have neglected the more i
   matters ....Mt 23:23
on to you as most i what I
   also 1Co 15:3
others as more i than
   yourselves..................Php 2:3

IMPOSSIBLE

Is anything i for the LORD?....Gn 18:14
It is i for God to do wrong,......Jb 34:10
Nothing will be i for you.......Mt 17:20
With man this is i, but with
   God ....Mt 19:26

IMPRISONED

For God has i all in
   disobedience,...............Rm 11:32
Scripture i everything under ...Gl 3:22

IMPURE

immoral or i or greedy
   person, ...Eph 5:5

IMPURITY

cleanse you from all
   your i-ies ....Ezk 36:25
as slaves to moral i,............Rm 6:19
and any i or greed should......Eph 5:3

INCALCULABLE

to the Gentiles the i riches of..Eph 3:8

INCENSE

an altar for the burning of i;......Ex 30:1
prayer be set before you as i, ..Ps 141:2

INCITED

against Israel and i David to
   count 1Ch 21:1

INCORRUPTIBLE

and the dead will be
   raised i,...................1Co 15:52

INCORRUPTION

Sown in corruption,
   raised in i; 1Co 15:42

INCREASE

If wealth i-s, don't set your
   heart on it...................Ps 62:10
said to the Lord, "I our faith."...Lk 17:5
He must i, but I must
   decrease. ....Jn 3:30

INDICATING

Christ within them was i
   when he 1Pt 1:11

INEXPRESSIBLE

heard i words, which a human being
   is not allowed to speak.....2Co 12:4
rejoice with i and glorious joy...1Pt 1:8

INFANT

mouths of i-s and nursing babies,..Ps 8:2
mouths of i-s and nursing
   babies? ....Mt 21:16
Like newborn i-s, desire the 1Pt 2:2

INFERIOR

myself in no way i to those
   "super-apostles".............2Co 11:5
the i is blessed by the superior. . Heb 7:7

INFINITE

His understanding is i..........Ps 147:5

INFLATE

Such people are i-d by empty..Col 2:18

INHERIT

You will i their land, since I ...Lv 20:24
the humble will i the land.......Ps 37:11
his household will i the wind,..Pr 11:29
blameless will i what is good. .Pr 28:10
humble, for they will i the earth..Mt 5:5
must I do to i eternal
   life?....................Lk 10:25; 18:18
will not i God's kingdom? 1Co 6:9

INHERITANCE

to be a people for his i,..........Dt 4:20
Levi has no i among his brothers, the
   LORD is his i,....................Dt 18:2
In him we have also received
   an i,...........................Eph 1:11
and into an i that is
   imperishable,..................1Pt 1:4

INIQUITY

you and did not conceal my i. ..Ps 32:5
crushed because of our i-ies;... Is 53:5
punished him for the i of us all..Is 53:6

INJURY

born prematurely but there is
   no i,.........................Ex 21:22

INJUSTICE

Is there i with God?...........Rm 9:14

INK

don't want to use paper and i. . . .2Jn 12

INN

him to an i, and took care. . . . . Lk 10:34

INNER

our i person is being renewed. .2Co 4:16
strengthened . . . in the i being. .Eph 3:16

INNKEEPER

two denarii, gave them to
   the i, ... Lk 10:35

INNOCENCE

wash my hands in i and go
   around . . . . .Ps 26:6
will they be incapable of i? . . . . . .Hs 8:5

INNOCENT

hands that shed i blood, ... Pr 6:17
as serpents and as i as doves. . Mt 10:16
sinned by betraying i blood, . . . Mt 27:4

INSANE

pretended to be i in their 1Sm 21:13

INSCRIBE

tablets i-d by the finger of
   God. . . . . .Ex 31:18
I have i-d you on the palms
   of my . . . . Is 49:16

INSCRIPTION

but none could read the i . . . . . . Dn 5:8
Whose image and i is this? . . .Mt 22:20

INSENSITIVITY

God gave them a spirit of i, ... Rm 11:8

INSIGHT

A man is praised for his i, ...Pr 12:8
to understand my i into the. . . . Eph 3:4

INSIST

I i on paying the full price, . . . 1Ch 21:24

INSPIRED

then that David, i by the Spirit . .Mt 22:43

All Scripture is i by God
   and is 2Tm 3:16

INSTALL

I have i-d my king on Zion, ...Ps 2:6

INSTITUTED

those that exist are i by God.. . . Rm 13:1

INSTRUCT

Your good Spirit to i them. . . . .Neh 9:20
I will i you and show you the . . .Ps 32:8
a wise person i-s its mouth; . . .Pr 16:23

INSTRUCTION

This book of i must not depart . Jos 1:8
his delight is in the LORD's i, ... Ps 1:2
The i of the LORD is perfect, ...Ps 19:7
see wondrous things from
   your i. . . . . Ps 119:18
but I delight in your i. . . . . Ps 119:70
Listen, my son, to your father's i, . . Pr 1:8
Listen to i and be wise; . . . . .Pr 8:33
who follows divine i will be
   happy. . . . . .Pr 29:18
For i will go out of Zion and . . . . . .Is 2:3
For i will go out of Zion and . . . .Mc 4:2
in the past was written for o
   ur i, ...Rm 15:4
were written for our i, ...1Co 10:11
the goal of our i is love. 1Tm 1:5

INSTRUCTOR

may have countless i-s in
   Christ, ...1Co 4:15

INSULT (N)

whoever ignores an i is
   sensible. Pr 12:16
there began to yell i-s at
   him:. . . . . Lk 23:39

INSULT (V)

of those who i you have fallen. .Ps 69:9
who mocks the poor i-s his
   Maker, ... Pr 17:5
blessed when they i you and. . . . . .Mt 5:11
of those who i you have fallen. . Rm 15:3
he was i-ed, but he did not I 1Pt 2:23

INTEGRITY

if you walk before me . . .
   with . . . i 1Kg 9:4

He still retains his i, even
   though you . . . . Jb 2:3
You desire i in the inner self . . . . Ps 51:6
The i of the upright guides
   them, ... Pr 11:3
with i and dignity in your
   teaching.. . . . . .Ti 2:7

INTELLIGENT

The woman was i and
   beautiful, ...1Sm 25:3

INTENSIFY

I will i your labor pains; . . . . Gn 3:16

INTENTION

and reveal the i-s of the
   hearts. 1Co 4:5

INTERCEDE

But Moses i-d with the
   LORD his . . . . .Ex 32:11
sins against the LORD, who
   can i 1Sm 2:25
sin of many and i-d for the
   rebels. . . . . Is 53:12
the Spirit himself i-s for us
   with . . . . Rm 8:26
He always lives to i for them. . Heb 7:25

INTERCESSION

perseverance and i for all the. . Eph 6:18
prayers, i-s, and thanksgivings . .1Tm 2:1

INTERCOURSE

has sexual i with an animal . . Ex 22:19
You are not to have sexual i
   with . . . . .Lv 18:9

INTEREST

you must not charge him i. . . . Ex 22:25
You may charge a foreigner i, . . .Dt 23:20
who does not lend his silver at i . .Ps 15:5
received my money back
   with i. . . . . .Mt 25:27
not only for his own i-s, but
   also . . . . .Php 2:4
has an unhealthy i in disputes. .1Tm 6:4

INTERMARRY

I with us; give your daughters . . Gn 34:9
You must not i with them, ...Dt 7:3
and i with the peoples who. . . .Ezr 9:14

INTERPRET

a dream, and no one can i it... Gn 41:15
and the ability to i dreams,......Dn 5:12
in other tongues? Do all i? ... 1Co 12:30
unless he i-s so that the
  church.......................1Co 14:5
and let someone i. 1Co 14:27

INTERPRETATION

Don't i-s belong to God? ....Gn 40:8
tell me the dream and its i, ... Dn 2:5
inscription and give me its i, .. Dn 5:16
to another, i of tongues. 1Co 12:10
from the prophet's own i, ...2Pt 1:20

INTERPRETER

But if there is no i, that
  person......................1Co 14:28

INTIMATE

The man was i with his wife
  Eve, ...Gn 4:1

INVADE

king of Assyria i-d the whole
  land, ...2Kg 17:5
For a nation has i-d my land, ... Jl 1:6

INVALIDATE

fine way of i-ing God's
  command ....Mk 7:9

INVESTIGATE

glory of kings to i a matter.......Pr 25:2
I have carefully i-d everything......Lk 1:3

INVISIBLE

His i attributes, that is, his .....Rm 1:20
He is the image of the i
  God,.........................Col 1:15
immortal, i, the only God,......1Tm 1:17

INVITE

Then i Jesse to the sacrifice, .. 1Sm 16:3
For many are i-d, but
  few are ....Mt 22:14
a banquet, i those who are
  poor,.........................Lk 14:13

INWARD

was you who created my i
  parts; ....Ps 139:13

INWARDLY

a person is a Jew who is one i,..Rm 2:29

IRON

it there, and made the i float.......2Kg 6:6
break them with an i scepter;..... Ps 2:9
I sharpens i, and one man...... Pr 27:17
legs were i, ... feet were partly i
  and ....Dn 2:33

IRREVERENT

the unholy and i, for those who ..1Tm 1:9

IRREVOCABLE

gracious gifts and calling
  are i. ....Rm 11:29

ISAAC

Son of Abraham and Sarah; fulfillment of a promise (Gn 17:17; 21:5). God tested Abraham by asking him to sacrifice Isaac (Gn 22; Heb 11:17-19). Married Rebekah (Gn 24). Heir to Abraham's promise (Gn 25:5,11; Ps 105:9; Rm 9:7). Father of Esau and Jacob (Gn 25:21-26); blessed Jacob (Gn 27). Lied to Abimelech in Gerar about Rebekah (26:7-11). Died in Hebron (35:27-29).

ISAIAH

Son of Amoz; prophet to four kings of Judah (Is 1:1). Called (Is 6). Sons' names were symbolic (7:3; 8:3).

ISH-BOSHETH

Saul's son; tried to become king (2Sm 2:8-17; 3:6-16); was murdered (2Sm 4).

ISHMAEL

Son of Abraham and Hagar (Gn 16:11-15). Received a blessing but not the promise (17:18-21). Descendants are perpetual opponents of Israel (25:18).

ISLAND

the many coasts and i-s be glad...Ps 97:1

ISRAEL

Name God gave Jacob (Gn 32:28; 35:10). Also his descendants—God's chosen people—and their land (Ex 3:16; 1Sm 13:19; 15:35; 1Kg 4:1; Mt 2:6,20; Php 3:5).

In the divided kingdom, the northern (1Kg 12:20).

ISRAELITE

about him, "Here truly is an I ... Jn 1:47
They are I-s, and to them
  belong ....Rm 9:4
For I too am an I, a descendant ..Rm 11:1
Are they I-s? So am I.......... 2Co 11:22

ISSACHAR

Son of Jacob and Leah (Gn 30:18). Tribe with territory from Jezreel to Tabor (Jos 19:17-23); its troops who rallied to David understood the times (1Ch 12:32).

ITCH

have an i to hear what they
  want.........................2Tm 4:3

ITHAMAR

Fourth son of Aaron (Ex 6:23; 28:1; Nm 26:20; 1Ch 6:3; 24:1); took over priesthood when their brothers died (Lv 10:6,12,16; Nm 3:4; 1Ch 24:2); in charge of the Levites (Ex 38:21; Nm 4:28,33; 7:8).

IVORY

from i palaces harps bring you..Ps 45:8
lie on beds inlaid with i, ...Am 6:4

J

JABEZ

Israelite who asked for and received a blessing (1Ch 4:9-10).

JABIN

A king of Canaan, whose commander Sisera was defeated by Israel (Jdg 4–5).

JACOB

Son of Isaac and Rebekah; younger twin brother of Esau (Gn 25:21-26). Took birthright (25:33); fled Esau (27:41–28:5). Received the promise (28:10-22). Worked for his wives (29:1-30). Wrestled with God (32:22-32); God changed his name to Israel (32:28; 49:2). Reconciled with Esau (33:4-16). Fathered the twelve tribes (29:21–30:24; 35:16-18).

Went to Egypt (46:1-7). Died there, buried in Hebron (49:29–50:14). Ancestor of Jesus (Mt 1:2).

Even so, I loved J, ...Mal 1:2
J-'s well was there, and Jesus....Jn 4:6
J I have loved, but Esau I have..Rm 9:13

JAIRUS

Synagogue leader whose daughter Jesus restored (Mk 5:22-43; Lk 8:41-56).

JAMES

1. Apostle; son of Zebedee; brother of John (Mt 4:21; 10:2). At transfiguration (17:1); in Gethsemane (26:36-37). Martyred (Ac 12:2).
2. Apostle; son of Alphaeus (Mt 10:3).
3. Brother of Jesus (Mt 13:55; Gl 1:19). Believed after the resurrection (Jn 7:3; Ac 1:14; 1Co 15:7). Leader of church in Jerusalem (Ac 15; 21:18; Gl 2:9). Author (Jms 1:1).

JAPHETH

Son of Noah (Gn 5:32; 9:18-27).

JAR

in the house except a j of oil......2Kg 4:2
an alabaster j of very
    expensive...................Mk 14:3
an alabaster j of perfume.......Lk 7:37
have this treasure in clay j-s, ..2Co 4:7

JAWBONE

He found a fresh j of a
    donkey,....................Jdg 15:15

JEALOUS

His brothers were j of him,......Gn 37:11
Lord your God, am a j God,......Ex 20:5
another God. He is a j God......Ex 34:14
is a consuming fire, a j God......Dt 4:24
and I will be j for my holy
    name ....Ezk 39:25
I will make you j of those
    who.......................Rm 10:19
For I am j for you with a godly..2Co 11:2

JEALOUSY

provoked his j with different
    gods ....Dt 32:16
For j enrages a husband,
    and he ....Pr 6:34
hatreds, strife, j, outbursts of ...Gl 5:20

JEBUSITES

Descendants of Canaan (Gn 10:16; 15:21; Ex 3:8; Dt 7:1; 20:17), inhabitants of Jebus (1Ch 11:4). Defeated by Judah and Benjamin, but not dispossessed (Jos 15:63; Jdg 1:8,21; 3:5); defeated by David (2Sm 5:6-9) and enslaved by Solomon (1Kg 9:20-21).

JEHOAHAZ

1. Son of Jehu; king of Israel (2Kg 13:1-9).
2. Son of Josiah; king of Judah (2Kg 23:30-34). Called Shallum (Jr 22:11).

JEHOASH

1. Alternate name of Joash son of Ahaziah, king of Judah (2Kg 12).
2. Son of Jehoahaz; king of Israel (2Kg 13:10–14:13).

JEHOIACHIN

Son of Jehoiakim; king of Judah (2Kg 24:6). Also called Jeconiah or Coniah (Jr 22:24; 24:1). Exiled (2Kg 24:10-17) but later favored (25:27-30).

JEHOIAKIM

Son of Josiah; king of Judah. Succeeded his brother Jehoahaz; name changed from Eliakim by Neco (2Kg 23:34). Burned Jeremiah's scroll (Jr 36). Became vassal of Babylon; later rebelled and was defeated (2Kg 24:1-6; Dn 1:2).

JEHORAM

1. Alternate form of Joram, son of Ahab; king of Israel (2Kg 3:1).
2. Son of Jehoshaphat; king of Judah (2Kg 8:16-24; 2Ch 21). Ahab's son-in-law (2Kg 8:18). Edom gained independence during his reign (8:20).

JEHOSHAPHAT

1. Son of Asa; king of Judah (1Kg 15:24). Initially faithful, strong, blessed (2Ch 17). Then married Ahab's daughter Athaliah and formed alliances with Ahab and Joram, kings of Israel (1Kg 22; 2Kg 3; 8:26; 2Ch 18; 20).
2. Valley of judgment (Jl 3:2,12).

JEHU

1. Son of Hanani; prophet against Baasha king of Israel (1Kg 16:1-12).

2. Son of Jehoshaphat; king of Israel. Anointed by Elisha's servant; executed Ahaziah king of Judah, Joram, Jezebel and the house of Ahab in Israel, and the worshipers of Baal (2Kg 9–10; cp. 1Kg 19:16-17).

JEPHTHAH

Gileadite judge who made rash vow affecting his daughter (Jdg 11–12; 1Sm 12:11; Heb 11:32).

JEREMIAH

Prophet to Judah in the time leading up to the exile (Jr 1:1-3). Put in stocks (20:1-3), threatened (Jr 26), opposed (Jr 28), imprisoned (32:2; 37), censured (Jr 36), and thrown into a cistern (Jr 38). Taken to Egypt against his will (Jr 43).

JERICHO

City near the Jordan River north of the Dead Sea (Nm 22:1). Spied out (Jos 2) and conquered (Jos 6; Heb 11:30) by Joshua; rebuilt by Hiel (1Kg 16:34). Visited by Jesus (Mt 20:29-34; Mk 10:46-52; Lk 18:35; 19:1-10).

JEROBOAM

1. Son of Nebat; Solomon's servant; rebelled; first king of Israel (1Kg 11:26–12:20). Judged for notorious idolatry (12:25–14:20).
2. Son of Joash, king of Israel (2Kg 14:23-29).

JERUSALEM

Formerly called Salem (Gn 14:18; Ps 76:2) or Jebus (Jos 18:28); 1Ch 11:4. David conquered it and made it his capital (2Sm 5:5-9); Solomon built temple, palace, and fortifications (1Kg 3:1). Conquered by Babylon (2Kg 24:10-12). Rebuilt and resettled after the exile (Ezr 1; Neh 12:27). Jesus visited (Mt 21:1; Jn 2:13); mourned (Mt 23:37). Important city in early church (Ac 15:4). New Jerusalem promised (Rv 3:12; 21:2,10).

in J he reigned thirty-three
    years........................2Sm 5:5
J, the city I chose for myself
    to put my name there.......1Kg 11:36
For a remnant will go out
    from J, ... 2Kg 19:31
Pray for the well-being of J:......Ps 122:6
If I forget you, J, may my right ..Ps 137:5

Speak tenderly to J, and
announce......................Is 40:2
From...rebuild J until an
Anointed ....Dn 9:25
J! J that kills the prophets
and ....Mt 23:37
say that the place to worship is
in J...........................Jn 4:20
you will be my witnesses in J,
in all.........................Ac 1:8
holy city, the new J, coming
down ....Rv 21:2

JESHUA

Son of Jozadak; high priest; returned with Zerubbabel (Ezr 3:2; Neh 7:7).

JESSE

David's father (Ru 4:17-22; 1Sm 16; 1Ch 2:12-16; Mt 1:5-6; Lk 3:32).

JESUS

Messiah and Lord (Ac 2:36; Eph 3:11; 1Pt 3:15). Born in Bethlehem (Mt 1:18-25; Lk 2:1-7) to a virgin, Mary (Mt 1:20; Lk 1:26-38). Genealogy (Mt 1:1-17; Lk 3:23-38). Raised in Nazareth (Mt 2:19-23; Lk 2:39-40). Visited the temple at age 12 (Lk 2:41-50).

Baptized by John (Mt 3:13-17; Lk 3:21). Tempted in the wilderness (Mt 4:1-11; Lk 4:1-13). Chose apostles (Lk 5:1-11,27-28; 6:12-16; Jn 1:35-51).

Transformation (Mt 17:1-9; Mk 9:2-10). Triumphal entry into Jerusalem (Mt 21:1-11; Lk 19:28-40). Betrayal and arrest (Mt 26:17-25,47-56; Mk 14:17-21,43-50; Lk 22:1-6,47-54), trial (Mt 26:57-66; 27:11-31; Mk 14:53-65; 15:1-20; Lk 22:66-23:25), crucifixion (Mt 27:32-56; Mk 15:21-39; Lk 23:32-49), and resurrection (Mt 28; Mk 16; Lk 24; Jn 20-21).

JETHRO

Priest of Midian; Moses's father-in-law and adviser (Ex 3:1; 4:18; 18). Also called Reuel (2:18).

JEW

He planned to destroy
all...the J-s,....................Est 3:6
has been born king of the J-s?.. Mt 2:2
Are you the king of the J-s?....Mt 27:11
How is it that you, a J, ask for a ..Jn 4:9
salvation is from the J-s.........Jn 4:22
first to the J, and also to the ...Rm 1:16

a person is a J who is one
inwardly, ...Rm 2:29
the God of J-s only? Is
he not. ....Rm 3:29
To the J-s I became like a J,.......1Co 9:20
There is no J or Greek,
slave or ....Gl 3:28

JEWEL

She is far more precious than
j-s. ....Pr 3:15

JEZEBEL

Wife of King Ahab of Israel, daughter of the king of Sidon; brought Baal worship to Israel (1Kg 16:31-33). Killed prophets and threatened Elijah (18:4,13; 19:1-2). Killed by Jehu (2Kg 9:30-37) in fulfillment of prophecy (1Kg 21). Name used as a label (Rv 2:20).

JOAB

Son of Zeruiah; David's nephew and commander of his troops (1Ch 2:16; 11:6). Killed Abner (2Sm 3:22-39), Absalom (2Sm 18), Amasa, and Sheba (2Sm 20). Sided with Adonijah (1Kg 1:7,19); David told Solomon to execute him (2:5-6,28-35).

JOASH

1. Son of Ahaziah; king of Judah (2Kg 12). Protected by Jehoiada (2Kg 11). Repaired temple (2Ch 24:4-14).
2. Alternate name of Jehoash son of Jehoahaz, king of Israel (2Kg 13:10).

JOB

Wealthy patriarch. His book tells of his testing (Jb 1-2), perseverance (Jb 3-37), rebuke (Jb 38-41), and vindication (Jb 42; Jms 5:11).

JOEL

1. Dishonest son of Samuel (2Sm 8:2).
2. Son of Pethuel; prophet who urged priests to call Judah to repentance; depicted calamities (Jl 1:1-2:11); predicted the Messiah (2:21-32; Ac 2:16).

JOHANAN

Commander; stayed in Judah and tried to protect Gedaliah (2Kg 25:23); forced Jeremiah to go to Egypt (Jr 40-43).

JOHN

1. The baptizer; Son of Zechariah; prophet. Annunciation and birth (Lk 1:5-25,57-66). Preached repentance, announced the coming Messiah (Mt 3:1-12; Mk 1:1-8; Lk 3:1-18; 7:27-28), and baptized Jesus (Mt 3:13-15; Mk 1:9; Lk 3:21-22). Fulfilled the role of Elijah (Mt 11:13-14; 17:12-13; Mk 9:12-13; Mt 3:4 cp. 2Kg 1:8). Asked Jesus to verify his identity (Mt 11:2-6; Lk 7:18-23). Beheaded by Herod Antipas (Mt 14:1-12; Mk 6:14-29; Lk 3:19-20; 9:7-9).
2. Apostle; Son of Zebedee; brother of James. Call (Mt 4:21-22; Mk 1:19-20). Among the inner three at special occasions (Mk 9:2; 14:32-33). With James, called "Sons of Thunder" (Mk 3:17); asked for places of honor (Mk 10:35-41). Often with Peter (Ac 1:13; 3:1-11; 4:13-20; 8:14); a leader in Jerusalem (Gl 2:9). In his gospel, called the disciple Jesus loved (Jn 13:23; 19:26; 20:2; 21:7,20); also wrote three letters and Revelation.
3. John Mark see MARK

JOIN

to house and j field to field ....Is 5:8
Then j them together into a...Ezk 37:17
what God has j-ed together,......Mt 19:6

JOINTS

soul and spirit, j and marrow...Heb 4:12

JOKING

or crude j are not suitable......Eph 5:4

JONAH

Son of Amittai; prophet at the time of Jeroboam II (2Kg 14:23-27). Rejected God's call to preach in Nineveh; swallowed by a great fish (Jnh 1). Prayed (Jnh 2); preached repentance in Nineveh (Jnh 3); scolded by God for his anger (Jnh 4). Used as an example (Mt 12:39-41; 16:4; Lk 11:29-32).

JONATHAN

Son of Saul; friend of David (1Sm 18:1-4; 19:1-7; 20; 23:16-18). Killed in battle (31:1-13); mourned by David (2Sm 1:17-27).

JORAM

1. Son of Ahab; king of Israel (2Kg 3). Succeeded his brother Ahaziah

(1:17). Attacked Moab with the help of Judah, Edom, and Elisha (3:4-27). Wounded by Arameans (8:28); killed by Jehu (9:14-26).
2. Alternate form of Jehoram, son of Jehoshaphat; king of Judah (2Kg 8:16-24; 2Ch 21).

JORDAN

Lot chose the entire plain of J. . Gn 13:11
the border will go down to
the J . . . . Nm 34:12
dry ground in the middle of
the J, ... Jos 3:17
himself in the J seven times,. . 2Kg 5:14
Jesus came . . . to John at the J, . .Mt 3:13

JOSEPH

1. Son of Jacob and Rachel. Sold into slavery in Egypt (Gn 37); imprisoned on false accusations (Gn 39); became Pharaoh's second in command (41:39-45); sold grain to brothers (Gn 42–45); enabled his father and brothers to move to Egypt (Gn 46–47). Sons Ephraim and Manasseh each became tribes (Gn 48). Died in Egypt, buried in Canaan (50:22-26; Ex 13:19; Jos 24:32; Ac 7:16).
2. Husband of Mary; foster father of Jesus (Mt 1:16,20; Lk 2:4; 3:23; 4:22; Jn 1:45; 6:42). Carpenter (Mt 13:55). Told in a dream not to divorce Mary (Mt 1:18-25); told in a dream to flee to Egypt (2:13-23).
3. Of Arimathea; a righteous member of the Sanhedrin who sought the kingdom of God; put Jesus's body in his tomb (Mt 27:57-60; Mk 15:43-46; Lk 23:50-53; Jn 19:38-42).

JOSHUA

Son of Nun; successor to Moses as leader of Israelites. Leader of Moses's army (Ex 17:8-13); Moses's servant on Mt. Sinai (32:17). Scouted Canaan and, along with Caleb, recommended invasion (Nm 13:30–14:38). Chosen, commissioned, and encouraged by God (Nm 27:15-23; Dt 31:14-15,23; Jos 1:1-9).
Conquered Canaan (Jos 2–11) and distributed the land (Jos 12–21). Renewed the covenant and charged the people (Jos 23–24).

JOSIAH

Son of Amon; king of Israel. Became king at age eight (2Kg 21:19–22:2).

Found the book of the law and instituted reforms (2Kg 22–23; 2Ch 34–35). Died resisting Pharaoh Neco (2Kg 23:29-30; 2Ch 35:20-25).

JOTHAM

1. Son of Gideon (Jdg 9).
2. Son of Uzziah/Azariah; coregent (2Kg 15:5), then king of Judah (15:32-38).

JOURNEY

like a man on a j, who left his. . Mk 13:34
On frequent j-s, I faced
dangers. 2Co 11:26

JOY

altar of God, to God, my greatest j. . Ps 43:4
Restore the j of your salvation. . . Ps 51:12
A wise son brings j to his father,. . Pr 10:1
crowned with unending j. . Is 35:10; 51:11
turn their mourning into j,. . . . . .Jr 31:13
immediately receives it with j. .Mt 13:20
Share your master's j!' . . . . Mt 25:21
news of great j that will be for . . Lk 2:10
will be more j in heaven over . . . Lk 15:7
but your sorrow will turn to j. . .Jn 16:20
peace, and j in the Holy Spirit. . Rm 14:17
fruit of the Spirit is love, j,
peace . . . . .Gl 5:22
make my j complete by thinking the
same. . . . . Php 2:2
For the j that lay before him . . Heb 12:2
Consider it a great j, my
brothers .Jms 1:2
inexpressible and glorious j,. 1Pt 1:8
I have no greater j than this:. 3Jn 4

JOYFUL

come before him with j songs. . Ps 100:2
A j heart is good medicine,. . . . . .Pr 17:22
In the day of prosperity be j,. . . . . .Ec 7:14
ate their food with a j and
sincere. . . . . Ac 2:46

JOYFULLY

Let the whole earth shout
j to God!. .Ps 66:1

JUBILEE

It will be your J, when . . . . .Lv 25:10

JUDAH

Son of Jacob and Leah (Gn 29:35); tribe with large territory west and south

of Jerusalem (Jos 15:20-63). Tricked by daughter-in-law (Gn 38). Ancestor of David and Jesus (Gn 49:10; 1Sm 17:12; Mt 1:3,6,16; Rv 5:5). Name of the southern part of the divided kingdom (2Kg 12:20; 14:21; 23:27; Ezk 37:15-23) and the Persian province in the restoration (Neh 5:14; Hg 1:1).

JUDAISM

my former way of life in J:. . . . . . Gl 1:13

JUDAS

1. Iscariot; apostle (Mt 10:4); treasurer, miser, thief (Jn 12:4-6). Betrayed Jesus (Mt 26:21-25,44-50; Lk 22:3-6; Jn 13:21-30); committed suicide (Mt 27:3-10; Ac 1:16-20).
2. Son of James; apostle; called Thaddaeus (Mt 10:3; Mk 3:18; Lk 6:16; Jn 14:22).
3. Brother of Jesus (Mt 13:55; Mk 6:3); also called Jude.

JUDE

Brother of Jesus; also called Judas; author (Mt 13:55; Jd 1).

JUDEA

Another name for the territory of Judah.
Jesus was born in Bethlehem
of J. . . . . .Mt 2:1
Pontius Pilate was governor of J, . .Lk 3:1
in Jerusalem, in all J and
Samaria,. .Ac 1:8

JUDGE (N)

Won't the J of the whole
earth do . . . . Gn 18:25
LORD raised up j-s, who saved. . Jdg 2:16
a j . . . who didn't fear God or. . . . . Lk 18:2

JUDGE (V)

May the LORD j between me
and . . . . Gn 16:5
He is coming to j the earth. . . 1Ch 16:33
He j-s the world with
righteousness;. . . . . Ps 9:8
There is a God who j-s on
earth!. . . . . .Ps 58:11
coming to j the earth.
He will j the. . . . . .Ps 96:13
Do not j, so that you won't be j-d. . .Mt 7:1
rather j according to righteous . .Jn 7:24
I did not come to j the world. . . Jn 12:47

the saints will j the world?......1Co 6:2
who is going to j the
living and................2Tm 4:1
who are you to j your
neighbor?..................Jms 4:12
the dead were j-d
according to...............Rv 20:12

JUDGMENT

the wicked will not stand
up in the j,...................Ps 1:5
my mouth, for I hope in
your j-s..................Ps 119:43
Teach me good j and
discernment,.............Ps 119:66
arrived and a j was given in ...Dn 7:22
Sodom on the day of j than for..Mt 11:24
not come under j but has
passed........................Jn 5:24
his j-s and untraceable.......Rm 11:33
eats and drinks j on himself...1Co 11:29
die once—and after this, j—..Heb 9:27
has come for j to begin with....1Pt 4:17
because his j-s are true and......Rv 19:2

JUDGMENT SEAT

will all stand before the j of
God.........................Rm 14:10
all appear before the j of
Christ, ...2Co 5:10

JUG

and the oil j will not run dry ..1Kg 17:14

JUST

Judge of the whole earth do
what is j? ....Gn 18:25
is holy and j and good..........Rm 7:12
whatever is j, whatever is pure..Php 4:8

JUSTICE

must not deny j to a poor
person.......................Ex 23:6
but he gives j to the oppressed. .Jb 36:6
The evil do not understand j, ...Pr 28:5
He will bring j to the nations.....Is 42:1
the LORD, showing faithful
love, j,......................Jr 9:24
But let j flow like water,........Am 5:24
will proclaim j to the nations..Mt 12:18
kind of herb, and you bypass j .Lk 11:42

JUSTIFICATION

and raised for our j............Rm 4:25
j leading to life for everyone. ..Rm 5:18

JUSTIFY

he had j-ied himself rather
than God....................Jb 32:2
righteous servant will j many, ..Is 53:11
But wanting to j himself, he ..Lk 10:29
down to his house j-ied rather
than ....Lk 18:14
who believes is j-ied through
him ....Ac 13:39
They are j-ied freely by his
grace ....Rm 3:24
a person is j-ied by faith apart..Rm 3:28
and those he called, he
also j-ied;..................Rm 8:30
God is the one who j-ies........Rm 8:33
no one is j-ied by the
works of the.................Gl 2:16
we might be j-ied by faith in
Christ......................Gl 2:16
that God would j the Gentiles by ..Gl 3:8
a person is j-ied by works and
not.......................Jms 2:24

JUSTLY

the LORD requires of you: to
act j, ...Mc 6:8

K

KADESH

Oasis, also called Kadesh-barnea.
Where Abraham fought the Amalekites (Gn 14:7). Where the Israelites
camped, they sent out spies, and Moses
struck the rock (Nm 13:26; 20:1,11; 27:14;
32:8; Dt 1:46; 9:23; Jdg 11:16-17). Southern
limit of Judah (Nm 34:4; Jos 10:41; 15:3).

KEEP

be with me, and k me from
harm......................1Ch 4:10
and in k-ing them there is an ..Ps 19:11
K your tongue from evil and
your ....Ps 34:13
How can a young man k his way
pure? By k-ing your word...Ps 119:9
K my commands and live......Pr 4:4; 7:2
fear God and k his commands,..Ec 12:13
K listening, but do not
understand; ....Is 6:9
You will k ...in perfect peace ..Is 26:3
"I have kept all these," the
young......................Mt 19:20
hates his life in this world
will k it ....Jn 12:25
loves me, he will k my word. ..Jn 14:23

the race, I have kept the faith. .2Tm 4:7
whoever k-s the entire law,...Jms 2:10
and unfading, kept in
heaven for....................1Pt 1:4
and those who k the words of ..Rv 22:9

KETURAH

Abraham's second wife (Gn 25:1-4).

KEY

give you the k-s of the
kingdom....................Mt 16:19
and I hold the k-s of death and..Rv 1:18
the One who has the k of
David,.....................Rv 3:7

KIDNAP

Whoever k-s a person must
be put......................Ex 21:16

KILL

his brother Abel and k-ed him. .Gn 4:8
Am I God, k-ing and giving
life 2Kg 5:7
a time to k and a time to heal; ...Ec 3:3
Don't fear those who k the body but
are not able to k the soul; ..Mt 10:28
k-ed, and be raised the third
day. ....Mt 16:21
way to arrest Jesus and k him..Mk 14:1
Why are you trying to k me?......Jn 7:19
You k-ed the source of life,......Ac 3:15
For the letter k-s, but the Spirit..2Co 3:6

KIND (ADJ)

Love is patient, love is k........1Co 13:4
And be k and compassionate
to ....Eph 4:32

KIND (N)

seed in it according to their k-s..Gn 1:11
the birds according to their
k-s,.......................Gn 6:20
asked, "What k of man is this?..Mt 8:27
is a root of all k-s of evil,......1Tm 6:10

KINDNESS

K to the poor is a loan to the......Pr 19:17
God's k is intended to lead
you to......................Rm 2:4
consider God's k and
severity: ....Rm 11:22
patience, k, goodness,
faithfulness ....Gl 5:22

KING

days there was no **k** in Israel;.. Jdg 17:6
said, "Give us a **k** to judge us... 1Sm 8:6
anointed David **k** over the
  house.........................2Sm 2:4
The **k-s** of the earth take their......Ps 2:2
The LORD is **K** forever and
  ever;...........................Ps 10:16
Who is this **K** of glory?.........Ps 24:8
It is by me that **k-s** reign and
  rulers.........................Pr 8:15
the glory of **k-s** to investigate ..Pr 25:2
my eyes have seen the **K**, ...Is 6:5
the living God and eternal **K**... Jr 10:10
Look, your **k** is coming to you;.. Zch 9:9
who has been born **k** of the
  Jews? ....Mt 2:2
See, your **K** is coming to you, .. Mt 21:5
JESUS, THE **K** OF THE JEWS....... Mt 27:37
Now to the **k** eternal,
  immortal 1Tm 1:17
for **k-s** and all those who
  are in........................1Tm 2:2
K of **k-s**, and the Lord of lords,..1Tm 6:15
K of **K-s** and Lord of ....Rv 19:16

KINGDOM *SEE ALSO* KINGDOM OF GOD; KINGDOM OF HEAVEN

you will be my **k** of priests and ..Ex 19:6
Your **k** is an everlasting **k**;......Ps 145:13
showed him all the **k-s** of the
  world.........................Mt 4:8
Your **k** come. Your will be done ..Mt 6:10
these are the children of the **k**.. Mt 13:38
I will give you the keys of
  the **k** ....Mt 16:19
nation, and **k** against **k**......... Mt 24:7
will give you, up to half my **k**...Mk 6:23
But seek his **k**, and these......Lk 12:31
my **k** is not from here." ....Jn 18:36
transferred us into the **k** of
  the Son ....Col 1:13
The **k** of the world has become ..Rv 11:15

KINGDOM OF GOD (GOD'S KINGDOM)

But seek first the **k** and his..... Mt 6:33
for a rich person to enter
  the **k**. ....Mt 19:24
for the **k** belongs to such as
  these.........................Mk 10:14
You are not far from the **k**.......Mk 12:34
you see, the **k** is in your
  midst..........................Lk 17:21
is born again, he cannot see
  the **k**. ....Jn 3:3
for the **k** is not eating
  drinking, ...Rm 14:17

KINGDOM OF HEAVEN

Repent, because the **k** has
  come near! ....Mt 3:2
poor in spirit, for the **k** is theirs...Mt 5:3
The **k** is like a mustard seed .. Mt 13:31
I will give you the keys of
  the **k**, ...Mt 16:19
k belongs to such as these. ... Mt 19:14

KINGSHIP

for **k** belongs to the LORD;......Ps 22:28

KISS (N)

but the **k-es** of an enemy are ...Pr 27:6
betraying the Son of Man
  with a **k**?.....................Lk 22:48
Greet one another with a
  holy **k**. ....Rm 16:16

KISS (V)

mouth that has not **k-ed**
  him..........................1Kg 19:18
that he would **k** me with the..... Sg 1:2
The One I **k**, he's the one;......Mt 26:48

KNEE

Every **k** will bow to me, every.. Is 45:23
the Lord, every **k** will bow to
  me ....Rm 14:11
name of Jesus every **k** will
  bow.........................Php 2:10

KNEEL

let us **k** before the LORD our......Ps 95:6
a stone's throw, **knelt** down,... Lk 22:41
For this reason I **k** before
  the.........................Eph 3:14

KNIFE

and took the **k** to slaughter
  his ....Gn 22:10

KNIT

k me together in my
  mother's....................Ps 139:13
fitted and **k** together by every. .Eph 4:16

KNOCK

K, and the door will be...........Mt 7:7
I stand at the door and **k**. ...... Rv 3:20

KNOW

be like God, **k-ing** good and
  evil...........................Gn 3:5
For now I **k** that you fear God, ..Gn 22:12
Egyptians will **k** that I am the
  LORD...........................Ex 7:5
But I **k** that my Redeemer lives,.. Jb 19:25
since he **k-s** the secrets of the.. Ps 44:21
and **k** that I am God, ...Ps 46:10
LORD **k-s** the thoughts of
  mankind; ....Ps 94:11
You have searched me and
  k-n me. ....Ps 139:1
You **k** when I sit down and
  when I ....Ps 139:2
Search me, God, and **k** my
  heart; ....Ps 139:23
for you don't **k** what a day
  might ....Pr 27:1
K the LORD, for they will all
  k me ....Jr 31:34
your left hand **k** what your
  right ....Mt 6:3
your Father **k-s** the things you
  need ....Mt 6:8
I never **knew** you! Depart
  from me,.....................Mt 7:23
that day and hour no one **k-s** ..Mt 24:36
you don't **k** what day your
  Lord ....Mt 24:42
I **k** my own, and my own **k** me, ..Jn 10:14
We **k** that his testimony is
  true..........................Jn 21:24
not for you to **k** times or.........Ac 1:7
For though they **knew** God,
  they...........................Rm 1:21
searches our hearts **k-s** the
  mind..........................Rm 8:27
We **k** that all things work..... Rm 8:28
Now I **k** in part, but then I will
  k fully, as I am fully **k-n**.....1Co 13:12
k Christ's love that surpasses ..Eph 3:19
is not how you came to **k**
  about ....Eph 4:20
the surpassing value of **k-ing**
  Christ ....Php 3:8
to **k** him and the power of his.. Php 3:10
I **k** whom I have believed in .. 2Tm 1:12
The Lord **k-s** those who are
  his,..........................2Tm 2:19
who says, "I have come to **k**
  him,"........................1Jn 2:4
to **k** love: he laid down his life ..1Jn 3:16

KNOWLEDGE

the tree of the **k** of good and
  evil...........................Gn 2:9
Can anyone teach God **k**, ...Jb 21:22
wondrous **k** is beyond me...... Ps 139:6
of the LORD is the beginning of **k**;.. Pr 1:7

The wise store up k, ... Pr 10:14
of the wisdom and the k of
  God! ....Rm 11:33
K inflates with pride, but love ..1Co 8:1
all mysteries and all k,.........1Co 13:2
Christ's love that surpasses k, ..Eph 3:19
In him are hidden ...
  wisdom and k.................Col 2:3
what is falsely called k. 1Tm 6:20
in the grace and k of our Lord..2Pt 3:18

KORAH

1. Led rebellion against Moses (Nm 16;
   Jd 11).
2. Kohathite Levite (Ex 6:21; 1Ch 6:22);
   ancestor of temple singers (2Ch 20:19;
   Pss 42; 44–49; 84–85; 87–88).

L

LABAN

Rebekah's brother (Gn 24:29); father of
Leah and Rachel (Gn 29:15-30).

LABOR (N)

that your l in the Lord is 1Co 15:58

LABOR (V)

You are to l six days and do all ..Ex 20:9
they don't l or spin thread...... Mt 6:28

LACK

but fools die for l of sense...... Pr 10:21
You l one thing: Go, sell all....Mk 10:21
Now if any of you l-s wisdom, ..Jms 1:5

LAKE

were thrown alive into the
  l of fire..................... Rv 19:20
second death, the l of fire..... Rv 20:14

LAMB

God himself will provide
  the l........................Gn 22:8
The wolf will dwell with the l,.....Is 11:6
He gathers the l-s in his arms..Is 40:11
Like a l led to the slaughter.....Is 53:7
you out like l-s among wolves. .Lk 10:3
L of God, who takes away the
  sin ....Jn 1:29
"Feed my l-s," he told him...... Jn 21:15
an unblemished and spotless l.. 1Pt 1:19

Worthy is the L who was
  slaughtered ....Rv 5:12
the marriage feast of the L!.....Rv 19:9
written in the L-'s book
  of life........................Rv 21:27

LAME

Then the l will leap like a deer, .. Is 35:6
receive their sight, the l walk, ..Mt 11:5

LAMENT

the following l for Saul and
  his 2Sm 1:17
You turned my l into dancing;..Ps 30:11
heard in Ramah, a l with
  bitter ....Jr 31:15
we sang a l, but you didn't..... Mt 11:17

LAMP

LORD, you light my l; ....Ps 18:28
Your word is a l for my
  feet and....................Ps 119:105
but the l of the wicked is
  put out. ....Pr 13:9
No one lights a l and puts it.... Mt 5:15
The eye is the l of the body..... Mt 6:22
like ten virgins who took
  their l-s .... Mt 25:1
the light of a l will never...... Rv 18:23

LAMPSTAND

a l out of pure, hammered
  gold. ....Ex 25:31
but rather on a l, and it gives
  light .... Mt 5:15
seven l-s are the seven
  churches....................Rv 1:20
and remove your l from its
  place..........................Rv 2:5

LAND

God called the dry l "earth," ....Gn 1:10
I will give this l to your ....Gn 12:7
a l flowing with milk and honey..Ex 3:8
So Joshua took the entire l, ... Jos 11:23
divide this l as an inheritance.. Jos 13:7
Judah went into exile
  from its l...................2Kg 25:21
forgive their sin, and heal
  their l. 2Ch 7:14
the humble will inherit the l... Ps 37:11
Woe to you, l, when your
  king is ....Ec 10:16
My flock from all the l-s
  where I ....Jr 23:3
and strike the l with a curse. .. Mal 4:6

those who owned l-s or
  houses sold.................. Ac 4:34
on the sea, his left on the l, ...Rv 10:2

LANGUAGE

The whole earth had the same l..Gn 11:1
He will speak ... in a foreign l...Is 28:11
and filthy l from your mouth. ..Col 3:8
every tribe and l and people.....Rv 5:9

LAPPED

with the three hundred men
  who l ....Jdg 7:7

LASHES

than a hundred l into a fool.... Pr 17:10
Five times I received forty l.. 2Co 11:24

LAST (ADJ)

These are the l words of
  David:......................2Sm 23:1
In the l days the mountain of......Is 2:2
are first will be l, and the l first...Mt 19:30
he must be l and servant of
  all. .... Mk 9:35
The l enemy to be abolished
  is 1Co 15:26
of an eye, at the l trumpet.... 1Co 15:52
In these l days, he has spoken...Heb 1:2
Children, it is the l hour........1Jn 2:18

LAST (N)

I am the first and I am the l...... Is 44:6
I am the First and the L,......... Rv 1:17

LAST (V)

For his anger l-s only a
  moment,.....................Ps 30:5

LATER

that in l times some will depart. .1Tm 4:1

LAUGH

Why did Sarah l, ... Gn 18:13
The one enthroned in
  heaven l-s;...................Ps 2:4
a time to weep and a time to l;...... Ec 3:4

LAUGHTER

Even in l a heart may be sad, .. Pr 14:13
Let your l be turned to
  mourning .... Jms 4:9

LAUNDERER

white as no l on earth could....Mk 9:3

LAW

the stone tablets with the l......Ex 24:12
Moses wrote down this l and
    gave it ....Dt 31:9
L after l, l after l, line after line,..Is 28:10
think that I came to abolish
    the L............................Mt 5:17
All the L and the Prophets
    depend ....Mt 22:40
stroke of a letter in the l to
    drop ....Lk 16:17
the l was given through Moses;..Jn 1:17
not under the l but under
    grace ....Rm 6:14
So then, the l is holy, and the...Rm 7:12
For Christ is the end of the l...Rm 10:4
The l, then, was our
    guardian until................Gl 3:24
For the whole l is fulfilled in ...Gl 5:14
I will put my l-s into their
    minds.....................Heb 8:10
Since the l has only a shadow..Heb 10:1
For whoever keeps the
    entire l,.....................Jms 2:10

LAWBREAKER

Depart from me, you l-s!.......Mt 7:23

LAWLESS

and then the l one will be......2Th 2:8

LAWLESSNESS

Because l will multiply, ...Mt 24:12
the mystery of l is already at ...2Th 2:7
who commits sin practices l....1Jn 3:4

LAY

Look, I have laid a stone in Zion,..Is 28:16
Man has no place to l his head..Mt 8:20
in cloth and laid him in a
    manger,......................Lk 2:7
I l down my life for the sheep..Jn 10:15
through the l-ing on of my
    hands.......................2Tm 1:6
ritual washings, l-ing on of
    hands.......................Heb 6:2
let us l aside every weight and..Heb 12:1
He laid down his life for us. ...1Jn 3:16

LAZARUS

1. Poor man in Jesus's parable (Lk
16:19-31).

2. Brother of Mary and Martha; friend
of Jesus (Jn 11:1-5). Died; revived by
Jesus (11:3-44). Endangered because
of fame (12:9-11,17).

LAZY

A l hunter doesn't roast his
    game,.......................Pr 12:27
and a l person will go
    hungry......................Pr 19:15
so that you won't become l ...Heb 6:12

LEAD

of cloud to l them on their
    way.........................Ex 13:21
way of the wicked l-s to ruin......Ps 1:6
He l-s me beside quiet waters...Ps 23:2
way, LORD, and l me on a level . Ps 27:11
L me to a rock that is high
    above me ....Ps 61:2
l me in the everlasting way... Ps 139:24
The fear of the LORD l-s to life;..Pr 19:23
and a child will l them. ....Is 11:6
Like a lamb led to the slaughter..Is 53:7
l astray, if possible, even the
    elect.........................Mt 24:24
and led him away to crucify
    him..........................Mt 27:31
sheep by name and l-s them
    out. ....Jn 10:3
is intended to l you to
    repentance? ....Rm 2:4
sin l-ing to death or of
    obedience ....Rm 6:16
All those led by God's
    Spirit are ....Rm 8:14
But if you are led by the Spirit,.. Gl 5:18

LEADER

He chose Judah as l,..........1Ch 28:4
For the l-s of the earth belong
    to ....Ps 47:9
of the synagogue l-s, named
    Jairus ....Mk 5:22
Obey your l-s and submit......Heb 13:17

LEADING (ADJ)

as a number of the l women. ...Ac 17:4

LEAF

they sewed fig l-ves together
    and ....Gn 3:7
and whose l does not wither .... Ps 1:3
becomes tender and sprouts
    l-ves,........................Mt 24:32
The l-ves of the tree are for......Rv 22:2

LEAH

Wife of Jacob; mother of Reuben, Simeon, Levi, Judah, Issachar, Zebulun, and
Dinah (Gn 29:16-35; 30:14-21).

LEAN

temple, so I can l against
    them. ....Jdg 16:26
So he l-ed back against Jesus
    and ....Jn 13:25

LEAP

with my God I can l over a
    wall. ....Ps 18:29
greeting, the baby l-ed inside
    her...........................Lk 1:41
walking, l-ing, and praising
    God..........................Ac 3:8

LEARN

will listen and l to fear the
    LORD ....Dt 31:13
that I could l your statutes.......Ps 119:71
and the inexperienced l a
    lesson; ....Pr 19:25
L to do what is good............. Is 1:17
take up my yoke and l from
    me,..........................Mt 11:29
for I have l-ed to be content in ..Php 4:11
A woman is to l quietly 1Tm 2:11
He l-ed obedience through
    what he.....................Heb 5:8

LEASE

He l-d it to tenant farmers
    and ....Mt 21:33

LEAST

are by no means l among the......Mt 2:6
will be called l in the kingdom.. Mt 5:19
you did for one of the l of
    these.........................Mt 25:40
For I am the l of the apostles,..1Co 15:9

LEATHER

man with a l belt around his ...2Kg 1:8
garment with a l belt
    around his....................Mt 3:4

LEAVE

This is why a man l-s his father..Gn 2:24
I will not l you or abandon you...Jos 1:5
Spirit of the LORD had left
    Saul, ...1Sm 16:14

LEAVEN

I alone am **left**, and they are..1Kg 19:10
do not I me or abandon me,......Ps 27:9
I your gift there in front of.....Mt 5:24
won't he I the ninety-nine on ..Mt 18:12
we have **left** everything and.. Mt 19:27
reason a man will I his father.. Mk 10:7
I will not I you as orphans;......Jn 14:18
of Hosts had not **left** us
   offspring,................... Rm 9:29
I will never I you or abandon..Heb 13:5

LEAVEN (N)

of heaven is like I that a
   woman .... Mt 13:33
beware of the I of the
   Pharisees.................... Mt 16:6
know that a little I 1Co 5:6

LEAVEN (V)

A little leaven I-s the whole
   batch .... Gl 5:9

LEBANON

Mountainous region of northern
promised land (Dt 1:7; 11:24). Known
for its cedars and lush growth (Jdg
9:15; 1Kg 5:6; 2Ch 2:8,16; Ps 72:16; 92:12;
Sg 4:11,15; Is 2:13; Ezk 27:5; 31:3). God is
greater (Ps 29:5-6; 104:16).

LEECH

The I has two daughters:
   "Give, ...Pr 30:15

LEFT

not to turn aside to the right
   or the I. ....Dt 5:32
Don't turn to the right or to
   the I; ....Pr 4:27
down on your I side and place.. Ezk 4:4
don't let your I hand know
   what...........................Mt 6:3
right and the other on your I, ..Mt 20:21
right and the goats on the I.......Mt 25:33

LEFT-HANDED

Ehud son of Gera, a I
   Benjaminite,................Jdg 3:15

LEFTOVER

up twelve baskets full of I
   pieces!.....................Mt 14:20
they collected the I pieces......Mt 15:37
Collect the I-s so that nothing......Jn 6:12

LEGAL

It's not I for us to put...........Jn 18:31
that are not I for us as
   Romans.....................Ac 16:21
Is it I for you to scourge a .....Ac 22:25

LEGION

here and now with more than
   twelve I-s of angels?........Mt 26:53
"My name is L," he answered
   him,..........................Mk 5:9

LEGS

its I were iron, and its feet...... Dn 2:33
they did not break his I since ..Jn 19:33

LEND

If you I silver to my people......Ex 22:25
who does not I his silver at......Ps 15:5
come to the one who I-s
   generously .... Ps 112:5
and I, expecting nothing in
   return.......................Lk 6:35

LENDER

borrower is a slave to the I...... Pr 22:7

LENGTH

I of days forever and ever....... Ps 21:4
Its I, width, and height are
   equal.........................Rv 21:16

LENGTHENING (ADJ)

I fade away like a I shadow; .. Ps 109:23

LEOPARD

and the I will lie down with the.. Is 11:6
his skin, or a I his spots?....... Jr 13:23

LEPROSY

a man with I came up and
   knelt......................... Mt 8:2
cleanse those with I,........... Mt 10:8

LESS

punished us I than our sins....Ezr 9:13
You made him little I than
   God ....Ps 8:5

LESSER

the I light to rule over...........Gn 1:16

LET

L there be light, ...Gn 1:3
L the little children come to
   me...........................Mk 10:14

LETTER

not the smallest I or one
   stroke........................ Mt 5:18
I kills, but the Spirit gives life... 2Co 3:6
His I-s are weighty and
   powerful, ... 2Co 10:10
Look at what large I-s I use ..... Gl 6:11
these things in all his I-s. 2Pt 3:16

LEVEL (ADJ)

My foot stands on I ground; ...Ps 26:12
Spirit lead me on I ground. ....Ps 143:10
The path of the righteous is I;... Is 26:7
and rough places into I
   ground.......................Is 42:16

LEVEL (V)

mountain and hill will be I-ed;.. Is 40:4

LEVI

1. Son of Jacob and Leah (Gn 29:34).
   Ancestor of priestly tribe (Ex 32:25-
   29; Nm 3:11-13; Dt 10:6-9); received
   no allotment of land, only scattered
   towns and cities of refuge (Nm 18:20;
   35:1-8; Jos 13:14,33); supported by
   tithes (Nm 18:21; Heb 7:5). Assisted
   descendants of Aaron in worship
   (Nm 3:5-9; 1Ch 6:16,31-32,49; 23:24-
   32; 2Ch 29:12-21); taught the word of
   God (2Ch 17:7-9; Neh 8:9-12).
2. Apostle, called Matthew (Mk 2:14; Lk
   5:27-29; cp. Mt 9:9).

LEVIATHAN

Can you pull in L with a hook or..Jb 41:1
You crushed the heads of L;......Ps 74:14

LEVITICAL

came through the I priesthood ..Heb 7:11

LIAR

alarm I said, "Everyone is a I.".. Ps 116:11
he is a I and the father of I-s.....Jn 8:44
be true, even though
   everyone is a I, ...Rm 3:4
we make him a I, and his
   word is 1Jn 1:10
and all I-s—their share will......Rv 21:8

LIBERTY

to proclaim l to the captives..... Is 61:1

LICK

the dogs will also l up your
    blood!.......................1Kg 21:19
The dogs l-ed up his blood, . . 1Kg 22:38

LIE (N)

one who utters l-s will not
    escape......................... Pr 19:9
They are prophesying a l to
    you........................... Jr 27:10
exchanged the truth of God for
    a l, ... Rm 1:25
because no l comes from the
    truth. 1Jn 2:21

LIE (V) (DECEIVE) *SEE ALSO* LYING

or l to one another. .... Lv 19:11
God is not a man, that he
    might l, ... Nm 23:19
your heart to l to the Holy Spirit . . Ac 5:3
Do not l to one another, since . . Col 3:9

LIE (V) (RECLINE)

when you l down and when
    you get........................ Dt 6:7
He lets me l down in green..... Ps 23:2
the leopard will l down with the . . Is 11:6
in cloth and l-ing in a
    manger......................Lk 2:12

LIFE

the breath of l into his .... Gn 2:7
the tree of l in the middle....... Gn 2:9
then you must give l for l, ...Ex 21:23
the l of a creature is in the
    blood,.......................Lv 17:11
Choose l so that you and your . . Dt 30:19
Remember that my l is but a
    breath........................ Jb 7:7
LORD is perfect, renewing
    one's l........................ Ps 19:7
will pursue me all the days of
    my l, ...Ps 23:6
the blessing—l forevermore. . Ps 133:3
preserve my l from the anger . . Ps 138:7
Guard it, for it is your l.......... Pr 4:13
the one who finds me finds l . . Pr 8:35
setting before you the way of
    l and the...................... Jr 21:8
awake, some to eternal l, and
    some........................ Dn 12:2
Don't worry about your l, ...Mt 6:25

gains whole world yet loses
    his l?........................ Mt 16:26
to give his l as a ransom for
    many. ....Mt 20:28
one's l is not in the
    abundance of...............Lk 12:15
In him was l, and that l was
    the light .... Jn 1:4
in him may have eternal l....... Jn 3:15
but has passed from death to l . . Jn 5:24
"I am the bread of l," Jesus told . . Jn 6:35
that they may have l and
    have it ....Jn 10:10
I am the resurrection and the l. . Jn 11:25
the way, the truth, and the l.......Jn 14:6
too may walk in newness of l . . . Rm 6:4
but the Spirit gives l............ 2Co 3:6
The l I now live in the body,......Gl 2:20
and your l is hidden with
    Christ........................Col 3:3
required for l and godliness 2Pt 1:3
lay down our **lives** for our
    brothers 1Jn 3:16
in the book of l of the Lamb
    who..........................Rv 13:8

LIFEBLOOD

not eat meat with its l in it. ...... Gn 9:4

LIFE-GIVING

last Adam became a l Spirit. . 1Co 15:45

LIFETIME

only a moment, but his
    favor, a l......................Ps 30:5

LIFT

and the One who l-s up my head . . . Ps 3:3
L up your heads, you gates!..... Ps 24:7
You have l-ed me up and have . . Ps 30:1
so the Son of Man must be
    l-ed up, ...Jn 3:14
When you l up the Son of Man, . . Jn 8:28
if I am l-ed up from the earth I . . Jn 12:32

LIGHT (N)

"Let there be l," and there was l. . Gn 1:3
The LORD is my l and my
    salvation..................... Ps 27:1
for my feet and a l on my
    path........................Ps 119:105
like the l of dawn, shining
    brighter .... Pr 4:18
let us walk in the LORD's l. ....Is 2:5
in darkness have seen a great l; . . . Is 9:2
people and a l to the nations .....Is 42:6

Arise, shine, for your l has
    come, ...Is 60:1
live in darkness have seen a
    great l, ... Mt 4:16
You are the l of the world. ..... Mt 5:14
a l for revelation to the
    Gentiles...................... Lk 2:32
I am the l of the world.......... Jn 8:12
walk in the l as he . . . is in the l. . .1Jn 1:7

LIGHT (V)

No one l-s a lamp and puts it......Mt 5:15
to horizon and l-s up the sky, . . Lk 17:24

LIGHTNING

was thunder and l, a thick
    cloud ....Ex 19:16
he hurled l bolts and routed
    them. .... Ps 18:14
For as the l comes from the
    east ....Mt 24:27
His appearance was like l, ... Mt 28:3

LIKE

you will be l God, knowing
    good .... Gn 3:5
I am God, and no one is l me.......Is 46:9
LORD, there is no one l you...... Jr 10:6
What is the kingdom of
    God l, ...Lk 13:18
spoke l a child, I thought l
    a child,..................... 1Co 13:11
He had to be l his brothers..... Heb 2:17

LIKE-MINDED

have no one else l who will . . . Php 2:20

LIKENESS

our image, according to
    our l.......................... Gn 1:26
united with him in the l of
    his death.....................Rm 6:5
servant, taking on the l of
    humanity..................... Php 2:7
curse people who are made in
    God's l .... Jms 3:9

LIMIT

when he set a l for the
    sea so......................Pr 8:29

LINE

l after l, l after l, a little
    here........................... Is 28:10

LINEN

on his l robe and l
   undergarments.............Lv 6:10
body, wrapped it in clean,
   fine l,......................Mt 27:59
tomb and saw the l cloths lying..Jn 20:6

LINTEL

and brush the l and the two .. Ex 12:22

LION

Judah is a young l.............Gn 49:9
and the l will eat straw like
   cattle.........................Is 11:7
will be thrown into the l-s' den...Dn 6:7
prowling around like a
   roaring l, ...1Pt 5:8
The l from the tribe of Judah,....Rv 5:5

LIPS

His praise will always
   be on my l....................Ps 34:1
a stranger, and not your own l.. Pr 27:2
I am a man of unclean l..........Is 6:5
people honors me with their l,..Mt 15:8
and by the l of foreigners,..... 1Co 14:21

LIP-SERVICE

honor me with l—yet their
   hearts.......................Is 29:13

LISTEN

L, Israel: The LORD our God;......Dt 6:4
Speak, for your servant is l-ing....1Sm
   3:10
LORD, l and be gracious to me;.. Ps 30:10
For the LORD l-s to the needy
   and ....Ps 69:33
L, sons, to a father's discipline, .. Pr 4:1
who gives an answer before
   he l-s.........................Pr 18:13
Keep l-ing, but do not
   understand; ....Is 6:9
You will l and l, but never..... Mt 13:14
whom I am well-pleased. L
   to him!.......................Mt 17:5
But if he won't l, take one or.. Mt 18:16
you cannot l to my word........Jn 8:43
and they will l to my voice...... Jn 10:16
Everyone should be quick to l,..Jms 1:19
not from God does not l to us... 1Jn 4:6

LITTLE

You made him l less than
   God and ....Ps 8:5

Better a l with the fear of the .. Pr 15:16
are you afraid, you of l faith?.. Mt 8:26
the one who is forgiven l, loves l. .Lk 7:47
know both how to make do
   with l,.......................Php 4:12
and he held a l scroll opened in ..Rv 10:2

LIVE

for humans cannot see me
   and l........................Ex 33:20
man does not l on bread alone ..Dt 8:3
But I know that my Redeemer
   l-s, ...Jb 19:25
The LORD l-s—blessed be my ..Ps 18:46
to my God as long as I l........Ps 146:2
Keep my commands and l ...... Pr 4:4;7:2
on those l-ing in the land of
   darkness........................Is 9:2
listen, so that you will l......... Is 55:3
the righteous one will l by
   his faith......................Hab 2:4
Man must not l on bread alone.. Mt 4:4
in me, even if he dies, will l .... Jn 11:25
Because I l, you will l too....... Jn 14:19
in him we l and move and......Ac 17:28
The righteous will l by faith.... Rm 1:17
the life he l-s, he l-s to God......Rm 6:10
If we l, we l for the Lord;.......Rm 14:8
I no longer l, but Christ l-s in me.
The life I now l in the body,
   I l by faith....................Gl 2:20
L as children of light...........Eph 5:8
to l is Christ and to die is gain...Php 1:21

LIVING (ADJ)

and the man became a l being.. Gn 2:7
the voice of the l God speaking ..Dt 5:26
flesh cry out for the l God.......Ps 84:2
let every l thing bless his ......Ps 145:21
me, the fountain of l water, and
   dug ....Jr 2:13
On that day l water will flow .. Zch 14:8
Messiah, the Son of the l God! ..Mt 16:16
and he would give you l water. . Jn 4:10
I am the l bread that came
   down ....Jn 6:51
your bodies as a l sacrifice,......Rm 12:1
word of God is l and effective. .Heb 4:12
into the hands of the l God... Heb 10:31

LIVING (N)

God of the dead, but of the l...Mt 22:32
to judge the l and the dead......1Pt 4:5

LOAD (N)

tie up heavy l-s that are
   hard to......................Mt 23:4

LOAD (V)

You l people with burdens t
   hat.........................Lk 11:46

LOAF

only have five l-ves and two
   fish ....Mt 14:17
took the seven l-ves and the
   fish,........................Mt 15:36

LOAN

to the poor is a l to the LORD, .. Pr 19:17
Don't ...put up security for
   l-s. ....Pr 22:26

LOCUST

I will bring l-s into your
   territory......................Ex 10:4
fruit of their labor to the l......Ps 78:46
What the devouring l has left, the ..Jl 1:4
his food was l-s and wild honey...Mt 3:4

LOFTY

It is l; I am unable to reach it. ..Ps 139:6
against all that is proud and l, ...Is 2:12
Lord seated on a high and l
   throne,........................Is 6:1

LONG (ADJ)

you may have a l life in the
   land.........................Ex 20:12
How l will you waver
   between 1Kg 18:21
How l will you hide your face .. Ps 13:1
How l, LORD? Will you hide......Ps 89:46
if a man has l hair it is a
   disgrace 1Co 11:14

LONG (V)

As a deer l-s for flowing streams,
   so ....Ps 42:1
I l for you in the night;.......... Is 26:9
He l-ed to eat his fill from the.. Lk 15:16

LOOK

But Lot's wife l-ed back and
   became ....Gn 19:26
he was afraid to l at God. ....Ex 3:6
Do not l at his appearance or ..1Sm 16:7
The LORD l-s down from
   heaven on ....Ps 14:2
L down from heaven and see;.. Ps 80:14
Let your eyes l forward; ....Pr 4:25
keep l-ing, but do not perceive....Is 6:9

that day people will l to their
Maker .... Is 17:7
that we should l at him,......... Is 53:2
eyes are too pure to l on evil,.. Hab 1:13
will l at me whom they
pierced....................Zch 12:10
everyone who l-s at a woman.. Mt 5:28
because l-ing they do not
see,......................... Mt 13:13
the plow and l-s back is fit for ..Lk 9:62
L at my hands and my feet, ... Lk 24:39
your eyes and l at the fields,...Jn 4:35
They will l at the one they......Jn 19:37
l-ing as in a mirror at the
glory........................ 2Co 3:18

LOOSE

whatever you l on earth
will have.................... Mt 16:19

LORD LD = LORD

The **Ld** our God, the **Ld** is One.... Dt 6:4
For the **Ld** your God is the
God of gods and L of l-s,..... Dt 10:17
Ld gives, and the **Ld** takes
away. ....Jb 1:21
The **Ld** is my shepherd; .... Ps 23:1
declaration of the **Ld** to my L:.. Ps 110:1
Give thanks to the L of l-s......Ps 136:3
l-s other than you have
owned us,................... Is 26:13
who says to me, 'L, L,' will
enter........................Mt 7:21
Son of Man is L of the Sabbath.. Mt 12:8
The L declared to my L, ...Mt 22:44
If David calls him 'L,' how
then ....Mt 22:45
The L our God, the L is one....Mk 12:29
you call me 'L, L,' and don't do.. Lk 6:46
You call me Teacher and L...... Jn 13:13
Thomas ... "My L and my
God!" .... Jn 20:28
crucified, both L and Messiah.".. Ac 2:36
with your mouth, "Jesus is L," ...Rm 10:9
are many "gods" and many "l-s" .1Co 8:5
one L, Jesus Christ.............1Co 8:6
can say, "Jesus is L," except by..1Co 12:3
Now the L is the Spirit;.......2Co 3:17
one L, one faith, one baptism, . Eph 4:5
confess that Jesus Christ is L, ...Php 2:11
King of kings, and the L of l-s,.. 1Tm 6:15
obeyed Abraham, calling him l. ..1Pt 3:6
but regard Christ the L as holy, ..1Pt 3:15
was in the Spirit on the L-'s day,.. Rv 1:10
King of Kings and L of L-s .....Rv 19:16

LORDING

not l it over those entrusted to...1Pt 5:3

LOSE

who finds his life will l it,..... Mt 10:39
but whoever l-s his life
because...................... Mt 16:25
a hundred sheep and l-s one ...Lk 15:4
that I should l none of those he ..Jn 6:39

LOSS

everything to be a l in view of .. Php 3:8

LOST (ADJ)

I wander like a l sheep; ...... Ps 119:176
and a time to count as l; ....Ec 3:6
My people were l sheep;........Jr 50:6
go to the l sheep of the house .. Mt 10:6
sent only to the l sheep of
the .... Mt 15:24
he was l and is found! ....Lk 15:24
them and not one of them is l, ..Jn 17:12

LOST (N)

I will seek the l, bring back .. Ezk 34:16
will not seek the l or heal the...Zch 11:16
come to seek and to save the l.. Lk 19:10

LOT

Abraham's nephew (Gn 11:27). Separated from Abraham; settled in Sodom
(13:1-13). Rescued from kings (14:1-16);
from Sodom (18:16–19:29; Lk 17:28-29;
2Pt 2:7-9). Fathered Moabites and Ammonites by his daughters (Gn 19:30-38).

LOT

The land is to be divided
by l;........................Nm 26:55
Cast the l between me and
my 1Sm 14:42
Pur—that is, the l—was cast... Est 3:7
and they cast l-s for my
clothing .... Ps 22:18
The l is cast into the lap, ...Pr 16:33
cast l-s, and the l singled
out Jonah. .... Jnh 1:7
His clothes by casting l-s...... Mt 27:35
Let's not tear it, but cast l-s
for it,........................Jn 19:24
and the l fell to Matthias........Ac 1:26

LOUD

neighbor with a l voice early .. Pr 27:14
Jesus cried out with a l
voice, ...Mt 27:46
I heard a l voice behind
me like....................... Rv 1:10

LOVE (N)

showing faithful l to a
thousand .... Ex 20:6
abounding in faithful l and
truth, ... Ex 34:6
not withdraw my faithful l
from .... Ps 89:33
His faithful l endures
forever....................Ps 136:1-26
but l covers all offenses........ Pr 10:12
have loved you with an
everlasting l; .... Jr 31:3
with human cords, with
ropes of l.....................Hs 11:4
No one has greater l than this:..Jn 15:13
God proves his own l for us
in that ....Rm 5:8
Let l must be without
hypocrisy. ....Rm 12:9
puffs up, but l builds up........1Co 8:1
L is patient, l is kind.
l does not...................1Co 13:4
For the l of money is a root of..1Tm 6:10
God is l, ...1Jn 4:16
abandoned the l you had at
first. ....Rv 2:4

LOVE (V)

but l your neighbor as
yourself;....................Lv 19:18
L the LORD your God with all......Dt 6:5
Your God l-d Israel enough to.. 2Ch 9:8
I l you, LORD, my strength....... Ps 18:1
He l-s righteousness and
justice;.......................Ps 33:5
I l the LORD because he has .... Ps 116:1
How I l your instruction!......Ps 119:97
LORD disciplines the one he l-s, ..Pr 3:12
I l those who l me, and those ... Pr 8:17
A friend l-s at all times, ...Pr 17:17
a time to l and a time to hate;....Ec 3:8
I have l-d you with an
everlasting .... Jr 31:3
When Israel was a child, I
l-d him, ... Hs 11:1
Hate evil and l good; ....Am 5:15
Even so, I l-d Jacob, ...Mal 1:2
l your enemies and pray for ... Mt 5:44
will hate one and l the other, .. Mt 6:24
L the Lord your God with all.. Mt 22:37
L your neighbor as yourself...Mt 22:39
is forgiven little, l-s little. ....Lk 7:47
For God l-d the world in this
way: .... Jn 3:16
a new command: l one
another. ....Jn 13:34
since God l-s a cheerful giver. . 2Co 9:7
Husbands, l your wives,
just as.......................Eph 5:25
He who l-s his wife l-s himself. . Eph 5:28

LOVELY (cont.)

Do not l the world or the
things.......................1Jn 2:15
l one another, because l is from
God............................1Jn 4:7
We l because he first l-d us.....1Jn 4:19
As many as I l, I rebuke and.....Rv 3:19

LOVELY

How l is your dwelling place,...Ps 84:1
I am dark ... yet I like the
curtains of....................Sg 1:5
whatever is pure, whatever is l,..Php 4:8

LOVER

will be l-s of self, l-s of money ..2Tm 3:2

LOW

and hill will be made l;...........Lk 3:5

LOWER

You made him l than the
angels ....Heb 2:7

LOWLY

He sets the l on high,...........Jb 5:11
thrones and exalted the l...........Lk 1:52

LOYALTY

keeps his gracious covenant l ... Dt 7:9
He shows l to his anointed, .. 2Sm 22:51
Never let l and faithfulness......Pr 3:3

LUKE

Companion of Paul (2Tm 4:11; Phm 24);
physician (Col 4:14); author of Luke and
Acts (note "we" in Ac 16:10; 28:16).

LUKEWARM

because you are l, and neither.. Rv 3:16

LUST (N)

the l of the flesh, the l of the
eyes..........................1Jn 2:16

LUST (V)

looks at a woman l has already.. Mt 5:28

LUXURY

L is not appropriate for a
fool— ....Pr 19:10

LYDIA

First Philippian convert; seller of purple (Ac 16:12-15,40).

LYING (ADJ)

go and become a l spirit 1Kg 22:22
arrogant eyes, a l tongue,
hands........................Pr 6:17

LYING (N)

Cursing, l, murder, stealing,......Hs 4:2
Therefore, putting away l,
speak ....Eph 4:25

LYRE

who knows how to play
the l........................1Sm 16:16
Praise the LORD with the l;.....Ps 33:2
we hung up our l-s on the
poplar ....Ps 137:2
flute, zither, l, harp, drum....... Dn 3:5

M

MAACAH

1. David's wife; mother of Absalom
(2Sm 3:3; 1Ch 3:2).
2. Mother of Judah's King Abijam (1Kg
15:2); promoted Asherah worship
(15:13).

MAD

Too much study is driving you
m!..........................Ac 26:24

MADMAN

He acted like a m around
them, ...1Sm 21:13
I'm talking like a m— 2Co 11:23

MADNESS

and knowledge, m and folly;.... Ec 1:17

MAGDALENE SEE MARY 2.

MAGIC

seems like a m stone to its...... Pr 17:8
practiced m collected their
books.......................Ac 19:19

MAGICIAN

summoned all the m-s of
Egypt ....Gn 41:8
the m-s of Egypt, and they also
did ....Ex 7:11

MAGNIFICENT

our Lord, how m is your name .. Ps 8:1
m acts of God in our own
tongues. ....Ac 2:11

MAGOG

Land ruled by Gog, an apocalyptic foe
from the north (Ezk 38:2; 39:6; Rv 20:8).

MAIMED

It is better for you to enter life
m ....Mt 18:8
invite those who are poor,
m, lame, ...Lk 14:13

MAJESTIC

All that he does is splendid and
m;..........................Ps 111:3
came to him from the M
Glory:........................2Pt 1:17

MAJESTY

Splendor and m are before
him;........................1Ch 16:27
and the splendor and the m ..1Ch 29:11
awesome m surrounds him....Jb 37:22
He is robed in m;..............Ps 93:1
right hand of the M on high.... Heb 1:3
we were eyewitnesses of
his m........................2Pt 1:16

MAKE

Let us m man in our image,.... Gn 1:26
The sea is his; he made it........Ps 95:5
He made us, and we are his......Ps 100:3
is the day the LORD has made;.. Ps 118:24
I have been ... wondrously
made........................Ps 139:14
forming it, 'What are you
m-ing?' ....Is 45:9
when I will m a new covenant.. Jr 31:31
and I will m you fish for
people! ....Mt 4:19
and m disciples of all nations,.. Mt 28:19
Sabbath was made for man
and not ....Mk 2:27
Why did you m me like this?.. Rm 9:20
made him lower than the
angels ....Heb 2:7

MAKER

a man be more pure than his
M?..........................Jb 4:17
kneel before the LORD our M....Ps 95:6
Indeed, your husband is
your M........................Is 54:5

MALACHI

Postexilic prophet (Mal 1:1).

MALE

he created them m and female.. Gn 1:27
made them m and female,..... Mt 19:4
m-s who have sex with m-s,....1Co 6:9
slave or free, m or female;.....Gl 3:28

MALICE

quarrels, deceit, and m........Rm 1:29
anger, wrath, m, slander, ...Col 3:8

MAN SEE ALSO MAN OF GOD

Let us make m in our image,... Gn 1:26
God formed the m out of the
dust..........................Gn 2:7
Egyptians are men, not God; ....Is 31:3
that he did not look like a m, .. Is 52:14
One like a son of m was coming
with ....Dn 7:13
I am God and not m, the
Holy One.....................Hs 11:9
M must not live on bread alone.. Mt 4:4
this reason a m will leave his.. Mt 19:5
will see the Son of M coming
on...........................Mt 24:30
for m and not m for the
Sabbath......................Mk 2:27
You—being a m—make
yourself ....Jn 10:33
your young men will see
visions, ...Ac 2:17
Men committed shameless
acts ....Rm 1:27
entered the world through
one m, ...Rm 5:12
Christ is the head of every m, and the
m is the head of the woman,..1Co 11:3
What is m, that you remember
him ....Heb 2:6
was one like the Son of M, ...Rv 1:13

MAN OF GOD

blessing that Moses, the m,
gave ....Dt 33:1
She said to Elijah, "M, what
do...........................1Kg 17:18
When Elisha the m heard......2Kg 5:8

word . . . came to Shemaiah,
the m:.......................2Ch 11:2
as David the m had
prescribed. ....Neh 12:24
you, m, flee from these
things, ...1Tm 6:11
so that the m may be
complete,...................2Tm 3:17

MANAGE

m his own household
competently................1Tm 3:4

MANASSEH

1. Son of Joseph and Asenath (Gn 41:50-
51). Adopted by Jacob as a tribe (Gn
48); allotted half of its territory east
of the Jordan from Gerasa to Mt.
Hermon in the far north and half
west of the Jordan to the Mediterranean from the Yarkon River to Mt.
Carmel (Nm 32:33-42; Jos 13:29-31; 17).
2. Son of Hezekiah; king of Judah (2Kg
21:1-18). Wickedness brought on God's
judgment (21:10-15; Jr 15:4).

MANGER

in cloth and lying in a m. ....Lk 2:12

MANIFESTATION

A m of the Spirit is given to
each 1Co 12:7

MANIFESTED

He was m in the flesh,
vindicated.................1Tm 3:16

MANNA

Israel named the substance m. . Ex 16:31
The m resembled coriander
seed, ...Nm 11:7
the land, the m ceased. .... Jos 5:12
ancestors ate the m in the......Jn 6:31,49

MANSLAUGHTER

could flee there who
committed m, ...Dt 4:42
for the one who
commits m,.............Jos 21:13-38

MANTLE

him and threw his m over
him..........................1Kg 19:19

picked up the m that had
fallen 2Kg 2:13

MANY

give his life as a ransom
for m........................Mt 20:28
For m are invited, but few are.. Mt 22:14
way we who are m are one
body ....Rm 12:5

MARCH

m around the city seven times, ..Jos 6:4

MARITAL

his m duty to his wife, ...1Co 7:3

MARK, JOHN

Missionary (Ac 12:12,25); Barnabas's
cousin (Col 4:10); cause of split between Paul and Barnabas (Ac 15:36-40);
later apparently reconciled to Paul
(Col 4:10; 2Tm 4:11; Phm 24). Also close
to Peter (1Pt 5:13). Wrote the Gospel of
Mark.

MARK

he placed a m on Cain so that ...Gn 4:15
If I don't see the m of the nails. .Jn 20:25
and receives a m on his
forehead.....................Rv 14:9
who accepted the m of the
beast........................Rv 19:20

MARKET

that is sold in the meat m......1Co 10:25

MARKETPLACE

My Father's house into a m!......Jn 2:16

MARRIAGE

nor are given in m but are
like.........................Mt 22:30
and giving in m, until the day..Mt 24:38
M is to be honored by all,..... Heb 13:4
the m of the Lamb has come, ...Rv 19:7

MARRIED (ADJ)

a m man is concerned about ..1Co 7:33

MARROW

soul and spirit, joints and m. . Heb 4:12

MARRY

who have **m-ied** foreign
    women .... Ezr 10:14
divorces...and **m-ies**
    another,...................... Mt 19:9
For all seven had **m-ied** her... Lk 20:33
the dead neither **m** nor are
    given...................... Lk 20:35
it is better to **m** than to burn ...1Co 7:9

MARTHA

Sister of Mary and Lazarus (Lk 10:38-42;
Jn 11:1–12:2).

MARVELOUS

of darkness into his **m** light...... 1Pt 2:9

MARY

1. Mother of Jesus (Mt 1:16; Lk 1:26-56;
2:1-20,34-35). Present at the cross (Jn
19:25-27); among the believers (Ac
1:14).
2. Magdalene; delivered from demons
(Lk 8:2); follower and supporter of
Jesus (Mk 15:40-41). Witness to the
crucifixion and resurrection (Mt
27:54–28:10; Mk 16:1-10; Lk 24:10; Jn
19:25–20:18).
3. Mother of James and Joseph/Joses;
follower and supporter of Jesus (Mk
15:40-41). Witness to the crucifixion
and resurrection (Mt 27:54–28:10;
Mk 16:1-8; Lk 24:10).
4. Sister of Martha and Lazarus (Jn 11);
anointed Jesus's feet (12:1-3).

MASSACRE

He gave orders to **m** all the
    boys .... Mt 2:16

MASTER (N)

And if I am a **m**, where is ...... Mal 1:6
No one can serve two **m-s** ..... Mt 6:24
is not greater than his **m**, ... Jn 13:16
doesn't know what his **m** is
    doing....................... Jn 15:15
obey your human **m-s** with
    fear .... Eph 6:5
m-s, treat your slaves the
    same way.................... Eph 6:9

MAT

lowered the **m** ... the
    paralytic.................... Mk 2:4
pick up your **m** and walk! .... Jn 5:8

MATERIAL

godliness is a way to **m** gain. ..1Tm 6:5

MATTHEW

Apostle; former tax collector (Mt 9:9;
10:3). Also called Levi son of Alphaeus
(Mk 2:14; cp. Lk 5:27-32). Wrote a Gospel.

MATTHIAS

Chosen to replace Judas (Ac 1:23-26).

MATURE

speak a wisdom among the **m**, ..1Co 2:6
let all of us who are **m** think.. Php 3:15
But solid food is for the **m** .... Heb 5:14

MATURITY

and go on to **m**, not laying..... Heb 6:1

MEAL

in exchange for a single **m**... Heb 12:16

MEANS

by every possible **m** save some.. 1Co 9:22

MEASURE (N)

a full and honest dry **m**, ... Dt 25:15
by the same **m** you use.......... Mt 7:2
a good **m**—pressed down,
    shaken...................... Lk 6:38
he gives the Spirit without **m**.. Jn 3:34

MEASURE (V)

Who has **m-d** the waters in the ..Is 40:12
He **m-d** the thickness of the .. Ezk 40:5
you will be **m-d** by the same...... Mt 7:2
He **m-d** the city with the rod at ..Rv 21:16

MEASUREMENTS

Do not be unfair in **m** .... Lv 19:35
These are the city's **m**: .... Ezk 48:16

MEASURING (ADJ)

will make justice the **m** line ....Is 28:17
and a **m** rod in his hand....... Ezk 40:3
was given a **m** reed like a rod ... Rv 11:1

MEAT

Lord will give you **m** to eat...... Ex 16:8
It is a good thing not to eat **m**, ..Rm 14:21

I will never again eat **m**,
    so that I 1Co 8:13

MEDES

People of Media, conquerors of Babylon (Is 13:17; 21:2; Jr 51:11,28); Darius (Dn
5:31; 9:1; 11:1); present at Pentecost (Ac
2:9).

MEDIA

Country of the Medes, north of Elam
and west of Assyria (Ezr 6:2); ally of
Persia (Est 1:3; Dn 5:28; 8:20); cursed by
Jeremiah (Jr 25:25).

MEDIATOR

through angels by means of
    a **m**........................... Gl 3:19
one God and one **m** between
    God 1Tm 2:5
He is the **m** of a better .... Heb 8:6

MEDICINE

A joyful heart is good **m**, ... Pr 17:22

MEDITATE

he **m-s** on it day and night. ...... Ps 1:2
I will **m** on your precepts..... Ps 119:15
in her heart and **m-ing** on
    them........................ Lk 2:19

MEDITATION

mouth and the **m** of my heart ..Ps 19:14
It is my **m** all day long......... Ps 119:97

MEDITERRANEAN SEA

Western border of Israel (Ex 23:31;
Nm 34:6; Dt 11:24; 34:2; Jos 1:4; 23:4; Ezk
47:15-20), including several of the tribal territories (Jos 15:4,11,12,47; 16:3,8;
17:9).

MEDIUM

Do not turn to **m-s** or consult.. Lv 19:31
A man or a woman who is a **m** ..Lv 20:27
a woman at En-dor who
    is a **m**...................... 1Sm 28:7

MEET

I will **m** with you there above..Ex 25:22
faithful God will come to
    m me;...................... Ps 59:10

Israel, prepare to **m** your God!. .Am 4:12
in the clouds to **m** the Lord in. . 1Th 4:17

MEETING (N)

In the tent of **m** outside the . . . . . .Ex 27:21

MELCHIZEDEK

King of Salem and priest (Gn 14:18);
represents undying priesthood (Ps
110:4; Heb 5:6,10; 6:20; 7).

MELT

The mountains **m** like wax at
the . . . . .Ps 97:5
elements will **m** with the heat. .2Pt 3:12

MEMBER

individually **m-s** of one another. . Rm 12:5
one **m** suffers, all the **m-s**
suffer 1Co 12:26
since we are **m-s** of his body. .Eph 5:30

MEMORY

All **m** of him perishes from the. . Jb 18:17
let him remove all **m** of them. . .Ps 109:15
will also be told in **m** of her. . . Mt 26:13

MENAHEM

King of Israel; obtained throne by
force (2Kg 15:10-16). Paid tribute to the
king of Assyria (15:19-20).

MENE

inscribed: M, M, Tekel, Parsin. . Dn 5:25

MENTION

that I constantly **m** you, ... Rm 1:9
shameful even to **m** what is
done . . . . Eph 5:12
my God when I **m** you in my. . . . . .Phm 4

MEPHIBOSHETH

1. Son of Jonathan; granted privilege in
   David's court (2Sm 4:4; 9; 16; 19).
2. Son of Saul whom David delivered
   to the Gibeonites (2Sm 21:1-9). His
   mother guarded his body until he
   was buried (21:10-14).

MERCIFUL

Blessed are the **m**, for they will be . .Mt 5:7

Be **m**, just as your Father also
is **m**. . . . . Lk 6:36
a **m** and faithful high priest . . Heb 2:17
is compassionate and **m**. . . . . . .Jms 5:11

MERCY

Make a **m** seat of pure gold, . . .Ex 25:17
in the cloud above the **m** seat. . .Lv 16:2
from above the **m** seat that
was . . . . Nm 7:89
LORD is waiting to show you **m** . .Is 30:18
for his **m-ies** never end. . . . . . . .Lm 3:22
In your wrath remember **m**!. . . Hab 3:2
merciful, for they will be
shown **m**. Mt 5:7
I desire **m** and not sacrifice. . . . Mt 9:13
of the law—justice, **m**, and
faith. . . . . .Mt 23:23
show **m** to whom I will
show **m**, .Rm 9:15
in view of the **m-ies** of God, . . . Rm 12:1
the Father of **m-ies** and the
God of 2Co 1:3
But God, who is rich in **m**, ... Eph 2:4
ark overshadowing the **m** seat. .Heb 9:5
M triumphs over judgment. . . Jms 2:13

MESSAGE

Their **m** has gone out to all the. .Ps 19:4
because his **m** had authority. . . Lk 4:32
Lord, who has believed our **m**?. .Jn 12:38
committed the **m** of
reconciliation 2Co 5:19

MESSENGER

or deaf like my **m** I am
sending? . . . . Is 42:19
See, I am going to send my **m**, . .Mal 3:1
am sending my **m** ahead of
you; . . . . .Mt 11:10
a **m** of Satan to torment me so . .2Co 12:7

MESSIAH *SEE ALSO* CHRIST

false **m-s** and false prophets . . Mt 24:24
was born for you, who is the **M**,. . Lk 2:11
M is coming" (. . . called Christ). . .Jn 4:25
that you may believe Jesus is
the **M** . . . . .Jn 20:31
been appointed for you as
the **M**. . . . . Ac 3:20

MICAH

1. Ephraimite idolater (Jdg 17–18).
2. Prophet to Israel and Judah in the
   days of kings Jotham, Ahaz, and
   Hezekiah of Judah (Jr 26:18; Mc 1:1).

MICAIAH

Son of Imlah; prophet against Ahab
(1Kg 22; 5–28; 2Ch 18:4-27).

MICHAEL

Archangel; guardian of Israel (Dn
10:13,21; 12:1). Disputed with the Devil (Jd
9); will fight the dragon (Rv 12:7).

MICHAL

Daughter of Saul (1Sm 14:49); offered
to David to endanger him (18:20-29);
warned David of a plot (19:11-17). Given
to Palti (25:44); taken back (2Sm 3:12-
16). Despised David dancing before the
Lord (6:14-23; 1Ch 15:29).

MIDDLE

tree in the **m** of the garden,. . . . . Gn 3:3

MIDWIFE

of Egypt said to the Hebrew
m-ves. . . . . .Ex 1:15

MIGHT

and will declare your **m** . . . . . . Ps 145:11
Not by strength or by **m**, but by
my . . . . Zch 4:6
who are greater in **m** and
power, ... 2Pt 2:11

MIGHTY

How the **m** have fallen! 2Sm 1:19
strong and **m**, the LORD,
m in battle. . . . . .Ps 24:8
and will proclaim your **m** acts. . . Ps 145:4
Counselor, **M** God, Eternal Father. . Is 9:6
because the **M** One has done
great. . . . . .Lk 1:49
Lord God who judges her is **m**. . Rv 18:8

MILE

if anyone forces you to go
one **m**, ... Mt 5:41

MILK

a land flowing with **m** and
honey. . . . . .Ex 3:8
churning of **m** produces
butter. . . . . Pr 30:33
gave you **m** to drink, not solid
food, ...1Co 3:2
You need **m**, not solid food. . . . Heb 5:12

MILL

desire the pure **m** of the word,......1Pt 2:2

MILL

while the sound of the **m**
  fades;..........................Ec 12:4
will be grinding . . . with a hand
  m;...........................Mt 24:41

MILLSTONE

the upper **m** as security for a ...Dt 24:6
better for him if a heavy **m**
  were.........................Mt 18:6

MINA

gave them ten **m-s**, and told
  them........................Lk 19:13

MIND

that he might change his **m**.. Nm 23:19
is not man who changes
  his **m**.......................1Sm 15:29
wholeheartedly and a
  willing **m,**...................1Ch 28:9
or gave the **m**
  understanding?............Jb 38:36
examine my heart and **m**.......Ps 26:2
I applied my **m** to examine .....Ec 1:13
Make the **m-s** of these people
  dull;...........................Is 6:10
will keep the **m** ... in perfect
  peace,........................Is 26:3
all your soul, and with all
  your **m**......................Mt 22:37
them over to a corrupt **m**......Rm 1:28
by the renewing of your **m,**......Rm 12:2
But we have the **m** of Christ....1Co 2:16
has blinded the **m-s** of the.....2Co 4:4
renewed in the spirit of your
  m-s;.........................Eph 4:23
Set your **m-s** on things above, ..Col 3:2
will put my laws into their
  m-s ....Heb 8:10
One who examines **m-s** and
  hearts,......................Rv 2:23

MIND-SET

Now the **m** of the flesh is death, ..Rm 8:6

MINISTER (N)

Levites to be **m-s** before the
  ark.........................1Ch 16:4
speak of you as **m-s** of our God. .Is 61:6
be a **m** of Christ Jesus to the ..Rm 15:16
as God's **m-s**, we commend....2Co 6:4
a **m** of the sanctuary and the ..Heb 8:2

MINISTER (V)

worn by Aaron whenever
  he **m-s** ....Ex 28:35

MINISTERING (N)

Are they not all **m** spirits sent ..Heb 1:14

MINISTRY

prayer and to the **m** of the word. . Ac 6:4
given us the **m** of
  reconciliation:.............2Co 5:18
the saints for the work of **m** .. Eph 4:12
an evangelist, fulfill your **m**....2Tm 4:5
has now obtained a superior
  m ....Heb 8:6

MINT

pay a tenth of **m**, dill, and
  cumin,......................Mt 23:23

MIRACLE

Pharaoh tells you, 'Perform a **m**,' ..Ex 7:9
and do many **m-s** in your
  name? ....Mt 7:22
For if the **m-s** that were
  done in ....Mt 11:21
was not able to do a **m** there,......Mk 6:5
extraordinary **m-s** by Paul's
  hands.......................Ac 19:11
testified by signs . . . various
  m-s,........................Heb 2:4

MIRIAM

Sister of Moses and Aaron; daughter
of Jochebed and Amram (Nm 26:59;
1Ch 6:3). Watched over baby Moses (Ex
2:4-8). Prophetess; led dancing at Red
Sea (15:20-21). Struck with skin disease
for criticizing Moses (Nm 12; Dt 24:9);
died in Kadesh (Nm 20:1).

MIRROR

as in a **m**, but then face to
  face.........................1Co 13:12
looking at his own face in
  a **m**.........................Jms 1:23

MISERABLE

You are all **m** comforters........ Jb 16:2
Be **m** and mourn and weep......Jms 4:9

MISERY

I have observed the **m** of my people. .Ex 3:7

MIST

Your love is like the
  morning **m** ....Hs 6:4

MISTAKE

do not say ... that it was a **m**...... Ec 5:6

MISTREAT

pray for those who **m** you.......Lk 6:28

MISTRESS

her **m** became contemptible
  to her........................Gn 16:4

MISUSE

Do not **m** the name of the
  LORD.........................Ex 20:7

MOABITE

No Ammonite or **M** may enter
  the...........................Dt 23:3

MOABITESS

her daughter-in-law Ruth the
  M............................Ru 1:22

MOCK

At noon Elijah **m-ed** them. 1Kg 18:27
Everyone who sees me **m-s**
  me;...........................Ps 22:7
He **m-s** those who **m**, but gives
  grace ....Pr 3:34
down before him and **m-ed**
  him:..........................Mt 27:29
God is not **m-ed**. For whatever a
  person........................Gl 6:7

MOCKER

or sit in the company of **m-s!**..... Ps 1:1
one who corrects a **m** will bring ..Pr 9:7
Wine is a **m**, beer is a brawler;.. Pr 20:1

MODEST

dress themselves in **m**
  clothing,.....................1Tm 2:9

MOMENT

For his anger lasts only a **m,**......Ps 30:5
I deserted you for a brief **m**..... Is 54:7
in a **m**, in the twinkling of an
  eye, ...1Co 15:52

MOMENTARY

For our **m** light affliction is....2Co 4:17

MONEY

and **m** is the answer for
   everything...................Ec 10:19
cannot serve both God
   and **m**.......................Mt 6:24
overturned the tables of the **m**..Mt 21:12
no traveling bag, no bread,
   no **m**;.........................Lk 9:3
a lot of wine, not greedy for **m**,..1Tm 3:8
For the love of **m** is a root of..1Tm 6:10
free from the love of **m**........Heb 13:5

MONEY-BAG

Don't carry a **m**, traveling bag, ..Lk 10:4
charge of the **m** and
   would steal...................Jn 12:6

MONSTER

all sea **m**-s and ocean depths,......Ps 148:7

MONTH

it is the first **m** of your year..... Ex 12:2
Each **m** they will bear fresh
   fruit........................ Ezk 47:12
producing its fruit every **m**......Rv 22:2

MOON

and this time the sun, **m**, and
   eleven stars................. Gn 37:9
sun stood still and the **m**
   stopped.................... Jos 10:13
the **m** and the stars, which
   you set.......................Ps 8:3
you by day or the **m** by night... Ps 121:6
the **m** to blood before the great.. Jl 2:31
and the **m** will not shed its
   light;.......................Mt 24:29
the **m** to blood before the great..Ac 2:20
another of the **m**, and
   another....................1Co 15:41

MORALS

Bad company corrupts
   good **m**.................... 1Co 15:33

MORDECAI

Cousin and legal guardian of Esther
(Est 2:7). Uncovered assassination plot
(2:21-23). Offended Haman (3:1-7); Haman sought genocide (3:7-15); Mordecai led Esther to thwart the attempt

(Est 4–5). Honored by the king (Est 6);
wrote revenge edict (Est 8).

MORNING

and there was **m**: one day........Gn 1:5
the **m** stars sang together ......Jb 38:7
but there is joy in the **m**.........Ps 30:5
a loud voice early in the **m**,..... Pr 27:14
They are new every **m**;........Lm 3:23
Very early in the **m**, on the
   first day ....Mk 16:2
and the **m** star rises in your
   hearts...................... 2Pt 1:19
of David, the bright **m** star.......Rv 22:16

MORON

'You **m**!' will be subject to
   hellfire..................... Mt 5:22

MORTAL

Do not let a mere **m** hinder you....2Ch
14:11
Can a **m** be righteous before ... Jb 4:17
What can mere **m**-s do to me? ..Ps 56:4
let sin reign in your **m** body, ...Rm 6:12
and this **m** body must be
   clothed 1Co 15:53

MORTALITY

that **m** may be swallowed up .. 2Co 5:4

MOSES

Leader of Israel; Levite; brother of Aaron
and Miriam (1Ch 6:3). Born under Egyptian oppression (Ex 1); set adrift on Nile;
rescued and raised by Pharaoh's daughter (2:1-10). Killed Egyptian; fled to Midian and married Zipporah (2:11-22). Called
by God from burning bush (Ex 3–4). Announced ten plagues (Ex 7–11).
   Divided the Red Sea (Ex 14). Brought
water from a rock (17:1-7); held up God's
staff and defeated Amalek (17:8-13). Delegated judging (18:13-26).
   God spoke to him at Sinai: law (Ex
19–23); tabernacle, equipment, and
garments (Ex 25–28; 30); consecration
of priests (Ex 29). Discovered golden
calf and broke tablets (Ex 32). Saw God's
glory (33:12–34:28). Ordained Aaron
and his sons (Lv 8–9).
   Opposed by Aaron and Miriam (Nm
12); opposed by Korah (Nm 16). Excluded from promised land for striking
rock (Nm 20:1-13; 27:12-14; Dt 32:51).
Made a bronze snake for healing (Nm

21:4-9; Jn 3:14). Wrote the book of the
law (Jos 23:6; 2Ch 34:14). Saw promised
land from a distance (Dt 3:23-27; 34:1-
4); commissioned Joshua as successor
(Nm 27:12-23); buried by God (34:5-8).

MOST

holy place and the **m** holy
   place........................ Ex 26:33
is the **m** important of all?......Mk 12:28
making the **m** of the time..... Eph 5:16

MOST HIGH

he was a priest to God **M**...... Gn 14:18
I call to God **M**, to God who......Ps 57:2
you are all sons of the **M**........Ps 82:6
under the protection of the **M**.. Ps 91:1
come from the mouth of
   the **M**?......................Lm 3:38
Jesus, Son of the **M** God?.......Mk 5:7
called the Son of the **M**,.........Lk 1:32
the **M** does not dwell in
   sanctuaries.................. Ac 7:48
of Salem, priest of the God **M**, ..Heb 7:1

MOTH

where **m** and rust destroy
   and .... Mt 6:19

MOTHER

a man leaves his father and **m** ..Gn 2:24
she was the **m** of all the living.. Gn 3:20
Honor your father and your
   m so .... Ex 20:12
Naked I came from my **m**-'s
   womb, ...Jb 1:21
the joyful **m** of children....... Ps 113:9
don't reject your **m**-'s teaching,.. Pr 1:8
pronouncement that his **m**
   taught .... Pr 31:1
As a **m** comforts her son, so I.. Is 66:13
father or **m** more than me is.. Mt 10:37
Who is my **m** and who are my..Mt 12:48
Honor your father and your **m**;..Mt 15:4
leave his father and **m** and
   be joined.................... Mt 19:5
not hate his own father and **m**..Lk 14:26
to the disciple, "Here is your
   m."..........................Jn 19:27

MOTHER-IN-LAW

a daughter-in-law is against
   her **m**; .... Mc 7:6
a daughter-in-law against
   her **m**; .... Mt 10:35
Simon's **m** was suffering from .. Lk 4:38

MOTIVES

but the LORD weighs m.......... Pr 16:2
whether from false m or ..... Php 1:18

MOUNT (N) *SEE ALSO*
CARMEL, MOUNT OF OLIVES,
SINAI, ZION

The LORD came down on M
　Sinai .... Ex 19:20
the blessing at M Gerizim and .. Dt 11:29
M Zion—the summit of
　Zaphon— .... Ps 48:2
M Zion, which he loved. .... Ps 78:68
The M of Olives will be split in.. Zch 14:4
was sitting on the M of Olives, .. Mt 24:3
they went out to the M of
　Olives. .... Mt 26:30
Now Hagar represents M Sinai.. Gl 4:25

MOUNT (V)

gentle, and m-ed on a donkey,.. Mt 21:5

MOUNT OF OLIVES

The M will be split in half...... Zch 14:4
psalms, they went out to
　the M....................... Mt 26:30
made his way as usual to
　the M,...................... Lk 22:39
But Jesus went to the M.......... Jn 8:1

MOUNTAIN

will be provided on the
　LORD's m................... Gn 22:14
came to Horeb, the m of God..... Ex 3:1
my king on Zion, my holy m...... Ps 2:6
The m-s melt like wax at the.... Ps 97:5
I lift my eyes toward the m-s... Ps 121:1
The m-s surround Jerusalem .. Ps 125:2
let us go up to the m of the LORD,... Is 2:3
beautiful on the m-s are the feet.. Is 52:7
became a great m and
　filled the.................... Dn 2:35
to a very high m and
　showed him .... Mt 4:8
up on a high m by themselves... Mt 17:1
will tell this m, 'Move from ... Mt 17:20
and every m and hill will be ..... Lk 3:5
all faith so that I can move m-s. .1Co 13:2

MOURN

a time to m and a time to dance;.. Ec 3:4
to comfort all who m,........... Is 61:2
will m for him as one m-s for .. Zch 12:10
Blessed are those who m, for...... Mt 5:4
Be miserable and m and weep.. Jms 4:9
of the earth will m over him..... Rv 1:7

MOURNING (N)

day long I go around in m....... Ps 38:6
festive oil instead of m,.......... Is 61:3
I will turn their m into joy,..... Jr 31:13

MOUTH

Who placed a m on .... Ex 4:11
from the m-s of infants.......... Ps 8:2
May the words of my m and... Ps 19:14
They have m-s but cannot
　speak,...................... Ps 115:5
from his m come knowledge
　and .... Pr 2:6
praise you, and not your
　own m....................... Pr 27:2
Do not let your m bring guilt on.. Ec 5:6
yet he did not open his m....... Is 53:7
that comes from the m of God.. Mt 4:4
If you confess with your m...... Rm 10:9
cursing come out of the
　same m. .... Jms 3:10

MOVE

M-ed with compassion, Jesus..Mt 20:34
so that I can m mountains..... 1Co 13:2

MUD

made some m from the saliva, .. Jn 9:6

MUDDY

out of the m clay, and
　set my feet................... Ps 40:2

MULTIPLY

Be fruitful, m, fill the earth,.... Gn 1:28
fruitful, increased rapidly,
　m-ied,...................... Ex 1:7
Yet the fool m-ies words. ...... Ec 10:14
The more they m-ied, the
　more they .... Hs 4:7
where sin m-ied, grace m-ied.. Rm 5:20
sin so that grace may m? .... Rm 6:1

MULTITUDE

M-s, m-s in the valley of
　decision!.................... Jl 3:14
and cover a m of sins.......... Jms 5:20
since love covers a m of sins...... 1Pt 4:8
there was a vast m from every .. Rv 7:9

MURDER

Do not m. .... Ex 20:13
Do not m, and whoever
　m-s will. .... Mt 5:21

whom you had m-ed by
　hanging .... Ac 5:30
adultery, also said, Do not m.. Jms 2:11

MURDERER

the m must be put to death. . Nm 35:16
He was a m from the beginning.. Jn 8:44
hates his brother or sister is
　a m,......................... 1Jn 3:15

MUSIC

in charge of the m in the
　LORD's 1Ch 6:31
sing and make m to the LORD....... Ps 27:6
harp and the m of a lyre........ Ps 92:3
house, he heard m and
　dancing. .... Lk 15:25
songs, singing and making m . Eph 5:19

MUSICAL

accompanied by m
　instruments 1Ch 15:16
the m instruments of the LORD,.. 2Ch 7:6
the m instruments of David... Neh 12:36

MUSTARD

is like a m seed that a man ...... Mt 13:31
faith the size of a m seed, ... Mt 17:20

MUTE

Who makes a person m or deaf, .. Ex 4:11

MUTUALLY

to be m encouraged by each... Rm 1:12

MUZZLE

Do not m an ox while it treads. .Dt 25:4
my mouth with a m as long as
　the.......................... Ps 39:1
Do not m an ox while it is..... 1Tm 5:18

MYRRH

My hands dripped with m, ... Sg 5:5
gold, frankincense, and m...... Mt 2:11

MYSTERY

I will speak m-ies from the past.. Ps 78:2
The m was then revealed to
　Daniel .... Dn 2:19
I am telling you a m:.......... 1Co 15:51
This m is profound, but I am.. Eph 5:32
the m hidden for ages and ..... Col 1:26

holding the **m** of the faith with . .1Tm 3:9
the **m** of godliness is great: . . . 1Tm 3:16

MYTHS

pay attention to **m** and endless . .1Tm 1:4
truth and will turn aside to **m**. . .2Tm 4:4
contrived **m** when we
    made known 2Pt 1:16

N

NAGGING (ADJ)

share a house with a **n** wife. . . . . .Pr 21:9
rainy day and a **n** wife are. . . . . .Pr 27:15

NAGGING (N)

a wife's **n** is an endless. . . . . Pr 19:13

NAHUM

Prophet against Nineveh (Nah 1:1).

NAIL (N)

finger into the mark of the **n-s**. .Jn 20:25

NAIL (V)

people to **n** him to a cross . . . . . Ac 2:23
away by **n-ing** it to the cross . .Col 2:14

NAKED

the man and his wife were **n** . . . . . .Gn 2:25
Who told you that you were **n**? . .Gn 3:11
N I came from my mother's
    womb, ...Jb 1:21
I was **n** and you clothed me; . .Mt 25:36
we will not be found **n**. 2Co 5:3

NAKEDNESS

they covered their father's **n**. . .Gn 9:23
or famine or **n** or danger or . . Rm 8:35

NAME (N)

The man gave **n-s** to all the . . . . . Gn 2:20
This is my **n** forever; . . . . .Ex 3:15
Do not misuse the **n** of the
    LORD. . . . . .Ex 20:7
the place to have his **n** dwell. . . Dt 12:11
people, who bear my **n**, ... 2Ch 7:14
magnificent is your **n** throughout . .Ps 8:1
we take pride in the **n** of the
    LORD . . . . .Ps 20:7

let us exalt his **n** together. . . . . . .Ps 34:3
within me, bless his holy **n**. . . . . . .Ps 103:1
who comes in the **n** of the
    LORD . . . . .Ps 118:26
n of the LORD is a strong
    tower; . . . . .Pr 18:10
A good **n** is to be chosen over . . Pr 22:1
I am the LORD. That is my **n**, ... Is 42:8
I had concern for my holy **n**, . .Ezk 36:21
Your **n** be honored as holy. . . . . . Mt 6:9
These are the **n-s** of the
    twelve . . . . Mt 10:2
that your **n-s** are written in
    heaven. . . . . Lk 10:20
have asked for nothing in
    my **n**. . . . . .Jn 16:24
calls on the **n** of the Lord will. . .Ac 2:21
there is no other **n** under
    heaven. .Ac 4:12
calls on the **n** of the Lord
    will . . . . .Rm 10:13
the **n** that is above every **n**, ... Php 2:9
whose **n-s** are in the book . . . . . Php 4:3
beast's **n** or the number of
    its **n**. . . . . Rv 13:17

NAME (V)

and you are to **n** him Jesus, ... Mt 1:21

NAOMI

Ruth's mother-in-law (Ru 1:2-4).

NAPHTALI

Son of Jacob and Bilhah (Gn 30:1-8).
Tribe with territory north and west of
the Sea of Galilee (Jos 19:32-39); praised
by Deborah (Jdg 5:18); produced Hiram
the craftsman (1Kg 7:13-14).

NARROW

Enter through the **n** gate. . . . . . .Mt 7:13

NATHAN

Prophet to David; told David he would
never fail to have a descendant on the
throne (2Sm 7:4-17); confronted David
about Bathsheba (2Sm 12:1-15). Anointed Solomon (1Kg 1).

NATHANAEL

Apostle "in whom is no deceit"; invited by Philip; asked if anything good
comes out of Nazareth (Jn 1:45-49; 21:2);
possibly also called Bartholomew (Mt
10:3).

NATION

I will make you into a great **n**. . Gn 12:2
kingdom of priests and my
    holy **n**. .Ex 19:6
Why do the **n-s** rage and the. . . . . Ps 2:1
Happy is the **n** whose God is . .Ps 33:12
Declare his glory among
    the **n-s** . . . . .Ps 96:3
Righteousness exalts a **n**,
    but sin . . . . .Pr 14:34
N will not take up the sword . . . . . .Is 2:4
proclaim my glory among the
    n-s. . . . . Is 66:19
For **n** will rise up against **n**, ... Mt 24:7
and make disciples of all **n-s** . .Mt 28:19
a royal priesthood, a holy **n**, ...1Pt 2:9
and language and people and **n**.. .Rv 5:9

NATURAL

exchanged **n** sexual relations . . Rm 1:26
did not spare the **n** branches, . .Rm 11:21
sown a **n** body, raised a 1Co 15:44

NATURE

His eternal power and
    divine **n**. . . . . .Rm 1:20
and against **n** were
    grafted into. . . . . .Rm 11:24
Does not even **n** itself
    teach you 1Co 11:14
you may share in the divine **n** . . 2Pt 1:4

NAZARENE

that he will be called a **N**. . . . . . . Mt 2:23
of the sect of the **N-s**! . . . . Ac 24:5

NAZARETH

Hometown of Jesus (Mt 2:23; Lk 2:51;
4:16; Jn 1:45-46).
"Jesus of **N**," they answered. . . . . Jn 18:5

NAZIRITE

a special vow, a **N** vow, ... Nm 6:2
boy will be a **N** to God from. . . .Jdg 13:5

NEAR

But the message is very
    n you, ...Dt 30:14
The LORD is **n** all who call out . .Ps 145:18
call to him while he is **n**. . . . . Is 55:6
The great day of the LORD is
    n, ...Zph 1:14
kingdom of heaven has
    come **n**! . . . . .Mt 3:2
The message is **n** you, in your. . . Rm 10:8

The Lord is n.................... Php 4:5
Draw n to God, and he will
    draw n....................... Jms 4:8
because the time is n......... Rv 22:10

NEARER

our salvation is n than
    when we.................... Rm 13:11

NEBUCHADNEZZAR

King of Babylon; defeated and exiled
Judah (2Kg 24–25; 1Ch 6:15; 2Ch 36; Jr 39).
Dreams interpreted by Daniel (Dn 2; 4);
threw Shadrach, Meshach, and Abednego into the furnace (Dn 3); temporarily insane (Dn 4); praised God (2:47; 3:28; 4:34-37).

NECK

you and adornment for your n. .Pr 3:22
Your n is like the tower of ....Sg 4:4

NEED (N)

a robber, your n, like a bandit. .Pr 24:34
supply all your n-s according. .Php 4:19
a fellow believer in n but
    withholds 1Jn 3:17

NEED (V)

Father knows the things you n ..Mt 6:8
It is not those who are well who n a
    doctor .... Mt 9:12
say to the hand, "I don't
    n you!"....................1Co 12:21

NEEDLE

the eye of a n than for a rich. .Mt 19:24

NEEDY

and lifts the n from the trash. .1Sm 2:8
I was a father to the n, ...Jb 29:16
He heard the outcry of the n. .Jb 34:28
is kind to the n honors him......Pr 14:31

NEGATIVE

a n report about the land .... Nm 14:36

NEGLECT

you have n-ed the more
    important ....Mt 23:23
Don't n the gift that is in you;...1Tm 4:14
we escape if we n such a great ..Heb 2:3
not n-ing to gather together ..Heb 10:25

NEHEMIAH

Cupbearer to King Artaxerxes of Babylon (Neh 1:11); obtained permission,
planned, and supervised rebuilding
Jerusalem's walls despite opposition
(Neh 2–6). Was appointed governor
of Judah (5:14). Dedicated wall (12:27-
43). Promoted reforms (Neh 8–10; 13).
Prayed frequently (1:4-11; 2:4; 4:4-5,9;
5:19; 6:9,14; 13:14,22,29,31).

NEIGHBOR

false testimony against
    your n........................ Ex 20:16
Do not covet your n-'s wife,......Ex 20:17
but love your n as yourself;..... Lv 19:18
better a n nearby than a
    brother ....Pr 27:10
one teach his n or his brother,. .Jr 31:34
to him who gives his n-s
    drink,...................... Hab 2:15
Love your n and hate your
    enemy .... Mt 5:43
and love your n as yourself... Mt 19:19
asked Jesus, "And who is
    my n?" .... Lk 10:29
Love your n as yourself. .... Gl 5:14

NEST (N)

your n is set in the cliffs...... Nm 24:21
and make your n among the stars. .Ob 4
and birds of the sky have n-s .. Mt 8:20

NEST (V)

sky come and n in its
    branches.................... Mt 13:32

NET

They prepared a n for my steps; . .Ps 57:6
to spread a n where any
    bird can......................Pr 1:17
street like an antelope in a n... Is 51:20
they left their n-s and followed. .Mt 4:20
Cast the n on the right side of . .Jn 21:6

NEVER

and they will n perish..........Jn 10:28
Love n ends....................1Co 13:8
I will n leave you or abandon. .Heb 13:5

NEW

A n king, who did not know......Ex 1:8
Sing a n song to him;...........Ps 33:3
He put a n song in my mouth, ..Ps 40:3
there is nothing n under the sun. .Ec 1:9

will create a n heaven and a
    n earth;.......................Is 65:17
I will make a n covenant with. . .Jr 31:31
you a n heart and put a n
    spirit...................... Ezk 36:26
And no one puts n wine
    into old ....Mt 9:17
A n teaching with authority! . . Mk 1:27
This cup is the n covenant......Lk 22:20
I give you a n command: Love. .Jn 13:34
in Christ, he is a n creation;....2Co 5:17
and have put on the n self...... Col 3:10
wait for n heavens and a n
    earth........................2Pt 3:13
I saw a n heaven and a n earth; . .Rv 21:1
I am making everything n."....Rv 21:5

NEWBORN

Like n infants, desire the 1Pt 2:2

NEWS

good n strengthens the bones. . Pr 15:30
who brings n of good things,..... Is 52:7
Then the n about him spread. . Mt 4:24
the poor are told the good n. ...Mt 11:5
Repent and believe in the
    good n! .... Mk 1:15

NICODEMUS

Pharisee and member of the Sanhedrin. Visited Jesus at night (Jn 3:1-21);
defended Jesus to the Sanhedrin (7:45-
52); helped prepare Jesus's body for
burial (19:39).

NIGHT

the darkness he called "n." ......Gn 1:5
earth forty days and forty n-s . . Gn 7:4
you are to meditate on it day
    and n .... Jos 1:8
he meditates on it day and n..... Ps 1:2
not fear the terror of the n ......Ps 91:5
fasted forty days and forty n-s ..Mt 4:2
watch at n over their flock.....Lk 2:8
man came to him at n and said,. .Jn 3:2
come just like a thief in the n. . .1Th 5:2
not belong to the n or the
    darkness.....................1Th 5:5
N will be no more; .... Rv 22:5

NILE

River of Egypt (Gn 41:1; Ex 1:22; 2:3; Is
7:18; 19:7-8; Ezk 29:3-10; Nah 3:8; Zch
10:11); floods periodically (Jr 46:7-8; Am
8:8; 9:5); struck by the plagues (Ex 7:20-
21; 8:3).

NINE

He was n feet, n inches tall ... 1Sm 17:4
ten cleansed? Where are
the n?......................... Lk 17:17
since it's only n in the
morning...................... Ac 2:15

NINETY-NINE

Abraham was n years old
when .... Gn 17:24
leave the n in the open field ..... Lk 15:4

NINETY-YEAR-OLD

Can Sarah, a n woman,
give birth?................... Gn 17:17

NINEVEH

Capital of Assyria (Gn 10:11-12; 2Kg 19:36; Is 37:37); Jonah preached against (Jnh 3:2-4) and the people repented (3:5-7; Mt 12:41; Lk 11:30-32); prophets condemned (Nah 1:1; Zph 2:13).

NOAH

Son of Lamech; descendant of Seth; a righteous man (Gn 5:28-29; 6:9; Ex 14:14; 2Pt 2:5; Heb 11:7). Built an ark, entered it with animals and his family, and survived the flood (Gn 6:14–8:19; 1Pt 3:20). Received God's promise (Gn 8:20–9:17). Got drunk and cursed Canaan (9:20-27). Flood a symbol of sudden judgment (Mt 24:37-38; Lk 17:26-27).

NOBLE (ADJ)

you are a woman of n
character.................... Ru 3:11
My heart is moved by a n
theme as I .... Ps 45:1
She has done a n thing for
me......................... Mt 26:10
powerful, not many of n
birth....................... 1Co 1:26

NOBLE (N)

Do not trust in n-s, in man, who .... Ps 146:3
when your king is a son of n-s ..Ec 10:17
slaughtered all Judah's n-s...... Jr 39:6

NOISE

Pharaoh king of Egypt was
all n; .... Jr 46:17
an end to the n of your
songs,...................... Ezk 26:13
from me the n of your songs!..Am 5:23
will pass away with a loud n ..2Pt 3:10

NORTH

the king of the N will come,......Dn 11:15

NOSE

and twisting a n draws blood,..Pr 30:33

NOSTRILS

the breath of life into his n ..... Gn 2:7
from God remains in my n ......Jb 27:3
blast of the breath of your n. .. Ps 18:15

NOTHING

N is too difficult for you!....... Jr 32:17
N will be impossible for you.. Mt 17:20
you can do n without me........ Jn 15:5
but do not have love, I am n...1Co 13:2
I didn't run or labor for n...... Php 2:16
For we brought n into the
world, ... 1Tm 6:7

NULLIFY

You n the word of God by
your tradition .... Mk 7:13

NUMBER (N)

and grew daily in n............Ac 16:5
it is the n of a person.
Its n is 666. ....Rv 13:18

NUMBER (V)

Teach us to n our days
carefully................... Ps 90:12
God has n-ed the days of
your .... Dn 5:26
who was n-ed among the
Twelve. .... Lk 22:3

NURSE

that Sarah would n children?...Gn 21:7
woman took the boy and
n-d him. .... Ex 2:9

NURSING (ADJ)

mouths of infants and n babies, ..Ps 8:2
a woman forget her n child,..... Is 49:15
mouths of infants and n
babies? .... Mt 21:16

O

OAK

live near the o-s of Mamre..... Gn 13:18
and he was as sturdy as
the o-s;..................... Am 2:9

OATH

The LORD swore an o to David, ..Ps 132:11
I tell you, don't take an o at all: .. Mt 5:34
by earth or with any other o. . Jms 5:12

OBADIAH

Prophet against Edom (Ob 1).

OBEDIENCE

through the one man's o the
many .... Rm 5:19
or of o leading to
righteousness?.............. Rm 6:16
He learned o through what he ..Heb 5:8

OBEDIENT

to Nazareth and was o to them. .Lk 2:51
becoming o to the point
of death—.................. Php 2:8

OBEY

to o is better than sacrifice,.. 1Sm 15:22
the winds and the sea o him! .. Mt 8:27
unclean spirits, and they
o him...................... Mk 1:27
We must o God rather than......Ac 5:29
Children, o your parents as.... Eph 6:1

OBLIGATED

are not o to the flesh to ....Rm 8:12

OBSCENE

O and foolish talking .... Eph 5:4

OBSERVE

You must o my Sabbaths, ...Ex 31:13
When I o your heavens, the
work....................... Ps 8:3
teaching them to o
everything I ....Mt 28:20
o-ing special days,
months,..................... Gl 4:10
they will o your
good works.................. 1Pt 2:12

OBTAIN

have o-ed righteousness ..... Rm 9:30

OBVIOUS

each one's work will
    become o 1Co 3:13
the works of the flesh are o: .... Gl 5:19
good works are o, and those
    that 1Tm 5:25

OFFEND

one who isn't o-ed by me........Mt 11:6

OFFENSE

but love covers all o-s. .... Pr 10:12
o-s will inevitably come,
    but woe to ....Mt 18:7
that case the o of the cross
    has...........................Gl 5:11

OFFENSIVE

if there is any o way in me; .. Ps 139:24

OFFER

o him there as a burnt
    offering......................Gn 22:2
if you are o-ing your gift on..... Mt 5:23
once for all time when he
    o-ed himself................ Heb 7:27
not do this to o himself
    many ....Heb 9:25

OFFERING (N)

take pleasure in burnt o-s ... as much
    as in obeying the LORD? ... 1Sm 15:22
You do not delight in
    sacrifice and o...............Ps 40:6
You make him a guilt o, ... Is 53:10
of God rather than burnt o-s......Hs 6:6
and fragrant o to God. .... Eph 5:2
You did not desire sacrifice
    and o, ...Heb 10:5

OFFSPRING

and between your o and her o...Gn 3:15
I will give this land to your o....Gn 12:7
said, 'For we are also his o.'..... Ac 17:28

OIL

and the o jug did not run dry, ..1Kg 17:16
You anoint my head with o;..... Ps 23:5
wise ones took o in their
    flasks ....Mt 25:4

OLD

I have been young and now
    I am o, ...Ps 37:25
even when he is o he will not...Pr 22:6
your o men will have dreams, .. Jl 2:28
puts new wine into o
    wineskins...................Mt 9:17
and your o men will dream
    dreams ....Ac 2:17
the o has passed away,........2Co 5:17
have put off the o self with its ..Col 3:9

OLDER

The o will serve the younger. . .Rm 9:12

OLIVE   *SEE ALSO* MOUNT OF OLIVES

was a plucked o leaf in its beak..Gn 8:11

OMEGA

the Alpha and the O...Rv 1:8; 21:6; 22:13

OMRI

Army commander; king of Israel; founded the city of Samaria (1Kg 16:15-28).

ONCE

He died to sin o for all; ....Rm 6:10
appointed for people to die o ..Heb 9:27

ONE   *SEE ALSO* ONE AND ONLY SON

and then morning: o day. ....Gn 1:5
the LORD our God, the LORD is o. . Dt 6:4
Are you the o who is to come, ..Mt 11:3
the two will become o flesh? .. Mt 19:5
I and the Father are o...........Jn 10:30
they may be o as we are o.......Jn 17:11
baptized by o Spirit into
    o body 1Co 12:13
you are all o in Christ Jesus...... Gl 3:28
o Lord, o faith, o baptism,......Eph 4:5
For there is o God and o
    mediator 1Tm 2:5
You believe that God is o. ..... Jms 2:19

ONE AND ONLY SON

glory as the o from the Father,.. Jn 1:14
No one has ever seen God. The o..Jn 1:18
He gave his o, so that everyone..Jn 3:16
not believed in the name of
    the o ....Jn 3:18
God sent his o into the world...1Jn 4:9

OPEN

eyes will be o-ed and you
    will be ....Gn 3:5
O my eyes so that I may .... Ps 119:18
what he o-s, no one can close; ..Is 22:22
yet he did not o his mouth. ...... Is 53:7
and the door will be o-ed to you..Mt 7:7
hears my voice and o-s the
    door, ... Rv 3:20
Who is worthy to o the scroll......Rv 5:2
and books were o-ed...........Rv 20:12

OPPORTUNITY

looking for a good o to betray
    him........................... Mt 26:16
and don't give the devil an o. . Eph 4:27

OPPRESS

He was o-ed and afflicted, ... Is 53:7
to the blind, to set free the o-ed,..Lk 4:18
Don't the rich o you and drag......Jms 2:6

ORACLE

The o of Balaam son of Beor,.. Nm 24:3
received living o-s to give to us.. Ac 7:38

ORDAIN

the way you will o Aaron and
    his .... Ex 29:9
unless the Lord has o-ed it?......Lm 3:37

ORDER

Set your house in o, ... 2Kg 20:1
give his angels o-s concerning ..Ps 91:11
give his angels o-s concerning...Mt 4:6
must be done decently and
    in o.......................... 1Co 14:40
according to the o of
    Melchizedek. .... Heb 5:6

ORDINANCE

the o-s of the LORD are reliable ..Ps 19:9

ORDINATION

the ram of Aaron's o .... Ex 29:26

ORGIES

drunkenness, o, carousing, ... 1Pt 4:3

ORIGINATE

Did the word of God o from
    you,........................ 1Co 14:36

ORNAN *SEE* ARAUNAH

ORPHANS

I will not leave you as o; .... Jn 14:18
to look after o and widows in.. Jms 1:27

OTHER

I am the LORD, and there is no o; ..Is 45:5
as you want o-s to do for you, ..Lk 6:31

OTHNIEL

Judge; defeated Arameans (Jdg 3:7-11);
Caleb's nephew (Jos 15:17; Jdg 1:13).

OUTDO

O one another in showing
honor. ....Rm 12:10

OUTER

though our o person is being ..2Co 4:16

OUTRAN

other disciple o Peter and got .. Jn 20:4

OUTSIDE

You clean the o of the cup
and ....Mt 23:25
person commits is o the body. . 1Co 6:18
Jesus also suffered o the
gate, ... Heb 13:12

OUTSIDER

Act wisely toward o-s, ...Col 4:5
properly in the presence
of o-s 1Th 4:12

OUTSTRETCHED

you with an o arm and
great acts ....Ex 6:6

OUTWARD

Stop judging according to o ....Jn 7:24
consist of o things like.......... 1Pt 3:3

OUTWARDLY

person is not a Jew who is
one o, ... Rm 2:28

OVERCOME

yet the darkness did not o it. ..... Jn 1:5

OVERFLOW

my cup o-s.....................Ps 23:5
speaks from the o of the
heart. ....Mt 12:34
to make every grace o to you,.. 2Co 9:8

OVERLOOK

having o-ed the times of
ignorance ....Ac 17:30

OVERPOWER

gates of Hades will not o it.... Mt 16:18

OVERSEE

not o-ing out of compulsion
but...........................1Pt 5:2

OVERSEER

If anyone aspires to be an o, ... 1Tm 3:1
an o of God's household ....Ti 1:7
Shepherd and O of your souls. . 1Pt 2:25

OVERSHADOW

of the Most High will o you. ....Lk 1:35

OVERTAKE

so that darkness doesn't o you. .Jn 12:35

OVERTURN

o-ed tables of the money
changers .... Mt 21:12

OVERWHELM

rivers, they will not o you....... Is 43:2

OWE

one who o-d ten thousand
talents .... Mt 18:24
not ... a gift, but as something
o-d. ....Rm 4:4
Do not o anyone anything,
except .... Rm 13:8
you o me even your very self... Phm 19

OWN (ADJ)

rely on your o understanding;... Pr 3:5
all have turned to our o way; ... Is 53:6

OWN (N)

He came to his o,.................Jn 1:11

Having loved his o who were in ..Jn 13:1
You are not your o,............1Co 6:19

OX

Do not muzzle an o while it
treads........................Dt 25:4
not muzzle an o while it treads.. 1Co 9:9

P

PAIN

I will intensify your labor p-s;.. Gn 3:16
so that I will not experience p. . 1Ch 4:10
and he carried our p-s; .... Is 53:4
if I cause you p, then who will ..2Co 2:2
and p will be no more, ...Rv 21:4

PALM

you on the p-s of my hands;......Is 49:16
they took p branches and went. Jn 12:13

PARABLE

He told them many things
in p-s .... Mt 13:3
Why are you speaking ... in
p-s?........................ Mt 13:10
tell them anything without
a p,.......................... Mt 13:34
I will open my mouth in p-s;.. Mt 13:35
but to the rest it is in p-s,
so that ....Lk 8:10

PARADISE

you will be with me in p ...... Lk 23:43
was caught up into p.......... 2Co 12:4

PARALYTIC

brought to him a p lying on a... Mt 9:2
told the p, "Son, your sins are...Mk 2:5

PARENT

who sinned, this man or his p-s,.. Jn 9:2
evil, disobedient to p-s,........Rm 1:30
Children, obey your p-s as..... Eph 6:1
obey your p-s in everything,.. Col 3:20
disobedient to p-s, ungrateful,.. 2Tm 3:2

PART

You who created my inward
p-s;.........................Ps 139:13
wash you, you have no p with me...Jn 13:8

as we have many **p-s** in one
   body,..........................Rm 12:4
your bodies are a **p** of Christ's..1Co 6:15
body is one and has many
   p-s,..........................1Co 12:12
know in **p**, and we prophesy
   in **p**..........................1Co 13:9

PARTIAL

A **p** hardening has come
   upon Israel..................Rm 11:25

PARTIALITY

Do not show **p** when deciding...Dt 1:17
not good to
   show **p**..........Pr 18:5; 24:23; 28:21
nor do you show
   p but teach ....Mk 12:14

PARTNER

Do not become **p-s** with 2Co 6:14

PARTNERSHIP

For what **p** is there between.. 2Co 6:14
because of your **p** in the gospel..Php 1:5

PASS

see the blood, I will **p** over you. .Ex 12:13
when you **p** through the
   waters,......................... Is 43:2
Heaven and earth will **p** away, but my
   words will never **p** away....Mt 24:35
let this cup **p** from me........Mt 26:39
he **p-ed** by on the other side. .Lk 10:31
but has **p-ed** from death to life. .Jn 5:24
God **p-ed** over the sins
   previously.................. Rm 3:25
For I **p-ed** on to you as most ...1Co 15:3
the old has **p-ed** away, ...2Co 5:17
we have **p-ed** from death to
   life 1Jn 3:14

PASSIONS

them over to disgraceful **p**.....Rm 1:26
Flee from youthful **p**, and
   pursue..................... 2Tm 2:22

PASSOVER

it is the LORD's **P**................ Ex 12:11
the **P** lamb had to be sacrificed. . Lk 22:7
eat this **P** with you before I
   suffer.........................Lk 22:15
For Christ our **P** lamb has
   been sacrificed. 1Co 5:7

PAST

Do not hold **p** iniquities
   against us; ....Ps 79:8
the cleansing from his **p** sins. .. 2Pt 1:9

PASTORS

some **p** and teachers, ...Eph 4:11

PASTURE

lets me lie down in green **p-s**; ..Ps 23:2
His people, the sheep of his **p**. .Ps 100:3
come in and go out and find **p**. . Jn 10:9

PATCH

No one sews a **p** of unshrunk..Mk 2:21

PATH

the right **p-s** for his name's......Ps 23:3
for my feet and a light on
   my **p**........................Ps 119:105
make his **p-s** straight! .... Mt 3:3
some seeds fell along the **p**, ... Mt 13:4
make straight **p-s** for your
   feet,....................... Heb 12:13

PATIENCE

endured with much **p** objects
   of .... Rm 9:22
love, joy, peace, **p**, kindness,...... Gl 5:22

PATIENT

Rejoice in hope; be **p** in
   affliction;................... Rm 12:12
Love is **p**, love is kind..........1Co 13:4
able to teach, and **p**,.......... 2Tm 2:24
but is **p** with you, not wanting
   any..........................2Pt 3:9

PATIENTLY

I waited **p** for the LORD,.........Ps 40:1

PATTERN

according to the **p** you have been
   shown on the mountain.... Ex 25:40
according to the **p** that was
   shown...................... Heb 8:5

PAUL

Early church missionary, theologian,
and writer. Also called Saul (Ac 13:9). Citizen of Tarsus, a Benjaminite, raised in
Jerusalem as a rabbinical student and

Pharisee (Ac 21:39; 22:3,28; 26:5; Gl 1:14;
Php 3:5). Persecuted Christians, including Stephen (Ac 8:1; 26:9-11); converted
on the way to Damascus (9:1-19); began
preaching Christ in Arabia and Damascus and was threatened (9:20-22; Gl 1:17;
2Co 11:32-33).
   Introduced to the church at Jerusalem by Barnabas (Ac 9:26-30); carried
money with Barnabas from Antioch
to Judea (11:27-30). Set apart with Barnabas to go through Cyprus and Galatia as missionaries (Ac 13–14); stoned
(Ac 14:19-20). Focused on Gentile evangelism (Ac 9:15; Gl 2:7; Eph 3:8). Attended Jerusalem council (Ac 15). Split with
Barnabas over John Mark (15:36-39).
   Traveled with Silas and Timothy
through Asia Minor and Greece (15:39–
16:3). Hindered by the Spirit from entering Bithynia; called to Macedonia in a
vision (16:7-10). Beaten, imprisoned, and
released in Philippi (16:16-40). Spoke at
Areopagus in Athens (17:19-34). Preached
at Corinth and Ephesus (Ac 18–19). Said
farewell in Ephesus (20:17-38).
   Arrested at riot in Jerusalem (21:26-
36); testified before the Sanhedrin
(23:1-10), Governors Felix and Festus
(24:10-21; 25:1-12), and King Agrippa
(Ac 26); appealed to Caesar (25:11).
Shipwrecked on the way to Rome (Ac
27); ministered in Malta, then Rome
(Ac 28).

PAY

until you have **paid** the last
   penny.......................Mt 5:26
Is it lawful to **p** taxes to
   Caesar .... Mt 22:17
P your obligations to
   everyone:................... Rm 13:7
not **p-ing** back evil for evil or .. 1Pt 3:9

PAYMENT

Spirit in our hearts as a
   down **p**...................... 2Co 1:22
gave us the Spirit as a down **p**. . 2Co 5:5
Spirit is the down **p** of our .....Eph 1:14

PEACE

favor on you and give you **p**... Nm 6:26
seek **p** and pursue it...........Ps 34:14
time for war and a time for **p**. ...Ec 3:8
Eternal Father, Prince of **P**. ....Is 9:6
You will keep ... in perfect **p**..... Is 26:3
who proclaims **p**, who brings
   news.......................... Is 52:7

P, p, when there is no **p**...... Jr 6:14; 8:11
I did not come to bring **p,**..... Mt 10:34
and **p** on earth to people he
   favors!........................Lk 2:14
P I leave with you. My **p** I give...Jn 14:27
we have **p** with God
   through our ....Rm 5:1
fruit of the Spirit is love,
   joy, **p,** ....Gl 5:22
For he is our **p,** who made
   both .... Eph 2:14
And the **p** of God, which
   surpasses...................Php 4:7
by making **p** through the
   blood ....Col 1:20
to take **p** from the earth,.........Rv 6:4

PEACEMAKERS

Blessed are the **p,** for they ...... Mt 5:9

PEARL

or toss your **p-s** before pigs,.... Mt 7:6
When he found one
   priceless **p**..................Mt 13:46
gate was made of a single **p**....Rv 21:21

PEKAH

King of Israel; assassin (2Kg 15:25-31).

PEKAHIAH

Son of Menahem; king of Israel; assassinated by his captain, Pekah (2Kg
15:22-26).

PENTECOST

When the day of **P** had arrived,.. Ac 2:1

PEOPLE

your **p** will be my **p,**..............Ru 1:16
and my **p,** who bear my name.. 2Ch 7:14
his **p,** the sheep of his pasture.. Ps 100:3
but sin is a disgrace to any **p**...Pr 14:34
They will be my **p,** and I will be.. Jr 24:7
will save his **p** from their sins...Mt 1:21
has God rejected his **p**?........Rm 11:1
God, and they will be my **p**..... 2Co 6:16
God, and they will be my **p**.... Heb 8:10
a holy nation, a **p** for his
   possession,....................1Pt 2:9
and language and **p** and nation.. Rv 5:9
will be his **p,** and God himself ..Rv 21:3

PEOPLE-PLEASERS

Don't work...as **p,** ....Eph 6:6

PERCEIVE

keep looking, but do not **p**. ....Is 6:9
look and look, but never **p**......Mt 13:14

PERFECT (ADJ)

The instruction of the LORD
   is **p,** ....Ps 19:7
You will keep...in **p** peace ..... Is 26:3
Be **p,** therefore, as your
   heavenly.....................Mt 5:48
pleasing, and **p** will of God.......Rm 12:2
But when the **p** comes,........1Co 13:10
good and **p** gift is from above,..Jms 1:17
instead, **p** love drives out fear,..1Jn 4:18

PERFECT (V)

for my power is **p-ed** in
   weakness. 2Co 12:9

PERFECTER

the source and **p** of our faith.. Heb 12:2

PERISH

If I **p,** I **p**.........................Est 4:16
one of these little ones **p**...... Mt 18:14
in him will not **p** but have ...... Jn 3:16
Don't work for the food
   that **p-es**.....................Jn 6:27
and they will never **p**..........Jn 10:28
foolishness to those who
   are **p-ing** 1Co 1:18
not wanting any to **p** but all to.. 2Pt 3:9

PERISHABLE

not of **p** seed but of 1Pt 1:23

PERMISSIBLE

"Everything is **p** for me,"......1Co 6:12
"Everything is **p,**" but not.....1Co 10:23

PERPLEXED

we are **p** but not in despair;..... 2Co 4:8

PERSECUTE

Princes have **p-d** me without..Ps 119:161
blessed when they insult you
   and **p** you....................Mt 5:11
and pray for those who **p** you,.. Mt 5:44
they **p-d** me, they will also **p**
   you...........................Jn 15:20
Saul, Saul, why are you
   p-ing me? ....Ac 9:4
Bless those who **p** you; ....Rm 12:14

we are **p-d** but not abandoned; ..2Co 4:9
in Christ Jesus will be **p-d**.....2Tm 3:12

PERSECUTION

When distress or **p** comes..... Mt 13:21
a severe **p** broke out against......Ac 8:1
or distress or **p** or famine or.. Rm 8:35

PERSEVERE

p in these things, for in doing.. 1Tm 4:16

PERSISTENT

be **p** in prayer..................Rm 12:12

PERSUADE

Are you going to **p** me to
   become.....................Ac 26:28
For I am **p-d** that neither
   death ....Rm 8:38
we seek to **p** people. 2Co 5:11
and am **p-d** that he is able..... 2Tm 1:12

PERVERSION

to mate with it; it is a **p**.........Lv 18:23

PERVERT

Does God **p** justice?..............Jb 8:3

PERVERTED (ADJ)

in a crooked and **p**
   generation, ... Php 2:15

PESTERING

because this widow keeps
   p me,.........................Lk 18:5

PESTILENCE

or the **p** that ravages at noon. ...Ps 91:6

PETER

Apostle; originally named Simon; also
called Simeon (Ac 15:14) and Cephas. A
fisherman in business with James and
John (Lk 5:2-3,10); married, lived in Capernaum (Mk 1:21,29-30).
   Walked on water (Mt 14:28-31). Confessed Jesus as Messiah (Mt 16:13-20;
Mk 8:27-30; Lk 9:18-21). At transfiguration (Mt 17:1-9; Mk 9:2-8; Lk 9:28-36; 2Pt
1:16-18). Jesus predicted he would deny
him (Mt 26:31-35; Mk 14:27-31; Lk 22:31-

34; Jn 13:36-38); denial (Mt 26:69-75; Mk 14:66-72; Lk 22:54-62; Jn 18:15-18,25-27); restoration to "feed my sheep" (Jn 21:15-19).

Spoke at Pentecost (Ac 2:14-40). Healed people (3:1-10; 5:15; 9:34); raised Tabitha from the dead (9:36-43). Arrested and forbidden to preach (4:1-31; 5:17-41). Saw vision: sent to Cornelius (Ac 10); reported Gentile conversions (Ac 11; 15); confronted by Paul for inconsistency (Gl 2:11-14). Imprisoned by Herod; freed by angel (Ac 12:1-19).

Focused on Jewish evangelism (Gl 2:7). Wrote two letters (1Pt 1:1; 2Pt 1:1).

PETITION

prayer and **p** with
  thanksgiving,................. Php 4:6
I urge that **p-s**, prayers, ... 1Tm 2:1

PHARAOH

Then **P** sent for Joseph, ... Gn 41:14
when I receive glory
  through **P**, ... Ex 14:18
For the Scripture tells **P**, ... Rm 9:17

PHARISEE

surpasses that of the scribes
  and **P-s**...................... Mt 5:20
Then the **P-s** went and
  plotted..................... Mt 22:15
woe to you, scribes and
  P-s,.......................... Mt 23:13
a **P** asked him to dine with
  him......................... Lk 11:37
one a **P** and the other a tax .... Lk 18:10
I am a **P**, a son of **P-s**!.......... Ac 23:6
regarding the law, a **P**; .... Php 3:5

PHILIP

1. Apostle (Mt 10:3; Jn 12:21-22). Invited Nathanael to "come and see" (Jn 1:43-51); questioned how to feed the five thousand (6:5-7); asked Jesus to show them the Father (14:8-9).
2. One of the first seven deacons (Ac 6:1-6); evangelized Simon the sorcerer in Samaria (8:5-13) and an Ethiopian eunuch (8:26-39).

PHILIPPI

City in Macedonia where Paul preached (Ac 16:12; 20:6; 1Th 2:2) and to whom he wrote (Php 1:1; 4:15).

PHILISTINES

People of Philistia (Gn 10:14; 26:1). Originated in Caphtor (Jr 47:4; Am 9:7) as the Casluh (Gn 10:14).

Enemies of Israel: Moses and Joshua did not defeat them (Ex 13:17; Jos 13:2; Jdg 3:1-3). In conflict with Shamgar (3:31); with Samson (13–16); with Samuel (1Sm 4–7); with Saul (13–14; 17; 23:27-28; 28:5,15; 31:1-6); with David (17:20-57; 18:20-27; 19:8; 23:1-5; 30:16; 2Sm 5:17-25; 8:1; 21:15-22; 23:9-13); with Jehoram (2Ch 21:16); with Uzziah (26:6-7); with Ahaz (28:18); and with Hezekiah (2Kg 18:8). David hid among them (1Sm 27:1,7,11; 29:11) but did not fight for them (27:8-12; 29:9).

Prophesied against (Is 11:14; 14:29-32; Jr 47; Ezk 25:15-17; Am 1:6-8; Ob 19; Zph 2:4-7; Zch 9:5-7).

PHILOSOPHY

captive through **p** and empty...Col 2:8

PHYSICIAN

Luke, the dearly loved **p**,.......Col 4:14

PIECE

weighed out thirty **p-s** of silver.....Mt 26:15

PIERCE

they **p-d** my hands and my
  feet.........................Ps 22:16
But he was **p-d** because of our.. Is 53:5
will look at me whom they
  p-d..........................Zch 12:10
a sword will **p** your own soul.. Lk 2:35
the soldiers **p-d** his side with..Jn 19:34
will look at the one they **p-d**. ..Jn 19:37

PIG

like a gold ring in a **p-'s** snout.. Pr 11:22
or toss your pearls before **p-s**,.. Mt 7:6
a large herd of **p-s** was
  feeding...................... Mt 8:30
him into his fields to feed **p-s**. Lk 15:15

PILATE, PONTIUS

Governor of Judea; presided over Jesus's trial and sentencing (Mt 27:11-26; Mk 15:1-15; Lk 23:1-25; Jn 18:28–19:16); warned by his wife (Mt 27:19); gave Jesus's body to Joseph of Arimathea (Mt 27:58; Mk 15:45; Lk 23:52;

Jn 19:38); assigned guards to the tomb (Mt 27:65).

PILLAR

back and became a **p** of salt... Gn 19:26
p of cloud by day and the **p** of
  fire.......................... Ex 13:22
the **p** and foundation of the
  truth......................... 1Tm 3:15

PINNACLE

stand on the **p** of the
  temple, ... Mt 4:5; Lk 4:9

PIT

redeems your life from the **P**;. .Ps 103:4
blind, both will fall into a **p**. .. Mt 15:14

PITIED (ADJ)

we should be **p** more than
  anyone................... 1Co 15:19

PLACE *SEE ALSO* HIGH PLACE, HOLY PLACE

Surely the LORD is in this **p**, ... Gn 28:16
going away to prepare a **p**
  for you........................ Jn 14:2
they now desire a better **p**..... Heb 11:16

PLAGUE

to send all my **p-s** against you,.. Ex 9:14
angels with the seven last **p-s**;.. Rv 15:1
add to him the **p-s** that are..... Rv 22:18

PLAIN

and the rough places, a **p**........ Is 40:4

PLAN

P-s fail when there is no ....Pr 15:22
A man's heart **p-s** his way,but ..Pr 16:9
Many **p-s** are in a man's heart,..Pr 19:21
I have **p-ned** it; I will also do it. .Is 46:11

PLANT (N)

will eat the **p-s** of the field. .... Gn 3:18
grew up before him like a
  young **p**...................... Is 53:2

PLANT (V)

LORD God **p-ed** a garden in
  Eden, ... Gn 2:8

like a tree **p-ed** beside flowing .. Ps 1:3
a time to **p** and a time to uproot;..Ec 3:2
I **p-ed**, Apollos watered, but
    God 1Co 3:6

PLATTER

the Baptist's head here on a **p**!.. Mt 14:8

PLAY

p skillfully on the strings,.......Ps 33:3
An infant will **p** beside the.......Is 11:8
p-ed the flute for you, but you.. Mt 11:17
eat and drink, and got up to **p**...1Co 10:7

PLEAD

We **p** on Christ's behalf:.......2Co 5:20

PLEASANT

have fallen for me in **p** places;.. Ps 16:6
How good and **p** it is when .... Ps 133:1

PLEASE

heaven and does whatever
    he **p-s**. ....Ps 115:3
does whatever he **p-s** in
    heaven......................Ps 135:6
the LORD was **p-d** to crush him..Is 53:10
it will accomplish what I **p** ......Is 55:11
I give it to anyone I **p**........... Jr 27:5
The wind blows where it **p-s**,......Jn 3:8
in the flesh cannot **p** God. ......Rm 8:8
even Christ did not **p** himself. .Rm 15:3
—how he may **p** his wife— ...1Co 7:33
as I also try to **p** everyone in. 1Co 10:33
am I striving to **p** people?....... Gl 1:10
God was **p-d** to have all his .... Col 1:19
obey ... for this **p-s** the Lord. . Col 3:20
in order to **p** men, but ....Col 3:22
it is impossible to **p** God,.......Heb 11:6

PLEASING (ADJ)

The sacrifice **p** to God is a ..... Ps 51:17
May my meditation be **p** to
    him;....................... Ps 104:34
living sacrifice, holy and **p** to
    God;........................ Rm 12:1
acceptable sacrifice, **p** to God. ..Php 4:18

PLEASURE

at your right hand are
    eternal **p-s**. .... Ps 16:11
since he takes **p** in him.........Ps 22:8
The one who loves **p** will
    become.................... Pr 21:17

I take no **p** in the death of the.. Ezk 18:32
according to his good **p**........ Eph 1:9
lovers of **p** rather than lovers.. 2Tm 3:4
enjoy the fleeting **p** of sin.... Heb 11:25

PLOT

and the peoples **p** in vain?....... Ps 2:1

PLOW (N)

swords into **p-s** and their
    spears ....Is 2:4
Beat your **p-s** into swords and...Jl 3:10
his hand to the **p** and looks
    back .... Lk 9:62

PLOW (V)

If you hadn't **p-ed** with my
    young......................Jdg 14:18
he who **p-s** ought to **p** in hope,.. 1Co 9:10

PLUMB LINE

I am setting a **p** among my
    people ....Am 7:8

POINT

obedient to the **p** of death ..... Php 2:8
yet stumbles in one **p**, is guilty. Jms 2:10

POISON

evil, full of deadly **p**. .... Jms 3:8

POISONOUS

the LORD sent **p** snakes among..Nm 21:6

POLLUTED

abstain from things **p**
    by idols,.................... Ac 15:20

POOL

your eyes like **p-s** in Heshbon......Sg 7:4
there is a **p**, called Bethesda......Jn 5:2

POOR

there will never cease to be **p**......Dt 15:11
He raises the **p** from the dust.. 1Sm 2:8
He raises the **p** from the dust.. Ps 113:7
Idle hands make one **p**, ...Pr 10:4
me to bring good news to the **p**.. Is 61:1
Blessed are the **p** in spirit, ... Mt 5:3
and the **p** are told the good
    news..........................Mt 11:5

You always have the **p** with
    you,......................... Mt 26:11
for your sake he became **p**,......2Co 8:9

PORE

You **p** over the Scriptures.......Jn 5:39

PORTION

But the LORD's **p** is his people, ..Dt 32:9
strength of my heart, my **p**
    forever.......................Ps 73:26
Jacob's **P** is not like these ......Jr 10:16
The LORD is my **p**, therefore I ..Lm 3:24
and brought a **p** of it and laid....Ac 5:2

POSSESS

to give you this land to **p**........Gn 15:7
nothing yet **p-ing** everything. . 2Co 6:10

POSSESSION

Canaan—as a permanent **p**, ...Gn 17:8
chosen you to be his own **p** ..Dt 7:6; 14:2
the ends of the earth your **p**.......Ps 2:8
Honor the LORD with your **p-s**... Pr 3:9
in the abundance of his **p-s**.... Lk 12:15
sold their **p-s** and property....Ac 2:45
a people for his own **p**,.......... Ti 2:14
a holy nation, a people for his **p**, ..1Pt 2:9

POSSIBLE

but with God all things are **p**.. Mt 19:26
If it is **p**, let this cup pass......Mt 26:39
Everything is **p** for the
    one who .... Mk 9:23
If **p**, as far as it depends
    on you,.....................Rm 12:18

POTTER

we are the clay, and you are
    our **p**; .... Is 64:8
Just like clay in the **p-'s** hand,......Jr 18:6
and bought the **p-'s** field
    with it .... Mt 27:7
Or has the **p** no right over the
    clay,...........................Rm 9:21

POUR

after day they **p** out speech; ....Ps 19:2
p out your hearts before him. ..Ps 62:8
I will **p** out my Spirit on your......Is 44:3
I will **p** out my Spirit on all...... Jl 2:28
of heaven and **p** out a
    blessing.................... Mal 3:10
that I will **p** out my Spirit on....Ac 2:17

even if I am **p-ed** out as a
   drink .... Php 2:17

POVERTY

your **p** will come like a.... Pr 6:11; 24:34
Give me neither **p** nor wealth;.. Pr 30:8
but she out of her **p** has
   put in .... Mk 12:44
so that by his **p** you might 2Co 8:9

POWER

this purpose: to show you my **p**.. Ex 9:16
Ascribe **p** to God. .... Ps 68:34
life are in the **p** of the tongue.. Pr 18:21
the Scriptures or the **p** of
   God........................... Mt 22:29
right hand of **P** and coming ..Mt 26:64
the kingdom of God come in **p**.. Mk 9:1
you will receive **p** when the Holy.. Ac 1:8
the Holy Spirit and with **p**,...... Ac 10:38
the **p** of God for salvation to ... Rm 1:16
his eternal **p** and divine
   nature .... Rm 1:20
or things to come, nor **p-s**,..... Rm 8:38
for **p** is perfected in
   weakness. 2Co 12:9
the cosmic **p-s** of this
   darkness. .... Eph 6:12
know him and the **p** of his...... Php 3:10
fear, but one of **p**, love,........ 2Tm 1:7
form of godliness but
   denying its **p**. 2Tm 3:5
His divine **p** has given us 2Pt 1:3
glory, and **p** belong to our God,.. Rv 19:1

POWERFUL

many **p**, not many of noble...... 1Co 1:26
are **p** through God for the..... 2Co 10:4

PRACTICE

they don't **p** what they teach... Mt 23:3
those who **p** such
   things................ Rm 1:32; Gl 5:21
and are not **p-ing** the truth..... 1Jn 1:6

PRAISE (N)

enthroned on the **p-s** of Israel. .Ps 22:3
his **p** will always be on my lips. .Ps 34:1
Sing **p** to God, sing **p**; .... Ps 47:6
and his courts with **p**........... Ps 100:4
have prepared **p** from the
   mouths .... Mt 21:16
For they loved human **p** more
   than .... Jn 12:43
to the **p** of his glorious grace .. Eph 1:6
up to God a sacrifice of **p**,..... Heb 13:15

PRAISE (V)

This is my God, and I will **p** him,.. Ex 15:2
LORD is great and highly **p-d**; ..1Ch 16:25
that breathes **p** the LORD........ Ps 150:6
Let another **p** you, and not
   your .... Pr 27:2
host with the angel, **p-ing** God..Lk 2:13

PRAY

against the LORD by ceasing
   to **p** 1Sm 12:23
my name, humble
   themselves, **p**............... 2Ch 7:14
we **p-ed** to our God and
   stationed .... Neh 4:9
P for the well-being of
   Jerusalem:................... Ps 122:6
and **p** for those who persecute
   you,........................... Mt 5:44
you should **p** like this: .... Mt 6:9
the mountain by himself to **p**... Mt 14:23
teach us to **p**, just as John........ Lk 11:1
I **p** for them. I am not **p-ing** for.. Jn 17:9
know what to **p** for as we
   should .... Rm 8:26
Every man who **p-s** or
   prophesies 1Co 11:4
P at all times in the Spirit ..... Eph 6:18
p constantly. 1Th 5:17
suffering? He should **p**........ Jms 5:13

PRAYER

the LORD accepts my **p**. .... Ps 6:9
a house of **p** for all nations...... Is 56:7
will be called a house of **p**..... Mt 21:13
be persistent in **p**.............. Rm 12:12
everything, through **p** and
   petition..................... Php 4:6
which are the **p-s** of the saints... Rv 5:8

PREACH

the world and **p** the gospel to.. Mk 16:15
how can they **p** unless they
   are .... Rm 10:15
but we **p** Christ crucified,...... 1Co 1:23
p Christ out of envy and strife.. Php 1:15
seen by angels, **p-ed** among
   the.......................... 1Tm 3:16

PREACHER

how can they hear without
   a **p**?......................... Rm 10:14

PRECIOUS

their lives are **p** in his sight....... Ps 72:14
She is more **p** than jewels; ...... Pr 3:15

She is far more **p** than jewels. . Pr 31:10
a tested stone, a **p** cornerstone.. Is 28:16
but with the **p** blood of Christ,.. 1Pt 1:19

PREDESTINED

your will had **p** to take place. .. Ac 4:28
He also **p** to be conformed..... Rm 8:29
a wisdom God **p** before the
   ages.......................... 1Co 2:7
He **p** us to be adopted as sons .. Eph 1:5
p according to the plan of the
   one .... Eph 1:11

PREGNANT

and hit a **p** woman so that
   her........................... Ex 21:22
that she was **p** from the Holy ...Mt 1:18
will become **p** and give
   birth to .... Mt 1:23
was engaged to him and was **p**. .Lk 2:5

PREPARE

You **p** a table before me in the ..Ps 23:5
P the way of the LORD in the .... Is 40:3
Israel, **p** to meet your God! ....Am 4:12
P the way for the Lord;........... Mt 3:3
he will **p** your way before you. .Mt 11:10
she has **p-d** me for burial. .... Mt 26:12
going away to **p** a place for you.. Jn 14:2
God **p-d** this for those who love. .1Co 2:9
which God **p-d** ahead of time. .Eph 2:10
but you **p-d** a body for me..... Heb 10:5

PRESENCE

the Bread of the **P** on the table.. Ex 25:30
in the **p** of my enemies;......... Ps 23:5
Do not banish me from your
   p or .... Ps 51:11
Where can I flee from your **p**?.. Ps 139:7
not only in my **p**, but now
   even .... Php 2:12
appear in the **p** of God for us... Heb 9:24

PRESENT (ADJ)

things **p** nor things to come,.. Rm 8:38
absent in body, I am **p** in spirit,.. 1Co 5:3

PRESENT (V)

I urge you to **p** your bodies as a .Rm 12:1
He did this to **p** the church to .Eph 5:27
Be diligent to **p** yourself 2Tm 2:15

PRESERVE

loses his life will **p** it............ Lk 17:33

PRESS

good measure—**p-ed** down,
 shaken...................... Lk 6:38

PREVIOUSLY

over the sins **p** committed.......Rm 3:25
in which you **p** lived according.. Eph 2:2

PRICE

I insist on paying the full **p**,.. 1Ch 21:24
the **p** of him whose **p** was
 set by .... Mt 27:9
for you were bought at a **p**.......1Co 6:20
You were bought at a **p**;........1Co 7:23

PRICELESS

When he found one **p** pearl, .. Mt 13:46

PRIDE

P comes before destruction,......Pr 16:18

PRIEST

he was a **p** to God Most High.. . Gn 14:18
be my kingdom of **p-s** and my
 holy..........................Ex 19:6
serve me as **p**—Aaron, his
 sons .... Ex 28:1
You are a **p** forever
 according to................. Ps 110:4
A **p** happened to be going ......Lk 10:31
a great high **p** who has passed. .Heb 4:14
You are a **p** forever according
 to .... Heb 5:6
but they will be **p-s** of God and.. Rv 20:6

PRIESTHOOD

a permanent **p** for them ...... Ex 40:15
he holds his **p** permanently. .. Heb 7:24
race, a royal **p**, a holy nation..... 1Pt 2:9

PRINCE

P-s have persecuted me
 without.................... Ps 119:161
Eternal Father, **P** of Peace........Is 9:6

PRISON

I was in **p** and you
 visited me'....................Mt 25:36
Peter was kept in **p**, but the
 church........................Ac 12:5
saw the doors of the **p**
 standing....................Ac 16:27
to the spirits in **p**.............. 1Pt 3:19

PRISONER

The LORD frees **p-s**............. Ps 146:7
and freedom to the **p-s**;......... Is 61:1
p of Christ Jesus on behalf..... Eph 3:1

PRIZE

but only one receives the **p**? .. 1Co 9:24
as my goal the **p** promised by.. Php 3:14

PROCLAIM

and I will **p** the name 'the
 Lord'....................... Ex 33:19
P his salvation from day to
 day......................... 1Ch 16:23
and the expanse **p-s** the work
 of his ....Ps 19:1
The heavens **p** his
 righteousness ....Ps 50:6
to **p** liberty to the captives....... Is 61:1
He has sent me to **p** release ..... Lk 4:18
you **p** the Lord's death
 until he 1Co 11:26

PRODUCE

A good tree can't **p** bad fruit; ...Mt 7:18
of your faith **p-s** endurance.... Jms 1:3

PROFANE

Do not **p** the name of your
 God;..........................Lv 18:21

PROFIT

who hates dishonest **p**
 prolongs....................Pr 28:16
and do business and make
 a **p**.......................... Jms 4:13

PROFITABLE

God and is **p** for teaching 2Tm 3:16

PROGRESS

for your **p** and joy in the faith, .. Php 1:25
so that your **p** may be
 evident to.................. 1Tm 4:15

PROMINENT

number of the **p** Greek
 women .... Ac 17:12

PROMISCUITY

Go and marry a woman of **p**......Hs 1:2
moral impurity, **p**,............. Gl 5:19

PROMISE (N)

not one **p** has failed...........Jos 23:14
For the **p** is for you and for ...... Ac 2:39
of God's **p-s** is "Yes" in him.......2Co 1:20
first commandment with a **p**,.. Eph 6:2
since it holds **p** for the present..1Tm 4:8
The Lord does not delay his **p**... 2Pt 3:9

PROMISE (V)

This is the land I **p-d** Abraham, ..Dt 34:4
since he who **p-d** is faithful. .Heb 10:23
did not receive what was **p-d**, ..Heb 11:39

PROMISED (ADJ)

from the Father the **p**
 Holy Spirit, ... Ac 2:33

PRONOUNCE

he could not **p** it correctly,......Jdg 12:6

PROOF

to them by many convincing **p-s**.. Ac 1:3
the **p** of what is not seen....... Heb 11:1

PROPER

Is it **p** for a woman to pray to. . 1Co 11:13
among you, as is **p** for saints... Eph 5:3

PROPERTY

wife Sapphira, sold a piece of **p**. .Ac 5:1

PROPHECY

miracles, to another, **p**, ...1Co 12:10
If I have the gift of **p** 1Co 13:2
But as for **p-ies**, they will
 come to.....................1Co 13:8
it was given to you through **p**,. .1Tm 4:14
No **p** of Scripture comes from.. 2Pt 1:20

PROPHESY

sons and your daughters will **p**, ..Jl 2:28
Lord, didn't we **p** in your name,. .Mt 7:22
P to us, Messiah! Who was it. .Mt 26:68
sons and your daughters will **p** ..Ac 2:17
and especially that you may **p**...1Co 14:1
to **p** for 1,260 days, dressed in... Rv 11:3

PROPHET

God will raise up for you a
 p like........................ Dt 18:15
A **p** is not without honor
 except .... Mt 13:57

be called a **p** of the Most High,.. Lk 1:76
No **p** is accepted in his
    hometown................... Lk 4:24
"Are you the **P**?" "No," .... Jn 1:21
first apostles, second **p-s**,.... 1Co 12:28
apostles, some **p-s**, some ......Eph 4:11
the beast and the false **p** are, .. Rv 20:10

PROPHETESS

There was also a **p**, Anna,...... Lk 2:36

PROPHETIC

known through the **p**
    Scriptures,.................Rm 16:26
also have the **p** word strongly ..2Pt 1:19

PROSPER

Whatever he does **p-s**. .... Ps 1:3
will **p** in what I send it to do.....Is 55:11

PROSPERITY

set before you life and **p**, ...Dt 30:15
I saw the **p** of the wicked........Ps 73:3

PROSTITUTE

a **p** named Rahab, and stayed
    there........................ Jos 2:1
p-s are entering the
    kingdom................... Mt 21:31
and make it part of a **p**?........1Co 6:15

PROTECT

P me as the pupil of your eye; .. Ps 17:8
He **p-s** his flock like a
    shepherd;....................Is 40:11
who is able to **p** you from........Jd 24

PROTECTION

lives under the **p** of the
    Most High .... Ps 91:1

PROUD

LORD, my heart is not **p**;....... Ps 131:1
downfall a person's heart is **p**,..Pr 18:12
arrogant, **p**, boastful,
    inventors ....Rm 1:30
money, boastful, **p**,
    demeaning 2Tm 3:2
God resists the **p**, but gives..... Jms 4:6

PROVE

But God **p-s** his own love for us. .Rm 5:8

PROVEN

endurance produces **p**
    character,....................Rm 5:4

PROVERB

Solomon spoke 3,000 **p-s**,..... 1Kg 4:32
The **p-s** of Solomon son of David,..Pr 1:1
you will quote this **p** to me:......Lk 4:23

PROVIDE

God himself will **p** the lamb...... Gn 22:8
all these things will be **p-d**
    for you.......................Mt 6:33
he will also **p** a way out.......1Co 10:13
own flesh but **p-s** and
    cares for it, ...Eph 5:29
if anyone does not **p** for his
    own..........................1Tm 5:8
richly **p-s** us with all things......1Tm 6:17

PROVOKE

tested God and **p-d** the
    Holy One.....................Ps 78:41

PROWLING

the devil is **p** around like a...... 1Pt 5:8

PRUNES

and he **p** every branch that ..... Jn 15:2

PSALM

and the **P-s** must be fulfilled. . Lk 24:44
speaking to one another in
    p-s,........................ Eph 5:19

PUBLIC

your attention to **p** reading, ...1Tm 4:13

PUBLICLY

not wanting to disgrace her **p** ..Mt 1:19
P rebuke those who sin,
    so that 1Tm 5:20

PUNISH

the LORD has **p-ed** him for the......Is 53:6
and **p-es** every son he
    receives..................... Heb 12:6

PUNISHMENT

My **p** is too great to bear! ...... Gn 4:13
p for our peace was on him,......Is 53:5

son won't suffer **p** for the
    father's .... Ezk 18:20
they will go away into
    eternal **p**, ...Mt 25:46
because fear involves **p**........ 1Jn 4:18

PUPIL

protected him as the **p** of
    his eye........................Dt 32:10
Protect me as the **p** of your
    eye; .... Ps 17:8

PURCHASED

which he **p** with his own
    blood........................Ac 20:28

PURE

The fear of the LORD is **p**, ... Ps 19:9
can a young man keep his
    way **p**? .... Ps 119:9
eyes are too **p** to look on
    evil, ... Hab 1:13
Blessed are the **p** in heart, ... Mt 5:8
whatever is just, whatever is **p**,..Php 4:8
To the **p**, everything is **p**, but to.. Ti 1:15
from a **p** heart love one
    another 1Pt 1:22

PURIFICATION

After making **p** for sins, he sat.. Heb 1:3

PURIFY

P me with hyssop, and I will be .. Ps 51:7
he will **p** the sons of Levi and.. Mal 3:3

PURIM

reason these days are called **P**,.. Est 9:26

PURITY

by **p**, by knowledge,
    by patience,.................. 2Co 6:6

PURPLE

crown of thorns and the **p** robe...Jn 19:5

PURPOSE

has prepared everything for
    his **p** ....Pr 16:4
because I was sent for this **p**. .....Lk 4:43
are called according to his **p**... Rm 8:28
so that God's **p** according to ... Rm 9:11
and to work out his good **p**. .. Php 2:13

PURSUE

seek peace and **p** it. . . . . Ps 34:14
who did not **p** righteousness, . . Rm 9:30
and **p** righteousness,
    godliness 1Tm 6:11
P peace with everyone, and . . Heb 12:14
Let him seek peace and **p** it, ... 1Pt 3:11

PURSUIT

futile, a **p** of the wind. . . . . Ec 1:14

PUT

But **p** on the Lord Jesus
    Christ, ... Rm 13:14
P on the full armor of God so. . Eph 6:11

Q

QUAIL

So at evening **q** came . . . . Ex 16:13

QUAKE

earth **q-d**, and the rocks were
    split. . . . . Mt 27:51

QUALITY

will test the **q** of each one's 1Co 3:13

QUARREL

The Lord's servant must
    not **q**, ... 2Tm 2:24

QUARRELSOME

but gentle, not **q**, not greedy . . . 1Tm 3:3

QUEEN

The **q** of Sheba heard about. . . . 1Kg 10:1
The **q** of the south will
    rise up . . . . Mt 12:42

QUICK

Everyone must be **q** to
    listen, ... Jms 1:19

QUICKLY

What you're doing, do **q**. . . . . Jn 13:27
I am coming **q**. Hold on to
    what . . . . Rv 3:11
Yes, I am coming **q**. . . . . Rv 22:20

QUIET

He leads me beside **q** waters. . . . Ps 23:2
a tranquil and **q** life in all 1Tm 2:2
of a gentle and **q** spirit, ... 1Pt 3:4

QUIVER

who has filled his **q** with
    them. . . . . Ps 127:5

QUOTA

require the same **q** of bricks. . . . . Ex 5:8

R

RABBI

do not be called '**R**,' because
    you . . . . Mt 23:8

RABBONI

she said to him in Aramaic, "**R!**" . . Jn 20:16

RACE (N)

the **r** is not to the swift, ... Ec 9:11
I have finished the **r**, I have
    kept. 2Tm 4:7
endurance the **r** that lies
    before . . . . Heb 12:1
you are a chosen **r**, a royal. 1Pt 2:9

RACE (V)

the runners in a stadium all **r**, . . 1Co 9:24

RACHEL

Daughter of Laban; wife and cousin
of Jacob (Gn 29:10,18-30); mother of
Joseph and Benjamin (30:24; 35:16-
20); stole her father's household idols
(31:19).
R weeping for her children; . . . . . . Mt 2:18

RADIANCE

The Son is the **r** of God's glory, . . Heb 1:3

RAGE (N)

king's **r** is like the roaring of a
    lion, ... Pr 19:12

RAGE (V)

Why do the Gentiles **r** and . . . . . Ac 4:25

RAHAB

Prostitute in Jericho who hid the Isra-
elite spies (Jos 2; Heb 11:31); spared by
Joshua (Jos 6:17,22-25). Mother of Boaz
(Mt 1:5).

RAIN (N)

and the **r** fell on the earth forty. . Gn 7:12
and sends **r** on the righteous
    and . . . . Mt 5:45

RAIN (V)

prayed . . . that it would not **r**, . . Jms 5:17

RAISE

I will **r** up for them a prophet. . Dt 18:18
LORD **r-d** up judges, who saved. . Jdg 2:16
God is able to **r** up children for. . . Mt 3:9
killed, and be **r-d** the third day. . Mt 16:21
and on the third day he will
    be **r**. . . . . Mt 20:19
and I will **r** it up in three days. . . Jn 2:19
and I will **r** him up on the last . . . Jn 6:40
God has **r** this Jesus. . . . . Ac 2:32
and **r-d** for our justification. . . Rm 4:25
that he was **r-d** on the third . . . 1Co 15:4
dead will be **r-d**
    incorruptible, ... 1Co 15:52
who **r-d** the Lord Jesus will **r** us . . . 2Co
    4:14
He also **r-d** us up with him and. . Eph 2:6

RAM

and saw a **r** caught in the
    thicket. . . . . Gn 22:13

RANSOM (N)

these cannot . . . pay his **r** to
    God . . . . Ps 49:7
to give his life as a **r** for many. . Mt 20:28
gave himself as a **r** for all, ... 1Tm 2:6

RANSOM (V)

for the LORD has **r-ed** Jaco band. . Jr 31:11

RASHLY

something **r** and later to
    reconsider. . . . . Pr 20:25

RAVEN

he sent out a **r**. . . . . Gn 8:7
The **r-s** kept bringing him
    bread 1Kg 17:6

Consider the r-s: They don't
   sow .... Lk 12:24

READ

Sabbath day and stood up to r. . Lk 4:16
you understand what you're
   r-ing? .... Ac 8:30
your attention to public r-ing, . . 1Tm 4:13
Blessed is the one who r-s aloud . . Rv 1:3

READY

R . . . to give a defense 1Pt 3:15

REALITY

faith is the r of what is hoped . . Heb 11:1

REALLY

Did God r say, 'You can't eat from . . Gn 3:1

REAP

sow in tears will r with shouts . . Ps 126:5
the wind and r the whirlwind. . . . Hs 8:7
They don't sow or r or gather . . Mt 6:26
a person sows he will also r, ... Gl 6:7
r, for the time to r has come, . . . Rv 14:15

REASON (N)

They hated me for no r . . . . Jn 15:25
asks you for a r for the hope 1Pt 3:15

REASON (V)

So he r-ed in the synagogue
   with .... Ac 17:17
a child, I r-ed like a child. 1Co 13:11

REBEKAH

Sister of Laban; wife of Isaac (Gn 24);
mother of Jacob and Esau (25:21-26).
Passed off as Isaac's sister (26:6-11).
Encouraged Jacob to secure Isaac's
blessing (27:1-17).

REBEL

Only don't r against the LORD, . . Nm 14:9
but they have r-led against me. . . . Is 1:2

REBELLION

For r is like the sin of
   divination, ... 1Sm 15:23
the wicked increase, r
   increases .... Pr 29:16

REBELLIOUS

a stubborn and r generation, . . . Ps 78:8
unbelieving and r generation! . . Mt 17:17

REBUILD

to go up and r the LORD's house. . Ezr 1:5
Come, let's r Jerusalem's wall . . Neh 2:17
and the ruins will be r-t. . . . . . Ezk 36:33
temple of God and r it in
   three days .... Mt 26:61

REBUKE

do not r me in your anger; . . . . Ps 6:1
The LORD r you, Satan! . . . . Zch 3:2
he got up and r-d the winds . . . Mt 8:26
go and r him in private .... Mt 18:15
Don't r an older man, ... 1Tm 5:1
Publicly r those who sin, ... 1Tm 5:20
profitable for teaching, for
   r-ing, ... 2Tm 3:16
r, correct, and encourage with . . 2Tm 4:2
him but said, "The Lord r you!" . . . . . Jd 9
many as I love, I r and
   discipline. .... Rv 3:19

RECEIVE

who asks r-s, and the one who . . Mt 7:8
But to all who did r him, he
   gave .... Jn 1:12
Ask and you will r, ... Jn 16:24
But you will r power when the . . Ac 1:8
is more blessed to give than
   to r .... Ac 20:35
What do you have that you
   didn't r? 1Co 4:7
For I r-d from the Lord what I . . 1Co 11:23
as you have r-d Christ Jesus ...... Col 2:6

RECOGNIZE

r-d his brothers, they did not
   r him .... Gn 42:8
opened, and they r-d him, but . . Lk 24:31
yet the world did not r him . . . . Jn 1:10

RECONCILE

First go and be r-d with your . . Mt 5:24
Christ's behalf, "Be r-d
   to God." 2Co 5:20
that he might r both to God . . . Eph 2:16
through him to r everything to . . Col 1:20

RECONCILIATION

we have now received this r . . . Rm 5:11
if their rejection brings r . . . . . Rm 11:15
has given us the ministry of r: . 2Co 5:18

RECONSIDER

rashly and later to r his
   vows. .... Pr 20:25

RECORD

does not keep a r of wrongs. . . . 1Co 13:5

RECRUCIFYING *SEE ALSO* CRUCIFYING

they are r the Son of God ...... Heb 6:6

RED

Don't gaze at wine because
   it is r, ... Pr 23:31
they are crimson r, ... Is 1:18
good weather because the
   sky is r.' .... Mt 16:2
another horse went out, a
   fiery r one, ... Rv 6:4

RED SEA

Crossed by Israel (Ex 13:18; 14:15-31; Nm
21:14; Dt 11:4; Jos 2:10; 4:23; 24:6; Neh 9:9;
Pss 106:7,9-11,22; 136:13-15; Ac 7:36; Heb
11:29); southern extent of the promised
land (Ex 23:31); location of Solomon's
fleet (1Kg 9:26).

REDEEM

I will r you with an outstretched
   arm .... Ex 6:6
to r a people for himself, ... 2Sm 7:23
the price of r-ing him is too
   costly, ... Ps 49:8
He r-s your life from the Pit; . . . Ps 103:4
Christ r-ed us from the curse . . . Gl 3:13
to r those under the law, ... Gl 4:5

REDEEMED (N)

Let the r of the LORD .... Ps 107:2
r of the LORD will return . . Is 35:10; 51:11

REDEEMER

I know that my R lives, ... Jb 19:25
LORD, my rock and my R. . . . . . Ps 19:14
for their R is strong, ... Pr 23:11
Your R is the Holy One of
   Israel .... Is 41:14

REDEMPTION

because your r is near! . . . . Lk 21:28
adoption, the r of our
   bodies .... Rm 8:23

In him we have **r** through his
blood,.............................Eph 1:7
We have **r**, the forgiveness of
sins............................ Col 1:14
having obtained eternal **r**..... Heb 9:12

REED

He will not break a bruised **r**,... Is 42:3
A **r** swaying in the wind? .... Mt 11:7
He will not break a bruised **r**.. Mt 12:20

REFINER

For he will be like a **r-'s** fire......Mal 3:2

REFRESHING (N)

that seasons of **r** may come......Ac 3:19

REFUGE

will include six cities of **r**,..... Nm 35:6
whose wings you have come
for **r**...........................Ru 2:12
God is our **r** and strength, ... Ps 46:1
shield to those who take **r** in
him............................Pr 30:5
we who have fled for **r** might.. Heb 6:18

REFUTE

For he vigorously **r-d** the
Jews in...................... Ac 18:28

REGARD (N)

The LORD had **r** for Abel and his...Gn 4:4

REGARD (V)

but we in turn **r-ed** him stricken,.. Is 53:4

REGENERATION

through the washing of **r** and..... Ti 3:5

REGION

In the same **r**, shepherds were ..Lk 2:8

REGISTER

that the whole empire should
be **r-ed**........................ Lk 2:1

REGRET

LORD **r-ted** that he had made
man............................ Gn 6:6
I **r** that I made Saul king,......1Sm 15:11

REGULATIONS

Why do you submit to **r**:...... Col 2:20

REHOBOAM

Son of Solomon; king of Judah (1Kg
11:43). Answered people harshly; the
kingdom was divided (12:1-19; 2Ch 10:1-
19).

REIGN

The LORD will **r** forever and
ever!..........................Ex 15:18
The LORD **r-s**! He is robed in......Ps 93:1
The LORD **r-s** forever; ....Ps 146:10
who says to Zion, "Your God
r-s!"............................ Is 52:7
He will **r** over the house of ......Lk 1:33
death **r-ed** from Adam to
Moses,........................Rm 5:14
do not let sin **r** in your
mortal.........................Rm 6:12
For he must **r** until he puts all..1Co 15:25
we will also **r** with him;......2Tm 2:12
and he will **r** forever and ever.. Rv 11:15
will **r** with him a thousand
years......................... Rv 20:6

REJECT

LORD, he has **r-ed** you as
king..........................1Sm 15:23
stone that the builders **r-ed**
has...........................Ps 118:22
He was despised and **r-ed** by
men,........................... Is 53:3
the builders **r-ed** has
become..................... Mt 21:42
Whoever **r-s** you **r-s** me........Lk 10:16
but the one who **r-s** the Son ......Jn 3:36
has God **r-ed** his people? ......Rm 11:1
r-ed by men but chosen and.... 1Pt 2:4

REJOICE

all who take refuge in you **r**;......Ps 5:11
let us **r** and be glad in it. ......Ps 118:24
R greatly, Daughter Zion! ...... Zch 9:9
but **r** that your names are
written .... Lk 10:20
R with those who **r**;..........Rm 12:15
but **r-s** in the truth.............1Co 13:6
R in the Lord always.
I will say it again: **R**! .... Php 4:4
R always,.......................1Th 5:16

RELATIONS

men ... left natural **r** with
women .... Rm 1:27

RELATIVE

The man is a close **r**........... Ru 2:20
in his hometown, among
his **r-s**, ...Mk 6:4

RELEASE

do you want me to **r** for you?.. Mt 27:21

RELENT

and **r** concerning this disaster.. Ex 32:12
but the LORD **r-ed**
concerning 2Sm 24:16
may turn and **r** and leave a
blessing........................Jl 2:14
so God **r-ed** from the disaster.. Jnh 3:10

RELIGION

and undefiled **r** before God... Jms 1:27

RELIGIOUS

are extremely **r** in every
respect......................Ac 17:22

RELY

He **r-ies** on the LORD; let him......Ps 22:8
do not **r** on your own
understanding;............... Pr 3:5
What are you **r-ing** on? .... Is 36:4
all who **r** on the works of the
law............................ Gl 3:10

REMAIN

the word of our God **r-s** forever.. Is 40:8
R in me, and I in you............. Jn 15:4
three **r**: faith, hope, and love. .1Co 13:13
they would have **r-ed**
with us...................... 1Jn 2:19

REMARKABLE

and look at this **r** sight. ....Ex 3:3

REMARKABLY

been **r** and wondrously made. .Ps 139:14

REMEMBER

God **r-ed** Noah,...................Gn 8:1
R the Sabbath day, to keep it
holy. .... Ex 20:8
human being that you **r** him,......Ps 8:4
made of, **r-ing** that we are
dust..........................Ps 103:14
So **r** your Creator in the days......Ec 12:1

REMEMBRANCE

own sake and r your sins no
more. . . . . Is 43:25
and never again r their sin. . . . . . . Jr 31:34
R Lot's wife!. Lk 17:32
asked only that we would
r the poor. Gl 2:10
R my chains. . . . . Col 4:18
I will never again r their sins. . . Heb 8:12

REMEMBRANCE

there is no r of you in death;. . . . . Ps 6:5
Do this in r of me. . . . . . . Lk 22:19; 1Co 11:24

REMIND

r you of everything I have
told you. . . . . Jn 14:26

REMINDER

there is a r of sins year after
year. . . . . Heb 10:3

REMNANT

For a r will go out from. 2Kg 19:31
our God to preserve a r for us . . Ezr 9:8
The r will return, the r of Jacob, . . Is 10:21
I will gather the r of my flock. . . Jr 23:3
only the r will be saved;. . . . . . . Rm 9:27

REMOTE

by boat to a r place to be
alone. . . . . Mt 14:13

REMOVAL

not as the r of the dirt from. 1Pt 3:21

REMOVE

R the sandals from your feet, . . Jos 5:15
so far has he r-d our . . . . Ps 103:12
I will r your heart of stone
and . . . . Ezk 36:26

RENEW

He r-s my life; he leads me
along . . . . Ps 23:3
and r a steadfast spirit
within me. . . . . Ps 51:10
youth is r-ed like the eagle. . . . . . Ps 103:5
the LORD will r their strength;. . . Is 40:31
by the r-ing of your mind, ... Rm 12:2
person is being r-ed day by
day. 2Co 4:16
is impossible to r to
repentance . . . . Heb 6:4

RENEWAL

regeneration and r by the
Holy Spirit. . . . . Ti 3:5

REPAY

Vengeance belongs to me;
I will r. . . . . Dt 32:35
deserve or repaid us
according to. . . . . Ps 103:10
Do not r anyone evil for evil. . Rm 12:17
I will r, says the Lord. . . . . Rm 12:19
that no one r-s evil for evil. 1Th 5:15

REPEAT

R them to your children. . . . . Dt 6:7

REPENT

R, because the kingdom of
heaven. . . . . Mt 3:2
who r-s than over ninety-nine . . Lk 15:7
R and be baptized, ... Ac 2:38
all people everywhere to r, ... Ac 17:30

REPENTANCE

fruit consistent with r. . . . . Mt 3:8
a baptism of r for the
forgiveness. . . . . Mk 1:4
righteous, but sinners to r. . . . . Lk 5:32
r for forgiveness of sins . . . . . . Lk 24:47
and do works worthy of r. . . . . . Ac 26:20
is intended to lead you to r?. . . . Rm 2:4
godly grief produces a r 2Co 7:10
any to perish but all to come
to r. 2Pt 3:9

REPRIMAND

Better an open r than
concealed . . . . Pr 27:5

REPROACH

must be above r, the husband
of 1Tm 3:2
he considered r for the sake
of . . . . Heb 11:26

REPUTATION

have a good r among
outsiders, ... 1Tm 3:7
you have a r for being alive, ... Rv 3:1

REQUEST

your r-s be made known to
God. . . . . Php 4:6

REQUIRE

what it is the LORD r-s of you:. . . Mc 6:8
much will be r-d;. . . . . Lk 12:48

REQUIREMENT

in order that the law's r
would. . . . . Rm 8:4

RESCUE

let the LORD r him, since he . . . . . . Ps 22:8
the LORD r-s him from
them all. . . . . Ps 34:19
R those being taken off to
death, ... Pr 24:11
He trusts in God; let God
r him. . . . . Mt 27:43
has r-d us from the
domain of . . . . Col 1:13
r-s us from the coming wrath. . 1Th 1:10
Lord knows how to r the
godly 2Pt 2:9

RESIDE

Christ's power may r in me. . . 2Co 12:9
has eternal life r-ing in him. . . . 1Jn 3:15

RESIDENCE

I will place my r among you, . . . Lv 26:11
a place for your r forever. 2Ch 6:2

RESIST

tell you, don't r an evildoer. . . . . Mt 5:39
are always r-ing the Holy Spirit. . Ac 7:51
For who can r his will? . . . . Rm 9:19
may be able to r in the evil
day. . . . . Eph 6:13
have not yet r-ed to the point . . Heb 12:4
R the devil, and he will flee . . . . . Jms 4:7

RESOUND

sea and all that fills it r. . . . . Ps 96:11
Praise him with r-ing
cymbals;. . . . . Ps 150:5

RESPECT (N)

r to those you owe r, ... Rm 13:7
masters as worthy of all r, ... 1Tm 6:1
do this with gentleness and r, . . 1Pt 3:16

RESPECT (V)

Each of you is to r his mother . . Lv 19:3
'They will r my son,' he said. . . Mt 21:37
the wife is to r her husband. . . Eph 5:33

REST (N)

be a Sabbath of complete r,......Ex 31:15
They will not enter my r........ Ps 95:11
and find r for yourselves........ Jr 6:16
and I will give you r. .... Mt 11:28
Sabbath r remains for God's
  people .... Heb 4:9

REST (V)

he r-ed on the seventh day ..... Gn 2:2

RESTORE

the LORD r-d his fortunes and.. Jb 42:10
R the joy of your salvation to
  me,.......................... Ps 51:12
is coming and will r
  everything, ... Mt 17:11
it out, and his hand was r-d. ....Mk 3:5
are you r-ing the kingdom
  to Israel....................... Ac 1:6
spiritual, r such a person .... Gl 6:1

RESTRAIN

know what currently r-s him,...2Th 2:6

RESTRAINT

because in his r God passed
  over......................... Rm 3:25

RESURRECTION

in the r ... whose wife will she
  be........................... Mt 22:28
the r of life ... the r of
  condemnation................Jn 5:29
I am the r and the life............ Jn 11:25
if there is no r of the dead,....1Co 15:13
know him and the power of
  his r......................... Php 3:10
This is the first r............... Rv 20:5

RETAIN

r the sins of any, they are r-ed.. Jn 20:23

RETURN

you are dust, and you will r to
  dust.......................... Gn 3:19
the spirit r-s to God who gave .. Ec 12:7
mouth will not r to me empty,..Is 55:11
Come, let us r to the LORD........ Hs 6:1

REUBEN

Son of Jacob and Leah; eldest (Gn
29:32). Lost birthright for sleeping

with father's concubine (35:22; 49:4;
1Ch 5:1). Tried to rescue Joseph (Gn
37:21-29); offered to protect Benjamin
(42:37). Tribe with territory east of the
Dead Sea, north of the Arnon River
(Nm 32; Jos 13:15-23).

REVEAL

the arm of the LORD been
  r-ed?..........................Is 53:1
whom the Son desires to r
  him...........................Mt 11:27
blood did not r this to you,......Mt 16:17
him and will r myself to him... Jn 14:21
of his heart will be r-ed, ... 1Co 14:25

REVELATION

Without r people run wild,..... Pr 29:18
light for r to the Gentiles ...... Lk 2:32
eagerly wait for the r of
  our Lord 1Co 1:7
has a hymn, a teaching, a r,.. 1Co 14:26
it came by a r of Jesus........... Gl 1:12
was made known to me by r, .. Eph 3:3
at the r of the Lord Jesus........2Th 1:7
at the r of Jesus Christ 1Pt 1:7
The r of Jesus Christ that
  God gave..................... Rv 1:1

REVERE

descendants of Israel, r him!...Ps 22:23

REVERENCE

serve God acceptably,
  with r..................... Heb 12:28

REVERENT

observe your pure, r lives....... 1Pt 3:2

REVILE

When we are r-d, we bless; 1Co 4:12

REVIVE

Will you not r us again so that..Ps 85:6

REWARD (N)

there is a r for the righteous! .. Ps 58:11
from the LORD, offspring, a r... Ps 127:3
and his r accompanies him......Is 40:10
your r is great in heaven. ...... Mt 5:12
they have their r............Mt 6:2,5,16
survives, he will receive a r. ...1Co 3:14
looking ahead to the r........ Heb 11:26

REWARD (V)

that he r-s those who seek
  him.......................... Heb 11:6

RIB

God made the r ... into a
  woman .... Gn 2:22

RICH

Don't wear yourself out to
  get r;........................ Pr 23:4
in a hurry to get r will not ..... Pr 28:20
hard for a r person to enter .. Mt 19:23
woe to you who are r,.......... Lk 6:24
who want to be r fall into......1Tm 6:9
r boast in his humiliation......Jms 1:10

RICHES

and you have not requested r .. 2Ch 1:11
in her left, r and honor......... Pr 3:16
make known the r of his glory..Rm 9:23
Oh, the depth of the r ....Rm 11:33
immeasurable r of his grace... Eph 2:7

RIDDLE

directly, openly, and not in r-s; ..Nm 12:8
"Let me tell you a r," Samson
  said .... Jdg 14:12
words of the wise, and their r-s. ..Pr 1:6

RIDE

humble and r-ing on a donkey,.. Zch 9:9

RIDER

horse and its r into the sea... Ex 15:1,21

RIGHT (ADJ)

So you are r when you pass..... Ps 51:4
Sit at my r hand until I make... Ps 110:1
way that seems r to
  a person,.............. Pr 14:12; 16:25
one on your r and the other
  on............................ Mt 20:21
Sit at my r hand until I put ....Mt 22:44
He will put the sheep on his r. .Mt 25:33
He also is at the r hand of God..Rm 8:34
Sit at my r hand until I make...Heb 1:13
sat down at the r hand of
  God.......................... Heb 10:12

RIGHT (N)

Defend the r-s of the fatherless. . Is 1:17
gave them the r to be children.. Jn 1:12

RIGHTEOUS (ADJ)

no one alive is r in your sight. . Ps 143:2
raise up a R Branch of David. . . . . . Jr 23:5
But the r one will live by his
    faith. . . . . Hab 2:4
Joseph, being a r man, and not. . Mt 1:19
saying, "This man really
    was r!" . . . . Lk 23:47
the coming of the R One, ... Ac 7:52
is no one r, not even one. . . . . . . Rm 3:10
But my r one will live by
    faith; . . . . Heb 10:38
Jesus Christ the r one. 1Jn 2:1

RIGHTEOUS (N)

watches over the way of the r . . . . . Ps 1:6
I have not seen the r
    abandoned . . . . Ps 37:25
The r will never be shaken, ... Pr 10:30
the r run to it and are
    protected. . . . . Pr 18:10
sends rain on the r and the . . . . Mt 5:45
I didn't come to call the r . . . . . . Mt 9:13
The r will live by faith. . . . . Rm 1:17
because the r will live by faith. . Gl 3:11

RIGHTEOUSLY

He will judge the world r . . . . Ps 98:9

RIGHTEOUSNESS

He credited it to him as r. . . . . . . Gn 15:6
He judges the world with r; . . . . . Ps 9:8
His r endures forever. . . . . Pss 111:3; 112:3
R exalts a nation, but sin is . . . . . . Pr 14:34
will be named: The LORD is
    Our R. . . . . Jr 23:6
those who hunger and thirst
    for r, ... Mt 5:6
kingdom of God and his r, ... Mt 6:33
apart from the law, the r of
    God . . . . Rm 3:21
it was credited to him for r. . . . . . Rm 4:3
end of the law for r to
    everyone . . . . Rm 10:4
His r endures forever. 2Co 9:9
r like armor on your chest, ... Eph 6:14
reserved for me the crown
    of r, ... 2Tm 4:8
was credited to him as r . . . . . . Jms 2:23

RING

is like a gold r in a pig's snout. . Pr 11:22

RISE

From the r-ing of the sun to its . . Ps 113:3
After three days I will r again. . Mt 27:63

For he has r, just as he said. . . . . . . Mt 28:6
He is r-n! He is not here! . . . . Mk 16:6
A great prophet has r-n
    among us, ... Lk 7:16
that Jesus died and rose again, . . 1Th 4:14
dead in Christ will r first. 1Th 4:16

RIVALRY

that there is r among you. 1Co 1:11
proclaim Christ out of r . . . . Php 1:17
Do nothing out of r or conceit, . . Php 2:3

RIVER

There is a r—its streams . . . . Ps 46:4
By the r-s of Babylon—there
    we . . . . Ps 137:1
make peace flow to her like a r, . . Is 66:12
were baptized by him in the
    Jordan R . . . . Mt 3:6
showed me the r of the water
    of life, ... Rv 22:1

ROAD

r broad that leads to
    destruction, ... Mt 7:13

ROAR

though its water r-s and foams. . Ps 46:3
The LORD r-s from on high; . . . . . . Jr 25:30
The LORD will r from Zion and. . . Jl 3:16

ROARING (ADJ)

prowling around like a r lion, . . 1Pt 5:8

ROAST

they should eat it, r-ed over the
    fire. . . . . Ex 12:8
A lazy hunter doesn't r his
    game, ... Pr 12:27

ROB

to meet a bear r-bed of her
    cubs . . . . Pr 17:12
Will a man r God? Yet you are . Mal 3:8

ROBBER

this house . . . become a den of
    r-s. . . . . Jr 7:11
and fell into the hands of r-s. . Lk 10:30

ROBE

and he made a r of many colors. . Gn 37:3

cut off the corner of Saul's r. . . 1Sm 24:4
hem of his r filled the temple. . . . . . Is 6:1
If I can just touch his r, ... Mt 9:21
and his r was as white as
    snow. . . . . Mt 28:3
crown of thorns and the
    purple r. Jn 19:5
He wore a r dipped in blood, . . Rv 19:13

ROBED (V)

He is r in majesty; . . . . Ps 93:1

ROCK

when you hit the r, water will . . Ex 17:6
will put you in the crevice of
    the r . . . . Ex 33:22
and struck the r twice with
    his . . . . Nm 20:11
The LORD is my r, ... Ps 18:2
LORD, my r and my Redeemer. . Ps 19:14
and set my feet on a r, ... Ps 40:2
and a r to trip over, ... Is 8:14
who built his house on the r. . . Mt 7:24
on this r I will build my
    church, ... Mt 16:18
Other seed fell on the r; . . . . Lk 8:6
and a r to trip over, ... Rm 9:33
drank from a spiritual r that followed
    them, and that r was Christ. . 1Co 10:4
and a r to trip over. 1Pt 2:8

ROCKY

Other seed fell on r ground, . . . Mt 13:5

ROD

your r and your staff—they. . . . Ps 23:4
not use the r hates his son, ... Pr 13:24
with a r, he will not die. . . . . Pr 23:13

ROLL

The sky will r up like a scroll, . . . Is 34:4
Who will r away the stone
    from . . . . Mk 16:3
very large—had been r-ed
    away. . . . . Mk 16:4

ROMAN

Tell me, are you a R citizen? . . . Ac 22:27

ROME

Italian city, capital of the Roman Empire; represented at Pentecost (Ac 2:10); Jews expelled (18:2); Paul addressed a letter to the church there (Rm 1:7,15)

and goes there (Ac 19:21; 23:11; 28:14-16; 2Tm 1:17).

ROOF

From the r he saw a woman.. 2Sm 11:2
went up on the r and lowered
    him ....Lk 5:19

ROOM

you pray, go into your private r,..Mt 6:6
there was no guest r available...Lk 2:7
Father's house are many r-s; ...Jn 14:2

ROOSTER

before the r crows, you will ..Mt 26:34

ROOT

On that day the r of Jesse will...Is 11:10
and like a r out of dry ground... Is 53:2
since it had no r, it withered... Mt 13:6
And if the r is holy, so are the. Rm 11:16
The r of Jesse will appear, ...Rm 15:12
r-ed and firmly established... Eph 3:17
r-ed and built up in him and......Col 2:7
of money is a r of all kinds..... 1Tm 6:10
and that no r of bitterness...... Heb 12:15
of Judah, the R of David, ...Rv 5:5

ROUGH

and the r places, a plain......... Is 40:4
straight, the r ways smooth,.....Lk 3:5

ROYAL

if you fulfill the r law
    prescribed...................Jms 2:8
a chosen race, a r priesthood, a..1Pt 2:9

RUIN (N)

his lips invites his own r. .... Pr 13:3
my house still lies in r-s..........Hg 1:9
desires, which plunge people
    into r 1Tm 6:9
leads to the r of those who
    listen......................2Tm 2:14

RUIN (V)

Woe is me for I am r-ed..........Is 6:5
and the skins are r-ed..........Mt 9:17

RULE (N)

when he abolishes all r
    and all 1Co 15:24

he competes according to
    the r-s......................2Tm 2:5

RULE (V)

They will r the fish of the sea.. Gn 1:26
He r-s forever by his might;......Ps 66:7
For sin will not r over you,......Rm 6:14

RULER

and the r-s conspire together
    against ....Ps 2:2
one will come from you to be r..Mc 5:2
know that the r-s of the
    Gentiles....................Mt 20:25
Now the r of this world will be ..Jn 12:31
death nor life, nor angels
    nor r-s,..................... Rm 8:38
but against the r-s, against ... Eph 6:12
Remind them to submit to r-s......Ti 3:1

RUMOR

to hear of wars and r-s of
    wars........................Mt 24:6

RUN

his word r-s swiftly...........Ps 147:15
righteous r to it and are
    protected. .... Pr 18:10
they will r and not become
    weary. .... Is 40:31
R in such a way to win the
    prize...................... 1Co 9:24
was not r-ning, and had not
    been r......................... Gl 2:2
You were r-ning well............ Gl 5:7
Let us r with endurance the
    race.......................Heb 12:1

RUNNER

the r-s in a stadium all race,
    but......................... 1Co 9:24

RUSH

sound ...of a violent r-ing wind ..Ac 2:2

RUST

where moth and r destroy and..Mt 6:19

RUTH

Moabitess; widowed daughter-in-law
of Naomi (Ru 1:1-5); married Boaz; ancestor of David and Christ (Ru 4:1; Mt
1:5-6,16).

RUTHLESSLY

They worked the Israelites r.... Ex 1:13

S

SABBATH

Remember the S day to keep it. .Ex 20:8
through the grainfields
    on the S. ....Mt 12:1
The S was made for man and
    not.........................Mk 2:27
Son of Man is Lord even of
    the S........................ Mk 2:28
whether he would heal him
    on the S. ....Mk 3:2
lawful to do good on the S or ...Mk 3:4
a S rest remains for God's
    people .... Heb 4:9

SACKCLOTH

with fasting, s, and ashes. ...... Dn 9:3
proclaimed a fast and dressed
    in s......................... Jnh 3:5
would have repented in s
    and ashes..................Mt 11:21

SACRED

you have known the s
    Scriptures,..................2Tm 3:15

SACRIFICE

is the Passover s to the LORD, ..Ex 12:27
to obey is better than s,......1Sm 15:22
You do not delight in s and
    offering;.....................Ps 40:6
You do not want a s, or I would..Ps 51:16
The s pleasing to God is a
    broken...................... Ps 51:17
faithful love and not s,..........Hs 6:6
I desire mercy and not s........ Mt 9:13
your bodies as a living s,....... Rm 12:1
our Passover lamb has
    been s-d.....................1Co 5:7
an acceptable s, pleasing to
    God.. .... Php 4:18
need to offer s-s every day, ... Heb 7:27
of sin by the s of himself.......Heb 9:26
offer up to God a s of praise,..Heb 13:15
offer spiritual s-s acceptable
    to 1Pt 2:5

SADDUCEES

of the leaven of the Pharisees
    and S....................... Mt 16:6

S, who say there is no
   resurrection...............Mt 22:23

SAFETY

The horse is a false hope for s;.. Ps 33:17

SAINT

intercedes for the s-s
   according ....Rm 8:27
glorious inheritance in the
   s-s,...........................Eph 1:18
Greet every s in Christ Jesus.. Php 4:21
to the s-s once for all...............Jd 3
are the prayers of the s-s.........Rv 5:8
the righteous acts of the s-s......Rv 19:8

SAKE

right paths for his name's s.......Ps 23:3
not for your s that I will
   act ....Ezk 36:22,32

SALOME

Wife of Zebedee, mother of James and
John (Mk 15:40; 16:1; cp. Mt 27:56); possibly Mary's sister (Jn 19:25).

SALT

back and became a pillar of s. .Gn 19:26
It is a permanent covenant
   of s...........................Nm 18:19
You are the s of the earth...... Mt 5:13
seasoned with s, so that you
   may...........................Col 4:6

SALVATION

Stand firm and see the
   LORD'S s......................Ex 14:13
He has become my s............Ex 15:2
Proclaim his s from day to
   day. 1Ch 16:23
The God of my s is exalted...... Ps 18:46
The LORD is my light and my s .. Ps 27:1
Restore the joy of your s to me,..Ps 51:12
He has become my s............Ps 118:14
who proclaims s, who says to .. Is 52:7
For my eyes have seen
   your s. ....Lk 2:30
everyone will see the s of God......Lk 3:6
There is s in no one else,........Ac 4:12
now is the day of s.............2Co 6:2
the helmet of s and the sword..Eph 6:17
work out your own s with
   fear........................Php 2:12
if we neglect such a great s?... Heb 2:3
S belongs to our God, who is......Rv 7:10

SAMARIA

Capital and namesake of the northern
kingdom (1Kg 13:32; 16:24; 2Kg 17:24; Is
7:9; Ezk 16:46; 23:4; Hos 8:5; Ob 19; Mc
1:1); captured by Assyria (2Kg 17:6).
   In NT times, region of central hill
country between Judah and Galilee
(Lk 17:11; Ac 1:8; 8:1,5,14, often shunned
by Jews (Jn 4:4-9); home of Samaritans.

SAMARITAN

But a S on his journey came
   up...........................Lk 10:33
thanking him. And he
   was a S.......................Lk 17:16
Jews do not associate with S-s...Jn 4:9

SAME

Jesus Christ is the s yesterday,..Heb 13:8

SAMSON

Son of Manoah; Danite judge. Birth
announced; to be a Nazirite (Jdg 13).
Rashly married a Philistine; posed a
riddle (Jdg 14). Took revenge on Philistines: set fire to fields; killed 1,000
with donkey's jawbone (Jdg 15). Married Delilah; was betrayed (16:4-21).
Slaughter in Dagon's temple (16:23-30;
Heb 11:32-34).

SAMUEL

Son of Elkanah and Hannah; Ephraimite judge, kingmaker, priest, and
prophet. Born in answer to prayer
(1Sm 1:1-20); raised at Shiloh by Eli (1:25-
28; 2:11); called (3:1-18). Served as military and judicial judge (1Sm 7). Warned
people about the nature of a king (8:10-
18; 10:25); anointed Saul (10:1); rejected
Saul (13:11-14; 15:10-29). Anointed David
(16:1-13); protected David from Saul
(19:18-24). Death (25:1); appearance to
Saul after death (28:3-19).

SANCTIFICATION

which results in s...........Rm 6:19,22
For this is God's will, your s:....1Th 4:3

SANCTIFY

S them by the truth;............Jn 17:17
washed, you were s-ied, you
   were.........................1Co 6:11
the God of peace himself s
   you 1Th 5:23

SANCTUARY

They are to make a s for me......Ex 25:8
up my hands toward your
   holy s.........................Ps 28:2
Praise God in his s.............Ps 150:1
and will set my s among
   them.......................Ezk 37:26
not enter a s made with
   hands.......................Heb 9:24

SAND

offspring like the s of the sea,..Gn 32:12
who built his house on the s... Mt 7:26

SANDAL

Remove the s-s from your feet,.. Ex 3:5
Remove the s-s from your feet,.. Jos 5:15
not worthy to remove his s-s....Mt 3:11

SARAH

Wife and half sister of Abraham; originally named Sarai (Gn 11:29-31; 20:12);
barren (11:30). Twice passed off as
Abraham's sister (12:10-20; 20). Gave
Hagar to Abraham, then sent her away
(Gn 16; 21:9-21). Laughed when she
heard the promise of a son (18:9-15).
Bore Isaac (21:1-7; Heb 11:11). Died; buried at Machpelah (Gn 23; 25:10; 49:31).

SATAN

LORD asked S, "Where have you .. Jb 1:7
Jesus told him, "Go away, S!..... Mt 4:10
If S drives out S, he is divided..Mt 12:26
told Peter, "Get behind me, S!..Mt 16:23
I watched S fall from heaven ...Lk 10:18
Then S entered Judas, called... Lk 22:3
and from the power of S to
   God,.........................Ac 26:18
S disguises himself as an
   angel........................2Co 11:14
messenger of S to torment
   me so 2Co 12:7
synagogue of S..............Rv 2:9; 3:9
who is called the devil and S,..Rv 12:9
S will be released from his..... Rv 20:7

SATISFY

your wages on what does not s?..Is 55:2

SAUL

1. First king of united Israel. Son of
Kish; tall, handsome Benjaminite
(1Sm 9:1-2). Met Samuel while looking for donkeys (9:3-27). Anointed

privately (10:1); chosen by lot and announced publicly (10:17-24); delivered Jabesh-gilead (11:1-11); confirmed king at Gilgal (11:12-15). Rebuked and rejected (13:8-15; 15:11-30). Attempted to kill David (18:11,17,25; 19:10-17; 23:8,25; 24:2; 26:2); spared by David (1Sm 24; 26). Among the prophets (10:9-13; 19:18-24). Consulted a medium to inquire of Samuel (1Sm 28). Killed by Philistines (1Sm 31).

2. Paul's Hebrew name. see PAUL

SAVE

and I was s-d from my enemies...Ps 18:3
and s those stumbling toward...Pr 24:11
Turn to me and be s-d, all the
ends .... Is 45:22
on the name of the LORD
will be s-d, ... Jl 2:32
Jesus, because he will s his
people .... Mt 1:21
whoever wants to s his life
will .... Mt 16:25
asked, "Then who can be s-d?"..Mt 19:25
cut short, no one would
be s-d........................ Mt 24:22
and is baptized will be s-d,....Mk 16:16
come to seek and to s the lost. .Lk 19:10
to s the world through him. .... Jn 3:17
name of the Lord will be s-d. ...Ac 2:21
Sirs, what must I do to
be s-d? .... Ac 16:30
on name of the Lord will
be s-d........................Rm 10:13
you are s-d by grace through
faith,........................ Eph 2:8
came into the world to s
sinners 1Tm 1:15
wants everyone to be s-d 1Tm 2:4
to this, now s-s you (not as
the......................... 1Pt 3:21

SAVIOR

They forgot God their S, ...Ps 106:21
Besides me, there is no S. ....Is 43:11
and no S exists besides me.....Hs 13:4
a S ... who is Messiah, the
Lord........................... Lk 2:11
God, who is the S of all
people,...................... 1Tm 4:10
appearing of our S Christ
Jesus, ... 2Tm 1:10
glory of our great God and S, ... Ti 2:13
of our Lord and S Jesus Christ. . 2Pt 3:18

SAY

"who do you s that I am?"..... Mt 16:15

SCALE

Dishonest s-s are detestable......Pr 11:1
something like s-s fell from his. .Ac 9:18
had a set of s-s in his hand.......Rv 6:5

SCARLET

Though your sins are s,..........Is 1:18
dressed him in a s robe.........Mt 27:28

SCATTER

sheep of the flock will be
s-ed......................... Mt 26:31
A man s-s seed on the ground;..Mk 4:26

SCEPTER

s will not depart from Judah ..Gn 49:10
break them with an iron s; ......Ps 2:9

SCHEMES

against the s of the devil. ......Eph 6:11

SCOFFERS

S will come in the last days 2Pt 3:3

SCORN

and s-ed the Rock of his
salvation....................Dt 32:15
s-ed by mankind and
despised by..................Ps 22:6

SCORPION

asks for an egg, will give
him a s?..................... Lk 11:12

SCOUT

Send men to s out the land......Nm 13:2

SCRIBE

authority, and not like their
s-s........................... Mt 7:29
woe to you, s-s and Pharisees,..Mt 23:13

SCRIPTURE

don't know the S-s or the
power ....Mt 22:29
Today ... this S has been
fulfilled. ....Lk 4:21
concerning himself in all
the S-s...................... Lk 24:27
You pore over the S-s
because you ....Jn 5:39

and the S cannot be broken....Jn 10:35
you have known the
sacred S-s, ...2Tm 3:15
All S is inspired by God and is ..2Tm 3:16
No prophecy of S comes from ..2Pt 1:20

SCROLL

Eat this s, then go and speak to..Ezk 3:1
open the s and break its seals? ..Rv 5:2

SEA

through the s on dry ground,..Ex 14:22
the winds and the s obey him!..Mt 8:27
toward them walking on
the s......................... Mt 14:25
Something like a s of glass, ...Rv 4:6

SEAL (N)

Set me as a s on your heart,......Sg 8:6
He has also put his s on us and
given........................ 2Co 1:22
the scroll and break its s-s?'......Rv 5:2

SEAL (V)

s the book until the time of the
end........................... Dn 12:4
were s-ed with the promised
Holy ....Eph 1:13
s-ed with seven seals............Rv 5:1
s the servants ... on their
foreheads.....................Rv 7:3

SEARCH

You have s-ed me and
known me..................... Ps 139:1
S me, God, and know
my heart; .... Ps 139:23
me when you s for me with all. .Jr 29:13
And he who s-es our hearts
knows ....Rm 8:27
since the Spirit s-es
everything, ...1Co 2:10

SEASON

that bears its fruit in its s .... Ps 1:3
days, months, s-s, and years......Gl 4:10
About the times and the s-s:....1Th 5:1

SEASONED

be gracious, s with salt, so......Col 4:6

SEAT (N)

Make a mercy s of pure gold, ..Ex 25:17

love the front s in the .... Lk 11:43

SEAT (V)

I saw the Lord s-ed on a high and . .Is 6:1
s-ed at the right hand of
  Power......................Mt 26:64
and s-ed us with him the
  heavens,................... Eph 2:6

SECOND

The s is like it: Love your......Mt 22:39
This is the s death, the lake of . .Rv 20:14

SECRET

He knows the s-s of the heart?. . Ps 44:21
Father who sees in s will
  reward you. .... Mt 6:4
things kept s from the .... Mt 13:35
judges what people have
  kept s,.........................Rm 2:16
The s-s of his heart will be......1Co 14:25
I have learned the s of being. . Php 4:12

SECRETLY

decided to divorce her s.........Mt 1:19
but s because of his fear of the . .Jn 19:38

SECURE

anchor for the soul, firm
  and s. .... Heb 6:19

SEE

humans cannot s me and live...Ex 33:20
They say, "The LORD doesn't s it. . Ps 94:7
they might s with their eyes......Is 6:10
darkness have s-n a great light,. .Mt 4:16
heart, for they will s God........ Mt 5:8
because looking they do not s,. .Mt 13:13
No one has ever s-n God. .... Jn 1:18
I was blind, and now I can s!......Jn 9:25
who has s-n me has s-n the
  Father.........................Jn 14:9
what we have s-n with our
  eyes,..............................1Jn 1:1
because we will s him as he is.. . 1Jn 3:2

SEED

who sowed good s in his field.. Mt 13:24
like a mustard s that a man
  took........................... Mt 13:31
faith the size of a mustard s,. . Mt 17:20
Other s fell on the rock;.........Lk 8:6
He does not say "and to s-s,"......Gl 3:16
not of perishable s but of 1Pt 1:23

SEEK

when you s him with
  all your ....Dt 4:29
If you s him, he will be found . .1Ch 28:9
pray and s my face, and turn...2Ch 7:14
s peace and pursue it..........Ps 34:14
S the LORD while he may be
  found; .... Is 55:6
But s first the kingdom of God. .Mt 6:33
S, and you will find..............Mt 7:7
come to s and to save the lost.. Lk 19:10
No one is to s his own good,...1Co 10:24
he rewards those who s him... Heb 11:6

SEEM

a way that s-s right to a
  person.................Pr 14:12; 16:25

SEIZE

Then they tried to s him.........Jn 7:30

SELF

put off the old s with its ....Col 3:9
For people will be lovers of s,. .2Tm 3:2

SELF-CONTROL

you because of your lack of s. . .1Co 7:5
gentleness, s. The law is not
  against ....Gl 5:23
knowledge with s, s with
  endurance, ... 2Pt 1:6

SELF-CONTROLLED

let us stay awake and be s.......1Th 5:6
sensible, righteous, holy, s,........Ti 1:8

SELF-INDULGENCE

not of any value in curbing s...Col 2:23

SELFISH

anger outbursts, s ambitions,
  slander 2Co 12:20
envy and s ambition ....Jms 3:14,16

SELL

and do not s—truth,
  wisdom ....Pr 23:23
"You were sold for nothing,
  and you.................... Is 52:3
joy he goes and s-s
  everything.................. Mt 13:44
s all you have and give to the
  poor .... Mk 10:21

sold his birthright in
  exchange .... Heb 12:16
one can buy or s unless he has. . Rv 13:17

SEND

I AM has sent me to you. ....Ex 3:14
Who should I s? ... Here I am.
  S me.............................Is 6:8
of the harvest to s out workers.. Mt 9:38
sent out these twelve after
  giving. .... Mt 10:5
me welcomes him who sent
  me............................ Mt 10:40
has sent me to proclaim
  release ....Lk 4:18
For God did not s his Son into . . Jn 3:17
the will of him who sent
  me.....................Jn 5:30; 6:38
If I go, I will s him to you. .... Jn 16:7
Father has sent me, I also s
  you..............................Jn 20:21
they preach unless they are
  sent?........................Rm 10:15
God sent his Son, born of a
  woman,....................... Gl 4:4
he loved us and sent his
  Son to be....................1Jn 4:10

SENSE

who commits adultery lacks s; . .Pr 6:32

SENSIBLE

who accepts correction is s..... Pr 15:5

SEPARATE (ADJ)

out from among them and
  be s,..........................2Co 6:17

SEPARATE (V)

and a gossip s-s close friends. . Pr 16:28
joined together, let no one s.... Mt 19:6
just as a shepherd s-s the
  sheep ....Mt 25:32
Who can s us from the love of . . Rm 8:35

SEPARATION

as far as the s of soul and
  spirit,........................ Heb 4:12

SERPENT

Now the s was the most
  cunning ....Gn 3:1
as shrewd as s-s and as
  innocent.................... Mt 10:16

as the s deceived Eve by his....2Co 11:3
the ancient s, who is called.....Rv 12:9

SERVANT

Speak, for your s is listening. . 1Sm 3:10
Give praise, you s-s of the LORD . .Ps 135:1
"This is my s; I strengthen him, . .Is 42:1
See, my s will be successful; . . . Is 52:13
Here is my s whom I have
    chosen, ...Mt 12:18
great among you must be
    your s, ...Mt 20:26
he must be last and s of all.... Mk 9:35
"I am the Lord's s," said Mary. . .Lk 1:38
s-s; we've only done our duty. . Lk 17:10
Where I am, there my s also
    will be ....Jn 12:26
I do not call you s-s anymore, because
    a s doesn't know what ......Jn 15:15

SERVE

S the LORD with gladness; ...... Ps 100:2
No one can s two masters, ...Mt 6:24
did not come to be s-d,
    but to s, ...Mt 20:28
am among you as the one
    who s-s.......................Lk 22:27
but s one another through love. . Gl 5:13
S with a good attitude, ... Eph 6:7

SERVICE

If s, use it in s; if teaching, in
    teaching; ....Rm 12:7

SET

S apart for me Barnabas and
    Saul..........................Ac 13:2
instrument, s apart, useful to. .2Tm 2:21

SEVEN

march around the city s times,. . Jos 6:4
the ruler, will be s weeks and
    sixty-two weeks. ....Dn 9:25
sins against me him? As many as s
    times? ....Mt 18:21
To the s churches in Asia.........Rv 1:4
s angels with the s last plagues; . .Rv 15:1

SEVEN HUNDRED

He had s wives who were......1Kg 11:3

SEVENTH

On the s day God had
    completed ....Gn 2:2

the s day is a Sabbath to the
    LORD.......................... Ex 20:10
And on the s day God rested
    from .... Heb 4:4

SEVENTY

until s years were fulfilled. . . 2Ch 36:21
When s years for Babylon ..... Jr 29:10
number of years ... would
    be s.............................Dn 9:2
S weeks are decreed about
    your ....Dn 9:24
but s times seven..............Mt 18:22

SEVENTY-TWO

The s returned with joy,
    saying,......................Lk 10:17

SEVERE

and s treatment of the body, . . .Col 2:23

SEW

so they s-ed fig leaves
    together .... Gn 3:7
No one s-s a patch of
    unshrunk....................Mk 2:21

SHADE

to provide s for his head....... Jnh 4:6
birds of the sky can nest
    in its s....................... Mk 4:32

SHADOW

Our days on earth are like a s, . .1Ch 29:15
hide me in the s of your wings ....Ps 17:8
person goes about like a
    mere s.......................Ps 39:6
dwells in the s of the Almighty. . Ps 91:1
in darkness and the s of death, . .Lk 1:79
least his s might fall on some.......Ac 5:15
as a copy and s of the heavenly. .Heb 8:5

SHAKE

established; it cannot be s-n. . 1Ch 16:30
of the LORD s-s the wilderness; . .Ps 29:8
The righteous will never be
    s-n, ...Pr 10:30
s the dust off your feet when
    you .... Mt 10:14
pressed down, s-n together, ... Lk 6:38
where they were assembled
    was s-n,......................Ac 4:31
once more I will s not only
    the . . ..Heb 12:26

SHALLUM

1. King of Israel; assassinated Zechariah; was assassinated by Menahem
   (2Kg 15:10-15).
2. Alternate name for Jehoahaz (2Kg
   23:30-34; Jr 22:11). see JEHOAHAZ

SHAME

were naked, yet felt no s. ...... Gn 2:25
hope in me will not be put to s. . Is 49:23
some to s and eternal
    contempt. .... Dn 12:2
on him will not be put to s. ... Rm 9:33
what is foolish ... to s the
    wise, ...1Co 1:27
their glory is in their s.......... Php 3:19
the cross, despising the s...... Heb 12:2
in him will never be put to s...... 1Pt 2:6

SHAMEFUL

For it is s even to mention
    what .... Eph 5:12

SHAMELESS

Men committed s acts with
    men.........................Rm 1:27

SHAMGAR

Judge; killed 600 Philistines with a cattle prod (Jdg 3:31; 5:6).

SHAPHAN

Josiah's court secretary or scribe (2Kg
22:3-14); his sons were friends of Jeremiah (Jr 26:24; 36:10; 39:14).

SHARE

S your master's joy.'.......... Mt 25:21
two shirts must s with
    someone.....................Lk 3:11

SHARES

let me inherit two s of your
    spirit........................ 2Kg 2:9

SHARP

They had such a s
    disagreement .... Ac 15:39

SHARPEN

s-s iron, and one man s-s
    another. .... Pr 27:17

SHARPER

s than any double-edged
    sword, ... Heb 4:12

SHAVE

If I am s-d, my strength will
    leave........................ Jdg 16:17
emissaries, s-d off half their. .2Sm 10:4
for them to get their heads
    s-d.......................... Ac 21:24
the same as having her head
    s-d........................... 1Co 11:5

SHEAF

shouts of joy, carrying his
    s-ves. .... Ps 126:6

SHEARER

a sheep silent before her s-s, ... Is 53:7
a lamb is silent before its s, ... Ac 8:32

SHEBA

Nation whose queen came to see
Solomon (1Kg 10; 2Ch 9); also called
Sabeans (Jb 1:15; Jl 3:8).

SHECHEM

1. City in the hill country of Ephraim.
Simeon and Levi destroyed the city in
revenge for the rape of Dinah (Gn 34);
Joshua renewed the covenant there
(Jos 24:1-28); served as first capital of
the northern kingdom (1Kg 12:25).
2. Son of Hamor; raped Dinah (Gn 34).

SHED

Whoever s-s human blood ..... Gn 9:6
without the s-ding of blood
    there.......................Heb 9:22

SHEEP

hills like s without a
    shepherd...................1Kg 22:17
people, the s of his pasture. ......Ps 100:3
We all went astray like s; .... Is 53:6
and like a s silent before her ...... Is 53:7
and the s will be scattered; ......Zch 13:7
like s without a shepherd...... Mt 9:36
go to the lost s of the house of ..Mt 10:6
someone has a hundred s,
    and .... Mt 18:12
separates the s from the
    goats.......................Mt 25:32
He calls his own s by name...... Jn 10:3

I lay down my life for the s..... Jn 10:15
My s hear my voice, I know
    them, ...Jn 10:27
"Feed my s," Jesus said. .... Jn 21:17
was led like a s to the
    slaughter,................... Ac 8:32

SHEET

a large s coming down, ... Ac 10:11

SHELTER

The Festival of S-s to the
    LORD........................ Lv 23:34
dwell in s-s during the
    festival.....................Neh 8:14
under the s of your wings....... Ps 61:4
I will set up three s-s here: ......Mt 17:4
Jewish Festival of S-s was near,. . Jn 7:2

SHEOL *SEE ALSO* HADES, HELL

You will not abandon
    me to S; .... Ps 16:10
make my bed in S, you are
    there.......................Ps 139:8
Her house is the road to S, ... Pr 7:27
S and Abaddon lie open before. . Pr 15:11
S, where is your sting?.........Hs 13:14

SHEPHERD (N)

hills like sheep without a s....1Kg 22:17
The LORD is my s; I have what... Ps 23:1
He protects his flock like a s; ...Is 40:11
prophesy against the s-s of
    Israel....................... Ezk 34:2
establish over them one s, ...Ezk 34:23
Strike the s, and the sheep will . .Zch 13:7
like sheep without a s .... Mt 9:36
I will strike the s, and the
    sheep .... Mt 26:31
s-s were staying out in the fields ..Lk 2:8
I am the good s. The good s lays. .Jn 10:11
the great S of the sheep ......Heb 13:20
And when the chief S appears, . . 1Pt 5:4

SHEPHERD (V)

You will s my people Israel 2Sm 5:2
overseers, to s the church of
    God,........................ Ac 20:28
S God's flock among you, not... 1Pt 5:2

SHIELD

He is a s to all who take
    refuge 2Sm 22:31
LORD is my strength and my s; . .Ps 28:7
situation take up the s of faith. .Eph 6:16

SHINE

LORD make his face s on you. . Nm 6:25
Arise, s, for your light has .... Is 60:1
let your light s before others, . . Mt 5:16
righteous will s like the sun . . Mt 13:43
and his face **shone** like the sun; . .Mt 17:2
glory of the Lord **shone**
    around them,................... Lk 2:9
That light s-s in the darkness, ... Jn 1:5
and Christ will s on you....... Eph 5:14

SHIPWRECK

Three times I was s-ed. 2Co 11:25
have s-ed their faith.......... 1Tm 1:19

SHIRT

to sue you and take away
    your s, ... Mt 5:40

SHOOT

a s will grow from the stump.... Is 11:1

SHORE

daybreak came, Jesus stood
    on the s. .... Jn 21:4

SHORT

the crowd, since he was a s
    man.......................Lk 19:3
sinned and fall s of the glory . .Rm 3:23

SHOULDERS

government will be on his s.......Is 9:6

SHOUT

until the time I say, 'S!' Then
    you .... Jos 6:10
Let the whole earth s to the
    LORD; ....Ps 98:4
s triumphantly to God, ... Ps 100:1
kept s-ing all the more,
    "Crucify him!" .... Mt 27:23
descend from heaven
    with a s,.....................1Th 4:16

SHOW

for they will be s-n mercy....... Mt 5:7
He s-ed them his hands and
    feet. .... Lk 24:40
s us the Father, and that's
    enough .... Jn 14:8
s mercy to whom I will s
    mercy, ... Rm 9:15

And I will **s** you an even
better.......................1Co 12:31
S me your faith without
works, ...Jms 2:18

SHOWERS

s in ... season—**s** of
blessing...................Ezk 34:26

SHREWD

crooked you prove
yourself **s**. ....Ps 18:26
Therefore be as **s** as
serpents ....Mt 10:16

SHUDDER

demons believe—and
they **s**.......................Jms 2:19

SHUT

and they have **s** their eyes;.... Mt 13:15
that every mouth may be **s** ....Rm 3:19

SICK

need a doctor, but those who
are **s**.......................... Mt 9:12
I was **s** and you took care
of me;.....................Mt 25:36
is why many are **s** and ill
among.....................1Co 11:30
Is anyone among you **s**? ...... Jms 5:14

SICKLE

Swing the **s** because the harvest.. Jl 3:13
and a sharp **s** in his hand.......Rv 14:14

SICKNESS

he himself bore our **s-es**, ... Is 53:4
healing every disease and
every **s**. ....Mt 9:35

SIDE

Though a thousand fall at
your **s**......................... Ps 91:7
the LORD had not been on
our **s**— ....Ps 124:1
pierced his **s** with a spear, ...Jn 19:34
showed them his hands and
his **s**......................... Jn 20:20

SIFT

has asked to **s** you like wheat.. Lk 22:31

SIGHT

The blind receive their **s**,.......Lk 7:22
For we walk by faith, not by **s** .. 2Co 5:7

SIGN

will give you a **s**: See, the virgin.. Is 7:14
demands a **s**, but no **s** will be given to
it except the **s** of ... Jonah. . Mt 12:39
s of your coming and of the
end ....Mt 24:3
This will be the **s** for you: ....Lk 2:12
the first of his **s-s**, in Cana of
Galilee.......................... Jn 2:11
Jesus performed many
other **s-s** .... Jn 20:30
them to do **s-s** and wonders ....Ac 14:3
Jews ask for **s-s** and the
Greeks.......................1Co 1:22
tongues, then, is intended
as a **s**, ... 1Co 14:22

SILAS

Early church leader and prophet; also
called Silvanus. Brought news from Jerusalem to Antioch (Ac 15:22,32); worked
with Paul and Peter in missions and writing letters (15:40-41; 16:19-40; 17:10-15;
18:5; 2Co 1:19; 1Th 1:1; 2Th 1:1; 1Pt 5:12).

SILENCE (N)

there was **s** in heaven for about .. Rv 8:1

SILENCE (V)

that he had **s-d** the Sadducees,. .Mt 22:34
said to the sea, "**S**! Be still!"......Mk 4:39

SILENT

If you keep **s** at this time, ... Est 4:14
When I kept **s**, my bones
became ....Ps 32:3
considered wise when he
keeps **s**, ...Pr 17:28
and like a sheep **s** before her ... Is 53:7
But Jesus kept **s**...............Mt 26:63
and as a lamb is **s** before its..... Ac 8:32
women should be **s** in the..... 1Co 14:34
instead, she is to be **s**..........1Tm 2:12

SILOAM

Pool in Jerusalem (Jn 9:7,11).

SILVER

return each man's **s** to his
sack, ...Gn 42:25

my instruction instead of **s**,......Pr 8:10
like gold apples in **s** settings... Pr 25:11
loves **s** is never satisfied
with **s**, ...Ec 5:10
you without **s**, come, buy, and
eat!............................Is 55:1
thirty pieces of **s** for him...... Mt 26:15
I don't have **s** or gold, but ....Ac 3:6

SIMEON

1. Son of Jacob and Leah (Gn 29:33);
with Levi, avenged Dinah's rape by
Shechem (34:25-31; 49:5); held as hostage by Joseph (42:24). Tribe with territory within Judah (Jos 19:1-9; Jdg 1:3,17).
2. Devout Jew who blessed the baby
Jesus (Lk 2:25-35).
3. Jewish variation of Simon (Ac 15:14;
2Pt 1:1). see PETER

SIMON

1. Apostle Peter's original name (Mt
4:18). see PETER
2. Apostle; called the Zealot (Mt 10:4;
Mk 3:18; Lk 6:15; Ac 1:13).
3. Leper who hosted Jesus (Mt 26:6-13).
4. Cyrenian forced to carry Jesus's
cross (Mk 15:21).
5. Sorcerer who wanted to buy the
power of the Spirit (Ac 8:9-24).
6. Tanner of Joppa who hosted Peter,
where Peter saw the vision (Ac 9:43).

SIN (N)

be sure your **s** will catch
up with ....Nm 32:23
forgive their **s**, and heal their
land. 2Ch 7:14
and my **s** is always before me... Ps 51:3
but **s** is a disgrace to any
people........................Pr 14:34
yet he bore the **s** of many ...... Is 53:12
authority on earth to
forgive **s-s** .... Mt 9:6
forgive us our **s-s**, for we ....Lk 11:4
takes away the **s** of the world!.. Jn 1:29
The one without **s** among you... Jn 8:7
just as **s** entered the world..... Rm 5:12
For the wages of **s** is death, ... Rm 6:23
Christ died for our **s-s**
according to.................1Co 15:3
who did not know **s** to be **s**
for us,........................ 2Co 5:21
way as we are, yet without **s**. . Heb 4:15
hindrance and the **s** that so
easily ....Heb 12:1
confess our **s-s**, he is faithful......1Jn 1:9
and **s** is lawlessness............1Jn 3:4

SIN (V)

you—you alone—I have s-ned . Ps 51:4
so that I may not s against
  you . . . . Ps 119:11
your right eye causes you to s, . . Mt 5:29
If your brother s-s against
  you, ... Mt 18:15
If your brother s-s, rebuke him, . . Lk 17:3
And if he s-s against you seven . . Lk 17:4
from now on do not s anymore. . . Jn 8:11
Rabbi, who s-ned, this man or . . . . Jn 9:2
For all have s-ned and fall
  short. . . . . Rm 3:23
say, "We have not s-ned," we . . . 1Jn 1:10
so that you may not s 1Jn 2:1

SINAI

Mountain where God revealed the
Law (Ex 19:20; 31:18; 34:32; Lv 25:1; Ac
7:38; Gl 4:25). The wilderness region
(Ex 19:1; Lv 7:38).

SINCERE

s brotherly love for each other, . . 1Pt 1:22

SINFUL

I was s when my mother
  conceived . . . . Ps 51:5
into the hands of s men, ... Lk 24:7

SING

I will s to the LORD, for he is . . . . Ex 15:1
Let the whole earth s to the
  LORD. 1Ch 16:23
the morning stars sang
  together . . . . Jb 38:7
S praise to God, s praise; . . . . Ps 47:6
S a new song to the LORD . . Pss 96:1; 98:1
After s-ing a hymn, they
  went out . . . . Mt 26:30
praying and s-ing hymns to
  God, ... Ac 16:25
songs, s-ing and making
  music . . . . Eph 5:19
s-ing to God with gratitude in . . Col 3:16
cheerful? He should s praises . . . Jms 5:13
they sang a new song: You are . . . Rv 5:9

SINGED

not a hair of their heads
  was s, ... Dn 3:27

SINGER

S-s lead the way, with
  musicians . . . . Ps 68:25

SINK

I have sunk in deep mud, ... Ps 69:2
And beginning to s he cried
  out, ... Mt 14:30

SINNER

or stand in the pathway of s-s . . . . . Ps 1:1
My son, if s-s entice you, don't . . . Pr 1:10
Don't let your heart envy s-s; . . Pr 23:17
to call the righteous, but s-s . . . . Mt 9:13
friend of tax collectors and
  s-s! . . . . Mt 11:19
Even s-s do that. . . . . Lk 6:33
in heaven over one s who
  repents . . . . Lk 15:7
while we were still s-s, Christ
  died . . . . Rm 5:8
came into the world to
  save s-s 1Tm 1:15

SISTER

say you're my s . . . . Gn 12:13
is my brother and s and
  mother. Mt 12:50
the younger women as s-s. 1Tm 5:2

SIT

the LORD s-s enthroned forever; . . Ps 9:7
S at my right hand until I make . Ps 110:1
You know when I s down and
  when . . . . Ps 139:2
But to s at my right and left is . Mt 20:23
into heaven and sat down at
  the . . . . Mk 16:19
S at my right hand until I
  make . . . . Heb 1:13

SIX

are to labor s days and do all . . Ex 20:9

SIX HUNDRED THOUSAND

about s soldiers on foot, ... Ex 12:37

SIXTY-TWO

seven weeks and s weeks. . . . . . Dn 9:25

SKILL

may my right hand forget its s . . Ps 137:5

SKIN

clothing from s-s for the man
  and . . . . Gn 3:21
unclean; he has a . . . s disease . . Lv 13:8

SKULL

Naaman . . . had a s disease 2Kg 5:1
"S for s!" Satan answered . . . . Jb 2:4
Even after my s has been
  destroyed, ... Jb 19:26
Can the Cushite change his s, . . Jr 13:23
Otherwise, the s-s burst, ... Mt 9:17

SKULL

Golgotha (which means Place
  of the S), ... Mt 27:33

SKY

God called the expanse "s." . . . . . Gn 1:8
good weather because the s is
  red. . . . . Mt 16:2
Son of Man will appear in
  the s, ... Mt 24:30
the s was split apart like a
  scroll . . . . Rv 6:14

SLACKER

Go to the ant, you s! . . . . Pr 6:6
by the field of a s and by the . . Pr 24:30

SLANDER (N)

and whoever spreads s is a
  fool. . . . . Pr 10:18
hypocrisy, envy, and all s 1Pt 2:1

SLANDER (V)

who does not s with his
  tongue, ... Ps 15:3
are s-ed, we respond
  graciously. 1Co 4:13
to s no one, to avoid fighting, . . . Ti 3:2

SLANDERER

worthy of respect, not s-s, ... 1Tm 3:11
behavior, not s-s, not slaves to . . . Ti 2:3

SLANDEROUSLY

as some people s claim we say, . . Rm 3:8

SLAP

if anyone s-s you on your right . . Mt 5:39

SLAUGHTER

are counted as sheep to be
  s-ed. . . . . Ps 44:22
save those stumbling toward s. . Pr 24:11
Like a lamb led to the s . . . . Is 53:7
was led like a sheep to the s, . . . Ac 8:32

are counted as sheep to be
　　s-ed. . . . . Rm 8:36
Worthy is the Lamb who was
　　s-ed. . . . . .Rv 5:12

SLAVE

Remember that you were a s in . . Dt 5:15
borrower is a s to the lender. . . . Pr 22:7
to my s, 'Do this!' and he
　　does it. . . . . Mt 8:9
first among you must be
　　your s; . . . . .Mt 20:27
Well done, good and
　　faithful s! . . . . Mt 25:21
who commits sin is a s of sin. . . .Jn 8:34
you used to be s-s of sin, ... Rm 6:17
no Jew or Greek, s or free, male . .Gl 3:28
by assuming the form of a s,. . . Php 2:7
but as God's s-s. Honor
　　everyone. 1Pt 2:16

SLAVERY

out of Egypt, out of the place
　　of s, ...Ex 13:3
you did not receive a spirit of s . .Rm 8:15
don't submit again to a yoke of s. . . Gl 5:1

SLEEP (N)

God caused a deep s to come
　　over. . . . . Gn 2:21
A little s, a little slumber, . . Pr 6:10; 24:33

SLEEP (V)

of Israel does not slumber or s. . .Ps 121:4
disciples and found them
　　s-ing. . . . . .Mt 26:40

SLEEPER

Get up, s, and rise up from the. .Eph 5:14

SLING

Philistine with a s and a
　　stone. 1Sm 17:50

SLOW

s to anger and abounding in
　　faithful . . . . Ex 34:6
to hear, s to speak, and s to
　　anger, ...Jms 1:19

SLUMBER

your Protector will not s. . . . . . . Ps 121:3
A little sleep, a little s, ... Pr 6:10; 24:33

SMALL

Four things on earth are s, . . . Pr 30:24
faithful in a very s matter, ... Lk 19:17

SMALLEST

It's the s of all the seeds, ... Mt 13:32

SMOKE

Sinai was . . . enveloped in s. . . .Ex 19:18
the temple was filled with s. . . . . .Is 6:4

SMOLDERING

He will not put out a s wick; . . . . Is 42:3
He will not put out a s wick, . . Mt 12:20

SMOOTH

S lips with an evil heart are. . . Pr 26:23
the uneven ground will
　　become s . . . . Is 40:4
straight, the rough ways s, ...Lk 3:5

SNAKE

the ground, it became a s, ...Ex 4:3
made a bronze s and
　　mounted it . . . . .Nm 21:9
In the end it bites like a s . . . . Pr 23:32
for a fish, will give him a s?. . . . . Mt 7:10
they will pick up s-s; . . . . .Mk 16:18
the authority to trample on
　　s-s . . . . .Lk 10:19
as Moses lifted up the s in the . . Jn 3:14

SNARE

their gods, it will be a s for you.. . . . . Ex 23:33
the s-s of death confronted me. . . 2Sm 22:6
will keep your foot from a s. . . . .Pr 3:26
The fear of mankind is a s,. . . . Pr 29:25

SNATCH

one comes and s-es away
　　what was . . . . Mt 13:19
No one will s them out of my . .Jn 10:28

SNOUT

like a gold ring in a pig's s. . . . . Pr 11:22

SNOW

and I will be whiter than s. . . . . . Ps 51:7
they will be as white as s; . . . . .Is 1:18
his clothing was as white as s. . Mt 28:3

SOAR

s-ing on the wings of the
　　wind. . . . . .Ps 18:10
will s on wings like eagles; . . . . Is 40:31

SOBER-MINDED

Be s! Be on the alert! 1Pt 5:8

SODOM

City on the plain, where Lot settled (Gn 10:19; 13:10; 14:11-12); destroyed along with Gomorrah by God (Gn 18:20; 19:24).

SOIL

quickly since the s wasn't deep.. Mt 13:5

SOLDIER

The s-s also mocked him. . . . . . Lk 23:36
No one serving as a s gets
　　entangled. 2Tm 2:4

SOLID

gave you milk to drink,
　　not s food, ...1Co 3:2
But s food is for the mature. . . Heb 5:14

SOLOMON

Son of David and Bathsheba; third king of Israel (2Sm 12:24; 1Kg 1:30-40). Asked for wisdom (1 Kg 3:5-15); knew many proverbs and songs (4:32; Pss 72; 127; Pr 1:1; 10:1; 25:1; Sg 1:1); wisdom demonstrated in child dispute (1Kg 3:16-28) and the visit of the Queen of Sheba (10:1-13). Built and dedicated the temple (1Kg 5–8). Accumulated vast wealth (9:26-28; 10:26-29); had many wives and concubines, who influenced him toward idolatry (11:1-8).

SON *SEE ALSO* SON OF DAVID, SON OF GOD, SON OF MAN, SONS OF GOD

"Take your s," he said, "your
　　only. . . . . Gn 22:2
and he will be my s. 2Sm 7:14
My s Absalom! My s, my s . . 2Sm 18:33
He said to me, "You are my S; . . . . . Ps 2:7
are all s-s of the Most High. . . . . .Ps 82:6
S-s are indeed a heritage from. .Ps 127:3
the virgin will conceive, have a s,. .Is 7:14
born for us, a s will be given to
　　us, ...Is 9:6

be called: S-s of the living God. . Hs 1:10
and out of Egypt I called my s... Hs 11:1
Out of Egypt I called my S...... Mt 2:15
This is my beloved S, with
 whom ....Mt 3:17
how then can he be his s?"......Mt 22:45
Truly this man was the S of
 God! .... Mt 27:54
called the S of the Most High,...Lk 1:32
longer worthy to be called
 your s.......................Lk 15:19
He gave his one and only S, ...Jn 3:16
believes in the S has eternal
 life,.........................Jn 3:36
by God's Spirit are God's s-s....Rm 8:14
conformed to the image of
 his S,....................... Rm 8:29
He did not even spare his
 own S....................... Rm 8:32
will be called s-s of the living..Rm 9:26
you will be s-s and
 daughters 2Co 6:18
slave but a s, and if a s, then God.. Gl 4:7
He has spoken to us by his S. .. Heb 1:2
that addresses you as s-s:..... Heb 12:5
one and only S into the world .. 1Jn 4:9
loved us and sent his S to be ... 1Jn 4:10
The one who has the S has life. .1Jn 5:12

SON OF DAVID

Have mercy on us, S!........... Mt 9:27
"Could this be the S?" .... Mt 12:23
Hosanna to the S! .... Mt 21:9

SON OF GOD

If you are the S, come down .. Mt 27:40
will be called the S. ....Lk 1:35
Are you, then, the S?.......... Lk 22:70
that this is the S. ....Jn 1:34
of the one and only S............Jn 3:18
appointed to be the
 powerful S ....Rm 1:4
confesses that Jesus is the S ... 1Jn 4:15
one who believes that Jesus is
 the S? 1Jn 5:5

SON OF MAN

s that you think of him? ....Ps 8:4
He said to me, "S,...............Ezk 2:1
one like a s was coming ....Dn 7:13
S has no place to lay his........ Mt 8:20
S coming in his kingdom...... Mt 16:28
When the S comes in his
 glory,..................... Mt 25:31
see the S seated at the right
 hand......................Mk 14:62
so the S must be lifted up,....... Jn 3:14
Who is this S? ....Jn 12:34

S standing at the right hand of
 God! .... Ac 7:56
One like the S was seated on...Rv 14:14

SONG

The LORD is my strength and
 my s;.......................Ex 15:2
Sing a new s to him;............Ps 33:3
He put a new s in my mouth, ...Ps 40:3
psalms, hymns, and spiritual
 s-s,................... Eph 5:19; Col 3:16
the s of the Lamb:...............Rv 15:3

SONS OF GOD

the s saw that the daughters of
 mankind.......................Gn 6:2
peacemakers ... will be
 called s........................ Mt 5:9
through faith you are all s in
 Christ..........................Gl 3:26

SORCERER

But Elymas the s...opposed them..Ac 13:8

SORCERY

interpret omens, practice s,.....Dt 18:10
idolatry, s, hatreds, strife,.......Gl 5:20

SORROW

For with much wisdom is
 much s;......................Ec 1:18
and s and sighing will flee. .....Is 35:10;
 51:11
but your s will turn to joy......Jn 16:20
I have great s and unceasing ...Rm 9:2

SOUL

with all your s, and with all
 strength......................Dt 6:5
to destroy both s and body in
 hell...........................Mt 10:28
with all your s, and with all... Mt 22:37
a sword will pierce your
 own s— .... Lk 2:35
Now my s is troubled...........Jn 12:27
separation of s and spirit,
 joints .... Heb 4:12
the salvation of your s-s.........1Pt 1:9
Shepherd and Overseer of
 your s-s. 1Pt 2:25

SOUND (N)

if the bugle makes an
 unclear s,....................1Co 14:8

voice like the s of cascading
 waters.........................Rv 1:15

SOUND (V)

s the alarm on my holy mountain!..Jl 2:1
the trumpet will s, and the
 dead 1Co 15:52

SOUR

The fathers have eaten s
 grapes,....................... Jr 31:29
The fathers eat s grapes, and ..Ezk 18:2

SOURCE

You killed the s of life, ...Ac 3:15
s and perfecter of our faith, .. Heb 12:2

SOVEREIGN

He is the blessed and only S, ..1Tm 6:15

SOW

those who s trouble reap the
 same. ....Jb 4:8
Those who s in tears will reap..Ps 126:5
who s-s injustice will reap
 disaster, ...Pr 22:8
They don't s or reap or gather..Mt 6:26
As he s-ed, some seeds fell .....Mt 13:4
a man who s-ed good seed......Mt 13:24
One s-s and another reaps...... Jn 4:37
we have sown spiritual things ..1Co 9:11
Sown in corruption,
 raised in 1Co 15:42
person who s-s sparingly will.. 2Co 9:6
whatever a person s-s he
 will also .... Gl 6:7

SOWER

Consider the s who went out to..Mt 13:3
The s sows the word...........Mk 4:14

SPARE

He did not even s his own Son..Rm 8:32
if God didn't s the angels who ..2Pt 2:4

SPARINGLY

person who sows s will also
 reap s, ... 2Co 9:6

SPARROW

are worth more than
 many s-s. .... Mt 10:31

SPEAK

He **spoke**, and it came into
   being;.........................Ps 33:9
to be silent and a time to s; ......Ec 3:7
the mouth of the LORD has
   spoken........................ Is 40:5
worry about . . . what you are
   to s. .... Mt 10:19
We s what we know............. Jn 3:11
began to s in different tongues,..Ac 2:4
If I s human or angelic tongues...1Co 13:1
was a child, I **spoke** like a
   child,........................1Co 13:11
But s-ing the truth in love, let..Eph 4:15
he has **spoken** to us by his Son.. Heb 1:2
instead, men **spoke** from God ..2Pt 1:21

SPEAR

their s-s into pruning
   knives..................Is 2:4; Mc 4:3
your pruning knives into s-s...... Jl 3:10
pierced his side with a s,.......Jn 19:34

SPECTACLE

We have become a s to the
   world.......................1Co 4:9

SPEECH

Day after day they pour out s; ..Ps 19:2
There is no s; there are no
   words;........................Ps 19:3
Let your s always be gracious,..Col 4:6

SPEND

gladly s and be **spent** for you..2Co 12:15

SPICES

cloths with the fragrant s,......Jn 19:40

SPIN

They don't labor or s..Mt 6:28; Lk 12:27

SPIRIT *SEE ALSO* HOLY SPIRIT, SPIRIT OF GOD, SPIRIT OF THE LORD

My S will not remain with
   mankind..................... Gn 6:3
an evil s sent from the LORD.. 1Sm 16:14
Into your hand I entrust my s; ..Ps 31:5
renew a steadfast s within me..Ps 51:10
or take your Holy S from me... Ps 51:11
pleasing to God is a broken s... Ps 51:17
Where can I go to escape
   your S?.......................Ps 139:7

Who knows if the s of the
   children ....Ec 3:21
the s returns to God who gave.. Ec 12:7
I have put my S on him;..........Is 42:1
and put a new s within you;..Ezk 36:26
pour out my S on all humanity.. Jl 2:28
but by my S,' says the LORD......Zch 4:6
Blessed are the poor in s, ... Mt 5:3
them authority over unclean
   s-s,...........................Mt 10:1
I will put my S on him, and he..Mt 12:18
against the S will not be ...... Mt 12:31
The s is willing, but the flesh .. Mt 26:41
open and the S descending
   to him .... Mk 1:10
into your hands I entrust
   my s.........................Lk 23:46
God is s, and those who worship
   him must worship in S and
   truth. ....Jn 4:24
He is the S of truth............. Jn 14:17
pour out my S on all people..... Ac 2:17
but the S of Jesus did not allow.. Ac 16:7
had a s by which she
   predicted.....................Ac 16:16
are not in the flesh, but in the S, .. Rm 8:9
testifies together with our s
   that we ....Rm 8:16
have the S as the firstfruits—.. Rm 8:23
S helps us in our weakness,... Rm 8:26
different gifts, but the same S.. 1Co 12:4
distinguishing between s-s, ..1Co 12:10
the S . . . as a down payment .. 2Co 1:22
walk by the S and you will...... Gl 5:16
There is one body and one S ... Eph 4:4
but be filled by the S:......... Eph 5:18
Don't stifle the S...............1Th 5:19
And may your whole s, soul,
   and 1Th 5:23
separation of soul and s,
   joints ....Heb 4:12
proclamation to the s-s in
   prison 1Pt 3:19
not believe every s, but test
   the s-s 1Jn 4:1

SPIRIT OF GOD

S was hovering over the surface ..Gn 1:2
He saw the S descending like a
   dove .... Mt 3:16

SPIRIT OF THE LORD

S came powerfully on David
   from 1Sm 16:13
The S GOD is on me, ...Is 61:1
S is on me . . . he has anointed
   me ....Lk 4:18
where the S is, there is
   freedom......................2Co 3:17

SPIRITIST

not turn to mediums or
   consult s-s, ...Lv 19:31

SPIRITUAL

explaining s things to s
   people......................1Co 2:13
a natural body, raised a s
   body......................... 1Co 15:44
who are s, restore such a
   person........................Gl 6:1
blessed us with every s
   blessing..................... Eph 1:3
psalms, hymns, and s
   songs,............. Eph 5:19; Col 3:16

SPIRITUALLY

since it is evaluated s..........1Co 2:14

SPIT

Then they **spat** in his face and
   beat.........................Mt 26:67
He s on the ground, made
   some mud ....Jn 9:6

SPLATTER

blood he s-ed on the altar...... Ex 24:8
s it on all sides of the altar..... Ex 29:16
present the blood and s it........ Lv 1:5

SPLENDOR

S and majesty are before
   him;........................1Ch 16:27
Worship the LORD in the s of....Ps 29:2
are clothed with majesty
   and s. .... Ps 104:1
not even Solomon in all his s
   was .... Mt 6:29

SPLINTER

the s in your brother's eye...... Mt 7:3

SPLIT

He s the rock, and water
   gushed...................... Is 48:21

SPONGE

a s full of sour wine on a
   hyssop......................Jn 19:29

SPOT

his skin, or a leopard his s-s? .. Jr 13:23

SPRAWL

without s or wrinkle or
anything....................Eph 5:27
without s or blemish in his
sight.........................2Pt 3:14

SPRAWL

with ivory, s-ed out on their ....Am 6:4
of those who s out will
come to.......................Am 6:7

SPREAD

s-ing out the sky like a
canopy, ...Ps 104:2
word...may s rapidly and......2Th 3:1

SPRING (N)

give...from the s of the water..Rv 21:6

SPRING (V)

S up, well—sing to it!.........Nm 21:17
well of water s-ing up in him...Jn 4:14

SPRINKLE

so he will s many nations. ......Is 52:15
will also s clean water on
you, ...Ezk 36:25
hearts s-d clean from an
evil..........................Heb 10:22
and to the s-d blood, which
says..........................Heb 12:24
s-d with the blood of Jesus
Christ........................1Pt 1:2

SPROUT

cause...Branch to s up for
David,........................Jr 33:15

SPY

to s on the freedom we have.....Gl 2:4

SQUANDERED

he s his estate in foolish living.. Lk 15:13

STAFF

threw down his s before
Pharaoh ....Ex 7:10
s of the man I choose will
sprout,.......................Nm 17:5
rod and your s—they
comfort me...................Ps 23:4
the manna, Aaron's s that
budded,......................Heb 9:4

STAIRWAY

A s was set on the ground
with ....Gn 28:12
the shadow...on s of Ahaz.. 2Kg 20:11

STAND

where you are s-ing is holy
ground........................Ex 3:5
place where you are s-ing is
holy..........................Jos 5:15
And the sun stood still and ...Jos 10:13
s still, and see the salvation.. 2Ch 20:17
Who may s in his holy place?...Ps 24:3
will be able to s when he
appears?......................Mal 3:2
against itself, that house
cannot s......................Mk 3:25
into this grace in which we s,...Rm 5:2
he s-s or falls. And he will s, because
the Lord is able to make
him s.........................Rm 14:4
thinks he s-s must be careful ..1Co 10:12
so that you can s against the .Eph 6:11
I s at the door and knock.......Rv 3:20

STAR

God made...as well as the s-s..Gn 1:16
numerous as the s-s of the
sky...........................Gn 22:17
the morning s-s sang together..Jb 38:7
moon and the s-s, which you set ..Ps 8:3
we saw his s in the east........Mt 2:2
you shine like s-s in the
world. ....Php 2:15
of David, the bright
morning s...................Rv 22:16

STARTED

He who s a good work in you.. Php 1:6

STATURE

look at his appearance or
his s........................1Sm 16:7
Jesus increased in wisdom
and s,.......................Lk 2:52

STAY

and s awake with me.........Mt 26:38

STEADFAST

me and renew a s spirit within. Ps 51:10

STEAL

Do not s.......................Ex 20:15

or I might have nothing and s,..Pr 30:9
where thieves break in and s.. Mt 6:19
adultery; do not s; do not bear ..Mt 19:18
comes only to s and to kill and.. Jn 10:10
the thief no longer s...........Eph 4:28

STEP

but the LORD determines his s-s. Pr 16:9
you should follow in his s-s...... 1Pt 2:21

STEPHEN

Foremost of the first seven deacons
(Ac 6:1-7). First Christian martyr (6:8–
7:60); Saul approved of his death (8:1;
22:20); start of persecution and dispersion (11:19).

STIFLE

Don't s the Spirit. 1Th 5:19

STILL

reflect in your heart and be s...... Ps 4:4
Silence! Be s!" The wind
ceased ....Mk 4:39

STING

Sheol, where is your s ?.......Hs 13:14
Where, death, is your s? 1Co 15:55

STIR

but a harsh word s-s up wrath.. Pr 15:1
my compassion is s-red!........Hs 11:8

STOLEN

S water is sweet, ... Pr 9:17

STOMACH

passes into the s and is
eliminated?..................Mt 15:17
"Food is for the s and the s
for food," 1Co 6:13
their god is their s;........... Php 3:19
a little wine because of your s. 1Tm 5:23

STONE (N)

s tablets inscribed by...God... Ex 31:18
five smooth s-s from the
wadi 1Sm 17:40
strike your foot against a s......Ps 91:12
The s that the builders
rejected....................Ps 118:22
a time to throw s-s and a time to.. Ec 3:5

He will be a **s** to stumble over ...Is 8:14
I have laid a **s** in Zion, a
tested **s**,....................... Is 28:16
remove your heart of **s** and
give ....Ezk 36:26
tell these **s-s** to become bread." ..Mt 4:3
strike your foot against a **s**...... Mt 4:6
for bread, will give him a **s**?...... Mt 7:9
The **s** that the builders
rejected..................... Mt 21:42
Who will roll away the **s**
from.......................... Mk 16:3
silent, the **s-s** would cry out!.. Lk 19:40
be the first to throw a **s** at her.... Jn 8:7
stumbled over the
stumbling **s**. .... Rm 9:32
not on tablets of **s** but on
tablets 2Co 3:3
to him, a living **s**—rejected by ...1Pt 2:4

STONE (V)

were **s-ing** Stephen, he called
out: .... Ac 7:59

STORE

Don't **s** up for yourselves
treasures .... Mt 6:19
have anywhere to **s** my crops?..Lk 12:17

STOREHOUSE

brings the wind from his
s-s.....................Jr 10:13; 51:16
Bring the full tenth into
the **s** .... Mal 3:10

STOREROOM

brings out of his **s**
treasures new .... Mt 13:52

STORM

and shelter from **s** and rain.......Is 4:6
such a great **s** arose on
the sea......................Jnh 1:4
a violent **s** arose on the sea, ... Mt 8:24

STRAIGHT

make a **s** highway for our
God in .... Is 40:3
the crooked will become **s**, ...Lk 3:5
Make **s** the way of the Lord ..... Jn 1:23

STRAIN

You **s** out a gnat, but gulp
down .... Mt 23:24

STRANGER

I was a **s** and you took me in;.. Mt 25:35
no longer foreigners and **s-s**,..Eph 2:19
I urge you as **s-s** and exiles......1Pt 2:11

STRANGLE

eating anything that has
been **s-d**,.................... Ac 15:20

STRAP

whose sandal **s** I'm not
worthy to .... Jn 1:27

STRAW

go and gather **s** for themselves. .Ex 5:7
costly stones, wood, hay, or **s**,..1Co 3:12

STREAM

planted beside flowing **s-s**....... Ps 1:3
its **s-s** delight the city of God,...Ps 46:4
s-s of living water flow from ...Jn 7:38

STREET

Wisdom calls out in the **s**; ......Pr 1:20
on the **s** corners to be seen by
people......................... Mt 6:5
s of the city was pure gold,...... Rv 21:21

STRENGTH

The LORD is my **s** and my song; ..Ex 15:2
all your soul, and with all your **s**...Dt 6:5
does not prevail by his own **s**. .1Sm 2:9
I love you, LORD, my **s**. .... Ps 18:1
The LORD is my **s** and my shield;..Ps 28:7
God is our refuge and **s**, a
helper ....Ps 46:1
ascribe to the LORD glory and **s**. .Ps 96:7
in the LORD will renew their **s**; ... Is 40:31
strong should not boast in his **s**;..Jr 9:23
Not by **s** or by might, but by my.. Zch 4:6
your mind, and with all
your **s**. ....Mk 12:30

STRENGTHEN

have turned back, **s** your
brothers.................... Lk 22:32
He will also **s** you to the end, ...1Co 1:8
speaks to people for their
s-ing, ...1Co 14:3
be **s-ed** by the Lord and by his. .Eph 6:10
things through him who
s-s me. .... Php 4:13
Lord who has **s-ed** me,........ 1Tm 1:12
Therefore **s** your tired hands.. Heb 12:12

STRICKEN

but we in turn regarded him **s**, ..Is 53:4

STRIFE

a house full of feasting with **s**....Pr 17:1
there is envy and **s**
among you, ...1Co 3:3
sorcery, hatreds, **s**, jealousy, ...Gl 5:20

STRIKE

s your head, and you will **s** his
heel. .... Gn 3:15
and **struck** the rock twice..... Nm 20:11
you will not **s** your foot
against .... Ps 91:12
The sun will not **s** you by day .. Ps 121:6
S the shepherd, and the sheep
will ....Zch 13:7
you will not **s** your foot
against ....Mt 4:6
I will **s** the shepherd, and the ..Mt 26:31
struck down but not
destroyed. 2Co 4:9

STRIP

They **s-ped** him, beat him up,.. Lk 10:30

STRIVE

Don't **s** for what you should
eat ....Lk 12:29
s-ing with his strength that
works........................Col 1:29

STROKE

or one **s** of a letter will pass
from .... Mt 5:18
than for one **s** of a letter ...
to drop...................... Lk 16:17

STRONG

Be **s** and courageous; ....Dt 31:6
be **s** and very courageous ....Jos 1:7
LORD, **s** and mighty, the
LORD, ...Ps 24:8
The name of the LORD is a **s**
tower;....................... Pr 18:10
Redeemer is **s**, and he will ..... Pr 23:11
Their Redeemer is **s**; the LORD.. Jr 50:34
can someone enter a **s** man's
house .... Mt 12:29
The boy grew up and
became **s**,.................Lk 2:40
Now we who are **s** have an .... Rm 15:1
For when I am weak, then
I am **s**..................... 2Co 12:10

STRONGER

God's weakness is s than
    human......................1Co 1:25

STRONGHOLD

David did capture the s of
    Zion,.........................2Sm 5:7
my salvation, my s, my
    refuge,.....................2Sm 22:3
the God of Jacob is our s......Ps 46:7,11
my rock and my salvation,
    my s;........................Ps 62:2,6
way of the LORD is a s for the ..Pr 10:29
for the demolition of s-s......2Co 10:4

STRUGGLE

our s is not against flesh and
    blood ....Eph 6:12
s-ing against sin, you have
    not..........................Heb 12:4

STUBBORN

a s and rebellious generation, ..Ps 78:8

STUDY

and much s wearies the body. . Ec 12:12
Too much s is driving you
    mad.........................Ac 26:24

STUMBLE

nothing makes them s........Ps 119:165
when you run, you will not s.....Pr 4:12
be a stone to s over and a rock. . Is 8:14
cause one of these little ones
    to s............................Lk 17:2
walks during the day, he
    doesn't s,.....................Jn 11:9
They s-d over the s-ing stone...Rm 9:32
for we all s in many ways. ......Jms 3:2
A stone to s over,................1Pt 2:8
who is able to protect you from
    s-ing..........................Jd 24

STUMBLING BLOCK

instead decide never to put
    a s...........................Rm 14:13
Christ crucified, a s to the
    Jews 1Co 1:23
this right ... in no way
    becomes a s 1Co 8:9

STUMP

shoot will grow from the s of
    Jesse, ...Is 11:1

STUPID

one who hates correction is s...Pr 12:1

SUBDUE

fill the earth, and s it. ....Gn 1:28

SUBJECT

the creation was s-ed to
    futility ....Rm 8:20
when everything is s to
    Christ,.....................1Co 15:28
s-ed everything under his feet. .Heb 2:8

SUBMISSION

learn quietly with full s. 1Tm 2:11

SUBMIT

he willingly s-ted to death,......Is 53:12
s to the governing authorities, ..Rm 13:1
don't s again to a yoke of slavery...Gl 5:1
Wives, s to your husbands......Eph 5:22
Why do you s to regulations: ..Col 2:20
Remind them s to rulers...........Ti 3:1
Therefore, s to God. Resist..... Jms 4:7
S to every human authority......1Pt 2:13
s yourselves to your own
    husbands.....................1Pt 3:1

SUCCESS

He stores up s for the upright;...Pr 2:7

SUDDENLY

you seek will s come to his
    temple, ...Mal 3:1

SUE

one who wants to s you and
    take...........................Mt 5:40

SUEZ

LORD will divide the Gulf of S. . . Is 11:15

SUFFER

Son of Man must s many
    things........................Mk 8:31
Passover with you before I s. ..Lk 22:15
s these things and enter into
    his ....Lk 24:26
Messiah would s and rise
    from.......................Lk 24:46
that his Messiah would s........Ac 3:18
we s with him so that we may. .Rm 8:17

one member s-s, all ... s
    with it;.....................1Co 12:26
share in s-ing for the gospel, ..2Tm 1:8
obedience from what he s-ed..Heb 5:8
Is anyone among you s-ing?...Jms 5:13
when you do what is good
    and s, ...1Pt 2:20
Christ also s-ed for you, ...1Pt 2:21
it is better to s for doing good,. .1Pt 3:17
Christ also s-ed for sins once...1Pt 3:18

SUFFERING (N)

man of s who knew what
    sickness ....Is 53:3
the s-s of this present time
    are not.......................Rm 8:18
the fellowship of his s-s, ...Php 3:10
share in the s-s of Christ........1Pt 4:13

SUFFICIENT

My grace is s for you, ...2Co 12:9

SUMMER

it prepares its provisions in s; ...Pr 6:8
leaves, you know that s is
    near........................Mt 24:32

SUN

And the s stood still...........Jos 10:13
the LORD God is a s and shield.. Ps 84:11
s will not strike you by day.....Ps 121:6
there is nothing new under
    the s..........................Ec 1:9
The s will be turned to
    darkness......................Jl 2:31
the s of righteousness will rise..Mal 4:2
For he causes his s to rise on . . Mt 5:45
The s will be darkened, ...Mt 24:29
Don't let the s go down on
    your ....Eph 4:26
His face was shining like the s. . Rv 1:16
not need the s or the moon to Rv 21:23

SUNRISE

they went to the tomb at s......Mk 16:2

SUPERIOR

became s to the angels. ....Heb 1:4
inferior is blessed by the s. .....Heb 7:7

SUPPER

took the cup after s and said, . . Lk 22:20
he took the cup after s, and
    said......................1Co 11:25

SUPPLY

And my God will s all your
   needs .... Php 4:19

SUPPORT

but the LORD was my s. 2Sm 22:19

SUPPRESS

unrighteousness s the truth, .. Rm 1:18

SURE

be s your sin will catch up
   with .... Nm 32:23
cornerstone, a s foundation;... Is 28:16

SURELY

to say to him, "S not I,
   Lord?" .... Mt 26:22

SURPASS

deeds, but you s them all!......Pr 31:29
unless your righteousness
   s-es .... Mt 5:20
love that s-es knowledge,..... Eph 3:19
view of the s-ing value of
   knowing.................... Php 3:8
peace of God, which s-es every ..Php 4:7

SURROUND

Many bulls s me;.............. Ps 22:12
large cloud of witnesses s-ing
   us,.......................... Heb 12:1

SURVIVE

built s-s, he will receive a
   reward......................1Co 3:14

SURVIVOR

of Armies had not left us a
   few s-s, ... Is 1:9

SUSTAIN

wake again because the
   LORD s-s me................... Ps 3:5
establish and s it with justice..... Is 9:7
not s the root, but the root
   s-s you. .... Rm 11:18
s-ing all things by his powerful. . Heb 1:3

SUSTAINER

the Lord is the s of my life....... Ps 54:4

SWALLOW

has been s-ed up in victory. ...1Co 15:54

SWEAR

By myself I have sworn, ... Gn 22:16
swore in my anger, "They will
   not........................... Ps 95:11
LORD swore an oath to David, ..Ps 132:11
Do not s by your head,......... Mt 5:36
swore in my anger, "They will
   not...........................Heb 3:11
to s by, he swore by himself: .. Heb 6:13
Lord has sworn and will not .. Heb 7:21
do not s, either by heaven or .. Jms 5:12

SWEAT

eat bread by the s of your brow ..Gn 3:19
His s became like drops of
   blood .... Lk 22:44

SWEEP

vacant, swept, and put in
   order..................... Mt 12:44
not light a lamp, s the house, ...Lk 15:8

SWEET

How s your word is to my
   taste— .... Ps 119:103
Stolen water is s,............... Pr 9:17
it was as s as honey in my
   mouth...................... Ezk 3:3
Does a spring pour out s and
   bitter .... Jms 3:11

SWIFT

that the race is not to the s,..... Ec 9:11
Their feet are s to shed blood;.. Rm 3:15

SWINDLER

or s-s will inherit God's
   kingdom.................... 1Co 6:10

SWORD

whirling s east of the garden
   of .... Gn 3:24
not by s ... that the LORD
   saves, ... 1Sm 17:47
Nation will not take up the
   s against.....................Is 2:4
Beat your plows into s-s ....Jl 3:10
will beat their s-s into plows, ... Mc 4:3
come to bring peace, but a s... Mt 10:34
He who take up the s will
   perish by a s. ....Mt 26:52

a s will pierce your own soul— ..Lk 2:35
does not carry the s for no
   reason......................Rm 13:4
and the s of the Spirit, ... Eph 6:17
sharper than any
   double-edged s, ... Heb 4:12
a s came from his mouth,....... Rv 1:16

SYCAMORE

he climbed up a s tree to see....Lk 19:4

SYMBOL

a s on your forehead...... Ex 13:16; Dt 6:8
should have a s of authority .. 1Co 11:10

SYMPATHIZE

a high priest who is unable
   to s.......................... Heb 4:15

SYNAGOGUE

teaching in their s-s,
   preaching .... Mt 4:23
He entered the s on the Sabbath..Lk 4:16
They will ban you from the s-s.. Jn 16:2
taught in the s and in the
   temple...................... Jn 18:20
reasoned in the s every
   Sabbath..................... Ac 18:4
but are a s of Satan..............Rv 2:9

T

TABERNACLE

the pattern of the t............. Ex 25:9
glory of the LORD filled the t. . Ex 40:34
more perfect t not made with.. Heb 9:11

TABLE

construct a t of acacia wood,.. Ex 25:23
You prepare a t before me in
   the...........................Ps 23:5
because all overturned the t-s of the
   money changers .... Mt 21:12
and drink at my t in my
   kingdom................... Lk 22:30
the Lord's t and the t of
   demons. 1Co 10:21

TABLET

that I may give you the
   stone t-s .... Ex 24:12
them on the t of yourheart... Pr 3:3; 7:3

engraved on the t of their
   hearts............................Jr 17:1
not on t-s of stone but on t-s... 2Co 3:3

TAKE

or t your Holy Spirit from me. . Ps 51:11
T up my yoke and learn
   from me,......................Mt 11:29
deny himself, t up his cross, . . Mt 16:24
one will be **taken** and one
   left.............................Mt 24:40
T and eat it; this is my body.... Mt 26:26
who t-s away the sin of the
   world! ....Jn 1:29
they've **taken** away my Lord, . .Jn 20:13
t up the full armor of God,......Eph 6:13

TALENTS

To one he gave five t;..........Mt 25:15

TALK

T about them when you sit in ... Dt 6:7

TALL

He was nine feet, nine inches t ..1Sm 17:4

TAMAR

1. Judah's daughter-in-law; widow of
   Er and Onan; mother of Judah's sons
   (Gn 38).
2. Daughter of David; raped by Amnon;
   avenged by Absalom (2Sm 13).

TAMBOURINE

Praise him with t and dance; . .Ps 150:4

TARSHISH

Distant Mediterranean port city
known for sea trade (1Kg 10:22; 22:48;
Pss 48:7; 72:10; Is 2:16; 23:1,6,10,14; 66:19;
Jr 10:9; Ezk 27:12,25; 38:13); Jonah fled
toward it (Jnh 1:3).

TASTE

T and see that the LORD is good. . Ps 34:8
if the salt should lose its t, ... Mt 5:13
who will not t death until
   they...........................Mt 16:28
he will never t death—ever!' . . .Jn 8:52
handle, don't t, don't touch"? . .Col 2:21
grace he might t death for......Heb 2:9
who t-d the heavenly gift,...... Heb 6:4
if you have t-d that the Lord 1Pt 2:3

TATTOO

not ... put t marks on
   yourselves; ....Lv 19:28

TAUNT

crucified with him t-ed him. . Mt 27:44

TAX SEE ALSO TAX
COLLECTOR

lawful to pay t-es to Caesar or
   not?..........................Mt 22:17
t-es to those you owe t-es,...... Rm 13:7

TAX COLLECTOR

Don't even the t-s do the
   same?.........................Mt 5:46
a friend of t-s and sinners! .....Mt 11:19
like an Gentile and a t to you...Mt 18:17
T-s and prostitutes are
   entering ....Mt 21:31
one a Pharisee and the other
   a t............................Lk 18:10
Zacchaeus who was a chief t,...Lk 19:2

TEACH

T them to your children ... Dt 4:9; 11:19
t me your paths...................Ps 25:4
T us to number our days.......Ps 90:12
No longer will one t his
   neighbor ....Jr 31:34
t-ing them to observe
   everything..................Mt 28:20
t-ing them as one having
   authority....................Mk 1:22
He **taught** them many things in..Mk 4:2
t us to pray, just as John also
   taught.........................Lk 11:1
Holy Spirit ... will t you all
   things........................Jn 14:26
allow a woman to t or to have . .1Tm 2:12
hospitable, able to t, ...1Tm 3:2
will be able to t others also.......2Tm 2:2
correctly t-ing the word of
   truth..........................2Tm 2:15
able to t, and patient, ... 2Tm 2:24
you don't need anyone to t
   you...........................1Jn 2:27

TEACHER

A disciple is not above his t, . . Mt 10:24
you have one T, and you are all. .Mt 23:8
Are you a t of Israel and don't . . Jn 3:10
if I, your Lord and T, have
   washed ....Jn 13:14
some pastors and t-s,..........Eph 4:11
will be false t-s among you.......2Pt 2:1

TEACHING (N)

I will put my t within them .... Jr 31:33
were astonished at his t..Mt 7:28; 22:33
is contrary to the sound t.....1Tm 1:10
and is profitable for t, ...2Tm 3:16

TEAR (N)

My t-s have been my food
   day and ....Ps 42:3
Put my t-s in your bottle..........Ps 56:8
Those who sow in t-s will
   reap..........................Ps 126:5
to wash his feet with her t-s.......Lk 7:38
away every t from their
   eyes........................Rv 7:17; 21:4

TEAR (V)

T your hearts, not just your ...... Jl 2:13
high priest **tore** his robes and. .Mt 26:65

TELL

t about all his wonderful
   works!........................Ps 105:2
he has **told** each of you what
   is good........................Mc 6:8
if not, I would have **told** you......Jn 14:2
I have **told** you now before it . .Jn 14:29

TEMPLE

The LORD is in his holy t; .... Ps 11:4
But the LORD is in his holy t; . .Hab 2:20
will suddenly come to his t,.....Mal 3:1
something greater than the
   t is here! .... Mt 12:6
they found him in the t
   complex .... Lk 2:46
Destroy this t, and I will raise... Jn 2:19
that you are God's t 1Co 3:16
your body is a t of the Holy......1Co 6:19
Almighty and the Lamb are
   its t......................... Rv 21:22

TEMPORARY

what is seen is t, but what is . . 2Co 4:18

TEMPT

wilderness to be t-ed by the
   devil...........................Mt 4:1
allow you to be t-ed beyond
   what 1Co 10:13
and he himself doesn't t
   anyone.......................Jms 1:13
when he was t-ed, he is able. . Heb 2:18
who has been t-ed in every
   way ....Heb 4:15

TEMPTATION

And do not bring us into t,..... Mt 6:13
pray, so that you won't enter
   into t. .... Mt 26:41
No t has come upon you
   except 1Co 10:13

TEMPTER

Then the t approached him and.. Mt 4:3

TEN

He wrote the T
   Commandments,........... Ex 34:28
will be like t virgins who took ..Mt 25:1
to the one who has t talents...Mt 25:28
Were not t cleansed?.......... Lk 17:17
The t horns you saw are t kings..Rv 17:12

TEN THOUSAND

one who owed t talents was .. Mt 18:24
than t words in another
   tongue. 1Co 14:19

TEND

I will t my flock and let them ..Ezk 34:15

TENDERLY

Speak t to Jerusalem, and....... Is 40:2

TENT

ark of God sits inside t
   curtains...................... 2Sm 7:2
dwell in your t forever and ..... .Ps 61:4
Enlarge the site of your t,....... Is 54:2

TENTH *SEE ALSO* TEN

Abram gave him a t of
   everything................. Gn 14:20
give to you a t of all that you
   give .... Gn 28:22
Bring the full t into the
   storehouse .... Mal 3:10
You pay a t of mint, dill, and ..Mt 23:23
I give a t of everything I get.......Lk 18:12

TERRIBLE

great and t day of the
   LORD.................. Jl 2:31; Mal 4:5

TERRIFY

around them, and they
   were t-ied.................... Lk 2:9

It is a t-ing thing to fall into ..Heb 10:31

TERROR

not fear the t of the night, ... Ps 91:5
are not a t to good conduct...... Rm 13:3

TEST

God t-ed Abraham............. Gn 22:1
Do not t the LORD your God ...... Dt 6:16
The LORD left them to t Israel, ..Jdg 3:4
t me and know my concerns.. Ps 139:23
but the LORD is the t-er of
   hearts....................... Pr 17:3
stone in Zion, a t-ed stone,..... Is 28:16
T me in this way," says the
   LORD....................... Mal 3:10
Do not t the Lord your God..... Mt 4:7
approached him to t him. ..... Mt 19:3
expert in the law stood up to
   t him...................... Lk 10:25
asked this to t him, for
   he ... knew .... Jn 6:6
did you agree to t the Spirit...... Ac 5:9
t all things. Hold on to what ...1Th 5:21
but t the spirits to see.......... 1Jn 4:1

TESTIFY

is another who t-ies about me, Jn 5:32
the Scriptures ...t about me. ...Jn 5:39
the Spirit ... he will t about
   me............................ Jn 15:26
Spirit himself t-ies together ...Rm 8:16
For there are three that t:....... 1Jn 5:7

TESTIMONY

Do not give false t against
   your .... Ex 20:16
based on the t of one
   witness.................... Nm 35:30
the t of the LORD is trustworthy, ..Ps 19:7
Bind up the t. Seal up the ....Is 8:16
looking for false t against
   Jesus...................... Mt 26:59
We know that his t is true..... Jn 21:24

THANKS

Give t to the LORD; call on...... 1Ch 16:8
Give t to the LORD, ... he is
   good. 1Ch 16:34
Give t to him and bless his
   name....................... Ps 100:4
Give t to the LORD, for he is
   good. .... Ps 136:1
gave t, broke them, and gave.. Mt 15:36
and after giving t, he gave it ..Mt 26:27
But t be to God, who gives us..1Co 15:57

Give t in everything; for this...1Th 5:18

THANKSGIVING

Let us enter his presence
   with t;....................... Ps 95:2
Enter his gates with t and .....Ps 100:4
I will offer you a sacrifice of t ..Ps 116:17
through prayer and petition
   with t,....................... Php 4:6

THIEF

and where t-ves don't break in
   and .... Mt 6:19
you are making it a den of
   t-ves! .... Mt 21:13
what time the t was coming, ..Mt 24:43
other way is a t and a robber.... Jn 10:1
Let the t no longer steal. ......Eph 4:28
come just like a t in the night. ..1Th 5:2
Look, I am coming like a t.......Rv 16:15

THING

all these t-s will be provided... Mt 6:33
with God all t-s are possible... Mt 19:26
kept all these t-s in her heart....Lk 2:51
But one t I do: Forgetting ..... Php 3:13
praiseworthy—dwell on these
   t-s.......................... Php 4:8
able to do all t-s through him.. Php 4:13

THINK *SEE ALSO* THOUGHT (N)

son of man, that you t of him?.. Ps 144:3
not to t of himself more
   highly than .... Rm 12:3
beyond all that we ask or t....Eph 3:20

THIRD

and on the t day he will raise ....Hs 6:2
killed, and be raised the t day...Mt 16:21
raised on the t day
   according to................. 1Co 15:4

THIRST

I t for God, the living God. ....Ps 42:2
who hunger and t for
   righteousness .... Mt 5:6
they will no longer t;........... Rv 7:16

THIRSTY

and if he is t, give him water...Pr 25:21
everyone who is t, come to the ..Is 55:1
was t and you gave me
   something.................. Mt 25:35
this water will get t again....... Jn 4:13

in me will ever be t again. ......Jn 6:35
If anyone is t, let him come .....Jn 7:37
Let the one who is t come......Rv 22:17

THIRTY

my wages, t pieces of silver...Zch 11:12
weighed out t pieces of silver... Mt 26:15
Jesus was about t years old and..Lk 3:23

THISTLES

produce thorns and t for you,...Gn 3:18

THOMAS

Apostle; sought evidence of resurrection; made confession of faith (Jn
20:24-29).

THORN

It will produce t-s and thistles ..Gn 3:18
fell among t-s, and the t-s came
  up...........................Mt 13:7
twisted together a crown of
  t-s,...........................Mt 27:29
t in the flesh was given to me, ..2Co 12:7

THOUGHT (N) *SEE ALSO* THINK

The LORD knows the t-s of
  mankind;..................... Ps 94:11
You understand my t-s from
  far ....Ps 139:2
My t-s are not your t-s, ... Is 55:8
Perceiving their t-s, Jesus said,.. Mt 9:4
a child, I t like a child,......... 1Co 13:11
take every t captive to obey .. 2Co 10:5

THOUSAND

his t-s, but David his tens of t-s..1Sm 18:7
the cattle on a t hills...........Ps 50:10
in your sight a t years are like ..Ps 90:4
one day is like a t years,........2Pt 3:8
and bound him for a t years.... Rv 20:2
reign with him for a t years.... Rv 20:6

THREATEN

he suffered, he did not t 1Pt 2:23

THREE

cord of t strands is not easily...Ec 4:12
the huge fish t days and t
  nights, ...Mt 12:40
For where two or t are
  gathered....................Mt 18:20

you will deny me t times." ....Mt 26:34
and rebuild it in t days. ....Mt 26:61
killed, and rise after t days......Mk 8:31
Now these t remain: faith,
  hope,.......................1Co 13:13
For there are t that testify:......1Jn 5:7

THRESHING FLOOR

David bought the t.......... 2Sm 24:24

THROAT

their t is an open grave;.........Ps 5:9
Their t is an open grave; ....Rm 3:13

THRONE

will establish the t of his
  kingdom....................2Sm 7:13
Your t, God, is forever and
  ever; ....Ps 45:6
seated on a high and lofty t, ...Is 6:1
He will reign on the t of David....Is 9:7
Heaven is my t, and earth is
  my ....Is 66:1
heaven, because it is God's t; .. Mt 5:34
will also sit on twelve t-s,..... Mt 19:28
whether t-s or dominions or .. Col 1:16
Your t, God, is forever and ..... Heb 1:8
let us approach the t of grace
  with ....Heb 4:16
cast their crowns before the t,..Rv 4:10
great white t and one seated
  on it.........................Rv 20:11

THROW

He has t-n the horse and its
  rider ....Ex 15:1
should be the first to t a stone
  at her..........................Jn 8:7

THUNDERCLOUD

I answered you from the t. ..... Ps 81:7

TIME

for such a t as this.............. Est 4:14
a t for every activity under
  heaven:........................Ec 3:1
for a t, t-s, and half a t......Dn 7:25; 12:7
Teacher says: My t is near;.....Mt 26:18
you will deny me three t-s! ...Mt 26:34
My t has not yet fully come,...... Jn 7:6
It is not for you to know t-s .....Ac 1:7
making the most of the t........Col 4:5
About the t-s and the
  seasons: 1Th 5:1
for a t, t-s, and half a t.........Rv 12:14

TIMOTHY

Companion of Paul (Ac 16–20; Rm
16:21; 2Co 1:1; 1Th 1:1; 2Th 1:1; Php 1:1;
Phm 1). Sent by Paul to Corinth (1Co
4:17); to Philippi (Php 2:19); to Thessalonica (1Th 3:2). Pastored Ephesian
church (1Tm 1:3). Received two letters
from Paul (1Tm 1:2; 2Tm 1:2) and a plea
to come (4:9).

TIRED

let us not get t of doing good,.... Gl 6:9

TITUS

Gentile coworker with Paul (Gl 2:1-3;
2Co 8:23). Sent to Corinth (2:1-4; 7:13-15;
8:16-17); in charge of church in Crete (Ti
1:5); went to Dalmatia (2Tm 4:10).

TOBIAH

Adversary against Nehemiah's efforts to rebuild Jerusalem's walls (Neh
2:10,19; 4:1-9; 6; 13:4-9).

TODAY

T, if you hear his voice: ....Ps 95:7
Give us t our daily bread........Mt 6:11
T you will be with me in
  paradise..................... Lk 23:43
t I have become your
  Father, ... Heb 1:5; 5:5
while it is still called t, ... Heb 3:13
T, if you hear his voice,
  do not.......................Heb 3:15
same yesterday, t, and
  forever. ....Heb 13:8

TOLA

Issacharite judge (Jdg 10:1-2).

TOLERABLE

It will be more t on the day of..Mt 10:15

TOLERATE

will not t sound doctrine,......2Tm 4:3
and that you cannot t evil
  people..........................Rv 2:2

TOMB

You are like whitewashed t-s, .Mt 23:27
he laid him in a t cut out of ...Mk 15:46
stone rolled away from the t... Lk 24:2
already been in the t four days.. Jn 11:17

TOMORROW

Don't boast about t, for you
don't............................ Pr 27:1
Let us eat and drink, for t we
die! .... Is 22:13
Therefore don't worry about t, ..Mt 6:34
us eat and drink, for t we die... 1Co 15:32
do not know what t will
bring—..................... Jms 4:14

TONGUE

Before a word is on my t, you..Ps 139:4
death are in the power of the t, ..Pr 18:21
every t will swear allegiance... Is 45:23
they will speak in new t-s;.... Mk 16:17
t-s like flames of fire that........Ac 2:3
in other t-s and declaring..... Ac 10:46
in other t-s and to prophesy.....Ac 19:6
interpretation of t-s...........1Co 12:10
If I speak human or angelic
t-s............................1Co 13:1
as for t-s, they will cease;......1Co 13:8
person who speaks in
another t 1Co 14:2
not forbid speaking in
other t-s 1Co 14:39
and every t will confess
that ....Php 2:11
but no man can tame the t. ..... Jms 3:8

TOOTH

eye for eye, t
for t.......Ex 21:24; Lv 24:20; Dt 19:21
for an eye and a t for a t........ Mt 5:38
weeping and gnashing of
teeth......................... Mt 8:12

TOP

was torn in two from t to
bottom,...................... Mt 27:51

TORCH

fire pot and a flaming t
appeared ....Gn 15:17

TORMENT

come here to t us before the
time? .... Mt 8:29
those t-ed by unclean spirits ...Lk 6:18
they will be t-ed day and
night....................... Rv 20:10

TORRENT

the t would have swept
over us;.....................Ps 124:4

TOSS

driven and t-ed by the wind.....Jms 1:6

TOUCH

You must not eat it or t it,....... Gn 3:3
t-ed my mouth with it and said: ..Is 6:7
If I can just t his robe,.......... Mt 9:21
in order that he might t
them, ...Mk 10:13
T me and see, because a ghost..Lk 24:39
Don't handle, don't taste,
don't t"?....................Col 2:21
and have t-ed with our hands,...1Jn 1:1

TOWEL

took a t, and tied it around
himself........................Jn 13:4

TOWER

a t with its top in the sky. ....Gn 11:4
name of the LORD is a strong t;..Pr 18:10

TOWN

and from the t of Bethlehem, ...Jn 7:42

TRADERS

When Midianite t passed by,.. Gn 37:28

TRADITION

nullify the word of God by
your t .... Mk 7:13
empty deceit based on
human t,....................Col 2:8
hold to the t-s you were
taught,.................... 2Th 2:15

TRAGEDY

a sickening t .... Ec 5:13,16
Here is a t I have observed....... Ec 6:1

TRAIN

who t-s my hands for battle
and ....Ps 144:1
will never again t for war.. Is 2:4; Mc 4:3

TRAINING

them up in the t and
instruction .... Eph 6:4
t of the body has a limited
benefit, ...1Tm 4:8
correcting, for t in
righteousness,.............2Tm 3:16

TRAITOR

Judas Iscariot, who became a t. . Lk 6:16

TRAMPLE

be thrown out and t-d under .. Mt 5:13
pearls before pigs, or they will t..Mt 7:6
Jerusalem will be t-d by the ...Lk 21:24
who has t-d on the Son of
God,........................Heb 10:29

TRAMPLING (N)

you—this t of my courts? ....Is 1:12

TRANSFIGURE

He was t-ed in front of them, ...Mt 17:2

TRANSFORM

be t-ed by the renewing of
your ....Rm 12:2
are being t-ed into the same
image......................... 2Co 3:18
He will t the body of our
humble .... Php 3:21

TRANSGRESSION

is the one whose t is forgiven, ..Ps 32:1
has he removed our t-s from
us...........................Ps 103:12
I—I sweep away your t-s ...... Is 43:25
where there is no law,
there is no t. ....Rm 4:15

TRANSLATE

law...t-ing and giving the
meaning..................... Neh 8:8
Immanuel...t-d "God is with
us."........................... Mt 1:23

TRAP

their gods will be a t for you. ....Jdg 2:3
to t him by what he said....... Mt 22:15
into disgrace and the devil's t.. 1Tm 3:7

TREAD

your foot t-s will be yours...... Dt 11:24
ox while it t-s out grain. . Dt 25:4; 1Co 9:9
ox while it is t-ing out the
grain, ...1Tm 5:18

TREASURE (N)

for yourselves t-s on earth, ... Mt 6:19
For where your t is, there your ..Mt 6:21

TREASURE

The kingdom of heaven
   is like t, ... Mt 13:44
and you will have t in
   heaven......................... Mt 19:21
Now we have this t in clay jars,.. 2Co 4:7
the t-s of wisdom and
   knowledge .... Col 2:3

TREASURE (V)

I have t-d your word in my
   heart......................... Ps 119:11
But Mary was t-ing up all
   these........................... Lk 2:19

TREATY

Make no t with them .... Dt 7:2
Please make a t with us. .... Jos 9:6

TREE SEE ALSO TREE OF LIFE

the t of the knowledge of good
   and .... Gn 2:9
hung on a t is under God's
   curse......................... Dt 21:23
He is like a t planted beside...... Ps 1:3
all the t-s of the forest will...... Ps 96:12
all the t-s of the field will
   clap........................... Is 55:12
every t that doesn't produce
   good .... Mt 3:10
for a t is known by its fruit.... Mt 12:33
At once the fig t withered..... Mt 21:19
Cursed is everyone ...
   hung on a t................... Gl 3:13
our sins in his body on the t;... 1Pt 2:24

TREE OF LIFE

the t in the middle of the
   garden, ... Gn 2:9
must not ... take from the
   t, eat,......................... Gn 3:22
She is a t to those who
   embrace her, ... Pr 3:18
The fruit of the righteous
   is a t,......................... Pr 11:30
the right to eat from the t, ... Rv 2:7
will take away his share of
   the t......................... Rv 22:19

TREMBLE

let the whole earth t before
   him......................... 1Ch 16:30

TREMBLING (N)

your own salvation with
   fear and t................... Php 2:12

TRESPASS

delivered up for our t-es and
   raised....................... Rm 4:25
by the one man's t the many
   died, ... Rm 5:15
not counting their t-es
   against 2Co 5:19
you were dead in your t-es and
   sins .... Eph 2:1
when you were dead in t-es ... Col 2:13

TRIAL

you experience various t-s,.... Jms 1:2

TRIBE

These are the t-s of Israel,
   twelve .... Gn 49:28
He chose instead the t of
   Judah, ... Ps 78:68
judging the twelve t-s of
   Israel....................... Mt 19:28
every t and language and
   people .... Rv 5:9
the names of the twelve t-s..... Rv 21:12

TRIBULATION

ones coming out of the great t.. Rv 7:14

TRIP

over and a rock to t over, ... Is 8:14
a rock to t over, and the one
   who.......................... Rm 9:33
and a rock to t over............. 1Pt 2:8

TRIUMPH

When the righteous t, there is
   great........................ Pr 28:12
He t-ed over them in him....... Col 2:15
Mercy t-s over judgment...... Jms 2:13

TROPHIMUS

and Tychicus and T from Asia.. Ac 20:4
previously seen T the
   Ephesian .... Ac 21:29
I left T sick at Miletus......... 2Tm 4:20

TROUBLE (N)

humans are born for t as surely
   as .... Jb 5:7
a refuge in times of t. .... Ps 9:9
is always found in times of t...... Ps 46:1
and our salvation in time of t. .. Is 33:2
Each day has enough t of its
   own.......................... Mt 6:34

TROUBLE (V)

Now my soul is t-d. What
   should .... Jn 12:27
Don't let your heart be t-d....... Jn 14:1
your heart be t-d or fearful. ... Jn 14:27

TRUE

He is righteous and t........... Dt 32:4
The t light that gives light to..... Jn 1:9
I am the t vine, and my Father .. Jn 15:1
you, the only t God, and the one.. Jn 17:3
his testimony is t........ Jn 19:35; 21:24
Let God be t, even though
   everyone .... Rm 3:4
whatever is t, whatever is ..... Php 4:8
these words are faithful
   and t. .... Rv 21:5; 22:6

TRULY

"T you are the Son of God."...... Mt 14:33

TRUMPET

priests carry seven
   ram's-horn t-s................ Jos 6:4
Praise him with t blast; .... Ps 150:3
give ... don't sound a t before
   you,......................... Mt 6:2
at the last t. For the t will
   sound,...................... 1Co 15:52
with the t of God, and the
   dead in..................... 1Th 4:16
seven t-s were given to them.... Rv 8:2

TRUST

When I am afraid, I will t in
   you.......................... Ps 56:3
in God I t; ... What can mere .. Ps 56:4,11
T in the LORD with all your ...... Pr 3:5
those who t in the LORD will
   renew...................... Is 40:31
He t-s in God; let God rescue.. Mt 27:43
Again, I will t in him.......... Heb 2:13

TRUSTWORTHY

the testimony of the LORD is t,.. Ps 19:7
The wounds of a friend are t,... Pr 27:6
This saying is t 1Tm 1:15; 3:1; 4:9

TRUTH

The entirety of your
   word is t, ... Ps 119:160
grace and t came through Jesus.. Jn 1:17
worship the Father in Spirit
   and t. .... Jn 4:23
the t, and the t will set you free. . Jn 8:32

am the way, the **t**, and the life. . . Jn 14:6
exchanged the **t** of God for a
   lie . . . . Rm 1:25
But speaking the **t** in love, ... Eph 4:15
teaching the word of **t**. 2Tm 2:15
and the **t** is not in us 1Jn 1:8

TUNIC

took the **t**, which was
   seamless, ... Jn 19:23

TURMOIL

Why are you in such **t**? Pss 42:5,11; 43:5

TURN

All have **t-ed** away; all alike
   have . . . . Ps 14:3
T my heart to your decrees
   and . . . . Ps 119:36
A gentle answer **t-s** away
   anger, ... Pr 15:1
t back, and be healed . . . . Is 6:10
we all have **t-ed** to our own
   way; . . . . Is 53:6
should **t** from his way and
   live . . . . Ezk 33:11
t to me with all your heart, ... Jl 2:12
And he will **t** the hearts of
   fathers . . . . Mal 4:6
right cheek, **t** the other to
   him . . . . Mt 5:39
to **t** the hearts of fathers to . . . . . Lk 1:17
All have **t-ed** away, all alike
   have . . . . Rm 3:12
that whoever **t-s** a sinner
   from . . . . Jms 5:20

TURTLEDOVE

may take two **t-s** or two
   young . . . . Lv 12:8
pair of **t-s** or two young
   pigeons . . . . Lk 2:24

TWELVE

Jacob had **t** sons: . . . . Gn 35:22
the names of the **t** apostles: . . . . . Mt 10:2
t thrones, judging the **t** tribes . . Mt 19:28
When he was **t** years old, they . . Lk 2:42
He appointed the **T**: . . . . Mk 3:16
t foundations, and the **t** names of
   the **t** apostles of the Lamb . . . Rv 21:14

TWENTY-FOUR

on the thrones sat **t** elders . . . . Rv 4:4
and the **t** elders fell down . . . . Rv 5:8

TWIN

were indeed **t-s** in her womb. . Gn 25:24

TWINKLING

in a moment, in the **t** of an
   eye, ... 1Co 15:52

TWIST

They **t** my words all daylong; . . . Ps 56:5
and unstable will **t** them to
   their 2Pt 3:16

TWO

into the ark **t** of all the living . . Gn 6:19
T are better than one because . . . Ec 4:9
No one can serve **t** masters, . . . Mt 6:24
where **t** or three are gathered . . Mt 18:20
are no longer **t**, but one flesh. . Mt 19:6
and the **t** will become one
   flesh. . . . . Eph 5:31

U

UNAPPROACHABLE

lives in **u** light, ... 1Tm 6:16

UNAUTHORIZED

and presented **u** fire before the. . Lv 10:1

UNBELIEF

And he was amazed at their **u**. . . Mk 6:6
I do believe; help my **u**! . . . . Mk 9:24
He rebuked their **u** and
   hardness . . . . Mk 16:14
they were broken off because
   of **u**, ... Rm 11:20

UNBELIEVER

But if the **u** leaves, let him
   leave. 1Co 7:15
not for believers but for **u-s**. . 1Co 14:22
faith and is worse than an **u**. . . 1Tm 5:8

UNBELIEVING (ADJ)

You **u** and perverse
   generation, ... Mt 17:17
If any brother has an **u** wife . . . 1Co 7:12

UNCIRCUMCISED

house of Israel is **u** in heart. . . . . Jr 9:26

A man who is physically
   u, ... Rm 2:27
called "the **u**" by those called . . Eph 2:11

UNCIRCUMCISION

matter and **u** does not matter, . . 1Co 7:19
circumcision nor **u**
   accomplishes . . . . Gl 5:6
circumcision and **u**, barbarian, . . Col 3:11

UNCLEAN

if someone touches anything **u**. . Lv 5:2
I am a man of **u** lips and live
   among . . . . Is 6:5
gave them authority over **u**
   spirits, ... Mt 10:1
Whenever the **u** spirits saw
   him . . . . Mk 3:11
I have never eaten
   anything . . . **u**! . . . . Ac 10:14
am persuaded . . . that
   nothing is **u** . . . . Rm 14:14

UNCLOTHED

do not want to be **u** but
   clothed, ... 2Co 5:4

UNCOVER

go in and **u** his feet, and lie
   down . . . . Ru 3:4
with her head **u-ed**
   dishonors her 1Co 11:5

UNDEFILED

and the marriage bed kept **u**, . . Heb 13:4

UNDER

no other name **u** heaven
   given to . . . . Ac 4:12
you are not **u** the law but
   u grace . . . . Rm 6:14

UNDERNEATH

and **u** are the everlasting
   arms. . . . . Dt 33:27

UNDERSTAND

then you will **u** the fear of the
   LORD . . . . Pr 2:5
Keep listening, but do not **u**; . . . . . Is 6:9
u with their hearts and turn
   back . . . . Mt 13:15
holy place" (let the reader **u**), . Mt 24:15

Then he opened their minds
to u .... Lk 24:45
but u what the Lord's will is... Eph 5:17
some matters that are hard
to u........................... 2Pt 3:16

UNDERSTANDING (N)

and do not rely on your own u; .. Pr 3:5

UNEDUCATED

that they were u and
untrained..................... Ac 4:13

UNFADING

and u, kept in heaven 1Pt 1:4
receive the u crown of glory. ... 1Pt 5:4

UNFRUITFUL

but my understanding is u.... 1Co 14:14

UNGODLY

time, Christ died for the u....... Rm 5:6

UNINFORMED

We do not want you to be u, ... 1Th 4:13

UNITED

were continually u in prayer, ... Ac 1:14

UNITY

until we all reach u in the
faith .... Eph 4:13
the perfect bond of u........... Col 3:14

UNJUST

Listen to what the u judge
says. .... Lk 18:6
For God is not u; he will not .. Heb 6:10

UNKNOWN

'To an U God.' .... Ac 17:23

UNLEAVENED

observe the Festival of U
Bread .... Ex 12:17
On the first day of U Bread ...... Mt 26:17

UNMARRIED

I say to the u and to widows: ... 1Co 7:8

UNNATURAL

natural sexual relations for u
ones........................... Rm 1:26

UNPUNISHED

will not leave the guilty u, ... Ex 34:7
that the wicked will not go u,.. Pr 11:21

UNQUENCHABLE

and go to hell, the u fire, ... Mk 9:43

UNRIGHTEOUS

rain on the righteous and
the u. .... Mt 5:45
whoever is u in very little is
also .... Lk 16:10
the righteous for the u, ... 1Pt 3:18

UNRIGHTEOUSNESS

and there is no u in him........ Ps 92:15
and to cleanse us from
all u........................... 1Jn 1:9

UNSEARCHABLE

How u his judgments and .... Rm 11:33

UNSEEN

temporary, but what is u is
eternal. 2Co 4:18

UNSHRUNK

an old garment with u
cloth, ... Mt 9:16

UNSTABLE

double-minded and u in all his
ways. .... Jms 1:8
They seduce u people.......... 2Pt 2:14

UNTIE

sandal strap I'm not worthy
to u.......................... Jn 1:27

UNTRACEABLE

his judgments and u his
ways! .... Rm 11:33

UNVEILED

We all, with u faces, are
looking 2Co 3:18

UNWORTHY

cup of the Lord in an u way... 1Co 11:27

UPRIGHT

The u will see his face. .... Ps 11:7
God made people u, but they ... Ec 7:29

UPROOT

Be u-ed and planted in the sea, .. Lk 17:6

UPSTAIRS

He will show you a large
room u, ... Mk 14:15

UR

City in lower Mesopotamia; birthplace
of Abraham (Gn 11:28,31; 15:7; Neh 9:7).

URIAH

Hethite; husband of Bathsheba. One of
David's warriors (2Sm 23:39); David arranged his death (2Sm 11).

URIM

Place the U and Thummim
in the .... Ex 28:30

USEFUL

now he is u both to you and to
me........................... Phm 11

USELESS

that faith without works is
u?........................... Jms 2:20

UZZIAH

Son of Amaziah; king of Judah; also
known as Azariah (2Kg 15:1-7). Made
king by popular acclaim (2Ch 26:1);
expanded and fortified Judah (26:6-
15); struck with skin disease when he
attempted to serve as priest (26:16-21).

V

VAIN

and the peoples plot in v? .... Ps 2:1
its builders labor over it in v; .. Ps 127:1
They worship me in v, ... Mt 15:9

labor in the Lord is not in **v**. . 1Co 15:58
and had not been running, in **v**. . Gl 2:2

VALLEY

when I go through the
    darkest **v**,......................Ps 23:4
Every **v** will be lifted up,........ Is 40:4
multitudes in the **v** of decision! . .Jl 3:14
Every **v** will be filled, and every . .Lk 3:5

VALUE

despised, and we didn't **v** him. . .Is 53:3
the surpassing **v** of knowing . . Php 3:8
any **v** in curbing
    self-indulgence..............Col 2:23

VANISH

the heavens will **v** like smoke,. . .Is 51:6

VEGETABLE

Let us be given **v-s** to eat and . . .Dn 1:12
one who is weak eats only **v-s**. .Rm 14:2

VEIL

he put a **v** over his face........ Ex 34:33
old covenant, the same **v**
    remains;.................... 2Co 3:14

VENGEANCE

V belongs to me; I will repay. . Dt 32:35
For the LORD has a day of **v**,..... Is 34:8
it is written: **V** belongs to me;. .Rm 12:19
who has said, **V** belongs
    to me,.....................Heb 10:30

VICTORY

has been swallowed up in **v**. . 1Co 15:54
Where, death, is your **v**? 1Co 15:55
gives us the **v** through
    our Lord 1Co 15:57
This is the **v** that has conquered . .1Jn 5:4

VINDICATE

wisdom is **v-d** by all her
    children.......................Lk 7:35

VINE

I am the true **v**, and my Father. . Jn 15:1

VINEGAR

thirst they gave me **v** to drink. . Ps 69:21

VINEYARD

to hire workers for his **v**. ...... Mt 20:1
who planted a **v**, put a fence. . Mt 21:33

VIOLENCE

because he had done no **v** ...... Is 53:9
of heaven has been
    suffering **v**,...................Mt 11:12

VIOLENT

and the **v** have been seizing it. . Mt 11:12

VIPER

he said to them, "Brood of **v-s**!. . Mt 3:7
Snakes! Brood of **v-s**!
    How can....................Mt 23:33

VIRGIN

The **v** will conceive, have a son,. .Is 7:14
the **v** will become pregnant
    and .... Mt 1:23
be like ten **v-s** who took their . Mt 25:1
The **v-**'s name was Mary.........Lk 1:27

VISIBLE

humans see what is **v**, but the
    LORD 1Sm 16:7
made from things that are
    not **v**. ....Heb 11:3

VISION

and your young men will see
    v-s...........................Jl 2:28
your young men will see **v-s**, . . .Ac 2:17
move on to **v-s** and
    revelations 2Co 12:1

VISIT

was in prison and you
    v-ed me....................Mt 25:36
God has **v-ed** his people.........Lk 7:16

VOICE

after the fire there was a **v**,
    a soft 1Kg 19:12
Today, if you hear his **v**:........Ps 95:7
A **v** of one crying out:........... Is 40:3
A **v** was heard in Ramah, a
    lament.......................Jr 31:15
A **v** was heard in Ramah,
    weeping,.................... Mt 2:18
And a **v** from heaven said:......Mt 3:17
and the sheep hear his **v**. ....Jn 10:3

Then a **v** came from heaven:. . .Jn 12:28
Their **v** has gone out to the . . .Rm 10:18
Today, if you hear his **v**,. .Heb 3:7,15; 4:7
If anyone hears my **v** and
    opens....................... Rv 3:20

VOMIT (N)

As a dog returns to its **v**,....... Pr 26:11
A dog returns to its own **v**,......2Pt 2:22

VOMIT (V)

I am going to **v** you out of my. . .Rv 3:16

VOW (N)

makes a special **v**, a Nazirite **v**, . .Nm 6:2
Jephthah made this **v** to the
    LORD: ....Jdg 11:30
I will fulfill my **v-s** before
    those .... Ps 22:25
and later to reconsider his **v-s**. .Pr 20:25

VOW (V)

Fulfill what you **v**. ....Ec 5:4

W

WAGE

the worker is worthy of his **w-s**. .Lk 10:7
For the **w-s** of sin is death,......Rm 6:23
the worker is worthy of his
    w-s..........................1Tm 5:18

WAIST

a leather belt around his **w**,......Mt 3:4

WAIT

W for the LORD; be strong .....Ps 27:14
creation eagerly **w-s** with .....Rm 8:19
we eagerly **w** for it with
    patience.................... Rm 8:25
as you eagerly **w** for the
    revelation 1Co 1:7
to **w** for his Son from heaven,. . .1Th 1:10

WALK

Enoch **w-ed** with God; then he
    was .... Gn 5:24
his sons did not **w** in his
    ways........................1Sm 8:3
to **w** in his ways and to keep....1Kg 2:3
they will **w** and not faint....... Is 40:31

and to **w** humbly with your
    God . . . . Mc 6:8
or to say, 'Get up and **w**'? . . . . Mt 9:5
saw him **w-ing** on the sea,. . . . .Mt 14:26
pick up your mat and **w**. . . . . Jn 5:8
we too may **w** in newness of
    life. . . . . .Rm 6:4
we **w** by faith, not by sight. 2Co 5:7
w by the Spirit and you will . . . . . Gl 5:16
If we **w** in the light as he 1Jn 1:7

WALL

shout, and the **w** collapsed. . . . .Jos 6:20
let's rebuild Jerusalem's **w**, . . . Neh 2:17
down the dividing **w** of
    hostility. Eph 2:14
By faith the **w-s** of Jericho
    fell . . . . Heb 11:30

WANDER

have **w-ed** away from the
    faith 1Tm 6:10

WANDERER

will be a restless **w** on the
    earth. . . . . Gn 4:12

WAR

makes **w-s** cease
    throughout the . . . . .Ps 46:9
a time for **w** and a time for . . . . . .Ec 3:8
will never again train for **w**. . . . . . .Is 2:4
hear of **w-s** and rumors of
    w-s. . . . . Mt 24:6
do not wage **w** according to the
    flesh,. 2Co 10:3

WARFARE

weapons of our **w** are not
    flesh, but 2Co 10:4

WARM

lie down together, they can
    keep **w**; . . . . Ec 4:11

WARN

if you **w** a wicked
    person. . . . . Ezk 3:19; 33:9
And being **w-ed** in a
    dream . . . . Mt 2:12,22
Who **w-ed** you to flee from
    the. . . . . .Mt 3:7
w-ing and teaching everyone
    with . . . . .Col 1:28

WARRIOR

LORD is a **w**; the LORD is his
    name. . . . . .Ex 15:3

WASH

Go **w** seven times in the
    Jordan 2Kg 5:10
w me, and I will be whiter than. .Ps 51:7
they don't **w** their hands
    when . . . . Mt 15:2
began to **w** his feet with her
    tears. . . . . .Lk 7:38
began to **w** his disciples' feet . . . Jn 13:5
and **w** away your sins by
    calling . . . . Ac 22:16
But you were **w-ed**, you were . .1Co 6:11
the **w-ing** of water by the
    word. . . . . .Eph 5:26
Blessed . . . who **w** their robes, . .Rv 22:14

WASTE

Why has this perfume been
    w-d? . . . . .Mk 14:4
my labor for you has been **w-d**. . .Gl 4:11

WATCH (N)

keeping **w** at night over their
    flock. . . . . .Lk 2:8
since they keep **w** over your
    souls. . . . . Heb 13:17

WATCH (V)

the LORD **w-es** over the way of . . Ps 1:6
unless the LORD **w-es** over a
    city, ... Ps 127:1
W! Be alert! For you don't
    know . . . . .Mk 13:33

WATCHMAN

the **w** stays alert in vain. . . . . . . Ps 127:1
more than **w-men** for the
    morning. . . . . .Ps 130:6
I have made you a **w** . . . . .Ezk 3:17; 33:7

WATER (N)

w covered the earth. . . . . Gn 7:6
I am poured out like **w**, ...Ps 22:14
He leads me beside quiet **w-s**. . .Ps 23:2
bread on the surface of the **w**, . . .Ec 11:1
who is thirsty, come to the **w**; . . .Is 55:1
abandoned . . . fountain of
    living **w**, .Jr 2:13
will also sprinkle clean **w** on
    you, ... Ezk 36:25
that day living **w** will flow out. .Zch 14:8

I baptize you with **w** for
    repentance, ...Mt 3:11
a cup of cold **w** to one of
    these. . . . . Mt 10:42
Peter started walking on
    the **w** . . . . Mt 14:29
is born of **w** and the Spirit, ...Jn 3:5
and he would give you living **w**. .Jn 4:10
of living **w** flow from deep . . . . . .Jn 7:38
the washing of **w** by the
    word. . . . . .Eph 5:26
the one who came by **w** and
    blood, ...1Jn 5:6
give to the thirsty from the
    spring of the **w** of life. . . . . .Rv 21:6

WATER (V)

I planted, Apollos **w-ed**, but
    God 1Co 3:6

WATERFALLS

calls to deep in the roar of
    your **w**; . . . . .Ps 42:7

WAVER

He did not **w** in unbelief at
    God's . . . . Rm 4:20
of our hope without **w-ing**, . . Heb 10:23

WAVES

was being swamped by the
    w— . . . . .Mt 8:24
even the winds and the **w**, ... Lk 8:25

WAX

my heart is like **w**, melting
    within . . . . .Ps 22:14

WAY

God—his **w** is perfect; 2Sm 22:31
watches over the **w** of the
    righteous. Ps 1:6
Commit your **w** to the LORD; . . . . .Ps 37:5
can a young man keep his
    w pure?. . . . . Ps 119:9
See if there is any offensive
    w in me; lead me in the
    everlasting **w**. . . . . Ps 139:24
There is a **w** that seems right . . Pr 14:12
youth out on his **w**; even when
    he. . . . . .Pr 22:6
Prepare the **w** of the LORD in
    the. . . . . Is 40:3
we all have turned to our
    own **w**; . . . . Is 53:6

and your **w-s** are not my **w-s**. . . Is 55:8
Prepare the **w** for the Lord;. . . . . Mt 3:3
God loved the world in this **w**:. . Jn 3:16
I am the **w**, the truth, and the
   life.. . . . . Jn 14:6
found any . . . who belonged
   to the **W** . . . . Ac 9:2
will also provide a **w** out 1Co 10:13
will show you an even
   better **w**. 1Co 12:31

WEAK

spirit is willing, but the flesh
   is **w**.. . . . . Mt 26:41
Accept anyone who is **w**in
   faith,. . . . . Rm 14:1
God has chosen . . . what is **w** .1Co 1:27
For when I am **w**, then I am. . 2Co 12:10

WEAKER

as with a **w** partner,. 1Pt 3:7

WEAKNESS

took our **w-es** and carried
   our. . . . . .Mt 8:17
Spirit also helps us in our **w**,. . Rm 8:26
sown in **w**, raised in
   power;. 1Co 15:43
for power is perfected in **w**. . . 2Co 12:9
to sympathize with our
   w-es . . . . Heb 4:15

WEALTH

They trust in their **w** . . . . .Ps 49:6
W is not profitable on a day of . . . .Pr 11:4
Give me neither poverty nor **w**;. . Pr 30:8
wealthy should not boast in
   his **w**. . . . . .Jr 9:23
deceitfulness of **w** choke the
   word, ... Mt 13:22
hard it is for those who have
   w to. . . . . .Mk 10:23

WEAPON

No **w** formed against you will . . Is 54:17
the **w-s** of our warfare are not. . 2Co 10:4

WEAR

about your body, what you
   will **w**. . . . . Mt 6:25
and **w-ing** gold jewelry 1Pt 3:3

WEARISOME

All things are **w**, more than . . . . . Ec 1:8

WEARY

they will run and not become
   w,. . . . . Is 40:31
Come to me, all of you who are
   w . . . . Mt 11:28
do not grow **w** in doing good.. .2Th 3:13

WEDDING

Can the **w** guests be sad while . .Mt 9:15
get in here without **w**
   clothes?' . . . . Mt 22:12
a **w** took place in Cana of
   Galilee.. . . . . Jn 2:1

WEEDS

w among the wheat,. . . . . Mt 13:25

WEEK

Observe the Festival of **W-s** . . . Ex 34:22
Seventy **w-s** are decreed. . . . . . . Dn 9:24
first day of the **w** was
   dawning, ... Mt 28:1

WEEP

W-ing may stay overnight, but . .Ps 30:5
wept when we remembered
   Zion. . . . . Ps 137:1
a time to **w** and a time to laugh;. . .Ec 3:4
Rachel **w-ing** for her children,. . .Jr 31:15
Rachel **w-ing** for her children;. . Mt 2:18
there will be **w-ing** and
   gnashing . . . . Mt 8:12
Jesus **wept**. . . . . Jn 11:35
who rejoice; **w** with those
   who **w**.. .Rm 12:15

WEIGH

you have been **w-ed** on the
   balance . . . . Dn 5:27

WEIGHT

honest balances, honest **w-s**, . .Lv 19:36
incomparable eternal **w** of
   glory.. . . . . .2Co 4:17

WELCOME

whoever **w-s** one child like
   this . . . . Mt 18:5

WELL

and I know this very **w**. . . . . . . .Ps 139:14
master said to him,
   'W done, ... Mt 25:21

WELL-BEING

plans for your **w**, not for
   disaster, .Jr 29:11

WENT *SEE* GO

WEST

far as the east is from the **w**,. .Ps 103:12

WHATEVER

W you ask in my name,
   I will do. . . . . Jn 14:13
w is true, **w** is honorable,
   w is just,. . . . . Php 4:8

WHEAT

sowed weeds among
   the **w**,. . . . . Mt 13:25
has asked to sift you like **w**. . . .Lk 22:31
Unless a grain of **w** falls to. . . . . .Jn 12:24

WHEEL

was like a **w** within a **w**. . . . . . . Ezk 1:16

WHIPPED

I will have him **w** and. . . . . .Lk 23:16

WHIRLWIND

Elijah up to heaven in a **w**. 2Kg 2:1
Lᴏʀᴅ answered Job from
   the **w**. . . . . .Jb 38:1
sow the wind and reap the **w**. . . .Hs 8:7

WHISPER

there was a voice, a soft **w**. . . .1Kg 19:12
What you hear in a **w**,
   proclaim.. . . . . Mt 10:27

WHITE

scarlet, they will be as **w** as
   snow;. . . . . .Is 1:18
make a single hair **w** or black.. Mt 5:36
his clothing was as **w** as
   snow. . . . . Mt 28:3
hair of his head were **w** as
   wool— . . . . Rv 1:14
I saw a great **w** throne and
   one . . . . Rv 20:11

WHITER

and I will be **w** than snow. . . . . . . Ps 51:7

WHITEWASH

You are like **w-ed** tombs, ... Mt 23:27

WHO

w do you say that I am?....... Mt 16:15

WHOLE

if he gains the **w** world yet
loses .... Mt 16:26

WICK

will not put out a smoldering **w**; ..Is 42:3
will not put out a
smoldering **w**, ... Mt 12:20

WICKED

w men of the city
surrounded................. Jdg 19:22
does not walk in the advice
of the **w**......................... Ps 1:1
He was assigned a grave with
the **w**, ... Is 53:9
no pleasure in the death of
the **w**, ... Ezk 33:11

WICKEDNESS

saw that human **w** was
widespread.................. Gn 6:5

WIDE

the gate is **w** and the road
broad .... Mt 7:13

WIDOW

Support **w-s** who are
genuinely in need........... 1Tm 5:3

WIFE

and mother and bonds with
his **w**, ... Gn 2:24
Do not covet your
neighbor's **w**, ... Ex 20:17
seven hundred **w-ves** ...
turned his heart 1Kg 11:3
pleasure in the **w** of your
youth........................ Pr 5:18
A man who finds a **w** finds a
good .... Pr 18:22
Who can find a **w** of noble
character?.................. Pr 31:10
should have ... with his own **w**, ..1Co 7:2
W-ves, submit to your .... Eph 5:22
Husbands, love your **w-ves**, ..Eph 5:25

husband of one **w**, ... 1Tm 3:2
the bride, the **w** of the Lamb. ...Rv 21:9

WILD

Without revelation people
run **w**, ... Pr 29:18
food was locusts and **w** honey. . Mt 3:4
you, though a **w** olive branch, ..Rm 11:17
in the same flood of **w** living ... 1Pt 4:4

WILDERNESS

Prepare the way of the Lord
in the **w**; .... Is 40:3
voice of one crying out in the **w**:..Mt 3:3
into the **w** to be tempted.........Mt 4:1
ancestors ate the manna in
the **w**, ... Jn 6:31,49

WILDFLOWERS

Consider how the **w** grow:..... Lk 12:27

WILL (N)

I delight to do your **w**, my God; Ps 40:8
Your **w** be done on earth as it is. ..Mt 6:10
one who does the **w** of my
Father .... Mt 7:21
Yet not as I **w**, but as you **w**.. ..Mt 26:39
My food is to do the **w** of him ..Jn 4:34
hand and your **w** had
predestined to take place ... Ac 4:28
it does not depend on
human **w** .... Rm 9:16
the good, pleasing, and
perfect **w** .... Rm 12:2
See, I have come to do your **w**.. Heb 10:9
ask anything according to
his **w**, ... 1Jn 5:14

WILL (V)

say, "If the Lord **w-s**, we will...... Jms 4:15

WILLING (ADJ)

giving me a **w** spirit........... Ps 51:12
her wings, but you were not
w!.......................... Mt 23:37
The spirit is **w**, but the flesh .. Mt 26:41
if you are **w**, take this cup
away........................ Lk 22:42

WIND

but the Lord was not in the **w**. .1Kg 19:11
soaring on the wings of the **w**..Ps 18:10
will inherit the **w**, ... Pr 11:29
they sow the **w** and reap the..... Hs 8:7

the **w-s** and the sea obey him! ..Mt 8:27
The **w** blows where it pleases,.......Jn 3:8
around by every **w** of
teaching, ... Eph 4:14

WINDSTORM

A great **w** arose, and the
waves........................ Mk 4:37

WINE

W is a mocker, beer is a
brawler,...................... Pr 20:1
and **w** to one whose life is
bitter........................ Pr 31:6
no one puts new **w** into old..... Mt 9:17
water (after it had become **w**),... Jn 2:9
said, "They're drunk on
new **w**!"..................... Ac 2:13
And don't get drunk with **w**,.. Eph 5:18
not drinking a lot of **w**, ..1Tm 3:3; Ti 1:7
a little **w** because of your
stomach 1Tm 5:23

WINESKIN

no one puts new wine into
old **w-s**.................... Mt 9:17

WING

I carried you on eagles' **w-s** ....Ex 19:4
under whose **w-s** you have
come......................... Ru 2:12
soaring on the **w-s** of the
wind. 2Sm 22:11
hide me in the shadow of your
w-s .... Ps 17:8
soaring on the **w-s** of the wind. ..... Ps
18:10
will soar on **w-s** like eagles; ... Is 40:31
rise with healing in its **w-s**,...... Mal 4:2
gathers her chicks under her
w-s, ... Mt 23:37

WINTER

Pray it won't happen in **w**..... Mk 13:18

WIPE

Lord God will **w** away the tears ..Is 25:8
She **w-d** his feet with the hair ..Lk 7:38
will **w** away every tear...... Rv 7:17; 21:4

WISDOM

God gave Solomon **w**,........ 1Kg 4:29
of the Lord is the beginning
of **w**, ... Pr 9:10

Yet **w** is vindicated by all her ...Lk 7:35
both of the **w** and the
knowledge ....Rm 11:33
I will destroy the **w** of the
wise,.........................1Co 1:19
able to give you **w** for
salvation....................2Tm 3:15
Now if any of you lacks **w**,.....Jms 1:5
and riches and **w** and strength..Rv 5:12

WISE

making the inexperienced **w**. .. Ps 19:7
is considered **w** when he
keeps ....Pr 17:28
w men from the east arrived ....Mt 2:1
hidden these things from
the **w** .... Mt 11:25
foolish ... to shame the **w**,.....1Co 1:27

WITHER

and whose leaf does not **w**....... Ps 1:3
The grass **w-s**, the flowers fade . .Is 40:7
it had no root, it **w-ed** away......Mt 13:6
At once the fig tree **w-ed**...... Mt 21:19
grass **w-s**, and the flower falls, ..1Pt 1:24

WITHHOLD

have not **w-held** your only
son........................ Gn 22:12,16

WITNESS

the testimony of two or three
w-es.........................Dt 19:15
two or three **w-es** every fact
may...................... Mt 18:16
many false **w-es** came
forward....................Mt 26:60
will be my **w-es** in Jerusalem, ...Ac 1:8
a good confession ... many
w-es.........................1Tm 6:12
large cloud of **w-es**
surrounding.................Heb 12:1
from Jesus Christ, the faithful **w**,..Rv 1:5
grant my two **w-es** authority...Rv 11:3

WOE

W is me for I am ruined..........Is 6:5
w to you, scribes and
Pharisees, ... Mt 23:13
W to you who are now full,.... Lk 6:25
And **w** to me if I do not preach..1Co 9:16
W! **W**! **W** to those who live on . .Rv 8:13

WOLF

The **w** will dwell with the lamb,. .Is 11:6

you out like sheep among
w-ves....................... Mt 10:16
savage **w-ves** will come in.... Ac 20:29

WOMAN

this one will be called "**w**,"..... Gn 2:23
w who fears the LORD ...
praised.......................Pr 31:30
who looks at a **w** lustfully ......Mt 5:28
There were also **w-en**
watching ....Mk 15:40
Blessed are you among **w-en**, ..Lk 1:42
brought a **w** caught in adultery. . Jn 8:3
for a man not to use a **w** for
sex." 1Co 7:1
the man is the head of the **w**, .. 1Co 11:3
w-en should be silent in the ..1Co 14:34
God sent his Son, born of a **w**,......Gl 4:4
I do not allow a **w** to teach......1Tm 2:12

WOMB

Two nations are in your **w**; ...Gn 25:23
Naked I came from my
mother's **w**,...................Jb 1:21
me together in my
mother's **w**..................Ps 139:13
me from the **w** to be his
servant,...................... Is 49:5
before I formed you in the **w**;......Jr 1:5
his mother's **w** a second time ...Jn 3:4

WONDERFUL

He will be named **W** Counselor, . .Is 9:6
and it is **w** in our eyes? .... Mt 21:42

WONDERS

God of Israel, who alone
does **w**. ....Ps 72:18
I will display **w** in the heaven...Ac 2:19

WONDROUS

tell about all his **w** works! .....Ps 105:2
it is **w** in our sight.............Ps 118:23
w things from your
instruction..................Ps 119:18
Your works are **w**, and I know ..Ps 139:14

WONDROUSLY

been remarkably and **w**
made........................Ps 139:14

WOOD

I bow down to a block of **w**?" .. Is 44:19
costly stones, **w**, hay, or straw, ..1Co 3:12

WOOL

made of both **w** and linen...... Dt 22:11
crimson red, they will be like **w**... Is 1:18
hair of his head was white
as **w**—......................... Rv 1:14

WORD

bread alone but on every **w** that. . Dt 8:3
the **w** of the LORD is pure.......Ps 18:30
May the **w-s** of my mouth
and the .... Ps 19:14
treasured your **w** in my heart
so ....Ps 119:11
Your **w** is a lamp for my feet ..Ps 119:105
Before a **w** is on my tongue, ...Ps 139:4
Every **w** of God is pure;........Pr 30:5
w of our God remains forever. . Is 40:8
my **w** ... not return to me
empty, ...Is 55:11
bread alone but on every **w** that..Mt 4:4
hears these **w-s** of mine and... Mt 7:24
but my **w-s** will never pass
away........................Mt 24:35
The sower sows the **w**.........Mk 4:14
beginning was the **W**, and the **W** was
with God, and the **W** was God.... Jn 1:1
The **W** became flesh and dwelt..Jn 1:14
You have the **w-s** of eternal life. .Jn 6:68
by the truth; your **w** is truth. ...Jn 17:17
the **w** of the cross is
foolishness 1Co 1:18
correctly teaching the **w** of
truth. 2Tm 2:15
For the **w** of God is living and. .Heb 4:12
name is called the **W** of God. ...Rv 19:13
who keeps the **w-s** of this book..Rv 22:9

WORK (N)

God had completed his **w** ...... Gn 2:2
six days and do all your **w**,.... Ex 20:9
heavens, the **w** of your fingers, ..Ps 8:3
w-s are wondrous, and I
know .... Ps 139:14
There is profit in all hard **w**,......Pr 14:23
we all are the **w** of your hands...Is 64:8
do even greater **w-s** than
these, ... Jn 14:12
faith apart from the **w-s** of
the law. .... Rm 3:28
if by grace, then it is not
by **w-s**;...................... Rm 11:6
test the quality of each
one's **w**....................1Co 3:13
because by the **w-s** of the
law no .... Gl 2:16
not from **w-s**, so that no
one can .... Eph 2:9
in Christ Jesus for good **w-s**, .. Eph 2:10
started a good **w** in you will..... Php 1:6

equipped for every good **w**. . .2Tm 3:17
have faith but does not have
   w-s? . . . . .Jms 2:14
I know your **w-s** . . . . . .Rv 2:2,19; 3:1,8,15
judged according to their
   w-s. . . . . Rv 20:13

WORK (V)

My Father is still **w-ing**, and I . . Jn 5:17
Don't **w** for the food that . . . . . . .Jn 6:27
that all things **w** together for. . Rm 8:28
w out your own salvation
   with . . . . Php 2:12
For it is God who is **w-ing** in
   you . . . . Php 2:13
isn't willing to **w**, he should not
   eat. 2Th 3:10

WORKER

abundant, but the **w-s** are few.. .Mt 9:37
the **w** is worthy of his wages. . . .Lk 10:7
The **w** is worthy of his wages.. .1Tm 5:18
a **w** who doesn't need to be. . .2Tm 2:15

WORKMANSHIP

we are his **w**, created in
   Christ. . . . . Eph 2:10

WORLD

He judges the **w** with
   righteousness;. . . . . .Ps 9:8
You are the light of the **w**. . . . . . Mt 5:14
gains the whole **w** yet loses
   his . . . . Mt 16:26
Go into all the **w** and preach
   the. . . . . .Mk 16:15
who takes away the sin of
   the **w**!. . . . . .Jn 1:29
For God loved the **w** in this
   way: . . . . Jn 3:16
I am the light of the **w**. . . . . . .Jn 8:12; 9:5
I have conquered the **w**. . . . . . .Jn 16:33
Do not love the **w** or the
   things. 1Jn 2:15
greater than the one who is
   in the **w**. 1Jn 4:4

WORM

But I am a **w** and not a man, ...Ps 22:6
for their **w** will never die,. . . . . . Is 66:24
God appointed a **w** that
   attacked . . . . .Jnh 4:7

WORMWOOD

The name of the star is **W**, ... Rv 8:11

WORRY

Don't **w** about your life,. . . . . Mt 6:25
don't **w** beforehand what you
   will . . . . Mk 13:11
Don't **w** about anything,
   but in . . . . Php 4:6

WORSHIP

W the Lᴏʀᴅ in the splendor
   of 1Ch 16:29
Come, let us **w** and bow down;. . Ps 95:6
those who **w** him must **w** in
   spirit. . . . . .Jn 4:24
this is your true **w**. . . . . Rm 12:1

WORSHIPERS

when the true **w** will worship . .Jn 4:23

WORTHLESS

not been raised, your faith
   is **w**;. 1Co 15:17

WORTHY

to the Lᴏʀᴅ, who is **w** of
   praise, ... 2Sm 22:4
and follow me is not **w** of me. . .Mt 10:38
I am not **w** to untie the strap of . .Lk 3:16
not **w** to be called an apostle,. . .1Co 15:9
you to live **w** of the calling . . . . . . Eph 4:1
W is the Lamb who was
   slaughtered . . . . .Rv 5:12

WOUND

and bandages their **w-s**. . . . . .Ps 147:3
The **w-s** of a friend are
   trustworthy, ...Pr 27:6
and we are healed by his **w-s**. . . Is 53:5
By his **w-s** you have been
   healed. 1Pt 2:24
but its fatal **w** was healed. . . . . . .Rv 13:3

WRAP

body, **w-ped** it in clean, fine
   linen, ... Mt 27:59
and she **w-ped** him tightly in
   cloth . . . . .Lk 2:7

WRATH

do not discipline me in your **w**. . . Ps 6:1
Even human **w** will praise
   you;. . . . . .Ps 76:10
is not profitable on a day of **w**,. . Pr 11:4
but a harsh word stirs up **w**. . . . . .Pr 15:1
you to flee from the coming **w**? . .Mt 3:7

For God's **w** is revealed from. . Rm 1:18
were by nature children
   under **w**,. . . . . Eph 2:3
and from the **w** of the Lamb,. . . . .Rv 6:16

WRESTLED

man **w** with him until
   daybreak. . . . . .Gn 32:24

WRETCHED

What a **w** man I am! Who will. .Rm 7:24
you don't realize that you
   are **w**,. . . . . .Rv 3:17

WRINKLE

without spot or **w** or
   anything. . . . . .Eph 5:27

WRITE

Moses **wrote** down all the
   words. . . . . Ex 24:4
w them on the tablet of your . . Pr 3:3; 7:3
within them and **w** it on
   their hearts. . . . . Jr 31:33
hand appeared and began
   w-ing, ... Dn 5:5
because he **wrote** about me. . . . . .Jn 5:46
are **w-ten** so that you may
   believe. . . . . .Jn 20:31
I will . . . **w** them on their
   hearts. . . . . .Heb 8:10

WRONG

this man has done nothing **w**. . Lk 23:41
Love does no **w** to a neighbor. . .Rm 13:10
does not keep a record of **w-s**. . .1Co 13:5

WRONGDOING

if someone is overtaken in
   any **w**, ... Gl 6:1

Y

YEAR

The fiftieth **y** will be your
   Jubilee; . . . . .Lv 25:11
a thousand **y-s** are like
   yesterday. . . . . .Ps 90:4
proclaim the **y** of the
   Lᴏʀᴅ's favor, ...Is 61:2
proclaim the **y** of the
   Lord's favor. . . . . .Lk 4:19

days, months, seasons, and **y-s**... Gl 4:10
continually offer **y** after **y**...... Heb 10:1
one day is like a thousand **y-s**,.. 2Pt 3:8
for a thousand **y-s**.......... Rv 20:2,4,6

YES

let your '**y**' mean '**y**,'............ Mt 5:37
God's promises is "**Y**" in him. . 2Co 1:20
your "**y**" mean "**y**," and your .. Jms 5:12

YESTERDAY

were born only **y** and know
  nothing........................ Jb 8:9
Jesus Christ is the same **y**,
  today,........................ Heb 13:8

YOKE

Your father made our **y**
  harsh........................1Kg 12:4
take up my **y** and learn from me, ... Mt
  11:29
submit again to a **y** of slavery....... Gl 5:1

YOUNG

How can a **y** man keep his way..Ps 119:9
and your **y** men will see visions... Jl 2:28
your **y** men will see visions, ... Ac 2:17

YOUNGER

The older will serve the **y**. .....Rm 9:12
y men as brothers,............. 1Tm 5:1

YOUTH

Do not remember the sins
  of my **y** .... Ps 25:7
y is renewed like the eagle.....Ps 103:5
take pleasure in the wife of
  your **y**........................ Pr 5:18
Start a **y** out on his way; ....Pr 22:6
your Creator in the days of
  your **y**:...................... Ec 12:1
Don't let anyone despise
  your **y**,..................... 1Tm 4:12

YOUTHFUL

Flee from **y** passions, ... 2Tm 2:22

Z

ZACCHAEUS

Tax collector who hosted Jesus and
was converted (Lk 19:2-9).

ZEAL

The **z** of the LORD of Armies
  will 2Kg 19:31
z for your house has consumed me,..Ps 69:9
z is not good without
  knowledge,................... Pr 19:2
The **z** of the LORD of Armies
  will .... Is 9:7; 37:32
Z for your house will consume me..Jn 2:17
that they have **z** for God, but...Rm 10:2
regarding **z**, persecuting
  the church; .... Php 3:6

ZEBULUN

Son of Jacob and Leah (Gn 30:20). Tribe
with territory between the Sea of Galilee and Mount Carmel (Jos 19:10-16).

ZECHARIAH

1. Son of Jeroboam II; king of Israel
   (2Kg 15:8-12).
2. Prophet after the exile; son of Berechiah; descendant of Iddo (Ezr 5:1;
   Zch 1:1).
3. Father of John the Baptist (Lk 1:5-23,
   59-79).

ZEDEKIAH

Son of Josiah; last king of Judah; originally called Mattaniah; sons blinded;
exiled (2Kg 24:17–25:7).

ZEPHANIAH

Prophet to Josiah; descendant of Hezekiah (Zph 1:1).

ZERUBBABEL

Leader of those returning from exile
to rebuild the temple (Ezr 2:2; 4:2; 5:2;

Hg 1:1). Descendant of David and Jehoiachin; ancestor of Jesus (1Ch 3:9-19;
Mt 1:13; Lk 3:27).

ZIMRI

Chariot commander; killed Elah king
of Israel; reigned seven days (1Kg 16:8-
20).

ZION

Specifically, the stronghold in Jerusalem; also refers to the temple, hill, city,
people, and heavenly city.
did capture the stronghold
  of **Z**,.......................... 2Sm 5:7
Mount **Z**—the summit
  of Zaphon—................... Ps 48:2
Sing us one of the songs of **Z**... Ps 137:3
laid a stone in **Z**, a tested
  stone, ... Is 28:16
Blow the horn in **Z**; sound
  the alarm....................... Jl 2:1
Rejoice greatly, Daughter **Z**!......Zch 9:9
Tell Daughter **Z**, "See, your King..Mt 21:5
Do not be afraid, Daughter **Z**; .. Jn 12:15
a stone in **Z** to stumble over, .. Rm 9:33
The Deliverer will come
  from **Z**;..................... Rm 11:26

#

430

lived in Egypt was **430** years. . Ex 12:40
which came **430** years later,...... Gl 3:17

666

of a person. Its number is **666**. . Rv 13:18

1,260

to prophesy for **1,260** days, ...Rv 11:3

144,000

144,000 sealed from every
  tribe .... Rv 7:4

PERMISSIONS

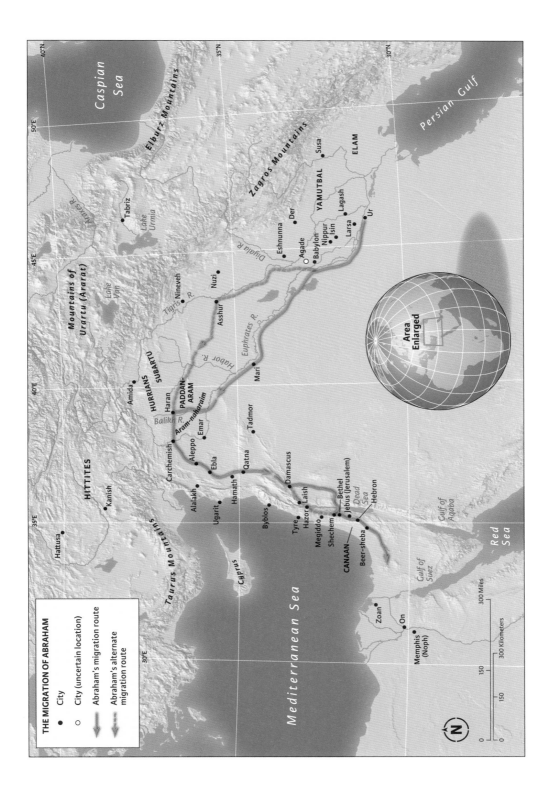

THE MIGRATION OF ABRAHAM

• City
○ City (uncertain location)
↓ Abraham's migration route
↓ Abraham's alternate migration route

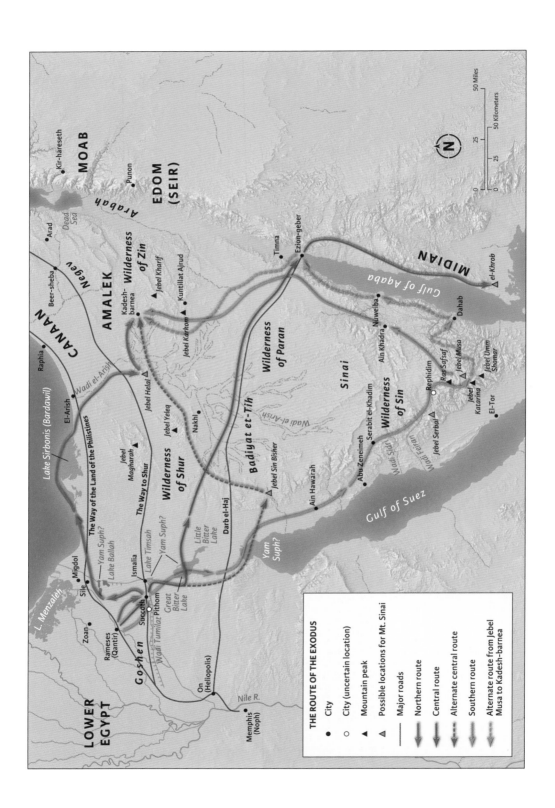

THE ROUTE OF THE EXODUS

- Gity
- ○ City (uncertain location)
- ▲ Mountain peak
- △ Possible locations for Mt. Sinai
- — Major roads
- Northern route
- Central route
- Alternate central route
- Southern route
- Alternate route from Jebel Musa to Kadesh-barnea

LOWER
EGYPT

Memphis
(Noph)

Nile R.

On
(Heliopolis)

Zoan

Rameses
(Qantir)

Wadi Tumilat

Goshen

L. Menzaleh

Sile

Migdol

Ismailia

Succoth
Pithom

Great
Bitter
Lake

Little
Bitter
Lake

Lake Timsah

Lake Ballah

Yam Suph?

Yam Suph?

Yam Suph?

Darb el-Haj

Lake Sirbonis (Bardawil)

The Way of the Land of the Philistines

El-Arish

Wadi el-Arish

Raphia

CANAAN

Beer-sheba

Negev

Arad

Dead
Sea

MOAB

Kir-hareseth

Punon

EDOM
(SEIR)

Arabah

AMALEK

Kadesh-
barnea

Wilderness
of Zin

Jebel Kharif

Kuntillat Ajrud

Jebel Karkom

Jebel Helal

Jebel Yeleq

The Way to Shur

Jebel
Magharah

Wilderness
of Shur

Nakhl

Badiyat et-Tih

Wadi el-Arish

Jebel Sin Bisher

Ain Hawarah

Gulf of Suez

Abu Zeneimeh

Serabit el-Khadim

Wadi Sidri

Wadi Feiran

Jebel Serbal

El-Tor

Wilderness
of Sin

Sinai

Wilderness
of Paran

Rephidim

Ras Safsaf

Jebel Musa

Jebel
Katarina

Jebel Umm
Shomar

Ain Khadra

Nuweiba

Dahab

Gulf of Aqaba

MIDIAN

el-Khrob

Timna

Ezion-geber

N

0   25   50 Miles

0   25   50 Kilometers

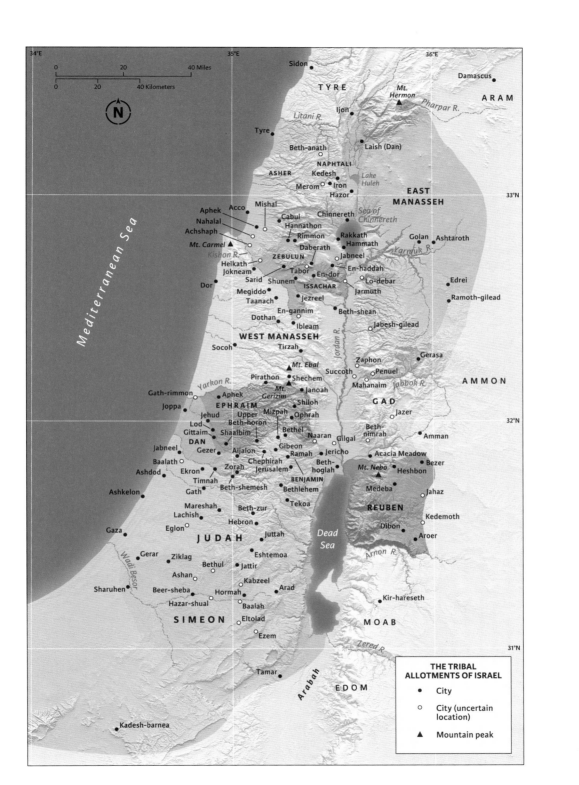

THE TRIBAL
ALLOTMENTS OF ISRAEL

- • City
- ○ City (uncertain location)
- ▲ Mountain peak

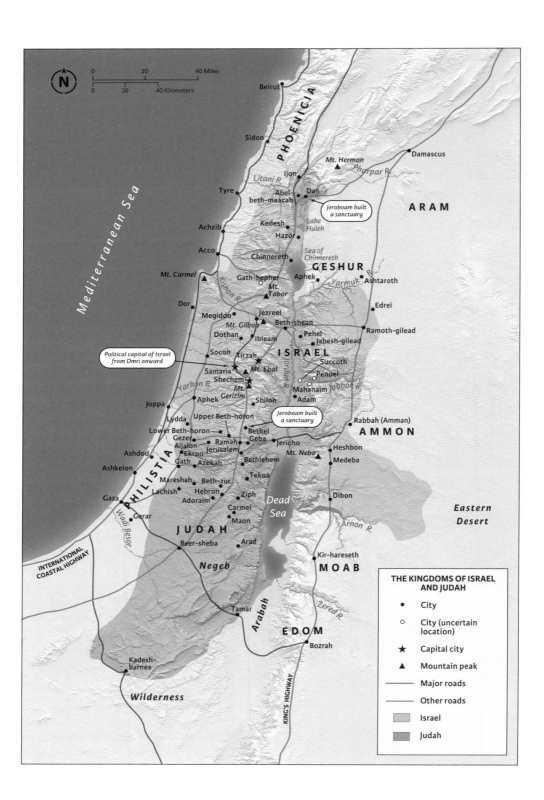

THE KINGDOMS OF ISRAEL
AND JUDAH

- ● City
- ○ City (uncertain location)
- ★ Capital city
- ▲ Mountain peak
- —— Major roads
- —— Other roads
- Israel
- Judah

Mediterranean Sea

PHOENICIA

Beirut

Sidon

Mt. Hermon ▲

Damascus

Ijon

Litani R.

Pharpar R.

Tyre

Abel-beth-maacah

Dan

Jeroboam built a sanctuary

ARAM

Achzib

Kedesh

Lake Huleh

Hazor

Acco

Chinnereth

Sea of Chinnereth

GESHUR

Mt. Carmel ▲

Gath-hepher ○

Aphek

Ashtaroth

Mt. Tabor ▲

Yarmuk R.

Dor

Kishon R.

Jezreel

Edrei

Megiddo

Mt. Gilboa

Beth-shean

Dothan

Ibleam

Pehel

Jabesh-gilead

Ramoth-gilead

Socoh

Tirzah ★

ISRAEL

Political capital of Israel from Omri onward

Samaria ★

Mt. Ebal ▲

Succoth

Shechem

Penuel

Mt. Gerizim ▲

Mahanaim ○

Jordan R.

Jabbok R.

Joppa

Adam

Aphek

Shiloh

Yarkon R.

Upper Beth-horon

Lydda

Bethel

Jeroboam built a sanctuary

Rabbah (Amman)

Lower Beth-horon

Geba

Gezer

Ramah

Jericho

AMMON

Aijalon

Ekron

Jerusalem

Heshbon

Ashdod

Gath

Azekah

Mt. Nebo ▲

Medeba

Ashkelon

Bethlehem

PHILISTIA

Mareshah

Beth-zur

Tekoa

Gaza

Lachish

Hebron

Ziph

Dibon

Gerar

Adoraim

Carmel

Dead Sea

Eastern Desert

Wadi Besor

JUDAH

Maon

Arnon R.

INTERNATIONAL COASTAL HIGHWAY

Beer-sheba

Arad

Kir-hareseth

Negeb

MOAB

Arabah

Zered R.

Tamar

EDOM

Bozrah

KING'S HIGHWAY

Kadesh-barnea

Wilderness

N

0   20   40 Miles
0   20   40 Kilometers

ISRAEL IN THE TIME OF JESUS

- City
- City (uncertain location)
- Decapolis city
- Decapolis city (uncertain location)
- ★ Administrative capital
- ▲ Mountain peak
- —— Major route
- —— Other route
- First procuratorship
- Territory of Antipas
- Territory of Philip
- Syrian territory

Coponius was named the first prefect and established the administrative capital at Caesarea Maritima

Mediterranean Sea

ABILENE

Sidon

Mt. Hermon

Damascus

ITUREA

Litani R.

Pharpar R.

Tyre

Caesarea-Philippi (Paneas)

Raphana

Cadasa (Kedesh)

Gischala (Gush Halav)

Lake Huleh

GAULANITIS

BATANEA

Ptolemais (Acco)

Jotapata

Bethsaida

Capernaum

TRACHONITIS

Mt. Carmel

Tiberias

Gergesa (Kursi)

Gamala

Yarmuk R.

Canatha

GALILEE

Nazareth

Hippos

Adraa (Edrei)

Dora

Mt. Tabor

Sea of Galilee

Gadara

Abila

AURANITIS

Legio (Megiddo)

Scythopolis (Beth-shean)

Dion

Bostra

Caesarea Maritima (Strato's Tower)

Ginae (Jenin)

Pella

Aenon Salim

Gerasa (Jerash)

DECAPOLIS

SAMARIA

Sebaste (Samaria)

Mt. Ebal

Amathus

Apollonia

Yarkon R.

Neapolis (Shechem)

Jabbok R.

Antipatris (Aphek)

Ephraim (Ophrah)

Alexandrium

PEREA

Gedor (Gadara)

Joppa

Lydda

Archelais

Philadelphia (Amman)

JUDEA

Jamnia

Azotus (Ashdod)

Emmaus (Nicopolis)

Jerusalem

Jericho

Esbus (Heshbon)

Mt. Nebo

Ascalon (Ashkelon)

Hyrcania

Mesad Hasidim (Qumran)

Medeba

Betogabris (Beth-guvrin)

Hebron

Callirrhoe (Zereth-shahar)

Machaerus

Gaza

En-gedi

Dead Sea

Arnon R.

IDUMEA

Masada

NABATEA

Raphia

Beer-sheba

Arad

Malatha

Arabah

Khirbet Tannur

Zered R.

INTERNATIONAL COASTAL HIGHWAY

Wadi Besor

KING'S HIGHWAY

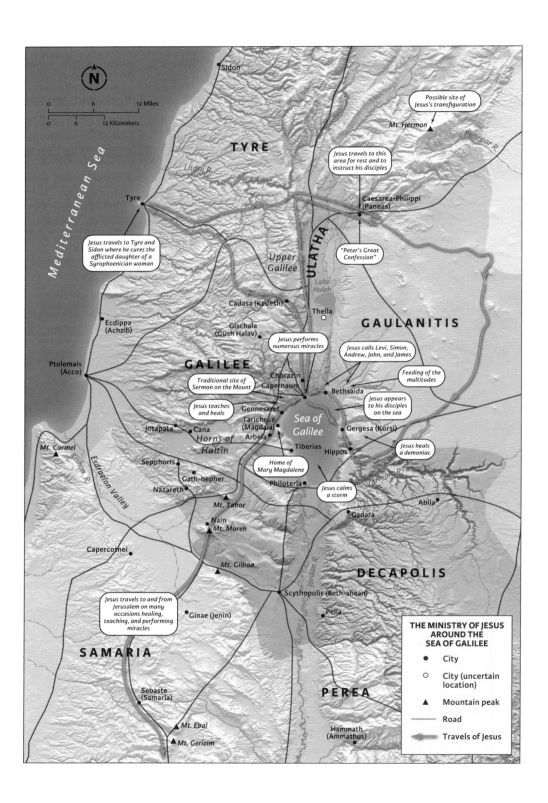

N

0   6   12 Miles

0   6   12 Kilometers

Mediterranean Sea

Sidon

TYRE

Litani R.

Pharpar R.

Possible site of Jesus's transfiguration

Mt. Hermon

Jesus travels to this area for rest and to instruct his disciples

Tyre

Caesarea-Philippi (Paneas)

Jesus travels to Tyre and Sidon where he cures the afflicted daughter of a Syrophoenician woman

Upper Galilee

ULATHA

Lake Huleh

"Peter's Great Confession"

Ecdippa (Achzib)

Cadasa (Kedesh)

Thella

GAULANITIS

Gischala (Gush Halav)

Jesus performs numerous miracles

Ptolemais (Acco)

GALILEE

Chorazin

Jesus calls Levi, Simon, Andrew, John, and James

Traditional site of Sermon on the Mount

Capernaum

Bethsaida

Feeding of the multitudes

Jesus teaches and heals

Gennesaret

Sea of Galilee

Jesus appears to his disciples on the sea

Jotapata

Cana

Taricheae (Magdala)

Gergesa (Kursi)

Horns of Hattin

Arbela

Jesus heals a demoniac

Tiberias

Sepphoris

Hippos

Mt. Carmel

Gath-hepher

Home of Mary Magdalene

Esdraelon Valley

Nazareth

Philoteria

Kishon R.

Jesus calms a storm

Abila

Mt. Tabor

Gadara

Nain

Mt. Moreh

Jordan R.

Yarmuk R.

Mt. Gilboa

DECAPOLIS

Capercotnei

Scythopolis (Beth-shean)

Jesus travels to and from Jerusalem on many occasions healing, teaching, and performing miracles

Ginae (Jenin)

Pella

SAMARIA

PEREA

Sebaste (Samaria)

Mt. Ebal

Hammath (Ammathus)

Mt. Gerizim

THE MINISTRY OF JESUS AROUND THE SEA OF GALILEE

● City

○ City (uncertain location)

▲ Mountain peak

— Road

⬅ Travels of Jesus

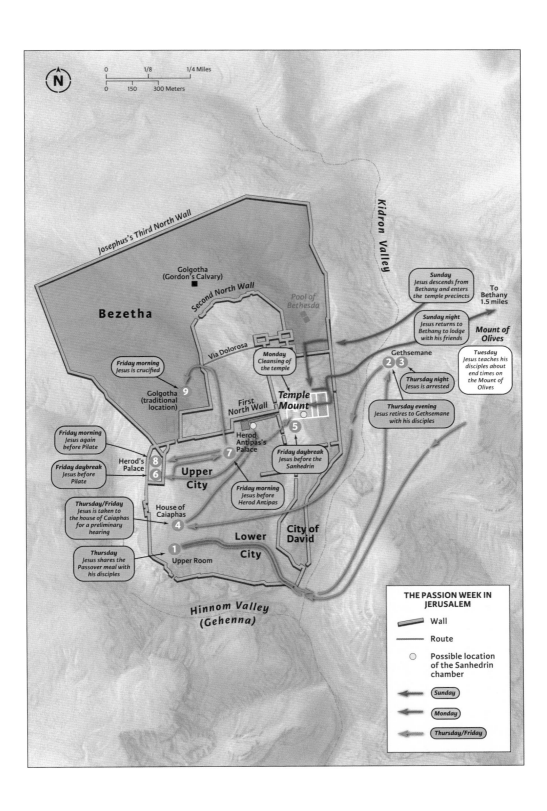

THE PASSION WEEK IN JERUSALEM

N

0   1/8   1/4 Miles
0   150   300 Meters

Josephus's Third North Wall

Bezetha

Golgotha
(Gordon's Calvary)

Second North Wall

Pool of
Bethesda

Via Dolorosa

Friday morning
Jesus is crucified

Golgotha
(traditional
location) **9**

Monday
*Cleansing of
the temple*

First
North Wall

**Temple
Mount**

5

Herod
Antipas's
Palace **7**

Friday daybreak
*Jesus before
the Sanhedrin*

Friday morning
*Jesus again
before Pilate* **8**

Herod's
Palace **6**

**Upper
City**

Friday daybreak
*Jesus before
Pilate*

Friday morning
*Jesus before
Herod Antipas*

Thursday/Friday
*Jesus is taken to
the house of Caiaphas
for a preliminary
hearing*

House of
Caiaphas **4**

**Lower
City**

**City of
David**

Thursday
*Jesus shares the
Passover meal with
his disciples* **1**

Upper Room

Hinnom Valley
(Gehenna)

Kidron Valley

Sunday
*Jesus descends from
Bethany and enters
the temple precincts*

To
Bethany
1.5 miles

Sunday night
*Jesus returns to
Bethany to lodge
with his friends*

**Mount of
Olives**

Gethsemane
2 **3**

Thursday night
Jesus is arrested

Tuesday
*Jesus teaches his
disciples about
end times on
the Mount of
Olives*

Thursday evening
*Jesus retires to Gethsemane
with his disciples*

**THE PASSION WEEK IN
JERUSALEM**

▬▬ Wall

—— Route

◯ Possible location
of the Sanhedrin
chamber

◀— Sunday

◀— Monday

◀— Thursday/Friday

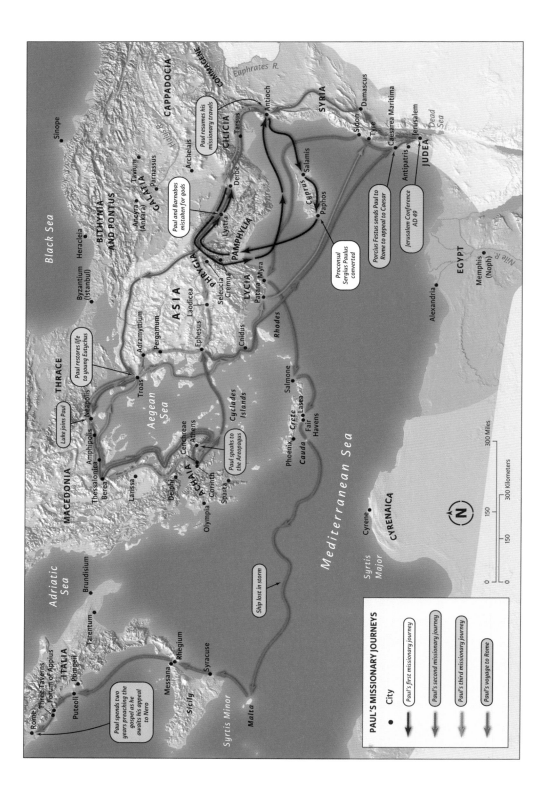

PAUL'S MISSIONARY JOURNEYS

- • City
- → Paul's first missionary journey
- → Paul's second missionary journey
- → Paul's third missionary journey
- → Paul's voyage to Rome

Paul spends two years preaching the gospel as he awaits his appeal to Nero

Luke joins Paul

Paul restores life to young Eutychus

Paul speaks to the Areopagus

Paul resumes his missionary travels

Paul and Barnabas mistaken for gods

Proconsul Sergius Paulus converted

Porcius Festus sends Paul to Rome to appeal to Caesar

Jerusalem Conference AD 49

Ship lost in storm

Black Sea

Sinope

Heraclea

Byzantium (Istanbul)

BITHYNIA AND PONTUS

CAPPADOCIA

COMMAGENE

Euphrates R.

Archelais

Tavium

Parnassus

Ancyra (Ankara)

GALATIA

CILICIA

Tarsus

Antioch

SYRIA

Damascus

Derbe

Lystra

Seleucia

Crema

PHRYGIA

PAMPHYLIA

LYCIA

Patara Myra

Salmone

Cyprus

Salamis

Paphos

Sidon

Tyre

Caesarea Maritima

Antipatris

Jerusalem

JUDEA

Dead Sea

THRACE

Neapolis

Amphipolis

Troas

Adramyttium

Pergamum

ASIA

Laodicea

Ephesus

Cnidus

Rhodes

Aegean Sea

MACEDONIA

Thessalonica

Berea

Larissa

Delphi

Olympia

ACHAIA

Athens

Cenchreae

Corinth

Sparta

Cyclades Islands

Crete

Phoenix

Lasea

Fair Havens

Cauda

Mediterranean Sea

Syrtis Major

CYRENAICA

Cyrene

EGYPT

Memphis (Noph)

Nile R.

Alexandria

Adriatic Sea

Brundisium

Tarentum

ITALIA

Pompeii

Puteoli

Three Taverns

Forum of Appius

Rome

Rhegium

Messana

Syracuse

Sicily

Malta

Syrtis Minor

N

0   150   300 Miles

0   150   300 Kilometers